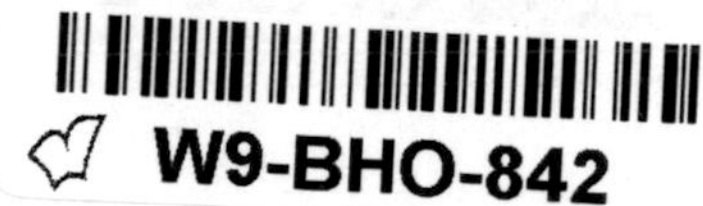

Goldmine Standard Catalog Of American Records 1950–1975

2nd Edition

Tim Neely

Published by

700 E. State Street • Iola, WI 54990-0001
Telephone: 715/445-2214

Please call or write for our free catalog of music publications.
Our toll-free number to place an order or obtain a free catalog is 800-258-0929
or please use our regular business telephone 715-445-2214
for editorial comment and further information.

Library of Congress Catalog Number: 98-84618

ISBN: 0-87341-934-0

Printed in the United States of America

Contents

Introduction

The readers have spoken.

The *Standard Catalog of American Records 1950-1975* has been a tremendous success. We've received some lavish praise for the book, everything from "just what the hobby needed" to "I've been waiting for a guide of this caliber to come along" to "...the best US guide I've seen in over 30 years of collecting."

The kind words have been heartwarming. We at Krause Publications have believed for years that a comprehensive price guide, one that attempts to cover record collecting in both breadth and depth, would be well received. And we were right; the first edition is a complete sellout, and we thank you.

We also heard you when you said you wanted even more information. You gave us lists of artists who we missed and you thought belonged in a book like this. You told us what you liked and didn't like about the first edition, and we're working to make some of those improvements. Some of them have come to fruition; others are in the works for future editions.

In case this is your first time...

What is the *Standard Catalog of American Records 1950-1975*, anyway?

Simply, this is a unique price guide for the record collecting hobby.

Both collectors and dealers have been clamoring for a book like this for years. I have been asked, "Why doesn't *Goldmine* have an all-encompassing price guide that actually lists the records?" People who aren't collectors and don't want to become collectors tell me, "I don't want to have to buy six or seven price guides, especially if I just want to get rid of my records."

Other price guides, including our own, have tried to cover one facet of collecting, be it 45s, albums, the British Invasion, jazz, comedy, picture sleeves, whatever. And we have no plans to discontinue publishing such books. There also are a couple of guides on the market that claim to have broad coverage but are useless to the novice collector, as they skimp on discographies – the lists of records that help someone determine what they have and what they are missing.

So we've tried to do the best of both worlds.

Inside we have approximately 150,000 (give or take a few hundred) listings of records of four different types – 45 rpm singles, LPs, extended play 7-inch singles, and 12-inch singles. We also list hundreds and hundreds of picture sleeves and promotional items. Thousands of records that are not listed in any other price guide can be found on these pages.

Also, we've included many artists who have never been covered in a price guide in such depth, at least not recently. Many of the "pop" artists that some collect, yet receive short shrift from other guides, are here. Almost everyone who had an album on the *Billboard* pop charts from 1955 to 1975 is in here. We have pop, rock, rhythm & blues, country, comedy, jazz, easy listening, even some big band listings.

Obviously, this has been an enormous task. The first edition was more than three years in the making, and we've never stopped adding to the database in the two years since the first edition was published. We've had help from hundreds of collectors and dealers from throughout the United States and the rest of the world – we received some great information from Canada, Great Britain, Italy and Australia, among other places – to try to make this the most accurate and up-to-date book possible.

We tried not to "assume" the existence of anything. As much as possible, we used the records themselves, or photocopies, pictures or computer scans of actual records, or reliable sales and auction lists, to confirm questionable information. We've compared our material to other published sources and found many errors and misconceptions elsewhere. We'd like to think that you can trust the information you find here.

We have made no "plants," listings that are deliberately false, that others use to trap would-be copyright infringers. Doing so hurts the hobby. I know of people who added false listings to their "want lists" based on a mention in a price guide, then spent 20 years vainly searching for a disc that only existed in someone's fertile imagination!

And we continue to find new material; some of which was too late to make our deadlines for this book. But you'll see some of that information reflected in other *Goldmine* price guides. (That's a good reason to keep buying them!)

We hope, too, that this book injects a dose of reality into the record collecting hobby. For the most part, this is not a place to make big money. Despite some well-publicized rarities, most records remain reasonably priced; only the rarest items are skyrocketing in value. So we list a lot of common items amidst the rare.

Focusing too much on the items that fetch four and five figures, as the mainstream media has a habit of doing, gives two impressions: Everything is worth that much, and collecting is getting out of the price range of the average person. Both are false, and we hope this book helps show that.

Another myth is that all of the "good" stuff has been found. Sure, it's not as easy to find certifiable rarities at yard sales, flea markets and thrift shops as it once was. But it's not impossible.

Just a few weeks ago, a local resident came by the Krause Publications offices with a record he had had since

the mid-1960s. He bought it when it came out, he said, and it was tough to find even then. He hadn't thought too much of it – until he saw it listed for a phenomenal price in one of our *Goldmine* price guides. His rare record? "My Bonnie" by Tony Sheridan and the Beat Brothers on Decca, one of the world's most sought-after 45s because it was the first American release by the Beatles!

What's new for 2000

For starters, we've added between 15,000 and 20,000 more listings for this edition. Some are records by artists who were listed in the first edition that we did not know about the last time or had not confirmed; some are by artists we omitted the last time but have chosen to include this time.

We've beefed up the extended play 45 listings. Many, many hundreds of items we formerly had listed as "contents unknown" are now known, thanks to many readers who generously jotted down or photocopied the information from their own collections. There are still many gaps here; see the **How you can help** section for advice on filling in these holes for us.

We've added several new sections in the back of the book. These are called "Original Cast Recordings," "Soundtracks," "Television Records" and "Various Artists Collections." Our research here is still in its infancy, especially in the various artists section.

Thousands of confirmed picture sleeves have been added, including some that are not listed in any other price guide. These have been verified either by seeing the actual sleeve, viewing a photocopy of the sleeve, or through confirmation by trusted experts who have the missing sleeve in their collection.

We've fixed most of the errors and omissions that readers saw. That said, I'm sure there are still more in here that we still haven't fixed.

One of the very few complaints we had with the first edition is how we treated multiple artists with the same name. Here's how we explained it in the first edition of the *Standard Catalog:*

"In the first edition of the *Goldmine Price Guide To 45 RPM Records*, when the same name was used by two or more artists, we listed every record under one heading with the mention that the below included, as our example does, 'several different groups' or 'more than one group.' We continue that in this book, because we've found that it makes the listings easier to find. We have made some exceptions when an artist is extremely popular, yet others used the name (usually earlier). Such exceptions include the Beach Boys, the Eagles, the Supremes and the Temptations."

Many of you, frankly, don't like this system. And we listened. So we've begun to break up this kind of listings. But we aren't going to do so willy-nilly. Obviously, much more research is necessary to make this work properly. If we haven't yet broken up a listing, it's because we don't have 100 percent proof about which listings belong together.

What's included

When the decision was made to create a "standard catalog" for records to join Krause Publications' long and distinguished line of such books in other collecting fields, the original idea was to do a "complete" book. But it quickly became apparent that such a book would be impossible. It would have to be narrowed down somehow to keep it within a reasonable size and cost.

So we decided to restrict the listings to those artists whose first record was released in the United States in or before 1975. As a result, many highly collectible artists of the 1980s and 1990s, such as Prince, Madonna, Garth Brooks and Nirvana, aren't in here. In the first edition, we mentioned the possibility of creating a *Standard Catalog of American Records 1976-Present*, and it looks as if that will happen in the fall of 2001.

Why did we choose 1975 as the cutoff year?

That covers 20 years of the so-called "rock era," which is said to begin when "Rock Around the Clock" by Bill Haley and His Comets hit number one on the national music charts. It predates most disco and new wave-punk rock. And it covers most of those really bad 1970s records – some of which have become collectible – that Rhino Records has immortalized in its Have a Good Day series of compact discs. Not to mention that it allows us to include such varied artists as Elton John, Barry Manilow, Bruce Springsteen, the Brady Bunch (!!) and Tanya Tucker, along with hundreds of others.

Though we decided to cut off new artists at 1975, we didn't cut off their listings at 1975. That's why you'll see hundreds of 12-inch singles, which weren't introduced in the United States until 1976, listed. Among others, Led Zeppelin, Merle Haggard, Eddy Arnold, and Richard Thompson have new 1999 or 2000 vinyl releases listed! Not much readily accessible information exists as to what does and doesn't exist on vinyl in the 1990s and 2000s; this book is certainly the most accurate source for such listings anywhere, at least among the artists who qualify for inclusion.

Although our "official" range of years starts at 1950, we didn't automatically exclude artists whose first record predates that. The 33 1/3 rpm record was introduced to the masses in 1948; the 45 rpm record followed in 1949. Those years are where the true boundaries of our listings are. You'll actually find at least one artist who was already dead for five years when his music began to appear on 45s and 33s – and most of those reissues are more valuable than most of the original 78s!

As we implied earlier, there is no value cutoff. In other words, all of an artist's records we were able to confirm, *regardless of value*, are listed.

What's not included

Even among artists included in this book's parameters, you'll probably find something missing if you look hard enough. For some artists, our data is woefully incomplete; others were the victims of deadlines and space limitations. If there's someone you believe belongs, be sure to let us know! See the **How you can help** section for more advice.

In areas of music for which we have a specialized catalog (jazz and country-western most prominently), we have not included everyone, but have tended to focus on those artists who had some popular crossover success.

Two areas that are not in here, with very few exceptions, are classical music and 78 rpm records.

It's possible that we can add some selected 78s in future editions, especially the highly collectible mid- to late-1950s rock and roll 78s. Compiling the more readily accessible formats of 45, LP and EP remains a much higher priority.

A couple artists who might be considered "classical" can be found in these pages, but wholesale classical listings aren't in here and are unlikely in the future. Certain items in the genre are highly collectible; the *Goldmine Record Album Price Guide* contains hundreds of listings of RCA Red Seal "Living Stereo" and Mercury "Living Presence" stereo LPs, two of the most desirable categories of classical records. But in this book, we will not include classical music unless the artist had popular success (for example, Van Cliburn) or is collectible for its pioneering use of electronics and-or synthesizers (*Switched-On Bach* and the like).

And by the way, we called this book *Standard Catalog of **American** Records* for a reason. Imports are not included. Nor will they be in the future. There is no current U.S.-published price guide on imports.

Record collecting questions

I've got a bunch of old records that I want to get rid of, and I suspect some of them might be worth something. How do I find out?

This, or variations thereof, is the most common question I am asked by callers. The answer can be as easy or as complicated as you want to make it.

The below is based on an essay that Jay Horman, formerly of Fast Hits Music, wrote for the vinyl collector and dealer newsgroup on Usenet (that's a cousin to the World Wide Web). It's called rec.music.collecting.vinyl, and it is for the discussion of records, not for buying and selling. You will be scolded (or "flamed" in computer parlance) if you try to sell items in that newsgroup! A separate newsgroup is set up for that purpose, rec.music.marketplace.vinyl. Most of the regulars are highly knowledgeable, and if you're not careful, you might see a post from the author of the *Standard Catalog of American Records* every once in a while.

Jay Horman is now out of the record-dealing business. Fast Hits Music still exists, though, and sells new 45 rpm records (as in current releases – yes, 45s are still being made, despite beliefs to the contrary in some circles). It does have some used stuff, though. You can contact FHM on the Web at www.fasthits.com.

The following is used with Jay's permission.

Let's assume for the moment that you've picked up this book more out of curiosity than anything else. You have an old stash of records from your youth, or you've inherited some from a deceased relative or maybe an older sibling who "upgraded" to compact discs. What to do now?

The first thing, the *very* first thing, is to decide how much time you wish to put into the effort of "cashing out". Simply put, the more time you put in, the more money you will get out of the collection.

If you choose to put virtually *no* time into it, just put the records in a box and take them to your local vinyl store, then take whatever offer is given. You might get 10 cents each, maybe 50 cents per LP, maybe even more. But you will be rid of them, and will hopefully cover the cost of the gas to get you to the store.

But you are reading this, so the assumption is that you'd rather not settle for the lowest price. The next level would be to get an idea of what the value of the records are, so you at least have some cards to play at the dealing table. You do that by buying a price guide.

Make sure that it is a relatively recent edition, and that it covers the items you have. You'll just be using the book for what it is: a guide. Then, go through and look up the records, and make a list of each one's value, based on the condition. Be conservative on condition, because any buyer will be.

Sometimes, you'll see different prices for very slight variations on the record or jacket. It is usually safe to assume that you have the less expensive (more common) version, unless there is definite evidence that you have the more valuable one.

At this stage, you are mostly looking to be sure that you don't have any relatively rare (worth more than say $50) records. If you do have some records like that, then the original collector was probably pretty discriminating in his/her purchases, and you may find a few others in the batch. But most collectors collected their favorite music, so don't be too disappointed if each record is valued at/below $10. The reason you bought the price guide in the first place was to avoid giving away a $1000 record for 10 cents. With any luck, you'll have found that the collection at this stage was worth the investment in the guide.

Let's assume the collection does have a bit of value, at least according to the price guide. You are again faced with the choice: The amount of time you continue to put into the

collection should increase the value of what you get at its sale.

You essentially have two options now: go to a vinyl dealer with your records, or sell them yourself directly to collectors, either wholly, or piece-by-piece.

If you choose to go to a dealer, you will save time, but won't get quite as much for the records. You might expect 10 percent to maybe 75 percent at the most, but probably at the low end, especially for the more common items. Remember that the guides typically show the high-end price of items sold by dealers to collectors. Being professionals, the dealers need to earn a living and pay the rent, so that's about all they can offer. But they are also typically the only people that buy your collection as a whole.

Don't limit yourself. Send a copy of your list to non-local dealers who may be interested. Shop around for offers a bit. And obviously, if you find an offer you like, take it.

Keep in mind that the rarities (and the knowledge that you have them) work in your favor. Use them as bargaining chips. You might even dump the more common items with the dealer, and sell the more valuable items yourself.

If you wish to get the highest price for your records, you'll probably want to sell directly to collectors. This will involve more effort, and possibly some additional costs. It will also take some time.

You must choose how to let people know (advertising by whatever medium), and how to sell the items (set sale, auction, best offer, etc.). The possibilities for what you'll make vary widely – you may not do better than 10 percent of the price guide, or you may find someone willing to pay twice what the guide says. Again, remember it's just a guide. People will often expect a little better deal from an individual vs. a dealer, but again, don't give away the $100 record for 10 cents. You've come too far!

Exactly what method of selling works best will depend on the type of items you have and how comfortable you are with selling.

I've got some of the items in here, but no one will give me what they are "worth"! They want to give me pennies on the dollar! What's up?

Too many people treat books like this way too literally, and with delusions of grandeur.

What the values in here reflect are **retail** prices – what a collector might pay for the item from a dealer, and **not** what a dealer will pay a collector for resale. Too many non-collectors (and even some collectors) don't understand that.

I know one dealer who has told me that he won't buy records from someone who tells him they consulted a price guide first. While that is extreme, it shows the distrust some dealers have for books like this and how the public uses (and abuses) them.

Just as importantly, the highest values are for records in the best condition (see the section on "Grading your records" below). And there is a reason for that: Truly pristine records are very difficult to find! Many collectors are willing to pay handsomely for them – but for many of the records in this book, Near Mint examples aren't even known to exist!

One reason we've expanded the price listing to three grades of condition is to reflect that. There's a tendency to look at the highest price listed for something and assume that's what your record is worth. More realistically, though, such a small percentage of records are truly Near Mint – especially from the 1950s and 1960s – that your own records, if you were a typical accumulator and not a collector, are considerably less than Near Mint. A well-known dealer of Beatles records has said that he's seen maybe two or three Near Mint copies, and only one Mint copy, of original Capitol pressings of *Sgt. Pepper's Lonely Hearts Club Band*, and he's looked at hundreds.

The price guide tells me that my Elvis records are worth something, but the used record store in the local strip mall treats them as if they are by Mantovani. What's up?

To get the most from a dealer, make sure the kind of music you're trying to sell matches his/her main inventory focus.

Many dealers today are specialists within the vast world of record collecting. For example, they only deal in 1950s and 1960s R&B and rock, or they only deal in soundtracks, or they only deal in 45s. And they aren't interested in other things, no matter how valuable they might be.

I know of a classical music dealer who intentionally undervalues Elvis Presley records in his "wanted to buy" lists for a very simple reason: His clientele doesn't buy them, so he doesn't want them! The same Elvis records would get a lot more from someone who focuses on Elvis. Keep that in mind when you try to sell your Rolling Stones records to a jazz shop, or your John Coltrane records to a rock store.

I still think I can get the most for what I have. How do I do so?

There is only one way you'll be able to get anything close to the prices listed for most items, and that's to sell them direct to the collector.

The "old-fashioned" way is through record collecting magazines. The oldest and most widely read remains *Goldmine*, which was founded in 1974. Published every two weeks, the magazine is loaded with ads from people selling records of all kinds and from all eras. *Goldmine* has advertising salespeople who will help you put your ad together for maximum impact. To see what *Goldmine* is about, pick up a copy. It is available at all Tower Records stores in the U.S., most Barnes and Noble and Borders bookstores and hundreds of independent record dealers. If you still can't find a copy, call 1-800-258-0929.

A rapidly growing way to sell records and other memorabilia is over the Internet. Some dealers have web sites;

others use some of the many online auction sites; some use both. I have bought records over the web, and have yet to have significant problems. It's faster than "snail mail" and less expensive than a long-distance telephone call. But it's not perfect: As a seller, you are reaching a larger audience than you would in a record collecting magazine, but also a much less targeted one. The 'Net seems to be a good place to sell lower-priced items that might take up valuable space in an expensive print ad. But many more valuable pieces sit or fetch less than they might through more traditional means.

As a buyer, you have to watch out for overgraded, under-described items. Photos of the items help. Also, buying from someone who deals in records as a primary area rather than as an obvious sideline to his/her Beanie Baby business is recommended. You can usually tell these sellers by the way they describe the records – they have no concept of any kind of grading system.

Now, one from the other side of the equation, the record seller.

I'm a dealer, and I can't sell my records at these prices. If I try, they just sit until I reduce them. What gives?

Basically, how much you get for a record depends on what kind of a dealer you are.

In general, the highest prices for records are obtained by those dealers who sell mostly or entirely through mail-order to a targeted audience. These are people who sell items through auctions in Goldmine and sometimes through their own private auction lists. They cater to record collectors, often those from abroad (who, like it or not, often set the prices on rare items because they have to have something more than an American does). They have built reputations for sterling customer service, and their clientele is willing to pay more for the knowledge that they, indeed, are getting what they bought. They will usually get something approaching the prices in this book, and often they can get more.

But most dealers don't fit in that category.

Anyone who sells records in a store or a stand, by definition, has a larger potential market than a mail-order dealer (an area's entire population that might want to buy music), but a less targeted one. Therefore, it's going to be difficult for Fred's Collectible Records in Keokuk, Iowa (a hypothetical example – there is no such store) to get the same for a record that a well-known, well-established dealer will. The average customer at our fictional Fred's will have little or no knowledge of what collectible records sell for from an educated dealer to an educated consumer.

That's why we have price guides: to help educate average people about what their records may sell for. And after all, that's all it is: a guide. (How many times have we said that now?) You may know from your own experience that you can't sell at these prices; adjust accordingly. You also may know that some of these prices are too low (it does happen); you know your market as well as anyone.

Now, some questions about specific albums that have received lots of publicity.

I have this old Beatles album. It's called Introducing the Beatles. It says stereophonic on it and it's on Vee Jay Records, etc. etc. I think I might have something valuable here. Do I?

The usual reply: "No."

Perhaps no album in the history of recorded music has been counterfeited as often as *Introducing The Beatles*. Exactly where they all came from is a matter of conjecture, but the truth is that they began to emerge not too long after the album was pulled from the market in late 1964, and they continued to appear well into the early 1980s. And they were available at even the most respectable kinds of record stores, including department stores that sold records.

It used to be easy to know if you had a fake, but now, even most of the fakes have been in collections for 20 or more years.

So in the interests of awareness, we'll give you some of the more obvious ways to tell whether that *Introducing The Beatles* you have is an original.

Check the cover first: If your back cover either has ads for other albums, is completely blank, or has a list of songs claiming that "Please Please Me" and "Ask Me Why" are on the record, it's probably authentic.

If your cover has a brown border around the front cover photo, stop right there; it's fake.

If there is no shadow accompanying George Harrison, who is at the far right of the cover photo, you have a fake.

If the cover has a yellow tint and has the word "Stereo" in the upper left, it's counterfeit.

There are some very well-done counterfeit covers; another giveaway is if you have a counterfeit record inside the jacket. Unless someone who owned both put an authentic record into a phony cover (it happens), a phony record implies a phony cover.

Raise a warning flag if the album claims to be "Stereo" or "Stereophonic" on the cover and has a list of songs on the back that include "Love Me Do" and "P.S. I Love You." This is the most common counterfeit version.

Is your copy still sealed? If so, and it has a "Stereophonic" banner across the top with the list of songs including "Love Me Do" and "P.S. I Love You," you have a 99 and 44/100 chance of having a counterfeit. No reputable dealer or knowledgeable collector will pay a premium for a sealed copy of *Introducing the Beatles* that matches the above description. So go ahead and unseal it, as the strongest counterfeit evidence can be found on the actual record.

Most authentic front covers don't say "Stereophonic" on them; in the lower right corner they will say "LP 1062."

Authentic copies of *Introducing The Beatles* in stereo have always been scarce; they were even scarce in 1964!

On The Record: Let's assume your record passes the above tests or you still have doubts. Now, check the record, because this is where the originals really stick out from the fakes.

First, does the record say "Stereo" on the label? If the album cover claims to be "stereophonic" and the record label does not have any mention of stereo, odds are it's a fake.

Second, where are the words "Introducing The Beatles" and "The Beatles"? Both real and phony copies have them. But on an authentic copy, the words "The Beatles" are directly underneath "Introducing The Beatles," and both lines are above the center hole. If the center hole separates "Introducing The Beatles" and "The Beatles," it's a counterfeit.

Almost all real copies of the record have some sort of machine stamping in the dead wax, usually the words "Audio Matrix," the letters "MR" in a circle, or the letters "ARP." Some (not all) originals also have a numerical date scrawled in the dead wax (such as 2-12-64). No phonies have any of the above. Also, phonies often will be on flimsy vinyl as opposed to the sturdier 1960s vinyl.

The Play Test: If you're still not sure whether your "stereo" *Introducing The Beatles* is the real thing, put Side 1, Song 1 on your turntable. "I Saw Her Standing There," as well as the next four tracks, will be in clean, crisp, true stereo, with plenty of separation. If the record is mono or very poorly rechanneled stereo, and the record doesn't say "Stereo" on it, it's an authentic mono copy or a phony.

I have an intriguing collection of papers, letters and other odds and sods relating to The Who. They look to be contracts and letters and things like that. What are they worth?

Not much. All of these "documents" exist hundreds of thousands of times over, although they look convincing enough to fool the novice.

In 1970, The Who released their first legitimate live album, *Live At Leeds*. Even by the standards of the day, it had quite elaborate packaging. The album cover itself was about as simple as it gets: The Decca originals were packaged like an advance press kit, with the album cover opening up into a 12x12 folder. The record, in a brown generic sleeve with a phony handwritten label, was in one of the two flaps inside the package. And in the other flap was an assortment of extremely well reproduced items from all phases of The Who's history. Among them:

- A contract for the band's appearance at Woodstock;
- A rejection letter from EMI Records to The High Numbers' manager, Kit Lambert, dated "22nd October 1964" (the High Numbers were the early Who);
- A lyric sheet for "My Generation";
- A letter informing the band of the cancellation of a ballroom gig in 1965;
- Notes of the payments for certain gigs.

The album also has a poster and photos, 12 items in all. Also, some copies have a rectangular sticker at the upper left corner of the front cover stating, "It Is The Best Live Rock Album Ever Made… – *The New York Times*."

It is not difficult to find Decca pressings of *Live At Leeds*. Finding one with all the pieces is a different matter entirely. The most likely missing item is the poster, as many consumers took it out of the package to hang it on their wall, thus irreparably separating it from its source. All in all, a near-mint copy of the entire package on Decca can go for $40 or so.

When MCA reissued the album in 1973, after consolidating all its labels (Decca, Kapp and Uni most prominent among them) into one, it deleted all the goodies and packaged the album in a more normal LP cover. So for more than 20 years, the *Live At Leeds* package was incomplete. In 1995, the original release was expanded to twice its prior length on a CD reissue; early pressings came in a 12x12 box that reproduced all the goodies that had been in the original LP, at full size no less, not postage-stamp CD size.

So no, these contracts and things are not a rare find. Presumably, the true originals reside wherever The Who keeps such items.

Grading your records

When it comes to records, and how much you'll get for them, remember this above all:

Condition is (almost) everything!

Yes, it's possible to get a high price for a beat-up record, if it's exceptionally rare. But for common material, if it's not in at least Very Good condition – and preferably closer to Near Mint – you won't get many buyers. Or at least you won't the second time around. So accurately grading your discs is important, whether you're selling your records to a dealer or selling them to another collector.

Visual or play grading? In an ideal world, every record would be played before it is graded. But the time involved makes it impractical for most dealers, and anyway, it's rare that you get a chance to hear a record before you buy through the mail. Some advertisers play-grade everything and say so. But unless otherwise noted, records are visually graded.

How to grade. Look at everything about a record -- its playing surface, its label, its edges -- under a strong light. Then, based on your overall impression, give it a grade based on the following criteria:

Mint (M): Absolutely perfect in every way -- certainly never played, possibly even still sealed. (More on still

CD LP CAS 45 78 10" EP CD LP CAS 45 78 10" EP
レコードカタログのオンラインサーチ
SEARCH OUR VINYL CATALOGUE ON-LINE
www.saturnrecords.com
SATURN RECORDS
WORLDS BEST VINYL ON THE INTERNET
2万枚以上の貴重盤にインターネットでアクセス
5488 COLLEGE AVE. OAKLAND, CA. 94618
PHONE (510)654-0335 FAX (510)654-4386
JAZZ CLASSICAL SOUL ROCK BLUES FOLK MOVIES VOCAL EASY LISTENING NOSTALGIA "STRANGE"
CD LP CAS 45 78 10 EP CD LP CAS 45 78 10 EP

sealed under "Other considerations.") Should be used sparingly as a grade, if at all.

Near Mint (NM or M-): A nearly perfect record. Many dealers won't give a grade higher than this, implying (perhaps correctly) that no record is ever truly perfect.

The record should show no obvious signs of wear. A 45 RPM or EP sleeve should have no more than the most minor defects, such as almost invisible ring wear or other signs of slight handling.

An LP jacket should have no creases, folds, seam splits or any other noticeable similar defect. No cut-out holes, either. And of course, the same should be true of any other inserts, such as posters, lyric sleeves and the like.

Basically, an LP in Near Mint condition looks as if you just got it home from a new record store and removed the shrink wrap.

Near Mint is the highest price listed in all *Goldmine* price guides. Anything that exceeds this grade, in the opinion of both buyer and seller, is worth significantly more than the highest *Goldmine* book value.

Very Good Plus (VG+): Generally worth 50 percent of the Near Mint value.

A Very Good Plus record will show some signs that it was played and otherwise handled by a previous owner who took good care of it.

Record surfaces may show some slight signs of wear and may have slight scuffs or very light scratches that don't affect one's listening experience. Slight warps that do not affect the sound are OK.

The label may have some ring wear or discoloration, but it should be barely noticeable. The center hole will not have been misshapen by repeated play.

Picture sleeves and LP inner sleeves will have some slight ring wear, lightly turned-up corners, or a slight seam split. An LP jacket may have slight signs of wear also and may be marred by a cut-out hole, indentation or corner indicating it was taken out of print and sold at a discount.

In general, if not for a couple minor things wrong with it, this would be Near Mint. All but the most mint-crazy collectors will find a Very Good Plus record highly acceptable.

A synonym used by some collectors and dealers for "Very Good Plus" is "Excellent."

Very Good (VG): Generally worth 25 percent of the Near Mint value.

Many of the defects found in a VG+ record will be more pronounced in a VG disc.

Surface noise will be evident upon playing, especially in soft passages and during a song's intro and fade, but will not overpower the music otherwise. Groove wear will start to be noticeable, as will light scratches (deep enough to feel with a fingernail) that will affect the sound.

Labels may be marred by writing, or have tape or stickers (or their residue) attached. The same will be true of picture sleeves or LP covers. However, it will not have all of these problems at the same time, only two or three of them.

This *Goldmine* price guide lists Very Good as the lowest price. This, not the Near Mint price, should be your guide when determining how much a record is worth, as that is the price a dealer will normally pay you for a Near Mint record.

Good (G), Good Plus (G+): Generally worth 10-15 percent of the Near Mint value.

Good does not mean Bad! A record in Good or Good Plus condition can be put onto a turntable and will play through without skipping. But it will have significant surface noise and scratches and visible groove wear (on a styrene record, the groove will be starting to turn white).

A jacket or sleeve will have seam splits, especially at the bottom or on the spine. Tape, writing, ring wear or other defects will start to overwhelm the object.

If it's a common item, you'll probably find another copy in better shape eventually. Pass it up. But if it's something you have been seeking for years, and the price is right, get it... but keep looking to upgrade.

Poor (P), Fair (F): Generally worth 0-5 percent of the Near Mint price.

The record is cracked, badly warped, and won't play through without skipping or repeating. The picture sleeve is water damaged, split on all three seams and heavily marred by wear and writing. The LP jacket barely keeps the LP inside it. Inner sleeves are fully seam split, crinkled, and written upon.

Except for impossibly rare records otherwise unattainable, records in this condition should be bought or sold for no more than a few cents each.

Other grading considerations. Most dealers give a separate grade to the record and its sleeve or cover. In an ad, a record's grade is listed first, followed by that of the sleeve or jacket.

With **Still Sealed (SS)** records, let the buyer beware, unless it's a U.S. pressing from the last 10-15 years or so. It's too easy to re-seal one. Yes, some legitimately never-opened LPs from the 1960s still exist. But if you're looking for a specific pressing, the only way you can know for sure is to open the record. Also, European imports are not factory-sealed, so if you see them advertised as sealed, someone other than the manufacturer sealed them.

Common collecting abbreviations

In addition to the letters used to designate a record's grade, it's not uncommon to see other abbreviations used in dealer advertisements. Knowing the more common ones helps to prevent confusion. Here are some:

boot: bootleg (illegal pressing)
cc: cut corner
co: cutout

coh: cut-out hole
cov, cv, cvr: cover
demo: demonstration record (synonym for promo, this is the more common term overseas)
dh: drill hole
dj: disc jockey (promotional) record
ep: extended play (can be used for both 45s and LPs)
gf: gatefold (cover)
imp: import
ins: insert
lbl: label
m, mo: monaural (mono)
m/s: mono/stereo (usually used to describe a promo single that has the same song on both sides, with the only difference in the type of sound)
nap: (does) not affect play
noc: number on cover
nol: number on label
obi: not actually an abbreviation, "obi" is the Japanese word for "sash" and is used to describe the strip of paper usually wrapped around Japanese (and occasional US) pressings of LPs.
orig: original
pr, pro, promo: promotional record
ps: picture sleeve (the cover that appears with some 45s and most 7-inch extended play singles).
q: quadraphonic
re: reissue
rec: record
repro: reproduction
ri: reissue
rw: ring wear
s: stereo
sl: slight
sm: saw mark
soc: sticker on cover
sol: sticker on label
ss: still sealed
s/t: self-titled
st: stereo
sw: shrink wrap
toc: tape on cover
tol: tape on label
ts: taped seam
w/: with
wlp: white label promo
wobc: writing on back cover
woc: writing on cover
wofc: writing on front cover
wol: writing on label
wr: wear
wrp: warp
xol: "x" on label

Some notes on the pricing

The prices listed in this book were determined from many sources.

The more common items reflect a consensus of used record shops and collectors, plus prices in ads over the past few months. In some ways, these items are more difficult to get a handle on; they sell without much publicity because of their low value, thus they aren't reported as often.

The rarer items are often the matter of conjecture because they so rarely come up for public sale. A high auction price for a truly rare piece can be the only way such an item's "worth" can be gauged, no matter what someone says about the value being inflated. Records, as with all collectibles, are only worth what someone will pay for them.

Because of the inexact nature of this undertaking, that's why we always urge you to use a book such as this as a guide and not as the final word on pricing.

We, too, can always use more input on the subject. See the **How you can help** section for more information.

And by the way, the publisher of the book does not engage in the buying and selling of records. So the prices listed in here should not be construed as "offers to buy" or "offers to sell" from Krause Publications.

Some notes on promotional records

To list every promotional version of every record in this book would be a consumption of space better used for unique listings. It would come close to doubling the length of the book. Some selected promos are listed, either because they are unique – in other words, the only version of the record is promotional – or because there is a significant, verifiable price difference between the promo and stock copies.

Obviously, not all promos are created equal.

It's probably easier to say which promotional copies are *not* going to fetch a premium. Those are copies that are otherwise identical to stock copies – the same label, the same number, the same everything – but are merely stamped on the front or back cover with (usually) a gold "For Promotion Only" indicator. There's nothing special about these records for the most part; any time the record company wants to create a promo, it can take a stock copy and gold-stamp it!

These are known as "designate promos" and rarely get more than 10 percent above the price of a regular stock copy, if that. For some sought-after rare items, such as Tori Amos' early album *Y Kant Tori Read*, designate promos go for much, much less than copies not so designated.

Some albums that appear to be "designate promos" do have collector value. These are copies pressed on special "audiophile vinyl," the most notable of which are the "Quiex II" pressings from the Warner-Reprise-Geffen family. Some of these fetch as much as 4-5 times the regular

editions! These will *always* be marked on the cover with a sticker advertising the "Quiex II" record within.

Other promos of little collector value are those with a hole punch in the corner. This was Capitol's preferred method of creating promos during much of the 1970s. These are never worth more than the stock copy, and usually go for less.

Also, Columbia for a time merely used a "timing strip" on the front or back cover to designate a promo; these, too, also have little extra value above the stock copy. There is a major exception, though: The earliest promos for Bruce Springsteen's *Greetings From Asbury Park, N.J.* included both an attached timing strip and a glossy 8 1/2 x 11 "Bruce Springsteen Fact Sheet" glued to the back cover along the top. By the way, no white-label promos were ever pressed of this title.

Promos that *do* attract interest are those with custom promotional labels. Most of the time, these are white versions of the regular label, thus the term "white label promo." Of course, the label isn't always white; sometimes it's yellow or blue or pink or some other color. But it will always have as part of the label typesetting, "Promotional Copy" or "Audition Copy" or "Demonstration" or some other such term. Sometimes, the label will be almost identical to the stock versions, but some sort of words alluding to the promotional nature of the record will have been added to the typeset copy.

What makes these promos special? They are far more likely to have been mastered from the actual master mixdown tape, rather than a several-generations-removed copy, thus making them of higher sonic quality than later editions. They are among the first to come off the presses – after all, promos get sent out before stock copies Sometimes they are specially mastered to sound better over the air or through a store's loudspeakers. Regardless, they are sought after, and their value ranges from the same as a stock copy to as much as twice that of a stock copy.

Another rule of thumb when it comes to promos: In most cases, the more valuable a stock copy is, the less valuable the promo is. That's because in these instances, there are fewer stock copies known to exist than the promos.

Finally, be cautious when selling promos over the Internet. At least one prominent online auction site treats promos as illegal to buy and sell, and it has been known to remove these items from its site. So until the operators wise up and realize that buying and selling these on the secondary market is not illegal, regardless what the record companies claim, use synonyms when selling promos on eBay.

Making sense of the listings

Below is a sample listing that might be found in this book. The entries are actually in here, though we have put them under one fictitious artist heading to better demonstrate how to use the listings.

ANYARTISTS, THE
Several different groups.

12-Inch Singles					
ELEKTRA					
ED 5370 [DJ]	If I Can Just Get Through the Night (same on both sides)	1989	---	3.00	6.00
ED 5383 [DJ]	Something Real (same on both sides)	1989	---	3.00	6.00
45s					
ARGO					
5316	Walking Along/Please Kiss This Letter	1958	7.50	15.00	30.00
MGM					
13221	Fool That I Am/Fair Weather Lover	1964	7.50	15.00	30.00
OLD TOWN					
1000	Blue Valentine/Wonder Boy	1954	125.00	250.00	500.00
1000	Blue Valentine/Wonder Boy	1954	200.00	400.00	800.00
-- *Red vinyl*					
1003	Chapel of St. Clair/If I Loved You	1954	---	---	---
-- *Unreleased?*					
7-Inch Extended Plays					
CAPITOL					
EAP 1-488	(contents unknown)	1954	5.00	10.00	20.00
EAP 1-488 [PS]	Songs for Young Lovers, Part I	1954	5.00	10.00	20.00
EAP 1-1348	Talk to Me/They Came to Cordura// When No One Cares/Where Do You Go?	1959	7.50	15.00	30.00
EAP 1-1348 [PS]	Talk to Me	1959	7.50	15.00	30.00
Albums					
COLUMBIA					
CL 2495 [M]	Come Alive	1966	5.00	10.00	20.00
CS 9295 [S]	Come Alive	1966	6.25	12.50	25.00
PC2 36854 [(2)]	The River	1980	3.00	6.00	12.00
DISCOVERY					
DS-883	Dream	1983	3.00	6.00	12.00
-- *With Bob Florence*					

The artists' names are in bold capital letters. They are alphabetized, for the most part, the way our computer did, so blame anything that seems way out of line on that. We did make some manual corrections – artists who have numbers in their names are listed as if they spelled out the name; artists with "Mr." are listed as if their name was "Mister," and the same with "St." and "Saint."

On the next line under some artists are cross-references or other information we feel is helpful. In some cases, we know that the artist name actually was used by several different acts. When we haven't been able to ascertain with certainty which ones are which, they are left together.

When we have separated the artists, the most famous (usually, but not always, the most collectible) will be listed first, usually with the number (1) in parentheses after it. The rest will be arranged alphabetically by record label and will be followed by the appropriate parenthetical number, (2), (3) and so on. This way, you'll know if there is more than one entry for the same artist name; only those names listed more than once will have the supplementary number. Any that we don't know where they go will be listed last with a (U) for Unknown after it.

Records are listed in four formats, in this order: "12-Inch Singles"; "45s"; "7-Inch Extended Plays"; "Albums."

These are defined for the purposes of this book as follows:

A **12-inch single** is meant to promote or make available one particular song. These rarely have a name other than that of the song being promoted. Album-sized records with three or four songs on them that are not meant to specifically "sell" one song are 12-inch extended plays, and are listed under "Albums." Sometimes we had to make a judgment call as to where to put some of these.

A **45** is a seven-inch record, usually with one song on each side. It need not have a big hole. It need not even play

at 45 rpm – for simplicity's sake, we've included Columbia Microgroove 33 1/3 rpm singles of the late 1940s and early 1950s in this category. They always have a note attached to them explaining what they are. Sometimes we list a 45 with more than one song on a side; either that's because the record was sold as a 45 or it was part of a record company's regular numbering system for 45s.

A **7-Inch Extended Play**, a product of the 1950s and early 1960s, is a hybrid. Most of the time they contain two songs on each side and had big holes, like 45s. But they almost always came with cardboard sleeves, like albums. Again, until only a few years ago, price guides always treated these items as inseparable. Consumers, however, often treated EPs like 45s – they threw out the covers. Reflecting that, all EP listings here have separate lines, and values, for the cover and the record.

An **album** is defined here as a 10- or 12-inch record (never 7 inches) that has a small hole and isn't a 12-inch single. Defining it any more than that is problematical. Some albums have only one song on a side, others have over a dozen; some play for 15 minutes, others for over an hour; some albums even play at 45 rpm rather than the standard 33 1/3 rpm. Unless noted, however, all albums are assumed to be 33 1/3s. No 78s are listed under albums.

Under each format listing, the records are sorted alphabetically by label, which are printed in all capital letters, then numerically within each label, ignoring prefixes. The one exception is with RCA Victor 45s, which are arranged with APBO issues first, then PB issues, then other issues in order of prefix. (Those who have the first edition will realize this is a different order than the last time. It's a computer glitch, and yes, we're working on it. If you have any preference on the order in which the RCA 45s should be listed, we'd like to know.)

After many of the numbers is a number or letter in brackets. These designate something special about the listing as follows:

DJ: some sort of promotional copy, usually for radio stations and not meant for public sale.

EP: extended play album. Only used with album listings for 12-inch releases with 4 to 6 tracks and not as long as a regular album.

M: mono record.

P: partially stereo record. Rarely are records advertised as such; the determination has been made by careful listening.

PD: picture disc (the artwork is actually part of the record; these proliferated in the late 1970s and early 1980s and tend to have inferior sound quality)

PS: picture sleeve (this is the value for the sleeve alone; combine the record and sleeve value to get an estimated worth for the two together).

Q: quadraphonic record.

R: rechanneled stereo record. These will usually be labeled with such terms as "Electronically Re-Channeled for Stereo"; "Enhanced for Stereo"; "Simulated Stereo"; or "Duophonic." But sometimes they aren't labeled as rechanneled.

S: stereo record.

10: a 10-inch LP.

(x) where x is a number: the number of records in a set. This is in parentheses inside the brackets so that in those rare instances where they exist, 10-record sets won't be confused with 10-inch LPs.

Most albums after 1968 do not have a stereo content designation. After 1968, if no designation is listed, it's probably stereo, though not necessarily. More importantly, it means that there was only one purchasing option available (except for the quadraphonic years of 1972-1977).

In the next, widest, column, we list the titles.

In the 12-inch single listings, we mention whether the version is extended, or how long it is, or something to identify it. We also mention, when known, whether a record has the same version on both sides.

For 45s, we list both the A- and B-side.

Each EP has two listings, one with its contents in order, one with the title of the EP as listed on the cover. In many cases, the title of the EP is found nowhere on the actual label – another reason to list the record and its sleeve separately.

If the contents of the EP are preceded by an asterisk (*), we know that these are the songs on this record, but we're not sure this is the correct order. Readers with this information are welcome to supply confirmation.

As most albums are almost worthless without a cover, they have one listing with the title as shown on the cover (assuming a title is shown on the cover). Most album listings have a prefix, usually from one to five letters. These prefixes often tell you whether your album is a first pressing and can have a considerable effect on an album's value. For proof, look up Bruce Springsteen and see what an album with a "KC" prefix goes for compared to the same title with a "PC" prefix.

The next column lists the year of release. Please note that the year of release and the year of recording are not necessarily the same! For example, if an album had several singles taken from it, the later singles may not have come out until another year, even though all of the singles have the same year on them. Most of the "corrections" we received in year of release were caused by this confusion.

That said, some of these may be off by a year; sometimes a record is released in December of the year before or January of the year after. Other years we can only guess the decade, and the year will have a question mark in it.

The next three columns are the values in very good, very good plus, and near mint condition. For all but the rarest pieces, the Very Good Plus value is twice the Very Good value, and the Near Mint value is twice the VG+ listing or four times the VG listing.

In some cases, dashes appear in the pricing column. That means that the VG or VG+ value is under two dollars (bargain bin, yard sale, thrift shop material). If all three columns have dashes, there is some other reason, and we mention that in the explanatory notes below the listing. Every item with no value listed in any column is explained. If not, it's our error.

Finally, many items have a descriptive line in italics under the entry. This often purveys important information that plays a role in the above record's value, such as label design, cover design or colored vinyl. Sometimes, relatively insignificant differences can make a huge difference in value. Just look at the Beatles or Elvis Presley listings for proof.

How you can help

Conservatively speaking, this book has 150,000 listings by thousands of artists. All of this information is located in a growing database of records, which will make both future price guides and *Goldmine* magazine better products in the long run.

But as you look through this edition of the *Standard Catalog of American Records,* you'll see that we need help in several areas. Certain parts of this book aren't as good as they could be, and we know you can help.

While any information is helpful, here are areas where the most help is needed:

Stereo and other unusual 7-inch pressings of the 1958-63 era. Record companies tried numerous 7-inch alternatives to regular mono 45s in this era. We know that many labels, including Columbia, RCA Victor, MGM, Warner Bros., ABC-Paramount, Roulette, King, and even Carlton and Big Top, released stereo singles in this period. All of these are collectible, almost without regard to artist.

Some of these are documented here, but we need more information.

Extended plays. Thousands of extended play 7-inch singles are listed in this book. Most of them are certainly collectible, and many fetch healthy sums. But some of them we still don't know about.

Anywhere you see the words "(contents unknown)," we'd like to know exactly what's on the record. What we need is side 1 and side 2, plus sleeve variations. As the titles of extended plays are often not listed on the records, we feel that actually listing the songs will be of greater help to the collector.

We received much good information in the past two years. But to make it even better, follow these guidelines:

-- Use the *record*, not the jacket, to determine the exact order of songs. Often, the titles on the sleeve are arranged to look better and don't necessarily correspond to the playing order.

-- Not all EPs list Side 1 and Side 2 explicitly. So how do you tell? Look for the master numbers, which are usually found below the main number. On most EPs, the master number for Side 1 is one smaller than the master number for Side 2. For example, one of the Perry Como EPs listed in these pages has a Side 1 master number of "E2PW-0173" and a Side 2 number of "E2PW-0174." Another example: One of the Joni James EPs has a Side 1 master number of "57-EP-291" and a Side 2 number of "57-EP-292." You get the idea.

Also, on those EP listings with an asterisk before the contents, we need confirmation of the exact order of tracks.

So if you're an EP collector, you can play a big role in helping us.

Picture sleeves. Again, we didn't list a sleeve we weren't sure about. If you have something we haven't listed, let us know.

Phantom picture sleeves. OK, so we goofed once in a while in the first edition. Among the top picture sleeve collectors, there is a strong suspicion that at least some picture sleeves that are said to exist really do not! Thus the designation "phantom sleeve."

As research continues, we'll probably come up with others that have always been assumed to exist but really don't. Also, one of these "phantom" sleeves, which we first mentioned in the second edition of the *Goldmine Price Guide to 45 RPM Records*, has turned up since then ("El Matador" by the Kingston Trio).

In here, we still list the ones we had in the first edition, but with no values attached to them and with the following notice: "Rumored to exist, but without conclusive evidence, we will delete this from future editions." And we will do so, if no one can prove beyond a shadow of a doubt that they own legitimate U.S.-made copies of these mystery sleeves.

B-sides. Some records are listed as "(B-side unknown)." In many cases, it's because a record never got past the promo stage; in others, the record just hasn't crossed too many paths. Again, readers filled in hundreds of these "unknown" B-sides. If you can make some of these other B-sides known, it would be appreciated.

Mitch Ryder's "Sock It To Me Baby!" It's a long-held story in record collecting circles: Originally the single had a line where Mitch Ryder is singing, "Feels like a punch," mumbling it to the point where the last word sounds obscene. According to the story, the line was hastily re-recorded to say "Hits me like a PUNCH!" with a very heavy emphasis on the last word.

We've confirmed that the first version really exists. But what we still don't know is how someone can tell which version they are getting without having to play the 45. We're looking for someone who has both variations in their collection so the two can be compared.

Our readers helped clear up the "Rhapsody in the Rain" mystery; maybe you can clear this one up also.

Very early 45s. We know that Capitol, MGM and

Columbia, to name three, used different 45 RPM numbering systems in 1949-50 than the ones that became standard. Our information on these is somewhat sketchy. Again, if you have any of these (not to mention Columbia Microgroove 7-inch 33s from the era), let us know.

Early 45s on colored vinyl. Many of the early, extremely rare R&B and blues records were pressed on both black and other colors of wax (usually red). Sources conflict as to which of these are on colored vinyl only, black vinyl only, or both. Most of these are so rare that I've never seen them myself. So any authoritative help on sorting these out would be appreciated.

Late mono LPs. In 1967 and 1968, record companies somewhat abruptly stopped making monaural albums. Some of the mono albums are quite rare now. We're interested in what might exist that we don't have. We're also interested in deleting listings of mono albums that really don't exist.

Also, we've found that the Mercury family of labels, including Philips, Smash and Fontana, consciously packaged stereo albums inside mono sleeves in 1967. These can be identified by the stamped number starting with "2/6" in the trail-off wax, instead of starting with simply "2" (mono) or "6" (stereo). Copies of these in "true mono" may be much more rare than previously thought. If you have any of these "2/6" albums, let us know so we can indicate them.

Quadraphonic LPs. The general guides were pretty good at keeping up with quad LPs, which often feature radically different mixes than their stereo counterparts. If it's not listed, we'd like to know about it.

Photos. Sending us photos, photocopies or computer scans of items helps us, as these serve to prove the existence of the item in question.

We hope that future editions of this, and all, *Goldmine* price guides can have some cool photos of rarities. We also can accept computer scans e-mailed to us as attachments or sent on a disc. Some of our photos in this book and others came from computer scans. You can contact us for more information if you think you have something that might be worth putting in a future edition of any of our books.

We receive many contributions and suggestions, so not everyone's help can be acknowledged. But rest assured that even your one little correction helps in the long run. By the way, if you sent us corrections for a prior edition of this, or any other, book I compiled, and they aren't reflected in here, there's no need to send them again; if they reached me, I still have them. Some submissions take more time to go through than others.

You may contact the author by mail:

Tim Neely
Goldmine Standard Catalog of American Records
700 E. State St.
Iola, WI 54990

or by phone:

(715) 445-2214 or 4612, ext. 782

or by e-mail:

neelyt@krause.com

If you write or e-mail, enclose a daytime phone number or return e-mail where I can reply in case I have any questions.

Acknowledgments

"With God all things are possible." (Matt.19:26) And so another edition of the *Standard Catalog of American Records* is complete.

But this book also would not have been possible without a large supply of help from all over, and not just from a benevolent deity.

First, here at Krause Publications, a big thanks to Greg Loescher, the former publisher and now editor of *Goldmine*. He brought me on board five years ago with a specific goal in mind: a *Standard Catalog* for record collecting. He has never been less than encouraging through the entire process, even as we at times expressed doubts that it was possible.

In the growing Krause book department, I wish to thank several people. Managing editor Don Gulbrandsen kept an eye on things as they went along, injected some realism into the process and was patient, as were the other people in books who were awaiting the final product.

Proofreading 150,000-plus lines of six-point type was a thankless task, but the Krause proofreaders were up to it. Thanks to all who had a hand in eliminating as many typos as humanly possible. Thanks also to Tom Dupuis for the cover design.

We used a new database system to put this book together. This process will allow for a more timely book, as what used to take 2-3 months to do now will take 2-3 weeks, and potentially even less once all the bugs are worked out. Thanks to Kathy Ott, Jeff Kenton and Bonnie Tetzlaff in our computer department for making this transition possible, if not always smooth. (We're getting there, though.)

Many of the illustrations came from my collection. Most of those that didn't came from Good Rockin' Tonight, which runs four auctions a year of rare and valuable records and memorabilia. Thanks to them for their continued cooperation in our price guides. For more information on Good Rockin' Tonight, call (800) 531-1899 or surf to www.collectors.com/grt.

Then there were the *Goldmine* readers, purchasers of prior price guides, dealers and collectors who filled in holes, corrected things, helped with pricing and, in general, made this a better book. I've received dozens, perhaps hundreds, of letters, e-mails, faxes and phone calls with suggestions for additions and corrections to errors in my other books. Some of the corrections were made immediately and are reflected within here. Others have taken some time, and should be reflected in future books. A sincere thank you to everyone who has taken the time out to contact me.

An unbelievable outpouring of information came from our readers. With apologies to anyone I left out, I wish to thank the following for helping to make the second edition more comprehensive and more accurate than the first:

Bob Anderson; James Anstey; Tom Arkle; Norb Aschom; David Barnett (Johnny Mathis info); Bob Barth; Steve Bartlett; Erma Benson; Charles Berger; Jack Berkus;

John Beznik; Harry Blesy; Susan Bowman; Dave Boyle; Gale Britton; Julie Burkbuckler; Betty Chrisman; Joseph A. Ciccone; Jeff Collins; Gary Conley;

Leo Costanzo; Jerry Crown; Scott Dietrich; Denise Duesterbeck; Bruce Dumais; Mark Erbach; Brett Fagerness; Mark Feldberg; Lou Ferraro; Bill Files;

Michael Forney; Russell Forsythe; Kerry Fowler; Rob Friedman; Michael Furmall; Ken Gadsberry; J.E. Gardner; Grant Gehlson; Larry Gerhard; Wayne Garrett;

Al Goodwin; Denise Gregoire; Tom Groff; Tom Grosh, Very English and Rolling Stone; Bill Hamilton; Derek Henderson; Donna Henley; Ed Hippo; Ron Holbach; Dave Holmes;

Joe Hood; Larry Hough; Stewart Joyner; Jack Juarez; Judy June; Stephen Kauffman; Mike Kearney; Peter Kuchenbrod; Steve Leafgren; Julius Levine;

Peter Lindberg; "Ug" Lippard; Alan Lowell (picture sleeves); Ernie Mabrey (late mono LPs); James Mains; Rick Malone; Jim Martin; Karen McAlister; Rich McCarty; Kent McCombs (Rick Nelson listings);

Mike McKenna; Chris McLeer; Richard Mertz; Chuck Miller; Ed Moench; Mike Monnat; Ken Mullen; Al Mundy; Dave Nelson; John F. Nielson, M.D.;

Randy Oakes; Craig Orkney; Nancy Parker; Dick Parr; Charles Pearce; Carlos Perez; Jef Michael Piehler (Neil Young listings); Steve Pimper; David Price; Randy Price;

David Pullen; Mark P. Rafter; George Ravelo; Sean Reilly; Peter Reinert; Jeff Richner; James Roberton; Ben Rogers; Dick Rosemont; Bob Schaefer;

Steve Schroeder; Malcolm Senior; Judy Shaffer; Michael Sharritt; Dan Shorr, POPS Resale & Consignment; Mal Sillett; Stephen E. Simon; Brian Sklut; Dave G. Smith; Ron Smith;

Tim Spies; Richard Spitznogle; Byron Stewart; Dave Stiles; Dave Stimson; Francine Stinson; James Stoick; Billy Streicher; Clay Summers; David Swadley;

John Tobler; David Town; Jeff Turkali; Keith Venturoni; Jim Vogan; John Wade; James Walker; John S. Weathers; Matt Weber; Rod Wells;

Kemper Whaley; Norman White; Bill Wood; Ed Worcester; Robert Ziella.

I'd also like to thank various family members for bearing with my lengthy periods of unavailability, especially my mother, Judith Neely.

Finally, as with the first edition of this book, I wish to dedicate this to two people who will never see this. Both of them died in 1997, before the first edition became a reality. Both of them played a key role in starting a young man off to a lifelong hobby of record collecting.

First is Dick Koffel of Koffel's Curiosity Shop in Telford, Pa. My record collecting began in his store in 1973 with a purchase of eight 45s for 10 cents each, one of which was a well-worn copy of Capitol 5112, "I Want to Hold Your Hand" / "I Saw Her Standing There" by the Beatles. He continued to encourage me by giving me deals he wouldn't give to his adult customers and giving me first dibs on new stashes of 45s and LPs. Even after adulthood set in, I continued to visit and buy, and sometimes he'd still give me good deals.

And second is my father, William Neely. He waited for me as I scrounged through piles of records at yard sales; he "loaned" me money for those large hauls, knowing that a 15-year-old could never repay, but he kept loaning anyway; he always looked for more records for my growing collection; and he remained encouraging right up until November 29, 1997, when he passed away.

I miss both of you greatly and always will.

Tim Neely
Iola,Wisconsin
September 1, 2000

A

A.F.O. EXECUTIVES WITH TAMI LYNN

Albums

A.F.O.

Number	Title (A Side/B Side)	Yr	VG	VG+	NM
5002 [M]	A Compendium	1962	37.50	75.00	150.00

ABBA

Also see BJORN AND BENNY.

45s

ATLANTIC

Number	Title (A Side/B Side)	Yr	VG	VG+	NM
PR 380 [DJ]	Happy New Year (mono/stereo)	1980	3.00	6.00	12.00
PR 390 [DJ]	Happy New Year	1980	3.00	6.00	12.00
—One-sided promo					
3035	Waterloo/Watch Out	1974	—	2.50	5.00
3035 [PS]	Waterloo	1974	3.75	7.50	15.00
—Sleeve is promo only					
3209	Honey Honey/Dance (While the Music Still Goes On)	1974	—	2.50	5.00
3240	Hasta Manana/Ring Ring	1975	—	2.50	5.00
3265	SOS/Man in the Middle	1975	—	2.50	5.00
3310	I Do, I Do, I Do, I Do, I Do/Bang-a-Boomerang	1975	—	2.50	5.00
3315	Mamma Mia/Tropical Loveland	1976	—	2.50	5.00
3346	Fernando/Rock Me	1976	—	2.00	4.00
3346	Fernando/Tropical Loveland	1976	—	2.00	4.00
3372	Dancing Queen/That's Me	1976	—	2.00	4.00
3387	Knowing Me, Knowing You/Happy Hawaii	1977	—	2.00	4.00
3387 [PS]	Knowing Me, Knowing You/Happy Hawaii	1977	—	2.50	5.00
3434	Money, Money, Money/Crazy World	1977	—	2.00	4.00
3434 [PS]	Money, Money, Money/Crazy World	1977	—	3.00	6.00
3449	The Name of the Game/I Wonder (Departure)	1977	—	2.00	4.00
3457	Take a Chance on Me/I'm a Marionette	1978	—	2.00	4.00
3457 [PS]	Take a Chance on Me/I'm a Marionette	1978	—	3.00	6.00
3574	Does Your Mother Know/Kisses of Fire	1979	—	2.00	4.00
3574 [PS]	Does Your Mother Know/Kisses of Fire	1979	—	2.50	5.00
3609	Voulez-Vous/Angeleyes	1979	—	2.00	4.00
3609 [PS]	Voulez-Vous/Angeleyes	1979	—	2.50	5.00
3629	Chiquitita/Lovelight	1979	—	2.00	4.00
3630	Chiquitita (Spanish Version)/I Have a Dream (Spanish Version)	1979	—	2.50	5.00
3652	Gimme! Gimme! Gimme! (A Man After Midnight)/The King Has Lost His Crown	1980	—	2.00	4.00
3776	The Winner Takes It All/Elaine	1980	—	2.00	4.00
3806	Super Trouper/The Piper	1981	—	2.00	4.00
3806 [PS]	Super Trouper/The Piper	1981	—	2.00	4.00
3826	On and On and On/Lay All Your Love on Me	1981	—	2.00	4.00
3889	When All Is Said and Done/Should I Laugh or Cry	1982	—	—	3.00
3889 [PS]	When All Is Said and Done/Should I Laugh or Cry	1982	—	—	3.00
4031	The Visitors/Head Over Heels	1982	—	—	3.00
4031 [PS]	The Visitors/Head Over Heels	1982	—	—	3.00
89881	One of Us/Should I Laugh or Cry	1983	—	—	3.00
89881 [PS]	One of Us/Should I Laugh or Cry	1983	—	2.00	4.00
89948	The Day Before You Came/Cassandra	1982	—	—	3.00

Albums

ATLANTIC

Number	Title (A Side/B Side)	Yr	VG	VG+	NM
PR 300 [DJ]	Abba	1978	7.50	15.00	30.00
PR 432 [DJ]	A Collection of Hits	1982	7.50	15.00	30.00
PR 436 [(2) DJ]	The Abba Special	1983	12.50	25.00	50.00
SD 16000	Voulez-Vous	1979	2.50	5.00	10.00
SD 16009	Greatest Hits, Vol. 2	1979	3.00	6.00	12.00
SD 16023	Super Trouper	1980	2.50	5.00	10.00
SD 18101	Waterloo	1974	3.00	6.00	12.00
SD 18146	Abba	1975	3.00	6.00	12.00
SD 18189	Greatest Hits	1976	3.00	6.00	12.00
SD 18207	Arrival	1977	3.00	6.00	12.00
SD 19114	Greatest Hits	1977	2.50	5.00	10.00
SD 19115	Arrival	1977	2.50	5.00	10.00
SD 19164	The Album	1978	2.50	5.00	10.00
SD 19332	The Visitors	1981	2.50	5.00	10.00
80036 [(2)]	The Singles — The First Ten Years	1982	3.75	7.50	15.00
80142	I Love Abba	1983	2.50	5.00	10.00
81675	Abba Live	1986	3.00	6.00	12.00

CBS INTERNATIONAL

Number	Title (A Side/B Side)	Yr	VG	VG+	NM
DAL 40301	Gracias Por La Musica	1980	10.00	20.00	40.00

—Spanish-language versions of some of their hits, this LP was pressed in the U.S.

K-TEL

Number	Title (A Side/B Side)	Yr	VG	VG+	NM
NU 9510	The Magic of Abba	1978	3.75	7.50	15.00

NAUTILUS

Number	Title (A Side/B Side)	Yr	VG	VG+	NM
NR-20	Arrival	1981	7.50	15.00	30.00

—Audiophile vinyl

ABBEY TAVERN SINGERS, THE

Albums

V.I.P.

Number	Title (A Side/B Side)	Yr	VG	VG+	NM
402 [M]	We're Off to Dublin in the Green	1966	10.00	20.00	40.00
S-402 [S]	We're Off to Dublin in the Green	1966	12.50	25.00	50.00

ABRAMS, MISS, AND THE STRAWBERRY POINT SCHOOL THIRD GRADE CLASS

Albums

REPRISE

Number	Title (A Side/B Side)	Yr	VG	VG+	NM
MS 2098	Abrams, Miss, and the Strawberry Point School Third Grade Class	1972	3.00	6.00	12.00

ABSTRACTS, THE

45s

POMPEII

Number	Title (A Side/B Side)	Yr	VG	VG+	NM
66679	Smell the Incense/See the Birdies	1968	5.00	10.00	20.00

Albums

POMPEII

Number	Title (A Side/B Side)	Yr	VG	VG+	NM
SD 6002	The Abstracts	1968	10.00	20.00	40.00

ACCENTS, THE

Several different groups.

45s

Number	Title (A Side/B Side)	Yr	VG	VG+	NM
ACCENT					
1036	Voice of the Boyous/Where Will You Be	1956	7.50	15.00	30.00
1037	The Name Song/This Ole Body	1956	7.50	15.00	30.00
BANGAR					
605	Wherever There's a Will/Howlin' for My Baby	1964	3.75	7.50	15.00
629	Searchin'/You Don't Love Me	1964	3.75	7.50	15.00
648	Road Runner/Why	1965	3.75	7.50	15.00
BRUNSWICK					
55100	Wiggle Waggle/Dreamin' and Schemin'	1958	3.75	7.50	15.00
55123	I Give My Heart to You/Ching-a-Ling	1959	3.75	7.50	15.00
C-R-C					
1017	I've Got Better Things to Do/Then He Starts to Cry	1964	5.00	10.00	20.00
—Featuring Sandi					
CHALLENGE					
59254	Tell Me/Better Watch Out Boy	1964	3.75	7.50	15.00
59294	Sweet Talk/Tell Me	1965	3.00	6.00	12.00
CHARTER					
1017	I've Got Better Things to Do/Then He Starts to Cry	1964	3.75	7.50	15.00
—Featuring Sandi					
COMMERCE					
5012	Tell Me/Better Watch Out Boy	1964	5.00	10.00	20.00
CORAL					
62151	Autumn Leaves/Anything You Want Me to Be	1959	3.75	7.50	15.00
GARRETT					
4008	Wherever There's a Will/Howlin' for My Baby	1964	5.00	10.00	20.00
4014	Road Runner/Why	1965	5.00	10.00	20.00
JERDEN					
728	Linda Lou/Stickey	1964	3.00	6.00	12.00
—Featurning Ron Peterson					
JUBILEE					
5353	Red Light/22 Del Rio Ave.	1958	3.75	7.50	15.00
KARATE					
529	He's the One/On the Run	1966	3.75	7.50	15.00
LIBERTY					
55813	I Really Love You/What Do You Want to Do (Little Darlin')	1965	3.00	6.00	12.00
M-PAC!					
7216	New Girl/Do You Need a Good Man	1964	5.00	10.00	20.00
MERCURY					
72154	Enchanted Garden/Tell Me Now	1963	2.50	5.00	10.00
ONE-DERFUL					
4833	You Better Think Again/Who You Gonna Love	1965	5.00	10.00	20.00
RCA VICTOR					
74-0127	Love Is a Many-Splendored Thing/Yours Until Tomorrow	1969	—	3.00	6.00
SULTAN					
5500	Rags to Riches/Where Can I Go?	1961	15.00	30.00	60.00
VEE JAY					
484	Our Wonderful Love/A Hundred Walkin' Cats	1963	2.00	4.00	8.00

ACE

45s

ANCHOR

Number	Title (A Side/B Side)	Yr	VG	VG+	NM
21000	How Long/Sniffin' About	1975	—	2.50	5.00
21002	Rock & Roll Runaway/Know How It Feels	1975	—	2.50	5.00

Albums

ANCHOR

Number	Title (A Side/B Side)	Yr	VG	VG+	NM
ANCL-2001	Five-a-Side (An Ace Album)	1975	3.00	6.00	12.00
ANCL-2013	Time for Another	1975	3.00	6.00	12.00
ANCL-2020	No Strings	1977	3.00	6.00	12.00

ACE, JOHNNY

45s

Number	Title (A Side/B Side)	Yr	VG	VG+	NM
DUKE					
102	My Song/Follow the Rule	1952	20.00	40.00	80.00
107	Cross My Heart/Angel	1953	15.00	30.00	60.00
112	The Clock/Ace's Wild	1953	15.00	30.00	60.00
118	Saving My Love for You/Yes Baby	1953	10.00	20.00	40.00
128	Please Forgive Me/You've Been Gone So Long	1954	10.00	20.00	40.00
132	Never Let Me Go/Burley Cutie	1954	10.00	20.00	40.00
136	Pledging My Love/No Money	1954	10.00	20.00	40.00
136	Pledging My Love/Anymore	1954	10.00	20.00	40.00
144	Anymore/How Can You Be So Mean	1955	10.00	20.00	40.00
148	So Lonely/I'm Crazy	1956	7.50	15.00	30.00
154	Still Love You So/Don't You Know	1956	7.50	15.00	30.00
FLAIR					
1015	Midnight Hours Journey/Trouble and Me	1953	37.50	75.00	150.00
—B-side by Earl Forrest					

7-Inch Extended Plays

DUKE

Number	Title (A Side/B Side)	Yr	VG	VG+	NM
80	(contents unknown)	1955	37.50	75.00	150.00
80 [PS]	Memorial Album	1955	37.50	75.00	150.00
81	(contents unknown)	1955	37.50	75.00	150.00
81 [PS]	Tribute to Johnny Ace	1955	37.50	75.00	150.00

Albums

Number	Title (A Side/B Side)	Yr	VG	VG+	NM
ABC DUKE					
DLPX-71	Memorial Album	1974	5.00	10.00	20.00
DUKE					
DLP-70 [10]	Memorial Album for Johnny Ace	1955	400.00	800.00	1200.
DLP-71 [M]	Memorial Album for Johnny Ace	1956	125.00	250.00	500.00
—With no playing card on front cover					
DLP-71 [M]	Memorial Album for Johnny Ace	1961	50.00	100.00	200.00
—With playing card on front cover					

Number	Title (A Side/B Side)	Yr	VG	VG+	NM
DLP-71 [M]	Memorial Album for Johnny Ace	1961	2000.	3000.	4000.
—Playing card cover; red vinyl					
MCA					
27014	Memorial Album	1983	2.00	4.00	8.00

ACE, SONNY

45s

Number	Title (A Side/B Side)	Yr	VG	VG+	NM
ATLANTIC					
2364	Wooleh Booleh/Chili Peppers	1966	2.50	5.00	10.00

ACE SPECTRUM

45s

Number	Title (A Side/B Side)	Yr	VG	VG+	NM
ATLANTIC					
3012	Don't Send Nobody Else/Don't Let Me Be Lonely Tonight	1974	—	2.50	5.00
3281	I Just Want to Spend the Night with You/Trust Me	1975	—	2.50	5.00
3296	Without You/Keep Holding On	1975	—	2.50	5.00
3353	Live and Learn/Just Like in the Movies	1976	—	2.50	5.00

Albums

Number	Title (A Side/B Side)	Yr	VG	VG+	NM
ATLANTIC					
SD 7299	Inner Spectrum	1974	3.00	6.00	12.00
SD 18143	Low Rent Rendezvous	1975	3.00	6.00	12.00
SD 18185	Just Like in the Movies	1976	3.00	6.00	12.00

ACKLES, DAVID

45s

Number	Title (A Side/B Side)	Yr	VG	VG+	NM
ELEKTRA					
45634	Down River/L.A. Route and Chicago	1968	2.00	4.00	8.00
45676	That's No Reason to Cry/Subway to the Country	1970	2.00	4.00	8.00
45712	One Night Stand/Be My Friend	1971	—	3.00	6.00
45797	Love's Enough/American Gothic	1972	—	3.00	6.00
45810	Oh California/One Night Stand	1972	—	3.00	6.00

Albums

Number	Title (A Side/B Side)	Yr	VG	VG+	NM
COLUMBIA					
KC 32466	Five & Dime	1973	3.00	6.00	12.00
ELEKTRA					
EKS-74022	David Ackles	1968	3.75	7.50	15.00
EKS-74060	Subway to the Country	1970	3.00	6.00	12.00
EKS-75032	American Gothic	1972	3.00	6.00	12.00

ACKLIN, BARBARA

45s

Number	Title (A Side/B Side)	Yr	VG	VG+	NM
BRUNSWICK					
55319	Fool, Fool, Fool (Look in the Mirror)/ Your Sweet Loving	1967	2.00	4.00	8.00
55355	I've Got You Baby/Old Matchmaker	1967	2.00	4.00	8.00
55379	Love Makes a Woman/Come and See My Baby	1968	2.00	4.00	8.00
55388	Just Ain't No Love/Please Sunrise Please	1968	2.00	4.00	8.00
55388 [PS]	Just Ain't No Love/Please Sunrise Please	1968	3.75	7.50	15.00
55399	Am I the Same Girl/Be By My Side	1969	2.00	4.00	8.00
55412	Seven Days of Night/Raggedy Ride	1969	2.00	4.00	8.00
55421	After You/More Ways Than One	1969	2.00	4.00	8.00
55433	Is It Me/Someone Else's Arms	1970	2.00	4.00	8.00
55440	I Did It/I'm Living with a Memory	1970	2.00	4.00	8.00
55447	I Can't Do My Thing/Make the Man Love You	1971	2.00	4.00	8.00
55465	Lady, Lady, Lady/Stop, Look and Listen	1971	2.00	4.00	8.00
55486	I Call It Trouble/Love You Are Mine Today	1972	2.00	4.00	8.00
55501	I'm Gonna Bake a Man/I Call It Trouble	1973	—	3.00	6.00
CAPITOL					
3892	Raindrops/Here You Come Again	1974	—	2.50	5.00
4013	Special Loving/You Gave Him Everything, But I Gave Him Love	1974	—	2.50	5.00
4061	Give Me Some of Your Sweet Love/Fire Love	1975	—	2.50	5.00

Albums

Number	Title (A Side/B Side)	Yr	VG	VG+	NM
BRUNSWICK					
BL 754129	Great Soul Hits	1967	6.25	12.50	25.00
BL 754137	Love Makes a Woman	1968	5.00	10.00	20.00
BL 754148	Seven Days of Night	1969	5.00	10.00	20.00
BL 754156	Someone Else's Arms	1970	5.00	10.00	20.00
BL 754166	I Did It	1971	5.00	10.00	20.00
BL 754187	I Call It Trouble	1972	5.00	10.00	20.00
CAPITOL					
ST-11377	A Place in the Sun	1975	3.00	6.00	12.00

ACORNS, THE

45s

Number	Title (A Side/B Side)	Yr	VG	VG+	NM
UNART					
2006	Angel/I'm Gonna Stick to You	1958	5.00	10.00	20.00
2015	Please Come Back/Your Name and Mine	1959	5.00	10.00	20.00

ACTION, THE

45s

Number	Title (A Side/B Side)	Yr	VG	VG+	NM
CAPITOL					
5949	Never Ever/24th Hour	1967	2.00	4.00	8.00

AD LIBS, THE

Probably all the same group.

45s

Number	Title (A Side/B Side)	Yr	VG	VG+	NM
AGP					
101	New York in the Dark/Human	1968	25.00	50.00	100.00
BLUE CAT					
102	The Boy from New York City/Kicked Around	1965	3.75	7.50	15.00
114	Ask Anybody/He Ain't No Angel	1965	2.50	5.00	10.00
119	On the Corner/Oo-Wee Oh Me Oh My	1965	2.50	5.00	10.00
123	Just a Down Home Girl/Johnny My Boy	1966	2.50	5.00	10.00
CAPITOL					
2944	Love Me/Know All About You	1970	—	3.00	6.00
JOHNNIE BOY					
01	Santa's On His Way/I Stayed Home (New Year's Eve)	19??	2.00	4.00	8.00

Number	Title (A Side/B Side)	Yr	VG	VG+	NM
KAREN					
1527	Think of Me/Every Boy and Girl	1966	5.00	10.00	20.00
PHILIPS					
40461	Don't Ever Leave Me/You're in Love	1967	2.00	4.00	8.00
SHARE					
101	You're Just a Rolling Stone/Show a Little Appreciation	1969	2.00	4.00	8.00
104	Giving Up/Appreciation	1969	2.00	4.00	8.00
106	The Boy from New York City/Nothing Worse Than Being Alone	1969	2.00	4.00	8.00

ADAM'S APPLES

45s

Number	Title (A Side/B Side)	Yr	VG	VG+	NM
BRUNSWICK					
55330	Don't Take It Out on This World/Don't You Want Me Home	1967	25.00	50.00	100.00
55367	You Are the One I Love/Stop Along the Way	1968	12.50	25.00	50.00

ADAM, MIKE AND TIM

45s

Number	Title (A Side/B Side)	Yr	VG	VG+	NM
PRESS					
9728	Little Baby/You're the Reason Why	1964	2.50	5.00	10.00

ADAMS, ART

45s

Number	Title (A Side/B Side)	Yr	VG	VG+	NM
CHERRY					
1004	Rock Crazy Baby/Indian Joe	1960	25.00	50.00	100.00
1018	Dancing Doll/She Don't Live Here Anymore	1960	25.00	50.00	100.00

ADAMS, BILLY

45s

Number	Title (A Side/B Side)	Yr	VG	VG+	NM
AMY					
893	You and Me/Go (Go On, Get Out of Here Now)	1963	3.00	6.00	12.00
APT					
25072	My Happiness/Big M	1962	3.00	6.00	12.00
CAPITOL					
4308	Count Every Star/Peggy's Party	1959	6.25	12.50	25.00
4373	Can't Get Enough/The Gods Were Angry With Me	1960	6.25	12.50	25.00
DECCA					
30724	Baby I'm Bugged/Short Hair and Turtle Neck Sweater	1958	7.50	15.00	30.00
DOT					
15689	You Heard Me Knocking/True Love Will Come Your Way	1958	7.50	15.00	30.00
FERN					
807	Darling Take My Hand/Tender Years	1961	6.25	12.50	25.00
808	Tattle Tale/Born to Be a Loser	1961	6.25	12.50	25.00
812	Rip Van Winkle/Sleep Baby Sleep	1961	6.25	12.50	25.00
813	Comic Strip/Call Me	1961	6.25	12.50	25.00
HOME OF THE BLUES					
239	Looking for My Baby/Had the Blues	1962	2.50	5.00	10.00
242	My Happiness/Big M	1962	5.00	10.00	20.00
NAU VOO					
802	You've Gotta Have a Duck Tail/Walking Star	1959	25.00	50.00	100.00
805	Return of the All American Boy/That's My Baby	1959	18.75	37.50	75.00
808	Blue Eyed Ella/Fun House	1959	18.75	37.50	75.00
QUINCY					
932	Rock Pretty Mama/(B-side unknown)	195?	500.00	1000.	1500.
SUN					
389	Got My Mojo Workin'/Betty and Dupree	1964	5.00	10.00	20.00
391	Trouble in My Mind/Lookin' for Mary Ann	1964	5.00	10.00	20.00
394	Reconsider Baby/Ruby Jane	1964	5.00	10.00	20.00
401	Open the Door, Richard/Rock Me Baby	1966	5.00	10.00	20.00

ADAMS, CLIFF

45s

Number	Title (A Side/B Side)	Yr	VG	VG+	NM
DOT					
16385	Funny Kind of Feeling/Keep Off My Mountain	1962	2.50	5.00	10.00

ADAMS, FAYE

45s

Number	Title (A Side/B Side)	Yr	VG	VG+	NM
ATLANTIC					
1007	Sweet Talk/Watch Out, I Told You	1953	12.50	25.00	50.00
HERALD					
416	Shake a Hand/I've Got to Leave You	1953	7.50	15.00	30.00
—Black vinyl					
416	Shake a Hand/I've Got to Leave You	1953	25.00	50.00	100.00
—Red vinyl					
419	I'll Be True/Happiness to My Soul	1953	6.25	12.50	25.00
423	Say a Prayer/Every Day	1954	6.25	12.50	25.00
429	Somebody, Somewhere, Someday /Crazy Mixed-Up World	1954	6.25	12.50	25.00
434	Hurts Me to My Heart/Ain't Gonna Tell	1954	6.25	12.50	25.00
439	I Owe My Heart to You/ Love Ain't Nothin' to Play With	1954	6.25	12.50	25.00
444	Anything for a Friend/Your Love Has My Heart Burning	1955	6.25	12.50	25.00
450	You Ain't Been True/My Greatest Desire	1955	6.25	12.50	25.00
457	Angels Tell Me/Tag Along	1955	6.25	12.50	25.00
462	No Way Out/Same Old Me	1955	6.25	12.50	25.00
470	Teen-Age Heart/Witness to the Crime	1956	6.25	12.50	25.00
480	Takin' You Back/Don't Forget to Smile	1956	6.25	12.50	25.00
489	Anytime, Anyplace, Anywhere/The Hammer Keeps Knockin'	1956	6.25	12.50	25.00
512	Shake a Hand/I'll Be True	1958	5.00	10.00	20.00
IMPERIAL					
5443	Keeper of My Heart/So Much	1957	5.00	10.00	20.00
5456	Johnny Lee/You're Crazy	1957	5.00	10.00	20.00
5471	I Have a Twinkle in My Eye/Someone Like You	1957	5.00	10.00	20.00
5525	When We Kiss/Everything	1958	5.00	10.00	20.00

Number	Title (A Side/B Side)	Yr	VG	VG+	NM
LIDO					
603	That's All Right/It Made Me Cry	1960	3.00	6.00	12.00
606	It Can't Be Wrong/I Waited So Long	1960	3.00	6.00	12.00
SAVOY					
1606	Cry, You Crazy Heart/Step Up and Rescue Me	1960	3.00	6.00	12.00
4357	Sinner Man/God	197?	—	2.50	5.00
WARWICK					
590	Shake a Hand/It Hurts to My Heart	1960	3.00	6.00	12.00
620	Johnny, Don't/Obey My Rules	1961	3.00	6.00	12.00
638	It Can't Be Wrong/It's Nice to Know	1961	3.00	6.00	12.00
Albums					
COLLECTABLES					
COL-5122	Golden Classics	1988	2.50	5.00	10.00
WARWICK					
W 2031 [M]	Shake a Hand	1961	150.00	300.00	600.00

ADAMS, MIKE, AND THE RED JACKETS

Number	Title (A Side/B Side)	Yr	VG	VG+	NM
Albums					
CROWN					
CST-255 [S]	Twist Contest	1962	7.50	15.00	30.00
CST-312 [S]	Surfer's Beat	1963	7.50	15.00	30.00
—Black vinyl					
CST-312 [S]	Surfer's Beat	1963	25.00	50.00	100.00
—Red vinyl					
CLP-5255 [M]	Twist Contest	1962	6.25	12.50	25.00
CLP-5312 [M]	Surfer's Beat	1963	6.25	12.50	25.00

ADAMS, RICHIE

Number	Title (A Side/B Side)	Yr	VG	VG+	NM
45s					
BELTONE					
1001	No Mistakin' It/The Right Way	1961	3.75	7.50	15.00
1011	Two Initials (In a Heart)/What Took You So Long	1961	3.75	7.50	15.00
CONGRESS					
217	I Understand/Lookin' for the Blues	1964	3.75	7.50	15.00
226	Are You Changing/The King	1964	3.75	7.50	15.00
232	Slippin' Away/What Am I	1965	3.75	7.50	15.00
248	Every Window in the City/I Ain't Gonna Make It Without You	1965	3.75	7.50	15.00
256	Road to Nowhere/I Can't Escape from You	1965	15.00	30.00	60.00
IMPERIAL					
5806	Something Inside of Me Died/I Got Eyes	1962	3.75	7.50	15.00
5838	My Prayer of Love/Pakistan	1962	3.75	7.50	15.00
5856	It's Worth It/Test of Love	1962	3.75	7.50	15.00
MCA					
41182	The Best of the Rest of Our Lives/Warm	1980	—	2.00	4.00
MGM					
13629	You Were Mine/Better Off Without You	1966	2.50	5.00	10.00
P.I.P.					
6519	Mamacita/Lisa Lisa	1976	—	2.00	4.00
RIBBON					
6910	Lonely One/Tell Me Baby Did You Wait	1960	3.00	6.00	12.00
6913	Back to School/Don't Go, My Love, Don't Go	1960	3.00	6.00	12.00

ADDEO, LEO

Number	Title (A Side/B Side)	Yr	VG	VG+	NM
Albums					
RCA CAMDEN					
CAL-510 [M]	Hawaii in Hi-Fi	1960	3.75	7.50	15.00
CAS-510 [S]	Hawaii in Stereo	1960	5.00	10.00	20.00
CAL-594 [M]	More Hawaii in Hi-Fi	1961	3.75	7.50	15.00
CAS-594 [S]	More Hawaii in Hi-Fi	1961	5.00	10.00	20.00
CAL-672 [M]	Great Standards with a Hawaiian Touch	1962	3.00	6.00	12.00
CAS-672 [S]	Great Standards with a Hawaiian Touch	1962	3.75	7.50	15.00
CAL-726 [M]	Organ and Chimes Play Christmas Carols	1962	3.00	6.00	12.00
CAS-726 [S]	Organ and Chimes Play Christmas Carols	1962	3.75	7.50	15.00
CAL-759 [M]	Songs of Hawaii	1963	3.00	6.00	12.00
CAS-759 [S]	Songs of Hawaii	1963	3.75	7.50	15.00
CAL-807 [M]	Calypso and Other Island Favorites	1963	3.00	6.00	12.00
CAS-807 [S]	Calypso and Other Island Favorites	1963	3.75	7.50	15.00
CAL-828 [M]	"Hello Dolly" and Other Favorites	1964	3.00	6.00	12.00
CAS-828 [S]	"Hello Dolly" and Other Favorites	1964	3.75	7.50	15.00
CAL-853 [M]	Hawaiian Paradise	1964	3.00	6.00	12.00
CAS-853 [S]	Hawaiian Paradise	1964	3.75	7.50	15.00
CAL-901 [M]	Far Away Places	1965	3.00	6.00	12.00
CAS-901 [S]	Far Away Places	1965	3.75	7.50	15.00
CAL-977 [M]	Musical Orchids from Hawaii	1966	3.00	6.00	12.00
CAS-977 [S]	Musical Orchids from Hawaii	1966	3.75	7.50	15.00
CAL-2134 [M]	"Love Is a Hurtin' Thing" and Other Favorites	1966	3.00	6.00	12.00
CAS-2134 [S]	"Love Is a Hurtin' Thing" and Other Favorites	1966	3.75	7.50	15.00
CAL-2211 [M]	The Magic of Hawaii	1967	3.00	6.00	12.00
CAS-2211 [S]	The Magic of Hawaii	1967	3.75	7.50	15.00
RCA VICTOR					
LPM-2414 [M]	Paradise Regained	1961	3.75	7.50	15.00
LSA-2414 [S]	Paradise Regained	1961	7.50	15.00	30.00

ADDEO, NICKY

Number	Title (A Side/B Side)	Yr	VG	VG+	NM
45s					
EARLS					
1533	Gloria/Bring Back Your Heart	19??	2.50	5.00	10.00
MELODY					
1417	Where There Is Love/You Can Depend on Me	1964	6.25	12.50	25.00
REVELATION					
7-101	Danny Boy/A Lovely Way to Spend An Evening	1964	125.00	250.00	500.00
SAVOY					
200	Gloria/Bring Back Your Heart	1963	50.00	100.00	200.00
—Black vinyl					
200	Gloria/Bring Back Your Heart	1963	100.00	200.00	400.00
—Red vinyl					
200	Gloria/Bring Back Your Heart	1963	75.00	150.00	300.00
—Green vinyl					
SELSOM					
104	Over the Rainbow/Fool #2	1965	50.00	100.00	200.00

ADDERLEY, CANNONBALL

Number	Title (A Side/B Side)	Yr	VG	VG+	NM
45s					
BLUE NOTE					
1737	Autumn Leaves (Part 1)/Autumn Leaves (Part 2)	1959	2.50	5.00	10.00
1738	Somethin' Else (Part 1)/Somethin' Else (Part 2)	1959	2.50	5.00	10.00
1739	One for Daddy-O (Part 1)/One for Daddy-O (Part 2)	1959	2.50	5.00	10.00
CAPITOL					
2064	Oh Babe/Games	1967	—	3.00	6.00
2299	Hamba Nami/Gumba Gumba	1968	—	3.00	6.00
2399	Zorba/Sweet Emma	1969	—	3.00	6.00
2698	Country Preacher/Hummin'	1970	—	2.50	5.00
2798	Marabi/Oh Babe	1970	—	2.50	5.00
2939	The Price You Got to Pay to Be Free/Run Away Sunshine	1970	—	2.50	5.00
3041	Down in Black Bottom/Get Up Off Your Knees	1971	—	2.50	5.00
5281	Goodbye Charlie/Little Boy with Sad Eyes	1964	2.00	4.00	8.00
5374	Matchmaker/Chavaleh	1965	2.00	4.00	8.00
5457	Shake a Lady/Cyclops	1965	2.00	4.00	8.00
5648	Money in the Pocket/Hear Me Talking to You	1966	—	3.00	6.00
5736	Sticks/Cannon's Theme	1966	—	3.00	6.00
5798	Mercy, Mercy, Mercy/Games	1966	—	3.50	7.00
5877	Why Am I Treated So Bad/I'm On My Way	1967	—	3.00	6.00
5968	Walk Tall/Do, Do, Do	1967	—	3.00	6.00
FANTASY					
706	Inside Straight/Saudade	1973	—	2.50	5.00
MERCURY					
71712	Limehouse Blues/Stars Fell on Alabama	1960	2.50	5.00	10.00
RIVERSIDE					
415	Things Are Getting Better (Part 1)/Things Are Getting Better (Part 2)	1958	3.00	6.00	12.00
428	Poor Butterfly (Part 1)/Poor Butterfly (Part 2)	1958	3.00	6.00	12.00
432	This Year (Part 1)/This Year (Part 2)	1959	3.00	6.00	12.00
442	Jeanine (Part 1)/Jeanine (Part 2)	1959	3.00	6.00	12.00
443	The Word Song/Sassier	1959	3.00	6.00	12.00
454	Sack of Woe (Part 1)/Sack of Woe (Part 2)	1960	2.50	5.00	10.00
457	African Waltz/Kelly Blue	1961	2.50	5.00	10.00
465	The Chant (Part 1)/The Chant (Part 2)	1961	2.50	5.00	10.00
4501	The Uptown/Something Different	1962	2.00	4.00	8.00
4509	Gemini (Part 1)/Gemini (Part 2)	1962	2.00	4.00	8.00
4528	Blue Brass Groove/This Here	1963	2.00	4.00	8.00
4541	The Jive Samba/Lillie	1963	2.00	4.00	8.00
4562	Brother John/Tengo Tango	1964	2.00	4.00	8.00
4573	Nippon Soul/Tengo Tango	1964	2.00	4.00	8.00
Albums					
ARCHIVE OF FOLK AND JAZZ					
261	Cannonball Adderley and John Coltrane	1973	3.00	6.00	12.00
—Abridged reissue of Limelight 86009					
BLUE NOTE					
BM-LA169-F	Somethin' Else	1973	2.50	5.00	10.00
—Reissue					
LT-169	Somethin' Else	1981	2.50	5.00	10.00
—Another reissue					
BLP-1595 [M]	Somethin' Else	1958	37.50	75.00	150.00
—"Deep groove" version (deep indentation under label on both sides)					
BLP-1595 [M]	Somethin' Else	1958	25.00	50.00	100.00
—Regular version with W. 63rd St. address on label					
BLP-1595 [M]	Somethin' Else	1963	6.25	12.50	25.00
—With New York, USA address on label					
BST-1595 [S]	Somethin' Else	1959	25.00	50.00	100.00
—"Deep groove" version (deep indentation under label on both sides)					
BST-1595 [S]	Somethin' Else	1959	18.75	37.50	75.00
—Regular version with W. 63rd St. address on label					
B1-46338	Somethin' Else	1997	5.00	10.00	20.00
—Audiophile reissue					
BST-81595	Somethin' Else	1984	2.50	5.00	10.00
—"The Finest in Jazz Since 1939" label					
BST-81595	Somethin' Else	199?	6.25	12.50	25.00
—Classic Records reissue					
BST-81595 [S]	Somethin' Else	1963	5.00	10.00	20.00
—With New York, USA address on label					
BST-81595 [S]	Somethin' Else	1966	3.75	7.50	15.00
—With "A Division of Liberty Records" on label					
CAPITOL					
ST-162	Cannonball in Person	1968	3.75	7.50	15.00
SKAO-404	Country Preacher	1970	3.75	7.50	15.00
ST-484	Experience in E, Tensity, Dialogues	1970	3.75	7.50	15.00
SWBB-636 [(2)]	The Price You Got to Pay to Be Free	1971	3.75	7.50	15.00
STBB-697 [(2)]	Walk Tall/Quiet Nights	1971	3.75	7.50	15.00
SWBO-812 [(2)]	Cannonball Adderley and Friends	1971	3.75	7.50	15.00
SWBO-846 [(2)]	The Black Messiah	1972	3.75	7.50	15.00
ST 2203 [S]	Domination	1964	5.00	10.00	20.00
T 2203 [M]	Domination	1964	3.75	7.50	15.00
ST 2216 [S]	Fiddler on the Roof	1965	5.00	10.00	20.00
T 2216 [M]	Fiddler on the Roof	1965	3.75	7.50	15.00
ST 2284 [S]	Live Session	1965	5.00	10.00	20.00
T 2284 [M]	Live Session	1965	3.75	7.50	15.00
SM-2399	Cannonball Adderley — Live!	1976	2.50	5.00	10.00
ST 2399 [S]	Cannonball Adderley — Live!	1965	5.00	10.00	20.00
T 2399 [M]	Cannonball Adderley — Live!	1965	3.75	7.50	15.00
ST 2531 [S]	Great Love Themes	1966	5.00	10.00	20.00
T 2531 [M]	Great Love Themes	1966	3.75	7.50	15.00
ST 2617 [S]	Why Am I Treated So Bad?	1966	5.00	10.00	20.00
T 2617 [M]	Why Am I Treated So Bad?	1966	3.75	7.50	15.00
SM-2663	Mercy, Mercy, Mercy!	1976	2.50	5.00	10.00
ST-8-2663 [S]	Mercy, Mercy, Mercy!	1967	5.00	10.00	20.00
—Capitol Record Club edition					
ST 2663 [S]	Mercy, Mercy, Mercy!	1967	3.75	7.50	15.00
T 2663 [M]	Mercy, Mercy, Mercy!	1967	6.25	12.50	25.00
ST 2822 [S]	74 Miles Away — Walk Tall	1967	3.75	7.50	15.00
T 2822 [M]	74 Miles Away — Walk Tall	1967	6.25	12.50	25.00
SKAO 2939	The Best of Cannonball Adderley	1968	3.75	7.50	15.00
ST 2987	Accent on Africa	1968	3.75	7.50	15.00

Number	Title (A Side/B Side)	Yr	VG	VG+	NM
ST-11008	Fiddler on the Roof	1972	3.00	6.00	12.00
—Reissue of 2216					
SABB-11120 [(2)]	The Soul of the Bible	1973	3.75	7.50	15.00
ST-11121	Happy People	1973	3.00	6.00	12.00
SVBB-11233 [(2)]	Cannonball Adderley and Friends	1974	3.00	6.00	12.00
—Reissue of 812					
ST-11484	Music, You All	1975	3.00	6.00	12.00
SM-11817	Cannonball Adderley and Friends, Vol. 1	1978	2.50	5.00	10.00
SM-11838	Cannonball Adderley and Friends, Vol. 2	1978	2.50	5.00	10.00
SN-16002	The Best of Cannonball Adderley	1979	2.00	4.00	8.00
SN-16153	Mercy, Mercy, Mercy!	1981	2.00	4.00	8.00
—Budget-line reissue					
DOBRE					
1008	Cannonball, Volume 1	1977	3.00	6.00	12.00
EMARCY					
EMS-2-404 [(2)]	Beginnings	1976	3.75	7.50	15.00
MG-36043 [M]	Julian "Cannonball" Adderley	1955	15.00	30.00	60.00
MG-36063 [M]	Julian "Cannonball" Adderley and Strings	1956	15.00	30.00	60.00
MG-36077 [M]	In the Land of Hi-Fi	1956	15.00	30.00	60.00
MG-36110 [M]	Sophisticated Swing	1957	15.00	30.00	60.00
MG-36135 [M]	Cannonball's Sharpshooters	1958	15.00	30.00	60.00
MG-36146 [M]	Jump for Joy	1958	15.00	30.00	60.00
FANTASY					
FSP 2 [DJ]	Big Man Sampler	1975	5.00	10.00	20.00
OJC-032	Things Are Getting Better	1982	2.50	5.00	10.00
OJC-035	Cannonball Adderley Quintet in San Francisco	1982	2.50	5.00	10.00
OJC-105	Know What I Mean?	1984	2.50	5.00	10.00
OJC-142	Cannonball Adderley Sextet in New York	1985	2.50	5.00	10.00
OJC-258	African Waltz	1987	2.50	5.00	10.00
OJC-306	The Cannonball Adderley Quintet Plus	1988	2.50	5.00	10.00
OJC-361	Portrait of Cannonball	1989	2.50	5.00	10.00
OJC-435	Nippon Soul	1990	3.00	6.00	12.00
9435	Inside Straight	1973	3.00	6.00	12.00
9445	Love, Sex and the Zodiac	1974	3.00	6.00	12.00
9455	Pyramid	1974	3.00	6.00	12.00
9505	Lovers	1975	3.00	6.00	12.00
79004 [(2)]	Phenix	1975	3.75	7.50	15.00
79006 [(2)]	Big Man	1976	3.75	7.50	15.00
LANDMARK					
LLP-1301	The Cannonball Adderley Collection Vol. 1: Them Dirty Blues	1987	2.50	5.00	10.00
LLP-1302	The Cannonball Adderley Collection Vol. 2: Cannonball's Bossa Nova	1987	2.50	5.00	10.00
LLP-1303	The Cannonball Adderley Collection Vol. 3: Jazz Workshop Revisited	1987	2.50	5.00	10.00
LLP-1304	The Cannonball Adderley Collection Vol. 4: Cannonball and the Poll-Winners	1987	2.50	5.00	10.00
LLP-1305	The Cannonball Adderley Collection Vol. 5: At the Lighthouse	1987	2.50	5.00	10.00
LLP-1306	The Cannonball Adderley Collection Vol. 6: Cannonball Takes Charge	1987	2.50	5.00	10.00
LLP-1307	The Cannonball Adderley Collection Vol. 7: Cannonball in Europe	1987	2.50	5.00	10.00
LIMELIGHT					
LM 82009 [M]	Cannonball and Coltrane	1964	6.25	12.50	25.00
—Reissue of Mercury 20449					
LS 86009 [S]	Cannonball and Coltrane	1964	5.00	10.00	20.00
—Reissue of Mercury 60449					
MERCURY					
MG-20449 [M]	Cannonball Adderley Quintet in Chicago	1959	12.50	25.00	50.00
MG-20530 [M]	Jump for Joy	1960	10.00	20.00	40.00
—Reissue of EmArcy 36146					
MG-20531 [M]	Cannonball's Sharpshooters	1960	10.00	20.00	40.00
—Reissue of EmArcy 36135					
MG-20616 [M]	Cannonball En Route	1961	10.00	20.00	40.00
MG-20652 [M]	The Lush Side of Cannonball Adderley	1961	10.00	20.00	40.00
—Reissue of EmArcy 36063					
SR-60449 [S]	Cannonball Adderley Quintet in Chicago	1960	10.00	20.00	40.00
SR-60530 [S]	Jump for Joy	1960	7.50	15.00	30.00
SR-60531 [S]	Cannonball's Sharpshooters	1960	7.50	15.00	30.00
SR-60616 [S]	Cannonball En Route	1961	7.50	15.00	30.00
SR-60652 [R]	The Lush Side of Cannonball Adderley	1961	7.50	15.00	30.00
MILESTONE					
9030	Cannonball Adderley in New Orleans	197?	3.00	6.00	12.00
9106	The Sextet	198?	2.50	5.00	10.00
47001 [(2)]	Eight Giants	1973	3.75	7.50	15.00
47029 [(2)]	The Japanese Concerts	1975	3.00	6.00	12.00
47039 [(2)]	Coast to Coast	1976	3.75	7.50	15.00
47053 [(2)]	What I Mean	1979	3.75	7.50	15.00
47059 [(2)]	Alabama/Africa	1982	3.00	6.00	12.00
PABLO LIVE					
2308238	What Is This Thing Called Soul	1984	2.50	5.00	10.00
RIVERSIDE					
RLP 12-269 [M]	Portrait of Cannonball	1958	12.50	25.00	50.00
RLP 12-286 [M]	Things Are Getting Better	1959	12.50	25.00	50.00
RLP 12-303 [M]	Cannonball Takes Charge	1959	12.50	25.00	50.00
RLP 12-311 [M]	Cannonball Adderley Quintet in San Francisco	1959	12.50	25.00	50.00
RLP 12-322 [M]	Them Dirty Blues	1960	12.50	25.00	50.00
RLP 344 [M]	Cannonball Adderley Quintet at the Lighthouse	1960	10.00	20.00	40.00
RLP 355 [M]	Cannonball Adderley and the Poll-Winners	1960	10.00	20.00	40.00
RLP 377 [M]	African Waltz	1961	10.00	20.00	40.00
RLP 388 [M]	Cannonball Adderley Quintet Plus	1961	10.00	20.00	40.00
RLP 404 [M]	Cannonball Adderley Sextet In New York	1962	7.50	15.00	30.00
RLP 416 [M]	Cannonball's Greatest Hits	1962	10.00	20.00	40.00
RLP 433 [M]	Know What I Mean?	1962	7.50	15.00	30.00
RLP 444 [M]	Jazz Workshop Revisited	1963	7.50	15.00	30.00
RLP 455 [M]	Cannonball's Bossa Nova	1963	7.50	15.00	30.00
RLP 477 [M]	Nippon Soul — Recorded in Concert in Tokyo	1964	6.25	12.50	25.00
RM 499 [M]	Cannonball in Europe	1967	5.00	10.00	20.00
RLP 1128 [S]	Things Are Getting Better	1959	10.00	20.00	40.00
RLP 1148 [S]	Cannonball Takes Charge	1959	10.00	20.00	40.00
RLP 1157 [S]	Cannonball Adderley Quintet in San Francisco	1959	10.00	20.00	40.00
RLP 1170 [S]	Them Dirty Blues	1960	10.00	20.00	40.00
RS 3038	The Best of Cannonball Adderley	1968	3.75	7.50	15.00
RS 3041	Planet Earth	1969	3.75	7.50	15.00
6051	Know What I Mean?	197?	3.00	6.00	12.00
—Reissue of 9433					
6062	Cannonball Adderley Quintet in San Francisco	197?	3.00	6.00	12.00
—Reissue of 1157					
6108	Cannonball Adderley Sextet in New York	197?	3.00	6.00	12.00
—Reissue of 9404					
6122	Things Are Getting Better	197?	3.00	6.00	12.00
—Reissue of 1128					
RS 9344 [S]	Cannonball Adderley Quintet at the Lighthouse	1960	7.50	15.00	30.00
RS 9355 [S]	Cannonball Adderley and the Poll-Winners	1960	7.50	15.00	30.00
RS 9377 [S]	African Waltz	1961	7.50	15.00	30.00
RS 9388 [S]	Cannonball Adderley Quintet Plus	1961	7.50	15.00	30.00
RS 9404 [S]	Cannonball Adderley Sextet In New York	1962	7.50	15.00	30.00
RS 9416 [S]	Cannonball's Greatest Hits	1962	7.50	15.00	30.00
RS 9433 [S]	Know What I Mean?	1962	7.50	15.00	30.00
RS 9444 [S]	Jazz Workshop Revisited	1963	7.50	15.00	30.00
RS 9455 [S]	Cannonball's Bossa Nova	1963	7.50	15.00	30.00
RS 9477 [S]	Nippon Soul — Recorded in Concert in Tokyo	1964	6.25	12.50	25.00
RS 9499 [S]	Cannonball in Europe	1967	3.75	7.50	15.00
SAVOY					
MG-12018 [M]	Presenting Cannonball	1955	20.00	40.00	80.00
—Band pictured on cover					
MG-12018 [M]	Presenting Cannonball	196?	10.00	20.00	40.00
—Cannonballs pictured on cover with band members merely listed					
SAVOY JAZZ					
SJC-401	Presenting Cannonball	1985	2.50	5.00	10.00
—Reissue of Savoy 12018					
SJL-1195	Discoveries	1989	2.50	5.00	10.00
SJL-2206	Spontaneous Combustion	1976	3.00	6.00	12.00
WONDERLAND/RIVERSIDE					
RLP 1435 [M]	A Child's Introduction to Jazz	196?	12.50	25.00	50.00
—Adderley narrates an album introducing the works of such artists as Armstrong, Monk, Waller, etc.					

ADDERLEY, CANNONBALL AND NAT

Albums

Number	Title (A Side/B Side)	Yr	VG	VG+	NM
LIMELIGHT					
LM 82032 [M]	Them Adderleys	1964	6.25	12.50	25.00
LS 86032 [S]	Them Adderleys	1964	5.00	10.00	20.00

ADDRISI, DICK

45s

Number	Title (A Side/B Side)	Yr	VG	VG+	NM
VALIANT					
742	You're Bad/Excuse Me	1966	3.00	6.00	12.00

ADDRISI BROTHERS, THE

45s

Number	Title (A Side/B Side)	Yr	VG	VG+	NM
BELL					
45434	Somebody Found Her/Who Do You Think I Am	1974	—	2.00	4.00
BRAD					
003	I'll Be True/Everybody's Happy	1958	8.75	17.50	35.00
BUDDAH					
566	Slow Dancin' Don't Turn Me On (Short)/Slow Dancin' Don't Turn Me On (Long)	1977	—	2.50	5.00
579	Does She Do It Like She Dances/Baby, Love Is a Two-Way Street	1977	—	2.00	4.00
587	Never My Love/Emergency	1977	—	2.00	4.00
COLUMBIA					
45521	We've Got to Get It On Again/You Make It All Worthwhile	1972	—	2.50	5.00
45610	One Last Time/I Can Feel You	1972	—	2.50	5.00
45705	Lifetime/I Can Count on You	1972	—	2.50	5.00
DEL-FI					
4116	Cherrystone/Lilies Grow High	1959	7.50	15.00	30.00
4120	Saving My Kisses/Un Jarro	1959	7.50	15.00	30.00
4125	It's Love/Back to the Old Salt Mine	1959	7.50	15.00	30.00
4130	Gonna See My Baby/Ven Ami	1959	6.25	12.50	25.00
ELEKTRA					
47203	Honey Come Home/Red-Eye Flight	1981	—	2.00	4.00
IMPERIAL					
5715	What a Night for Love/Poor Little Girls	1960	5.00	10.00	20.00
POM POM					
4160	The Dance Is Over/Socialite	1962	6.25	12.50	25.00
PRIVATE STOCK					
45012	Wait for Me/You Made All the Difference	1975	—	2.00	4.00
SCOTTI BROTHERS					
500	Ghost Dancer/Ghost Dancer	1979	—	2.00	4.00
500 [PS]	Ghost Dancer/Ghost Dancer	1979	—	3.00	6.00
—Promo-only title sleeve					
506	As Long As the Music Keeps Playing/(B-side unknown)	1979	—	2.00	4.00
VALIANT					
720	Mr. Love/Side by Side	1965	3.00	6.00	12.00
6047	Love Me Baby/The Way You Look at Him	1964	3.00	6.00	12.00
6058	C'mon Home Baby/Little Miss Sad	1964	3.75	7.50	15.00
WARNER BROS.					
5268	The Dance Is Over (Dance with Me)/Sleeping Beauty	1962	3.75	7.50	15.00
7249	Time to Love/Good News	1968	2.50	5.00	10.00

Albums

Number	Title (A Side/B Side)	Yr	VG	VG+	NM
BUDDAH					
BDS-5694	Addrisi Brothers	1977	2.50	5.00	10.00
COLUMBIA					
KC 31296	We've Got to Get It On Again	1972	3.00	6.00	12.00

ADELPHIS, THE

45s

Number	Title (A Side/B Side)	Yr	VG	VG+	NM
RIM					
2020	Darlin' It's You/Kathleen	1958	37.50	75.00	150.00
—Artist's name listed as "Adelphies"					
2020	Darlin' It's You/Kathleen	1958	25.00	50.00	100.00
—Artist's name spelled correctly as "Adelphis"					

Number	Title (A Side/B Side)	Yr	VG	VG+	NM

ADLIBS, THE

Not to be confused with THE AD LIBS, this is a British group.

Number	Title (A Side/B Side)	Yr	VG	VG+	NM
45s					
INTERPHON					
7717	Neighbour, Neighbour/Lovely Ladies	1965	2.50	5.00	10.00

ADMIRALS, THE

Number	Title (A Side/B Side)	Yr	VG	VG+	NM
45s					
KING					
4772	Oh Yes/Left with a Broken Heart	1955	62.50	125.00	250.00
4782	Close Your Eyes/Give Me Love	1955	62.50	125.00	250.00
4792	It's a Sad, Sad Feeling/Ow	1955	12.50	25.00	50.00
—With Lucky Millinder					

ADMIRATIONS, THE

More than one group.

Number	Title (A Side/B Side)	Yr	VG	VG+	NM
45s					
ATOMIC					
12871	Dear Lady/Memories Are Here to Stay	195?	50.00	100.00	200.00
BRUNSWICK					
55332	Hey Mama/Lonely Street	1967	5.00	10.00	20.00
HULL					
1202	Moonlight/Ain't It Funny	1965	50.00	100.00	200.00
KELLWAY					
108	Over the Rainbow/In My Younger Days	196?	2.50	5.00	10.00
MERCURY					
71521	The Bells of Roja Rita/Little Bo Poop	1959	10.00	20.00	40.00
71883	To the Aisle/Hey Senorita	1962	50.00	100.00	200.00
ONE-DERFUL					
4849	Wait Till I Get to Know You/(Instrumental)	1967	6.25	12.50	25.00
4851	Don't Leave Me/All for You	1967	6.25	12.50	25.00

ADORABLES, THE

Number	Title (A Side/B Side)	Yr	VG	VG+	NM
45s					
GOLDEN WORLD					
4	Daddy Please/Deep Freeze	1964	6.25	12.50	25.00
10	School's All Over/Be	1964	6.25	12.50	25.00
25	Ooh Boy!/Devil in His Eyes	1965	10.00	20.00	40.00
PEACOCK					
1924	The Drive/Baby, Come and Get It	1963	3.00	6.00	12.00

ADRIAN AND THE SUNSETS

Number	Title (A Side/B Side)	Yr	VG	VG+	NM
45s					
SUNSET					
602	Breakthrough/Cherry Pie	1963	10.00	20.00	40.00
602 [PS]	Breakthrough/Cherry Pie	1963	30.00	60.00	120.00
Albums					
SUNSET					
63-601 [M]	Breakthrough	1963	20.00	40.00	80.00
—Black vinyl					
63-601 [M]	Breakthrough	1963	37.50	75.00	150.00
—Multi-color vinyl					
SD 63-601 [S]	Breakthrough	1963	37.50	75.00	150.00
—Black vinyl					
SD 63-601 [S]	Breakthrough	1963	75.00	150.00	300.00
—Multi-color vinyl					

ADVANCEMENT, THE

Number	Title (A Side/B Side)	Yr	VG	VG+	NM
Albums					
PHILIPS					
PHS 600328	The Advancement	1969	10.00	20.00	40.00

ADVENTURERS, THE (1)

Number	Title (A Side/B Side)	Yr	VG	VG+	NM
45s					
COLUMBIA					
42227	Rock and Roll Uprising/My Mama Done Told Me	1961	10.00	20.00	40.00
Albums					
COLUMBIA					
CL 1747 [M]	Can't Stop Twistin'	1961	15.00	30.00	60.00
CS 8547 [S]	Can't Stop Twistin'	1961	20.00	40.00	80.00

ADVENTURERS, THE (U)

Number	Title (A Side/B Side)	Yr	VG	VG+	NM
45s					
BLUE ROCK					
4071	Something Bad (Is Happening)/Nobody Can Save Me	1968	2.00	4.00	8.00
CAPITOL					
F-4292	Rip Van Winkle/Trail Blazer	1959	3.75	7.50	15.00
COMPASS					
7010	Easy Baby/(These Days) A Good Girl Is So Hard to Find	1967	2.00	4.00	8.00
MECCA					
A-11	2 O'Clock Express/Shaggin'	1960	10.00	20.00	40.00
MIRACLE					
1	2 O'Clock Express/October Days	1960	5.00	10.00	20.00

AEROSMITH

Number	Title (A Side/B Side)	Yr	VG	VG+	NM
12-Inch Singles					
GEFFEN					
PRO-A-2882 [DJ]	Dude (Looks Like a Lady) (4 versions)	1987	2.00	4.00	8.00
45s					
COLUMBIA					
08536	Chip Away the Stone/S.O.S.	1989	—	2.00	4.00
10034	Train Kept a-Rollin'/Spaced	1974	—	3.00	6.00
10105	S.O.S. (Too Bad)/Lord of the Thighs	1975	—	3.00	6.00
10155	Sweet Emotion/Pandora's Box	1975	—	2.50	5.00
10206	Walk This Way/Round and Round	1975	—	3.00	6.00
10253	Toys in the Attic/You See Me Crying	1975	—	3.00	6.00
10278	Dream On/Somebody	1975	—	2.50	5.00
—Contains the full-length version of A-side					
10359	Last Child/Combination	1976	—	2.50	5.00
10407	Home Tonight/Pandora's Box	1976	—	2.50	5.00
10449	Walk This Way/Uncle Salty	1976	—	2.50	5.00
10516	Back in the Saddle/Nobody's Fault	1977	—	2.50	5.00
10637	Draw the Line/Bright, Light, Fright	1977	—	2.50	5.00
10699	Kings and Queens/Critical Mass	1978	—	2.50	5.00
10727	Get It Up/Milk Cow Blues	1978	—	2.50	5.00
10802	Come Together/Kings and Queens	1978	—	2.50	5.00
10880	Chip Away the Stone (Studio)//S.O.S./Chip Away the Stone (Live)	1979	—	3.00	6.00
11181	Remember (Walking in the Sand)/Bone to Bone (Coney Island White Fish Boy)	1980	—	2.50	5.00
45894	Dream On/Somebody	1973	—	3.00	6.00
—Contains a remixed, edited version of A-side					
46029	Pandora's Box/Same Old Song and Dance	1974	—	3.00	6.00
78499	Falling in Love (Is Hard on the Knees)/Fall Together	1997	—	—	2.00
—Small hole					
78499 [PS]	Falling in Love (Is Hard on the Knees)/Fall Together	1997	—	—	2.00
78569	Hole in My Soul/Falling Off	1997	—	—	2.00
78569 [PS]	Hole in My Soul/Falling Off	1997	—	—	2.00
78592	I Don't Want to Miss a Thing/Animal Crackers//Taste of India (Rock Remix)	1998	—	—	2.00
78592 [PS]	I Don't Want to Miss a Thing/Animal Crackers//Taste of India (Rock Remix)	1998	—	—	2.00
GEFFEN					
19143	Livin' on the Edge/Don't Stop	1993	—	—	3.00
19256	Cryin'/Walk On Down	1993	—	—	3.00
19264	Amazing/Fever	1993	—	—	3.00
19267	Crazy/Gotta Love It	1994	—	—	3.00
19377	Blind Man/Head First	1994	—	—	3.00
19927	The Other Side/My Girl	1990	—	—	3.00
19946	What It Takes/Monkey on My Back	1990	—	—	3.00
22845	Love in an Elevator/Young Lust	1989	—	—	3.00
22845 [PS]	Love in an Elevator/Young Lust	1989	—	—	3.00
27915	Rag Doll/St. John	1988	—	—	3.00
27915 [PS]	Rag Doll/St. John	1988	—	—	3.00
28240	Dude (Looks Like a Lady)/Simoriah	1987	—	—	3.00
28240 [PS]	Dude (Looks Like a Lady)/Simoriah	1987	—	—	3.00
28249	Angel/Girl Keeps Coming Apart	1987	—	—	3.00
28249 [PS]	Angel/Girl Keeps Coming Apart	1987	—	—	3.00
28814	Shela/Gypsy Boots	1986	—	2.00	4.00
Albums					
COLUMBIA					
A3S 187 [DJ]	Pure Gold from Rock 'n' Roll's Golden Boys	1976	12.50	25.00	50.00
—Promo-only compilation of the first three albums					
JC 32005	Aerosmith	1977	2.00	4.00	8.00
KC 32005	Aerosmith	1973	5.00	10.00	20.00
—Orange cover with back cover typo "Walking The Dig"					
KC 32005	Aerosmith	1973	3.75	7.50	15.00
—Orange cover with correct title "Walking The Dog"					
KC 32005	Aerosmith	1973	3.00	6.00	12.00
—Light blue cover, most (if not all) of which say "Featuring 'Dream On' " on front					
PC 32005	Aerosmith	1976	2.50	5.00	10.00
—Without bar code					
PC 32005	Aerosmith	1984	2.00	4.00	8.00
—With bar code					
JC 32847	Get Your Wings	1977	2.00	4.00	8.00
KC 32847	Get Your Wings	1974	3.00	6.00	12.00
KCQ 32847 [Q]	Get Your Wings	1974	6.25	12.50	25.00
PC 32847	Get Your Wings	1976	2.50	5.00	10.00
—Without bar code					
PC 32847	Get Your Wings	1984	2.00	4.00	8.00
—With bar code					
JC 33479	Toys in the Attic	1977	2.50	5.00	10.00
PC 33479	Toys in the Attic	1975	3.00	6.00	12.00
—Without bar code					
PC 33479	Toys in the Attic	1984	2.00	4.00	8.00
—With bar code					
PCQ 33479 [Q]	Toys in the Attic	1975	6.25	12.50	25.00
JC 34165	Rocks	1976	2.50	5.00	10.00
—Some copies have "Rocks" in quotes on the cover, others don't; no difference in value					
PC 34165	Rocks	1976	3.00	6.00	12.00
—Without bar code. Some copies have "Rocks" in quotes on the cover, others don't; no difference in value					
PC 34165	Rocks	1984	2.00	4.00	8.00
—With bar code					
PCQ 34165 [Q]	Rocks	1976	6.25	12.50	25.00
JC 34856	Draw the Line	1977	3.00	6.00	12.00
PC 34856	Draw the Line	198?	2.00	4.00	8.00
PC2 35564 [(2)]	Live! Bootleg	1978	3.75	7.50	15.00
FC 36050	Night in the Ruts	1979	2.50	5.00	10.00
PC 36050	Night in the Ruts	1984	2.00	4.00	8.00
FC 36865	Aerosmith's Greatest Hits	1980	2.50	5.00	10.00
PC 36865	Aerosmith's Greatest Hits	1984	2.00	4.00	8.00
FC 38061	Rock in a Hard Place	1982	2.50	5.00	10.00
PC 38061	Rock in a Hard Place	1984	2.00	4.00	8.00
FC 40329	Classics Live	1986	2.50	5.00	10.00
FC 40855	Classics Live, Vol. 2	1987	2.50	5.00	10.00
FC 44487	Gems (1973-1982)	1989	2.50	5.00	10.00
GEFFEN					
GHS 24091	Done with Mirrors	1985	2.50	5.00	10.00
GHS 24162	Permanent Vacation	1987	2.50	5.00	10.00
GHS 24254	Pump	1989	2.50	5.00	10.00

AESOP'S FABLES

Number	Title (A Side/B Side)	Yr	VG	VG+	NM
45s					
ATCO					
6508	Girl, I've Got News for You/Yes I'm Back	1967	2.00	4.00	8.00
6523	Take a Step/What's a Man to Do	1967	2.00	4.00	8.00
6565	Slow and Easy/The Truth	1968	2.00	4.00	8.00

Number	Title (A Side/B Side)	Yr	VG	VG+	NM
CADET CONCEPT					
7011	Temptation 'Bout to Get Me/What Is Love	1909	2.00	4.00	8.00
7016	I'm Gonna Make You Love Me/They Go Out and Get It	1968	2.00	4.00	8.00
7016	And When It's Over/What Is Love	1969	2.00	4.00	8.00
Albums					
CADET CONCEPT					
LPS-323	In Due Time	1969	5.00	10.00	20.00
AFDEM, JEFF, AND THE SPRINGFIELD FLUTE					
Albums					
BURDETTE					
5162	Something	1969	10.00	20.00	40.00
AFFECTION COLLECTION, THE					
45s					
EVOLUTION					
1004	Girl/I'll Be There	1969	3.00	6.00	12.00
1013	Watch Her Walk/I Don't Mind	1969	3.00	6.00	12.00
UNITED ARTISTS					
50268	In Apple Blossom Time/Time Rests Heavy on My Hands	1968	2.50	5.00	10.00
Albums					
EVOLUTION					
2007	The Affection Collection	1969	5.00	10.00	20.00
AFFINITY					
Albums					
PARAMOUNT					
PAS-5027	Affinity	1970	6.25	12.50	25.00
AFRIQUE					
45s					
MAINSTREAM					
5542	Soul Makossa/Hot Mud	1973	—	2.50	5.00
5547	Kumbo Coming/Hot Mud	1973	—	2.50	5.00
Albums					
MAINSTREAM					
S-394	Soul Makossa	1973	3.00	6.00	12.00
AGAPE					
Albums					
MARK					
MRS-2170	Gospel Hard Rock	1971	30.00	60.00	120.00
RENRUT					
101	Victims of Tradition	1972	30.00	60.00	120.00
AGE OF REASON, THE					
Albums					
GEORGETOWNE					
(no #)	The Age of Reason	1969	37.50	75.00	150.00
AGGREGATION, THE					
45s					
LHI					
1209	Sunshine Superman/Maharish	1968	7.50	15.00	30.00
Albums					
LHI					
12008	Mind Odyssey	1967	100.00	200.00	400.00
AHBEZ, EDEN					
45s					
DEL-FI					
4131	Tobago/The Old Boat	1959	3.75	7.50	15.00
Albums					
DEL-FI					
DFLP-1211 [M]	Eden's Island	1960	37.50	75.00	150.00
DFST-1211 [S]	Eden's Island	1960	50.00	100.00	200.00
AKENS, JEWEL					
45s					
AMERICAN INT'L					
110	When Something Is Wrong with My Baby/I Just Can't Turn My Habit into Love	196?	—	3.00	6.00
CAPEHART					
5007	(Dancing) The Mashed Potatoes/Wee Bit More of Your Lovin'	1962	3.00	6.00	12.00
COLGEMS					
66-1025	It's a Sin to Tell a Lie/You Better Move On	1968	2.00	4.00	8.00
CREST					
1098	(Dancing) The Mashed Potatoes/Wee Bit More of Your Lovin'	1962	2.50	5.00	10.00
ERA					
104	Buenos Aires/Mississippi Syrup Sopper	1969	—	3.00	6.00
3141	The Birds and the Bees/Tic Tac Toe	1964	3.75	7.50	15.00
3142	Georgie Porgie/Around the Corner	1965	2.50	5.00	10.00
3147	You Sure Know How to Hurt a Guy/It's the Only Way to Fly	1965	2.50	5.00	10.00
3154	You Don't Need a Crowd/I've Arrived	1965	2.50	5.00	10.00
3156	A Slice of the Pie/You Better Believe It	1965	2.50	5.00	10.00
3164	My First Lonely Night/Mama Take Your Daughter Back	1966	2.50	5.00	10.00
3207	A Slice of the Pie/A Land Where Animals Are People	1969	2.00	4.00	8.00
MDM					
191	Christine/Please God	1988	—	2.00	4.00
—As "Jewel Akens, Mr. Birds and Bees"					

Number	Title (A Side/B Side)	Yr	VG	VG+	NM
Albums					
ERA					
EL-110 [M]	The Birds and the Bees	1965	7.50	15.00	30.00
ES-110 [S]	The Birds and the Bees	1965	25.00	50.00	100.00
AKKERMAN, JAN					
Also see BRAINBOX; FOCUS.					
45s					
ATLANTIC					
3478	Crackers/(B-side unknown)	1978	—	2.00	4.00
Albums					
ATCO					
SD 7032	Tabernakel	1974	3.00	6.00	12.00
ATLANTIC					
SD 18210	Eli	1977	2.50	5.00	10.00
SD 19159	Jan Akkerman	1978	2.50	5.00	10.00
SIRE					
SAS 7407	Profile	1973	3.75	7.50	15.00
ALABAMA					
45s					
BNA					
65312	Angels Among Us/Make a Miracle	1997	—	—	3.00
—B-side credited to "Various Artists"					
GRT					
129	I Wanna Be with You Tonight/Lovin' You Is Killin' Me	1977	3.75	7.50	15.00
129 [PS]	I Wanna Be with You Tonight/Lovin' You Is Killin' Me	1977	5.00	10.00	20.00
MDJ					
1002-JB	My Home's in Alabama/Some Other Time, Some Other Place	1980	2.50	5.00	10.00
—Jukebox pressing with one B-side					
1002-R	My Home's in Alabama//Some Other Time, Some Other Place/Why Lady Why	1980	3.00	6.00	12.00
—Regular pressing with two B-sides					
7906	I Wanna' Come Over/Get It While It's Hot	1979	3.00	6.00	12.00
RCA					
2519-7-R	Pass It On Down/The Borderline	1990	—	—	3.00
2519-7-R [PS]	Pass It On Down/The Borderline	1990	—	2.00	4.00
2643-7-R	Jukebox in My Mind/Fire on Fire	1990	—	—	3.00
2706-7-R	Forever's As Far As I'll Go/Starting Tonight	1990	—	2.50	5.00
2778-7-R	Down Home/Goodbye (Kelly's Song)	1991	—	—	3.00
2828-7-R	Here We Are/Gulf of Mexico	1991	—	—	3.00
5003-7-R	Touch Me When We're Dancing/Hanging Up My Travelin' Shoes	1986	—	—	3.00
5051-7-R	Christmas in Dixie/Tennessee Christmas	1986	—	2.00	4.00
5081-7-R	"You've Got" The Touch/True, True Housewife	1987	—	—	3.00
5222-7-R	Tar Top/If I Could Just See You Now	1987	—	—	3.00
—Promo-only sleeve					
5222-7-R [PS]	Tar Top/If I Could Just See You Now	1987	2.00	4.00	8.00
—Promo-only sleeve					
5328-7-R	Face to Face/Vacation	1987	—	—	3.00
6902-7-R	Fallin' Again/I Saw the Time	1988	—	—	3.00
8744-7-R	Song of the South/(I Wish It Could Always Be) '55	1988	—	—	3.00
8817-7-R	If I Had You/I Showed Her	1988	—	—	3.00
8937-7-R	Fallin' Again/Song of the South	1989	—	—	3.00
—Gold Standard Series reissue					
8948-7-R	High Cotton/"Ole" Baugh Road	1989	—	—	3.00
9083-7-R	Southern Star/Barefootin'	1989	—	—	3.00
PB-12008	My Home's in Alabama/I Wanna Come Over	1980	—	2.00	4.00
PB-12008 [PS]	My Home's in Alabama/I Wanna Come Over	1980	—	3.00	6.00
PB-12018	Tennessee River/Can't Forget About You	1980	—	2.00	4.00
PB-12091	Why Lady Why/I Wanna Come Over	1980	—	2.00	4.00
PB-12091 [PS]	Why Lady Why/I Wanna Come Over	1980	—	2.50	5.00
PB-12169	Old Flame/I'm Stoned	1981	—	2.00	4.00
PB-12236	Feels So Right/See the Embers, Feel the Flame	1981	—	2.00	4.00
PB-12288	Love in the First Degree/Ride the Train	1981	—	2.00	4.00
GB-12310	Why Baby Why/My Home's in Alabama	1981	—	—	3.00
—Gold Standard Series reissue					
GB-12369	Tennessee River/Old Flame	1981	—	—	3.00
—Gold Standard Series reissue					
PB-13019	Mountain Music/Never Be One	1981	—	2.00	4.00
PB-13019 [PS]	Mountain Music/Never Be One	1981	—	2.50	5.00
PB-13210	Take Me Down/Lovin' You Is Killin' Me	1982	—	2.00	4.00
PB-13294	Close Enough to Perfect/Fantasy	1982	—	2.00	4.00
PB-13358	Christmas in Dixie/Christmas Is Just a Song for Us This Year	1982	—	2.50	5.00
—B-side by Louise Mandrell and R.C. Bannon					
PB-13446	Dixieland Delight/A Very Special Love	1983	—	2.00	4.00
GB-13489	Feels So Right/Mountain Music	1983	—	—	3.00
—Gold Standard Series reissue					
GB-13492	Take Me Down/Close Enough to Perfect	1983	—	—	3.00
—Gold Standard Series reissue					
PB-13524	The Closer You Get/You Turn Me On	1983	—	2.00	4.00
PB-13590	Lady Down on Love/Lovin' Man	1983	—	2.00	4.00
PB-13664	Christmas in Dixie/Never Be One	1983	—	2.00	4.00
PB-13716	Roll On (Eighteen Wheeler)/Food on the Table	1984	—	2.00	4.00
PB-13763	When We Make Love/Oklahoma Mountain Dew	1984	—	2.00	4.00
GB-13786	Dixieland Delight/Lady Down on Love	1984	—	—	3.00
—Gold Standard Series reissue					
PB-13840	If You're Gonna Play in Texas (You Gotta Have a Fiddle in the Band)/I'm Not That Way Anymore	1984	—	2.00	4.00
PB-13926	(There's A) Fire in the Night/Rock on the Bayou	1984	—	2.00	4.00
PB-13992	There's No Way/The Boy	1985	—	2.00	4.00
GB-14067	Roll On (Eighteen Wheeler)/When We Make Love	1985	—	—	3.00
—Gold Standard Series reissue					
PB-14085	Forty Hour Week (For a Livin')/As Right Now	1985	—	2.00	4.00
PB-14085 [PS]	Forty Hour Week (For a Livin')/As Right Now	1985	—	2.50	5.00
PB-14165	Can't Keep a Good Man Down/If It Ain't Dixie (It Won't Do)	1985	—	2.00	4.00
GB-14174	Love in the First Degree/The Closer You Get	1985	—	—	3.00
—Gold Standard Series reissue					

Number	Title (A Side/B Side)	Yr	VG	VG+	NM
GB-14176	(There's a) Fire in the Night/If You're Gonna Play in Texas (You Gotta Have a Fiddle in the Band)	1985	—	—	3.00
—Gold Standard Series reissue					
PB-14213	Thistlehair the Christmas Bear/Santa Claus (I Still Believe in You)	1985	—	—	—
—Unreleased					
PB-14219	Joseph and Mary's Boy/Santa Claus (I Still Believe in You)	1985	—	2.00	4.00
PB-14281	She and I/The Fans	1986	—	2.00	4.00
PB-14281 [PS]	She and I/The Fans	1986	—	2.50	5.00
GB-14347	There's No Way/(There's a) Fire in the Night	1986	—	—	3.00
—Gold Standard Series reissue					
GB-14350	Forty Hour Week (For a Livin')/Can't Keep a Good Man Down	1986	—	—	3.00
—Gold Standard Series reissue					
60211	We Made Love/Small Stuff	2000	—	—	3.00
62059	Then Again/Hats Off	1991	—	—	3.00
62168	Born Country/Until It Happens to You	1991	—	—	3.00
62253	Take a Little Trip/Pictures and Memories	1992	—	—	3.00
62336	I'm In a Hurry (And Don't Know Why)/Sometimes Out of Touch	1992	—	—	3.00
62428	Once Upon a Lifetime/American Pride	1992	—	—	3.00
62495	Hometown Honeymoon/Homesick Fever	1993	—	—	3.00
62623	The Cheap Seats/This Love's on Me	1994	—	—	3.00
62636	Reckless/Clean Water Blues	1993	—	—	3.00
62643	Angels Among Us/Santa Claus (I Still Believe in You)	1993	—	2.00	4.00
62712	T.L.C.A.S.A.P./That Feeling	1993	—	—	3.00
62894	We Can't Love Like This Anymore/Still Goin' Strong	1994	—	—	3.00
64273	Give Me One More Shot/Jukebox in My Mind	1995	—	—	3.00
64346	She Ain't Your Ordinary Girl/Heartbreak Express	1995	—	—	3.00
64419	In Pictures/Between the Two of Them	1995	—	—	3.00
64436	Christmas in Dixie/Thistlehair the Christmas Bear	1995	—	—	3.00
—Reissue with edit of A-side					
64473	It Works/Katy Brought My Guitar Back Today	1996	—	—	3.00
64543	Say I/My Love Belongs to You	1996	—	—	3.00
64588	The Maker Said Take Her/Nothing Comes Close	1996	—	—	3.00
64775	Sad Lookin' Moon/Give Me One More Shot	1997	—	—	3.00
64849	Dancin', Shaggin' on the Boulevard/Very Special Love	1997	—	—	3.00
64965	Of Course I'm Alright/(I Wish It Could Always Be) '55	1997	—	—	3.00
65409	She's Got That Look in Her Eyes/That Feeling	1998	—	—	3.00
65561	How Do You Fall in Love/Keepin' Up	1998	—	—	3.00
65759	God Must Have Spent a Little More Time on You/Sad Lookin' Moon	1999	—	2.00	4.00
65935	Small Stuff/God Must Have Spent a Little More Time on You	1999	—	—	3.00
SUN					
1173 [DJ]	I Wanna Be with You Tonight (Standard Version/Edited Version)	1982	7.50	15.00	30.00
—Promo only on yellow vinyl; stock copies were not released					
Albums					
ALABAMA					
ALA-78-9-01	The Alabama Band	1978	100.00	200.00	400.00
HEARTLAND					
HL 1186/7 [(2)]	The Very Best of Alabama	1992	3.75	7.50	15.00
LSI					
0177	Deuces Wild	1977	300.00	600.00	1200.
—As "Wild Country"					
0275	Wild Country	1975	750.00	1125.	1500.
—As "Wild Country"					
PLANTATION					
44	Wild Country	1981	15.00	30.00	60.00
RCA					
5649-1-R	The Touch	1986	2.00	4.00	8.00
6495-1-R	Just Us	1987	2.00	4.00	8.00
6825-1-R	Alabama Live	1988	2.00	4.00	8.00
8587-1-R	Southern Star	1989	2.00	4.00	8.00
9574-1-RDJ [DJ]	Open-Ended Interview	1988	7.50	15.00	30.00
RCA VICTOR					
AHL1-3644	My Home's in Alabama	1980	3.75	7.50	15.00
AYL1-3644	My Home's in Alabama	1986	2.00	4.00	8.00
—"Best Buy Series" reissue					
AHL1-3930	Feels So Right	1981	2.00	4.00	8.00
AHL1-4229	Mountain Music	1982	2.00	4.00	8.00
AHL1-4663	The Closer You Get	1983	2.00	4.00	8.00
AHL1-4939	Roll On	1984	2.00	4.00	8.00
AHL1-5339	40 Hour Week	1985	2.00	4.00	8.00
ASL1-7014	Christmas	1985	3.00	6.00	12.00
—Original copies have gold embossed letters on cover					
ASL1-7014	Christmas	1986	2.50	5.00	10.00
—Later copies have white non-embossed letters on cover					
AHL1-7170	Greatest Hits	1986	2.00	4.00	8.00

ALABAMA CHRISTIAN MOVEMENT FOR HUMAN RIGHTS CHOIR

Number	Title (A Side/B Side)	Yr	VG	VG+	NM
45s					
TCF					
2	Do You Hear What I Hear?/The Virgin Mary	1963	3.00	6.00	12.00

ALADDINS, THE

Number	Title (A Side/B Side)	Yr	VG	VG+	NM
45s					
ALADDIN					
3275	Remember/Cry Baby Cry	1955	50.00	100.00	200.00
3298	I Had a Dream Last Night/Get Off My Feet	1955	50.00	100.00	200.00
3314	All My Life/So Long, Farewell, Bye Bye	1956	50.00	100.00	200.00
3358	Help Me/Lord, Show Me	1957	50.00	100.00	200.00
FRANKIE					
6	Dot, My Love/My Charlene	1958	100.00	200.00	400.00
WITCH					
109	Please Love Me/Munch	1962	12.50	25.00	50.00
111	Our Love Will Be/Simple Simon	1962	12.50	25.00	50.00

ALAIMO, CHUCK

Number	Title (A Side/B Side)	Yr	VG	VG+	NM
45s					
MGM					
12449	Leap Frog/That's My Desire	1957	3.75	7.50	15.00
12508	Local 60-6/How I Love You	1957	3.75	7.50	15.00
12589	Where's My Baby/Lovers Again	1957	3.75	7.50	15.00
12636	Hop in My Jalop/Rockin' in G	1958	3.75	7.50	15.00

ALAIMO, STEVE

Also see THE REDCOATS; THE UNKNOWNS.

Number	Title (A Side/B Side)	Yr	VG	VG+	NM
45s					
ABC					
10805	So Much Love/Truer Than True	1966	3.00	6.00	12.00
10833	Happy/On the Beach	1966	3.00	6.00	12.00
10873	Pardon Me (It's My First Day Alone)/Savin' All My Love	1966	3.00	6.00	12.00
10917	You Don't Love Me/You Don't Know Like I Know	1967	2.50	5.00	10.00
ABC-PARAMOUNT					
10540	Love's Gonna Live Here/Let Her Go	1964	3.00	6.00	12.00
10553	Love Is a Many Splendored Thing/Fade Out	1964	3.00	6.00	12.00
10580	I Don't Know/That's What Love Will Do	1964	3.00	6.00	12.00
10605	Happy/Everybody Knows But Her	1964	3.00	6.00	12.00
10620	Real Live Girl/Need You	1965	3.00	6.00	12.00
10643	Laughing on the Outside/Tomorrow Is Another Day	1965	3.00	6.00	12.00
10680	Cast Your Fate to the Wind/Mais Oui	1965	3.00	6.00	12.00
10712	Blowin' in the Wind/Lady of the House	1965	3.00	6.00	12.00
10764	Bright Lights Big City/Once a Day	1966	3.00	6.00	12.00
ATCO					
6512	New Orleans/Ooh Poo Pah Doo	1967	2.00	4.00	8.00
6560	Cuando Yo Vuelvo Ami Tierra/Todavia	1968	2.50	5.00	10.00
6561	Denver/I Do	1968	2.00	4.00	8.00
6589	1 x 1 Ain't 2/My Friend	1968	2.00	4.00	8.00
6620	Thank You for the Sunshine Days/Watching the Trains Go	1968	2.00	4.00	8.00
6659	I'm Thankful/Afetr the Smoke Is Gone	1969	2.00	4.00	8.00
—With Betty Wright					
6710	One Woman/And Then I Tripped Over Your Goodbye	1969	2.00	4.00	8.00
6732	Melissa/Smilin' in My Sleep	1970	—	3.00	6.00
6797	Can't You See/(On the) Wild Side of Life	1971	—	3.00	6.00
CHECKER					
981	Big Bad Beulah/I Cried All the Way Home	1961	3.00	6.00	12.00
989	All Night Long/I'm Thankful	1961	3.00	6.00	12.00
998	The Waiting's So Hard/You Got Me Whistling	1961	3.00	6.00	12.00
1006	Mashed Potatoes/Mashed Potatoes (Part 2)	1962	3.00	6.00	12.00
1018	My Friend/Going Back to Mary	1962	3.00	6.00	12.00
1024	Cry Myself to Sleep/One Good Reason	1962	3.00	6.00	12.00
1032	Every Day I Have to Cry/Little Girl	1962	3.00	6.00	12.00
1042	A Lifetime of Loneliness/It's a Long, Long Way to Happiness	1963	3.00	6.00	12.00
1047	Don't Let the Sun Catch You Cryin'/I Told You So	1963	3.00	6.00	12.00
1054	Michael — Pt. 1/Michael — Pt. 2	1963	3.00	6.00	12.00
DADE					
1800	Home by Eleven/I Wanna Kiss You	1959	12.50	25.00	50.00
1805	Love Letters/You Can Fall in Love	1959	12.50	25.00	50.00
DICKSON					
6444/5	Blue Fire/My Heart Never Said Goodbye	1960	5.00	10.00	20.00
ENTRANCE					
7501	When My Little Girl Is Smiling/Gemini	1971	—	2.50	5.00
7503	Thorn in Our Roses/Nobody's Fool	1971	—	2.50	5.00
7507	Amerikan Music/Nobody's Fool	1972	—	2.50	5.00
7513	Sand in My Pocket/Gemini	1972	—	2.50	5.00
IMPERIAL					
5699	My Heart Never Said Goodbye/Blue Fire	1960	3.75	7.50	15.00
5717	Unchained Melody/It Happens Ev'ry Time	1961	3.75	7.50	15.00
66003	Gotta Lotta Love/Happy Pappy	1963	3.00	6.00	12.00
LIFETIME					
6112/3	Jelly/The Girl Can't Help It	1957	20.00	40.00	80.00
MARLIN					
6064	I Want You to Love Me/Blue Skies	1959	7.50	15.00	30.00
6065	The Weekend's Over/Girls! Girls! Girls!	1959	6.25	12.50	25.00
6067	She's My Baby/Should I Care?	1959	6.25	12.50	25.00
6103	Spooky/The Redcoats Are Coming	1961	7.50	15.00	30.00
—As "Count Stephen"					
TONE LATINO					
5051	Yo No Se Que Voy A Hacer Sin Ti/No Quiero Dejaria Ya	1970	2.00	4.00	8.00
7-Inch Extended Plays					
CHECKER					
EP-5135	Don't Cry/I Wake Up Crying//Cry/Don't Let the Sun Catch You Crying	1963	20.00	40.00	80.00
EP-5135 [PS]	(title unknown)	1963	20.00	40.00	80.00
Albums					
ABC-PARAMOUNT					
501 [M]	Starring Steve Alaimo	1965	10.00	20.00	40.00
S-501 [S]	Starring Steve Alaimo	1965	12.50	25.00	50.00
531 [M]	Where the Action Is	1965	10.00	20.00	40.00
S-531 [S]	Where the Action Is	1965	12.50	25.00	50.00
551 [M]	Steve Alaimo Sings and Swings	1966	10.00	20.00	40.00
S-551 [S]	Steve Alaimo Sings and Swings	1966	12.50	25.00	50.00
CHECKER					
LP-2981 [M]	Twist with Steve Alaimo	1962	37.50	75.00	150.00
LP-2983 [M]	Mashed Potatoes	1962	37.50	75.00	150.00
LP-2986 [M]	Every Day I Have to Cry	1963	37.50	75.00	150.00
CROWN					
CST-382 [R]	Steve Alaimo	1963	3.75	7.50	15.00
CLP-5382 [M]	Steve Alaimo	1963	6.25	12.50	25.00

ALAMO, TONY

45s

MGM

Number	Title (A Side/B Side)	Yr	VG	VG+	NM
11390	Merry Christmas Darling/It's Christmas Time	1952	5.00	10.00	20.00

ALAN, LEE

45s

LEE ALAN PRESENTS

Number	Title (A Side/B Side)	Yr	VG	VG+	NM
(no #)	A Trip to Miami	1964	125.00	250.00	500.00

—Interviews with the Beatles; a giveaway with Lee Alan's two-page story of his trip ($200 NM)

ALBERT, MORRIS

45s

RCA

Number	Title (A Side/B Side)	Yr	VG	VG+	NM
GB-10937	Feelings/Memories	1977	—	—	3.00
—Gold Standard Series					
PB-10958	Never Let You Go/Conversation	1977	—	—	3.00
PB-11089	Someone, Somehow/So Good to Me	1977	—	—	3.00

RCA VICTOR

Number	Title (A Side/B Side)	Yr	VG	VG+	NM
PB-10279	Feelings/This World Today Is a Mess	1975	—	2.00	4.00
PB-10437	Sweet Loving Man/Christine	1975	—	2.00	4.00
PB-10626	Summer in Paris/She's My Girl	1976	—	2.00	4.00
PB-10706	Memories/The Same Things	1976	—	2.00	4.00

Albums

RCA VICTOR

Number	Title (A Side/B Side)	Yr	VG	VG+	NM
APL1-1018	Feelings	1975	2.00	4.00	8.00
APL1-1496	Morris Albert	1976	2.00	4.00	8.00

ALBERT, THE

Albums

PERCEPTION

Number	Title (A Side/B Side)	Yr	VG	VG+	NM
9	The Albert	1971	5.00	10.00	20.00

ALBERTS, AL

Also see FOUR ACES.

45s

COLUMBIA

Number	Title (A Side/B Side)	Yr	VG	VG+	NM
42737	Fly Me to the Moon/Before Tomorrow Is Yesterday	1963	2.00	4.00	8.00

CORAL

Number	Title (A Side/B Side)	Yr	VG	VG+	NM
62035	Things I Didn't Say/God's Greatest Gifts	1958	2.50	5.00	10.00
62061	My Love/Willingly	1958	2.50	5.00	10.00
62083	How Soon/Love Is the Tomorrow	1959	2.50	5.00	10.00
62090	How Soon/Taking a Chance on Love	1959	2.50	5.00	10.00
62113	By You/High School	1959	2.50	5.00	10.00

DECCA

Number	Title (A Side/B Side)	Yr	VG	VG+	NM
28807	Please Tell Me/Endless	1953	3.75	7.50	15.00

MGM

Number	Title (A Side/B Side)	Yr	VG	VG+	NM
12836	Imagination/Handful of Gold	1959	2.50	5.00	10.00
12884	South of the Border/No Love But Your Love	1960	2.50	5.00	10.00
12922	Handful of Gold/Blue Bird of Happiness	1960	2.50	5.00	10.00

PRESIDENT

Number	Title (A Side/B Side)	Yr	VG	VG+	NM
711	Don't Wait for the Hearse/Heaven Needed an Angel	1961	2.00	4.00	8.00
712	Only on Sunday/Heaven Needed an Angel	1961	2.00	4.00	8.00
715	Blue O'Clock in the Morning/Till Then (I'll Never Again)	1962	2.00	4.00	8.00
719	Fly Me to the Moon/Before Tomorrow Is Yesterday	1963	3.00	6.00	12.00

SWAN

Number	Title (A Side/B Side)	Yr	VG	VG+	NM
4067	Oh My Papa/Alone	1961	2.50	5.00	10.00
4191	Mr. Sandman/Summertime in Venice	1964	2.50	5.00	10.00

VEE JAY

Number	Title (A Side/B Side)	Yr	VG	VG+	NM
568	One Has My Name, The Other Has My Heart/Mala Femina	1963	3.75	7.50	15.00

Albums

CORAL

Number	Title (A Side/B Side)	Yr	VG	VG+	NM
CRL 57259 [M]	A Man Has Got to Sing	1959	6.25	12.50	25.00
CRL 757259 [S]	A Man Has Got to Sing	1959	7.50	15.00	30.00

ALDA, ALEX

Actually Nick Massi of THE FOUR SEASONS.

45s

ONE WAY

Number	Title (A Side/B Side)	Yr	VG	VG+	NM
224	The Ballad of Mr. Nixon/Little Pony	1976	—	2.50	5.00

TOPIX

Number	Title (A Side/B Side)	Yr	VG	VG+	NM
6007 [DJ]	Little Pony (one-sided)	1961	25.00	50.00	100.00

ALDRICH, RONNIE

Albums

LONDON

Number	Title (A Side/B Side)	Yr	VG	VG+	NM
LL 3348 [M]	The Romantic Pianos of Ronnie Aldrich	1964	3.00	6.00	12.00
LL 3383 [M]	Christmas with Ronnie	1964	2.50	5.00	10.00

LONDON PHASE 4

Number	Title (A Side/B Side)	Yr	VG	VG+	NM
22 [(2)]	Love Story	1971	3.75	7.50	15.00
SP-44007 [S]	Melody and Percussion for Two Pianos	1961	3.75	7.50	15.00
SP 44018 [S]	Ronnie Aldrich and His Two Pianos	1962	3.75	7.50	15.00
SP-44029 [S]	The Magnificent Pianos of Ronnie Aldrich	1963	3.75	7.50	15.00
SP-44042 [S]	The Romantic Pianos of Ronnie Aldrich	1964	3.75	7.50	15.00
SP 44051 [S]	Christmas with Ronnie	1964	3.75	7.50	15.00
SP-44062 [S]	Magic Moods	1965	3.00	6.00	12.00
SP-44070 [S]	That Aldrich Feeling	1966	3.00	6.00	12.00
SP-44081 [S]	All-Time Piano Hits	1967	3.00	6.00	12.00

ALEXANDER, ARTHUR

45s

BUDDAH

Number	Title (A Side/B Side)	Yr	VG	VG+	NM
492	Every Day I Have to Cry Some/Everybody Needs Somebody to Love	1975	—	2.50	5.00
522	Sharing the Night Together/She'll Throw Stones at You	1976	—	2.50	5.00
602	Sharing the Night Together/She'll Throw Stones at You	1978	—	2.00	4.00

DOT

Number	Title (A Side/B Side)	Yr	VG	VG+	NM
16309	You Better Move On/A Shot of Rhythm and Blues	1962	5.00	10.00	20.00
16357	Soldier of Love/Where Have You Been	1962	5.00	10.00	20.00
16387	Anna/I Hang My Head and Cry	1962	5.00	10.00	20.00
16425	You're the Reason/Go Home Girl	1963	3.75	7.50	15.00
16454	I Wonder Where You Are Tonight/Dream Girl	1963	3.75	7.50	15.00
16509	Pretty Girls Everywhere/Baby Baby	1963	3.75	7.50	15.00
16554	Where Did Sally Go/Keep Her Guessin'	1963	3.75	7.50	15.00
16616	Black Knight/Ole John Amos	1964	3.00	6.00	12.00
16737	Detroit City/You Don't Care	1965	3.00	6.00	12.00

JUDD

Number	Title (A Side/B Side)	Yr	VG	VG+	NM
1020	Sally Sue Brown/The Girl That Radiates That Charm	1960	12.50	25.00	50.00

—As "June Alexander"

MONUMENT

Number	Title (A Side/B Side)	Yr	VG	VG+	NM
1060	I Need You Baby/Spanish Harlem	1968	2.00	4.00	8.00

SOUND STAGE 7

Number	Title (A Side/B Side)	Yr	VG	VG+	NM
2556	The Other Woman/(Baby) For You	1965	2.50	5.00	10.00
2572	Turn Around (And Try Me)/Show Me the Road	1966	2.50	5.00	10.00
2619	Set Me Free/Love's Where Life Begins	1968	2.00	4.00	8.00
2626	Bye Bye Love/Another	1969	2.00	4.00	8.00
2652	Glory Road/Cry Like a Baby	1970	2.00	4.00	8.00

WARNER BROS.

Number	Title (A Side/B Side)	Yr	VG	VG+	NM
7571	I'm Comin' Home/It Hurts to Want It So Bad	1972	—	3.00	6.00
7633	Mr. John/You Got Me Knockin'	1972	—	3.00	6.00
7658	Burning Love/It Hurts to Want It So Bad	1972	—	3.00	6.00

Albums

DOT

Number	Title (A Side/B Side)	Yr	VG	VG+	NM
DLP 3434 [M]	You Better Move On	1962	25.00	50.00	100.00
DLP 25434 [S]	You Better Move On	1962	40.00	80.00	160.00

WARNER BROS.

Number	Title (A Side/B Side)	Yr	VG	VG+	NM
BS 2592	Arthur Alexander	1972	6.25	12.50	25.00

ALEXANDER, JOE, AND THE CUBANS

With a pre-Chess CHUCK BERRY in the band.

45s

BALLAD

Number	Title (A Side/B Side)	Yr	VG	VG+	NM
1008	Oh Maria/I Hope These Words Will FInd You Well	1954	500.00	1000.	1500.

ALEXANDER, JUNE

See ARTHUR ALEXANDER.

ALEXANDER, MAX

45s

CAPROCK

Number	Title (A Side/B Side)	Yr	VG	VG+	NM
116	Little Rome/Rock, Rock, Rock Everybody	1959	50.00	100.00	200.00

ALEXANDER'S TIMELESS BLOOZBAND

45s

KAPP

Number	Title (A Side/B Side)	Yr	VG	VG+	NM
967	Maybe Baby/Power of Your Love	1969	3.00	6.00	12.00

MATAMAT

Number	Title (A Side/B Side)	Yr	VG	VG+	NM
101	Love So Strong/Horn Song	1967	5.00	10.00	20.00

UNI

Number	Title (A Side/B Side)	Yr	VG	VG+	NM
55044	Love So Strong/Horn Song	1967	3.75	7.50	15.00

Albums

SMASK

Number	Title (A Side/B Side)	Yr	VG	VG+	NM
1001 [M]	Alexander's Timeless Bloozband	1967	50.00	100.00	200.00

UNI

Number	Title (A Side/B Side)	Yr	VG	VG+	NM
73021	For Sale	1968	6.25	12.50	25.00

ALEXANDER AND THE GREATS

45s

ARVEE

Number	Title (A Side/B Side)	Yr	VG	VG+	NM
5064	Swanee Stomp/Waterlogged	1963	10.00	20.00	40.00

LIMELIGHT

Number	Title (A Side/B Side)	Yr	VG	VG+	NM
3040	Do the Mustang/Hot Dang Mustang	1964	10.00	20.00	40.00

ALFI AND HARRY

45s

LIBERTY

Number	Title (A Side/B Side)	Yr	VG	VG+	NM
55008	The Trouble with Harry/Little Beauty	1955	6.25	12.50	25.00
55016	The Word Game Song/Persian on Excursion	1956	6.25	12.50	25.00
55066	Safari/Cloding Time	1957	6.25	12.50	25.00

ALICE JEAN AND THE MONDELLOS

See THE MONOELLOS.

ALIOTTA-HAYNES-JEREMIAH

45s

AMPEX

Number	Title (A Side/B Side)	Yr	VG	VG+	NM
11012	Pitter Patter/(B-side unknown)	1970	2.00	4.00	8.00
—As "Aliotta Haynes"					
11026	Tomorrow's Another Day/One Night Stand	1971	2.00	4.00	8.00
—As "Aliotta Haynes"					

SNOW QUEEN

Number	Title (A Side/B Side)	Yr	VG	VG+	NM
1000	Lake Shore Drive/(B-side unknown)	1973	5.00	10.00	20.00

Albums

AMPEX

Number	Title (A Side/B Side)	Yr	VG	VG+	NM
A-10108	Aliotta-Haynes Music	1970	5.00	10.00	20.00
—As "Aliota-Haynes"					
A-10119	Aliotta-Haynes-Jeremiah	1970	5.00	10.00	20.00

BIG FOOT

Number	Title (A Side/B Side)	Yr	VG	VG+	NM
714	Lake Shore Drive	1978	6.25	12.50	25.00

Number	Title (A Side/B Side)	Yr	VG	VG+	NM
LITTLE FOOT					
711	Slippin' Away	1977	5.00	10.00	20.00

ALIVE AND KICKING

45s

Number	Title (A Side/B Side)	Yr	VG	VG+	NM
ROULETTE					
7078	Tighter, Tighter/Sunday Morning	1970	—	2.50	5.00
7087	Just Let It Come/Mother Carey's Chicken	1970	—	2.50	5.00
7094	London Bridge/You Gave Me Something	1971	—	2.50	5.00
7113	Good Ole Lovin' Back Home/Jordan	1971	—	2.50	5.00

ALL AMERICAN RUMBLERS, THE

Albums

Number	Title (A Side/B Side)	Yr	VG	VG+	NM
GONE					
LP-5006 [M]	Destination Dixie	1959	12.50	25.00	50.00

ALL STARS, THE

Albums

Number	Title (A Side/B Side)	Yr	VG	VG+	NM
GRAMOPHONE					
20192	Boogie Woogie	196?	12.50	25.00	50.00

ALLAN, CHAD

Member of the early GUESS WHO.

45s

Number	Title (A Side/B Side)	Yr	VG	VG+	NM
MALA					
12033	Thru the Looking Glass/Ramon's Hourglass	1968	—	3.00	6.00
REPRISE					
1003	On the Back Step/West Coast Girl	1971	—	3.00	6.00

ALLAN, DAVIE, AND THE ARROWS

45s

Number	Title (A Side/B Side)	Yr	VG	VG+	NM
CUDE					
101	War Path/Beyond the Blue	1963	25.00	50.00	100.00
GET HIP					
GH-209	The Born Losers Theme/The Glory Stompers	1997	—	—	2.00
GH-209 [PS]	The Born Losers Theme/The Glory Stompers	1997	—	—	2.00
MARC					
3223	War Path/Beyond the Blue	1963	12.50	25.00	50.00
MGM					
14299	It's the Little Things You Do/Haven't You Heard	1971	2.00	4.00	8.00
14374	Head Over Heels/Here It Comes	1972	2.00	4.00	8.00
14432	Dawn of the 7th Cavalry/Little Big Horn	1972	2.00	4.00	8.00
14560	And Evil Did Too/Pleasure Girl	1973	2.00	4.00	8.00
14650	Apache '73/Run of the Arrow	1973	2.00	4.00	8.00
MRC					
0901	Stoked on Surf/Flashback	1984	—	2.50	5.00
PRIVATE STOCK					
45001	Touch Too Much/We Can Make It Together	1974	—	3.00	6.00
SIDEWALK					
1	Apache '65/Blue Guitar	1965	5.00	10.00	20.00
TOWER					
116	Apache '65/Blue Guitar	1965	3.75	7.50	15.00
133	Moon Dawg '65/Dance the Freddie	1965	3.00	6.00	12.00
142	Baby Ruth/I'm Looking Over a Four Leaf Clover	1965	3.00	6.00	12.00
158	Space Hop/Granny Goose	1965	3.00	6.00	12.00
267	Wild Angels Theme/UFO	1966	3.00	6.00	12.00
295	Blue's Theme/Bongo Party	1966	3.00	6.00	12.00
341	Devil's Angels/Cody's Theme	1967	3.00	6.00	12.00
381	Cycle-Delic/Blue Rides Again	1967	3.00	6.00	12.00
446	Wild in the Streets/Shape of Things to Come	1968	3.00	6.00	12.00

Albums

Number	Title (A Side/B Side)	Yr	VG	VG+	NM
TOWER					
DT 5002 [R]	Apache '65	1965	7.50	15.00	30.00
T 5002 [M]	Apache '65	1965	10.00	20.00	40.00
DT 5043 [R]	The Wild Angels	1966	5.00	10.00	20.00
T 5043 [M]	The Wild Angels	1966	7.50	15.00	30.00
DT 5056 [R]	The Wild Angels, Vol. II	1967	5.00	10.00	20.00
T 5056 [M]	The Wild Angels, Vol. II	1967	7.50	5.00	30.00
DT 5074 [R]	Devil's Angel	1967	5.00	10.00	20.00
T 5074 [M]	Devil's Angel	1967	7.50	15.00	30.00
DT 5078 [R]	Blues Theme	1967	10.00	20.00	40.00
T 5078 [M]	Blues Theme	1967	12.50	25.00	50.00
DT 5083 [R]	Mondo Hollywood	1968	5.00	10.00	20.00
T 5083 [M]	Mondo Hollywood	1968	7.50	15.00	30.00
DT 5094 [R]	Cycle-Delic Sounds	1968	12.50	25.00	50.00
T 5094 [M]	Cycle-Delic Sounds	1968	25.00	50.00	100.00

ALLAN & THE FLAMES

45s

Number	Title (A Side/B Side)	Yr	VG	VG+	NM
CAMPBELL					
225	Winter Wonderland/Till The End Of Time	1960	12.50	25.00	50.00
COLONIAL					
7006	Winter Wonderland/Till The End of Time	1960	12.50	25.00	50.00

ALLEN, BILLY

45s

Number	Title (A Side/B Side)	Yr	VG	VG+	NM
EL DORADO					
505	Butterfly/Oo Wee Baby	1957	5.00	10.00	20.00
—As "Bill Allen"					
IMPERIAL					
5500	Please Give Me Something/Since I Have You	1958	25.00	50.00	100.00

ALLEN, DAVE

Albums

Number	Title (A Side/B Side)	Yr	VG	VG+	NM
INTERNATIONAL ARTISTS					
11	Color Blind	1969	15.00	30.00	60.00
—Original pressing					
11	Color Blind	1979	5.00	10.00	20.00
—Repressing with "RE2" and "Masterfonics" in dead wax					

ALLEN, DAYTON

Albums

Number	Title (A Side/B Side)	Yr	VG	VG+	NM
GRAND AWARD					
GA 33-424 [M]	Why Not?	1960	6.25	12.50	25.00

ALLEN, JESSE

45s

Number	Title (A Side/B Side)	Yr	VG	VG+	NM
ALADDIN					
3129	Rock This Morning/Gonna Move Away from Town	1953	50.00	100.00	200.00
BAYOU					
011	Dragnet/Take It Easy	1953	25.00	50.00	100.00
CORAL					
65078	My Suffering/Let's Party	1952	50.00	100.00	200.00
IMPERIAL					
5256	Gotta Call That Number/Gonna Tell My Mama	1953	50.00	100.00	200.00
—With Audrey Walker					
5285	Sittin' and Wonderin'/I Wonder What's the Matter	1954	62.50	125.00	250.00
5303	What a Party/The Things I'm Gonna Do	1954	50.00	100.00	200.00
5315	Rockin' and Rollin'/I Love You So	1954	50.00	100.00	200.00

ALLEN, JIMMY, AND TOMMY BARTELLA

45s

Number	Title (A Side/B Side)	Yr	VG	VG+	NM
AL-BRITE					
1300	When Santa Comes Over The Brooklyn Bridge/What Would You Like To Have For Christmas?	1959	10.00	20.00	40.00

ALLEN, LEE

45s

Number	Title (A Side/B Side)	Yr	VG	VG+	NM
ALADDIN					
3334	Shimmy/Rockin' at Cosmos	1956	6.25	12.50	25.00
EMBER					
1027	Walkin' with Mr. Lee/Promenade	1957	6.25	12.50	25.00
1031	Strollin' with Mr. Lee/Boppin' at the Hop	1958	5.00	10.00	20.00
1039	Tic Toc/Chuggin'	1958	5.00	10.00	20.00
1047	Jim Jam/Short Circuit	1958	5.00	10.00	20.00
1057	Cat Walk/Creole Alley	1959	5.00	10.00	20.00
1082	Twistin' with Mr. Lee/Twist Around the Clock	1962	3.75	7.50	15.00

7-Inch Extended Plays

Number	Title (A Side/B Side)	Yr	VG	VG+	NM
EMBER					
103	(contents unknown)	1958	50.00	100.00	200.00
103 [PS]	Walkin' with Mr. Lee	1958	50.00	100.00	200.00

Albums

Number	Title (A Side/B Side)	Yr	VG	VG+	NM
EMBER					
ELP-200 [M]	Walkin' with Mr. Lee	1958	125.00	250.00	500.00
—Red label					
ELP-200 [M]	Walkin' with Mr. Lee	1959	50.00	100.00	200.00
—White "logs" label					
ELP-200 [M]	Walkin' with Mr. Lee	1961	25.00	50.00	100.00
—Red and black label					

ALLEN, MILTON

45s

Number	Title (A Side/B Side)	Yr	VG	VG+	NM
RCA VICTOR					
47-6994	Love A Love A Lover/Just Look, Don't Touch, She's Mine	1957	7.50	15.00	30.00
47-7116	Don't Bug Me Baby/Jamboree	1957	12.50	25.00	50.00

ALLEN, RAY, AND THE UPBEATS

45s

Number	Title (A Side/B Side)	Yr	VG	VG+	NM
BLAST					
204	Peggy Sue/La Bamba	1962	7.50	15.00	30.00

Albums

Number	Title (A Side/B Side)	Yr	VG	VG+	NM
BLAST					
BLP-6804 [M]	A Tribute to Six	1962	30.00	60.00	120.00

ALLEN, RICHIE

45s

Number	Title (A Side/B Side)	Yr	VG	VG+	NM
ERA					
3058	Blue Holiday/Goochie Bamba	1961	5.00	10.00	20.00
IMPERIAL					
5683	Stranger from Durango/Redskin	1960	5.00	10.00	20.00
5701	Sally Ann/Why Did It End	1960	3.75	7.50	15.00
—As "Dickie Allen"					
5720	Haunted Guitar/In a Persian Market	1961	5.00	10.00	20.00
5846	Mr. Hobbs (Theme)/Comin' Back to You	1962	3.75	7.50	15.00
5865	Not So Quiet/A Touch of Blue	1962	3.75	7.50	15.00
5872	Cave Man/Room 304	1962	5.00	10.00	20.00
5885	Kick Off/Undercurrent	1962	5.00	10.00	20.00
5917	Butterscotch/Sunday Picnic	1963	3.75	7.50	15.00
5929	Foot Stomp U.S.A./Skag Along Pete	1963	5.00	10.00	20.00
5941	Surf Beater/The Rising Surf	1963	3.75	7.50	15.00
5984	The Quiet Surf/Ballad of the Surf	1963	3.75	7.50	15.00
TOWER					
273	Stranger from Durango/Nothing Good	1966	3.00	6.00	12.00

Albums

Number	Title (A Side/B Side)	Yr	VG	VG+	NM
IMPERIAL					
LP-9212 [M]	Stranger from Durango	1962	10.00	20.00	40.00
LP-9229 [M]	The Rising Surf	1963	20.00	40.00	80.00
LP-9243 [M]	Surfer's Slide	1963	20.00	40.00	80.00
LP-12212 [S]	Stranger from Durango	1962	12.50	25.00	50.00
LP-12229 [S]	The Rising Surf	1963	37.50	75.00	150.00
LP-12243 [S]	Surfer's Slide	1963	37.50	75.00	150.00

ALLEN, RONNIE

45s

Number	Title (A Side/B Side)	Yr	VG	VG+	NM
DAPT					
205	Flip You Over/Ronnie's Swanee	1961	10.00	20.00	40.00
SAN					
208	Juvenile Delinquent/River of Love	1959	20.00	40.00	80.00

Number	Title (A Side/B Side)	Yr	VG	VG+	NM
209	High School Love/(B-side unknown)	1959	20.00	40.00	80.00
300	Gonna Get My Baby/(B-side unknown)	1960	20.00	40.00	80.00

ALLEN, STEVE

45s

Number	Title (A Side/B Side)	Yr	VG	VG+	NM
BRUNSWICK					
80228	Cinderella/Goldilocks and the Three Bears	1953	3.75	7.50	15.00
80230	But Officer/But Baby	1953	3.75	7.50	15.00
80231	Jack and the Beanstalk/Snow White and the Seven Dwarfs	1953	3.75	7.50	15.00
CORAL					
61368	The Ballad of Davy Crockett/Very Square Dance	1955	3.00	6.00	12.00
61375	Tonight/Just Stay a Little While	1955	3.00	6.00	12.00
61376	I'm Glad There Is You/It Can't Be Wrong	1955	3.00	6.00	12.00
61445	The Goo Goo Doll Song/Old Betsy	1955	3.00	6.00	12.00
61485	Autumn Leaves/High and Dry	1955	3.00	6.00	12.00
61542	What Is a Wife/Memories of You	1956	3.00	6.00	12.00
61565	Don't Be That Way/Sing, Sing, Sing	1956	3.00	6.00	12.00
61566	Let's Dance/Goodbye	1956	3.00	6.00	12.00
61573	What Is a Freem?/I Never Harmed an Onion	1956	3.00	6.00	12.00
61620	Theme from "Picnic"/My Nita, Juanita	1956	3.00	6.00	12.00
61681	Lola's Theme/Conversation	1956	3.00	6.00	12.00
61707	Star Dust/The Golden Wedding Waltz	1956	3.00	6.00	12.00
61839	Do You Ever Think of Me/I Love You	1957	2.50	5.00	10.00
61877	Gotta Have Something in the Bank, Frank/The Disc-Jockey's Theme Song	1957	2.50	5.00	10.00
61909	Pretend You Don't See Him/But I Haven't Got Him	1957	2.50	5.00	10.00
61995	You're So Influential/When You're Smiling	1958	2.50	5.00	10.00
DOT					
15831	Hula Hoop/Love Theme from "Houseboat"	1958	2.50	5.00	10.00
15891	St. Louis Blues/Ida Sweet as Apple Cider	1959	2.50	5.00	10.00
15947	Hawaiian Punch/Follow the Leader	1959	2.50	5.00	10.00
16408	Mah Mah Limbo/Dream	1962	2.00	4.00	8.00
16457	Gravy Waltz/Preacherman	1963	2.00	4.00	8.00
16507	Quando Caliente El Sol/Leave It to Me	1963	2.00	4.00	8.00
16613	I Am the Greatest/Mouth to Mouth Resuscitation	1964	2.00	4.00	8.00
16645	Theme from "The Magic Fountain"/Who's Your Sister	1964	2.00	4.00	8.00
DUNHILL					
4097	Here Comes Sgt. Pepper/Flowers and Love	1967	3.75	7.50	15.00
4127	Dance Time/Impossible	1968	—	3.00	6.00
SIGNATURE					
12003	Flattery/I Remember It Well	1959	2.50	5.00	10.00
—With Jayne Meadows					
12044	Dance Time/Impossible	1960	2.50	5.00	10.00

Albums

Number	Title (A Side/B Side)	Yr	VG	VG+	NM
CASABLANCA					
811366-1	Funny Fone Calls	1983	2.00	4.00	8.00
—Reissue of Dot 3472					
811367-1	More Funny Fone Calls	1983	2.00	4.00	8.00
—Reissue of Dot 3517					
CORAL					
CRL 57004 [M]	Music for Tonight	1955	6.25	12.50	25.00
CRL 57015 [M]	Tonight at Midnight	1956	6.25	12.50	25.00
CRL 57018 [M]	Jazz for Tonight	1956	6.25	12.50	25.00
CRL 57019 [M]	Steve Sings	1956	6.25	12.50	25.00
CRL 57028 [M]	Let's Dance	1956	6.25	12.50	25.00
CRL 57048 [M]	Allen Plays Allen	1956	6.25	12.50	25.00
CRL 57070 [M]	The Steve Allen Show	1957	6.25	12.50	25.00
CRL 57138 [M]	Romantic Rendezvous	1957	5.00	10.00	20.00
CRL 57442 [M]	Songs Everybody Knows	1964	3.75	7.50	15.00
CRL 757442 [R]	Songs Everybody Knows	1964	3.00	6.00	12.00
DECCA					
DL 8151 [M]	Steve Allen's All Star Jazz Concert, Vol. 1	1955	7.50	15.00	30.00
DL 8152 [M]	Steve Allen's All Star Jazz Concert, Vol. 2	1955	7.50	15.00	30.00
DOT					
DLP 3472 [M]	Funny Fone Calls	1963	5.00	10.00	20.00
DLP 3473 [M]	12 Greatest Hits	1963	5.00	10.00	20.00
DLP 3480 [M]	Bossa Nova Jazz	1963	3.75	7.50	15.00
DLP 3515 [M]	Gravy Waltz and 11 Current Hits!	1963	3.75	7.50	15.00
DLP 3517 [M]	More Funny Fone Calls	1963	5.00	10.00	20.00
DLP 3519 [M]	Steve Allen Plays the Piano Greats	1963	3.75	7.50	15.00
DLP 3530 [M]	Steve Allen Sings	1963	3.75	7.50	15.00
DLP 3538 [M]	Cuano Caliente El Sol and More	1963	3.75	7.50	15.00
DLP 3560 [M]	Great Ragtime Hits	1963	3.75	7.50	15.00
DLP 3587 [M]	Songs from the Steve Allen TV Show	1964	3.00	6.00	12.00
DLP 3597 [M]	Steve Allen, His Piano and Orchestra	1964	3.00	6.00	12.00
DLP 3624 [M]	I Play for You	1965	3.00	6.00	12.00
DLP 3683 [M]	Rhythm and Blues	1966	3.00	6.00	12.00
DLP 25380 [S]	Bossa Nova Jazz	1963	5.00	10.00	20.00
DLP 25515 [S]	Gravy Waltz and 11 Current Hits!	1963	5.00	10.00	20.00
DLP 25519 [S]	Steve Allen Plays the Piano Greats	1963	5.00	10.00	20.00
DLP 25530 [S]	Steve Allen Sings	1963	5.00	10.00	20.00
DLP 25538 [S]	Cuano Caliente El Sol and More	1963	5.00	10.00	20.00
DLP 25560 [S]	Great Ragtime Hits	1963	5.00	10.00	20.00
DLP 25587 [S]	Songs from the Steve Allen TV Show	1964	3.75	7.50	15.00
DLP 25597 [S]	Steve Allen, His Piano and Orchestra	1964	3.75	7.50	15.00
DLP 25624 [S]	I Play for You	1965	3.75	7.50	15.00
DLP 25683 [S]	Rhythm and Blues	1966	3.75	7.50	15.00
FORUM					
F-9014 [M]	Steve Allen at the Round Table	196?	5.00	10.00	20.00
FS-9014 [S]	Steve Allen at the Round Table	196?	3.75	7.50	15.00
HAMILTON					
HLP 132 [M]	Some of My Favorites	196?	3.00	6.00	12.00
HLP 12132 [S]	Some of My Favorites	196?	3.75	7.50	15.00
ROULETTE					
R-25053 [M]	Steve Allen at the Round Table	1959	6.25	12.50	25.00
SR-25053 [S]	Steve Allen at the Round Table	1959	5.00	10.00	20.00
SIGNATURE					
1004 [M]	Man in the Street	1959	7.50	15.00	30.00

ALLEN, STEVE, AND MANNY ALBAM

Albums

Number	Title (A Side/B Side)	Yr	VG	VG+	NM
DOT					
DLP 3194 [M]	...And All That Jazz	1959	6.25	12.50	25.00
DLP 25194 [S]	...And All That Jazz	1959	5.00	10.00	20.00

ALLEN, TONY

Also see THE ORIGINALS (4).

45s

Number	Title (A Side/B Side)	Yr	VG	VG+	NM
ALADDIN					
3403	Time Won't Wait on You/Holy Smoke, Baby	1957	5.00	10.00	20.00
BETHLEHEM					
3002	Come-A, Come-A Baby/Just Like Before	1961	3.00	6.00	12.00
3004	It Hurts Me So/The Trakey-Doo	1962	3.00	6.00	12.00
DIG					
104	It Hurts Me So/Check Yourself	1955	5.00	10.00	20.00
109	I Found An Angel/I'm Dreaming	1956	12.50	25.00	50.00
EBB					
115	Come Back/Why in the World	1957	5.00	10.00	20.00
IMPERIAL					
5523	Strange Talk/Call My Name	1958	3.75	7.50	15.00
5547	Forgive Me/Rockin' Shoes	1958	3.75	7.50	15.00
JAMIE					
1143	Train of Love/God Gave Me You	1959	3.75	7.50	15.00
KENT					
364	Dreaming/Be My Love, Be My Love	1961	3.00	6.00	12.00
SPECIALTY					
560	Nite Owl/I	1955	12.50	25.00	50.00
570	Check Yourself Baby/Especially	1956	7.50	15.00	30.00
TAMPA					
157	Be My Love, Be My Love/Tell Me	195?	7.50	15.00	30.00
—As "The Wonders"					
ULTRA					
104	It Hurts Me So/Check Yourself	1955	7.50	15.00	30.00
UNITED ARTISTS					
50190	Now Is Forever/Triple Cross	1967	2.00	4.00	8.00

Albums

Number	Title (A Side/B Side)	Yr	VG	VG+	NM
CROWN					
CST-240 [S]	Rock and Roll with Tony Allen	1961	25.00	50.00	100.00
CLP-5231 [M]	Rock and Roll with Tony Allen	1960	25.00	50.00	100.00
—Black label					
CLP-5231 [M]	Rock and Roll with Tony Allen	1961	15.00	30.00	60.00
—Gray label					

ALLEN, WOODY

Albums

Number	Title (A Side/B Side)	Yr	VG	VG+	NM
BELL					
6008	The Wonderful Wacky World of Woody Allen	1967	5.00	10.00	20.00
CAPITOL					
ST 2986	The Third Woody Allen Album	1968	6.25	12.50	25.00
CASABLANCA					
NBLP2-7145 [(2)]	Woody Allen: Stand-Up Comic 1964-1968	1979	3.75	7.50	15.00
—Compilation of material from Colpix and Capitol LPs (different from either UA collection)					
COLPIX					
CP 488 [M]	Woody Allen 2	1965	7.50	15.00	30.00
SCP 488 [R]	Woody Allen 2	1965	6.25	12.50	25.00
CP 518 [M]	Woody Allen	1964	7.50	15.00	30.00
UNITED ARTISTS					
UA-LA849-J2 [(2)]	Woody Allen: Stand-Up Comic 1964-1968	1977	5.00	10.00	20.00
—Compilation of material from Colpix and Capitol LPs (different from UA 9968)					
UAS 9968 [(2)]	Woody Allen: The Nightclub Years	1972	5.00	10.00	20.00
—Compilation of material from Colpix and Capitol LPs					

ALLENS, ARVEE

See RITCHIE VALENS.

ALLEY CATS, THE

45s

Number	Title (A Side/B Side)	Yr	VG	VG+	NM
EPIC					
9778	Lily of the West/I Should Have Stayed at Home Tonight	1965	3.00	6.00	12.00
PHILLES					
108	Puddin N' Tain (Ask Me Again, I'll Tell You the Same)/Feel So Good	1962	6.25	12.50	25.00
PHILLES/COLLECTABLES					
3201	Puddin' and Tain/Then He Kissed Me	1985	—	3.00	6.00
—Red vinyl; part of box set "Phil Spector Wall of Sound Series Vol. 2"; B-side by the Crystals					
3201	Puddin' and Tain/Then He Kissed Me	1986	—	2.50	5.00
—Black vinyl; B-side by the Crystals					
WHIPPET					
202	This Thing Called Love/Spang-a-Lang	1957	5.00	10.00	20.00
209	Snap, Crackle and Pop/Last Night	1958	5.00	10.00	20.00

ALLIES, THE

45s

Number	Title (A Side/B Side)	Yr	VG	VG+	NM
REPRISE					
674	I Would Love You/The Sound of Children	1968	5.00	10.00	20.00
VALIANT					
748	I'll Sell My Soul/Burning Glass	1966	10.00	20.00	40.00

ALLISON, GENE

45s

Number	Title (A Side/B Side)	Yr	VG	VG+	NM
CHAMPION					
1008	Goodbye My Love/If Things Don't Change	196?	3.00	6.00	12.00
1019	Now We're Together/Understand	196?	3.00	6.00	12.00
1022	You're Gonna Be Sorry/I Know We Can Make It	196?	3.00	6.00	12.00
DECCA					
30185	You're My Baby/Somebody Somewhere	1957	3.75	7.50	15.00
MONUMENT					
876	Ev'rybody's Got a Little Problem/Now Hear This	1965	2.00	4.00	8.00

Number	Title (A Side/B Side)	Yr	VG	VG+	NM
REF-O-REE					
703	Having a Party/Almost Sundown	196?	2.50	5.00	10.00
709	I Understand/Somebody Somewhere	196?	2.50	5.00	10.00
727	How Long's the Train Been Gone/You Can Make It If You Try & Have Faith	196?	2.50	5.00	10.00
729	I Understand/Almost Sundown	196?	2.50	5.00	10.00
VEE JAY					
256	You Can Make It If You Try/Hey, Hey, I Love You	1957	5.00	10.00	20.00
273	Have Faith/My Heart Remembers	1958	3.75	7.50	15.00
286	I Don't Know Why/Let's Sit and Talk	1958	3.75	7.50	15.00
299	Everything Will Be Alright/I'm a Fool Wanting You	1958	3.75	7.50	15.00
305	Tell Me the Truth/Reap What You Sow	1959	3.75	7.50	15.00
317	Everybody But Me/I Believe in Myself	1959	3.75	7.50	15.00
329	I'll Be Waiting for You/Let There Be Women	1959	3.75	7.50	15.00
341	Why Do You Treat Me So Cold/Oh Yeah I'm in Love	1960	3.75	7.50	15.00
365	Ask/Tell Me Sugar Baby	1960	3.75	7.50	15.00
Albums					
VEE JAY					
LP-1009 [M]	Gene Allison	1959	75.00	150.00	300.00
—Maroon label					
LP-1009 [M]	Gene Allison	196?	25.00	50.00	100.00
—Black label, oval or brackets logo					

ALLISON, KEITH

Number	Title (A Side/B Side)	Yr	VG	VG+	NM
45s					
AMY					
11024	Who Do You Love/Don't Want Nobody But You	1968	3.00	6.00	12.00
COLUMBIA					
43619	Look at Me/I Ain't Blaming You	1966	3.00	6.00	12.00
43619 [PS]	Look at Me/I Ain't Blaming You	1966	6.25	12.50	25.00
43900	Action/Glitter and Gold	1966	3.00	6.00	12.00
44028	Louise/Freeborn Man	1967	3.00	6.00	12.00
44028 [PS]	Louise/Freeborn Man	1967	6.25	12.50	25.00
44853	Birds of a Feather/To Know Her Is to Love Her	1969	2.50	5.00	10.00
45115	Everybody/Wednesday's Child	1970	2.50	5.00	10.00
WARNER BROS.					
5681	Sweet Little Rock and Roller/The Girl Can't Help It	1965	3.00	6.00	12.00
5681 [PS]	Sweet Little Rock and Roller/The Girl Can't Help It	1965	6.25	12.50	25.00
Albums					
COLUMBIA					
CL 2641 [M]	Keith Allison In Action	1967	6.25	12.50	25.00
CS 9441 [S]	Keith Allison In Action	1967	6.25	12.50	25.00

ALLISON, LUTHER

Number	Title (A Side/B Side)	Yr	VG	VG+	NM
45s					
GORDY					
7128	The Little Red Rooster/Raggedy and Dirty	1973	—	2.50	5.00
7137	Part Time Love/Now You Got It	1974	—	2.50	5.00
Albums					
DELMARK					
DS-625	Love Me, Mama	1969	6.25	12.50	25.00
GORDY					
G-964	Bad News Is Coming	1973	2.50	5.00	10.00
G-967	Luther's Blues	1974	2.50	5.00	10.00
G-974	Night Life	1976	2.50	5.00	10.00

ALLISONS, THE

Number	Title (A Side/B Side)	Yr	VG	VG+	NM
45s					
COLUMBIA					
42034	Words/Blue Tears	1961	2.50	5.00	10.00
LONDON					
1977	Are You Sure/There's One Thing More	1961	2.50	5.00	10.00
1977 [PS]	Are You Sure/There's One Thing More	1961	6.25	12.50	25.00
SMASH					
1749	Lessons in Love/Oh My Love	1962	2.50	5.00	10.00

ALLMAN, DUANE

Of THE ALLMAN BROTHERS BAND and THE ALLMAN JOYS.

Number	Title (A Side/B Side)	Yr	VG	VG+	NM
Albums					
CAPRICORN					
2CP 0108 [(2)]	An Anthology	1972	5.00	10.00	20.00
2CP 0139 [(2)]	An Anthology, Vol. II	1974	5.00	10.00	20.00
POLYDOR					
PD-1-6338	The Best of Duane Allman	1981	3.00	6.00	12.00
827563-1	The Best of Duane Allman	1984	2.00	4.00	8.00

ALLMAN, DUANE AND GREGG

Of THE ALLMAN BROTHERS BAND and THE ALLMAN JOYS.

Number	Title (A Side/B Side)	Yr	VG	VG+	NM
45s					
BOLD					
200	Morning Dew/Morning Dew	1973	2.50	5.00	10.00
200 [DJ]	Morning Dew/Morning Dew	1973	5.00	10.00	20.00
—Promo on red vinyl					
Albums					
BOLD					
33-301	Duane and Gregg Allman	1972	6.25	12.50	25.00
—Gatefold cover					
33-301	Duane and Gregg Allman	197?	3.00	6.00	12.00
—Non-gatefold cover					

ALLMAN, GREGG

Of THE ALLMAN BROTHERS BAND and THE ALLMAN JOYS.

Number	Title (A Side/B Side)	Yr	VG	VG+	NM
45s					
CAPRICORN					
0035	Midnight Rider/Multi-Colored Lady	1973	—	2.50	5.00
0042	Don't Mess Up a Good Thing/Please Call Home	1974	—	2.00	4.00
0053	Midnight Rider/Don't Mess Up a Good Thing	1975	—	2.00	4.00
—Back to Back Hits series					
0279	Cryin' Shame/One More Try	1977	—	2.00	4.00
EPIC					
06998	I'm No Angel/Lead Me On	1987	—	2.00	4.00
07215	Can't Keep Running/Anything Goes	1987	—	—	3.00
07430	Evidence of Love/Anything Goes	1987	—	—	3.00
08041	Slip Away/Every Hungry Woman	1988	—	—	3.00
Albums					
CAPRICORN					
CP 0116	Laid Back	1973	3.00	6.00	12.00
2CP 0141 [(2)]	The Gregg Allman Tour	1974	3.75	7.50	15.00
CP 0181	Playin' Up a Storm	1977	3.00	6.00	12.00
EPIC					
FE 40531	I'm No Angel	1987	2.50	5.00	10.00
OE 44033	Just Before the Bullets Fly	1988	2.50	5.00	10.00

ALLMAN, SHELDON

Number	Title (A Side/B Side)	Yr	VG	VG+	NM
45s					
HIFI					
593	Walk on the Ground/Radioactive Mama	1960	3.00	6.00	12.00
ORIGINAL SOUND					
25	Heartbreak Boulevard/Little Black Things	1963	2.50	5.00	10.00

ALLMAN AND WOMAN

GREGG ALLMAN and CHER.

Number	Title (A Side/B Side)	Yr	VG	VG+	NM
45s					
WARNER BROS.					
8504	Love Me/Move Me	1977	—	2.50	5.00
Albums					
WARNER BROS.					
BSK 3120	Two the Hard Way	1977	2.50	5.00	10.00

ALLMAN BROTHERS BAND, THE

Also see ALLMAN AND WOMAN; THE ALLMAN JOYS; DUANE ALLMAN; DUANE AND GREGG ALLMAN; GREGG ALLMAN; DICKIE BETTS; THE HOUR GLASS.

Number	Title (A Side/B Side)	Yr	VG	VG+	NM
45s					
ARISTA					
0555	Angeline/So Long	1980	—	2.00	4.00
0584	Mystery Woman/Hell and High Water	1981	—	2.00	4.00
0618	Straight from the Heart/Leavin'	1981	—	2.00	4.00
0618 [PS]	Straight from the Heart/Leavin'	1981	—	2.00	4.00
0643	Two Rights/Never Knew How Much	1981	—	2.00	4.00
CAPRICORN					
0003	Ain't Wastin' Time No More/Melissa	1972	—	2.50	5.00
0007	Melissa/Blue Sky	1972	—	2.50	5.00
0014	One Way Out/Standback	1972	—	2.50	5.00
0027	Ramblin Man/Pony Boy	1973	—	2.50	5.00
0036	Jessica/Come and Go Blues	1973	—	2.50	5.00
0050	Ain't Wastin' Time No More/Blue Sky	1974	—	2.00	4.00
—Back to Back Hits series					
0051	Ramblin Man/Jessica	1974	—	2.00	4.00
—Back to Back Hits series					
0246	Nevertheless/Louisiana Lou and Three Card Monty John	1975	—	2.00	4.00
0320	Crazy Love/Just Ain't Easy	1979	—	2.00	4.00
0326	Can't Take It With You/Sail Away	1979	—	2.00	4.00
8003	Black Hearted Woman/Every Hungry Woman	1970	—	3.00	6.00
8011	Revival (Love Is Everywhere)/Leave My Blues at Home	1971	—	2.50	5.00
8014	Whipping Post/Midnight Rider	1971	—	2.50	5.00
EPIC					
73504	Good Clean Fun/Seven Turns	1990	—	2.00	4.00
Albums					
ARISTA					
AL 9535	Reach for the Sky	1980	2.50	5.00	10.00
AL 9564	Brothers of the Road	1981	2.50	5.00	10.00
ATCO					
SD 33-308	The Allman Brothers Band	1969	3.75	7.50	15.00
SD 33-342	Idlewild South	1970	3.75	7.50	15.00
SD 2-805 [(2)]	Beginnings	1973	5.00	10.00	20.00
CAPRICORN					
2CP 0102 [(2)]	Eat a Peach	1972	3.75	7.50	15.00
CPN2 0102 [(2)]	Eat a Peach	198?	3.00	6.00	12.00
CX4 0102 [(2) Q]	Eat a Peach	1974	7.50	15.00	30.00
CP 0111	Brothers and Sisters	1973	3.00	6.00	12.00
CPN 0111	Brothers and Sisters	198?	2.00	4.00	8.00
2CP 0131 [(2)]	The Allman Brothers Band at Fillmore East	1974	3.75	7.50	15.00
CPN2 0131 [(2)]	The Allman Brothers Band at Fillmore East	198?	3.00	6.00	12.00
CX4 0131 [(2) Q]	The Allman Brothers Band at Fillmore East	1974	7.50	15.00	30.00
2CX 0132 [(2)]	Beginnings	1974	3.75	7.50	15.00
CPN2 0132 [(2)]	Beginnings	198?	3.00	6.00	12.00
CP 0156	Win, Lose or Draw	1975	2.50	5.00	10.00
CPN 0156	Win, Lose or Draw	198?	2.00	4.00	8.00
2CX 0164 [(2)]	The Road Goes On Forever	1975	3.00	6.00	12.00
2CX 0177 [(2)]	Wipe the Windows, Check the Oil, Dollar Gas	1976	3.00	6.00	12.00
CPN 0196	The Allman Brothers Band	1978	2.50	5.00	10.00
CPN 0197	Idlewild South	1978	2.50	5.00	10.00
CPN 0218	Enlightened Rogues	1979	2.50	5.00	10.00
2-802 [(2) M]	The Allman Brothers Band at Fillmore East	1971	20.00	40.00	80.00
—Promo only; sticker on front cover says "Promotional DJ Copy Monaural Not for Sale"					
SD 2-802 [(2)]	The Allman Brothers Band at Fillmore East	1971	5.00	10.00	20.00
EPIC					
E 46144	Seven Turns	1990	3.75	7.50	15.00
MOBILE FIDELITY					
1-157 [(2)]	Eat a Peach	1984	50.00	100.00	200.00
—Audiophile vinyl					
1-213	Brothers and Sisters	1994	7.50	15.00	30.00
—Audiophile vinyl					
NAUTILUS					
NR-30 [(2)]	The Allman Brothers Band at Fillmore East	1982	25.00	50.00	100.00
—Audiophile vinyl					
POLYDOR					
PD-1-6339	The Best of the Allman Brothers Band	1981	2.50	5.00	10.00
823273-1 [(2)]	The Allman Brothers Band at Fillmore East	1984	2.50	5.00	10.00

Number	Title (A Side/B Side)	Yr	VG	VG+	NM
823653-1	The Allman Brothers Band	1984	2.00	4.00	8.00
823654-1 [(2)]	Eat a Peach	1984	2.50	5.00	10.00
823708-1	The Best of the Allman Brothers Band	1984	2.00	4.00	8.00
825092-1	Brothers and Sisters	1985	2.00	4.00	8.00
839417-1 [(6)]	Dreams	1989	10.00	20.00	40.00

ALLMAN JOYS, THE

Early ALLMAN BROTHERS BAND.

45s

Number	Title (A Side/B Side)	Yr	VG	VG+	NM
DIAL					
4046	Spoonful/You Deserve Each Other	1966	10.00	20.00	40.00

Albums

Number	Title (A Side/B Side)	Yr	VG	VG+	NM
DIAL					
DL 6005	Early Allman	1973	3.75	7.50	15.00

ALLSUP, TOMMY

45s

Number	Title (A Side/B Side)	Yr	VG	VG+	NM
GRT					
38	I'll See Him Through/Snowbird	1971	—	3.00	6.00

Albums

Number	Title (A Side/B Side)	Yr	VG	VG+	NM
GRT					
20004	Tommy Allsup and the Tennessee Saxes Play the Hits of Tammy Wynette	1970	5.00	10.00	20.00
METROMEDIA					
MM 1004	Tommy Allsup and the Nashville Survey Play the Hits of Charley Pride	1969	6.25	12.50	25.00
REPRISE					
R 6182 [M]	Tommy Allsup Plays the Buddy Holly Songbook	1965	10.00	20.00	40.00
RS 6182 [S]	Tommy Allsup Plays the Buddy Holly Songbook	1965	12.50	25.00	50.00

ALMA-KEYS, THE

45s

Number	Title (A Side/B Side)	Yr	VG	VG+	NM
KISKI					
2056	Please Come Back to Me/Jumpin' Twist	1962	75.00	150.00	300.00

ALMEIDA, LAURINDO

Also see STAN GETZ.

45s

Number	Title (A Side/B Side)	Yr	VG	VG+	NM
CAPITOL					
3298	Volcano/The Naked Sea	1955	3.75	7.50	15.00
5496	Morituri Theme/Forget Domani	1965	2.00	4.00	8.00

Albums

Number	Title (A Side/B Side)	Yr	VG	VG+	NM
ANGEL					
S-36050	Duets with the Spanish Guitar	197?	3.00	6.00	12.00
S-36051	Duets with the Spanish Guitar, Vol. 2	197?	3.00	6.00	12.00
S-36064	Clair de Lune	197?	2.50	5.00	10.00
S-36076	Duets with the Spanish Guitar, Vol. 3	197?	3.00	6.00	12.00
S-37322	Prelude	197?	2.50	5.00	10.00
CAPITOL					
H-193 [10]	Guitar Concert	1950	20.00	40.00	80.00
SM-1759	Viva Bossa Nova!	197?	2.50	5.00	10.00
ST 1759 [S]	Viva Bossa Nova!	1962	5.00	10.00	20.00
T 1759 [M]	Viva Bossa Nova!	1962	3.75	7.50	15.00
ST 1872 [S]	Ole! Bossa Nova	1963	5.00	10.00	20.00
T 1872 [M]	Ole! Bossa Nova	1963	3.75	7.50	15.00
ST 1946 [S]	It's a Bossa Nova World	1963	5.00	10.00	20.00
T 1946 [M]	It's a Bossa Nova World	1963	3.75	7.50	15.00
ST 2063 [S]	Broadway Solo Guitar	1964	3.75	7.50	15.00
T 2063 [M]	Broadway Solo Guitar	1964	3.00	6.00	12.00
ST 2197 [S]	Guitar from Ipanema	1964	3.75	7.50	15.00
T 2197 [M]	Guitar from Ipanema	1964	3.00	6.00	12.00
T 2345 [M]	Suenos (Dreams)	1965	3.00	6.00	12.00
ST 2419 [S]	New Broadway-Hollywood Hits	1965	3.75	7.50	15.00
T 2419 [M]	New Broadway-Hollywood Hits	1965	3.00	6.00	12.00
SM-2701	A Man and a Woman	197?	2.50	5.00	10.00
ST 2701 [S]	A Man and a Woman	1967	3.75	7.50	15.00
T 2701 [M]	A Man and a Woman	1967	3.00	6.00	12.00
ST 2866	The Look of Love	1968	3.00	6.00	12.00
P 8295 [M]	Guitar Music of Spain	196?	3.75	7.50	15.00
P 8367 [M]	Vistas d'Espana	196?	3.75	7.50	15.00
P 8406 [M]	Duets with the Spanish Guitar	196?	3.00	6.00	12.00
—Regular cover					
PAO 8406 [M]	Duets with the Spanish Guitar	196?	3.75	7.50	15.00
—Gatefold cover					
P 8461 [M]	For My True Love	196?	3.00	6.00	12.00
SP 8461 [S]	For My True Love	196?	3.75	7.50	15.00
P 8482 [M]	Songs of Enchantment	196?	3.75	7.50	15.00
SP 8482 [S]	Songs of Enchantment	196?	5.00	10.00	20.00
P 8497 [M]	Music of the Spanish Guitar	196?	3.00	6.00	12.00
SP 8497 [S]	Music of the Spanish Guitar	196?	3.75	7.50	15.00
P 8521 [M]	The Spanish Guitars of Laurindo Almeida	196?	3.00	6.00	12.00
SP 8521 [S]	The Spanish Guitars of Laurindo Almeida	196?	3.75	7.50	15.00
P 8532 [M]	Conversations with the Guitar	196?	3.00	6.00	12.00
P 8546 [M]	The Guitar Worlds of Laurindo Almeida	196?	3.00	6.00	12.00
SP 8546 [S]	The Guitar Worlds of Laurindo Almeida	196?	3.75	7.50	15.00
SP 8562 [S]	Conversations with the Guitar	196?	3.75	7.50	15.00
P 8571 [M]	Reverie	196?	3.00	6.00	12.00
SP 8571 [S]	Reverie	196?	3.75	7.50	15.00
P 8625 [M]	Concerto de Copacabana	196?	3.00	6.00	12.00
SP 8625 [S]	Concerto de Copacabana	196?	3.75	7.50	15.00
DP 8686 [R]	The Best of Laurindo Almeida	1969	3.00	6.00	12.00
CONCORD CONCERTO					
CC-2001	First Concerto for Guitar and Orchestra	197?	2.50	5.00	10.00
CC-2003	Laurindo Almeida with Bud Shank	198?	2.50	5.00	10.00
CONCORD JAZZ					
CJ-84	Chamber Jazz	197?	2.50	5.00	10.00
CJ-328	Artistry in Rhythm	1984	2.50	5.00	10.00
CORAL					
CRL 56049 [10]	A Guitar Recital of Famous Serenades	1952	20.00	40.00	80.00
CRL 56086 [10]	Latin Melodies	1952	20.00	40.00	80.00
CRL 57056 [M]	A Guitar Recital of Famous Serenades	1956	12.50	25.00	50.00
CRYSTAL CLEAR					
CCS-8001	Virtuoso Guitar	1978	6.25	12.50	25.00
—Direct-to-disc recording; plays at 45 rpm					
CCS-8007	New Directions	1979	6.25	12.50	25.00
—Direct-to-disc recording					
DOBRE					
1000	Latin Guitar	1977	2.50	5.00	10.00
1024	Trio	197?	2.50	5.00	10.00
INNER CITY					
6031	Concierto de Aranjuez	1979	2.50	5.00	10.00
ORION					
7259	The Art of Laurindo Almeida	197?	2.50	5.00	10.00
PACIFIC JAZZ					
PJLP-7 [10]	Laurindo Almeida Quartet	1953	30.00	60.00	120.00
PJLP-13 [10]	Laurindo Almeida Quartet, Vol. 2	1954	30.00	60.00	120.00
PJ-1204 [M]	Laurindo Almeida Quartet Featuring Bud Shank	1955	20.00	40.00	80.00
—Reissue of 10-inch Pacific Jazz LPs					
PAUSA					
9009	Brazilliance	1983	2.50	5.00	10.00
—Reissue					
PRO ARTE					
PAD-235	3 Guitars 3	1985	2.50	5.00	10.00
—With Sharon Isbin and Larry Coryell					
WORLD PACIFIC					
WP-1204 [M]	Laurindo Almeida Quartet Featuring Bud Shank	1958	12.50	25.00	50.00
—Reissue of Pacific Jazz 1204					
WP-1412 [M]	Brazilliance, Vol. 1	1962	7.50	15.00	30.00
—Reissue of World Pacific 1204					
ST-1419 [S]	Brazilliance, Vol. 2	1962	6.25	12.50	25.00
WP-1419 [M]	Brazilliance, Vol. 2	1962	7.50	15.00	30.00
ST-1425 [S]	Brazilliance, Vol. 3	1962	6.25	12.50	25.00
WP-1425 [M]	Brazilliance, Vol. 3	1962	7.50	15.00	30.00

ALMEIDA, LAURINDO, AND CHARLIE BYRD

Also see each artist's individual listings.

Albums

Number	Title (A Side/B Side)	Yr	VG	VG+	NM
CONCORD PICANTE					
P-150	Brazilian Soul	198?	2.50	5.00	10.00
P-211	Latin Odyssey	1983	2.50	5.00	10.00
CJ-290	Tango	1986	2.50	5.00	10.00

ALMOND, JOHNNY

45s

Number	Title (A Side/B Side)	Yr	VG	VG+	NM
DERAM					
85052	Music Machine to R.K./Solar Level	1969	2.00	4.00	8.00

Albums

Number	Title (A Side/B Side)	Yr	VG	VG+	NM
DERAM					
DES 18030	Music Machine	1969	3.75	7.50	15.00

ALPERT, DORE

See HERB ALPERT.

ALPERT, HERB

12-Inch Singles

Number	Title (A Side/B Side)	Yr	VG	VG+	NM
A&M					
SP-12022	Rise/Aranjuez (Mon Amour)	1979	3.75	7.50	15.00
—Clear vinyl					

45s

Number	Title (A Side/B Side)	Yr	VG	VG+	NM
ANDEX					
4036	Summer School/Hully Gully	1959	2.50	5.00	10.00
—As "Herbie Alpert Sextet"					
A&M					
714	Dina/You're Doin' What You Did with Me with Him	1963	2.50	5.00	10.00
—As "Dore Alpert"					
729	I'd Do It All Again/Special Kind of Love	1964	2.00	4.00	8.00
—As "Dore Alpert"					
1231	I Need You/The Lady in My Life	1988	—	—	3.00
1446	3 O'Clock Jump/Kalimba	1989	—	—	3.00
2107	Foreign Natives/Mama Way	1979	—	2.00	4.00
—With Hugh Masekela					
2151	Rise/Aranjuez (Mon Amour)	1979	—	2.00	4.00
2202	Rotation/Angelina	1979	—	2.00	4.00
2202 [PS]	Rotation/Angelina	1979	—	2.50	5.00
2221	Street Life/1980	1980	—	2.00	4.00
2246	Beyond/Keep It Goin'	1980	—	2.00	4.00
2246 [PS]	Beyond/Keep It Goin'	1980	—	2.00	4.00
2268	Kamali/Interlude (For Erica)	1980	—	2.00	4.00
2289	Reach for the Stars/Interlude (For Erica)	1980	—	2.00	4.00
2356	Magic Man/Fantasy Island	1981	—	2.00	4.00
2356 [PS]	Magic Man/Fantasy Island	1981	—	2.50	5.00
2375	Manhattan Melody/You Smile, The Song Begins	1981	—	2.00	4.00
2422	Route 101/Angel	1982	—	2.00	4.00
2426	Fandango/The Lonely Bull	1982	—	—	—
—Unreleased?					
2441	Fandango/Coco Loco	1982	—	2.00	4.00
2515	Love Me the Way I Am (Quiereme Tal Como Say)/California Blues	1982	—	2.00	4.00
2562	Garden Party/Oriental Eyes	1983	—	2.00	4.00
2573	Sundown/Garden Party	1983	—	2.00	4.00
2593	Red Hot/Sundown	1983	—	2.00	4.00
2621	Oriental Eyes/Sundown	1984	—	2.00	4.00
2632	We Could Be Flying/Come What May	1984	—	2.00	4.00
—With Lani Hall					
2655	Bullish/Oriental Eyes	1984	—	2.00	4.00
—As "Herb Alpert Tijuana Brass"					
2655 [PS]	Bullish/Oriental Eyes	1984	—	2.00	4.00
2690	Struttin' on Five/Blow Your Own Horn	1984	—	2.00	4.00
—As "Herb Alpert Tijuana Brass"					
2757	"#8" Ball/Lady Love	1985	—	—	3.00
2779	You Are the One/Lady Love	1985	—	—	3.00
—With Brenda Russell					
2802	African Flame/Lady Love	1985	—	—	3.00
2915	Keep Your Eye on Me/Our Song	1987	—	—	3.00

Number	Title (A Side/B Side)	Yr	VG	VG+	NM
2915 [PS]	Keep Your Eye on Me/Our Song	1987	—	—	3.00
2929	Diamonds/African Flame	1987	—	—	3.00
2929 [PS]	Diamonds/African Flame	1987	—	2.50	5.00
2949	Making Love in the Rain/Rocket to the Moon	1987	—	—	3.00
2949 [PS]	Making Love in the Rain/Rocket to the Moon	1987	—	—	3.00
2973	Our Song/African Flame	1987	—	—	3.00
CARNIVAL					
701	Tell It to the Birds/Fallout Shelter	1962	2.50	5.00	10.00
—As "Dore Alpert"					
CAROL					
700	Sweet Georgia Brown/Vipers Blues	1961	2.50	5.00	10.00
DOT					
16396	Fallout Shelter/Tell It to the Birds	1962	2.50	5.00	10.00
—As "Dore Alpert"					
RCA VICTOR					
47-7918	Gotta Get a Girl/Dreamland	1961	3.00	6.00	12.00
—As "Dore Alpert"					
47-7988	Little Lost Lover/Won't You Be My Valentine	1962	3.00	6.00	12.00
—As "Dore Alpert"					
Albums					
A&M					
SP-3714	Rise	1980	2.00	4.00	8.00
—Reissue of 4790					
SP-3717	Beyond	1980	2.00	4.00	8.00
SP-3728	Magic Man	1981	2.00	4.00	8.00
SP-3731	Fandango	1982	2.00	4.00	8.00
SP-4591	Just You and Me	1976	2.50	5.00	10.00
SP-4790	Rise	1979	2.50	5.00	10.00
SP-4949	Blow Your Own Horn	1983	2.00	4.00	8.00
SP-5082	Wild Romance	1985	2.00	4.00	8.00
SP-5125	Keep Your Eye on Me	1987	2.00	4.00	8.00
SP-5209	Under a Spanish Moon	1988	2.00	4.00	8.00
SP-5273	My Abstract Heart	1989	2.00	4.00	8.00
75021 5345 1	North on South Street	1991	3.00	6.00	12.00
MOBILE FIDELITY					
1-053	Rise	1981	6.25	12.50	25.00
—Audiophile vinyl					

ALPERT, HERB, AND THE TIJUANA BRASS

Number	Title (A Side/B Side)	Yr	VG	VG+	NM
45s					
A&M					
703	The Lonely Bull (El Solo Torro)/Acapulco 1922	1962	2.50	5.00	10.00
—With pale brown label and no horn logo					
705	Marching Through Madrid/Struttin' with Maria	1963	2.00	4.00	8.00
711	Mexican Corn/Let It Be Me	1963	2.00	4.00	8.00
721	Spanish Harlem/A-Mer-I-Ca	1963	2.00	4.00	8.00
732	Mexican Drummer Man/Great Manolete	1963	2.00	4.00	8.00
742	The Mexican Shuffle/Numero Cinco	1964	2.00	4.00	8.00
751	All My Loving/El Presidente	1964	2.00	4.00	8.00
755	South of the Border/Up Cherry Street	1965	—	3.00	6.00
760	Whipped Cream/Las Mananitas	1965	—	3.00	6.00
767	El Garbanzo/Mae	1965	—	3.00	6.00
775	Taste of Honey/Third Man Theme	1965	—	3.00	6.00
787	Zorba the Greek/Tijuana Taxi	1965	—	3.00	6.00
792	What Now My Love/Spanish Flea	1966	—	3.00	6.00
792 [PS]	What Now My Love/Spanish Flea	1966	2.50	5.00	10.00
805	The Work Song/Plucky	1966	—	3.00	6.00
805 [PS]	The Work Song/Plucky	1966	2.50	5.00	10.00
813	Flamingo/So What's New	1966	—	3.00	6.00
813 [PS]	Flamingo/So What's New	1966	2.50	5.00	10.00
823	Mame/Our Day Will Come	1966	—	3.00	6.00
823 [PS]	Mame/Our Day Will Come	1966	2.50	5.00	10.00
840	Wade in the Water/Mexican Road Race	1967	—	2.50	5.00
840 [PS]	Wade in the Water/Mexican Road Race	1967	2.00	4.00	8.00
850	Casino Royale/Wall Street Rag	1967	—	2.50	5.00
850 [PS]	Casino Royale/Wall Street Rag	1967	2.00	4.00	8.00
860	The Happening/Town Without Pity	1967	—	2.50	5.00
860 [PS]	The Happening/Town Without Pity	1967	2.00	4.00	8.00
870	A Banda/Miss Frenchy Brown	1967	—	2.50	5.00
870 [PS]	A Banda/Miss Frenchy Brown	1967	2.00	4.00	8.00
890	Carmen/A Love So Fine	1967	—	2.50	5.00
890 [PS]	Carmen/A Love So Fine	1967	2.00	4.00	8.00
925	Cabaret/Slick	1968	—	2.50	5.00
925 [PS]	Cabaret/Slick	1968	2.00	4.00	8.00
929	This Guy's in Love with You/A Quiet Tear	1968	—	2.50	5.00
929 [PS]	This Guy's in Love with You/A Quiet Tear	1968	2.00	4.00	8.00
960	Yo Doy Ese Amor (This Guy's in Love with You)/ A Love So Fine	1968	—	3.00	6.00
964	To Wait for Love/Bud	1968	—	2.50	5.00
964 [PS]	To Wait for Love/Bud	1968	2.00	4.00	8.00
1001	My Favorite Things/The Christmas Song	1968	—	3.00	6.00
1001 [PS]	My Favorite Things/The Christmas Song	1968	2.50	5.00	10.00
1015	She Touched Me/My Favorite Things	1969	—	2.50	5.00
1028	Monday, Monday/Treasure of San Miguel	1969	—	2.50	5.00
1043	Zazueira/Treasure of San Miguel	1969	—	2.50	5.00
1043 [PS]	Zazueira/Treasure of San Miguel	1969	—	3.00	6.00
1065	Without Her/Sandbox	1969	—	2.50	5.00
1065 [PS]	Without Her/Sandbox	1969	—	3.00	6.00
1094	Ob-La-Di, Ob-La-Da/Girl Talk	1969	—	2.50	5.00
1100	Marjorine/Warm	1969	—	2.50	5.00
1102	Marjorine/Ob-La-Di, Ob-La-Da	1969	—	2.50	5.00
1143	Good Morning Mr. Sunshine/You Are My Life	1969	—	2.50	5.00
1159	The Maltese Melody/Country Lake	1969	—	2.50	5.00
1194	Brasilia/Love Potion #9	1970	—	2.00	4.00
1225	Jerusalem/Strike Up the Band	1970	—	2.00	4.00
1225 [PS]	Jerusalem/Strike Up the Band	1970	—	2.50	5.00
1237	The Bell That Couldn't Jingle/Las Mananitas	1970	—	2.50	5.00
1261	Hurt So Bad/Summertime	1971	—	2.00	4.00
1284	Montezuma's Revenge/Darlin'	1971	—	2.00	4.00
1337	Zazuiera/Without Her	1972	—	2.00	4.00
1420	Last Tango in Paris/Fire and Rain	1973	—	2.00	4.00
1423	The Nicest Things Happen/Last Tango in Paris	1973	—	2.00	4.00
1526	Fox Hunt/I Can't Go On Living, Baby, Without You	1974	—	2.00	4.00
1542	You Smile, the Song Begins/Save the Sunlight	1974	—	2.00	4.00
1688	Coney Island/Ratatouille	1975	—	2.00	4.00
1714	El Bimbo/Catfish	1975	—	2.00	4.00
1762	The Whistle Song (Whistlestar)/Carmine	1975	—	2.00	4.00
1852	Promenade/Musique	1976	—	2.00	4.00
1962	African Summer/You in Me	1977	—	2.00	4.00
7-Inch Extended Plays					
A&M					
SP 410 [PS]	Whipped Cream and Other Delights	1965	2.50	5.00	10.00
SP 410 [S]	(A-side unknown)//Bittersweet Samba/Lollipops and Roses/El Garbanzo	1965	2.50	5.00	10.00
—33 1/3 rpm, small hole					
Albums					
A&M					
SP-101 [M]	The Lonely Bull	1962	3.00	6.00	12.00
SP-103 [M]	Herb Alpert's Tijuana Brass, Volume 2	1963	3.00	6.00	12.00
SP-108 [M]	South of the Border	1964	3.00	6.00	12.00
SP-110 [M]	Whipped Cream & Other Delights	1965	2.50	5.00	10.00
SP-112 [M]	Going Places	1965	2.50	5.00	10.00
SP-114 [M]	What Now My Love	1966	2.50	5.00	10.00
SP-119 [M]	S.R.O.	1966	2.50	5.00	10.00
SP-124 [M]	Sounds Like	1967	2.50	5.00	10.00
SP-3101	The Lonely Bull	198?	2.00	4.00	8.00
—Reissue					
SP-3113	Christmas Album	198?	2.00	4.00	8.00
—Reissue of SP-4166					
SP-3157	Whipped Cream & Other Delights	198?	2.00	4.00	8.00
—Reissue					
SP-3263	South of the Border	1984	2.00	4.00	8.00
SP-3264	Going Places	1984	2.00	4.00	8.00
—Reissue					
SP-3265	What Now My Love	1984	2.00	4.00	8.00
SP-3266	The Beat of the Brass	1984	2.00	4.00	8.00
—Reissue					
SP-3267	Greatest Hits	1984	2.00	4.00	8.00
—Reissue					
SP-3268	Solid Brass	1984	2.00	4.00	8.00
SP-3269	Greatest Hits, Vol. 2	1984	2.00	4.00	8.00
SP-3521 [(2)]	Foursider	1973	3.00	6.00	12.00
SP-3620	You Smile — The Song Begins	1974	2.50	5.00	10.00
SP-4101 [S]	The Lonely Bull	1962	3.75	7.50	15.00
SP-4103 [S]	Herb Alpert's Tijuana Brass, Volume 2	1963	3.75	7.50	15.00
SP-4108 [S]	South of the Border	1964	3.75	7.50	15.00
SP-4110 [S]	Whipped Cream & Other Delights	1965	3.00	6.00	12.00
SP-4112 [S]	Going Places	1965	3.00	6.00	12.00
SP-4114 [S]	What Now My Love	1966	3.00	6.00	12.00
SP-4119 [S]	S.R.O.	1966	3.00	6.00	12.00
SP-4124 [S]	Sounds Like	1967	3.00	6.00	12.00
SP-4134	Herb Alpert's Ninth	1967	2.50	5.00	10.00
SP-4146	The Beat of the Brass	1968	2.50	5.00	10.00
SP-4166	Christmas Album	1968	3.00	6.00	12.00
SP-4190	Warm	1969	2.50	5.00	10.00
SP-4228	The Brass Are Comin'	1969	2.50	5.00	10.00
SP-4245	Greatest Hits	1970	2.50	5.00	10.00
SP-4314	Summertime	1971	2.50	5.00	10.00
SP-4341	Solid Brass	1972	2.50	5.00	10.00
SP-4521	Coney Island	1975	2.50	5.00	10.00
SP-4627	Greatest Hits, Vol. 2	1976	2.50	5.00	10.00
SP-5022	Bullish	1984	2.00	4.00	8.00
SP-6011 [(2)]	Foursider	197?	2.50	5.00	10.00
—Reissue					
LP-9004 [DJ]	The Best from Herb Alpert & The Tijuana Brass	196?	3.75	7.50	15.00
—Promo-only compilation					
ST-90387 [S]	Whipped Cream & Other Delights	1965	3.75	7.50	15.00
—Capitol Record Club edition					

ALPERT, HERB/HUGH MASEKELA

Also see each artist's individual listings.

Number	Title (A Side/B Side)	Yr	VG	VG+	NM
45s					
HORIZON					
115	Skokiaan/African Summer	1978	—	2.00	4.00
116	Lobo/African Summer	1978	—	2.00	4.00
Albums					
A&M					
SP-3150	Herb Alpert/Hugh Masekela	198?	2.00	4.00	8.00
HORIZON					
728	Herb Alpert/Hugh Masekela	1978	2.50	5.00	10.00

ALTAIRS, THE

GEORGE BENSON was a member.

Number	Title (A Side/B Side)	Yr	VG	VG+	NM
45s					
AMY					
803	If You Love Me/Groove Time	1960	5.00	10.00	20.00

ALTON AND JIMMY

Number	Title (A Side/B Side)	Yr	VG	VG+	NM
45s					
SUN					
323	Have Faith in My Love/No More Crying the Blues	1959	6.25	12.50	25.00

ALVIN AND BILL

Number	Title (A Side/B Side)	Yr	VG	VG+	NM
45s					
FERNWOOD					
124	Typing Jive/How Long	1960	15.00	30.00	60.00

AMAZING RHYTHM ACES

Number	Title (A Side/B Side)	Yr	VG	VG+	NM
45s					
ABC					
12078	Third Rate Romance/Mystery Train	1975	—	2.50	5.00
12142	Amazing Grace (Used to Be Her Favorite Song)/ Beautiful Lie	1975	—	2.00	4.00
12202	Same Ol' Me/The End Is Not in Sight	1976	—	2.00	4.00
12242	Dancin' the Night Away/If I Just Knew What to Say	1976	—	2.00	4.00
12272	Two Can Do It Too/Living in a World Unknown	1977	—	2.00	4.00
12287	Just Between You and Me and the Wall/Never Been to the Islands	1977	—	2.00	4.00

Number	Title (A Side/B Side)	Yr	VG	VG+	NM
12359	Burning the Ballroom Down/All That I Had Left (With You)	1978	—	2.00	4.00
12369	Ashes of Love/All That I Had Left (With You)	1978	—	2.00	4.00
12454	Lipstick Traces (On a Cigarette)/Whispering in the Night	1979	—	2.00	4.00
COLUMBIA					
10983	Love and Happiness/Homestead in My Heart	1979	—	2.00	4.00
WARNER BROS.					
49543	Living on Borrowed Time/What Kind of Love Is This	1980	—	2.00	4.00
49600	I Musta Died and Gone to Texas/Give Me Flowers While I'm Living	1980	—	2.00	4.00
Albums					
ABC					
D-913	Stacked Deck	1975	5.00	10.00	20.00
D-940	Too Stuffed to Jump	1976	3.75	7.50	15.00
AB-1005	Toucan Do It Too	1977	3.75	7.50	15.00
AA-1063	Burning the Ballroom Down	1978	3.75	7.50	15.00
AA-1123	The Amazing Rhythm Aces	1979	5.00	10.00	20.00
COLUMBIA					
JC 36083	The Amazing Rhythm Aces	1979	3.00	6.00	12.00
—Reissue of ABC 1123					
WARNER BROS.					
BSK 3476	How the Hell Do You Spell Rythum?	1980	3.00	6.00	12.00

AMBASSADORS, THE (1)

Male vocal group from Philadelphia.

Number	Title (A Side/B Side)	Yr	VG	VG+	NM
45s					
ARCTIC					
150	Ain't Got the Love of One Girl/Music Makes You Wanna Dance	1969	2.50	5.00	10.00
153	Storm Warning/I Dig You Baby	1969	2.50	5.00	10.00
156	Can't Take My Eyes Off You/A.W.O.L.	1969	2.50	5.00	10.00
ATLANTIC					
2442	(I've Got to Find) Happiness)/I'm So Proud of My Baby	1967	2.50	5.00	10.00
2491	Good Love Gone Bad/Happiness	1968	2.50	5.00	10.00
2547	We Got Love/Never Get Tired of Loving You	1968	2.50	5.00	10.00
Albums					
ARCTIC					
ALPS-1005	Soul Summit	1969	6.25	12.50	25.00

AMBASSADORS, THE (2)

British band known as The Saints in the U.K.

Number	Title (A Side/B Side)	Yr	VG	VG+	NM
45s					
DOT					
16528	Surfin' John Brown/Big Breaker	1963	7.50	15.00	30.00

AMBASSADORS, THE (U)

More than one group. Some of these may go with (1) above.

Number	Title (A Side/B Side)	Yr	VG	VG+	NM
45s					
CUCA					
1022	Christmas Polka/Little Drummer Boy	1960	3.00	6.00	12.00
SOUND STAGE 7					
2588	If You Don't Know (You Better Ask Somebody)/ There's Something on My Baby's Mind	1967	2.50	5.00	10.00
TIMELY					
1001	Darling I'm Sorry/Willa-Bea	1954	100.00	200.00	400.00
UPTOWN					
734	I Need Someone/Bear With Me	1965	6.25	12.50	25.00

AMBOY DUKES, THE

Also see TED NUGENT.

Number	Title (A Side/B Side)	Yr	VG	VG+	NM
45s					
DISCREET					
1199	Sweet Revenge/Ain't It the Truth	1974	—	3.00	6.00
—As "Ted Nugent and the Amboy Dukes"					
MAINSTREAM					
676	Baby Please Don't Go/Psalms of Aftermath	1968	3.00	6.00	12.00
684	Journey to the Center of the Mind/Mississippi Murderer	1968	3.75	7.50	15.00
693	You Talk Sunshine, I Breathe Fire/Scottish Tea	1968	3.00	6.00	12.00
700	Prodigal Man/Good Natured Emma	1969	3.00	6.00	12.00
704	For His Namesake/Loaded for Bear	1969	3.00	6.00	12.00
711	Flight of the Byrd/Ivory Castles	1969	3.00	6.00	12.00
Albums					
DISCREET					
DS 2181	Call of the Wild	1974	3.75	7.50	15.00
—As "Ted Nugent and the Amboy Dukes"					
DS 2203	Tooth, Fang and Claw	1974	3.75	7.50	15.00
—As "Ted Nugent and the Amboy Dukes"					
MAINSTREAM					
S-414	Dr. Slingshot	1975	3.75	7.50	15.00
S-421	Ted Nugent and the Amboy Dukes	1976	7.50	15.00	30.00
—Reissue of early material					
S-2-801 [(2)]	Journeys and Migrations	1974	7.50	15.00	30.00
—Reissue of 6112 and 6118					
S-6104 [S]	The Amboy Dukes	1967	10.00	20.00	40.00
S-6112	Journey to the Center of the Mind	1968	10.00	20.00	40.00
S-6118	Migration	1968	10.00	20.00	40.00
S-6125	The Best of the Original Amboy Dukes	1969	7.50	15.00	30.00
56104 [M]	The Amboy Dukes	1967	20.00	40.00	80.00
POLYDOR					
24-4012	Marriage on the Rocks/Rock Bottom	1970	6.25	12.50	25.00
24-4035	Survival of the Fittest/Live	1971	6.25	12.50	25.00
—As "Ted Nugent and the Amboy Dukes"					

AMBROSE SLADE

See SLADE.

AMBROSIA

Number	Title (A Side/B Side)	Yr	VG	VG+	NM
45s					
20TH CENTURY					
2207	Holdin' On to Yesterday/Make Us All Aware	1975	—	2.50	5.00
2244	Nice, Nice, Very Nice/Lover Arrive	1975	—	2.00	4.00
2310	Can't Let a Woman/The Brunt	1976	—	2.00	4.00
2327	Magical Mystery Tour/Cowboy Star	1977	—	2.50	5.00
FULL MOON					
49654	Outside/I Can't Tell You Why	1981	—	2.50	5.00
—B-side by Eagles					
SCEPTER					
12373	Shine On/Listen To Her Sing	1973	2.00	4.00	8.00
WARNER BROS.					
8640	How Much I Feel/Ready for Amarillo	1978	—	2.50	5.00
—With "Burbank..." palm trees label					
8640	How Much I Feel/Ready for Amarillo	1978	—	2.00	4.00
—With white label					
8699	Life Beyond L.A./Angola	1978	—	2.00	4.00
8817	If Heaven Could Find Me/Apothecary	1979	—	2.00	4.00
29937	Feelin' Alive Again/For Openers	1982	—	2.00	4.00
29996	How Can You Love Me/Still Not Satisfied	1982	—	2.00	4.00
49225	Biggest Part of Me/Livin' on My Own	1980	—	2.00	4.00
49508	You're the Only Woman (You & I)/Shape I'm In	1980	—	2.00	4.00
49590	Cryin' in the Rain/No Big Deal	1980	—	2.00	4.00
Albums					
20TH CENTURY					
T-434	Ambrosia	1975	3.00	6.00	12.00
—Original cover with black border					
T-434	Ambrosia	1975	2.50	5.00	10.00
—New cover without black border					
T-510	Somewhere I've Never Traveled	1976	3.00	6.00	12.00
—Fold-open cover in the shape of a pyramid					
T-510	Somewhere I've Never Traveled	1976	2.50	5.00	10.00
—Standard cover					
NAUTILUS					
NR-23	Life Beyond L.A.	1981	7.50	5.00	30.00
—Audiophile vinyl					
WARNER BROS.					
BSK 3135	Life Beyond L.A.	1978	2.50	5.00	10.00
BSK 3181	Ambrosia	1978	2.00	4.00	8.00
—Reissue of 20th Century 434					
BSK 3368	One Eighty	1980	2.50	5.00	10.00
BSK 3638	Road Island	1982	2.50	5.00	10.00

AMECHE, DON, AND FRANCES LANGFORD

Number	Title (A Side/B Side)	Yr	VG	VG+	NM
Albums					
COLUMBIA					
CL 1692	The Bickersons	1962	5.00	10.00	20.00
—Live-in-the-studio recordings from 1961					
CL 1883	The Bickersons Fight Back	1962	5.00	10.00	20.00
—More live-in-the-studio recordings from 1961					
G 30523 [(2)]	The Bickersons Rematch	1970	3.75	7.50	15.00
—Compilation of the earlier Columbia LPs					
RADIOLA					
MR 1115	The Bickersons	198?	3.00	6.00	12.00
—Compilation of radio shows					
RADIOLA/MURRAY HILL					
3MH 36721 [(3)]	Return of the Bickersons	1987	5.00	10.00	20.00
—Compilation of radio shows					

AMECHE, JIM

Number	Title (A Side/B Side)	Yr	VG	VG+	NM
45s					
DELTONE					
5016	The First Christmas Tree (Part 1)/The First Christmas Tree (Part 2)	1964	2.50	5.00	10.00
RIC					
137	The First Christmas Tree (Part 1)/The First Christmas Tree (Part 2)	1964	2.50	5.00	10.00
137 [PS]	The First Christmas Tree (Part 1)/The First Christmas Tree (Part 2)	1964	3.00	6.00	12.00

AMELIO, JOHNNY

Number	Title (A Side/B Side)	Yr	VG	VG+	NM
45s					
BLUE MOON					
405	Jugue/Downbeat	1957	37.50	75.00	150.00
408	Jo-Ann, Jo-Ann/I'll Forever Love You	1958	25.00	50.00	100.00
410	Jugue/Jo-Ann, Jo-Ann	1958	20.00	40.00	80.00

AMEN CORNER

Number	Title (A Side/B Side)	Yr	VG	VG+	NM
45s					
DERAM					
7521	Run, Run, Run/High in the Sky	1968	2.50	5.00	10.00
85014	Gin House Blues/I Know	1967	3.00	6.00	12.00
85021	Nema/World of Broken Hearts	1967	3.00	6.00	12.00
IMMEDIATE					
5013	If Paradise Is Half As Nice/Hey Hey Girl	1968	2.50	5.00	10.00

AMERICA

Number	Title (A Side/B Side)	Yr	VG	VG+	NM
45s					
AMERICAN INT'L.					
700	California Dreamin'/See It My Way	1979	—	2.50	5.00
—B-side by FDR					
700 [PS]	California Dreamin'/See It My Way	1979	—	2.50	5.00
CAPITOL					
4752	Only Game in Town/High in the City	1979	—	2.00	4.00
4777	All My Life/One Morning	1979	—	2.00	4.00
4817	All Around/1960	1980	—	2.00	4.00
4915	Catch That Train/He Could Have Been the One	1980	—	2.00	4.00
4950	One in a Million/Hangover	1980	—	2.00	4.00

Number	Title (A Side/B Side)	Yr	VG	VG+	NM
B-5142	You Can Do Magic/Even the Score	1982	—	2.00	4.00
B-5177	Right Before Your Eyes/Inspector Mills	1982	—	—	3.00
B-5177 [PS]	Right Before Your Eyes/Inspector Mills	1982	—	—	3.00
B-5236	The Border/Sometimes Lovers	1983	—	—	3.00
B-5236 [PS]	The Border/Sometimes Lovers	1983	—	—	3.00
B-5275	My Dear/Cost the Spirit	1983	—	—	3.00
B-5398	Special Girl/Unconditional Love	1984	—	—	3.00
B-5430	(Can't Fall Asleep to a) Lullaby/Fallin' Off the World	1984	—	—	3.00
WARNER BROS.					
7555	A Horse with No Name/Everyone I Meet Is From California	1972	—	3.00	6.00
7580	I Need You/Riverside	1972	—	2.50	5.00
7580 [PS]	I Need You/Riverside	1972	—	3.00	6.00
7641	Ventura Highway/Saturn Nights	1972	—	2.50	5.00
7650	A Horse with No Name/I Need You	1973	—	2.00	4.00
—"Back to Back Hits" series					
7670	Don't Cross the River/To Each His Own	1972	—	2.50	5.00
7694	Only in Your Heart/Moon Song	1973	—	2.50	5.00
7725	Muskrat Love/Cornwall Blank	1973	—	2.50	5.00
7760	Rainbow Song/Willow Tree Lullaby	1973	—	2.50	5.00
7785	She's Gonna Let You Down/Green Monkey	1974	—	2.50	5.00
7839	Tin Man/In the Country	1974	—	2.50	5.00
8014	Tin Man/In the Country	1974	—	2.00	4.00
8048	Lonely People/Mad Dog	1974	—	2.50	5.00
8048 [PS]	Lonely People/Mad Dog	1974	—	3.00	6.00
8086	Sister Golden Hair/Midnight	1975	—	2.50	5.00
8118	Daisy Jane/Tomorrow	1975	—	2.50	5.00
8157	Woman Tonight/Bell Tree	1975	—	2.50	5.00
8212	Today's the Day/Hideaway (Part 2)	1976	—	2.50	5.00
8238	Amber Cascades/Who Loves You	1976	—	2.50	5.00
8285	She's Beside You/She's a Liar	1976	—	2.50	5.00
8373	God of the Sun/Down to the Water	1977	—	2.50	5.00
8397	Don't Cry Baby/Monster	1977	—	2.50	5.00
Albums					
CAPITOL					
SO-11950	Silent Letter	1979	2.50	5.00	10.00
SOO-12098	Alibi	1980	2.50	5.00	10.00
ST-12209	View from the Ground	1982	2.50	5.00	10.00
ST-12277	Your Move	1983	2.50	5.00	10.00
ST-12370	Perspective	1984	2.50	5.00	10.00
ST-12422	In Concert	1985	2.50	5.00	10.00
SN-16275	Alibi	1982	2.00	4.00	8.00
SN-16350	View from the Ground	1985	2.00	4.00	8.00
SN-16361	Your Move	1985	2.00	4.00	8.00
WARNER BROS.					
BS 2576	America	1971	6.25	12.50	25.00
—Allegedly, first pressings omit "A Horse with No Name."					
BS 2576	America	1972	3.00	6.00	12.00
—With "A Horse with No Name"; green label					
BS 2655	Homecoming	1972	3.00	6.00	12.00
BS 2728	Hat Trick	1973	3.00	6.00	12.00
BS 2808	Holiday	1974	3.00	6.00	12.00
BS4 2808 [Q]	Holiday	1974	5.00	10.00	20.00
BS 2852	Hearts	1975	3.00	6.00	12.00
BS4 2852 [Q]	Hearts	1975	5.00	10.00	20.00
BS 2894	History/America's Greatest Hits	1975	3.00	6.00	12.00
BS 2932	Hideaway	1976	3.00	6.00	12.00
BSK 3017	Harbor	1977	3.00	6.00	12.00
BSK 3110	History/America's Greatest Hits	1977	2.50	5.00	10.00
—With "Burbank" palm trees label (later white labels are $8 NM)					
BSK 3136	America/Live	1977	3.00	6.00	12.00

AMERICAN BEATLES, THE

Number	Title (A Side/B Side)	Yr	VG	VG+	NM
45s					
BYP					
1001	She's Mine/Theme of the American Beetles	1964	5.00	10.00	20.00
—As "The American Beetles"					
ROULETTE					
4550	You Did It to Me/Don't Be Unkind	1964	3.75	7.50	15.00
4559	School Days/Hey Hey Girl	1964	3.75	7.50	15.00

AMERICAN BLUES, THE

Early incarnation of ZZ TOP.

Number	Title (A Side/B Side)	Yr	VG	VG+	NM
45s					
AMY					
997	Your Love Is True/Say So	1967	6.25	12.50	25.00
KARMA					
1001	If I Were a Carpenter/(B-side unknown)	1967	10.00	20.00	40.00
Albums					
KARMA					
1001	The American Blues Is Here	1967	100.00	200.00	400.00
UNI					
73044	The American Blues Do Their Thing	1968	15.00	30.00	60.00

AMERICAN BLUES EXCHANGE, THE

Number	Title (A Side/B Side)	Yr	VG	VG+	NM
Albums					
TAYL					
TLS-1	Blueprint	1969	100.00	200.00	400.00

AMERICAN BREED, THE

Members of this band later formed RUFUS.

Number	Title (A Side/B Side)	Yr	VG	VG+	NM
45s					
ACTA					
802	I Don't Think You Know/Give Two Young Lovers a Chance	1967	2.00	4.00	8.00
804	Step Out of Your Mind/Same Old Thing	1967	2.50	5.00	10.00
808	Don't Forget About Me/Short Skirts	1967	2.00	4.00	8.00
811	Bend Me, Shape Me/Mindrocker	1967	3.00	6.00	12.00
821	Green Light/Don't It Make You Cry	1968	2.00	4.00	8.00
821 [PS]	Green Light/Don't It Make You Cry	1968	5.00	10.00	20.00
824	Ready, Willing and Able/Take Me If You Want Me	1968	2.00	4.00	8.00
827	Anyway You Want Me/Master of My Fate	1968	2.00	4.00	8.00
830	Private Zoo/Keep the Faith	1968	2.00	4.00	8.00
833	Hunky Funky/Enter Her Majesty	1969	2.00	4.00	8.00
836	Room at the Top/Walls	1969	2.00	4.00	8.00
837	Cool It/The Brain	1969	2.00	4.00	8.00
PARAMOUNT					
0040	When I'm With You/Can't Make It Without You	1970	—	3.00	6.00
Albums					
ACTA					
8002 [M]	The American Breed	1967	5.00	10.00	20.00
8003 [M]	Bend Me, Shape Me	1968	5.00	10.00	20.00
38002 [S]	The American Breed	1967	6.25	12.50	25.00
38003 [S]	Bend Me, Shape Me	1968	6.25	12.50	25.00
38006	Pumpkin, Powder, Scarlet & Green	1968	5.00	10.00	20.00
38008	Lonely Side of the City	1969	5.00	10.00	20.00

AMERICAN DREAM, THE

Number	Title (A Side/B Side)	Yr	VG	VG+	NM
45s					
AMPEX					
11001	Goodnews/I Ain't Searchin'	1970	2.50	5.00	10.00
Albums					
AMPEX					
A-10101	The American Dream	1970	5.00	10.00	20.00
—Produced by Todd Rundgren					

AMERICAN EAGLE

Number	Title (A Side/B Side)	Yr	VG	VG+	NM
45s					
DECCA					
32788	Family/Gospel	1971	2.00	4.00	8.00
32833	Ballad of a Well-Known Gun/On the Rack	1971	2.50	5.00	10.00
Albums					
DECCA					
DL 75258	American Eagle	1971	5.00	10.00	20.00

AMERICAN FOUR, THE

With Arthur Lee, future leader of LOVE.

Number	Title (A Side/B Side)	Yr	VG	VG+	NM
45s					
SELMA					
2001	Luci Baines/Soul Food	1964	12.50	25.00	50.00

AMERICAN REVOLUTION

Number	Title (A Side/B Side)	Yr	VG	VG+	NM
Albums					
FLICK DISC					
FLS-45,002	American Revolution	1968	6.25	12.50	25.00

AMERICAN SPRING

Formed by ex-members of THE HONEYS. Also see SPRING.

Number	Title (A Side/B Side)	Yr	VG	VG+	NM
45s					
COLUMBIA					
45834	Fallin' in Love/Shyin' Away	1973	7.50	15.00	30.00
45834 [PS]	Fallin' in Love/Shyin' Away	1973	15.00	30.00	60.00

AMES, ED

Also see THE AMES BROTHERS.

Number	Title (A Side/B Side)	Yr	VG	VG+	NM
45s					
HELLO LYNDON					
RPKM-4426	Hello, Lyndon!/Hello, Lyndon! (Chorus)	1964	6.25	12.50	25.00
RPKM-4426 [PS]	Hello, Lyndon!/Hello, Lyndon! (Chorus)	1964	12.50	25.00	50.00
—Promotional item for Lyndon Johnson's 1964 election campaign					
RCA VICTOR					
SP-45-188 [DJ]	The Ballad Of The Christmas Donkey/Let It Snow! Let It Snow! Let It Snow!	1968	2.00	4.00	8.00
47-6791	The Bean Song/I'd Give You the World	1957	3.00	6.00	12.00
—As "Eddie Ames"					
47-8231	My Love Is Yours/Somewhere	1963	2.00	4.00	8.00
47-8245	Before I Kiss the World Goodbye/They Were You	1963	2.00	4.00	8.00
47-8320	It Only Takes a Moment/The Time Has Come	1964	2.00	4.00	8.00
47-8393	Give Me Back My Life/Monica (Love Theme from "The Carpetbaggers")	1964	2.00	4.00	8.00
47-8483	Try to Remember/Love Is Here to Stay	1964	2.00	4.00	8.00
47-8547	Dio Mio/Weaver, Weaver	1965	2.00	4.00	8.00
47-8700	Pretty Is/Melinda	1965	2.00	4.00	8.00
47-8752	River Boy/A Man and a Woman	1965	2.00	4.00	8.00
47-8871	Gone/There's a Time for Everything	1966	2.00	4.00	8.00
47-9002	My Cup Runneth Over/It Seems a Long, Long Time	1966	2.00	4.00	8.00
47-9178	One Little Girl at a Time/Time, Time	1967	—	3.00	6.00
47-9249	Ballad of the War Wagon/Time, Time	1967	—	3.00	6.00
47-9319	Let Me So Love/When the Snow Is On the Roses	1967	—	3.00	6.00
47-9400	Who Will Answer/My Love Is Gone from Me	1967	—	3.00	6.00
47-9400 [PS]	Who Will Answer/My Love Is Gone from Me	1967	3.00	6.00	12.00
47-9517	Apologize/The Wind Will Change Tomorrow	1968	—	3.00	6.00
47-9589	I'll Stay Lonely/All My Love's Laughter	1968	—	3.00	6.00
47-9647	Kiss Her Now/Gloves, Pictures, Dreams (Doors, Mirrors and Heartaches)	1968	—	3.00	6.00
47-9682	Away in a Manger/Carry the Lord to Jerusalem	1968	—	—	—
—Unreleased					
47-9726	Changing, Changing/Six Words	1969	—	3.00	6.00
47-9864	Chippewa Town/Sing Away the World	1970	—	3.00	6.00
74-0156	2001/Son of a Preacher Man	1969	—	3.00	6.00
74-0253	Love of the Common People/Leave Them a Flower	1969	—	3.00	6.00
74-0296	Thing Called Love/Today Is the First Day of the Rest of Our Lives	1969	—	3.00	6.00
74-0329	Honey, What's the Matter/Three Good Reasons	1970	—	2.50	5.00
74-0398	The Answer Is/Sweet, Sweet Reason	1970	—	2.50	5.00
74-0498	More Than Ever Before/The Day	1971	—	2.50	5.00
74-0551	He Gives Us All His Love/Angelica	1971	—	2.50	5.00
74-0678	And I Love You So/The Ship	1972	—	2.00	4.00
74-0726	Distant Drums/Blue Side of Lonesome	1972	—	2.00	4.00
74-0800	Lost Horizon/Question Me an Answer	1972	—	2.00	4.00
74-0883	Butterflies Are Free/The World Is a Circle	1973	—	2.00	4.00

Number	Title (A Side/B Side)	Yr	VG	VG+	NM
Albums					
RCA VICTOR					
LPM-2781 [M]	Opening Night	1963	3.00	6.00	12.00
LSP-2781 [S]	Opening Night	1963	3.75	7.50	15.00
LPM-2944 [M]	The Ed Ames Album	1964	3.00	6.00	12.00
LSP-2944 [S]	The Ed Ames Album	1964	3.75	7.50	15.00
LPM-3390 [M]	My Kind of Songs	1965	3.00	6.00	12.00
LSP-3390 [S]	My Kind of Songs	1965	3.75	7.50	15.00
LPM-3460 [M]	It's a Man's World	1965	3.00	6.00	12.00
LSP-3460 [S]	It's a Man's World	1965	3.75	7.50	15.00
LPM-3636 [M]	More I Cannot Wish You	1966	2.50	5.00	10.00
LSP-3636 [S]	More I Cannot Wish You	1966	3.00	6.00	12.00
LPM-3774 [M]	My Cup Runneth Over	1967	2.50	5.00	10.00
LSP-3774 [S]	My Cup Runneth Over	1967	3.00	6.00	12.00
LPM-3834 [M]	Time, Time	1967	3.00	6.00	12.00
LSP-3834 [S]	Time, Time	1967	2.50	5.00	10.00
LPM-3838 [M]	Christmas with Ed Ames	1967	3.75	7.50	15.00
LSP-3838 [S]	Christmas with Ed Ames	1967	3.00	6.00	12.00
—Same as above, but in stereo					
LPM-3913 [M]	When the Snow Is On the Roses	1967	3.00	6.00	12.00
LSP-3913 [S]	When the Snow Is On the Roses	1967	2.50	5.00	10.00
LPM-3961 [M]	Who Will Answer? And Other Songs of Our Time	1968	3.75	7.50	15.00
LSP-3961 [S]	Who Will Answer? And Other Songs of Our Time	1968	2.50	5.00	10.00
LPM-4028 [M]	Apologize	1968	5.00	10.00	20.00
LSP-4028 [S]	Apologize	1968	2.50	5.00	10.00
LSP-4079	The Hits of Broadway and Hollywood	1968	2.50	5.00	10.00
LSP-4128	A Time for Living, A Time for Hope	1969	2.50	5.00	10.00
LSP-4172	The Windmills of Your Mind	1969	2.50	5.00	10.00
LSP-4184	The Best of Ed Ames	1969	2.50	5.00	10.00
LSP-4249	Love of the Common People	1969	2.50	5.00	10.00
LSP-4381	Sing Away the World	1970	2.50	5.00	10.00
LSP-4453	The Songs of Bacharach and David	1971	2.50	5.00	10.00

AMES, NANCY

Number	Title (A Side/B Side)	Yr	VG	VG+	NM
45s					
ABC					
11100	On Green Dolphin Street/Something's Gotten Hold of My Heart	1968	—	3.00	6.00
EPIC					
9845	Shake a Hand/Funny Thing About It	1965	2.00	4.00	8.00
9874	I've Got a Lot of Love (Left in Me)/Friends and Lovers Forever	1965	2.00	4.00	8.00
9885	Dear Hearts and Gentle People/Friends and Lovers Forever	1966	2.00	4.00	8.00
10003	He Wore the Green Beret/War Is a Card Game	1966	2.00	4.00	8.00
10056	I Don't Want to Talk About It/Cry Softly	1966	3.00	6.00	12.00
10149	Love's Like Wine/My Story Book	1967	2.00	4.00	8.00
LIBERTY					
55548	Bonsoir Cher/Cu Cu Ru Cu Cu Paloma	1963	2.50	5.00	10.00
55598	An Elizabethan Ballad (Part 1)/An Elizabethan Ballad (Part 2)	1963	2.50	5.00	10.00
55737	Malaguena Salerosa/Cu Cu Ru Cu Cu Paloma	1964	2.50	5.00	10.00
55762	It Scares Me/Let Tonight Linger On	1965	2.50	5.00	10.00
Albums					
EPIC					
LN 24189 [M]	Latin Pulse	1966	3.00	6.00	12.00
LN 24197 [M]	As Time Goes By	1967	3.00	6.00	12.00
LN 24238 [M]	Spiced with Brazil	1967	3.00	6.00	12.00
BN 26189 [S]	Latin Pulse	1966	3.75	7.50	15.00
BN 26197 [S]	As Time Goes By	1967	3.75	7.50	15.00
BN 26238 [S]	Spiced with Brazil	1967	3.75	7.50	15.00
BN 26378	Nancy Ames at the Americana	1968	3.00	6.00	12.00
LIBERTY					
LRP-3276 [M]	The Incredible Nancy Ames	1963	3.75	7.50	15.00
LRP-3299 [M]	Portrait of Nancy	1963	3.75	7.50	15.00
LRP-3329 [M]	I Never Will Marry	1964	3.75	7.50	15.00
LRP-3369 [M]	This Is the Girl That Is	1964	3.75	7.50	15.00
LRP-3400 [M]	Let It Be Me	1965	3.75	7.50	15.00
LST-7276 [S]	The Incredible Nancy Ames	1963	5.00	10.00	20.00
LST-7299 [S]	Portrait of Nancy	1963	5.00	10.00	20.00
LST-7329 [S]	I Never Will Marry	1964	5.00	10.00	20.00
LST-7369 [S]	This Is the Girl That Is	1964	5.00	10.00	20.00
LST-7400 [S]	Let It Be Me	1965	5.00	10.00	20.00
SUNSET					
SUM-1109 [M]	The Versatile Nancy Ames	196?	3.00	6.00	12.00
SUS-5109 [S]	The Versatile Nancy Ames	196?	3.75	7.50	15.00

AMES BROTHERS, THE

Also see ED AMES.

Number	Title (A Side/B Side)	Yr	VG	VG+	NM
45s					
CORAL					
60173	Sentimental Me/Blue Prelude	1950	3.75	7.50	15.00
—Ames Brothers records on Coral before 60173 are unconfirmed on 45 rpm.					
60185	Dormi, Dormi/Marianna	1950	3.75	7.50	15.00
60209	Hoop-De-Doo/Stars Are the Windows of Heaven	1950	3.75	7.50	15.00
60212	Blue Prelude/Lorelei	1950	3.75	7.50	15.00
60255	Can Anyone Explain?/Sittin', Starin', and Rockin'	1950	3.75	7.50	15.00
60267	The Twelve Days of Christmas/Wassail Song	1950	3.75	7.50	15.00
60268	Silent Night/Adeste Fideles	1950	3.75	7.50	15.00
60269	Hark! The Herald Angels Sing/It Came Upon a Midnight Clear	1950	3.75	7.50	15.00
60270	Oh, Little Town of Bethlehem/God Rest Ye Merry Gentlemen	1950	3.75	7.50	15.00
60300	Thirsty for Your Kisses/I Don't Mind Being All Alone	1950	3.75	7.50	15.00
60327	Oh Babe/To Think You've Chosen Me	1950	3.75	7.50	15.00
60333	The Thing/Music by the Angels (Lyrics by the Lord)	1950	3.75	7.50	15.00
60336	Just a Dream of You, Dear/In the Evening in the Moonlight	1950	3.75	7.50	15.00
60337	Till We Meet Again/Tell Me Your Dream	1950	3.75	7.50	15.00
60338	Meet Me Tonight in Dreamland/Moonlight Bay	1950	3.75	7.50	15.00
60339	Because/Love's Old Sweet Song	1950	3.75	7.50	15.00
60352	Loving Is Believing/Music by the Angels (Lyrics by the Lord)	1951	3.75	7.50	15.00
60363	Three Dollars and Ninety-Eight Cents/More Than I Care to Remember	1951	3.75	7.50	15.00
60385	Sentimental Me/Dormi, Dormi	1951	3.75	7.50	15.00
60386	Can Anyone Explain?/Lingering Down the Lane (Ah! La Petit Vin Blanc)	1951	3.75	7.50	15.00
60387	Lorelei/To Think You've Chosen Me	1951	3.75	7.50	15.00
60388	Stars Are the Window of Heaven/I Don't Mind Being All Alone (When I'm Alone with You)	1951	3.75	7.50	15.00
60397	Rag Mop/Hoop-De-Doo	1951	3.75	7.50	15.00
60398	Marianna/(Lift Your Glass) Sing Until the Cows Come Home	1951	3.75	7.50	15.00
60399	Clancey Lowered the Boom/More Beer	1951	3.75	7.50	15.00
60400	Noah's Ark/Bar Room Polka	1951	3.75	7.50	15.00
60404	My Love Serenade/I Love You Much Too Much	1951	3.75	7.50	15.00
60452	Too Many Women/Sometimes There Must Be Happiness	1951	3.75	7.50	15.00
60489	Wang Wang Blues/Who'll Take My Love	1951	3.75	7.50	15.00
60510	Hawaiian War Chant/Sweet Leilani	1951	3.75	7.50	15.00
60511	My Little Grass Shack/To You, Sweetheart, Aloha	1951	3.75	7.50	15.00
60512	Sing Me a Song of the Islands/Song of the Islands	1951	3.75	7.50	15.00
60513	Blue Hawaii/Moon of Manakoora	1951	3.75	7.50	15.00
60549	Only, Only You/Everything's Gonna Be Alright	1951	3.75	7.50	15.00
60566	Sentimental Journey/Undecided	1951	3.75	7.50	15.00
60572	Jolly Old St. Nicholas/Ting-a-Ling-a-Jingle	1951	3.75	7.50	15.00
60617	I Wanna Love You/I'll Still Love You	1952	3.00	6.00	12.00
60628	Mother, At Your Feet Is Kneeling/Lovely Lady Dressed in Blue	1952	3.00	6.00	12.00
60633	Deep River/Dry Bones	1952	3.00	6.00	12.00
60634	Shadrack/Swing Low, Sweet Chariot	1952	3.00	6.00	12.00
60635	Joshua Fit De Battle of Jericho/Go Down Moses	1952	3.00	6.00	12.00
60636	Blind Barnabas/Who Built the Ark	1952	3.00	6.00	12.00
60680	The Shiek of Araby/And So I Waited	1952	3.00	6.00	12.00
60751	Stardust/Crazy 'Cause I Love You	1952	3.00	6.00	12.00
60773	Auf Wiedersehn Sweetheart/Break the Bonds That Bind Me	1952	3.00	6.00	12.00
60804	Absence Makes the Heart Grow Fonder (For Someone Else)/String Along	1952	3.00	6.00	12.00
60846	My Favorite Song/Al-Lee-O! Al-Lee-Ay!	1952	3.00	6.00	12.00
60861	Sing a Song of Santa Claus/Winter's Here Again	1952	3.00	6.00	12.00
60870	Do Nothin' Till You Hear from Me/No Moon at All	1952	3.00	6.00	12.00
60885	Home on the Range/Wagon Wheels	1952	3.00	6.00	12.00
60886	Rye Whiskey/You Are My Sunshine	1952	3.00	6.00	12.00
60887	Old Faithful/Tumbling Tumbleweeds	1952	3.00	6.00	12.00
60888	The Last Round-Up/The Strawberry Roan	1952	3.00	6.00	12.00
60926	Lonely Wine/Can't I	1953	3.00	6.00	12.00
60967	At the End of a Rainbow/Candy Bar Boogie	1953	3.00	6.00	12.00
61005	Always in My Dreams/This Is Fiesta	1953	3.00	6.00	12.00
61060	Lazy River/Stardust	1953	3.00	6.00	12.00
61127	Don't Believe a Word They Say/Helen Polka	1954	3.00	6.00	12.00
61145	Don't Lie to Me/Don't Believe a Word They Say	1954	3.00	6.00	12.00
61723	Mother At Your Feet Is Kneeling/Lovely Lady Dressed in Blue	1956	3.00	6.00	12.00
EPIC					
9530	Love Me with All Your Heart/Love Is an Ocean of Emotion	1962	2.00	4.00	8.00
9591	Surrender, Surrender/Wrong Man	1963	2.00	4.00	8.00
9630	Washington Square/Knees Up, Mother Brown	1963	2.00	4.00	8.00
MCA					
60002	Rag Mop/Sentimental Me	1973	—	2.00	4.00
60005	Sentimental Journey/Undecided	1973	—	2.00	4.00
—With Les Brown					
RCA VICTOR					
WY 491	There'll Always Be a Christmas/I Got a Cold for Christmas	1954	2.50	5.00	10.00
—From the "Little Nipper" children's series					
WY 491 [PS]	There'll Always Be a Christmas/I Got a Cold for Christmas	1954	3.00	6.00	12.00
47-5325	You You You/Once Upon a Time	1953	3.00	6.00	12.00
47-5404	My Love, My Life, My Happiness/If You Want My Heart	1953	3.00	6.00	12.00
47-5530	I Can't Believe That You're in Love with Me/ Boogie Woogie Maxine	1953	3.00	6.00	12.00
47-5644	Man Is for the Woman Made/The Man with the Banjo	1954	2.50	5.00	10.00
47-5764	Leave It to Your Heart/Let's Walk and Talk	1954	2.50	5.00	10.00
47-5840	One More Time/Hopelessly	1954	2.50	5.00	10.00
47-5897	The Naughty Lady of Shady Lane/Addio	1954	2.50	5.00	10.00
47-5929	There'll Always Be a Christmas/I Got a Cold for Christmas	1954	2.50	5.00	10.00
47-6051	Sympathetic Eyes/Sweet Brown-Eyed Baby	1955	2.50	5.00	10.00
47-6117	Gotta Be This or That/Southern Cross	1955	2.50	5.00	10.00
47-6156	Wrong Again/Merci Beaucoup	1955	2.50	5.00	10.00
47-6208	My Bonnie Lassie/So Will I	1955	2.50	5.00	10.00
47-6323	My Love, Your Love/The Next Time It Happens	1955	2.50	5.00	10.00
47-6400	Forever Darling/I'm Gonna Love You	1956	2.50	5.00	10.00
47-6481	It Only Hurts for a Little While/If You Wanna See Mamie Tonight	1956	2.50	5.00	10.00
47-6566	I Couldn't Sleep a Wink Last Night/(B-side unknown)	1956	2.50	5.00	10.00
47-6608	49 Shades of Green/Summer Sweetheart	1956	2.50	5.00	10.00
47-6720	I Saw Esau/The Game of Love	1956	2.50	5.00	10.00
47-6821	I Only Know One Way to Love You/Did You Ever Get the Roses	1957	2.50	5.00	10.00
47-6851	Yeah, Yeah, Yeah/Man on Fire	1957	2.50	5.00	10.00
47-6930	Tammy/Rockin' Shoes	1957	2.50	5.00	10.00
47-7046	Melodie D'Amour/So Little Time	1957	2.50	5.00	10.00
47-7142	Little Gypsy/In Love	1958	2.50	5.00	10.00
47-7167	A Very Precious Love/Don't Leave Me Now	1958	2.50	5.00	10.00
47-7268	Stay/Little Serenade	1958	2.50	5.00	10.00
47-7315	Pussy Cat/No One But You	1958	2.50	5.00	10.00
47-7365	It's Only a Paper Moon/I Don't Know Why	1958	2.50	5.00	10.00
47-7413	Red River Rose/When the Summer Comes Again	1958	2.50	5.00	10.00
47-7474	Dancin' in the Streets/(Yes I Need) Only Your Love	1959	2.50	5.00	10.00

Number	Title (A Side/B Side)	Yr	VG	VG+	NM
47-7526	Someone to Come Home To/Mason-Dixon Line	1959	2.50	5.00	10.00
47-7565	Now Hear This/Now It's Me	1959	2.50	5.00	10.00
47-7604	Take Me Along/What Do I Hear	1959	2.50	5.00	10.00
47-7655	China Doll/Chritsopher Sunday	1959	2.50	5.00	10.00
47-7655 [PS]	China Doll/Chritsopher Sunday	1959	3.75	7.50	15.00
47-7680	Quizas, Quizas, Quizas/Me Lo Digo Adela	1960	2.00	4.00	8.00
47-7742	A Hayy Pair/Carnival	1960	2.00	4.00	8.00
47-7766	Ring Them Bells/You Are My Love	1960	2.00	4.00	8.00
47-7801	Suzie Wong/There the Hot Winds Blow	1960	2.00	4.00	8.00
47-7836	Kiss from Cuba/Asking for You	1961	2.00	4.00	8.00

7-Inch Extended Plays

CORAL

Number	Title (A Side/B Side)	Yr	VG	VG+	NM
EC 81000	*Star Dust/Lazy River/Wang Wang Blues/The Sheik of Araby	1953	5.00	10.00	20.00
EC 81000 [PS]	Song Time	1953	5.00	10.00	20.00
EC 81041	*White Christmas/Winter Wonderland/Jolly Old St. Nicholas/Ting-a-Ling-a-Jingle	1954	5.00	10.00	20.00
EC 81041 [PS]	Christmas Greetings from the Ames Brothers	1954	5.00	10.00	20.00
EC 81042	*My Favorite Song/Blue Prelude/Cruising Down the River/Oh, You Sweet One	1954	5.00	10.00	20.00
EC 81042 [PS]	Favorite Songs, Vol. 1	1954	5.00	10.00	20.00
EC 81043	*Absence Makes the Heart Grow Fonder (For Someone Else)/String Along/Auf Wiederseh'n Sweetheart/Thirsty for Your Kisses	1954	5.00	10.00	20.00
EC 81043 [PS]	Favorite Songs, Vol. 2	1954	5.00	10.00	20.00
EC 81053	*In the Evening by the Moonlight/Just a Dream of You Dear/Till We Meet Again/You Tell Me Your Dream, I'll Tell You Mine	1954	5.00	10.00	20.00
EC 81053 [PS]	In the Evening by the Moonlight	1954	5.00	10.00	20.00
EC 81054	*Sweet Leilani/Hawaiian War Chant/To You Sweetheart, Aloha/My Little Grass Shack in Kealakekua, Hawaii	1954	5.00	10.00	20.00
EC 81054 [PS]	Sweet Leilani	1954	5.00	10.00	20.00
EC 81060	*Home on the Range/Wagon Wheels/Rye Whiskey/You Are My Sunshine	1955	5.00	10.00	20.00
EC 81060 [PS]	Home on the Range	1955	5.00	10.00	20.00
EC 81100	Dry Bones/Deep River//Shadrack/Swing Low Sweet Chariot	1956	5.00	10.00	20.00
EC 81100 [PS]	Favorite Spirituals	1956	5.00	10.00	20.00
83010 [DJ]	Sing a Song of Santa Claus/Winter's Here Again//Let's Have an Old Fashioned Christmas/I've Got The Christmas Spirit	195?	3.75	7.50	15.00

—B-side by Don Cornell

RCA VICTOR

Number	Title (A Side/B Side)	Yr	VG	VG+	NM
SP-45-48	Moonglow/Rag Mop/Seventeen//Two Sleepy People/When My Sugar Walks Down My Street/I Can't Give You Anything But Love	1958	5.00	10.00	20.00
SP-45-48 [PS]	French's Mustard Invites You to a Platter Party with the Ames Brothers	1958	5.00	10.00	20.00
LPC-112	(contents unknown)	1961	5.00	10.00	20.00

—Compact 33 Double

Number	Title (A Side/B Side)	Yr	VG	VG+	NM
LPC-112 [PS]	The Ames Brothers Sing the Best of the Bands	1961	5.00	10.00	20.00
547-0329	Gotta Be This or That/Anniversary Song//Love Your Magic Spell Is Everywhere/I Can't Give You Anything But Love	1953	3.75	7.50	15.00

—Part of 2-EP set, EPB-3186

Number	Title (A Side/B Side)	Yr	VG	VG+	NM
EPA-571	(contents unknown)	1955	3.75	7.50	15.00
EPA-571 [PS]	The Man with the Banjo	1955	3.75	7.50	15.00
EPA-680	(contents unknown)	1955	3.75	7.50	15.00
EPA-680 [PS]	Exactly Like You	1955	3.75	7.50	15.00
EPA-790	(contents unknown)	1956	3.75	7.50	15.00
EPA-790 [PS]	The Ames Brothers	1956	3.75	7.50	15.00
EPA-819	(contents unknown)	1956	3.75	7.50	15.00
EPA-819 [PS]	Four Brothers, Vol. 1	1956	3.75	7.50	15.00
EPA-820	(contents unknown)	1956	3.75	7.50	15.00
EPA-820 [PS]	Four Brothers, Vol. 2	1956	3.75	7.50	15.00
EPA 1-1541	Silver Bells/The Christmas Song//Jingle Bells/There'll Always Be a Christmas	1957	3.75	7.50	15.00
EPA 1-1541 [PS]	There'll Always Be a Christmas, Vol. 1	1957	3.75	7.50	15.00
EPA 2-1541	(contents unknown)	1957	3.75	7.50	15.00
EPA 2-1541 [PS]	There'll Always Be a Christmas, Vol. 2	1957	3.75	7.50	15.00
EPA 3-1541	(contents unknown)	1957	3.75	7.50	15.00
EPA 3-1541 [PS]	There'll Always Be a Christmas, Vol. 3	1957	3.75	7.50	15.00
EPB 3186 [PS]	It Must Be True	1953	3.75	7.50	15.00

—Two-pocket jacket for two-EP set

Number	Title (A Side/B Side)	Yr	VG	VG+	NM
EPA-4096	(contents unknown)	1957	3.75	7.50	15.00
EPA-4096 [PS]	Tammy	1957	3.75	7.50	15.00
EPA-4173	(contents unknown)	1957	3.75	7.50	15.00
EPA-4173 [PS]	Melodie D'Amour	1957	3.75	7.50	15.00
EPA-4213	(contents unknown)	1958	3.75	7.50	15.00
EPA-4213 [PS]	Sentimental Mood	1958	3.75	7.50	15.00
EPA-4227	(contents unknown)	1958	3.75	7.50	15.00
EPA-4227 [PS]	Destination Moon	1958	3.75	7.50	15.00
EPA-4320	(contents unknown)	1958	3.75	7.50	15.00
EPA-4320 [PS]	The Best of the Ames Brothers	1958	3.75	7.50	15.00
EPA-5020	(contents unknown)	1959	3.75	7.50	15.00
EPA-5020 [PS]	The Ames Brothers	1959	3.75	7.50	15.00

Albums

CORAL

Number	Title (A Side/B Side)	Yr	VG	VG+	NM
CRL 56014 [10]	Sing a Song of Christmas	1950	12.50	25.00	50.00
CRL 56017 [10]	In the Evening by the Moonlight	1951	12.50	25.00	50.00
CRL 56024 [10]	Sentimental Me	1951	12.50	25.00	50.00
CRL 56025 [10]	Hoop-De-Hoo	1951	12.50	25.00	50.00
CRL 56042 [10]	Sweet Leilani	1951	12.50	25.00	50.00
CRL 56050 [10]	Favorite Spirituals	1952	12.50	25.00	50.00
CRL 56079 [10]	Home on the Range	1952	12.50	25.00	50.00
CRL 56080 [10]	Merry Christmas	1952	12.50	25.00	50.00
CRL 56097 [10]	Favorite Songs	1954	12.50	25.00	50.00
CRL 57031 [M]	Ames Brothers Concert	1956	7.50	15.00	30.00
CRL 57054 [M]	Love's Old Sweet Song	1956	7.50	15.00	30.00
CRL 57166	Sounds of Christmas Harmony	1957	7.50	15.00	30.00
CRL 57176 [M]	Love Serenade	1958	7.50	15.00	30.00
CRL 57338 [M]	Our Golden Favorites	1960	7.50	15.00	30.00

EPIC

Number	Title (A Side/B Side)	Yr	VG	VG+	NM
LN 24036 [M]	Hello Italy	1962	3.75	7.50	15.00
LN 24069 [M]	Knees Up Mother Brown	1963	3.75	7.50	15.00
BN 26036 [S]	Hello Italy	1962	5.00	10.00	20.00
BN 26069 [S]	Knees Up Mother Brown	1963	5.00	10.00	20.00

MCA

Number	Title (A Side/B Side)	Yr	VG	VG+	NM
1510 [R]	The Ames Brothers	197?	2.50	5.00	10.00

RCA CAMDEN

Number	Title (A Side/B Side)	Yr	VG	VG+	NM
CAL-571 [M]	The Ames Brothers — Sweet and Swing	1958	3.75	7.50	15.00

RCA VICTOR

Number	Title (A Side/B Side)	Yr	VG	VG+	NM
LPM-1142 [M]	Exactly Like You	1955	7.50	15.00	30.00
LPM-1157 [M]	Four Brothers	1955	7.50	15.00	30.00
LPM-1228 [M]	The Ames Brothers with Hugo Winterhalter	1956	7.50	15.00	30.00
LPM-1487 [M]	Sweet Seventeen	1957	7.50	15.00	30.00
LPM-1541 [M]	There'll Always Be a Christmas	1957	7.50	15.00	30.00
LPM-1680 [M]	Destination Moon	1958	6.25	12.50	25.00
LSP-1680 [S]	Destination Moon	1958	7.50	15.00	30.00
LPM-1855 [M]	Smoochin' Time	1958	6.25	12.50	25.00
LSP-1855 [S]	Smoochin' Time	1958	7.50	15.00	30.00
LPM-1859 [M]	The Best of the Ames Brothers	1958	6.25	12.50	25.00
LSP-1859(e) [R]	The Best of the Ames Brothers	196?	5.00	10.00	20.00
LPM-1954 [M]	Famous Hits of Famous Quartets	1959	5.00	10.00	20.00
LSP-1954 [S]	Famous Hits of Famous Quartets	1959	6.25	12.50	25.00
LPM-1998 [M]	The Ames Brothers Sing the Best in the Country	1959	5.00	10.00	20.00
LSP-1998 [S]	The Ames Brothers Sing the Best in the Country	1959	6.25	12.50	25.00
LPM-2009 [M]	Words and Music	1959	5.00	10.00	20.00
LSP-2009 [S]	Words and Music	1959	6.25	12.50	25.00
LPM-2100 [M]	Hello, Amigos	1960	5.00	10.00	20.00
LSP-2100 [S]	Hello, Amigos	1960	6.25	12.50	25.00
LPM-2182 [M]	The Blend and the Beat	1960	5.00	10.00	20.00
LSP-2182 [S]	The Blend and the Beat	1960	6.25	12.50	25.00
LPM-2273 [M]	The Best of the Bands	1960	5.00	10.00	20.00
LSP-2273 [S]	The Best of the Bands	1960	6.25	12.50	25.00
LPM-2876 [M]	For Sentimental Reasons	1964	3.00	6.00	12.00
LSP-2876 [S]	For Sentimental Reasons	1964	3.75	7.50	15.00
LPM-2981 [M]	Down Memory Lane with the Ames Brothers	1964	3.00	6.00	12.00
LSP-2981 [S]	Down Memory Lane with the Ames Brothers	1964	3.75	7.50	15.00
LPM-3186 [10]	It Must Be True	1954	12.50	25.00	50.00

VOCALION

Number	Title (A Side/B Side)	Yr	VG	VG+	NM
VL 3617 [M]	The Ames Brothers	196?	3.75	7.50	15.00
VL 73788 [R]	Christmas Harmony	196?	3.00	6.00	12.00

—Reissue of some Coral tracks

Number	Title (A Side/B Side)	Yr	VG	VG+	NM
VL 73818	The Ames Brothers Featuring Ed Ames	196?	2.50	5.00	10.00

AMISH, THE

Albums

SUSSEX

Number	Title (A Side/B Side)	Yr	VG	VG+	NM
SUX-7016	The Amish	1972	6.25	12.50	25.00

AMMONS, GENE

45s

ARGO

Number	Title (A Side/B Side)	Yr	VG	VG+	NM
5417	I Can't Stop Loving You/My Babe	1962	2.50	5.00	10.00

PRESTIGE

Number	Title (A Side/B Side)	Yr	VG	VG+	NM
112	The Happy Blues (Part 1)/The Happy Blues (Part 2)	196?	2.50	5.00	10.00
140	Blue Greens and Beans (Part 1)/Blue Greens and Beans (Part 2)	196?	2.50	5.00	10.00
166	Woofin' and Tweetin' (Part 1)/Woofin' and Tweetin' (Part 2)	196?	2.50	5.00	10.00
176	Hit the Jug/Canadian Sunset	196?	2.50	5.00	10.00
189	Ol' Man River/Exactly Like You	196?	2.50	5.00	10.00
201	Miss Lucy/Namely You	196?	2.50	5.00	10.00
206	The Breeze and I/Uptight	196?	2.50	5.00	10.00
214	Twisting the Jug (Part 1)/Twisting the Jug (Part 2)	1962	3.00	6.00	12.00
226	I Sold My Heart to the Junkman/Moonglow	1962	2.50	5.00	10.00
227	Anna/Pagan Love Song	1962	2.50	5.00	10.00
229	Ca' Purange (Part 1)/Ca' Purange (Part 2)	196?	2.50	5.00	10.00
245	Molto Mato Grosso (Part 1)/Molto Mato Grosso (Part 2)	196?	2.50	5.00	10.00
253	On the Street of Dreams/You'd Be So Nice to Come Home To	196?	2.50	5.00	10.00
276	Let It Be You/Seed Shack	196?	2.50	5.00	10.00
294	Tuby/Love I've Found You	196?	2.50	5.00	10.00
319	The Party's Over/I Wanna Be Loved	196?	2.50	5.00	10.00
336	Velvet Soul/Stranger in Town	196?	2.50	5.00	10.00
371	Angel Eyes (Part 1)/Angel Eyes (Part 2)	196?	2.00	4.00	8.00
390	Seed Shack/Canadian Sunset	196?	2.00	4.00	8.00
403	Rock Roll/Sock	196?	2.00	4.00	8.00
441	Don't Go to Strangers/Carbow	196?	2.00	4.00	8.00
707	Jungle Soul (Part 1)/Jungle Soul (Part 2)	196?	—	3.00	6.00
713	Bye Bye/Let It Be	1951	3.75	7.50	15.00
717	I Wanna Be Loved/Gravy	1951	3.75	7.50	15.00
721	La Vie En Rose/Who Put the Sleeping Pills in Rip Van Winkle's Coffee	195?	3.75	7.50	15.00
721	Angel Eyes (Part 1)/Angel Eyes (Part 2)	196?	—	3.00	6.00
729	Jungle Boss (Part 1)/Jungle Boss (Part 2)	196?	—	3.00	6.00
731	I Can't Give You Anything But My Love/Sweet Jennie Lou	195?	3.75	7.50	15.00
734	Didn't We/Son of a Preacher Man	1970	—	3.00	6.00
735	Jug/Around About One A.M.	195?	3.75	7.50	15.00
737	Jungle Strut/Madame Queen	197?	—	3.00	6.00
741	Blue & Sentimental/Chabootie	195?	3.75	7.50	15.00
742	Jug Eyes/He's a Real Gone Guy	197?	—	3.00	6.00
745	Something/The Black Cat	197?	—	3.00	6.00
753	My Way/Chicago Breakdown	197?	—	3.00	6.00
754	Hot Stuff/When the Saints Go Marching In	195?	3.75	7.50	15.00
757	Lady Sings the Blues/Play Me	1973	—	3.00	6.00
805	Wow/When I Dream of You	195?	3.75	7.50	15.00
844	Jug/La Vie En Rose	195?	3.00	6.00	12.00
845	Bye Bye/I Can't Give You Anything But Love	195?	3.00	6.00	12.00
907	Cara Mia/Count Your Blessings	195?	3.00	6.00	12.00
910	This Is Always/I've Had My Last Affair	195?	3.00	6.00	12.00
911	Sock/Blue Roller	195?	3.00	6.00	12.00
916	What I Say/Our Love Is Here to Stay	195?	3.00	6.00	12.00
921	Undecided/Until the Real Thing Comes Along	195?	3.00	6.00	12.00

Number	Title (A Side/B Side)	Yr	VG	VG+	NM
UNITED					
137	Street of Dreams/The Beat	1954	3.75	7.50	15.00
149	Red Top/Just Chips	1955	3.75	7.50	15.00
164	Stairway to the Stars/Jim Dog	1955	3.75	7.50	15.00
175	Big Slam (Part 1)/Big Slam (Part 2)	1955	3.75	7.50	15.00
185	Traveling Light/Fuzzy	1956	3.75	7.50	15.00
Albums					
ARGO					
697 [M]	Dig Him	1962	7.50	15.00	30.00
S-697 [S]	Dig Him	1962	6.25	12.50	25.00
698 [M]	Just Jug	1962	7.50	15.00	30.00
S-698 [S]	Just Jug	1962	6.25	12.50	25.00
CADET					
LP-783 [M]	Make It Happen	1967	6.25	12.50	25.00
LPS-783 [S]	Make It Happen	1967	3.75	7.50	15.00
CHESS					
LP 1442 [M]	Soulful Saxophone	1959	10.00	20.00	40.00
CH2-92514 [(2)]	Early Visions	198?	3.00	6.00	12.00
EMARCY					
EMS-2-400 [(2)]	The "Jug" Sessions	197?	3.00	6.00	12.00
MG-26031 [10]	With or Without	1954	30.00	60.00	120.00
ENJA					
3093	Gene Ammons in Sweden	198?	2.50	5.00	10.00
FANTASY					
OJC-013	The Happy Blues	198?	2.50	5.00	10.00
OJC-014	All-Star Sessions	198?	2.50	5.00	10.00
OJC-129	Jammin' in Hi-Fi	198?	2.50	5.00	10.00
OJC-192	Blue Gene	1985	2.50	5.00	10.00
OJC-211	Jammin' with Gene	1986	2.50	5.00	10.00
OJC-244	Funky	1987	2.50	5.00	10.00
OJC-297	Boss Tenor	1988	2.50	5.00	10.00
OJC-351	Bad! Bossa Nova	198?	2.50	5.00	10.00
OJC-395	Live in Chicago	198?	2.50	5.00	10.00
OJC-651	The Big Sound	1991	3.00	6.00	12.00
OJC-6005	Gene Ammons' Greatest Hits, Vol. 1: The Sixties	1988	3.00	6.00	12.00
MOODSVILLE					
MVLP-18 [M]	Nice and Cool	1961	12.50	25.00	50.00
—Originals have green label					
MVLP-18 [M]	Nice and Cool	1965	6.25	12.50	25.00
—Second editions have blue label with trident at right					
MVLP-28 [M]	The Soulful Moods of Gene Ammons	1963	12.50	25.00	50.00
—Originals have green label					
MVLP-28 [M]	The Soulful Moods of Gene Ammons	1965	6.25	12.50	25.00
—Second editions have blue label with trident at right					
MVST-28 [S]	The Soulful Moods of Gene Ammons	1963	10.00	20.00	40.00
PRESTIGE					
PRLP-107 [10]	Gene Ammons	1951	50.00	100.00	200.00
PRLP-112 [10]	Tenor Sax Favorites, Volume 1	1951	50.00	100.00	200.00
PRLP-127 [10]	Gene Ammons Favorites, Volume 2	1952	50.00	100.00	200.00
PRLP-149 [10]	Gene Ammons Favorites, Volume 3	1953	50.00	100.00	200.00
PRLP-211 [10]	Gene Ammons Jazz Session	1955	50.00	100.00	200.00
2514	Blue Groove	198?	2.50	5.00	10.00
PRLP-7039 [M]	Hi Fidelity Jam Session	1956	25.00	50.00	100.00
PRLP-7039 [M]	The Happy Blues	1960	12.50	25.00	50.00
—Retitled version of "Hi Fidelity Jam Session"					
PRLP-7050 [M]	Gene Ammons All Star Session	1956	25.00	50.00	100.00
—Compilation of Prestige 107 and 127					
PRLP-7050 [M]	Woofin' and Tweetin'	1960	12.50	25.00	50.00
—Retitled version of "Gene Ammons All Star Session"					
PRLP-7060 [M]	Jammin' with Gene	1956	25.00	50.00	100.00
PRLP-7060 [M]	Not Really the Blues	1960	12.50	25.00	50.00
—Retitled version of "Jammin' with Gene"					
PRLP-7083 [M]	Funky	1957	25.00	50.00	100.00
—Originals have yellow label, "W. 50th St., NYC" address					
PRLP-7110 [M]	Jammin' in Hi-Fi with Gene Ammons	1957	25.00	50.00	100.00
—Originals have yellow label, "W. 50th St., NYC" address					
PRLP-7132 [M]	The Big Sound	1958	25.00	50.00	100.00
—Originals have yellow label, "W. 50th St., NYC" address					
PRLP-7146 [M]	Blue Gene	1958	12.50	25.00	50.00
—Originals have yellow label, Bergenfield, N.J. address					
PRLP-7176 [M]	The Twister	1960	12.50	25.00	50.00
—Originals have yellow label, Bergenfield, N.J. address; reissue of 7110					
PRLP-7180 [M]	Boss Tenor	1960	12.50	25.00	50.00
—Originals have yellow label, Bergenfield, N.J. address					
PRST-7180 [S]	Boss Tenor	1960	10.00	20.00	40.00
—Originals have silver label					
PRLP-7192 [M]	Jug	1960	12.50	25.00	50.00
—Originals have yellow label, Bergenfield, N.J. address					
PRST-7192 [S]	Jug	1960	10.00	20.00	40.00
—Originals have silver label					
PRLP-7201 [M]	Groove Blues	1961	12.50	25.00	50.00
—Originals have yellow label, Bergenfield, N.J. address					
PRLP-7208 [M]	Up Tight!	1961	12.50	25.00	50.00
—Originals have yellow label, Bergenfield, N.J. address					
PRST-7208 [S]	Up Tight!	1961	10.00	20.00	40.00
—Originals have silver label					
PRLP-7238 [M]	Twistin' the Jug	1962	12.50	25.00	50.00
—Originals have yellow label, Bergenfield, N.J. address					
PRST-7238 [S]	Twistin' the Jug	1962	10.00	20.00	40.00
—Originals have silver label					
PRLP-7257 [M]	Bad! Bossa Nova	1962	7.50	15.00	30.00
—Originals have yellow label, Bergenfield, N.J. address; some copies have a cover calling this "Jungle Soul! (ca' purange)"					
PRST-7257 [S]	Bad! Bossa Nova	1962	10.00	20.00	40.00
—Originals have silver label					
PRLP-7270 [M]	Preachin'	1963	7.50	15.00	30.00
—Originals have yellow label, Bergenfield, N.J. address					
PRST-7270 [S]	Preachin'	1963	10.00	20.00	40.00
—Originals have silver label					
PRLP-7275 [M]	Soul Summit, Volume 2	1963	7.50	15.00	30.00
—Originals have yellow label, Bergenfield, N.J. address					
PRST-7275 [S]	Soul Summit, Volume 2	1963	10.00	20.00	40.00
—Originals have silver label					
PRLP-7287 [M]	Late Hour Special	1964	7.50	15.00	30.00
—Originals have yellow label, Bergenfield, N.J. address					

Number	Title (A Side/B Side)	Yr	VG	VG+	NM
PRST-7287 [S]	Late Hour Special	1964	10.00	20.00	40.00
—Originals have silver label					
PRLP-7320 [M]	Velvet Soul	1964	7.50	15.00	30.00
—Originals have yellow label, Bergenfield, N.J. address					
PRST-7320 [S]	Velvet Soul	1964	10.00	20.00	40.00
—Originals have silver label					
PRLP-7369 [M]	Angel Eyes	1965	6.25	12.50	25.00
—Originals have blue label with trident at right					
PRST-7369 [S]	Angel Eyes	1965	7.50	15.00	30.00
—Originals have blue label with trident at right					
PRLP-7400 [M]	Sock!	1966	6.25	12.50	25.00
—Originals have blue label with trident at right					
PRST-7400 [S]	Sock!	1966	7.50	15.00	30.00
—Originals have blue label with trident at right					
PRLP-7445 [M]	Boss Soul!	1967	6.25	12.50	25.00
—Originals have blue label with trident at right					
PRST-7445 [S]	Boss Soul!	1967	7.50	15.00	30.00
—Originals have blue label with trident at right					
PRLP-7495 [M]	Gene Ammons Live in Chicago	1967	5.00	10.00	20.00
—Originals have blue label with trident at right					
PRST-7495 [S]	Gene Ammons Live in Chicago	1967	6.25	12.50	25.00
—Originals have blue label with trident at right					
PRLP-7534 [M]	Boss Tenor	1967	6.25	12.50	25.00
—Originals have blue label with trident at right					
PRST-7534 [S]	Boss Tenor	1967	5.00	10.00	20.00
—Originals have blue label with trident at right					
PRST-7552	Jungle Soul	1968	5.00	10.00	20.00
—Reissue of 7257					
PRST-7654	The Happy Blues — Jam Session, Vol. 1	1969	3.75	7.50	15.00
—Second reissue of 7039					
PRST-7708	The Best of Gene Ammons for Beautiful People	1969	5.00	10.00	20.00
PRST-7739	The Boss Is Back!	1970	5.00	10.00	20.00
PRST-7771	Jammin' Jam Sessions, Vol. 2	1970	3.00	6.00	12.00
PRST-7774	The Best of Gene Ammons	1970	5.00	10.00	20.00
P-7862	Night Lights	1985	2.50	5.00	10.00
10006	Black Cat	197?	3.75	7.50	15.00
10010	Chase	197?	3.75	7.50	15.00
10019	You Talk That Talk!	197?	3.75	7.50	15.00
10021	Brother Jug	197?	3.75	7.50	15.00
10022	My Way	197?	3.75	7.50	15.00
10023	The Boss Is Back	197?	3.00	6.00	12.00
—Reissue of 7739					
10040	Free Again	197?	3.00	6.00	12.00
10058	Got My Own	197?	3.00	6.00	12.00
10070	Big Bad Jug	197?	3.00	6.00	12.00
10078	Gene Ammons and Friends at Montreux	197?	3.00	6.00	12.00
10080	Brasswind	197?	3.00	6.00	12.00
10084	Greatest Hits	197?	3.00	6.00	12.00
10093	Goodbye	197?	3.00	6.00	12.00
24036 [(2)]	Juganthology	197?	3.75	7.50	15.00
24058 [(2)]	The Gene Ammons Story: The 78 Era	197?	3.75	7.50	15.00
24071 [(2)]	The Gene Ammons Story: Organ Combos	197?	3.75	7.50	15.00
24079 [(2)]	The Gene Ammons Story: Gentle Jug	197?	3.75	7.50	15.00
24098 [(2)]	The Big Sound of Gene Ammons	1981	3.00	6.00	12.00
SAVOY					
SJL-1103	Red Top	197?	3.00	6.00	12.00
MG-14033 [M]	Golden Saxophone	1961	7.50	15.00	30.00
STATUS					
18	Nice & Cool	197?	3.00	6.00	12.00
UPFRONT					
UPF-116	Nothing But Soul	1968	3.00	6.00	12.00
—Reissue of Vee-Jay material					
VEE JAY					
LP-3024 [M]	Juggin' Around	1961	10.00	20.00	40.00
LPS-3024 [S]	Juggin' Around	1961	7.50	15.00	30.00
WING					
MGW-12156 [M]	Light, Bluesy and Moody	1963	3.75	7.50	15.00
—Reissue of EmArcy 10-inch LP					
SRW-16156 [R]	Light, Bluesy and Moody	1963	2.50	5.00	10.00

AMMONS, GENE, AND RICHARD "GROOVE" HOLMES

Number	Title (A Side/B Side)	Yr	VG	VG+	NM
Albums					
PACIFIC JAZZ					
PJ-32 [M]	Groovin' with Jug	1961	10.00	20.00	40.00
ST-32 [S]	Groovin' with Jug	1961	7.50	15.00	30.00

AMMONS, GENE, AND SONNY STITT

Also see each artist's individual listings.

Number	Title (A Side/B Side)	Yr	VG	VG+	NM
45s					
PRESTIGE					
709	Blues Up and Down/You Can Depend On Me	1951	5.00	10.00	20.00
748	Stringin' the Jugs (Part 1)/Stringin' the Jugs (Part 2)	195?	3.75	7.50	15.00
877	New Blues Up and Down (Part 1)/New Blues Up and Down (Part 2)	195?	3.00	6.00	12.00
Albums					
CADET					
LP-785 [M]	Jug and Sonny	1967	5.00	10.00	20.00
LPS-785 [S]	Jug and Sonny	1967	3.75	7.50	15.00
CHESS					
LP 1455 [M]	Jug and Sonny	1960	10.00	20.00	40.00
CH-91549	Jug and Sonny	198?	2.50	5.00	10.00
PRESTIGE					
PRLP-7234 [M]	Soul Summit	1962	12.50	25.00	50.00
PRST-7234 [S]	Soul Summit	1962	10.00	20.00	40.00
PRLP-7454 [M]	Soul Summit	1967	5.00	10.00	20.00
PRST-7454 [S]	Soul Summit	1967	3.75	7.50	15.00
PRST-7606	We'll Be Together Again	1969	3.75	7.50	15.00
PRST-7823	Blues Up	197?	3.00	6.00	12.00
10019	You Talk That Talk	197?	3.75	7.50	15.00
10100	Together Again for the Last Time	197?	3.00	6.00	12.00
VERVE					
V-8426 [M]	Boss Tenors	1962	5.00	10.00	20.00
V6-8426 [S]	Boss Tenors	1962	6.25	12.50	25.00

Number	Title (A Side/B Side)	Yr	VG	VG+	NM
V-8468 [M]	Boss Tenors in Orbit	1962	5.00	10.00	20.00
V6-8468 [S]	Boss Tenors in Orbit	1962	6.25	12.50	25.00

AMON DUUL

Albums

Number	Title (A Side/B Side)	Yr	VG	VG+	NM
PROPHESY					
PHS-1003	Amon Duul	1969	6.25	12.50	25.00

AMON DUUL II

45s

Number	Title (A Side/B Side)	Yr	VG	VG+	NM
LIBERTY					
56196	Soda Shop Rock/Archangel's Thunderbird	1970	—	3.00	6.00
UNITED ARTISTS					
XW419	Pigman/Mozambique	1974	—	2.50	5.00

Albums

Number	Title (A Side/B Side)	Yr	VG	VG+	NM
ATCO					
SD 36-108	Hijack	1975	2.50	5.00	10.00
SD 36-119	Made in Germany	1976	2.50	5.00	10.00
UNITED ARTISTS					
UA-LA017-F	Wolf City	1973	3.00	6.00	12.00
UA-LA198-F	Viva La Trance	1974	3.00	6.00	12.00
UAS-5586	Carnival in Babylon	1972	3.00	6.00	12.00
UAS-9954 [(2)]	Dance of the Lemmings	1971	3.75	7.50	15.00

ANASTASIA

45s

Number	Title (A Side/B Side)	Yr	VG	VG+	NM
LAURIE					
3066	Time Bomb/That's My Kind of Love	1960	6.25	12.50	25.00
STASI					
1000	Every Road I Walk Along/Bicycle Hop	196?	50.00	100.00	200.00
1001	Seven Days a Week/Nothing Beats My Girl	196?	37.50	75.00	150.00

ANCIENT GREASE

Albums

Number	Title (A Side/B Side)	Yr	VG	VG+	NM
MERCURY					
SR-61305	Women and Children First	1970	7.50	15.00	30.00

ANDANTES, THE

45s

Number	Title (A Side/B Side)	Yr	VG	VG+	NM
DOT					
16495	My Baby's Gone/No Yo Ru	1963	6.25	12.50	25.00
V.I.P.					
25006	If You Were Mine/(Like a) Nightmare	1964	625.00	1250.	2500.

—One of the rarest of all Motown-related 45s

ANDERS, BERNIE

45s

Number	Title (A Side/B Side)	Yr	VG	VG+	NM
KING					
4833	My Heart Believes/Too Late I Learned	1955	12.50	25.00	50.00

ANDERS & PONCIA

45s

Number	Title (A Side/B Side)	Yr	VG	VG+	NM
KAMA SUTRA					
240	So It Goes/Virgin of the Night	1967	3.00	6.00	12.00
WARNER BROS.					
7271	Take His Love/I'm Beginning to Touch You	1969	2.00	4.00	8.00
7294	Make a Change (To Something Better)/Lucky	1969	2.00	4.00	8.00

Albums

Number	Title (A Side/B Side)	Yr	VG	VG+	NM
WARNER BROS.					
WS 1778	The Anders & Poncia Album	1969	7.50	15.00	30.00

ANDERSEN, ERIC

45s

Number	Title (A Side/B Side)	Yr	VG	VG+	NM
ARISTA					
0121	Ol' 55/Can't Get You Out of My Life	1975	—	2.00	4.00
0141	Be True to You/(B-side unknown)	1975	—	2.00	4.00
COLUMBIA					
45637	Is It Really Love at All/Pearl's Goodtime Blues	1972	—	2.50	5.00
45730	Blue River/More Often Than Not	1972	—	2.50	5.00
WARNER BROS.					
7231	Think About It/So Hard to Fall	1968	—	3.00	6.00
7408	Lie with Me/Secrets	1970	—	3.00	6.00
7435	Sittin' in the Sunshine/Sunshine & Flowers	1970	—	3.00	6.00
7459	Born Again/Rocky Mountain Red	1971	—	3.00	6.00

Albums

Number	Title (A Side/B Side)	Yr	VG	VG+	NM
ARISTA					
AL 4037	Be True to You	1975	2.50	5.00	10.00
AL 4075	Sweet Surprise	1976	2.50	5.00	10.00
AL 4128	The Best Songs	1977	2.50	5.00	10.00
COLUMBIA					
KC 31062	Blue River	1972	2.50	5.00	10.00
PC 31062	Blue River	197?	2.00	4.00	8.00
—Reissue					
VANGUARD					
VSD 7/8 [(2)]	The Best of Eric Andersen	1971	3.75	7.50	15.00
VSD 6540	A Country Dream	1969	3.75	7.50	15.00
VRS 9157 [M]	Today Is the Highway	1965	3.75	7.50	15.00
VRS 9206 [M]	'Bout Changes and Things	1966	3.75	7.50	15.00
VSD 79157 [S]	Today Is the Highway	1965	5.00	10.00	20.00
VSD 79206 [S]	'Bout Changes and Things	1966	5.00	10.00	20.00
VSD 79236	'Bout Changes and Things, Take 2	1968	3.75	7.50	15.00
VSD 79271	More Hits from Tin Can Alley	1969	3.75	7.50	15.00
WARNER BROS.					
WS 1748	Avalanche	1968	3.75	7.50	15.00
WS 1806	Eric Andersen	1969	3.75	7.50	15.00

ANDERSON, BILL

45s

Number	Title (A Side/B Side)	Yr	VG	VG+	NM
CURB					
76855	Deck of Cards/Thank You Darling	1991	—	2.50	5.00
DECCA					
9-30773	That's What It's Like to Be Lonesome/Thrill of My Life	1958	3.75	7.50	15.00
9-30914	Ninety-Nine/Back Where I Started From	1959	3.75	7.50	15.00
9-30993	Dead or Alive/It's Not the End of Everything	1959	3.75	7.50	15.00
31092	The Tip of My Fingers/No Man's Land	1960	3.00	6.00	12.00
31168	Walk Out Backwards/The Best of Strangers	1960	3.00	6.00	12.00
31262	Po' Folks/Goodbye Cruel World	1961	3.00	6.00	12.00
31358	Get a Little Dirt on Your Hands/Down Came the Rain	1962	3.00	6.00	12.00
31404	Mama Sang a Song/On and On and On	1962	2.50	5.00	10.00
31458	Still/You Make It Easy	1963	2.50	5.00	10.00
31521	8 x 10/One Mile Over — Two Miles Back	1963	2.50	5.00	10.00
31521 [PS]	8 x 10/One Mile Over — Two Miles Back	1963	5.00	10.00	20.00
31577	Five Little Fingers/Easy Come — Easy Go	1964	2.50	5.00	10.00
31630	Me/Cincinnati, Ohio	1964	2.50	5.00	10.00
31681	In Case You Ever Change Your Mind/Three A.M.	1964	2.50	5.00	10.00
31743	Certain/You Can Have Her	1965	2.50	5.00	10.00
31825	Bright Lights and Country Music/Born	1965	2.50	5.00	10.00
31890	Bright Guitar/I Love You Drops	1966	2.50	5.00	10.00
31999	I Get the Fever/The First Mrs. Jones	1966	2.00	4.00	8.00
32077	Get While the Gettin's Good/Something to Believe In	1967	2.00	4.00	8.00
32146	No One's Gonna Hurt You Anymore/Papa	1967	2.00	4.00	8.00
32215	Stranger on the Run/Happiness	1967	2.00	4.00	8.00
32276	Wild Week-End/Fun While It Lasted	1968	2.00	4.00	8.00
32360	Happy State of Mind/Time's Been Good to Me	1968	2.00	4.00	8.00
32417	Po' Folks' Christmas/Christmas Time's a-Coming	1968	2.00	4.00	8.00
32417 [PS]	Po' Folks' Christmas/Christmas Time's a-Coming	1968	3.75	7.50	15.00
32445	My Life (Throw It Away If I Want To)/To Be Alone	1969	—	3.50	7.00
32514	But You Know I Love You/A Picture from Life's Other Side	1969	—	3.50	7.00
32643	Love Is a Sometimes Thing/And I'm Still Missing You	1970	—	3.50	7.00
32744	Where Have All Our Heroes Gone/Loving a Memory	1970	—	3.50	7.00
32793	Always Remember/You Can Change the World	1971	—	3.50	7.00
32850	Quits/I'll Live for You	1971	—	3.50	7.00
32930	All the Lonely Women in the World/It Was Time for Me to Move Anyway	1972	—	3.50	7.00
33002	Don't She Look Good/I'm Just Gone	1972	—	3.50	7.00
MCA					
40004	If You Can Live With It (I Can Live Without It)/Let's Fall Apart	1973	—	2.00	4.00
40070	The Corner of My Life/Home and Things	1973	—	2.00	4.00
40164	World of Make Believe/Gonna Shine on It Again	1973	—	2.00	4.00
40243	Can I Come Home to You/I'm Happily Married	1974	—	2.00	4.00
40304	Every Time I Turn the Radio On/You Are My Story	1974	—	2.00	4.00
40351	I Still Feel the Same About You/Talk to Me Ohio	1975	—	2.00	4.00
40404	Country D.J./We Made Love	1975	—	2.00	4.00
40443	Thanks/Why's the Last Time Have to Be the Best	1975	—	2.00	4.00
40595	Peanuts and Diamonds/Your Love Blows Me Away	1976	—	2.00	4.00
40661	Liars One, Believers Zero/Let Me Whisper Darling One More Time	1976	—	2.00	4.00
40713	Head to Toe/Love Song for Jackie	1977	—	2.00	4.00
40794	Still the One/This Ole Suitcase	1977	—	2.00	4.00
40893	I Can't Wait Any Longer/Joanna	1978	—	2.00	4.00
40964	Double S/Married Lady	1978	—	2.00	4.00
40992	This Is a Love Song/Remembering the Good	1979	—	2.00	4.00
41060	The Dream Never Dies/One More Sexy Lady	1979	—	2.00	4.00
41150	More Than a Bedroom Thing/Love Me and I'll Be Your Best Friend	1979	—	2.00	4.00
41212	Mike Mine Night Time/Old Me and You	1980	—	2.00	4.00
41297	Rock 'N' Roll to Rock of Ages/I'm Used to the Rain	1980	—	2.00	4.00
51017	I Want That Feelin' Again/She Made Me Remember	1980	—	2.00	4.00
51052	Mister Peepers/How Married Are You, Mary Ann	1981	—	2.00	4.00
51150	Homebody/One Man Band	1981	—	2.00	4.00
51204	Whiskey Made Me Stumble (The Devil Made Me Fall)/All That Keeps Me Goin'	1981	—	2.00	4.00
SOUTHERN TRACKS					
1007	Southern Fried/You Turn the Light On	1982	—	2.00	4.00
1011	Laid Off/Lovin' Tonight	1982	—	2.00	4.00
1014	Thank You Darling/Lovin' Tonight	1983	—	2.00	4.00
1021	Son of the South/20th Century Fox	1983	—	2.00	4.00
1026	Your Eyes/I Never Get Enough of You	1984	—	2.00	4.00
1030	Speculation/We May Never Pass This Way Again	1984	—	2.00	4.00
1067	Sheet Music/Maybe Go Down	1986	—	—	3.00
1077	No Ordinary Memory/Sheet Music	1987	—	—	3.00
SWANEE					
4013	Wino the Clown/(B-side unknown)	1985	—	—	3.00
5015	Pity Party/(B-side unknown)	1985	—	—	3.00
5018	When You Leave That Way, You Can Never Go Back/(B-side unknown)	1985	—	—	3.00
TNT					
9015	City Lights/No Song to Sing	1958	20.00	40.00	80.00

Albums

Number	Title (A Side/B Side)	Yr	VG	VG+	NM
DECCA					
DL 4192 [M]	Bill Anderson Sings Country Songs	1962	5.00	10.00	20.00
DL 4427 [M]	Still	1963	5.00	10.00	20.00
DL 4499 [M]	Bill Anderson Sings	1964	3.75	7.50	15.00
DL 4600 [M]	Bill Anderson Showcase	1964	3.75	7.50	15.00
DL 4646 [M]	From This Pen	1965	3.75	7.50	15.00
DL 4686 [M]	Bright Lights and Country Music	1965	3.75	7.50	15.00
DL 4771 [M]	I Love You Drops	1966	3.75	7.50	15.00
DL 4855 [M]	Get While the Gettin's Good	1967	3.75	7.50	15.00
DL 4859 [M]	Bill Anderson's Greatest Hits	1967	5.00	10.00	20.00
DL 4886 [M]	I Can Do Nothing Alone	1967	6.25	12.50	25.00
DXSA 7198 [(2)]	The Bill Anderson Story	1969	3.75	7.50	15.00
DL 74192 [S]	Bill Anderson Sings Country Songs	1962	6.25	12.50	25.00
DL 74427 [S]	Still	1963	6.25	12.50	25.00
DL 74499 [S]	Bill Anderson Sings	1964	5.00	10.00	20.00
DL 74600 [S]	Bill Anderson Showcase	1964	5.00	10.00	20.00
DL 74646 [S]	From This Pen	1965	5.00	10.00	20.00

Number	Title (A Side/B Side)	Yr	VG	VG+	NM
DL 74686 [S]	Bright Lights and Country Music	1965	5.00	10.00	20.00
DL 74771 [S]	I Love You Drops	1966	5.00	10.00	20.00
DL 74855 [S]	Get While the Gettin's Good	1967	5.00	10.00	20.00
DL 74859 [S]	Bill Anderson's Greatest Hits	1967	5.00	10.00	20.00
DL 74886 [S]	I Can Do Nothing Alone	1967	5.00	10.00	20.00
DL 74998	Wild Weekend	1968	3.75	7.50	15.00
DL 75056	Happy State of Mind	1968	3.75	7.50	15.00
DL 75142	My Life/But You Know I Love You	1969	3.75	7.50	15.00
DL 75161	Bill Anderson's Christmas	1969	3.75	7.50	15.00
DL 75206	Love Is a Sometimes Thing	1970	3.00	6.00	12.00
DL 75254	Where Have All Our Heroes Gone?	1971	3.00	6.00	12.00
DL 75275	Always Remember	1971	3.00	6.00	12.00
DL 75315	Bill Anderson's Greatest Hits, Vol. 2	1971	3.00	6.00	12.00
DL 75339	Singing His Praise	1972	3.00	6.00	12.00
DL 75344	Bill Anderson Sings For "All the Lonely Women in the World"	1972	3.00	6.00	12.00
DL 75383	Don't She Look Good	1972	3.00	6.00	12.00

MCA

Number	Title (A Side/B Side)	Yr	VG	VG+	NM
13	Bill Anderson's Greatest Hits	1973	2.50	5.00	10.00
—Reissue of Decca 74859					
320	Bill	1973	3.00	6.00	12.00
416	"Whispering" Bill Anderson	1974	3.00	6.00	12.00
454	Every Time I Turn the Radio On/Talk to Me Ohio	1974	2.50	5.00	10.00
693	Love and Other Sad Stories	198?	2.00	4.00	8.00
—Reissue					
694	Ladies' Choice	198?	2.00	4.00	8.00
—Reissue					
766	Nashville Mirrors	198?	2.00	4.00	8.00
—Reissue					
2222	Peanuts & Diamonds & Other Jewels	1975	2.50	5.00	10.00
2264	Scorpio	1976	2.50	5.00	10.00
2371	Love and Other Sad Stories	1977	2.50	5.00	10.00
3075	Ladies' Choice	1979	2.50	5.00	10.00
3214	Nashville Mirrors	1980	2.50	5.00	10.00
4001 [(2)]	The Bill Anderson Story	1973	3.00	6.00	12.00
—Reissue of Decca 7198					
35032	Whispering	197?	2.50	5.00	10.00

MCA CORAL

Number	Title (A Side/B Side)	Yr	VG	VG+	NM
20002	I Can Do Nothing	1973	2.50	5.00	10.00

VOCALION

Number	Title (A Side/B Side)	Yr	VG	VG+	NM
VL 3835 [M]	Bill Anderson's Country Style	196?	3.00	6.00	12.00
VL 73835 [S]	Bill Anderson's Country Style	196?	3.75	7.50	15.00
VL 73927	Just Plain Bill	197?	2.50	5.00	10.00

ANDERSON, BILL, AND JAN HOWARD

45s

DECCA

Number	Title (A Side/B Side)	Yr	VG	VG+	NM
31884	I Know You're Married (But I Love You Still)/Time Out	1966	2.50	5.00	10.00
32197	For Loving You/The Untouchables	1967	2.00	4.00	8.00
32511	If It's All the Same to You/I Thank God for You	1969	2.00	4.00	8.00
32689	Someday We'll Be Together/Who's the Biggest Fool	1970	2.00	4.00	8.00
32877	Dis-Satisfied/Knowing You're Mine	1971	2.00	4.00	8.00

Albums

DECCA

Number	Title (A Side/B Side)	Yr	VG	VG+	NM
DL 4959 [M]	For Loving You	1967	6.25	12.50	25.00
DL 74959 [S]	For Loving You	1967	5.00	10.00	20.00
DL 75184	If It's All the Same to You	1970	5.00	10.00	20.00
DL 75293	Bill & Jan (Or Jan & Bill)	1972	5.00	10.00	20.00

ANDERSON, BILL, AND MARY LOU TURNER

45s

MCA

Number	Title (A Side/B Side)	Yr	VG	VG+	NM
40488	Sometimes/Circle in a Triangle	1975	—	2.00	4.00
40533	That's What Made Me Love You/Can We Still Be Friends	1976	—	2.00	4.00
40753	Where Are You Going, Billy Boy/Sad Ole Shade of Gray	1977	—	2.00	4.00
40852	I'm Way Ahead of You/Just Enough to Make Me Want It All	1978	—	2.00	4.00

Albums

MCA

Number	Title (A Side/B Side)	Yr	VG	VG+	NM
2182	Sometimes	1976	3.00	6.00	12.00
2298	Billy Boy & Mary Lou	1977	3.00	6.00	12.00

ANDERSON, BROTHER JAMES

45s

SUN

Number	Title (A Side/B Side)	Yr	VG	VG+	NM
406	I'm Gonna Move in the Room with the Lord/My Soul Needs Resting	1967	12.50	25.00	50.00

ANDERSON, ERNESTINE

45s

MERCURY

Number	Title (A Side/B Side)	Yr	VG	VG+	NM
71354	My Man/Wrap Your Troubles in Dreams	1958	2.50	5.00	10.00
71423	I Don't See Me in Your Eyes Anymore/Be Mine	1959	2.50	5.00	10.00
71500	I Can Dream, Can't I/I Heard You Cried Last Night	1959	2.50	5.00	10.00
71536	Call Me Darling/My Love Will Last	1959	2.50	5.00	10.00
71559	There Are Such Things/You, You, You	1960	2.00	4.00	8.00
71604	A Kiss to Build a Dream On/Come On Baby, Let's Go	1960	2.00	4.00	8.00
71772	A Lover's Question/That's All I Want from You	1961	2.00	4.00	8.00
71919	See See Rider/Mound Bayou	1961	2.00	4.00	8.00
71960	Hurry Hurry/After the Lights Go Down Low	1962	2.00	4.00	8.00

SUE

Number	Title (A Side/B Side)	Yr	VG	VG+	NM
10-004	You Deserve the Best/You're Not the Guy for Me	1968	—	3.00	6.00
115	I Pity the Fool/You're Not the Guy for Me	1964	2.00	4.00	8.00
793	Keep an Eye on Love/Continental Mind	1963	2.00	4.00	8.00
803	The Best Is Yet to Come/Will I Find My Love Today	1964	2.00	4.00	8.00

Albums

CONCORD JAZZ

Number	Title (A Side/B Side)	Yr	VG	VG+	NM
CJ-31	Hello Like Before	1977	3.00	6.00	12.00
CJ-54	Live from Concord to London	1978	3.00	6.00	12.00
CJ-109	Sunshine	1980	2.50	5.00	10.00
CJ-147	Never Make Your Move Too Soon	1982	2.50	5.00	10.00
CJ-214	Big City	1983	2.50	5.00	10.00
CJ-263	When the Sun Goes Down	1985	2.50	5.00	10.00
CJ-319	Be Mine Tonight	1987	2.50	5.00	10.00

MERCURY

Number	Title (A Side/B Side)	Yr	VG	VG+	NM
MG-20354 [M]	Hot Cargo	1958	10.00	20.00	40.00
MG-20400 [M]	Ernestine Anderson	1959	10.00	20.00	40.00
MG-20492 [M]	Fascinating Ernestine	1959	10.00	20.00	40.00
MG-20496 [M]	My Kinda Swing	1959	10.00	20.00	40.00
MG-20582 [M]	Moanin'	1960	10.00	20.00	40.00
SR-60074 [S]	Ernestine Anderson	1959	12.50	25.00	50.00
SR-60171 [S]	Fascinating Ernestine	1959	12.50	25.00	50.00
SR-60175 [S]	My Kinda Swing	1959	12.50	25.00	50.00
SR-60242 [S]	Moanin'	1960	12.50	25.00	50.00

SUE

Number	Title (A Side/B Side)	Yr	VG	VG+	NM
LP 1015 [M]	The New Sound of Ernestine Anderson	1963	5.00	10.00	20.00

WING

Number	Title (A Side/B Side)	Yr	VG	VG+	NM
MGW-12281 [M]	Ernestine Anderson	1964	3.00	6.00	12.00
SRW-16281 [S]	Ernestine Anderson	1964	3.75	7.50	15.00

ANDERSON, LYNN

45s

CHART

Number	Title (A Side/B Side)	Yr	VG	VG+	NM
1001	Too Much of You/If This Is Love	1967	—	2.50	5.00
—Reissue of 1475					
1010	Promises, Promises/It Makes You Happy	1967	—	2.50	5.00
1026	No Another Time/The Worst Is Yet to Come	1968	—	2.50	5.00
1042	Big Girls Don't Cry/I Keep Forgettin'	1968	—	2.50	5.00
1059	Flattery Will Get You Everywhere/A Million Shades of Blue	1968	—	2.50	5.00
1330	My Heart Keeps Walking the Floor/In Person	1966	—	3.00	6.00
1375	Ride, Ride, Ride/Tear By Tear	1966	—	3.00	6.00
1430	If I Kiss You (Will You Go Away)/Then Go	1967	—	3.00	6.00
1475	Too Much of You/If This Is Love	1967	—	3.00	6.00
5001	Our House Is Not a Home (If It's Never Been Loved In)/Wave Bye-Bye to the Man	1969	—	2.50	5.00
5013	Where's the Playground Bobby/There Oughta Be a Law	1969	—	2.50	5.00
5021	That's a No No/If Silence Is Golden	1969	—	2.50	5.00
5040	He'd Still Love Me/All You Add Is Love	1969	—	2.50	5.00
5053	I've Been Everywhere/Penny for Your Thoughts	1970	—	2.50	5.00
5068	Rocky Top/Take Me Home	1970	—	2.50	5.00
5098	I'm Alright/Pick of the Week	1970	—	2.50	5.00
5113	It Wasn't God Who Made Honky Tonk Angels/Be Quiet Mind	1971	—	2.50	5.00
5125	Jim Dandy/Strangers	1971	—	2.50	5.00
5136	He Even Woke Me Up to Say Goodbye/A Pillow That Whispers	1971	—	2.50	5.00
5146	Love of the Common People/Simple Words	1971	—	2.50	5.00
5151	There Oughta Be a Law/Too Much of You	1972	—	2.50	5.00

COLUMBIA

Number	Title (A Side/B Side)	Yr	VG	VG+	NM
AE7 1056 [DJ]	Frosty The Snowman/Don't Wish Me Merry Christmas	1972	—	3.00	6.00
10041	What a Man, My Man Is/Everything's Falling in Place	1974	—	2.00	4.00
10100	He Turns It Into Love Again/Someone to Finish What You Started	1975	—	2.00	4.00
10160	I've Never Loved Anyone More/He Worshipped Me	1975	—	2.00	4.00
10240	Paradise/You've Got It All Together Now	1975	—	2.00	4.00
10280	All the King's Horses/If All I Have to Do Is Just Love You	1975	—	2.00	4.00
10337	Rodeo Cowboy/Dixieland, You Will Never Die	1976	—	2.00	4.00
10401	Sweet Talkin' Man/A Good Old Country Song	1976	—	2.00	4.00
10467	Wrap Your Love All Around Your Man/I Couldn't Be Lonely (Even If I Wanted To)	1976	—	2.00	4.00
10545	I Love What Love Is Doing to Me/Will I Ever Hear Those Church Bells Ring	1977	—	2.00	4.00
10597	He Ain't You/It's Your Love What Keeps Me Going	1977	—	2.00	4.00
10650	We Got Love/Sunshine Man	1977	—	2.00	4.00
10721	Rising Above It All/My World Begins and Ends with You	1978	—	2.00	4.00
10809	Last Love of My Life/When You Marry for Money	1978	—	2.00	4.00
10909	Isn't It Always Love/A Child with You Tonight	1979	—	2.00	4.00
11006	I Love How You Love Me/Come As You Are	1979	—	2.00	4.00
11104	Sea of Heartbreak/Say You Will	1979	—	2.00	4.00
11296	Even Cowgirls Get the Blues/See Through Me	1980	—	2.00	4.00
11374	Blue Baby Blue/The Lonely Hearts Café	1980	—	2.00	4.00
45101	Stay There 'Til I Get There/I'd Run a Mile to You	1970	—	2.50	5.00
45190	No Love at All/I Found You Just in Time	1970	—	2.50	5.00
45251	Don't Wish Me Merry Christmas/Ding-a-Ling the Christmas Bell	1970	—	3.00	6.00
45251 [PS]	Don't Wish Me Merry Christmas/Ding-a-Ling the Christmas Bell	1970	2.00	4.00	8.00
45252	Rose Garden/Nothing Between Us	1970	—	2.50	5.00
45356	You're My Man/I'm Gonna Write a Song	1971	—	2.00	4.00
45429	How Can I Unlove You/Don't Say Things You Don't Mean	1971	—	2.00	4.00
45527	Don't Wish Me Merry Christmas/Ding-a-Ling the Christmas Bell	1971	—	2.50	5.00
45529	Cry/Simple Words	1972	—	2.00	4.00
45615	Listen to a Country Song/That's What Loving You Has Meant to Me	1972	—	2.00	4.00
45692	Fool Me/What's Made Milwaukee Famous	1972	—	2.00	4.00
45768	Keep Me in Mind/Rodeo	1973	—	2.00	4.00
45843	Sing About Love/Home Is Where I Hang My Head	1973	—	—	—
—Canceled?					
45857	Top of the World/I Wish I Was a Little Girl Again	1973	—	2.00	4.00
45918	Sing About Love/Fickle Fortune	1973	—	2.00	4.00
46009	Smile for Me/A Man Like Your Daddy	1974	—	2.00	4.00

Number	Title (A Side/B Side)	Yr	VG	VG+	NM
46056	Talkin' to the Wall/I Want to Be a Part of You	1974	—	2.00	4.00
MCA					
52408	Running from the Real Thing/The Heart of the Matter	1984	—	—	3.00
MERCURY					
870528-7	Under the Boardwalk/Turn the Page	1988	—	—	3.00
872154-7	The Angel Song (Glory to God in the Highest)/ When a Child Is Born	1988	—	—	3.00
—With Butch Baker					
872220-7	What He Does Best/It Goes Without Saying	1988	—	—	3.00
872602-7	How Many Hearts/How Many Hearts (Long Version)	1989	—	—	3.00
888209-7	Didn't We Shine/We Must Be Doing It Right	1986	—	—	3.00
888597-7	It Goes Without Saying/So Little Love in the World	1987	—	—	3.00
888839-7	Read Between the Lines/If This Ain't Love	1987	—	—	3.00
PERMIAN					
82000	You Can't Lose What You Never Had/(B-side unknown)	1983	—	2.00	4.00
82001	What I Learned from Loving You/(B-side unknown)	1983	—	2.00	4.00
82003	You're Welcome To Tonight/(B-side unknown)	1983	—	2.00	4.00
—A-side with Gary Morris					

Albums

Number	Title (A Side/B Side)	Yr	VG	VG+	NM
CHART					
CHM-1001 [M]	Ride, Ride, Ride	1967	5.00	10.00	20.00
CHS-1001 [S]	Ride, Ride, Ride	1967	3.75	7.50	15.00
CHM-1004 [M]	Promises, Promises	1968	5.00	10.00	20.00
CHS-1004 [S]	Promises, Promises	1968	3.75	7.50	15.00
CHS-1008	Big Girls Don't Cry	1969	3.75	7.50	15.00
CHS-1009	The Best of Lynn Anderson	1969	3.75	7.50	15.00
CHS-1013	With Love, From Lynn	1969	3.75	7.50	15.00
CHS-1017	At Home with Lynn	1969	3.75	7.50	15.00
CHS-1022	Songs That Made Country Girls Famous	1970	3.00	6.00	12.00
CHS-1028	Uptown Country Girl	1970	3.00	6.00	12.00
CHS-1032	Songs My Mother Wrote	1970	3.00	6.00	12.00
CHS-1037	I'm Alright	1970	3.00	6.00	12.00
CHS-1040	Lynn Anderson's Greatest Hits	1971	3.00	6.00	12.00
CHS-1043	Lynn Anderson with Strings	1971	3.00	6.00	12.00
CHS-1050 [(2)]	Lynn Anderson	1972	3.75	7.50	15.00
COLUMBIA					
CS 1025	Stay There 'Til I Get There	1970	3.00	6.00	12.00
C 30099	No Love at All	1970	3.00	6.00	12.00
C 30411	Rose Garden	1970	2.50	5.00	10.00
PC 30411	Rose Garden	197?	2.00	4.00	8.00
—Reissue					
KC 30793	You're My Man	1971	2.50	5.00	10.00
CG 30902 [(2)]	The World of Lynn Anderson	1971	3.00	6.00	12.00
KC 30925	How Can I Unlove You	1971	2.50	5.00	10.00
3C 30957	Christmas Album	198?	2.00	4.00	8.00
—Reissue of KC 30957					
KC 30957	Christmas Album	1971	3.00	6.00	12.00
KC 31316	Cry	1972	2.50	5.00	10.00
KC 31641	Lynn Anderson's Greatest Hits	1972	2.50	5.00	10.00
PC 31641	Lynn Anderson's Greatest Hits	197?	2.00	4.00	8.00
—Reissue					
KC 31647	Listen to a Country Song	1972	2.50	5.00	10.00
KC 32078	Keep Me in Mind	1973	2.50	5.00	10.00
KC 32429	Top of the World	1973	2.50	5.00	10.00
KC 32719	Queens of Country	1974	2.50	5.00	10.00
KC 32941	Smile for Me	1974	2.50	5.00	10.00
KC 33293	What a Man, My Man Is	1974	2.50	5.00	10.00
KC 33691	I've Never Loved Anyone More	1975	2.50	5.00	10.00
PC 34089	All the King's Horses	1976	2.50	5.00	10.00
PC 34308	Lynn Anderson's Greatest Hits Volume II	1976	2.50	5.00	10.00
PC 34439	Wrap Your Love All Around Your Man	1977	2.50	5.00	10.00
JC 34871	I Love What Love Is Doing to Me/He Ain't You	1977	2.50	5.00	10.00
JC 35776	Outlaw Is Just a State of Mind	1979	2.50	5.00	10.00
JC 36568	Even Cowgirls Get the Blues	1980	2.50	5.00	10.00
FC 37354	Encore	1981	2.50	5.00	10.00
PC 37354	Encore	1983	2.00	4.00	8.00
—Budget-line reissue					
HARMONY					
KH 32433	Singing My Song	1973	2.00	4.00	8.00
MERCURY					
834625-1	What She Does Best	1988	2.00	4.00	8.00
MOUNTAIN DEW					
7047	Lynn Anderson	197?	2.50	5.00	10.00
PERMIAN					
8205	Back	1983	2.50	5.00	10.00
PICKWICK					
PTP-2049 [(2)]	Lynn Anderson	1973	3.00	6.00	12.00
SPC-3267	Flower of Love	197?	2.00	4.00	8.00
SPC-3296	It Makes You Happy	197?	2.00	4.00	8.00

ANDERSON, LYNN, AND JERRY LANE

45s

Number	Title (A Side/B Side)	Yr	VG	VG+	NM
CHART					
1003	Keeping Up Appearances/You've Gotta Be the Greatest	1967	—	2.50	5.00
—Reissue of 1425					
1300	For Better or For Worse/We're Different	1965	—	3.00	6.00
1425	Keeping Up Appearances/You've Gotta Be the Greatest	1967	—	3.00	6.00

ANDERSON, MILDRED

45s

Number	Title (A Side/B Side)	Yr	VG	VG+	NM
BLUESVILLE					
804	Person to Person/Connections	1960	3.75	7.50	15.00

Albums

Number	Title (A Side/B Side)	Yr	VG	VG+	NM
BLUESVILLE					
BVLP-1004 [M]	Person to Person	1960	12.50	25.00	50.00
—Blue and silver label					
BVLP-1004 [M]	Person to Person	1964	6.25	12.50	25.00
—Blue label with trident logo					
BVLP-1017 [M]	No More in Life	1961	12.50	25.00	50.00
—Blue and silver label					
BVLP-1017 [M]	No More in Life	1964	6.25	12.50	25.00
—Blue label with trident logo					

ANDERSON, SONNY

45s

Number	Title (A Side/B Side)	Yr	VG	VG+	NM
IMPERIAL					
5634	Yes, I'm Gonna Love You/Lonely, Lonely Train	1959	12.50	25.00	50.00
5689	Our Love Could Never Be/Fool	1960	12.50	25.00	50.00

ANDERSON, VICKI

Also see JAMES BROWN.

45s

Number	Title (A Side/B Side)	Yr	VG	VG+	NM
BROWNSTONE					
4202	I'm Too Tough for Mr. Big Stuff/Sound Funky	1971	—	3.00	6.00
4204	I'll Work It Out/In the Land of Milk and Honey	1971	—	3.00	6.00
4307	Don't Throw Your Love in the Garbage Can/In the Land of Milk and Honey	1972	—	3.00	6.00
DELUXE					
6201	Wide Awake in a Dream/Nobody Cares	1966	2.00	4.00	8.00
FONTANA					
1527	Never, Never Let You Go (Part 1)/Never, Never Let You Go (Part 2)	1965	3.00	6.00	12.00
KING					
6066	You Send Me/Unchain My Heart	1967	2.00	4.00	8.00
6091	Think/Nobody Cares	1967	2.50	5.00	10.00
—A-side: With James Brown					
6109	Tears of Joy/If You Don't Give Me	1967	2.00	4.00	8.00
6138	That Feelin' Is Real/Baby Don't You Know	1967	2.00	4.00	8.00
6152	You've Got the Power/What the World Needs Now Is Love	1968	2.50	5.00	10.00
—A-side: With James Brown					
6221	What the World Needs Now Is Love/I'll Work It Out	1969	2.00	4.00	8.00
6251	The Answer to Mother Popcorn (I Got a Mother for You)/I'll Work It Out	1969	2.00	4.00	8.00
6274	Wide Awake in a Dream/I Want to Be in the Land of Milk and Honey	1969	2.00	4.00	8.00
6293	Let It Be Me/No More Heartaches, No More Pain	1970	2.50	5.00	10.00
—A-side: With James Brown					
6314	Never Find a Love Like Mine/No More Heartaches, No More Pain	1970	2.00	4.00	8.00
6377	Message from the Soul Sisters Part 1/Yesterday	1971	2.00	4.00	8.00
SMASH					
1985	I Love You/Nobody Cares	1965	2.50	5.00	10.00
TUFF					
420	I Can't Stop Loving You/I Lost a Good Man	1964	2.50	5.00	10.00

ANDREWS, CHRIS

45s

Number	Title (A Side/B Side)	Yr	VG	VG+	NM
ATCO					
6385	Yesterday Man/Too Bad You Don't Want Me	1965	2.50	5.00	10.00
6414	Something On My Mind/To Whom It May Concern	1966	2.50	5.00	10.00
RCA VICTOR					
47-9746	Pretty Belinda/Maker of Mistakes	1969	2.00	4.00	8.00

ANDREWS, LEE, AND THE HEARTS

45s

Number	Title (A Side/B Side)	Yr	VG	VG+	NM
ARGO					
1000	Tear Drops/The Girl Around the Corner	1957	12.50	25.00	50.00
CASINO					
110	Baby, Come Back/I Wonder	1958	7.50	15.00	30.00
452	Try the Impossible/Nobody's Home	1958	200.00	400.00	600.00
—With playing cards on label					
452	Try the Impossible/Nobody's Home	1958	50.00	100.00	200.00
—All-black label					
CHESS					
1665	Long Lonely Nights/The Clock	1957	10.00	20.00	40.00
—Sliver-top "chess pieces" label					
1665	Long Lonely Nights/The Clock	1957	3.75	7.50	15.00
—All-blue label					
1675	Tear Drops/The Girl Around the Corner	1957	5.00	10.00	20.00
—All-blue label (if a "chess pieces" label exists, we aren't aware of it)					
CRIMSON					
1002	Oh My Love/'Island of Love	1967	2.00	4.00	8.00
1009	Nevertheless/Island of Love	1967	2.00	4.00	8.00
1015	I've Had It/Little Bird	1968	2.00	4.00	8.00
GOTHAM					
318	Bluebird of Happiness/Show Me the Meringue	1956	50.00	100.00	200.00
320	Lonely Room/Leona	1956	75.00	150.00	300.00
321	Just Suppose/It's Me!	1956	75.00	150.00	300.00
GRAND					
156	Teardrops/The Girl Around the Corner	1962	3.00	6.00	12.00
157	Long Lonely Nights/The Clock	1962	3.00	6.00	12.00
LANA					
110	Long Lonely Nights/The Clock	196?	—	3.00	6.00
—Lana records are reissues					
111	Try the Impossible/Nobody's Home	196?	—	3.00	6.00
112	Teardrops/The Girl Around the Corner	196?	—	3.00	6.00
LOST-NITE					
104	The Fairest/Much Too Much	196?	—	3.00	6.00
106	The Bells of St. Mary/Much Too Much	196?	—	3.00	6.00
108	The White Cliffs of Dover/Much Too Much	196?	—	3.00	6.00
110	Maybe You'll Be There/Baby Come Back	196?	—	3.00	6.00
135	The Bluebird of Happiness/Show Me the Meringue	196?	—	3.00	6.00
136	Lonely Room/Leona	196?	—	3.00	6.00
137	Just Suppose/It's Me	196?	—	3.00	6.00
176	Teardrops/The Girl Around the Corner	196?	—	3.00	6.00
190	Long Lonely Nights/The Clock	196?	—	3.00	6.00

Number	Title (A Side/B Side)	Yr	VG	VG+	NM
193	Try the Impossible/Nobody's Home	196?	—	3.00	6.00
216	All I Ask Is Love/Maybe You'll Be There	196?	—	3.00	6.00
234	Glad to Be Here/Why Do I	196?	—	3.00	6.00
—All the above Lost-Nite records (three-digit numbers) are reissues					
1001	Cold Gray Dawn/All You Can Do	1968	2.00	4.00	8.00
1004	Oh My Love/Can't Do Without You	1968	2.00	4.00	8.00
1005	Quiet As It's Kept/Island of Love	1968	2.00	4.00	8.00
—The above three are NOT reissues					
MAIN LINE					
102	Long Lonely Nights/The Clock	1957	100.00	200.00	400.00
—Green label, no address					
102	Long Lonely Nights/The Clock	1957	50.00	100.00	200.00
—Black label, Philadelphia address on label					
102	Long Lonely Nights/The Clock	1962	7.50	15.00	30.00
—Black label, no address					
105	Teardrops/The Girl Around the Corner	1962	3.00	6.00	12.00
PARKWAY					
860	I'm Sorry, Pillow/Gee, But I'm Lonesome	1962	3.75	7.50	15.00
866	Looking Back/Operator	1963	3.75	7.50	15.00
RAINBOW					
252	Maybe You'll Be There/Baby Come Back	1954	100.00	200.00	400.00
—Black vinyl					
252	Maybe You'll Be There/Baby Come Back	1954	200.00	400.00	800.00
—Red vinyl					
252	Maybe You'll Be There/Baby Come Back	1962	2.50	5.00	10.00
—Reissue with large print					
256	White Cliffs of Dover/Much Too Much	1954	375.00	750.00	1500.
—Yellow label original					
256	White Cliffs of Dover/Much Too Much	1962	2.50	5.00	10.00
—Blue label reissue					
259	The Bells of St. Mary's/The Fairest	1954	150.00	300.00	600.00
—Yellow label original					
259	The Bells of St. Mary's/The Fairest	1962	2.50	5.00	10.00
—Blue label reissue					
RCA VICTOR					
47-8929	Quiet As It's Kept/You're Taking a Long Time Coming Back	1966	2.50	5.00	10.00
SWAN					
4065	I Miss You So/I've Got to Cry	1960	25.00	50.00	100.00
4076	A Night Like This/You Gave to Me	1961	37.50	75.00	150.00
4087	P.S. I Love You/I Cried	1961	50.00	100.00	200.00
UNITED ARTISTS					
123	Try the Impossible/Nobody's Home	1958	6.25	12.50	25.00
136	Why Do I/Glad to Be Here	1958	5.00	10.00	20.00
151	Maybe You'll Be There/All I Ask Is Love	1958	5.00	10.00	20.00
162	Boom/Just Suppose	1959	5.00	10.00	20.00
592	Try the Impossible/Nobody's Home	1963	3.75	7.50	15.00
Albums					
COLLECTABLES					
COL-5003	Gotham Recording Sessions	1982	3.00	6.00	12.00
COL-5028	Biggest Hits	198?	3.00	6.00	12.00
LOST-NITE					
LLP-1 [10]	Lee Andrews and the Hearts	1981	3.00	6.00	12.00
—Red vinyl					
LLP-2 [10]	Lee Andrews and the Hearts	1981	3.00	6.00	12.00
—Red vinyl					
LP-101 [M]	Biggest Hits	1964	25.00	50.00	100.00
—Yellow vinyl					
LP-101 [M]	Biggest Hits	1964	12.50	25.00	50.00
—Black vinyl					
LP-113 [M]	Lee Andrews and the Hearts Live	1965	12.50	25.00	50.00

ANDREWS SISTERS, THE

Also see BING CROSBY.

Number	Title (A Side/B Side)	Yr	VG	VG+	NM
45s					
CAPITOL					
F-3567	Crazy Arms/I Want to Linger	1956	3.00	6.00	12.00
F-3583	A Child's Christmas Song/Silver Bells	1956	3.75	7.50	15.00
F-3658	Rum and Coca Cola/No Baby	1957	3.00	6.00	12.00
F-3707	Give Me Back My Heart/Stars, Stars	1957	3.00	6.00	12.00
F-3784	By His Word/I'm Goin' Home	1957	3.00	6.00	12.00
F-3869	One Mistake/Melancholy Moon	1957	3.00	6.00	12.00
F-3965	Torero/Sunshine	1958	3.00	6.00	12.00
F-4144	I've Got an Invitation to a Dance/My Love Is a Kitten	1959	2.50	5.00	10.00
DECCA					
23605	Bei Mir Bist Du Schoen/Joseph! Joseph!	1950	3.75	7.50	15.00
23606	Hold Tight, Hold Tight/Well Alright	1950	3.75	7.50	15.00
23607	Beat Me Daddy, Eight to the Bar/Scrub Me Mama with a Boogie Beat	1950	3.75	7.50	15.00
23608	(I'll Be With You) In Apple Blossom Time/Rhumba Boogie	1950	3.75	7.50	15.00
—The above four comprise a box set (9-23) originally issued on 78s					
23722	Christmas Island/Winter Wonderland	1950	3.75	7.50	15.00
—With Guy Lombardo and His Royal Canadians; lines label					
23722	Christmas Island/Winter Wonderland	1955	3.00	6.00	12.00
—With Guy Lombardo and His Royal Canadians; star label					
23722	Christmas Island/Winter Wonderland	1960	2.50	5.00	10.00
—With Guy Lombardo and His Royal Canadians; color bars label					
24705	I Can Dream, Can't I?/The Wedding of Lili Marlene	1950	5.00	10.00	20.00
—78 released in 1949					
24748	Merry Christmas Polka/Christmas Candles	1950	3.75	7.50	15.00
—With Guy Lombardo and His Royal Canadians; 78 released in 1949, may not exist on 45					
27007	I Wanna Be Loved/I've Just Got to Get Out of the Habit	1950	3.75	7.50	15.00
27115	Can't We Talk It Over/There Will Never Be Another You	1950	3.75	7.50	15.00
27202	The Glory of Love/A Rainy Day Refrain	1950	3.75	7.50	15.00
—With Guy Lombardo and His Royal Canadians					
27242	Jing-a-Ling/Parade of the Wooden Soldiers	1950	3.75	7.50	15.00
27251	I'd Like to Hitch a Ride with Santa Claus/(Sweet Angie) The Christmas Tree Angel	1950	3.75	7.50	15.00
27252	A Bushel and a Peck/Guys and Dolls	1950	3.75	7.50	15.00
27310	Sleigh Ride/Telephone Song	1950	5.00	10.00	20.00
27349	Go West, Young Man/Along the Navaho Trail	1950	3.75	7.50	15.00
27414	A Penny a Kiss — A Penny A Hug/Zing Zing, Zoom Zoom	1951	3.75	7.50	15.00
27421	Between Two Trees/I Wish I Knew	1951	3.75	7.50	15.00
27432	Three O'Clock in the Morning/Lullaby of Broadway	1951	3.75	7.50	15.00
27537	I Remember Mama/My Mom	1951	3.75	7.50	15.00
27635	It Never Entered My Mind/I'm in Love Again	1951	3.75	7.50	15.00
27652	Night on the Waters/Dimples and Cherry Cheeks	1951	3.75	7.50	15.00
27700	How Many Times/I Used to Love You	1951	3.75	7.50	15.00
—With Tommy Dorsey and His Orchestra					
27715	Can We Talk It Over/There Will Never Be Another You	1951	3.75	7.50	15.00
27757	Carioca/Daddy	1951	3.75	7.50	15.00
27760	Lying in the Way/Love Is Such a Cheat	1951	3.75	7.50	15.00
27834	Nobody's Darling But Mine/Goodbye, Darling	1951	3.75	7.50	15.00
27858	The Three Bells/The Windmill Song	1951	3.75	7.50	15.00
27878	Blonde Sailor/All the World to Me	1951	3.75	7.50	15.00
27894	Down in the Valley/Red River Valley	1951	3.75	7.50	15.00
27910	I'm on a Seesaw of Love/Play Me a Hurtin' Tune	1951	3.75	7.50	15.00
—With Guy Lombardo and His Royal Canadians					
27979	Wondering/Poor Whip-Poor-Will	1952	3.75	7.50	15.00
28042	Why Worry/That Ever Lovin' Rag	1952	3.75	7.50	15.00
28116	Dreams Come Tumbling Down/Music Lessons	1952	3.75	7.50	15.00
28143	Linger Awhile/Wabash Blues	1952	3.75	7.50	15.00
—With Russ Morgan and His Orchestra					
28163	Where Is Your Wandering Mother Tonight/Hang Your Head in Shame	1952	3.75	7.50	15.00
—A-side with Red Foley					
28276	Idle Chatter/One for the Wonder	1952	3.75	7.50	15.00
28294	Isle of Golden Dreams/Nalani	1952	3.00	6.00	12.00
28295	Kings Serenade/Cockeyed Mayor of Kannakakai	1952	3.00	6.00	12.00
28296	Fair Hawaii/Ke Kali Nei Au	1952	3.00	6.00	12.00
28297	Good Night, Aloha/Malihini Mele	1952	3.00	6.00	12.00
—Above 4 with Alfred Apaka and His Orchestra					
28342	Adios/Carmen's Boogie	1952	3.75	7.50	15.00
28480	Don't Be That Way/Sing, Sing, Sing	1952	3.00	6.00	12.00
28481	Piccolo Pete/If I Had a Boy Like You	1952	3.00	6.00	12.00
28482	East of the Sun/In the Mood	1952	3.00	6.00	12.00
28483	Old Don Juan/The Mambo Man	1952	3.00	6.00	12.00
28680	Fugue for Tinhorns/Now That I'm in Love	1953	3.75	7.50	15.00
28773	You Too, You Too?/Tegucigalpa	1953	3.75	7.50	15.00
28929	This Little Piggie Went to Market/Love Sends a Little Gift of Roses	1953	3.75	7.50	15.00
29149	My Love, The Blues and Me/There's a Rainbow in the Valley	1954	3.75	7.50	15.00
29995	Rum and Coca Cola/Jack, Jack, Jack	1956	3.00	6.00	12.00
DOT					
16433	Pistol Packin' Mama/Ti-Pi-Tin	1963	2.00	4.00	8.00
16497	Mr. Bass Man/My Midnight Prison	1963	2.00	4.00	8.00
KAPP					
309	One, Two, Three, Four/I've Got to Pass Your House	1959	2.50	5.00	10.00
MCA					
60012	Beer Barrel Polka/Pennsylvania Polka	1973	—	2.00	4.00
60040	Boogie Woogie Bugle Boy/Rum and Coca-Cola	1974	—	2.00	4.00
60041	Bei Mir Bist Du Schoen/(I'll Be With You) In Apple Blossom Time	1974	—	2.00	4.00
60042	Don't Sit Under the Apple Tree/I Can Dream, Can't I?	1974	—	2.00	4.00
65016	Take Me Out to the Ball Game/In the Good Old Summertime	1973	—	2.00	4.00
65020	Christmas Island/Winter Wonderland	1973	—	2.00	4.00
—With Guy Lombardo and His Royal Canadians; black label with rainbow					
65020	Christmas Island/Winter Wonderland	1980	—	—	3.00
—With Guy Lombardo and His Royal Canadians; blue label with rainbow					
PARAMOUNT					
0257	Rum and Coca-Cola/Pennsylvania Polka	1973	—	2.50	5.00
7-Inch Extended Plays					
DECCA					
ED 2006	I Can Dream, Can't I?/I Wanna Be Loved//I Don't Know Why/Jealous	195?	3.75	7.50	15.00
ED 2006 [PS]	The Andrews Sisters, Vol. 1	195?	3.75	7.50	15.00
Albums					
ABC					
4003	16 Great Performances	1975	3.00	6.00	12.00
CAPITOL					
T 790 [M]	The Andrews Sisters in Hi-Fi	1957	7.50	15.00	30.00
T 860 [M]	Fresh and Fancy Free	1957	7.50	15.00	30.00
T 973 [M]	The Dancing Twenties	1957	7.50	15.00	30.00
DT 1924 [R]	The Hits of the Andrews Sisters	1963	3.00	6.00	12.00
T 1924 [M]	The Hits of the Andrews Sisters	1963	5.00	10.00	20.00
DECCA					
DL 4019 [M]	Curtain Call	1956	7.50	15.00	30.00
DL 5065 [10]	Tropical Songs	1950	10.00	20.00	40.00
DL 5120 [10]	The Andrews Sisters	1951	10.00	20.00	40.00
DL 5155 [10]	Club 15	1951	10.00	20.00	40.00
DL 5264 [10]	Berlin Songs	1951	10.00	20.00	40.00
DL 5282 [10]	Christmas Cheer	1950	10.00	20.00	40.00
—Also see "Crosby, Bing"					
DL 5306 [10]	I Love to Tell the Story	1952	10.00	20.00	40.00
DL 5423 [10]	My Isle of Golden Dreams	1953	10.00	20.00	40.00
DL 5438 [10]	Sing, Sing, Sing	1953	10.00	20.00	40.00
DL 8354 [M]	Jingle Bells	1956	7.50	15.00	30.00
DL 8360 [M]	The Andrews Sisters — By Popular Demand	1957	7.50	15.00	30.00
DOT					
DLP 3406 [M]	The Andrews Sisters' Greatest Hits	1962	3.75	7.50	15.00
DLP 3452 [M]	Great Golden Hits	1962	3.75	7.50	15.00
DLP 3529 [M]	Present	1963	3.00	6.00	12.00
DLP 3567 [M]	Great Country Hits	1963	3.00	6.00	12.00
DLP 3632 [M]	The Andrews Sisters Go Hawaiian	1964	3.00	6.00	12.00
DLP 25406 [S]	The Andrews Sisters' Greatest Hits	1962	5.00	10.00	20.00
DLP 25452 [S]	Great Golden Hits	1962	5.00	10.00	20.00

Number	Title (A Side/B Side)	Yr	VG	VG+	NM
DLP 25529 [S]	Present	1963	3.75	7.50	15.00
DLP 25567 [S]	Great Country Hits	1963	3.75	7.50	15.00
DLP 25632 [S]	The Andrews Sisters Go Hawaiian	1964	3.75	7.50	15.00
HAMILTON					
HLP 124 [M]	Pennsylvania Polka	196?	3.00	6.00	12.00
HLP 12124 [S]	Pennsylvania Polka	196?	3.75	7.50	15.00
MCA					
739	Near You	198?	2.00	4.00	8.00
—Reissue of Vocalion album					
908	Rarities	198?	2.00	4.00	8.00
2-4024	The Best of the Andrews Sisters	1973	3.75	7.50	15.00
2-4093 [(2)]	The Best of the Andrews Sisters, Vol. 2	197?	3.75	7.50	15.00
24015	Christmas	1987	2.00	4.00	8.00
—Reissue					
27081	16 Great Performances	1980	2.00	4.00	8.00
—Reissue of ABC 4003					
27082	Boogie Woogie Bugle Girls	1980	2.00	4.00	8.00
—Reissue of Paramount 6075					
PARAMOUNT					
PAS-1023	In the Mood	1974	3.75	7.50	15.00
PAS-6075	Boogie Woogie Bugle Girls	1973	3.00	6.00	12.00
PICKWICK					
SPC-3382	Sing! Sing! Sing!	197?	2.50	5.00	10.00
VOCALION					
VL 3611 [M]	Near You	196?	3.00	6.00	12.00

ANGEL

Number	Title (A Side/B Side)	Yr	VG	VG+	NM
45s					
CASABLANCA					
853	Rock and Rollers/(B-side unknown)	1976	—	2.50	5.00
878	That Magic Touch/Big Boy (Let's Do It Again)	1977	—	2.50	5.00
903 DJ [DJ]	The Winter Song/The Christmas Song	1978	—	3.00	6.00
903	Winter Song/Can You Feel It	1977	—	2.50	5.00
914	My Angel Flying with Broken Wings//Under Suspicion/I Ain't Gonna Eat Out My Heart Anymore	1978	—	2.50	5.00
933	Stick Like Glue/Don't Leave Me Lonely	1978	—	2.50	5.00
963	Bad Time/Don't Take Your Love	1979	—	2.00	4.00
2240	20th Century Woman/Can You Feel It	1980	—	2.00	4.00
Albums					
CASABLANCA					
NBLP 7021	Angel	1975	3.00	6.00	12.00
NBLP 7028	Helluva Band	1976	3.00	6.00	12.00
NBLP 7043	On Earth As It Is in Heaven	1977	3.00	6.00	12.00
NBLP 7085	White Hot	1977	3.00	6.00	12.00
—Contains one Christmas song:					
NBLP 7127	Sinful	1979	3.00	6.00	12.00
NBLP 7203 [(2)]	Live Without a Net	1980	3.75	7.50	15.00

ANGEL, JOHNNY

Number	Title (A Side/B Side)	Yr	VG	VG+	NM
45s					
EXCELLO					
2077	I Realize/Baby I'm Confessin'	1956	6.25	12.50	25.00
FELSTED					
8633	Lady of Spain/Without Her Heart	1961	5.00	10.00	20.00
8646	Mashed Potatoe Stomp/One More Tomorrow	1962	5.00	10.00	20.00
8659	Looking for a Fool/Roller Motion	1962	5.00	10.00	20.00
GARDENA					
117	All Night Party/Baby, You've Got Soul	1961	3.75	7.50	15.00
IMPERIAL					
5673	Falling Teardrops/Doubt	1960	10.00	20.00	40.00
JAF					
2024	Lonely Nights/Seven Words	1961	3.75	7.50	15.00
LIBERTY					
55895	Summertime Blues/Biggest Part of Me	1966	2.00	4.00	8.00
POWER					
250	Starlight/The Story of Love	1959	30.00	60.00	120.00
SWAN					
4263	This Is the Night for Love/You've Been Wrong	1966	10.00	20.00	40.00
VIN					
1004	Teenage Wedding/Baby, It's Love	1958	6.25	12.50	25.00

ANGEL, JOHNNY T.

Number	Title (A Side/B Side)	Yr	VG	VG+	NM
45s					
BELL					
45472	Tell Laura I Love Her/The Way I Feel Tonight	1974	—	2.00	4.00
YORKSVILLE					
45090	Tell Laura I Love Her/The Way I Feel Tonight	1974	—	3.00	6.00

ANGEL, MARIAN

Number	Title (A Side/B Side)	Yr	VG	VG+	NM
45s					
JUBILEE					
5508	It's Gonna Be Alright/Tomorrow's Fool	1965	2.50	5.00	10.00

ANGELOU, MAYA

Number	Title (A Side/B Side)	Yr	VG	VG+	NM
Albums					
LIBERTY					
LRP-3028 [M]	Miss Calypso	1958	12.50	25.00	50.00

ANGELS, THE (1)

Female vocal group.

Number	Title (A Side/B Side)	Yr	VG	VG+	NM
45s					
CAPRICE					
107	'Til/A Moment Ago	1961	7.50	15.00	30.00
—With horizontal "Caprice" logo; B-side listed as "A Moment Ago" but plays "Cotton Fields"					
107	'Til/A Moment Ago	1961	5.00	10.00	20.00
—With semicircular "Caprice" logo					
112	Cry Baby Cry/That's All I Ask of You	1962	5.00	10.00	20.00
116	Everybody Loves a Lover/Blow Joe	1962	3.75	7.50	15.00
118	You Should Have Told Me/I'd Be Good for You	1962	3.75	7.50	15.00
121	Cotton Fields/A Moment Ago	1963	3.75	7.50	15.00
POLYDOR					
14222	You're All I Need to Get By/Poppa's Side of the Bed	1974	—	2.50	5.00
RCA VICTOR					
47-9129	I Had a Dream I Lost You/What to Do	1967	2.50	5.00	10.00
47-9246	Go Out and Play/You'll Never Get to Heaven (If You Break My Heart)	1967	2.50	5.00	10.00
47-9404	You're the Cause of It/With Love	1967	2.50	5.00	10.00
47-9541	The Medley: Moments to Remember-Theme from A Summer Place-One Summer Night/If I Didn't Love You	1968	2.50	5.00	10.00
47-9612	But for Love/The Man with the Green Eyes	1968	2.50	5.00	10.00
47-9681	Merry Go Round/So Nice (Samba De Verao)	1968	2.50	5.00	10.00
SMASH					
1834	My Boyfriend's Back/(Love Me) Now	1963	4.00	8.00	16.00
1854	I Adore Him/Thank You and Goodnight	1963	3.75	7.50	15.00
1854 [PS]	I Adore Him/Thank You and Goodnight	1963	15.00	30.00	60.00
1870	Wow Wow Wee (He's the Boy for Me)/Snowflakes and Teardrops	1964	3.75	7.50	15.00
1885	Little Beatle Boy/Java	1964	5.00	10.00	20.00
1915	Jamaica Joe/Dream Boy	1964	3.75	7.50	15.00
1915 [PS]	Jamaica Joe/Dream Boy	1964	15.00	30.00	60.00
1931	World Without Love/The Boy from Crosstown	1964	3.75	7.50	15.00
1931 [PS]	World Without Love/The Boy from Crosstown	1964	20.00	40.00	80.00
—The existence of this sleeve has been confirmed!					
Albums					
ASCOT					
AM 13009 [M]	Twelve of Their Greatest Hits	1964	6.25	12.50	25.00
AS 16009 [S]	Twelve of Their Greatest Hits	1964	7.50	15.00	30.00
CAPRICE					
LP 1001 [M]	...And the Angels Sing	1962	30.00	60.00	120.00
SLP 1001 [S]	...And the Angels Sing	1962	50.00	100.00	200.00
COLLECTABLES					
COL-5085	My Boyfriend's Back: Golden Classics	198?	2.50	5.00	10.00
SMASH					
MGS-27039 [M]	My Boyfriend's Back	1963	10.00	20.00	40.00
MGS-27048 [M]	A Halo to You	1964	10.00	20.00	40.00
SRS-67039 [S]	My Boyfriend's Back	1963	15.00	30.00	60.00
SRS-67048 [S]	A Halo to You	1964	15.00	30.00	60.00

ANGELS, THE (2)

Male vocal group.

Number	Title (A Side/B Side)	Yr	VG	VG+	NM
45s					
GEE					
1024	Glory of Love/It's You I Love Best	1956	15.00	30.00	60.00
GRAND					
115	Wedding Bells/Times Have Changed	1954	100.00	200.00	400.00
—With no address on label					
115	Wedding Bells/Times Have Changed	1954	12.50	25.00	50.00
—With address on label					
121	A Lovely Way to Spend An Evening/You're Still My Baby	1954	125.00	250.00	500.00
—With no address on label					
121	A Lovely Way to Spend An Evening/You're Still My Baby	1954	12.50	25.00	50.00
—With address on label					

ANGELS, THE (3)

Different male vocal group than (2). Also see THE SAFARIS.

Number	Title (A Side/B Side)	Yr	VG	VG+	NM
45s					
TAWNY					
101	A Lover's Poem (To Him)/A Lover's Poem (To Her)	1959	10.00	20.00	40.00

ANGELS, THE (U)

Number	Title (A Side/B Side)	Yr	VG	VG+	NM
45s					
ASCOT					
2139	Irresistible/Cotton Fields	1963	3.00	6.00	12.00
CAMEO					
250	You Turn Me On/Raining Teardrops	1963	3.75	7.50	15.00

ANGIE AND THE CHICKLETTES

Number	Title (A Side/B Side)	Yr	VG	VG+	NM
45s					
APT					
25080	Treat Him Tender Maureen (Now That Ringo Belongs to You)/Tommy	1965	7.50	15.00	30.00

ANGLO-AMERICANS, THE

Number	Title (A Side/B Side)	Yr	VG	VG+	NM
45s					
CHATTAHOOCHIE					
705	The Music Never Stops/Are You Ready for This?	1966	7.50	15.00	30.00

ANGLOS, THE

Number	Title (A Side/B Side)	Yr	VG	VG+	NM
45s					
ORBIT					
201	Incense/You're Fooling Me	1965	12.50	25.00	50.00
—Steve Winwood is on this record, his first					
SCEPTER					
12204	Since You've Been Gone/A Small Town Boy	1967	5.00	10.00	20.00

ANIMALS, THE

Includes "Eric Burdon and the Animals." Also see ERIC BURDON; ERIC BURDON AND WAR; ALAN PRICE; HILTON VALENTINE.

Number	Title (A Side/B Side)	Yr	VG	VG+	NM
45s					
ABKCO					
4025	House of the Rising Sun/Bring It On Home to Me	1973	—	2.50	5.00
—Contains the full-length version of A-side					
4026	We Gotta Get Out of This Place/It's My Life	1973	—	2.00	4.00
4037	Don't Let Me Be Misunderstood/Talkin' About You	1973	—	2.00	4.00
4038	I'm Cryin'/Boom Boom	1973	—	2.00	4.00

Number	Title (A Side/B Side)	Yr	VG	VG+	NM
I.R.S.					
9920	The Night/No John No	1983	—	2.50	5.00
9923	Love Is For All Time/It's Too Late	1983	—	2.50	5.00
JET					
XW-1070	Fire on the Sun/Riverside County	1977	—	3.00	6.00
MGM					
CS-11-5	Celebrity Scene: The Animals	1967	20.00	40.00	80.00
—Box set of five singles (13791-13795). Price includes box, all 5 singles, jukebox title strips, bio. Records are sometimes found by themselves, so they are also listed separately.					
KGC 178	Gonna Take You Back to Walker/Baby Let Me Take You Home	196?	2.00	4.00	8.00
—Reissue label					
KGC 179	The House of the Rising Sun/I'm Crying	196?	2.50	5.00	10.00
—Reissue label; A-side, despite being labeled 2:58, actually plays 4:29					
KGC 180	Don't Let Me Be Misunderstood/Boom Boom	196?	2.00	4.00	8.00
—Reissue label					
KGC 181	We Gotta Get Out of This Place/Don't Bring Me Down	196?	2.00	4.00	8.00
—Reissue label					
KGC 182	It's My Life/Inside Looking Out	196?	2.00	4.00	8.00
—Reissue label					
13242	Gonna Send You Back to Walker (Gonna Send You Back to Georgia)/Baby, Let Me Take You Home	1964	3.75	7.50	15.00
13264	The House of the Rising Sun/Talkin' About You	1964	3.75	7.50	15.00
13264 [PS]	The House of the Rising Sun/Talkin' About You	1964	7.50	15.00	30.00
13274	I'm Crying/Take It Easy Baby	1964	3.75	7.50	15.00
13274 [PS]	I'm Crying/Take It Easy Baby	1964	6.25	12.50	25.00
13298	Boom Boom/Blue Feeling	1964	3.75	7.50	15.00
13298 [PS]	Boom Boom/Blue Feeling	1964	6.25	12.50	25.00
13311	Don't Let Me Be Misunderstood/Club A-Go-Go	1964	3.75	7.50	15.00
13339	Bring It On Home to Me/For Miss Caulker	1965	3.00	6.00	12.00
13339 [PS]	Bring It On Home to Me/For Miss Caulker	1965	6.25	12.50	25.00
13382	We Gotta Get Out of This Place/I Can't Believe It	1965	3.00	6.00	12.00
13414	It's My Life/I'm Going to Change the World	1965	3.00	6.00	12.00
13468	Inside-Looking Out/You're On My Mind	1966	3.00	6.00	12.00
13514	Don't Bring Me Down/Cheating	1966	3.00	6.00	12.00
13582	See See Rider/She'll Return It	1966	2.50	5.00	10.00
—Starting here, records are by "Eric Burdon and the Animals"					
13636	Help Me Girl/That Ain't Where It's At	1966	2.50	5.00	10.00
13721	When I Was Young/A Girl Called Sandoz	1967	2.50	5.00	10.00
13769	San Franciscan Nights/Good Times	1967	2.50	5.00	10.00
13769 [PS]	San Franciscan Nights/Good Times	1967	6.25	12.50	25.00
13791	Don't Bring Me Down/When I Was Young	1967	3.00	6.00	12.00
13792	See See Rider/Hey Gyp	1967	3.00	6.00	12.00
13793	Inside-Looking Out/Help Me Girl	1967	3.00	6.00	12.00
13794	San Franciscan Nights/Good Times	1967	3.00	6.00	12.00
13795	It's All Meat/The Other Side of This Life	1967	3.00	6.00	12.00
13868	Monterey/Ain't That So	1967	2.50	5.00	10.00
13868 [PS]	Monterey/Ain't That So	1967	6.25	12.50	25.00
13917	Anything/It's All Meat	1968	2.50	5.00	10.00
13939	Sky Pilot (Part 1)/Sky Pilot (Part 2)	1968	2.50	5.00	10.00
—First pressings have black labels					
13939	Sky Pilot (Part 1)/Sky Pilot (Part 2)	1968	2.00	4.00	8.00
—Second pressings have blue and gold labels					
14013	River Deep, Mountain High/White Houses	1968	2.00	4.00	8.00
Albums					
ABKCO					
AB-4226 [(2)]	The Best of the Animals	1973	3.00	6.00	12.00
AB-4324 [M]	The Best of the Animals	1987	2.50	5.00	10.00
—With alternate version of "We Gotta Get Out of This Place"					
ACCORD					
SN-7193	Looking Back	1981	2.00	4.00	8.00
SN-7235	The Animals with Eric Burdon	1982	2.00	4.00	8.00
I.R.S.					
SP 70037	The Ark	1983	2.50	5.00	10.00
SP 70043	Rip It to Shreds: Their Greatest Hits Live	1984	2.50	5.00	10.00
JET/UA					
JT-LA780-H	Before We Were So Rudely Interrupted	1977	2.50	5.00	10.00
—As "The Original Animals"					
MGM					
E-4264 [M]	The Animals	1964	7.50	15.00	30.00
—"The House of the Rising Sun" is the edited 45 version					
E-4264 [M-DJ]	The Animals	1964	25.00	50.00	100.00
—Yellow label promo					
SE-4264 [R]	The Animals	1964	6.25	12.50	25.00
—"The House of the Rising Sun" is the edited 45 version (rechanneled, like the rest of the LP)					
E-4281 [M]	The Animals On Tour	1965	7.50	15.00	30.00
E-4281 [M-DJ]	The Animals On Tour	1965	25.00	50.00	100.00
—Yellow label promo					
SE-4281 [R]	The Animals On Tour	1965	6.25	12.50	25.00
E-4305 [M]	Animal Tracks	1965	10.00	20.00	40.00
E-4305 [M-DJ]	Animal Tracks	1965	37.50	75.00	150.00
—Yellow label promo					
SE-4305 [R]	Animal Tracks	1965	7.50	15.00	30.00
E-4324 [M]	The Best of the Animals	1966	5.00	10.00	20.00
—This album was the first to contain the full-length version of "House of the Rising Sun."					
E-4324 [M-DJ]	The Best of the Animals	1966	20.00	40.00	80.00
—Yellow label promo					
SE-4324 [R]	The Best of the Animals	1966	6.25	12.50	25.00
E-4384 [M]	Animalization	1966	6.25	12.50	25.00
E-4384 [M-DJ]	Animalization	1966	25.00	50.00	100.00
—Yellow label promo					
SE-4384 [P]	Animalization	1966	7.50	15.00	30.00
—All stereo except "Inside Looking Out," which is rechanneled.					
E-4414 [M]	Animalism	1966	6.25	12.50	25.00
E-4414 [M-DJ]	Animalism	1966	25.00	50.00	100.00
—Yellow label promo					
SE-4414 [S]	Animalism	1966	7.50	15.00	30.00
E-4433 [M]	Eric Is Here	1967	3.75	7.50	15.00
SE-4433 [S]	Eric Is Here	1967	5.00	10.00	20.00
E-4454 [M]	The Best of Eric Burdon and the Animals, Vol. 2	1967	5.00	10.00	20.00
SE-4454 [P]	The Best of Eric Burdon and the Animals, Vol. 2	1967	5.00	10.00	20.00
E-4484 [M]	Winds of Change	1967	5.00	10.00	20.00
SE-4484 [S]	Winds of Change	1967	6.25	12.50	25.00

Number	Title (A Side/B Side)	Yr	VG	VG+	NM
E-4537 [M]	The Twain Shall Meet	1968	5.00	10.00	20.00
SE-4537 [S]	The Twain Shall Meet	1968	6.25	12.50	25.00
SE-4553	Every One of Us	1968	6.25	12.50	25.00
SE-4591 [(2)]	Love Is	1968	12.50	25.00	50.00
SE-4602	Greatest Hits of Eric Burdon and the Animals	1969	3.75	7.50	15.00
ST 90414 [R]	The Animals on Tour	1965	10.00	20.00	40.00
—Capitol Record Club edition					
T 90414 [M]	The Animals on Tour	1965	12.50	25.00	50.00
—Capitol Record Club edition					
T 90571 [M]	Animal Tracks	1965	12.50	25.00	50.00
—Capitol Record Club edition					
KAO 90622 [M]	The Best of the Animals	1966	10.00	20.00	40.00
—Capitol Record Club edition					
SKAO 90622 [R]	The Best of the Animals	1966	10.00	20.00	40.00
—Capitol Record Club edition					
T 90687 [M]	The Animals	1966	12.50	25.00	50.00
—Capitol Record Club edition					
ST 90923 [P]	Animalization	1966	12.50	25.00	50.00
—Capitol Record Club edition					
T 90923 [M]	Animalization	1966	12.50	25.00	50.00
—Capitol Record Club edition					
PICKWICK					
SPC-3330	The Early Animals with Eric Burdon	1971	2.00	4.00	8.00
POLYDOR					
829091-1 [M]	Animalization	1986	2.00	4.00	8.00
SCEPTER CITATION					
18026	The Best of the Animals	1972	2.00	4.00	8.00
SPRINGBOARD					
SPB-4025	The Best of the Animals	1972	2.00	4.00	8.00
SPB-4065	The Night Time Is the Right Time	1973	2.00	4.00	8.00
WAND					
WDS-690	In the Beginning	1970	2.50	5.00	10.00

ANIMATED EGG, THE

Albums

Number	Title (A Side/B Side)	Yr	VG	VG+	NM
ALSHIRE					
SF-32700	The Animated Egg	1967	12.50	25.00	50.00

ANKA, PAUL

45s

Number	Title (A Side/B Side)	Yr	VG	VG+	NM
ABC-PARAMOUNT					
45-PRO-104	(You Can) Share Your Love/I Talk to You (On the Telephone)	1958	7.50	15.00	30.00
—Evidently a custom pressing for Paul Anka's fan club					
S 296-1 [S]	(All of a Sudden) My Heart Sings/(B-side unknown)	1959	10.00	20.00	40.00
S 296-2 [S]	(titles unknown)	1959	10.00	20.00	40.00
S 296-3 [S]	C'est Si Bon/Comme Ci, Comme Ca	1959	10.00	20.00	40.00
S 296-4 [S]	Melodie D'Amour/I Miss You So	1959	10.00	20.00	40.00
S 296-5 [S]	I Love Paris/If You Love Me, Really Love Me	1959	10.00	20.00	40.00
—The above five are jukebox singles excerpting the LP "My Heart Sings"					
9831	Diana/Don't Gamble with Love	1957	5.00	10.00	20.00
9855	I Love You, Baby/Tell Me That You Love Me	1957	7.50	15.00	30.00
9880	You Are My Destiny/When I Stop Loving You	1958	5.00	10.00	20.00
9907	Crazy Love/Let the Bells Keep Ringing	1958	5.00	10.00	20.00
9937	Midnight/Verboten!	1958	5.00	10.00	20.00
9956	Just Young/So It's Goodbye	1958	5.00	10.00	20.00
9956 [PS]	Just Young/So It's Goodbye	1958	—	—	—
—Rumored to exist, but without conclusive evidence, we will delete this from future editions					
9987 [M]	(All of a Sudden) My Heart Sings/That's Love	1958	5.00	10.00	20.00
S-9987 [S]	(All of a Sudden) My Heart Sings/That's Love	1958	12.50	25.00	50.00
10011 [M]	I Miss You So/Late Last Night	1959	3.75	7.50	15.00
10011 [PS]	I Miss You So/Late Last Night	1959	6.25	12.50	25.00
S-10011 [S]	I Miss You So/Late Last Night	1959	12.50	25.00	50.00
10022 [M]	Lonely Boy/Your Love	1959	3.75	7.50	15.00
S-10022 [S]	Lonely Boy/Your Love	1959	12.50	25.00	50.00
10040 [M]	Put Your Head on My Shoulder/Don't Ever Leave Me	1959	3.75	7.50	15.00
10040 [PS]	Put Your Head on My Shoulder/Don't Ever Leave Me	1959	6.25	12.50	25.00
S-10040 [S]	Put Your Head on My Shoulder/Don't Ever Leave Me	1959	12.50	25.00	50.00
10064 [M]	It's Time to Cry/Something Has Changed Me	1959	3.75	7.50	15.00
10064 [PS]	It's Time to Cry/Something Has Changed Me	1959	6.25	12.50	25.00
S-10064 [S]	It's Time to Cry/Something Has Changed Me	1959	12.50	25.00	50.00
10082 [M]	Puppy Love/Adam and Eve	1960	3.75	7.50	15.00
10082 [PS]	Puppy Love/Adam and Eve	1960	6.25	12.50	25.00
S-10082 [S]	Puppy Love/Adam and Eve	1960	12.50	25.00	50.00
10106 [M]	My Home Town/Something Happened	1960	3.75	7.50	15.00
10106 [PS]	My Home Town/Something Happened	1960	6.25	12.50	25.00
S-10106 [S]	My Home Town/Something Happened	1960	12.50	25.00	50.00
10132 [M]	Hello Young Lovers/I Love You in the Same Old Way	1960	3.75	7.50	15.00
10132 [PS]	Hello Young Lovers/I Love You in the Same Old Way	1960	6.25	12.50	25.00
S-10132 [S]	Hello Young Lovers/I Love You in the Same Old Way	1960	12.50	25.00	50.00
10147 [M]	Summer's Gone/I'd Have to Share	1960	3.75	7.50	15.00
10147 [PS]	Summer's Gone/I'd Have to Share	1960	5.00	10.00	20.00
S-10147 [S]	Summer's Gone/I'd Have to Share	1960	12.50	25.00	50.00
10163	Rudolph, the Red-Nosed Reindeer/I Saw Mommy Kissing Santa Claus	1960	6.25	12.50	25.00
10168 [M]	The Story of My Love/Don't Say You're Sorry	1960	3.75	7.50	15.00
10168 [PS]	The Story of My Love/Don't Say You're Sorry	1960	6.25	12.50	25.00
S-10168 [S]	The Story of My Love/Don't Say You're Sorry	1960	12.50	25.00	50.00
10169	It's Christmas Everywhere/Rudolph, the Red-Nosed Reindeer	1960	4.00	8.00	16.00
10169 [PS]	It's Christmas Everywhere/Rudolph, the Red-Nosed Reindeer	1960	6.25	12.50	25.00
10194	Tonight My Love, Tonight/I'm Just a Fool Anyway	1961	3.00	6.00	12.00
10194 [PS]	Tonight My Love, Tonight/I'm Just a Fool Anyway	1961	6.25	12.50	25.00
10220	Dance On Little Girl/I Talk to You	1961	3.00	6.00	12.00
10220 [PS]	Dance On Little Girl/I Talk to You	1961	6.25	12.50	25.00
10239	Kissin' on the Phone/Cinderella	1961	3.00	6.00	12.00

Number	Title (A Side/B Side)	Yr	VG	VG+	NM
10239 [PS]	Kissin' on the Phone/Cinderella	1961	6.25	12.50	25.00
10279	Loveland/The Bells at My Wedding	1961	3.00	6.00	12.00
10282	The Fools Hall of Fame/Far from the Lights of Town	1961	3.00	6.00	12.00
10311	I'll Never Find Another You/Uh Huh	1962	2.50	5.00	10.00
10338	I'm Coming Home/Why	1962	2.50	5.00	10.00
BARNABY					
2027	You're Some Kind of Friend/Why Are You Leaning on Me, Sir	1971	—	3.00	6.00
BUDDAH					
252	Do I Love You/So Long City	1971	—	2.50	5.00
294	Everything's Been Changed/Jubilation	1972	—	2.50	5.00
314	Something Good Is Coming/Life Song	1972	—	2.50	5.00
337	While We're Still Young/This Is Your Song	1973	—	2.50	5.00
349	Hey Girl/You and Me Today	1973	—	2.50	5.00
COLUMBIA					
03897	Hold Me 'Til the Mornin' Comes/This Is the First Time	1983	—	—	3.00
03897 [PS]	Hold Me 'Til the Mornin' Comes/This Is the First Time	1983	—	2.00	4.00
04187	Gimme the Word/No Way Out	1983	—	—	3.00
—A-side: With Karla DeVito					
04407	Second Chance/Walk a Fine Line	1984	—	—	3.00
07358	No Way Out/Just for Once	1987	—	—	3.00
—A-side: Paul Anka and Julia Migenas; B-side: Migenas solo					
EPIC					
50298	You/Make It Up to Me in Love	1976	—	2.00	4.00
—With Odia Coates					
ERIC					
200	Diana/Don't Gamble with Love	197?	—	2.00	4.00
200 [PS]	Diana/Don't Gamble with Love	197?	—	2.50	5.00
FAME					
XW-345	Flashback/Let Me Get to Know You	1973	—	2.00	4.00
RCA					
PB-11351	Lovely Lady/Brought Up in New York	1978	—	2.00	4.00
PB-11351 [PS]	Lovely Lady/Brought Up in New York	1978	—	2.50	5.00
PB-11395	This Is Love/I'm By Myself Again	1978	—	2.00	4.00
PB-11662	As Long As We Keep Believing/Headlines	1979	—	2.00	4.00
PB-11957	Rainbow/After All	1980	—	—	—
—Unreleased					
PB-12184	We Love Each Other/Think I'm in Love Again	1981	—	—	3.00
PB-12225	I've Been Waiting for You All My Life/Think I'm in Love Again	1981	—	—	3.00
PB-12262	Lady Lay Down/You're Still a Part of Me	1981	—	—	3.00
RCA VICTOR					
VP1-2502 [S]	Young, Alive and In Love/Young and Foolish	1962	10.00	20.00	40.00
VP2-2502 [S]	Younger Than Springtime/You Make Me Feel So Young	1962	10.00	20.00	40.00
VP3-2502 [S]	This Life of Mine/Life Is Just a Bowl of Cherries	1962	10.00	20.00	40.00
VP4-2502 [S]	I Love Life/Aren't You Glad You're You?	1962	10.00	20.00	40.00
VP5-2502 [S]	Falling in Love with You/You're Just in Love	1962	10.00	20.00	40.00
—The above five are 33 1/3 rpm, small hole jukebox singles excerpting the LP "Young, Alive and In Love"					
GB-10180	Diana/Put Your Head on My Shoulders	1975	—	2.00	4.00
—Gold Standard Series					
GB-10181	Puppy Love/Lonely Boy	1975	—	2.00	4.00
—Gold Standard Series					
GB-10182	You Are My Destiny/Tonight, My Love, Tonight	1975	—	2.00	4.00
—Gold Standard Series					
37-7977	Love Me Warm and Tender/I'd Like to Know	1962	6.25	12.50	25.00
—"Compact Single 33" (small hole, plays at LP speed)					
47-7977	Love Me Warm and Tender/I'd Like to Know	1962	2.50	5.00	10.00
47-7977 [PS]	Love Me Warm and Tender/I'd Like to Know	1962	5.00	10.00	20.00
47-8030	A Steel Guitar and a Glass of Wine/I Never Knew Your Name	1962	2.50	5.00	10.00
47-8030 [PS]	A Steel Guitar and a Glass of Wine/I Never Knew Your Name	1962	5.00	10.00	20.00
47-8068	Every Night (Without You)/There You Go	1962	2.50	5.00	10.00
47-8068 [PS]	Every Night (Without You)/There You Go	1962	5.00	10.00	20.00
47-8097	Eso Beso (That Kiss!)/Give Me Back My Heart	1962	2.50	5.00	10.00
47-8097 [PS]	Eso Beso (That Kiss!)/Give Me Back My Heart	1962	5.00	10.00	20.00
47-8115	Love (Makes the World Go 'Round)/Crying in the Wind	1962	2.50	5.00	10.00
47-8115 [PS]	Love (Makes the World Go 'Round)/Crying in the Wind	1962	5.00	10.00	20.00
47-8158	Think About It/At Night	1963	—	—	—
—Unreleased					
47-8170	Remember Diana/At Night	1963	2.50	5.00	10.00
47-8170 [PS]	Remember Diana/At Night	1963	5.00	10.00	20.00
47-8195	Hello Jim/You've Got the Nerve to Call This Love	1963	2.50	5.00	10.00
47-8195 [PS]	Hello Jim/You've Got the Nerve to Call This Love	1963	5.00	10.00	20.00
47-8237	Wondrous Are the Ways of Love/Hurry Up and Tell Me	1963	2.50	5.00	10.00
47-8237 [PS]	Wondrous Are the Ways of Love/Hurry Up and Tell Me	1963	5.00	10.00	20.00
47-8272	Did You Have a Happy Birthday/For No Good Reason at All	1963	2.50	5.00	10.00
47-8272 [PS]	Did You Have a Happy Birthday/For No Good Reason at All	1963	5.00	10.00	20.00
47-8311	From Rocking Horse to Rocking Chair/Cheer Up	1964	2.00	4.00	8.00
47-8311 [PS]	From Rocking Horse to Rocking Chair/Cheer Up	1964	3.75	7.50	15.00
47-8349	My Baby's Comin' Home/No, No	1964	2.00	4.00	8.00
47-8349 [PS]	My Baby's Comin' Home/No, No	1964	3.75	7.50	15.00
47-8396	In My Imagination/It's Easy to Say	1964	2.00	4.00	8.00
47-8396 [PS]	In My Imagination/It's Easy to Say	1964	3.75	7.50	15.00
47-8441	Cindy Go Home/Ogni Volta	1964	2.00	4.00	8.00
47-8441 [PS]	Cindy Go Home/Ogni Volta	1964	3.75	7.50	15.00
47-8493	Sylvia/Behind My Smile	1965	2.00	4.00	8.00
47-8595	Dream Me Happy/The Loneliest Boy in the World	1965	2.00	4.00	8.00
47-8662	Every Day a Heart Is Broken/As If There Were No Tomorrow	1965	2.00	4.00	8.00
47-8764	Truly Yours/Oh, Such a Stranger	1965	2.00	4.00	8.00
47-8839	I Wish/I Went to Your Wedding	1966	2.00	4.00	8.00
47-8893	I Can't Help Loving You/Can't Get Along Very Well Without Her	1966	2.00	4.00	8.00

Number	Title (A Side/B Side)	Yr	VG	VG+	NM
47-9032	Poor Old World/I'd Rather Be a Stranger	1966	2.00	4.00	8.00
47-9128	Until It's Time for You to Go/Would You Still Be My Baby	1967	2.00	4.00	8.00
47-9228	A Woman Is a Sentimental Thing/That's How Love Goes	1967	2.00	4.00	8.00
47-9457	Can't Get You Out of My Mind/When We Get There	1968	2.00	4.00	8.00
47-9648	Goodnight My Love/This Crazy World	1968	2.00	4.00	8.00
47-9767	Happy/Can't Get You Out of My Mind	1969	2.00	4.00	8.00
47-9846	Midnight Mistress/Before It's Too Late-This Land Is Your Land	1970	2.00	4.00	8.00
74-0126	In the Still of the Night/Pickin' Up the Pieces	1969	2.00	4.00	8.00
74-0164	Sincerely/Next Year	1969	2.00	4.00	8.00
RPM					
472	I Confess/Blau-Wile Deveest Fontaine	1956	20.00	40.00	80.00
499	I Confess/Blau-Wile Deveest Fontaine	1957	7.50	15.00	30.00
UNITED ARTISTS					
XW-454	(You're) Having My Baby/Papa	1974	—	2.00	4.00
XW-569	One Man Woman/One Woman Man//Let Me Get to Know You	1974	—	2.00	4.00
—A-side: With Odia Coates					
XW-615	I Don't Like to Sleep Alone/How Can Anything Be Beautiful After You	1975	—	2.00	4.00
XW-615 [PS]	I Don't Like to Sleep Alone/How Can Anything Be Beautiful After You	1975	—	2.00	4.00
XW-685	(I Believe) There's Nothing Stronger Than Our Love/Today I Became a Fool	1975	—	2.00	4.00
XW-737	Times of Your Life/Water Runs Deep	1975	—	2.00	4.00
XW-737 [PS]	Times of Your Life/Water Runs Deep	1975	—	2.00	4.00
XW-789	Anytime (I'll Be There)/Something About You	1976	—	2.00	4.00
XW-896	Happier/Closing Doors	1976	—	3.00	6.00
—Canada-only release					
XW-911	Happier/Closing Doors	1976	—	2.00	4.00
XW-945	I'll Help You/Never Gonna Fall in Love Like I Fell in Love with You	1977	—	2.00	4.00
XW-972	My Best Friend's Wife/Never Gonna Fall in Love Like I Fell in Love with You	1977	—	2.00	4.00
XW-1018	Tonight/Everybody Ought to Be in Love	1977	—	2.00	4.00
XW-1157	(You're) Having My Baby//One Man Woman/One Woman Man	1978	—	—	3.00
—Reissue					
XW-1158	I Don't Like to Sleep Alone/Times of Your Life	1978	—	—	3.00
—Reissue					
Albums					
ABC-PARAMOUNT					
240 [M]	Paul Anka	1958	12.50	25.00	50.00
296 [M]	My Heart Sings	1959	7.50	15.00	30.00
S-296 [S]	My Heart Sings	1959	12.50	25.00	50.00
323 [M]	Paul Anka Sings His Big 15	1960	12.50	25.00	50.00
S-323 [R]	Paul Anka Sings His Big 15	196?	7.50	15.00	30.00
347 [M]	Paul Anka Swings for Young Lovers	1960	7.50	15.00	30.00
S-347 [S]	Paul Anka Swings for Young Lovers	1960	10.00	20.00	40.00
353 [M]	Anka at the Copa	1960	7.50	15.00	30.00
S-353 [S]	Anka at the Copa	1960	10.00	20.00	40.00
ABC 360 [M]	It's Christmas Everywhere	1960	7.50	15.00	30.00
ABCS 360 [S]	It's Christmas Everywhere	1960	10.00	20.00	40.00
371 [M]	Strictly Instrumental	1961	7.00	15.00	30.00
S-371 [S]	Strictly Instrumental	1961	10.00	20.00	40.00
390 [M]	Paul Anka Sings His Big 15, Vol. 2	1961	7.50	15.00	30.00
S-390 [S]	Paul Anka Sings His Big 15, Vol. 2	1961	10.00	20.00	40.00
409 [M]	Paul Anka Sings His Big 15, Vol. 3	1962	6.25	12.50	25.00
S-409 [S]	Paul Anka Sings His Big 15, Vol. 3	1962	7.50	15.00	30.00
420 [M]	Diana	1962	6.25	12.50	25.00
S-420 [S]	Diana	1962	7.50	15.00	30.00
ACCORD					
SN-7117	She's a Lady	1981	2.00	4.00	8.00
BUDDAH					
BDS 5093	Paul Anka	1971	3.00	6.00	12.00
BDS 5114	Jubilation	1972	3.00	6.00	12.00
BDS 5622 [(2)]	This Is Anka	1974	3.75	7.50	15.00
BDS 5667 [(2)]	The Essential Paul Anka	1974	3.75	7.50	15.00
COLUMBIA					
FC 38442	Walk a Fine Line	1983	2.00	4.00	8.00
FC 39323	Paul Anka Live	1984	2.00	4.00	8.00
LIBERTY					
LN-10000	Paul Anka: His Best	1980	2.00	4.00	8.00
—Budget-line reissue					
LN-10001	The Times of Your Life	1980	2.00	4.00	8.00
—Budget-line reissue					
LN-10149	Feelings	1982	2.00	4.00	8.00
—Budget-line reissue					
LN-10220	The Painter	1983	2.00	4.00	8.00
—Budget-line reissue					
PAIR					
PDL2-1129 [(2)]	Songs I Write and Sing	1986	3.00	6.00	12.00
PICKWICK					
PTP-2087 [(2)]	Paul Anka Way	197?	2.50	5.00	10.00
SPC-3508	Puppy Love	1975	2.00	4.00	8.00
SPC-3523	She's a Lady	1975	2.00	4.00	8.00
RANWOOD					
8203	The Very Best of Paul Anka	1981	2.00	4.00	8.00
RCA CAMDEN					
ACL1-0616	My Way	1974	2.00	4.00	8.00
RCA VICTOR					
ANL1-0896	Remember Diana	1975	2.50	5.00	10.00
ANL1-1054	She's a Lady	1975	2.50	5.00	10.00
ANL1-1584	Paul Anka Sings His Favorites	1976	2.50	5.00	10.00
ANL1-2482	Songs I Wish I'd Written	1977	2.50	5.00	10.00
LPM-2502 [M]	Young, Alive and In Love!	1962	6.25	12.50	25.00
—With portrait of Paul Anka on front cover					
LPM-2502 [M]	Young, Alive and In Love!	1962	3.75	7.50	15.00
—With portrait of Paul Anka on back cover					
LSP-2502 [S]	Young, Alive and In Love!	1962	7.50	15.00	30.00
—With portrait of Paul Anka on front cover					

Number	Title (A Side/B Side)	Yr	VG	VG+	NM
LSP-2502 [S]	Young, Alive and In Love!	1962	5.00	10.00	20.00
—With portrait of Paul Anka on back cover					
LPM-2575 [M]	Let's Sit This One Out	1962	5.00	10.00	20.00
LSP-2575 [S]	Let's Sit This One Out	1962	6.25	12.50	25.00
LPM-2614 [M]	Our Man Around the World	1963	5.00	10.00	20.00
LSP-2614 [S]	Our Man Around the World	1963	6.25	12.50	25.00
LPM-2691 [M]	Paul Anka's 21 Golden Hits	1963	5.00	10.00	20.00
LSP-2691 [S]	Paul Anka's 21 Golden Hits	1963	6.25	12.50	25.00
—LPM/LSP-2691 has re-recorded versions of ABC-Paramount hits					
LPM-2744 [M]	Songs I Wish I'd Written	1963	3.75	7.50	15.00
LSP-2744 [S]	Songs I Wish I'd Written	1963	5.00	10.00	20.00
AFL1-2892	Listen to Your Heart	1978	2.50	5.00	10.00
LPM-2996 [M]	Excitement on Park Avenue	1964	3.75	7.50	15.00
LSP-2996 [S]	Excitement on Park Avenue	1964	5.00	10.00	20.00
AFL1-3382	Headlines	1979	2.50	5.00	10.00
LPM-3580 [M]	Strictly Nashville	1966	3.75	7.50	15.00
LSP-3580 [S]	Strictly Nashville	1966	5.00	10.00	20.00
AYL1-3808	Paul Anka's 21 Golden Hits	1980	2.00	4.00	8.00
—"Best Buy Series" reissue					
LPM-3875 [M]	Paul Anka Live	1967	3.75	7.50	15.00
LSP-3875 [S]	Paul Anka Live	1967	5.00	10.00	20.00
AFL1-3926	Both Sides of Love	1981	2.50	5.00	10.00
LSP-4142	Goodnight My Love	1969	3.75	7.50	15.00
LSP-4203	Sincerely	1969	3.75	7.50	15.00
LSP-4250	Life Goes On	1969	3.75	7.50	15.00
LSP-4300	Paul Anka 70s	1970	3.75	7.50	15.00
RHINO					
RNLP-70220	The Best of Paul Anka (14 Original Hits, 1957-1961)	1986	2.50	5.00	10.00
RIVIERA					
0047 [M]	Paul Anka and Others	1959	37.50	75.00	150.00
—With Paul Anka's RPM recordings plus tracks by other artists					
SIRE					
SASH-3704 [(2)]	Paul Anka Gold	1974	3.75	7.50	15.00
SBK 6043 [(2)]	The Vintage Years 1957-1961	1978	3.00	6.00	12.00
UNITED ARTISTS					
UA-LA314-G	Anka	1974	2.50	5.00	10.00
UA-LA367-G	Feelings	1975	2.50	5.00	10.00
UA-LA569-G	Times of Your Life	1975	2.50	5.00	10.00
UA-LA653-G	The Painter	1976	2.50	5.00	10.00
UA-LA746-H	The Music Man	1977	2.50	5.00	10.00
UA-LA922-H	Paul Anka: His Best	1978	2.50	5.00	10.00

ANKA, PAUL/GEORGE HAMILTON IV/JOHNNY NASH

Also see each artist's individual listings.

45s

Number	Title (A Side/B Side)	Yr	VG	VG+	NM
ABC-PARAMOUNT					
9974	The Teen Commandments/If You Learn to Pray	1958	6.25	12.50	25.00

ANN-MARGRET

Also see JOHN GARY; AL HIRT.

45s

Number	Title (A Side/B Side)	Yr	VG	VG+	NM
ARIOLA					
7511	Love Rush/For You	1979	—	3.00	6.00
AVCO EMBASSY					
4547	Today/Today	1970	3.75	7.50	15.00
—B-side by Lenny Stack					
LHI					
1	It's a Nice World to Visit/You Turned My Head Around	1969	—	3.00	6.00
2	Chico/Sleep in the Grass	1969	—	3.00	6.00
—With Lee Hazlewood					
5	The Dark End of the Street/Victims of the Night	1969	—	3.00	6.00
—With Lee Hazlewood					
11	Walk Out of My Mind/Hangin' In	1970	—	3.00	6.00
—With Lee Hazlewood					
MCA					
41186	Love Rush/For You	1980	—	2.50	5.00
41223	Midnight Message/For You	1980	—	2.50	5.00
RCA VICTOR					
VP1-2551 [S]	Jim Dandy/Thirteen Men	1962	10.00	20.00	40.00
VP2-2551 [S]	Rock and Roll Waltz/There'll Be Some Changes Made	1962	10.00	20.00	40.00
VP3-2551 [S]	Make Love to Me/Tell Me, Tell Me	1962	10.00	20.00	40.00
VP4-2551 [S]	C'est Si Bon/Please Don't Talk About Me When I'm Gone	1962	10.00	20.00	40.00
VP5-2551 [S]	Inka Dinka Doo/Begin the Beguine	1962	10.00	20.00	40.00
—The above five are 33 1/3 rpm, small hole jukebox singles excerpting the LP "The Vivacious One"					
37-7857	I Ain't Got Nobody/Lost Love	1961	6.25	12.50	25.00
—"Compact Single 33" (small hole, plays at LP speed)					
37-7894	I Just Don't Understand/I Don't Hurt Anymore	1961	6.25	12.50	25.00
—"Compact Single 33" (small hole, plays at LP speed)					
37-7952	It Do Me So Good/Gimme Love	1961	6.25	12.50	25.00
—"Compact Single 33" (small hole, plays at LP speed)					
47-7857	I Ain't Got Nobody/Lost Love	1961	3.00	6.00	12.00
47-7894	I Just Don't Understand/I Don't Hurt Anymore	1961	3.75	7.50	15.00
47-7894 [PS]	I Just Don't Understand/I Don't Hurt Anymore	1961	6.25	12.50	25.00
47-7952	It Do Me So Good/Gimme Love	1961	2.50	5.00	10.00
47-7952 [PS]	It Do Me So Good/Gimme Love	1961	6.25	12.50	25.00
47-7986	What Am I Supposed to Do/Let's Stop Kidding Each Other	1962	2.50	5.00	10.00
47-7986 [PS]	What Am I Supposed to Do/Let's Stop Kidding Each Other	1962	6.25	12.50	25.00
47-8061	Jim Dandy/I Was Only Kidding	1962	2.50	5.00	10.00
47-8061 [PS]	Jim Dandy/I Was Only Kidding	1962	6.25	12.50	25.00
47-8130	No More/So Did I	1963	2.50	5.00	10.00
47-8130 [PS]	No More/So Did I	1963	6.25	12.52	25.00
47-8168	Bye Bye Birdie/Take All the Kisses	1963	2.50	5.00	10.00
47-8168 [PS]	Bye Bye Birdie/Take All the Kisses	1963	6.25	12.50	25.00
47-8295	Hey Little Star/Man's Favorite Sport	1963	2.50	5.00	10.00
47-8446	He's My Man/Someday Soon	1964	2.50	5.00	10.00
47-8446 [PS]	He's My Man/Someday Soon	1964	7.50	15.00	30.00
47-8734	Mister Kiss Kiss Bang Bang/What Did I Have That I Don't Have Now	1965	2.50	5.00	10.00
47-9013	The Swinger/You've Come a Long Way from St. Louis	1966	2.50	5.00	10.00

Albums

Number	Title (A Side/B Side)	Yr	VG	VG+	NM
MCA					
3226	Ann-Margret	1980	3.00	6.00	12.00
RCA VICTOR					
LPM-2399 [M]	And Here She Is...	1961	7.50	15.00	30.00
LSP-2399 [S]	And Here She Is...	1961	10.00	20.00	40.00
LPM-2453 [M]	On the Way Up	1961	7.50	15.00	30.00
LSP-2453 [S]	On the Way Up	1961	10.00	20.00	40.00
LPM-2551 [M]	The Vivacious One	1962	7.50	15.00	30.00
LSP-2551 [S]	The Vivacious One	1962	10.00	20.00	40.00
LPM-2659 [M]	Bachelor's Paradise	1963	7.50	15.00	30.00
LSP-2659 [S]	Bachelor's Paradise	1963	10.00	20.00	40.00
LPM-3710 [M]	Songs from The Swinger and Others	1966	15.00	30.00	60.00
LSP-3710 [S]	Songs from The Swinger and Others	1966	20.00	40.00	80.00

ANNETTE

Also see FRANKIE AVALON AND ANNETTE FUNICELLO.

45s

Number	Title (A Side/B Side)	Yr	VG	VG+	NM
BUENA VISTA					
336	Jo Jo the Dog Faced Boy/Lonely Guitar	1959	5.00	10.00	20.00
336	Jo Jo the Dog Faced Boy/Love Me Forever	1959	3.75	7.50	15.00
339	Wild Willie/Lonely Guitar	1959	3.75	7.50	15.00
339 [PS]	Wild Willie/Lonely Guitar	1959	7.50	15.00	30.00
344	Especially for You/My Heart Became of Age	1959	3.75	7.50	15.00
349	First Name Initial/My Heart Became of Age	1959	3.75	7.50	15.00
349 [PS]	First Name Initial/My Heart Became of Age	1959	7.50	15.00	30.00
354	O Dio Mio/It Took Dreams	1960	3.75	7.50	15.00
354 [PS]	O Dio Mio/It Took Dreams	1960	7.50	15.00	30.00
359	Train of Love/Tell Me Who's the Girl	1960	3.75	7.50	15.00
359 [PS]	Train of Love/Tell Me Who's the Girl	1960	10.00	20.00	40.00
362	Pineapple Princess/Luau Cha Cha Cha	1960	3.75	7.50	15.00
362 [PS]	Pineapple Princess/Luau Cha Cha Cha	1960	7.50	15.00	30.00
369	Talk to Me Baby/I Love You Baby	1960	3.75	7.50	15.00
369 [PS]	Talk to Me Baby/I Love You Baby	1960	7.50	15.00	30.00
374	Dream Boy/Please, Please Signore	1961	3.75	7.50	15.00
374 [PS]	Dream Boy/Please, Please Signore	1961	7.50	15.00	30.00
375	Indian Giver/Mama, Mama Rosa (Where's the Spumoni)	1961	3.75	7.50	15.00
375 [PS]	Indian Giver/Mama, Mama Rosa (Where's the Spumoni)	1961	7.50	15.00	30.00
384	Hawaiian Love Talk/Blue Muu Muu	1961	3.75	7.50	15.00
384 [PS]	Hawaiian Love Talk/Blue Muu Muu	1961	12.50	25.00	50.00
388	Dreamin' About You/Strummin' Song	1961	3.75	7.50	15.00
388 [PS]	Dreamin' About You/Strummin' Song	1961	7.50	15.00	30.00
392	That Crazy Place From Outer Space/Seven Moons (Of Batalayre)	1962	3.75	7.50	15.00
—B-side by Danny Saval and Tom Tryon					
392 [PS]	That Crazy Place From Outer Space/Seven Moons (Of Batalayre)	1962	10.00	20.00	40.00
394	The Truth About Youth/I Can't Do the Sum	1962	3.75	7.50	15.00
394 [PS]	The Truth About Youth/I Can't Do the Sum	1962	10.00	20.00	40.00
400	My Little Grass Shack/Hukilau	1962	3.75	7.50	15.00
405	He's My Ideal/Mr. Piano Man	1962	3.75	7.50	15.00
405 [PS]	He's My Ideal/Mr. Piano Man	1962	7.50	15.00	30.00
407	Bella Bella Florence/Canzone d'Amoure	1962	3.75	7.50	15.00
—With Marcochi					
407 [PS]	Bella Bella Florence/Canzone d'Amoure	1962	37.50	75.00	150.00
414	Teenage Wedding/Walkin' and Talkin'	1962	5.00	10.00	20.00
414 [PS]	Teenage Wedding/Walkin' and Talkin'	1962	150.00	300.00	600.00
427	Treat Him Nicely/Promise Me Anything	1963	3.75	7.50	15.00
427 [PS]	Treat Him Nicely/Promise Me Anything	1963	15.00	30.00	60.00
431	Merlin Jones/The Scrambled Egghead	1964	3.00	6.00	12.00
—With Tommy Kirk					
431 [PS]	Merlin Jones/The Scrambled Egghead	1964	7.50	15.00	30.00
432	Custom City/Rebel Rider	1964	5.00	10.00	20.00
432 [PS]	Custom City/Rebel Rider	1964	20.00	40.00	60.00
433	Muscle Beach Party/I Dream About Frankie	1964	3.75	7.50	15.00
433 [PS]	Muscle Beach Party/I Dream About Frankie	1964	7.50	15.00	30.00
436	Bikini Beach Party/The Clyde	1964	3.75	7.50	15.00
436 [PS]	Bikini Beach Party/The Clyde	1964	10.00	20.00	40.00
437	The Wah-Watusi/The Clyde	1964	3.00	6.00	12.00
438	Something Borrowed, Something Blue/How Will I Know My Love	1965	3.75	7.50	15.00
438 [PS]	Something Borrowed, Something Blue/How Will I Know My Love	1965	20.00	40.00	80.00
440	The Monkey's Uncle/How Will I Know My Love	1965	3.00	6.00	12.00
—With the Beach Boys backing up					
440 [PS]	The Monkey's Uncle/How Will I Know My Love	1965	5.00	10.00	20.00
442	The Boy to Love/No One Else Could Be Prouder	1965	3.00	6.00	12.00
450	No Way to Go But Up/Crystal Ball	1966	3.00	6.00	12.00
475	The Computer Wore Tennis Shoes/Merlin Jones	1970	2.00	4.00	8.00
DISNEYLAND					
102	How Will I Know My Love/Don't Jump to Conclusions	1958	6.25	15.00	30.00
102 [PS]	How Will I Know My Love/Don't Jump to Conclusions	1958	12.50	25.00	50.00
114	That Crazy Place in Outer Space/Gold Doubloons and Pieces of Eight	1958	10.00	20.00	40.00
—B-side: "Theme from the Hardy Boys"					
118	Tall Paul/Ma, He's Making Eyes at Me	1959	5.00	10.00	20.00
786	That Crazy Place From Outer Space/Happy Glow	196?	2.50	5.00	10.00
—No artist credit on label, but A-side is the same recording as Disneyland 114					
EPIC					
9829	Baby Needs Me Now/Moment of Silence	1965	6.25	12.50	25.00
—With Cecil Null					
STARVIEW					
3001	The Promised Land/In Between and Out of Love	1983	2.50	5.00	10.00
3001 [PS]	The Promised Land/In Between and Out of Love	1983	2.50	5.00	10.00
TOWER					
326	What's a Girl to Do/When You Get What You Want	1967	7.50	15.00	30.00

Number	Title (A Side/B Side)	Yr	VG	VG+	NM

Albums

BUENA VISTA

Number	Title (A Side/B Side)	Yr	VG	VG+	NM
BV-3301 [M]	Annette	1959	30.00	60.00	120.00
BV-3302 [M]	Annette Sings Anka	1960	25.00	50.00	100.00
BV-3303 [M]	Hawaiiannette	1960	18.75	37.50	75.00
BV-3304 [M]	Italiannette	1960	18.75	37.50	75.00
BV-3305 [M]	Dance Annette	1961	18.75	37.50	75.00
BV-3312 [M]	The Story of My Teens	1962	18.75	37.50	75.00
BV-3313 [M]	Teen Street	1962	18.75	37.50	75.00
BV-3314 [M]	Muscle Beach Party	1963	18.75	37.50	75.00
STER-3314 [S]	Muscle Beach Party	1963	37.50	75.00	150.00
BV-3316 [M]	Beach Party	1963	15.00	30.00	60.00
STER-3316 [S]	Beach Party	1963	25.00	50.00	100.00
BV-3320 [M]	Annette on Campus	1964	12.50	25.00	50.00
STER-3320 [S]	Annette on Campus	1964	25.00	50.00	100.00
BV-3324 [M]	Annette at Bikini Beach	1964	12.50	25.00	50.00
STER-3324 [S]	Annette at Bikini Beach	1964	25.00	50.00	100.00
BV-3325 [M]	Annette's Pajama Party	1964	10.00	20.00	40.00
STER-3325 [S]	Annette's Pajama Party	1964	25.00	50.00	100.00
BV-3327 [M]	Annette Sings Golden Surfin' Hits	1964	25.00	50.00	100.00
STER-3327 [S]	Annette Sings Golden Surfin' Hits	1964	37.50	75.00	150.00
BV-3328 [M]	Something Borrowed, Something Blue	1964	15.00	30.00	60.00
STER-3328 [P]	Something Borrowed, Something Blue	1964	25.00	50.00	100.00
BV-4037	Annette Funicello	1972	12.50	25.00	50.00

RHINO

Number	Title (A Side/B Side)	Yr	VG	VG+	NM
RNDF-206	The Best of Annette	1984	3.00	6.00	12.00
RNLP-702 [PD]	The Best of Annette	1984	6.25	12.50	25.00

ANNETTE / HAYLEY MILLS

Albums

DISNEYLAND

Number	Title (A Side/B Side)	Yr	VG	VG+	NM
DL-3508 [M]	Annette and Hayley Mills (Singing 10 of Their Greatest All-Time Hits)	1964	250.00	500.00	1000.

—TV offer; issued with paper jacket. Though the cover says "Buena Vista Records Presents," the label is the yellow Disneyland label

ANNIE AND THE ORPHANS

45s

CAPITOL

Number	Title (A Side/B Side)	Yr	VG	VG+	NM
5144	My Girl's Been Bitten by the Beatle Bug/A Place Called Happiness	1964	5.00	10.00	20.00
5144 [PS]	My Girl's Been Bitten by the Beatle Bug/A Place Called Happiness	1964	6.25	12.50	25.00

ANONYMOUS

Albums

A-MAJOR

Number	Title (A Side/B Side)	Yr	VG	VG+	NM
AMLS-1002	Inside the Shadow	1976	62.50	125.00	250.00

ANT TRIP CEREMONY

Albums

C.R.C.

Number	Title (A Side/B Side)	Yr	VG	VG+	NM
2129	24 Hours	1970	150.00	300.00	600.00

ANTELL, PETE

45s

BOUNTY

Number	Title (A Side/B Side)	Yr	VG	VG+	NM
103	The Times They Are a-Changin'/Yesterrday and Tomorrow	1965	3.75	7.50	15.00

CAMEO

Number	Title (A Side/B Side)	Yr	VG	VG+	NM
234	Night Time/Something About You	1962	5.00	10.00	20.00
264	You in Disguise/Keep It Up	1963	3.75	7.50	15.00

NEW VOICE

Number	Title (A Side/B Side)	Yr	VG	VG+	NM
818	Wanting/Warm Smoke	1967	2.50	5.00	10.00

ANTHEM

Albums

BUDDAH

Number	Title (A Side/B Side)	Yr	VG	VG+	NM
BDS-5071	Anthem	1971	5.00	10.00	20.00

ANTHONY, LAMONT

See LAMONT DOZIER.

ANTHONY, MARK

45s

LA BELLE

Number	Title (A Side/B Side)	Yr	VG	VG+	NM
779	Mama's Twistin' with Santa/Music from Studio "D"	1962	3.00	6.00	12.00

ANTHONY, NICK

45s

ABC-PARAMOUNT

Number	Title (A Side/B Side)	Yr	VG	VG+	NM
9919	More Than Ever/You're Real Keen, Jelly Bean	1958	5.00	10.00	20.00
9985	Forbidden Love/My Baby's Gone	1958	5.00	10.00	20.00

ANTHONY, RAY

45s

CAPITOL

Number	Title (A Side/B Side)	Yr	VG	VG+	NM
F-794	Sitting by the Window/Dixie	1949	3.75	7.50	15.00
F-819	I'll See You In My Dreams/My Baby Is Blue	1950	3.00	6.00	12.00
F-859	Count Every Star/Bamboo	1950	3.00	6.00	12.00
F-923	Sentimental Me/Spaghetti Rag	1950	3.00	6.00	12.00
F-933	Where in the World/Candy & Cake	1950	3.00	6.00	12.00
F-945	Why/Little Peach from East Orange	1950	3.00	6.00	12.00
F-958	In the Mood/Way Down Yonder	1950	3.00	6.00	12.00
F-968	Autumn Nocturne/Tenderly	1950	3.00	6.00	12.00
F-979	Count Every Star/The Darktown Strutters Ball	1950	3.00	6.00	12.00
F-1001	Roses/National Emblem March	1950	3.00	6.00	12.00
F-1020	The Girl That I Marry/They Say It's Wonderful	1950	3.00	6.00	12.00
F-1040	Skip to My Lou/Scattered Toys	1950	3.00	6.00	12.00
F-1051	Francie/Mama Teach Me to Do the Charleston	1950	3.00	6.00	12.00
F-1073	Lazy Old Tune/Lackawanna Local	1950	3.00	6.00	12.00
F-1131	Can Anyone Explain/Shy Coach	1950	3.00	6.00	12.00
F-1169	Dixie Doodle/All of a Sudden (My Heart Sings)	1950	3.00	6.00	12.00
F-1190	Harbor Lights/Nevertheless (I'm in Love with You)	1950	3.00	6.00	12.00
F-1196	A Marshmallow World/Where Do I Go from You	1950	3.75	7.50	15.00
F-1249	My Heart Is Out of Town/Harlem Nocturne	1950	3.00	6.00	12.00
F-1280	Autumn Leaves/Mr. Anthony's Boogie	1950	3.00	6.00	12.00
F-1310	The Night Is Young and You're So Beautiful/All Anthony No Cleopatra	1950	3.00	6.00	12.00
F-1352	Be My Love/I Wonder What's Become of Sally	1951	3.00	6.00	12.00
F-1367	More Than I Care to Remember/Columbia, The Gem of the Ocean	1951	3.00	6.00	12.00
F-1490	I'll Never Know Why/Faithfully Yours	1951	3.00	6.00	12.00
F-1522	These Things I Offer You (For a Lifetime)/Here's To Your Illusions	1951	3.00	6.00	12.00
F-1556	Villa/Melancholy Rhapsody	1951	3.00	6.00	12.00
F-1574	Believing You/One Dance with You	1951	3.00	6.00	12.00
F-1583	My Truly, Truly Fair/Pretty Eyed Baby	1951	3.00	6.00	12.00
F-1622	Star Dust/Man with a Horn	1951	3.00	6.00	12.00
F-1654	Tenderly/Autumn Nocturne	1951	3.00	6.00	12.00
F-1664	What Is This Thing Called Love/Harlem Nocturne	1951	3.00	6.00	12.00
F-1678	As Time Goes By/At Last	1954	2.50	5.00	10.00
—Reissue					
F-1679	Mr. Anthony's Boogie/I Wonder What's Become of Sally	1954	2.50	5.00	10.00
—Reissue					
F-1723	I Love the Sunshine in Your Smile/You Blew Out the Flame	1951	3.00	6.00	12.00
F-1739	Mary Rose/Ho Ho	1951	3.00	6.00	12.00
F-1758	The Fox/Rollin' Home	1951	3.00	6.00	12.00
F-1810	Deep Night/With All My Heart and Soul	1951	3.00	6.00	12.00
F-1824	Undecided/Just a Moment More	1951	3.00	6.00	12.00
F-1835	My Concerto/I'll Remember April	1951	3.00	6.00	12.00
F-1857	Brother Fats/I Remember Harlem	1951	3.00	6.00	12.00
F-1884	Honeydriper/Busman's Holiday	1951	3.00	6.00	12.00
F-1912	At Last/I'll See You in My Dreams	1952	2.50	5.00	10.00
F-1956	Bermuda/Broken Hearted	1952	2.50	5.00	10.00
F-1957	Singin' in the Rain/I Let a Song Go Out of My Heart	1952	2.50	5.00	10.00
F-1973	I Hear a Rhapsody/For Dancers Only	1952	2.50	5.00	10.00
F-2002	There Are Such Things/Moonlight Savings Time	1952	2.50	5.00	10.00
F-2058	Trumpet Boogie/You're Driving Me Crazy	1952	2.50	5.00	10.00
6F-2085	Slaughter on Tenth Avenue (Part I)/Slaughter on Tenth Avenue (Part II)	1952	2.50	5.00	10.00
—Has a maroon rather than purple label					
F-2104	As Time Goes By/Scatterbrain	1952	2.50	5.00	10.00
F-2194	Make Believe Dreams/Loaded with Love	1952	2.50	5.00	10.00
F-2207	Marilyn/Randles Island	1952	5.00	10.00	20.00
F-2251	Bunny Hop/Blow, Man, Blow	1952	3.00	6.00	12.00
F-2293	Idaho/People in Love	1952	2.50	5.00	10.00
F-2327	On the Trail/Street Scene	1953	2.50	5.00	10.00
F-2349	You're a Heartbreaker/Wild Horses	1953	2.50	5.00	10.00
F-2393	True Blue Lou/They Didn't Believe Me	1953	2.50	5.00	10.00
F-2427	The Hokey Pokey/Bunny Hop	1953	3.00	6.00	12.00
F-2451	Piccadilly Circus/Thunderbird	1953	2.50	5.00	10.00
F-2488	When the Saints Go Marching In/That's My Weakness Now	1953	2.50	5.00	10.00
F-2532	Jersey Bounce/I Guess It Was You All the Time	1953	2.50	5.00	10.00
F-2562	Dragnet/Dancing in the Dark	1953	3.75	7.50	15.00
F-2637	Sound Off/Another Dawn, Another Day	1953	2.50	5.00	10.00
F-2678	O Mein Papa (O! My Papa)/Secret Love	1953	2.50	5.00	10.00
F-2699	Tuxedo Junction/In the Mood	1954	2.50	5.00	10.00
F-2728	Sign Post/Air Express	1954	2.50	5.00	10.00
F-2777	Dance My Heart/Somewhere Beyond Tonight	1954	2.50	5.00	10.00
F-2860	I Don't Hurt Anymore/Cat Dancin'	1954	2.50	5.00	10.00
F-2896	Skokiaan/Say Hey	1954	2.50	5.00	10.00
F-2936	A Woman's World/Jambo	1954	2.50	5.00	10.00
F-3029	Heat Wave/Juke Box Special	1955	2.50	5.00	10.00
F-3096	Sluefoot/Something's Gotta Give	1955	2.50	5.00	10.00
F-3147	Learning the Blues/Mmmm Marie	1955	2.50	5.00	10.00
F-3176	Pete Kelly's Blues/D.C. 7	1955	2.50	5.00	10.00
F-3261	Flip Flop/Hurricane Anthony	1955	2.50	5.00	10.00
F-3319	Bullfighter Lament/Rockin' Thru Dixie	1955	2.50	5.00	10.00
F-3335	Madeira/Show Me the Way to Go Home	1955	2.50	5.00	10.00
F-3416	Chubasco (Mexican Storm Song)/Sleepwalker	1956	2.00	4.00	8.00
F-3500	I Am in Love/I Love You Samantha	1956	2.00	4.00	8.00
F-3593	Love Is Just Around the Corner/Danciong Lovers	1956	2.00	4.00	8.00
F-3646	Calypso Dance/Plymouth Rock	1957	2.00	4.00	8.00
F-3676	The Incredible Shrinking Man/This Could Be the Night	1957	2.00	4.00	8.00
F-3739	Lonely Trumpet/Cello-Phane	1957	2.00	4.00	8.00
F-3897	Till There Was You/Big Record	1958	2.00	4.00	8.00
F-4041	Peter Gunn/Tango for Two	1958	2.50	5.00	10.00
F-4176	Walkin' to Mother's/Bunny Hop	1959	2.50	5.00	10.00
F-4227	Fly Now Pay Later/707	1959	2.00	4.00	8.00
F-4275	Room 45/Stockholm Blues	1959	2.00	4.00	8.00
4358	Just in Time/Tres Chic	1960	2.00	4.00	8.00
4440	Atsa Nice-a/You Know It, You Know It, You Know It	1960	2.00	4.00	8.00
4513	Gurney Slade Theme/Return to Me	1961	2.00	4.00	8.00
4603	Moliendo Café/Champs Elysses	1961	2.00	4.00	8.00
4728	Bunny Hop Twist/Tequila with a Twist	1962	2.00	4.00	8.00
4742	Worried Mind/Al Di La	1962	2.00	4.00	8.00
4834	I Almost Lost My Mind/Trouble in Mind	1962	2.00	4.00	8.00
4876	Let Me Entertain You/Wishing Star	1962	2.00	4.00	8.00
4972	Heartaches/Mexican Market Day	1963	—	3.00	6.00
5026	Toys in the Attic/Oh Steal Away	1963	—	3.00	6.00
5070	Candy Wrapper/Mr. Novak	1963	—	3.00	6.00
5149	Let's All Do the Swim/Everybody Do the Swim	1964	—	3.00	6.00
5320	Lady Bird/Tiger Tail	1964	—	3.00	6.00
5418	Skunk in a Trunk/Sabor Ami	1965	—	3.00	6.00
5468	Seventh Son/Meeting Over Yonder	1965	—	3.00	6.00
5589	It's Such a Happy Day/Bah-Yoop	1966	—	3.00	6.00
5654	Goodbye My Love/Merci Cherie	1966	—	3.00	6.00
5714	Danke Schoen/Huapango Mexicana	1966	—	3.00	6.00
5836	Gallant Men/Around the World	1967	—	2.50	5.00

7-Inch Extended Plays

Number	Title (A Side/B Side)	Yr	VG	VG+	NM
CAPITOL					
EAP 1-373	I Wonder What's Become of Sally/Mr. Anthony's Boogie//The Man with the Horn/Mr. Anthony's Blues	195?	3.00	6.00	12.00
EAP 1-373 [PS]	(title unknown)	195?	3.00	6.00	12.00
EAP 2-373	For Dancers Only/Harlem Nocturne//Tenderly/Stardust	195?	3.00	6.00	12.00
EAP 2-373 [PS]	(title unknown)	195?	3.00	6.00	12.00
EBF 373 [PS]	(title unknown)	195?	3.00	6.00	12.00
—Gatefold cover for some versions of 1-373 and 2-373					
EAP 1-504	Cooks Tour Idaho//Jersey Bounce/Thunderbird	1955	2.50	5.00	10.00
EAP 1-504 [PS]	Ray Anthony Plays for Dancing	1955	2.50	5.00	10.00

Albums

Number	Title (A Side/B Side)	Yr	VG	VG+	NM
AERO SPACE					
1007	Around the World	197?	2.50	5.00	10.00
CAPITOL					
H 292 [10]	Houseparty Hop	195?	10.00	20.00	40.00
H 476 [10]	I Remember Glenn Miller	1954	10.00	20.00	40.00
T 563 [M]	Golden Horn	1955	3.75	7.50	15.00
T 723 [M]	Dream Dancing	1956	3.75	7.50	15.00
T 749 [M]	Jam Session at the Tower	1956	10.00	20.00	40.00
T 831 [M]	Star Dancing	1957	3.75	7.50	15.00
T 866 [M]	Young Ideas	1957	3.75	7.50	15.00
T 917 [M]	Moments Together	1958	3.75	7.50	15.00
T 969 [M]	The Dream Girl	1958	3.75	7.50	15.00
T 1029 [M]	Dancing Over the Waves	1958	3.75	7.50	15.00
T 1066 [M]	Ray Anthony Plays Steve Allen	1958	3.75	7.50	15.00
T 1200 [M]	Sound Spectacular	1959	3.75	7.50	15.00
ST 1252 [S]	More Dream Dancing	1959	3.75	7.50	15.00
T 1252 [M]	More Dream Dancing	1959	3.00	6.00	12.00
ST 1304 [S]	Like Wild!	1959	3.75	7.50	15.00
T 1304 [M]	Like Wild!	1959	3.00	6.00	12.00
T 1371 [M]	Arthur Murray Favorites — Fox Trots	1960	3.00	6.00	12.00
ST 1420 [S]	Dancing Alone Together	1960	3.75	7.50	15.00
T 1420 [M]	Dancing Alone Together	1960	3.00	6.00	12.00
ST 1421 [S]	The New Ray Anthony Show	1960	3.75	7.50	15.00
T 1421 [M]	The New Ray Anthony Show	1960	3.00	6.00	12.00
T 1477 [M]	The Hits of Ray Anthony	1960	3.00	6.00	12.00
ST 1608 [S]	Dream Dancing Medley	1961	3.75	7.50	15.00
T 1608 [M]	Dream Dancing Medley	1961	3.00	6.00	12.00
ST 1668 [S]	Twist with Ray Anthony	1961	3.75	7.50	15.00
T 1668 [M]	Twist with Ray Anthony	1961	3.00	6.00	12.00
ST 1752 [S]	Worried Mind	1962	3.75	7.50	15.00
T 1752 [M]	Worried Mind	1962	3.00	6.00	12.00
ST 1783 [S]	I Almost Lost My Mind	1962	3.75	7.50	15.00
T 1783 [M]	I Almost Lost My Mind	1962	3.00	6.00	12.00
ST 1917 [S]	Smash Hits of '63	1963	3.75	7.50	15.00
T 1917 [M]	Smash Hits of '63	1963	3.00	6.00	12.00
ST 2043 [S]	Charade and Other Top Themes	1964	3.75	7.50	15.00
T 2043 [M]	Charade and Other Top Themes	1964	3.00	6.00	12.00
ST 2150 [S]	My Love, Forgive Me	1964	3.75	7.50	15.00
T 2150 [M]	My Love, Forgive Me	1964	3.00	6.00	12.00
ST 2188 [S]	Swim, Swim, C'mon, Let's Swim	1964	3.75	7.50	15.00
T 2188 [M]	Swim, Swim, C'mon, Let's Swim	1964	3.00	6.00	12.00
ST 2457 [S]	Dream Dancing Today	1966	3.75	7.50	15.00
T 2457 [M]	Dream Dancing Today	1966	3.00	6.00	12.00
ST 2530 [S]	Hit Songs to Remember	1966	3.75	7.50	15.00
T 2530 [M]	Hit Songs to Remember	1966	3.00	6.00	12.00
M-11978	Fox Trots	1979	2.50	5.00	10.00
CIRCLE					
CLP-96	Sweet and Swingin' 1949-1953	1987	2.50	5.00	10.00
HINDSIGHT					
HSR-240	Young Man with a Horn	1988	2.50	5.00	10.00
RANWOOD					
8059	Love Is for the Two of Us	197?	2.50	5.00	10.00
8082	Now	197?	2.50	5.00	10.00
8083	I Get the Blues When It Rains	197?	2.50	5.00	10.00
8153	Golden Hits	197?	2.50	5.00	10.00

ANTHONY, RAYBURN

45s

Number	Title (A Side/B Side)	Yr	VG	VG+	NM
SUN					
333	Alice Blue Gown/St. Louis Blues	1959	5.00	10.00	20.00
339	There's No Tomorrow/Who's Gonna Shoe Your Pretty Foot	1960	5.00	10.00	20.00
373	Big Dream/How Well I Know	1962	5.00	10.00	20.00

ANTHONY, TONY

45s

Number	Title (A Side/B Side)	Yr	VG	VG+	NM
HERALD					
533	Peek-a-Boo/Lonely One	1959	7.50	15.00	30.00

ANTHONY AND THE SOPHOMORES

Also see THE DYNAMICS (3).

45s

Number	Title (A Side/B Side)	Yr	VG	VG+	NM
ABC					
10844	Heartbreak/I'll Go Through Life Loving You	1966	5.00	10.00	20.00
ABC-PARAMOUNT					
10737	Gee (But I'd Give the World)/It Depends On You	1965	5.00	10.00	20.00
10770	Get Back to You/Wild for Her	1966	5.00	10.00	20.00
GRAND					
163	Embraceable You/Beautiful Dreamer	1963	15.00	30.00	60.00
JAMIE					
1330	Serenade (From The Student Prince)/Work Out	1967	3.75	7.50	15.00
1340	One Summer Night/Work Out	1967	3.75	7.50	15.00
JASON SCOTT					
18	Embraceable You/Beautiful Dreamer	1978	—	2.00	4.00
MERCURY					
72103	Play Those Oldies Mr. D.J./Clap Your Hands	1963	15.00	30.00	60.00
72168	Swingin' at the Chariot/Better Late Than Never	1963	7.50	15.00	30.00

ANTWINETTES, THE

45s

Number	Title (A Side/B Side)	Yr	VG	VG+	NM
RCA VICTOR					
47-7398	Johnny/Kill It	1958	10.00	20.00	40.00

AORTA

45s

Number	Title (A Side/B Side)	Yr	VG	VG+	NM
ATLANTIC					
2545	Strange/Shape of Things to Come	1968	5.00	10.00	20.00
COLUMBIA					
44870	Strange/Ode to Missy Mztsfpklk	1969	2.50	5.00	10.00
HAPPY TIGER					
567	Sandcastles/Willie Jean	1970	3.75	7.50	15.00

Albums

Number	Title (A Side/B Side)	Yr	VG	VG+	NM
COLUMBIA					
CS 9785	Aorta	1969	7.50	15.00	30.00
HAPPY TIGER					
HT-1010	Aorta 2	1970	10.00	20.00	40.00

APHRODITE'S CHILD

45s

Number	Title (A Side/B Side)	Yr	VG	VG+	NM
PHILIPS					
40536	Other People/Plastics Nevermore	1968	5.00	10.00	20.00
40587	End of the World/You Always Stand in My Way	1969	5.00	10.00	20.00
POLYDOR					
15005	Magic Mirror/I Want to Live	1969	2.00	4.00	8.00
VERTIGO					
107	Babylon/Break	1973	—	3.00	6.00

Albums

Number	Title (A Side/B Side)	Yr	VG	VG+	NM
VERTIGO					
VEL-2-500 [(2)]	666 (The Apocalypse of John)	1972	5.00	10.00	20.00

APOLLO 100

45s

Number	Title (A Side/B Side)	Yr	VG	VG+	NM
MEGA					
0050	Joy/Exercise in A Minor	1971	—	2.50	5.00
0069	Reach for the Sky/Symphony #4, 2nd Movement	1972	—	2.00	4.00
0080	Minuet for a Funky Lady/Telstar	1972	—	2.00	4.00

Albums

Number	Title (A Side/B Side)	Yr	VG	VG+	NM
MEGA					
1010	Joy	1972	2.50	5.00	10.00

APPALACHIANS, THE

45s

Number	Title (A Side/B Side)	Yr	VG	VG+	NM
ABC-PARAMOUNT					
10419	Bony Maronie/It Takes a Man	1963	2.50	5.00	10.00
10464	Big Betty/Hilly-Billy-Ding-Dong-Choo-Choo	1963	2.00	4.00	8.00
10498	Lawdy Miss Clawdy/Over Yonder	1963	2.00	4.00	8.00

APPALOOSA

Albums

Number	Title (A Side/B Side)	Yr	VG	VG+	NM
COLUMBIA					
CS 9819	Appaloosa	1969	3.75	7.50	15.00
—Produced by Al Kooper					

APPELL, DAVE

See THE APPLEJACKS (1).

APPLE PIE MOTHERHOOD BAND, THE

45s

Number	Title (A Side/B Side)	Yr	VG	VG+	NM
ATLANTIC					
2477	Flight Path/Long Live Apple Pie	1968	2.00	4.00	8.00

Albums

Number	Title (A Side/B Side)	Yr	VG	VG+	NM
ATLANTIC					
SD 8189	The Apple Pie Motherhood Band	1968	6.25	12.50	25.00
SD 8233	Apple Pie	1969	6.25	12.50	25.00

APPLEJACKS, THE (1)

Essentially Dave Appell. The below includes his "solo" records.

45s

Number	Title (A Side/B Side)	Yr	VG	VG+	NM
B.T. PUPPY					
554	The Son of a Preacher Man/Girl of the Skies	1970	2.00	4.00	8.00
—As "Dave Appell"					
CAMEO					
110	Love in the Jungle/Chitter Chatter Baby	1957	5.00	10.00	20.00
132	Dinner with Drac/No Name Theme	1958	6.25	12.50	25.00
138	Moonlight Serenade/Walk On	1958	5.00	10.00	20.00
149	Mexican Hat Rock/Sophisticated Swing	1958	5.00	10.00	20.00
149	Mexican Hat Rock/Stop! Red Light	1958	4.00	8.00	16.00
155	Rocka-Tonga/Am I Blue	1958	5.00	10.00	20.00
—First pressing contains a typographical error on A-side					
155	Rocka-Conga/Am I Blue	1958	4.00	8.00	16.00
—Later pressings have correct A-side title					
158	Bunny Hop/Night Train Stroll	1959	4.00	8.00	16.00
170	Circle Dance/Love Scene	1959	4.00	8.00	16.00
177	The Untouchables/Memories Are Made of This	1960	4.00	8.00	16.00
184	Theme from The Young Ones/September Song	1960	3.75	7.50	15.00
—As "Dave Appell and His Orchestra"					
203	Mexican Hat Twist/Let's Continental	1961	3.75	7.50	15.00
207	Happy Jose/Noivous	1961	3.75	7.50	15.00
—As "Dave Appell and His Orchestra"					
222	Struttin' in the Summertime/Any Time	1962	3.75	7.50	15.00
248	Hippies Waltz/Back in 60 Seconds	1963	3.75	7.50	15.00
283	Hot Toddy/Dance of the Hours	1963	3.75	7.50	15.00
321	She Loves You/Bongo Beach	1964	3.75	7.50	15.00
—As "Dave Appell and His Orchestra"					

Albums

Number	Title (A Side/B Side)	Yr	VG	VG+	NM
CAMEO					
C-1004 [M]	Alone Together	1958	12.50	25.00	50.00
—As "Dave Appell"					

APPLEJACKS, THE (2)

British band.

45s

LONDON

Number	Title (A Side/B Side)	Yr	VG	VG+	NM
9658	Baby Jane/Tell Me When	1964	3.00	6.00	12.00
9681	Like Dreamers Do/Everybody Fall Down	1964	3.75	7.50	15.00
9709	You're the One for Me/Three Little Words	1964	3.00	6.00	12.00
9709	You're the One for Me/Send Me Love	1964	3.00	6.00	12.00

APPLEJACKS, THE (U)

45s

DECCA

Number	Title (A Side/B Side)	Yr	VG	VG+	NM
9-29218	Smarter/My Heart Will Wait for You	1954	5.00	10.00	20.00
9-29330	Sweet Patootie Pie/Reunion	1954	5.00	10.00	20.00

PRESIDENT

Number	Title (A Side/B Side)	Yr	VG	VG+	NM
1005	Ring Around My Baby/Love Express	1956	5.00	10.00	20.00
1006	Teenage Meeting/Ooh Baby Ooh	1956	5.00	10.00	20.00
1011	Rock and Roll Story/Rainbow of Love	1956	5.00	10.00	20.00

APPLETREE THEATRE CO.

45s

VERVE FORECAST

Number	Title (A Side/B Side)	Yr	VG	VG+	NM
5071	Hightower Square/Who Do You Think I Am	1967	3.00	6.00	12.00
5082	Lotus Flower/What a Way to Go	1968	3.00	6.00	12.00

Albums

VERVE FORECAST

Number	Title (A Side/B Side)	Yr	VG	VG+	NM
FTS-3042	Playback	1968	7.50	15.00	30.00
—RICK NELSON appears on this album					

APPRECIATIONS, THE

45s

JUBILEE

Number	Title (A Side/B Side)	Yr	VG	VG+	NM
5525	Afraid of Love/Far from Your Love	1966	3.00	6.00	12.00

SPORT

Number	Title (A Side/B Side)	Yr	VG	VG+	NM
108	There's a Place in My Heart/She Never Really Believed Me	1967	25.00	50.00	100.00
112	It's Better to Cry/Gimme Back My Soul	1967	50.00	100.00	200.00

APRIL WINE

45s

BIG TREE

Number	Title (A Side/B Side)	Yr	VG	VG+	NM
133	You Could Have Been a Lady/Teacher	1972	—	3.00	6.00
142	Bad Side of the Moon/Believe in Me	1972	—	2.50	5.00
15006	Come On Along/I'm on Fire for You Baby	1974	—	2.50	5.00
16010	Just Like That/Weeping Willow	1973	—	2.50	5.00
16036	Oowatanite/(B-side unknown)	1975	—	2.50	5.00

CAPITOL

Number	Title (A Side/B Side)	Yr	VG	VG+	NM
4660	Roller/Right Down to It	1978	—	2.00	4.00
4728	Get Ready for Love/Comin' Right Down on Top of Me	1979	—	2.00	4.00
4802	Before the Dawn/Say Hello	1979	—	2.00	4.00
4828	I Like to Rock/Babes in Arms	1980	—	2.00	4.00
4859	Lady's Man/Tonite	1980	—	2.00	4.00
4975	Just Between You and Me/Big City Girls	1981	—	2.00	4.00
4975 [PS]	Just Between You and Me/Big City Girls	1981	2.00	4.00	8.00
—Fold-out poster sleeve					
4975 [PS]	Just Between You and Me/Big City Girls	1981	—	2.50	5.00
—Regular sleeve					
A-5001	Sign of the Gypsy Queen/Crash and Burn	1981	—	2.00	4.00
A-5001 [PS]	Sign of the Gypsy Queen/Crash and Burn	1981	—	2.50	5.00
B-5133	Enough Is Enough/Ain't Got Your Love	1982	—	2.00	4.00
B-5133 [PS]	Enough Is Enough/Ain't Got Your Love	1982	—	2.00	4.00
B-5153	If You See Kay/Blood Money	1982	—	2.50	5.00
B-5168	Tell Me Why/Runners in the Night	1982	—	2.00	4.00
B-5319	This Could Be the Right One/Really Don't Want Your Love	1984	—	—	3.00
B-5319 [PS]	This Could Be the Right One/Really Don't Want Your Love	1984	—	2.00	4.00
B-5506	Rock Myself to Sleep/All It Will Ever Be	1985	—	—	3.00

LONDON

Number	Title (A Side/B Side)	Yr	VG	VG+	NM
245	Shot Down/(B-side unknown)	1976	—	2.50	5.00
255	You Won't Dance with Me/Shot Down	1976	—	2.50	5.00
265	I'm Alive/Rock and Roll Is a Vicious Game	1977	—	2.50	5.00

Albums

AQUARIUS

Number	Title (A Side/B Side)	Yr	VG	VG+	NM
AQR 504	Electric Jewels	1973	3.75	7.50	15.00
AQR 505	Live	1974	3.75	7.50	15.00

ATLANTIC

Number	Title (A Side/B Side)	Yr	VG	VG+	NM
SD 19303	Stand Back	1981	2.50	5.00	10.00
—Reissue of Big Tree 89506					

BIG TREE

Number	Title (A Side/B Side)	Yr	VG	VG+	NM
BTS 2012	April Wine	1972	5.00	10.00	20.00
89506	Stand Back	1975	3.75	7.50	15.00

CAPITOL

Number	Title (A Side/B Side)	Yr	VG	VG+	NM
ST-11852	First Glance	1979	3.00	6.00	12.00
ST-12013	Harder...Faster	1979	2.50	5.00	10.00
SOO-12125	The Nature of the Beast	1981	2.50	5.00	10.00
ST-12218	Power Play	1982	2.50	5.00	10.00
ST-12311	Animal Grace	1984	2.50	5.00	10.00
SN-16245	First Glance	1982	2.00	4.00	8.00
—Budget-line reissue					
SN-16322	Harder...Faster	1984	2.00	4.00	8.00
—Budget-line reissue					
SN-16344	Power Play	1984	2.00	4.00	8.00
—Budget-line reissue					
SN-16379	The Nature of the Beast	1986	2.00	4.00	8.00
—Budget-line reissue					
C1-48418	Walking Through Fire	1988	3.00	6.00	12.00

LONDON

Number	Title (A Side/B Side)	Yr	VG	VG+	NM
PS 675	The Whole World's Goin' Crazy	1976	3.75	7.50	15.00
PS 699	Live at the El Mocambo	1977	3.75	7.50	15.00

AQUARIANS

45s

UNI

Number	Title (A Side/B Side)	Yr	VG	VG+	NM
55124	Abela/Jungle Grass	1969	—	3.00	6.00

Albums

UNI

Number	Title (A Side/B Side)	Yr	VG	VG+	NM
73053	Jungle Grass	1969	3.75	7.50	15.00

AQUATONES, THE

45s

FARGO

Number	Title (A Side/B Side)	Yr	VG	VG+	NM
1001	You/She's the One for Me	1958	6.25	12.50	25.00
1002	Say You'll Be Mine/So Fine	1958	6.25	12.50	25.00
1003	Our First Kiss/The Drive-In	1958	6.25	12.50	25.00
1005	My Treasure/My One Desire	1959	6.25	12.50	25.00
1015	Every Time/There's a Long, Long Trail	1960	6.25	12.50	25.00
1016	Wanted/Crazy for You	1961	6.25	12.50	25.00
1022	My Treasure/Say You'll Be Mine	1961	6.25	12.50	25.00
1111	My Darling/For You, For You	196?	5.00	10.00	20.00

Albums

FARGO

Number	Title (A Side/B Side)	Yr	VG	VG+	NM
3001 [M]	The Aquatones Sing	1964	125.00	250.00	500.00

RELIC/FARGO

Number	Title (A Side/B Side)	Yr	VG	VG+	NM
5033 [M]	The Aquatones Sing	198?	2.00	4.00	8.00

ARBORS, THE

45s

CARNEY

Number	Title (A Side/B Side)	Yr	VG	VG+	NM
1011	A Symphony for Susan/Love Is the Light	1966	6.25	12.50	25.00

DATE

Number	Title (A Side/B Side)	Yr	VG	VG+	NM
1529	A Symphony for Susan/Love Is the Light	1966	2.50	5.00	10.00
1546	Dreamer Girl/Just Let It Happen	1967	2.50	5.00	10.00
1561	Graduation Day/I Win the Whole Wide World	1967	2.50	5.00	10.00
1570	Love for All Seasons/With You Girl	1967	2.50	5.00	10.00
1581	Valley of the Dolls/You Are the Music	1967	2.50	5.00	10.00
1601	That's the Way It Is/Graduation Day	1968	2.50	5.00	10.00
1638	The Letter/Most of All	1969	3.00	6.00	12.00
1645	I Can't Quit Her/Lovin' Tonight (Maybe Tonight)	1969	2.50	5.00	10.00
1651	Touch Me/Motet	1969	2.50	5.00	10.00
1672	Julie I Tried/Okalona River Bottom Band	1970	2.50	5.00	10.00

MERCURY

Number	Title (A Side/B Side)	Yr	VG	VG+	NM
72456	Anybody Here for Love/The Girl with the Heather Green Eyes	1965	3.00	6.00	12.00

Albums

DATE

Number	Title (A Side/B Side)	Yr	VG	VG+	NM
TEM 3003 [M]	A Symphony for Susan	1967	3.75	7.50	15.00
TEM 3011 [M]	Valley of the Dolls	1967	5.00	10.00	20.00
TES 4003 [S]	A Symphony for Susan	1967	3.75	7.50	15.00
TES 4011 [S]	Valley of the Dolls	1967	3.75	7.50	15.00
TES 4017	The Arbors Featuring I Can't Quit Her and The Letter	1969	3.75	7.50	15.00

ARCHERS, THE

45s

LAURIE

Number	Title (A Side/B Side)	Yr	VG	VG+	NM
3207	Hey Rube/Unwind It	1963	3.75	7.50	15.00

SUMMER

Number	Title (A Side/B Side)	Yr	VG	VG+	NM
502	Motorcycle Michael/Golden Girl	196?	7.50	15.00	30.00

ARCHIBALD

45s

IMPERIAL

Number	Title (A Side/B Side)	Yr	VG	VG+	NM
5212	Early Morning Blues/Great Big Eyes	1953	750.00	1125.	1500.
5358	Stack-O-Lee (Part 1)/Stack-O-Lee (Part 2)	1955	25.00	50.00	100.00

ARCHIES, THE

Also see RON DANTE.

45s

CALENDAR

Number	Title (A Side/B Side)	Yr	VG	VG+	NM
63-1006	Bang-Shang-a-Lang/Truck Driver	1968	2.00	4.00	8.00
63-1006 [PS]	Bang-Shang-a-Lang/Truck Driver	1968	4.00	8.00	16.00
63-1007	Feelin' So Good (S.K.O.O.B.Y.-D.O.O.)/Love Light	1968	2.00	4.00	8.00
63-1007 [PS]	Feelin' So Good (S.K.O.O.B.Y.-D.O.O.)/Love Light	1968	4.00	8.00	16.00
63-1008	Sugar Sugar/Melody Hill	1969	2.50	5.00	10.00

KIRSHNER

Number	Title (A Side/B Side)	Yr	VG	VG+	NM
63-1009	Sunshine/Over and Over	1970	2.00	4.00	8.00
63-5002	Jingle Jangle/Justine	1969	2.00	4.00	8.00
63-5003	Who's Your Baby/Senorita Rita	1970	2.00	4.00	8.00
63-5009	Everything's Alright/Together We Two	1970	2.00	4.00	8.00
63-5011	Throw a Little Love My Way/This Is Love	1971	2.00	4.00	8.00
63-5014	A Summer Prayer for Peace/Maybe I'm Wrong	1971	2.00	4.00	8.00
63-5014 [PS]	A Summer Prayer for Peace/Maybe I'm Wrong	1971	4.00	8.00	16.00
63-5018	Love Is Living in You/Hold On to Lovin'	1972	2.00	4.00	8.00
63-5021	Strangers in the Morning/Plum Crazy	1972	2.00	4.00	8.00

Albums

51 WEST

Number	Title (A Side/B Side)	Yr	VG	VG+	NM
16002	The Archies	1979	2.50	5.00	10.00

ACCORD

Number	Title (A Side/B Side)	Yr	VG	VG+	NM
SN-7149	Straight A's	1981	2.50	5.00	10.00

CALENDAR

Number	Title (A Side/B Side)	Yr	VG	VG+	NM
KES-101	The Archies	1968	6.25	12.50	25.00
KES-103	Everything's Archie	1969	6.25	12.50	25.00

KIRSHNER

Number	Title (A Side/B Side)	Yr	VG	VG+	NM
KES-103 [DJ]	Everything's Archie Box	1969	25.00	50.00	100.00
—Box with LP, photos, press kit and buttons					
KES-105	Jingle Jangle	1969	6.25	12.50	25.00
KES-107	Sunshine	1970	6.25	12.50	25.00
KES-109	The Archies Grestest Hits	1970	6.25	12.50	25.00

ARDELLS, THE

Number	Title (A Side/B Side)	Yr	VG	VG+	NM
45s					
EPIC					
9621	Eefananny/Lonely Valley	1963	3.75	7.50	15.00
MARCO					
102	Every Day of the Week/Roll On	1961	7.50	15.00	30.00
SELMA					
4001	Seven Lonely Nights/You Can Fall in Love	1963	6.25	12.50	25.00

AREA CODE 615

Number	Title (A Side/B Side)	Yr	VG	VG+	NM
45s					
POLYDOR					
14012	Why Ask Why/Ruby	1969	—	3.00	6.00
14215	Stone Fox Chase/Sligo	1973	—	2.50	5.00
Albums					
POLYDOR					
24-4002	Area Code 615	1969	5.00	10.00	20.00
24-4025	A Trip in the Country	1970	5.00	10.00	20.00

ARENA BRASS, THE

Number	Title (A Side/B Side)	Yr	VG	VG+	NM
Albums					
EPIC					
LN 24039 [M]	The Lonely Bull	1962	3.00	6.00	12.00
BN 26039 [S]	The Lonely Bull	1962	3.75	7.50	15.00

ARGENT

Rod Argent's group after THE ZOMBIES broke up. Also see RUSS BALLARD.

Number	Title (A Side/B Side)	Yr	VG	VG+	NM
45s					
DATE					
1659	Liar/Schoolgirl	1970	2.50	5.00	10.00
EPIC					
10718	Rejoice/Sweet Mary	1971	—	3.00	6.00
10746	Celebration/Kingdom	1971	—	3.00	6.00
10852	Hold Your Head Up/Closer to Heaven	1972	2.00	4.00	8.00
10919	Tragedy/He's a Dynamo	1972	—	2.50	5.00
10972	God Gave Rock and Roll To You/Christmas for the Free	1973	—	2.50	5.00
11019	It's Only Money, Part 2/Losing Hold	1973	—	2.50	5.00
11137	Man for All Seasons/Music from the Spheres	1974	—	2.50	5.00
50025	The Coming of Kohoutek/Thunder and Lightning	1974	—	2.50	5.00
Albums					
EPIC					
BN 26525	Argent	1970	5.00	10.00	20.00
—Yellow label					
BN 26525	Argent	1973	3.00	6.00	12.00
—Orange label					
E 30128	A Ring of Hands	1971	5.00	10.00	20.00
—Yellow label					
KE 30128	A Ring of Hands	1973	3.00	6.00	12.00
—Orange label					
KE 31556	All Together Now	1972	5.00	10.00	20.00
—Yellow label					
KE 31556	All Together Now	1973	3.00	6.00	12.00
—Orange label					
KE 32195	In Deep	1973	5.00	10.00	20.00
—Orange label					
KE 32195	In Deep	1973	6.25	12.50	25.00
—Yellow label					
PEQ 32195 [Q]	In Deep	1974	7.50	15.00	30.00
PE 32573	Nexus	1974	5.00	10.00	20.00
—Orange label					
PEG 33079 [(2)]	Encore — Live in Concert	1975	5.00	10.00	20.00
—Orange labels					
PE 33422	Circus	1975	5.00	10.00	20.00
—Orange label					
PE 33955	Anthology	1976	3.75	7.50	15.00
—Orange label					
PE 33955	Anthology	1979	2.50	5.00	10.00
—Dark blue label					
UNITED ARTISTS					
UA-LA560-G	Counterpoint	1975	3.00	6.00	12.00

ARGYLES, THE (1)

See THE HOLLYWOOD ARGYLES.

ARGYLES, THE (2)

Number	Title (A Side/B Side)	Yr	VG	VG+	NM
45s					
BALLY					
1030	Moonbeam/Every Time You Smile	1957	10.00	20.00	40.00

ARIELS, THE

Number	Title (A Side/B Side)	Yr	VG	VG+	NM
45s					
BRENT					
7060	Feels Like I'm Cryin'/I Love You	1967	15.00	30.00	60.00

ARISTOCATS, THE

Number	Title (A Side/B Side)	Yr	VG	VG+	NM
Albums					
HIFI					
J-610 [M]	Boogie and Blues	1959	7.50	15.00	30.00
JS-610 [S]	Boogie and Blues	1959	10.00	20.00	40.00

ARISTOCRATS, THE

Number	Title (A Side/B Side)	Yr	VG	VG+	NM
45s					
ARGO					
5275	Maid of the Mist/Vagabonds	1957	6.25	12.50	25.00
ESSEX					
366	Believe Me/I'm Waiting for Ships	1954	15.00	30.00	60.00

ARLINGTON, BRUCE

Number	Title (A Side/B Side)	Yr	VG	VG+	NM
45s					
KING					
5918	You Made Me Cry/How Could You Know	1964	7.50	15.00	30.00

ARMAGEDDON (1)

Number	Title (A Side/B Side)	Yr	VG	VG+	NM
Albums					
AMOS					
73075	Armageddon	1970	6.25	12.50	25.00

ARMAGEDDON (2)

With KEITH RELF, ex-member of THE YARDBIRDS; his last material before his death.

Number	Title (A Side/B Side)	Yr	VG	VG+	NM
Albums					
A&M					
SP-4513	Armageddon	1975	5.00	10.00	20.00

ARMATRADING, JOAN

Number	Title (A Side/B Side)	Yr	VG	VG+	NM
45s					
A&M					
1235	Living for You/I Really Must Be Going	1988	—	2.00	4.00
1452	Lonely Lady/Together in Words and Music	1973	—	2.00	4.00
1865	Love and Affection/Help Yourself	1976	—	2.50	5.00
1898	Down to Zero/Like Fire	1976	—	2.00	4.00
1914	Water with the Wine/People	1977	—	2.00	4.00
1994	Show Some Emotion/No Way Out	1977	—	2.00	4.00
2018	Warm Love/No Way Out	1978	—	2.00	4.00
2102	Bottom to the Top/Your Letter	1978	—	2.00	4.00
2113	Barefoot and Pregnant/Your Letter	1979	—	2.00	4.00
2210	Rosie/Show Some Emotion	1979	—	2.00	4.00
2224	He Wants Up/Show Some Emotion	1980	—	2.00	4.00
2240	Me Myself I/Friends	1980	—	2.00	4.00
2262	Is It Tomorrow Yet/Ma-Me-O-Beach	1980	—	2.00	4.00
2381	Weakness in Me/Crying	1981	—	2.00	4.00
2400	I Wanna Hold You/Crying	1982	—	2.00	4.00
2538	Business Is Business/Drop the Pilot	1983	—	2.00	4.00
2564 [DJ]	Call Me Names (same on both sides)	1983	—	2.50	5.00
—Stock copies do not exist					
2622	Frustration/Heaven	1984	—	2.00	4.00
2712	Temptation/Talking to the Wall	1985	—	2.00	4.00
2751	Love Grows/Thinking Man	1985	—	2.00	4.00
2837	Kind Words (And a Real Good Heart)/Figure of Speech	1986	—	2.00	4.00
2868	Angel Man/Rivers on Fire	1986	—	2.00	4.00
Albums					
A&M					
SP-3141	Back to the Night	1980	2.00	4.00	8.00
—Reissue					
SP-3227	Whatever's For Us	1984	2.00	4.00	8.00
—Reissue					
SP-3228	Joan Armatrading	1984	2.00	4.00	8.00
—Reissue					
SP-3273	Show Some Emotion	1984	2.00	4.00	8.00
—Reissue					
SP-3302 [EP]	How Cruel	1979	2.00	4.00	8.00
SP-4382	Whatever's For Us	1974	3.00	6.00	12.00
SP-4525	Back to the Night	1975	3.00	6.00	12.00
SP-4588	Joan Armatrading	1976	2.50	5.00	10.00
SP-4663	Show Some Emotion	1977	2.50	5.00	10.00
SP-4732	To the Limit	1978	2.50	5.00	10.00
SP-4809	Me Myself I	1980	2.50	5.00	10.00
SP-4876	Walk Under Ladders	1981	2.50	5.00	10.00
SP-4912	The Key	1983	2.50	5.00	10.00
SP-4987	Track Record	1984	2.50	5.00	10.00
SP-5040	Secret Secrets	1985	2.50	5.00	10.00
SP-5130	Sleight of Hand	1986	2.50	5.00	10.00
SP-5211	The Shouting Stage	1988	2.50	5.00	10.00
75021 5298 1	Hearts and Flowers	1990	3.75	7.50	15.00
SP-8414 [DJ]	Joan Armatrading Live at Bijou Café	1977	5.00	10.00	20.00
—Promo-only "Superstars Radio Network" issue					
SP-12400 [EP]	How Cruel	1984	—	3.00	6.00
—Reissue					

ARMSTRONG, BRICE, AND THE AMERICAN GHOULS

Number	Title (A Side/B Side)	Yr	VG	VG+	NM
45s					
DUCHESS					
1020	The Fright Before Christmas/Happy Ghoul Tide	1962	5.00	10.00	20.00

ARMSTRONG, LOUIS

Also see BING CROSBY; ELLA FITZGERALD.

Number	Title (A Side/B Side)	Yr	VG	VG+	NM
45s					
ABC					
10982	What a Wonderful World/Cabaret	1967	2.00	4.00	8.00
11075	Hellzapoppin/The Sunshine of Love	1968	—	3.00	6.00
11126	Hello Brother/The Sunshine of Love	1968	—	3.00	6.00
AMSTERDAM					
85013	We Shall Overcome/(Instrumental)	1970	—	3.00	6.00
85016	Give Peace a Chance/The Creator Has a Master Plan	1970	2.00	4.00	8.00
85017 [DJ]	Here Is My Heart For Christmas/His Father Wore Long Hair	1970	2.50	5.00	10.00
85019	Everybody's Talkin'/(B-side unknown)	1970	—	2.50	5.00
85021	What a Wonderful World/His Father Wore Long Hair	1971	—	2.50	5.00
AUDIO FIDELITY					
097	Ain't Gonna Give Nobody None of My Jelly Roll/Frankie & Johnny	196?	2.00	4.00	8.00
173	Bill Bailey/The Creator Has a Master Plan	1971	—	3.00	6.00
AVCO EMBASSY					
4562	Miller's Cave/You Can Have Her	1971	—	3.00	6.00
A&M					
3010	What a Wonderful World/Game of Love	1988	—	2.00	4.00
—B-side by Wayne Fontana and the Mindbenders					

Number	Title (A Side/B Side)	Yr	VG	VG+	NM
3010 [PS]	What a Wonderful World/Game of Love	1988	—	2.00	4.00
—"Good Morning Vietnam" sleeve					
BRUNSWICK					
55318	Daydream/Northern Boulevard Blues	1967	—	3.00	6.00
55328	Louie's Dream/Step Down, Brother, Next Case	1967	—	3.00	6.00
55350	Rosie/You'll Never Walk Alone	1967	—	3.00	6.00
55360	Happy Time/Willkomen	1968	—	3.00	6.00
55380	Talk to the Animals/I Will Wait for You	1968	—	3.00	6.00
55395	I Believe/Sunrise, Sunset	1968	—	3.00	6.00
55457	I Believe/You'll Never Walk Alone	1971	—	2.50	5.00
55474	Willkomen/Sunrise, Sunset	1972	—	2.50	5.00
55534	'Twas the Night Before Christmas/(B-side unknown)	1976	2.00	4.00	8.00
BUENA VISTA					
F-465	Ten Feet Off the Ground/'Bout Time	1968	3.75	7.50	15.00
F-465 [PS]	Ten Feet Off the Ground/'Bout Time	1968	6.25	12.50	25.00
F-466	The Bare Necessities/Louis	1968	3.75	7.50	15.00
F-469	Bibbidi-Bobbidi-Boo/Zip-a-Dee-Doo-Dah	1968	3.75	7.50	15.00
F-470	Heigh-Ho/When You Wish Upon a Star	1968	3.75	7.50	15.00
F-471	The Ballad of Davy Crocket/Chim-Chim-Cheree	1968	5.00	10.00	20.00
F-489	When You Wish Upon a Star/Zip-a-Dee-Doo-Dah	1972	2.50	5.00	10.00
COLUMBIA					
40587	A Theme from the Threepenny Opera (Mack the Knife)Back O' Town Blues	1956	3.75	7.50	15.00
40662	When the Red, Red Robin Comes Bob, Bob, Bobbin' Along/Six Foot Four	1956	3.00	6.00	12.00
40711	The Faithful Hussar/Six Foot Four	1956	3.00	6.00	12.00
41471	Mack the Knife/The Faithful Hussar	1959	2.50	5.00	10.00
CONTINENTAL					
1001	The Night Before Christmas/When the Saints Go Marching In	1971	—	2.50	5.00
1001 [PS]	The Night Before Christmas/When the Saints Go Marching In	1971	—	2.50	5.00
—With sticker: "Only 25 cents with purchase" of one of four brands of cigarette					
1001 [PS]	The Night Before Christmas/When The Saints Go Marching In	1971	—	3.00	6.00
—With sticker: "Free with purchase" of six-pack of Fresca					
DECCA					
27059	New Orleans Function (Part 1)/New Orleans Function (Part 2)	1950	5.00	10.00	20.00
27113	La Vie En Rose/C'est Si Bon	1950	5.00	10.00	20.00
27187	That's for Me (Part 1)/Russian Lullaby (Part 2)	1950	3.00	6.00	12.00
27188	That's for Me (Part 2)/Russian Lullaby (Part 1)	1950	3.00	6.00	12.00
27189	Fine and Dandy/I Surrender Dear (Part 2)	1950	3.00	6.00	12.00
27190	Baby Won't You Please Come Home/I Surrender Dear (Part 1)	1950	3.00	6.00	12.00
27191	Panama (Part 1)/Bugle Call Rag (Part 3)	1950	3.00	6.00	12.00
27192	Panama (Part 2)/Bugle Call Rag (Part 2)	1950	3.00	6.00	12.00
27193	New Orleans Function (Part 1)/Bugle Call Rag (Part 1)	1950	3.00	6.00	12.00
27194	New Orleans Function (Part 2)/My Bucket's Got a Hole In It	1950	3.00	6.00	12.00
27254	Sit Down You're Rockin' the Boat/That's What the Man Said	1950	5.00	10.00	20.00
27481	If/You're Just in Love	1951	3.75	7.50	15.00
27616	Unless/That's for Me	1951	3.75	7.50	15.00
27720	(When We Are Dancing) I Get Ideas/A Kiss to Buid a Dream On	1951	3.75	7.50	15.00
27816	Because of You/Cold, Cold Heart	1951	3.75	7.50	15.00
27899	When It's Sleepy Time Down South/It's All in the Game	1952	3.75	7.50	15.00
—With Gordon Jenkins and His Orchestra					
27931	You're the Apple of My Eye/Big Butter and Egg Man	1952	3.75	7.50	15.00
28095	Royal Garden Blues (Part 2)/Muskrat Ramble (Part 1)	1952	3.00	6.00	12.00
28096	Royal Garden Blues (Part 1)/Muskrat Ramble (Part 2)	1952	3.00	6.00	12.00
—Above two with Edward "Kid" Ory					
28097	Lover/Black and Blue	1952	3.00	6.00	12.00
28098	Mahogany Hall Stomp/Since I Fell for You	1952	3.00	6.00	12.00
28099	I Cried for You (Part 1)/Tea for Two (Part 2)	1952	3.00	6.00	12.00
28100	I Cried for You (Part 2)/Tea for Two (Part 1)	1952	3.00	6.00	12.00
—Above two with Velma Middleton					
28101	Stars Fell on Alabama (Part 1)/Stars Fell on Alabama (Part 2)	1952	3.00	6.00	12.00
28102	Boff Boff/C Jam Blues	1952	3.00	6.00	12.00
28103	Body and Soul (Part 1)/How High the Moon (Part 2)	1952	3.00	6.00	12.00
28104	Body and Soul (Part 2)/How High the Moon (Part 1)	1952	3.00	6.00	12.00
—Above two with Barney B					
28105	On the Sunny Side of the Street (Part 1)/That's My Desire (Part 2)	1952	3.00	6.00	12.00
28106	On the Sunny Side of the Street (Part 2)/That's My Desire (Part 1)	1952	3.00	6.00	12.00
28107	High Society/Baby Won't You Please Come Home	1952	3.00	6.00	12.00
28108	Steak Face (Part 1)/Steak Face (Part 2)	1952	3.00	6.00	12.00
28169	Back Home Again in Indiana (Part 1)/Way Down Yonder in New Orleans (Part 2)	1952	3.00	6.00	12.00
28170	Back Home Again in Indiana (Part 2)/Way Down Yonder in New Orleans (Part 1)	1952	3.00	6.00	12.00
28171	The Hucklebuck/Stardust (Part 2)	1952	3.00	6.00	12.00
28172	Baby It's Cold Outside/Stardust (Part 1)	1952	3.00	6.00	12.00
28173	Honeysuckle Rose/That's a Plenty	1952	3.00	6.00	12.00
28174	My Monday Date (Part 1)/My Monday Date (Part 4)	1952	3.00	6.00	12.00
28175	My Monday Date (Part 2)/My Monday Date (Part 3)	1952	3.00	6.00	12.00
28176	Big Daddy Blues/You Can Depend on Me	1952	3.00	6.00	12.00
28177	Kiss of Fire/Delicado	1952	3.75	7.50	15.00
28306	Once in a While/Confessin'	1952	3.75	7.50	15.00
28372	That's My Desire/Baby It's Cold Outside	1952	3.75	7.50	15.00
28394	Takes Two to Tango/I Laughed at Love	1952	3.75	7.50	15.00

Number	Title (A Side/B Side)	Yr	VG	VG+	NM
28443	White Christmas/Winter Wonderland	1952	3.75	7.50	15.00
28524	Chlo-E/Listen to the Mocking Bird	1953	3.75	7.50	15.00
28628	Your Cheatin' Heart/Congratulations to Someone	1953	3.75	7.50	15.00
28704	April in Portugal/Ramona	1953	3.75	7.50	15.00
28803	The Dummy Song/Sittin' in the Sun	1953	3.75	7.50	15.00
28943	'Zat You, Santa Claus?/Cool Yule	1953	3.75	7.50	15.00
28995	The Gypsy/I Can't Afford to Miss This Dream	1954	3.75	7.50	15.00
29102	Basin Street Blues (Part 1)/Basin Street Blues (Part 2)	1954	3.75	7.50	15.00
29117	On a Coconut Island/To You Sweetheart Aloha	1954	3.75	7.50	15.00
29153	The Whiffenpoof Song/Bye and Bye	1954	3.75	7.50	15.00
—With Gordon Jenkins and His Orchestra					
29256	Skokiaan (Part 1)/Skokiaan (Part 2)	1954	3.75	7.50	15.00
29280	Muskrat Ramble/Someday You'll Be Sorry	1954	3.75	7.50	15.00
29352	Trees/Spooks	1954	3.75	7.50	15.00
29421	Sincerely/Pledging My Love	1955	3.75	7.50	15.00
29546	Pretty Little Missy/Baby Your Sleep Is Showing	1955	3.75	7.50	15.00
29694	Only You (And You Alone)/Moments to Remember	1955	3.75	7.50	15.00
29710	Christmas Night in Harlem/Christmas in New Orleans	1955	3.75	7.50	15.00
29921	Lazy Bones/Easy Street	1956	3.00	6.00	12.00
—With Gary Crosby					
30091	Blueberry Hill/That Lucky Old Sun	1956	3.00	6.00	12.00
30188	This Younger Generation/In Pursuit of Happiness	1957	2.50	5.00	10.00
30309	The Prisoner's Song/You're a Heavenly Thing	1957	2.50	5.00	10.00
30624	Nobody Knows the Trouble I've Seen/When You're Smiling	1958	2.50	5.00	10.00
30771	I Love Jazz/Mardi Gras March	1958	2.50	5.00	10.00
30860	I'll String Along with You/On My Way (Out on My Traveling Shoes)	1959	2.50	5.00	10.00
30980	Only You (And You Alone)/Onkel Satchmo's Lullaby	1960	2.50	5.00	10.00
DOT					
15941	The Five Pennies Saints/Just the Blues	1959	2.50	5.00	10.00
—With Danny Kaye					
15991	Battle Hymn of the Republic/Lullaby in Ragtime	1959	2.50	5.00	10.00
—With Red Nichols					
KAPP					
573	Hello, Dolly!/A Lot of Livin' to Do	1964	—	3.00	6.00
573 [PS]	Hello, Dolly!/A Lot of Livin' to Do	1964	2.50	5.00	10.00
597	I Still Get Jealous/Someday	1964	—	3.00	6.00
597 [PS]	I Still Get Jealous/Someday	1964	2.50	5.00	10.00
901	You Are Woman, I Am Man/Life of the Party	1968	—	3.00	6.00
977	Kinda Love Song/Someday	1969	—	3.00	6.00
2145	That's All I Want the World to Remember Me By/Hello, Dolly!	1971	—	2.50	5.00
MERCURY					
72338	So Long Dearie/Pretty Little Missy	1964	2.00	4.00	8.00
72338 [PS]	So Long Dearie/Pretty Little Missy	1964	3.00	6.00	12.00
72371	By and By/Faith	1964	2.00	4.00	8.00
72495	Circle of Your Arms/Short But Sweet	1965	2.00	4.00	8.00
72574	Mame/Tin Roof Blues	1966	2.00	4.00	8.00
72593	Cheesecake/Bye 'N' Bye	1966	2.00	4.00	8.00
MGM					
12809	Someday You'll Be Sorry/The Beat Generation	1959	3.00	6.00	12.00
RCA VICTOR					
47-4004	Rockin' Chair/Save It, Pretty Mama	1950	3.75	7.50	15.00
47-4005	Ain't Misbehavin'/Pennies from Heaven	1950	3.75	7.50	15.00
47-4006	Saint James Infirmary/Back o' Town Blues	1950	3.75	7.50	15.00
UNITED ARTISTS					
50251	No Time Is Good Goodbye Time/We're a Home	1968	—	3.00	6.00
50617	We Have All the Time in the World/Pretty Little Missy	1969	—	3.00	6.00
VERVE					
10182	Nobody Knows the Troubles I've Seen/That Old Feeling	1959	3.00	6.00	12.00

7-Inch Extended Plays

Number	Title (A Side/B Side)	Yr	VG	VG+	NM
COLUMBIA					
B-2540	*Mack the Knife/Ain't Misbehavin'/St, Louis Blues	1958	5.00	10.00	20.00
B-2540 [PS]	Louis Armstrong (Hall of Fame Series)	1958	5.00	10.00	20.00
DECCA					
ED 2012	Kiss of Fire/I'll Walk Alone//Takes Two to Tango/Sit Down, You're Rocking the Boat	195?	3.75	7.50	15.00
ED 2012 [PS]	Louis Armstrong, Vol. 1	195?	3.75	7.50	15.00

Albums

Number	Title	Yr	VG	VG+	NM
ABC					
S-650	What a Wonderful World	1968	7.50	15.00	30.00
ACCORD					
SN-7161	Mr. Music	1982	2.50	5.00	10.00
AMSTERDAM					
AMS 12009	Louis Armstrong and His Friends	1970	3.75	7.50	15.00
ARCHIVE OF FOLK AND JAZZ					
258	Louis "Satchmo" Armstrong	197?	3.00	6.00	12.00
312	Louis Armstrong, Vol. 2	197?	2.50	5.00	10.00
AUDIO FIDELITY					
AFLP-1930 [M]	Louis Armstrong Plays King Oliver	1960	7.50	15.00	30.00
AFLP-2128 [M]	Ain't Gonna Give Nobody None of My Jelly Roll	1964	3.75	7.50	15.00
AFLP-2132 [M]	The Best of Louis Armstrong	1964	3.75	7.50	15.00
AFSD-5930 [S]	Louis Armstrong Plays King Oliver	1960	10.00	20.00	40.00
AFSD-6128 [S]	Ain't Gonna Give Nobody None of My Jelly Roll	1964	5.00	10.00	20.00
AFSD-6132 [S]	The Best of Louis Armstrong	1964	5.00	10.00	20.00
AFSD-6241	Louis Armstrong	196?	3.75	7.50	15.00
BIOGRAPH					
C-5	Great Soloists	1973	3.00	6.00	12.00
C-6	Louis Armstrong Plays the Blues	1973	3.00	6.00	12.00
BLUEBIRD					
AXM2-5519 [(2)]	Young Louis (1932-1933)	1984	3.00	6.00	12.00
5920-1-RB [(2)]	Pops: The 1940s Small Band Sides	1987	3.75	7.50	15.00
8310-1-RB	What a Wonderful World	1988	2.50	5.00	10.00
9759-1-RB	Louis Armstrong & His Orchestra 1932-33: Laughin' Louie	1989	3.00	6.00	12.00

Number	Title (A Side/B Side)	Yr	VG	VG+	NM
BRUNSWICK					
BL 58004 [10]	Armstrong Classics	1950	25.00	50.00	100.00
BL 754136	I Will Wait for You	1968	3.75	7.50	15.00
BUENA VISTA					
BV-4044	Disney Swings the Satchmo Way	1968	10.00	20.00	40.00
CHIAROSCURO					
2002	Snake Rag	1977	3.00	6.00	12.00
2003	Great Alternatives	1977	3.00	6.00	12.00
2006	Sweetheart	1977	3.00	6.00	12.00
COLUMBIA					
CL 591 [M]	Louis Armstrong Plays W.C. Handy	1954	10.00	20.00	40.00
CL 708 [M]	Satch Plays Fats	1955	10.00	20.00	40.00
CL 840 [M]	Ambassador Satch	1956	10.00	20.00	40.00
CL 851 [M]	The Louis Armstrong Story, Volume 1	1956	7.50	15.00	30.00
CL 852 [M]	The Louis Armstrong Story, Volume 2	1956	7.50	15.00	30.00
CL 853 [M]	The Louis Armstrong Story, Volume 3	1956	7.50	15.00	30.00
CL 854 [M]	The Louis Armstrong Story, Volume 4	1956	7.50	15.00	30.00
CL 1077 [M]	Satchmo the Great	1957	7.50	15.00	30.00
CL 2638 [M]	Louis Armstrong's Greatest Hits	1967	5.00	10.00	20.00
ML 4383 [M]	The Louis Armstrong Story, Volume 1	1951	12.50	25.00	50.00
ML 4384 [M]	The Louis Armstrong Story, Volume 2	1951	12.50	25.00	50.00
ML 4385 [M]	The Louis Armstrong Story, Volume 3	1951	12.50	25.00	50.00
ML 4386 [M]	The Louis Armstrong Story, Volume 4	1951	12.50	25.00	50.00
CL 6335 [10]	Louis Armstrong Plays W.C. Handy, Volume 2	1955	10.00	20.00	40.00
CS 9438 [R]	Louis Armstrong's Greatest Hits	1967	3.00	6.00	12.00
PC 9438 [R]	Louis Armstrong's Greatest Hits	198?	2.00	4.00	8.00
—Budget-line reissue					
CG 30416 [(2)]	The Genius of Louis Armstrong, Vol. 1	1971	3.75	7.50	15.00
COLUMBIA MUSICAL TREASURIES					
P4M 5676 [(4)]	40 Greatest Hits	197?	5.00	10.00	20.00
DECCA					
DX 108 [(2) M]	Satchmo at Symphony Hall	1954	18.75	37.50	75.00
—Black labels, silver print					
DX 155 [(4) M]	Satchmo, A Musical Autobiography	1956	25.00	50.00	100.00
—Black labels, silver print					
DXM 155 [(4) M]	Satchmo, A Musical Autobiography	1960	10.00	20.00	40.00
—Black labels with color bars					
DXB 183 [(2) M]	The Best of Louis Armstrong	196?	7.50	15.00	30.00
DL 4137 [M]	Satchmo's Golden Favorites	1961	5.00	10.00	20.00
DL 4227 [M]	I Love Jazz	1962	5.00	10.00	20.00
DL 4230 [M]	Satchmo, A Musical Autobiography, 1926-1927	1962	6.25	12.50	25.00
DL 4245 [M]	King Louis	1962	5.00	10.00	20.00
DL 4330 [M]	Satchmo, A Musical Autobiography, 1928-1930	1962	6.25	12.50	25.00
DL 4331 [M]	Satchmo, A Musical Autobiography, 1930-1934	1962	6.25	12.50	25.00
DL 5225 [10]	New Orleans to New York	1950	18.75	37.50	75.00
DL 5279 [10]	New Orleans Days	1950	18.75	37.50	75.00
DL 5280 [10]	Jazz Concert	1950	18.75	37.50	75.00
DL 5401 [10]	Satchmo Serenades	1952	18.75	37.50	75.00
DL 5532 [10]	Latter-Day Louis	1954	18.75	37.50	75.00
DL 5536 [10]	Louis Armstrong-Gordon Jenkins	1954	18.75	37.50	75.00
DXSB 7183 [(2) R]	The Best of Louis Armstrong	196?	3.75	7.50	15.00
DL 8037 [M]	Satchmo at Symphony Hall, Volume 1	1954	10.00	20.00	40.00
—Black label, silver print					
DL 8037 [M]	Satchmo at Symphony Hall, Volume 1	1960	3.75	7.50	15.00
—Black label with color bars					
DL 8038 [M]	Satchmo at Symphony Hall, Volume 2	1954	10.00	20.00	40.00
—Black label, silver print					
DL 8038 [M]	Satchmo at Symphony Hall, Volume 2	1960	3.75	7.50	15.00
—Black label with color bars					
DL 8041 [M]	Satchmo at Pasadena	1954	10.00	20.00	40.00
—Black label, silver print					
DL 8041 [M]	Satchmo at Pasadena	1960	3.75	7.50	15.00
—Black label with color bars					
DL 8126 [M]	Satchmo Sings	1955	10.00	20.00	40.00
—Black label, silver print					
DL 8126 [M]	Satchmo Sings	1960	3.75	7.50	15.00
—Black label with color bars					
DL 8168 [M]	Louis Armstrong at the Crescendo, Volume 1	1955	10.00	20.00	40.00
—Black label, silver print					
DL 8169 [M]	Louis Armstrong at the Crescendo, Volume 2	1955	10.00	20.00	40.00
—Black label, silver print					
DL 8211 [M]	Satchmo Serenades	1956	10.00	20.00	40.00
—Black label, silver print					
DL 8211 [M]	Satchmo Serenades	1960	3.75	7.50	15.00
—Black label with color bars					
DL 8283 [M]	New Orleans Jazz	1956	10.00	20.00	40.00
—Black label, silver print					
DL 8283 [M]	New Orleans Jazz	1960	3.75	7.50	15.00
—Black label with color bars					
DL 8284 [M]	Jazz Classics	1956	10.00	20.00	40.00
—Black label, silver print					
DL 8284 [M]	Jazz Classics	1960	3.75	7.50	15.00
—Black label with color bars					
DL 8327 [M]	Satchmo's Collector's Items	1957	10.00	20.00	40.00
—Black label, silver print					
DL 8327 [M]	Satchmo's Collector's Items	1960	3.75	7.50	15.00
—Black label with color bars					
DL 8329 [M]	New Orleans Nights	1957	10.00	20.00	40.00
—Black label, silver print					
DL 8329 [M]	New Orleans Nights	1960	3.75	7.50	15.00
—Black label with color bars					
DL 8329 [M]	New Orleans Nights	1960	3.75	7.50	15.00
—Black label with color bars					
DL 8330 [M]	Satchmo on Stage	1957	10.00	20.00	40.00
—Black label, silver print					
DL 8330 [M]	Satchmo on Stage	1960	3.75	7.50	15.00
—Black label with color bars					
DL 8488 [M]	Louis and the Angels	1957	10.00	20.00	40.00
—Black label, silver print					
DL 8488 [M]	Louis and the Angels	1960	3.75	7.50	15.00
—Black label with color bars					
DL 8741 [M]	Louis and the Good Book	1958	10.00	20.00	40.00
—Black label, silver print					
DL 8741 [M]	Louis and the Good Book	1960	3.75	7.50	15.00
—Black label with color bars					

Number	Title (A Side/B Side)	Yr	VG	VG+	NM
DL 8840 [M]	Satchmo in Style	1958	10.00	20.00	40.00
—Black label, silver print					
DL 8840 [M]	Satchmo in Style	1960	3.75	7.50	15.00
—Black label with color bars					
DL 8963 [M]	Satchmo, A Musical Autobiography, 1923-1925	1960	6.25	12.50	25.00
DL 9225 [M]	Rare Items (1935-1944)	196?	5.00	10.00	20.00
DL 9233 [M]	Young Louis the Sideman (1924-1927)	196?	5.00	10.00	20.00
DL 74137 [R]	Satchmo's Golden Favorites	1961	3.00	6.00	12.00
DL 74227 [R]	I Love Jazz	1962	3.00	6.00	12.00
DL 74245 [R]	King Louis	1962	3.00	6.00	12.00
DL 74330 [R]	A Musical Autobiography, 1928-1930	1962	3.00	6.00	12.00
DL 78963 [R]	Satchmo, A Musical Autobiography, 1923-1925	196?	3.00	6.00	12.00
DL 79225 [R]	Rare Items (1935-1944)	196?	3.00	6.00	12.00
DL 79233 [R]	Young Louis the Sideman (1924-1927)	196?	3.00	6.00	12.00
GNP CRESCENDO					
9050	Pasadena Concert, Vol. II	1987	2.50	5.00	10.00
11001 [(2)]	An Evening with Louis Armstrong	1977	3.75	7.50	15.00
HARMONY					
HS 11316	Louis Armstrong	197?	3.00	6.00	12.00
KH 31236	The Louis Armstrong Saga	1971	3.00	6.00	12.00
KAPP					
KL-1364 [M]	Hello, Dolly!	1964	3.00	6.00	12.00
KS-3364 [S]	Hello, Dolly!	1964	3.75	7.50	15.00
MCA					
538	Hello, Dolly!	197?	2.50	5.00	10.00
—Reissue of Kapp LP					
1300	Louis and the Good Book	197?	2.50	5.00	10.00
—Reissue of Decca 8741					
1301	Young Louis the Sideman	197?	2.50	5.00	10.00
—Reissue of Decca 9233					
1304	Back in New York	197?	2.50	5.00	10.00
1306	Louis with Guest Stars	197?	2.50	5.00	10.00
1312	Swing That Music!	197?	2.50	5.00	10.00
1316	Satchmo Serenades	197?	2.50	5.00	10.00
—Reissue of Decca 8211					
1322	Satchmo's Collector's Items	197?	2.50	5.00	10.00
—Reissue of Decca 8327					
1334	Satchmo For Ever!	197?	2.50	5.00	10.00
1335	Old Favorites	197?	2.50	5.00	10.00
2-4013 [(2)]	Louis Armstrong at the Crescendo	197?	3.00	6.00	12.00
—Reissue of Decca 8168/8169 in one sleeve					
2-4035 [(2)]	The Best of Louis Armstrong	197?	3.00	6.00	12.00
—Reissue of Decca 7183					
2-4057 [(2)]	Satchmo at Symphony Hall	197?	3.00	6.00	12.00
—Reissue of Decca 108					
10006 [(4)]	Satchmo, A Musical Autobiography	197?	6.25	12.50	25.00
—Reissue of Decca 155					
25204	What a Wonderful World	1988	2.50	5.00	10.00
—Reissue of ABC 650					
42328	Louis Armstrong of New Orleans	1990	3.00	6.00	12.00
MERCURY					
MG-21081 [M]	Louis Armstrong Sings Louis Armstrong	1965	3.00	6.00	12.00
SR-61081 [S]	Louis Armstrong Sings Louis Armstrong	1965	3.75	7.50	15.00
METRO					
M-510 [M]	Hello, Louis	1965	3.00	6.00	12.00
MS-510 [S]	Hello, Louis	1965	3.75	7.50	15.00
MILESTONE					
2010	Early Portrait	197?	2.50	5.00	10.00
47017 [(2)]	Louis Armstrong and King Oliver	197?	3.00	6.00	12.00
MOSAIC					
MQ8-146 [(8)]	The Complete Decca Studio Recordings of Louis Armstrong and the All-Stars	199?	37.50	75.00	150.00
MURRAY HILL					
930633 [(2)]	Louis Armstrong Plays Dixieland Trumpet	197?	3.75	7.50	15.00
PABLO					
2310941	Mack the Knife	1990	3.00	6.00	12.00
PAIR					
PDL2-1042 [(2)]	The Jazz Legend	1986	3.00	6.00	12.00
PAUSA					
9018	The Greatest of Louis Armstrong	1983	2.50	5.00	10.00
RCA VICTOR					
LPT 7 [10]	Louis Armstrong Town Hall Concert	1951	20.00	40.00	80.00
LJM-1005 [M]	Louis Armstrong Sings the Blues	1954	12.50	25.00	50.00
LPM-1443 [M]	Town Hall Concert Plus	1957	12.50	25.00	50.00
LPM-2322 [M]	A Rare Batch of Satch	1961	6.25	12.50	25.00
LPM-2971 [M]	Louis Armstrong in the '30s/in the '40s	1964	5.00	10.00	20.00
LSP-2971(e) [R]	Louis Armstrong in the '30s/in the '40s	1964	3.00	6.00	12.00
VPM-6044 [(2)]	July 4, 1900/July 6, 1971	1971	5.00	10.00	20.00
RIVERSIDE					
RLP 12-101 [M]	The Young Louis Armstrong	1956	20.00	40.00	80.00
—White label, blue print					
RLP 12-101 [M]	The Young Louis Armstrong	195?	10.00	20.00	40.00
—Blue label					
RLP 12-122 [M]	Louis Armstrong 1923	1956	20.00	40.00	80.00
—White label, blue print					
RLP 12-122 [M]	Louis Armstrong 1923	195?	10.00	20.00	40.00
—Blue label					
RLP-1001 [10]	Louis Armstrong Plays the Blues	1953	25.00	50.00	100.00
RLP-1029 [10]	Louis Armstrong with King Oliver's Creole Jazz Band 1923	1953	25.00	50.00	100.00
SEAGULL					
LG-8206	Greatest Hits: Live in Concert	198?	3.00	6.00	12.00
STORYVILLE					
4012	Louis Armstrong and His All-Stars	1980	2.50	5.00	10.00
SWING					
SW-8450	Louis and the Big Bands	1984	2.50	5.00	10.00
VANGUARD					
VSD 91/92 [(2)]	Essential Louis Armstrong	1977	3.75	7.50	15.00
VMS 73129	Essential Louis Armstrong, Vol. 1	1986	2.00	4.00	8.00
VERVE					
MGV-4012 [M]	Louis Under the Stars	1957	12.50	25.00	50.00
MGVS-4012	Louis Under the Stars	199?	6.25	12.50	25.00
—Classic Records reissue					

Number	Title (A Side/B Side)	Yr	VG	VG+	NM
V-4012 [M]	Louis Under the Stars	1961	5.00	10.00	20.00
V6-4012 [S]	Louis Under the Stars	1961	3.75	7.50	15.00
MGV-4035 [M]	I've Got the World on a String	1959	12.50	25.00	50.00
MGVS-4035	I've Got the World on a String	199?	6.25	12.50	25.00
—Classic Records reissue					
V-4035 [M]	I've Got the World on a String	1961	5.00	10.00	20.00
V6-4035 [S]	I've Got the World on a String	1961	3.75	7.50	15.00
MGVS-6044 [S]	Louis Under the Stars	1960	10.00	20.00	40.00
MGVS-6101 [S]	I've Got the World on a String	1960	10.00	20.00	40.00
V-8569 [M]	The Essential Louis A.	1963	3.00	6.00	12.00
V6-8569 [S]	The Essential Louis A.	1963	3.75	7.50	15.00
V-8595 [M]	The Best of Louis Armstrong	1964	3.00	6.00	12.00
V6-8595 [S]	The Best of Louis Armstrong	1964	3.75	7.50	15.00
VOCALION					
VL 3851 [M]	Here's Louis Armstrong	196?	3.75	7.50	15.00
VL 73851 [R]	Here's Louis Armstrong	196?	2.50	5.00	10.00
VL 73871 [R]	The One and Only Louis Armstrong	1968	2.50	5.00	10.00
WING					
SR-16381	Great Louis	196?	2.50	5.00	10.00

ARMSTRONG, LOUIS, AND SIDNEY BECHET

Albums

Number	Title (A Side/B Side)	Yr	VG	VG+	NM
JOLLY ROGER					
5029 [M]	Louis Armstrong and Sidney Bechet	195?	10.00	20.00	40.00

ARMSTRONG, LOUIS, AND DUKE ELLINGTON

Also see each artist's individual listings.

Albums

Number	Title (A Side/B Side)	Yr	VG	VG+	NM
MOBILE FIDELITY					
2-155 [(2)]	The Great Reunion	1984	20.00	40.00	80.00
—Audiophile vinyl					
PICKWICK					
PC-3033	Louis Armstrong and Duke Ellington	196?	2.50	5.00	10.00
ROULETTE					
RE-108 [(2)]	The Duke Ellington-Louis Armstrong Era	1973	3.75	7.50	15.00
R 52074 [M]	Together for the First Time	1961	6.25	12.50	25.00
SR 52074 [S]	Together for the First Time	1961	5.00	10.00	20.00
R 52103 [M]	The Great Reunion	1963	5.00	10.00	20.00
SR 52103 [S]	The Great Reunion	1963	6.25	12.50	25.00

ARMSTRONG, LOUIS, AND THE MILLS BROTHERS

Also see each artist's individual listings.

45s

Number	Title (A Side/B Side)	Yr	VG	VG+	NM
DECCA					
28984	My Walking Stick/Marie	1953	3.75	7.50	15.00

Albums

Number	Title (A Side/B Side)	Yr	VG	VG+	NM
DECCA					
DL 5509 [10]	Louis Armstrong and the Mills Brothers	1954	15.00	30.00	60.00

ARMSTRONG, LOUIS, AND OSCAR PETERSON

Also see each artist's individual listings.

Albums

Number	Title (A Side/B Side)	Yr	VG	VG+	NM
VERVE					
MGVS-6062 [S]	Louis Armstrong Meets Oscar Peterson	1960	10.00	20.00	40.00
MGV-8322 [M]	Louis Armstrong Meets Oscar Peterson	1959	12.50	25.00	50.00
V-8322 [M]	Louis Armstrong Meets Oscar Peterson	1961	5.00	10.00	20.00
V6-8322 [S]	Louis Armstrong Meets Oscar Peterson	1961	3.75	7.50	15.00

ARNAZ, DESI

45s

Number	Title (A Side/B Side)	Yr	VG	VG+	NM
COLUMBIA					
4-39937	I Love Lucy/There's a Brand New Baby	1953	10.00	20.00	40.00
RCA VICTOR					
47-2865	Tabu/Cuban Pete	1949	3.75	7.50	15.00
47-2866	Babalu/Brazil	1949	3.75	7.50	15.00
47-2867	Tico Tico/Peanut Vendor	1949	3.75	7.50	15.00
—The above three comprise a box set					

Albums

Number	Title (A Side/B Side)	Yr	VG	VG+	NM
RCA VICTOR					
LPM-3096 [10]	Babalu!	1954	30.00	60.00	120.00

ARNOLD, BILLY BOY

See BILLY BOY.

ARNOLD, EDDY

45s

Number	Title (A Side/B Side)	Yr	VG	VG+	NM
CURB					
73088	Cattle Call (with LeAnn Rimes)/I Walk Alone	1999	—	—	3.00
MGM					
14478	So Many Ways/Once in a While	1972	—	2.50	5.00
14535	If the Whole World Stopped Lovin'/My Son, I Wish You Everything	1973	—	2.00	4.00
14600	Oh, Oh, I'm Falling in Love Again/Anyway You Want Me	1973	—	2.00	4.00
14672	She's Got Everything I Need/I'm Glad You Happened to Me	1973	—	2.00	4.00
14711	Just for Old Times Sake/I Got This Thing About You	1974	—	2.00	4.00
14734	I Wish That I Had Loved You Better/Let It Be Love	1974	—	2.00	4.00
14769	Butterfly/If You Could Only Love Me Now	1974	—	2.00	4.00
14780	Red Roses for a Blue Lady/I Will	1975	—	2.00	4.00
14827	Middle of a Memoryl Just Had You on My Mind	1975	—	2.00	4.00
RCA					
2750-7-R	You Don't Miss a Thing/Just One Time	1990	—	2.00	4.00
PB-10794	Put Me Back Into Your World/Goodnight Irene	1976	—	2.00	4.00
PB-10899	(I Need You) All the Time/I've Never Loved Anyone More	1977	—	2.00	4.00
PB-11031	Freedom Ain't the Same as Being Free/Till You Can Make It On Your Own	1977	—	2.00	4.00
PB-11133	Where Lonely People Go/Penny Arcade	1977	—	2.00	4.00
PB-11257	Country Lovin'/I've So Much to Be Thankful For	1978	—	2.00	4.00
PB-11319	I'm the South/You Are My Sunshine	1978	—	2.00	4.00
PB-11422	If Everyone Had Someone Like You/You're a Beautiful Place to Be	1978	—	2.00	4.00
PB-11537	What In Her World Did I Do/Love of My Life	1979	—	2.00	4.00
PB-11668	Goodbye/You're So Good At Lovin' Me	1979	—	2.00	4.00
PB-11752	If I Ever Had to Say Goodbye to You/Love of My Life	1979	—	2.00	4.00
PB-11918	Let's Get It While the Gettin's Good/You Cared Enough (To Give Your Very Best)	1980	—	2.00	4.00
PB-12039	That's What I Get for Loving You/Undivided Love	1980	—	2.00	4.00
PB-12136	Don't Look Now (But We Just Fell in Love)/There's Women (Then There's My Woman)	1980	—	2.00	4.00
PB-12226	Bally-Hoo Days/Two Hearts Beat Better Than One	1981	—	2.00	4.00
PB-13000	All I'm Missing Is You/Don't It Break Your Heart	1981	—	2.00	4.00
PB-13094	Don't Give Up on Me/In Love with Loving You	1982	—	2.00	4.00
PB-13339	The Valley Below/Make the World Go Away	1982	—	2.00	4.00
PB-13452	The Blues Don't Care Who's Got 'Em/Wooden Heart	1983	—	2.00	4.00
62598	Out of the Blue/On a Night Like This	1993	—	2.00	4.00
RCA VICTOR					
PB-10701	Cowboy/Don't Let the Good Times Roll Away	1976	—	2.00	4.00
47-2729	Anytime/What a Fool I Was	1949	7.50	15.00	30.00
47-2730	Bouquet of Roses/Texarkana Baby	1949	7.50	15.00	30.00
47-2776	I'm Thinking Tonight of My Blue Eyes/Rockin' Alone	1949	7.50	15.00	30.00
47-2777	It Makes No Difference Now/Molly Darling	1949	7.50	15.00	30.00
47-2778	The Prisoner's Song/Seven Years with the Wrong Woman	1949	7.50	15.00	30.00
47-3310	That's How Much I Love You/Chained to a Memory	1949	6.25	12.50	25.00
47-3311	Will the Circle Be Unbroken/Who, At My Door, Is Standing	1949	6.25	12.50	25.00
47-4243	When My Blue Moon Turns to Gold Again/White Azaleas	1951	5.00	10.00	20.00
47-4244	When You and I Were Young, Maggie/Roll Along Kentucky Moon	1951	5.00	10.00	20.00
47-4245	That Little Boy of Mine/Sinner's Prayer	1951	5.00	10.00	20.00
47-4273	Somebody's Been Beating My Time/Heart Strings	1951	5.00	10.00	20.00
47-4413	Bundle of Southern Sunshine/Call Her Your Sweetheart	1951	5.00	10.00	20.00
47-4490	Take My Hand, Precious Lord/Open Thy Merciful Arms	1952	5.00	10.00	20.00
47-4569	Easy on the Eyes/Anything That's Part of You	1952	5.00	10.00	20.00
47-4597	Bouquet of Roses/Texarkana Baby	1952	5.00	10.00	20.00
47-4598	It's a Sin/Anytime	1952	5.00	10.00	20.00
47-4599	That's How Much I Love You/A Heart Full of Love	1952	5.00	10.00	20.00
47-4600	I'll Hold You in My Heart (Till I Can Hold You in My Arms)/Don't Rob Another Man's Castle	1952	5.00	10.00	20.00
47-4787	A Full Time Job/Shephard of My Heart	1952	5.00	10.00	20.00
47-4954	Older and Bolder/I'd Trade All My Tomorrows (For Just One Yesterday)	1952	5.00	10.00	20.00
47-5020	My Desire/I Want to Thank You Lord	1952	5.00	10.00	20.00
47-5108	Eddy's Song/Condemned Without a Trial	1952	5.00	10.00	20.00
47-5189	When Your Hair Has Turned to Silver/Angry	1953	5.00	10.00	20.00
47-5192	Moonlight and Roses/Missouri Waltz	1953	5.00	10.00	20.00
47-5193	You Always Hurt the One You Love/I'm Gonna Lock My Heart	1953	5.00	10.00	20.00
47-5196	The Old Rugged Cross/Have Thine Own Way, Lord	1953	5.00	10.00	20.00
47-5197	Someday Somewhere/When I've Done My Best	1953	5.00	10.00	20.00
47-5305	Free Home Demonstration/How's the World Treating You	1953	5.00	10.00	20.00
47-5415	Mama, Come Get Your Baby Boy/If I Never Get to Heaven	1953	5.00	10.00	20.00
47-5525	I Really Don't Want to Know/I'll Never Get Over You	1953	5.00	10.00	20.00
47-5601	Rose of Calvary/Prayer	1954	5.00	10.00	20.00
47-5634	My Everything/Second Fling	1954	5.00	10.00	20.00
47-5753	Chapel on the Hill/A Touch of God's Hand	1954	5.00	10.00	20.00
47-5805	This Is the Thanks I Get (For Loving You)/Hep Cat Baby	1954	5.00	10.00	20.00
47-5905	Christmas Can't Be Far Away/I'm Your Private Santa Claus	1954	5.00	10.00	20.00
47-6000	I've Been Thinking/Don't Forget	1955	3.75	7.50	15.00
47-6001	It Took a Miracle/I Always Have Someone to Turn To	1955	3.75	7.50	15.00
47-6069	Two Kinds of Love/In Time	1955	3.75	7.50	15.00
47-6139	The Cattle Call/The Kentuckian Song	1955	5.00	10.00	20.00
47-6198	Just Call Me Lonesome/That Do Make It Nice	1955	3.75	7.50	15.00
47-6290	The Richest Man/I Walked Alone Last Night	1955	3.75	7.50	15.00
47-6365	Trouble in Mind/When You Say Goodbye	1955	3.75	7.50	15.00
47-6407	Bayou Baby/Do You Know Where God Lives	1956	3.75	7.50	15.00
47-6502	You Don't Know Me/The Rockin' Mockin' Bird	1956	3.75	7.50	15.00
47-6601	Casey Jones (The Brave Engineer)/You Were Mine for Awhile	1956	3.75	7.50	15.00
47-6699	The Ballad of Wes Tancred/I Wouldn't Know Where to Begin	1956	3.75	7.50	15.00
47-6708	Mutual Admiration Society/If'n	1956	3.75	7.50	15.00
—With Jaye P. Morgan					
47-6773	A Dozen Hearts/A Good Lookin' Blonde	1956	3.75	7.50	15.00
47-6842	One/Do You Love Me	1957	3.00	6.00	12.00
—With Jaye P. Morgan					
47-6905	Gonna Find Me a Bluebird/Little Bit	1957	3.00	6.00	12.00
47-6975	Crazy Dream/Open Your Heart	1957	3.00	6.00	12.00
47-7040	Little Miss Sunbeam/When He Was Young	1957	3.00	6.00	12.00
47-7089	Wagon Wheels/You're Made Up for Everything	1957	3.00	6.00	12.00
47-7143	Too Soon to Know/I Need Somebody	1958	3.00	6.00	12.00
47-7221	Peck a Cheek/Before You Know It	1958	3.00	6.00	12.00
47-7292	The Day You Left Me/Real Love	1958	3.00	6.00	12.00
47-7340	Till You Come Back Again/I'm a Good Boy	1958	3.00	6.00	12.00
47-7435	Chip Off the Old Block/I'll Hold You in My Heart (Till I Can Hold You in My Arms)	1959	2.50	5.00	10.00
47-7542	Tennessee Stud/What's the Good (Of All This Love)	1959	2.50	5.00	10.00

Number	Title (A Side/B Side)	Yr	VG	VG+	NM
47-7619	Did It Rain/Sittin' By Sittin' Bull	1959	2.50	5.00	10.00
47-7661	Boot Hill/Johnny Reb, That's Me	1959	2.50	5.00	10.00
47-7727	Little Sparrow/My Arms Are a House	1960	2.50	5.00	10.00
47-7794	Before This Day Ends/Just Out of Reach	1960	2.50	5.00	10.00
47-7861	(Jim) I Wore a Tie Today/Just Call Me Lonesome	1961	2.50	5.00	10.00
47-7926	One Grain of Sand/The Worst Night of My Life	1961	2.50	5.00	10.00
47-7984	Tears Broke Out on Me/I'll Do As Much for You Someday	1962	2.00	4.00	8.00
47-8048	A Little Heartache/After Loving You	1962	2.00	4.00	8.00
47-8102	Does He Mean That Much to You/Tender Touch	1962	2.00	4.00	8.00
47-8160	Yesterday's Memories/Lonely Balladeer	1963	2.00	4.00	8.00
47-8160 [PS]	Yesterday's Memories/Lonely Balladeer	1963	3.75	7.50	15.00
47-8207	A Million Years or So/Just a Ribbon	1963	2.00	4.00	8.00
47-8253	Jealous Hearted Me/I Met Her Today	1963	2.00	4.00	8.00
47-8296	Molly/The Song of the Coo Coo	1963	2.00	4.00	8.00
47-8363	Sweet Adorable You/Why	1964	—	3.00	6.00
47-8445	I Thank My Lucky Stars/I Don't Cry No More	1964	—	3.00	6.00
47-8516	What's He Doing in My World/Laura Lee	1965	—	3.00	6.00
47-8632	I'm Letting You Go/The Days Gone By	1965	—	3.00	6.00
47-8679	Make the World Go Away/The Easy Way	1965	2.00	4.00	8.00
47-8679 [PS]	Make the World Go Away/The Easy Way	1965	3.75	7.50	15.00
47-8749	I Want to Go With You/Better Stop Tellin' Lies (About Me)	1965	2.00	4.00	8.00
47-8749 [PS]	I Want to Go With You/Better Stop Tellin' Lies (About Me)	1965	3.75	7.50	15.00
47-8818	The Last Word in Lonesome Is Me/Mary Claire Melvina Rebecca Jane	1966	—	3.00	6.00
47-8818 [PS]	The Last Word in Lonesome Is Me/Mary Claire Melvina Rebecca Jane	1966	3.00	6.00	12.00
47-8869	The Tip of My Fingers/Long, Long Friendship	1966	—	3.00	6.00
47-8869 [PS]	The Tip of My Fingers/Long, Long Friendship	1966	3.00	6.00	12.00
47-8965	Somebody Like Me/Taking Chances	1966	—	3.00	6.00
47-8965 [PS]	Somebody Like Me/Taking Chances	1966	3.00	6.00	12.00
47-9027	The Angel and the Stranger/The First Word	1966	—	3.00	6.00
47-9080	Lonely Again/Love on My Mind	1967	—	3.00	6.00
47-9182	Misty Blue/Calling Mary Names	1967	—	3.00	6.00
47-9265	Turn the World Around/The Long Ride Home	1967	—	3.00	6.00
47-9368	Here Comes Heaven/Baby That's Loving	1967	—	3.00	6.00
47-9387	Jolly Old St. Nicholas/This World of Ours	1967	2.00	4.00	8.00
47-9437	Here Comes the Rain, Baby/The World I Used to Know	1968	—	3.00	6.00
47-9525	It's Over/No Matter Whose Baby You Are	1968	—	3.00	6.00
47-9606	Then You Can Tell Me Goodbye/Apples, Raisins and Roses	1968	—	3.00	6.00
47-9667	They Don't Make Love Like They Used To/What a Wonderful World	1968	—	3.00	6.00
47-9801	Soul Deep/(Today) I Started Loving You Again	1969	—	3.00	6.00
47-9848	A Man's Kind of Woman/Living Under Pressure	1970	—	2.50	5.00
47-9889	From Heaven to Heartache/Ten Times Forever More	1970	—	2.50	5.00
47-9935	Portrait of My Woman/I Really Don't Want to Know	1970	—	2.50	5.00
47-9968	A Part of America Died/Call Me	1971	—	2.50	5.00
47-9993	Welcome to My World/It Ain't No Big Thing	1971	—	2.50	5.00
48-0001	Bouquet of Roses/Texarkana Baby	1949	12.50	25.00	50.00
—Originals on green vinyl					
48-0001	Bouquet of Roses/Texarkana Baby	1949	6.25	12.50	25.00
—Second pressings: Green label, black vinyl					
48-0001 [PS]	Bouquet of Roses/Texarkana Baby	1949	20.00	40.00	80.00
—Brown and dark brown title sleeve					
48-0002	Anytime/What a Fool I Was	1949	6.25	12.50	25.00
—Second pressings: Green label, black vinyl					
48-0002	Anytime/What a Fool I Was	1949	12.50	25.00	50.00
—Originals on green vinyl					
48-0016	I'm Thinking Tonight of My Blue Eyes/Rockin' Alone	1949	12.50	25.00	50.00
—Originals on green vinyl					
48-0016	I'm Thinking Tonight of My Blue Eyes/Rockin' Alone	1949	6.25	12.50	25.00
—Second pressings: Green label, black vinyl					
48-0017	It Makes No Difference Now/Molly Darling	1949	6.25	12.50	25.00
—Second pressings: Green label, black vinyl					
48-0017	It Makes No Difference Now/Molly Darling	1949	12.50	25.00	50.00
—Originals on green vinyl					
48-0018	The Prisoner's Song/Seven Years with the Wrong Woman	1949	12.50	25.00	50.00
—Originals on green vinyl					
48-0018	The Prisoner's Song/Seven Years with the Wrong Woman	1949	6.25	12.50	25.00
—Second pressings: Green label, black vinyl					
48-0019	Will the Circle Be Unbroken/Who at My Door Is Standing	1949	6.25	12.50	25.00
—Second pressings: Green label, black vinyl					
48-0019	Will the Circle Be Unbroken/Who at My Door Is Standing	1949	12.50	25.00	50.00
—Originals on green vinyl					
48-0025	A Heart Full of Love (For a Handful of Kisses)/Then I Turned and Walked Slowly Away	1949	12.50	25.00	50.00
—Originals on green vinyl					
48-0025	A Heart Full of Love (For a Handful of Kisses)/Then I Turned and Walked Slowly Away	1949	6.25	12.50	25.00
—Second pressings: Green label, black vinyl					
48-0026	Just a Little Lovin' (Will Go a Long, Long Way)/My Daddy Is Only a Picture	1949	12.50	25.00	50.00
—Originals on green vinyl					
48-0026	Just a Little Lovin' (Will Go a Long, Long Way)/My Daddy Is Only a Picture	1949	6.25	12.50	25.00
—Second pressings: Green label, black vinyl					
48-0030	I'll Hold You in My Heart (Till I Can Hold You in My Arms)/Don't Bother to Cry	1949	12.50	25.00	50.00
—Originals on green vinyl					
48-0030	I'll Hold You in My Heart (Till I Can Hold You in My Arms)/Don't Bother to Cry	1949	6.25	12.50	25.00
—Second pressings: Green label, black vinyl					
48-0042	There's Not a Thing (I Wouldn't Do for You)/Don't Rob Another Man's Castle	1949	12.50	25.00	50.00
—Originals on green vinyl					
48-0042	There's Not a Thing (I Wouldn't Do for You)/Don't Rob Another Man's Castle	1949	6.25	12.50	25.00
—Second pressings: Green label, black vinyl					
48-0080	I'm Throwing Rice (At the Girl That I Love)/Show Me the Way Back to Your Heart	1949	12.50	25.00	50.00
—Originals on green vinyl					
48-0080	I'm Throwing Rice (At the Girl That I Love)/Show Me the Way Back to Your Heart	1949	6.25	12.50	25.00
—Second pressings: Green label, black vinyl					
48-0127	C-H-R-I-S-T-M-A-S/Will Santa Come to Shanty Town	1949	12.50	25.00	50.00
—Originals on green vinyl					
48-0127	C-H-R-I-S-T-M-A-S/Will Santa Come to Shanty Town	1949	6.25	12.50	25.00
—Second pressings: Green label, black vinyl					
48-0136	The Nearest Thing to Heaven/The Cattle Call	1949	12.50	25.00	50.00
—Originals on green vinyl					
48-0136	The Nearest Thing to Heaven/The Cattle Call	1949	6.25	12.50	25.00
—Second pressings: Green label, black vinyl					
48-0137	There's No Wings on My Angel/You Know How Talk Gets Around	1949	12.50	25.00	50.00
—Originals on green vinyl					
48-0137	There's No Wings on My Angel/You Know How Talk Gets Around	1949	6.25	12.50	25.00
—Second pressings: Green label, black vinyl					
48-0138	Just a Little Lovin' (Will Go a Long, Long Way)/I'm Throwing Rice (At the Girl That I Love)	1949	12.50	25.00	50.00
—Originals on green vinyl					
48-0138	Just a Little Lovin' (Will Go a Long, Long Way)/I'm Throwing Rice (At the Girl That I Love)	1949	6.25	12.50	25.00
—Second pressings: Green label, black vinyl					
48-0150	Take Me in Your Arms and Hold Me/Mama and Daddy Broke My Heart	1949	12.50	25.00	50.00
—Originals on green vinyl					
48-0150	Take Me in Your Arms and Hold Me/Mama and Daddy Broke My Heart	1949	6.25	12.50	25.00
—Second pressings: Green label, black vinyl					
48-0165	The Lily of the Valley/Evil, Tempt Me Not	1950	12.50	25.00	50.00
—Originals on green vinyl					
48-0165	The Lily of the Valley/Evil, Tempt Me Not	1950	6.25	12.50	25.00
—Second pressings: Green label, black vinyl					
48-0166	When Jesus Beckons Me Home/Beautiful Isle	1950	12.50	25.00	50.00
—Originals on green vinyl					
48-0166	When Jesus Beckons Me Home/Beautiful Isle	1950	6.25	12.50	25.00
—Second pressings: Green label, black vinyl					
48-0167	Hills of Tomorrow/Softly and Tenderly	1950	12.50	25.00	50.00
—Originals on green vinyl					
48-0167	Hills of Tomorrow/Softly and Tenderly	1950	6.25	12.50	25.00
—Second pressings: Green label, black vinyl					
48-0174	That Wonderful Mother of Mine/Mother	1950	12.50	25.00	50.00
—Originals on green vinyl					
48-0174	That Wonderful Mother of Mine/Mother	1950	6.25	12.50	25.00
—Second pressings: Green label, black vinyl					
48-0175	Bring Roses to Her Now/I Wish I Had a Girl	1950	12.50	25.00	50.00
—Originals on green vinyl					
48-0175	Bring Roses to Her Now/I Wish I Had a Girl	1950	6.25	12.50	25.00
—Second pressings: Green label, black vinyl					
48-0176	My Mother's Sweet Voice/I Wouldn't Trade the Silver	1950	12.50	25.00	50.00
—Originals on green vinyl					
48-0176	My Mother's Sweet Voice/I Wouldn't Trade the Silver	1950	6.25	12.50	25.00
—Second pressings: Green label, black vinyl					
48-0197	To My Sorrow/Easy Rockin' Chair	1950	12.50	25.00	50.00
—Originals on green vinyl					
48-0197	To My Sorrow/Easy Rockin' Chair	1950	6.25	12.50	25.00
—Second pressings: Green label, black vinyl					
48-0198	It's a Sin/I Couldn't Believe It Was True	1950	12.50	25.00	50.00
—Originals on green vinyl					
48-0198	It's a Sin/I Couldn't Believe It Was True	1950	6.25	12.50	25.00
—Second pressings: Green label, black vinyl					
48-0199	What Is Life Without Love/Be Sure There's No Mistake	1950	12.50	25.00	50.00
—Originals on green vinyl					
48-0199	What Is Life Without Love/Be Sure There's No Mistake	1950	6.25	12.50	25.00
—Second pressings: Green label, black vinyl					
48-0300	Little Angel with the Dirty Face/Why Should I Cry?	1950	12.50	25.00	50.00
—Originals on green vinyl					
48-0300	Little Angel with the Dirty Face/Why Should I Cry?	1950	6.25	12.50	25.00
—Second pressings: Green label, black vinyl					
48-0342	Cuddle Buggin' Baby/Enclosed, One Broken Heart	1950	12.50	25.00	50.00
—Originals on green vinyl					
48-0342	Cuddle Buggin' Baby/Enclosed, One Broken Heart	1950	6.25	12.50	25.00
—Second pressings: Green label, black vinyl					
48-0382	The Lovebug Itch/A Prison Without Walls	1950	12.50	25.00	50.00
—Originals on green vinyl					
48-0382	The Lovebug Itch/A Prison Without Walls	1950	6.25	12.50	25.00
—Second pressings: Green label, black vinyl					
48-0390	White Christmas/Santa Claus Is Comin' to Town	1950	12.50	25.00	50.00
—Originals on green vinyl					
48-0390	White Christmas/Santa Claus Is Comin' to Town	1950	6.25	12.50	25.00
—Second pressings: Green label, black vinyl					
48-0412	There's Been a Change in Me/Tie Me to Your Apron Strings Again	1950	12.50	25.00	50.00
—Originals on green vinyl					
48-0412	There's Been a Change in Me/Tie Me to Your Apron Strings Again	1950	6.25	12.50	25.00
—Second pressings: Green label, black vinyl					

Number	Title (A Side/B Side)	Yr	VG	VG+	NM
48-0425	May the Good Lord Bless and Keep You/I'm Writing a Letter to the Lord	1951	12.50	25.00	50.00
—Originals on green vinyl					
48-0425	May the Good Lord Bless and Keep You/I'm Writing a Letter to the Lord	1951	5.00	10.00	20.00
—Second pressings: Green label, black vinyl					
48-0444	Kentucky Waltz/A Million Miles from Your Heart	1951	12.50	25.00	50.00
—Originals on green vinyl					
48-0444	Kentucky Waltz/A Million Miles from Your Heart	1951	5.00	10.00	20.00
—Second pressings: Green label, black vinyl					
48-0476	I Wanna Play House with You/Something Old, Something New	1951	6.25	12.50	25.00
48-0495	Jesus and the Atheist/He Knows	1951	6.25	12.50	25.00
74-0120	Please Don't Go/Heaven Below	1969	—	2.50	5.00
74-0175	But For Love/My Lady of Love	1969	—	2.50	5.00
74-0226	You Fool/You Don't Need Me Anymore	1969	—	2.50	5.00
74-0282	Since December/Morning of Our Mind	1969	—	2.50	5.00
74-0559	I Love You Dear/Long Life, Lots of Happiness	1971	—	2.50	5.00
74-0641	Lonely People/If It's Alright with You	1972	—	2.50	5.00
74-0705	Poison Red Berries/Just Out of Reach	1972	—	2.50	5.00
74-0747	Lucy/The Last Letter	1972	—	2.50	5.00
74-0842	An Angel Sleeps Beside Me/Sweet Bunch of Daisies	1972	—	—	—
—Unreleased					

7-Inch Extended Plays

RCA VICTOR

Number	Title (A Side/B Side)	Yr	VG	VG+	NM
547-0100	I'll Hold You in My Heart (Till I Can Hold You in My Arms)/A Heart Full of Love (For a Handful of Kisses)//Anytime/Texarkana Baby	1952	5.00	10.00	20.00
—Part of 2-EP set EPB-3027					
EPA 260	The Cattle Call/The Nearest Thing to Heaven//I'm Throwing Rice (At the Girl That I Love)/Just a Little Lovin' (Will Go a Long, Long Way)	195?	5.00	10.00	20.00
EPA 260 [PS]	Eddy Arnold Sings	195?	5.00	10.00	20.00
EPB 3027 [PS]	Anytime (Country Classics)	1952	5.00	10.00	20.00
—Two-pocket jacket for two-EP set					

Albums

MGM

Number	Title (A Side/B Side)	Yr	VG	VG+	NM
SE-4878	If the World Stopped Loving	1973	3.00	6.00	12.00
SE-4912	She's Got Everything I Need	1974	3.00	6.00	12.00
SE-4916	I Wish I Had Loved You Better	1974	3.00	6.00	12.00
MG-1-4992	The Wonderful World of Eddy Arnold	1975	3.00	6.00	12.00
MJB-5107 [(2)]	World of Hits	1976	3.00	6.00	12.00

PAIR

Number	Title (A Side/B Side)	Yr	VG	VG+	NM
PDL2-1000 [(2)]	The Mellow Side of Eddy Arnold	1986	3.00	6.00	12.00

RCA

Number	Title (A Side/B Side)	Yr	VG	VG+	NM
9963-1-R	Hand-Holdin' Songs	1990	3.75	7.50	15.00

RCA CAMDEN

Number	Title (A Side/B Side)	Yr	VG	VG+	NM
CAL-471 [M]	Eddy Arnold (That's How Much I Love You)	1959	5.00	10.00	20.00
CAS-471(e) [R]	Eddy Arnold (That's How Much I Love You)	1966	2.50	5.00	10.00
CAL-563 [M]	More Eddy Arnold	1960	5.00	10.00	20.00
CAS-563(e) [R]	More Eddy Arnold	1966	2.50	5.00	10.00
CAL-741 [M]	Country Songs I Love to Sing	1963	3.75	7.50	15.00
CAS-741(e) [R]	Country Songs I Love to Sing	1966	2.50	5.00	10.00
CAL-799 [M]	Eddy's Songs	1964	3.75	7.50	15.00
CAS-799(e) [R]	Eddy's Songs	1966	2.50	5.00	10.00
CAL-897 [M]	I'm Throwing Rice (At the Girl That I Love) And Other Favorites	1966	3.75	7.50	15.00
CAS-897(e) [R]	I'm Throwing Rice (At the Girl That I Love) And Other Favorites	1966	2.50	5.00	10.00

RCA VICTOR

Number	Title (A Side/B Side)	Yr	VG	VG+	NM
APL1-0239	The World of Eddy Arnold	1973	3.00	6.00	12.00
PRS-346	Christmas with Eddy Arnold	1971	3.75	7.50	15.00
—Special-products issue					
ANL1-1078	Pure Gold	1975	2.50	5.00	10.00
LPM-1111 [M]	Wanderin' with Eddy Arnold	1955	12.50	25.00	50.00
LPM-1223 [M]	All-Time Favorites	1955	12.50	25.00	50.00
—New version of LPM 3117					
LPM-1224 [M]	Anytime	1955	12.50	25.00	50.00
—New version of LPM 3027					
LPM-1225 [M]	The Chapel on the Hill	1955	12.50	25.00	50.00
—New version of LPM 3031					
LPM-1293 [M]	A Dozen Hits	1956	12.50	25.00	50.00
LPM-1377 [M]	A Little on the Lonely Side	1956	12.50	25.00	50.00
LPM-1484 [M]	When They Were Young	1956	12.50	25.00	50.00
LPM-1575 [M]	My Darling, My Darling	1957	10.00	20.00	40.00
LPM-1733 [M]	Praise Him, Praise Him	1958	10.00	20.00	40.00
APL1-1817	Eddy	1976	3.00	6.00	12.00
LPM-1928 [M]	Have Guitar, Will Travel	1959	6.25	12.50	25.00
LSP-1928 [S]	Have Guitar, Will Travel	1959	7.50	15.00	30.00
LPM-2036 [M]	Thretby Hangs a Tale	1959	6.25	12.50	25.00
LSP-2036 [S]	Thretby Hangs a Tale	1959	7.50	15.00	30.00
LPM-2185 [M]	Eddy Arnold Sings Them Again	1960	6.25	12.50	25.00
LSP-2185 [S]	Eddy Arnold Sings Them Again	1960	7.50	15.00	30.00
LPM-2268 [M]	You Gotta Have Love	1960	6.25	12.50	25.00
LSP-2268 [S]	You Gotta Have Love	1960	7.50	15.00	30.00
APL1-2277	I Need You All the Time	1977	3.00	6.00	12.00
LPM-2337 [M]	Let's Make Memories Tonight	1961	5.00	10.00	20.00
LSP-2337 [S]	Let's Make Memories Tonight	1961	6.25	12.50	25.00
LPM-2471 [M]	One More Time	1961	5.00	10.00	20.00
LSP-2471 [S]	One More Time	1961	6.25	12.50	25.00
LPM-2554 [M]	Christmas with Eddy Arnold	1962	5.00	10.00	20.00
LSP-2554 [S]	Christmas with Eddy Arnold	1962	6.25	12.50	25.00
LPM-2578 [M]	Cattle Call	1962	6.25	12.50	25.00
LSP-2578 [S]	Cattle Call	1962	7.50	15.00	30.00
LPM-2596 [M]	Our Man Down South	1962	6.25	12.50	25.00
LSP-2596 [S]	Our Man Down South	1962	7.50	15.00	30.00
LPM-2629 [M]	Faithfully Yours	1963	6.25	12.50	25.00
LSP-2629 [S]	Faithfully Yours	1963	7.50	15.00	30.00
LPM-2811 [M]	Folk Song Book	1964	5.00	10.00	20.00
LSP-2811 [S]	Folk Song Book	1964	6.25	12.50	25.00
LPM-2909 [M]	Sometimes I'm Happy, Sometimes I'm Blue	1964	5.00	10.00	20.00
LSP-2909 [S]	Sometimes I'm Happy, Sometimes I'm Blue	1964	6.25	12.50	25.00
LPM-2951 [M]	Pop Hits from the Country Side	1964	5.00	10.00	20.00
LSP-2951 [S]	Pop Hits from the Country Side	1964	6.25	12.50	25.00
LPM-3027 [10]	Anytime	1952	30.00	60.00	120.00
—Label calls this "Country Classics"					
LPM-3031 [10]	All-Time Hits from the Hills	1952	25.00	50.00	100.00
LPM-3117 [10]	All-Time Favorites	1953	25.00	50.00	100.00
LPM-3219 [10]	The Chapel on the Hill	1954	25.00	50.00	100.00
LPM-3230	An American Institution Booklet	1954	12.50	25.00	50.00
LPM-3230 [10]	An American Institution	1954	25.00	50.00	100.00
AHL1-3358	Somebody	1979	2.50	5.00	10.00
LPM-3361 [M]	The Easy Way	1965	3.75	7.50	15.00
LSP-3361 [S]	The Easy Way	1965	5.00	10.00	20.00
LPM-3466 [M]	My World	1965	3.00	6.00	12.00
LSP-3466 [S]	My World	1965	3.75	7.50	15.00
LPM-3507 [M]	I Want to Go with You	1966	3.00	6.00	12.00
LSP-3507 [S]	I Want to Go with You	1966	3.75	7.50	15.00
LPM-3565 [M]	The Best of Eddy Arnold	1967	5.00	10.00	20.00
LSP-3565 [S]	The Best of Eddy Arnold	1967	3.75	7.50	15.00
AHL1-3606	A Legend and His Lady	1980	2.50	5.00	10.00
LPM-3622 [M]	The Last Word in Lonesome	1966	3.00	6.00	12.00
LSP-3622 [S]	The Last Word in Lonesome	1966	3.75	7.50	15.00
AYL1-3675	The Best of Eddy Arnold	1980	2.00	4.00	8.00
—"Best Buy Series" reissue					
LPM-3715 [M]	Somebody Like Me	1966	3.00	6.00	12.00
LSP-3715 [S]	Somebody Like Me	1966	3.75	7.50	15.00
LPM-3753 [M]	Lonely Again	1967	5.00	10.00	20.00
LSP-3753 [S]	Lonely Again	1967	3.75	7.50	15.00
LPM-3869 [M]	Turn the World Around	1967	5.00	10.00	20.00
LSP-3869 [S]	Turn the World Around	1967	3.75	7.50	15.00
AHL1-3914	A Man for All Seasons	1980	2.50	5.00	10.00
LPM-3931 [M]	The Everlovin' World of Eddy Arnold	1968	10.00	20.00	40.00
LSP-3931 [S]	The Everlovin' World of Eddy Arnold	1968	3.75	7.50	15.00
AYL1-3937	The Best of Eddy Arnold, Volume II	1981	2.00	4.00	8.00
—"Best Buy Series" reissue					
LSP-4009	The Romantic World of Eddy Arnold	1968	3.75	7.50	15.00
LSP-4089	Walkin' in Love Land	1968	3.75	7.50	15.00
LSP-4110	Songs of the Young World	1969	3.75	7.50	15.00
LSP-4179	The Glory of Love	1969	3.75	7.50	15.00
LSP-4231	The Warmth of Eddy	1969	3.75	7.50	15.00
AHL1-4263	Don't Give Up on Me	1981	2.50	5.00	10.00
LSP-4304	Love & Guitars	1970	3.00	6.00	12.00
LSP-4320	The Best of Eddy Arnold, Volume II	1970	3.00	6.00	12.00
LSP-4471	Portrait of My Woman	1971	3.00	6.00	12.00
LSP-4625	Loving Her Was Easier	1971	3.00	6.00	12.00
AHL1-4661	Close Enough to Love	1983	2.50	5.00	10.00
LSP-4738	Eddy Arnold Sings for Housewives and Other Ladies	1972	3.00	6.00	12.00
CPL2-4885 [(2)]	The Legendary Performances (1945-1971)	1983	3.00	6.00	12.00
AHL1-5467	Collector's Series	1985	2.50	5.00	10.00
VPS-6032 [(2)]	This Is Eddy Arnold	1972	3.75	7.50	15.00

ARNOLD, EDDY & JO ANN

45s

RCA VICTOR

Number	Title (A Side/B Side)	Yr	VG	VG+	NM
490	A Present For Santa Claus/Sittin' On Santa Claus' Lap	195?	—	2.50	5.00
490 [PS]	A Present For Santa Claus/Sittin' On Santa Claus' Lap	195?	—	2.50	5.00

ARNOLD, P.P.

45s

ATLANTIC

Number	Title (A Side/B Side)	Yr	VG	VG+	NM
2674	Bury Me Down by the River/Give a Hand, Take a Hand	1969	—	3.00	6.00

IMMEDIATE

Number	Title (A Side/B Side)	Yr	VG	VG+	NM
1901	The First Cut Is the Deepest/Speak to Me	1967	2.50	5.00	10.00
5006	If You Think You're Groovy/It Hurts Me Badly	1968	2.50	5.00	10.00

Albums

IMMEDIATE

Number	Title (A Side/B Side)	Yr	VG	VG+	NM
Z12 52016	Kafunta	1968	3.75	7.50	15.00

ARNOLD, VANCE, AND THE AVENGERS

See JOE COCKER.

ARRIBIANS, THE

45s

J.O.B.

Number	Title (A Side/B Side)	Yr	VG	VG+	NM
1116	To Look at a Star/Working and Gambling	1958	200.00	400.00	800.00

ARROGANTS, THE

45s

LUTE

Number	Title (A Side/B Side)	Yr	VG	VG+	NM
6226	Mirror Mirror/Canadian Sunset	1963	7.50	15.00	30.00

ARS NOVA

45s

ATLANTIC

Number	Title (A Side/B Side)	Yr	VG	VG+	NM
2625	Sunshine and Shadows/Walk on the Sand	1969	—	3.00	6.00

ELEKTRA

Number	Title (A Side/B Side)	Yr	VG	VG+	NM
45627	Pavan for My Lady (Fall Winter Summer and Spring)/Zoroaster	1968	2.00	4.00	8.00
45631	Fields of People/March of the Mad Duke's Circus	1968	2.00	4.00	8.00

Albums

ATLANTIC

Number	Title (A Side/B Side)	Yr	VG	VG+	NM
SD 8221	Sunshine and Shadows	1969	3.75	7.50	15.00

ELEKTRA

Number	Title (A Side/B Side)	Yr	VG	VG+	NM
EKS-74020	Ars Nova	1968	3.75	7.50	15.00

ART OF LOVIN'

45s

MAINSTREAM

Number	Title (A Side/B Side)	Yr	VG	VG+	NM
687	Good Times/You've Got the Power	1968	6.25	12.50	25.00

Number	Title (A Side/B Side)	Yr	VG	VG+	NM

Albums
MAINSTREAM

Number	Title (A Side/B Side)	Yr	VG	VG+	NM
S-6113	Art of Lovin'	1968	50.00	100.00	200.00

ARTHUR
Albums
LHI

Number	Title (A Side/B Side)	Yr	VG	VG+	NM
12000	Dreams and Images	1968	10.00	20.00	40.00

ARTISTICS, THE
45s
BRUNSWICK

Number	Title (A Side/B Side)	Yr	VG	VG+	NM
55301	I'm Gonna Miss You/Hope We Have	1966	2.00	4.00	8.00
55315	Girl I Need You/Glad I Met You	1967	2.00	4.00	8.00
55326	Love Song/I'll Always Love You	1967	2.00	4.00	8.00
55342	The Chase Is On/One Last Chance	1967	2.00	4.00	8.00
55353	You Make Me Happy/Nothing But Heartaches	1967	2.00	4.00	8.00
55370	Hard to Carry On/Trouble, Heartaches and Pain	1968	2.00	4.00	8.00
55384	Lonely Old World/You Left Me	1968	2.00	4.00	8.00
55404	Walking Tall/What Happened	1969	2.00	4.00	8.00
55416	Price of Love/Yesterday's Girl	1969	2.00	4.00	8.00
55431	Just Another Heartache/Ain't It Strange	1970	2.00	4.00	8.00
55444	(I Want You To) Make My Life Over/Sugar Cane	1971	2.00	4.00	8.00
55477	Being in Love/It's Those Little Things That Count	1972	2.00	4.00	8.00
55493	She's Heaven/Look Out I'm Gonna Get You	1973	2.00	4.00	8.00

OKEH

Number	Title (A Side/B Side)	Yr	VG	VG+	NM
7177	I Need Your Love/What'll I Do	1963	2.50	5.00	10.00
7193	Get My Hands on Some Lovin'/I'll Leave It Up to You	1964	2.50	5.00	10.00
7217	In Another Man's Arms/Patty Cake	1965	2.50	5.00	10.00
7232	This Heart of Mine/I'll Come Running	1965	2.50	5.00	10.00
7243	Loveland/So Much Love in My Heart	1966	2.50	5.00	10.00

Albums
BRUNSWICK

Number	Title (A Side/B Side)	Yr	VG	VG+	NM
BL 54123 [M]	I'm Gonna Miss You	1967	6.25	12.50	25.00
BL 754123 [S]	I'm Gonna Miss You	1967	6.25	12.50	25.00
BL 754139	The Articulate Artistics	1968	6.25	12.50	25.00
BL 754153	What Happened	1969	6.25	12.50	25.00
BL 754168	I Want You to Make My Life Over	1970	6.25	12.50	25.00
BL 754195	Look Out	1973	5.00	10.00	20.00

OKEH

Number	Title (A Side/B Side)	Yr	VG	VG+	NM
OKM-12119 [M]	Get My Hands on Some Lovin'	1967	20.00	40.00	80.00
OKS-14119 [S]	Get My Hands on Some Lovin'	1967	20.00	40.00	80.00

ARZACHEL
Albums
ROULETTE

Number	Title (A Side/B Side)	Yr	VG	VG+	NM
SR 42036	Arzachel	1969	37.50	75.00	150.00

ASCOTS, THE
More than one group.

45s
ACE

Number	Title (A Side/B Side)	Yr	VG	VG+	NM
650	I'm Touched/Perfect Love	1962	6.25	12.50	25.00

ARROW

Number	Title (A Side/B Side)	Yr	VG	VG+	NM
736	Easier Said Than Done/Is It Really You	1958	7.50	15.00	30.00

BETHLEHEM

Number	Title (A Side/B Side)	Yr	VG	VG+	NM
3046	Hip Talk/She Did	1962	3.75	7.50	15.00

DUAL-TONE

Number	Title (A Side/B Side)	Yr	VG	VG+	NM
1120	Acapulco Run/The Gladiator	1963	15.00	30.00	60.00

J&S

Number	Title (A Side/B Side)	Yr	VG	VG+	NM
1628/9	What Love Can Do/Everything Will Be Alright	1958	7.50	15.00	30.00

KING

Number	Title (A Side/B Side)	Yr	VG	VG+	NM
5679	I Don't Care One Bit/Tonight	1962	7.50	15.00	30.00

SUPER

Number	Title (A Side/B Side)	Yr	VG	VG+	NM
102	Monkey See, Monkey Do/You Can't Do That	1966	5.00	10.00	20.00
103	Midnight Hour/Midnight Hour (Part 2)	1966	5.00	10.00	20.00
104	Put Your Arms Around Me/Sookie Sookie	1966	5.00	10.00	20.00

ASGAERD
45s
THRESHOLD

Number	Title (A Side/B Side)	Yr	VG	VG+	NM
67010	Friends/Children of a New Born Age	1972	2.50	5.00	10.00

Albums
THRESHOLD

Number	Title (A Side/B Side)	Yr	VG	VG+	NM
THS 6	In the Realm of Asgaerd	1972	5.00	10.00	20.00

ASHES
45s
VAULT

Number	Title (A Side/B Side)	Yr	VG	VG+	NM
924	Is There Anything I Can Do/Every Little Prayer	1966	3.00	6.00	12.00
936	Dark on You Now/Roses Gone	1967	3.00	6.00	12.00
973	Homeward Bound/Sleeping Serenade	1971	2.50	5.00	10.00

Albums
VAULT

Number	Title (A Side/B Side)	Yr	VG	VG+	NM
125	Ashes	1968	12.50	25.00	50.00

ASHFORD, NICK
Also see ASHFORD AND SIMPSON.

45s
ABC

Number	Title (A Side/B Side)	Yr	VG	VG+	NM
11260	Let's Go Get Stoned/Dead End Kids	1970	—	3.00	6.00

VERVE

Number	Title (A Side/B Side)	Yr	VG	VG+	NM
10463	I Don't Need No Doctor/Young Emotions	1966	2.50	5.00	10.00
10493	When I Feel the Need/Young Emotions	1967	2.50	5.00	10.00
10599	California Soul/Young Emotions	1968	2.00	4.00	8.00

ASHFORD AND SIMPSON
Also see NICK ASHFORD; VALERIE SIMPSON.

45s
CAPITOL

Number	Title (A Side/B Side)	Yr	VG	VG+	NM
B-5109	Street Corner/Make It Work Again	1982	—	—	3.00
B-5109 [PS]	Street Corner/Make It Work Again	1982	—	—	3.00
B-5146	Love It Away/Street Opera (Part 2)	1982	—	—	3.00
B-5190	I'll Take the Whole World On/Mighty Mighty Love	1982	—	—	3.00
B-5250	High-Rise/(Instrumental)	1983	—	—	3.00
B-5250 [PS]	High-Rise/(Instrumental)	1983	—	—	3.00
B-5284	It's Much Deeper/Working Man	1983	—	—	3.00
B-5284 [PS]	It's Much Deeper/Working Man	1983	—	—	3.00
B-5310	I'm Not That Tough/Side Effect	1984	—	—	3.00
B-5310 [PS]	I'm Not That Tough/Side Effect	1984	—	—	3.00
B-5397	Solid/Solid (Dub Version)	1984	—	—	3.00
B-5397 [PS]	Solid/Solid (Dub Version)	1984	—	—	3.00
B-5435	Outta the World/Outta the World (Dub)	1985	—	—	3.00
B-5435 [PS]	Outta the World/Outta the World (Dub)	1985	—	—	3.00
B-5468	Babies/Street Corner	1985	—	—	3.00
B-5468 [PS]	Babies/Street Corner	1985	—	—	3.00
B-5598	Count Your Blessings/Side Effect	1986	—	—	3.00
B-5598 [PS]	Count Your Blessings/Side Effect	1986	—	—	3.00
B-5637	What Becomes of Love/It's a Rush	1986	—	—	3.00
B-5666	Nobody Walks in L.A./Way Ah Way Ahead	1987	—	—	3.00
B-44326	I'll Be There for You/Way Ahead	1989	—	—	3.00
B-44326 [PS]	I'll Be There for You/Way Ahead	1989	—	—	3.00

HOPSACK & SILK

Number	Title (A Side/B Side)	Yr	VG	VG+	NM
96-398	Been Found/I Remember All	1996	—	—	3.00

—With Maya Angelou

WARNER BROS.

Number	Title (A Side/B Side)	Yr	VG	VG+	NM
7745	(I'd Know You) Anywhere/I'm Determined	1973	—	2.00	4.00
7781	Have You Ever Tried It/Time	1974	—	2.00	4.00
7811	Main Line/Don't Fight It	1974	—	2.00	4.00
8030	Everybody's Got to Give It Up/Over to Where You Are	1974	—	2.00	4.00
8070	Bend Me/Ain't Nothin' But a Name	1975	—	2.00	4.00
8179	It'll Come, It'll Come, It'll Come/Caretaker	1976	—	2.00	4.00
8216	Somebody Told a Lie/It Came to Me	1976	—	2.00	4.00
8286	Tried, Tested and Found True/Believe in Me	1976	—	2.00	4.00
8337	So So Satisfied/Maybe I Can Find It	1977	—	2.00	4.00
8391	Over and Over/It's You	1977	—	2.00	4.00
8453	Send It/Couldn't Get Enough	1977	—	2.00	4.00
8514	Don't Cost You Nothing/Let Love Use Me	1978	—	2.00	4.00
8571	By Way of Love's Express/Too Bad	1978	—	2.00	4.00
8651	It Seems to Hang On/Too Bad	1978	—	2.00	4.00
8710	Is It Still Good to Ya/As Long As It Holds You	1978	—	2.00	4.00
8775	Flashback/Ain't It a Shame	1979	—	2.00	4.00
8870	Found a Cure/You Always Could	1979	—	2.00	4.00
49099	Nobody Knows/Crazy	1979	—	2.00	4.00
49269	Love Don't Make It Right/Finally Got to Me	1980	—	2.00	4.00
49269 [PS]	Love Don't Make It Right/Finally Got to Me	1980	—	2.50	5.00
49594	Happy Endings/Make It to the Sky	1980	—	2.00	4.00
49646	Get Out Your Handkerchief/You Never Left Me Alone	1980	—	2.00	4.00
49805	It Shows in the Eyes/Enough	1981	—	2.00	4.00
49867	I Need Your Light/It's the Long Run	1981	—	2.00	4.00

Albums
CAPITOL

Number	Title (A Side/B Side)	Yr	VG	VG+	NM
ST-12207	Street Opera	1982	2.00	4.00	8.00
ST-12282	High Rise	1983	2.00	4.00	8.00
ST-12366	Solid	1984	2.00	4.00	8.00
ST-12469	Real Love	1986	2.00	4.00	8.00
C1-46946	Love Or Physical	1989	2.50	5.00	10.00

WARNER BROS.

Number	Title (A Side/B Side)	Yr	VG	VG+	NM
BS 2739	Gimme Something Real	1973	2.50	5.00	10.00
BS 2789	I Wanna Be Selfish	1974	2.50	5.00	10.00
BS 2858	Come As You Are	1976	2.50	5.00	10.00
BS 2992	So So Satisfied	1977	2.50	5.00	10.00
BS 3088	Send It	1977	2.50	5.00	10.00
BSK 3219	Is It Still Good to Ya	1978	2.50	5.00	10.00
BSK 3357	Stay Free	1979	2.50	5.00	10.00
HS 3458	A Musical Affair	1980	2.50	5.00	10.00
2BS 3524 [(2)]	Performance	1981	3.00	6.00	12.00

ASHKAN
Albums
SIRE

Number	Title (A Side/B Side)	Yr	VG	VG+	NM
SES-97107	In from the Cold	1970	6.25	12.50	25.00

ASHLEY, DEL
See DAVID GATES.

ASHLEY, JOHN
45s
CAPEHART

Number	Title (A Side/B Side)	Yr	VG	VG+	NM
5006	Little Lou/I Need Your Lovin'	1961	12.50	25.00	50.00

DOT

Number	Title (A Side/B Side)	Yr	VG	VG+	NM
15775	Born to Rock/Pickin' on the Wrong Chicken	1958	12.50	25.00	50.00
15878	My Story/Let the Good Times Roll	1958	3.75	7.50	15.00

INTRO

Number	Title (A Side/B Side)	Yr	VG	VG+	NM
6097	Bermuda/Let Yourself Go Go Go	196?	7.50	15.00	30.00

SILVER

Number	Title (A Side/B Side)	Yr	VG	VG+	NM
1002	I Want to Hear It from You/Seriously in Love	1959	6.25	12.50	25.00
1005	Cry of the Wild Goose/One Love	1960	6.25	12.50	25.00

ASHLEY, ROBERT
45s
MERCURY

Number	Title (A Side/B Side)	Yr	VG	VG+	NM
71365	Comic Strip Rock and Roll/The Baby	1957	12.50	25.00	50.00

Number	Title (A Side/B Side)	Yr	VG	VG+	NM

ASHLEY, TONY

45s

DECCA

Number	Title (A Side/B Side)	Yr	VG	VG+	NM
32240	I'll Never Be Satisfied/All Along I've Loved You	1967	5.00	10.00	20.00
32342	We Must Have Love/I Can't Put You Down	1968	5.00	10.00	20.00
32520	I'll Go Crazy/Just a Taste	1969	15.00	30.00	60.00

ASHTON, GARDNER AND DYKE

45s

CAPITOL

Number	Title (A Side/B Side)	Yr	VG	VG+	NM
2981	Hymn to Everyone/Mister Freako	1970	—	2.50	5.00
3060	Resurrection Shuffle/I'm Your Spiritual Breadman	1971	—	3.00	6.00
3206	Can You Get It/Oh Lord	1971	—	2.50	5.00
3288	Delirium/Still Got a Long Way to Go	1972	—	2.50	5.00

Albums

CAPITOL

Number	Title (A Side/B Side)	Yr	VG	VG+	NM
SMAS-862	What a Bloody Long Day It's Been	1972	3.00	6.00	12.00

ASLEEP AT THE WHEEL

45s

ARISTA

Number	Title (A Side/B Side)	Yr	VG	VG+	NM
2045	Keepin' Me Up Nights/Pedernales Stroll	1990	—	—	3.00
2122	That's the Way Love Is/Beat Me, Daddy (Eight to the Bar)	1990	—	—	3.00
2178	Dance With Who Brung You/Quittin' Time	1991	—	—	3.00

CAPITOL

Number	Title (A Side/B Side)	Yr	VG	VG+	NM
4115	The Letter That Johnny Walker Read/(B-side unknown)	1975	—	2.00	4.00
4187	Bump Bounce Boogie/Fat Boy Rag	1975	—	2.00	4.00
4238	Nothin' Takes the Place of You/Tonight the Bartender Is on the Wrong Side of the Bar	1976	—	2.00	4.00
4319	Route 66/Shout Wa Hey	1976	—	2.00	4.00
4357	Miles and Miles of Texas/Blues for Dixie	1976	—	2.00	4.00
4393	The Trouble with Lovin' Today/Ragtime Annie	1977	—	2.00	4.00
4438	Somebody Stole His Body/Let's Face Up	1977	—	2.00	4.00
4601	Ghost Dancer/Louisiana	1978	—	2.00	4.00
4659	Texas Me & You/One O'Clock Jump	1978	—	2.00	4.00
4725	Choo Choo Ch'Boogie/Too Many Bad Habits	1979	—	2.00	4.00

CAPITOL NASHVILLE

Number	Title (A Side/B Side)	Yr	VG	VG+	NM
S7-18844	Lay Down Sally/Hightower	1995	—	2.00	4.00

EPIC

Number	Title (A Side/B Side)	Yr	VG	VG+	NM
06671	Way Down Texas Way/String of Pars	1987	—	—	3.00
07125	House of Blue Lights/Big Foot Stomp	1987	—	—	3.00
07610	Boogie Back to Texas/(B-side unknown)	1987	—	—	3.00
07659	Blowin' Like a Bandit/String of Pars	1987	—	—	3.00
07966	Walk On By/Sugarfoot Rag	1988	—	—	3.00
08087	Hot Rod Lincoln/String of Pars	1988	—	—	3.00
08461	House of Blue Lights/Blowin' Like a Bandit	1988	—	—	3.00
—Reissue					
50045	Choo Choo Ch'Boogie/Our Names Aren't Mentioned	1974	—	2.00	4.00

LIBERTY

Number	Title (A Side/B Side)	Yr	VG	VG+	NM
S7-17715	Red Wing/Bring It On Down to My House	1993	—	2.00	4.00
S7-17970	Blues for Dixie/Got a Letter from My Kid Today	1993	—	2.00	4.00

MCA

Number	Title (A Side/B Side)	Yr	VG	VG+	NM
51020	Cool as a Breeze/Don't Get Caught Out in the Rain	1980	—	2.00	4.00

UNITED ARTISTS

Number	Title (A Side/B Side)	Yr	VG	VG+	NM
XW-245	Take Me Back to Tulsa/Before You Stop Loving Me	1973	—	2.50	5.00
XW-344	Daddy's Advice/Drivin' Nails in My Coffin	1973	—	2.50	5.00

Albums

ARISTA

Number	Title (A Side/B Side)	Yr	VG	VG+	NM
AL-8550	Keepin' Me Up Nights	1990	3.00	6.00	12.00

CAPITOL

Number	Title (A Side/B Side)	Yr	VG	VG+	NM
ST-11441	Texas Gold	1975	3.00	6.00	12.00
ST-11548	Wheelin' and Dealin'	1976	3.00	6.00	12.00
ST-11620	The Wheel	1977	3.00	6.00	12.00
SW-11726	Collision Course	1978	3.00	6.00	12.00
ST-11945	Served Live	1979	3.00	6.00	12.00
SN-16306	Served Live	1984	2.00	4.00	8.00
—Budget-line reissue					

CAPITOL SPECIAL MARKETS

Number	Title (A Side/B Side)	Yr	VG	VG+	NM
SL-8138	Drivin'	1980	3.00	6.00	12.00

DOT/MCA

Number	Title (A Side/B Side)	Yr	VG	VG+	NM
39036	Asleep at the Wheel	1985	2.50	5.00	10.00

EPIC

Number	Title (A Side/B Side)	Yr	VG	VG+	NM
KE 33097	Asleep at the Wheel	1974	3.75	7.50	15.00
PE 33097	Asleep at the Wheel	197?	2.00	4.00	8.00
—Reissue					
BG 33782 [(2)]	Fathers and Sons	1974	6.25	12.50	25.00
—With Bob Wills					
EG 33782 [(2)]	Fathers and Sons	197?	3.00	6.00	12.00
—Reissue					
BFE 40681	10	1987	2.00	4.00	8.00
FE 44213	Western Standard Time	1988	2.00	4.00	8.00

LIBERTY

Number	Title (A Side/B Side)	Yr	VG	VG+	NM
LN-10296	Comin' Right At Ya!	1986	2.00	4.00	8.00
—Budget-line reissue					

MCA

Number	Title (A Side/B Side)	Yr	VG	VG+	NM
742	Framed	1982	2.00	4.00	8.00
—Reissue of 5131					
5131	Framed	1980	2.50	5.00	10.00

UNITED ARTISTS

Number	Title (A Side/B Side)	Yr	VG	VG+	NM
UA-LA038-F	Comin' Right At Ya!	1973	5.00	10.00	20.00

ASSEMBLED MULTITUDE, THE

45s

ATLANTIC

Number	Title (A Side/B Side)	Yr	VG	VG+	NM
2737	Overture from Tommy (A Rock Opera)/Mud	1970	—	2.00	4.00
2764	Woodstock/Mr. Peppercorn	1970	—	2.00	4.00
2780	Medley from "Superstar" (A Rock Opera)/Where the Wood Bine Twineth	1971	—	2.00	4.00
2870	Godfather Waltz/Mac Arthur Park	1972	—	2.00	4.00

Albums

ATLANTIC

Number	Title (A Side/B Side)	Yr	VG	VG+	NM
SD 8262	The Assembled Multitude	1970	3.00	6.00	12.00

ASSOCIATION, THE

45s

COLUMBIA

Number	Title (A Side/B Side)	Yr	VG	VG+	NM
45602	Indian Wells Woman/Darling Be Home Soon	1972	—	2.50	5.00
45654	Come the Fall/Kicking the Gong Around	1972	—	2.50	5.00

ELEKTRA

Number	Title (A Side/B Side)	Yr	VG	VG+	NM
47094	Dreamer/You Turn the Light On	1980	—	2.00	4.00
47146	Small Town Lovers/Across the Persian Gulf	1981	—	2.00	4.00

JUBILEE

Number	Title (A Side/B Side)	Yr	VG	VG+	NM
5505	Babe I'm Gonna Leave You/Baby Can't You Hear Me Call Your Name	1965	6.25	12.50	25.00

MUMS

Number	Title (A Side/B Side)	Yr	VG	VG+	NM
6016	Names, Tags, Numbers & Labels/Rainbows Bent	1973	—	2.00	4.00

RCA VICTOR

Number	Title (A Side/B Side)	Yr	VG	VG+	NM
PB-10217	One Sunday Morning/Life Is a Carnival	1975	—	2.00	4.00

VALIANT

Number	Title (A Side/B Side)	Yr	VG	VG+	NM
730	Too Many Mornings/Forty Times	1965	3.75	7.50	15.00
741	Along Comes Mary/Your Own Love	1966	3.00	6.00	12.00
747	Cherish/Don't Blame It On Me	1966	3.00	6.00	12.00
755	Pandora's Golden Heebie Jeebies/Standing Still	1966	2.50	5.00	10.00
755 [PS]	Pandora's Golden Heebie Jeebies/Standing Still	1966	5.00	10.00	20.00
758	No Fair at All/Looking Glass	1967	2.50	5.00	10.00

WARNER BROS.

Number	Title (A Side/B Side)	Yr	VG	VG+	NM
7040	Pandora's Golden Heebie Jeebies/Standing Still	1967	2.00	4.00	8.00
7041	Windy/Sometime	1967	2.50	5.00	10.00
7074	Never My Love/Requiem for the Masses	1967	2.50	5.00	10.00
—A picture sleeve is rumored to exist					
7105	Along Comes Mary/Cherish	1968	2.00	4.00	8.00
—"Back to Back Hits" series on "W7" label					
7119	Windy/Never My Love	1968	2.00	4.00	8.00
—"Back to Back Hits" series on "W7" label					
7163	Everything That Touches You/We Love Us	1968	2.00	4.00	8.00
—Orange "WB" label					
7195	Time for Livin'/Birthday Morning	1968	2.00	4.00	8.00
7229	Six Man Band/Like Always	1968	2.00	4.00	8.00
7267	Goodbye Columbus/The Time It Is Today	1969	2.00	4.00	8.00
7277	Under Branches/Hear in Here	1969	2.00	4.00	8.00
7305	Yes, I Will/I Am Up for Europe	1969	2.00	4.00	8.00
7349	Are You Ready/Dubuque Blues	1969	2.00	4.00	8.00
7372	Just About the Same/Look at Me, Look at You	1970	—	3.00	6.00
7429	Along the Way/Traveler's Guide	1970	—	3.00	6.00
7471	P.F. Sloan/Traveler's Guide	1971	—	3.00	6.00
7515	Bring Yourself Home/It's Gotta Be Real	1971	—	3.00	6.00
7524	That's Racin'/Makes Me Cry (Funny Kind of Song)	1971	—	3.00	6.00

Albums

COLUMBIA

Number	Title (A Side/B Side)	Yr	VG	VG+	NM
KC 31348	Waterbeds in Trinidad	1972	2.50	5.00	10.00

PAIR

Number	Title (A Side/B Side)	Yr	VG	VG+	NM
PDL2-1061 [(2)]	Songs That Made Them Famous	1986	3.00	6.00	12.00

VALIANT

Number	Title (A Side/B Side)	Yr	VG	VG+	NM
VLM-5002 [M]	And Then...Along Comes The Association	1966	5.00	10.00	20.00
VLM-5004 [M]	Renaissance	1966	5.00	10.00	20.00
—With no blurb for "No Fair at All" on cover					
VLM-5004 [M]	Renaissance	1967	3.75	7.50	15.00
—With blurb for "No Fair at All" on cover					
VLS-25002 [S]	And Then...Along Comes The Association	1966	6.25	12.50	25.00
VLS-25004 [S]	Renaissance	1966	6.25	12.50	25.00
—With no blurb for "No Fair at All" on cover					
VLS-25004 [S]	Renaissance	1967	5.00	10.00	20.00
—With blurb for "No Fair at All" on cover					

WARNER BROS.

Number	Title (A Side/B Side)	Yr	VG	VG+	NM
W 1696 [M]	Insight Out	1967	3.75	7.50	15.00
WS 1696 [S]	Insight Out	1967	5.00	10.00	20.00
—Gold label					
WS 1696 [S]	Insight Out	1968	3.00	6.00	12.00
—With "W7" logo on green label					
W 1702 [M]	And Then...Along Comes the Association	1967	5.00	10.00	20.00
WS 1702	And Then...Along Comes the Association	1967	3.00	6.00	12.00
—With "W7" logo on green label					
WS 1702 [S]	And Then...Along Comes the Association	1967	5.00	10.00	20.00
—Gold label					
WS 1704	Renaissance	1967	3.00	6.00	12.00
WS 1733	Birthday	1968	3.00	6.00	12.00
—With "W7" logo on green label					
WS 1767	Greatest Hits	1968	3.00	6.00	12.00
—With "W7" logo on green label					
WS 1767	Greatest Hits	197?	2.00	4.00	8.00
—Any later pressing (LP in print until the late 1980s)					
WS 1786	Goodbye Columbus	1969	3.00	6.00	12.00
—With "W7" logo on green label					
WS 1800	The Association	1969	3.00	6.00	12.00
—With "W7" logo on green label					
2WS 1868 [(2)]	The Association "Live"	1970	3.00	6.00	12.00
WS 1927	Stop Your Motor	1971	3.00	6.00	12.00
ST-91586	Greatest Hits	1968	5.00	10.00	20.00
—Capitol Record Club edition					

ASTORS, THE

45s

STAX

Number	Title (A Side/B Side)	Yr	VG	VG+	NM
139	What Can It Be/Just Enough to Hurt Me	1963	20.00	40.00	80.00
170	Candy/I Found Out	1965	6.25	12.50	25.00
179	Mystery Woman/In the Twilight Zone	1965	6.25	12.50	25.00
232	Daddy Didn't Tell You/More Power to You	1967	3.00	6.00	12.00

ASTRO JETS, THE

45s

IMPERIAL

Number	Title (A Side/B Side)	Yr	VG	VG+	NM
5760	Hide and Seek/Boom-A-Lay	1961	5.00	10.00	20.00

ASTRONAUTS, THE (1)

Best known as a surf-instrumental group.

45s

RCA VICTOR

Number	Title (A Side/B Side)	Yr	VG	VG+	NM
47-8194	Baja/Kuk	1963	5.00	10.00	20.00
47-8224	Hot Doggin'/Everyone But Me	1963	5.00	10.00	20.00
47-8224 [PS]	Hot Doggin'/Everyone But Me	1963	15.00	30.00	60.00
47-8298	Competition Coupe/Surf Party	1963	5.00	10.00	20.00
47-8364	Go Fight for Her/Swim Little Mermaid	1964	5.00	10.00	20.00
47-8419	Main Title from Ride the Wild Surf/Around and Around	1964	5.00	10.00	20.00
47-8463	I'm a Fool/Can't You See I Do	1964	5.00	10.00	20.00
47-8499	Almost Grown/My Sin Is Pride	1965	5.00	10.00	20.00
47-8545	Tomorrow's Gonna Be Another Day/Razza Matazz	1965	5.00	10.00	20.00
47-8628	It Doesn't Matter Anymore/The La La La Song	1965	5.00	10.00	20.00
47-8885	In My Car/Main Street	1966	3.75	7.50	15.00
47-9109	I Know You Rider/Better Things	1967	3.75	7.50	15.00

Albums

RCA VICTOR

Number	Title (A Side/B Side)	Yr	VG	VG+	NM
PRM-183 [M]	Rockin' with the Astronauts	1965	7.50	15.00	30.00
LPM-2760 [M]	Surfin' with the Astronauts	1963	15.00	30.00	60.00
LSP-2760 [S]	Surfin' with the Astronauts	1963	20.00	40.00	80.00
LPM-2782 [M]	Everything Is A-OK!	1964	12.50	25.00	50.00
LSP-2782 [S]	Everything Is A-OK!	1964	15.00	30.00	60.00
LPM-2858 [M]	Competition Coupe	1964	15.00	30.00	60.00
LSP-2858 [S]	Competition Coupe	1964	20.00	40.00	80.00
LPM-2903 [M]	The Astronauts Orbit Kampus	1964	10.00	20.00	40.00
LSP-2903 [S]	The Astronauts Orbit Kampus	1964	12.50	25.00	50.00
LPM-3307 [M]	The Astronauts Go, Go, Go	1965	7.50	15.00	30.00
LSP-3307 [S]	The Astronauts Go, Go, Go	1965	10.00	20.00	40.00
LPM-3359 [M]	Favorites for You from Us	1965	7.50	15.00	30.00
LSP-3359 [S]	Favorites for You from Us	1965	10.00	20.00	40.00
LPM-3454 [M]	Down the Line	1966	7.50	15.00	30.00
LSP-3454 [S]	Down the Line	1966	10.00	20.00	40.00
LPM-3733 [M]	Travelin' Men	1967	12.50	25.00	50.00
LSP-3733 [S]	Travelin' Men	1967	7.50	15.00	30.00

ASTRONAUTS, THE (1) / THE LIVERPOOL FIVE

Albums

RCA VICTOR

Number	Title (A Side/B Side)	Yr	VG	VG+	NM
PRS-251 [S]	Stereo Festival	1967	25.00	50.00	100.00
—Special-prodcuts edition					

ASTRONAUTS, THE (U)

45s

Number	Title (A Side/B Side)	Yr	VG	VG+	NM
JAN ELL					
459	Geneva Twist/Take 17	1962	7.50	15.00	30.00
LUNEY					
100	Ridge Route/Blast Off	1962	7.50	15.00	30.00
MERCURY					
71675	Alabama Jubilee/Gadabout	1960	3.00	6.00	12.00
PALLADIUM					
610	Come Along Baby/Trying to Get to You	1962	25.00	50.00	100.00
TRIAL					
3521	Farewell/Chili Charlene	1960	50.00	100.00	200.00
VANRUS					
1000	Ski Lift/Blues Beat	1962	7.50	15.00	30.00

ASYLUM CHOIR

See LEON RUSSELL AND MARC BENNO.

ATKINS, CHET

45s

Number	Title (A Side/B Side)	Yr	VG	VG+	NM
COLUMBIA					
AE7 1776 [DJ]	East Tennessee Christmas/Winter Wonderland	1983	—	2.00	4.00
03984	Run Don't Walk/Walk Me Home	1983	—	—	3.00
04859	The Boot and the Stone/Sunrise	1985	—	—	3.00
05662	Please Stay Tuned/Some Leather and Lace	1985	—	—	3.00
06165	The Official Beach Music/Alicia	1986	—	—	3.00
07929	I Still Can't Say Goodbye/The Mockingbird	1988	—	—	3.00
RCA					
PB-10902	La Chicana/Four in the Morning	1977	—	2.00	4.00
—With Danny Davis and Floyd Cramer					
PB-11071	Me and My Guitar/Cascade	1977	—	2.00	4.00
PB-11892	Blind Willie/Dance with Me	1980	—	2.00	4.00
PB-12064	I Can Hear Kentucky Calling Me/Strawberry Man	1980	—	2.00	4.00
PB-12263	Orange Blossom Special/Ready for the Times to Get Better	1981	—	2.00	4.00
RCA VICTOR					
APBO-0146	Fiddlin' Around/Paramaribo	1973	—	2.00	4.00
PB-10046	The Entertainer/Dizzy Fingers	1974	—	2.00	4.00
PB-10346	The Night Atlanta Burned/Old Folks of Okracoke	1975	—	2.00	4.00
—As "The Atkins String Co."					
PB-10448	Sonora/Mostly Mozart	1975	—	2.00	4.00
—As "The Atkins String Co."					
PB-10614	Frog Kissin'/Bill Cheatham	1976	—	2.00	4.00
47-4377	In the Mood/Sweet Bunch of Daisies	1951	6.25	12.50	25.00
47-4491	Goodbye Blues/Rainbow	1952	6.25	12.50	25.00
47-4684	Spanish Fandango/Your Mean Little Heart	1952	6.25	12.50	25.00
47-4896	Meet Mr. Callaghan/Chinatown, My Chinatown	1952	6.25	12.50	25.00
47-4922	Gallopin' on the Guitar/(B-side unknown)	1952	6.25	12.50	25.00
47-4931	Tennessee Rag/My Little Girl	1952	6.25	12.50	25.00
47-5010	Midnight/Rustic Dance	1952	6.25	12.50	25.00
47-5100	Guitar Polka/Dream Train	1952	5.00	10.00	20.00
—With Rosalie Allen					
47-5181	Fig Leaf Rag/High Rockin' Swing	1953	5.00	10.00	20.00
47-5300	Country Gentlemen/The Bells of St. Mary's	1953	5.00	10.00	20.00
47-5484	Three O'Clock in the Morning/City Slicker	1953	5.00	10.00	20.00
47-5565	Barber Shop Rag/Centipede Boogie	1953	5.00	10.00	20.00
47-5638	Wildwood Flower/Simple Simon	1954	5.00	10.00	20.00
47-5650	Georgia Camp Meeting/Jealous Hearted Me	1954	5.00	10.00	20.00
—With Minnie Pearl					
47-5704	Downhill Drag/Kentucky Derby	1954	5.00	10.00	20.00
47-5813	San Antonio Rose/Mister Misery	1954	5.00	10.00	20.00
—With Red Kirk					
47-5956	Mr. Sandman/Set a Spell	1954	5.00	10.00	20.00
47-5995	Silver Bells/Old Spinning Wheel	1954	5.00	10.00	20.00
—With Hank Snow					
47-6108	Hey Mr. Guitar/Unchained Melody	1955	3.75	7.50	15.00
47-6199	Somebody Stole My Gal/Shine On Harvest Moon	1955	3.75	7.50	15.00
47-6314	Christmas Carols/Jingle Bells	1955	3.75	7.50	15.00
47-6366	Jean's Song/Honey	1955	3.75	7.50	15.00
47-6550	Cecilia/The Lady Loves	1956	3.75	7.50	15.00
47-6796	Trambone/Blue Echo	1957	3.75	7.50	15.00
47-6808	Tricky/Peanut Vendor	1957	3.75	7.50	15.00
—With the Rhythm Rockers					
47-6919	Martinique/Dig These Blues	1957	3.75	7.50	15.00
—With the Rhythm Rockers					
47-7048	Hidden Charms/Colonial Ballroom	1957	3.75	7.50	15.00
47-7589	Boo Boo Stick Beat/Django's Castle	1959	3.00	6.00	12.00
47-7684	One Mint Julep/Teensville	1960	3.00	6.00	12.00
47-7747	Slinkey/Rainbow's End	1960	3.00	6.00	12.00
47-7796	Hocus Pocus/Theme from The Dark at the End of the Stairs	1960	3.00	6.00	12.00
47-7847	The Slop/Hot Mocking Bird	1961	3.00	6.00	12.00
47-7891	Man of Mystery/Windy and Warm	1961	3.00	6.00	12.00
47-7971	Jingle Bells/Jingle Bell Rock	1961	3.00	6.00	12.00
47-8029	Down Home/Melissa	1962	3.00	6.00	12.00
47-8246	Guitar Country/Waitin' for the Evening Train	1963	3.00	6.00	12.00
—With the Anita Kerr Quartet					
47-8342	Freight Train/Dobro	1964	3.00	6.00	12.00
47-8492	Travelin'/Cloudy and Cool	1965	2.50	5.00	10.00
47-8590	Yakety Axe/Letter Edged in Black	1965	2.50	5.00	10.00
47-8781	From Nashville with Love/Rhythm Guitar	1966	2.50	5.00	10.00
47-8829	Tennessee Waltz/Country Gentleman	1966	2.50	5.00	10.00
47-8927	Prissy/La Fiesta	1966	2.50	5.00	10.00
47-9116	Charlie Brown/What'd I Say	1967	2.50	5.00	10.00
47-9229	Country Gentleman/Chet's Tune	1967	2.50	5.00	10.00
—With "Some of Chet's Friends"					
47-9229 [PS]	Country Gentleman/Chet's Tune	1967	3.75	7.50	15.00
—With "Some of Chet's Friends"					
47-9578	Huntin' Boots/Blue Angel	1968	2.00	4.00	8.00
47-9672	Light My Fire/Mrs. Robinson	1968	2.00	4.00	8.00
47-9725	Theme from Zorba the Greek/Those Were the Days	1969	—	3.00	6.00
47-9803	Wheels/Difficult	1969	—	3.00	6.00
—With Hank Snow					
47-9824	Love Beads/Passion Flower	1969	—	3.00	6.00
47-9827	Steeplechase Lane/Love Beads	1970	—	2.50	5.00
47-9890	Tennessee Stud/Cannonball Rag	1970	—	2.50	5.00
—With Jerry Reed					
47-9956	Snowbird/Chaplain in New Shoes	1971	—	2.50	5.00
48-0062	Guitar Waltz/Barber Shop Rag	1949	12.50	25.00	50.00
—Originals on green vinyl					
48-0062	Guitar Waltz/Barber Shop Rag	1949	6.25	12.50	25.00
—Second pressings: Green label, black vinyl					
48-0089	Dance of the Goldenrod/Telling My Troubles to My Old Guitar	1949	12.50	25.00	50.00
—Originals on green vinyl					
48-0089	Dance of the Goldenrod/Telling My Troubles to My Old Guitar	1949	6.25	12.50	25.00
—Second pressings: Green label, black vinyl					
48-0142	Centipede Boogie/Wednesday Night Waltz	1949	12.50	25.00	50.00
—Originals on green vinyl					
48-0142	Centipede Boogie/Wednesday Night Waltz	1949	6.25	12.50	25.00
—Second pressings: Green label, black vinyl					
48-0173	One More Chance/Old Buck Dance	1950	6.25	12.50	25.00
—Originals on green vinyl					
48-0173	One More Chance/Old Buck Dance	1950	6.25	12.50	25.00
—Second pressings: Green label, black vinyl					
48-0329	Main Street Breakdown/Under the Hickory Nut Tree	1950	12.50	25.00	50.00
—Originals on green vinyl					
48-0329	Main Street Breakdown/Under the Hickory Nut Tree	1950	6.25	12.50	25.00
—Second pressings: Green label, black vinyl					
48-0367	Boogie Man Boogie/Was Bitten By the Same Bug Twice	1950	12.50	25.00	50.00
—Originals on green vinyl					
48-0367	Boogie Man Boogie/Was Bitten By the Same Bug Twice	1950	6.25	12.50	25.00
—Second pressings: Green label, black vinyl					
48-0402	The Birth of the Blues/Confusin'	1950	12.50	25.00	50.00
—Originals on green vinyl					
48-0402	The Birth of the Blues/Confusin'	1950	6.25	12.50	25.00
—Second pressings: Green label, black vinyl					
48-0428	Indian Love Call/Music in My Heart	1951	12.50	25.00	50.00
—Originals on green vinyl					
48-0428	Indian Love Call/Music in My Heart	1951	6.25	12.50	25.00
—Second pressings: Green label, black vinyl					
48-0439	My Life with You/A Trinket of Shiny Gold	1951	6.25	12.50	25.00
—With the Carter Sisters					
48-0440	You're Always Brand New/Mountain Melody	1951	6.25	12.50	25.00
48-0471	Jitterbug Waltz/My Crazy Heart	1951	6.25	12.50	25.00
48-0500	Crazy Rhythm/Hybrid Corn	1951	6.25	12.50	25.00
74-0236	Delilah/Ode to Billie Joe	1969	—	2.50	5.00
—With Arthur Fiedler and the Boston Pops					
74-0536	Black Magic Woman/Wabash Blues	1971	—	2.50	5.00
74-0696	Red, White and Blue Medley/Kentucky	1972	—	2.50	5.00
74-0775	Nashtownville/Jerry's Breakdown	1972	—	2.50	5.00
—With Jerry Reed					

Number	Title (A Side/B Side)	Yr	VG	VG+	NM
74-0799	Chet's Tune (Part 1)/Chet's Tune (Part 2)	1972	—	2.50	5.00
—As "Some of Chet's Friends"					
74-0914	Ruby, Are You Mad at Your Man/Somewhere, My Love	1973	—	2.00	4.00

7-Inch Extended Plays

RCA VICTOR

Number	Title (A Side/B Side)	Yr	VG	VG+	NM
EPA-685	Arkansaw Traveler/Londonderry Air//Ouch Chornya/La Golondrina	195?	5.00	10.00	20.00
EPA-685 [PS]	Chet Atkins in 3 Dimensions Vol. 1: Folk	1955	5.00	10.00	20.00
EPA-687	Minuet and Prelude No. 2/Intermezzo//Schon Rosmarin/Minute Waltz	195?	5.00	10.00	20.00
EPA-687 [PS]	Chet Atkins in 3 Dimensions Vol. 3: Classical	195?	5.00	10.00	20.00
EPA-796	(title unknown)	195?	5.00	10.00	20.00
EPA-796 [PS]	Indian Love Call/Memphis Blues//St. Louis Blues/ Black Mountain Rag	195?	5.00	10.00	20.00
547-0919	Oh By Jingo/Indian Love Call//Alice Blue Gown/ The 3rd Man Theme	1956	5.00	10.00	20.00
—One record of 2-EP set EPB 1236					
547-0920	Memphis Blues/12th Street Rag//Gallopin' Guitar/St. Louis Blues	1956	5.00	10.00	20.00
—One record of 2-EP set EPB 1236					
EPB 1236 [PS]	Stringin' Along with Chet Atkins	1956	5.00	10.00	20.00
EPA-4194	Say "Si Si"/Villa//Yankee Doodle Dandy/You're Just in Love	1958	3.75	7.50	15.00
EPA-4194 [PS]	Chet Atkins at Home	1958	3.75	7.50	15.00
EPA-5052	The Poor People of Paris/Chinatown, My Chinatown//San Antonio Rose/Country Gentlemen	195?	3.75	7.50	15.00
EPA-5052 [PS]	(title unknown)	195?	3.75	7.50	15.00

Albums

COLUMBIA

Number	Title (A Side/B Side)	Yr	VG	VG+	NM
FC 38536	Work It Out with Chet Atkins C.G.P.	1983	2.50	5.00	10.00
PC 38536	Work It Out with Chet Atkins C.G.P.	1985	2.00	4.00	8.00
—Budget-line reissue					
PC 39003	East Tennessee Christmas	1983	2.50	5.00	10.00
FC 39591	Stay Tuned	1985	2.50	5.00	10.00
FC 40256	Street Dreams	1986	2.00	4.00	8.00
FC 40593	Sails	1987	2.00	4.00	8.00
FC 44323	Chet Atkins, C.G.P.	1989	2.00	4.00	8.00

DOLTON

Number	Title (A Side/B Side)	Yr	VG	VG+	NM
BLP-16506 [M]	Play Guitar with Chet Atkins	1967	6.25	12.50	25.00
BST-17506 [S]	Play Guitar with Chet Atkins	1967	7.50	15.00	30.00

PAIR

Number	Title (A Side/B Side)	Yr	VG	VG+	NM
PDL2-1047 [(2)]	Tennessee Guitar Man	1985	3.00	6.00	12.00
PDL2-1115 [(2)]	Guitar for All Seasons	1986	3.00	6.00	12.00

RCA CAMDEN

Number	Title (A Side/B Side)	Yr	VG	VG+	NM
CAL-659 [M]	Chet Atkins and His Guitar	196?	3.75	7.50	15.00
CAS-659(e) [R]	Chet Atkins and His Guitar	1964	3.00	6.00	12.00
CAL-753 [M]	Guitar Genius	196?	3.75	7.50	15.00
CAS-753(e) [R]	Guitar Genius	196?	3.00	6.00	12.00
CAL-981 [M]	Music from Nashville, My Home Town	196?	3.00	6.00	12.00
CAS-981 [S]	Music from Nashville, My Home Town	196?	3.75	7.50	15.00
CAL-2182 [M]	Chet	196?	3.00	6.00	12.00
CAS-2182 [S]	Chet	196?	3.75	7.50	15.00
CAS-2296	Relaxin' with Chet	1969	3.00	6.00	12.00
CAS-2523	Chet 'n Boots	1972	3.00	6.00	12.00
CAS-2555	Nashville Gold	1972	3.00	6.00	12.00
CAS-2600	Finger Pickin' Good	1973	2.50	5.00	10.00
ACL1-7042	Love Letters	197?	2.50	5.00	10.00

RCA RED SEAL

Number	Title (A Side/B Side)	Yr	VG	VG+	NM
LM-2870 [M]	The "Pops" Goes Country	1966	3.75	7.50	15.00
LSC-2870 [S]	The "Pops" Goes Country	1966	5.00	10.00	20.00
—Above two with the Boston Pops Orchestra, Arthur Fiedler, conductor					
LSC-3104	Chet Picks On the Pops	1969	3.75	7.50	15.00
—With the Boston Pops Orchestra, Arthur Fiedler, conductor					

RCA VICTOR

Number	Title (A Side/B Side)	Yr	VG	VG+	NM
APL1-0159	Alone	1973	3.00	6.00	12.00
APL1-0329	Superpickers	1974	3.00	6.00	12.00
APL1-0545	Chet Atkins Picks On Jerry Reed	1974	3.00	6.00	12.00
APL1-0645	Chat Atkins Goes to the Movies	1973	3.00	6.00	12.00
ANL1-0981	Chet Atkins Picks the Best	1975	2.50	5.00	10.00
LPM-1090 [M]	A Session with Chet Atkins	1954	15.00	30.00	60.00
—Red cover					
LPM-1090 [M]	A Session with Chet Atkins	1961	5.00	10.00	20.00
—Woman and guitars cover					
LSP-1090(e) [R]	A Session with Chet Atkins	1967	2.50	5.00	10.00
LPM-1197 [M]	Chet Atkins in Three Dimensions	1956	12.50	52.00	50.00
—Black-and-white guitar cover					
LPM-1197 [M]	Chet Atkins in Three Dimensions	1961	5.00	10.00	20.00
—Red guitar cover					
LSP-1197(e) [R]	Chet Atkins in Three Dimensions	1967	2.50	5.00	10.00
APL1-1233	The Night Atlanta Burned	1975	3.00	6.00	12.00
LPM-1236 [M]	Stringin' Along with Chet Atkins	1956	12.50	25.00	50.00
—Orange cover					
LPM-1236 [M]	Stringin' Along with Chet Atkins	1961	5.00	10.00	20.00
—Full-color cover					
LSP-1236(e) [R]	Stringin' Along with Chet Atkins	1967	2.50	5.00	10.00
LPM-1383 [M]	Finger Style Guitar	1956	12.50	25.00	50.00
—Chet's face not visible on cover					
LPM-1383 [M]	Finger Style Guitar	1961	5.00	10.00	20.00
—Chet's face visible on cover					
LSP-1383(e) [R]	Finger Style Guitar	1962	3.00	6.00	12.00
LPM-1544 [M]	Chet Atkins at Home	1957	12.50	25.00	50.00
—Title in block letters on cover					
LPM-1544 [M]	Chet Atkins at Home	1961	5.00	10.00	20.00
—Title in script on cover					
LSP-1544(e) [R]	Chet Atkins at Home	1967	2.50	5.00	10.00
LPM-1577 [M]	Hi-Fi in Focus	1957	12.50	25.00	50.00
—No guitars on cover					
LPM-1577 [M]	Hi-Fi in Focus	1957	5.00	10.00	20.00
—Guitar on cover					
LSP-1577(e) [R]	Hi-Fi in Focus	196?	2.50	5.00	10.00
ANL1-1935	Christmas with Chet Atkins	1976	2.00	4.00	8.00
—Reissue of LSP-2423					
APL1-1985	The Best of Chet Atkins	1975	3.00	6.00	12.00
LPM-1993 [M]	Chet Atkins in Hollywood	1959	7.50	15.00	30.00
—Night-time cover					
LPM-1993 [M]	Chet Atkins in Hollywood	1961	5.00	10.00	20.00
—Daylight "blonde" cover					
LSP-1993 [S]	Chet Atkins in Hollywood	1959	12.50	25.00	50.00
—Night-time cover					
LSP-1993 [S]	Chet Atkins in Hollywood	1961	7.50	15.00	30.00
—Daylight "blonde" cover					
LPM-2025 [M]	Hum & Strum Along	1959	6.25	12.50	25.00
—Add $10 NM if instruction book is included					
LSP-2025 [S]	Hum & Strum Along	1959	10.00	20.00	40.00
—Add $10 NM if instruction book is included					
LPM-2103 [M]	Mister Guitar	1959	7.50	15.00	30.00
—Lone guitar on cover					
LPM-2103 [M]	Mister Guitar	1961	5.00	10.00	20.00
—Guitar and woman on cover					
LSP-2103 [S]	Mister Guitar	1959	12.50	25.00	50.00
—Lone guitar on cover					
LSP-2103 [S]	Mister Guitar	1961	7.50	15.00	30.00
—Guitar and woman on cover					
LPM-2161 [M]	Teensville	1960	7.50	15.00	30.00
—Title overlaps cover photo					
LPM-2161 [M]	Teensville	1961	5.00	10.00	20.00
—Title in black strip at top of cover photo					
LSP-2161 [S]	Teensville	1960	12.50	25.00	50.00
—Title overlaps cover photo					
LSP-2161 [S]	Teensville	1961	7.50	15.00	30.00
—Title in black strip at top of cover photo					
LPM-2175 [M]	The Other Chet Atkins	1960	5.00	10.00	20.00
LSP-2175 [S]	The Other Chet Atkins	1960	7.50	15.00	30.00
LPM-2232 [M]	Chet Atkins' Workshop	1961	5.00	10.00	20.00
LSP-2232 [S]	Chet Atkins' Workshop	1961	7.50	15.00	30.00
LPM-2346 [M]	The Most Popular Guitar	1961	5.00	10.00	20.00
LSP-2346 [S]	The Most Popular Guitar	1961	7.50	15.00	30.00
AHL1-2405	My Guitar	1977	3.00	6.00	12.00
LPM-2423 [M]	Christmas with Chet Atkins	1961	5.00	10.00	20.00
LSP-2423 [S]	Christmas with Chet Atkins	1961	7.50	15.00	30.00
LPM-2450 [M]	Down Home	1962	5.00	10.00	20.00
LSP-2450 [S]	Down Home	1962	6.25	12.50	25.00
CPL1-2503	A Legendary Performer	1977	3.00	6.00	12.00
LPM-2549 [M]	Caribbean Guitar	1962	5.00	10.00	20.00
LSP-2549 [S]	Caribbean Guitar	1962	6.25	12.50	25.00
LPM-2601 [M]	Back Home Hymns	1962	5.00	10.00	20.00
LSP-2601 [S]	Back Home Hymns	1962	6.25	12.50	25.00
LPM-2616 [M]	Our Man in Nashville	1963	5.00	10.00	20.00
LSP-2616 [S]	Our Man in Nashville	1963	6.25	12.50	25.00
LPM-2678 [M]	Travelin'	1963	5.00	10.00	20.00
LSP-2678 [S]	Travelin'	1963	6.25	12.50	25.00
LPM-2719 [M]	Teen Scene	1963	5.00	10.00	20.00
LSP-2719 [S]	Teen Scene	1963	6.25	12.50	25.00
LPM-2783 [M]	Guitar Country	1964	3.75	7.50	15.00
LSP-2783 [S]	Guitar Country	1964	5.00	10.00	20.00
LPM-2887 [M]	The Best of Chet Atkins	1964	3.75	7.50	15.00
LSP-2887 [S]	The Best of Chet Atkins	1964	5.00	10.00	20.00
LPM-2908 [M]	Progressive Pickin'	1964	3.75	7.50	15.00
LSP-2908 [S]	Progressive Pickin'	1964	5.00	10.00	20.00
LPM-3079 [10]	Chet Atkins' Gallopin' Guitar	1952	37.50	75.00	150.00
LPM-3169 [10]	Stringin' Along with Chet Atkins	1953	25.00	50.00	100.00
AHL1-3302	The First Nashville Guitar Quartet	1979	3.00	6.00	12.00
LPM-3316 [M]	My Favorite Guitars	1965	3.75	7.50	15.00
LSP-3316 [S]	My Favorite Guitars	1965	5.00	10.00	20.00
LPM-3429 [M]	More of That "Guitar Country"	1965	3.75	7.50	15.00
LSP-3429 [S]	More of That "Guitar Country"	1965	5.00	10.00	20.00
AHL1-3505	The Best of Chet On The Road...Live	1980	3.00	6.00	12.00
LPM-3531 [M]	Chet Atkins Picks On the Beatles	1966	6.25	12.50	25.00
LSP-3531 [S]	Chet Atkins Picks On the Beatles	1966	7.50	15.00	30.00
LPM-3558 [M]	The Best of Chet Atkins, Volume 2	1966	3.00	6.00	12.00
LSP-3558 [S]	The Best of Chet Atkins, Volume 2	1966	3.75	7.50	15.00
LPM-3647 [M]	From Nashville with Love	1966	3.00	6.00	12.00
LSP-3647 [S]	From Nashville with Love	1966	3.75	7.50	15.00
LPM-3728 [M]	It's a Guitar World	1967	7.50	15.00	30.00
LSP-3728 [S]	It's a Guitar World	1967	3.00	6.00	12.00
AYL1-3741	The First Nashville Guitar Quartet	1981	2.00	4.00	8.00
—"Best Buy Series" reissue					
LPM-3818 [M]	Chet Atkins Picks the Best	1967	7.50	15.00	30.00
LSP-3818 [S]	Chet Atkins Picks the Best	1967	3.00	6.00	12.00
LPM-3885 [M]	Class Guitar	1967	7.50	15.00	30.00
LSP-3885 [S]	Class Guitar	1967	3.00	6.00	12.00
LPM-3992 [M]	Solo Flights	1968	12.50	25.00	50.00
LSP-3992 [S]	Solo Flights	1968	3.00	6.00	12.00
LSP-4017	Hometown Guitar	1968	3.75	7.50	15.00
AHL1-4044	Still Country — After All These Years	1981	2.50	5.00	10.00
LSP-4061	Solid Gold '68	1968	3.75	7.50	15.00
LSP-4135	Lover's Guitar	1968	3.75	7.50	15.00
LSP-4244	Solid Gold '69	1969	3.00	6.00	12.00
LSP-4331	Yestergroovin'	1970	3.00	6.00	12.00
LSP-4396	Me & Jerry	1971	3.75	7.50	15.00
—With Jerry Reed					
LSP-4464	For the Good Times	1971	3.75	7.50	15.00
AHL1-4724	Great Hits of the Past	1983	2.50	5.00	10.00
LSP-4754	Chet Atkins Picks the Hits	1973	3.75	7.50	15.00
AHL1-5495	Collector's Series	1985	2.50	5.00	10.00
VPS-6030 [(2)]	This Is Chet Atkins	1972	3.75	7.50	15.00
VPXS-6079 [(2)]	Now & Then	1972	3.75	7.50	15.00

TIME-LIFE

Number	Title (A Side/B Side)	Yr	VG	VG+	NM
117	Country Music	1981	3.00	6.00	12.00

ATKINS, CHET, AND LES PAUL

Also see each artist's individual listings.

45s

RCA

Number	Title (A Side/B Side)	Yr	VG	VG+	NM
PB-11330	I'm Your Greatest Fan/Hot Toddy	1978	—	2.00	4.00

RCA VICTOR

Number	Title (A Side/B Side)	Yr	VG	VG+	NM
PB-10642	Moonglow/Avalon	1976	—	2.50	5.00

Number	Title (A Side/B Side)	Yr	VG	VG+	NM

Albums

RCA VICTOR

Number	Title (A Side/B Side)	Yr	VG	VG+	NM
APL1-1167	Chester and Lester	1976	3.00	6.00	12.00
APL1-2786	Guitar Monsters	1978	3.00	6.00	12.00
AYL1-3682	Chester and Lester	1980	2.00	4.00	8.00

—"Best Buy Series" reissue

ATKINS, CHET, AND DOC WATSON

Also see each artist's individual listings.

45s

RCA

Number	Title (A Side/B Side)	Yr	VG	VG+	NM
PB-12138	Medley-Tennessee Rag & Beaumont Rag/On My Way to Canaan's Land	1981	—	2.00	4.00

Albums

RCA VICTOR

Number	Title (A Side/B Side)	Yr	VG	VG+	NM
AHL1-3701	Reflections	1980	2.50	5.00	10.00

ATLANTA RHYTHM SECTION

Formed by ex-members of THE CANDYMEN and CLASSICS IV.

45s

COLUMBIA

Number	Title (A Side/B Side)	Yr	VG	VG+	NM
18-02471	Alien/Southern Exposure	1981	—	2.00	4.00

DECCA

Number	Title (A Side/B Side)	Yr	VG	VG+	NM
32928	All in Your Mind/Can't Stand It No More	1972	2.00	4.00	8.00
32948	Earnestine/Another Man's Woman	1972	2.00	4.00	8.00
33051	Back Up Against the Wall/It Must Be Done	1973	2.00	4.00	8.00

MCA

Number	Title (A Side/B Side)	Yr	VG	VG+	NM
40059	Cold Turkey, Tennessee/Conversation	1973	—	3.00	6.00
40719	All in Your Mind/Earnestine	1977	—	2.50	5.00

POLYDOR

Number	Title (A Side/B Side)	Yr	VG	VG+	NM
2001	Spooky/It's Only Music	1979	—	2.50	5.00
2039	Back Up Against the Wall/Large Time	1980	—	2.50	5.00
2079	Conversation/Indigo Passion	1980	—	2.50	5.00
2125	Putting My Faith in Love/I Ain't Much	1980	—	2.50	5.00
2142	Silver Eagle/Strictly R & R	1981	—	2.50	5.00
14248	Doraville/Who Are You Going to Run To	1974	—	2.50	5.00
14262	Angel (What in the World's Come Over Us)/Help Yourself	1975	—	2.50	5.00
14273	Get Your Head Out of Your Heart/Jesus Hearted People	1975	—	2.50	5.00
14289	Bless My Soul/Crazy	1975	—	2.50	5.00
14323	Jukin'/Beautiful Dreamer	1976	—	2.50	5.00
14339	Free Spirit/Police Police	1976	—	2.50	5.00
14373	So In to You/Everybody Gotta Go	1977	—	2.50	5.00
14397	Neon Nites/Don't Miss the Message	1977	—	2.50	5.00
14411	Dog Days/Cuban Crisis	1977	—	2.50	5.00
14459	Imaginary Lover/Silent Treatment	1978	—	2.50	5.00
14484	I'm Not Gonna Let It Bother Me Tonight/Ballad of Lois Malone	1978	—	2.50	5.00
14504	Champagne Jam/Great Escape	1978	—	2.50	5.00
14568	Do It or Die/My Song	1979	—	2.50	5.00
14582	Spooky/It's Only Music	1979	—	—	—

—Unreleased?

Albums

COLUMBIA

Number	Title (A Side/B Side)	Yr	VG	VG+	NM
FC 37550	Quinella	1981	2.50	5.00	10.00
PC 37550	Quinella	1982	2.00	4.00	8.00

—Budget-line reissue

DECCA

Number	Title (A Side/B Side)	Yr	VG	VG+	NM
DL 75265	Atlanta Rhythm Section	1972	6.25	12.50	25.00
DL 75390	Back Up Against the Wall	1973	6.25	12.50	25.00

MCA

Number	Title (A Side/B Side)	Yr	VG	VG+	NM
2-4114 [(2)]	Atlanta Rhythm Section	1977	3.00	6.00	12.00

—Combines the two Decca LPs into one package

MOBILE FIDELITY

Number	Title (A Side/B Side)	Yr	VG	VG+	NM
1-038	Champagne Jam	1981	10.00	20.00	40.00

—Audiophile vinyl

POLYDOR

Number	Title (A Side/B Side)	Yr	VG	VG+	NM
PD 6027	Third Annual Pipe Dream	1974	2.50	5.00	10.00
PD 6041	Dog Days	1975	2.50	5.00	10.00
PD-1-6060	Red Tape	1976	2.50	5.00	10.00
PD-1-6080	A Rock and Roll Alternative	1977	2.50	5.00	10.00
PD-1-6134	Champagne Jam	1978	2.50	5.00	10.00
PD-1-6200	Underdog	1979	2.50	5.00	10.00
PD-2-6236 [(2)]	Are You Ready!	1979	3.00	6.00	12.00
PD-1-6285	The Boys from Doraville	1980	2.50	5.00	10.00

ATLANTICS, THE

More than one group.

45s

COLUMBIA

Number	Title (A Side/B Side)	Yr	VG	VG+	NM
42877	Greensleeves/Bombera	1963	5.00	10.00	20.00
43023	War of the World/Bow Man	1964	5.00	10.00	20.00

LINDA

Number	Title (A Side/B Side)	Yr	VG	VG+	NM
103	Boo-Hoo-Hoo/Everything Is Gonna Be All Right	1961	6.25	12.50	25.00
107	Remember the Night/Flame of Love	1962	20.00	40.00	80.00

RAMPART

Number	Title (A Side/B Side)	Yr	VG	VG+	NM
614	Let Me Call You Sweetheart/Home on the Range	1964	3.00	6.00	12.00
643	Beaver Shot/Fine, Fine, Fine	1965	2.50	5.00	10.00
647	Slopp Dance/Sonny and Cher	1965	2.50	5.00	10.00

ATOMIC ROOSTER

45s

ELEKTRA

Number	Title (A Side/B Side)	Yr	VG	VG+	NM
45727	Tomorrow Night/Play the Game	1971	—	2.50	5.00
45745	Devil's Answer/The Rock	1971	—	2.50	5.00
45766	Save Me/Never to Lose	1972	—	2.50	5.00
45800	Stand By Me/Never to Lose	1972	—	2.50	5.00

Albums

ELEKTRA

Number	Title (A Side/B Side)	Yr	VG	VG+	NM
EKS-74094	Death Walks Behind You	1971	5.00	10.00	20.00
EKS-74109	In Hearing Of Atomic Rooster	1971	5.00	10.00	20.00
EKS-75039	Made in England	1972	5.00	10.00	20.00
EKS-75074	Atomic Rooster IV	1973	3.75	7.50	15.00

ATTILA

BILLY JOEL was a member.

Albums

BACK-TRAC

Number	Title (A Side/B Side)	Yr	VG	VG+	NM
P 18808	Attila	1985	2.50	5.00	10.00

EPIC

Number	Title (A Side/B Side)	Yr	VG	VG+	NM
E 30030	Attila	1970	7.50	15.00	30.00

ATTITUDES

45s

DARK HORSE

Number	Title (A Side/B Side)	Yr	VG	VG+	NM
8404	Sweet Summer Music/If We Want To	1977	—	2.00	4.00
8452	Good News/In a Stranger's Arms	1977	—	2.00	4.00
10004	Ain't Love Enough/The Whole World's Crazy	1975	—	2.50	5.00
10008	Lend a Hand/Honey Don't Leave L.A.	1976	—	2.50	5.00
10011	Sweet Summer Music/If We Want To	1976	—	2.50	5.00

Albums

DARK HORSE

Number	Title (A Side/B Side)	Yr	VG	VG+	NM
DH 3021	Good News	1977	2.50	5.00	10.00
SP-22008	Attitudes	1976	3.00	6.00	12.00

ATTRACTIONS, THE

45s

BELL

Number	Title (A Side/B Side)	Yr	VG	VG+	NM
659	Destination You/Find Me	1967	5.00	10.00	20.00
674	New Girl in the Neighborhood/That Girl Is Mine	1967	5.00	10.00	20.00
690	Why Shouldn't a Man Cry/Some of Your Time	1967	5.00	10.00	20.00

JUNE BUG

Number	Title (A Side/B Side)	Yr	VG	VG+	NM
697/8	You Don't Know, Boy/Think Back	1966	6.25	12.50	25.00

ATWELL, WINIFRED

45s

COLUMBIA

Number	Title (A Side/B Side)	Yr	VG	VG+	NM
43472	Snow Bells/Flea Circus	1965	—	3.00	6.00

ATWOOD THE ELECTRIC ICEMAN

Actually the SIR DOUGLAS QUINTET with Atwood Allen.

45s

UNI

Number	Title (A Side/B Side)	Yr	VG	VG+	NM
55216	Bossier City/Michoacan	1970	—	3.00	6.00

AUDIENCE

45s

ELEKTRA

Number	Title (A Side/B Side)	Yr	VG	VG+	NM
45732	Indian Summer/It Brings a Tear	1971	—	2.50	5.00
45756	I Put a Spell on You/Nancy	1971	—	2.50	5.00
45788	Stand By the Door/Seven Sore Bruises	1972	—	2.50	5.00

Albums

ELEKTRA

Number	Title (A Side/B Side)	Yr	VG	VG+	NM
EKS-74100	House on the Hill	1971	3.00	6.00	12.00
EKS-75026	Lunch	1972	3.00	6.00	12.00

AUDREY

45s

PLUS

Number	Title (A Side/B Side)	Yr	VG	VG+	NM
104	Dear Elvis/Dear Elvis (Part 2)	1956	20.00	40.00	80.00

—Black vinyl; a red vinyl pressing has been reported but is unconfirmed

AUGER, BRIAN, TRINITY

Includes "Brian Auger's Oblivion Express."

45s

ATCO

Number	Title (A Side/B Side)	Yr	VG	VG+	NM
6593	This Wheel's On Fire/A Kind of Love-In	1968	2.00	4.00	8.00
—With Julie Driscoll					
6611	Black Cat/In and Out	1968	2.00	4.00	8.00
6629	Shadows of You/Road to Cairo	1968	2.00	4.00	8.00
—With Julie Driscoll					
6656	A Day in the Life/Bumpin' On Sunset	1969	2.00	4.00	8.00
6685	Save the Country/The Flesh Failures (Let the Sun Shine In)	1969	2.00	4.00	8.00
6685	Save the Country/Light My Fire	1969	2.00	4.00	8.00
6685 [DJ]	Save the Country (long/short versions)	1969	3.00	6.00	12.00

RCA VICTOR

Number	Title (A Side/B Side)	Yr	VG	VG+	NM
APBO-0085	Happiness Is Just Around the Bend/Inner City Blues	1973	—	2.50	5.00
APBO-0282	Straight Ahead/Beginning Again	1974	—	2.50	5.00
74-0381	I Wanna Take You Higher/Listen Here	1970	—	3.00	6.00
74-0579	Maria's Wedding/Trouble	1971	—	2.50	5.00
—Group becomes "Oblivion Express"					
74-0735	Second Wind/Freedom Jazz Dance	1972	—	2.50	5.00

Albums

ATCO

Number	Title (A Side/B Side)	Yr	VG	VG+	NM
33-258 [M]	Open	1968	5.00	10.00	20.00
—White label promo; no stock copies were issued in mono					
SD 33-258 [S]	Open	1968	3.00	6.00	12.00
SD 33-273	Definitely What!	1969	3.00	6.00	12.00
SD 2-701 [(2)]	Streetnoise	1969	5.00	10.00	20.00

CAPITOL

Number	Title (A Side/B Side)	Yr	VG	VG+	NM
DT-136 [R]	Jools & Brian	1969	3.00	6.00	12.00

—American issue of pre-Atco material

HEADFIRST

Number	Title (A Side/B Side)	Yr	VG	VG+	NM
9702	Search Party	1981	3.75	7.50	15.00

POLYDOR

Number	Title (A Side/B Side)	Yr	VG	VG+	NM
PD-1-6505	Genesis	1975	3.00	6.00	12.00

RCA VICTOR

Number	Title (A Side/B Side)	Yr	VG	VG+	NM
AFL1-0140	Closer To It	197?	2.00	4.00	8.00

—Reissue

Number	Title (A Side/B Side)	Yr	VG	VG+	NM
APL1-0140	Closer To It	1973	2.50	5.00	10.00
AFL1-0454	Straight Ahead	197?	2.00	4.00	8.00
—Reissue					
CPL1-0454	Straight Ahead	1974	2.50	5.00	10.00
CPL1-0645	Live Oblivion	1974	2.50	5.00	10.00
APL1-1210	Reinforcements	1975	2.50	5.00	10.00
CPL2-1230 [(2)]	Live Oblivion, Vol. 2	1976	3.75	7.50	15.00
AFL1-2249	The Best of Brian Auger	1977	2.50	5.00	10.00
ANL1-2481	Live Oblivion	1977	2.00	4.00	8.00
—Reissue					
LSP-4372	Befour	1970	2.50	5.00	10.00
AFL1-4462	Brian Auger's Oblivion Express	197?	2.00	4.00	8.00
—Reissue					
LSP-4462	Brian Auger's Oblivion Express	1971	2.50	5.00	10.00
—Starting here, group is "Oblivion Express"					
LSP-4540	A Better Land	1971	2.50	5.00	10.00
AFL1-4703	Second Wind	197?	2.00	4.00	8.00
—Reissue					
LSP-4703	Second Wind	1972	2.50	5.00	10.00
SPRINGBOARD					
SPB-4044	Brian Auger	1973	2.00	4.00	8.00
—Reissue of early material					
WARNER BROS.					
BS 2981	Happiness Heartaches	1977	2.50	5.00	10.00
BSK 3153	Encore	1978	2.50	5.00	10.00

AUGUST AND DENEEN

45s

Number	Title (A Side/B Side)	Yr	VG	VG+	NM
ABC					
11082	We Go Together/Can't Get You Out of My Head	1968	15.00	30.00	60.00

AUM

Albums

Number	Title (A Side/B Side)	Yr	VG	VG+	NM
FILLMORE					
Z 30002	Resurrection	1970	7.50	15.00	30.00
SIRE					
SES-97007	Bluesvibes	1969	10.00	20.00	40.00

AUSTIN, DONALD

45s

Number	Title (A Side/B Side)	Yr	VG	VG+	NM
EASTBOUND					
603	Crazy Legs/Nan Zee	1973	2.00	4.00	8.00
608	Sex Plot/Can't Understand the Strain	1973	2.00	4.00	8.00

Albums

Number	Title (A Side/B Side)	Yr	VG	VG+	NM
EASTBOUND					
EB-9005	Crazy Legs	1973	7.50	15.00	30.00

AUSTIN, PATTI

45s

Number	Title (A Side/B Side)	Yr	VG	VG+	NM
ABC					
11104	Music to My Heart/Love 'Em and Leave 'Em Kind of Love	1968	3.75	7.50	15.00
COLUMBIA					
45337	Are We Ready for Love/Now That I Know What Loneliness Is	1971	—	2.50	5.00
45410	Black California/All Good Gifts-Day by Day	1971	—	2.50	5.00
45499	God Only Knows/Can't Forget the One I Love	1971	—	2.50	5.00
45592	Day by Day/Didn't Say a Word	1972	—	2.50	5.00
45785	Come to Him/Turn On the Music	1973	—	2.50	5.00
45906	Being with You/Take a Closer Look	1973	—	2.50	5.00
CORAL					
62455	He's Good Enough for Me/Earl	1965	5.00	10.00	20.00
62471	I Wanna Be Loved/A Most Unusual Boy	1965	5.00	10.00	20.00
62478	Someone's Gonna Cry/You'd Better Know What You're Getting	1966	25.00	50.00	100.00
62491	Take Your Time/Take Away the Pain Stain	1966	5.00	10.00	20.00
62500	Leave a Little Love/My Lovelight Ain't Gonna Shine	1966	5.00	10.00	20.00
62511	Got to Check You Out/What a Difference a Day Makes	1967	5.00	10.00	20.00
62518	Only All the Time/Oh How I Need You Joe	1967	5.00	10.00	20.00
62541	I'll Keep Loving You/You're Too Much a Part of Me	1967	5.00	10.00	20.00
62548	(I've Given) All My Love/Why Can't We Try It Again	1968	5.00	10.00	20.00
CTI					
7	In My Life (Part 1)/In My Life (Part 2)	1973	—	2.50	5.00
—With Jerry Butler					
33	Say You Love Me/In My Life	1976	—	2.00	4.00
41	We're in Love/Golden Oldies	1977	—	2.00	4.00
51	Love Me by Name/You Fooled Me	1978	—	2.00	4.00
59	What's at the End of the Rainbow/In My Life	1978	—	2.00	4.00
9600	Body Language/People in Love	1980	—	2.00	4.00
9601	I Want You Tonight/Love Me Again	1980	—	2.00	4.00
QWEST					
27718	Smoke Gets In Your Eyes/How Long Has This Been Goin' On?	1988	—	—	3.00
27718 [PS]	Smoke Gets In Your Eyes/How Long Has This Been Goin' On?	1988	—	—	3.00
28573	Only a Breath Away/Summer Is the Coldest Time of Year	1986	—	—	3.00
28659	Gettin' Away with Murder/Anything Can Happen Here	1986	—	—	3.00
28788	The Heat of Heat/Hot in the Flames of Love	1986	—	—	3.00
28935	Honey for the Bees/Hot in the Flames of Love	1985	—	—	3.00
29136	All Behind Us Now/Fine Fine Fella (Got to Have You)	1984	—	2.00	4.00
29234	Shoot the Moon/Change Your Attitude	1984	—	2.00	4.00
29305	Rhythm of the Street/Solero	1984	—	2.00	4.00
29373	It's Gonna Be Special/Solero	1984	—	2.00	4.00
29618	How Do You Keep the Music Playing/same (Long Version)	1983	—	2.00	4.00
29727	Every Home Should Have One/Solero	1983	—	2.00	4.00
49754	Do You Love Me/Solero	1981	—	2.00	4.00
49854	Every Home Should Have One/Solero	1981	—	2.50	5.00
50036	Baby, Come to Me/Solero	1982	—	2.00	4.00
—With James Ingram					
UNITED ARTISTS					
50520	The Family Tree/Magical Boy	1969	2.00	4.00	8.00
50588	I Will Wait for You/Big Mouth	1969	2.00	4.00	8.00
50640	Your Love Made a Difference in Me/It's Easier to Laugh Than Cry	1970	2.00	4.00	8.00

Albums

Number	Title (A Side/B Side)	Yr	VG	VG+	NM
CTI					
5001	End of a Rainbow	1976	2.50	5.00	10.00
5006	Havana Candy	1977	2.50	5.00	10.00
7086	Live at the Bottom Line	1979	2.50	5.00	10.00
JZ 36503	Body Language	1980	2.50	5.00	10.00
PZ 36503	Body Language	198?	2.00	4.00	8.00
—Budget-line reissue					
GRP					
GR-9603	Love Is Gonna Getcha	1990	2.50	5.00	10.00
QWEST					
QWS 3591	Every Home Should Have One	1981	2.00	4.00	8.00
23974	Patti Austin	1984	2.00	4.00	8.00
25276	Gettin' Away with Murder	1985	2.00	4.00	8.00
25698	The Real Me	1988	2.00	4.00	8.00

AUTOSALVAGE

45s

Number	Title (A Side/B Side)	Yr	VG	VG+	NM
RCA VICTOR					
47-9506	Parahighway/Rampant Generalities	1968	3.00	6.00	12.00

Albums

Number	Title (A Side/B Side)	Yr	VG	VG+	NM
RCA VICTOR					
LPM-3940 [M]	Autosalvage	1968	10.00	20.00	40.00
LSP-3940 [S]	Autosalvage	1968	10.00	20.00	40.00

AUTRY, GENE

45s

Number	Title (A Side/B Side)	Yr	VG	VG+	NM
CHALLENGE					
1009	No Back Door to Heaven/You're the Only Good Thing	1957	3.00	6.00	12.00
1010	Rudolph the Red-Nosed Reindeer/Here Come Santa Claus	1957	3.00	6.00	12.00
—Re-recordings of originals on Columbia					
59030	Rudolph, the Red-Nosed Reindeer/Here Come Santa Claus	1958	3.00	6.00	12.00
59030 [PS]	Rudolph, the Red-Nosed Reindeer/Here Come Santa Claus	1958	5.00	10.00	20.00
COLUMBIA					
4-56	Rudolph, the Red-Nosed Reindeer/If It Doesn't Snow on Christmas	1951	5.00	10.00	20.00
—Yellow label, red print; second number on label is 90049					
4-56 [PS]	Rudolph, the Red-Nosed Reindeer/If It Doesn't Snow on Christmas	1951	6.25	12.50	25.00
—Sleeve was manufactured with a hole in the middle					
4-68	Peter Cottontail/Funny Little Bunny	1950	5.00	10.00	20.00
—Yellow label, red print; second number on label is unknown					
4-68 [PS]	Peter Cottontail/Funny Little Bunny	1950	6.25	12.50	25.00
—Sleeve was manufactured with a hole in the middle					
4-75	Frosty the Snow Man/When Santa Claus Gets Your Letter	1951	5.00	10.00	20.00
—Yellow label, red print; second number on label is 90072					
4-75 [PS]	Frosty the Snow Man/When Santa Claus Gets Your Letter	1951	6.25	12.50	25.00
—Sleeve was manufactured with a hole in the middle					
4-84	Here Comes Santa Claus/He's a Chubby Little Fellow	1951	5.00	10.00	20.00
—Yellow label, red print; second number on label is 90088					
4-84 [PS]	Here Comes Santa Claus/He's a Chubby Little Fellow	1951	6.25	12.50	25.00
—Sleeve was manufactured with a hole in the middle					
4-121	Thirty-Two Feet — Eight Little Tails/(Hedrock, Coco and Joe) The Three Little Dwarfs	1952	5.00	10.00	20.00
—Yellow label, red print; second number on label is 90135					
4-121 [PS]	Thirty-Two Feet — Eight Little Tails/(Hedrock, Coco and Joe) The Three Little Dwarfs	1952	6.25	12.50	25.00
—Sleeve was manufactured with a hole in the middle					
4-122	Poppy the Puppy/He'll Be Coming Down the Chimney (Like He Always Did Before)	1952	5.00	10.00	20.00
—Yellow label, red print; second number on label is 90136					
4-122 [PS]	Poppy the Puppy/He'll Be Coming Down the Chimney (Like He Always Did Before)	1952	6.25	12.50	25.00
—Sleeve was manufactured with a hole in the middle					
4-150	Merry Texas Christmas, You All!/The Night Before Christmas (In Texas, That Is)	1953	3.75	7.50	15.00
—Yellow label, red print; second number on label is 90172					
4-150 [PS]	Merry Texas Christmas, You All!/The Night Before Christmas (In Texas, That Is)	1953	5.00	10.00	20.00
—Sleeve was manufactured with a hole in the middle					
4-176	Santa Claus Is Comin' to Town/Up on the Housetop (Ho! Ho! Ho!)	1954	3.75	7.50	15.00
—Yellow label, red print					
4-176 [PS]	Santa Claus Is Comin' to Town/Up on the Housetop (Ho! Ho! Ho!)	1954	5.00	10.00	20.00
2-210 (?)	Ellie Mae/Sun Flower	1949	10.00	20.00	40.00
—Microgroove 33 1/3 rpm single					
2-270 (?)	My Empty Heart/I Wish I Had Stayed Over Yonder	1949	10.00	20.00	40.00
—Microgroove 33 1/3 rpm single					
2-320 (?)	Santa, Santa, Santa/He's a Chubby Little Fellow	1949	10.00	20.00	40.00
—Microgroove 33 1/3 rpm single					
2-340 (?)	When the Silver Colorado Turns to Gold/Whirlwinds	1949	10.00	20.00	40.00
—Microgroove 33 1/3 rpm single					
2-370 (?)	Riders in the Sky/Cowboy Trademarks	1949	10.00	20.00	40.00
—Microgroove 33 1/3 rpm single					

Number	Title (A Side/B Side)	Yr	VG	VG+	NM
1-375	Rudolph, the Red-Nosed Reindeer/If It Doesn't Snow on Christmas	1949	10.00	20.00	40.00
—Microgroove 33 1/3 rpm single					
6-375	Rudolph, the Red-Nosed Reindeer/If It Doesn't Snow on Christmas	1950	6.25	12.50	25.00
—Reissue on 45 of a single originally on 33 1/3 Microgroove single					
2-430 (?)	Mule Train/Cowboy Serenade	1950	10.00	20.00	40.00
—Microgroove 33 1/3 rpm single					
2-480 (?)	Poison Ivy/A New Star Is Shining	1950	10.00	20.00	40.00
—Microgroove 33 1/3 rpm single					
2-550 (?)	Take Me Back to My Boots and Saddle/Dust	1950	10.00	20.00	40.00
—Microgroove 33 1/3 rpm single					
1-575	Peter Cottontail/Funny Little Bunny	1950	10.00	20.00	40.00
—Microgroove 33 1/3 rpm single					
1-630 (?)	Roses/The Roses I Picked for Our Wedding	1950	10.00	20.00	40.00
—Microgroove 33 1/3 rpm single					
1-741 (?)	Blue Canadian Rockies/Onteora	1950	10.00	20.00	40.00
—Microgroove 33 1/3 rpm single					
6-741 (?)	Blue Canadian Rockies/Onteora	1950	6.25	12.50	25.00
1-742	Frosty the Snow Man/When Santa Claus Gets Your Letter	1950	10.00	20.00	40.00
—Microgroove 33 1/3 rpm single					
6-742	Frosty the Snow Man/When Santa Claus Gets Your Letter	1950	5.00	10.00	20.00
1-765 (?)	Goodnight Irene/Texans Never Cry	1950	10.00	20.00	40.00
—Microgroove 33 1/3 rpm single					
6-765 (?)	Goodnight Irene/Texans Never Cry	1950	6.25	12.50	25.00
1-810 (?)	Little Johnny Pilgrim/Guffy the Goofy Gobbler	1950	10.00	20.00	40.00
—Microgroove 33 1/3 rpm single					
6-810 (?)	Little Johnny Pilgrim/Guffy the Goofy Gobbler	1950	6.25	12.50	25.00
38-06189	The Statue in the Bay/God Bless America	1986	—	2.00	4.00
20377	Here Comes Santa Claus (Down Santa Claus Lane)/An Old-Fashioned Tree	1950	5.00	10.00	20.00
—Reissue on 45 of a single originally on 78					
20709	I Love You Because/The Last Straw	1950	6.25	12.50	25.00
20727	Silver Haired Daddy/Mississippi Valley Blues	1950	6.25	12.50	25.00
20763	Rose Colored Memories/Let Me Cry on Your Shoulder	1950	6.25	12.50	25.00
20775	The Statue in the Bay/The Place Where I Worship	1951	5.00	10.00	20.00
20814	At Mail Call Today/I'll Be Back	1951	5.00	10.00	20.00
20865	When It's Springtime in the Rockies/I Don't Want to Set the World on Fire	1951	5.00	10.00	20.00
20899	Heartsick Soldier/I'm Learning to Live	1952	3.75	7.50	15.00
20904	Am I a Pastime/I Was Just Walkin'	1952	3.75	7.50	15.00
20929	Diesel Smoke/Stop Your Gambling	1952	3.75	7.50	15.00
21035	I've Lived a Lifetime for You/Story Book of Love	1952	3.75	7.50	15.00
21144	Love Is So Misleadin'/Don't Send Your Love	1953	3.75	7.50	15.00
21207	Bimbo/Roly Poly	1954	3.75	7.50	15.00
21229	Angels in the Sky/A Voice in the Choir	1954	3.75	7.50	15.00
21252	Closing the Book/My Lazy Day	1954	3.75	7.50	15.00
21269	20-20 Vision/You're the Only Good Thing	1954	3.75	7.50	15.00
21280	I'm a Fool to Care/A Broken Promise Means a Broken Heart	1954	3.75	7.50	15.00
21304	When He Grows Tired of You/It Just Don't Seem Like Home	1954	3.75	7.50	15.00
21329	Barney the Bashful Bullfrog/Little Peter Pumpkin Eater	1954	3.75	7.50	15.00
21358	I'm Innocent/You're an Angel	1955	3.75	7.50	15.00
21481	You've Got to Take the Bitter with the Sweet/Two Cheaters in Love	1956	3.75	7.50	15.00
21527	God's in the Saddle/If Today Were the End of the World	1956	3.75	7.50	15.00
33023	Back in the Saddle Again/Tumbling Tumbleweeds	196?	2.00	4.00	8.00
—"Hall of Fame" reissue; red and black label					
33165	Rudolph, the Red-Nosed Reindeer/Here Comes Santa Claus (Down Santa Claus Lane)	1970	—	2.50	5.00
—"Hall of Fame" reissue; red and black label					
33165	Rudolph, the Red-Nosed Reindeer/Here Comes Santa Claus (Down Santa Claus Lane)	198?	—	—	3.00
—"Hall of Fame" reissue; gray label					
38610	Rudolph, the Red-Nosed Reindeer/If It Doesn't Snow On Christmas	1951	3.75	7.50	15.00
—Second 45 issue of this song					
38907	Frosty The Snowman/When Santa Claus Gets Your Letter	1951	3.75	7.50	15.00
—Second 45 issue of this song					
3-39086	My Heart Cries for You/Teardrops from My Eyes	1950	7.50	15.00	30.00
—Microgroove 33 1/3 rpm single					
4-39086	My Heart Cries for You/Teardrops from My Eyes	1950	5.00	10.00	20.00
39217	Sonny the Bunny/Bunny Roundup Time	1951	5.00	10.00	20.00
39347	Crime Will Never Pay/Gold Can Buy Anything	1951	3.75	7.50	15.00
39371	Mr. and Mississippi/How Long Is Forever	1951	3.75	7.50	15.00
39405	Old Soldiers Never Die/God Bless America	1951	3.75	7.50	15.00
39461	Frosty the Snow Man/An Old-Fashioned Tree	1951	3.00	6.00	12.00
39462	When Santa Claus Gets Your Letter/He's a Chubby Little Fellow	1951	3.00	6.00	12.00
39463	Rudolph, the Red-Nosed Reindeer/Here Comes Santa Claus (Down Santa Claus Lane)	1951	3.00	6.00	12.00
39464	Santa, Santa, Santa/If It Doesn't Snow on Christmas	1951	3.00	6.00	12.00
39542	Poppy the Puppy/He'll Be Coming Down the Chimney (Like He Always Did Before)	1951	3.75	7.50	15.00
39543	Thirty-Two Feet — Eight Little Tails/(Hedrock, Coco and Joe) The Three Little Dwarfs	1951	3.75	7.50	15.00
39808	Don't Believe a Word They Say/God's Little Candles	1952	3.75	7.50	15.00
39876	The Night Before Christmas Song/Look Out the Window	1952	3.75	7.50	15.00
—With Rosemary Clooney					
40092	Where Did My Snowman Go?/Freddie the Little Fir Tree	1953	3.75	7.50	15.00
40135	I Wish My Mom Would Marry Santa Claus/Sleigh Bells	1953	3.75	7.50	15.00
40167	Easter Morning/The Horse with the Easter Bonnet	1954	3.75	7.50	15.00
40589	Round, Round the Christmas Tree/Merry Christmas Tree	1955	3.75	7.50	15.00
40790	Everyone's a Child at Christmas/You Can See Old Santa Claus	1956	3.75	7.50	15.00
40960	Half Your Heart/Darlin' What More Can I Do	1957	3.00	6.00	12.00
44632	Back in the Saddle Again/Home on the Range	1968	2.00	4.00	8.00
CRICKET					
CX-6	Rudolph, the Red-Nosed Reindeer/Tinker Town Santa Claus	196?	3.00	6.00	12.00
—B-side by the Cricketones					
MISTLETOE					
801	Rudolph, The Red-Nosed Reindeer/Up On The House Top	196?	2.00	4.00	8.00
REPUBLIC					
001	Back in the Saddle Again/The Last Round-Up	1977	—	2.50	5.00
326	Rudolph the Red-Nosed Reindeer/Here Comes Santa Claus	1976	—	2.00	4.00
1405	Rudolph the Red-Nosed Reindeer/Here Comes Santa Claus	1969	2.00	4.00	8.00
2001	Nine Little Reindeer/Buon Natale (Means Merry Christmas)	1959	3.00	6.00	12.00
2001 [PS]	Nine Little Reindeer/Buon Natale (Means Merry Christmas)	1959	3.00	6.00	12.00
2002	Santa's Comin' in a Whirlybird/Jingle Bells	1959	3.00	6.00	12.00
Albums					
CHALLENGE					
CHL-600 [M]	Christmas with Gene Autry	1958	12.50	25.00	50.00
COLUMBIA					
CL 677 [M]	Gene Autry and Champion — Western Adventures	1955	30.00	60.00	120.00
CL 1575 [M]	Gene Autry's Greatest Hits	1961	7.50	15.00	30.00
—Red and black label with six "eye" logos					
CL 2547 [10]	Merry Christmas with Gene Autry	1954	30.00	60.00	120.00
—"House Party Series" release					
CL 2568 [10]	Gene Autry Sings Peter Cottontail	1955	30.00	60.00	120.00
CL 6020 [10]	Easter Favorites	1949	37.50	75.00	150.00
CL 6137 [10]	Merry Christmas	1950	37.50	75.00	150.00
JL 8001 [10]	Gene Autry at the Rodeo	1949	37.50	75.00	150.00
JL 8009 [10]	Stampede	1949	37.50	75.00	150.00
JL 8012 [10]	Champion	1950	37.50	75.00	150.00
CL 9001 [10]	Western Classics, Volume 1	1949	37.50	75.00	150.00
CL 9002 [10]	Western Classics, Volume 2	1949	37.50	75.00	150.00
COLUMBIA SPECIAL PRODUCTS					
P 15766	Christmas Favorites	1981	3.00	6.00	12.00
GRAND PRIX					
KX-11 [M]	The Original Gene Autry Sings Rudolph the Red-Nosed Reindeer and Other Christmas Favorites	1961	3.75	7.50	15.00
KS- [S]	The Original Gene Autry Sings Rudolph the Red-Nosed Reindeer and Other Christmas Favorites	1961	5.00	10.00	20.00
GUSTO					
1038	Christmas Classics	19??	2.50	5.00	10.00
HARMONY					
HL 7332 [M]	Gene Autry's Great Western Hits	1965	7.50	15.00	30.00
HL 7376 [M]	Back in the Saddle Again	1966	5.00	10.00	20.00
HL 7399 [M]	Gene Autry Sings	1966	5.00	10.00	20.00
HL 9505 [M]	Gene Autry and Champion — Western Adventures	1959	7.50	15.00	30.00
HL 9550 [M]	The Original Rudolph the Red-Nosed Reindeer and Other Children's Christmas Favorites	1964	6.25	12.50	25.00
HS 14450 [R]	The Original Rudolph the Red-Nosed Reindeer and Other Children's Christmas Favorites	1964	3.00	6.00	12.00
MELODY RANCH					
101 [M]	Melody Ranch	1965	10.00	20.00	40.00
MURRAY HILL					
897296 [(4)]	Melody Ranch Radio Show	197?	15.00	30.00	60.00
—Compilation of some of Gene's radio shows in a box set					
RCA VICTOR					
LPM-2623 [M]	Gene Autry's Golden Hits	1962	7.50	15.00	30.00
LSP-2623 [S]	Gene Autry's Golden Hits	1962	10.00	20.00	40.00
REPUBLIC					
6011	South of the Border, All American Cowboy	1976	5.00	10.00	20.00
6012	Cowboy Hall of Fame	1976	5.00	10.00	20.00
RLP 6018 [M]	Christmas with Gene Autry	1976	3.00	6.00	12.00

AVALANCHES, THE

45s

Number	Title (A Side/B Side)	Yr	VG	VG+	NM
WARNER BROS.					
5407	Baby, It's Cold Outside/Avalanche	1964	3.75	7.50	15.00
Albums					
WARNER BROS.					
W 1525 [M]	Ski Surfin'	1963	10.00	20.00	40.00
WS 1525 [S]	Ski Surfin'	1963	15.00	30.00	60.00

AVALON, FRANKIE

45s

Number	Title (A Side/B Side)	Yr	VG	VG+	NM
AMOS					
127	The Star/Woman Cryin'	1969	—	2.50	5.00
BOBCAT					
4103	Such a Miracle/You're the Miracle	1983	—	2.00	4.00
CHANCELLOR					
11FX 1	Christmas Holiday/Dear Gesu Bambino	196?	5.00	10.00	20.00
G-1 [DJ]	Shy Guy/Too Young	1959	10.00	20.00	40.00
—Promo-only record made for "Acnecare"					
1004	Cupid/Jivin' with the Saints	1957	5.00	10.00	20.00
1006	Shy Guy/Teacher's Pet	1957	5.00	10.00	20.00
1011	Dede Dinah/Ooh La La	1958	3.75	7.50	15.00
1016	You Excite Me/Darlin'	1958	3.75	7.50	15.00
1021	Ginger Bread/Blue Betty	1958	3.75	7.50	15.00
1021 [PS]	Ginger Bread/Blue Betty	1958	10.00	20.00	40.00
1026	I'll Wait for You/What Little Girl	1958	3.75	7.50	15.00
1026 [PS]	I'll Wait for You/What Little Girl	1958	10.00	20.00	40.00
1031 [M]	Venus/I'm Broke	1959	5.00	10.00	20.00

Number	Title (A Side/B Side)	Yr	VG	VG+	NM
1031 [PS]	Venus/I'm Broke	1959	10.00	20.00	40.00
S-1031 [S]	Venus/I'm Broke	1959	10.00	20.00	40.00
1036 [M]	Bobby Sox to Stockings/A Boy Without a Girl	1959	5.00	10.00	20.00
—Originals have pink labels					
1036 [M]	Bobby Sox to Stockings/A Boy Without a Girl	1959	3.00	6.00	12.00
—Reissues have black labels					
1036 [PS]	Bobby Sox to Stockings/A Boy Without a Girl	1959	10.00	20.00	40.00
S-1036 [S]	Bobby Sox to Stockings/A Boy Without a Girl	1959	10.00	20.00	40.00
1040 [M]	Just Ask Your Heart/Two Fools	1959	3.75	7.50	15.00
1040 [PS]	Just Ask Your Heart/Two Fools	1959	7.50	15.00	30.00
S-1040 [S]	Just Ask Your Heart/Two Fools	1959	10.00	20.00	40.00
1045 [M]	Why/Swingin' on a Rainbow	1959	3.75	7.50	15.00
1045 [PS]	Why/Swingin' on a Rainbow	1959	7.50	15.00	30.00
S-1045 [S]	Why/Swingin' on a Rainbow	1959	10.00	20.00	40.00
1048	Don't Throw Away All Those Teardrops/Talk, Talk, Talk	1960	3.75	7.50	15.00
1048 [PS]	Don't Throw Away All Those Teardrops/Talk, Talk, Talk	1960	7.50	15.00	30.00
1052	Where Are You/Tuxedo Junction	1960	3.75	7.50	15.00
1052 [PS]	Where Are You/Tuxedo Junction	1960	7.50	15.00	30.00
1056	Togetherness/Don't Let Love Pass You By	1960	3.75	7.50	15.00
1056 [PS]	Togetherness/Don't Let Love Pass You By	1960	7.50	15.00	30.00
1065	A Perfect Love/The Puppet Song	1960	3.75	7.50	15.00
1065 [PS]	A Perfect Love/The Puppet Song	1960	7.50	15.00	30.00
1071	All of Everything/Call Me Anytime	1961	3.00	6.00	12.00
1071 [PS]	All of Everything/Call Me Anytime	1961	6.25	12.50	25.00
1077	Who Else But You/Gotta Get a Girl	1961	3.00	6.00	12.00
1081	Voyage to the Bottom of the Sea/Summer of '61	1961	3.00	6.00	12.00
1081 [PS]	Voyage to the Bottom of the Sea/Summer of '61	1961	6.25	12.50	25.00
1087	True, True Love/Married	1961	2.50	5.00	10.00
1087 [PS]	True, True Love/Married	1961	5.00	10.00	20.00
1095	Sleeping Beauty/The Lonely Bit	1961	2.50	5.00	10.00
1095 [PS]	Sleeping Beauty/The Lonely Bit	1961	5.00	10.00	20.00
1101	After You've Gone/If You Don't Think I'm Leaving	1962	2.50	5.00	10.00
1101 [PS]	After You've Gone/If You Don't Think I'm Leaving	1962	5.00	10.00	20.00
1107	You Are Mine/Ponchinello	1962	2.50	5.00	10.00
1107	You Are Mine/Italiano	1962	3.00	6.00	12.00
1107 [PS]	You Are Mine/Ponchinello	1962	5.00	10.00	20.00
1114	Venus/I'm Broke	1962	2.50	5.00	10.00
1115	A Miracle/Don't Let Me Stand in Your Way	1962	2.50	5.00	10.00
1115 [PS]	A Miracle/Don't Let Me Stand in Your Way	1962	5.00	10.00	20.00
1125	Dance the Bossa Nova/Welcome Home	1962	2.50	5.00	10.00
1125 [PS]	Dance the Bossa Nova/Welcome Home	1962	5.00	10.00	20.00
1131	My Ex-Best Friend/First Love Never Dies	1963	2.50	5.00	10.00
1134	Come Fly with Me/Girl Back Home	1963	2.50	5.00	10.00
1135	Cleopatra/Heartbeats	1963	2.50	5.00	10.00
1139	Beach Party/Don't Stop Now	1963	3.75	7.50	15.00
DE-LITE					
907	Beauty School Dropout/Midnight Lady	1978	—	2.00	4.00
907 [PS]	Beauty School Dropout/Midnight Lady	1978	—	2.50	5.00
1578	Venus/Venus (Disco Version)	1976	—	2.00	4.00
1578 [PS]	Venus/Venus (Disco Version)	1976	2.00	4.00	8.00
1582	Thank You for That Extra Sunrise/It's His Game	1976	—	2.00	4.00
1584	It's Never Too Late/Where ILeave Off (And You Begin)	1976	—	2.00	4.00
1589	Midnight Lady/Does She Wonder Where I Am	1977	—	2.00	4.00
1591	Splish Splash/When I Said I Love You	1977	—	2.00	4.00
1595	Roses Grow Beyond the Wall/Midnight Lady	1977	—	2.00	4.00
METROMEDIA					
181	Come On Back to Me Baby/Empty	1970	—	2.50	5.00
192	Heart of Everything/I Want You Near Me	1970	—	2.50	5.00
REGALIA					
5508	I'm in the Mood for Love/It's the Same Old Dream	1972	—	2.50	5.00
REPRISE					
0697	Dancing on the Stars/But I Do	1968	2.00	4.00	8.00
0796	Don't You Do It/It's Over	1968	2.00	4.00	8.00
0826	For Your Love/Why Don't They Understand	1969	2.00	4.00	8.00
UNITED ARTISTS					
728	Again/Don't Make Fun of Me	1964	2.50	5.00	10.00
748	My Love Is Here to Stay/New-Fangled, Jingle-Jangle, Swimming Suit from Paris	1964	2.50	5.00	10.00
748 [PS]	My Love Is Here to Stay/New-Fangled, Jingle-Jangle, Swimming Suit from Paris	1964	5.00	10.00	20.00
800	Moon River/Every Girl Should Get Married	1964	2.50	5.00	10.00
895	There'll Be Rainbows Again/I'll Take Sweden	1965	2.50	5.00	10.00
"X"					
0006	Trumpet Sorrento/The Rock	1954	12.50	25.00	50.00
0026	Trumpet Tarantella/Dormi, Dormi	1954	12.50	25.00	50.00

7-Inch Extended Plays

Number	Title (A Side/B Side)	Yr	VG	VG+	NM
CHANCELLOR					
B-5000	Shy Guy/The One I Love//Trumpet Instrumental/Undecided	1959	12.50	25.00	50.00
B-5000 [PS]	The Young Frankie Avalon	1959	12.50	25.00	50.00

Albums

Number	Title (A Side/B Side)	Yr	VG	VG+	NM
ABC					
X-803	16 Greatest Hits	1974	3.00	6.00	12.00
CHANCELLOR					
CHL 5001 [M]	Frankie Avalon	1958	12.50	25.00	50.00
—Pink label					
CHL 5001 [M]	Frankie Avalon	1959	10.00	20.00	40.00
—Black label					
CHL 5002 [M]	The Young Frankie Avalon	1959	12.50	25.00	50.00
—Pink label					
CHL 5002 [M]	The Young Frankie Avalon	1959	10.00	20.00	40.00
—Black label					
CHLS 5002 [S]	The Young Frankie Avalon	1959	15.00	30.00	60.00
—Pink label					
CHLS 5002 [S]	The Young Frankie Avalon	1959	12.50	25.00	50.00
—Black label					
CHLX 5004 [M]	Swingin' on a Rainbow	1959	10.00	20.00	40.00
CHLXS 5004 [S]	Swingin' on a Rainbow	1959	12.50	25.00	50.00
CHL 5011 [M]	Summer Scene	1960	7.50	15.00	30.00
CHLS 5011 [S]	Summer Scene	1960	10.00	20.00	40.00
CHL 5018 [M]	A Whole Lotta Frankie	1961	7.50	15.00	30.00
CHL 5022 [M]	And Now About Mr. Avalon	1961	7.50	15.00	30.00
CHLS 5022 [S]	And Now About Mr. Avalon	1961	10.00	20.00	40.00
CHL 5025 [M]	Italiano	1962	7.50	15.00	30.00
CHLS 5025 [S]	Italiano	1962	10.00	20.00	40.00
CHL 5027 [M]	You're Mine	1962	7.50	15.00	30.00
CHLS 5027 [S]	You're Mine	1962	10.00	20.00	40.00
CHL 5031 [M]	Frankie Avalon's Christmas Album	1962	7.50	15.00	30.00
CHLS 5031 [S]	Frankie Avalon's Christmas Album	1962	10.00	20.00	40.00
CHL 5032 [M]	Cleopatra Plus 13 Other Great Hits	1963	7.50	15.00	30.00
CHLS 5032 [S]	Cleopatra Plus 13 Other Great Hits	1963	10.00	20.00	40.00
69801 [M]	Young and In Love	1960	20.00	40.00	80.00
—LP in felt cover and 3-D portrait, all in box					
69801 [M]	Young and In Love	1960	10.00	20.00	40.00
—LP without the box					
DE-LITE					
2020	Venus	1976	3.75	7.50	15.00
9504	You're My Life	1977	3.75	7.50	15.00
EVEREST					
4187	Greatest Hits	1982	2.50	5.00	10.00
LIBERTY					
LN-10193	Songs from Muscle Beach Party	1981	2.00	4.00	8.00
—Budget-line reissue					
MCA					
27096	The Best of Frankie Avalon	1985	2.00	4.00	8.00
METROMEDIA					
MD-1034	I Want You Near Me	1970	3.75	7.50	15.00
SUNSET					
SUS-5244	Frankie Avalon	1969	3.75	7.50	15.00
TRIP					
1621	16 Greatest Hits of Frankie Avalon	1977	2.50	5.00	10.00
UNITED ARTISTS					
UA-LA450-F	The Very Best of Frankie Avalon	1975	3.00	6.00	12.00
UAL-3371 [M]	Songs from Muscle Beach Party	1964	6.25	12.50	25.00
UAL-3382 [M]	Frankie Avalon's 15 Greatest Hits	1964	5.00	10.00	20.00
UAS-6371 [S]	Songs from Muscle Beach Party	1964	7.50	15.00	30.00
UAS-6382 [S]	Frankie Avalon's 15 Greatest Hits	1964	6.25	12.50	25.00

AVALON, FRANKIE, AND ANNETTE FUNICELLO

Also see each artist's individual listings.

45s

Number	Title (A Side/B Side)	Yr	VG	VG+	NM
PACIFIC STAR					
569	(Together We Can Make a) Merry Christmas/The Night Before Christmas	1981	—	2.50	5.00
—Red vinyl					
569 [PS]	(Together We Can Make a) Merry Christmas/The Night Before Christmas	1981	—	2.50	5.00

AVALONS, THE

45s

Number	Title (A Side/B Side)	Yr	VG	VG+	NM
ALADDIN					
3336	I Miss You/Love Me	1956	7.50	15.00	30.00
CASINO					
108	You Do Something to Me/You Can Count on Me	1959	50.00	100.00	200.00
DICE					
90/91	Louella/You Broke Our Hearts	1958	37.50	75.00	150.00
GROOVE					
0141	Chains Around My Heart/Och! She Flew	1956	37.50	75.00	150.00
—Black vinyl					
0141	Chains Around My Heart/Och! She Flew	1956	125.00	250.00	500.00
—Green vinyl					
0174	It's Funny But It's True/Sugar Sugar	1956	37.50	75.00	150.00
NPC					
302	Begin the Beguine/Malanese	1964	6.25	12.50	25.00
ROULETTE					
4568	Is It the End/Many Things from Your Window	1964	3.00	6.00	12.00
UNART					
2007	Hearts Desire/Ebbtide	1958	30.00	60.00	120.00

AVANT-GARDE, THE

Game-show host Chuck Woolery was in this group.

45s

Number	Title (A Side/B Side)	Yr	VG	VG+	NM
COLUMBIA					
44388	Yellow Beads/Honey and Gall	1967	2.00	4.00	8.00
44590	Naturally Stoned/Honey and Gall	1968	2.00	4.00	8.00
44701	Fly with Me/Revelations Revelations	1968	2.00	4.00	8.00

—While not issued with a picture sleeve, some stock copies came with a lyric insert. Triple the value if this is included.

AVANTIS, THE

Probably more than one group.

45s

Number	Title (A Side/B Side)	Yr	VG	VG+	NM
ARGO					
5436	Keep On Dancing/I Want to Dance	1963	3.75	7.50	15.00
ASTRA					
1006	Gypsy Surfer/Wax 'Em Down	1963	10.00	20.00	40.00
CHANCELLOR					
1144	Gypsy Surfer/Wax 'Em Down	1963	6.25	12.50	25.00
IKON					
115	Too Much/Mid-Night Blues	196?	6.25	12.50	25.00
PEPPER					
435	You Got a Funny Way/One Man's Poison	196?	3.00	6.00	12.00
REGENCY					
108	Do the Surfin' Granny/Surfin' Granny	1964	10.00	20.00	40.00
110	Phantom Surfer/Lucille	1964	10.00	20.00	40.00

AVENGERS VI, THE

Albums

Number	Title (A Side/B Side)	Yr	VG	VG+	NM
MARK 56					
(# unknown)	Good Humor Presents Real Cool Hits	1966	62.50	125.00	250.00

—Custom pressing for the Good Humor ice cream company

Voulez-Vous/Angeleyes

ABBA

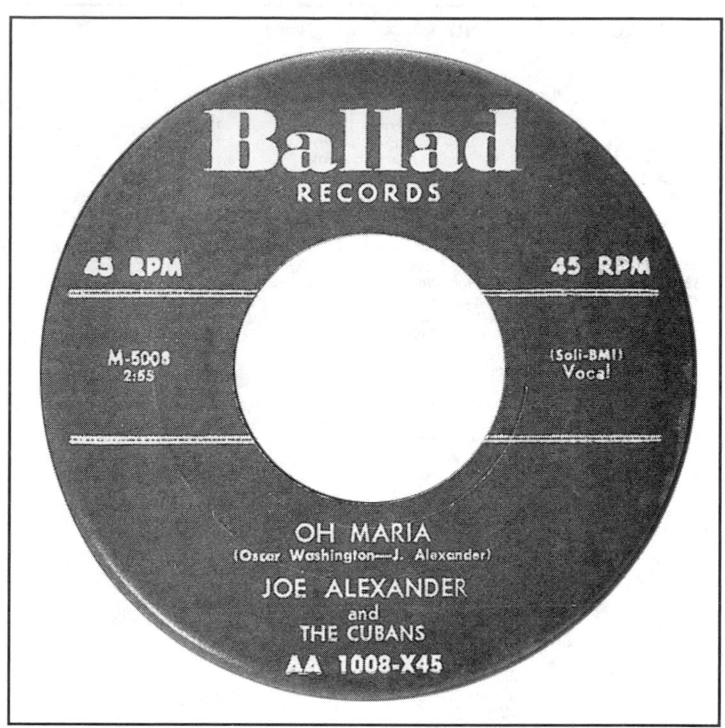

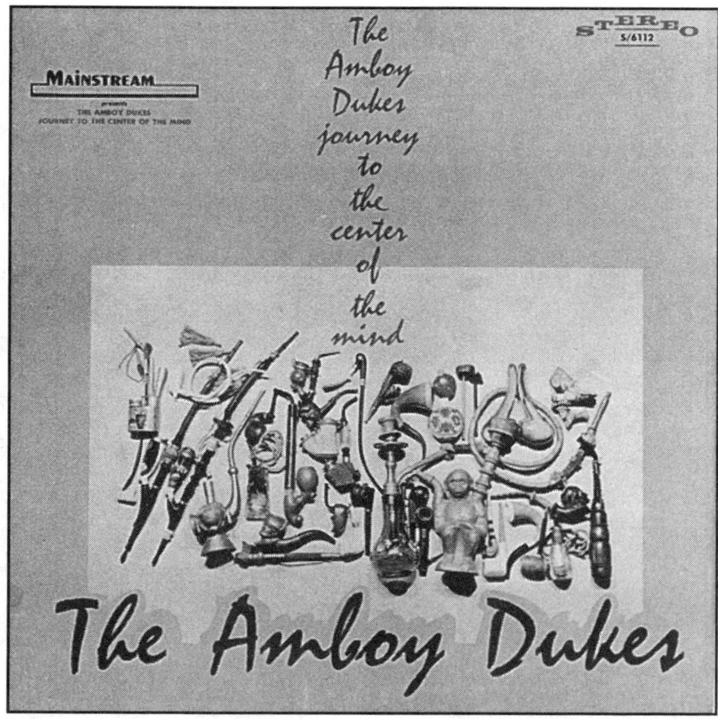

(Top left) Though hardly a one-hit wonder, Abba was never as successful in the United States as in the rest of the world. Many of their worldwide hits are pretty obscure in America, including "Voulez-Vouz," the followup to their 1979 hit "Does Your Mother Know." (Top right) Joe Alexander and the Cubans were a St. Louis band that would have remained forever obscure except for one thing: This 45 on the Ballad label includes the first appearance on record by Chuck Berry! (Bottom left) Before he got cat scratch fever or became an outspoken advocate for hunters' rights, Ted Nugent was in a band called The Amboy Dukes. Their only hit single was "Journey to the Center of the Mind," which appeared in all its sterophonic glory on this tough-to-find album on the Mainstream label. (Bottom right) How many fans of the movie *Grease* are familiar with this one? Frankie Avalon's recording of "Beauty School Dropout" was actually released as a single in 1978 to almost no attention.

AVERAGE WHITE BAND

45s

Number	Title (A Side/B Side)	Yr	VG	VG+	NM
ARISTA					
0515	Let's Go Round Again/Shine	1980	—	2.00	4.00
0553	For You, For Love/Whatcha 'Gonna Do for Me	1980	—	2.00	4.00
0580	Into the Night/(B-side unknown)	1980	—	2.00	4.00
0679	Easier Said Than Done/(B-side unknown)	1982	—	2.00	4.00
1022	Cupid's in Fashion/(B-side unknown)	1982	—	2.00	4.00
ATLANTIC					
3044	Nothing You Can Do/I Just Can't Give You Up	1974	—	2.00	4.00
3229	Pick Up the Pieces/Work to Do	1974	—	2.50	5.00
3261	Cut the Cake/Person to Person	1975	—	2.00	4.00
3285	If I Ever Lose This Heaven/High Flyin' Woman	1975	—	2.00	4.00
3304	School Boy Crush/Groovin' the Night Away	1975	—	2.00	4.00
3354	Queen of My Soul/Would You Stay	1976	—	2.00	4.00
3363	Soul Searching/Love of Your Own	1976	—	2.00	4.00
3388	Cloudy/Love Your Life	1977	—	2.00	4.00
3402	Get It Up/Keepin' It To Myself	1977	—	2.00	4.00
—With Ben E. King					
3427	A Star in the Ghetto/What Is Soul?	1977	—	2.00	4.00
—With Ben E. King					
3444	Fool for You Anyway/The Message	1977	—	2.00	4.00
—With Ben E. King					
3481	Your Love Is a Miracle/One Look	1978	—	2.00	4.00
3500	Big City Lights/She's a Dream	1978	—	2.00	4.00
3563	Walk On By/Too Late to Cry	1979	—	2.00	4.00
3581	Feel No Fret/Fire Burning	1979	—	2.00	4.00
3614 [DJ]	When Will You Be Mine (same on both sides)	1979	—	2.00	4.00
—May be promo only					
MCA					
40168	This World Has Music/The Jugglers	1973	—	2.50	5.00
40196	Twilight Zone/How Can You Go Home	1974	—	2.50	5.00

Albums

Number	Title	Yr	VG	VG+	NM
ARISTA					
AB 9523	Shine	1980	2.50	5.00	10.00
AB 9594	Cupid's in Fashion	1981	2.50	5.00	10.00
ATLANTIC					
SD 2-1002 [(2)]	Person to Person	1977	3.00	6.00	12.00
QD 7308 [Q]	Average White Band	1975	5.00	10.00	20.00
SD 7308	Average White Band	1974	2.50	5.00	10.00
SD 18140	Cut the Cake	1975	2.50	5.00	10.00
SD 18179	Soul Searching	1976	2.50	5.00	10.00
SD 19105	Benny and Us	1977	2.50	5.00	10.00
—With Ben E. King					
SD 19116	Average White Band	1977	2.00	4.00	8.00
—Reissue					
SD 19162	Warmer Communications	1978	2.50	5.00	10.00
SD 19207	Feel No Fret	1979	2.50	5.00	10.00
SD 19266	Volume VIII	1980	2.50	5.00	10.00
MCA					
345	Show Your Hands	1973	6.25	12.50	25.00
475	Put It Where You Want It	1975	2.50	5.00	10.00
—Reissue of MCA 345					
MOBILE FIDELITY					
1-245	Average White Band	1996	5.00	10.00	20.00
—Audiophile vinyl					

AVONS, THE (1)

Male vocal group.

45s

Number	Title (A Side/B Side)	Yr	VG	VG+	NM
ASTRA					
1023	Baby/Whisper (Softly)	1966	7.50	15.00	30.00
—Reissue of Hull material					
HULL					
717	Our Love Will Never End/I'm Sending S.O.S.	1956	50.00	100.00	200.00
—Black label					
717	Our Love Will Never End/I'm Sending S.O.S.	1956	12.50	25.00	50.00
—Red label					
722	Baby/Bonnie	1957	37.50	75.00	150.00
726	You Are So Close to Me/Gonna Catch You Nappin'	1958	30.00	60.00	120.00
728	What Will I Do/Please Come Back to Me	1958	30.00	60.00	120.00
731	What Love Can Do/On the Island	1958	30.00	60.00	120.00
744	Whisper (Softly)/If I Just (Had My Way)	1961	25.00	50.00	100.00
—White label					
744	Whisper (Softly)/If I Just (Had My Way)	1961	25.00	50.00	100.00
—Pink label					
744	Whisper (Softly)/If I Just (Had My Way)	196?	20.00	40.00	80.00
—Brown label					
754	A Girl to Call My Own/The Grass Is Greener on the Other Side	1962	37.50	75.00	150.00
—White label					
754	A Girl to Call My Own/The Grass Is Greener on the Other Side	1962	20.00	40.00	80.00
—Brown label					

Albums

Number	Title	Yr	VG	VG+	NM
HULL					
HLP-1000 [M]	The Avons	1960	175.00	350.00	700.00

AVONS, THE (U)

45s

Number	Title (A Side/B Side)	Yr	VG	VG+	NM
ABET					
9419	Talk to Me/Got to Get Used to You	1967	2.00	4.00	8.00
EXCELLO					
2296	Since I Met You Baby/He's My Hero	1968	2.00	4.00	8.00
GROOVE					
58-0022	Oh, Gee Baby/Push a Little Harder	1963	3.75	7.50	15.00
58-0022 [PS]	Oh, Gee Baby/Push a Little Harder	1963	7.50	15.00	30.00
58-0033	Words Written on Water/Rolling Stone	1964	3.00	6.00	12.00
58-0039	Whatever Happened to Our Love/Tonight Kiss Your Baby Goodbye	1964	3.00	6.00	12.00
MERCURY					
71618	We Fell in Love/Pickin' Petals	1960	3.75	7.50	15.00
REF-O-REE					
700	Tell Me Baby/A Sample of My Love	196?	5.00	10.00	20.00
SOUND STAGE 7					
2561	Be Good to Your Baby/Just As Long As I Live	1966	2.50	5.00	10.00

AXTON, HOYT

45s

Number	Title (A Side/B Side)	Yr	VG	VG+	NM
20TH FOX					
6648	Five Dollar Bill/Smoky	1966	2.50	5.00	10.00
A&M					
1437	Sweet Misery/Less Than the Song	1973	—	2.50	5.00
1497	When the Morning Comes/Billie's Theme	1974	—	2.50	5.00
1607	Boney Fingers/Life Machine	1974	—	2.50	5.00
1657	Nashville/Speed Trap	1974	—	2.50	5.00
1683	Lion in the Winter/No No Song	1975	—	2.50	5.00
1713	In a Young Girl's Mind/Southbound	1975	—	2.50	5.00
1811	Flash of Fire/Paid in Advance	1976	—	2.00	4.00
BRIAR					
100	Georgia Hoss Soldier/Drinking Gourd	1961	3.75	7.50	15.00
CAPITOL					
3121	Alice in Wonderland/Have a Nice Day	1971	—	3.00	6.00
3167	California Women/Ease Your Pain	1971	—	3.00	6.00
3259	Speed Traps/Hey, Mr. Pilot Man	1972	—	3.00	6.00
COLGEMS					
66-1005	San Fernando/Ten Thousand Sunsets	1967	2.50	5.00	10.00
COLUMBIA					
44810	Snowblind Friend/It's All Right Now	1969	—	3.50	7.00
44850	Way Before the Time of Towns/It's All Right Now	1969	—	3.50	7.00
ELEKTRA					
47133	Flo's Yellow Rose/Lion in the Winter	1981	—	2.00	4.00
HORIZON					
2	Grizzly Bear/Gypsy Woman	1963	2.50	5.00	10.00
6	The Happy Song/We'll Sing in the Sunshine	1963	2.50	5.00	10.00
351	Greenback Dollar/Crawdad Song	1962	3.75	7.50	15.00
360	Grizzly Bear/Gypsy Woman	1963	3.00	6.00	12.00
361	This Little Light/Thunder 'N' Lightnin'	1963	3.00	6.00	12.00
362	One More Round/Greenback Dollar	1963	3.00	6.00	12.00
JEREMIAH					
1000	Della and the Dealer/A Young Girl's Mind	1979	—	2.00	4.00
1001	A Rusty Old Halo/Keep Rollin'	1979	—	2.00	4.00
1003	Wild Bull Rider/Torpedo	1979	—	2.00	4.00
1005	Evangelina/So Hard to Give It All Up	1980	—	2.00	4.00
1006	Boozers Are Losers (When the Benders Don't End)/Politicians	1980	—	2.00	4.00
1008	Where Did the Money Go/Smile As You Go By	1980	—	2.00	4.00
1011	The Devil/Jealous Man	1981	—	2.00	4.00
1012	Win This One/Ease Your Pain	1981	—	2.00	4.00
1014	She's Too Lazy to Be Crazy/You Do Not Tango	1982	—	2.00	4.00
1015	There Stands the Glass/James Dean and the Junkman	1982	—	2.00	4.00
1016	Pistol Packin' Mama/Fearless the Wonderdog	1982	—	2.00	4.00
1017	Warm Storms and Wild Flowers/Don't Fence Me In	1983	—	2.00	4.00
1018	If You're a Cowboy/I Collect Hearts	1983	—	2.00	4.00
MCA					
40711	You're the Hangnail in My Life/Never Been to Spain	1977	—	2.00	4.00
40731	Little White Moon/Funeral of the King	1977	—	2.50	5.00
VEE JAY					
604	L.A. Town/Double Double Dare	1964	3.00	6.00	12.00
619	Bring Your Lovin'/Tiger in the Closet	1964	3.00	6.00	12.00
659	Hush Hush Sweet Charlotte/After You've Gone	1965	2.50	5.00	10.00

Albums

Number	Title	Yr	VG	VG+	NM
ACCORD					
SN-7197	Heartbreak Hotel	1982	2.50	5.00	10.00
ALLEGIANCE					
AV-5023	Down and Out	1984	2.50	5.00	10.00
A&M					
SP-3155	Life Machine	198?	2.00	4.00	8.00
—Budget-line reissue					
SP-3182	Road Songs	198?	2.00	4.00	8.00
—Budget-line reissue					
SP-4376	Less Than a Song	1973	2.50	5.00	10.00
SP-4402	Life Machine	1974	2.50	5.00	10.00
SP-4510	Southbound	1975	2.50	5.00	10.00
SP-4571	Fearless	1976	2.50	5.00	10.00
SP-4669	Road Songs	1977	2.50	5.00	10.00
BRYLEN					
BN 4400	Double Dare	1982	3.00	6.00	12.00
CAPITOL					
ST-788	Joy to the World	1971	3.00	6.00	12.00
SMAS-850	Country Anthem	1971	3.00	6.00	12.00
COLUMBIA					
CS 9766	My Griffin Is Gone	1969	3.75	7.50	15.00
KC 33103	My Griffin Is Gone	1975	2.50	5.00	10.00
PC 33103	My Griffin Is Gone	1979	2.00	4.00	8.00
—Budget-line reissue					
EXODUS					
EX-301 [M]	Hoyt Axton Sings Bessie Smith	1966	5.00	10.00	20.00
EXS-321 [M]	Saturday's Child	1966	5.00	10.00	20.00
—Cover says stereo, record plays mono					
HORIZON					
WP-1601 [M]	The Balladeer	1962	6.25	12.50	25.00
—Black label					
WP-1601 [M]	Greenback Dollar	1963	5.00	10.00	20.00
—Black label; two fewer songs than "The Balladeer"					
WP-1601 [S]	The Balladeer	1962	7.50	15.00	30.00
—Same number as mono, but with blue label					
WP-1601 [S]	Greenback Dollar	1963	6.25	12.50	25.00
—Blue label; two fewer songs than "The Balladeer"					
SWP-1613 [S]	Thunder 'N Lightnin'	1963	7.50	15.00	30.00
WP-1613 [M]	Thunder 'N Lightnin'	1963	6.25	12.50	25.00

Number	Title (A Side/B Side)	Yr	VG	VG+	NM
SWP-1621 [S]	Saturday's Child	1963	7.50	15.00	30.00
WP-1621 [M]	Saturday's Child	1963	6.25	12.50	25.00
JEREMIAH					
JH-5000	A Rusty Old Halo	1979	3.00	6.00	12.00
JH-5001	Where Did the Money Go?	1980	3.00	6.00	12.00
MCA					
647	Snow Blind Friend	198?	2.00	4.00	8.00
—Budget-line reissue					
648	Free Sailin'	198?	2.00	4.00	8.00
—Budget-line reissue					
2263	Snow Blind Friend	1977	2.50	5.00	10.00
2319	Free Sailin'	1978	2.50	5.00	10.00
SURREY					
S-1005 [M]	Mr. Greenback Dollar Man	1965	5.00	10.00	20.00
SS-1005 [S]	Mr. Greenback Dollar Man	1965	6.25	12.50	25.00
VEE JAY					
LP-1098 [M]	Hoyt Axton Explodes!	1964	6.25	12.50	25.00
LPS-1098 [R]	Hoyt Axton Explodes!	1964	5.00	10.00	20.00
LP-1118 [M]	The Best of Hoyt Axton	1965	5.00	10.00	20.00
LPS-1118 [S]	The Best of Hoyt Axton	1965	6.25	12.50	25.00
LP-1126 [M]	Greenback Dollar	1965	5.00	10.00	20.00
LPS-1126 [S]	Greenback Dollar	1965	6.25	12.50	25.00
LP-1127 [M]	Saturday's Child	1965	5.00	10.00	20.00
LPS-1127 [S]	Saturday's Child	1965	6.25	12.50	25.00
—Reissue of Horizon 1621					
LP-1128 [M]	Thunder 'N Lightnin'	1965	5.00	10.00	20.00
LPS-1128 [S]	Thunder 'N Lightnin'	1965	6.25	12.50	25.00
—Reissue of Horizon 1613					
VEE JAY INTERNATIONAL					
VJS-2-1005 [(2)]	Gold	1974	5.00	10.00	20.00
—Compilation of older Vee Jay material					
LP-6001	Long Old Road	1977	3.75	7.50	15.00
VEE JAY/DYNASTY					
VJS-7306	Bessie Smith... My Way	1974	3.75	7.50	15.00

AYERS, ROY

Includes "Roy Ayers Ubiquity."

45s

Number	Title (A Side/B Side)	Yr	VG	VG+	NM
COLUMBIA					
04653	In the Dark/Love Is in the Field	1984	—	—	3.00
04821	Poo Poo La La/Sexy Sexy Sexy	1985	—	—	3.00
05613	Slip n' Slide/Can I See You	1985	—	—	3.00
05752	Hot/Virgo	1985	—	—	3.00
05874	Programmed for Love/For You	1986	—	—	3.00
ICHIBAN					
149	Fast Money/(Instrumental)	1987	—	2.00	4.00
157	D.C. City/(Instrumental)	1987	—	2.00	4.00
POLYDOR					
2020	Fever/I Wanna Feel It	1979	—	2.00	4.00
2037	Don't Stop the Feeling/Don't Hide Your Love	1979	—	2.00	4.00
2066	What You Won't Do for Love/Shack Up, Pack Up, It's Up (When I'm Gone)_	1980	—	2.00	4.00
2138	Rock Your Roll/Sigh & Feel the Vibration	1981	—	2.00	4.00
2154	Love Fantasy/Baby Bubba	1981	—	2.00	4.00
2185	There's a Master Plan/Land of Fruit and Honey	1981	—	2.00	4.00
2198	Turn Me Loose/Ooh	1982	—	2.00	4.00
2204	Fire Up the Funk/Let's Stay Together	1982	—	2.00	4.00
14078	Pretty Brown Skin/He Gives Us All His Love	1971	—	2.50	5.00
14111	He's a Superstar (Part 1)/He's a Superstar (Part 2)	1972	—	2.50	5.00
14165	Will Your Soul Be Free (Henceforth)/Rhythms of Your Mind	1973	—	2.50	5.00
14171	Red, Black and Green/Will Your Soul Be Free (Henceforth)	1973	—	2.50	5.00
14275	Magic Lady/No Question	1975	—	2.00	4.00
14294	Way of the World/2000 Black	1975	—	2.00	4.00
14316	Mystic Voyage/(B-side unknown)	1976	—	2.00	4.00
14337	The Golden Rod/Tongue Power	1976	—	2.00	4.00
14349	You and Me My Love/Hey-Uh-What You Say Come On	1976	—	2.00	4.00
14370	Vibrations/Domelo (Give It to Me)	1977	—	2.00	4.00
14379	Searching/Come Out and Play	1977	—	2.00	4.00
14415	Running Away/Cincinnati Growl	1977	—	2.00	4.00
14451	Freaky Deaky/You Came Into My Life	1978	—	2.00	4.00
14477	Let's Do It/Melody Maker	1978	—	2.00	4.00
14509	Get On Up, Get On Down/And Don't You Say No	1978	—	2.00	4.00
14573	Love Will Bring Us Back Together/Leo	1979	—	2.00	4.00

Albums

Number	Title (A Side/B Side)	Yr	VG	VG+	NM
ATLANTIC					
1488 [M]	Virgo Vibes	1967	5.00	10.00	20.00
SD 1488 [S]	Virgo Vibes	1967	3.75	7.50	15.00
SD 1514	Stoned Soul Picnic	1968	5.00	10.00	20.00
SD 1538	Daddy Bug	1969	5.00	10.00	20.00
COLUMBIA					
FC 39422	In the Dark	1984	2.50	5.00	10.00
ICHIBAN					
ICH-1028	Drive	198?	2.50	5.00	10.00
ICH-1040	Wake Up	198?	2.50	5.00	10.00
POLYDOR					
PD 5022	He's Coming	1972	3.00	6.00	12.00
PD 5045	Red, Black and Green	1973	3.00	6.00	12.00
PD 6016	Virgo Red	1973	3.00	6.00	12.00
PD 6032	Change Up the Groove	1974	2.50	5.00	10.00
PD 6046	A Tear to a Smile	1975	2.50	5.00	10.00
PD 6057	Mystic Voyage	1976	2.50	5.00	10.00
PD-1-6070	Everybody Loves the Sunshine	1976	2.50	5.00	10.00
PD-1-6078	Red, Black and Green	1976	2.50	5.00	10.00
—Reissue of 5045					
PD-1-6091	Vibrations	1977	2.50	5.00	10.00
PD-1-6108	Lifeline	1977	2.50	5.00	10.00
PD-1-6126	Let's Do It	1978	2.50	5.00	10.00
PD-1-6159	You Send Me	1978	2.50	5.00	10.00
PD-1-6204	Fever	1979	2.50	5.00	10.00
PD-1-6246	No Stranger to Love	1979	2.50	5.00	10.00
PD-1-6301	Love Fantasy	1980	2.50	5.00	10.00
PD-1-6327	Africa, Center of the World	1981	2.50	5.00	10.00
PD-1-6348	Feeling Good	1982	2.50	5.00	10.00
UNITED ARTISTS					
UAL-3325 [M]	West Coast Vibes	1964	5.00	10.00	20.00
UAS-6325 [S]	West Coast Vibes	1964	6.25	12.50	25.00

AYERS, ROY, AND WAYNE HENDERSON

45s

Number	Title (A Side/B Side)	Yr	VG	VG+	NM
POLYDOR					
2114	You Make Me Feel Like (Rockin' with You)/Million Dollar Baby (Feel So Real)	1980	—	2.00	4.00
2127	Weekend Lover/Thank You, Thank You	1980	—	—	—
—Canceled					
14523	Heat of the Beat/No Deposit No Return	1978	—	2.00	4.00
14545	Ooh Baby/Step Into Our Life	1979	—	2.00	4.00
14559	No Deposit No Return/Step Into Our Life	1979	—	2.00	4.00

Albums

Number	Title (A Side/B Side)	Yr	VG	VG+	NM
POLYDOR					
PD-1-6179	Step Into Our Life	1978	2.50	5.00	10.00
PD-1-6276	Prine Time	1980	2.50	5.00	10.00

AZALEAS, THE

45s

Number	Title (A Side/B Side)	Yr	VG	VG+	NM
ROMULUS					
3001	Hands Off/One Drummer Can't Keep Time	1963	7.50	15.00	30.00

AZTECA

45s

Number	Title (A Side/B Side)	Yr	VG	VG+	NM
COLUMBIA					
45762	Peace Everybody/Mamita Linda	1973	—	3.00	6.00
45808	Ain't Got No Special Woman/Can't Take the Funk Out of Me	1973	—	3.00	6.00
45962	Night in Nazca/Whatcha Gonna Do	1973	—	2.50	5.00

Albums

Number	Title (A Side/B Side)	Yr	VG	VG+	NM
COLUMBIA					
CQ 31776 [Q]	Azteca	1974	5.00	10.00	20.00
KC 31776	Azteca	1972	3.00	6.00	12.00
KC 32451	Pyramid of the Sun	1973	3.00	6.00	12.00

AZTECS, THE

45s

Number	Title (A Side/B Side)	Yr	VG	VG+	NM
WORLD ARTISTS					
1029	Da Doo Ron Ron/Hi-Hel Sneakers	1964	3.00	6.00	12.00

Albums

Number	Title (A Side/B Side)	Yr	VG	VG+	NM
WORLD ARTISTS					
WAM-2001 [M]	Live at the Ad Lib Club of London	1964	15.00	30.00	60.00

AZTEX

45s

Number	Title (A Side/B Side)	Yr	VG	VG+	NM
STAFF					
(# unknown)	I Said Move/(B-side unknown)	196?	625.00	1250.	2500.
ERA BACK TO BACK HITS					
023	Dance with Me/Land of 1000 Dances	197?	—	2.50	5.00
—B-side by Cannibal and the Headhunters					
RAMPART					
641	La La La La La/Huggies Bunnies	1964	6.25	12.50	25.00
REPRISE					
0291	La La La La La/Huggies Bunnies	1964	5.00	10.00	20.00
0340	Dance with Me/Get Your Baby	1965	5.00	10.00	20.00

B

B. BUMBLE AND THE STINGERS

45s

Number	Title (A Side/B Side)	Yr	VG	VG+	NM
DYMO					
13	Pollywog/Slumber Party	196?	2.50	5.00	10.00
ERA BACK TO BACK HITS					
038	Bumble Boogie/Angel Baby	197?	—	3.00	6.00
—B-side by Rosie and the Originals					
ERIC					
297	Nut Rocker/Bumble Boogie	197?	—	2.00	4.00
GOLDIES 45					
2465	Bumble Boogie/School Day Blues	1973	—	2.50	5.00
2466	Nut Rocker/Nautilus	1973	—	2.50	5.00
GOLDISC					
3106	Nut Rocker/Bumble Boogie	198?	—	2.00	4.00
HI OLDIES					
409	Nut Rocker/Nautilus	197?	—	2.50	5.00
HIGHLAND					
2001	Bumble Boogie/School Day Blues	196?	2.50	5.00	10.00
MERCURY					
72614	Green Hornet Theme/Flight of the Hornet	1966	2.50	5.00	10.00
72665	Silent Movies/Twelfth Street Rag	1967	2.50	5.00	10.00
OLDIES 45					
37	Nut Rocker/Nautilus	1964	2.00	4.00	8.00
065	Nut Rocker/Baby I Love You	197?	—	2.50	5.00
—B-side by Joe Weaver and the Don Juans					
RENDEZVOUS					
140	Bumble Boogie/School Day Blues	1961	5.00	10.00	20.00
151	Boogie Woogie/Near You	1961	3.75	7.50	15.00
160	Bee Hive/Caravan	1961	3.75	7.50	15.00
166	Nut Rocker/Nautilus	1962	3.75	7.50	15.00
174	Rockin-On-And-Off/Mashed #5	1962	3.00	6.00	12.00
179	Apple Knocker/The Moon and the Sea	1962	3.00	6.00	12.00
182	Dawn Cracker/Scales	1962	3.00	6.00	12.00
186	12th Street Rag/Canadian Sunset	1962	3.00	6.00	12.00
192	Baby Mash/Night Time Madness	1962	3.00	6.00	12.00
210	In the Mood/Chicken Chow Mein	1963	3.00	6.00	12.00
TRIAD					
778	Chariots from the Stars/Funky Mud	197?	—	3.00	6.00
WAX					
13	Pollywog/Slumber Party	196?	2.50	5.00	10.00
—"Wax" in small vertical print					
13	Pollywog/Slumber Party	196?	2.00	4.00	8.00
—"Wax" in large sideways print					

B.J. AND THE GEMINIS

45s

Number	Title (A Side/B Side)	Yr	VG	VG+	NM
ATCO					
6364	Scratch My Back Part 1/Scratch My Back Part 2	1965	6.25	12.50	25.00

B.R.A.T.T.S., THE

45s

Number	Title (A Side/B Side)	Yr	VG	VG+	NM
TOLLIE					
9024	Secret Weapon (The British Are Coming)/Jealous Kinda Woman	1964	5.00	10.00	20.00

B.T. EXPRESS

12-Inch Singles

Number	Title (A Side/B Side)	Yr	VG	VG+	NM
COAST TO COAST					
02631	Let Yourself Go/Cowboy Dancer	1981	2.00	4.00	8.00

45s

Number	Title (A Side/B Side)	Yr	VG	VG+	NM
COAST TO COAST					
02630	Let Yourself Go/Cowboy Dancer	1981	—	2.00	4.00
02994	Keep It Up/Dancin' Dreams	1982	—	2.00	4.00
COLUMBIA					
10346	Can't Stop Groovin' Now, Wanna Do It Some More/Herbs	1976	—	2.00	4.00
10399	Energy to Burn/Make Your Body Move	1976	—	2.00	4.00
10582	Funky Music (Don't Laugh at My Funk)/We Got It Together	1977	—	2.00	4.00
10649	Shout It Out/Ride On B.T.	1977	—	2.00	4.00
10752	You Got Something/What You Do in the Dark	1978	—	2.00	4.00
11200	Heart of Fire/Better Late Than Never	1980	—	2.00	4.00
11249	Give Up the Funk (Let's Dance)/Better Late Than Never	1980	—	2.00	4.00
11336	Does It Feel Good/Have Some Fun	1980	—	2.00	4.00
11400	Stretch/Just Want to Hold You	1980	—	2.00	4.00
60518	Let Me Be the One/Midnight Beat	1981	—	2.00	4.00
ROADSHOW					
7001	Express/Express (Disco Mix)	1975	—	2.00	4.00
7003	Give It What You Got/Peace Pipe	1975	—	2.00	4.00
SCEPTER					
12395	Do It ('Til You're Satisfied)/Do It ('Til You're Satisfied) Long Version	1974	—	2.50	5.00

Albums

Number	Title (A Side/B Side)	Yr	VG	VG+	NM
COAST TO COAST					
FZ 38001	Keep It Up	1982	2.50	5.00	10.00
COLLECTABLES					
COL-5190	Golden Classics: Express	198?	2.50	5.00	10.00
COLUMBIA					
PC 34178	Energy to Burn	1976	2.50	5.00	10.00
PCQ 34178 [Q]	Energy to Burn	1976	3.75	7.50	15.00
PC 34702	Function at the Junction	1977	2.50	5.00	10.00
JC 35078	Shout!	1978	2.50	5.00	10.00
JC 36333	B.T. Express 1980	1980	2.50	5.00	10.00
JC 36923	Greatest Hits	1980	2.50	5.00	10.00
ROADSHOW					
41001	Non-Stop	1975	3.00	6.00	12.00
ROADSHOW/SCEPTER					
5117	Do It ('Til You're Satisfied)	1974	3.00	6.00	12.00

BABE RUTH

45s

Number	Title (A Side/B Side)	Yr	VG	VG+	NM
CAPITOL					
4219	Say No More/Elusive	1976	—	2.00	4.00
HARVEST					
3553	Wells Fargo/Theme from "For A Few Dollars More"	1973	—	2.50	5.00

Albums

Number	Title (A Side/B Side)	Yr	VG	VG+	NM
CAPITOL					
ST-11515	Kids Stuff	1976	2.50	5.00	10.00
HARVEST					
SW-11151	First Base	1973	3.75	7.50	15.00
ST-11275	Amar Caballero	1974	3.00	6.00	12.00
ST-11367	Babe Ruth	1975	2.50	5.00	10.00
ST-11451	Stealin' Home	1975	2.50	5.00	10.00

BABIES, THE

45s

Number	Title (A Side/B Side)	Yr	VG	VG+	NM
ABC DUNHILL					
4148	I Wanna Testify/Party Time	1968	3.00	6.00	12.00
DUNHILL					
4085	You Make Me Feel Like Someone/The Hand of Fate	1967	4.00	8.00	16.00
4085 [PS]	You Make Me Feel Like Someone/The Hand of Fate	1967	7.50	15.00	30.00
4101	I'm Not Asking for the World/Goodbye My Love, Goodbye	1967	3.75	7.50	15.00

BABY

45s

Number	Title (A Side/B Side)	Yr	VG	VG+	NM
CHELSEA					
3057	Where Did All the Money Go/(B-side unknown)	1976	—	2.50	5.00
3068	Fallen Angel/Baton Rouge	1977	—	2.50	5.00

Albums

Number	Title (A Side/B Side)	Yr	VG	VG+	NM
CHELSEA					
CHL-517	Where Did All the Money Go	1976	2.50	5.00	10.00
LONE STARR					
9782	Baby	1974	6.25	12.50	25.00

BABY BUGS, THE

45s

Number	Title (A Side/B Side)	Yr	VG	VG+	NM
VEE JAY					
594	Bingo/Bingo's Bongo Bingo Party	1964	6.25	12.50	25.00
594 [PS]	Bingo/Bingo's Bongo Bingo Party	1964	18.75	37.50	75.00

BABY DOLLS, THE

45s

Number	Title (A Side/B Side)	Yr	VG	VG+	NM
BOOM					
60002	I Will Do It ('Cause He Wants Me To)/Now That I've Lost You	1966	2.50	5.00	10.00
GAMBLE					
213	Please Don't Rush Me/There You Are	1968	2.00	4.00	8.00
HOLLYWOOD					
1111	Got to Get You Into My Life/Why Can't I Make Him Like You	1960	10.00	20.00	40.00
MASKE					
103	Go Away Baby/I'm Lonely	1960	12.50	25.00	50.00
701	Thanks, Mr. DJ/What a Wonderful Love	1961	30.00	60.00	120.00
RCA VICTOR					
47-7296	Tutti Frutti/Cause I'm in Love	1958	3.75	7.50	15.00
WARNER BROS.					
5086	Hey Baby/Quiet	1959	3.00	6.00	12.00

BABY HUEY

45s

Number	Title (A Side/B Side)	Yr	VG	VG+	NM
CURTOM					
1939	Mighty Mighty Children/Mighty Mighty Children (Part 2)	1969	2.50	5.00	10.00
1962	Hard Times/Listen to Me	1971	2.50	5.00	10.00
SATELLITE					
2013	Messin' with the Kid/Monkey Man	196?	5.00	10.00	20.00
U.S.A.					
801	Messin' with the Kid/Just Being Careful	196?	5.00	10.00	20.00

Albums

Number	Title (A Side/B Side)	Yr	VG	VG+	NM
CURTOM					
CRS-8007	The Living Legend	1970	10.00	20.00	40.00

BABY JANE AND THE ROCKABYES

45s

Number	Title (A Side/B Side)	Yr	VG	VG+	NM
PORT					
3013	Heartbreak Shop/Dance Till My Feet Get Tired	1964	7.50	15.00	30.00
UNITED ARTISTS					
505	If You Wanna/Oh Johnny	1962	5.00	10.00	20.00
560	How Much is That Doggie in the Window/My Boy John	1963	5.00	10.00	20.00
593	Get Me to the Church on Time/Hickory Dickory Dock	1963	3.75	7.50	15.00

BABY RAY

45s

Number	Title (A Side/B Side)	Yr	VG	VG+	NM
IMPERIAL					
66216	There's Something On Your Mind/House on Soul Hill	1966	3.75	7.50	15.00
66232	Elvira/Just Because	1967	3.75	7.50	15.00
66256	Your Sweet Love/Yours Until Tomorrow	1967	3.75	7.50	15.00

Albums

IMPERIAL

Number	Title (A Side/B Side)	Yr	VG	VG+	NM
LP-9335 [M]	Where Soul Lives	1967	6.25	12.50	25.00
LP-12335 [S]	Where Soul Lives	1967	7.50	15.00	30.00

BABY RAY AND THE FERNS

An early production of FRANK ZAPPA.

45s

DONNA

Number	Title (A Side/B Side)	Yr	VG	VG+	NM
1378	How's Your Bird/The World's Greatest Sinner	1963	50.00	100.00	200.00

BACHARACH, BURT

45s

A&M

Number	Title (A Side/B Side)	Yr	VG	VG+	NM
845	Alfie/Bond Street	1967	2.00	4.00	8.00
888	The Look of Love/Reach Out for Me	1967	2.00	4.00	8.00
931	Are You There (With Another Girl)/Message to Michael	1968	—	3.00	6.00
1004	The Bell That Couldn't Jingle/What the World Needs Now Is Love	1968	—	3.00	6.00
1064	I'll Never Fall in Love Again/Pacific Coast Highway	1969	—	3.00	6.00
1153	Come Touch the Sun/Raindrops Keep Fallin' on My Head	1969	—	3.00	6.00
1222	A House Is Not a Home/Any Day Now	1970	—	2.50	5.00
1241	All Kinds of People/She's Gone Away	1971	—	2.50	5.00
1290	One Less Bell to Answer/Freefall	1971	—	2.50	5.00
1290 [PS]	One Less Bell to Answer/Freefall	1971	2.00	4.00	8.00
1489	Living Together, Growing Together/Something Big	1973	—	2.00	4.00
1512	Living Together, Growing Together/Reflections	1974	—	2.00	4.00
1921	I Took My Strength from You (I Had None)/Time and Tenderness	1977	—	2.00	4.00
1960	No One Remembers My Name/Futures	1977	—	2.00	4.00
2161	New York Lady/Riverboat	1979	—	2.00	4.00

KAPP

Number	Title (A Side/B Side)	Yr	VG	VG+	NM
532	Saturday Sunshine/And So Goodbye My Love	1963	2.00	4.00	8.00
657	Don't Go Breaking My Heart/Trains and Boats and Planes	1965	2.00	4.00	8.00
685	My Little Red Book/What's New Pussycat	1965	2.00	4.00	8.00

LIBERTY

Number	Title (A Side/B Side)	Yr	VG	VG+	NM
55934	Juanita's Place/Nikki	1966	2.00	4.00	8.00

UNITED ARTISTS

Number	Title (A Side/B Side)	Yr	VG	VG+	NM
50123	The Fox Trot/Ukeatalia	1967	2.00	4.00	8.00

Albums

A&M

Number	Title (A Side/B Side)	Yr	VG	VG+	NM
SP-131 [M]	Reach Out	1967	3.00	6.00	12.00
SP-3501	Burt Bacharach	1971	2.50	5.00	10.00
SP-3527	Living Together	1973	2.50	5.00	10.00
SP-3661	Burt Bacharach's Greatest Hits	1973	2.50	5.00	10.00
SP-4131 [S]	Reach Out	1967	3.00	6.00	12.00
SP-4188	Make It Easy on Yourself	1969	2.50	5.00	10.00
SP-4622	Futures	1977	2.50	5.00	10.00

KAPP

Number	Title (A Side/B Side)	Yr	VG	VG+	NM
KS-3577	Burt Bacharach Plays His Hits	1969	3.00	6.00	12.00

MCA

Number	Title (A Side/B Side)	Yr	VG	VG+	NM
65	Burt Bacharach Plays His Hits	1973	2.00	4.00	8.00

—Reissue of Kapp LP

BACHELORS, THE (1)

British Invasion male vocal group.

45s

LONDON

Number	Title (A Side/B Side)	Yr	VG	VG+	NM
9584	Charmaine/Old Bill	1963	3.00	6.00	12.00
9623	Faraway Places/Is There a Chance	1964	3.00	6.00	12.00
9632	Whispering/No Light in the Window	1964	3.00	6.00	12.00
9639	Diane/Happy Land	1964	3.00	6.00	12.00
9639	Diane/I Believe	1964	3.75	7.50	15.00
9672	I Believe/Sweet Lullaby	1964	3.00	6.00	12.00
9672 [PS]	I Believe/Sweet Lullaby	1964	6.25	12.50	25.00
9693	I Wouldn't Trade You for the World/Beneath the Willow Tree	1964	3.00	6.00	12.00
9693 [PS]	I Wouldn't Trade You for the World/Beneath the Willow Tree	1964	6.25	12.50	25.00
9724	No Arms Can Ever Hold You/Oh Samuel, Don't Die	1964	3.00	6.00	12.00
9762	Marie/You Can Tell	1965	2.50	5.00	10.00
9793	Chapel in the Moonlight/The Old Wishing Well	1965	2.50	5.00	10.00
9793 [PS]	Chapel in the Moonlight/The Old Wishing Well	1965	5.00	10.00	20.00
9828	Love Me with All of Your Heart/There's No Room in My Heart	1966	2.50	5.00	10.00
20010	Can I Trust You/My Girl	1966	2.50	5.00	10.00
20018	Walk with Faith in Your Heart/Queen Molly Malone of Ireland	1966	2.50	5.00	10.00
20027	Marta/Oh How I Miss You	1967	2.00	4.00	8.00
20033	Learn to Live Without You/3 O'Clock Flamingo Street	1967	2.00	4.00	8.00
20051	Punky's Dilemma/It's a Beautiful Day	1968	2.00	4.00	8.00
20063	Love Is All/The Colours of Love	1970	—	3.00	6.00
20071	Diamonds Are Forever/Where There's a Heartache	1971	—	3.00	6.00

Albums

LONDON

Number	Title (A Side/B Side)	Yr	VG	VG+	NM
PS 353 [S]	Presenting the Bachelors	1964	5.00	10.00	20.00
PS 393 [P]	Back Again	1964	5.00	10.00	20.00
—"I Wouldn't Trade You for the World" is rechanneled.					
PS 418 [S]	No Arms Can Ever Hold You	1965	5.00	10.00	20.00
PS 435 [P]	Marie	1965	5.00	10.00	20.00
—"Marie" is rechanneled					
PS 460 [S]	Hits of the 60's	1966	5.00	10.00	20.00
PS 491 [P]	The Bachelors' Girls	1966	3.75	7.50	15.00
—"Marie" is rechanneled					
PS 518 [P]	Golden All Time Hits	1967	3.75	7.50	15.00
PS 528	Bachelors '68	1968	3.00	6.00	12.00
PS 611	Under and Over	1972	2.50	5.00	10.00
LL 3353 [M]	Presenting the Bachelors	1964	3.75	7.50	15.00
LL 3393 [M]	Back Again	1964	3.75	7.50	15.00
LL 3418 [M]	No Arms Can Ever Hold You	1965	3.75	7.50	15.00
LL 3435 [M]	Marie	1965	3.75	7.50	15.00
LL 3460 [M]	Hits of the 60's	1966	3.75	7.50	15.00
LL 3491 [M]	The Bachelors' Girls	1966	3.00	6.00	12.00
LL 3518 [M]	Golden All Time Hits	1967	3.75	7.50	15.00

BACHELORS, THE (2)

American male vocal group.

45s

ALADDIN

Number	Title (A Side/B Side)	Yr	VG	VG+	NM
3210	Pretty Baby/Can't Help Loving You	1953	625.00	1250.	2500.

ROYAL ROOST

Number	Title (A Side/B Side)	Yr	VG	VG+	NM
620	I Found Love/You've Lied	1952	75.00	150.00	300.00

BACHELORS, THE (U)

None of these are group (1), though some could be group (2).

45s

EPIC

Number	Title (A Side/B Side)	Yr	VG	VG+	NM
9369	Do the Madison/Bachelor's Club	1960	3.00	6.00	12.00

MERCURY

Number	Title (A Side/B Side)	Yr	VG	VG+	NM
8159	Yesterday's Roses/Hereafter	1949	75.00	150.00	300.00

MGM

Number	Title (A Side/B Side)	Yr	VG	VG+	NM
12668	Sometimes/Teenage Memory	1958	5.00	10.00	20.00

NATIONAL

Number	Title (A Side/B Side)	Yr	VG	VG+	NM
104	From Your Heart/A Million Teardrops	1957	6.25	12.50	25.00
115	Today, Tomorrow, Forever/I Want a Girl	1957	6.25	12.50	25.00

POPLAR

Number	Title (A Side/B Side)	Yr	VG	VG+	NM
101	After/You Know, I Know (I Love You)	1957	12.50	25.00	50.00

SMASH

Number	Title (A Side/B Side)	Yr	VG	VG+	NM
1723	The Day I Met You/Hey Little Girl	1961	3.00	6.00	12.00

BACHMAN-TURNER OVERDRIVE

Also see BRAVE BELT; THE GUESS WHO.

45s

COMPLEAT

Number	Title (A Side/B Side)	Yr	VG	VG+	NM
127	For the Weekend/Just Look at Me Now	1984	—	2.00	4.00
133	My Sugaree/Service with a Smile	1984	—	2.00	4.00
137	My Sugaree/(B-side unknown)	1985	—	2.00	4.00

MERCURY

Number	Title (A Side/B Side)	Yr	VG	VG+	NM
73383	Gimmie Your Money Please/Little Gandy Dancer	1973	—	2.50	5.00
73417	Blue Collar/Hold Back the Water	1973	—	2.50	5.00
73457	Let It Ride/Tramp	1974	—	2.00	4.00
73487	Takin' Care of Business/Stonegates	1974	—	2.00	4.00
73622	You Ain't Seen Nothin' Yet/Free Wheelin'	1974	—	2.00	4.00
73656	Roll On Down the Highway/Sledgehammer	1975	—	2.00	4.00
73683	Hey You/Flat Broke Love	1975	—	2.00	4.00
73724	Down to the Line/She's a Devil	1975	—	2.00	4.00
73724 [PS]	Down to the Line/She's a Devil	1975	2.00	4.00	8.00
73766	Take It Like a Man/Woncha Take Me for a While	1976	—	2.00	4.00
73784	Looking Out for #1/Find Out About Love	1976	—	2.00	4.00
73843	Gimme Your Money Please/Four Wheel Drive	1976	—	2.00	4.00
73903	Freeways/My Wheels Won't Turn	1977	—	2.00	4.00
73926	Shotgun Rider/Down, Down	1977	—	2.00	4.00
73951	Life Still Goes On (I'm Lonely)/Just for You	1977	—	2.00	4.00
73987	Down the Road/A Long Time for a Little While	1978	—	2.00	4.00
74046	Heaven Tonight/Heartaches	1979	—	2.00	4.00
74062	End of the Line/Jamaica	1979	—	2.00	4.00

Albums

COMPLEAT

Number	Title (A Side/B Side)	Yr	VG	VG+	NM
CPL1-1010	Bachman-Turner Overdrive	1984	2.00	4.00	8.00

MCA/CURB

Number	Title (A Side/B Side)	Yr	VG	VG+	NM
5760	Live! Live! Live!	1986	2.00	4.00	8.00

MERCURY

Number	Title (A Side/B Side)	Yr	VG	VG+	NM
SRM-1-673	Bachman-Turner Overdrive	1973	3.00	6.00	12.00
—Red label					
SRM-1-673	Bachman-Turner Overdrive	1974	2.50	5.00	10.00
—Chicago skyline label					
SRM-1-696	Bachman-Turner Overdrive II	1973	3.00	6.00	12.00
—Red label					
SRM-1-696	Bachman-Turner Overdrive II	1974	2.50	5.00	10.00
—Chicago skyline label					
SRM-1-1004	Not Fragile	1974	2.50	5.00	10.00
SRM-1-1027	Four Wheel Drive	1975	2.50	5.00	10.00
SRM-1-1067	Head On	1975	2.50	5.00	10.00
SRM-1-1101	Best of B.T.O. (So Far)	1976	2.50	5.00	10.00
SRM-1-3700	Freeways	1977	2.50	5.00	10.00
SRM-1-3713	Street Action	1978	2.50	5.00	10.00
SRM-1-3748	Rock N' Roll Nights	1979	2.50	5.00	10.00
822786-1	Best of B.T.O. (So Far)	1984	2.00	4.00	8.00
—Reissue of 1101					

BACHS, THE

Albums

RAIO

Number	Title (A Side/B Side)	Yr	VG	VG+	NM
(no #)	Out of the Bachs	1967	2000.	3000.	4000.

BACK BEAT

45s

LAURIE

Number	Title (A Side/B Side)	Yr	VG	VG+	NM
3092	Rock and Roll Symphony, 1st and 2nd Movements	1961	5.00	10.00	20.00

BACK PORCH MAJORITY, THE

45s

EPIC

Number	Title (A Side/B Side)	Yr	VG	VG+	NM
9689	Friends/Hand-Me-Down Things	1964	2.50	5.00	10.00
9754	Hey Nelly Nelly/Ol' Dan Tucker	1965	2.50	5.00	10.00
9769	Smash Flops/Jack O'Diamonds	1965	2.50	5.00	10.00

Number	Title (A Side/B Side)	Yr	VG	VG+	NM
9809	Good-Time Joe/Ramblin' Man	1965	2.50	5.00	10.00
9850	The Mighty Mississippi/Song of Hope	1965	2.50	5.00	10.00
9879	Second Hand Man/That's the Way It's Gonna Be	1965	2.50	5.00	10.00
10036	Honey and Wine/Brother John	1966	2.00	4.00	8.00
10079	Once Again/Slippery Sal and Dirty Dan, the Oyster Man	1966	2.00	4.00	8.00
10129	Southtown U.S.A./This Little Light	1967	2.00	4.00	8.00
Albums					
EPIC					
LN 24134 [M]	Live from Ledbetter's	1965	3.75	7.50	15.00
LN 24149 [M]	Riverboat Days	1965	3.75	7.50	15.00
LN 24184 [M]	That's the Way It's Gonna Be	1966	3.75	7.50	15.00
LN 24319 [M]	Willy Nilly Wonder of Illusion	1967	5.00	10.00	20.00
BN 26134 [S]	Live from Ledbetter's	1965	5.00	10.00	20.00
BN 26149 [S]	Riverboat Days	1965	5.00	10.00	20.00
BN 26184 [S]	That's the Way It's Gonna Be	1966	5.00	10.00	20.00
BN 26319 [S]	Willy Nilly Wonder of Illusion	1967	3.75	7.50	15.00

BACK STREET CRAWLER

Number	Title (A Side/B Side)	Yr	VG	VG+	NM
Albums					
ATCO					
SD 36-125	The Band Plays On	1975	3.00	6.00	12.00
SD 36-138	2nd Street	1976	3.00	6.00	12.00
EPIC					
PE 34900	Crawler	1977	2.50	5.00	10.00
—Epic titles as "Crawler"					
JE 35482	Snake, Rattle and Roll	1978	2.50	5.00	10.00

BACKUS, JIM

Number	Title (A Side/B Side)	Yr	VG	VG+	NM
45s					
DICO					
101	I Was a Teenage Reindeer/The Office Party	1959	5.00	10.00	20.00
DORE					
899	Dirty Old Man/Frigid	1974	—	2.50	5.00
JUBILEE					
5330	Delicious!/I Need a Vacation	1958	3.75	7.50	15.00
—As "Jim Bakus and Friend"					
5351	Cave Man/Why Don't You Go Home for Christmas	1958	3.00	6.00	12.00
5361	Cave Man/Rock on the Roof	1959	3.00	6.00	12.00
Albums					
RCA VICTOR					
LPM-1362 [M]	Mr. Magoo in Hi-Fi	1957	12.50	25.00	50.00

BACON, GAR

Number	Title (A Side/B Side)	Yr	VG	VG+	NM
45s					
BATON					
248	There's Gonna Be Rockin' Tonight/Y-I-O-U	1957	15.00	30.00	60.00
250	Justice/Pucker Up	1958	10.00	20.00	40.00
DALE					
105	Chains of Love/Mary Jane	1957	6.25	12.50	25.00
108	Dutch Treat/I'll Never Fail You	1958	7.50	15.00	30.00
OKEH					
7115	Marshall, Marshall/Too Young to Love	1959	5.00	10.00	20.00
RKO UNIQUE					
395	Lonesome Wail/You and Your Love	1957	5.00	10.00	20.00

BACON FAT

Number	Title (A Side/B Side)	Yr	VG	VG+	NM
Albums					
BLUE HORIZON					
BH-4807	Grease One for Me	1970	6.25	12.50	25.00

BAD COMPANY

Also see BOZ; FREE.

Number	Title (A Side/B Side)	Yr	VG	VG+	NM
45s					
ATCO					
98463	This Could Be the One/How About That	1992	—	2.00	4.00
—Also see BOZ BURRELL.					
ATLANTIC					
88939	Shake It Up/Dangerous Age	1989	—	—	3.00
89035	No Smoke Without a Fire/Love Attack	1988	—	—	3.00
89299	If I'm Sleeping/That Girl	1987	—	—	3.00
89355 [DJ]	This Tell It Like It Is (same on both sides)	1986	—	2.00	4.00
—May be promo only					
SWAN SONG					
70015	Can't Get Enough/Little Miss Fortune	1974	—	2.50	5.00
70101	Movin' On/Easy on My Soul	1974	—	2.00	4.00
70103	Good Lovin' Gone Bad/Whiskey Bottle	1975	—	2.00	4.00
70106	Feel Like Makin' Love/Wild Fire Woman	1975	—	2.50	5.00
70108	Young Blood/Do Right...Woman	1976	—	2.00	4.00
70109	Honey Child/Fade Away	1976	—	2.00	4.00
70112	Burnin' Sky/Everything I Need	1976	—	2.00	4.00
70119	Rock 'N' Roll Fantasy/Crazy Circles	1979	—	2.00	4.00
70119 [PS]	Rock 'N' Roll Fantasy/Crazy Circles	1979	—	3.00	6.00
71000	Gone, Gone, Gone/Take the Time	1979	—	2.00	4.00
99966	Electricland/Untie the Knot	1982	—	2.00	4.00
Albums					
ATCO					
91371	Holy Water	1990	3.75	7.50	15.00
ATLANTIC					
81625	10 from 6 (The Best of Bad Company)	1986	2.50	5.00	10.00
81684	Fame and Fortune	1987	2.50	5.00	10.00
81884	Dangerous Age	1988	2.50	5.00	10.00
SWAN SONG					
SS 8410	Bad Company	1974	2.50	5.00	10.00
SS 8413	Straight Shooter	1975	2.50	5.00	10.00
SS 8415	Run with the Pack	1976	2.50	5.00	10.00
SS 8500	Burnin' Sky	1977	2.50	5.00	10.00
SS 8501	Bad Company	1977	2.00	4.00	8.00
SS 8502	Straight Shooter	1977	2.00	4.00	8.00
SS 8503	Run with the Pack	1977	2.00	4.00	8.00
SS 8506	Desolation Angels	1979	2.50	5.00	10.00
90001	Rough Diamonds	1982	2.50	5.00	10.00

BADD BOYS, THE

Number	Title (A Side/B Side)	Yr	VG	VG+	NM
45s					
EPIC					
10119	Never Going Back to Georgia/River Deep Mountain High	1967	12.50	25.00	50.00
10165	Folks in a Hurry/I Told You So	1967	15.00	30.00	60.00

BADFINGER

Also see GEORGE HARRISON AND FRIENDS.

Number	Title (A Side/B Side)	Yr	VG	VG+	NM
45s					
APPLE					
1803	Maybe Tomorrow/And Her Daddy's a Millionaire	1969	7.50	15.00	30.00
—By "The Iveys"; with star on label					
1803	Maybe Tomorrow/And Her Daddy's a Millionaire	1969	5.00	10.00	20.00
—By "The Iveys"; without star on label					
1815	Come and Get It/Rock of All Ages	1969	—	3.00	6.00
1815	Come and Get It/Rock of All Ages	1969	2.00	4.00	8.00
—With Capitol logo on B-side bottom					
1822	No Matter What/Carry On Till Tomorrow	1970	—	3.00	6.00
1822	No Matter What/Carry On Till Tomorrow	1970	5.00	10.00	20.00
—With star on A-side label					
1841	Day After Day/Money	1971	5.00	10.00	20.00
—With star on A-side label					
1841	Day After Day/Money	1971	—	3.00	6.00
1841 [DJ]	Day After Day/Money	1971	30.00	60.00	120.00
—White label					
1844	Baby Blue/Flying	1972	—	3.00	6.00
1844 [DJ]	Baby Blue/Flying	1972	30.00	60.00	120.00
—White label					
1844 [PS]	Baby Blue/Flying	1972	3.75	7.50	15.00
1864	Apple of My Eye/Blind Owl	1973	—	3.00	6.00
P-1864 [DJ]	Apple of My Eye (mono/stereo)	1973	6.25	12.50	25.00
APPLE/AMERICOM					
1803P/M-300	Maybe Tomorrow/And Her Daddy's a Millionaire	1969	150.00	300.00	600.00
—By "The Iveys"; four-inch flexidisc sold from vending machines					
CAPITOL					
S7-17487	Baby Blue/Day After Day	1993	—	—	3.00
—Blue vinyl					
S7-17487	Baby Blue/Day After Day	1993	—	2.50	5.00
—Black vinyl					
ELEKTRA					
46022	Lost Inside Your Love/Come Down Hard	1979	—	2.50	5.00
46025	Love Is Gonna Come At Last/Sail Away	1979	—	2.50	5.00
RADIO					
3793	Hold On/Passin' Time	1981	—	2.50	5.00
3815	I Got You/Rock and Roll Contract	1981	—	2.50	5.00
3833	Because I Love You/Too Hung Up on You	1981	—	2.50	5.00
WARNER BROS.					
7801	I Miss You/Shine On	1974	—	3.00	6.00
Albums					
APPLE					
ST-3355	Maybe Tomorrow	1969	500.00	1000.	2000.
—As "The Iveys"; album not released in US; price is for an LP slick, which does exist					
ST 3364	Magic Christian Music	1970	7.50	15.00	30.00
—With Capitol logo on Side 2 bottom					
ST 3364	Magic Christian Music	1970	5.00	10.00	20.00
SKAO 3367	No Dice	1970	7.50	15.00	30.00
SW 3387	Straight Up	1971	15.00	30.00	60.00
SW 3411	Ass	1973	5.00	10.00	20.00
ELEKTRA					
6E-175	Airwaves	1979	3.00	6.00	12.00
RADIO					
RR 16030	Say No More	1981	2.50	5.00	10.00
RYKO ANALOGUE					
RALP 10189	Day After Day	1990	5.00	10.00	20.00
—Limited edition on clear vinyl with obi					
WARNER BROS.					
BS 2762	Badfinger	1974	3.75	7.50	15.00
BS 2827	Wish You Were Here	1974	3.75	7.50	15.00

BADGER

Number	Title (A Side/B Side)	Yr	VG	VG+	NM
Albums					
ATCO					
SD 7022	One Live Badger	1973	3.00	6.00	12.00
EPIC					
KE 32831	White Lady	1974	3.00	6.00	12.00

BAEZ, JOAN

Number	Title (A Side/B Side)	Yr	VG	VG+	NM
45s					
A&M					
1334	Song of Bangladesh/Prison Trilogy (Billy Rose)	1972	—	2.50	5.00
1334 [PS]	Song of Bangladesh/Prison Trilogy (Billy Rose)	1972	2.50	5.00	10.00
1362	In the Quiet Morning/To Bobby	1972	—	2.00	4.00
1362 [PS]	In the Quiet Morning/To Bobby	1972	2.00	4.00	8.00
1393	Love Song to a Stranger/Tumbleweed	1972	—	2.00	4.00
1454	The Best of Friends/Mary Call	1973	—	2.00	4.00
1472	Less Than the Song/Windrose	1973	—	2.00	4.00
1516	Forever Young/Guantanamera	1974	—	2.00	4.00
1703	Blue Sky/Dida	1975	—	2.00	4.00
1737	Diamonds and Rust/Winds of the Old Days	1975	—	2.50	5.00
1802	Please Come to Boston/Love Song to a Stranger	1976	—	2.00	4.00
1820	Never Dreamed You'd Leave in Summer/Children and All That Jazz	1976	—	2.00	4.00
1884	Caruso/Time Is Passing Us By	1976	—	2.00	4.00
1906	O Brother/Still Waters at Night	1977	—	2.00	4.00
DECCA					
32890	Silent Running/Rejoice in the Sun	1971	—	3.00	6.00
GUARDIAN					
S7-19727	No Mermaid/Diamonds and Rust	1997	—	—	3.00

Number	Title (A Side/B Side)	Yr	VG	VG+	NM
PHILCO-FORD					
HP-36	There But For Fortune/Pack Up Your Sorrows	1969	5.00	10.00	20.00
—4-inch plastic "Hip Pocket Record" with color sleeve					
PORTRAIT					
70006	I'm Blowing Away/The Altar Boy and the Sheep	1977	—	2.00	4.00
70009	Time Rag/Miracles	1977	—	2.00	4.00
70032	Light a Light/Michael	1979	—	2.00	4.00
RCA VICTOR					
74-0568	The Ballad of Sacco and Vanzetti/Here's to You	1971	—	3.00	6.00
VANGUARD					
35012	Banks of the Ohio/Old Blue	1962	2.00	4.00	8.00
35013	Lonesome Road/Pal of Mine	1962	2.00	4.00	8.00
35018	What Have They Done to the Rain/Danger Waters	1963	2.00	4.00	8.00
35023	We Shall Overcome/What Have They Done to the Rain	1963	2.00	4.00	8.00
35026	Medley: With God on Our Side/Railroad Bill//Rambler Gambler	1964	2.00	4.00	8.00
35031	There But for Fortune/Daddy You Been On My Mind	1965	2.00	4.00	8.00
35031 [PS]	There But for Fortune/Daddy You Been On My Mind	1965	7.50	15.00	30.00
35040	Pack Up Your Sorrows/Swallow Song	1966	2.00	4.00	8.00
35046	Little Drummer Boy/Cantique de Noel	1966	2.50	5.00	10.00
35055	Be Not Too Hard/The North	1967	2.00	4.00	8.00
35088	Love Is Just a Four-Letter Word/Love Minus Zero-No Limit	1969	2.00	4.00	8.00
35092	If I Knew/Rock Salt and Nails	1969	2.00	4.00	8.00
35098	Four Days Gone/Hickory Wind	1969	2.00	4.00	8.00
35103	No Expectations/One Day at a Time	1970	—	3.00	6.00
35106	Sweet Sir Galahad/The Ghetto	1970	—	3.00	6.00
35114	Carry It On/Rock Salt and Nails	1970	—	3.00	6.00
35138	The Night They Drove Old Dixie Down/When Time Is Stolen	1971	2.00	4.00	8.00
35145	Let It Be/Poor Wayfaring Stranger	1971	—	3.00	6.00
35148	Will the Circle Be Unbroken/Just a Closer Walk with Thee	1972	—	2.50	5.00
35158	Blessed Are/The Brand New Tennessee Waltz	1972	—	2.50	5.00
Albums					
A&M					
SP-3103	Come from the Shadows	198?	2.00	4.00	8.00
—Budget-line reissue					
SP-3233	Diamonds and Rust	198?	2.00	4.00	8.00
—Budget-line reissue					
SP-3234	The Best of Joan C. Baez	198?	2.00	4.00	8.00
—Budget-line reissue					
SP-3614	Gracias A La Vida	1974	3.00	6.00	12.00
SP-3704 [(2)]	From Every Stage	1976	3.00	6.00	12.00
SP-4339	Come From the Shadows	1972	2.50	5.00	10.00
SP-4390	Where Are You Now, My Son?	1973	2.50	5.00	10.00
SP-4527	Diamonds and Rust	1975	2.50	5.00	10.00
SP-4603	Gulf Winds	1976	2.50	5.00	10.00
SP-4668	The Best of Joan C. Baez	1977	2.50	5.00	10.00
SP-6506 [(2)]	From Every Stage	198?	2.50	5.00	10.00
—Reissue					
QU-54339 [Q]	Come From the Shadows	1974	5.00	10.00	20.00
QU-54527 [Q]	Diamonds and Rust	1975	5.00	10.00	20.00
GOLD CASTLE					
D1-71309	Recently	1989	3.00	6.00	12.00
—Reissue of 171 009					
D1-71321	Diamonds and Rust in the Castle	1989	3.00	6.00	12.00
D1-71324	Speaking of Dreams	1989	3.00	6.00	12.00
171009	Recently	1988	2.50	5.00	10.00
MOBILE FIDELITY					
1-238	Diamonds and Rust	1996	15.00	30.00	60.00
—Audiophile vinyl					
NAUTILUS					
NR-12	Diamonds and Rust	1980	10.00	20.00	40.00
—Audiophile vinyl					
PORTRAIT					
PR 34697	Blowin' Away	1977	2.50	5.00	10.00
JR 35766	Honest Lullaby	1979	2.50	5.00	10.00
SQUIRE					
SQ-33001 [M]	The Best of Joan Baez	1963	5.00	10.00	20.00
VANGUARD					
VSD-41/42 [(2)]	The Joan Baez Ballad Book	1972	3.00	6.00	12.00
VSD-49/50 [(2)]	The Contemporary Ballad Book	1974	3.00	6.00	12.00
VSD-79/80 [(2)]	The Love Song Album	197?	3.00	6.00	12.00
VSD-105/6 [(2)]	The Country Music Album	1979	3.00	6.00	12.00
VSD-2077 [S]	Joan Baez	1960	6.25	12.50	25.00
VSD-2097 [S]	Joan Baez, Vol. 2	1961	6.25	12.50	25.00
VSD-2122 [S]	Joan Baez In Concert	1962	6.25	12.50	25.00
VSD-2123 [S]	Joan Baez In Concert, Part 2	1963	6.25	12.50	25.00
VSD-6560/1 [(2)]	The First 10 Years	1970	3.75	7.50	15.00
VSD-6570/1 [(2)]	Blessed Are	1971	3.75	7.50	15.00
VRS-9078 [M]	Joan Baez	1960	5.00	10.00	20.00
VRS-9094 [M]	Joan Baez, Vol. 2	1961	5.00	10.00	20.00
VRS-9112 [M]	Joan Baez In Concert	1962	5.00	10.00	20.00
VRS-9113 [M]	Joan Baez In Concert, Part 2	1963	5.00	10.00	20.00
VRS-9160 [M]	Joan Baez/5	1964	3.75	7.50	15.00
VRS-9200 [M]	Farewell, Angelina	1965	3.75	7.50	15.00
VRS-9230 [M]	Noel	1966	3.75	7.50	15.00
VRS-9240 [M]	Joan	1967	3.75	7.50	15.00
VSQ-40001/2 [(2) Q]	Blessed Are	1973	6.25	12.50	25.00
VSQ-40032 [Q]	Hits/Greatest & Others	1973	5.00	10.00	20.00
VMS-73107	The Joan Baez Ballad Book, Vol. 1	1985	2.50	5.00	10.00
VMS-73115	The Joan Baez Ballad Book, Vol. 2	1985	2.50	5.00	10.00
VMS-73119	The Night They Drove Old Dixie Down	198?	2.50	5.00	10.00
VSD-79160 [S]	Joan Baez/5	1964	5.00	10.00	20.00
VSD-79200 [S]	Farewell, Angelina	1965	5.00	10.00	20.00
VSD-79230 [S]	Noel	1966	5.00	10.00	20.00
VSD-79240 [S]	Joan	1967	5.00	10.00	20.00
VSD-79275	Baptism	1968	5.00	10.00	20.00
VSD-79306/7 [(2)]	Any Day Now	1969	6.25	12.50	25.00

Number	Title (A Side/B Side)	Yr	VG	VG+	NM
VSD-79308	David's Album	1969	3.00	6.00	12.00
VSD-79310	One Day at a Time	1970	3.00	6.00	12.00
VSD-79313	Carry It On	1971	3.00	6.00	12.00
VSD-79332	Hits/Greatest & Others	1973	2.50	5.00	10.00
VSD-79446/7	Very Early Joan	1981	3.00	6.00	12.00

BAG, THE

Number	Title (A Side/B Side)	Yr	VG	VG+	NM
45s					
DECCA					
32279	Nobody's Child/Nickels 'N Dimes	1968	2.00	4.00	8.00
32409	Down and Out/Up in the Mornin'	1968	2.00	4.00	8.00
32463	Red, Purple and Blue/I Want You By My Side	1969	2.00	4.00	8.00
Albums					
DECCA					
DL 75057	Real	1968	3.75	7.50	15.00

BAGDASARIAN, ROSS

Real name of DAVID SEVILLE, who also invented THE CHIPMUNKS.

Number	Title (A Side/B Side)	Yr	VG	VG+	NM
45s					
CORAL					
60544	Come On-a My House/Oh Beauty	1951	7.50	15.00	30.00
60597	The Girl with the Tambourine/He Says Mu-Humm	1951	6.25	12.50	25.00
IMPERIAL					
66379	Jone-Cone-Phone/Spanish Pizza	1969	2.50	5.00	10.00
66414	You've Got Me on a Merry-Go-Round/You Better Open Your Eyes	1969	2.50	5.00	10.00
LIBERTY					
55013	The Bold and the Brave/See a Teardrop Fall	1956	5.00	10.00	20.00
55193	Judy/Maria from Madrid	1959	4.00	8.00	16.00
55239	Lotta Bull/(B-side unknown)	1959	4.00	8.00	16.00
55275	Lazy Lovers/One Finger Waltz	1960	4.00	8.00	16.00
55462	Armen's Theme/Russian Roulette	1962	3.75	7.50	15.00
55557	Cecelia/Gotta Get to Your House	1963	3.75	7.50	15.00
55619	Lucy, Lucy/Scalliwags and Sinners	1963	3.75	7.50	15.00
55810	La Noche/Naval Maneuver	1965	3.00	6.00	12.00
55837	Come On-a My House/Gotta Get to Your House	1965	3.00	6.00	12.00
56004	Walking Birds of Carnaby/Red Wine	1967	3.00	6.00	12.00
56043	Yallah/Naval Maneuver	1968	—	—	—
—Unreleased					
56048	When I Look in Your Eyes/Sands of Time	1968	3.00	6.00	12.00
56165	I Treasure Thee/Lie Lie	1969	3.00	6.00	12.00
MERCURY					
70254	Let's Have a Merry, Merry Christmas/Hey Brother, Pour the Wine	1953	6.25	12.50	25.00
Albums					
LIBERTY					
LRP-3451 [M]	The Crazy, Mixed-Up World of Ross Bagdasarian	1966	10.00	20.00	40.00
LST-7451 [S]	The Crazy, Mixed-Up World of Ross Bagdasarian	1966	12.50	25.00	50.00

BAGELS, THE

Number	Title (A Side/B Side)	Yr	VG	VG+	NM
45s					
WARNER BROS.					
5420	I Wanna Hold Your Hair/Yeah, Yeah, Yeah, Yeah	1964	3.75	7.50	15.00

BAGGYS, THE

Number	Title (A Side/B Side)	Yr	VG	VG+	NM
45s					
PIPELINE					
501	El Surfer/El Seagull	1963	10.00	20.00	40.00

BAILEY, DIANE

Number	Title (A Side/B Side)	Yr	VG	VG+	NM
45s					
SWAN					
4079	Golden Idol/Someone Else's Hands	1961	3.00	6.00	12.00
4086	True Blue Love/There's a Time	1961	3.00	6.00	12.00

BAILEY, J.R.

Number	Title (A Side/B Side)	Yr	VG	VG+	NM
45s					
CALLA					
158	Love Won't Wear Off/(Instrumental)	1968	—	3.00	6.00
MALA					
12015	Hold Back the Dawn/Too Late	1968	2.00	4.00	8.00
MAM					
3635	I'll Always Be Your Lover/Not Too Long Ago	1974	—	2.50	5.00
3639	Everything I Want I See in You/I Can't See Me Without You	1974	—	2.50	5.00
MIDLAND INT'L					
PB-10305	The Entertainer (If They Could Only See Me Now)/You Pass My Love (Like a Moving Train)	1975	—	2.50	5.00
RCA					
PB-10799	Super Loser/Love Still Remains	1976	—	2.50	5.00
SPRING					
3038	I'm Still in Love with You/(B-side unknown)	1984	—	2.00	4.00
TOY					
3801	Love, Love, Love/(B-side unknown)	1972	—	3.00	6.00
3805	After Hours/(B-side unknown)	1972	—	3.00	6.00
UNITED ARTISTS					
XW-1215	Alone in the Morning/Stella by Starlight	1978	—	2.00	4.00
Albums					
MAM					
9	Just Me 'N' You	1974	3.00	6.00	12.00

BAILEY, THOMAS

Number	Title (A Side/B Side)	Yr	VG	VG+	NM
45s					
FEDERAL					
12559	Fran/Just Won't Move	1969	3.00	6.00	12.00
12567	Wish I Was Back/Percy's Place	1970	25.00	50.00	100.00

BAINES, VICKI

45s

Number	Title (A Side/B Side)	Yr	VG	VG+	NM
LOMA					
2078	We Can Find True Love/Sweeter Than Sweet Things	1967	3.00	6.00	12.00
PARKWAY					
957	Losing You/Got to Run	1965	6.25	12.50	25.00
966	Country Girl/Are You Kidding	1966	25.00	50.00	100.00

BAJA MARIMBA BAND, THE

Also includes records as "Julius Wechter and the Baja Marimba Band."

45s

Number	Title (A Side/B Side)	Yr	VG	VG+	NM
ALMO					
201	Comin' In the Back Door/December's Child	1963	2.00	4.00	8.00
203	Moonglow & Theme from Picnic/Acapulco 1922	1964	—	3.00	6.00
206	Pedro's Pouch/Wincle Lamoyan Coan	1964	—	3.00	6.00
207	Up Cherry Street/Woody Woodpecker Song	1964	—	3.00	6.00
211	Baja Ska/Samba De Orfeu	1964	—	3.00	6.00
216	Juarez/Guacamole	1965	—	3.00	6.00
218	Goin' Out the Side Door/Brasilia	1965	—	3.00	6.00
228	Yellow Bird/For Animals Only	1966	—	3.00	6.00
231	(How Much Is That) Doggie in the Window/Puff (The Magic Dragon)	1966	—	3.00	6.00
A&M					
XMAS 1 [DJ]	The 12 Days Of Christmas/My Favorite Things	1968	3.00	6.00	12.00
—B-side by We Five					
XMAS 1 [PS]	The 12 Days Of Christmas/My Favorite Things	1968	3.75	7.50	15.00
—B-side by We Five					
816	The Telephone Song/Portuguese Washerwoman	1966	—	2.50	5.00
824	Ghost Riders in the Sky/Sabor A Mi	1966	—	2.50	5.00
833	The Cry of the Wild Goose/Spanish Moss	1967	—	2.50	5.00
843	Georgy Girl/Cabeza Arriba (Heads Up)	1967	—	2.50	5.00
862	Along Comes Mary/Wall Street Rag	1967	—	2.00	4.00
862 [PS]	Along Comes Mary/Wall Street Rag	1967	—	2.50	5.00
892	Foul Play/The Sounds of Silence	1967	—	2.00	4.00
913	Fiddler on the Roof/Sunday Mornin'	1968	—	2.00	4.00
937	Brasilia/Yes Sir, That's My Baby	1968	—	2.00	4.00
975	Little Prayer/Do You Know the Way to San Jose	1968	—	2.00	4.00
—Artist credit: "Julius Wechter & The Baja Marimba Band"					
1005	Flyin' High/Les Bicyclettes de Belsize	1968	—	2.00	4.00
1047	Big Red/Ruby '68	1969	—	2.00	4.00
1078	I'll Marimba You/I Don't Wanna Walk Without You	1969	—	2.00	4.00
—Artist credit: "Julius Wechter & The Baja Marimba Band"					
1126	Fresh Air/Wave	1969	—	2.00	4.00
1136	Can You Dig It Part 1/Can You Dig It Part 2	1969	—	2.00	4.00
1186	Picasso Summer/Samba Nuevo	1970	—	2.00	4.00
1281	Spanish Flea/As Time Goes By	1971	—	2.00	4.00
—Artist credit: "Julius Wechter & The Baja Marimba Band"					
BELL					
45339	Theme from "Deep Throat"/Do You Want to Dance	1973	—	2.50	5.00
45376	Anytime of the Year/Taco Belle	1973	—	2.00	4.00

Albums

Number	Title (A Side/B Side)	Yr	VG	VG+	NM
A&M					
SP-104 [M]	Baja Marimba Band	1964	2.50	5.00	10.00
SP-109 [M]	Baja Marimba Band Rides Again	1965	2.50	5.00	10.00
SP-113 [M]	For Animals Only	1965	2.50	5.00	10.00
SP-118 [M]	Watch Out!	1966	2.50	5.00	10.00
SP-123 [M]	Heads Up	1967	2.50	5.00	10.00
SP-3523 [(2)]	Foursider	1972	3.00	6.00	12.00
SP-4104 [S]	Baja Marimba Band	1964	3.00	6.00	12.00
SP-4109 [S]	Baja Marimba Band Rides Again	1965	3.00	6.00	12.00
SP-4113 [S]	For Animals Only	1965	3.00	6.00	12.00
SP-4118 [S]	Watch Out!	1966	3.00	6.00	12.00
SP-4123 [S]	Heads Up	1967	3.00	6.00	12.00
SP-4136	Fowl Play	1968	2.50	5.00	10.00
SP-4150	Do You Know the Way to San Jose?	1968	2.50	5.00	10.00
SP-4167	Those Were the Days	1969	2.50	5.00	10.00
SP-4200	Fresh Air	1969	2.50	5.00	10.00
SP-4248	Greatest Hits	1970	2.50	5.00	10.00
SP-4298	As Time Goes By	1971	2.50	5.00	10.00

BAKER, BOBBY

45s

Number	Title (A Side/B Side)	Yr	VG	VG+	NM
SWAN					
4037	Baby Blue Eyes/Hush Our Secret	1959	3.75	7.50	15.00

BAKER, CHARLIE

45s

Number	Title (A Side/B Side)	Yr	VG	VG+	NM
LIBERTY					
55226	Star of Wonder/You Crack Me Up	1959	6.25	12.50	25.00
MUNRAB					
106	Star of Wonder/You Crack Me Up	1959	37.50	75.00	150.00

BAKER, DONNIE, AND THE DEMENSIONALS

45s

Number	Title (A Side/B Side)	Yr	VG	VG+	NM
RAINBOW					
219	Drinkin' Pop Sodee-Odee (Pop Pop)/Sleepy Time Gal	1953	15.00	30.00	60.00
—Black vinyl					
219	Drinkin' Pop Sodee-Odee (Pop Pop)/Sleepy Time Gal	1953	37.50	75.00	150.00
—Red vinyl					

BAKER, GEORGE, SELECTION

45s

Number	Title (A Side/B Side)	Yr	VG	VG+	NM
COLOSSUS					
112	Little Gren Bag/Pretty Little Dreamer	1970	—	2.50	5.00
117	Dear Ann/Fly	1970	—	2.00	4.00
124	I Wanna Love You/Impressions	1970	—	2.00	4.00
WARNER BROS.					
8115	Paloma Blanca/Dreamboat	1975	—	2.00	4.00
8207	Baby Blue/Morning Sky	1976	—	2.00	4.00

Albums

Number	Title (A Side/B Side)	Yr	VG	VG+	NM
COLOSSUS					
CS-1002	Little Green Bag	1970	5.00	10.00	20.00
WARNER BROS.					
BS 2905	Paloma Blanca	1975	3.75	7.50	15.00

BAKER, GINGER, 'S AIR FORCE

Includes records credited only to Ginger Baker. Also see BLIND FAITH; CREAM.

45s

Number	Title (A Side/B Side)	Yr	VG	VG+	NM
ATCO					
6750	Man of Constant Sorrow/Doin' It	1970	—	2.50	5.00
6816	Atunde! (We Are Here) Part 1/Atunde! (We Are Here) Part 2	1971	—	2.50	5.00

Albums

Number	Title (A Side/B Side)	Yr	VG	VG+	NM
ATCO					
SD 33-343	Ginger Baker's Air Force 2	1971	3.00	6.00	12.00
SD 2-703 [(2)]	Ginger Baker's Air Force	1970	5.00	10.00	20.00
SD 7012	Stratavarious	1972	3.00	6.00	12.00
AXIOM					
539864-1	Middle Passage	1990	3.75	7.50	15.00
CELLULOID					
CEL-6126	Horses and Trees	1986	2.50	5.00	10.00
POLYDOR					
3504 [(2)]	Ginger Baker At His Best	1973	3.75	7.50	15.00
SIRE					
SASD-7532	Eleven Sides of Baker	1977	2.50	5.00	10.00

BAKER, LAVERN

45s

Number	Title (A Side/B Side)	Yr	VG	VG+	NM
ATLANTIC					
1004	How Can You Leave a Man Like This/Soul on Fire	1953	12.50	25.00	50.00
1030	I Can't Hold Out Any Longer/I'm Living My Life for You	1954	10.00	20.00	40.00
1047	Tweedlee Dee/Tomorrow Night	1954	10.00	20.00	40.00
1057	Bop-Ting-a-Ling/That's All I Need	1955	10.00	20.00	40.00
1075	Play It Fair/That Lucky Old Sun	1955	10.00	20.00	40.00
1087	Get Up Get Up (You Sleepyhead)/My Happiness Forever	1956	6.25	12.50	25.00
1093	Fee Fee Fi Fo Fum/I'll Do the Same for You	1956	6.25	12.50	25.00
1104	I Can't Love You Enough/Still	1956	6.25	12.50	25.00
1116	Jim Dandy/Tra La La	1956	6.25	12.50	25.00
1136	Jim Dandy Got Married/The Game of Love	1957	6.25	12.50	25.00
1150	Humpty Dumpty Heart/Love Me Right	1957	6.25	12.50	25.00
1163	St.Louis Blues/Miracles	1957	6.25	12.50	25.00
1176	Substitute/Learning to Love	1958	6.25	12.50	25.00
1189	Harbor Lights/Whipper Snapper	1958	6.25	12.50	25.00
2001	It's So Fine/Why Baby Why	1958	6.25	12.50	25.00
2007	I Cried a Tear/Dix-A-Billy	1958	6.25	12.50	25.00
2021	I Waited Too Long/You're Teasing Me	1959	5.00	10.00	20.00
2033	So High So Low/If You Love Me	1959	5.00	10.00	20.00
2041	Tiny Tim/For the Love of You	1959	5.00	10.00	20.00
2048	Shake a Hand/Manana	1960	5.00	10.00	20.00
2059	Wheel of Fortune/Shadows of Love	1960	3.75	7.50	15.00
2067	A Help-Each-Other Romance/How Often	1960	3.75	7.50	15.00
—With Ben E. King					
2077	Bumble Bee/My Time Will Come	1960	3.75	7.50	15.00
2090	You're the Boss/I'll Never Be Free	1961	3.75	7.50	15.00
—With Jimmy Ricks					
2099	Saved/Don Juan	1961	3.75	7.50	15.00
2109	I Didn't Know I Was Crying/Hurtin' Inside	1961	3.75	7.50	15.00
2119	Hey, Memphis/Voodoo Voodoo	1961	3.75	7.50	15.00
2137	Must I Cry Again/No Love So True	1962	3.00	6.00	12.00
2167	See See Rider/The Story of My Love	1962	3.00	6.00	12.00
2186	Trouble in Mind/Half of Your Love	1963	3.00	6.00	12.00
2203	Itty Bitty Girl/Oh, Johnny Oh, Johnny	1963	3.00	6.00	12.00
2234	You'd Better Find Yourself Another Fool/Go Away	1964	2.50	5.00	10.00
2267	Fly Me to the Moon/Ain't Gonna Cry No More	1965	2.50	5.00	10.00
BRUNSWICK					
55285	Let Me Belong to You/Pledging My Love	1965	2.00	4.00	8.00
55287	Think Twice/Please Don't Hurt Me	1965	2.00	4.00	8.00
—With Jackie Wilson					
55291	One Monkey (Don't Stop the Show)/Baby	1966	2.00	4.00	8.00
55297	Batman to the Rescue/Call Me Darling	1966	2.50	5.00	10.00
55311	Nothing Like Being in Love/Wrapped, Tied and Tangled	1967	2.00	4.00	8.00
55341	Born to Lose/I Need You So	1967	2.00	4.00	8.00
55408	I'm the One to Do It/Baby	1969	—	3.00	6.00
KING					
4556	Trying/Snuff Dipper	1952	12.50	25.00	50.00
—B-side by Todd Rhodes					
4583	Must I Cry Again/Hog Maw and Cabbage Slaw	1952	12.50	25.00	50.00
—B-side by Todd Rhodes					
4601	Lost Child/Thunderball Boogie	1953	12.50	25.00	50.00
—B-side by Todd Rhodes					

7-Inch Extended Plays

Number	Title (A Side/B Side)	Yr	VG	VG+	NM
ATLANTIC					
566	(contents unknown)	1956	50.00	100.00	200.00
566 [PS]	LaVern Baker: Tweedle Dee	1956	25.00	50.00	100.00
588	*Jim Dandy/Still/Play It Fair/Tra La La	1957	20.00	40.00	80.00
588 [PS]	LaVern Baker: Jim Dandy	1957	37.50	75.00	150.00
617	(contents unknown)	1958	20.00	40.00	80.00
617 [PS]	LaVern Baker: I Cried a Tear	1958	37.50	75.00	150.00

Albums

Number	Title (A Side/B Side)	Yr	VG	VG+	NM
ATCO					
SD 33-372	Her Greatest Recordings	1971	3.00	6.00	12.00
ATLANTIC					
1281 [M]	LaVern Baker Sings Bessie Smith	1958	30.00	60.00	120.00
—Black label					

Number	Title (A Side/B Side)	Yr	VG	VG+	NM
1281 [M]	LaVern Baker Sings Bessie Smith	1960	7.50	15.00	30.00
—Red and purple label, "fan" logo in white					
1281 [M]	LaVern Baker Sings Bessie Smith	1960	5.00	10.00	20.00
—Red and purple label, "fan" logo in black					
SD 1281 [S]	LaVern Baker Sings Bessie Smith	1959	37.50	75.00	150.00
—Green label					
SD 1281 [S]	LaVern Baker Sings Bessie Smith	1960	10.00	20.00	40.00
—Green and blue label, "fan" logo in white					
SD 1281 [S]	LaVern Baker Sings Bessie Smith	1963	6.25	12.50	25.00
—Green and blue label, "fan" logo in black					
8002 [M]	LaVern	1956	62.50	125.00	250.00
—Black label					
8002 [M]	LaVern	1960	7.50	15.00	30.00
—Red and purple label, "fan" logo in white					
8002 [M]	LaVern	1963	5.00	10.00	20.00
—Red and purple label, "fan" logo in black					
8007 [M]	LaVern Baker	1957	62.50	125.00	250.00
—Black label					
8007 [M]	LaVern Baker	1960	7.50	15.00	30.00
—Red and purple label, "fan" logo in white					
8007 [M]	LaVern Baker	1963	5.00	10.00	20.00
—Red and purple label, "fan" logo in black					
8030 [M]	Blues Ballads	1959	50.00	100.00	200.00
—Black label					
8030 [M]	Blues Ballads	1960	37.50	75.00	150.00
—White "bullseye" label					
8030 [M]	Blues Ballads	1960	7.50	15.00	30.00
—Red and purple label, "fan" logo in white					
8030 [M]	Blues Ballads	1960	5.00	10.00	20.00
—Red and purple label, "fan" logo in black					
8036 [M]	Precious Memories	1959	50.00	100.00	200.00
—Black label					
8036 [M]	Precious Memories	1960	37.50	75.00	150.00
—White "bullseye" label					
8036 [M]	Precious Memories	1960	7.50	15.00	30.00
—Red and purple label, "fan" logo in white					
8036 [M]	Precious Memories	1963	5.00	10.00	20.00
—Red and purple label, "fan" logo in black					
SD 8036 [S]	Precious Memories	1959	75.00	150.00	300.00
—Green label					
SD 8036 [S]	Precious Memories	1960	50.00	100.00	200.00
—White "bullseye" label					
SD 8036 [S]	Precious Memories	1960	10.00	20.00	40.00
—Green and blue label, "fan" logo in white					
SD 8036 [S]	Precious Memories	1963	6.25	12.50	25.00
—Green and blue label, "fan" logo in black					
8050 [M]	Saved	1961	25.00	50.00	100.00
—Red and purple label, "fan" logo in white					
8050 [M]	Saved	1963	5.00	10.00	20.00
—Red and purple label, "fan" logo in black					
SD 8050 [S]	Saved	1961	37.50	75.00	150.00
—Green and blue label, "fan" logo in white					
SD 8050 [S]	Saved	1963	6.25	12.50	25.00
—Green and blue label, "fan" logo in black					
8071 [M]	See See Rider	1962	25.00	50.00	100.00
—Red and purple label, "fan" logo in white					
8071 [M]	See See Rider	1963	5.00	10.00	20.00
—Red and purple label, "fan" logo in black					
SD 8071 [S]	See See Rider	1962	37.50	75.00	150.00
—Green and blue label, "fan" logo in white					
SD 8071 [S]	See See Rider	1963	6.25	12.50	25.00
—Green and blue label, "fan" logo in black					
8078 [M]	The Best of LaVern Baker	1963	37.50	75.00	150.00
—Red and purple label, "fan" logo in black					
90980	LaVern Baker Sings Bessie Smith	1989	3.00	6.00	12.00
—Reissue of SD 1281					
BRUNSWICK					
BL 754160	Let Me Belong to You	1970	5.00	10.00	20.00

BAKER, MICKEY "GUITAR"

Also see MICKEY AND SYLVIA.

Number	Title (A Side/B Side)	Yr	VG	VG+	NM
45s					
ATLANTIC					
2042	Third Man Theme/Baia	1959	3.00	6.00	12.00
KING					
5951	Side Show/Steam Roller	1964	2.50	5.00	10.00
5979	Do What You Do/Night Blue	1965	2.50	5.00	10.00
MGM					
12418	Spinnin' Rock Boogie/Tricky	1957	5.00	10.00	20.00
RAINBOW					
288	Shake Walkin'/Greasy Spoon	1955	7.50	15.00	30.00
299	Bandstand Stomp/Rock with a Sock	1955	7.50	15.00	30.00
303	Old Devil Moon/Guitarambo	1955	7.50	15.00	30.00
SAVOY					
867	Guitar Mambo/Riverboat	1952	12.50	25.00	50.00
874	Love Me Baby/Oh Happy Day	1953	12.50	25.00	50.00
Albums					
ATLANTIC					
8035 [M]	The Wildest Guitar	1959	37.50	75.00	150.00
—Black label					
8035 [M]	The Wildest Guitar	1960	12.50	25.00	50.00
—Red and purple label, "fan" logo in white					
SD 8035 [S]	The Wildest Guitar	1959	62.50	125.00	250.00
—Green label					
SD 8035 [S]	The Wildest Guitar	1960	20.00	40.00	80.00
—Green and blue label, "fan" logo in white					
KICKING MULE					
140	The Jazz Rock Guitar of Mickey Baker	1978	3.00	6.00	12.00
142	The Blues and Jazz Guitar of Mickey Baker	1978	3.00	6.00	12.00
KING					
839 [M]	But Wild	1963	100.00	200.00	400.00
—Black label, no crown					
839 [M]	But Wild	196?	20.00	40.00	80.00
—Blue label with crown					
S-839 [R]	But Wild	196?	10.00	20.00	40.00

BAKER, PENNY, AND THE PILLOWS

Number	Title (A Side/B Side)	Yr	VG	VG+	NM
45s					
WITCH					
123	Bring Back the Beatles/Gonna Win Him	1964	5.00	10.00	20.00
123 [PS]	Bring Back the Beatles/Gonna Win Him	1964	5.00	10.00	20.00

BAKER, RONNIE

Number	Title (A Side/B Side)	Yr	VG	VG+	NM
45s					
LAURIE					
3128	My Story/I Want to Be Loved	1962	15.00	30.00	60.00
3164	Land of Love/Time Told Me	1963	5.00	10.00	20.00
3250	See You in September/Young at Heart	1964	5.00	10.00	20.00

BAKER, YVONNE

Also see THE SENSATIONS.

Number	Title (A Side/B Side)	Yr	VG	VG+	NM
45s					
JAMIE					
1290	What a Difference Love Makes/Funny What Time Can Do	1965	3.00	6.00	12.00
MODERN					
1055	A Woman Needs a Man/My Baby Needs Me	196?	2.50	5.00	10.00
PARKWAY					
140	You Didn't Say a Word/To Prove My Love Is True	1967	25.00	50.00	100.00

BAKER GURVITZ ARMY, THE

Number	Title (A Side/B Side)	Yr	VG	VG+	NM
45s					
ATCO					
7043	People/(B-side unknown)	1976	—	2.50	5.00
JANUS					
248	4 Phil/Help Me	1975	—	2.50	5.00
Albums					
ATCO					
SD 36-123	Elysian Encounters	1975	2.50	5.00	10.00
SD 36-137	Hearts On Fire	1976	2.50	5.00	10.00
JANUS					
JXS-7015	The Baker Gurvitz Army	1975	3.00	6.00	12.00

BAKER SISTERS, THE

Number	Title (A Side/B Side)	Yr	VG	VG+	NM
45s					
MERCURY					
70839	Too Many Teardrops/Break the String	1956	5.00	10.00	20.00
70980	Little Monster/One By One	1956	5.00	10.00	20.00
71074	Trinidaddy/Careless Love	1957	5.00	10.00	20.00
UNIQUE					
324	Last Bus Home/If You're Ever Gonna Leave Me	1956	3.75	7.50	15.00

BALDRY, LONG JOHN

Number	Title (A Side/B Side)	Yr	VG	VG+	NM
45s					
ASCOT					
2229	Bring My Baby Back to Me/Cuckoo	1967	2.50	5.00	10.00
2236	Only a Fool Breaks His Own Heart/Let Him Go	1967	2.50	5.00	10.00
A&M					
974	When the Sun Comes Shining Through/Wise to the Ways of the World	1968	2.00	4.00	8.00
1041	It's Too Late Now/Long and Lonely Nights	1969	2.00	4.00	8.00
EMI AMERICA					
8018	You've Lost That Lovin' Feelin'/Baldry's Out	1979	—	2.00	4.00
—A-side: With Kathi McDonald					
8018 [PS]	You've Lost That Lovin' Feelin'/Baldry's Out	1979	—	3.00	6.00
8024	A Thrill Is a Thrill/Find You	1979	—	2.00	4.00
UNITED ARTISTS					
50141	Bring My Baby Back to Me/Cuckoo	1967	2.50	5.00	10.00
WARNER BROS.					
7098	Hey Lord You Made the Night Too Long/Let the Heartaches Begin	1967	2.00	4.00	8.00
7184	Hold Back the Daybreak/Since I Lost You Baby	1968	—	3.00	6.00
7506	Don't Try to Lay No Boogie-Woogie on the King of Rock N Roll/Mr. Rubin	1971	—	3.00	6.00
7516	Don't Try to Lay No Boogie-Woogie on the King of Rock N Roll/same (Part 2)	1971	—	3.00	6.00
7597	Iko Iko/You Can't Judge a Book by Its Cover	1972	—	3.00	6.00
7617	Mother Ain't Dead/You Can't Judge a Book by Its Cover	1972	—	3.00	6.00
Albums					
ASCOT					
AM-13022 [M]	Long John's Blues	1965	12.50	25.00	50.00
AS-16022 [R]	Long John's Blues	1965	10.00	20.00	40.00
CASABLANCA					
NBLP 7012	Good to Be Alive	1975	3.00	6.00	12.00
NBLP 7035	Welcome to the Club	1976	3.00	6.00	12.00
EMI AMERICA					
SW-17015	Baldry's Out	1979	2.50	5.00	10.00
SW-17038	Long John Baldry	1980	2.50	5.00	10.00
UNITED ARTISTS					
UAS-5543 [M]	Long John's Blues	1971	3.00	6.00	12.00
—Reissue of Ascot 13022					
WARNER BROS.					
WS 1921	It Ain't Easy	1971	3.75	7.50	15.00
BS 2614	Everything Stops for Tea	1973	3.00	6.00	12.00

BALDWIN, CLIVE

Number	Title (A Side/B Side)	Yr	VG	VG+	NM
45s					
MERCURY					
73680	Now It's Paul McCartney, Stevie Wonder, Alice Cooper, Elton John/The Disco Rag	1975	2.00	4.00	8.00

BALIN, MARTY

Also see BODACIOUS D.F.; JEFFERSON AIRPLANE; JEFFERSON STARSHIP.

45s

CHALLENGE

Number	Title (A Side/B Side)	Yr	VG	VG+	NM
9146	Nobody But You/You Made Me Fall	1962	12.50	25.00	50.00
9156	I Specialize in Love/You're Alive with Love	1962	12.50	25.00	50.00

EMI AMERICA

Number	Title (A Side/B Side)	Yr	VG	VG+	NM
8084	Hearts/Freeway	1981	—	2.00	4.00
8084 [PS]	Hearts/Freeway	1981	—	2.50	5.00
8093	Atlanta Lady (Something About Your Love)/Lydia	1981	—	2.00	4.00
8153	What Love Is/Will You Forever	1983	—	2.00	4.00
8153 [PS]	What Love Is/Will You Forever	1983	—	2.50	5.00
8160	Do It for Love/Heart of Stone	1983	—	2.00	4.00
8160 [PS]	Do It for Love/Heart of Stone	1983	—	2.50	5.00

Albums

EMI AMERICA

Number	Title (A Side/B Side)	Yr	VG	VG+	NM
SPRO-9673 [DJ]	Balin	1981	5.00	10.00	20.00
—Red vinyl					
ST-17054	Balin	1981	2.50	5.00	10.00
ST-17088	Lucky	1983	2.50	5.00	10.00

BALL, KENNY

45s

BELL

Number	Title (A Side/B Side)	Yr	VG	VG+	NM
45412	Make Love to Me/Smile, Smile, Smile	1973	—	2.50	5.00

DECCA

Number	Title (A Side/B Side)	Yr	VG	VG+	NM
32083	Greenback Theme/Red Square	1967	2.00	4.00	8.00
32104	Rosie/Harmonize	1967	2.00	4.00	8.00
—With Max Bygraves					

GUYDEN

Number	Title (A Side/B Side)	Yr	VG	VG+	NM
2054	Samantha/I Still Love You All	1961	3.75	7.50	15.00

JERDEN

Number	Title (A Side/B Side)	Yr	VG	VG+	NM
776	900 Miles/(I Wonder) What Becomes of Life	1965	5.00	10.00	20.00

KAPP

Number	Title (A Side/B Side)	Yr	VG	VG+	NM
442	Midnight in Moscow/American Patrol	1962	3.00	6.00	12.00
451	March of the Siamese Children/Villa	1962	2.50	5.00	10.00
460	The Green Leaves of Summer/I Shall Not Be Moved	1962	2.50	5.00	10.00
483	So Do I/All Through the Night	1962	2.50	5.00	10.00
494	The Payoff/Coronet Chop Suey	1962	2.50	5.00	10.00
509	Sukiyaki/Hazelmere	1963	2.50	5.00	10.00
509	Sukiyaki/Nuages	1963	2.50	5.00	10.00
531	55 Days at Peking/Rondo	1963	2.50	5.00	10.00
554	Heartaches/High Hopes	1963	2.50	5.00	10.00
581	From Russia with Love/Acapulco 1922	1964	2.50	5.00	10.00

Albums

JAZZOLOGY

Number	Title (A Side/B Side)	Yr	VG	VG+	NM
65	In Concert in the USA, Volume 1	1979	2.50	5.00	10.00
66	In Concert in the USA, Volume 2	1979	2.50	5.00	10.00

KAPP

Number	Title (A Side/B Side)	Yr	VG	VG+	NM
KL-1276 [M]	Midnight in Moscow	1962	5.00	10.00	20.00
KL-1285 [M]	It's Trad	1962	5.00	10.00	20.00
KL-1294 [M]	Recorded Live	1962	5.00	10.00	20.00
KL-1314 [M]	More	1963	3.75	7.50	15.00
KL-1340 [M]	Big Ones	1963	3.75	7.50	15.00
KL-1348 [M]	Washington Square and the Best of Kenny Ball	1964	3.75	7.50	15.00
KL-1392 [M]	For the Jet Set	1964	3.75	7.50	15.00
KS-3276 [S]	Midnight in Moscow	1962	5.00	10.00	20.00
KS-3285 [S]	It's Trad	1962	5.00	10.00	20.00
KS-3294 [S]	Recorded Live	1962	5.00	10.00	20.00
KS-3314 [S]	More	1963	5.00	10.00	20.00
KS-3340 [S]	Big Ones	1963	5.00	10.00	20.00
KS-3348 [S]	Washington Square and the Best of Kenny Ball	1964	5.00	10.00	20.00
KS-3392 [S]	For the Jet Set	1964	5.00	10.00	20.00

BALLACK, ROBERT JOHN

45s

ROULETTE

Number	Title (A Side/B Side)	Yr	VG	VG+	NM
7122	Sweet Sounds of Music/I'm Comin' to Get You	1972	—	2.50	5.00
7133	Ain't No Use/Givin' Up Givin' You Up	1972	—	2.50	5.00

BALLARD, FLORENCE

Former member of THE SUPREMES.

45s

ABC

Number	Title (A Side/B Side)	Yr	VG	VG+	NM
11074	Goin' Out of My Head/It Doesn't Matter How I Say It	1968	7.50	15.00	30.00
11144	Love Ain't Love/Forever Faithful	1968	7.50	15.00	30.00

BALLARD, FRANK

Albums

PHILLIPS INTERNATIONAL

Number	Title (A Side/B Side)	Yr	VG	VG+	NM
1985 [M]	Rhythm-Blues Party	1962	2500.	3750.	5000.

BALLARD, HANK, AND THE MIDNIGHTERS

Includes records credited only to Hank Ballard. Also see THE MIDNIGHTERS; THE ROYALS (1).

45s

CHESS

Number	Title (A Side/B Side)	Yr	VG	VG+	NM
2111	Love, Why Is It Taking You So Long/I'm a Junkie for My Baby's Love	1971	—	3.00	6.00

KING

Number	Title (A Side/B Side)	Yr	VG	VG+	NM
5171	Teardrops on Your Letter/The Twist	1959	7.50	15.00	30.00
5195 [M]	Kansas City/I'll Keep You Happy	1959	6.25	12.50	25.00
S-5195 [S]	Kansas City/I'll Keep You Happy	1959	12.50	25.00	50.00
5215 [M]	Sugaree/Rain Down Tears	1959	6.25	12.50	25.00
S-5215 [S]	Sugaree/Rain Down Tears	1959	12.50	25.00	50.00
5245	Cute Little Ways/A House with No Windows	1959	6.25	12.50	25.00
5275	I Could Love You/Never Knew	1959	6.25	12.50	25.00
5289	Look at Little Sister/I Said I Wouldn't Beg You	1959	6.25	12.50	25.00
5312	The Coffee Grind/Waiting	1960	6.25	12.50	25.00
5341	Finger Poppin' Time/I Love You, I Love You So-o-o	1960	6.25	12.50	25.00
5400	Let's Go, Let's Go, Let's Go/If You'd Forgive Me	1960	6.25	12.50	25.00
5430	The Hoochi Coochi Coo/I'm Thinking of You	1960	5.00	10.00	20.00
5459	Let's Go Again (Where We Went Last Night)/ Deep Blue Sea	1961	5.00	10.00	20.00
5491	The Continental Walk/What Is This I See	1961	5.00	10.00	20.00
5491 [PS]	The Continental Walk/What Is This I See	1961	20.00	40.00	80.00
5510	The Switch-A-Roo/The Float	1961	3.75	7.50	15.00
5513	The Big Frog/Doin' Everything	1961	3.75	7.50	15.00
—B-side by Henry Moore					
5535	Nothing But Good/Keep On Dancing	1961	3.75	7.50	15.00
5550	Big Red Sunset/Can't You See — I Need a Friend	1961	3.75	7.50	15.00
5578	Do You Remember/I'm Gonna Miss You	1961	3.75	7.50	15.00
5593	Do You Know How to Twist/Broadway	1962	3.75	7.50	15.00
5601	It's Twistin' Time/Autumn Breeze	1962	3.75	7.50	15.00
5635	Good Twistin' Tonight/I'm Young	1962	3.75	7.50	15.00
5655	I Want to Thank You/Excuse Me	1962	3.75	7.50	15.00
5677	Dream World/When I Need You	1962	3.75	7.50	15.00
5693	Shaky Mae/I Love and Care for You	1962	3.75	7.50	15.00
5703	Bring Me Your Love/She's the One	1962	3.75	7.50	15.00
5713	All the Things in Life That Please You/The Rising Tide	1963	3.75	7.50	15.00
5719	The House on the Hill/That Low-Down Move	1963	3.75	7.50	15.00
5729	Christmas Time for Everyone But Me/Santa Claus Is Coming	1963	3.75	7.50	15.00
5746	How Could You Leave Your Man Alone/Walkin' and Talkin'	1963	3.75	7.50	15.00
5798	Those Lonely, Lonely Feelings/It's Love, Baby	1963	3.75	7.50	15.00
5821	Buttin' In/I'm Leavin'	1963	3.75	7.50	15.00
5835	Don't Let Temptation Turn You Around/Have Mercy, Have a Little Pity	1964	3.75	7.50	15.00
5860	Don't Fall in Love with Me/I'm So Mad with You	1964	3.75	7.50	15.00
5884	I Don't Know How to Do But One Thing/These Young Girls	1964	3.75	7.50	15.00
5901	Stay Away from My Baby/She's Got a Whole Lot of Soul	1964	3.75	7.50	15.00
5931	Daddy Rolling Stone/What's Your Name	1964	3.75	7.50	15.00
5954	Let's Get the Show on the Road/A Winner Never Quits	1964	3.75	7.50	15.00
5963	One Monkey Don't Stop No Show/What Can I Tell You	1964	3.75	7.50	15.00
5974	The Handwriting on the Wall/I Done It	1964	3.75	7.50	15.00
5996	Poppin' the Whip/You, Just You	1965	3.00	6.00	12.00
6001	I'm Just a Fool and Everybody Knows/Do It Zulu Style	1965	3.00	6.00	12.00
6018	Sloop and Slide/My Sun Is Going Down	1966	3.00	6.00	12.00
6031	I'm Ready/Togetherness	1966	3.00	6.00	12.00
6055	I Was Born to Move/He Came Alone	1966	3.00	6.00	12.00
6092	Here Comes the Hurt/Dance Till It Hurt Cha	1967	3.00	6.00	12.00
6119	You're in Real Good Hands/Unwind Yourself	1967	3.00	6.00	12.00
6131	Funky's Soul Train/Which Way Should I Turn	1967	3.00	6.00	12.00
6177	I'm Back to Stay/Come On Wit' It	1968	3.00	6.00	12.00
6196	How You Gonna Get Respect (When You Haven't Cut Your Process Yet)/Teardrops on Your Letter	1968	2.50	5.00	10.00
—As "Hank Ballard Along With The Dapps"					
6215	You're So Sexy/Thrill on the Hill	1969	2.50	5.00	10.00
—As "Hank Ballard Along With The Dapps"					
6228	Are You Lonely for Me Baby/With Our Sweet Lovin' Self	1969	2.50	5.00	10.00
6244	Butter Your Popcorn/Funky Soul Train	1969	3.75	7.50	15.00
6246	Come On with It/Blackenized	1969	3.75	7.50	15.00
6332	Work With Me Annie/Sexy Ways	1970	2.50	5.00	10.00

PEOPLE

Number	Title (A Side/B Side)	Yr	VG	VG+	NM
604	Teardrops on Your Letter/Annie Had a Baby	1972	—	2.50	5.00
606	With Your Sweet Lovin' Self/Finger Poppin' Time	1972	—	2.50	5.00

POLYDOR

Number	Title (A Side/B Side)	Yr	VG	VG+	NM
14128	Finger Poppin' Time/From the Love Side	1972	—	2.50	5.00
14166	Going to Get a Thrill/(B-side unknown)	1973	—	2.50	5.00

SILVER FOX

Number	Title (A Side/B Side)	Yr	VG	VG+	NM
23	Sunday Morning Coming Down/Love Made a Fool of Me	1970	—	3.00	6.00

STANG

Number	Title (A Side/B Side)	Yr	VG	VG+	NM
5053	Let's Go Streaking/Let's Go Streaking (Part 2)	1974	—	2.50	5.00
5058	Hey There Sexy Lady/(Instrumental)	1975	—	2.50	5.00
5061	Let's Go Skinny Dipping/Love On Love	1975	—	2.50	5.00

7-Inch Extended Plays

KING

Number	Title (A Side/B Side)	Yr	VG	VG+	NM
435	Teardrops on Your Letter/The Twist//Cute Little Ways/House with No Windows	1959	30.00	60.00	120.00
435 [PS]	Singin' and Swingin', Vol. 1	1959	30.00	60.00	120.00
436	(contents unknown)	1959	30.00	60.00	120.00
436 [PS]	Singin' and Swingin', Vol. 2	1959	30.00	60.00	120.00

Albums

KING

Number	Title (A Side/B Side)	Yr	VG	VG+	NM
618 [M]	Singin' and Swingin'	1959	62.50	125.00	250.00
674 [M]	The One and Only Hank Ballard	1959	62.50	125.00	250.00
—Brown cover					
674 [M]	The One and Only Hank Ballard	1960	37.50	75.00	150.00
—Green cover					
700 [M]	Finger Poppin' Time	1960	37.50	75.00	150.00
740 [M]	Spotlight on Hank Ballard	1961	37.50	75.00	150.00
KS-740 [S]	Spotlight on Hank Ballard	1961	75.00	150.00	300.00
748 [M]	Let's Go Again	1961	30.00	60.00	120.00
759 [M]	Dance Along	1961	30.00	60.00	120.00
781 [M]	The Twistin' Fools	1962	25.00	50.00	100.00
793 [M]	Jumpin' Hank Ballard	1962	25.00	50.00	100.00
815 [M]	The 1963 Sound of Hank Ballard	1963	25.00	50.00	100.00
867 [M]	Biggest Hits	1963	25.00	50.00	100.00
896 [M]	A Star in Your Eyes	1964	25.00	50.00	100.00
913 [M]	Those Lazy, Lazy Days	1965	17.50	35.00	70.00
927 [M]	Glad Songs, Sad Songs	1965	17.50	35.00	70.00
950 [M]	24 Hit Tunes	1966	15.00	30.00	60.00
981 [M]	24 Great Songs	1968	10.00	20.00	40.00
KSD-1052	You Can't Keep a Good Man Down	1969	12.50	25.00	50.00

BALLARD, KENNY

Number	Title (A Side/B Side)	Yr	VG	VG+	NM
45s					
GENIE					
101	Lady of Stone/(B-side unknown)	196?	7.50	15.00	30.00
KAPP					
602	Mr. Magic/Oh How I Cried	1964	6.25	12.50	25.00
ROULETTE					
4716	Your Letter/I'm Losing You	1966	3.75	7.50	15.00

BALLARD, RUSS

Member of ARGENT.

Number	Title (A Side/B Side)	Yr	VG	VG+	NM
45s					
EMI AMERICA					
8204	Living Without You/Voices	1984	—	2.00	4.00
8217	Two Silhouettes/Playing with Fire	1984	—	2.00	4.00
8275	The Fire Still Burns/Hold On	1985	—	—	3.00
EPIC					
50085	You Can Do Voodoo/Danger Zone Part 2	1975	—	2.00	4.00
50211	Winning/Here I Am	1976	—	2.00	4.00
50542	Treat Her Right/What Does It Take	1978	—	2.00	4.00
50883	On the Rebound/Riding with the Angels	1980	—	2.00	4.00
51002	Breakdown/Rock and Roll Lover	1981	—	2.00	4.00
Albums					
EMI AMERICA					
ST-17108	Russ Ballard	1984	2.00	4.00	8.00
ST-17162	The Fire Still Burns	1985	2.00	4.00	8.00
EPIC					
KE 33252	Russ Ballard	1974	2.50	5.00	10.00
PE 34093	Winning	1976	2.50	5.00	10.00
JE 35035	At the Third Stroke	1978	2.50	5.00	10.00
JE 36186	Russ Ballard & the Barnet Dogs	1980	2.50	5.00	10.00
JE 36993	Into the Fire	1981	2.50	5.00	10.00

BALLIN' JACK

Number	Title (A Side/B Side)	Yr	VG	VG+	NM
45s					
COLUMBIA					
45312	Super Highway/Only a Tear	1971	—	2.50	5.00
45464	Ballin' the Jack/Hold On	1971	—	2.50	5.00
45698	Playin' the Game/I'm the One You Need	1972	—	2.00	4.00
MERCURY					
73401	Thunder/Try to Relax	1973	—	2.50	5.00
73429	Sunday Morning/This Song	1973	—	2.50	5.00
Albums					
COLUMBIA					
C 30344	Ballin' Jack	1971	2.50	5.00	10.00
KC 31468	Buzzard Luck	1972	2.50	5.00	10.00
MERCURY					
SRM-1-672	Special Pride	1973	2.50	5.00	10.00

BALLOON FARM, THE

Number	Title (A Side/B Side)	Yr	VG	VG+	NM
45s					
LAURIE					
3405	A Question of Tempature/Hurtin' for Your Lovin'	1967	5.00	10.00	20.00
—First pressing has misspelled A-side					
3405	A Question of Temperature/Hurtin' for Your Lovin'	1967	2.50	5.00	10.00
—Second pressing corrects A-side spelling					
3445	Hurry Up Sundown/Farmer Brown	1968	2.50	5.00	10.00

BALTIMORE AND OHIO MARCHING BAND, THE

Number	Title (A Side/B Side)	Yr	VG	VG+	NM
45s					
JUBILEE					
5592	Lapland/Condition Red	1967	—	3.00	6.00
5614	The B&O Marching Band Song/The Wanderer	1968	—	2.50	5.00
5644	Sgt. Crunch/Typsy Gypsy	1968	—	2.50	5.00
5672	Little Arrows/(B-side unknown)	1969	—	2.50	5.00
Albums					
JUBILEE					
JGS-8008	Lapland	1968	3.75	7.50	15.00

BALTINEERS, THE

Number	Title (A Side/B Side)	Yr	VG	VG+	NM
45s					
TEENAGE					
1000	Moments Like This/New Love	1956	75.00	150.00	300.00
1002	Tears in My Eyes/Joe's Calypso	1956	75.00	150.00	300.00

BAN-LONS, THE

Number	Title (A Side/B Side)	Yr	VG	VG+	NM
45s					
FIDELITY					
4051	Highest Mountain/Hey Baby	1959	50.00	100.00	200.00
4056	I Like It/Hey Good Lookin'	1959	50.00	100.00	200.00

BANANA AND THE BUNCH

Number	Title (A Side/B Side)	Yr	VG	VG+	NM
45s					
WARNER BROS.					
7621	My True Life Blues/Vanderbilt's Lament	1972	—	2.50	5.00
7626	Back in the U.S.A./My True Life Blues	1972	—	2.50	5.00
Albums					
WARNER BROS.					
BS 2626	Mid Mountain Ranch	1972	3.00	6.00	12.00

BANANA BOYS

Number	Title (A Side/B Side)	Yr	VG	VG+	NM
45s					
UNI					
55194	Come Into My Life/What Will Your Mama Say	1970	—	3.00	6.00

BANANA SPLITS, THE

Number	Title (A Side/B Side)	Yr	VG	VG+	NM
45s					
DECCA					
32391	We're the Banana Splits/Wait Til Tomorrow	1968	3.00	6.00	12.00
32429	The Tra-La-La Song (One Banana, Two Banana)/Toy Piano Melody	1968	3.00	6.00	12.00
32429 [PS]	The Tra-La-La Song (One Banana, Two Banana)/Toy Piano Melody	1968	6.25	12.50	25.00
32536	Pretty Painted Carousel/Long Live Love	1969	3.00	6.00	12.00
32536 [PS]	Pretty Painted Carousel/Long Live Love	1969	6.25	12.50	25.00
7-Inch Extended Plays					
KELLOGG'S/HANNA-BARBERA					
34578	The Tra La La Song/That's the Pretty Part of You //It's a Good Day for a Parade/The Very First Kid on My Block	1969	5.00	10.00	20.00
34578 [PS]	Kellogg's Presents The Banana Splits, Vol. 1	1969	5.00	10.00	20.00
34579	Doin' the Banana Split/I Enjoy Being a Boy (In Love with You)//The Beautiful Calliopa/Let Me Remember You Smiling	1969	5.00	10.00	20.00
34579 [PS]	Kellogg's Presents The Banana Splits, Vol. 2	1969	5.00	10.00	20.00
Albums					
DECCA					
DL 75075	We're the Banana Splits	1969	50.00	100.00	200.00

BANBARRA

Number	Title (A Side/B Side)	Yr	VG	VG+	NM
45s					
UNITED ARTISTS					
XW-734	Shack Up Part 1/Shack Up Part 2	1975	—	2.00	4.00

BANCHEE

Number	Title (A Side/B Side)	Yr	VG	VG+	NM
45s					
ATLANTIC					
2708	I Just Don't Know/Train of Life	1970	2.50	5.00	10.00
POLYDOR					
14104	Searcher's Life//3/4 Song	1971	2.50	5.00	10.00
Albums					
ATLANTIC					
SD 8240	Banchee	1969	5.00	10.00	20.00
POLYDOR					
24-4066	Thinkin'	1971	12.50	25.00	50.00

BAND, THE

Also see BOB DYLAN; RONNIE HAWKINS AND THE HAWKS; LEVON AND THE HAWKS.

Number	Title (A Side/B Side)	Yr	VG	VG+	NM
45s					
CAPITOL					
2269	The Weight/I Shall Be Released	1968	2.00	4.00	8.00
—First pressing credits "Jaime Robbie Robertson, Rick Danko, Richard Manuel, Garth Hudson, Levon Helm"					
2635	Up on Cripple Creek/The Night They Drove Old Dixie Down	1969	—	3.00	6.00
2705	Rag Mama Rag/The Unfaithful Servant	1969	—	3.00	6.00
2705 [PS]	Rag Mama Rag/The Unfaithful Servant	1969	—	3.00	6.00
2870	Time to Kill/The Shape I'm In	1970	—	3.00	6.00
3199	Life Is a Carnival/The Moon Struck One	1971	—	3.00	6.00
3249	When I Paint My Masterpiece/Where Do We Go from Here	1971	—	—	—
—Unreleased?					
3433	Don't Do It/Rag Mama Rag	1972	—	2.50	5.00
3500	Hang Up My Rock & Roll Shoes/Caledonia Mission	1972	—	2.50	5.00
3758	Ain't Got No Home/Get Up Jake	1973	—	2.50	5.00
3828	Third Man Theme/W.S. Walcott Medicine Show	1974	—	2.50	5.00
4230	Ophelia/Hobo Jungle	1976	—	2.00	4.00
4316	Twilight/Acadian Driftwood	1976	—	2.00	4.00
4361	Georgia on My Mind/The Night They Drove Old Dixie Down	1976	—	2.00	4.00
WARNER BROS.					
8592	Out of the Blue/The Well	1978	—	2.00	4.00
Albums					
CAPITOL					
STAO-132	The Band	1969	3.75	7.50	15.00
SW-425	Stage Fright	1970	3.75	7.50	15.00
—Includes tear-off wraparound cover					
SW-425	Stage Fright	1970	2.50	5.00	10.00
—Without tear-off wraparound cover					
SMAS-651	Cahoots	1971	3.75	7.50	15.00
SKAO 2955	Music from Big Pink	1968	6.25	12.50	25.00
—Black label with colorband					
SKAO 2955	Music from Big Pink	1969	3.75	7.50	15.00
—Lime green label					
SABB-11045 [(2)]	Rock of Ages	1972	5.00	10.00	20.00
SW-11214	Moondog Matinee	1973	3.75	7.50	15.00
—Includes tear-off wraparound cover					
SW-11214	Moondog Matinee	1973	2.50	5.00	10.00
—Without tear-off wraparound cover					
ST-11440	Northern Lights-Southern Cross	1975	3.00	6.00	12.00
ST-11553	The Best of the Band	1976	3.00	6.00	12.00
SO-11602	Islands	1977	3.00	6.00	12.00
SKBO-11856 [(2)]	Anthology	1978	3.75	7.50	15.00
SN-16003	Cahoots	1980	2.00	4.00	8.00
—Budget-line reissue					
SN-16004	Moondog Matinee	1980	2.00	4.00	8.00
—Budget-line reissue					
SN-16005	Northern Lights-Southern Cross	1980	2.00	4.00	8.00
—Budget-line reissue					
SN-16006	Stage Fright	1980	2.00	4.00	8.00
—Budget-line reissue					
SN-16007	Islands	1980	2.00	4.00	8.00
—Budget-line reissue					
SN-16008	Rock of Ages, Volume 1	1980	2.00	4.00	8.00
—Budget-line reissue					
SN-16009	Rock of Ages, Volume 2	1980	2.00	4.00	8.00
—Budget-line reissue					
SN-16010	Anthology, Volume 1	1980	2.00	4.00	8.00
—Budget-line reissue					
SN-16011	Anthology, Volume 2	1980	2.00	4.00	8.00
—Budget-line reissue					

Number	Title (A Side/B Side)	Yr	VG	VG+	NM
SN-16296	The Band	198?	2.00	4.00	8.00
—Budget-line reissue					
SN-16331	The Best of the Band	198?	2.00	4.00	8.00
—Budget-line reissue					
MOBILE FIDELITY					
1-039	Music from Big Pink	1981	12.50	25.00	50.00
—Audiophile vinyl					
WARNER BROS.					
PRO-A-737 [DJ]	The Last Waltz Sampler	1978	5.00	10.00	20.00
3WS 3146 [(3)]	The Last Waltz	1978	5.00	10.00	20.00

BAND WITHOUT A NAME, THE

Number	Title (A Side/B Side)	Yr	VG	VG+	NM
45s					
SIDEWALK					
913	Theme from "Thunder Alley"/Time After Time	1967	5.00	10.00	20.00
TOWER					
246	Turn On Your Love Light/Perfect Girl	1966	3.75	7.50	15.00
246 [PS]	Turn On Your Love Light/Perfect Girl	1966	7.50	15.00	30.00

BANDS OF GOLD

Number	Title (A Side/B Side)	Yr	VG	VG+	NM
45s					
SMASH					
2058	It's Over/You Won't Change Me	1966	6.25	12.50	25.00

BANDWAGON, THE

Also includes records credited to "Johnny Johnson and the Bandwagon."

Number	Title (A Side/B Side)	Yr	VG	VG+	NM
45s					
BELL					
902	Sweet Inspiration/Pride Comes Before Fall	1970	—	3.00	6.00
953	(Blame It) On the Pony Express/Never Let Her Go	1971	—	3.00	6.00
EPIC					
10255	Baby Make Your Own Sweet Music/On the Day We Fell in Love	1967	2.00	4.00	8.00
10352	Breakin' Down the Walls of Heartache/Dancin' Master	1968	2.00	4.00	8.00
10412	I Ain't Lying/You	1968	2.00	4.00	8.00
—Artist credit: "Johnny Johnson and the Bandwagon"					
10442	Don't Let It In/When Love Has Gone Away	1969	2.00	4.00	8.00
10473	You Blew Your Cool (And Lost Your Fool)/Let's Hang On	1969	2.00	4.00	8.00
—Artist credit: "Johnny Johnson and the Bandwagon"					
Albums					
EPIC					
BN 26426	Johnny Johnson and the Bandwagon	1969	5.00	10.00	20.00

BANG

Number	Title (A Side/B Side)	Yr	VG	VG+	NM
45s					
CAPITOL					
3304	Questions/Future Shock	1972	—	2.50	5.00
3386	Keep On/Redman	1972	—	2.00	4.00
3474	No Sugar Tonight/Idealist Realist	1972	—	2.00	4.00
3622	Must Be Love/Love Sonnet	1973	—	2.00	4.00
3816	Feels Nice/Slow Down	1974	—	2.00	4.00
Albums					
CAPITOL					
ST-11015	Bang	1972	3.75	7.50	15.00
SMAS-11110	Mother/Bow to the Music	1972	3.75	7.50	15.00
ST-11190	Music	1973	5.00	10.00	20.00

BANGOR FLYING CIRCUS

Number	Title (A Side/B Side)	Yr	VG	VG+	NM
45s					
ABC DUNHILL					
4220	Come On People/A Change in Our Lives	1969	—	3.00	6.00
4223	Mama Don't You Know/Someday I'll Find	1970	—	3.00	6.00
Albums					
ABC DUNHILL					
DS-50069	Bangor Flying Circus	1969	3.75	7.50	15.00

BANKS, BESSIE

Number	Title (A Side/B Side)	Yr	VG	VG+	NM
45s					
BLUE CAT					
106	Go Now/It Sounds Like My Baby	1965	2.50	5.00	10.00
SPOKANE					
4009	Do It Now/(You Should Have Been a) Doctor	1963	3.75	7.50	15.00
TIGER					
102	Go Now/It Sounds Like My Baby	1964	5.00	10.00	20.00
VERVE					
10519	I Can't Make It (Without You Baby)/Need You	1967	2.00	4.00	8.00
VOLT					
4112	Ain't No Easy Way/Try to Leave Me If You Can	1974	—	3.00	6.00
WAND					
163	Do It Now/(You Should Have Been a) Doctor	1964	3.00	6.00	12.00

BANKS, DARRELL

Number	Title (A Side/B Side)	Yr	VG	VG+	NM
45s					
ATCO					
6471	Here Come the Tears/I've Got That Feeling	1967	6.25	12.50	25.00
6484	Angel Baby Don't You Leave Me/Look Into the Eyes of a Fool	1967	6.25	12.50	25.00
COTILLION					
44006	I Wanna Go Home/Love of My Woman	1968	2.50	5.00	10.00
REVILOT					
201	Open the Door to Your Heart/Our Love Is In the Pocket	1966	3.75	7.50	15.00
203	Somebody (Somewhere) Needs You/Baby Whatcha Got (For Me)	1966	3.75	7.50	15.00
VOLT					
4014	Just Because Your Love Has Gone/I'm the One Who Loves You	1969	2.50	5.00	10.00
4026	Beautiful Feeling/No One Blinder	1969	2.50	5.00	10.00
Albums					
ATCO					
33-216 [M]	Darrell Banks Is Here	1967	6.25	12.50	25.00
SD 33-216 [S]	Darrell Banks Is Here	1967	7.50	15.00	30.00
VOLT					
VOS-6002	Here to Stay	1969	6.25	12.50	25.00

BANKS, DICK

Number	Title (A Side/B Side)	Yr	VG	VG+	NM
45s					
LIBERTY					
55145	Dirty Dog/Too Late	1958	10.00	20.00	40.00
55507	Just Like You/Be Faithful to Me	1962	5.00	10.00	20.00

BANKS, DOUG

Number	Title (A Side/B Side)	Yr	VG	VG+	NM
45s					
ARGO					
5483	I Just Keep Dancing/Baby Since You Went Away	1964	15.00	30.00	60.00
GUYDEN					
2082	Ain't That Just Like a Woman/Never Say Goodbye	1963	15.00	30.00	60.00

BANKS, EDDIE

Number	Title (A Side/B Side)	Yr	VG	VG+	NM
45s					
JOSIE					
804	Sugar Diabetes/Rock-a-Bye Blues	1956	10.00	20.00	40.00

BANKS, HOMER

Number	Title (A Side/B Side)	Yr	VG	VG+	NM
45s					
GENIE					
1000	Hooked by Love/Lady of Stone	1966	12.50	25.00	50.00
MINIT					
32008	Do You Know What/60 Minutes of Your Love	1966	6.25	12.50	25.00
32020	Hooked by Love/Lady of Stone	1967	6.25	12.50	25.00

BANKS, PETER

Number	Title (A Side/B Side)	Yr	VG	VG+	NM
Albums					
CAPITOL/SOVEREIGN					
SMAS-11217	Two Sides of Peter Banks	1973	3.75	7.50	15.00

BANNED, THE

Number	Title (A Side/B Side)	Yr	VG	VG+	NM
45s					
FONTANA					
1604	My Life Is My Own/Nothing Matters But You	1967	2.50	5.00	10.00
1616	It Couldn't Happen Here/Annie Went to Ohio	1968	2.50	5.00	10.00
1616 [PS]	It Couldn't Happen Here/Annie Went to Ohio	1968	5.00	10.00	20.00
1621	Goodbye, Groovy, Goodbye/A Blanket of Sound	1968	2.50	5.00	10.00

BANTAMS, THE

Number	Title (A Side/B Side)	Yr	VG	VG+	NM
45s					
DECCA					
31040	My Swing Is Broke/Windows of Blue	1959	3.75	7.50	15.00
WARNER BROS.					
5695	Follow Me/Meet Me Tonight Little Girl	1966	2.50	5.00	10.00
5868	Good Lovin' Girl/I'm So Lucky	1966	2.50	5.00	10.00
Albums					
WARNER BROS.					
W 1625 [M]	Beware the Bantams	1966	5.00	10.00	20.00
WS 1625 [S]	Beware the Bantams	1966	6.25	12.50	25.00

BAR-KAYS, THE

Number	Title (A Side/B Side)	Yr	VG	VG+	NM
45s					
HIGH STACKS					
9801	Body Fine/Hey Rufus!	1999	—	—	3.00
—B-side by Rufus Thomas; artist listed as "The Barkays"					
MERCURY					
73833	Shake Your Rump to the Funk/Summer of Our Love	1976	—	2.00	4.00
73888	Too Hot to Stop (Pt. 1)/Bang Bang (Stick 'Em Up)	1977	—	2.00	4.00
73915	Spellbound/You're So Sexy	1977	—	2.00	4.00
73971	Let's Have Some Fun/Cozy	1977	—	2.00	4.00
73994	Attitudes/Can't Keep My Hands Off You	1978	—	2.00	4.00
74039	I'll Dance/Angel Eyes	1978	—	2.00	4.00
74048	Shine/Are You Being Real	1979	—	2.00	4.00
76015	Move Your Boogie Body/Love's What It's All About	1979	—	2.00	4.00
76036	Today is the Day/Loving You Is My Occupation	1980	—	2.00	4.00
76088	Boogie Body Land/Running In and Out of My Life	1980	—	2.00	4.00
76097	Body Fever/Deliver Us	1981	—	2.00	4.00
76123	Hit and Run/Say It Through Love	1981	—	2.00	4.00
76143	Freaky Behavior/Backseat Driver	1982	—	2.00	4.00
76187	Do It (Let Me See You Shake)/Feels Like I'm Falling in Love	1982	—	2.00	4.00
810435-7	She Talks to Me with Her Body/Anticipation	1983	—	2.00	4.00
818631-7	Freakshow on the Dance Floor/Lovers Should Never Fall in Love	1984	—	2.00	4.00
870018-7	Don't Hang Up/Contagious	1988	—	—	3.00
870018-7 [PS]	Don't Hang Up/Contagious	1988	—	—	3.00
870214-7	Many Mistakes/Contagious	1988	—	—	3.00
872102-7	Struck by You/Your Place or Mine	1989	—	—	3.00
872102-7 [PS]	Struck by You/Your Place or Mine	1989	—	—	3.00
872954-7	Animal/Time Out	1989	—	—	3.00
872954-7 [PS]	Animal/Time Out	1989	—	—	3.00
880045-7	Dirty Dancer/Dirty Dancer	1984	—	—	3.00
880255-7	Sexomatic/(B-side unknown)	1984	—	—	3.00
880966-7	Your Place or Mine/(B-side unknown)	1985	—	—	3.00
884232-7	Banging the Walls/Gina	1985	—	—	3.00
888837-7	Certified True/It Be That Way Sometimes	1987	—	—	3.00
STAX					
3216	Holy Ghost/Monster	1978	—	2.50	5.00
VOLT					
148	Soul Finger/Knucklehead	1967	2.00	4.00	8.00

Number	Title (A Side/B Side)	Yr	VG	VG+	NM
154	Give Everybody Some/Don't Do That	1967	—	3.00	6.00
158	A Hard Day's Night/I Want Someone	1968	—	3.00	6.00
4007	Copy Cat/In the Middle	1968	—	3.00	6.00
4011	Don't Stop Dancing/Don't Stop Dancing (Part 2)	1969	—	3.00	6.00
4019	Midnight Cowboy/A.J. The Housefly	1969	—	3.00	6.00
4033	Song and Dance/I Thank You	1970	—	3.00	6.00
4050	Montego Bay/Humpin'	1971	—	2.50	5.00
4073	Son of Shaft/Song and Dance	1972	—	2.50	5.00
4081	Dance, Dance, Dance/Memphis at Sunrise	1972	—	2.50	5.00
4092	You're the Best Thing That Ever Happened to Me/ You're Still My Brother	1973	—	2.50	5.00
4097	God Is Watching/It Ain't Easy	1973	—	2.50	5.00
Albums					
ATCO					
SD 33-289	Soul Finger	1968	6.25	12.50	25.00
MERCURY					
SRM-1-1099	Too Hot to Stop	1976	2.50	5.00	10.00
SRM-1-1181	Flying High on Your Love	1977	2.50	5.00	10.00
SRM-1-3732	Light of Life	1978	2.50	5.00	10.00
SRM-1-3781	Injoy	1979	2.50	5.00	10.00
SRM-1-3844	As One	1980	2.50	5.00	10.00
SRM-1-4028	Nightcruising	1981	2.50	5.00	10.00
SRM-1-4065	Propositions	1982	2.50	5.00	10.00
818478-1	Dangerous	1984	2.50	5.00	10.00
824727-1	Banging the Wall	1985	2.50	5.00	10.00
830305-1	Contagious	1987	2.50	5.00	10.00
836774-1	Animal	1989	2.50	5.00	10.00
STAX					
4106	Money Talks	1978	2.50	5.00	10.00
4130	Gotta Groove	1979	2.50	5.00	10.00
MPS-8510	Cold Blooded	1981	2.50	5.00	10.00
MPS-8542	The Best of the Bar-Kays	1988	2.50	5.00	10.00
VOLT					
417 [M]	Soul Finger	1967	10.00	20.00	40.00
S-417 [S]	Soul Finger	1967	10.00	20.00	40.00
6004	Gotta Groove	1969	7.50	15.00	30.00
6011	Black Rock	1971	6.25	12.50	25.00
VOS-8001	Do You See What I See	1972	6.25	12.50	25.00
9504	Cold Blooded	1974	6.25	12.50	25.00

BARA, TONY

Number	Title (A Side/B Side)	Yr	VG	VG+	NM
45s					
ATCO					
6172	Rambling/Long Gone Mare	1960	3.00	6.00	12.00

BARBARA AND THE BELIEVERS

Number	Title (A Side/B Side)	Yr	VG	VG+	NM
45s					
CAPITOL					
5866	When You Wish Upon a Star/What Can Happen to Me Now	1967	4.00	8.00	16.00

BARBARA AND THE BOYS

Number	Title (A Side/B Side)	Yr	VG	VG+	NM
45s					
DOT					
15794	Hooty Sapperticker/Cobra	1958	3.75	7.50	15.00

BARBARA AND THE BROWNS

Number	Title (A Side/B Side)	Yr	VG	VG+	NM
45s					
STAX					
150	Big Party/You Belong to Her	1964	5.00	10.00	20.00
158	Please Be Honest with Me/In My Heart	1964	3.75	7.50	15.00
164	I Don't Want Trouble/My Lover	1965	3.75	7.50	15.00

BARBARIANS, THE

Number	Title (A Side/B Side)	Yr	VG	VG+	NM
45s					
JOY					
290	Hey Little Bird/You've Got to Understand	1964	12.50	25.00	50.00
LAURIE					
3308	Are You a Boy or Are You a Girl/Take It or Leave It	1965	5.00	10.00	20.00
3321	Susie Q/What the New Breed Say	1965	5.00	10.00	20.00
3326	Moulty/I'll Keep On Seeing You	1965	5.00	10.00	20.00
Albums					
LAURIE					
LLP-2033 [M]	Are You a Boy or Are You a Girl?	1966	37.50	75.00	150.00
SLP-2033 [S]	Are You a Boy or Are You a Girl?	1966	50.00	100.00	200.00
RHINO					
RNLP 008	The Barbarians	1979	3.00	6.00	12.00

BARBARY, RICHARD

Number	Title (A Side/B Side)	Yr	VG	VG+	NM
45s					
A&M					
1019	Call On Me/Like You, Babe	1969	—	3.00	6.00
SPRING					
701	Get Right/When Johnny Comes Marching Home	1967	2.00	4.00	8.00
Albums					
A&M					
SP-3010	Soul Machine	1969	5.00	10.00	20.00

BARBEES, THE

Early version of THE VELVELETTES.

Number	Title (A Side/B Side)	Yr	VG	VG+	NM
45s					
STEPP					
236	The Wind/Que Pasa	1963	50.00	100.00	200.00

BARBER, CHRIS

Number	Title (A Side/B Side)	Yr	VG	VG+	NM
45s					
ATLANTIC					
2016	Hush-a-Bye/You Don't Understand	1959	3.00	6.00	12.00
LAURIE					
3022	Petite Fleur/Wild Cat Blues	1958	3.75	7.50	15.00
3022 [PS]	Petite Fleur/Wild Cat Blues	1958	6.25	12.50	25.00
3026	Rugged Cross/Thriller Rag	1959	3.00	6.00	12.00
3057	Swanee River/ Lonesome	1960	3.00	6.00	12.00
3154	It Looks Like a Big Night Tonight/King Kong	1963	3.00	6.00	12.00
LONDON					
9571V	The Loneliness of the Long Distance Runner/ Valley of Roses	1963	3.00	6.00	12.00
Albums					
ATLANTIC					
1292 [M]	Here Is Chris Barber	1959	10.00	20.00	40.00
COLPIX					
CP-404 [M]	Petite But Great	1959	7.50	15.00	30.00
GHB					
GHB-40 [M]	Collaboration	1967	3.75	7.50	15.00
LAURIE					
1001 [M]	Petite Fleur	1959	10.00	20.00	40.00
LLP-1003 [M]	Trad Jazz Volume 1	1960	7.50	15.00	30.00
LLP-1009 [M]	Chris Barber's "American" Jazz Band	1962	7.50	15.00	30.00

BARBER BROTHERS, THE

Number	Title (A Side/B Side)	Yr	VG	VG+	NM
45s					
DECCA					
30753	Well All Right/How Can You Tell If It's Love	1958	3.75	7.50	15.00

BARBIERI, GATO

Number	Title (A Side/B Side)	Yr	VG	VG+	NM
45s					
A&M					
1885	Behind the Rain/Fiesta	1976	—	2.00	4.00
1916	Don't Cry Rochelle/Europa (Earth's Cry Heaven's Smile)	1977	—	2.00	4.00
2006	Midnight Tango/Nostalgia	1978	—	2.00	4.00
2066	Evil Eyes/Poinciana (Song of the Tree)	1978	—	2.00	4.00
2141	Firepower/Lions Also Cry	1979	—	2.00	4.00
2189	Secret Fiesta/Sophia	1979	—	2.00	4.00
UNITED ARTISTS					
XW-175	Last Tango in Paris/Return Tango	1973	—	2.00	4.00
Albums					
ABC IMPULSE!					
AS-9248	Chapter One — Latin America	1973	3.00	6.00	12.00
AS-9263	Chapter Two — Hasta Siempre	1974	3.00	6.00	12.00
AS-9279	Chapter Three — Viva Emiliano Zapata	1974	3.00	6.00	12.00
AS-9303	Chapter Four — Alive in New York	1975	3.00	6.00	12.00
A&M					
SP-3029	Fire and Passion	198?	2.50	5.00	10.00
SP-3188	Euphoria	198?	2.00	4.00	8.00
—Budget-line reissue					
SP-3247	Caliente!	198?	2.00	4.00	8.00
—Budget-line reissue					
SP-4597	Caliente!	1976	2.50	5.00	10.00
SP-4655	Ruby, Ruby	1977	2.50	5.00	10.00
SP-4710	Tropico	1978	2.50	5.00	10.00
SP-4774	Euphoria	1979	2.50	5.00	10.00
DR. JAZZ					
W2X 39204 [(2)]	Gato...Para Los Amigos	1985	3.00	6.00	12.00
FW 40183	Apasionado	1986	2.50	5.00	10.00
ESP-DISK'					
1049	In Search of the Mystery	1968	5.00	10.00	20.00
FLYING DUTCHMAN					
BDL1-0550	Yesterdays	1974	3.00	6.00	12.00
BDL1-1147	El Gato	1976	3.00	6.00	12.00
BXL1-2826	3rd World	1978	2.50	5.00	10.00
—Reissue of 10117					
BXL1-2827	Fenix	1978	2.50	5.00	10.00
—Reissue of 10144					
BXL1-2828	El Pampero	1978	2.50	5.00	10.00
—Reissue of 10151					
BXL1-2829	Under Fire	1978	2.50	5.00	10.00
—Reissue of 10156					
BXL1-2830	Bolivia	1978	2.50	5.00	10.00
—Reissue of 10158					
AYL1-3815	3rd World	1980	2.00	4.00	8.00
—Budget-line reissue					
AYL1-3816	Yesterdays	1980	2.00	4.00	8.00
—Budget-line reissue					
AYL1-3817	El Gato	1980	2.00	4.00	8.00
—Budget-line reissue					
FD 10117	3rd World	1970	3.75	7.50	15.00
FD 10144	Fenix	1972	3.75	7.50	15.00
FD 10151	El Pampero	1973	3.75	7.50	15.00
FD 10156	Under Fire	1973	3.00	6.00	12.00
FD 10158	Bolivia	1973	3.00	6.00	12.00
FD 10165	Legend	1974	3.00	6.00	12.00
MCA					
29002	Chapter Two — Hasta Siempre	1981	2.00	4.00	8.00
—Reissue of Impulse 9263					
29003	Chapter Four — Alive in New York	1981	2.00	4.00	8.00
—Reissue of Impulse 9303					
UNITED ARTISTS					
UA-LA045-F	Last Tango in Paris	1973	3.00	6.00	12.00

BARBIERI, GATO & DOLLAR BRAND

Number	Title (A Side/B Side)	Yr	VG	VG+	NM
Albums					
ARISTA FREEDOM					
AL 1003	Confluence	1975	3.00	6.00	12.00

BARBOUR, KEITH

Number	Title (A Side/B Side)	Yr	VG	VG+	NM
45s					
BARNABY					
2036	A Pound of Peaches/Music Sweet Music	1971	—	2.50	5.00
EPIC					
10486	Echo Park/Here I Am Losing You	1969	—	3.00	6.00
10575	Bake Me a Woman/If I Could Only Touch You	1970	—	3.00	6.00

Number	Title (A Side/B Side)	Yr	VG	VG+	NM
10598	Alicia/Sweet Mary Sunday	1970	—	3.00	6.00
10652	In the Quiet of Your Love/My God and I	1970	—	3.00	6.00
Albums					
EPIC					
BN 26485	Echo Park	1969	5.00	10.00	20.00

BARBRA AND NEIL

BARBRA STREISAND and NEIL DIAMOND.

Number	Title (A Side/B Side)	Yr	VG	VG+	NM
45s					
COLUMBIA					
3-10840	You Don't Bring Me Flowers/(Instrumental)	1978	—	2.50	5.00

BARCLAY JAMES HARVEST

Number	Title (A Side/B Side)	Yr	VG	VG+	NM
45s					
HARVEST					
3501	Thank You/Medicine Man	1972	—	2.50	5.00
MCA					
40690	Rock 'N' Roll Star/Polk Street Rag	1977	—	2.00	4.00
40795	Hymn/Our Kid's Kid	1977	—	2.00	4.00
POLYDOR					
14546	Loving Is Easy (Fantasy)/Turning in Circles	1979	—	2.00	4.00
15104	Crazy City/Child of the Universe	1975	—	2.00	4.00
15118	Titles/(B-side unknown)	197?	—	2.00	4.00
SIRE					
4105	Early Morning/Mr. Sunshine	1969	2.00	4.00	8.00
4112	Brother Thrush/Poor Wages	1969	2.00	4.00	8.00
Albums					
HARVEST					
SW-11145	Baby James Harvest	1973	3.75	7.50	15.00
MCA					
2234	Octoberon	1976	2.50	5.00	10.00
2302	Gone to Earth	1977	2.50	5.00	10.00
POLYDOR					
PD-1-6173	XII	1978	2.50	5.00	10.00
PD-1-6267	Eyes of the Universe	1980	2.50	5.00	10.00
PD-6508	Everyone Is Everybody Else	1974	3.00	6.00	12.00
PD-6517	Time Honoured Ghosts	1975	3.00	6.00	12.00
SIRE					
SI-4904	Back Again	1971	3.75	7.50	15.00
SI-5904	Other Short Stories	1972	3.75	7.50	15.00
SES-97026	Barclay James Harvest	1970	5.00	10.00	20.00

BARD, ANNETTE

One of THE TEDDY BEARS.

Number	Title (A Side/B Side)	Yr	VG	VG+	NM
45s					
IMPERIAL					
5643	What Difference Does It Make/Alibi	1960	12.50	25.00	50.00

BARDS, THE

Number	Title (A Side/B Side)	Yr	VG	VG+	NM
45s					
BURDETTE					
103	I Want You/Freedom Catcher	1971	2.00	4.00	8.00
CAPITOL					
2041	The Jabberwocky/Never Too Much Love	1967	2.50	5.00	10.00
2148	The Owl and the Pussycat/The Light of Love	1968	2.50	5.00	10.00
2148 [PS]	The Owl and the Pussycat/The Light of Love	1968	5.00	10.00	20.00
DAWN					
208	I'm a Wine Drinker/Easy Going Baby	1954	62.50	125.00	250.00
209	Gravy/Avalon	1954	62.50	125.00	250.00
JERDEN					
907	Good Time Charlie's Got the Blues/Tunesmith	1969	3.00	6.00	12.00
PARROT					
337	Good Time Charlie's Got the Blues/Tunesmith	1969	2.50	5.00	10.00
344	Our Love/Jubilation	1970	2.50	5.00	10.00
351	Day by Day/Wadda Wadda	1970	2.50	5.00	10.00
PICCADILLY					
224	The Owl and the Pussycat/The Light of Love	1966	5.00	10.00	20.00
232	The Jabberwocky/My Generation	1966	3.00	6.00	12.00
242	Our Love/Jubilation	1967	3.00	6.00	12.00

BARE, BOBBY

By record-company accident, he also recorded as BILL PARSONS.

Number	Title (A Side/B Side)	Yr	VG	VG+	NM
45s					
CAPITOL					
F3557	Down on the Corner of Love/Another Love Has Ended	1956	7.50	15.00	30.00
F3686	Darling Don't/Life of a Fool	1957	7.50	15.00	30.00
F3771	The Livin' End/Beggar	1957	7.50	15.00	30.00
COLUMBIA					
02577	Dropping Out of Sight/She Is Gone	1981	—	2.00	4.00
02690	Let Him Roll/New Cut Road	1982	—	2.00	4.00
02895	If You Ain't Got Nothing (You've Got Nothing To Lose)/Golden Memories	1982	—	2.00	4.00
03135	New Cut Road/Numbers	1982	—	—	3.00
—Reissue					
03149	(I'm Not) A Candle in the Wind/Cold Day in Hell	1982	—	2.00	4.00
03334	Praise the Lord and Send Me the Money/I've Been Rained On Too	1982	—	2.00	4.00
03628	It's a Dirty Job/Caught in the Spotlight	1983	—	2.00	4.00
—A-side: With Lacy J. Dalton					
03809	Gravy Train/The Jogger	1983	—	2.00	4.00
04092	Diet Song/Stacy Brown Got Two	1983	—	2.00	4.00
10690	Too Many Nights Alone/A Yard Full of Rusty Cars	1978	—	2.50	5.00
10831	Sleep Tight, Good Night Man/Hot Afternoon	1978	—	2.50	5.00
10891	Healin'/Love Is a Cold Wind	1979	—	2.00	4.00
10998	Till I Gain Control Again/I'll Feel a Whole Lot Better	1979	—	2.00	4.00
11045	No Memories Hangin' Round/This Has Happened Before	1979	—	2.00	4.00
—With Roseanne Cash					
11170	Numbers/When Hippies Get Older	1980	—	2.00	4.00
11259	Tequila Sheila/Quaaludes Again	1980	—	2.00	4.00
11365	Used Cars/Food Blues	1980	—	2.00	4.00
11408	Willie Jones/If That Ain't Love	1980	—	2.00	4.00
EMI AMERICA					
8279	When I Get Home/Party of the First Part	1985	—	—	3.00
8296	Reno and Me/Party of the First Part	1985	—	—	3.00
8317	Better Not Look Down/Wait Until Tomorrow	1986	—	—	3.00
8333	Real Good/Wait Until Tomorrow	1986	—	—	3.00
FRATERNITY					
861	I'm Hanging Up My Rifle/That's Where I Wanna Be	1959	10.00	20.00	40.00
867	Sweet Singing Sam/More Than a Poor Boy Could Give	1960	7.50	15.00	30.00
871	No Letter from My Baby/Lynchin' Party	1960	5.00	10.00	20.00
878	Book of Love/Lorena	1961	5.00	10.00	20.00
885	Sailor Man/Island of Love	1961	5.00	10.00	20.00
890	Zigzag Twist/Brooklyn Bridge	1961	5.00	10.00	20.00
892	The Day My Rainbow Fell/That Mean Old Clock	1961	5.00	10.00	20.00
MERCURY					
73097	It's Freezing in El Paso/How I Got to Memphis	1970	—	3.00	6.00
73148	Come Sundown/Woman You Have Been a Friend to Me	1970	—	3.00	6.00
73203	Please Don't Tell Me How the Story Ends/Where Have All the Seasons Gone	1971	—	3.00	6.00
73236	A Million Miles to the City/Short and Sweet	1971	—	3.00	6.00
73279	Love Forever/What Am I Gonna Do	1972	—	3.00	6.00
73317	Sylvia's Mother/Music City U.S.A.	1972	—	3.00	6.00
RCA					
PB-10718	Put a Little Lovin' on Me/Those City Lights	1976	—	2.50	5.00
PB-10790	Drop Kick Me, Jesus/Baby Wants to Boogie	1976	—	3.00	6.00
PB-10852	Vegas/The Shelter of Your Eyes	1976	—	2.50	5.00
—Bobby and Jeannie Bare					
PB-10902	If You Think I'm Crazy/Look Who I'm Cheatin' On Tonight	1977	—	2.50	5.00
PB-11037	Red Neck Hippie Romance/Bottom Dollar	1977	—	2.50	5.00
PB-11673	Hurricane Shirley/Crazy Arms	1979	—	2.50	5.00
—B-side by Willie Nelson					
RCA VICTOR					
APBO-0063	You Know Who/Send Tomorrow to the Moon	1973	—	2.50	5.00
AMAO-0119	Shame on Me/Above and Beyond	1973	—	2.50	5.00
APBO-0197	Daddy What If/Restless Wind	1973	—	2.50	5.00
APBO-0261	Marie Laveau/Mermaid	1974	—	2.50	5.00
PB-10037	Where'd I Come From/Scarlet Ribbons	1974	—	2.50	5.00
PB-10096	You Are/Singin' in the Kitchen	1974	—	2.50	5.00
—Bobby Bare and Family					
GB-10166	Daddy What If/Ride Me Down Easy	1975	—	—	3.00
—Gold Standard Series issue					
PB-10223	Warm and Free/Back in Huntsville Again	1975	—	2.50	5.00
PB-10318	Alimony/Daddy's Been Around the House Too Long	1975	—	2.50	5.00
PB-10409	Cowboys and Daddys/High Plains Jamboree	1975	—	2.50	5.00
GB-10495	Singin' in the Kitchen/You Are	1975	—	—	3.00
—Gold Standard Series issue					
GB-10496	Marie Laveau/Mermaid	1975	—	—	3.00
—Gold Standard Series issue					
GB-10497	Where'd I Come From/Scarlet Ribbons	1975	—	—	3.00
—Gold Standard Series issue					
PB-10556	Up Against the Wall Redneck Mother/The Winner	1976	—	2.50	5.00
47-8032	Shame on Me/Above and Beyond	1962	3.00	6.00	12.00
47-8083	I Don't Believe I'll Fall in Love Today/To Whom It May Concern	1962	3.00	6.00	12.00
47-8083 [PS]	I Don't Believe I'll Fall in Love Today/To Whom It May Concern	1962	6.25	12.50	25.00
47-8146	Dear Waste Basket/I'd Fight the World	1963	3.00	6.00	12.00
47-8183	Detroit City/Heart of Ice	1963	3.75	7.50	15.00
47-8183 [PS]	Detroit City/Heart of Ice	1963	6.25	12.50	25.00
47-8238	500 Miles Away from Home/It All Depends On Linda	1963	3.75	7.50	15.00
47-8294	Miller's Cave/Jeannie's Last Kiss	1963	3.00	6.00	12.00
47-8358	Have I Stayed Away Too Long/More Than a Poor Boy Can Give	1964	3.00	6.00	12.00
47-8395	He Was a Friend of Mine/When I'm Gone	1964	3.00	6.00	12.00
47-8443	Four Strong Winds/Take Me Home	1964	3.00	6.00	12.00
47-8509	Times Are Gettin' Hard/One Day at a Time	1965	2.50	5.00	10.00
47-8571	It's Alright/She Picked a Perfect Day	1965	2.50	5.00	10.00
47-8654	Just to Satisfy You/Memories	1965	2.50	5.00	10.00
47-8699	Talk Me Some Sense/Delia's Gone	1965	2.50	5.00	10.00
47-8758	In the Same Old Way/Long Black Veil	1965	2.50	5.00	10.00
47-8851	The Streets of Baltimore/She Took My Sunshine Away	1966	2.50	5.00	10.00
47-8988	Homesick/Guess I'll Move On Down the Line	1966	2.50	5.00	10.00
47-9098	Charleston Railroad Tavern/Vincennes	1967	2.00	4.00	8.00
47-9191	Come Kiss Me Love/Sandy's Crying Again	1967	2.00	4.00	8.00
47-9314	The Piney Wood Hills/They Covered Up the Old Swimmin' Hole	1967	2.00	4.00	8.00
47-9450	Find Out What's Happening/When Am I Ever Gonna Settle Down	1968	2.00	4.00	8.00
47-9568	A Little Bit Farther On Down the Line/Don't Do Like I Done, Son	1968	2.00	4.00	8.00
47-9643	The Town That Broke My Heart/My Baby	1968	2.00	4.00	8.00
74-0110	(Margie's At) Lincoln Park Inn/Rainy Day in Richmond	1969	—	3.00	6.00
74-0202	Which One Will It Be/My Frame of Mind	1969	—	3.00	6.00
74-0264	God Bless America Again/Baby, What Else Can I Do	1969	—	3.00	6.00
74-0866	Fallin' Apart/I Hate Goodbyes	1973	—	3.00	6.00
74-0918	Ride Me Down Easy/A Train That Never Runs	1973	—	3.00	6.00
RICE					
5057	Christian Soldier/Dropping Out of Sight	1973	—	2.50	5.00
5060	Love Forever/A Million Miles to the City	1973	—	2.50	5.00
5066	I Took a Memory to Lunch/It's Freezing in St. Paul	1974	—	2.50	5.00
Albums					
COLUMBIA					
KC 35314	Bare	1977	2.50	5.00	10.00
JC 36323	Down & Dirty	1978	2.50	5.00	10.00

Number	Title (A Side/B Side)	Yr	VG	VG+	NM
PC 36323	Down & Dirty	198?	2.00	4.00	8.00
—*Budget-line reissue*					
JC 36785	Drunk & Crazy	1980	2.50	5.00	10.00
FC 37157	As Is	1981	2.50	5.00	10.00
FC 37351	Encore	1981	2.50	5.00	10.00
PC 37351	Encore	198?	2.00	4.00	8.00
—*Budget-line reissue*					
FC 37719	Ain't Got Nothin' to Lose	1982	2.50	5.00	10.00
FC 38311	Biggest Hits	1982	2.50	5.00	10.00
FC 38670	Drinkin' from the Bottle, Singin' from the Heart	1983	2.50	5.00	10.00
HILLTOP					
6026	Tender Years	196?	3.00	6.00	12.00
MERCURY					
SR-61290	This Is Bare Country	1970	5.00	10.00	20.00
SR-61316	Where Have All the Seasons Gone	1971	5.00	10.00	20.00
SR-61363	What Am I Gonna Do?	1972	5.00	10.00	20.00
RCA CAMDEN					
ACL1-0150	Memphis, Tennessee	1973	3.00	6.00	12.00
CAS-2290	Folsom Prison Blues	1969	3.00	6.00	12.00
CAS-2465	I'm a Long Way from Home	1971	3.00	6.00	12.00
RCA VICTOR					
APL1-0040	I Hate Goodbyes/Ride Me Down Easy	1973	3.75	7.50	15.00
CPL2-0290 [(2)]	Bobby Bare Sings Lullabys, Legends and Lies	1973	5.00	10.00	20.00
ANL1-0560	Sunday Morning	1974	2.50	5.00	10.00
APL1-0700	Singin' in the Kitchen	1974	3.75	7.50	15.00
APL1-0906	Hard Time Hungrys	1975	3.00	6.00	12.00
APL1-1222	Cowboys and Daddys	1975	3.00	6.00	12.00
APL1-1786	The Winner and Other Losers	1976	3.00	6.00	12.00
APL1-2179	Me and McDill	1977	3.00	6.00	12.00
LPM-2776 [M]	"Detroit City" and Other Hits	1963	5.00	10.00	20.00
LSP-2776 [S]	"Detroit City" and Other Hits	1963	6.25	12.50	25.00
LPM-2835 [M]	500 Miles Away from Home	1964	5.00	10.00	20.00
LSP-2835 [S]	500 Miles Away from Home	1964	6.25	12.50	25.00
LPM-2955 [M]	The Travelin' Bare	1964	5.00	10.00	20.00
LSP-2955 [S]	The Travelin' Bare	1964	6.25	12.50	25.00
LPM-3395 [M]	Constant Sorrow	1965	5.00	10.00	20.00
LSP-3395 [S]	Constant Sorrow	1965	6.25	12.50	25.00
LPM-3479 [M]	The Best of Bobby Bare	1965	5.00	10.00	20.00
LSP-3479 [S]	The Best of Bobby Bare	1965	6.25	12.50	25.00
LPM-3515 [M]	Talk Me Some Sense	1966	5.00	10.00	20.00
LSP-3515 [S]	Talk Me Some Sense	1966	6.25	12.50	25.00
LPM-3618 [M]	The Streets of Baltimore	1966	5.00	10.00	20.00
LSP-3618 [S]	The Streets of Baltimore	1966	6.25	12.50	25.00
LPM-3688 [M]	This I Believe	1966	5.00	10.00	20.00
LSP-3688 [S]	This I Believe	1966	6.25	12.50	25.00
LPM-3831 [M]	A Bird Named Yesterday	1967	6.25	12.50	25.00
LSP-3831 [S]	A Bird Named Yesterday	1967	5.00	10.00	20.00
LPM-3896 [M]	The English Country Side	1967	10.00	20.00	40.00
LSP-3896 [S]	The English Country Side	1967	5.00	10.00	20.00
LPM-3994 [M]	The Best of Bobby Bare — Volume 2	1968	10.00	20.00	40.00
LSP-3994 [S]	The Best of Bobby Bare — Volume 2	1968	5.00	10.00	20.00
AYL1-4118	Greatest Hits	1982	2.00	4.00	8.00
LSP-4177	(Margie's At) The Lincoln Park Inn (And Other Controversial Country Songs)	1969	5.00	10.00	20.00
LSP-4422	Real Thing	1970	3.75	7.50	15.00
AHL1-5469	Collector's Series	1985	2.50	5.00	10.00
VPS-6090 [(2)]	This Is Bobby Bare	1972	5.00	10.00	20.00
UNITED ARTISTS					
UA-LA621-G	Bare Country	1977	3.00	6.00	12.00

BARE, BOBBY, AND SKEETER DAVIS

Also see each artist's individual listings.

Number	Title (A Side/B Side)	Yr	VG	VG+	NM
45s					
RCA VICTOR					
47-8496	A Dear John Letter/Too Used to Being with You	1965	2.50	5.00	10.00
47-9789	Your Husband, My Wife/Before the Sunshine	1969	—	3.00	6.00
Albums					
RCA VICTOR					
LPM-3336 [M]	Tunes for Two	1965	5.00	10.00	20.00
LSP-3336 [S]	Tunes for Two	1965	6.25	12.50	25.00
LSP-4335	Your Husband, My Wife	1970	3.75	7.50	15.00

BARE, BOBBY, NORMA JEAN, & LIZ ANDERSON

Number	Title (A Side/B Side)	Yr	VG	VG+	NM
45s					
RCA VICTOR					
47-8963	The Game of Triangles/Bye Bye Bye	1966	2.50	5.00	10.00
Albums					
RCA VICTOR					
LPM-3764 [M]	The Game of Triangles	1967	6.25	12.50	25.00
LSP-3764 [S]	The Game of Triangles	1967	5.00	10.00	20.00

BARGE, GENE

Number	Title (A Side/B Side)	Yr	VG	VG+	NM
45s					
CHECKER					
839	Way Down Home/Country	1954	7.50	15.00	30.00
1110	Fine Twine/The "In" Crowd	1965	2.50	5.00	10.00
LEGRAND					
1006	Thinking of You/Autumn Leaves	1961	10.00	20.00	40.00
PARAMOUNT					
0160	Love Theme from "The Godfather"/Gina	1972	—	2.50	5.00
Albums					
CHECKER					
LP-2994 [M]	Dance with Daddy G	1965	12.50	25.00	50.00

BARIN, PETE

Number	Title (A Side/B Side)	Yr	VG	VG+	NM
45s					
SABINA					
504	So Wrong/Broken Heart	1962	12.50	25.00	50.00
512	Loneliest Guy in the World/Look Out for Cindy	1962	7.50	15.00	30.00

BARITONES, THE

Number	Title (A Side/B Side)	Yr	VG	VG+	NM
45s					
DORE					
501	After School Rock/Sentimental Baby	1958	10.00	20.00	40.00

BARKER, DELBERT

Number	Title (A Side/B Side)	Yr	VG	VG+	NM
45s					
KING					
4951	That's a Sin/No Good, Robin Hood	1956	7.50	15.00	30.00
5008	Wild Heart/There Must Be a Way	1957	7.50	15.00	30.00
5031	Amanda/Broken Heart	1957	7.50	15.00	30.00
6042	It Can't Last Long/Color Me Gone	1966	2.50	5.00	10.00

BARNABY BYE

Number	Title (A Side/B Side)	Yr	VG	VG+	NM
45s					
ATLANTIC					
2984	I Think I'm Gonna Like It/Dreamer	1973	—	2.50	5.00
3244	Take Me With You/Blonde	1975	—	2.50	5.00
3266	Can't Live This Way/Happy Was the Day We Met	1975	—	2.50	5.00
Albums					
ATLANTIC					
SD 7273	Room to Grow	1973	3.00	6.00	12.00
SD 18104	Touch	1974	3.00	6.00	12.00

BARNES, BENNY

Number	Title (A Side/B Side)	Yr	VG	VG+	NM
45s					
D					
1052	Gold Records in the Snow/Happy Little Blue Bird	1959	15.00	30.00	60.00
HALL-WAY					
1203	A Bar with No Beer/Headed for Heartbreak	1964	2.50	5.00	10.00
1207	It's Good to Be Home/For a Minute There	1965	2.50	5.00	10.00
KAPP					
859	A Bar with No Beer/Headed for Heartbreak	1967	2.00	4.00	8.00
912	Sweet Suzannah/It's My Mind That's Broken	1968	2.00	4.00	8.00
MEGA					
0071	Woman, Leave My Mind Alone/I'm Just Here to Get My Baby Off My Mind	1972	—	2.50	5.00
MERCURY					
71048	A Poor Man's Riches/Those Who Know	1957	5.00	10.00	20.00
71057	Poor Old Me/Penalty	1957	5.00	10.00	20.00
71119	Nickels Worth of Dreams/Mine All Mine	1957	5.00	10.00	20.00
71188	King for a Day/Your Old Stand By	1957	5.00	10.00	20.00
71284	Moon Over My Shoulder/Lonely Street	1958	6.25	12.50	25.00
71552	Beggar to a King/The Fastest Gun Alive	1959	3.75	7.50	15.00
71600	That-a Boy Willie/Token of Love	1960	3.75	7.50	15.00
71637	Pretty Little Girl/Message in the Wind	1960	3.75	7.50	15.00
71717	You're Still on My Mind/I Think I'll Take a Walk and Disappear	1960	3.75	7.50	15.00
71806	Go On, Go On/Yearning	1961	3.75	7.50	15.00
71896	The World's Worst Loser/I Changed My Mind	1961	3.75	7.50	15.00
MUSICOR					
1100	Let Me Live As Long As I Can/Tea Leaves Don't Lie	1965	2.00	4.00	8.00
1127	Have We Really Tried/Heartache's Comin'	1965	2.00	4.00	8.00
1169	Diesel Smoke/That's How I Need You	1966	2.00	4.00	8.00
1194	Stand By Your Window/You're Not There	1966	2.00	4.00	8.00
1223	What's the Matter with Me/Third Time Down	1966	2.00	4.00	8.00
1247	I'm Her Lover/Same Old Boat	1967	2.00	4.00	8.00
1277	Let One Call Do It All/Rosanna Martin	1967	2.00	4.00	8.00
PLAYBOY					
5808	I've Got Some Gettin' Over You to Do/I'll Drink to That	1977	—	3.00	6.00
RCA VICTOR					
47-9830	An Old Memory Got in My Eye/You're Everywhere	1970	—	3.00	6.00
74-0271	Pressure Cooker/To the Ones I Love	1969	—	3.00	6.00
STARDAY					
236	Once Again/No Fault of Mine	1956	5.00	10.00	20.00
262	A Poor Man's Riches/Those Who Know	1956	5.00	10.00	20.00
401	You Gotta Pay/Heads You Win	1958	3.75	7.50	15.00

BARNES, BILLY

Number	Title (A Side/B Side)	Yr	VG	VG+	NM
45s					
LIBERTY					
55421	Until/To Prove My Love	1962	6.25	12.50	25.00
UNITED ARTISTS					
148	You'd Have to Fall in Love/If You But Knew	1958	5.00	10.00	20.00
157	I'm Coming to See You/What Am I Supposed to Do	1959	5.00	10.00	20.00
218	Home Again/I Wish I Didn't Love You So	1960	5.00	10.00	20.00
311	C.C. Rider/Here Am I	1961	5.00	10.00	20.00

BARNES, DENA

Number	Title (A Side/B Side)	Yr	VG	VG+	NM
45s					
INFERNO					
2002	Who Am I/(B-side unknown)	196?	62.50	125.00	250.00

BARNES, GEORGE

Number	Title (A Side/B Side)	Yr	VG	VG+	NM
45s					
DECCA					
30398	Tammy/Around the World	1957	5.00	10.00	20.00
MERCURY					
71968	Transville/Spooky	1962	7.50	15.00	30.00

BARNES, J.J.

Number	Title (A Side/B Side)	Yr	VG	VG+	NM
45s					
BUDDAH					
120	Evidence/I'll Keep Coming Back	1969	3.75	7.50	15.00
CONTEMPO					
7003	How Long/The Erroll Flynn	1977	—	2.50	5.00

Number	Title (A Side/B Side)	Yr	VG	VG+	NM
GROOVESVILLE					
1006	Baby Please Come Back Home/Chains of Love	1967	3.75	7.50	15.00
1008	Now That I Got You Back/Forgive Me	1967	3.75	7.50	15.00
1009	Easy Living/(B-side unknown)	1967	4.00	8.00	16.00
INVASION					
1001	My Baby/(You Still) My Baby	1970	2.50	5.00	10.00
KABLE					
437	Won't You Let Me Know/My Love Came Tumbling Down	1960	12.50	25.00	50.00
MAGIC TOUCH					
1000	To An Early Grave/Cloudy Days	1970	2.50	5.00	10.00
MICKAY'S					
3004	Just One More Time/Hey Child, I Love You	1963	20.00	40.00	80.00
4472	Get a Hold of Yourself/Lonely No More	1964	20.00	40.00	80.00
PERCEPTION					
546	Just a Living Doll/Touching You	1974	—	3.00	6.00
REVILOT					
216	Hold On to It/Now She's Gone	1968	3.75	7.50	15.00
218	I'll Keep Coming Back/Sad Day a-Comin'	1968	3.75	7.50	15.00
222	Our Love Is in the Pocket/All Your Goodies Are Gone	1968	20.00	40.00	80.00
225	So-Called Friends/Now She's Gone	1968	3.75	7.50	15.00
RIC-TIC					
106	Please Let Me In/I Think I Found a Love	1965	3.75	7.50	15.00
110	Real Humdinger/I Ain't Gonna Do It	1966	3.75	7.50	15.00
115	Day Tripper/Don't Bring Me Bad News	1966	3.75	7.50	15.00
117	Deeper in Love/Say It	1966	3.75	7.50	15.00
RICH					
1005	Won't You Let Me Know/My Love Came Tumbling Down	1960	25.00	50.00	100.00
1737	Won't You Let Me Know/My Love Came Tumbling Down	1962	6.25	12.50	25.00
RING					
101	She Ain't Ready/Poor-Unfortunate Me	1964	6.25	12.50	25.00
SCEPTER					
1266	Just One More Time/Hey Child, I Love You	1964	7.50	15.00	30.00
VOLT					
4027	Got to Get Rid of You/Snowflakes	1969	3.75	7.50	15.00
Albums					
VOLT					
VOS-6001	Rare Stamps	1969	7.50	15.00	30.00
—With Steve Mancha					

BARNES, SIDNEY

Number	Title (A Side/B Side)	Yr	VG	VG+	NM
45s					
BLUE CAT					
125	I Hurt on the Other Side/Switchy Walk	1966	37.50	75.00	150.00
CHESS					
2094	Baloney/Old Times	1970	2.50	5.00	10.00
PARACHUTE					
521	Hold On I'm Coming/Your Love Is So Good to Me	1978	—	2.00	4.00
RED BIRD					
10-039	You'll Always Be in Style/I'm So Glad	1965	10.00	20.00	40.00
10-054	I Hurt on the Other Side/Switchy Walk	1966	10.00	20.00	40.00
Albums					
PARACHUTE					
9009	Footstomp'n Music	1978	3.00	6.00	12.00

BARNES, TAWANDA

Number	Title (A Side/B Side)	Yr	VG	VG+	NM
45s					
A&M					
1141	(You Better) Find Someone to Love/You Don't Mean It	1969	6.25	12.50	25.00

BARNUM, H.B.

Number	Title (A Side/B Side)	Yr	VG	VG+	NM
45s					
CAPITOL					
2036	Baby, Love Me/The Bad Luck's on Me	1967	3.00	6.00	12.00
2139	Vaya Con Dios/What Did Sister Do	1968	2.50	5.00	10.00
2317	Happiness/It's Just a Game, Love	1968	2.50	5.00	10.00
5391	I'm a Man/The Record	1965	3.00	6.00	12.00
5440	Gimme Some/Don't Forget 127th Street	1965	3.00	6.00	12.00
5477	I Can't Help It/Dance with Me	1965	3.00	6.00	12.00
5748	Gotta Go/Nobody Wants to Hear Nobody's Trouble	1966	3.00	6.00	12.00
5932	Heartbreaker/Searchin' for My Soul	1967	5.00	10.00	20.00
DECCA					
32892	Run to Daylight/Howard Hardsell	1971	—	2.50	5.00
—B-side by Tom Patchett and Jay Tarses					
ELDO					
111	Lost Love/Hallelujah	1960	3.75	7.50	15.00
IMPERIAL					
5530	Blue Moon/Tia-Juana	1958	10.00	20.00	40.00
66011	Backstage/Rented Tuxedo	1964	3.00	6.00	12.00
66046	Skakiaan (Skokiaan)/Ska Drums	1964	3.00	6.00	12.00
66063	Calpyso Blues/Three Room Flat	1964	3.00	6.00	12.00
66074	Eternal Love/So What	1964	3.00	6.00	12.00
RCA VICTOR					
47-7960	Baby Baby Baby (All the Time)/How Many More Times	1961	3.75	7.50	15.00
47-8014	Call On Me/Oh My Achin' Back	1962	3.75	7.50	15.00
47-8112	Lonely Hearts/It Hurts Too Much to Cry	1962	15.00	30.00	60.00
UNITED ARTISTS					
XW338	Theme from "5 on the Back Hand Side"/Keep It Comin'	1973	—	2.50	5.00
Albums					
CAPITOL					
ST 2278 [S]	Golden Boy	1965	5.00	10.00	20.00
T 2278 [M]	Golden Boy	1965	3.75	7.50	15.00
ST 2289 [S]	Big Hits of Detroit	1965	5.00	10.00	20.00
T 2289 [M]	Big Hits of Detroit	1965	3.75	7.50	15.00
ST 2583 [S]	Pop and Ice Cream Sodas	1966	5.00	10.00	20.00
T 2583 [M]	Pop and Ice Cream Sodas	1966	3.75	7.50	15.00

BARONS, THE

Several different groups.

Number	Title (A Side/B Side)	Yr	VG	VG+	NM
45s					
BELLAIRE					
103	The Bandit/Wanderin'	1963	5.00	10.00	20.00
BROWNFIELD					
1035	Hope I Please You/Don't Burn It	196?	12.50	25.00	50.00
DART					
126	Lonely Loretta/Lula Mae	1959	6.25	12.50	25.00
134	Perfect Love/Until the Thirteenth Chime	1960	6.25	12.50	25.00
DECCA					
29293	Exactly Like You/Forget About Me	1954	30.00	60.00	120.00
48323	A Year and a Day/My Baby's Gone	1954	30.00	60.00	120.00
DEMON					
1520	Gravel Gert/The Fight	1959	3.75	7.50	15.00
EPIC					
9586	Don't Go Away (Pretty Little Girl)/Pledge of a Fool	1963	7.50	15.00	30.00
9747	Lucky Star/Remember Rita	1964	37.50	75.00	150.00
10093	Don't Go Away (Pretty Little Girl)/Pledge of a Fool	1966	3.75	7.50	15.00
IMPERIAL					
5343	Eternally Yours/Boom Boom	1955	30.00	60.00	120.00
5343	Eternally Yours/Boom Boom	1955	75.00	150.00	300.00
—Red vinyl, probably promo only					
5359	I Know I Was Wrong/My Dream, My Love	1955	30.00	60.00	120.00
5370	Cold Kisses/Searching for You	1955	30.00	60.00	120.00
5383	So Long My Darling/Crying for You Baby	1956	30.00	60.00	120.00
5397	Don't Walk Out/Once in a Lifetime	1956	20.00	40.00	80.00
66057	Silence/I Just Go Wild Inside	1964	3.75	7.50	15.00
RCA VICTOR					
47-9034	Since You're Gone/My Smile Is Bigger (Than Your Smile)	1966	6.25	12.50	25.00
SPARTAN					
400	I've Been Hurt/Willow Weep for Me	196?	3.75	7.50	15.00
TENDER					
511	Drawbridge/(B-side unknown)	1958	3.75	7.50	15.00

BAROQUE ENSEMBLE OF THE MERSEYSIDE KAMMERMUSIKGESELLSCHAFT, THE

Number	Title (A Side/B Side)	Yr	VG	VG+	NM
45s					
ELEKTRA					
45602	You've Got to Hide Your Love Away/Ticket to Ride	1966	3.00	6.00	12.00
Albums					
ELEKTRA					
EKL-306 [M]	The Baroque Beatles Book	1966	6.25	12.50	25.00
EKS-7306 [S]	The Baroque Beatles Book	1966	7.50	15.00	30.00

BAROQUES, THE

Number	Title (A Side/B Side)	Yr	VG	VG+	NM
45s					
CHESS					
2001	Mary Jane/Iowa, A Girl's Name	1967	3.75	7.50	15.00

BARRABAS

Number	Title (A Side/B Side)	Yr	VG	VG+	NM
45s					
ATCO					
7027	Hi Jack/Susie Wong	1975	—	2.50	5.00
7036	Mellow Blue (Long)/Checkmate	1975	—	2.50	5.00
7059	Desperately/If	1976	—	2.50	5.00
POLYDOR					
14267	Hi Jack	1974	—	—	—
—Unreleased					
Albums					
ATCO					
SD 36-110	Barrabas	1974	2.50	5.00	10.00
SD 36-118	Heart of the City	1975	2.50	5.00	10.00
SD 36-136	Watch Out	1976	2.50	5.00	10.00
RCA VICTOR					
LSP-4861	Wild Safari	1973	3.00	6.00	12.00

BARRACUDA

Number	Title (A Side/B Side)	Yr	VG	VG+	NM
45s					
RCA VICTOR					
47-9660	The Dance of St. Francis/Lady Fingers	1968	5.00	10.00	20.00
47-9660 [PS]	The Dance of St. Francis/Lady Fingers	1968	10.00	20.00	40.00
47-9743	Julie (The Song I Sing Is To You)/Sleeping Out the Storm	1969	3.00	6.00	12.00

BARRACUDAS, THE

Number	Title (A Side/B Side)	Yr	VG	VG+	NM
Albums					
JUSTICE					
JLP-143	A Plane View	1968	125.00	250.00	500.00

BARRAN, BOB

Number	Title (A Side/B Side)	Yr	VG	VG+	NM
45s					
SILVER STREAK					
311	Tom Tom Rock/Mother Goose Hop	1960	37.50	75.00	150.00

BARRETT, RICHARD

Number	Title (A Side/B Side)	Yr	VG	VG+	NM
45s					
20TH FOX					
150	Lovely One/The Snake and the Bookworm	1959	3.75	7.50	15.00
ATLANTIC					
2142	Some Other Guy/Tricky Dicky	1962	3.75	7.50	15.00
—As "Richie Barrett"					
CRACKERJACK					
4012	Summer's Love/Let Me Down Easy	1963	3.75	7.50	15.00

Number	Title (A Side/B Side)	Yr	VG	VG+	NM
GONE					
5056	Come Softly to Me/Walking Through Dreamland	1959	7.50	15.00	30.00
—With the Chantels					
5060	Summer's Love/All Is Forgiven	1959	7.50	15.00	30.00
—With the Chantels					
METRO					
20006	Lovable/Only One Way	1959	3.75	7.50	15.00
MGM					
12616	Smoke Gets In Your Eyes/Remember Me	1958	7.50	15.00	30.00
12659	Body and Soul/The Party	1958	7.50	15.00	30.00
SEVILLE					
104	Dream On/I Am Yours	1960	3.75	7.50	15.00

BARRETT, SUSAN

Number	Title (A Side/B Side)	Yr	VG	VG+	NM
45s					
PHILIPS					
40147	Between Two Loves/Chico's Girl	1963	6.25	12.50	25.00
40247	The Love We Never Knew/No One But You	1964	6.25	12.50	25.00
RCA VICTOR					
47-8888	A Grain of Sand/She Gets Everything She Wants	1966	5.00	10.00	20.00
47-9017	Walking Happy/How Can You Hold On to a Dream	1966	5.00	10.00	20.00
47-9296	What's It Gonna Be/It's No Secret	1967	12.50	25.00	50.00
47-9384	Sunny/Ev'ry Time We Say Goodbye	1967	5.00	10.00	20.00
Albums					
RCA VICTOR					
LPM-3738 [M]	Susan Barrett	1967	10.00	20.00	40.00
LSP-3738 [S]	Susan Barrett	1967	7.50	15.00	30.00

BARRETT, SYD

Member of the earliest incarnation of PINK FLOYD.

Number	Title (A Side/B Side)	Yr	VG	VG+	NM
7-Inch Extended Plays					
CAPITOL					
NR-58186	Terrapin/Octopus//Baby Lemonade/ Effervescent Elephant	1994	—	3.00	6.00
—Pink vinyl					
NR-58186 [PS]	Crazy Diamond	1994	—	3.00	6.00
Albums					
CAPITOL					
C1-91206	Opel	1989	5.00	10.00	20.00
HARVEST					
SABB-11314 [(2)]	The Madcap Laughs/Barrett	1974	6.25	12.50	25.00

BARRI, STEVE

Number	Title (A Side/B Side)	Yr	VG	VG+	NM
45s					
RONA					
1003	Down Around the Corner/Please Let It Be You	1961	10.00	20.00	40.00
1004	I Want Your Love/Story of the Ring	1961	10.00	20.00	40.00
1005	Two Different Worlds/Don't Run Away from Love	1962	10.00	20.00	40.00
1006	Never Before/Whenever You Kiss Me	1962	10.00	20.00	40.00

BARRIX, BILLY

Number	Title (A Side/B Side)	Yr	VG	VG+	NM
45s					
CHESS					
1662	Cool Off Baby/Almost	1958	5000.	7500.	10000.
—Outrageously rare rockabilly record					

BARRON KNIGHTS, THE

Number	Title (A Side/B Side)	Yr	VG	VG+	NM
45s					
DECCA					
32160	Lazy Fat People/In the Night	1967	2.50	5.00	10.00
EPIC					
9835	Pop Go the Workers Part 1/Part 2	1965	3.00	6.00	12.00
50755	The Topical Song/The Big V-asectomy	1979	—	2.00	4.00
MERCURY					
73302	Nothin' Doin'/You're All I Need	1972	—	2.50	5.00

BARRY, GENE

Number	Title (A Side/B Side)	Yr	VG	VG+	NM
45s					
FELSTED					
8648	Moonlight Gambler/Red Silk Stockings and Green Perfume	1961	3.00	6.00	12.00
Albums					
RCA VICTOR					
LPM-2975 [M]	The Star of "Burke's Law" Sings of Love and Things	1964	6.25	12.50	25.00
LSP-2975 [S]	The Star of "Burke's Law" Sings of Love and Things	1964	7.50	15.00	30.00

BARRY, JAY

Number	Title (A Side/B Side)	Yr	VG	VG+	NM
45s					
ABC-PARAMOUNT					
10154	A Picture of You/Sherry	1960	3.75	7.50	15.00
10226	Love Bank/Love Spell	1961	3.75	7.50	15.00

BARRY, JEFF

Also see THE RAINDROPS.

Number	Title (A Side/B Side)	Yr	VG	VG+	NM
45s					
A&M					
1422	Walkin' in the Sun/Whatcha Wanna Do	1973	—	2.50	5.00
BELL					
45140	Sweet Saviour/Love Has Never Let Me Down	1971	—	3.00	6.00
DECCA					
31037	Never Never/It Won't Hurt	1959	5.00	10.00	20.00
31089	Lenore/Why Does the Feeling Go Away	1960	5.00	10.00	20.00
RCA VICTOR					
47-7477	It's Called Rock & Roll/Hip Couples	1959	6.25	12.50	25.00
47-7797	The Face from Outer Space/Lovely Lips	1960	6.25	12.50	25.00
47-7821	All You Need Is a Quarter/Teen Quartet	1960	6.25	12.50	25.00
RED BIRD					
10-026	I'll Still Love You/Our Love Can Still Be Saved	1965	4.00	8.00	16.00
UNITED ARTISTS					
440	We Got Love Money Can't Buy/Welcome Home	1962	4.00	8.00	16.00
50529	Much Too Young/Where It's At	1969	2.00	4.00	8.00
Albums					
A&M					
SP-4393	Walkin' in the Sun	1973	3.75	7.50	15.00

BARRY, JOHN

Number	Title (A Side/B Side)	Yr	VG	VG+	NM
45s					
20TH FOX					
472	Theme from "Man in the Middle"/Barney's Blues	1964	3.00	6.00	12.00
CAPITOL					
F4212	Snap 'N Whistle/Long Long	1959	3.75	7.50	15.00
COLUMBIA					
43320	A Man Alone/Barbara's Theme	1965	2.00	4.00	8.00
43360	The Knack (And How to Get It)/The Knack (And How to Get It)	1965	2.50	5.00	10.00
—B-side by Johnny DeLittle					
43544	The Chase/Saturday Night Philosopher	1966	2.50	5.00	10.00
43801	Theme from Born Free/Goldfinger	1966	2.50	5.00	10.00
43951	Wednesday's Child/Sleep Well, My Darling	1966	2.50	5.00	10.00
44167	You Only Live Twice/The Girl with the Sun in Her Hair	1967	2.00	4.00	8.00
44721	The Lion in Winter/To Rome	1968	2.00	4.00	8.00
44891	Midnight Cowboy/Fun City	1969	—	3.00	6.00
45062	On Her Majesty's Secret Service/We Have All the Time in the World	1970	—	3.00	6.00
45140	Theme from "The Appointment"/The More Things Change	1970	—	3.00	6.00
DECCA					
31815	A Man Alone (Jazz Version)/A Man Alone (Latin Version)	1965	2.50	5.00	10.00
EPIC					
10865	The Persuaders/The Girl with the Sun in Her Hair	1972	—	3.00	6.00
KING					
5495	Black Stockings/Get Lost Jack Frost	1961	3.75	7.50	15.00
MERCURY					
72261	From Russia with Love/007	1964	3.00	6.00	12.00
MGM					
13591	Born Free/Elsa at Play	1966	2.00	4.00	8.00
UNITED ARTISTS					
581	James Bond Theme/March of the Mandarins	1963	3.75	7.50	15.00
743	Big Shield/Zulu Stomp	1964	2.50	5.00	10.00
791	Goldfinger/Troubadour	1964	2.50	5.00	10.00
863	From Russia with Love/James Bond Theme	1965	2.50	5.00	10.00
WARNER BROS.					
7230	Highway 101/Petula	1968	—	3.00	6.00
Albums					
BULLDOG					
BDL-1036	Bond by Barry	198?	2.50	5.00	10.00
COLUMBIA					
C 1003	Ready When You Are, Mr. J.B.	1970	2.50	5.00	10.00
CL 2493 [M]	Great Movie Sounds of John Barry	1966	3.75	7.50	15.00
CL 2708 [M]	You Only Live Twice	1967	3.75	7.50	15.00
CS 9293 [S]	Great Movie Sounds of John Barry	1966	5.00	10.00	20.00
CS 9508 [S]	You Only Live Twice	1967	5.00	10.00	20.00
UNITED ARTISTS					
UAL 3424 [M]	Goldfinger and Other Favorites	1965	3.00	6.00	12.00
UAS 6424 [S]	Goldfinger and Other Favorites	1965	3.75	7.50	15.00

BARRY, LEN

Former member of THE DOVELLS.

Number	Title (A Side/B Side)	Yr	VG	VG+	NM
45s					
AMY					
11026	4-5-6 (Now I'm Alone)/Funky Night	1968	—	3.00	6.00
11037	You're My Picasso, Baby/Christopher Columbus	1968	—	3.00	6.00
11047	The Child Is Born/Wouldn't It Be Beautiful	1968	—	3.00	6.00
BUDDAH					
284	Just the Two of Us/Diggin' Life	1972	—	2.50	5.00
284 [PS]	Just the Two of Us/Diggin' Life	1972	—	3.00	6.00
CAMEO					
303	Jim Dandy/Don't Come Back	1964	3.00	6.00	12.00
318	Little White House/Hearts Are Trump	1964	3.00	6.00	12.00
DECCA					
31788	Lip Sync (To the Tongue Twisters)/At the Hop '65	1965	2.50	5.00	10.00
31827	1-2-3/Bullseye	1965	3.75	7.50	15.00
31889	Like a Baby/Happiness (Is a Girl Like You)	1966	2.50	5.00	10.00
31923	Somewhere/It's a Crying Shame	1966	2.50	5.00	10.00
31969	It's That Time of the Year/Happily Ever After	1966	2.50	5.00	10.00
32011	I Struck It Rich/Love Is	1966	2.50	5.00	10.00
32054	Would I Love You/You Baby	1966	2.50	5.00	10.00
MERCURY					
72299	Let's Do It Again/Happy Days	1964	3.00	6.00	12.00
PARAMOUNT					
0206	Heaven Plus Earth/I'm Marching to the Music	1973	—	2.50	5.00
PARKWAY					
969	Little White House/Hearts Are Trump	1966	2.00	4.00	8.00
RCA VICTOR					
47-9150	Our Song/The Moving Finger Writes	1967	2.00	4.00	8.00
47-9275	All Those Memories/Rainy Side of the Street	1967	2.00	4.00	8.00
47-9348	The ABC's of Love/Come Rain or Shine	1967	2.00	4.00	8.00
47-9464	Sweet and Funny/I Like the Way	1968	2.00	4.00	8.00
SCEPTER					
12251	Put Out the Fire/Spread It On Like Butter	1969	2.00	4.00	8.00
12263	Keem-O-Sabe/This Old World	1969	2.00	4.00	8.00
12284	Bob & Carol & Ted & Alice/In My Present State of Mind	1970	—	3.00	6.00

Number	Title (A Side/B Side)	Yr	VG	VG+	NM
Albums					
BUDDAH					
BDS-5105	Ups & Downs	1972	3.75	7.50	15.00
DECCA					
DL 4720 [M]	1-2-3	1965	7.50	15.00	30.00
DL 74720 [S]	1-2-3	1965	10.00	20.00	40.00
RCA VICTOR					
LPM-3823 [M]	My Kind of Soul	1967	6.25	12.50	25.00
LSP-3823 [S]	My Kind of Soul	1967	5.00	10.00	20.00

BARRY, SANDRA

Number	Title (A Side/B Side)	Yr	VG	VG+	NM
45s					
PARKWAY					
943	We Were Lovers/The End of the Line	1965	2.50	5.00	10.00
954	Question/You Can Take It from Me	1965	2.50	5.00	10.00

BARRY AND BARRY

See BARRY McGUIRE AND BARRY KANE.

BARRY AND THE TAMERLANES

Also see BARRY DeVORZON.

Number	Title (A Side/B Side)	Yr	VG	VG+	NM
45s					
VALIANT					
703	I Wonder What She's Doing Tonight/Roberta	1965	3.00	6.00	12.00
6034	I Wonder What She's Doing Tonight/Don't Go	1963	5.00	10.00	20.00
6040	Roberta/Butterfly	1964	3.75	7.50	15.00
6046	Lucky Guy/I Don't Want to Be Your Clown	1964	3.75	7.50	15.00
6050	A Date with Judy/Pretty Things	1964	3.75	7.50	15.00
6059	Gee/Don't Cry Cindy	1964	3.75	7.50	15.00
Albums					
VALIANT					
LP-406 [M]	I Wonder What She's Doing Tonight	1963	37.50	75.00	150.00
LPS-406 [S]	I Wonder What She's Doing Tonight	1963	75.00	150.00	300.00

BARTEL, LOU

Number	Title (A Side/B Side)	Yr	VG	VG+	NM
45s					
ABC-PARAMOUNT					
9801	Natural, Natural Baby/My Idea of Heaven	1957	6.25	12.50	25.00
9877	Blue Moon/I'm Gonna Kiss My Baby Goodnight	1957	6.25	12.50	25.00
APOLLO					
473	I Pray/(Zoom) Give Me Your Tonight	1954	37.50	75.00	150.00

BARTHOLOMEW, DAVE

Number	Title (A Side/B Side)	Yr	VG	VG+	NM
45s					
DECCA					
48216	Tra La La/Teejim	1951	30.00	60.00	120.00
IMPERIAL					
5210	Who Drank the Beer While I Was in the Rear/The Rest of My Life	1952	30.00	60.00	120.00
—Dave Bartholomew records on Imperial before 5210 are unconfirmed on 45 rpm					
5249	No More Black Nights/Air Tight	1953	30.00	60.00	120.00
5273	Texas Hop/When the Saints Go Marchin' In Boogie	1954	37.50	75.00	150.00
5308	Cat Music/Jump Children	1954	30.00	60.00	120.00
5322	Another Mule/I Want to Be with Her	1955	12.50	25.00	50.00
5350	Every Night, Every Day/Four Winds	1955	12.50	25.00	50.00
5373	Shrimp and Gumbo/An Old Cowhand from a Blues Band	1956	10.00	20.00	40.00
5390	Would You/Turn Your Lamp Down Low	1956	10.00	20.00	40.00
5408	Lovin' You/Three Time Loser	1956	7.50	15.00	30.00
5438	The Monkey/The Shuffling	1957	6.25	12.50	25.00
5460	How Could You/Barrel House	1957	6.25	12.50	25.00
5481	Hard Times (The Slop)/Cinderella	1957	6.25	12.50	25.00
5560	Button Blues/Short Subjects	1959	5.00	10.00	20.00
5702	I Cried/Somebody New	1960	5.00	10.00	20.00
5714	People Are Talking/Yeah, Yeah	1961	5.00	10.00	20.00
5803	I'm Walkin'/Going to the River	1962	3.75	7.50	15.00
5835	A Sunday Kind of Love/Honky Tonk Trumpet	1962	3.75	7.50	15.00
KING					
4482	Sweet Home Blues/Twins	1951	37.50	75.00	150.00
4508	In the Alley/I'll Never Be the Same	1952	50.00	100.00	200.00
4523	Lawdy, Lawdy, Lawd (Part 1)/Lawdy, Lawdy, Lawd (Part 2)	1952	37.50	75.00	150.00
4544	My Ding-a-Ling/Bad Habit	1952	62.50	125.00	250.00
4559	The Golden Rule/Mother Knows Best	1952	25.00	50.00	100.00
4585	High Flying Woman/Stormy Weather	1953	25.00	50.00	100.00
Albums					
IMPERIAL					
LP-9162 [M]	Fats Domino Presents Dave Bartholomew	1961	25.00	50.00	100.00
LP-9217 [M]	New Orleans House Party	1963	25.00	50.00	100.00
LP-12076 [S]	Fats Domino Presents Dave Bartholomew	1961	37.50	75.00	150.00
LP-12217 [S]	New Orleans House Party	1963	37.50	75.00	150.00

BARTON, ERNIE

Number	Title (A Side/B Side)	Yr	VG	VG+	NM
45s					
PHILLIPS INTERNATIONAL					
3528	Stairway of Love/Raining the Blues	1958	5.00	10.00	20.00
3541	Open the Door Richard/Shut Your Mouth	1959	37.50	75.00	150.00

BASH, OTTO

Number	Title (A Side/B Side)	Yr	VG	VG+	NM
45s					
HDS					
2008	My Babe/Straighten Up and Fly Right	1956	5.00	10.00	20.00
RCA VICTOR					
47-6426	Later Alligator/Lookout Mountain	1956	6.25	12.50	25.00
47-6585	The Elvis Blues/Later	1956	12.50	25.00	50.00

BASIC BLACK AND PEARL

Number	Title (A Side/B Side)	Yr	VG	VG+	NM
45s					
POLYDOR					
15111	There'll Come a Time, There'll Come a Day/He's a Rebel	1975	—	2.50	5.00

BASIE, COUNT

Also see TONY BENNETT; TERESA BREWER; ELLA FITZGERALD; ARTHUR PRYSOCK; FRANK SINATRA; SARAH VAUGHAN; JACKIE WILSON.

Number	Title (A Side/B Side)	Yr	VG	VG+	NM
45s					
BRUNSWICK					
55344	Bright Lights, Big City/Mercy, Mercy, Mercy	1967	—	3.00	6.00
55352	Green Onions/Hang On Sloopy	1967	—	3.00	6.00
CAPITOL					
S7-57888	Jingle Bells/Let It Snow! Let It Snow! Let It Snow!	1992	—	2.00	4.00
—B-side by Lena Horne					
CLEF					
89070	Blee Blop Blues/Small Hotel	1953	3.75	7.50	15.00
89086	Tippin' on the QT/Bread	1953	3.75	7.50	15.00
89101	Count's Organ Blues/Basie Beat	1954	3.75	7.50	15.00
89102	K.C. Organ Blues/Stan Shorthair	1954	3.75	7.50	15.00
89112	Basie Goes Wess/Softly, With Feeling	1954	3.75	7.50	15.00
89120	Cherry Point/Right On	1954	3.75	7.50	15.00
89126	You for Me/Slow But Sure	1955	3.75	7.50	15.00
89131	Two for the Blues/Soft Drink	1955	3.75	7.50	15.00
89137	Stereophonie/I Feel Like a New Man	1955	3.75	7.50	15.00
89147	Ska-Di-De-Dee-Oo/16 Men Swinging	1955	3.75	7.50	15.00
89149	Every Day/The Comeback	1955	3.75	7.50	15.00
89151	The Comeback (Part 1)/The Comeback (Part 2)	1955	3.75	7.50	15.00
89167	Teach Me Tonight/My Baby Upsets Me	1956	3.00	6.00	12.00
89169	Big Red/Smack Dab in the Middle	1956	3.00	6.00	12.00
89171	Amazing Love/Magic	1956	3.00	6.00	12.00
89172	April in Paris/Party Blues	1956	3.00	6.00	12.00
COLUMBIA					
1-709	Bluebeard Blues/Golden Bullet	1950	7.50	15.00	30.00
—Microgroove 7-inch, 33 1/3 rpm single					
6-709	Bluebeard Blues/Golden Bullet	1950	5.00	10.00	20.00
1-930 (?)	Danny Boy/Neal's Deal	1950	7.50	15.00	30.00
—Microgroove 7-inch, 33 1/3 rpm single					
6-930 (?)	Danny Boy/Neal's Deal	1950	5.00	10.00	20.00
39406	Little Pony/Beaver Junction	1951	5.00	10.00	20.00
DOT					
17201	Hay Burner/That Warm Feeling	1969	—	2.50	5.00
MERCURY					
89014	Paradise Squat/Hot Nail Boogie	1953	5.00	10.00	20.00
89028	Goin' to Chicago/Sent for You Yesterday and Here You Come Today	1953	5.00	10.00	20.00
89033	I Want a Little Girl/Oh, Lady Be Good	1953	5.00	10.00	20.00
89061	Song of the Islands/Royal Garden Blues	1953	5.00	10.00	20.00
OKEH					
6895	Jump the Blues Away/Wiggle Woogie	1952	5.00	10.00	20.00
RCA VICTOR					
47-2915	Cheek to Cheek/Bran' New Dolly	1949	5.00	10.00	20.00
47-2990	Did You See Jackie Robinson Hit That Ball?/Shoutin' Blues	1949	10.00	20.00	40.00
47-3032	She's a Wine-O/Slider	1949	5.00	10.00	20.00
47-3065	Rocky Mountain Blues/Walking Slow Behind You	1949	5.00	10.00	20.00
47-3107	St. Louis Baby/Normania	1949	5.00	10.00	20.00
REPRISE					
0240	I Left My Heart in San Francisco/Walk Don't Run	1963	2.50	5.00	10.00
20170	I Can't Stop Loving You/Nice & Easy	1963	2.50	5.00	10.00
ROULETTE					
4040	Lil' Darlin'/The Kid from Red Bank	1957	2.50	5.00	10.00
4088	Going to Chicago Blues/Swingin' the Blues	1958	2.50	5.00	10.00
4109	M Squad Theme/Late Late Show	1958	2.50	5.00	10.00
4124	Jumpin' at the Woodside/Rusty Dusty Blues	1958	2.50	5.00	10.00
4166	Rat Race/The Big Walk	1959	2.50	5.00	10.00
4226	How Am I to Know/It Had to Be You	1960	2.50	5.00	10.00
4286	Ol' Man River Part 1/Ol' Man River Part 2	1960	2.50	5.00	10.00
4403	The Basie Twist/Trot	1962	3.00	6.00	12.00
4409	Song of the Islands/Summertime	1962	2.50	5.00	10.00
4465	Basie's Jingle Bells/Lullabye of Birdland	1962	2.50	5.00	10.00
UNITED ARTISTS					
50002	Double-O-Seven/Kingston Calypso	1966	2.00	4.00	8.00
VERVE					
10318	All of Me/On the Road to Mandalay	1964	2.00	4.00	8.00
10329	Li'l Ol' Groove Maker/Pleasingly Plump	1964	2.00	4.00	8.00
10350	My Kind of Town/Watermelon Man	1965	2.00	4.00	8.00
89177	Only Forever/Move	1957	3.00	6.00	12.00
Albums					
ABC					
570 [M]	Basie's Swingin' — Voices Singin'	1966	5.00	10.00	20.00
S-570 [S]	Basie's Swingin' — Voices Singin'	1966	6.25	12.50	25.00
4001	16 Great Performances	1974	3.00	6.00	12.00
ABC IMPULSE!					
AS-15 [S]	Count Basie and the Kansas City Seven	1968	3.00	6.00	12.00
IA-9351 [(2)]	Retrospective Sessions	1978	3.00	6.00	12.00
ACCORD					
SN-7183	Command Performance	1981	2.50	5.00	10.00
AMERICAN RECORDING SOCIETY					
G-401 [M]	Count Basie	1956	10.00	20.00	40.00
G-402 [M]	The Band That Swings the Blues	1956	10.00	20.00	40.00
G-422 [M]	Basie's Best	1957	10.00	20.00	40.00
G-435 [M]	Mainstream Jazz Swing	1957	10.00	20.00	40.00
ARCHIVE OF FOLK AND JAZZ					
318	Savoy Ballroom 1937	197?	2.50	5.00	10.00
BASF					
25111 [(2)]	Basic Basie	1973	3.75	7.50	15.00
BRIGHT ORANGE					
XBO-702	Count Basie Featuring B.B. King	196?	5.00	10.00	20.00
BRUNSWICK					
BL 54012 [M]	Count Basie	1957	10.00	20.00	40.00

Number	Title (A Side/B Side)	Yr	VG	VG+	NM
BL 754127	Basie's in the Bag	196?	3.75	7.50	15.00
BULLDOG					
BDL-2020	20 Golden Pieces of Count Basie	198?	2.50	5.00	10.00
CLEF					
MCG-120 [10]	Count Basie and His Orchestra Collates	1953	50.00	100.00	200.00
MCG-146 [10]	Count Basie Sextet	1954	50.00	100.00	200.00
MGC-148 [10]	Count Basie Big Band	1954	50.00	100.00	200.00
MGC-626 [M]	Count Basie Dance Session #1	1954	25.00	50.00	100.00
MGC-633 [M]	Basie Jazz	1954	25.00	50.00	100.00
MGC-647 [M]	Count Basie Jazz Session #2	1955	25.00	50.00	100.00
MGC-666 [M]	Basie	1955	25.00	50.00	100.00
MGC-685 [M]	The Count	1956	20.00	40.00	80.00
MGC-706 [M]	The Swinging Count	1956	15.00	30.00	60.00
MGC-722 [M]	The Band of Distinction	1956	15.00	30.00	60.00
MGC-723 [M]	Basie Roars Again	1956	15.00	30.00	60.00
MGC-724 [M]	The King of Swing	1956	15.00	30.00	60.00
MGC-729 [M]	Basie Rides Again!	1956	15.00	30.00	60.00
MGC-749 [M]	Basie in Europe	1956	—	—	—
—Canceled; released as Verve 8199					
COLISEUM					
51003	The Happiest Millionaire	1968	3.75	7.50	15.00
COLUMBIA					
CL 754 [M]	Classics	1955	10.00	20.00	40.00
CL 901 [M]	Blues By Basie	1956	10.00	20.00	40.00
CL 997 [M]	One O'Clock Jump	1956	10.00	20.00	40.00
CL 2560 [10]	Basie Bash	1956	20.00	40.00	80.00
CL 6079 [10]	Dance Parade	1949	25.00	50.00	100.00
G 31224 [(2)]	Suoer Chief	1972	3.75	7.50	15.00
COLUMBIA JAZZ MASTERPIECES					
CJ 40608	The Essential Count Basie, Volume 1	1987	2.50	5.00	10.00
CJ 40835	The Essential Count Basie, Volume 2	1987	2.50	5.00	10.00
CJ 44150	The Essential Count Basie, Volume 3	1988	2.50	5.00	10.00
COLUMBIA JAZZ ODYSSEY					
PC 36824	Blues by Basie	1981	2.00	4.00	8.00
COLUMBIA SPECIAL PRODUCTS					
P 14355	The Count	198?	2.00	4.00	8.00
COMMAND					
33-905 [M]	Broadway Basie's...Way	1966	3.00	6.00	12.00
SD 905 [S]	Broadway Basie's...Way	1966	3.75	7.50	15.00
33-912 [M]	Hollywood Basie's Way	1967	3.75	7.50	15.00
SD 912 [S]	Hollywood Basie's Way	1967	3.00	6.00	12.00
CQ-40004 [Q]	Broadway Basie's...Way	1972	5.00	10.00	20.00
DAYBREAK					
2005	Have a Nice Day	1971	3.00	6.00	12.00
DECCA					
DXB 170 [(2) M]	The Best of Count Basie	196?	6.25	12.50	25.00
DL 5111 [10]	Count Basie at the Piano	1950	25.00	50.00	100.00
DXSB 7170 [(2) R]	The Best of Count Basie	196?	3.75	7.50	15.00
DL 8049 [M]	Count Basie and His Orchestra	1954	12.50	25.00	50.00
DL 78049 [R]	Count Basie and His Orchestra	196?	3.00	6.00	12.00
DOCTOR JAZZ					
FW 39520	Afrique	1985	2.00	4.00	8.00
DOT					
DLP-25902	Straight Ahead	1969	3.75	7.50	15.00
DLP-25938	Standing Ovation	1969	3.75	7.50	15.00
EMARCY					
MG-26023 [10]	Jazz Royalty	1954	17.50	35.00	70.00
EPIC					
LG 1021 [10]	The Old Count and the New Count — Basie	1954	17.50	35.00	70.00
LN 1117 [10]	Rock the Blues	1955	17.50	35.00	70.00
LN 3107 [M]	Lester Leaps In	1955	12.50	25.00	50.00
—With Lester Young					
LN 3168 [M]	Let's Go to Prez	1955	12.50	25.00	50.00
—With Lester Young					
LN 3169 [M]	Basie's Back in Town	1955	12.50	25.00	50.00
FANTASY					
OJC-379	Basie Big Band Montreux '77	1989	2.50	5.00	10.00
—Reissue of Pablo Live 2308 209					
OJC-449	Kansas City 6	1990	3.00	6.00	12.00
—Reissue of Pablo 2310 871					
OJC-600	Kansas City 3/For the Second Time	1991	3.00	6.00	12.00
—Reissue of Pablo 2310 878					
FLYING DUTCHMAN					
FD 10138	Afrique	1972	3.00	6.00	12.00
FORUM					
F-9032 [M]	Kansas City Suite	196?	3.00	6.00	12.00
SF-9032 [S]	Kansas City Suite	196?	3.75	7.50	15.00
—Reissue of Roulette 52056					
F-9060 [M]	One More Time	196?	3.00	6.00	12.00
SF-9060 [S]	One More Time	196?	3.75	7.50	15.00
—Reissue of Roulette 52024					
F-9063 [M]	Not Now — I'll Tell You When	196?	3.00	6.00	12.00
SF-9063 [S]	Not Now — I'll Tell You When	196?	3.75	7.50	15.00
—Reissue of Roulette 52044					
GROOVE MERCHANT					
2001	Evergreens	1972	3.00	6.00	12.00
HAPPY TIGER					
1007	Basie on the Beatles	196?	6.25	12.50	25.00
HARMONY					
HL 7229 [M]	Basie's Best	1960	3.75	7.50	15.00
HS 11371	Just in Time	1970	3.00	6.00	12.00
IMPULSE!					
A-15 [M]	Count Basie and the Kansas City Seven	1962	7.50	15.00	30.00
AS-15 [S]	Count Basie and the Kansas City Seven	1962	10.00	20.00	40.00
INTERMEDIA					
QS-5028	The Deacon	198?	2.50	5.00	10.00
QS-5039	The Classic Count	198?	2.50	5.00	10.00
JAZZ ARCHIVES					
JA-16	The Count at the Chatterbox, 1937	198?	2.50	5.00	10.00
JA-41	At the Famous Door, 1938-1939	198?	2.50	5.00	10.00
JAZZ MAN					
5006	Ain't It the Truth	198?	2.50	5.00	10.00

Number	Title (A Side/B Side)	Yr	VG	VG+	NM
JAZZ PANORAMA					
1803 [10]	Count Basie and Lester Young	1951	25.00	50.00	100.00
MCA					
718	16 Greatest Performances	198?	2.00	4.00	8.00
4050 [(2)]	The Best of Count Basie	197?	3.00	6.00	12.00
4108 [(2)]	Good Morning Blues	197?	3.00	6.00	12.00
4130 [(2)]	Retrospective Sessions	198?	2.50	5.00	10.00
4163 [(2)]	Showtime	198?	2.50	5.00	10.00
29003	Count Basie and the Kansas City Seven	198?	2.00	4.00	8.00
29004	Straight Ahead	198?	2.00	4.00	8.00
29005	Standing Ovation	198?	2.00	4.00	8.00
42324	One O'Clock Jump	1990	3.00	6.00	12.00
MCA/IMPULSE!					
5656	Count Basie and the Kansas City Seven	1986	2.00	4.00	8.00
MERCURY					
MGC-120 [10]	Count Basie and His Orchestra Collates	1952	55.00	110.00	220.00
MG-25105 [10]	Count Basie and His Kansas City Seven	1952	25.00	50.00	100.00
METRO					
M-516 [M]	Count Basie	1965	3.75	7.50	15.00
MS-516 [S]	Count Basie	1965	3.00	6.00	12.00
MGM					
GAS-126	Count Basie (Golden Archive Series)	1970	3.75	7.50	15.00
MOBILE FIDELITY					
1-129	Basie Plays Hefti	1985	20.00	40.00	80.00
—Audiophile vinyl					
1-237	April in Paris	1995	10.00	20.00	40.00
—Audiophile vinyl					
MOSAIC					
MR12-135 [(12)]	The Complete Roulette Live Recordings of Count Basie and His Orchestra	199?	50.00	100.00	200.00
M15Q-149 [(15)]	The Complete Roulette Studio Recordings of Count Basie and His Orchestra	199?	50.00	100.00	200.00
PABLO					
2310709	The Bosses	1974	3.00	6.00	12.00
2310712	Trio	1974	3.00	6.00	12.00
2310718	Basie Jam	1975	3.00	6.00	12.00
2310745	Basie and Zoot	1976	3.00	6.00	12.00
2310750	Basie Jam/Montreux '75	1976	3.00	6.00	12.00
2310756	Basie Big Band	1975	3.00	6.00	12.00
2310767	I Told You So	1976	3.00	6.00	12.00
2310786	Basie Jam #2	1977	3.00	6.00	12.00
2310797	Prime Time	1977	3.00	6.00	12.00
2310840	Basie Jam #3	1979	2.50	5.00	10.00
2310852	The Best of Basie	1980	2.50	5.00	10.00
2310859	Kansas City Shout	1980	3.00	6.00	12.00
—With Joe Turner and Eddie "Cleanhead" Vinson					
2310871	Kansas City 6	198?	2.50	5.00	10.00
2310874	Farmers Market Barbecue	1982	2.50	5.00	10.00
2310891	Me & You	1983	2.50	5.00	10.00
2310901	88 Basie Street	1987	2.50	5.00	10.00
2310919	Mostly Blues...And Some Others	1987	2.50	5.00	10.00
2310920	Fancy Pants	1987	2.50	5.00	10.00
2310924	Count Basie Get Together	1987	2.50	5.00	10.00
2310925	Basie and His Friends	1988	2.50	5.00	10.00
2405408	The Best of the Count Basie Band	198?	2.50	5.00	10.00
PABLO LIVE					
2308207	Basie Big Band Montreux '77	1977	3.00	6.00	12.00
2308209	Basie Jam/Montreux '77	1977	3.00	6.00	12.00
2308246	Live in Japan, 1978	198?	2.50	5.00	10.00
PABLO TODAY					
2312112	On the Road	1980	2.50	5.00	10.00
2312126	Kansas City 5	198?	2.50	5.00	10.00
2312131	Warm Breeze	198?	2.50	5.00	10.00
PAIR					
PDL2-1045 [(2)]	Basic Basie	1986	3.00	6.00	12.00
PAUSA					
7105	High Voltage	198?	2.50	5.00	10.00
PICKWICK					
PC-3028 [M]	His Hits of the 60's	196?	3.75	7.50	15.00
SPC-3028 [S]	His Hits of the 60's	196?	3.00	6.00	12.00
SPC-3500	Everything's Coming Up Roses	197?	2.50	5.00	10.00
PRESTIGE					
24109 [(2)]	Reunions	197?	3.00	6.00	12.00
QUINTESSENCE					
25151	Everything's Coming Up Roses	197?	2.50	5.00	10.00
RCA CAMDEN					
CAL-395 [M]	The Count	1958	6.25	12.50	25.00
CAL-497 [M]	Basie's Basement	1959	6.25	12.50	25.00
CAL-514 [M]	Count Basie in Kansas City	1959	6.25	12.50	25.00
RCA VICTOR					
LPV-514 [M]	Count Basie in Kansas City	196?	3.75	7.50	15.00
LPM-1112 [M]	Count Basie	1955	12.50	25.00	50.00
AFM1-5180	Kansas City Style	1985	2.50	5.00	10.00
REPRISE					
R-6070 [M]	This Time by Basie! Hits of the 50's and 60's	1963	5.00	10.00	20.00
R9-6070 [S]	This Time by Basie! Hits of the 50's and 60's	1963	6.25	12.50	25.00
R-6153 [M]	Pop Goes the Basie	1965	3.75	7.50	15.00
RS-6153 [S]	Pop Goes the Basie	1965	5.00	10.00	20.00
ROULETTE					
RB-1 [(2) M]	The Count Basie Story	1960	10.00	20.00	40.00
SRB-1 [(2) S]	The Count Basie Story	1960	12.50	25.00	50.00
RE-102 [(2)]	Echoes of an Era (The Count Basie Years)	1971	3.75	7.50	15.00
RE-107 [(2)]	Echoes of an Era (The Vocal Years)	1971	3.75	7.50	15.00
RE-118 [(2)]	The Best of Count Basie	1971	3.75	7.50	15.00
RE-124 [(2)]	Kansas City Suite/Easin' It	1973	3.75	7.50	15.00
SR 42009	Fantail	1968	3.75	7.50	15.00
SR 42015	The Kid from Red Bank	1968	3.75	7.50	15.00
R 52003 [M]	Basie	1958	7.50	15.00	30.00
SR 52003 [S]	Basie	1958	7.50	15.00	30.00
—Black vinyl					
SR 52003 [S]	Basie	1958	25.00	50.00	100.00
—Red vinyl					
R 52011 [M]	Basie Plays Hefti	1958	7.50	15.00	30.00

Number	Title (A Side/B Side)	Yr	VG	VG+	NM
SR 52011 [S]	Basie Plays Hefti	1958	7.50	15.00	30.00
R 52024 [M]	One More Time	1959	7.50	15.00	30.00
SR 52024 [S]	One More Time	1959	7.50	15.00	30.00
R 52028 [M]	Breakfast, Dance & Barbeque	1959	7.50	15.00	30.00
SR 52028 [S]	Breakfast, Dance & Barbeque	1959	7.50	15.00	30.00
R 52032 [M]	Chairman of the Board	1959	7.50	15.00	30.00
SR 52032 [S]	Chairman of the Board	1959	7.50	15.00	30.00
R 52036 [M]	Dance Along with Basie	1959	7.50	15.00	30.00
SR 52036 [S]	Dance Along with Basie	1959	7.50	15.00	30.00
R 52044 [M]	Not Now — I'll Tell You When	1960	6.25	12.50	25.00
SR 52044 [S]	Not Now — I'll Tell You When	1960	7.50	15.00	30.00
R 52051 [M]	String Along with Basie	1960	6.25	12.50	25.00
SR 52051 [S]	String Along with Basie	1960	7.50	15.00	30.00
R 52056 [M]	Benny Carter's Kansas City Suite	1960	6.25	12.50	25.00
SR 52056 [S]	Benny Carter's Kansas City Suite	1960	7.50	15.00	30.00
R 52065 [M]	Basie at Birdland	1961	6.25	12.50	25.00
SR 52065 [S]	Basie at Birdland	1961	7.50	15.00	30.00
R 52081 [M]	The Best of Basie	1962	3.75	7.50	15.00
SR 52081 [S]	The Best of Basie	1962	5.00	10.00	20.00
R 52086 [M]	The Legend	1962	5.00	10.00	20.00
SR 52086 [S]	The Legend	1962	6.25	12.50	25.00
R 52089 [M]	The Best of Basie, Volume 2	1962	3.75	7.50	15.00
SR 52089 [S]	The Best of Basie, Volume 2	1962	5.00	10.00	20.00
R 52099 [M]	Count Basie in Sweden	1963	5.00	10.00	20.00
SR 52099 [S]	Count Basie in Sweden	1963	6.25	12.50	25.00
R 52106 [M]	Easin' It	1963	5.00	10.00	20.00
SR 52106 [S]	Easin' It	1963	6.25	12.50	25.00
R 52111/3 [(2) M]	The World of Count Basie	1964	10.00	20.00	40.00
SR 52111/3 [(2) S]	The World of Count Basie	1964	12.50	25.00	50.00
R 52113 [M]	Back with Basie	1964	5.00	10.00	20.00
SR 52113 [S]	Back with Basie	1964	6.25	12.50	25.00
SOLID STATE					
18032	Basie Meets Bond	1968	3.75	7.50	15.00
—Reissue of United Artists LP					
UNITED ARTISTS					
UAL-3480 [M]	Basie Meets Bond	1966	6.25	12.50	25.00
UAS-6480 [S]	Basie Meets Bond	1966	7.50	15.00	30.00
UPFRONT					
UPF-142	Count Basie and His Orchestra	1969	3.00	6.00	12.00
VEE JAY					
VJS-3054	I Got Rhythm	198?	3.00	6.00	12.00
VERVE					
VSP-12 [M]	Inside Basie, Outside	1966	3.75	7.50	15.00
VSPS-12 [S]	Inside Basie, Outside	1966	5.00	10.00	20.00
VE-2-2517 [(2)]	16 Men Swinging	197?	3.00	6.00	12.00
VE-2-2542 [(2)]	Paradise Squat	197?	3.00	6.00	12.00
UMV-1-2619	Count Basie at Newport	198?	2.50	5.00	10.00
UMV-1-2641	April in Paris	198?	2.50	5.00	10.00
MGVS-6024 [S]	Count Basie at Newport	1960	12.50	25.00	50.00
MGV-8012 [M]	April in Paris	1957	12.50	25.00	50.00
V-8012 [M]	April in Paris	1961	5.00	10.00	20.00
MGV-8018 [M]	Basie Roars Again	1957	12.50	25.00	50.00
—Reissue of Clef 723					
V-8018 [M]	Basie Roars Again	1961	5.00	10.00	20.00
MGV-8070 [M]	The Count	1957	12.50	25.00	50.00
—Reissue of Clef 120					
V-8070 [M]	The Count	1961	5.00	10.00	20.00
MGV-8090 [M]	The Swinging Count!	1957	12.50	25.00	50.00
—Reissue of Clef 706					
V-8090 [M]	The Swinging Count!	1961	5.00	10.00	20.00
MGV-8103 [M]	The Band of Distinction	1957	12.50	25.00	50.00
—Reissue of Clef 722					
V-8103 [M]	The Band of Distinction	1961	5.00	10.00	20.00
MGV-8104 [M]	The King of Swing	1957	12.50	25.00	50.00
—Reissue of Clef 724					
V-8104 [M]	The King of Swing	1961	5.00	10.00	20.00
MGV-8108 [M]	Basie Rides Again!	1957	12.50	25.00	50.00
—Reissue of Clef 729					
V-8108 [M]	Basie Rides Again!	1961	5.00	10.00	20.00
MGV-8199 [M]	Basie in London	1957	12.50	25.00	50.00
V-8199 [M]	Basie in London	1961	5.00	10.00	20.00
MGV-8243 [M]	Count Basie at Newport	1958	12.50	25.00	50.00
V-8243 [M]	Count Basie at Newport	1961	5.00	10.00	20.00
V6-8243 [S]	Count Basie at Newport	1961	5.00	10.00	20.00
MGV-8291 [M]	Hall of Fame	1958	12.50	25.00	50.00
V-8291 [M]	Hall of Fame	1961	5.00	10.00	20.00
V-8407 [M]	The Essential Count Basie	1961	3.75	7.50	15.00
V6-8407 [S]	The Essential Count Basie	1961	5.00	10.00	20.00
V-8511 [M]	On My Way and Shoutin' Again!	1963	3.75	7.50	15.00
V6-8511 [S]	On My Way and Shoutin' Again!	1963	5.00	10.00	20.00
V-8549 [M]	Li'l Ol' Groovemaker...Basie!	1963	3.75	7.50	15.00
V6-8549 [S]	Li'l Ol' Groovemaker...Basie!	1963	5.00	10.00	20.00
V-8563 [M]	More Hits of the 50's and 60's	1963	3.75	7.50	15.00
V6-8563 [S]	More Hits of the 50's and 60's	1963	5.00	10.00	20.00
V-8596 [M]	Verve's Choice — Best of Count Basie	1964	3.75	7.50	15.00
V6-8596 [S]	Verve's Choice — Best of Count Basie	1964	5.00	10.00	20.00
V-8597 [M]	Basie Land	1964	3.75	7.50	15.00
V6-8597 [S]	Basie Land	1964	5.00	10.00	20.00
V-8616 [M]	Basie Picks the Winners	1965	3.75	7.50	15.00
V6-8616 [S]	Basie Picks the Winners	1965	5.00	10.00	20.00
V-8659 [M]	Basie's Beatle Bag	1966	7.50	15.00	30.00
V6-8659 [S]	Basie's Beatle Bag	1966	10.00	20.00	40.00
V-8687 [M]	Basie's Beat	1967	5.00	10.00	20.00
V6-8687 [S]	Basie's Beat	1967	3.75	7.50	15.00
V6-8783	Basie	1969	3.75	7.50	15.00
V6-8831	The Newport Years	1973	3.00	6.00	12.00
821291-1	Basic Basie	198?	2.50	5.00	10.00
825194-1	High Voltage (Basic Basie Vol. 2)	198?	2.50	5.00	10.00

BASIE, COUNT, AND SAMMY DAVIS, JR.

Also see each artist's individual listings.

Number	Title (A Side/B Side)	Yr	VG	VG+	NM
45s					
VERVE					
10349	She's a Woman/You're Nobody 'Til Somebody Loves You	1965	—	3.00	6.00
Albums					
VERVE					
V-8605 [M]	Our Shining Hour	1965	3.75	7.50	15.00
V6-8605 [S]	Our Shining Hour	1965	5.00	10.00	20.00

BASIE, COUNT, AND BILLY ECKSTINE

Also see each artist's individual listings.

Number	Title (A Side/B Side)	Yr	VG	VG+	NM
Albums					
ROULETTE					
SR 42017	Count Basie and Billy Eckstine	1968	3.75	7.50	15.00
—Reissue					
R 52029 [M]	Basie/Eckstine, Incorporated	1959	6.25	12.50	25.00
SR 52029 [S]	Basie/Eckstine, Incorporated	1959	7.50	15.00	30.00

BASIE, COUNT, AND DUKE ELLINGTON

Also see each artist's individual listings.

Number	Title (A Side/B Side)	Yr	VG	VG+	NM
Albums					
ACCORD					
SN-7200	Heads of State	1982	2.50	5.00	10.00

BASIE, COUNT, AND MAYNARD FERGUSON

Number	Title (A Side/B Side)	Yr	VG	VG+	NM
Albums					
ROULETTE					
R 52117 [M]	Big Band Scene '65	1965	5.00	10.00	20.00
SR 52117 [S]	Big Band Scene '65	1965	6.25	12.50	25.00

BASIE, COUNT, AND DIZZY GILLESPIE

Number	Title (A Side/B Side)	Yr	VG	VG+	NM
Albums					
PABLO					
2310833	The Gifted Ones	1979	2.50	5.00	10.00
VERVE					
V-8560 [M]	The Count Basie Band and the Dizzy Gillespie Band at Newport	1963	5.00	10.00	20.00
V6-8560 [S]	The Count Basie Band and the Dizzy Gillespie Band at Newport	1963	6.25	12.50	25.00

BASIE, COUNT, AND THE MILLS BROTHERS

Also see each artist's individual listings.

Number	Title (A Side/B Side)	Yr	VG	VG+	NM
Albums					
DOT					
DLP-25838	The Board of Directors	1968	3.75	7.50	15.00

BASIE, COUNT, AND OSCAR PETERSON

Also see each artist's individual listings.

Number	Title (A Side/B Side)	Yr	VG	VG+	NM
Albums					
PABLO					
2310722	"Satch" and "Josh"	1975	3.00	6.00	12.00
2310802	Satch and Josh Again	1978	2.50	5.00	10.00
2310843	Night Rider	1979	2.50	5.00	10.00
2310896	The Timekeepers	198?	3.00	6.00	12.00
2310923	Yessir, That's My Baby	1987	2.50	5.00	10.00

BASIE, COUNT, AND JOE WILLIAMS

Number	Title (A Side/B Side)	Yr	VG	VG+	NM
45s					
CLEF					
89152	Alright, Okay, You Win/When the Sun Goes Down	1955	3.75	7.50	15.00
89162	April in Paris/Roll 'Em Pete	1956	3.75	7.50	15.00
Albums					
CLEF					
MGC-678 [M]	Count Basie Swings/Joe Williams Sings	1955	12.50	25.00	50.00
ROULETTE					
R 52021 [M]	Memories Ad Lib	1959	7.50	15.00	30.00
SR 52021 [S]	Memories Ad Lib	1959	10.00	20.00	40.00
R 52033 [M]	Everyday I Have the Blues	1959	7.50	15.00	30.00
SR 52033 [S]	Everyday I Have the Blues	1959	10.00	20.00	40.00
R 52054 [M]	Just the Blues	1960	7.50	15.00	30.00
SR 52054 [S]	Just the Blues	1960	10.00	20.00	40.00
R 52093 [M]	Back to Basie and Blues	1963	6.25	12.50	25.00
SR 52093 [S]	Back to Basie and Blues	1963	7.50	15.00	30.00
VANGUARD					
VRS-8508 [M]	A Night at Count Basie's	1955	12.50	25.00	50.00
VERVE					
MGV-2016 [M]	The Greatest! Count Basie Swings/Joe Williams Sings Standards	1956	12.50	25.00	50.00
UMV-1-2650	The Greatest	198?	2.50	5.00	10.00
MGVS-6006 [S]	The Greatest! Count Basie Swings/Joe Williams Sings Standards	1960	10.00	20.00	40.00
MGV-8063 [M]	Count Basie Swings/Joe Williams Sings	1957	10.00	20.00	40.00
—Reissue of Clef 678					
V-8488 [M]	Count Basie Swings/Joe Williams Sings	1962	6.25	12.50	25.00
—Reissue of 8063					
V6-8488 [R]	Count Basie Swings/Joe Williams Sings	1962	3.00	6.00	12.00

BASIE, COUNT; JOE WILLIAMS; LAMBERT, HENDRICKS AND ROSS

Number	Title (A Side/B Side)	Yr	VG	VG+	NM
Albums					
ROULETTE					
R 52018 [M]	Sing Along with Basie	1959	5.00	10.00	20.00
SR 52018 [S]	Sing Along with Basie	1959	6.25	12.50	25.00

BASIL, TONI

Number	Title (A Side/B Side)	Yr	VG	VG+	NM
12-Inch Singles					
CHRYSALIS					
AS 1615 [DJ]	Nobody/Rock On	1983	—	3.00	6.00
42708	Street Beat (Club Mix)/Street Beat (Dub)	1983	—	3.00	6.00
45s					
A&M					
791	Breakaway/I'm 28	1966	50.00	100.00	200.00
CHRYSALIS					
2638	Mickey/Thief on the Loose	1982	—	—	3.00
2638 [PS]	Mickey/Thief on the Loose	1982	—	—	3.00

Number	Title (A Side/B Side)	Yr	VG	VG+	NM
2665	Mickey (Spanish)/Thief on the Loose	1982	—	2.00	4.00
2665 [PS]	Mickey (Spanish)/Thief on the Loose	1982	—	2.00	4.00
03537	Shoppin' from A to Z/Time After Time	1983	—	—	3.00
03537 [PS]	Shoppin' from A to Z/Time After Time	1983	—	—	3.00
03539	Mickey/Thief on the Loose	1983	—	—	3.00
—Reissue					
42711	Street Beat/(B-side unknown)	1983	—	—	3.00
42753	Over My Head/Best Performance	1983	—	—	3.00
42753 [PS]	Over My Head/Best Performance	1983	—	—	3.00
RAZOR & TIE					
93018-07507	Mickey (Radio Remix)/Mickey ("Killa Klub" Edit)	1999	—	—	3.00
Albums					
CHRYSALIS					
CHR 1410	Word of Mouth	1982	3.00	6.00	12.00
FV 41410	Word of Mouth	1983	2.50	5.00	10.00
—Reissue					
PV 41410	Word of Mouth	1986	2.00	4.00	8.00
—Reissue with new prefix					
FV 41449	Toni Basil	1983	2.50	5.00	10.00
PV 41449	Toni Basil	1986	2.00	4.00	8.00
—Reissue with new prefix					

BASKERVILLE HOUNDS, THE

Number	Title (A Side/B Side)	Yr	VG	VG+	NM
45s					
AVCO EMBASSY					
4504	Hold Me/Here I Come, Miami	1968	2.50	5.00	10.00
BUDDAH					
17	Caroline/Last Night on the Back Porch	1967	2.50	5.00	10.00
DOT					
17004	Space Rock, Part 1/Space Rock, Part 2	1967	2.50	5.00	10.00
17017	Debbie/Jackie's Theme	1967	2.50	5.00	10.00
17037	Baby, Am I Losing/Never on Sunday	1967	2.50	5.00	10.00
TEMA					
125	Debbie/Jackie's Theme	1966	3.75	7.50	15.00
128	Space Rock, Part 1/Space Rock, Part 2	1966	3.75	7.50	15.00
131	Christmas Is Here (But Not For Long)/Make Me Your Man	1966	3.75	7.50	15.00
131 [PS]	Christmas Is Here (But Not For Long)/Make Me Your Man	1966	12.50	25.00	50.00
132	All You Had to Do Was Ask/Who Does She Love	1967	3.75	7.50	15.00
135	Hold Me/Here I Come, Miami	1967	3.75	7.50	15.00
Albums					
DOT					
DLP-3823 [M]	The Baskerville Hounds (Featuring Space Rock, Part 2)	1967	12.50	25.00	50.00
DLP-25823 [S]	The Baskerville Hounds (Featuring Space Rock, Part 2)	1967	20.00	40.00	80.00

BASS, FONTELLA

Number	Title (A Side/B Side)	Yr	VG	VG+	NM
45s					
BOBBIN					
134	I Don't Hurt Anymore/Brand New Love	1962	3.75	7.50	15.00
140	Honey Bee/Bad Boy	1963	3.75	7.50	15.00
CHECKER					
1097	Don't Mess Up a Good Thing/Baby, What You Want Me to Do	1965	2.50	5.00	10.00
—With Bobby McClure					
1111	You'll Miss Me (When I'm Gone)/Don't Jump	1965	2.50	5.00	10.00
—With Bobby McClure					
1120	Rescue Me/Soul of the Man	1965	5.00	10.00	20.00
—Red label with "Checker" vertically on left					
1120	Rescue Me/Soul of the Man	1965	3.75	7.50	15.00
—Light blue label with red and black checkers					
1131	Recovery/Leave It in the Hands of Love	1965	2.50	5.00	10.00
1137	I Surrender/I Can't Rest	1966	2.50	5.00	10.00
1147	Safe and Sound/You'll Never Ever Know	1966	2.50	5.00	10.00
1183	Lucky in Love/Sweet Lovin' Daddy	1967	2.50	5.00	10.00
EPIC					
50341	Soon as I Touched Him/You Can Betcha in Love	1977	—	2.00	4.00
PAULA					
360	Who You Gonna Blame/Hold On This Time	1972	—	2.50	5.00
367	I Need to Be Loved/I Want Everyone to Know	1972	—	2.50	5.00
376	It Sure Is Good/I'm Leaving the Choice to You	1973	—	2.50	5.00
389	Home Wrecker/Now That I've Found a Good Thing	1973	—	2.50	5.00
393	Talking About Freedom/It's Hard to Get Back In	1974	—	2.50	5.00
Albums					
CHECKER					
LP-2997 [M]	The "New" Look	1966	15.00	30.00	60.00
—Blue label with red and black checkers					
LP-2997 [M]	The "New" Look	1967	7.50	15.00	30.00
—Blue and white label					
LPS-2997 [S]	The "New" Look	1966	20.00	40.00	80.00
—Blue label with red and black checkers					
LPS-2997 [S]	The "New" Look	1967	10.00	20.00	40.00
—Blue and white label					
PAULA					
LPS-2203	Free	1971	3.00	6.00	12.00

BASS, FONTELLA, AND TINA TURNER

Number	Title (A Side/B Side)	Yr	VG	VG+	NM
45s					
VESUVIUS					
1002	This Would Make Me Happy/Poor Little Fool	1963	6.25	12.50	25.00

BASS, MARTHA AND FONTELLA

Number	Title (A Side/B Side)	Yr	VG	VG+	NM
Albums					
SOUL NOTE					
SN-1006	From the Root to the Source	197?	3.00	6.00	12.00

BASSEY, SHIRLEY

Number	Title (A Side/B Side)	Yr	VG	VG+	NM
45s					
COLUMBIA					
40848	Tonight My Heart Is Crying/If I Had a Needle and Thread	1957	3.75	7.50	15.00
EPIC					
9303	As I Love You/Kiss Me Honey, Honey Kiss Me	1959	3.00	6.00	12.00
MERCURY					
874412-7	No Tengo Nada (I Who Have Nothing)/Sin Ti (Without You)	1989	—	—	3.00
MGM					
12919	'S Wonderful/The Party's Over	1960	3.00	6.00	12.00
UNITED ARTISTS					
0146	Diamonds Are Forever/This Is My Love	1973	—	2.00	4.00
—Silver Spotlight Series issue					
XW211	Never, Never, Never/Day by Day	1973	—	2.00	4.00
XW318	This Is My Life/Make the World a Little Younger	1973	—	2.00	4.00
363	Reach for the Stars/You'll Never Know	1961	2.50	5.00	10.00
XW387	Davy/The Trouble with Hello	1974	—	2.00	4.00
404	I'll Get By/Climb Ev'ry Mountain	1962	2.50	5.00	10.00
421	Climb Ev'ry Mountain/Where Are You	1962	2.50	5.00	10.00
503	What Kind of Fool Am I/What Now My Love	1962	2.50	5.00	10.00
XW508	Goldfinger/How Can I Tell	1974	—	2.00	4.00
XW509	Never, Never, Never (Grande, Grande, Grande)/Something	1974	—	2.00	4.00
511	Above All Others/As Long As He Needs Me	1962	2.50	5.00	10.00
681	Theme from "The Victors"/How Can You Tell	1964	2.00	4.00	8.00
699	I Who Have Nothing/Imagination	1964	2.00	4.00	8.00
XW717	Send In the Clowns/Living	1975	—	2.00	4.00
790	Goldfinger/Strange How Love Can Be	1964	2.50	5.00	10.00
XW854	Everything That Touches You/If I Never Sing Another Song	1976	—	2.00	4.00
872	No Regrets/See-Saw Dreams	1965	2.00	4.00	8.00
XW923	What I Did for Love/Feelings	1976	—	2.00	4.00
956	It's Yourself/Secrets	1965	2.00	4.00	8.00
X1303	Copacabana/This Is My Life (La Vita)	1979	—	2.00	4.00
X1308	Moonraker-Main Title/Moonraker-End Title	1979	—	2.00	4.00
50031	Don't Take the Lovers from the World/Take Away	1966	—	3.00	6.00
50071	Give Me Your Love/Who Could Love Me	1966	—	3.00	6.00
50099	The Liquidator/Sunshine	1966	—	3.00	6.00
50105	I (Who Have Nothing)/Shirley	1966	—	3.00	6.00
50125	The Impossible Dream/They	1967	—	—	—
—Unreleased					
50129	The Impossible Dream/Do I Look Like a Fool	1967	—	3.00	6.00
50229	Big Spender/Dangerous Games	1967	—	3.00	6.00
50312	Funny Girl/This Is My Life (La Vita)	1968	—	—	—
—Unreleased					
50459	Funny Girl/This Is My Life (La Vita)	1968	—	2.50	5.00
50502	Medley: Goin' Out of My Head-You Go to My Head/I Must Know	1969	—	2.50	5.00
50544	Does Anybody Miss Me/We	1969	—	2.50	5.00
50606	Fa Fa Fa (Live for Today)/A Bus That Never Comes	1969	—	2.50	5.00
50682	Sea and Sand/What About Today	1970	—	2.00	4.00
50698	Something/What Are You Doing the Rest of Your Life	1970	—	2.00	4.00
50770	Breakfast in Bed/Pieces of Dreams	1971	—	2.00	4.00
50833	For All We Know/What's Done Is Done Is Done	1971	—	2.00	4.00
50845	Diamonds Are Forever/For the Love of Him	1971	—	2.00	4.00
50961	And I Love You So/Jezebel	1972	—	2.00	4.00
Albums					
EPIC					
LN 3834 [M]	The Bewitching Shirley Bassey	1962	5.00	10.00	20.00
LIBERTY					
LWB-111 [(2)]	Live at Carnegie Hall	198?	2.50	5.00	10.00
LWB-715 [(2)]	Greatest Hits	198?	2.50	5.00	10.00
LW-847	Yesterdays	198?	2.00	4.00	8.00
LM-1013	Something Else	198?	2.00	4.00	8.00
LN-10012	The Magic Is You	1980	2.00	4.00	8.00
LN-10104	The Best of Shirley Bassey	1980	2.00	4.00	8.00
LN-10180	I, Capricorn	198?	2.00	4.00	8.00
LN-10252	Greatest Hits	198?	2.00	4.00	8.00
LN-10262	Shirley Means Bassey	198?	2.00	4.00	8.00
MERCURY					
838033-1	La Mujer	1989	3.00	6.00	12.00
MGM					
E-3862 [M]	The Fabulous Shirley Bassey	1960	5.00	10.00	20.00
SE-3862 [S]	The Fabulous Shirley Bassey	1960	6.25	12.50	25.00
E-4301 [M]	Golden Sound	1965	3.00	6.00	12.00
SE-4301 [S]	Golden Sound	1965	3.75	7.50	15.00
PAIR					
PDL2-1057 [(2)]	Sassy Bassey	1986	3.00	6.00	12.00
PHILIPS					
PHM 200168 [M]	Spectacular Shirley Bassey	1965	3.00	6.00	12.00
PHS 600168 [S]	Spectacular Shirley Bassey	1965	3.75	7.50	15.00
UNITED ARTISTS					
UA-LA055-F	Never, Never, Never	1973	2.50	5.00	10.00
UA-LA111-H2 [(2)]	Live at Carnegie Hall	1973	3.75	7.50	15.00
UA-LA214-G	Nobody Does It Like Me	1974	2.50	5.00	10.00
UA-LA542-G	Good, Bad But Beautiful	1975	2.50	5.00	10.00
UA-LA715-H2 [(2)]	Greatest Hits	1976	3.75	7.50	15.00
UA-LA751-H	You Take My Heart Away	1977	2.50	5.00	10.00
UA-LA847-H	Yesterdays	1977	2.50	5.00	10.00
LM-1013	Something Else	1979	2.50	5.00	10.00
UAL 3169 [M]	Shirley Bassey	1962	3.75	7.50	15.00
UAL 3237 [M]	Shirley Bassey Sings the Hits from "Oliver"	1962	3.75	7.50	15.00
UAL 3419 [M]	Shirley Bassey Belts the Best	1965	3.00	6.00	12.00
UAL 3463 [M]	In Person	1965	3.00	6.00	12.00
UAL 3545 [M]	Shirley Means Bassey	1966	3.00	6.00	12.00
UAL 3565 [M]	And We Were Lovers	1967	3.00	6.00	12.00
UAS 5565	I, Capricorn	1971	2.50	5.00	10.00
UAS 5643	And I Love You So	1972	2.50	5.00	10.00
UAS 6169 [S]	Shirley Bassey	1962	5.00	10.00	20.00

Number	Title (A Side/B Side)	Yr	VG	VG+	NM
UAS 6237 [S]	Shirley Bassey Sings the Hits from "Oliver"	1962	5.00	10.00	20.00
UAS 6419 [S]	Shirley Bassey Belts the Best	1965	3.75	7.50	15.00
UAS 6463 [S]	In Person	1965	3.75	7.50	15.00
UAS 6545 [S]	Shirley Means Bassey	1966	3.75	7.50	15.00
UAS 6565 [S]	And We Were Lovers	1967	3.75	7.50	15.00
UAS 6675	This Is My Life	1969	3.00	6.00	12.00
UAS 6713	Does Anybody Miss Me?	1969	3.00	6.00	12.00
UAS 6765	Shirley Bassey Is Really "Something"	1970	2.50	5.00	10.00
UAS 6797	Something Else	1971	2.50	5.00	10.00

BASTILLES, THE

45s

PHILIPS

Number	Title (A Side/B Side)	Yr	VG	VG+	NM
40453	Tenderly/Vengeance	1967	5.00	10.00	20.00

BATDORF & RODNEY

45s

ARISTA

Number	Title (A Side/B Side)	Yr	VG	VG+	NM
0132	You Are a Song/Another Part of Me	1975	—	2.00	4.00
0159	Somewhere in the Night/Ain't It Like Home	1975	—	2.00	4.00

ASYLUM

Number	Title (A Side/B Side)	Yr	VG	VG+	NM
11011	All I Need/Between the Ages	1972	—	2.50	5.00
11012	Home Again/Between the Ages	1972	—	2.50	5.00

ATLANTIC

Number	Title (A Side/B Side)	Yr	VG	VG+	NM
2850	Oh My Surprise/Farm	1972	—	2.50	5.00
2863	Can You See Him/Never See His Face Again	1972	—	2.50	5.00

BATS, THE

45s

FLAME

Number	Title (A Side/B Side)	Yr	VG	VG+	NM
5155	Batmobile/Batusi	1966	10.00	20.00	40.00

HBR

Number	Title (A Side/B Side)	Yr	VG	VG+	NM
445	Big Bright Eyes/Nothing at All	1965	2.50	5.00	10.00

PARROT

Number	Title (A Side/B Side)	Yr	VG	VG+	NM
40013	Listen to My Heart/You Look Good Together	1967	2.50	5.00	10.00

BATTERED ORNAMENTS

Albums

HARVEST

Number	Title (A Side/B Side)	Yr	VG	VG+	NM
SKAO-422	Mantle-Piece	1970	10.00	20.00	40.00

BATTIN, SKIP

Mamber of later versions of THE BYRDS.

45s

AURORA

Number	Title (A Side/B Side)	Yr	VG	VG+	NM
159	The Dating Game Theme/Night Time Girl	1966	3.75	7.50	15.00

GROOVE

Number	Title (A Side/B Side)	Yr	VG	VG+	NM
58-0055	Searchin'/She Acts Like We Never Have Met	1965	10.00	20.00	40.00
58-0065	Ten Feet Tall/What's Mine Is Mine	1965	10.00	20.00	40.00

SIGNPOST

Number	Title (A Side/B Side)	Yr	VG	VG+	NM
70010 [DJ]	Ballad of Dick Clark (mono/stereo)	1973	—	3.00	6.00

—May be promo only

Albums

SIGNPOST

Number	Title (A Side/B Side)	Yr	VG	VG+	NM
SP 8408	Skip Battin	1972	3.00	6.00	12.00

BAUM, ALLEN

45s

RED ROBIN

Number	Title (A Side/B Side)	Yr	VG	VG+	NM
124	My Kinda Woman/Too Much Competition	1954	100.00	200.00	400.00

BAXTER

45s

PARAMOUNT

Number	Title (A Side/B Side)	Yr	VG	VG+	NM
0194	Give It All/197 Three	1973	2.00	4.00	8.00

Albums

PARAMOUNT

Number	Title (A Side/B Side)	Yr	VG	VG+	NM
PAS-6050	Baxter	1973	5.00	10.00	20.00

BAXTER, LES

45s

AMERICAN INT'L.

Number	Title (A Side/B Side)	Yr	VG	VG+	NM
143	Dunwich/Necronomicon	1970	—	2.50	5.00
145	Dock at Papeete/Bora Bora	1970	—	2.50	5.00

A/S

Number	Title (A Side/B Side)	Yr	VG	VG+	NM
4511	La La La/Girl on the Boulevard	1970	—	2.50	5.00
4515	Soolaimon/A Taste of Soul	1970	—	2.50	5.00

CAPITOL

Number	Title (A Side/B Side)	Yr	VG	VG+	NM
F1299	Somewhere, Somehow, Someday/Tamberina	1950	3.75	7.50	15.00
F1381	The Roving Kind/So Long	1951	3.75	7.50	15.00
F1390	Zing Zing Zoom Zoom/When You Return	1951	3.75	7.50	15.00
F1493	Because of You/Unless	1951	3.75	7.50	15.00
F1546	Roller Coaster/On Top of the Ferris Wheel	1951	3.75	7.50	15.00
F1584	Vanity/The World Is Mine	1951	3.75	7.50	15.00
F1596	How Many Times/Bacoa	1951	3.75	7.50	15.00
F1681	Because of You/Blue Tango	195?	3.00	6.00	12.00
F1731	Longing for You/Sarah Kelly from Plumb Nelly	1951	3.75	7.50	15.00
F1760	Somewhere, Somehow, Someday/Because of You	195?	3.00	6.00	12.00
F1785	Be Mine Tonight/California Moon	1951	3.75	7.50	15.00
F1818	When/If You've Forgotten Me	1951	3.75	7.50	15.00
F1839	I Remember You Love/I Only Have One Life to Live	1951	3.75	7.50	15.00
F1873	Jalousie/Shrimp Boats	1951	3.75	7.50	15.00
F1887	Somebody's Been Beatin' My Time/I Can't Help It	1951	3.75	7.50	15.00
F1966	Blue Tango/Please Mr. Sun	1952	3.00	6.00	12.00
F2005	Festival/Invitation	1952	3.00	6.00	12.00
F2018	Wondering/God's Little Candles	1952	3.00	6.00	12.00
F2053	Green Grow the Lilacs/A Day Away from You	1952	3.00	6.00	12.00
F2102	I'm Yours/Kiss of Fire	1952	3.00	6.00	12.00
F2106	Lonely Wine/Lost in Meditation	1952	3.00	6.00	12.00
F2117	Tears/Please Say You Love Me	1952	3.00	6.00	12.00
F2143	Auf Wiedersehn Sweetheart/Padam Padam	1952	3.00	6.00	12.00
F2205	Till the End of the World/The Two-Faced Clock	1952	3.00	6.00	12.00
F2225	Quiet Village/Indian Summer	1952	3.00	6.00	12.00
F2274	Yours/Flute Salad	1952	3.00	6.00	12.00
F2275	Santa Claus' Party/Hang Your Wishes on the Tree	1952	3.00	6.00	12.00
F2328	Vieni, Vieni/As Long As You Care	1953	3.00	6.00	12.00
F2374	Aprin in Portugal/Suddenly	1953	3.00	6.00	12.00
F2375	The Lord Is My Shepherd/My Name Is God	1953	3.00	6.00	12.00
F2405	No More Goodbyes/Dance of the Flutes	1953	3.00	6.00	12.00
F2457	A Little Love/Ruby	1953	3.00	6.00	12.00
F2479	I Love Paris/Gigi	1953	3.00	6.00	12.00
F2568	Tropicana/Julie	1953	3.00	6.00	12.00
F2579	Cornflakes/Elaine	1953	3.00	6.00	12.00
F2632	Love Theme from The Robe/Manhattan	1953	3.00	6.00	12.00
F2705	Atlantis/The Flirtation Waltz	1954	3.00	6.00	12.00
F2748	If You Were Mine/Douchka	1954	3.00	6.00	12.00
F2799	Venezuela/Sea Song	1954	3.00	6.00	12.00
F2845	The High and the Mighty/More Love Than Your Love	1954	3.00	6.00	12.00
F2918	Romantic Rio/When You're in Love	1954	3.00	6.00	12.00
F2950	Midnight on the Cliffs/Dream Rhapsody	1954	3.00	6.00	12.00

—With Leonard Pennario

Number	Title (A Side/B Side)	Yr	VG	VG+	NM
F3002	Earth Angel)Will You Be Mine)/Happy Baby	1954	3.00	6.00	12.00
F3040	I Ain't Mad at You/Blue Mirage	1955	3.00	6.00	12.00
F3055	Unchained Melody/Medic	1955	3.00	6.00	12.00
F3120	Walke the Town and Tell the People/I'll Never Stop Loving You	1955	3.00	6.00	12.00
F3195	Toy Tiger/Shrike	1955	3.00	6.00	12.00
F3259	Song of the Bayou/Monika	1955	3.00	6.00	12.00
F3291	The Trouble with Harry/Havana	1955	3.00	6.00	12.00
F3336	The Poor People of Paris/Theme from "Helen of Troy"	1956	3.75	7.50	15.00
F3404	Tango of the Drums/Sinner Man	1956	2.50	5.00	10.00
F3478	Foreign Interlude/Melodia Loca	1956	2.50	5.00	10.00
F3526	Giant/There's Never Been Anyone Else But You	1956	2.50	5.00	10.00
F3573	The Left Arm of Buddah/What Happens in Buenos Aires	1956	2.50	5.00	10.00
F3599	Dream Rhapsody/Midnight on the Cliffs	1956	2.50	5.00	10.00
F3606	Stealin'/I'd Love to Fall Asleep	1956	2.50	5.00	10.00

—With Line Renaud

Number	Title (A Side/B Side)	Yr	VG	VG+	NM
F3624	Clown on the Eiffel Tower/Woman's Devotion	1957	2.50	5.00	10.00
F3653	Rain on My Window/I Dance When I Walk	1957	2.50	5.00	10.00
F3704	Blue Echo/Designing Woman	1957	2.50	5.00	10.00
F3728	The Lonely Whistler/Ruby Lips	1957	2.50	5.00	10.00
F3768	La Panse/Manhattan	1957	2.50	5.00	10.00
F3798	Search for Paradise/Ricordate Marcellino	1957	2.50	5.00	10.00
F3841	Invisible Boy/I Never Had a Dream Like This Before	1957	2.50	5.00	10.00
F3887	A Farewell to Arms/The Dance from Bonjour Tristesse	1958	2.50	5.00	10.00
F4011	Love Song from Houseboat/Lily of Laguna	1958	2.50	5.00	10.00
F4032	Dance, Everyone, Dance/A Chance Is All I Ask	1958	2.50	5.00	10.00
F4091	Come Prima/My Heart's in Portugal	1958	2.50	5.00	10.00
F4206	Tell Me, Margarita/Piccolissima Serenata	1959	2.50	5.00	10.00
F4249	Sabre Dance/Milord	1959	2.50	5.00	10.00
4322	Prelude & Ben-Hur Theme/Till Tomorrow	1959	2.50	5.00	10.00
4374	Boomada/Cochi Baba	1960	2.50	5.00	10.00
4489	Pepe/Dolce Par Niente	1960	2.50	5.00	10.00
4523	Angelina/Follow Me	1961	2.50	5.00	10.00

GNP CRESCENDO

Number	Title (A Side/B Side)	Yr	VG	VG+	NM
313	Linin' Track/Baion	1964	2.00	4.00	8.00
382	And We Were Lovers/Balan Samba	1967	2.00	4.00	8.00
399	Live for Life/Free Again	1967	2.00	4.00	8.00
425	Flame Tree/Girl from Uganda	1969	—	3.00	6.00

RCA VICTOR

Number	Title (A Side/B Side)	Yr	VG	VG+	NM
47-3305	Toujours Moi/Fame	1949	5.00	10.00	20.00
47-3306	Jet/Tzezane	1949	5.00	10.00	20.00
47-3307	L'Ardente Nuit/Possession	1949	5.00	10.00	20.00

—RCA sides by "Leslie Baxter and His Orchestra"

REPRISE

Number	Title (A Side/B Side)	Yr	VG	VG+	NM
0243	How Shall I Send Thee/Have Yourself a Merry Little Christmas	1963	5.00	10.00	20.00

—B-side by Frank Sinatra

Number	Title (A Side/B Side)	Yr	VG	VG+	NM
20120	Theme from "The Manchurian Candidate"/The Manchurian Beat	1962	2.50	5.00	10.00
20120 [PS]	Theme from "The Manchurian Candidate"/The Manchurian Beat	1962	12.50	25.00	50.00
20159	Theme from "How the West Was Won"/Theme from "Lawrence of Arabia"	1963	2.50	5.00	10.00
20165	Sail Away Ladies/Due Bonita Bandera	1963	2.50	5.00	10.00

7-Inch Extended Plays

CAPITOL

Number	Title (A Side/B Side)	Yr	VG	VG+	NM
EAP 1-147	April in Portugal/Blue Tango//Ruby/Quiet Village	195?	3.00	6.00	12.00
EAP 1-147 [PS]	(title unknown)	195?	3.00	6.00	12.00
EAP 1-474	Little White Lies/Miss You//Nevertheless/Mine	195?	3.00	6.00	12.00
EAP 1-474 [PS]	Thinking of You, Part 1	195?	3.00	6.00	12.00
EAP 2-474	Thinking of You/Speak Low//With My Eyes Wide Open I'm Dreaming/The Nearness of You	195?	3.00	6.00	12.00
EAP 2-474 [PS]	Thinking of You, Part 2	195?	3.00	6.00	12.00
EBF-474 [PS]	Thinking of You	195?	3.00	6.00	12.00

—Gatefold sleeve with some versions of 1-474 and 2-474

Number	Title (A Side/B Side)	Yr	VG	VG+	NM
EAP 1-599	Blue Mirage/Lonely Wine//Unchained Melody/If You've Forgotten Me	195?	3.00	6.00	12.00
EAP 1-599 [PS]	(title unknown)	195?	3.00	6.00	12.00
EAP 1-672	"Wake the Town and Tell the People/The Shrike/Toy Tiger/I'll Never Stop Loving You	1955	3.00	6.00	12.00
EAP 1-672 [PS]	Wake the Town and Tell the People	1955	3.00	6.00	12.00

Albums

CAPITOL

Number	Title (A Side/B Side)	Yr	VG	VG+	NM
H 288 [10]	Le Sacre Du Sauvage	1952	20.00	40.00	80.00
T 288 [M]	Le Sacre Du Sauvage	1954	10.00	20.00	40.00
T 390 [M]	Music Out of the Moon/Music for Peace of Mind	1954	10.00	20.00	40.00
H 474 [10]	Thinking of You	1954	12.50	25.00	50.00

Number	Title (A Side/B Side)	Yr	VG	VG+	NM
T 474 [M]	Thinking of You	1954	10.00	20.00	40.00
LAL 486 [M]	The Passions	1954	10.00	20.00	40.00
T 594 [M]	Kaleidoscope	1955	10.00	20.00	40.00
T 655 [M]	Tamboo!	1955	10.00	20.00	40.00
T 733 [M]	Caribbean Moonlight	1956	10.00	20.00	40.00
T 774 [M]	Skins!	1957	10.00	20.00	40.00
T 780 [M]	'Round the World	1957	10.00	20.00	40.00
T 843 [M]	Midnight on the Cliffs	1957	10.00	20.00	40.00
T 868 [M]	Ports of Pleasure	1957	10.00	20.00	40.00
T 968 [M]	Space Escapade	1958	10.00	20.00	40.00
T 1012 [M]	Selections from "South Pacific"	1958	10.00	20.00	40.00
T 1088 [M]	Love Is a Fabulous Thing	1958	10.00	20.00	40.00
DT 1388 [R]	Baxter's Best	1960	3.75	7.50	15.00
SM-1388	Baxter's Best	197?	2.00	4.00	8.00
T 1388 [M]	Baxter's Best	1960	7.50	15.00	30.00
ST 1537 [S]	Jewels of the Sea	1961	7.50	15.00	30.00
T 1537 [M]	Jewels of the Sea	1961	6.25	12.50	25.00
ST 1661 [S]	The Sensational Les Baxter	1962	7.50	15.00	30.00
T 1661 [M]	The Sensational Les Baxter	1962	6.25	12.50	25.00
ST 1846 [S]	The Original Quiet Village	1963	6.25	12.50	25.00
T 1846 [M]	The Original Quiet Village	1963	5.00	10.00	20.00
H 2000 [10]	Music Out of the Moon	1953	20.00	40.00	80.00
T 10015 [M]	La Femme	1956	10.00	20.00	40.00
M-11702	Ritual of the Savage	1977	2.50	5.00	10.00
SQBO-90984 [(2)]	The Sounds of Adventure	1967	7.50	15.00	30.00
H (# unknown) [10]	Music for Peace of Mind	1953	20.00	40.00	80.00

GNP CRESCENDO

Number	Title (A Side/B Side)	Yr	VG	VG+	NM
GNP-2036 [M]	Brazil Now	1967	3.75	7.50	15.00
GNPS-2036 [S]	Brazil Now	1967	3.00	6.00	12.00
GNPS-2042	Love Is Blue	1968	3.00	6.00	12.00
GNPS-2047	African Blue	1969	3.00	6.00	12.00
GNPS-2053	Moon Rock	1969	3.00	6.00	12.00

PICKWICK

Number	Title (A Side/B Side)	Yr	VG	VG+	NM
PC-3011 [M]	The Fabulous Sounds of Les Baxter	196?	3.75	7.50	15.00
SPC-3011 [S]	The Fabulous Sounds of Les Baxter	196?	3.75	7.50	15.00
PC-3048 [M]	I Could Have Danced All Night	196?	3.75	7.50	15.00
SPC-3048 [S]	I Could Have Danced All Night	196?	3.00	6.00	12.00

REPRISE

Number	Title (A Side/B Side)	Yr	VG	VG+	NM
R-6036 [M]	Voices in Rhythm	1961	3.75	7.50	15.00
R9-6036 [S]	Voices in Rhythm	1961	5.00	10.00	20.00
R-6048 [M]	The Primitive and the Passionate	1962	3.75	7.50	15.00
R9-6049 [S]	The Primitive and the Passionate	1962	5.00	10.00	20.00
R-6079 [M]	Academy Award Winners '63	1963	3.75	7.50	15.00
R9-6079 [S]	Academy Award Winners '63	1963	5.00	10.00	20.00
R-6100 [M]	The Soul of the Drums	1963	3.75	7.50	15.00
R9-6100 [S]	The Soul of the Drums	1963	5.00	10.00	20.00

BAXTER, RONNIE

45s

ATCO

Number	Title (A Side/B Side)	Yr	VG	VG+	NM
6093	Drivin' Me Out of My Mind/Afraid of Love	1957	10.00	20.00	40.00

GONE

Number	Title (A Side/B Side)	Yr	VG	VG+	NM
5036	Someone to Love Me/Gates of Heaven	1958	7.50	15.00	30.00
5041	Gates of Heaven/Prisoner of Love	1958	7.50	15.00	30.00
5050	Is It Because/I Finally Found You	1958	7.50	15.00	30.00
5058	Is It Because/I Finally Found You	1959	7.50	15.00	30.00
5084	It's Magic/If You Let Me	1960	6.25	12.50	25.00

MARK-X

Number	Title (A Side/B Side)	Yr	VG	VG+	NM
8001	It's Magic/If You Let Me	1959	3.00	6.00	12.00

BAY CITY 5

See LUIGI MARTINI AND THE BAY CITY 5.

BAY CITY ROLLERS

45s

ARISTA

Number	Title (A Side/B Side)	Yr	VG	VG+	NM
0120	Bye Bye Baby/It's for You	1975	—	2.50	5.00
0149	Saturday Night/Marlina	1975	—	2.00	4.00
0149 [PS]	Saturday Night/Marlina	1975	—	3.00	6.00
0170	Money Honey/Maryanne	1976	—	2.00	4.00
0170 [PS]	Money Honey/Maryanne	1976	—	3.00	6.00
0185	Rock and Roll Love Letter/Shanghai'd in Love	1976	—	2.00	4.00
0193	Don't Stop the Music (Long)/Don't Stop the Music (Short)	1976	—	2.50	5.00
0205	I Only Want to Be with You/Write a Letter	1976	—	2.00	4.00
0216	Yesterday's Hero/My Lisa	1976	—	2.00	4.00
0233	Dedication/Rock N' Roller	1977	—	2.00	4.00
0233 [PS]	Dedication/Rock N' Roller	1977	—	2.50	5.00
0256	You Made Me Believe in Magic/Dance Dance Dance	1977	—	2.00	4.00
0272	The Way I Feel Tonight/Love Power	1977	—	2.50	5.00
0272	The Way I Feel Tonight/Sweet Virginia	1977	—	2.50	5.00
0363	Where Will I Be Now/If You Were My Woman	1978	—	2.00	4.00
0476	Turn On the Radio/Hello and Welcome Home	1979	—	2.00	4.00

—As "The Rollers"

BELL

Number	Title (A Side/B Side)	Yr	VG	VG+	NM
45169	Keep On Dancing/Alright	1972	—	3.00	6.00
45274	Manana/I Heard You Singing Your Song	1972	—	3.00	6.00
45481	Shang-a-Lang/(B-side unknown)	1974	—	3.00	6.00
45607	Summerlove Sensation/(B-side unknown)	1974	—	3.00	6.00
45618	All of Me Loves All of You/(B-side unknown)	1974	—	3.00	6.00

Albums

ARISTA

Number	Title (A Side/B Side)	Yr	VG	VG+	NM
AL 4049	Bay City Rollers	1975	2.50	5.00	10.00
AL 4071	Rock N' Roll Love Letter	1976	2.50	5.00	10.00
AL 4093	Dedication	1976	2.50	5.00	10.00
AB 4158	Greatest Hits	1977	2.50	5.00	10.00
AB 4194	Strangers in the Wind	1978	2.50	5.00	10.00
AB 4241	Elevator	1979	2.50	5.00	10.00

—As "The Rollers"

Number	Title (A Side/B Side)	Yr	VG	VG+	NM
AB 7004	It's a Game	1977	2.50	5.00	10.00

BAY RIDGE, THE

45s

ATLANTIC

Number	Title (A Side/B Side)	Yr	VG	VG+	NM
2431	Back Track/I Can't Get Her Out of My Mind	1967	2.50	5.00	10.00

BAYOU BOYS, THE

45s

CHECKER

Number	Title (A Side/B Side)	Yr	VG	VG+	NM
765	Dinah/Bambalays	1952	37.50	75.00	150.00

BAYSIDERS, THE

45s

EVEREST

Number	Title (A Side/B Side)	Yr	VG	VG+	NM
19366	Over the Rainbow/My Bonnie	1960	3.75	7.50	15.00
19386	Trees/Look for the Silver Lining	1960	3.75	7.50	15.00
19393	The Bells of St. Mary's/Comin' Thru the Rye	1961	3.75	7.50	15.00

Albums

EVEREST

Number	Title (A Side/B Side)	Yr	VG	VG+	NM
BRST-1124 [S]	Over the Rainbow	1961	75.00	150.00	300.00
LPBR-5124 [M]	Over the Rainbow	1961	50.00	100.00	200.00

BAZUKA, TONY CAMILLO'S

45s

A&M

Number	Title (A Side/B Side)	Yr	VG	VG+	NM
1666	Dynomite Part 1/Dynomite Part 2	1975	—	2.00	4.00
1744	Bazuka Limited/Love Explosion	1975	—	2.00	4.00
1840	Theme from "Policeman"/Walkin' Tall	1976	—	2.00	4.00

VENTURE

Number	Title (A Side/B Side)	Yr	VG	VG+	NM
110	(C'est) Le Rock/Rock the Night Away	1979	—	2.00	4.00

Albums

A&M

Number	Title (A Side/B Side)	Yr	VG	VG+	NM
SP-3406	Tomy Camillo's Bazuka	1975	2.50	5.00	10.00

BE-BOP DELUXE

45s

HARVEST

Number	Title (A Side/B Side)	Yr	VG	VG+	NM
4151	Sister Seagull/Maid in Heaven	1975	—	2.00	4.00
4244	Crying to the Sky/Ships in the Night	1976	—	2.00	4.00
4571	Panic in the World/Blue As a Jewel	1978	—	2.00	4.00

Albums

CAPITOL

Number	Title (A Side/B Side)	Yr	VG	VG+	NM
SPRO-8486 [DJ]	Sunburst Finish	1975	6.25	12.50	25.00
—Specially banded version for radio					
SN-16022	Sunburst Finish	1980	2.00	4.00	8.00
—Reissue of Harvest 11478					
SN-16023	Drastic Plastic	1980	2.00	4.00	8.00
—Reissue of Harvest 11750					
SN-16024	Futurama	1980	2.00	4.00	8.00
—Reissue of Harvest 11432					
SN-16025	Axe Victim	1980	2.00	4.00	8.00
—Reissue of Harvest 11689					
SN-16026	Modern Music	1980	2.00	4.00	8.00
—Reissue of Harvest 11575					

HARVEST

Number	Title (A Side/B Side)	Yr	VG	VG+	NM
SPRO-8531 [DJ]	Be-Bop's Biggest	1978	7.50	15.00	30.00
—Promo-only compilation					
ST-11432	Futurama	1975	2.50	5.00	10.00
ST-11478	Sunburst Finish	1975	2.50	5.00	10.00
ST-11575	Modern Music	1976	2.50	5.00	10.00
SKBB-11666 [(2)]	Live! In the Air Age	1977	3.00	6.00	12.00
SM-11689	Axe Victim	1977	2.50	5.00	10.00
—Their first UK album; first US issue has "SM" prefix					
SW-11750	Drastic Plastic	1978	2.50	5.00	10.00
SKBO-11870 [(2)]	The Best Of & The Rest Of Be-Bop Deluxe	1979	3.00	6.00	12.00

BEACH, BILL

45s

KING

Number	Title (A Side/B Side)	Yr	VG	VG+	NM
4940	Peg Pants/You're Gonna Like My Baby	1956	37.50	75.00	150.00

BEACH BOYS, THE

Also see GLEN CAMPBELL; BRUCE JOHNSTON; BRIAN WILSON; BRIAN WILSON AND MIKE LOVE.

12-Inch Singles

CARIBOU

Number	Title (A Side/B Side)	Yr	VG	VG+	NM
9028	Here Comes the Night/(Instrumental)	1979	2.50	5.00	10.00

45s

BROTHER

Number	Title (A Side/B Side)	Yr	VG	VG+	NM
1001	Heroes and Villains/You're Welcome	1967	3.00	6.00	12.00
1001 [PS]	Heroes and Villains/You're Welcome	1967	25.00	50.00	100.00
—Not to be confused with Capitol 5826, which is a completely different sleeve					

BROTHER/REPRISE

Number	Title (A Side/B Side)	Yr	VG	VG+	NM
0101	Wouldn't It Be Nice/Sloop John B	1973	—	2.50	5.00
—"Back to Back Hits" series					
0102	God Only Knows/Caroline, No	1973	—	2.50	5.00
—"Back to Back Hits" series					
0103	Good Vibrations/Heroes and Villains	1973	—	2.50	5.00
—"Back to Back Hits" series					
0104	Darlin'/Wild Honey	1973	—	2.50	5.00
—"Back to Back Hits" series					
0105	Friends/Be Here in the Morning	1973	—	2.50	5.00
—"Back to Back Hits" series					
0106	Do It Again/Cottonfields	1973	—	2.50	5.00
—"Back to Back Hits" series					
0107	I Can Hear Music/Bluebirds Over the Mountain	1973	—	2.50	5.00
—"Back to Back Hits" series					
0118	Rock and Roll Music/It's O.K.	1977	—	2.00	4.00
—"Back to Back Hits" series					
0894	Add Some Music to Your Day/Susie Cincinnati	1970	2.00	4.00	8.00
0929	Slip On Through/This Whole World	1970	2.50	5.00	10.00
0957	It's About Time/Tears in the Morning	1970	5.00	10.00	20.00

Number	Title (A Side/B Side)	Yr	VG	VG+	NM
0998	Cool, Cool Water/Forever	1971	20.00	40.00	80.00
1015	Long Promised Road/Deirdre	1971	5.00	10.00	20.00
1047	Long Promised Road/'Til I Die	1971	5.00	10.00	20.00
1058	Surf's Up/Don't Go Near the Water	1971	12.50	25.00	50.00
1091	You Need a Mess of Help to Stand Alone/Cuddle Up	1972	7.50	15.00	30.00
1101	Marcella/Hold On Dear Brother	1972	7.50	15.00	30.00
1138	Sail On Sailor/Only With You	1972	2.50	5.00	10.00
1156	California Saga (On My Way to Sunny Californ-I-A)/Funky Pretty	1973	2.50	5.00	10.00
1310	I Can Hear Music/Let the Wind Blow	1974	2.50	5.00	10.00
1321	Child of Winter (Christmas Song)/Susie Cincinnati	1974	12.50	25.00	50.00
1321 [DJ]	Child of Winter (Christmas Song) (mono/stereo)	1974	6.25	12.50	25.00
1325	Sail On Sailor/Only With You	1975	2.00	4.00	8.00
1336	Wouldn't It Be Nice/Caroline, No	1975	3.00	6.00	12.00
1354	Rock and Roll Music/The T M Song	1976	—	2.00	4.00
1368	It's O.K./Had to Phone Ya	1976	—	2.00	4.00
1375	Everyone's In Love with You/Susie Cincinnati	1976	—	2.00	4.00
1389	Honkin' Down the Highway/Solar System	1977	—	2.00	4.00
1394	Peggy Sue/Hey Little Tomboy	1978	—	2.00	4.00

CANDIX

Number	Title (A Side/B Side)	Yr	VG	VG+	NM
301	Surfin'/Luau	1961	50.00	100.00	200.00
—Label says "Distributed by Era Records Sales, Inc."					
301	Surfin'/Luau	1961	75.00	150.00	300.00
—No mention of Era Records on label					
331	Surfin'/Luau	1962	50.00	100.00	200.00

CAPITOL

Number	Title (A Side/B Side)	Yr	VG	VG+	NM
2028	Wild Honey/Wind Chimes	1967	3.00	6.00	12.00
2068	Darlin'/Here Today	1967	3.00	6.00	12.00
2068 [PS]	Darlin'/Here Today	1967	5.00	10.00	20.00
2160	Friends/Little Bird	1968	3.00	6.00	12.00
2239	Do It Again/Wake the World	1968	3.00	6.00	12.00
2360	Bluebirds Over the Mountain/Never Learn Not to Love	1968	3.00	6.00	12.00
2432	I Can Hear Music/All I Want to Do	1969	3.00	6.00	12.00
2530	Break Away/Celebrate the News	1969	3.00	6.00	12.00
2765	Cottonfields/The Nearest Faraway Place	1970	5.00	10.00	20.00
3924	Surfin' U.S.A./The Warmth of the Sun	1974	—	2.50	5.00
4093	Little Honda/Hawaii	1975	—	2.50	5.00
4110	Barbara Ann/Little Honda	1975	—	2.50	5.00
4334	Be True to Your School/Graduation Day	1976	—	2.50	5.00
4777	Surfin' Safari/409	1962	6.25	12.50	25.00
4777 [PS]	Surfin' Safari/409	1962	20.00	40.00	80.00
4880	Ten Little Indians/County Fair	1962	7.50	15.00	30.00
4880 [PS]	Ten Little Indians/County Fair	1962	50.00	100.00	200.00
4932	Surfin' U.S.A./Shut Down	1963	6.25	12.50	25.00
—Version 1: Brian Wilson listed as composer of "Surfin' U.S.A."					
4932	Surfin' U.S.A./Shut Down	1963	6.25	12.50	25.00
—Version 2: Chuck Berry listed as composer of "Surfin' U.S.A."					
5009	Surfer Girl/Little Deuce Coupe	1963	6.25	12.50	25.00
A-5030	The Beach Boys Medley/God Only Knows	1981	—	2.50	5.00
5069	Be True to Your School/In My Room	1963	6.25	12.50	25.00
5096	Little Saint Nick/The Lord's Prayer	1963	7.50	15.00	30.00
—Orange and yellow swirl label					
5096	Little Saint Nick/The Lord's Prayer	1969	4.50	9.00	18.00
—Red and orange "target" label					
5096	Little Saint Nick/The Lord's Prayer	1972	3.75	7.50	15.00
—Orange label with "Capitol" at bottom of label					
5096	Little Saint Nick/The Lord's Prayer	1978	—	2.50	5.00
—Purple label					
5096	Little Saint Nick/The Lord's Prayer	1982	—	2.50	5.00
—Black label with colorband					
5118	Fun, Fun, Fun/Why Do Fools Fall in Love	1964	6.25	12.50	25.00
—A-side songwriter listed as "Brian Wilson"					
5118	Fun, Fun, Fun/Why Do Fools Fall in Love	1964	5.00	10.00	20.00
—A-side songwriter listed as "Brian Wilson-Mike Love"					
5118 [PS]	Fun, Fun, Fun/Why Do Fools Fall in Love	1964	10.00	20.00	40.00
5174	I Get Around/Don't Worry Baby	1964	6.25	12.50	25.00
—Orange and yellow swirl label					
5174	I Get Around/Don't Worry Baby	1969	3.00	6.00	12.00
—Red and orange "target" label					
5174	I Get Around/Don't Worry Baby	1972	2.00	4.00	8.00
—Orange label with "Capitol" at bottom					
5174	I Get Around/Don't Worry Baby	1978	—	2.50	5.00
—Purple label					
5174	I Get Around/Don't Worry Baby	1982	—	2.50	5.00
—Black label with colorband					
5174 [PS]	I Get Around/Don't Worry Baby	1964	10.00	20.00	40.00
5245	When I Grow Up (To Be a Man)/She Knows Me Too Well	1964	6.25	12.50	25.00
5245 [PS]	When I Grow Up (To Be a Man)/She Knows Me Too Well	1964	12.50	25.00	50.00
—With green border					
5245 [PS]	When I Grow Up (To Be a Man)/She Knows Me Too Well	1964	10.00	20.00	40.00
—With blue border					
R-5267	Wendy/Don't Back Down//Little Honda/Hushabye	1964	15.00	30.00	60.00
R-5267 [PS]	4-By the Beach Boys	1964	15.00	30.00	60.00
5306	Dance, Dance, Dance/The Warmth of the Sun	1964	6.25	12.50	25.00
5306 [PS]	Dance, Dance, Dance/The Warmth of the Sun	1964	30.00	60.00	120.00
5312	The Man with All the Toys/Blue Christmas	1964	7.50	15.00	30.00
5372	Do You Wanna Dance/Please Let Me Wonder	1965	5.00	10.00	20.00
5372 [PS]	Do You Wanna Dance/Please Let Me Wonder	1965	10.00	20.00	40.00
5395	Help Me, Rhonda/Kiss Me, Baby	1965	6.25	12.50	25.00
5395 [PS]	Help Me, Rhonda/Kiss Me, Baby	1965	10.00	20.00	40.00
5464	California Girls/Let Him Run Wild	1965	6.25	12.50	25.00
—Orange and yellow swirl label					
5464	California Girls/Let Him Run Wild	1969	2.50	5.00	10.00
—Red and orange "target" label					
5464	California Girls/Let Him Run Wild	1973	2.00	4.00	8.00
—Orange label with "Capitol" at bottom of label					
5464	California Girls/Let Him Run Wild	1978	—	2.50	5.00
—Purple label					
5464 [PS]	California Girls/Let Him Run Wild	1965	10.00	20.00	40.00
5540	The Little Girl I Once Knew/There's No Other (Like My Baby)	1965	5.00	10.00	20.00
5540 [PS]	The Little Girl I Once Knew/There's No Other (Like My Baby)	1965	10.00	20.00	40.00
5561	Barbara Ann/Girl Don't Tell Me	1965	5.00	10.00	20.00
5561 [PS]	Barbara Ann/Girl Don't Tell Me	1965	37.50	75.00	150.00
—Glossy finish					
5561 [PS]	Barbara Ann/Girl Don't Tell Me	1965	50.00	100.00	200.00
—Non-glossy finish					
B-5595	Rock and Roll to the Rescue/Good Vibrations (Live in London)	1986	—	—	3.00
B-5595 [PS]	Rock and Roll to the Rescue/Good Vibrations (Live in London)	1986	—	2.00	4.00
5602	Sloop John B/You're So Good to Me	1966	5.00	10.00	20.00
—Orange and yellow swirl label					
5602	Sloop John B/You're So Good to Me	1969	2.50	5.00	10.00
—Red and orange "target" label					
5602	Sloop John B/You're So Good to Me	1973	2.00	4.00	8.00
—Orange label with "Capitol" at bottom of label					
5602	Sloop John B/You're So Good to Me	1978	—	2.50	5.00
—Purple label					
5602 [PS]	Sloop John B/You're So Good to Me	1966	7.50	15.00	30.00
B-5630	California Dreamin'/Lady Liberty	1986	—	—	3.00
5676	Good Vibrations/Let's Go Away for Awhile	1966	5.00	10.00	20.00
5676 [PS]	Good Vibrations/Let's Go Away for Awhile	1966	7.50	15.00	30.00
5706	Wouldn't It Be Nice/God Only Knows	1966	5.00	10.00	20.00
—Even though it has a higher number, this single was released before "Good Vibrations."					
5826 [PS]	Heroes and Villains	1967	100.00	200.00	400.00
—U.S. picture sleeve for unreleased record. This sleeve, however, was exported and used in other countries.					
S7-17521	409/Punchline	1993	—	2.00	4.00
S7-17522	Be True to Your School/Things We Did Last Summer	1993	—	2.00	4.00
S7-17523	Do You Wanna Dance/Ruby Baby	1993	—	2.00	4.00
S7-18205	Merry Christmas, Baby/Santa's Beard	1994	—	2.00	4.00
—Green vinyl					
S7-19765	The Man with All the Toys/We Three Kings of Orient Are	1997	—	—	3.00
B-44297	Don't Worry Baby/Tequila Dreams	1989	—	2.00	4.00
—A-side: With the Everly Brothers; B-side by Dave Grusin					
B-44297 [PS]	Don't Worry Baby/Tequila Dreams	1989	2.50	5.00	10.00
S7-57886	Frosty the Snowman/Little Saint Nick	1992	—	2.50	5.00
—Originals on black vinyl					
S7-57886	Frosty the Snowman/Little Saint Nick	1993	—	2.00	4.00
—Second pressing on green vinyl					
58745	Child of Winter (Christmas Song)/Winter Symphony	1998	—	2.00	4.00
58746	Christmas Is Here Again/Auld Lang Syne	1998	—	2.00	4.00
58747	I'll Be Home for Christmas/Little Saint Nick (Alternate Version)	1998	—	2.00	4.00
7PRO-79789 [DJ]	Still Cruisin' (same on both sides)	1989	15.00	30.00	60.00
—Vinyl is promo only					
7PRO-79841 [DJ]	Somewhere Near Japan (same on both sides)	1989	15.00	30.00	60.00
—Vinyl is promo only					

CAPITOL CUSTOM

Number	Title (A Side/B Side)	Yr	VG	VG+	NM
(no #)	Spirit of America/Boogie Woodie	1963	50.00	100.00	200.00
(no #) [PS]	Spirit of America/Boogie Woodie	1963	150.00	300.00	600.00
—Promo for KFWB and opening day of Wallich's Music City South Bay store					
2936/7	Salt Lake City/Amusemant Parks U.S.A.	1965	50.00	100.00	200.00

CAPITOL STARLINE

Number	Title (A Side/B Side)	Yr	VG	VG+	NM
6059	Be True to Your School/In My Room	1965	3.75	7.50	15.00
—Originals have green swirl labels					
6060	Ten Little Indians/She Knows Me Too Well	1965	3.75	7.50	15.00
—Originals have green swirl labels					
6081	Help Me, Rhonda/Do You Wanna Dance?	1966	3.75	7.50	15.00
—Originals have green swirl labels					
6094	Surfin' U.S.A./Shut Down	1966	3.75	7.50	15.00
—Originals have green swirl labels					
6095	Surfin' Safari/409	1966	3.75	7.50	15.00
—Originals have green swirl labels					
6105	Dance, Dance, Dance/The Warmth of the Sun	1967	3.00	6.00	12.00
—Originals have red and white "target" labels					
6106	Fun, Fun, Fun/Why Do Fools Fall in Love	1967	3.00	6.00	12.00
—Originals have red and white "target" labels					
6107	Surfer Girl/Little Deuce Coupe	1967	3.00	6.00	12.00
—Originals have red and white "target" labels					
6132	Good Vibrations/Barbara Ann	1968	3.00	6.00	12.00
—Originals have red and white "target" labels					
6204	When I Grow Up (To Be a Man)/She Knows Me Too Well	197?	—	2.50	5.00
—Originals have grayish labels					
6205	Wendy/Little Honda	197?	—	2.50	5.00
—Originals have grayish labels					
6259	Barbara Ann/Little Honda	1978	—	2.00	4.00
—Originals have grayish labels					
6277	Little Saint Nick/The Lord's Prayer	1981	—	—	3.00
—Originals have blue labels					
6280	I Get Around/Don't Worry Baby	1981	—	—	3.00
—Originals have blue labels					
6289	California Girls/Let Him Run Wild	1981	—	—	3.00
—Originals have blue labels					
6295	Sloop John B/You're So Good to Me	1981	—	—	3.00
—Originals have blue labels					

CARIBOU

Number	Title (A Side/B Side)	Yr	VG	VG+	NM
02633	Come Go with Me/Don't Go Near the Water	1981	—	—	3.00
04913	Getcha Back/Male Ego	1985	—	—	3.00
04913 [PS]	Getcha Back/Male Ego	1985	—	—	3.00
05433	It's Gettin' Late/It's OK	1985	—	—	3.00
05433 [PS]	It's Gettin' Late/It's OK	1985	—	—	3.00
05624	She Believes in Love Again/It's Just a Matter of Time	1985	—	—	3.00
05624 [PS]	She Believes in Love Again/It's Just a Matter of Time	1985	—	—	3.00
9026	Here Comes the Night/Baby Blue	1979	—	2.00	4.00
9029	Good Timin'/Love Surrounds Me	1979	—	2.00	4.00
9030	Lady Lynda/Full Sail	1979	—	2.00	4.00

Number	Title (A Side/B Side)	Yr	VG	VG+	NM
9031	It's a Beautiful Day/Sumahama	1979	—	2.00	4.00
9032	Goin' On/Endless Harmony	1980	—	2.00	4.00
9033	Livin' with a Heartache/Santa Ana Winds	1980	—	2.00	4.00
9034	School Day (Ring! Ring! Goes the Bell)/When Girls Get Together	1980	—	—	—
—Not known to exist					
9034 [DJ]	School Day (Ring! Ring! Goes the Bell) (same on both sides)	1980	50.00	125.00	250.00
CRITIQUE					
99392	Happy Endings/California Girls	1987	—	—	3.00
—A-side: With Little Richard					
ELEKTRA					
69385	Kokomo/Tutti-Frutti	1988	—	—	3.00
—B-side by Little Richard					
ERA BACK TO BACK HITS					
042	Surfer Girl/The Freeze	197?	2.00	4.00	8.00
—A-side is from the Hite Morgan sessions; B-side by Tony & Jo					
043	Surfin'/Surfin' Safari	197?	2.00	4.00	8.00
—Both sides from the Hite Morgan sessions					
FBI					
7701	East Meets West/Rhapsody	1986	5.00	10.00	20.00
—With Frankie Valli and the Four Seasons					
ODE					
66016	Wouldn't It Be Nice/The Times They Are a-Changing	1971	7.50	15.00	30.00
—B-side by Merry Clayton					
SUB POP					
363	I Just Wasn't Made for These Times/Wouldn't It Be Nice//Here Today	1996	—	2.50	5.00
—Newly released versions from the Pet Sounds box set					
363 [PS]	I Just Wasn't Made for These Times/Wouldn't It Be Nice//Here Today	1996	—	2.50	5.00
—Not seam sealed (folded piece of cardboard)					
X					
301	Surfin'/Luau	1961	250.00	500.00	1000.
7-Inch Extended Plays					
CAPITOL					
SXA-1981 [DJ]	Your Summer Dream/Our Car Club/Surfer Girl// Catch a Wave/In My Room/Hawaii	1963	37.50	75.00	150.00
—Small hole, 33 1/3 rpm jukebox EP					
SXA-1981 [PS]	Surfer Girl	1963	37.50	75.00	150.00
Albums					
ASYLUM					
R 113793	Surf's Up	1972	37.50	75.00	150.00
—RCA Record Club edition, pressed with wrong labels					
BROTHER					
ST 9001 [R]	Smiley Smile	1967	5.00	10.00	20.00
—No mention of Barry Turnbull on cover					
ST 9001 [R]	Smiley Smile	1967	3.75	7.50	15.00
—"Title for this album by Barry Turnbull" on back cover					
T 9001 [M]	Smiley Smile	1967	10.00	20.00	40.00
—No mention of Barry Turnbull on cover					
T 9001 [M]	Smiley Smile	1967	7.50	15.00	30.00
—"Title for this album by Barry Turnbull" on back cover					
BROTHER/REPRISE					
2MS 2083 [(2)]	Carl and the Passions "So Tough"/Pet Sounds	1972	7.50	15.00	30.00
2MS 2083 [(2) DJ]	Carl and the Passions "So Tough"/Pet Sounds	1972	12.50	25.00	50.00
—White label promo					
MS 2118	Holland	1973	3.75	7.50	15.00
—Includes bonus stock-copy EP, "Mount Vernon and Fairway," in picture sleeve, taped to back cover					
MS 2118 [DJ]	Holland	1973	10.00	20.00	40.00
—White label promo; includes bonus white-label promo EP, "Mount Vernon and Fairway," in picture sleeve, taped to back cover					
MS 2118 [DJ]	Holland	1973	125.00	250.00	500.00
—Test pressing with "We Got Love," deleted from promos and stock copies					
2MS 2166 [(2)]	Wild Honey & 20/20	1974	3.75	7.50	15.00
2MS 2167 [(2)]	Friends & Smiley Smile	1974	3.75	7.50	15.00
MS 2197 [M]	Pet Sounds	1974	5.00	10.00	20.00
MS 2223	Good Vibrations — Best of the Beach Boys	1975	3.00	6.00	12.00
MS 2251	15 Big Ones	1976	3.00	6.00	12.00
MSK 2258	Love You	1977	3.00	6.00	12.00
MSK 2268	M.I.U. Album	1978	3.00	6.00	12.00
MSK 2280	Good Vibrations — Best of the Beach Boys	1978	2.50	5.00	10.00
RS-6382	Sunflower	1970	6.25	12.50	25.00
RS-6382 [DJ]	Sunflower	1970	12.50	25.00	50.00
—White label promo					
RS 6453	Surf's Up	1971	5.00	10.00	20.00
RS 6453 [DJ]	Surf's Up	1971	10.00	20.00	40.00
—White label promo					
2RS 6484 [(2)]	The Beach Boys In Concert	1973	5.00	10.00	20.00
2RS 6484 [(2) DJ]	The Beach Boys In Concert	1973	10.00	20.00	40.00
—White label promo					
SKAO-93352	Sunflower	1970	50.00	100.00	200.00
—Capitol Record Club edition					
R 113793	Surf's Up	1972	6.25	12.50	25.00
—RCA Record Club edition					
R 130223	15 Big Ones	1976	3.75	7.50	15.00
—RCA Record Club edition					
R 223569 [(2)]	The Beach Boys In Concert	1973	6.25	12.50	25.00
—RCA Record Club edition					
CAPITOL					
SKAO-133	20/20	1969	5.00	10.00	20.00
—Black label with colorband					
SKAO-133	20/20	1969	3.75	7.50	15.00
—"Starline" label					
SKAO-8-0133	20/20	1969	7.50	15.00	30.00
—Capitol Record Club edition; black label					
SKAO-8-0133	20/20	1970	10.00	20.00	40.00
—Capitol Record Club edition; lime label					
SWBB-253 [(2)]	Close-Up	1969	7.50	15.00	30.00
—Reissue of "Surfin' U.S.A." and "All Summer Long" in one package; black labels with colorband					
SWBB-253 [(2)]	Close-Up	1970	10.00	20.00	40.00
—Lime labels					

Number	Title (A Side/B Side)	Yr	VG	VG+	NM
ST-442	Good Vibrations	1970	5.00	10.00	20.00
—Lime label (original)					
ST-442	Good Vibrations	1972	6.25	12.50	25.00
—Red or orange label					
ST-8-0442	Good Vibrations	1970	7.50	15.00	30.00
—Capitol Record Club edition					
STBB-500 [(2)]	All Summer Long/California Girls	1970	5.00	10.00	20.00
—Lime labels; "Special Double Play" pack; two separate LPs (abridged versions of "All Summer Long" and "Summer Days [And Summer Nights!!]") bound together					
STBB-500 [(2)]	All Summer Long/California Girls	1971	6.25	12.50	25.00
—Red labels; "Special Double Play" pack; two separate LPs (abridged versions of "All Summer Long" and "Summer Days [And Summer Nights!!]") bound together					
SF-501	All Summer Long	1970	2.50	5.00	10.00
—Individual record from above set					
SF-8-0501	All Summer Long	1971	2.50	5.00	10.00
—Capitol Record Club edition					
SF-502	California Girls	1970	2.50	5.00	10.00
—Individual record from above set					
SF-8-0502	California Girls	1971	2.50	5.00	10.00
—Capitol Record Club edition					
STBB-701 [(2)]	Fun, Fun, Fun/Dance, Dance, Dance	1970	5.00	10.00	20.00
—Lime labels; "Special Double Play" pack; two separate LPs (abridged versions of "Shut Down, Volume 2" and "The Beach Boys Today!") bound together					
STBB-701 [(2)]	Fun, Fun, Fun/Dance, Dance, Dance	1971	6.25	12.50	25.00
—Red labels; "Special Double Play" pack; two separate LPs (abridged versions of "Shut Down, Volume 2" and "The Beach Boys Today!") bound together					
SF-702	Fun, Fun, Fun	1971	2.50	5.00	10.00
—Individual record from above set					
SF-8-0702	Fun, Fun, Fun	1971	2.50	5.00	10.00
—Capitol Record Club edition					
SF-703	Dance, Dance, Dance	1971	2.50	5.00	10.00
—Individual record from above set					
SF-8-0703	Dance, Dance, Dance	1971	2.50	5.00	10.00
—Capitol Record Club edition					
DT 1808 [R]	Surfin' Safari	1962	20.00	40.00	80.00
—With "Capitol Full Dimensional Stereo" banner under the "Duophonic" banner					
DT 1808 [R]	Surfin' Safari	1962	6.25	12.50	25.00
—With only the "Duophonic" banner at top					
SM-1808 [R]	Surfin' Safari	197?	2.50	5.00	10.00
T 1808 [M]	Surfin' Safari	1962	10.00	20.00	40.00
SM-1890 [S]	Surfin' U.S.A.	197?	2.50	5.00	10.00
ST 1890 [S]	Surfin' U.S.A.	1963	12.50	25.00	50.00
T 1890 [M]	Surfin' U.S.A.	1963	10.00	20.00	40.00
SM-1981 [S]	Surfer Girl	197?	2.50	5.00	10.00
ST 1981 [S]	Surfer Girl	1963	12.50	25.00	50.00
—With reference to The Four Freshmen in liner notes					
ST 1981 [S]	Surfer Girl	1963	12.50	25.00	50.00
—With reference to "their other new single record, 'Little Deuce Coupe'" in liner notes					
T 1981 [M]	Surfer Girl	1963	10.00	20.00	40.00
—With reference to The Four Freshmen in liner notes					
T 1981 [M]	Surfer Girl	1963	10.00	20.00	40.00
—With reference to "their other new single record, 'Little Deuce Coupe'" in liner notes					
SM-1998 [S]	Little Deuce Coupe	197?	2.50	5.00	10.00
ST 1998 [S]	Little Deuce Coupe	1963	10.00	20.00	40.00
T 1998 [M]	Little Deuce Coupe	1963	10.00	20.00	40.00
ST 2027 [P]	Shut Down, Volume 2	1964	10.00	20.00	40.00
T 2027 [M]	Shut Down, Volume 2	1964	10.00	20.00	40.00
ST 2110 [S]	All Summer Long	1964	12.50	25.00	50.00
—With "Don't Break Down" erroneously listed on front cover					
ST 2110 [S]	All Summer Long	1964	7.50	15.00	30.00
—With "Don't Back Down" correctly listed on front cover					
T 2110 [M]	All Summer Long	1964	12.50	25.00	50.00
—With "Don't Break Down" erroneously listed on front cover					
T 2110 [M]	All Summer Long	1964	7.50	15.00	30.00
—With "Don't Back Down" correctly listed on front cover					
SM-2164	The Beach Boys' Christmas Album	197?	2.50	5.00	10.00
ST 2164 [S]	The Beach Boys' Christmas Album	1964	12.50	25.00	50.00
T 2164 [M]	The Beach Boys' Christmas Album	1964	12.50	25.00	50.00
SM-2198	Beach Boys Concert	197?	2.50	5.00	10.00
STAO-8-2198 [S]	Beach Boys Concert	196?	20.00	40.00	80.00
—Capitol Record Club edition					
STAO 2198 [S]	Beach Boys Concert	1964	7.50	15.00	30.00
—With bound-in booklet					
TAO 2198 [M]	Beach Boys Concert	1964	7.50	15.00	30.00
—With bound-in booklet					
DT-8-2269 [R]	The Beach Boys Today!	1965	20.00	40.00	80.00
—Capitol Record Club edition					
DT 2269 [R]	The Beach Boys Today!	1965	6.25	12.50	25.00
T 2269 [M]	The Beach Boys Today!	1965	7.50	15.00	30.00
DT 2354 [R]	Summer Days (And Summer Nights!!)	1965	12.50	25.00	50.00
—With "New Improved Full Dimensional Stereo" banner					
DT 2354 [R]	Summer Days (And Summer Nights!!)	1965	6.25	12.50	25.00
—With "Duophonic" banner					
T 2354 [M]	Summer Days (And Summer Nights!!)	1965	7.50	15.00	30.00
DMAS 2398 [R]	Beach Boys Party!	1965	7.50	15.00	30.00
—With sheet of photos					
DMAS 2398 [R]	Beach Boys Party!	1965	6.25	12.50	25.00
—Without sheet of photos					
MAS 2398 [M]	Beach Boys Party!	1965	10.00	20.00	40.00
—With sheet of photos					
MAS 2398 [M]	Beach Boys Party!	1965	7.50	15.00	30.00
—Without sheet of photos					
DT 2458 [R]	Pet Sounds	1966	7.50	15.00	30.00
T 2458 [M]	Pet Sounds	1966	10.00	20.00	40.00
DT 2545 [P]	Best of the Beach Boys	1966	3.75	7.50	15.00
—Black label with colorband					
DT 2545 [P]	Best of the Beach Boys	1966	3.00	6.00	12.00
—Black "The Star Line" label					
DT 2545 [P]	Best of the Beach Boys	1967	3.75	7.50	15.00
—Red and white "Starline" label					
DT 2545 [P]	Best of the Beach Boys	1970	3.00	6.00	12.00
—Green "Starline" label					
DT 2545 [P]	Best of the Beach Boys	1973	2.50	5.00	10.00
—Orange label, "Capitol" on bottom					
DT 2545 [P]	Best of the Beach Boys	1978	2.50	5.00	10.00
—Purple label, large Capitol logo					

Number	Title (A Side/B Side)	Yr	VG	VG+	NM
DT 2545 [P]	Best of the Beach Boys	1983	2.50	5.00	10.00
—Black label, print in colorband					
T 2545 [M]	Best of the Beach Boys	1966	5.00	10.00	20.00
—Black label with colorband					
T 2545 [M]	Best of the Beach Boys	1966	3.75	7.50	15.00
—Black "The Star Line" label					
T 2545 [M]	Best of the Beach Boys	1967	7.50	15.00	30.00
—Red and white "Starline" label					
T/DT 2580	Smile	1966	250.00	500.00	1000.
—Unreleased; price is for cover slick, which has been counterfeited					
T/DT 2580	Smile Booklet	1966	75.00	150.00	300.00
—Printed for insertion into unreleased "Smile" LP; counterfeits exist					
DT 2706 [P]	Best of the Beach Boys, Vol. 2	1967	3.75	7.50	15.00
—Red and while "Starline" label					
DT 2706 [P]	Best of the Beach Boys, Vol. 2	1970	3.00	6.00	12.00
—Green "Starline" label					
DT 2706 [P]	Best of the Beach Boys, Vol. 2	1973	2.50	5.00	10.00
—Orange label, "Capitol" on bottom					
DT 2706 [P]	Best of the Beach Boys, Vol. 2	1978	2.50	5.00	10.00
—Purple label, large Capitol logo					
T 2706 [M]	Best of the Beach Boys, Vol. 2	1967	6.25	12.50	25.00
DTCL-8-2813 [(3) R]	The Beach Boys Deluxe Set	1967	37.50	75.00	150.00
—Capitol Record Club edition; blue border on box; custom pressings of LPs with "DTCL" prefixes					
DTCL 2813 [(3) R]	The Beach Boys Deluxe Set	1967	12.50	25.00	50.00
—Maroon border on box; custom pressings of LPs with "DTCL" prefixes					
TCL 2813 [(3) M]	The Beach Boys Deluxe Set	1967	62.50	125.00	250.00
—Black border on box; albums have "T" prefixes					
ST 2859 [S]	Wild Honey	1967	5.00	10.00	20.00
T 2859 [M]	Wild Honey	1967	10.00	20.00	40.00
ST-8-2891 [R]	Smiley Smile	1968	75.00	150.00	300.00
—Capitol Record Club edition					
DKAO-8-2893	Stack-o-Tracks	1968	50.00	100.00	200.00
—Capitol Record Club edition					
DKAO 2893	Stack-o-Tracks	1968	25.00	50.00	100.00
—With sheet music booklet					
DKAO 2893	Stack-o-Tracks	1968	12.50	25.00	50.00
—Without sheet music booklet					
ST 2895	Friends	1968	6.25	12.50	25.00
DKAO 2945 [P]	The Best of the Beach Boys, Vol. 3	1968	3.75	7.50	15.00
—Black label with colorband					
DKAO 2945 [P]	The Best of the Beach Boys, Vol. 3	1969	5.00	10.00	20.00
—"Starline" label					
PRO 3133 [DJ]	Silver Platter Service from Hollywood: The Beach Boys Christmas Special	1964	50.00	100.00	200.00
SVBB-11307 [(2)]	Endless Summer	1974	5.00	10.00	20.00
—Orange labels, "Capitol" on bottom; with poster					
SVBB-11307 [(2)]	Endless Summer	1978	3.75	7.50	15.00
—Purple labels, large Capitol logo					
SVBB-11307 [(2)]	Endless Summer	1983	3.00	6.00	12.00
—Black labels, print in colorband					
SVBB-11307 [(2)]	Endless Summer	1988	3.00	6.00	12.00
—Purple labels, small Capitol logo					
SVBB-11384 [(2)]	Spirit of America	1975	3.75	7.50	15.00
—Orange labels, "Capitol" on bottom					
SVBB-11384 [(2)]	Spirit of America	1978	3.00	6.00	12.00
—Purple labels, large Capitol logo					
SVBB-11384 [(2)]	Spirit of America	1983	2.50	5.00	10.00
—Black labels, print in colorband					
SVBB-11384 [(2)]	Spirit of America	1988	2.50	5.00	10.00
—Purple labels, small Capitol logo					
ST-11584	Beach Boys '69 (The Beach Boys Live in London)	1976	3.00	6.00	12.00
SN-12011	Beach Boys '69 (The Beach Boys Live in London)	1979	2.50	5.00	10.00
SVBB-12220 [(2)]	Sunshine Dream	1982	3.00	6.00	12.00
ST-12293	Rarities	1983	3.75	7.50	15.00
STBK-12396 [(2)]	Made in U.S.A.	1986	3.00	6.00	12.00
N-16012 [M]	Surfin' Safari	1980	2.00	4.00	8.00
SN-16013 [S]	Little Deuce Coupe	1980	2.00	4.00	8.00
SN-16014 [S]	Surfer Girl	1980	2.00	4.00	8.00
SN-16015 [S]	Surfin' U.S.A.	1980	2.00	4.00	8.00
SN-16016 [S]	All Summer Long	1980	2.00	4.00	8.00
DN-16017 [R]	California Girls	1980	2.00	4.00	8.00
SN-16018 [P]	Fun, Fun, Fun	1980	2.00	4.00	8.00
—Reissue of "Shut Down, Vol. 2"					
DN-16019 [R]	Dance, Dance, Dance	1981	2.00	4.00	8.00
SN-16134	Beach Boys '69 (The Beach Boys Live in London)	1981	2.00	4.00	8.00
SN-16156 [M]	Pet Sounds	1981	2.00	4.00	8.00
SN-16157	Friends	1981	2.00	4.00	8.00
SN-16158 [M]	Smiley Smile	1981	2.00	4.00	8.00
SN-16159 [S]	Wild Honey	1981	2.00	4.00	8.00
DN-16272 [R]	Beach Boys Party!	1982	2.00	4.00	8.00
N-16273	Be True to Your School	1983	2.00	4.00	8.00
DN-16318 [R]	Best of the Beach Boys, Vol. 2	1984	2.00	4.00	8.00
C1-21241 [S]	Pet Sounds	1999	3.75	7.50	15.00
—True stereo version on heavyweight vinyl					
C1-29628 [S]	Surfer Girl	1994	3.75	7.50	15.00
C1-29629 [M]	Shut Down, Volume 2	1994	3.75	7.50	15.00
C1-29630 [S]	Little Deuce Coupe	1994	3.75	7.50	15.00
C1-29631 [S]	All Summer Long	1994	3.75	7.50	15.00
C1-29632 [M]	The Beach Boys Today!	1994	3.75	7.50	15.00
C1-29633 [M]	Summer Days (And Summer Nights!!)	1994	3.75	7.50	15.00
C1-29634	Beach Boys '69 (The Beach Boys Live in London)	1994	3.75	7.50	15.00
C1-29635 [M]	Smiley Smile	1994	3.75	7.50	15.00
C1-29636 [S]	Wild Honey	1994	3.75	7.50	15.00
C1-29637	Friends	1994	3.75	7.50	15.00
C1-29638	20/20	1994	3.75	7.50	15.00
C1-29640 [M]	Beach Boys Party!	1994	3.75	7.50	15.00
C1-29641	Stack-o-Tracks	1994	3.75	7.50	15.00
C1-29661 [M]	Surfin' Safari	1994	3.75	7.50	15.00
C1-48421 [M]	Pet Sounds	1994	3.75	7.50	15.00
C1-48422 [S]	Surfin' U.S.A.	1994	3.75	7.50	15.00
C1-90427	Beach Boys Concert	1994	3.75	7.50	15.00
C1-91318 [R]	Best of the Beach Boys	1988	3.00	6.00	12.00
—Purple label, small Capitol logo					
C1-92639	Still Cruisin'	1989	3.00	6.00	12.00
R 123946	Best of the Beach Boys	197?	3.75	7.50	15.00
—RCA Music Service edition					
R 133854	The Beach Boys' Christmas Album	197?	3.75	7.50	15.00
—RCA Music Service edition					
R 223559 [(2)]	Endless Summer	197?	6.25	12.50	25.00
—RCA Music Service edition					
R 233593 [(2)]	American Summer	1975	6.25	12.50	25.00
—RCA Music Service exclusive					
SF-500501	All Summer Long	1971	2.50	5.00	10.00
—Columbia Record Club edition					
SF-500502	California Girls	1971	2.50	5.00	10.00
—Columbia Record Club edition					
DT-502545 [P]	Best of the Beach Boys	197?	3.75	7.50	15.00
—Columbia Record Club edition					
DT-502706 [P]	Best of the Beach Boys, Vol. 2	197?	3.75	7.50	15.00
—Columbia Record Club edition					
SVBB-511307 [(2)]	Endless Summer	197?	6.25	12.50	25.00
—Columbia Record Club edition					
SVBB-511384 [(2)]	Spirit of America	1975	5.00	10.00	20.00
—Columbia Record Club edition					
CAPITOL SPECIAL MARKETS					
SLB-6994 [(2)]	Golden Years of the Beach Boys	1975	5.00	10.00	20.00
SL-8114	Beach Boys Super Hits	1978	2.50	5.00	10.00
SLB-8134 [(2)]	The Beach Boys	1980	5.00	10.00	20.00
SL-9431	Good Vibrations from the Beach Boys	1986	3.75	7.50	15.00
—Special issue for Sunkist					
CARIBOU					
JZ 35752	L.A. (Light Album)	1979	2.50	5.00	10.00
JZ 35752 [DJ]	L.A. (Light Album)	1979	3.75	7.50	15.00
—White label promo					
PZ 35752	L.A. (Light Album)	1980	2.00	4.00	8.00
—Budget-line reissue					
FZ 36283	Keepin' the Summer Alive	1980	2.50	5.00	10.00
FZ 36283 [DJ]	Keepin' the Summer Alive	1980	3.75	7.50	15.00
—White label promo					
Z2X 37445 [(2)]	Ten Years of Harmony (1970-1980)	1981	3.00	6.00	12.00
BFZ 39946	The Beach Boys	1985	2.50	5.00	10.00
PZ 39946	The Beach Boys	1988	2.00	4.00	8.00
—Budget-line reissue					
DCC COMPACT CLASSICS					
LPZ-2006 [M]	Pet Sounds	1995	6.25	12.50	25.00
—Audiophile vinyl					
ERA					
HTE-805 [M]	The Beach Boys' Biggest Beach Hits	1969	3.75	7.50	15.00
—Also contains non-Beach Boys filler					
EVEREST					
4108 [M]	Rare Early Recordings	1981	2.00	4.00	8.00
GATEWAY					
GSLP-10104 [M]	Surfing with the Beach Boys, the Marketts and the Frogmen	1979	2.00	4.00	8.00
MOBILE FIDELITY					
1-116	Surfer Girl	1984	7.50	15.00	30.00
—Audiophile vinyl					
ORBIT					
OR 688 [M]	The Beach Boys' Greatest Hits 1961-1963	1972	3.00	6.00	12.00
—Also contains non-Beach Boys filler					
PAIR					
PDL2-1068 [(2)]	For All Seasons	1986	3.75	7.50	15.00
PDL2-1084 [(2)]	Golden Harmonies	1986	3.75	7.50	15.00
PICKWICK					
PTP-2059 [(2)]	High Water	1973	3.00	6.00	12.00
SPC-3221	Summertime Blues	1970	2.50	5.00	10.00
SPC-3269	Good Vibrations	1971	2.50	5.00	10.00
SPC-3309	Wow! Great Concert!	1972	2.50	5.00	10.00
SPC-3351	Surfer Girl	1973	2.50	5.00	10.00
SPC-3562	Little Deuce Coupe	1975	2.50	5.00	10.00
SCEPTER					
CTN-18004 [M]	The Best of the Beach Boys (1961-1963)	1972	3.00	6.00	12.00
—Also contains non-Beach Boys filler					
SEARS					
SPS-609	Summertime Blues	1970	12.50	25.00	50.00
SPRINGBOARD					
SPB-4021 [M]	The Beach Boys 1961	1977	2.00	4.00	8.00
—Also contains non-Beach Boys filler					
SUNDAZED					
LP 5005 [B]	Lost & Found!	1991	3.00	6.00	12.00
—Yellow vinyl; first LP issue of the 1961 sessions from the master tapes; three tracks are stereo					
TIME-LIFE					
SRNR-03 [(2)]	The Beach Boys: 1963-1967	1986	3.75	7.50	15.00
—2 LPs in box with fold-open liner notes; second cover has a portrait of the Beach Boys					
SRNR-03 [(2)]	The Beach Boys: 1963-1967	1986	6.25	12.50	25.00
—2 LPs in box with fold-open liner notes; original cover portrays the Beach Boys surfing					
WAND					
WDS-688 [M]	The Beach Boys' Greatest Hits 1961-1963	1972	3.00	6.00	12.00
—Also contains non-Beach Boys filler					

BEACH BOYS, THE (2)

No relation to the group that became famous.

45s

Number	Title (A Side/B Side)	Yr	VG	VG+	NM
KAPP					
289	Bathing Beauty/On the Beach at Sunset	1959	6.25	12.50	25.00

BEACH BUMS, THE

Early BOB SEGER.

45s

Number	Title (A Side/B Side)	Yr	VG	VG+	NM
ARE YOU KIDDING ME?					
1010	Florida Time/The Ballad of the Yellow Beret	1966	15.00	30.00	60.00
—Early Bob Seger; B-side credited to "D. Dodger"					

BEACH GIRLS, THE

45s

Number	Title (A Side/B Side)	Yr	VG	VG+	NM
DYNO-VOX					
202	Goin' Places/Skiing in the Snow	1965	6.25	12.50	25.00
VAULT					
905	He's My Surfin' Guy/Bobby's the Boy	1963	7.50	15.00	30.00

BEACH NUTS, THE

45s

BANG

Number	Title (A Side/B Side)	Yr	VG	VG+	NM
504	Out in the Sun (Hey-O)/Someday Soon	1965	12.50	25.00	50.00

CORONADO

Number	Title (A Side/B Side)	Yr	VG	VG+	NM
131	Surf Ride '65/The Last Ride	1965	12.50	25.00	50.00
131 [PS]	Surf Ride '65/The Last Ride	1965	15.00	30.00	60.00

BEACON STREET UNION, THE

45s

MGM

Number	Title (A Side/B Side)	Yr	VG	VG+	NM
13865	South End Incident/Speed Kills	1967	2.50	5.00	10.00
13935	Blue Suede Shoes/Four Hundred and Five	1968	2.50	5.00	10.00
14012	May I Light Your Cigarette/Mayola	1968	2.50	5.00	10.00

Albums

MGM

Number	Title (A Side/B Side)	Yr	VG	VG+	NM
E-4517 [M]	The Eyes of the Beacon Street Union	1967	7.50	15.00	30.00
SE-4517 [S]	The Eyes of the Beacon Street Union	1967	6.25	12.50	25.00
E-4568 [M]	The Clown Died in Marvin Gardens	1968	12.50	25.00	50.00
—May be promo only (yellow label)					
SE-4568 [S]	The Clown Died in Marvin Gardens	1968	6.25	12.50	25.00

BEAGLES, THE

45s

ERA

Number	Title (A Side/B Side)	Yr	VG	VG+	NM
3132	Let's All Sing Like the Birdies Sing/Deep in the Heart of Texas	1964	3.75	7.50	15.00
3132 [PS]	Let's All Sing Like the Birdies Sing/Deep in the Heart of Texas	1964	6.25	12.50	25.00

HIT

Number	Title (A Side/B Side)	Yr	VG	VG+	NM
113	Can't Buy Me Love/White on White	1964	3.00	6.00	12.00
—B-side by Fred York					

BEALE STREET BOYS, THE

45s

OBA

Number	Title (A Side/B Side)	Yr	VG	VG+	NM
101	Next Christmas/There's Nothing Greater Than A Prayer	1960	15.00	30.00	60.00

BEAN, YOUNG BILLY

See BILLY BURNETTE.

BEANS

45s

AVALANCHE

Number	Title (A Side/B Side)	Yr	VG	VG+	NM
36011	Bleecker Street Rain/Honky Tonk Refrigerator	1972	2.00	4.00	8.00

Albums

AVALANCHE

Number	Title (A Side/B Side)	Yr	VG	VG+	NM
9200	Beans	1971	5.00	10.00	20.00

BEARD, DEAN

45s

ATLANTIC

Number	Title (A Side/B Side)	Yr	VG	VG+	NM
1137	On My Mind Again/Rakin' and Scrapin'	1957	10.00	20.00	40.00
1162	Party Party/Stand By Me	1957	10.00	20.00	40.00
1182	Take Time to Love Me/Hold Me Close	1958	7.50	15.00	30.00

CANDIX

Number	Title (A Side/B Side)	Yr	VG	VG+	NM
341	The Day That I Lost You/Villa Acuna	1962	3.00	6.00	12.00

CHALLENGE

Number	Title (A Side/B Side)	Yr	VG	VG+	NM
59033	Egad, Charlie Brown/Keeper of the Key	1958	6.25	12.50	25.00
59048	Holding On to a Memory/Little Lover	1959	6.25	12.50	25.00

EDMORAL

Number	Title (A Side/B Side)	Yr	VG	VG+	NM
1011	On My Mind Again/Rakin' and Scrapin'	1956	37.50	75.00	150.00

JOED

Number	Title (A Side/B Side)	Yr	VG	VG+	NM
715	Coffee Break/Tropical Nights	1962	6.25	12.50	25.00

SIMS

Number	Title (A Side/B Side)	Yr	VG	VG+	NM
299	(Are There) Honkytonks in Heaven/Pocketful of Stardust	1966	2.50	5.00	10.00

WINSTON

Number	Title (A Side/B Side)	Yr	VG	VG+	NM
1063	I Don't Know How/The Red Rose	1962	3.00	6.00	12.00
1073	Don't Let the Stars Get In Your Eyes/That's How It Gets Sun Up	1963	3.00	6.00	12.00
1075	Smile Pretty for Me Temper/To Me	1963	3.00	6.00	12.00
—With Bill Graham					

BEARFOOT

45s

EPIC

Number	Title (A Side/B Side)	Yr	VG	VG+	NM
11018	Right On/Mark Twain	1973	—	2.50	5.00

Albums

EPIC

Number	Title (A Side/B Side)	Yr	VG	VG+	NM
KE 32146	Bearfoot	1973	3.00	6.00	12.00

BEASLEY, JIMMY

45s

MODERN

Number	Title (A Side/B Side)	Yr	VG	VG+	NM
991	Ella Jane/No Love for Me	1956	6.25	12.50	25.00
996	Don't Feel Sorry for Me/Little Coquette	1956	6.25	12.50	25.00
1009	My Happiness/Jambalaya	1956	6.25	12.50	25.00
1014	Near You/I'm So Blue	1956	6.25	12.50	25.00
1018	Thinking of You/You Were Fooling	1956	6.25	12.50	25.00
1021	Johnny's House Party (Part 1)/Johnny's House Party (Part 2)	1957	6.25	12.50	25.00
1023	I Want My Baby/We Three	1957	6.25	12.50	25.00

BEAST

45s

EVOLUTION

Number	Title (A Side/B Side)	Yr	VG	VG+	NM
1028	Communication/Move Mountain	1970	—	3.00	6.00

Albums

COTILLION

Number	Title (A Side/B Side)	Yr	VG	VG+	NM
SD 9012	Beast	1969	3.75	7.50	15.00

EVOLUTION

Number	Title (A Side/B Side)	Yr	VG	VG+	NM
2017	Beast	1970	3.75	7.50	15.00

BEAT BROTHERS, THE

45s

MGM

Number	Title (A Side/B Side)	Yr	VG	VG+	NM
13201	Nick Nack Hully Gully/Lantern Hully Gully	1963	4.00	8.00	16.00

BEAT MERCHANTS, THE

45s

TOWER

Number	Title (A Side/B Side)	Yr	VG	VG+	NM
127	So Fine/You Were Made for Me	1965	3.75	7.50	15.00
—B-side by Freddie and the Dreamers					

BEAT OF THE EARTH, THE

Albums

ARDISH

Number	Title (A Side/B Side)	Yr	VG	VG+	NM
AS-001	The Beat of the Earth	1968	75.00	150.00	300.00
AS-0001	The Beat of the Earth	1968	100.00	200.00	400.00

BEATIN' PATH, THE

45s

FONTANA

Number	Title (A Side/B Side)	Yr	VG	VG+	NM
1583	The Original Nothing People/I Waited So Long	1967	5.00	10.00	20.00

BEATLE-ETTES, THE

45s

ASSAULT

Number	Title (A Side/B Side)	Yr	VG	VG+	NM
1893	Yes, You Can Hold My Hand/Yes, You Can Hold My Hand (Part 2)	1964	5.00	10.00	20.00

JAMIE

Number	Title (A Side/B Side)	Yr	VG	VG+	NM
1270	Dance, Beatle, Dance/We Were Meant to Be Married	1964	5.00	10.00	20.00

JUBILEE

Number	Title (A Side/B Side)	Yr	VG	VG+	NM
5472	Only Seventeen/Now We're Together	1964	5.00	10.00	20.00

BEATLE BUDDIES, THE

Albums

DIPLOMAT

Number	Title (A Side/B Side)	Yr	VG	VG+	NM
D-2313 [M]	The Beatle Buddies	1964	3.75	7.50	15.00
DS-2313 [S]	The Beatle Buddies	1964	5.00	10.00	20.00

BEATLES, THE

Also see PETE BEST; GEORGE HARRISON; JOHN LENNON; PAUL McCARTNEY; RINGO STARR.

12-Inch Singles

(NO LABEL)

Number	Title (A Side/B Side)	Yr	VG	VG+	NM
(no #) [DJ]	Merry Christmas and Happy New Year	1965	125.00	250.00	500.00
—Promo item from KYA Radio, San Francisco; B-side is blank					

45s

APPLE

Number	Title (A Side/B Side)	Yr	VG	VG+	NM
Promo-1970 [DJ]	Dialogue from the Beatles' Motion Picture "Let It Be"	1970	15.00	30.00	60.00
2056	Hello Goodbye/I Am the Walrus	1971	7.50	15.00	30.00
—With star on A-side label					
2056	Hello Goodbye/I Am the Walrus	1971	2.50	5.00	10.00
—Without star on A-side label					
2056	Hello Goodbye/I Am the Walrus	1975	5.00	10.00	20.00
—With "All Rights Reserved" disclaimer					
2138	Lady Madonna/The Inner Light	1971	7.50	15.00	30.00
—With star on A-side label					
2138	Lady Madonna/The Inner Light	1971	2.50	5.00	10.00
—Without star on A-side label					
2138	Lady Madonna/The Inner Light	1975	5.00	10.00	20.00
—With "All Rights Reserved" disclaimer					
2276	Hey Jude/Revolution	1968	3.75	7.50	15.00
—Original: With small Capitol logo on bottom of B-side label					
2276	Hey Jude/Revolution	1968	2.50	5.00	10.00
—With "Mfd. by Apple" on label					
2276	Hey Jude/Revolution	1975	5.00	10.00	20.00
—With "All Rights Reserved" disclaimer					
2490	Get Back/Don't Let Me Down	1969	2.50	5.00	10.00
—Original: With small Capitol logo on bottom of B-side label					
2490	Get Back/Don't Let Me Down	1969	2.50	5.00	10.00
—With "Mfd. by Apple" on label					
2490	Get Back/Don't Let Me Down	1975	5.00	10.00	20.00
—With "All Rights Reserved" disclaimer					
2531	The Ballad of John and Yoko/Old Brown Shoe	1969	2.50	5.00	10.00
—Original: With small Capitol logo on bottom of B-side label					
2531	The Ballad of John and Yoko/Old Brown Shoe	1969	2.50	5.00	10.00
—With "Mfd. by Apple" on label					
2531	The Ballad of John and Yoko/Old Brown Shoe	1975	15.00	10.00	20.00
—With "All Rights Reserved" disclaimer					
2531 [PS]	The Ballad of John and Yoko/Old Brown Shoe	1969	25.00	50.00	100.00
2654	Something/Come Together	1969	25.00	50.00	100.00
—Original: With small Capitol logo on bottom of B-side label					
2654	Something/Come Together	1969	2.50	5.00	10.00
—With "Mfd. by Apple" on label					
2654	Something/Come Together	1975	5.00	10.00	20.00
—With "All Rights Reserved" disclaimer					
2764	Let It Be/You Know My Name (Look Up My Number)	1970	3.00	6.00	12.00
—Original: With small Capitol logo on bottom of B-side label					
2764	Let It Be/You Know My Name (Look Up My Number)	1970	2.50	5.00	10.00
—With "Mfd. by Apple" on label					
2764	Let It Be/You Know My Name (Look Up My Number)	1975	5.00	10.00	20.00
—With "All Rights Reserved" disclaimer					

Number	Title (A Side/B Side)	Yr	VG	VG+	NM
2764 [PS]	Let It Be/You Know My Name (Look Up the Number)	1970	25.00	50.00	100.00
2832	The Long and Winding Road/For You Blue	1970	5.00	10.00	20.00
—Original: With small Capitol logo on bottom of B-side label					
2832	The Long and Winding Road/For You Blue	1970	2.50	5.00	10.00
—With "Mfd. by Apple" on label					
2832	The Long and Winding Road/For You Blue	1975	5.00	10.00	20.00
—With "All Rights Reserved" disclaimer					
2832 [PS]	The Long and Winding Road/For You Blue	1970	25.00	50.00	100.00
5112	I Want to Hold Your Hand/I Saw Her Standing There	1971	7.50	15.00	30.00
—With star on label					
5112	I Want to Hold Your Hand/I Saw Her Standing There	1971	2.50	5.00	10.00
—Without star on label					
5112	I Want to Hold Your Hand/I Saw Her Standing There	1975	5.00	10.00	20.00
—With "All Rights Reserved" disclaimer on label					
5150	Can't Buy Me Love/You Can't Do That	1971	7.50	15.00	30.00
—With star on A-side label					
5150	Can't Buy Me Love/You Can't Do That	1971	2.50	5.00	10.00
—Without star on A-side label					
5150	Can't Buy Me Love/You Can't Do That	1975	3.75	7.50	15.00
—With "All Rights Reserved" disclaimer on label					
5222	A Hard Day's Night/I Should Have Known Better	1971	7.50	15.00	30.00
—With star on A-side label					
5222	A Hard Day's Night/I Should Have Known Better	1971	2.50	5.00	10.00
—Without star on A-side label					
5222	A Hard Day's Night/I Should Have Known Better	1975	3.75	7.50	15.00
—With "All Rights Reserved" disclaimer					
5234	I'll Cry Instead/I'm Happy Just to Dance with You	1971	7.50	15.00	30.00
—With star on A-side label					
5234	I'll Cry Instead/I'm Happy Just to Dance with You	1971	2.50	5.00	10.00
—Without star on A-side label					
5234	I'll Cry Instead/I'm Happy Just to Dance with You	1975	3.75	7.50	15.00
—With "All Rights Reserved" disclaimer					
5235	And I Love Her/If I Fell	1971	7.50	15.00	30.00
—With star on A-side label					
5235	And I Love Her/If I Fell	1971	2.50	5.00	10.00
—Without star on A-side label					
5235	And I Love Her/If I Fell	1975	3.75	7.50	15.00
—With "All Rights Reserved" disclaimer					
5255	Matchbox/Slow Down	1971	7.50	15.00	30.00
—With star on A-side label					
5255	Matchbox/Slow Down	1971	2.50	5.00	10.00
—Without star on A-side label					
5255	Matchbox/Slow Down	1975	3.75	7.50	15.00
—With "All Rights Reserved" disclaimer					
5327	I Feel Fine/She's a Woman	1971	7.50	15.00	30.00
—With star on A-side label					
5327	I Feel Fine/She's a Woman	1971	2.50	5.00	10.00
—Without star on A-side label					
5327	I Feel Fine/She's a Woman	1975	3.75	7.50	15.00
—With "All Rights Reserved" disclaimer					
5371	Eight Days a Week/I Don't Want to Spoil the Party	1971	7.50	15.00	30.00
—With star on A-side label					
5371	Eight Days a Week/I Don't Want to Spoil the Party	1971	2.50	5.00	10.00
—Without star on A-side label					
5371	Eight Days a Week/I Don't Want to Spoil the Party	1975	3.75	7.50	15.00
—With "All Rights Reserved" disclaimer					
5407	Ticket to Ride/Yes It Is	1971	7.50	15.00	30.00
—With star on A-side label					
5407	Ticket to Ride/Yes It Is	1971	2.50	5.00	10.00
—Without star on A-side label					
5407	Ticket to Ride/Yes It Is	1975	3.75	7.50	15.00
—With "All Rights Reserved" disclaimer					
5476	Help!/I'm Down	1971	7.50	15.00	30.00
—With star on A-side label					
5476	Help!/I'm Down	1971	2.50	5.00	10.00
—Without star on A-side label					
5476	Help!/I'm Down	1975	3.75	7.50	15.00
—With "All Rights Reserved" disclaimer					
5498	Yesterday/Act Naturally	1971	7.50	15.00	30.00
—With star on A-side label					
5498	Yesterday/Act Naturally	1971	2.50	5.00	10.00
—Without star on A-side label					
5498	Yesterday/Act Naturally	1975	3.75	7.50	15.00
—With "All Rights Reserved" disclaimer					
5555	We Can Work It Out/Day Tripper	1971	7.50	15.00	30.00
—With star on A-side label					
5555	We Can Work It Out/Day Tripper	1971	2.50	5.00	10.00
—Without star on A-side label					
5555	We Can Work It Out/Day Tripper	1975	3.75	7.50	15.00
—With "All Rights Reserved" disclaimer					
5587	Nowhere Man/What Goes On	1971	7.50	15.00	30.00
—With star on A-side label					
5587	Nowhere Man/What Goes On	1971	2.50	5.00	10.00
—Without star on A-side label					
5587	Nowhere Man/What Goes On	1975	3.75	7.50	15.00
—With "All Rights Reserved" disclaimer					
5651	Paperback Writer/Rain	1971	7.50	15.00	30.00
—With star on A-side label					
5651	Paperback Writer/Rain	1971	2.50	5.00	10.00
—Without star on A-side label					
5651	Paperback Writer/Rain	1975	3.75	7.50	15.00
—With "All Rights Reserved" disclaimer					
5715	Yellow Submarine/Eleanor Rigby	1971	7.50	15.00	30.00
—With star on A-side label					
5715	Yellow Submarine/Eleanor Rigby	1971	2.50	5.00	10.00
—Without star on A-side label					
5715	Yellow Submarine/Eleanor Rigby	1975	3.75	7.50	15.00
—With "All Rights Reserved" disclaimer					
5810	Penny Lane/Strawberry Fields Forever	1971	7.50	15.00	30.00
—With star on A-side label					
5810	Penny Lane/Strawberry Fields Forever	1971	2.50	5.00	10.00
—Without star on A-side label					
5810	Penny Lane/Strawberry Fields Forever	1975	3.75	7.50	15.00
—With "All Rights Reserved" disclaimer					
5964	All You Need Is Love/Baby, You're a Rich Man	1971	7.50	15.00	30.00
—With star on A-side label					
5964	All You Need Is Love/Baby, You're a Rich Man	1971	2.50	5.00	10.00
—Without star on A-side label					
5964	All You Need Is Love/Baby, You're a Rich Man	1975	3.75	7.50	15.00
—With "All Rights Reserved" disclaimer					
58348	Baby It's You/I'll Follow the Sun//Devil in Her Heart/Boys	1995	—	2.00	4.00
—All 4 tracks from BBC sessions					
58348 [PS]	Baby It's You/I'll Follow the Sun//Devil in Her Heart/Boys	1995	—	2.00	4.00
58497	Free as a Bird/Christmas Time (Is Here Again)	1995	—	2.00	4.00
—Small center hole; all with large hole were "dinked" somewhere other than when manufactured and have little, if any, value					
58497 [PS]	Free as a Bird/Christmas Time (Is Here Again)	1995	—	2.00	4.00
58544	Real Love/Baby's in Black (Live)	1996	—	—	3.00
—Small center hole; all with large hole were "dinked" somewhere other than when manufactured and have little, if any, value					
58544 [PS]	Real Love/Baby's in Black (Live)	1996	—	—	3.00
APPLE/AMERICOM					
2276/M-221	Hey Jude/Revolution	1969	75.00	150.00	300.00
—Four-inch flexi-disc sold in vending machines; "Hey Jude" is edited to 3:25					
2490/M-335	Get Back/Don't Let Me Down	1969	250.00	500.00	1000.
—Four-inch flexi-disc sold in vending machines					
2531/M-382	The Ballad of John and Yoko/Old Brown Shoe	1969	200.00	400.00	800.00
—Four-inch flexi-disc sold in vending machines					
5715	Yellow Submarine/Eleanor Rigby	1969	1000.	1500.	2000.
—Four-inch flexi-disc sold in vending machines					
ATCO					
6302	Sweet Georgia Brown/Take Out Some Insurance On Me Baby	1964	50.00	100.00	200.00
6308	Ain't She Sweet/Nobody's Child	1964	12.50	25.00	50.00
—With "Vocal by John Lennon" on left of label					
6308	Ain't She Sweet/Nobody's Child	1964	15.00	30.00	60.00
—With "Vocal by John Lennon" under "The Beatles"					
6308 [PS]	Ain't She Sweet/Nobody's Child	1964	125.00	250.00	500.00
—Sleeves with black and green print are reproductions					
ATLANTIC					
OS-13243	Ain't She Sweet/Sweet Georgia Brown	1983	2.50	5.00	10.00
—"Oldies Series"					
BACKSTAGE					
1112 [DJ]	Like Dreamers Do/Love of the Loved	1982	6.25	12.50	25.00
—Promotional 45 from "Oui" magazine					
1122 [DJ]	Love of the Loved/Memphis	1983	6.25	12.50	25.00
—Promotional picture disc					
1133 [DJ]	Like Dreamers Do/Three Cool Cats	1983	6.25	12.50	25.00
—Promotional picture disc					
1155 [DJ]	Crying, Waiting, Hoping/Take Good Care of My Baby	1983	6.25	12.50	25.00
BEATLES FAN CLUB					
(1964)	Season's Greetings from the Beatles	1964	75.00	150.00	300.00
—Tri-fold soundcard					
(1965)	The Beatles Third Christmas Record	1965	20.00	40.00	80.00
—Flexi-disc					
(1965) [PS]	The Beatles Third Christmas Record	1965	25.00	50.00	100.00
(1966)	Everywhere It's Christmas	1966	37.50	75.00	150.00
—Postcard					
(1967)	Christmastime Is Here Again	1967	37.50	75.00	150.00
—Postcard					
(1968) H-2041	The Beatles 1968 Christmas Record	1968	15.00	30.00	60.00
—Flexi-disc					
(1968) H-2041 [PS]	The Beatles 1968 Christmas Record	1968	17.50	35.00	70.00
(1969) H-2565	Happy Christmas 1969	1969	10.00	20.00	40.00
—Flexi-disc					
(1969) H-2565 [PS]	Happy Christmas 1969	1969	15.00	30.00	60.00
CAPITOL					
2056	Hello Goodbye/I Am the Walrus	1967	7.50	15.00	30.00
—Original: Orange and yellow swirl, without "A Subsidiary Of"... in perimeter label print; publishing credited to "Maclen" (we're not sure which came first)					
2056	Hello Goodbye/I Am the Walrus	1967	7.50	15.00	30.00
—Original: Orange and yellow swirl, without "A Subsidiary Of"... in perimeter label print; publishing credited to "Comet" (we're not sure which came first)					
2056	Hello Goodbye/I Am the Walrus	1968	12.50	25.00	50.00
—Orange and yellow swirl label with "A Subsidiary Of" in perimeter print					
2056	Hello Goodbye/I Am the Walrus	1969	15.00	30.00	60.00
—Red and orange "target" label with Capitol dome logo					
2056	Hello Goodbye/I Am the Walrus	1969	5.00	10.00	20.00
—Red and orange "target" label with Capitol round logo					
2056	Hello Goodbye/I Am the Walrus	1976	—	3.00	6.00
—Orange label with "Capitol" at bottom					
2056	Hello Goodbye/I Am the Walrus	1978	2.00	4.00	8.00
—Purple label; label has reeded edge					
2056	Hello Goodbye/I Am the Walrus	1983	—	3.00	6.00
—Black label with colorband					
2056	Hello Goodbye/I Am the Walrus	1988	—	2.50	5.00
—Purple label; label has smooth edge					
2056 [PS]	Hello Goodbye/I Am the Walrus	1967	25.00	50.00	100.00
P 2056 [DJ]	Hello Goodbye/I Am the Walrus	1967	62.50	125.00	250.00
—Light green label promo					
2138	Lady Madonna/The Inner Light	1968	7.50	15.00	30.00
—Original: Orange and yellow swirl, without "A Subsidiary Of"... in perimeter label print					
2138	Lady Madonna/The Inner Light	1968	12.50	25.00	50.00
—Orange and yellow swirl label with "A Subsidiary Of" in perimeter print					
2138	Lady Madonna/The Inner Light	1969	15.00	30.00	60.00
—Red and orange "target" label with Capitol dome logo					
2138	Lady Madonna/The Inner Light	1969	5.00	10.00	20.00
—Red and orange "target" label with Capitol round logo					
2138	Lady Madonna/The Inner Light	1976	—	3.00	6.00
—Orange label with "Capitol" at bottom					
2138	Lady Madonna/The Inner Light	1978	2.00	4.00	8.00
—Purple label; label has reeded edge					
2138	Lady Madonna/The Inner Light	1983	—	3.00	6.00
—Black label with colorband					

Number	Title (A Side/B Side)	Yr	VG	VG+	NM
2138	Lady Madonna/The Inner Light	1988	—	2.50	5.00
—Purple label; label has smooth edge					
2138 [PS]	Lady Madonna/The Inner Light	1968	25.00	50.00	100.00
2138 [PS]	Lady Madonna/The Inner Light	1968	5.00	10.00	20.00
—"Beatles Fan Club" insert that was issued with above sleeve. Originals are glossy.					
P 2138 [DJ]	Lady Madonna/The Inner Light	1968	50.00	100.00	200.00
—Light green label promo					
2276	Hey Jude/Revolution	1976	—	3.00	6.00
—Orange label with "Capitol" at bottom					
2276	Hey Jude/Revolution	1978	2.00	4.00	8.00
—Purple label; label has reeded edge					
2276	Hey Jude/Revolution	1983	—	3.00	6.00
—Black label with colorband					
2276	Hey Jude/Revolution	1988	—	2.50	5.00
—Purple label; label has smooth edge					
2490	Get Back/Don't Let Me Down	1976	—	3.00	6.00
—Orange label with "Capitol" at bottom					
2490	Get Back/Don't Let Me Down	1978	2.00	4.00	8.00
—Purple label; label has reeded edge					
2490	Get Back/Don't Let Me Down	1983	—	3.00	6.00
—Black label with colorband; "Get Back" replaced by LP version as on Let It Be					
2490	Get Back/Don't Let Me Down	1988	—	2.50	5.00
—Purple label; label has smooth edge; "Get Back" replaced by LP version as on Let It Be					
2531	The Ballad of John and Yoko/Old Brown Shoe	1976	—	—	—
—Orange label with "Capitol" at bottom; should exist, but not known to exist					
2531	The Ballad of John and Yoko/Old Brown Shoe	1978	—	3.00	6.00
—Purple label; label has reeded edge					
2531	The Ballad of John and Yoko/Old Brown Shoe	1983	—	3.50	7.00
—Black label with colorband					
2531	The Ballad of John and Yoko/Old Brown Shoe	1988	—	3.00	6.00
—Purple label; label has smooth edge					
2654	Something/Come Together	1976	—	3.00	6.00
—Orange label with "Capitol" at bottom					
2654	Something/Come Together	1978	—	3.00	6.00
—Purple label; label has reeded edge					
2654	Something/Come Together	1983	—	3.00	6.00
—Black label with colorband					
2654	Something/Come Together	1988	—	2.50	5.00
—Purple label; label has smooth edge					
2764	Let It Be/You Know My Name (Look Up My Number)	1976	—	3.00	6.00
—Orange label with "Capitol" at bottom					
2764	Let It Be/You Know My Name (Look Up My Number)	1978	2.00	4.00	8.00
—Purple label; label has reeded edge					
2764	Let It Be/You Know My Name (Look Up My Number)	1983	—	3.00	6.00
—Black label with colorband					
2764	Let It Be/You Know My Name (Look Up My Number)	1988	—	2.50	5.00
—Purple label; label has smooth edge					
2832	The Long and Winding Road/For You Blue	1976	—	3.00	6.00
—Orange label with "Capitol" at bottom					
2832	The Long and Winding Road/For You Blue	1978	2.00	4.00	8.00
—Purple label; label has reeded edge					
2832	The Long and Winding Road/For You Blue	1983	—	3.00	6.00
—Black label with colorband					
2832	The Long and Winding Road/For You Blue	1988	—	2.50	5.00
—Purple label; label has smooth edge					
4274	Got to Get You Into My Life/Helter Skelter	1976	—	3.00	6.00
—Original: Orange label with "Capitol" at bottom, George Martin's name not on label					
4274	Got to Get You Into My Life/Helter Skelter	1976	2.50	5.00	10.00
—Orange label with "Capitol" at bottom, George Martin's name is on label					
4274	Got to Get You Into My Life/Helter Skelter	1978	—	3.00	6.00
—Purple label; label has reeded edge					
4274	Got to Get You Into My Life/Helter Skelter	1983	—	3.00	6.00
—Black label with colorband					
4274	Got to Get You Into My Life/Helter Skelter	1988	—	2.50	5.00
—Purple label; label has smooth edge					
4274 [PS]	Got to Get You Into My Life/Helter Skelter	1976	—	2.50	5.00
P-4274 [DJ]	Got to Get You Into My Life (mono/stereo)	1976	10.00	20.00	40.00
P-4274 [DJ]	Helter Skelter (mono/stereo)	1976	10.00	20.00	40.00
4347	Ob-La-Di, Ob-La-Da/Julia	1976	2.00	4.00	8.00
—Original: Orange label with "Capitol" at bottom					
4347	Ob-La-Di, Ob-La-Da/Julia	1978	2.00	4.00	8.00
—Purple label; label has reeded edge					
4347	Ob-La-Di, Ob-La-Da/Julia	1983	—	3.00	6.00
—Black label with colorband					
4347	Ob-La-Di, Ob-La-Da/Julia	1988	—	2.50	5.00
—Purple label; label has smooth edge					
4347 [PS]	Ob-La-Di, Ob-La-Da/Julia	1976	2.00	4.00	8.00
—Sleeves are individually numbered; very low numbers (under 1000) can fetch premium prices					
P-4347 [DJ]	Ob-La-Di, Ob-La-Da (mono/stereo)	1976	10.00	20.00	40.00
4506 [PS]	Girl/You're Going to Lose That Girl	1977	3.75	7.50	15.00
—Sleeve for a single that was never pressed					
P-4506 [DJ]	Girl (mono/stereo)	1977	50.00	100.00	200.00
—Promo only; all colored vinyl versions are counterfeits					
4612	Sgt. Pepper's Lonely Hearts Club Band-With a Little Help from My Friends/A Day in the Life	1978	2.00	4.00	8.00
—Original: Purple label; label has reeded edge					
4612	Sgt. Pepper's Lonely Hearts Club Band-With a Little Help from My Friends/A Day in the Life	1983	—	3.00	6.00
—Black label with colorband					
4612	Sgt. Pepper's Lonely Hearts Club Band-With a Little Help from My Friends/A Day in the Life	1988	—	2.50	5.00
—Purple label; label has smooth edge					
4612 [PS]	Sgt. Pepper's Lonely Hearts Club Band-With a Little Help from My Friends/A Day in the Life	1978	5.00	10.00	20.00
P-4612 [DJ]	Sgt. Pepper's Lonely Hearts Club Band-With a Little Help from My Friends (mono/stereo)	1978	10.00	20.00	40.00
B-5100	The Beatles' Movie Medley/Fab Four on Film	1982	12.50	25.00	50.00
—Stock copy; not officially released, but some got out by mistake					
B-5100 [PS]	The Beatles' Movie Medley/Fab Four on Film	1982	5.00	10.00	20.00
PB-5100 [DJ]	The Beatles' Movie Medley/Fab Four on Film	1982	6.25	12.50	25.00
B-5107	The Beatles' Movie Medley/I'm Happy Just to Dance with You	1982	—	2.50	5.00

Number	Title (A Side/B Side)	Yr	VG	VG+	NM
B-5107 [PS]	The Beatles' Movie Medley/I'm Happy Just to Dance with You	1982	—	2.50	5.00
5112	I Want to Hold Your Hand/I Saw Her Standing There	1964	10.00	20.00	40.00
—First pressing credits "Walter Hofer" as B-side publisher					
5112	I Want to Hold Your Hand/I Saw Her Standing There	1964	8.75	17.50	35.00
—Second pressing credits "George Pincus and Sons" as B-side publisher					
5112	I Want to Hold Your Hand/I Saw Her Standing There	1964	7.50	15.00	30.00
—Third (and all later) pressings credit "Gil Music" as B-side publisher					
5112	I Want to Hold Your Hand/I Saw Her Standing There	1968	15.00	30.00	60.00
—Orange and yellow swirl label with "A Subsidiary Of" in perimeter print					
5112	I Want to Hold Your Hand/I Saw Her Standing There	1969	6.25	12.50	25.00
—Red and orange "target" label, round logo					
5112	I Want to Hold Your Hand/I Saw Her Standing There	1969	15.00	30.00	60.00
—Red and orange "target" label, dome logo					
5112	I Want to Hold Your Hand/I Saw Her Standing There	1976	2.50	5.00	10.00
—Orange label, "Capitol" logo on bottom					
5112	I Want to Hold Your Hand/I Saw Her Standing There	1978	3.75	7.50	15.00
—Purple label					
5112	I Want to Hold Your Hand/I Saw Her Standing There	1984	—	2.50	5.00
—20th anniversary reissue; black print on perimeter of label (1964 pressings are white)					
5112	I Want to Hold Your Hand/I Saw Her Standing There	1994	—	2.50	5.00
—30th anniversary reissue; has "NR-58123" engraved in record's trail-off area					
5112 [PS]	I Want to Hold Your Hand/I Saw Her Standing There	1964	25.00	50.00	100.00
—Die-cut, crops George Harrison's head in photo					
5112 [PS]	I Want to Hold Your Hand/I Saw Her Standing There	1964	25.00	50.00	100.00
—Straight cut, shows all of George Harrison's head					
5112 [PS]	I Want to Hold Your Hand/WMCA Good Guys	1964	500.00	1000.	2000.
—Giveaway from New York radio station with photo of WMCA DJs on rear					
5112 [PS]	I Want to Hold Your Hand/I Saw Her Standing There	1984	—	3.00	6.00
—Same as 1964 sleeve except has "1984" in small print, and Paul McCartney's cigarette is airbrushed out					
5112 [PS]	I Want to Hold Your Hand/I Saw Her Standing There	1994	—	2.00	4.00
—Same as 1964 sleeve except "Reg. U.S. Pat. Off." has periods (1964s do not). Also came with a plastic sleeve with a "30th Anniversary" and UPC stickers (add 25%)					
5150	Can't Buy Me Love/You Can't Do That	1964	7.50	15.00	30.00
—Original: Orange and yellow swirl, without "A Subsidiary Of"... in perimeter label print					
5150	Can't Buy Me Love/You Can't Do That	1964	2000.	3000.	4000.
—Yellow vinyl (unauthorized); value is conjecture					
5150	Can't Buy Me Love/You Can't Do That	1964	1000.	1500.	2000.
—Yellow and black vinyl (unauthorized); value is conjecture					
5150	Can't Buy Me Love/You Can't Do That	1968	12.50	25.00	50.00
—Orange and yellow swirl label with "A Subsidiary Of" in perimeter print					
5150	Can't Buy Me Love/You Can't Do That	1969	6.25	12.50	25.00
—Red and orange "target" label, dome logo					
5150	Can't Buy Me Love/You Can't Do That	1969	15.00	30.00	60.00
—Red and orange "target" label, round logo					
5150	Can't Buy Me Love/You Can't Do That	1976	—	3.00	6.00
—Orange label with "Capitol" at bottom					
5150	Can't Buy Me Love/You Can't Do That	1978	3.75	7.50	15.00
—Purple label					
5150 [PS]	Can't Buy Me Love/You Can't Do That	1964	200.00	400.00	800.00
—One of the rarest Beatles picture sleeves. Numerous counterfeits exist; if in doubt, see an expert.					
B-5189	Love Me Do/P.S. I Love You	1982	—	2.50	5.00
—Original: Orange and yellow swirl label, black print					
B-5189	Love Me Do/P.S. I Love You	1983	—	3.00	6.00
—Black label with colorband					
B-5189	Love Me Do/P.S. I Love You	1988	—	2.00	4.00
—Purple label; label has smooth edge					
B-5189 [PS]	Love Me Do/P.S. I Love You	1982	—	2.50	5.00
PB-5189 [DJ]	Love Me Do (same on both sides)	1982	3.75	7.50	15.00
5222	A Hard Day's Night/I Should Have Known Better	1964	7.50	15.00	30.00
—Original: Orange and yellow swirl, without "A Subsidiary Of"... in perimeter label print; first version credited both "Unart" and "Maclen" as publishers					
5222	A Hard Day's Night/I Should Have Known Better	1964	7.50	15.00	30.00
—Orange and yellow swirl, without "A Subsidiary Of"... in perimeter label print; second version credited only "Maclen" as publishers					
5222	A Hard Day's Night/I Should Have Known Better	1968	12.50	25.00	50.00
—Orange and yellow swirl with "A Subsidiary Of"... on perimeter print in white					
5222	A Hard Day's Night/I Should Have Known Better	1968	25.00	50.00	100.00
—Orange and yellow swirl with "A Subsidiary Of"... on perimeter print in black					
5222	A Hard Day's Night/I Should Have Known Better	1969	15.00	30.00	60.00
—Red and orange "target" label with Capitol dome logo					
5222	A Hard Day's Night/I Should Have Known Better	1969	5.00	10.00	20.00
—Red and orange "target" label with Capitol round logo					
5222	A Hard Day's Night/I Should Have Known Better	1976	—	3.00	6.00
—Orange label with "Capitol" at bottom					
5222	A Hard Day's Night/I Should Have Known Better	1978	3.75	7.50	15.00
—Purple label					
5222 [PS]	A Hard Day's Night/I Should Have Known Better	1964	25.00	50.00	100.00
5234	I'll Cry Instead/I'm Happy Just to Dance with You	1964	10.00	20.00	40.00
—Original: Orange and yellow swirl, without "A Subsidiary Of"... in perimeter label print					
5234	I'll Cry Instead/I'm Happy Just to Dance with You	1968	15.00	30.00	60.00
—Orange and yellow swirl label with "A Subsidiary Of" in perimeter print					
5234	I'll Cry Instead/I'm Happy Just to Dance with You	1969	17.50	35.00	70.00
—Red and orange "target" label with Capitol dome logo					
5234	I'll Cry Instead/I'm Happy Just to Dance with You	1969	5.00	10.00	20.00
—Red and orange "target" label with Capitol round logo					
5234	I'll Cry Instead/I'm Happy Just to Dance with You	1976	—	3.00	6.00
—Orange label with "Capitol" at bottom					
5234	I'll Cry Instead/I'm Happy Just to Dance with You	1978	3.75	7.50	15.00
—Purple label					
5234 [PS]	I'll Cry Instead/I'm Happy Just to Dance with You	1964	37.50	75.00	150.00

Number	Title (A Side/B Side)	Yr	VG	VG+	NM
5235	And I Love Her/If I Fell	1964	7.50	15.00	30.00
—Original: Orange and yellow swirl, without "A Subsidiary Of"... in perimeter label print; publishers listed as "Unart" and "Maclen"					
5235	And I Love Her/If I Fell	1964	7.50	15.00	30.00
—Original: Orange and yellow swirl, without "A Subsidiary Of"... in perimeter label print; publishers listed as "Maclen" only					
5235	And I Love Her/If I Fell	1968	12.50	25.00	50.00
—Orange and yellow swirl with "A Subsidiary Of"... on perimeter print in white					
5235	And I Love Her/If I Fell	1968	18.75	37.50	75.00
—Orange and yellow swirl with "A Subsidiary Of"... on perimeter print in black					
5235	And I Love Her/If I Fell	1969	5.00	10.00	20.00
—Red and orange "target" label with Capitol dome logo					
5235	And I Love Her/If I Fell	1969	15.00	30.00	60.00
—Red and orange "target" label with Capitol round logo					
5235	And I Love Her/If I Fell	1976	—	3.00	6.00
—Orange label with "Capitol" at bottom					
5235	And I Love Her/If I Fell	1978	3.75	7.50	15.00
—Purple label					
5235 [PS]	And I Love Her/If I Fell	1964	30.00	60.00	120.00
5255	Matchbox/Slow Down	1964	7.50	15.00	30.00
—Original: Orange and yellow swirl, without "A Subsidiary Of"... in perimeter label print					
5255	Matchbox/Slow Down	1968	12.50	25.00	50.00
—Orange and yellow swirl label with "A Subsidiary Of" in perimeter print					
5255	Matchbox/Slow Down	1969	15.00	30.00	60.00
—Red and orange "target" label with Capitol dome logo					
5255	Matchbox/Slow Down	1969	5.00	10.00	20.00
—Red and orange "target" label with Capitol round logo					
5255	Matchbox/Slow Down	1976	—	3.00	6.00
—Orange label with "Capitol" at bottom					
5255	Matchbox/Slow Down	1978	3.75	7.50	15.00
—Purple label					
5255 [PS]	Matchbox/Slow Down	1964	37.50	75.00	150.00
5327	I Feel Fine/She's a Woman	1964	7.50	15.00	30.00
—Original: Orange and yellow swirl, without "A Subsidiary Of"... in perimeter label print					
5327	I Feel Fine/She's a Woman	1968	12.50	25.00	50.00
—Orange and yellow swirl label with "A Subsidiary Of" in perimeter print					
5327	I Feel Fine/She's a Woman	1969	5.00	10.00	20.00
—Red and orange "target" label with Capitol dome logo					
5327	I Feel Fine/She's a Woman	1969	15.00	30.00	60.00
—Red and orange "target" label with Capitol round logo					
5327	I Feel Fine/She's a Woman	1976	—	3.00	6.00
—Orange label with "Capitol" at bottom					
5327	I Feel Fine/She's a Woman	1978	3.75	7.50	15.00
—Purple label					
5327 [PS]	I Feel Fine/She's a Woman	1964	20.00	40.00	80.00
5371	Eight Days a Week/I Don't Want to Spoil the Party	1965	7.50	15.00	30.00
—Original: Orange and yellow swirl, without "A Subsidiary Of"... in perimeter label print					
5371	Eight Days a Week/I Don't Want to Spoil the Party	1968	12.50	25.00	50.00
—Orange and yellow swirl label with "A Subsidiary Of" in perimeter print					
5371	Eight Days a Week/I Don't Want to Spoil the Party	1969	15.00	30.00	60.00
—Red and orange "target" label with Capitol dome logo					
5371	Eight Days a Week/I Don't Want to Spoil the Party	1969	5.00	10.00	20.00
—Red and orange "target" label with Capitol round logo					
5371	Eight Days a Week/I Don't Want to Spoil the Party	1976	—	3.00	6.00
—Orange label with "Capitol" at bottom					
5371	Eight Days a Week/I Don't Want to Spoil the Party	1978	3.75	7.50	15.00
—Purple label					
5371 [PS]	Eight Days a Week/I Don't Want to Spoil the Party	1965	6.25	12.50	25.00
—Die-cut sleeve					
5371 [PS]	Eight Days a Week/I Don't Want to Spoil the Party	1965	18.75	37.50	75.00
—Straight-cut sleeve					
5407	Ticket to Ride/Yes It Is	1965	7.50	15.00	30.00
—Original: Orange and yellow swirl, without "A Subsidiary Of"... in perimeter label print					
5407	Ticket to Ride/Yes It Is	1968	12.50	25.00	50.00
—Orange and yellow swirl with "A Subsidiary Of"... on perimeter print in white					
5407	Ticket to Ride/Yes It Is	1968	25.00	50.00	100.00
—Orange and yellow swirl with "A Subsidiary Of"... on perimeter print in black					
5407	Ticket to Ride/Yes It Is	1969	15.00	30.00	60.00
—Red and orange "target" label with Capitol dome logo					
5407	Ticket to Ride/Yes It Is	1969	5.00	10.00	20.00
—Red and orange "target" label with Capitol round logo					
5407	Ticket to Ride/Yes It Is	1976	—	3.00	6.00
—Orange label with "Capitol" at bottom					
5407	Ticket to Ride/Yes It Is	1978	3.75	7.50	15.00
—Purple label					
5407 [PS]	Ticket to Ride/Yes It Is	1965	25.00	50.00	100.00
B-5439 [PS]	Leave My Kitten Alone/Ob-La-Di, Ob-La-Da	1985	12.50	25.00	50.00
—Sleeve for a record that was never released, not even as a promo					
5476	Help!/I'm Down	1965	7.50	15.00	30.00
—Original: Orange and yellow swirl, without "A Subsidiary Of"... in perimeter label print					
5476	Help!/I'm Down	1968	12.50	25.00	50.00
—Orange and yellow swirl with "A Subsidiary Of"... on perimeter print in white					
5476	Help!/I'm Down	1968	25.00	50.00	100.00
—Orange and yellow swirl with "A Subsidiary Of"... on perimeter print in black					
5476	Help!/I'm Down	1969	15.00	30.00	60.00
—Red and orange "target" label with Capitol dome logo					
5476	Help!/I'm Down	1969	5.00	10.00	20.00
—Red and orange "target" label with Capitol round logo					
5476	Help!/I'm Down	1976	—	3.00	6.00
—Orange label with "Capitol" at bottom					
5476	Help!/I'm Down	1978	3.75	7.50	15.00
—Purple label					
5476 [PS]	Help!/I'm Down	1965	18.75	37.50	75.00
5498	Yesterday/Act Naturally	1965	7.50	15.00	30.00
—Original: Orange and yellow swirl, without "A Subsidiary Of"... in perimeter label print					
5498	Yesterday/Act Naturally	1968	12.50	25.00	50.00
—Orange and yellow swirl with "A Subsidiary Of"... on perimeter print in white					
5498	Yesterday/Act Naturally	1968	25.00	50.00	100.00
—Orange and yellow swirl with "A Subsidiary Of"... on perimeter print in black					
5498	Yesterday/Act Naturally	1969	15.00	30.00	60.00
—Red and orange "target" label with Capitol dome logo					
5498	Yesterday/Act Naturally	1969	5.00	10.00	20.00
—Red and orange "target" label with Capitol round logo					
5498	Yesterday/Act Naturally	1976	—	3.00	6.00
—Orange label with "Capitol" at bottom					

Number	Title (A Side/B Side)	Yr	VG	VG+	NM
5498	Yesterday/Act Naturally	1978	3.75	7.50	15.00
—Purple label					
5498 [PS]	Yesterday/Act Naturally	1965	25.00	50.00	100.00
5555	We Can Work It Out/Day Tripper	1965	7.50	15.00	30.00
—Original: Orange and yellow swirl, without "A Subsidiary Of"... in perimeter label print					
5555	We Can Work It Out/Day Tripper	1968	12.50	25.00	50.00
—Orange and yellow swirl label with "A Subsidiary Of" in perimeter print					
5555	We Can Work It Out/Day Tripper	1969	15.00	30.00	60.00
—Red and orange "target" label with Capitol dome logo					
5555	We Can Work It Out/Day Tripper	1969	5.00	10.00	20.00
—Red and orange "target" label with Capitol round logo					
5555	We Can Work It Out/Day Tripper	1969	500.00	1000.	1500.
—Red and white "Starline" label (mispress)					
5555	We Can Work It Out/Day Tripper	1976	—	3.00	6.00
—Orange label with "Capitol" at bottom					
5555	We Can Work It Out/Day Tripper	1978	3.75	7.50	15.00
—Purple label					
5555 [PS]	We Can Work It Out/Day Tripper	1978	15.00	30.00	60.00
5587	Nowhere Man/What Goes On	1966	6.25	12.50	25.00
—Original: Orange and yellow swirl, without "A Subsidiary Of"... in perimeter label print; composers of B-side listed as "John Lennon-Paul McCartney"					
5587	Nowhere Man/What Goes On	1966	12.50	25.00	50.00
—Orange and yellow swirl, without "A Subsidiary Of"... in perimeter label print; B-side composers listed as "Lennon-McCartney-Starkey"					
5587	Nowhere Man/What Goes On	1968	12.50	25.00	50.00
—Orange and yellow swirl label with "A Subsidiary Of" in perimeter print					
5587	Nowhere Man/What Goes On	1969	15.00	30.00	60.00
—Red and orange "target" label with Capitol dome logo					
5587	Nowhere Man/What Goes On	1969	5.00	10.00	20.00
—Red and orange "target" label with Capitol round logo					
5587	Nowhere Man/What Goes On	1976	—	3.00	6.00
—Orange label with "Capitol" at bottom					
5587	Nowhere Man/What Goes On	1978	3.75	7.50	15.00
—Purple label					
5587 [PS]	Nowhere Man/What Goes On	1966	10.00	20.00	40.00
B-5624	Twist and Shout/There's a Place	1986	—	2.50	5.00
—Black label with colorband					
B-5624	Twist and Shout/There's a Place	1988	—	2.50	5.00
—Purple label; label has smooth edge					
P-B-5624 [DJ]	Twist and Shout (same on both sides)	1986	3.75	7.50	15.00
5651	Paperback Writer/Rain	1966	6.25	12.50	25.00
—Original: Orange and yellow swirl, without "A Subsidiary Of"... in perimeter label print					
5651	Paperback Writer/Rain	1968	12.50	25.00	50.00
—Orange and yellow swirl with "A Subsidiary Of"... on perimeter print in white					
5651	Paperback Writer/Rain	1968	25.00	50.00	100.00
—Orange and yellow swirl with "A Subsidiary Of"... on perimeter print in black					
5651	Paperback Writer/Rain	1969	15.00	30.00	60.00
—Red and orange "target" label with Capitol dome logo					
5651	Paperback Writer/Rain	1969	5.00	10.00	20.00
—Red and orange "target" label with Capitol round logo					
5651	Paperback Writer/Rain	1976	—	3.00	6.00
—Orange label with "Capitol" at bottom					
5651	Paperback Writer/Rain	1978	3.75	7.50	15.00
—Purple label					
5651 [PS]	Paperback Writer/Rain	1966	18.75	37.50	75.00
5715	Yellow Submarine/Eleanor Rigby	1966	6.25	12.50	25.00
—Original: Orange and yellow swirl, without "A Subsidiary Of"... in perimeter label print; print on perimeter is white					
5715	Yellow Submarine/Eleanor Rigby	1966	12.50	25.00	50.00
—Orange and yellow swirl, without "A Subsidiary Of"... in perimeter label print; print on perimeter is yellow (mispress)					
5715	Yellow Submarine/Eleanor Rigby	1968	12.50	25.00	50.00
—Orange and yellow swirl label with "A Subsidiary Of" in perimeter print					
5715	Yellow Submarine/Eleanor Rigby	1969	5.00	10.00	20.00
—Red and orange "target" label with Capitol dome logo					
5715	Yellow Submarine/Eleanor Rigby	1969	15.00	30.00	60.00
—Red and orange "target" label with Capitol round logo					
5715	Yellow Submarine/Eleanor Rigby	1976	—	3.00	6.00
—Orange label with "Capitol" at bottom					
5715	Yellow Submarine/Eleanor Rigby	1978	3.75	7.50	15.00
—Purple label					
5715 [PS]	Yellow Submarine/Eleanor Rigby	1966	25.00	50.00	100.00
5810	Penny Lane/Strawberry Fields Forever	1967	6.25	12.50	25.00
—Original: Orange and yellow swirl, without "A Subsidiary Of"... in perimeter label print; "Penny Lane" time listed as 3:00					
5810	Penny Lane/Strawberry Fields Forever	1967	7.50	15.00	30.00
—Orange and yellow swirl, without "A Subsidiary Of"... in perimeter label print; "Penny Lane" time listed as 2:57					
5810	Penny Lane/Strawberry Fields Forever	1968	12.50	25.00	50.00
—Orange and yellow swirl label with "A Subsidiary Of" in perimeter print					
5810	Penny Lane/Strawberry Fields Forever	1969	15.00	30.00	60.00
—Red and orange "target" label with Capitol dome logo					
5810	Penny Lane/Strawberry Fields Forever	1969	5.00	10.00	20.00
—Red and orange "target" label with Capitol round logo					
5810	Penny Lane/Strawberry Fields Forever	1976	—	3.00	6.00
—Orange label with "Capitol" at bottom					
5810	Penny Lane/Strawberry Fields Forever	1978	3.75	7.50	15.00
—Purple label					
5810 [PS]	Penny Lane/Strawberry Fields Forever	1967	25.00	50.00	100.00
P 5810 [DJ]	Penny Lane/Strawberry Fields Forever	1967	75.00	150.00	300.00
—Light green promo; most copies have an extra trumpet solo at the end of "Penny Lane"					
P 5810 [DJ]	Penny Lane/Strawberry Fields Forever	1967	150.00	300.00	600.00
—Light green promo; a few copies have no trumpet solo at the end of "Penny Lane"					
5964	All You Need Is Love/Baby, You're a Rich Man	1967	6.25	12.50	25.00
—Original: Orange and yellow swirl, without "A Subsidiary Of"... in perimeter label print					
5964	All You Need Is Love/Baby, You're a Rich Man	1968	12.50	25.00	50.00
—Orange and yellow swirl label with "A Subsidiary Of" in perimeter print					
5964	All You Need Is Love/Baby, You're a Rich Man	1969	18.75	37.50	75.00
—Red and orange "target" label with Capitol dome logo					
5964	All You Need Is Love/Baby, You're a Rich Man	1969	5.00	10.00	20.00
—Red and orange "target" label with Capitol round logo					
5964	All You Need Is Love/Baby, You're a Rich Man	1976	—	3.00	6.00
—Orange label with "Capitol" at bottom					
5964	All You Need Is Love/Baby, You're a Rich Man	1978	3.75	7.50	15.00
—Purple label					
5964 [PS]	All You Need Is Love/Baby, You're a Rich Man	1967	10.00	20.00	40.00

Number	Title (A Side/B Side)	Yr	VG	VG+	NM
P 5964 [DJ]	All You Need Is Love/Baby, You're a Rich Man	1967	62.50	125.00	250.00
—Light green label promo					
S7-17488	Birthday/Taxman	1994	12.50	25.00	50.00
—Black vinyl "error" pressing					
S7-17488	Birthday/Taxman	1994	—	2.00	4.00
—Green vinyl					
S7-17688	She Loves You/I'll Get You	1994	—	2.00	4.00
—Red vinyl					
S7-17689	I Want to Hold Your Hand/This Boy	1994	—	2.00	4.00
—Clear vinyl					
S7-17690	Can't Buy Me Love/You Can't Do That	1994	—	2.00	4.00
—Gren vinyl					
S7-17691	Help!/I'm Down	1994	—	2.00	4.00
—White vinyl					
S7-17692	A Hard Day's Night/Things We Said Today	1994	—	2.00	4.00
—White vinyl					
S7-17693	All You Need Is Love/Baby You're a Rich Man	1994	—	2.00	4.00
—Pink vinyl					
S7-17694	Hey Jude/Revolution	1994	—	2.00	4.00
—Blue vinyl					
S7-17695	Let It Be/You Know My Name (Look Up My Number)	1994	—	2.00	4.00
—Yellow vinyl					
S7-17696	Yellow Submarine/Eleanor Rigby	1994	—	2.00	4.00
—Yellow vinyl					
S7-17697	Strawberry Fields Forever/Penny Lane	1994	—	2.00	4.00
—Red vinyl					
S7-17698	Something/Come Together	1994	—	2.00	4.00
—Blue vinyl					
S7-17699	Twist and Shout/There's a Place	1994	—	2.00	4.00
—Pink vinyl					
S7-17700	Here Comes the Sun/Octopus's Garden	1994	—	2.00	4.00
—Gold/orange vinyl					
S7-17701	Sgt. Pepper's Lonely Hearts Club Band-With a Little Help from My Friends/A Day in the Life	1994	—	2.00	4.00
—Clear vinyl					
S7-18888	Norwegian Wood/If I Needed Someone	1995	12.50	25.00	50.00
—Green vinyl; 1,000 pressed, given by Collectors' Choice Music to buyers of Beatles reissue LPs					
S7-18889	You've Got to Hide Your Love Away/I've Just Seen a Face	1996	—	2.00	4.00
—Gold/orange vinyl					
S7-18890	Magical Mystery Tour/The Fool on the Hill	1996	—	2.00	4.00
—Yellow vinyl					
S7-18891	Across the Universe/Two of Us	1996	—	2.00	4.00
—Clear vinyl					
S7-18892	While My Guitar Gently Weeps/Blackbird	1996	—	2.00	4.00
—Blue vinyl					
S7-18893	It's All Too Much/Only a Northern Song	1996	—	2.00	4.00
—Blue vinyl					
S7-18894	Nowhere Man/What Goes On	1996	—	2.00	4.00
—Green vinyl					
S7-18895	We Can Work It Out/Day Tripper	1996	—	2.00	4.00
—Pink vinyl					
S7-18896	Lucy in the Sky with Diamonds/When I'm 64	1996	—	2.00	4.00
—Red vinyl					
S7-18897	Here, There and Everywhere/Good Day Sunshine	1996	—	2.00	4.00
—Yellow vinyl					
S7-18898	The Long and Winding Road/For You Blue	1996	—	2.00	4.00
—Blue vinyl					
S7-18899	Got to Get You Into My Life/Helter Skelter	1996	—	2.00	4.00
—Gold/orange vinyl					
S7-18900	Ob-La-Di, Ob-La-Da/Julia	1996	—	2.00	4.00
—Clear vinyl					
S7-18901	Yesterday/Act Naturally	1996	—	2.00	4.00
—Pink vinyl					
S7-18902	Paperback Writer/Rain	1996	—	2.00	4.00
—Red vinyl					
S7-19341	Norwegian Wood (This Bird Has Flown)/If I Needed Someone	1996	—	—	3.00
S7-56785	Love Me Do/P.S. I Love You	1992	—	2.00	4.00
S7-56785	Love Me Do/P.S. I Love You	1992	7.50	15.00	30.00
—Small pressing on red vinyl "by mistake"					
72133	Roll Over Beethoven/Please Mister Postman	1964	12.50	25.00	50.00
—Orange and yellow swirl; Canadian release that was heavily imported to the U.S.					
72144	All My Loving/This Boy	1964	12.50	25.00	50.00
—Orange and yellow swirl; Canadian release that was heavily imported to the U.S.					
72144	All My Loving/This Boy	1971	25.00	50.00	100.00
—Canadian number with U.S. labels (red and orange "target" label)					
7PRO-79551/2 [DJ]	Love Me Do/P.S. I Love You	1992	6.25	12.50	25.00
7PRO-79551/2 [PS]	Love Me Do/P.S. I Love You	1992	6.25	12.50	25.00

CAPITOL STARLINE

Number	Title (A Side/B Side)	Yr	VG	VG+	NM
6061	Twist and Shout/There's a Place	1965	30.00	60.00	120.00
—Green swirl label					
6062	Love Me Do/P.S. I Love You	1965	30.00	60.00	120.00
—Green swirl label					
6063	Please Please Me/From Me to You	1965	30.00	60.00	120.00
—Green swirl label					
6064	Do You Want to Know a Secret/Thank You Girl	1965	30.00	60.00	120.00
—Green swirl label					
6065	Roll Over Beethoven/Misery	1965	30.00	60.00	120.00
—Green swirl label					
6065	Roll Over Beethoven/Misery	1971	7.50	15.00	30.00
—Red and orange "target" label					
6066	Boys/Kansas City	1965	20.00	40.00	80.00
—Green swirl label					
6066	Boys/Kansas City	1971	7.50	15.00	30.00
—Red and orange "target" label					
6278	I Want to Hold Your Hand/I Saw Her Standing There	1981	5.00	10.00	20.00
—Originals have blue labels					
6279	Can't Buy Me Love/You Can't Do That	1981	2.00	4.00	8.00
—Originals have blue labels					
6281	A Hard Day's Night/I Should Have Known Better	1981	2.00	4.00	8.00
—Originals have blue labels					
6282	I'll Cry Instead/I'm Happy Just to Dance with You	1981	2.00	4.00	8.00
—Originals have blue labels					
6283	And I Love Her/If I Fell	1981	2.00	4.00	8.00
—Originals have blue labels					
6284	Matchbox/Slow Down	1981	2.00	4.00	8.00
—Originals have blue labels					
6286	I Feel Fine/She's a Woman	1981	2.00	4.00	8.00
—Originals have blue labels					
6287	Eight Days a Week/I Don't Want to Spoil the Party	1981	2.00	4.00	8.00
—Originals have blue labels					
6288	Ticket to Ride/Yes It Is	1981	2.00	4.00	8.00
—Originals have blue labels					
6290	Help!/I'm Down	1981	2.00	4.00	8.00
—Originals have blue labels					
6291	Yesteday/Act Naturally	1981	2.00	4.00	8.00
—Originals have blue labels					
6293	We Can Work It Out/Day Tripper	1981	2.00	4.00	8.00
—Originals have blue labels					
6294	Nowhere Man/What Goes On	1981	2.00	4.00	8.00
—Originals have blue labels					
6296	Paperback Writer/Rain	1981	2.00	4.00	8.00
—Originals have blue labels					
6297	Yeloow Submarine/Eleanor Rigby	1981	2.00	4.00	8.00
—Originals have blue labels					
6299	Penny Lane/Strawberry Fields Forever	1981	2.00	4.00	8.00
—Originals have blue labels					
6300	All You Need Is Love/Baby You're a Rich Man	1981	2.00	4.00	8.00
—Originals have blue labels					

CAPITOL/EVATONE

Number	Title (A Side/B Side)	Yr	VG	VG+	NM
420826cs	All My Loving/You've Got to Hide Your Love Away	1982	2.50	5.00	10.00
—Flexi-disc issued as giveaway by The Musicland Group; "Musicland" version					
420826cs	All My Loving/You've Got to Hide Your Love Away	1982	5.00	10.00	20.00
—Flexi-disc issued as giveaway by The Musicland Group; "Discount" version					
420826cs	All My Loving/You've Got to Hide Your Love Away	1982	6.25	12.50	25.00
—Flexi-disc issued as giveaway by The Musicland Group; "Sam Goody" version					
420827cs	Magical Mystery Tour/Here Comes the Sun	1982	2.50	5.00	10.00
—Flexi-disc issued as giveaway by The Musicland Group; "Musicland" version					
420827cs	Magical Mystery Tour/Here Comes the Sun	1982	5.00	10.00	20.00
—Flexi-disc issued as giveaway by The Musicland Group; "Discount" version					
420827cs	Magical Mystery Tour/Here Comes the Sun	1982	6.25	12.50	25.00
—Flexi-disc issued as giveaway by The Musicland Group; "Sam Goody" version					
420828cs	Rocky Raccoon/Why Don't We Do It in the Road?	1982	2.50	5.00	10.00
—Flexi-disc issued as giveaway by The Musicland Group; "Musicland" version					
420828cs	Rocky Raccoon/Why Don't We Do It in the Road?	1982	5.00	10.00	20.00
—Flexi-disc issued as giveaway by The Musicland Group; "Discount" version					
420828cs	Rocky Raccoon/Why Don't We Do It in the Road?	1982	6.25	12.50	25.00
—Flexi-disc issued as giveaway by The Musicland Group; "Sam Goody" version					
830771 X	Till There Was You/Three Cool Cats	1983	—	3.00	6.00
—Flexi-disc issued as giveaway with a book					
1214825cs	German Medley	1983	15.00	30.00	60.00
—Flexi-disc given away by House of Guitars in New York					

CICADELIC/BIODISC

Number	Title (A Side/B Side)	Yr	VG	VG+	NM
001	A Hard Day's Night Open End Interview	1990	3.75	7.50	15.00
—Limited edition of 700; lower numbers increase value substantially					
001	A Hard Day's Night Open End Interview	1990	7.50	15.00	30.00
—"Records Etc." pressing					
002	Help! Open End Interview	1990	—	2.50	5.00
002 [PS]	Help! Open End Interview	1990	—	2.50	5.00

COLLECTABLES

Number	Title (A Side/B Side)	Yr	VG	VG+	NM
1501	I'm Gonna Sit Right Down and Cry Over You/Roll Over Beethoven	1982	—	—	3.00
1501 [PS]	I'm Gonna Sit Right Down and Cry Over You/Roll Over Beethoven	1982	—	—	3.00
1502	Hippy Hippy Shake/Sweet Little Sixteen	1982	—	—	3.00
1502 [PS]	Hippy Hippy Shake/Sweet Little Sixteen	1982	—	—	3.00
1503	Lend Me Your Comb/Your Feets Too Big	1982	—	—	3.00
1503 [PS]	Lend Me Your Comb/Your Feets Too Big	1982	—	—	3.00
1504	Where Have You Been All My Life/Mr. Moonlight	1982	—	—	3.00
1504 [PS]	Where Have You Been All My Life/Mr. Moonlight	1982	—	—	3.00
1505	A Taste of Honey/Besame Mucho	1982	—	—	3.00
1505 [PS]	A Taste of Honey/Besame Mucho	1982	—	—	3.00
1506	Till There Was You/Everybody's Trying to Be My Baby	1982	—	—	3.00
1506 [PS]	Till There Was You/Everybody's Trying to Be My Baby	1982	—	—	3.00
1507	Kansas City-Hey Hey Hey Hey/Ain't Nothing Shakin Like the Leaves on a Tree	1982	—	—	3.00
1507 [PS]	Kansas City-Hey Hey Hey Hey/Ain't Nothing Shakin Like the Leaves on a Tree	1982	—	—	3.00
1508	To Know Her Is To Love Her/Little Queenie	1982	—	—	3.00
1508 [PS]	To Know Her Is To Love Her/Little Queenie	1982	—	—	3.00
1509	Falling in Love Again/Sheila	1982	—	—	3.00
1509 [PS]	Falling in Love Again/Sheila	1982	—	—	3.00
1510	Be-Bop-a-Lula/Hallelujah I Love Her So	1982	—	—	3.00
1510 [PS]	Be-Bop-a-Lula/Hallelujah I Love Her So	1982	—	—	3.00
1511	Red Sails in the Sunset/Matchbox	1982	—	—	3.00
1511 [PS]	Red Sails in the Sunset/Matchbox	1982	—	—	3.00
1512	Talkin' Bout You/Shimmy Shake	1982	—	—	3.00
1512 [PS]	Talkin' Bout You/Shimmy Shake	1982	—	—	3.00
1513	Long Tall Sally/I Remember You	1982	—	—	3.00
1513 [PS]	Long Tall Sally/I Remember You	1982	—	—	3.00
1514	Ask Me Why/Twist and Shout	1982	—	—	3.00
1514 [PS]	Ask Me Why/Twist and Shout	1982	—	—	3.00
1515	I Saw Her Standing There/Can't Help It "Blue Angel"	1982	—	—	3.00
—B-side is actually "Reminiscing"					
1515 [PS]	I Saw Her Standing There/Can't Help It "Blue Angel"	1982	—	—	3.00
1516	I'll Try Anyway/I Don't Know Why I Do (I Just Do)	1987	2.50	5.00	10.00
—Despite label credit to The Beatles, both are Peter Best recordings					
1517	She's Not the Only Girl in Town/More Than I Need Myself	1987	2.50	5.00	10.00
—Despite label credit to The Beatles, both are Peter Best recordings					
1518	I'll Have Everything Too/I'm Checking Out Now Baby	1987	2.50	5.00	10.00
—Despite label credit to The Beatles, both are Peter Best recordings					

Number	Title (A Side/B Side)	Yr	VG	VG+	NM
1519	How'd You Get to Know Her Name/If You Can't Get Her	1987	2.50	5.00	10.00
—Despite label credit to The Beatles, both are Peter Best recordings					
1520	Cry for a Shadow/Rock and Roll Music	1987	—	2.50	5.00
—Despite label credit to The Beatles, B-side is a Peter Best recording					
1521	Let's Dance/If You Love Me Baby	1987	—	3.00	6.00
—Despite label credit to The Beatles, A-side is a Tony Sheridan solo recording					
1522	What'd I Say/Sweet Georgia Brown	1987	—	3.00	6.00
—Despite label credit to The Beatles, A-side is a Tony Sheridan solo recording					
1523	Ruby Baby/Ya Ya	1987	—	3.00	6.00
—Despite label credit to The Beatles, both are by Tony Sheridan without the Fab Four					
1524	Why/I'll Try Anyway	1987	—	3.00	6.00
—Despite label credit to The Beatles, B-side is a Peter Best recording					
DECCA					
31382	My Bonnie/The Saints	1962	7500.	11250.	15000.
—By "Tony Sheridan and the Beat Brothers"; black label with color bars (all-black label with star under "Decca" should be a counterfeit)					
31382 [DJ]	My Bonnie/The Saints	1962	1000.	2000.	3000.
—By "Tony Sheridan and the Beat Brothers"; ' pink label, star on label under "Decca"					
EVA-TONE					
830771X [DJ]	Til There Was You/Three Cool Cats (both on same side)	1983	—	3.00	6.00
—Red plastic flexidisc; issued as giveaway with a Beatles price guide					
MGM					
13213	My Bonnie (My Bonnie Lies Over the Ocean)/The Saints (When the Saints Go Marching In)	1964	10.00	20.00	40.00
—The Beatles with Tony Sheridan; no reference to LP on label					
13213	My Bonnie (My Bonnie Lies Over the Ocean)/The Saints (When the Saints Go Marching In)	1964	12.50	25.00	50.00
—The Beatles with Tony Sheridan; LP number on label					
13213 [DJ]	My Bonnie (My Bonnie Lies Over the Ocean)/The Saints (When the Saints Go Marching In)	1964	75.00	150.00	300.00
—The Beatles with Tony Sheridan					
13213 [PS]	My Bonnie (My Bonnie Lies Over the Ocean)/The Saints (When the Saints Go Marching In)	1964	30.00	60.00	120.00
—The Beatles with Tony Sheridan					
13227	Why/Cry for a Shadow	1964	37.50	75.00	150.00
—The Beatles with Tony Sheridan					
13227 [DJ]	Why/Cry for a Shadow	1964	62.50	125.00	250.00
—The Beatles with Tony Sheridan					
13227 [PS]	Why/Cry for a Shadow	1964	100.00	200.00	400.00
—The Beatles with Tony Sheridan					
OLDIES 45					
#149	Do You Want to Know a Secret/Thank You Girl	1965	3.75	7.50	15.00
#150	Please Please Me/From Me to You	1965	3.75	7.50	15.00
#151	Love Me Do/P.S. I Love You	1965	3.75	7.50	15.00
#152	Twist and Shout/There's a Place	1965	3.75	7.50	15.00
SWAN					
4152	She Loves You/I'll Get You	1963	150.00	300.00	600.00
—Semi-glossy white label/red print; "Don't Drop Out" not on label					
4152	She Loves You/I'll Get You	1963	162.50	325.00	650.00
—Flat white label/red print, "Don't Drop Out" not on label					
4152	She Loves You/I'll Get You	1963	162.50	325.00	650.00
—Semi-glossy white label/red print, "Don't Drop Out" on label					
4152	She Loves You/I'll Get You	1963	150.00	300.00	600.00
—Semi-glossy white label/blue printing					
4152	She Loves You/I'll Get You	1964	10.00	20.00	40.00
—Black label, silver print, "Don't Drop Out" not on label					
4152	She Loves You/I'll Get You	1964	7.50	15.00	30.00
—Black label, silver print, "Don't Drop Out" on label					
4152	She Loves You/I'll Get You	1964	12.50	25.00	50.00
—Black label, silver print, "Produced by George Martin" on both labels					
4152	She Loves You/I'll Get You	1964	12.50	25.00	50.00
—Black label, silver print, "Produced by George Martin" on only one label					
4152	She Loves You/I'll Get You	196?	5.00	10.00	20.00
—Black label, silver print, "Don't Drop Out" not on label, smaller numbers in trailoff area					
4152	She Loves You/I'll Get You	196?	12.50	25.00	50.00
—White label, red or maroon print, same as above					
4152 [DJ]	She Loves You/I'll Get You	1963	125.00	250.00	500.00
—Thick print, no "Don't Drop Out" on label					
4152 [DJ]	She Loves You/I'll Get You	1963	112.50	225.00	450.00
—Thin print, "Don't Drop Out" on label					
4152 [DJ]	She Loves You/I'll Get You	1963	125.00	250.00	500.00
—Flat white label, no "Don't Drop Out" on label					
4152 [DJ]	I'll Get You (one-sided)	1964	200.00	400.00	600.00
4152 [PS]	She Loves You/I'll Get You	1964	30.00	60.00	120.00
4182	Sie Liebt Dich (She Loves You)/I'll Get You	1964	37.50	75.00	150.00
—White label, "Sie Liebt Dich (She Loves You)" on one line					
4182	Sie Liebt Dich (She Loves You)/I'll Get You	1964	37.50	75.00	150.00
—White label, "(She Loves You)" under "Sie Liebt Dich," narrow print					
4182	Sie Liebt Dich (She Loves You)/I'll Get You	1964	37.50	75.00	150.00
—White label, "(She Loves You)" under "Sie Liebt Dich," wide red print					
4182	Sie Liebt Dich (She Loves You)/I'll Get You	1964	43.75	87.50	175.00
—White label, "(She Loves You)" under "Sie Liebt Dich," wide orange print					
4182 [DJ]	Sie Liebt Dich (She Loves You)/I'll Get You	1964	100.00	200.00	400.00
—White label, "(She Loves You)" under "Sie Liebt Dich"					
4182 [DJ]	Sie Liebt Dich (She Loves You)/I'll Get You	1964	112.50	225.00	450.00
—White label, "Sie Liebt Dich (She Loves You)" on one line					
TOLLIE					
9001	Twist and Shout/There's a Place	1964	12.50	25.00	50.00
—Yellow label, green print, "tollie" lowercase					
9001	Twist and Shout/There's a Place	1964	12.50	25.00	50.00
—Yellow label, black print, "TOLLIE" stands alone					
9001	Twist and Shout/There's a Place	1964	12.50	25.00	50.00
—Yellow label, black print, black "tollie" in box					
9001	Twist and Shout/There's a Place	1964	15.00	30.00	60.00
—Yellow label, black print, purple "tollie" in box					
9001	Twist and Shout/There's a Place	1964	12.50	25.00	50.00
—Yellow label, black print, black "TOLLIE" in thin box					
9001	Twist and Shout/There's a Place	1964	18.75	37.50	75.00
—Yellow label, black print, "TOLLIE" in brackets					
9001	Twist and Shout/There's a Place	1964	15.00	30.00	60.00
—Yellow label, blue print					
9001	Twist and Shout/There's a Place	1964	20.00	40.00	80.00
—Yellow label, purple print					
9001	Twist and Shout/There's a Place	1964	20.00	40.00	80.00
—Yellow label, green print, "TOLLIE" uppercase					
9001	Twist and Shout/There's a Place	1964	15.00	30.00	60.00
—Black label, silver print					
9008	Love Me Do/P.S. I Love You	1964	12.50	25.00	50.00
—Yellow label, black print (any logo or print variation)					
9008	Love Me Do/P.S. I Love You	1964	12.50	25.00	50.00
—Yellow label, blue/green print					
9008	Love Me Do/P.S. I Love You	1964	15.00	30.00	60.00
—Black label, silver print					
9008 [DJ]	Love Me Do/P.S. I Love You	1964	100.00	200.00	400.00
9008 [PS]	Love Me Do/P.S. I Love You	1964	37.50	75.00	150.00
UNITED ARTISTS					
SP-2357 [DJ]	A Hard Day's Night Theatre Lobby Spot	1964	500.00	1000.	1500.
UAEP 10029 [DJ]	A Hard Day's Night Open End Interview	1964	500.00	1000.	1500.
ULP-42370	Let It Be Radio Spots	1970	400.00	800.00	1200.
VEE JAY					
(no #) [PS]	We Wish You a Merry Christmas and a Happy New Year	1964	20.00	40.00	80.00
—Used with any Vee Jay or Tollie Beatles single in 1964-65 holiday season					
Spec. DJ No. 8	Ask Me Why/Anna	1964?	5000.	7500.	10000.
—One of the more controversial items in Beatles collecting, but it is nonetheless authentic					
498	Please Please Me/Ask Me Why	1963	800.00	1200.	1600.
—Misspelled "The Beattles"; number is "#498"					
498	Please Please Me/Ask Me Why	1963	750.00	1125.	1500.
—Misspelled "The Beattles"; number is "VJ 498"					
498	Please Please Me/Ask Me Why	1963	800.00	1200.	1600.
—Correct spelling; number is "#498"					
498	Please Please Me/Ask Me Why	1963	300.00	600.00	900.00
—Correct spelling; number is "VJ 498"; thick print					
498	Please Please Me/Ask Me Why	1963	1000.	1500.	2000.
—Correct spelling; number is "VJ 498"; brackets label					
498 [DJ]	Please Please Me/Ask Me Why	1963	550.00	825.00	1100.
—Misspelled "The Beattles"					
522	From Me to You/Thank You Girl	1963	150.00	300.00	600.00
—Black rainbow label; "Vee Jay" in oval					
522	From Me to You/Thank You Girl	1963	300.00	600.00	900.00
—Black rainbow label; "VJ" in brackets					
522	From Me to You/Thank You Girl	1963	200.00	400.00	800.00
—Plain black label					
522 [DJ]	From Me to You/Thank You Girl	1963	125.00	250.00	500.00
581	Please Please Me/From Me to You	1964	12.50	25.00	50.00
—Black rainbow label, oval logo					
581	Please Please Me/From Me to You	1964	11.25	22.50	45.00
—Plain black label with two horizontal lines					
581	Please Please Me/From Me to You	1964	18.75	37.50	75.00
—Plain black label, brackets logo					
581	Please Please Me/From Me to You	1964	18.75	37.50	75.00
—Yellow label					
581	Please Please Me/From Me to You	1964	40.00	80.00	160.00
—White label					
581	Please Please Me/From Me to You	1964	62.50	125.00	250.00
—Purple label					
581	Please Please Me/From Me to You	1964	15.00	30.00	60.00
—Plain black label, "VEE JAY" stands alone					
581	Please Please Me/From Me to You	1964	16.25	32.50	65.00
—Plain black label, "VJ" stands alone					
581	Please Please Me/From Me to You	1964	15.00	30.00	60.00
—Black rainbow label, brackets logo					
581	Please Please Me/From Me to You	1964	15.00	30.00	60.00
—Plain black label, oval logo					
581 [DJ]	Please Please Me/From Me to You	1964	200.00	400.00	600.00
—White label, blue print; "Promotional Copy" on label					
581 [DJ]	Please Please Me/From Me to You	1964	300.00	600.00	900.00
—White label, blue print; no "Promotional Copy" on label					
581 [PS]	Please Please Me/From Me to You	1964	1250.	1875.	2500.
—Special "The Record That Started Beatlemania" promo-only sleeve					
581 [PS]	Please Please Me/From Me to You	1964	125.00	250.00	500.00
587	Do You Want to Know a Secret/Thank You Girl	1964	12.50	25.00	50.00
—Black rainbow label, oval logo					
587	Do You Want to Know a Secret/Thank You Girl	1964	16.25	32.50	65.00
—Plain black label; "Vee Jay" in oval					
587	Do You Want to Know a Secret/Thank You Girl	1964	16.25	32.50	65.00
—Plain black label; "VJ" in brackets					
587	Do You Want to Know a Secret/Thank You Girl	1964	16.25	32.50	65.00
—Plain black label; "VJ" stands alone					
587	Do You Want to Know a Secret/Thank You Girl	1964	12.50	25.00	50.00
—Plain black label; "VEE JAY" stands alone					
587	Do You Want to Know a Secret/Thank You Girl	1964	11.25	22.50	45.00
—Plain black label with two horizontal lines; "VJ" in brackets					
587	Do You Want to Know a Secret/Thank You Girl	1964	16.25	32.50	65.00
—Yellow label					
587	Do You Want to Know a Secret/Thank You Girl	1964	10.00	20.00	40.00
—Black rainbow label, brackets logo					
587 [DJ]	Do You Want to Know a Secret/Thank You Girl	1964	150.00	300.00	600.00
587 [PS]	Do You Want to Know a Secret/Thank You Girl	1964	30.00	60.00	120.00
(NO LABEL)					
MBRF-55551	Decade	1974	—	—	—
—A clever bootleg of radio spots for the Beatles' back catalog, compiled without authorization by two former Capitol employees.					

7-Inch Extended Plays

Number	Title (A Side/B Side)	Yr	VG	VG+	NM
CAPITOL					
SXA-2047 [PS]	Meet the Beatles	1964	150.00	300.00	600.00
—With all jukebox title strips intact (deduct 33 percent if missing, deduct less if material is there but not intact)					
SXA-2047 [S]	(contents unknown)	1964	100.00	200.00	400.00
—33 1/3 rpm, small hole jukebox edition					
SXA-2080 [PS]	The Beatles' Second Album	1964	150.00	300.00	600.00
—With all jukebox title strips intact (deduct 33 percent if missing, deduct less if material is there but not intact)					
SXA-2080 [S]	(contents unknown)	1964	100.00	200.00	400.00
—33 1/3 rpm, small hole jukebox edition					
SXA-2108 [PS]	Something New	1964	150.00	300.00	600.00
—With all jukebox title strips intact (deduct 33 percent if missing, deduct less if material is there but not intact)					

Number	Title (A Side/B Side)	Yr	VG	VG+	NM
SXA-2108 [S]	(contents unknown)	1964	100.00	200.00	400.00
—33 1/3 rpm, small hole jukebox edition					
EAP 1-2121	Roll Over Beethoven/This Boy//All My Loving/ Please Mr. Postman	1964	25.00	50.00	100.00
EAP 1-2121 [PS]	Four by the Beatles	1964	75.00	150.00	300.00
PRO-2548/9 [DJ]	Open End Interview with the Beatles	1964	200.00	400.00	800.00
—33 1/3 rpm, small hole. Authentic copies have colorband along outside of label.					
PRO-2548/9 [PS]	Open End Interview with the Beatles	1964	250.00	500.00	1000.
—Contains script for interview. Authentic copies are glossy and have a die-cut thumb tab.					
PRO-2598/9 [DJ]	The Beatles Second Album Open End Interview	1964	200.00	400.00	800.00
—33 1/3 rpm, small hole; interview plus three songs from the LP					
PRO-2598/9 [PS]	The Beatles Second Album Open End Interview	1964	250.00	500.00	1000.
—Contains script for interview					
R-5365	Honey Don't/I'm a Loser//Mr. Moonlight/ Everybody's Trying to Be My Baby	1965	20.00	40.00	80.00
R-5365 [PS]	4-By the Beatles	1965	50.00	100.00	200.00
POLYDOR					
PRO 1113-7 [DJ]	Ain't She Sweet/Cry for a Shadow//My Bonnie/ The Saints	1994	6.25	12.50	25.00
PRO 1113-7 [PS]	Backbeat	1994	6.25	12.50	25.00
—Picture sleeve for above sampler					
VEE JAY					
1-903	Misery/Taste of Honey//Ask Me Why/Anna	1964	10.00	20.00	40.00
—Black rainbow label, oval logo					
1-903	Misery/Taste of Honey//Ask Me Why/Anna	1964	31.25	62.50	125.00
—Plain black label, oval logo					
1-903	Misery/Taste of Honey//Ask Me Why/Anna	1964	31.25	62.50	125.00
—Black rainbow label, brackets logo, "Ask Me Why" in much larger print					
1-903	Misery/Taste of Honey//Ask Me Why/Anna	1964	22.50	45.00	90.00
—Black rainbow label, brackets logo, all titles the same size					
1-903	Misery/Taste of Honey//Ask Me Why/Anna	1964	50.00	100.00	200.00
—Plain black label, brackets logo					
1-903	Misery/Taste of Honey//Ask Me Why/Anna	1964	37.50	75.00	150.00
—Plain black label, "VEE JAY" stands alone					
1-903 [DJ]	Misery/Taste of Honey//Ask Me Why/Anna	1964	100.00	200.00	400.00
—White and blue label, all titles the same size					
1-903 [DJ]	Misery/Taste of Honey//Ask Me Why/Anna	1964	75.00	150.00	300.00
—White and blue label, "Ask Me Why" in much larger print					
1-903 [PS]	Souvenir of Their Visit to America	1964	15.00	30.00	60.00
—Cardboard sleeve					
1-903 [PS]	Souvenir of Their Visit to America	1964	4000.	6000.	8000.
—"Ask Me Why/The Beatles" plugged on promo-only sleeve					

Albums

Number	Title (A Side/B Side)	Yr	VG	VG+	NM
APPLE					
SBC-100 [M]	The Beatles' Christmas Album	1970	100.00	200.00	400.00
—Fan club issue of the seven Christmas messages; very good counterfeits exist					
SWBO-101 [(2)]	The Beatles	1968	37.50	75.00	200.00
—Numbered copy; includes four individual photos and large poster (included in value); because the white cover shows ring wear so readily, this is an EXTREMELY difficult album to find in near-mint condition					
SWBO-101 [(2)]	The Beatles	1975	17.50	35.00	70.00
—With "All Rights Reserved" on labels; title in black on cover; photos and poster of thinner stock than originals					
SWBO-101 [(2)]	The Beatles	197?	15.00	30.00	60.00
—Un-numbered copy; includes four individual photos and large poster (included in value)					
SW-153 [P]	Yellow Submarine	1969	12.50	25.00	50.00
—With Capitol logo on Side 2 bottom. "Only a Northern Song" is rechanneled.					
SW-153 [P]	Yellow Submarine	1971	5.00	10.00	20.00
—With "Mfd. by Apple" on label					
SW-153 [P]	Yellow Submarine	1975	6.25	12.50	25.00
—With "All Rights Reserved" on label					
SO-383	Abbey Road	1969	18.75	37.50	75.00
—With Capitol logo on Side 2 bottom; "Her Majesty" is NOT listed on either the jacket or the label					
SO-383	Abbey Road	1969	10.00	20.00	40.00
—With Capitol logo on Side 2 bottom; "Her Majesty" IS listed on both the jacket and the label					
SO-383	Abbey Road	1969	5.00	10.00	20.00
—With "Mfd. by Apple" on label; "Her Majesty" is NOT listed on the label					
SO-383	Abbey Road	1969	5.00	10.00	20.00
—With "Mfd. by Apple" on label; "Her Majesty" IS listed on the label					
SO-383	Abbey Road	1975	6.25	12.50	25.00
—With "All Rights Reserved" on label					
SO-385 [DJ]	The Beatles Again	1970	4000.	6000.	8000.
—Prototypes with "The Beatles Again" on cover; not released to the general public					
SW-385	Hey Jude	1970	10.00	20.00	40.00
—Label calls the LP "The Beatles Again"; record is "SO-385" (this could be found in retail stores as late as 1973)					
SW-385	Hey Jude	1970	6.25	12.50	25.00
—Label calls the LP "The Beatles Again"; record is "SW-385"					
SW-385	Hey Jude	1970	18.75	37.50	75.00
—With Capitol logo on Side 2 bottom; label calls the LP "Hey Jude"					
SW-385	Hey Jude	1970	5.00	10.00	20.00
—With "Mfd. by Apple" on label; label calls the LP "Hey Jude"					
SW-385	Hey Jude	1975	6.25	12.50	25.00
—With "All Rights Reserved" on label; label calls the LP "Hey Jude"					
SKBO-3403 [P]	The Beatles 1962-1966	1973	7.50	15.00	30.00
—Custom red Apple labels. "Love Me Do" and "I Want to Hold Your Hand" are rechanneled; "She Loves You," "A Hard Day's Night," "I Feel Fine" and "Ticket to Ride" are mono; "From Me to You," "Can't Buy Me Love" and everything else is stereo.					
SKBO-3403 [P]	The Beatles 1962-1966	1975	12.50	25.00	50.00
—Custom red Apple labels with "All Rights Reserved" on labels					
SKBO-3404 [B]	The Beatles 1967-1970	1973	7.50	15.00	30.00
—Custom blue Apple labels. "Hello Goodbye" and "Penny Lane" are mono, all others stereo.					
SKBO-3404 [B]	The Beatles 1967-1970	1975	12.50	25.00	50.00
—Custom blue Apple labels with "All Rights Reserved" on labels					
SPRO 11206/7 [EP]	Anthology 2 Sampler	1996	37.50	75.00	150.00
—Promo-only collection sent to college radio stations					
C1-8-31796 [(2)]	Live at the BBC	1994	12.50	25.00	50.00
AR-34001	Let It Be	1970	6.25	12.50	25.00
—Red Apple label; originals have "Bell Sound" stamped in trail-off area, counterfeits do not					
C1-8-34445 [(3)]	Anthology 1	1995	10.00	20.00	40.00
—All copies distributed in the U.S. were manufactured in the U.K. with no distinguishing marks (some LPs imported directly from the U.K. have "Made in England" stickers, which can be removed easily)					
C1-8-34448 [(3)]	Anthology 2	1996	10.00	20.00	40.00
C1-8-34451 [(3)]	Anthology 3	1996	7.50	15.00	30.00

Number	Title (A Side/B Side)	Yr	VG	VG+	NM
C1-97036 [B]	The Beatles 1962-1966	1993	6.25	12.50	25.00
—Custom red Apple labels; red vinyl; all copies pressed in U.K; U.S. versions have a bar-code sticker over the international bar code on back cover. "Love Me Do," "Please Please Me," "From Me to You" and "She Loves You" are mono; all others are stereo.					
C1-97039	The Beatles 1967-1970	1993	6.25	12.50	25.00
—Custom blue Apple labels; blue vinyl; all copies pressed in U.K.; U.S. versions have a bar-code sticker over the international bar code on back cover					
APPLE FILMS					
KAL 004 [DJ]	The Yellow Submarine (A United Artists Release)	1969	1000.	1500.	2000.
—One-sided LP with radio spots for movie					
APPLE/CAPITOL					
(no #) [(10)]	The Beatles Special Limited Edition	1974	300.00	600.00	1200.
(no #) [(17)]	The Beatles 10th Anniversary Box Set	1974	1000.	1500.	2000.
ST 2047 [P]	Meet the Beatles!	1968	10.00	20.00	40.00
—With Capitol logo on Side 2 bottom					
ST 2047 [P]	Meet the Beatles!	1971	5.00	10.00	20.00
—With "Mfd. by Apple" on label					
ST 2047 [P]	Meet the Beatles!	1975	6.25	12.50	25.00
—With "All Rights Reserved" on label					
ST 2080 [P]	The Beatles' Second Album	1968	10.00	20.00	40.00
—With Capitol logo on Side 2 bottom					
ST 2080 [P]	The Beatles' Second Album	1971	5.00	10.00	20.00
—With "Mfd. by Apple" on label					
ST 2080 [P]	The Beatles' Second Album	1975	6.25	12.50	25.00
—With "All Rights Reserved" on label					
ST 2108 [S]	Something New	1968	10.00	20.00	40.00
—With Capitol logo on Side 2 bottom					
ST 2108 [S]	Something New	1971	5.00	10.00	20.00
—With "Mfd. by Apple" on label					
ST 2108 [S]	Something New	1975	6.25	2.50	25.00
—With "All Rights Reserved" on label					
STBO 2222 [(2) P]	The Beatles' Story	1968	12.50	25.00	50.00
—With Capitol logo on bottom of B-side of both records					
STBO 2222 [(2) P]	The Beatles' Story	1971	7.50	15.00	30.00
—With "Mfd. by Apple" on labels					
STBO 2222 [(2) P]	The Beatles' Story	1975	10.00	20.00	40.00
—With "All Rights Reserved" on labels					
ST 2228 [P]	Beatles '65	1968	10.00	20.00	40.00
—With Capitol logo on Side 2 bottom					
ST 2228 [P]	Beatles '65	1971	5.00	10.00	20.00
—With "Mfd. by Apple" on label					
ST 2228 [P]	Beatles '65	1975	6.25	12.50	25.00
—With "All Rights Reserved" on label					
ST 2309 [P]	The Early Beatles	1969	10.00	20.00	40.00
—With Capitol logo on Side 2 bottom					
ST 2309 [P]	The Early Beatles	1971	5.00	10.00	20.00
—With "Mfd. by Apple" on label					
ST 2309 [P]	The Early Beatles	1975	6.25	12.50	25.00
—With "All Rights Reserved" on label					
ST 2358 [P]	Beatles VI	1969	10.00	20.00	40.00
—With Capitol logo on Side 2 bottom					
ST 2358 [P]	Beatles VI	1971	5.00	10.00	20.00
—With "Mfd. by Apple" on label					
ST 2358 [P]	Beatles VI	1975	6.25	12.50	25.00
—With "All Rights Reserved" on label					
SMAS 2386 [P]	Help!	1969	10.00	20.00	40.00
—With Capitol logo on Side 2 bottom					
SMAS 2386 [P]	Help!	1971	5.00	10.00	20.00
—With "Mfd. by Apple" on label					
SMAS 2386 [P]	Help!	1975	6.25	12.50	25.00
—With "All Rights Reserved" on label					
ST 2442 [S]	Rubber Soul	1969	10.00	20.00	40.00
—With Capitol logo on Side 2 bottom					
ST 2442 [S]	Rubber Soul	1971	5.00	10.00	20.00
—With "Mfd. by Apple" on label					
ST 2442 [S]	Rubber Soul	1975	6.25	12.50	25.00
—With "All Rights Reserved" on label					
ST 2553 [P]	Yesterday and Today	1969	10.00	20.00	40.00
—With Capitol logo on Side 2 bottom					
ST 2553 [P]	Yesterday and Today	1971	5.00	10.00	20.00
—With "Mfd. by Apple" on label					
ST 2553 [P]	Yesterday and Today	1975	6.25	12.50	25.00
—With "All Rights Reserved" on label					
ST 2553 [S]	Yesterday and Today	1971	6.25	12.50	25.00
—With "Mfd. by Apple" on label; all 11 tracks are in true stereo. Check for a triangle in the record's trail-off area.					
ST 2576 [S]	Revolver	1969	10.00	20.00	40.00
—With Capitol logo on Side 2 bottom					
ST 2576 [S]	Revolver	1971	5.00	10.00	20.00
—With "Mfd. by Apple" on label					
ST 2576 [S]	Revolver	1975	6.25	12.50	25.00
—With "All Rights Reserved" on label					
SMAS 2653 [S]	Sgt. Pepper's Lonely Hearts Club Band	1969	10.00	20.00	40.00
—With Capitol logo on Side 2 bottom					
SMAS 2653 [S]	Sgt. Pepper's Lonely Hearts Club Band	1971	6.25	12.50	25.00
—With "Mfd. by Apple" on label					
SMAS 2653 [S]	Sgt. Pepper's Lonely Hearts Club Band	1975	6.25	12.50	25.00
—With "All Rights Reserved" on label					
SMAL 2835 [P]	Magical Mystery Tour	1969	10.00	20.00	40.00
—With Capitol logo on Side 2 bottom; with 24-page booklet					
SMAL 2835 [P]	Magical Mystery Tour	1971	5.00	10.00	20.00
—With "Mfd. by Apple" on label; with 24-page booklet					
SMAL 2835 [P]	Magical Mystery Tour	1975	6.25	12.50	25.00
—With "All Rights Reserved" on label; with 24-page booklet					
ATCO					
33-169 [M]	Ain't She Sweet	1964	50.00	100.00	200.00
33-169 [M-DJ]	Ain't She Sweet	1964	250.00	500.00	1000.
—White label promo					
SD 33-169 [P]	Ain't She Sweet	1964	100.00	200.00	400.00
—Tan and purple label; all four Beatles tracks are rechanneled					
SD 33-169 [P]	Ain't She Sweet	1969	125.00	250.00	500.00
—Yellow label					
AUDIO RARITIES					
AR-2452 [M]	The Complete Silver Beatles	1982	3.75	7.50	15.00
—Contains 12 Decca audition tracks					

Number	Title (A Side/B Side)	Yr	VG	VG+	NM
AUDIOFIDELITY					
PD-339 [M]	First Movement	1982	7.50	15.00	30.00
—Contains eight Decca audition tracks; picture disc					
PHX-339 [M]	First Movement	1982	3.00	6.00	12.00
—Contains eight Decca audition tracks					
BACKSTAGE					
2-201 [(2) M]	Like Dreamers Do	1982	10.00	20.00	40.00
—Gatefold package, individually numbered (numbers under 100 increase value significantly)					
2-201 [(2) M]	Like Dreamers Do	1982	12.50	25.00	50.00
—Non-gatefold package					
BSR-1111 [DJ]	Like Dreamers Do	1982	12.50	25.00	50.00
—White vinyl promo in white sleeve					
BSR-1111 [DJ]	Like Dreamers Do	1982	12.50	25.00	50.00
—Gray vinyl promo in white sleeve					
BSR-1111 [(3) M]	Like Dreamers Do	1982	15.00	30.00	60.00
—Two picture discs (10 of 15 Decca audition tracks on one, interviews on the other) and one white-vinyl record (same contests as musical picture disc)					
BSR-1111 [(3) M]	Like Dreamers Do	1982	25.00	50.00	100.00
—Same as above, except colored-vinyl LP is gray					
BSR-1165 [PD]	The Beatles Talk with Jerry G.	1982	6.25	12.50	25.00
—Picture disc					
BSR-1175 [PD]	The Beatles Talk with Jerry G., Vol. 2	1983	6.25	12.50	25.00
—Picture disc					
CAPITOL					
(no #) [(18)]	The Beatles Collection Platinum Series	1984	200.00	400.00	800.00
BC-13 [(14)]	The Beatles Collection	1978	62.50	125.00	250.00
—American versions have "EMI" and "BC-13" on box spine; imports go for less					
SWBO-101 [(2)]	The Beatles	1976	7.50	15.00	30.00
—Orange label; with photos and poster					
SWBO-101 [(2)]	The Beatles	1978	7.50	15.00	30.00
—Purple label, large Capitol logo; with photos and poster (some copies have four photos as one perforated sheet)					
SWBO-101 [(2)]	The Beatles	1983	10.00	20.00	40.00
—Black label, print in colorband; with photos and poster (some copies have four photos as one perforated sheet)					
SW-153 [P]	Yellow Submarine	1976	3.00	6.00	12.00
—Orange label					
SW-153 [P]	Yellow Submarine	1978	2.50	5.00	10.00
—Purple label, large Capitol logo					
SW-153 [P]	Yellow Submarine	1983	3.75	7.50	15.00
—Black label, print in colorband					
SJ-383	Abbey Road	1984	7.50	15.00	30.00
—New prefix; black label, print in colorband					
SO-383	Abbey Road	1976	3.00	6.00	12.00
—Orange label					
SO-383	Abbey Road	1978	2.50	5.00	10.00
—Purple label, large Capitol logo					
SO-383	Abbey Road	1983	3.75	7.50	15.00
—Black label, print in colorband					
SJ-385	Hey Jude	1984	7.50	15.00	30.00
—New prefix; black label, print in colorband					
SW-385	Hey Jude	1976	3.00	6.00	12.00
—Orange label (all Capitol label versions call the LP "Hey Jude")					
SW-385	Hey Jude	1978	2.50	5.00	10.00
—Purple label, large Capitol logo					
SW-385	Hey Jude	1983	12.50	25.00	50.00
—Black label, print in colorband					
ST-8-2047 [P]	Meet the Beatles!	1964	125.00	250.00	500.00
—Capitol Record Club edition; black label with colorband					
ST-8-2047 [P]	Meet the Beatles!	1969	50.00	100.00	200.00
—Capitol Record Club edition; lime green label					
ST 2047 [P]	Meet the Beatles!	1964	37.50	75.00	150.00
—Black label with colorband; "Beatles!" on cover in tan to brown print. "I Want to Hold Your Hand" and "This Boy" are rechanneled, the other 10 tracks are true stereo					
ST 2047 [P]	Meet the Beatles!	1964	18.75	37.50	75.00
—Black label with colorband; "Beatles!" on cover in green print					
ST 2047 [P]	Meet the Beatles!	1969	10.00	20.00	40.00
—Lime green label					
ST 2047 [P]	Meet the Beatles!	1976	3.00	6.00	12.00
—Orange label					
ST 2047 [P]	Meet the Beatles!	1978	2.50	5.00	10.00
—Purple label, large Capitol logo					
ST 2047 [P]	Meet the Beatles!	1983	3.75	7.50	15.00
—Black label, print in colorband					
T 2047 [M]	Meet the Beatles!	1964	50.00	100.00	200.00
—Black label with colorband; "Beatles!" on cover in tan to brown print					
T 2047 [M]	Meet the Beatles!	1964	25.00	50.00	100.00
—Black label with colorband; "Beatles!" on cover in green print					
ST-8-2080 [P]	The Beatles' Second Album	1964	125.00	250.00	500.00
—Capitol Record Club edition; black label with colorband					
ST-8-2080 [P]	The Beatles' Second Album	1969	75.00	150.00	300.00
—Capitol Record Club edition; lime green label					
ST 2080 [P]	The Beatles' Second Album	1964	25.00	50.00	100.00
—Black label with colorband. "She Loves You," "I'll Get You" and "You Can't Do That" are rechanneled					
ST 2080 [P]	The Beatles' Second Album	1969	10.00	20.00	40.00
—Lime green label					
ST 2080 [P]	The Beatles' Second Album	1976	3.00	6.00	12.00
—Orange label					
ST 2080 [P]	The Beatles' Second Album	1978	2.50	5.00	10.00
—Purple label, large Capitol logo					
ST 2080 [P]	The Beatles' Second Album	1983	3.75	7.50	15.00
—Black label, print in colorband					
T 2080 [M]	The Beatles' Second Album	1964	45.00	90.00	180.00
ST-8-2108 [S]	Something New	1964	75.00	150.00	300.00
—Capitol Record Club edition; black label with colorband					
ST-8-2108 [S]	Something New	1969	37.50	75.00	150.00
—Capitol Record Club edition; lime green label					
ST-8-2108 [S]	Something New	1969	75.00	150.00	300.00
—Longines Symphonette edition (will be stated on label); lime green label					
ST 2108 [S]	Something New	1964	20.00	40.00	80.00
—Black label with colorband					
ST 2108 [S]	Something New	1969	10.00	20.00	40.00
—Lime green label					
ST 2108 [S]	Something New	1976	3.00	6.00	12.00
—Orange label					
ST 2108 [S]	Something New	1978	2.50	5.00	10.00
—Purple label, large Capitol logo					
ST 2108 [S]	Something New	1983	3.75	7.50	15.00
—Black label, print in colorband					
T 2108 [M]	Something New	1964	37.50	75.00	150.00
STBO 2222 [(2) P]	The Beatles' Story	1964	37.50	75.00	150.00
—Black label with colorband. Some of the musical snippets are rechanneled.					
STBO 2222 [(2) P]	The Beatles' Story	1969	12.50	25.00	50.00
—Lime green label					
STBO 2222 [(2) P]	The Beatles' Story	1976	5.00	10.00	20.00
—Orange label					
STBO 2222 [(2) P]	The Beatles' Story	1978	5.00	10.00	20.00
—Purple label, large Capitol logo					
STBO 2222 [(2) P]	The Beatles' Story	1983	10.00	20.00	40.00
—Black label, print in colorband					
TBO 2222 [(2) M]	The Beatles' Story	1964	50.00	100.00	200.00
ST 2228 [P]	Beatles '65	1964	20.00	40.00	80.00
—Black label with colorband. "She's a Woman" and "I Feel Fine" are rechanneled.					
ST 2228 [P]	Beatles '65	1969	10.00	20.00	40.00
—Lime green label					
ST 2228 [P]	Beatles '65	1976	3.00	6.00	12.00
—Orange label					
ST 2228 [P]	Beatles '65	1978	2.50	5.00	10.00
—Purple label, large Capitol logo					
ST 2228 [P]	Beatles '65	1983	3.75	7.50	15.00
—Black label, print in colorband					
T 2228 [M]	Beatles '65	1964	30.00	60.00	120.00
ST 2309 [P]	The Early Beatles	1965	25.00	50.00	100.00
—Black label with colorband. "Love Me Do" and "P.S. I Love You" are rechanneled.					
ST 2309 [P]	The Early Beatles	1969	10.00	20.00	40.00
—Lime green label					
ST 2309 [P]	The Early Beatles	1976	3.00	6.00	12.00
—Orange label					
ST 2309 [P]	The Early Beatles	1978	2.50	5.00	10.00
—Purple label, large Capitol logo					
ST 2309 [P]	The Early Beatles	1983	6.25	12.50	25.00
—Black label, print in colorband					
T 2309 [M]	The Early Beatles	1965	50.00	100.00	200.00
ST-8-2358 [P]	Beatles VI	1965	125.00	250.00	500.00
—Capitol Record Club edition; black label with colorband					
ST-8-2358 [P]	Beatles VI	1969	100.00	200.00	400.00
—Capitol Record Club edition; lime green label					
ST 2358 [M]	Beatles VI	1983	3.75	7.50	15.00
—Black label, print in colorband; plays in mono despite label designation					
ST 2358 [M]	Beatles VI	1988	20.00	40.00	80.00
—Purple label, small Capitol logo; plays in mono despite label designation					
ST 2358 [P]	Beatles VI	1965	20.00	40.00	80.00
—Black label with colorband; with "See label for correct playing order" on back cover					
ST 2358 [P]	Beatles VI	1965	18.75	37.50	75.00
—Black label with colorband; with song titles listed in correct order on back cover. "Yes It Is" is rechanneled.					
ST 2358 [P]	Beatles VI	1969	10.00	20.00	40.00
—Lime green label					
ST 2358 [P]	Beatles VI	1976	3.00	6.00	12.00
—Orange label					
ST 2358 [P]	Beatles VI	1978	2.50	5.00	10.00
—Purple label, large Capitol logo					
T 2358 [M]	Beatles VI	1965	30.00	60.00	120.00
—With "See label for correct playing order" on back cover					
T 2358 [M]	Beatles VI	1965	25.00	50.00	100.00
—With song titles listed in correct order on back cover					
MAS 2386 [M]	Help!	1965	37.50	75.00	150.00
SMAS-8-2386 [P]	Help!	1965	100.00	200.00	400.00
—Capitol Record Club edition; black label with colorband; no "8" on cover					
SMAS-8-2386 [P]	Help!	1965	150.00	300.00	600.00
—Capitol Record Club edition; black label with colorband; with "8" on cover					
SMAS-8-2386 [P]	Help!	1969	50.00	100.00	200.00
—Capitol Record Club edition; lime green label; no "8" on cover					
SMAS-8-2386 [P]	Help!	1969	100.00	200.00	400.00
—Capitol Record Club edition; lime green label; with "8" on cover					
SMAS-8-2386 [P]	Help!	197?	175.00	350.00	700.00
—Longines Symphonette edition; with "Mfd. by Longines" and "8" on cover					
SMAS 2386 [P]	Help!	1965	18.75	37.50	75.00
—Black label with colorband. Has incidental music by George Martin. "Ticket to Ride" is rechanneled.					
SMAS 2386 [P]	Help!	1969	10.00	20.00	40.00
—Lime green label					
SMAS 2386 [P]	Help!	1976	3.00	6.00	12.00
—Orange label					
SMAS 2386 [P]	Help!	1978	2.50	5.00	10.00
—Purple label, large Capitol logo					
SMAS 2386 [P]	Help!	1983	3.75	7.50	15.00
—Black label, print in colorband					
ST-8-2442 [S]	Rubber Soul	1965	75.00	150.00	300.00
—Capitol Record Club edition; black label with colorband					
ST-8-2442 [S]	Rubber Soul	1969	50.00	100.00	200.00
—Capitol Record Club edition; lime green label					
ST-8-2442 [S]	Rubber Soul	1969	62.50	125.00	250.00
—Longines Symphonette edition (will be stated on label); lime green label					
ST 2442 [S]	Rubber Soul	1965	15.00	30.00	60.00
—Black label with colorband					
ST 2442 [S]	Rubber Soul	1969	10.00	20.00	40.00
—Lime green label					
ST 2442 [S]	Rubber Soul	1976	3.00	6.00	12.00
—Orange label					
SW 2442 [S]	Rubber Soul	1978	2.50	5.00	10.00
—Purple label, large Capitol logo					
SW 2442 [S]	Rubber Soul	1983	3.75	7.50	15.00
—Black label, print in colorband					
T 2442 [M]	Rubber Soul	1965	30.00	60.00	120.00
ST-8-2553 [P]	Yesterday and Today	1966	75.00	150.00	300.00
—Capitol Record Club edition; black label with colorband					
ST-8-2553 [S]	Yesterday and Today	1969	37.50	75.00	150.00
—Capitol Record Club edition; lime green label; all 11 tracks are in true stereo! (We don't know if the same is true of the black label version.)					

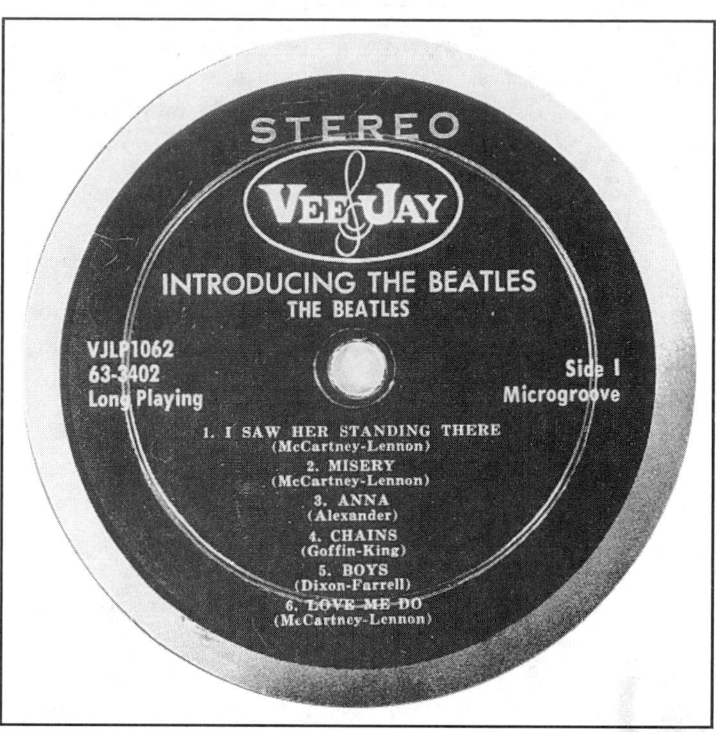

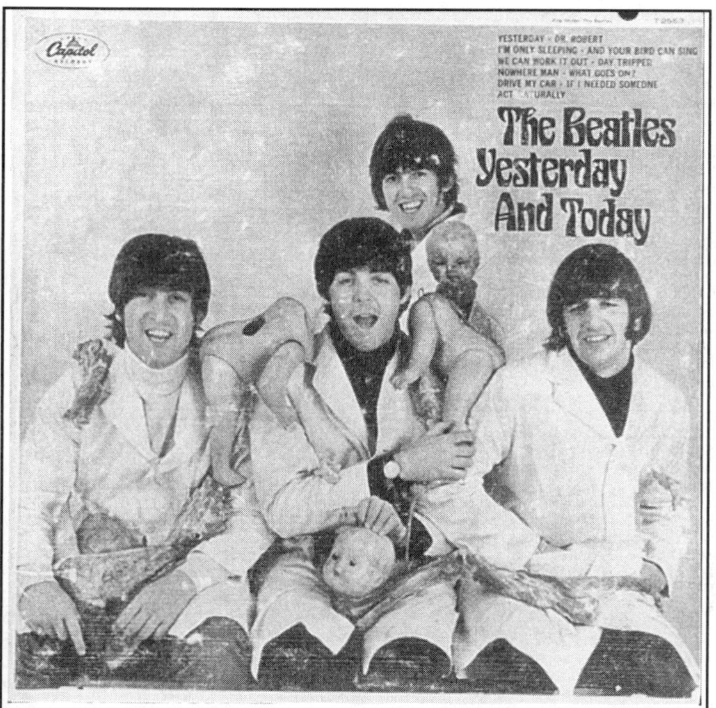

(Top left) It's one of the world's most sought-after records. In 1962, Decca issued "My Bonnie" by a group called Tony Sheridan and the Beat Brothers. As most collectors know, the Beat Brothers were really the Beatles. As rare as this 45 is, there are two distinct label variations. One, as shown, has the catalog number information in the rainbow area at right. Another variation has the number information in the black area below "Decca." Both are legitimate. (Top right) Here's a legitimate stereo copy of *Introducting the Beatles* with "Love Me Do" as the last song on side 1. The overwhelming majority of "stereo" copies that exist are counterfeits. (Bottom left) A mono peeled copy of the legendary *Yesterday and Today* "butcher cover." Stereo copies go for more, as do copies pasted over the butcher photo. (Bottom right) One of the last extended-play 45s issued on Capitol on its old turquoise-green label was *Four by the Beatles*, issued in 1964 and compiling two Canada-only single releases onto one record.

Number	Title (A Side/B Side)	Yr	VG	VG+	NM
ST 2553 [P]	Yesterday and Today	1966	4000.	6000.	8000.
—"First state" butcher cover (never had other cover on top); cover will be the same size as other Capitol Beatles LPs					
ST 2553 [P]	Yesterday and Today	1966	500.00	750.00	1000.
—"Second state" butcher cover (trunk cover pasted over original cover)					
ST 2553 [P]	Yesterday and Today	1966	375.00	750.00	1500.
—"Third state" butcher cover (trunk cover removed, leaving butcher cover intact); cover will be about 3/16-inch narrower than other Capitol Beatles LPs; value is highly negotiable depending upon the success of removing the paste-over					
ST 2553 [P]	Yesterday and Today	1966	20.00	40.00	80.00
—Trunk cover; black label with colorband (all later variations have the trunk cover). "I'm Only Sleeping," "Dr. Robert" and "And Your Bird Can Sing" are rechanneled.					
ST 2553 [P]	Yesterday and Today	1969	10.00	20.00	40.00
—Lime green label					
ST 2553 [P]	Yesterday and Today	1976	3.00	6.00	12.00
—Orange label; it's possible that this and all future pressings have all 11 tracks in true stereo, but we don't know.					
ST 2553 [P]	Yesterday and Today	1978	2.50	5.00	10.00
—Purple label, large Capitol logo					
ST 2553 [P]	Yesterday and Today	1983	3.75	7.50	15.00
—Black label, print in colorband					
T 2553 [M]	Yesterday and Today	1966	2000.	3000.	4000.
—"First state" butcher cover (never had other cover on top); cover will be the same size as other Capitol Beatles LPs					
T 2553 [M]	Yesterday and Today	1966	250.00	500.00	1000.
—"Second state" butcher cover (trunk cover pasted over original cover)					
T 2553 [M]	Yesterday and Today	1966	400.00	800.00	1200.
—"Third state" butcher cover (trunk cover removed, leaving butcher cover intact); cover will be about 3/16-inch narrower than other Capitol Beatles LPs; value is highly negotiable depending upon the success of removing the paste-over					
T 2553 [M]	Yesterday and Today	1966	37.50	75.00	150.00
—Trunk cover					
ST-8-2576 [S]	Revolver	1966	100.00	200.00	400.00
—Capitol Record Club edition; black label with colorband					
ST-8-2576 [S]	Revolver	1969	30.00	60.00	120.00
—Capitol Record Club edition; lime green label					
ST-8-2576 [S]	Revolver	1973?	50.00	100.00	200.00
—Capitol Record Club edition; orange label (a very late issue, as Capitol Record Club closed in 1973)					
ST 2576 [S]	Revolver	1966	25.00	50.00	100.00
—Black label with colorband					
ST 2576 [S]	Revolver	1969	10.00	20.00	40.00
—Lime green label					
ST 2576 [S]	Revolver	1970	75.00	150.00	300.00
—Red label with "target" Capitol at top (same design as lime green label)					
ST 2576 [S]	Revolver	1976	3.00	6.00	12.00
—Orange label					
SW 2576 [S]	Revolver	1978	2.50	5.00	10.00
—Purple label, large Capitol logo					
SW 2576 [S]	Revolver	1983	3.75	7.50	15.00
—Black label, print in colorband					
T 2576 [M]	Revolver	1966	50.00	100.00	200.00
2653	Sgt. Pepper's Lonely Hearts Club Band Cut-Out Inserts	1967	—	—	3.00
2653	Sgt. Pepper's Lonely Hearts Club Band Special Inner Sleeve	1967	3.75	7.50	15.00
—Red-pink psychedelic sleeve only issued with 1967 (mono and stereo) editions					
MAS 2653 [M]	Sgt. Pepper's Lonely Hearts Club Band	1967	75.00	150.00	300.00
SMAS 2653 [S]	Sgt. Pepper's Lonely Hearts Club Band	1967	25.00	50.00	100.00
—Black label with colorband					
SMAS 2653 [S]	Sgt. Pepper's Lonely Hearts Club Band	1969	12.50	25.00	50.00
—Lime green label					
SMAS 2653 [S]	Sgt. Pepper's Lonely Hearts Club Band	1976	3.00	6.00	12.00
—Orange label					
SMAS 2653 [S]	Sgt. Pepper's Lonely Hearts Club Band	1978	2.50	5.00	10.00
—Purple label, large Capitol logo. Many copies from 1978 had a "The Original Classic" sticker on shrink wrap; it was added at the time of the release of the bomb movie version of Sgt. Pepper. Double the value if the sticker is still there.					
SMAS 2653 [S]	Sgt. Pepper's Lonely Hearts Club Band	1983	3.75	7.50	15.00
—Black label, print in colorband; some of these had "The Original Classic" stickers, too. Add $10 to value if it is there.					
MAL 2835 [M]	Magical Mystery Tour	1967	75.00	150.00	300.00
—With 24-page book bound into center of gatefold					
SMAL 2835 [P]	Magical Mystery Tour	1967	25.00	50.00	100.00
—Black label with colorband; with 24-page booklet. "Penny Lane," "Baby You're a Rich Man" and "All You Need Is Love" is rechanneled, as is the second half of "I Am the Walrus" (every "stereo" version of "Walrus" is this way)					
SMAL 2835 [P]	Magical Mystery Tour	1969	12.50	25.00	50.00
—Lime green label; with 24-page booklet					
SMAL 2835 [P]	Magical Mystery Tour	1976	3.00	6.00	12.00
—Orange label; with 24-page booklet					
SMAL 2835 [P]	Magical Mystery Tour	1978	2.50	5.00	10.00
—Purple label, large Capitol logo; this edition did not come with booklet					
SMAL 2835 [P]	Magical Mystery Tour	1983	3.75	7.50	15.00
—Black label, print in colorband; no booklet					
SKBO-3403 [P]	The Beatles 1962-1966	1976	5.00	10.00	20.00
—Red labels					
SKBO-3403 [P]	The Beatles 1962-1966	1976	7.50	15.00	30.00
—Blue labels (error pressing)					
SKBO-3404 [B]	The Beatles 1967-1970	1976	5.00	10.00	20.00
—Blue labels					
SPRO-8969	Rarities	1978	12.50	25.00	50.00
—Purple label, large Capitol logo; part of the U.S. box set The Beatles Collection (BC-13)					
SKBO-11537 [(2)]	Rock 'n' Roll Music	1976	6.25	12.50	25.00
SMAS-11638	The Beatles at the Hollywood Bowl	1977	5.00	10.00	20.00
—Originals with embossed title and ticket on front cover					
SMAS-11638	The Beatles at the Hollywood Bowl	1980	3.75	7.50	15.00
—Second pressing without embossed title and ticket					
SMAS-11638	The Beatles at the Hollywood Bowl	1989	10.00	20.00	40.00
—With UPC code on back cover					
SMAS-11638 [DJ]	The Beatles at the Hollywood Bowl	1977	125.00	250.00	500.00
—Advance tan label promo in plain white jacket					
SKBL-11711 [(2) P]	Love Songs	1977	5.00	10.00	20.00
—With booklet and embossed, leather-like cover. "P.S. I Love You" and "Yes It Is" are rechanneled.					
SKBL-11711 [(2) P]	Love Songs	1988	7.50	15.00	30.00
—With booklet, but without embossed cover					
SEAX-11840 [PD]	Sgt. Pepper's Lonely Hearts Club Band	1978	5.00	10.00	20.00
—Picture disc; deduct 25% for cut-outs					
SEBX-11841 [(2)]	The Beatles	1978	12.50	25.00	50.00
—White vinyl; with photos and poster (with number "SEBX-11841" on each)					
SEBX-11842 [P]	The Beatles 1962-1966	1978	10.00	20.00	40.00
—Red vinyl					
SEBX-11843 [B]	The Beatles 1967-1970	1978	10.00	20.00	40.00
—Blue vinyl					
SEAX-11900 [PD]	Abbey Road	1978	10.00	20.00	40.00
—Picture disc; deduct 25% for cut-outs					
SW-11921 [P]	A Hard Day's Night	1979	3.00	6.00	12.00
—Purple label, large Capitol logo					
SW-11921 [P]	A Hard Day's Night	1983	3.75	7.50	15.00
—Black label, print in colorband					
SW-11921 [P]	A Hard Day's Night	1988	6.25	12.50	25.00
—Purple label, small Capitol logo					
SW-11922	Let It Be	1979	3.75	7.50	15.00
—Purple label, large Capitol logo; with poster and custom innersleeve					
SW-11922	Let It Be	1983	3.75	7.50	15.00
—Black label, print in colorband; add 33% if poster is included					
SW-11922	Let It Be	1988	6.25	12.50	25.00
—Purple label, small Capitol logo; add 20% if poster and custom innersleeve are included					
SN-12009 [DJ]	Rarities	1979	75.00	150.00	300.00
—Green label; withdrawn before official release; all known copies have a plain white sleeve					
SHAL-12080 [B]	Rarities	1980	5.00	10.00	20.00
—Completely different LP than 12009; black label with colorband. First pressing says that "There's a Place" debuts in stereo (false) and that the screaming at the end of "Helter Skelter" was a "classic Lennon statement" (it's actually Ringo).					
SHAL-12080 [B]	Rarities	1980	3.75	7.50	15.00
—Same as above, with errors deleted and "Produced by George Martin" added to back cover					
SV-12199	Reel Music	1982	2.50	5.00	10.00
—Standard issue with 12-page booklet					
SV-12199 [DJ]	Reel Music	1982	10.00	20.00	40.00
—Yellow vinyl promo; numbered back cover with 12-page booklet					
SV-12199 [DJ]	Reel Music	1982	5.00	10.00	20.00
—Yellow vinyl promo; plain white cover with 12-page booklet					
SV-12245 [P]	20 Greatest Hits	1982	5.00	10.00	20.00
—Purple label, large Capitol logo. "Love Me Do" and "She Loves You" are rechanneled, the other 18 tracks are stereo					
SV-12245 [P]	20 Greatest Hits	1983	5.00	10.00	20.00
—Black label, print in colorband					
SV-12245 [P]	20 Greatest Hits	1988	6.25	12.50	25.00
—Purple label, small Capitol logo					
SN-16020	Rock 'n' Roll Music, Volume 1	1980	2.50	5.00	10.00
SN-16021	Rock 'n' Roll Music, Volume 2	1980	2.50	5.00	10.00
C1-46435 [M]	Please Please Me	1995	3.00	6.00	12.00
—New prefix; Apple logo on back cover					
CLJ-46435 [M]	Please Please Me	1987	5.00	10.00	20.00
—Black label, print in colorband; first Capitol version of original British LP					
CLJ-46435 [M]	Please Please Me	1988	6.25	12.50	25.00
—Purple label, small Capitol logo					
C1-46436 [M]	With the Beatles	1995	3.00	6.00	12.00
—New prefix; Apple logo on back cover					
CLJ-46436 [M]	With the Beatles	1987	5.00	10.00	20.00
—Black label, print in colorband; first Capitol version of original British LP					
CLJ-46436 [M]	With the Beatles	1988	6.25	12.50	25.00
—Purple label, small Capitol logo					
C1-46437 [M]	A Hard Day's Night	1995	3.00	6.00	12.00
—New prefix; Apple logo on back cover					
CLJ-46437 [M]	A Hard Day's Night	1987	5.00	10.00	20.00
—Black label, print in colorband; first Capitol version of original British LP					
CLJ-46437 [M]	A Hard Day's Night	1988	6.25	12.50	25.00
—Purple label, small Capitol logo					
C1-46438 [M]	Beatles for Sale	1995	3.00	6.00	12.00
—New prefix; Apple logo on back cover					
CLJ-46438 [M]	Beatles for Sale	1987	5.00	10.00	20.00
—Black label, print in colorband; first Capitol version of original British LP					
CLJ-46438 [M]	Beatles for Sale	1988	6.25	12.50	25.00
—Purple label, small Capitol logo					
C1-46439 [S]	Help!	1995	3.00	6.00	12.00
—New prefix; Apple logo on back cover					
CLJ-46439 [S]	Help!	1987	5.00	10.00	20.00
—Black label, print in colorband; first Capitol version of original British LP					
CLJ-46439 [S]	Help!	1988	6.25	12.50	25.00
—Purple label, small Capitol logo					
C1-46440 [S]	Rubber Soul	1995	3.00	6.00	12.00
—New prefix; Apple logo on back cover					
CLJ-46440 [S]	Rubber Soul	1987	5.00	10.00	20.00
—Black label, print in colorband; first Capitol version of original British LP					
CLJ-46440 [S]	Rubber Soul	1988	6.25	12.50	25.00
—Purple label, small Capitol logo					
C1-46441 [S]	Revolver	1995	3.00	6.00	12.00
—New prefix; Apple logo on back cover					
CLJ-46441 [S]	Revolver	1987	5.00	10.00	20.00
—Black label, print in colorband; first Capitol version of original British LP					
CLJ-46441 [S]	Revolver	1988	6.25	12.50	25.00
—Purple label, small Capitol logo					
C1-46442 [S]	Sgt. Pepper's Lonely Hearts Club Band	1988	6.25	12.50	25.00
—New number; purple label, small Capitol logo					
C1-46442 [S]	Sgt. Pepper's Lonely Hearts Club Band	1995	3.00	6.00	12.00
—With Apple logo on back cover					
C1-46443 [(2)]	The Beatles	1988	12.50	25.00	50.00
—New number; purple label, small Capitol logo; with photos and poster (some copies have four photos as one perforated sheet)					
C1-46443 [(2)]	The Beatles	1995	5.00	10.00	20.00
—With Apple logo on back cover					
C1-46445 [P]	Yellow Submarine	1988	6.25	12.50	25.00
—New number; purple label, small Capitol logo					
C1-46445 [P]	Yellow Submarine	1995	3.00	6.00	12.00
—Reissue has the British liner notes, which include a review of the White Album.					
C1-46446	Abbey Road	1988	6.25	12.50	25.00
—New number; purple label, small Capitol logo					
C1-46446	Abbey Road	1995	3.00	6.00	12.00
—Apple logo restored to back cover on reissue					
C1-46447	Let It Be	1995	3.00	6.00	12.00
—New number (the only 1995 reissue with a completely new number)					
C1-48062 [P]	Magical Mystery Tour	1988	6.25	12.50	25.00
—New number; purple label, small Capitol logo; no booklet					

Number	Title (A Side/B Side)	Yr	VG	VG+	NM
C1-48062 [P]	Magical Mystery Tour	1992	3.00	6.00	12.00
—With Apple logo on back cover; reissue restores booklet to package					
C1-90435 [P]	The Beatles 1962-1966	1988	7.50	15.00	30.00
—New number; purple labels, small Capitol logo					
C1-90438 [B]	The Beatles 1967-1970	1988	7.50	15.00	30.00
—New number; purple labels, small Capitol logo					
C1-90441 [P]	Meet the Beatles!	1988	6.25	12.50	25.00
—New number; purple label, small Capitol logo					
C1-90442	Hey Jude	1988	6.25	12.50	25.00
—New number; purple label, small Capitol logo					
C1-90443 [S]	Something New	1988	6.25	12.50	25.00
—New number; purple label, small Capitol logo					
C1-90444 [P]	The Beatles' Second Album	1988	6.25	12.50	25.00
—New number; purple label, small Capitol logo					
C1-90445 [M]	Beatles VI	1988	6.25	12.50	25.00
—New number; purple label, small Capitol logo; plays in mono despite label designation					
C1-90446 [P]	Beatles '65	1988	6.25	12.50	25.00
—New number; purple label, small Capitol logo					
C1-90447 [P]	Yesterday and Today	1988	6.25	12.50	25.00
—New number; purple label, small Capitol logo; stereo content uncertain					
C1-90452 [S]	Revolver	1988	6.25	12.50	25.00
—New number; purple label, small Capitol logo					
C1-90453 [S]	Rubber Soul	1988	6.25	12.50	25.00
—New number; purple label, small Capitol logo					
C1-90454 [P]	Help!	1988	6.25	12.50	25.00
—New number; purple label, small Capitol logo					
C1-91135 [(2) B]	Past Masters Volume 1 and 2	1988	6.25	12.50	25.00
—Some early tracks are in mono, but "This Boy," "She's a Woman," "Yes It Is," and "The Inner Light" are in stereo.					
BBX1-91302 [(14)]	The Beatles Deluxe Box Set	1988	75.00	150.00	300.00
CICADELIC					
1960	Moviemania	1987	3.00	6.00	12.00
1961	Not a Second Time	1987	3.00	6.00	12.00
1962	Things We Said Today	1986	3.00	6.00	12.00
1963	All Our Loving	1986	3.00	6.00	12.00
1964	East Coast Invasion	1985	3.00	6.00	12.00
1965	Round the World	1986	3.00	6.00	12.00
1966	West Coast Invasion	1985	3.00	6.00	12.00
1967	From Britain with Beat!	1987	3.00	6.00	12.00
1968	Here, There and Everywhere	1988	3.00	6.00	12.00
CLARION					
601 [M]	The Amazing Beatles and Other Great English Group Sounds	1966	25.00	50.00	100.00
SD 601 [P]	The Amazing Beatles and Other Great English Group Sounds	1966	50.00	100.00	200.00
—All four Beatles tracks are rechanneled					
GREAT NORTHWEST					
GNW 4007	Beatle Talk	1978	2.50	5.00	10.00
GNW 4007	Beatle Talk	1978	12.50	25.00	50.00
—Columbia Record Club edition; "CRC" on spine					
HALL OF MUSIC					
HM-1-2200 [(2) M]	Live 1962, Hamburg, Germany	1981	12.50	25.00	50.00
—Only American LP with the original Eurpoean contents -- "I Saw Her Standing There," "Twist and Shout," "Ask Me Why" and "Reminiscing" replace the four songs listed with the Lingasong issue					
I-N-S RADIO NEWS					
DOC-1 [DJ]	Beatlemania Tour Coverage	1964	750.00	1125.	1500.
—Promo-only open-end interview with script in plain white jacket					
LINGASONG					
LS-2-7001 [(2) DJ]	Live at the Star Club in Hamburg, Germany, 1962	1977	75.00	150.00	300.00
—Promo only on blue vinyl					
LS-2-7001 [(2) DJ]	Live at the Star Club in Hamburg, Germany, 1962	1977	50.00	100.00	200.00
—Promo only on red vinyl					
LS-2-7001 [(2) DJ]	Live at the Star Club in Hamburg, Germany, 1962	1977	10.00	20.00	40.00
—Promo on black vinyl; "D.J. Copy Not for Sale" on labels					
LS-2-7001 [(2) R]	Live at the Star Club in Hamburg, Germany, 1962	1977	5.00	10.00	20.00
—American version contains "I'm Gonna Sit Right Down and Cry," "Where Have You Been All My Life," "Till There Was You," and "Sheila," not on imports					
LLOYDS					
ER-MC-LTD	The Great American Tour — 1965 Live Beatlemania Concert	1965	150.00	300.00	600.00
—Another interview album from the Ed Rudy people, with a live Beatles show in the background and the songs poorly overdubbed by the Liverpool Lads					
METRO					
M-563 [M]	This Is Where It Started	1966	25.00	50.00	100.00
—Reissue of MGM album with two of the "others" tracks deleted					
MS-563 [R]	This Is Where It Started	1966	37.50	75.00	150.00
—In stereo cover					
MS-563 [R]	This Is Where It Started	1966	50.00	100.00	200.00
—In mono cover with "Stereo" sticker					
MGM					
E-4215 [M]	The Beatles with Tony Sheridan and Their Guests	1964	50.00	100.00	200.00
—Without "And Guests" on cover					
E-4215 [M]	The Beatles with Tony Sheridan and Their Guests	1964	62.50	125.00	250.00
—With "And Guests" on cover					
SE-4215 [R]	The Beatles with Tony Sheridan and Their Guests	1964	150.00	300.00	600.00
—With "And Guests" on cover					
SE-4215 [R]	The Beatles with Tony Sheridan and Their Guests	1964	200.00	400.00	800.00
—Without "And Guests" on cover					
MOBILE FIDELITY					
BC-1 [(13)]	The Beatles Collection	1982	125.00	250.00	500.00
1-023	Abbey Road	1979	12.50	25.00	50.00
—Audiophile vinyl					
1-047 [P]	Magical Mystery Tour	1980	15.00	30.00	60.00
—Audiophile vinyl; yes, this contains the rechanneled stereo versions of "Penny Lane," "Baby You're a Rich Man" and "All You Need Is Love"					
2-072 [(2)]	The Beatles	1982	12.50	25.00	50.00
—Audiophile vinyl; not issued with photos or poster					
1-100 [S]	Sgt. Pepper's Lonely Hearts Club Band	1985	10.00	20.00	40.00
—Audiophile vinyl					
UHQR 1-100 [S]	Sgt. Pepper's Lonely Hearts Club Band	1982	75.00	150.00	300.00
—Ultra High Quality release with special cover; numbered edition of 5,000; numbers under 100 fetch even more					

Number	Title (A Side/B Side)	Yr	VG	VG+	NM
1-101 [P]	Please Please Me	1986	10.00	20.00	40.00
—Audiophile vinyl; British version of album. "Love Me Do" and "P.S. I Love You" are rechanneled.					
1-102 [S]	With the Beatles	1986	37.50	75.00	150.00
—Audiophile vinyl; British version of album. Limited run because of a damaged stamper that was not replaced.					
1-103 [S]	A Hard Day's Night	1987	10.00	20.00	40.00
—Audiophile vinyl; British version of album					
1-104 [S]	Beatles for Sale	1986	10.00	20.00	40.00
—Audiophile vinyl; British version of album					
1-105 [S]	Help!	1985	10.00	20.00	40.00
—Audiophile vinyl; British version of album					
1-106 [S]	Rubber Soul	1985	10.00	20.00	40.00
—Audiophile vinyl; British version of album					
1-107 [S]	Revolver	1986	10.00	20.00	40.00
—Audiophile vinyl; British version of album					
1-108 [P]	Yellow Submarine	1987	15.00	30.00	60.00
—Audiophile vinyl					
1-109	Let It Be	1987	10.00	20.00	40.00
—Audiophile vinyl; gatefold cover					
1-109	Let It Be	1987	50.00	100.00	200.00
—Audiophile vinyl; regular cover					
ORANGE					
ORC-12880 [DJ]	The Silver Beatles	1985	75.00	150.00	300.00
—Test pressing; white cover with title sticker					
ORC-12880 [DJ]	The Silver Beatles	1985	100.00	200.00	400.00
—Test pressing; full cover cover slick folded around a white cover. Both contain all 15 Decca audition tracks					
PBR INTERNATIONAL					
7005/6 [(2)]	The David Wigg Interviews (The Beatles Tapes)	1978	20.00	40.00	80.00
—Blue vinyl					
7005/6 [(2)]	The David Wigg Interviews (The Beatles Tapes)	1980	15.00	30.00	60.00
—Black vinyl					
PHOENIX					
PHX-352 [M]	Silver Beatles, Volume 1	1982	3.00	6.00	12.00
—Contains seven Decca audition tracks					
PHX-353 [M]	Silver Beatles, Volume 2	1982	3.00	6.00	12.00
—Contains seven Decca audition tracks (different seven than Phoenix 352)					
P20-623	20 Hits, Beatles	1983	5.00	10.00	20.00
—With 12 Decca audition tracks, four Beatles/Tony Sheridan tracks, and four Tony Sheridan solo tracks					
P20-629	20 Hits, Beatles	1983	5.00	10.00	20.00
—With 20 live Hamburg tracks					
PICKWICK					
PTP-2098 [(2) M]	The Historic First Live Recordings	1980	4.50	9.00	18.00
—Same contents as Lingasong LP, plus "Hully Gully"					
SPC-3661 [M]	The Beatles' First Live Recordings, Volume 1	1979	3.00	6.00	12.00
SPC-3662 [M]	The Beatles' First Live Recordings, Volume 2	1979	3.00	6.00	12.00
BAN-90051 [M]	Recorded Live in Hamburg, Vol. 1	1978	7.50	15.00	30.00
BAN-90061 [M]	Recorded Live in Hamburg, Vol. 2	1978	7.50	15.00	30.00
BAN-90071 [M]	Recorded Live in Hamburg, Vol. 3	1978	10.00	20.00	40.00
POLYDOR					
24-4504 [P]	The Beatles — Circa 1960 — In the Beginning Featuring Tony Sheridan	1970	6.25	12.50	25.00
—Originals have gatefold cover					
24-4504 [P]	The Beatles — Circa 1960 — In the Beginning Featuring Tony Sheridan	197?	10.00	20.00	40.00
—Some copies of the record contain only the title "The Beatles -- In the Beginning"					
PD-4504 [P]	The Beatles — Circa 1960 — In the Beginning Featuring Tony Sheridan	1981	3.00	6.00	12.00
—Reissue without gatefold cover					
SKAO-93199 [P]	The Beatles — Circa 1960 — In the Beginning Featuring Tony Sheridan	1970	10.00	20.00	40.00
—Capitol Record Club edition					
825073-1 [P]	The Beatles — Circa 1960 — In the Beginning Featuring Tony Sheridan	1988	5.00	10.00	20.00
—Reissue with new number					
RADIO PULSEBEAT NEWS					
2	The American Tour with Ed Rudy	1964	25.00	50.00	100.00
—Yellow label; some copies came with a special edition of Teen Talk magazine (add 50%)					
2	The American Tour with Ed Rudy	1980	6.25	12.50	25.00
—Blue label; authorized reissue with Beatles' photo on cover					
3	1965 Talk Album — Ed Rudy with New U.S. Tour	1965	37.50	75.00	150.00
—"The Beatles" in black print under front cover photo (other versions appear to be bootlegs)					
RAVEN/PVC					
8911	Talk Downunder	1981	2.50	5.00	10.00
8911 [DJ]	Talk Downunder	1981	20.00	40.00	80.00
—Promo only in white cover with title sticker. Label reads "For Radio Play Only"					
SAVAGE					
BM-69 [M]	The Savage Young Beatles	1964	37.50	75.00	150.00
—Orange label; no legitimate copy says "Stereo" on cover					
BM-69 [M]	The Savage Young Beatles	1964	375.00	750.00	1500.
—Yellow label, glossy orange cover					
SILHOUETTE					
SM-10004 [PD]	Timeless	1981	5.00	10.00	20.00
—Picture disc with all interviews					
SM-10004 [PD]	Timeless	1981	6.25	12.50	25.00
—Picture disc with interviews plus remakes of "Imagine" and "Let It Be" (by non-Beatles)					
SM-10010 [PD]	Timeless II	1982	5.00	10.00	20.00
—Picture disc with mostly interviews					
SM-10013	The British Are Coming	1984	3.75	7.50	15.00
—Interview album with numbered sticker (very low numbers increase the value)					
SM-10013	The British Are Coming	1984	20.00	40.00	80.00
—Same as above, but on red vinyl					
SM-10013 [DJ]	The British Are Coming	1984	10.00	20.00	40.00
—White label promo; no numbered sticker					
SM-10015	Golden Beatles	1985	3.75	7.50	15.00
SM-10015	Golden Beatles	1985	20.00	40.00	80.00
—Gold vinyl					
PD-83010 [PD]	The British Are Coming	1985	7.50	15.00	30.00
—Picture disc					
STERLING					
8895-6481	I Apologize	1966	100.00	200.00	400.00
—One-sided LP with John Lennon's "apology" for supposed anti-Christian remarks; includes photo					
8895-6481	I Apologize	1966	75.00	150.00	300.00
—Same as above, but without photo					

Number	Title (A Side/B Side)	Yr	VG	VG+	NM
UNITED ARTISTS					
SP-2359/60 [DJ]	United Artists Presents A Hard Day's Night	1964	1000.	1500.	2000.
—Open-end interview with script					
SP-2362/3 [DJ]	United Artists Presents A Hard Day's Night	1964	375.00	750.00	1500.
—Radio spots for movie					
UAL 3366 [M]	A Hard Day's Night	1964	50.00	100.00	200.00
—With "I Cry Instead" listing					
UAL 3366 [M]	A Hard Day's Night	1964	62.50	125.00	250.00
—With "I'll Cry Instead" listing					
UAL 3366 [M-DJ]	A Hard Day's Night	1964	750.00	1500.	3000.
—White label promo					
UAS 6366 [P]	A Hard Day's Night	1964	50.00	100.00	200.00
—With "I Cry Instead" listing					
UAS 6366 [P]	A Hard Day's Night	1964	62.50	125.00	250.00
—With "I'll Cry Instead" listing. Has incidental music by George Martin. All eight Beatles tracks are rechanneled; Martin's are in true stereo.					
UAS 6366 [P]	A Hard Day's Night	1964	6000.	9000.	12000.
—Pink vinyl; only one copy known, probably privately (and secretly) done by a pressing-plant employee					
UAS 6366 [P]	A Hard Day's Night	1968	12.50	25.00	50.00
—Pink and orange label					
UAS 6366 [P]	A Hard Day's Night	1970	12.50	25.00	50.00
—Black and orange label					
UAS 6366 [P]	A Hard Day's Night	1971	5.00	10.00	20.00
—Tan label					
UAS 6366 [P]	A Hard Day's Night	1975	5.00	10.00	20.00
—Tan label with "All Rights Reserved" in perimeter print					
UAS 6366 [P]	A Hard Day's Night	1977	5.00	10.00	20.00
—Sunrise label. Note: Any of the variations from 1968 on can have titles of songs incorrectly listed as "I Cry Instead" and "Tell Me Who," or only one can be wrong, or neither can be wrong. No difference in value at this time.					
ST-90828 [P]	A Hard Day's Night	1964	187.50	375.00	750.00
—Capitol Record Club edition					
T-90828 [M]	A Hard Day's Night	1964	750.00	1125.	1500.
—Capitol Record Club edition					
UA-Help-A/B [DJ]	United Artists Presents Help!	1965	500.00	1000.	1500.
—Radio spots for movie					
UA-Help-INT [DJ]	United Artists Presents Help!	1965	1000.	1500.	2000.
—Open-end interview with script (red label)					
UA-Help-Show [DJ]	United Artists Presents Help!	1965	1500.	2250.	3000.
—One-sided interview with script (blue label)					
UNITED DISTRIBUTORS					
UDL-2333 [M]	Dawn of the Silver Beatles	1981	15.00	30.00	60.00
—Hand-stamped numbers on back cover and label; contains 10 Decca audition tracks					
UDL-2333 [M]	Dawn of the Silver Beatles	1981	12.50	25.00	50.00
—With numbered registration card (deduct 20% if missing)					
UDL-2382 [M]	Lightning Strikes Twice	1981	15.00	30.00	60.00
—Side 1 has five Beatles' Decca audition tracks; Side 2 has live Elvis Presley performances from 1955					
VEE JAY					
DX-30 [(2) M]	The Beatles vs. The Four Seasons	1964	200.00	400.00	800.00
—Combines "Introducing the Beatles" with "Golden Hits of the Four Seasons" (Vee Jay 1065)					
DXS-30 [(2) S]	The Beatles vs. The Four Seasons	1964	1500.	2250.	3000.
—Combines "Introducing the Beatles" with "Golden Hits of the Four Seasons" (Vee Jay 1065)					
DX(S)-30	The Beatles vs. The Four Seasons Poster	1964	75.00	150.00	300.00
202 [M]	Hear the Beatles Tell All	1964	75.00	150.00	300.00
—Without "PRO" prefix on label					
PRO 202 [DJ]	Hear the Beatles Tell All	1964	6000.	12000.	18000.
—White label promo with blue print					
PRO 202 [M]	Hear the Beatles Tell All	1964	50.00	100.00	200.00
—With "PRO" prefix on label					
PRO 202 [PD]	Hear the Beatles Tell All	1987	5.00	10.00	20.00
—Shaped picture disc with same recordings as the black vinyl versions					
PRO 202 [S]	Hear the Beatles Tell All	1979	2.50	5.00	10.00
—Authorized reissue in stereo					
LP 1062 [M]	Introducing the Beatles	1964	1500.	2750.	4000.
—"Ad back" cover; with "Love Me Do" and "P.S. I Love You"; oval Vee Jay logo with colorband only!					
LP 1062 [M]	Introducing the Beatles	1964	400.00	800.00	1200.
—Blank back cover; with "Love Me Do" and "P.S. I Love You"; oval Vee Jay logo with colorband only!					
LP 1062 [M]	Introducing the Beatles	1964	250.00	500.00	1000.
—Blank back cover; with "Please Please Me" and "Ask Me Why"; oval Vee Jay logo with colorband only!					
LP 1062 [M]	Introducing the Beatles	1964	200.00	400.00	800.00
—Song titles cover; with "Love Me Do" and "P.S. I Love You"; oval Vee Jay logo with colorband only!					
LP 1062 [M]	Introducing the Beatles	1964	75.00	150.00	300.00
—Song titles cover; with "Please Please Me" and "Ask Me Why"; oval Vee Jay logo with colorband					
LP 1062 [M]	Introducing the Beatles	1964	62.50	125.00	250.00
—Song titles cover; with "Please Please Me" and "Ask Me Why"; brackets Vee Jay logo with colorband (most common authentic version)					
LP 1062 [M]	Introducing the Beatles	1964	62.50	125.00	250.00
—Song titles cover; with "Please Please Me" and "Ask Me Why"; plain Vee Jay logo on solid black label					
LP 1062 [M]	Introducing the Beatles	1964	75.00	150.00	300.00
—Song titles cover; with "Please Please Me" and "Ask Me Why"; oval Vee Jay logo on solid black label					
LP 1062 [M]	Introducing the Beatles	1964	250.00	500.00	1000.
—Song titles cover; with "Please Please Me" and "Ask Me Why"; brackets Vee Jay logo on solid black label					
SR 1062 [B]	Introducing the Beatles	1964	4000.	8000.	12000.
—"Ad back" cover; with "Love Me Do" and "P.S. I Love You" (both mono); oval Vee Jay logo with colorband only!					
SR 1062 [B]	Introducing the Beatles	1964	625.00	1250.	2500.
—Blank back cover; with "Love Me Do" and "P.S. I Love You"; oval Vee Jay logo with colorband only!					
SR 1062 [B]	Introducing the Beatles	1964	3000.	5500.	8000.
—Song titles cover; with "Love Me Do" and "P.S. I Love You"; oval Vee Jay logo with colorband only! Only two authentic copies are known, with hundreds of thousands of counterfeits					
SR 1062 [S]	Introducing the Beatles	1964	400.00	800.00	1600.
—Song titles cover; with "Please Please Me" and "Ask Me Why"; oval Vee Jay logo with colorband					
SR 1062 [S]	Introducing the Beatles	1964	375.00	750.00	1500.
—Song titles cover; with "Please Please Me" and "Ask Me Why"; brackets Vee Jay logo with colorband					
SR 1062 [S]	Introducing the Beatles	1964	400.00	800.00	1600.
—Song titles cover; with "Please Please Me" and "Ask Me Why"; plain Vee Jay logo on solid black label					
LP 1085 [M]	Jolly What! The Beatles and Frank Ifield on Stage	1964	62.50	125.00	250.00
—Man in Beatle wig cover; originals have printing on spine and a dark blue/purple background (counterfeits have a black background and no spine print)					
LP 1085 [M]	The Beatles and Frank Ifield on Stage	1964	2000.	3500.	5000.
—Portrait of Beatles cover; counterfeits are poorly reproduced and have no spine print					
SR 1085 [B]	Jolly What! The Beatles and Frank Ifield on Stage	1964	125.00	250.00	500.00
—Man in Beatle wig cover; "Stereo" on both cover and label. "From Me to You" is mono.					
SR 1085 [B]	The Beatles and Frank Ifield on Stage	1964	4000.	8000.	12000.
—Portrait of Beatles cover; "Stereo" on both cover and label					
LP 1092 [M]	Songs, Pictures and Stories of the Fabulous Beatles	1964	125.00	250.00	500.00
—All copies have gatefold cover with 2/3 width on front; also, all copies have "Introducing the Beatles" records. Oval Vee Jay logo with colorband.					
LP 1092 [M]	Songs, Pictures and Stories of the Fabulous Beatles	1964	125.00	250.00	500.00
—See above; brackets Vee Jay logo with colorband					
LP 1092 [M]	Songs, Pictures and Stories of the Fabulous Beatles	1964	125.00	250.00	500.00
—See above; plain Vee Jay logo on solid black label					
LP 1092 [M]	Songs, Pictures and Stories of the Fabulous Beatles	1964	125.00	250.00	500.00
—See above; oval Vee Jay logo on solid black label					
VJS 1092 [S]	Songs, Pictures and Stories of the Fabulous Beatles	1964	800.00	1600.	2400.
—All copies have gatefold cover with 2/3 width on front; also, all copies have "Introducing the Beatles" records. Oval Vee Jay logo with colorband.					
VJS 1092 [S]	Songs, Pictures and Stories of the Fabulous Beatles	1964	800.00	1600.	2400.
—See above; brackets Vee Jay logo with colorband					
VJS 1092 [S]	Songs, Pictures and Stories of the Fabulous Beatles	1964	800.00	1600.	2400.
—See above; plain Vee Jay logo on solid black label. NOTE: Any non-gatefold copy or any copy called "Songs and Pictures of the Fabulous Beatles" is a counterfeit.					

BEATSTALKERS, THE

45s

Number	Title (A Side/B Side)	Yr	VG	VG+	NM
PRESS					
5001	Left, Right, Left/Get a Better Hold On	1966	3.75	7.50	15.00

BEAU BRUMMELS, THE

Also see RON ELLIOTT; SAL VALENTINO.

45s

Number	Title (A Side/B Side)	Yr	VG	VG+	NM
AUTUMN					
8	Laugh, Laugh/Still in Love with You Baby	1965	3.75	7.50	15.00
—White label					
8	Laugh, Laugh/Still in Love with You Baby	1965	3.00	6.00	12.00
—Tan label					
10	Just a Little/They'll Make You Cry	1965	3.75	7.50	15.00
16	You Tell Me Why/I Want You	1965	2.00	4.00	8.00
20	Don't Talk to Strangers/In Good Time	1965	2.00	4.00	8.00
24	Good Time Music/Sad Little Girl	1965	2.00	4.00	8.00
RHINO					
RNOR 4506	Laugh, Laugh/Just a Little	1984	—	2.00	4.00
RNOR 4506 [PS]	Laugh, Laugh/Just a Little	1984	—	2.00	4.00
WARNER BROS.					
5813	One Too Many Mornings/She Reigns	1966	2.00	4.00	8.00
5848	Fine with Me/Here We Are Again	1966	2.00	4.00	8.00
7014	Don't Make Promises/Two Days 'Til Tomorrow	1967	2.00	4.00	8.00
7079	Magic Hollow/Lower Level	1967	2.00	4.00	8.00
7204	Are You Happy/Lift Me	1968	—	3.00	6.00
7218	I'm a Sleeper/Long Walking Down to Misery	1968	—	3.00	6.00
7260	Cherokee Girl/Deep Water	1969	—	3.00	6.00
8119	You Tell Me Why/Down to the Bottom	1975	—	2.50	5.00

Albums

Number	Title (A Side/B Side)	Yr	VG	VG+	NM
ACCORD					
SN-7175	Just a Little	1982	2.50	5.00	10.00
AUTUMN					
LP 103 [M]	Introducing the Beau Brummels	1965	12.50	25.00	50.00
SLP 103 [S]	Introducing the Beau Brummels	1965	15.00	30.00	60.00
SLP 103 [S]	The Beau Brummels, Volume 2	1965	12.50	25.00	50.00
LP 104 [M]	The Beau Brummels, Volume 2	1965	10.00	20.00	40.00
JAS					
5000	Original Hits of the Beau Brummels	1976	3.75	7.50	15.00
POST					
6000	The Beau Brummels Sing	196?	3.75	7.50	15.00
RHINO					
RNLP-101	The Best of the Beau Brummels	1981	2.50	5.00	10.00
RNLP-102	Introducing the Beau Brummels	1981	2.50	5.00	10.00
RNLP-104	From the Vaults	1981	3.00	6.00	12.00
RNLP-70171	The Best of the Beau Brummels (Golden Archive Series)	1986	2.50	5.00	10.00
VAULT					
LP-114 [M]	Best of the Beau Brummels	1967	6.25	12.50	25.00
SLP-114 [S]	Best of the Beau Brummels	1967	6.25	12.50	25.00
SLP-121	Beau Brummels, Vol. 44	1968	6.25	12.50	25.00
WARNER BROS.					
W 1644 [M]	Beau Brummels '66	1966	5.00	10.00	20.00
WS 1644 [S]	Beau Brummels '66	1966	6.25	12.50	25.00
W 1692 [M]	Triangle	1967	5.00	10.00	20.00
WS 1692 [S]	Triangle	1967	6.25	12.50	25.00
WS 1760	Bradley's Barn	1968	6.25	12.50	25.00
BS 2842	The Beau Brummels	1975	5.00	10.00	20.00

BEAU-K'S, THE

45s

Number	Title (A Side/B Side)	Yr	VG	VG+	NM
MERCURY					
72157	Packin' Up/Forget Me Not	1963	2.50	5.00	10.00
72224	A Rose and a Star/What Else Could I Do But Cry	1963	2.50	5.00	10.00

BEAU-MARKS, THE

45s

Number	Title (A Side/B Side)	Yr	VG	VG+	NM
MAINSTREAM					
688	Clap Your Hands/Daddy Said	1968	2.50	5.00	10.00
PORT					
70029	Little Miss Twist/Lovely Little Lady	1962	3.75	7.50	15.00

Number	Title (A Side/B Side)	Yr	VG	VG+	NM
RUST					
5035	School Is Out/Classmates	1961	5.00	10.00	20.00
5050	I'll Never Be the Same/Tender Years	1962	5.00	10.00	20.00
SHAD					
5017	Clap Your Hands/Daddy Said	1960	5.00	10.00	20.00
5021	Cause We're in Love/Billy Went a-Walkin'	1960	5.00	10.00	20.00
TIME					
1032	Oh Joan/Rockin' Blues	1961	7.50	15.00	30.00

BEAUMONT, JIMMY

Of THE SKYLINERS.

Number	Title (A Side/B Side)	Yr	VG	VG+	NM
45s					
BANG					
510	Tell Me/I Feel Like I'm Falling in Love	1965	5.00	10.00	20.00
525	I Never Loved Her Anyway/You Got Too Much Going for You	1966	7.50	15.00	30.00
COLPIX					
607	The End of a Story/Baion Rhythms	1961	7.50	15.00	30.00
GALLANT					
3007	Please Send Me Someone to Love/There Is No Other Love	196?	5.00	10.00	20.00
3012	Love Is a Dangerous Game/Just a Little Closer	196?	3.00	6.00	12.00
MAY					
112	Ev'rybody's Cryin'/Camera	1961	6.25	12.50	25.00
115	I Should Have Listened to Mama/Juarez	1962	6.25	12.50	25.00
120	Never Say Goodbye/I'm Gonna Try My Wings	1962	6.25	12.50	25.00
136	I'll Always Be in Love with You/Give Her My Best	1963	6.25	12.50	25.00

BEAUREGARDE

Number	Title (A Side/B Side)	Yr	VG	VG+	NM
45s					
INTERNATIONAL ARTISTS					
123	Popcorn Popper/Mama Never Taught Me How to Jelly Roll	1968	6.25	12.50	25.00
Albums					
EMPIRE					
(no #)	Beauregarde	1969	25.00	50.00	100.00
SOUND					
7104	Beauregarde	1969	20.00	40.00	80.00

BEAVER, PAUL

Number	Title (A Side/B Side)	Yr	VG	VG+	NM
Albums					
RAPTURE					
11111	Perchance to Dream	196?	12.50	25.00	50.00

BEAVER AND KRAUSE

Number	Title (A Side/B Side)	Yr	VG	VG+	NM
45s					
WARNER BROS.					
7414	People's Park/Salute to the Vanishing Bald Eagle	1970	—	3.00	6.00
7485	Walkin' By the River/The Saga of the Blue Beaver	1971	—	3.00	6.00
7642	Bluebird Canyon Stomp/Real Slow Drag	1972	—	3.00	6.00
Albums					
LIMELIGHT					
86069	Ragnarok — Electronic Funk	1969	7.50	15.00	30.00
WARNER BROS.					
WS 1850	In a Wild Sanctuary	1969	3.75	7.50	15.00
WS 1909	Gandharva	1970	3.75	7.50	15.00
BS 2624	All Good Men	1972	3.75	7.50	15.00

BEAVERS, THE

Number	Title (A Side/B Side)	Yr	VG	VG+	NM
45s					
CAPITOL					
F3956	Sack Dress/Rockin' at the Drive-In	1958	6.25	12.50	25.00
F4015	The Road to Happiness/Low As I Can Be	1958	5.00	10.00	20.00

BECK, BECKY LEE

Number	Title (A Side/B Side)	Yr	VG	VG+	NM
45s					
CHALLENGE					
59272	I Want a Beatle for Christmas/Puppy Dog	1964	5.00	10.00	20.00

BECK, BOBBY

Number	Title (A Side/B Side)	Yr	VG	VG+	NM
45s					
ABC-PARAMOUNT					
10099	Isle of Capri/Swinging on a Chandelier	1960	5.00	10.00	20.00
10148	The Door Is Always Open/You Got All My Love	1960	5.00	10.00	20.00

BECK, JEFF

Includes the Jeff Beck Group, of whom ROD STEWART was lead singer. Also see BECK, BOGERT AND APPICE; THE YARDBIRDS.

Number	Title (A Side/B Side)	Yr	VG	VG+	NM
45s					
EPIC					
05595	Gets Us All in the End/You Know We Know	1985	—	—	3.00
10157	Beck's Bolero/Hi-Ho Silver Lining	1967	4.00	8.00	16.00
10218	Rock My Plimsoul/Tally Man	1967	4.00	8.00	16.00
10390	Blues De Luxe/Ol' Man River	1968	3.00	6.00	12.00
10484	Jailhouse Rock/Plynth (Water Down the Drain)	1969	3.00	6.00	12.00
10814	Got the Feeling/Situation	1971	2.50	5.00	10.00
10938	Definitely Maybe/Hi Ho Silver Lining	1973	2.50	5.00	10.00
50112	Constipated Duck/You Know What I Mean	1975	—	3.00	6.00
50276	Come Dancing/Head for Backstage Pass	1976	—	2.00	4.00
50914	Too Much to Lose/The FInal Peace	1980	—	2.00	4.00
Albums					
ACCORD					
SN-7141	Early Anthology	1981	2.50	5.00	10.00
EPIC					
AS 151 [DJ]	Everything You Always Wanted to Hear by Jeff Beck But Were Afraid to Ask For	1977	5.00	10.00	20.00
—Promo-only sampler					
A2S 850 [(2) DJ]	Then and Now	1981	6.25	12.50	25.00
—Promo-only sampler					
BN 26413	Truth	1968	3.75	7.50	15.00
—Yellow label					
BN 26413	Truth	1973	2.50	5.00	10.00
—Orange label					
PE 26413	Truth	198?	2.00	4.00	8.00
—Reissue with new prefix					
BN 26478	Beck-Ola	1969	3.75	7.50	15.00
—Yellow label					
BN 26478	Beck-Ola	1973	2.50	5.00	10.00
—Orange label					
PE 26478	Beck-Ola	197?	2.00	4.00	8.00
—Reissue with new prefix					
EQ 30973 [Q]	Rough and Ready	1972	5.00	10.00	20.00
KE 30973	Rough and Ready	1971	3.75	7.50	15.00
—Yellow label					
KE 30973	Rough and Ready	1973	2.50	5.00	10.00
—Orange label					
PE 30973	Rough and Ready	198?	2.00	4.00	8.00
—Budget-line reissue					
EQ 31331 [Q]	Jeff Beck Group	1972	5.00	10.00	20.00
KE 31331	Jeff Beck Group	1972	3.75	7.50	15.00
—Yellow label					
KE 31331	Jeff Beck Group	1973	2.50	5.00	10.00
—Orange label					
PE 31331	Jeff Beck Group	198?	2.00	4.00	8.00
—Budget-line reissue					
PE 33409	Blow by Blow	1975	2.50	5.00	10.00
—Orange label, no bar code on cover					
PE 33409	Blow by Blow	198?	2.00	4.00	8.00
—Reissue with dark blue label and bar code on cover					
PEQ 33409 [Q]	Blow by Blow	1975	5.00	10.00	20.00
BG 33779 [(2)]	Truth/Beck-Ola	1975	3.00	6.00	12.00
PE 33849	Wired	1976	2.50	5.00	10.00
—Orange label, no bar code on cover					
PE 33849	Wired	198?	2.00	4.00	8.00
—Reissue with dark blue label and bar code on cover					
PEQ 33849 [Q]	Wired	1976	5.00	10.00	20.00
PE 34433	Jeff Beck with the Jan Hammer Group Live	1977	2.50	5.00	10.00
—Orange label, no bar code on cover					
PE 34433	Jeff Beck with the Jan Hammer Group Live	198?	2.00	4.00	8.00
—Reissue with dark blue label and bar code on cover					
FE 35684	There and Back	1980	2.50	5.00	10.00
PE 35684	There and Back	1985	2.00	4.00	8.00
—Budget-line reissue					
FE 39483	Flash	1985	2.50	5.00	10.00
HE 43409	Blow by Blow	1980	7.50	15.00	30.00
—Half-speed mastered edition					
HE 43849	Wired	198?	7.50	15.00	30.00
—Half-speed mastered edition					
FE 44313	Jeff Beck's Guitar Shop	1989	3.75	7.50	15.00

BECK, JEFF, AND ROD STEWART

Also see each artist's individual listings.

Number	Title (A Side/B Side)	Yr	VG	VG+	NM
45s					
EPIC					
05416	People Get Ready/Back on the Street	1985	—	—	3.00
05416 [PS]	People Get Ready/Back on the Street	1985	—	—	3.00

BECK, JOE

Number	Title (A Side/B Side)	Yr	VG	VG+	NM
45s					
POLYDOR					
14384	Dr. Lee/Stand Up and Be Someone	1977	—	2.00	4.00
Albums					
CTI					
8002	Beck & Sanborn	1979	2.50	5.00	10.00
—Reissue of Kudu 21 with new title					
CTI/CBS ASSOCIATED					
FZ 40805	Beck & Sanborn	1987	2.50	5.00	10.00
KUDU					
21	Beck	1975	3.00	6.00	12.00
POLYDOR					
PD-1-6092	Watch the Time	1976	2.50	5.00	10.00

BECK, BOGERT & APPICE

Also see JEFF BECK; VANILLA FUDGE.

Number	Title (A Side/B Side)	Yr	VG	VG+	NM
45s					
EPIC					
10998	I'm So Proud/Oh to Love You	1973	2.00	4.00	8.00
11027	Lady/Oh to Love You	1973	2.00	4.00	8.00
Albums					
EPIC					
CQ 32140 [Q]	Beck, Bogert & Appice	1973	5.00	10.00	20.00
KE 32140	Beck, Bogert & Appice	1973	3.75	7.50	15.00
—Yellow label					
KE 32140	Beck, Bogert & Appice	1973	2.50	5.00	10.00
—Orange label					
PE 32140	Beck, Bogert & Appice	198?	2.00	4.00	8.00
—Budget-line reissue					

BECKHAM, BOB

Number	Title (A Side/B Side)	Yr	VG	VG+	NM
45s					
DECCA					
30617	Tomorrow/I'm Tired of Everyone But You	1958	3.00	6.00	12.00
30861	Just As Much As Ever/Your Sweet Love	1959	3.00	6.00	12.00
31029	Crazy Arms/Beloved	1959	3.00	6.00	12.00
31089	Only the Broken Hearted/Mais Oui	1960	2.50	5.00	10.00
31132	Two Wrongs Don't Make a Right/Nothing Is Forever	1960	2.50	5.00	10.00
31163	Meet Me Halfway/One More Time	1960	2.50	5.00	10.00
31239	Forget It/Like a Fool	1961	2.50	5.00	10.00
31285	How Soon (Will I Be Seeing You)/I'm Wondering	1961	2.50	5.00	10.00
31337	10,000 Teardrops (And One Broken Heart)/Just Friends	1961	2.50	5.00	10.00

Number	Title (A Side/B Side)	Yr	VG	VG+	NM
31391	I Cry Like a Baby/I'll Take My Chances	1962	2.00	4.00	8.00
31432	Building Memories/Memory Mountain	1962	2.00	4.00	8.00
31493	Footprints/Midnight	1963	2.00	4.00	8.00
31547	Grabbing at Rainbows/My Heart Would Know	1963	2.00	4.00	8.00
31607	Helpless/I'll Be Around	1964	2.00	4.00	8.00
MONUMENT					
1018	Cherokee Strip/You Really Know How to Hurt a Guy	1967	—	3.00	6.00
1030	Lily White/Look at Them	1967	—	3.00	6.00
SMASH					
1990	Slowly Dying/It's My Heart	1965	2.00	4.00	8.00

BECKY AND THE LOLLIPOPS

45s

Number	Title (A Side/B Side)	Yr	VG	VG+	NM
EPIC					
9736	I Don't Care (What They Say)/My Boyfriend	1964	3.00	6.00	12.00

BED BUGS, THE

45s

Number	Title (A Side/B Side)	Yr	VG	VG+	NM
LIBERTY					
55679	Yeah Yeah/Lucy Lucy	1964	6.25	12.50	25.00

BEDLAM

Albums

Number	Title (A Side/B Side)	Yr	VG	VG+	NM
CHRYSALIS					
CHR-1048	Bedlam	1973	6.25	12.50	25.00

BEE BEE TWINS, THE

45s

Number	Title (A Side/B Side)	Yr	VG	VG+	NM
LIBERTY					
55173	The Night Before Christmas/Yuletide Tango	1958	3.75	7.50	15.00

BEE GEES

Also see BARRY GIBB; MAURICE GIBB; ROBIN GIBB.

45s

Number	Title (A Side/B Side)	Yr	VG	VG+	NM
ATCO					
6487	New York Mining Disaster 1941/I Can't See Nobody	1967	3.00	6.00	12.00
6487	New York Mining Disaster 1941 Have You Seen My Wife, Mr. Jones/I Can't See Nobody	1967	2.50	5.00	10.00
6487 [DJ]	New York Mining Disaster 1941/I Can't See Nobody	1967	6.25	12.50	25.00
—Artist not listed on label.					
6503	To Love Somebody/Close Another Door	1967	2.50	5.00	10.00
6521	Holiday/Every Christian Lion Hearted Man Will Show You	1967	2.50	5.00	10.00
6532	(The Lights Went Out in) Massachusetts/Sir Geoffrey Saved the World	1967	2.50	5.00	10.00
6548	Words/Sinking Ships	1968	2.50	5.00	10.00
6570	Jumbo/The Singer Sang His Song	1968	2.00	4.00	8.00
6603	I've Gotta Get a Message to You/Kitty Can	1968	2.00	4.00	8.00
6639	I Started a Joke/Kilburn Towers	1969	2.00	4.00	8.00
6657	First of May/Lamplight	1969	2.00	4.00	8.00
6682	Tomorrow Tomorrow/Sun in My Morning	1969	2.00	4.00	8.00
6702	Don't Forget to Remember/The Lord	1969	2.50	5.00	10.00
6702	Don't Forget to Remember/I Lay Down and Die	1969	2.00	4.00	8.00
6741	If Only I Had My Mind on Something Else/Sweetheart	1970	2.00	4.00	8.00
6752	I.O.I.O./Then You Left Me	1970	2.00	4.00	8.00
6795	Lonely Days/Man for All Seasons	1971	—	3.00	6.00
6824	How Can You Mend a Broken Heart/Country Woman	1971	—	3.00	6.00
6847	Don't Wanna Live Inside Myself/Walking Back to Waterloo	1971	—	3.00	6.00
6871	My World/On Time	1972	—	2.50	5.00
6896	Run to Me/Road to Alaska	1972	—	2.50	5.00
6909	Alive/Paper Mache, Cabbages and Kings	1972	—	2.50	5.00
EMMC					
(no #)	A Personal Message from the Bee Gees/The Rescue of Bonnie Prince Wally	1979	2.50	5.00	10.00
—Official Bee Gees Fan Club record; small hole, plays at 33 1/3 rpm					
POLYDOR					
31457 1006 7	Alone/How Deep Is Your Love	1997	—	—	3.00
RSO					
401	Saw a New Morning/My Life Has Been a Song	1973	—	3.00	6.00
404	Wouldn't I Be Someone/Elisa	1973	—	3.00	6.00
408	Mr. Natural/It Doesn't Matter Much Anymore	1974	—	3.00	6.00
410	Throw a Penny/I Can't Let Go	1974	—	3.00	6.00
501	Charade/Heavy Breathing	1974	—	3.00	6.00
510	Jive Talkin'/Wind of Change	1975	—	2.00	4.00
515	Nights on Broadway/Edge of the Universe	1975	—	2.00	4.00
519	Fanny (Be Tender With My Love)/Country Lanes	1975	—	2.00	4.00
853	You Should Be Dancing/Subway	1976	—	2.00	4.00
859	Love So Right/You Stepped Into My Life	1976	—	2.00	4.00
867	Boogie Child/Lovers	1976	—	2.00	4.00
880	Edge of the Universe/Words	1977	—	2.00	4.00
882	How Deep Is Your Love/Can't Keep a Good Man Down	1977	—	2.00	4.00
885	Stayin' Alive/If I Can't Have You	1977	—	2.00	4.00
889	Night Fever/Down the Road	1978	—	2.00	4.00
907	She's Leaving Home/Oh! Darling	1978	—	2.00	4.00
—B-side by Robin Gibb solo					
913	Too Much Heaven/Rest Your Love on Me	1978	—	2.00	4.00
918	Tragedy/Until	1979	—	2.00	4.00
925	Love You Inside Out/I'm Satisfied	1979	—	2.00	4.00
1066	He's a Liar/(Instrumental)	1981	—	—	3.00
1067	Living Eyes/I Still Love You	1981	—	—	3.00
8001	Come On Over/Jive Talkin'	1980	—	2.00	4.00
—Reissue series; first time on 45 for A-side					
8019	More Than a Woman/Night Fever	1980	—	2.00	4.00
—Reissue series; first time on 45 for A-side					
813373-7	The Woman in You/Stayin' Alive	1983	—	—	3.00
813373-7 [PS]	The Woman in You/Stayin' Alive	1983	—	3.00	6.00
815235-7	Someone Belonging to Someone/I Love You Too Much	1983	—	—	3.00
815235-7 [PS]	Someone Belonging to Someone/I Love You Too Much	1983	—	3.00	6.00
WARNER BROS.					
22733	You Win Again/Will You Ever Let Me	1989	—	2.50	5.00
22889	One/Wing and a Prayer	1989	—	—	3.00
22889 [PS]	One/Wing and a Prayer	1989	—	—	3.00
28139	E.S.P./Overnight	1987	—	—	3.00
28139 [PS]	E.S.P./Overnight	1987	—	2.00	4.00
28351	You Win Again/Backtafunk	1987	—	—	3.00
28351 [PS]	You Win Again/Backtafunk	1987	—	—	3.00

Albums

Number	Title (A Side/B Side)	Yr	VG	VG+	NM
ATCO					
33-223 [M]	Bee Gees' 1st	1967	7.50	15.00	30.00
SD 33-223	Bee Gees' 1st	1969	2.50	5.00	10.00
—Yellow label reissue					
SD 33-223 [S]	Bee Gees' 1st	1967	5.00	10.00	20.00
—Brown and purple label original					
33-233 [M]	Horizontal	1968	7.50	15.00	30.00
SD 33-233	Horizontal	1969	2.50	5.00	10.00
—Yellow label reissue					
SD 33-233 [S]	Horizontal	1968	5.00	10.00	20.00
—Brown and purple label original					
33-253 [M]	Idea	1968	12.50	25.00	50.00
—White label promo only					
SD 33-253	Idea	1969	2.50	5.00	10.00
—Yellow label reissue					
SD 33-253 [S]	Idea	1968	5.00	10.00	20.00
—Brown and purple label original					
33-264 [M]	Rare, Precious & Beautiful	1968	7.50	15.00	30.00
—White label promo only					
SD 33-264	Rare, Precious & Beautiful	1969	2.50	5.00	10.00
—Yellow label reissue					
SD 33-264 [R]	Rare, Precious & Beautiful	1968	3.75	7.50	15.00
—Brown and purple label original					
33-292 [M]	Best of Bee Gees	1969	7.50	15.00	30.00
—White label promo only					
SD 33-292 [S]	Best of Bee Gees	1969	3.00	6.00	12.00
33-321 [M]	Rare, Precious & Beautiful, Volume 2	1970	7.50	15.00	30.00
—White label promo only					
SD 33-321 [R]	Rare, Precious & Beautiful, Volume 2	1970	3.00	6.00	12.00
SD 33-327	Cucumber Castle	1970	3.00	6.00	12.00
SD 33-353	2 Years On	1971	3.00	6.00	12.00
SD 2-702 [(2)]	Odessa	1969	10.00	20.00	40.00
—Red felt cover					
SD 2-702 [(2)]	Odessa	1969	20.00	40.00	80.00
—Record club editions with plain red cover					
SD 7003	Trafalgar	1971	3.00	6.00	12.00
SD 7012	To Whom It May Concern	1972	3.00	6.00	12.00
MOBILE FIDELITY					
1-263	Trafalgar	1996	10.00	20.00	40.00
—Audiophile vinyl					
NAUTILUS					
NR-17	Spirits Having Flown	1981	7.50	15.00	30.00
NR-42	Living Eyes	1982	25.00	50.00	100.00
—Record was never released; value is for test pressings					
RSO					
SMP-1 [DJ]	The Words and Music of Maurice, Barry and Robin Gibb	1979	12.50	25.00	50.00
—Promo-only publisher's sampler					
PRO 033 [DJ]	Saturday Night Fever Special Disco Versions	1978	12.50	25.00	50.00
—Promo-only sampler; contains an otherwise unavailable extended version of "Stayin' Alive"					
SO 870	Life in a Tin Can	1973	2.50	5.00	10.00
SO 875	Best of Bee Gees, Vol. 2	1973	2.50	5.00	10.00
PUB-1000 [DJ]	Unichappell Publisher's Sampler	1980	12.50	25.00	50.00
RS-1-3003	Children of the World	1976	2.50	5.00	10.00
RS-1-3006	Bee Gees Gold, Volume One	1976	2.50	5.00	10.00
RS-1-3007	Odessa	1976	2.50	5.00	10.00
—Condensed version of Atco original					
RS-1-3024	Main Course	1977	2.00	4.00	8.00
RS-1-3041	Spirits Having Flown	1979	2.50	5.00	10.00
—Some pressings have a cardboard innersleeve, others a paper innersleeve. No difference in value.					
RS-1-3042 [PD]	Spirits Having Flown	1979	3.75	7.50	15.00
RS-1-3098	Living Eyes	1981	2.50	5.00	10.00
RS-2-3901 [(2)]	Here At Last...Bee Gees...Live	1977	3.00	6.00	12.00
RS-2-4200 [(2)]	Bee Gees' Greatest	1979	3.00	6.00	12.00
SO 4800	Mr. Natural	1974	2.50	5.00	10.00
SO 4807	Main Course	1975	2.50	5.00	10.00
823274-1 [(2)]	Here At Last...Bee Gees...Live	1984	2.50	5.00	10.00
823658-1	Children of the World	1984	2.00	4.00	8.00
823659-1	Bee Gees Gold, Volume One	1984	2.00	4.00	8.00
825390-1 [(2)]	Bee Gees' Greatest	1984	2.50	5.00	10.00
—Gatefold replaced by single-pocket cover					
PRO ??? [DJ]	Select Disco Cuts from "Spirits Having Flown"	1979	7.50	15.00	30.00
WARNER BROS.					
25541	E.S.P.	1987	2.50	5.00	10.00
25887	One	1989	3.00	6.00	12.00

BEE JAY

45s

Number	Title (A Side/B Side)	Yr	VG	VG+	NM
CLOCK					
1743	I'll Go On/There's No One for Me	1962	6.25	12.50	25.00

BEEFEATERS, THE

Early version of THE BYRDS.

45s

Number	Title (A Side/B Side)	Yr	VG	VG+	NM
ELEKTRA					
45013	Please Let Me Love You/It Won't Be Long	1964	125.00	250.00	500.00
45013 [DJ]	Please Let Me Love You/It Won't Be Long	1964	62.50	125.00	250.00

BEEHIVES, THE

45s

Number	Title (A Side/B Side)	Yr	VG	VG+	NM
KING					
5881	I Want to Hold Your Hand/She Loves You	1964	3.75	7.50	15.00

BEES, THE

At least two different groups.

45s

Number	Title (A Side/B Side)	Yr	VG	VG+	NM
FINCH					
506	So Jealous/(B-side unknown)	196?	18.75	37.50	75.00
IMPERIAL					
5314	Toy Bell/Snatchin' Back	1954	50.00	100.00	200.00
5320	I Want to Be Loved/Get Away Baby	1954	75.00	150.00	300.00
LIVERPOOL					
62225	Voices Green and Purple/(B-side unknown)	1966	20.00	40.00	80.00
62225 [PS]	Voices Green and Purple/(B-side unknown)	1966	25.00	50.00	100.00
MIRWOOD					
5503	She's An Artist/Leave Me Be	1965	6.25	12.50	25.00

BEETHOVEN SOUL

45s

Number	Title (A Side/B Side)	Yr	VG	VG+	NM
DOT					
17031	Good Time Gal/The Walls Are High	1967	2.00	4.00	8.00

Albums

Number	Title (A Side/B Side)	Yr	VG	VG+	NM
DOT					
DLP-3821 [M]	Beethoven Soul	1967	6.25	12.50	25.00
DLP-25821 [S]	Beethoven Soul	1967	6.25	12.50	25.00

BEETLES, THE

45s

Number	Title (A Side/B Side)	Yr	VG	VG+	NM
BLUE CAT					
115	Ain't That Love/Welcome to My Heart	1965	3.75	7.50	15.00
—Also issued as "The Bouquets"					

BEGINNING OF THE END, THE

45s

Number	Title (A Side/B Side)	Yr	VG	VG+	NM
ALSTON					
4595	Funky Nassau- Part 1/Funky Nassau - Part 2	1971	—	2.50	5.00
4599	Hey Pretty Girl/Monkey Tamarind	1971	—	2.00	4.00
4604	Come Down Baby - Part 1/Come Down Baby - Part 2	1971	—	2.00	4.00
4605	Gee Whiz, It's Christmas/Surrey Ride	1971	—	2.00	4.00
4607	Doin' the Funky Do/Fishman	1972	—	2.00	4.00

Albums

Number	Title (A Side/B Side)	Yr	VG	VG+	NM
ALSTON					
SD 33-379	Funky Nassau	1971	5.00	10.00	20.00

BEL-AIRE GIRLS, THE

Albums

Number	Title (A Side/B Side)	Yr	VG	VG+	NM
EVEREST					
STBR-1081 [S]	The Bel-Aire Girls Sing Along with the Teen-Agers	1960	20.00	40.00	80.00
LPBR-5081 [M]	The Bel-Aire Girls Sing Along with the Teen-Agers	1960	15.00	30.00	60.00

BEL-AIRE POPS ORCHESTRA, THE

Albums

Number	Title (A Side/B Side)	Yr	VG	VG+	NM
LIBERTY					
LRP-3414 [M]	Jan and Dean's Pop Symphony No. 1	1965	30.00	60.00	120.00
LST-7414 [S]	Jan and Dean's Pop Symphony No. 1	1965	50.00	100.00	200.00

BEL-AIRES, THE

45s

Number	Title (A Side/B Side)	Yr	VG	VG+	NM
CROWN					
126	Cherry Pie/Tick Tock	1954	12.50	25.00	50.00
DECCA					
30631	My Yearbook/Rockin' An' Strollin'	1958	7.50	15.00	30.00
FLIP					
303	This Paradise/Let's Party Awhile	1954	25.00	50.00	100.00
—Maroon label					
303	This Paradise/Let's Party Awhile	1954	12.50	25.00	50.00
—Blue label					
304	White Port and Lemon Juice/This Is Goodbye	1955	25.00	50.00	100.00
MERCURY					
71763	Knock Knock Knock (Knocking on My Door)/Wear My Class Ring on a Ribbon	1961	3.00	6.00	12.00
NU SOUND					
1022	Palmeras/Pony Rock	1962	3.00	6.00	12.00

BELAFONTE, HARRY

45s

Number	Title (A Side/B Side)	Yr	VG	VG+	NM
CAPITOL					
F1018	A Farewell to Arms/I Still Get a Thrill	1950	7.50	15.00	30.00
COLUMBIA					
02396	Forever Young/Something to Hold On To	1981	—	2.00	4.00
GEFFEN					
27859	Day-O/Main Titles	1988	—	—	3.00
—B-side: instrumental from the "Beetlejuice" soundtrack					
27859 [PS]	Day-O/Main Titles	1988	—	—	3.00
JUBILEE					
5158	Venezuela/Annabelle Lee	1954	5.00	10.00	20.00
RCA VICTOR					
APBO-0093	Morningside/So Close	1973	—	2.00	4.00
47-4676	A-Roving/Chimney Smoke	1952	3.75	7.50	15.00
47-4892	Man Smart (Woman Smarter)/Jerry	1952	3.75	7.50	15.00
47-5051	Scarlet Ribbons (For Her Hair)/Shenandoah	1952	3.75	7.50	15.00
47-5210	Springfield Mountain/Gomen-Nasai	1953	3.75	7.50	15.00
47-5311	Matilda, Matilda/Suzanne	1953	3.75	7.50	15.00
47-5617	Hold 'Em Joe/I'm Just a Country Boy	1954	3.75	7.50	15.00
47-5722	Pretty As A Rainbow/Acorn in the Meadow	1954	3.75	7.50	15.00
47-5722 [PS]	Pretty As A Rainbow/Acorn in the Meadow	1954	7.50	15.00	30.00
47-5872	John Henry/(B-side unknown)	1954	3.75	7.50	15.00
47-6249	Troubles/Hello Everybody	1955	3.00	6.00	12.00
47-6458	The Blues Is Man (Part 1)/The Blues Is Man (Part 2)	1956	3.00	6.00	12.00
47-6663	Jamaica Farewell/Once Was	1956	3.00	6.00	12.00
47-6663 [PS]	Jamaica Farewell/Once Was	1956	6.25	12.50	25.00
47-6735	Mary's Boy Child/Venezuela	1956	3.00	6.00	12.00
47-6735 [PS]	Mary's Boy Child/Venezuela	1956	6.25	12.50	25.00
47-6771	Banana Boat (Day-O)/Star-O	1956	3.00	6.00	12.00
47-6771 [PS]	Banana Boat (Day-O)/Star-O	1956	6.25	12.50	25.00
47-6780	John Henry/Tol' My Captain	1956	2.50	5.00	10.00
47-6781	Mo Mary/Lord Randall	1956	2.50	5.00	10.00
47-6782	Man Piaba/The Fox	1956	2.50	5.00	10.00
47-6782 [PS]	Man Piaba/The Fox	1956	5.00	10.00	20.00
47-6783	Man Smart (Woman Smarter)/Chimney Smoke	1956	2.50	5.00	10.00
47-6784	Unchained Melody/A-Roving	1956	2.50	5.00	10.00
47-6785	Jump Down-Spin Around/In That Great Gettin' Up Mornin'	1956	2.50	5.00	10.00
47-6786	Will His Love Be Like His Rum?/Dolly Dawn	1956	2.50	5.00	10.00
47-6787	Hosanna/I Adore Her	1956	2.50	5.00	10.00
47-6788	Come Back Liza/Brown Skin Girl	1956	2.50	5.00	10.00
47-6789	Water Boy/Noah	1956	2.50	5.00	10.00
47-6790	Danny Boy/Take My Mother Home	1956	2.50	5.00	10.00
47-6830	Mama Look at Bubu/Don't Ever Love Me	1957	3.00	6.00	12.00
47-6830	Mama Look a Boo Boo (Shut Your Mouth - Go Away)/Don't Ever Love Me	1957	3.00	6.00	12.00
—Same recording as above, but new A-side title					
47-6830 [PS]	Mama Look at Bubu/Don't Ever Love Me	1957	6.25	12.50	25.00
47-6885	Island in the Sun/Cocoanut Woman	1957	2.50	5.00	10.00
47-7176	The Marching Saints/Did You Hear About Jerry?	1958	2.00	4.00	8.00
47-7289	Ain't That Love/The Waiting Game	1958	2.00	4.00	8.00
47-7425	I Heard the Bells on Christmas Day/Mary, Mary	1958	2.00	4.00	8.00
47-7425 [PS]	I Heard the Bells on Christmas Day/Mary, Mary	1958	3.75	7.50	15.00
47-7445	Gotta Travel On/Tarrytown	1959	2.00	4.00	8.00
47-7491	Darlin' Cora/Turn Around	1959	2.00	4.00	8.00
47-7550	Fifteen/'Round the Bay of Mexico	1959	2.00	4.00	8.00
47-7681	March Down to Jordan/Oh Freedom	1960	2.00	4.00	8.00
47-8513	Hallelujah I Love You So/In the Even' Mama	1965	—	3.00	6.00
47-8717	Little Bit of Rain/Roll On, Buddy	1965	—	3.00	6.00
47-9075	Hurry Sundown/Mama Look At Bubu	1967	—	3.00	6.00
47-9263	Sunflower/A Strange Song	1967	—	3.00	6.00
47-9406	Annie Love/I'm Just a Country Boy	1967	—	3.00	6.00
47-9542	By the Time I Get to Phoenix/Sleep Late, My Lady Friend	1968	—	3.00	6.00
74-0145	Lullabye/The Train Song	1969	—	2.50	5.00
—With Miriam Makeba					
74-0428	Circle 'Round the Sun/Something in the Way She Moves	1971	—	2.50	5.00
74-0628	Women/Pastures of Plenty	1971	—	2.50	5.00
447-0320	Suzanne/Matilda, Matilda!	195?	2.50	5.00	10.00
—Black label, dog on top					
447-0321	Shenandoah/Scarlet Ribbons	195?	2.50	5.00	10.00
—Black label, dog on top					
447-0321 [PS]	Shenandoah/Scarlet Ribbons	195?	5.00	10.00	20.00
447-0322	Hold 'Em Joe/I'm Just a Country Boy	195?	2.50	5.00	10.00
—Black label, dog on top					
447-0323	Mary's Boy Child/Venezuela	195?	2.50	5.00	10.00
—Black label, dog on top					
447-0324	Banana Boat (Day-O)/Jamaica Farewell	195?	2.50	5.00	10.00
—Black label, dog on top					
447-0325	Mama Look A Boo Boo/Don't Ever Love Me	195?	2.50	5.00	10.00
—Black label, dog on top					

7-Inch Extended Plays

Number	Title (A Side/B Side)	Yr	VG	VG+	NM
CAPITOL					
EAP-619	(contents unknown)	1955	3.75	7.50	15.00
EAP-619 [PS]	Close Your Eyes	1955	3.75	7.50	15.00
RCA VICTOR					
SPD-24 [PS]	The Best of Belafonte	1956	5.00	10.00	20.00
—Box for 10-EP set plus liner-note booklet					
SP-45-67	(contents unknown)	195?	5.00	10.00	20.00
SP-45-67 [PS]	RCA Victor Presents Harry Belafonte	195?	5.00	10.00	20.00
547-0404	Mark Twain/Man Piaba//Mo Mary/Lord Randall	1954	2.50	5.00	10.00
—Record 1 of 2-EP set EPB 1022					
547-0405	John Henry/Tol' My Captain//Soldier, Soldier/The Next Big River	1954	2.50	5.00	10.00
—Record 2 of 2-EP set EPB 1022					
EPA 412	Shenandoah/Scarlet Ribbons (For Her Hair)//Man Smart (Woman Smarter)/Jerry (This Timber Got to Roll)	1952	3.00	6.00	12.00
EPA 412 [PS]	Harry Belafonte Sings "Man Smart" and Other Folk Songs	1952	3.00	6.00	12.00
EPA 559	Delia/The Fox//Kalenda Rock/The Drummer and the Cook	195?	3.00	6.00	12.00
EPA 559 [PS]	Harry Belafonte	195?	3.00	6.00	12.00
EPA 693	Take My Mother Home//Unchained Melody/Matilda	1956	3.00	6.00	12.00
EPA 693 [PS]	Belafonte, Act 1	1956	3.00	6.00	12.00
EPA 694	Sylvie//In That Great Gettin' Up Mornin'/Jump Down, Spin Around	1955	3.00	6.00	12.00
—With dog on label					
EPA 694	Sylvie//In That Great Gettin' Up Mornin'/Jump Down, Spin Around	1955	3.75	7.50	15.00
—No dog on label					
EPA 694 [PS]	Belafonte, Act 2	1955	3.00	6.00	12.00
EPA 768	Day O/Will His Love Be Like His Rum?//Jamaica Farewell/Dolly Dawn	1956	3.00	6.00	12.00
EPA 768 [PS]	Calypso	1956	3.00	6.00	12.00
547-0899	Day-O/I Do Adore Her//Brown Skin Girl/Dolly Dawn	1956	2.50	5.00	10.00
—Record 1 of 2-EP set EPB 1248					
547-0900	Jamaica Farewell/Will His Love Be Like His Rum?//Star O/Hosanna	1956	2.50	5.00	10.00
—Record 2 of 2-EP set EPB 1248					
EPB 1022 [PS]	"Mark Twain" and Other Folk Favorites	1954	5.00	10.00	20.00
—Two-pocket jacket for two-EP set					

Number	Title (A Side/B Side)	Yr	VG	VG+	NM
EPB 1248 [PS]	Calypso	1956	5.00	10.00	20.00
—Two-pocket jacket for two-EP set					
EPA 1-1402	*Merci Bon Dieu/The Drummer and the Cook/ Danny Boy	1956	3.00	6.00	12.00
EPA 1-1402 [PS]	An Evening with Belafonte, Vol. 1	1956	3.00	6.00	12.00
EPA 2-1402	Cu Cu Ru Cu Cu/Paloma//Hava Negela/When the Saints Go Marching In	1956	3.00	6.00	12.00
EPA 2-1402 [PS]	An Evening with Belafonte, Vol. 2	1956	3.00	6.00	12.00
EPA 3-1402	(contents unknown)	1956	3.00	6.00	12.00
EPA 3-1402 [PS]	An Evening with Belafonte, Vol. 3	1956	3.00	6.00	12.00
EPA 1-1505	Haiti Cherie/Love, Love Alone//Lucy's Door/ Scratch, Scratch	1957	2.50	5.00	10.00
EPA 1-1505 [PS]	Belafonte Sings of the Caribbean, Vol. 1	1957	2.50	5.00	10.00
EPA 2-1505	(contents unknown)	1957	2.50	5.00	10.00
EPA 2-1505 [PS]	Belafonte Sings of the Caribbean, Vol. 2	1957	2.50	5.00	10.00
EPA 4217	Cordella Brown/Judy Drownded//Lead Man Holler/Angelique-O	1958	3.00	6.00	12.00
EPA 4217 [PS]	Ballads by Belafonte	1958	3.00	6.00	12.00
599-9126	Day-O/I Do Adore Her//Jamaica Farewell/Will His Love Be Like His Rum?	1956	2.00	4.00	8.00
—Side 1 and 20 of 10-EP set SPD-24					
599-9127	Dolly Dawn/Star O//The Jack-Ass Song/Hosanna	1956	2.00	4.00	8.00
—Side 2 and 19 of 10-EP set SPD-24					
599-9128	Come Back Liza/Brown Skin Girl//Man Smart (Woman Smarter)/Matilda	1956	2.00	4.00	8.00
—Side 3 and 18 of 10-EP set SPD-24					
599-9129	Waterboy/Suzanne (Every Night When the Sun Goes Down)//Troubles/In That Great Gettin' Up Mornin'	1956	2.00	4.00	8.00
—Side 4 and 17 of 10-EP set SPD 24					
599-9130	Noah/Jump Down, Spin Around//Take My Mother Home	1956	2.00	4.00	8.00
—Side 5 and 16 of 10-EP set SPD-24					
599-9131	Sylvie//Scarlet Ribbons (For Her Hair)/ Unchained Melody	1956	2.00	4.00	8.00
—Side 6 and 15 of 10-EP set SPD-24					
599-9132	Mark Twain/Tol' My Captain//Man Piaba/The Drummer and the Cook	1956	2.00	4.00	8.00
—Side 7 and 14 of 10-EP set SPD-24					
599-9133	John Henry/Kalenda Rock//The Fox/Soldier, Soldier/The Next Big River	1956	2.00	4.00	8.00
—Side 8 and 13 of 10-EP set SPD-24					
599-9134	Mo Mary/Lord Randall//Delia/Shenandoah	1956	2.00	4.00	8.00
—Side 9 and 12 of 10-EP set SPD-24					
599-9135	Jerry (The Timber Got to Roll)/The Blues Is Man - Part I//Acorn in the Meadow/Hello Everybody	1956	2.00	4.00	8.00
—Side 10 and 11 of 10-EP set SPD-24					

Albums

COLUMBIA

Number	Title (A Side/B Side)	Yr	VG	VG+	NM
FC 37489	Loving You Is Where I Belong	1981	2.50	5.00	10.00

DCC COMPACT CLASSICS

Number	Title (A Side/B Side)	Yr	VG	VG+	NM
LPZ-2039	Jump Up Calypso	1997	6.25	12.50	25.00
—Audiophile vinyl					

EMI

Number	Title (A Side/B Side)	Yr	VG	VG+	NM
E1-92247	Belafonte '89	1989	3.00	6.00	12.00

EMI MANHATAN

Number	Title (A Side/B Side)	Yr	VG	VG+	NM
E1-46971	Paradise in Gazankulu	1988	3.00	6.00	12.00

PAIR

Number	Title (A Side/B Side)	Yr	VG	VG+	NM
PDL2-1060 [(2)]	The Belafonte Song Book	1986	3.00	6.00	12.00

RCA CAMDEN

Number	Title (A Side/B Side)	Yr	VG	VG+	NM
ACL1-0502	Abraham, Martin and John	1974	2.50	5.00	10.00
CAS-2599	Harry	1972	2.50	5.00	10.00

RCA CUSTOM EDITION

Number	Title (A Side/B Side)	Yr	VG	VG+	NM
DRL1-0068	I Wish You a Merry Christmas	1973	3.75	7.50	15.00
—Reissue of LSP-2424 with two tracks deleted					

RCA VICTOR

Number	Title (A Side/B Side)	Yr	VG	VG+	NM
APL1-0094	Play Me	1973	3.00	6.00	12.00
ANL1-0979	Pure Gold	1975	2.50	5.00	10.00
LPM-1006 [M]	Belafonte Sings the Blues	1954	12.50	25.00	50.00
—Reissued in 1958 with the same number, then re-recorded in 1959					
LPM-1022 [M]	"Mark Twain" and Other Folk Favorites	1954	12.50	25.00	50.00
LSP-1022(e) [R]	"Mark Twain" and Other Folk Favorites	196?	3.00	6.00	12.00
LPM-1150 [M]	Belafonte	1955	12.50	25.00	50.00
LSP-1150(e) [R]	Belafonte	196?	3.00	6.00	12.00
AFL1-1248	Calypso	1977	2.50	5.00	10.00
—Reissue with new prefix					
LPM-1248 [M]	Calypso	1956	7.50	15.00	30.00
LSP-1248(e) [R]	Calypso	196?	3.00	6.00	12.00
LPM-1402 [M]	An Evening with Belafonte	1957	6.25	12.50	25.00
LSP-1402(e) [R]	An Evening with Belafonte	1960	3.00	6.00	12.00
—Dog on top					
LSP-1402(e) [R]	An Evening with Belafonte	1969	2.50	5.00	10.00
—Orange label					
ANL1-1434	An Evening with Belafonte	1976	2.50	5.00	10.00
—Reissue of LSP-1402					
LPM-1505 [M]	Belafonte Sings of the Caribbean	1957	7.50	15.00	30.00
LSP-1505(e) [R]	Belafonte Sings of the Caribbean	196?	3.00	6.00	12.00
LOC-1507 [M]	Porgy and Bess	1959	5.00	10.00	20.00
LSO-1507 [S]	Porgy and Bess	1959	6.25	12.50	25.00
—With Lena Horne					
LPM-1887 [M]	To Wish You a Merry Christmas	1958	6.25	12.50	25.00
LSP-1887 [S]	To Wish You a Merry Christmas	1958	10.00	20.00	40.00
LPM-1927 [M]	Love Is a Gentle Thing	1959	5.00	10.00	20.00
LSP-1927 [S]	Love Is a Gentle Thing	1959	6.25	12.50	25.00
LPM-1972 [M]	Belafonte Sings the Blues	1959	5.00	10.00	20.00
LSP-1972	Belafonte Sings the Blues	199?	6.25	12.50	25.00
—Classic Records reissue on audiophile vinyl					
LSP-1972 [S]	Belafonte Sings the Blues	1959	6.25	12.50	25.00
LPM-2022 [M]	My Lord What a Mornin'	1960	5.00	10.00	20.00
LSP-2022 [S]	My Lord What a Mornin'	1960	6.25	12.50	25.00
LPM-2194 [M]	Swing Dat Hammer	1961	5.00	10.00	20.00
LSP-2194 [S]	Swing Dat Hammer	1961	6.25	12.50	25.00
LPM-2309 [M]	At Home and Abroad	1961	5.00	10.00	20.00
LSP-2309 [S]	At Home and Abroad	1961	6.25	12.50	25.00
ANL1-2324	The Midnight Special	1976	2.50	5.00	10.00
—Reissue of LSP-2449					
LPM-2388 [M]	Jump Up Calypso	1961	5.00	10.00	20.00
LSP-2388 [S]	Jump Up Calypso	1961	6.25	12.50	25.00
LPM-2449 [M]	The Midnight Special	1962	7.50	15.00	30.00
LSP-2449 [S]	The Midnight Special	1962	10.00	20.00	40.00
—The above LP features Bob Dylan on harmonica on the title track, his first appearance on record					
CPL1-2469	A Legendary Performer	1977	2.50	5.00	10.00
LPM-2574 [M]	The Many Moods of Belafonte	1962	5.00	10.00	20.00
LSP-2574 [S]	The Many Moods of Belafonte	1962	6.25	12.50	25.00
LPM-2626 [M]	To Wish You a Merry Christmas	1962	5.00	10.00	20.00
—Reissue of LPM-1887 with new cover and one additional track					
LSP-2626 [S]	To Wish You a Merry Christmas	1962	6.25	12.50	25.00
LPM-2695 [M]	Streets I Have Walked	1963	5.00	10.00	20.00
LSP-2695 [S]	Streets I Have Walked	1963	6.25	12.50	25.00
LPM-2953 [M]	Ballads, Blues and Boasters	1964	3.75	7.50	15.00
LSP-2953 [S]	Ballads, Blues and Boasters	1964	5.00	10.00	20.00
LPM-3415 [M]	An Evening with Belafonte/Mouskouri	1966	3.75	7.50	15.00
LSP-3415 [S]	An Evening with Belafonte/Mouskouri	1966	5.00	10.00	20.00
—With Nana Mouskouri					
LPM-3420 [M]	An Evening with Belafonte/Makeba	1965	3.75	7.50	15.00
LSP-3420 [S]	An Evening with Belafonte/Makeba	1965	5.00	10.00	20.00
—With Miriam Makeba					
LPM-3571 [M]	In My Quiet Room	1966	3.00	6.00	12.00
LSP-3571 [S]	In My Quiet Room	1966	3.75	7.50	15.00
LPM-3658 [M]	Calypso in Brass	1967	3.00	6.00	12.00
LSP-3658 [S]	Calypso in Brass	1967	3.75	7.50	15.00
LPM-3779 [M]	Belafonte on Campus	1967	3.00	6.00	12.00
LSP-3779 [S]	Belafonte on Campus	1967	3.75	7.50	15.00
AYL1-3801(e) [R]	Calypso	1980	2.00	4.00	8.00
AYL1-3860(e) [R]	Pure Gold	1980	2.00	4.00	8.00
LPM-3938 [M]	Belafonte Sings of Love	1968	3.75	7.50	15.00
LSP-3938 [S]	Belafonte Sings of Love	1968	3.75	7.50	15.00
LSP-4255	Homeward Bound	1969	3.75	7.50	15.00
LSP-4301	By Request	1970	3.00	6.00	12.00
LSP-4481	Warm Touch	1971	3.00	6.00	12.00
LSP-4521	Calypso Carnival	1971	3.00	6.00	12.00
LOC-6006 [(2) M]	Belafonte at Carnegie Hall	1959	6.25	12.50	25.00
LSO-6006 [(2)]	Belafonte at Carnegie Hall	1996	10.00	20.00	40.00
—Classic Records reissue on audiophile vinyl					
LSO-6006 [(2) S]	Belafonte at Carnegie Hall	1959	12.50	25.00	50.00
LSO-6006 [(2) S]	Belafonte at Carnegie Hall	199?	10.00	20.00	40.00
—Classic Records reissue					
LOC-6007 [(2) M]	Belafonte Returns to Carnegie Hall	1960	5.00	10.00	20.00
LSO-6007 [(2)]	Belafonte Returns to Carnegie Hall	1996	10.00	20.00	40.00
—Classic Records reissue on audiophile vinyl					
LSO-6007 [(2) S]	Belafonte Returns to Carnegie Hall	1960	15.00	30.00	60.00
—The above LP also has tracks by Odetta, Miriam Makeba and The Chad Mitchell Trio (the latter for the first time on record)					
LSO-6007 [(2) S]	Belafonte Returns to Carnegie Hall	199?	10.00	20.00	40.00
—Classic Records reissue					
LOC-6009 [(2) M]	Belafonte at the Greek Theatre	1964	5.00	10.00	20.00
LSO-6009 [(2) S]	Belafonte at the Greek Theatre	1964	10.00	20.00	40.00
VPS-6024 [(2)]	This Is Harry Belafonte	1970	3.75	7.50	15.00
VPSX-6077 [(2)]	Belafonte Live	1972	3.75	7.50	15.00

BELAIRS, THE

45s

ARVEE

Number	Title (A Side/B Side)	Yr	VG	VG+	NM
A-5034	Mr. Moto/Little Brown Jug	1961	10.00	20.00	40.00
A-5054	Volcanic Action/Runaway	1962	7.50	15.00	30.00

BELFAST GYPSIES, THE

Also see THEM.

45s

LOMA

Number	Title (A Side/B Side)	Yr	VG	VG+	NM
2051	Gloria's Dream/Secret Police	1966	3.75	7.50	15.00
2060	Portland Town/People, Let's Freak Out	1966	3.75	7.50	15.00

BELL, ARCHIE, AND THE DRELLS

45s

ATLANTIC

Number	Title (A Side/B Side)	Yr	VG	VG+	NM
2478	Tighten Up/Tighten Up — Part 2	1968	2.00	4.00	8.00
2478	Tighten Up/Dog Eat Dog	1968	3.00	6.00	12.00
2534	I Can't Stop Dancing/You're Such a Beautiful Child	1968	—	3.50	7.00
2559	Do the Choo Choo/Love Will Rain on You	1968	—	3.50	7.00
2583	(There's Gonna Be A) Showdown/Go for What You Know	1968	—	3.50	7.00
2612	I Love My Baby/Just a Little Closer	1969	—	3.50	7.00
2644	Girl You're Too Young/Do the Hand Jive	1969	—	3.50	7.00
2663	My Balloon's Going Up/Giving Up Dancing	1969	—	3.50	7.00
2693	A World Without Music/Here I Go Again	1969	—	3.50	7.00
2721	Don't Let the Music Slip Away/Houston, Texas	1970	—	3.50	7.00
2744	I Wish/Get from the Bottom	1970	—	3.50	7.00
2769	Wrap It Up/Deal with Him	1970	—	3.50	7.00
2793	I Just Want to Fall in Love/Love at First Sight	1971	—	3.00	6.00
2829	Let the World Know/Archie's in Love	1971	—	3.00	6.00
2855	Green Power/I Can't Face You Baby	1972	—	3.00	6.00

BECKET

Number	Title (A Side/B Side)	Yr	VG	VG+	NM
45-4	Any Time Is Right/(B-side unknown)	1981	—	2.00	4.00

EAST WEST

Number	Title (A Side/B Side)	Yr	VG	VG+	NM
2048	She's My Woman/The Yankee Dance	1968	—	3.50	7.00

GLADES

Number	Title (A Side/B Side)	Yr	VG	VG+	NM
1707	Dancing to Your Music/Count the Ways	1973	—	3.00	6.00
1711	Ain't Nothing for a Man in Love/You Never Know What's On a Woman's Mind	1973	—	3.00	6.00
1718	Girls Grow Up Faster Than Boys/Love's Gonna Rain on You	1973	—	3.00	6.00

OVIDE

Number	Title (A Side/B Side)	Yr	VG	VG+	NM
228	Tighten Up/Dog Eat Dog	1967	7.50	15.00	30.00

PHILADELPHIA INT'L

Number	Title (A Side/B Side)	Yr	VG	VG+	NM
3605	Nothing Comes Easy/Right Here Is Where I Want to Be	1976	—	2.50	5.00

Number	Title (A Side/B Side)	Yr	VG	VG+	NM
3615	Everybody Have a Good Time/I Bet I Can Do That Dance You're Doin'	1977	—	2.50	5.00
3632	Glad You Can Make It/There's No Other Like You	1977	—	2.50	5.00
3637	I've Been Missing You/It's Hard Not to Love You	1977	—	2.50	5.00
3651	Old People/On the Radio	1978	—	2.50	5.00
TSOP					
4767	I Could Dance All Night/King of the Castle	1975	—	2.50	5.00
4774	The Soul City Walk/King of the Castle	1975	—	2.50	5.00
4775	Let's Groove (Part 1)/Let's Groove (Part 2)	1976	—	2.50	5.00
WMOT					
03057	Touchin' You/(Instrumental)	1982	—	2.50	5.00
Albums					
ATLANTIC					
8181 [M]	Tighten Up	1968	12.50	25.00	50.00
SD 8181 [S]	Tighten Up	1968	7.50	15.00	30.00
SD 8204	I Can't Stop Dancing	1968	7.50	15.00	30.00
SD 8226	There's Gonna Be a Showdown	1969	7.50	15.00	30.00
PHILADELPHIA INT'L.					
PZ 34323	Where Will...	1976	2.50	5.00	10.00
PZ 34855	Hard Not to Like It	1977	2.50	5.00	10.00
JZ 36096	Strategy	1979	2.50	5.00	10.00
TSOP					
PZ 33844	Dance Your Troubles Away	1975	2.50	5.00	10.00

BELL, CARL, AND THE NORVAIRS

Number	Title (A Side/B Side)	Yr	VG	VG+	NM
45s					
LAURIE					
3014	Birth of the Beat/Open House in Your Heart	1958	6.25	12.50	25.00

BELL, FREDDIE, AND THE BELL BOYS

Number	Title (A Side/B Side)	Yr	VG	VG+	NM
45s					
MERCURY					
70919	Stay Loose, Mother Goose/All Right, OK, You Win	1956	5.00	10.00	20.00
71075	Take the First Train Out of Town/Hey There You	1957	5.00	10.00	20.00
71105	Rockin' Is My Business/You're Gonna Be Sorry	1957	10.00	20.00	40.00
TEEN					
101	Hound Dog/Move Me Baby	1955	12.50	25.00	50.00
103	Old Town Hall/5-10-15 Hours	1955	7.50	15.00	30.00
WING					
90066	Giddy Up a Ding Dong/I Said It and I'm Glad	1956	10.00	20.00	40.00
90082	The Hucklebuck/Rompin' and Stompin'	1956	10.00	20.00	40.00
Albums					
20TH FOX					
TF-4146 [M]	Bells Are Swinging	1964	6.25	12.50	25.00
TFS-4146 [S]	Bells Are Swinging	1964	7.50	15.00	30.00
MERCURY					
MG-20289 [M]	Rock and Roll... All Flavors	1957	50.00	100.00	200.00

BELL, MADELINE

Also see BLUE MINK.

Number	Title (A Side/B Side)	Yr	VG	VG+	NM
45s					
ASCOT					
2156	You Don't Love Me No More/Don't Cross Over to My Side of the Street	1964	2.50	5.00	10.00
2180	Don't Cry My Heart/Daytime	1965	2.50	5.00	10.00
BRUT					
808	All That Love Went to Waste/A Touch of Class	1973	—	2.50	5.00
MOD					
1007	I'm Gonna Make You Love Me/Picture Me Gone	1967	3.00	6.00	12.00
PHILIPS					
40517	I'm Gonna Make You Love Me/Picture Me Gone	1968	2.00	4.00	8.00
40539	Finding You, Loving You/Doing Things Together with You	1968	—	3.00	6.00
40582	Step Inside Love/What I'm Supposed to Do	1969	—	3.00	6.00
PYE					
71061	I Always Seem to Wind Up Loving You/Your Smile	1976	—	2.00	4.00
Albums					
PHILIPS					
PHS 600271	I'm Gonna Make You Love Me	1968	3.00	6.00	12.00

BELL, MAGGIE

Also see STONE THE CROWS.

Number	Title (A Side/B Side)	Yr	VG	VG+	NM
45s					
ATLANTIC					
3018	After Midnight/Souvenirs	1974	—	2.50	5.00
3040	Caddo Queen/Oh My My	1974	—	2.50	5.00
SWAN SONG					
70105	Wishing Well/Comin' On Strong	1975	—	2.50	5.00
99907	Here, There and Everywhere/Put Angels Around You	1983	—	2.00	4.00
—With Bobby Whitlock					
Albums					
ATLANTIC					
SD 7293	Queen of the Night	1974	3.00	6.00	12.00
SWAN SONG					
SS 8412	Suicide Sal	1975	3.00	6.00	12.00

BELL, TRUDY

Number	Title (A Side/B Side)	Yr	VG	VG+	NM
45s					
PHILIPS					
40021	Willie/This Friend of Mine	1962	3.00	6.00	12.00
40055	I Remember Jimmy/A Promise and a Kiss Goodnight	1962	3.00	6.00	12.00

BELL, VINCENT

Number	Title (A Side/B Side)	Yr	VG	VG+	NM
45s					
DECCA					
32224	Eleanor/Goin' Out of My Head	1967	—	3.00	6.00
32418	California Summer/A Sinner Kissed An Angel	1968	—	3.00	6.00
32483	Good Morning Starshine/Because of You	1969	—	2.50	5.00
32530	Les Bicyclettes De Belsize/The Ballad of John and Yoko	1969	—	2.50	5.00
32659	Airport Love Theme/Marilyn's Theme	1970	—	2.50	5.00
32695	Darling Lili/Nikki	1970	—	2.50	5.00
INDEPENDENT					
102	Quicksand/(B-side unknown)	1960	10.00	20.00	40.00
MUSICOR					
1068	Just a Little Kiss/Baker Street Mystery	1965	3.00	6.00	12.00
VERVE					
10308	Shindig/Whistle Stop	1963	3.00	6.00	12.00
Albums					
DECCA					
DL 4938 [M]	Pop Goes the Electric Sitar	1967	5.00	10.00	20.00
DL 74938 [S]	Pop Goes the Electric Sitar	1967	3.75	7.50	15.00
DL 75212	Airport Love Theme	1970	3.75	7.50	15.00
MUSICOR					
MM-3009 [M]	51 Motion Picture Favorites	1963	3.75	7.50	15.00
MS-3009 [S]	51 Motion Picture Favorites	1963	5.00	10.00	20.00
MM-3047 [M]	Big 16 Guitar Favorites	1965	3.75	7.50	15.00
MS-3047 [S]	Big 16 Guitar Favorites	1965	5.00	10.00	20.00
VERVE					
V-8574 [M]	Whistle Stop	1964	3.75	7.50	15.00
V6-8574 [S]	Whistle Stop	1964	5.00	10.00	20.00

BELL, WILLIAM

Number	Title (A Side/B Side)	Yr	VG	VG+	NM
45s					
ATLANTIC					
13154	Everyday Will Be Like A Holiday/Winner	197?	—	2.00	4.00
—Oldies Series reissue					
KAT FAMILY					
03502	Bad Time to Break Off/The Truth in Your Eyes	1983	—	2.00	4.00
03995	Playing Hard to Get/The Truth in Your Eyes	1983	—	2.00	4.00
MERCURY					
73839	Tryin' to Love Two/If Sex Was All We Had	1976	—	2.50	5.00
73922	Coming Back for More/You I Absolutely Positively Love	1977	—	2.00	4.00
73961	Your Love Keeps Me Goin'/Easy Comin' Out	1977	—	2.00	4.00
STAX					
0005	Private Number/Love-Eye-Tis	1968	—	2.50	5.00
—With Judy Clay					
0015	I Forgot to Be Your Lover/Bring the Curtains Down	1968	—	3.00	6.00
0017	Left-Over Love/My Baby Specializes	1968	—	2.50	5.00
—With Judy Clay					
0032	My Whole World Is Falling Down/All God's Children Got Soul	1969	—	2.50	5.00
0038	My Kind of Girl/Happy	1969	—	2.50	5.00
0043	Love's Sweet Sensation/Strung Out	1969	—	2.50	5.00
—With Mavis Staples					
0044	I Can't Stop/I Need You Woman	1969	—	2.50	5.00
—With Carla Thomas					
0054	Born Under a Bad Sign/A Smile Can't Hide a Broken Heart	1969	—	2.50	5.00
0067	All I Have to Do Is Dream/Leave the Girl Alone	1970	—	2.50	5.00
—With Carla Thomas					
0070	Lonely Soldier/Let Me Ride	1970	—	2.50	5.00
0092	A Penny for Your Thoughts/Till My Back Ain't Got No Bone	1971	—	2.50	5.00
0106	All for the Love of a Woman/I'll Be Home	1971	—	2.50	5.00
116	You Don't Miss Your Water/Formula of Love	1961	5.00	10.00	20.00
128	Any Other Way/Please Help Me I'm Falling	1962	5.00	10.00	20.00
0128	If You Really Love Him/Save Us	1972	—	2.50	5.00
132	I Told You So/What'Cha Gonna Do	1963	3.75	7.50	15.00
135	Just As I Thought/I'm Waiting on You	1963	3.75	7.50	15.00
138	Somebody Mentioned Your Name/What Can I Do to Forget	1963	3.75	7.50	15.00
141	I'll Show You/Monkeying Around	1963	3.75	7.50	15.00
146	Don't Make Something Out of Nothing/Who Will It Be Tomorrow	1964	3.00	6.00	12.00
0157	Livin' on Borrowed Time/The Man in the Street	1973	—	2.50	5.00
174	Crying All By Myself/Don't Stop Now	1965	3.00	6.00	12.00
0175	You've Got the Kind of Love I Need/I've Got to Go On Without You	1973	—	2.50	5.00
191	Share What You Got/Marching Off to War	1966	2.50	5.00	10.00
0198	All I Need Is Your Love/Gettin' What You Want	1974	—	2.50	5.00
199	Soldier's Goodbye/Never Like This Before	1966	2.50	5.00	10.00
212	Everybody Loves a Winner/You're Such a Sweet Thing	1967	2.00	4.00	8.00
0221	Get It While It's Hot/Nobody Walks Away from Love Unhurt	1974	—	2.50	5.00
227	One Plus One/Eloise (Hang On In There)	1967	2.00	4.00	8.00
237	Everyday Will Be Like a Holiday/Ain't Got No Girl	1967	2.00	4.00	8.00
248	A Tribute to a King (Otis Redding)/Every Man Oughta Have a Woman	1968	—	3.00	6.00
WRC					
202	I Don't Want to Wake Up (Feelin' Guilty)/(B-side unknown)	1986	—	2.50	5.00
—With Janice Bullock					
204	Headline News/(B-side unknown)	1986	—	2.50	5.00
Albums					
KAT FAMILY					
FZ 38643	Survivor	1983	2.50	5.00	10.00
MERCURY					
SRM-1-1146	Coming Back for More	1977	2.50	5.00	10.00
SRM-1-1193	It's Time You Took Another Listen	1978	2.50	5.00	10.00
STAX					
719 [M]	Soul of a Bell	1967	10.00	20.00	40.00
S-719 [S]	Soul of a Bell	1967	12.50	25.00	50.00
ST-2014 [M]	Bound to Happen	1969	12.50	25.00	50.00
—Mono is promo only					
STS-2014 [S]	Bound to Happen	1969	7.50	15.00	30.00
STS-2037	Wow...	1971	7.50	15.00	30.00

Number	Title (A Side/B Side)	Yr	VG	VG+	NM
STS-3005	Phases of Reality	1973	5.00	10.00	20.00
STS-5502	Relating	1974	5.00	10.00	20.00
MPS-8541	The Best of William Bell	1988	2.50	5.00	10.00
WRC					
WL-3007	On a Roll	1986	3.00	6.00	12.00

BELL HOPS, THE
Probably two different groups.

45s

Number	Title (A Side/B Side)	Yr	VG	VG+	NM
BARB					
100	Angela/Ring Dang Doo Ting-a-Ling	1958	6.25	12.50	25.00
101/2	Teenage Years/Carmella	1958	6.25	12.50	25.00
DECCA					
48208	For the Rest of My Life/It Would Take a Million Years	1951	25.00	50.00	100.00
48239	I'm All Yours/Where Is Love	1951	25.00	50.00	100.00
TIN PAN ALLEY					
153	Please Don't Say No to Me/Merchant Street Blues	1956	37.50	75.00	150.00

BELL NOTES, THE
45s

Number	Title (A Side/B Side)	Yr	VG	VG+	NM
AUTOGRAPH					
204	Little Girl in Blue/Too Young or Too Old	1960	6.25	12.50	25.00
CLOCK					
71889	There She Goes/My Pledge to You	1961	5.00	10.00	20.00
MADISON					
136	Shortnin' Bread/To Each His Own	1960	5.00	10.00	20.00
141	Real Wild Child/Friendly Star	1960	5.00	10.00	20.00
TIME					
1004	I've Had It/Be Mine	1958	7.50	15.00	30.00
—First pressing on blue labels					
1004	I've Had It/Be Mine	1959	6.25	12.50	25.00
—Later pressings on red labels					
1010	Old Spanish Town/She Went Thataway	1959	6.25	12.50	25.00
1013	That's Right/Betty Dear	1959	6.25	12.50	25.00
1015	You're a Big Girl Now/Don't Ask Me Why	1959	6.25	12.50	25.00
1017	White Buckskin Sneakers and Checkerboard Socks/No Dice	1959	6.25	12.50	25.00

BELL TONES, THE
45s

Number	Title (A Side/B Side)	Yr	VG	VG+	NM
RAMA					
170	Heart to Heart/The Wedding	1955	50.00	100.00	200.00

BELLAMY, DAVID
One-half of THE BELLAMY BROTHERS.

45s

Number	Title (A Side/B Side)	Yr	VG	VG+	NM
WARNER BROS.					
8123	Baby, You're Not a Legend/Nothin' Heavy	1975	—	2.50	5.00

BELLAMY BROTHERS, THE
Also see DAVID BELLAMY.

45s

Number	Title (A Side/B Side)	Yr	VG	VG+	NM
ATLANTIC					
87650	Anyway I Can/All in the Name of Love	1991	—	2.00	4.00
87748	She Don't Know That She's Perfect/I Make Her Laugh	1991	—	2.00	4.00
ELEKTRA					
47431	For All the Wrong Reasons/This Time	1982	—	2.00	4.00
69850	When I'm Away from You/Long Distance Love Affair	1983	—	2.00	4.00
69999	Get Into Reggae Cowboy/We're Just a Little Ole Country Band	1982	—	2.00	4.00
MCA CURB					
52380	Forget About Me/We're Having Some Fun Now	1984	—	—	3.00
52446	The World's Greatest Lover/Rock-A-Dash	1984	—	—	3.00
52518	I Need More of You/Diesel Cafe	1984	—	—	3.00
52579	Old Hippie/Wheels	1985	—	—	3.00
52668	Lie to You for Your Love/Season of the Wind	1985	—	—	3.00
52747	Feelin' the Feelin'/The Single Man and His Wife	1985	—	—	3.00
52834	Country Rap/One Too Many Times	1986	—	—	3.00
52917	Too Much Is Not Enough/Restless	1986	—	—	3.00
—A-side: With The Forrester Sisters					
53018	Kids of the Baby Boom/Hard on a Heart	1987	—	—	3.00
53154	Crazy from the Heart/White Trash	1987	—	—	3.00
53222	Santa Fe/White Trash	1987	—	—	3.00
53310	I'll Give You All My Love Tonight/Ying Yang	1988	—	—	3.00
53399	Rebels Without a Clue/A Little Naive	1988	—	—	3.00
53478	Big Love/The Courthouse	1988	—	—	3.00
53642	Hillbilly Hell/You're My Favorite Star	1989	—	—	3.00
53672	You'll Never Be Sorry/Hillbilly Hell	1989	—	—	3.00
53719	The Center of My Universe/Hillbilly Hell	1989	—	—	3.00
79019	I Could Be Persuaded/What's This World Coming To	1990	—	—	3.00
WARNER BROS.					
8169	Let Your Love Flow/Inside My Guitar	1975	—	2.50	5.00
8220	Hell Cat/I'm the Only Man Left Alive	1976	—	2.00	4.00
8248	Rainy, Windy, Sunshine (Roadeo Road)/Satin Sheets	1976	—	2.00	4.00
8284	Livin' in the West/Highway 2-18 (Hang On to Your Dreams)	1976	—	2.00	4.00
8350	Crossfire/Tiger Lily Lover	1977	—	2.00	4.00
8401	Can Somebody Hear Me Now/You Made Me	1977	—	2.00	4.00
8462	Hard Rockin'/Memorabilia	1977	—	2.00	4.00
8521	Bird Dog/Make Me Over	1978	—	2.00	4.00
8558	Let's Give Love a Try/Slipping Away	1978	—	2.00	4.00
8627	Tumbleweed and Rosalee/Wild Honey	1978	—	2.00	4.00
8692	Lovin' on/My Shy Anne	1978	—	2.00	4.00
8790	If I Said You Have a Beautiful Body Would You Hold It Against Me/Make Me Over	1979	—	2.00	4.00
29514	Strong Weakness/Doin' It the Hard Way	1983	—	2.00	4.00
29645	I Love Her Mind/Lazy Eyes	1983	—	2.00	4.00
29923	Redneck Girl/Let Your Love Flow	1982	—	2.00	4.00
49032	You Ain't Just Whistlin' Dixie/Blue Ribbons	1979	—	2.00	4.00
49160	Sugar Daddy/I Could Be Makin' Love to You	1980	—	2.00	4.00
49241	Dancin' Cowboys/Dead Aim	1980	—	2.00	4.00
49573	Classic Case of the Blues/Lovers Live Longer	1980	—	2.00	4.00
49639	Do You Love As Good As You Look/Givin' In to Love Again	1980	—	2.00	4.00
49729	They Could Put Me in Jail/Endangered Species	1981	—	2.00	4.00
49815	You're My Favorite Star/It's Hard to Be a Cowboy These Days	1981	—	2.00	4.00
49875	It's So Close to Christmas/Let Me Waltz Into Your Heart	1981	—	2.00	4.00

Albums

Number	Title (A Side/B Side)	Yr	VG	VG+	NM
ELEKTRA					
60099	When We Were Boys	1982	2.50	5.00	10.00
60210	Strong Weakness	1982	2.50	5.00	10.00
MCA CURB					
1441	Restless	1985	2.00	4.00	8.00
—Reissue of MCA 5489					
1462	Greatest Hits	1985	2.00	4.00	8.00
—Reissue of Warner Bros. 23697					
5489	Restless	1984	2.50	5.00	10.00
5586	Howard & David	1985	2.50	5.00	10.00
5721	Country Rap	1987	2.50	5.00	10.00
5812	Greatest Hits Volume Two	1986	2.50	5.00	10.00
42039	Crazy from the Heart	1987	2.50	5.00	10.00
42224	Rebels Without a Clue	1988	2.50	5.00	10.00
42298	Greatest Hits Volume III	1989	2.50	5.00	10.00
WARNER BROS.					
BS 2941	Let Your Love Flow	1976	2.50	5.00	10.00
BS 3034	Plain & Fancy	1977	2.50	5.00	10.00
BSK 3176	Friends	1978	2.50	5.00	10.00
BSK 3347	The Two and Only	1979	2.50	5.00	10.00
BSK 3408	You Can Get Crazy	1980	2.50	5.00	10.00
BSK 3491	Sons of the Sun	1980	2.50	5.00	10.00
23697	Greatest Hits	1982	2.50	5.00	10.00
60210	Strong Weakness	1983	2.00	4.00	8.00
—Reissue of Elektra 60210					

BELLAND & SOMERVILLE
45s

Number	Title (A Side/B Side)	Yr	VG	VG+	NM
BARNABY					
2009	Sure Seems a Lot Like Sunday/When She's Lovin'	1969	2.00	4.00	8.00

BELLS, THE (1)
Canadian band with male and female lead singers.

45s

Number	Title (A Side/B Side)	Yr	VG	VG+	NM
MGM					
14533	Child of Mine/He Was Me, He Was You	1973	—	2.00	4.00
14624	Love Once Removed/The Singer	1973	—	2.00	4.00
POLYDOR					
15016	Fly Little White Dove, Fly/Follow the Sun	1970	—	2.00	4.00
15023	Stay Awhile/Sing a Song of Freedom	1971	—	2.50	5.00
15025	Je Vais Rester/Blanc Petit Ois Eau Blanc	1970	—	2.00	4.00
15027	I Love You Lady Dawn/Rain	1971	—	2.00	4.00
15029	She's a Lady/Sweet Sounds of Music	1971	—	2.00	4.00
15031	To Know You Is To Love You/For Better For Worse	1971	—	2.00	4.00
15036	Oh My Love/You You You	1972	—	2.00	4.00
15039	Lord, Don't You Think It's Time/Easier Said Than Done	1972	—	2.00	4.00
15063	Kris Collection/Simple Song of Freedom	1973	—	2.00	4.00

Albums

Number	Title (A Side/B Side)	Yr	VG	VG+	NM
POLYDOR					
24-4510	Fly, Little White Dove, Fly	1971	3.75	7.50	15.00
24-5503	Love, Luck & Lollypops	1972	3.75	7.50	15.00

BELLS, THE (2)
Male vocal group.

45s

Number	Title (A Side/B Side)	Yr	VG	VG+	NM
RAMA					
166	What Can I Tell Her Now/Let Me Love You, Love You	1955	125.00	250.00	500.00

BELLTONES, THE
45s

Number	Title (A Side/B Side)	Yr	VG	VG+	NM
GRAND					
102	Estelle/Promise Love	1954	2000.	3000.	4000.

BELLUS, TONY
45s

Number	Title (A Side/B Side)	Yr	VG	VG+	NM
ERA BACK TO BACK HITS					
048	Robbin' the Cradle/Rockin' Little Angel	197?	—	2.50	5.00
—B-side by Ray Smith					
KING					
5973	Mustang/Goodbye Baby, Goodbye	1964	3.00	6.00	12.00
NRC					
023	Robbin' the Cradle/Valentine Girl	1959	5.00	10.00	20.00
—Available with the letters "NRC" with no background, with the title of the song in either orange or blue letters; also with each letter of "NRC" in a background box. No difference in value.					
035	Hey Little Darlin'/Only Your Heart	1959	5.00	10.00	20.00
040	Little Dreams/Young Girls	1959	5.00	10.00	20.00
045	Hey Little Darlin'/Young Girls	1959	5.00	10.00	20.00
051	The End of My Love/The Echo of An Old Song	1960	5.00	10.00	20.00
—Available on both white and tan labels, no difference in value					
058	The Great Pretender/Give Me a Heart	1960	5.00	10.00	20.00

Albums

Number	Title (A Side/B Side)	Yr	VG	VG+	NM
NRC					
LPA-8 [M]	Robbin' the Cradle	1960	50.00	100.00	200.00
—Blue label					

Number	Title (A Side/B Side)	Yr	VG	VG+	NM
LPA-8 [M]	Robbin' the Cradle	1960	25.00	50.00	100.00
—Black label					

BELMONTS, THE

Also see DION AND THE BELMONTS; BUDDY SHEPPARD AND THE HOLIDAYS.

45s

Number	Title (A Side/B Side)	Yr	VG	VG+	NM
DOT					
17173	Reminiscing/She Only Wants to Do Her Thing	1968	3.75	7.50	15.00
17257	Have You Heard-The Worst That Could Happen/ Answer Me My Love	1969	3.75	7.50	15.00
LAURIE					
3080	We Belong Together/Such a Long Way	1961	7.50	15.00	30.00
3631	A Brand New Song/Story Teller	1975	—	2.50	5.00
3698	Medley/You're the Only Girl for Me	198?	—	2.50	5.00
—B-side by Ernie Maresca					
SABINA					
502	I Need Some One/That American Dance	1961	6.25	12.50	25.00
503	Hombre/I Confess	1962	6.25	12.50	25.00
505	Come On Little Angel/How About Me	1962	6.25	12.50	25.00
—Black label					
505	Come On Little Angel/How About Me	1962	5.00	10.00	20.00
—Greenish label					
507	Diddle-Dee-Dum (What Happens When Your Love Has Gone)/Farewell	1962	5.00	10.00	20.00
509	Ann Marie/Ac-Cent-Tchu-Ate the Positive	1963	5.00	10.00	20.00
513	Let's Call It a Day/Walk On Boy	1963	5.00	10.00	20.00
517	More Important Things to Do/Walk On Boy	1963	5.00	10.00	20.00
519	C'mon Everybody/Why	1964	5.00	10.00	20.00
521	Summertime/Nothing in Return	1964	5.00	10.00	20.00
SABRINA					
500	Tell Me Why/Smoke from Your Cigarette	1961	6.25	12.50	25.00
501	Searching for a New Love/Don't Get Around Much Anymore	1961	6.25	12.50	25.00
STRAWBERRY					
106	Cheek to Cheek/Voyager	1976	—	2.50	5.00
SURPRISE					
1000	Tell Me Why/Smoke from Your Cigarette	1961	25.00	50.00	100.00
UNITED ARTISTS					
809	Wintertime/I Don't Know Why, I Just Do	1965	5.00	10.00	20.00
904	(Then) I Walked Away/Today My Love Has Gone Away	1965	5.00	10.00	20.00
966	I Got a Feeling/To Be with You	1965	5.00	10.00	20.00
S7-19769	Wintertime/Please Come Home for Christmas	1997	—	2.00	4.00
—B-side by Dion on The Right Stuff					
50007	Come with Me/You're Like a Mystery	1966	6.25	12.50	25.00

Albums

Number	Title (A Side/B Side)	Yr	VG	VG+	NM
BUDDAH					
BDS-5123	Cigars, Acapella, Candy	1972	12.50	25.00	50.00
DOT					
DLP-25949	Summer Love	1969	7.50	15.00	30.00
SABINA					
SALP-5001 [M]	The Belmonts' Carnival of Hits	1962	37.50	75.00	150.00
STRAWBERRY					
6001	Cheek to Cheek	1978	3.75	7.50	15.00

BELVIN, ANDY

45s

Number	Title (A Side/B Side)	Yr	VG	VG+	NM
ATCO					
6289	Travelin' Mood/Flip Flip	1964	3.00	6.00	12.00
CANDIX					
338	Walking the Blues/Prettiest Girl	1962	5.00	10.00	20.00
VAULT					
908	Travelin' Mood/Flip Flop	1964	3.75	7.50	15.00

BELVIN, JESSE

Also see THE CLIQUES; JESSE AND MARVIN.

45s

Number	Title (A Side/B Side)	Yr	VG	VG+	NM
ALADDIN					
3431	Let Me Dream/Sugar Doll	1958	10.00	20.00	40.00
CASH					
1056	Dry Your Tears/Beware	1957	25.00	50.00	100.00
—Black and silver label					
1056	Dry Your Tears/Beware	1957	6.25	12.50	25.00
—Orange and black label					
CLASS					
267	I'm Confessin'/Deep in My Heart	1960	6.25	12.50	25.00
HOLLYWOOD					
1059	Betty My Darling/Dear Heart	1956	100.00	200.00	400.00
IMPACT					
23	Tonight My Love/Looking for Love	1962	3.75	7.50	15.00
JAMIE					
1145	Goodnight My Love (Pleasant Dreams)/My Desire	1959	5.00	10.00	20.00
KENT					
326	Sentimental Reasons/Senorita	1959	6.25	12.50	25.00
KNIGHT					
2012	Little Darling/Deacon Dan Tucker	1959	10.00	20.00	40.00
MODERN					
1005	Goodnight My Love (Pleasant Dreams)/Let Me Love You Tonight	1956	10.00	20.00	40.00
1005	Goodnight My Love (Pleasant Dreams)/I Want You With Me Xmas	1956	10.00	20.00	40.00
1013	I Need You So/Senorita	1957	7.50	15.00	30.00
1015	By My Side/Don't Close the Door	1957	7.50	15.00	30.00
1020	Sad and Lonesome/I'm Not Free	1957	7.50	15.00	30.00
1025	You Send Me/Summertime	1957	7.50	15.00	30.00
1027	My Satellite/Just to Say Hello	1957	7.50	15.00	30.00
MONEY					
208	I'm Only a Fool/Trouble and Misery	1955	15.00	30.00	60.00
RCA VICTOR					
47-7310	Volare/Ever Since We Met	1958	5.00	10.00	20.00
47-7387	Funny/Pledging My Love	1958	5.00	10.00	20.00
47-7469	Guess Who/My Girl Is Just Enough Woman for Me	1959	5.00	10.00	20.00
47-7543	Here's a Heart/It Could've Been Worse	1959	5.00	10.00	20.00
47-7596	Give Me Love/I'll Never Be Lonely Again	1959	5.00	10.00	20.00
47-7675	Something Happens to Me/The Door Is Always Open	1960	5.00	10.00	20.00
47-8040	Guess Who/Funny	1962	3.75	7.50	15.00
61-7469	Guess Who/My Girl Is Just Enough Woman for Me	1959	12.50	25.00	50.00
—"Living Stereo" (large hole, plays at 45 rpm)					
RECORDED IN HOLLYWOOD					
120	Dream Girl/Hang Your Tears Out to Dry	1951	150.00	300.00	600.00
412	Love Comes Tumbling Down/(B-side unknown)	1953	100.00	200.00	400.00
SPECIALTY					
435	Confusin' Blues/Baby Don't Go	1952	20.00	40.00	80.00
550	Gone/One Little Blessing	1955	12.50	25.00	50.00
559	Where's My Girl/Love, Love of My Life	1955	12.50	25.00	50.00

Albums

Number	Title (A Side/B Side)	Yr	VG	VG+	NM
CROWN					
CLP-5145 [M]	The Casual Jesse Belvin	1959	17.50	35.00	70.00
—Black label					
CLP-5145 [M]	The Casual Jesse Belvin	196?	3.75	7.50	15.00
—Gray label					
CLP-5187 [M]	The Unforgettable Jesse Belvin	1959	17.50	35.00	70.00
—Black label					
CLP-5187 [M]	The Unforgettable Jesse Belvin	196?	3.75	7.50	15.00
—Gray label					
RCA CAMDEN					
CAL-960 [M]	Jesse Belvin's Best	1966	3.00	6.00	12.00
CAS-960 [S]	Jesse Belvin's Best	1966	3.75	7.50	15.00
RCA VICTOR					
LPM-2089 [M]	Just Jesse Belvin	1959	10.00	20.00	40.00
LSP-2089 [S]	Just Jesse Belvin	1959	15.00	30.00	60.00
LPM-2105 [M]	Mr. Easy	1960	7.50	15.00	30.00
LSP-2105 [S]	Mr. Easy	1960	10.00	20.00	40.00
SPECIALTY					
SP-7003	The Blues Balladeer	1990	3.75	7.50	15.00

BEN, LA BRENDA

45s

Number	Title (A Side/B Side)	Yr	VG	VG+	NM
GORDY					
7009	Camel Walk/The Chaperone	1962	12.50	25.00	50.00
7021	I Can't Help It, I Gotta Dance/Just Be Yourself	1963	12.50	25.00	50.00
MOTOWN					
1033	Camel Walk/Chaperone	1962	100.00	200.00	400.00

BENET, VICKI

45s

Number	Title (A Side/B Side)	Yr	VG	VG+	NM
DECCA					
30044	Sam's Song (The Happy Tune)/Tea for Two	1956	3.75	7.50	15.00
LIBERTY					
55100	After My Laughter Came Tears/Always in My Heart	1957	3.75	7.50	15.00
55186	Heartstring Melody/Love Me	1959	3.00	6.00	12.00

Albums

Number	Title (A Side/B Side)	Yr	VG	VG+	NM
DECCA					
DL 8233 [M]	Woman of Paris	1956	10.00	20.00	40.00
DL 8381 [M]	The French Touch	1957	10.00	20.00	40.00
DL 8987 [M]	Vicki Benet a Paris	1959	7.50	15.00	30.00
DL 78987 [S]	Vicki Benet a Paris	1959	10.00	20.00	40.00
LIBERTY					
LRP-3103 [M]	Sing to Me of Love	1960	6.25	12.50	25.00
LST-7103 [S]	Sing to Me of Love	1960	7.50	15.00	30.00

BENNETT, BOYD

45s

Number	Title (A Side/B Side)	Yr	VG	VG+	NM
KING					
1413	Waterloo/I've Had Enough	1954	8.75	17.50	35.00
1432	Poison Ivy/You Upset Me Baby	1955	8.75	17.50	35.00
1443	Everlovin'/Boogie at Midnight	1955	8.75	17.50	35.00
1470	Seventeen/Little Old You-All	1955	8.75	17.50	35.00
—Maroon label					
1470	Seventeen/Little Old You-All	1955	6.25	12.50	25.00
—Blue label					
1475	Tennessee Rock and Roll/Oo, Oo, Oo	1955	6.25	12.50	25.00
1494	My Boy-Flat Top/Banjo Rock and Roll	1955	6.25	12.50	25.00
4853	Desperately/The Most	1955	6.25	12.50	25.00
4874	Right Around the Corner/Partners for Life	1956	6.25	12.50	25.00
4903	Blue Suede Shoes/Mumbles Blues	1956	6.25	12.50	25.00
4925	Let Me Love You/Groovy Age	1956	6.25	12.50	25.00
4953	Hit That Jive, Jack/Rabbit-Eye Pink and Charcoal Black	1956	6.25	12.50	25.00
4985	Rockin' Up a Storm/A Lock of Your Hair	1956	6.25	12.50	25.00
5021	I'm Moving On/Big Jay Shuffle	1957	6.25	12.50	25.00
5049	Big Boy/Put the Chain on the Door	1957	6.25	12.50	25.00
5097	Sentimental Journey/Boy Meets Girl	1957	6.25	12.50	25.00
5113	Signed, Sealed and Delivered/Her Momma Doesn't Think It's Right	1958	6.25	12.50	25.00
5115	Click Clack/Move	1958	6.25	12.50	25.00
5282	High School Hop/Cool Disc Jockey	1959	6.25	12.50	25.00
5374	Seventeen/My Boy Flat Top	1960	6.25	12.50	25.00
5738	Teenage Years/Hear Me Talking	1963	3.75	7.50	15.00
MERCURY					
71409	Tight Tights/Tear It Up	1959	5.00	10.00	20.00
71479	Boogie Bear/A Boy Can Tell	1959	5.00	10.00	20.00
71537	Naughty Rock and Roll/Lover's Night	1959	5.00	10.00	20.00
71605	It's Wonderful/Amo, Amas, Amat	1960	5.00	10.00	20.00
71648	Seventeen/Sarasota	1960	5.00	10.00	20.00
71724	Hershey Bar/Big Junior	1960	5.00	10.00	20.00
71813	Coffee Break/The Brain	1961	5.00	10.00	20.00

Number	Title (A Side/B Side)	Yr	VG	VG+	NM

7-Inch Extended Plays

KING

Number	Title (A Side/B Side)	Yr	VG	VG+	NM
377	(contents unknown)	1956	50.00	100.00	200.00
377 [PS]	Boyd Bennett	1956	75.00	150.00	300.00
383	(contents unknown)	1956	50.00	100.00	200.00
383 [PS]	Rock & Roll with Boyd Bennett & the Rockets	1956	75.00	150.00	300.00

Albums

KING

Number	Title (A Side/B Side)	Yr	VG	VG+	NM
395-594 [M]	Boyd Bennett	1955	1500.	2750.	4000.

BENNETT, CLIFF, AND THE REBEL ROUSERS

45s

Number	Title (A Side/B Side)	Yr	VG	VG+	NM
ABC					
10842	Got to Get You Into My Life/Baby Each Day	1966	3.75	7.50	15.00
AMY					
930	If Only You'd Reply/Three Rooms with Running Water	1965	3.75	7.50	15.00
ASCOT					
2146	Everybody Loves a Lover/My Old Stand By	1964	3.75	7.50	15.00
CAPITOL					
4621	I'm in Love with You/You've Got What I Like	1961	12.50	25.00	50.00
5309	One Way Love/I'm in Love with You	1964	3.75	7.50	15.00

BENNETT, JOE, AND THE SPARKLETONES

45s

Number	Title (A Side/B Side)	Yr	VG	VG+	NM
ABC-PARAMOUNT					
9837	Black Slacks/Boppin' Rock Boogie	1957	7.50	15.00	30.00
9867	Penny Loafers and Bobby Socks/Rocket	1957	7.50	15.00	30.00
9885	Cotton Pickin' Rocker/I Dig You Baby	1958	7.50	15.00	30.00
9929	Little Turtle/We've Had It	1958	7.50	15.00	30.00
9959	Do the Stop/Late Again	1958	7.50	15.00	30.00
PARIS					
530	Bayou Rock/Beautiful One	1959	7.50	15.00	30.00
537	Boys Do Cry/What the Heck	1959	6.25	12.50	25.00
546	Softly/What the Heck	1960	6.25	12.50	25.00

BENNETT, TONY

45s

Number	Title (A Side/B Side)	Yr	VG	VG+	NM
COLUMBIA					
AE 28 [DJ]	My Favorite Things/I Love the Winter Weather	1970	2.00	4.00	8.00
AE 28 [PS]	My Favorite Things/I Love the Winter Weather	1970	3.00	6.00	12.00
—Theme Song for 1970 Christmas Seals Campaign					
1-640 (?)	The Boulevard of Broken Dreams/I Wanna Be Loved	1950	6.25	12.50	25.00
—Microgroove 7-inch 33 1/3 rpm single					
1-670 (?)	Let's Make Love/I Can't Give You Anything But Love, Baby	1950	6.25	12.50	25.00
—Microgroove 7-inch 33 1/3 rpm single					
1-800 (?)	Sing You Sinners/Kiss You	1950	6.25	12.50	25.00
—Microgroove 7-inch 33 1/3 rpm single					
6-800 (?)	Sing You Sinners/Kiss You	1950	5.00	10.00	20.00
06138	Why Do People Fall in Love/Moments Like This	1986	—	—	3.00
07658	White Christmas/All of My Life	1987	—	—	3.00
07658 [PS]	White Christmas/All of My Life	1987	—	—	3.00
31272 [S]	(contents unknown)	1961	3.00	6.00	12.00
31273 [S]	(contents unknown)	1961	3.00	6.00	12.00
31274 [S]	(contents unknown)	1961	3.00	6.00	12.00
31275 [S]	(contents unknown)	1961	3.00	6.00	12.00
31276 [S]	(contents unknown)	1961	3.00	6.00	12.00
31563 [S]	(contents unknown)	1962	3.00	6.00	12.00
31564 [S]	(contents unknown)	1962	3.00	6.00	12.00
31565 [S]	(contents unknown)	1962	3.00	6.00	12.00
31566 [S]	(contents unknown)	1962	3.00	6.00	12.00
31567 [S]	(contents unknown)	1962	3.00	6.00	12.00
—Anyone who can fill in these gaps -- the above 10 all are Columbia "Stereo 7" singles -- please let us know.					
39187	Once There Lived a Fool/I Can't Give You Anything But Love, Baby	1951	3.75	7.50	15.00
39209	Beautiful Madness/Valentino Tango	1951	3.75	7.50	15.00
3-39209	Beautiful Madness/Valentino Tango	1951	6.25	12.50	25.00
—Microgroove 7-inch 33 1/3 rpm single					
39362	Because of You/I Won't Cry Anymore	1951	3.00	6.00	12.00
39449	Cold, Cold Heart/While We're Young	1951	3.00	6.00	12.00
39555	Blue Velvet/Solitaire	1951	3.00	6.00	12.00
39635	Silly Dreamer/Since My Love Has Gone	1952	3.00	6.00	12.00
39745	Here in My Heart/I'm Lost Again	1952	3.00	6.00	12.00
39764	Have a Good Time/Please My Love	1952	3.00	6.00	12.00
39815	You Could Make Me Smile Again/Roses of Yesterday	1952	3.00	6.00	12.00
39824	Because of You/I Won't Cry Anymore	1952	2.50	5.00	10.00
39825	The Boulevard of Broken Dreams/I Wanna Be Loved	1952	2.50	5.00	10.00
39826	Once There Lived a Fool/The Valentine Tango	1952	2.50	5.00	10.00
39827	Cold, Cold Heart/While We're Young	1952	2.50	5.00	10.00
39910	Congratulations to Someone/Take Me	1953	3.00	6.00	12.00
39964	I'm the King of Broken Hearts/No One Will Ever Know	1953	3.00	6.00	12.00
40004	Someone Turned the Moon Upside Down/I'll Go	1953	3.00	6.00	12.00
40048	Rags to Riches/Here Comes That Heartache Again	1953	3.00	6.00	12.00
40121	Stranger in Paradise/Why Does It Have to Be Me	1953	3.00	6.00	12.00
40169	There'll Be No Teardrops Tonight/My Heart Won't Say Goodbye	1954	3.00	6.00	12.00
40213	Until Yesterday/Please Driver, Once Around the Park Again	1954	3.00	6.00	12.00
40272	Cinnamon Sinner/Take Me Back Again	1954	3.00	6.00	12.00
40376	Funny Thing/My Pretty Shoo-Gah	1954	3.00	6.00	12.00
40427	It's Too Soon to Know/Close Your Eyes	1955	2.50	5.00	10.00
40491	What Will I Tell My Heart/Punch and Judy Love	1955	2.50	5.00	10.00
40523	May I Never Love Again/Don't Tell Me Why	1955	2.50	5.00	10.00
40567	How Can I Replace You/Tell Me That You Love Me	1955	2.50	5.00	10.00
40632	Sing You Sinners/Capri in May	1956	2.50	5.00	10.00
40667	Can You Find It in Your Heart/Forget Her	1956	2.50	5.00	10.00
40726	From the Candy Store on the Corner to the Chapel on the Hill/Happiness Street (Corner Sunshine Square)	1956	2.50	5.00	10.00
40770	The Autumn Waltz/Just in Time	1956	2.50	5.00	10.00
40849	One Kiss Away from Heaven/Sold to the Man with the Broken Heart	1957	2.50	5.00	10.00
40907	One for My Baby (And One More for the Road)/No Hard Feelings	1957	2.50	5.00	10.00
40965	In the Middle of An Island/I Am	1957	2.50	5.00	10.00
41032	Ca, C'est L'amour/I Never Felt More Like Falling in Love	1957	2.50	5.00	10.00
41086	Love Song from Beauty and the Beast/Weary Blues From Waitin'	1957	2.50	5.00	10.00
41127	You're So Right for Me/Alone at Last	1958	2.50	5.00	10.00
41157	Crazy Rhythm/The Beat of My Heart	1958	2.50	5.00	10.00
41172	Young and Warm and Wonderful/Now I Lay Me Down to Sleep	1958	2.50	5.00	10.00
41237	Firefly/The Night That Heaven Fell	1958	2.50	5.00	10.00
41237 [PS]	Firefly/The Night That Heaven Fell	1958	5.00	10.00	20.00
41298	Love, Look Away/Blue Moon	1958	2.50	5.00	10.00
41341	It's So Peaceful in the Country/Being True to One Another	1959	2.50	5.00	10.00
41381	The Cool School/You'll Never Get Away from Me	1959	2.50	5.00	10.00
41434	Smile/You Can't Love 'Em All	1959	2.50	5.00	10.00
41520	Climb Ev'ry Mountain/Ask Anyone in Love	1959	2.50	5.00	10.00
41595	I'll Bring You a Rainbow/Ask Me (I Know)	1960	2.00	4.00	8.00
41691	Put On a Happy Face/Baby, Talk to Me	1960	2.00	4.00	8.00
41770	Till/I Am	1960	2.00	4.00	8.00
41860	Marriage-Go-Round/Somebody	1960	2.00	4.00	8.00
41874	Ramona/Follow Me	1960	2.00	4.00	8.00
41965	The Best Is Yet to Come/Marry Young	1961	2.00	4.00	8.00
42003	Toot Toot Tootsie (Goodbye)/I'm Coming Virginia	1961	2.00	4.00	8.00
42135	Close Your Eyes/Rules of the Road	1961	2.00	4.00	8.00
42219	Tender Is the Night/Comes Once in a Lifetime	1961	2.00	4.00	8.00
42332	I Left My Heart In San Francisco/Once Upon a Time	1962	2.00	4.00	8.00
42332 [PS]	I Left My Heart In San Francisco/Once Upon a Time	1962	3.75	7.50	15.00
42395	Candy Kisses/Have I Told You Lately That I Love You	1962	2.00	4.00	8.00
42634	I Wanna Be Around/I Will Live My Life for You	1962	2.00	4.00	8.00
42779	The Good Life/Spring in Manhattan	1963	2.00	4.00	8.00
42820	This Is All I Ask/True Blue Lou	1963	2.00	4.00	8.00
42886	Don't Wait Too Long/Limehouse Blues	1963	2.00	4.00	8.00
42931	The Little Boy/The Moment of Truth	1963	2.00	4.00	8.00
42996	When Joanna Loved Me/The Kid's a Dreamer	1964	2.00	4.00	8.00
43073	It's a Sin to Tell a Lie/A Taste of Honey	1964	2.00	4.00	8.00
43141	Who Can I Turn To (When Nobody Needs Me)/Waltz for Debby	1964	2.00	4.00	8.00
43202	The Best Thing to Be Is a Person/The Brightest Smile in Town	1964	2.00	4.00	8.00
43220	If I Ruled the World/Take the Moment	1965	—	3.00	6.00
43331	Fly Me to the Moon (In Other Words)/How Insensitive	1965	—	3.00	6.00
43431	The Shadow of Your Smile/I'll Only Miss Her When I Think of Her	1965	—	3.00	6.00
43508	Song from The Oscar/Baby Dream Your Dream	1966	—	3.00	6.00
43508 [PS]	Song from The Oscar/Baby Dream Your Dream	1966	2.50	5.00	10.00
43715	Georgia Rose/The Very Thought	1966	—	3.00	6.00
43768	A Time for Love/Touch the Earth	1966	—	3.00	6.00
43954	What Makes It Happen/Country Girl	1966	—	3.00	6.00
43954 [DJ]	What Makes It Happen/Country Girl	1966	3.75	7.50	15.00
—Orange-vinyl promo issue					
44154	Keep Smiling at Trouble/Days of Love	1967	—	2.50	5.00
44258	For Once in My Life/How Do You Say Auf Wiedersehn	1967	—	3.00	6.00
44443	The Glory of Love/A Fool of Fools	1968	—	2.50	5.00
44510	Yesterday I Heard the Rain/Sweet Georgie Fame	1968	—	2.50	5.00
44584	Hushabye Mountain/Hi-Ho	1968	—	2.50	5.00
44688	Where Is Love/My Favorite Things	1968	—	2.50	5.00
44755	People/They All Laughed	1969	—	2.50	5.00
44824	Whoever You Are, I Love You/A Place Over the Sun	1969	—	2.50	5.00
44855	What the World Needs Now Is Love/Play It Again Sam	1969	—	2.50	5.00
44947	I've Gotta Be Me/A Lonely Place	1969	—	2.50	5.00
45032	MacArthur Park/Before We Say Goodbye	1969	—	2.50	5.00
45073	Little Green Apples/Coco	1970	—	2.50	5.00
45109	Something/Eleanor Rigby	1970	—	2.50	5.00
45157	Everybody's Talkin'/Think How It's Gonna Be	1970	—	2.50	5.00
45205	Something/Think How It's Gonna Be	1970	—	2.50	5.00
45255	I'll Begin Again/I Do Not Know a Day I Did Not Love You	1970	—	2.50	5.00
45316	(Where Do I Begin) Love Story/I'll Begin Again	1971	—	2.50	5.00
45376	I Want to Be Happy/Tea for Two	1971	—	2.50	5.00
45411	More and More/I'm Losing My Mind	1971	—	2.50	5.00
45449	Walkabout/How Beautiful Is Night	1971	—	2.50	5.00
45493	Remind Me/The Riviera	1971	—	2.50	5.00
45523	Somewhere Along the Line/The Summer Knows	1972	—	2.50	5.00
45573	Twilight World/Easy Come, Easy Go	1972	—	2.50	5.00
45613	Love/Maybe This Time	1972	—	2.50	5.00
JZSP 112321 [DJ]	Love Theme from "The Sandpiper" (The Shadow of Your Smile) (same on both sides)	1965	2.00	4.00	8.00
—Black vinyl promo					
MGM					
14607	My Love/(B-side unknown)	1973	—	2.00	4.00
VERVE					
10690	Living Together, Growing Together/The Good Things in Life	1972	—	2.00	4.00
10702	O Solo Mio/The Good Things in Life	1973	—	2.00	4.00
10714	Tell Her It's Snowing/If I Could Go Back	1973	—	2.00	4.00

7-Inch Extended Plays

Number	Title (A Side/B Side)	Yr	VG	VG+	NM
COLUMBIA					
B-2582	*One for My Baby/I Can't Give You Anything But Love/Solitaire/Once There Lived a Fool	1959	2.50	5.00	10.00

Number	Title (A Side/B Side)	Yr	VG	VG+	NM
B-2582	Tony Bennett (Hall of Fame Series)	1959	2.50	5.00	10.00
7-9173 [PS]	Tony Bennett's Greatest Hits Volume III	1964	3.00	6.00	12.00
7-9173 [S]	I Left My Heart in San Francisco/I Wanna Be Around/Quiet Nights of Quiet Stars//The Good Life/A Taste of Honey/The Best Is Yet to Come	1964	2.50	5.00	10.00
—33 1/3 rpm, small hole, "Special Coin Operator Release"					
B-9382	*These Foolish Things/I Can't Give You Anything But Love/Boulevard of Broken Dreams/I'll Be Seeing You	1957	2.50	5.00	10.00
B-9382 [PS]	Tony	1957	2.50	5.00	10.00
ZTEP 26851/2	Because of You/In the Middle of an Island/Cold, Cold Heart//From Rags to Riches/Come Next Spring/Can You Find It in Your Heart	1957	6.25	12.50	25.00
—Coca-Cola promotional item					
ZTEP 26851/2 [PS]	Tony Bennett Autographed Edition of Hits	1957	6.25	12.50	25.00
—Coca-Cola promotional item					
Albums					
COLUMBIA					
GP 14 [(2)]	Love Songs	1969	3.75	7.50	15.00
C2L 23 [(2) M]	Tony Bennett at Carnegie Hall	1962	5.00	10.00	20.00
CL 621 [M]	Cloud Seven	1955	10.00	20.00	40.00
C2S 823 [(2) S]	Tony Bennett at Carnegie Hall	1962	6.25	12.50	25.00
CL 938 [M]	Tony	1956	7.50	15.00	30.00
CL 1079 [M]	The Beat of My Heart	1957	7.50	15.00	30.00
CL 1186 [M]	Long Ago and Far Away	1958	7.50	15.00	30.00
CL 1229 [M]	Tony's Greatest Hits	1958	7.50	15.00	30.00
CL 1292 [M]	Blue Velvet	1958	7.50	15.00	30.00
CL 1301 [M]	Hometown, My Hometown	1959	6.25	12.50	25.00
CL 1429 [M]	To My Wonderful One	1960	6.25	12.50	25.00
CL 1446 [M]	Tony Sings for Two	1960	6.25	12.50	25.00
CL 1471 [M]	Alone Together	1960	6.25	12.50	25.00
CL 1535 [M]	More Tony's Greatest Hits	1961	5.00	10.00	20.00
CL 1559 [M]	A String of Harold Arlen	1961	5.00	10.00	20.00
CL 1658 [M]	My Heart Sings	1961	5.00	10.00	20.00
CL 1763 [M]	Mr. Broadway	1962	3.75	7.50	15.00
CL 1869 [M]	I Left My Heart in San Francisco	1962	3.75	7.50	15.00
CL 2000 [M]	I Wanna Be Around	1963	3.75	7.50	15.00
CL 2056 [M]	This Is All I Ask	1963	3.75	7.50	15.00
CL 2141 [M]	The Many Moods of Tony	1964	3.75	7.50	15.00
CL 2175 [M]	When Lights Are Low	1964	3.75	7.50	15.00
CL 2285 [M]	Who Can I Turn To	1964	3.75	7.50	15.00
CL 2343 [M]	If I Ruled the World — Songs for the Jet Set	1965	3.00	6.00	12.00
CL 2373 [M]	Tony's Greatest Hits, Volume III	1965	3.00	6.00	12.00
CL 2472 [M]	The Movie Song Album	1966	3.00	6.00	12.00
CL 2507 [10]	Alone at Last with Tony Bennett	1955	15.00	30.00	60.00
CL 2550 [10]	Because of You	1956	15.00	30.00	60.00
CL 2560 [M]	A Time for Love	1966	3.00	6.00	12.00
CL 2653 [M]	Tony Makes It Happen!	1967	3.75	7.50	15.00
CL 6221 [10]	Because of You	1952	20.00	40.00	80.00
CS 8107 [S]	Hometown, My Hometown	1959	10.00	20.00	40.00
CS 8226 [S]	To My Wonderful One	1960	10.00	20.00	40.00
CS 8242 [S]	Tony Sings for Two	1960	10.00	20.00	40.00
CS 8262 [S]	Alone Together	1960	10.00	20.00	40.00
CS 8335 [S]	More Tony's Greatest Hits	1961	6.25	12.50	25.00
CS 8359 [S]	A String of Harold Arlen	1961	6.25	12.50	25.00
CS 8458 [S]	My Heart Sings	1961	6.25	12.50	25.00
CS 8563 [S]	Mr. Broadway	1962	5.00	10.00	20.00
CS 8652 [R]	Tony's Greatest Hits	1962	3.75	7.50	15.00
CS 8669 [S]	I Left My Heart in San Francisco	1962	5.00	10.00	20.00
PC 8669	I Left My Heart in San Francisco	198?	2.00	4.00	8.00
—Reissue with new prefix					
CS 8800 [S]	I Wanna Be Around	1963	6.25	12.50	25.00
CS 8856 [S]	This Is All I Ask	1963	5.00	10.00	20.00
CS 8941 [S]	The Many Moods of Tony	1964	5.00	10.00	20.00
CS 8975 [S]	When Lights Are Low	1964	5.00	10.00	20.00
CS 9085 [S]	Who Can I Turn To	1964	5.00	10.00	20.00
CS 9143 [S]	If I Ruled the World — Songs for the Jet Set	1965	3.75	7.50	15.00
CS 9173 [S]	Tony's Greatest Hits, Volume III	1965	3.75	7.50	15.00
CS 9272 [S]	The Movie Song Album	1966	3.75	7.50	15.00
CS 9360 [S]	A Time for Love	1966	3.75	7.50	15.00
CS 9453 [S]	Tony Makes It Happen!	1967	3.75	7.50	15.00
CS 9573	For Once in My Life	1967	3.75	7.50	15.00
CS 9678	Yesterday I Heard the Rain	1968	3.75	7.50	15.00
CS 9739	Snowfall: The Tony Bennett Christmas Album	1968	3.00	6.00	12.00
CS 9814	Tony Bennett's Greatest Hits, Volume IV	1969	3.75	7.50	15.00
CS 9882	I've Gotta Be Me	1969	3.75	7.50	15.00
CS 9980	Tony Sings the Great Hits of Today!	1970	3.00	6.00	12.00
C 30240	All Time Hall of Fame Hits	1971	3.00	6.00	12.00
C 30280	Tony Bennett's "Something"	1971	3.00	6.00	12.00
C 30558	Love Story	1971	3.00	6.00	12.00
C 31216	Summer of '42	1972	3.00	6.00	12.00
KC 31460	With Love	1972	3.00	6.00	12.00
KG 31494 [(2)]	Tony Bennett's All-Time Greatest Hits	1972	3.75	7.50	15.00
CG 33612 [(2)]	I Left My Heart in San Francisco/Tony Sings the Great Hits of Today!	1975	3.75	7.50	15.00
FC 40344	The Art of Excellence	1986	2.50	5.00	10.00
CG 40424 [(2)]	Tony Bennett Jazz	1987	3.00	6.00	12.00
FC 44029	Bennett/Berlin	1987	2.50	5.00	10.00
COLUMBIA LIMITED EDITION					
LE 10057	For Once in My Life	197?	2.50	5.00	10.00
COLUMBIA SPECIAL PRODUCTS					
CSM 552 [M]	Singer Presents Tony Bennett	1966	3.75	7.50	15.00
CSS 552 [S]	Singer Presents Tony Bennett	1966	5.00	10.00	20.00
DRG					
MRS-910	Make Magnificent Music	1985	2.50	5.00	10.00
DARC-2-2102 [(2)]	The Rodgers and Hart Songbook	1986	3.75	7.50	15.00
HARMONY					
HS 11340	Just One of Those Things	1969	2.50	5.00	10.00
KH 32171	Tony	1973	2.50	5.00	10.00
IMPROV					
7112	Life Is Beautiful	197?	3.00	6.00	12.00
7113	Tony Bennett Sings Rodgers and Hart	197?	3.00	6.00	12.00
7120	Tony Bennett Sings More Rodgers and Hart	1978	3.00	6.00	12.00
7123	Beautiful Music	1979	3.00	6.00	12.00
MGM					
SE-4929	Greatest Hits, Vol. 7	1973	3.00	6.00	12.00
PAIR					
PDL2-1102 [(2)]	All-Time Favorites	1986	3.00	6.00	12.00
VERVE					
MV-5088	The Good Things in Life	1972	3.00	6.00	12.00
MV-5094	Listen Easy	1973	3.00	6.00	12.00

BENNETT, TONY, AND COUNT BASIE

Also see each artist's individual listings.

Number	Title (A Side/B Side)	Yr	VG	VG+	NM
Albums					
COLUMBIA					
CL 1294 [M]	Tony Bennett In Person	1959	6.25	12.50	25.00
CS 8104 [S]	Tony Bennett In Person	1959	10.00	20.00	40.00
ROULETTE					
R 25072 [M]	Count Basie Swings/Tony Bennett Sings	1961	6.25	12.50	25.00
SR 25072 [S]	Count Basie Swings/Tony Bennett Sings	1961	7.50	15.00	30.00
R 25231 [M]	Bennett and Basie Strike Up the Band	1963	5.00	10.00	20.00
SR 25231 [S]	Bennett and Basie Strike Up the Band	1963	6.25	12.50	25.00

BENNETT, TONY, AND BILL EVANS

Number	Title (A Side/B Side)	Yr	VG	VG+	NM
Albums					
DRG					
MRS-901	Together Again	1985	2.00	4.00	8.00
FANTASY					
9489	The Tony Bennett/Bill Evans Album	197?	3.00	6.00	12.00
IMPROV					
7117	Together Again	1978	3.00	6.00	12.00
MOBILE FIDELITY					
1-117	The Tony Bennett/Bill Evans Album	1981	10.00	20.00	40.00
—Audiophile vinyl					

BENNIS, BARBARA

Number	Title (A Side/B Side)	Yr	VG	VG+	NM
45s					
MALA					
468	Here's My Shoulder/I Wonder What He'll Say	1963	3.00	6.00	12.00

BENNO, MARC

Also see LEON RUSSELL AND MARC BENNO.

Number	Title (A Side/B Side)	Yr	VG	VG+	NM
45s					
A&M					
1327	Baby, I Love You/Speak Your Mind	1972	—	3.00	6.00
1387	Southern Woman/Jive Fade Jive	1972	—	3.00	6.00
2184	Chasin' Rainbows/(B-side unknown)	1979	—	3.00	6.00
Albums					
A&M					
SP-4273	Marc Benno	1970	3.00	6.00	12.00
SP-4303	Minnows	1971	3.00	6.00	12.00
SP-4364	Ambush	1972	3.00	6.00	12.00
SP-4767	Lost in Austin	1979	2.50	5.00	10.00

BENNY AND THE BEDBUGS

Number	Title (A Side/B Side)	Yr	VG	VG+	NM
45s					
DCP					
1008	The Beatle Beat/Roll Over Beethoven	1964	3.75	7.50	15.00
1008 [PS]	The Beatle Beat/Roll Over Beethoven	1964	6.25	12.50	25.00

BENSON, GEORGE

Also see THE ALTAIRS.

Number	Title (A Side/B Side)	Yr	VG	VG+	NM
45s					
ARISTA					
251	The Greatest Love of All/Ali's Theme	1977	—	2.00	4.00
—B-side by Michael Masser					
251 [PS]	The Greatest Love of All/Ali's Theme	1977	—	3.00	6.00
A&M					
1003	Chattanooga Choo Choo/The Shape of Things to Come	1968	—	3.00	6.00
1057	Don't Let Me Lose This Dream Part 1/Part 2	1969	—	3.00	6.00
1076	Jackie All/My Woman's Good to Me	1969	—	3.00	6.00
1124	My Cherie Amour/Tell It Like It Is	1969	—	3.00	6.00
1128	I Got a Woman Part 1/I Got a Woman Part 2	1969	—	3.00	6.00
8395	Golden Slumbers-You Never Give Me Your Money (Medley)/(B-side unknown)	1971	—	3.00	6.00
—May be promo only					
COLUMBIA					
43684	Summertime/Ain't That Peculiar	1966	2.50	5.00	10.00
43998	The Man from Toledo/Georgia Stick	1967	2.50	5.00	10.00
CTI					
25	Supership/My Latin Brother	1975	—	3.00	6.00
30	Summertime & 2001 (Part 1)/Summertime & 2001 (Part 2)	1977	—	2.50	5.00
47	Hold On, I'm Comin'/Gone	1978	—	2.50	5.00
GROOVE					
0024	It Should Have Been Me #2/She Makes Me Mad	1954	10.00	20.00	40.00
PRESTIGE					
317	Just Another Sunday/Shadow Dancers	1964	3.00	6.00	12.00
WARNER BROS.					
8209	This Masquerade/Lady	1976	—	2.50	5.00
8268	Breezin'/Six to Four	1976	—	2.00	4.00
8360	Everything Must Change/The Wind and I	1977	—	2.00	4.00
8377	Gonna Love You More/Valdez in the Country	1977	—	2.00	4.00
8542	On Broadway/We As Love	1978	—	2.00	4.00
8542 [PS]	On Broadway/We As Love	1978	—	2.50	5.00
8604	Lady Blue/California P.M.	1978	—	2.00	4.00
8759	Love Ballad/You're Never Too Far from Me	1979	—	2.00	4.00
8759 [PS]	Love Ballad/You're Never Too Far from Me	1979	—	2.50	5.00
8843	Unchained Melody/Before You Go	1979	—	2.00	4.00
27537	Good Habit/Stephanie	1989	—	—	3.00
27658	Twice the Love/(Instrumental)	1989	—	—	3.00
27658 [PS]	Twice the Love/(Instrumental)	1989	—	—	3.00
27780	Let's Do It Again/Let Go	1988	—	—	3.00

Number	Title (A Side/B Side)	Yr	VG	VG+	NM
27780 [PS]	Let's Do It Again/Let Go	1988	—	—	3.00
28410	Did You Hear Thunder/Teaser	1987	—	—	3.00
28523	Shiver/Love Is Here Tonight	1986	—	—	3.00
28640	Kisses in the Moonlight/Open Your Eyes (Instrumental)	1986	—	—	3.00
28640 [PS]	Kisses in the Moonlight/Open Your Eyes (Instrumental)	1986	—	—	3.00
28969	New Day/No One Emotion	1985	—	—	3.00
29042	I Just Wanna Hang Around You/Beyond the Sea (La Mer)	1985	—	—	3.00
29120	20-20/Shark Bite	1984	—	2.00	4.00
29120 [PS]	20-20/Shark Bite	1984	—	2.00	4.00
29442	In Your Eyes/Never Too Far to Fall	1983	—	2.00	4.00
29563	Lady Love Me (One More Time)/Being with You	1983	—	2.00	4.00
29649	Inside Love (So Personal)/In Search of a Dream	1983	—	2.00	4.00
29649 [PS]	Inside Love (So Personal)/In Search of a Dream	1983	—	2.00	4.00
49051	Hey Girl/Welcome Into My World	1979	—	2.00	4.00
49505	Give Me the Night/Dinorah, Dinorah	1980	—	2.00	4.00
49505 [PS]	Give Me the Night/Dinorah, Dinorah	1980	—	2.50	5.00
49570	Love Dance/Love X Love	1980	—	2.00	4.00
49637	Midnight Love Affair/Turn Off the Lamplight	1980	—	2.00	4.00
49846	Turn Your Love Around/Nature Boy	1981	—	2.00	4.00
49846 [PS]	Turn Your Love Around/Nature Boy	1981	—	2.00	4.00
50005	Never Give Up on a Good Thing/Livin' Inside Your Love	1982	—	2.00	4.00
50005 [PS]	Never Give Up on a Good Thing/Livin' Inside Your Love	1982	—	2.00	4.00

Albums

Number	Title (A Side/B Side)	Yr	VG	VG+	NM
A&M					
SP-3014	Shape of Things to Come	1969	5.00	10.00	20.00
—Brown label					
SP-3014	Shape of Things to Come	1976	3.00	6.00	12.00
—Silvery label					
SP-3014	Shape of Things to Come	198?	3.75	7.50	15.00
—Audiophile reissue					
SP-3020	Tell It Like It Is	1969	5.00	10.00	20.00
—Brown label					
SP-3020	Tell It Like It Is	1976	3.00	6.00	12.00
—Silvery label					
SP-3020	Tell It Like It Is	198?	3.75	7.50	15.00
—Audiophile reissue					
SP-3028	The Other Side of Abbey Road	1970	6.25	12.50	25.00
—Brown label					
SP-3028	The Other Side of Abbey Road	1976	3.00	6.00	12.00
—Silvery label					
SP-3028	The Other Side of Abbey Road	198?	3.75	7.50	15.00
—Audiophile reissue					
SP-3203	The Best of George Benson	1983	2.50	5.00	10.00
COLUMBIA					
CL 2525 [M]	The Most Exciting New Guitarist on the Jazz Scene Today — It's Uptown	1966	5.00	10.00	20.00
CL 2613 [M]	The George Benson Cook Book	1967	5.00	10.00	20.00
CS 9325	The Most Exciting New Guitarist on the Jazz Scene Today — It's Uptown	1976	2.50	5.00	10.00
—Orange label					
CS 9325 [S]	The Most Exciting New Guitarist on the Jazz Scene Today — It's Uptown	1966	5.00	10.00	20.00
—Red "360 Sound" label					
PC 9325	The Most Exciting New Guitarist on the Jazz Scene Today — It's Uptown	198?	2.00	4.00	8.00
—Reissue with new prefix					
CS 9413	The George Benson Cook Book	1976	2.50	5.00	10.00
—Orange label					
CS 9413 [S]	The George Benson Cook Book	1967	5.00	10.00	20.00
—Red "360 Sound" label					
PC 9413	The George Benson Cook Book	198?	2.00	4.00	8.00
—Reissue with new prefix					
CG 33569 [(2)]	Benson Burner	1976	3.00	6.00	12.00
CTI					
6009	Beyond the Blue Horizon	1971	3.00	6.00	12.00
6015	White Rabbit	1972	3.00	6.00	12.00
6033	Body Talk	1973	3.00	6.00	12.00
6045	Bad Benson	1974	3.00	6.00	12.00
6062	Good King Bad	1976	3.00	6.00	12.00
6069	Benson & Farrell	1976	3.00	6.00	12.00
6072	George Benson In Concert — Carnegie Hall	1976	3.00	6.00	12.00
8009	White Rabbit	198?	2.50	5.00	10.00
8014	Take Five	198?	2.50	5.00	10.00
8030	Cast Your Fate to the Wind	1982	2.50	5.00	10.00
8031	Summertime: In Concert	198?	2.50	5.00	10.00
FANTASY					
OJC-461	New Boss Guitar	1990	3.00	6.00	12.00
—Reissue of Prestige 7310					
MOBILE FIDELITY					
1-11	Breezin'	1979	15.00	30.00	60.00
—Audiophile vinyl					
POLYDOR					
PD-1-6084	Blue Benson	1976	2.50	5.00	10.00
PRESTIGE					
PRLP-7310 [M]	The New Boss Guitar of George Benson	1964	6.25	12.50	25.00
PRST-7310 [S]	The New Boss Guitar of George Benson	1964	7.50	15.00	30.00
24072 [(2)]	George Benson & Jack McDuff	1976	3.75	7.50	15.00
VERVE					
V6-8749	Giblet Gravy	1968	5.00	10.00	20.00
V6-8771	Goodies	1969	5.00	10.00	20.00
WARNER BROS.					
BS 2919	Breezin'	1976	3.75	7.50	15.00
—With no mention of "This Masquerade" on front cover					
BS 2919	Breezin'	1976	2.50	5.00	10.00
—With "Contains This Masquerade" on front cover					
BSK 2983	In Flight	1977	2.50	5.00	10.00
BSK 3111	Breezin'	1977	2.00	4.00	8.00
—Reissue of 2919					
2WS 3139 [(2)]	Weekend in L.A.	1978	3.00	6.00	12.00
2BSK 3277	Livin' Inside Your Love	1979	3.00	6.00	12.00
HS 3453	Give Me the Night	1980	2.50	5.00	10.00
2HS 3577 [(2)]	The George Benson Collection	1981	3.00	6.00	12.00
23744	In Your Eyes	1983	2.50	5.00	10.00
25178	20/20	1985	2.50	5.00	10.00
25475	While the City Sleeps...	1986	2.50	5.00	10.00
25705	Twice the Love	1988	2.50	5.00	10.00
25907	Tenderly	1989	3.00	6.00	12.00
26295	Big Boss Band	1990	3.75	7.50	15.00

BENSON, GEORGE, AND EARL KLUGH

45s

Number	Title (A Side/B Side)	Yr	VG	VG+	NM
WARNER BROS.					
27975	Since You're Gone/Love Theme from "Romeo and Juliet"	1988	—	—	3.00
28244	Dreamin'/Love Theme from "Romeo and Juliet"	1987	—	—	3.00

Albums

Number	Title (A Side/B Side)	Yr	VG	VG+	NM
WARNER BROS.					
25580	Collaboration	1987	2.50	5.00	10.00

BENSON, JANE

45s

Number	Title (A Side/B Side)	Yr	VG	VG+	NM
ATCO					
6151	Growing Up/Surrendering	1959	3.75	7.50	15.00

BENTLEYS, THE

45s

Number	Title (A Side/B Side)	Yr	VG	VG+	NM
SMASH					
1967	She's My Hot Rod Queen/Why Does Everybody Want to Hold My Baby	1965	6.25	12.50	25.00
1988	Did Anybody Lose a Tear/Why Didn't I Listen to Mother	1965	6.25	12.50	25.00

BENTON, BROOK

Also see THE SANDMEN (2); DINAH WASHINGTON AND BROOK BENTON.

45s

Number	Title (A Side/B Side)	Yr	VG	VG+	NM
ALL PLATINUM					
2364	Can't Take My Eyes Off You/Weekend with Feathers	1976	—	2.50	5.00
BRUT					
810	Lay Lady Lay/A Touch of Class	1973	—	2.50	5.00
816	South Carolina/(B-side unknown)	1973	—	2.50	5.00
COTILLION					
44007	I Just Don't Know What to Do with Myself/Do Your Own Thing	1968	2.00	4.00	8.00
44031	She Knows What to Do with 'Em/Touch 'Em with Love	1969	2.00	4.00	8.00
44034	Nothing Can Take the Place of You/Woman Without Love	1969	2.00	4.00	8.00
44057	Rainy Night in Georgia/Where Do You Go from Here	1969	2.50	5.00	10.00
44072	My Way/A Little Bit of Soap	1970	—	3.00	6.00
44078	Don't It Make You Want to Go Home/I've Gotta Be Me	1970	—	3.00	6.00
44093	Shoes/Let Me Fix It	1970	—	3.00	6.00
44110	Whoever Finds This, I Love You/Heaven Help Us All	1971	—	3.00	6.00
44119	Take a Look at Your Hands/If You Think God Is Dead	1971	—	3.00	6.00
44130	Please Send Me Someone to Love/She Even Woke Me Up to Say Goodbye	1971	—	3.00	6.00
44138	A Black Child Can't Smile/If You Think God Is Dead	1971	—	3.00	6.00
44141	Soul Santa/Let Us All Get Together with the Lord	1971	2.00	4.00	8.00
44152	Movin' Day/Poor Make Believer	1972	—	3.00	6.00
EPIC					
9177	Love Made Me Your Fool/Give Me a Sign	1956	6.25	12.50	25.00
9199	The Wall/All My Love Belongs to You	1957	6.25	12.50	25.00
MERCURY					
30101	Merry Christmas, Happy New Year/This Time Of The Year	196?	2.00	4.00	8.00
—Reissue					
71394	It's Just a Matter of Time/Hurtin' Inside	1959	3.75	7.50	15.00
71443	Endlessly/So Close	1959	3.75	7.50	15.00
71478	Thank You Pretty Baby/With All of My Heart	1959	3.75	7.50	15.00
71512	So Many Ways/I Want You Forever	1959	3.75	7.50	15.00
71554	This Time of the Year/Nothing in the World	1959	3.75	7.50	15.00
71558	This Time of the Year/How Many Times	1959	3.75	7.50	15.00
71566	The Ties That Bind/Hither, Thither and Yon	1960	3.00	6.00	12.00
71566 [PS]	The Ties That Bind/Hither, Thither and Yon	1960	5.00	10.00	20.00
71652	Kiddio/The Same One	1960	3.00	6.00	12.00
71652 [PS]	Kiddio/The Same One	1960	5.00	10.00	20.00
71722	Fools Rush In (Where Angels Fear to Tread)/Someday You'll Want Me to Want You	1960	3.00	6.00	12.00
71722 [PS]	Fools Rush In (Where Angels Fear to Tread)/Someday You'll Want Me to Want You	1960	5.00	10.00	20.00
71730	This Time of the Year/Merry Christmas, Happy New Year	1960	3.00	6.00	12.00
71774	Think Twice/For My Baby	1961	3.00	6.00	12.00
71774 [PS]	Think Twice/For My Baby	1961	5.00	10.00	20.00
71820	The Boll Weevil Song/Your Eyes	1961	3.00	6.00	12.00
71820 [PS]	The Boll Weevil Song/Your Eyes	1961	5.00	10.00	20.00
71859	Frankie and Johnny/It's Just a House Without You	1961	3.00	6.00	12.00
71859 [PS]	Frankie and Johnny/It's Just a House Without You	1961	5.00	10.00	20.00
71903	Revenge/Really Really	1961	3.00	6.00	12.00
71903 [PS]	Revenge/Really Really	1961	5.00	10.00	20.00
71912	Shadrack/The Lost Penny	1961	3.00	6.00	12.00
71912 [PS]	Shadrack/The Lost Penny	1961	5.00	10.00	20.00
71925	Walk on the Wild Side/Somewhere in the Used to Be	1962	2.50	5.00	10.00
71925 [PS]	Walk on the Wild Side/Somewhere in the Used to Be	1962	5.00	10.00	20.00
71962	Hit Record/Thanks to the Fool	1962	2.50	5.00	10.00
71962 [PS]	Hit Record/Thanks to the Fool	1962	5.00	10.00	20.00

Number	Title (A Side/B Side)	Yr	VG	VG+	NM
72009	Two Tickets to Paradise/It's Alright	1962	—	—	—
—Unreleased					
72024	Lie to Me/With the Touch of Your Hand	1962	2.50	5.00	10.00
72024 [PS]	Lie to Me/With the Touch of Your Hand	1962	5.00	10.00	20.00
72055	Hotel Happiness/Still Waters Run Deep	1962	2.50	5.00	10.00
72055 [PS]	Hotel Happiness/Still Waters Run Deep	1962	5.00	10.00	20.00
72099	I Got What I Wanted/Dearer Than Life	1963	2.50	5.00	10.00
72099 [PS]	I Got What I Wanted/Dearer Than Life	1963	5.00	10.00	20.00
72135	My True Confession/Tender Years	1963	2.50	5.00	10.00
72135 [PS]	My True Confession/Tender Years	1963	5.00	10.00	20.00
72177	Two Tickets to Paradise/Don't Hate Me	1963	2.50	5.00	10.00
72177 [PS]	Two Tickets to Paradise/Don't Hate Me	1963	5.00	10.00	20.00
72214	This Time of the Year/You're All I Want for Christmas	1963	2.50	5.00	10.00
72214 [DJ]	You're All I Want For Christmas/This Time Of The Year	1963	2.50	5.00	10.00
72230	Going, Going, Gone/After Midnight	1963	2.50	5.00	10.00
72230 [PS]	Going, Going, Gone/After Midnight	1963	5.00	10.00	20.00
72266	Too Late to Turn Back Now/Another Cup of Coffee	1964	2.50	5.00	10.00
72266 [PS]	Too Late to Turn Back Now/Another Cup of Coffee	1964	5.00	10.00	20.00
72303	A House Is Not a Home/Come On Back	1964	2.50	5.00	10.00
72303 [PS]	A House Is Not a Home/Come On Back	1964	5.00	10.00	20.00
72333	Lumberjack/Don't Do What I Did (Do What I Say)	1964	2.50	5.00	10.00
72333 [PS]	Lumberjack/Don't Do What I Did (Do What I Say)	1964	5.00	10.00	20.00
72365	Do It Right/Please, Please Make It Easy	1964	2.50	5.00	10.00
72365 [PS]	Do It Right/Please, Please Make It Easy	1964	5.00	10.00	20.00
72398	Special Years/Where There's a Will (There's a Way)	1965	2.50	5.00	10.00
72446	Love Me Now/A-Sleepin' at the End of the Bed	1965	2.50	5.00	10.00
872796-7	It's Just a Matter of Time/Hurtin' Inside	1989	—	2.00	4.00
872798-7	Endlessly/So Many Ways	1989	—	2.00	4.00
MGM					
14440	If You've Got the Time/You Take Me Home Honey	1972	—	2.50	5.00
OKEH					
7058	The Kentuckian Song/Ooh	1955	6.25	12.50	25.00
7065	Bring Me Love/Some of My Best Friends	1956	6.25	12.50	25.00
OLDE WORLD					
1100	Makin' Love Is Good for You/Better Times	1977	—	2.50	5.00
1107	Soft/Glow Love	1978	—	2.50	5.00
POLYDOR					
2015	I Cried for You/Love Me a Little	1979	—	2.00	4.00
RCA VICTOR					
47-7489	Only Your Love/(B-side unknown)	1959	—	—	—
—Unreleased?					
47-8693	Mother Nature, Father Time/You're Mine	1965	2.50	5.00	10.00
47-8693 [PS]	Mother Nature, Father Time/You're Mine	1965	5.00	10.00	20.00
47-8768	Where There's Life/Only a Girl Like You	1965	2.50	5.00	10.00
47-8830	Too Much Good Lovin'/A Sailor Boy's Love Song	1966	2.50	5.00	10.00
47-8879	Break Her Heart/In the Evening in the Moonlight	1966	2.50	5.00	10.00
47-8944	Where Does a Man Go to Cry/The Roach Song	1966	2.50	5.00	10.00
47-8995	So True in Life, So True in Love/If You Only Knew	1966	2.50	5.00	10.00
47-9031	Our First Christmas Together/Silent Night	1966	3.00	6.00	12.00
47-9096	Wake Up/All My Love Belongs to You	1967	2.00	4.00	8.00
47-9105	Keep the Faith Baby/Going to Soulsville	1967	2.00	4.00	8.00
REPRISE					
0611	You're the Reason I'm Living/Laura (Tell Me What He's Got That I Ain't Got)	1967	2.00	4.00	8.00
0649	Glory of Love/Weakness in a Man	1967	2.00	4.00	8.00
0676	Instead (Of Loving You)/Lonely Street	1968	2.00	4.00	8.00
STAX					
0231	Winds of Change/I Keep Thinking to Myself	1974	—	2.50	5.00
VIK					
0285	I Wanna Do Everything for You/Come On Be Nice	1957	5.00	10.00	20.00
0311	A Million Miles from Nowhere/Devoted	1957	5.00	10.00	20.00
0325	Because You Love Me/Crinoline Skirt	1958	5.00	10.00	20.00
0336	Crazy in Love with You/I'm Coming Back to You	1958	5.00	10.00	20.00

Albums

Number	Title	Yr	VG	VG+	NM
ALL PLATINUM					
3015	This Is Brook Benton	1976	3.00	6.00	12.00
ALLEGIANCE					
AV-5033	Memories Are Made of This	1986	2.50	5.00	10.00
COTILLION					
SD 9002	Do Your Own Thing	1969	3.00	6.00	12.00
SD 9018	Brook Benton Today	1970	3.00	6.00	12.00
SD 9028	Home Style	1970	3.00	6.00	12.00
SD 9050	Story Teller	1971	3.00	6.00	12.00
SD 9058	The Gospel Truth	1972	3.00	6.00	12.00
EPIC					
LN 3573 [M]	Brook Benton At His Best	1959	12.50	25.00	50.00
HARMONY					
HL 7346 [M]	The Soul of Brook Benton	196?	3.00	6.00	12.00
HS 11146 [R]	The Soul of Brook Benton	196?	3.00	6.00	12.00
HMC					
830724	Beautiful Memories of Christmas	1983	3.00	6.00	12.00
MERCURY					
MG-20421 [M]	It's Just a Matter of Time	1959	10.00	20.00	40.00
MG-20464 [M]	Endlessly	1959	7.50	15.00	30.00
MG-20565 [M]	So Many Ways I Love You	1960	7.50	15.00	30.00
MG-20602 [M]	Songs I Love to Sing	1960	7.50	15.00	30.00
MG-20607 [M]	Golden Hits	1961	5.00	10.00	20.00
MG-20619 [M]	If You Believe	1961	5.00	10.00	20.00
MG-20641 [M]	The Boll Weevil Song and 11 Other Great Hits	1961	5.00	10.00	20.00
MG-20673 [M]	There Goes That Song Again	1962	5.00	10.00	20.00
MG-20740 [M]	Singing the Blues — Lie to Me	1962	5.00	10.00	20.00
MG-20774 [M]	Golden Hits, Volume 2	1963	5.00	10.00	20.00
MG-20830 [M]	Best Ballads of Broadway	1963	5.00	10.00	20.00
MG-20886 [M]	Born to Sing the Blues	1964	5.00	10.00	20.00
MG-20918 [M]	On the Country Side	1964	3.75	7.50	15.00
MG-20934 [M]	This Bitter Earth	1964	3.75	7.50	15.00
SR-60077 [S]	It's Just a Matter of Time	1959	12.50	25.00	50.00
SR-60146 [S]	Endlessly	1959	10.00	20.00	40.00
SR-60225 [S]	So Many Ways I Love You	1960	10.00	2.00	40.00
SR-60602 [S]	Songs I Love to Sing	1960	10.00	20.00	40.00
SR-60607 [S]	Golden Hits	1961	7.50	15.00	30.00
SR-60619 [S]	If You Believe	1961	7.50	15.00	30.00
SR-60641 [S]	The Boll Weevil Song and 11 Other Great Hits	1961	7.50	15.00	30.00
SR-60673 [S]	There Goes That Song Again	1962	7.50	15.00	30.00
SR-60740 [S]	Singing the Blues — Lie to Me	1962	7.50	15.00	30.00
SR-60774 [S]	Golden Hits, Volume 2	1963	7.50	15.00	30.00
SR-60830 [S]	Best Ballads of Broadway	1963	6.25	12.50	25.00
SR-60886 [S]	Born to Sing the Blues	1964	6.25	12.50	25.00
SR-60918 [S]	On the Country Side	1964	5.00	10.00	20.00
SR-60934 [S]	This Bitter Earth	1964	5.00	10.00	20.00
822321-1	It's Just a Matter of Time: His Greatest Hits	1984	2.50	5.00	10.00
MGM					
SE-4874	Something for Everyone	1973	3.00	6.00	12.00
MUSICOR					
4603 [(2)]	The Best of Brook Benton	1977	3.00	6.00	12.00
PAIR					
PDL2-1100 [(2)]	Brook Benton's Best	1986	3.00	6.00	12.00
RCA CAMDEN					
CAL-564 [M]	Brook Benton	1960	3.75	7.50	15.00
CAS-2431	I Wanna Be with You	1970	3.00	6.00	12.00
RCA VICTOR					
APL1-1044	Book Benton Sings a Love Story	1975	2.50	5.00	10.00
LPM-3514 [M]	That Old Feeling	1966	3.75	7.50	15.00
LSP-3514 [S]	That Old Feeling	1966	5.00	10.00	20.00
LPM-3526 [M]	Mother Nature, Father Time	1965	3.75	7.50	15.00
LSP-3526 [S]	Mother Nature, Father Time	1965	5.00	10.00	20.00
LPM-3590 [M]	My Country	1966	3.75	7.50	15.00
LSP-3590 [S]	My Country	1966	5.00	10.00	20.00
REPRISE					
R-6268 [M]	Laura (What's He Got That I Ain't Got)	1967	5.00	10.00	20.00
RS-6268 [S]	Laura (What's He Got That I Ain't Got)	1967	3.75	7.50	15.00
RHINO					
RNFP 71497 [(2)]	The Brook Benton Anthology (1959-1970)	1986	3.00	6.00	12.00
WING					
MGW-12314 [M]	Brook Benton	1966	3.00	6.00	12.00
SRW-16314 [S]	Brook Benton	1966	3.00	6.00	12.00

BENTON, BROOK, AND DAMITA JO

Also see each artist's individual listings.

45s

Number	Title (A Side/B Side)	Yr	VG	VG+	NM
MERCURY					
72196	Yaba-Taba-Do/Almost Persuaded	1963	—	—	—
—Unreleased					
72207	Baby You Got It Made/Stop Foolin'	1963	2.50	5.00	10.00

BERBERIAN, JOHN, WITH THE ROCK EAST ENSEMBLE

Albums

Number	Title	Yr	VG	VG+	NM
MAINSTREAM					
S-6123	Impressions East	1969	30.00	60.00	120.00
VERVE FORECAST					
FTS-3073	Middle Eastern Rock	1969	12.50	25.00	50.00

BERG, GERTRUDE

Albums

Number	Title	Yr	VG	VG+	NM
AMY					
8007 [M]	How to Be a Jewish Mother	1965	6.25	12.50	25.00

BERGEN, POLLY

45s

Number	Title (A Side/B Side)	Yr	VG	VG+	NM
COLUMBIA					
41342	He Didn't Call/I Feel Sorry for the Boy	1959	3.00	6.00	12.00
41617	It Might As Well Be Spring/Four Seasons	1960	2.50	5.00	10.00
41675	Do It Yourself/The Party's Over	1960	2.50	5.00	10.00
41971	Bye Bye Blackbird/The Happiest Girl in the World	1961	2.50	5.00	10.00
JUBILEE					
5230	No One Else Will Ever Know/Let's Make Love	1956	3.75	7.50	15.00
RCA VICTOR					
47-3886	Oh Them Dudes/I Got Tookin'	1950	3.75	7.50	15.00
47-3958	Just the Way You Are/I Put My Head in the Lion's Mouth	1950	3.75	7.50	15.00
47-4022	Out of Sight/Tonda Wanda Hey	1951	3.75	7.50	15.00

Albums

Number	Title	Yr	VG	VG+	NM
COLUMBIA					
CL 994 [M]	Bergen Sings Morgan	1957	7.50	15.00	30.00
CL 1031 [M]	The Party's Over	1957	7.50	15.00	30.00
CL 1138 [M]	Polly and Her Pop	1958	6.25	12.50	25.00
CL 1218 [M]	My Heart Sings	1959	5.00	10.00	20.00
CL 1300 [M]	All Alone by the Telephone	1959	5.00	10.00	20.00
CL 1451 [M]	Four Seasons of Love	1960	5.00	10.00	20.00
CL 1632 [M]	"Do Re Mi" and "Annie Get Your Gun"	1961	5.00	10.00	20.00
CS 8018 [S]	My Heart Sings	1959	6.25	12.50	25.00
CS 8246 [S]	Four Seasons of Love	1960	6.25	12.50	25.00
CS 8432 [S]	"Do Re Mi" and "Annie Get Your Gun"	1961	6.25	12.50	25.00
CS (# unknown) [S]	All Alone by the Telephone	1959	6.25	12.50	25.00
JUBILEE					
JGL-14 [10]	Polly Bergen	1955	12.50	25.00	50.00
PHILIPS					
PHM 200084 [M]	Act One — Sing, Too	1963	3.75	7.50	15.00
PHS 600084 [S]	Act One — Sing, Too	1963	5.00	10.00	20.00

BERMAN, SHELLEY

Albums

Number	Title	Yr	VG	VG+	NM
METRO					
M-546 [M]	Let Me Tell You a Funny Story	1965	3.75	7.50	15.00
MS-546 [R]	Let Me Tell You a Funny Story	1965	3.00	6.00	12.00
VERVE					
MGV-15003 [M]	Inside Shelley Berman	1959	6.25	12.50	25.00
V-15003 [M]	Inside Shelley Berman	1962	3.75	7.50	15.00
V6-15003 [R]	Inside Shelley Berman	196?	3.00	6.00	12.00

Number	Title (A Side/B Side)	Yr	VG	VG+	NM
MGV-15007 [M]	Outside Shelley Berman	1959	6.25	12.50	25.00
V-15007 [M]	Outside Shelley Berman	1962	3.75	7.50	15.00
V6-15007 [R]	Outside Shelley Berman	196?	3.00	6.00	12.00
MGV-15008-2 [(2) M]	Inside and Outside Shelley Berman	1959	7.50	15.00	30.00
V-15008-2 [(2) M]	Inside and Outside Shelley Berman	1962	5.00	10.00	20.00
MGV-15013 [M]	The Edge of Shelley Berman	1960	6.25	12.50	25.00
V-15013 [M]	The Edge of Shelley Berman	1962	3.75	7.50	15.00
V6-15013 [R]	The Edge of Shelley Berman	196?	3.00	6.00	12.00
MGV-15027 [M]	A Personal Appearance	1961	5.00	10.00	20.00
V-15027 [M]	A Personal Appearance	1962	3.75	7.50	15.00
V6-15027 [R]	A Personal Appearance	196?	3.00	6.00	12.00
V-15036 [M]	The New Sides of Shelley Berman	1962	3.75	7.50	15.00
V6-15036 [R]	The New Sides of Shelley Berman	196?	3.00	6.00	12.00
V-15043 [M]	The Sex Life of the Primate (And Other Bits of Gossip)	1964	5.00	10.00	20.00
V6-15043 [R]	The Sex Life of the Primate (And Other Bits of Gossip)	1964	3.75	7.50	15.00
V-15048 [M]	Great Moments in Comedy	1965	5.00	10.00	20.00
V6-15048 [R]	Great Moments in Comedy	1965	3.75	7.50	15.00

BERMUDAS, THE

45s

Number	Title (A Side/B Side)	Yr	VG	VG+	NM
ERA					
3125	Donnie/Chu Sen Ling	1964	3.00	6.00	12.00

BERNA-DEAN

45s

Number	Title (A Side/B Side)	Yr	VG	VG+	NM
IMPERIAL					
5792	I Walk in My Sleep/Little Willie	1961	5.00	10.00	20.00
5840	He's Mine/One Gal in Town, Five Men Hagin' Around	1962	5.00	10.00	20.00
5877	Morning, Noon and Night/The World Keeps Changing	1962	5.00	10.00	20.00
5950	The President Says Walk/I Wonder	1963	5.00	10.00	20.00
5978	Hello/Sleepless Nights	1963	5.00	10.00	20.00

BERNARD, ROD

45s

Number	Title (A Side/B Side)	Yr	VG	VG+	NM
ARBEE					
101	Recorded in England/Somebody Wrote That Song for My Baby	1965	2.50	5.00	10.00
104	Gimme Back My Cadillac/Don't You Think I've Paid Enough	1965	2.50	5.00	10.00
105	Those Were Our Songs/Just Another Lie	1966	2.50	5.00	10.00
ARGO					
5327	This Should Go On Forever/Pardon Mr. Gordon	1959	5.00	10.00	20.00
5338	You're On My Mind/My Life Is a Mystery	1959	5.00	10.00	20.00
CARL					
(# unknown)	Linda Gail/Little Bitta Mama	1957	6.25	12.50	25.00
CRAZY CAJUN					
9020	Papa Thibodeaux/My Little Jollie Blonde	1978	—	2.50	5.00
HALLWAY					
1806	I Had a Girl/Wedding Bells	1963	3.75	7.50	15.00
1902	Who's Gonna Rock My Baby/Colinda	1962	3.75	7.50	15.00
1906	New Orleans Jail/Fais Do-Do	1962	3.75	7.50	15.00
1915	Forgive/I Want Somebody	1963	3.75	7.50	15.00
1917	Diggy Liggy Lo/The Clock	1963	3.75	7.50	15.00
1919	Loneliness/Boss Man's Son	1964	3.75	7.50	15.00
1922	My Own Mother-in-Law/I Might As Well	1964	3.75	7.50	15.00
JIN					
105	This Should Go On Forever/Pardon, Mr. Gordon	1958	10.00	20.00	40.00
232	Congratulations to You Darling/You're the Reason I'm in Love	1968	2.00	4.00	8.00
237	To Have and Hold/Cajun Honey	1968	2.00	4.00	8.00
240	Big Mamou/New Orleans Jail	1969	2.00	4.00	8.00
307	Don't You Think I've Paid Enough/Somebody Wrote That Song for Me	1974	—	2.50	5.00
325	Breaking Up Is Hard to Do/Sometimes I Walk in My Sleep	1975	—	2.50	5.00
338	This Should Go On Forever/I Spent a Week There Last Night	1975	—	2.50	5.00
350	A Winner in Love/I Forgot I Had These Memories of You	1975	—	2.50	5.00
373	Mardi Gras in New Orleans/Oh Mother Dear	1976	—	2.50	5.00
376	Go On, Go On/I Naver Had the One I Wanted	1976	—	2.50	5.00
MERCURY					
71507	Shedding Teardrops Over You/One More Chance	1959	5.00	10.00	20.00
71592	One of These Days/Let's Get Together Tonight	1960	5.00	10.00	20.00
71654	Two Young Fools in Love/Dance Fool Dance	1960	5.00	10.00	20.00
71689	Sttrange Kisses/Just a Memory	1960	5.00	10.00	20.00
71767	Lonely Hearts Club/Who Knows	1961	4.00	8.00	16.00
71842	(Tell Me) Sometime/I'm Not Lonely Anymore	1961	4.00	8.00	16.00
SCEPTER					
12195	Those Were Our Songs/Recorded in England	1967	4.00	8.00	16.00
TEAR DROP					
3044	Our Teenage Love/Doing the Oo-Wa-Woo	1966	2.50	5.00	10.00
3052	You're the Reason I'm in Love/My Jole Blon	1966	2.50	5.00	10.00
3060	No Money Down/Little Green Man	1967	2.50	5.00	10.00
3117	This Should Go On Forever/Recorded in England	1969	2.00	4.00	8.00

Albums

Number	Title (A Side/B Side)	Yr	VG	VG+	NM
JIN					
LP-4007 [M]	Rod Bernard	196?	15.00	30.00	60.00

BERRY, BROOKS, AND SCRAPPER BLACKWELL

Albums

Number	Title (A Side/B Side)	Yr	VG	VG+	NM
BLUESVILLE					
BVLP-1074 [M]	My Heart Struck Sorrow	1963	20.00	40.00	80.00
—Blue label, silver print					
BVLP-1074 [M]	My Heart Struck Sorrow	1964	6.25	12.50	25.00
—Blue label with trident logo					

BERRY, CHUCK

Also see JOE ALEXANDER AND THE CUBANS; BO DIDDLEY/CHUCK BERRY.

45s

Number	Title (A Side/B Side)	Yr	VG	VG+	NM
ATCO					
7203	Oh What a Thrill/California	1979	—	2.00	4.00
CHESS					
1604	Maybellene/Wee Wee Hours	1955	12.50	25.00	50.00
1610	Thirty Days (To Come Back Home)/Together	1955	12.50	25.00	50.00
1615	No Money Down/Down Bound Train	1956	12.50	25.00	50.00
1626	Roll Over Beethoven/Drifting Heart	1956	12.50	25.00	50.00
1635	Too Much Monkey Business/Brown Eyed Handsome Man	1956	12.50	25.00	50.00
1645	You Can't Catch Me/Havana Moon	1956	12.50	25.00	50.00
1653	School Day (Ring! Ring! Goes the Bell)/Deep Feeling	1957	12.50	25.00	50.00
1664	Oh Baby Doll/La Jaunda	1957	12.50	25.00	50.00
1671	Rock & Roll Music/Blue Feeling	1957	7.50	15.00	30.00
1683	Sweet Little Sixteen/Reelin' and Rockin'	1958	7.50	15.00	30.00
1691	Johnny B. Goode/Around and Around	1958	7.50	15.00	30.00
1697	Beautiful Delilah/Vacation Time	1958	7.50	15.00	30.00
1700	Carol/Hey Pedro	1958	7.50	15.00	30.00
1709	Sweet Little Rock and Roll/Joe Joe Gun	1958	7.50	15.00	30.00
1714	Run Rudolph Run/Merry Christmas Baby	1958	10.00	20.00	40.00
1716	Anthony Boy/That's My Desire	1959	7.50	15.00	30.00
1722	Almost Grown/Little Queenie	1959	7.50	15.00	30.00
1729	Back in the U.S.A./Memphis Tennessee	1959	7.50	15.00	30.00
1737	Broken Arrow/Childhood Sweetheart	1959	10.00	20.00	40.00
1747	Too Pooped to Pop ("Casey")/Let It Rock	1960	6.25	12.50	25.00
1754	Bye Bye Johnny/Worried Life Blues	1960	6.25	12.50	25.00
1763	I Got to Find My Baby/Mad Lad	1960	6.25	12.50	25.00
1767	Our Little Rendezvous/Jaguar and Thunderbird	1960	6.25	12.50	25.00
1779	I'm Talking About You/Little Star	1961	6.25	12.50	25.00
1799	Come On/Go-Go-Go	1961	5.00	10.00	20.00
1853	I'm Talking About You/Diploma for Two	1963	5.00	10.00	20.00
1866	Memphis/Sweet Little Sixteen	1963	5.00	10.00	20.00
1883	Nadine (Is It You?)/O Rangutang	1964	5.00	10.00	20.00
1898	No Particular Place to Go/You Two	1964	5.00	10.00	20.00
1898 [PS]	No Particular Place to Go/You Two	1964	12.50	25.00	50.00
1906	You Never Can Tell/Brenda Lee	1964	5.00	10.00	20.00
1906 [PS]	You Never Can Tell/Brenda Lee	1964	10.00	20.00	40.00
1912	Little Marie/Go Bobby Soxer	1964	3.75	7.50	15.00
1912 [PS]	Little Marie/Go Bobby Soxer	1964	10.00	20.00	40.00
1916	Promised Land/Things I Used to Do	1964	3.75	7.50	15.00
1916 [PS]	Promised Land/Things I Used to Do	1964	12.50	25.00	50.00
1926	Dear Dad/Lonely School Days	1965	3.75	7.50	15.00
1943	It Wasn't Me/Welcome Back Pretty Girl	1965	3.75	7.50	15.00
1943 [PS]	It Wasn't Me/Welcome Back Pretty Girl	1965	7.50	15.00	30.00
1963	Ramona Say Yes/Lonely School Days	1966	3.75	7.50	15.00
1963	Ramona Say Yes/Havana Moon	1966	3.75	7.50	15.00
2090	Tulane/Have Mercy Judge	1970	—	3.00	6.00
2131	My Ding-a-Ling/Johnny B. Goode	1972	—	3.00	6.00
—All-blue label					
2131	My Ding-a-Ling/Johnny B. Goode	1972	—	2.00	4.00
—Orange and blue label					
2136	Reelin' & Rockin'/Let's Boogie	1972	—	2.00	4.00
2140	Roll 'Em Pete/Bio	1973	—	2.00	4.00
2169	Baby What You Want Me to Do/Shake, Rattle and Roll	1975	—	2.00	4.00
COLLECTABLES					
3437	Run Rudolph Run/Merry Christmas Baby	199?	—	—	3.00
MERCURY					
30143	Maybellene/Sweet Little Sixteen	196?	—	3.00	6.00
30144	Memphis/School Day (Ring, Ring Goes the Bell)	196?	—	3.00	6.00
30145	Back in the U.S.A./Roll Over Beethoven	196?	—	3.00	6.00
30146	Johnny B. Goode/Rock and Roll Music	196?	—	3.00	6.00
—The Mercury 30000 series are re-recordings of the Chess hits					
72643	Club Nitty Gritty/Laugh and Cry	1966	2.50	5.00	10.00
72680	Back to Memphis/I Do Really Love You	1967	2.50	5.00	10.00
72748	It Hurts Me Too/Feelin' It	1967	2.50	5.00	10.00
72840	Louie to Frisco/Ma Dear	1968	2.50	5.00	10.00
72963	It's Too Dark in There/Good Looking Woman	1969	5.00	10.00	20.00
72963 [PS]	It's Too Dark in There/Good Looking Woman	1969	7.50	15.00	30.00
PHILCO-FORD					
HP-34	Maybellene/Roll Over Beethoven	1969	5.00	10.00	20.00
—4-inch plastic "Hip Pocket Record" with color sleeve					

7-Inch Extended Plays

Number	Title (A Side/B Side)	Yr	VG	VG+	NM
CHESS					
CH-5118	School Day (Ring, Ring Goes the Bell)/Wee Wee Hours//Brown Eyed Handsome Man/Too Much Monkey Business	1957	30.00	60.00	120.00
CH-5118 [PS]	Head Over Heels	1957	50.00	100.00	200.00
CH-5119	(contents unknown)	1957	25.00	50.00	100.00
CH-5119 [PS]	Rock and Roll Music	1957	50.00	100.00	200.00
CH-5121	Sweet Little Sixteen/Rockin' at the Philharmonic //Reelin' and Rockin'/Guitar Boogie	1958	25.00	50.00	100.00
CH-5121 [PS]	Sweet Little Sixteen	1958	50.00	100.00	200.00
CH-5124	(contents unknown)	1958	25.00	50.00	100.00
CH-5124 [PS]	Pickin' Berries	1958	50.00	100.00	200.00
CH-5126	(contents unknown)	1958	25.00	50.00	100.00
CH-5126 [PS]	Sweet Little Rock and Roller	1958	50.00	100.00	200.00

Albums

Number	Title (A Side/B Side)	Yr	VG	VG+	NM
ACCORD					
SN-7171	Toronto Rock 'N' Roll Revival, Vol. 2	1982	2.50	5.00	10.00
SN-7172	Toronto Rock 'N' Roll Revival, Vol. 3	1982	2.50	5.00	10.00
ARCHIVE OF FOLK AND JAZZ					
321	Greatest Hits	197?	2.50	5.00	10.00
ATCO					
SD 38-118	Rockit	1979	3.00	6.00	12.00
CHESS					
LP-1426 [M]	After School Session	1958	50.00	100.00	200.00
LPS-1426 [R]	After School Session	196?	3.00	6.00	12.00
LP-1432 [M]	One Dozen Berrys	1958	50.00	100.00	200.00
LPS-1432 [R]	One Dozen Berrys	196?	3.00	6.00	12.00
LP-1435 [M]	Chuck Berry Is On Top	1959	45.00	90.00	180.00

Number	Title (A Side/B Side)	Yr	VG	VG+	NM
LPS-1435 [R]	Chuck Berry Is On Top	196?	3.00	6.00	12.00
LP-1448 [M]	Rockin' at the Hops	1960	45.00	90.00	180.00
LP-1456 [M]	New Juke Box Hits	1961	45.00	90.00	180.00
LP-1465 [M]	Chuck Berry Twist	1962	25.00	50.00	100.00
LP-1465 [M]	More Chuck Berry	1963	30.00	60.00	120.00
—Retitled version of above					
LPS-1465 [R]	More Chuck Berry	196?	3.00	6.00	12.00
LP-1480 [M]	Chuck Berry On Stage	1963	30.00	60.00	120.00
LPS-1480 [R]	Chuck Berry On Stage	196?	3.00	6.00	12.00
LP-1485 [M]	Chuck Berry's Greatest Hits	1964	30.00	60.00	120.00
LPS-1485 [R]	Chuck Berry's Greatest Hits	196?	3.00	6.00	12.00
LP-1488 [M]	St. Louis to Liverpool	1964	15.00	30.00	60.00
LPS-1488 [S]	St. Louis to Liverpool	1964	20.00	40.00	80.00
LP-1495 [M]	Chuck Berry in London	1965	7.50	15.00	30.00
LPS-1495 [S]	Chuck Berry in London	1965	10.00	20.00	40.00
LP-1498 [M]	Fresh Berry's	1965	7.50	15.00	30.00
LPS-1498 [S]	Fresh Berry's	1965	10.00	20.00	40.00
2CH-1514 [(2) R]	Chuck Berry's Golden Decade	1972	3.75	7.50	15.00
—New cover has a pink radio					
LP-1514 [(2) M]	Chuck Berry's Golden Decade	1967	10.00	20.00	40.00
LPS-1514 [(2) R]	Chuck Berry's Golden Decade	1967	5.00	10.00	20.00
—Old cover does not have a pink radio					
LPS-1550	Back Home	1970	5.00	10.00	20.00
CH-9171	New Juke Box Hits	1986	2.50	5.00	10.00
—Reissue of 1456					
CH-9186	St. Louis to Liverpool	1988	2.50	5.00	10.00
—Reissue of 1488					
CH-9190	More Rock 'n' Roll Rarities	1986	2.50	5.00	10.00
CH-9256	Chuck Berry Is On Top	1987	2.50	5.00	10.00
—Reissue of 1435					
CH-9259	Rockin' at the Hop	1987	2.50	5.00	10.00
—Reissue of 1448					
CH-9284	After School Session	1989	2.50	5.00	10.00
—Reissue of 1426					
CH-9295	The London Chuck Berry Sessions	1989	2.50	5.00	10.00
—Reissue of 60020					
CH-9318	Missing Berries: Rarities, Volume 3	1990	2.50	5.00	10.00
CH-50008	San Fransisco Dues	1971	5.00	10.00	20.00
CH-50043	Chuck Berry/Bio	1973	5.00	10.00	20.00
CH-60020	The London Chuck Berry Sessions	1972	5.00	10.00	20.00
2CH-60023 [(2)]	Chuck Berry's Golden Decade, Vol. 2	1973	6.25	12.50	25.00
2CH-60028 [(2)]	Chuck Berry's Golden Decade, Vol. 3	1974	6.25	12.50	25.00
CH6-80001 [(6)]	The Chess Box	1989	12.50	25.00	50.00
CH2-92500 [(2)]	The Great Twenty-Eight	1983	3.00	6.00	12.00
CH2-92521 [(2)]	Rock 'n' Roll Rarities	1986	3.75	7.50	15.00
GUSTO					
0004	The Best of the Best of Chuck Berry	198?	2.50	5.00	10.00
MERCURY					
SRM-2-6501 [(2)]	St. Louis to Frisco to Memphis	1972	5.00	10.00	20.00
MG-21103 [M]	Chuck Berry's Golden Hits	1967	3.75	7.50	15.00
MG-21123 [M]	Chuck Berry in Memphis	1967	3.75	7.50	15.00
MG-21138 [M]	Love at the Fillmore Auditorium	1967	5.00	10.00	20.00
SR-61103 [S]	Chuck Berry's Golden Hits	1967	3.75	7.50	15.00
SR-61123 [S]	Chuck Berry in Memphis	1967	3.75	7.50	15.00
SR-61138 [S]	Love at the Fillmore Auditorium	1967	5.00	10.00	20.00
SR-61176	From St. Louis to Frisco	1968	5.00	10.00	20.00
SR-61223	Concerto in B Goode	1969	5.00	10.00	20.00
826256-1	Chuck Berry's Golden Hits	1985	2.00	4.00	8.00
—Reissue					
PICKWICK					
PTP-2061 [(2)]	Flashback	1975	3.00	6.00	12.00
SPC-3327	Johnny B. Goode	1973	2.50	5.00	10.00
SPC-3345	Sweet Little Rock and Roller	1974	2.50	5.00	10.00
SPC-3392	Wild Berrys	1974	2.50	5.00	10.00
QUICKSILVER					
QS-1017	Live Hits	198?	2.50	5.00	10.00
SSS INTERNATIONAL					
36	Chuck Berry Live	1981	2.50	5.00	10.00

BERRY, DAVE

Number	Title (A Side/B Side)	Yr	VG	VG+	NM
45s					
LONDON					
9666	Memphis Tennessee/My Baby Left Me	1964	3.75	7.50	15.00
9698	The Crying Game/Don't Gimme No Lip Child	1964	4.00	8.00	16.00
9781	This Strange Effect/Now	1965	3.75	7.50	15.00
20038	Do I Still Figure in Your Life/Latisha	1968	2.00	4.00	8.00
PARROT					
40010	Picture Me Gone/Baby's Gone	1967	2.50	5.00	10.00

BERRY, JAN

Includes records as "Jan Barry" and "I Jan I." Also see JAN AND DEAN.

Number	Title (A Side/B Side)	Yr	VG	VG+	NM
45s					
A&M					
1957	Little Queenie/That's the Way It Is	1977	3.75	7.50	15.00
2020	Skateboard Surfin' U.S.A. (Sidewalk Surfin' with Me)/How How I Love You	1978	3.75	7.50	15.00
LIBERTY					
55845	The Universal Coward/I Can't Wait to Love You	1965	5.00	10.00	20.00
55845 [PS]	The Universal Coward/I Can't Wait to Love You	1965	75.00	150.00	300.00
ODE					
66023	Mother Earth/Blue Moon Shuffle	1972	5.00	10.00	20.00
66034	Don't You Just Know It/Blue Moon Shuffle	1973	10.00	20.00	40.00
—With Brian Wilson on co-lead vocals on A-side					
66050	Tinsel Town/Blow Up Music	1974	5.00	10.00	20.00
—As "I Jan I"					
66120	Sing Sang a Song/Sing Sang a Song (Singalong Version)	1976	5.00	10.00	20.00
RIPPLE					
6101	Tomorrow's Teardrops/My Midsummer Night's Dream	1961	25.00	50.00	100.00
—As "Jan Barry"					

BERRY, JOHN

Number	Title (A Side/B Side)	Yr	VG	VG+	NM
45s					
DOT					
16132	Dance with Me Darlin'/Lucy Lou	1960	3.00	6.00	12.00

BERRY, KEN

Number	Title (A Side/B Side)	Yr	VG	VG+	NM
45s					
BARNABY					
2020	Lonely Street/Ain't That a Shame	1970	2.00	4.00	8.00
2034	Everyday with You/He'll Have to Go	1971	2.00	4.00	8.00
Albums					
BARNABY					
Z 30014	R.F.D.	1970	6.25	12.50	25.00
Z 30094	Ken Berry, R.F.D.	1970	7.50	15.00	30.00

BERRY, MIKE

Number	Title (A Side/B Side)	Yr	VG	VG+	NM
45s					
CORAL					
62341	A Tribute to Buddy Holly/Every Little Kiss	1962	15.00	30.00	60.00
62357	Don't You Think It's Time/Loneliness	1963	7.50	15.00	30.00
62483	Gonna Fall in Love/It Comes and Goes	1966	4.00	8.00	16.00
EPIC					
50748	I Am a Rocker/Boogaloo Dues	1979	—	2.00	4.00
50913	Stay Close to Me/One by One	1980	—	2.00	4.00
MCA					
40432	Don't Be Cruel/It's All Over	1975	—	2.50	5.00
Albums					
EPIC					
JE 36071	I'm a Rocker	1979	2.50	5.00	10.00
SIRE					
SASD 7524	Rocks in My Head	1976	3.75	7.50	15.00

BERRY, RICHARD

Number	Title (A Side/B Side)	Yr	VG	VG+	NM
45s					
FLAIR					
1016	I'm Still in Love with You/One Little Prayer	1953	20.00	40.00	80.00
1052	Bye Bye/At Last	1954	15.00	30.00	60.00
—With the Dreamers					
1055	What You Do to Me/The Big Break	1954	15.00	30.00	60.00
1058	Daddy Daddy/Baby Darling	1954	15.00	30.00	60.00
—With the Dreamers					
1064	Please Tell Me/Oh Oh Get Out of the Car	1955	12.50	25.00	50.00
1068	God Gave Me You/Doncha Go	1955	12.50	25.00	50.00
1071	Next Time/Crazy Lover	1955	12.50	25.00	50.00
1075	Together/Jelly Roll	1955	12.50	25.00	50.00
FLIP					
318	Take the Key/No Kissin' and Huggin'	1956	10.00	20.00	40.00
321	Louie, Louie/You Are My Sunshine	1957	15.00	30.00	60.00
321	Louie, Louie/Rock, Rock, Rock	1957	10.00	20.00	40.00
327	Sweet Sugar You/Rock, Rock, Rock	1957	10.00	20.00	40.00
331	You're the Girl/You Look So Good	1958	10.00	20.00	40.00
336	Heaven on Wheels/The Mess Around	1958	10.00	20.00	40.00
339	Besame Mucho/Do I, Do I	1958	7.50	15.00	30.00
349	Have Love, Will Travel/No Room	1960	7.50	15.00	30.00
352	I'll Never Ever Love Again/Somewhere There's a Rainbow	1961	7.50	15.00	30.00
360	You Look So Good/You Are My Sunshine	1962	7.50	15.00	30.00
HAPPY TIGER					
5063	Louie Louie/Rock Rock Rock	1972	2.00	4.00	8.00
K&G					
9001	I'm Your Fool/In a Really Big Way	1961	7.50	15.00	30.00
RPM					
448	Rockin' Man/Big John	1955	25.00	50.00	100.00
452	Pretty Brown Eyes/I Am Bewildered	1956	7.50	15.00	30.00
465	Angel of My Life/Yama Yama Pretty Mama	1956	25.00	50.00	100.00
477	Wait for Me/Good Love	1956	7.50	15.00	30.00
SMASH					
1789	What Good Is a Heart/Everybody's Got a Lover But Me	1963	3.00	6.00	12.00
1811	I'm Learning/Empty Chair	1963	3.00	6.00	12.00
WARNER BROS.					
5164	Walk Right In/It's All Right	1960	12.50	25.00	50.00
Albums					
CROWN					
CST-371 [R]	Richard Berry and the Dreamers	1963	7.50	15.00	30.00
CLP-5371 [M]	Richard Berry and the Dreamers	1963	15.00	30.00	60.00
PAM					
1001	Live at the Century Restaurant	1968	10.00	20.00	40.00
1002	Wild Berry	196?	10.00	20.00	40.00

BERRY KIDS, THE

Number	Title (A Side/B Side)	Yr	VG	VG+	NM
45s					
MGM					
12379	Go, Go, Go, Right Into Town/Love Me, Love	1956	20.00	40.00	80.00
12496	Rootie Tootie/Yo're My Teenage Baby	1957	20.00	40.00	80.00

BEST, BILLY, AND THE DITALIANS

Number	Title (A Side/B Side)	Yr	VG	VG+	NM
45s					
MERCURY					
72923	Baby That Takes the Cake/Time Is Getting Hard Josephine	1969	2.00	4.00	8.00

BEST, PETER (1)

Former drummer with THE BEATLES.

Number	Title (A Side/B Side)	Yr	VG	VG+	NM
45s					
CAMEO					
391	Boys/Kansas City	1965	20.00	40.00	80.00
391 [PS]	Boys/Kansas City	1965	25.00	50.00	100.00
HAPPENING					
405	If You Can't Get Her/Don't Play with Me	1964	45.00	90.00	180.00

Number	Title (A Side/B Side)	Yr	VG	VG+	NM
1117/8	If You Can't Get Her/The Way I Feel About You	1966	37.50	75.00	150.00
—Label credit: "Best of the Beatles (Peter Best)"					
MR. MAESTRO					
711	I Can't Do Without You Now/Keys to My Heart	1965	50.00	100.00	200.00
—Label credit: "Best of the Beatles"; black vinyl					
711	I Can't Do Without You Now/Keys to My Heart	1965	37.50	75.00	150.00
—Label credit: "Best of the Beatles"; blue vinyl					
712	Casting My Spell/I'm Blue	1965	37.50	75.00	150.00
—Black vinyl					
712	Casting My Spell/I'm Blue	1965	50.00	100.00	200.00
—Blue vinyl					
ORIGINAL BEATLES DRUMMER					
800	(I'll Try) Anyway/I Wanna Be There	1964	45.00	90.00	180.00
Albums					
PHOENIX					
PHX-340	The Beatle That Time Forgot	1982	3.00	6.00	12.00
SAVAGE					
BM-71	Best of the Beatles	1966	50.00	100.00	200.00

—Authentic copies have white circle around the word "Savage" and white circle around Pete Best's head on the album cover.

BEST, PETER (2)
This Peter Best is from Australia.

Number	Title (A Side/B Side)	Yr	VG	VG+	NM
45s					
CAPITOL					
2092	Carousel of Love/Want You	1968	7.50	15.00	30.00

BEST THINGS, THE

Number	Title (A Side/B Side)	Yr	VG	VG+	NM
45s					
UNITED ARTISTS					
50027	Chicks Are for Kids/You May See Me Cry	1966	2.50	5.00	10.00

BETH, KAREN

Number	Title (A Side/B Side)	Yr	VG	VG+	NM
Albums					
DECCA					
DL 75148	The Joys of Life	1969	3.75	7.50	15.00
DL 75247	Harvest	1970	3.75	7.50	15.00

BETTS, DICKEY
Also see THE ALLMAN BROTHERS BAND.

Number	Title (A Side/B Side)	Yr	VG	VG+	NM
45s					
ARISTA					
0255	Nothing You Can Do	1977	—	2.00	4.00
0269	Bougainvilla/Sweet Virginia	1977	—	2.00	4.00
0333	Atlanta's Burning Down/Mr. Blues Man	1978	—	2.00	4.00
CAPRICORN					
0213	Kissimmee Kid/Long Time Gone	1974	—	2.50	5.00
0221	Highway Call/Rain	1975	—	2.50	5.00
Albums					
ARISTA					
AL 4123	Dickey Betts & Great Southern	1977	2.50	5.00	10.00
AL 4168	Atlanta's Burning Down	1978	2.50	5.00	10.00
CAPRICORN					
CP 0123	Highway Call	1974	3.00	6.00	12.00
—As "Richard Betts"					
EPIC					
FE 44289	Pattern Disruptive	1988	2.50	5.00	10.00

BEVEL, CHARLES

Number	Title (A Side/B Side)	Yr	VG	VG+	NM
45s					
A&M					
1481	Making a Decision/Meet "Mississippi Charles Bevel"	1973	—	2.50	5.00
1481	Black Santa Claus/Making A Decision (Bring On Sunshine)	1973	—	3.00	6.00
1501	Sally B. White/Porcupine Meat	1974	—	2.50	5.00
1608	Don't Lie to Me/It Ain't Magic	1974	—	2.50	5.00
AM-8725	Black Santa Claus/Sally B. White	199?	—	—	3.00
—Reissue					
Albums					
A&M					
SP-4412	Meet "Mississippi Charles"	1973	3.00	6.00	12.00

BEVERLY SISTERS, THE

Number	Title (A Side/B Side)	Yr	VG	VG+	NM
45s					
LONDON					
1703	Greensleeves/I'll See You in My Dreams	1956	3.00	6.00	12.00
1731	Blow the Wind Southerly/Doodle Doo Doo	1957	3.00	6.00	12.00
1757	Old Enough to Know/I Remember Mama	1957	3.00	6.00	12.00
1783	Long Black Nylons/Young Cavalier	1958	3.00	6.00	12.00
1862	The Little Drummer Boy/Strawberry Fair	1958	3.00	6.00	12.00
1891	Little Donkey/Toy Dream	1960	3.00	6.00	12.00
MERCURY					
71671	Oh Ricky/Only Me	1960	3.00	6.00	12.00
ROULETTE					
4350	Flight 1203/(B-side unknown)	1961	3.00	6.00	12.00

BIDDU ORCHESTRA

Number	Title (A Side/B Side)	Yr	VG	VG+	NM
12-Inch Singles					
EPIC					
50397	Funky Tropical/Boogietown	1977	2.00	4.00	8.00
45s					
COLOSSUS					
125	The Sooner I Get to You/(B-side unknown)	1970	2.00	4.00	8.00
—As "Biddu"					
EPIC					
50139	Summer of '42/Northern Dancer	1975	1.00	2.00	4.00
50173	I Could Have Danced All Night/Jump for Joy	1975	1.00	2.00	4.00
50212	Rainforest/Hot Ice	1976	—	2.00	4.00
50387	Funky Tropical/Nirvana	1977	—	2.00	4.00
50439	Soal Coaxing/Nirvana	1977	—	2.00	4.00
Albums					
EPIC					
PE 33903	Biddu Orchestra	1975	2.50	5.00	10.00
PE 34230	Rain Forest	1976	2.50	5.00	10.00
PE 34723	Eastern Man	1977	2.50	5.00	10.00

BIG BEATS, THE
Also see TRINI LOPEZ.

Number	Title (A Side/B Side)	Yr	VG	VG+	NM
45s					
COLUMBIA					
41072	Clark's Expedition/Big Boy	1958	6.25	12.50	25.00
—Trini Lopez was a member					
41179	Rush Me/Sentimental Journey	1958	6.25	12.50	25.00
Albums					
LIBERTY					
LRP-3407 [M]	The Big Beats Live	1965	7.50	15.00	30.00
LST-7407 [S]	The Big Beats Live	1965	10.00	20.00	40.00

BIG BLACK
No relation to the 1980s-1990s punk band of the same name.

Number	Title (A Side/B Side)	Yr	VG	VG+	NM
45s					
UNI					
55051	The Snakecharmer/Come On and Get It Baby	1968	2.00	4.00	8.00
55099	Come On Down to the Beach/Love, Sweet Like Sugarcane	1968	2.00	4.00	8.00
55293	Long Hair/Diggin' What You're Doing	1971	—	3.00	6.00
55337	Mellow/Diggin' What You're Doing	1972	—	3.00	6.00
Albums					
UNI					
73018	Elements of Now	1968	3.75	7.50	15.00
73033	Lion Walk	1969	3.75	7.50	15.00
73134	Big Black and the Blues	1972	3.75	7.50	15.00

BIG BOPPER

Number	Title (A Side/B Side)	Yr	VG	VG+	NM
45s					
D					
1008	Chantilly Lace/The Purple People Eater Meets the Witch Doctor	1958	62.50	125.00	250.00
MERCURY					
71219	Beggar to a King/Crazy Blue	1957	15.00	30.00	60.00
—As "Jape Richardson"					
71312	A Teenage Mom/Monkey Song	1958	15.00	30.00	60.00
—As "Jape Richardson"					
71343	Chantilly Lace/The Purple People Eater Meets the Witch Doctor	1958	5.00	10.00	20.00
71375	Big Bopper's Wedding/Little Red Riding Hood	1958	3.75	7.50	15.00
71416	Someone's Watching Over You/Walking Through My Dreams	1959	3.75	7.50	15.00
71451	It's the Truth, Ruth/That's What I'm Talkin' About	1959	3.75	7.50	15.00
71482	Pink Petticoats/Time Clock	1959	3.75	7.50	15.00
Albums					
MERCURY					
MG-20402 [M]	Chantilly Lace	1959	125.00	250.00	500.00
—Black label					
MG-20402 [M]	Chantilly Lace	1964	50.00	100.00	200.00
—Red label with black or black & white Mercury logo at top					
MG-20402 [M]	Chantilly Lace	196?	6.25	12.50	25.00
—Red label with twelve Mercury logos on label edge					
MG-20402 [M]	Chantilly Lace	1975	3.75	7.50	15.00
—Chicago skyline label					
832902-1 [M]	Chantilly Lace	1988	3.75	7.50	15.00
—New number, black label					
PICKWICK					
SPC-3365	Chantilly Lace	1973	3.75	7.50	15.00
RHINO					
R1-70164	Helloooo Baby! The Best of the Big Bopper 1954-1959	1989	3.00	6.00	12.00

BIG BROTHER

Number	Title (A Side/B Side)	Yr	VG	VG+	NM
45s					
ALL AMERICAN					
5718	E.S.P./Brother, Where Are You	1970	10.00	20.00	40.00
Albums					
ALL-AMERICAN					
5770	Big Brother	1970	37.50	75.00	150.00

BIG BROTHER AND THE HOLDING COMPANY
Also see JANIS JOPLIN.

Number	Title (A Side/B Side)	Yr	VG	VG+	NM
45s					
COLUMBIA					
44626	Piece of My Heart/Turtle Blues	1968	2.50	5.00	10.00
45284	Keep On/Home on the Strange	1970	—	3.00	6.00
45502	Black Widow Spider/Nu Boogaloo Jam	1971	—	3.00	6.00
MAINSTREAM					
657	All Is Loneliness/Blindman	1967	3.00	6.00	12.00
662	Down on Me/Call On Me	1967	3.00	6.00	12.00
666	Bye Bye Baby/Intruder	1968	3.00	6.00	12.00
675	Women Is Losers/Caterpillar	1968	3.00	6.00	12.00
675	Women Is Losers/Light Is Faster Than Sound	1968	3.00	6.00	12.00
678	Coo Coo/The Last Time	1968	3.00	6.00	12.00
Albums					
COLUMBIA					
KCL 2900 [M]	Cheap Thrills	1968	75.00	150.00	300.00
—Red label stock copy has been confirmed					
KCS 9700	Cheap Thrills	1970	3.00	6.00	12.00
—Orange label					
KCS 9700 [M]	Cheap Thrills	1968	25.00	50.00	100.00
—White label "Special Mono Radio Station Copy" with stereo number					
KCS 9700 [S]	Cheap Thrills	1968	6.25	12.50	25.00
—Red "360 Sound" label					

Number	Title (A Side/B Side)	Yr	VG	VG+	NM
PC 9700	Cheap Thrills	198?	2.00	4.00	8.00
—Reissue with new prefix					
C 30222	Be a Brother	1970	5.00	10.00	20.00
C 30631	Big Brother and the Holding Company	1971	5.00	10.00	20.00
—Reissue of Mainstream LP with two extra tracks					
C 30738	How Hard It Is	1971	5.00	10.00	20.00
COLUMBIA SPECIAL PRODUCTS					
P 13313	Big Brother and the Holding Company	197?	3.75	7.50	15.00
MAINSTREAM					
S-6099 [S]	Big Brother and the Holding Company	1967	12.50	25.00	50.00
56099 [M]	Big Brother and the Holding Company	1967	25.00	50.00	100.00

BIG DADDY AND HIS BOYS

Number	Title (A Side/B Side)	Yr	VG	VG+	NM
45s					
KING					
5013	Bacon Fat/Bad Boy	1957	6.25	12.50	25.00

BIG ED AND HIS COMBO

See EDDIE BURNS.

BIG FOOT

Number	Title (A Side/B Side)	Yr	VG	VG+	NM
Albums					
WINRO					
1004	Big Foot	1969	7.50	15.00	30.00

BIG FRANK AND THE ESSENCES

Number	Title (A Side/B Side)	Yr	VG	VG+	NM
45s					
BLUE ROCK					
4012	Secret/I Won't Let Her See Me Cry	1965	50.00	100.00	200.00
PHILIPS					
40283	Secret/I Won't Let Her See Me Cry	1965	25.00	50.00	100.00

BIG GUYS, THE

Number	Title (A Side/B Side)	Yr	VG	VG+	NM
45s					
PALETTE					
5110	Walkin' the Board/Faith 7	1963	6.25	12.50	25.00
5114	Propulsion/(B-side unknown)	1964	6.25	12.50	25.00
WARNER BROS.					
7047	Hang My Head and Cry/Mr. Cupid (Don't You Call on Me)	1967	12.50	25.00	50.00

BIG MAYBELLE

Number	Title (A Side/B Side)	Yr	VG	VG+	NM
45s					
BRUNSWICK					
55234	Candy/Cry	1962	3.00	6.00	12.00
55242	Cold, Cold Heart/Why Was I Born	1963	3.00	6.00	12.00
55256	Everybody's Got a Home But Me/How Deep Is the Ocean	1963	3.00	6.00	12.00
CHESS					
1967	It's a Man's Man's Man's World/Big Maybelle Sings the Blues	1966	2.50	5.00	10.00
OKEH					
6931	Gabbin' Blues/Rain Down Rain	1953	10.00	20.00	40.00
6955	Way Back Home/Just Want Your Love	1953	10.00	20.00	40.00
6998	Send for Me/Jimmy Mule	1953	10.00	20.00	40.00
7009	My Country Man/Maybelle's Blues	1953	10.00	20.00	40.00
7026	I've Got a Feelin'/You'll Never Know	1954	7.50	15.00	30.00
7042	My Big Mistake/I'm Gettin' 'Long Alright	1954	7.50	15.00	30.00
7053	Ain't No Use/Don't Leave Poor Me	1955	7.50	15.00	30.00
7060	Whole Lotta Shakin' Goin' On/One Monkey Don't Stop No Show	1955	7.50	15.00	30.00
7066	Such a Cutie/The Other Night	1956	7.50	15.00	30.00
7069	Gabbin' Blues/New Kind of Mambo	1956	7.50	15.00	30.00
PARAMOUNT					
0237	Blame It on Your Love/See See Rider	1973	—	3.00	6.00
PORT					
3002	Let Me Go/No Better for You	1965	3.00	6.00	12.00
ROJAC					
112	96 Tears/That's Life	1966	2.50	5.00	10.00
115	I Can't Wait Any Longer/Turn the World Around the Other Way	1967	2.00	4.00	8.00
116	Mama (He Treats Your Daughter Mean)/Keep That Man	1967	2.00	4.00	8.00
118	Quittin' Time/I Can't Wait Any Longer	1967	2.00	4.00	8.00
121	Heaven Will Welcome You, Dr. King/Eleanor Rigby	1968	2.50	5.00	10.00
124	How It Lies/Old Love Never Dies	1968	2.00	4.00	8.00
1003	Careless Love/My Mother's Eyes	196?	2.00	4.00	8.00
1969	Don't Pass Me By/It's Been Raining	1966	2.50	5.00	10.00
SAVOY					
1195	Candy/That's a Pretty Good Love	1956	5.00	10.00	20.00
1500	Mean to Me/Tell Me Who	1956	3.75	7.50	15.00
1512	I Don't Want to Cry/All of Me	1957	3.75	7.50	15.00
1519	Rock House/Jim	1957	3.75	7.50	15.00
1527	So Long/Ring Dang Dilly	1957	3.75	7.50	15.00
1536	Blues Early, Early (Part 1)/Blues Early, Early (Part 2)	1958	3.75	7.50	15.00
1541	White Christmas/Silent Night	1958	3.75	7.50	15.00
1558	Baby Won't You Please Come Home/Say It Isn't Do	1959	3.75	7.50	15.00
1572	A Good Man Is Hard to Find/Pitiful	1959	3.75	7.50	15.00
1576	Some of These Days/I Understand	1959	3.75	7.50	15.00
1583	I Got It Bad and That Ain't Good/Ramblin' Blues	1960	3.75	7.50	15.00
1583	I Got It Bad and That Ain't Good/Until the Real Thing Comes Along	1960	3.75	7.50	15.00
1595	I Ain't Got Nobody/Going Home Baby	1961	3.75	7.50	15.00
SCEPTER					
1288	I Don't Want to Cry/Yesterday's Kisses	1965	3.00	6.00	12.00
Albums					
BRUNSWICK					
BL 54107 [M]	What More Can a Woman Do	1962	12.50	25.00	50.00
BL 754107 [S]	What More Can a Woman Do	1962	17.50	35.00	70.00
BL 754142	The Gospel Soul of Big Maybelle	1968	10.00	20.00	40.00
EPIC					
EE 22011 [M]	Gabbin' Blues	196?	7.50	15.00	30.00
—Reissue of Okeh recordings					
PARAMOUNT					
PAS-1011 [(2)]	The Last of Big Maybelle	1973	6.25	12.50	25.00
ROJAC					
RS 123	Saga of the Good Life and Hard Times	196?	10.00	20.00	40.00
R 522 [M]	Got a Brand New Bag	1967	10.00	20.00	40.00
RS 522 [S]	Got a Brand New Bag	1967	10.00	20.00	40.00
SAVOY					
MG-14005 [M]	Big Maybelle Sings	1957	75.00	150.00	300.00
MG-14011 [M]	Blues, Candy and Big Maybelle	1958	75.00	150.00	300.00
SAVOY JAZZ					
SJL-1143	Roots of Rock 'n' Roll Vol. 13: Blues & Early Soul	1985	2.50	5.00	10.00
SJL-1168	Blues, Candy and Big Maybelle	1986	2.50	5.00	10.00
—Reissue of 14011					
SCEPTER					
S-522 [M]	The Soul of Big Maybelle	1964	10.00	20.00	40.00
SS-522 [S]	The Soul of Big Maybelle	1964	12.50	25.00	50.00

BIG STAR

Alex Chilton, formerly of THE BOX TOPS, was lead singer.

Number	Title (A Side/B Side)	Yr	VG	VG+	NM
45s					
ARDENT					
2902	When My Baby's Beside Me/In the Street	1972	6.25	12.50	25.00
2904	Watch the Sunrise/Don't Lie to Me	1972	6.25	12.50	25.00
—With correct song on B-side. Label has the number "AS-01180" on it.					
2904	Watch the Sunrise/Don't Lie to Me	1972	12.50	25.00	50.00
—B-side plays the song "Thirteen" in error. Label has the number "AS-01127" on it.					
2909	O My Soul/Morphatoo—I'm in Love with a Girl	1974	5.00	10.00	20.00
2912	September Girls/(B-side unknown)	1974	5.00	10.00	20.00
Albums					
ARDENT					
ADS-1501	Radio City	1974	7.50	15.00	30.00
ADS-2803	#1 Record	1972	6.25	12.50	25.00
PVC					
7903	Big Star's Third	1978	6.25	12.50	25.00
8933	Sister Lovers	1985	3.75	7.50	15.00
—Reissue of PVC 7903 with new title					

BIG THREE, THE

Also see CASS ELLIOT.

Number	Title (A Side/B Side)	Yr	VG	VG+	NM
45s					
ROULETTE					
4689	Nora's Dove (Dink's Song)/Grandfather's Clock	1966	2.50	5.00	10.00
TOLLIE					
9006	Winkin' Blinkin' and Nod/The Banjo Song	1964	3.00	6.00	12.00
Albums					
FM					
307 [M]	The Big Three	1963	7.50	15.00	30.00
S-307 [S]	The Big Three	1963	10.00	20.00	40.00
311 [M]	Live at the Recording Studio	1964	7.50	15.00	30.00
S-311 [S]	Live at the Recording Studio	1964	10.00	20.00	40.00
ROULETTE					
R-42000 [M]	The Big Three Featuring Cass Elliot	1967	5.00	10.00	20.00
SR-42000 [S]	The Big Three Featuring Cass Elliot	1967	6.25	12.50	25.00

BIG WHEELIE AND THE HUB CAPS

Number	Title (A Side/B Side)	Yr	VG	VG+	NM
45s					
MCA					
40951	Sh-Boom (Life Could Be a Dream)/Touch and Go	1978	—	2.50	5.00
SCEPTER					
12375	Elvis Presley Medley/Chuck Berry Medley	1973	2.50	5.00	10.00
12385	Little Richard Medley/Over the Mountain	1973	2.50	5.00	10.00
12392	Leader of the Pack/Redneck Rock and Rollers	1974	2.00	4.00	8.00
Albums					
SCEPTER					
SPS-5109	Solid Grease!	1973	3.00	6.00	12.00

BIKINIS, THE

Number	Title (A Side/B Side)	Yr	VG	VG+	NM
45s					
DOT					
15808	Fatima the Dreamer/Kitchy Koo	1958	6.25	12.50	25.00
15872	Chop Stick Rock/A'Right, A'Ready	1958	10.00	20.00	40.00
ROULETTE					
4073	Bikini/Boogie Rock 'n' Roll	1958	6.25	12.50	25.00
TOP RANK					
2032	Crazy Vibrations/Spunky	1959	6.25	12.50	25.00

BILK, ACKER

Number	Title (A Side/B Side)	Yr	VG	VG+	NM
45s					
ATCO					
6160	Summer Set/Acker's Away	1960	2.50	5.00	10.00
6190	Buona Sera/Corinne, Corinna	1961	2.50	5.00	10.00
6217	Stranger on the Shore/Cieleto Lindo	1962	3.00	6.00	12.00
6230	Above the Stars/Soft Sands	1962	2.50	5.00	10.00
6238	Lonely/Lime Light	1962	2.50	5.00	10.00
6247	A Taste of Honey/Only You (& You Alone)	1963	2.00	4.00	8.00
6264	Underneath the Arches/Lady of the Lake	1963	2.00	4.00	8.00
6269	Moonlight Tango/Never Love a Stranger	1963	2.00	4.00	8.00
6282	The Harem/Train Song	1964	2.00	4.00	8.00
6311	Dream Ska/Ska Face	1964	2.00	4.00	8.00
6323	The Good Life/Theme from Warsaw Concerto	1964	2.00	4.00	8.00
6441	La Playa/When You Are There	1966	—	3.00	6.00
6514	Limehouse Blues/Wot Cher (Knocked 'Em In the Old Kent Road)	1967	—	3.00	6.00
PYE					
71078	Aria/The Fool on the Hill	1976	—	2.00	4.00
REPRISE					
20090	Dardenella Part 1/Dardenella Part 2	1962	3.75	7.50	15.00

Number	Title (A Side/B Side)	Yr	VG	VG+	NM
Albums					
ATCO					
33-129 [M]	Stranger on the Shore	1961	3.75	7.50	15.00
SD 33-129 [S]	Stranger on the Shore	1961	5.00	10.00	20.00
33-144 [M]	Above the Stars	1962	3.75	7.50	15.00
SD 33-144 [S]	Above the Stars	1962	5.00	10.00	20.00
33-150 [M]	Only You	1963	3.75	7.50	15.00
SD 33-150 [S]	Only You	1963	5.00	10.00	20.00
33-158 [M]	Call Me Mister	1963	3.75	7.50	15.00
SD 33-158 [S]	Call Me Mister	1963	5.00	10.00	20.00
33-168 [M]	A Touch of Latin	1964	3.00	6.00	12.00
SD 33-168 [S]	A Touch of Latin	1964	3.75	7.50	15.00
33-170 [M]	Great Themes from Great Foreign Films	1965	3.00	6.00	12.00
SD 33-170 [S]	Great Themes from Great Foreign Films	1965	3.75	7.50	15.00
33-181 [M]	Acker Bilk in Paris	1966	3.00	6.00	12.00
SD 33-181 [S]	Acker Bilk in Paris	1966	3.75	7.50	15.00
GNP CRESCENDO					
GNPS-2116	The Best of Acker Bilk: His Clarinet and Strings	198?	2.50	5.00	10.00
GNPS-2171	The Best of Acker Bilk: His Clarinet and Strings, Volume 2	198?	2.50	5.00	10.00
GNPS-2191	Acker Bilk Plays Lennon and McCartney	1988	3.00	6.00	12.00
REPRISE					
R-6031 [M]	A Stranger No More	1962	5.00	10.00	20.00
RS-6031 [R]	A Stranger No More	1962	3.75	7.50	15.00

BILK, ACKER, AND KEN COLYER

Number	Title (A Side/B Side)	Yr	VG	VG+	NM
Albums					
STOMP OFF					
SOS-1119	It Looks Like a Big Time Tonight	198?	2.50	5.00	10.00

BILK, ACKER, AND BENT FABRIC

Also see each artist's individual listings.

Number	Title (A Side/B Side)	Yr	VG	VG+	NM
45s					
ATCO					
6378	Alley Cat/Stranger on the Shore	1965	—	3.00	6.00
Albums					
ATCO					
33-175 [M]	Together	1965	3.00	6.00	12.00
SD 33-175 [S]	Together	1965	3.75	7.50	15.00

BILLY AND LILLIE

Also see LILLIE BRYANT; BILLY FORD.

Number	Title (A Side/B Side)	Yr	VG	VG+	NM
45s					
ABC-PARAMOUNT					
10421	Love Me Sincerely/Whip It To Me Baby	1963	7.50	15.00	30.00
10489	Carry Me Across the Threshold/Why I Love Billy (Lillie)	1963	7.50	15.00	30.00
CAMEO					
412	Nothing Moves (Without a Little Push)/The Two of Us	1966	2.50	5.00	10.00
435	You Got Me by the Heart/Hear You Better Hear	1966	2.50	5.00	10.00
SWAN					
4002	La Dee Dah/The Monster	1957	7.50	15.00	30.00
—"SWAN" in all capital letters; B-side by Billy Ford and the Thunderbirds					
4002	La Dee Dah/The Monster	1958	5.00	10.00	20.00
—Only the S in "Swan" is capitalized; B-side by Billy Ford and the Thunderbirds					
4005	Happiness/Creepin' Crawlin' Cryin'	1958	5.00	10.00	20.00
4011	The Greasy Spoon/Hanging On to You	1958	5.00	10.00	20.00
4020	Lucky Ladybug/I Promise You	1958	6.25	12.50	25.00
4030	Tumbled Down/A.H. Thomas the Cat	1959	3.75	7.50	15.00
4036	Bells, Bells, Bells/Honeymoonin'	1959	3.75	7.50	15.00
4042	Terrific Together/Swampy	1959	3.75	7.50	15.00
4051	Free for All/The Ins and Outs of Love	1960	3.75	7.50	15.00
4058	That's the Way the Cookie Crumbles (Ah-So)/ Over the Mountain, Across the Sea	1960	3.75	7.50	15.00
4069	Ain't Comin' Back (To You)/Bananas	1961	3.75	7.50	15.00

BILLY AND THE BEATERS

See BILLY VERA.

BILLY AND THE ESSENTIALS

Number	Title (A Side/B Side)	Yr	VG	VG+	NM
45s					
CAMEO					
344	Remember Me Baby/The Actor	1965	100.00	200.00	400.00
JAMIE					
1229	The Dance Is Over/Steady Girl	1962	7.50	15.00	30.00
1239	Over the Weekend/Maybe You'll Be There	1962	7.50	15.00	30.00
LANDA					
691	The Dance Is Over/Steady Girl	1962	12.50	25.00	50.00
MERCURY					
72127	Young at Heart/Lonely Weekend	1963	6.25	12.50	25.00
72210	Last Dance/Yes Sir, That's My Baby	1963	6.25	12.50	25.00
SMASH					
2045	Babalu's Wedding Day/My Way of Saying	1966	3.75	7.50	15.00
2071	Don't Cry (Sing Along with the Music)/Baby Go Away	1966	3.00	6.00	12.00
SSS INTERNATIONAL					
706	I Wrote a Song/Oh What a Feeling	1967	3.00	6.00	12.00

BILLY BOY

Number	Title (A Side/B Side)	Yr	VG	VG+	NM
45s					
VEE JAY					
146	I Wish You the World/I Was Fooled	1955	20.00	40.00	80.00
171	I Ain't Got You/Don't Stay Out All Night	1956	20.00	40.00	80.00
—Label lists artist as "Billy Boy Arnold"					
192	Here's My Picture/You've Got Me Wrong	1956	10.00	20.00	40.00
238	Kissing at Midnight/My Heart Is Crying	1957	10.00	20.00	40.00
260	Rockinitis/Prisoner's Plea	1957	10.00	20.00	40.00

BILLY JOE AND THE CHECKMATES

Number	Title (A Side/B Side)	Yr	VG	VG+	NM
45s					
DORE					
620	Percolator (Twist)/Round & Round & Round & Round	1961	3.75	7.50	15.00
636	Rocky's Theme/Twist That Thing	1962	3.00	6.00	12.00
643	The Chester Drag/Laughing Machine Gunner	1962	3.00	6.00	12.00
652	Chalypso Dancer/My Friend, the Rain	1962	3.00	6.00	12.00
664	Solid Gold Hubcaps/Laughing Woodpecker	1963	3.00	6.00	12.00
668	Bossville/One More Cup	1963	3.00	6.00	12.00
680	Shake, Shake, Shake/Summertime in Venice	1963	3.00	6.00	12.00
685	Last Dance/My Friend the Rain	1963	3.00	6.00	12.00
694	The Drifter/Nashville West (One More Time)	1963	3.00	6.00	12.00
697	Forbidden Planet/Slauson, Baby, Slauson	1964	3.00	6.00	12.00
703	Spotlight Dance/Zip Code	1964	3.00	6.00	12.00
720	C'mopn Everybody (Part 1)/C'mon Everybody (Part 2)	1964	3.00	6.00	12.00
728	Bells of Rome/Shadows	1965	2.50	5.00	10.00
747	Clair de Looney/Holding Hands	1966	2.50	5.00	10.00
756	Voyage to the Bottom of the Sea/Nutty Dance Instructor	1966	2.50	5.00	10.00
791	A Man and a Woman/Floatin'	1967	2.50	5.00	10.00
857	Ambrosia/Newport Beach Concerto	1971	—	3.00	6.00
871	Try It, You'll Like It/Topless Dancer	1972	—	2.50	5.00
884	Aphrodisiac (Part 1)/Aphrodisiac (Part 2)	1973	—	2.50	5.00
892	Flaky (same on both sides)	1974	—	2.50	5.00
982	Raindrops, Mem'ries, and Tears/Liuvio, Memorias, y Lagramas	1985	—	2.00	4.00

BILLY THE KID

Number	Title (A Side/B Side)	Yr	VG	VG+	NM
45s					
KAPP					
261	Apron Strings/I Hardly Know You	1959	3.00	6.00	12.00

BINGHAM, J.B.

Number	Title (A Side/B Side)	Yr	VG	VG+	NM
45s					
UNITED ARTISTS					
XW816	All Alone by the Telephone/Live and You Learn	1976	3.75	7.50	15.00
XW872	She's Gone/Keep On Walking	1976	3.75	7.50	15.00
WARNER BROS.					
7775	Sunshine/Peek-A-Boo	1974	2.50	5.00	10.00

BINKLEY, JIMMY

Number	Title (A Side/B Side)	Yr	VG	VG+	NM
45s					
ALADDIN					
3193	Night Life/Hot Smoke	1953	30.00	60.00	120.00
CHANCE					
1134	Hey, Hey Sugar Ray/Midnite Wail	1953	50.00	100.00	200.00
CHECKER					
789	Wine, Wine, Wine/Boogie On the Hour	1954	50.00	100.00	200.00
835	Messin' Around/You Made a Boo-Boo	1956	25.00	50.00	100.00
NOTE					
10002	Why Oh Why/Blue Moon	1957	75.00	150.00	300.00

BIRD WATCHERS, THE

Number	Title (A Side/B Side)	Yr	VG	VG+	NM
45s					
LAURIE					
3399	Turn Around Girl/You Got It	1967	3.00	6.00	12.00
MALA					
527	Girl I've Got News for You/Eddie's Tune	1966	7.50	15.00	30.00
536	I'm Gonna Love You Anyway/A Little Bit of Lovin'	1966	7.50	15.00	30.00
548	I'm Gonna Do It to You/I Have No Worried Mind	1966	7.50	15.00	30.00
555	Mary Mary (It's to You That I Belong)/Cry a Little Bit	1967	7.50	15.00	30.00

BIRDSONG, EDWIN

Number	Title (A Side/B Side)	Yr	VG	VG+	NM
12-Inch Singles					
PHILADELPHIA INT'L					
3671	Phiss-Phizz/Goldmine	1979	2.00	4.00	8.00
45s					
PHILADELPHIA INT'L					
3659	Kunta Dance Part 1/Kunta Dance Part 2	1978	—	2.00	4.00
3670	Phiss-Phizz/Goldmine	1979	—	2.00	4.00
POLYDOR					
14058	The Old Messiah/Use What You Got	1970	—	2.50	5.00
—With Doug McClure					
14095	It Ain't No Fun Being a Welfare Recipient/Uncle Tom Game	1971	—	2.50	5.00
14118	My Father Preaches That God Is the Father of Us All/The Spirit of Do Do	1972	—	2.50	5.00
14186	Rising Sign/Rising Sign Climax	1973	—	2.50	5.00
14192	Rising Sign/Grow Some Flowers, You Will Learn to Love the Rain	1973	—	2.50	5.00
14224	Turn Around Hate (Communicate)/Down on the Beat	1974	—	2.50	5.00
SALSOUL					
2135	Rapper Dapper Snapper/(Instrumental)	1981	—	2.00	4.00
7019	Funtaztik/Win Tonight	1982	—	2.00	4.00
7024	She's Wrapped Too Tight (She's a Button Buster)/ (Instrumental)	1982	—	2.00	4.00
Albums					
ABC DUNHILL					
DSX-51036	Can't Stop the Madness	1974	3.75	7.50	15.00
PHILADELPHIA INT'L.					
JZ 35758	Edwin Birdsong	1978	2.50	5.00	10.00
POLYDOR					
24-4071	What It Is	1971	3.00	6.00	12.00
PD-5057	Super Natural	1973	3.00	6.00	12.00
SALSOUL					
SA-8550	Funktaztic	1981	2.50	5.00	10.00

BIRKIN, JANE, AND SERGE GAINSBOURG

Number	Title (A Side/B Side)	Yr	VG	VG+	NM
45s					
FONTANA					
1665	Je T'Aime...Moi Non Plus/Jane B	1969	2.00	4.00	8.00
1684	La Decadanse/Les Langues de Chat	1969	—	2.50	5.00
Albums					
FONTANA					
SRF-67610	Je T'aime	1970	5.00	10.00	20.00

BIRTH CONTROL

Number	Title (A Side/B Side)	Yr	VG	VG+	NM
Albums					
PROPHESY					
PRS-1002	Birth Control: A New German Rock Group	1970	7.50	15.00	30.00

BISCAYNES, THE

Number	Title (A Side/B Side)	Yr	VG	VG+	NM
45s					
NORTHRIDGE					
1001	Church Key/Moment of Truth	1963	15.00	30.00	60.00
—B-side by the Surfaris					
REPRISE					
20180	Church Key/Moment of Truth	1963	7.50	15.00	30.00
—B-side by the Surfaris					

BISHOP, EDDIE

Number	Title (A Side/B Side)	Yr	VG	VG+	NM
45s					
ABC					
10858	Candy Man/What You're Doing to Me	1966	6.25	12.50	25.00
ABC-PARAMOUNT					
10799	What Did He Say?/Call Me	1966	15.00	30.00	60.00

BISHOP, ELVIN

Number	Title (A Side/B Side)	Yr	VG	VG+	NM
45s					
CAPRICORN					
0054	Fooled Around and Fell in Love/Struttin' My Stuff	197?	—	2.00	4.00
—Hall of Fame Series					
0202	Fishin'/Travelin' Blues	1974	—	2.00	4.00
0222	Can't Go Back/Let It Flow	1975	—	2.00	4.00
0237	Arkansas Line/Sure Feels Good	1975	—	2.00	4.00
0243	Calling All Cows/Juke Joint Jump	1975	—	2.00	4.00
0248	Silent Night (Vocal Version)/Silent Night (Instrumental Version)	1975	—	3.00	6.00
0252	Fooled Around and Fell in Love/Have a Good Time	1976	—	2.50	5.00
—This is actually the second pressing, bit it's harder to find than the first					
0252	Fooled Around and Fell in Love/Slick Titty Boom	1976	—	2.00	4.00
0256	Struttin' My Stuff/Grab All the Love	1976	—	2.00	4.00
0266	Spend Some Time/Sugar Dumplin	1976	—	2.00	4.00
0269	Keep It Cool/Yes Sir	1976	—	2.00	4.00
0285	Rock My Soul/Yes Sir	1978	—	2.00	4.00
0296	Fooled Around and Fell in Love/Travelin' Shoes	1978	—	2.00	4.00
0313	It's a Feeling/Right Now Is the Hour	1979	—	2.00	4.00
EPIC					
10926	Rock My Soul/Holler and Shout	1973	—	2.50	5.00
11022	Last Mile/Stealin' Watermelons	1973	—	2.50	5.00
FILLMORE					
7002	So Fine/(B-side unknown)	1971	—	3.00	6.00
7003	Don't Fight It, Feel It/(B-side unknown)	1971	—	3.00	6.00
7004	I Just Can't Go On/(B-side unknown)	1971	—	3.00	6.00
Albums					
ALLIGATOR					
AL-4767	Big Fun	1987	2.50	5.00	10.00
CAPRICORN					
CP 0134	Let It Flow	1974	3.00	6.00	12.00
CP 0151	Juke Joint Jump	1975	3.00	6.00	12.00
CP 0165	Struttin' My Stuff	1975	3.00	6.00	12.00
CPN-0165	Struttin' My Stuff	1980	2.50	5.00	10.00
—Reissue with revised prefix and Polygram distribution					
CP 0176	Hometown Boy Makes Good!	1976	3.00	6.00	12.00
2CP 0185 [(2)]	Live! Raisin' Hell	1977	3.75	7.50	15.00
CP 0215	Hog Heaven	1978	3.00	6.00	12.00
EPIC					
KE 31563	Rock My Soul	1972	3.75	7.50	15.00
PE 33693	The Best of Elvin Bishop	1975	3.00	6.00	12.00
FILLMORE					
F 30001	Elvin Bishop Group	1969	5.00	10.00	20.00
Z 30239	Feel It	1970	5.00	10.00	20.00

BISHOP, JOEY

Number	Title (A Side/B Side)	Yr	VG	VG+	NM
Albums					
ABC					
ABCS-656	Joey Bishop Sings Country and Western	1968	7.50	15.00	30.00

BIT 'A SWEET

Number	Title (A Side/B Side)	Yr	VG	VG+	NM
45s					
ABC					
11125	The Second Time/2086	1968	5.00	10.00	20.00
MGM					
13695	Out of Sight, Out of Mind/It Is On, It Is Off	1967	6.25	12.50	25.00
Albums					
ABC					
S-640	Hypnotic 1	1968	10.00	20.00	40.00

BJORN AND BENNY

Early ABBA.

Number	Title (A Side/B Side)	Yr	VG	VG+	NM
45s					
PLAYBOY					
50014	Merry-Go-Round/People Need Love	1972	7.50	15.00	30.00
50018	Another Town, Another Train/I Am Just a Girl	1973	7.50	15.00	30.00
50025	Rock 'N Roll Band/Another Town, Another Train	1973	7.50	15.00	30.00

BLACK, BILL, 'S COMBO

Number	Title (A Side/B Side)	Yr	VG	VG+	NM
45s					
COLUMBIA					
44867	But It's Alright/Slow Action	1969	—	2.50	5.00
44983	California Dreamin'/Funky Train	1969	—	2.50	5.00
45092	Heaven Knows/One Five One Eight Chelsea	1970	—	2.50	5.00
45162	Keep the Customer Satisfied/One Five One Eight Chelsea	1970	—	2.50	5.00
HI					
2018	Smokie (Part 2)/Smokie (Part 1)	1959	5.00	10.00	20.00
2021	White Silver Sands/The Wheel	1960	5.00	10.00	20.00
2022	Josephine/Dry Bones	1960	3.75	7.50	15.00
2022 [PS]	Josephine/Dry Bones	1960	6.25	12.50	25.00
2026	Don't Be Cruel/Rollin'	1960	3.75	7.50	15.00
2026 [PS]	Don't Be Cruel/Rollin'	1960	6.25	12.50	25.00
2027	Blue Tango/Willie	1960	3.75	7.50	15.00
2027 [PS]	Blue Tango/Willie	1960	6.25	12.50	25.00
2028	Hearts of Stone/Royal Blue	1961	3.00	6.00	12.00
2029	Old Time Religion/He's Got the Whole World in His Hands	1961	10.00	20.00	40.00
—Stereo single, small hole, plays at 33 1/3 rpm					
2030	Do Lord/When the Roll Is Called Up Yonder	1961	10.00	20.00	40.00
—Stereo single, small hole, plays at 33 1/3 rpm					
2031	Down by the Riverside/It Is No Secret (What God Can Do)	1961	10.00	20.00	40.00
—Stereo single, small hole, plays at 33 1/3 rpm					
2032	When the Saints Go Marching In/(B-side unknown)	1961	10.00	20.00	40.00
—Stereo single, small hole, plays at 33 1/3 rpm					
2033	Just a Closer Walk with Thee/This Old House	1961	10.00	20.00	40.00
—Stereo single, small hole, plays at 33 1/3 rpm					
2036	Ole Buttermilk Sky/Yogi	1961	3.00	6.00	12.00
2036 [PS]	Ole Buttermilk Sky/Yogi	1961	6.25	12.50	25.00
2038	Movin'/Honky Train	1961	3.00	6.00	12.00
2042	Twist-Her/My Girl Josephine	1961	3.00	6.00	12.00
2045	Twist-Her/Night Train	1962	10.00	20.00	40.00
—Stereo single, small hole, plays at 33 1/3 rpm					
2046	The Hucklebuck/Corrina, Corrina	1962	10.00	20.00	40.00
—Stereo single, small hole, plays at 33 1/3 rpm					
2047	Johnny B. Goode/(B-side unknown)	1962	10.00	20.00	40.00
—Stereo single, small hole, plays at 33 1/3 rpm					
2048	Josephine/My Girl Josephine	1962	10.00	20.00	40.00
—Stereo single, small hole, plays at 33 1/3 rpm					
2049	Slippin' and Slidin'/Twist with Me, Baby	1962	10.00	20.00	40.00
—Stereo single, small hole, plays at 33 1/3 rpm					
2052	Twistin' — White Silver Sands/My Babe	1962	3.00	6.00	12.00
2052 [PS]	Twistin' — White Silver Sands/My Babe	1962	6.25	12.50	25.00
2055	So What/Blues for the Red Boy	1962	3.00	6.00	12.00
2059	Joey's Song/Hot Taco	1962	3.00	6.00	12.00
2064	Do It — Rat Now/Little Jasper	1963	3.00	6.00	12.00
2069	Monkey-Shine/Love Gone	1963	3.00	6.00	12.00
2072	Comin' On/Soft Winds	1964	3.00	6.00	12.00
2077	Tequila/Raunchy	1964	3.00	6.00	12.00
2079	Little Queenie/Boo Ray	1964	3.00	6.00	12.00
2085	Come On Home/He'll Have to Go	1964	2.50	5.00	10.00
2094	Spootin'/Crazy Feeling	1965	2.50	5.00	10.00
2106	Hey, Good Lookin'/Mountain of Love	1966	2.50	5.00	10.00
2115	Rambler/You Call Everybody Darling	1966	2.50	5.00	10.00
2124	Son of Smokie/Peg Leg	1967	2.00	4.00	8.00
2145	Turn On Your Love Life/Ribbon of Darkness	1968	—	3.00	6.00
2153	Red Light/Bright Lights, Big City	1968	—	3.00	6.00
2168	Creepin' Around/The Son of Hickory Holler's Tramp	1969	—	3.00	6.00
2185	No More/Closin' Time	1971	—	2.50	5.00
2208	Daylite/Four A.M.	1972	—	2.50	5.00
2234	Smokey Bourbon Street/Mighty Fine	1973	—	2.50	5.00
2277	Soul Serenade/Pickin'	1974	—	2.00	4.00
2283	Truck Stop/Boilin' Cabbage	1975	—	2.00	4.00
2291	Almost Persuaded/Back Up and Push	1975	—	2.00	4.00
2301	Fire on the Bayou/Memphis Soul	1976	—	2.00	4.00
2311	I Can Help/Jump Back Joe	1976	—	2.00	4.00
2317	Redneck Rock/Yakety Sax	1976	—	2.00	4.00
78508	Cashin' In (A Tribute to Luther Perkins)/L.A. Blues	1978	—	2.00	4.00
MEGA					
0036	Rings/Cotton Carnival	1971	—	2.50	5.00
0052	Oh Happy Day/Sugar Cured	1971	—	2.50	5.00
0070	Harlem Nocturne/Sassy Parts	1972	—	2.50	5.00
0086	Night Train/Bluff City	1972	—	2.50	5.00
0113	Listen to the Music/Memphis Shuffle	1973	—	2.50	5.00
0117	Satin Sheets/Memphis Shuffle	1973	—	2.50	5.00
201	Smokie Part 2/Tequila	1973	—	2.50	5.00
207	Oh Happy Day/Listen to the Music	1974	—	2.00	4.00
7-Inch Extended Plays					
HI					
HSP 2 [PS]	(title unknown)	1962	3.75	7.50	15.00
HSP 2 [S]	My Babe/40 Miles of Bad Road/Ain't That Lovin' You Baby//What'd I Say/The Walk/Witchcraft	1962	3.75	7.50	15.00
—33 1/3 rpm jukebox single, small hole					
SBG 26 [PS]	Bill Black's Combo Goes Big Band	196?	2.50	5.00	10.00
SBG 26 [S]	T.D.'s Boogie Woogie/Tuxedo Junction/ Canadian Sunset//Leap Frog/In the Mood/So Rare	196?	2.50	5.00	10.00
—33 1/3 rpm jukebox single, small hole					
HE 22002	Honky Tonk/Cherry Pink//Singing the Blues/You Win Again	1961	10.00	20.00	40.00
HE 22002 [PS]	Solid and Raunchy	1961	10.00	20.00	40.00
Albums					
COLUMBIA					
CS 1055	Basic Black	1970	3.00	6.00	12.00
CS 9848	Black with Sugar	1969	3.00	6.00	12.00
CS 9957	Raindrops Keep Fallin' on My Head	1970	3.00	6.00	12.00
HI					
6005	Award Winners	1978	2.50	5.00	10.00
8004	Memphis Tennessee	1977	2.50	5.00	10.00

Number	Title (A Side/B Side)	Yr	VG	VG+	NM
HL-12001 [M]	Smokie	1960	15.00	30.00	60.00
—Black label with red and silver logo					
HL-12001 [M]	Smokie	1960	10.00	20.00	40.00
—Orange and white label					
HL-12002 [M]	Saxy Jazz	1960	10.00	20.00	40.00
HL-12003 [M]	Solid and Raunchy	1960	10.00	20.00	40.00
HL-12004 [M]	That Wonderful Feeling	1961	5.00	10.00	20.00
HL-12005 [M]	Movin'	1961	5.00	10.00	20.00
HL-12006 [M]	Bill Black's Record Hop	1961	6.25	12.50	25.00
HL-12006 [M]	Let's Twist Her	1961	3.75	7.50	15.00
—Retitled version of above					
HL-12009 [M]	The Untouchable Sound of Bill Black	1962	3.75	7.50	15.00
HL-12012 [M]	Bill Black's Greatest Hits	1963	3.75	7.50	15.00
HL-12013 [M]	Bill Black's Combo Goes West	1963	3.75	7.50	15.00
HL-12015 [M]	Bill Black Plays the Blues	1964	3.75	7.50	15.00
HL-12017 [M]	Bill Black Plays Tunes by Chuck Berry	1964	3.75	7.50	15.00
HL-12020 [M]	Bill Black's Combo Goes Big Band	1964	3.75	7.50	15.00
HL-12023 [M]	More Solid and Raunchy	1965	3.75	7.50	15.00
HL-12027 [M]	Mr. Beat	1965	3.75	7.50	15.00
HL-12032 [M]	All Timers	1966	3.00	6.00	12.00
HL-12033 [M]	Black Lace	1966	3.00	6.00	12.00
HL-12036 [M]	King of the Road	1966	3.00	6.00	12.00
HL-12041 [M]	The Beat Goes On	1967	3.75	7.50	15.00
HL-12044 [M]	Turn Your Lovelight On	1967	3.75	7.50	15.00
HL-12047 [M]	Soulin' the Blues	1968	3.75	7.50	15.00
SHL-32001 [R]	Smokie	1964	5.00	10.00	20.00
SHL-32002 [R]	Saxy Jazz	1964	5.00	10.00	20.00
SHL-32003 [R]	Solid and Raunchy	1964	5.00	10.00	20.00
SHL-32004 [S]	That Wonderful Feeling	1961	6.25	12.50	25.00
SHL-32005 [S]	Movin'	1961	6.25	12.50	25.00
SHL-32006 [S]	Bill Black's Record Hop	1961	7.50	15.00	30.00
SHL-32006 [S]	Let's Twist Her	1961	5.00	10.00	20.00
—Retitled version of above					
SHL-32009 [S]	The Untouchable Sound of Bill Black	1962	5.00	10.00	20.00
SHL-32012 [S]	Bill Black's Greatest Hits	1963	5.00	10.00	20.00
SHL-32013 [S]	Bill Black's Combo Goes West	1963	5.00	10.00	20.00
SHL-32015 [S]	Bill Black Plays the Blues	1964	5.00	10.00	20.00
SHL-32017 [S]	Bill Black Plays Tunes by Chuck Berry	1964	5.00	10.00	20.00
SHL-32020 [S]	Bill Black's Combo Goes Big Band	1964	5.00	10.00	20.00
SHL-32023 [S]	More Solid and Raunchy	1965	5.00	10.00	20.00
SHL-32027 [S]	Mr. Beat	1965	5.00	10.00	20.00
SHL-32032 [S]	All Timers	1966	3.75	7.50	15.00
SHL-32033 [S]	Black Lace	1966	3.75	7.50	15.00
SHL-32036 [S]	King of the Road	1966	3.75	7.50	15.00
SHL-32041 [S]	The Beat Goes On	1967	3.75	7.50	15.00
SHL-32044 [S]	Turn Your Lovelight On	1967	3.75	7.50	15.00
SHL-32047 [S]	Soulin' the Blues	1968	3.75	7.50	15.00
SHL-32052	Solid and Raunchy The 3rd	1969	3.75	7.50	15.00
SHL-32061	More Magic	1971	3.00	6.00	12.00
XSHL-32078	Bill Black's Greatest Hits, Vol. 2	1973	3.00	6.00	12.00
XSHL-32088	Solid and Country	1974	3.00	6.00	12.00
SHL-32093	The World's Greatest Honky Tonk Band	1975	3.00	6.00	12.00
SHL-32104	It's Honky Tonk Time	1976	3.00	6.00	12.00

MEGA

Number	Title (A Side/B Side)	Yr	VG	VG+	NM
MLPS-600	Bill Black Is Back	1973	3.00	6.00	12.00
31-1008	The Memphis Scene	1971	3.00	6.00	12.00
31-1014	Juke Box Favorites	1972	3.00	6.00	12.00
51-5008	Rock 'n' Roll Forever	1973	3.00	6.00	12.00

BLACK, CILLA

45s

BELL

Number	Title (A Side/B Side)	Yr	VG	VG+	NM
726	Step Inside Love/I Couldn't Take My Eyes Off You	1968	5.00	10.00	20.00

CAPITOL

Number	Title (A Side/B Side)	Yr	VG	VG+	NM
5196	You're My World/Suffer Now I Must	1964	3.75	7.50	15.00
5258	It's for You/He Won't Ask Me	1964	3.00	6.00	12.00
5373	One Little Voice/Is It Love	1965	3.00	6.00	12.00
5414	I've Been Wrong Before/My Love Came Home	1965	3.00	6.00	12.00
5595	Love's Just a Broken Heart/Yesterday	1966	3.00	6.00	12.00
5595 [PS]	Love's Just a Broken Heart/Yesterday	1966	7.50	15.00	30.00
5674	Alfie/Night Time Is Here	1966	3.00	6.00	12.00
5763	Don't Answer Me/The Right One Is Left	1966	3.00	6.00	12.00
5782	A Fool Am I/For No One	1966	3.00	6.00	12.00

DJM

Number	Title (A Side/B Side)	Yr	VG	VG+	NM
70007	What the World Needs Now Is Love/Only Forever Will Do	1969	2.00	4.00	8.00
70011	Without Him/It'll Never Happen Again	1969	2.00	4.00	8.00
70012	Surround Yourself with Sorrow/It'll Never Happen Again	1969	2.00	4.00	8.00
70014	Conversations/London Bridge	1969	2.00	4.00	8.00
70015	If I Thought You'd Ever Change Your Mind/It Feels So Good	1970	2.00	4.00	8.00
70016	If I Thought You'd Ever Change Your Mind/Conversations	1970	2.00	4.00	8.00
70018 [DJ]	Across the Universe (mono/stereo)	1970	3.00	6.00	12.00

EMI

Number	Title (A Side/B Side)	Yr	VG	VG+	NM
4003	He Was a Writer/I'll Never Run Out of You	1974	—	3.00	6.00

PRIVATE STOCK

Number	Title (A Side/B Side)	Yr	VG	VG+	NM
45040	I'll Take a Tango/To Know Him Is To Love Him	1975	—	2.50	5.00
45077	Fantasy/It's Now	1976	—	2.50	5.00

Albums

CAPITOL

Number	Title (A Side/B Side)	Yr	VG	VG+	NM
ST 2308 [S]	Is It Love?	1965	10.00	20.00	40.00
T 2308 [M]	Is It Love?	1965	6.25	12.50	25.00

BLACK, JAY

The second "Jay" of JAY AND THE AMERICANS.

12-Inch Singles

MILLENNIUM

Number	Title (A Side/B Side)	Yr	VG	VG+	NM
20614	Love Is In the Air/Please Stay	1978	3.75	7.50	15.00

ROULETTE

Number	Title (A Side/B Side)	Yr	VG	VG+	NM
2005	One Night Affair/Fill Me Up	1976	3.75	7.50	15.00
—B-side by Caress					

45s

ATLANTIC

Number	Title (A Side/B Side)	Yr	VG	VG+	NM
3273	Dolphins/Running Scared	1975	—	2.50	5.00

MIDSONG INT'L

Number	Title (A Side/B Side)	Yr	VG	VG+	NM
72012	The Part of Me That Needs You Most/You Stole the Music	1980	—	2.00	4.00

MILLENNIUM

Number	Title (A Side/B Side)	Yr	VG	VG+	NM
618	Love Is In the Air/Please Stay	1978	—	2.50	5.00

PRIVATE STOCK

Number	Title (A Side/B Side)	Yr	VG	VG+	NM
45058	Every Time You Walk in the Room/I'd Build a Bridge	1975	—	2.50	5.00

ROULETTE

Number	Title (A Side/B Side)	Yr	VG	VG+	NM
7198	One Night Affair/Between Two Worlds	1976	—	3.00	6.00

UNITED ARTISTS

Number	Title (A Side/B Side)	Yr	VG	VG+	NM
50116	What Will My Mary Say/Return to Me	1967	3.00	6.00	12.00
50116 [PS]	What Will My Mary Say/Return to Me	1967	6.25	12.50	25.00

BLACK, OSCAR

45s

ATLANTIC

Number	Title (A Side/B Side)	Yr	VG	VG+	NM
956	Love, Love, Love/Troubled Man Blues	1952	37.50	75.00	150.00

GROOVE

Number	Title (A Side/B Side)	Yr	VG	VG+	NM
0012	I'll Get By/Hold Me Baby	1954	15.00	30.00	60.00
—With Sue Allen					
0102	Be My Baby/Ain't Nobody Home But Me	1955	15.00	30.00	60.00
—With Sue Allen					
0115	Baby, Please Don't Go/I'll Live My Life Alone	1955	15.00	30.00	60.00
—With Sue Allen					
0130	Think of Tomorrow/Set a Wedding Day	1955	15.00	30.00	60.00
—With Sue Allen and the Four Students					
0168	Into Each Heart (Some Tears Must Fall)/If I Cry Tomorrow	1956	12.50	25.00	50.00
—With Sue Allen					

SAVOY

Number	Title (A Side/B Side)	Yr	VG	VG+	NM
1600	I Got a Feeling/I'm a Fool to Care	1961	3.75	7.50	15.00

BLACK, TERRY

45s

DUNHILL

Number	Title (A Side/B Side)	Yr	VG	VG+	NM
4005	How Many Guys/Only Sixteen	1965	2.50	5.00	10.00
4046	Ordinary Girl/Baby's Gone	1966	2.50	5.00	10.00

TOLLIE

Number	Title (A Side/B Side)	Yr	VG	VG+	NM
9026	Unless You Care/Can't We Go Somewhere	1964	3.00	6.00	12.00
9041	Say It Again/Everyone Can Tell	1965	3.00	6.00	12.00
9041 [PS]	Say It Again/Everyone Can Tell	1965	5.00	10.00	20.00

BLACK, TERRY, AND LAUREL WARD

45s

KAMA SUTRA

Number	Title (A Side/B Side)	Yr	VG	VG+	NM
540	Oh Babe/Goin' Down	1972	—	2.50	5.00

BLACK, ZELL

45s

MOTOWN

Number	Title (A Side/B Side)	Yr	VG	VG+	NM
1281	I'd Hate Myself in the Morning/Take My Word	1973	—	2.50	5.00
1290	I Been Had by the Devil/Confession	1974	—	2.50	5.00

WARNER BROS.

Number	Title (A Side/B Side)	Yr	VG	VG+	NM
8138	Fly Me Part 1/You Make the Sun Keep Shining	1975	—	2.00	4.00
8202	Fly Me/Ride On Rider	1976	—	2.00	4.00

BLACK HEAT

45s

ATLANTIC

Number	Title (A Side/B Side)	Yr	VG	VG+	NM
2890	Street of Tears/Ship's Funk	1972	—	2.50	5.00
2934	The Jungle Part 1/The Jungle Part 2	1973	—	2.50	5.00
2987	No Time to Burn/Supercool	1973	—	2.50	5.00
3033	Check It All Out/M & M's	1974	—	2.50	5.00
3258	Drive My Car/Questions and Conclusions	1975	—	2.50	5.00

Albums

ATLANTIC

Number	Title (A Side/B Side)	Yr	VG	VG+	NM
SD 7237	Black Heat	1972	3.00	6.00	12.00
SD 7294	No Time to Burn	1974	3.00	6.00	12.00
SD 18128	Keep On Burnin'	1975	3.00	6.00	12.00

BLACK IVORY

45s

BUDDAH

Number	Title (A Side/B Side)	Yr	VG	VG+	NM
443	Will We Ever Come Together/Warm Inside	1975	—	2.00	4.00
489	Feel It/Daily News	1975	—	2.00	4.00
506	Love Won't You Stay/Daily News	1975	—	2.00	4.00
561	You Mean Everything to Me/White Wind	1977	—	2.00	4.00
610	Mainline/(B-side unknown)	1979	—	2.00	4.00
616	You Turned My Whole World Around/(B-side unknown)	1979	—	2.00	4.00

KWANZA/WB

Number	Title (A Side/B Side)	Yr	VG	VG+	NM
7800	No One Else Will Do/What Goes Around	1974	—	2.50	5.00

PANORAMIC

Number	Title (A Side/B Side)	Yr	VG	VG+	NM
200	You Are My Lover/(B-side unknown)	1984	—	2.00	4.00

PERCEPTION

Number	Title (A Side/B Side)	Yr	VG	VG+	NM
508	You and I/Our Future	1972	—	3.00	6.00

TODAY

Number	Title (A Side/B Side)	Yr	VG	VG+	NM
1501	Don't Turn Around/I Keep Asking You Questions	1971	—	2.50	5.00
1508	You and I/Our Future	1972	—	2.50	5.00
1511	I'll Find A Way (Loneliest Man in Town)/Surrender	1972	—	2.50	5.00
1516	Time Is Love/Got to Be There	1972	—	2.50	5.00
1520	Spinning Around/Find the One Who Loves You	1973	—	2.50	5.00
1524	We Made It/Just Leave Me Some	1973	—	2.50	5.00

Albums

BUDDAH

Number	Title (A Side/B Side)	Yr	VG	VG+	NM
BDS-5644	Feel It	1975	2.50	5.00	10.00
BDS-5658	Black Ivory	1976	2.50	5.00	10.00

Number	Title (A Side/B Side)	Yr	VG	VG+	NM
BDS-5722	Hangin' Heavy	1979	2.50	5.00	10.00
TODAY					
1005	Don't Turn Around	1972	3.00	6.00	12.00
1008	Baby, Won't You Change Your Mind	1972	3.00	6.00	12.00

BLACK LIGHTNING

Albums

Number	Title (A Side/B Side)	Yr	VG	VG+	NM
TOWER					
ST 5129	Shades of Black Lightning	1968	5.00	10.00	20.00

BLACK MERDA

45s

Number	Title (A Side/B Side)	Yr	VG	VG+	NM
CHESS					
2095	Reality/Cynthy-Ruth	1970	3.00	6.00	12.00

Albums

Number	Title (A Side/B Side)	Yr	VG	VG+	NM
CHESS					
LP-1551	Black Merda	1970	12.50	25.00	50.00

BLACK OAK ARKANSAS

45s

Number	Title (A Side/B Side)	Yr	VG	VG+	NM
ATCO					
6829	Lord Have Mercy on My Soul/Uncle Lijah	1971	—	2.50	5.00
6849	Singing the Blues/Hot and Nasty	1971	—	2.50	5.00
6878	Keep the Faith/The Big One's Still Coming	1972	—	2.00	4.00
6893	Full Moon Ride/We Help Each Other	1972	—	2.00	4.00
6925	Hot and Nasty/Hot Rod	1973	—	2.00	4.00
6948	Jim Dandy/Red Hot Lovin'	1973	—	2.50	5.00
7003	Hey Y'all/Sting Me	1974	—	2.00	4.00
7015	Taxman/Dixie	1975	—	2.00	4.00
7019	Back Door Man/Good Stuff	1975	—	2.00	4.00
CAPRICORN					
0284	Not Fade Away/Feels So Good	1978	—	2.00	4.00
—Label lists artist as "Black Oak"					
0305	Ride with Me/Wind in Our Sails	1978	—	2.00	4.00
—Label lists artist as "Black Oak"					
ENTERPRISE					
9010	King's Row/Older Than Grandpa	1970	2.50	5.00	10.00
MCA					
40496	Ace in the Hole/Strong Enough to Be Gentle	1975	—	2.00	4.00
40536	Great Balls of Fire/Highway Pirate	1976	—	2.00	4.00
40586	A Fistful of Love/Storm of Passion	1976	—	2.00	4.00
40621	When the Band Was Singin' "Shakin' All Over"/ Bad Boy's Back in School	1976	—	2.00	4.00

Albums

Number	Title (A Side/B Side)	Yr	VG	VG+	NM
ATCO					
SD 36-101	Street Party	1974	3.00	6.00	12.00
SD 36-111	Ain't Life Grand	1975	3.00	6.00	12.00
SD 36-128	Live! Mutha	1976	3.00	6.00	12.00
SD 36-150	The Best of Black Oak Arkansas	1976	3.00	6.00	12.00
SD 33-354	Black Oak Arkansas	1971	3.75	7.50	15.00
SD 33-381	Keep the Faith	1972	3.75	7.50	15.00
SD 7008	If An Angel Came to See You, Would You Make Her Feel at Home?	1972	3.75	7.50	15.00
QD 7019 [Q]	Raunch 'n' Roll/Live	1974	5.00	10.00	20.00
SD 7019	Raunch 'n' Roll/Live	1973	3.75	7.50	15.00
SD 7035	High on the Hog	1973	3.75	7.50	15.00
CAPRICORN					
CP 0191	Race with the Devil	1977	3.00	6.00	12.00
CP 0207	I'd Rather Be Sailing	1978	3.00	6.00	12.00
MCA					
704	X-Rated	198?	2.00	4.00	8.00
—Budget-line reissue					
2155	X-Rated	1975	3.00	6.00	12.00
2199	Balls of Fire	1976	3.00	6.00	12.00
2224	10 Year Overnight Success	1977	3.00	6.00	12.00
STAX					
STS-5504	Early Times	1974	3.75	7.50	15.00

BLACK PEARL

45s

Number	Title (A Side/B Side)	Yr	VG	VG+	NM
ATLANTIC					
2657	White Devil/Mr. Soul Satisfaction	1969	2.00	4.00	8.00

Albums

Number	Title (A Side/B Side)	Yr	VG	VG+	NM
ATLANTIC					
SD 8220	Black Pearl	1969	6.25	12.50	25.00
PROPHESY					
PRS-1001	Black Pearl — Live!	1970	6.25	12.50	25.00

BLACK SABBATH

45s

Number	Title (A Side/B Side)	Yr	VG	VG+	NM
WARNER BROS.					
7437	Paranoid/Wizard	1970	2.50	5.00	10.00
7530	Iron Man/Electric Funeral	1971	2.00	4.00	8.00
7625	Laguna Sunrise/Tomorrow's Dream	1972	2.00	4.00	8.00
7764	Sabbath, Bloody Sabbath/Changes	1973	2.00	4.00	8.00
7802	Iron Man/Electric Funeral	1974	2.00	4.00	8.00
8315	Rock 'N' Roll Doctor/It's Alright	1976	—	3.00	6.00
29434	Stonehenge/Trashed	1983	—	3.00	6.00
49549	Lady Evil/Children of the Sea	1980	—	3.00	6.00

Albums

Number	Title (A Side/B Side)	Yr	VG	VG+	NM
I.R.S.					
82002	Headless Cross	1989	2.50	5.00	10.00
WARNER BROS.					
WS 1871	Black Sabbath	1970	3.75	7.50	15.00
—Green label					
WS 1871	Black Sabbath	1973	2.50	5.00	10.00
—"Burbank" palm trees label					
WS 1871	Black Sabbath	1979	2.00	4.00	8.00
—White or tan label					
WS 1887	Paranoid	1971	3.75	7.50	15.00
—Green label					
WS 1887	Paranoid	1973	2.50	5.00	10.00
—"Burbank" palm trees label					
WS4 1887 [Q]	Paranoid	1974	7.50	15.00	30.00
—All quad copies have "Burbank" palm trees label					
BS 2562	Master of Reality	1971	3.75	7.50	15.00
—Green label					
BS 2562	Master of Reality Poster	1971	6.25	12.50	25.00
BS 2562	Master of Reality	1973	2.50	5.00	10.00
—"Burbank" palm trees label					
BS 2562	Master of Reality	1979	2.00	4.00	8.00
—White or tan label					
BS 2602	Black Sabbath, Vol. 4	1972	3.75	7.50	15.00
—Green label					
BS 2602	Black Sabbath, Vol. 4	1973	2.50	5.00	10.00
—"Burbank" palm trees label					
BS 2602	Black Sabbath, Vol. 4	1979	2.00	4.00	8.00
—White or tan label					
BS 2695	Sabbath Bloody Sabbath	1974	3.75	7.50	15.00
—"Burbank" palm trees label					
BS 2695	Sabbath Bloody Sabbath	1979	2.00	4.00	8.00
—White or tan label					
BS 2822	Sabotage	1975	3.75	7.50	15.00
—"Burbank" palm trees label					
BS 2822	Sabotage	1979	2.00	4.00	8.00
—White or tan label					
2BS 2923 [(2)]	We Sold Our Souls for Rock 'N' Roll	1975	5.00	10.00	20.00
—"Burbank" palm trees label					
2BS 2923 [(2)]	We Sold Our Souls for Rock 'N' Roll	1979	2.50	5.00	10.00
—White or tan label					
BS 2969	Technical Ecstasy	1976	3.75	7.50	15.00
—"Burbank" palm trees label					
BS 2969	Technical Ecstasy	1979	2.00	4.00	8.00
—White or tan label					
BSK 3104	Paranoid	1978	2.50	5.00	10.00
—Reissue; "Burbank" palm trees label					
BSK 3104	Paranoid	1979	2.00	4.00	8.00
—Reissue; white or tan label					
BSK 3186	Never Say Die!	1978	3.00	6.00	12.00
BSK 3372	Heaven and Hell	1980	3.00	6.00	12.00
BSK 3605	Mob Rules	1981	3.00	6.00	12.00
23742 [(2)]	Live Evil	1983	3.75	7.50	15.00
23978	Born Again	1983	2.50	5.00	10.00
25337	Seventh Star	1986	2.50	5.00	10.00
25548	The Eternal Idol	1987	2.50	5.00	10.00

BLACK SATIN

See THE FIVE SATINS.

BLACK SHEEP

With Lou Gramm, pre-Foreigner.

45s

Number	Title (A Side/B Side)	Yr	VG	VG+	NM
CAPITOL					
4012	A Little or a Lot/Broken Promises	1974	—	2.50	5.00
CHRYSALIS					
2038	Stick Around/Cruisin'	1974	—	2.50	5.00

Albums

Number	Title (A Side/B Side)	Yr	VG	VG+	NM
CAPITOL					
ST-11369	Black Sheep	1974	5.00	10.00	20.00
ST-11447	Encouraging Words	1975	5.00	10.00	20.00

BLACK VELVET

45s

Number	Title (A Side/B Side)	Yr	VG	VG+	NM
EMBER					
702	Peace and Love Is the Message/The Clown	1970	2.50	5.00	10.00
OKEH					
7330	Come On Heart/Just Came Back	1969	3.75	7.50	15.00

Albums

Number	Title (A Side/B Side)	Yr	VG	VG+	NM
OKEH					
OKS 14130	Love City	1969	6.25	12.50	25.00

BLACKBURN, LOU

45s

Number	Title (A Side/B Side)	Yr	VG	VG+	NM
IMPERIAL					
5943	Grand Prix/Jazz-a-Nova	1963	7.50	15.00	30.00
5998	Two Note Samba/17 Richmond Park	1963	5.00	10.00	20.00

BLACKBYRDS, THE

Also see DONALD BYRD.

45s

Number	Title (A Side/B Side)	Yr	VG	VG+	NM
FANTASY					
729	Do It, Fluid/Summer Love	1974	—	2.50	5.00
736	Walking in Rhythm/The Baby	1975	—	2.00	4.00
747	Flyin' High/All I Ask	1975	—	2.00	4.00
762	Happy Music/Love So Fine	1976	—	2.00	4.00
771	Rock Creek Park/Thankful 'Bout Yourself	1976	—	2.00	4.00
787	Time Is Movin'/Lady	1977	—	2.00	4.00
794	Party Land/In Life	1977	—	2.00	4.00
809	Soft and Easy/Something Special	1977	—	2.00	4.00
819	Supernatural Feeling/Looking Ahead	1978	—	2.00	4.00
904	What We Have Is Right/What's On Your Mind	1980	—	2.00	4.00
910	Love Don't Strike Twice/Don't Know What to Say	1981	—	2.00	4.00
914	Dancin' Dancin'/Lonelies for Your Love	1981	—	2.00	4.00

Albums

Number	Title (A Side/B Side)	Yr	VG	VG+	NM
FANTASY					
FPM-4004 [Q]	Flying Start	1975	6.25	12.50	25.00
F-9444	The Blackbyrds	1974	3.75	7.50	15.00
F-9472	Flying Start	1974	3.75	7.50	15.00
F-9490	City Life	1975	3.75	7.50	15.00
F-9518	Unfinished Business	1976	3.75	7.50	15.00
F-9535	Action	1977	3.00	6.00	12.00
F-9570	Night Grooves	1978	3.00	6.00	12.00
F-9602	Better Days	1980	3.00	6.00	12.00

BLACKFOOT, J.D.

Number	Title (A Side/B Side)	Yr	VG	VG+	NM
45s					
FANTASY					
741	Twilight/Done on the Ocean	1975	2.00	4.00	8.00
PHILIPS					
40625	Epitaph for a Head/Who's Nuts, Alfred	1969	3.00	6.00	12.00
40679	I've Never Seen You/One Time Woman	1970	3.00	6.00	12.00
Albums					
FANTASY					
F-9468	Song of Crazy Horse	1974	5.00	10.00	20.00
F-9487	Southbound and Gone	1975	5.00	10.00	20.00
MERCURY					
SR-61288	The Ultimate Prophecy	1970	15.00	30.00	60.00

BLACKMAN, HONOR

Number	Title (A Side/B Side)	Yr	VG	VG+	NM
Albums					
LONDON					
PS 408 [S]	Everything I've Got	1964	10.00	20.00	40.00
LL 3408 [M]	Everything I've Got	1964	7.50	15.00	30.00

BLACKWELL, OTIS

Number	Title (A Side/B Side)	Yr	VG	VG+	NM
45s					
ATLANTIC					
1165	Make Ready for Love/When You're Around	1957	10.00	20.00	40.00
1178	Turtle Dove/What a Coincidence	1958	10.00	20.00	40.00
CUB					
9092	Jeannie's Wedding/I'd Rather Kiss You Than Eat	1961	5.00	10.00	20.00
9107	Sister Twister/Ga Ga	1962	5.00	10.00	20.00
DATE					
1006	Don't Run Away/Handle with Care	1958	7.50	15.00	30.00
EPIC					
10654	Just Keep It Up/It's All Over Me	1970	6.25	12.50	25.00
GROOVE					
0034	Oh, What a Babe/Here I Am	1954	10.00	20.00	40.00
JAY-DEE					
784	Daddy Rolling Stone/Tears! Tears! Tears!	1953	12.50	25.00	50.00
787	You're My Love/Bartender Fill It Up Again	1954	12.50	25.00	50.00
791	On That Power Line/Don't You Know How I Love You	1954	12.50	25.00	50.00
792	I'm Standing at the Doorway/Nobody Met the Train	1954	12.50	25.00	50.00
794	My Josephine/Ain't Got No Time	1954	12.50	25.00	50.00
798	Go Away Mr. Blues/I'm Comin' Back Baby	1955	12.50	25.00	50.00
802	You Move Me Baby/My Poor Broken Heart	1955	12.50	25.00	50.00
808	Oh What a Wonderful Time/Let the Daddy Hold You	1955	12.50	25.00	50.00
MGM					
13090	Kiss Away/Grandaddy of Them All	1962	5.00	10.00	20.00
RCA VICTOR					
47-5069	Wake You Fool/Please Help Me Find	1952	12.50	25.00	50.00
47-5225	The Fool That I Be/Number 000	1953	12.50	25.00	50.00
Albums					
DAVIS					
109 [M]	Singin' the Blues	1956	125.00	250.00	500.00
INNER CITY					
1032	These Are My Songs	1977	5.00	10.00	20.00

BLACKWELL, SCRAPPER

Number	Title (A Side/B Side)	Yr	VG	VG+	NM
Albums					
BLUESVILLE					
BVLP-1047	Mr. Scrapper's Blues	1962	45.00	90.00	180.00
—Blue label, silver print					
BVLP-1047	Mr. Scrapper's Blues	1964	10.00	20.00	40.00
—Blue label with trident logo					

BLADES, CAROL

Number	Title (A Side/B Side)	Yr	VG	VG+	NM
45s					
GEE					
1029	When Will I Know/What Did I Do Wrong	1957	50.00	100.00	200.00

BLADES OF GRASS, THE

Number	Title (A Side/B Side)	Yr	VG	VG+	NM
45s					
JUBILEE					
5582	Happy/That's What a Boy Likes	1967	2.00	4.00	8.00
5590	Just Another Face/Baby You're a Real Good Friend of Mine	1967	2.00	4.00	8.00
5605	Help/Justah	1967	2.00	4.00	8.00
5616	You Won't Find That Girl/Charlie and Fred	1968	2.00	4.00	8.00
5622	The Way You'll Never Be/You Turned Off the Sun	1968	2.00	4.00	8.00
5635	I Love You, Alice B. Toklas/That's What a Boy Likes	1968	2.00	4.00	8.00
5662	Love Her and Cherish Her/Pageant	1969	2.00	4.00	8.00
Albums					
JUBILEE					
JGS-8007	The Blades of Grass Are Not for Smoking	1968	3.75	7.50	15.00

BLAINE, HAL

Number	Title (A Side/B Side)	Yr	VG	VG+	NM
45s					
ABC DUNHILL					
4181	Beverly Drive/Midnight at Fink's	1969	3.00	6.00	12.00
DUNHILL					
4006	La Bamba/Topsy '65	1965	3.75	7.50	15.00
4021	Secret Agent Man/Midnight at Pink's	1966	3.75	7.50	15.00
4049	Bang Bang Rhythm/Drums A-Go-Go	1966	3.75	7.50	15.00
4074	The Swinger/Drums A-Go-Go	1967	3.75	7.50	15.00
4091	Love-In (December)/Wiggy (November)	1967	3.75	7.50	15.00
4102	The Invaders/Secret Agent Man	1967	3.75	7.50	15.00
4142	Allegro from "Mac Arthur Park"/Drums A-Go-Go	1968	3.75	7.50	15.00
MELODY HOUSE					
100	Slow Gate/South of Shreveport	1962	10.00	20.00	40.00
RCA VICTOR					
47-8147	Hawaii 1963/East Side Story	1963	6.25	12.50	25.00
47-8223	Dance with the Surfin' Band/The Drummer Plays for Me	1963	6.25	12.50	25.00
47-8282	Challenger II/Gear Stripper	1963	6.25	12.50	25.00
ROCK-IT					
1000	Alamo Rock/Alamo Rock (Part 2)	1959	12.50	25.00	50.00
Albums					
ABC DUNHILL					
DS-50035	Have Fun!!! Play Drums!!!	1968	12.50	25.00	50.00
—With instruction booklet					
DS-50035	Have Fun!!! Play Drums!!!	1968	10.00	20.00	40.00
—Without instruction booklet					
DUNHILL					
D-50002 [M]	Drums! Drums! A-Go-Go	1966	7.50	15.00	30.00
DS-50002 [S]	Drums! Drums! A-Go-Go	1966	10.00	20.00	40.00
D-50019 [M]	Psychedelic Percussion	1967	10.00	20.00	40.00
DS-50019 [S]	Psychedelic Percussion	1967	15.00	30.00	60.00
RCA VICTOR					
LPM-2834 [M]	Deuces, "T's," Roadsters & Drums	1963	25.00	50.00	100.00
LSP-2834 [S]	Deuces, "T's," Roadsters & Drums	1963	37.50	75.00	150.00

BLAIR, TOM

Number	Title (A Side/B Side)	Yr	VG	VG+	NM
45s					
DECCA					
31223	West Coast/With My Hand on My Heart	1961	7.50	15.00	30.00
31344	Dolar Bills/Since You Are Gone	1961	7.50	15.00	30.00
DOT					
16095	Rock It/You Name It	1960	12.50	25.00	50.00
TEEN TUNES					
767	Rock It/You Name It	1960	25.00	50.00	100.00

BLAKE, TOMMY

Number	Title (A Side/B Side)	Yr	VG	VG+	NM
45s					
BUDDY					
107	I'm a Fool/Kool It	1958	7.50	15.00	30.00
CHANCELLOR					
101	I Gotta Be Somewhere/Three Cheers for the Red, White and Blue	19??	2.50	5.00	10.00
RCA VICTOR					
47-6925	Freedom/Mr. Hoody	1957	12.50	25.00	50.00
SUN					
278	Flatfoot Sam/Lordy Hoody	1957	25.00	50.00	100.00
300	Sweetie Pie/I Dig You	1958	75.00	150.00	300.00

BLAKELY, WELLINGTON

Number	Title (A Side/B Side)	Yr	VG	VG+	NM
45s					
VEE JAY					
104	Sailor Joe/Gypsy with a Broken Heart	1953	100.00	200.00	400.00

BLANC, MEL

Number	Title (A Side/B Side)	Yr	VG	VG+	NM
45s					
CAPITOL					
F1360	I Tawt I Taw a Puddy Tat/Yosemite Sam	1951	7.50	15.00	30.00
F1441	K-K-K-Katy/Flying Saucers	1951	7.50	15.00	30.00
F1727	10 Little Bottles in the Sink/OKMNX	1951	7.50	15.00	30.00
F1853	I Tan't Wait Till Quithmuth/Christmas Chopsticks	1951	7.50	15.00	30.00
F1948	That's All Folks!/Wontcha Ever	1952	7.50	15.00	30.00
F2048	Lord Bless His Soul/Morris	1952	7.50	15.00	30.00
F2261	The Misses Wouldn't Approve/I Tell My Troubles to Joe	1952	7.50	15.00	30.00
F2470	Somebody Stole My Gal/I Love Me	1953	6.25	12.50	25.00
F2619	Ya, Das Ist Ein Christmas Tree/I Tan't Wait Till Quithmuth	1953	7.50	15.00	30.00
F2635	I'm in the Mood for Love/My Kinda Love	1953	6.25	12.50	25.00
F2718	I Dess I Dotta Doe/The Lady Bird Song	1954	7.50	15.00	30.00
F2764	Money/Polly Pretty Polly	1954	6.25	12.50	25.00
F3902	The Hat I Got for Christmas Is Too Beeg/Pancho's Christmas	1959	6.25	12.50	25.00
WARNER BROS.					
5129	Tweety's Twistmas Troubles/I Keep Hearing Those Bells	1959	6.25	12.50	25.00
5156	Blimey/I Can't Fool My Heart	1960	6.25	12.50	25.00
Albums					
CAPITOL					
H-436 [10]	Party Panic	1953	25.00	50.00	100.00

BLANCHARD, JACK, AND MISTY MORGAN

Number	Title (A Side/B Side)	Yr	VG	VG+	NM
45s					
EPIC					
11030	Cockroach Stomp/Carolina Sundown Red	1973	—	2.00	4.00
11058	Just One More Song/Why Did I Sleep So Long	1973	—	2.00	4.00
50023	Down to the End of the Wine/You Can't Say I Didn't Try	1974	—	2.00	4.00
50082	Chorus/House	1975	—	2.00	4.00
50122	Because We Love/It's Me	1975	—	2.00	4.00
50181	Let's Pretend/I'm High on You	1975	—	2.00	4.00
50205	47 Miles (to the Georgia Line)/Motel Time	1976	—	2.00	4.00
MEGA					
0031	There Must Be More to Life/Fire Hydrant #79	1971	—	2.00	4.00
0046	Somewhere in Virginia in the Rain/If Eggs Had Legs	1971	—	2.00	4.00
0063	The Legendary Chicken Fairy/The Night We Heard the Voice	1972	—	2.00	4.00
0082	Miami Sidewalks/Washin' Harry Down the Sink	1972	—	2.00	4.00
0089	Second Tuesday in December/Don't It Make You Want to Go Home	1972	—	2.00	4.00
0101	A Handful of Dimes/It Seems Like There Ain't No Going Home	1973	—	2.00	4.00
0114	Shadows of the Leaves/Sweet Memories	1973	—	2.00	4.00

Number	Title (A Side/B Side)	Yr	VG	VG+	NM
UNITED ARTISTS					
XW1004	Tennessee Birdwalk/Living Together	1977	—	2.00	4.00
XW1067	Heartaches/You Come So Easy to Me	1977	—	2.00	4.00
WAYSIDE					
000	Big Black Bird (Spirit of Our Love)/Autumn Song (On a Yellow Day)	1969	—	2.50	5.00
—Reissue of 1028					
007	Changin' Times/Poor Jody	1969	—	2.50	5.00
010	Tennessee Bird Walk/The Clock of St. James	1970	—	2.50	5.00
013	Humphrey the Camel/A Place in My Mind	1970	—	2.50	5.00
015	You've Got Your Troubles (I've Got Mine)/How I Lost 31 Pounds in 17 Days	1970	—	2.50	5.00
1024	Bethlehem Steel/No Sign of Love	1969	—	3.00	6.00
1028	Big Black Bird (Spirit of Our Love)/Autumn Song (On a Yellow Day)	1969	—	3.00	6.00
Albums					
MEGA					
31-1009	Two Sides	1972	3.00	6.00	12.00
WAYSIDE					
33-1	Birds of a Feather	1970	3.75	7.50	15.00

BLAND, BILLY

Number	Title (A Side/B Side)	Yr	VG	VG+	NM
45s					
OLD TOWN					
1016	Chicken in the Basket/The Fat Man	1956	5.00	10.00	20.00
1022	Chicken Hop/Oh You for Me	1956	5.00	10.00	20.00
1035	If I Could Be Your Man/I Had a Dream	1957	5.00	10.00	20.00
1076	Let the Little Girl Dance/Sweet Thing	1960	6.25	12.50	25.00
1082	You Were Born to Be Loved/Pardon Me	1960	3.75	7.50	15.00
1088	Make Believe Lover/Harmonys	1960	3.75	7.50	15.00
1093	Everything That Shines Ain't Gold/Keep Talkin' That Sweet Talk	1960	3.75	7.50	15.00
1098	I Cross My Heart/Steady Kind	1961	3.75	7.50	15.00
1105	My Heart's On Fire/Can't Stop Her from Dancing	1961	3.75	7.50	15.00
1109	Do the Bug with Me/Uncle Bud	1962	3.75	7.50	15.00
1114	Busy Little Boy/All I Want to Do Is Cry	1961	3.75	7.50	15.00
1124	Mama Stole the Chicken/I Spent My Life Loving You	1962	3.75	7.50	15.00
1128	Darling Won't You Think of Me/How Many Hearts	1962	3.75	7.50	15.00
1143	Doing the Mule/Farmer in the Dell	1963	3.75	7.50	15.00
1151	A Little Touch of Your Love/Little Boy Blue	1963	3.75	7.50	15.00
ST. LAWRENCE					
1005	She's Already Married/My Divorce	1965	3.00	6.00	12.00
TIP TOP					
708	Chicken in the Basket/Chicken Hop	1958	5.00	10.00	20.00

BLAND, BOBBY

Includes records by "Bobby 'Blue' Bland."

Number	Title (A Side/B Side)	Yr	VG	VG+	NM
45s					
ABC					
12105	Yolanda/When You Come to the End of Your Road	1975	—	2.00	4.00
12134	I Take It On Home/You've Never Been This Far Before	1975	—	2.00	4.00
12156	Today I Started Loving You Again/Too Far Gone	1976	—	2.00	4.00
12189	It Ain't the Real Thing/Who's Foolin' Who	1976	—	2.00	4.00
12280	The Soul of a Man/If I Weren't a Gambler	1977	—	2.00	4.00
12330	Sittin' on a Poor Man's Throne/I Intend to Take Your Place	1978	—	2.00	4.00
12360	Love to See You Smile/I'm Just Your Man	1978	—	2.00	4.00
12405	Come Fly with Me/Ain't God Something	1978	—	2.00	4.00
ABC DUNHILL					
4369	This Time I'm Gone for Good/Where Baby Went	1973	—	2.50	5.00
4379	Goin' Down Slow/Up and Down World	1974	—	2.50	5.00
15003	Ain't No Love in the Heart of the City/Twenty-Four Hour Blues	1974	—	2.50	5.00
15015	I Wouldn't Treat a Dog (The Way You Treated Me)/I Ain't Gonna Be the First to Cry	1974	—	2.50	5.00
DUKE					
105	Lovin' Blues/I.O.U. Blues	1952	75.00	150.00	300.00
115	Army Blues/No Blow, No Show	1953	50.00	100.00	200.00
141	Time Out/It's My Life Baby	1955	15.00	30.00	60.00
146	You or None/Woke Up Screaming	1955	15.00	30.00	60.00
153	I Can't Put You Down/You've Got Bad Intentions	1956	12.50	25.00	50.00
160	I Learned My Lesson/I Don't Believe	1956	10.00	20.00	40.00
160	I Learned My Lesson/Lead Us On	1956	10.00	20.00	40.00
167	Don't Want No Woman/I Smell Trouble	1957	7.50	15.00	30.00
170	Farther Up the Road/Sometime Tomorrow	1957	7.50	15.00	30.00
182	Teach Me/Bobby's Blues	1957	6.25	12.50	25.00
185	You Got Me Where You Want Me/Loan a Helping Hand	1958	6.25	12.50	25.00
196	Little Boy Blue/Last Night	1958	6.25	12.50	25.00
300	You Did Me Wrong/I Lost Sight of the World	1959	6.25	12.50	25.00
303	Wishing Well/I'm Not Ashamed	1959	6.25	12.50	25.00
310	Is It Real/Someday	1959	6.25	12.50	25.00
314	I'll Take Care of You/That's Why	1959	6.25	12.50	25.00
318	Lead Me On/Hold Me Tenderly	1960	6.25	12.50	25.00
327	Cry Cry Cry/I've Been Wrong So Long	1960	6.25	12.50	25.00
332	I Pity the Fool/Close to You	1961	5.00	10.00	20.00
336	Don't Cry No More/How Does a Cheating Woman Feel	1961	5.00	10.00	20.00
338	Ain't That Loving You/Jelly, Jelly, Jelly	1961	5.00	10.00	20.00
340	Don't Cry No More/Saint James Infirmary	1961	5.00	10.00	20.00
344	Turn On Your Love Light/You're the One (That I Need)	1961	5.00	10.00	20.00
347	Who Will the Next Fool Be/Blue Moon	1962	5.00	10.00	20.00
352	Yield Not to Temptation/How Does a Cheating Woman Feel	1962	5.00	10.00	20.00
355	Stormy Monday Blues/Your Friends	1962	5.00	10.00	20.00
360	That's the Way Love Is/Call On Me	1962	5.00	10.00	20.00
366	Sometimes You Gotta Cry a Little/You're Worth It All	1963	3.75	7.50	15.00
369	Ain't It a Good Thing/Queen for a Day	1963	3.75	7.50	15.00
370	The Feeling Is Gone/I Can't Stop Singing	1963	3.75	7.50	15.00
375	Ain't Nothing You Can Do/Honey Child	1964	3.75	7.50	15.00
377	Share Your Love with Me/After It's Too Late	1964	2.50	5.00	10.00
383	Ain't Doing Too Bad (Part 1)/Ain't Doing Too Bad (Part 2)	1964	2.50	5.00	10.00
385	These Hands (Small But Mighty)/Today	1965	2.50	5.00	10.00
386	Blind Man/Black Night	1965	2.50	5.00	10.00
390	Dust Got in Daddy's Eyes/Ain't No Telling	1965	2.50	5.00	10.00
393	I'm Too Far Gone (To Turn Around)/If You Could Read My Mind	1965	2.50	5.00	10.00
402	Good Time Charlie/Good Time Charlie (Part 2)	1966	2.00	4.00	8.00
407	Poverty/Building a Fire with Hair	1966	2.00	4.00	8.00
412	Back in the Same Old Bag Again/I Ain't Myself Anymore	1966	2.00	4.00	8.00
416	You're All I Need/Deep in My Soul	1967	2.00	4.00	8.00
421	That Did It/Getting Used to the Blues	1967	2.00	4.00	8.00
426	A Touch of the Blues/Shoes	1967	2.00	4.00	8.00
432	Driftin' Blues/You Could Read My Mind	1968	2.00	4.00	8.00
433	Honey Child/A Piece of Gold	1968	2.00	4.00	8.00
435	Save Your Love for Me/Share Your Love with Me	1968	2.00	4.00	8.00
440	Rockin' in the Same Old Boat/Wouldn't You Rather Have Me	1968	2.00	4.00	8.00
447	Gotta Get to Know You/Baby I'm On My Way	1969	2.00	4.00	8.00
449	Chains of Love/Ask Me 'Bout Nothing (But the Blues)	1969	2.00	4.00	8.00
458	If You've Got a Heart/Sad Feeling	1970	2.00	4.00	8.00
460	Lover with a Reputation/If Love Ruled the World	1970	2.00	4.00	8.00
464	Keep On Loving Me (You'll See the Change)/I Just Got to Forget About You	1970	2.00	4.00	8.00
466	I'm Sorry/Yum Yum Tree	1971	2.00	4.00	8.00
471	Shape Up or Ship Out/The Love That We Share (Is True)	1971	2.00	4.00	8.00
472	Do What You Set Out to Do/Ain't Nothing You Can Do	1972	2.00	4.00	8.00
477	I'm So Tired/If You Could Read My Mind	1972	2.00	4.00	8.00
480	That's All There Is/I Don't Want Another Mountain to Climb	1973	2.00	4.00	8.00
KENT					
378	Love You Baby/Drifting	1962	2.50	5.00	10.00
—With Ike Turner					
MALACO					
2122	Members Only/I Just Got to Know	1985	—	—	3.00
2126	Can We Make Love Tonight/In the Ghetto	1986	—	—	3.00
2133	Angel/I Hear You Thinkin'	1986	—	—	3.00
MCA					
41140	Tit for Tat/Come Fly with Me	1979	—	2.00	4.00
41197	Soon as the Weather Breaks/To Be Friends	1980	—	2.00	4.00
51068	You'd Be a Millionaire/Swat Vibrator	1981	—	—	3.00
51181	What a Difference A Day Makes/Givin' Up the Streets for Love	1982	—	—	3.00
52085	Recess in Heaven/Exactly, Where It's At	1982	—	—	3.00
52136	Here We Go Again/You're About to Win	1982	—	—	3.00
52180	Is This the Blues/You're About to Win	1983	—	—	3.00
52270	If It Ain't One Thing/Tell Mr. Bland	1983	—	—	3.00
52436	Looking Back/You Got Me Loving You	1984	—	—	3.00
52482	Get Real Clean/It's Too Bad	1984	—	—	3.00
52508	You Are My Christmas/New Merry Christmas Baby	1984	—	—	3.00
WAND					
1102	Honey, You've Been On My Mind/You've Got Time	1965	3.75	7.50	15.00
Albums					
ABC					
D-895	Get On Down with Bobby Bland	1975	3.00	6.00	12.00
AB-1018	Reflections in Blue	1977	2.50	5.00	10.00
AA-1075	Come Fly with Me	1978	2.50	5.00	10.00
ABC DUKE					
DLPS-74	Two Steps from the Blues	197?	3.00	6.00	12.00
DLP-75	Here's the Man!!!	1974	3.00	6.00	12.00
DLP-77	Call On Me/That's the Way Love Is	1974	3.00	6.00	12.00
DLP-78	Ain't Nothing You Can Do	1974	3.00	6.00	12.00
DLP-79	The Soul of the Man	1974	3.00	6.00	12.00
DLP-84	The Best of Bobby Bland	1974	3.00	6.00	12.00
DLP-86	The Best of Bobby Bland, Volume 2	1974	3.00	6.00	12.00
DLP-88	A Touch of the Blues	1974	3.00	6.00	12.00
DLP-89	Spotlighting the Man	1974	3.00	6.00	12.00
DLP 92-2 [(2)]	Introspective of the Early Years	1974	5.00	10.00	20.00
ABC DUNHILL					
DSX-50163	His California Album	1973	3.75	7.50	15.00
DSX-50169	Dreamer	1974	3.75	7.50	15.00
BLUESWAY					
BLS-6065	Call On Me	197?	3.75	7.50	15.00
DUKE					
DLP-74 [M]	Two Steps from the Blues	1961	62.50	125.00	250.00
—Purple and yellow label					
DLP-74 [M]	Two Steps from the Blues	1962	62.50	125.00	250.00
—Orange label, red vinyl					
DLP-74 [M]	Two Steps from the Blues	1962	25.00	50.00	100.00
—Orange label, black vinyl					
DLPS-74 [R]	Two Steps from the Blues	196?	15.00	30.00	60.00
DLP-75 [M]	Here's the Man!!!	1962	50.00	100.00	200.00
—Purple and yellow label					
DLP-75 [M]	Here's the Man!!!	1962	25.00	50.00	100.00
—Orange label					
DLPS-75 [S]	Here's the Man!!!	1962	50.00	100.00	200.00
—With spoken intro to "36-22-36"					
DLPS-75 [S]	Here's the Man!!!	196?	25.00	50.00	100.00
—Without spoken intro to "36-22-36"					
DLP-77 [M]	Call On Me/That's the Way Love Is	1963	25.00	50.00	100.00
DLPS-77 [S]	Call On Me/That's the Way Love Is	1963	37.50	75.00	150.00
DLP-78 [M]	Ain't Nothing You Can Do	1964	20.00	40.00	80.00
DLPS-78 [S]	Ain't Nothing You Can Do	1964	30.00	60.00	120.00
DLP-79 [M]	The Soul of the Man	1966	20.00	40.00	80.00
DLPS-79 [S]	The Soul of the Man	1966	30.00	60.00	120.00
DLP-84 [M]	The Best of Bobby Bland	1967	5.00	10.00	20.00

Number	Title (A Side/B Side)	Yr	VG	VG+	NM
DLPS-84 [P]	The Best of Bobby Bland	1967	6.25	12.50	25.00
DLP-86 [M]	The Best of Bobby Bland, Volume 2	1968	6.25	12.50	25.00
DLPS-86 [P]	The Best of Bobby Bland, Volume 2	1968	5.00	10.00	20.00
DLP-88 [M]	A Touch of the Blues	1968	6.25	12.50	25.00
DLPS-88 [S]	A Touch of the Blues	1968	5.00	10.00	20.00
DLPS-89	Spotlighting the Man	1969	5.00	10.00	20.00
DLPS-90	If Loving You Is Wrong	1970	5.00	10.00	20.00
MCA					
3157	I Feel Good, I Feel Fine	1979	2.50	5.00	10.00
4172 [(2)]	Introspective of the Early Years	198?	2.50	5.00	10.00
—Reissue of Duke 92					
5145	Sweet Vibrations	1980	2.50	5.00	10.00
5233	Try Me, I'm Real	1981	2.50	5.00	10.00
5297	Here We Go Again	1982	2.50	5.00	10.00
5425	Tell Mr. Bland	1983	2.50	5.00	10.00
5503	You've Got Me Loving You	1984	2.50	5.00	10.00
27013	The Best of Bobby Bland	198?	2.00	4.00	8.00
—Reissue of Duke 84					
27036	Two Steps from the Blues	198?	2.00	4.00	8.00
—Reissue of Duke 74					
27038	Here's the Man!!!	198?	2.00	4.00	8.00
—Reissue of Duke 75					
27040	Ain't Nothing You Can Do	198?	2.00	4.00	8.00
—Reissue of Duke 78					
27041	The Soul of the Man	1984	2.00	4.00	8.00
—Reissue of Duke 79					
27042	Call On Me/That's the Way Love Is	1984	2.00	4.00	8.00
—Reissue of Duke 77					
27043	Reflections in Blue	1984	2.00	4.00	8.00
—Reissue of ABC 1018					
27044	Come Fly with Me	1984	2.00	4.00	8.00
—Reissue of ABC 1075					
27045	The Best of Bobby Bland, Volume 2	1984	2.00	4.00	8.00
—Reissue of Duke 86					
27047	A Touch of the Blues	1984	2.00	4.00	8.00
—Reissue of Duke 88					
27048	Spotlighting the Man	1984	2.00	4.00	8.00
—Reissue of Duke 89					
27073	I Feel Good, I Feel Fine	1985	2.00	4.00	8.00
—Reissue of MCA 3157					
27076	Sweet Vibrations	198?	2.00	4.00	8.00
—Reissue of 5145					

BLAND, BOBBY, AND B.B. KING

Also see each artist's individual listings.

Number	Title (A Side/B Side)	Yr	VG	VG+	NM
45s					
ABC IMPULSE					
31006	Let the Good Times Roll/Strange Things	1976	—	2.00	4.00
31009	Everyday I Have the Blues/The Thrill Is Gone	1976	—	2.00	4.00
Albums					
ABC DUNHILL					
DSY-50190 [(2)]	Together for the First Time...Live	1974	3.75	7.50	15.00
ABC IMPULSE!					
9317	Together Again...Live	1976	3.00	6.00	12.00
COMMAND					
CQDY-40012 [(2) Q]	Together for the First Time...Live	1974	6.25	12.50	25.00
MCA					
4160 [(2)]	Together for the First Time...Live	198?	2.50	5.00	10.00
—Reissue of ABC Dunhill 50190					
27012	Together Again...Live	198?	2.00	4.00	8.00
—Reissue of ABC Impulse! 9317					

BLANDERS, THE

Number	Title (A Side/B Side)	Yr	VG	VG+	NM
45s					
SMASH					
2005	Jitterbug/Desert Sands	1965	12.50	25.00	50.00

BLANE, MARCIE

Number	Title (A Side/B Side)	Yr	VG	VG+	NM
45s					
SEVILLE					
120	Bobby's Girl/Time to Dream	1962	5.00	10.00	20.00
—Exists with "Seville" logo straight across the top of the label, and with the "Seville" logo curving around the top of the label. No difference in value has yet been noted.					
123	What Does a Girl Do?/How Can I Tell Him	1963	4.00	8.00	16.00
126	Little Miss Fool/Rag Time Sound	1963	4.00	8.00	16.00
128	You Gave My Number to Billy/Told You So	1963	4.00	8.00	16.00
130	Why Can't I Get a Guy/Who's Going to Take My Daddy's Place	1963	4.00	8.00	16.00
133	Bobby Did/After the Laughter	1964	4.00	8.00	16.00
137	The Hurtin' Kind/She'll Break the String	1965	4.00	8.00	16.00

BLAVAT, JERRY

Number	Title (A Side/B Side)	Yr	VG	VG+	NM
45s					
CAMEO					
393	Discophonic Walk/Back to School One More Time	1965	3.00	6.00	12.00
EPIC					
10193	Jerry's Theme/Let's Love Again	1967	3.00	6.00	12.00
FAVOR					
100	Discophonic Walk/Back to School One More Time	1965	3.75	7.50	15.00
ROULETTE					
7085	Tasty (To Me)/Oh Be Joyous	1970	2.00	4.00	8.00
—With the Geatorettes					

BLAZER BOY

Number	Title (A Side/B Side)	Yr	VG	VG+	NM
45s					
IMPERIAL					
5199	Mornin'Train/Joe's Kid Sister	1952	25.00	50.00	100.00
5244	Surprise Blues/Waiting for My Baby	1953	25.00	50.00	100.00
5801	New Orleans Twist/That's Where It's At	1962	5.00	10.00	20.00

BLENDELLS, THE

Number	Title (A Side/B Side)	Yr	VG	VG+	NM
45s					
COTILLION					
44020	Night After Night/The Love That I Needed	1968	2.50	5.00	10.00
ERA BACK TO BACK HITS					
023	Dance with Me/Land of 1000 Dances	197?	—	2.50	5.00
—B-side by Cannibal and the Headhunters					
RAMPART					
641	La La La La La/Huggies Bunnies	1964	6.25	12.50	25.00
REPRISE					
0291	La La La La La/Huggies Bunnies	1964	5.00	10.00	20.00
0340	Dance with Me/Get Your Baby	1965	5.00	10.00	20.00

BLENDERS, THE

Several different groups.

Number	Title (A Side/B Side)	Yr	VG	VG+	NM
45s					
AFO					
305	Graveyard/It Takes Time	1962	75.00	150.00	300.00
ALADDIN					
3449	Two Loves/Soda Shop	1959	250.00	500.00	1000.
CLASS					
236	My Heart's Desire/Little Rose	1958	10.00	20.00	40.00
CORTLAND					
102	Love Is a Treasure/Fisherman	1962	3.00	6.00	12.00
103	Everybody's Got a Right/What Have You Got	1962	3.00	6.00	12.00
DECCA					
27403	The Masquerade Is Over/Little Small Town Girl	1951	100.00	200.00	400.00
27587	All I Gotta Do Is Think of You/The Busiest Corner	1951	75.00	150.00	300.00
28092	Just a Little Walk with Me/I'd Be a Fool Again	1952	75.00	150.00	300.00
28241	Never in a Million Years/Memories of You	1952	75.00	150.00	300.00
48156	Gone/Honeysuckle Rose	1950	75.00	150.00	300.00
48158	Count Every Star/Would I Still Be the One in Your Heart	1950	75.00	150.00	300.00
48183	I'm So Crazy for Love/What About Tonight	1950	75.00	150.00	300.00
48244	My Heart Will Never Forget/You Do the Dreaming	1951	75.00	150.00	300.00
JAY DEE					
780	Don't Play Around with You/You'll Never Smile Again	1953	50.00	100.00	200.00
MAR-V-LUS					
6010	Your Love Has Got Me Down/Love Is a Good Thing Going	1966	50.00	100.00	200.00
MGM					
11488	I Don't Miss You Anymore/If That's the Way You Want It Baby	1953	100.00	200.00	400.00
11531	Please Take Me Back/Isn't It a Shame	1953	100.00	200.00	400.00
RCA VICTOR					
47-6591	I've Told Every Little Star/Cecilia	1956	15.00	30.00	60.00
47-6712	Wake Up to Music/New Sensations in Sound	1956	12.50	25.00	50.00
47-7009	I'm Following You/Since I Kissed My Baby Goodbye	1957	12.50	25.00	50.00
WANGER					
189	Angel/Old MacDonald	1959	6.25	12.50	25.00
WITCH					
114	Daughter/Everybody's Got a Right	1963	4.00	8.00	16.00
117	Boys Think/Squat and Squirm	1963	3.75	7.50	15.00
123	One Time/(B-side unknown)	1964	3.75	7.50	15.00

BLESSED END

Number	Title (A Side/B Side)	Yr	VG	VG+	NM
Albums					
TNS					
248	Movin' On	1971	75.00	150.00	300.00

BLESSING, MICHAEL

See MICHAEL NESMITH.

BLEU LIGHTS, THE

Number	Title (A Side/B Side)	Yr	VG	VG+	NM
45s					
BAYSOUND					
67003	Forever/They Don't Know My Heart	1968	10.00	20.00	40.00
67007	Bony Moronie/Lonely Man's Prayer	1968	7.50	15.00	30.00
67010	Yes I Do/The End of My Dreams	1969	7.50	15.00	30.00

BLEVINS, CHUCK

Number	Title (A Side/B Side)	Yr	VG	VG+	NM
45s					
FOXIE					
7006	Sleigh Bell Rock/(B-side unknown)	1959	5.00	10.00	20.00

BLIND FAITH

Also see GINGER BAKER'S AIR FORCE; ERIC CLAPTON; STEVE WINWOOD.

Number	Title (A Side/B Side)	Yr	VG	VG+	NM
45s					
POLYDOR					
871798-7	Presence of the Lord/Can't Find My Way Home	1989	—	2.00	4.00
RSO					
873	Presence of the Lord/Can't Find My Way Home	1977	2.00	4.00	8.00
—First single release from 1969 self-titled album					
Albums					
ATCO					
33-304A [M]	Blind Faith	1969	50.00	100.00	200.00
—White label promo only					
SD 33-304A [S]	Blind Faith	1969	6.25	12.50	25.00
—Cover with naked girl on Side 1 and same scene without girl on Side 2					
SD 33-304B [S]	Blind Faith	1969	3.75	7.50	15.00
—Cover with band photo on Side 1 and song lyrics on Side 2					
MOBILE FIDELITY					
1-186	Blind Faith	1985	10.00	20.00	40.00
—Audiophile vinyl					
RSO					
RS-1-3016	Blind Faith	1977	2.50	5.00	10.00
—Reissue with naked girl on one side and band photo on the other					
825094-1	Blind Faith	1986	2.00	4.00	8.00

BLINKY

45s

Number	Title (A Side/B Side)	Yr	VG	VG+	NM
MOTOWN					
1134	I Wouldn't Change the Man He Is/I'll Always Love You	1968	2.00	4.00	8.00
1168	How You Gonna Keep It/This Time Last Summer	1970	25.00	50.00	100.00
1233	You Get a Tangle in Your Life Line/This Man of Mine	1973	—	3.00	6.00
MOWEST					
5019	For Your Precious Love/So Tired	1972	—	3.00	6.00
5033	T'Ain't Nobody's Bizness If I Do/What More Can I Do	1973	—	2.50	5.00
SOUL					
35089	How You Gonna Keep It/This Time Last Summer	1971	—	3.00	6.00

BLISTERS, THE

45s

Number	Title (A Side/B Side)	Yr	VG	VG+	NM
LIBERTY					
55577	Shortnin' Bread/Cookie Rockin' in Her Stockings	1963	3.00	6.00	12.00
55647	Rich in My Pocket, Poor in My Heart/Friendly Loans	1963	3.00	6.00	12.00
TITANIC					
5005	Fifty Mile Hike/Recitation	1963	5.00	10.00	20.00

BLODWYN PIG

45s

Number	Title (A Side/B Side)	Yr	VG	VG+	NM
A&M					
1158	Dear Jill/Summer Day	1969	—	3.00	6.00

Albums

Number	Title (A Side/B Side)	Yr	VG	VG+	NM
A&M					
SP-3180	Ahead Rings Out	1982	2.00	4.00	8.00
—Budget-line reissue					
SP-4210	Ahead Rings Out	1969	3.75	7.50	15.00
SP-4243	Getting to This	1970	3.75	7.50	15.00

BLOND

45s

Number	Title (A Side/B Side)	Yr	VG	VG+	NM
FONTANA					
1673	Deep Inside My Heart/I Will Bring You Flowers in the Morning	1969	3.00	6.00	12.00
1673 [PS]	Deep Inside My Heart/I Will Bring You Flowers in the Morning	1969	4.00	8.00	16.00

Albums

Number	Title (A Side/B Side)	Yr	VG	VG+	NM
FONTANA					
SRF-67067	Blond	1969	5.00	10.00	20.00

BLONDE ON BLONDE

Albums

Number	Title (A Side/B Side)	Yr	VG	VG+	NM
JANUS					
JLP-3003	Contrasts	1969	6.25	12.50	25.00

BLOOD, SWEAT AND TEARS

Also see DAVID CLAYTON-THOMAS; AL KOOPER.

45s

Number	Title (A Side/B Side)	Yr	VG	VG+	NM
ABC					
12310	Blue Street/Somebody I Trusted	1977	—	2.00	4.00
COLUMBIA					
10151	Got to Get You Into My Life/Naked Man	1975	—	2.50	5.00
10189	No Show/Yesterday's Music	1975	—	2.50	5.00
10400	You're the One/Heavy Blue	1976	—	2.50	5.00
44559	I Can't Quit Her/House in the Country	1968	2.00	4.00	8.00
44776	You've Made Me So Very Happy/Blues — Part 2	1969	—	3.00	6.00
44871	Spinning Wheel/More and More	1969	—	3.00	6.00
45008	And When I Die/Sometimes in Winter	1969	—	3.00	6.00
45204	Hi-De-Ho/The Battle	1970	—	2.50	5.00
45235	Lucretia Mac Evil/Lucretia's Reprise	1970	—	2.50	5.00
45427	Go Down Gamblin'/Valentine's Day	1971	—	2.50	5.00
45427 [PS]	Go Down Gamblin'/Valentine's Day	1971	2.00	4.00	8.00
45477	Lisa, Listen to Me/Cowboys and Indians	1971	—	2.50	5.00
45661	So Long Dixie/Alone	1972	—	2.50	5.00
45661 [PS]	So Long Dixie/Alone	1972	2.00	4.00	8.00
45755	Velvet/I Can't Move No Mountains	1973	—	2.50	5.00
45937	Roller Coaster/Inner Crisis	1973	—	2.50	5.00
45965	Save Our Ship/Song for John	1973	—	2.50	5.00
46059	Tell Me That I'm Wrong/Rock Reprise	1974	—	2.50	5.00
MCA					
41198	Nuclear Blues/Agitato	1980	—	2.00	4.00

7-Inch Extended Plays

Number	Title (A Side/B Side)	Yr	VG	VG+	NM
COLUMBIA					
7-30590 [PS]	Blood, Sweat and Tears 4	1971	3.00	6.00	12.00
7-30590 [S]	*Redemption/Lisa, Listen to Me/A Look to My Heart (duet)/A Look to My Heart (inst.)/For My Lady/Mama Gets High	1971	2.50	5.00	10.00
—33 1/3 rpm, small hole jukebox release					

Albums

Number	Title (A Side/B Side)	Yr	VG	VG+	NM
ABC					
1015	Brand New Day	1977	2.50	5.00	10.00
COLUMBIA					
CS 9616	Child Is Father to the Man	1968	3.75	7.50	15.00
—Red "360 Sound" label					
CS 9616	Child Is Father to the Man	1970	2.50	5.00	10.00
—Orange label					
PC 9619	Child Is Father to the Man	1980	2.00	4.00	8.00
CS 9720	Blood, Sweat and Tears	1969	3.75	7.50	15.00
—Red "360 Sound" label					
CS 9720	Blood, Sweat and Tears	1970	2.50	5.00	10.00
—Orange label					
PC 9720	Blood, Sweat and Tears	1980	2.00	4.00	8.00
KC 30090	Blood, Sweat and Tears 3	1970	2.50	5.00	10.00
PC 30090	Blood, Sweat and Tears 3	1986	2.00	4.00	8.00
KC 30590	BS&T: 4	1971	2.50	5.00	10.00
CQ 30994 [Q]	Blood, Sweat and Tears	1972	5.00	10.00	20.00
CQ 31170 [Q]	Blood, Sweat and Tears' Greatest Hits	1972	5.00	10.00	20.00
KC 31170	Blood, Sweat and Tears' Greatest Hits	1972	2.50	5.00	10.00
—With the single versions of "You've Made Me So Very Happy," "Spinning Wheel," and "And When I Die" (all in mono)					
PC 31170	Blood, Sweat and Tears' Greatest Hits	1980	2.00	4.00	8.00
KC 31780	New Blood	1972	2.50	5.00	10.00
KC 32180	No Sweat	1973	2.50	5.00	10.00
CQ 32929 [Q]	Mirror Image	1974	5.00	10.00	20.00
PC 32929	Mirror Image	1974	2.50	5.00	10.00
PC 33484	New City	1975	2.50	5.00	10.00
PC 34233	More Than Ever	1976	2.50	5.00	10.00
HC 49619	Child Is Father to the Man	1981	12.50	25.00	50.00
—Half-speed mastered edition					
DIRECT DISK					
SD-16605	Blood, Sweat and Tears	1981	15.00	30.00	60.00
MCA					
L33-1865 [DJ]	Nuclear Blues	1980	3.75	7.50	15.00
—Promo only on gold vinyl					
3061	Nuclear Blues	1980	2.50	5.00	10.00
3227	Blood, Sweat and Tears	1981	—	—	—
—Canceled?					
MOBILE FIDELITY					
1-251	Blood, Sweat and Tears	1996	30.00	60.00	120.00
—Audiophile vinyl; fewer than 2,000 pressed					

BLOODROCK

45s

Number	Title (A Side/B Side)	Yr	VG	VG+	NM
CAPITOL					
2736	Fatback/Gotta Find a Way	1970	—	3.00	6.00
3009	D.O.A./Children's Heritage	1971	2.00	4.00	8.00
3089	You Gotta Roll/A Certain Kind	1971	—	3.00	6.00
3161	Jessica/You Gotta Roll	1971	—	3.00	6.00
3227	Rock and Roll Candy Man/Don't Eat the Children	1971	—	3.00	6.00
3320	Erosion/Castle of Thoughts	1972	—	2.50	5.00
3399	Castle of Thoughts/D.O.A.	1972	—	2.50	5.00
3451	Help Is On the Way/Thank You Daniel Ellsburg	1972	—	2.50	5.00
3770	Voices/Thank You Daniel Ellsburg	1973	—	2.50	5.00

Albums

Number	Title (A Side/B Side)	Yr	VG	VG+	NM
CAPITOL					
ST-435	Bloodrock	1970	3.75	7.50	15.00
ST-491	Bloodrock 2	1970	3.75	7.50	15.00
SM-645	Bloodrock U.S.A.	197?	2.50	5.00	10.00
—Reissue with new prefix					
SMAS-645	Bloodrock U.S.A.	1971	3.75	7.50	15.00
SM-765	Bloodrock 3	197?	2.50	5.00	10.00
—Reissue with new prefix					
ST-765	Bloodrock 3	1971	3.75	7.50	15.00
SVBB-11038 [(2)]	Bloodrock Live	1972	5.00	10.00	20.00
SW-11109	Bloodrock Passage	1972	3.75	7.50	15.00
SMAS-11259	Whirlwind Tongues	1973	3.75	7.50	15.00
SM-11417	Bloodrock 'N' Roll	1975	3.00	6.00	12.00

BLOODSTONE

45s

Number	Title (A Side/B Side)	Yr	VG	VG+	NM
EPIC					
50437	Got to Find Myself Another Baby/Weeping Willow Tree	1977	—	2.00	4.00
LONDON					
1038	Girl/Judy, Judy	1972	—	2.50	5.00
1042	That's the Way We Make Our Music/This Thing Is Heavy	1972	—	2.50	5.00
1046	Natural High/Peter's Jones	1973	—	2.50	5.00
1051	Never Let You Go/You Know We've Learned	1973	—	2.50	5.00
1052	Outside Woman/Dumb Dude	1974	—	2.50	5.00
1055	That's Not How It Goes/Everybody Needs Love	1974	—	2.50	5.00
1059	I Believe You Now/I Need Time	1974	—	2.50	5.00
1061	My Little Lady/Loving You Is Just a Pastime	1975	—	2.50	5.00
1062	Give Me Your Heart/Something's Missing	1975	—	2.50	5.00
1062 [PS]	Give Me Your Heart/Something's Missing	1975	2.50	5.00	10.00
1064	Do You Wanna Do a Thing/Save Me	1976	—	2.50	5.00
1067	Just Like in the Movies/Little Linda	1976	—	2.50	5.00
MOTOWN					
1458	Just Wanna Get the Feel of It/It's Been a Long Time	1978	—	2.00	4.00
T-NECK					
02825	We Go a Long Way Back/Nite Time Fun	1982	—	2.00	4.00
03049	Go On and Cry/(Instrumental)	1982	—	2.00	4.00
03394	My Love Grows Stronger/(Instrumental)	1982	—	2.00	4.00
04465	Instant Love/It Feels So Good	1984	—	2.00	4.00
04592	Bloodstone's Party/Feel the Heat	1984	—	2.00	4.00

Albums

Number	Title (A Side/B Side)	Yr	VG	VG+	NM
LONDON					
XPS 620	Natural High	1973	3.00	6.00	12.00
XPS 634	Unreal	1973	3.00	6.00	12.00
APS 647	I Need Time	1974	3.00	6.00	12.00
PS 654	Riddle of the Sphinx	1975	3.00	6.00	12.00
PS 671	Do a Thing?	1976	3.00	6.00	12.00
MOTOWN					
M7-909	Don't Stop!	1978	2.50	5.00	10.00
T-NECK					
FZ 38115	We Go a Long Way Back	1982	2.50	5.00	10.00
FZ 39146	Bloodstone's Party	1984	2.50	5.00	10.00
PZ 40016	Greatest Hits	1985	2.00	4.00	8.00
PZ 40042	Lullaby of Broadway	1985	2.00	4.00	8.00

BLOODY MARY

Albums

Number	Title (A Side/B Side)	Yr	VG	VG+	NM
FAMILY PRODUCTIONS					
FPS-2707	Bloody Mary	1972	6.25	12.50	25.00

BLOOM, BOBBY

Number	Title (A Side/B Side)	Yr	VG	VG+	NM
45s					
KAMA SUTRA					
210	Heart of Town/Make the Radio a Little Louder	1966	3.00	6.00	12.00
—As "Bobby Mann"					
Albums					
BUDDAH					
BDS-5072	Where Are We Going	1971	3.00	6.00	12.00
L&R					
1035	The Bobby Bloom Album	1970	3.75	7.50	15.00

BLOOMFIELD, MIKE

Number	Title (A Side/B Side)	Yr	VG	VG+	NM
Albums					
COLUMBIA					
CS 9883	It's Not Killing Me	1969	3.75	7.50	15.00
—Red "360 Sound" label					
C2 37578 [(2)]	Bloomfield	1982	3.00	6.00	12.00
HARMONY					
KH 30395	It's Not Killing Me	1971	2.50	5.00	10.00
TAKOMA					
C-1059	Analine	1977	2.50	5.00	10.00
C-1063	Michael Bloomfield	1978	2.50	5.00	10.00
C-1070	Between a Hard Place and the Ground	1979	2.50	5.00	10.00
TAK-7059	Analine	198?	2.00	4.00	8.00
TAK-7063	Michael Bloomfield	198?	2.00	4.00	8.00
TAK-7070	Between a Hard Place and the Ground	198?	2.00	4.00	8.00
TAK-7091	Cruisin' for a Bruisin'	198?	2.00	4.00	8.00
WATERHOUSE					
11	Living in the Fast Lane	1981	2.50	5.00	10.00

BLOOMFIELD, MIKE, AND NICK GRAVENITES

Number	Title (A Side/B Side)	Yr	VG	VG+	NM
Albums					
COLUMBIA					
CS 9899	My Labors	1969	3.00	6.00	12.00
—Red "360 Sound" label					
CS 9899	My Labors	1970	2.50	5.00	10.00
—Orange label					

BLOOMFIELD, MIKE/JOHN PAUL HAMMOND/DR. JOHN

Number	Title (A Side/B Side)	Yr	VG	VG+	NM
45s					
COLUMBIA					
45887	I Yi Yi/Pretty Thing	1973	—	3.00	6.00
Albums					
COLUMBIA					
KC 32172	Triumvirate	1973	3.00	6.00	12.00

BLOOMFIELD, MIKE, AND AL KOOPER

Also see each artist's individual listings.

Number	Title (A Side/B Side)	Yr	VG	VG+	NM
45s					
COLUMBIA					
44678	The Weight/Mama's Temptation	1968	—	3.00	6.00
Albums					
COLUMBIA					
KGP 6 [(2)]	The Live Adventures of Mike Bloomfield & Al Kooper	1969	6.25	12.50	25.00
—Red "360 Sound" labels					
PG 6 [(2)]	The Live Adventures of Mike Bloomfield & Al Kooper	197?	3.00	6.00	12.00
—Reissue with new prefix					

BLOOMFIELD, MIKE/AL KOOPER/STEVE STILLS

Also see each artist's individual listings.

Number	Title (A Side/B Side)	Yr	VG	VG+	NM
45s					
COLUMBIA					
44657	Season of the Witch/Albert's Shuffle	1968	—	3.00	6.00
Albums					
COLUMBIA					
CS 9701	Super Session	1968	5.00	10.00	20.00
—Red "360 Sound" label					
CS 9701	Super Session	1970	2.50	5.00	10.00
—Orange label					
PC 9701	Super Session	198?	2.00	4.00	8.00
—Reissue with new prefix					
CQ 30991 [Q]	Super Session	1971	5.00	10.00	20.00
MOBILE FIDELITY					
1-178	Super Session	198?	10.00	20.00	40.00
—Audiophile vinyl					

BLOSSOMS, THE

Probably all the same group.

Number	Title (A Side/B Side)	Yr	VG	VG+	NM
Albums					
LION					
1007	Shockwave	1972	3.75	7.50	15.00

BLUE, DAVID

Number	Title (A Side/B Side)	Yr	VG	VG+	NM
Albums					
ASYLUM					
7E-1043	Comin' Back for More	1975	2.50	5.00	10.00
7E-1077	Cupid's Arrow	1976	2.50	5.00	10.00
SD 5052	Stories	1972	3.00	6.00	12.00
SD 5066	The Nice Baby and the Angel	1973	3.00	6.00	12.00
ELEKTRA					
EKM-4003 [M]	David Blue	1966	5.00	10.00	20.00
EKS-74003 [S]	David Blue	1966	5.00	10.00	20.00
REPRISE					
RS 6296	These 23 Days in September	1968	3.75	7.50	15.00

BLUE BARONS, THE

Number	Title (A Side/B Side)	Yr	VG	VG+	NM
Albums					
PHILIPS					
PHM 200017 [M]	Twist to the Great Blues Hits	1962	5.00	10.00	20.00
PHS 600017 [S]	Twist to the Great Blues Hits	1962	6.25	12.50	25.00

BLUE BELLES, THE

Also see PATTI LaBELLE AND THE BLUE BELLES.

Number	Title (A Side/B Side)	Yr	VG	VG+	NM
45s					
ATLANTIC					
987	The Story of a Fool/Cancel the Call	1953	37.50	75.00	150.00

BLUE CHEER

Number	Title (A Side/B Side)	Yr	VG	VG+	NM
45s					
MERCURY					
872804-7	Summertime Blues/Just a Little Bit	1989	—	2.00	4.00
—Reissue					
PHILIPS					
40516	Summertime Blues/Out of Focus	1968	3.00	6.00	12.00
40516 [PS]	Summertime Blues/Out of Focus	1968	6.25	12.50	25.00
40541	Just a Little Bit/Gypsy Ball	1968	2.50	5.00	10.00
40561	Sun Cycle/Albert's Shuffle	1968	2.50	5.00	10.00
40561	Sun Cycle/Feathers from Our Tree	1968	2.50	5.00	10.00
40602	West Coast Child of Sunshine/When It All Gets Old	1969	2.00	4.00	8.00
40651	All Night Long/Fortunes	1969	2.00	4.00	8.00
40664	Hello L.A., Bye-Bye Birmingham/Natural Man	1970	2.00	4.00	8.00
40682	Ain't That the Way/Fool	1970	2.00	4.00	8.00
40691	Babji (Twilight Raga)/Pilot	1971	2.00	4.00	8.00
40691	Babji (Twilight Raga)/Fool	1971	2.50	5.00	10.00
Albums					
MEGAFORCE/CAROLINE					
CAROL-1395-1	The Beast Is Back	198?	3.00	6.00	12.00
PHILIPS					
PHM 200264 [M]	Vincebus Eruptum	1968	20.00	40.00	80.00
PHS 600264 [S]	Vincebus Eruptum	1968	10.00	20.00	40.00
PHS 600278	Outsideinside	1968	10.00	20.00	40.00
PHS 600305	New! Improved! Blue Cheer	1969	10.00	20.00	40.00
PHS 600333	Blue Cheer	1970	10.00	20.00	40.00
PHS 600347	The Original Human Being	1970	10.00	20.00	40.00
PHS 600350	Oh! Pleasant Hope	1971	10.00	20.00	40.00
RHINO					
RNLP 70130	Louder Than God (The Best of Blue Cheer, 1968-1969)	1986	2.50	5.00	10.00

BLUE DIAMONDS, THE

With Ernie Kador (later ERNIE K-DOE)

Number	Title (A Side/B Side)	Yr	VG	VG+	NM
45s					
SAVOY					
1134	Honey Baby/No Money	1954	15.00	30.00	60.00

BLUE HAZE

Number	Title (A Side/B Side)	Yr	VG	VG+	NM
45s					
A&M					
1357	Smoke Gets In Your Eyes/Anna Roseanna	1972	—	2.00	4.00
1426	Take Away My Heart Teresa/You'll Never Walk Alone	1973	—	2.00	4.00

BLUE JAYS, THE (1)

Los Angeles-based male vocal group.

Number	Title (A Side/B Side)	Yr	VG	VG+	NM
45s					
MILESTONE					
2008	Lover's Island/You're Gonna Cry	1961	10.00	20.00	40.00
—Dark blue label					
2008	Lover's Island/You're Gonna Cry	1961	7.50	15.00	30.00
—Light blue and white label					
2008	Lover's Island/You're Gonna Cry	1961	7.50	15.00	30.00
—Green label					
2009	Tears Are Falling/Tree Tall Men	1961	7.50	15.00	30.00
2010	Let's Make Love/Rock, Rock, Rock	1962	5.00	10.00	20.00
2012	The Right to Love/Rock, Rock, Rock	1962	5.00	10.00	20.00
2014	Venus, My Love/Tall Len	1962	15.00	30.00	60.00
Albums					
MILESTONE					
1001 [M]	The Blue Jays Meet Little Caesar and the Romans	1962	25.00	50.00	100.00

BLUE JAYS, THE (2)

Chicago-based (probably) male vocal group.

Number	Title (A Side/B Side)	Yr	VG	VG+	NM
45s					
CHECKER					
782	White Cliffs of Dover/Hey Poppa	1953	1000.	1500.	2000.

BLUE JAYS, THE (U)

Number	Title (A Side/B Side)	Yr	VG	VG+	NM
45s					
LAURIE					
3037	Sweet Georgia Brown/J.J.'s Blues	1959	6.25	12.50	25.00
MAP CITY					
300	Hang On/Hard Thing to Accept	1969	—	3.00	6.00
307	Freedom (Where Have You Gone)/(B-side unknown)	1971	—	3.00	6.00
311	Jackson/Wacka Wacka	1971	—	3.00	6.00
PHILIPS					
40186	Who (Will I Be Today)?/Come On Baby	1964	3.75	7.50	15.00
ROULETTE					
4169	Practical Joker/Barbara	1959	5.00	10.00	20.00
4264	Kum Ba Yah/Cave Man Love	1960	5.00	10.00	20.00
WARNER BROS.					
7299	Edgy/I'm Only Dreaming	1969	—	3.00	6.00

BLUE MAGIC

12-Inch Singles

Number	Title (A Side/B Side)	Yr	VG	VG+	NM
ATCO					
99914	Magic Number/See Through	1983	2.00	4.00	8.00

45s

Number	Title (A Side/B Side)	Yr	VG	VG+	NM
ATCO					
6910	Spell/Guess Who	1972	—	3.00	6.00
6930	Look Me Up/What's Come Over Me	1973	—	3.00	6.00
6949	Stop to Start/Where Have You Been	1973	—	3.00	6.00
6961	Sideshow/Just Don't Want to Be Lonely	1974	—	3.00	6.00
7004	Three Ring Circus/Welcome to the Club	1974	—	3.00	6.00
7014	Love Has Found Its Way to Me/When Ya Coming Home	1975	—	3.00	6.00
7031	Chasing Rainbows/You Won't Have to Tell Me Goodbye	1975	—	2.50	5.00
7046	Grateful Part 1/Grateful Part 2	1976	—	2.50	5.00
7052	Freak-N-Stein/Stop and Get a Hold of Yourself	1976	—	2.50	5.00
7061	Teach Me (It's Something About Love)/Spark of Love	1976	—	2.50	5.00
7090	I Waited/Can't Get You Out of My Mind	1978	—	2.00	4.00
CAPITOL					
4977	Land of Make Believe/Remember November	1981	—	2.00	4.00
DEF JAM					
68566	Romeo and Juliet/Couldn't Get to Sleep Last Night	1989	—	2.00	4.00
LIBERTY					
56146	Can I Say I Love You/One, Two, Three	1969	2.50	5.00	10.00
MIRAGE					
99843	See Through/(B-side unknown)	1983	—	2.00	4.00
99869	Since You Been Gone/If You Move You Lose	1983	—	2.00	4.00
OBR					
68900	It's Like Magic/Couldn't Get to Sleep Last Night	1989	—	2.00	4.00
69016	You Are My Everything/Feels So Good	1989	—	2.00	4.00
WMOT					
4003	Summer Snow/(B-side unknown)	1976	—	2.50	5.00

Albums

Number	Title (A Side/B Side)	Yr	VG	VG+	NM
ATCO					
SD 36-103	The Magic of the Blue	1974	3.00	6.00	12.00
SD 38-104	The Message	1977	3.00	6.00	12.00
SD 36-120	Thirteen Blue Magic Lane	1975	3.00	6.00	12.00
SD 36-140	Mystic Dragons	1976	3.00	6.00	12.00
SD 7038	Blue Magic	1974	3.00	6.00	12.00
CAPITOL					
ST-12143	Welcome Back	1981	2.50	5.00	10.00
COLLECTABLES					
COL-5031	The Magic of the Blue: Greatest Hits	198?	2.50	5.00	10.00
MIRAGE					
90074	Migiac #	1983	2.50	5.00	10.00
OBR					
45097	From Out of the Blue	1989	2.50	5.00	10.00
OMNI					
90527	Greatest Hits	1986	2.50	5.00	10.00

BLUE MINK

Also see MADELINE BELL.

45s

Number	Title (A Side/B Side)	Yr	VG	VG+	NM
MCA					
40031	I Can't Find the Answer/By the Devil I Was Tempted	1973	—	2.50	5.00
40091	Randy/Another Without You Day	1973	—	2.50	5.00
40230	Get Up/Loneliness	1974	—	2.50	5.00
PHILIPS					
40658	Melting Pot/But Not Forever	1969	2.00	4.00	8.00
40672	Can You Feel It Baby/(B-side unknown)	1970	2.00	4.00	8.00
40678	Good Morning Freedom/Mary Jane	1970	—	—	—
—Canceled					
40686	Our World/Respects to Mrs. Jones	1970	2.00	4.00	8.00
40697	Gasoline Alley Bred/We Have All Been Saved	1971	2.00	4.00	8.00

Albums

Number	Title (A Side/B Side)	Yr	VG	VG+	NM
MCA					
332	Blue Mink	1973	3.00	6.00	12.00
PHILIPS					
PHS 600323	Melting Pot	1970	3.75	7.50	15.00
PHS 600339	Real Mink	1970	3.75	7.50	15.00

BLUE NOTES, THE (1)

This group evolved into HAROLD MELVIN AND THE BLUE NOTES.

45s

Number	Title (A Side/B Side)	Yr	VG	VG+	NM
3 SONS					
103	WPLJ/While I'm Away	1962	7.50	15.00	30.00
COLLECTABLES					
1113	Winter Wonderland/O Holy Night	198?	—	2.00	4.00
—Reissue					
JOSIE					
800	If You Love Me/There's Something in Your Eyes, Eloise	1956	50.00	100.00	200.00
814	Letters/With This Pen	1957	30.00	60.00	120.00
—As "Todd Randall and the Blue Notes"					
823	The Retribution Blues/Wagon Wheels	1957	37.50	75.00	150.00
PORT					
70021	If You Love Me/There's Something in Your Eyes, Eloise	1958	15.00	30.00	60.00
RED TOP					
135	My Hero/A Good Woman	1963	7.50	15.00	30.00
UNI					
55132	Got Chills and Cold Thrills/Never Gonna Leave You	1969	3.00	6.00	12.00
55201	This Time Will Be Different/Lucky Me	1970	3.00	6.00	12.00
VAL-UE					
213	My Hero/A Good Woman	1960	20.00	40.00	80.00
215	Winter Wonderland/O Holy Night	1960	20.00	40.00	80.00

Albums

Number	Title (A Side/B Side)	Yr	VG	VG+	NM
COLLECTABLES					
COL-5006	The Early Years	1982	3.00	6.00	12.00

BLUE NOTES, THE (2)

Earlier male vocal group, no relation to (1).

45s

Number	Title (A Side/B Side)	Yr	VG	VG+	NM
RAMA					
25	If You'll Be Mine/Too Hot to Handle	1953	50.00	100.00	200.00

BLUE NOTES, THE (U)

None of these appear to be by (1) or (2), but we don't know how many different groups are represented below.

45s

Number	Title (A Side/B Side)	Yr	VG	VG+	NM
20TH CENTURY					
1213	Blue Star/(B-side unknown)	1961	3.75	7.50	15.00
DOT					
15692	My Steady Girl/Mighty Lou	1958	6.25	12.50	25.00
—B-side by Henry Wilson					
15720	Darling of Mine/I Love Her So	1958	6.25	12.50	25.00
TNT					
150	Darling of Mine/I Love Her So	1958	7.50	15.00	30.00

BLUE ORCHIDS, THE

45s

Number	Title (A Side/B Side)	Yr	VG	VG+	NM
LONDON					
9637	Love Hit Me/Don't Make Me Mad	1964	2.50	5.00	10.00
9669	Oo-Chang-a-Lang/I've Got That Feeling	1964	2.50	5.00	10.00

BLUE OYSTER CULT

45s

Number	Title (A Side/B Side)	Yr	VG	VG+	NM
COLUMBIA					
02415	Burnin' for You/Vengeance (The Fact)	1981	—	2.00	4.00
02415 [PS]	Burnin' for You/Vengeance (The Fact)	1981	—	2.50	5.00
03137	(Don't Fear) The Reaper/Burnin' for You	1982	—	2.00	4.00
—Reissue					
04298	Shooting Shark/Dragon Lady	1984	—	—	3.00
04435	Take Me Away/Let Go	1984	—	—	3.00
05845	Dancin' in the Ruins/Shadow Warrior	1986	—	—	3.00
06199	Perfect Water/Spy in the House of Knight	1986	—	—	3.00
10046	Dominance and Submission/Career of Evil	1974	—	3.00	6.00
10169	Born to Be Wild/Born to Be Wild	1975	—	3.00	6.00
10384	(Don't Fear) The Reaper/Tattoo Vampire	1976	—	3.00	6.00
10560	Debby Denise/This Ain't the Summer of Love	1977	—	2.50	5.00
10659	Goin' Through the Motions/Searchin' for Celine	1977	—	2.50	5.00
10697	Godzilla/Nosferatu	1978	—	2.50	5.00
10725	Godzilla (Live)/Godzilla	1978	—	2.50	5.00
10841	We Gotta Get Out of This Place/E.T.I. (Extra Terrestrial Intelligence)	1978	—	2.50	5.00
11055	In There/Lonely Teardrops	1979	—	2.00	4.00
11145	You're Not the One (I Was Looking For)/Moon Crazy	1979	—	2.00	4.00
11401	Here's Johnny (The Marshall Plan)/Divine Wind	1980	—	2.00	4.00
45598	Cities on Flame with Rock and Roll/Before the Kiss, A Redcap	1972	2.50	5.00	10.00
45879	Hot Rods to Hell/Seven Screaming Diz Busters	1973	—	3.00	6.00
45879 [PS]	Hot Rods to Hell/Seven Screaming Diz Busters	1973	3.00	6.00	12.00
74716	(Don't Fear) The Reaper/Burnin' for You	1992	—	—	3.00
—Reissue					

Albums

Number	Title (A Side/B Side)	Yr	VG	VG+	NM
COLUMBIA					
C 31063	Blue Oyster Cult	1972	3.00	6.00	12.00
PC 31063	Blue Oyster Cult	197?	2.00	4.00	8.00
—Reissue with new prefix					
CQ 32017 [Q]	Tyranny and Mutation	1973	7.50	15.00	30.00
KC 32017	Tyranny and Mutation	1973	3.00	6.00	12.00
PC 32017	Tyranny and Mutation	197?	2.00	4.00	8.00
—Reissue with new prefix					
CQ 32858 [Q]	Secret Treaties	1974	7.50	15.00	30.00
KC 32858	Secret Treaties	1974	3.00	6.00	12.00
PC 32858	Secret Treaties	197?	2.00	4.00	8.00
—Reissue with new prefix					
KG 33371 [(2)]	On Your Feet or On Your Knees	1975	3.75	7.50	15.00
PC 34164	Agents of Fortune	1976	2.50	5.00	10.00
—Original gatefold with no bar code on cover					
PC 34164	Agents of Fortune	198?	2.00	4.00	8.00
—Budget-line reissue with bar code					
JC 35019	Spectres	1977	2.50	5.00	10.00
PC 35019	Spectres	198?	2.00	4.00	8.00
—Budget-line reissue					
JC 35563	Some Enchanted Evening	1978	2.50	5.00	10.00
PC 35563	Some Enchanted Evening	198?	2.00	4.00	8.00
—Budget-line reissue					
JC 36009	Mirrors	1979	2.50	5.00	10.00
PC 36009	Mirrors	198?	2.00	4.00	8.00
—Budget-line reissue					
JC 36550	Cultosaurus Erectus	1980	2.50	5.00	10.00
PC 36550	Cultosaurus Erectus	198?	2.00	4.00	8.00
—Budget-line reissue					
FC 37389	Fire of Unknown Origin	1981	2.50	5.00	10.00
PC 37389	Fire of Unknown Origin	1984	2.00	4.00	8.00
—Budget-line reissue					
KG 37946 [(2)]	Extraterrestrial Live	1982	3.00	6.00	12.00
FC 38947	The Revolution by Night	1983	2.50	5.00	10.00
PC 38947	The Revolution by Night	1985	2.00	4.00	8.00
—Budget-line reissue					
FC 39979	Club Ninja	1986	2.50	5.00	10.00
FC 40618	Imaginos	1988	2.50	5.00	10.00

BLUE RIDGE RANGERS, THE

See JOHN FOGERTY.

BLUE RONDOS, THE

45s

PARKWAY

Number	Title (A Side/B Side)	Yr	VG	VG+	NM
937	Little Baby/Baby I Go for You	1964	3.00	6.00	12.00

BLUE STARS

45s

MERCURY

Number	Title (A Side/B Side)	Yr	VG	VG+	NM
70742	Lullaby of Birdland/That's My Girl	1955	2.50	5.00	10.00
70808	Mambo Italiano/Speak Low	1956	2.50	5.00	10.00
70924	Jumpin' at the Woodside/Hernando's Hideaway	1956	2.50	5.00	10.00

BLUE STARS, THE

Albums

EMARCY

Number	Title (A Side/B Side)	Yr	VG	VG+	NM
MG-36067 [M]	Lullaby of Birdland	1956	10.00	20.00	40.00

BLUE SWEDE

45s

CAPITOL

Number	Title (A Side/B Side)	Yr	VG	VG+	NM
3627	Hooked on a Feeling/Gotta Have Your Love	1973	2.00	4.00	8.00

EMI

Number	Title (A Side/B Side)	Yr	VG	VG+	NM
3627	Hooked on a Feeling/Gotta Have Your Love	1974	—	2.50	5.00
3893	Silly Milly/Lonely Sunday Afternoon	1974	—	2.00	4.00
3938	Never My Love/Pinewood Rally	1974	—	2.00	4.00
3938 [PS]	Never My Love/Pinewood Rally	1974	—	3.00	6.00
4029	Hush-I'm Alive/Lonely Summer Afternoon	1975	—	2.00	4.00
4065	Dr. Rock and Roll/Gotta Have Your Love	1975	—	2.00	4.00

Albums

EMI

Number	Title (A Side/B Side)	Yr	VG	VG+	NM
ST-11266	Hooked on a Feeling	1974	2.50	5.00	10.00
ST-11346	Out of the Blue	1975	2.50	5.00	10.00

BLUE THINGS, THE

45s

RCA VICTOR

Number	Title (A Side/B Side)	Yr	VG	VG+	NM
47-8692	La Do Da Da/I Must Be Doing Something Wrong	1965	6.25	12.50	25.00
47-8860	Doll House/Man on the Street	1966	6.25	12.50	25.00
47-8998	Orange Rooftop of Your Mind/One Hour Cleaners	1966	6.25	12.50	25.00
47-9203	Twist and Shout/You Can Live in Our Tree	1967	6.25	12.50	25.00
47-9308	Yes, My Friend/Somebody Help Me	1967	6.25	12.50	25.00

RUFF

Number	Title (A Side/B Side)	Yr	VG	VG+	NM
1000	Mary Lou/Your Turn to Cry	1965	10.00	20.00	40.00
1002	Pretty Thing/Just Two Days Ago	1965	10.00	20.00	40.00

Albums

RCA VICTOR

Number	Title (A Side/B Side)	Yr	VG	VG+	NM
LPM-3603 [M]	The Blue Things	1966	30.00	60.00	120.00
LSP-3603 [S]	The Blue Things	1966	45.00	90.00	180.00

BLUE TONES, THE

45s

BLUE JAY

Number	Title (A Side/B Side)	Yr	VG	VG+	NM
101	I'll Love You Till the End of Time/(Instrumental)	1965	37.50	75.00	150.00

—Reissued on Swan 4200 by "The Royal Teens"

BLUE VELVET BAND, THE

45s

WARNER BROS.

Number	Title (A Side/B Side)	Yr	VG	VG+	NM
7320	Hitch-Hiker/Sittin' on Top of the World	1969	2.00	4.00	8.00

Albums

WARNER BROS.

Number	Title (A Side/B Side)	Yr	VG	VG+	NM
WS 1802	Sweet Moments	1969	7.50	15.00	30.00

BLUENOTES, THE

Probably not related to any of the groups called THE BLUE NOTES, they were a white male vocal group from North Carolina.

45s

BROOKE

Number	Title (A Side/B Side)	Yr	VG	VG+	NM
111	I Don't Know What It Is/You Can't Get Away from Love	1959	4.00	8.00	16.00
116	Forever on My Mind/I'm Gonna Find Out	1960	3.75	7.50	15.00
119	It Had to be You/Summer Love	1960	3.75	7.50	15.00

BLUES CLIMAX

Albums

HORNE

Number	Title (A Side/B Side)	Yr	VG	VG+	NM
JC-333	Blues Climax	1969	15.00	30.00	60.00

BLUES IMAGE

45s

ATCO

Number	Title (A Side/B Side)	Yr	VG	VG+	NM
6718	Lay Your Sweet Love on Me/Outside Was Night	1969	—	2.00	4.00
6746	Ride Captain Ride/Pay My Dues	1970	—	2.50	5.00
6777	Gas Lamps and Clay/Running the Water	1970	—	2.00	4.00
6798	Rise Up/Take Me Back	1971	—	2.00	4.00
6814	Behind Every Man/It's the Truth	1971	—	2.00	4.00

Albums

ATCO

Number	Title (A Side/B Side)	Yr	VG	VG+	NM
SD 33-300	Blues Image	1969	6.25	12.50	25.00
SD 33-317	Open	1970	5.00	10.00	20.00
SD 33-346	Red, White and Blues Image	1971	5.00	10.00	20.00

BLUES MAGOOS

45s

ABC

Number	Title (A Side/B Side)	Yr	VG	VG+	NM
11226	Heartbreak Hotel/I Can Feel It (Feelin' Time)	1969	2.00	4.00	8.00
11250	Never Goin' Back to Georgia/Feelin' Time	1969	2.00	4.00	8.00
11283	Gulf Coast Bound/Sea Breeze Express	1970	2.00	4.00	8.00

GANIM

Number	Title (A Side/B Side)	Yr	VG	VG+	NM
1000	Who Do You Love/Let Your Love Ride	1968	10.00	20.00	40.00

MERCURY

Number	Title (A Side/B Side)	Yr	VG	VG+	NM
72590	Tobacco Road/Sometimes I Think About You	1966	3.75	7.50	15.00
72622	(We Ain't Got) Nothin' Yet/Gotta Get Away	1966	5.00	10.00	20.00
72660	Pipe Dream/There's a Chance We Can Make It	1967	3.75	7.50	15.00
72660 [PS]	Pipe Dream/There's a Chance We Can Make It	1967	7.50	15.00	30.00
72692	One by One/Dante's Inferno	1967	3.75	7.50	15.00
72692 [PS]	One by One/Dante's Inferno	1967	7.50	15.00	30.00
72707	I Wanna Be There/Summer Is the Man	1967	2.50	5.00	10.00
72729	Life Is Just a Cher O'Bowlies/There She Goes	1967	2.50	5.00	10.00
72762	Jingle Bells/Santa Claus Is Coming to Town	1967	2.50	5.00	10.00
72838	I Can Hear the Grass Grow/Yellow Rose	1968	2.50	5.00	10.00
872806-7	(We Ain't Got) Nothin' Yet/Pipedream	1989	—	—	3.00

—Reissue

VERVE FOLKWAYS

Number	Title (A Side/B Side)	Yr	VG	VG+	NM
5006	People Had No Faces/So I'm Wrong and You Are Right	1966	5.00	10.00	20.00

—As "The Bloos Magoos"

Number	Title (A Side/B Side)	Yr	VG	VG+	NM
5006	People Had No Faces/So I'm Wrong and You Are Right	1966	3.75	7.50	15.00
5044	People Had No Faces/So I'm Wrong and You Are Right	1967	3.75	7.50	15.00

Albums

ABC

Number	Title (A Side/B Side)	Yr	VG	VG+	NM
S-697	Never Goin' Back to Georgia	1969	5.00	10.00	20.00
S-710	Gulf Coast Bound	1970	5.00	10.00	20.00

MERCURY

Number	Title (A Side/B Side)	Yr	VG	VG+	NM
MG-21096 [M]	Psychedelic Lollipop	1966	10.00	20.00	40.00

—With "21096" in trail-off; this record is mono

Number	Title (A Side/B Side)	Yr	VG	VG+	NM
MG-21096 [S]	Psychedelic Lollipop	1966	10.00	20.00	40.00

—With "2/61096" in trail-off; this record plays stereo, though labeled mono

Number	Title (A Side/B Side)	Yr	VG	VG+	NM
21104/61104	Electric Comic Book Comic Book	1967	3.75	7.50	15.00
MG-21104 [M]	Electric Comic Book	1967	7.50	15.00	30.00
SR-61096	Psychedelic Lollipop	197?	3.00	6.00	12.00

—Reissue on Chicago skyline label

Number	Title (A Side/B Side)	Yr	VG	VG+	NM
SR-61096 [S]	Psychedelic Lollipop	1966	12.50	25.00	50.00
SR-61104 [S]	Electric Comic Book	1967	10.00	20.00	40.00
SR-61167	Basic Blues Magoos	1968	7.50	15.00	30.00

BLUES PROJECT, THE

45s

CAPITOL

Number	Title (A Side/B Side)	Yr	VG	VG+	NM
3374	Crazy Girl/Easy Lady	1972	2.00	4.00	8.00

MCA

Number	Title (A Side/B Side)	Yr	VG	VG+	NM
40154	Fly Away/Louisiana Blues	1973	—	2.50	5.00

VERVE FOLKWAYS

Number	Title (A Side/B Side)	Yr	VG	VG+	NM
5004	Back Door Man/Violets of Dawn	1966	3.75	7.50	15.00
5013	Catch the Wind/I Want to Be Your Driver	1966	3.75	7.50	15.00
5019	Where There's Smoke There's Fire/Goin' Down Louisiana	1966	3.75	7.50	15.00
5019 [PS]	Where There's Smoke There's Fire/Goin' Down Louisiana	1966	6.25	12.50	25.00
5032	I Can't Keep from Crying Sometimes/The Way My Baby Walks	1966	3.75	7.50	15.00
5040	No Time Like the Right Time/Steve's Song	1967	3.00	6.00	12.00

VERVE FORECAST

Number	Title (A Side/B Side)	Yr	VG	VG+	NM
5063	Gentle Dreams/Lost in the Shuffle	1967	3.00	6.00	12.00

Albums

CAPITOL

Number	Title (A Side/B Side)	Yr	VG	VG+	NM
ST-782	Lazarus	1971	3.00	6.00	12.00
SMAS-11017	The Blues Project	1972	3.00	6.00	12.00

MCA

Number	Title (A Side/B Side)	Yr	VG	VG+	NM
8003 [(2)]	Reunion in Central Park	1975	3.75	7.50	15.00

—Reissue of Sounds of the South LP; black rainbow labels

MGM

Number	Title (A Side/B Side)	Yr	VG	VG+	NM
GAS-118	The Blues Project	1970	3.00	6.00	12.00
M3G-4953	Archetypes	1974	3.00	6.00	12.00

RHINO

Number	Title (A Side/B Side)	Yr	VG	VG+	NM
R1-70165	No Time Like the Right Time: The Best of the Blues Project	1989	3.00	6.00	12.00

SOUNDS OF THE SOUTH

Number	Title (A Side/B Side)	Yr	VG	VG+	NM
MCA2-8003 [(2)]	Reunion in Central Park	1973	5.00	10.00	20.00

—Yellow labels

VERVE

Number	Title (A Side/B Side)	Yr	VG	VG+	NM
827918-1	Projections	1986	2.00	4.00	8.00

—Reissue

VERVE FOLKWAYS

Number	Title (A Side/B Side)	Yr	VG	VG+	NM
FT-3000 [M]	Live at the Café a Go Go	1966	5.00	10.00	20.00
FTS-3000 [S]	Live at the Café a Go Go	1966	6.25	12.50	25.00
FT-3008 [M]	Projections	1966	5.00	10.00	20.00
FTS-3008 [S]	Projections	1966	6.25	12.50	25.00

VERVE FORECAST

Number	Title (A Side/B Side)	Yr	VG	VG+	NM
FT-3000 [M]	Live at the Café a Go Go	1967	3.75	7.50	15.00

—Reissue of Verve Folkways 3000

Number	Title (A Side/B Side)	Yr	VG	VG+	NM
FTS-3000 [S]	Live at the Café a Go Go	1967	5.00	10.00	20.00

—Reissue of Verve Folkways 3000

Number	Title (A Side/B Side)	Yr	VG	VG+	NM
FT-3008 [M]	Projections	1967	3.75	7.50	15.00

—Reissue of Verve Folkways 3008

Number	Title (A Side/B Side)	Yr	VG	VG+	NM
FTS-3008 [S]	Projections	1967	5.00	10.00	20.00

—Reissue of Verve Folkways 3008

Number	Title (A Side/B Side)	Yr	VG	VG+	NM
FT-3025 [M]	The Blues Project Live at Town Hall	1967	5.00	10.00	20.00
FTS-3025 [S]	The Blues Project Live at Town Hall	1967	3.75	7.50	15.00
FTS-3046	Planned Obsolescence	1968	3.75	7.50	15.00
FTS-3069	Flanders/Kalb/Katz, Etc.	1969	3.75	7.50	15.00
FTS-3077	Best of the Blues Project	1969	3.75	7.50	15.00

BLUNSTONE, COLIN
Also see THE ZOMBIES.

45s

Number	Title (A Side/B Side)	Yr	VG	VG+	NM
EPIC					
10826	Caroline Goodbye/Misty Roses	1972	—	2.50	5.00
10868	Say You Don't Mind/Though You Are Far Away	1972	—	2.50	5.00
10948	I Don't Believe in Miracles/I've Always Had You	1973	—	2.50	5.00
10981	Pay Me Later/I Want Some More	1973	—	2.50	5.00
11004	Andorra/Carolina Goodbye	1973	—	2.50	5.00
ROCKET					
PB-11356	I'll Never Forget You/You Are the Way for Me	1978	—	2.00	4.00
PB-11412	Photograph/Touch and Go	1978	—	2.00	4.00

Albums

Number	Title (A Side/B Side)	Yr	VG	VG+	NM
EPIC					
E 30974	One Year	1972	3.00	6.00	12.00
KE 31994	Ennismore	1972	3.00	6.00	12.00
KE 32962	Journey	1974	3.00	6.00	12.00
ROCKET					
BXL1-2093	Never Even Thought	1978	2.50	5.00	10.00

BO GRUMPUS

Albums

Number	Title (A Side/B Side)	Yr	VG	VG+	NM
ATCO					
33-246 [M]	Bo Grumpus	1968	7.50	15.00	30.00
SD 33-246 [S]	Bo Grumpus	1968	5.00	10.00	20.00

BO PETE
See NILSSON.

BOA

Albums

Number	Title (A Side/B Side)	Yr	VG	VG+	NM
SNAKEFIELD					
SN-001	Wrong Road	1969	62.50	125.00	250.00

BOB AND EARL

45s

Number	Title (A Side/B Side)	Yr	VG	VG+	NM
CHENE					
103	The Sissy/(B-side unknown)	1964	2.50	5.00	10.00
CLASS					
213	That's My Desire/You Made a Boo-Boo	1957	10.00	20.00	40.00
231	Gee Whiz/When She Walks	1958	7.50	15.00	30.00
232	Chains of Love/Sweet Pea	1958	7.50	15.00	30.00
247	That's My Desire/You Made a Boo-Boo	1959	6.25	12.50	25.00
LOMA					
2004	Everybody Jerk/Just One Look in Your Eyes	1964	2.50	5.00	10.00
MARC					
104	Harlem Shuffle/I'll Come Running	1963	5.00	10.00	20.00
MIRWOOD					
5517	Baby It's Over/Dancin' Everywhere	1966	2.00	4.00	8.00
5526	I'll Keep Running Back/Baby, Your Time Is My Time	1966	2.00	4.00	8.00
TEMPE					
102	Don't Ever Leave Me/Oh Baby Doll	1962	3.75	7.50	15.00
UNI					
55196	Uh Uh No No/(Pickin' Up) Love's Vibrations	1970	—	3.00	6.00
55248	Get Ready for the New Day/Honey, Sugar, My Sweet Thing	1970	—	3.00	6.00
WHITE WHALE					
310	Harlem Shuffle/I'll Come Running	1969	3.00	6.00	12.00

Albums

Number	Title (A Side/B Side)	Yr	VG	VG+	NM
CRESTVIEW					
CRS-3055	Bob & Earl	1969	6.25	12.50	25.00
TIP					
TLP-1011 [M]	Harlem Shuffle	1964	7.50	15.00	30.00
TLS-9011 [S]	Harlem Shuffle	1964	12.50	25.00	50.00

BOB AND LUCILLE

45s

Number	Title (A Side/B Side)	Yr	VG	VG+	NM
DITTO					
121	What's the Password/Demon Lover	1962	20.00	40.00	80.00
126	Eeny-Meeny-Miney-Moe/The Big Kiss	1962	20.00	40.00	80.00
KING					
5631	Eeny-Meeny-Miney-Moe/The Big Kiss	1962	7.50	15.00	30.00

BOB AND SHERI

45s

Number	Title (A Side/B Side)	Yr	VG	VG+	NM
SAFARI					
101	The Surfer Moon/Humpty Dumpty	1962	2000.	3000.	4000.
—Light blue label (other colors and colored vinyl are reproductions or counterfeits)					
101 [DJ]	The Surfer Moon/Humpty Dumpty	1962	250.00	500.00	1000.
—White label					

BOB B. SOXX AND THE BLUE JEANS

45s

Number	Title (A Side/B Side)	Yr	VG	VG+	NM
PHILLES					
107	Zip-a-Dee-Doo-Dah/Flip and Nitty	1962	5.00	10.00	20.00
110	Why Do Lovers Brak Each Other's Heart?/Dr. Kaplan's Office	1963	5.00	10.00	20.00
113	Not Too Young to Get Married/Annette	1963	5.00	10.00	20.00
PHILLES/COLLECTABLES					
3207	Not Too Young to Get Married/There's No Other (Like My Baby)	1985	—	3.00	6.00
—Gold vinyl; part of box set "Phil Spector Wall of Sound Series Vol. 1"; B-side by the Crystals					
3207	Not Too Young to Get Married/There's No Other (Like My Baby)	1986	—	2.50	5.00
—Black vinyl; B-side by the Crystals					

Albums

Number	Title (A Side/B Side)	Yr	VG	VG+	NM
PHILLIES					
PHLP-4002 [M]	Zip-a-Dee Doo-Dah	1963	125.00	250.00	500.00

BOBBETTES, THE

45s

Number	Title (A Side/B Side)	Yr	VG	VG+	NM
ATLANTIC					
1144	Mr. Lee/Look at the Stars	1957	6.25	12.50	25.00
1159	Speedy/Come-a Come-a	1957	5.00	10.00	20.00
1181	Zoomy/Rock and Ree-Ah-Zole	1958	5.00	10.00	20.00
1194	The Dream/Um Bow Bow	1958	5.00	10.00	20.00
2027	Don't Say Goodnight/You Are My Sweetheart	1959	5.00	10.00	20.00
2069	I Shot Mr. Lee/Untrue Love	1960	7.50	15.00	30.00
DIAMOND					
133	Row, Row, Row/Teddy	1963	3.00	6.00	12.00
142	Close Your Eyes/Somebody Bad Stole De Wedding Bell	1963	3.00	6.00	12.00
156	My Mamma Said/Sandman	1964	3.00	6.00	12.00
166	I'm Climbing a Mountain/In Paradise	1964	3.00	6.00	12.00
181	You Ain't Seen Nothing Yet/I'm Climbing a Mountain	1965	3.00	6.00	12.00
189	Love Is Blind/Teddy	1965	3.00	6.00	12.00
END					
1093	Mr. Johnny Q/Teach Me Tonight	1961	5.00	10.00	20.00
1095	I Don't Like It Like That (Part 1)/I Don't Like It Like That (Part 2)	1961	5.00	10.00	20.00
GALLANT					
1006	Oh, My Papa/I Cried	1960	5.00	10.00	20.00
GONE					
5112	I Don't Like It Like That (Part 1)/Mr. Johnny Q	1961	3.75	7.50	15.00
JUBILEE					
5427	Over There/Loneliness	1962	3.00	6.00	12.00
5442	The Broken Heart/Mama, Papa	1962	3.00	6.00	12.00
KING					
5490	Oh My Papa/Dance With Me Georgie	1961	3.75	7.50	15.00
5551	Are You Satisfied/Looking for a Lover	1961	3.75	7.50	15.00
5623	I'm Stepping Out Tonight/My Dearest	1962	3.75	7.50	15.00
RCA VICTOR					
47-8832	I've Gotta Face the World/Having Fun	1966	3.75	7.50	15.00
47-8983	It's All Over/Happy-Go-Lucky Me	1966	3.75	7.50	15.00
TRIPLE-X					
104	I Shot Mr. Lee/Billy	1960	5.00	10.00	20.00
106	Have Mercy Baby/Dance with Me Georgie	1960	5.00	10.00	20.00

BOBBIE JEAN

45s

Number	Title (A Side/B Side)	Yr	VG	VG+	NM
SUN					
342	You Burned the Bridges/Cheaters Never Win	1960	5.00	10.00	20.00

BOBBIE & BOOBIE

45s

Number	Title (A Side/B Side)	Yr	VG	VG+	NM
DICE					
480	Cool, Cool Christmas/Teenage Party	195?	50.00	100.00	200.00

BOBBY AND HIS ORBITS

45s

Number	Title (A Side/B Side)	Yr	VG	VG+	NM
GONE					
5126	Your Cheatin' Heart/I Don't Stand a Chance	1962	6.25	12.50	25.00
SEECO					
6005	Felicia/Bandstand Dancing	1959	20.00	40.00	80.00
6030	Teen Age Love/What Do I Say (When I'm Close to You)	1960	12.50	25.00	50.00

BOBBY AND THE DUKES

45s

Number	Title (A Side/B Side)	Yr	VG	VG+	NM
PHILIPS					
40293	Ah, Ah, Ah/Come Go with Me	1965	5.00	10.00	20.00

BOBBY THE POET
See SENATOR BOBBY.

BOBO, WILLIE

45s

Number	Title (A Side/B Side)	Yr	VG	VG+	NM
BLUE NOTE					
XW977	Kojak Theme/Dreamin'	1977	—	2.50	5.00
CAPITOL					
4253	Funky Sneakers/Funky Sneakers (Part 2)	1976	—	2.00	4.00
COLUMBIA					
10862	Fairytales for Two/Always There	1978	—	2.00	4.00
VERVE					
CS?-5	Celebrity Scene: Willie Bobo	1967	12.50	25.00	50.00
—Box set of five singles (10472-10476). Price includes box, all 5 singles, jukebox title strips, bio. Records are sometimes found by themselves, so they are also listed separately.					
10374	Hurt So Bad/It's Not Unusual	1966	2.00	4.00	8.00
10400	1-2-3 (Uno, Dos, Tres)/Fried Neckbones and Home Fries	1966	2.00	4.00	8.00
10448	Sockit To Me/Sunshine Superman	1967	2.00	4.00	8.00
10472	Sunshine Superman/Call Me	1967	2.00	4.00	8.00
10473	Hurt So Bad/Boogaloo in Room 802	1967	2.00	4.00	8.00
10474	Blues in the Closet/Spanish Grease	1967	2.00	4.00	8.00
10475	Sockit To Me/1-2-3 (Uno, Dos, Tres)	1967	2.00	4.00	8.00
10476	Fried Neckbones and Home Fries/Feelin' So Good	1967	2.00	4.00	8.00
10482	Shing-a-Ling Baby/Juicy	1967	—	3.00	6.00
10518	Ain't Too Proud to Beg/Knock on Wood	1967	—	3.00	6.00
10550	Evil Ways/Up, Up and Away	1967	—	3.00	6.00
10593	Move It On Over/Tweedlee Dee	1968	—	3.00	6.00

Albums

Number	Title (A Side/B Side)	Yr	VG	VG+	NM
BLUE NOTE					
BN-LA711-G	Tomorrow Is Here	1977	3.00	6.00	12.00
COLUMBIA					
JC 35734	Hell of an Act to Follow	1978	3.00	6.00	12.00
MGM					
10007	Spanish Grease	197?	3.00	6.00	12.00
10011	Uno, Dos, Tres	197?	3.00	6.00	12.00

Number	Title (A Side/B Side)	Yr	VG	VG+	NM
10012	Spanish Blues Band	197?	3.00	6.00	12.00
ROULETTE					
R-52097 [M]	Bobo's Beat	1962	6.25	12.50	25.00
SR-52097 [S]	Bobo's Beat	1962	7.50	15.00	30.00
SUSSEX					
SUS-7003	Do What You Want to Do	1971	3.00	6.00	12.00
TICO					
ST-1108 [S]	Do That Thing	1963	7.50	15.00	30.00
T-1108 [M]	Do That Thing	1963	6.25	12.50	25.00
TRIP					
5013	Latin Beat	1974	2.50	5.00	10.00
VERVE					
V-8631 [M]	Spanish Grease	1965	3.75	7.50	15.00
V6-8631 [S]	Spanish Grease	1965	5.00	10.00	20.00
V-8648 [M]	Uno, Dos, Tres	1966	3.75	7.50	15.00
V6-8648 [S]	Uno, Dos, Tres	1966	5.00	10.00	20.00
V-8669 [M]	Feelin' So Good	1966	3.75	7.50	15.00
V6-8669 [S]	Feelin' So Good	1966	5.00	10.00	20.00
V-8685 [M]	Juicy	1967	5.00	10.00	20.00
V6-8685 [S]	Juicy	1967	5.00	10.00	20.00
V-8699 [M]	Bobo Motion	1967	5.00	10.00	20.00
V6-8699 [S]	Bobo Motion	1967	5.00	10.00	20.00
V6-8736	Spanish Blues Band	1968	5.00	10.00	20.00
V6-8772	A New Dimension	1969	3.75	7.50	15.00
V6-8781	Evil Ways	1969	3.75	7.50	15.00

BOCEPHUS

See HANK WILLIAMS, JR.

BOCKY AND THE VISIONS

45s

Number	Title (A Side/B Side)	Yr	VG	VG+	NM
PHILIPS					
40224	Mojo Hanna/Spirit of '64	1964	6.25	12.50	25.00
40242	I'm Pickin' Petals/I'm Not Worth It	1964	6.25	12.50	25.00

BODACIOUS D.F.

MARTY BALIN was in this group.

Albums

Number	Title (A Side/B Side)	Yr	VG	VG+	NM
RCA VICTOR					
AFL1-0206	Bodacious D.F.	1977	2.50	5.00	10.00
APL1-0206	Bodacious D.F.	1973	3.75	7.50	15.00
AYL1-4243	Bodacious D.F.	1982	2.00	4.00	8.00
—"Best Buy Series" reissue					

BOENZEE CRYQUE

With Rusty Young, later of POCO.

45s

Number	Title (A Side/B Side)	Yr	VG	VG+	NM
CHICORY					
406	Sky Gone Gray/Still in Love with You Baby	1966	7.50	15.00	30.00
UNI					
55012	Sky Gone Gray/Still in Love with You Baby	1967	5.00	10.00	20.00
55022	Watch the Time/You Won't Believe It's True	1967	5.00	10.00	20.00

BOETCHER, CURT

45s

Number	Title (A Side/B Side)	Yr	VG	VG+	NM
ELEKTRA					
45834	I Love You More Each Day/Such a Lady	1973	—	2.50	5.00

Albums

Number	Title (A Side/B Side)	Yr	VG	VG+	NM
ELEKTRA					
EKS-75037	There's an Innocent Face	1972	5.00	10.00	20.00

BOFFALONGO

45s

Number	Title (A Side/B Side)	Yr	VG	VG+	NM
UNITED ARTISTS					
50607	Tomorrow Not Today/Mr. Go Away	1969	2.00	4.00	8.00
50656	Please Stay/Mr. Go Away	1970	2.00	4.00	8.00
50699	Dancing in the Moonlight/Endless Question	1970	2.00	4.00	8.00

Albums

Number	Title (A Side/B Side)	Yr	VG	VG+	NM
UNITED ARTISTS					
UAS-6726	Boffalongo	1969	5.00	10.00	20.00
UAS-6770	Beyond Your Head	1970	5.00	10.00	20.00

BOHANNON

12-Inch Singles

Number	Title (A Side/B Side)	Yr	VG	VG+	NM
PHASE II					
02133	Goin' for Another One/The Happy Dance	1981	3.00	6.00	12.00
02146	Foot Stompin' in the Summertime/(Instrumental)	1981	3.00	6.00	12.00
02876	I've Got the Dance Fever (With Rap Intro)/I've Got the Dance Fever (Without Intro)	1982	2.50	5.00	10.00

45s

Number	Title (A Side/B Side)	Yr	VG	VG+	NM
COMPLEAT					
103	Make Your Body Move/Come Back My Love	1983	—	2.00	4.00
107	Funkville/Don't Leave Me	1983	—	2.00	4.00
114	Wake Up/Enjoy Your Day	1983	—	2.00	4.00
118	Rock Your Body/(Instrumental)	1983	—	2.00	4.00
148	South Africa/South Africa (Special Mix)	1984	—	2.00	4.00
DAKAR					
4518	Save Their Souls/Stop and Go	1973	—	3.00	6.00
4521	The Pimpwalk/Happiness	1973	—	3.00	6.00
4525	Run It On Down Mr. DJ (Part 1)/Run It On Down Mr. DJ (Part 2)	1973	—	3.00	6.00
4528	Fat Man/Red Bone	1974	—	3.00	6.00
4534	Happiness/Truck Stop	1974	—	3.00	6.00
4535	Keep On Dancin' (Part 1)/Keep On Dancin' (Part 2)	1974	—	3.00	6.00
4539	South African Music (Pt. 1)/Have a Good Day	1974	—	2.50	5.00
4544	Foot Stompin' Music/Dance with Your Partner	1975	—	2.50	5.00
4549	Disco Stomp (Part 1)/Disco Stomp (Part 2)	1975	—	2.50	5.00
4551	Bohannon's Beat (Pt. 1)/East Coast Groove	1975	—	2.50	5.00
4554	Dance Your Ass Off/Happy Feeling	1976	—	2.50	5.00
4560	Gittin' Off/Come Winter	1976	—	2.50	5.00
MCA					
53685	House Train/(Instrumental)	1989	—	—	3.00
53766	The Gang's All Here/Over the Rainbow	1989	—	—	3.00
MERCURY					
73939	Bohannon Disco Symphony/Moving Fast	1977	—	2.00	4.00
73946	Just Doing My Thing/Andrea	1977	—	2.00	4.00
74015	Let's Start the Dance/I Wonder Why	1978	—	2.00	4.00
74035	Me and the Gang/Summertime Groove	1978	—	2.00	4.00
74044	Cut Loose/Listen to the Children Play	1979	—	2.00	4.00
74085	The Groove Machine/Love Floats	1979	—	2.00	4.00
76040	Feel Like Dancin'/Funk Walk	1980	—	2.00	4.00
76054	Baby I'm for Real/Hurry Mr. Sunshine	1980	—	2.00	4.00
888143-7	Jammin' in the Street/(B-side unknown)	1986	—	—	3.00
PHASE II					
02062	Goin' for Another One/Do What Cha Wanna Do	1981	—	2.00	4.00
02145	Foot Stompin' in the Summertime/(Instrumental)	1981	—	2.00	4.00
02573	Let's Start II Dance Again/Let's Start the Dance	1981	—	2.00	4.00
02897	I've Got the Dance Fever (With Rap Intro)/I've Got the Dance Fever (Without Intro)	1982	—	2.00	4.00
02998	The Party Train (Parts I & II)/Thoughts and Wishes	1982	—	2.00	4.00
5650	Throw Down the Groove (Part I)/Throw Down the Groove (Part II)	1980	—	2.00	4.00
5651	Dance, Dance, Dance All Night/(B-side unknown)	1980	—	2.00	4.00
5654	Don't Be Ashame to Call My Name/(B-side unknown)	1981	—	2.00	4.00

Albums

Number	Title (A Side/B Side)	Yr	VG	VG+	NM
COMPLEAT					
CPL-1-1003	Make Your Body Move	1983	2.50	5.00	10.00
CPL-1-1005	The Bohannon Drive	1984	2.50	5.00	10.00
DAKAR					
6910	Keep On Dancing	1973	3.00	6.00	12.00
76916	Insides Out	1974	3.00	6.00	12.00
76917	Bohannon	1975	3.00	6.00	12.00
76919	Dance Your Ass Off	1976	3.00	6.00	12.00
MCA					
42310	Here Comes Bohannon	1989	3.00	6.00	12.00
MERCURY					
SRM-1-1159	Phase II	1977	2.50	5.00	10.00
SRM-1-3710	On My Way	1978	2.50	5.00	10.00
SRM-1-3728	Summertime Groove	1978	2.50	5.00	10.00
SRM-1-3762	Cut Loose	1979	2.50	5.00	10.00
SRM-1-3778	Too Hot to Hold	1979	2.50	5.00	10.00
SRM-1-3813	Music in the Air	1980	2.50	5.00	10.00
PHASE II					
JW 36867	One Step Ahead	1980	2.50	5.00	10.00
FZ 37695	Alive	1981	2.50	5.00	10.00
FZ 38113	Bohannon Fever	1982	2.50	5.00	10.00

BOHEMIAN VENDETTA

45s

Number	Title (A Side/B Side)	Yr	VG	VG+	NM
MAINSTREAM					
681	Riddles and Fairytales/I Wanna Touch Your Heart	1968	5.00	10.00	20.00
UNITED ARTISTS					
50174	Talk the Time/Enough	1967	6.25	12.50	25.00

Albums

Number	Title (A Side/B Side)	Yr	VG	VG+	NM
MAINSTREAM					
S-6106 [S]	Bohemian Vendetta	1968	50.00	100.00	200.00
56106 [M]	Bohemian Vendetta	1968	30.00	60.00	120.00

BOLDER DAMN

Albums

Number	Title (A Side/B Side)	Yr	VG	VG+	NM
HIT					
HRI-5061	Mourning	1971	250.00	500.00	1000.

BOLIN, TOMMY

Also see THE JAMES GANG; ZEPHYR.

45s

Number	Title (A Side/B Side)	Yr	VG	VG+	NM
NEMPEROR					
004	The Grind/Homeward Strut	1976	2.00	4.00	8.00
005	Savannah Woman/Marching Power	1976	2.00	4.00	8.00

Albums

Number	Title (A Side/B Side)	Yr	VG	VG+	NM
COLUMBIA					
PC 34329	Private Eyes	1976	3.00	6.00	12.00
—Original with no bar code on cover					
PC 34329	Private Eyes	198?	2.00	4.00	8.00
—With bar code on cover					
GEFFEN					
3GHS 24248 [(3)]	The Ultimate Tommy Bolin	1989	7.50	15.00	30.00
NEMPEROR					
NE 436	Teaser	1975	3.00	6.00	12.00
PZ 37534	Teaser	1982	2.00	4.00	8.00

BOLTON, MICHAEL

Includes records as "Michael Bolotin."

45s

Number	Title (A Side/B Side)	Yr	VG	VG+	NM
COLUMBIA					
03800	Fighting for My Life/Fool's Game	1983	—	2.00	4.00
04154	I Almost Believed You/She Did the Same Thing	1983	—	2.00	4.00
04823	Everybody's Crazy/She Did the Same Thing	1985	—	—	3.00
07322	That's What Love Is All About/Take a Look at My Face	1987	—	—	3.00
07680	(Sittin' On) The Dock of the Bay/Call My Name	1988	—	—	3.00
07680 [PS]	(Sittin' On) The Dock of the Bay/Call My Name	1988	—	—	3.00
07794	Wait on Love/I Almost Believed You	1988	—	—	3.00
07794 [PS]	Wait on Love/I Almost Believed You	1988	—	—	3.00
07983	Walk Away/The Hunger	1988	—	—	3.00
68909	Soul Provider/The Hunger	1989	—	—	3.00
73017	How Am I Supposed to Live Without You/Forever Eyes	1989	—	—	3.00

Number	Title (A Side/B Side)	Yr	VG	VG+	NM
73257	How Can We Be Lovers/That's What Love Is All About	1990	—	—	3.00
73342	When I'm Back on My Feet Again/Walk Away	1990	—	—	3.00
73490	Georgia on My Mind/Take a Look at My Face	1990	—	—	3.00
73719	Love Is a Wonderful Thing/Soul Provider	1991	—	—	3.00
73889	Time, Love and Tenderness/That's What Love Is All About	1991	—	—	3.00
74020	When a Man Loves a Woman/Save Me	1991	—	—	3.00
74184	Missing You Now/It's Only My Heart	1992	—	—	3.00
74798	Reach Out I'll Be There/White Christmas	1992	—	2.00	4.00
77260	Said I Loved You...But I Lied/Soul Provider	1993	—	—	3.00
77376	Completely/That's What Love Is All About	1994	—	—	3.00
77941	Can I Touch You...There?/Ain't Got Nothing If You Ain't Got Love	1995	—	—	3.00
RCA					
PB-10650	You Make Me Feel Like Lovin' You/If I Had Your Lovin'	1976	2.50	5.00	10.00
—As "Michael Bolotin"					
RCA VICTOR					
PB-10283	Your Love/Dream While You Can	1975	2.50	5.00	10.00
—As "Michael Bolotin"					

Albums

Number	Title	Yr	VG	VG+	NM
COLUMBIA					
BFC 38357	Michael Bolton	1983	2.50	5.00	10.00
PC 38357	Michael Bolton	1985	—	3.00	6.00
—Reissue with new prefix					
BFC 39328	Everybody's Crazy	1985	2.50	5.00	10.00
FC 40473	The Hunger	1987	2.00	4.00	8.00
OC 45012	Soul Provider	1989	2.50	5.00	10.00
C 46771	Time, Love and Tenderness	1991	3.75	7.50	15.00
RCA VICTOR					
APL1-0992	Michael Bolotin	1975	5.00	10.00	20.00
—As "Michael Bolotin"					
APL1-1551	Every Day of My Life	1976	5.00	10.00	20.00
—As "Michael Bolotin"					

BON-AIRS, THE

45s

Number	Title	Yr	VG	VG+	NM
KING					
4975	Stop the World/Bermuda	1956	7.50	15.00	30.00

BON BONS, THE

45s

Number	Title	Yr	VG	VG+	NM
CORAL					
62402	What's Wrong with Ringo/Come On Baby	1964	15.00	30.00	60.00
62435	Everybody Wants My Boyfriend/Each Time	1964	12.50	25.00	50.00

BONADUCE, DANNY

One of the stars of the TV series "The Partridge Family," but he doesn't appear on any of the records.

45s

Number	Title	Yr	VG	VG+	NM
LION					
145	Blueberry You/Dreamland	1973	2.50	5.00	10.00

Albums

Number	Title	Yr	VG	VG+	NM
LION					
LN-1015	Danny Bonaduce	1973	15.00	30.00	60.00

BONAIRS, THE

45s

Number	Title	Yr	VG	VG+	NM
DOOTONE					
325	It's Christmas/I'm Alone Tonight	1953	37.50	75.00	150.00
—B-side by Ernie Tavares Trio					

BOND, ANGELO

45s

Number	Title	Yr	VG	VG+	NM
ABC					
12077	Reach for the Moon (Poor People)/I Never Sang for My Baby	1975	—	2.50	5.00
12135	I Love You for What You Are/Eve	1975	—	2.50	5.00
12153	He Gained the World (But Lost His Soul)/I Love You for What You Are	1976	—	2.50	5.00

Albums

Number	Title	Yr	VG	VG+	NM
ABC					
D-889	Bondage	1975	2.50	5.00	10.00

BOND, GRAHAM

45s

Number	Title	Yr	VG	VG+	NM
ASCOT					
2211	St. James Infirmary/Wade in the Water	1966	2.50	5.00	10.00
PULSAR					
2405	Love Is the Law/The Naz	1969	2.00	4.00	8.00
2409	Crossroads of Time/Moving Towards the Light	1969	2.00	4.00	8.00
2415	Stiffened Chicken/Water, Water	1969	2.00	4.00	8.00

Albums

Number	Title	Yr	VG	VG+	NM
MERCURY					
SRM-1-612	We Put Our Magick on You	1971	5.00	10.00	20.00
SR-61327	Holy Magick	1970	5.00	10.00	20.00
PULSAR					
10604	Love Is the Law	1969	6.25	12.50	25.00
10606	Mighty Graham Bond	1969	6.25	12.50	25.00
WARNER BROS.					
2LS 2555 [(2)]	Solid Bond	1971	5.00	10.00	20.00

BOND, JOHNNY

45s

Number	Title (A Side/B Side)	Yr	VG	VG+	NM
20TH FOX					
156	Gold Rush/The Long Tall Shadow	1959	3.00	6.00	12.00
231	Jealous Lad/A Kid Named Bell	1960	3.00	6.00	12.00
COLUMBIA					
2-100 (?)	Tennessee Saturday Night/A Heart Full of Love	1949	6.25	12.50	25.00
—Microgroove 7-inch, 33 1/3 rpm single					
2-100 (?)	Take It or Leave It Baby/Till the End of the World	1949	6.25	12.50	25.00
—Microgroove 7-inch, 33 1/3 rpm single					
2-200 (?)	Read It and Weep/Somebody Loves You	1950	6.25	12.50	25.00
—Microgroove 7-inch, 33 1/3 rpm single					
2-210 (?)	I'm Biting My Fingernails/I Wish I Had a Nickel	1949	6.25	12.50	25.00
—Microgroove 7-inch, 33 1/3 rpm single					
2-300 (?)	Drowning My Sorrows/Women Make a Fool Out of Me	1950	6.25	12.50	25.00
—Microgroove 7-inch, 33 1/3 rpm single					
2-400 (?)	A Petal from a Faded Rose/Put Me to Bed #2	1950	6.25	12.50	25.00
—Microgroove 7-inch, 33 1/3 rpm single					
2-532	Love Song in 32 Bars/Tennessee Kentucky & Alabam'	1950	6.25	12.50	25.00
—Microgroove 7-inch, 33 1/3 rpm single					
2-600 (?)	Cherokee Waltz/Mean Mama Boogie	1950	6.25	12.50	25.00
—Microgroove 7-inch, 33 1/3 rpm single					
20726	Under the Red, White and Blue/Star Spangled Waltz	1950	5.00	10.00	20.00
20734	Barrel House Bessie/It Ain't Gonna Happen to Me	1950	5.00	10.00	20.00
20738	There's a Gold Moon Shining/Cream of Kentucky	1950	5.00	10.00	20.00
20756	I Wanna Do Something For Santa/Jingle Bell Boogie	1950	5.00	10.00	20.00
20787	Set 'Em Up Joe/Glad Rags	1951	5.00	10.00	20.00
20808	Sick, Sober and Sorry/Tennessee Walking Horse	1951	5.00	10.00	20.00
20844	Ten Trips to the Altar/Keep Your Cotton Pickin' Hands	1951	5.00	10.00	20.00
20876	Broke, Disgusted and Sad/In Old New Mexico	1952	3.75	7.50	15.00
20909	I Found You Out/Alabama Boogie Boy	1952	3.75	7.50	15.00
20948	Louisiana Lucy/The Man Behind the Throttle	1952	3.75	7.50	15.00
21007	I Went to Your Wedding/Our Love Isn't Legal	1952	3.75	7.50	15.00
21041	Back Street Affair/Our Love Isn't Legal	1952	3.75	7.50	15.00
21042	Born to Be Bad/#9 Blues	1952	3.75	7.50	15.00
21066	Wildcat Boogie/Let Me Go, Devil	1953	3.75	7.50	15.00
21082	Anybody's Baby/Hills of Kentucky	1953	3.75	7.50	15.00
21113	Peace Be Still/Ninety & Nine	1953	3.75	7.50	15.00
21150	Live and Let Live/I Wonder Where You Are Tonight	1953	3.75	7.50	15.00
21160	Wildcat Boogie/Let Me Go, Devil	1953	3.75	7.50	15.00
21186	Sweet Mama Tree Top Tall/Put a Little Sweetness in Your Love	1953	3.75	7.50	15.00
21187	Thanks/I Dreamed I Searched Heaven	1953	3.75	7.50	15.00
21222	10 Little Bottles/They Got Me	1954	3.75	7.50	15.00
21243	Firewater/Old Man Blues	1954	3.75	7.50	15.00
21294	Stealin'/My Darling Lola Lee	1954	3.75	7.50	15.00
21335	I Lose Again/Everybody Knew the Truth But Me	1954	3.75	7.50	15.00
21369	Cherokee Waltz/Glad Rags	1955	3.75	7.50	15.00
21383	Jim, Johnny & Jonas/Louisiana Swing	1955	3.75	7.50	15.00
21424	Somebody's Pushin'/Carolina Waltz	1955	3.75	7.50	15.00
21448	Remember the Alamo/Livin' It Up	1955	3.75	7.50	15.00
21494	Loaded for Bear/Six of One, Half a Dozen of the Other	1956	3.75	7.50	15.00
21521	Little Rock and Roll/I'll Be Here	1956	12.50	25.00	50.00
21565	Lonesome Train/Laughing Back the Heartaches	1956	3.75	7.50	15.00
40080	Santa Got Stuck in the Chimney/I Said a Prayer for Santa Claus	1953	3.75	7.50	15.00
—With Jimmy Boyd					
40842	Honky Tonk Fever/Lay It on the Line	1957	3.75	7.50	15.00
40973	All I Can Do Is Cry/Sale of Broken Hearts	1957	3.75	7.50	15.00
41034	That's Just What I'll Do/Broken Doll	1957	3.75	7.50	15.00
DITTO					
120	The Tijuana Jail/Fools Paradise	1959	3.00	6.00	12.00
MGM					
14596	Rose of Reynosa/Who Stole the Juke Box	1973	—	2.50	5.00
REPUBLIC					
2005	Hot Rod Lincoln/Five Minute Love Affair	1960	3.00	6.00	12.00
2008	X-15/The Way a Star Is Born	1960	3.00	6.00	12.00
2010	Side Car Cycle/Like Nothin' Man	1961	3.00	6.00	12.00
2022	Sadie Was a Lady/Buck Private's Lament	1961	3.00	6.00	12.00
SMASH					
1761	I'll Step Aside/Mister Sun	1962	2.50	5.00	10.00
STARDAY					
618	How to Succeed with Girls (Without Half-Way Trying)/Don't Mention Her Name	1963	2.00	4.00	8.00
635	True Love (Is Hard to Find)/Cimarron	1963	2.00	4.00	8.00
649	Three Sheets in the Wind/Let the Tears Begin	1963	2.00	4.00	8.00
665	Have You Seen My Baby/What Have You Done for Me Lately	1964	2.00	4.00	8.00
678	Hot Rod Surfin' Hootlebeatnanny/Don't Mama Count Anymore	1964	3.75	7.50	15.00
690	My Wicked, Wicked Ways/Bachelor Bill	1964	2.00	4.00	8.00
704	10 Little Bottles/Let It Be Me	1964	2.00	4.00	8.00
721	Sick, Sober & Sorry/The Man Who Comes Around	1965	2.00	4.00	8.00
731	The Great Figure Eight Race/Sadie Was a Lady	1965	2.00	4.00	8.00
749	They Got Me/Silent Walls	1966	2.00	4.00	8.00
758	Fireball/Over the Hill	1966	2.00	4.00	8.00
776	Hell's Angels/A Way of Life	1966	2.00	4.00	8.00
803	Your Old Love Letters/Si Si	1967	2.00	4.00	8.00
813	I Ain't Gonna Go/Don't Bite the Hand That's Feeding You	1967	2.00	4.00	8.00
826	Bottom of the Bottle/I'm Gonna Raise Cain (While I'm Able)	1968	2.00	4.00	8.00
847	Down to Your Last Fool/Invitation to the Blues	1968	2.00	4.00	8.00
893	It Only Hurts When I Cry/The Girl Who Carried the Torch for Me	1970	—	3.00	6.00
916	Here Come the Elephants/Take Me Back to Tulsa	1970	—	3.00	6.00
931	The Bottle's Empty/The Late and Great Myself	1971	—	3.00	6.00
951	Put the Country Back in Country Music/Fly Me, Try Me	1972	—	3.00	6.00
7021	Hot Rod Lincoln/Barrel House Betsy	197?	—	2.50	5.00
7027	Divorce Me C.O.D./Three Sheets in the Wind	197?	—	2.50	5.00
7033	Tennessee, Kentucky and Alabam'/Glad Rags	197?	—	2.50	5.00

7-Inch Extended Plays

Number	Title	Yr	VG	VG+	NM
COLUMBIA					
B-2820	(contents unknown)	1958	7.50	15.00	30.00

Number	Title (A Side/B Side)	Yr	VG	VG+	NM
B-2820 [PS]	Johnny Bond and His Red River Boys	1958	7.50	15.00	30.00
REPUBLIC					
100	(contents unknown)	1960	5.00	10.00	20.00
100 [PS]	Hot Rod Lincoln	1960	5.00	10.00	20.00
Albums					
CMH					
6212	The Singing Cowboy Again	1981	2.50	5.00	10.00
6213	The Return of the Singing Cowboy	1981	2.50	5.00	10.00
HARMONY					
HL 7308 [M]	Johnny Bond's Best	1964	5.00	10.00	20.00
HL 7353 [M]	Bottled in Bond	1965	5.00	10.00	20.00
NASHVILLE					
2054	Three Sheets to the Wind	196?	3.75	7.50	15.00
STARDAY					
SLP-147 [M]	That Wild, Wicked But Wonderful Wesy	1961	12.50	25.00	50.00
SLP-227 [M]	Songs That Made Him Famous	1963	10.00	20.00	40.00
SLP-298 [M]	Hot Rod Lincoln	1964	12.50	25.00	50.00
333 [M]	Ten Little Bottles	1965	10.00	20.00	40.00
SLP-333 [S]	Ten Little Bottles	1965	7.50	15.00	30.00
354 [M]	Famous Hot Rodders I Have Known	1965	20.00	40.00	80.00
SLP-354 [S]	Famous Hot Rodders I Have Known	1965	10.00	20.00	40.00
368 [M]	The Man Who Comes Around	1966	5.00	10.00	20.00
SLP-368 [S]	The Man Who Comes Around	1966	6.25	12.50	25.00
378 [M]	Bottles Up	1966	5.00	10.00	20.00
SLP-378 [S]	Bottles Up	1966	6.25	12.50	25.00
388 [M]	The Branded Stock of Johnny Bond	1966	3.75	7.50	15.00
SLP-388 [S]	The Branded Stock of Johnny Bond	1966	5.00	10.00	20.00
402 [M]	Ten Nights in a Barroom	1967	3.75	7.50	15.00
SLP-402 [S]	Ten Nights in a Barroom	1967	5.00	10.00	20.00
SLP-416	Drink Up and Go Home	1968	3.75	7.50	15.00
SLP-444	The Best of Johnny Bond	1969	3.75	7.50	15.00
SLP-456	Old, New, Patriotic and Blue	1970	3.75	7.50	15.00
SLP-472	Here Come the Elephants	1971	3.75	7.50	15.00
954	The Best of Johnny Bond	1976	2.50	5.00	10.00

BOND, JOHNNY, AND LEFTY FRIZZELL

45s

Number	Title (A Side/B Side)	Yr	VG	VG+	NM
COLUMBIA					
40934	Sick, Sober and Sorry/Lover By Appointment	1957	3.75	7.50	15.00

BOND, JOHNNY, AND RED SOVINE

Also see each artist's individual listings.

45s

Number	Title (A Side/B Side)	Yr	VG	VG+	NM
STARDAY					
790	The Gearjammer and the Hobo/Sweet Nellie	1966	2.50	5.00	10.00

BONDS, GARY U.S.

45s

Number	Title (A Side/B Side)	Yr	VG	VG+	NM
ATCO					
6689	The Star/You Need a Personal Manager	1969	—	3.00	6.00
BLUFF CITY					
221	My Love Song/Blue Grass	1974	—	2.50	5.00
BOTANIC					
1002	I'm Glad You're Back/Funky Lies	1968	2.00	4.00	8.00
EMI AMERICA					
8079	This Little Girl/Way Back When	1981	—	2.00	4.00
8079 [PS]	This Little Girl/Way Back When	1981	—	2.50	5.00
8089	Jole Blon/Just Like a Child	1981	—	2.00	4.00
8099	Your Love/Just Like a Child	1981	—	2.00	4.00
8117	Out of Work/Bring Her Back	1982	—	2.00	4.00
8117 [PS]	Out of Work/Bring Her Back	1982	—	2.50	5.00
8133	Love's on the Line/Way Back When	1982	—	2.00	4.00
8145	Turn the Music Down/Way Back When	1982	—	2.00	4.00
LEGRAND					
1003	New Orleans/Please Forgive Me	1960	5.00	10.00	20.00
—Original lists artist as "By-U.S. Bonds"; purple label					
1003	New Orleans/Please Forgive Me	1960	3.75	7.50	15.00
—Gold and red label					
1005	Not Me/Give Me One More Chance	1961	5.00	10.00	20.00
—Artist listed as "U.S. Bonds"; purple label					
1005	Not Me/Give Me One More Chance	1961	3.75	7.50	15.00
—Gold and red label					
1008	Quarter to Three/Time Ole Story	1961	10.00	20.00	40.00
—Artist listed as "U.S. Bonds"; purple label					
1008	Quarter to Three/Time Ole Story	1961	3.75	7.50	15.00
—Artist listed as "U.S. Bonds"; gold and red label					
1008 [PS]	Quarter to Three/Time Ole Story	1961	10.00	20.00	40.00
1009	School Is Out/One Million Years	1961	5.00	10.00	20.00
—Artist listed as "U.S. Bonds"					
1009	School Is Out/One Million Years	1961	3.75	7.50	15.00
—Artist listed as "Gary (U.S.) Bonds" as are all later Legrand singles					
1009 [PS]	School Is Out/One Million Years	1961	10.00	20.00	40.00
1012	School Is In/Trip to the Moon	1961	3.75	7.50	15.00
1015	Dear Lady/Havin' So Much Fun	1961	5.00	10.00	20.00
—Original title of A-side					
1015	Dear Lady Twist/Havin' So Much Fun	1962	3.75	7.50	15.00
1018	Twist, Twist Senora/Food of Love	1962	3.75	7.50	15.00
1019	Seven Day Weekend/Gettin' a Groove	1962	3.75	7.50	15.00
1020	Copy Cat/I'll Change That Too	1962	3.75	7.50	15.00
1022	Mixed Up Faculty/I Dig This Station	1962	3.75	7.50	15.00
1025	Do the Limbo with Me/Where Did That Naughty Little Girl Go	1962	3.75	7.50	15.00
1027	I Don't Wanta Wait/What a Dream	1963	3.00	6.00	12.00
1029	No More Homework/She's Alright	1963	3.00	6.00	12.00
1030	Perdido Part 1/Perdido Part 2	1963	3.00	6.00	12.00
1031	King Kong's Monkey/My Sweet Ruby Rose	1964	3.00	6.00	12.00
1032	The Music Goes Round and Round/Ella Is Yella	1964	3.00	6.00	12.00
1034	You Little Angel You/My Little Miss America	1964	3.00	6.00	12.00
1035	Oh Yeah, Oh Yeah/Let Oh Yeah, Oh Yeah/Let Me Go Lover	1965	2.50	5.00	10.00
1039	Beaches U.S.A./Do the Bumpsie	1965	2.50	5.00	10.00
1040	Take Me Back to New Orleans/I'm That Kind of Guy	1966	2.50	5.00	10.00
1041	Due to Circumstances Under My Control/Slow Motion	1966	2.50	5.00	10.00
1043	Send Her Back to Me/Workin' for My Baby	1967	2.50	5.00	10.00
1045	Call Me for Christmas/Mixed Up Faculty	1967	3.00	6.00	12.00
1046	Sarah Jane/What a Crazy World	1967	2.50	5.00	10.00
MCA					
52335	One More Time Around the Block, Ophelia/Deadline U.S.A.	1984	—	2.00	4.00
—B-side by Shalamar					
52400	New Orleans/Rhythm of the Rain	1984	—	2.00	4.00
—With Neil Sedaka					
PRODIGAL					
0612	Grandma's Washboard/Believing You	1975	—	2.50	5.00
SUE					
17	One Broken Heart/Can't Use You in My Business	1970	—	3.00	6.00
Albums					
EMI AMERICA					
SO-17051	Dedication	1981	2.50	5.00	10.00
SO-17068	On the Line	1982	2.50	5.00	10.00
LEGRAND					
LLP-3001 [M]	Dance 'Til Quarter to Three	1961	25.00	50.00	100.00
LLP-3002 [M]	Twist Up Calypso	1962	17.50	35.00	70.00
LLP-3003 [M]	Greatest Hits of Gary U.S. Bonds	1962	17.50	35.00	70.00
MCA					
905	The Best of Gary U.S. Bonds	1984	2.50	5.00	10.00
RHINO					
RNLP-805	Certified Soul	1981	2.50	5.00	10.00

BONFIRE, MARS

Real name: Dennis McCrohan. Also see SPARROW; STEPPENWOLF.

45s

Number	Title (A Side/B Side)	Yr	VG	VG+	NM
COLUMBIA					
44772	Faster Than the Speed of Life/She	1969	2.50	5.00	10.00
44888	In Christina's Arms/Lady Moon Walker	1969	2.50	5.00	10.00
Albums					
COLUMBIA					
CS 9834	Faster Than the Speed of Life	1969	3.75	7.50	15.00
UNI					
73027	Mars Bonfire	1968	5.00	10.00	20.00

BONNEVILLES, THE

More than one group.

45s

Number	Title (A Side/B Side)	Yr	VG	VG+	NM
BARRY					
104	Lorraine/Zu Zu	1962	12.50	25.00	50.00
CAPRI					
102	Give Me Your Love/Until You Say We're Through	1959	12.50	25.00	50.00
CORAL					
62273	Johnny/Freeway U.S.A.	1961	5.00	10.00	20.00
MUNICH					
103	Lorraine/Zu Zu	1960	75.00	150.00	300.00
—Red label					
103	Lorraine/Zu Zu	1960	25.00	50.00	100.00
—Black label					
WHITEHALL					
30002	I Do/Make Believe Lovin'	1959	7.50	15.00	30.00
Albums					
DRUM BOY					
DLM-1001 [M]	Meet the Bonnevilles	1963	25.00	50.00	100.00
DLS-1001 [S]	Meet the Bonnevilles	1963	37.50	75.00	150.00
JUSTICE					
JLP-146	Bringing It Home	196?	125.00	250.00	500.00

BONNEY, GRAHAM

45s

Number	Title (A Side/B Side)	Yr	VG	VG+	NM
CAPITOL					
2221	I'll Be Your Baby Tonight/Back from Baltimore	1968	—	3.00	6.00
5624	Super Girl/Hill of Lovin'	1966	2.00	4.00	8.00
MIKE					
4009	Baby's Gone/Later Tonight	1966	2.00	4.00	8.00

BONNIE AND THE BUTTERFLYS

45s

Number	Title (A Side/B Side)	Yr	VG	VG+	NM
SMASH					
1878	I Saw Him Standing There/Dust Storm	1964	5.00	10.00	20.00

BONNIE AND THE TREASURES

45s

Number	Title (A Side/B Side)	Yr	VG	VG+	NM
PABLO					
7014	Davey, I'm So Glad It Rained/The Lonely Surfer	1964	10.00	20.00	40.00
—B-side by the Mid-Americans					
PHI-DAN					
5005	Home of the Brave/Our Song	1965	10.00	20.00	40.00

BONNIE LOU

45s

Number	Title (A Side/B Side)	Yr	VG	VG+	NM
FRATERNITY					
808	No One Ever Lost More/Have You Ever Been Lonely	1958	2.50	5.00	10.00
812	Friction Heat/I Give My Love to You	1958	2.50	5.00	10.00
KING					
1192	Seven Lonely Days/Just Out of Reach	1953	3.75	7.50	15.00
1213	Scrap of Paper/Dancin' with Someone	1953	3.75	7.50	15.00
1237	Tennessee Wig Walk/Hand Me Down Heart	1953	3.75	7.50	15.00
1272	Papaya Mama/Since You Said Goodbye	1953	3.75	7.50	15.00
1279	Texas Polka/No Heart at All	1953	3.75	7.50	15.00
1318	Welcome Mat/Don't Stop Kissing Me Goodnight	1954	3.00	6.00	12.00
1341	Huckleberry Pie/No One	1954	3.00	6.00	12.00
1365	Wait for Me Darling/Blue Tennessee Rain	1954	3.00	6.00	12.00

Number	Title (A Side/B Side)	Yr	VG	VG+	NM
1373	Two Step Side Step/Please Don't Laugh When I Cry	1954	3.00	6.00	12.00
1384	Tell the World/Darlin' Why	1954	3.00	6.00	12.00
1414	Tennessee Mambo/Train Whistle Blues	1955	3.00	6.00	12.00
1436	Tweedle Dee/Finger of Suspicion	1955	3.00	6.00	12.00
1445	Danger, Heartbreak Ahead/A Rusty Old Halo	1955	3.00	6.00	12.00
1476	Drop Me a Line/Old Faithful	1955	3.00	6.00	12.00
1506	Barnyard Hop/Miss the Love	1955	3.00	6.00	12.00
4835	Daddy-O/Dancing in My Socks	1955	3.00	6.00	12.00
4864	Daddy-O/Miss the Love	1956	2.50	5.00	10.00
4895	Little Miss Bobby Sox/Beyond the Shadow of a Doubt	1956	2.50	5.00	10.00
4900	Bo Weevil/Chaperon	1956	2.50	5.00	10.00
4919	I Turn to You/Lonesome Lover	1956	2.50	5.00	10.00
4948	No Rock 'N' Roll Tonight/One Track Love	1956	2.50	5.00	10.00
5009	I Want You/Easy Love, Easy Kisses	1957	2.50	5.00	10.00
5033	Kit 'N Caboodle/Takes Two	1957	2.50	5.00	10.00
5063	Teeange Wedding/Runnin' Away	1957	2.50	5.00	10.00
5094	I'm Available/Waiting in Vain	1957	2.50	5.00	10.00
5425	Tweedle Dee/Daddy-O	1960	2.00	4.00	8.00
5865	Seven Lonely Days/Tennessee Wig Walk	1964	—	3.00	6.00
Albums					
KING					
595 [M]	Bonnie Lou Sings	1958	35.00	70.00	140.00

BONNIWELL, T.S.

Sean Bonniwell of THE MUSIC MACHINE.

Number	Title (A Side/B Side)	Yr	VG	VG+	NM
45s					
CAPITOL					
2551	Sleep/Where Am I to Go	1969	2.50	5.00	10.00
Albums					
CAPITOL					
ST-277	Close	1969	12.50	25.00	50.00

BONNIWELL'S MUSIC MACHINE

See THE MUSIC MACHINE.

BONO, SONNY

See SONNY; SONNY AND CHER.

BONZO DOG BAND, THE

Number	Title (A Side/B Side)	Yr	VG	VG+	NM
45s					
IMPERIAL					
66345	I'm the Urban Spaceman/Canyons of Your Mind	1969	3.75	7.50	15.00
—As "The Bonzo Dog Doo-Dah Band"					
66373	Mr. Apollo/Ready Made	1969	3.75	7.50	15.00
—As "The Bonzo Dog Doo-Dah Band"					
UNITED ARTISTS					
50809	I'm the Urban Spaceman/Canyons of Your Mind	1971	2.50	5.00	10.00
50943	Slush/King of Scurf	1972	3.75	7.50	15.00
—Stock copy has been confirmed					
Albums					
IMPERIAL					
LP 9370 [M]	Gorilla	1968	7.50	15.00	30.00
—With booklet					
LP 9370 [M]	Gorilla	1968	5.00	10.00	20.00
—Without booklet					
LP 12370 [S]	Gorilla	1968	7.50	15.00	30.00
—With booklet					
LP 12370 [S]	Gorilla	1968	5.00	10.00	20.00
—Without booklet					
LP 12432	Urban Spaceman	1968	7.50	15.00	30.00
—With booklet					
LP 12432	Urban Spaceman	1968	5.00	10.00	20.00
—Without booklet					
LP 12445	Tadpoles	1969	5.00	10.00	20.00
LP 12457	Keynsham	1969	5.00	10.00	20.00
LIBERTY					
LN-10206	Some of the Best of the Bonzo Dog Band	1983	2.00	4.00	8.00
UNITED ARTISTS					
UA-LA321-H2 [(2)]	The History of the Bonzos	1974	3.75	7.50	15.00
UAS 5517	The Beast of the Bonzos	1971	3.75	7.50	15.00
UAS 5584	Let's Make Up and Be Friendly	1972	3.75	7.50	15.00

BOOGIE KINGS, THE

Number	Title (A Side/B Side)	Yr	VG	VG+	NM
45s					
MONTEL					
939	Crying Man/Two Steps from the Blues	1965	3.00	6.00	12.00
984	When She Touches Me/Philly Walk	196?	2.50	5.00	10.00
995	Elaine/Philly Walk	196?	2.50	5.00	10.00
PAULA					
260	Tell It Like It Is/Philly Walk	1967	2.50	5.00	10.00
272	Bony Maronie/I've Got Your Number	1967	2.50	5.00	10.00
PIC 1					
121	The Band Doll/She	196?	3.75	7.50	15.00
129	This Is Blue Eyed Soul/Do 'Em All	196?	3.75	7.50	15.00
133	Let It Be Me/That's Really Some Good	196?	3.75	7.50	15.00
Albums					
MONTEL					
LP-104 [M]	The Boogie Kings	1966	6.25	12.50	25.00
LP-109 [M]	Blue Eyed Soul	1967	6.25	12.50	25.00

BOOKENDS, THE

Number	Title (A Side/B Side)	Yr	VG	VG+	NM
45s					
CAPITOL					
4667	Christmas Kisses/Let Me Walk with You	1961	3.75	7.50	15.00

BOOKER, JOHN LEE

See JOHN LEE HOOKER.

BOOKER T. AND PRISCILLA

Also see BOOKER T. AND THE MG'S.

Number	Title (A Side/B Side)	Yr	VG	VG+	NM
45s					
A&M					
1298	The Wedding Song/She	1971	—	2.50	5.00
1487	Crippled Crow/Wild Fox	1973	—	2.50	5.00
Albums					
A&M					
SP-3504 [(2)]	Booker T. and Priscilla	1971	3.75	7.50	15.00
SP-4351	Home Grown	1972	2.50	5.00	10.00
SP-4413	Chronicles	1973	2.50	5.00	10.00

BOOKER T. AND THE MG'S

Also see BOOKER T. AND PRISCILLA; STEVE CROPPER.

Number	Title (A Side/B Side)	Yr	VG	VG+	NM
45s					
ASYLUM					
45392	Sticky Stuff/The Stick	1977	—	2.00	4.00
45424	Grab Bag/Reincarnation	1977	—	2.00	4.00
A&M					
2100	Knockin' on Heaven's Door/Let's Go Dancin'	1978	—	2.00	4.00
—As "Booker T. Jones"					
2234	The Best of You/Let's Go Dancin'	1980	—	2.00	4.00
—As "Booker T. Jones"					
2279	Will You Be the One/Cookie	1980	—	2.00	4.00
—As "Booker T. Jones"					
2374	I Want You/You're the Best	1981	—	2.00	4.00
2394	Don't Stop Your Love/I Came to Love You	1982	—	2.00	4.00
COLUMBIA					
77526	Cruisin'/Just My Imagination	1994	—	2.00	4.00
EPIC					
50031	Evergreen/Song for Casey	1974	—	2.00	4.00
50078	Front Street Rag/Mama Stewart	1975	—	2.00	4.00
50149	Life Is Funny/Tennessee Voodoo	1975	—	2.00	4.00
STAX					
0001	Soul-Limbo/Heads Or Tails	1968	2.00	4.00	8.00
0013	Hang 'Em High/Over Easy	1968	2.00	4.00	8.00
0028	Time Is Tight/Johnny I Love You	1969	2.00	4.00	8.00
0037	Mrs. Robinson/Soul Clap '69	1969	2.00	4.00	8.00
0049	Slum Baby/Meditation	1969	2.00	4.00	8.00
0073	Something/Sunday Sermon	1970	—	3.00	6.00
0082	Melting Pot/Kinda Easy Like	1970	—	3.00	6.00
127	Green Onions/Behave Yourself	1962	5.00	10.00	20.00
—Gray label					
127	Green Onions/Behave Yourself	1962	4.00	8.00	16.00
—Blue label					
131	Jellybread/Aw' Mercy	1963	3.00	6.00	12.00
134	Big Train/Home Grown	1963	3.00	6.00	12.00
134	Big Train/Burnt Biscuits	1963	3.00	6.00	12.00
137	Chinese Checkers/Plum Nellie	1963	3.00	6.00	12.00
142	Mo' Onions/Tic Tac Toe	1963	3.00	6.00	12.00
142	Mo' Onions/Fannie Mae	1963	3.00	6.00	12.00
153	Soul Dressing/MG Party	1964	2.50	5.00	10.00
161	Can't Be Still/Terrible Thing	1964	2.50	5.00	10.00
169	Boot-Leg/Outrage	1965	2.50	5.00	10.00
0169	Sugarcane/Blackride	1973	—	2.50	5.00
—As "The MG's"					
182	Red Beans and Rice/Be My Lady	1965	2.50	5.00	10.00
196	Booker-Loo/My Sweet Potato	1966	2.50	5.00	10.00
0200	Breezy/Neckbone	1974	—	2.50	5.00
—As "The MG's"					
203	Jingle Bells/Winter Wonderland	1966	3.00	6.00	12.00
211	Hip-Hug-Her/Summertime	1967	2.50	5.00	10.00
224	Groovin'/Slim Jenkin's Place	1967	2.50	5.00	10.00
236	Silver Bells/Winter Snow	1967	3.00	6.00	12.00
VOLT					
102	Green Onions/Behave Yourself	1962	7.50	15.00	30.00
Albums					
ASYLUM					
7E-1093	Universal Language	1977	2.50	5.00	10.00
ATLANTIC					
SD 8202	The Best of Booker T. and the MG's	1968	5.00	10.00	20.00
81285	The Best of Booker T. and the MG's	1985	2.00	4.00	8.00
A&M					
SP-4720	Try and Love Again	1978	2.50	5.00	10.00
—As "Booker T. Jones"					
SP-4798	The Best of You	1979	2.50	5.00	10.00
—As "Booker T. Jones"					
SP-4874	I Want You	1981	2.50	5.00	10.00
—As "Booker T. Jones"					
EPIC					
KE 33143	Evergreen	1974	3.00	6.00	12.00
MCA					
6282	The Runaway	1989	3.00	6.00	12.00
—As "Booker T. Jones"					
STAX					
ST-701 [M]	Green Onions	1962	17.50	35.00	70.00
STS-701 [R]	Green Onions	1966	12.50	25.00	50.00
ST-705 [M]	Soul Dressing	1965	17.50	35.00	70.00
STS-705 [R]	Soul Dressing	1966	12.50	25.00	50.00
ST-711 [M]	And Now...Booker T. and the MG's	1966	12.50	25.00	50.00
STS-711 [S]	And Now...Booker T. and the MG's	1966	20.00	40.00	80.00
ST-713 [M]	In the Christmas Spirit	1966	100.00	200.00	400.00
—Fingers and piano keys cover					
ST-713 [M]	In the Christmas Spirit	1967	50.00	100.00	200.00
—Same as above; Santa Claus cover					
STS-713 [S]	In the Christmas Spirit	1966	100.00	200.00	400.00
—Fingers and piano keys cover					
STS-713 [S]	In the Christmas Spirit	1967	50.00	100.00	200.00
—Santa Claus cover					
ST-717 [M]	Hip Hug-Her	1967	10.00	20.00	40.00

Number	Title (A Side/B Side)	Yr	VG	VG+	NM
STS-717 [S]	Hip Hug-Her	1967	12.50	25.00	50.00
STS-724	Doin' Our Thing	1968	12.50	25.00	50.00
STS-2001	Soul Limbo	1968	6.25	12.50	25.00
STS-2006	Uptight	1969	6.25	12.50	25.00
STS-2009	The Booker T. Set	1969	6.25	12.50	25.00
STS-2027	McLemore Avenue	1970	6.25	12.50	25.00
STS-2033	Booker T. and the MG's Greatest Hits	1970	3.75	7.50	15.00
STS-2035	Melting Pot	1971	3.75	7.50	15.00
STX-4104	Free Ride	1978	2.50	5.00	10.00
STX-4113	Soul Limbo	198?	2.50	5.00	10.00
—Reissue of 2001					
MPS-8505	Booker T. and the MG's Greatest Hits	1981	2.50	5.00	10.00
MPS-8521	Melting Pot	198?	2.50	5.00	10.00
—Reissue of 2035					
MPS-8531	The Booker T. Set	1987	2.50	5.00	10.00
—Reissue of 2009					
MPS-8552	McLemore Avenue	1990	3.00	6.00	12.00
—Reissue of 2027					

BOOMERANG

45s

RCA VICTOR

Number	Title (A Side/B Side)	Yr	VG	VG+	NM
74-0508	Mockingbird/Montreal Jail	1971	2.00	4.00	8.00
74-0580	Juke It/Hard Times	1971	2.00	4.00	8.00

Albums

RCA VICTOR

Number	Title (A Side/B Side)	Yr	VG	VG+	NM
LSP-4577	Boomerang	1971	5.00	10.00	20.00

BOONE, DANIEL

45s

EPIC

Number	Title (A Side/B Side)	Yr	VG	VG+	NM
10787	Daddy Don't You Walk So Fast/Tiger Woman	1971	—	2.50	5.00

MERCURY

Number	Title (A Side/B Side)	Yr	VG	VG+	NM
73281	Beautiful Sunday/Truly Julie	1972	—	2.50	5.00
73339	Annabelle/Sleepyhead	1972	—	2.00	4.00
73357	Crying/Sunshine Lover	1973	—	2.00	4.00
73428	Skydiver/Do You Thank the Lord	1973	—	2.00	4.00
73461	Love Spell/Lilly, I Love You	1974	—	2.00	4.00

PYE

Number	Title (A Side/B Side)	Yr	VG	VG+	NM
71007	A Rock 'N Roll Band/Singing Backing Vocal with a Rock 'N Roll Band	1975	—	2.00	4.00
71011	Run, Tell the People/Rock 'N' Roll Bum	1975	—	2.00	4.00
71041	Run, Tell the People/(B-side unknown)	1976	—	2.00	4.00
71052	I Think of You/(B-side unknown)	1976	—	2.00	4.00

Albums

MERCURY

Number	Title (A Side/B Side)	Yr	VG	VG+	NM
SRM-1-649	Beautiful Sunday	1972	2.50	5.00	10.00

BOONE, PAT

Also see THE BOONES.

45s

BUENA VISTA

Number	Title (A Side/B Side)	Yr	VG	VG+	NM
487	Little Green Tree/The Sounds of Christmas	1973	—	3.50	7.00

CAPITOL

Number	Title (A Side/B Side)	Yr	VG	VG+	NM
2763	What Are You Doing the Rest of Your Life/Now I'm Saved	1970	—	2.50	5.00
2860	Picking Up Pebbles/Oh My God	1970	—	2.50	5.00

DOT

Number	Title (A Side/B Side)	Yr	VG	VG+	NM
S-200 [S]	With the Wind and the Rain in Your Hair/Good Rockin' Tonight	1959	10.00	20.00	40.00
S-203 [S]	For a Penny/The Wang Dang Taffy Apple Tango	1959	10.00	20.00	40.00
S-207 [S]	Twixt Twlve and Twenty/Rock Boll Weevil	1959	10.00	20.00	40.00
S-211 [S]	Fools Hall of Fame/The Brightest Wishing Star	1959	10.00	20.00	40.00
S-218 [S]	Beyond the Sunset/My Faithful Heart	1959	10.00	20.00	40.00
S-220 [S]	(Welcome) New Lovers/Words	1960	10.00	20.00	40.00
S-221 [S]	Walking the Floor Over You/Spring Rain	1960	10.00	20.00	40.00
S-228 [S]	Delia Gone/Candy Street	1960	10.00	20.00	40.00
15338	Two Hearts/Tra La La	1955	5.00	10.00	20.00
15377	Ain't That a Shame/Tennessee Saturday Night	1955	5.00	10.00	20.00
15422	At My Front Door/No Other Arms	1955	5.00	10.00	20.00
15435	Gee Whittakers!/Take the Time	1955	5.00	10.00	20.00
15443	Tutti Frutti/I'll Be Home	1956	5.00	10.00	20.00
15457	Long Tall Sally/Just As Long As I'm with You	1956	5.00	10.00	20.00
15472	I Almost Lost My Mind/I'm in Love with You	1956	5.00	10.00	20.00
15490	Friendly Persuasion (Thee I Love)/Chains of Love	1956	5.00	10.00	20.00
—Original on maroon label					
15490	Friendly Persuasion (Thee I Love)/Chains of Love	1956	3.75	7.50	15.00
—Second pressing on black label					
15521	Don't Forbid Me/Anastasia	1956	3.75	7.50	15.00
15545	Why Baby Why/I'm Waiting Just for You	1957	3.75	7.50	15.00
15570	Love Letters in the Sand/Bernardine	1957	3.75	7.50	15.00
15570 [PS]	Love Letters in the Sand/Bernardine	1957	7.50	15.00	30.00
15602	Remember You're Mine/There's a Gold Mine in the Sky	1957	3.75	7.50	15.00
15660	April Love/When the Swallows Come Back to Capistrano	1957	3.75	7.50	15.00
15690	It's Too Soon to Know/A Wonderful Time Up There	1958	3.75	7.50	15.00
15750	Sugar Moon/Cherie, I Love You	1958	3.75	7.50	15.00
15750 [PS]	Sugar Moon/Cherie, I Love You	1958	7.50	15.00	30.00
15785	If Dreams Came True/That's How Much I Love You	1958	3.75	7.50	15.00
15825	Gee, But It's Lonely/For My Good Fortune	1958	3.75	7.50	15.00
15840	I'll Remember Tonight/The Mardi Gras March	1958	3.75	7.50	15.00
15840 [PS]	I'll Remember Tonight/The Mardi Gras March	1958	7.50	15.00	30.00
15888 [M]	With the Wind and the Rain in Your Hair/Good Rockin' Tonight	1959	3.75	7.50	15.00
15914 [M]	For a Penny/The Wang Dang Taffy Apple Tango	1959	3.75	7.50	15.00
15955 [M]	Twixt Twlve and Twenty/Rock Boll Weevil	1959	3.75	7.50	15.00
15955 [PS]	Twixt Twlve and Twenty/Rock Boll Weevil	1959	7.50	15.00	30.00
15982 [M]	Fools Hall of Fame/The Brightest Wishing Star	1959	3.75	7.50	15.00
15982 [PS]	Fools Hall of Fame/The Brightest Wishing Star	1959	7.50	15.00	30.00
16006 [M]	Beyond the Sunset/My Faithful Heart	1959	3.75	7.50	15.00
16015	To the Center of the Earth Part 1/Part 2	1959	5.00	10.00	20.00
16028	Ain't That a Shame/I'll Be Home	1960	2.50	5.00	10.00
16033	I Almost Lost My Mind/Friendly Persuasion	1960	2.50	5.00	10.00
16034	Don't Forbid Me/April Love	1960	2.50	5.00	10.00
16035	Love Letters in the Sand/A Wonderful Time Up There	1960	2.50	5.00	10.00
16048	(Welcome) New Lovers/Words	1960	3.00	6.00	12.00
16048 [PS]	(Welcome) New Lovers/Words	1960	5.00	10.00	20.00
16073	Walking the Floor Over You/Spring Rain	1960	3.00	6.00	12.00
16073 [PS]	Walking the Floor Over You/Spring Rain	1960	5.00	10.00	20.00
16122	Delia Gone/Candy Street	1960	3.00	6.00	12.00
16152	Dear John/Alabam	1960	3.00	6.00	12.00
16176	The Exodus Song (This Land Is Mine)/There's a Moon Out Tonight	1961	3.00	6.00	12.00
16190	Cherry Pink and Apple Blossom White/On Both Sides	1961	3.00	6.00	12.00
16209	Moody River/A Thousand Years	1961	3.75	7.50	15.00
16244	Big Cold Wind/That's My Desire	1961	3.00	6.00	12.00
16278	Louella/(B-side unknown)	1961	—	—	—
—Unreleased?					
16284	Johnny Will/Just Let Me Dream	1961	3.00	6.00	12.00
16312	I'll See You in My Dreams/Pictures in the Fire	1961	3.00	6.00	12.00
16349	Quando, Quando, Quando (Tell Me When)/Willing and Eager	1962	2.50	5.00	10.00
16368	Speedy Gonzales/The Locket	1962	3.00	6.00	12.00
16391	Ten Lonely Guys/Lover's Lane	1962	2.50	5.00	10.00
16416	In the Room/Mexican Joe	1963	2.50	5.00	10.00
16439	Days of Wine and Roses/Meditation	1963	2.50	5.00	10.00
16474	Always You and Me/Main Attraction	1963	2.50	5.00	10.00
16494	Tie Me Kangaroo Down Sport/I Feel Like Crying	1963	2.50	5.00	10.00
16498	Amore Baciami/Gondoli Gondola	1963	2.50	5.00	10.00
16498	Main Attraction/Si Si Si	1963	2.50	5.00	10.00
16525	Love Me/Mr. Moon	1963	2.50	5.00	10.00
16547	Santa's Coming in a Whirleybird/Oh Holy Night	1963	2.50	5.00	10.00
16559	Some Enchanted Evening/That's Me	1963	2.50	5.00	10.00
16576	I Like What You Do/Never Put It in Writing	1964	2.00	4.00	8.00
16598	I Understand (Just How You Feel)/Rosemarie	1964	2.00	4.00	8.00
16626	Side by Side/I'll Never Be Free	1964	2.00	4.00	8.00
—By "Pat and Shirley Boone"					
16641	Sincerely/Don't You Just Know It	1964	2.00	4.00	8.00
16658	Beach Girl/Little Honda	1964	7.50	15.00	30.00
16668	Goodbye, Charlie/Love, Who Needs It	1964	2.00	4.00	8.00
16684	I'd Rather Die Young/I Want It That Way	1964	2.00	4.00	8.00
16699	Blueberry Hill/Heartaches	1965	2.00	4.00	8.00
16707	Baby Elephant Walk/Say Goodbye	1965	2.00	4.00	8.00
16728	Pearly Shells/Crazy Arms	1965	2.00	4.00	8.00
16738	Mickey Mouse/Time Marches On	1965	2.00	4.00	8.00
16738	Mickey Mouse/(Welcome) New Lovers	1965	2.00	4.00	8.00
16754	Rainy Days/With My Eyes Wide Open I'm Dreaming	1965	2.00	4.00	8.00
16785	I Love You So Much It Hurts/Meet Me Tonight in Dreamland	1965	2.00	4.00	8.00
16808	A Man Alone/Run to Me, Baby	1966	2.00	4.00	8.00
16825	As Tears Go By/Judith	1966	2.00	4.00	8.00
16836	It Seems Like Yesterday/Well Remembered, Highly Thought Of Love Affair	1966	2.00	4.00	8.00
16871	Five Miles from Home/Don't Put Your Feet in the Lemonade	1966	2.00	4.00	8.00
16903	Wrath of Grapes/You Don't Need Me Anymore	1966	2.00	4.00	8.00
16933	Wish You Were Here, Buddy/Love for You	1966	2.00	4.00	8.00
16998	Hurry Sundown/What If They Gave a War and Nobody Came	1967	—	3.00	6.00
17018	Have You Heard (It's All Over)/Me	1967	—	3.00	6.00
17027	In the Mirror of Your Mind/Swanee Is a River	1967	—	3.00	6.00
17045	By the Time I Get to Phoenix/Ride Ride Ride	1967	—	3.00	6.00
17056	The Green Kentucky Hills of Home/You Mean All the World to Me	1967	—	3.00	6.00
17076	It's a Happening World/Emily	1968	—	3.00	6.00
17098	500 Miles/I Had a Dream	1968	—	3.00	6.00
17122	Gonna Find Me a Bluebird/Deafening Roar of Silence	1968	—	3.00	6.00
17156	Beyond One Memory/September Blues	1968	—	3.00	6.00

HITSVILLE

Number	Title (A Side/B Side)	Yr	VG	VG+	NM
6037	Texas Woman/It's Gone	1976	—	2.50	5.00
6042	Oklahoma Sunshine/Won't Be Home Tonight	1976	—	2.50	5.00
6047	Country Days and Country Nights/Lovelight Comes a-Shining	1976	—	2.50	5.00
6054	Colorado Country Morning/Don't Want to Fall Away from You	1977	—	2.50	5.00

LAMB & LION

Number	Title (A Side/B Side)	Yr	VG	VG+	NM
818	It's OK to Be a Kid at Christmas/Don't Let the Season Pass You By	1979	—	2.50	5.00

LION

Number	Title (A Side/B Side)	Yr	VG	VG+	NM
106	Mr. Blue/Song of the Children of Israel (Exodus)	1972	—	2.50	5.00
—With the Boone Girls					
119	I Believe in Music/Children Learn What They Live	1972	—	2.50	5.00
—With the Boone Family					
126	Empty Chairs/If You're Gonna Make a Fool of Somebody	1972	—	2.50	5.00

MELODYLAND

Number	Title (A Side/B Side)	Yr	VG	VG+	NM
6001	Candy Lips/Young Girl	1974	—	2.50	5.00
6005	Indiana Girl/Young Girl	1975	—	2.50	5.00
6018	I'd Do It with You/Yester-Me, Yester-You, Yesterday	1975	—	2.50	5.00
—A-side with Shirley Boone					
6029	Glory Train/U.F.O.	1976	—	2.50	5.00

MGM

Number	Title (A Side/B Side)	Yr	VG	VG+	NM
14242	All for the Love of Sunshine/M.I.A-P.O.W.	1971	—	2.50	5.00
14282	C'mon, Give a Hand/Where There's a Heartache	1971	—	2.50	5.00
14470	I Saw the Light/Great Speckled Bird	1972	—	2.50	5.00
14521	Tying the Pieces Together/Hayden Carter	1973	—	2.00	4.00
14521 [PS]	Tying the Pieces Together/Hayden Carter	1973	—	2.50	5.00
14601	Everything Begins and Ends with You/Golden Rocket	1973	—	2.00	4.00

Number	Title (A Side/B Side)	Yr	VG	VG+	NM
M.C.					
5001	Whatever Happened to the Good Old Honky Tonk/Ain't Going Down in the Ground Before My Time	1977	—	2.50	5.00
REPUBLIC					
7049	My Heart Belongs to You/Until You Tell Me So	1953	6.25	12.50	25.00
7062	Remember to Be Mine/Half Way Chance with You	1953	6.25	12.50	25.00
7084	I Need Someone/Loving You Madly	1954	6.25	12.50	25.00
7119	My Heart Belongs to You/I Need Someone	1955	5.00	10.00	20.00
TETRAGRAMMATON					
1516	July, You're a Woman/Break My Mind	1969	—	2.50	5.00
1529	Never Goin' Back/What's Gnawing at Me	1969	—	2.50	5.00
1540	You Win Again/Good Morning, Dear	1969	—	2.50	5.00
WARNER BROS.					
49097	Midnight/Can You Feel the Love	1979	—	2.00	4.00
—By "Pat and Shirley Boone"					
49255	Hostage Prayer/Love's Got a Way of Hanging On	1980	—	2.00	4.00
49596	Colorado Country Morning/Whatever Happened to the Good Old Honky Tonk	1980	—	2.00	4.00
49691	Won't Be Home Tonight/Throw It Away	1981	—	2.00	4.00
7-Inch Extended Plays					
DOT					
DEP-1049	At My Front Door/Tennessee Saturday Night//Ain't That a Shame/Two Hearts	1956	5.00	10.00	20.00
DEP-1049 [PS]	Pat Boone	1956	5.00	10.00	20.00
DEP-1053	Treasure of Love/B-I-N-G-O//Hoboken Baby/Am I Seeing Angels	1956	5.00	10.00	20.00
DEP-1053 [PS]	Pat On Mike	1956	5.00	10.00	20.00
DEP-1054	Coax Me A Little/The Mocking Bird In The Willow Tree//Indiana Holiday/Marry Me, Marry Me	1956	5.00	10.00	20.00
DEP-1054 [PS]	Pat Boone Sings Songs from Friendly Persuasion	1956	5.00	10.00	20.00
DEP-1055	Don't Forbid Me/Why Did I Choose You?//Rock Me Baby/The Fat Man	1957	5.00	10.00	20.00
DEP-1055 [PS]	A Date with Pat Boone	1957	5.00	10.00	20.00
DEP-1056	Just a Closer Walk with Thee/Peace in the Valley//He'll Understand/Steal Away	1957	5.00	10.00	20.00
DEP-1056 [PS]	A Closer Walk with Thee	1957	5.00	10.00	20.00
DEP-1057	Technique/Cathedral in the Pines//Louella/Without My Love	1957	5.00	10.00	20.00
DEP-1057 [PS]	Four by Pat	1957	5.00	10.00	20.00
DEP-1062	White Christmas/Silent Night//Jingle Bells/Santa Claus Is Comin' to Town	1957	7.50	15.00	30.00
DEP-1062 [PS]	... And a Very Merry Christmas	1957	7.50	15.00	30.00
DEP-1064	Chattanooga Shoe Shine Boy/Harbor Lights//Tutti Frutti/I'll Be Home	195?	3.75	7.50	15.00
DEP-1064 [PS]	Tutti Frutti	195?	3.75	7.50	15.00
DEP-1068	The Lord's Prayer/I Believe//Ave Maria/He	195?	3.75	7.50	15.00
DEP-1068 [PS]	The Lord's Prayer	195?	3.75	7.50	15.00
DEP-1069	Autumn Leaves/Blueberry Hill//Cold, Cold Heart/St. Louis Blues	1958	5.00	10.00	20.00
DEP-1069 [PS]	Star Dust	1958	5.00	10.00	20.00
DEP-1075	Loyalty/Bourbon Street Blues//Bigger Than Texas/A Fiddle, A Rifle, An Axe and a Bible	1958	3.75	7.50	15.00
DEP-1075 [PS]	Mardi Gras	1958	3.75	7.50	15.00
DEP-1076	*You Can't Be True, Dear/My Happiness//Now Is the Hour/Side by Side	1959	3.75	7.50	15.00
DEP-1076 [PS]	Side by Side	1959	3.75	7.50	15.00
—By "Pat & Shirley Boone"					
DEP-1081	Beyond The Sunset/It Is No Secret//My God Is Real (Yes, God Is Real)/Yield Not To Temptation	195?	3.75	7.50	15.00
DEP-1081 [PS]	Hymns We Love	195?	3.75	7.50	15.00
DEP-1082	*Tenderly/Fascination/True Love/Maybe You'll Be There	196?	3.75	7.50	15.00
DEP-1082 [PS]	Tenderly	196?	3.75	7.50	15.00
DEP-1083	(contents unknown)	196?	3.75	7.50	15.00
DEP-1083 [PS]	Pat's Great Hits	196?	3.75	7.50	15.00
DEP-1086	(contents unknown)	196?	3.75	7.50	15.00
DEP-1086 [PS]	I'm In the Mood for Love	196?	3.75	7.50	15.00
DEP-1090	(contents unknown)	196?	3.75	7.50	15.00
DEP-1090 [PS]	Beyond the Sunset	196?	3.75	7.50	15.00
DEP-1091	(contents unknown)	196?	3.75	7.50	15.00
DEP-1091 [PS]	Journey to the Center of the Earth	196?	3.75	7.50	15.00
DEP-1098	(contents unknown)	196?	3.75	7.50	15.00
DEP-1098 [PS]	All Hands On Deck	196?	3.75	7.50	15.00
Albums					
ABC					
4006	16 Great Performances	1975	2.50	5.00	10.00
BIBLE VOICE					
7076	The Solution to Crisis-America	1970	3.00	6.00	12.00
DOT					
DLP-3012 [M]	Pat Boone	1956	12.50	25.00	50.00
—Maroon label					
DLP-3012 [M]	Pat Boone	1957	6.25	12.50	25.00
—Black label					
DLP-3030 [M]	Howdy!	1956	12.50	25.00	50.00
—Maroon label					
DLP-3030 [M]	Howdy!	1957	6.25	12.50	25.00
—Black label					
DLP-3050 [M]	Pat	1957	6.25	12.50	25.00
DLP-3068 [M]	Hymns We Love	1957	6.25	12.50	25.00
DLP-3071 [M]	Pat's Great Hits	1957	6.25	12.50	25.00
DLP-3077 [M]	Pat Boone Sings Irving Berlin	1958	5.00	10.00	20.00
DLP-3118 [M]	Star Dust	1958	5.00	10.00	20.00
DLP-3121 [M]	Yes Indeed!	1958	5.00	10.00	20.00
DLP-3158 [M]	Pat Boone Sings	1959	5.00	10.00	20.00
DLP-3180 [M]	Tenderly	1959	5.00	10.00	20.00
DLP-3199 [M]	Side by Side	1959	5.00	10.00	20.00
DLP-3222 [M]	White Christmas	1959	6.25	12.50	25.00
DLP-3234 [M]	He Leadeth Me	1960	3.75	7.50	15.00
DLP-3261 [M]	Pat's Great Hits Volume 2	1960	3.75	7.50	15.00
DLP-3270 [M]	Moonglow	1960	3.75	7.50	15.00
DLP-3285 [M]	This and That	1960	3.75	7.50	15.00
DLP-3346 [M]	Great! Great! Great!	1961	3.75	7.50	15.00
DLP-3384 [M]	Moody River	1961	3.00	6.00	12.00
DLP-3386 [M]	My God and I	1961	3.00	6.00	12.00
DLP-3399 [M]	I'll See You in My Dreams	1961	3.00	6.00	12.00
DLP-3402 [M]	Pat Boone Reads from the Holy Bible	1962	3.75	7.50	15.00
DLP-3455 [M]	Pat Boone's Golden Hits	1962	3.00	6.00	12.00
DLP-3475 [M]	I Love You Truly	1962	3.00	6.00	12.00
DLP-3501 [M]	Pat Boone Sings Guess Who?	1963	12.50	25.00	50.00
DLP-3504 [M]	Pat Boone Sings "Days of Wine and Roses" and Other Great Movie Themes	1963	3.00	6.00	12.00
DLP-3513 [M]	Sing Along Without Pat Boone	1963	3.00	6.00	12.00
DLP-3520 [M]	The Star Spangled Banner	1963	3.00	6.00	12.00
DLP-3534 [M]	Tie Me Kangaroo Down, Sport	1963	3.00	6.00	12.00
DLP-3546 [M]	The Touch of Your Lips	1963	3.00	6.00	12.00
DLP-3582 [M]	The Lord's Prayer And Other Great Hymns	1964	3.00	6.00	12.00
DLP-3594 [M]	Boss Beat	1964	3.00	6.00	12.00
DLP-3601 [M]	Blest Be the Tie That Binds	1965	3.00	6.00	12.00
DLP-3606 [M]	Near You	1965	3.00	6.00	12.00
DLP-3626 [M]	The Golden Era of Country Hits	1965	3.00	6.00	12.00
DLP-3650 [M]	My 10th Anniversary with Dot Records	1965	3.00	6.00	12.00
DLP-3667 [M]	Winner of the Reader's Digest Poll	1965	3.00	6.00	12.00
DLP-3685 [M]	Great Hits of 1965	1965	3.00	6.00	12.00
DLP-3748 [M]	Memories	1966	3.00	6.00	12.00
DLP-3764 [M]	Wish You Were Here, Buddy	1966	3.00	6.00	12.00
DLP-3770 [M]	Christmas Is a-Comin'	1966	3.00	6.00	12.00
DLP-3798 [M]	How Great Thou Art	1967	3.75	7.50	15.00
DLP-3805 [M]	I Was Kaiser Bill's Batman	1967	3.75	7.50	15.00
DLP-3814 [M]	15 Hits of Pat Boone	1967	3.75	7.50	15.00
DLP-3876 [M]	Look Ahead	1968	3.75	7.50	15.00
DLP-25068 [S]	Hymns We Love	1959	7.50	15.00	30.00
DLP-25071 [P]	Pat's Great Hits	1959	7.50	15.00	30.00
DLP-25077 [S]	Pat Boone Sings Irving Berlin	1959	6.25	12.50	25.00
DLP-25118 [S]	Star Dust	1959	6.25	12.50	25.00
DLP-25121 [S]	Yes Indeed!	1959	6.25	12.50	25.00
DLP-25158 [S]	Pat Boone Sings	1959	6.25	12.50	25.00
DLP-25180 [S]	Tenderly	1959	6.25	12.50	25.00
DLP-25199 [S]	Side by Side	1959	6.25	12.50	25.00
DLP-25222 [S]	White Christmas	1959	7.50	15.00	30.00
DLP-25234 [S]	He Leadeth Me	1960	5.00	10.00	20.00
DLP-25261 [S]	Pat's Great Hits Volume 2	1960	5.00	10.00	20.00
DLP-25270 [S]	Moonglow	1960	5.00	10.00	20.00
—Black vinyl					
DLP-25270 [S]	Moonglow	1960	12.50	25.00	50.00
—Blue vinyl					
DLP-25285 [S]	This and That	1960	5.00	10.00	20.00
DLP-25346 [S]	Great! Great! Great!	1961	5.00	10.00	20.00
DLP-25384 [S]	Moody River	1961	3.75	7.50	15.00
DLP-25386 [S]	My God and I	1961	3.75	7.50	15.00
DLP-25399 [S]	I'll See You in My Dreams	1961	3.75	7.50	15.00
DLP-25455 [S]	Pat Boone's Golden Hits	1962	3.75	7.50	15.00
DLP-25475 [S]	I Love You Truly	1962	3.75	7.50	15.00
DLP-25501 [S]	Pat Boone Sings Guess Who?	1963	20.00	40.00	80.00
DLP-25504 [S]	Pat Boone Sings "Days of Wine and Roses" and Other Great Movie Themes	1963	3.75	7.50	15.00
DLP-25513 [S]	Sing Along Without Pat Boone	1963	3.75	7.50	15.00
DLP-25520 [S]	The Star Spangled Banner	1963	3.75	7.50	15.00
DLP-25534 [S]	Tie Me Kangaroo Down, Sport	1963	3.75	7.50	15.00
DLP-25546 [S]	The Touch of Your Lips	1963	3.75	7.50	15.00
DLP-25573 [R]	Pat Boone	1964	3.00	6.00	12.00
DLP-25582 [S]	The Lord's Prayer And Other Great Hymns	1964	3.75	7.50	15.00
DLP-25594 [S]	Boss Beat	1964	3.75	7.50	15.00
DLP-25601 [S]	Blest Be the Tie That Binds	1965	3.75	7.50	15.00
DLP-25606 [S]	Near You	1965	3.75	7.50	15.00
DLP-25626 [S]	The Golden Era of Country Hits	1965	3.75	7.50	15.00
DLP-25650 [S]	My 10th Anniversary with Dot Records	1965	3.75	7.50	15.00
DLP-25667 [S]	Winner of the Reader's Digest Poll	1965	3.75	7.50	15.00
DLP-25685 [S]	Great Hits of 1965	1965	3.75	7.50	15.00
DLP-25748 [S]	Memories	1966	3.75	7.50	15.00
DLP-25764 [S]	Wish You Were Here, Buddy	1966	3.75	7.50	15.00
DLP-25770 [S]	Christmas Is a-Comin'	1966	3.75	7.50	15.00
DLP-25798 [S]	How Great Thou Art	1967	3.00	6.00	12.00
DLP-25805 [S]	I Was Kaiser Bill's Batman	1967	3.00	6.00	12.00
DLP-25814 [S]	15 Hits of Pat Boone	1967	3.00	6.00	12.00
DLP-25876 [S]	Look Ahead	1968	3.00	6.00	12.00
HAMILTON					
HLP-118 [M]	12 Great Hits	196?	3.00	6.00	12.00
HLP-12118 [S]	12 Great Hits	196?	3.00	6.00	12.00
HITSVILLE					
H6-405	Texas Woman	1976	3.00	6.00	12.00
LAMB & LION					
1002	New Songs of the Jesus People	197?	3.00	6.00	12.00
1004	Pat Boone and the First Nashville Jesus Band	197?	3.00	6.00	12.00
1005	Christian People, Vol. 1	197?	2.50	5.00	10.00
1006	The Family Who Prays	197?	2.50	5.00	10.00
1007	Born Again	197?	2.50	5.00	10.00
1008	All in the Boone Family	1972	2.50	5.00	10.00
1013	S-A-V-E-D	197?	2.50	5.00	10.00
1016	Songs from the Inner Court	197?	2.50	5.00	10.00
5000	The Pat Boone Family in the Holy Land	197?	2.50	5.00	10.00
MCA					
658	16 Great Performances	1980	2.00	4.00	8.00
6020 [(2)]	The Best of Pat Boone	1980	3.00	6.00	12.00
15028 [S]	White Christmas	198?	2.50	5.00	10.00
—Reissue of Dot LP					
MELODYLAND					
6-501	The Country Side of Pat Boone	1975	3.00	6.00	12.00
MGM					
SE-4899	I Love You More and More Every Day	1973	2.50	5.00	10.00
PARAMOUNT					
1024 [(2)]	Pat Boone's Greatest Hymns	1974	3.75	7.50	15.00
1043 [(2)]	Pat Boone's Greatest Hits	1974	3.75	7.50	15.00
PICKWICK					
SPC-1024	White Christmas	1979	2.50	5.00	10.00
SPC-3079	True Love	196?	2.50	5.00	10.00
SPC-3107	Love Me Tender	196?	2.50	5.00	10.00
SPC-3123	Canadian Sunset	196?	2.50	5.00	10.00
SPC-3145	Favorite Hymns	197?	2.50	5.00	10.00

Number	Title (A Side/B Side)	Yr	VG	VG+	NM
SPC-3219	You've Lost That Lovin' Feeling	197?	2.50	5.00	10.00
SPC-3568	The Old Rugged Cross	1978	2.00	4.00	8.00
SPC-3597	Great Hits	1978	2.00	4.00	8.00
SUPREME					
SS-2060	Rapture	1970	3.00	6.00	12.00
TETRAGRAMMATON					
T-118	Departure	1969	3.00	6.00	12.00
WORD					
WST-8536	The Pat Boone Family	1970	2.50	5.00	10.00
WST-8664	Hymns We Love	197?	2.50	5.00	10.00
WST-8711	He Leadeth Me	197?	2.50	5.00	10.00
WST-8725	The Star-Spangled Banner	197?	2.50	5.00	10.00
WST-8738	I Believe	198?	2.00	4.00	8.00

BOONES, THE

45s

Number	Title (A Side/B Side)	Yr	VG	VG+	NM
MOTOWN					
1314	Please Mr. Postman/Friend	1974	—	2.50	5.00
—As "The Pat Boone Family"					
1334	When The Lovelight Starts Shining Through His Eyes/Viva Espana	1975	—	2.50	5.00
1389	My Guy/When the Lovelight Starts Shining Through His Eyes	1976	—	2.50	5.00
WARNER BROS.					
8385 [DJ]	Hasta Manana (mono/stereo)	1977	—	2.50	5.00
—Stock copy not known to exist					
8446	He's a Rebel/You Light Up My Life	1977	—	3.00	6.00
—B-side by Debby Boone					

BOOT

45s

Number	Title (A Side/B Side)	Yr	VG	VG+	NM
AGAPE					
9008	Hey Little Girl/Liza Brown	1972	2.00	4.00	8.00

Albums

Number	Title (A Side/B Side)	Yr	VG	VG+	NM
AGAPE					
2601	Boot	1972	6.25	12.50	25.00

BOOTLES, THE

45s

Number	Title (A Side/B Side)	Yr	VG	VG+	NM
GNP CRESCENDO					
311	I'll Let You Hold My Hand/Never Till Now	1964	3.75	7.50	15.00

BOP-A-LOOS, THE

45s

Number	Title (A Side/B Side)	Yr	VG	VG+	NM
MERCURY					
70552	Teach Me Tonight/South Parkway Mambo	1955	5.00	10.00	20.00
70553	Tweedle Dee/Bongo Mambo	1955	5.00	10.00	20.00
70568	Hearts of Stone/Miracle Mambo	1955	5.00	10.00	20.00
70569	Sincerely/Cuban Carnival	1955	5.00	10.00	20.00

BORDERSONG

With Ann and Nancy Wilson, later of HEART.

45s

Number	Title (A Side/B Side)	Yr	VG	VG+	NM
GREAT NORTHWEST					
704	She's a Good Woman/Morning	1976	6.25	12.50	25.00

Albums

Number	Title (A Side/B Side)	Yr	VG	VG+	NM
REAL GOOD					
1001	Morning	1975	17.50	35.00	70.00

BOSSTONES, THE

45s

Number	Title (A Side/B Side)	Yr	VG	VG+	NM
BOSS					
401	Mope-Itty Mope/Wings of an Angel	1959	25.00	50.00	100.00
—As "Boss Tones"					
501	Mope-Itty Mope/Wings of an Angel	1959	50.00	100.00	200.00
—As "Bosstones"					
V-TONE					
208	Mope-Itty Mope/Wings of an Angel	1960	15.00	30.00	60.00

BOSTIC, EARL

45s

Number	Title (A Side/B Side)	Yr	VG	VG+	NM
KING					
4444	Sleep/September Song	1951	7.50	15.00	30.00
4454	Always/How Could It Have Been You and I	1951	7.50	15.00	30.00
4475	Flamingo/I'm Getting Sentimental Over You	1951	7.50	15.00	30.00
4491	I Got Loaded/Chains of Love	1951	10.00	20.00	40.00
4511	The Moon Is Low/Lover Come Back to Me	1952	6.25	12.50	25.00
4536	Linger Awhile/Velvet Sunset	1952	6.25	12.50	25.00
4550	Moonglow/Ain't Misbehavin'	1952	6.25	12.50	25.00
4570	For You/Smoke Gets In Your Eyes	1952	6.25	12.50	25.00
4586	You Go to My Head/Hour of Parting	1953	6.25	12.50	25.00
4603	The Sheik of Araby/Steamwhistle Jump	1953	6.25	12.50	25.00
4623	Cherokee/The Song Is Ended	1953	6.25	12.50	25.00
4644	Melancholy Serenade/What, No Pearls?	1953	6.25	12.50	25.00
4653	The Very Thought of You/Memories	1953	6.25	12.50	25.00
4674	Deep Purple/Smoke Rings	1953	6.25	12.50	25.00
4683	Off Shore/Don't You Do It	1953	6.25	12.50	25.00
4699	My Heart at Thy Sweet Voice/Cracked Ice	1954	5.00	10.00	20.00
4708	Jungle Drums/Danube Waves	1954	5.00	10.00	20.00
4723	Blue Skies/Mambolino	1954	5.00	10.00	20.00
4730	These Foolish Things/Mambostic	1954	5.00	10.00	20.00
4741	Ubangi Stomp/Time on My Hands	1954	5.00	10.00	20.00
4754	Song of the Islands/Liebestraum	1954	5.00	10.00	20.00
4765	Embraceable You/Night and Day	1955	5.00	10.00	20.00
4776	Melody of Love/Sweet Lorraine	1955	5.00	10.00	20.00
4790	Cocktails for Two/When Your Lover Has Gone	1955	5.00	10.00	20.00
4799	Remember/Cherry Bean	1955	5.00	10.00	20.00
4815	East of the Sun/Dream	1955	5.00	10.00	20.00
4829	For All We Know/Beyond the Blue Horizon	1955	5.00	10.00	20.00
4845	O Solo Mio/Poeme	1955	5.00	10.00	20.00
4883	I Love You Truly/'Cause You're My Lover	1956	3.75	7.50	15.00
4905	Bugle Call Rag/I'll String Along with You	1956	3.75	7.50	15.00
4943	Roses of Picardy/Where or When	1956	3.75	7.50	15.00
4978	Harlem Nocturne/I Hear a Rhapsody	1956	3.75	7.50	15.00
5025	Too Fine for Crying/Avalon	1957	3.75	7.50	15.00
5041	Temptation/September Song	1957	3.75	7.50	15.00
5056	She's Funny That Way/Exercise	1957	3.75	7.50	15.00
5071	Vienna, City of My Dreams/Just Too Shy	1957	3.75	7.50	15.00
5081	A Gay Day/Answer Me	1957	3.75	7.50	15.00
5092	Josephine/Jeannie I Dream of Lilac Time	1957	3.75	7.50	15.00
5106	Southern Fried/No Name Jive	1958	3.75	7.50	15.00
5120	Lester Leaps In/Pompton Turnpike	1958	3.75	7.50	15.00
5127	Honeysuckle Rose/Back Beat	1958	3.75	7.50	15.00
5133	Woodchopper's Ball/John's Idea	1958	3.75	7.50	15.00
5136	Twilight Time/Over Waves Rock	1958	3.75	7.50	15.00
5144	Pinkie/Home Sweet Home Rock	1958	3.75	7.50	15.00
5152	Goodnight Sweetheart/Indian Boogie Woogie	1958	3.75	7.50	15.00
5161	Red Skin Cha Cha/Rockin' with Richard	1958	3.75	7.50	15.00
5175	My Reverie Cha Cha/Barcarole	1959	3.00	6.00	12.00
5190	Up There in Orbit/Sweet Pea	1959	3.00	6.00	12.00
5203	Up There in Orbit (Part 1)/Up There in Orbit (Part 2)	1959	3.00	6.00	12.00
5209	La Cucaracha Cha Cha/Dancing in the Dark	1959	3.00	6.00	12.00
5229	Who Cares/Feeling Cool	1959	3.00	6.00	12.00
5252	White Horse/Dark Eyes	1959	3.00	6.00	12.00
5263	Gondola/Once in a While	1959	3.00	6.00	12.00
5290	Tut-Strut/All the Things You Are	1959	3.00	6.00	12.00
5301	Ebb Tide/Hildegarde	1959	3.00	6.00	12.00
5309	Let's Move Out/I Burned Your Letter	1960	3.00	6.00	12.00
5314	Off Shore/Hello '60	1960	3.00	6.00	12.00
5317	Elegie/Out of Nowhere	1960	3.00	6.00	12.00
5345	Make Believe/A Gay Day	1960	3.00	6.00	12.00
5362	Tuxedo Junction/Polonaise	1960	3.00	6.00	12.00
5402	720 in the Books/Just in Time	1960	3.00	6.00	12.00
5454	That Old Black Magic/Full Moon and Empty Arms	1961	2.50	5.00	10.00
5477	Jersey Bounce/Because of You	1961	2.50	5.00	10.00
5564	The Thrill Is Gone/April in Portugal	1961	2.50	5.00	10.00
5600	How Deep Is the Ocean/Wrap It	1962	2.50	5.00	10.00
5636	Dark Eyes/People Will Say We're in Love	1962	2.50	5.00	10.00
5661	More Than You Know/Don't Blame Me	1962	2.50	5.00	10.00
5683	Ducky/Deep in My Heart	1962	2.50	5.00	10.00
5699	Autumn Leaves/Anita's Theme	1962	2.50	5.00	10.00
5711	El Choclo Bossa Nova/My Reverie	1963	2.50	5.00	10.00
5742	Cherry Pink (And Apple Blossom White)/Your Cheatin' Heart	1963	2.50	5.00	10.00
5776	Love Letters in the Sand/Tammy	1963	2.50	5.00	10.00
5819	Apple Cake/Don't Do It Please	1963	2.50	5.00	10.00
5839	Telstar Drive/Fast Track	1964	2.00	4.00	8.00
5861	Let's Dance Little Girl/Summertime	1964	2.00	4.00	8.00
5900	Make Believe/Star Gazer	1964	2.00	4.00	8.00
5925	The Pink Panther/Lawrence of Arabia	1964	2.00	4.00	8.00
5944	From Russia with Love/My Special Dream	1964	2.00	4.00	8.00
5955	Theme from The Unforgiven/Dominique	1964	2.00	4.00	8.00
5961	Hello Dolly/Walk on the Wild Side	1964	2.00	4.00	8.00
5977	More/Charade	1965	2.00	4.00	8.00
6254	September Song/Harlem Nocturne	1969	—	2.50	5.00

7-Inch Extended Plays

Number	Title (A Side/B Side)	Yr	VG	VG+	NM
KING					
EP-200	Flamingo/Swing Low Sweet Boogie//I Can't Give You Anything But Love/The Moon Is Low	195?	6.25	12.50	25.00
EP-200 [PS]	Earl Bostic and His Alto Sax, Vol. 1	195?	6.25	12.50	25.00
EP 201	*Sleep/Earl's Imagination/Lover Come Back to Me/I'm Gettin' Sentimental Over You	1953	6.25	12.50	25.00
EP 201 [PS]	Earl Bostic and His Alto Sax, Vol. 2	1953	6.25	12.50	25.00
EP 202	*Always/Linger Awhile/Merry Widow/Earl Blows a Fuse	1953	6.25	12.50	25.00
EP 202 [PS]	Earl Bostic and His Alto Sax, Vol. 3	1953	6.25	12.50	25.00
EP 203	*Deep Purple/Velvet Sunset/Choppin' It Down/You Go to My Head	1953	6.25	12.50	25.00
EP 203 [PS]	Earl Bostic and His Alto Sax, Vol. 4	1953	6.25	12.50	25.00
EP 204	*Cherokee/Seven Steps/No Name Blues/Don't You Do It	1953	6.25	12.50	25.00
EP 204 [PS]	Earl Bostic and His Alto Sax, Vol. 5	1953	6.25	12.50	25.00
EP 205	*Moonglow/For You/Blip Boogie/Wrap It Up	1953	6.25	12.50	25.00
EP 205 [PS]	Earl Bostic and His Alto Sax, Vol. 6	1953	6.25	12.50	25.00
EP 206	*Filibuster/The Sheik of Araby/Smoke Gets in Your Eyes/The Hour of Parting	1953	6.25	12.50	25.00
EP 206 [PS]	Earl Bostic and His Alto Sax, Vol. 7	1953	6.25	12.50	25.00
EP 207	*Serenade/Ain't Misbehavin'/Smoke Rings/Steamwhistle Jump	1953	6.25	12.50	25.00
EP 207 [PS]	Earl Bostic and His Alto Sax, Vol. 8	1953	6.25	12.50	25.00
EP 284	*Jungle Drums/The Song Is Ended/Off Shore/Cracked Ice	1954	5.00	10.00	20.00
EP 284 [PS]	Earl Bostic and His Alto Sax, Vol. 10	1954	5.00	10.00	20.00
EP 285	*Danube Waves/My Heart at Thy Sweet Voice/Poeme/O Sole Mio	1954	5.00	10.00	20.00
EP 285 [PS]	Earl Bostic and His Alto Sax, Vol. 11	1954	5.00	10.00	20.00
EP 347	*Mambostic/Time on My Hands/Mambolino/Ven-A-Mi	1955	5.00	10.00	20.00
EP 347 [PS]	Earl Bostic and His Alto Sax, Vol. 12	1955	5.00	10.00	20.00
EP 350	*Blue Skies/These Foolish Things/Song of the Islands/Ubangi Stomp	1955	5.00	10.00	20.00
EP 350 [PS]	Earl Bostic and His Alto Sax, Vol. 13	1955	5.00	10.00	20.00
EP 355	*Cherry Bean/Liebestraum/Night and Day/Embraceable You	1955	5.00	10.00	20.00
EP 355 [PS]	Earl Bostic and His Alto Sax, Vol. 14	1955	5.00	10.00	20.00
EP 363	*Melody of Love/Cocktails for Two/Blue Moon/Remember	1955	5.00	10.00	20.00
EP 363 [PS]	Earl Bostic and His Alto Sax, Vol. 15	1955	5.00	10.00	20.00
EP 375	*Dream/Beyond the Blue Horizon/East of the Sun/For All We Know	1956	5.00	10.00	20.00
EP 375 [PS]	Earl Bostic with Strings, Vol. 16	1956	5.00	10.00	20.00
EP 381	*Bugle Call Rag/I'll String Along with You/I Love You Truly/'Cause You're My Lover	1956	5.00	10.00	20.00
EP 381 [PS]	Bostic Blows, Vol. 17	1956	5.00	10.00	20.00
KEP 398	Harlem Nocturne/I Hear a Rhapsody//Roses of Picardy/Where or When	1957	5.00	10.00	20.00
KEP 398 [PS]	Earl Bostic, Vol. 18	1957	5.00	10.00	20.00

Number	Title (A Side/B Side)	Yr	VG	VG+	NM
EP-417	(contents unknown)	1958	5.00	10.00	20.00
EP-417 [PS]	Showcase of Swinging Dance Hits, Vol. 1	1958	5.00	10.00	20.00
EP-418	Two O'Clock Jump/Back Beat//John's Idea/Royal Garden Blues	1958	5.00	10.00	20.00
EP-418 [PS]	Showcase of Swinging Dance Hits, Vol. 2	1958	5.00	10.00	20.00
EP-420	Twilight Time/Stairway to the Stars//Rockin' with Richard/Be My Love	1958	5.00	10.00	20.00
EP-420 [PS]	Alto Magic in Hi Fi, Vol. 1	1958	5.00	10.00	20.00
EP-421	(contents unknown)	1958	5.00	10.00	20.00
EP-421 [PS]	Alto Magic in Hi Fi, Vol. 2	1958	5.00	10.00	20.00
EP-422	C Jam Blues/Wee-Gee Board//The Wrecking Rock/Home Sweet Home Rock	1958	5.00	10.00	20.00
EP-422 [PS]	Alto Magic in Hi Fi, Vol. 3	1958	5.00	10.00	20.00
ROYALE					
EP 367	The Man I Love/All On//Hurricane Blues/The Major and the Minor	195?	3.75	7.50	15.00
EP 367 [PS]	His Saxophone and Orchestra	195?	3.75	7.50	15.00

Albums

Number	Title (A Side/B Side)	Yr	VG	VG+	NM
GRAND PRIX					
K-404 [M]	The Grand Prix Series	196?	3.75	7.50	15.00
KS-404 [R]	The Grand Prix Series	196?	3.00	6.00	12.00
K-416 [M]	Wild Man	196?	3.75	7.50	15.00
KS-416 [R]	Wild Man	196?	3.00	6.00	12.00
KING					
295-64 [10]	Earl Bostic and His Alto Sax	1951	50.00	100.00	200.00
—Black vinyl					
295-64 [10]	Earl Bostic and His Alto Sax	1951	100.00	200.00	400.00
—Red vinyl					
295-65 [10]	Earl Bostic and His Alto Sax	1951	50.00	100.00	200.00
—Black vinyl					
295-65 [10]	Earl Bostic and His Alto Sax	1951	100.00	200.00	400.00
—Red vinyl					
295-66 [10]	Earl Bostic and His Alto Sax	1951	50.00	100.00	200.00
—Black vinyl					
295-66 [10]	Earl Bostic and His Alto Sax	1951	100.00	200.00	400.00
—Red vinyl					
295-72 [10]	Earl Bostic and His Alto Sax	1952	50.00	100.00	200.00
295-76 [10]	Earl Bostic and His Alto Sax	1952	50.00	100.00	200.00
295-77 [10]	Earl Bostic and His Alto Sax	1952	50.00	100.00	200.00
295-78 [10]	Earl Bostic and His Alto Sax	1952	50.00	100.00	200.00
295-79 [10]	Earl Bostic and His Alto Sax	1952	50.00	100.00	200.00
295-95 [10]	Earl Bostic Plays the Old Standards	1954	50.00	100.00	200.00
295-103 [10]	Earl Bostic and His Alto Sax	1954	50.00	100.00	200.00
395-500 [M]	Dance to the Best of Bostic	1956	25.00	50.00	100.00
—Original cover with Earl Bostic pictured					
395-500 [M]	Dance to the Best of Bostic	195?	20.00	40.00	80.00
—Second cover with girl in a swimsuit pictured					
395-503 [M]	Bostic for You	1956	25.00	50.00	100.00
395-515 [M]	Alto-Tude	1956	25.00	50.00	100.00
395-525 [M]	Dance Time	1956	20.00	40.00	80.00
395-529 [M]	Let's Dance with Earl Bostic	1956	20.00	40.00	80.00
395-547 [M]	Invitation to Dance	1956	20.00	40.00	80.00
558 [M]	C'mon and Dance with Earl Bostic	1956	20.00	40.00	80.00
KS-558 [S]	C'mon and Dance with Earl Bostic	1959	37.50	75.00	150.00
571 [M]	Hits of the Swing Age	1957	20.00	40.00	80.00
583 [M]	Showcase of Swinging Dance Hits	1958	20.00	40.00	80.00
597 [M]	Alto Magic in Hi-Fi	1958	20.00	40.00	80.00
KS-597 [S]	Alto Magic in Hi-Fi	1959	37.50	75.00	150.00
602 [M]	Sweet Tunes of the Fantastic Fifties	1959	12.50	25.00	50.00
KS-602 [S]	Sweet Tunes of the Fantastic Fifties	1959	25.00	50.00	100.00
613 [M]	Bostic Workshop	1959	12.50	25.00	50.00
KS-613 [S]	Bostic Workshop	1959	25.00	50.00	100.00
620 [M]	Sweet Tunes from the Roaring Twenties	1959	12.50	25.00	50.00
KS-620 [S]	Sweet Tunes from the Roaring Twenties	1959	25.00	50.00	100.00
632 [M]	Sweet Tunes of the Swinging Thirties	1959	12.50	25.00	50.00
KS-632 [S]	Sweet Tunes of the Swinging Thirties	1959	25.00	50.00	100.00
640 [M]	Sweet Tunes of the Sentimental Forties	1960	12.50	25.00	50.00
KS-640 [S]	Sweet Tunes of the Sentimental Forties	1960	20.00	40.00	80.00
662 [M]	Musical Pearls	1960	12.50	25.00	50.00
KS-662 [S]	Musical Pearls	1960	20.00	40.00	80.00
705 [M]	Hit Tunes of Big Broadway Shows	1960	12.50	25.00	50.00
KS-705 [S]	Hit Tunes of Big Broadway Shows	1960	20.00	40.00	80.00
786 [M]	By Popular Demand	1961	12.50	25.00	50.00
827 [M]	Earl Bostic Plays Bossa Nova	1963	12.50	25.00	50.00
838 [M]	Songs of the Fantastic Fifties, Volume 2	1963	12.50	25.00	50.00
846 [M]	Jazz As I Feel It	1963	12.50	25.00	50.00
881 [M]	The Best of Earl Bostic, Volume 2	1964	12.50	25.00	50.00
900 [M]	The New Sound	1964	12.50	25.00	50.00
921 [M]	The Great Hits of 1964	1964	12.50	25.00	50.00
947 [M]	24 Songs That Earl Loved the Most	1966	10.00	20.00	40.00
KS-1048 [S]	Harlem Nocturne	1969	6.25	12.50	25.00
K-5010X	14 Original Greatest Hits	1977	3.00	6.00	12.00
PHILIPS					
PHM 200262 [M]	The Song Is Not Ended	1967	6.25	12.50	25.00
PHS 600262 [S]	The Song Is Not Ended	1967	6.25	12.50	25.00

BOSTIC, EARL, AND BILL DOGGETT

Also see each artist's individual listings.

45s

Number	Title (A Side/B Side)	Yr	VG	VG+	NM
KING					
4930	Mean to Me/Bo-Do Rock	1956	3.75	7.50	15.00
4954	Indiana/Bubbins Rock	1956	3.75	7.50	15.00
5427	Special Delivery Stomp/Earl's Dog	1960	2.50	5.00	10.00

BOSTIC, EARL/JIMMY LUNCEFORD

Albums

Number	Title (A Side/B Side)	Yr	VG	VG+	NM
ALLEGRO ELITE					
4053 [10]	Earl Bostic/Jimmy Lunceford Orchestras	195?	10.00	20.00	40.00

BOSTICK, CALVIN

45s

Number	Title (A Side/B Side)	Yr	VG	VG+	NM
CHESS					
1530	Christmas Won't Be Christmas Without You/Four-Eleven Boogie	1952	37.50	75.00	150.00

BOSTON CRABS, THE

45s

Number	Title (A Side/B Side)	Yr	VG	VG+	NM
CAPITOL					
5493	Down in Mexico/Who?	1965	2.50	5.00	10.00
TOWER					
368	Gin House/Leave My Woman Alone	1967	2.50	5.00	10.00

BOTKIN, PERRY, JR.

45s

Number	Title (A Side/B Side)	Yr	VG	VG+	NM
A&M					
1856	Nadia's Theme (The Young and the Restless)/Down the Line	1976	2.50	5.00	10.00
—Original issue; Barry DeVorzon's name was added after he threatened legal action					
1856 [PS]	Nadia's Theme (The Young and the Restless)/Down the Line	1976	2.50	5.00	10.00
—Sleeve with only Perry Botkin Jr.'s name on it (see above listing)					
1967	Looking for Home/Lovers	1977	—	2.00	4.00
1990	Bridges/Love Theme from Aspen	1977	—	2.00	4.00
DECCA					
30912	The Execution Theme/Waltz of the Hunter	1959	3.00	6.00	12.00
MGM					
14357	Soley Soley/(B-side unknown)	1972	—	2.50	5.00
—As "Perry Botkin, Inc."					
14379	Bless the Beasts and Children/Lost	1972	—	2.50	5.00
PRIDE					
1005	Journey to Moscow/Ellie's Theme	1972	—	2.50	5.00
VALIANT					
719	Where Does Love Go (Instrumental)/Where Does Love Go (Vocal)	1965	2.00	4.00	8.00
—B-side by Charles Boyer					
6025	Careless Love/Wabash Cannonball	1962	2.50	5.00	10.00

BOUCHER, PEGI

45s

Number	Title (A Side/B Side)	Yr	VG	VG+	NM
HIBACK					
101	The Christmas Clock/Christmas Tree Heaven	1966	2.00	4.00	8.00
101 [PS]	The Christmas Clock/Christmas Tree Heaven	1966	3.75	7.50	15.00

BOUGALIEU

45s

Number	Title (A Side/B Side)	Yr	VG	VG+	NM
ROULETTE					
4767	Let's Do Wrong/When I Was a Child	1967	6.25	12.50	25.00
4776	Let's Do Wrong/When I Was a Child	1967	3.75	7.50	15.00

BOUQUETS

45s

Number	Title (A Side/B Side)	Yr	VG	VG+	NM
BLUE CAT					
115	Welcome to My Heart/Ain't That Love	1965	7.50	15.00	30.00
MALA					
472	I Love Him So/No Love at All	1964	3.75	7.50	15.00
VEST					
8000	Yeah Babe/Girls, Girls	1963	3.75	7.50	15.00

BOW STREET RUNNERS, THE

Albums

Number	Title (A Side/B Side)	Yr	VG	VG+	NM
B.T. PUPPY					
BTPS-1026	The Bow Street Runners	1969	500.00	750.00	1000.
SUNDAZED					
LP 5029	The Bow Street Runners	199?	2.50	5.00	10.00
—Reissue of B.T. Puppy LP					

BOWEN, JIMMY

45s

Number	Title (A Side/B Side)	Yr	VG	VG+	NM
CAPEHART					
5005	Teenage Dreamworld/It's Against the Law	1962	5.00	10.00	20.00
5005 [PS]	Teenage Dreamworld/It's Against the Law	1962	12.50	25.00	50.00
CREST					
1085	Don't Drop It/Somebody to Love	1961	5.00	10.00	20.00
REPRISE					
0264	The Biggest Lover in Town/The Big Bus	1964	2.50	5.00	10.00
0358	The Golden Eagle/Spanish Cricket	1965	2.50	5.00	10.00
0450	Wonder Mother/Captain Gorgeous	1966	2.50	5.00	10.00
0592	Raunchy/It's Such a Pretty World Today	1967	2.50	5.00	10.00
ROULETTE					
4001	I'm Stickin' With You/Ever Lovin' Fingers	1957	5.00	10.00	20.00
—With the Rhythm Orchids					
4010	Warm Up to Me Baby/I Trusted You	1957	5.00	10.00	20.00
4017	Ever Since That Night/Don't Tell Me Your Troubles	1957	5.00	10.00	20.00
4023	Cross Over/It's Shameful	1957	5.00	10.00	20.00
4057	Can She Kiss/Keeping You	1958	5.00	10.00	20.00
4083	By the Light of the Silvery Moon/The Two Step	1958	5.00	10.00	20.00
4102	My Kind of Woman/Blue Moon	1958	5.00	10.00	20.00
4122	Always Faithful/Wish I Were Tied to You	1958	5.00	10.00	20.00
4175	You're Just Wasting Your Time/Walkin' on Air	1959	5.00	10.00	20.00
4224	Oh Yeah! Oh Yeah! Mm Mm/Your Loving Arms	1960	5.00	10.00	20.00
TRIPLE D					
798	I'm Stickin' With You/Party Doll	1956	250.00	500.00	1000.
—B-side by Buddy Knox					

7-Inch Extended Plays

Number	Title (A Side/B Side)	Yr	VG	VG+	NM
ROULETTE					
302	(contents unknown)	1957	50.00	100.00	200.00
302 [PS]	Jimmy Bowen	1957	50.00	100.00	200.00

Albums

Number	Title (A Side/B Side)	Yr	VG	VG+	NM
REPRISE					
R-6210 [M]	Sunday Morning with the Comics	1966	7.50	15.00	30.00
RS-6210 [S]	Sunday Morning with the Comics	1966	10.00	20.00	40.00
ROULETTE					
R 25004 [M]	Jimmy Bowen	1957	75.00	150.00	300.00
—Black and silver label					

Number	Title (A Side/B Side)	Yr	VG	VG+	NM
R 25004 [M]	Jimmy Bowen	1958	37.50	75.00	150.00
—Red label					
R 25004 [M]	Jimmy Bowen	198?	3.00	6.00	12.00
—Reissue for Publishers Central Bureau (it says so on the jacket)					

BOWENS, PRIVATE CHARLES

45s

ROJAC

Number	Title (A Side/B Side)	Yr	VG	VG+	NM
111	Christmas In Viet Nam/(B-side unknown)	196?	15.00	30.00	60.00

BOWIE, DAVID

12-Inch Singles

Number	Title (A Side/B Side)	Yr	VG	VG+	NM
BACKSTREET					
L33-1759 [DJ]	Cat People (Putting Out Fire) (same on both sides)	1982	3.75	7.50	15.00
EMI					
SPRO-04532 [DJ]	Fame 90 (4 mixes)	1990	3.75	7.50	15.00
56163	Fame 90 (5 versions, including Queen Latifah mix)	1990	2.00	4.00	8.00
93492	Fame 90 (5 mixes)	1990	—	3.00	6.00
EMI AMERICA					
7805	Let's Dance/Cat People (Putting Out Fire)	1983	2.50	5.00	10.00
7809	China Girl/Shake It	1983	2.50	5.00	10.00
7811	Modern Love/Modern Love (Live)	1983	2.50	5.00	10.00
7838	Blue Jean/Dancing with the Big Boys	1984	2.50	5.00	10.00
7846	Tonight (2 versions)/Tumble and Twirl	1984	2.50	5.00	10.00
7858	Loving the Alien (2 versions)/Don't Look Down	1985	3.00	6.00	12.00
—With gatefold sleeve and poster					
SPRO-9222 [DJ]	Blue Jean/Dancing with the Big Boys	1984	3.75	7.50	15.00
SPRO-9295 [DJ]	Tonight (same on both sides)	1984	3.75	7.50	15.00
SPRO 9670 [DJ]	Underground (Long)/Underground (Short)	1986	3.00	6.00	12.00
SPRO-9904 [DJ]	Let's Dance (same on both sides)	1983	3.00	6.00	12.00
SPRO-9952 [DJ]	China Girl (Long)/Shake It (Long)	1983	3.75	7.50	15.00
SPRO-9985 [DJ]	Day In Day Out (same on both sides)	1987	2.50	5.00	10.00
SPRO-9996 [DJ]	Day In Day Out (4 versions)	1987	3.75	7.50	15.00
19205	Absolute Beginners (Full Length)/Absolute Beginners (Dub)	1986	2.50	5.00	10.00
19210	Underground (3 versions)	1986	2.00	4.00	8.00
19217	Magic Dance (2 versions)/Within You	1986	2.00	4.00	8.00
19234	Day In Day Out (2 versions)/Julie	1987	2.50	5.00	10.00
19239	Day In Day Out (3 versions)	1984	3.75	7.50	15.00
19247	Time Will Crawl (2 versions)/Girls (2 versions)	1987	2.50	5.00	10.00
19255	Never Let Me Down (5 versions)/87 and Cry	1987	2.50	5.00	10.00
SPRO-79090 [DJ]	Never Let Me Down (same on both sides)	1987	3.00	6.00	12.00
RCA					
DJL1-3255 [DJ]	Star/What in the World/Breaking Glass	1978	6.25	12.50	25.00
—White vinyl promo					
DJL1-3795 [DJ]	Space Oddity/Ashes to Ashes (2 versions)	1980	7.50	15.00	30.00
—With set of stamps					
DJL1-3795 [DJ]	Space Oddity/Ashes to Ashes (2 versions)	1980	5.00	10.00	20.00
—Without stamps					
JD-11151	Heroes (Unedited)/Heroes (Edited)	1977	6.25	12.50	25.00
PC-11204 [DJ]	Beauty and the Beast/Fame	1978	7.50	15.00	30.00
JD-11306 [DJ]	Peter and the Wolf (Part 1)/Peter and the Wolf (Part 2)	1978	7.50	15.00	30.00
PB-11886	John I'm Only Dancing (Again) 1975/Golden Years	1980	5.00	10.00	20.00
JD-12079	Ashes to Ashes/Fashion	1980	—	—	—
—Unreleased					
JD-12140 [DJ]	Fashion (long)/Fashion (short)	1981	3.00	6.00	12.00
PD-12145	Fashion/Scream Like a Baby	1980	3.00	6.00	12.00
PB-12249	Up the Hills Backwards/Crystal Japan	1981	5.00	10.00	20.00
PB-13770	1984/TVC 15	1984	2.00	4.00	8.00
SAVAGE					
50039 [DJ]	Jump They Say (5 versions)/Pallas Athena	1993	3.75	7.50	15.00
50042	Jump They Say (5 versions)/Pallas Athena	1993	2.00	4.00	8.00
50045 [DJ]	Black Tie White Noise (7 versions)	1993	3.75	7.50	15.00

45s

Number	Title (A Side/B Side)	Yr	VG	VG+	NM
BACKSTREET					
52024	Cat People/Paul's Theme	1982	—	—	3.00
—B-side by Georgio Moroder					
52024 [PS]	Cat People/Paul's Theme	1982	—	—	3.00
DERAM					
85009	Rubber Band/There Is a Happy Land	1967	25.00	50.00	100.00
85016	Love You Till Tuesday/Did You Ever Have a Dream	1967	25.00	50.00	100.00
EMI AMERICA					
8158	Let's Dance/Cat People (Putting Out Fire)	1983	—	—	3.00
8158 [PS]	Let's Dance/Cat People (Putting Out Fire)	1983	—	—	3.00
8165	China Girl/Shake It	1983	—	—	3.00
8165 [PS]	China Girl/Shake It	1983	—	2.50	5.00
8177	Modern Love/Modern Love (Live)	1983	—	—	3.00
8177 [PS]	Modern Love/Modern Love (Live)	1983	—	—	3.00
8190	Without You/Criminal Law	1984	—	—	3.00
8190 [PS]	Without You/Criminal Law	1984	—	—	3.00
8231	Blue Jean/Dancin' with the Big Boys	1984	2.00	4.00	8.00
—First pressing on blue vinyl					
8231	Blue Jean/Dancin' with the Big Boys	1984	—	—	2.00
8231 [PS]	Blue Jean/Dancin' with the Big Boys	1984	—	—	2.00
—Both colors of vinyl have the same picture sleeve					
8246	Tonight/Tumble and Twirl	1984	—	—	3.00
8246 [PS]	Tonight/Tumble and Twirl	1984	—	2.50	5.00
—Fold-out poster sleeve					
8251	This Is Not America/(Instrumental)	1984	—	—	3.00
8251 [PS]	This Is Not America/(Instrumental)	1984	—	—	3.00
—With the Pat Metheny Group					
8271	Loving the Alien/Don't Look Down	1985	—	—	3.00
8271 [PS]	Loving the Alien/Don't Look Down	1985	—	—	3.00
8308	Absolute Beginners/Absolute Beginnners (Dub Mix)	1986	—	—	3.00
8308 [PS]	Absolute Beginners/Absolute Beginnners (Dub Mix)	1986	—	—	3.00
8323	Underground/(instrumental)	1986	—	—	3.00
8323 [PS]	Underground/(instrumental)	1986	—	—	3.00
8380	Day In Day Out/Day In Day Out	1987	—	—	3.00
8380 [PS]	Day In Day Out/Day In Day Out	1987	—	—	3.00
43020	Time Will Crawl/Time Will Crawl	1987	—	—	3.00
43020 [PS]	Time Will Crawl/Time Will Crawl	1987	2.50	5.00	10.00
43031	Never Let Me Down/Never Let Me Down	1987	—	—	3.00
43031 [PS]	Never Let Me Down/Never Let Me Down	1987	—	—	3.00
LONDON					
20079	The Laughing Gnome/The Gospel According to Tony Day	1973	12.50	25.00	50.00
MERCURY					
72949	Space Oddity/Wild-Eyed Boy from Freecloud	1969	12.50	25.00	50.00
73075	Memory of a Free Festival Part 1/Part 2	1970	50.00	100.00	200.00
73173 [DJ]	All the Madmen (mono/stereo)	1971	37.50	75.00	150.00
—May be promo only					
RCA					
PB-10664	TVC 15/We Are the Dead	1976	—	2.50	5.00
PB-10736	Stay/Word on a Wing	1976	—	2.50	5.00
PB-10905	Sound and Vision/A New Career in a New Town	1977	—	2.50	5.00
GB-10938	Fame/Golden Years	1977	—	—	3.00
—Gold Standard Series issue					
GB-10938	Fame/Golden Years	1977	—	—	3.00
—Gold Standard Series issue					
PB-11017	Be My Wife/The Speed of Life	1977	—	2.50	5.00
PB-11121	Heroes/V-2 Schneider	1977	—	2.50	5.00
PB-11190	Beauty and the Beast/Sense of Doubt	1978	—	2.50	5.00
PB-11585	Boys Keep Swinging/Fantastic Voyage	1979	—	2.50	5.00
PB-11661	D.J./Fantastic Voyage	1979	—	2.50	5.00
PB-11724	Look Back in Anger/Repetition	1979	—	2.50	5.00
PB-11887	John I'm Only Dancing 1972/Joe the Lion	1980	—	2.50	5.00
JH-12078 [PS]	Ashes to Ashes/It's No Game	1980	3.75	7.50	15.00
—Promo-only sleeve of Bowie holding a shoe and looking down at it					
PB-12078	Ashes to Ashes/It's No Game	1980	—	2.50	5.00
PB-12078 [PS]	Ashes to Ashes/It's No Game	1980	—	2.50	5.00
JE-12087 [DJ]	Fashion/It's No Game/Teenage Wildlife	1980	100.00	200.00	400.00
PB-12134	Fashion/Scream Like a Baby	1980	—	2.50	5.00
PB-12134 [PS]	Fashion/Scream Like a Baby	1980	—	2.50	5.00
PH-13400	Peace on Earth-Little Drummer Boy/Fantastic Voyage	1982	—	2.50	5.00
—A-side with Bing Crosby					
PH-13400 [PS]	Peace on Earth-Little Drummer Boy/Fantastic Voyage	1982	2.50	5.00	10.00
—A-side with Bing Crosby					
PB-13660	White Light-White Heat/Cracked Actor	1983	—	2.50	5.00
PB-13660 [PS]	White Light-White Heat/Cracked Actor	1983	—	2.50	5.00
PB-13769	1984/TVC 15	1984	—	2.50	5.00
PB-13769 [PS]	1984/TVC 15	1984	—	2.50	5.00
RCA VICTOR					
APBO-0001	Time/The Prettiest Star	1973	—	3.00	6.00
APBO-0001 [PS]	Time/The Prettiest Star	1973	200.00	400.00	800.00
APBO-0028	Let's Spend the Night Together/Lady Grinning Soul	1973	—	3.00	6.00
APBO-0160	Sorrow/Amsterdam	1973	—	3.00	6.00
APBO-0287	Rebel Rebel/Lady Grinning Soul	1974	2.50	5.00	10.00
—All copies contain an alternate mix of "Rebel, Rebel"					
APBO-0293	Diamond Dogs/Holy Holy	1974	2.50	5.00	10.00
—Part of U.S. numbering system, but released only outside the U.S.					
PB-10026	1984/Queen Bitch	1974	—	3.00	6.00
PB-10105	Rock and Roll with Me/Panic in Detroit	1974	—	3.00	6.00
PB-10152	Young Americans/Knock on Wood	1975	—	3.00	6.00
—Tan label (Indianapolis pressing)					
PB-10152	Young Americans/Knock on Wood	1975	—	3.00	6.00
—Orange label (West Coast pressing)					
PB-10320	Fame/Right	1975	—	3.00	6.00
—Tan label (Indianapolis pressing)					
PB-10320	Fame/Right	1975	—	3.00	6.00
—Orange label (West Coast pressing)					
PB-10441	Golden Years/Can You Hear Me	1975	—	3.00	6.00
GB-10468	Changes/Andy Warhol	1975	—	2.00	4.00
—Gold Standard Series issue					
GB-10469	Young Americans/Knock on Wood	1975	—	2.00	4.00
—Gold Standard Series issue					
GB-10470	Space Oddity/The Man Who Sold the World	1975	—	2.00	4.00
—Gold Standard Series issue					
74-0605	Changes/Andy Warhol	1971	2.50	5.00	10.00
—Orange label (original)					
74-0605	Changes/Andy Warhol	1974	—	3.00	6.00
—Tan or gray label					
74-0719	Starman/Suffragette City	1972	—	3.00	6.00
74-0719 [PS]	Starman/Suffragette City	1972	7.50	15.00	30.00
74-0838	The Jean Genie/Hang On to Yourself	1972	—	3.00	6.00
74-0876	Space Oddity/The Man Who Sold the World	1973	—	3.00	6.00
74-0876 [PS]	Space Oddity/The Man Who Sold the World	1973	5.00	10.00	20.00
VIRGIN					
S7-19517	Dead Man Walking/Little Wonder	1997	—	2.00	4.00
58833	Changes/Rebel Rebel	2000	—	2.00	4.00
58834	Fame/Golden Years	2000	—	2.00	4.00
—Both are full-length versions, not the single edits					
58835	Let's Dance (single edit)/Modern Love	2000	—	2.00	4.00
WARNER BROS.					
5815	Can't Stop Thinking About Me/And I Say to Myself	1966	100.00	200.00	400.00
—As "David Bowie and the Lower Third"					

7-Inch Extended Plays

Number	Title (A Side/B Side)	Yr	VG	VG+	NM
RCA VICTOR					
45-103 [DJ]	Space Oddity/Moonage Daydream//(B-side unknown)	1972	5.00	10.00	20.00
45-103 [PS]	David Bowie	1972	5.00	10.00	20.00

Albums

Number	Title (A Side/B Side)	Yr	VG	VG+	NM
DERAM					
DE 16003 [M]	David Bowie	1967	30.00	60.00	120.00
DES 18003 [S]	David Bowie	1967	37.50	75.00	150.00
EMI AMERICA					
SPRO 9960/1 [(2) DJ]	Let's Talk	1983	6.25	12.50	25.00
—Promo-only interview album					
SO-17093	Let's Dance	1983	2.50	5.00	10.00

Number	Title (A Side/B Side)	Yr	VG	VG+	NM
SJ-17138	Tonight	1984	2.50	5.00	10.00
PJ-17267	Never Let Me Down	1987	2.50	5.00	10.00
SPRO-79112/3 [DJ]	Never Let Me Down: The Interview	1987	6.25	12.50	25.00
R 153730	Let's Dance	1983	3.00	6.00	12.00
—RCA Music Service edition					
R 174212	Never Let Me Down	1987	3.00	6.00	12.00
—BMG Direct Marketing edition					
LONDON					
PS 628/9 [(2)]	Images 1966-1967	1973	12.50	25.00	50.00
—Original pressings have dark blue and silver labels. Later pressings, if any, are worth at least 50% less.					
50007	Starting Point	1977	3.00	6.00	12.00
MERCURY					
SR 61246	Man of Words, Man of Music	1969	37.50	75.00	150.00
SR 61325	The Man Who Sold the World	1970	10.00	20.00	40.00
—An often-counterfeited album; originals have matrix numbers stamped in the trail-off area					
MOBILE FIDELITY					
1-064	The Rise and Fall of Ziggy Stardust and the Spiders from Mars	1983	12.50	25.00	50.00
—Audiophile vinyl					
1-083	Let's Dance	1984	7.50	15.00	30.00
—Audiophile vinyl					
RCA RED SEAL					
ARL1-2743	Peter and the Wolf	1978	5.00	10.00	20.00
—With the Philadelphia Orchestra conducted by Eugene Ormandy; green vinyl					
ARL1-2743	Peter and the Wolf	1978	5.00	10.00	20.00
—With the Philadelphia Orchestra conducted by Eugene Ormandy; black vinyl					
RCA VICTOR					
AFL1-0291	Pin Ups	1978	2.50	5.00	10.00
—Reissue					
APL1-0291	Pin Ups	1973	5.00	10.00	20.00
CPL1-0576	Diamond Dogs	1974	1000.	2000.	4000.
—Original copies have cover with dog's genitals clearly visible. Almost all were destroyed prior to release.					
CPL1-0576	Diamond Dogs	1974	5.00	10.00	20.00
—Standard issue, with dog's genitals airbrushed					
CPL2-0771 [(2)]	David Live	1974	5.00	10.00	20.00
—At time of release, available with either orange or tan labels					
CPL2-0771 [(2)]	David Live	1976	3.00	6.00	12.00
—Reissue with black label, dog near top					
APL1-0998	Young Americans	1975	3.00	6.00	12.00
—At time of release, available with either orange or tan label					
APL1-0998	Young Americans	1976	2.50	5.00	10.00
—Black label					
AQK1-0998	Young Americans	1984	2.50	5.00	10.00
—Reissue					
APL1-1327	Station to Station	1976	3.00	6.00	12.00
—Originals have a brown label					
APL1-1327	Station to Station	1976	2.50	5.00	10.00
—Black label					
AQK1-1327	Station to Station	1984	2.50	5.00	10.00
—Reissue					
AFL1-1732	Changesonebowie	1978	2.50	5.00	10.00
—Reissue					
APL1-1732	Changesonebowie	1976	—	—	—
—With alternate version of "John, I'm Only Dancing." Released in England this way, and long rumored to exist as a US pressing, but no US version has ever turned up.					
APL1-1732	Changesonebowie	1976	2.50	5.00	10.00
—With common take of "John, I'm Only Dancing"					
AQL1-1732	Changesonebowie	1984	2.50	5.00	10.00
—Reissue					
APL1-2030	Low	1977	2.50	5.00	10.00
AFL1-2522	"Heroes"	1977	2.50	5.00	10.00
DJL1-2697 [DJ]	Bowie Now	1978	18.75	37.50	75.00
CPL2-2913 [(2)]	Stage	1978	5.00	10.00	20.00
DJL1-3016 [DJ]	An Evening with David Bowie	1978	12.50	25.00	50.00
—Live concert for "Superstars Radio Network"					
AQL1-3254	Lodger	1979	2.50	5.00	10.00
DJL1-3545 [DJ]	1980 All Clear	1980	5.00	10.00	20.00
AQL1-3647	Scary Monsters	1980	2.50	5.00	10.00
DJL1-3829 [DJ]	Special Radio Series, Volume 1	1980	6.25	12.50	25.00
DJL1-3840 [DJ]	Scary Monsters Interview	1980	5.00	10.00	20.00
AYL1-3843	The Rise and Fall of Ziggy Stardust and the Spiders from Mars	1980	2.00	4.00	8.00
—Reissue					
AYL1-3844	Hunky Dory	1980	2.00	4.00	8.00
—Reissue					
AYL1-3856	Low	1980	2.00	4.00	8.00
—Reissue					
AYL1-3857	"Heroes"	1980	2.00	4.00	8.00
—Reissue					
AYL1-3889	Diamond Dogs	1980	2.00	4.00	8.00
—Reissue					
AYL1-3890	Aladdin Sane	1980	2.00	4.00	8.00
—Reissue					
AFL1-4202	Changestwobowie	1981	2.50	5.00	10.00
AYL1-4234	Lodger	1981	2.00	4.00	8.00
—Reissue					
CPL1-4346	David Bowie in Berthold Brecht's Baal	1982	2.50	5.00	10.00
LSP-4623	Hunky Dory	1972	5.00	10.00	20.00
AYL1-4653	Pin Ups	1982	2.00	4.00	8.00
—Reissue					
AFL1-4702	The Rise and Fall of Ziggy Stardust and the Spiders from Mars	1977	2.50	5.00	10.00
—Reissue					
LSP-4702	The Rise and Fall of Ziggy Stardust and the Spiders from Mars	1972	5.00	10.00	20.00
—Orange label					
LSP-4702	The Rise and Fall of Ziggy Stardust and the Spiders from Mars	1975	3.00	6.00	12.00
—Tan label					
AFL1-4792	Golden Years	1983	2.50	5.00	10.00
LSP-4813	Space Oddity	1973	5.00	10.00	20.00
—Reissue of Mercury SR-61246; add 1/3 if bonus poster is enclosed					
LSP-4816	The Man Who Sold the World	1973	5.00	10.00	20.00
—Reissue of Mercury SR-61325; add 1/3 if bonus poster is enclosed					
AFL1-4852	Aladdin Sane	1977	2.50	5.00	10.00
—Reissue					
LSP-4852	Aladdin Sane	1973	5.00	10.00	20.00
—Orange label is original (deduct 50% for tan labels)					
CPL2-4862 [(2)]	Ziggy Stardust, The Motion Picture	1983	5.00	10.00	20.00
CPL2-4862 [(2) DJ]	Ziggy Stardust, The Motion Picture	1983	12.50	25.00	50.00
—Promo version on clear vinyl					
AFL1-4919	Fame and Fashion	1984	2.50	5.00	10.00
9503/4 [DJ]	David Bowie Special	1976	—	—	—
—This album has been listed elsewhere, but we can't confirm its existence. The numbering doesn't even make sense.					
RYKO ANALOGUE					
RALP 0120/1/2 [(6)]	Sound + Vision	1989	20.00	40.00	80.00
—Six-LP box set on clear vinyl with three gatefold cardboard inner sleeves					
RALP 0131 [(2)]	Space Oddity	1990	5.00	10.00	20.00
—Clear vinyl with "Limited Edition" obi					
RALP 0132 [(2)]	The Man Who Sold the World	1990	5.00	10.00	20.00
—Clear vinyl with "Limited Edition" obi					
RALP 0133 [(2)]	Hunky Dory	1990	5.00	10.00	20.00
—Clear vinyl with "Limited Edition" obi					
RALP 0134 [(2)]	The Rise and Fall of Ziggy Stardust and the Spiders from Mars	1990	5.00	10.00	20.00
—Clear vinyl with "Limited Edition" obi					
RALP 0135	Aladdin Sane	1990	5.00	10.00	20.00
—Clear vinyl with "Limited Edition" obi					
RALP 0136	Pin Ups	1990	5.00	10.00	20.00
—Clear vinyl with "Limited Edition" obi					
RALP 0137	Diamond Dogs	1990	5.00	10.00	20.00
—Clear vinyl with "Limited Edition" obi; genitals on dog are restored					
RALP 0138/9 [(2)]	David Live	1990	5.00	10.00	20.00
—Clear vinyl with "Limited Edition" obi					
RALP 0171 [(2)]	Changesbowie	1990	5.00	10.00	20.00
—Clear vinyl with "Limited Edition" obi					
LSD-4702 [DJ]	The Rise and Fall of Ziggy Stardust and the Spiders from Mars	1990	25.00	50.00	100.00
—Special promo-only package with both the LP and CD versions					

BOX TOPS, THE

Lead singer Alex Chilton was later in BIG STAR.

45s

Number	Title (A Side/B Side)	Yr	VG	VG+	NM
ARISTA					
9488	Sweet Cream Ladies/Neon Rainbow	1986	—	—	3.00
—"Flashback" oldies series					
BELL					
865	Come On Honey/You Keep Tightening Up on Me	1970	2.00	4.00	8.00
923	Let Me Go/Got to Hold On to You	1970	2.00	4.00	8.00
981	King's Highway/Since I've Been Gone	1971	2.00	4.00	8.00
GUSTO					
2112	The Letter/Cry Like a Baby	1981	—	2.00	4.00
—Re-recordings					
HI					
2228	It's All Over/Sugar Creek Woman	1972	—	3.00	6.00
2242	Hold On Girl/Angel	1973	—	3.00	6.00
MALA					
565	The Letter/Happy Times	1967	3.00	6.00	12.00
580	Neon Rainbow/Everything I Am	1967	2.50	5.00	10.00
593	Cry Like a Baby/The Door You Closed to Me	1968	3.00	6.00	12.00
12005	Choo Choo Train/Fields of Clover	1968	2.50	5.00	10.00
12017	I Met Her in Church/People Gonna Talk	1968	2.50	5.00	10.00
12035	Sweet Cream Ladies, Forward March/I See Only Sunshine	1968	2.50	5.00	10.00
12038	I Shall Be Released/I Must Be the Devil	1969	2.50	5.00	10.00
12040	Soul Deep/The Happy Song	1969	2.50	5.00	10.00
12042	Turn On a Dream/Together	1969	2.50	5.00	10.00
PHILCO-FORD					
HP-27	The Letter/Happy Times	1968	5.00	10.00	20.00
—4-inch plastic "Hip Pocket Record" with color sleeve					
SPHERE SOUND					
77001	The Letter/Happy Times	1969	2.50	5.00	10.00
—Blue label; reissue					
77001	The Letter/Happy Times	1970	2.00	4.00	8.00
—Silver label; reissue					
77002	Cry Like a Baby/The Door You Closed to Me	1970	2.00	4.00	8.00
—Silver label; reissue					
STAX					
0199	It's Gonna Be O.K./Willobee and Dale	1974	—	3.00	6.00

Albums

Number	Title (A Side/B Side)	Yr	VG	VG+	NM
BELL					
6011 [M]	The Letter/Neon Rainbow	1967	6.25	12.50	25.00
S-6011 [S]	The Letter/Neon Rainbow	1967	5.00	10.00	20.00
S-6017	Cry Like a Baby	1968	5.00	10.00	20.00
S-6023	Non-Stop	1968	5.00	10.00	20.00
S-6025	The Box Tops Super Hits	1968	5.00	10.00	20.00
S-6032	Dimensions	1969	5.00	10.00	20.00
RHINO					
RNLP-161	The Greatest Hits	1982	3.00	6.00	12.00

BOXER, KARL

45s

Number	Title (A Side/B Side)	Yr	VG	VG+	NM
DOT					
16853	Hava Nagila/A Piece of the Action	1966	5.00	10.00	20.00

BOYCE, TOMMY

Also see TOMMY BOYCE AND BOBBY HART.

45s

Number	Title (A Side/B Side)	Yr	VG	VG+	NM
A&M					
809	Sunday, The Day Before Monday/The Green Grass (Is Turning Brown)	1966	3.75	7.50	15.00
826	In Case the Wind Should Blow/Simon Smith and the Amazing Dancing Bear	1966	6.25	12.50	25.00
CAPITOL					
3136	Alice My Sweet/Eve Laurain	1971	—	2.50	5.00

Number	Title (A Side/B Side)	Yr	VG	VG+	NM
CHELSEA					
BCBO-0101	Thank God for Rock and Roll/Krush on Kris	1973	—	2.50	5.00
—As "Christopher Cloud"					
78-0118	Zip-a-Dee-Doo-Dah/Interpretation of War	1973	—	2.50	5.00
—As "Christopher Cloud"					
COLPIX					
794	Let's Go Where the Action Is/(Instrumental)	1966	5.00	10.00	20.00
DOT					
16117	The Gypsy Song/Give Me the Clue	1960	5.00	10.00	20.00
MGM					
13400	Pretty Thing (You Look Out of Sight Tonight)/I Don't Have to Worry 'Bout You	1965	3.75	7.50	15.00
13429	Little Suzy Somethin'/Pee's N' Que's	1965	3.75	7.50	15.00
R-DELL					
111	Betty Jean/I'm Not Sure	1960	6.25	12.50	25.00
RCA VICTOR					
47-7975	Along Came Linda/You Look So Lonely	1961	5.00	10.00	20.00
47-8025	Come Here Joanne/The Way I Used to Do	1962	5.00	10.00	20.00
47-8074	I'll Remember Carol/Too Late for Tears	1962	5.00	10.00	20.00
47-8126	Have You Had a Change of Heart/Sweet Little Baby, I Care	1963	5.00	10.00	20.00
47-8208	Don't Be Afraid/A Million Things to Say	1963	5.00	10.00	20.00
WOW					
345	Is It True/Little One	1961	5.00	10.00	20.00
Albums					
RCA CAMDEN					
CAL-2202 [M]	Tommy Boyce	1967	5.00	10.00	20.00
CAS-2202 [S]	Tommy Boyce	1967	6.25	12.50	25.00

BOYCE, TOMMY, AND BOBBY HART

Also see each artist's individual listings.

Number	Title (A Side/B Side)	Yr	VG	VG+	NM
45s					
AQUARIAN					
380	I'll Blow You a Kiss in the Wind/Smilin'	1970	—	2.00	4.00
380 [PS]	I'll Blow You a Kiss in the Wind/Smilin'	1970	—	3.00	6.00
A&M					
858	Out and About/My Little Chickadee	1967	2.50	5.00	10.00
858 [PS]	Out and About/My Little Chickadee	1967	5.00	10.00	20.00
874	Sometimes She's a Little Girl/Love Every Day	1967	2.50	5.00	10.00
874 [PS]	Sometimes She's a Little Girl/Love Every Day	1967	5.00	10.00	20.00
893	I Wonder What She's Doing Tonight/The Ambushers	1967	3.00	6.00	12.00
893 [PS]	I Wonder What She's Doing Tonight/The Ambushers	1967	5.00	10.00	20.00
919	Goodbye Baby (I Don't Want to See You Cry)/Where Angels Go, Trouble Follows	1968	2.50	5.00	10.00
919 [PS]	Goodbye Baby (I Don't Want to See You Cry)/Where Angels Go, Trouble Follows	1968	5.00	10.00	20.00
948	Alice Long (You're Still My Favorite Girlfriend)/P.O. Box 9847	1968	2.50	5.00	10.00
948 [PS]	Alice Long (You're Still My Favorite Girlfriend)/P.O. Box 9847	1968	5.00	10.00	20.00
993	We're All Going to the Same Place/6 + 6	1968	2.50	5.00	10.00
993 [PS]	We're All Going to the Same Place/6 + 6	1968	2.50	5.00	10.00
1017	Maybe Somebody Heard/It's All Happening on the Inside	1969	2.00	4.00	8.00
1031	L.U.V. (Let Us Vote)/I Wanna Be Free	1969	2.00	4.00	8.00
1031 [PS]	L.U.V. (Let Us Vote)/I Wanna Be Free	1969	3.75	7.50	15.00
Albums					
A&M					
LP-126 [M]	Test Patterns	1967	5.00	10.00	20.00
LP-143 [M]	I Wonder What She's Doing Tonite?	1968	7.50	15.00	30.00
SP-4126 [S]	Test Patterns	1967	5.00	10.00	20.00
SP-4143 [S]	I Wonder What She's Doing Tonite?	1968	5.00	10.00	20.00
SP-4162	It's All Happening on the Inside	1968	5.00	10.00	20.00

BOYD, EDDIE

Number	Title (A Side/B Side)	Yr	VG	VG+	NM
45s					
ART TONE					
832	I'm Comin' Home/Operator	1962	3.75	7.50	15.00
BEA & BABY					
101	I'm Comin' Home/Thank You Baby	1959	3.75	7.50	15.00
107	Blue Monday Blues/The Blues Is Here to Stay	1959	3.75	7.50	15.00
108	Come Home/You've Got to Reap What You Sow	1959	3.75	7.50	15.00
CHESS					
1523	Cool Kind Treatment/Rosa Lee Swing	1952	25.00	50.00	100.00
1533	24 Hours/The Tickler	1953	25.00	50.00	100.00
—Black vinyl					
1533	24 Hours/The Tickler	1953	100.00	200.00	400.00
—Red vinyl					
1541	Third Degree/Back Beat	1953	50.00	100.00	200.00
—Black vinyl					
1541	Third Degree/Back Beat	1953	125.00	250.00	500.00
—Red vinyl					
1552	That's When I Miss You So/Tortured Soul	1953	20.00	40.00	80.00
1561	Nothing But Trouble/Picture in the Frame	1954	15.00	30.00	60.00
1573	Hush Baby, Don't You Cry/Came Home This Morning	1954	15.00	30.00	60.00
1576	Driftin'/Rattin' and Runnin' Around	1954	15.00	30.00	60.00
1582	The Story of Bill/Please Help Me	1954	15.00	30.00	60.00
1595	The Nightmare Is Over/Real Good Feeling	1955	12.50	25.00	50.00
1606	I'm a Prisoner/I've Been Deceived	1955	12.50	25.00	50.00
1621	Don't/Life Gets to Be a Burden	1956	10.00	20.00	40.00
1634	Just a Fool/Four Leaf Clover	1956	10.00	20.00	40.00
1660	I Got a Woman/Hotel Blues	1957	10.00	20.00	40.00
1674	I Got the Blues/She's the One	1957	10.00	20.00	40.00
HERALD					
406	Lonesome for My Baby/I'm Goin' Downtown	1953	100.00	200.00	400.00
J.O.B.					
1007	Five Long Years/Blue Coat Man	1952	37.50	75.00	150.00
—Black vinyl					
1007	Five Long Years/Blue Coat Man	1952	75.00	150.00	300.00
—Red vinyl					
1009	It's Miserable to Be Alone/I'm Pleading	1953	75.00	150.00	300.00
1114	I Love You/Save Her Doctor	1957	15.00	30.00	60.00
RCA VICTOR					
50-0006	What Makes These Things Happen/Chicago Is Just That Way	1950	30.00	60.00	120.00
—Gray label, orange vinyl					

BOYD, JIMMY

Also see ROSEMARY CLOONEY; FRANKIE LAINE.

Number	Title (A Side/B Side)	Yr	VG	VG+	NM
45s					
CAPITOL					
4967	Day Dreamer/I've Got It Made	1963	2.50	5.00	10.00
COLUMBIA					
4-152	I Saw Mommy Kissing Santa Claus/Thumbelina	1952	5.00	10.00	20.00
—Yellow-label Children's Series issue; alternate number is 90174					
4-152 [PS]	I Saw Mommy Kissing Santa Claus/Thumbelina	1952	6.25	12.50	25.00
4-183	Santa Got Stuck In The Chimney/I Said A Prayer For Santa Claus	1953	3.75	7.50	15.00
—Yellow-label Children's Series issue					
4-183 [PS]	Santa Got Stuck In The Chimney/I Said A Prayer For Santa Claus	1953	5.00	10.00	20.00
21571	Rockin' Down the Mississippi/Crazy Mixed Up Blues	1956	12.50	25.00	50.00
39696	God's Little Candles/Owl Lullaby	1952	3.75	7.50	15.00
39733	Little Train A-Chuggin'/Needle In, Needle Out	1952	3.75	7.50	15.00
39871	I Saw Mommy Kissing Santa Claus/Thumbelina	1952	3.75	7.50	15.00
39927	Early Bird/I'll Stay in the House	1953	3.75	7.50	15.00
39955	My Bunny and My Sister Sue/Two Easter Sunday Sweethearts	1953	3.75	7.50	15.00
40007	Playmates/Shoo Fly Pie and Apple Pan Dowdy	1953	3.75	7.50	15.00
40049	Marco, the Polo Pony/God Bless Us All	1953	3.75	7.50	15.00
40070	I Saw Mommy Kissing Santa Claus/Santa Claus Is Coming to Town	1953	3.00	6.00	12.00
40071	Winter Wonderland/Here Comes Santa Claus	1953	3.00	6.00	12.00
40072	Silent Night, Holy Night/Frosty the Snowman	1953	3.00	6.00	12.00
40073	The Little Match Girl/Rudolph, the Red-Nosed Reindeer	1953	3.00	6.00	12.00
40080	Santa Got Stuck in the Chimney/I Said a Prayer for Santa Claus	1953	3.75	7.50	15.00
—With Johnny Bond					
40138	I've Got Those "Wake Up Seven-Thirty, Wash Your Ears They're Dirty, Eat Your Eggs and Oatmeal, Rush to School" Blues/Jelly on My Head	1954	5.00	10.00	20.00
40181	Little Bonny Bunny/Jimmy, Roll Me Gently	1954	3.75	7.50	15.00
40218	I'm So Glad (I'm a Little Boy and You're a Little Girl)/Kitty in the Basket	1954	3.75	7.50	15.00
—With Gayla Peevey					
40253	Ma I Miss Your Apple Pie/Shepherd Boy	1954	3.75	7.50	15.00
40304	Little Sir Echo/The Little White Duck	1954	3.75	7.50	15.00
40365	I Saw Mommy Do the Mambo (With You Know Who)/Santa Claus Blues	1954	3.75	7.50	15.00
40504	I Want a Haircut with a Moon on Top/How Come	1955	3.00	6.00	12.00
40601	Reindeer Rock/A Kiss for Christmas	1955	5.00	10.00	20.00
40756	Don't Forget to Say Your Prayers/Little Dog	1956	3.00	6.00	12.00
40881	I Wanna Go Steady/Gonna Take My Heart on a Hayride	1957	3.00	6.00	12.00
DOT					
16126	Dusty/Jambalaya	1960	3.00	6.00	12.00
IMPERIAL					
66166	I Would Never Do That/Lazy Me	1966	2.00	4.00	8.00
66206	She Chased Me/Will I Cry	1966	2.00	4.00	8.00
66233	So Young and So Fine/I Would Never Do That	1967	2.00	4.00	8.00
MGM					
12788	Cream Puff/I Love You So Much	1959	15.00	30.00	60.00
VEE JAY					
620	All Alone/In Love In Vain	1964	2.50	5.00	10.00
686	That's What I'll Give to You/My Home Town	1965	2.50	5.00	10.00
7-Inch Extended Plays					
COLUMBIA					
B-1913	I Saw Mommy Kissing Santa Claus/Jingle Bells/I Said A Prayer For Santa Claus/Santa Got Stuck In The Chimney	195?	3.00	6.00	12.00
B-1913 [PS]	Jimmy Boyd	195?	3.75	7.50	15.00
Albums					
COLUMBIA					
CL 2543 [10]	I Saw Mommy Kissing Santa Claus	1955	10.00	20.00	40.00
—"House Party Series" reissue					
CL 6270 [10]	Christmas with Jimmy Boyd	1953	25.00	50.00	100.00

BOYD, MICKEY, AND THE PLAIN VIEWERS

See THE STRING-A-LONGS.

BOYFRIENDS, THE

Also known as THE FIVE DISCS.

Number	Title (A Side/B Side)	Yr	VG	VG+	NM
45s					
KAPP					
569	Let's Fall in Love/Oh Lana	1964	25.00	50.00	100.00

BOZ

Boz Burrell, later of KING CRIMSON and BAD COMPANY.

Number	Title (A Side/B Side)	Yr	VG	VG+	NM
45s					
EPIC					
10097	Baby Song/Pinocchio	1966	2.50	5.00	10.00
10097 [PS]	Baby Song/Pinocchio	1966	3.75	7.50	15.00

BOZE, CALVIN

Number	Title (A Side/B Side)	Yr	VG	VG+	NM
45s					
ALADDIN					
3045	Waiting and Drinking/If You Ever Had the Blues	1950	37.50	75.00	150.00
3055	Safronia Blues/Angel City Blues	1950	37.50	75.00	150.00
3065	Lizzie Lou/Lizzie Lou (Part 2)	1950	37.50	75.00	150.00

Number	Title (A Side/B Side)	Yr	VG	VG+	NM
3072	Stinkin' from Drinkin'/Look Out for Tomorrow Today	1950	25.00	50.00	100.00
3079	Beat Street on Saturday Night/Choo Choo Ch'Boogieing My Baby Back Home	1951	25.00	50.00	100.00
3086	Slippin' and Slidin'/Baby, You're Tops with Me	1951	25.00	50.00	100.00
3100	I've Got News for You/I Can't Stop Crying	1951	20.00	40.00	80.00
3110	I'm Gonna Steam Off the Stamp/Fish Tail	1952	20.00	40.00	80.00
3122	Hey, Lawdy Miss Clawdy/My Friend Told Me	1952	20.00	40.00	80.00
3132	Good Time Sue/Keep Your Nose Out of My Business	1952	15.00	30.00	60.00
3142	The Blue Tango/The Glory of Love	1952	15.00	30.00	60.00
3143	Blue Shuffle/Popside	1952	15.00	30.00	60.00
3147	Looped/Blow Man Blow	1952	15.00	30.00	60.00
3160	Havin' a Time/Shamrock	1953	12.50	25.00	50.00
3181	That Other Woman/Shoot De Pistol	1953	12.50	25.00	50.00
IMPERIAL					
5844	Shamrock/Safronia B	1962	3.00	6.00	12.00

BRACELETS, THE

45s

Number	Title (A Side/B Side)	Yr	VG	VG+	NM
20TH CENTURY-FOX					
539	You Better Move On/You're Just Fooling Yourself	1964	3.00	6.00	12.00
CONGRESS					
104	I'll Play Along/Waddle, Waddle	1962	4.00	8.00	16.00

BRADEN, JOHN

45s

Number	Title (A Side/B Side)	Yr	VG	VG+	NM
A&M					
1066	What a Friend We Have in Jesus/Hand Me Down Man	1969	2.50	5.00	10.00

Albums

Number	Title (A Side/B Side)	Yr	VG	VG+	NM
A&M					
SP-4172	John Braden	1969	3.75	7.50	15.00

BRADLEY, JAN

45s

Number	Title (A Side/B Side)	Yr	VG	VG+	NM
CHESS					
1845	Mama Didn't Lie/Lovers Like Me	1962	2.50	5.00	10.00
1851	These Tears/Baby What Can I Do	1963	2.00	4.00	8.00
1884	Curfew Blues/Pack My Things	1964	2.00	4.00	8.00
1897	Please Mr. D.J./Two of a Kind	1964	2.00	4.00	8.00
1919	I'm Over You/The Brush-Off	1964	2.00	4.00	8.00
1975	Just a Summer Memory/He'll Wait for Me	1966	—	3.00	6.00
1996	Trust Me/Things a Woman Needs	1967	—	3.00	6.00
2023	Your Kind of Love/It's Just Your Way	1967	—	3.00	6.00
2043	You Have Me What's Missing/Nights in New York City	1968	—	3.00	6.00
FORMAL					
1044	Mama Didn't Lie/Lovers Like Me	1962	50.00	100.00	200.00
1048	Dear Sears and Roebuck/(B-side unknown)	1963	3.00	6.00	12.00
HOOTENANNY					
1	Christmas Time (Part 1)/Christmas Time (Part 2)	1962	3.00	6.00	12.00

BRADSHAW, JACK

45s

Number	Title (A Side/B Side)	Yr	VG	VG+	NM
DECCA					
29654	My Heart, My Heart/Flirting with You	1955	6.25	12.50	25.00
GLENN					
754	No, No/Welcome Heart	1955	15.00	30.00	60.00
755	I Got What You Need/You Hurt Me	195?	15.00	30.00	60.00
MAR-VEL					
750	Don't Tease Me/Don't Cause Me to Hate You	1954	25.00	50.00	100.00
751	Searchin'/My Heart, My Heart	1955	15.00	30.00	60.00
752	It Just Ain't Right/Naughty Girls	1955	15.00	30.00	60.00
753	Jo Jo/Men Are Weak	1955	25.00	50.00	100.00
756	Saturday Night Special/Out of the Picture	195?	15.00	30.00	60.00

BRADSHAW, TINY

45s

Number	Title (A Side/B Side)	Yr	VG	VG+	NM
KING					
4376	After You've Gone/Boogie Green	1950	15.00	30.00	60.00
4397	Butterfly/I'm Going to Have Myself a Ball	1950	15.00	30.00	60.00
4417	Breaking Up the House/If You Don't Love Me, Tell Me So	1950	15.00	30.00	60.00
4427	Walk That Mess/One, Two, Three, Kick Blues	1951	15.00	30.00	60.00
4447	Brad's Blues/Two Dry Bones on the Pantry Shelf	1951	15.00	30.00	60.00
4457	Bradshaw Boogie/Walkin' the Chalk Line	1951	15.00	30.00	60.00
4467	I'm a High Ballin' Daddy/You Came By	1951	15.00	30.00	60.00
4487	T-99/Long Time Baby	1951	50.00	100.00	200.00
4497	The Train Kept a-Rollin'/Knockin' Blues	1951	50.00	100.00	200.00
4537	Mailman's Sack/Newspaper Boy Blues	1952	50.00	100.00	200.00
4547	Rippin' and Runnin'/Lay It on the Line	1952	50.00	100.00	200.00
4577	Strange/Soft	1952	12.50	25.00	50.00
4713	Don't Worry 'Bout Me/Overflow	1954	10.00	20.00	40.00
4727	Spider Web/The Gypsey	1954	10.00	20.00	40.00
4747	A Stack of Dollars/Cat Fruit	1954	10.00	20.00	40.00
4757	Light/Choice	1954	10.00	20.00	40.00
4777	Cat Nap/Stomping Room Only	1955	10.00	20.00	40.00
4787	Phantom Turnpike/Come On	1955	10.00	20.00	40.00
5114	Short Shorts/Bushes	1958	6.25	12.50	25.00

7-Inch Extended Plays

Number	Title (A Side/B Side)	Yr	VG	VG+	NM
KING					
EP 248	Off and On/Free for All//South of the Orient/Later	195?	10.00	20.00	40.00
EP 248 [PS]	Tiny Bradshaw, Vol. 2	195?	10.00	20.00	40.00

Albums

Number	Title (A Side/B Side)	Yr	VG	VG+	NM
KING					
295-74 [10]	Off and On	1955	250.00	500.00	1000.
395-501 [M]	Selections	1956	175.00	350.00	700.00
653 [M]	Great Composer	1960	75.00	150.00	300.00
953 [M]	24 Great Songs	1966	10.00	20.00	40.00

BRADY, JUNE AND GEORGE

45s

Number	Title (A Side/B Side)	Yr	VG	VG+	NM
ABC-PARAMOUNT					
9893	Sweetheart, Sweetheart/You're My Love	1958	5.00	10.00	20.00

BRADY BUNCH, THE

Also see CHRIS KNIGHT; MIKE LOOKINLAND; MAUREEN McCORMICK; EVE PLUMB; BARRY WILLIAMS.

45s

Number	Title (A Side/B Side)	Yr	VG	VG+	NM
PARAMOUNT					
0062	Frosty the Snowman/Silver Bells	1970	3.00	6.00	12.00
0062 [PS]	Frosty the Snowman/Silver Bells	1970	7.50	15.00	30.00
0141	We Can Make the World a Whole Lot Brighter/Time to Change	1972	3.00	6.00	12.00
0167	Time to Change/We'll Always Be Friends	1972	3.00	6.00	12.00
0205	Zuckerman's Famous Pig/Charlotte's Web	1973	3.00	6.00	12.00
0205 [PS]	Zuckerman's Famous Pig/Charlotte's Web	1973	5.00	10.00	20.00
0229	I'd Love You to Want Me/Everything I Do	1973	3.00	6.00	12.00

—As "The Brady Bunch Kids"

Albums

Number	Title (A Side/B Side)	Yr	VG	VG+	NM
PARAMOUNT					
PAS-5026	Merry Christmas from the Brady Bunch	1971	20.00	40.00	80.00
PAS-6032	Meet the Brady Bunch	1972	12.50	25.00	50.00
PAS-6037	The Kids from the Brady Bunch	1972	10.00	20.00	40.00
PAS-6058	The Brady Bunch Phonograph Record	1973	20.00	40.00	80.00

BRAINBOX

With JAN AKKERMAN, later of FOCUS.

45s

Number	Title (A Side/B Side)	Yr	VG	VG+	NM
CAPITOL					
2943	Alpha & Omega/Cruel Train	1970	2.00	4.00	8.00
ELEKTRA					
45673	Woman's Gone/Down Man	1969	2.00	4.00	8.00

Albums

Number	Title (A Side/B Side)	Yr	VG	VG+	NM
CAPITOL					
ST-596	Brainbox	1970	3.75	7.50	15.00

BRAMLETT, BONNIE

Half of DELANEY AND BONNIE.

45s

Number	Title (A Side/B Side)	Yr	VG	VG+	NM
CAPRICORN					
0229	Higher and Higher/It's Time	1975	—	2.00	4.00
0262	Let's Go, Let's Go, Let's Go/Never Gonna Give You Up	1976	—	2.00	4.00
0306	Except for Real/I've Just Seen a Face	1978	—	2.00	4.00
COLUMBIA					
45897	Good Vibrations/How Glad I Am	1973	—	2.50	5.00

Albums

Number	Title (A Side/B Side)	Yr	VG	VG+	NM
CAPRICORN					
CP 0148	It's Time	1975	3.00	6.00	12.00
CP 0169	Lady's Choice	1976	3.00	6.00	12.00
CP 0190	Memories	1978	3.00	6.00	12.00
COLUMBIA					
KC 31786	Sweet Bonnie Bramlett	1973	3.75	7.50	15.00

BRAMLETT, DELANEY

Half of DELANEY AND BONNIE.

45s

Number	Title (A Side/B Side)	Yr	VG	VG+	NM
COLUMBIA					
45696	I'm Not Your Lover, I'm Your Lover/Over and Over	1972	—	2.50	5.00
45781	We Can't Be Seen Together/Thank God	1973	—	2.50	5.00
45950	Are You a Beatle or a Rolling Stone/California Rain	1973	2.50	5.00	10.00
CREAM					
8147	What's a Little Love/I Love to Love You	1981	—	2.00	4.00
—By "Delaney and Bekka Bramlett"					
GNP CRESCENDO					
328	Heartbreak Hotel/You Never Looked Sweeter	1964	3.75	7.50	15.00
339	Liverpool Lou/You Have No Choice	1965	3.75	7.50	15.00
363	Without Your Love/A Better Man Than Me	1965	3.75	7.50	15.00
INDEPENDENCE					
76	Guess I Must Be Dreaming/Don't Let It	1967	3.75	7.50	15.00

Albums

Number	Title (A Side/B Side)	Yr	VG	VG+	NM
COLUMBIA					
KC 31631	Some Things Coming	1972	3.00	6.00	12.00
KC 32420	Moblus Strip	1973	3.00	6.00	12.00
MGM					
M3G-5011	Giving Birth to a Song	1975	2.50	5.00	10.00
PRODIGAL					
P6-10017S1	Class Reunion	1977	2.50	5.00	10.00

BRANT, BOBBY

45s

Number	Title (A Side/B Side)	Yr	VG	VG+	NM
EASTWEST					
124	Piano Nellie/I Found a New Love	1959	25.00	50.00	100.00
WHITE ROCK					
1114	Piano Nellie/I Found a New Love	1959	37.50	75.00	150.00

BRASS RING, THE

45s

Number	Title (A Side/B Side)	Yr	VG	VG+	NM
ABC DUNHILL					
4164	For the Love of Ivy/The Theme from The Odd Couple	1968	—	3.00	6.00
DUNHILL					
4023	The Phoenix Love Theme (Sensa Fine)/Lightning Bug	1966	—	3.00	6.00
4036	Lara's Theme/Secret Love	1966	—	3.00	6.00
4047	California Dreamin'/Samba de Orfeu	1966	—	3.00	6.00
4059	Lapland/Patricia	1966	—	3.00	6.00
4065	The Dis-Advantages of You/The Dating Game	1967	—	3.00	6.00

Number	Title (A Side/B Side)	Yr	VG	VG+	NM
4090	Love in the Open Air/Wait for Me	1967	5.00	10.00	20.00
4090 [PS]	Love in the Open Air/Wait for Me	1967	7.50	15.00	30.00
—Sleeve says this is "Paul McCartney's first non-Beatles song"					
4108	Monday, Monday/Flower Ring	1967	—	3.00	6.00
4132	Cherry Pink & Apple Blossom White/Adoro (Don't Tempt Me)	1968	—	3.00	6.00

7-Inch Extended Plays

Number	Title (A Side/B Side)	Yr	VG	VG+	NM
ABC DUNHILL					
LP-DS-50044 [DJ]	Mrs. Robinson/This Guy's in Love with You/For Love of Ivy//Do You Know the Way to San Jose/Love Is Blue/Honey	1969	3.00	6.00	12.00
—Small hole, 33 1/3 rpm jukebox EP					
LP-DS-50044 [PS]	Only Love	1969	3.00	6.00	12.00

Albums

Number	Title (A Side/B Side)	Yr	VG	VG+	NM
ABC DUNHILL					
DS-50034	Gazpacho	1968	3.00	6.00	12.00
DS-50044	Only Love	1969	3.00	6.00	12.00
DS-50051	The Best of the Brass Ring	1970	2.50	5.00	10.00
DUNHILL					
D 50008 [M]	Love Theme from The Flight of the Phoenix	1966	3.00	6.00	12.00
DS 50008 [S]	Love Theme from The Flight of the Phoenix	1966	3.75	7.50	15.00
D 50012 [M]	Lara's Theme	1966	3.00	6.00	12.00
DS 50012 [S]	Lara's Theme	1966	3.75	7.50	15.00
D 50015 [M]	Sunday Night at the Movies	1967	3.00	6.00	12.00
DS 50015 [S]	Sunday Night at the Movies	1967	3.75	7.50	15.00
D 50017 [M]	The Dis-Advantages of You	1967	3.00	6.00	12.00
DS 50017 [S]	The Dis-Advantages of You	1967	3.75	7.50	15.00
D 50023 [M]	The Now Sound	1967	3.00	6.00	12.00
DS 50023 [S]	The Now Sound	1967	3.75	7.50	15.00
PROJECT 3					
5067	The Brass Ring	1972	2.50	5.00	10.00

BRAUTIGAN, RICHARD

Albums

Number	Title (A Side/B Side)	Yr	VG	VG+	NM
HARVEST					
ST-424	Listening to Richard Brautigan	1970	7.50	15.00	30.00

BRAVE BELT

Also see BACHMAN-TURNER OVERDRIVE.

45s

Number	Title (A Side/B Side)	Yr	VG	VG+	NM
REPRISE					
1039	Holy Train/Crazy Arms-Crazy Eyes	1971	—	2.50	5.00
1061	Never Comin' Home/Can You Feel It	1971	—	2.50	5.00
1083	Another Way Out/Dunrobin's Gone	1972	—	2.50	5.00

Albums

Number	Title (A Side/B Side)	Yr	VG	VG+	NM
REPRISE					
MS 2057	Brave Belt II	1972	3.00	6.00	12.00
MS 2210	Bachman-Turner-Bachman As Brave Belt	1974	2.50	5.00	10.00
RS 6447	Brave Belt	1971	3.00	6.00	12.00

BRAVE NEW WORLD

45s

Number	Title (A Side/B Side)	Yr	VG	VG+	NM
EPIC					
10123	It's Tomorrow/Cried	1967	5.00	10.00	20.00

BREAD

Also see DAVID GATES; JIMMY GRIFFIN.

45s

Number	Title (A Side/B Side)	Yr	VG	VG+	NM
ELEKTRA					
45365	Lost Without Your Love/Change of Heart	1976	—	2.00	4.00
45389	Hooked on You/Our Lady of Sorrow	1977	—	2.00	4.00
45666	Dismal Day/Anyway You Want Me	1969	2.00	4.00	8.00
45668	Could I/You Can't Measure the Cost	1969	—	3.00	6.00
45686	Make It With You/Why Do You Keep Me Waiting	1970	—	2.00	4.00
—Red, black and white label					
45686	Make It With You/Why Do You Keep Me Waiting	1970	—	2.00	4.00
—Yellow and black label					
45701	It Don't Matter to Me/Call on Me	1970	—	2.00	4.00
45701 [PS]	It Don't Matter to Me/Call on Me	1970	2.00	4.00	8.00
45711	Let Your Love Go/Too Much Love	1971	—	2.00	4.00
45720	If/Take Comfort	1971	—	2.00	4.00
45720 [PS]	If/Take Comfort	1971	2.00	4.00	8.00
45740	Mother Freedom/Life in Your Love	1971	—	2.00	4.00
45751	Baby I'm-a Want You/Truckin'	1971	—	2.00	4.00
45765	Everything I Own/I Don't Love You	1972	—	2.00	4.00
45784	Diary/Down on My Knees	1972	—	2.00	4.00
45803	The Guitar Man/Just Like Yesterday	1972	—	2.00	4.00
45818	Sweet Surrender/Make It By Yourself	1972	—	2.00	4.00
45832	Aubrey/Didn't Even Know Her Name	1973	—	2.00	4.00

Albums

Number	Title (A Side/B Side)	Yr	VG	VG+	NM
ELEKTRA					
BRD-1 [DJ]	Bread	1971	5.00	10.00	20.00
—In-store sampler; very similar to the future LP "The Best of Bread"					
6E-108	The Best of Bread	1977	2.00	4.00	8.00
—Reissue of 75056					
6E-110	The Best of Bread, Volume 2	1977	2.00	4.00	8.00
—Reissue of 7E-1005					
7E-1005	The Best of Bread, Volume 2	1974	3.00	6.00	12.00
7E-1094	Lost Without Your Love	1976	2.50	5.00	10.00
EQ-5015 [Q]	Baby I'm-a Want You	1974	5.00	10.00	20.00
EQ-5056 [Q]	The Best of Bread	1973	5.00	10.00	20.00
60414	Anthology of Bread	1985	2.50	5.00	10.00
EKS-74044	Bread	1969	3.75	7.50	15.00
—Red label with large stylized "E"					
EKS-74044	Bread	1971	2.50	5.00	10.00
—Butterfly label					
EKS-74076	On the Waters	1970	3.75	7.50	15.00
—Red label with large stylized "E"					
EKS-74076	On the Waters	1971	2.50	5.00	10.00
—Butterfly label					
EKS-74086	Manna	1971	3.00	6.00	12.00
EKS-75015	Baby I'm-a Want You	1971	3.75	7.50	15.00
—Gatefold with raised photo on front					
EKS-75015	Baby I'm-a Want You	197?	2.50	5.00	10.00
—Front photo is not raised					
EKS-75047	Guitar Man	1972	3.00	6.00	12.00
EKS-75056	The Best of Bread	1973	3.00	6.00	12.00

BREAD, LOVE AND DREAMS

Albums

Number	Title (A Side/B Side)	Yr	VG	VG+	NM
LONDON					
PS 566	Bread, Love and Dreams	1969	7.50	15.00	30.00

BREAKAWAYS, THE

45s

Number	Title (A Side/B Side)	Yr	VG	VG+	NM
CAMEO					
323	That's How It Goes/He Doesn't Love Me	1964	3.75	7.50	15.00
LONDON INT'L.					
10526	That Boy of Mine/Here She Comes	1963	3.00	6.00	12.00
MELBOURNE					
1805	Granada/The Flipper	1964	3.00	6.00	12.00

BREAKERS, THE

45s

Number	Title (A Side/B Side)	Yr	VG	VG+	NM
AMY					
938	Don't Send Me No Flowers (I Ain't Dead Yet)/Love of My Life	1965	3.75	7.50	15.00
BRANA					
1001/2	Kama-Kaze/Surf Breaker	1963	15.00	30.00	60.00
DJB					
116	Jet Stream/Beach Head	1964	12.50	25.00	50.00
116	Super Jet Rumble/Beach Head	1964	12.50	25.00	50.00
—Revised A-side title					
IMPACT					
14	Surfin' Tragedy/Surf Bird	1963	6.25	12.50	25.00
—Black vinyl					
14	Surfin' Tragedy/Surf Bird	1963	20.00	40.00	80.00
—Gold vinyl					
JERDEN					
789	All My Nights, All My Days/Better for the Both of Us	1966	5.00	10.00	20.00
MARSH					
206	Balboa Memories/Long Way Home	1963	12.50	25.00	50.00
RIVERTON					
102	All My Nights, All My Days/Better for the Both of Us	1966	10.00	20.00	40.00

BRECKER BROTHERS, THE

45s

Number	Title (A Side/B Side)	Yr	VG	VG+	NM
ARISTA					
0122	Sneakin' Up Behind You/Sponge	1975	—	2.00	4.00
0182	If You Wanna Boogie...Forget It/Slick Stuff	1976	—	2.00	4.00
0253	Finger Lickin' Good/Don't Stop the Music	1977	—	2.00	4.00
0365	East River (La-Di-Da)/Funky Sea, Funky Do	1978	—	2.00	4.00
0533	You Ga (Ta Give It)/(B-side unknown)	1980	—	2.00	4.00

Albums

Number	Title (A Side/B Side)	Yr	VG	VG+	NM
ARISTA					
AL 4037	The Brecker Brothers	1975	2.50	5.00	10.00
AL 4061	Back to Back	1976	2.50	5.00	10.00
AL 4122	Don't Stop the Music	1977	2.50	5.00	10.00
AL 4185	Heavy Metal Be-Bop	1978	2.50	5.00	10.00
AB 4272	Détente	1979	2.50	5.00	10.00
AL 9550	Straphangin'	1981	2.50	5.00	10.00

BREEDLOVE, JIMMY

45s

Number	Title (A Side/B Side)	Yr	VG	VG+	NM
ATCO					
6094	That's My Baby/Over Somebody Else's Shoulder	1957	6.25	12.50	25.00
6105	I Can Still Hear You Say You Love Me/I Wish I Were Twins	1957	6.25	12.50	25.00
DIAMOND					
144	Jealous Fool/Lil' Ol' Me	1963	7.50	15.00	30.00
EPIC					
9270	Could This Be Love/This Too Shall Pass Away	1958	5.00	10.00	20.00
9283	Love Is All We Need/Lovable	1958	5.00	10.00	20.00
9289	Love Is All We Need/Oo-Wee Good Gosh A-Mighty	1958	5.00	10.00	20.00
9319	All Is Forgiven/I Say Hello	1959	5.00	10.00	20.00
9360	To Belong/Waiting for You	1960	5.00	10.00	20.00
JUBILEE					
5551	Jealous Fool/The Greatest Love (Nothing Less, Nothing More)	1966	2.50	5.00	10.00
OKEH					
7145	Anytime You Want Me/My Guardian Angel	1962	3.00	6.00	12.00
7152	Don't Let It Happen/Queen Bee	1962	3.00	6.00	12.00
ROULETTE					
7010	I Can't Help Lovin' You/I Saw You	1968	2.00	4.00	8.00

7-Inch Extended Plays

Number	Title (A Side/B Side)	Yr	VG	VG+	NM
RCA CAMDEN					
CEP-447	(contents unknown)	1958	6.25	12.50	25.00
CEP-447 [PS]	Rock 'N' Roll Music	1958	6.25	12.50	25.00

Albums

Number	Title (A Side/B Side)	Yr	VG	VG+	NM
RCA CAMDEN					
CAL-430 [M]	Rock 'N' Roll Hits	1958	10.00	20.00	40.00

BREEN, BOBBY

45s

Number	Title (A Side/B Side)	Yr	VG	VG+	NM
CHIC					
1003	If the Night Could Tell You/Wait	1956	3.75	7.50	15.00
1013	We Will Make Love/Rainbow	1957	3.75	7.50	15.00

Number	Title (A Side/B Side)	Yr	VG	VG+	NM
LYRIC					
105	It's a Sin/Valley of Romance	196?	5.00	10.00	20.00
MOTOWN					
1053	How Can We Tell Him/Better Late Than Never	1964	6.25	12.50	25.00
1059	You're Just Like You/Here Comes That Heartache	1964	6.25	12.50	25.00
1059 [PS]	You're Just Like You/Here Comes That Heartache	1964	10.00	20.00	40.00
NRC					
055	Hawaii Calls/Theme from A Summer Place	1960	2.50	5.00	10.00
Albums					
LONDON					
LB 270 [10]	Songs at Yuletide	1953	12.50	25.00	50.00

BREMERS, BEVERLY

Number	Title (A Side/B Side)	Yr	VG	VG+	NM
45s					
COLUMBIA					
10180	What I Did for Love/You're Precious to Me	1975	—	2.50	5.00
10451	The Prisoner/Flight 309 to Tennessee	1976	—	2.50	5.00
SCEPTER					
12315	Don't Say You Don't Remember/Get Smart Girl	1971	—	3.00	6.00
12332	When Michael Calls/Toy Girl	1971	—	2.50	5.00
12348	We're Free/Colors of Love	1972	—	2.50	5.00
12363	I'll Make You Music/I Made a Man Out of You, Jimmy	1972	—	2.50	5.00
12370	Heaven Help Us/All That's Left Is the Music	1973	—	2.50	5.00
12378	Run to Her/Baby I Don't Know You	1973	—	2.50	5.00
12380	Daddy's Coming Home/A Little Bit of Love	1973	—	2.50	5.00
12391	Sing a Happy Song/Get Smart Girl	1974	—	2.50	5.00
12399	One Day at a Time/Get Up in the Morning	1975	—	2.50	5.00
Albums					
SCEPTER					
SPS-5102	I'll Make You Music	1972	2.50	5.00	10.00

BRENDA AND THE TABULATIONS

Number	Title (A Side/B Side)	Yr	VG	VG+	NM
45s					
CHOCOLATE CITY					
004	Home to Myself/Leave Me Alone	1976	—	2.00	4.00
009	(I'm a) Superstar/Take It or Leave It	1977	—	2.00	4.00
012	Let's Go All the Way (Down)/I Keep Coming Back for More	1977	—	2.00	4.00
DIONN					
500	Dry Your Eyes/The Wash	1967	2.50	5.00	10.00
501	Who's Lovin' You/Stay Together Young Lovers	1967	2.50	5.00	10.00
503	Just Once in a Lifetime/Hey Boy	1967	2.50	5.00	10.00
504	When You're Gone/Hey Boy	1967	2.50	5.00	10.00
507	To the One I Love/Baby You're So Right	1968	2.50	5.00	10.00
509	I Can't Get Over You/That's in the Past	1968	2.50	5.00	10.00
511	Reason to Live/Hey Boy	1968	2.50	5.00	10.00
512	That's the Price You Have to Pay/I Wish I Hadn't Done What I Did	1969	2.50	5.00	10.00
EPIC					
10898	Little Bit of Love/Let Me Be Happy	1972	—	3.00	6.00
10954	One Girl Too Late/The Magic of Your Love	1973	—	3.00	6.00
11000	Key to My Heart/Love Is Just a Carnival	1973	—	3.00	6.00
11059	I'm in Love/Walk On In	1973	—	3.00	6.00
50081	Let Me Be Happy/Little Bit of Love	1975	—	2.00	4.00
PHILCO-FORD					
HP-40	Dry Your Eyes/When You're Gone	1969	5.00	10.00	20.00
—4-inch plastic "Hip Pocket Record" with color sleeve					
TOP & BOTTOM					
401	The Touch of You/Stop Sneaking Around	1969	2.00	4.00	8.00
403	And My Heart Sang (Tra La La)/Lies, Lies, Lies	1970	2.00	4.00	8.00
404	Don't Make Me Over/You've Changed	1970	2.00	4.00	8.00
406	A Child No One Wanted/Scuse Us All	1970	2.00	4.00	8.00
407	Right on the Tip of My Tongue/Always and Forever	1971	2.00	4.00	8.00
408	A Part of You/Where There's a Will	1971	2.00	4.00	8.00
411	Why Didn't I Think of That/A Love You Can Depend On	1971	2.00	4.00	8.00
Albums					
CHOCOLATE CITY					
2002	I Keep Coming Back for More	1977	2.50	5.00	10.00
DIONN					
LPM-2000 [M]	Dry Your Eyes	1967	10.00	20.00	40.00
LPS-2000 [S]	Dry Your Eyes	1967	12.50	25.00	50.00
TOM & BOTTOM					
100	Brenda and the Tabulations	1970	5.00	10.00	20.00

BRENNAN, WALTER

Number	Title (A Side/B Side)	Yr	VG	VG+	NM
45s					
DOT					
16066	Dutchman's Gold/Back to the Farm	1960	3.00	6.00	12.00
16066 [PS]	Dutchman's Gold/Back to the Farm	1960	5.00	10.00	20.00
16136	Space Mice/The Thievin' Stranger	1960	3.00	6.00	12.00
16348	Tribute to a Dog/Life Gets Tee-Jus Don't It	1962	3.00	6.00	12.00
EVEREST					
19365	Noah's Ark (Part 1)/Noah's Ark (Part 2)	1960	3.00	6.00	12.00
KAPP					
2126	Grandad/Man Needs to Know	1971	—	3.00	6.00
LIBERTY					
55436	Old Rivers/The Epic Ride of John B. Glenn	1962	3.00	6.00	12.00
55477	Houdini/The Old Kelly Place	1962	3.00	6.00	12.00
55477 [PS]	Houdini/The Old Kelly Place	1962	5.00	10.00	20.00
55508	Mama Sang a Song/Who Will Take Gramma	1962	3.00	6.00	12.00
55518	Henry Had A Merry Christmas/White Christmas	1962	3.00	6.00	12.00
55518 [PS]	Henry Had A Merry Christmas/White Christmas	1962	5.00	10.00	20.00
55617	Keep a-Movin' Old Man/Waiting for a Train	1963	3.00	6.00	12.00
LONDON					
141	Yesterday, When I Was Young/Time	1970	—	3.00	6.00
RPC					
502	Knight in Bright Armor/The Soul of Big Jack Dunn	1961	3.00	6.00	12.00
UNITED ARTISTS					
0055	Old Rivers/Mama Sang a Song	1973	—	2.00	4.00
—Silver Spotlight Series issue					
Albums					
DOT					
DLP-3309 [M]	Dutchman's Gold	1960	6.25	12.50	25.00
DLP-25309 [S]	Dutchman's Gold	1960	7.50	15.00	30.00
EVEREST					
SDBR-1103 [S]	World of Miracles	1960	7.50	15.00	30.00
SDBR-1123 [S]	The President: A Musical Biography of Our Chief Executive	1960	7.50	15.00	30.00
LPBR-5103 [M]	World of Miracles	1960	6.25	12.50	25.00
LPBR-5123 [M]	The President: A Musical Biography of Our Chief Executive	1960	6.25	12.50	25.00
HAMILTON					
HLP-159 [M]	Dutchman's Gold	1965	3.00	6.00	12.00
HLP-12159 [S]	Dutchman's Gold	1965	3.00	6.00	12.00
LIBERTY					
LRP-3233 [M]	Old Rivers	1962	5.00	10.00	20.00
LRP-3241 [M]	The President: A Musical Biography of Our Chief Executive	1962	3.75	7.50	15.00
—Reissue of Everest 5123					
LRP-3244 [M]	World of Miracles	1962	3.75	7.50	15.00
—Reissue of Everest 5103					
LRP-3257 [M]	'Twas the Night Before Christmas Back Home	1962	5.00	10.00	20.00
LRP-3266 [M]	Mama Sang a Song	1963	5.00	10.00	20.00
LRP-3317 [M]	Talkin' from the Heart	1964	5.00	10.00	20.00
LRP-3372 [M]	Gunfight at the O.K. Corral	1964	5.00	10.00	20.00
LST-7233 [S]	Old Rivers	1962	6.25	12.50	25.00
LST-7241 [S]	The President: A Musical Biography of Our Chief Executive	1962	5.00	10.00	20.00
—Reissue of Everest 1123					
LST-7244 [S]	World of Miracles	1962	5.00	10.00	20.00
—Reissue of Everest 1103					
LST-7257 [S]	'Twas the Night Before Christmas Back Home	1962	6.25	12.50	25.00
LST-7266 [S]	Mama Sang a Song	1963	6.25	12.50	25.00
LST-7317 [S]	Talkin' from the Heart	1964	6.25	12.50	25.00
LST-7372 [S]	Gunfight at the O.K. Corral	1964	6.25	12.50	25.00
LONDON					
PS 577	Yesterday, When I Was Young	1970	3.75	7.50	15.00
R.P.C.					
108S [S]	By the Fireside	1961	10.00	20.00	40.00
108 [M]	By the Fireside	1961	7.50	15.00	30.00
SUNSET					
SUM-1100 [M]	Country Heart	1966	3.00	6.00	12.00
SUS-5100 [S]	Country Heart	1966	3.00	6.00	12.00
SUS-5269	God and Country	1970	2.50	5.00	10.00
UNITED ARTISTS					
UA-LA438-E	The Very Best of Walter Brennan	1975	3.00	6.00	12.00

BRENSTON, JACKIE

Number	Title (A Side/B Side)	Yr	VG	VG+	NM
45s					
CHESS					
1458	Rocket "88"/Come Back Where You Belong	1951	5000.	7500.	10000.
—Early rockabilly classic; obscenely rare, even though the 45s were pressed later					
1469	In My Real Gone Rocket/Tuckered Out	1951	500.00	750.00	1000.
1472	Juiced/Independent Woman	1951	500.00	750.00	1000.
1496	Leo the Louse/Hi-Ho Baby	1952	125.00	250.00	500.00
1532	Blues Got Me Again/Starvation	1953	62.50	125.00	250.00
FEDERAL					
12283	What Can It Be/Gonna Wait for My Chance	1956	12.50	25.00	50.00
12291	Much Later/The Mistreater	1957	12.50	25.00	50.00
SUE					
736	Trouble Up the Road/You Ain't the One	1961	5.00	10.00	20.00

BRENT, RONNIE

Number	Title (A Side/B Side)	Yr	VG	VG+	NM
45s					
COLT 45					
101	Crazy Feeling/Shirley Ann	1959	6.25	12.50	25.00
109	Cowboys and Indians/Flow Gently	1959	6.25	12.50	25.00
UNITED ARTISTS					
108	My Sweet Verlene/Love	1958	10.00	20.00	40.00

BRENT, TONY

Number	Title (A Side/B Side)	Yr	VG	VG+	NM
45s					
ROULETTE					
4113	Girl of My Dreams/Don't Play That Melody	1958	3.00	6.00	12.00

BREWER, TERESA

Number	Title (A Side/B Side)	Yr	VG	VG+	NM
45s					
ABC					
10909	Jimmy/Thoroughly Modern Millie	1967	—	2.50	5.00
AMSTERDAM					
85024	Day by Day/Somewhere There's Someone Who Loves You	1972	—	2.00	4.00
85025	A Simple Song/Singing a Doo-Dah Song	1973	—	2.00	4.00
85027	Music, Music, Music/School Days	1973	—	2.00	4.00
85028	Music to the Man/Another Useless Day	1973	—	2.00	4.00
85029	Bo Weevil/Bei Mir Bist Du Schoen (Means That You're Grand)	1974	—	2.00	4.00
CORAL					
60591	Sing, Sing, Sing/I Don't Care	1952	3.00	6.00	12.00
60645	Lovin' Machine/Noodlin' Bay	1952	3.00	6.00	12.00
60676	Gonna Get Along Without You Now/Roll Them Roly-Poly Eyes	1952	3.00	6.00	12.00
60755	I Hear the Bluebells/Kisses on Paper	1952	3.00	6.00	12.00
60775	Rhode Island Red/En-Thuz-E-Uz-E-As-M	1952	3.00	6.00	12.00
—With Eileen Barton					
60873	Till I Waltz Again with You/Hello Bluebird	1952	3.00	6.00	12.00
60953	Breakin' the Blues/Dancing with Someone	1953	3.00	6.00	12.00

Number	Title (A Side/B Side)	Yr	VG	VG+	NM
60994	Too Much Mustard/Into Each Life Some Rain Must Fall	1953	3.00	6.00	12.00
61043	Ricochet (Rick O'Shay)/Too Young to Tango	1953	3.00	6.00	12.00
61066	Bell Bottom Blues/Our Heartbreaking Waltz	1953	3.00	6.00	12.00
61067	I Guess It Was You All the Time/Baby, Baby, Baby	1953	3.00	6.00	12.00
61078	I Saw Mommy Kissing Santa Claus/Ebenezer Scrooge	1953	3.00	6.00	12.00
61079	I Just Can't Wait Till Christmas/Too Fat for the Chimney	1953	3.00	6.00	12.00
61152	Jilted/Le Grand Tour de L'Amour	1954	3.00	6.00	12.00
61197	Skinnie Minnie (Fish Tart)/I Had Someone Else Before I Had You	1954	3.00	6.00	12.00
61225	Au Revoir/Danger Signs	1954	3.00	6.00	12.00
61286	Time/My Sweetie Went Away	1954	3.00	6.00	12.00
61315	Let Me Go, Lover/The Moon Is On Fire	1954	3.00	6.00	12.00
61339	I Gotta Go Get My Baby/What More Is There to Say	1955	3.00	6.00	12.00
61362	How Important Can It Be?/Pledging My Love	1955	3.00	6.00	12.00
61366	Tweedlee Dee/Rock Love	1955	3.00	6.00	12.00
61394	Silver Dollar/I Don't Want to Be Lonely Tonight	1955	3.00	6.00	12.00
61448	The Banjo's Back in Town/How to Be Very, Very Popular	1955	3.00	6.00	12.00
61500	Baby Be My Toy/So Doggone Lonely	1955	3.00	6.00	12.00
61528	Shoot It Again/You're Telling Our Secrets	1955	3.00	6.00	12.00
61548	A Good Man Is Hard to Find/It's Siesta Time	1956	2.50	5.00	10.00
61590	A Tear Fell/Bo Weevil	1956	2.50	5.00	10.00
61636	A Sweet Old Fashioned Girl/Goodbye John	1956	2.50	5.00	10.00
61700	I Love Mickey/Keep Your Cotton Pickin' Hands Off My Baby	1956	6.25	12.50	25.00
61700 [PS]	I Love Mickey/Keep Your Cotton Pickin' Hands Off My Baby	1956	12.50	25.00	50.00
61737	Mutual Admiration Society/Crazy with Love	1956	2.50	5.00	10.00
61776	How Lonely Can One Be/I'm Drowning My Sorrows	1957	2.50	5.00	10.00
61805	Empty Arms/The Ricky Tick Song	1957	2.50	5.00	10.00
61850	Lula Rock-a Hula/Teardrops in My Heart	1957	2.50	5.00	10.00
61878	It's the Same Old Jazz/Born to Love	1957	2.50	5.00	10.00
61898	You Send Me/Would I Wear	1957	2.50	5.00	10.00
61912	Listen My Children/Hush-a-Bye, Wink-a-Bye	1957	2.50	5.00	10.00
61944	Lost a Little Puppy/Because Him Is a Baby	1958	2.50	5.00	10.00
61948	There's Nothing As Lonesome As Saturday Night/Whirlpool	1958	2.50	5.00	10.00
61983	Saturday Dance/I Think the World of You	1958	2.50	5.00	10.00
62013	Pickle Up a Doodle/The Rain Falls on Everybody	1958	2.50	5.00	10.00
62033	The Hula Hoop Song/So Shy	1958	2.50	5.00	10.00
62057	The One Rose (That's Left in My Heart)/Satellite	1958	2.50	5.00	10.00
62058	Jingle Bell Rock/I Like Christmas	1958	2.50	5.00	10.00
62084	Heavenly Lover/Fair Weather Sweetheart	1959	2.50	5.00	10.00
62126	Bye Bye Baby Goodbye/Chain of Friendship	1959	2.50	5.00	10.00
62150	Mexicali Rose/If You Like-A Me	1959	2.50	5.00	10.00
62167	Peace of Mind/Venetian Sunset	1960	2.00	4.00	8.00
62167 [PS]	Peace of Mind/Venetian Sunset	1960	2.50	5.00	10.00
62197	If There Are Stars in My Eyes/How Do You Know It's Love	1960	2.00	4.00	8.00
62219	Anymore/That Piano Man	1960	2.00	4.00	8.00
62219 [PS]	Anymore/That Piano Man	1960	2.50	5.00	10.00
62236	Have You Ever Been Lonely (Have You Ever Been Blue)/When Do You Love Me	1960	2.00	4.00	8.00
62253	Whippoorwill/Older and Wiser	1961	2.00	4.00	8.00
62265	Milord/I've Got My Fingers Crossed	1961	2.00	4.00	8.00
62278	Sea Shell/Little Miss Belong to No One	1961	2.00	4.00	8.00
62299	Step Right Up/Pretty Lookin' Boy	1961	2.00	4.00	8.00
62306	Another/I Want You to Worry	1962	2.00	4.00	8.00
62316	You Came a Long Way from St. Louis/One Heart Less to Break	1962	2.00	4.00	8.00
62428	Cry Baby/I Hear the Angels Singing	1964	—	3.00	6.00
69039	Too Fat For The Chimney/I Just Can't Wait Till Christmas	1953	3.75	7.50	15.00

—Maroon label with silver print

DR. JAZZ

Number	Title (A Side/B Side)	Yr	VG	VG+	NM
03835	Classic Medley #1/Jimmy Dorsey Medley	1983	—	2.00	4.00
04114	No Way Conway/Sittin' Here Cryin'	1983	—	2.00	4.00

LONDON

Number	Title (A Side/B Side)	Yr	VG	VG+	NM
1083	Oceana Roll/Wang Wang Blues	1951	3.75	7.50	15.00
1085	If You Don't Marry Me/I Wish I Wuz	1951	3.75	7.50	15.00
1086	Longing for You/Jazz Me Blues	1951	3.75	7.50	15.00
30023	Music! Music! Music! (Put Another Nickel In)/Copenhagen	1950	3.75	7.50	15.00
30100	Choo'n Gum/(B-side unknown)	1950	3.75	7.50	15.00

PHILIPS

Number	Title (A Side/B Side)	Yr	VG	VG+	NM
40077	The Ballad of Lover's Hill/Not Like a Sister	1962	2.00	4.00	8.00
40095	She'll Never Love You/The Thrill Is Gone	1963	2.00	4.00	8.00
40120	Second Hand Love/Stand-In	1963	2.00	4.00	8.00
40135	He Understands Me/Just Before We Say Goodbye	1963	2.00	4.00	8.00
40177	Come On In/Simple Things	1964	—	3.00	6.00
40227	Dang Me (Dern You)/Mama Never Told Me	1964	—	3.00	6.00
40253	Goldfinger/Make Room for One More Fool	1965	—	3.00	6.00
40282	Supercalifragilisticexpialidocious/I've Grown Accustomed to His Face	1965	—	3.00	6.00
40310	Say Something Sweet to Your Sweetheart/What About Time	1965	—	3.00	6.00
40345	Little Bitty Grain of Sand/Little Buddy	1965	—	3.00	6.00
40367	Handle with Care/I Can't Remember Ever Loving You	1966	—	3.00	6.00
40389	Evil on Your Mind/Ain't Had No Lovin'	1966	—	3.00	6.00

PROJECT 3

Number	Title (A Side/B Side)	Yr	VG	VG+	NM
#100	Come Follow the Band/(B-side unknown)	1982	—	2.00	4.00

SIGNATURE

Number	Title (A Side/B Side)	Yr	VG	VG+	NM
04654	The Pilgrim (Chapter #33)/School Days	1984	—	2.00	4.00
PB-10100	Am I Asking Too Much of You/Willie Burgundy	1974	—	2.00	4.00
PB-10173	Unliberated Woman/(B-side unknown)	1975	—	2.00	4.00
PB-10609	Music, Music, Music/Where Did the Good Times Go	1976	—	2.00	4.00

SSS INTERNATIONAL

Number	Title (A Side/B Side)	Yr	VG	VG+	NM
735	Live a Little/Step to the Rear	1968	—	2.50	5.00
744	Ride-A-Roo/A Woman's World	1968	—	2.50	5.00

TERESA BREWER

Number	Title (A Side/B Side)	Yr	VG	VG+	NM
TB-1 [DJ]	Take a Message to Jesus (same on both sides)	198?	—	2.00	4.00

7-Inch Extended Plays

CORAL

Number	Title (A Side/B Side)	Yr	VG	VG+	NM
EC 81008	(contents unknown)	195?	3.00	6.00	12.00
EC 81008 [PS]	Sing, Sing, Sing	195?	3.00	6.00	12.00
EC 81034	(contents unknown)	195?	3.00	6.00	12.00
EC 81034 [PS]	'Til I Waltz Again with You	195?	3.00	6.00	12.00
EC 81072	(contents unknown)	195?	3.00	6.00	12.00
EC 81072 [PS]	Teresa Brewer	195?	3.00	6.00	12.00
EC 81085	(contents unknown)	195?	3.00	6.00	12.00
EC 81085 [PS]	A Bouquet of Hits from Teresa Brewer, Part 1	195?	3.00	6.00	12.00
EC 81086	(contents unknown)	195?	3.00	6.00	12.00
EC 81086 [PS]	A Bouquet of Hits from Teresa Brewer, Part 2	195?	3.00	6.00	12.00
EC 81108	(contents unknown)	195?	3.00	6.00	12.00
EC 81108 [PS]	Teresa Brewer Favorites	195?	3.00	6.00	12.00
EC 81115	(contents unknown)	195?	3.00	6.00	12.00
EC 81115 [PS]	Rock Love	195?	3.00	6.00	12.00
EC 81162	(contents unknown)	195?	3.00	6.00	12.00
EC 81162 [PS]	Miss Music	195?	3.00	6.00	12.00
EC 81175	(contents unknown)	1959	3.00	6.00	12.00
EC 81175 [PS]	When Your Lover Has Gone	1959	3.00	6.00	12.00
EC 81176 [M]	(contents unknown)	1959	3.00	6.00	12.00
EC 81176 [PS]	Teresa Brewer and the Dixieland Band	1959	3.00	6.00	12.00
EC7-81176 [PS]	Teresa Brewer and the Dixieland Band	1959	5.00	10.00	20.00
EC7-81176 [S]	(contents unknown)	1959	5.00	10.00	20.00
EC 81178	(contents unknown)	195?	3.00	6.00	12.00
EC 81178 [PS]	Kiss Me	195?	3.00	6.00	12.00
EC 82023	(contents unknown)	195?	3.00	6.00	12.00
EC 82023 [PS]	Music, Music, Music	195?	3.00	6.00	12.00

LONDON

Number	Title (A Side/B Side)	Yr	VG	VG+	NM
BEP 6039	Music, Music, Music/Copenhagen/Honky Tonkin'/Ol' Man Mose	1952	5.00	10.00	20.00
BEP 6039 [PS]	Teresa Brewer	1952	5.00	10.00	20.00
BEP 6041	*The Jazz Me Blues/Longing for You/I Wish I Wuz/If You Don't Marry Me	1952	5.00	10.00	20.00
BEP 6041 [PS]	Teresa Brewer, Vol. 2	1952	5.00	10.00	20.00

RCA

Number	Title (A Side/B Side)	Yr	VG	VG+	NM
ZE-11882	Jingle Bells/Santa Claus Is Comin' to Town-The Christmas Song//Deck The Halls/Away in a Manger	1979	2.50	5.00	10.00

—Name of EP is "Merry Christmas From Teresa Brewer"; picture label, no PS

Albums

AMSTERDAM

Number	Title (A Side/B Side)	Yr	VG	VG+	NM
12012	The Doo Dah Song	1973	2.50	5.00	10.00
12013	Music, Music, Music	1973	2.50	5.00	10.00
12015	Teresa Brewer In London	1974	2.50	5.00	10.00

COLUMBIA

Number	Title (A Side/B Side)	Yr	VG	VG+	NM
FC 37363	A Sophisticated Lady	1981	2.50	5.00	10.00
PC 37363	A Sophisticated Lady	198?	2.00	4.00	8.00

—Budget-line reissue

CORAL

Number	Title (A Side/B Side)	Yr	VG	VG+	NM
CXB 7 [(2) M]	The Best of Teresa Brewer	1965	5.00	10.00	20.00
CXSB 7 [(2) P]	The Best of Teresa Brewer	1965	5.00	10.00	20.00
CRL 56072 [10]	A Bouquet of Hits	1952	10.00	20.00	40.00
CRL 56093 [10]	Till I Waltz Again with You	1953	10.00	20.00	40.00
CRL 57027 [M]	Music, Music, Music	1955	7.50	15.00	30.00
CRL 57053 [M]	Teresa	1956	7.50	15.00	30.00
CRL 57135 [M]	For Teenagers in Love	1957	7.50	15.00	30.00
CRL 57144 [M]	Teresa Brewer At Christmas Time	1957	7.50	15.00	30.00
CRL 57179 [M]	Miss Music	1958	7.50	15.00	30.00
CRL 57232 [M]	Time for Teresa	1958	7.50	15.00	30.00
CRL 57245 [M]	Teresa Brewer and the Dixieland Band	1958	5.00	10.00	20.00
CRL 57297 [M]	When Your Lover Has Gone	1959	5.00	10.00	20.00
CRL 57315 [M]	Ridin' High	1960	5.00	10.00	20.00
CRL 57329 [M]	Naughty, Naughty, Naughty	1960	5.00	10.00	20.00
CRL 57351 [M]	My Golden Favorites	1960	5.00	10.00	20.00
CRL 57361 [M]	Songs Everybody Knows	1961	5.00	10.00	20.00
CRL 57374 [M]	Aloha from Teresa	1961	5.00	10.00	20.00
CRL 57414 [M]	Don't Mess with Tess	1962	5.00	10.00	20.00
CRL 757245 [S]	Teresa Brewer and the Dixieland Band	1958	7.50	15.00	30.00
CRL 757297 [S]	When Your Lover Has Gone	1959	7.50	15.00	30.00
CRL 757315 [S]	Ridin' High	1960	6.25	12.50	25.00
CRL 757329 [S]	Naughty, Naughty, Naughty	1960	6.25	12.50	25.00
CRL 757351 [R]	My Golden Favorites	1960	5.00	10.00	20.00
CRL 757361 [S]	Songs Everybody Knows	1961	6.25	12.50	25.00
CRL 757374 [S]	Aloha from Teresa	1961	6.25	12.50	25.00
CRL 757414 [S]	Don't Mess with Tess	1962	6.25	12.50	25.00

DOCTOR JAZZ

Number	Title (A Side/B Side)	Yr	VG	VG+	NM
ASLP 804	Good News	198?	2.50	5.00	10.00
FW 38534	I Dig Big Band Singers	1983	2.50	5.00	10.00
W2X 39521 [(2)]	Live at Carnegie Hall and Montreux, Switzerland	1984	3.00	6.00	12.00
FW 40232	Midnight Café	1986	2.50	5.00	10.00
FW 40951	Good News	198?	2.00	4.00	8.00

FLYING DUTCHMAN

Number	Title (A Side/B Side)	Yr	VG	VG+	NM
BSL1-0577	Good News	1974	3.00	6.00	12.00

LONDON

Number	Title (A Side/B Side)	Yr	VG	VG+	NM
APB-1006 [10]	Teresa Brewer	1951	12.50	25.00	50.00

PHILIPS

Number	Title (A Side/B Side)	Yr	VG	VG+	NM
PHM 200062 [M]	Teresa Brewer's Greatest Hits	1962	3.75	7.50	15.00
PHM 200099 [M]	Terrific Teresa	1963	3.75	7.50	15.00
PHM 200119 [M]	Moments to Remember	1964	3.00	6.00	12.00
PHM 200147 [M]	Golden Hits of 1964	1964	3.00	6.00	12.00
PHM 200163 [M]	Dear Heart/Goldfinger	1965	3.00	6.00	12.00
PHM 200200 [M]	Songs for Our Fighting Men	1966	3.00	6.00	12.00
PHM 200216 [M]	Gold Country	1966	3.00	6.00	12.00
PHM 200230 [M]	Texas Leather and Mexican Lace	1967	3.75	7.50	15.00
PHS 600062 [S]	Teresa Brewer's Greatest Hits	1962	5.00	10.00	20.00
PHS 600099 [S]	Terrific Teresa	1963	5.00	10.00	20.00
PHS 600119 [S]	Moments to Remember	1964	3.75	7.50	15.00
PHS 600147 [S]	Golden Hits of 1964	1964	3.75	7.50	15.00

Number	Title (A Side/B Side)	Yr	VG	VG+	NM
PHS 600163 [S]	Dear Heart/Goldfinger	1965	3.75	7.50	15.00
PHS 600200 [S]	Songs for Our Fighting Men	1966	3.75	7.50	15.00
PHS 600216 [S]	Gold Country	1966	3.75	7.50	15.00
PHS 600230 [S]	Texas Leather and Mexican Lace	1967	3.00	6.00	12.00
PROJECT 3					
5108	Come Follow the Band	1982	2.50	5.00	10.00
RCA VICTOR					
ANL1-1131	The Best of Teresa Brewer	1975	2.50	5.00	10.00
SIGNATURE					
FW 39421	Teresa Brewer In London	1984	2.00	4.00	8.00
—Reissue of Amsterdam 12015					
PW 40113	Teresa Brewer At Christmas Time	1985	2.50	5.00	10.00
—Reissue of Coral 57144					
VOCALION					
VL 3693 [M]	Teresa Brewer	1966	3.00	6.00	12.00
VL 73847 [R]	Here's Teresa Brewer	1969	2.50	5.00	10.00

BREWER, TERESA, AND SVEND ASMUSSEN

Albums

Number	Title (A Side/B Side)	Yr	VG	VG+	NM
DOCTOR JAZZ					
FW 40233	On the Good Ship Lollipop	1987	2.50	5.00	10.00

BREWER, TERESA, AND COUNT BASIE

Also see each artist's individual listings.

Albums

Number	Title (A Side/B Side)	Yr	VG	VG+	NM
DOCTOR JAZZ					
FW 38836	Songs of Bessie Smith	1984	2.00	4.00	8.00
FLYING DUTCHMAN					
FD 10161	Songs of Bessie Smith	1973	3.00	6.00	12.00

BREWER, TERESA, AND DON CORNELL

Also see each artist's individual listings.

45s

Number	Title (A Side/B Side)	Yr	VG	VG+	NM
CORAL					
60829	You'll Never Get Away/The Hookey Song	1952	3.00	6.00	12.00
61027	The Glad Song/What Happened to the Music	1953	3.00	6.00	12.00

7-Inch Extended Plays

Number	Title (A Side/B Side)	Yr	VG	VG+	NM
CORAL					
EC 81073	(contents unknown)	195?	3.00	6.00	12.00
EC 81073 [PS]	Don Cornell and Teresa Brewer	195?	3.00	6.00	12.00

BREWER, TERESA, AND MERCER ELLINGTON

Albums

Number	Title (A Side/B Side)	Yr	VG	VG+	NM
DOCTOR JAZZ					
FW 40031	The Cotton Connection	1985	2.50	5.00	10.00

BREWER, TERESA, AND STEPHANE GRAPPELLI

Albums

Number	Title (A Side/B Side)	Yr	VG	VG+	NM
DOCTOR JAZZ					
FW 38448	On the Road Again	198?	2.50	5.00	10.00

BREWER AND SHIPLEY

45s

Number	Title (A Side/B Side)	Yr	VG	VG+	NM
A&M					
905	The Keeper of the Keys/I Can't See Her	1968	2.00	4.00	8.00
—Artist reads "Michael Brewer and Tom Shipley"					
938	Green Bamboo/Truly Right	1968	2.00	4.00	8.00
—Artist reads "Michael Brewer and Tom Shipley"					
996	Dreamin' in the Shade/Tame and Changes	1968	2.00	4.00	8.00
BUDDAH					
154	Rise Up Easy Rider/Boomerang	1970	—	2.00	4.00
CAPITOL					
3933	Fair Play/How Are You	1974	—	2.00	4.00
4105	Brain Damage/Rock and Roll Hostage	1975	—	2.00	4.00
KAMA SUTRA					
512	People Love Each Other/Witchi-Tai-To	1970	—	2.00	4.00
516	One Toke Over the Line/Oh Mommy	1970	—	2.50	5.00
524	Tarkio Road/Seems Like a Long Time	1971	—	2.00	4.00
539	Shake Off the Demon/Indian Summer	1972	—	2.00	4.00
547	Natural Child/Yankee Lady	1972	—	2.00	4.00
567	Black Sky/Fly, Fly Fly	1972	—	2.00	4.00

Albums

Number	Title (A Side/B Side)	Yr	VG	VG+	NM
A&M					
SP-4154	Down in L.A.	1968	3.75	7.50	15.00
CAPITOL					
ST-11261	ST-11261	1974	2.50	5.00	10.00
ST-11402	Welcome to Riddle Bridge	1975	2.50	5.00	10.00
KAMA SUTRA					
KSBS-2016	Weeds	1969	3.00	6.00	12.00
KSBS-2024	Tarkio	1970	3.00	6.00	12.00
KSBS-2039	Shake Off the Demon	1971	3.00	6.00	12.00
KSBS-2058	Rural Space	1972	3.00	6.00	12.00

BRIDGE, THE

See THE BROOKLYN BRIDGE.

BRIGADE, THE

Albums

Number	Title (A Side/B Side)	Yr	VG	VG+	NM
BAND'N VOCAL					
1066	Last Laugh	1970	1000.	1500.	2000.

BRIGADIERS, THE

45s

Number	Title (A Side/B Side)	Yr	VG	VG+	NM
MALA					
441	The Cry of the Wild Goose/Dixie Brigade	1961	5.00	10.00	20.00

BRIGANDS, THE

45s

Number	Title (A Side/B Side)	Yr	VG	VG+	NM
EPIC					
10011	(Would I Still Be) Her Big Man/I'm a Patient Man	1966	5.00	10.00	20.00

BRIGG

Albums

Number	Title (A Side/B Side)	Yr	VG	VG+	NM
SUSQUEHANNA					
LP-301	Brigg	1973	45.00	90.00	180.00

BRIGGS, LILLIAN

45s

Number	Title (A Side/B Side)	Yr	VG	VG+	NM
ABC-PARAMOUNT					
10253	I Want You to Be My Baby/I'm Burning for You	1961	2.50	5.00	10.00
CORAL					
62108	Rag Mop/Smile for the People	1959	2.50	5.00	10.00
62136	Blues in the Night/Is There a Man in the House	1959	2.50	5.00	10.00
62156	Hooray for the Rock/Diddy Boppers	1959	2.50	5.00	10.00
62193	Be Mine/Not a Soul	1960	2.50	5.00	10.00
62223	I Care for You/That's What It's Like to Be Lonesome	1960	2.50	5.00	10.00
EPIC					
9115	I Want You to Be My Baby/Don't Stay Away Too Long	1955	7.50	15.00	30.00
9120	Give Me a Band and My Baby/It Could've Been Me	1955	7.50	15.00	30.00
9138	Rock and Roll-y Poly Santa Claus/Can't Stop	1955	7.50	15.00	30.00
9141	Follow the Leader/That's the Only Way to Live	1956	5.00	10.00	20.00
9151	Eddie, My Love/Teens in Jeans from New Orleans	1956	5.00	10.00	20.00
9166	The Gypsy Goofed/Too Close for Comfort	1956	5.00	10.00	20.00
9190	I'll Be Gone/Mean Words	1956	5.00	10.00	20.00
9214	Sugar Blues/Boogie Blues	1957	3.75	7.50	15.00
9249	She Sells Sea Shells/I	1957	3.75	7.50	15.00
SUNBEAM					
104	Come Home/Till We Meet Again	1958	3.00	6.00	12.00
114	Hey Ba Ba Re Bop/I've Got Your Heart	1958	3.00	6.00	12.00

7-Inch Extended Plays

Number	Title (A Side/B Side)	Yr	VG	VG+	NM
EPIC					
B-7163	(contents unknown)	1956	10.00	20.00	40.00
B-7163 [PS]	High Priestess of Rock 'n' Roll	1956	10.00	20.00	40.00

BRIGHTONES, THE

45s

Number	Title (A Side/B Side)	Yr	VG	VG+	NM
WARNER BROS.					
5472	Swim, Swim, Swim/Rumors	1964	5.00	10.00	20.00

BRIGMAN, GEORGE

Albums

Number	Title (A Side/B Side)	Yr	VG	VG+	NM
SOLID					
SR-001	Jungle Rot	1975	30.00	60.00	120.00

BRIKS, THE

45s

Number	Title (A Side/B Side)	Yr	VG	VG+	NM
BISMARK					
1013	Foolish Baby/Can You See Me	1966	50.00	100.00	200.00
DOT					
16876	Foolish Baby/Can You See Me	1966	6.25	12.50	25.00

BRIMSTONE

Albums

Number	Title (A Side/B Side)	Yr	VG	VG+	NM
BRIMSTONE					
(no #)	Paper Winged Dreams	1968	50.00	100.00	200.00

BRIMSTONES, THE

45s

Number	Title (A Side/B Side)	Yr	VG	VG+	NM
MGM					
13653	It's All Over But the Crying/What Is This Life	1966	5.00	10.00	20.00
WORLD PACIFIC					
77834	Cold Hearted Woman/I'm in Misery	1966	7.50	15.00	30.00

BRINSLEY SCHWARZ

Featuring Nick Lowe and Ian Gomm.

45s

Number	Title (A Side/B Side)	Yr	VG	VG+	NM
CAPITOL					
3004	Rock and Roll Women/Hymn to Be	1970	2.00	4.00	8.00
UNITED ARTISTS					
50915	Nightingale/Silver Pistol	1972	—	3.00	6.00
50976	Nervous on the Road/Happy Doing What We're Doing	1972	—	3.00	6.00

Albums

Number	Title (A Side/B Side)	Yr	VG	VG+	NM
CAPITOL					
ST-589	Brinsley Schwarz	1970	5.00	10.00	20.00
ST-744	Despite It All	1971	5.00	10.00	20.00
SWBC-11869 [(2)]	Brinsley Schwarz	1978	3.75	7.50	15.00
LIBERTY					
LN 10145	Silver Pistol	1980	2.50	5.00	10.00
—10-track reissue					
LN 10146	Nervous on the Road	1981	2.50	5.00	10.00
—10-track reissue					
UNITED ARTISTS					
UAS-5566	Silver Pistol	1972	3.75	7.50	15.00
UAS-5647	Nervous on the Road	1972	3.75	7.50	15.00

BRISTOL, JOHNNY

Also see JOHNNY AND JACKIE.

45s

Number	Title (A Side/B Side)	Yr	VG	VG+	NM
ATLANTIC					
3360	Do It to My Mind/Love to Take a Chance to Taste the Wine	1976	—	2.00	4.00
3391	I Sho Like Groovin' with You/You Turn Me On to Love	1977	—	2.00	4.00
3421	Waiting on Love/She's So Amazing	1977	—	2.00	4.00
3501	When He Comes (You Will Know)/Strangers in the Dark Corners	1978	—	2.00	4.00

Number	Title (A Side/B Side)	Yr	VG	VG+	NM
3526	Why Stop Now/When He Comes (You Will Know)	1978	—	2.00	4.00
HANDSHAKE					
02594	Take Me Down/Loving and Free	1981	—	2.00	4.00
5300	My Guy/My Girl//(B-side unknown)	1980	—	2.00	4.00
—With Amii Stewart					
5304	Love No Longer Has a Hold on Me/(B-side unknown)	1981	—	2.00	4.00
MGM					
14715	Hang On In There Baby/Take Care of You for Me	1974	—	2.50	5.00
14762	You and I/It Don't Hurt No More	1974	—	2.50	5.00
14792	Leave My World/All Goodbyes Aren't Good	1975	—	2.50	5.00
14814	Love Takes Tears/Go On and Dream	1975	—	2.50	5.00
POLYDOR					
813982-7	Hang On In There Baby/Stand By Me	1983	—	—	3.00
—Reissue					
Albums					
ATLANTIC					
SD 18197	Bristol's Creme	1976	2.50	5.00	10.00
SD 19184	Strangers	1978	2.50	5.00	10.00
HANDSHAKE					
FW 37666	Free to Be Me	1981	2.50	5.00	10.00
MGM					
M3G-4959	Hang On In There Baby	1974	3.00	6.00	12.00
M3G-4983	Feeling the Magic	1975	3.00	6.00	12.00

BRITISH CASUALS, THE

See THE CASUALS (3).

BROGUES, THE

Two members became part of QUICKSILVER MESSENGER SERVICE.

Number	Title (A Side/B Side)	Yr	VG	VG+	NM
45s					
CHALLENGE					
59311	But Now I'm Fine/Someday	1965	7.50	15.00	30.00
59316	I Ain't No Miracle Worker/Don't Shoot Me Down	1965	7.50	15.00	30.00
TWILIGHT					
408	But Now I'm Fine/Someday	1965	10.00	20.00	40.00
408	But Now I'm Fine/Early Bird	1965	10.00	20.00	40.00

BROMBERG, DAVID

Number	Title (A Side/B Side)	Yr	VG	VG+	NM
45s					
COLUMBIA					
45612	The Holdup/Suffer to Sing the Blues	1972	—	3.00	6.00
45767	Sharon/Hardworkin' John	1973	2.00	4.00	8.00
FANTASY					
785	Such a Night/Bluebirds	1977	—	2.00	4.00
812	Battle of Bull Run Medley/I Want to Go Home	1978	—	2.00	4.00
854	Don't Let Your Deal Go Down/My Own House	1979	—	2.00	4.00
Albums					
COLUMBIA					
C 31104	David Bromberg	1972	3.00	6.00	12.00
PC 31104	David Bromberg	198?	2.00	4.00	8.00
—Budget-line reissue					
KC 31753	Demon in Disguise	1973	3.00	6.00	12.00
PC 31753	Demon in Disguise	198?	2.00	4.00	8.00
—Budget-line reissue					
KC 32717	Wanted Dead or Alive	1974	3.00	6.00	12.00
PC 33397	Midnight on the Water	1975	3.00	6.00	12.00
—Original with no bar code					
PC 33397	Midnight on the Water	198?	2.00	4.00	8.00
—Budget-line reissue with bar code					
PC 34467	The Best of David Bromberg: Out of the Blues	1976	3.00	6.00	12.00
—Original with no bar code					
PC 34467	The Best of David Bromberg: Out of the Blues	198?	2.00	4.00	8.00
—Budget-line reissue with bar code					
FANTASY					
9540	Reckless Abandon	1977	3.00	6.00	12.00
9555	Bandit in a Bathing Suit	1978	2.50	5.00	10.00
9572	My Own House	1979	2.50	5.00	10.00
9590	You Should See the Rest of the Band	1980	2.50	5.00	10.00
79007 [(2)]	How Late'll Ya Play 'Til?	1976	3.75	7.50	15.00
ROUNDER					
3110	Sideman Serenade	1989	3.00	6.00	12.00

BRONZETTES, THE

Number	Title (A Side/B Side)	Yr	VG	VG+	NM
45s					
PARKWAY					
929	Hot Spot/Run, Run, You Little Fool	1964	3.00	6.00	12.00

BROOKLYN BRIDGE, THE

Also see JOHNNY MAESTRO.

Number	Title (A Side/B Side)	Yr	VG	VG+	NM
45s					
BUDDAH					
60	Little Red Boat by the River/From My Window	1968	—	3.00	6.00
75	Worst That Could Happen/Your Kite, My Kite	1968	2.00	4.00	8.00
95	Welcome Me Love/Blessed Is the Rain	1969	—	3.00	6.00
126	Your Husband, My Wife/Upside Down	1969	—	3.00	6.00
139	You'll Never Walk Alone/Minstrel Sunday	1969	—	3.00	6.00
162	Free as the Wind/He's Not a Happy Man	1970	—	3.00	6.00
179	Down by the River/Look Again	1970	—	3.00	6.00
193	Day Is Done/Opposites	1970	—	3.00	6.00
193	Day Is Done/Easy Way	1970	—	3.00	6.00
199	Nights in White Satin/Cynthia	1971	2.00	4.00	8.00
230	Wednesday in Your Garden (mono/stereo)	1971	2.00	4.00	8.00
—Stock copy unknown					
293	Man in a Band/Bruno's Place	1972	2.00	4.00	8.00
317	I Feel Free (mono/stereo)	1972	2.50	5.00	10.00
—As "The Bridge"; stock copy unknown					
COLLECTABLES					
3997	Have Yourself A Merry Little Christmas/A Christmas Long Ago (Jingle Jingle)	199?	—	—	3.00
—As "Johnny Maestro and the Brooklyn Bridge"; B-side by the Echelons					
Albums					
BUDDAH					
BDS-5034	Brooklyn Bridge	1969	5.00	10.00	20.00
BDS-5042	The Second Brooklyn Bridge	1969	5.00	10.00	20.00
BDS-5065	The Brooklyn Bridge	1970	5.00	10.00	20.00
BDS-5107	Bridge in Blue	1972	5.00	10.00	20.00
COLLECTABLES					
COL-5015	The Greatest Hits	198?	3.00	6.00	12.00
—As "Johnny Maestro and the Brooklyn Bridge"					

BROOKS, CHUCK, AND THE SHARPIES

Number	Title (A Side/B Side)	Yr	VG	VG+	NM
45s					
DUB					
2844	Spinning My Wheels/You Make Me Feel Mean	1958	75.00	150.00	300.00

BROOKS, DONNIE

Number	Title (A Side/B Side)	Yr	VG	VG+	NM
45s					
CHALLENGE					
59331	I Call Your Name/Be Fair	1966	2.00	4.00	8.00
59344	Pink Carousel/Mission Man	1966	2.00	4.00	8.00
ERA					
3004	Lil' Sweetheart/If You're Lookin'	1959	5.00	10.00	20.00
3007	White Orchid/Sway and Move with the Beat	1959	5.00	10.00	20.00
3014	The Devil Ain't a Man/How Long	1960	5.00	10.00	20.00
3018	Mission Bell/Do It for Me	1960	5.00	10.00	20.00
3028	Doll House/Round Robin	1960	3.75	7.50	15.00
3028 [PS]	Doll House/Round Robin	1960	6.25	12.50	25.00
3042	Memphis/That's Why	1961	3.75	7.50	15.00
3042 [PS]	Memphis/That's Why	1961	6.25	12.50	25.00
3049	All I Can Give/Wishbone	1961	3.75	7.50	15.00
3052	Boomerang/How Long	1961	3.75	7.50	15.00
3059	Sweet Lorraine/Up to My Ears in Tears	1961	3.75	7.50	15.00
3063	Goodnight Judy/Your Little Boy's Gone Home	1961	3.75	7.50	15.00
3071	My Favorite Kind of Face/He Stole Flo	1962	3.75	7.50	15.00
3077	Oh You Beautiful Doll/Just a Bystander	1962	3.75	7.50	15.00
3095	Cries My Heart/It's Not That Easy	1962	3.75	7.50	15.00
3194	Blue Soldier/Love Is Funny That Way	1968	2.00	4.00	8.00
HAPPY TIGER					
526	Abracadabra/I Know You as a Woman	1970	—	2.50	5.00
544	Hush/I Know You as a Woman	1970	—	2.50	5.00
551	My God and I/Pink Carousel	1970	—	2.50	5.00
566	(I Wanna) Have You for Myself/Rub-a-Dub-Dub	1971	—	2.50	5.00
579	I'm Gonna Make You Love Me/Pink Carousel	1971	—	2.50	5.00
MIDSONG INT'L.					
1007	Big John/Get Fame, Son	1978	—	2.00	4.00
OAK					
1019	The Song That I Sing Is For You/Country Dude	1971	—	2.50	5.00
REPRISE					
0261	Gone/Girl Machine	1964	2.50	5.00	10.00
0311	Can't Help Lovin' You/Pickin' Up the Pieces	1964	2.50	5.00	10.00
0363	Hey, Little Girl/I Never Get to Love You	1965	2.50	5.00	10.00
YARDBIRD					
8006	Sunglasses on the Sand/Sunshine, Summertime and Love	1968	—	3.00	6.00
8008	Hush/Sunshine, Summertime and Love	1968	—	3.00	6.00
8010	Tree Trimming Time/(Instrumental)	1968	—	3.00	6.00
Albums					
ERA					
EL-105 [M]	The Happiest	1961	37.50	75.00	150.00

BROOKS, DUSTY, AND HIS TONES WITH JUANITA BROWN

Number	Title (A Side/B Side)	Yr	VG	VG+	NM
45s					
SUN					
182	Heaven or Fire/Tears and Wine	1953	1500.	2250.	3000.

BROOKS, ELKIE

Number	Title (A Side/B Side)	Yr	VG	VG+	NM
45s					
A&M					
1781	Where Do We Go from Here (Rich Man's Woman)/Roll Me Over	1976	—	2.50	5.00
1935	You Did Something for Me/Pearl's a Singer	1977	—	2.50	5.00
1953	Sunshine After the Rain/You Did Something for Me	1977	—	2.50	5.00
1968	Love Potion No. 9/Honey, Can I Put On Your Clothes	1977	—	2.50	5.00
2068	Since You Went Away/Too Precious	1978	—	2.00	4.00
2271	Paint Your Pretty Pictures/Pull On the Rope	1980	—	2.00	4.00
PARROT					
9699	Nothin' Left to Do But Cry/Strange Tho It Seems	1964	2.50	5.00	10.00
Albums					
A&M					
SP-4554	Rich Man's Woman	1975	2.50	5.00	10.00
SP-4631	Two Days Away	1977	2.50	5.00	10.00
SP-4695	Shooting Star	1977	2.50	5.00	10.00

BROOKS BROTHERS, THE

Number	Title (A Side/B Side)	Yr	VG	VG+	NM
45s					
LONDON					
1987	Warpaint/Sometimes	1961	3.75	7.50	15.00
9668	Once in Awhile/Poor Plan	1964	2.50	5.00	10.00
—As "The Brooks"					
LONDON INT'L.					
10501	Ain't Gonna Wash for a Week/One Last Kiss	1962	3.00	6.00	12.00
10515	Too Scared/Tell Tale	1962	3.00	6.00	12.00

BROONZY, BIG BILL

Number	Title (A Side/B Side)	Yr	VG	VG+	NM
45s					
CHESS					
1546	Little City Woman/Lonesome	1953	100.00	200.00	400.00

Number	Title (A Side/B Side)	Yr	VG	VG+	NM
MERCURY					
8160	You've Been Mistreating Me/I Stay Blue All the Time	1951	7.50	15.00	30.00
—Released on 78 in 1949					
8261	Willie Mae Blues/Hollerin' the Blues	1951	7.50	15.00	30.00
8271	Hey Hey/Walkin' the Lonesome Road	1952	7.50	15.00	30.00
8284	Mopper's Blues/I Know She Will	1952	7.50	15.00	30.00
70039	South Bound Train/Leavin' Day	1953	6.25	12.50	25.00
71352	Tomorrow/Hey Hey	1958	5.00	10.00	20.00
Albums					
ARCHIVE OF FOLK AND JAZZ					
213	Big Bill Broonzy	1967	3.00	6.00	12.00
BIOGRAPH					
C-15	Big Bill Broonzy 1932-1942	197?	2.50	5.00	10.00
CHESS					
LP-1468 [M]	Big Bill Broonzy and Washboard Sam	1962	40.00	80.00	160.00
COLUMBIA					
WL 111 [M]	Big Bill's Blues	1958	25.00	50.00	100.00
DIAL					
LP-306 [10]	Blues Concert	1952	37.50	75.00	150.00
EMARCY					
MG-26034 [10]	Folk Blues	1954	30.00	60.00	120.00
MG-36137 [M]	Blues by Broonzy	1958	25.00	50.00	100.00
EPIC					
EE 22017 [M]	Big Bill's Blues	196?	5.00	10.00	20.00
FOLKWAYS					
FA-2315 [M]	Big Bill Broonzy	1957	12.50	25.00	50.00
FA-2326 [M]	Country Blues	1957	12.50	25.00	50.00
FG-3586 [M]	His Songs and Story	195?	12.50	25.00	50.00
31005 [R]	Big Bill Sings Country Blues	196?	3.75	7.50	15.00
GNP CRESCENDO					
10004	Feeling Low Down	1974	2.50	5.00	10.00
10009	Lonesome Road Blues	1975	2.50	5.00	10.00
MERCURY					
MG-20822 [M]	Big Bill Broonzy — Memorial	1963	7.50	15.00	30.00
MG-20905 [M]	Remembering Big Bill Broonzy	1964	7.50	15.00	30.00
SR-60822 [R]	Big Bill Broonzy — Memorial	1963	5.00	10.00	20.00
SR-60905 [R]	Remembering Big Bill Broonzy	1964	5.00	10.00	20.00
PERIOD					
SLP-1114 [M]	Big Bill Broonzy Sings (Blues)	1956	37.50	75.00	150.00
SLP-1209 [M]	Big Bill Broonzy Sings and Josh White Comes a-Visiting	1958	17.50	35.00	70.00
PORTRAIT MASTERS					
RJ 44089	Big Bill's Blues	1988	3.75	7.50	15.00
—Reissue of Columbia 111					
SMITHSONIAN FOLKWAYS					
SF-40023	Big Bill Broonzy Sings Folk Songs	1989	3.00	6.00	12.00
VERVE					
MGV-3000-5 [(5) M]	The Big Bill Broonzy Story	1959	50.00	100.00	200.00
MGV-3001 [M]	Last Session, Vol. 1	1959	12.50	25.00	50.00
MGV-3002 [M]	Last Session, Vol. 2	1959	12.50	25.00	50.00
MGV-3003 [M]	Last Session, Vol. 3	1959	12.50	25.00	50.00
YAZOO					
L-1011	The Young Big Bill Broonzy	1969	3.75	7.50	15.00
L-1035	Do That Guitar Rag	197?	3.75	7.50	15.00

BROTH

Number	Title (A Side/B Side)	Yr	VG	VG+	NM
Albums					
MERCURY					
SR-61298	Broth	1970	5.00	10.00	20.00

BROTHER FOX AND TAR BABY

Number	Title (A Side/B Side)	Yr	VG	VG+	NM
45s					
CAPITOL					
2940	Electric Chair/Steel Dog Man	1970	2.50	5.00	10.00
Albums					
CAPITOL					
ST-544	Brother Fox and Tar Baby	1970	7.50	15.00	30.00
ORACLE					
1001	Brother Fox and Tar Baby	1969	7.50	15.00	30.00

BROTHER SISTERS, THE

Number	Title (A Side/B Side)	Yr	VG	VG+	NM
45s					
MERCURY					
71195	Alone (Why Must I Be Alone)/Pass Me the Mustard	1957	5.00	10.00	20.00
71678	Strawberry Shortcake/Crystal Ball	1960	5.00	10.00	20.00

BROTHERHOOD OF MAN, THE

Number	Title (A Side/B Side)	Yr	VG	VG+	NM
45s					
BELL					
45456	When Love Catches Up on You/(B-side unknown)	1974	—	2.00	4.00
DERAM					
85056	Love One Another/A Little Bit of Heaven	1970	—	3.00	6.00
85059	United We Stand/Say a Prayer	1970	—	3.00	6.00
85065	Where Are You Going To My Love/Living in the Land of Love	1970	—	2.50	5.00
85070	This Boy/You Can Depend on Me	1971	—	2.50	5.00
85073	Reach Out Your Hand/A Better Tomorrow	1971	—	2.50	5.00
85077	Sing in the Sunshine/You and I	1971	—	2.50	5.00
85078	California Sunday Morning/Do Your Thing	1972	—	2.50	5.00
85081	Say a Prayer/Follow Me	1972	—	2.50	5.00
MERCURY					
882118-7	United We Stand/My Baby Loves Lovin'	1986	—	2.00	4.00
—Reissue; B-side by White Plains					
PRIVATE STOCK					
45148	Oh Boy (The Mood I'm In)	1977	—	2.00	4.00
45165	Angelo/All Night	1977	—	2.00	4.00
PYE					
70176	Sweet Lady from Georgia/Sugar Honey Love	1976	—	2.00	4.00
71043	Spring of 1912/(B-side unknown)	1976	—	2.00	4.00
71066	Save Your Kisses for Me/Let's Love Together	1976	—	2.00	4.00
Albums					
DERAM					
DES 18046	United We Stand	1970	3.75	7.50	15.00

BROTHERS, THE

Number	Title (A Side/B Side)	Yr	VG	VG+	NM
45s					
ARGO					
5318	Lazy Susan/Deep Sleep	1958	5.00	10.00	20.00
5329	Sioux City Sue/Deep Sleep	1959	5.00	10.00	20.00
CHECKER					
995	My True Love/One Lonely Heart	1961	3.75	7.50	15.00

BROTHERS CAIN, THE

Number	Title (A Side/B Side)	Yr	VG	VG+	NM
45s					
ACTA					
810	Better Times/Pupil Alexander	1967	6.25	12.50	25.00
820	It Sure Is Groovy/Anyway You Like It	1968	6.25	12.50	25.00
MERCURY					
72437	In Love with One/Two Wrongs	1965	6.25	12.50	25.00

BROTHERS FOUR, THE

Number	Title (A Side/B Side)	Yr	VG	VG+	NM
45s					
COLUMBIA					
31089 [S]	(contents unknown)	1961	3.00	6.00	12.00
31090 [S]	(contents unknown)	1961	3.00	6.00	12.00
31091 [S]	(contents unknown)	1961	3.00	6.00	12.00
31092 [S]	(contents unknown)	1961	3.00	6.00	12.00
31093 [S]	(contents unknown)	1961	3.00	6.00	12.00
—Anyone who can fill in these gaps -- the above 5 all are Columbia "Stereo 7" singles -- please let us know.					
41461	Chicka Mucha Hi Di/Darlin' Won't You Wait	1959	2.50	5.00	10.00
41571	Greenfields/Angelique-O	1960	2.00	4.00	8.00
41571 [PS]	Greenfields/Angelique-O	1960	3.00	6.00	12.00
41692	My Tani/Ellie Lou	1960	2.00	4.00	8.00
41692 [PS]	My Tani/Ellie Lou	1960	3.00	6.00	12.00
41808	The Green Leaves of Summer/Beautiful Brown Eyes	1960	2.00	4.00	8.00
41808 [PS]	The Green Leaves of Summer/Beautiful Brown Eyes	1960	3.00	6.00	12.00
41958	Frogg/Sweet Rosyanne	1961	2.00	4.00	8.00
41958 [PS]	Frogg/Sweet Rosyanne	1961	3.00	6.00	12.00
42142	My Woman Left Me/Nobody Knows	1961	2.00	4.00	8.00
42235	What Child Is This/Christmas Bells	1961	2.50	5.00	10.00
42256	Blue Water Line/Summer Days Alone	1962	2.00	4.00	8.00
42256 [PS]	Blue Water Line/Summer Days Alone	1962	3.00	6.00	12.00
42391	Darlin' Sporty Jenny/Slowly, Slowly	1962	2.00	4.00	8.00
42450	This Train/Summertime	1962	2.00	4.00	8.00
42586	The Tavern Song/25 Minutes to Go	1962	2.00	4.00	8.00
42756	Ringing Bells/Welcome Home Sally	1963	2.00	4.00	8.00
42787	55 Days at Peking/All for the Love of a Girl	1963	2.00	4.00	8.00
42888	Four Strong Winds/John B. Sails	1963	2.00	4.00	8.00
42927	Hootenanny Saturday Night/Across the Sea	1963	2.00	4.00	8.00
43025	Seven Daffodils/San Francisco Bay Blues	1964	2.00	4.00	8.00
43147	Take This Hammer/Little Play Soldier	1964	2.00	4.00	8.00
43211	Somewhere/Turn Around	1965	—	3.00	6.00
43317	Come Kiss Me Love/Lazy Harry's	1965	—	3.00	6.00
43404	Try to Remember/Sakura	1965	—	3.00	6.00
43493	It Was a Very Good Year/Wild Colonial Boy	1965	—	3.00	6.00
43547	Ratman and Bobbin in the Clipper Caper/Muleskinner	1966	3.75	7.50	15.00
43621	Nowhere Man/If I Fell	1966	2.50	5.00	10.00
43825	Changes/For Emily, Whenever I May Find Her	1966	—	3.00	6.00
43919	I'll Be Home for Christmas/'Twas the Night Before Christmas	1966	2.00	4.00	8.00
43984	All I Need Is You/And Then the Sun Came Down	1967	—	3.00	6.00
44058	Ain't No More Cane on the Brazos/Shenandoah	1967	—	3.00	6.00
44175	The First Time Ever/Walkin' Backwards Down the Road	1967	—	3.00	6.00
44278	Here Today and Gone Tomorrow/No Sad Songs from Me	1967	—	3.00	6.00
44578	I'm Falling Down/Sweet Dreams, Sweet Runaway Child	1968	—	2.50	5.00
44832	Skip a Rope/Strangest Dream	1969	—	2.50	5.00
FANTASY					
640	Going Back to Big Sur/Here I Go Again	1970	—	2.50	5.00
Albums					
COLUMBIA					
CL 1402 [M]	The Brothers Four	1960	3.00	6.00	12.00
CL 1479 [M]	Rally 'Round the Brothers Four	1960	3.00	6.00	12.00
CL 1578 [M]	B.M.O.C. (Best Music On/Off Campus)	1961	3.00	6.00	12.00
CL 1625 [M]	Roamin'	1961	3.00	6.00	12.00
CL 1697 [M]	The Brothers Four Song Book	1961	3.00	6.00	12.00
CL 1803 [M]	The Brothers Four's Greatest Hits	1962	3.00	6.00	12.00
CL 1828 [M]	The Brothers Four: In Person	1962	3.00	6.00	12.00
CL 1946 [M]	Cross Country Concert	1963	3.00	6.00	12.00
CL 2033 [M]	The Big Folk Hits	1963	3.00	6.00	12.00
CL 2128 [M]	The Brothers Four Sing of Our Times	1964	3.00	6.00	12.00
CL 2213 [M]	More Big Folk Hits	1964	3.00	6.00	12.00
CL 2305 [M]	The Honey Wind Blows	1965	3.00	6.00	12.00
CL 2379 [M]	Try to Remember	1965	3.00	6.00	12.00
CL 2502 [M]	A Beatles' Songbook (The Brothers Four Sing Lennon/McCartney)	1966	3.75	7.50	15.00
CL 2702 [M]	A New World's Record	1967	3.75	7.50	15.00
CS 8197 [S]	The Brothers Four	1960	3.75	7.50	15.00
CS 8270 [S]	Rally 'Round the Brothers Four	1960	3.75	7.50	15.00
CS 8378 [S]	B.M.O.C. (Best Music On/Off Campus)	1961	3.75	7.50	15.00
CS 8425 [S]	Roamin'	1961	3.75	7.50	15.00
CS 8497 [S]	The Brothers Four Song Book	1961	3.75	7.50	15.00
CS 8603	The Brothers Four's Greatest Hits	1970	2.50	5.00	10.00
—Orange label					
CS 8603 [S]	The Brothers Four's Greatest Hits	1962	3.75	7.50	15.00
—Red "360 Sound" label					

Number	Title (A Side/B Side)	Yr	VG	VG+	NM
PC 8603	The Brothers Four's Greatest Hits	198?	2.00	4.00	8.00
—Reissue with new prefix					
CS 8628 [S]	The Brothers Four: In Person	1962	3.75	7.50	15.00
CS 8746 [S]	Cross Country Concert	1963	3.75	7.50	15.00
CS 8833 [S]	The Big Folk Hits	1963	3.75	7.50	15.00
CS 8928 [S]	The Brothers Four Sing of Our Times	1964	3.75	7.50	15.00
CS 9013 [S]	More Big Folk Hits	1964	3.75	7.50	15.00
CS 9105 [S]	The Honey Wind Blows	1965	3.75	7.50	15.00
CS 9179 [S]	Try to Remember	1965	3.75	7.50	15.00
CS 9302 [S]	A Beatles' Songbook (The Brothers Four Sing Lennon/McCartney)	1966	5.00	10.00	20.00
CS 9502 [S]	A New World's Record	1967	3.00	6.00	12.00
CS 9818	Let's Get Together	1969	3.00	6.00	12.00
FANTASY					
8400	The Brothers Four 1970	1970	2.50	5.00	10.00
FIRST AMERICAN					
7705	The Brothers Four Now	1978	2.50	5.00	10.00
7722 [(2)]	Greenfields and Other Gold	1980	3.00	6.00	12.00
7728	New Gold	1981	2.50	5.00	10.00
HARMONY					
HS 11341	Four Strong Winds	1969	2.50	5.00	10.00
H 31505	Great Songs of Our Times	1972	2.50	5.00	10.00

BROTHERS GRIMM, THE

45s

Number	Title (A Side/B Side)	Yr	VG	VG+	NM
MERCURY					
72512	A Man Needs Love/Looky, Looky	1966	2.50	5.00	10.00

BROWN, AL

45s

Number	Title (A Side/B Side)	Yr	VG	VG+	NM
AMY					
804	The Madison/Mo' Madison	1960	6.25	12.50	25.00
806	It's True 'Bout Love/Sweet Little Love	1960	5.00	10.00	20.00
811	Take Me Back/Mention Me	1960	5.00	10.00	20.00
829	Route 66/Shimmy Swing	1961	5.00	10.00	20.00

Albums

Number	Title (A Side/B Side)	Yr	VG	VG+	NM
AMY					
A-1 [M]	Madison Dance Party	1960	10.00	20.00	40.00
AS-1 [S]	Madison Dance Party	1960	12.50	25.00	50.00

BROWN, ARTHUR, THE CRAZY WORLD OF

45s

Number	Title (A Side/B Side)	Yr	VG	VG+	NM
ATLANTIC					
2556	Fire/Rest Cure	1968	2.50	5.00	10.00
MERCURY					
873504-7	Fire/Rest Cure	1990	—	—	3.00
—Reissue					
TRACK					
2582	I Put a Spell on You/Nightmare	1968	2.00	4.00	8.00

Albums

Number	Title (A Side/B Side)	Yr	VG	VG+	NM
GULL					
GU6-405	Dance	1975	3.00	6.00	12.00
PASSPORT					
98003	Journey	1974	3.00	6.00	12.00
TRACK					
SD 8198	The Crazy World of Arthur Brown	1968	6.25	12.50	25.00

BROWN, BILLY

45s

Number	Title (A Side/B Side)	Yr	VG	VG+	NM
CHALLENGE					
59396	One of the Ten Most Wanted Women/Open Arms	1969	2.00	4.00	8.00
COLUMBIA					
41029	Did We Have a Party/It's Love	1957	10.00	20.00	40.00
41100	Meet Me in the Alley, Sally/I Wanted You	1958	12.50	25.00	50.00
41297	Flip Out/Echo Mountain	1958	10.00	20.00	40.00
41380	Run 'Em Off/He'll Have to Go	1959	10.00	20.00	40.00
DECCA					
29559	Drunk-Drunk Again/High Heels But No Soul	1955	5.00	10.00	20.00
REPUBLIC					
2004	The Last Letter/Be Honest with Me	1960	3.75	7.50	15.00
2007	Just Out of Reach/Lost Weekend	1960	3.75	7.50	15.00
2012	Look Out Heart (Here Comes Love)/It Don't Take Long to Learn	1961	3.75	7.50	15.00

BROWN, BUSTER

45s

Number	Title (A Side/B Side)	Yr	VG	VG+	NM
FIRE					
507	Sugar Babe/I'm Going — But I'll Be Back	1962	5.00	10.00	20.00
516	Raise a Rucks Tonight/Gonna Love My Baby	1962	5.00	10.00	20.00
1008	Fannie Mae/Lost in a Dream	1959	6.25	12.50	25.00
1020	The Madison Shuffle/John Henry	1960	5.00	10.00	20.00
1023	Is You Is or Is You Ain't My Baby/Don't Dog Your Woman	1960	5.00	10.00	20.00
1032	Sincerely/Doctor Brown	1960	5.00	10.00	20.00
1040	Blues When It Rains/Good News	1961	5.00	10.00	20.00
2021	Sugar Babe/Don't Dog Your Woman	1962	3.75	7.50	15.00
RCA VICTOR					
PB-10023	Eloise/Fallin' Out of Love	1974	—	2.50	5.00
WHITE WHALE					
316	The Proud One/I've Got It Made	1969	2.50	5.00	10.00

Albums

Number	Title (A Side/B Side)	Yr	VG	VG+	NM
COLLECTABLES					
COL-5110	Golden Classics: The New King of the Blues	198?	2.50	5.00	10.00
FIRE					
FLP-102 [M]	The New King of the Blues	1961	175.00	350.00	700.00
—White and red label					
FLP-102 [M]	The New King of the Blues	1961	100.00	200.00	400.00
—Red and black label, purple cover					
FLP-102 [M]	The New King of the Blues	1961	75.00	150.00	300.00
—Red and black label, white cover					

Number	Title (A Side/B Side)	Yr	VG	VG+	NM
SOUFFLE					
2014	Get Down	1973	3.00	6.00	12.00

BROWN, CHARLES

45s

Number	Title (A Side/B Side)	Yr	VG	VG+	NM
ACE					
561	Educated Fool/I Want to Go Back Home	1959	3.00	6.00	12.00
—With Amos Milburn					
599	Love's Like a River/Boys Will Be Boys	1960	3.00	6.00	12.00
599	Love's Like a River/Sing My Blues Tonight	1960	3.00	6.00	12.00
ALADDIN					
3076	Black Night/Once There Was a Fool	1951	37.50	75.00	150.00
—Charles Brown records on Aladdin prior to 3076 are unconfirmed on 45 rpm					
3091	I'll Always Be in Love with You/The Message	1951	20.00	40.00	80.00
3092	Seven Long Days/Don't Fool with My Heart	1951	20.00	40.00	80.00
3116	Hard Times/Tender Heart	1952	20.00	40.00	80.00
3120	Still Water/My Last Affair	1952	20.00	40.00	80.00
3138	See/Without Your Love	1952	20.00	40.00	80.00
3157	Rollin' Like a Pebble in the Sand/Alley Batting	1952	20.00	40.00	80.00
3163	Evening Shadows/Moonrise	1953	15.00	30.00	60.00
3176	Take Me/Rising Sun	1953	15.00	30.00	60.00
3191	Lonesome Feeling/I Lost Everything	1953	15.00	30.00	60.00
3200	All My Life/Don't Leave Me Poor	1953	15.00	30.00	60.00
3209	P.S. I Love You/Cryin' and Driftin' Blues	1953	15.00	30.00	60.00
3220	Everybody's Got Trouble/I Fool Around with You	1954	10.00	20.00	40.00
3235	Let's Walk/Crying Mercy	1954	10.00	20.00	40.00
3254	My Silent Love/Foolish	1954	10.00	20.00	40.00
3272	By the Bend of the River/Honey Slipper	1955	7.50	15.00	30.00
3284	Night After Night/Walk with Me	1955	7.50	15.00	30.00
3290	Hot Lips and Seven Kisses/Fools' Paradise	1955	7.50	15.00	30.00
3296	My Heart Is Mended/Trees, Trees	1955	7.50	15.00	30.00
3316	Please Don't Drive Me Away/One Minute to One	1956	6.25	12.50	25.00
3342	Soothe Me/I'll Always Be in Love with You	1956	6.25	12.50	25.00
3348	Merry Christmas, Baby/Black Night	1956	6.25	12.50	25.00
3366	Please Believe Me/It's a Sin to Tell a Lie	1957	5.00	10.00	20.00
3423	Hard Times/Ooh, Ooh Sugar	1958	5.00	10.00	20.00
BLUES SPECTRUM					
17	Merry Christmas, Baby/Rockin' Blues	197?	—	3.00	6.00
BLUESWAY					
61031	Merry Christmas, Baby/Rainy, Rainy Day	1969	—	3.00	6.00
CASH					
1052	Lost in the Night/I Sold My Heart to the Junkman	1957	7.50	15.00	30.00
—B-side by the Basin Street Boys					
CHARLENA					
001	Please Come Home For Christmas/Santa Claus Santa Claus	197?	—	2.00	4.00
001 [PS]	Please Come Home For Christmas/Santa Claus Santa Claus	197?	—	2.50	5.00
EASTWEST					
106	When Did You Leave Heaven/We've Got a Lot in Common	1958	5.00	10.00	20.00
EMI					
S7-18213	Please Come Home for Christmas/Merry Christmas Baby	1994	—	2.00	4.00
—Green vinyl					
GALAXY					
762	I'm Gonna Push On/Cry No More	1968	2.50	5.00	10.00
766	Abraham, Martin, and John/(B-side unknown)	1968	2.50	5.00	10.00
HOLLYWOOD					
1006	Pleading for Your Love/The Best I Can Do	1954	10.00	20.00	40.00
1021	Merry Christmas Baby/Sleigh Ride	1954	5.00	10.00	20.00
—Charles Brown's first recording of the A-side, released on 78 on Exclusive 254 (1946); B-side by Lloyd Glenn; maroon label					
1021	Merry Christmas Baby/Sleigh Ride	196?	2.00	4.00	8.00
—B-side by Lloyd Glenn; color label					
1021	Merry Christmas Baby/Sleigh Ride	197?	—	2.50	5.00
—B-side by Lloyd Glenn; black label					
IMPERIAL					
5830	Fool's Paradise/Lonesome Feeling	1962	2.50	5.00	10.00
5902	Merry Christmas Baby/I Lost Everything	1962	2.50	5.00	10.00
5905	Black Night/Drifting Blues	1963	2.50	5.00	10.00
5961	I'm Savin' My Love for You/Please Don't Drive Me Away	1963	2.50	5.00	10.00
JEWEL					
814	Christmas in Heaven/Just a Blessing	1970	—	3.00	6.00
815	Merry Christmas Baby/Please Come Home for Christmas	1970	—	3.00	6.00
830	I Don't Know/For You	1972	—	2.50	5.00
838	I've Got Your Love/I Just Can't Get Over You	1973	—	2.50	5.00
847	Please Come Home for Christmas/Christmas in Heaven	1974	—	2.50	5.00
KENT					
501	Merry Christmas Baby/3 O'Clock Blues	1968	2.50	5.00	10.00
KING					
5405	Please Come Home for Christmas/Christmas (Comes But Once a Year)	1960	3.00	6.00	12.00
—B-side by Amos Milburn; original blue label					
5405	Please Come Home for Christmas/Christmas (Comes But Once a Year)	1970	—	3.00	6.00
—B-side by Amos Milburn; black label					
5439	Angel Baby/Baby Oh Baby	1961	3.00	6.00	12.00
5464	I Wanna Go Back Home/My Little Baby	1961	3.00	6.00	12.00
—With Amos Milburn					
5523	Butterfly/This Fool Has Learned	1961	3.00	6.00	12.00
5530	Christmas in Heaven/It's Christmas All Year 'Round	1961	3.00	6.00	12.00
5570	Without a Friend/If You Play with Cats	1961	3.00	6.00	12.00
5722	I'm Just a Drifter/I Don't Want Your Rambling Letters	1963	2.50	5.00	10.00
5726	It's Christmas Time/Christmas Finds Me Lonely	1963	2.50	5.00	10.00
5731	Christmas Questions/Wrap Yourself in a Christmas Package	1963	2.50	5.00	10.00
5802	If You Don't Believe I'm Crying/I Wanna Be Close	1963	2.50	5.00	10.00
5825	Lucky Dreamer/Too Fine for Crying	1963	2.50	5.00	10.00

Number	Title (A Side/B Side)	Yr	VG	VG+	NM
5852	Blow Out All the Candles/Come Home	1964	2.50	5.00	10.00
5946	Christmas Blues/My Most Miserable Christmas	1964	2.50	5.00	10.00
5947	Christmas Comes (But Once a Year)/Bringin' In a Brand New Year	1964	2.50	5.00	10.00
6094	Regardless/The Plan	1967	2.00	4.00	8.00
6192	Hang On a Little Longer/Black Night	1968	2.00	4.00	8.00
6194	Merry Christmas, Baby/Let's Make Every Day Christmas	1968	2.00	4.00	8.00
6420	For the Good Times/Lonesome and Driftin'	1973	—	2.50	5.00
LIBERTY					
1393	Merry Christmas, Baby/Silent Night	1980	—	2.50	5.00
—B-side by Baby Washington					
5902	Merry Christmas, Baby/I Lost Everything	196?	2.00	4.00	8.00
—Reissue of Imperial 5902					
LILLY					
506	Bon Voyage/Bye and Bye	1962	2.50	5.00	10.00
MAINSTREAM					
607	Pledging My Love/Tomorrow Night	1965	2.00	4.00	8.00
NOLA					
702	Standing on the Outside/I'll Love You (If You Let Me)	1965	2.00	4.00	8.00
SWING TIME					
238	Merry Christmas, Baby/Lost In The Night	195?	25.00	50.00	100.00
—Originally released on 78, but a 45 does exist					
253	I'll Miss You/New Orleans Blues	1952	30.00	60.00	120.00
259	Be Fair with Me/Sunny Road	1952	30.00	60.00	120.00
TEEM					
1008	Merry Christmas Baby/Christmas Finds Me Oh So Sad	19??	—	3.00	6.00
UNITED ARTISTS					
0085	Drifting Blues/Black Night	1973	—	2.00	4.00
—Silver Spotlight Series issue					
0086	I Lost Everything/Lonesome Feeling	1973	—	2.00	4.00
—Silver Spotlight Series issue					
XW582	Merry Christmas Baby/(B-side unknown)	1974	—	2.50	5.00
UPSIDE					
PRO 002	Santa Claus Boogie (one-sided)	1986	—	2.00	4.00
—Flexidisc					
PRO 002 [PS]	Santa Claus Boogie	1986	—	2.00	4.00

Albums

Number	Title	Yr	VG	VG+	NM
ALADDIN					
LP-702 [10]	Mood Music	1953	3000.	5250.	7500.
—Red vinyl					
LP-702 [10]	Mood Music	1953	1500.	2750.	4000.
—Black vinyl					
LP-809 [M]	Mood Music	1956	—	—	—
—Unreleased?					
ALLIGATOR					
AL-4771	One More for the Road	1989	3.00	6.00	12.00
BIG TOWN					
1003	Merry Christmas Baby	1977	3.00	6.00	12.00
1005	Music Maestro Please	1978	2.50	5.00	10.00
BLUESWAY					
BLS-6039	Charles Brown — Legend	1970	6.25	12.50	25.00
BULLSEYE BLUES					
BB-9501	All My Life	1990	5.00	10.00	20.00
IMPERIAL					
LP-9178 [M]	Charles Brown Sings Million Sellers	1961	100.00	200.00	400.00
JEWEL					
5006	Blues 'N' Brown	1972	3.00	6.00	12.00
KING					
775 [M]	Charles Brown Sings Christmas Songs	1961	37.50	75.00	150.00
KS-775 [S]	Charles Brown Sings Christmas Songs	1963	75.00	150.00	300.00
—Stereo copies (whether true stereo or rechanneled, we don't know) exist on blue labels with "King" in block letters (no crown)					
878 [M]	The Great Charles Brown	1963	50.00	100.00	200.00
MAINSTREAM					
S-6007 [S]	Boss of the Blues	1965	7.50	15.00	30.00
S-6035 [S]	Ballads My Way	1965	7.50	15.00	30.00
56007 [M]	Boss of the Blues	1965	5.00	10.00	20.00
56035 [M]	Ballads My Way	1965	5.00	10.00	20.00
SCORE					
SLP-4011 [M]	Driftin' Blues	1958	100.00	200.00	400.00
SLP-4036 [M]	More Blues with Charles Brown	1959	—	—	—
—Unreleased					

BROWN, CLARENCE "GATEMOUTH"

45s

Number	Title	Yr	VG	VG+	NM
PEACOCK					
1600	Baby Take It Easy/Just Got Lucky	1952	100.00	200.00	400.00
1607	Dirty Work at the Crossroads/You Got Money	1952	62.50	125.00	250.00
1617	Boogie Uproar/Hurry Back Good News	1953	50.00	100.00	200.00
1619	Please Tell Me Baby/Gate Walks to Board	1953	50.00	100.00	200.00
1633	Midnight Hour/For Now So Long	1954	37.50	75.00	150.00
1637	Okie Dokie Stomp/Depression Blues	1954	37.50	75.00	150.00
1653	Gate's Salty Blues/Rock My Blues Away	1955	25.00	50.00	100.00
1662	Ain't That Dandy/September Song	1956	20.00	40.00	80.00
1692	Just Before Dawn/Swinging the Gate	1958	10.00	20.00	40.00

BROWN, ESTELLE

One of the SWEET INSPIRATIONS.

45s

Number	Title	Yr	VG	VG+	NM
UNITED ARTISTS					
727	You Got Just What You Asked For/Stick Close	1964	2.50	5.00	10.00

BROWN, GENE

45s

Number	Title	Yr	VG	VG+	NM
DOT					
15709	Playing with My Heart Again/Big Door	1958	15.00	30.00	60.00

BROWN, GEORGE WASHINGTON

See VAN DYKE PARKS.

BROWN, JAMES

Also see VICKI ANDERSON; BOBBY BYRD; LYN COLLINS; FRED WESLEY AND THE JB'S.

45s

Number	Title (A Side/B Side)	Yr	VG	VG+	NM
AUGUSTA SOUND					
94023	Bring It On ... Bring It On/The Night Time Is the Right Time (To Be With the One That You Love)	1983	—	2.00	4.00
A&M					
3022	I Got You (I Feel Good)/Nowhere to Run	1988	—	2.00	4.00
—B-side by Martha and the Vandellas					
3022 [PS]	I Got You (I Feel Good)/Nowhere to Run	1988	—	2.00	4.00
—"Good Morning Vietnam" sleeve					
BACKSTREET					
52215	King of Soul/Theme from Doctor Detroit	1983	—	—	3.00
—B-side by Devo					
BETHLEHEM					
3089	I Loves You Porgy/Yours and Mine	1969	3.75	7.50	15.00
3098	A Man Has to Go Back to the Crossroads/The Drunk	1969	3.75	7.50	15.00
FEDERAL					
12258	Please, Please, Please/Why Do You Do Me?	1956	10.00	20.00	40.00
12264	I Don't Know/I Feel That Old Feeling Coming On	1956	6.25	12.50	25.00
12277	No, No, No, No/Hold My Baby's Hand	1956	6.25	12.50	25.00
12289	Just Won't Do Right/Let's Make It	1957	6.25	12.50	25.00
12290	I Won't Plead No More/Chonnie On Chon	1957	6.25	12.50	25.00
12292	Gonna Try/Can't Be the Same	1957	6.25	12.50	25.00
12295	Love or a Game/Messing with the Blues	1957	6.25	12.50	25.00
12300	I Walked Alone/You're Mine, You're Mine	1957	6.25	12.50	25.00
12311	Baby Cries Over the Ocean/That Dood It	1957	6.25	12.50	25.00
12316	Begging, Begging/That's When I Lost My Heart	1958	6.25	12.50	25.00
12337	Try Me/Tell Me What I Did Wrong	1958	7.50	15.00	30.00
12348	I Want You So Bad/There Must Be a Reason	1959	5.00	10.00	20.00
12352 [M]	I've Got to Change/It Hurts to Tell You	1959	5.00	10.00	20.00
S-12352 [S]	I've Got to Change/It Hurts to Tell You	1959	12.50	25.00	50.00
12361 [M]	Don't Let It Happen to Me/Good Good Lovin'	1959	5.00	10.00	20.00
S-12361 [S]	Don't Let It Happen to Me/Good Good Lovin'	1959	12.50	25.00	50.00
12364	It Was You/Got to Cry	1959	5.00	10.00	20.00
12369	I'll Go Crazy/I Know It's True	1960	5.00	10.00	20.00
12370	Think/You've Got the Power	1960	5.00	10.00	20.00
12378	This Old Heart/I Wonder When You're Coming Home	1960	5.00	10.00	20.00
KING					
5423	The Bells/And I Do Just What I Want	1960	3.75	7.50	15.00
5438	The Scratch/Hold It	1961	3.75	7.50	15.00
5442	Bewildered/If You Want Me	1961	3.75	7.50	15.00
5466	I Don't Mind/Love Don't Love Nobody	1961	3.75	7.50	15.00
5485	Sticky/Suds	1961	3.75	7.50	15.00
5519	Night Flying/Cross Firing	1961	3.75	7.50	15.00
5524	Baby You're Right/I'll Never, Never Let You Go	1961	3.75	7.50	15.00
5547	Just You and Me, Darling/I Love You, Yes I Do	1961	3.75	7.50	15.00
5573	Lost Someone/Cross Firing	1961	3.75	7.50	15.00
5614	Night Train/Why Does Everything Happen to Me	1962	3.75	7.50	15.00
5654	Tell Me Why/Say So Long	1962	3.75	7.50	15.00
—With Yvonne Fair					
5657	Shout and Shimmy/Come Over Here	1962	3.75	7.50	15.00
5672	Mashed Potatoes U.S.A./You Don't Have to Go	1962	3.75	7.50	15.00
5687	It Hurts to Be in Love/You Can Make It If You Try	1962	3.75	7.50	15.00
—With Yvonne Fair					
5698	(Can You) Feel It Part 1/(Can You) Feel It Part 2	1962	3.75	7.50	15.00
5701	Three Hearts in a Tangle/I've Got Money	1962	3.75	7.50	15.00
5710	Like a Baby/Every Beat of My Heart	1963	3.75	7.50	15.00
5739	Prisoner of Love/Choo Choo	1963	3.75	7.50	15.00
5767	These Foolish Things/Can You Feel It — Part 1	1963	3.75	7.50	15.00
5803	Signed, Sealed and Delivered/Waiting in Vain	1963	3.75	7.50	15.00
5829	The Bells/I've Got to Change	1963	3.75	7.50	15.00
5842	Oh Baby Don't You Weep (Part 1)/Oh Baby Don't You Weep (Part 2)	1964	3.75	7.50	15.00
5842 [PS]	Oh Baby Don't You Weep (Part 1)/Oh Baby Don't You Weep (Part 2)	1964	6.25	12.50	25.00
5853	Please, Please, Please/In the Wee Wee Hours	1964	3.75	7.50	15.00
5876	How Long Darling/Again	1964	3.75	7.50	15.00
5899	So Long/Dancin' Little Thing	1964	3.75	7.50	15.00
5922	Tell Me What You're Gonna Do/I Don't Care	1964	3.75	7.50	15.00
5952	Think/Try Me	1964	3.75	7.50	15.00
5956	Fine Old Foxy Self/Medley	1964	3.75	7.50	15.00
5968	Have Mercy Baby/Just Won't Do Right	1964	3.75	7.50	15.00
5995	This Old Heart/It Was You	1965	3.00	6.00	12.00
5999	Papa's Got a Brand New Bag Part I/Papa's Got a Brand New Bag Part II	1965	3.75	7.50	15.00
6015	I Got You (I Feel Good)/I Can't Help It (I Just Do, Do, Do)	1965	3.75	7.50	15.00
6020	I'll Go Crazy/Lost Someone	1966	3.00	6.00	12.00
6025	Ain't That a Groove Part I/Ain't That a Groove Part II	1966	3.00	6.00	12.00
6029	Prisoner of Love/I've Got to Change	1966	3.00	6.00	12.00
6033	Come Over Here/Tell Me What You're Gonna Do	1966	3.00	6.00	12.00
6035	It's a Man's Man's Man's World/Is It Yes Or Is It No?	1966	3.00	6.00	12.00
6037	I've Got Money/Just Won't Do Right	1966	3.00	6.00	12.00
6040	I Don't Care/It Was You	1966	3.00	6.00	12.00
6044	This Old Heart/How Long Darling	1966	3.00	6.00	12.00
6048	Money Won't Change You Part 1/Money Won't Change You Part 2	1966	3.00	6.00	12.00
6056	Don't Be a Drop-Out/Tell Me That You Love Me	1966	3.00	6.00	12.00
6064	The Christmas Song (Version 1)/The Christmas Song (Version 2)	1966	3.75	7.50	15.00
6065	Sweet Little Baby Boy (Part 1)/Sweet Little Baby Boy (Part 2)	1966	3.00	6.00	12.00
6071	Bring It Up/Nobody Knows	1967	3.00	6.00	12.00
6072	Let's Make Christmas Mean Something This Year (Part 1)/Let's Make Christmas Mean Something This Year (Part 2)	1967	3.00	6.00	12.00
6086	Kansas City/Stone Fox	1967	3.00	6.00	12.00

Number	Title (A Side/B Side)	Yr	VG	VG+	NM
6091	Think/Nobody Cares	1967	3.00	6.00	12.00
—A-side: With Vicki Anderson; B-side: Vicki Anderson solo					
6100	Let Yourself Go/Good Rockin' Tonight	1967	3.00	6.00	12.00
6110	Cold Sweat — Part 1/Cold Sweat — Part 2	1967	3.00	6.00	12.00
6111	Mona Lisa/It Won't Be Me	1967	15.00	30.00	60.00
—Evidently not released or pulled shortly after release					
6112	America Is My Home — Part 1/America Is My Home — Part 2	1967	3.00	6.00	12.00
6122	Get It Together (Part 1)/Get It Together (Part 2)	1967	3.00	6.00	12.00
6133	The Soul of J.B./Funky Soul #1	1967	3.00	6.00	12.00
6141	I Guess I'll Have to Cry, Cry, Cry/Just Plain Funk	1967	3.00	6.00	12.00
6144	I Can't Stand Myself (When You Touch Me)/There Was a Time	1967	3.00	6.00	12.00
6151	You've Got to Change Your Mind/I'll Lose My Mind	1968	3.00	6.00	12.00
—A-side: With Bobby Byrd; B-side: Bobby Byrd solo					
6152	You've Got the Power/What the World Needs Now Is Love	1968	3.00	6.00	12.00
—A-side: With Vicki Anderson; B-side: Vicki Anderson solo					
6155	I Got the Feelin'/If I Ruled the World	1968	3.00	6.00	12.00
6164	Here I Go/Shhhh	1968	3.00	6.00	12.00
6166	Licking Stick — Licking Stick (Part 1)/Licking Stick — Licking Stick (Part 2)	1968	3.00	6.00	12.00
6187	Say It Loud — I'm Black and I'm Proud (Part 1)/ Say It Loud — I'm Black and I'm Proud (Part 2)	1968	2.50	5.00	10.00
6187	Say It Loud — I'm Black But I'm Proud (Part 1)/ Say It Loud — I'm Black But I'm Proud (Part 2)	1968	6.25	12.50	25.00
—Some copies have the above erroneous title on both sides					
6198	Goodbye My Love/Shades of Brown	1968	2.50	5.00	10.00
6203	Santa Claus Go Straight to the Ghetto/You Know It	1968	2.50	5.00	10.00
6204	Believers Shall Enjoy/Tit for Tat (Ain't No Turning Back)	1968	2.50	5.00	10.00
6205	Let's Unite the World at Christmas/In the Middle (Part 1)	1968	2.50	5.00	10.00
6206	In the Middle (Part 2)/Tit for Tat (Ain't No Turning Back)	1969	2.50	5.00	10.00
—A-side: With Marva Whitney					
6213	Give It Up or Turnit A Loose/I'll Lose My Mind	1969	2.50	5.00	10.00
6216	Shades of Brown (Part 2)/A Talk with the News	1969	2.50	5.00	10.00
—B-side by Steve Soul					
6218	You Got to Have a Job/I'm Tired, I'm Tired, I'm Tired	1969	2.50	5.00	10.00
—A-side with Marva Whitney; B-side: Marva Whitney solo					
6222	Soul Pride (Part 1)/Soul Pride (Part 2)	1969	2.50	5.00	10.00
6223	You've Got to Have a Mother for Me (Part 1)/ You've Got to Have a Mother for Me (Part 2)	1969	2.50	5.00	10.00
6224	I Don't Want Nobody to Give Me Nothing (Open Up the Door, I'll Get It Myself) Part 1/Part 2	1969	2.50	5.00	10.00
6235	Little Groove Maker (Part 1)/Any Day Now	1969	2.50	5.00	10.00
6235	Little Groove Maker (Part 1)/I'm Shook	1969	2.50	5.00	10.00
6240	The Popcorn/The Chicken	1969	2.50	5.00	10.00
6245	Mother Popcorn (You Got to Have a Mother for Me) Part 1/Mother Popcorn (You Got to Have a Mother for Me) Part 2	1969	2.50	5.00	10.00
6250	Lowdown Popcorn/Top of the Stack	1969	2.50	5.00	10.00
6255	Let a Man Come In and Do the Popcorn Part One/ Sometime	1969	2.50	5.00	10.00
6258	World (Part 1)/World (Part 2)	1969	2.50	5.00	10.00
6273	I'm Not Demanding (Part 1)/I'm Not Demanding (Part 2)	1969	2.50	5.00	10.00
6275	Part Two (Let a Man Come In and Do the Popcorn)/Get a Little Hipper	1969	2.50	5.00	10.00
6277	It's Christmas Time (Part 1)/It's Christmas Time (Part 2)	1969	2.50	5.00	10.00
6280	Ain't It Funky Now (Part 1)/Ain't It Funky Now (Part 2)	1970	2.00	4.00	8.00
6290	Funky Drummer (Part 1)/Funky Drummer (Part 2)	1970	2.00	4.00	8.00
6292	It's a New Day (Part 1)/It's a New Day (Part 2)	1970	2.00	4.00	8.00
6293	Let It Be Me/No More Heartaches, No More Pain	1970	2.00	4.00	8.00
—A-side: With Vicki Anderson; B-side: Vicki Anderson solo					
6300	Talkin' Loud and Sayin' Nothing (Part 1)/Talkin' Loud and Sayin' Nothing (Part 2)	1970	2.00	4.00	8.00
6310	Brother Rapp (Part 1)/Brother Rapp (Part 2)	1970	2.00	4.00	8.00
6318	Get Up (I Feel Like Being A) Sex Machine (Part 1)/Get Up (I Feel Like Being A) Sex Machine (Part 2)	1970	2.00	4.00	8.00
6322	I'm Not Demanding (Part 1)/I'm Not Demanding (Part 2)	1970	2.00	4.00	8.00
6329	Call Me Super Bad (Part 1 & Part 2)/Bewitched	1970	5.00	10.00	20.00
—First pressing: Note longer title					
6329	Super Bad (Part 1 & Part 2)/Bewitched	1970	2.00	4.00	8.00
6339	Hey America/(Instrumental)	1970	2.00	4.00	8.00
6339 [PS]	Hey America/(Instrumental)	1970	3.75	7.50	15.00
6340	Santa Claus Is Definitely Here to Stay/ (Instrumental)	1970	2.00	4.00	8.00
6340 [PS]	Santa Claus Is Definitely Here to Stay/ (Instrumental)	1970	7.50	15.00	30.00
6347	Get Up, Get Into It, Get Involved Pt. 1/Get Up, Get Into It, Get Involved Pt. 2	1971	2.00	4.00	8.00
6359	Talking Loud and Saying Nothing — Part 1/ Talking Loud and Saying Nothing — Part 2	1971	2.00	4.00	8.00
6363	I Cried/World (Part 2)	1971	2.00	4.00	8.00
6366	Spinning Wheel (Part 1)/Spinning Wheel (Part 2)	1971	2.00	4.00	8.00
6368	Soul Power Pt. 1/Soul Power Pt 2 & Pt. 3	1971	2.00	4.00	8.00
MERCURY					
885190-7	Prisoner of Love/Please, Please, Please	1986	—	2.00	4.00
—Reissue					
885194-7	Get on the Good Foot/Give It Up or Turnit A Loose	1986	—	2.00	4.00
—Reissue					
PEOPLE					
664	Everybody Wanna Be Funky One More Time Pt. 1/Everybody Wanna Be Funky One More Time Pt. 2	1976	—	2.50	5.00
2500	Escape-ism (Part 1)/Escape-ism (Parts 2 & 3)	1971	—	3.00	6.00
2501	Hot Pants Pt. 1 (She Got to Use What She Got to Get What She Wants)/Hot Pants Pt. 2	1971	—	3.00	6.00
POLYDOR					
2005	Star Generation/Women Are Something Else	1979	—	2.50	5.00
2034	The Original Disco Man/Let the Boogie Do the Rest	1979	—	2.50	5.00
2054	Regrets/Stone Cold Drag	1979	—	2.50	5.00
2078	Let the Funk Flow/Sometimes That's All There Is	1980	—	2.50	5.00
2129	Get Up Offa That Thing/It's Too Funky in Here	1980	—	2.50	5.00
2167	Give the Bass Player Some Part 1/Part 2	1981	—	2.50	5.00
14088	Make It Funky Part 1/Make It Funky Part 2	1971	—	3.00	6.00
14098	My Part/Make It Funky, Part 3//Make It Funky, Part 4	1971	—	3.00	6.00
14100	I'm a Greedy Man Part 1/I'm a Greedy Man Part 2	1971	—	3.00	6.00
14109	Talking Loud and Saying Nothing Part 1/Part 2	1972	—	3.00	6.00
14110	Nothing Beats a Try But a Fail/Hot Pants Road	1972	—	—	—
—Unreleased					
14116	King Heroin/Theme from King Heroin	1972	—	3.00	6.00
14116 [PS]	King Heroin/Theme from King Heroin	1972	2.50	5.00	10.00
14125	There It Is Part 1/There It Is Part 2	1972	—	3.00	6.00
14129	Honky Tonk Part 1/Honky Tonk Part 2	1972	—	3.00	6.00
—Artist credit: "James Brown Soul Train"					
14139	Get On the Good Foot Part 1/Get On the Good Foot Part 2	1972	—	3.00	6.00
14153	I Got a Bag of My Own/Public Enemy #1	1972	—	3.00	6.00
14155	I Got a Bag of My Own/I Know It's True	1972	7.50	15.00	30.00
—Manufactured in U.S. for export					
14157	What My Baby Needs Now Is a Little More Lovin'/ This Guy-This Girl's in Love	1972	—	3.00	6.00
—With Lyn Collins					
14161	Santa Claus Goes Straight to the Ghetto/Sweet Little Baby Boy	1972	—	3.00	6.00
14162	I Got Ants in My Pants (and I want to dance) Part 1/Part 2	1973	—	2.50	5.00
14168	Down and Out in New York City/Mama's Dead	1973	—	2.50	5.00
14169	The Boss/Like It Is, Like It Was	1973	—	2.50	5.00
14177	Think/Something	1973	—	2.50	5.00
14185	Think/Something	1973	—	2.50	5.00
14193	Woman Part 1/Woman Part 2	1973	—	2.50	5.00
14194	Sexy, Sexy, Sexy/Slaughter Theme	1973	—	2.50	5.00
14199	Let It Be Me/It's All Right	1973	—	2.50	5.00
—With Lyn Collins					
14206	I Got a Good Thing Part 1/I Got a Good Thing Part 2	1973	—	2.50	5.00
14210	Stoned to the Bone Part 1/Stoned to the Bone Part 2	1973	—	2.50	5.00
—Notice corrected title					
14210	Stone to the Bone Part 1/Stone to the Bone Part 2	1973	2.50	5.00	10.00
14223	The Payback Part 1/The Payback Part 2	1974	—	2.50	5.00
14223 [PS]	The Payback Part 1/The Payback Part 2	1974	2.50	5.00	10.00
14244	My Thang/Public Enemy No. 1	1974	—	2.50	5.00
14255	Papa Don't Take No Mess Part 1/Part 2	1974	—	2.50	5.00
14258	Funky President (People It's Bad)/Coldblooded	1974	—	2.50	5.00
14268	Reality/I Need Your Love So Bad	1975	—	2.50	5.00
14270	Sex Machine Part 1/Sex Machine Part 2	1975	—	2.50	5.00
14274	Thank You For Letting Me Be Myself And... Part 1/Part 2	1975	—	2.50	5.00
14279	Dead On It Part 1/Dead On It Part 2	1975	—	—	—
—Unreleased					
14281	Hustle (Dead On It) Part 1/Hustle (Dead On It) Part 2	1975	—	2.50	5.00
14295	Superbad, Superslick Part 1/Superbad, Superslick Part 2	1975	—	2.50	5.00
14301	Hot (I Need to Be Loved, Loved, Loved, Loved)/ Superbad, Superslick	1975	—	2.50	5.00
14302	Dooley's Junkyard Dogs Part 1/Part 2	1975	—	2.50	5.00
14303	(I Love You) For Sentimental Reasons/Goodnight My Love	1975	—	2.50	5.00
14326	Get Up Offa That Thing/Release the Pressure	1976	—	2.50	5.00
14354	I Refuse to Lose/Home Again	1976	—	2.50	5.00
14360	Bodyheat Part 1/Bodyheat Part 2	1976	—	2.50	5.00
14388	Kiss in 77/Woman	1977	—	2.50	5.00
14409	Give Me Some Skin/People Wake Up and Live	1977	—	2.50	5.00
—With the J.B.'s					
14433	Take Me Higher and Groove Me/Summertime	1977	—	2.50	5.00
—B-side by Martha and James					
14438	If You Don't Give a Doggone About It/People Who Criticize	1977	—	2.50	5.00
—With the New J.B.'s					
14460	Love Me Tender/Have a Happy Day	1978	—	2.50	5.00
—With the New J.B.'s					
14465	Eyesight/I Never Never Never Will Forget	1978	—	2.50	5.00
14487	The Spank/Love Me Tender	1978	—	2.50	5.00
14512	Nature Part 1/Nature Part 2	1978	—	2.50	5.00
14522	For Goodness Sakes, Look at Those Cakes Part 1/Part 2	1979	—	2.50	5.00
14540	Someone to Talk To Part 1/Someone to Talk To Part 2	1979	—	2.50	5.00
14557	It's Too Funky in Here/Are We Really Dancing	1979	—	2.50	5.00
871804-7	Think/Lost Someone	1989	—	—	3.00
—Reissue					
871808-7	Out of Sight/Maybe the Last Time	1989	—	—	3.00
—Reissue					
871810-7	I Got You (I Feel Good)/Papa's Got a Brand New Bag	1989	—	—	3.00
—Reissue					
887500-7	(Get Up I Feel Like Being a) Sex Machine/ Vincent's Theme	1988	—	—	3.00
—B-side by Ethan James					
887500-7 [PS]	(Get Up I Feel Like Being a) Sex Machine/ Vincent's Theme	1988	—	2.00	4.00
—B-side by Ethan James					
SCOTTI BROS.					
05682	Living in America/Farewell	1985	—	—	3.00
—B-side by Vince Di Cola					
05682 [PS]	Living in America/Farewell	1985	—	—	3.00

Number	Title (A Side/B Side)	Yr	VG	VG+	NM
06275	Gravity/Gravity (Dub Mix)	1986	—	—	3.00
06275 [PS]	Gravity/Gravity (Dub Mix)	1986	—	—	3.00
06568	How Do You Stop/House of Rock	1987	—	—	3.00
06568 [PS]	How Do You Stop/House of Rock	1987	—	—	3.00
07090	Let's Get Personal/Repeat the Bat	1987	—	—	3.00
07783	I'm Real/Gravity	1988	—	—	3.00
07783 [PS]	I'm Real/Gravity	1988	—	—	3.00
07975	Static/Godfather Runnin' the Joint	1988	—	—	3.00
08088	Time to Get Busy/Busy J.B.	1988	—	—	3.00
68559	It's Your Money $/You and Me	1989	—	—	3.00
75286	(So Tired of Standing Still We Got to) Move On/ You Are My Everything	1991	—	2.00	4.00

SMASH

Number	Title (A Side/B Side)	Yr	VG	VG+	NM
1898	Caledonia/Evil	1964	3.00	6.00	12.00
1898	Caldonia/Evil	1964	3.00	6.00	12.00
1898 [PS]	Caledonia/Evil	1964	6.25	12.50	25.00
1908	The Things That I Used to Do/Out of the Blue	1964	3.00	6.00	12.00
1908 [PS]	The Things That I Used to Do/Out of the Blue	1964	10.00	20.00	40.00
1919	Out of Sight/Maybe the Last Time	1964	3.00	6.00	12.00
1919 [PS]	Out of Sight/Maybe the Last Time	1964	10.00	20.00	40.00
1949	Who's Afraid of Virginia Woolf? Part 1/Part 2	1964	—	—	—
—Unreleased					
1975	Devil's Hideaway/Who's Afraid of Virginia Woolf?	1965	2.50	5.00	10.00
1989	I Got You/Only You	1965	12.50	25.00	50.00
—Withdrawn					
2008	Try Me/Papa's Got a Brand New Bag	1965	2.50	5.00	10.00
2028	New Breed Part 1/New Breed Part 2	1966	2.50	5.00	10.00
2042	James Brown's Boo-Ga-Loo/Lost in the Mood of Changes	1966	2.50	5.00	10.00
2064	Let's Go Get Stoned/Our Day Will Come	1966	2.50	5.00	10.00
2093	Jimmy Mack/What Do You Like	1967	2.50	5.00	10.00

T.K.

Number	Title (A Side/B Side)	Yr	VG	VG+	NM
1039	Rapp Payback (Where Iz Moses) Part 1/Part 2	1980	—	2.00	4.00
1042	Stay with Me/Smokin' and Drinkin'	1981	—	2.00	4.00

7-Inch Extended Plays

KING

Number	Title (A Side/B Side)	Yr	VG	VG+	NM
430	(contents unknown)	1959	50.00	100.00	200.00
430 [PS]	Please, Please, Please	1959	100.00	200.00	400.00
826	(contents unknown)	1963	20.00	40.00	80.00
826 [PS]	Live at the Apollo	1963	30.00	60.00	120.00

Albums

HRB

Number	Title (A Side/B Side)	Yr	VG	VG+	NM
1004 [(2)]	The Fabulous James Brown	1974	6.25	12.50	25.00

KING

Number	Title (A Side/B Side)	Yr	VG	VG+	NM
610 [M]	Please Please Please	1958	300.00	600.00	1200.
—"Woman's and man's legs" cover; "King" on label is two inches wide					
610 [M]	Please Please Please	1961	250.00	500.00	1000.
—"Woman's and man's legs" cover; "King" on label is three inches wide					
635 [M]	Try Me!	1959	225.00	450.00	900.00
—"Woman with cigarette and gun" cover; "King" on label is two inches wide					
635 [M]	Try Me!	1961	150.00	300.00	600.00
—"Woman with cigarette and gun" cover; "King" on label is three inches wide					
683 [M]	Think!	1960	225.00	450.00	900.00
—"Baby" cover; "King" on label is two inches wide					
683 [M]	Think!	1961	150.00	300.00	600.00
—"Baby" cover; "King" on label is three inches wide					
683 [M]	Think!	1963	25.00	50.00	100.00
—James Brown photo cover; "crownless" King label					
683 [M]	Think!	1966	12.50	25.00	50.00
—James Brown photo cover; "crown" King label					
743 [M]	The Amazing James Brown	1961	125.00	250.00	500.00
—"James Brown in suit" cover					
743 [M]	The Amazing James Brown	1963	37.50	75.00	150.00
—White title cover; "crownless" King label					
743 [M]	The Amazing James Brown	1966	125.00	250.00	500.00
—White title cover with "James Brown" in huge letters; "crown" King label					
771 [M]	Night Train	1961	75.00	150.00	300.00
—Original title					
771 [M]	Twist Around	1962	62.50	125.00	250.00
—Second title					
771 [M]	Jump Around	1963	50.00	100.00	200.00
—Third title					
KS-771 [S]	Jump Around	1963	75.00	150.00	300.00
—Stereo copies of King 771 only exist with this title					
780 [M]	Shout and Shimmy	1962	62.50	125.00	250.00
—"Shout and Shimmy" on both cover and label					
780 [M]	Good Good Twistin'	1962	50.00	100.00	200.00
—"Good Good Twistin' " on either label or cover, or both					
780 [M]	Excitement	1963	37.50	75.00	150.00
—Third title; "crownless" King label					
780 [M]	Excitement	1966	12.50	25.00	50.00
—Third title; "crown" King label					
804 [M]	James Brown & His Famous Flames Tour the U.S.A.	1962	37.50	125.00	250.00
—"Crownless" King label					
804 [M]	James Brown & His Famous Flames Tour the U.S.A.	1966	12.50	25.00	50.00
—"Crown" King label					
826 [M]	Live at the Apollo	1963	50.00	100.00	200.00
—Custom back cover; "crownless" King label					
826 [M]	Live at the Apollo	1963	37.50	75.00	150.00
—Other King albums on back cover; "crownless" King label					
826 [M]	Live at the Apollo	1966	12.50	25.00	50.00
—"Crown" King label					
KS-826 [S]	Live at the Apollo	1963	75.00	150.00	300.00
—Custom back cover; "crownless" King label					
KS-826 [S]	Live at the Apollo	1963	50.00	100.00	200.00
—Other King albums on back cover; "crownless" King label					
KS-826 [S]	Live at the Apollo	1966	17.50	35.00	70.00
—"Crown" King label					
851 [M]	Prisoner of Love	1963	50.00	100.00	200.00
—Custom back cover; "crownless" King label					
851 [M]	Prisoner of Love	1963	25.00	50.00	100.00
—Other King albums on back cover; "crownless" King label					
851 [M]	Prisoner of Love	1966	12.50	25.00	50.00
—"Crown" King label					
883 [M]	Pure Dynamite! Live at the Royal	1964	50.00	100.00	200.00
—"Crownless" King label					
883 [M]	Pure Dynamite! Live at the Royal	1966	12.50	25.00	50.00
—"Crown" King label					
883 [M-DJ]	Pure Dynamite! Live at the Royal	1964	200.00	400.00	800.00
—White label promo; banded for airplay					
909 [M]	Please Please Please	1964	25.00	50.00	100.00
—Reissue of 610; "crownless" King label					
909 [M]	Please Please Please	1966	12.50	25.00	50.00
—"Crown" King label					
919 [M]	The Unbeatable James Brown — 16 Hits	1964	25.00	50.00	100.00
—Reissue of 635; "crownless" King label					
919 [M]	The Unbeatable James Brown — 16 Hits	1966	12.50	25.00	50.00
—"Crown" King label					
938 [M]	Papa's Got a Brand New Bag	1965	20.00	40.00	80.00
—Red cover; "crownless" King label					
938 [M]	Papa's Got a Brand New Bag	1966	12.50	25.00	50.00
—Green cover; "crownless" King label					
938 [M]	Papa's Got a Brand New Bag	1966	10.00	20.00	40.00
—"Crown" King label					
LPS-938 [P]	Papa's Got a Brand New Bag	1965	25.00	50.00	100.00
—Red cover; "crownless" King label					
LPS-938 [P]	Papa's Got a Brand New Bag	1966	15.00	30.00	60.00
—Green cover; "crownless" King label					
LPS-938 [P]	Papa's Got a Brand New Bag	1966	12.50	25.00	50.00
—"Crown" King label					
946 [M]	I Got You (I Feel Good)	1966	25.00	50.00	100.00
—"Crownless" King label					
946 [M]	I Got You (I Feel Good)	1966	10.00	20.00	40.00
—"Crown" King label					
LPS-946 [S]	I Got You (I Feel Good)	1966	37.50	75.00	150.00
—"Crownless" King label					
LPS-946 [S]	I Got You (I Feel Good)	1966	12.50	25.00	50.00
—"Crown" King label					
961 [M]	Mighty Instrumentals	1966	25.00	50.00	100.00
LPS-961 [S]	Mighty Instrumentals	1966	37.50	75.00	150.00
985 [M]	It's a Man's Man's Man's World	1966	12.50	25.00	50.00
KS-985 [S]	It's a Man's Man's Man's World	1966	17.50	35.00	70.00
1010 [M]	Christmas Songs	1966	25.00	50.00	100.00
—Wreath on gray wall, no song titles on back					
1010 [M]	Christmas Songs	1967	20.00	40.00	80.00
—Wreath on white wall, song titles are on back					
KS-1010 [S]	Christmas Songs	1966	37.50	75.00	150.00
—Wreath on gray wall, no song titles on back					
KS-1010 [S]	Christmas Songs	1967	25.00	50.00	100.00
—Wreath on white wall, song titles are on back					
1016 [M]	Raw Soul	1967	12.50	25.00	50.00
KS-1016 [P]	Raw Soul	1967	17.50	35.00	70.00
1018 [M]	Live at the Garden	1967	100.00	200.00	400.00
—Black label promo; banded for airplay					
1018 [M]	Live at the Garden	1967	20.00	40.00	80.00
KS-1018 [S]	Live at the Garden	1967	25.00	50.00	100.00
1020 [M]	Cold Sweat	1967	12.50	25.00	50.00
KS-1020 [S]	Cold Sweat	1967	17.50	35.00	70.00
LPS-1022 [(2)]	Live at the Apollo, Volume II	1968	17.50	35.00	70.00
LPS-1024	James Brown Presents His Show of Tomorrow	1968	12.50	25.00	50.00
—Various-artists album					
LPS-1030	I Can't Stand Myself (When You Touch Me)	1968	12.50	25.00	50.00
LPS-1031	I Got the Feelin'	1968	12.50	25.00	50.00
LPS-1034	James Brown Plays Nothing But Soul	1968	12.50	25.00	50.00
LPS-1038	Thinking About Little Willie John and a Few Nice Things	1968	12.50	25.00	50.00
KS-1040	A Soulful Christmas	1968	20.00	40.00	80.00
KS-1047	Say It Loud — I'm Black and I'm Proud	1969	12.50	25.00	50.00
KS-1051	Gettin' Down To It	1969	12.50	25.00	50.00
KSD-1055	James Brown Plays & Directs The Popcorn	1969	10.00	20.00	40.00
KSD-1063	It's a Mother	1969	10.00	20.00	40.00
KSD-1092	Ain't It Funky	1970	10.00	20.00	40.00
KSD-1095	It's a New Day So Let a Man Come In	1970	10.00	20.00	40.00
KSD-1100	Soul on Top	1970	10.00	20.00	40.00
KSD-1110	Sho Is Funky Down Here	1971	10.00	20.00	40.00
KSD-1115 [(2)]	Sex Machine	1970	12.50	25.00	50.00
KSD-1124	Hey America!	1970	10.00	20.00	40.00
KSD-1127	Super Bad	1971	10.00	20.00	40.00

POLYDOR

Number	Title (A Side/B Side)	Yr	VG	VG+	NM
25-3003 [(2)]	Revolution of the Mind — Live at the Apollo, Volume III	1971	15.00	30.00	60.00
PD2-3004 [(2)]	Get On the Good Foot	1972	15.00	30.00	60.00
PD2-3007 [(2)]	The Payback	1973	12.50	25.00	50.00
24-4054	Hot Pants	1971	10.00	20.00	40.00
PD-5028	There It Is	1972	10.00	20.00	40.00
SC-5401	James Brown Soul Classics	1972	6.25	12.50	25.00
SC-5402	Soul Classics, Volume 2	1973	6.25	12.50	25.00
PD-6014	Black Caesar	1973	12.50	25.00	50.00
PD-6015	Slaughter's Big Rip-Off	1973	12.50	25.00	50.00
PD-1-6039	Reality	1975	10.00	20.00	40.00
PD-1-6042	Sex Machine Today	1975	10.00	20.00	40.00
PD-1-6054	Everybody's Doin' the Hustle & Dead On the Double Bump	1975	10.00	20.00	40.00
PD-1-6059	Hot	1976	10.00	20.00	40.00
PD-1-6071	Get Up Offa That Thing	1976	10.00	20.00	40.00
PD-1-6093	Bodyheat	1976	10.00	20.00	40.00
PD-1-6111	Mutha's Nature	1977	10.00	20.00	40.00
PD-1-6140	Jam/1980s	1978	10.00	20.00	40.00
PD-1-6181	Take a Look at Those Cakes	1978	7.50	15.00	30.00
PD-1-6212	The Original Disco Man	1979	7.50	15.00	30.00
PD-1-6258	People	1980	7.50	15.00	30.00
PD-2-6290 [(2)]	James Brown...Live/Hot on the One	1980	12.50	25.00	50.00
PD-1-6318	Nonstop!	1981	7.50	15.00	30.00
PD-1-6340	The Best of James Brown	1981	5.00	10.00	20.00
PD-2-9001 [(2)]	Hell	1974	20.00	40.00	80.00
PD-2-9004 [(2)]	Sex Machine Live	1976	12.50	25.00	50.00
821231-1	Ain't That a Groove: The James Brown Story 1966-1969	1984	3.75	7.50	15.00

Number	Title (A Side/B Side)	Yr	VG	VG+	NM
821232-1	Doing It to Death: The James Brown Story 1970-1973	1984	3.75	7.50	15.00
823275-1	The Best of James Brown	1984	3.00	6.00	12.00
—Reissue of 6340					
827439-1	Dead on the Heavy Funk: The James Brown Story 1974-1978	1985	3.75	7.50	15.00
829254-1 [(2)]	Solid Gold: 30 Golden Hits	1985	5.00	10.00	20.00
829417-1	James Brown's Funky People	1986	3.75	7.50	15.00
—Various-artists LP					
829624-1	In the Jungle Groove	1986	3.75	7.50	15.00
835857-1	James Brown's Funky People 2	1988	3.75	7.50	15.00
—Various-artists compilation					
837126-1	Motherlode	1988	3.75	7.50	15.00
RHINO					
RNLP-217	Live at the Apollo, Volume 2, Part 1	1985	3.75	7.50	15.00
RNLP-218	Live at the Apollo, Volume 2, Part 2	1985	3.75	7.50	15.00
RNLP-219	Greatest Hits (1964-1968)	1986	3.75	7.50	15.00
R1 70194	Santa's Got a Brand New Bag	1986	2.50	5.00	10.00
—Reissue of King material					
R1-70217	Live at the Apollo, Volume 2, Part 1	1988	3.00	6.00	12.00
—Reissue of 217					
R1-70218	Live at the Apollo, Volume 2, Part 2	1988	3.00	6.00	12.00
—Reissue of 218					
R1-70219	Greatest Hits (1964-1968)	1988	3.00	6.00	12.00
—Reissue of 219					
SCOTTI BROTHERS					
FZ 40380	Gravity	1986	3.00	6.00	12.00
FZ 44241	I'm Real	1988	3.00	6.00	12.00
FZ 45164	Soul Session Live	1989	3.75	7.50	15.00
75225-1	Love Overdue	1991	5.00	10.00	20.00
SMASH					
MGS-27054 [M]	Showtime	1964	7.50	15.00	30.00
MGS-27057 [M]	Grits & Soul	1965	7.50	15.00	30.00
MGS-27058 [M]	Out of Sight	1965	25.00	50.00	100.00
MGS-27072 [M]	James Brown Plays James Brown — Today & Yesterday	1965	7.50	15.00	30.00
MGS-27080 [M]	James Brown Plays New Breed	1966	7.50	15.00	30.00
MGS-27084 [M]	Handful of Soul	1966	7.50	15.00	30.00
MGS-27087 [M]	The James Brown Show	1967	7.50	15.00	30.00
—Various-artists LP					
MGS-27093 [M]	James Brown Plays the Real Thing	1967	7.50	15.00	30.00
SRS-67054 [S]	Showtime	1964	10.00	2.00	40.00
SRS-67057 [S]	Grits & Soul	1965	10.00	20.00	40.00
SRS-67058 [S]	Out of Sight	1965	37.50	75.00	150.00
SRS-67072 [S]	James Brown Plays James Brown — Today & Yesterday	1965	10.00	20.00	40.00
SRS-67080 [S]	James Brown Plays New Breed	1966	10.00	2.00	40.00
SRS-67084 [S]	Handful of Soul	1966	10.00	20.00	40.00
SRS-67087 [S]	The James Brown Show	1967	10.00	2.00	40.00
—Various-artists LP					
SRS-67093 [S]	James Brown Plays the Real Thing	1967	10.00	20.00	40.00
SRS-67109	James Brown Sings Out of Sight	1968	7.50	15.00	30.00
—Abridged reissue of 67058					
SOLID SMOKE					
SS-8006	Live and Lowdown at the Apollo, Vol. 1	1980	3.00	6.00	12.00
SS-8013	Can Your Heart Stand It	1981	3.00	6.00	12.00
SS-8023	The Federal Years, Part 1	198?	3.00	6.00	12.00
SS-8024	The Federal Years, Part 2	198?	3.00	6.00	12.00
T.K.					
615	Soul Syndrome	1980	7.50	15.00	30.00

BROWN, JAMES (2)

The MGM James Brown is not the same person as the others.

45s

Number	Title (A Side/B Side)	Yr	VG	VG+	NM
MGM					
11987	The Berry Tree/I Lost When I Found You	1955	3.00	6.00	12.00
12011	The Kentuckian Song/The Man from Laramie	1955	3.00	6.00	12.00
12080	The White Buffalo/It's Lonesome Out Tonight	1955	3.00	6.00	12.00

BROWN, JERICHO

45s

Number	Title (A Side/B Side)	Yr	VG	VG+	NM
DEL-FI					
4103	I Need You/Lonesome Drifter	1958	6.25	12.50	25.00
RKO UNIQUE					
412	Little Neva/Darling I Love Thee	1957	7.50	15.00	30.00
WARNER BROS.					
5161	Look for a Star/Don't You Know	1960	3.00	6.00	12.00
5213	Rovin' Eye/Someday She'll Come Along	1961	2.50	5.00	10.00
5381	Lonely Birthday/Paper Rose and Candy Ring	1963	2.50	5.00	10.00
5408	I'll Be Gone/He's Taken My Baby	1964	2.50	5.00	10.00
5458	I'm Watching You/Wisdom of a Fool	1964	2.50	5.00	10.00

BROWN, JIM ED

Also see THE BROWNS.

45s

Number	Title (A Side/B Side)	Yr	VG	VG+	NM
RCA					
PB-10619	Let Me Love You Where It Hurts/I Love You All Over Again	1976	—	2.00	4.00
PB-10786	I've Rode with the Best/Close the Door	1976	—	2.00	4.00
PB-11134	When I Touch Her There/Mexican Joe	1977	—	2.00	4.00
PB-11742	You're the Part of Me/Changes	1979	—	2.00	4.00
RCA VICTOR					
APBO-0059	Broad-Minded Man/Helpin' You Get Over Him	1973	—	2.50	5.00
APBO-0180	Sometime Sunshine/Louisiana Woman	1973	—	2.50	5.00
APBO-0267	It's That Time of Night/If Wishes Were Horses	1974	—	2.50	5.00
PB-10047	Get Up I Think I Love You/A Nickel for the Fiddler	1974	—	2.50	5.00
PB-10131	Don Junior/Who's Gonna Love Me	1974	—	2.50	5.00
PB-10233	Barroom Pal, Goodtime Gals/Nearer My Love to You	1975	—	2.50	5.00
PB-10370	Fine Time to Get the Blues/Sweet Song	1975	—	2.50	5.00
PB-10531	Another Morning/An Old Flame Never Dies	1975	—	2.50	5.00
47-8566	I Heard from a Memory Last Night/Just to Satisfy You	1965	2.00	4.00	8.00
47-8644	I'm Just a Country Boy/To Be or Not to Be	1965	2.00	4.00	8.00
47-8766	Regular on My Mind/The Mounties	1966	2.00	4.00	8.00
47-8867	A Taste of Heaven/Paint Me the Color of Your Wall	1966	2.00	4.00	8.00
47-8997	The Last Laugh/Party Girl	1966	2.00	4.00	8.00
47-9077	You Can Have Her/If You Were Mine, Mary	1967	2.00	4.00	8.00
47-9192	Pop a Top/Too Good to Be True	1967	2.00	4.00	8.00
47-9329	Bottle, Bottle/It Doesn't Know Any Better	1967	2.00	4.00	8.00
47-9434	The Cajun Stripper/You'll Never Know	1968	2.00	4.00	8.00
47-9518	The Enemy/I Just Came from There	1968	2.00	4.00	8.00
47-9616	Jack and Jill/Honky Tonkin'	1968	2.00	4.00	8.00
47-9677	Longest Beer of the Night/What's a Girl Like You	1968	—	3.00	6.00
47-9810	Lift Ring, Pull Open/Going Up the Country	1970	—	3.00	6.00
47-9858	Baby, I Tried/The City Cries at Night	1970	—	3.00	6.00
47-9909	Morning/How to Lose a Good Woman	1970	—	3.00	6.00
47-9965	Angel's Sunday/Every Mile of the Way	1971	—	3.00	6.00
74-0114	Man and Wife Time/Healing Hands of Time	1969	—	3.00	6.00
74-0190	The Three Bells/Beyond the Shadow	1969	—	3.00	6.00
74-0274	Ginger Is Gentle and Waiting for Me/Drink Boys Drink	1969	—	3.00	6.00
74-0509	She's Leavin' (Bonnie, Please Don't Go)/Love Is Worth the Tryin'	1971	—	3.00	6.00
74-0642	Evening/You Keep Right On Loving Me	1972	—	3.00	6.00
74-0712	How I Love Them Old Songs/Close	1972	—	3.00	6.00
74-0785	All I Had to Do/Triangle	1972	—	3.00	6.00
74-0846	Unbelievable Love/If Her Blue Eyes Don't Get You	1972	—	3.00	6.00
74-0928	Southern Loving/How Long Does It Take a Memory to Drown	1973	—	3.00	6.00

Albums

Number	Title (A Side/B Side)	Yr	VG	VG+	NM
RCA CAMDEN					
ACL1-0197	Hey Good Lookin'	1973	2.50	5.00	10.00
ACL1-0618	The Three Bells	1974	2.50	5.00	10.00
CAS-2496	Gentle on My Mind	1971	2.50	5.00	10.00
CAS-2549	Country Cream	1972	2.50	5.00	10.00
RCA VICTOR					
APL1-0172	Bar-Rooms & Pop-A-Tops	1973	3.75	7.50	15.00
APL1-0324	Best of Jim Ed Brown	1973	3.75	7.50	15.00
APL1-0572	It's That Time of Night	1974	3.75	7.50	15.00
ANL1-1215	It's That Time of Night	1975	2.50	5.00	10.00
—Reissue of 0572					
LPM-3569 [M]	Alone with You	1966	5.00	10.00	20.00
LSP-3569 [S]	Alone with You	1966	6.25	12.50	25.00
LPM-3744 [M]	Just Jim	1967	6.25	12.50	25.00
LSP-3744 [S]	Just Jim	1967	5.00	10.00	20.00
LPM-3853 [M]	Gems by Jim	1967	6.25	12.50	25.00
LSP-3853 [S]	Gems by Jim	1967	5.00	10.00	20.00
LPM-3942 [M]	Bottle, Bottle	1968	10.00	20.00	40.00
LSP-3942 [S]	Bottle, Bottle	1968	5.00	10.00	20.00
LSP-4011	Country's Best on Record	1968	5.00	10.00	20.00
LSP-4130	This Is My Best!	1968	5.00	10.00	20.00
LSP-4175	Jim Ed Sings the Browns	1969	5.00	10.00	20.00
LSP-4262	Going Up the Country	1970	3.75	7.50	15.00
LSP-4366	Just for You	1970	3.75	7.50	15.00
LSP-4461	Morning	1971	3.75	7.50	15.00
LSP-4525	Angel's Sunday	1971	3.75	7.50	15.00
LSP-4614	She's Leavin'	1971	3.75	7.50	15.00
LSP-4713	Evening	1972	3.75	7.50	15.00
LSP-4755	Brown Is Blue	1972	3.75	7.50	15.00

BROWN, JOE, AND THE BRUVVERS

45s

Number	Title (A Side/B Side)	Yr	VG	VG+	NM
BELL					
45364 [DJ]	Hey Mama (mono/stereo)	1973	—	3.00	6.00
—May be promo only					
CAMEO					
241	It Only Took a Minute/All Things Bright and Beautiful	1963	3.00	6.00	12.00
DOT					
16508	Hava Nagila/That's What Love Will Do	1963	3.00	6.00	12.00
HICKORY					
1329	Sally Ann/Little Ukulele	1965	2.50	5.00	10.00
JAMIE					
1298	Lonely Circus/Teardrops in the Rain	1965	2.50	5.00	10.00
1327	Sea of Heartbreak/Mrs. O's Theme	1966	2.50	5.00	10.00
KAPP					
2068	Adieu, Monsieur Le Professeur/Diamonds of Dew	1969	—	3.00	6.00
LONDON INT'L.					
10507	What a Crazy World We're Living In/Popcorn	1962	3.75	7.50	15.00
10517	A Picture of You/A Lay-About's Lament	1962	3.75	7.50	15.00
10522	Your Tender Look/The Other Side of Town	1962	3.75	7.50	15.00
STELLAR					
1504	Hava Nagila/That's What Love Will Do	1963	3.75	7.50	15.00
VERTIGO					
201	I Was Lost/Cincinnati Floor	1974	—	2.50	5.00
—As "Brown's Home Brew"					
WARNER BROS.					
7055	With a Little Help from My Friends/Won't You Show Me Around	1967	2.00	4.00	8.00

BROWN, MAXINE

45s

Number	Title (A Side/B Side)	Yr	VG	VG+	NM
ABC-PARAMOUNT					
10235	I Don't Need You No More/Think of Me	1961	3.00	6.00	12.00
10255	After All We've Been Through Together/My Life	1961	3.00	6.00	12.00
10290	I Got a Funny Kind of Feeling/What I Don't Know	1962	3.00	6.00	12.00
10315	Forget Him/A Man	1962	3.00	6.00	12.00
10327	No Time for Cryin'/Wanting You	1962	3.00	6.00	12.00
10343	I Kneel at Your Throne/If I Knew Then	1962	3.00	6.00	12.00
10370	Promise Me Anything/Am I Falling in Love	1962	3.00	6.00	12.00
10388	Life Goes On Just the Same/If You Have No Real Objections	1962	3.00	6.00	12.00

Number	Title (A Side/B Side)	Yr	VG	VG+	NM
AVCO					
4585	Always and Forever/Make Love to Me	1971	—	2.50	5.00
4604	Treat Me Like a Lady/I.O.U.	1972	—	2.50	5.00
4612	Picked Up, Packed and Went Away/(B-side unknown)	1972	—	2.50	5.00
COMMONWEALTH UNITED					
3001	We'll Cry Together/Darling Be Home Soon	1969	—	3.00	6.00
3008	I Can't Get Along Without You/Reason to Believe	1970	—	3.00	6.00
EPIC					
10334	Seems You've Forsaken My Love/Plum Outa Sight	1968	2.50	5.00	10.00
10424	Love in Them There Hills/From Loving You	1968	2.50	5.00	10.00
NOMAR					
103	All in My Mind/Harry, Let's Marry	1960	3.75	7.50	15.00
106	Funny/Now That You've Gone	1961	3.75	7.50	15.00
107	Heaven in Your Arms/Maxine's Place	1961	3.75	7.50	15.00
—B-side by Frankie and the Flips					
WAND					
135	Ask Me/Yesterday's Kisses	1963	2.50	5.00	10.00
135 [PS]	Ask Me/Yesterday's Kisses	1963	12.50	25.00	50.00
142	Coming Back to You/Since I Found You	1963	2.50	5.00	10.00
152	Little Girl Lost/You Upset My Soul	1964	2.00	4.00	8.00
158	I Cry Alone/Put Yourself in My Place	1964	2.00	4.00	8.00
162	Oh No Not My Baby/You Upset My Soul	1964	3.00	6.00	12.00
173	It's Gonna Be Alright/You Do Something to Me	1965	2.00	4.00	8.00
185	Anything for a Laugh/One Step at a Time	1965	2.00	4.00	8.00
1104	If You Gotta Make a Fool of Somebody/You're in Love	1965	2.00	4.00	8.00
1117	One in a Million/Anything You Do Is Alright	1966	2.00	4.00	8.00
1128	We Can Work It Out/Let Me Give You My Lovin'	1966	2.00	4.00	8.00
1145	I Don't Need Anything/The Secret of Livin'	1967	2.00	4.00	8.00
1179	Soul Serenade/He's the Only Guy I'll Ever Love	1968	2.00	4.00	8.00
Albums					
COLLECTABLES					
COL-5116	Golden Classics	198?	3.00	6.00	12.00
COMMONWEALTH UNITED					
CU-6001	We'll Cry Together	1969	5.00	10.00	20.00
GUEST STAR					
GS-1911 [M]	Maxine Brown	1964	3.00	6.00	12.00
WAND					
WD-656 [M]	The Fabulous Sound of Maxine Brown	1963	12.50	25.00	50.00
WDS-656 [S]	The Fabulous Sound of Maxine Brown	1963	15.00	30.00	60.00
WD-663 [M]	Spotlight on Maxine Brown	1965	7.50	15.00	30.00
WDS-663 [S]	Spotlight on Maxine Brown	1965	10.00	20.00	40.00
WD-684 [M]	Maxine Brown's Greatest Hits	1967	5.00	10.00	20.00
WDS-684 [S]	Maxine Brown's Greatest Hits	1967	6.25	12.50	25.00

BROWN, NAPPY

45s

Number	Title (A Side/B Side)	Yr	VG	VG+	NM
ICHIBAN					
206	Lemon Squeezin' Daddy/Small Red Apples	1989	—	2.50	5.00
SAVOY					
1129	That Man/I Wonder	1954	7.50	15.00	30.00
1135	Is It True, Is It True/Two-Faced Woman	1954	7.50	15.00	30.00
1155	Don't Be Angry/It's Really You	1955	6.25	12.50	25.00
1162	Piddly Patter Patter/There'll Come a Day	1955	6.25	12.50	25.00
1176	Doodle I Love You/Sittin' in the Dark	1955	6.25	12.50	25.00
1187	Open Up That Door/Pleasing You	1956	6.25	12.50	25.00
1196	Am I/Love Baby	1956	6.25	12.50	25.00
1506	Little by Little/I'm Getting Lonesome	1956	5.00	10.00	20.00
1511	Pretty Girl (Yea Yea Yea)/I'm Gonna Get You	1957	5.00	10.00	20.00
1514	Goody Goody Gum Drops/Bye Bye Baby	1957	5.00	10.00	20.00
1525	The Right Time/Oh You Don't Know	1957	5.00	10.00	20.00
1530	If You Need Some Lovin'/I'm in the Mood	1958	5.00	10.00	20.00
1547	Skidy Wo/I Cried Like a Baby	1958	5.00	10.00	20.00
1551	It Don't Hurt No More/My Baby	1958	5.00	10.00	20.00
1555	You're Going to Need Someone/Skiddy Woe	1958	5.00	10.00	20.00
1562	A Long Time/All Right Now	1959	5.00	10.00	20.00
1569	This Is My Confession/For Those Who Love	1959	5.00	10.00	20.00
1575	I Cried Like a Baby/So Deep	1959	5.00	10.00	20.00
1579	Give Me Your Love/Too Shy	1959	5.00	10.00	20.00
1582	Down in the Alley/My Baby Knows	1960	3.75	7.50	15.00
1587	Baby, Cry, Cry, Cry, Baby/What's Come Over You	1960	3.75	7.50	15.00
1588	Apple of My Eye/Baby I Got News for You	1960	3.75	7.50	15.00
1592	The Hole I'm In/Nobody Can Say	1960	3.75	7.50	15.00
1594	Coal Miner/Honnie-Bonnie	1961	3.75	7.50	15.00
1598	Don't Be Angry/Any Time Is the Right Time	1961	3.75	7.50	15.00
1616	Didn't You Know/I've Had My Fun	1962	3.75	7.50	15.00
1621	Lock on the Door/So Glad I Don't Have to Cry No More	1963	3.75	7.50	15.00
Albums					
BLACK TOP					
BT-1039	Something Gonna Jump Out the Bushes	1988	3.00	6.00	12.00
ICHIBAN					
ICH-1056	Apples and Lemons	198?	3.00	6.00	12.00
KING SNAKE					
ICH-9006	Aw! Shucks	1991	3.75	7.50	15.00
SAVOY					
MG-14002 [M]	Nappy Brown Sings	1958	100.00	200.00	400.00
MG-14025 [M]	The Right Time	1960	62.50	125.00	250.00
14427	Nappy Brown	1977	3.00	6.00	12.00
SAVOY JAZZ					
SJL-1149	Don't Be Angry	198?	2.50	5.00	10.00

BROWN, ODELL

45s

Number	Title (A Side/B Side)	Yr	VG	VG+	NM
CADET					
5570	Mellow Yellow/Quiet Village	1967	2.00	4.00	8.00
5591	The Look of Love/No More Water in the Well	1968	2.00	4.00	8.00
5624	The Weight/Think About It	1968	2.00	4.00	8.00
Albums					
CADET					
LP-775 [M]	Raising the Roof	1966	3.75	7.50	15.00
LPS-775 [S]	Raising the Roof	1966	5.00	10.00	20.00
LP-788 [M]	Mellow Yellow	1967	5.00	10.00	20.00
LPS-788 [S]	Mellow Yellow	1967	3.75	7.50	15.00
LP-800 [M]	Ducky	1967	5.00	10.00	20.00
LPS-800 [S]	Ducky	1967	3.75	7.50	15.00
LPS-823	Odell Brown Plays Otis Redding	1969	3.75	7.50	15.00
LPS-838	Free Delivery	1970	3.75	7.50	15.00
PAULA					
4005	Odell Brown	1974	3.00	6.00	12.00

BROWN, RAY, AND THE WHISPERS

45s

Number	Title (A Side/B Side)	Yr	VG	VG+	NM
GNP CRESCENDO					
357	Fool, Fool, Fool/Pride	1965	5.00	10.00	20.00
PARKWAY					
951	20 Miles/Devoted to You	1965	7.50	15.00	30.00

BROWN, ROY

45s

Number	Title (A Side/B Side)	Yr	VG	VG+	NM
BLUESWAY					
61002	New Orleans Women/Standing on Broadway (Watching the Girls)	1967	2.00	4.00	8.00
DELUXE					
3318	Big Town/Train Time Blues	1951	50.00	100.00	200.00
—Roy Brown singles on DeLuxe before 3318 are unconfirmed on 45 rpm					
3318	Big Town/Train Time Blues	1951	100.00	200.00	400.00
—Blue vinyl					
3319	Bar Room Blues/Good Rockin' Man	1951	50.00	100.00	200.00
—Black vinyl					
3319	Bar Room Blues/Good Rockin' Man	1951	100.00	200.00	400.00
—Blue vinyl					
3323	I've Got the Last Laugh Now/Brown Angel	1951	50.00	100.00	200.00
—Black vinyl					
3323	I've Got the Last Laugh Now/Brown Angel	1951	100.00	200.00	400.00
—Blue vinyl					
HOME OF THE BLUES					
107	Don't Break My Heart/A Man with the Blues	1960	6.25	12.50	25.00
110	Tired of Being Alone/Rocking All the Time	1960	6.25	12.50	25.00
115	Oh So Wonderful/Sugar Baby	1961	6.25	12.50	25.00
122	Rock and Roll Jamboree/I Need a Friend	1961	6.25	12.50	25.00
IMPERIAL					
5422	Everybody/Saturday Night	1957	7.50	15.00	30.00
5427	Party Doll/I'm Sticking with You	1957	7.50	15.00	30.00
5439	Let the Four Winds Blow/Diddy-Y-Diddy-O	1957	7.50	15.00	30.00
5455	I'm Convicted of Love/I'm Ready to Play	1957	7.50	15.00	30.00
5469	Tick of the Clock/Slow Down Little Eva	1957	7.50	15.00	30.00
5489	Ain't Gonna Do It/Sail On Little Girl	1958	7.50	15.00	30.00
5510	Hip Shakin' Baby/Be My Love Tonight	1958	7.50	15.00	30.00
5969	Let the Four Winds Blow/Diddy-Yi-Diddy-Yo	1963	5.00	10.00	20.00
KING					
4602	Travelin' Man/Hurry, Hurry Baby	1953	15.00	30.00	60.00
4609	Grandpa Stole My Baby/Money Can't Buy Love	1953	15.00	30.00	60.00
4704	Trouble at Midnight/Bootlegging Baby	1954	15.00	30.00	60.00
4715	Up Jumped the Devil/This Is My Last Goodbye	1954	15.00	30.00	60.00
4722	No Love at All/Don't Let It Rain	1954	15.00	30.00	60.00
4731	Ain't It a Shame/Gal from Kokomo	1954	15.00	30.00	60.00
4743	Worried Life Blues/Black Diamond	1954	15.00	30.00	60.00
4761	Fannie Brown Got Married/Queen of Diamonds	1955	12.50	25.00	50.00
4816	Shake 'Em Up Baby/Letter to Baby	1955	12.50	25.00	50.00
4834	My Little Angel Child/She's Gone Too Long	1955	12.50	25.00	50.00
5178	La-Dee-Dah-Dee/Melinda	1959	5.00	10.00	20.00
5207	I Never Had It So Good/Rinky Dinky Doo	1959	5.00	10.00	20.00
5218	Hard Luck Blues/Good Looking and Forty	1959	5.00	10.00	20.00
5247	School Bell Rock/Ain't No Rocking No More	1959	5.00	10.00	20.00
5333	Ain't Got No Blues Today/Adorable One	1960	5.00	10.00	20.00
5521	Mighty Mighty Man/Good Man Blues	1961	5.00	10.00	20.00
MERCURY					
73166	It's My Fault Darling/Love for Sale	1970	—	3.00	6.00
73219	Mail Man Blues/Hunky Funky Woman	1971	—	3.00	6.00
Albums					
BLUESWAY					
BLS-6019	The Blues Are Brown	1968	6.25	12.50	25.00
BLS-6056	Hard Times	1973	6.25	12.50	25.00
EPIC					
E 30473	Live at Monterey	1971	6.25	12.50	25.00
INTERMEDIA					
QS-5027	Good Rockin' Tonight	198?	2.50	5.00	10.00
KING					
956 [M]	Roy Brown Sings 24 Hits	1966	12.50	25.00	50.00
KS-956 [R]	Roy Brown Sings 24 Hits	1966	12.50	25.00	50.00
KS-1130	Hard Luck Blues	1971	6.25	12.50	25.00

BROWN, ROY / WYNONIE HARRIS

Albums

Number	Title (A Side/B Side)	Yr	VG	VG+	NM
KING					
607 [M]	Battle of the Blues	1958	150.00	300.00	600.00
627 [M]	Battle of the Blues, Volume 2	1959	200.00	400.00	800.00

BROWN, ROY / WYNONIE HARRIS / EDDIE VINSON

Albums

Number	Title (A Side/B Side)	Yr	VG	VG+	NM
KING					
668 [M]	Battle of the Blues, Volume 4	1960	625.00	1250.	2500.

BROWN, RUTH

45s

Number	Title (A Side/B Side)	Yr	VG	VG+	NM
ATLANTIC					
919	Teardrops from My Eyes/Am I Making the Same Mistake	1950	100.00	200.00	400.00
—This and Atlantic 914 were the label's first two 45s.					

Number	Title (A Side/B Side)	Yr	VG	VG+	NM
948	Shine On—Big Bright Moon Shine On/Without My Love	1951	15.00	30.00	60.00
—Ruth Brown records on Atlantic before 948 (except 919) are unconfirmed on 45 rpm					
962	5-10-15 Hours/Be Anything But Be Mine	1952	12.50	25.00	50.00
973	Daddy Daddy/Have a Good Time	1952	12.50	25.00	50.00
978	Three Letters/Good for Nothing Joe	1952	12.50	25.00	50.00
986	(Mama) He Treats Your Daughter Mean/R.B. Blues	1953	15.00	30.00	60.00
993	Wild Wild Young Men/Mend Your Ways	1953	10.00	20.00	40.00
1005	The Tears Keep Tumblin' Down/I Would If I Could	1953	7.50	15.00	30.00
1018	Love Contest/If You Don't Want Me	1954	7.50	15.00	30.00
1023	Sentimental Journey/It's All in Your Mind	1954	7.50	15.00	30.00
1027	If I Had Any Sense/Hello Little Boy	1954	7.50	15.00	30.00
1036	Oh What a Dream/Please Don't Freeze	1954	7.50	15.00	30.00
1044	Somebody Touch Me/Mambo Baby	1954	7.50	15.00	30.00
1051	Ever Since My Baby's Been Gone/Bye Bye Young Men	1955	7.50	15.00	30.00
1059	I Can See Everybody's Baby/As Long As I'm Moving	1955	7.50	15.00	30.00
1072	What'd I Say/It's Love Baby (24 Hours of the Day)	1955	7.50	15.00	30.00
1077	Love Has Joined Us Together/I Gotta Have You	1955	7.50	15.00	30.00
—With Clyde McPhatter					
1082	Old Man River/I Want to Do More	1956	6.25	12.50	25.00
1091	Sweet Baby of Mine/I'm Getting Right	1956	6.25	12.50	25.00
1102	I Want to Be Loved/Mom, Oh Mom	1956	6.25	12.50	25.00
1113	Smooth Operator/I Still Love You	1956	6.25	12.50	25.00
1125	Lucky Lips/My Heart Is Breaking Over You	1957	6.25	12.50	25.00
1140	When I Get You Baby/One More Time	1957	6.25	12.50	25.00
1153	Show Me/I Hope We Meet	1957	6.25	12.50	25.00
1166	A New Love/Look Me Up	1957	6.25	12.50	25.00
1177	Book of Lies/Just Too Much	1958	6.25	12.50	25.00
1197	This Little Girl's Gone/Why Me	1958	6.25	12.50	25.00
2008	Mama, He Treats Your Daughter Mean/I'll Step Aside	1958	5.00	10.00	20.00
2015	5-10-15 Hours/Itty Bitty Girl	1959	5.00	10.00	20.00
2026	Jack O'Diamonds/I Can't Hear a Word You Say	1959	5.00	10.00	20.00
2035	I Don't Know/Papa Daddy	1959	5.00	10.00	20.00
2052	Don't Deceive Me/I Burned Your Letter	1960	5.00	10.00	20.00
2064	The Door Is Still Open/What I Wouldn't Give	1960	5.00	10.00	20.00
2075	Taking Care of Business/Honey Boy	1960	5.00	10.00	20.00
2088	Sure 'Nuff/Here He Comes	1961	3.75	7.50	15.00
2104	It Tears Me All to Pieces/Anyone But You	1961	3.75	7.50	15.00
DECCA					
31598	What Happened to You/Yes Sir That's My Baby	1964	2.50	5.00	10.00
31640	Come a Little Closer/I Love Him and I Know It	1964	2.50	5.00	10.00
MAINSTREAM					
611	On the Good Ship Lollipop/Hurry On Down	1965	2.50	5.00	10.00
PHILIPS					
40028	Shake a Hand/Say It Again	1962	3.00	6.00	12.00
40056	Mama He Treats Your Daughter Mean/Hold My Hand	1962	3.00	6.00	12.00
40086	He Tells Me with His Eyes/If You Don't Tell Nobody	1963	3.00	6.00	12.00
40119	Satisfied/If You Don't Tell Nobody	1963	3.00	6.00	12.00
7-Inch Extended Plays					
ATLANTIC					
505	Teardrops from My Eyes/5-10-15//Mama He Treats Your Daughter Mean/So Long	1953	25.00	50.00	100.00
505 [PS]	Ruth Brown Sings	1953	37.50	75.00	150.00
585	*Lucky Lips/Mambo Baby/Smooth Operator/Oh What a Dream	1957	15.00	30.00	60.00
585 [PS]	Ruth Brown	1957	30.00	60.00	120.00
Albums					
ATLANTIC					
1308 [M]	Last Date with Ruth Brown	1959	50.00	100.00	200.00
—Black label					
1308 [M]	Last Date with Ruth Brown	1961	12.50	25.00	50.00
—Red and purple label, "fan" logo in white					
SD 1308 [S]	Last Date with Ruth Brown	1959	75.00	150.00	300.00
—Green label					
SD 1308 [S]	Last Date with Ruth Brown	1961	15.00	30.00	60.00
—Blue and green label, "fan" logo in white					
8004 [M]	Ruth Brown	1957	50.00	100.00	200.00
—Black label					
8004 [M]	Ruth Brown	1960	37.50	75.00	150.00
—White "bullseye" label					
8004 [M]	Ruth Brown	1961	12.50	25.00	50.00
—Red and purple label, "fan" logo in white					
8026 [M]	Miss Rhythm	1959	50.00	100.00	200.00
—Black label					
8026 [M]	Miss Rhythm	1960	37.50	75.00	150.00
—White "bullseye" label					
8026 [M]	Miss Rhythm	1961	12.50	25.00	50.00
—Red and purple label, "fan" logo in white					
8080 [M]	The Best of Ruth Brown	1963	10.00	20.00	40.00
DOBRE					
1041	You Don't Know Me	1978	3.00	6.00	12.00
FANTASY					
F-9661	Have a Good Time	1988	3.00	6.00	12.00
F-9662	Blues on Broadway	1989	3.00	6.00	12.00
MAINSTREAM					
369	Softly	1972	3.00	6.00	12.00
S-6034 [S]	Ruth Brown '65	1965	7.50	15.00	30.00
56034 [M]	Ruth Brown '65	1965	6.25	12.50	25.00
PHILIPS					
PHM 200028 [M]	Along Comes Ruth	1962	10.00	20.00	40.00
PHM 200065 [M]	Gospel Time	1962	7.50	15.00	30.00
PHS 600028 [S]	Along Comes Ruth	1962	12.50	25.00	50.00
PHS 600065 [S]	Gospel Time	1962	10.00	20.00	40.00
SDEG					
4023	Brown, Black and Beautiful	198?	3.00	6.00	12.00
SKYE					
LP-13	Black Is Brown and Brown Is Beautiful	1970	3.75	7.50	15.00

BROWN, SKIPPY

Number	Title (A Side/B Side)	Yr	VG	VG+	NM
45s					
CHANCE					
1129	So Many Days/Tale of Woe	1953	62.50	125.00	250.00

BROWN, TOMMY

Number	Title (A Side/B Side)	Yr	VG	VG+	NM
45s					
ABC-PARAMOUNT					
10632	Ain't So/Well, There Goes My Heart	1965	3.00	6.00	12.00
DOT					
16130	Tra-La-La/Weepin' and Cryin'	1960	3.75	7.50	15.00
GROOVE					
0132	Don't Leave Me/Won't You Forgive Me	1955	7.50	15.00	30.00
0143	The Thrill Is Gone/Gambler's Prayer	1956	7.50	15.00	30.00
IMPERIAL					
5476	Rock Away My Blues/Someday, Somewhere	1957	12.50	25.00	50.00
5533	Just for You/A Heart with No Feeling	1958	7.50	15.00	30.00
KING					
4658	How Much Do You Think I Can Stand/Fore Day Train	1953	37.50	75.00	150.00
4679	Goodbye, I'm Gone/Since You Left Me Dear	1953	15.00	30.00	60.00
UNITED					
183	Remember Me/Southern Woman	1956	37.50	75.00	150.00

BROWN, WINI

Number	Title (A Side/B Side)	Yr	VG	VG+	NM
45s					
COLUMBIA					
1-872	A Good Man Is Hard to Find/This Is the Last Time	1950	10.00	20.00	40.00
—Microgroove 7-inch, 33 1/3 rpm single					
6-872	A Good Man Is Hard to Find/This Is the Last Time	1950	7.50	15.00	30.00
JARO					
77018	Gone Again/Johnny with the Gentle Hand	1960	5.00	10.00	20.00
MERCURY					
5870	Here in My Heart/Your Happiness Is Mine	1952	50.00	100.00	200.00
8270	Be Anything — Be Mine/Heaven Knows Why	1952	50.00	100.00	200.00
70062	Tear Down the Sky/Can't Stand No More	1953	25.00	50.00	100.00
RCA VICTOR					
47-6970	Available Lover/It's All in Your Mind	1957	5.00	10.00	20.00
Albums					
SAVOY JAZZ					
SJL-1163 [M]	Miss Brown for You	1986	2.50	5.00	10.00

BROWN'S HOME BREW

See JOE BROWN AND THE BRUVVERS.

BROWNE, JACKSON

Number	Title (A Side/B Side)	Yr	VG	VG+	NM
45s					
ASYLUM					
11004	Doctor My Eyes/Looking Into You	1972	—	2.50	5.00
11006	Rock Me on the Water/Something Fine	1972	—	2.00	4.00
11023	Redneck Friend/Those Times You've Come	1973	—	2.00	4.00
11030	Ready or Not/Take It Easy	1974	—	2.00	4.00
45227	Walking Slow/Before the Deluge	1975	—	2.00	4.00
45242	Fountains of Sorrow/The Late Show	1975	—	2.00	4.00
45379	Here Come Those Tears Again/Linda Paloma	1976	—	2.00	4.00
45399	The Pretender/Daddy's Tune	1977	—	2.00	4.00
45460	Running on Empty/Nothing But Time	1978	—	2.00	4.00
45460 [PS]	Running on Empty/Nothing But Time	1978	—	2.50	5.00
45485 A/B	Stay/Rosie	1978	—	2.50	5.00
45485 A/B [PS]	Stay/Rosie	1978	—	2.50	5.00
45485 A/C	Stay/The Load-Out	1978	—	2.00	4.00
45543	You Love the Thunder/The Road	1978	—	2.00	4.00
45543 [PS]	You Love the Thunder/The Road	1978	—	2.50	5.00
47003	Boulevard/Call It a Loan	1980	—	2.00	4.00
47003 [PS]	Boulevard/Call It a Loan	1980	—	2.50	5.00
47036	That Girl Could Sing/Of Missing Persons	1980	—	2.00	4.00
69543	In the Shape of a Heart/Voice of America	1986	—	—	3.00
69566	For America/Till I Go Down	1986	—	—	3.00
69566 [PS]	For America/Till I Go Down	1986	—	—	3.00
69764	For a Rocker/Downtown	1984	—	—	3.00
69764 [PS]	For a Rocker/Downtown	1984	—	—	3.00
69791	Tender Is the Night/On the Day	1983	—	—	3.00
69791 [PS]	Tender Is the Night/On the Day	1983	—	—	3.00
69826	Lawyers in Love/Say It Isn't True	1983	—	—	3.00
69826 [PS]	Lawyers in Love/Say It Isn't True	1983	—	—	3.00
69982	Somebody's Baby/The Crow on the Cradle [w/ Graham Nash & David Lindley]	1982	—	2.00	4.00
69982 [PS]	Somebody's Baby/The Crow on the Cradle [w/ Graham Nash & David Lindley]	1982	—	2.00	4.00
ELEKTRA					
69292	World in Motion/My Personal Revenge	1989	—	2.00	4.00
Albums					
ASYLUM					
6E-107	The Pretender	1977	2.50	5.00	10.00
—Reissue of 7E-1079					
6E-113	Running on Empty	1977	2.50	5.00	10.00
5E-511	Hold Out	1979	2.50	5.00	10.00
7E-1017	Late for the Sky	1974	3.00	6.00	12.00
EQ-1017 [Q]	Late for the Sky	1974	7.50	15.00	30.00
7E-1079	The Pretender	1976	3.00	6.00	12.00
SD 5051	Jackson Browne (Saturate Before Using)	1972	5.00	10.00	20.00
—Burlap cover, opens at top; white label with "Asylum Records" logo in a circle at top					
SD 5051	Jackson Browne (Saturate Before Using)	1972	4.00	8.00	16.00
—Burlap cover, opens at right side; white label with "Asylum Records" logo in a circle at top					
SD 5051	Jackson Browne (Saturate Before Using)	1972	3.00	6.00	12.00
—Burlap cover; "clouds" label					
SD 5051	Jackson Browne (Saturate Before Using)	1972	2.00	4.00	8.00
—Standard cover					
SD 5067	For Everyman	1973	3.00	6.00	12.00
60268	Lawyers in Love	1983	2.50	5.00	10.00
60457	Lives in the Balance	1986	2.50	5.00	10.00

Number	Title (A Side/B Side)	Yr	VG	VG+	NM
ELEKTRA					
60830	World in Motion	1989	2.50	5.00	10.00
MOBILE FIDELITY					
1-055	The Pretender	1981	6.25	12.50	25.00
—Audiophile vinyl					
(NO LABEL)					
(no #) [(2)]	"Jackson Browne's First Album"	1967	1000.	1500.	2000.
—Publisher's demo in plain cardboard jacket					

BROWNETTES, THE

45s

Number	Title (A Side/B Side)	Yr	VG	VG+	NM
KING					
6153	Baby, Don't You Know/Never Find a Love Like Mine	1968	5.00	10.00	20.00

BROWNS, THE

Also see JIM ED BROWN.

45s

Number	Title (A Side/B Side)	Yr	VG	VG+	NM
FABOR					
107	Rio De Janeiro/Lookin' Back to See	1954	6.25	12.50	25.00
—All on Fabor as "Jim Edward and Maxine Brown"					
112	Why Am I Falling/Itsy Witsy Bitsy Me	1954	6.25	12.50	25.00
118	Here Today and Gone Tomorrow/Draggin' Main Street	1955	6.25	12.50	25.00
122	Do Memories Haunt You/Jungle Magic	1955	6.25	12.50	25.00
126	You Thought I Thought/Here Today and Gone Tomorrow	1955	6.25	12.50	25.00
RCA VICTOR					
37-7866	Ground Hog/Angel's Dolly	1961	6.25	12.50	25.00
—"Compact Single 33" (small hole, plays at LP speed)					
37-7917	Whispering Wine/My Baby's Gone	1961	6.25	12.50	25.00
—"Compact Single 33" (small hole, plays at LP speed)					
37-7969	Foolish Pride/Alpha and Omega	1961	6.25	12.50	25.00
—"Compact Single 33" (small hole, plays at LP speed)					
47-6480	I Take the Chance/Goo Goo Da Da	1956	5.00	10.00	20.00
—As "Jim Edward and Maxine Brown"					
47-6628	Here Today and Gone Tomorrow/Looking Back to See	1956	5.00	10.00	20.00
47-6629	Do Memories Haunt You/Draggin' Main Street	1956	5.00	10.00	20.00
47-6631	Just As Long As You Love Me/Don't Tell Me Your Troubles	1956	5.00	10.00	20.00
—As "Jim Edward, Maxine and Bonnie Brown"					
47-6730	A Man with a Plan/Just a Lot of Sweet Talk	1956	5.00	10.00	20.00
—As "Jim, Maxine and Bonnie Brown"					
47-6823	Money/It Takes a Long Train with a Red Caboose	1957	3.75	7.50	15.00
47-6918	I'm in Heaven/Getting Used to Being Lonely	1957	3.75	7.50	15.00
—As "Jim, Maxine and Bonnie Brown"					
47-6995	I Heard the Bluebirds Sing/The Last Thing I Want	1957	3.75	7.50	15.00
—As "Jim, Maxine and Bonnie Brown"					
47-7110	The Man in the Moon/True Love Goes Far Beyond	1957	3.75	7.50	15.00
47-7208	Crazy Dreams/Ain't No Way in the World	1958	3.75	7.50	15.00
47-7311	Would You Care?/The Trot	1958	3.75	7.50	15.00
47-7427	Beyond the Shadow/This Time I Would Know	1958	3.75	7.50	15.00
47-7555	The Three Bells/Heaven Fell Last Night	1959	3.00	6.00	12.00
47-7614	Scarlet Ribbons (For Her Hair)/Blue Bells Ring	1959	3.00	6.00	12.00
47-7700	The Old Lamplighter/Teen-Ex	1960	3.00	6.00	12.00
47-7700 [PS]	The Old Lamplighter/Teen-Ex	1960	6.25	12.50	25.00
47-7755	Lonely Little Robin/Margo (The Ninth of May)	1960	3.00	6.00	12.00
47-7755 [PS]	Lonely Little Robin/Margo (The Ninth of May)	1960	6.25	12.50	25.00
47-7780	The Whiffenpoof Song/Brighten the Corner Where You Are	1960	3.00	6.00	12.00
47-7780 [PS]	The Whiffenpoof Song/Brighten the Corner Where You Are	1960	6.25	12.50	25.00
47-7804	Send Me the Pillow You Dream On/You're So Much a Part of Me	1960	3.00	6.00	12.00
47-7820	Blue Christmas/Greenwillow Christmas	1960	3.00	6.00	12.00
47-7866	Ground Hog/Angel's Dolly	1961	2.50	5.00	10.00
47-7917	Whispering Wine/My Baby's Gone	1961	2.50	5.00	10.00
47-7969	Foolish Pride/Alpha and Omega	1961	2.50	5.00	10.00
47-7997	Buttons and Bows/Remember Me	1962	2.50	5.00	10.00
47-8066	It's Just a Little Heartache/The Old Master Painter	1962	2.50	5.00	10.00
47-8198	The Twelfth Rose/Watching My World Fall Apart	1963	2.50	5.00	10.00
47-8242	Oh, No!/Dear Teresa	1963	2.50	5.00	10.00
47-8348	Then I'll Stop Loving You/I Know My Place	1964	2.00	4.00	8.00
47-8423	Everybody's Darlin', Plus Mine/The Outskirts of Town	1964	2.00	4.00	8.00
47-8495	I Feel Like Crying/No Sad Songs for Me	1965	2.00	4.00	8.00
47-8603	You Can't Grow Peaches on a Cherry Tree/A Little Too Much to Dream	1965	2.00	4.00	8.00
47-8714	Meadowgreen/One Take Away One	1965	2.00	4.00	8.00
47-8838	I'd Just Be Fool Enough/Springtime	1966	2.00	4.00	8.00
47-8942	Coming Back to You/Gigawachem	1966	2.00	4.00	8.00
47-9153	I Hear It Now/He Will Set Your Fields on Fire	1967	2.00	4.00	8.00
47-9364	Big Daddy/I Will Bring You Water	1967	2.00	4.00	8.00
61-7555 [S]	The Three Bells/Heaven Fell Last Night	1959	6.25	12.50	25.00
—"Living Stereo" (large hole, plays at 45 rpm)					
61-7614 [S]	Scarlet Ribbons (For Her Hair)/Blue Bells Ring	1959	6.25	12.50	25.00
—"Living Stereo" (large hole, plays at 45 rpm)					
61-7700 [S]	The Old Lamplighter/Teen-Ex	1960	6.25	12.50	25.00
—"Living Stereo" (large hole, plays at 45 rpm)					
61-7755 [S]	Lonely Little Robin/Margo (The Ninth of May)	1960	6.25	12.50	25.00
—"Living Stereo" (large hole, plays at 45 rpm)					
61-7780 [S]	The Whiffenpoof Song/Brighten the Corner Where You Are	1960	6.25	12.50	25.00
—"Living Stereo" (large hole, plays at 45 rpm)					
61-7804 [S]	Send Me the Pillow You Dream On/You're So Much a Part of Me	1960	6.25	12.50	25.00
—"Living Stereo" (large hole, plays at 45 rpm)					

7-Inch Extended Plays

Number	Title (A Side/B Side)	Yr	VG	VG+	NM
RCA VICTOR					
EPA-4347	The Three Bells/Be My Love//The Man in the Moon/This Time I Would Know	1959	3.75	7.50	15.00
EPA-4347 [PS]	The Browns Sing The 3 Bells	1959	3.75	7.50	15.00
EPA-4352	Scarlet Ribbons/I Still Do//Love Me Tender/We Should Be Together	1959	3.75	7.50	15.00
EPA-4352 [PS]	Scarlet Ribbons	1959	3.75	7.50	15.00
EPA-4364	The Old Lamplighter/Oh! My Pa-Pa//True Love/The Enchanted Sea	1960	3.75	7.50	15.00
EPA-4364 [PS]	The Old Lamplighter	1960	3.75	7.50	15.00

Albums

Number	Title (A Side/B Side)	Yr	VG	VG+	NM
RCA CAMDEN					
CAL-885 [M]	I Heard the Bluebirds Sing	1965	3.00	6.00	12.00
CAS-885 [S]	I Heard the Bluebirds Sing	1965	3.00	6.00	12.00
CAL-2142 [M]	Big Ones from the Country	1967	3.00	6.00	12.00
CAS-2142 [S]	Big Ones from the Country	1967	2.50	5.00	10.00
CAS-2262	The Browns Sing a Harvest of Country Songs	1968	2.50	5.00	10.00
RCA VICTOR					
ANL1-1083	The Best of the Browns	1975	2.50	5.00	10.00
LPM-1438 [M]	Jim Edward, Maxine and Bonnie Brown	1957	12.50	25.00	50.00
LPM-2144 [M]	Sweet Sounds by the Browns	1959	7.50	15.00	30.00
LSP-2144 [S]	Sweet Sounds by the Browns	1959	10.00	20.00	40.00
LPM-2174 [M]	Town and Country	1960	5.00	10.00	20.00
LSP-2174 [S]	Town and Country	1960	6.25	12.50	25.00
LPM-2260 [M]	The Browns Sing Their Hits	1960	5.00	10.00	20.00
LSP-2260 [S]	The Browns Sing Their Hits	1960	6.25	12.50	25.00
LPM-2333 [M]	Our Favorite Folk Songs	1961	5.00	10.00	20.00
LSP-2333 [S]	Our Favorite Folk Songs	1961	6.25	12.50	25.00
LPM-2345 [M]	The Little Brown Church Hymnal	1961	5.00	10.00	20.00
LSP-2345 [S]	The Little Brown Church Hymnal	1961	6.25	12.50	25.00
LPM-2784 [M]	Grand Ole Opry Favorites	1963	3.75	7.50	15.00
LSP-2784 [S]	Grand Ole Opry Favorites	1963	5.00	10.00	20.00
LPM-2860 [M]	This Young Land	1964	3.75	7.50	15.00
LSP-2860 [S]	This Young Land	1964	5.00	10.00	20.00
LPM-2987 [M]	Three Shades of Brown	1964	3.75	7.50	15.00
LSP-2987 [S]	Three Shades of Brown	1964	5.00	10.00	20.00
LPM-3423 [M]	When Love Is Gone	1965	3.75	7.50	15.00
LSP-3423 [S]	When Love Is Gone	1965	5.00	10.00	20.00
LPM-3561 [M]	The Best of the Browns	1966	3.75	7.50	15.00
LSP-3561 [S]	The Best of the Browns	1966	5.00	10.00	20.00
LPM-3668 [M]	Our Kind of Country	1966	3.75	7.50	15.00
LSP-3668 [S]	Our Kind of Country	1966	5.00	10.00	20.00
LPM-3798 [M]	The Old Country Church	1967	5.00	10.00	20.00
LSP-3798 [S]	The Old Country Church	1967	3.75	7.50	15.00

BROWNSVILLE STATION

45s

Number	Title (A Side/B Side)	Yr	VG	VG+	NM
BIG TREE					
144	Rock with the Music/(B-side unknown)	1972	—	2.50	5.00
156	The Red Back Spider/Rock with the Music	1972	—	2.50	5.00
161	Let Your Yeah Be Yeah/Mister Robert	1973	—	2.50	5.00
15005	I'm the Leader of the Gang/Meet Me on the Fourth Floor	1974	—	2.00	4.00
15005	I'm the Leader of the Gang/Fast Phyllis	1974	—	2.00	4.00
16001	Kings of the Party/Ostrich	1974	—	2.00	4.00
16011	Smokin' in the Boy's Room/Barefootin'	1973	—	2.50	5.00
16029	I Got It Bad for You/Mama Don't Allow No Parkin'	1974	—	2.00	4.00
EPIC					
50695	Love Stealer/Fever	1979	—	2.00	4.00
—As "Brownsville"					
HIDEOUT					
1957	Rock and Roll Holiday/Jailhouse Rock	1969	3.00	6.00	12.00
POLYDOR					
14017	Rock and Roll Holiday/Jailhouse Rock	1969	—	2.50	5.00
PRIVATE STOCK					
45149	Lady (Put the Light on Me)/Rockers and Rollers	1977	—	2.00	4.00
45167	The Martian Boogie/Mr. Johnson Sez	1977	—	2.00	4.00
WARNER BROS.					
7441	Be-Bop Confidential/City Life	1970	2.00	4.00	8.00
7456	Roadrunner/Do the Bosco	1971	2.00	4.00	8.00
7501	That's Fine/Tell Me All About It	1971	2.00	4.00	8.00

Albums

Number	Title (A Side/B Side)	Yr	VG	VG+	NM
BIG TREE					
BTS-2010	A Night on the Town	1972	3.00	6.00	12.00
BTS-2102	Yeah!	1973	3.00	6.00	12.00
BT 89500	School Punks	1974	3.00	6.00	12.00
BT 89510	Motor City Connection	1975	3.00	6.00	12.00
EPIC					
JE 35606	Air Special	1978	2.50	5.00	10.00
JE 35606 [DJ]	Air Special	1978	5.00	10.00	20.00
—Orange vinyl promo					
PALLADIUM					
P-1004	Brownsville Station	1970	7.50	15.00	30.00
PRIVATE STOCK					
PS-2026	Brownsville Station	1977	2.50	5.00	10.00
WARNER BROS.					
WS 1888	No B.S.	1970	3.75	7.50	15.00

BRUBECK, DAVE

45s

Number	Title (A Side/B Side)	Yr	VG	VG+	NM
ATLANTIC					
3015	Three to Get Ready/Blue Rondo (A La Turk)	1974	—	2.00	4.00
COLUMBIA					
30719 [S]	(contents unknown)	1960	3.00	6.00	12.00
30720 [S]	(contents unknown)	1960	3.00	6.00	12.00
30721 [S]	(contents unknown)	1960	3.00	6.00	12.00
30722 [S]	(contents unknown)	1960	3.00	6.00	12.00
30723 [S]	(contents unknown)	1960	3.00	6.00	12.00
30899 [S]	(contents unknown)	1961	3.00	6.00	12.00
30900 [S]	(contents unknown)	1961	3.00	6.00	12.00
30901 [S]	(contents unknown)	1961	3.00	6.00	12.00
30902 [S]	(contents unknown)	1961	3.00	6.00	12.00
30903 [S]	(contents unknown)	1961	3.00	6.00	12.00
31312 [S]	(contents unknown)	1962	3.00	6.00	12.00
31313 [S]	(contents unknown)	1962	3.00	6.00	12.00
31314 [S]	(contents unknown)	1962	3.00	6.00	12.00
31315 [S]	(contents unknown)	1962	3.00	6.00	12.00

Number	Title (A Side/B Side)	Yr	VG	VG+	NM
31316 [S]	(contents unknown)	1962	3.00	6.00	12.00
—Anyone who can fill in these gaps -- the above 15 all are Columbia "Stereo 7" singles -- please let us know.					
31443 [S]	Charles Matthew Hallelujah/Maria	1962	3.00	6.00	12.00
31444 [S]	Someday My Prince Will Come/I'm in a Dancing Mood	1962	3.00	6.00	12.00
31445 [S]	Tangerine/The Duke	1962	3.00	6.00	12.00
31446 [S]	Far More Blue/Gone with the Wind	1962	3.00	6.00	12.00
31447 [S]	Take the "A" Train/Camptown Races	1962	3.00	6.00	12.00
40776	Lover/I'm in a Dancin' Mood	1956	3.00	6.00	12.00
41479	Take Five/Blue Rondo A La Turk	1960	3.00	6.00	12.00
41485	Camptown Races/Shortnin' Bread	1959	3.00	6.00	12.00
42068	Paradiddle Joe/Briar Bush	1961	2.50	5.00	10.00
42228	Unsquare Dance/It's a Raggy Waltz	1961	2.50	5.00	10.00
42404	Countdown/Eleven Four	1962	2.50	5.00	10.00
42651	Bossa Nova U.S.A./This Can't Be Love	1962	2.50	5.00	10.00
42675	Bossa Nova U.S.A./Camptown Races	1963	2.00	4.00	8.00
42804	Summer Song/Three to Get Ready	1963	2.00	4.00	8.00
42920	Cable Car/Theme from Elementals	1963	2.00	4.00	8.00
43091	Unisphere/Toki's Theme	1964	2.00	4.00	8.00
43133	Mr. Broadway/Toki's Theme	1964	2.00	4.00	8.00
43409	Happy Bandito/Bag O' Heat	1965	2.00	4.00	8.00
43663	Three to Get Ready/Done Her Wrong	1966	2.00	4.00	8.00
44345	Raga Theme for Ragu/Do Not Fold, Staple, Spindle or Mutilate	1968	2.00	4.00	8.00
44834	Broke Blues/Blues Roots	1969	—	3.00	6.00

FANTASY

Number	Title (A Side/B Side)	Yr	VG	VG+	NM
501	Lullaby in Rhythm/You Stepped Out of a Dream	1952	3.75	7.50	15.00
502	Singing in the Rain/I'll Remember April	1952	3.75	7.50	15.00
503	Body & Soul/Let's Fall in Love	1952	3.75	7.50	15.00
504	Indiana/Laura	1952	3.75	7.50	15.00
—The above four records comprised a box set					
505	Blue Moon/Tea for Two	1952	3.75	7.50	15.00
506	Undecided/That Old Black Magic	1952	3.75	7.50	15.00
507	September Song/Sweet Georgia Brown	1952	3.75	7.50	15.00
508	'S Wonderful/Spring Is Here	1952	3.75	7.50	15.00
—The above four records comprised a box set					
509	The Way You Look Tonight/Love Walked In	1953	3.75	7.50	15.00
510	September in the Rain/What Is This Thing Called Love	1953	3.75	7.50	15.00
511	Prelude/Fugue on Bob's Theme	1953	3.75	7.50	15.00
512	Ipca/Let's Fall in Love	1953	3.75	7.50	15.00
—The above four records comprised a box set					
513	Avalon/Perfidia	1953	3.75	7.50	15.00
514	Always/I Didn't Know What Time It Was	1953	3.75	7.50	15.00
515	Squeeze Me/How High the Moon	1953	3.75	7.50	15.00
516	Too Marvelous for Words/Heart and Soul	1953	3.75	7.50	15.00
—The above four records comprised a box set					
517	Somebody Loves Me/Crazy Chris	1953	3.75	7.50	15.00
518	A Foggy Day/Lyons Bust (Theme)	1953	3.75	7.50	15.00
519	Mam'selle/Me and My Shadow	1953	3.75	7.50	15.00
520	At a Perfume Counter/Frenesi	1953	3.75	7.50	15.00
—The above four records comprised a box set					
521	This Can't Be Love/Look for the Silver Lining	1953	3.75	7.50	15.00
523	Just One of Those Things/My Romance	1953	3.75	7.50	15.00
524	Stardust/Lulu's Back in Town	1953	3.75	7.50	15.00
526	Alice in Wonderland/All the Things You Are	1953	3.75	7.50	15.00
527	On a Little Street in Singapore/I May Be Wrong	195?	3.75	7.50	15.00
530	The Trolley Song/My Heart Stood Still	195?	3.75	7.50	15.00
535	The Trolley Song/The Trolley Song Rehearsal	195?	5.00	10.00	20.00
549	The Piper/Soliloquy	195?	3.75	7.50	15.00
558	The Trolley Song/Crazy Chris	1961	3.00	6.00	12.00

7-Inch Extended Plays

COLUMBIA

Number	Title (A Side/B Side)	Yr	VG	VG+	NM
B-699 [PS]	Jazz Red Hot and Cool	1956	3.00	6.00	12.00
—Triple-pocket sleeve for 2280, 2281 and 2282					
5-2280	Lover/Love Walked In	1956	3.00	6.00	12.00
5-2281	Little Girl Blue/Indiana	1956	3.00	6.00	12.00
5-2282	*The Duke/Fare Thee Well, Annabelle/Sometimes I'm Happy	1956	3.00	6.00	12.00

Albums

ATLANTIC

Number	Title (A Side/B Side)	Yr	VG	VG+	NM
SD 2-317 [(2)]	The Art of Dave Brubeck: The Fantasy Years	1975	3.75	7.50	15.00
SD 1606	Truth Is Fallen	1972	3.00	6.00	12.00
SD 1607	The Last Set at Newport	1972	3.00	6.00	12.00
SD 1641	We're All Together Again for the First Time	1973	3.00	6.00	12.00
SD 1645	Two Generations of Brubeck	1974	3.00	6.00	12.00
SD 1660	Brother, The Great Spirit Made Us All	1974	3.00	6.00	12.00
SD 1684	All the Things We Are	1976	3.00	6.00	12.00

COLUMBIA

Number	Title (A Side/B Side)	Yr	VG	VG+	NM
C2L 26 [(2) M]	The Dave Brubeck Quartet at Carnegie Hall	1963	6.25	12.50	25.00
—Red "Guaranteed High Fidelity" label					
C2L 26 [(2) M]	The Dave Brubeck Quartet at Carnegie Hall	1966	3.75	7.50	15.00
—Red "360 Sound" label					
CL 566 [M]	Jazz Goes to College	1954	20.00	40.00	80.00
—Dark red label, gold print; released at the same time as 6321 and 6322					
CL 566 [M]	Jazz Goes to College	1955	12.50	25.00	50.00
—Red/black label with six "eye" logos					
CL 566 [M]	Jazz Goes to College	1962	5.00	10.00	20.00
—Red "Guaranteed High Fidelity" label					
CL 566 [M]	Jazz Goes to College	1966	3.00	6.00	12.00
—Red "360 Sound" label					
CL 590 [M]	Dave Brubeck at Storyville: 1954	1954	20.00	40.00	80.00
—Dark red label, gold print; released at the same time as 6330 and 6331					
CL 590 [M]	Dave Brubeck at Storyville: 1954	1955	12.50	25.00	50.00
—Red/black label with six "eye" logos					
CL 590 [M]	Dave Brubeck at Storyville: 1954	1962	5.00	10.00	20.00
—Red "Guaranteed High Fidelity" label					
CL 590 [M]	Dave Brubeck at Storyville: 1954	1966	3.00	6.00	12.00
—Red "360 Sound" label					
CL 622 [M]	Brubeck Time	1955	15.00	30.00	60.00
—Red/black label with six "eye" logos					
CL 622 [M]	Brubeck Time	1962	5.00	10.00	20.00
—Red "Guaranteed High Fidelity" label					
CL 622 [M]	Brubeck Time	1966	3.00	6.00	12.00
—Red "360 Sound" label					
CL 699 [M]	Jazz: Red Hot and Cool	1955	15.00	30.00	60.00
—Red/black label with six "eye" logos					
CL 699 [M]	Jazz: Red Hot and Cool	1962	5.00	10.00	20.00
—Red "Guaranteed High Fidelity" label					
CL 699 [M]	Jazz: Red Hot and Cool	1966	3.00	6.00	12.00
—Red "360 Sound" label					
C2S 826 [(2)]	The Dave Brubeck Quartet at Carnegie Hall	1971	3.75	7.50	15.00
—Orange label					
C2S 826 [(2) S]	The Dave Brubeck Quartet at Carnegie Hall	1963	7.50	15.00	30.00
—Red label, "360 Sound" in black					
C2S 826 [(2) S]	The Dave Brubeck Quartet at Carnegie Hall	1966	5.00	10.00	20.00
—Red label, "360 Sound" in white					
CL 878 [M]	Brubeck Plays Brubeck	1956	15.00	30.00	60.00
—Red/black label with six "eye" logos					
CL 878 [M]	Brubeck Plays Brubeck	1962	5.00	10.00	20.00
—Red "Guaranteed High Fidelity" label					
CL 878 [M]	Brubeck Plays Brubeck	1966	3.00	6.00	12.00
—Red "360 Sound" label					
CL 932 [M]	American Jazz Festival at Newport '56	1956	12.50	25.00	50.00
—Red/black label with six "eye" logos					
CL 932 [M]	American Jazz Festival at Newport '56	1962	5.00	10.00	20.00
—Red "Guaranteed High Fidelity" label					
CL 984 [M]	Jazz Impressions of the U.S.A.	1957	12.50	25.00	50.00
—Red/black label with six "eye" logos					
CL 984 [M]	Jazz Impressions of the U.S.A.	1962	5.00	10.00	20.00
—Red "Guaranteed High Fidelity" label					
CL 984 [M]	Jazz Impressions of the U.S.A.	1966	3.00	6.00	12.00
—Red "360 Sound" label					
CL 1034 [M]	Jazz Goes to Junior College	1957	10.00	20.00	40.00
—Red/black label with six "eye" logos					
CL 1034 [M]	Jazz Goes to Junior College	1962	5.00	10.00	20.00
—Red "Guaranteed High Fidelity" label					
CL 1034 [M]	Jazz Goes to Junior College	1966	3.00	6.00	12.00
—Red "360 Sound" label					
CL 1059 [M]	Dave Digs Disney	1957	10.00	20.00	40.00
—Red/black label with six "eye" logos					
CL 1059 [M]	Dave Digs Disney	1962	5.00	10.00	20.00
—Red "Guaranteed High Fidelity" label					
CL 1059 [M]	Dave Digs Disney	1966	3.00	6.00	12.00
—Red "360 Sound" label					
CL 1169 [M]	Dave Brubeck Quartet in Europe	1958	10.00	20.00	40.00
—Red/black label with six "eye" logos					
CL 1169 [M]	Dave Brubeck Quartet in Europe	1962	5.00	10.00	20.00
—Red "Guaranteed High Fidelity" label					
CL 1169 [M]	Dave Brubeck Quartet in Europe	1966	3.00	6.00	12.00
—Red "360 Sound" label					
CL 1249 [M]	Newport 1958	1958	10.00	20.00	40.00
—Red/black label with six "eye" logos					
CL 1249 [M]	Newport 1958	1962	5.00	10.00	20.00
—Red "Guaranteed High Fidelity" label					
CL 1249 [M]	Newport 1958	1966	3.00	6.00	12.00
—Red "360 Sound" label					
CL 1251 [M]	Jazz Impressions of Eurasia	1958	10.00	20.00	40.00
—Red/black label with six "eye" logos					
CL 1251 [M]	Jazz Impressions of Eurasia	1962	5.00	10.00	20.00
—Red "Guaranteed High Fidelity" label					
CL 1251 [M]	Jazz Impressions of Eurasia	1966	3.00	6.00	12.00
—Red "360 Sound" label					
CL 1347 [M]	Gone with the Wind	1959	10.00	20.00	40.00
—Red/black label with six "eye" logos					
CL 1347 [M]	Gone with the Wind	1962	5.00	10.00	20.00
—Red "Guaranteed High Fidelity" label					
CL 1347 [M]	Gone with the Wind	1966	3.00	6.00	12.00
—Red "360 Sound" label					
CL 1397 [M]	Time Out	1960	6.25	12.50	25.00
—Red/black label with six "eye" logos					
CL 1397 [M]	Time Out Featuring "Take Five"	1962	3.75	7.50	15.00
—Red "Guaranteed High Fidelity" label; beginning with this issue, the cover was altered to emphasize the hit					
CL 1397 [M]	Time Out Featuring "Take Five"	1966	3.00	6.00	12.00
—Red "360 Sound" label					
CL 1439 [M]	Southern Scene	1960	6.25	12.50	25.00
—Red/black label with six "eye" logos					
CL 1439 [M]	Southern Scene	1962	3.75	7.50	15.00
—Red "Guaranteed High Fidelity" label					
CL 1439 [M]	Southern Scene	1966	3.00	6.00	12.00
—Red "360 Sound" label					
CL 1454 [M]	The Riddle	1960	6.25	12.50	25.00
—Red/black label with six "eye" logos					
CL 1454 [M]	The Riddle	1962	3.75	7.50	15.00
—Red "Guaranteed High Fidelity" label					
CL 1454 [M]	The Riddle	1966	3.00	6.00	12.00
—Red "360 Sound" label					
CL 1466 [M]	Bernstein Plays Brubeck Plays Bernstein	1960	6.25	12.50	25.00
—Red/black label with six "eye" logos					
CL 1466 [M]	Bernstein Plays Brubeck Plays Bernstein	1962	3.75	7.50	15.00
—Red "Guaranteed High Fidelity" label					
CL 1466 [M]	Bernstein Plays Brubeck Plays Bernstein	1966	3.00	6.00	12.00
—Red "360 Sound" label					
CL 1553 [M]	Brubeck and Rushing	1961	6.25	12.50	25.00
—Red/black label with six "eye" logos					
CL 1553 [M]	Brubeck and Rushing	1962	3.75	7.50	15.00
—Red "Guaranteed High Fidelity" label					
CL 1553 [M]	Brubeck and Rushing	1966	3.00	6.00	12.00
—Red "360 Sound" label					
CL 1609 [M]	Tonight Only!	1961	6.25	12.50	25.00
—Red/black label with six "eye" logos					
CL 1609 [M]	Tonight Only!	1962	3.75	7.50	15.00
—Red "Guaranteed High Fidelity" label					
CL 1609 [M]	Tonight Only!	1966	3.00	6.00	12.00
—Red "360 Sound" label					
CL 1690 [M]	Time Further Out	1961	6.25	12.50	25.00
—Red/black label with six "eye" logos					

Number	Title (A Side/B Side)	Yr	VG	VG+	NM
CL 1690 [M]	Time Further Out	1962	3.75	7.50	15.00
—Red "Guaranteed High Fidelity" label					
CL 1690 [M]	Time Further Out	1966	3.00	6.00	12.00
—Red "360 Sound" label					
CL 1775 [M]	Countdown — Time in Outer Space	1962	7.50	15.00	30.00
—Red/black label with six "eye" logos					
CL 1775 [M]	Countdown — Time in Outer Space	1962	3.75	7.50	15.00
—Red "Guaranteed High Fidelity" label					
CL 1775 [M]	Countdown — Time in Outer Space	1966	3.00	6.00	12.00
—Red "360 Sound" label					
CL 1963 [M]	Brandenburg Gate Revisited	1963	5.00	10.00	20.00
—Red "Guaranteed High Fidelity" label					
CL 1963 [M]	Brandenburg Gate Revisited	1966	3.00	6.00	12.00
—Red "360 Sound" label					
CL 1998 [M]	Bossa Nova U.S.A.	1963	5.00	10.00	20.00
—Red "Guaranteed High Fidelity" label					
CL 1998 [M]	Bossa Nova U.S.A.	1966	3.00	6.00	12.00
—Red "360 Sound" label					
CL 2127 [M]	Time Changes	1964	5.00	10.00	20.00
—Red "Guaranteed High Fidelity" label					
CL 2127 [M]	Time Changes	1966	3.00	6.00	12.00
—Red "360 Sound" label					
CL 2212 [M]	Jazz Impressions of Japan	1964	5.00	10.00	20.00
—Red "Guaranteed High Fidelity" label					
CL 2212 [M]	Jazz Impressions of Japan	1966	3.00	6.00	12.00
—Red "360 Sound" label					
CL 2275 [M]	Jazz Impressions of New York	1965	5.00	10.00	20.00
—Red "Guaranteed High Fidelity" label					
CL 2275 [M]	Jazz Impressions of New York	1966	3.00	6.00	12.00
—Red "360 Sound" label					
CL 2316 [M]	Take Five	1965	5.00	10.00	20.00
—Red "Guaranteed High Fidelity" label					
CL 2316 [M]	Take Five	1966	3.00	6.00	12.00
—Red "360 Sound" label					
CL 2348 [M]	Angel Eyes	1965	5.00	10.00	20.00
—Red "Guaranteed High Fidelity" label					
CL 2348 [M]	Angel Eyes	1966	3.00	6.00	12.00
—Red "360 Sound" label					
CL 2437 [M]	My Favorite Things	1966	3.75	7.50	15.00
CL 2484 [M]	Dave Brubeck's Greatest Hits	1966	3.75	7.50	15.00
CL 2512 [M]	Time In	1966	3.75	7.50	15.00
CL 2602 [M]	Anything Goes! Dave Brubeck Quartet Plays Cole Porter	1966	3.75	7.50	15.00
CL 2695 [M]	Bravo Brubeck!	1967	5.00	10.00	20.00
CL 2712 [M]	Jackpot	1967	5.00	10.00	20.00
CL 6321 [10]	Jazz Goes to College, Volume 1	1954	25.00	50.00	100.00
CL 6322 [10]	Jazz Goes to College, Volume 2	1954	25.00	50.00	100.00
CL 6330 [10]	Dave Brubeck at Storyville: 1954, Volume 1	1954	20.00	40.00	80.00
CL 6331 [10]	Dave Brubeck at Storyville: 1954, Volume 2	1954	20.00	40.00	80.00
CS 8058 [S]	Jazz Impressions of Eurasia	1959	12.50	25.00	50.00
—Red/black label with six "eye" logos					
CS 8058 [S]	Jazz Impressions of Eurasia	1962	6.25	12.50	25.00
—Red label, "360 Sound" in black					
CS 8058 [S]	Jazz Impressions of Eurasia	1966	3.75	7.50	15.00
—Red label, "360 Sound" in white					
CS 8082 [S]	Newport 1958	1959	12.50	25.00	50.00
—Red/black label with six "eye" logos					
CS 8082 [S]	Newport 1958	1962	6.25	12.50	25.00
—Red label, "360 Sound" in black					
CS 8082 [S]	Newport 1958	1966	3.75	7.50	15.00
—Red label, "360 Sound" in white					
CS 8090 [S]	Dave Digs Disney	1959	12.50	25.00	50.00
—Red/black label with six "eye" logos					
CS 8090 [S]	Dave Digs Disney	1962	6.25	12.50	25.00
—Red label, "360 Sound" in black					
CS 8090 [S]	Dave Digs Disney	1966	3.75	7.50	15.00
—Red label, "360 Sound" in white					
CS 8156	Gone with the Wind	1971	3.00	6.00	12.00
—Orange label					
CS 8156 [S]	Gone with the Wind	1959	12.50	25.00	50.00
—Red/black label with six "eye" logos					
CS 8156 [S]	Gone with the Wind	1962	6.25	12.50	25.00
—Red label, "360 Sound" in black					
CS 8156 [S]	Gone with the Wind	1966	3.75	7.50	15.00
—Red label, "360 Sound" in white					
CS 8192	Time Out Featuring "Take Five"	1971	3.00	6.00	12.00
—Orange label					
CS 8192	Time Out	1995	6.25	12.50	25.00
—Audiophile vinyl, distributed by Classic Records					
CS 8192 [S]	Time Out	1960	7.50	15.00	30.00
—Red/black label with six "eye" logos					
CS 8192 [S]	Time Out Featuring "Take Five"	1962	5.00	10.00	20.00
—Red label, "360 Sound" in black; beginning with this issue, the cover was altered to emphasize the hit					
CS 8192 [S]	Time Out Featuring "Take Five"	1966	3.75	7.50	15.00
—Red label, "360 Sound" in white					
PC 8192	Time Out	1981	2.00	4.00	8.00
—Reissue with new prefix					
CS 8235 [S]	Southern Scene	1960	7.50	15.00	30.00
—Red/black label with six "eye" logos					
CS 8235 [S]	Southern Scene	1962	5.00	10.00	20.00
—Red label, "360 Sound" in black					
CS 8235 [S]	Southern Scene	1966	3.75	7.50	15.00
—Red label, "360 Sound" in white					
CS 8248 [S]	The Riddle	1960	7.50	15.00	30.00
—Red/black label with six "eye" logos					
CS 8248 [S]	The Riddle	1962	5.00	10.00	20.00
—Red label, "360 Sound" in black					
CS 8248 [S]	The Riddle	1966	3.75	7.50	15.00
—Red label, "360 Sound" in white					
CS 8257	Brubeck Plays Bernstein Plays Brubeck	1971	3.00	6.00	12.00
—Orange label					
CS 8257 [S]	Brubeck Plays Bernstein Plays Brubeck	1960	7.50	15.00	30.00
—Red/black label with six "eye" logos					
CS 8257 [S]	Brubeck Plays Bernstein Plays Brubeck	1962	5.00	10.00	20.00
—Red label, "360 Sound" in black					
CS 8257 [S]	Brubeck Plays Bernstein Plays Brubeck	1966	3.75	7.50	15.00
—Red label, "360 Sound" in white					
CS 8353 [S]	Brubeck and Rushing	1961	7.50	15.00	30.00
—Red/black label with six "eye" logos					
CS 8353 [S]	Brubeck and Rushing	1962	5.00	10.00	20.00
—Red label, "360 Sound" in black					
CS 8353 [S]	Brubeck and Rushing	1966	3.75	7.50	15.00
—Red label, "360 Sound" in white					
CS 8409 [S]	Tonight Only!	1961	7.50	15.00	30.00
—Red/black label with six "eye" logos					
CS 8409 [S]	Tonight Only!	1962	5.00	10.00	20.00
—Red label, "360 Sound" in black					
CS 8409 [S]	Tonight Only!	1966	3.75	7.50	15.00
—Red label, "360 Sound" in white					
CS 8490	Time Further Out	1971	3.00	6.00	12.00
—Orange label					
CS 8490 [S]	Time Further Out	1961	7.50	15.00	30.00
—Red/black label with six "eye" logos					
CS 8490 [S]	Time Further Out	1962	5.00	10.00	20.00
—Red label, "360 Sound" in black					
CS 8490 [S]	Time Further Out	1966	3.75	7.50	15.00
—Red label, "360 Sound" in white					
PC 8490	Time Further Out	1981	2.00	4.00	8.00
—Reissue with new prefix					
CS 8575 [S]	Countdown — Time in Outer Space	1962	10.00	20.00	40.00
—Red/black label with six "eye" logos					
CS 8575 [S]	Countdown — Time in Outer Space	1962	5.00	10.00	20.00
—Red label, "360 Sound" in black					
CS 8575 [S]	Countdown — Time in Outer Space	1966	3.75	7.50	15.00
—Red label, "360 Sound" in white					
CS 8645 [R]	Jazz: Red Hot and Cool	1963	3.75	7.50	15.00
—Red label, "360 Sound" in black					
CS 8645 [R]	Jazz: Red Hot and Cool	1966	3.00	6.00	12.00
—Red label, "360 Sound" in white					
CS 8763 [S]	Brandenburg Gate Revisited	1963	6.25	12.50	25.00
—Red label, "360 Sound" in black					
CS 8763 [S]	Brandenburg Gate Revisited	1966	3.75	7.50	15.00
—Red label, "360 Sound" in white					
CS 8798 [S]	Bossa Nova U.S.A.	1963	6.25	12.50	25.00
—Red label, "360 Sound" in black					
CS 8798 [S]	Bossa Nova U.S.A.	1966	3.75	7.50	15.00
—Red label, "360 Sound" in white					
CS 8927 [S]	Time Changes	1964	6.25	12.50	25.00
—Red label, "360 Sound" in black					
CS 8927 [S]	Time Changes	1966	3.75	7.50	15.00
—Red label, "360 Sound" in white					
CS 9012	Jazz Impressions of Japan	1971	3.00	6.00	12.00
—Orange label					
CS 9012 [S]	Jazz Impressions of Japan	1964	6.25	12.50	25.00
—Red label, "360 Sound" in black					
CS 9012 [S]	Jazz Impressions of Japan	1966	3.75	7.50	15.00
—Red label, "360 Sound" in white					
PC 9012	Jazz Impressions of Japan	1981	2.00	4.00	8.00
—Reissue with new prefix					
CS 9075	Jazz Impressions of New York	1971	3.00	6.00	12.00
—Orange label					
CS 9075 [S]	Jazz Impressions of New York	1965	6.25	12.50	25.00
—Red label, "360 Sound" in black					
CS 9075 [S]	Jazz Impressions of New York	1966	3.75	7.50	15.00
—Red label, "360 Sound" in white					
PC 9075	Jazz Impressions of New York	1981	2.00	4.00	8.00
—Reissue with new prefix					
CS 9116 [S]	Take Five	1965	6.25	12.50	25.00
—Red label, "360 Sound" in black					
CS 9116 [S]	Take Five	1966	3.75	7.50	15.00
—Red label, "360 Sound" in white					
CS 9148 [S]	Angel Eyes	1965	6.25	12.50	25.00
—Red label, "360 Sound" in black					
CS 9148 [S]	Angel Eyes	1966	3.75	7.50	15.00
—Red label, "360 Sound" in white					
CS 9237 [S]	My Favorite Things	1966	5.00	10.00	20.00
—Red "360 Sound" label					
CS 9284	Dave Brubeck's Greatest Hits	1971	3.00	6.00	12.00
—Orange label					
CS 9284 [S]	Dave Brubeck's Greatest Hits	1966	5.00	10.00	20.00
—Red "360 Sound" label					
PC 9284	Dave Brubeck's Greatest Hits	1981	2.00	4.00	8.00
—Reissue with new prefix					
CS 9312	Time In	1971	3.00	6.00	12.00
—Orange label					
CS 9312 [S]	Time In	1966	5.00	10.00	20.00
—Red "360 Sound" label					
PC 9312	Time In	1981	2.00	4.00	8.00
—Reissue with new prefix					
CS 9402	Anything Goes! Dave Brubeck Quartet Plays Cole Porter	1971	3.00	6.00	12.00
—Orange label					
CS 9402 [S]	Anything Goes! Dave Brubeck Quartet Plays Cole Porter	1966	5.00	10.00	20.00
—Red "360 Sound" label					
PC 9402	Anything Goes! Dave Brubeck Quartet Plays Cole Porter	1981	2.00	4.00	8.00
—Reissue with new prefix					
CS 9495	Bravo Brubeck!	1971	3.00	6.00	12.00
—Orange label					
CS 9495 [S]	Bravo Brubeck!	1967	3.75	7.50	15.00
—Red "360 Sound" label					
CS 9512 [S]	Jackpot	1967	3.75	7.50	15.00
—Red "360 Sound" label					
CS 9572	The Last Time We Saw Paris	1971	3.00	6.00	12.00
—Orange label					
CS 9672	The Last Time We Saw Paris	1968	3.75	7.50	15.00
—Red "360 Sound" label					
CS 9704	Compadres	1968	3.75	7.50	15.00
—Red "360 Sound" label					

Number	Title (A Side/B Side)	Yr	VG	VG+	NM
CS 9704	Compadres	1971	3.00	6.00	12.00
—Orange label					
CS 9749	Blues Roots	1969	3.75	7.50	15.00
—Red "360 Sound" label					
CS 9749	Blues Roots	1971	3.00	6.00	12.00
—Orange label					
CS 9897	Brubeck in Amsterdam	1969	3.75	7.50	15.00
—Red "360 Sound" label					
CS 9897	Brubeck in Amsterdam	1971	3.00	6.00	12.00
—Orange label					
C 30522	The Summit Sessions	1971	3.00	6.00	12.00
G 30625 [(2)]	Adventures in Time	1971	3.75	7.50	15.00
KG 31298 [(2)]	Brubeck On Campus	1972	3.75	7.50	15.00
KC 32143	Brubeck at the Berlin Philharmonic	1973	3.00	6.00	12.00
KG 32761 [(2)]	All-Time Greatest Hits	1974	3.75	7.50	15.00
CG 33666 [(2)]	Gone with the Wind/Time Out	1975	3.75	7.50	15.00
PC 37022	A Place in Time	1981	2.50	5.00	10.00
—Reissue of Odyssey LP					
COLUMBIA JAZZ MASTERPIECES					
CJ 40455	The Dave Brubeck Quartet Plays Music from West Side Story and Other Shows and Films	1987	2.50	5.00	10.00
CJ 40585	Time Out	1987	2.50	5.00	10.00
CJ 40627	Gone with the Wind	1987	2.50	5.00	10.00
CJ 45149	Jazz Goes to College	1989	2.50	5.00	10.00
CONCORD JAZZ					
CJ-103	Back Home	1979	2.50	5.00	10.00
CJ-129	Tritonis	1980	2.50	5.00	10.00
CJ-178	Paper Moon	1982	2.50	5.00	10.00
CJ-198	Concord on a Summer Night	1982	2.50	5.00	10.00
CJ-259	For Iola	1985	2.50	5.00	10.00
CJ-299	Reflections	1986	2.50	5.00	10.00
CJ-317	Blue Rondo	1987	2.50	5.00	10.00
CJ-353	Moscow Night	1988	2.50	5.00	10.00
CROWN					
CLP-5406 [M]	The Greats	196?	3.75	7.50	15.00
CLP 5470 [M]	Dave Brubeck and the George Nielson Quartet	196?	3.75	7.50	15.00
DECCA					
DL 710156 [(2)]	The Light in the Wilderness	1968	3.75	7.50	15.00
DL 710175	The Gates of Justice	1969	3.00	6.00	12.00
DL 710181	Brubeck/Mulligan/Cincinnati	1972	3.00	6.00	12.00
DIRECT DISK					
106 [(2)]	A Cut Above	1979	6.25	12.50	25.00
FANTASY					
3-1 [10]	Dave Brubeck Trio	1951	37.50	75.00	150.00
3-2 [10]	Dave Brubeck Trio	1951	37.50	75.00	150.00
3-3 [10]	Dave Brubeck Octet	1951	37.50	75.00	150.00
3-4 [10]	Dave Brubeck Trio	1952	37.50	75.00	150.00
3-5 [10]	Dave Brubeck Quartet with Paul Desmond	1952	37.50	75.00	150.00
3-7 [10]	Dave Brubeck Quartet with Paul Desmond	1952	37.50	75.00	150.00
3-8 [10]	Jazz at Storyville	1953	37.50	75.00	150.00
3-10 [10]	Jazz at the Blackhawk	1953	37.50	75.00	150.00
3-11 [10]	Jazz at Oberlin	1953	37.50	75.00	150.00
3-13 [10]	Jazz at the College of the Pacific	1954	37.50	75.00	150.00
3-16 [10]	Old Sounds from San Francisco	1954	37.50	75.00	150.00
3-20 [10]	Paul and Dave's Jazz Interwoven	1955	37.50	75.00	150.00
OJC-46	Jazz at Oberlin	198?	2.50	5.00	10.00
—Reissue of 3245					
OJC-47	Jazz at the College of the Pacific	198?	2.50	5.00	10.00
—Reissue of 3223					
OJC-101	The Dave Brubeck Octet	198?	2.50	5.00	10.00
—Reissue of Fantasy 3239					
OJC-150	Re-Union	198?	2.50	5.00	10.00
OJC-200	Brubeck A La Mode	1985	2.50	5.00	10.00
OJC-236	Near Myth	1986	2.50	5.00	10.00
—Reissue of Fantasy 3319					
3204 [M]	Dave Brubeck Trio	1956	25.00	50.00	100.00
—Dark red vinyl; reissue of 3-1					
3204 [M]	Dave Brubeck Trio	195?	15.00	30.00	60.00
—Black vinyl, red label, non-flexible vinyl					
3204 [M]	Dave Brubeck Trio	196?	10.00	20.00	40.00
—Black vinyl, red label, flexible vinyl					
3205 [M]	Dave Brubeck Trio: Distinctive Rhythm Instrumentals	1956	25.00	50.00	100.00
—Dark red vinyl; reissue of 3-2					
3205 [M]	Dave Brubeck Trio: Distinctive Rhythm Instrumentals	195?	15.00	30.00	60.00
—Black vinyl, red label, non-flexible vinyl					
3205 [M]	Dave Brubeck Trio: Distinctive Rhythm Instrumentals	196?	10.00	20.00	40.00
—Black vinyl, red label, flexible vinyl					
3210 [M]	Jazz at the Blackhawk	1956	25.00	50.00	100.00
—Dark red vinyl; reissue of 3-10					
3210 [M]	Jazz at the Blackhawk	195?	15.00	30.00	60.00
—Black vinyl, red label, non-flexible vinyl					
3210 [M]	Jazz at the Blackhawk	196?	10.00	20.00	40.00
—Black vinyl, red label, flexible vinyl					
3223 [M]	Jazz at the College of the Pacific	1956	25.00	50.00	100.00
—Dark red vinyl; reissue of 3-13					
3223 [M]	Jazz at the College of the Pacific	195?	15.00	30.00	60.00
—Black vinyl, red label, non-flexible vinyl					
3223 [M]	Jazz at the College of the Pacific	196?	10.00	20.00	40.00
—Black vinyl, red label, flexible vinyl					
3229 [M]	Brubeck-Desmond	1956	25.00	50.00	100.00
—Dark red vinyl; reissue of 3-5					
3229 [M]	Brubeck-Desmond	195?	15.00	30.00	60.00
—Black vinyl, red label, non-flexible vinyl					
3229 [M]	Brubeck-Desmond	196?	10.00	20.00	40.00
—Black vinyl, red label, flexible vinyl					
3230 [M]	Dave Brubeck Quartet	1956	25.00	50.00	100.00
—Dark red vinyl; reissue of 3-7					
3230 [M]	Dave Brubeck Quartet	195?	15.00	30.00	60.00
—Black vinyl, red label, non-flexible vinyl					
3230 [M]	Dave Brubeck Quartet	196?	10.00	20.00	40.00
—Black vinyl, red label, flexible vinyl					
3239 [M]	Dave Brubeck Octet	1956	25.00	50.00	100.00
—Dark red vinyl; reissue of 3-3					
3239 [M]	Dave Brubeck Octet	195?	15.00	30.00	60.00
—Black vinyl, red label, non-flexible vinyl					
3239 [M]	Dave Brubeck Octet	196?	10.00	20.00	40.00
—Black vinyl, red label, flexible vinyl					
3240 [M]	Brubeck Desmond: Jazz at Storyville	1957	25.00	50.00	100.00
—Dark red vinyl; reissue of 3-8					
3240 [M]	Brubeck Desmond: Jazz at Storyville	195?	15.00	30.00	60.00
—Black vinyl, red label, non-flexible vinyl					
3240 [M]	Brubeck Desmond: Jazz at Storyville	196?	10.00	20.00	40.00
—Black vinyl, red label, flexible vinyl					
3245 [M]	Jazz at Oberlin	1957	25.00	50.00	100.00
—Dark red vinyl; reissue of 3-11					
3245 [M]	Jazz at Oberlin	195?	15.00	30.00	60.00
—Black vinyl, red label, non-flexible vinyl					
3245 [M]	Jazz at Oberlin	196?	10.00	20.00	40.00
—Black vinyl, red label, flexible vinyl					
3249 [M]	Brubeck & Desmond at Wilshire-Ebell	1957	25.00	50.00	100.00
—Dark red vinyl					
3249 [M]	Brubeck & Desmond at Wilshire-Ebell	195?	15.00	30.00	60.00
—Black vinyl, red label, non-flexible vinyl					
3249 [M]	Brubeck & Desmond at Wilshire-Ebell	196?	10.00	20.00	40.00
—Black vinyl, red label, flexible vinyl					
3259 [M]	Dave Brubeck Plays and Plays and Plays and Plays and...	1958	15.00	30.00	60.00
—Red vinyl					
3259 [M]	Dave Brubeck Plays and Plays and Plays and Plays and...	195?	10.00	20.00	40.00
—Black vinyl, red label, non-flexible vinyl					
3259 [M]	Dave Brubeck Plays and Plays and Plays and Plays and...	196?	7.50	15.00	30.00
—Black vinyl, red label, flexible vinyl					
3268 [M]	Re-Union	1958	15.00	30.00	60.00
—Red vinyl					
3268 [M]	Re-Union	195?	10.00	20.00	40.00
—Black vinyl, red label, non-flexible vinyl					
3268 [M]	Re-Union	196?	7.50	15.00	30.00
—Black vinyl, red label, flexible vinyl					
3298 [M]	Two Knights at the Black Hawk	1959	15.00	30.00	60.00
—Red vinyl					
3298 [M]	Two Knights at the Black Hawk	1959	10.00	20.00	40.00
—Black vinyl, red label, non-flexible vinyl					
3298 [M]	Two Knights at the Black Hawk	196?	7.50	15.00	30.00
—Black vinyl, red label, flexible vinyl					
3301 [M]	Brubeck A La Mode	1960	15.00	30.00	60.00
—Red vinyl					
3301 [M]	Brubeck A La Mode	1960	10.00	20.00	40.00
—Black vinyl, red label, non-flexible vinyl					
3301 [M]	Brubeck A La Mode	196?	7.50	15.00	30.00
—Black vinyl, red label, flexible vinyl					
3319 [M]	Near-Myth	1961	15.00	30.00	60.00
—Red vinyl					
3319 [M]	Near-Myth	1961	10.00	20.00	40.00
—Black vinyl, red label, non-flexible vinyl					
3319 [M]	Near-Myth	196?	7.50	15.00	30.00
—Black vinyl, red label, flexible vinyl					
3331 [M]	Dave Brubeck Trio Featuring Cal Tjader	1962	15.00	30.00	60.00
—Red vinyl					
3331 [M]	Dave Brubeck Trio Featuring Cal Tjader	1962	10.00	20.00	40.00
—Black vinyl, red label, non-flexible vinyl					
3331 [M]	Dave Brubeck Trio Featuring Cal Tjader	196?	7.50	15.00	30.00
—Black vinyl, red label, flexible vinyl					
3332 [M]	Brubeck Tjader	1962	15.00	30.00	60.00
—Red vinyl					
3332 [M]	Brubeck Tjader	1962	10.00	20.00	40.00
—Black vinyl, red label, non-flexible vinyl					
3332 [M]	Brubeck Tjader	196?	7.50	15.00	30.00
—Black vinyl, red label, flexible vinyl					
MPF-4528	Greatest Hits from the Fantasy Years	198?	2.50	5.00	10.00
8007 [S]	Re-Union	1962	12.50	25.00	50.00
—Blue vinyl					
8007 [S]	Re-Union	196?	7.50	15.00	30.00
—Black vinyl, blue label, non-flexible vinyl					
8007 [S]	Re-Union	196?	5.00	10.00	20.00
—Black vinyl, blue label, flexible vinyl					
8047 [S]	Brubeck A La Mode	1962	12.50	25.00	50.00
—Blue vinyl					
8047 [S]	Brubeck A La Mode	196?	7.50	15.00	30.00
—Black vinyl, blue label, non-flexible vinyl					
8047 [S]	Brubeck A La Mode	196?	5.00	10.00	20.00
—Black vinyl, blue label, flexible vinyl					
8063 [S]	Near-Myth	1962	12.50	25.00	50.00
—Blue vinyl					
8063 [S]	Near-Myth	196?	7.50	15.00	30.00
—Black vinyl, blue label, non-flexible vinyl					
8063 [S]	Near-Myth	196?	5.00	10.00	20.00
—Black vinyl, blue label, flexible vinyl					
8069 [R]	Jazz at Oberlin	1962	10.00	20.00	40.00
—Blue vinyl					
8069 [R]	Jazz at Oberlin	196?	5.00	10.00	20.00
—Black vinyl, blue label, non-flexible vinyl					
8069 [R]	Jazz at Oberlin	196?	3.75	7.50	15.00
—Black vinyl, blue label, flexible vinyl					
8073 [R]	Dave Brubeck Trio Featuring Cal Tjader	1962	10.00	20.00	40.00
—Blue vinyl					
8073 [R]	Dave Brubeck Trio Featuring Cal Tjader	1962	5.00	10.00	20.00
—Black vinyl, blue label, non-flexible vinyl					
8073 [R]	Dave Brubeck Trio Featuring Cal Tjader	196?	3.75	7.50	15.00
—Black vinyl, blue label, flexible vinyl					
8074 [R]	Brubeck Tjader	1962	10.00	20.00	40.00
—Blue vinyl					
8074 [R]	Brubeck Tjader	1962	5.00	10.00	20.00
—Black vinyl, blue label, non-flexible vinyl					
8074 [R]	Brubeck Tjader	196?	3.75	7.50	15.00
—Black vinyl, blue label, flexible vinyl					

Number	Title (A Side/B Side)	Yr	VG	VG+	NM
8078 [R]	Jazz at the College of the Pacific	1962	10.00	20.00	40.00
—Blue vinyl					
8078 [R]	Jazz at the College of the Pacific	196?	5.00	10.00	20.00
—Black vinyl, blue label, non-flexible vinyl					
8078 [R]	Jazz at the College of the Pacific	196?	3.75	7.50	15.00
—Black vinyl, blue label, flexible vinyl					
8080 [R]	Jazz at Storyville	1962	10.00	20.00	40.00
—Blue vinyl					
8080 [R]	Jazz at Storyville	1962	5.00	10.00	20.00
—Black vinyl, blue label, non-flexible vinyl					
8080 [R]	Jazz at Storyville	196?	3.75	7.50	15.00
—Black vinyl, blue label, flexible vinyl					
8081 [R]	Two Knights at the Blackhawk	1962	10.00	20.00	40.00
—Blue vinyl					
8081 [R]	Two Knights at the Blackhawk	1962	5.00	10.00	20.00
—Black vinyl, blue label, non-flexible vinyl					
8081 [R]	Two Knights at the Blackhawk	196?	3.75	7.50	15.00
—Black vinyl, blue label, flexible vinyl					
8092 [R]	Brubeck-Desmond	1962	10.00	20.00	40.00
—Blue vinyl					
8092 [R]	Brubeck-Desmond	1962	5.00	10.00	20.00
—Black vinyl, blue label, non-flexible vinyl					
8092 [R]	Brubeck-Desmond	196?	3.75	7.50	15.00
—Black vinyl, blue label, flexible vinyl					
8093 [R]	Dave Brubeck Quartet	1962	10.00	2.00	40.00
—Blue vinyl					
8093 [R]	Dave Brubeck Quartet	1962	5.00	10.00	20.00
—Black vinyl, blue label, non-flexible vinyl					
8093 [R]	Dave Brubeck Quartet	196?	3.75	7.50	15.00
—Black vinyl, blue label, flexible vinyl					
8094 [R]	Dave Brubeck Octet	1962	10.00	20.00	40.00
—Blue vinyl					
8094 [R]	Dave Brubeck Octet	1962	5.00	10.00	20.00
—Black vinyl, blue label, non-flexible vinyl					
8094 [R]	Dave Brubeck Octet	196?	3.75	7.50	15.00
—Black vinyl, blue label, flexible vinyl					
8095 [S]	Brubeck and Desmond at Wilshire-Ebell	1962	12.50	25.00	50.00
—Blue vinyl					
8095 [S]	Brubeck and Desmond at Wilshire-Ebell	1962	7.50	15.00	30.00
—Black vinyl, blue label, non-flexible vinyl					
8095 [S]	Brubeck and Desmond at Wilshire-Ebell	196?	5.00	10.00	20.00
—Black vinyl, blue label, flexible vinyl					
24726 [(2)]	The Dave Brubeck Trio	198?	3.75	7.50	15.00
24727 [(2)]	Brubeck-Desmond	1982	3.75	7.50	15.00
24728 [(2)]	Stardust	198?	3.75	7.50	15.00
HARMONY					
HS 11253	Instant Brubeck	1968	3.00	6.00	12.00
HS 11336	Gone with the Wind	1969	3.00	6.00	12.00
HORIZON					
SP-703	1975: The Duets	1975	3.00	6.00	12.00
SP-714	The Dave Brubeck Quartet 25th Anniversary	1976	3.00	6.00	12.00
JAZZTONE					
J-1272 [M]	Best of Brubeck	195?	10.00	20.00	40.00
MOBILE FIDELITY					
1-216	We're All Together Again for the First Time	1994	15.00	30.00	60.00
—Audiophile vinyl					
MOON					
028	St. Louis Blues	1992	5.00	10.00	20.00
ODYSSEY					
32160248	A Place in Time	197?	3.00	6.00	12.00
TOMATO					
7018	The New Brubeck Quartet at Montreux	1978	3.00	6.00	12.00

BRUCE, ED

45s

Number	Title (A Side/B Side)	Yr	VG	VG+	NM
EPIC					
50424	When I Die, Just Let Me Go to Texas/I've Not Forgotten Marie	1977	—	2.00	4.00
50475	Star Studded Nights/Wedding Dress	1977	—	2.00	4.00
50503	Love Somebody to Death/I Can't Seem to Get the Hang of Telling Her Goodbye	1977	—	2.00	4.00
50544	Man Made of Glass/Never Take Candy from a Stranger	1978	—	2.00	4.00
50613	The Man That Turned My Mama On/Give My Old Memory a Call	1978	—	2.00	4.00
50645	Angeline/Give My Old Memory a Call	1978	—	2.00	4.00
MCA					
41201	Diane/Blue Umbrella	1980	—	—	3.00
41273	The Last Cowboy Song/The Outlaw and the Stranger	1980	—	—	3.00
51018	Girls, Women & Ladies/The Last Thing She Said	1980	—	—	3.00
51076	Evil Angel/Easy Temptations	1981	—	—	3.00
51139	(When You Fall in Love) Everything's a Waltz/Thirty-Nine and Holding	1982	—	—	3.00
51210	You're the Best Break This Old Heart Ever Had/It Just Makes Me Want You More	1982	—	—	3.00
52036	Love's Found You and Me/I Take the Chance	1982	—	—	3.00
52109	Ever, Never Lovin' You/Theme from "Bret Maverick"	1982	—	—	3.00
52156	My First Taste of Texas/One More Shot of "Old Back Home Again"	1983	—	—	3.00
52210	You're Not Leaving Here Tonight/I Think I'm in Love	1983	—	—	3.00
52251	If It Was Easy/You've Got Her Eyes	1983	—	—	3.00
52295	After All/It Would Take a Fool	1983	—	—	3.00
52433	Tell 'Em I've Gone Crazy/Birds of Paradise	1984	—	—	3.00
MONUMENT					
1118	Song for Jenny/Puzzles	1968	—	3.00	6.00
1138	Everybody Wants to Get to Heaven/When a Man Becomes a Man	1969	—	3.00	6.00
1155	Hey Porter/The Love of My Heart	1969	—	3.00	6.00
RCA					
5005-7-R	Fools for Each Other/Memphis Roots	1986	—	—	3.00
—A-side with Lynn Anderson					
5077-7-R	Quietly Crazy/Memphis Routes	1986	—	—	3.00
PB-13937	You Turn Me On Like a Radio/If It Ain't Love	1984	—	—	3.00
PB-14037	When Givin' Up Was Easy/Texas Girl, I'm Closing In on You	1985	—	—	3.00
PB-14150	If It Ain't Love/The Migrant	1985	—	—	3.00
PB-14305	Nights/Fifteen to Forty-Three (Man in the Middle)	1986	—	—	3.00
RCA VICTOR					
47-7842	Flight 303/Spun Gold	1961	3.75	7.50	15.00
47-9044	Walker's Woods/Lonesome Is Me	1966	2.00	4.00	8.00
47-9155	Last Train to Clarksville/I'm Getting Better	1967	2.00	4.00	8.00
47-9315	The Price I Pay to Stay/If I Could Just Go Home	1967	2.00	4.00	8.00
47-9394	Shadows of Her Mind/Her Sweet Love and the Baby	1967	2.00	4.00	8.00
47-9553	Painted Girls and Wine/Ninety-Seven More to Go	1968	2.00	4.00	8.00
61-7842 [S]	Flight 303/Spun Gold	1961	7.50	15.00	30.00
—"Living Stereo" (large hole, plays at 45 rpm)					
SUN					
276	Rock Boppin' Baby/More Than Yesterday	1957	7.50	15.00	30.00
—As "Edwin Bruce"					
292	Sweet Woman/Part of My Life	1958	10.00	20.00	40.00
—As "Edwin Bruce"					
UNITED ARTISTS					
XW204	A House in New Orleans/Good Jelly Jones	1973	—	2.00	4.00
XW353	July, You're a Woman/The Rain in Baby's Life	1973	—	2.00	4.00
XW403	It's Not What She Done/The Devil Ain't a Lonely Woman's Friend	1974	—	2.00	4.00
XW732	Mammas Don't Let Your Babies Grow Up to Be Cowboys/It's Not What She's Done (It's What You Didn't Do)	1975	—	2.50	5.00
XW774	The Littlest Cowboy Rides Again/The Feel of Being Gone	1976	—	2.00	4.00
XW811	Sleep All Mornin'/Working Man's Prayer	1976	—	2.00	4.00
XW862	For Love's Own Sake/When Wide Open Spaces and Cowboys Are Gone	1976	—	2.00	4.00
WAND					
136	It's Coming to Me/The Greatest Man	1963	3.00	6.00	12.00
156	I'm Gonna Have a Party/Half a Love	1964	3.00	6.00	12.00

Albums

Number	Title (A Side/B Side)	Yr	VG	VG+	NM
EPIC					
KE 35043	Tennesseean	1977	2.50	5.00	10.00
KE 35541	Cowboys and Dreamers	1978	2.50	5.00	10.00
MCA					
3242	Ed Bruce	1980	2.50	5.00	10.00
5188	One to One	1981	2.50	5.00	10.00
5323	I Write It Down	1982	2.50	5.00	10.00
5416	You're Not Leaving Here Tonight	1983	2.50	5.00	10.00
5511	Tell 'Em I've Gone Crazy	1984	2.50	5.00	10.00
5577	Greatest Hits	1985	2.50	5.00	10.00
27068	Ed Bruce	198?	2.00	4.00	8.00
—Reissue of 3242					
MONUMENT					
SLP-18118	Shades	1969	5.00	10.00	20.00
RCA VICTOR					
LPM-3948 [M]	If I Could Just Go Home	1968	12.50	25.00	50.00
LSP-3948 [S]	If I Could Just Go Home	1968	6.25	12.50	25.00
AHL1-5324	Homecoming	1985	2.50	5.00	10.00
AHL1-5808	Night Things	1986	2.50	5.00	10.00
UNITED ARTISTS					
UA-LA613-G	Ed Bruce	1976	3.00	6.00	12.00

BRUCE, JACK

Ex-member of CREAM.

45s

Number	Title (A Side/B Side)	Yr	VG	VG+	NM
RSO					
507	Keep It Down/Keep On Wondering	1975	—	2.50	5.00

Albums

Number	Title (A Side/B Side)	Yr	VG	VG+	NM
ATCO					
SD 33-306	Songs for a Tailor	1969	3.75	7.50	15.00
SD 33-349	Things We Like	1971	3.75	7.50	15.00
SD 33-365	Harmony Row	1971	3.75	7.50	15.00
EPIC					
JE 36827	I've Always Wanted to Do This	1980	2.50	5.00	10.00
FE 45279	A Question of Time	1989	3.75	7.50	15.00
POLYDOR					
PD2-3505 [(2)]	Jack Bruce At His Best	1972	3.75	7.50	15.00
RSO					
RS-1-3021	How's Tricks	1977	2.50	5.00	10.00
SO 4805	Out of the Storm	1974	2.50	5.00	10.00

BRUCE, JACK/ROBIN TROWER

Also see each artist's individual listings.

Albums

Number	Title (A Side/B Side)	Yr	VG	VG+	NM
CHRYSALIS					
CHR 1352	Truce	1982	2.50	5.00	10.00
PV 41352	Truce	1983	2.00	4.00	8.00
—Reissue					

BRUCE, LENNY

Albums

Number	Title (A Side/B Side)	Yr	VG	VG+	NM
BIZARRE					
2XS 6329 [(2)]	The Berkeley Concert	1969	6.25	12.50	25.00
DOUGLAS					
2	To Is a Preposition, Come Is a Verb	196?	5.00	10.00	20.00
788	The Essential Lenny Bruce Politics	1968	5.00	10.00	20.00
Z 30872	What I Was Arrested For	1971	3.75	7.50	15.00
—Reissue of 2					
FANTASY					
7001 [M]	Interviews of Our Times	1959	25.00	50.00	100.00
—Opaque, non-flexible red vinyl; tan cover with Lenny Bruce's name blacked out throughout the back					
7001 [M]	Interviews of Our Times	1959	10.00	20.00	40.00
—Non-flexible black vinyl; cover changed to blue tint					

Number	Title (A Side/B Side)	Yr	VG	VG+	NM
7001 [M]	Interviews of Our Times	1962	10.00	20.00	40.00
—Translucent, flexible red vinyl					
7001 [M]	Interviews of Our Times	1962	5.00	10.00	20.00
—Flexible black vinyl					
7003 [M]	The Sick Humor of Lenny Bruce	1959	25.00	50.00	100.00
—Opaque, non-flexible red vinyl					
7003 [M]	The Sick Humor of Lenny Bruce	1959	10.00	20.00	40.00
—Non-flexible black vinyl					
7003 [M]	The Sick Humor of Lenny Bruce	1962	10.00	20.00	40.00
—Translucent, flexible red vinyl					
7003 [M]	The Sick Humor of Lenny Bruce	1962	5.00	10.00	20.00
—Flexible black vinyl					
7007 [M]	I Am Not a Nut, Elect Me	1960	25.00	50.00	100.00
—Opaque, non-flexible red vinyl					
7007 [M]	I Am Not a Nut, Elect Me	1960	10.00	20.00	40.00
—Non-flexible black vinyl					
7007 [M]	I Am Not a Nut, Elect Me	1962	10.00	20.00	40.00
—Translucent, flexible red vinyl					
7007 [M]	I Am Not a Nut, Elect Me	1962	5.00	10.00	20.00
—Flexible black vinyl					
7011 [M]	Lenny Bruce, American	1961	25.00	50.00	100.00
—Opaque, non-flexible red vinyl					
7011 [M]	Lenny Bruce, American	1961	10.00	20.00	40.00
—Non-flexible black vinyl					
7011 [M]	Lenny Bruce, American	1962	10.00	20.00	40.00
—Translucent, flexible red vinyl					
7011 [M]	Lenny Bruce, American	1962	5.00	10.00	20.00
—Flexible black vinyl					
7012 [M]	The Best of Lenny Bruce	1962	12.50	25.00	50.00
—Red vinyl					
7012 [M]	The Best of Lenny Bruce	1962	5.00	10.00	20.00
—Black vinyl					
7017	Thank You Masked Man	1971	3.75	7.50	15.00
34201 [(3)]	Lenny Bruce at the Curran Theater	1971	10.00	20.00	40.00
79003 [(2)]	The Real Lenny Bruce	1975	5.00	10.00	20.00
LENNY BRUCE					
LB-3001/2 [M]	Lenny Bruce Is Out Again	196?	75.00	150.00	300.00
—Privately pressed version with white labels and Lenny's address on cover					
LB-9001/2 [10]	Warning: Sale of This Album...	1962	125.00	250.00	500.00
—Privately pressed LP with routines used as evidence in Lenny's obscenity trial					
PHILLIES					
PHLP-4010 [M]	Lenny Bruce Is Out Again	1966	25.00	50.00	100.00
—Reissue of Lenny Bruce 3001/2					
UNITED ARTISTS					
UAL 3580 [M]	The Midnight Concert	1967	6.25	12.50	25.00
UAS 6580	The Midnight Concert	1967	5.00	10.00	20.00
UAS 6794	The Midnight Concert	1972	3.75	7.50	15.00
—Reissue of 6580					
UAS 9800 [(3)]	Lenny Bruce/Carnegie Hall	1972	6.25	12.50	25.00
WARNER/SPECTOR					
SP 9101	The Law, the Language and Lenny Bruce	1975	3.75	7.50	15.00

BRUCE, TOMMY

45s

Number	Title (A Side/B Side)	Yr	VG	VG+	NM
CAPITOL					
4403	Ain't Misbehavin'/Got the Water Boilin'	1960	3.00	6.00	12.00
5354	It's Driving Me Wild/Over Suzanne	1965	2.50	5.00	10.00

BRUCE AND TERRY

BRUCE JOHNSTON and TERRY MELCHER.

45s

Number	Title (A Side/B Side)	Yr	VG	VG+	NM
COLUMBIA					
42956	Custom Machine/Makaha at Midnight	1964	5.00	10.00	20.00
43055	Summer Means Fun/Yeah!	1964	5.00	10.00	20.00
43238	I Love You Model T/Carmen	1965	5.00	10.00	20.00
43378	Raining in My Heart/Four Strong Winds	1965	4.00	8.00	16.00
43479	Thank You Baby/Come Love	1965	4.00	8.00	16.00
43582	Don't Run Away/Girl It's All Right Now	1966	4.00	8.00	16.00
EQUINOX					
PB-10238	Rebecca/Take It to Mexico	1975	2.50	5.00	10.00
—As "Bruce Johnston and Terry Melcher"					

BRUINS, THE

45s

Number	Title (A Side/B Side)	Yr	VG	VG+	NM
COMET					
2167	Nobody But You/One More Try	1964	6.25	12.50	25.00
GENERAL AMERICAN					
721	Go On and Cry/Can't Believe That You've Grown Up	1965	10.00	20.00	40.00
ROULETTE					
4566	Believe Me/The Slide	1964	5.00	10.00	20.00

BRUNO, BRUCE

45s

Number	Title (A Side/B Side)	Yr	VG	VG+	NM
ROULETTE					
4386	Hey Little One/Some Time, Some Place	1961	5.00	10.00	20.00
4427	Venus in Blue Jeans/Dear Joanne	1962	5.00	10.00	20.00

BRUTE FORCE

45s

Number	Title (A Side/B Side)	Yr	VG	VG+	NM
B.T. PUPPY					
561	War/Overture to Hello	1970	2.00	4.00	8.00
COLUMBIA					
44091	Cudd'ly/In Jim's Garage	1967	2.00	4.00	8.00
44371	Brute's Party/Toys for Tots	1967	2.00	4.00	8.00
WARNER BROS.					
7224	Adam & Evening/The Purpose of a Circus	1968	2.00	4.00	8.00

Albums

Number	Title (A Side/B Side)	Yr	VG	VG+	NM
B.T. PUPPY					
BTPS-1015	Extemporaneous	1971	1000.	1500.	2000.
COLUMBIA					
CL 2615 [M]	I, Brute Force — Confections of Love	1967	5.00	10.00	20.00
CS 9415 [S]	I, Brute Force — Confections of Love	1967	5.00	10.00	20.00
EMBRYO					
522	Brute Force	1970	5.00	10.00	20.00

BRYAN, BILLY

See GENE PITNEY.

BRYAN, WES

45s

Number	Title (A Side/B Side)	Yr	VG	VG+	NM
CLOCK					
1013	Honey Baby/So Blue Over You	1959	5.00	10.00	20.00
ROULETTE					
4289	I Guess I'll Never Know/Melodie D'Amour	1960	3.75	7.50	15.00
UNITED ARTISTS					
102	Tiny Spacemen/Lonesome Love	1957	7.50	15.00	30.00
122	Wait for Me Baby/Freeze!	1958	6.25	12.50	25.00

BRYANT, ANITA

45s

Number	Title (A Side/B Side)	Yr	VG	VG+	NM
CARLTON					
ST 118-1 [S]	Just in Time/Till There Was You	1959	3.75	7.50	15.00
ST 118-2 [S]	Hello Young Lovers/Mr. Wonderful	1959	3.75	7.50	15.00
ST 118-3 [S]	Anyone Would Love You/The Party's Over	1959	3.75	7.50	15.00
ST 118-4 [S]	Promise Me a Rose/Wouldn't It Be Lovely	1959	3.75	7.50	15.00
ST 118-5 [S]	Small World/Love Look Away	1959	3.75	7.50	15.00
—The above five are jukebox singles excerpting the LP "Anita Bryant"					
473	Be Good, Be Careful, Be Mine/Dance On	1958	3.75	7.50	15.00
512	Till There Was You/Little George	1959	2.50	5.00	10.00
518	Six Boys and Seven Girls/The Blessings of Love	1959	2.50	5.00	10.00
523	Promise Me a Rose (A Slight Detail)/Do-Re-Mi	1959	2.50	5.00	10.00
528	Paper Roses/Mixed Emotions	1960	2.00	4.00	8.00
530	In My Little Corner of the World/Anyone Would Love You	1960	2.00	4.00	8.00
535	One of the Lucky Ones/Love Look Away	1960	2.00	4.00	8.00
537	Wonderland by Night/Pictures	1960	2.00	4.00	8.00
538	A Texan and a Girl from Mexico/He's Not Good Enough for You	1961	2.00	4.00	8.00
547	I Can't Do It By Myself/An Angel Cried	1961	2.00	4.00	8.00
553	Lonesome for You Mama/A Place Called Happiness	1961	2.00	4.00	8.00
COLUMBIA					
31570 [S]	(contents unknown)	1962	2.50	5.00	10.00
31571 [S]	(contents unknown)	1962	2.50	5.00	10.00
31572 [S]	(contents unknown)	1962	2.50	5.00	10.00
31573 [S]	(contents unknown)	1962	2.50	5.00	10.00
31574 [S]	(contents unknown)	1962	2.50	5.00	10.00
—Anyone who can fill in these gaps -- the above 5 all are Columbia "Stereo 7" singles -- please let us know.					
42148	The Wedding/Seven Kinds of Lonesome	1961	2.00	4.00	8.00
42257	Step by Step, Little By Little/Cold, Cold Winter	1962	—	3.00	6.00
42257 [PS]	Step by Step, Little By Little/Cold, Cold Winter	1962	2.50	5.00	10.00
42438	One More Time with Billy/Free	1962	—	3.00	6.00
42629	A-Sleepin' at the Foot of the Bed/Wishing It Was You	1962	—	3.00	6.00
42739	Our Winter Love/Honest John	1963	—	3.00	6.00
42803	A Wound Time Can't Erase/Will I Cry in September	1963	—	3.00	6.00
42847	Hey Good Lookin'/You're the Only Star (In My Blue Heaven)	1963	—	3.00	6.00
43037	The World of Lonely People/It's Better to Cry Today Than Cry Tomorrow	1964	—	3.00	6.00
43106	Laughing on the Outside/Welcome, Welcome Home	1964	—	3.00	6.00
43205	Tell Me/I Don't Understand	1965	—	3.00	6.00
43436	My Mind's Playing Tricks on Me Again/Just Say Auf Wiedersehn	1965	—	3.00	6.00
43928	Battle Hymn of the Republic/The Star-Spangled Banner	1966	—	3.00	6.00
44067	Sticks and Stones/Tomorrow Belongs to Me	1967	—	2.50	5.00
44193	The Man in the Raincoat/Love Is (Everything You Are)	1967	—	2.50	5.00
44247	Some Sunday in the Middle of the Week/Little Love Words	1967	—	2.50	5.00
44324	I Don't See Me in Your Eyes Anymore/Happy Time	1967	—	2.50	5.00
44341	Do You Hear What I Hear/Away in the Manger	1967	2.00	4.00	8.00
44341 [PS]	Do You Hear What I Hear/Away in the Manger	1967	2.50	5.00	10.00
44427	Something in Your Smile/Yellow Days	1968	—	2.50	5.00
44471	Try to Remember/My Cup Runneth Over	1968	—	2.50	5.00
44569	Blue Summer/Silver and Blue	1968	—	2.50	5.00
44654	Let the Heartaches Begin/Sister Sarah	1968	—	2.50	5.00
DISNEYLAND					
DL-560	The Orange Bird Song/Orange Tree	1971	2.00	4.00	8.00
DL-560 [PS]	The Orange Bird Song/Orange Tree	1971	3.75	7.50	15.00

Albums

Number	Title (A Side/B Side)	Yr	VG	VG+	NM
CARLTON					
LP-118 [M]	Anita Bryant	1959	5.00	10.00	20.00
STLP-118 [S]	Anita Bryant	1959	7.50	15.00	30.00
LP-127 [M]	Hear Anita Bryant in Your Home Tonight	1960	5.00	10.00	20.00
STLP-127 [S]	Hear Anita Bryant in Your Home Tonight	1960	6.25	12.50	25.00
LP-132 [M]	In My Little Corner of the World	1961	5.00	10.00	20.00
STLP-132 [S]	In My Little Corner of the World	1961	6.25	12.50	25.00
COLUMBIA					
CL 1719 [M]	Kisses Sweeter Than Wine	1961	3.75	7.50	15.00
CL 1767 [M]	Abiding Love	1962	3.75	7.50	15.00
CL 1885 [M]	In a Velvet Mood	1962	3.00	6.00	12.00
CL 1956 [M]	Anita Bryant's Greatest Hits	1963	3.00	6.00	12.00
CL 2035 [M]	As Long As He Needs Me	1963	3.00	6.00	12.00
CL 2069 [M]	Country's Best	1964	3.00	6.00	12.00
CL 2222 [M]	World of Lonely People	1964	3.00	6.00	12.00
CL 2573 [M]	Mine Eyes Have Seen the Glory	1966	3.00	6.00	12.00
CL 2706 [M]	I Believe	1967	3.75	7.50	15.00
CL 2720 [M]	Do You Hear What I Hear?	1967	3.75	7.50	15.00
CS 8519 [S]	Kisses Sweeter Than Wine	1961	5.00	10.00	20.00

Number	Title (A Side/B Side)	Yr	VG	VG+	NM
CS 8567 [S]	Abiding Love	1962	5.00	10.00	20.00
CS 8685 [S]	In a Velvet Mood	1962	3.75	7.50	15.00
CS 8756 [S]	Anita Bryant's Greatest Hits	1963	3.75	7.50	15.00
CS 8835 [S]	As Long As He Needs Me	1963	3.75	7.50	15.00
CS 8869 [S]	Country's Best	1964	3.75	7.50	15.00
CS 9022 [S]	World of Lonely People	1964	3.75	7.50	15.00
CS 9373 [S]	Mine Eyes Have Seen the Glory	1966	3.75	7.50	15.00
CS 9506 [S]	I Believe	1967	3.00	6.00	12.00
CS 9520 [S]	Do You Hear What I Hear?	1967	2.50	5.00	10.00
CS 9607	In Remembrance of You (The Story of a Love Affair)	1968	3.00	6.00	12.00
CS 9642	How Great Thou Art	1968	3.00	6.00	12.00
COLUMBIA SPECIAL PRODUCTS					
CSS 900	The Sunshine Tree	1970	3.00	6.00	12.00
HARMONY					
HL 9557 [M]	ABC Stories of Jesus	196?	3.00	6.00	12.00
HS 11280	Anita Bryant	1968	2.50	5.00	10.00
HS 11330	Little Things Mean a Lot	1969	2.50	5.00	10.00
HS 11395	A World Without Love	1970	2.50	5.00	10.00
H 31181	You'll Never Walk Alone	1972	2.50	5.00	10.00
MYRRH					
MSB-6513	Naturally	197?	3.00	6.00	12.00
WORD					
WST-8532	Abide with Me	1970	3.00	6.00	12.00
WST-8540	Love Lifted Me	1971	3.00	6.00	12.00
WST-8558	The Miracle of Christmas	197?	2.50	5.00	10.00
WST-8571	Battle Hymn of the Republic	1972	3.00	6.00	12.00
WST-8631	This Is My Story	1975	3.00	6.00	12.00
WST-8652	Hymns	1976	3.00	6.00	12.00
WST-8670	Old Fashioned Prayin'	1977	3.00	6.00	12.00
8785	Singing a New Song	198?	2.50	5.00	10.00

BRYANT, LILLIE

Of BILLY AND LILLIE.

45s

Number	Title (A Side/B Side)	Yr	VG	VG+	NM
SWAN					
4029	Smokey Grey Eyes/I'll Never Be Free	1959	3.00	6.00	12.00

BRYANT, RAY

45s

Number	Title (A Side/B Side)	Yr	VG	VG+	NM
ATLANTIC JAZZ					
5102	Let It Be/Shake-A-Lady	1971	—	2.00	4.00
CADET					
5535	Gotta Travel On/It Was a Very Good Year	1966	—	3.00	6.00
5558	If You Go Away/Slow Freight	1967	—	3.00	6.00
5575	Ode to Billie Joe/Ramblin'	1967	—	3.00	6.00
5580	City Tribal Dance/Little Suzie	1967	—	3.00	6.00
5587	Pata Pata/Doing My Thing	1968	—	3.00	6.00
5598	To Sir with Love/Dinner on the Grounds	1968	—	2.50	5.00
5615	Mrs. Robinson/Poochie	1968	—	2.50	5.00
5625	Little Green Apples/Up Above the Rock	1968	—	2.50	5.00
5639	After Hours/Quizas, Quizas, Quizas	1969	—	2.50	5.00
COLUMBIA					
31339 [S]	(contents unknown)	1961	3.00	6.00	12.00
31340 [S]	(contents unknown)	1961	3.00	6.00	12.00
31341 [S]	(contents unknown)	1961	3.00	6.00	12.00
31342 [S]	(contents unknown)	1961	3.00	6.00	12.00
31343 [S]	(contents unknown)	1961	3.00	6.00	12.00
—Anyone who can fill in these gaps -- the above 5 all are Columbia "Stereo 7" singles -- please let us know.					
41553	Little Suzie (Part 1)/Little Suzie (Part 2)	1960	2.50	5.00	10.00
41628	The Madison Time (Part 1)/The Madison Time (Part 2)	1960	2.50	5.00	10.00
41628 [PS]	The Madison Time (Part 1)/The Madison Time (Part 2)	1960	3.75	7.50	15.00
41761	C Jam Blues (Part 1)/C Jam Blues (Part 2)	1960	2.50	5.00	10.00
41940	Sack O' Woe/Walk No More	1961	2.50	5.00	10.00
42015	Moonrise/First Lady	1961	2.50	5.00	10.00
42390	After Hours/Tonk	1962	2.50	5.00	10.00
NEW JAZZ					
505	Joy/Stocking Feet	1959	3.00	6.00	12.00
SIGNATURE					
12026	Little Suzie (Part 2)/Little Suzie (Part 4)	1960	3.00	6.00	12.00
SUE					
108	Shake a Lady/Blues March	1964	2.00	4.00	8.00
125	Goldfinger/Adalia	1965	2.00	4.00	8.00
801	Glissamba/Joey	1963	2.00	4.00	8.00

Albums

Number	Title (A Side/B Side)	Yr	VG	VG+	NM
ATLANTIC					
SD 1564	MCMLXX	1970	3.75	7.50	15.00
SD 1626	Alone at Montreux	1972	3.00	6.00	12.00
CADET					
LP-767 [M]	Gotta Travel On	1966	3.75	7.50	15.00
LPS-767 [S]	Gotta Travel On	1966	5.00	10.00	20.00
LP-778 [M]	Lonesome Traveler	1966	3.75	7.50	15.00
LPS-778 [S]	Lonesome Traveler	1966	5.00	10.00	20.00
LP-781 [M]	Slow Freight	1967	3.75	7.50	15.00
LPS-781 [S]	Slow Freight	1967	5.00	10.00	20.00
LP-793 [M]	The Ray Bryant Touch	1967	5.00	10.00	20.00
LPS-793 [S]	The Ray Bryant Touch	1967	3.75	7.50	15.00
LP-801 [M]	Take a Bryant Step	1967	5.00	10.00	20.00
LPS-801 [S]	Take a Bryant Step	1967	3.75	7.50	15.00
LPS-818	Up Above the Rock	1968	3.75	7.50	15.00
LPS-830	Sound Ray	1969	3.75	7.50	15.00
50038 [(2)]	It Was a Very Good Year	1973	3.75	7.50	15.00
50052	In the Cut	1974	3.00	6.00	12.00
CLASSIC JAZZ					
130	Hot Turkey	198?	2.50	5.00	10.00
COLUMBIA					
CL 1449 [M]	Little Susie	1960	5.00	10.00	20.00
CL 1476 [M]	The Madison Time	1960	6.25	12.50	25.00
CL 1633 [M]	Con Alma	1961	5.00	10.00	20.00
CL 1746 [M]	Dancing the Big Twist	1962	5.00	10.00	20.00
CL 1867 [M]	Hollywood Jazz Beat	1962	5.00	10.00	20.00
CS 8244 [S]	Little Susie	1960	6.25	12.50	25.00
CS 8276 [S]	The Madison Time	1960	7.50	15.00	30.00
CS 8433 [S]	Con Alma	1961	6.25	12.50	25.00
CS 8546 [S]	Dancing the Big Twist	1962	6.25	12.50	25.00
CS 8667 [S]	Hollywood Jazz Beat	1962	6.25	12.50	25.00
COLUMBIA JAZZ MASTERPIECES					
CJ 44058	Con Alma	1988	2.50	5.00	10.00
EMARCY					
832235-1	Ray Bryant Plays Basie and Ellington	1987	3.00	6.00	12.00
832589-1	The Ray Bryant Trio Today	1988	3.00	6.00	12.00
836368-1	Golden Earrings	1989	3.00	6.00	12.00
EPIC					
LN 3279 [M]	Ray Bryant Trio	1956	17.50	35.00	70.00
FANTASY					
OJC-213	Alone with the Blues	1987	2.50	5.00	10.00
—Reissue					
OJC-371	Montreux '77	1989	2.50	5.00	10.00
—Reissue of Pablo Live 2308 201					
NEW JAZZ					
NJLP-8213 [M]	Alone with the Blues	1959	12.50	25.00	50.00
—Purple label					
NJLP-8213 [M]	Alone with the Blues	1965	6.25	12.50	25.00
—Blue label with trident logo					
NJLP-8227 [M]	Ray Bryant Trio	1959	12.50	25.00	50.00
—Purple label; reissue of Prestige 7098					
NJLP-8227 [M]	Ray Bryant Trio	1965	6.25	12.50	25.00
—Blue label with trident logo					
PABLO					
2310764	Here's Ray Bryant	1976	2.50	5.00	10.00
2310798	Solo Piano	1976	2.50	5.00	10.00
2310820	All Blues	1978	2.50	5.00	10.00
2310860	Potpourri	1981	2.50	5.00	10.00
2405402	The Best of Ray Bryant	198?	2.50	5.00	10.00
PABLO LIVE					
2308201	Montreux '77	1977	2.50	5.00	10.00
PRESTIGE					
PRLP-7098 [M]	Ray Bryant Trio	1957	17.50	35.00	70.00
PRLP-7837	Alone with the Blues	1971	3.75	7.50	15.00
—Reissue of New Jazz 8213					
24038 [(2)]	Me and the Blues	1973	3.75	7.50	15.00
SIGNATURE					
SM-6008 [M]	Ray Bryant Plays	1960	50.00	100.00	200.00
SS-6008 [S]	Ray Bryant Plays	1960	62.50	125.00	250.00
SUE					
LP-1016 [M]	Groove House	1963	10.00	20.00	40.00
LPS-1016 [S]	Groove House	1963	12.50	25.00	50.00
LP-1019 [M]	Live at Basin Street	1964	10.00	20.00	40.00
LPS-1019 [S]	Live at Basin Street	1964	12.50	25.00	50.00
LP-1032 [M]	Cold Turkey	1964	10.00	20.00	40.00
LPS-1032 [S]	Cold Turkey	1964	12.50	25.00	50.00
LP-1036 [M]	Ray Bryant Soul	1965	10.00	20.00	40.00
LPS-1036 [S]	Ray Bryant Soul	1965	12.50	25.00	50.00

BRYNDLE

Andrew Gold, Karla Bonoff, Wendy Waldman, Kenny Edwards.

45s

Number	Title (A Side/B Side)	Yr	VG	VG+	NM
A&M					
1252	Let's Go Home and Start Again/Woke Up This Morning	1971	2.50	5.00	10.00

BUBBLE PUPPY, THE

Also see DEMIAN.

45s

Number	Title (A Side/B Side)	Yr	VG	VG+	NM
INTERNATIONAL ARTISTS					
128	Hot Smoke and Sasafrass/Lonely	1969	5.00	10.00	20.00
133	Beginning/If I Had a Reason	1969	6.25	12.50	25.00
136	Days of Our Time/Thinkin' About Thinkin'	1969	6.25	12.50	25.00
138	What Do You See/Hurry Sundown	1970	6.25	12.50	25.00
138 [DJ]	What Do You See/Hurry Sundown	1970	12.50	25.00	50.00
—Green vinyl promo					

Albums

Number	Title (A Side/B Side)	Yr	VG	VG+	NM
INTERNATIONAL ARTISTS					
10	A Gathering of Promises	1969	25.00	50.00	100.00
—Original does not have "Masterfonics" in the dead wax					
10	A Gathering of Promises	1979	6.25	12.50	25.00
—Reissue has "Masterfonics" in the dead wax					

BUBI AND BOB

45s

Number	Title (A Side/B Side)	Yr	VG	VG+	NM
SPHINX					
1201	The Mummy/Biscayne Beat	1959	7.50	15.00	30.00

BUCCANEERS, THE

45s

Number	Title (A Side/B Side)	Yr	VG	VG+	NM
RAINBOW					
211	Dear Ruth/Fine Brown Flame	1953	200.00	400.00	800.00
RAMA					
21	The Stars Will Remember/Come Back My Love	1954	500.00	1000.	2000.
24	In the Mission of St. Augustine/You Did Me Wrong	1954	500.00	1000.	2000.
SOUTHERN					
101	Dear Ruth/Fine Brown Flame	1953	2000.	3000.	4000.
—All copies are on red vinyl					

BUCHANAN, BILL

Also see BUCHANAN AND ANCELL; BUCHANAN AND CELLA; BUCHANAN AND GOODMAN; BUCHANAN AND GREENFIELD.

45s

Number	Title (A Side/B Side)	Yr	VG	VG+	NM
GONE					
5032	The Thing/Happy Day	1958	7.50	15.00	30.00
UNITED ARTISTS					
531	The Night Before Halloween/Beware	1962	3.75	7.50	15.00

BUCHANAN, ROY

Number	Title (A Side/B Side)	Yr	VG	VG+	NM
45s					
ATLANTIC					
3342	Keep What You Got/Caruso	1976	—	2.00	4.00
3414	The Circle/Green Onions	1977	—	2.00	4.00
3433	The Circle/(B-side unknown)	1977	—	2.00	4.00
POLYDOR					
14149	Haunted House/Cajun	1972	—	2.50	5.00
14174	Filthy Teddy/Thank You Lord	1973	—	2.50	5.00
14178	Sweet Dreams/John's Blues	1973	—	2.50	5.00
14265	Rescue Me/I'm a Ram	1974	—	2.50	5.00
SWAN					
4088	Mule Train Stomp/Pretty Please	1961	3.00	6.00	12.00
Albums					
ALLIGATOR					
AL-4741	When a Guitar Plays the Blues	1985	2.50	5.00	10.00
AL-4747	Dancing on the Edge	1986	2.50	5.00	10.00
AL-4756	Hot Wires	1988	2.50	5.00	10.00
ATLANTIC					
SD 18170	A Street Called Straight	1976	3.00	6.00	12.00
SD 18219	Loading Zone	1977	3.00	6.00	12.00
SD 19138	Loading Zone	1978	2.00	4.00	8.00
—Reissue of 18219					
SD 19170	You're Not Alone	1978	3.00	6.00	12.00
BIOYA					
MM-519	Buch and the Snake Stretchers	1971	50.00	100.00	200.00
POLYDOR					
PD-5033	Roy Buchanan	1972	3.75	7.50	15.00
PD-5046	Second Album	1973	3.75	7.50	15.00
PD-6020	That's What I Am Here For	1974	3.75	7.50	15.00
PD-6035	In the Beginning	1974	3.75	7.50	15.00
PD-6048	Live Stock	1975	3.75	7.50	15.00
WATERHOUSE					
12	My Babe	1981	2.50	5.00	10.00

BUCHANAN AND ANCELL

Also see BILL BUCHANAN.

Number	Title (A Side/B Side)	Yr	VG	VG+	NM
45s					
FLYING SAUCER					
501	The Creature/Meet the Creature	1957	10.00	20.00	40.00

BUCHANAN AND CELLA

Also see BILL BUCHANAN.

Number	Title (A Side/B Side)	Yr	VG	VG+	NM
45s					
ABC-PARAMOUNT					
10033	String Along with Pal-O-Mine/More and More String Along with Pal-O-Mine	1959	6.25	12.50	25.00

BUCHANAN AND GOODMAN

Also see BILL BUCHANAN; DICKIE GOODMAN.

Number	Title (A Side/B Side)	Yr	VG	VG+	NM
45s					
COMIC					
500	Flying Saucer the Third/The Cha Cha Lesson	1959	10.00	20.00	40.00
LUNIVERSE					
101X	Back to Earth Part 1/Back to Earth Part 2	1956	50.00	100.00	200.00
101	The Flying Saucer Part 1/The Flying Saucer Part 2	1956	12.50	25.00	50.00
—Most labels have the entire word "Luniverse" typeset					
101	The Flying Saucer Part 1/The Flying Saucer Part 2	1956	18.75	37.50	75.00
—Original labels have a handwritten "L" at the beginning of the printed word "Universe"					
102X	Public Opinion Part 1/Public Opinion Part 2	1956	—	—	—
—Not known to exist					
102	Buchanan and Goodman On Trial/Crazy	1956	10.00	20.00	40.00
103	The Banana Boat Story/The Mystery (In Slow Motion)	1957	10.00	20.00	40.00
105	Flying Saucer The 2nd/Martian Melody	1957	10.00	20.00	40.00
107	Santa and the Satellite Part 1/Santa and the Satellite Part 2	1957	10.00	20.00	40.00
108	The Flying Saucer Goes West/Saucer Serenade	1958	10.00	20.00	40.00
NOVELTY					
301	Frankenstein of '59/Frankenstein Returns	1959	10.00	20.00	40.00

BUCHANAN AND GREENFIELD

Also see BILL BUCHANAN.

Number	Title (A Side/B Side)	Yr	VG	VG+	NM
45s					
NOVEL					
711	The Invasion/What a Lovely Party	1964	7.50	15.00	30.00
—Originals have all-red labels					
711	The Invasion/What a Lovely Party	1972	2.00	4.00	8.00
—Red and white label reissue					

BUCHANAN BROTHERS

Early version of CASHMAN, PISTILLI AND WEST.

Number	Title (A Side/B Side)	Yr	VG	VG+	NM
45s					
EVENT					
201	Get Down with the People/You Don't Know	1970	—	3.00	6.00
205	Don't Stop Now/You Don't Know	1971	—	3.00	6.00
3302	Medicine Man (Part 1)/Medicine Man (Part 2)	1969	—	3.00	6.00
3305	Son of a Lovin' Man/I'll Never Get Enough	1969	—	3.00	6.00
3307	A Feeling That I Get/The Last Time	1969	—	3.00	6.00
3308	Sad Song with a Happy Soul/Rusianna	1970	—	3.00	6.00
Albums					
EVENT					
ES-101	Medicine Man	1969	6.25	12.50	25.00

BUCK, CHARLIE

Number	Title (A Side/B Side)	Yr	VG	VG+	NM
45s					
TAD					
104	I Wish I Were A Christmas Tree/We Can't Miss This Christmas	1962	3.00	6.00	12.00

BUCKEYES, THE

Number	Title (A Side/B Side)	Yr	VG	VG+	NM
45s					
DELUXE					
6110	Since I Fell for You/My Only You	1957	75.00	150.00	300.00
6126	Dottie Baby/Begging You Please	1957	100.00	200.00	400.00

BUCKINGHAM NICKS

Lindsey Buckingham and Stephanie (later known as Stevie) Nicks. Also see FLEETWOOD MAC.

Number	Title (A Side/B Side)	Yr	VG	VG+	NM
45s					
POLYDOR					
14209	Don't Let Me Down Again/The Races Are Run	1973	12.50	25.00	50.00
14229	Crying in the Night/Without a Leg to Stand On	1974	12.50	25.00	50.00
14335	Don't Let Me Down Again/Crystal	1976	7.50	15.00	30.00
14428	Crying in the Night/Stephanie	1977	7.50	15.00	30.00
14428 [PS]	Crying in the Night/Stephanie	1977	15.00	30.00	60.00
Albums					
POLYDOR					
PD-5058	Buckingham Nicks	1973	10.00	20.00	40.00
—Gatefold cover					
PD-5058	Buckingham Nicks	1975	3.00	6.00	12.00
—Regular cover					

BUCKINGHAMS, THE (1)

Chicago band. Also see THE FALLING PEBBLES.

Number	Title (A Side/B Side)	Yr	VG	VG+	NM
45s					
COLUMBIA					
44053	Don't You Care/Why Don't You Love Me	1967	2.00	4.00	8.00
44053 [PS]	Don't You Care/Why Don't You Love Me	1967	3.00	6.00	12.00
44182	Mercy, Mercy, Mercy/You Are Gone	1967	2.00	4.00	8.00
44182 [PS]	Mercy, Mercy, Mercy/You Are Gone	1967	3.00	6.00	12.00
44254	Hey Baby (They're Playing Our Song)/And Our Love	1967	2.00	4.00	8.00
44254 [PS]	Hey Baby (They're Playing Our Song)/And Our Love	1967	3.00	6.00	12.00
44378	Susan/Foreign Policy	1967	2.00	4.00	8.00
44378 [PS]	Susan/Foreign Policy	1967	3.00	6.00	12.00
44533	Back in Love Again/You Misunderstand Me	1968	2.00	4.00	8.00
44533 [PS]	Back in Love Again/You Misunderstand Me	1968	3.00	6.00	12.00
44672	Where Did You Come From/Song of the Breeze	1968	2.00	4.00	8.00
44672 [PS]	Where Did You Come From/Song of the Breeze	1968	3.00	6.00	12.00
44790	This Is How Much I Love You/Can't You Find the Words	1969	2.00	4.00	8.00
44790 [PS]	This Is How Much I Love You/Can't You Find the Words	1969	3.00	6.00	12.00
44923	It's a Beautiful Day/Difference of Opinion	1969	2.00	4.00	8.00
45066	It Took Forever/I Got a Feelin'	1970	2.00	4.00	8.00
PHILCO-FORD					
HP-14	Kind of a Drag/Lawdy Miss Clawdy	1968	5.00	10.00	20.00
—4-inch plastic "Hip Pocket Record" with color sleeve					
RED LABEL					
71001	Veronica/Can We Talk About It	1985	—	2.00	4.00
71001 [PS]	Veronica/Can We Talk About It	1985	—	2.50	5.00
SPECTRASOUND					
4618	Sweets for My Sweet/Beginner's Love	1967	5.00	10.00	20.00
U.S.A.					
844	I'll Go Crazy/I Don't Wanna Cry	1966	3.00	6.00	12.00
848	I Call Your Name/Makin' Up and Breakin' Up	1966	3.00	6.00	12.00
853	I've Been Wrong/Love Ain't Enough	1966	3.00	6.00	12.00
860	Kind of a Drag/You Make Me Feel So Good	1966	3.75	7.50	15.00
—Light blue label with all dark blue printing					
860	Kind of a Drag/You Make Me Feel So Good	1966	3.75	7.50	15.00
—Light blue label with red, white, blue and black printing					
869	Lawdy Miss Clawdy/I Call Your Name	1967	3.00	6.00	12.00
869	Lawdy Miss Clawdy/Making Up and Breaking Up	1967	3.00	6.00	12.00
873	Summertime/Don't Want to Cry	1967	3.00	6.00	12.00
Albums					
COLUMBIA					
CL 2669 [M]	Time & Charges	1967	6.25	12.50	25.00
CL 2798 [M]	Portraits	1968	6.25	12.50	25.00
CS 9469 [S]	Time & Charges	1967	5.00	10.00	20.00
CS 9598 [S]	Portraits	1968	5.00	10.00	20.00
CS 9703	In One Ear and Gone Tomorrow	1968	5.00	10.00	20.00
CS 9812	The Buckinghams Greatest Hits	1969	5.00	10.00	20.00
—Red "360 Sound" label					
CS 9812	The Buckinghams Greatest Hits	1970	3.00	6.00	12.00
—Orange label					
PC 9812	The Buckinghams Greatest Hits	198?	2.00	4.00	8.00
—Reissue with new prefix					
U.S.A.					
107 [M]	Kind of a Drag	1967	150.00	300.00	600.00
—With "I'm a Man"					
107 [M]	Kind of a Drag	1967	7.50	15.00	30.00
—Without "I'm a Man"					
107 [S]	Kind of a Drag	1967	10.00	20.00	40.00
—No known stereo copy has "I'm a Man"					

BUCKINGHAMS, THE (2)

These two records are not by group (1).

Number	Title (A Side/B Side)	Yr	VG	VG+	NM
45s					
LAURIE					
3258	Gonna Say Goodbye/Many Times	1964	2.50	5.00	10.00
SEG-WAY					
1004	Lobo Lobo/Rockin' Piper	1962	2.50	5.00	10.00

BUCKLEY, LORD

Number	Title (A Side/B Side)	Yr	VG	VG+	NM
Albums					
CRESTVIEW					
CRV-801 [M]	The Best of Lord Buckley	1963	12.50	25.00	50.00
CRV7-801 [S]	The Best of Lord Buckley	1963	15.00	30.00	60.00
ELEKTRA					
EKS-74047	The Best of Lord Buckley	1969	6.25	12.50	25.00
—Reissue of Crestview 7-801					

Number	Title (A Side/B Side)	Yr	VG	VG+	NM
RCA VICTOR					
LPM-3246 [10]	Hipsters, Flipsters and Finger Poppin' Daddies, Knock Me Your Lobes	1955	75.00	150.00	300.00
REPRISE					
RS 6389	A Most Immaculately Hip Aristocrat	1970	6.25	12.50	25.00
—Reissue of Straight 1054					
STRAIGHT					
STS-1054	A Most Immaculately Hip Aristocrat	1970	10.00	20.00	40.00
VAYA					
101/2 [M]	Euphoria, Volume 1	1955	37.50	75.00	150.00
107/8 [M]	Euphoria, Volume 2	1955	50.00	100.00	200.00
1715 [10]	Euphoria	195?	75.00	150.00	300.00
—Red vinyl					
WORLD PACIFIC					
WP-1279 [M]	The Way Out Humor of Lord Buckley	1959	30.00	60.00	120.00
—With "Far Out Humor" on the back cover					
WP-1279 [M]	The Way Out Humor of Lord Buckley	1959	25.00	50.00	100.00
—With correct "Way Out Humor" on the back cover					
WP-1815 [M]	Lord Buckley in Concert	1964	12.50	25.00	50.00
—Reissue of 1279					
WP-1849 [M]	Blowing His Mind (and Yours, Too)	1966	12.50	25.00	50.00
WPS-21879	Buckley's Best	1968	10.00	20.00	40.00
WPS-21889	Bad Rapping of the Marquis de Sade	1969	7.50	15.00	30.00

BUCKLEY, TIM

Number	Title (A Side/B Side)	Yr	VG	VG+	NM
45s					
DISCREET					
1187	Quicksand/Stone in Love	1973	—	3.00	6.00
1189	Dolphins/Honey Man	1974	—	3.00	6.00
1311	Wanda Lu/Who Could Deny You	1974	—	3.00	6.00
ELEKTRA					
45606	Grief in My Soul/Wings	1966	2.00	4.00	8.00
45612	Aren't You the Girl/Strange Street Affair Down Under	1967	2.00	4.00	8.00
45618	Once Upon a Time/Lady Give Me Your Heart	1967	2.00	4.00	8.00
45623	Morning Glory/Once I Was	1967	2.00	4.00	8.00
WARNER BROS.					
7623	Move with Me/Nighthawkin'	1972	—	3.00	6.00
Albums					
DISCREET					
MS 2157	Sefronia	1973	3.75	7.50	15.00
DS 2201	Look at the Fool	1974	3.75	7.50	15.00
ELEKTRA					
EKL-4004 [M]	Tim Buckley	1966	3.75	7.50	15.00
EKL-4018 [M]	Goodbye and Hello	1967	6.25	12.50	25.00
EKS-74004 [S]	Tim Buckley	1966	5.00	10.00	20.00
EKS-74018 [S]	Goodbye and Hello	1967	5.00	10.00	20.00
EKS-74045	Happy Sad	1969	5.00	10.00	20.00
EKS-74074	Lorca	1970	5.00	10.00	20.00
RHINO					
RNLP-112	The Best of Tim Buckley	1985	2.50	5.00	10.00
STRAIGHT					
STS-1060	Blue Afternoon	1969	7.50	15.00	30.00
WARNER BROS.					
WS 1842	Blue Afternoon	1970	3.75	7.50	15.00
WS 1881	Starsailor	1970	3.75	7.50	15.00
BS 2631	Greetings from L.A.	1972	3.75	7.50	15.00

BUCKNER, JOE

Number	Title (A Side/B Side)	Yr	VG	VG+	NM
45s					
VEE JAY					
141	Why Don't Cha/How Can I Let Her Go	1955	6.25	12.50	25.00
172	One More Mile/Straight and Ready	1956	6.25	12.50	25.00
—B-side by Tommy Dean					

BUCKWHEAT

Number	Title (A Side/B Side)	Yr	VG	VG+	NM
Albums					
LONDON					
PS 595	Buckwheat	1971	3.75	7.50	15.00
PS 609	Movin' On	1972	3.00	6.00	12.00
XPS 621	Charade	1972	3.00	6.00	12.00
XPS 635	Hot Tracks	1973	3.00	6.00	12.00

BUD AND TRAVIS

Number	Title (A Side/B Side)	Yr	VG	VG+	NM
45s					
LIBERTY					
55202	Truly Do/Bonsoir Dame	1959	2.50	5.00	10.00
55221	Poor Boy/Jenny on a Horse	1959	2.50	5.00	10.00
55235	Cloudy Summer Afternoon/E Labas	1959	2.50	5.00	10.00
55259	Come to the Dance/Carmen Carmelia	1960	2.00	4.00	8.00
55284	Ballad of the Alamo/The Green Leaves of Summer	1960	2.00	4.00	8.00
55612	Tomorrow Is a Long Time/Haiti	1963	—	3.00	6.00
55681	Maria Cristina/Sabras Que Te Quiero	1964	—	3.00	6.00
55713	How Long, How Long Blues/Gimme Some	1964	—	3.00	6.00
55764	I Talk to the Trees/Moment in the Sun	1965	—	3.00	6.00
55803	Cold Summer/Girl Sittin' Up in a Tree	1965	—	3.00	6.00
WORLD PACIFIC					
801	Raspberries Strawberries/Mexican Wedding Song	1959	3.00	6.00	12.00
Albums					
LIBERTY					
LRP-3125 [M]	Bud and Travis	1959	7.50	15.00	30.00
LRP-3138 [M]	Spotlight On Bud and Travis	1960	5.00	10.00	20.00
LRP-3222 [M]	Bud and Travis...In Concert, Volume 2	1961	5.00	10.00	20.00
LRP-3295 [M]	Naturally	1963	5.00	10.00	20.00
LRP-3341 [M]	Perspective on Bud and Travis	1964	5.00	10.00	20.00
LRP-3386 [M]	Bud and Travis In Person (At the Cellar Door)	1964	5.00	10.00	20.00
LRP-3398 [M]	The Latin Album	1965	5.00	10.00	20.00
LST-7125 [S]	Bud and Travis	1959	10.00	20.00	40.00
LST-7138 [S]	Spotlight On Bud and Travis	1960	6.25	12.50	25.00
LST-7222 [S]	Bud and Travis...In Concert, Volume 2	1961	6.25	12.50	25.00
LST-7295 [S]	Naturally	1963	6.25	12.50	25.00
LST-7341 [S]	Perspective on Bud and Travis	1964	6.25	12.50	25.00
LST-7386 [S]	Bud and Travis In Person (At the Cellar Door)	1964	6.25	12.50	25.00
LST-7398 [S]	The Latin Album	1965	6.25	12.50	25.00
LDM-11001 [(2) M]	Bud and Travis...In Concert	1960	6.25	12.50	25.00
LDS-12001 [(2) S]	Bud and Travis...In Concert	1960	7.50	15.00	30.00
SUNSET					
SUM-1154 [M]	Bud and Travis	1967	3.00	6.00	12.00
SUS-5154 [S]	Bud and Travis	1967	3.00	6.00	12.00

BUDDIES, THE

Several different groups.

Number	Title (A Side/B Side)	Yr	VG	VG+	NM
45s					
COMET					
2143	Hully Gully Baby/Must Be True Love	1961	6.25	12.50	25.00
DECCA					
29840	The Most Happy Fella/Two Skeletons on a Tin Roof	1956	3.75	7.50	15.00
29953	Bag of Bones/Every Time the Phone Rings	1956	3.75	7.50	15.00
30355	A Prom and a Promise/The Lottery	1957	3.75	7.50	15.00
31920	Duckman Part 1/Duckman Part 2	1966	2.00	4.00	8.00
GLORY					
230	I Stole Your Heart/I Waited	1955	37.50	75.00	150.00
OKEH					
7123	Castle of Love/Give Me Your Love	1959	3.75	7.50	15.00
SWAN					
4073	Spooky Spider/Lebone Delada	1961	3.75	7.50	15.00
4170	The Beatle/Pulsebeat	1964	6.25	12.50	25.00
TIARA					
6121	She's a Loser/Heartless	1959	6.25	12.50	25.00
Albums					
WING					
MGW-12293 [M]	The Buddies and the Compacts	1965	12.50	25.00	50.00
MGW-12306 [M]	Go Go with the Buddies	1965	12.50	25.00	50.00
SRW-16293 [S]	The Buddies and the Compacts	1965	20.00	40.00	80.00
SRW-16306 [S]	Go Go with the Buddies	1965	20.00	40.00	80.00

BUDGIE

Number	Title (A Side/B Side)	Yr	VG	VG+	NM
45s					
KAPP					
2152	Nude Disintegrating Parachutist Woman/Crash Course	1971	—	2.50	5.00
2185	Stranded/Whiskey River	1972	—	2.50	5.00
MCA					
40367	Honey/I Ain't No Mountain	1975	—	2.50	5.00
Albums					
A&M					
SP-4593	If I Were Brittania I'd Waive the Rules	1976	3.75	7.50	15.00
SP-4618	Bandolier	1977	3.75	7.50	15.00
SP-4675	Impeckable	1978	3.75	7.50	15.00
KAPP					
KS-3656	Budgie	1971	7.50	15.00	30.00
KS-3669	Squawk	1972	7.50	15.00	30.00
MCA					
429	In for the Kill	1973	5.00	10.00	20.00

BUFFALO NICKEL JUGBAND, THE

Number	Title (A Side/B Side)	Yr	VG	VG+	NM
Albums					
HAPPY TIGER					
1018	The Buffalo Nickel Jugband	1971	6.25	12.50	25.00

BUFFALO SPRINGFIELD

Also see DEWEY MARTIN AND MEDICINE BALL; JIM MESSINA; STEPHEN STILLS; NEIL YOUNG.

Number	Title (A Side/B Side)	Yr	VG	VG+	NM
45s					
ATCO					
6428	Nowadays Clancy Can't Even Sing/Go And Say Goodbye	1966	5.00	10.00	20.00
6452	Everybody's Wrong/Burned	1966	5.00	10.00	20.00
6459	For What It's Worth/Do I Have to Come Right Out and Say It	1967	3.75	7.50	15.00
6459	For What It's Worth (Stop, Hey, What's That Sound)/Do I Have to Come Right Out and Say It	1967	3.00	6.00	12.00
6499	Bluebird/Mr. Soul	1967	5.00	10.00	20.00
6519	Rock 'N' Roll Woman/A Child's Claim to Fame	1967	2.50	5.00	10.00
6545	Expecting to Fly/Everydays	1968	2.50	5.00	10.00
6572	Uno Mundo/Merry-Go-Round	1968	2.50	5.00	10.00
6602	Special Care/Kind Woman	1968	2.50	5.00	10.00
6615	Four Days Gone/On the Way Home	1968	2.50	5.00	10.00
Albums					
ATCO					
SD 38-105 [S]	Retrospective/The Best of Buffalo Springfield	197?	2.00	4.00	8.00
—Reissue of 33-283					
33-200 [M]	Buffalo Springfield	1967	50.00	100.00	200.00
—With "Baby Don't Scold Me"					
33-200A [M]	Buffalo Springfield	1967	6.25	12.50	25.00
—With "For What It's Worth" replacing "Baby Don't Scold Me"					
SD 33-200 [S]	Buffalo Springfield	1967	50.00	100.00	200.00
—With "Baby Don't Scold Me"					
SD 33-200A [S]	Buffalo Springfield	1967	6.25	12.50	25.00
—With "For What It's Worth" replacing "Baby Don't Scold Me"; purple and brown label					
SD 33-200A [S]	Buffalo Springfield	1969	3.75	7.50	15.00
—Reissue on yellow label					
SD 33-200A [S]	Buffalo Springfield	197?	2.00	4.00	8.00
—Later white or gray label					
33-226 [M]	Buffalo Springfield Again	1967	20.00	40.00	80.00
SD 33-226 [S]	Buffalo Springfield Again	1967	6.25	12.50	25.00
—Purple and brown label					
SD 33-226 [S]	Buffalo Springfield Again	1969	3.75	7.50	15.00
—Reissue on yellow label					
SD 33-226 [S]	Buffalo Springfield Again	197?	2.00	4.00	8.00
—Later white or gray label					

Number	Title (A Side/B Side)	Yr	VG	VG+	NM
33-256 [M]	Last Time Around	1968	30.00	60.00	120.00
—White label promo only					
SD 33-256 [S]	Last Time Around	1968	7.50	15.00	30.00
—Purple and brown label					
SD 33-256 [S]	Last Time Around	1969	3.75	7.50	15.00
—Reissue on yellow label					
SD 33-256 [S]	Last Time Around	197?	2.00	4.00	8.00
—Later white or gray label					
33-283 [M]	Retrospective/The Best of Buffalo Springfield	1969	25.00	50.00	100.00
—White label promo only					
SD 33-283 [S]	Retrospective/The Best of Buffalo Springfield	1969	5.00	10.00	20.00
—Yellow label					
SD 2-806 [(2)]	Buffalo Springfield	1973	5.00	10.00	20.00
—Yellow label					
SD 2-806 [(2)]	Buffalo Springfield	197?	3.00	6.00	12.00
—Later white or gray label					

BUFFETT, JIMMY

45s

Number	Title (A Side/B Side)	Yr	VG	VG+	NM
ABC					
11399	You Went to Paris/Peanut Butter Conspiracy	1973	—	—	—
—Unreleased? (Assigned by mistake?)					
12113	Door Number Three/Dallas	1975	—	2.50	5.00
12143	Big Red/Havana Daydreamin'	1975	—	2.50	5.00
12175	The Captain and the Kid/Cliches	1976	—	2.50	5.00
12200	Something So Feminine About a Mandolin/ Woman Goin' Crazy on Caroline Street	1976	—	2.50	5.00
12254	Margaritaville/Miss You So Badly	1977	—	2.00	4.00
12305	Changes in Latitudes, Changes in Attitudes/ Landfall	1977	—	2.00	4.00
12305 [PS]	Changes in Latitudes, Changes in Attitudes/ Landfall	1977	—	3.00	6.00
12358	Cheeseburger in Paradise/African Friend	1978	—	2.00	4.00
12391	Livingston Saturday Night/Cowboy in the Jungle	1978	—	2.00	4.00
12428	Manana/The Coast of Marsailles	1978	—	2.00	4.00
ABC DUNHILL					
4348	The Great Filling Station Hold Up/Why Don't We Get Drunk	1973	2.00	4.00	8.00
4353	The Great Filling Station Hold Up/They Can't Dance Like Carmen No More	1973	—	2.00	4.00
4359	Grapefruit-Juicy Fruit/I Found Me a Home	1973	—	2.00	4.00
4372	You Went to Paris/Peanut Butter Conspiracy	1973	—	2.00	4.00
4378	Ringling: Ringling/Saxophones	1974	—	2.00	4.00
4385	Come Monday/The Wino and I Know	1974	—	2.50	5.00
15008	Come Monday/The Wino and I Know	1974	—	2.00	4.00
15011	Brand New Country Star/Pencil Thin Moustache	1974	—	2.00	4.00
15029	Presents to Send You/A Pirate Looks at Forty	1975	—	2.00	4.00
ASYLUM					
69890	I Don't Know (Spicoli's Theme)/She's My Baby (And She's Out of Control)	1982	—	2.00	4.00
—B-side by Palmer & Jost					
BARNABY					
2013	The Christian/Richard Frost	1970	2.50	5.00	10.00
2019	He Ain't Free/There Ain't Nothing Soft About Hard Times	1970	2.50	5.00	10.00
2023	Captain America/Truckstop Salvation	1970	2.50	5.00	10.00
FULL MOON					
49659	Survive/Send Me Somebody to Love	1981	—	2.00	4.00
—B-side by Kathy Walker					
FULL MOON/ASYLUM					
47073	Hello Texas/Lyin' Eyes [by the Eagles]	1980	—	2.50	5.00
ISLAND					
562144-7	Pacing the Cage/I Will Play for Gumbo	1999	—	—	3.00
MCA					
S45-17084 [DJ]	Christmas In The Caribbean (same on both sides)	1985	—	2.50	5.00
41109	Fins/Dreamsicle	1979	—	2.00	4.00
41161	Volcano/Stranded on a Sandbar	1979	—	2.00	4.00
41199	Boat Drinks/Survive	1980	—	2.00	4.00
51061	It's My Job/Little Miss Magic	1981	—	2.00	4.00
51105	Stars Fell on Alabama/Growing Older But Not Up	1981	—	2.00	4.00
52013	It's Midnight And I'm Not Famous Yet/When Salome Plays the Drum	1982	—	2.00	4.00
52050	If I Could Just Get It on Paper/Where's the Party	1982	—	2.00	4.00
52298	One Particular Harbour/Distantly in Love	1983	—	2.00	4.00
52333	Brown Eyed Girl/Twelve Volt Man	1984	—	2.00	4.00
52438	When the Wild Life Betrays Me/Ragtop Day	1984	—	2.00	4.00
52499	Come to the Moon/Bigger Than the Both of Us	1984	—	2.00	4.00
52550	Who's the Blond Stranger/She's Going Out of My Mind	1985	—	—	3.00
52607	Gypies in the Palace/Jolly Mon Sing	1985	—	—	3.00
52664	If the Phone Doesn't Ring, It's Me/Frank and Lola	1985	—	—	3.00
52752	Please Bypass This Heart/Beyond the End	1986	—	—	3.00
52849	I Love the Now/No Plane on Sunday	1986	—	—	3.00
52932	Creola/You'll Never Work in Dis Bidness Again	1986	—	—	3.00
53035	Take It Back/Floridays	1987	—	—	3.00
53360	Homemade Music/L'air de la Louisiane	1988	—	—	3.00
53396	Bring Back the Magic/That's What Living Is to Me	1988	—	—	3.00
53675	Take Another Road/Off to See the Lizard	1989	—	—	3.00
54680	Another Saturday Night/Souvenirs	1993	—	—	3.00

Albums

Number	Title (A Side/B Side)	Yr	VG	VG+	NM
ABC					
SPDJ-43 [DJ]	Special Jimmy Buffett Sampler	1978	5.00	10.00	20.00
D-914	Havana Daydreamin'	1976	3.00	6.00	12.00
AB-990	Changes in Latitudes, Changes in Attitudes	1977	3.00	6.00	12.00
AK-1008 [(2)]	You Had to Be There	1978	3.75	7.50	15.00
AA-1046	Son of a Son of a Sailor	1978	3.00	6.00	12.00
ABC DUNHILL					
DS-50132	Living and Dying in 3/4 Time	1973	3.75	7.50	15.00
DSX-50150	A White Sport Coat and a Pink Crustaceon	1974	3.75	7.50	15.00
DS-50183	A1A	1975	3.75	7.50	15.00
BARNABY					
BR-6014	High Cumberland Jubilee	1975	10.00	20.00	40.00
Z 30093	Down to Earth	1970	25.00	50.00	100.00
MCA					
5102	Volcano	1979	2.50	5.00	10.00
5169	Coconut Telegraph	1981	2.50	5.00	10.00
5285	Somewhere Over China	1982	2.50	5.00	10.00
5447	One Particular Harbour	1983	2.50	5.00	10.00
5512	Riddles in the Sand	1984	2.50	5.00	10.00
5600	Last Mango in Paris	1985	2.50	5.00	10.00
5633	Songs You Know By Heart — Jimmy Buffett's Greatest Hit(s)	1985	2.50	5.00	10.00
5730	Floridays	1986	2.50	5.00	10.00
2-6005 [(2)]	You Had to Be There	1981	2.50	5.00	10.00
6314	Off to See the Lizard	1989	2.50	5.00	10.00
37023	Havana Daydreamin'	1981	2.00	4.00	8.00
37024	Son of a Son of a Sailor	1981	2.00	4.00	8.00
37025	Living and Dying in 3/4 Time	1981	2.00	4.00	8.00
37026	A White Sport Coat and a Pink Crustaceon	1981	2.00	4.00	8.00
37027	A1A	1981	2.00	4.00	8.00
37150	Changes in Latitudes, Changes in Attitudes	1982	2.00	4.00	8.00
37156	Volcano	1982	2.00	4.00	8.00
37246	Somewhere Over China	1984	2.00	4.00	8.00
42093	Hot Water	1988	2.50	5.00	10.00

BUG COLLECTORS, THE

45s

Number	Title (A Side/B Side)	Yr	VG	VG+	NM
CATCH					
103	The Beatle Bug/Thief in the Night	1964	5.00	10.00	20.00

BUG MEN, THE

See THE STRING-A-LONGS.

BUGALOOS, THE

45s

Number	Title (A Side/B Side)	Yr	VG	VG+	NM
CAPITOL					
2946	Senses of Our World/For a Friend	1970	3.00	6.00	12.00

Albums

Number	Title (A Side/B Side)	Yr	VG	VG+	NM
CAPITOL					
SW-621	The Bugaloos	1970	7.50	15.00	30.00

BUGGS, THE

45s

Number	Title (A Side/B Side)	Yr	VG	VG+	NM
SOMA					
1413	The Buggs vs. The Beatles/She Loves You	1964	6.25	12.50	25.00

Albums

Number	Title (A Side/B Side)	Yr	VG	VG+	NM
CORONET					
CX-212 [M]	The Beatle Beat	1964	5.00	10.00	20.00
CXS-212 [R]	The Beatle Beat	1964	3.00	6.00	12.00

BULLDOG

With Gene Cornish and Dino Danelli, ex-members of THE RASCALS.

45s

Number	Title (A Side/B Side)	Yr	VG	VG+	NM
BUDDAH					
414	Bad Bad Girl/I Tried to Sleep	1974	—	2.00	4.00
DECCA					
32996	Good Times Are Comin'/No	1972	—	2.00	4.00
GUYDEN					
5001	Man of Constant Sorrow/Inner Spring	1971	—	2.50	5.00
MCA					
40014	I'm a Madman/Are You Really Happy Together	1973	—	2.00	4.00
40050	I Tip My Hat/I'm a Madman	1973	—	2.00	4.00

Albums

Number	Title (A Side/B Side)	Yr	VG	VG+	NM
BUDDAH					
BDS-5600	Smasher	1974	3.75	7.50	15.00
DECCA					
DL 75370	Bulldog	1972	5.00	10.00	20.00

BULLDOGS, THE

45s

Number	Title (A Side/B Side)	Yr	VG	VG+	NM
MERCURY					
72262	John, Paul, George and Ringo/What Do I See	1964	5.00	10.00	20.00

BUNCH, THE

Albums

Number	Title (A Side/B Side)	Yr	VG	VG+	NM
A&M					
SP-4354	The Bunch	1973	6.25	12.50	25.00

BUNKERS, THE

45s

Number	Title (A Side/B Side)	Yr	VG	VG+	NM
RCA VICTOR					
74-0962	They Can't Take That Away from Me/Oh Babe, What Would You Say	1973	—	3.00	6.00
74-0962 [PS]	They Can't Take That Away from Me/Oh Babe, What Would You Say	1973	2.50	5.00	10.00

Albums

Number	Title (A Side/B Side)	Yr	VG	VG+	NM
RCA VICTOR					
APL1-0102	Archie and Edith Side by Side	1973	5.00	10.00	20.00

BUONO, VICTOR

45s

Number	Title (A Side/B Side)	Yr	VG	VG+	NM
DORE					
864	Fat Man's Prayer/Bless Me Doctor	1971	—	3.00	6.00

Albums

Number	Title (A Side/B Side)	Yr	VG	VG+	NM
DORE					
325	Heavy!	1971	3.75	7.50	15.00

BUOYS, THE

45s

Number	Title (A Side/B Side)	Yr	VG	VG+	NM
POLYDOR					
14201	Liza's Last Ride/Downtown Singer	1973	—	3.00	6.00

Number	Title (A Side/B Side)	Yr	VG	VG+	NM
SCEPTER					
12254	These Days/Don't You Know It's Over	1969	2.00	4.00	8.00
12275	Timothy/It Feels Good	1970	2.50	5.00	10.00
12275 [PS]	Timothy/It Feels Good	1970	5.00	10.00	20.00
12318	Give Up Your Guns/Prince of Thieves	1971	2.00	4.00	8.00
12331	Tell Me Heaven Is Here/Bloodknot	1971	2.00	4.00	8.00
Albums					
SCEPTER					
SPS-593	Timothy	1971	6.25	12.50	25.00

BURDEN, RAY

Number	Title (A Side/B Side)	Yr	VG	VG+	NM
45s					
CULLMAN					
6407	Christmas Is Here At Last/Santa, Bring Me A Gal	1958	12.50	25.00	50.00

BURDETTE, LEW

Number	Title (A Side/B Side)	Yr	VG	VG+	NM
45s					
DOT					
15672	Three Strikes and You're Out/Mary Lou	1957	6.25	12.50	25.00

BURDON, ERIC

Also see THE ANIMALS; ERIC BURDON AND WAR.

Number	Title (A Side/B Side)	Yr	VG	VG+	NM
45s					
CAPITOL					
3997	The Real Me/Letter from the County Farm	1974	—	2.50	5.00
4007	Ring of Fire/The Real Me	1974	—	2.50	5.00
MGM					
14296	Headin' for Home/Soledad	1971	—	2.50	5.00
—With Jimmy Witherspoon					
UNITED ARTISTS					
50842	Headin' for Home/Soledad	1971	—	—	—
—With Jimmy Witherspoon; assigned to MGM					
Albums					
CAPITOL					
ST-11359	Sun Secrets	1974	3.00	6.00	12.00
ST-11426	Stop	1975	3.00	6.00	12.00
—Regular square cover					
S?A?11426	Stop	1975	5.00	10.00	20.00
—Cover shaped like a hexagon					
GNP CRESCENDO					
GNPS-2194	Wicked Man	1988	2.50	5.00	10.00
LAX					
PW 37110	Sun Secrets	1981	2.50	5.00	10.00
—Reissue of Capitol 11359					
STRIPED HORSE					
SHL 2006	I Used to Be an Animal	1988	2.50	5.00	10.00

BURDON, ERIC, AND THE ANIMALS

See THE ANIMALS.

BURDON, ERIC, AND WAR

Also see ERIC BURDON; WAR.

Number	Title (A Side/B Side)	Yr	VG	VG+	NM
45s					
ABC					
12244	Magic Mountain/Home Dream	1977	—	2.50	5.00
MGM					
14118	Spill the Wine/Magic Mountain	1970	—	3.00	6.00
14118 [PS]	Spill the Wine/Magic Mountain	1970	3.00	6.00	12.00
14196	They Can't Take Away Our Music/Home Cookin'	1970	—	2.50	5.00
Albums					
ABC					
D-988	Love Is All Around	1976	3.00	6.00	12.00
—As "War Featuring Eric Burdon"					
LAX					
PW 37109	Spill the Wine	1981	2.50	5.00	10.00
—Reissue of MGM 4663 with new title					
MGM					
SE-4663	Eric Burdon Declares "War"	1970	3.75	7.50	15.00
SE-4710	The Black Man's Burdon	1970	5.00	10.00	20.00

BURGESS, DAVE

Also see THE CHAMPS.

Number	Title (A Side/B Side)	Yr	VG	VG+	NM
45s					
CHALLENGE					
1001	Don't Cry. For You I Love/Fire in the Eyes	1957	6.25	12.50	25.00
—As "Dave Dupree"					
1002	Flame of Love/Well, It Isn't Fair	1957	6.25	12.50	25.00
—As "Dave Dupree"					
1005	A Job Well Done/Our Tomorrow	1957	6.25	12.50	25.00
—As "Dave Dupree"					
1008	I'm Available/Who's Gonna Cry	1957	6.25	12.50	25.00
1018	Take This Love/Maybelle	1958	5.00	10.00	20.00
—As "Dave Burgess and the Champs"					
59032	Lovey Dovey Baby/I Hang My Head and Cry	1958	5.00	10.00	20.00
59037	I Don't Want to Know/Lulu	1959	5.00	10.00	20.00
59045	Everlovin'/Just for Me	1959	5.00	10.00	20.00
59101	Without You/Are You Teasing Me	1961	5.00	10.00	20.00
OKEH					
7002	Don't Put a Dent in My Heart/Judalina	1953	6.25	12.50	25.00
7044	Gratefully Yours/Too Late for Tears	1954	6.25	12.50	25.00
TAMPA					
104	Down, Down/Don't Turn Your Back on Love	1955	6.25	12.50	25.00
105	I Love Paris/Five Foot Two, Eyes of Blue	1955	6.25	12.50	25.00

BURGESS, SONNY

Number	Title (A Side/B Side)	Yr	VG	VG+	NM
45s					
PHILLIPS INT'L.					
3551	Sadie's Back in Town/Kiss Goodnight	1960	7.50	15.00	30.00
SUN					
247	Red Headed Woman/We Wanna Boogie	1956	37.50	75.00	150.00
263	Ain't Got a Thing/Restless	1957	20.00	40.00	80.00
285	My Bucket's Got a Hole in It/Sweet Misery	1958	12.50	25.00	50.00
304	Thunderbird/Itchy	1958	7.50	15.00	30.00

BURKE, BUDDY

Number	Title (A Side/B Side)	Yr	VG	VG+	NM
45s					
BULLSEYE					
1002	That Big Old Moon/Street of Sorrows	195?	37.50	75.00	150.00

BURKE, SOLOMON

Number	Title (A Side/B Side)	Yr	VG	VG+	NM
45s					
ABC DUNHILL					
4388	Midnight and You/I Have a Dream	1974	—	2.50	5.00
15009	Midnight and You/I Have a Dream	1974	—	2.00	4.00
AMHERST					
736	Please Don't You Say Goodbye to Me/See That Girl	1978	—	2.00	4.00
APOLLO					
485	Christmas Presents/When I'm All Alone	1955	7.50	15.00	30.00
487	I'm in Love/Why Do Me That Way	1956	6.25	12.50	25.00
491	I'm All Alone/To Thee	1956	6.25	12.50	25.00
500	No Man Walks Alone/Walking in a Dream	1956	6.25	12.50	25.00
505	A Picture of You/You Can Run But You Can't Hide	1957	6.25	12.50	25.00
511	I Need You Tonight/This Is It	1957	6.25	12.50	25.00
512	For You and You Alone/You Are My One Love	1957	6.25	12.50	25.00
522	They Always Say/Don't Cry	1958	6.25	12.50	25.00
527	My Heart Is a Chapel/This Is It	1958	6.25	12.50	25.00
ATLANTIC					
2089	Keep the Magic Working/How Many Times	1961	5.00	10.00	20.00
2114	Just Out of Reach (Of My Two Open Arms)/Be-Bop Grandma	1961	5.00	10.00	20.00
2131	Cry to Me/I Almost Lost My Mind	1962	5.00	10.00	20.00
2147	Down in the Valley/I'm Hanging Up My Heart for You	1962	3.75	7.50	15.00
2157	I Really Don't Want to Know/Tonight My Heart She Is Crying (Love Is a Bird)	1962	3.75	7.50	15.00
2170	Go On Back to Him/I Said I Was Sorry	1962	3.75	7.50	15.00
2180	Words/Home in Your Heart	1963	3.75	7.50	15.00
2185	If You Need Me/You Can Make It If You Try	1963	3.75	7.50	15.00
2196	Can't Nobody Love You/Stupidity	1963	3.75	7.50	15.00
2205	You're Good for Me/Beautiful Brown Eyes	1963	3.75	7.50	15.00
2218	He'll Have to Go/Rockin' Soul	1964	3.75	7.50	15.00
2226	Goodbye Baby (Baby Goodbye)/Someone to Love Me	1964	3.75	7.50	15.00
2241	Everybody Needs Somebody to Love/Looking for My Baby	1964	3.75	7.50	15.00
2254	Yes I Do/Won't You Give Him (One More Chance)	1964	3.75	7.50	15.00
2259	The Price/More Rockin' Soul	1964	3.75	7.50	15.00
2276	Got to Get You Off My Mind/Peepin'	1965	3.75	7.50	15.00
2288	Tonight's the Night/Maggie's Farm	1965	3.75	7.50	15.00
2299	Someone Is Watching/Dance, Dance, Dance	1965	3.00	6.00	12.00
2308	Only Love (Can Save Me Now)/A Little Girl That Loves Me	1965	3.00	6.00	12.00
2314	Baby Come On Home/(No, No, No) Can't Stop Lovin' You Now	1965	3.00	6.00	12.00
2327	I Feel a Sin Coming On/Mountain of Pride	1966	2.50	5.00	10.00
2345	Lawdy Miss Clawdy/Suddenly	1966	2.50	5.00	10.00
2349	Keep Looking/Don't Want You No More	1966	2.50	5.00	10.00
2359	When She Touches Me/Woman How Do You Make Me Love You Like I Do	1966	2.50	5.00	10.00
2369	Presents for Christmas/A Tear Fell	1966	3.00	6.00	12.00
2378	Keep a Light in the Window Till I Come Home/Time Is a Thief	1967	2.50	5.00	10.00
2416	Take Me (Just As I Am)/Stayed Away Too Long	1967	2.50	5.00	10.00
2459	It's Been a Change/Detroit City	1967	2.50	5.00	10.00
2483	Party People/Need Your Love So Bad	1968	2.50	5.00	10.00
2507	I Wish I Knew (How It Would Feel to Be Free)/It's Just a Matter of Time Baby	1968	2.50	5.00	10.00
2527	Save it/Meet Me in Church	1968	2.50	5.00	10.00
2566	Get Out of My Life Woman/What'd I Say	1968	2.50	5.00	10.00
BELL					
759	Up Tight Good Woman/I Can't Stop	1969	2.00	4.00	8.00
783	Proud Mary/What Am I Living For	1969	2.00	4.00	8.00
806	That Lucky Old Sun/How Big a Fool	1969	2.00	4.00	8.00
829	I'm Gonna Stay Right Here/Generation of Revelations	1969	2.00	4.00	8.00
891	God Knows I Love You/In the Ghetto	1970	—	3.00	6.00
CHESS					
2159	You and Your Baby Blues/I'm Leaving on That Late, Late Train	1975	—	2.00	4.00
2172	Let Me Wrap My Arms Around You/Everlasting Love	1975	—	2.00	4.00
INFINITY					
50046	Sidewalks, Fences and Walls/Boo-Hoo-Hoo (Cra-Cra-Craya)	1979	—	2.50	5.00
MALA					
420	This Little Ring/I'm Not Afraid	1960	5.00	10.00	20.00
MCI					
712842	You're All I Want For Christmas/No Place Like Home	19??	2.00	4.00	8.00
—B-side by Rayne					
MGM					
14185	Lookin' Out My Back Door/All for the Love of Sunshine	1970	—	3.00	6.00
14221	The Electronic Magnetism (That's Heavy, Baby)/Bridge of Life	1971	—	3.00	6.00
14279	J.C. I Know Who You Are/The Things Love Will Make You Do	1971	—	3.00	6.00
14302	The Night They Drove Old Dixie Down/PSR 1983	1971	—	3.00	6.00
14353	Love's Street and Fool's Road/I Got to Tell It	1972	—	3.00	6.00
14402	We're Almost Home/Fight Back	1972	—	3.00	6.00
14425	Get Up and Do Something for Yourself/We're Almost Home	1972	—	3.00	6.00
14571	Shambala/Love Thy Neighbor	1973	—	3.00	6.00
14651	Georgia Up North/Here Comes the Train	1973	—	3.00	6.00

Number	Title (A Side/B Side)	Yr	VG	VG+	NM
POINTBLANK					
S7-19520	Ooooooyou/Today Is Your Birthday	1997	—	2.00	4.00
PRIDE					
1017	I Can't Stop Loving You (Part 1)/I Can't Stop Loving You (Part 2)	1972	—	3.00	6.00
1022	All I Want for Christmas/I Can't Stop Loving You (Part 1)	1972	—	3.00	6.00
1028	My Prayer/Ookie Bookie Man	1973	—	3.00	6.00
1038	Sentimental Journey/Vaya Con Dios	1973	—	3.00	6.00
—With Lady Lee					

Albums

Number	Title (A Side/B Side)	Yr	VG	VG+	NM
ABC DUNHILL					
DSX-50161	I Have a Dream	1974	3.00	6.00	12.00
AMHERST					
AMH-1018	Please Don't You Say Goodbye to Me	1978	3.00	6.00	12.00
APOLLO					
ALP-498 [M]	Solomon Burke	1962	125.00	250.00	500.00
ATLANTIC					
8067 [M]	Solomon Burke's Greatest Hits	1962	12.50	25.00	50.00
SD 8067 [S]	Solomon Burke's Greatest Hits	1962	20.00	40.00	80.00
8085 [M]	If You Need Me	1963	12.50	25.00	50.00
SD 8085 [S]	If You Need Me	1963	20.00	40.00	80.00
8096 [M]	Rock N' Soul	1964	12.50	25.00	50.00
SD 8096 [S]	Rock N' Soul	1964	20.00	40.00	80.00
8109 [M]	The Best of Solomon Burke	1965	7.50	15.00	30.00
SD 8109 [S]	The Best of Solomon Burke	1965	10.00	20.00	40.00
SD 8158	King Solomon	1968	6.25	12.50	25.00
SD 8185	I Wish I Knew	1968	6.25	12.50	25.00
BELL					
6033	Proud Mary	1969	5.00	10.00	20.00
CHESS					
CH-19002	Back to My Roots	1976	3.00	6.00	12.00
CH-60042	Music to Make Love By	1975	3.00	6.00	12.00
CLARION					
607 [M]	I Almost Lost My Mind	1966	5.00	10.00	20.00
SD 607 [S]	I Almost Lost My Mind	1966	6.25	12.50	25.00
INFINITY					
INF-9024	Sidewalks, Fences and Walls	1979	3.00	6.00	12.00
KENWOOD					
LP-498 [M]	Solomon Burke	1964	50.00	100.00	200.00
—Reissue of Apollo 498					
MGM					
SE-4767	Electronic Magnetism	1971	3.75	7.50	15.00
SE-4830	King Heavy	1972	3.75	7.50	15.00
PRIDE					
0011	The History of Solomon Burke	1972	3.75	7.50	15.00
ROUNDER					
2042/3 [(2)]	Soul Alive!	1984	3.00	6.00	12.00
2053	A Change Is Gonna Come	1986	2.50	5.00	10.00
SAVOY					
14660	Solomon Burke	1981	2.50	5.00	10.00
14679	Into My Life	1982	2.50	5.00	10.00
14717	Take Me, Shake Me	1983	2.50	5.00	10.00

BURKE, SONNY

45s

Number	Title (A Side/B Side)	Yr	VG	VG+	NM
DECCA					
30815	Bye Bye Blues/Theme from "Auntie Mame"	1959	—	—	—
REPRISE					
0318	Theme from "Of Human Bondage"/Theme from "Peyton Place"	1964	—	—	—

BURLAND, SASCHA & THE SKIPJACK CHOIR

45s

Number	Title (A Side/B Side)	Yr	VG	VG+	NM
COLUMBIA					
42009	Gorilla Walk/Hole in My Soul	1960	5.00	10.00	20.00
RCA VICTOR					
47-8277	Have Yourself a Merry Little Christmas/The Chickens Are in the Chimes	1963	7.50	15.00	30.00
47-8277 [PS]	Have Yourself a Merry Little Christmas/The Chickens Are in the Chimes	1963	10.00	20.00	40.00

BURNETT, FRANCES

45s

Number	Title (A Side/B Side)	Yr	VG	VG+	NM
CORAL					
62092	Come to Me/So Many Tears	1959	25.00	50.00	100.00
62127	Please Remember Me/How I Miss You So	1959	25.00	50.00	100.00
62164	I Love Him So/Too Proud	1960	25.00	50.00	100.00
62214	She Was Taking My Baby/Sweetie	1960	25.00	50.00	100.00
DECCA					
30571	Spin the Wheel/A Promise Made a Fool of Me	1958	30.00	60.00	120.00

BURNETTE, BILLY

Also see FLEETWOOD MAC. Not to be confused with Billy Joe Burnette.

45s

Number	Title (A Side/B Side)	Yr	VG	VG+	NM
A&M					
743	Just Because We're Kids/Little Girl, Big Love	1964	6.25	12.50	25.00
—As "Young Billy Bean"; A-side written by Dr. Seuss!					
1794	Baby/Just Another Love Song	1976	—	2.50	5.00
CAPRICORN					
18525	I Still Remember (How to Miss You)/I Recovered, I Survived	1993	—	—	3.00
18751	Tangled Up in Texas/Into the Storm	1992	—	—	3.00
COLUMBIA					
02527	Let the New Love Begin/I Don't Know Why	1981	—	2.00	4.00
02699	The Bigger the Love/I Don't Know Why	1982	—	2.00	4.00
11380	Don't Say No/Rockin' L.A.	1980	—	2.00	4.00
11432	Oh Susan/Sittin' On Ready	1981	—	2.00	4.00
ENTRANCE					
7515	Broken Hearted/I'm Always Wondering	1972	—	2.50	5.00
MCA CURB					
52626	Ain't It Just Like Love/Guitar Bug	1985	—	—	3.00
52710	Who's Using Your Heart Tonight/It Ain't Over	1985	—	—	3.00
52749	It's Not Easy/Try Me	1985	—	—	3.00
52852	Soldier of Love/Guitar Bug	1986	—	—	3.00
POLYDOR					
2024	What's a Little Love Between Friends/Precious Times	1979	—	2.00	4.00
14530	Dreamin' My Way Back to You/Shoo-Be-Doo	1979	—	2.00	4.00
14549	Believe What You Say/Mississippi Line	1979	—	2.00	4.00
WARNER BROS.					
7327	Frog Prince/One Extreme to the Other	1969	2.00	4.00	8.00
19042	Nothin' to Do (And All Night to Do It)/Can't Get Over You	1992	—	—	3.00

Albums

Number	Title (A Side/B Side)	Yr	VG	VG+	NM
COLUMBIA					
JC 36792	Billy Burnette	1980	2.50	5.00	10.00
FC 37460	Gimme You	1981	2.50	5.00	10.00
ENTRANCE					
Z 31228	Billy Burnette	1972	5.00	10.00	20.00
MCA CURB					
5604	Try Me	1985	2.50	5.00	10.00
POLYDOR					
PD-1-6187	Billy Burnette	1979	2.50	5.00	10.00

BURNETTE, DORSEY

Also see DORSEY AND JOHNNY BURNETTE.

45s

Number	Title (A Side/B Side)	Yr	VG	VG+	NM
ABBOTT					
188	Let's Fall in Love/The Devil's Queen	1956	12.50	25.00	50.00
190	At a Distance/Jungle Magic	1957	12.50	25.00	50.00
CALLIOPE					
8004	Things I Treasure/One Mornin'	1977	—	3.00	6.00
8012	Soon As I Touched Her/Dear Hearted Children	1977	—	3.00	6.00
CAPITOL					
3073	New Orleans Woman/After the Long Drive Home	1971	—	2.50	5.00
3190	Shelby County Penal Farm/Children of the Universe	1971	—	2.50	5.00
3307	In the Spring (The Roses Always Turn Red)/The Same Old You, The Same Old Me	1972	—	2.50	5.00
3404	I Just Couldn't Let Her Walk Away/Church Bells	1972	—	2.50	5.00
3463	Cry Mama/Lonely to Be Alone	1972	—	2.50	5.00
3529	I Let Another Good One Get Away/Take Your Weapons, Lay 'Em Down	1973	—	2.50	5.00
3588	Keep Out of My Dreams/Mama, Mama	1973	—	2.50	5.00
3678	Darlin' (Don't Come Back)/Sweet Lovin' Woman	1973	—	2.50	5.00
3796	It Happens Every Time/Mr. Jukebox, Sing a Lullaby	1973	—	2.50	5.00
3829	Bob, All the Playboys, and Me/The Bootleggers	1974	—	2.50	5.00
3887	Daddy Loves You Honey/True Love Means Forgiving	1974	—	2.50	5.00
3963	What Ladies Can Do (When They Want To)/ Tangerine	1974	—	2.50	5.00
CEE-JAM					
16	Bertha Lou/'Til the Law Says Stop	1957	20.00	40.00	80.00
DOT					
16230	Rainin' in My Heart/A Full House	1961	4.00	8.00	16.00
16265	The Feminine Touch/Sad Boy	1961	4.00	8.00	16.00
16305	A Country Boy in the Army/A Dying Ember	1961	4.00	8.00	16.00
ELEKTRA					
46513	Here I Go Again/What Would It Profit Me	1979	—	2.00	4.00
46586	B.J. Kick-a-Beaux/What Would It Profit Me	1980	—	2.00	4.00
ERA					
3012	(There Was a)Tall Oak Tree/Juarez Town	1960	5.00	10.00	20.00
3019	Hey Little One/Big Rock Candy Mountain	1960	4.00	8.00	16.00
3025	The Ghost of Billy Malloo/Red Roses	1960	4.00	8.00	16.00
3033	The River and the Mountain/This Hotel	1960	4.00	8.00	16.00
3033 [PS]	The River and the Mountain/This Hotel	1960	10.00	20.00	40.00
3041	Hard Rock Mine/(It's No) Sin	1961	4.00	8.00	16.00
3045	Great Shakin' Fever/That's Me Without You	1961	4.00	8.00	16.00
HAPPY TIGER					
546	To Be a Man/Fly Away and Hurry Home	1970	—	3.00	6.00
563	One Lump Sum/Call Me Lowdown	1970	—	3.00	6.00
HICKORY					
1458	The House That Jack Built/Ain't That Fine	1967	2.00	4.00	8.00
IMPERIAL					
5561	Try/You Came as a Miracle	1959	6.25	12.50	25.00
5597	Lonely Train/Misery	1959	6.25	12.50	25.00
5668	Way in the Middle of the Night/Your Love	1960	6.25	12.50	25.00
5756	House with a Tin Roof Top/Circle Rock	1961	6.25	12.50	25.00
5987	House with a Tin Roof Top/Circle Rock	1963	3.75	7.50	15.00
LIBERTY					
56087	The Greatest Love/Thin Little Simple Little Plain Little Girl	1969	—	3.00	6.00
MEL-O-DY					
113	Little Acorn/Cold As Usual	1964	3.75	7.50	15.00
116	Jimmy Brown/Everybody's Angel	1964	3.75	7.50	15.00
118	Long Long Time Ago/Ever Since the World Began	1964	3.75	7.50	15.00
MELODYLAND					
6007	Molly (I Ain't Gettin' Any Younger)/She's Feeling Low	1975	—	2.50	5.00
6019	Lyin' in Her Arms Again/Doggone the Dogs	1975	—	2.50	5.00
6031	Ain't No Heartbreak/I Dreamed I Saw	1976	—	2.50	5.00
MERCURY					
72546	To Remember/In the Morning	1966	—	—	—
—Unreleased?					
MUSIC FACTORY					
417	I'll Walk Away/Son, You've Got to Make It Alone	1968	2.00	4.00	8.00
REPRISE					
0246	Four for Texas/Foolish Pride	1963	3.75	7.50	15.00
0246 [PS]	Four for Texas/Foolish Pride	1963	10.00	20.00	40.00
20093	Castle in the Sky/Boys Keep Hanging Around	1962	3.75	7.50	15.00

Number	Title (A Side/B Side)	Yr	VG	VG+	NM
20121	Darling Jane/I'm a Waitin' For Ya Baby	1962	3.75	7.50	15.00
20177	Invisible Chains/Pebbles	1963	3.75	7.50	15.00
20208	One of the Lonely/Where's the Girl	1963	3.75	7.50	15.00
SMASH					
2029	To Remember/In the Morning	1966	2.50	5.00	10.00
2039	If You Want to Love Somebody/Teach Me Little Children	1966	2.50	5.00	10.00
2062	Tall Oak Tree/I Just Can't Be Tamed	1966	2.50	5.00	10.00
U.S. NAVY					
(# unknown)	Be a Navy Man	196?	10.00	20.00	40.00
(# unknown) [PS]	Be a Navy Man	196?	5.00	10.00	20.00
Albums					
CALLIOPE					
CAL 7006	Things I Treasure	1977	3.00	6.00	12.00
CAPITOL					
ST-11094	Here and Now	1972	3.75	7.50	15.00
ST-11219	Dorsey Burnette	1973	3.75	7.50	15.00
DOT					
DLP-3456 [M]	Dorsey Burnette Sings	1963	10.00	20.00	40.00
DLP-25456 [S]	Dorsey Burnette Sings	1963	12.50	25.00	50.00
ERA					
EL-102 [M]	Tall Oak Tree	1960	37.50	75.00	150.00
ES-102 [S]	Tall Oak Tree	1960	75.00	150.00	300.00
ES-800 [M]	Dorsey Burnette's Greatest Hits	1969	6.25	12.50	25.00
GUSTO					
0050	The Golden Hits of Dorsey Burnette	197?	3.00	6.00	12.00

BURNETTE, DORSEY AND JOHNNY

Also see each artist's individual listings.

Number	Title (A Side/B Side)	Yr	VG	VG+	NM
45s					
CORAL					
62190	Blues Stay Away from Me/Midnight Train	1960	50.00	100.00	200.00
—As "Johnny and Dorsey Burnette"					
IMPERIAL					
5509	Warm Love/My Honey	1958	25.00	50.00	100.00
—As "Burnette Brothers"					
REPRISE					
20153	It Don't Take Much/Hey Sue	1963	5.00	10.00	20.00
Albums					
SOLID SMOKE					
SS-8005	Together Again	1978	3.75	7.50	15.00

BURNETTE, JOHNNY

Includes the Rock 'N' Roll Trio. Also see DORSEY AND JOHNNY BURNETTE.

Number	Title (A Side/B Side)	Yr	VG	VG+	NM
45s					
CAPITOL					
5023	All Week Long/It Isn't There	1963	3.75	7.50	15.00
5114	You Taught Me the Way to Love You/The Opposite	1964	3.75	7.50	15.00
5176	Walkin' Talkin' Doll/Sweet Suzie	1964	3.75	7.50	15.00
CHANCELLOR					
1116	I Wanna Thank Your Folks/The Giant	1962	3.75	7.50	15.00
1123	Party Girl/Tag Along	1962	3.75	7.50	15.00
1129	Remember Me/Time Is Not Enough	1962	3.75	7.50	15.00
CORAL					
61651	Tear It Up/You're Undecided	1956	75.00	150.00	300.00
61675	Midnight Train/Oh Baby Babe	1956	75.00	150.00	300.00
61719	The Train Kept a-Rollin'/Honey Hush	1956	62.50	125.00	250.00
61758	Lonesome Train/I Just Found Out	1956	75.00	150.00	300.00
61829	Eager Beaver Baby/Touch Me	1957	75.00	150.00	300.00
61869	Drinkin' Wine Spo-Dee-O-Dee/Butterfingers	1957	75.00	150.00	300.00
61918	Rock Billy Boogie/If You Want It Enough	1957	75.00	150.00	300.00
FREEDOM					
44001	I'm Restless/Kiss Me	1958	20.00	40.00	80.00
44011	Gumbo/Me and the Bear	1959	20.00	40.00	80.00
44017	Sweet Baby Doll/I'll Never Love Again	1959	20.00	40.00	80.00
LIBERTY					
55222	Settin' the Woods on Fire/Kentucky Waltz	1959	5.00	10.00	20.00
55243	Don't Do It/Patrick Henry	1959	5.00	10.00	20.00
55258	Dreamin'/Cincinnati Fireball	1960	5.00	10.00	20.00
55285	You're Sixteen/I Beg Your Pardon	1960	5.00	10.00	20.00
55285 [PS]	You're Sixteen/I Beg Your Pardon	1960	12.50	25.00	50.00
55298	Little Boy Sad/(I Go) Down to the River	1961	3.75	7.50	15.00
55298 [PS]	Little Boy Sad/(I Go) Down to the River	1961	10.00	20.00	40.00
55318	Big Big World/Ballad of the One Eyed Jacks	1961	3.75	7.50	15.00
55318 [PS]	Big Big World/Ballad of the One Eyed Jacks	1961	10.00	20.00	40.00
55345	Girls/I've Got a Lot of Things to Do	1961	3.75	7.50	15.00
55377	Honestly I Do/Fools Like Me	1961	3.75	7.50	15.00
55379	God, Country and My Baby/Honestly I Do	1961	3.75	7.50	15.00
55416	Clown Shoes/The Way I Am	1962	3.75	7.50	15.00
55448	The Fool of the Year/The Poorest Boy in Town	1962	3.75	7.50	15.00
55489	Damn the Defiant/Lonesome Waters	1962	3.75	7.50	15.00
MAGIC LAMP					
515	Bigger Man/Less Than a Heartache	1964	12.50	25.00	50.00
515 [PS]	Bigger Man/Less Than a Heartache	1964	75.00	150.00	300.00
SAHARA					
512	Fountain of Love/What a Summer Day	1964	3.75	7.50	15.00
UNITED ARTISTS					
0018	Dreamin'/Little Boy Sad	1973	—	2.00	4.00
—Silver Spotlight Series issue					
0019	You're Sixteen/God, Country and My Baby	1973	—	2.00	4.00
—Silver Spotlight Series issue					
VON					
1006	You're Undecided/Go, Mule, Go	1954	1500.	2250.	3000.
7-Inch Extended Plays					
LIBERTY					
LSX-1004	(contents unknown)	1960	25.00	50.00	100.00
LSX-1004 [PS]	Dreamin'	1960	37.50	75.00	150.00
LSX-1011	Little Boy Sad/Don't Do It//You're Sixteen/I Go Down to the River	1961	25.00	50.00	100.00
LSX-1011 [PS]	Johnny Burnette's Hits	1961	37.50	75.00	150.00
Albums					
CORAL					
CRL 57080 [M]	Johnny Burnette & the Rock 'N' Roll Trio	1956	2000.	4000.	6000.
—Originals have maroon labels, printing on jacket's spine and "Made in U.S.A." in lower right of back cover					
LIBERTY					
LRP-3179 [M]	Dreamin'	1960	10.00	20.00	40.00
LRP-3183 [M]	Johnny Burnette	1961	10.00	20.00	40.00
LRP-3190 [M]	Johnny Burnette Sings	1961	10.00	20.00	40.00
LRP-3206 [M]	Johnny Burnette's Hits and Other Favorites	1962	10.00	20.00	40.00
LRP-3255 [M]	Roses Are Red	1962	10.00	20.00	40.00
LRP-3389 [M]	The Johnny Burnette Story	1964	10.00	20.00	40.00
LST-7179 [S]	Dreamin'	1960	15.00	30.00	60.00
LST-7183 [S]	Johnny Burnette	1961	15.00	30.00	60.00
LST-7190 [S]	Johnny Burnette Sings	1961	15.00	30.00	60.00
LST-7206 [S]	Johnny Burnette's Hits and Other Favorites	1962	12.50	25.00	50.00
LST-7255 [S]	Roses Are Red	1962	12.50	25.00	50.00
LST-7389 [S]	The Johnny Burnette Story	1964	12.50	25.00	50.00
MCA					
1513	Listen to Johnny Burnette and the Rock 'N' Roll Trio	1982	2.50	5.00	10.00
SOLID SMOKE					
SS-8001	Tear It Up	1978	7.50	15.00	30.00
—Blue vinyl					
SS-8001	Tear It Up	1978	3.75	7.50	15.00
—Black viinyl					
SUNSET					
SUM-1179 [M]	Dreamin'	1967	3.75	7.50	15.00
SUS-5179 [S]	Dreamin'	1967	5.00	10.00	20.00
UNITED ARTISTS					
UA-LA432-G	The Very Best of Johnny Burnette	1975	2.50	5.00	10.00

BURNETTE BROTHERS

See DORSEY AND JOHNNY BURNETTE.

BURNING BUSH, THE

Number	Title (A Side/B Side)	Yr	VG	VG+	NM
45s					
MERCURY					
72657	Keep On Burning/Evil Eye	1967	5.00	10.00	20.00

BURNS, EDDIE

Number	Title (A Side/B Side)	Yr	VG	VG+	NM
45s					
CHECKER					
790	Biscuit Baking Mama/Superstition	1954	75.00	150.00	300.00
—As "Big Ed and His Combo"					
CHESS					
1672	Treat Me Like I Treat You/Don't Cha Leave Me Baby	1957	10.00	20.00	40.00
DELUXE					
6024	Hello Miss Jessie Lee/Dealing with the Devil	1953	50.00	100.00	200.00
HARVEY					
111	Orange Driver/Hard Hearted Woman	1962	25.00	50.00	100.00
115	The Thing to Do/Mean and Evil (Baby)	1962	7.50	15.00	30.00
118	Orange Driver/Messin' with My Bread	1962	7.50	15.00	30.00
JVB					
82	Treat Me Like I Treat You/Don't Cha Leave Me Baby	1957	25.00	50.00	100.00

BURNS, RANDY

Number	Title (A Side/B Side)	Yr	VG	VG+	NM
45s					
MERCURY					
73198	Living in the Country/17 Years on the River	1971	—	3.00	6.00
POLYDOR					
14143	Hold On/Country Rain	1972	—	3.00	6.00
Albums					
ESP-DISK'					
1039	Songs of Love and War	1966	6.25	12.50	25.00
1089	Evening of the Magician	1968	6.25	12.50	25.00
2007	Song for an Uncertain Lady	1971	3.75	7.50	15.00
MERCURY					
SR-61329	Randy Burns and the Skydog Band	1971	3.00	6.00	12.00
POLYDOR					
PD-5030	I'm a Lover, Not a Fool	1972	3.00	6.00	12.00
PD-5049	Still On Our Feet	1973	3.00	6.00	12.00

BURNT SUITE

Number	Title (A Side/B Side)	Yr	VG	VG+	NM
Albums					
B.J.W.					
9	Burnt Suite	1967	50.00	100.00	200.00

BURRAGE, HAROLD

Number	Title (A Side/B Side)	Yr	VG	VG+	NM
45s					
ALADDIN					
3194	Sweet Brown Gal/Way Down Boogie	1953	15.00	30.00	60.00
COBRA					
5004	One More Dance/You Eat Too Much	1956	12.50	25.00	50.00
5012	Messed Up/I Don't Care Who Knows	1957	12.50	25.00	50.00
5018	Satisfied/Stop for the Red Light	1957	12.50	25.00	50.00
5022	She Knocks Me Out/A Heart	1958	12.50	25.00	50.00
5026	Betty Jean/I Cry for You	1958	12.50	25.00	50.00
DECCA					
48175	Hi Ya/I Need You Baby	1950	25.00	50.00	100.00
M-PAC!					
7201	The Master Key/Faith and Understanding	1963	2.50	5.00	10.00
7204	Long Ways Together/I'll Take One	1963	2.50	5.00	10.00
7210	That's a Friend/Everybody's Dancing	1964	2.50	5.00	10.00
7211	Baby I'm Alright/Fifty-Fifty	1964	2.50	5.00	10.00
7222	Your Friend/Take Me Now	1965	2.50	5.00	10.00
7225	Got to Find a Way/How You Fix Your Mouth	1965	3.00	6.00	12.00
7229	More Power to You/A Long Way Together	1966	2.50	5.00	10.00
7234	Take Me Now/You Make Me So Happy	1966	2.50	5.00	10.00

Number	Title (A Side/B Side)	Yr	VG	VG+	NM
STATES					
144	Feel So Fine/You're Gonna Cry	1955	62.50	125.00	250.00
—Red vinyl					
144	Feel So Fine/You're Gonna Cry	1955	30.00	60.00	120.00
—Black vinyl					
VEE JAY					
318	What You Don't Know/Crying for My Baby	1959	6.25	12.50	25.00
VIVID					
102	Betty Jean/I Cry for You	1959	10.00	20.00	40.00

BURRELL, KENNY

45s

Number	Title (A Side/B Side)	Yr	VG	VG+	NM
BLUE NOTE					
1653	Delilah/The Dream's On Me	195?	2.50	5.00	10.00
1716	Yes Baby (Part 1)/Yes Baby (Part 2)	195?	2.50	5.00	10.00
1717	Rock Salt (Part 1)/Rock Salt (Part 2)	195?	2.50	5.00	10.00
1884	Good Life/Loie	196?	2.50	5.00	10.00
1885	Chittlins Con Carne (Part 1)/Chittlins Con Carne (Part 2)	196?	2.50	5.00	10.00
1886	Wavy Gravy (Part 1)/Wavy Gravy (Part 2)	196?	2.50	5.00	10.00
CADET					
5548	Hot Bossa/Mother-in-Law	1966	—	3.00	6.00
5555	The Little Drummer Boy/Silent Night	1966	2.00	4.00	8.00
5597	Blues Fuse/Recapitulation	1968	—	3.00	6.00
PRESTIGE					
110	Don't Cry Baby (Part 1)/Don't Cry Baby (Part 2)	195?	2.50	5.00	10.00
238	Montuno Blues/Out of This World	196?	2.00	4.00	8.00
260	I Thought About You/It's Gettin' Dark	196?	2.00	4.00	8.00
281	Freight Trane (Part 1)/Freight Trane (Part 2)	1963	2.00	4.00	8.00
VERVE					
10375	Downstairs/Loie	1966	2.00	4.00	8.00

Albums

Number	Title (A Side/B Side)	Yr	VG	VG+	NM
ARGO					
LP-655 [M]	A Night at the Vanguard	1959	7.50	15.00	30.00
LPS-655 [S]	A Night at the Vanguard	1959	10.00	20.00	40.00
BLUE NOTE					
BLP-1523 [M]	Introducing Kenny Burrell	1956	50.00	100.00	200.00
—"Deep groove" version (deep indentation under label on both sides)					
BLP-1523 [M]	Introducing Kenny Burrell	1956	37.50	75.00	150.00
—Regular version, Lexington Ave. address on label					
BLP-1523 [M]	Introducing Kenny Burrell	1957	12.50	25.00	50.00
—W. 63rd St., NYC address on label					
BLP-1523 [M]	Introducing Kenny Burrell	1963	6.25	12.50	25.00
—New York, USA address on label					
BLP-1543 [M]	Kenny Burrell, Volume 2	1957	50.00	100.00	200.00
—"Deep groove" version (deep indentation under label on both sides)					
BLP-1543 [M]	Kenny Burrell, Volume 2	1957	37.50	75.00	150.00
—Regular version, Lexington Ave. address on label					
BLP-1543 [M]	Kenny Burrell, Volume 2	1957	12.50	25.00	50.00
—W. 63rd St., NYC address on label					
BLP-1543 [M]	Kenny Burrell, Volume 2	1963	6.25	12.50	25.00
—New York, USA address on label					
BLP-1596 [M]	Blue Lights, Volume 1	1958	25.00	50.00	100.00
—"Deep groove" version (deep indentation under label on both sides)					
BLP-1596 [M]	Blue Lights, Volume 1	1958	17.50	35.00	70.00
—Regular version, W. 63rd St., NYC address on label					
BLP-1596 [M]	Blue Lights, Volume 1	1963	6.25	12.50	25.00
—New York, USA address on label					
BST-1596 [S]	Blue Lights, Volume 1	1959	25.00	50.00	100.00
—"Deep groove" version (deep indentation under label on both sides)					
BST-1596 [S]	Blue Lights, Volume 1	1959	17.50	35.00	70.00
—Regular version, W. 63rd St., NYC address on label					
BST-1596 [S]	Blue Lights, Volume 1	1963	6.25	12.50	25.00
—New York, USA address on label					
BLP-1597 [M]	Blue Lights, Volume 2	1958	25.00	50.00	100.00
—"Deep groove" version (deep indentation under label on both sides)					
BLP-1597 [M]	Blue Lights, Volume 2	1958	17.50	35.00	70.00
—Regular version, W. 63rd St., NYC address on label					
BLP-1597 [M]	Blue Lights, Volume 2	1963	6.25	12.50	25.00
—New York, USA address on label					
BST-1597 [S]	Blue Lights, Volume 2	1959	25.00	50.00	100.00
—"Deep groove" version (deep indentation under label on both sides)					
BST-1597 [S]	Blue Lights, Volume 2	1959	17.50	35.00	70.00
—Regular version, W. 63rd St., NYC address on label					
BST-1597 [S]	Blue Lights, Volume 2	1963	6.25	12.50	25.00
—New York, USA address on label					
BLP-4021 [M]	On View at the Five Spot Café	1960	25.00	50.00	100.00
—"Deep groove" version (deep indentation under label on both sides)					
BLP-4021 [M]	On View at the Five Spot Café	1960	17.50	35.00	70.00
—Regular version, W. 63rd St., NYC address on label					
BLP-4021 [M]	On View at the Five Spot Café	1963	6.25	12.50	25.00
—New York, USA address on label					
BLP-4123 [M]	Midnight Blue	1963	7.50	15.00	30.00
—New York, USA address on label					
BST-81523 [R]	Introducing Kenny Burrell	1967	3.00	6.00	12.00
—"A Division of Liberty Records" on label					
BST-81543 [R]	Kenny Burrell, Volume 2	1967	3.00	6.00	12.00
—"A Division of Liberty Records" on label					
BST-81596 [S]	Blue Lights, Volume 1	1967	3.75	7.50	15.00
—"A Division of Liberty Records" on label					
BST-81597 [S]	Blue Lights, Volume 2	1967	3.75	7.50	15.00
—"A Division of Liberty Records" on label					
BST-84021 [S]	On View at the Five Spot Café	1960	15.00	30.00	60.00
—W. 63rd St., NYC address on label					
BST-84021 [S]	On View at the Five Spot Café	1963	6.25	12.50	25.00
—New York, USA address on label					
BST-84021 [S]	On View at the Five Spot Café	1967	3.75	7.50	15.00
—"A Division of Liberty Records" on label					
BST-84123	Midnight Blue	1985	2.50	5.00	10.00
—"The Finest in Jazz Since 1939" reissue					
BST-84123 [S]	Midnight Blue	1963	10.00	20.00	40.00
—New York, USA address on label					
BST-84123 [S]	Midnight Blue	1967	3.75	7.50	15.00
—"A Division of Liberty Records" on label					
B1-85137	Generation	1987	2.50	5.00	10.00
B1-90260	Pieces of Blue and the Blues	1988	2.50	5.00	10.00
CADET					
LP-769 [M]	Men at Work	1965	3.75	7.50	15.00
—Reissue of Argo 655					
LPS-769 [S]	Men at Work	1965	5.00	10.00	20.00
—Reissue of Argo 655					
LP-772 [M]	The Tender Gender	1966	3.75	7.50	15.00
LPS-772 [S]	The Tender Gender	1966	5.00	10.00	20.00
LP-779 [M]	Have Yourself a Soulful Little Christmas	1966	3.75	7.50	15.00
LPS-779 [S]	Have Yourself a Soulful Little Christmas	1966	5.00	10.00	20.00
LP-798 [M]	Ode to 52nd Street	1967	5.00	10.00	20.00
LPS-798 [S]	Ode to 52nd Street	1967	3.75	7.50	15.00
CHESS					
CH-9316	A Night at the Vanguard	1990	3.00	6.00	12.00
—Reissue of Argo 655					
CH-60019 [(2)]	Cool Cookin'	1973	3.75	7.50	15.00
CH2-92509 [(2)]	Recapitulation	198?	3.00	6.00	12.00
COLUMBIA					
CL 1703 [M]	Weaver of Dreams	1961	5.00	10.00	20.00
CS 8503 [S]	Weaver of Dreams	1961	6.25	12.50	25.00
CONCORD JAZZ					
CJ-45	Tin Tin Deo	1978	2.50	5.00	10.00
CJ-83	When Lights Are Low	1978	2.50	5.00	10.00
CJ-121	Moon and Sand	1980	2.50	5.00	10.00
CONTEMPORARY					
C-14058	Guiding Spirit	1990	3.00	6.00	12.00
CTI					
6011	God Bless the Child	1970	3.00	6.00	12.00
DENON					
7533	Lush Life	1979	3.75	7.50	15.00
7541	'Round Midnight	1979	3.75	7.50	15.00
FANTASY					
OJC-019	Kenny Burrell	198?	2.50	5.00	10.00
—Reissue of Prestige 7088					
OJC-216	Two Guitars	198?	2.50	5.00	10.00
OJC-427	All Night Long	1990	3.00	6.00	12.00
OJC-456	All Day Long	1990	3.00	6.00	12.00
MPF-4506	For Duke	1981	2.50	5.00	10.00
F-9417	'Round Midnight	1972	3.00	6.00	12.00
F-9427	Both Feet on the Ground	1973	3.00	6.00	12.00
F-9458	Up the Street	1974	3.00	6.00	12.00
F-9514	Sky Street	1975	3.00	6.00	12.00
F-9558	Stormy Monday	1977	3.00	6.00	12.00
79005 [(2)]	Ellington Is Forever	197?	3.75	7.50	15.00
79008 [(2)]	Ellington Is Forever, Vol. 2	197?	3.75	7.50	15.00
KAPP					
KL-1326 [M]	Lotta Bossa Nova	1962	5.00	10.00	20.00
KS-3326 [S]	Lotta Bossa Nova	1962	6.25	12.50	25.00
MOODSVILLE					
MVLP-29 [M]	Bluesy Burrell	1963	10.00	20.00	40.00
—Green label					
MVLP-29 [M]	Bluesy Burrell	1965	5.00	10.00	20.00
—Blue label with trident logo					
MVST-29 [S]	Bluesy Burrell	1963	10.00	20.00	40.00
—Green label					
MVST-29 [S]	Bluesy Burrell	1965	6.25	12.50	25.00
—Blue label with trident logo					
MUSE					
5144	Handcrafted	1979	2.50	5.00	10.00
5216	Live at the Village Vanguard	1979	2.50	5.00	10.00
5241	Kenny Burrell in New York	1982	2.50	5.00	10.00
5264	Listen to the Dawn	1982	2.50	5.00	10.00
5281	Groovin' High	1983	2.50	5.00	10.00
5317	A La Carte	1984	2.50	5.00	10.00
PAUSA					
9000	Midnight	198?	2.50	5.00	10.00
PRESTIGE					
PRLP-7073 [M]	All Night Long	1957	25.00	50.00	100.00
—Actually an all-star session; reissued as a Kenny Burrell album, thus it is listed here					
PRLP-7081 [M]	All Day Long	1957	25.00	50.00	100.00
—Actually an all-star session; reissued as a Kenny Burrell album, thus it is listed here					
PRLP-7088 [M]	Kenny Burrell	1957	20.00	40.00	80.00
PRLP-7277 [M]	All Day Long	1963	12.50	25.00	50.00
—Reissue of 7081					
PRST-7277 [R]	All Day Long	1963	5.00	10.00	20.00
PRLP-7289 [M]	All Night Long	1964	12.50	25.00	50.00
—Reissue of 7073					
PRST-7289 [R]	All Night Long	1964	5.00	10.00	20.00
PRLP-7308 [M]	Blue Moods	1964	7.50	15.00	30.00
—Reissue of 7088					
PRST-7308 [R]	Blue Moods	1964	5.00	10.00	20.00
PRLP-7315 [M]	Soul Call	1964	6.25	12.50	25.00
PRST-7315 [S]	Soul Call	1964	7.50	15.00	30.00
PRLP-7347 [M]	Crash	1964	6.25	12.50	25.00
PRST-7347 [S]	Crash	1964	7.50	15.00	30.00
PRLP-7448 [M]	The Best of Kenny Burrell	1967	7.50	15.00	30.00
PRST-7448 [S]	The Best of Kenny Burrell	1967	5.00	10.00	20.00
PRST-7578	Out of This World	1968	3.75	7.50	15.00
—Reissue of Moodsville 29					
24025 [(2)]	All Day Long & All Night Long	197?	3.75	7.50	15.00
—Reissue of both albums in one package					
SAVOY JAZZ					
SJL-1121	Monday Stroll	198?	2.50	5.00	10.00
—Reissue					
VERVE					
UMV-2070	Guitar Forms	198?	2.50	5.00	10.00
—Reissue of 8612					
V-8553 [M]	Blue Bash!	1963	5.00	10.00	20.00
V6-8553 [S]	Blue Bash!	1963	6.25	12.50	25.00
V-8612 [M]	Guitar Forms	1965	3.75	7.50	15.00
V6-8612 [S]	Guitar Forms	1965	5.00	10.00	20.00
V-8656 [M]	A Generation Ago Today	1966	3.75	7.50	15.00
V6-8656 [S]	A Generation Ago Today	1966	5.00	10.00	20.00

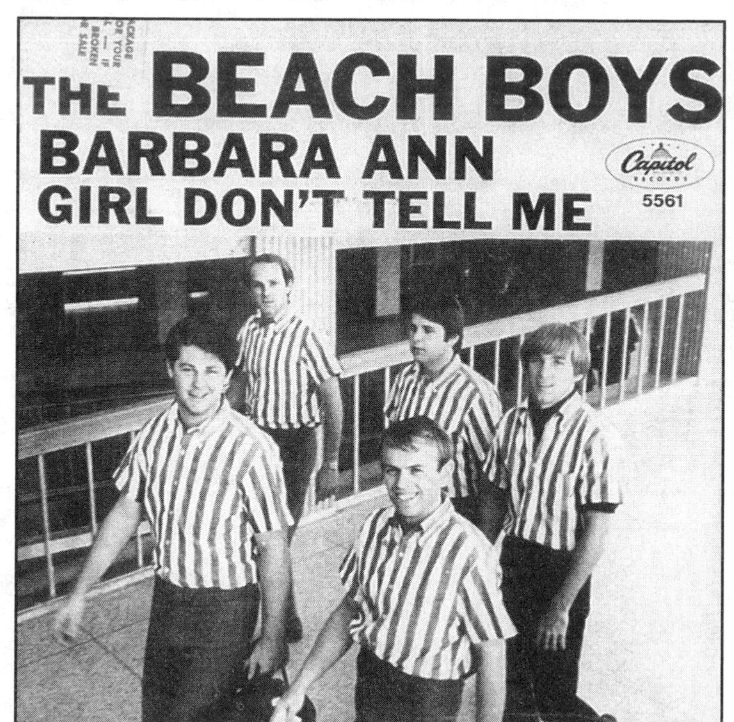

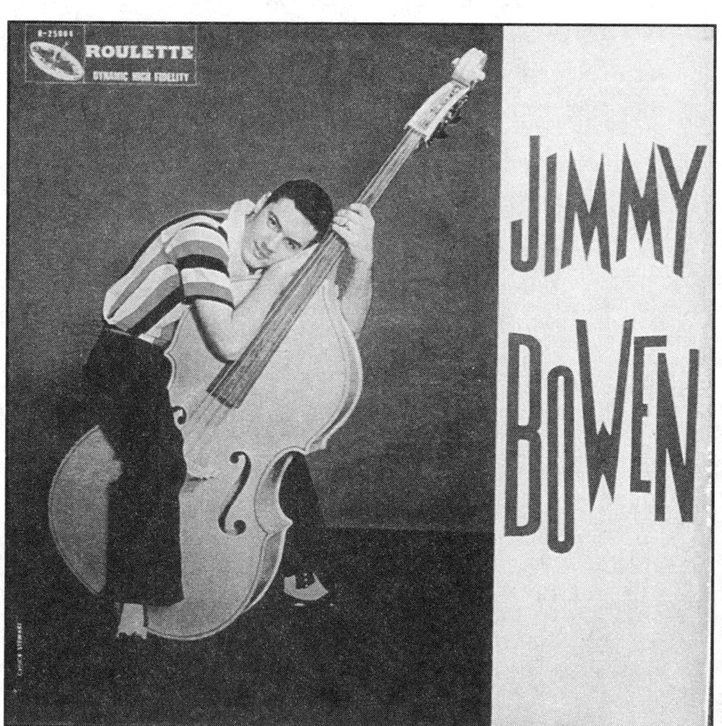

(Top left) "Barbara Ann" was a left-field hit taken from a "live in the studio" album, *Beach Boys' Party!* In fact, it's not even a Beach Boy singing lead; it's Dean Torrence of Jan and Dean. This picture sleeve is one of the Beach Boys' rarest. (Top right) J.P. Richardson, known to most as The Big Bopper, was around long enough in 1958 to record an entire album, a luxury that was quite rare for a man with only one hit record. The album actually went in and out of print several times in the vinyl era, but the original is the rarest and most collected. (Bottom left) Jimmy Bowen later became a producer and record-company executive, but first he was a rockabilly singer. Here is his rare LP on the Roulette label. (Bottom right) All of the original 45s by Johnny Burnette and the Rock 'N Roll Trio on Coral are highly collectible. Here is one of them, "Tear It Up," which is rare as a stock copy.

Number	Title (A Side/B Side)	Yr	VG	VG+	NM
V-8746 [M]	Blues— The Common Ground	1968	5.00	10.00	20.00
V6-8746 [S]	Blues— The Common Ground	1968	3.75	7.50	15.00
V6-8751	Night Song	1968	3.75	7.50	15.00
V6-8773	Asphalt Canyon Suite	1969	3.75	7.50	15.00
VOSS					
VLP1-42930	Heritage	1988	2.50	5.00	10.00

BURRELL, KENNY, AND JOHN COLTRANE
Also see each artist's individual listings.

Albums

Number	Title (A Side/B Side)	Yr	VG	VG+	NM
FANTASY					
OJC-079	The Cats	198?	2.50	5.00	10.00
—Reissue of New Jazz 8217					
OJC-300	Kenny Burrell and John Coltrane	1987	2.50	5.00	10.00
NEW JAZZ					
NJLP-8217 [M]	The Cats	1959	20.00	40.00	80.00
—Purple label					
NJLP-8217 [M]	The Cats	1965	6.25	12.50	25.00
—Blue label with trident logo					
NJLP-8276 [M]	Kenny Burrell with John Coltrane	1962	15.00	30.00	60.00
—Purple label					
NJLP-8276 [M]	Kenny Burrell with John Coltrane	1965	6.25	12.50	25.00
—Blue label with trident logo					
PRESTIGE					
PRLP-7532 [M]	Kenny Burrell Quintet with John Coltrane	1967	7.50	15.00	30.00
PRST-7532 [S]	Kenny Burrell Quintet with John Coltrane	1967	5.00	10.00	20.00
24059 [(2)]	Kenny Burrell & John Coltrane	197?	3.75	7.50	15.00
—Reissue of New Jazz and Prestige LPs in one package					

BURRELL, KENNY; TINY GRIMES; BILL JENNINGS

Albums

Number	Title (A Side/B Side)	Yr	VG	VG+	NM
STATUS					
ST-8318 [M]	Guitar Soul	1965	10.00	20.00	40.00

BURRELL, KENNY, AND JIMMY RANEY

Albums

Number	Title (A Side/B Side)	Yr	VG	VG+	NM
PRESTIGE					
PRLP-7119 [M]	Two Guitars	1957	20.00	40.00	80.00

BURRELL, KENNY, AND GROVER WASHINGTON. JR.
Also see each artist's individual listings.

Albums

Number	Title (A Side/B Side)	Yr	VG	VG+	NM
BLUE NOTE					
BT-85106	Togethering	1985	2.50	5.00	10.00

BURRITO BROTHERS, THE
See THE FLYING BURRITO BROTHERS.

BURROUGHS, WILLIAM

Albums

Number	Title (A Side/B Side)	Yr	VG	VG+	NM
ESP-DISK'					
1050 [M]	Call Me Burroughs	1967	25.00	50.00	100.00

BURTON, JAMES

45s

Number	Title (A Side/B Side)	Yr	VG	VG+	NM
PHILIPS					
40137	Swamp Surfer/Everybody Listen to the Dobro	1963	10.00	20.00	40.00
—As "Jimmy Dobro"					

BUSH, DICK

45s

Number	Title (A Side/B Side)	Yr	VG	VG+	NM
ERA					
1067	Hollywood Party/Exactly	1957	12.50	25.00	50.00

BUSTERS, THE

45s

Number	Title (A Side/B Side)	Yr	VG	VG+	NM
ARLEN					
735	Bust Out/Astronaut's	1963	5.00	10.00	20.00
740	All American Surfer/Pine Tree Hop	1963	5.00	10.00	20.00
745	Heartaches/Torrid Zone	1964	5.00	10.00	20.00
UNITED ARTISTS					
0145	Bust Out/The Green Mosquito	1973	—	2.50	5.00
—Silver Spotlight Series issue; B-side by the Tune Rockers					

BUTLER, CARL
Also see CARL BUTLER AND PEARL.

45s

Number	Title (A Side/B Side)	Yr	VG	VG+	NM
CAPITOL					
F-1399	Plastic Man/Country Mile	1951	6.25	12.50	25.00
F-1454	Shake, Rattle & Roll/No Guarantee on My Heart	1951	6.25	12.50	25.00
F1541	Our Last Rendezvous/I Live My Life Alone	1951	5.00	10.00	20.00
F1813	A String of Empties/You Plus Me	1951	5.00	10.00	20.00
F1891	Blue Million Tears/River of Love	1951	5.00	10.00	20.00
F1996	Alone Without You/Vicious Lies	1952	5.00	10.00	20.00
F2084	Penny for Your Thoughts/Everything Will Be the Same	1952	5.00	10.00	20.00
F2158	Stepping on My Heart/I Need You So	1952	5.00	10.00	20.00
COLUMBIA					
4-21353	Angel Band/Hallelujah We Shall Rise	1955	5.00	10.00	20.00
4-21407	Wedding Day/If I Could Spend My Heartaches	1955	5.00	10.00	20.00
4-21455	It's My Sin/Borrowed Love	1955	5.00	10.00	20.00
4-40874	Your Cold Heart Told Me So/I Know What It Means to Be Lonesome	1957	3.75	7.50	15.00
40994	River of Tears/Cry, You Fool, Cry	1957	3.00	6.00	12.00
41119	If You've Got the Money (I've Got the Time)/ Nothing I'd Rather Do	1958	2.50	5.00	10.00
41205	Jealous Heart/So Close	1958	2.50	5.00	10.00
41263	Baby I'm a-Waitin'/My Cajun Baby	1958	2.50	5.00	10.00
41368	I Like to Pretend/Oh, How I Miss You	1959	2.50	5.00	10.00
41475	Remember the Alamo/Grief in My Heart	1959	2.50	5.00	10.00
41560	You Jes' Don't Steal from a Poor Man/Cry, You Fool, Cry	1960	2.50	5.00	10.00
41674	The Door/I Know Why I Cry	1960	2.50	5.00	10.00
41869	I'm a Prisoner of Love/For the First Time	1960	2.50	5.00	10.00
41997	Honky Tonkitis/You Were the Orchid	1961	2.50	5.00	10.00
42306	Have You Run Out of Lies/If I Had Only Met You First	1962	2.50	5.00	10.00
42593	Don't Let Me Cross Over/Wonder Drug	1962	2.50	5.00	10.00
OKEH					
18003	Just for Fooling Around/You Can't Insure a House of Dreams	1954	3.75	7.50	15.00
18012	Crowded Out/My Heart Tells Me	1954	3.75	7.50	15.00
18018	So Close/It's Wrong to Be Jealous	1954	3.75	7.50	15.00
18032	A Victim of Lies/I Just Said Goodbye to My Dreams	1955	3.75	7.50	15.00
18039	That's All Right/I'll Go Steppin' Too	1955	5.00	10.00	20.00
18052	Kisses Don't Lie/I Wouldn't Change You If I Could	1955	3.75	7.50	15.00

Albums

Number	Title (A Side/B Side)	Yr	VG	VG+	NM
COLUMBIA					
CL 2002 [M]	Don't Let Me Cross Over	1963	5.00	10.00	20.00
CS 8802 [S]	Don't Let Me Cross Over	1963	6.25	12.50	25.00
HARMONY					
HL 7385 [M]	The Great Carl Butler Sings	1966	3.00	6.00	12.00
HS 11185 [S]	The Great Carl Butler Sings	1966	3.75	7.50	15.00
H 30674	For the First Time	1971	3.00	6.00	12.00

BUTLER, CARL, AND PEARL
Also see CARL BUTLER.

45s

Number	Title (A Side/B Side)	Yr	VG	VG+	NM
CHART					
5145	Temptation Keeps Twisting Her Arm/I'm So Close to Loving You	1972	—	2.00	4.00
5160	She Didn't Come Home/Two of a Kind	1972	—	2.00	4.00
5191	Heartaches for Lunch/Fifteen Years Ago	1973	—	2.00	4.00
COLUMBIA					
42778	Loving Arms/You'll Be Next	1963	2.00	4.00	8.00
42892	Too Late to Try Again/My Tears Don't Show	1963	2.00	4.00	8.00
43030	I'm Hanging Up the Phone/Just a Message	1964	2.00	4.00	8.00
43102	Forbidden Street/When the Door Swings Shut	1964	2.00	4.00	8.00
43210	Just Thought I'd Let You Know/We'd Destroy Each Other	1965	2.00	4.00	8.00
43335	Beers and Tears/Can I Draw the Line	1965	2.00	4.00	8.00
43433	Our Ship of Love/It's Called Cheating	1965	2.00	4.00	8.00
43536	Little Mac/Wrong Generation	1966	2.00	4.00	8.00
43685	Little Pedro/Cell 29	1966	2.00	4.00	8.00
43869	Same Old Me Lovin' Same Old You/Dreaming of a Little Cabin	1966	2.00	4.00	8.00
44043	Wild Goose Chase/Lost	1967	—	3.00	6.00
44252	Guilty of Love/For a Minute	1967	—	3.00	6.00
44447	If You Should Ever Stop Loving Me/If I'd Only Met You First	1968	—	3.00	6.00
44587	Punish Me Tomorrow/Goodbye Tennessee	1968	—	3.00	6.00
44694	I Never Got Over You/I Started Loving You Again	1968	—	3.00	6.00
44862	We'll Sweep Out the Ashes in the Morning/Your Way of Life	1969	—	3.00	6.00
45112	Used to Own This Train/Caution	1970	—	2.50	5.00
45228	Bottoms Up/Let the Sun Shine on the People	1970	—	2.50	5.00

Albums

Number	Title (A Side/B Side)	Yr	VG	VG+	NM
CHART					
1051	Temptation Keeps Twistin' Her Arm	1972	3.75	7.50	15.00
COLUMBIA					
CS 1039	Carl and Pearl Butler's Greatest Hits	1970	3.75	7.50	15.00
CL 2125 [M]	Loving Arms	1964	5.00	10.00	20.00
CL 2308 [M]	The Old and the New	1965	3.75	7.50	15.00
CL 2640 [M]	Avenue of Prayer	1967	5.00	10.00	20.00
CS 8925 [S]	Loving Arms	1964	6.25	12.50	25.00
CS 9108 [S]	The Old and the New	1965	5.00	10.00	20.00
CS 9440 [S]	Avenue of Prayer	1967	3.75	7.50	15.00
CS 9651	Our Country World	1968	3.75	7.50	15.00
CS 9769	Honky Tonkin'	1969	3.75	7.50	15.00
HARMONY					
H 31182	Watch and Pray	1972	3.00	6.00	12.00

BUTLER, FREDDIE

Albums

Number	Title (A Side/B Side)	Yr	VG	VG+	NM
KAPP					
KS-3519	With a Dab of Soul	1968	7.50	15.00	30.00

BUTLER, JERRY
Also see GENE CHANDLER; BETTY EVERETT; THE IMPRESSIONS.

45s

Number	Title (A Side/B Side)	Yr	VG	VG+	NM
ABNER					
1024	Lost/One by One	1959	7.50	15.00	30.00
1028	Hold Me Darling/Rainbow Valley	1959	7.50	15.00	30.00
1030	I Was Wrong/Couldn't Go to Sleep	1959	7.50	15.00	30.00
1035	A Lonely Soldier/I Found a Love	1960	7.50	15.00	30.00
FOUNTAIN					
400	No Love Without Changes/All the Way	1982	—	3.00	6.00
ICHIBAN					
269	Angel Flying Too Close to the Ground/You're the Only One	1992	—	—	3.00
290	Need to Belong/Sure Feels Good	1993	—	—	3.00
MCA					
52177	Let's Talk It Over/Especially You	1983	—	2.00	4.00
—With Stix Hooper; B-side by Stix Hooper solo					
MERCURY					
72592	Love (Oh How Sweet It Is)/Loneliness	1966	2.50	5.00	10.00
72625	You Make Me Feel Like Someone/For What You Made of Me	1966	2.50	5.00	10.00
72648	I Dig You Baby/Some Kinda Magic	1966	2.50	5.00	10.00
72676	Why Do I Lose You/You Walked Into My Life	1967	2.50	5.00	10.00

Number	Title (A Side/B Side)	Yr	VG	VG+	NM
72698	You Don't Know What You've Got Until You Lose It/The Way I Love You	1967	2.50	5.00	10.00
72721	Mr. Dream Merchant/'Cause I Love You So	1967	2.50	5.00	10.00
72764	Lost/You Don't Know What You've Got Until You Lose It	1968	2.00	4.00	8.00
72798	Never Give You Up/Beside You	1968	2.00	4.00	8.00
72850	Hey, Western Union Man/Just Can't Forget About You	1968	2.00	4.00	8.00
72876	Are You Happy/I Still Love You	1968	2.00	4.00	8.00
72898	Only the Strong Survive/Just Because I Really Love You	1969	2.00	4.00	8.00
72929	Moody Woman/Go Away — Find Yourself	1969	2.00	4.00	8.00
72960	What's the Use of Breaking Up/Brand New Me	1969	2.00	4.00	8.00
72991	Don't Let Love Hang You Up/Walking Around in Teardrops	1969	2.00	4.00	8.00
73015	Got to See If I Can't Get Mommy (To Come Back Home)/I Forgot to Remember	1970	2.00	4.00	8.00
73045	I Could Write a Book/Since I Lost You, Baby	1970	2.00	4.00	8.00
73101	Where Are You Going/You Can Fly	1970	2.00	4.00	8.00
73131	How Does It Feel/Special Memory	1970	2.00	4.00	8.00
73169	If It's Real What I Feel/Why Are You Leaving Me	1971	—	3.00	6.00
73210	How Did We Lose It baby/Do You Finally Need a Friend	1971	—	3.00	6.00
73241	Walk Easy My Son/Let Me Be	1971	—	3.00	6.00
73290	I Only Have Eyes for You/A Prayer	1972	—	3.00	6.00
73335	One Night Affair/Life's Unfortunate Song	1972	—	3.00	6.00
73443	Power of Love/What Do You Do on a Sunday Afternoon	1973	—	3.00	6.00
73459	That's How Heartaches Are Made/Too Many Danger Signs	1974	—	3.00	6.00
73495	Take the Time to Tell Her/High Stepper	1974	—	3.00	6.00
73629	You and Me Against the World/Playing on You	1974	—	3.00	6.00
872914-7	Only the Strong Survive/Lost	1989	—	—	3.00
—Reissue					
872916-7	Never Give You Up/Hey, Western Union Man	1989	—	—	3.00
—Reissue					
MISTLETOE					
803	Silent Night/O Holy Night	1974	—	2.50	5.00
MOTOWN					
1403	The Devil in Mrs. Jones/Don't Wanna Be Reminded	1976	—	2.50	5.00
1403 [PS]	The Devil in Mrs. Jones/Don't Wanna Be Reminded	1976	2.50	5.00	10.00
1414	I Wanna Do It to You/I Don't Wanna Be Reminded	1977	—	2.50	5.00
1421	Chalk It Up/I Don't Want Nobody to Know	1977	—	2.50	5.00
1422	It's a Lifetime Thing/Kiss Me Now	1977	—	2.50	5.00
—With Thelma Houston					
PHILADELPHIA INT'L					
3113	Don't Be Ashamed/Best Love I Ever Had	1980	—	2.00	4.00
3117	Tell Me Girl (Why It Has to End)/We've Got This Feeling Again	1980	—	2.00	4.00
3656	(I'm Just Thinking About) Cooling Out/Are You Lonely Tonight	1978	—	2.00	4.00
3664	(I'm Just Thinking About) Cooling Out/Are You Lonely Tonight	1978	—	2.00	4.00
3673	I'm Glad to Be Back/Nothing Says I Love You Like I Love You	1979	—	2.00	4.00
3683	Let's Make Love/Dream World	1979	—	2.00	4.00
VEE JAY					
354	He Will Break Your Heart/Thanks to You	1960	5.00	10.00	20.00
371	Silent Night/O Holy Night	1960	5.00	10.00	20.00
375	Find Another Girl/When Trouble Calls	1961	3.75	7.50	15.00
390	I See a Fool/I'm a Telling You	1961	3.75	7.50	15.00
396	For Your Precious Love/Sweet Was the Wine	1961	3.75	7.50	15.00
405	Moon River/Aware of Love	1961	3.75	7.50	15.00
426	Isle of Sirens/Chi Town	1962	3.75	7.50	15.00
451	Make It Easy on Yourself/It's Too Late	1962	3.75	7.50	15.00
463	You Can Run/I'm the One	1962	3.75	7.50	15.00
475	Theme from Taras Bulba (Wishing Star)/You Go Right Through Me	1963	3.00	6.00	12.00
475 [PS]	Theme from Taras Bulba (Wishing Star)/You Go Right Through Me	1963	10.00	20.00	40.00
486	You Won't Be Sorry/Whatever You Want	1963	3.00	6.00	12.00
526	Strawberries/I Almost Lost My Head	1963	3.00	6.00	12.00
534	Where's the Girl?/How Beautifully You Lie	1963	3.00	6.00	12.00
556	Just a Little Bit/A Woman with Soul	1963	3.00	6.00	12.00
567	Need to Belong/Give Me Your Love	1963	3.00	6.00	12.00
588	Giving Up on Love/I've Been Trying	1964	3.00	6.00	12.00
598	I Stand Accused/I Don't Want to Hear Anymore	1964	3.00	6.00	12.00
598 [PS]	I Stand Accused/I Don't Want to Hear Anymore	1964	7.50	15.00	30.00
651	Good Times/I've Grown Accustomed to Her Face	1965	3.00	6.00	12.00
696	I Can't Stand to See You Cry/Nobody Needs Your Love	1965	3.00	6.00	12.00
707	Believe in Me/Just for You	1965	3.00	6.00	12.00
711	Moon River/Make It Easy on Yourself	1966	3.00	6.00	12.00
715	For Your Precious Love/Give It Up	1966	3.00	6.00	12.00
Albums					
ABNER					
R-2001 [M]	Jerry Butler, Esquire	1959	100.00	200.00	400.00
BUDDAH					
BDS-4001	The Very Best of Jerry Butler	1969	3.75	7.50	15.00
FOUNTAIN					
FR 2-82-1	Ice 'n Hot	1982	2.50	5.00	10.00
MERCURY					
SRM-1-689	The Power of Love	1973	3.75	7.50	15.00
SRM-1-1006	Sweet Sixteen	1974	3.75	7.50	15.00
SRM-2-7502 [(2)]	The Spice of Life	1972	5.00	10.00	20.00
MG-21005 [M]	The Soul Artistry of Jerry Butler	1967	5.00	10.00	20.00
MG-21146 [M]	Mr. Dream Merchant	1967	5.00	10.00	20.00
SR-61005 [S]	The Soul Artistry of Jerry Butler	1967	3.75	7.50	15.00
SR-61146 [S]	Mr. Dream Merchant	1967	3.75	7.50	15.00
SR-61151	Jerry Butler's Golden Hits Live	1968	3.75	7.50	15.00
SR-61171	The Soul Goes On	1968	3.75	7.50	15.00
SR-61198	The Ice Man Cometh	1968	3.75	7.50	15.00
SR-61234	Ice On Ice	1969	3.75	7.50	15.00
SR-61269	You & Me	1970	3.75	7.50	15.00
SR-61281	The Best of Jerry Butler	1970	3.75	7.50	15.00
SR-61320	Jerry Butler Sings Assorted Sounds	1971	3.75	7.50	15.00
SR-61347	The Sagittarius Movement	1971	3.75	7.50	15.00
810369-1	The Best of Jerry Butler	1983	2.50	5.00	10.00
822212-1	Only the Strong Survive: The Great Philadelphia Hits	1984	2.50	5.00	10.00
MOTOWN					
M6-850	Love's on the Menu	1976	3.00	6.00	12.00
M6-878	Suite for the Single Girl	1977	2.50	5.00	10.00
M6-892	It All Comes Out in My Songs	1977	2.50	5.00	10.00
PHILADELPHIA INT'L.					
JZ 35510	Nothing Says I Love You Like I Love You	1978	2.50	5.00	10.00
JZ 36413	The Best Love I Ever Had	1979	2.50	5.00	10.00
RHINO					
RNLP-216	The Best of Jerry Butler (1958-1969)	1984	2.50	5.00	10.00
TRADITION					
TLP-2068	Starring Jerry Butler	1969	3.75	7.50	15.00
TRIP					
8011 [(2)]	All Time Hits	1972	3.75	7.50	15.00
UNITED ARTISTS					
UA-LA498-E	The Very Best of Jerry Butler	1975	2.50	5.00	10.00
VEE JAY					
VJLP2-1003 [(2)]	Jerry Butler Gold	198?	3.75	7.50	15.00
LP-1027 [M]	Jerry Butler, Esquire	1960	37.50	75.00	150.00
—Reissue of Abner 2001					
LP-1029 [M]	He Will Break Your Heart	1960	20.00	40.00	80.00
LP-1034 [M]	Love Me	1961	12.50	25.00	50.00
—Reissue of 1027					
LP-1038 [M]	Aware of Love	1961	10.00	20.00	40.00
SR-1038 [S]	Aware of Love	1961	12.50	25.00	50.00
LP-1046 [M]	Moon River	1962	10.00	20.00	40.00
SR-1046 [S]	Moon River	1962	12.50	25.00	50.00
VJLP-1046	Moon River	1985	2.50	5.00	10.00
—Reissue of original 1046; has softer vinyl					
LP-1048 [M]	The Best of Jerry Butler	1962	6.25	12.50	25.00
SR-1048 [P]	The Best of Jerry Butler	1962	7.50	15.00	30.00
VJLP-1048	The Best of Jerry Butler	1985	2.50	5.00	10.00
—Reissue of original 1048; has softer vinyl					
LP-1057 [M]	Folk Songs	1963	6.25	12.50	25.00
SR-1057 [S]	Folk Songs	1963	7.50	15.00	30.00
LP-1075 [M]	For Your Precious Love	1963	6.25	12.50	25.00
SR-1075 [S]	For Your Precious Love	1963	7.50	15.00	30.00
LP-1076 [M]	Giving Up On Love/Need to Belong	1963	6.25	12.50	25.00
VJS-1076 [S]	Giving Up On Love/Need to Belong	1963	7.50	15.00	30.00
LP-1119 [M]	More of the Best of Jerry Butler	1965	6.25	12.50	25.00
VJS-1119 [S]	More of the Best of Jerry Butler	1965	7.50	15.00	30.00
D1-74807	He Will Break Your Heart	1989	3.00	6.00	12.00

BUTLER, JERRY, AND BRENDA LEE EAGER

Also see each artist's individual listings.

Number	Title (A Side/B Side)	Yr	VG	VG+	NM
45s					
MERCURY					
73255	Ain't Understading Mellow/Windy City Soul	1971	—	3.00	6.00
73301	(They Long to Be) Close to You/You Can't Always Tell	1972	—	3.00	6.00
73395	Can't Understand It/How Long Will It Last	1973	—	3.00	6.00
73422	We Were Lovers, We Were Friends/The Love We Had Stays On My Mind	1973	—	3.00	6.00
Albums					
MERCURY					
SRM-1-660	The Love We Have	1973	3.75	7.50	15.00

BUTLER, JERRY, AND THE IMPRESSIONS

See THE IMPRESSIONS.

BUTLER, JIMMY

Number	Title (A Side/B Side)	Yr	VG	VG+	NM
45s					
GEM					
222	Trim Your Tree/Cruelty For Kindness	1954	12.50	25.00	50.00

BUTTERFIELD, PAUL

Number	Title (A Side/B Side)	Yr	VG	VG+	NM
45s					
BEARSVILLE					
49706	Living in Memphis/Footprints on the Windshield (Upside Down)	1981	—	2.00	4.00
ELEKTRA					
45016	Got My Mojo Working/Mellow Down Easy	1964	2.50	5.00	10.00
45609	Come On In/I Got a Mind to Give Up Living	1967	2.50	5.00	10.00
45620	Run Out of Time/One More Heartache	1967	2.50	5.00	10.00
45620 [PS]	Run Out of Time/One More Heartache	1967	5.00	10.00	20.00
45643	In My Own Dream/(B-side unknown)	1968	3.00	6.00	12.00
45658	Where Did My Baby Go/In My Own Dream	1969	2.50	5.00	10.00
45692	Love March/(B-side unknown)	1970	3.00	6.00	12.00
Albums					
AMHERST					
AMH-3305	The Legendary Paul Butterfield Rides Again	1986	3.00	6.00	12.00
BEARSVILLE					
BR 2119	Paul Butterfield's Better Days	1973	3.00	6.00	12.00
BR 2170	It All Comes Back	1973	3.00	6.00	12.00
BR 6960	Put It In Your Ear	1976	3.00	6.00	12.00
BRK 6995	North-South	1978	3.00	6.00	12.00
ELEKTRA					
EKL-294 [M]	The Paul Butterfield Blues Band	1965	5.00	10.00	20.00
—Gold label with guitar player					
EKL-294 [M]	The Paul Butterfield Blues Band	1966	3.75	7.50	15.00
—Brown label					
EKL-315 [M]	East-West	1966	5.00	10.00	20.00
—Gold label with guitar player					
EKL-315 [M]	East-West	1967	3.75	7.50	15.00
—Brown label					
7E-2001 [(2)]	The Butterfield Blues Band/Live	1970	6.25	12.50	25.00

Number	Title (A Side/B Side)	Yr	VG	VG+	NM
7E-2005 [(2)]	Golden Butter/The Best of the Paul Butterfield Blues Band	1972	6.25	12.50	25.00
EKL-4015 [M]	The Resurrection of Pigboy Crabshaw	1967	7.50	15.00	30.00
EKS-7294 [S]	The Paul Butterfield Blues Band	1965	6.25	12.50	25.00
—Gold label with guitar player					
EKS-7294 [S]	The Paul Butterfield Blues Band	1966	5.00	10.00	20.00
—Brown label					
EKS-7294 [S]	The Paul Butterfield Blues Band	1969	3.75	7.50	15.00
—Red label with large stylized "E"					
EKS-7294 [S]	The Paul Butterfield Blues Band	1971	3.00	6.00	12.00
—Butterfly label					
EKS-7315 [S]	East-West	1966	6.25	12.50	25.00
—Gold label with guitar player					
EKS-7315 [S]	East-West	1967	5.00	10.00	20.00
—Brown label					
EKS-7315 [S]	East-West	1969	3.75	7.50	15.00
—Red label with large stylized "E"					
EKS-7315 [S]	East-West	1971	3.00	6.00	12.00
—Butterfly label					
EKS-74015 [S]	The Resurrection of Pigboy Crabshaw	1967	5.00	10.00	20.00
—Brown label					
EKS-74015 [S]	The Resurrection of Pigboy Crabshaw	1969	3.75	7.50	15.00
—Red label with large stylized "E"					
EKS-74015 [S]	The Resurrection of Pigboy Crabshaw	1971	3.00	6.00	12.00
—Butterfly label					
EKS-74025	In My Own Dream	1968	5.00	10.00	20.00
—Brown label					
EKS-74025	In My Own Dream	1969	3.75	7.50	15.00
—Red label with large stylized "E"					
EKS-74025	In My Own Dream	1971	3.00	6.00	12.00
—Butterfly label					
EKS-74053	Keep On Moving	1969	5.00	10.00	20.00
—Red label with large stylized "E"					
EKS-74053	Keep On Moving	1971	3.00	6.00	12.00
—Butterfly label					
EKS-75013	Sometimes I Just Feel Like Smilin'	1971	5.00	10.00	20.00
RHINO					
RNLP-70877	Paul Butterfield's Better Days	1987	2.00	4.00	8.00
—Reissue of Bearsville 2119					
RNLP-70878	It All Comes Back	1987	2.00	4.00	8.00
—Reissue of Bearsville 2170					
RNLP-70879	Put It In Your Ear	1987	2.00	4.00	8.00
—Reissue of Bearsville 6960					
RNLP-70880	North-South	1987	2.00	4.00	8.00
—Reissue of Bearsville 6995					

BUTTERFLYS, THE

45s

Number	Title (A Side/B Side)	Yr	VG	VG+	NM
RED BIRD					
10-009	Goodnight Baby/The Swim	1964	6.25	12.50	25.00
10-016	I Wonder/Gee, Baby, Gee	1964	6.25	12.50	25.00

BUTTS BAND

With Robbie Krieger and John Densmore of THE DOORS.

45s

Number	Title (A Side/B Side)	Yr	VG	VG+	NM
BLUE THUMB					
242	Pop a Top/Baja Bus	1973	2.00	4.00	8.00
252	I Won't Be Alone Anymore/Kansas City	1974	2.00	4.00	8.00
263	Get Up, Stand Up/Mike's Blues	1975	2.00	4.00	8.00

Albums

Number	Title (A Side/B Side)	Yr	VG	VG+	NM
BLUE THUMB					
BTS-53	Butts Band	1973	3.00	6.00	12.00
—With Robby Krieger and John Densmore of THE DOORS.					
BTS-6018	Hear and Now	1975	3.00	6.00	12.00

BYE BYES, THE

45s

Number	Title (A Side/B Side)	Yr	VG	VG+	NM
MERCURY					
71530	Blonde Hair, Blue Eyes, Ruby Red Lips/Do You	1959	3.75	7.50	15.00

BYRD, BOBBY

Two different artists have this name. For records on the Cash, Jamie and Sage & Sand labels, see BOBBY DAY.

45s

Number	Title (A Side/B Side)	Yr	VG	VG+	NM
ABC					
11134	Here Is My Everything/Loving You	1968	—	—	—
—With Vicki Anderson					
BANG					
562	Whatcha Gonna Do About It/If She's There	1968	—	3.00	6.00
BROWNSTONE					
4203	Hot Pants - I'm Coming, Coming, I'm Coming	1971	—	3.00	6.00
4205	Keep On Doin' What You're Doin'/Let Me Know	1971	—	3.00	6.00
4206	If You Got a Love You Better (Hold On to It)/You Have Got to Change Your Mind	1972	—	3.00	6.00
4208	Never Get Enough/My Concerto	1972	—	3.00	6.00
4209	Sayin' It and Doin' It Are Two Different Things/ Never Get Enough	1972	—	3.00	6.00
4210	Signed, Sealed and Delivered/I Need Help (I Can't Do It Alone)	1973	—	3.00	6.00
FEDERAL					
12486	They Are Sayin'/I Found Out	1963	3.75	7.50	15.00
INTERNATIONAL BROTHERS					
901	Back from the Dead/(B-side unknown)	1975	—	3.00	6.00
KING					
6069	I Found Out/I'll Keep Pressing On	1967	—	3.00	6.00
6126	Funky Soul #1 (Part 1)/Funky Soul #1 (Part 2)	1967	—	3.00	6.00
6151	You've Got to Change Your Mind/I'll Lose My Mind	1968	2.50	5.00	10.00
—A-side with James Brown					
6165	You Gave My Heart a Brand New Song/Concerto	1968	—	3.00	6.00
6289	You Gave My Heart a New Song/Hang-Ups We Don't Need	1970	—	3.00	6.00
6308	I'm Not to Blame/It's I Who Loves You (It's Not Him Anymore)	1970	—	3.00	6.00
6323	I Need Help (Part 1)/I Need Help (Part 2)	1970	—	3.00	6.00
6342	You've Got to Change Your Mind/You Got to Have a Job (If You Don't Work You Can't Eat)	1970	—	3.00	6.00
6378	I Know You Got Soul/It's I Who Love You (It's Not Him Anymore)	1971	—	3.00	6.00
KWANZA/WB					
7703	On the Move/Try It Again	1973	—	3.00	6.00
SMASH					
1884	Baby, Baby, Baby/Baby, Baby, Baby (Instrumental)	1964	2.00	4.00	8.00
—With Anna King					
1903	Write Me a Letter/I Love You So	1964	2.00	4.00	8.00
1928	I'm Lonely/I've Got a Girl	1964	2.00	4.00	8.00
1964	No One Like My Baby/We Are In Love	1965	2.00	4.00	8.00
1984	Time Will Make a Change/The Way I Feel	1965	2.00	4.00	8.00
2003	You're Gonna Need My Lovin'/Let Me Know	1965	2.00	4.00	8.00
2018	Lost in the Mood of Changes/Oh, What a Nite	1966	2.00	4.00	8.00
2052	Ain't No Use/Let Me Know	1966	2.00	4.00	8.00

Albums

Number	Title (A Side/B Side)	Yr	VG	VG+	NM
KING					
KS-1118	I Need Help	1970	50.00	100.00	200.00

BYRD, BOBBY, AND THE IMPALAS

See BOBBY DAY.

BYRD, CHARLIE

45s

Number	Title (A Side/B Side)	Yr	VG	VG+	NM
COLUMBIA					
43504	Baby Love/Walk Right In	1966	2.00	4.00	8.00
—With the Lady Byrds					
43834	The Work Song/Tomorrow Belongs to Me	1966	2.00	4.00	8.00
44214	Zona Sul/Caper of the Golden Bulls	1967	2.00	4.00	8.00
44411	Empty Streets/Far Off, Close By	1967	—	3.00	6.00
44669	Lullaby from Rosemary's Baby/Happy Together	1969	—	3.00	6.00
44782	Wichita Lineman/I Don't Have to Take It	1969	—	3.00	6.00
45099	I'll Never Fall in Love Again/I'll Walk with the Rain	1970	—	2.50	5.00
RIVERSIDE					
4529	The Duck/One Note Samba	1962	2.50	5.00	10.00
4544	Meditation (Meditacao)/Little Boat (O Barquinho)	1962	2.50	5.00	10.00
4556	Longing for Bahia/Softly	1963	2.50	5.00	10.00

Albums

Number	Title (A Side/B Side)	Yr	VG	VG+	NM
COLUMBIA					
CS 1053	Let It Be	1970	3.00	6.00	12.00
CL 2337 [M]	Brazilian Byrd	1965	3.75	7.50	15.00
—"Guaranteed High Fidelity" on label					
CL 2337 [M]	Brazilian Byrd	1965	3.00	6.00	12.00
—"360 Sound Mono" on label					
CL 2435 [M]	Travellin' Man Recorded Live	1966	3.00	6.00	12.00
CL 2504 [M]	A Touch of Gold	1966	3.00	6.00	12.00
CL 2555 [M]	Christmas Carols for Solo Guitar	1966	3.75	7.50	15.00
CL 2592 [M]	Byrdland	1967	5.00	10.00	20.00
CL 2652 [M]	Hollywood Byrd	1967	5.00	10.00	20.00
CL 2692 [M]	More Brazilian Byrd	1967	5.00	10.00	20.00
CS 9137	Brazilian Byrd	1971	2.50	5.00	10.00
—Orange label					
CS 9137 [S]	Brazilian Byrd	1965	5.00	10.00	20.00
—Red label, "360 Sound" in black					
CS 9137 [S]	Brazilian Byrd	1965	3.75	7.50	15.00
—Red label, "360 Sound" in white					
PC 9137	Brazilian Byrd	198?	2.00	4.00	8.00
—Reissue with new prefix					
CS 9235 [S]	Travellin' Man Recorded Live	1966	3.75	7.50	15.00
CS 9304 [S]	A Touch of Gold	1966	3.75	7.50	15.00
CS 9355 [S]	Christmas Carols for Solo Guitar	1966	5.00	10.00	20.00
CS 9392 [S]	Byrdland	1967	3.75	7.50	15.00
CS 9452 [S]	Hollywood Byrd	1967	3.75	7.50	15.00
CS 9492 [S]	More Brazilian Byrd	1967	3.75	7.50	15.00
CS 9582	Sketches of Brazil (Music of Villa Lobos)	1968	3.75	7.50	15.00
CS 9627 [M]	Hit Trip	1968	6.25	12.50	25.00
—"Special Mono Radio Station Copy" with white label					
CS 9627 [S]	Hit Trip	1968	3.75	7.50	15.00
CS 9667	Delicately	1968	3.75	7.50	15.00
CS 9747	The Great Byrd	1968	3.75	7.50	15.00
CS 9841	Aquarius	1969	3.75	7.50	15.00
CS 9869	Let Go	1969	3.75	7.50	15.00
CS 9970	The Greatest Hits of the 60's	1970	3.00	6.00	12.00
C 30380	A Stroke of Genius	1971	3.00	6.00	12.00
G 30622 [(2)]	For All We Know	1971	3.75	7.50	15.00
C 31025	Onda Nuevo	1972	3.00	6.00	12.00
CG 31967 [(2)]	The World of Charlie Byrd	1972	3.75	7.50	15.00
CONCORD JAZZ					
CJ-82	Blue Byrd	1979	2.50	5.00	10.00
CJ-252	Isn't It Romantic	1984	2.50	5.00	10.00
CJ-304	Byrd & Brass	1986	2.50	5.00	10.00
CJ-374	It's a Wonderful World	1989	3.00	6.00	12.00
CONCORD PICANTE					
P-114	Sugarloaf Suite	1980	2.50	5.00	10.00
P-173	Brazilville	1981	2.50	5.00	10.00
CRYSTAL CLEAR					
8002	Charlie Byrd	1979	7.50	15.00	30.00
—Direct-to-disc recording; plays at 45 rpm					
FANTASY					
OJC-107	Bossa Nova Pelos Passaros	198?	2.50	5.00	10.00
—Reissue of Riverside 436					
OJC-262	Byrd at the Gate	1987	2.50	5.00	10.00
—Reissue of Riverside 9467					
F-9429	Crystal Silence	1973	3.00	6.00	12.00
F-9466	Byrd by the Sea	1974	3.00	6.00	12.00
F-9496	Top Hat	1975	3.00	6.00	12.00
IMPROV					
7116	Charlie Byrd Swings Downtown	1977	3.00	6.00	12.00

Number	Title (A Side/B Side)	Yr	VG	VG+	NM
MILESTONE					
47005 [(2)]	Latin Byrd	1973	3.75	7.50	15.00
47049 [(2)]	Charlie Byrd in Greenwich Village	1978	3.75	7.50	15.00
MOBILE FIDELITY					
1-515	Byrd at the Gate	1982	10.00	20.00	40.00
—Audiophile vinyl					
OFFBEAT					
OJ-3001 [M]	Jazz at the Show Boat, Volume 1	1959	6.25	12.50	25.00
OJ-3005 [M]	Jazz at the Show Boat, Volume 2	1959	6.25	12.50	25.00
OJ-3006 [M]	Jazz at the Show Boat, Volume 3	1959	6.25	12.50	25.00
OJ-3007 [M]	Charlie's Choice	1960	6.25	12.50	25.00
OLP-3009 [M]	Blues Sonata	1960	6.25	12.50	25.00
OS-93001 [S]	Jazz at the Show Boat, Volume 1	1959	7.50	15.00	30.00
OS-93005 [S]	Jazz at the Show Boat, Volume 2	1959	7.50	15.00	30.00
OS-93006 [S]	Jazz at the Show Boat, Volume 3	1959	7.50	15.00	30.00
OS-93007 [S]	Charlie's Choice	1960	7.50	15.00	30.00
OS-93009 [S]	Blues Sonata	1960	7.50	151.00	30.00
PICKWICK					
SPC-3042	Byrd and the Herd	196?	3.00	6.00	12.00
RIVERSIDE					
RM-427 [M]	Latin Impressions	1962	5.00	10.00	20.00
RM-436 [M]	Bossa Nova Pelos Passaros	1962	5.00	10.00	20.00
RM-448 [M]	Byrd's Word	1963	5.00	10.00	20.00
RM-449 [M]	Byrd in the Wind	1963	5.00	10.00	20.00
RM-450 [M]	Mr. Guitar	1963	5.00	10.00	20.00
RM-451 [M]	The Guitar Artistry of Charlie Byrd	1963	5.00	10.00	20.00
RM-452 [M]	Charlie Byrd at the Village Vanguard	1963	5.00	10.00	20.00
RM-453 [M]	Blues Sonata	1963	5.00	10.00	20.00
RM-454 [M]	Once More! Bossa Nova	1963	5.00	10.00	20.00
RM-467 [M]	Byrd at the Gate	1964	5.00	10.00	20.00
RM-481 [M]	Byrd Song	1966	3.75	7.50	15.00
RM-498 [M]	Solo Flight	1967	5.00	10.00	20.00
RS-3005	The Guitar Artistry of Charlie Byrd	1968	3.75	7.50	15.00
RS-3044	Byrd Man with Strings	1969	3.75	7.50	15.00
6054	Blues Sonata	197?	2.50	5.00	10.00
RS-9427 [S]	Latin Impressions	1962	6.25	12.50	25.00
RS-9436 [S]	Bossa Nova Pelos Passaros	1962	6.25	12.50	25.00
RS-9448 [S]	Byrd's Word	1963	6.25	12.50	25.00
RS-9449 [S]	Byrd in the Wind	1963	6.25	12.50	25.00
RS-9450 [S]	Mr. Guitar	1963	6.25	12.50	25.00
RS-9451 [S]	The Guitar Artistry of Charlie Byrd	1963	6.25	12.50	25.00
RS-9452 [S]	Charlie Byrd at the Village Vanguard	1963	6.25	12.50	25.00
RS-9453 [S]	Blues Sonata	1963	6.25	12.50	25.00
RS-9454 [S]	Once More! Bossa Nova	1963	6.25	12.50	25.00
RS-9467 [S]	Byrd at the Gate	1964	6.25	12.50	25.00
RS-9481 [S]	Byrd Song	1966	5.00	10.00	20.00
RS-9498 [S]	Solo Flight	1967	3.75	7.50	15.00
SAVOY					
MG-12099 [M]	Jazz Recital	1957	10.00	20.00	40.00
MG-12116 [M]	Blues for Night People	1957	10.00	20.00	40.00
SAVOY JAZZ					
SJL-1121	Midnight Guitar	1980	2.50	5.00	10.00
SJL-1131	First Flight	1980	2.50	5.00	10.00

BYRD, CHARLIE, AND FATHER MALCOLM BOYD

Number	Title (A Side/B Side)	Yr	VG	VG+	NM
45s					
COLUMBIA					
43942	It's Christmas Again, Jesus/It's Morning, Jesus	1966	2.00	4.00	8.00
Albums					
COLUMBIA					
CL 2548 [M]	Are You Running With Me, Jesus?	1966	3.75	7.50	15.00
CL 2657 [M]	Happening Prayers for Now	1967	3.75	7.50	15.00
CS 9348 [S]	Are You Running With Me, Jesus?	1966	5.00	10.00	20.00
CS 9457 [S]	Happening Prayers for Now	1967	3.75	7.50	15.00

BYRD, CHARLIE, HERB ELLIS & BARNEY KESSEL

Number	Title (A Side/B Side)	Yr	VG	VG+	NM
Albums					
CONCORD JAZZ					
C-4	The Great Guitars	197?	3.00	6.00	12.00
C-23	The Great Guitars	197?	3.00	6.00	12.00
CJ-131	The Great Guitars at the Winery	1981	2.50	5.00	10.00
CJ-209	The Great Guitars at Charlie's Georgetown	1982	2.50	5.00	10.00
CJD-1002	Straight Tracks	1986	5.00	10.00	20.00
—Direct-to-disc recording					

BYRD, CURTIS

Number	Title (A Side/B Side)	Yr	VG	VG+	NM
45s					
CANDIX					
340	Pretty Woman/Turn Some More Lights On	1962	6.25	12.50	25.00

BYRD, DONALD

Also see THE BLACKBYRDS.

Number	Title (A Side/B Side)	Yr	VG	VG+	NM
45s					
BLUE NOTE					
XW212	Black Byrd/Slop Jar Blues	1973	—	2.50	5.00
XW309	Flight Time/Mr. Thomas	1973	—	2.50	5.00
XW445	Witch Hunt/Woman of the World	1974	—	2.50	5.00
XW510	Cristo Redentor/Black Byrd	1974	—	2.50	5.00
XW650	Think Twice/We're Together	1975	—	2.50	5.00
XW726	Change (Makes You Want to Hustle) Part 1/Part 2	1975	—	2.50	5.00
XW783	Just My Imagination (Runnin' Away with Me)/ (Fallin' Like) Dominoes	1976	—	2.50	5.00
XW965	Dancing in the Street/Onward 'Til Morning	1977	—	2.50	5.00
1763	Here Am I (Part 1)/Here Am I (Part 2)	196?	2.00	4.00	8.00
1764	Amen/Fuego	196?	2.00	4.00	8.00
1798	Gate City/Little Boy Blue	196?	2.00	4.00	8.00
1799	Bo-Blue/Ghana	196?	2.00	4.00	8.00
1853	Hush/6 M's	196?	2.00	4.00	8.00
1854	Jorgie's (Part 1)/Jorgie's (Part 2)	196?	2.00	4.00	8.00
1916	Brother Isaac/I've Longed and Searched for My Mother	196?	2.00	4.00	8.00
1973	The Emperor (Part 1)/The Emperor (Part 2)	196?	2.00	4.00	8.00
ELEKTRA					
45545	Loving You/Thank You for Funking Up My Life	1978	—	2.00	4.00
46019	Christo Redentor/Loving You	1979	—	2.00	4.00
46601	Veronica/Pretty Baby	1980	—	2.00	4.00
47168	Love Has Come Around/Love for Sale	1981	—	2.00	4.00
47241	I Love Your Love/Falling	1981	—	2.00	4.00
47419	Butterfly/I Feel Like Lovin' You	1982	—	2.00	4.00
69972	Sexy Dancer/Midnight	1982	—	2.00	4.00
VERVE					
10344	Blind Man, Blind Man/You've Been Talkin' 'Bout My Baby	1965	2.00	4.00	8.00
Albums					
AMERICAN RECORDING SOCIETY					
G-437 [M]	Modern Jazz	1957	10.00	20.00	40.00
BLUE NOTE					
BN-LA047-F	Black Byrd	1973	3.75	7.50	15.00
LO-047	Black Byrd	1981	2.00	4.00	8.00
—Reissue of LA047					
BN-LA140-G	Street Lady	1974	3.75	7.50	15.00
BN-LA368-G	Sleeping Into Tomorrow	1975	3.75	7.50	15.00
BN-LA549-G	Places and Spaces	1975	3.75	7.50	15.00
LW-549	Places and Spaces	1981	2.00	4.00	8.00
—Reissue of LA549					
BN-LA633-G	Caricatures	1976	3.75	7.50	15.00
BN-LA700-G	Donald Byrd's Best	1976	3.75	7.50	15.00
LT-991	Chant	1980	3.00	6.00	12.00
LT-1096	Creeper	1981	3.00	6.00	12.00
BLP-4007 [M]	Off to the Races	1959	30.00	60.00	120.00
—"Deep groove" version (deep indentation under label on both sides)					
BLP-4007 [M]	Off to the Races	1959	20.00	40.00	80.00
—W. 63rd St., NYC address on label					
BLP-4007 [M]	Off to the Races	1963	6.25	12.50	25.00
—"New York, USA" address on label					
BST-4007 [S]	Off to the Races	1959	20.00	40.00	80.00
—"Deep groove" version (deep indentation under label on both sides)					
BST-4007 [S]	Off to the Races	1959	15.00	30.00	60.00
—W. 63rd St., NYC address on label					
BST-4007 [S]	Off to the Races	1963	6.25	12.50	25.00
—"New York, USA" address on label					
BLP-4019 [M]	Byrd in Hand	1959	30.00	60.00	120.00
—"Deep groove" version (deep indentation under label on both sides)					
BLP-4019 [M]	Byrd in Hand	1959	20.00	40.00	80.00
—W. 63rd St., NYC address on label					
BLP-4019 [M]	Byrd in Hand	1963	6.25	12.50	25.00
—"New York, USA" address on label					
BLP-4026 [M]	Fuego	1960	30.00	60.00	120.00
—"Deep groove" version (deep indentation under label on both sides)					
BLP-4026 [M]	Fuego	1960	20.00	40.00	80.00
—W. 63rd St., NYC address on label					
BLP-4026 [M]	Fuego	1963	6.25	12.50	25.00
—"New York, USA" address on label					
BLP-4048 [M]	Byrd in Flight	1960	30.00	60.00	120.00
—"Deep groove" version (deep indentation under label on both sides)					
BLP-4048 [M]	Byrd in Flight	1960	20.00	40.00	80.00
—W. 63rd St., NYC address on label					
BLP-4048 [M]	Byrd in Flight	1963	6.25	12.50	25.00
—"New York, USA" address on label					
BLP-4060 [M]	Donald Byrd at the Half Note Café, Volume 1	1961	20.00	40.00	80.00
—W. 63rd St., NYC address on label					
BLP-4060 [M]	Donald Byrd at the Half Note Café, Volume 1	1963	6.25	12.50	25.00
—"New York, USA" address on label					
BLP-4061 [M]	Donald Byrd at the Half Note Café, Volume 2	1961	20.00	40.00	80.00
—W. 63rd St., NYC address on label					
BLP-4061 [M]	Donald Byrd at the Half Note Café, Volume 2	1963	6.25	12.50	25.00
—"New York, USA" address on label					
BLP-4075 [M]	The Cat Walk	1961	20.00	40.00	80.00
—61st St, New York address on label					
BLP-4075 [M]	The Cat Walk	1963	6.25	12.50	25.00
—"New York, USA" address on label					
BLP-4101 [M]	Royal Flush	1962	5.00	10.00	20.00
BLP-4118 [M]	Free Form	1963	5.00	10.00	20.00
BLP-4124 [M]	A New Perspective	1964	5.00	10.00	20.00
BLP-4188 [M]	I'm Tryin' to Get Home	1965	5.00	10.00	20.00
BLP-4238 [M]	Mustang!	1966	5.00	10.00	20.00
BLP-4259 [M]	Blackjack	1967	6.25	12.50	25.00
LN-10054	Street Lady	1981	2.00	4.00	8.00
—Budget-line reissue					
B1-31875	Kofi	1995	3.75	7.50	15.00
B1-36195	Electric Byrd	1996	3.75	7.50	15.00
BST-84007 [S]	Byrd in Hand	1967	3.00	6.00	12.00
—"A Division of Liberty Records" on label					
BST-84019	Byrd in Hand	198?	2.50	5.00	10.00
—"The Finest in Jazz Since 1939" reissue					
BST-84019 [S]	Byrd in Hand	1959	15.00	30.00	60.00
—W. 63rd St., NYC address on label					
BST-84019 [S]	Byrd in Hand	1963	6.25	12.50	25.00
—"New York, USA" address on label					
BST-84019 [S]	Byrd in Hand	1967	3.00	6.00	12.00
—"A Division of Liberty Records" on label					
BST-84026 [S]	Fuego	1959	15.00	30.00	60.00
—W. 63rd St., NYC address on label					
BST-84026 [S]	Fuego	1963	6.25	12.50	25.00
—"New York, USA" address on label					
BST-84026 [S]	Fuego	1967	3.00	6.00	12.00
—"A Division of Liberty Records" on label					
BST-84048 [S]	Byrd in Flight	1960	15.00	30.00	60.00
—W. 63rd St., NYC address on label					
BST-84048 [S]	Byrd in Flight	1963	6.25	12.50	25.00
—"New York, USA" address on label					
BST-84048 [S]	Byrd in Flight	1967	3.00	6.00	12.00
—"A Division of Liberty Records" on label					
BST-84060 [S]	Donald Byrd at the Half Note Café, Volume 1	1961	15.00	30.00	60.00
—W. 63rd St., NYC address on label					
BST-84060 [S]	Donald Byrd at the Half Note Café, Volume 1	1963	6.25	12.50	25.00
—"New York, USA" address on label					

Number	Title (A Side/B Side)	Yr	VG	VG+	NM
BST-84060 [S]	Donald Byrd at the Half Note Café, Volume 1	1967	3.00	6.00	12.00
—"A Division of Liberty Records" on label					
BST-84061 [S]	Donald Byrd at the Half Note Café, Volume 2	1961	15.00	30.00	60.00
—W. 63rd St., NYC address on label					
BST-84061 [S]	Donald Byrd at the Half Note Café, Volume 2	1963	6.25	12.50	25.00
—"New York, USA" address on label					
BST-84061 [S]	Donald Byrd at the Half Note Café, Volume 2	1967	3.00	6.00	12.00
—"A Division of Liberty Records" on label					
BST-84075 [S]	The Cat Walk	1961	15.00	30.00	60.00
—61st St, New York address on label					
BST-84075 [S]	The Cat Walk	1963	6.25	12.50	25.00
—"New York, USA" address on label					
BST-84075 [S]	The Cat Walk	1967	3.00	6.00	12.00
—"A Division of Liberty Records" on label					
BST-84101 [S]	Royal Flush	1962	6.25	12.50	25.00
—"New York, USA" address on label					
BST-84101 [S]	Royal Flush	1967	3.00	6.00	12.00
—"A Division of Liberty Records" on label					
BST-84118	Free Form	1986	2.50	5.00	10.00
—"The Finest in Jazz Since 1939" reissue					
BST-84118 [S]	Free Form	1963	6.25	12.50	25.00
—"New York, USA" address on label					
BST-84118 [S]	Free Form	1967	3.00	6.00	12.00
—"A Division of Liberty Records" on label					
BST-84124	A New Perspective	198?	2.50	5.00	10.00
—"The Finest in Jazz Since 1939" reissue					
BST-84124 [S]	A New Perspective	1964	6.25	12.50	25.00
—"New York, USA" address on label					
BST-84124 [S]	A New Perspective	1967	3.00	6.00	12.00
—"A Division of Liberty Records" on label					
BST-84188	I'm Tryin' to Get Home	1986	2.50	5.00	10.00
—"The Finest in Jazz Since 1939" reissue					
BST-84188 [S]	I'm Tryin' to Get Home	1965	6.25	12.50	25.00
—"New York, USA" address on label					
BST-84188 [S]	I'm Tryin' to Get Home	1967	3.00	6.00	12.00
—"A Division of Liberty Records" on label					
BST-84238 [S]	Mustang!	1966	6.25	12.50	25.00
—"New York, USA" address on label					
BST-84238 [S]	Mustang!	1967	3.00	6.00	12.00
—"A Division of Liberty Records" on label					
BST-84259 [S]	Blackjack	1967	5.00	10.00	20.00
BST-84292	Slow Drag	1968	5.00	10.00	20.00
BST-84319	Fancy Free	1969	5.00	10.00	20.00
BST-84349	Electric	1970	5.00	10.00	20.00
BST-84380	Ethiopian Nights	1972	5.00	10.00	20.00
B1-89796	Fancy Free	1993	3.75	7.50	15.00
DELMARK					
DS-407	First Flight	1990	3.00	6.00	12.00
DISCOVERY					
869	September Afternoon	198?	2.50	5.00	10.00
ELEKTRA					
6E-144	Thank You for F.U.M.L. (Funking Up My Life)	1978	2.50	5.00	10.00
6E-247	Donald Byrd and 125th St., N.Y.C.	1980	2.50	5.00	10.00
5E-531	Love Byrd	1981	2.50	5.00	10.00
60188	Words, Sounds, Colors and Shapes	1982	2.50	5.00	10.00
LANDMARK					
LLP-1516	Harlem Blues	1988	2.50	5.00	10.00
LLP-1523	Getting Down to Business	1990	3.00	6.00	12.00
SAVOY					
MG-12032 [M]	Byrd's Word	1956	25.00	50.00	100.00
MG-12064 [M]	The Jazz Message of Donald Byrd	1956	30.00	60.00	120.00
SAVOY JAZZ					
SJL-1101	Long Green	198?	2.50	5.00	10.00
SJL-1114	Star Eyes	198?	2.50	5.00	10.00
TRANSITION					
TRLP-4 [M]	Byrd's Eye View	1956	150.00	300.00	600.00
TRLP-5 [M]	Byrd Jazz	1956	150.00	300.00	600.00
TRLP-17 [M]	Byrd Blows on Beacon Hill	1956	150.00	300.00	600.00
TRIP					
5000 [(2)]	Two Sides of Donald Byrd	1974	3.75	7.50	15.00
VERVE					
V-8609 [M]	Up with Donald Byrd	1965	5.00	10.00	20.00
V6-8609 [S]	Up with Donald Byrd	1965	6.25	12.50	25.00

BYRD, DONALD; HANY MOBLEY; KENNY BURRELL

Albums

STATUS

Number	Title (A Side/B Side)	Yr	VG	VG+	NM
ST-8317 [M]	Donald Byrd, Hank Mobley & Kenny Burrell	1965	10.00	20.00	40.00

BYRD, ROBERT, AND THE BIRDIES

See BOBBY DAY.

BYRDS, THE

Also see SKIP BATTIN; THE BEEFEATERS; DAVID CROSBY; GENE CLARK; ROGER McGUINN; GRAM PARSONS.

45s

Number	Title (A Side/B Side)	Yr	VG	VG+	NM
ASYLUM					
11016	Full Circle/Long Live the King	1973	—	2.50	5.00
11019	Cowgirl in the Sand/Long Live the King	1973	—	2.50	5.00
COLUMBIA					
43271	Mr. Tambourine Man/I Knew I'd Want You	1965	3.75	7.50	15.00
43271 [DJ]	Mr. Tambourine Man (same on both sides)	1965	37.50	75.00	150.00
—Red vinyl promo					
43271 [PS]	Mr. Tambourine Man	1965	75.00	150.00	300.00
—Promo-only sleeve promoting the Byrds' appeance on the TV show Hullabaloo					
43332	All I Really Want to Do/I'll Feel a Whole Lot Better	1965	3.75	7.50	15.00
43332 [DJ]	All I Really Want to Do (same on both sides)	1965	25.00	50.00	100.00
—Red vinyl promo					
43332 [DJ]	I'll Feel a Whole Lot Better (same on both sides)	1965	30.00	60.00	120.00
—Red vinyl promo					
43424	Turn! Turn! Turn! (To Everything There Is a Season)/She Don't Care About Time	1965	3.75	7.50	15.00
43424 [DJ]	Turn! Turn! Turn! (To Everything There Is a Season) (same on both sides)	1965	25.00	50.00	100.00
—Red vinyl promo					
43501	It Won't Be Wrong/Set You Free This Time	1965	3.00	6.00	12.00
43578	Eight Miles High/Why	1966	3.00	6.00	12.00
43578 [PS]	Eight Miles High/Why	1966	15.00	30.00	60.00
43702	5 D (Fifth Dimension)/Captain Soul	1966	3.00	6.00	12.00
43766	Mr. Spaceman/What's Happening	1966	3.00	6.00	12.00
43987	So You Want to Be a Rock 'N' Roll Star/Everybody's Been Burned	1967	3.00	6.00	12.00
44054	My Back Pages/Renaissance Fair	1967	3.00	6.00	12.00
44157	Have You Seen Her Face/Don't Make Waves	1967	2.50	5.00	10.00
44157 [PS]	Have You Seen Her Face/Don't Make Waves	1967	10.00	20.00	40.00
44230	Lady Friend/Old John Robertson	1967	2.50	5.00	10.00
44362	Goin' Back/Change Is Now	1967	2.00	4.00	8.00
44499	Artificial Energy/You Ain't Going Nowhere	1968	2.00	4.00	8.00
44643	Pretty Boy Floyd/I Am a Pilgrim	1968	2.00	4.00	8.00
44746	Drug Store Truck Drivin' Man/Bad Night at the Whiskey	1969	2.00	4.00	8.00
44868	Lay Lady Lay/Old Blue	1969	2.00	4.00	8.00
44990	Ballad of Easy Rider/Oil in My Lamp	1969	2.50	5.00	10.00
44990	Wasn't Born to Follow/Ballad of Easy Rider	1969	2.00	4.00	8.00
45071	Jesus Is Just Alright/It's All Over Now, Baby Blue	1970	2.00	4.00	8.00
45259	Chestnut Mare/Just a Season	1970	—	3.00	6.00
45440	Glory Glory/Citizen Kane	1971	—	3.00	6.00
45514	America's Great National Pastime/Farther Along	1971	—	3.00	6.00
45761	Jesus Is Just Alright/Mr. Spaceman	1973	2.50	5.00	10.00
JZSP 116476 [DJ]	He Was a Friend of Mine (same on both sides)	1966	10.00	20.00	40.00

7-Inch Extended Plays

COLUMBIA/SCHOLASTIC

Number	Title (A Side/B Side)	Yr	VG	VG+	NM
CV 10287	Lover of the Bayou/So You Want to Be a Rock and Roll Star//Chimes of Freedom/Goin' Back	1971	7.50	15.00	30.00
CV 10287 [PS]	The Byrds	1971	7.50	15.00	30.00

Albums

Number	Title (A Side/B Side)	Yr	VG	VG+	NM
ASYLUM					
SD 5058	Byrds	1973	3.00	6.00	12.00
COLUMBIA					
CL 2372 [M]	Mr. Tambourine Man	1965	10.00	20.00	40.00
—"Guaranteed High Fidelity" on label					
CL 2372 [M]	Mr. Tambourine Man	1966	7.50	15.00	30.00
—"360 Sound Mono" on label					
CL 2454 [M]	Turn! Turn! Turn!	1965	7.50	15.00	30.00
CL 2549 [M]	Fifth Dimension (5D)	1966	7.50	15.00	30.00
CL 2642 [M]	Younger Than Yesterday	1967	7.50	15.00	30.00
CL 2716 [M]	The Byrds' Greatest Hits	1967	7.50	15.00	30.00
CL 2775 [M]	The Notorious Byrd Brothers	1968	12.50	25.00	50.00
CS 9172 [S]	Mr. Tambourine Man	1965	10.00	20.00	40.00
—Red label, "360 Sound" in black					
CS 9172 [S]	Mr. Tambourine Man	1966	6.25	12.50	25.00
—Red label, "360 Sound" in white					
CS 9172 [S]	Mr. Tambourine Man	1971	2.50	5.00	10.00
—Orange label					
PC 9172 [S]	Mr. Tambourine Man	198?	2.00	4.00	8.00
—Reissue with new prefix					
CS 9254 [S]	Turn! Turn! Turn!	1965	6.25	12.50	25.00
—Red "360 Sound" label					
CS 9254 [S]	Turn! Turn! Turn!	1971	2.50	5.00	10.00
—Orange label					
PC 9254 [S]	Turn! Turn! Turn!	198?	2.00	4.00	8.00
—Reissue with new prefix					
CS 9349 [S]	Fifth Dimension (5D)	1966	6.25	12.50	25.00
—Red "360 Sound" label					
CS 9349 [S]	Fifth Dimension (5D)	1971	2.50	5.00	10.00
—Orange label					
PC 9349 [S]	Fifth Dimension (5D)	198?	2.00	4.00	8.00
—Reissue with new prefix					
CS 9442 [S]	Younger Than Yesterday	1967	6.25	12.50	25.00
—Red "360 Sound" label					
CS 9442 [S]	Younger Than Yesterday	1971	2.50	5.00	10.00
—Orange label					
PC 9442 [S]	Younger Than Yesterday	198?	2.00	4.00	8.00
—Reissue with new prefix					
CS 9516 [S]	The Byrds' Greatest Hits	1967	5.00	10.00	20.00
—Red "360 Sound" label					
KCS 9516 [S]	The Byrds' Greatest Hits	1971	2.50	5.00	10.00
—Orange label					
PC 9516 [S]	The Byrds' Greatest Hits	197?	2.00	4.00	8.00
—Reissue with another new prefix					
CS 9575 [S]	The Notorious Byrd Brothers	1968	5.00	10.00	20.00
—Red "360 Sound" label					
CS 9575 [S]	The Notorious Byrd Brothers	1971	2.50	5.00	10.00
—Orange label					
PC 9575 [S]	The Notorious Byrd Brothers	198?	2.00	4.00	8.00
—Reissue with new prefix					
CS 9670 [M]	Sweetheart of the Rodeo	1968	25.00	50.00	100.00
—"Special Mono Radio Station Copy" with white label					
CS 9670 [S]	Sweetheart of the Rodeo	1968	5.00	10.00	20.00
—Red "360 Sound" label					
CS 9670 [S]	Sweetheart of the Rodeo	1971	2.50	5.00	10.00
—Orange label					
PC 9670 [S]	Sweetheart of the Rodeo	198?	2.00	4.00	8.00
—Reissue with new prefix					
CS 9755 [S]	Dr. Byrds and Mr. Hyde	1969	5.00	10.00	20.00
—Red "360 Sound" label					
CS 9755 [S]	Dr. Byrds and Mr. Hyde	1971	2.50	5.00	10.00
—Orange label					
PC 9755 [S]	Dr. Byrds and Mr. Hyde	198?	2.00	4.00	8.00
—Reissue with new prefix					
CS 9942 [S]	Ballad of Easy Rider	1969	5.00	10.00	20.00
—Red "360 Sound" label					
CS 9942 [S]	Ballad of Easy Rider	1971	2.50	5.00	10.00
—Orange label					
PC 9942	Ballad of Easy Rider	1984	2.00	4.00	8.00
—Reissue with new prefix					

Number	Title (A Side/B Side)	Yr	VG	VG+	NM
G 30127 [(2)]	The Byrds (Untitled)	1970	5.00	10.00	20.00
—With "Kathleen" listed on back cover (it is not on the set)					
G 30127 [(2)]	The Byrds (Untitled)	1970	3.75	7.50	15.00
—Without "Kathleen" listed on back cover					
KC 30640	Byrdmaniax	1971	3.00	6.00	12.00
C 31050	Farther Along	1971	3.00	6.00	12.00
C 31795	The Best of the Byrds (Greatest Hits, Volume II)	197?	2.50	5.00	10.00
—Reissue with new prefix					
KC 31795	The Best of the Byrds (Greatest Hits, Volume II)	1972	3.00	6.00	12.00
PC 31795	The Best of the Byrds (Greatest Hits, Volume II)	198?	2.00	4.00	8.00
—Reissue with another new prefix					
C 32183	Preflyte	197?	2.50	5.00	10.00
—Reissue with new prefix					
KC 32183	Preflyte	1973	3.00	6.00	12.00
—Reissue of Together LP					
CG 33645 [(2)]	Mr. Tambourine Man/Turn! Turn! Turn!	1976	3.75	7.50	15.00
PC 36293	The Byrds Play Dylan	1980	2.50	5.00	10.00
FC 37335	The Original Singles Volume 1 (1965-1967)	1981	2.50	5.00	10.00
PC 37335	The Original Singles Volume 1 (1965-1967)	1985	2.00	4.00	8.00
—Budget-line reissue					
PAIR					
PDL2-1040 [(2)]	The Very Best of the Byrds	1986	3.00	6.00	12.00
RE-FLYTE					
MH-70318	Never Before	1987	3.00	6.00	12.00
—Released by Muuray Hill Records via mail order					
RHINO					
R1-70244	In the Beginning	1988	2.50	5.00	10.00
SUNDAZED					
LP 5057	Mr. Tambourine Man	1999	3.75	7.50	15.00
—Reissue on 180-gram vinyl					
LP 5058	Turn! Turn! Turn!	1999	3.75	7.50	15.00
—Reissue on 180-gram vinyl					
LP 5059	Fifth Dimension	1999	3.75	7.50	15.00
—Reissue on 180-gram vinyl					
LP 5060	Younger Than Yesterday	1999	3.75	7.50	15.00
—Reissue on 180-gram vinyl					
LP 5061	Sanctuary	2000	3.00	6.00	12.00
TOGETHER					
ST-1-1001	Preflyte	1969	6.25	12.50	25.00

BYRNES, EDD

45s

Number	Title (A Side/B Side)	Yr	VG	VG+	NM
WARNER BROS.					
5047 [M]	Kookie, Kookie (Lend Me Your Comb)/You're the Top	1959	5.00	10.00	20.00
—A-side by Edward Byrnes and Connie Stevens; B-side by Edward Byrnes					
5047 [PS]	Kookie, Kookie (Lend Me Your Comb)/You're the Top	1959	10.00	20.00	40.00
—A-side by Edward Byrnes and Connie Stevens; B-side by Edward Byrnes					
S-5047 [S]	Kookie, Kookie (Lend Me Your Comb)/You're the Top	1959	12.50	25.00	50.00
5087	Like I Love You/Kookie's Mad Pad	1959	4.00	8.00	16.00
—Artist credit: "Edd Byrnes and Friend"					
5087 [PS]	Like I Love You/Kookie's Mad Pad	1959	10.00	20.00	40.00
—Artist credit: "Edd Byrnes and Friend"					
5114	Kookie's Love Song Part 1/Kookie's Love Song Part 2	1959	4.00	8.00	16.00
—With the Mary Kay Trio					
5114 [PS]	Kookie's Love Song Part 1/Kookie's Love Song Part 2	1959	10.00	20.00	40.00
—With the Mary Kay Trio					
5121	Yulesville/Lonely Christmas	1959	4.00	8.00	16.00
5121 [PS]	Yulesville/Lonely Christmas	1959	10.00	20.00	40.00

7-Inch Extended Plays

Number	Title (A Side/B Side)	Yr	VG	VG+	NM
WARNER BROS.					
EA 1309	Hot Broad Rock/I Don't Dig You, Kookie//Saturday Night on Sunset Strip/The Kookie Cha-Cha-Cha	1959	12.50	25.00	50.00
EA 1309 [PS]	Kookie	1959	12.50	25.00	50.00

Albums

Number	Title (A Side/B Side)	Yr	VG	VG+	NM
WARNER BROS.					
W 1309 [M]	Kookie	1959	25.00	50.00	100.00
WS 1309 [S]	Kookie	1959	30.00	60.00	120.00
W/WS 1309	Kookie Bonus Photo	1959	12.50	25.00	50.00

BYRON, LORD DOUGLAS

45s

Number	Title (A Side/B Side)	Yr	VG	VG+	NM
DOT					
16685	Surfin' Santa/The Drink That Makes You Shrink	1964	7.50	15.00	30.00
UNION					
505	Big Bad Ho-Dad/Coffee House	1962	10.00	20.00	40.00
—B-side by the Continentals					

C

C.A. QUINTET, THE

Number	Title (A Side/B Side)	Yr	VG	VG+	NM
45s					
CANDY FLOSS					
102	Smooth as Silk/Dr. of Philosophy	1968	20.00	40.00	80.00
FALCON					
70	Mickey's Monkey/I Want You to Love Me Girl	1967	25.00	50.00	100.00
71	Blow to My Soul/She's Got to Be True	1967	25.00	50.00	100.00
Albums					
CANDY FLOSS					
7764	A Trip Through Hell	1969	500.00	1000.	1500.
SUNDAZED					
LP-5037 [(2)]	Trip Thru Hell	1997	3.75	7.50	15.00

C.C.S.

Number	Title (A Side/B Side)	Yr	VG	VG+	NM
45s					
BELL					
45396	The Band Played the Boogie/Hang It On Me	1973	—	2.00	4.00
RAK					
4501	Whole Lotta Love/Boom Boom	1971	—	3.00	6.00
4502	Walking/Lookin' for Fun	1971	—	2.50	5.00
4507	Save the World/The Tap Turns On the Water	1972	—	2.50	5.00
Albums					
RAK					
Z 30559	Whole Lotta Love	1971	5.00	10.00	20.00
KZ 31569	C.C.S.	1972	5.00	10.00	20.00

C.K. STRONG

Number	Title (A Side/B Side)	Yr	VG	VG+	NM
45s					
EPIC					
5-10534	Stormbird/Daddy	1969	2.50	5.00	10.00
Albums					
EPIC					
BN 26473	C.K. Strong	1969	5.00	10.00	20.00

C.L. AND THE PICTURES

Also see CURTIS LEE.

Number	Title (A Side/B Side)	Yr	VG	VG+	NM
45s					
DUNES					
2010	I'm Asking Forgiveness/Let's Take a Ride	1962	6.25	12.50	25.00
2017	Afraid/Mary Go 'Round	1962	6.25	12.50	25.00
2023	I'm Sorry/That's What's Happening	1963	6.25	12.50	25.00
JAMIE					
1398	You Really Slipped One By Me/The Same People (That You Meet Going Up, You Meet Coming Down)	1971	3.75	7.50	15.00
—As "C.L. Weldon and the Pictures"					
MONUMENT					
854	He'll Only Hurt You/Talking About My Baby	1964	5.00	10.00	20.00
888	Could This Be Magic/Yolanda	1965	5.00	10.00	20.00
958	Baby, Not Now/Jigsaw Puzzle	1966	5.00	10.00	20.00

C-NOTES, THE

Number	Title (A Side/B Side)	Yr	VG	VG+	NM
45s					
EVERLAST					
5005	On Your Mark/From Now On	1957	12.50	25.00	50.00

C.O.D.'S, THE

Number	Title (A Side/B Side)	Yr	VG	VG+	NM
45s					
KELLMAC					
1003	Michael/Cry No More	1965	3.00	6.00	12.00
1005	Pretty Baby/I'm a Good Guy	1965	5.00	10.00	20.00
1012	Coming Back Girl/It Must Be Love	1966	25.00	50.00	100.00

C-QUENTS, THE

Number	Title (A Side/B Side)	Yr	VG	VG+	NM
45s					
CAPETOWN					
4027	All I Want For Christmas Is You/Merry Christmas, Baby	1962	75.00	150.00	300.00
ESSICA					
4	Dearest One/It's You and Me	196?	7.50	15.00	30.00

CABINEERS, THE

Number	Title (A Side/B Side)	Yr	VG	VG+	NM
45s					
PRESTIGE					
904	Each Time/(B-side unknown)	1952	75.00	150.00	300.00
917	Baby Mine/(B-side unknown)	1953	100.00	200.00	400.00

CABOT, SEBASTIAN

Number	Title (A Side/B Side)	Yr	VG	VG+	NM
45s					
MGM					
13650	It Ain't Me Babe/And Mostly They Sing	1966	3.75	7.50	15.00
Albums					
MGM					
E-4431 [M]	Sebastian Cabot, Actor; Bob Dylan, Poet: A Dramatic Reading with Music	1967	7.50	15.00	30.00
SE-4431 [S]	Sebastian Cabot, Actor; Bob Dylan, Poet: A Dramatic Reading with Music	1967	10.00	20.00	40.00

CACTUS

With Tim Bogert and Carmen Appice, ex-VANILLA FUDGE.

Number	Title (A Side/B Side)	Yr	VG	VG+	NM
45s					
ATCO					
6782	Brother Bill/You Can't Judge a Book By Its Cover	1971	2.00	4.00	8.00
6811	Long Tall Sally/Rock 'n' Roll Christian	1971	2.00	4.00	8.00
6842	Token Chokin'/Alaska	1971	2.00	4.00	8.00
6872	The Booger Man/Cold Bear	1972	—	3.00	6.00
6901	Bringing Me Down/Bad Mother Boogie	1972	—	3.00	6.00
Albums					
ATCO					
SD 33-340	Cactus	1970	5.00	10.00	20.00
SD 33-356	One Way...Or Another	1971	5.00	10.00	20.00
SD 33-377	Restrictions	1971	5.00	10.00	20.00
SD 7011	'Ot 'N' Sweaty	1972	5.00	10.00	20.00

CADETS, THE

Also see THE JACKS.

Number	Title (A Side/B Side)	Yr	VG	VG+	NM
45s					
JAN-LAR					
102	Don't/Car Crash	1960	15.00	30.00	60.00
MODERN					
956	Don't Be Angry/I Cried	1955	12.50	25.00	50.00
960	Rollin' Stone/Fine Lookin' Baby	1955	12.50	25.00	50.00
963	I Cried/Fine Lookin' Baby	1955	10.00	20.00	40.00
969	Annie Met Henry/So Will I	1955	10.00	20.00	40.00
971	Do You Wanna Rock/If It Is Wrong	1956	25.00	50.00	100.00
985	Church Bells May Ring/Heartbreak Hotel	1956	10.00	20.00	40.00
994	Stranded in the Jungle/I Want You	1956	10.00	20.00	40.00
1000	I Got Loaded/Dancin' Dan	1956	10.00	20.00	40.00
1006	Fools Rush In/I'll Be Spinning	1956	10.00	20.00	40.00
1012	Heaven Help Me/Love Bandit	1957	10.00	20.00	40.00
1017	Wiggle Waggle Woo/You Belong to Me	1957	10.00	20.00	40.00
1019	Pretty Evey/Rum, Jamaica Rum	1957	12.50	25.00	50.00
—As "Aaron Collins and the Cadets"					
1024	Hands Across the Table/Love Can Do Most Anything	1957	10.00	20.00	40.00
—As "Will Jones and the Cadets"					
1026	Ring Chimes/Baby Ya Know	1957	10.00	20.00	40.00
SHERWOOD					
211	One More Chance/I'm Looking for a Job	1960	12.50	25.00	50.00
Albums					
CROWN					
CST-370 [R]	The Cadets	1963	25.00	50.00	100.00
CLP-5015 [M]	Rockin' 'n' Reelin'	1957	62.50	125.00	250.00
—Black label					
CLP-5370 [M]	The Cadets	1963	37.50	75.00	150.00
MODERN					
LPM-1215 [M]	Rockin' 'n' Reelin'	1956	—	—	—
—Canceled					
RELIC					
5025	The Cadets' Greatest Hits	197?	3.00	6.00	12.00

CADILLACS, THE

Number	Title (A Side/B Side)	Yr	VG	VG+	NM
45s					
ARTIC					
101	Fool/The Right Kind of Lovin'	1964	25.00	50.00	100.00
CAPITOL					
4825	Groovy, Groovy Love/White Gardenia	1962	5.00	10.00	20.00
4935	La Bomba/I Saw You	1963	5.00	10.00	20.00
—As "Bobby Ray and the Cadillacs"					
JOSIE					
765	Gloria/I Wonder Why	1954	175.00	350.00	700.00
765	Gloria/I Wonder Why	196?	6.25	12.50	25.00
—Reissue with 1960s label					
769	Wishing Well/I Want to Know About Love	1954	125.00	250.00	500.00
773	Sympathy/No Chance	1955	25.00	50.00	100.00
778	Widow Lady/Down the Road	1955	50.00	100.00	200.00
785	Speedo/Let Me Explain	1955	15.00	30.00	60.00
792	Zoom/You Are	1956	12.50	25.00	50.00
798	Woe Is Me/Betty My Love	1956	12.50	25.00	50.00
805	The Girl I Love/That's All I Need	1956	25.00	50.00	100.00
807	Rudolph the Red-Nosed Reindeer/Shack-a Doo	1956	10.00	20.00	40.00
812	Sugar Sugar/About That Girl Named Lou	1957	10.00	20.00	40.00
820	My Girl Friend/Broken Heart	1957	12.50	25.00	50.00
821	Lucy/Hurry Home	1957	10.00	20.00	40.00
—As "The Original Cadillacs"					
829	Buzz-Buzz-Buzz/Yes, Yes Baby	1957	10.00	20.00	40.00
—As "The Original Cadillacs"					
836	Speedo Is Back/A' Looka Here	1958	7.50	15.00	30.00
842	Holy Smoke Baby/I Want to Know	1958	7.50	15.00	30.00
846	Peek-a-Book/Oh, Oh Lolita	1958	7.50	15.00	30.00
857	Copy Cat/Jay Walker	1959	7.50	15.00	30.00
861	Cool It Fool/Please Mr. Johnson	1959	7.50	15.00	30.00
866 [M]	Romeo/Always My Darling	1959	7.50	15.00	30.00
870	Dumbell/Bad Dan McGoon	1959	7.50	15.00	30.00
876	Tell Me Today/It's Love	1960	7.50	15.00	30.00
883	That's Why/The Boogie Man	1960	7.50	15.00	30.00
915	Wayward Wanderer/I'll Never Let You Go	1963	5.00	10.00	20.00
—As "The Original Cadillacs"					
JUBILEE					
8010 [S]	Romeo/Always My Darling	1959	15.00	30.00	60.00
LANA					
118	Speedo/Baby It's All Right	196?	—	3.00	6.00
—Reissue					
119	Gloria/Hey Bob E Re Bob	196?	—	3.00	6.00
—Reissue					
MERCURY					
71738	I'm Willing/Thrill Me So	1961	25.00	50.00	100.00
POLYDOR					
14031	Deep in the Heart of the Ghetto (Part 1)/Deep in the Heart of the Ghetto (Part 2)	1969	3.75	7.50	15.00
—As "The Original Cadillacs"					
ROULETTE					
4654	Let's Get Together/She's My Connection	1965	5.00	10.00	20.00
SMASH					
1712	You Are to Blame/What to Bet	1961	6.25	12.50	25.00
Albums					
HARLEM HIT PARADE					
5009	Cruisin' with the Cadillacs	197?	2.50	5.00	10.00

Number	Title (A Side/B Side)	Yr	VG	VG+	NM
JUBILEE					
JGM-1045 [M]	The Fabulous Cadillacs	1957	100.00	200.00	400.00
—*Blue label*					
JGM-1045 [M]	The Fabulous Cadillacs	1959	62.50	125.00	250.00
—*Flat black label*					
JGM-1045 [M]	The Fabulous Cadillacs	1960	25.00	50.00	100.00
—*Glossy black label*					
JGM-1089 [M]	The Crazy Cadillacs	1959	75.00	150.00	300.00
—*Flat black label*					
JGM-1089 [M]	The Crazy Cadillacs	1960	25.00	50.00	100.00
—*Glossy black label*					
JGM-5009 [M]	Twisting with the Cadillacs	1962	50.00	100.00	200.00
MURRAY HILL					
1195	The Very Best of the Cadillacs	198?	3.75	7.50	15.00
1285 [(5)]	The Cadillacs	198?	10.00	20.00	40.00
—*Box set*					

CADILLACS, THE/ THE ORIOLES

Also see each artist's individual listings.

Albums

Number	Title (A Side/B Side)	Yr	VG	VG+	NM
JUBILEE					
JGM-1117 [M]	The Cadillacs Meet the Orioles	1961	50.00	100.00	200.00

CAESAR AND CLEO

See SONNY AND CHER.

CAGLE, WADE

45s

Number	Title (A Side/B Side)	Yr	VG	VG+	NM
SUN					
360	Groovy Train/Highland Rock	1961	6.25	12.50	25.00

CAHPERONES, THE

See THE CHAPERONES.

CAIN

Albums

Number	Title (A Side/B Side)	Yr	VG	VG+	NM
A.S.I.					
204	A Pound of Flesh	1974	15.00	30.00	60.00
214	Stinger	1975	10.00	20.00	40.00

CAIOLA, AL

45s

Number	Title (A Side/B Side)	Yr	VG	VG+	NM
AVALANCHE					
XW290	And I Love You So/Live and Let Die	1973	—	2.50	5.00
RCA VICTOR					
47-5252	Anna/Cachita	1953	3.75	7.50	15.00
47-5315	Pianola/The Donkey Serenade	1953	3.75	7.50	15.00
47-5400	Cumana/El Cumbanchero	1953	3.75	7.50	15.00
47-5949	Steel Guitar Rag/Stardust	1954	3.75	7.50	15.00
47-6101	A Song of India (Mambo)/Rapid Fire (Samba)	1955	3.75	7.50	15.00
47-6404	Antilles/Corsage (Her First Corsage)	1955	3.75	7.50	15.00
REGENT					
7500	Flamenco Love/(B-side unknown)	1956	3.75	7.50	15.00
UNITED ARTISTS					
261	The Magnificent Seven/The Lonely Rebel	1960	3.00	6.00	12.00
302	Bonanza/Bounty Hunter	1961	2.50	5.00	10.00
347	Autumn in Cheyenne/Speak Low	1961	2.00	4.00	8.00
400	Rollerama/Stampede	1962	2.00	4.00	8.00
438	Experiment in Terror/Sergeants Three March	1962	2.50	5.00	10.00
499	Katusha/Love Is Like Champagne	1962	2.00	4.00	8.00
545	Guitar Boogie/Kalinka	1963	2.00	4.00	8.00
577	Mexicali Rose/Mexicali Rose	1963	2.00	4.00	8.00
586	Gunsmoke/Ciao	1963	2.50	5.00	10.00
608	James Bond Theme/(B-side unknown)	1963	3.00	6.00	12.00
646	La Donna Nel Mondo/Redigo	1963	2.00	4.00	8.00
677	Burke's Law Theme/Smoke Signals	1963	2.50	5.00	10.00
711	From Russia with Love/Mexican Summer	1964	2.50	5.00	10.00
736	The Guns of Navarone/Theme from A Summer Place	1964	—	—	—
—*Canceled*					
740	Theme from The World of the Brothers Grimm/ Baby Elephant Walk	1964	—	—	—
—*Canceled*					
747	On the Trail/Wheels West	1964	2.00	4.00	8.00
787	Tuff Guitar/Hound Dog	1964	2.00	4.00	8.00
814	Brash Brannigan/Hunky Funky	1965	2.00	4.00	8.00
855	Gabrielle/Ring of Fire	1965	2.00	4.00	8.00
882	Forget Domani/Glory Boys	1965	2.00	4.00	8.00
932	Theme from "The Trials of O'Brien"/Walkin' Down the Line	1965	2.00	4.00	8.00
983	Batman Theme/Karelia	1966	3.00	6.00	12.00
50037	Duel at Diablo/Sugar Me Sweet	1966	—	3.00	6.00
50070	Hill Country Theme/Quedate Un Rato Mas	1966	—	3.00	6.00
50098	Return of the Seven/The Rat Patrol	1966	2.00	4.00	8.00
50159	Eight on the Lam/Sailor from Gibraltar	1967	—	3.00	6.00
50214	Tiny Bubbles/Stag or Drag	1967	—	3.00	6.00
50231	Never Pick Up a Stranger/Sleep Walk	1967	—	3.00	6.00
50237	Bossa Nova Noel/Holiday on Skis	1967	2.50	5.00	10.00
—*With Riz Ortolani*					
50252	Here Is Where I Belong/The Sound of Music	1968	—	2.50	5.00
50288	Scalphunter's Theme/Theme for November	1968	—	2.50	5.00
50471	The High Chaparral/Master Jack	1969	—	3.00	6.00
50519	Infinity Blue/Soul American	1969	—	2.50	5.00
50571	Stiletto/Guitar Woman	1969	—	2.50	5.00

Albums

Number	Title (A Side/B Side)	Yr	VG	VG+	NM
ATCO					
33-117 [M]	Music for Space Squirrels	1960	6.25	12.50	25.00
SD 33-117 [S]	Music for Space Squirrels	1960	7.50	15.00	30.00
AVALANCHE					
AV-LA058-F	The Magnificent Seven Ride '73	1973	2.50	5.00	10.00
9201	The Magnificent Seven	1972	3.00	6.00	12.00
AVCO EMBASSY					
33019	Bonanza Guitars/50 Years of the Greatest Country Music	1971	2.50	5.00	10.00
BAINBRIDGE					
1010	Soft Guitars	198?	2.00	4.00	8.00
1023	Italian Guitars	198?	2.00	4.00	8.00
1030	Guitar of Plenty	198?	2.00	4.00	8.00
CHANCELLOR					
CHL-5008 [M]	Great Pickin'	1960	6.25	12.50	25.00
CHS-5008 [S]	Great Pickin'	1960	7.50	15.00	30.00
PICKWICK					
SPC-3034	Italian Style	196?	3.00	6.00	12.00
RCA CAMDEN					
CAL-710 [M]	The Guitar Style of Al Caiola	1962	3.00	6.00	12.00
CAS-710 [S]	The Guitar Style of Al Caiola	1962	3.75	7.50	15.00
CAS-2569	Music from "The Godfather"	1972	2.50	5.00	10.00
RCA VICTOR					
LPM-2031 [M]	High Strung	1959	6.25	12.50	25.00
LSP-2031 [S]	High Strung	1959	7.50	15.00	30.00
ROULETTE					
R 25108 [M]	Salute Italia	1960	5.00	10.00	20.00
SR 25108 [S]	Salute Italia	1960	6.25	12.50	25.00
SR-42008	Roman Guitar	1968	2.50	5.00	10.00
SAVOY					
MG-12033 [M]	Deep in a Dream	1955	10.00	20.00	40.00
MG-12057 [M]	Serenade in Blue	1956	10.00	20.00	40.00
SUNSET					
SUS-5292	Guitar in Love	1970	2.50	5.00	10.00
TIME					
S-2000 [S]	Percussion and Guitars	1960	6.25	12.50	25.00
S-2006 [S]	Percussion Espanol	1960	6.25	12.50	25.00
S-2026 [S]	Percussion Espanol, Vol. 2	1960	6.25	12.50	25.00
S-2039 [S]	Spanish Guitars	1960	6.25	12.50	25.00
S-2101 [S]	Gershwin and Guitars	1961	6.25	12.50	25.00
52000 [M]	Percussion and Guitars	1960	5.00	10.00	20.00
52006 [M]	Percussion Espanol	1960	5.00	10.00	20.00
52026 [M]	Percussion Espanol, Vol. 2	1960	5.00	10.00	20.00
52039 [M]	Spanish Guitars	1960	5.00	10.00	20.00
52101 [M]	Gershwin and Guitars	1961	5.00	10.00	20.00
UNITED ARTISTS					
UAL-3133 [M]	The Magnificent Seven	1960	5.00	10.00	20.00
UAL-3142 [M]	Golden Instrumental Hits	1961	3.00	6.00	12.00
UAL-3161 [M]	Hit Instrumentals from TV Westerns	1961	3.75	7.50	15.00
UAL-3180 [M]	Solid Gold Guitar	1962	3.00	6.00	12.00
UAL-3228 [M]	Midnight Dance Party	1962	3.00	6.00	12.00
UAL-3240 [M]	Golden Guitar	1962	3.00	6.00	12.00
UAL-3255 [M]	City Guy Goes Country	1963	3.00	6.00	12.00
UAL-3256 [M]	Acapulco 1922 and The Lonely Bull	1963	3.00	6.00	12.00
UAL-3263 [M]	Paradise Village	1963	3.00	6.00	12.00
UAL-3276 [M]	Ciao	1963	3.00	6.00	12.00
UAL-3280 [M]	Give Me the Simple Life	1963	3.00	6.00	12.00
UAL-3299 [M]	Cleopatra and All That Jazz	1963	6.25	12.50	25.00
UAL-3310 [M]	The Best of Al Caiola	1964	3.00	6.00	12.00
UAL-3330 [M]	50 Fabulous Guitar Favorites	1964	3.00	6.00	12.00
UAL-3354 [M]	50 Fabulous Italian Favorites	1964	3.00	6.00	12.00
UAL-3362 [M]	On the Trail	1964	3.00	6.00	12.00
UAL-3389 [M]	Tuff Guitar	1965	3.00	6.00	12.00
UAL-3403 [M]	Guitar for Lovers	1965	3.00	6.00	12.00
UAL-3405 [M]	Have Guitar Will Travel	1965	3.00	6.00	12.00
UAL-3418 [M]	Solid Gold Guitar Goes Hawaiian	1965	3.00	6.00	12.00
UAL-3435 [M]	Sounds for Spies and Private Eyes	1965	3.75	7.50	15.00
UAL-3454 [M]	Tuff Guitar English Style	1966	3.00	6.00	12.00
UAS-6133 [S]	The Magnificent Seven	1960	6.25	12.50	25.00
UAS-6142 [S]	Golden Instrumental Hits	1961	3.75	7.50	15.00
UAS-6161 [S]	Hit Instrumentals from TV Westerns	1961	5.00	10.00	20.00
UAS-6180 [S]	Solid Gold Guitar	1962	3.75	7.50	15.00
UAS-6228 [S]	Midnight Dance Party	1962	3.75	7.50	15.00
UAS-6240 [S]	Golden Guitar	1962	3.75	7.50	15.00
UAS-6255 [S]	City Guy Goes Country	1963	3.75	7.50	15.00
UAS-6256 [S]	Acapulco 1922 and The Lonely Bull	1963	3.75	7.50	15.00
UAS-6263 [S]	Paradise Village	1963	3.75	7.50	15.00
UAS-6276 [S]	Ciao	1963	3.75	7.50	15.00
UAS-6280 [S]	Give Me the Simple Life	1963	3.75	7.50	15.00
UAS-6299 [S]	Cleopatra and All That Jazz	1963	7.50	15.00	30.00
UAS-6310 [S]	The Best of Al Caiola	1964	3.75	7.50	15.00
UAS-6330 [S]	50 Fabulous Guitar Favorites	1964	3.75	7.50	15.00
UAS-6354 [S]	50 Fabulous Italian Favorites	1964	3.75	7.50	15.00
UAS-6362 [S]	On the Trail	1964	3.75	7.50	15.00
UAS-6389 [S]	Tuff Guitar	1965	3.75	7.50	15.00
UAS-6403 [S]	Guitar for Lovers	1965	3.75	7.50	15.00
UAS-6405 [S]	Have Guitar Will Travel	1965	3.75	7.50	15.00
UAS-6418 [S]	Solid Gold Guitar Goes Hawaiian	1965	3.75	7.50	15.00
UAS-6435 [S]	Sounds for Spies and Private Eyes	1965	5.00	10.00	20.00
UAS-6454 [S]	Tuff Guitar English Style	1966	3.75	7.50	15.00
UAS-6712	Let the Sunshine In	1969	2.50	5.00	10.00

CAKE, THE

45s

Number	Title (A Side/B Side)	Yr	VG	VG+	NM
DECCA					
32179	Mockingbird/Baby That's Me	1967	2.50	5.00	10.00
32212	You Can Have Him/I Know	1967	2.50	5.00	10.00
32235	Fire Fly/Rainbow Wood	1967	2.50	5.00	10.00
32347	PT 280/Have You Heard the News 'Bout Miss Molly	1968	2.50	5.00	10.00

Albums

Number	Title (A Side/B Side)	Yr	VG	VG+	NM
DECCA					
DL 4927 [M]	The Cake	1967	5.00	10.00	20.00
DL 74927 [S]	The Cake	1967	6.25	12.50	25.00
DL 75039	A Slice of the Cake	1968	6.25	12.50	25.00

CALDWELL, LOUISE HARRISON

Albums

Number	Title (A Side/B Side)	Yr	VG	VG+	NM
RECAR					
2012 [M]	All About the Beatles	1965	50.00	100.00	200.00
—With insert					
2012 [M]	All About the Beatles	1965	37.50	75.00	150.00
—Without insert					

CALE, J.J.

45s

Number	Title (A Side/B Side)	Yr	VG	VG+	NM
LIBERTY					
55840	Dick Tracy/It's a Go-Go Place	1965	3.75	7.50	15.00
55881	Outside Lookin' In/In Our Time	1966	3.75	7.50	15.00
55931	After Midnight/Slow Motion	1966	3.75	7.50	15.00
MCA					
51095	Carry On/Deep Dark Dungeon	1981	—	2.00	4.00
MERCURY					
76145	Devil in Disguise/Drifter's Wife	1982	—	—	3.00
814497-7	Losers/Reality	1983	—	—	3.00
SHELTER					
7306	Magnolia/Crazy Mama	1971	2.00	4.00	8.00
7314	Crazy Mama/Don't Go to Strangers	1971	—	3.00	6.00
7321	After Midnight/Crying Eyes	1972	—	3.00	6.00
7326	Lies/Riding Home	1972	—	3.00	6.00
7332	Going Down/Louisiana Women	1973	—	3.00	6.00
40238	Cajun Moon/Starbound	1974	—	2.50	5.00
40290	I'll Be There/Precious Memories	1974	—	2.50	5.00
40366	I Got the Same Old Blues/Rock and Roll Records	1975	—	2.50	5.00
62002	Hey Baby/Cocaine	1976	—	3.00	6.00

Albums

Number	Title (A Side/B Side)	Yr	VG	VG+	NM
MCA					
5158	Shades	1981	2.50	5.00	10.00
37102	5	1981	2.00	4.00	8.00
—Reissue of Shelter 3163					
37103	Troubadour	1981	2.00	4.00	8.00
—Reissue of Shelter 52002					
37104	Naturally	1981	2.00	4.00	8.00
—Reissue of Shelter 52009					
37105	Really	1981	2.00	4.00	8.00
—Reissue of Shelter 52012					
37106	Okie	1981	2.00	4.00	8.00
—Reissue of Shelter 52019					
MERCURY					
SRM-1-4038	Grasshopper	1982	2.50	5.00	10.00
810313-1	5	1983	—	3.00	6.00
—Reissue of MCA 37102					
810314-1	Really	1983	—	3.00	6.00
—Reissue of MCA 37105					
811152-1	#8	1983	2.50	5.00	10.00
818633-1	Special Edition	1984	2.50	5.00	10.00
822888-1	Grasshopper	1985	—	3.00	6.00
—Reissue of 4038					
SHELTER					
2107	Okie	1974	3.75	7.50	15.00
2122	Naturally	1974	3.00	6.00	12.00
—Reissue of SW-8908					
2123	Really	1974	3.00	6.00	12.00
—Reissue of 8912					
3163	5	1979	3.00	6.00	12.00
SW-8908	Naturally	1971	3.75	7.50	15.00
SW-8912	Really	1972	3.75	7.50	15.00
52002	Troubadour	1976	3.75	7.50	15.00
52009	Naturally	1977	2.50	5.00	10.00
—Reissue of 2122					
52012	Really	1977	2.50	5.00	10.00
—Reissue of 2123					
52015	Okie	1977	2.50	5.00	10.00
—Reissue of 2107					
SILVERTONE					
1306-1-J	Travel-Log	1990	3.00	6.00	12.00

CALE, JOHN

Also see THE VELVET UNDERGROUND.

12-Inch Singles

Number	Title (A Side/B Side)	Yr	VG	VG+	NM
A&M					
17154 [DJ]	Dead or Alive/Honi Soit	1981	—	3.00	6.00

45s

Number	Title (A Side/B Side)	Yr	VG	VG+	NM
A&M					
2329	Dead or Alive/Honi Soit	1981	—	—	3.00
COLUMBIA					
45266	Big White Cloud/Gideon's Bible	1970	—	3.00	6.00
REPRISE					
1108	Legs Larry at Television Center/Days of Steam	1972	—	3.00	6.00
SPY/I.R.S.					
9008	Mercenaries/Rosegarden Funeral of Sores	1979	—	3.00	6.00
9008 [PS]	Mercenaries/Rosegarden Funeral of Sores	1979	—	3.00	6.00

Albums

Number	Title (A Side/B Side)	Yr	VG	VG+	NM
ANTILLES					
AN-7063	Guts	198?	2.50	5.00	10.00
—Reissue of Island 9459					
IT-8401	Caribbean Sunset	1984	2.50	5.00	10.00
IT-8402	John Cale Comes Alive	1984	2.50	5.00	10.00
A&M					
SP-4849	Honi Soit	1981	2.50	5.00	10.00
COLUMBIA					
CS 1037	Vintage Violence	1970	5.00	10.00	20.00
—Red "360 Sound" label; orange labels go for less					
C 30131	Church of Anthrax	1971	3.75	7.50	15.00
ISLAND					
IXP-2 [DJ]	Hear Fear	1975	12.50	25.00	50.00
—Promo-only interview album					
ILPS 9301	Fear	1975	5.00	10.00	20.00
ILPS 9317	Slow Dazzle	1975	3.75	7.50	15.00
ILPS 9459	Guts	1977	5.00	10.00	20.00
I.R.S.					
SP-004	Sabotage/Live	1980	3.75	7.50	15.00
REPRISE					
MS 2079	The Academy in Peril	1972	3.75	7.50	15.00
MS 2131	Paris, 1919	1973	6.25	12.50	25.00
WARNER BROS./OPAL					
26024	Words for the Dying	1989	2.50	5.00	10.00
ZE/PASSPORT					
60019	Music for a New Society	1982	3.00	6.00	12.00

CALIFORNIA

45s

Number	Title (A Side/B Side)	Yr	VG	VG+	NM
LAURIE					
3612	See You in September/Ivy Ivy	1974	—	2.00	4.00
3639	Song of a Thousand Voices/Abraham, Martin and John	1976	—	2.00	4.00
3647	Jeans On/Doo-Wop Music	1976	—	2.00	4.00
3651	I'm Just Thinking of You/Doo-Wop Music	1977	—	2.00	4.00
3695	Summer Fun Medley/Paris	1981	—	2.00	4.00
RCA					
PB-11769	Everybody Needs a Little Help/I'm a Poet	1979	2.50	5.00	10.00
RSO					
901	I Can Hear Music/Love's Supposed to Be That Way	1978	2.50	5.00	10.00
WARNER BROS.					
8253	Happy in Hollywood/Music, Music, Music	1976	2.50	5.00	10.00
8307	(Just to Let You Know) I Love You So/Happy in Hollywood	1977	2.50	5.00	10.00

CALIFORNIA, RANDY

Also see SPIRIT.

45s

Number	Title (A Side/B Side)	Yr	VG	VG+	NM
EPIC					
10927	Walkin' the Dog/Live for the Day	1972	2.00	4.00	8.00

Albums

Number	Title (A Side/B Side)	Yr	VG	VG+	NM
EPIC					
KE 31755	Kapt. Kopter & the Fabulous Twirly Birds	1972	6.25	12.50	25.00
—Yellow label					
KE 31755	Kapt. Kopter & the Fabulous Twirly Birds	1973	3.00	6.00	12.00
—Orange label					

CALIFORNIA MUSIC

45s

Number	Title (A Side/B Side)	Yr	VG	VG+	NM
EQUINOX					
PB-10120	Don't Worry Baby/Ten Years' Harmony	1974	3.75	7.50	15.00
PB-10363	Why Do Fools Fall in Love/Don't Worry Baby	1975	3.75	7.50	15.00
PB-10572	Jamaica Farewell/California Music	1976	3.75	7.50	15.00

CALIFORNIA POPPY PICKERS, THE

Albums

Number	Title (A Side/B Side)	Yr	VG	VG+	NM
ALSHIRE					
S-5153	Hair-Aquarius	1969	7.50	15.00	30.00
S-5167	Honky Tonk Women	1970	10.00	20.00	40.00

CALIFORNIANS, THE (1)

45s

Number	Title (A Side/B Side)	Yr	VG	VG+	NM
CRAZY HORSE					
1318	Nausea Beast/Glass Disguise	1969	2.50	5.00	10.00

CALIFORNIANS, THE (2)

JESSE BELVIN appears on this record.

45s

Number	Title (A Side/B Side)	Yr	VG	VG+	NM
FEDERAL					
12231	My Angel/Heavenly Ruby	1955	75.00	150.00	300.00

CALLENDER, BOBBY

45s

Number	Title (A Side/B Side)	Yr	VG	VG+	NM
CORAL					
62517	You've Really Got a Hold on Me/I Can't Get Over You	1967	2.50	5.00	10.00
62528	Sweet Song of Life/Vicissitude (Or a Day at Jaffry's)	1967	2.50	5.00	10.00
MGM					
13965	Rainbow/Symphonic Pictures	1968	3.00	6.00	12.00
ROULETTE					
4471	Little Star/Love and Kisses	1963	4.00	8.00	16.00

CALVANES, THE

45s

Number	Title (A Side/B Side)	Yr	VG	VG+	NM
DECK					
579	Dreamworld/5, 7 or 9	1958	25.00	50.00	100.00
580	My Love Song/Horror Pictures	1958	25.00	50.00	100.00
DOOTONE					
371	Crazy Over You/Don't Take Your Love from Me	1956	50.00	100.00	200.00
380	One More Kiss/Florabelle	1956	50.00	100.00	200.00

7-Inch Extended Plays

Number	Title (A Side/B Side)	Yr	VG	VG+	NM
DOOTONE					
205	(contents unknown)	1956	100.00	200.00	400.00
205 [PS]	Voices for Lovers	1956	150.00	300.00	600.00

CAMBRIDGE, GODFREY

Albums

Number	Title (A Side/B Side)	Yr	VG	VG+	NM
EPIC					
FLM 13101 [M]	Ready or Not...Here's Godfrey Cambridge	1964	5.00	10.00	20.00
FLM 13102 [M]	Them Cotton Pickin' Days Is Over	1965	5.00	10.00	20.00
FLM 13108 [M]	Godfrey Cambridge Toys with the World	1966	5.00	10.00	20.00
FLM 13115 [M]	The Godfrey Cambridge Show Live at the Aladdin	1968	5.00	10.00	20.00
FLS 15101 [S]	Ready or Not...Here's Godfrey Cambridge	1964	5.00	10.00	20.00

Number	Title (A Side/B Side)	Yr	VG	VG+	NM
FLS 15102 [S]	Them Cotton Pickin' Days Is Over	1965	5.00	10.00	20.00
FLS 15108 [S]	Godfrey Cambridge Toys with the World	1966	5.00	10.00	20.00
FLS 15115 [S]	The Godfrey Cambridge Show Live at the Aladdin	1968	5.00	10.00	20.00

CAMEL

45s

JANUS

Number	Title (A Side/B Side)	Yr	VG	VG+	NM
262	Another Night/Lunar Sea	1976	—	3.00	6.00

Albums

ARISTA

Number	Title (A Side/B Side)	Yr	VG	VG+	NM
AB 4206	Breathless	1979	2.50	5.00	10.00
AB 4254	I Can See Your House from Here	1980	2.50	5.00	10.00

JANUS

Number	Title (A Side/B Side)	Yr	VG	VG+	NM
7009	Mirage	1974	3.00	6.00	12.00
7016	The Snow Goose	1975	3.00	6.00	12.00
7024	Moonmadness	1976	3.00	6.00	12.00
7035	Rain Dances	1977	3.00	6.00	12.00

LONDON

Number	Title (A Side/B Side)	Yr	VG	VG+	NM
820166-1	Pressure Points	1987	2.50	5.00	10.00

PASSPORT

Number	Title (A Side/B Side)	Yr	VG	VG+	NM
PB-6008	Nude	198?	2.50	5.00	10.00
PB-6013	The Single Factor	198?	2.50	5.00	10.00
PB-9855	Mirage	198?	2.00	4.00	8.00
—Reissue of Janus 7009					
PB-9856	The Snow Goose	198?	2.00	4.00	8.00
—Reissue of Janus 7016					
PB-9857	Moonmadness	198?	2.00	4.00	8.00
—Reissue of Janus 7024					
PB-9858	Rain Dances	198?	2.00	4.00	8.00
—Reissue of Janus 7035					

CAMELOTS, THE

45s

AANKO

Number	Title (A Side/B Side)	Yr	VG	VG+	NM
1001	Your Way/Don't Leave Me Baby	1963	20.00	40.00	80.00
1004	Sunday Kind of Love/My Imagination	1963	20.00	40.00	80.00

CAMEO

Number	Title (A Side/B Side)	Yr	VG	VG+	NM
334	Don't Leave Me Baby/Love Call	1964	7.50	15.00	30.00
—B-side by the Ebonaires					

COMET

Number	Title (A Side/B Side)	Yr	VG	VG+	NM
930	Scratch/Charge	1962	3.75	7.50	15.00

CRIMSON

Number	Title (A Side/B Side)	Yr	VG	VG+	NM
1001	Don't Leave Me Baby/The Letter	1963	7.50	15.00	30.00

DREAM

Number	Title (A Side/B Side)	Yr	VG	VG+	NM
1001	Your Way/I Wonder	1967	2.00	4.00	8.00

EMBER

Number	Title (A Side/B Side)	Yr	VG	VG+	NM
1108	Pocahontas/Searching for My Baby	1964	5.00	10.00	20.00

LAURIE

Number	Title (A Side/B Side)	Yr	VG	VG+	NM
3239	Marie/Daddy's Going Away Again	1964	5.00	10.00	20.00
—As "The Harps"					

NIX

Number	Title (A Side/B Side)	Yr	VG	VG+	NM
101	Lulu/Never Been in Love Before	1961	5.00	10.00	20.00

RELIC

Number	Title (A Side/B Side)	Yr	VG	VG+	NM
530	Chain of Broken Hearts/Rat Race	196?	2.00	4.00	8.00
—B-side by the Bootleggers					
541	Dance Girl/That's My Baby	1965	2.00	4.00	8.00
—B-side by the Suns					

TIMES SQUARE

Number	Title (A Side/B Side)	Yr	VG	VG+	NM
32	Dance Girl/That's My Baby	1964	2.50	5.00	10.00
—B-side by the Suns					

7-Inch Extended Plays

CLIFTON/UGHA

Number	Title (A Side/B Side)	Yr	VG	VG+	NM
EP 507/1	Music to My Ears/Daddy's Going Away//Pocahontas/Don't Leave Me Baby	1981	—	2.50	5.00
EP 507/1 [PS]	(title unknown)	1981	—	2.50	5.00

CAMEO

45s

ATLANTA ARTISTS

Number	Title (A Side/B Side)	Yr	VG	VG+	NM
812054-7	Style/(B-side unknown)	1983	—	—	3.00
812472-7	Can't Help Falling in Love/For You	1983	—	—	3.00
814077-7	Slow Movin'/For You	1983	—	—	3.00
818384-7	She's Strange/Tribute to Bob Marley	1984	—	—	3.00
818870-7	Talkin' Out the Side of Your Neck/Leve-Toi	1984	—	—	3.00
870587-7	You Make Me Work/DKWIG	1988	—	—	3.00
870587-7 [PS]	You Make Me Work/DKWIG	1988	—	—	3.00
872314-7	Skin I'm In/Honey	1988	—	—	3.00
872314-7 [PS]	Skin I'm In/Honey	1988	—	—	3.00
872918-7	Single Life/She's Strange	1989	—	—	3.00
—Reissue					
874050-7	Pretty Girls/Pretty Girls (Dub)	1989	—	—	3.00
874050-7 [PS]	Pretty Girls/Pretty Girls (Dub)	1989	—	—	3.00
875668-7	I Want It Now/DKWIG	1990	—	—	3.00
878196-7	Close Quarters/Honey	1990	—	—	3.00
880169-7	Hangin' Downtown/(B-side unknown)	1984	—	—	3.00
880744-7	Attack Me With Your Love/Love You Anyway	1985	—	—	3.00
884010-7	Single Life/I've Got Your Image	1985	—	—	3.00
884270-7	A Good-Bye/Little Boys-Dangerous Toys	1985	—	—	3.00
884933-7	Word Up/Urban Warrior	1986	—	—	3.00
884933-7 [PS]	Word Up/Urban Warrior	1986	—	—	3.00
888193-7	Candy/She's Strange	1986	—	—	3.00
888193-7 [PS]	Candy/She's Strange	1986	—	—	3.00
888385-7	Back and Forth/You Can Have the World	1987	—	—	3.00
888385-7 [PS]	Back and Forth/You Can Have the World	1987	—	—	3.00
888711-7	Don't Be Lonely/I've Got Your Image	1987	—	—	3.00
888876-7	She's Mine/I've Got Your Image	1987	—	—	3.00

CHOCOLATE CITY

Number	Title (A Side/B Side)	Yr	VG	VG+	NM
001	Find My Way/Good Company	1975	—	2.50	5.00
005	Rigor Mortis/Stand By My Side	1976	—	2.50	5.00
008	Find My Way/Rigor Mortis	1977	—	2.00	4.00
010	Post Mortem/Smile	1977	—	2.00	4.00
011	Funk Funk/Good Time	1977	—	2.00	4.00
013	It's Serious/Inflation	1978	—	2.00	4.00
014	It's Over/Inflation	1978	—	2.00	4.00
016	Insane/I Want You	1978	—	2.00	4.00
018	Give Love a Chance/Two of Us	1979	—	2.00	4.00
019	I Just Want to Be/The Rock	1979	—	2.00	4.00
3202	Sparkle/Macho	1979	—	2.00	4.00
3206	We're Goin' Out Tonight/One the One	1980	—	2.00	4.00
3210	Shake Your Pants/I Came for You	1980	—	2.00	4.00
3219	Keep It Hot/I Came for You	1980	—	2.00	4.00
3222	Feel Me/Is This the Way	1981	—	2.00	4.00
3225	Freaky Dancin'/Better Days	1981	—	2.00	4.00
3227	I Like It/The Sound Table	1981	—	2.00	4.00
3231	Just Be Yourself/Use It or Lose It	1982	—	2.00	4.00
3233	Flirt/Owe It All to You	1982	—	2.00	4.00
3235	Alligator Woman/Soul Away	1982	—	2.00	4.00

Albums

ATLANTA ARTISTS

Number	Title (A Side/B Side)	Yr	VG	VG+	NM
811072-1	Style	1983	2.50	5.00	10.00
814984-1	She's Strange	1984	2.50	5.00	10.00
824546-1	Single Life	1985	2.50	5.00	10.00
830265-1	Word Up!	1986	2.50	5.00	10.00
836002-1	Machismo	1988	2.50	5.00	10.00
846297-1	Real Men..Wear Black	1990	3.00	6.00	12.00

CHOCOLATE CITY

Number	Title (A Side/B Side)	Yr	VG	VG+	NM
CCLP 2003	Cardiac Arrest	1977	3.00	6.00	12.00
CCLP 2004	We All Know Who We Are	1978	3.00	6.00	12.00
CCLP 2006	Ugly Ego	1978	3.00	6.00	12.00
CCLP 2008	Secret Omen	1979	3.00	6.00	12.00
CCLP 2011	Cameosis	1980	3.00	6.00	12.00
CCLP 2016	Feel Me	1980	3.00	6.00	12.00
CCLP 2019	Knights of the Sound Table	1981	3.00	6.00	12.00
CCLP 2021	Alligator Woman	1982	3.00	6.00	12.00

CAMEOS, THE

45s

CAMEO

Number	Title (A Side/B Side)	Yr	VG	VG+	NM
123	Merry Christmas/New Year's Eve	1957	37.50	75.00	150.00
123	Merry Christmas/New Year's Eve	197?	2.50	5.00	10.00
—Reproduction of the original 1957 release					

CAMERON, JIMMY AND VELLA

45s

REPRISE

Number	Title (A Side/B Side)	Yr	VG	VG+	NM
0483	Lovin' You Is Such a Groove/I Know a Place	1966	7.50	15.00	30.00

UNLIMITED GOLD

Number	Title (A Side/B Side)	Yr	VG	VG+	NM
1422	Mornin' Time/There Is No Other Love	1980	—	2.00	4.00

CAMP, THE

45s

SCEPTER

Number	Title (A Side/B Side)	Yr	VG	VG+	NM
12159	Marching/Long Long Trail	1966	20.00	40.00	80.00

CAMPBELL, CHOKER

45s

APT

Number	Title (A Side/B Side)	Yr	VG	VG+	NM
25011	Walk Awhile/Walking on Thin-Soled Shoes	1958	15.00	30.00	60.00

ATLANTIC

Number	Title (A Side/B Side)	Yr	VG	VG+	NM
1014	Last Call for Whiskey/How Could You Do This	1953	10.00	20.00	40.00
1038	Have You Seen My Baby/Jackie Mambo	1954	10.00	20.00	40.00

FORTUNE

Number	Title (A Side/B Side)	Yr	VG	VG+	NM
808	Frankie and Johnny/Rocking and Jumping	1953	15.00	30.00	60.00

MOTOWN

Number	Title (A Side/B Side)	Yr	VG	VG+	NM
1072	Come See About Me/Pride and Joy	1964	6.25	12.50	25.00

Albums

MOTOWN

Number	Title (A Side/B Side)	Yr	VG	VG+	NM
M-620 [M]	Hits of the Sixties	1964	25.00	50.00	100.00

CAMPBELL, GLEN

Also see THE BEACH BOYS; THE CHAMPS; GEE CEES.

45s

ATLANTIC AMERICA

Number	Title (A Side/B Side)	Yr	VG	VG+	NM
99525	Call Home/Sweet 16	1986	—	—	3.00
99559	Cowpoke/Rag Doll	1986	—	—	3.00
99600	It's Just a Matter of Time/Gene Autry, My Hero	1985	—	—	3.00
99600 [PS]	It's Just a Matter of Time/Gene Autry, My Hero	1985	—	2.00	4.00
99647	(Love Always) Letter to Home/An American Trilogy	1985	—	—	3.00
99691	A Lady Like You/Tennessee	1984	—	—	3.00
99768	Faithless Love/Scene of the Crime	1984	—	—	3.00
99930	I Love How You Love Me/Hang On Baby (Ease My Mind)	1983	—	—	3.00
99967	Old Home Town/Heartache #3	1982	—	2.00	4.00

CAPEHART

Number	Title (A Side/B Side)	Yr	VG	VG+	NM
5008	Death Valley/Nothin' Better Than a Pretty Woman	1961	6.25	12.50	25.00

CAPITOL

Number	Title (A Side/B Side)	Yr	VG	VG+	NM
2015	By the Time I Get to Phoenix/You've Still Got a Place in My Heart	1967	—	2.50	5.00
2076	Hey Little One/My Baby's Gone	1968	—	2.50	5.00
2076 [PS]	Hey Little One/My Baby's Gone	1968	2.50	5.00	10.00
2146	I Wanna Live/That's All That Matters	1968	—	2.50	5.00
2224	Dreams of the Everyday Housewife/Kelli Ho-Down	1968	—	2.50	5.00
2302	Wichita Lineman/Fate of Man	1968	—	2.50	5.00
2336	Christmas Is for Children/There's No Place Like Home	1968	—	2.50	5.00
2428	Galveston/How Come Every Time I Itch I Wind Up Scratchin' You	1969	—	2.50	5.00
2494	Where's the Playground Susie/Arkansas	1969	—	2.50	5.00
2573	True Grit/Hava Nagila	1969	—	2.50	5.00
2659	Try a Little Kindness/Lonely My Lonely Friend	1969	—	2.50	5.00
2718	Honey Come Back/Where Do You Go	1970	—	2.50	5.00
2787	Oh Happy Day/Someone Above	1970	—	2.50	5.00

Number	Title (A Side/B Side)	Yr	VG	VG+	NM
2843	Everything a Man Could Ever Need/Norwood (Me and My Guitar)	1970	—	2.50	5.00
2905	It's Only Make Believe/Pave Your Way Into Tomorrow	1970	—	2.50	5.00
3062	Dream Baby (How Long Must I Dream)/Here and Now	1971	—	2.50	5.00
3123	The Last Time I Saw Her/Bach Talk	1971	—	2.50	5.00
3254	Oklahoma Sunday Morning/Everybody's Got to Go There Sometime	1972	—	2.00	4.00
3305	Manhattan, Kansas/Wayfaring Stranger	1972	—	2.00	4.00
3382	We All Pull the Load/Wherefore and Why	1972	—	2.00	4.00
3411	I Will Never Pass This Way Again/We All Pull the Load	1972	—	2.00	4.00
3483	One Last Time/All My Tomorrows	1972	—	2.00	4.00
3509	I Believe in Christmas/New Snow on the Roof	1972	—	2.00	4.00
3548	I Knew Jesus (Before He Was a Star)/On This Road	1973	—	2.00	4.00
3669	Bring Back My Yesterday/Beautiful Love Song	1973	—	2.00	4.00
3735	Wherefore and Why/Give Me Back That Old Familiar Feeling	1973	—	2.00	4.00
3808	Houston (I'm Coming to See You)/Honestly Love	1973	—	2.00	4.00
3926	Bonaparte's Retreat/Too Many Mornings	1974	—	2.00	4.00
3988	It's a Sin When You Love Somebody/If I Were Loving You	1974	—	2.00	4.00
4095	Rhinestone Cowboy/Lovelight	1975	—	2.00	4.00
4155	Country Boy (You Got Your Feet in L.A.)/Record Collector's Dream	1975	—	2.00	4.00
4245	Then You Can Tell Me Goodbye-Don't Pull Your Love/I Miss You Tonight	1976	—	2.00	4.00
4288	See You on Sunday/Bloodline	1976	—	2.00	4.00
4376	Southern Nights/William Tell Overture	1976	—	2.00	4.00
4445	Sunflower/How High Did We Go	1977	—	2.00	4.00
4515	God Must Have Blessed America/Amazing Grace	1977	—	2.00	4.00
4584	Another Fine Mess/Can You Fool	1978	—	2.00	4.00
4638	Can You Fool/Let's All Sing a Song About It	1978	—	2.00	4.00
4682	I'm Gonna Love You/Love Takes You Higher	1979	—	2.00	4.00
4715	California/Never Tell You No Lies	1979	—	2.00	4.00
4769	Hound Dog Man/Tennessee Home	1979	—	2.00	4.00
4783	Too Late to Worry — Too Blue to Cry/How Do I Tell My Heart Not to Break	1962	2.50	5.00	10.00
4799	My Prayer/Don't Lose Me in the Confusion	1979	—	2.00	4.00
4856	Long Black Limousine/Here I Am	1962	2.50	5.00	10.00
4856 [PS]	Long Black Limousine/Here I Am	1962	5.00	10.00	20.00
4865	Somethin' 'Bout You Baby I Like/Late Night Confession	1980	—	2.00	4.00
—With Rita Coolidge					
4867	Truck Driving Man/Kentucky Means Paradise	1962	2.50	5.00	10.00
4909	Hollywood Smiles/Hooked on Love	1980	—	2.00	4.00
4925	Oh My Darling/Prima Donna	1963	2.50	5.00	10.00
4959	I Don't Want to Know Your Name/Daisy a Day	1981	—	2.00	4.00
4986	Why Don't We Just Sleep on It Tonight/It's Your World	1981	—	2.00	4.00
—With Tanya Tucker					
4990	Divorce Me C.O.D./Dark As a Dungeon	1963	2.50	5.00	10.00
5037	As Far As I'm Concerned/Same Old Places	1963	2.50	5.00	10.00
5172	Let Me Tell You About Mary/Through the Eyes of a Child	1964	2.50	5.00	10.00
5279	Summer, Winter, Spring and Fall/Heartaches Can Be Fun	1964	2.50	5.00	10.00
5279 [PS]	Summer, Winter, Spring and Fall/Heartaches Can Be Fun	1964	5.00	10.00	20.00
5360	It's a Woman's World/Tomorrow Never Comes	1965	2.50	5.00	10.00
5441	Guess I'm Dumb/That's All Right	1965	25.00	50.00	100.00
—A Brian Wilson "Pet Sounds"-like production					
5504	The Universal Soldier/Spanish Shades	1965	2.00	4.00	8.00
5545	Less of Me/Private John Q	1965	2.00	4.00	8.00
5638	Can't You See I'm Tryin'/Satisfied Mind	1966	—	3.00	6.00
5773	Burning Bridges/Only the Lonely	1966	—	3.00	6.00
5854	Just to Satisfy You/I Gotta Have My Baby Back	1967	—	3.00	6.00
5939	Gentle on My Mind/Just Another Man	1967	—	2.50	5.00
—Orange and yellow swirl, without "A Subsidiary Of"... in perimeter label print					
5939	Gentle on My Mind/Just Another Man	1968	—	3.00	6.00
—Orange and yellow swirl label with "A Subsidiary Of" in perimeter print					
7PRO-79107 [DJ]	On a Good Night (same on both sides)	1990	—	3.00	6.00
—Vinyl is promo only					
7PRO-79279 [DJ]	Somebody's Leavin' (same on both sides)	1990	—	3.00	6.00
—Vinyl is promo only					
7PRO-79966 [DJ]	Walkin' in the Sun (same on both sides)	1990	—	3.00	6.00
—Vinyl is promo only					
CENECO					
1324	Dreams for Sale/I've Got to Win	1961	6.25	12.50	25.00
1356	I Wonder/You, You, You	1961	5.00	10.00	20.00
COMPLEAT					
113	Letting Go/(Instrumental)	1983	—	2.00	4.00
CREST					
1087	Turn Around, Look at Me/Brenda	1961	5.00	10.00	20.00
1096	The Miracle of Love/Once More	1962	3.75	7.50	15.00
EVEREST					
2500	Delight, Arkansas/Walk Right In	1969	—	3.00	6.00
LIBERTY					
S7-18214	Blue Christmas/Feliz Navidad	1994	—	2.00	4.00
—B-side on EMI Latin by Jose Feliciano; red vinyl					
MCA					
41323	Dream Lover/Bronco	1980	—	2.00	4.00
—A-side with Tanya Tucker					
53108	The Hand That Rocks the Cradle/Arkansas	1987	—	—	3.00
—A-side with Steve Wariner					
53172	Still Within the Sound of My Voice/In My Life	1987	—	—	3.00
53218	I Have You/I'm a One Woman Man	1987	—	—	3.00
53245	I Remember You/For Sure, For Certain, Forever, For Always	1988	—	—	3.00
53426	Heart of the Matter/Light Years	1988	—	—	3.00
53493	More Than Enough/Our Movie	1989	—	—	3.00
MIRAGE					
3845	I Love My Truck/Melody's Melody	1981	—	2.00	4.00

Number	Title (A Side/B Side)	Yr	VG	VG+	NM
STARDAY					
853	For the Love of a Woman/Smokey Blue Eyes	1968	—	3.00	6.00
UNIVERSAL					
UVL-66024	She's Gone, Gone, Gone/William Tell Overture	1989	—	2.00	4.00
WARNER BROS.					
49609	Any Which Way You Can/Medley from Any Which Way You Can	1980	—	2.00	4.00
—B-side by Texas Opera Company					
Albums					
ATLANTIC AMERICA					
90016	Old Home Town	1983	2.00	4.00	8.00
90164	Letter to Home	1984	2.00	4.00	8.00
90483	It's Just a Matter of Time	1985	2.00	4.00	8.00
CAPITOL					
SM-103	Wichita Lineman	1977	2.00	4.00	8.00
—Reissue with new prefix					
ST-103	Wichita Lineman	1968	3.75	7.50	15.00
ST-210	Galveston	1969	3.75	7.50	15.00
STBO-268	Glen Campbell — "Live"	1969	5.00	10.00	20.00
SM-389	Try a Little Kindness	1977	2.00	4.00	8.00
—Reissue with new prefix					
SW-389	Try a Little Kindness	1970	3.00	6.00	12.00
SW-443	Oh Happy Day	1970	3.00	6.00	12.00
SW-493	The Glen Campbell Goodtime Album	1970	3.00	6.00	12.00
SM-733	The Last Time I Saw Her	1977	2.00	4.00	8.00
—Reissue with new prefix					
SW-733	The Last Time I Saw Her	1971	3.00	6.00	12.00
SW-752	Glen Campbell's Greatest Hits	1971	3.00	6.00	12.00
ST 1810 [S]	Big Bluegrass Special	1962	25.00	50.00	100.00
—As "The Green River Boys Featuring Glen Campbell"					
T 1810 [M]	Big Bluegrass Special	1962	20.00	40.00	80.00
—As "The Green River Boys Featuring Glen Campbell"					
ST 1881 [S]	Too Late to Worry, Too Blue to Cry	1963	6.25	12.50	25.00
T 1881 [M]	Too Late to Worry, Too Blue to Cry	1963	5.00	10.00	20.00
ST 2023 [S]	The Astounding 12-String Guitar of Glen Campbell	1964	5.00	10.00	20.00
T 2023 [M]	The Astounding 12-String Guitar of Glen Campbell	1964	3.75	7.50	15.00
ST 2392 [S]	The Big Bad Rock Guitar of Glen Campbell	1965	5.00	10.00	20.00
T 2392 [M]	The Big Bad Rock Guitar of Glen Campbell	1965	3.75	7.50	15.00
ST 2679 [S]	Burning Bridges	1967	3.75	7.50	15.00
T 2679 [M]	Burning Bridges	1967	3.75	7.50	15.00
ST 2809 [S]	Gentle on My Mind	1967	3.75	7.50	15.00
T 2809 [M]	Gentle on My Mind	1967	3.75	7.50	15.00
ST 2851 [S]	By the Time I Get to Phoenix	1967	3.75	7.50	15.00
T 2851 [M]	By the Time I Get to Phoenix	1967	3.75	7.50	15.00
ST 2878	Hey, Little One	1968	3.75	7.50	15.00
ST 2907	A New Place in the Sun	1968	3.75	7.50	15.00
ST 2978	That Christmas Feeling	1968	3.75	7.50	15.00
SW-11117	Glen Travis Campbell	1972	2.50	5.00	10.00
SW-11185	I Knew Jesus (Before He Was a Star)	1973	2.50	5.00	10.00
SW-11253	I Remember Hank Williams	1973	2.50	5.00	10.00
SW-11293	Hosuton (I'm Comin' to See You)	1974	2.50	5.00	10.00
SW-11336	Reunion (The Songs of Jimmy Webb)	1974	2.50	5.00	10.00
SM-11407	Arkansas	1977	2.00	4.00	8.00
—Reissue with new prefix					
SW-11407	Arkansas	1975	2.50	5.00	10.00
SW-11430	Rhinestone Cowboy	1975	2.50	5.00	10.00
SW-11516	Bloodline	1976	2.50	5.00	10.00
ST-11577	The Best of Glen Campbell	1976	2.50	5.00	10.00
SO-11601	Southern Nights	1977	2.50	5.00	10.00
SWBC-11707 [(2)]	Live at the Royal Festival Hall	1977	3.00	6.00	12.00
SW-11722	Basic	1978	2.50	5.00	10.00
SM-11960	Gentle on My Mind	1979	2.00	4.00	8.00
—Reissue of 2809					
SOO-12008	Highwayman	1979	2.50	5.00	10.00
SM-12040	By the Time I Get to Phoenix	1979	2.00	4.00	8.00
—Reissue of 2851					
SOO-12075	Somethin' 'Bout You Baby I Like	1980	2.50	5.00	10.00
SOO-12124	It's the World Gone Crazy	1981	2.50	5.00	10.00
SN-16029	Rhinestone Cowboy	1980	—	3.00	6.00
—Budget-line reissue					
SN-16030	Southern Nights	1980	—	3.00	6.00
—Budget-line reissue					
SN-16031	Glen Travis Campbell	1980	—	3.00	6.00
—Budget-line reissue					
SN-16160	Wichita Lineman	1981	—	3.00	6.00
—Budget-line reissue					
SN-16258	Hey Little Girl	1982	—	3.00	6.00
—Budget-line reissue					
SN-16259	Galveston	1982	—	3.00	6.00
—Budget-line reissue					
SN-16297	Glen Campbell's Greatest Hits	1984	—	3.00	6.00
—Budget-line reissue					
SN-16335	The Best of Glen Campbell	1984	—	3.00	6.00
—Budget-line reissue					
SWAK-93157	Limited Collector's Edition	1970	5.00	10.00	20.00
—Capitol Record Club exclusive; includes tour program					
MCA					
42009	Still Within the Sound of My Voice	1987	2.00	4.00	8.00
42210	Light Years	1988	2.00	4.00	8.00
PAIR					
PDL2-1089 [(2)]	All-Time Favorites	1986	3.00	6.00	12.00
PICKWICK					
PTP-2048 [(2)]	Only the Lonely	197?	2.50	5.00	10.00
SPC-3052	The 12 Strings of Glen Campbell	196?	2.50	5.00	10.00
SPC-3134	A Satisfied Mind	197?	2.00	4.00	8.00
SPC-3274	The Glen Campbell Album	197?	2.00	4.00	8.00
SPC-3346	I'll Paint You a Song	197?	2.00	4.00	8.00
STARDAY					
424	Country Soul	1968	3.75	7.50	15.00
437	Country Music Star #1	1969	3.75	7.50	15.00

CAMPBELL, GLEN, AND BOBBIE GENTRY

Also see each artist's individual listings.

Number	Title (A Side/B Side)	Yr	VG	VG+	NM
45s					
CAPITOL					
2314	Less of Me/Morning Glory	1968	—	2.50	5.00
2387	Let It Be Me/Little Green Apples	1969	—	2.50	5.00
2745	All I Have to Do Is Dream/Less of Me	1970	—	2.50	5.00
Albums					
CAPITOL					
ST 2928	Bobbie Gentry & Glen Campbell	1968	3.75	7.50	15.00

CAMPBELL, JO ANN

Number	Title (A Side/B Side)	Yr	VG	VG+	NM
45s					
ABC-PARAMOUNT					
10134 [M]	A Kookie Little Paradise/Bobby, Bobby, Bobby	1960	6.25	12.50	25.00
S-10134 [S]	A Kookie Little Paradise/Bobby, Bobby, Bobby	1960	12.50	25.00	50.00
10172	But Maybe This Year/Crazy Daisy	1960	5.00	10.00	20.00
10200	Motorcycle Michael/Puka Puka Pants	1961	5.00	10.00	20.00
10224	Eddie My Love/It Wasn't Right	1961	5.00	10.00	20.00
10258	Mama Don't Wait/Duane	1961	5.00	10.00	20.00
10300	I Changed My Mind Jack/You Made Me Love You	1962	5.00	10.00	20.00
10335	Amateur Night/I Wish It Would Rain All Summer	1962	5.00	10.00	20.00
CAMEO					
223	I'm the Girl from Wolverton Mountain/Sloppy Joe	1962	5.00	10.00	20.00
237	Let Me Do It My Way/Mr. Fix-It Man	1962	5.00	10.00	20.00
249	Mother Please/Waitin' for Love	1963	5.00	10.00	20.00
EL DORADO					
504	Forever Young/Come On Baby	1957	10.00	20.00	40.00
509	Funny Thing/I Can't Give You Anything But Love	1957	10.00	20.00	40.00
GONE					
5014	Wait a Minute/It's True	1957	10.00	20.00	40.00
5014	Wait a Minute/I'm in Love with You	1957	7.50	15.00	30.00
5021	You're Driving Me Mad/Rock and Roll Love	1958	7.50	15.00	30.00
5027	Whassa Matter with You/You-Oo	1958	7.50	15.00	30.00
5037	I Really, Really Love You/I'm Nobody's Baby Now	1958	7.50	15.00	30.00
5049	Happy New Year Baby/Tall Boy	1958	7.50	15.00	30.00
5055	Mama/Nervous	1959	7.50	15.00	30.00
5068	Beach Comber/I Ain't Got No Steady Date	1959	7.50	15.00	30.00
POINT					
4	I'm Coming Home Late Tonight/Wherever You Go	1956	10.00	20.00	40.00
RORI					
711	Jim Dandy/Five Minutes More	1962	5.00	10.00	20.00
Albums					
ABC-PARAMOUNT					
393 [M]	Twistin' and Listenin'	1962	20.00	40.00	80.00
S-393 [S]	Twistin' and Listenin'	1962	25.00	50.00	100.00
CAMEO					
C-1026 [M]	All the Hits of Jo Ann Campbell	1962	12.50	25.00	50.00
SC-1026 [S]	All the Hits of Jo Ann Campbell	1962	25.00	50.00	100.00
CORONET					
CX-199 [M]	Starring Jo Ann Campbell	196?	5.00	10.00	20.00
CXS-199 [R]	Starring Jo Ann Campbell	196?	3.00	6.00	12.00
END					
LP-306 [M]	I'm Nobody's Baby	1959	37.50	75.00	150.00

CAMPERS, THE

Includes SONNY CURTIS and THE CRICKETS (1).

Number	Title (A Side/B Side)	Yr	VG	VG+	NM
45s					
PARKWAY					
974	The Ballad of Batman/The Batmobile	1966	7.50	15.00	30.00
974	The Ballad of Batman/The Batmobile	1966	8.75	17.50	35.00
—Original label credit: "The Camps"					

CAMPI, RAY

Number	Title (A Side/B Side)	Yr	VG	VG+	NM
45s					
COLPIX					
166	French Fries/Hear What I Wanna Hear	1960	3.75	7.50	15.00
D					
1047	The Ballad of Donna and Peggy Sue/A Man I Met (Tribute to The Big Bopper)	1959	10.00	20.00	40.00
DOMINO					
700	My Screamin' Screamin' Meemie/With You	1958	7.50	15.00	30.00
DOT					
15617	It Ain't Me/Give That Love to Me	1957	15.00	30.00	60.00
ROLLIN' ROCK					
006	Eager Boy/Dobroggie	1978	—	2.50	5.00
008	Tore Up/If It's All the Same to You	1978	—	2.50	5.00
014	Sixteen Chicks/Pan American Boogie	1979	—	2.50	5.00
019	My Baby Left Me/A Li'l Bit of Heartache	1979	—	2.50	5.00
027	Wrong, Wrong, Wrong/Booze It	1980	—	2.00	4.00
029	Scrumptious Baby/I Didn't Mean to Be Mean	1980	—	2.00	4.00
031	Merle's Boogie-Woogie-Missouri/Sweet Temptation Guitar Rag	1980	—	2.00	4.00
—With Merle Travis					
038	Rockin' at the Ritz/Quit Your Triplin'	1981	—	2.00	4.00
044	Rattlin' Daddy/Wild One	1981	—	2.00	4.00
046	Texas Sands/How Long Can You Feel	1982	—	2.00	4.00
047	Sweet Woman Blues/The Newest Wave	1982	—	2.00	4.00
052	Rockabilly Man/Hollywood Cats	1983	—	2.00	4.00
TNT					
145	Caterpillar/Play It Cool	1958	75.00	150.00	300.00
WINSOR					
6401	Billie Jean/Shenandoah	1964	7.50	15.00	30.00
Albums					
ROLLIN' ROCK					
023	Rockabilly Music	1979	3.00	6.00	12.00
ROUNDER					
3046	Rockin' at the Ritz	198?	2.50	5.00	10.00
3047	Gone, Gone, Gone	198?	2.50	5.00	10.00

CAMPS, THE

See THE CAMPERS.

CANADIAN BEADLES, THE

Number	Title (A Side/B Side)	Yr	VG	VG+	NM
45s					
TIDE					
2203	I Think I'm Gonna Cry/I'll Show You the Way	1964	3.75	7.50	15.00
2206	I'm Coming Home/Love Walk Away	1964	3.75	7.50	15.00
—As "Vic, Paul and Bruce"					
Albums					
TIDE					
2005 [M]	Three Faces North	1964	12.50	25.00	50.00

CANARIES, THE

Number	Title (A Side/B Side)	Yr	VG	VG+	NM
45s					
B.T. PUPPY					
557	I'll Cry Again/Baby Don't Surprise Me	1970	2.00	4.00	8.00
DIMENSION					
1047	I'm Sorry Baby/Runaround Ronnie	1965	3.75	7.50	15.00
Albums					
B.T. PUPPY					
BTS-1007	Flying High with the Canaries	1970	25.00	50.00	100.00

CANDLELIGHTERS, THE

Number	Title (A Side/B Side)	Yr	VG	VG+	NM
45s					
DELTA					
203	Would You Do the Same for Me/(B-side unknown)	1958	200.00	400.00	800.00

CANDY AND THE KISSES

Number	Title (A Side/B Side)	Yr	VG	VG+	NM
45s					
CAMEO					
336	The 81/Two Happy People	1964	5.00	10.00	20.00
355	Soldier Boy (Of Mine)/Shakin' Time	1964	5.00	10.00	20.00
DECCA					
32415	Chains of Love/Someone Out There	1968	—	3.00	6.00
SCEPTER					
12106	Keep On Searchin'/Together	1965	3.75	7.50	15.00
12125	Sweet and Lovely/Out in the Streets Again	1965	3.75	7.50	15.00
12136	Tonight's the Night/The Last Time	1966	3.00	6.00	12.00

CANDY STORE, THE

Number	Title (A Side/B Side)	Yr	VG	VG+	NM
Albums					
DECCA					
DL 75147	Turned-On Christmas	1969	6.25	12.50	25.00

CANDYMEN, THE

Number	Title (A Side/B Side)	Yr	VG	VG+	NM
45s					
ABC					
10995	Georgia Pines/Movies in My Mind	1967	2.00	4.00	8.00
11023	Deep in the Night/Stone Blues Man	1967	2.00	4.00	8.00
11048	Sentimental Lady/Ways	1968	2.00	4.00	8.00
11077	Candy Man/Crowded Room	1968	2.00	4.00	8.00
11141	Go and Tell the People/It's Gonna Get Good in a Minute	1968	2.00	4.00	8.00
11175	I'll Never Forget/Lonely Eyes	1969	2.00	4.00	8.00
LIBERTY					
56172	Happy Tonight/Papers	1970	2.00	4.00	8.00
Albums					
ABC					
616 [M]	The Candymen	1967	6.25	12.50	25.00
S-616 [S]	The Candymen	1967	5.00	10.00	20.00
S-633	The Candymen Bring You Candypower	1968	5.00	10.00	20.00

CANNED HEAT

Number	Title (A Side/B Side)	Yr	VG	VG+	NM
45s					
ALA					
1996	C.C. Shooter/Harley Davidson Blues	1984	—	2.50	5.00
—As "Heat Brothers '84"					
ATLANTIC					
3010	One More River to Cross/Highway 401	1974	—	2.00	4.00
3236	The Harder They Come/Rock 'N' Roll Show	1975	—	2.00	4.00
CAPITOL					
S7-57890	Christmas Blues/Christmas Is the Time to Say "I Love You"	1992	—	2.00	4.00
—B-side by Billy Squier					
LIBERTY					
55979	Rolin' and Tumblin'/Bullfrog Blues	1967	2.00	4.00	8.00
56005	Evil Woman/The World Is a Jug	1967	2.00	4.00	8.00
56038	On the Road Again/Boogie Music	1968	—	3.00	6.00
56077	Going Up the Country/One Kind Favor	1968	—	3.00	6.00
56077 [PS]	Going Up the Country/One Kind Favor	1968	3.75	7.50	15.00
56079	Christmas Blues/The Chipmunk Song	1968	6.25	12.50	25.00
—B-side with the Chipmunks					
56097	Time Was/Low Down	1969	—	3.00	6.00
56127	Sic 'Em Pigs/Poor Man	1969	—	3.00	6.00
56140	Change My Ways/Get Off My Back	1969	—	3.00	6.00
56151	Let's Work Together/I'm Her Man	1970	—	3.00	6.00
56180	Future Blues/Going Up the Country	1970	—	3.00	6.00
56217	My TIme Ain't Long/Wooly Bully	1970	—	3.00	6.00
UNITED ARTISTS					
0058	On the Road Again/This Was	1973	—	2.00	4.00
—"Silver Spotlight Series" reissue					
0059	Going Up the Country/Let's Work Together	1973	—	2.00	4.00
—"Silver Spotlight Series" reissue					
XW167	Rock and Roll Music/Lookin' for My Rainbow	1973	—	2.50	5.00
XW243 [DJ]	Harley Davidson Blues (mono/stereo)	1973	—	3.00	6.00
—Stock copy apparently does not exist					
50831	Long Way from L.A./Hill's Stomp	1971	—	2.50	5.00
50892	Rockin' with the King/I Don't Care What You Tell Me	1972	—	2.50	5.00
50927	Sneakin' Around/Cherokee Dance	1972	—	2.50	5.00

Number	Title (A Side/B Side)	Yr	VG	VG+	NM
Albums					
ACCORD					
SN-7144	Captured Live	1981	2.50	5.00	10.00
ATLANTIC					
SD 7289	One More River to Cross	1973	3.75	7.50	15.00
DALI					
DCLP-89022	Reheated	1990	3.75	7.50	15.00
JANUS					
JLS-3009	Vintage — Canned Heat	1969	3.75	7.50	15.00
LIBERTY					
LRP-3526 [M]	Canned Heat	1967	6.25	12.50	25.00
LST-7526 [S]	Canned Heat	1967	5.00	10.00	20.00
LST-7541	Boogie with Canned Heat	1968	5.00	10.00	20.00
LST-7618	Hallelujah	1969	5.00	10.00	20.00
LN-10105	Boogie with Canned Heat	1981	2.00	4.00	8.00
—Budget-line reissue					
LN-10106	Canned Heat Cook Book (The Best of Canned Heat)	1981	2.00	4.00	8.00
—Budget-line reissue					
LST-11000	Canned Heat Cook Book (The Best of Canned Heat)	1969	5.00	10.00	20.00
LST-11002	Future Blues	1970	3.75	7.50	15.00
LST-27200 [(2)]	Living the Blues	1968	6.25	12.50	25.00
PICKWICK					
SPC-3364	Live at Topanga Canyon	197?	2.50	5.00	10.00
SPC-3614	Boogie	1978	2.50	5.00	10.00
SCEPTER					
CTN-18017	The Best of Canned Heat	1972	2.50	5.00	10.00
SUNSET					
SUS-5298	Collage	1971	2.50	5.00	10.00
TAKOMA					
7066	The Human Condition	1980	3.00	6.00	12.00
UNITED ARTISTS					
UA-LA049-F	The New Age	1973	3.75	7.50	15.00
LM-1015	Boogie with Canned Heat	1980	3.00	6.00	12.00
—Reissue of Liberty 7541					
UAS-5509	Canned Heat Concert (Recorded Live in Europe)	1971	3.75	7.50	15.00
UAS-5557	Historical Figures and Ancient Heads	1972	3.75	7.50	15.00
UAS-9955 [(2)]	Living the Blues	1971	5.00	10.00	20.00
—Reissue of Liberty 27200					
WAND					
WDS-693	Live at Topanga Canyon	1970	6.25	12.50	25.00

CANNED HEAT AND JOHN LEE HOOKER

See JOHN LEE HOOKER AND CANNED HEAT

CANNIBAL AND THE HEADHUNTERS

Number	Title (A Side/B Side)	Yr	VG	VG+	NM
45s					
AIRES					
1001	Mean So Much/Dance By the Light	1968	3.75	7.50	15.00
CAPITOL					
2393	Get It On Up (Get Up the Courage)/Mean So Much	1969	3.75	7.50	15.00
DATE					
1516	La Bamba/Zulu King	1966	3.75	7.50	15.00
1525	Land of 1,000 Dances/Love Bird	1966	3.75	7.50	15.00
ERA BACK TO BACK HITS					
023	Land of 1,000 Dances/Dance with Me	197?	—	2.50	5.00
—B-side by the Blendells					
RAMPART					
642	Land of 1,000 Dances/I'll Show You How to Love Me	1964	5.00	10.00	20.00
644	Here Comes Love/Nau Ninny Nau	1965	3.75	7.50	15.00
646	I Need Your Loving/Follow the Music	1965	3.75	7.50	15.00
654	Out of Sight/Please Baby Please	1965	3.75	7.50	15.00
Albums					
DATE					
TEM 3001 [M]	Land of 1000 Dances	1966	7.50	15.00	30.00
TES 4001 [S]	Land of 1000 Dances	1966	10.00	20.00	40.00
RAMPART					
RM-3302 [M]	Land of 1000 Dances	1965	12.50	25.00	50.00
RS-3302 [S]	Land of 1000 Dances	1965	17.50	35.00	70.00

CANNON, ACE

Number	Title (A Side/B Side)	Yr	VG	VG+	NM
45s					
FERNWOOD					
117	Big Shot/Rest	1960	7.50	15.00	30.00
—As "Johnny Cannon"					
135	Summertime/Hoe Down Rock	1963	5.00	10.00	20.00
137	Big Shot/Tie Me to Your Apron Strings Again	1964	5.00	10.00	20.00
HI					
2040	Tuff/Sittin' Tight	1961	4.00	8.00	16.00
2051	Blues (Stay Away from Me)/Blues in My Heart	1962	3.75	7.50	15.00
2057	Volare/Looking Back	1962	3.00	6.00	12.00
2063	Love Letters/Since I Met You Baby	1963	3.00	6.00	12.00
2065	Cottonfields/Mildew	1963	3.00	6.00	12.00
2065 [PS]	Cottonfields/Mildew	1963	5.00	10.00	20.00
2070	Swanee River/Moanin' the Blues	1963	3.00	6.00	12.00
2070 [PS]	Swanee River/Moanin' the Blues	1963	5.00	10.00	20.00
2074	Searchin'/Love Letters in the Sand	1964	2.50	5.00	10.00
2078	The Great Pretender/Gone	1964	2.50	5.00	10.00
2081	Empty Arms/Sunday Blues	1964	2.50	5.00	10.00
2084	Blue Christmas/Here Comes Santa Claus	1964	2.50	5.00	10.00
2089	Sea Cruise/Gold Coins	1965	2.00	4.00	8.00
2096	Up Shore/Ishapan	1965	2.00	4.00	8.00
2101	Funny (How Time Slips Away)/Saxy Lullaby	1966	2.00	4.00	8.00
2107	Mockingbird Hill/Dedicated to the One I Love	1966	2.00	4.00	8.00
2111	More/Spanish Eyes	1966	2.00	4.00	8.00
2117	Wonderland by Night/As Time Goes By	1966	2.00	4.00	8.00
2127	I Walk the Line/Memory	1967	2.00	4.00	8.00
2136	White Silver Sands/San Antonio Rose	1967	2.00	4.00	8.00
2144	Sleep Walk/By the Time I Get to Phoenix	1968	—	3.00	6.00
2148	Alley Cat/Cannonball	1968	—	3.00	6.00
2155	If I Had a Hammer/Soul for Sale	1969	—	3.00	6.00
2166	Amen/Down By the Riverside	1969	—	3.00	6.00
2174	Ruby, Don't Take Your Love to Town/I Can't Stop Loving You	1970	—	3.00	6.00
2180	Rainy Night in Georgia/Lodi	1970	—	3.00	6.00
2187	Chicken Fried Soul/Chunck	1971	—	2.50	5.00
2192	Me and Bobby McGee/Sweet Caroline	1971	—	2.50	5.00
2199	Easy Loving/Misty Blue	1971	—	2.50	5.00
2210	Lovesick Blues/Cold, Cold Heart	1972	—	2.50	5.00
2220	Wabash Cannonball/To Get to You	1972	—	2.50	5.00
2231	Tuffer Than Tuff/The Green Door	1973	—	2.00	4.00
2238	Ruff/Baby Don't Get Hooked on Me	1973	—	2.00	4.00
2256	Country Comfort/Closin' Time's a Downer	1973	—	2.00	4.00
2261	Last Date/Methilda	1974	—	2.00	4.00
2273	There Goes My Everything/Tennessee Saturday Night	1974	—	2.00	4.00
2286	Peace in the Valley/Raunchy	1975	—	2.00	4.00
2299	Walk On By/Malt Liquor	1975	—	2.00	4.00
2313	Blue Eyes Crying in the Rain/I'll Fly Away	1976	—	2.00	4.00
78516	It Was Almost Like a Song/(B-side unknown)	1978	—	2.00	4.00
78526	Don't It Make My Brown Eyes Blue/Blanket on the Ground	1978	—	2.00	4.00
LOUIS (LOUISE?)					
2001	Tuff/Sittin' Tight	1961	7.50	15.00	30.00
SANTO					
503	Sugar Blues/38 Special	1962	3.75	7.50	15.00
506	Big Shot/Rest	1962	3.75	7.50	15.00
Albums					
ALLEGIANCE					
AV-5024	Ace in the Whole	1986	2.00	4.00	8.00
HI					
6006	After Hours	1978	2.50	5.00	10.00
8003	Sax Man	1977	2.50	5.00	10.00
8008	Cannon Country	1979	2.50	5.00	10.00
HL-12007 [M]	Tuff Sax	1962	6.25	12.50	25.00
HL-12008 [M]	Looking Back	1962	6.25	12.50	25.00
HL-12014 [M]	The Moanin' Sax of Ace Cannon	1963	6.25	12.50	25.00
HL-12016 [M]	Aces Hi	1964	5.00	10.00	20.00
HL-12019 [M]	The Great Show Tunes	1964	5.00	10.00	20.00
HL-12022 [M]	Christmas Cheer	1964	5.00	10.00	20.00
HL-12025 [M]	Ace Cannon Live	1965	3.75	7.50	15.00
HL-12028 [M]	Nashville Hits	1965	3.75	7.50	15.00
HL-12030 [M]	Sweet and Tuff	1966	3.75	7.50	15.00
HL-12035 [M]	The Misty Sax of Ace Cannon	1967	5.00	10.00	20.00
HL-12040 [M]	Memphis Golden Hits	1967	5.00	10.00	20.00
SHL-32007 [S]	Tuff Sax	1962	7.50	15.00	30.00
SHL-32008 [S]	Looking Back	1962	7.50	15.00	30.00
SHL-32014 [S]	The Moanin' Sax of Ace Cannon	1963	7.50	15.00	30.00
SHL-32016 [S]	Aces Hi	1964	6.25	12.50	25.00
SHL-32019 [S]	The Great Show Tunes	1964	6.25	12.50	25.00
SHL-32022 [S]	Christmas Cheer	1964	6.25	12.50	25.00
SHL-32025 [S]	Ace Cannon Live	1965	5.00	10.00	20.00
SHL-32028 [S]	Nashville Hits	1965	5.00	10.00	20.00
SHL-32030 [S]	Sweet and Tuff	1966	5.00	10.00	20.00
SHL-32035 [S]	The Misty Sax of Ace Cannon	1967	3.75	7.50	15.00
SHL-32040 [S]	Memphis Golden Hits	1967	3.75	7.50	15.00
SHL-32043	The Incomparable Sax of Ace Cannon	1968	3.75	7.50	15.00
SHL-32046	In the Spotlight	1968	3.75	7.50	15.00
SHL-32051	The Ace of Sax	1969	3.75	7.50	15.00
SHL-32057	The Happy and Mellow Sax of Ace Cannon	1970	3.00	6.00	12.00
SHL-32060	Cool 'n Saxy	1971	3.00	6.00	12.00
SHL-32067	Blowing Wild	1971	3.00	6.00	12.00
SHL-32071	Cannon Country	1972	3.00	6.00	12.00
SHL-32072/3 [(2)]	Aces Back to Back	1972	3.75	7.50	15.00
SHL-32076	Baby Don't Get Hooked on Me	1973	2.50	5.00	10.00
SHL-32080	Country Comfort	1974	2.50	5.00	10.00
SHL-32086	That Music City Feeling	1974	2.50	5.00	10.00
SHL-32090	Super Sax Country Style	1975	2.50	5.00	10.00
SHL-32101	Peace in the Valley	1976	2.50	5.00	10.00

CANNON, FREDDIE

Number	Title (A Side/B Side)	Yr	VG	VG+	NM
45s					
AMHERST					
201	Dance to the Bop/(She's a) Mean Rebel Rouser	1983	—	2.00	4.00
327	Rockin' in My Socks/Rockin' in My Socks	1988	—	3.00	6.00
BUDDAH					
242	Rockin' Robin/Red Valley	1971	2.50	5.00	10.00
CLARIDGE					
401	Palisades Park/Way Down Yonder in New Orleans	1975	—	3.00	6.00
416	Sugar/Sugar (Part 2)	1976	—	3.00	6.00
HQ					
(no #) [DJ]	Kennywood Park/With a Little Love	1987	—	3.00	6.00
(no #) [PS]	Kennywood Park/With a Little Love	1987	2.00	4.00	8.00
—Promotional item for KDKA Radio, Pittsburgh, Pa.					
MCA					
40269	Rock and Roll ABC's/Superman	1974	3.75	7.50	15.00
METROMEDIA					
262	If You've Got the Time/Take Me Back	1972	2.50	5.00	10.00
MIASOUND					
1002	Let's Put the Fun Back in Rock and Roll/Your Mama Ain't Always Right	1981	—	2.50	5.00
—With the Belmonts					
RADIO ACTIVE GOLD					
64	Rockin' Robin/Red Valley	197?	—	2.50	5.00
ROYAL AMERICAN					
2	Charged-Up, Turned-On Rock-N-Roll Singer/I Ain't Much, But I'm Yours	1970	2.50	5.00	10.00
11	Nite Time Lady/I Ain't Much, But I'm Yours	1970	2.50	5.00	10.00
288	Strawberry Wine/Blossom Dear	1969	2.50	5.00	10.00
SIRE					
4103	Beautiful Downtown Burbank/If You Give Me a Title	1969	2.50	5.00	10.00

SWAN

Number	Title (A Side/B Side)	Yr	VG	VG+	NM
4031	Tallahassee Lassie/You Know	1959	5.00	10.00	20.00
4038	Okefenokee/Kookie Hat	1959	5.00	10.00	20.00
4043	Way Down Yonder in New Orleans/Fractured	1959	5.00	10.00	20.00
4043 [PS]	Way Down Yonder in New Orleans/Fractured	1959	7.50	15.00	30.00
4050	Chattanooga Shoe Shine Boy/Boston "My Home Town"	1960	3.75	7.50	15.00
4050 [PS]	Chattanooga Shoe Shine Boy/Boston "My Home Town"	1960	7.50	15.00	30.00
4053	Jump Over/The Urge	1960	3.75	7.50	15.00
4053 [PS]	Jump Over/The Urge	1960	7.50	15.00	30.00
4057	Happy Shades of Blue/Chattanooga Choo Choo	1960	3.75	7.50	15.00
4057 [PS]	Happy Shades of Blue/Chattanooga Choo Choo	1960	7.50	15.00	30.00
4061	Humdinger/My Blue Heaven	1960	3.75	7.50	15.00
4061 [PS]	Humdinger/My Blue Heaven	1960	7.50	15.00	30.00
4066	Muskrat Ramble/Two Thousand-88	1961	3.75	7.50	15.00
4066 [PS]	Muskrat Ramble/Two Thousand-88	1961	7.50	15.00	30.00
4071	Buzz Buzz A-Diddle It/Opportunity	1961	3.75	7.50	15.00
4078	Transistor Sister/Walk to the Moon	1961	3.75	7.50	15.00
4078 [PS]	Transistor Sister/Walk to the Moon	1961	7.50	15.00	30.00
4083	For Me and My Gal/Blue Plate Special	1961	3.75	7.50	15.00
4096	Teen Queen of the Week/Wild Guy	1962	3.75	7.50	15.00
4106	Palisades Park/June, July and August	1962	4.00	8.00	16.00
4117	What's Gonna Happen When Summer's Done/Broadway	1962	3.75	7.50	15.00
4122	If You Were a Rock and Roll Record/The Truth, Ruth	1962	3.75	7.50	15.00
4132	Come On and Love Me/Four Letter Man	1963	3.00	6.00	12.00
4139	Patty Baby/Betty Jean	1963	3.00	6.00	12.00
4149	Everybody Monkey/Oh Gloria	1963	6.25	12.50	25.00
4155	Do What the Hippies Do/That's the Way Girls Are	1963	3.00	6.00	12.00
4168	What a Party/Sweet Georgia Brown	1964	3.00	6.00	12.00
4178	The Ups and Downs of Love/It's Been Nice	1964	6.25	12.50	25.00

WARNER BROS.

Number	Title (A Side/B Side)	Yr	VG	VG+	NM
5409	Abigail Beecher/All American Girl	1964	3.00	6.00	12.00
5434	OK Wheeler, The Used Car Dealer/Odie Cologne	1964	3.00	6.00	12.00
5448	Summertime U.S.A./Gotta Good Thing Goin'	1964	3.00	6.00	12.00
5487	Little Autograph Seeker/Too Much Monkey Business	1964	3.00	6.00	12.00
5615	Little Miss A-Go-Go/In the Night	1965	3.00	6.00	12.00
5615 [PS]	Little Miss A-Go-Go/In the Night	1965	6.25	12.50	25.00
5645	Action/Beachwood City	1965	3.75	7.50	15.00
5666	Let Me Show You Where It's At/The Old Rag Man	1965	3.00	6.00	12.00
5673	She's Something Else/Little Bitty Corrine	1965	3.00	6.00	12.00
5693	The Dedication Song/Come On, Come On	1966	3.00	6.00	12.00
5810	The Greatest Show on Earth/Hokie Pokie Girl	1966	3.00	6.00	12.00
5832	The Laughing Song/Natalie	1966	3.00	6.00	12.00
5859	Run for the Sun/Use Your Imagination	1966	3.00	6.00	12.00
5876	A Happy Clown/In My Wildest Dreams	1966	6.25	12.50	25.00
7019	Maverick's Flat/Run to the Poet Man	1967	6.25	12.50	25.00
7075	20th Century Fox/Cincinnati Woman	1967	6.25	12.50	25.00

WE MAKE ROCK & ROLL

Number	Title (A Side/B Side)	Yr	VG	VG+	NM
1601	Rock Around the Clock/Sock It to the Judge	1968	—	3.00	6.00
1604	Sea Cruise/She's a Friday Night Fox	1968	—	3.00	6.00

Albums

RHINO

Number	Title (A Side/B Side)	Yr	VG	VG+	NM
RNLP-210	14 Booming Hits	1982	2.50	5.00	10.00

SWAN

Number	Title (A Side/B Side)	Yr	VG	VG+	NM
LP-502 [M]	The Explosive! Freddy Cannon	1960	30.00	60.00	120.00
LPS-502 [S]	The Explosive! Freddy Cannon	1960	75.00	150.00	300.00
LP-504 [M]	Happy Shades of Blue	1960	37.50	75.00	150.00
LP-505 [M]	Solid Gold Hits	1961	37.50	75.00	150.00
LP-507 [M]	Freddy Cannon at Palisades Park	1962	37.50	75.00	150.00
LP-511 [M]	Freddy Cannon Steps Out	1963	37.50	75.00	150.00

WARNER BROS.

Number	Title (A Side/B Side)	Yr	VG	VG+	NM
W 1544 [M]	Freddie Cannon	1964	7.50	15.00	30.00
WS 1544 [S]	Freddie Cannon	1964	10.00	20.00	40.00
W 1612 [M]	Action!	1965	7.50	15.00	30.00
WS 1612 [S]	Action!	1965	10.00	20.00	40.00
W 1628 [M]	Freddie Cannon's Greatest Hits	1966	7.50	15.00	30.00
WS 1628 [S]	Freddie Cannon's Greatest Hits	1966	10.00	20.00	40.00

CANNON, GUS

Albums

STAX

Number	Title (A Side/B Side)	Yr	VG	VG+	NM
ST-702 [M]	Walk Right In	1962	150.00	300.00	600.00

CANNON, JACKIE

45s

CHAN

Number	Title (A Side/B Side)	Yr	VG	VG+	NM
103	Proof of Your Love/Chill Bumps	1961	10.00	20.00	40.00

CHESS

Number	Title (A Side/B Side)	Yr	VG	VG+	NM
1807	Proof of Your Love/Chill Bumps	1961	3.75	7.50	15.00

CANNON, JOHNNY

See ACE CANNON.

CANO, EDDIE

45s

DUNHILL

Number	Title (A Side/B Side)	Yr	VG	VG+	NM
4072	Monday, Monday/Slip Slip	1967	—	3.00	6.00
4075	Amy's Theme/La Bamba	1967	—	3.00	6.00

GNP CRESCENDO

Number	Title (A Side/B Side)	Yr	VG	VG+	NM
172	La Casita/Hava Nagilah	1962	2.00	4.00	8.00
187	Line for Lyons/Tin Tin Deo	1962	2.00	4.00	8.00

REPRISE

Number	Title (A Side/B Side)	Yr	VG	VG+	NM
0237	Danke Schoen/Our Day Will Come	1963	2.00	4.00	8.00
0254	What Now My Love/Theme from Snow Angel	1963	2.00	4.00	8.00
0382	Tortilla Flats (Part 1)/Tortilla Flats (Part 2)	1965	2.00	4.00	8.00
20075	A Taste of Honey/Panchita	1962	2.00	4.00	8.00
20113	Barsonova Brown/Greenfields	1962	2.00	4.00	8.00
20147	Days of Wine and Roses/Our Day Will Come	1963	2.00	4.00	8.00

Albums

ATCO

Number	Title (A Side/B Side)	Yr	VG	VG+	NM
33-184 [M]	On Broadway	1966	2.50	5.00	10.00
SD 33-184 [S]	On Broadway	1966	3.00	6.00	12.00

DUNHILL

Number	Title (A Side/B Side)	Yr	VG	VG+	NM
D-50018 [M]	Brought Back Live from P.J.'s	1967	3.00	6.00	12.00
DS-50018 [S]	Brought Back Live from P.J.'s	1967	2.50	5.00	10.00

GNP CRESCENDO

Number	Title (A Side/B Side)	Yr	VG	VG+	NM
GNP-77 [M]	A Taste of Cano	1963	3.00	6.00	12.00
GNPS-77 [S]	A Taste of Cano	1963	3.75	7.50	15.00

PICKWICK

Number	Title (A Side/B Side)	Yr	VG	VG+	NM
SPC-3017	25 Latin Dance Favorites	196?	2.50	5.00	10.00

REPRISE

Number	Title (A Side/B Side)	Yr	VG	VG+	NM
R-6030 [M]	Eddie Cano at P.J.'s	1962	3.00	6.00	12.00
R9-6030 [S]	Eddie Cano at P.J.'s	1962	3.75	7.50	15.00
R-6055 [M]	Here Is the Fabulous Eddie Cano	1963	3.00	6.00	12.00
R9-6055 [S]	Here Is the Fabulous Eddie Cano	1963	3.75	7.50	15.00
R-6068 [M]	Cano Plays Mancini	1963	3.00	6.00	12.00
R9-6068 [S]	Cano Plays Mancini	1963	3.75	7.50	15.00
R-6105 [M]	Danke Schoen	1963	3.00	6.00	12.00
R9-6105 [S]	Danke Schoen	1963	3.75	7.50	15.00
R-6124 [M]	Broadway — Right Now!	1964	3.00	6.00	12.00
R9-6124 [S]	Broadway — Right Now!	1964	3.75	7.50	15.00
R-6145 [M]	The Sound of Music	1965	3.00	6.00	12.00
RS-6145 [S]	The Sound of Music	1965	3.75	7.50	15.00

CANTRELL, LANA

45s

POLYDOR

Number	Title (A Side/B Side)	Yr	VG	VG+	NM
14261	Like a Sunday Morning/Good Times	1974	—	2.00	4.00

RCA VICTOR

Number	Title (A Side/B Side)	Yr	VG	VG+	NM
47-8978	Breakfast at Tiffany's/Since I Fell for You	1966	—	3.00	6.00
47-9089	Confession/Theme from The Sand Pebbles	1967	—	3.00	6.00
47-9205	Sunshine/How Can I Hurt You	1967	—	3.00	6.00
47-9391	On the Good Ship Lollipop/When You Wish Upon a Star	1967	—	3.00	6.00
47-9526	The Music Played/Just a Little Lovin'	1968	—	3.00	6.00
47-9619	The Good Times We Had/Catch the Wind	1968	—	3.00	6.00
74-0103	Your Mother Should Know/Mr. Bojangles	1969	—	3.00	6.00
74-0173	All the Things You Are/If I Say No	1969	—	3.00	6.00
74-0268	I Let the Moment Slip By/Tomorrow Is the First Day of the Rest of My Life	1969	—	3.00	6.00

Albums

RCA VICTOR

Number	Title (A Side/B Side)	Yr	VG	VG+	NM
LPM-3755 [M]	And Then There Was Lana	1967	3.75	7.50	15.00
LSP-3755 [S]	And Then There Was Lana	1967	3.00	6.00	12.00
LPM-3862 [M]	Another Shade of Lana	1967	3.75	7.50	15.00
LSP-3862 [S]	Another Shade of Lana	1967	3.00	6.00	12.00
LPM-3947 [M]	Act III	1968	3.75	7.50	15.00
LSP-3947 [S]	Act III	1968	3.00	6.00	12.00
LSP-4026	Lana!	1968	3.00	6.00	12.00
LSP-4121	Now or Then	1969	3.00	6.00	12.00
LSP-4263	The 6th Lana	1970	3.00	6.00	12.00

CAP-TANS, THE

45s

ANNA

Number	Title (A Side/B Side)	Yr	VG	VG+	NM
1122	I'm Afraid/Tight Skirts and Crazy Sweaters	1960	75.00	15.00	30.00

CORAL

Number	Title (A Side/B Side)	Yr	VG	VG+	NM
65071	Asking/Who Can I Turn To	1951	75.00	150.00	300.00

DOT

Number	Title (A Side/B Side)	Yr	VG	VG+	NM
15114	I'm So Crazy for Love/With All My Love	1953	25.00	50.00	100.00

GOTHAM

Number	Title (A Side/B Side)	Yr	VG	VG+	NM
233	My, My, My, Ain't She Pretty/Never Be Lonely	1950	100.00	200.00	400.00
268	I Thought I Could Forget You/Waiting at the Station	1951	75.00	150.00	300.00

CAPALDI, JIM

Also see TRAFFIC.

45s

ATLANTIC

Number	Title (A Side/B Side)	Yr	VG	VG+	NM
89625	I'll Keep Holding On/Tales of Power	1984	—	2.00	4.00
89783 [DJ]	Tonight You're Mine (same on both sides)	1983	—	2.00	4.00
—May be promo only					
89799	Living on the Edge/Gifts of Unknown Things	1983	—	—	3.00
89849	That's Love/Runaway	1983	—	—	3.00
89849 [PS]	That's Love/Runaway	1983	—	2.00	4.00

ISLAND

Number	Title (A Side/B Side)	Yr	VG	VG+	NM
003	It's All Right/Whale Meat Again	1974	—	2.50	5.00
025	It's All Up to You/I've Got So Much Lovin'	1975	—	2.50	5.00
045	Love Hurts/Sugar Honey	1976	—	2.00	4.00
055	Goodbye Love/(B-side unknown)	1976	—	2.00	4.00
067	Goodnight and Good Morning/Short Cut Draw Blood	1976	—	2.00	4.00
1204	Eve/Going Down Slow All the Way	1972	—	3.00	6.00
1205	Oh How We Danced/Open Your Heart	1972	—	3.00	6.00
1216	Tricky Dicky Rides Again/Love Is All You Can Try	1973	—	2.50	5.00
99220	Some Came Running/Favela Music	1989	—	—	3.00
99220 [PS]	Some Came Running/Favela Music	1989	—	—	3.00
99266	Something So Strong/Child in the Storm	1988	—	—	3.00
99266 [PS]	Something So Strong/Child in the Storm	1988	—	—	3.00

RSO

Number	Title (A Side/B Side)	Yr	VG	VG+	NM
912	Daughter of the Night/I'm Gonna Do It	1978	—	2.00	4.00

Albums

ANTILLIES

Number	Title (A Side/B Side)	Yr	VG	VG+	NM
7050	Short Cut Draw Blood	198?	2.00	4.00	8.00
—Reissue of Island 9336					

ATLANTIC

Number	Title (A Side/B Side)	Yr	VG	VG+	NM
80059	Fierce Heart	1983	2.50	5.00	10.00
80182	One Man Mission	1984	2.50	5.00	10.00

ISLAND

Number	Title (A Side/B Side)	Yr	VG	VG+	NM
ILPS 9254	Whale Meat Again	1974	2.50	5.00	10.00

Number	Title (A Side/B Side)	Yr	VG	VG+	NM
SW-9314	Oh How We Danced	1972	3.00	6.00	12.00
ILPS 9336	Short Cut Draw Blood	1976	2.50	5.00	10.00
91024	Some Came Running	1988	2.50	5.00	10.00
RSO					
RS-1-3037	Daughter of the Night	1978	2.50	5.00	10.00
RS-1-3050	Electric Nights	1979	2.50	5.00	10.00

CAPEHART, JERRY

45s

Number	Title (A Side/B Side)	Yr	VG	VG+	NM
CASH					
1021	Walkin' Stick Boogie/Rollin'	1956	50.00	100.00	200.00
—With Eddie and Hank Cochran					
CREST					
1101	Song of New Orleans/The Young and Blue (Theme)	1962	12.50	25.00	50.00

CAPERS, THE

45s

Number	Title (A Side/B Side)	Yr	VG	VG+	NM
DORE					
587	Rockin' Round the Mountain/What Is This Thing Called Love	1961	3.00	6.00	12.00
VEE JAY					
297	Miss You My Dear/Early One Morning	1958	6.25	12.50	25.00
315	Candy Store Blues/High School Diploma	1959	6.25	12.50	25.00

CAPITAL CITY ROCKETS

45s

Number	Title (A Side/B Side)	Yr	VG	VG+	NM
ELEKTRA					
45855	Breakfast in Bed/Grab Your Honey	1973	2.00	4.00	8.00
45872	Little Bit O' Fun/Ten Hole Dollars	1973	2.00	4.00	8.00
Albums					
ELEKTRA					
EKS-75079	Capital City Rockets	1973	5.00	10.00	20.00

CAPITOLS, THE (1)

Detroit-based R&B vocal group.

45s

Number	Title (A Side/B Side)	Yr	VG	VG+	NM
KAREN					
1524	Cool Jerk/Hello Stranger	1966	3.75	7.50	15.00
1525	I Got to Handle It/Zig Zagging	1966	2.50	5.00	10.00
1526	We Got a Thing That's In the Groove/Tired Running from You	1966	2.50	5.00	10.00
1534	Patty Cake/Take a Chance on Me Baby	1967	2.50	5.00	10.00
1536	Cool Pearl/Don't Say Maybe Baby	1967	2.50	5.00	10.00
1537	Cool Jerk '68/Afro Twist	1968	2.50	5.00	10.00
1543	Soul Brother, Soul Sister/Ain't That Terrible	1968	2.50	5.00	10.00
1546	Soul Soul/When You're in Trouble	1969	2.50	5.00	10.00
1549	I Thought She Loved Me/When You're in Trouble	1969	2.50	5.00	10.00
Albums					
ATCO					
33-190 [M]	Dance the Cool Jerk	1966	10.00	20.00	40.00
SD 33-190 [S]	Dance the Cool Jerk	1966	12.50	25.00	50.00
33-201 [M]	We Got a Thing That's In the Groove	1966	10.00	20.00	40.00
SD 33-201 [S]	We Got a Thing That's In the Groove	1966	12.50	25.00	50.00
COLLECTABLES					
COL-5105	Golden Classics	1988	2.50	5.00	10.00
SOLID SMOKE					
8019	The Capitols: Their Greatest Hits	1983	3.00	6.00	12.00

CAPITOLS, THE (2)

Not group (1).

45s

Number	Title (A Side/B Side)	Yr	VG	VG+	NM
CARLTON					
461	I Let Her Go/I've Got a Girl	1958	150.00	300.00	600.00

CAPITOLS, THE (U)

None of these is by group (1), though it's possible that one or more is by group (2).

45s

Number	Title (A Side/B Side)	Yr	VG	VG+	NM
CINDY					
3002	Rosemary/Millie	1957	50.00	100.00	200.00
GATEWAY					
721	Day By Day/Little Things	1964	75.00	150.00	300.00
PET					
807	Angel of Love/'Cause I Love You	1958	50.00	100.00	200.00
TRIUMPH					
601	Three O'Clock Rock/Write Me a Love Letter	1959	7.50	15.00	30.00

CAPONE, SUSAN

45s

Number	Title (A Side/B Side)	Yr	VG	VG+	NM
PILGRIM					
704	I'll Be Dancing/Four or Five Hundred Kisses	1956	6.25	12.50	25.00
718	Click-I-Dee, Click-I-Dee/Maybe Someday	1956	6.25	12.50	25.00

CAPRIS, THE (1)

Italian male vocal group from New York.

45s

Number	Title (A Side/B Side)	Yr	VG	VG+	NM
20TH CENTURY					
1201	My Weakness/Yes, My Baby, Please!	1957	15.00	30.00	60.00
AMBIENT SOUND					
02697	There's a Moon Out Again/Morse Code of Love	1982	—	3.00	6.00
CANDLELITE					
422	Oh, My Darling/Rock Pretty Baby	196?	3.00	6.00	12.00
LIFETIME					
1001/2	Oh My Darling/Rock Pretty Baby	1961	25.00	50.00	100.00
LOST-NITE					
101	There's a Moon Out Tonight/Indian Girl	1961	17.50	35.00	70.00
—Pink label original					
101	There's a Moon Out Tonight/Indian Girl	196?	2.00	4.00	8.00
—Yellow label reissue					
148	Little Girl/When	196?	2.00	4.00	8.00
MR. PEEKE					
118	Limbo/From the Vine Came the Grape	1963	5.00	10.00	20.00
OLD TOWN					
1094	There's a Moon Out Tonight/Indian Girl	1961	7.50	15.00	30.00
—Light blue label					
1094	There's a Moon Out Tonight/Indian Girl	1962	5.00	10.00	20.00
—Mostly black label					
1099	Where I Fell in Love/Some People Think	1961	7.50	15.00	30.00
1103	Tears in My Eyes/Why Do I Cry	1961	7.50	15.00	30.00
1107	Girl in My Dreams/My Island in the Sun	1961	7.50	15.00	30.00
PLANET					
1010	There's a Moon Out Tonight/Indian Girl	1958	400.00	800.00	1200.
SABRE					
201/2	My Promise to You/Bop! Bop! Bop!	1959	37.50	75.00	150.00
TROMMERS					
101	There's a Moon Out Tonight/Indian Girl	1961	6.25	12.50	25.00
—Red label					
101	There's a Moon Out Tonight/Indian Girl	1961	6.25	12.50	25.00
—White label (not a promo)					
Albums					
AMBIENT SOUND					
FW 37714	There's a Moon Out Again	1982	3.75	7.50	15.00
COLLECTABLES					
COL-5016	There's a Moon Out Tonight	198?	3.00	6.00	12.00

CAPRIS, THE (2)

Different male vocal group than (1).

45s

Number	Title (A Side/B Side)	Yr	VG	VG+	NM
GOTHAM					
304	God Only Knows/That's What You're Doing to Me	1954	150.00	300.00	600.00
—Blue label					
304	God Only Knows/That's What You're Doing to Me	1954	30.00	60.00	120.00
—Red label					
304	God Only Knows/That's What You're Doing to Me	1956	20.00	40.00	80.00
—Yellow label					
306	It Was Moonglow/Too Poor to Love	1955	50.00	100.00	200.00
308	It's a Miracle/Let's Linger Awhile	1956	30.00	60.00	120.00
Albums					
COLLECTABLES					
COL-5000	Gotham Recording Stars	198?	3.00	6.00	12.00

CAPTAIN AND TENNILLE

45s

Number	Title (A Side/B Side)	Yr	VG	VG+	NM
A&M					
1624	The Way I Want to Touch You/Disney Girls	1974	—	3.00	6.00
1672	Love Will Keep Us Together/Gentle Stranger	1975	—	2.00	4.00
1672 [PS]	Love Will Keep Us Together/Gentle Stranger	1975	—	3.00	6.00
1715	Por Amor Vivremos (Love Will Keep Us Together)/Broddy Bounce	1975	—	2.50	5.00
1725	The Way I Want to Touch You/Broddy Bounce	1975	—	2.00	4.00
1725 [PS]	The Way I Want to Touch You/Broddy Bounce	1975	—	3.00	6.00
1774	Como Yo Quiero Sentorte (The Way I Want to Touch You)/El Rebote de Broddy	1975	—	2.50	5.00
1782	Lonely Night (Angel Face)/Smile for Me One More Time	1976	—	2.00	4.00
1782 [PS]	Lonely Night (Angel Face)/Smile for Me One More Time	1976	—	3.00	6.00
1817	Shop Around/Butterscotch Castle	1976	—	2.00	4.00
1817 [PS]	Shop Around/Butterscotch Castle	1976	—	3.00	6.00
1870	Muskrat Love/Honey Come Love Me	1976	—	2.00	4.00
1870 [PS]	Muskrat Love/Honey Come Love Me	1976	—	3.00	6.00
1894	Song of Joy/Wedding Song (There Is Love)	1976	—	—	—
—Unreleased					
1912	Can't Stop Dancin'/Mis Canciones (The Good Songs)	1977	—	2.00	4.00
1912 [PS]	Can't Stop Dancin'/Mis Canciones (The Good Songs)	1977	—	3.00	6.00
1944	Come In from the Rain/We Never Really Said Goodbye	1977	—	2.00	4.00
1944 [PS]	Come In from the Rain/We Never Really Said Goodbye	1977	—	3.00	6.00
1970	Circles/1954 Boogie Blues	1977	—	2.00	4.00
2027	I'm On My Way/We Never Really Said Goodbye	1978	—	2.00	4.00
2027 [PS]	I'm On My Way/We Never Really Said Goodbye	1978	—	3.00	6.00
2063	You Never Done It Like That/"D" Keyboard Blues	1978	—	2.00	4.00
2063 [PS]	You Never Done It Like That/"D" Keyboard Blues	1978	—	3.00	6.00
2106	You Need a Woman Tonight/Love Me Like a Baby	1978	—	2.00	4.00
2106 [PS]	You Need a Woman Tonight/Love Me Like a Baby	1978	—	3.00	6.00
8600	Lonely Night (Angel Face)/Shop Around	1977	—	2.00	4.00
—Originals on green and yellow labels (later issues $3 NM)					
8600 [PS]	Lonely Night (Angel Face)/Shop Around	1977	—	3.00	6.00
8601	Song of Joy/Wedding Song (There Is Love)	1977	—	2.00	4.00
—Originals on green and yellow labels (later issues $3 NM)					
8601 [PS]	Song of Joy/Wedding Song (There Is Love)	1977	—	3.00	6.00
BUTTERSCOTCH CASTLE					
001	The Way I Want to Tocuh You/Disney Girls	1974	20.00	40.00	80.00
CASABLANCA					
2215	Do That To Me One More Time/Deep in the Dark	1979	—	2.00	4.00
2243	Love on a Shoestring/How Can You Be So Cold	1980	—	2.00	4.00
2247	Amame Una Vez Mas (Do That To Me One More Time)/Deep in the Dark	1980	—	2.00	4.00
2264	Baby You Still Got It/Happy Together (A Fantasy)	1980	—	2.00	4.00
2320	This Is Not the First Time/Gentle Stranger	1980	—	2.00	4.00
2328	Don't Forget Me/Keep Our Love Warm	1981	—	2.00	4.00
JOYCE					
101	The Way I Want to Tocuh You/Disney Girls	1974	10.00	20.00	40.00
PUREBRED					
0001	Tahoe Snow/Here Comes Santa Claus	198?	—	2.50	5.00
0001 [PS]	Tahoe Snow/Here Comes Santa Claus	198?	—	3.00	5.00
Albums					
A&M					
SP-3105	Captain & Tennille's Greatest Hits	198?	2.00	4.00	8.00
—Reissue of 4667					

Number	Title (A Side/B Side)	Yr	VG	VG+	NM
SP-3405	Love Will Keep Us Together	1975	3.00	6.00	12.00
SP-4552	Love Will Keep Us Together	1975	2.50	5.00	10.00
—Reissue of 3405					
SP-4561	Por Amor Vivremos	1975	3.00	6.00	12.00
SP-4570	Song of Joy	1976	2.50	5.00	10.00
SP-4667	Captain & Tennille's Greatest Hits	1977	2.50	5.00	10.00
SP-4700	Come In From the Rain	1977	2.50	5.00	10.00
SP-4707	Dream	1978	2.50	5.00	10.00
QU-54552 [Q]	Love Will Keep Us Together	1975	3.75	7.50	15.00
CASABLANCA					
NBLP 7188	Make Your Move	1979	2.50	5.00	10.00
NBLP 7250	Keeping Our Love Warm	1980	2.50	5.00	10.00

CAPTAIN BEEFHEART

Also see FRANK ZAPPA.

45s

Number	Title (A Side/B Side)	Yr	VG	VG+	NM
A&M					
794	Diddy Wah Diddy/Who Do You Think You're Fooling	1966	10.00	20.00	40.00
818	Moonchild/Here I Am, Here I Always Am	1966	12.50	25.00	50.00
BUDDAH					
9	Yellow Brick Road/Abba Zaba	1967	3.75	7.50	15.00
108	Plastic Factory/Where There's Woman	1969	3.75	7.50	15.00
EPIC					
03190	Ice Cream for Crow/Light Reflected Off the Oceans of the Moon	1982	—	2.50	5.00
03190 [PS]	Ice Cream for Crow/Light Reflected Off the Oceans of the Moon	1982	—	3.00	6.00
MERCURY					
73494	I Got Love on My Mind/Upon the My-O-My	1974	2.00	4.00	8.00
REPRISE					
1068	Click Clack/I'm Gonna Boogalize You Baby	1972	3.75	7.50	15.00
1133	Too Much Time/My Head Is My Only House Unless It Rains	1972	3.75	7.50	15.00

Albums

Number	Title (A Side/B Side)	Yr	VG	VG+	NM
A&M					
SP-12510 [EP]	The Legendary A&M Sessions	1984	2.50	5.00	10.00
BLUE THUMB					
BTS-1	Strictly Personal	1968	12.50	25.00	50.00
—Black label, unbanded sides					
BTS-1	Strictly Personal	1969	7.50	15.00	30.00
—White label, unbanded sides					
BTS-1	Strictly Personal	197?	5.00	10.00	20.00
—White label, banded sides					
BUDDAH					
1001/5001	Safe As Milk "Baby Jesus" Bumper Sticker	1967	6.25	12.50	25.00
BDM-1001 [M]	Safe As Milk	1967	25.00	50.00	100.00
BDS-5001 [S]	Safe As Milk	1967	15.00	30.00	60.00
BDS-5063	Safe As Milk	1969	6.25	12.50	25.00
BDS-5077	Mirror Man	1971	12.50	25.00	50.00
—Die-cut gatefold cover					
BDS-5077	Mirror Man	197?	6.25	12.50	25.00
—Regular cover					
MERCURY					
SRM-1-709	Unconditionally Guaranteed	1974	3.75	7.50	15.00
SRM-1-1018	Bluejeans and Moonbeams	1975	5.00	10.00	20.00
REPRISE					
2MS 2027 [(2)]	Trout Mask Replica	1970	7.50	15.00	30.00
—Stock copy with 2027 labels and 2027 jacket					
MS 2050	The Spotlight Kid	1971	5.00	10.00	20.00
MS 2115	Clear Spot	1972	5.00	10.00	20.00
RS 6420	Lick My Decals Off, Baby	1970	5.00	10.00	20.00
STRAIGHT					
2 STS-1053 [(2)]	Trout Mask Replica	1969	62.50	125.00	250.00
—Stock copy with 1053 labels (this has been confirmed to exist)					
2 STS-1053 [(2) DJ]	Trout Mask Replica	1969	50.00	100.00	200.00
—White label promo with 1053 labels					
2MS 2027 [(2)]	Trout Mask Replica	1969	15.00	30.00	60.00
—Stock copy with 2027 labels inside 1053 jacket					
2MS 2027 [(2) DJ]	Trout Mask Replica	1969	37.50	75.00	150.00
—White label promo with 2027 labels inside 1053 jacket					
RS 6420	Lick My Decals Off, Baby	1970	12.50	25.00	50.00
VERVE FORECAST					
FTS-3054	Captain Beefheart and the Magic Band	1968	—	—	—
—Canceled					
VIRGIN					
VA 13148	Doc at the Radar Station	1980	3.00	6.00	12.00
ARE 38274	Ice Cream for Crow	1982	3.00	6.00	12.00
WARNER BROS.					
(no #)	Bat Chain Puller	1978	100.00	200.00	400.00
—Test pressing with different selections than stock version					
BSK 3256	Shiny Beast (Bat Chain Puller)	1978	3.00	6.00	12.00

CAPTAIN BEYOND

45s

Number	Title (A Side/B Side)	Yr	VG	VG+	NM
CAPRICORN					
0013	As the Moon Speaks (Return)/A Thousand Days of Yesterdays (Time Since Come & Gone)	1972	—	3.00	6.00
0029	Drifting in Space/Sufficiently Breathless	1973	—	3.00	6.00

Albums

Number	Title (A Side/B Side)	Yr	VG	VG+	NM
CAPRICORN					
CP 0105	Captain Beyond	1972	7.50	15.00	30.00
—Original covers are 3-D					
CP 0105	Captain Beyond	1972	3.75	7.50	15.00
—Later covers are normal					
CP 0115	Sufficiently Breathless	1973	3.75	7.50	15.00
WARNER BROS.					
BS 3047	Dawn Explosion	1977	2.50	5.00	10.00

CAPTAIN ZAP AND THE MOTORTOWN CUT-UPS

45s

Number	Title (A Side/B Side)	Yr	VG	VG+	NM
MOTOWN					
1151	The Luney Landing/The Luney Take-Off	1969	5.00	10.00	20.00

CAPTIVATIONS, THE

45s

Number	Title (A Side/B Side)	Yr	VG	VG+	NM
GARPAX					
44179	Red Hot Scrambler-Go/Speed Shift	1964	7.50	15.00	30.00
PENTACLE					
1635	Red Hot Scramblers-Go/Speed Shift	1964	15.00	30.00	60.00

CARAVAN

45s

Number	Title (A Side/B Side)	Yr	VG	VG+	NM
LONDON					
20065	Love to Love You/Golf Girl	1971	—	3.00	6.00
20080	Headloss/(B-side unknown)	1973	—	3.00	6.00
VERVE FORECAST					
5102	A Place of My Own/Ride	1969	2.50	5.00	10.00

Albums

Number	Title (A Side/B Side)	Yr	VG	VG+	NM
ARISTA					
AL 4088	Blind Dog	1976	2.50	5.00	10.00
BTM					
5000	Cunning Stunts	1975	2.50	5.00	10.00
LONDON					
PS 582	If I Could Do It All Over Again...	1971	3.75	7.50	15.00
PS 593	In the Land of the Grey & Pink	1971	3.75	7.50	15.00
XPS 615	Waterloo Lily	1972	3.75	7.50	15.00
XPS 637	For Girls Who Grow Plump in the Night	1973	3.75	7.50	15.00
XPS 650	Caravan and the New Symphonia	1974	3.75	7.50	15.00
LC 50011	The Best of Caravan	1978	2.50	5.00	10.00
VERVE FORECAST					
FTS-3066	Caravan	1969	10.00	20.00	40.00

CARAVAN, JIMMY

Albums

Number	Title (A Side/B Side)	Yr	VG	VG+	NM
TOWER					
ST 5103	Look Into the Flower	1968	5.00	10.00	20.00
VAULT					
9007	Hey Jude	1969	5.00	10.00	20.00

CARAVELLES, THE (1)

British female vocal group.

45s

Number	Title (A Side/B Side)	Yr	VG	VG+	NM
SMASH					
1852	You Don't Have to Be a Baby to Cry/The Last One to Know	1963	3.75	7.50	15.00
1869	Have You Ever Been Lonely/Don't Blow Your Cool	1964	3.00	6.00	12.00
1901	You Are Here/How Can I Be Sure	1964	3.00	6.00	12.00
1958	I Don't Care If the Sun Don't Shine/I Like a Man	1964	3.00	6.00	12.00

Albums

Number	Title (A Side/B Side)	Yr	VG	VG+	NM
SMASH					
MGS-27044 [M]	You Don't Have to Be a Baby to Cry	1963	15.00	30.00	60.00
SRS-67044 [R]	You Don't Have to Be a Baby to Cry	1963	15.00	30.00	60.00

CARAVELLES, THE (U)

These may or may not be the same group, but they are definitely not group (1).

45s

Number	Title (A Side/B Side)	Yr	VG	VG+	NM
JOEY					
301	Falling for You/Shake Baby	1963	37.50	75.00	150.00
6208	One Little Kiss/Twistin' Marie	1962	25.00	50.00	100.00
STARMAKER					
1925	Pink Lips/Angry Angel	1961	6.25	12.50	25.00

CARBO, CHUCK

Also see THE SPIDERS.

45s

Number	Title (A Side/B Side)	Yr	VG	VG+	NM
ACE					
631	Tears, Tears and More Tears/I Shouldn't, But I Do	1961	3.00	6.00	12.00
666	Out on a Limb/Getting Out	1962	3.00	6.00	12.00
IMPERIAL					
5405	That's the Way to Win My Heart/Goodbye	1956	6.25	12.50	25.00
5423	Honey Bee/That's My Desire	1957	7.50	15.00	30.00
5452	The Bells Are Ringing/Poor Boy	1957	5.00	10.00	20.00
5479	I Miss You/The Times	1957	5.00	10.00	20.00
INSTANT					
3240	In the Night/Run. Henry	1962	3.00	6.00	12.00
3254	Two Tables Away/What Does It Take	1962	3.00	6.00	12.00
REX					
1003	Promises/Be My Girl	1959	3.75	7.50	15.00
1011	Lucy Brown/A Picture of You	1960	3.75	7.50	15.00
1012	Blue Velvet/It's You	1960	3.75	7.50	15.00

CARDBOARD ZEPPELIN

Supposedly a pseudonym for THE REGENTS.

45s

Number	Title (A Side/B Side)	Yr	VG	VG+	NM
LAURIE					
3433	City Lights/Ten Story Building	1968	6.25	12.50	25.00

CARDINALS, THE (1)

Baltimore-based male vocal group.

45s

Number	Title (A Side/B Side)	Yr	VG	VG+	NM
ATLANTIC					
952	I'll Always Love You/Pretty Baby Blues	1952	100.00	200.00	400.00
—Cardinals records on Atlantic before 952 are unconfirmed on 45 rpm					
958	Wheel of Fortune/Kiss Me Baby	1952	150.00	300.00	600.00
972	The Bump/She Rocks	1952	75.00	150.00	300.00
995	You Are My Only Love/Lovie Darling	1953	100.00	200.00	400.00
1025	Please Baby/Under a Blanket of Blue	1954	50.00	100.00	200.00

Number	Title (A Side/B Side)	Yr	VG	VG+	NM
1054	The Door Is Still Open/Misirlou	1955	20.00	40.00	80.00
1067	Come Back My Love/Two Things I Love	1955	25.00	50.00	100.00
1079	Lovely Girl/There Goes My Heart to You	1955	25.00	50.00	100.00
1090	Choo Choo/Off Shore	1956	12.50	25.00	50.00
1103	The End of the Story/I Won't Make You Cry Anymore	1956	12.50	25.00	50.00
1126	Near You/One Love	1957	10.00	20.00	40.00

CARDINALS, THE (2)

45s

CHA CHA

Number	Title (A Side/B Side)	Yr	VG	VG+	NM
740	I Want You/Tomato Juice	1966	7.50	15.00	30.00
740 [PS]	I Want You/Tomato Juice	1966	12.50	25.00	50.00
741	Go Go Baby/Hatchet Face	1966	6.25	12.50	25.00
742	Saturday Night/I'm Gonna Tell on You	1966	6.25	12.50	25.00
748	When You're Away/I'm Gonna Tell on You	1966	6.25	12.50	25.00

CARE PACKAGE

45s

JUBILEE

Number	Title (A Side/B Side)	Yr	VG	VG+	NM
5599	To Discover/World of Thursday	1967	2.50	5.00	10.00

Albums

LIBERTY

Number	Title (A Side/B Side)	Yr	VG	VG+	NM
LST-7647	Keep On Keepin' On	1970	6.25	12.50	25.00

CAREFREES, THE

45s

LONDON INT'L.

Number	Title (A Side/B Side)	Yr	VG	VG+	NM
10614	We Love You Beatles/Hot Blooded Lover	1964	5.00	10.00	20.00
—Red label					
10614	We Love You Beatles/Hot Blooded Lover	1964	5.00	10.00	20.00
—Gold label					
10614 [PS]	We Love You Beatles/Hot Blooded Lover	1964	10.00	20.00	40.00
10615	Paddy Whack/Aren't You Glad You're You	1964	3.75	7.50	15.00

Albums

LONDON

Number	Title (A Side/B Side)	Yr	VG	VG+	NM
PS 379 [S]	From England! The Carefrees	1964	25.00	50.00	100.00
LL 3379 [M]	From England! The Carefrees	1964	20.00	40.00	80.00

CARETAKERS, THE

45s

ABC

Number	Title (A Side/B Side)	Yr	VG	VG+	NM
11110	Get Off My Tulips/Bee Side Blues	1968	3.00	6.00	12.00

CARGILL, HENSON

45s

ARCO

Number	Title (A Side/B Side)	Yr	VG	VG+	NM
6605	Big Town/How Long Is Never	1967	2.00	4.00	8.00

ATLANTIC

Number	Title (A Side/B Side)	Yr	VG	VG+	NM
4007	Some Old California Memory/A Writer of Verses and a Singer of Songs	1973	—	2.00	4.00
4016	She Still Comes to Me (To Pour the Wine)/But You Know I Love You	1974	—	2.00	4.00
4021	Stop and Smell the Roses/Strawberry Wine	1974	—	2.00	4.00

COPPER MOUNTAIN

Number	Title (A Side/B Side)	Yr	VG	VG+	NM
201	Silence on the Line/(B-side unknown)	1979	—	2.00	4.00
589	Have a Good Day/(B-side unknown)	1980	—	2.00	4.00

ELEKTRA

Number	Title (A Side/B Side)	Yr	VG	VG+	NM
45234	Deep in the Heart of Dixie/It Hurts the Man	1975	—	2.00	4.00
45273	Something to Hold On To/Now and Then	1975	—	2.00	4.00

MEGA

Number	Title (A Side/B Side)	Yr	VG	VG+	NM
0030	Pencil Marks on the Wall/Momma's Waiting	1971	—	2.50	5.00
0043	Naked and Crying/Afraid to Rock the Boat	1971	—	2.50	5.00
0060	I Can't Face the Bed Alone/Daddy Don't You Walk So Fast	1972	—	2.50	5.00
0074	Oklahoma Hell/She Likes Warm Summer Days	1972	—	2.50	5.00
0090	Red Skies Over Georgia/1932	1972	—	2.50	5.00

MONUMENT

Number	Title (A Side/B Side)	Yr	VG	VG+	NM
1041	Skip a Rope/Very Well Traveled Man	1967	—	3.00	6.00
1065	Row Row Row/Six White Horses	1968	—	3.00	6.00
1084	She Thinks I'm On That Train/It Just Don't Take Me Long to Say Goodbye	1968	—	3.00	6.00
1106	A Candle for Amy/Wild Flower	1968	—	3.00	6.00
1122	None of My Business/So Many Ways of Saying She's Gone	1969	—	3.00	6.00
1142	This Generation Shall Not Pass/Little Girls and Little Boys	1969	—	3.00	6.00
1158	Then the Baby Came/Hemphill, Kentucky, Consolidated Coal Mine	1969	—	3.00	6.00
1178	Silver Bells/The Little Drummer Boy	1969	2.00	4.00	8.00
1184	Me & Bobby McGee/What's My Name	1970	—	3.00	6.00
1198	The Most Uncomplicated Goodbye I've Ever Heard/Four Shades of Love	1970	—	3.00	6.00
1209	Bless 'Em All/How Much Do Memories Cost	1970	—	3.00	6.00

TOWER

Number	Title (A Side/B Side)	Yr	VG	VG+	NM
400	Picking White Cotton/Joe, Jesse and I	1968	2.00	4.00	8.00

Albums

ATLANTIC

Number	Title (A Side/B Side)	Yr	VG	VG+	NM
SD 7279	This Is Henson Cargill Country	1973	3.00	6.00	12.00

HARMONY

Number	Title (A Side/B Side)	Yr	VG	VG+	NM
KH 31397	Welcome to My World	1972	2.50	5.00	10.00

MEGA

Number	Title (A Side/B Side)	Yr	VG	VG+	NM
31-1016	On the Road	1972	3.75	7.50	15.00

MONUMENT

Number	Title (A Side/B Side)	Yr	VG	VG+	NM
SLP-18094	Skip a Rope	1968	5.00	10.00	20.00
SLP-18103	Coming On Strong	1968	5.00	10.00	20.00
SLP-18117	None of My Business	1969	5.00	10.00	20.00
SLP-18137	Uncomplicated	1970	5.00	10.00	20.00

CARIANS, THE

Also see THE CORDIALS.

45s

INDIGO

Number	Title (A Side/B Side)	Yr	VG	VG+	NM
136	She's Gone/Snooty Friends	1961	25.00	50.00	100.00

MAGENTA

Number	Title (A Side/B Side)	Yr	VG	VG+	NM
04	Only a Dream/Girls	1961	12.50	25.00	50.00

CARLA AND RUFUS

See RUFUS AND CARLA.

CARLE, BOBBY, AND THE BLENDAIRES

45s

DECCA

Number	Title (A Side/B Side)	Yr	VG	VG+	NM
30938	I Got It Bad and That Ain't Good/Guaranteed	1959	7.50	15.00	30.00

CARLIN, GEORGE

45s

LITTLE DAVID

Number	Title (A Side/B Side)	Yr	VG	VG+	NM
720	Eleven O'Clock News (Part 1)/Eleven O'Clock News (Part 2)	1971	—	3.00	6.00
731	New News (Part 1)/New News (Part 2)	1974	—	3.00	6.00
736	Head Lines (Part 1)/Head Lines (Part 2)	1977	—	3.00	6.00

RCA VICTOR

Number	Title (A Side/B Side)	Yr	VG	VG+	NM
47-9110	Winderful WINO/Al Sleet, Your Hippy Dippy Weatherman	1967	2.50	5.00	10.00

7-Inch Extended Plays

ATLANTIC

Number	Title (A Side/B Side)	Yr	VG	VG+	NM
EP-PR-409 [DJ]	*Have a Nice Day/Rice Krispies/Second, Third, Fifth, Sixth Announcements/Join the Book Club/Ice Box Man	197?	2.50	5.00	10.00
EP-PR-409 [PS]	A Place for My Stuff	197?	2.50	5.00	10.00

Albums

ATLANTIC

Number	Title (A Side/B Side)	Yr	VG	VG+	NM
SD 19326	A Place for My Stuff	1981	2.50	5.00	10.00

EARDRUM

Number	Title (A Side/B Side)	Yr	VG	VG+	NM
1001	Carlin On Campus	1984	2.50	5.00	10.00
90523	Playin' with Your Head	1986	2.50	5.00	10.00
90972	What Am I Doing in New Jersey?	1988	2.50	5.00	10.00

ERA

Number	Title (A Side/B Side)	Yr	VG	VG+	NM
EL 103 [M]	George Carlin and Jack Burns At the Playboy Club Tonight	1960	6.25	12.50	25.00
E 600	The Original George Carlin	1972	3.00	6.00	12.00

LAFF

Number	Title (A Side/B Side)	Yr	VG	VG+	NM
A 219	Killer Carlin	197?	2.50	5.00	10.00
—Reissue of Era material					

LITTLE DAVID

Number	Title (A Side/B Side)	Yr	VG	VG+	NM
LD 1004	Class Clown	1972	2.50	5.00	10.00
LD 1005	Occupation: Foole	1973	2.50	5.00	10.00
LD 1008	An Evening with Wally Londo	1975	2.50	5.00	10.00
LD 1075	On the Road	1977	2.50	5.00	10.00
LD 1076	Indecent Exposure (Some of the Best of George Carlin)	1978	2.50	5.00	10.00
LD 3003	Toledo Window Box	1974	2.50	5.00	10.00
LD 7214	FM & AM	1972	2.50	5.00	10.00
90129	Toledo Window Box	1983	2.00	4.00	8.00
—Reissue of 3003					
90241	The George Carlin Collection	1984	2.00	4.00	8.00

RCA CAMDEN

Number	Title (A Side/B Side)	Yr	VG	VG+	NM
CAS-2566	Take-Offs and Put-Ons	1972	2.50	5.00	10.00

RCA VICTOR

Number	Title (A Side/B Side)	Yr	VG	VG+	NM
LPM-3772 [M]	Take-Offs and Put-Ons	1967	5.00	10.00	20.00
LSP-3772 [S]	Take-Offs and Put-Ons	1967	3.75	7.50	15.00

CARLO

45s

LAURIE

Number	Title (A Side/B Side)	Yr	VG	VG+	NM
3063	Happy Time/Rockin' Rocket	1960	5.00	10.00	20.00
—As "Carlo and Jimmy"					
3151	Baby Doll/Write Me a Letter	1962	7.50	15.00	30.00
3157	Little Orphan Girl/Mairzy Doats	1963	7.50	15.00	30.00
3175	Five Minutes More/The Story of Love	1963	7.50	15.00	30.00
3227	Ring-a-Ling/Stranger in My Arms	1964	12.50	25.00	50.00

RAFTIS

Number	Title (A Side/B Side)	Yr	VG	VG+	NM
110	Claudine/Fever	1970	3.00	6.00	12.00

CARLOS, WALTER

In the early 1980s, he became a she (Wendy Carlos). It's possible that many of the early LPs were reissued with the new name on them, but we have not confirmed this.

45s

COLUMBIA

Number	Title (A Side/B Side)	Yr	VG	VG+	NM
8-3322 [PS]	A Second Chance for Bach!	1969	5.00	10.00	20.00
—Promo-only sleeve that came with JZSP 139195/6					
44803	Brandenberg Concerto No. 3 in G Major/Two-Part Invention in F Major	1969	2.50	5.00	10.00
45033	Third Movement, Brandenburg Concerto No. 4 in D Major/Scarliotta Sonata	1969	2.50	5.00	10.00
JZSP 139195/6 [DJ]	Third Movement, Brandenburg Concerto No. 3 (mono/stereo)	1969	3.00	6.00	12.00

Albums

CBS MASTERWORKS

Number	Title (A Side/B Side)	Yr	VG	VG+	NM
M 39340	Digital Moonscapes	1984	2.50	5.00	10.00
—As "Wendy Carlos"					

COLUMBIA

Number	Title (A Side/B Side)	Yr	VG	VG+	NM
KG 31236 [(2)]	Sonic Seasonings	1972	3.75	7.50	15.00
KC 31480	Walter Carlos' Clockwork Orange	1972	3.00	6.00	12.00

COLUMBIA MASTERWORKS

Number	Title (A Side/B Side)	Yr	VG	VG+	NM
MS 7194	Switched-On Bach	1968	3.75	7.50	15.00
—Gray label with "360 Sound Stereo"					
MS 7194	Switched-On Bach	1970	3.00	6.00	12.00
—Gray label with orange Columbia logos and no "360 Sound Stereo"					

Number	Title (A Side/B Side)	Yr	VG	VG+	NM
MS 7286	The Well-Tempered Synthesizer	1969	3.75	7.50	15.00
—Gray label with "360 Sound Stereo"					
MS 7286	The Well-Tempered Synthesizer	1970	3.00	6.00	12.00
—Gray label with orange Columbia logos and no "360 Sound Stereo"					
M 32088	Walter Carlos By Request	1973	3.00	6.00	12.00
KM 32659	More Switched-On Bach	1974	3.00	6.00	12.00
M2X 35895 [(2)]	Switched-On Brandenburgs	1979	3.75	7.50	15.00
HM 45950	Switched-On Brandenburgs Vol. 1	1980	25.00	50.00	100.00
—Half-speed mastered edition					
HS 47194	Switched-On Bach	198?	7.50	15.00	30.00
—Half-speed mastered edition					

CARLTON, CARL

12-Inch Singles

Number	Title (A Side/B Side)	Yr	VG	VG+	NM
RCA					
PD-13314	Baby I Need Your Loving/Everyone Can Be a Star	1982	2.00	4.00	8.00
PD-13407	Swing That Sexy Thang/Just One Kiss	1982	2.00	4.00	8.00

45s

Number	Title (A Side/B Side)	Yr	VG	VG+	NM
20TH CENTURY					
2459	This Feeling's Rated X-Tra/Fighting in the Name of Love	1980	—	2.00	4.00
2488	She's a Bad Mama Jama (She's Built, She's Stacked)/This Feeling's Rated X-Tra	1981	—	2.00	4.00
2513	Let Me Love You Till the Morning Comes/Sexy Lady	1982	—	2.00	4.00
2601	I Think It's Gonna Be Alright/Let Me Love You Till the Morning Comes	1982	—	2.00	4.00
ABC					
11378	You Can't Stop a Man in Love/You Times Me Plus Love	1973	—	2.50	5.00
12059	Smokin' Room/Signed, Sealed, Delivered, I'm Yours	1974	—	2.50	5.00
12089	Morning, Noon and Nightime/Our Day Will Come	1975	—	2.50	5.00
12166	Ain't Gonna Tell Nobody (About You)/Live for Today, Not for Tomorrow	1976	—	2.50	5.00
12226	Let's Groove/Live for Today, Not for Tomorrow	1976	—	2.50	5.00
BACK BEAT					
588	Competition Ain't Nothin'/Three Way Love	1968	—	3.00	6.00
—As "Little Carl Carlton"					
598	46 Drums — 1 Guitar/Why Don't They Leave Us Alone	1968	—	3.00	6.00
—As "Little Carl Carlton"					
603	Look at Mary Wonder (How I Got Over)/Bad for Each Other	1969	—	3.00	6.00
—As "Little Carl Carlton"					
610	Don't Walk Away/Hold On a Little Longer	1969	—	3.00	6.00
613	Drop By My Place/Two Timer	1970	—	3.00	6.00
—As "Little Carl Carlton"					
617	I Can Feel It/You've Got So Much (To Learn About Love)	1970	—	3.00	6.00
619	Sure Miss Loving You/Wild Child	1970	—	3.00	6.00
621	Wild Child/Look at Mary Wonder (How I Got Over)	1971	—	3.00	6.00
624	The Generation Gap/Where Have You Been	1972	—	3.00	6.00
627	I Won't Let That Chump Break Your Heart/Why Don't They Leave Us Alone	1972	—	3.00	6.00
629	It Ain't Been Easy/I Wanna Be Your Main Squeeze	1973	—	3.00	6.00
630	Everlasting Love/I Wanna Be Your Main Squeeze	1974	2.00	4.00	8.00
27001	Everlasting Love/I Wanna Be Your Main Squeeze	1974	—	2.50	5.00
CASABLANCA					
880949-7	Private Property/Mama's Boy	1985	—	—	3.00
884274-7	Slipped, Tripped (Fooled Around and Fell in Love)/Hot	1986	—	—	3.00
GOLDEN WORLD					
23	Nothin' No Sweeter Than Love/I Love True Love	1965	6.25	12.50	25.00
LANDO					
8527	So What/(B-side unknown)	1965	12.50	25.00	50.00
MERCURY					
73969	Something's Wrong/You, You	1977	—	2.00	4.00
RCA					
PB-13313	Baby I Need Your Loving/Everyone Can Be a Star	1982	—	2.00	4.00
PB-13406	Swing That Sexy Thang/Just One Kiss	1982	—	2.00	4.00

Albums

Number	Title (A Side/B Side)	Yr	VG	VG+	NM
20TH CENTURY					
T-628	Carl Carlton	1981	2.50	5.00	10.00
ABC					
D-857	Everlasting Love	1974	3.00	6.00	12.00
D-910	I Wanna Be with You	1975	3.00	6.00	12.00
BACK BEAT					
BBLX-71	Can't Stop a Man in Love	1973	3.75	7.50	15.00
CASABLANCA					
822705-1	Private Property	1985	2.50	5.00	10.00
RCA VICTOR					
AFL1-4425	The Bad C.C.	1982	2.50	5.00	10.00

CARLTON, LARRY

45s

Number	Title (A Side/B Side)	Yr	VG	VG+	NM
BLUE THUMB					
227	An American Family/(B-side unknown)	1973	2.00	4.00	8.00
MCA					
52844	Smiles and Smiles to Go/Carrying You	1986	—	—	3.00
UNI					
55080	The Odd Couple/Monday, Monday	1968	2.50	5.00	10.00
55120	Moon People/Son of a Preacher Man	1969	2.00	4.00	8.00
WARNER BROS.					
8694	Room 335/Where Did You Come From	1978	—	2.00	4.00
29590	Tequila/L.A., N.Y.	1983	—	2.00	4.00
29977	Song for Katie/10:00 P.M.	1982	—	2.00	4.00
50019	Sleepwalk/Frenchman's Flat	1982	—	2.00	4.00

Albums

Number	Title (A Side/B Side)	Yr	VG	VG+	NM
BLUE THUMB					
BTS-46	Singing/Playing	1972	3.75	7.50	15.00
GRP					
9611	Collection	1990	3.00	6.00	12.00
MCA					
5689	Alone/But Never Alone	1986	2.00	4.00	8.00
6237	On Solid Ground	1988	2.00	4.00	8.00
6322	Christmas at Our House	1989	2.50	5.00	10.00
42003	Discovery	1987	2.00	4.00	8.00
UNI					
73036	With a Little Help from My Friends	1968	5.00	10.00	20.00
WARNER BROS.					
BSK 3221	Larry Carlton	1978	2.50	5.00	10.00
BSK 3380	Strikes Twice	1980	2.50	5.00	10.00
BSK 3635	Sleepwalk	1981	2.50	5.00	10.00
23834	Friends	1983	2.00	4.00	8.00

CARMEL SISTERS, THE

Also see CAROL CONNORS.

45s

Number	Title (A Side/B Side)	Yr	VG	VG+	NM
COLPIX					
767	Go, Go, G.T.O./Sunny Winter	1965	75.00	150.00	300.00
—As "Carol and Cheryl"					
JUBILEE					
5464	Joey's Comin' Home/The Rumor	1963	5.00	10.00	20.00

CARMEN, ERIC

Also see CYRUS ERIE; RASPBERRIES.

45s

Number	Title (A Side/B Side)	Yr	VG	VG+	NM
ARISTA					
0165	All By Myself/Everything	1975	—	2.00	4.00
0184	Never Gonna Fall in Love Again/No Hard Feelings	1976	—	2.00	4.00
0200	Sunrise/My Girl	1976	—	2.00	4.00
0266	She Did It/Someday	1977	—	2.00	4.00
0266 [PS]	She Did It/Someday	1977	—	3.00	6.00
0295	Boats Against the Current/Take It or Leave It	1977	—	2.00	4.00
0319	Marathon Man/I Think I Found Myself	1978	—	2.00	4.00
0354	Change of Heart/Hey Deanie	1978	—	2.00	4.00
0384	Baby I Need Your Lovin'/Heaven Can Wait	1979	—	2.00	4.00
0435	Haven't We Come a Long Way/End of the World	1979	—	2.00	4.00
0506	It Hurts Too Much/You Need Some Lovin'	1980	—	2.00	4.00
0550	All for Love/Tonight You're Mine	1980	—	2.00	4.00
9686	Make Me Lose Control/That's Rock 'N' Roll	1988	—	—	3.00
9686 [PS]	Make Me Lose Control/That's Rock 'N' Roll	1988	—	—	3.00
9736	Boats Against the Current/No Hard Feelings	1988	—	—	3.00
9746	Reason to Try/Sunrise	1988	—	—	3.00
9746 [PS]	Reason to Try/Sunrise	1988	—	—	3.00
COOL					
101	The Rock Stops Here/(Instrumental)	1988	—	—	3.00
101 [PS]	The Rock Stops Here/(Instrumental)	1988	—	—	3.00
EPIC					
10669	I'll Hold Out My Hand/It Won't Be the Same Without You	1970	—	—	—
—Not known to exist					
GEFFEN					
29032	I'm Through with Love/Maybe My Baby	1985	—	—	3.00
29032 [PS]	I'm Through with Love/Maybe My Baby	1985	—	—	3.00
29118	I Wanna Hear It from Your Lips/Spotlight	1985	—	—	3.00
29118 [PS]	I Wanna Hear It from Your Lips/Spotlight	1985	—	—	3.00
RCA					
5315-7-R	Hungry Eyes/Where Are You Tonight	1987	—	—	3.00

Albums

Number	Title (A Side/B Side)	Yr	VG	VG+	NM
ARISTA					
AL 4057	Eric Carmen	1975	3.00	6.00	12.00
—Shiny, simulated gold foil cover					
AL 4057	Eric Carmen	1975	2.00	4.00	8.00
—Regular non-shiny gold cover					
AQ 4057 [Q]	Eric Carmen	1975	4.50	9.00	18.00
AL 4124	Boats Against the Current	1977	2.00	4.00	8.00
AB 4184	Change of Heart	1978	2.00	4.00	8.00
AL 8547	The Best of Eric Carmen	1988	3.75	7.50	15.00
—Original copies do not contain "Make Me Lose Control"					
AL 8547	The Best of Eric Carmen	1988	2.00	4.00	8.00
—Reissues add "Make Me Lose Control"					
AL 9513	Tonight You're Mine	1980	2.00	4.00	8.00
GEFFEN					
GHS 24042	Eric Carmen	1985	2.00	4.00	8.00

CARNATIONS, THE

Several different groups.

45s

Number	Title (A Side/B Side)	Yr	VG	VG+	NM
DERBY					
789	Tree in the Meadow/Clown of the Masquerade	1952	100.00	200.00	400.00
ENRICA					
1001	Gimme, Gimme, Gimme/Love, Open My Heart	1959	6.25	12.50	25.00
FRATERNITY					
863	Red Wing/Casual	1960	6.25	12.50	25.00
LAURIE					
3163	Punctuation/Funny Time	1963	6.25	12.50	25.00
LESCAY					
3002	Long Tall Girl/Is There Such a World	1961	25.00	50.00	100.00
SAVOY					
1172	Angels Sent You to Me/Night Time Is the Right Time	1955	15.00	30.00	60.00
TERRY-TONE					
199	Barbary Coast/Sleepy Hollow	1960	10.00	20.00	40.00
UNIVERSITY					
606	Leap Year/A Wing and a Prayer	1960	6.25	12.50	25.00

CARNE, JUDY

Number	Title (A Side/B Side)	Yr	VG	VG+	NM
45s					
REPRISE					
0680	Sock It To Me/Right, Said Fred	1968	2.50	5.00	10.00

CARNES, KIM

Also see GENE COTTON; KENNY ROGERS; BARBRA STREISAND.

Number	Title (A Side/B Side)	Yr	VG	VG+	NM
45s					
AMOS					
165	I Won't Call You Back/To Love	1971	2.00	4.00	8.00
166	To Love Somebody/Fell in Love with a Poet	1971	2.00	4.00	8.00
167	It's Love That Keeps It All Together/Long and Lonely Memeories	1971	2.00	4.00	8.00
—With Dave Ellingson					
A&M					
1748	Somewhere in the Night/Hang On to Your Airplane (Honeymoon)	1975	—	2.50	5.00
1767	You're a Part of Me/Hang On to Your Airplane (Honeymoon)	1975	—	2.50	5.00
1807 [DJ]	Bad Seed (mono/stereo)	1976	—	2.50	5.00
—No stock copies issued					
1902	The Last Thing You Ever Wanted to Do/Let Your Love Come Easy	1977	—	2.50	5.00
1943	Sailin'/He'll Come Home	1977	—	2.50	5.00
EMI AMERICA					
8010	Losing Love/Looking for a Big Night	1979	—	2.50	5.00
8011	It Hurts So Bad/Lookin' for a Big Night	1979	—	2.50	5.00
8014	Goodnight Moon/What Am I Gonna Do	1979	—	2.50	5.00
8045	More Love/Changin'	1980	—	2.00	4.00
8045 [PS]	More Love/Changin'	1980	—	3.00	6.00
8058	Cry Like a Baby/In the Chill of the Night	1980	—	2.00	4.00
8069	Mas Amor/Changin'	1980	—	3.00	6.00
8077	Bette Davis Eyes/Miss You Tonight	1981	—	2.00	4.00
8077 [PS]	Bette Davis Eyes/Miss You Tonight	1981	—	2.00	4.00
8088	Draw of the Cards/Break the Rules Tonite (Out of School)	1981	—	2.00	4.00
8088 [PS]	Draw of the Cards/Break the Rules Tonite (Out of School)	1981	—	2.00	4.00
8098	Mistaken Identity/Jamaica Sunday Morning	1981	—	2.00	4.00
8098 [PS]	Mistaken Identity/Jamaica Sunday Morning	1981	—	2.00	4.00
8127	Voyeur/Thrill of the Grill	1982	—	—	3.00
8127 [PS]	Voyeur/Thrill of the Grill	1982	—	—	3.00
8147	Does It Make You Remember/Take It on the Chin	1982	—	—	3.00
8147 [PS]	Does It Make You Remember/Take It on the Chin	1982	—	—	3.00
8154	Say You Don't Know Me/Breakin' Away from Society	1983	—	—	3.00
8181	Invisible Hands/I'll Be Here Where the Heart Is	1983	—	—	3.00
8181 [PS]	Invisible Hands/I'll Be Here Where the Heart Is	1983	—	—	3.00
8191	You Make My Heart Beat Faster (And That's All That Matters)/Hangin' On by a Thread	1984	—	—	3.00
8191 [PS]	You Make My Heart Beat Faster (And That's All That Matters)/Hangin' On by a Thread	1984	—	—	3.00
8202	I Pretend/Hurricane	1984	—	—	3.00
8202 [PS]	I Pretend/Hurricane	1984	—	—	3.00
8250	Invitation to Dance/Breakthrough	1984	—	—	3.00
—B-side by Haven					
8250 [PS]	Invitation to Dance/Breakthrough	1984	—	—	3.00
8267	Crazy in the Night (Barking at Airplanes)/Oliver (Voice on the Radio)	1985	—	—	3.00
8267 [PS]	Crazy in the Night (Barking at Airplanes)/Oliver (Voice on the Radio)	1985	—	—	3.00
8281	Abadabadango/He Makes the Sun Rise (Orpheus)	1985	—	—	3.00
8281 [PS]	Abadabadango/He Makes the Sun Rise (Orpheus)	1985	—	—	3.00
8290	Begging for Favors (Learning How Things Work)/Rough Edges	1985	—	—	3.00
8322	Divided Hearts/You Say You Love Me (But I Know You Don't)	1986	—	—	3.00
8322 [PS]	Divided Hearts/You Say You Love Me (But I Know You Don't)	1986	—	—	3.00
8335	Black and White/I'd Lie to You for Your Love	1986	—	—	3.00
MCA					
53387	Speed of the Sound of Loneliness/Blood from the Bandit	1988	—	—	3.00
53433	Crazy in Love/Blood from the Bandit	1988	—	—	3.00
53494	Fantastic Fire of Love/Brass and Batons	1989	—	—	3.00
Albums					
AMOS					
AAS 7016	Rest on Me	1971	5.00	10.00	20.00
A&M					
SP-3114	Sailin'	198?	2.00	4.00	8.00
—Budget-line reissue					
SP-3204	The Best of Kim Carnes	1982	2.50	5.00	10.00
SP-4548	Kim Carnes	1975	3.00	6.00	12.00
SP-4606	Sailin'	1976	3.00	6.00	12.00
EMI AMERICA					
SW-17004	St. Vincent's Court	1978	2.50	5.00	10.00
SW-17030	Romance Dance	1980	2.50	5.00	10.00
SO-17052	Mistaken Identity	1981	2.50	5.00	10.00
SO-17078	Voyeur	1982	2.50	5.00	10.00
SO-17107	Café Racers	1983	2.50	5.00	10.00
SO-17159	Barking at Airplanes	1985	2.50	5.00	10.00
ST-17198	Light House	1986	2.00	4.00	8.00
MCA					
914	The Early Years	1984	2.00	4.00	8.00
42200	View from the House	1988	2.00	4.00	8.00
MOBILE FIDELITY					
1-073	Mistaken Identity	1982	6.25	12.50	25.00
—Audiophile vinyl					

CARNIVAL

Number	Title (A Side/B Side)	Yr	VG	VG+	NM
45s					
UNITED ARTISTS					
50749	Where There's a Heartache (There Must Be a Heart)/The Truth About It	1971	—	2.50	5.00
WORLD PACIFIC					
77932	Laia Ladaia/Calito de Carnival	1969	—	3.00	6.00
Albums					
WORLD PACIFIC					
ST-21894	The Carnival	1969	3.00	6.00	12.00

CARO, NYDIA

Number	Title (A Side/B Side)	Yr	VG	VG+	NM
45s					
ROULETTE					
4588	Ask Me What I Want for Christmas/Hey Johnny What	1964	3.00	6.00	12.00
4588 [PS]	Ask Me What I Want for Christmas/Hey Johnny What	1964	5.00	10.00	20.00

CAROL AND CHERYL

See THE CARMEL SISTERS.

CAROL AND GERRI

Number	Title (A Side/B Side)	Yr	VG	VG+	NM
45s					
MGM					
13568	How Can I Ever Find the Way/On You, Heartache Looks Good	1966	10.00	20.00	40.00

CAROL, LINDA AND CATHY

Number	Title (A Side/B Side)	Yr	VG	VG+	NM
45s					
UNITED					
216	Merry Christmas/I Don't Wanna Be Last On Santa's List	1957	5.00	10.00	20.00

CAROLINA SLIM

Number	Title (A Side/B Side)	Yr	VG	VG+	NM
Albums					
SHARP					
2002 [M]	Blues from the Cotton Fields	195?	62.50	125.00	250.00

CAROLS, THE (1)

Female group.

Number	Title (A Side/B Side)	Yr	VG	VG+	NM
45s					
LAMP					
2001	My Search Is Over/Keko	1957	12.50	25.00	50.00

CAROLS, THE (2)

Male group.

Number	Title (A Side/B Side)	Yr	VG	VG+	NM
45s					
SAVOY					
896	Fifty Million Women/I Got a Feelin'	1953	37.50	75.00	150.00

CAROUSEL, THE

Number	Title (A Side/B Side)	Yr	VG	VG+	NM
45s					
ABC					
10953	One Mistake/Only One for Me	1967	3.00	6.00	12.00
TEEN TOWN					
108	I've Been with You/What Will You Do for Me	1969	3.75	7.50	15.00
116	To Say Goodbye/I Get Along Indefinitely	1969	3.75	7.50	15.00

CAROUSELS, THE

Possibly more than one group.

Number	Title (A Side/B Side)	Yr	VG	VG+	NM
45s					
ABC-PARAMOUNT					
10233	Symptoms of Love/The Hush of Love	1961	6.25	12.50	25.00
AUTUMN					
13	Beneath the Willow/Sail Away	1965	2.50	5.00	10.00
GONE					
5118	You Can Come If You Want To/Pretty Little Thing	1961	12.50	25.00	50.00
5118	If You Want To/Pretty Little Thing	1961	7.50	15.00	30.00
5131	Never Let Him Go/Dirty Tricks	1962	6.25	12.50	25.00
GUYDEN					
2102	I Wanna Fly/Something Else	1964	3.00	6.00	12.00
JAGUAR					
3029	Drive-In Movie/Rendezvous	1959	15.00	30.00	60.00
SPRY					
116	I've Cried Enough/Did I Cry Enough	1962	37.50	75.00	150.00

CARP

Actor Gary Busey was in this group.

Number	Title (A Side/B Side)	Yr	VG	VG+	NM
45s					
EPIC					
10632	Save the Delta Queen/Mammoth Mountain Blues	1970	2.00	4.00	8.00
10647	Pine Creek Bridge/Page 258	1970	2.00	4.00	8.00
Albums					
EPIC					
E 30212	Carp	1970	6.25	12.50	25.00

CARPENTERS

Number	Title (A Side/B Side)	Yr	VG	VG+	NM
45s					
A&M					
1142	Ticket to Ride/Your Wonderful Parade	1969	2.50	5.00	10.00
1183	(They Long to Be) Close to You/IKept On Loving You	1970	—	2.50	5.00
1217	We've Only Just Begun/All of My Life	1970	—	2.50	5.00
1217 [PS]	We've Only Just Begun/All of My Life	1970	—	3.00	6.00
1236	Merry Christmas Darling/Mr. Guder	1970	—	3.00	6.00
—A-side vocal is different than later releases of this song					
1236 [PS]	Merry Christmas Darling/Mr. Guder	1970	2.00	4.00	8.00
1243	For All We Know/Don't Be Afraid	1971	—	2.00	4.00

Number	Title (A Side/B Side)	Yr	VG	VG+	NM
1243 [PS]	For All We Know/Don't Be Afraid	1971	—	3.00	6.00
1260	Rainy Days and Mondays/Saturday	1971	—	2.00	4.00
1260 [PS]	Rainy Days and Mondays/Saturday	1971	—	3.00	6.00
1289	Superstar/Bless the Beasts and Children	1971	—	2.00	4.00
1289 [PS]	Superstar/Bless the Beasts and Children	1971	—	3.00	6.00
1322	Hurting Each Other/Maybe It's You	1972	—	2.00	4.00
1322 [PS]	Hurting Each Other/Maybe It's You	1972	—	3.00	6.00
1351	It's Going to Take Some Time/Flat Baroque	1972	—	2.00	4.00
1351 [PS]	It's Going to Take Some Time/Flat Baroque	1972	—	3.00	6.00
1367	Goodbye to Love/Crystal Lullaby	1972	—	2.00	4.00
1367 [PS]	Goodbye to Love/Crystal Lullaby	1972	—	3.00	6.00
1391	Top of the World/Druscilla Penny	1972	—	—	—
—Unreleased					
1413	Sing/Druscilla Penny	1973	—	2.00	4.00
1413 [PS]	Sing/Druscilla Penny	1973	—	3.00	6.00
1446	Yesterday Once More/Road Ode	1973	—	2.00	4.00
1446 [PS]	Yesterday Once More/Road Ode	1973	—	3.00	6.00
1468	Top of the World/Heather	1973	—	2.00	4.00
—Originals have brown labels					
1468	Top of the World/Heather	1973	—	—	3.00
—Second pressings have silvery labels					
1468 [PS]	Top of the World/Heather	1973	—	3.00	6.00
1521	I Won't Last a Day Without You/One Love	1974	—	2.00	4.00
1521 [PS]	I Won't Last a Day Without You/One Love	1974	—	3.00	6.00
1646	Please Mister Postman/This Masquerade	1974	—	2.00	4.00
1646 [PS]	Please Mister Postman/This Masquerade	1974	—	3.00	6.00
1648	Santa Claus Is Coming to Town/Merry Christmas Darling	1974	—	2.50	5.00
1648 [PS]	Santa Claus Is Coming to Town/Merry Christmas Darling	1974	2.50	5.00	10.00
1677	Only Yesterday/Happy	1975	—	2.00	4.00
1677 [PS]	Only Yesterday/Happy	1975	—	3.00	6.00
1721	Solitaire/Love Me for What I Am	1975	—	2.00	4.00
1721 [PS]	Solitaire/Love Me for What I Am	1975	—	3.00	6.00
1800	There's a Kind of Hush (All Over the World)/(I'm Caught Between) Goodbye and I Love You	1976	—	2.00	4.00
1800 [PS]	There's a Kind of Hush (All Over the World)/(I'm Caught Between) Goodbye and I Love You	1976	—	3.00	6.00
1828	I Need to Be in Love/Sandy	1976	—	2.00	4.00
1859	Goofus/Boat to Sail	1976	—	2.00	4.00
1940	All You Get from Love Is a Love Song/I Have You	1977	—	2.00	4.00
1978	Calling Occupants of Interplanetary Craft/Can't Smile Without You	1977	—	2.00	4.00
1978 [PS]	Calling Occupants of Interplanetary Craft/Can't Smile Without You	1977	—	3.00	6.00
1991	The Christmas Song/Merry Christmas Darling	1977	—	2.50	5.00
1991 [PS]	The Christmas Song/Merry Christmas Darling	1977	2.00	4.00	8.00
2008	Sweet, Sweet Smile/I Have You	1978	—	2.00	4.00
2097	I Believe You/B'wana She No Home	1978	—	2.00	4.00
2344	Touch Me When We're Dancing/Because We Are in Love (The Wedding Song)	1981	—	2.00	4.00
2344 [PS]	Touch Me When We're Dancing/Because We Are in Love (The Wedding Song)	1981	—	2.00	4.00
2370	(Want You) Back in My Life Again/Somebody's Been Lyin'	1981	—	2.00	4.00
2386	Those Good Old Dreams/When It's Gone	1981	—	2.00	4.00
2405	Beechwood 4-5789/Two Sides	1982	—	2.00	4.00
2585	Make Believe It's Your First Time/Look to Your Dreams	1983	—	2.00	4.00
2585 [PS]	Make Believe It's Your First Time/Look to Your Dreams	1983	—	2.50	5.00
2620	Sailing on the Tide/Your Baby Doesn't Love You Anymore	1984	—	2.00	4.00
2700	Do You Hear What I Hear/Little Altar Boy	1984	2.50	5.00	10.00
2735	Yesterday Once More/(They Long to Be) Close to You-We've Only Just Begun	1985	5.00	10.00	20.00
2735 [PS]	Yesterday Once More/(They Long to Be) Close to You-We've Only Just Begun	1985	5.00	10.00	20.00
8620	The Christmas Song/Merry Christmas Darling	1982	—	2.50	5.00
8620 [PS]	The Christmas Song/Merry Christmas Darling	1982	2.50	5.00	10.00
MAGIC LAMP					
704	I'll Be Yours/Looking for Love	1967	500.00	1000.	2000.
—As "Karen Carpenter", but Richard also was on this record					

Albums

Number	Title	Yr	VG	VG+	NM
A&M					
SP-3184	Close to You	1982	2.00	4.00	8.00
—Reissue of 4271					
SP-3197	A Kind of Hush	1982	2.00	4.00	8.00
—Reissue of 4581					
SP-3199	Passage	1982	2.00	4.00	8.00
—Reissue of 4703					
SP-3210	Christmas Portrait	198?	2.00	4.00	8.00
—Reissue of SP-4726					
SP-3270	An Old-Fashioned Christmas	1984	2.50	5.00	10.00
SP-3502	Carpenters	1971	3.00	6.00	12.00
SP-3511	A Song for You	1972	3.00	6.00	12.00
SP-3519	Now & Then	1973	3.00	6.00	12.00
SP-3601	The Singles 1969-1973	1973	3.00	6.00	12.00
SP-3723	Made in America	1981	3.00	6.00	12.00
SP-4205	Offering	1969	20.00	40.00	80.00
SP-4205	Ticket to Ride	1970	3.00	6.00	12.00
—Reissue of "Offering" with new title and cover					
SP-4271	Close to You	1970	3.00	6.00	12.00
SP-4530	Horizon	1975	3.00	6.00	12.00
SP-4581	A Kind of Hush	1976	3.00	6.00	12.00
SP-4703	Passage	1977	3.00	6.00	12.00
SP-4726	Christmas Portrait	1978	3.75	7.50	15.00
SP-4954	Voice of the Heart	1983	3.00	6.00	12.00
SP-5172	An Old Fashioned Christmas	1987	2.00	4.00	8.00
—Reissue of 3270 (record still says 3270 but cover is 5172)					
SP-6601 [(2)]	Yesterday Once More	1985	3.75	7.50	15.00
QU-53502 [Q]	Carpenters	1974	5.00	10.00	20.00
QU-53511 [Q]	A Song for You	1974	5.00	10.00	20.00
QU-53519 [Q]	Now & Then	1974	5.00	10.00	20.00
QU-53601 [Q]	The Singles 1969-1973	1974	5.00	10.00	20.00
QU-54271 [Q]	Close to You	1974	5.00	10.00	20.00
QU-54530 [Q]	Horizon	1975	5.00	10.00	20.00

CARPETS, THE

45s

Number	Title (A Side/B Side)	Yr	VG	VG+	NM
FEDERAL					
12257	Why Do I/Let Her Go	1956	50.00	100.00	200.00
12269	Lonely Me/Chicken Backs	1956	50.00	100.00	200.00

CARR, CATHY

45s

Number	Title (A Side/B Side)	Yr	VG	VG+	NM
CORAL					
60907	Heartbroken/Half Pink Boogie	1953	3.00	6.00	12.00
60988	I Just Can't Get That Melody Out of My Mind/Somebody Told You a Lie	1953	3.00	6.00	12.00
61092	I'll Cry at Your Wedding/Cryin' for the Caroline's	1953	3.00	6.00	12.00
61646	I'll Cry at Your Wedding/Heartbroken	1956	2.50	5.00	10.00
FRATERNITY					
718	Morning, Noon and Night/Toward Evening	1955	5.00	10.00	20.00
734	Ivory Tower/Please Please Believe Me	1956	3.75	7.50	15.00
743	Heart Hideaway/The Boy on Page 35	1956	3.75	7.50	15.00
750	Oh Baby/Waltzing to the Blues	1956	3.75	7.50	15.00
757	It Looks Like Love/Una Momenta	1957	3.00	6.00	12.00
765	Wild Honey/Speak for Yourself John	1957	3.00	6.00	12.00
782	House of Heartache/Presents from the Past	1957	3.00	6.00	12.00
793	Doll Baby/Don't Come to My Party	1958	3.00	6.00	12.00
LAURIE					
3133	Ivory Tower/Should I Believe Him	1962	2.50	5.00	10.00
3147	Sailorboy/Next Time a Band Plays a Waltz	1962	2.50	5.00	10.00
3161	I Waded in the Water/In Place of You	1963	2.50	5.00	10.00
3206	My Favorite Song/The Ghost of a Broken Heart	1963	2.50	5.00	10.00
3378	When You Come Home Again/The Ghost of a Broken Heart	1967	—	3.00	6.00
ROULETTE					
4107	To Know Him Is to Love Him/Put Away the Invitation	1958	3.00	6.00	12.00
4125	First Anniversary/With Love	1959	3.00	6.00	12.00
4152 [M]	I'm Gonna Change Him/The Little Things You Do	1959	3.00	6.00	12.00
SSR-4152 [S]	I'm Gonna Change Him/The Little Things You Do	1959	7.50	15.00	30.00
4187	Shy/Personal Secret	1959	3.00	6.00	12.00
4219	Little Sister/Dark River	1960	3.00	6.00	12.00
4248	A Little Time/What Do I Do Now	1960	3.00	6.00	12.00
4296	I Want to Be Your Pet/Golden Locket	1960	3.00	6.00	12.00
4323	Johnny's Song/Someone Told You a Lie	1961	3.00	6.00	12.00
4367	Yearning/Baseball He Loves	1961	3.00	6.00	12.00
4383	I Can't Begin to Tell You/You're Breaking My Heart	1961	3.00	6.00	12.00
SMASH					
1726	Footprints in the Snow/Nein. Nein, Fraulein	1961	3.00	6.00	12.00

Albums

Number	Title	Yr	VG	VG+	NM
DOT					
DLP-3674 [M]	Ivory Tower	1966	6.25	12.50	25.00
DLP-25674 [S]	Ivory Tower	1966	6.25	12.50	25.00
FRATERNITY					
1005 [M]	Ivory Tower	1957	30.00	60.00	120.00
ROULETTE					
R 25077 [M]	Shy	1959	10.00	20.00	40.00
SR 25077 [S]	Shy	1959	12.50	25.00	50.00

CARR, JAMES

45s

Number	Title (A Side/B Side)	Yr	VG	VG+	NM
ATLANTIC					
2803	Hold On/I'll Put It to You	1971	3.00	6.00	12.00
GOLDWAX					
108	You Don't Want Me/Only Fools Run Away	1965	7.50	15.00	30.00
112	I Can't Make It/Lovers' Competition	1965	7.50	15.00	30.00
119	He's Better Than You/Talk Talk	1965	7.50	15.00	30.00
302	You've Got My Mind Messed Up/That's What I Want to Know	1966	5.00	10.00	20.00
309	Love Attack/Come Back to Me Baby	1966	3.75	7.50	15.00
311	Pouring Water on a Drowning Man/Forgetting You	1966	3.75	7.50	15.00
317	The Dark End of the Street/Lovable Girl	1967	4.00	8.00	16.00
323	Let It Happen/A Losing Game	1967	3.75	7.50	15.00
328	I'm a Fool for You/Gonna Send You Back to Georgia	1967	3.75	7.50	15.00
332	A Man Needs a Woman/Stronger Than Love	1968	3.75	7.50	15.00
335	Life Turned Her That Way/A Message to Young Lovers	1968	3.75	7.50	15.00
338	Freedom Train/That's the Way Love Turned Out for Me	1968	3.75	7.50	15.00
340	To Love Somebody/These Ain't Teardrops	1969	3.75	7.50	15.00
343	Everybody Needs Somebody/Row, Row Your Boat	1969	3.75	7.50	15.00

Albums

Number	Title	Yr	VG	VG+	NM
GOLDWAX					
3001S	You Got My Mind Messed Up	1968	37.50	75.00	150.00
3002S	A Man Needs a Woman	1968	37.50	75.00	150.00

CARR, VIKKI

45s

Number	Title (A Side/B Side)	Yr	VG	VG+	NM
COLUMBIA					
AS 85 [DJ]	It Came Upon A Midnight Clear/Wind Me Up	1971	—	2.00	4.00
AS 85 [PS]	It Came Upon A Midnight Clear/Wind Me Up	1971	2.00	4.00	8.00
10058	One Hell of a Woman/Wind Me Up	1974	—	2.00	4.00
10122	Hoy (Today)/El Pajaro Herido	1975	—	2.00	4.00
10214	Puttin' Myself in Your Hands (Gettin' Ready to Move)/I Don't Want a Sometimes Man	1975	—	2.00	4.00
45208	Ain't No Mountain High Enough/Call My Heart Your Home	1970	—	2.50	5.00
45296	I'll Be Home/Call My Heart Your Home	1971	—	2.00	4.00
45403	Six Weeks Every Summer (Christmas Every Day)/If You Could Read My Mind	1971	—	2.00	4.00

Number	Title (A Side/B Side)	Yr	VG	VG+	NM
45454	I Can't Give Back the Love I Feel for You/I've Never Been a Woman Before	1971	—	2.00	4.00
45510	I'd Do It All Again/I'm Gonna Love You	1971	—	2.00	4.00
45622	Cabaret/The Big Hurt	1972	—	2.00	4.00
45658	Y Volvere/Grande, Grande, Grande	1972	—	2.50	5.00
45750	Reflections/Let the Band Play On	1973	—	2.00	4.00
45809	Ms. America/We Didn't Know the Time of Day	1973	—	2.00	4.00
45955	Have You Heard the News/Leave a Little Room	1973	—	2.50	5.00
46033	Borrowed Time/Sleeping Between Two People	1974	—	2.00	4.00

LIBERTY

Number	Title (A Side/B Side)	Yr	VG	VG+	NM
55465	I'll Walk the Rest of the Way/Beside a Bridge	1962	2.50	5.00	10.00
55493	He's a Rebel/Be My Love	1962	5.00	10.00	20.00

—Recorded about the same time, and with many of the same musicians, as The Crystals' classic version.

Number	Title (A Side/B Side)	Yr	VG	VG+	NM
55564	The Rose and the Butterfly/From 9 to 5	1963	2.50	5.00	10.00
55620	San Francisco/Irma La Douce	1963	2.50	5.00	10.00
55620	San Francisco/Look Again	1963	2.50	5.00	10.00
55640	Right Kind of Woman/Poor Butterfly, Stay	1963	2.50	5.00	10.00
55736	Forget You/Her Little Heart Went to Loveland	1964	2.00	4.00	8.00
55783	Should I Follow/Don't Talk to Me (Spanish)	1965	2.00	4.00	8.00
55804	Theme from "Peyton Place"/Unforgettable	1965	2.00	4.00	8.00
55839	I Only Have Eyes for You/None But the Lonely Heart	1965	2.00	4.00	8.00
55857	The Silencers/Santiago	1966	—	3.00	6.00
55869	Heartaches/True Love's a Blessing	1966	—	3.00	6.00
55897	My Heart Reminds Me (Part 1)/My Heart Reminds Me (Part 2)	1966	—	3.00	6.00
55917	It Must Be Him/So Nice	1966	2.00	4.00	8.00
55937	Until Today/Now I Know the Feeling	1966	—	3.00	6.00
55976	Fly Away/Sunshine	1967	—	3.00	6.00
55986	It Must Be Him/That's All	1967	—	3.00	6.00
56012	The Lesson/One More Mountain	1968	—	2.50	5.00
56012 [PS]	The Lesson/One More Mountain	1968	2.50	5.00	10.00
56026	She'll Be There/Your Heart Is Free Just Like the Wind	1968	—	2.50	5.00
56039	Nothing to Lose/Don't Break My Pretty Balloon	1968	—	2.50	5.00
56062	Happy Together/Dissatisfied Man	1968	—	2.50	5.00
56092	With Pen in Hand/Can't Take My Eyes Off You	1969	—	2.50	5.00
56132	Eternity/I Will Wait for Love	1969	—	2.50	5.00
56185	Make It Rain/Singing My Song	1970	—	2.50	5.00

UNITED ARTISTS

Number	Title (A Side/B Side)	Yr	VG	VG+	NM
0097	It Must Be Him/The Lesson	1973	—	2.00	4.00

—"Silver Spotlight Series" reissue

Number	Title (A Side/B Side)	Yr	VG	VG+	NM
0098	With Pen in Hand/Eternity	1973	—	2.00	4.00

—"Silver Spotlight Series" reissue

Albums

COLUMBIA

Number	Title	Yr	VG	VG+	NM
C 30662	Vikki Carr's Love Story	1971	2.50	5.00	10.00
C 31040	Superstar	1971	2.50	5.00	10.00
KC 31453	The First Time Ever (I Saw Your Face)	1972	2.50	5.00	10.00
KC 31470	Canta En Espanol	1972	2.50	5.00	10.00
KC 32251	Ms. America	1973	2.50	5.00	10.00
KG 32656 [(2)]	Live at the Greek Theatre	1973	3.00	6.00	12.00
KC 32860	One Hell of a Woman	1974	2.50	5.00	10.00
PC 33340	Hoy (Today)	1975	2.50	5.00	10.00
CG 33609 [(2)]	Love Story/The First Time Ever	1976	3.00	6.00	12.00

LIBERTY

Number	Title	Yr	VG	VG+	NM
LRP-3314 [M]	Color Her Great	1963	3.75	7.50	15.00
LRP-3354 [M]	Discovery!	1964	3.75	7.50	15.00
LRP-3383 [M]	Discovery! Volume Two	1964	3.75	7.50	15.00
LRP-3420 [M]	The Anatomy of Love	1965	3.75	7.50	15.00
LRP-3456 [M]	The Way of Today	1966	3.75	7.50	15.00
LRP-3506 [M]	Intimate Excitement	1967	5.00	10.00	20.00
LRP-3533 [M]	It Must Be Him	1967	5.00	10.00	20.00
LST-7314 [S]	Color Her Great	1963	5.00	10.00	20.00
LST-7354 [S]	Discovery!	1964	5.00	10.00	20.00
LST-7383 [S]	Discovery! Volume Two	1964	5.00	10.00	20.00
LST-7420 [S]	The Anatomy of Love	1965	5.00	10.00	20.00
LST-7456 [S]	The Way of Today	1966	5.00	10.00	20.00
LST-7506 [S]	Intimate Excitement	1967	3.75	7.50	15.00
LST-7533 [S]	It Must Be Him	1967	3.75	7.50	15.00
LST-7548	Vikki	1968	3.75	7.50	15.00
LST-7604	For Once in My Life	1969	3.75	7.50	15.00
LN-10108	The Best of Vikki Carr	1981	2.00	4.00	8.00
LST-11001	Nashville by Carr	1970	3.75	7.50	15.00

PAIR

Number	Title	Yr	VG	VG+	NM
PDL2-1082 [(2)]	From the Heart	1986	3.00	6.00	12.00

PICKWICK

Number	Title	Yr	VG	VG+	NM
SPC-3587	Intimate	1978	2.00	4.00	8.00
SPC-3613	Unforgettable	1978	2.00	4.00	8.00

SUNSET

Number	Title	Yr	VG	VG+	NM
SUS-5228	That's All	1969	2.50	5.00	10.00
SUS-5293	Unforgettable	1971	2.50	5.00	10.00

UNITED ARTISTS

Number	Title	Yr	VG	VG+	NM
UA-LA089-G [(2)]	Vikki Carr's Golden Songbook/Superpak	1973	3.00	6.00	12.00
UA-LA244-G	The Very Best of Vikki Carr	1974	2.50	5.00	10.00
LM-1006	It Must Be Him	1980	2.50	5.00	10.00

—Abridged reissue of Liberty 7533

Number	Title	Yr	VG	VG+	NM
UAS-5581 [(2)]	The Best of Vikki Carr	1972	3.00	6.00	12.00
UAS-6813	The Ways to Love a Man	1972	2.50	5.00	10.00

CARROLL, ANDREA

45s

BIG TOP

Number	Title (A Side/B Side)	Yr	VG	VG+	NM
515	The Doolang/This Time Tomorrow	1964	10.00	20.00	40.00
3156	It Hurts to Be Sixteen/Why Am I So Shy	1963	5.00	10.00	20.00

EPIC

Number	Title (A Side/B Side)	Yr	VG	VG+	NM
9438	I've Got a Date with Frankie/Young and Lonely	1961	25.00	50.00	100.00
9450	Please Don't Talk to the Lifeguard/Room of Memories	1961	5.00	10.00	20.00
9471	Gee Dad/The Charm on My Arm	1961	5.00	10.00	20.00
9471 [PS]	Gee Dad/The Charm on My Arm	1961	10.00	20.00	40.00
9523	Miss Happiness/Fifteen Shades of Pink	1962	5.00	10.00	20.00

RCA VICTOR

Number	Title (A Side/B Side)	Yr	VG	VG+	NM
47-8618	Mr. Music Man/Sally Fool	1965	5.00	10.00	20.00

UNITED ARTISTS

Number	Title (A Side/B Side)	Yr	VG	VG+	NM
982	The World Isn't Big Enough/She Gets Everything She Wants	1966	5.00	10.00	20.00
50039	Hey, Beach Boy/Why Should We Take the Easy Way Out	1966	7.50	15.00	30.00

CARROLL, ANDREA /BEVERLY WARREN

Also see each artist's individual listings.

Albums

B.T. PUPPY

Number	Title	Yr	VG	VG+	NM
BTS-1017	Andrea Carroll and Beverly Warren Side By Side	1971	37.50	75.00	150.00

CARROLL, BERNADETTE

45s

JULIA

Number	Title (A Side/B Side)	Yr	VG	VG+	NM
1106	My Heart Stood Still/Sweet Sugar Sweet	1962	3.75	7.50	15.00

LAURIE

Number	Title (A Side/B Side)	Yr	VG	VG+	NM
3217	Nicky/All the Way Home I Cried	1964	3.75	7.50	15.00

—The Four Seasons sing backup on this record

Number	Title (A Side/B Side)	Yr	VG	VG+	NM
3238	Party Girl/I Don't Wanna Know	1964	3.75	7.50	15.00
3268	Happy Birthday/Homecoming Party	1964	3.75	7.50	15.00
3278	The Hero/One Little Lie	1964	3.75	7.50	15.00
3311	Circus Girl/Don't Hurt Me	1965	3.75	7.50	15.00
3320	He's Just a Playboy/Try Your Luck	1965	3.75	7.50	15.00

CARROLL, DELORES, AND THE FOUR TOPS

Also see THE FOUR TOPS.

45s

CHATEAU

Number	Title (A Side/B Side)	Yr	VG	VG+	NM
2002	Everybody Knows/I Just Can't Keep the Tears from Tumblin' Down	1956	75.00	150.00	300.00

CARROLL, JIM

Not the same Jim Carroll as the Jim Carroll Band ("People Who Died" in 1981).

45s

A&M

Number	Title (A Side/B Side)	Yr	VG	VG+	NM
1329	On and On/I Don't Know	1972	—	2.50	5.00
1360	Save Me/I Got Plenty	1972	—	2.50	5.00

Albums

A&M

Number	Title	Yr	VG	VG+	NM
SP-4323	Jim Carroll	1971	3.00	6.00	12.00

CARROLL, JOHNNY

45s

DECCA

Number	Title (A Side/B Side)	Yr	VG	VG+	NM
29940	Rock and Roll Ruby/Tryin' to Get to You	1956	37.50	75.00	150.00
29941	Wild, Wild Women/Corrine, Corrina	1956	37.50	75.00	150.00
30013	Hot Rock/Crazy, Crazy	1956	37.50	75.00	150.00

PHILLIPS INT'L.

Number	Title (A Side/B Side)	Yr	VG	VG+	NM
3520	That's the Way I Love/I'll Wait	1957	50.00	100.00	200.00

SARG

Number	Title (A Side/B Side)	Yr	VG	VG+	NM
144	I'll Think of You/Stars Come Down	1956	20.00	40.00	80.00

WARNER BROS.

Number	Title (A Side/B Side)	Yr	VG	VG+	NM
5042	Bandstand Doll/The Swing	1959	7.50	15.00	30.00
5080	Lost Without You/Sugar	1959	7.50	15.00	30.00

Albums

HMG/HIGHTONE

Number	Title	Yr	VG	VG+	NM
HT 6602	Texabilly	1997	2.50	5.00	10.00

CARROLL, RONNIE

45s

PHILIPS

Number	Title (A Side/B Side)	Yr	VG	VG+	NM
40110	Say Wonderful Things/Please Tell Me Your Name	1963	3.00	6.00	12.00
40388	Tomorrow/Wait for Me	1966	2.50	5.00	10.00

CARROLL, WAYNE

45s

KING

Number	Title (A Side/B Side)	Yr	VG	VG+	NM
5123	Chicken Out/Cindy Lee	1958	12.50	25.00	50.00
5134	Rockin' Chair Momma/There's Been a Change in Me	1958	12.50	25.00	50.00
5146	He Cheated/Wall Around Your Heart	1958	12.50	25.00	50.00

CARROLL BROTHERS, THE

45s

CAMEO

Number	Title (A Side/B Side)	Yr	VG	VG+	NM
140	(My Gal Is) Red Hot/Dearly Beloved	1959	20.00	40.00	80.00
213	Don't Knock the Twist/Bo Diddley	1962	5.00	10.00	20.00
221	Sweet Georgia Brown/Boot It	1962	5.00	10.00	20.00

FELSTED

Number	Title (A Side/B Side)	Yr	VG	VG+	NM
8550	Movin' Day/I Found You	1959	5.00	10.00	20.00

Albums

CAMEO

Number	Title	Yr	VG	VG+	NM
C-1015 [M]	College Twist Party	1962	6.25	12.50	25.00
SC-1015 [S]	College Twist Party	1962	10.00	20.00	40.00

CARSON, MARTHA

45s

CAPITOL

Number	Title (A Side/B Side)	Yr	VG	VG+	NM
F1900	Satisfied/Hide Me Rock of Ages	1951	3.75	7.50	15.00
F1982	Weighed the Balance/You Sure Do Need Him Now	1952	3.75	7.50	15.00
F2077	I Wanna Rest/Old Blind Barnabas	1952	3.75	7.50	15.00
F2145	Beyond the Shadow/I'm Gonna Walk and Talk with the Lord	1952	3.75	7.50	15.00
F2180	He Will Set Your Fields on Fire/When God Dips His Love	1952	3.75	7.50	15.00

Number	Title (A Side/B Side)	Yr	VG	VG+	NM
F2252	Fear Not/Cryin' Holy Unto the Lord	1952	3.75	7.50	15.00
F2342	There's a Higher Power/Inspiration from Above	1953	3.75	7.50	15.00
F2477	Ask and You Shall Receive/I Feel It in My Soul	1953	3.75	7.50	15.00
F2634	Singing on the Other Side/I've Got a Better Place to Go	1953	3.75	7.50	15.00
F2740	Lazarus/Bye & Bye	1954	3.75	7.50	15.00
F2825	I Bowed Down/He'll Part the Water	1954	3.75	7.50	15.00
F2969	Christmas Time Is Here/Peace On Earth (At Christmas Time)	1954	3.75	7.50	15.00
F3045	It's Alright/Counting My Blessings	1955	3.75	7.50	15.00
RCA VICTOR					
47-6293	Laugh a Little More/Let the Light Shine on Me	1955	5.00	10.00	20.00
47-6413	David and Goliath/I Want to Rest a Little While	1956	5.00	10.00	20.00
47-6510	Dixieland Roll/Music Drives Me Crazy	1956	5.00	10.00	20.00
47-6603	All These Things/Faith Is the Key	1956	5.00	10.00	20.00
47-6724	Get That Golden Key/He Was There	1956	5.00	10.00	20.00
47-6861	Satisfied/Let the Light Shine on Me	1957	3.75	7.50	15.00
47-6948	Now Stop/Just Whistle or Call	1957	3.75	7.50	15.00
Albums					
CAPITOL					
ST 1507 [S]	Satisfied	1960	7.50	15.00	30.00
T 1507 [M]	Satisfied	1960	6.25	12.50	25.00
ST 1607 [S]	A Talk with the Lord	1961	7.50	15.00	30.00
T 1607 [M]	A Talk with the Lord	1961	6.25	12.50	25.00
RCA VICTOR					
LPM-1145 [M]	Journey to the Sky	1955	10.00	20.00	40.00
LPM-1490 [M]	Rock-a My Soul	1957	12.50	25.00	50.00
SIMS					
LP-100 [M]	Martha Carson	196?	6.25	12.50	25.00

CARTER, CLARENCE

Number	Title (A Side/B Side)	Yr	VG	VG+	NM
45s					
ABC					
12050	Warning/On Your Way Down	1974	—	2.00	4.00
12094	Everything Comes Up Roses/A Very Special Love Song	1975	—	2.00	4.00
12130	I Got Caught/Take It All Off	1975	—	2.00	4.00
12162	Dear Abby/Love Ain't Here No More	1976	—	2.00	4.00
12224	Heart Full of Song/All Messed Up	1976	—	2.00	4.00
ATLANTIC					
2461	I Can't See Myself/Looking for a Fox	1967	—	3.00	6.00
2508	Slip Away/Funky Fever	1968	2.00	4.00	8.00
2569	Too Weak to Fight/Let Me Comfort You	1968	—	3.00	6.00
2576	Back Door Santa/That Old Time Feeling	1968	2.00	4.00	8.00
2605	Snatching It Back/Making Love	1969	—	3.00	6.00
2642	The Feeling Is Right/You Can't Miss What You Can't Measure	1969	—	3.00	6.00
2660	Doin' Our Thing/I Smell a Rat	1969	—	3.00	6.00
2702	Take It Off Him and Put It On Me/A Few Troubles I've Had	1970	—	3.00	6.00
2726	I Can't Leave Your Love Alone/Devil Woman	1970	—	3.00	6.00
2748	Patches/Say It One More Time	1970	—	3.00	6.00
2774	It's All in Your Mind/Till I Can't Take It Anymore	1970	—	3.00	6.00
2801	The Court Room/Getting the Bills	1971	—	3.00	6.00
2818	Slipped, Tripped, and Fell in Love/I Hate to Love and Run	1971	—	3.00	6.00
2842	I'm the One/Scratch My Back	1971	—	3.00	6.00
2875	If You Can't Beat 'Em/Lonesomest Lonesome	1972	—	3.00	6.00
—With Candi Carter					
FAME					
XW179	Put On Your Shoes and Walk/I Found Somebody New	1973	—	2.50	5.00
XW250	Sixty Minute Man/Mother-in-Law	1973	—	2.50	5.00
XW330	I'm the Midnight Special/I Got Another Woman	1973	—	2.50	5.00
XW415	Love's Trying to Come to You/Heartbreak Woman	1974	—	2.50	5.00
1010	Tell Daddy/I Stayed Away Too Long	1966	3.00	6.00	12.00
1013	Thread the Needle/Don't Make My Baby Cry	1967	3.00	6.00	12.00
1016	Road of Love/She Ain't Gonna Do Right	1967	3.00	6.00	12.00
91006	Back in Your Arms/Holdin' Out	1972	—	2.50	5.00
ICHIBAN					
101	Messin' with My Mind/I Was in the Neighborhood	1986	—	—	3.00
106	If You Let Me Take You Home/So You're Leaving Me	1986	—	—	3.00
108	Strokin'/Love Me with Feelin'	1987	2.00	4.00	8.00
116	Doctor C.C./I Stayed Away Too Long	1987	—	—	3.00
131	Grandpa Can't Find His Kate/What'd I Say	1988	—	—	3.00
135	Trying to Sleep Tonight/(B-side unknown)	1988	—	—	3.00
158	I'm Just Not Good/I'm the Best	1989	—	—	3.00
164	Why Do I Stay Here and Take This Shit fro You/It's a Man Down There	1989	—	—	3.00
213	In Between a Rock and a Hard Place/Dance to the Blues	1990	—	—	3.00
222	Things Ain't Like They Used to Be/Pickin' 'Em Up, Layin' 'Em Down	1990	—	—	3.00
238	I Ain't Leaving, Girl/If You See My Lady	1991	—	—	3.00
262	"G" Spot/Hot Dog	1992	—	—	3.00
275	Hand Me Down Love/Let's Get a Quickie	1992	—	—	3.00
RONN					
90	I Couldn't Refuse Your Love/What Was I Supposed to Do?	1977	—	2.50	5.00
VENTURE					
130	Jimmy's Disco/Searching	1980	—	2.00	4.00
141	Let's Burn/If I Stay	1980	—	2.00	4.00
145	It's a Monster Thang/If I Were Yours	1981	—	2.00	4.00
147	Can We Slip Away Again/If I Were Yours	1981	—	2.00	4.00
Albums					
ABC					
X-833	Real	1974	3.75	7.50	15.00
X-896	Loneliness & Temptation	1975	3.75	7.50	15.00
X-943	A Heart Full of Song	1976	3.75	7.50	15.00
ATLANTIC					
SD 8192	This Is Clarence Carter	1968	7.50	15.00	30.00
SD 8199	The Dynamic Clarence Carter	1969	7.50	15.00	30.00
SD 8238	Testifyin'	1969	7.50	15.00	30.00
SD 8267	Patches	1970	7.50	15.00	30.00
SD 8282	The Best of Clarence Carter	1971	5.00	10.00	20.00
FAME					
FM-LA186-F	Sixty Minutes	1973	3.75	7.50	15.00
ICHIBAN					
ICH-1001	Messin' with My Mind	1986	3.00	6.00	12.00
ICH-1003	Dr. C.C.	1986	3.00	6.00	12.00
ICH-1016	Hooked on Love	1987	3.00	6.00	12.00
ICH-1032	Touch of Blues	1988	3.00	6.00	12.00
ICH-1068	Between a Rock and a Hard Place	1989	3.00	6.00	12.00
ICH-1116	The Best of Clarence Carter: The Dr.'s Greatest Presciptions	1991	3.00	6.00	12.00
VENTURE					
VL 1005	Let's Burn	1980	2.50	5.00	10.00
VL 1009	Mr. Clarence Carter In Person	1981	2.50	5.00	10.00

CARTER, MEL

Number	Title (A Side/B Side)	Yr	VG	VG+	NM
45s					
AMOS					
132	Everything Stops for a Little While/This Is My Life	1970	—	3.00	6.00
139	Kiss Tomorrow Goodbye/This Is My Life	1970	—	3.00	6.00
ARWIN					
123	Sugar/I'm Coming Home	1960	3.75	7.50	15.00
BELL					
743	Didn't We/I Pretend	1968	—	3.00	6.00
775	Another Saturday Night/Coming From You	1969	—	3.00	6.00
CREAM					
8041	You Changed My Life Again/(B-side unknown)	1980	—	2.00	4.00
8143	Who's Right, Who's Wrong/I Don't Wanna Get Over You	1981	—	2.00	4.00
DERBY					
1003	When a Boy Falls in Love/So Wonderful	1963	3.00	6.00	12.00
1005	Time of Young Love/Wonderful Love	1963	3.00	6.00	12.00
1008	Why I Call Her Mine/After the Party, the Meeting Is Sweeter	1964	3.00	6.00	12.00
IMPERIAL					
66052	'Deed I Do/What's On Your Mind	1964	2.00	4.00	8.00
66078	I'll Never Be Free/The Richest Man Alive	1964	2.00	4.00	8.00
66101	High Noon/I Just Can't Imagine	1965	2.00	4.00	8.00
66113	Hold Me, Thrill Me, Kiss Me/Sweet Little Girl	1965	2.50	5.00	10.00
66138	(All of a Sudden) My Heart Sings/When I Hold the Hand of the One I Love	1965	2.00	4.00	8.00
66148	Love Is All We Need/I Wish I Didn't Love You So	1965	2.00	4.00	8.00
66165	Band of Gold/Detour	1966	2.00	4.00	8.00
66183	You You You/If You Lose Her	1966	2.00	4.00	8.00
66208	Take Good Care of Her/Tar and Cement	1966	2.00	4.00	8.00
66228	As Time Goes By/Look to the Rainbow	1966	2.00	4.00	8.00
LIBERTY					
MLC-1 [DJ]	The Star Spangled Banner (same on both sides)	196?	3.00	6.00	12.00
—Promo only; "This record is issued by Liberty Records as a Public Service" on label					
55970	Edelweiss/For Once in My Life	1968	—	3.00	6.00
55987	Star Dust/Enter Laughing	1967	—	3.00	6.00
56000	Be My Love/Look Into My Love	1967	—	3.00	6.00
56015	Excuse Me/The Other Woman	1968	—	3.00	6.00
PRIVATE STOCK					
45057	Put a Little Love Away/Dancing for Dimes	1975	—	2.00	4.00
45087	My Coloring Book	1976	—	2.00	4.00
ROMAR					
711	She Is Me/Do Me Wrong, But Do Me	1973	—	2.00	4.00
714	Treasure of Love/Do Me Wrong, But Do Me	1973	—	2.00	4.00
716	I Only Have Eyes for You/Treasure of Love	1974	—	2.00	4.00
Albums					
AMOS					
7010	This Is My Life	1971	3.00	6.00	12.00
DERBY					
LPM-702 [M]	When a Boy Falls in Love	1963	75.00	150.00	300.00
IMPERIAL					
LP-9289 [M]	Hold Me, Thrill Me, Kiss Me	1965	3.75	7.50	15.00
LP-9300 [M]	All of a Sudden My Heart Sings	1966	3.75	7.50	15.00
LP-9319 [M]	Easy Listening	1966	3.75	7.50	15.00
LP-12289 [S]	Hold Me, Thrill Me, Kiss Me	1965	5.00	10.00	20.00
LP-12300 [S]	All of a Sudden My Heart Sings	1966	5.00	10.00	20.00
LP-12319 [S]	Easy Listening	1966	5.00	10.00	20.00
SUNSET					
SUS-5227	Mel Carter	1968	2.50	5.00	10.00
SUS-5295	Easy Goin'	1970	2.50	5.00	10.00

CARTER, SONNY

Number	Title (A Side/B Side)	Yr	VG	VG+	NM
45s					
CARLTON					
481	Crying Over You/My Lonely Life	1959	—	—	—
—Unreleased?					
DOT					
15921	Crying Over You/My Lonely Life	1959	7.50	15.00	30.00
KING					
4739	There Is No Greater Love/Oh Baby	1954	12.50	25.00	50.00
4756	It's Strange but True/I Solemnly Swear	1954	12.50	25.00	50.00

CARTEY, RIC

Number	Title (A Side/B Side)	Yr	VG	VG+	NM
45s					
ABC-PARAMOUNT					
10415	Poor Me/Something in My Eye	1963	3.00	6.00	12.00
NRC					
503	My Heart Belongs to You/Scratching on the Screen	1959	12.50	25.00	50.00
RCA VICTOR					
47-6751	Young Love/Oooh-Eee	1956	20.00	40.00	80.00
47-6828	Heart Throb/I Wancha to Know	1957	20.00	40.00	80.00
47-6920	Let Me Tell You About Love/Born to Love One Woman	1957	30.00	60.00	120.00
47-7011	My Babe/Hello Down Easy	1957	30.00	60.00	120.00

Number	Title (A Side/B Side)	Yr	VG	VG+	NM
STARS					
539	Young Love/Oooh-Eee	1956	37.50	75.00	150.00

CARTOONE

45s

Number	Title (A Side/B Side)	Yr	VG	VG+	NM
ATLANTIC					
2598	Mr. Poor Man/Knik Knak Man	1969	2.00	4.00	8.00
2630	Reflections on a Common Theme/Penny for the Sun	1969	—	3.00	6.00

Albums

Number	Title (A Side/B Side)	Yr	VG	VG+	NM
ATLANTIC					
SD 8219	Cartoone	1969	5.00	10.00	20.00

CARVETTES, THE

45s

Number	Title (A Side/B Side)	Yr	VG	VG+	NM
COPA					
200-1/2	A Lover's Prayer/Never Gonna Leave Me	1959	200.00	400.00	800.00

CASANOVAS, THE

45s

Number	Title (A Side/B Side)	Yr	VG	VG+	NM
APOLLO					
471	That's All/Are You for Real	1955	25.00	50.00	100.00
474	It's Been a Long Time/Hush-a-Mecca	1955	37.50	75.00	150.00
477	I Don't Want You to Go/Please Be My Love	1955	37.50	75.00	150.00
483	My Baby's Love/Sleepy Head Mama	1956	37.50	75.00	150.00
519	Please Be Mine/For You and You Alone	1957	25.00	50.00	100.00
523	(I Got a) Good Lookin' Baby/You Are My Queen	1957	25.00	50.00	100.00

CASCADES, THE

Probably all the same group.

45s

Number	Title (A Side/B Side)	Yr	VG	VG+	NM
ARWIN					
132	Cheryl's Going Home/Truly Julie's Blues	1966	2.00	4.00	8.00
—The group on Renee is different than the others.					
134	Midnight Lace/All's Fair in Love and War	1966	2.00	4.00	8.00
CANBASE					
714	I Started a Joke/Sweet America	1972	—	2.50	5.00
CHARTER					
1018	She Was Never Really Mine (To Lose)/My Best Girl	1964	5.00	10.00	20.00
1018	She Was Never Mine (To Really Lose)/My Best Girl	1964	3.75	7.50	15.00
ERA BACK TO BACK HITS					
027	Rhythm of the Rain/Harlem Shuffle	197?	—	2.50	5.00
—A-side is a re-recording; B-side by Bob and Earl					
LIBERTY					
55822	She'll Love Again/I Bet You Won't Stay	1965	2.50	5.00	10.00
LONDON					
177	Two-Sided Man/The Woman's A Girl	1972	—	2.50	5.00
PROBE					
453	Two-Sided Man/Everyone Is Blossoming	1968	2.00	4.00	8.00
453 [PS]	Two-Sided Man/Everyone Is Blossoming	1968	3.75	7.50	15.00
RCA VICTOR					
47-8206	Cinderella/A Little Like Lovin'	1963	3.75	7.50	15.00
47-8268	For Your Sweet Love/Jeannie	1963	3.00	6.00	12.00
47-8321	Little Betty Falling Star/Those Were the Good Old Days	1964	3.75	7.50	15.00
47-8402	I Dare You to Cry/Awake	1964	3.00	6.00	12.00
RENEE					
105	Pains in My Heart/One That I Can Spare	19??	5.00	10.00	20.00
SMASH					
2083	Hey Little Girl of Mine/Blue Hours	1967	2.00	4.00	8.00
2101	Flying on the Ground/Main Street	1967	2.00	4.00	8.00
UNI					
55152	Maybe the Rain Will Fall/Naggin' Cries	1969	2.00	4.00	8.00
55169	Indian River/Big City Country Boy	1969	2.00	4.00	8.00
55200	But For Love/Hazel Autumn Cocoa Brown	1970	2.00	4.00	8.00
55231	April, May, June and July/Big Ugly Sky	1970	2.00	4.00	8.00
VALIANT					
6021	There's a Reason/Second Chance	1962	6.25	12.50	25.00
6026	Rhythm of the Rain/Let Me Be	1962	5.00	10.00	20.00
6028	Shy Girl/The Last Leaf	1963	3.75	7.50	15.00
6032	I Wanna Be Your Lover/My First Day Alone	1963	3.75	7.50	15.00
WARNER BROS.					
7114	Rhythm of the Rain/The Last Leaf	1968	—	2.50	5.00
—"Back to Back Hits" series; originals on green "W7" label					

Albums

Number	Title (A Side/B Side)	Yr	VG	VG+	NM
UNI					
73069	Maybe the Rain Will Fall	1969	6.25	12.50	25.00
VALIANT					
W 405 [M]	Rhythm of the Rain	1963	37.50	75.00	150.00
WS 405 [S]	Rhythm of the Rain	1963	75.00	150.00	300.00

CASEY, AL

Also see DUANE EDDY.

45s

Number	Title (A Side/B Side)	Yr	VG	VG+	NM
BLUE HORIZON					
925	Cookin'/Hot Foot	1962	6.25	12.50	25.00
DOT					
15524	A Fool's Blues/Juice	1956	7.50	15.00	30.00
15563	Guitar Man/Come What May	1957	10.00	20.00	40.00
HIGHLAND					
1002	Got the Teenage Blues/(B-side unknown)	1959	10.00	20.00	40.00
1004	Night Beat/The Stinger	1960	6.25	12.50	25.00
LIBERTY					
55117	Willa Mae/She Gotta Shake	1957	5.00	10.00	20.00
MCI					
1005	Pink Panther/If I Told You	1965	3.75	7.50	15.00
STACY					
925	Cookin'/Hot Foot	1962	3.75	7.50	15.00
936	Jivin' Around/Doin' the Shotish	1962	3.75	7.50	15.00
950	Laughin'/Chicken Feathers	1962	3.75	7.50	15.00
956	Doin' It/Monte Carlo	1963	3.75	7.50	15.00
961	Full House/Indian Love Call	1963	3.75	7.50	15.00
962	Surfin' Hootenanny/Easy Pickin'	1963	5.00	10.00	20.00
—Black vinyl					
962	Surfin' Hootenanny/Easy Pickin'	1963	10.00	20.00	40.00
—Red vinyl					
964	Surfin' Blues/Guitars, Guitars, Guitars	1963	3.75	7.50	15.00
971	Cookin'/What Are We Gonna Do in '64	1964	3.75	7.50	15.00
UNITED ARTISTS					
158	The Stinger/Keep Talking	1959	6.25	12.50	25.00
494	Jivin' Around/Doin' the Shotish	1962	6.25	12.50	25.00

Albums

Number	Title (A Side/B Side)	Yr	VG	VG+	NM
MOODSVILLE					
MVLP-12 [M]	The Al Casey Quartet	1960	12.50	25.00	50.00
—Green label					
MVLP-12 [M]	The Al Casey Quartet	1965	6.25	12.50	25.00
—Blue label, trident logo at right					
STACY					
STM-100 [M]	Surfin' Hootenanny	1963	75.00	150.00	300.00
STS-100 [S]	Surfin' Hootenanny	1963	100.00	200.00	400.00
SUNDAZED					
LP-5026	Surfin' Hootenanny	1996	2.50	5.00	10.00
SWINGVILLE					
SVLP-2007 [M]	Buck Jumpin'	1960	12.50	25.00	50.00
—Purple label					
SVLP-2007 [M]	Buck Jumpin'	1965	6.25	12.50	25.00
—Blue label, trident logo at right					

CASH, ALVIN

45s

Number	Title (A Side/B Side)	Yr	VG	VG+	NM
CHESS					
2098	Getaway/Saddle Up	1970	2.00	4.00	8.00
DAKAR					
4559	Doin' the Ali Shuffle/The Feeling	1976	—	2.50	5.00
MAR-V-LUS					
6002	Twine Time/The Bump	1964	3.75	7.50	15.00
6005	The Barracuda/Do It One More Time	1965	2.50	5.00	10.00
6006	Un-Wind the Twine/The Penguin	1965	2.50	5.00	10.00
6009	Boston Monkey/Unwind the Twine	1965	2.50	5.00	10.00
6012	The Philly Freeze/No Deposit No Return	1966	2.50	5.00	10.00
6014	Alvin's Boo-Ga-Loo/Let's Do Some Good Timing	1966	2.50	5.00	10.00
6015	Doin' the Ali Shuffle/Feel So Good	1967	2.50	5.00	10.00
6019	Different Strokes for Different Folks/The Change	1967	2.50	5.00	10.00
SEVENTY-7					
112	Alvin's Doing His Thing/It's a Party	1972	—	3.00	6.00
118	Doin' the Creep/Party Time	1972	—	3.00	6.00
SOUND STAGE 7					
1509	Funky Washing Machine/I Don't Want It	1973	—	3.00	6.00
TODDLIN' TOWN					
104	Alvin's Bag/Whip It On Me	1968	2.00	4.00	8.00
111	Keep On Dancing/(Instrumental)	1968	2.00	4.00	8.00
119	Funky '69/Moaning and Groaning	1969	2.00	4.00	8.00
124	Poppin' Popcorn/(Instrumental)	1969	2.00	4.00	8.00
WESTBOUND					
159	Stone Thing (Part 1)/Stone Thing (Part 2)	1970	2.00	4.00	8.00

Albums

Number	Title (A Side/B Side)	Yr	VG	VG+	NM
MAR-V-LUS					
1827 [M]	Twine Time	1965	7.50	15.00	30.00

CASH, BOBBY

45s

Number	Title (A Side/B Side)	Yr	VG	VG+	NM
KING					
5844	Mona Lisa/Teen Love	1964	7.50	15.00	30.00
5864	Only Make Believe/Run, Fool, Run	1964	7.50	15.00	30.00
5894	The Answer to My Dreams/I Don't Need Your Love and Kisses	1964	7.50	15.00	30.00

CASH, EDDIE

45s

Number	Title (A Side/B Side)	Yr	VG	VG+	NM
PEAK					
1001	Doing All Right/Land of Promises	1958	30.00	60.00	120.00
1010	Come On Home/(B-side unknown)	1960	3.75	7.50	15.00
ROULETTE					
4380	Stormy Weather/Lonely Island	1961	3.00	6.00	12.00
TODD					
1057	Thinkin' Man/Livin' Lovin' Temptation	1960	3.00	6.00	12.00

CASH, JOHNNY

12-Inch Singles

Number	Title (A Side/B Side)	Yr	VG	VG+	NM
COLUMBIA					
AS 921 [DJ]	Without Love (one-sided)	1980	3.75	7.50	15.00
—Black B-side has etched autographs of Johnny Cash and Nick Lowe					

45s

Number	Title (A Side/B Side)	Yr	VG	VG+	NM
AMERICAN					
18091	Drive On/Delia's Gone	1994	—	2.00	4.00
A&M					
2291	The Death of Me/One More Shot	1980	—	2.00	4.00
—With Levon Helm					
CACHET					
4504	Wings in the Morning/What on Earth	1980	—	2.50	5.00
4504 [PS]	Wings in the Morning/What on Earth	1980	—	2.50	5.00
COLUMBIA					
02189	Mobile Bay/The Hard Way	1981	—	2.00	4.00
02669	The Reverend Mr. Black/Chattanooga City Limit Sign	1982	—	2.00	4.00
03058	Georgia on a Fast Train/Sing a Song	1982	—	2.00	4.00
03317	Fair Weather Friends/Ain't Gonna Hobo No More	1982	—	2.00	4.00
03524	I'll Cross Over Jordan Some Day/We Must Believe in Magic	1983	—	2.00	4.00

Number	Title (A Side/B Side)	Yr	VG	VG+	NM
04060	I'm Ragged, But I'm Right/Brand New Dance	1983	—	2.00	4.00
04227	Johnny 99/New Cut Road	1983	—	—	3.00
04428	That's the Truth/Joshua Gone Barbados	1984	—	—	3.00
04513	The Chicken in Black/The Battle of Nashville	1984	—	—	3.00
04740	They Killed Him/The Three Bells	1985	—	—	3.00
—With the Carter Family					
04860	Crazy Old Soldier/It Ain't Gonna Worry My Mind	1985	—	—	3.00
—A-side: Ray Charles and Johnny Cash; B-side: Ray Charles and Mickey Gilley					
04881	Highwayman/The Human Condition	1985	—	—	3.00
—A-side: Willie Nelson/Waylon Jennings/Johnny Cash/Kris Kristofferson; B-side: Nelson, Cash					
04881 [PS]	Highwayman/The Human Condition	1985	—	2.50	5.00
—A-side: Willie Nelson/Waylon Jennings/Johnny Cash/Kris Kristofferson; B-side: Nelson, Cash					
05594	Desperadoes Waiting for a Train/The Twentieth Century Is Almost Over	1985	—	—	3.00
—A-side: Willie Nelson/Waylon Jennings/Johnny Cash/Kris Kristofferson; B-side: Nelson, Cash					
05672	I'm Leaving Now/Easy Street	1985	—	—	3.00
05896	American by Birth/Even Cowgirls Get the Blues	1986	—	—	3.00
—A-side: Johnny Cash/Waylon Jennings					
08406	Highwayman/Desperadoes Waiting for a Train	1988	—	—	3.00
—Waylon Jennings/Willie Nelson/Johnny Cash/Kris Kristofferson; reissue					
10011	The Junkie and the Juicehead/Crystal Chandeliers and Burgundy	1974	—	2.50	5.00
10048	Father and Daughter, Father and Son/Don't Take Your Love to Town	1974	—	2.50	5.00
—With Rosey Nix					
10066	The Lady Came from Baltimore/Lonesome to the Bone	1974	—	2.50	5.00
10116	My Old Kentucky Home (Turpentine and Dandelion Wine)/Hard Times Comin'	1975	—	2.50	5.00
10177	Look at Them Beans/All Around Cowboy	1975	—	2.50	5.00
10237	Texas — 1947/I Hardly Ever Sing Beer Drinking Songs	1975	—	2.50	5.00
10279	Strawberry Cake/I Got Stripes	1975	—	2.50	5.00
10321	One Piece at a Time/Go On Blues	1976	—	2.50	5.00
10381	Sold Out of Flagpoles/Mountain Lady	1976	—	2.50	5.00
10424	It's All Over/Ridin' on the Cotton Belt	1976	—	2.50	5.00
10483	The Last Gunfighter Ballad/City Jail	1977	—	2.50	5.00
10587	Lady/Hit the Road and Go	1977	—	2.50	5.00
10623	After the Ball/Calilou	1977	—	2.50	5.00
10681	I Would Like to See You Again/Lately	1978	—	2.50	5.00
10742	There Ain't No Good Chain Gang/I Wish I Was Crazy Again	1978	—	2.50	5.00
—With Waylon Jennings					
10817	Gone Girl/I'm Alright Now	1978	—	2.50	5.00
10855	It'll Be Her/It Comes and Goes	1978	—	2.50	5.00
10888	I Will Rock and Roll with You/A Song for the Life	1979	—	2.50	5.00
10961	(Ghost) Riders in the Sky/I'm Gonna Sit on the Porch and Pick on My Guitar	1979	—	2.50	5.00
10961 [PS]	(Ghost) Riders in the Sky/I'm Gonna Sit on the Porch and Pick on My Guitar	1979	—	3.00	6.00
11103	I'll Say It's True/Cocaine Blues	1979	—	2.50	5.00
11237	Bull Rider/Lonesome to the Bone	1980	—	2.00	4.00
11283	Song of a Patriot/She's a Go-er	1980	—	2.00	4.00
11340	Cold Lonesome Morning/The Cowboy Who Started the Fight	1980	—	2.00	4.00
11399	The Last Time/Rockabilly Blues (Texas 1965)	1980	—	2.00	4.00
11424	Without Love/It Ain't Nothing New Babe	1981	—	2.00	4.00
30843 [S]	Loading Coal/Slow Rider	1960	7.50	15.00	30.00
30844 [S]	Lumberjack/Dorrance of Ponchartrain	1960	7.50	15.00	30.00
30845 [S]	When Papa Played the Dobro/Going to Memphis	1960	7.50	15.00	30.00
30846 [S]	Old Doc Brown/Boss Jack	1960	7.50	15.00	30.00
—The above four are "Stereo Seven" 33 1/3 rpm jukebox singles from "JS 7-12" and the album "Ride This Train"					
30847 [S]	One More Ride/Run Softly, Blue River	1960	7.50	15.00	30.00
—"Stereo Seven" 33 1/3 rpm jukebox single from "JS 7-12," but from the album "The Fabulous Johnny Cash"					
31109 [S]	Seasons of My Heart/I Couldn't Keep from Crying	1961	7.50	15.00	30.00
31110 [S]	My Shoes Keep Walking Back to You/Time Changes Everything	1961	7.50	15.00	30.00
31111 [S]	Transfusion Blues/I'd Just Be Fool Enough (To Fall)	1961	7.50	15.00	30.00
31112 [S]	I'm So Lonesome I Could Cry/I Will Miss You When You Go	1961	7.50	15.00	30.00
31113 [S]	Just One More/Honky Tonk Girl	1961	7.50	15.00	30.00
—The above five are "Stereo Seven" 33 1/3 rpm jukebox singles from "JS 7-29" and the album "Now There Was a Song"					
3-38990	Hey Porter/Big River	1964	7.50	15.00	30.00
—Stereo jukebox single, plays at 33 1/3 rpm; rather than the usual rainbow "target" label of Columbia "Stereo Seven" singles, this one has green labels					
41251	All Over Again/What Do I Care	1958	3.75	7.50	15.00
41251 [PS]	All Over Again/What Do I Care	1958	10.00	20.00	40.00
41313	Don't Take Your Guns to Town/I Still Miss Someone	1959	3.75	7.50	15.00
41313 [PS]	Don't Take Your Guns to Town/I Still Miss Someone	1959	10.00	20.00	40.00
41371	Frankie's Man, Johnny/You, Dreamer, You	1959	3.75	7.50	15.00
41427	I Got Stripes/Five Feet High and Rising	1959	3.75	7.50	15.00
41481	The Little Drummer Boy/I'll Remember You	1959	3.75	7.50	15.00
41481 [PS]	The Little Drummer Boy/I'll Remember You	1959	10.00	20.00	40.00
41618	Seasons of My Heart/Smiling Bill McCall	1960	3.75	7.50	15.00
41707	Second Honemoon/Honky Tonk Girl	1960	3.75	7.50	15.00
41804	Going to Memphis/Loading Coal	1960	3.75	7.50	15.00
41920	Girl in Saskatoon/Locomotive Man	1960	3.75	7.50	15.00
41995	The Rebel-Johnny Yuma/Forty Shades of Green	1961	3.00	6.00	12.00
41995 [PS]	The Rebel-Johnny Yuma/Forty Shades of Green	1961	6.25	12.50	25.00
42147	Tennessee Flat Top Box/Tall Men	1961	3.00	6.00	12.00
42147 [PS]	Tennessee Flat Top Box/Tall Men	1961	6.25	12.50	25.00
42301	The Big Battle/What I've Learned	1962	3.00	6.00	12.00
42301 [PS]	The Big Battle/What I've Learned	1962	6.25	12.50	25.00
42425	In the Jailhouse Now/A Little at a Time	1962	3.00	6.00	12.00
42425 [PS]	In the Jailhouse Now/A Little at a Time	1962	6.25	12.50	25.00
42512	Bonanza!/Pick a Bale o' Cotton	1962	3.00	6.00	12.00
42615	Peace in the Valley/Were You There	1962	3.00	6.00	12.00
—With the Carter Family					
42665	Busted/Send a Picture of Mother	1963	2.50	5.00	10.00
42665 [PS]	Busted/Send a Picture of Mother	1963	6.25	12.50	25.00

Number	Title (A Side/B Side)	Yr	VG	VG+	NM
42788	Ring of Fire/I'd Still Be There	1963	2.50	5.00	10.00
42788 [DJ]	Ring of Fire (same on both sides)	1963	10.00	20.00	40.00
—Red vinyl promo					
42788 [PS]	Ring of Fire/I'd Still Be There	1963	7.50	15.00	30.00
42880	The Matador/Still in Town	1963	2.50	5.00	10.00
42880 [PS]	The Matador/Still in Town	1963	5.00	10.00	20.00
42964	Understand Your Man/Dark as a Dungeon	1964	2.50	5.00	10.00
43058	The Ballad of Ira Hayes/Bad News	1964	2.50	5.00	10.00
43145	It Ain't Me, Babe/Time and Time Again	1964	2.50	5.00	10.00
43206	Orange Blossom Special/All of God's Children Ain't Free	1965	2.00	4.00	8.00
43313	Mister Garfield/Streets or Laredo	1965	2.00	4.00	8.00
43342	The Sons of Katie Elder/A Certain Kinda Hurtin'	1965	2.00	4.00	8.00
43420	Happy to Be with You/Pickin' Time	1965	2.00	4.00	8.00
43496	The One on the Right Is On the Left/Cotton Pickin' Hands	1965	2.00	4.00	8.00
43673	Everybody Loves a Nut/Austin Prison	1966	—	3.00	6.00
43763	Boa Constrictor/Bottom of a Mountain	1966	—	3.00	6.00
43921	You Beat All I Ever Saw/Put the Sugar to Bill	1966	—	3.00	6.00
44288	The Wind Changes/Red Velvet	1967	—	3.00	6.00
44373	Rosanna's Going Wild/Roll Call	1967	—	3.00	6.00
44373 [PS]	Rosanna's Going Wild/Roll Call	1967	2.50	5.00	10.00
44513	Folsom Prison Blues/The Folk Singer	1968	—	3.00	6.00
44513 [PS]	Folsom Prison Blues/The Folk Singer	1968	2.50	5.00	10.00
44689	Daddy Sang Bass/He Turned the Water Into Wine	1968	—	3.00	6.00
44944	A Boy Named Sue/San Quentin	1969	—	3.00	6.00
45020	Blistered/See Ruby Fall	1969	—	3.00	6.00
45134	What Is Truth/Sing a Traveling Song	1970	—	2.50	5.00
45211	Sonday Morning Coming Down/I'm Gonna Try to Be That Way	1970	—	2.50	5.00
45269	Flesh and Blood/This Side of the Law	1970	—	2.50	5.00
45339	Man in Black/Little Bit of Yesterday	1971	—	2.50	5.00
45393	Singing in Viet Nam Talking Blues/You've Got a New Light Shining	1971	—	2.50	5.00
45460	Papa Was a Good Man/I Promise You	1971	—	2.50	5.00
45534	A Thing Called Love/Daddy	1972	—	2.50	5.00
45590	Kate/Miracle Man	1972	—	2.50	5.00
45660	Oney/Country Trash	1972	—	2.50	5.00
45679	The World Needs a Melody/A Bird with Broken Wings Can't Fly	1972	—	2.50	5.00
—With the Carter Family					
45740	Any Old Wind That Blows/Kentucky Straight	1972	—	2.50	5.00
45786	Children/Last Summer	1973	—	2.50	5.00
45938	Pick the Wildwood Flower/Diamonds in the Rough	1973	—	2.50	5.00
—With Mother Maybelle and the Carter Family					
45979	Christmas As I Knew It/That Christmasy Feeling	1973	—	2.50	5.00
—With Tommy Cash					
45997	Orleans Parish Prison/Jacob Green	1974	—	2.50	5.00
46028	Ragged Old Flag/Don't Go Near the Water	1974	—	2.50	5.00
60516	The Baron/I Will Dance with You	1981	—	2.00	4.00
69067	Ragged Old Flag/I'm Leaving Now	1989	—	—	3.00
73233	America Remains/Silver Stallion	1990	—	—	3.00
—Waylon Jennings/Willie Nelson/Johnny Cash/Kris Kristofferson					
73381	Born and Raised in Black and White/Texas	1990	—	—	3.00
—The Highwaymen (Waylon Jennings/Willie Nelson/Johnny Cash/Kris Kristofferson)					
73572	American Remains/Texas	1990	—	—	3.00
—The Highwaymen (Waylon Jennings/Willie Nelson/Johnny Cash/Kris Kristofferson)					

EPIC

Number	Title (A Side/B Side)	Yr	VG	VG+	NM
50778	There Ain't No Good Chain Gang/I Wish I Was Crazy Again	1979	—	2.50	5.00
—Johnny Cash/Waylon Jennings					

LIBERTY

Number	Title (A Side/B Side)	Yr	VG	VG+	NM
S7-18486	It Is What It Is/The Devil's Right Hand	1995	—	—	3.00
—By The Highwaymen					

MERCURY

Number	Title (A Side/B Side)	Yr	VG	VG+	NM
870010-7	W. Lee O'Daniel (And the Light Crust Dough Boys)/Letters from Homes	1987	—	—	3.00
870237-7	Cry, Cry, Cry/Get Rhythm	1988	—	—	3.00
870688-7	Tennessee Flat Top Box/That Old Wheel	1988	—	—	3.00
—A-side with Hank Williams, Jr.					
872420-7	Ballad of a Teenage Queen/Get Rhythm	1988	—	—	3.00
—With Roseanne Cash and the Everly Brothers					
874562-7	The Last of the Drifters/(B-side unknown)	1989	—	—	3.00
—With Tom T. Hall					
875626-7	Cat's in the Cradle/I Love You, Love You	1990	—	—	3.00
878292-7	Goin' By the Book/Beans for Breakfast	1990	—	—	3.00
878710-7	The Greatest Cowboy of Them All/Hey Porter	1990	—	—	3.00
878968-7	The Mystery of Life/I'm an Easy Rider	1990	—	—	3.00
888459-7	The Night Hank Williams Came to Town/I'd Rather Have You	1987	—	—	3.00
888719-7	Sixteen Tons/The Ballad of Barbara	1987	—	—	3.00
888838-7	Let Him Roll/My Ship Will Sail	1987	—	—	3.00

SCOTTI BROS.

Number	Title (A Side/B Side)	Yr	VG	VG+	NM
02803	The General Lee/Duelin' Dukes	1982	—	2.00	4.00
—Narration on B-side: Sorrell Booke					

SMASH

Number	Title (A Side/B Side)	Yr	VG	VG+	NM
884934-7	Sixteen Candles/Rock & Roll (Fais-Do-Do)	1986	—	2.00	4.00
—With Jerry Lee Lewis, Roy Orbison and Carl Perkins					
888142-7	We Remember the King/Class of '55	1987	—	2.00	4.00
—With Jerry Lee Lewis, Roy Orbison and Carl Perkins; B-side by Carl Perkins solo					

SUN

Number	Title (A Side/B Side)	Yr	VG	VG+	NM
221	Hey Porter/Cry, Cry, Cry	1955	10.00	20.00	40.00
232	Folsom Prison Blues/So Doggone Lonesome	1956	7.50	15.00	30.00
241	I Walk the Line/Get Rhythm	1956	10.00	20.00	40.00
258	Train of Love/There You Go	1956	7.50	15.00	30.00
266	Next in Line/Don't Make Me Go	1957	7.50	15.00	30.00
279	Home of the Blues/Give My Love to Rose	1957	7.50	15.00	30.00
283	Ballad of a Teenage Queen/Big River	1958	6.25	12.50	25.00
295	Guess Things Happen That Way/Come In Stranger	1958	6.25	12.50	25.00
295 [PS]	Guess Things Happen That Way/Come In Stranger	1958	10.00	20.00	40.00
302	The Ways of a Woman in Love/The Nearest Thing to Heaven	1958	6.25	12.50	25.00

Number	Title (A Side/B Side)	Yr	VG	VG+	NM
309	It's Just About Time/Just Thought You'd Like to Know	1958	6.25	12.50	25.00
316	Luther Played the Boogie/Thanks a Lot	1959	5.00	10.00	20.00
321	Katy Too/I Forgot to Remember to Forget	1959	5.00	10.00	20.00
331	Goodbye Little Darlin'/You Tell Me	1959	5.00	10.00	20.00
334	Straight A's in Love/I Love You Because	1960	5.00	10.00	20.00
343	Story of a Broken Heart/Down the Street to 301	1960	5.00	10.00	20.00
347	Mean Eyed Cat/Port of Lonely Hearts	1960	5.00	10.00	20.00
355	Oh Lonesome Me/Life Goes On	1961	5.00	10.00	20.00
363	Sugartime/My Treasurer	1961	5.00	10.00	20.00
376	Born to Lose/Blue Train	1962	5.00	10.00	20.00
392	Wide Open Road/Belshazar	1964	5.00	10.00	20.00
1103	Get Rhythm/Hey Porter	1969	—	3.00	6.00
1111	Rock Island Line/Next in Line	1970	—	3.00	6.00
1121	Big River/Come In Stranger	1971	—	2.50	5.00

WARNER BROS.

Number	Title (A Side/B Side)	Yr	VG	VG+	NM
28979	I Will Dance with You/Too Bad for Love	1985	—	—	3.00

—With Karen Brooks

7-Inch Extended Plays

COLUMBIA

Number	Title (A Side/B Side)	Yr	VG	VG+	NM
B-2155	The Rebel — Johnny Yuma/Remember the Alamo//The Ballad of Boot Hill/Lorena	1961	3.75	7.50	15.00
B-2155 [PS]	The Rebel — Johnny Yuma	1961	3.75	7.50	15.00
B-12531	Run Softly, Blue River/That's All Over//I Still Miss Someone/Supper-Time	1958	3.00	6.00	12.00
B-12531 [PS]	The Fabulous Johnny Cash, Vol. I	1958	3.00	6.00	12.00
B-12532	Frankie's Man, Johnny/The Troubadour//Don't Take Your Guns to Town/That's Enough	1958	3.00	6.00	12.00
B-12532 [PS]	The Fabulous Johnny Cash, Vol. II	1958	3.00	6.00	12.00
B-12533	(A-side unknown)//Pickin' Time/Shepherd of My Heart	1958	3.00	6.00	12.00
B-12533 [PS]	The Fabulous Johnny Cash, Vol. III	1958	3.00	6.00	12.00
B-12861	It Was Jesus/I Saw a Man//Are All the Children In?/The Old Account	1959	3.00	6.00	12.00
B-12861 [PS]	Hymns by Johnny Cash, Vol. I	1959	3.00	6.00	12.00
B-12862	Lead Me Gently Home/Swing Low, Sweet Chariot//Snow in His Hair/Lead Me Father	1959	3.00	6.00	12.00
B-12862 [PS]	Hymns by Johnny Cash, Vol. II	1959	3.00	6.00	12.00
B-12863	I Call Him/These Things Shall Pass//He'll Be a Friend/God Will	1959	3.00	6.00	12.00
B-12863 [PS]	Hymns by Johnny Cash, Vol. III	1959	3.00	6.00	12.00
B-13391	(contents unknown)	1959	3.00	6.00	12.00
B-13391 [PS]	Songs of Our Soil, Vol. I	1959	3.00	6.00	12.00
B-13392	(contents unknown)	1959	3.00	6.00	12.00
B-13392 [PS]	Songs of Our Soil, Vol. II	1959	3.00	6.00	12.00
B-13393	Old Apache Squaw/Don't Step on Mother's Roses//My Grandfather's Clock/It Could Be You	1959	3.00	6.00	12.00
B-13393 [PS]	Songs of Our Soil, Vol. III	1959	3.00	6.00	12.00
B-14631	Seasons of My Heart/I Feel Better All Over//I Couldn't Keep from Crying/Time Changes Everything	1960	3.00	6.00	12.00
B-14631 [PS]	Now, There Was a Song, Vol. I	1960	3.00	6.00	12.00
B-14632	My Shoes Just Keep Walking Back to You/I'd Just Be Fool Enough (To Fall)//Transfusion Blues/Why Do You Punish Me	1960	3.00	6.00	12.00
B-14632 [PS]	Now, There Was a Song, Vol. II	1960	3.00	6.00	12.00
B-14633	I Will Miss You When You Go/I'm So Lonesome I Could Cry//Just One More/Honky Tonk Girl	1960	3.00	6.00	12.00
B-14633 [PS]	Now, There Was a Song, Vol. III	1960	3.00	6.00	12.00

SUN

Number	Title (A Side/B Side)	Yr	VG	VG+	NM
EPA-111	I Can't Help It/You Win Again//Hey Good Lookin'/I Could Never Be Ashamed	1956	10.00	20.00	40.00
EPA-111 [PS]	Johnny Cash Sings Hank Williams	1956	15.00	30.00	60.00
EPA-112	Rock Island Line/I Heard That Lonesome Whistle//Country Boy/If the Good Lord's Willin'	1956	7.50	15.00	30.00
EPA-112 [PS]	Country Boy	1956	12.50	25.00	50.00
EPA-113	I Walk the Line/The Wreck of the Old '97//Folsom Prison Blues/Doin' My Time	1958	7.50	15.00	30.00
EPA-113 [PS]	I Walk the Line	1958	12.50	25.00	50.00
EPA-114	The Ways of a Woman in Love/Next in Line//Guess Things Happen That Way/Train of Love	1958	7.50	15.00	30.00
EPA-114 [PS]	His Top Hits	1958	12.50	25.00	50.00
SEP-116	Home of the Blues/Big River//You're the Nearest Thing to Heaven/I Can't Help It	1959	7.50	15.00	30.00
SEP-116 [PS]	Home of the Blues	1959	12.50	25.00	50.00
SEP-117	So Doggone Lonesome/I Was There When It Happened//Cry, Cry, Cry/Remember Me	1958	7.50	15.00	30.00
SEP-117 [PS]	Johnny Cash	1958	12.50	25.00	50.00

Albums

ACCORD

Number	Title	Yr	VG	VG+	NM
SN-7134	I Walk the Line	1983	2.50	5.00	10.00
SN-7208	Years Gone By	1983	2.50	5.00	10.00

ALLEGIANCE

Number	Title	Yr	VG	VG+	NM
AV-5017	The First Years	1986	2.50	5.00	10.00

AMERICAN

Number	Title	Yr	VG	VG+	NM
43097	Unchained	1996	3.00	6.00	12.00
45220	American Recordings	1994	3.00	6.00	12.00

ARCHIVE OF FOLK MUSIC

Number	Title	Yr	VG	VG+	NM
278	Johnny Cash	198?	3.00	6.00	12.00

CACHET

Number	Title	Yr	VG	VG+	NM
9001	A Believer Sings the Truth	1979	3.75	7.50	15.00

COLUMBIA

Number	Title	Yr	VG	VG+	NM
GP 29 [(2)]	The World of Johnny Cash	1970	3.75	7.50	15.00
C2L 38 [(2) M]	Ballads of the True West	1965	6.25	12.50	25.00
C2S 838 [(2) S]	Ballads of the True West	1965	6.25	12.50	25.00
CL 1253 [M]	The Fabulous Johnny Cash	1958	5.00	10.00	20.00
CL 1284 [M]	Hymns by Johnny Cash	1959	6.25	12.50	25.00
CL 1339 [M]	Songs of Our Soil	1959	6.25	12.50	25.00
CL 1463 [M]	Now, There Was a Song!	1960	6.25	12.50	25.00
CL 1464 [M]	Ride This Train	1960	6.25	12.50	25.00
CL 1622 [M]	The Lure of the Grand Canyon	1961	10.00	20.00	40.00
—Cash narrates; with Andre Kostelanetz and His Orchestra					
CL 1722 [M]	Hymns from the Heart	1962	5.00	10.00	20.00
CL 1802 [M]	The Sound of Johnny Cash	1962	5.00	10.00	20.00
CL 1930 [M]	Blood, Sweat & Tears	1963	5.00	10.00	20.00
CL 2052 [M]	Ring of Fire (The Best of Johnny Cash)	1963	5.00	10.00	20.00
CL 2117 [M]	The Christmas Spirit	1963	6.25	12.50	25.00
CL 2190 [M]	I Walk the Line	1964	3.75	7.50	15.00
CL 2248 [M]	Bitter Tears (Ballads of the American Indian)	1964	3.75	7.50	15.00
CL 2309 [M]	Orange Blossom Special	1965	3.75	7.50	15.00
CL 2446 [M]	Mean as Hell	1965	3.75	7.50	15.00
CL 2492 [M]	Everybody Loves a Nut	1966	3.75	7.50	15.00
CL 2537 [M]	That's What You Get for Lovin' Me	1966	3.75	7.50	15.00
CL 2647 [M]	From Sea to Shining Sea	1967	5.00	10.00	20.00
CL 2678 [M]	Johnny Cash's Greatest Hits, Volume 1	1967	5.00	10.00	20.00
CS 8122 [S]	The Fabulous Johnny Cash	1959	10.00	20.00	40.00
CS 8125 [S]	Hymns by Johnny Cash	1959	10.00	20.00	40.00
CS 8148 [S]	Songs of Our Soil	1959	10.00	20.00	40.00
CS 8254 [S]	Now, There Was a Song!	1960	10.00	20.00	40.00
CS 8255 [S]	Ride This Train	1960	10.00	20.00	40.00
CS 8422 [S]	The Lure of the Grand Canyon	1961	12.50	25.00	50.00
—Cash narrates; with Andre Kostelanetz and His Orchestra					
CS 8522 [S]	Hymns from the Heart	1962	7.50	15.00	30.00
CS 8602 [S]	The Sound of Johnny Cash	1962	7.50	15.00	30.00
CS 8730 [S]	Blood, Sweat & Tears	1963	6.25	12.50	25.00
CS 8852 [S]	Ring of Fire (The Best of Johnny Cash)	1963	6.25	12.50	25.00
CS 8917 [S]	The Christmas Spirit	1963	7.50	15.00	30.00
CS 8990 [S]	I Walk the Line	1964	5.00	10.00	20.00
CS 9048 [S]	Bitter Tears (Ballads of the American Indian)	1964	5.00	10.00	20.00
CS 9109 [S]	Orange Blossom Special	1965	5.00	10.00	20.00
CS 9246 [S]	Mean as Hell	1965	5.00	10.00	20.00
CS 9292 [S]	Everybody Loves a Nut	1966	5.00	10.00	20.00
CS 9337 [S]	That's What You Get for Lovin' Me	1966	5.00	10.00	20.00
CS 9447 [S]	From Sea to Shining Sea	1967	5.00	10.00	20.00
CS 9478 [S]	Johnny Cash's Greatest Hits, Volume 1	1967	5.00	10.00	20.00
CS 9639	Johnny Cash at Folsom Prison	1968	5.00	10.00	20.00
KCS 9726	The Holy Land	1969	3.75	7.50	15.00
CS 9827	Johnny Cash at San Quentin	1969	3.00	6.00	12.00
KCS 9943	Hello, I'm Johnny Cash	1970	3.00	6.00	12.00
C 30100	The Johnny Cash Show	1970	3.00	6.00	12.00
S 30397	I Walk the Line	1970	3.00	6.00	12.00
—Soundtrack from movie					
KC 30550	Man in Black	1971	3.00	6.00	12.00
KC 30887	The Johnny Cash Collection (His Greatest Hits, Volume II)	1971	3.00	6.00	12.00
CQ 30961 [Q]	Johnny Cash at San Quentin	1971	5.00	10.00	20.00
KC 31256	Give My Love to Rose	1972	3.00	6.00	12.00
KC 31332	A Thing Called Love	1972	3.00	6.00	12.00
KC 31645	Johnny Cash: America (A 200-Year Salute in Story and Song)	1972	3.00	6.00	12.00
KC 32091	Any Old Wind That Blows	1973	3.00	6.00	12.00
C 32240	Sunday Morning Coming Down	1973	3.00	6.00	12.00
C 32253	The Gospel Road	1973	3.00	6.00	12.00
CG 32253 [(2)]	The Gospel Road	1973	6.25	12.50	25.00
KC 32898	Children's Album	1974	3.00	6.00	12.00
C 32917	The Ragged Old Flag	1974	3.00	6.00	12.00
C 32951	Five Feet High and Rising	1974	3.00	6.00	12.00
KC 33086	The Junkie and the Juicehead	1974	3.00	6.00	12.00
C 33087	Johnny Cash Sings Precious Memories	1974	3.00	6.00	12.00
KC 33370	John R. Cash	1975	3.00	6.00	12.00
CG 33639 [(2)]	Johnny Cash at Folsom Prison/Johnny Cash at San Quentin	1974	3.75	7.50	15.00
KC 33814	Look at Them Beans	1975	3.00	6.00	12.00
KC 34088	Strawberry Cake	1976	3.00	6.00	12.00
KC 34193	One Piece at a Time	1976	3.00	6.00	12.00
JC 34314	The Last Gunfighter Ballad	1977	3.00	6.00	12.00
JC 34833	The Rambler	1977	3.00	6.00	12.00
KC 35313	I Would Like to See You Again	1978	2.50	5.00	10.00
JC 35637	Johnny Cash's Greatest Hits, Volume 3	1978	3.00	6.00	12.00
JC 36086	Silver	1979	3.00	6.00	12.00
JC 36779	Rockabilly Blues	1980	2.50	5.00	10.00
JC 36866	Classic Christmas	1980	3.00	6.00	12.00
FC 37179	The Baron	1981	2.50	5.00	10.00
FC 37355	Encore	1981	2.50	5.00	10.00
PC 38074	A Believer Sings the Truth	1985	2.00	4.00	8.00
—Reissue of Priority 38074					
FC 38094	The Adventures of Johnny Cash	1982	2.50	5.00	10.00
FC 38317	Johnny Cash's Biggest Hits	1982	2.50	5.00	10.00
FC 38696	Johnny 99	1983	2.50	5.00	10.00
PC 38696	Johnny 99	1986	2.00	4.00	8.00
—Budget-line reissue					
FC 39951	Rainbow	1985	2.50	5.00	10.00

COLUMBIA SPECIAL PRODUCTS

Number	Title	Yr	VG	VG+	NM
363	Legends and Love Songs	196?	5.00	10.00	20.00
P 13832	Hello, I'm Johnny Cash	1977	3.00	6.00	12.00

DORAL/CSP

Number	Title	Yr	VG	VG+	NM
(# unknown)	Doral Presents Johnny Cash	1972	10.00	20.00	40.00

—Mail-order offer from Doral cigarettes

EVEREST

Number	Title	Yr	VG	VG+	NM
276	Johnny Cash	19??	3.00	6.00	12.00

HARMONY

Number	Title	Yr	VG	VG+	NM
HS 11249	Golden Sounds of Country Music	1968	3.00	6.00	12.00
HS 11342	Johnny Cash	1969	3.00	6.00	12.00
KH 30916	Understand Your Man	1971	3.00	6.00	12.00
KH 31602	The Johnny Cash Songbook	1972	3.00	6.00	12.00
KH 32388	Ballads of the American Indian	1973	3.00	6.00	12.00

MERCURY

Number	Title	Yr	VG	VG+	NM
832031-1	Johnny Cash Is Coming to Town	1987	2.50	5.00	10.00
834778-1	Water from the Wells of Home	1988	2.50	5.00	10.00

PAIR

Number	Title	Yr	VG	VG+	NM
PDL2-1107 [(2)]	Classic Cash	1986	3.75	7.50	15.00

POWER PAK

Number	Title	Yr	VG	VG+	NM
246	Country Gold	198?	2.50	5.00	10.00

PRIORITY

Number	Title	Yr	VG	VG+	NM
UG 32253 [(2)]	The Gospel Road	1981	3.75	7.50	15.00
—Reissue of Columbia album of the same name					
PU 33087	Johnny Cash Sings Precious Memories	1982	3.00	6.00	12.00
—Reissue of Columbia album of the same name					

Number	Title (A Side/B Side)	Yr	VG	VG+	NM
PU 38074	A Believer Sings the Truth	1982	3.00	6.00	12.00
—Reissue of Cachet album					
RHINO					
RNLP 70229	The Vintage Years	1987	3.00	6.00	12.00
SHARE					
5000	I Walk the Line	197?	3.00	6.00	12.00
5001	Folsom Prison Blues	197?	3.00	6.00	12.00
5002	The Blue Train	197?	3.00	6.00	12.00
5003	Johnny Cash Sings the Greatest Hits	197?	3.00	6.00	12.00
SUN					
LP-100	Original Golden Hits, Volume I	1969	3.00	6.00	12.00
LP-101	Original Golden Hits, Volume II	1969	3.00	6.00	12.00
LP-104	Story Songs of the Trains and Rivers	1969	3.00	6.00	12.00
LP-105	Get Rhythm	1969	3.00	6.00	12.00
LP-106	Showtime	1969	3.00	6.00	12.00
LP-115	The Singing Story Teller	1970	3.00	6.00	12.00
LP-118 [(2)]	Johnny Cash — The Legend	1970	5.00	10.00	20.00
LP-122	Rough Cut King of Country	1971	3.00	6.00	12.00
LP-126 [(2)]	Johnny Cash: The Man, The World, His Music	1971	5.00	10.00	20.00
LP-127	Original Golden Hits, Volume III	1972	3.00	6.00	12.00
LP-139	I Walk the Line	1979	2.50	5.00	10.00
LP-140	Folsom Prison Blues	1979	2.50	5.00	10.00
LP-141	The Blue Train	1979	2.50	5.00	10.00
LP-142	Johnny Cash Sings the Greatest Hits	1979	2.50	5.00	10.00
1002	Superbilly (1955-58)	198?	2.50	5.00	10.00
1006	The Original Johnny Cash	1980	2.50	5.00	10.00
SLP-1220 [M]	Johnny Cash with His Hot and Blue Guitar	1956	25.00	50.00	100.00
SLP-1235 [M]	The Songs That Made Him Famous	1958	25.00	50.00	100.00
SLP-1240 [M]	Johnny Cash's Greatest!	1959	12.50	25.00	50.00
SLP-1245 [M]	Johnny Cash Sings Hank Williams	1960	12.50	25.00	50.00
SLP-1255 [M]	Now Here's Johnny Cash	1961	12.50	25.00	50.00
SLP-1270 [M]	All Aboard the Blue Train	1963	12.50	25.00	50.00
SLP-1275 [M]	The Original Sun Sound of Johnny Cash	1965	12.50	25.00	50.00
WORD					
WR 8333	Believe in Him	1986	3.00	6.00	12.00

CASH, JOHNNY, AND JUNE CARTER

45s

Number	Title (A Side/B Side)	Yr	VG	VG+	NM
COLUMBIA					
10436	Old Time Feeling/Far Side Banks of Jordan	1976	—	2.50	5.00
44011	Jackson/Pack Up Your Sorrows	1967	—	3.00	6.00
44158	Long-Legged Guitar Pickin' Man/You'll Be All Right	1967	—	3.00	6.00
45064	If I Were a Carpenter/'Cause I Love You	1970	—	2.50	5.00
45431	No Need to Worry/I'll Be Loving You	1971	—	2.50	5.00
45631	If I Had a Hammer/I Gotta Go	1972	—	2.50	5.00
45758	The Loving Gift/Help Me Make It Through the Night	1973	—	2.50	5.00
45890	Praise the Lord and Pass the Soup/The Ballad of Barbara	1973	—	2.50	5.00
45929	Allegheny/We're for Love	1973	—	2.50	5.00

Albums

Number	Title (A Side/B Side)	Yr	VG	VG+	NM
COLUMBIA					
CL 2728 [M]	Carryin' On with Johnny Cash and June Carter	1967	5.00	10.00	20.00
CS 9528 [S]	Carryin' On with Johnny Cash and June Carter	1967	5.00	10.00	20.00

CASHMAN, TERRY

Also see BUCHANAN BROTHERS; CASHMAN AND WEST; CASHMAN, PISTILLI AND WEST.

45s

Number	Title (A Side/B Side)	Yr	VG	VG+	NM
BOOM					
60005	Try Me/Pretty Face	1966	3.75	7.50	15.00
LIFESONG					
45015	Baby, Baby I Love You/We'll Be Together	1976	—	2.00	4.00
45021	Football U.S.A./The Dreamer	1977	—	2.00	4.00
45086	Willie, Mickey and "The Duke" (Talkin' Baseball)/It's So Easy to Sing a Love Song	1980	—	2.50	5.00
45096	Talkin' Baseball (Philadelphia Phillies Version)/Baby, Baby I Love You	1982	—	2.00	4.00
45096 [PS]	Talkin' Baseball (Philadelphia Phillies Version)/Baby, Baby I Love You	1982	—	2.00	4.00
—Green "Talkin' Baseball" sleeve with custom sticker					
45097	Talkin' Baseball (New York Yankees Version)/Baby, Baby I Love You	1982	—	2.00	4.00
45097 [PS]	Talkin' Baseball (New York Yankees Version)/Baby, Baby I Love You	1982	—	2.00	4.00
—Green "Talkin' Baseball" sleeve with custom sticker					
45098	Talkin' Baseball (Los Angeles Dodgers Version)/Baby, Baby I Love You	1982	—	2.00	4.00
45098 [PS]	Talkin' Baseball (Los Angeles Dodgers Version)/Baby, Baby I Love You	1982	—	2.00	4.00
—Green "Talkin' Baseball" sleeve with custom sticker					
45099	Talkin' Baseball (Cleveland Indians Version)/Baby, Baby I Love You	1982	—	2.00	4.00
45099 [PS]	Talkin' Baseball (Cleveland Indians Version)/Baby, Baby I Love You	1982	—	2.00	4.00
—Green "Talkin' Baseball" sleeve with custom sticker					
45100	Talkin' Baseball (Texas Rangers Version)/Baby, Baby I Love You	1982	—	2.00	4.00
45100 [PS]	Talkin' Baseball (Texas Rangers Version)/Baby, Baby I Love You	1982	—	2.00	4.00
—Green "Talkin' Baseball" sleeve with custom sticker					
45101	Talkin' Baseball (Cincinnati Reds Version)/Baby, Baby I Love You	1982	—	2.00	4.00
45101 [PS]	Talkin' Baseball (Cincinnati Reds Version)/Baby, Baby I Love You	1982	—	2.00	4.00
—Green "Talkin' Baseball" sleeve with custom sticker					
45102	Talkin' Baseball (San Francisco Giants Version)/Baby, Baby I Love You	1982	—	2.00	4.00
45102 [PS]	Talkin' Baseball (San Francisco Giants Version)/Baby, Baby I Love You	1982	—	2.00	4.00
—Green "Talkin' Baseball" sleeve with custom sticker					
45103	Talkin' Baseball (Detroit Tigers Version)/Baby, Baby I Love You	1982	—	2.00	4.00
45103 [PS]	Talkin' Baseball (Detroit Tigers Version)/Baby, Baby I Love You	1982	—	2.00	4.00
—Green "Talkin' Baseball" sleeve with custom sticker					
45104	Talkin' Baseball (Chicago Cubs Version)/Baby, Baby I Love You	1982	—	2.00	4.00
45104 [PS]	Talkin' Baseball (Chicago Cubs Version)/Baby, Baby I Love You	1982	—	2.00	4.00
—Green "Talkin' Baseball" sleeve with custom sticker					
45105	Talkin' Baseball (Baltimore Orioles Version)/Baby, Baby I Love You	1982	—	2.00	4.00
45105 [PS]	Talkin' Baseball (Baltimore Orioles Version)/Baby, Baby I Love You	1982	—	2.00	4.00
—Green "Talkin' Baseball" sleeve with custom sticker					
45105 [PS]	Talkin' Baseball (Baltimore Orioles Version)/Baby, Baby I Love You	1982	—	2.50	5.00
—Sleeve with photo of Cal Ripken Jr.					
45106	Talkin' Baseball (Boston Red Sox Version)/Baby, Baby I Love You	1982	—	2.00	4.00
45106 [PS]	Talkin' Baseball (Boston Red Sox Version)/Baby, Baby I Love You	1982	—	2.00	4.00
—Green "Talkin' Baseball" sleeve with custom sticker					
45107	Talkin' Baseball (St. Louis Cardinals Version)/Baby, Baby I Love You	1982	—	2.00	4.00
45107 [PS]	Talkin' Baseball (St. Louis Cardinals Version)/Baby, Baby I Love You	1982	—	2.00	4.00
—Green "Talkin' Baseball" sleeve with custom sticker					
45108	Talkin' Baseball (New York Mets Version)/Baby, Baby I Love You	1982	—	2.00	4.00
45108 [PS]	Talkin' Baseball (New York Mets Version)/Baby, Baby I Love You	1982	—	2.00	4.00
—Green "Talkin' Baseball" sleeve with custom sticker					
45109	Talkin' Baseball (Pittsburgh Pirates Version)/Baby, Baby I Love You	1982	—	2.00	4.00
45109 [PS]	Talkin' Baseball (Pittsburgh Pirates Version)/Baby, Baby I Love You	1982	—	2.00	4.00
—Green "Talkin' Baseball" sleeve with custom sticker					
45110	Talkin' Baseball (Atlanta Braves Version)/Baby, Baby I Love You	1982	—	2.00	4.00
45110 [PS]	Talkin' Baseball (Atlanta Braves Version)/Baby, Baby I Love You	1982	—	2.00	4.00
—Green "Talkin' Baseball" sleeve with custom sticker					
45111	Talkin' Baseball (Kansas City Royals Version)/Baby, Baby I Love You	1982	—	2.00	4.00
45111 [PS]	Talkin' Baseball (Kansas City Royals Version)/Baby, Baby I Love You	1982	—	2.00	4.00
—Green "Talkin' Baseball" sleeve with custom sticker					
45112	Talkin' Baseball (Houston Astros Version)/Baby, Baby I Love You	1982	—	2.00	4.00
45112 [PS]	Talkin' Baseball (Houston Astros Version)/Baby, Baby I Love You	1982	—	2.00	4.00
—Green "Talkin' Baseball" sleeve with custom sticker					
45113	Talkin' Baseball (Milwaukee Brewers Version)/Baby, Baby I Love You	1982	—	2.00	4.00
45113 [PS]	Talkin' Baseball (Milwaukee Brewers Version)/Baby, Baby I Love You	1982	—	2.00	4.00
—Green "Talkin' Baseball" sleeve with custom sticker					
45114	Talkin' Baseball (Minnesota Twins Version)/Baby, Baby I Love You	1982	—	2.00	4.00
45114 [PS]	Talkin' Baseball (Minnesota Twins Version)/Baby, Baby I Love You	1982	—	2.00	4.00
—Green "Talkin' Baseball" sleeve with custom sticker					
45115	Talkin' Baseball (Montreal Expos Version)/Baby, Baby I Love You	1982	—	2.00	4.00
45115 [PS]	Talkin' Baseball (Montreal Expos Version)/Baby, Baby I Love You	1982	—	2.00	4.00
—Green "Talkin' Baseball" sleeve with custom sticker					
45117	Cooperstown (The Town Where Baseball Lives)/Baseball Ballet	1983	—	2.00	4.00
45119	The Earl of Baltimore/Baseball Ballet	1983	—	2.00	4.00
45121 [DJ]	Football U.S.A. (same on both sides)	1983	—	2.00	4.00
—May be promo only					

Albums

Number	Title (A Side/B Side)	Yr	VG	VG+	NM
LIFESONG					
LS 6006	Terry Cashman	1976	3.00	6.00	12.00
PZ 34999	Terry Cashman	1977	2.50	5.00	10.00
—Reissue of 6006					

CASHMAN AND WEST

Also see TERY CASHMAN.

45s

Number	Title (A Side/B Side)	Yr	VG	VG+	NM
ABC DUNHILL					
4324	American City Suite/I Belong to You	1972	—	3.00	6.00
4324 [PS]	American City Suite/I Belong to You	1972	2.00	4.00	8.00
4333	Songman/If You Were a Rainbow	1972	—	2.50	5.00
4349	The King of Rock 'N Roll/Somebody Stole the Sun	1973	—	2.50	5.00
4380	Is It Raining in New York City/Will You Be My Baby	1973	—	2.50	5.00
15021	Lifesong/I Could Feel the Morning	1974	—	2.50	5.00
LIFESONG					
45000	American City Suite/A Friend Is Dying	1975	—	2.50	5.00

Albums

Number	Title (A Side/B Side)	Yr	VG	VG+	NM
ABC DUNHILL					
DSX-50126	A Song or Two	1972	3.00	6.00	12.00
DSX-50141	Moondog Serenade	1973	3.00	6.00	12.00
DSX-50179	Lifesong	1974	3.00	6.00	12.00

CASHMAN, PISTILLI AND WEST

Also see BUCHANAN BROTHERS; TERRY CASHMAN; CASHMAN AND WEST; GENE PISTILLI.

45s

Number	Title (A Side/B Side)	Yr	VG	VG+	NM
ABC					
11047	But for Love/Song That Never Comes	1968	2.00	4.00	8.00
11079	Spring Has a Tear in Her Eye/Little Girl	1968	2.00	4.00	8.00
11111	My Side of the Sky/You Can Write a Song	1968	2.00	4.00	8.00
CAPITOL					
2462	Some of My Best Friends Are People/Sausalito	1969	—	3.00	6.00

Number	Title (A Side/B Side)	Yr	VG	VG+	NM
2582	Proud Mary-Dock of the Bay/Sister John	1969	—	3.00	6.00
2671	Signs/Dolphins	1969	—	3.00	6.00
2747	She Never Looked Better/Goodbye Jo	1970	—	3.00	6.00
2863	Midnight Man/Automatic Pilot	1970	—	3.00	6.00
Albums					
ABC					
ABCS-629	Bound to Happen	1968	5.00	10.00	20.00
CAPITOL					
ST-211	Cashman, Pistilli, and West	1969	3.75	7.50	15.00

CASHMERES, THE
Possibly more than one group.

Number	Title (A Side/B Side)	Yr	VG	VG+	NM
45s					
HERALD					
474	Little Dream Girl/Do I Upset You	1956	20.00	40.00	80.00
JOSIE					
894	Life Line/Where Have You Been	1961	3.00	6.00	12.00
LAKE					
703	Everything's Gonna Be Alright/Four Lonely Nights	1960	7.50	15.00	30.00
705	Satisfied/Satisfied (Part 2)	1961	6.25	12.50	25.00
LAURIE					
3078	I Believe in St. Nick/A Very Special Birthday	1960	10.00	20.00	40.00
3088	I Gotta Go/Singing Waters	1961	6.25	12.50	25.00
3105	Poppa Said/Bobby Come On Home	1961	6.25	12.50	25.00
MERCURY					
70501	My Sentimental Heart/Yes, Yes, Yes	1954	20.00	40.00	80.00
70617	Don't Let It Happen Again/Boom Mag-Azeno-Vip Vay	1955	20.00	40.00	80.00
70679	There's a Rumor/Second Hand Heart	1955	20.00	40.00	80.00
RELIC					
1005	Satisfied/Satisfied (Part 2)	1970	—	3.00	6.00

CASINOS, THE (1)
Male vocal group from Cincinnati.

Number	Title (A Side/B Side)	Yr	VG	VG+	NM
45s					
BUCCANEER					
3000	Then You Can Tell Me Goodbye/I Still Love You	196?	2.00	4.00	8.00
—Reissue of Fraternity release					
FRATERNITY					
944	She's Out of Sight/The Gallop	1965	2.50	5.00	10.00
949	Right There Beside You/The Gallop	1965	2.50	5.00	10.00
977	Then You Can Tell Me Goodbye/I Still Love You	1967	3.00	6.00	12.00
985	It's All Over Now/Tailor Made	1967	2.50	5.00	10.00
987	Forever and a Night/How Long Has It Been	1967	2.50	5.00	10.00
995	When I Stop Dreaming/Please Love	1967	2.50	5.00	10.00
997	Bye Bye Love/Walk Through This World with Me	1967	2.50	5.00	10.00
1020	These Are the Things We'll Share/Casinos Having Fun	1969	2.50	5.00	10.00
1028	I Wish I Were Anyone But Me/I Just Want to Stay Here	1969	2.50	5.00	10.00
1200	Father John/The Old Saloon	1970	2.50	5.00	10.00
1201	Wisdom of Love/My House	1970	2.50	5.00	10.00
1250	Loving Her Was Easier/A Restless Wind	1971	2.50	5.00	10.00
MILLION					
13	I'm Walking Behind You/Angels Were All Asleep	1972	2.50	5.00	10.00
—As "Gene Hughes and the Casinos"					
UNITED ARTISTS					
50255	Here I Am/Peggy	1968	2.50	5.00	10.00
—As "Gene Hughes and the Casinos"					
50313	Nobody's Child/Leaving Makes the Rain Come Down	1968	2.50	5.00	10.00
—As "Gene Hughes and the Casinos"					
Albums					
FRATERNITY					
LP-1019 [M]	Then You Can Tell Me Goodbye	1967	10.00	20.00	40.00
LPS-1019 [S]	Then You Can Tell Me Goodbye	1967	15.00	30.00	60.00

CASINOS, THE (U)
Some of these no doubt are group (1), but not all of them are, and we're not sure which is which.

Number	Title (A Side/B Side)	Yr	VG	VG+	NM
45s					
AIRTOWN					
002	That's the Way/Too Good to Be True	1967	3.75	7.50	15.00
ALTO					
2002	I Like It Like That/Baby Don't Do It	1961	7.50	15.00	30.00
CASINO					
111	My Love for You/Why Am I a Fool	1960	10.00	20.00	40.00
CERTRON					
10015	Coal River/(B-side unknown)	1970	—	3.00	6.00
ITZY					
2	Do You Recall?/The Swim	1964	12.50	25.00	50.00
NAME					
7739	Do You Recall?/The Swim	1962	62.50	125.00	250.00
OLIMPIC					
251	Do You Recall?/The Swim	1963	37.50	75.00	150.00
SIMS					
306	Moon River/Soul Serenade	1966	3.00	6.00	12.00
TERRY					
115	Gee Whiz/Lovely One	1964	15.00	30.00	60.00
116	That's the Way/Too Good to Be True	1964	12.50	25.00	50.00

CASSIDY, DAVID
Also see THE PARTRIDGE FAMILY.

Number	Title (A Side/B Side)	Yr	VG	VG+	NM
45s					
BELL					
45150	Cherish/All I Want to Do Is Touch You	1971	—	2.50	5.00
45150 [PS]	Cherish/All I Want to Do Is Touch You	1971	—	3.00	6.00
45187	Could It Be Forever/Blind Hope	1972	—	2.00	4.00
45187 [PS]	Could It Be Forever/Blind Hope	1972	—	3.00	6.00
45220	How Can I Be Sure/Ricky's Tune	1972	—	2.00	4.00
45260	Rock Me Baby/Two Time Loser	1972	—	2.00	4.00
45386	Daydream/Can't Go Home Again	1973	—	2.00	4.00
45413	Daydreamer/The Puppy Song	1973	—	2.00	4.00
45605	Breaking Up Is Hard to Do/Please Please Me	1974	—	2.00	4.00
MCA					
41101	Hurt So Bad/Once a Fool	1979	—	2.00	4.00
RCA					
PB-10788	I'll Have to Go Away (Saying Goodbye)/Gettin' It in the Streets	1976	2.00	4.00	8.00
PB-10921	Saying Goodbye Ain't Easy (We'll Have to Go Away)/Rosa's Cantina	1977	2.00	4.00	8.00
RCA VICTOR					
PB-10321	Get It Up for Love/Love In Bloom	1975	2.50	5.00	10.00
PB-10405	This Could Be the Night/Darlin'	1975	2.50	5.00	10.00
PB-10585	Tomorrow/Bedtime	1976	2.50	5.00	10.00
PB-10647	Breakin' Down Again/On Fire	1976	2.50	5.00	10.00
Albums					
BELL					
1109	Rock Me Baby	1972	5.00	10.00	20.00
1132	Dreams Are Nothing More Than Wishes	1973	5.00	10.00	20.00
1312	Cassidy Live	1974	6.25	12.50	25.00
1321	David Cassidy's Greatest Hits	1974	3.75	7.50	15.00
6070	Cherish	1972	5.00	10.00	20.00
RCA VICTOR					
APL1-1066	The Higher They Climb...	1975	3.75	7.50	15.00
—Black vinyl					
APL1-1066	The Higher They Climb...	1975	25.00	50.00	100.00
—Blue vinyl					
APL1-1309	Home Is Where the Heart Is	1976	3.75	7.50	15.00
APL1-1852	Gettin' It in the Street	1976	10.00	20.00	40.00

CASTALEERS, THE

Number	Title (A Side/B Side)	Yr	VG	VG+	NM
45s					
DONNA					
1349	That's Why I Cry/My Baby's All Right	1961	6.25	12.50	25.00
FELSTED					
8504	Come Back/Hi-Fi Baby	1958	12.50	25.00	50.00
8512	Lonely Boy/My Bull Fightin' Baby	1958	10.00	20.00	40.00
8585	You're My Dream/I'll Be Around	1959	15.00	30.00	60.00
PLANET					
44	That's Why I Cry/My Baby's All Right	1961	10.00	20.00	40.00

CASTANETS, THE

Number	Title (A Side/B Side)	Yr	VG	VG+	NM
45s					
TCF					
1	I Love Him/Funky Wunky Piano	1963	2.50	5.00	10.00

CASTAWAYS, THE (1)
Garage rock band from Minnesota.

Number	Title (A Side/B Side)	Yr	VG	VG+	NM
45s					
BEAR					
2000	I Feel So Fine/Hit the Road Jack	1967	10.00	20.00	40.00
ERA BACK TO BACK HITS					
016	Liar, Liar/Surfin' Bird	197?	—	2.50	5.00
—B-side by the Trashmen					
ERIC					
247	Liar, Liar/Surfin' Bird	197?	—	2.50	5.00
—B-side by the Trashmen; reissue					
FONTANA					
1615	Walking in Different Circles/Just On High	1968	3.75	7.50	15.00
1626	Lavender Popcorn/What Kind of Face	1968	3.75	7.50	15.00
LANA					
151	Liar, Liar/Sam	196?	2.00	4.00	8.00
—Reissue					
SOMA					
1433	Liar, Liar/Sam	1965	3.75	7.50	15.00
1442	Goodbye Babe/A Man's Gotta Be a Man	1965	3.00	6.00	12.00
1461	Girl in Love/Should Happen to Me	1966	3.00	6.00	12.00
1469	Liar, Liar/Surfin' Bird	1966	3.00	6.00	12.00
—B-side by the Trashmen					
TAUNAH					
7745	(I) Feel So Fine/Hit the Road Jack	1967	3.00	6.00	12.00

CASTAWAYS, THE (2)
Not sure who they are, but they are not (1), (3) or (4).

Number	Title (A Side/B Side)	Yr	VG	VG+	NM
45s					
CAPITOL					
4340	The Twitch/Vibrations	1960	3.00	6.00	12.00

CASTAWAYS, THE (3)
Not sure who they are, but they are not (1), (2) or (4).

Number	Title (A Side/B Side)	Yr	VG	VG+	NM
45s					
EXCELLO					
2038	I Wish/Teasin'	1954	10.00	20.00	40.00

CASTAWAYS, THE (4)
Different group, probably from California.

Number	Title (A Side/B Side)	Yr	VG	VG+	NM
45s					
GNP CRESCENDO					
302	Tarzan/Wild Boy	1963	2.50	5.00	10.00
310	Moritat/Pass It Around	1964	2.50	5.00	10.00

CASTAWAYS, THE (U)
May go with (4) above, or possibly not.

Number	Title (A Side/B Side)	Yr	VG	VG+	NM
45s					
WITCH					
124	Don't You Just Know It/I Go Ape	1964	7.50	15.00	30.00

CASTELLES, THE

Number	Title (A Side/B Side)	Yr	VG	VG+	NM
45s					
ATCO					
6069	Happy and Gay/Hey Baby Baby	1956	25.00	50.00	100.00

Number	Title (A Side/B Side)	Yr	VG	VG+	NM
CLASSIC ARTISTS					
114	At Christmas Time/One Little Teardrop	1989	—	2.00	4.00
GRAND					
101	My Girl Awaits Me/Sweetness	1954	500.00	1000.	2000.
—Blue label original					
103	This Silver Ring/Wonder Why	1954	500.00	1000.	2000.
—Glossy yellow label original					
105	Do You Remember/If You Were the Only Girl	1954	375.00	750.00	1500.
—Glossy yellow label original					
109	Baby Can't You See/Over a Cup of Coffee	1954	500.00	1000.	2000.
—Blue label original					
114	Marcella/I'm a Fool to Care	1955	400.00	800.00	1200.
—Cream label original					
122	My Wedding Day/Heavenly Father	1955	1750.	3500.	7000.
—Cream label original					
Albums					
COLLECTABLES					
COL-5002	The Sweet Sounds of the Castelles	198?	3.00	6.00	12.00

CASTELLS, THE

Number	Title (A Side/B Side)	Yr	VG	VG+	NM
45s					
BLACK GOLD					
306	Save a Chance/Children Who Dream	196?	2.00	4.00	8.00
DECCA					
31834	Just Walk Away/An Angel Cried	1965	3.75	7.50	15.00
31967	Life Goes On/I Thought You'd Like That	1966	3.75	7.50	15.00
ERA					
3038	Little Sad Eyes/Romeo	1961	6.25	12.50	25.00
3048	Sacred/I Get Dreamy	1961	6.25	12.50	25.00
3057	My Miracle/Make Believe Wedding	1961	5.00	10.00	20.00
3064	The Vision of You/Stiki De Boom Boom	1961	5.00	10.00	20.00
3073	So This Is Love/On the Streets of Tears	1962	5.00	10.00	20.00
3083	Oh, What It Seemed to Be/Stand There, Mountain	1962	5.00	10.00	20.00
3089	Echoes in the Night/The Only One	1962	5.00	10.00	20.00
3098	Clown Prince/Eternal Spring, Eternal Love	1962	5.00	10.00	20.00
3102	Little Sad Eyes/Initials	1963	5.00	10.00	20.00
3107	Some Enchanted Evening/What Do Little Girls Dream Of	1963	5.00	10.00	20.00
LAURIE					
3444	I'd Like to Know/Rocky Ridges	1968	2.50	5.00	10.00
UNITED ARTISTS					
50324	Two Lovers/Jerusalem	1968	2.50	5.00	10.00
WARNER BROS.					
5421	I Do/Teardrops	1964	20.00	40.00	80.00
—A-side written and produced by Brian Wilson					
5445	Could This Be Magic/Shinny Up Your Own Side	1964	7.50	15.00	30.00
5486	Love Finds a Way/Tell Her If I Could	1964	5.00	10.00	20.00
Albums					
ERA					
EL-109 [M]	So This Is Love	1962	30.00	60.00	120.00
ES-109 [S]	So This Is Love	1962	100.00	200.00	400.00

CASTLE, JOEY

Number	Title (A Side/B Side)	Yr	VG	VG+	NM
45s					
HEADLINE					
1008	Rock and Roll Daddy-O/Wild Love	1959	100.00	200.00	400.00
RCA VICTOR					
47-7283	That Ain't Nothin' But Right/Come A Little Closer Baby	1958	15.00	30.00	60.00

CASTLE, TONY

Number	Title (A Side/B Side)	Yr	VG	VG+	NM
45s					
EASTWEST					
107	Terry/Young and In Love	1958	7.50	15.00	30.00
GONE					
5099	Salty/Salty, Part 2	1961	5.00	10.00	20.00
5099	Salty/Hi Lili, Hi Lo	1961	6.25	12.50	25.00
5105	Sincerely/Tara's Themes	1961	5.00	10.00	20.00
5107	Seems Like Old Times/The Loneliest Girl in the World	1961	5.00	10.00	20.00
TREY					
3002	Kiss Me Goodnight/The Fool	1960	6.25	12.50	25.00

CASTLE KINGS, THE

Number	Title (A Side/B Side)	Yr	VG	VG+	NM
45s					
ATLANTIC					
2107	You Can Get Him Frankenstein/Loch Lomond	1961	7.50	15.00	30.00
—Produced by Phil Spector					
2158	Jeanette/The Caissons Go Rolling Along	1962	3.75	7.50	15.00

CASTON, BOBBY

Number	Title (A Side/B Side)	Yr	VG	VG+	NM
45s					
ATLAS					
1103	Call Me Darling/Why Wasn't I Told	1958	25.00	50.00	100.00

CASTOR, JIMMY, BUNCH

Also see THE CLINTONIAN CUBS.

Number	Title (A Side/B Side)	Yr	VG	VG+	NM
45s					
ATLANTIC					
3011	Maggie (Part 1)/Maggie (Part 2)	1974	—	2.50	5.00
3045	Everything Man (E-Man)/Heaven Kissed	1974	—	2.50	5.00
3232	The Bertha Butt Boogie (Part 1)/The Bertha Butt Boogie (Part 2)	1975	—	2.50	5.00
3270	Potential/Daniel	1975	—	2.50	5.00
3295	King Kong (Part 1)/King Kong (Part 2)	1975	—	2.50	5.00
3302	The Christmas Song (Chestnuts Roasting on an Open Fire)/Merry Christmas	1975	—	3.50	7.00
3316	Supersound/Drifting	1976	—	2.00	4.00
3331	Bom Bom/What's Best	1976	—	2.00	4.00
3362	Everything Is Beautiful to Me/The Magic Is in the Music	1976	—	2.00	4.00
3369 [DJ]	I Don't Wanna Lose You (mono/stereo)	1976	—	2.50	5.00
—May be promo-only					
3375	Space Age/Dracula	1976	—	2.00	4.00
3396	I Love a Mellow Groove/I Don't Want to Lose You	1977	—	2.00	4.00
3424	The Return of Leroy (Part 1)/The Return of Leroy (Part 2)	1977	—	2.00	4.00
3451	Magnolia/TR-7	1978	—	2.00	4.00
3455	Maximum Stimulation/It Was You	1978	—	2.00	4.00
ATOMIC					
100	Somebody Mentioned Your Name/This Girl of Mine	1957	125.00	250.00	500.00
CAPITOL					
2358	Hey Shorty (Part 1)/Hey Shorty (Part 2)	1968	2.00	4.00	8.00
2487	Psycho Man/The Real McCoy	1969	2.00	4.00	8.00
2634	Helpless/Make Me	1969	2.00	4.00	8.00
CATAWBA					
05676	Godzilla/(Instrumental)	1985	—	—	3.00
COMPASS					
7019	Soul Sister/Rattlesnake	1968	2.00	4.00	8.00
COTILLION					
44253	Don't Do That!/Don't Do That! (Part 2)	1979	—	2.00	4.00
45004	Party People/I Just Wanna Stop	1979	—	2.00	4.00
DECCA					
31963	In a Boogaloo Bag (Part 1)/In a Boogaloo Bag (Part 2)	1966	2.50	5.00	10.00
DRIVE					
6271	Bertha Butt Encounters Vadar/(B-side unknown)	1978	—	2.00	4.00
6276	You Light Up My Life/Let It Out	1978	—	2.00	4.00
HULL					
758	Poor Loser/Oh Suzzana	1963	5.00	10.00	20.00
LONG DISTANCE					
702	Can't Help Falling in Love/Stay with Me (Spend the Night)	1980	—	2.50	5.00
RCA VICTOR					
APBO-0047	How Beautiful You Are/I'm Not a Child Anymore	1973	—	2.50	5.00
AMBO-0120	Troglodyte (Cave Man)/Luther the Anthropod	1973	—	2.00	4.00
—Gold Standard Series					
48-1024	Say Leroy (The Creature from the Black Lagoon Is Your Father) (Parts 1 & 2)	1972	—	2.50	5.00
48-1029	Troglodyte (Cave Man)/I Promise to Remember	1972	—	3.00	6.00
74-0583	My Brightest Day/You Better Be Good	1971	—	2.50	5.00
74-0763	Luther the Anthropod/Party Life	1972	—	2.50	5.00
74-0836	Paradise/The First Time Ever I Saw Your Face	1972	—	2.50	5.00
74-0953	Soul Serenade/Purple Haze-Foxey Lady (Tribute to Jimi Hendrix)	1973	—	2.50	5.00
SALSOUL					
7018	E-Man Boogie '82/Any Way, Any Where, Any Time	1982	—	2.00	4.00
7058	E-Man Boogie '83/It's Just Begun	1983	—	2.00	4.00
SMASH					
2069	Hey, Leroy, Your Mama's Calling You/Ham Hocks Espanol	1966	2.00	4.00	8.00
2085	Just You Girl/Magic Saxophone	1967	2.00	4.00	8.00
2099	Leroy Is In the Army/Dry	1967	2.00	4.00	8.00
2120	Jamaica Farewell/Mini-Sonata	1967	2.00	4.00	8.00
WING					
90078	I Promise/I Know the Meaning of Love	1956	30.00	60.00	120.00
Albums					
ATLANTIC					
SD 7305	The Everything Man	1974	2.50	5.00	10.00
SD 18124	Butt Of Course	1975	2.50	5.00	10.00
SD 18150	Supersound	1975	2.50	5.00	10.00
SD 18186	E-Man Groovin'	1976	2.50	5.00	10.00
SD 19111	Maximum Stimulation	1977	2.50	5.00	10.00
COTILLION					
SD 5215	The Jimmy Castor Bunch	1979	3.00	6.00	12.00
DRIVE					
407	Let It Out	1978	3.00	6.00	12.00
LONG DISTANCE					
1201	C	1980	3.00	6.00	12.00
RCA VICTOR					
APD1-0103 [Q]	Dimension III	1973	5.00	10.00	20.00
APL1-0103	Dimension III	1973	3.75	7.50	15.00
APL1-0313	The Everything Man	1974	3.75	7.50	15.00
LSP-4640	It's Just Begun	1972	3.75	7.50	15.00
LSP-4783	Phase Two	1972	3.75	7.50	15.00
SMASH					
MGS-27091 [M]	Hey Leroy!	1967	10.00	20.00	40.00
SRS-67091 [S]	Hey Leroy!	1967	10.00	20.00	40.00

CASTROES, THE

Number	Title (A Side/B Side)	Yr	VG	VG+	NM
45s					
GRAND					
2002	Dearest Darling/Dance with Me	1959	37.50	75.00	150.00

CASUALAIRS, THE

Number	Title (A Side/B Side)	Yr	VG	VG+	NM
45s					
AUTUMN					
21	Just For You/This Is a Mean World	1965	6.25	12.50	25.00
CRAIG					
5001	Bossa Nova Twist/Cruising	1962	10.00	20.00	40.00
MONA-LEE					
136	At the Dance/Satsfied	1959	10.00	20.00	40.00

CASUALS, THE (1)

See THE ORIGINAL CASUALS.

CASUALS, THE (2)

Number	Title (A Side/B Side)	Yr	VG	VG+	NM
45s					
DOT					
15557	Somebody Help Me/My Love Song for You	1957	6.25	12.50	25.00

Number	Title (A Side/B Side)	Yr	VG	VG+	NM
15671	Hello Love/Till You Come Back to Me	1957	6.25	12.50	25.00

CASUALS, THE (3)
British group.

Number	Title (A Side/B Side)	Yr	VG	VG+	NM
45s					
MAINSTREAM					
692	I've Got Something Too/Jesamine (A Butterfly Child)	1968	2.50	5.00	10.00
697	Touched/Toy	1968	2.50	5.00	10.00
—As "The British Casuals"					

CASUALS, THE (4)

Number	Title (A Side/B Side)	Yr	VG	VG+	NM
45s					
MINARET					
109	Money/Big Hammer	1963	3.75	7.50	15.00
MONUMENT					
905	Promise Her Anything (But Give Her Love)/Walk	1965	3.00	6.00	12.00
937	Walk Away/If You Don't	1966	3.00	6.00	12.00
SOUND STAGE 7					
2534	Mustang 2 + 2/Play Me a Sad Song	1964	3.75	7.50	15.00

CAT MOTHER AND THE ALL NIGHT NEWS BOYS

Number	Title (A Side/B Side)	Yr	VG	VG+	NM
45s					
POLYDOR					
14002	Good Old Rock 'N Roll/Bad News	1969	2.00	4.00	8.00
14007	Can You Dance to It/Marie	1969	—	3.00	6.00
—Both of the above were produced by Jimi Hendrix					
14029	Last Go-Round/I Must Be Dreaming	1970	—	3.00	6.00
14126	Letter to the President/Ode to Oregon	1972	—	3.00	6.00
14138	She Came from a Different World/Three and Me	1972	—	3.00	6.00
Albums					
POLYDOR					
24-4001	The Street Giveth...And the Street Taketh Away	1969	6.25	12.50	25.00
—Produced by Jimi Hendrix					
24-4023	Albion Doo-Wah	1970	3.75	7.50	15.00
PD-5017	Cat Mother	1971	3.75	7.50	15.00
PD-5042	Last Chance Dance	1972	3.75	7.50	15.00

CATALINAS, THE (1)
Studio band of Los Angeles session pros.

Number	Title (A Side/B Side)	Yr	VG	VG+	NM
45s					
RIC					
113	Banzai Wipeout/Beach Walkin'	1964	6.25	12.50	25.00
164	Boss Barracuda/Surfer Boy	1965	6.25	12.50	25.00
SIMS					
134	Bail Out/Bulletin	1963	3.75	7.50	15.00
Albums					
RIC					
M-1006 [M]	Fun, Fun, Fun	1964	25.00	50.00	100.00
S-1006 [S]	Fun, Fun, Fun	1964	37.50	75.00	150.00

CATALINAS, THE (2)
Five-man vocal group.

Number	Title (A Side/B Side)	Yr	VG	VG+	NM
45s					
LITTLE					
811/2	Give Me Your Love/Castle of Love	1957	50.00	100.00	200.00

CATALINAS, THE (U)

Number	Title (A Side/B Side)	Yr	VG	VG+	NM
45s					
20TH FOX					
286	Sweetheart/Unchained Melody	1962	7.50	15.00	30.00
299	Safari/Pretty Little Nashville Girl	1962	7.50	15.00	30.00
BACK BEAT					
513	Speechless/Flying Formation with You	1958	7.50	15.00	30.00
DEE JAY					
1010	Bail Out/Bulletin	1963	10.00	20.00	40.00
DIAL					
3008	Cha Cha Joe/Echo One	1963	3.00	6.00	12.00
GLORY					
285	Marlene/With Your Girl — Yeah!	1958	5.00	10.00	20.00
ORIGINAL SOUND					
48	Your Tender Lips/Gonna Tell	1964	3.00	6.00	12.00
RITA					
1006	Ring of Stars/Wooly Wooly Willie	1960	5.00	10.00	20.00
SCEPTER					
12188	Tick Tock/You Haven't the Right	1967	3.75	7.50	15.00

CATANOOGA CATS, THE

Number	Title (A Side/B Side)	Yr	VG	VG+	NM
Albums					
FORWARD					
ST-F-1018	The Catanooga Cats	1969	10.00	20.00	40.00

CATHY JEAN AND THE ROOMATES
Also see THE ROOMATES.

Number	Title (A Side/B Side)	Yr	VG	VG+	NM
45s					
PHILIPS					
40106	My Hert Belongs to Only You/I Only Want You	1963	5.00	10.00	20.00
—As "Cathy Jean"					
40143	Double Trouble/Believe Me	1963	5.00	10.00	20.00
—As "Cathy Jean"					
VALMOR					
007	Please Love Me Forever/Canadian Sunset	1961	6.25	12.50	25.00
—Sleeve is promo only					
007	Please Love Me Forever/Canadian Sunset	1961	3.75	7.50	15.00
—Black label					
007 [PS]	Please Love Me Forever/Canadian Sunset	1961	17.50	35.00	70.00
—Sleeve is promo only					
009	Make Me Smile Again/Sugar Cake	1961	6.25	12.50	25.00
011	I Only Want You/One Love	1961	5.00	10.00	20.00
016	Please Tell Me/Sugar Cake	1962	5.00	10.00	20.00
Albums					
VALMOR					
78 [M]	Great Oldies	1962	200.00	400.00	800.00
—Reissue of 789 with titles on cover and no group shot					
789 [M]	At the Hop!	1961	225.00	450.00	900.00

CAVALIERE, FELIX
Also see FELIX AND THE ESCORTS; THE RASCALS.

Number	Title (A Side/B Side)	Yr	VG	VG+	NM
45s					
BEARSVILLE					
0300	High Price to Pay/Mountain Men	1974	—	2.50	5.00
0302	Everlasting Love/Future Train	1975	—	2.50	5.00
0305	Never Felt Love Before/Love Came	1975	—	2.50	5.00
EPIC					
50785	Castles in the Air/Outside Your Window	1979	—	2.00	4.00
50829	Only a Lonely Heart Sees/You Turned Me Around	1980	—	2.00	4.00
50880	Dancin' the Night Away/Good to Have Love Back	1980	—	2.00	4.00
Albums					
BEARSVILLE					
BR 6955	Felix Cavaliere	1974	3.00	6.00	12.00
BR 6958	Destiny	1975	3.00	6.00	12.00
EPIC					
JE 35990	Castles in the Air	1979	2.50	5.00	10.00

CAVALIERS, THE
Probably several different groups.

Number	Title (A Side/B Side)	Yr	VG	VG+	NM
45s					
APT					
25004	Dance, Dance, Dance/Play By the Rules of Love	1958	10.00	20.00	40.00
CORAL					
62245	Teen Fever/Funky	1961	3.00	6.00	12.00
DECCA					
29556	Somewhere, Sometime, Someday/Honor Bright	1955	3.75	7.50	15.00
GALENA					
1277	Blowin' Smoke/Ten More Miles	1962	5.00	10.00	20.00
MUSIC WORLD					
101	The Magic Age of Sixteen/So Young, So Warm, So Beautiful	1963	7.50	15.00	30.00
NRC					
028	Dreamy Bikini/Charm Bracelet	1959	3.75	7.50	15.00
RCA VICTOR					
47-9054	Dance Little Girl/Hold On to My Baby	1966	7.50	15.00	30.00
47-9321	I Really Love You/I've Gotta Find Her	1967	5.00	10.00	20.00

CAVE DWELLERS, THE

Number	Title (A Side/B Side)	Yr	VG	VG+	NM
45s					
ABC-PARAMOUNT					
10735	Sinking Feeling/Sling My Rock	1965	5.00	10.00	20.00

CELEBRATION FEATURING MIKE LOVE
Also see THE BEACH BOYS.

Number	Title (A Side/B Side)	Yr	VG	VG+	NM
45s					
MCA					
S45-1986 [DJ]	Almost Summer/Almost Summer (KRTH Version)	1978	2.50	5.00	10.00
—Special promo for Los Angeles radio station					
40891	Almost Summer/Lookin' Good	1978	—	2.50	5.00
40930	Summer in the City/Island Girl	1978	—	2.00	4.00
PACIFIC ARTS					
105	Gettin' Hungry/Star Baby	1979	2.50	5.00	10.00
Albums					
PACIFIC ARTS					
122	Celebration	1979	3.75	7.50	15.00

CELEBRITYS, THE

Number	Title (A Side/B Side)	Yr	VG	VG+	NM
45s					
CAROLINE					
2301	Juanita/(B-side unknown)	1956	150.00	300.00	600.00
2302	Absent Minded/We Made Romance	1956	150.00	300.00	600.00

CELLOS, THE

Number	Title (A Side/B Side)	Yr	VG	VG+	NM
45s					
APOLLO					
510	Rang Tang Ding Dong/You Took My Love	1957	20.00	40.00	80.00
510	Rang Tang Ding Dong (I Am the Japanese Sandman)/You Took My Love	1957	6.25	12.50	25.00
515	Under Your Spell/The Juicy Crocodile	1957	12.50	25.00	50.00
516	The Be-Bop Mouse/Girlie That I Love	1957	12.50	25.00	50.00
524	I Beg for Your Love/What's the Matter with You	1958	15.00	30.00	60.00

CELTICS, THE

Number	Title (A Side/B Side)	Yr	VG	VG+	NM
45s					
AL-JACK'S					
0002	Can You Remember/Send Me Someone to Love	1958	2500.	3750.	5000.
WAR CONN					
2216	Darline, Darling/Only the Lonely	1962	100.00	200.00	400.00

CENTIPEDE

Number	Title (A Side/B Side)	Yr	VG	VG+	NM
Albums					
RCA VICTOR					
CPL2-5042 [(2)]	Septober Energy	1974	12.50	25.00	50.00

CENTRAL NERVOUS SYSTEM

Number	Title (A Side/B Side)	Yr	VG	VG+	NM
45s					
LAURIE					
3421	It Takes All Kinds/I'm Still Hung Up on You	1968	2.50	5.00	10.00
3446	Alice in Wonderland/Something Happened to Me	1968	2.50	5.00	10.00

Number	Title (A Side/B Side)	Yr	VG	VG+	NM
Albums					
MUSIC FACTORY					
MF-12003 [M]	I Could Have Danced All Night	1968	7.50	15.00	30.00
—White label promo only (no stock copies were issued in mono)					
MFS-12003 [S]	I Could Have Danced All Night	1968	5.00	10.00	20.00

CENTURIONS, THE

Number	Title (A Side/B Side)	Yr	VG	VG+	NM
Albums					
DEL-FI					
DFLP-1228 [M]	Surfer's Pajama Party	1963	25.00	50.00	100.00
DFST-1228 [S]	Surfer's Pajama Party	1963	50.00	100.00	200.00
—Above has the same title and number, and almost the same cover, as the album of the same name by Bruce Johnston, but the contents are different					

CESANA

Number	Title (A Side/B Side)	Yr	VG	VG+	NM
Albums					
MODERN					
M-100 [M]	Tender Emotions	1964	5.00	10.00	20.00

CEYLEIB PEOPLE, THE

Number	Title (A Side/B Side)	Yr	VG	VG+	NM
45s					
VAULT					
940	Changes/Ceyladd Seyta	1968	5.00	10.00	20.00
Albums					
VAULT					
LP-117	Tanyet	1968	15.00	30.00	60.00

CHAD AND JEREMY

Also see CHAD AND JILL STUART.

Number	Title (A Side/B Side)	Yr	VG	VG+	NM
45s					
CAPITOL STARLINE					
6087	A Summer Song/Willow Weep for Me	1966	2.00	4.00	8.00
—Green and white swirl label					
COLUMBIA					
43277	Before and After/Fare Thee Well	1965	2.50	5.00	10.00
43277 [DJ]	Before and After/Fare Thee Well	1965	10.00	20.00	40.00
—Red vinyl					
43339	I Don't Wanna Lose You Baby/Pennies	1965	2.00	4.00	8.00
43339 [PS]	I Don't Wanna Lose You Baby/Pennies	1965	5.00	10.00	20.00
43414	I Have Dreamed/Should I?	1966	2.00	4.00	8.00
43490	Teenage Failure/Early Morning Rain	1965	2.00	4.00	8.00
43490 [PS]	Teenage Failure/Early Morning Rain	1965	5.00	10.00	20.00
43682	Distant Shores/Last Night	1966	2.00	4.00	8.00
43682 [PS]	Distant Shores/Last Night	1966	5.00	10.00	20.00
43807	You Are She/I Won't Cry	1966	2.00	4.00	8.00
43807 [PS]	You Are She/I Won't Cry	1966	5.00	10.00	20.00
44131	Rest in Peace/Family Way	1967	2.00	4.00	8.00
44379	Painted Dayglow Smile/Editorial	1967	2.00	4.00	8.00
44525	Sister Marie/Rest in Peace	1968	2.00	4.00	8.00
44660	Paxton Quigley's Had the Course/You Need Feet	1968	2.00	4.00	8.00
44660 [PS]	Paxton Quigley's Had the Course/You Need Feet	1968	4.00	8.00	16.00
—Promo-only sleeve of a Nazi military rally					
ROCSHIRE					
95046	Bite the Bullet/How Many Trains	1983	—	2.00	4.00
95050 [DJ]	Bite the Bullet/Interview	1983	3.00	6.00	12.00
95061	Dreams/Zanzibar Sunset	1983	—	2.00	4.00
WORLD ARTISTS					
1021	Yesterday's Gone/Lemon Tree	1964	2.50	5.00	10.00
—As "Chad Stuart and Jeremy Clyde"					
1027	A Summer Song/No Tears for Johnny	1964	2.50	5.00	10.00
—As "Chad Stuart and Jeremy Clyde"					
1034	Willow Weep for Me/If She Was Mine	1964	2.50	5.00	10.00
1034 [PS]	Willow Weep for Me/If She Was Mine	1964	5.00	10.00	20.00
1041	If I Loved You/Donna, Donna	1965	2.50	5.00	10.00
1041 [PS]	If I Loved You/Donna, Donna	1965	5.00	10.00	20.00
1052	What Do You Want from Me/A Very Good Year	1965	2.50	5.00	10.00
—As "Chad Stuart and Jeremy Clyde"					
1056	From a Window/My Coloring Book	1965	2.50	5.00	10.00
1060	September in the Rain/Only for the Young	1965	2.50	5.00	10.00
Albums					
CAPITOL					
ST 2470 [P]	The Best of Chad and Jeremy	1966	3.00	6.00	12.00
—Black label with colorband					
ST 2470 [P]	The Best of Chad and Jeremy	1967	2.50	5.00	10.00
—"Starline" label					
T 2470 [M]	The Best of Chad and Jeremy	1966	2.50	5.00	10.00
—Black label with colorband					
T 2470 [M]	The Best of Chad and Jeremy	1967	2.00	4.00	8.00
—"Starline" label					
STT 2546 [P]	More Chad and Jeremy	1966	3.00	6.00	12.00
TT 2546 [M]	More Chad and Jeremy	1966	2.50	5.00	10.00
SN-16135 [P]	The Best of Chad and Jeremy	1980	2.00	4.00	8.00
—Budget-line reissue					
COLUMBIA					
CL 2374 [M]	Before and After	1965	5.00	10.00	20.00
CL 2398 [M]	I Don't Want to Lose You Baby	1966	6.25	12.50	25.00
CL 2564 [M]	Distant Shores	1966	5.00	10.00	20.00
CL 2671 [M]	Of Cabbages and Kings	1967	5.00	10.00	20.00
CL 2899 [M]	The Ark	1968	6.25	12.50	25.00
CS 9174 [S]	Before and After	1965	7.50	15.00	30.00
CS 9198 [S]	I Don't Want to Lose You Baby	1966	10.00	20.00	40.00
CS 9364 [P]	Distant Shores	1966	6.25	12.50	25.00
—"Distant Shores" is rechanneled					
CS 9471 [S]	Of Cabbages and Kings	1967	6.25	12.50	25.00
CS 9699 [S]	The Arc	1968	6.25	12.50	25.00
—Some copies spell the LP title this way on the cover					
CS 9699 [S]	The Ark	1968	6.25	12.50	25.00
—Correct spelling of LP title on cover					
FIDU					
FM-101 [M]	5 + 10 = 15 Fabulous Hits	1966	2.50	5.00	10.00
FS-101 [P]	5 + 10 = 15 Fabulous Hits	1966	3.00	6.00	12.00
HARMONY					
HS 11357 [S]	Chad and Jeremy	1973	2.00	4.00	8.00
ROCSHIRE					
XR-22018	Chad Stuart and Jeremy Clyde	1983	2.50	5.00	10.00
WORLD ARTISTS					
WAM-2002 [M]	Yesterday's Gone	1964	3.00	6.00	12.00
WAM-2005 [M]	Chad and Jeremy Sing for You	1965	3.00	6.00	12.00
WAS-3002 [P]	Yesterday's Gone	1964	3.75	7.50	15.00
—"Yesterday's Gone" is rechanneled.					
WAS-3005 [S]	Chad and Jeremy Sing for You	1965	3.75	7.50	15.00

CHAFFIN, ERNIE

Number	Title (A Side/B Side)	Yr	VG	VG+	NM
45s					
SUN					
262	Feelin' Low/Lonesome for My Baby	1957	7.50	15.00	30.00
275	Laughin' and Jokin'/I'm Lonesome	1957	7.50	15.00	30.00
307	Nothing Can Change My Love for You/Born to Lose	1958	6.25	12.50	25.00
320	Don't Ever Leave Me/Miracle of You	1959	6.25	12.50	25.00

CHAIN REACTION

This Chain Reaction includes Steve Tallarico, later known as Steve Tyler of AEROSMITH.

Number	Title (A Side/B Side)	Yr	VG	VG+	NM
45s					
DATE					
1538	When I Needed You/The Sun	1966	7.50	15.00	30.00

CHAIRMEN OF THE BOARD

Number	Title (A Side/B Side)	Yr	VG	VG+	NM
45s					
INVICTUS					
1251	Finder's Keepers/Finder's Keepers (Part 2)	1973	—	2.50	5.00
1263	Life & Death/Love with Me, Love with Me	1974	—	2.50	5.00
1268	Everybody Party All Night/Morning Glory	1974	—	2.50	5.00
1271	Let's Have Some Fun/Love at First Sight	1974	—	2.50	5.00
1276	The Skin I'm In/Love at First Sight	1975	—	2.50	5.00
1278	You've Got Extra Added Power in Your Love/Someone Just Like You	1975	—	2.50	5.00
9074	Give Me Just a Little More Time/Since the Days of Pigtails	1970	—	3.00	6.00
9078	(You've Got Me) Dangling on a String/I'll Come Crawling	1970	—	2.50	5.00
9079	Everything's Tuesday/Patches	1970	—	2.50	5.00
9081	Pay to the Piper/Bless You	1970	—	2.50	5.00
9081 [PS]	Pay to the Piper/Bless You	1970	2.50	5.00	10.00
9086	Chairman of the Board/When Will She Tell Me She Needs Me	1971	—	2.50	5.00
9089	Hanging On (To) A Memory/Tracked and Trapped	1971	—	2.50	5.00
9099	Try On My Love for Size/Working on a Building of Love	1971	—	2.50	5.00
9103	Men Are Getting Scarce/Bravo! Hurray!	1971	—	2.50	5.00
9106	Bittersweet/Elmo James	1972	—	2.50	5.00
9122	Everybody's Got a Song to Sing/Working on a Building of Love	1972	—	2.50	5.00
9126	Let Me Down Easy/I Can't Find Myself	1972	—	2.50	5.00
Albums					
INVICTUS					
ST-7300	Give Me Just a Little More Time	1970	10.00	20.00	40.00
SKAO-7304	In Session	1970	10.00	20.00	40.00
ST-9801	Bittersweet	1972	10.00	20.00	40.00
KZ 32526	The Skin I'm In	1974	10.00	20.00	40.00

CHAKACHAS, THE

Number	Title (A Side/B Side)	Yr	VG	VG+	NM
45s					
AVCO					
4596	Judas Kiss/Stories	1972	—	2.50	5.00
JANUS					
237	Africa Yama (Part 1)/Africa Yama (Part 2)	1974	—	2.50	5.00
POLYDOR					
15030	Jungle Fever/Cha Ka Cha	1972	—	3.00	6.00
15102	Jungle Fever '75/Liza (And Brook)	1975	—	2.00	4.00
Albums					
POLYDOR					
PD-5504	Jungle Fever	1972	3.75	7.50	15.00

CHAKIRIS, GEORGE

Number	Title (A Side/B Side)	Yr	VG	VG+	NM
45s					
CAPITOL					
4844	Maria/Once Upon a Time	1962	2.00	4.00	8.00
4892	My Coloring Book/I've Got Your Number	1962	2.00	4.00	8.00
5113	My Place/Love Being Here with You	1964	2.00	4.00	8.00
5209	Invisible Tears/Not for Me	1964	2.00	4.00	8.00
5426	Days of the Waltz/Finding Words for Spring	1965	2.00	4.00	8.00
5458	Blue Summer/Ship of Fools	1965	2.00	4.00	8.00
HORIZON					
356	But Not for Me/Embraceable You	1962	3.00	6.00	12.00
363	Cool/Embraceable You	1962	3.00	6.00	12.00
Albums					
CAPITOL					
ST 1750 [S]	George Chakiris	1962	5.00	10.00	20.00
T 1750 [M]	George Chakiris	1962	3.75	7.50	15.00
ST 1813 [S]	Memories Are Made of These	1963	5.00	10.00	20.00
T 1813 [M]	Memories Are Made of These	1963	3.75	7.50	15.00
ST 2391 [S]	It's Been a Swingin' Summer	1965	3.75	7.50	15.00
T 2391 [M]	It's Been a Swingin' Summer	1965	3.00	6.00	12.00
HORIZON					
ST-1610 [S]	The Gershwin Songbook	1962	5.00	10.00	20.00
WP-1610 [M]	The Gershwin Songbook	1962	3.75	7.50	15.00

CHAKRAS, THE

Number	Title (A Side/B Side)	Yr	VG	VG+	NM
45s					
REPRISE					
0838	Things We Said Today/Just with You	1969	3.75	7.50	15.00
0859	Agnes Vandalism/City Boy	1969	3.75	7.50	15.00

CHALETS, THE

45s

Number	Title (A Side/B Side)	Yr	VG	VG+	NM
DART					
1026	Who's Laughing-Who's Crying/Fat Fat Fat! Mom-Mi-O	1961	6.25	12.50	25.00
LAURIE					
3348	She's Not the Marrying Type/(Theme from) She's Not the Marrying Type	1966	3.00	6.00	12.00
MUSICNOTE					
1001	Who's Laughing-Who's Crying/Fat Fat Fat! Mom-Mi-O	1962	5.00	10.00	20.00
TRU-LITE					
1001	Who's Laughing-Who's Crying/Mom-Mia	1961	12.50	25.00	50.00

CHALLENGERS, THE (1)

California surf and instrumental group.

45s

Number	Title (A Side/B Side)	Yr	VG	VG+	NM
GNP CRESCENDO					
362	The Man from U.N.C.L.E./The Streets of London	1965	2.50	5.00	10.00
362	The Man from U.N.C.L.E./Summer Nights	1965	2.50	5.00	10.00
368	Walk with Me/How Could It	1966	2.50	5.00	10.00
376	Wipe Out/North Beach	1966	2.50	5.00	10.00
380	Milord/What If It Should Rain	1966	2.50	5.00	10.00
396	The Water Country/Everything to Me	1967	2.50	5.00	10.00
400	Color Me In/Before You	1968	2.50	5.00	10.00
412	Chitty Chitty Bang Bang/Lonely Little Girl	1968	2.50	5.00	10.00
TRIUMPH					
112	Pipeline/Asphalt Spinner	1966	7.50	15.00	30.00
VAULT					
900	Bull Dog/Torquay	1963	5.00	10.00	20.00
902	Moondawg/Tidal Wave	1963	5.00	10.00	20.00
904	Foot Tapper/On the Move	1963	5.00	10.00	20.00
910	Hot Rod Hootenanny/Maybellene	1964	7.50	15.00	30.00
913	Hot Rod Show/K-39	1964	7.50	15.00	30.00
918	Channel Nine/Can't Seem to Make You Mine	1965	5.00	10.00	20.00

Albums

Number	Title (A Side/B Side)	Yr	VG	VG+	NM
FANTASY					
F-9443	Where Were You in the Summer of '62	1973	3.00	6.00	12.00
GNP CRESCENDO					
GNP-609 [(2) M]	25 Great Instrumental Hits	1967	6.25	12.50	25.00
GNPS-609 [(2) S]	25 Great Instrumental Hits	1967	5.00	10.00	20.00
GNP-2010 [M]	The Challengers at the Teenage Fair	1965	5.00	10.00	20.00
GNPS-2010 [S]	The Challengers at the Teenage Fair	1965	6.25	12.50	25.00
GNP-2018 [M]	The Man from U.N.C.L.E.	1965	5.00	10.00	20.00
GNPS-2018 [S]	The Man from U.N.C.L.E.	1965	6.25	12.50	25.00
GNP-2025 [M]	California Kicks	1966	5.00	10.00	20.00
GNPS-2025 [S]	California Kicks	1966	6.25	12.50	25.00
GNP-2030 [M]	Billy Strange and the Challengers	1966	5.00	10.00	20.00
GNPS-2030 [S]	Billy Strange and the Challengers	1966	6.25	12.50	25.00
GNP-2031 [M]	Wipe Out	1966	5.00	10.00	20.00
GNPS-2031 [S]	Wipe Out	1966	6.25	12.50	25.00
GNPS-2045	Light My Fire with Classical Gas	1968	5.00	10.00	20.00
GNPS-2056	Vanilla Funk	1970	5.00	10.00	20.00
GNPS-2093	Sidewalk Surfing	1975	3.00	6.00	12.00
RHINO					
RNLP-053	Best of the Challengers	1982	2.50	5.00	10.00
TRIUMPH					
TR-100 [M]	The Challengers Go Sidewalk Surfing	1965	5.00	10.00	20.00
TRS-100 [S]	The Challengers Go Sidewalk Surfing	1965	6.25	12.50	25.00
VAULT					
LP-100 [M]	Surfbeat	1963	12.50	25.00	50.00
VS-100 [S]	Surfbeat	1963	20.00	40.00	80.00
—Black vinyl					
VS-100 [S]	Surfbeat	1963	62.50	12.50	250.00
—Orange vinyl					
VS-100 [S]	Surfbeat	1963	62.50	125.00	250.00
—Red vinyl					
VS-100 [S]	Surfbeat	1963	62.50	125.00	250.00
—Yellow vinyl					
LP-101 [M]	Lloyd Thaxton Goes Surfin' with the Challengers	1963	15.00	30.00	60.00
—Original title					
LP-101 [M]	Surfin' with the Challengers	1963	12.50	25.00	50.00
—Altered title					
VS-101 [S]	Lloyd Thaxton Goes Surfin' with the Challengers	1963	25.00	50.00	100.00
—Original title; black vinyl					
VS-101 [S]	Surfin' with the Challengers	1963	20.00	40.00	80.00
—Altered title; black vinyl					
VS-101 [S]	(Lloyd Thaxton Goes) Surfin' with the Challengers	1963	62.50	125.00	250.00
—Either title; orange vinyl					
VS-101 [S]	(Lloyd Thaxton Goes) Surfin' with the Challengers	1963	62.50	125.00	250.00
—Either title; red vinyl					
VS-101 [S]	(Lloyd Thaxton Goes) Surfin' with the Challengers	1963	62.50	125.00	250.00
—Either title; yellow vinyl					
VS-101 [S]	(Lloyd Thaxton Goes) Surfin' with the Challengers	1963	62.50	125.00	250.00
—Either title; blue vinyl					
LP-102 [M]	The Challengers On The Move	1963	10.00	20.00	40.00
VS-102 [S]	The Challengers On The Move	1963	15.00	30.00	60.00
LP-107 [M]	K-39	1964	20.00	40.00	80.00
LP-109 [M]	The Surf's Up	1965	10.00	20.00	40.00
VS-109 [S]	The Surf's Up	1965	15.00	30.00	60.00
LP-110 [M]	The Challengers A-Go-Go	1966	7.50	15.00	30.00
VS-110 [S]	The Challengers A-Go-Go	1966	10.00	20.00	40.00
LP-111 [M]	The Challengers' Greatest Hits	1967	6.25	12.50	25.00
VS-111 [S]	The Challengers' Greatest Hits	1967	6.25	12.50	25.00

CHALLENGERS, THE (2)

Mid-1960s R&B group.

45s

Number	Title (A Side/B Side)	Yr	VG	VG+	NM
CHESS					
1957	Tossin' and Turnin'/Don;t You Know It	1966	2.50	5.00	10.00

CHALLENGERS, THE (3)

Members of this group later recorded as THE OLYMPICS.

45s

Number	Title (A Side/B Side)	Yr	VG	VG+	NM
MELATONE					
1002	I Can Tell/The Mambo Beat	1956	75.00	150.00	300.00

CHALLENGERS, THE (4)

Members of this group later recorded as UNDERGROUND SUNSHINE.

45s

Number	Title (A Side/B Side)	Yr	VG	VG+	NM
NIGHT OWL					
6794	I Wanna Hold You/The Challengers Take a Ride on the Jefferson Airplane	1967	7.50	15.00	30.00

CHALLENGERS, THE (5)

British group.

45s

Number	Title (A Side/B Side)	Yr	VG	VG+	NM
TRIODEX					
102	Goofus/Lazy Twist	1960	5.00	10.00	20.00
107	Deadline/Cry of the Wild Goose	1961	5.00	10.00	20.00

CHALLENGERS, THE (U)

May be another record by group (2), but we're not sure.

45s

Number	Title (A Side/B Side)	Yr	VG	VG+	NM
CUCA					
1500	Hear My Message/I Wanna Hold You	1968	2.00	4.00	8.00

CHALLENGERS III, THE

45s

Number	Title (A Side/B Side)	Yr	VG	VG+	NM
TRI-PHI					
1012	Stay/Honey, Honey, Honey	1962	12.50	25.00	50.00
—As "The Challengers III"					
1012	Stay/Honey, Honey, Honey	1962	7.50	15.00	30.00
—As "The Challengers"					
1020	Every Day/I Hear an Echo	1963	12.50	25.00	50.00

CHAMAELEON CHURCH

Chevy Chase was in this group.

45s

Number	Title (A Side/B Side)	Yr	VG	VG+	NM
MGM					
13929	Your Golden Love/Camillia I Changing	1968	3.00	6.00	12.00

Albums

Number	Title (A Side/B Side)	Yr	VG	VG+	NM
MGM					
SE-4574	Chamaeleon Church	1968	5.00	10.00	20.00

CHAMBERLAIN, RICHARD

45s

Number	Title (A Side/B Side)	Yr	VG	VG+	NM
MCA					
40691	Secret Kingdom/The Slipper and the Rose Waltz	1977	—	2.00	4.00
MGM					
13075	Theme from Dr. Kildare (Three Stars Will Shine Tonight)/A Kiss to Build a Dream On	1962	2.50	5.00	10.00
13075 [PS]	Theme from Dr. Kildare (Three Stars Will Shine Tonight)/A Kiss to Build a Dream On	1962	5.00	10.00	20.00
13097	Love Me Tender/All I Do Is Dream of You	1962	2.50	5.00	10.00
13097 [PS]	Love Me Tender/All I Do Is Dream of You	1962	5.00	10.00	20.00
13121	All I Have to Do Is Dream/Hi-Lili, Hi-Lo	1963	2.50	5.00	10.00
13121 [PS]	All I Have to Do Is Dream/Hi-Lili, Hi-Lo	1963	5.00	10.00	20.00
13148	I Will Love You/True Love	1963	2.50	5.00	10.00
13148 [PS]	I Will Love You/True Love	1963	5.00	10.00	20.00
13170	Blue Guitar/They Long to Be Close to You	1963	2.50	5.00	10.00
13170 [PS]	Blue Guitar/They Long to Be Close to You	1963	5.00	10.00	20.00
13205	Stella By Starlight/Georgia on My Mind	1964	2.00	4.00	8.00
13285	Rome Will Never Leave You/You Always Hurt the One You Love	1964	2.00	4.00	8.00
13285 [PS]	Rome Will Never Leave You/You Always Hurt the One You Love	1964	3.75	7.50	15.00
13340	Joy in the Morning/April Love	1965	2.00	4.00	8.00

Albums

Number	Title (A Side/B Side)	Yr	VG	VG+	NM
METRO					
M-564 [M]	Richard Chamberlain Sings	1966	3.00	6.00	12.00
MS-564 [S]	Richard Chamberlain Sings	1966	3.00	6.00	12.00
MGM					
E-4088 [M]	Richard Chamberlain Sings	1962	3.75	7.50	15.00
SE-4088 [S]	Richard Chamberlain Sings	1962	5.00	10.00	20.00
E-4185 [M]	Twilight of Honor	1963	3.75	7.50	15.00
SE-4185 [S]	Twilight of Honor	1963	5.00	10.00	20.00
E-4287 [M]	Joy in the Morning	1965	3.75	7.50	15.00
SE-4287 [S]	Joy in the Morning	1965	5.00	10.00	20.00
ST 90512 [S]	Richard Chamberlain Sings	1965	7.50	15.00	30.00
—Capitol Record Club edition					
T 90512 [M]	Richard Chamberlain Sings	1965	6.25	12.50	25.00
—Capitol Record Club edition					

CHAMBERLAIN, WILT "THE STILT"

45s

Number	Title (A Side/B Side)	Yr	VG	VG+	NM
END					
1066	By the River/That's Easy to Say	1960	6.25	12.50	25.00

CHAMBERS BROTHERS, THE

45s

Number	Title (A Side/B Side)	Yr	VG	VG+	NM
AVCO					
4632	Let's Go, Let's Go, Let's Go/Do You Believe in Magic	1974	—	2.00	4.00
4638	1-2-3/Looking Back	1974	—	2.00	4.00
4657	Miss Lady Brown/Stealin' Watermelons	1975	—	2.00	4.00
COLUMBIA					
43816	Time Has Come Today/Dinah	1966	3.00	6.00	12.00
43957	All Strung Out Over You/Falling in Love	1967	—	3.00	6.00
44080	Please Don't Leave Me/I Can't Stand It	1967	—	3.00	6.00
44296	Uptown/Love Me Like the Rain	1967	—	3.00	6.00
44414	Time Has Come Today/People Get Ready	1968	2.00	4.00	8.00

Number	Title (A Side/B Side)	Yr	VG	VG+	NM
44679	I Can't Turn You Loose/Do Your Thing	1968	—	3.00	6.00
44679 [PS]	I Can't Turn You Loose/Do Your Thing	1968	2.50	5.00	10.00
44779	Are You Ready/You Got the Power to Turn Me On	1969	—	3.00	6.00
44890	Wake Up/Everybody Needs Someone	1969	—	3.00	6.00
44986	Have a Little Faith/Baby Takes Care of Business	1969	—	2.50	5.00
45055	Merry Christmas, Happy New Year/Did You Stop to Pray This Morning	1969	—	3.00	6.00
45088	Love, Peace and Happiness/If You Want Me To	1970	—	2.50	5.00
45146	To Love Somebody/Let's Do It	1970	—	2.50	5.00
45277	Love, Peace and Happiness/Funky	1970	—	2.50	5.00
45394	When the Evening Comes/New Generation	1971	—	2.50	5.00
45488	Heaven/(By the Hair on) My Chinny Chin Chin	1971	—	3.00	6.00
45518	Merry Christmas, Happy New Year/Did You Stop to Pray This Morning	1971	—	3.00	6.00
45837	Boogie Children/You Make the Magic	1973	—	3.00	6.00
ROXBURY					
2034	Bring It On Down Front Pretty Mama/Midnight Blue	1976	—	2.50	5.00
VAULT					
920	Call Me/Seventeen	1965	3.75	7.50	15.00
923	Pretty Girls Everywhere/Love Me Like the Rain	1966	3.00	6.00	12.00
945	Shout Part 1/Shout Part 2	1968	2.00	4.00	8.00
955	Just a Closer Walk with Thee/Girls We Love You	1969	—	3.00	6.00
967	House of the Rising Sun/Blues Get Off My Shoulder	1970	—	3.00	6.00

Albums

Number	Title (A Side/B Side)	Yr	VG	VG+	NM
AVCO					
11013	Unbonded	1974	3.00	6.00	12.00
69003	Night Move	1975	5.00	10.00	20.00
COLUMBIA					
KGP 20 [(2)]	Love, Peace and Happiness	1969	6.25	12.50	25.00
CL 2722 [M]	The Time Has Come	1967	7.50	15.00	30.00
CS 9522	The Time Has Come	1971	3.00	6.00	12.00
—Orange label					
CS 9522 [S]	The Time Has Come	1967	5.00	10.00	20.00
—Red "360 Sound" label					
PC 9522	The Time Has Come	198?	2.00	4.00	8.00
—Reissue with new prefix					
CS 9671	A New Time — A New Day	1968	5.00	10.00	20.00
C 30032	New Generation	1970	3.75	7.50	15.00
C 30871	The Chambers Brothers' Greatest Hits	1971	3.75	7.50	15.00
PC 30871	The Chambers Brothers' Greatest Hits	198?	2.00	4.00	8.00
—Reissue with new prefix					
KC 31158	Oh My God	1972	—	—	—
—Canceled					
CG 33642 [(2)]	The Time Has Come/A New Time — A New Day	1975	3.75	7.50	15.00
FANTASY					
24718 [(2)]	The Best of the Chambers Brothers	1973	3.75	7.50	15.00
FOLKWAYS					
31008	Groovin' Time	1968	3.75	7.50	15.00
ROXBURY					
RLX-106	Live In Concert on Mars	1976	7.50	15.00	30.00
VAULT					
LP-115 [M]	The Chambers Brothers Now	1967	3.75	7.50	15.00
VS-115 [S]	The Chambers Brothers Now	1967	3.75	7.50	15.00
VS-120	The Chambers Brothers Shout	1968	3.75	7.50	15.00
VS-128	Feelin' the Blues	1969	3.75	7.50	15.00
VS-135 [(2)]	The Chambers Brothers Greatest Hits	1970	5.00	10.00	20.00
LP-9003 [M]	People Get Ready	1966	5.00	10.00	20.00
LPS-9003 [S]	People Get Ready	1966	6.25	12.50	25.00

CHAMP, BILLY

45s

Number	Title (A Side/B Side)	Yr	VG	VG+	NM
ABC-PARAMOUNT					
10518	Believe Me/Hush-A-Bye	1964	7.50	15.00	30.00

CHAMPLAINS, THE

FRED PARRIS of THE FIVE SATINS is the lead voice.

45s

Number	Title (A Side/B Side)	Yr	VG	VG+	NM
UNITED ARTISTS					
346	Ding Dong/Have You Changed Your Mind	1961	10.00	20.00	40.00

CHAMPS, THE

Also see DAVE BURGESS; GLEN CAMPBELL; CHICK RIO; SEALS AND CROFTS.

45s

Number	Title (A Side/B Side)	Yr	VG	VG+	NM
CHALLENGE					
1016	Tequila/Train to Nowhere	1958	6.25	12.50	25.00
1016	Tequila/Train to Nowhere	1958	150.00	300.00	600.00
—Blue vinyl (one known to exist)					
9113	The Shoddy Shoddy/Sombrero	1961	5.00	10.00	20.00
9116	Cantina/Panic Button	1961	5.00	10.00	20.00
9131	Tequila Twist/Limbo Rock	1961	5.00	10.00	20.00
9140	Experiment in Terror/La Cucaracha	1962	3.75	7.50	15.00
9143	What a Country/I've Just Seen Her	1962	3.75	7.50	15.00
9162	Limbo Dance/Latin Limbo	1962	3.75	7.50	15.00
9174	Varsity Rock/That Did It	1962	3.75	7.50	15.00
9180	Mr. Cool//3/4 Mash	1963	3.75	7.50	15.00
9189	Nik Nak/Shades	1963	3.75	7.50	15.00
9199	Cactus Juice/Roots	1963	3.75	7.50	15.00
59007	El Rancho Rock/Midnighter	1958	5.00	10.00	20.00
59018	Chariot Rock/Subway	1958	5.00	10.00	20.00
59026	Turnpike/Rockin' Mary	1958	5.00	10.00	20.00
59035	Gone Train/Beatnik	1958	5.00	10.00	20.00
59043	Moonlight Bay/Caramba	1959	5.00	10.00	20.00
59049	Night Train/The Rattler	1959	5.00	10.00	20.00
59053	Sky High/Double Eagle Rock	1959	5.00	10.00	20.00
59063	Too Much Tequila/Twenty Thousand Leagues	1960	5.00	10.00	20.00
59076	Red Eye/The Little Matador	1960	5.00	10.00	20.00
59086	Alley Cat/Coconut Grove	1960	5.00	10.00	20.00
59097	The Face/Tough Train	1960	5.00	10.00	20.00
59103	Hokey Pokey/Jumping Bean	1961	5.00	10.00	20.00
59219	San Juan/Jalisco	1963	3.75	7.50	15.00
59236	Switzerland/Only the Young	1964	3.75	7.50	15.00
59263	Fraternity Waltz/Kahlua	1964	3.75	7.50	15.00
59276	French 75/Bright Lights, Big City	1965	3.75	7.50	15.00
59314	The Man from Durango/Red Pepper	1965	3.75	7.50	15.00
59322	Anna/Buckaroo	1965	3.75	7.50	15.00
REPUBLIC					
246	Tequila '76 (Long)/Tequila '76 (Short)	1976	2.00	4.00	8.00
246 [PS]	Tequila '76 (Long)/Tequila '76 (Short)	1976	2.00	4.00	8.00
WE'RE BACK					
1	Tequila '77/From Me to You	1977	2.00	4.00	8.00

7-Inch Extended Plays

Number	Title (A Side/B Side)	Yr	VG	VG+	NM
CHALLENGE					
7100	Tequila/Train to Nowhere//Lollipop/I'll Be There	1958	37.50	75.00	150.00
7100 [PS]	Tequila	1958	37.50	75.00	150.00

Albums

Number	Title (A Side/B Side)	Yr	VG	VG+	NM
CHALLENGE					
CHL-601 [M]	Go Champs Go	1958	800.00	1600.	2400.
—Blue vinyl					
CHL-601 [M]	Go Champs Go	1958	62.50	125.00	250.00
CHL-605 [M]	Everybody's Rockin' with the Champs	1959	50.00	100.00	200.00
CHL-613 [M]	Great Dance Hits	1962	30.00	60.00	120.00
CHL-614 [M]	All American Music from the Champs	1962	30.00	60.00	120.00
CHS-2500 [S]	Everybody's Rockin' with the Champs	1959	75.00	150.00	300.00
CHS-2513 [S]	Great Dance Hits	1962	50.00	100.00	200.00
CHS-2514 [S]	All American Music from the Champs	1962	50.00	100.00	200.00

CHANCE, NOLAN

45s

Number	Title (A Side/B Side)	Yr	VG	VG+	NM
CONSTELLATION					
144	She's Gone/If He Makes You	1965	6.25	12.50	25.00
161	Don't Use Me/Just Like the Weather	1965	30.00	60.00	120.00

CHANCERS, THE

45s

Number	Title (A Side/B Side)	Yr	VG	VG+	NM
DOT					
15870	Shirley Ann/My One	1958	7.50	15.00	30.00

CHANDELLES, THE

45s

Number	Title (A Side/B Side)	Yr	VG	VG+	NM
DOT					
16553	El Gato/Jetster	1963	6.25	12.50	25.00

CHANDLER, DENIECE

See DENIECE WILLIAMS.

CHANDLER, GENE

Includes records as "The Duke of Earl." Also see THE DUKAYS.

45s

Number	Title (A Side/B Side)	Yr	VG	VG+	NM
20TH CENTURY					
2411	When You're #1/I'll Remember You	1979	—	2.00	4.00
2428	Do What Comes So Natural/That Funky Disco Rhythm	1979	—	2.00	4.00
BRUNSWICK					
55312	Girl Don't Care/My Love	1967	2.00	4.00	8.00
55339	There Goes the Lover/Tell Me What I Can Do	1967	2.00	4.00	8.00
55383	There Was a Time/Those Were the Good Old Days	1968	2.00	4.00	8.00
55394	Teacher, Teacher/Pit of Loneliness	1968	2.00	4.00	8.00
55413	Eleanor Rigby/Familiar Footsteps	1969	2.00	4.00	8.00
55425	This Bitter Earth/Suicide	1969	2.00	4.00	8.00
CHECKER					
1155	I Fooled You This Time/Such a Pretty Thing	1966	2.00	4.00	8.00
1165	To Be a Lover/After the Laughter	1967	2.00	4.00	8.00
1190	I Won't Need You/No Peace, No Satisfaction	1967	2.00	4.00	8.00
1199	River of Tears/It's Time to Settle Down	1968	2.00	4.00	8.00
1220	Go Back Home/In My Baby's House	1969	2.00	4.00	8.00
CHI-SOUND					
1001	I'll Make the Living If You Make the Loving Worthwhile/(B-side unknown)	1982	—	2.50	5.00
1168	Give Me the Cue/Tomorrow We May Not Feel the Same	1978	—	2.00	4.00
2386	Get Down/I'm the Traveling Kind	1978	—	2.00	4.00
2404	Please Sunrise/Greatest Love Ever Known	1979	—	2.00	4.00
2411	When You're #1/I'll Remember You	1979	—	2.50	5.00
2451	Does She Have a Friend?/Let Me Make Love to You	1980	—	2.00	4.00
2468	Lay Me Gently/You've Been So Good to Me	1980	—	2.00	4.00
2480	Rainbow '80/I'll Be There	1980	—	2.00	4.00
2494	I'm Attracted to You/I've Got to Meet You	1981	—	2.00	4.00
2507	Love Is the Answer/Godsend	1981	—	2.00	4.00
CONSTELLATION					
104	From Day to Day/It's No Good for Me	1963	2.50	5.00	10.00
110	Pretty Little Girl/A Little Like Lovin'	1963	2.50	5.00	10.00
112	Think Nothing About It/Wish You Were Here	1964	2.50	5.00	10.00
114	Soul Hootenanny (Part 1)/Soul Hootenanny (Part 2)	1964	2.50	5.00	10.00
124	A Song Called Soul/You Left Me	1964	2.50	5.00	10.00
130	Just Be True/A Song Called Soul	1964	2.50	5.00	10.00
136	Bless Our Love/London Town	1964	2.50	5.00	10.00
141	What Now/If You Can't Be True	1964	2.50	5.00	10.00
146	You Can't Hurt Me No More/Everybody Let's Dance	1965	2.00	4.00	8.00
149	Nothing Can Stop Me/The Big Lie	1965	2.00	4.00	8.00
158	Rainbow '65 (Part 1)/Rainbow '65 (Part 2)	1965	2.00	4.00	8.00
160	Good Times/No One Can Love You	1965	2.00	4.00	8.00
164	Here Come the Tears/Soul Hootenanny (Part 2)	1965	2.00	4.00	8.00
166	Baby That's Love/Bet You Never Thought	1966	2.00	4.00	8.00
167	(I'm Just a) Fool for You/Buddy Ain't It a Shame	1966	2.00	4.00	8.00
169	I Can Take Care of Myself/If I Can't Save It	1966	2.00	4.00	8.00
172	Mr. Big Shot/I Hate to Be the One to Say	1966	2.00	4.00	8.00
CURTOM					
1979	Don't Have to Be Lyin' Babe (Part 1)/Don't Have to Be Lyin' Babe (Part 2)	1973	—	2.50	5.00

Number	Title (A Side/B Side)	Yr	VG	VG+	NM
1986	Baby I Still Love You/I Understand	1973	—	2.50	5.00
1992	Without You Here/Just Be There	1973	—	2.50	5.00
FASTFIRE					
7003	Haven't Heard That Line Before/(B-side unknown)	1985	—	2.00	4.00
7005	Lucy/(B-side unknown)	1986	—	2.00	4.00
MERCURY					
73083	Groovy Situation/Not the Marrying Kind	1970	—	3.00	6.00
73121	Simply Call It Love/Give Me a Chance	1970	—	3.00	6.00
73206	You're a Lady/Stone Cold Feeling	1971	—	3.00	6.00
73258	Yes I'm Ready (If I Don't Get to Go)/Pillars of Glass	1971	—	3.00	6.00
SALSOUL					
7051	You're the One/I Keep Comin' Back for More	1983	—	2.00	4.00
—With Jaime Lynn					
VEE JAY					
416	Duke of Earl/Kissin' in the Kitchen	1961	6.25	12.50	25.00
416	Duke of Earl/Kissin' in the Kitchen	1962	5.00	10.00	20.00
—Some later pressings as "The Duke of Earl"					
440	Walk On with the Duke/London Town	1962	3.75	7.50	15.00
—As "The Duke of Earl"					
450	Daddy's Home/The Big Lie	1962	3.75	7.50	15.00
—As "The Duke of Earl"					
455	I'll Follow You/You Left Me	1962	3.75	7.50	15.00
—As "The Duke of Earl"					
461	Tear for Tear/Miracle After Miracle	1962	3.75	7.50	15.00
468	You Threw a Lucky Punch/Rainbow	1962	3.75	7.50	15.00
511	Check Yourself/Forgive Me	1963	3.75	7.50	15.00
536	Baby, That's Love/Man's Temptation	1963	3.75	7.50	15.00
Albums					
20TH CENTURY					
T-605	Gene Chandler '80	1980	2.50	5.00	10.00
T-625	Ear Candy	1980	2.50	5.00	10.00
T-629	Here's to Love	1981	2.50	5.00	10.00
BRUNSWICK					
BL 54124 [M]	The Girl Don't Care	1967	6.25	12.50	25.00
BL 754124 [S]	The Girl Don't Care	1967	5.00	10.00	20.00
BL 754131	There Was a Time	1968	5.00	10.00	20.00
BL 754149	The Two Sides of Gene Chandler	1969	5.00	10.00	20.00
CHECKER					
LP-3003 [M]	The Duke of Soul	1967	12.50	25.00	50.00
LPS-3003 [R]	The Duke of Soul	1967	7.50	15.00	30.00
CHI-SOUND					
T-578	Get Down	1978	2.50	5.00	10.00
CONSTELLATION					
LP 1421 [M]	Greatest Hits by Gene Chandler	1964	12.50	25.00	50.00
LP 1423 [M]	Just Be True	1964	12.50	25.00	50.00
LP 1425 [M]	Gene Chandler — Live On Stage in '65	1965	12.50	25.00	50.00
MERCURY					
SR-61304	The Gene Chandler Situation	1970	3.75	7.50	15.00
SOLID SMOKE					
SS-8027	Stroll On with the Duke	198?	2.50	5.00	10.00
VEE JAY					
LP-1040 [M]	The Duke of Earl	1962	30.00	60.00	120.00
SR-1040 [S]	The Duke of Earl	1962	200.00	400.00	800.00
—"Stereophonic" on front cover; top back cover contains note that begins: "Important Notice...This Is a Stereophonic Record"; "Stereo" on record labels					
SR-1040 [S]	The Duke of Earl	1962	62.50	125.00	250.00
—"Stereo" sticker on mono cover; "Stereo" on record labels					
SR-1040 [S/M]	The Duke of Earl	196?	12.50	25.00	50.00
—"Stereophonic" on front; no "Important Notice..." on back; record plays mono. Most labels are all-black with "VJ" in brackets. This was a semi-authorized reissue after ex-Vee Jay executives bought the company's remnants in bankruptcy court in 1966.					
VJLP-1040	The Duke of Earl	198?	2.50	5.00	10.00
—Mid-1980s authorized reissue					

CHANDLER, GENE, AND BARBARA ACKLIN

Also see each artist's individual listings.

Number	Title (A Side/B Side)	Yr	VG	VG+	NM
45s					
BRUNSWICK					
55366	Love Won't Start/Show Me the Way to Go	1968	2.00	4.00	8.00
55387	From the Teacher to the Preacher/Anywhere But Nowhere	1968	2.00	4.00	8.00
55405	Little Green Apples/Will I Find You	1969	2.00	4.00	8.00

CHANDLER, GENE, AND JERRY BUTLER

Also see each artist's individual listings.

Number	Title (A Side/B Side)	Yr	VG	VG+	NM
45s					
MERCURY					
73163	You Just Can't Win (By Making the Same Mistake)/The Show Is Grooving	1971	—	3.00	6.00
73195	Two and Two (Take This Woman Off the Corner)/Everybody Is Waiting	1971	—	3.00	6.00
Albums					
MERCURY					
SR-61330	Gene & Jerry — One & One	1971	3.75	7.50	15.00

CHANDLER, JEFF

Number	Title (A Side/B Side)	Yr	VG	VG+	NM
45s					
DECCA					
9-29004	I Should Care/More Than Anyone	1954	3.75	7.50	15.00
9-29175	Lamplight/That's All She's Waiting to Hear	1954	3.00	6.00	12.00
9-29345	Always/Everything Happens to Me	1955	3.00	6.00	12.00
9-29405	My Prayer/When Spring Comes	1955	3.00	6.00	12.00
9-29532	Shaner Maidel/Foxfire	1955	3.00	6.00	12.00
9-29600	Only the Very Young/A Little Love Can Go a Long, Long Way	1955	3.00	6.00	12.00
LIBERTY					
55092	Half of My Heart/Hold Me	1957	2.50	5.00	10.00
Albums					
LIBERTY					
LRP-3067 [M]	Jeff Chandler Sings to You	1957	10.00	20.00	40.00
LRP-3074 [M]	Warm and Easy	1958	10.00	20.00	40.00
SUNSET					
SUS-5127	Sincerely Yours	1969	3.00	6.00	12.00

CHANDLER, KENNY

Number	Title (A Side/B Side)	Yr	VG	VG+	NM
45s					
AMY					
890	I Don't Know Why/Happy to Be Unhappy	1963	2.50	5.00	10.00
CORAL					
62309	It Might Have Been/Yours and Yours Alone	1962	2.50	5.00	10.00
EPIC					
9758	Come Softly to Me/S.O.S. (Sweet On Susie)	1965	2.00	4.00	8.00
10009	I'll Be Coming Back/Sunshine Sweetheart	1966	2.00	4.00	8.00
LAURIE					
3140	Man on the Run/Leave Me If You Want To	1962	2.50	5.00	10.00
3158	Heart/Wait for Me	1963	2.50	5.00	10.00
3181	I Tell Myself/I Can't Stand Tears at a Party	1963	2.50	5.00	10.00
TOWER					
354	Sleep/Nickles and Dimes	1967	2.00	4.00	8.00
405	Beyond Love/Charity	1968	2.00	4.00	8.00
UNITED ARTISTS					
342	The Magic Ring/Drums	1961	3.00	6.00	12.00
384	Please Mr. Mountain/What Kind of Love Is Yours	1961	3.00	6.00	12.00

CHANDLER, LORRAINE

Number	Title (A Side/B Side)	Yr	VG	VG+	NM
45s					
GIANT					
703	What Can I Do/Tell Me You're Mine	1966	15.00	30.00	60.00
RCA VICTOR					
47-8810	What Can I Do/Tell Me You're Mine	1966	7.50	15.00	30.00
47-8980	I Can't Hold On/She Don't Want You	1966	7.50	15.00	30.00
47-9349	I Can't Change/Oh How I Need Your Love	1967	12.50	25.00	50.00

CHANGIN' TIMES, THE

Number	Title (A Side/B Side)	Yr	VG	VG+	NM
45s					
BELL					
675	Free Spirit/You Just Seem to Know	1967	5.00	10.00	20.00
711	Show Me the Way to Go Home/When the Good Sun Shines	1968	5.00	10.00	20.00
PHILIPS					
40320	Pied Piper/Thank You Babe	1965	5.00	10.00	20.00
40341	How Is the Air Up There/Young and Innocent Girl	1965	5.00	10.00	20.00
40368	Goin' Lovin' with You/I Should Have Brought Her Home	1966	3.75	7.50	15.00
40401	Aladdin/All in the Mind of a Young Girl	1966	3.75	7.50	15.00

CHANGING SCENE, THE

Number	Title (A Side/B Side)	Yr	VG	VG+	NM
45s					
FONTANA					
1669	Is It Really Worth It/Sing Me Something Pretty	1969	3.00	6.00	12.00

CHANNEL, BRUCE

Number	Title (A Side/B Side)	Yr	VG	VG+	NM
45s					
ELEKTRA					
46587	One More Last Chance/That's the Truth, Ruth	1980	—	2.00	4.00
KING					
5294	Will I Ever Love Again/Blow Down Baby	1959	7.50	15.00	30.00
5331	Now or Never/Boy, This Stuff Kills Me	1960	7.50	15.00	30.00
5620	Now or Never/Will I Ever Love Again	1962	5.00	10.00	20.00
LE CAM					
122	Going Back to Louisiana/Forget Me Not	1964	2.50	5.00	10.00
125	My Baby/Blue Monday	1964	2.50	5.00	10.00
953	Hey! Baby/Dream Girl	1961	10.00	20.00	40.00
1117	A Presley Medley/A Man Without a Woman	1977	—	2.50	5.00
7277	The King Is Free (Love Me)/Funky Dude (Andy and the Dude)	1977	—	2.50	5.00
MALA					
579	Mr. Bus Driver/It's Me	1967	2.50	5.00	10.00
592	Keep On/Barbara Allen	1968	2.50	5.00	10.00
12011	California/Water the Family Tree	1968	2.50	5.00	10.00
12027	Try Me/Nobody	1968	2.50	5.00	10.00
12041	The Web/Mrs. P	1969	2.50	5.00	10.00
MANCO					
1035	Run Romance, Run/Don't Leave Me	1962	5.00	10.00	20.00
MEL-O-DY					
112	That's What's Happenin'/Satisfied Mind	1964	3.75	7.50	15.00
114	You Make Me Happy/You Never Looked Better	1964	3.75	7.50	15.00
SMASH					
1731	Hey! Baby/Dream Girl	1962	5.00	10.00	20.00
1752	Number One Man/If Only I Had Known	1962	3.75	7.50	15.00
1769	Come On Baby/Mine Exclusively	1962	3.75	7.50	15.00
1780	Stand Tough/Somewhere in This Town	1962	3.75	7.50	15.00
1780 [PS]	Stand Tough/Somewhere in This Town	1962	7.50	15.00	30.00
1792	Oh Baby/Let's Hurt Together	1962	3.75	7.50	15.00
1826	No Other Baby/Night People	1963	3.75	7.50	15.00
1826 [PS]	No Other Baby/Night People	1963	7.50	15.00	30.00
1838	The Dipsy Doodle/Send Her Home	1963	3.75	7.50	15.00
1838 [PS]	The Dipsy Doodle/Send Her Home	1963	7.50	15.00	30.00
TEENAGER					
601	Run Romance, Run/Don't Leave Me	1960	7.50	15.00	30.00
Albums					
SMASH					
MGS-27008 [M]	Hey! Baby (And 11 Other Songs About Your Baby)	1962	25.00	50.00	100.00
SRS-67008 [R]	Hey! Baby (And 11 Other Songs About Your Baby)	1962	15.00	30.00	60.00

CHANNELLS, THE
See THE CHANNELS (2).

CHANNELS, THE (1)
Group led by Earl Lewis.

45s

Number	Title (A Side/B Side)	Yr	VG	VG+	NM
CHANNEL					
1000	Gloria/You Said You Loved Me	1971	2.50	5.00	10.00
1001	We Belong Together/Hey Girl, I'm in Love with You	1972	2.50	5.00	10.00
1002	You Got What It Takes/Crazy Mixed-Up World	1972	2.50	5.00	10.00
1003	Close Your Eyes/Work with Me Annie	1973	2.50	5.00	10.00
1004	Over Again/In My Arms to Stay	1973	2.50	5.00	10.00
1006	A Thousand Miles Away/Don't Let the Green Grass Fool You	1974	2.50	5.00	10.00
FIRE					
1001	My Heart Is Sad/The Girl Next Door	1959	12.50	25.00	50.00
—As "Earl Lewis and the Channels"					
FURY					
1021	Bye Bye Baby/My Love Will Never Die	1959	12.50	25.00	50.00
1071	Bye Bye Baby/My Love Will Never Die	1963	10.00	20.00	40.00
GONE					
5012	That's My Desire/Stay As You Are	1957	15.00	30.00	60.00
5019	Altar of Love/All Alone	1957	15.00	30.00	60.00
PORT					
70014	The Closer You Are/Now You Know	1960	6.25	12.50	25.00
—Reissue of Whirlin' Disc 100					
70017	The Gleam in Your Eyes/Stars in the Sky	1960	6.25	12.50	25.00
—Reissue of Whirlin' Disc 102					
70022	Flames in My Heart/My Lovin' Baby	1961	6.25	12.50	25.00
—Reissue of Whirlin' Disc 109					
70023	I Really Love You/What Do You Do	1961	6.25	12.50	25.00
—Reissue of Whirlin' Disc 107					
RARE BIRD					
5017	She Blew My Mind/Breaking Up Is Hard to Do	1971	2.50	5.00	10.00
WHIRLIN' DISC					
100	The Closer You Are/Now You Know	1956	62.50	125.00	250.00
—Block-letter label name; publisher listed as "Bob-Dan Music"					
100	The Closer You Are/Now You Know	1956	50.00	100.00	200.00
—Block-letter label name; publisher listed as "Spinning Wheel Music"					
100	The Closer You Are/Now You Know	1956	25.00	50.00	100.00
—Label name is all caps, but not in block letters					
102	The Gleam in Your Eyes/Stars in the Sky	1956	50.00	100.00	200.00
107	I Really Love You/What Do You Do	1957	50.00	100.00	200.00
109	Flames in My Heart/My Lovin' Baby	1957	50.00	100.00	200.00

Albums

Number	Title (A Side/B Side)	Yr	VG	VG+	NM
COLLECTABLES					
COL-5012	New York's Finest: The Best of Earl Lewis and the Channels	198?	3.00	6.00	12.00
LOST-NITE					
LLP-15 [10]	The Channels	1981	3.00	6.00	12.00
—Red vinyl					
LLP-16 [10]	The Channels	1981	3.00	6.00	12.00
—Red vinyl					

CHANNELS, THE (2)
Group led by Tony and Gene Williams.

45s

Number	Title (A Side/B Side)	Yr	VG	VG+	NM
ENJOY					
2001	Sad Song/My Love	1963	6.25	12.50	25.00
GROOVE					
58-0046	Anything You Do/I've Got My Eyes on You	1964	6.25	12.50	25.00
58-0061	Old Chinatown/You Can Count on Me	1965	6.25	12.50	25.00
HIT RECORD					
700	In My Arms to Stay/You Hurt Me	1963	10.00	20.00	40.00
—As "The Channells"					

CHANNELS, THE (3)
Neither of the above.

45s

Number	Title (A Side/B Side)	Yr	VG	VG+	NM
MERCURY					
71501	Earthquake/Jungle Lights	1959	3.00	6.00	12.00

CHANTAY'S

45s

Number	Title (A Side/B Side)	Yr	VG	VG+	NM
DOT					
145	Pipeline/Move It	1966	2.00	4.00	8.00
—Reissue; black label					
145	Pipeline/Move It	1969	—	3.00	6.00
—Reissue; orange-red label					
16440	Pipeline/Move It	1963	6.25	12.50	25.00
16492	Monsoon/Scotch Highs	1963	5.00	10.00	20.00
DOWNEY					
104	Pipeline/Move It	1963	15.00	30.00	60.00
108	Monsoon/Scotch Highs	1963	7.50	15.00	30.00
116	Space Probe/Continental Missile	1964	5.00	10.00	20.00
120	Only If You Care/Love Can Be Cruel	1964	5.00	10.00	20.00
126	Beyond/I'll Be Back Someday	1964	5.00	10.00	20.00
130	Three Coins in the Fountain/Greens	1965	5.00	10.00	20.00

Albums

Number	Title (A Side/B Side)	Yr	VG	VG+	NM
DOT					
DLP 3516 [M]	Pipeline	1963	12.50	25.00	50.00
DLP 3771 [M]	Two Sides of the Chantays	1966	12.50	25.00	50.00
DLP 25516 [S]	Pipeline	1963	20.00	40.00	80.00
DLP 25771 [S]	Two Sides of the Chantays	1966	20.00	40.00	80.00
DOWNEY					
DLP-1002 [M]	Pipeline	1963	55.00	110.00	220.00
DLPS-1002 [S]	Pipeline	1963	87.50	175.00	350.00

CHANTECLAIRS, THE

45s

Number	Title (A Side/B Side)	Yr	VG	VG+	NM
DOT					
1227	Baby Please/Someday Love Will Come My Way	1954	18.75	37.50	75.00
15404	Believe Me, Beloved/I've Never Been There	1955	15.00	30.00	60.00

CHANTELS, THE
Also see ARLENE SMITH; THE VENEERS.

45s

Number	Title (A Side/B Side)	Yr	VG	VG+	NM
CARLTON					
555	Look in My Eyes/Glad to Be Back	1961	5.00	10.00	20.00
564	Still/Well, I Told You	1961	5.00	10.00	20.00
569	Summertime/Here It Comes Again	1962	5.00	10.00	20.00
END					
1001	He's Gone/The Plea	1957	20.00	40.00	80.00
—Black label					
1005	Maybe/Come My Little Baby	1957	20.00	40.00	80.00
—Black label					
1005	Maybe/Come My Little Baby	1958	10.00	20.00	40.00
—Gray (white) label					
1005	Maybe/Come My Little Baby	1959	5.00	10.00	20.00
—Multi-color label					
1015	Every Night/Whoever You Are	1958	7.50	15.00	30.00
—Gray (white) label					
1015	Every Night/Whoever You Are	1959	5.00	10.00	20.00
—Multi-color label					
1020	I Love You So/How Could You Call It Off	1958	10.00	20.00	40.00
1026	Prayer/Sure of Love	1958	6.25	12.50	25.00
1030	If You Try/Congratulations	1958	6.25	12.50	25.00
1037	Never Let Go/I Can't Take It	1959	6.25	12.50	25.00
1048	I'm Confessin'/Goodbye to Love	1959	6.25	12.50	25.00
1069	Whoever You Are/How Could You Call It Off	1960	6.25	12.50	25.00
1103	Believe Me (My Angel)/I	1961	15.00	30.00	60.00
—Originally released on Princeton 102 as "The Veneers"					
1105	There's Our Song Again/I'm the Girl	1961	6.25	12.50	25.00
LUDIX					
101	Eternally/Swamp Water	1963	5.00	10.00	20.00
106	That's Why I'm Happy/Some Tears Fall Dry	1963	5.00	10.00	20.00
RCA VICTOR					
74-0347	I'm Gonna Win Him Back/Love Makes All the Difference in the World	1970	2.50	5.00	10.00
ROULETTE					
7064	Maybe/He's Gone	1969	2.50	5.00	10.00
TCF HALL					
123	Take Me As I Am/There's No Forgetting Me	1965	3.75	7.50	15.00
VERVE					
10387	You're Welcome to My Heart/Soul of a Soldier	1966	3.75	7.50	15.00
10435	Indian Giver/It's Just Me	1966	3.75	7.50	15.00

7-Inch Extended Plays

Number	Title (A Side/B Side)	Yr	VG	VG+	NM
END					
201	(contents unknown)	1958	37.50	75.00	150.00
201 [PS]	I Love You So	1958	62.50	125.00	250.00
202	(contents unknown)	1958	25.00	50.00	100.00
202 [PS]	C'est Si Bon	1958	50.00	100.00	200.00

Albums

Number	Title (A Side/B Side)	Yr	VG	VG+	NM
CARLTON					
LP-144 [M]	The Chantels On Tour/Look in My Eyes	1962	50.00	100.00	200.00
STLP-144 [S]	The Chantels On Tour/Look in My Eyes	1962	100.00	200.00	400.00
END					
LP-301 [M]	We're the Chantels	1958	500.00	1000.	1500.
—Group photo on front cover					
LP-301 [M]	We're the Chantels	1959	100.00	200.00	400.00
—Jukebox on front cover, "1962" not in trail-off wax					
LP-301 [M]	We're the Chantels	1962	50.00	100.00	200.00
—Jukebox on front cover, "1962" in trail-off wax					
LP-312 [M]	There's Our Song Again	1962	30.00	60.00	120.00
FORUM					
F-9104 [M]	The Chantels Sing Their Favorites	1964	12.50	25.00	50.00
FS-9104 [R]	The Chantels Sing Their Favorites	1964	6.25	12.50	25.00

CHANTERS, THE (1)

45s

Number	Title (A Side/B Side)	Yr	VG	VG+	NM
COMBO					
78	Why/Watts	1954	125.00	250.00	500.00
92	I Love You/Hot Mamma	1955	100.00	200.00	400.00
DELUXE					
6162	My My Darling/I Need Your Tenderness (I Love You Darling)	1958	12.50	25.00	50.00
6166	Row Your Boat/Stars in the Skies	1958	10.00	20.00	40.00
—Black label					
6166	Row Your Boat/Stars in the Skies	1958	5.00	10.00	20.00
—Yellow label					
6172	Angel Darling/Five Little Kisses	1958	12.50	25.00	50.00
6177	No, No, No/Over the Rainbow	1958	10.00	20.00	40.00
6191	No, No, No/I Make This Pledge (To You)	1961	7.50	15.00	30.00
6194	My My Darling/At My Door	1961	10.00	20.00	40.00
6200	Row Your Boat/No, No, No	1963	7.50	15.00	30.00
KEM					
2740	Lonesome Me/Golden Apple	1955	75.00	150.00	300.00
RPM					
415	Tell Me, Thrill Me/She Wants to Mambo	1954	75.00	150.00	300.00

CHANTERS, THE (2)

45s

Number	Title (A Side/B Side)	Yr	VG	VG+	NM
MGM					
13750	Free As A Bird/Bongo, Bongo	1967	—	3.00	6.00

CHANTEURS, THE
With Eugene Record, later of THE CHI-LITES.

Number	Title (A Side/B Side)	Yr	VG	VG+	NM
45s					
VEE JAY					
519	You've Got a Great Love/The Grizzly Bear	1963	5.00	10.00	20.00

CHANTONES, THE

Number	Title (A Side/B Side)	Yr	VG	VG+	NM
45s					
CAPITOL					
4661	Stormy Weather/Sweet Georgia Brown	1961	6.25	12.50	25.00
CARLTON					
485	Five Little Numbers/It's Just a Summer Love	1958	7.50	15.00	30.00
TOP RANK					
2066	Don't Open That Door/Tangerock	1960	6.25	12.50	25.00

CHANTS, THE (1)
British soul group.

Number	Title (A Side/B Side)	Yr	VG	VG+	NM
45s					
CAMEO					
277	I Don't Care/Come Go with Me	1963	5.00	10.00	20.00
297	I Could Write a Book/A Thousand Stars	1964	5.00	10.00	20.00
INTERPHON					
7703	She's Mine/Then I'll Be Home	1964	3.75	7.50	15.00

CHANTS, THE (U)
None of these are by group (1), but we doubt all of them are by the same group.

Number	Title (A Side/B Side)	Yr	VG	VG+	NM
45s					
CAPITOL					
F-3949	Lost and Found/Close Friends	1958	5.00	10.00	20.00
CHECKER					
1209	Surfside/Chicken 'N' Gravy	1968	2.00	4.00	8.00
EKO					
3567/77	Respectable/Kiss Me Goodbye	1961	7.50	15.00	30.00
MGM					
13008	Respectable/Kiss Me Goodbye	1961	5.00	10.00	20.00
NITE OWL					
40	Heaven and Paradise/When I'm With You	1960	75.00	150.00	300.00
—Maroon label original					
40	Heaven and Paradise/When I'm With You	1960	10.00	20.00	40.00
—Black label, black vinyl					
40	Heaven and Paradise/When I'm With You	196?	5.00	10.00	20.00
—Red vinyl					
40	Heaven and Paradise/When I'm With You	196?	5.00	10.00	20.00
—Blue vinyl					
40	Heaven and Paradise/When I'm With You	196?	5.00	10.00	20.00
—Yellow vinyl					
U.W.R.					
4243	Rockin' Santa/Respectable	1962	6.25	12.50	25.00
VERVE					
10244	Dick Tracy/Choo Choo	1961	5.00	10.00	20.00

CHAPEL, JEAN

Number	Title (A Side/B Side)	Yr	VG	VG+	NM
45s					
CHALLENGE					
59350	Tell It Like It Is/I'm Your Woman	1966	2.00	4.00	8.00
59362	You Can Take Me/Stamp Out Loneliness	1967	2.00	4.00	8.00
59370	In the Reach of Your Arms/This Waltz Is Mine	1967	2.00	4.00	8.00
59376	Hungry Eyes/Green Paper	1967	2.00	4.00	8.00
59381	Dino's TV Door/If I Never Get You	1967	2.00	4.00	8.00
59386	See and Ye Shall Find/I Really Go for You	1968	2.00	4.00	8.00
KAPP					
2034	Bluebird Ridge/I Started Loving You Again	1969	—	3.00	6.00
2082	I'm Your Woman/The Roll Call	1970	—	3.00	6.00
RCA VICTOR					
47-6681	I Won't Be Rockin' Tonight/Welcome to the Club	1956	10.00	20.00	40.00
47-6892	Oo-Ba La Baby/I Had a Dream	1957	6.25	12.50	25.00
SMASH					
1829	Don't Let Go/Your Tender Love	1963	3.00	6.00	12.00
SUN					
244	I Won't Be Rockin' Tonight/Welcome to the Club	1956	12.50	25.00	50.00

CHAPERONES, THE

Number	Title (A Side/B Side)	Yr	VG	VG+	NM
45s					
JOSIE					
880	Dance with Me/Cruise to the Moon	1960	37.50	75.00	150.00
—With typographical error listing group as "The Cahperones"					
880	Dance with Me/Cruise to the Moon	1960	6.25	12.50	25.00
—With correct group name on label					
885	Shining Star/My Shadow and Me	1960	6.25	12.50	25.00
891	Man from the Moon/Blueberry Sweet	1961	12.50	25.00	50.00

CHAPIN, HARRY
Also see THE CHAPINS.

Number	Title (A Side/B Side)	Yr	VG	VG+	NM
45s					
BOARDWALK					
NB7-11-119	Story of a Love/Salt and Pepper	1981	—	2.00	4.00
5700	Sequel/I Finally Found It Sandy	1980	—	2.00	4.00
5705	Remember When the Music/Northwest 222	1981	—	2.00	4.00
ELEKTRA					
45203	Cat's in the Cradle/Vacancy	1974	—	2.00	4.00
45236	I Wanna Learn a Love Song/She Sings Songs Without Words	1975	—	2.00	4.00
45264	Dreams Go By/Sandy	1975	—	2.00	4.00
45285	Tangled-Up Puppet/Dirt Get Under the Fingernails	1975	—	2.00	4.00
45304	Star Tripper/The Rock	1976	—	2.00	4.00
45327	Better Place to Be (Part 1)/Better Place to Be (Part 2)	1976	—	2.00	4.00
45368	Corey's Coming/If My Mary Were Here	1976	—	2.00	4.00
45426	Dance Band on the Titanic/I Wonder What Happened to Him	1977	—	2.00	4.00
45445	My Old Lady/I'd Do It for You, Jane	1977	—	2.00	4.00
45497	I Wonder What Would Happen to This World/If You Want to Feel	1978	—	2.00	4.00
45524	Flowers Are Red/Jenny	1978	—	2.00	4.00
45770	Taxi/Empty	1972	—	2.50	5.00
45792	Could You Put Your Light On, Please?/Any Old Kind of Day	1972	—	2.00	4.00
45811	Sunday Morning Sunshine/Burning Herself	1972	—	2.00	4.00
45828	Better Place to Be/Winter Song	1973	—	2.00	4.00
45874	WOLD/Short Stories	1973	—	2.00	4.00
45893	What Made America Famous/Old College Avenue	1974	—	2.00	4.00
Albums					
BOARDWALK					
FW 36872	Sequel	1980	2.50	5.00	10.00
ELEKTRA					
6E-142	Living Room Suite	1978	2.50	5.00	10.00
9E-301 [(2)]	Dance Band on the Titanic	1977	3.00	6.00	12.00
BB-703 [(2)]	Legends of the Lost and Found — New Greatest Stories Live	1979	3.00	6.00	12.00
7E-1012	Verities & Balderdash	1974	2.50	5.00	10.00
7E-1041	Portrait Gallery	1975	2.50	5.00	10.00
7E-1082	On the Road to Kingdom Come	1976	2.50	5.00	10.00
7E-2009 [(2)]	Greatest Stories Live	1976	3.00	6.00	12.00
8E-6003 [(2)]	Greatest Stories Live	1978	2.50	5.00	10.00
—Reissue of 7E-2009					
60413	Anthology of Harry Chapin	1985	2.50	5.00	10.00
EKS-75023	Heads and Tales	1972	2.50	5.00	10.00
EKS-75042	Sniper and Other Love Songs	1972	2.50	5.00	10.00
EKS-75065	Short Stories	1973	2.50	5.00	10.00

CHAPINS, THE
HARRY CHAPIN; Steve Chapin; Tom Chapin.

Number	Title (A Side/B Side)	Yr	VG	VG+	NM
45s					
EPIC					
10761	Workin' On My Life/The Only Thing (You Ever Really Have to Do Is Die)	1971	3.00	6.00	12.00
ROCK-LAND					
664	Old Time Movies/Not Your Kind	1966	3.75	7.50	15.00
664 [PS]	Old Time Movies/Not Your Kind	1966	6.25	12.50	25.00
Albums					
ROCK-LAND					
RR-66 [M]	Chapin Music	1966	7.50	15.00	30.00
—As "The Chapin Brothers"					

CHAPMAN, GRADY

Number	Title (A Side/B Side)	Yr	VG	VG+	NM
45s					
IMPERIAL					
5591	Garden of Memories/Tell Me That You Care	1959	3.00	6.00	12.00
5611	Come Away/Let's Talk About Us	1959	3.00	6.00	12.00
KNIGHT					
2003	Say You Will Be Mine/Starlight, Starbright	1958	7.50	15.00	30.00
MERCURY					
71632	Sweet Thing/I Know What I Want	1960	3.00	6.00	12.00
71698	Ambush/My Life Would Be Worth Living	1960	12.50	25.00	50.00
71771	I'll Never Question Your Love/This, That, 'N the Other	1961	3.00	6.00	12.00
MONEY					
204	I Need You So/Don't Blooper	1955	75.00	150.00	300.00
ZEPHYR					
016	My Love Will Never Change/Smiling	1957	7.50	15.00	30.00

CHARGERS, THE
Also see JESSE BELVIN.

Number	Title (A Side/B Side)	Yr	VG	VG+	NM
45s					
RCA VICTOR					
47-7301	Old MacDonald/Dandelion	1958	7.50	15.00	30.00

CHARIOT

Number	Title (A Side/B Side)	Yr	VG	VG+	NM
Albums					
NATIONAL GENERAL					
NG-2003	Chariot	1971	12.50	25.00	50.00

CHARIOTEERS, THE
Also see BILLY WILLIAMS.

Number	Title (A Side/B Side)	Yr	VG	VG+	NM
45s					
COLUMBIA					
1-168	A Kiss and a Rose/A Cottage in Old Donegal	1949	150.00	300.00	600.00
—Microgroove 7-inch, 33 1/3 rpm single					
1-363	This Side of Heaven/Hawaiian Sunset	1949	150.00	300.00	600.00
—Microgroove 7-inch, 33 1/3 rpm single					
JOSIE					
787	I've Got My Heart on My Sleeve/Don't Play No Mambo	1955	20.00	40.00	80.00
MGM					
12569	The Candles/I Didn't Mean to Be Mean to You	1957	20.00	40.00	80.00
RCA VICTOR					
47-6098	Easy Does It/Tremble, Tremble, Tremble	1955	20.00	40.00	80.00
Albums					
COLUMBIA					
CL 6014 [10]	Sweet and Low	1949	75.00	150.00	300.00
HARMONY					
HL 7089 [M]	The Charioteers with Billy Williams	1957	25.00	50.00	100.00

CHARISMA

Number	Title (A Side/B Side)	Yr	VG	VG+	NM
45s					
ROULETTE					
7075	What's It Like/(B-side unknown)	1970	2.00	4.00	8.00
7096	Bizwambi/(B-side unknown)	1971	2.00	4.00	8.00

Albums

ROULETTE

Number	Title (A Side/B Side)	Yr	VG	VG+	NM
SR-42037	Charisma	1970	5.00	10.00	20.00

CHARITY

45s

Number	Title (A Side/B Side)	Yr	VG	VG+	NM
PHILIPS					
40614	Never Change Your Mind/Windy City Woman	1969	2.50	5.00	10.00
UNI					
55159	Never Change Your Mind/I Still Love You	1969	2.00	4.00	8.00

Albums

Number	Title (A Side/B Side)	Yr	VG	VG+	NM
UNI					
73061	Charity Now	1969	6.25	12.50	25.00

CHARLATANS, THE

45s

Number	Title (A Side/B Side)	Yr	VG	VG+	NM
KAPP					
779	The Shadow Knows/32-20	1967	12.50	25.00	50.00
779 [PS]	The Shadow Knows/32-20	1967	20.00	40.00	80.00
PHILIPS					
40610	High Coin/When I Go Sailin' By	1969	10.00	20.00	40.00
40610 [PS]	High Coin/When I Go Sailin' By	1969	20.00	40.00	80.00
—Sleeve is promo only					
44824 [DJ]	Date: May 19, 1969	1969	15.00	30.00	60.00
—One-sided, promo only					

Albums

Number	Title (A Side/B Side)	Yr	VG	VG+	NM
PHILIPS					
PHS 600309	The Charlatans	1969	25.00	50.00	100.00

CHARLENE

45s

Number	Title (A Side/B Side)	Yr	VG	VG+	NM
ARIOLA AMERICA					
7696	Are You Free/We Know	1977	—	2.50	5.00
MOTOWN					
1262	Give It One More Try/Relove	1973	2.00	4.00	8.00
1285	All That Love Went to Waste/Give It One More Try	1973	2.00	4.00	8.00
1492	Hungry/I Won't Remember Ever Loving You	1980	—	2.00	4.00
1611	I've Never Been to Me/Somewhere in My Life	1982	—	—	3.00
1621	Nunca He Ido A Mi/If I Could See Myself	1982	—	2.00	4.00
1663	I Want to Go Back There Again/Richie's Song	1983	—	—	3.00
1734	We're Both in Love with You/I Want the World to Know He's Mine	1984	—	—	3.00
1761	Hit and Run Lover/Last Song	1984	—	—	3.00
PRODIGAL					
0632	It Ain't Easy Coming Down/On My Way to You	1977	—	2.50	5.00
0633	Freddie/(B-side unknown)	1977	—	2.50	5.00
0633 [PS]	Freddie/(B-side unknown)	1977	2.00	5.00	10.00
0636	I've Never Been to Me/It's Really Nice to Be in Love Again	1977	5.00	10.00	20.00

Albums

Number	Title (A Side/B Side)	Yr	VG	VG+	NM
MOTOWN					
6007 ML	Charlene	1981	2.50	5.00	10.00
6027 ML	Used to Be	1982	2.50	5.00	10.00
6090 ML	Hit and Run Lover	1985	2.50	5.00	10.00
PRODIGAL					
P6-10015	Charlene	1976	5.00	10.00	20.00
P6-10018	Songs of Love	1977	5.00	10.00	20.00

CHARLENE WITH STEVIE WONDER

Also see each artist's individual listings.

45s

Number	Title (A Side/B Side)	Yr	VG	VG+	NM
MOTOWN					
1650	Used to Be/I Want to Come Back As A Song	1982	—	—	3.00
1650 [PS]	Used to Be/I Want to Come Back As A Song	1982	—	—	3.00

CHARLES, BOBBY

45s

Number	Title (A Side/B Side)	Yr	VG	VG+	NM
BEARSVILLE					
0010	Small Town Talk/Save Me Jesus	1973	—	2.00	4.00
CHESS					
1609	Later Alligator/On Bended Knee	1955	12.50	25.00	50.00
1617	Why Did You Leave/Don't You Know I Love You	1956	12.50	25.00	50.00
1628	Only Time Will Tell/Take It Easy. Greasy	1956	12.50	25.00	50.00
1638	Laura Lee/No Use Knocking	1956	12.50	25.00	50.00
1647	Put Your Arms Around Me/Why Can't You, Honey	1957	10.00	20.00	40.00
1658	No More/You Can Suit Yourself	1957	10.00	20.00	40.00
1670	One Eyed Jack/Yea Yea Baby	1957	10.00	20.00	40.00
IMPERIAL					
5542	Since She's Gone/At the Jamboree	1958	5.00	10.00	20.00
5557	Oh Yeah/Since I Lost You	1958	5.00	10.00	20.00
5579	The Town Is Talking/What Can I Do	1959	5.00	10.00	20.00
5642	Bye Bye Baby/Those Eyes	1960	5.00	10.00	20.00
5681	What a Party/I Just Want You	1960	5.00	10.00	20.00
5691	Four Winds/Nothing Sweet As You	1960	5.00	10.00	20.00
JEWEL					
728	Everybody's Laughing/Everybody Knows	1964	2.50	5.00	10.00
729	Goodnight Irene/I Hope	1964	2.50	5.00	10.00
735	Ain't Misbehavin'/Preacher's Daughter	1964	2.50	5.00	10.00
740	Oh Lonesome Me/One More Glass of Wine	1964	2.50	5.00	10.00
PAULA					
226	The Walk/Worrying Over You	1965	2.50	5.00	10.00

CHARLES, DON

45s

Number	Title (A Side/B Side)	Yr	VG	VG+	NM
WORLD ARTISTS					
1031	She's Mine/Big Talk from a Little Man	1964	2.50	5.00	10.00

CHARLES, JIMMY

45s

Number	Title (A Side/B Side)	Yr	VG	VG+	NM
PROMO					
1002	A Million to One/Hop Scotch Hop	1960	3.75	7.50	15.00
1003	The Age for Love/Follow the Swallow	1960	3.75	7.50	15.00
1003 [PS]	The Age for Love/Follow the Swallow	1960	5.00	10.00	20.00
1004	Santa Won't Be Blue This Christmas/I Saw Mommy Kissing Santa Claus	1960	3.75	7.50	15.00
1004 [PS]	Santa Won't Be Blue This Christmas/I Saw Mommy Kissing Santa Claus	1960	5.00	10.00	20.00
1005	Christmasville U.S.A./A Little White Mouse Called Steve	1960	3.75	7.50	15.00
1005 [PS]	Christmasville U.S.A./A Little White Mouse Called Steve	1960	5.00	10.00	20.00

CHARLES, RAY

Also see BILLY JOEL.

45s

Number	Title (A Side/B Side)	Yr	VG	VG+	NM
ABC					
10808	Let's Go Get Stoned/At the Train	1966	2.00	4.00	8.00
10840	I Chose to Sing the Blues/Hopelessly	1966	2.00	4.00	8.00
10865	Please Say You're Fooling/I Don't Need No Doctor	1966	2.00	4.00	8.00
10901	I Want to Talk About You/Something Inside Me	1967	2.00	4.00	8.00
10938	Here We Go Again/Somebody Ought to Write a Book About It	1967	2.00	4.00	8.00
10970	In the Heat of the Night/Somebody's Got to Change	1967	2.00	4.00	8.00
11009	Yesterday/Never Had Enough of Nothing Yet	1967	2.00	4.00	8.00
11045	That's a Lie/Go On Home	1968	2.00	4.00	8.00
11045 [PS]	That's a Lie/Go On Home	1968	3.75	7.50	15.00
11090	Eleanor Rigby/Understanding	1968	2.00	4.00	8.00
11133	Sweet Young Thing Like You/Listen, They're Playing Our Song	1968	2.00	4.00	8.00
11170	If It Wasn't for Bad Luck/When I Stop Dreaming	1969	2.00	4.00	8.00
—With Jimmy Lewis					
11193	I'll Be Your Servant/I Don't Know What Time It Was	1969	2.00	4.00	8.00
11213	Let Me Love You/I'm Satisfied	1969	2.00	4.00	8.00
11239	We Can Make It/I Can't Stop Loving You Baby	1969	2.00	4.00	8.00
11251	Someone to Watch Over Me/Claudie Mae	1969	2.00	4.00	8.00
11259	Laughin' and Clownin'/That Thing Called Love	1970	2.00	4.00	8.00
11271	If You Were Mine/Till I Can't Take It Anymore	1970	2.00	4.00	8.00
11291	Don't Change on Me/Sweet Memories	1971	2.00	4.00	8.00
11308	Feel So Bad/Your Love Is So Doggone Good	1971	—	3.00	6.00
11317	What Am I Living For/Tired of My Tears	1971	—	3.00	6.00
11329	Look What They've Done to My Song, Ma/America the Beautiful	1972	—	3.00	6.00
11337	Hey Mister/There'll Be No Peace Without All Men as One	1972	—	3.00	6.00
11344	Every Saturday Night/Take Me Home, Country Roads	1973	—	3.00	6.00
11351	I Can Make It Through the Days (But Oh Those Lonely Nights)/Ring of Fire	1973	—	3.00	6.00
ABC-PARAMOUNT					
4801 [S]	Don't Cry Baby/Teardrops from My Eyes	1964	5.00	10.00	20.00
4802 [S]	Baby, Don't You Cry/Cry Me a River	1964	5.00	10.00	20.00
4803 [S]	I Cried for You/Cry	1964	5.00	10.00	20.00
4804 [S]	A Tear Fell/No One to Cry To	1964	5.00	10.00	20.00
4805 [S]	You've Got Me Crying Again/After My Laughter Came Tears	1964	5.00	10.00	20.00
—The above five are 33 1/3 rpm, small hole jukebox singles excerpted from the LP "Sweet and Sour Tears"					
10081	My Baby/Who You Gonna Love	1960	3.75	7.50	15.00
10118	Sticks and Stones/Worried Life Blues	1960	3.00	6.00	12.00
10135	Georgia on My Mind/Carry Me Back to Old Virginny	1960	3.75	7.50	15.00
10141	Them That Got/I Wonder	1960	3.00	6.00	12.00
10164	Ruby/Heard Hearted Woman	1960	3.00	6.00	12.00
10244	Hit the Road Jack/The Danger Zone	1961	3.75	7.50	15.00
10266	Unchain My Heart/But on the Other Hand, Baby	1961	3.75	7.50	15.00
10314	Hide 'Nor Hair/At the Club	1962	3.00	6.00	12.00
10330	I Can't Stop Loving You/Born to Lose	1962	3.75	7.50	15.00
10345	You Don't Know Me/Careless Love	1962	3.75	7.50	15.00
10375	You Are My Sunshine/Your Cheating Heart	1962	3.00	6.00	12.00
10405	Don't Set Me Free/The Brightest Smile in Town	1963	3.00	6.00	12.00
10435	Take These Chains from My Heart/No Letter Today	1963	3.75	7.50	15.00
10453	No One/Without Love (There Is Nothing)	1963	3.00	6.00	12.00
10481	Busted/Making Believe	1963	3.75	7.50	15.00
10509	That Lucky Old Sun/Old Man Time	1963	2.50	5.00	12.00
10530	Baby Don't You Cry/My Heart Cries for You	1964	3.00	6.00	12.00
10557	My Baby Don't Dig Me/Something's Wrong	1964	3.00	6.00	12.00
10571	No One to Cry To/A Tear Fell	1964	3.00	6.00	12.00
10588	Smack Dab in the Middle/I Wake Up Crying	1964	3.00	6.00	12.00
10609	Makin' Whoopee/(Instrumental)	1964	3.00	6.00	12.00
10615	Cry/Teardrops from My Eyes	1965	3.00	6.00	12.00
10649	I Gotta Woman (Part 1)/I Gotta Woman (Part 2)	1965	3.00	6.00	12.00
10663	Without a Song (Part 1)/Without a Song (Part 2)	1965	3.00	6.00	12.00
10700	I'm a Fool to Care/Love's Gonna Live Here	1965	3.00	6.00	12.00
10720	The Cincinnati Kid/That's All I Am to You	1965	3.00	6.00	12.00
10739	Crying Time/When My Dreamboat Comes Home	1965	3.75	7.50	15.00
10785	Together Again/You're Just About to Lose Your Clown	1966	3.00	6.00	12.00
ATLANTIC					
976	Roll with Me Baby/The Midnight Hour	1952	125.00	250.00	500.00
984	The Sun's Gonna Shine Again/Jumpin' in the Morning	1953	100.00	200.00	400.00
999	Mess Around/Funny (But I Still Love You)	1953	50.00	100.00	200.00
1008	Feelin' Sad/Heartbreaker	1953	25.00	50.00	100.00
1021	It Should've Been Me/Sinner's Prayer	1954	12.50	25.00	50.00
1037	Don't You Know/Losing Hand	1954	7.50	15.00	30.00
1050	I've Got a Woman/Come Back	1954	12.50	25.00	50.00
1063	This Little Girl of Mine/A Fool for You	1955	7.50	15.00	30.00
1076	Blackjack/Greenbacks	1955	7.50	15.00	30.00
1085	Drown in My Own Tears/Mary Ann	1956	6.25	12.50	25.00
1096	Hallelujah, I Love Her So/What Would I Do Without You	1956	5.00	10.00	20.00
1108	Lonely Avenue/Leave My Woman Alone	1956	5.00	10.00	20.00

Number	Title (A Side/B Side)	Yr	VG	VG+	NM
1124	I Want to Know/Ain't That Love	1957	5.00	10.00	20.00
1143	It's All Right/Get On the Right Track Baby	1957	5.00	10.00	20.00
1154	Swanee River Rock (Talkin' 'Bout That River)/I Want a Little Girl	1957	5.00	10.00	20.00
1172	Talkin' 'Bout You/What Kind of a Man Are You	1958	3.75	7.50	15.00
1180	Yes Indeed/I Had a Dream	1958	3.75	7.50	15.00
—With the Cookies					
1196	My Bonnie/You Be My Baby	1958	3.75	7.50	15.00
2006	Rockhouse (Part 1)/Rockhouse (Part 2)	1958	3.75	7.50	15.00
2010	(Night Time Is) The Right Time/Tell All the World About You	1959	3.75	7.50	15.00
2022	Tell Me How Do You Feel/That's Enough	1959	3.75	7.50	15.00
2031	What'd I Say (Part I)/What'd I Say (Part II)	1959	5.00	10.00	20.00
2043	I'm Movin' On/I Believe to My Soul	1959	3.00	6.00	12.00
2047	Let the Good Times Roll/Don't Let the Sun Catch You Cryin'	1960	3.00	6.00	12.00
2055	Heartbreaker/Just for a Thrill	1960	3.00	6.00	12.00
2068	Tell the Truth/Sweet Sixteen Bars	1960	3.00	6.00	12.00
2084	Come Rain or Come Shine/Tell Me You'll Wait for Me	1960	3.00	6.00	12.00
2094	Early in the Morning/A Bit of Soul	1961	3.00	6.00	12.00
2106	Am I Blue/It Should've Been Me	1961	3.00	6.00	12.00
2118	I Wonder Who/Hard Times (No One Knows Better Than I)	1961	3.00	6.00	12.00
2174	Carryin' That Load/Feelin' Sad	1963	2.50	5.00	10.00
2239	Talkin' 'Bout You/In a Little Spanish Town	1964	2.50	5.00	10.00
2470	Come Rain or Come Shine/Tell Me You'll Wait for Me	1968	2.50	5.00	10.00
3443	I Can See Clearly Now/Anonymous Love	1977	—	2.50	5.00
3473	A Peace That We Never Could Enjoy/Game Number Nine	1978	—	2.50	5.00
3527	Riding Thumb/You Forgot Your Memories	1978	—	2.50	5.00
3549 [DJ]	Christmas Time (same on both sides)	1978	—	3.00	6.00
—May be promo-only					
3611	Some Enchanted Evening/20th Century Fox	1979	—	2.50	5.00
3634	Just Because/Love Me or Set Me Free	1979	—	2.50	5.00
3762	Compared To What/Now That We've Found Each Other	1980	—	2.50	5.00
5005	Doodlin' (Part 1)/Doodlin' (Part 2)	1960	3.75	7.50	15.00
BARONET					
7111	See See Rider/I Used to be So Happy	1960	3.00	6.00	12.00
7111 [PS]	See See Rider/I Used to be So Happy	1960	6.25	12.50	25.00
COLUMBIA					
03429	String Bean/Born to Love Me	1982	—	2.00	4.00
03810	You Feel Good All Over/ 3/4 Time	1983	—	—	3.00
04083	Ain't Your Memory Got No Pride at All/I Don't Want No Strangers Sleeping in My Bed	1983	—	—	3.00
04297	We Didn't See a Thing/I Wish You Were Here Tonight	1983	—	—	3.00
—A-side with George Jones and Chet Atkins					
04420	Do I Ever Cross Your Mind/They Call It Love	1984	—	—	3.00
04500	Woman (Sensuous Woman)/I Was On Georgia Time	1984	—	—	3.00
04531	Rock and Roll Shoes/Then I'll Be Over You	1984	—	—	3.00
—Ray Charles and B.J. Thomas					
04715	Seven Spanish Angels/Who Cares	1984	—	—	3.00
—A-side with Willie Nelson; B-side with Janie Frickie					
04860	It Ain't Gonna Worry My Mind/Crazy Old Soldier	1985	—	—	3.00
—A-side with Mickey Gilley; B-side with Johnny Cash					
05575	Two Old Cats Like Us/Little Hotel Room	1985	—	—	3.00
—A-side with Hank Williams, Jr.					
06172	Pages of My Mind/Slip Away	1986	—	—	3.00
06370	Dixie Moon/A Little Bit of Heaven	1986	—	—	3.00
08393	Seven Spanish Angels/It Ain't Gonna Worry My Mind	1988	—	—	3.00
—Reissue; A-side with Willie Nelson, B-side with Mickey Gilley					
CROSSOVER					
973	Come Live with Me/Everybody Sing	1973	—	2.50	5.00
974	Louise/Somebody	1974	—	2.50	5.00
981	Living for the City/Then We'll Be Home	1975	—	2.50	5.00
985	America the Beautiful/Sunshine	1976	—	3.00	6.00
—A-side is a different recording than that on the B-side of ABC 11329					
IMPULSE!					
200	One Mint Julep/Let's Go	1961	2.50	5.00	10.00
202	I've Got News for You/I'm Gonna Move to the Outskirts of Town	1961	2.50	5.00	10.00
RCA					
PB-10800	Oh Lawd, I'm On My Way/Oh Bess, Where's My Bess	1976	—	2.50	5.00
ROCKIN'					
504	Walkin' and Talkin' (To Myself)/I'm Wonderin' and Wonderin'	1952	75.00	150.00	300.00
SITTIN' IN WITH					
641	Baby Let Me Hear You Call My Name/Guitar Blues	1952	75.00	150.00	300.00
651	I Can't Do No More/Roly Poly	1952	—	—	—
—Unconfirmed on 45 rpm					
SWING TIME					
250	Baby, Let Me Hold Your Hand/Lonely Boy	1951	125.00	250.00	500.00
—Ray Charles records on Swing Time before 250 are unconfirmed on 45 rpm					
274	Kissa Me Baby/I'm Glad for Your Sake	1952	125.00	250.00	500.00
297	Baby Won't You Please Come Home/Hey Now	1952	—	—	—
—Unconfirmed on 45 rpm					
300	Baby Let Me Hear You Call My Name/Guitar Blues	1952	125.00	250.00	500.00
326	The Snow Is Falling/Misery in My Heart	1953	125.00	250.00	500.00
TANGERINE					
1015	Booty Butt/Sidewinder	1971	—	3.00	6.00
TIME					
1026	I Found My Baby/Guitar Blues	1960	3.75	7.50	15.00
1054	Why Did You Go/Back Home	1962	3.00	6.00	12.00
WARNER BROS.					
18611	A Song for You/I Can't Get Enough	1993	—	—	3.00
49608	Beers to You/Cotton-Eyed Clint	1980	—	2.50	5.00
—A-side: With Clint Eastwood; B-side by Texas Opera Company					

7-Inch Extended Plays

Number	Title (A Side/B Side)	Yr	VG	VG+	NM
ATLANTIC					
EP 587	*Ain't That Love/Greenbacks/Drown in My Own Tears/Hallelujah I Love Her So	1956	25.00	50.00	100.00
EP 587 [PS]	Ray Charles	1956	25.00	50.00	100.00
EP 597	(contents unknown)	1957	25.00	50.00	100.00
EP 597 [PS]	The Great Ray Charles	1957	25.00	50.00	100.00
EP 607	(contents unknown)	1958	25.00	50.00	100.00
EP 607 [PS]	Rock with Ray Charles	1958	25.00	50.00	100.00
EP 619	*Let the Good Times Roll/Come Rain or Come Shine/Don't Let the Sun Catch You Cryin'/Alexander's Ragtime Band	1959	25.00	50.00	100.00
EP 619 [PS]	The Genius of Ray Charles	1959	25.00	50.00	100.00

Albums

Number	Title (A Side/B Side)	Yr	VG	VG+	NM
ABC					
S-335 [S]	The Genius Hits the Road	1967	3.00	6.00	12.00
S-355 [S]	Dedicated to You	1967	3.00	6.00	12.00
S-410 [S]	Modern Sounds in Country and Western Music	1967	3.00	6.00	12.00
S-415 [S]	Ray Charles' Greatest Hits	1967	3.00	6.00	12.00
S-435 [S]	Modern Sounds in Country and Western Music (Volume Two)	1967	3.00	6.00	12.00
S-465 [S]	Ingredients in a Recipe for Soul	1967	3.00	6.00	12.00
S-480 [S]	Sweet & Sour Tears	1967	3.00	6.00	12.00
S-495 [S]	Have a Smile with Me	1967	3.00	6.00	12.00
S-500 [S]	Ray Charles Live in Concert	1967	3.00	6.00	12.00
S-520 [S]	Together Again	1967	3.00	6.00	12.00
—Retitled version of "Country and Western Meets Rhythm and Blues"					
S-544 [S]	Crying Time	1967	3.00	6.00	12.00
550 [M]	Ray's Moods	1966	3.00	6.00	12.00
S-550 [S]	Ray's Moods	1966	3.75	7.50	15.00
590X [(2) M]	A Man and His Soul	1967	3.75	7.50	15.00
S-590X [(2) S]	A Man and His Soul	1967	5.00	10.00	20.00
595 [M]	Ray Charles Invites You to Listen	1967	5.00	10.00	20.00
S-595 [S]	Ray Charles Invites You to Listen	1967	3.75	7.50	15.00
S-625	A Portrait of Ray	1968	3.00	6.00	12.00
S-675	I'm All Yours — Baby!	1969	3.00	6.00	12.00
S-695	Doing His Thing	1969	3.00	6.00	12.00
S-707	Love Country Style	1971	3.00	6.00	12.00
S-726	Volcanic Action of My Soul	1971	3.00	6.00	12.00
H-731 [(2)]	A 25th Anniversary in Show Business Salute to Ray Charles	1971	3.75	7.50	15.00
X-755	A Message from the People	1972	3.00	6.00	12.00
X-765	Through the Eyes of Love	1972	3.00	6.00	12.00
X-781/2 [(2)]	All-Time Great Country & Western Hits	1973	3.75	7.50	15.00
SQBO-91036 [(2)]	The Ray Charles Story	1967	6.25	12.50	25.00
—Capitol Record Club exclusive					
ST-91233 [S]	Ray Charles Invites You to Listen	1967	3.75	7.50	15.00
—Capitol Record Club edition					
ABC-PARAMOUNT					
335 [M]	The Genius Hits the Road	1960	5.00	10.00	20.00
S-335 [S]	The Genius Hits the Road	1960	7.50	15.00	30.00
355 [M]	Dedicated to You	1961	5.00	10.00	20.00
S-355 [S]	Dedicated to You	1961	7.50	15.00	30.00
410 [M]	Modern Sounds in Country and Western Music	1962	6.25	12.50	25.00
S-410 [S]	Modern Sounds in Country and Western Music	1962	7.50	15.00	30.00
415 [M]	Ray Charles' Greatest Hits	1962	5.00	10.00	20.00
S-415 [S]	Ray Charles' Greatest Hits	1962	6.25	12.50	25.00
435 [M]	Modern Sounds in Country and Western Music (Volume Two)	1962	5.00	10.00	20.00
S-435 [S]	Modern Sounds in Country and Western Music (Volume Two)	1962	6.25	12.50	25.00
465 [M]	Ingredients in a Recipe for Soul	1963	5.00	10.00	20.00
S-465 [S]	Ingredients in a Recipe for Soul	1963	6.25	12.50	25.00
480 [M]	Sweet & Sour Tears	1964	5.00	10.00	20.00
S-480 [S]	Sweet & Sour Tears	1964	6.25	12.50	25.00
495 [M]	Have a Smile with Me	1964	5.00	10.00	20.00
S-495 [S]	Have a Smile with Me	1964	6.25	12.50	25.00
500 [M]	Ray Charles Live in Concert	1965	3.75	7.50	15.00
S-500 [S]	Ray Charles Live in Concert	1965	5.00	10.00	20.00
520 [M]	Country & Western Meets Rhythm & Blues	1965	3.75	7.50	15.00
S-520 [S]	Country & Western Meets Rhythm & Blues	1965	5.00	10.00	20.00
544 [M]	Crying Time	1966	3.75	7.50	15.00
S-544 [S]	Crying Time	1966	5.00	10.00	20.00
ST-90144 [S]	Ray Charles Live in Concert	1965	5.00	10.00	20.00
—Capitol Record Club edition					
T-90144 [M]	Ray Charles Live in Concert	1965	5.00	10.00	20.00
—Capitol Record Club edition					
ST-90625 [S]	Crying Time	1966	5.00	10.00	20.00
—Capitol Record Club edition					
T-90625 [M]	Crying Time	1966	5.00	10.00	20.00
—Capitol Record Club edition					
ABC IMPULSE!					
AS-2 [S]	Genius + Soul = Jazz	1968	3.00	6.00	12.00
ARCHIVE OF FOLK AND JAZZ					
244	Ray Charles	1970	3.00	6.00	12.00
292	Ray Charles, Vol. 2	197?	2.50	5.00	10.00
358	Rockin' with Ray	1979	2.50	5.00	10.00
ATLANTIC					
SD 2-503 [(2)]	Ray Charles Live	1973	3.75	7.50	15.00
2-900 [(2) M]	The Ray Charles Story	1962	10.00	20.00	40.00
1259 [M]	The Great Ray Charles	1957	12.50	25.00	50.00
—Black label					
1259 [M]	The Great Ray Charles	1960	6.25	12.50	25.00
—Red and white label, white fan logo on right					
1259 [M]	The Great Ray Charles	1962	5.00	10.00	20.00
—Red and white label, black fan logo on right					
SD 1259 [S]	The Great Ray Charles	1959	12.50	25.00	50.00
—Green label					
SD 1259 [S]	The Great Ray Charles	1960	6.25	12.50	25.00
—Blue and green label, white fan logo on right					
SD 1259 [S]	The Great Ray Charles	1962	5.00	10.00	20.00
—Blue and green label, black fan logo on right					
1289 [M]	Ray Charles at Newport	1958	12.50	25.00	50.00
—Black label					

Number	Title (A Side/B Side)	Yr	VG	VG+	NM
1289 [M]	Ray Charles at Newport	1960	6.25	12.50	25.00
—Red and white label, white fan logo on right					
1289 [M]	Ray Charles at Newport	1962	5.00	10.00	20.00
—Red and white label, black fan logo on right					
SD 1289 [S]	Ray Charles at Newport	1959	12.50	25.00	50.00
—Green label					
SD 1289 [S]	Ray Charles at Newport	1960	6.25	12.50	25.00
—Blue and green label, white fan logo on right					
SD 1289 [S]	Ray Charles at Newport	1962	5.00	10.00	20.00
—Blue and green label, black fan logo on right					
1312 [M]	The Genius of Ray Charles	1960	10.00	20.00	40.00
—Black label					
1312 [M]	The Genius of Ray Charles	1960	10.00	20.00	40.00
—White "bullseye" label					
1312 [M]	The Genius of Ray Charles	1960	6.25	12.50	25.00
—Red and white label, white fan logo on right					
1312 [M]	The Genius of Ray Charles	1962	5.00	10.00	20.00
—Red and white label, black fan logo on right					
SD 1312 [S]	The Genius of Ray Charles	1960	12.50	25.00	50.00
—Green label					
SD 1312 [S]	The Genius of Ray Charles	1960	12.50	25.00	50.00
—White "bullseye" label					
SD 1312 [S]	The Genius of Ray Charles	1960	6.25	12.50	25.00
—Blue and green label, white fan logo on right					
SD 1312 [S]	The Genius of Ray Charles	1962	5.00	10.00	20.00
—Blue and green label, black fan logo on right					
SD 1312 [S]	The Genius of Ray Charles	1968	5.00	10.00	20.00
—Brown and purple label					
1369 [M]	The Genius After Hours	1961	6.25	12.50	25.00
—Red and white label, white fan logo on right					
1369 [M]	The Genius After Hours	1962	5.00	10.00	20.00
—Red and white label, black fan logo on right					
SD 1369 [S]	The Genius After Hours	1961	7.50	15.00	30.00
—Blue and green label, white fan logo on right					
SD 1369 [S]	The Genius After Hours	1962	6.25	12.50	25.00
—Blue and green label, black fan logo on right					
SD 1543	The Best of Ray Charles	1970	3.00	6.00	12.00
3700 [(6)]	Ray Charles: A Life in Music	198?	12.50	25.00	50.00
SD 7101 [S]	The Great Hits of Ray Charles Recorded on 8-Track Stereo	1966	6.25	12.50	25.00
8006 [M]	Ray Charles (Rock and Roll)	1957	22.50	45.00	90.00
—Black label					
8006 [M]	Ray Charles (Rock and Roll)	1960	6.25	12.50	25.00
—Red and white label, white fan logo on right					
8006 [M]	Hallelujah! I Love Her So	1962	5.00	10.00	20.00
—Red and white label, black fan logo on right; retitled version					
8025 [M]	Yes, Indeed!	1958	12.50	25.00	50.00
—Black label; cover has screaming girls					
8025 [M]	Yes, Indeed!	1960	6.25	12.50	25.00
—Red and white label, white fan logo on right; cover has screaming girls					
8025 [M]	Yes, Indeed!	1962	5.00	10.00	20.00
—Red and white label, black fan logo on right; cover has Ray on it					
8029 [M]	What'd I Say	1959	12.50	25.00	50.00
—Black label					
8029 [M]	What'd I Say	1960	10.00	20.00	40.00
—White "bullseye" label					
8029 [M]	What'd I Say	1960	6.25	12.50	25.00
—Red and white label, white fan logo on right					
8029 [M]	What'd I Say	1962	5.00	10.00	20.00
—Red and white label, black fan logo on right					
8039 [M]	Ray Charles In Person	1960	10.00	20.00	40.00
—Black label					
8039 [M]	Ray Charles In Person	1960	6.25	12.50	25.00
—Red and white label, white fan logo on right					
8039 [M]	Ray Charles In Person	1962	5.00	10.00	20.00
—Red and white label, black fan logo on right					
8052 [M]	The Genius Sings the Blues	1961	6.25	12.50	25.00
—Red and white label, white fan logo on right					
8052 [M]	The Genius Sings the Blues	1962	5.00	10.00	20.00
—Red and white label, black fan logo on right					
8054 [M]	Do the Twist!	1961	6.25	12.50	25.00
—Red and white label, white fan logo on right					
8054 [M]	Do the Twist!	1962	5.00	10.00	20.00
—Red and white label, black fan logo on right					
8063 [M]	The Ray Charles Story, Volume 1	1962	5.00	10.00	20.00
8064 [M]	The Ray Charles Story, Volume 2	1962	5.00	10.00	20.00
8083 [M]	The Ray Charles Story, Volume 3	1963	5.00	10.00	20.00
8094 [M]	The Ray Charles Story, Volume 4	1964	5.00	10.00	20.00
SD 8094 [S]	The Ray Charles Story, Volume 4	1964	6.25	12.50	25.00
SD 19142	True to Life	1977	3.00	6.00	12.00
SD 19199	Love and Peace	1978	3.00	6.00	12.00
SD 19251	Ain't It So	1979	3.00	6.00	12.00
SD 19281	Brother Ray Is At It Again	1980	3.00	6.00	12.00
90464	The Genius After Hours	1986	2.50	5.00	10.00
—Reissue					
BARONET					
B-111 [M]	The Artistry of Ray Charles	196?	3.00	6.00	12.00
BS-111 [R]	The Artistry of Ray Charles	196?	2.50	5.00	10.00
B-117 [M]	The Great Ray Charles	196?	3.00	6.00	12.00
BS-117 [R]	The Great Ray Charles	196?	2.50	5.00	10.00
BLUESWAY					
6053	The Genius Live	1973	3.00	6.00	12.00
COLUMBIA					
AS 1920 [DJ]	Friendship Radio Show	1984	5.00	10.00	20.00
FC 38293	Wish You Were Here Tonight	1983	2.50	5.00	10.00
PC 38293	Wish You Were Here Tonight	1985	2.00	4.00	8.00
—Budget-line reissue					
FC 38990	Do I Ever Cross Your Mind	1984	2.50	5.00	10.00
FC 39415	Friendship	1985	2.50	5.00	10.00
FC 40125	The Spirit of Christmas	1985	2.50	5.00	10.00
FC 40338	From the Pages of My Mind	1986	2.50	5.00	10.00
FC 45062	Seven Spanish Angels and Other Hits (1982-1986)	1989	3.00	6.00	12.00
CORONET					
CX-173 [M]	Ray Charles	196?	3.00	6.00	12.00
CXS-173 [R]	Ray Charles	196?	2.50	5.00	10.00
CROSSOVER					
9000	Come Live with Me	1974	3.00	6.00	12.00
9005	Renaissance	1975	3.00	6.00	12.00
9007	My Kind of Jazz, Part 3	1976	3.00	6.00	12.00
DCC COMPACT CLASSICS					
LPZ-2012	Greatest Country and Western Hits	1995	17.50	35.00	70.00
—Audiophile vinyl					
DUNHILL COMPACT CLASSICS					
DZL-038	Genius + Soul = Jazz	1988	3.75	7.50	15.00
—Clear vinyl reissue					
HOLLYWOOD					
504 [M]	The Original Ray Charles	1959	37.50	75.00	150.00
505 [M]	The Fabulous Ray Charles	1959	37.50	75.00	150.00
IMPULSE!					
A-2 [M]	Genius + Soul = Jazz	1961	6.25	12.50	25.00
AS-2 [S]	Genius + Soul = Jazz	1961	7.50	15.00	30.00
INTERMEDIA					
QS-5013	Goin' Down Slow	198?	2.50	5.00	10.00
LONGINES SYMPHONETTE					
95647 [(5)]	The Greatest Hits of Ray Charles	1974	10.00	20.00	40.00
PAIR					
PDL2-1139 [(2)]	The Real Ray Charles	1986	3.00	6.00	12.00
PREMIER					
PM 2004 [M]	The Great Ray Charles	196?	3.00	6.00	12.00
PS 2004 [R]	The Great Ray Charles	196?	2.50	5.00	10.00
PS-6001 [R]	Fantastic Ray Charles	196?	2.50	5.00	10.00
RHINO					
R1-70097	Greatest Hits, Volume 1	1988	2.50	5.00	10.00
R1-70098	Greatest Hits, Volume 2	1988	2.50	5.00	10.00
R1-70099	Modern Sounds in Country and Western Music	1988	2.50	5.00	10.00
TANGERINE					
1512	My Kind of Jazz	1970	3.00	6.00	12.00
1516	My Kind of Jazz No. II	1973	3.00	6.00	12.00
WARNER BROS.					
26343	Would You Believe?	1990	3.75	7.50	15.00

CHARLES, RAY / HARRY BELAFONTE

Also see each artist's individual listings.

Albums

Number	Title (A Side/B Side)	Yr	VG	VG+	NM
CORONET					
CX-203 [M]	The Greatest Ever	196?	3.00	6.00	12.00
CXS-203 [R]	The Greatest Ever	196?	2.50	5.00	10.00

CHARLES, RAY, AND BETTY CARTER

45s

Number	Title (A Side/B Side)	Yr	VG	VG+	NM
ABC-PARAMOUNT					
10298	Baby It's Cold Outside/We'll Be Together Again	1962	2.50	5.00	10.00

Albums

Number	Title (A Side/B Side)	Yr	VG	VG+	NM
ABC					
S-385 [S]	Ray Charles and Betty Carter	1967	5.00	10.00	20.00
—Reissue of ABC-Paramount ABCS-385					
ABC-PARAMOUNT					
ABC-385 [M]	Ray Charles and Betty Carter	1961	10.00	20.00	40.00
ABCS-385 [S]	Ray Charles and Betty Carter	1961	15.00	30.00	60.00
DCC COMPACT CLASSICS					
LPZ-2005	Ray Charles and Betty Carter	1995	20.00	40.00	80.00
—Audiophile vinyl					
DUNHILL COMPACT CLASSICS					
DZL-039	Ray Charles and Betty Carter	1988	3.75	7.50	15.00
—Clear vinyl reissue					

CHARLES, RAY/IVORY JOE HUNTER/JIMMY RUSHING

Also see RAY CHARLES; IVORY JOE HUNTER.

Albums

Number	Title (A Side/B Side)	Yr	VG	VG+	NM
DESIGN					
DLP-909 [M]	Three of a Kind	196?	3.00	6.00	12.00
DLS-909 [R]	Three of a Kind	196?	2.50	5.00	10.00

CHARLES, RAY, AND MILT JACKSON

Albums

Number	Title (A Side/B Side)	Yr	VG	VG+	NM
ATLANTIC					
1279 [M]	Soul Brothers	1958	12.50	25.00	50.00
—Black label					
1279 [M]	Soul Brothers	1960	6.25	12.50	25.00
—Red and white label, white fan logo on right					
1279 [M]	Soul Brothers	1962	5.00	10.00	20.00
—Red and white label, black fan logo on right					
SD 1279 [S]	Soul Brothers	1959	12.50	25.00	50.00
—Green label					
SD 1279 [S]	Soul Brothers	1960	6.25	12.50	25.00
—Blue and green label, white fan logo on right					
SD 1279 [S]	Soul Brothers	1962	5.00	10.00	20.00
—Blue and green label, black fan logo on right					
1360 [M]	Soul Meeting	1961	6.25	12.50	25.00
—Red and white label, white fan logo on right					
1360 [M]	Soul Meeting	1962	5.00	10.00	20.00
—Red and white label, black fan logo on right					
SD 1360 [S]	Soul Meeting	1961	7.50	15.00	30.00
—Blue and green label, white fan logo on right					
SD 1360 [S]	Soul Meeting	1962	6.25	12.50	25.00
—Blue and green label, black fan logo on right					

CHARLES, RAY, AND CLEO LAINE

Albums

Number	Title (A Side/B Side)	Yr	VG	VG+	NM
RCA VICTOR					
CPL2-1831 [(2)]	Porgy & Bess	1976	3.75	7.50	15.00
DJL1-2163	Porgy & Bess	1976	5.00	10.00	20.00
—Promo-only excerpts from 2-record set					

CHARLES, RAY, SINGERS

No relation to the above Ray Charles.

45s

COMMAND

Number	Title (A Side/B Side)	Yr	VG	VG+	NM
4046	Love Me with All Your Heart/Sweet Little Mountain Bird	1964	2.50	5.00	10.00
—The LP title "Something Special for Young Lovers" is in bold, with "The Ray Charles Singers" in tiny print at bottom					
4046	Love Me with All Your Heart/Sweet Little Mountain Bird	1964	—	3.00	6.00
—With the Ray Charles Singers receiving a more "apt" credit					
4049	Al Di La/Till the End of Time	1964	—	3.00	6.00
4057	One More Time/Bluesette	1964	—	3.00	6.00
4059	This Is My Prayer/A Toy for a Boy	1965	—	3.00	6.00
4070	Hey, Pretty Pussycat/The Nut Song	1965	—	3.00	6.00
4073	My Love, Forgive Me/My Guitar and My Song	1965	—	3.00	6.00
4074	Christmas Is a Birthday/A Toy for a Boy	1965	2.50	5.00	10.00
4079	One of Those Songs/To You	1966	—	2.50	5.00
4082	Blue Roses/My World (Il Mondo)	1966	—	2.50	5.00
4085	It's Time to Sing/Promises	1966	—	2.50	5.00
4086	Minneapolis/The Bells	1966	—	2.50	5.00
4090	Don't Cry/There's No Place Like Home	1967	—	2.50	5.00
4092	Birds of a Feather/Step By Step	1967	—	2.50	5.00
4096	Bless Your Heart/Little By Little and Step By Step	1967	—	2.50	5.00
4103	Then You Can Tell Me Goodbye/Blame It on Me	1968	—	2.50	5.00
4105	Take Me Along/Walkin' Lonely	1968	—	2.50	5.00
4115	I Can See It Now/Quiz Me	1968	—	2.50	5.00
4123	I Wish I Knew How It Would Feel to Be Free/Let Go	1969	—	2.00	4.00
4130	Holly/Summer Warning	1969	—	2.00	4.00
4135	Move Me, O Wondrous Music/I'll Fly Away	1969	—	2.00	4.00

DECCA

Number	Title (A Side/B Side)	Yr	VG	VG+	NM
30834	Hip Hop/A Touch of Pink	1959	2.50	5.00	10.00

MGM

Number	Title (A Side/B Side)	Yr	VG	VG+	NM
12068	Autumn Leaves/Early Autumn	1955	2.50	5.00	10.00
12108	Autumn in New York/Autumn in Rome	1955	2.50	5.00	10.00
12217	Spring Is Here/Spring! Spring! Spring!	1956	2.50	5.00	10.00
12274	June Night/When the Red, Red Robin Comes Bob, Bob, Bobbin' Along	1956	2.50	5.00	10.00
12333	September in the Rain/'Tis Autumn	1956	2.50	5.00	10.00
12363	Moonlight in Vermont/Button Up Your Overcoat	1956	2.50	5.00	10.00
12413	I've Got My Love to Keep Me Warm/When Winter Comes	1957	2.50	5.00	10.00
12445	Mam'selle/Madamoiselle de Paris	1957	2.50	5.00	10.00
12470	When It's Springtime in the Rockies/Lovelier Than Ever	1957	2.50	5.00	10.00
12507	Around the World/Take a Trip to Memory Lane	1957	2.50	5.00	10.00
12524	Lazy Afternoon/Mountain Greenery	1957	2.50	5.00	10.00
12563	The Things We Did Last Summer/Shine On Harvest Moon	1957	2.50	5.00	10.00
12606	Let It Snow, Let It Snow, Let It Snow/You're My Girl	1957	3.00	6.00	12.00

7-Inch Extended Plays

MGM

Number	Title (A Side/B Side)	Yr	VG	VG+	NM
X-1503	Here's to My Lady/You Must Have Been a Beautiful Baby//The Very Thought of You/You're Getting to Be a Habit with Me	1957	2.50	5.00	10.00
X-1503 [PS]	Here's to My Lady, Vol. 1	1957	2.50	5.00	10.00

Albums

ABC

Number	Title (A Side/B Side)	Yr	VG	VG+	NM
X-772	Moods of Love	1973	2.50	5.00	10.00

ATCO

Number	Title (A Side/B Side)	Yr	VG	VG+	NM
SD 33-263	Memories of a Middle-Aged Movie Fan	1970	2.50	5.00	10.00

COMMAND

Number	Title (A Side/B Side)	Yr	VG	VG+	NM
33-827 [M]	Something Wonderful	1961	2.50	5.00	10.00
SD 827 [S]	Something Wonderful	1961	3.00	6.00	12.00
33-839 [M]	Rome Revisited	1962	2.50	5.00	10.00
SD 839 [S]	Rome Revisited	1962	3.00	6.00	12.00
33-845 [M]	Paradise Islands	1962	2.50	5.00	10.00
SD 845 [S]	Paradise Islands	1962	3.00	6.00	12.00
33-866 [M]	Something Special for Young Lovers	1964	2.50	5.00	10.00
SD 866 [S]	Something Special for Young Lovers	1964	3.00	6.00	12.00
33-870 [M]	Al-Di-La and Other Extra Special Songs for Young Lovers	1964	2.50	5.00	10.00
SD 870 [S]	Al-Di-La and Other Extra Special Songs for Young Lovers	1964	3.00	6.00	12.00
33-874 [M]	Songs for Lonesome Lovers	1964	2.50	5.00	10.00
SD 874 [S]	Songs for Lonesome Lovers	1964	3.00	6.00	12.00
33-876 [M]	Command Performances	1965	2.50	5.00	10.00
SD 876 [S]	Command Performances	1965	3.00	6.00	12.00
33-886 [M]	Songs for Latin Lovers	1965	2.50	5.00	10.00
SD 886 [S]	Songs for Latin Lovers	1965	3.00	6.00	12.00
33-890 [M]	Young Lovers on Broadway	1965	2.50	5.00	10.00
SD 890 [S]	Young Lovers on Broadway	1965	3.00	6.00	12.00
33-896 [M]	Command Performances Vol. 2	1966	2.50	5.00	10.00
SD 896 [S]	Command Performances Vol. 2	1966	3.00	6.00	12.00
33-898 [M]	One of Those Songs	1966	2.50	5.00	10.00
SD 898 [S]	One of Those Songs	1966	3.00	6.00	12.00
33-903 [M]	What the World Needs Now Is Love	1966	2.50	5.00	10.00
SD 903 [S]	What the World Needs Now Is Love	1966	3.00	6.00	12.00
33-914 [M]	Special Something	1967	3.00	6.00	12.00
SD 914 [S]	Special Something	1967	2.50	5.00	10.00
SD 923	At the Movies	1968	2.50	5.00	10.00
SD 926	Take Me Along	1968	2.50	5.00	10.00
SD 936	MacArthur Park	1969	2.50	5.00	10.00
SD 949	Move Me, O Wondrous Music	1969	2.50	5.00	10.00
CQ-40005 [Q]	Love Me with All of Your Heart	1972	3.75	7.50	15.00

DECCA

Number	Title (A Side/B Side)	Yr	VG	VG+	NM
DL 8787 [M]	Highest Fidelity — Love and Marriage	1958	3.00	6.00	12.00
DL 8838 [M]	Sunrise Serenade	1958	3.00	6.00	12.00
DL 8874 [M]	In the Evening by the Moonlight	1959	3.00	6.00	12.00
DL 8940 [M]	We Gather Together — Beloved Hymns	1959	3.00	6.00	12.00
DL 8988 [M]	Deep Night	1960	3.00	6.00	12.00
DL 78787 [S]	Highest Fidelity — Love and Marriage	1958	3.75	7.50	15.00
DL 78838 [S]	Sunrise Serenade	1958	3.75	7.50	15.00
DL 78874 [S]	In the Evening by the Moonlight	1959	3.75	7.50	15.00
DL 78940 [S]	We Gather Together — Beloved Hymns	1959	3.75	7.50	15.00
DL 78988 [S]	Deep Night	1960	3.75	7.50	15.00

MCA

Number	Title (A Side/B Side)	Yr	VG	VG+	NM
4162 [(2)]	The Best of the Ray Charles Singers	1980	2.50	5.00	10.00

METRO

Number	Title (A Side/B Side)	Yr	VG	VG+	NM
M-507 [M]	Spring, Spring, Spring	1965	2.50	5.00	10.00
MS-507 [S]	Spring, Spring, Spring	1965	2.50	5.00	10.00

MGM

Number	Title (A Side/B Side)	Yr	VG	VG+	NM
E-3387 [M]	Winter Wonderland	1956	3.75	7.50	15.00
—Yellow label					
E-3387 [M]	Winter Wonderland	1960	3.00	6.00	12.00
—Black label					
E-3568 [M]	Here's to My Lady	1957	3.75	7.50	15.00
—Yellow label					
E-3568 [M]	Here's to My Lady	1960	3.00	6.00	12.00
—Black label					
E-4163 [M]	Autumn Moods	1963	3.00	6.00	12.00
SE-4163 [S]	Autumn Moods	1963	3.00	6.00	12.00
E-4164 [M]	Songs for a Lazy Summer Afternoon	1963	3.00	6.00	12.00
SE-4164 [S]	Songs for a Lazy Summer Afternoon	1963	3.00	6.00	12.00
E-4165 [M]	We Love Paris	1963	3.00	6.00	12.00
SE-4165 [S]	We Love Paris	1963	3.00	6.00	12.00
E-4166 [M]	Christmas at Home	1963	3.00	6.00	12.00
SE-4166 [S]	Christmas at Home	1963	3.00	6.00	12.00
E-4257 [M]	The Very Best of the Ray Charles Singers	1964	3.00	6.00	12.00
SE-4257 [S]	The Very Best of the Ray Charles Singers	1964	3.00	6.00	12.00

SOMERSET

Number	Title (A Side/B Side)	Yr	VG	VG+	NM
P-21400 [M]	Quiet Moments for Young Lovers	196?	2.50	5.00	10.00
SF-21400 [S]	Quiet Moments for Young Lovers	196?	2.50	5.00	10.00
P-21500 [M]	Young Lovers in Far Away Places	196?	2.50	5.00	10.00
SF-21500 [S]	Young Lovers in Far Away Places	196?	2.50	5.00	10.00

VOCALION

Number	Title (A Side/B Side)	Yr	VG	VG+	NM
VL 3784 [M]	Love Is a Many-Splendored Thing	196?	2.50	5.00	10.00
VL 73784 [S]	Love Is a Many-Splendored Thing	196?	2.50	5.00	10.00

CHARLES, SONNY

Also see THE CHECKMATES LTD.

45s

FRATERNITY

Number	Title (A Side/B Side)	Yr	VG	VG+	NM
935	Speechless/These Two Feet	1964	4.00	8.00	12.00

HIGHRISE

Number	Title (A Side/B Side)	Yr	VG	VG+	NM
2001	Put It in a Magazine/Week-End Father Song	1982	—	2.00	4.00
2006	Always on My Mind/One-Eyed Jacks	1983	—	2.00	4.00

RCA VICTOR

Number	Title (A Side/B Side)	Yr	VG	VG+	NM
74-0645	It's Alright in the City/Nicasio	1972	—	3.00	6.00

Albums

HIGHRISE

Number	Title (A Side/B Side)	Yr	VG	VG+	NM
102	The Sun Still Shines	1982	2.50	5.00	10.00

CHARLES AND CARL

45s

RED ROBIN

Number	Title (A Side/B Side)	Yr	VG	VG+	NM
137	Lucky Star/One More Chance	1955	25.00	50.00	100.00

CHARLES RIVER VALLEY BOYS, THE

Albums

ELEKTRA

Number	Title (A Side/B Side)	Yr	VG	VG+	NM
EKL-4006 [M]	Beatle Country	1967	5.00	10.00	20.00
EKS-74006 [S]	Beatle Country	1967	6.25	12.50	25.00

CHARLETTES, THE

45s

ANGIE

Number	Title (A Side/B Side)	Yr	VG	VG+	NM
1002	The Fight's Not Over/Whatever Happened to Our Love	1963	6.25	12.50	25.00

CHARMAINES, THE

45s

DOT

Number	Title (A Side/B Side)	Yr	VG	VG+	NM
16351	Where Is the Boy Tonight/On the Wagon	1961	5.00	10.00	20.00

CHARMERS, THE (1)

Female group.

45s

ALADDIN

Number	Title (A Side/B Side)	Yr	VG	VG+	NM
3337	All Alone/Johnny My Dear	1956	15.00	30.00	60.00
3341	He's Gone/Oh! Yes	1956	15.00	30.00	60.00

IMPERIAL

Number	Title (A Side/B Side)	Yr	VG	VG+	NM
5957	All Alone/Johnny My Dear	1963	3.00	6.00	12.00
—Reissue of Aladdin 3337					

CHARMERS, THE (2)

Another female group, but not the same as group (1).

45s

CENTRAL

Number	Title (A Side/B Side)	Yr	VG	VG+	NM
1002	The Beating of My Heart/Why Does It Have to Be Me	1954	200.00	400.00	800.00
1006	Tony, My Darling/In the Rain	1954	250.00	500.00	1000.

TIMELY

Number	Title (A Side/B Side)	Yr	VG	VG+	NM
1009	I Was Wrong/The Mambo	1955	250.00	500.00	1000.
1011	The Church on the Hill/Battle Axe	1955	250.00	500.00	1000.

CHARMERS, THE (U)

Probably none of these are group (1) or (2), but which ones go together, we don't yet know.

45s

CO-REC

Number	Title (A Side/B Side)	Yr	VG	VG+	NM
101	The Letter/Watch What You Do	1963	5.00	10.00	20.00

JAF

Number	Title (A Side/B Side)	Yr	VG	VG+	NM
2021	Little Fool/Hard to Get	1961	6.25	12.50	25.00

Number	Title (A Side/B Side)	Yr	VG	VG+	NM
LAURIE					
3142	My Kind of Love/Johnny	1962	5.00	10.00	20.00
3173	Shy Guy/I Cried	1963	5.00	10.00	20.00
3203	Work It Out/Sweet Talk	1963	5.00	10.00	20.00
LOUIS					
6806	It's a Funny Way We Met/Where's the Boy	1965	3.00	6.00	12.00
PIP					
8000	Looking for Trouble/After You Walk Me Home	1964	3.00	6.00	12.00
SILHOUETTE					
522	Rock, Rhythm and Blues/Letters Don't Have Arms	1957	15.00	30.00	60.00
SURE SHOT					
104	Lessons from the Stars/My Love	1963	75.00	150.00	300.00
TERRACE					
7512	Visiting Day/Whatever Happened to Baby Jane	1962	6.25	12.50	25.00

CHARMETTES, THE

45s

Number	Title (A Side/B Side)	Yr	VG	VG+	NM
FEDERAL					
12345	Johnny, Johnny/School Letter	1959	10.00	20.00	40.00
HI					
2003	My Love with All My Heart/Skating in Blue Light	1958	5.00	10.00	20.00
KAPP					
547	Please Don't Kiss Me Again/What Is a Tear	1963	7.50	15.00	30.00
570	Oozi-Oozi-Ooh/He's a Wise Guy	1964	6.25	12.50	25.00
MALA					
491	My Lover Is a Boy Scout/Mailbox	1964	3.00	6.00	12.00
TRI-DISC					
103	Why Oh Why/On a Night Like Tonight	1962	6.25	12.50	25.00
WORLD ARTISTS					
1053	Stop the Wedding (Preacher Man)/Sugar Boy	1965	6.25	12.50	25.00

CHARMS, THE

Also see OTIS WILLIAMS AND THE CHARMS.

45s

Number	Title (A Side/B Side)	Yr	VG	VG+	NM
CHART					
608	Love's Our Inspiration/Love, Love Stick Stov	1956	10.00	20.00	40.00
613	Heart of a Rose/I Offer You	1956	10.00	20.00	40.00
623	I'll Be True/Boom Diddy Boom Boom	1956	10.00	20.00	40.00
DELUXE					
6000	Heaven Only Knows/Loving Baby	1953	125.00	250.00	500.00
6014	Happy Are We/What Do You Know About That	1953	100.00	200.00	400.00
6034	Bye Bye Baby/Please Believe in Me	1954	100.00	200.00	400.00
6050	Quiet Please/55 Seconds	1954	100.00	200.00	400.00
6056	Come to Me Baby/My Baby, Dearest Darling	1954	50.00	100.00	200.00
6062	Hearts of Stone/Who Knows	1954	12.50	25.00	50.00
6065	Two Hearts/The First Time We Met	1954	12.50	25.00	50.00
6072	Crazy, Crazy Love/Mambo Sh-Mambo	1955	12.50	25.00	50.00
6076	Ling, Ting, Tong/Bazoom (I Need Your Lovin')	1955	12.50	25.00	50.00
6080	Ko Ko Mo (I Love You So)/Whadya Want?	1955	12.50	25.00	50.00
6082	Whadya Want?/Crazy, Crazy Love	1955	10.00	20.00	40.00
6087	When We Get Married/Let the Happenings Happen	1955	10.00	20.00	40.00
6089	One Fine Day/It's You, You, You	1955	10.00	20.00	40.00
ROCKIN'					
516	Heaven Only Knows/Loving Baby	1953	200.00	400.00	800.00

CHARTERS, THE

May all be the same group.

45s

Number	Title (A Side/B Side)	Yr	VG	VG+	NM
ALVA					
1001	I Lost You/My Little Girl	1963	75.00	150.00	300.00
MEL-O-DY					
104	Trouble Lover/Show Me Some Sign	1962	500.00	1000.	2000.
MERRY-GO-ROUND					
103	Lost in a Dream/This Makes Me Mad	1963	15.00	30.00	60.00
TARX					
1003	My Rose/El Merengue	1962	25.00	50.00	100.00

CHARTS, THE

45s

Number	Title (A Side/B Side)	Yr	VG	VG+	NM
EVERLAST					
5001	Deserie/Zoop	1957	20.00	40.00	80.00
5002	Dance Girl/Why Do You Cry	1957	20.00	40.00	80.00
5006	You're the Reason (I'm in Love)/I've Been Wondering	1958	15.00	30.00	60.00
5008	I Told You So/All Because of Love	1958	15.00	30.00	60.00
5010	My Diane/All Because of You	1958	17.50	35.00	70.00
5026	Deserie/Zoop	1963	6.25	12.50	25.00
GUYDEN					
2021	For the Birds/Ooba-Gooba	1959	5.00	10.00	20.00
WAND					
1112	Deserie/Fell in Love with Your Baby	1966	6.25	12.50	25.00
1124	Livin' the Night Life/Nobody Made You Love Me	1966	15.00	30.00	60.00

Albums

Number	Title (A Side/B Side)	Yr	VG	VG+	NM
COLLECTABLES					
COL-5029	Greatest Hits	1986	3.00	6.00	12.00
LOST-NITE					
LLP-10 [10]	The Charts	1981	3.00	6.00	12.00
—Red vinyl					

CHASE

45s

Number	Title (A Side/B Side)	Yr	VG	VG+	NM
EPIC					
10738	Get It On/River	1971	—	2.50	5.00
10775	Handbags and Gladrags/Open Up Wide	1971	—	2.00	4.00
10806	So Many People/Paint It Sad	1971	—	2.00	4.00
10853	I Can Feel It/Cronus (Saturn)	1972	—	2.00	4.00
11113	Run Back to Mama/Weird Song Number 1	1974	—	2.00	4.00
50027	Love Is on the Way/Bochawa	1974	—	2.00	4.00

Albums

Number	Title (A Side/B Side)	Yr	VG	VG+	NM
EPIC					
E 30472	Chase	1971	3.00	6.00	12.00
EQ 30472 [Q]	Chase	1973	5.00	10.00	20.00
KE 31097	Ennea	1972	3.00	6.00	12.00
EQ 32572 [Q]	Pure Music	1974	5.00	10.00	20.00
KE 32572	Pure Music	1974	3.00	6.00	12.00
EG 33737 [(2)]	Chase/Ennea	1976	3.75	7.50	15.00

CHAVELLES, THE

45s

Number	Title (A Side/B Side)	Yr	VG	VG+	NM
VITA					
127	Valley of Love/Red Tape	1956	37.50	75.00	150.00

CHAVIS BROTHERS, THE

45s

Number	Title (A Side/B Side)	Yr	VG	VG+	NM
ASCOT					
2177	Torture Me/Humpty Dumpty Time	1965	3.00	6.00	12.00
CLOCK					
1025	I Love You/So Tired	1960	6.25	12.50	25.00
CORAL					
62270	Old Time Rock and Roll/Baby, Don't Leave Me	1961	7.50	15.00	30.00
—As "The Five Chavis Brothers"					
PARKWAY					
851	Slippin' and Slidin'/Good Old Mountain Dew	1962	3.75	7.50	15.00

CHECKER, CHUBBY

Also see BOBBY RYDELL; DEE DEE SHARP.

45s

Number	Title (A Side/B Side)	Yr	VG	VG+	NM
20TH CENTURY					
2040	Reggae My Way/Gypsy	1973	—	2.50	5.00
2075	She's a Bad Woman/Happiness Is a Girl Like You	1974	—	2.50	5.00
ABKCO					
4001	The Twist/Loddy Lo	1972	—	2.50	5.00
4002	The Hucklebuck/Pony Time	1972	—	2.50	5.00
4003	Limbo Rock/Let's Limbo Some More	1972	—	2.50	5.00
4004	Hey Bobba Needle/Hooka Tooka	1972	—	2.50	5.00
4027	Slow Twistin'/Birdland	1973	—	2.50	5.00
AMHERST					
716	The Rub/Move It	1976	—	2.00	4.00
BUDDAH					
100	Back in the U.S.S.R./Windy Cream	1969	3.00	6.00	12.00
MCA					
51233	Running/Is Tonight the Night	1982	—	2.50	5.00
52015	Running/Is Tonight the Night	1982	—	2.00	4.00
52043	Harder Than Diamond/Your Love	1982	—	2.00	4.00
PARKWAY					
003 [DJ]	Never on Sunday/Alouette	1962	10.00	20.00	40.00
—Yellow label, black print, promo only					
004 [DJ]	Love Is Like a Twist/Peppermint Twist	1962	10.00	20.00	40.00
—Yellow label, black print, promo only					
005 [DJ]	Your Lips and Mine/Dear Lady Twist	1962	10.00	20.00	40.00
—Yellow label, black print, promo only					
006 [DJ]	The Jet/The Ray Charles-ton	1962	7.50	15.00	30.00
105	You Got the Power/Looking at Tomorrow	1966	3.75	7.50	15.00
112	Karate Monkey/Her Heart	1966	3.75	7.50	15.00
804	The Class/Schooldays, Oh Schooldays	1959	7.50	15.00	30.00
808	Samson and Delilah/Whole Lotta Laughin'	1959	6.25	12.50	25.00
810	Dancing Dinosaur/Those Private Eyes (Keep Watchin' Me)	1960	6.25	12.50	25.00
—The existence of both 808 and 810 has been confirmed since the last edition					
811	The Twist/Toot	1960	7.50	15.00	30.00
—First pressings have white label with blue print					
811	The Twist/Toot	1960	5.00	10.00	20.00
—Second pressings have orange label with black print					
811	The Twist/Twistin' U.S.A.	1961	3.75	7.50	15.00
811 [DJ]	The Twist/Twistin' U.S.A.	1961	50.00	100.00	200.00
—Promo copy on red vinyl					
811 [DJ]	The Twist/Twistin' U.S.A.	1961	37.50	75.00	150.00
—Promo copy on yellow vinyl					
811 [PS]	The Twist/Twistin' U.S.A.	1961	6.25	12.50	25.00
813	The Hucklebuck/Whole Lotta Shakin' Goin' On	1960	3.75	7.50	15.00
818	Pony Time/Oh, Susannah	1960	3.75	7.50	15.00
822	Dance the Mess Around/Good, Good Lovin'	1961	3.75	7.50	15.00
824	Let's Twist Again/Everything's Gonna Be Alright	1961	3.75	7.50	15.00
824 [PS]	Let's Twist Again/Everything's Gonna Be Alright	1961	6.25	12.50	25.00
830	The Fly/That's the Way It Goes	1961	3.75	7.50	15.00
830 [PS]	The Fly/That's the Way It Goes	1961	6.25	12.50	25.00
835	Slow Twistin'/La Paloma Twist	1962	3.75	7.50	15.00
—Features female vocal by Dee Dee Sharp					
835 [PS]	Slow Twistin'/La Paloma Twist	1962	6.25	12.50	25.00
842	Dancin' Party/Gotta Get Myself Together	1962	3.75	7.50	15.00
842 [PS]	Dancin' Party/Gotta Get Myself Together	1962	6.25	12.50	25.00
849	Limbo Rock/Popeye The Hitch-Hiker	1962	3.75	7.50	15.00
849 [PS]	Limbo Rock/Popeye The Hitch-Hiker	1962	6.25	12.50	25.00
862	Twenty Miles/Let's Limbo Some More	1963	3.75	7.50	15.00
862 [PS]	Twenty Miles/Let's Limbo Some More	1963	6.25	12.50	25.00
873	Birdland/Black Cloud	1963	3.75	7.50	15.00
873 [PS]	Birdland/Black Cloud	1963	6.25	12.50	25.00
879	Surf Party/Twist It Up	1963	3.75	7.50	15.00
879 [PS]	Surf Party/Twist It Up	1963	6.25	12.50	25.00
890	Loddy Lo/Everything's Gonna Be Alright	1963	4.00	8.00	16.00
890	Loddy Lo/Hooka Tooka	1963	3.75	7.50	15.00
890 [PS]	Loddy Lo/Everything's Gonna Be Alright	1963	7.00	14.00	28.00
890 [PS]	Loddy Lo/Hooka Tooka	1963	6.25	12.50	25.00
907	Hey Bobba Needle/Spread Joy	1964	3.75	7.50	15.00
907 [PS]	Hey Bobba Needle/Spread Joy	1964	6.25	12.50	25.00
920	Lazy Elsie Molly/Rosie	1964	3.75	7.50	15.00
920 [PS]	Lazy Elsie Molly/Rosie	1964	6.25	12.50	25.00
922	She Wants T'Swim/You Better Believe It, Baby	1964	3.00	6.00	12.00
922 [PS]	She Wants T'Swim/You Better Believe It, Baby	1964	6.25	12.50	25.00
936	Lovely, Lovely (Loverly, Loverly)/The Weekend's Here	1964	3.00	6.00	12.00

Number	Title (A Side/B Side)	Yr	VG	VG+	NM
936 [PS]	Lovely, Lovely (Loverly, Loverly)/The Weekend's Here	1964	6.25	12.50	25.00
949	Let's Do the Freddie/(At the) Discoteque	1965	3.00	6.00	12.00
959	Everything's Wrong/Cu Me La Be-Stay	1965	3.00	6.00	12.00
965	You Just Don't Know/Two Hearts Make One Love	1965	50.00	100.00	200.00
989	Hey You! Little Boo-Ga-Loo/Pussy Cat	1966	3.00	6.00	12.00
SEA BRIGHT					
5128	Read You Like a Book/(B-side unknown)	1986	—	2.00	4.00
TIN PAN APPLE					
887571-7	The Twist (Yo, Twist!)/The Twist (Buffapella)	1988	—	—	3.00
—"Stupid def vocals" on a Fat Boys record					
887571-7 [PS]	The Twist (Yo, Twist!)/The Twist (Buffapella)	1988	—	—	3.00

7-Inch Extended Plays

Number	Title (A Side/B Side)	Yr	VG	VG+	NM
PARKWAY					
5001	The Ray Charles-ton/The Mess Around//The Jet/ The Continental Walk	1961	15.00	30.00	60.00
—Small hole, plays at 33 1/3 rpm					
5001 [PS]	Chubby Checker	1961	15.00	30.00	60.00
—Paper die-cut sleeve					

Albums

Number	Title (A Side/B Side)	Yr	VG	VG+	NM
ABKCO					
4219 [(2)]	Chubby Checker's Greatest Hits	1972	5.00	10.00	20.00
EVEREST					
4111	Chubby Checker's Greatest Hits	1981	3.00	6.00	12.00
MCA					
5291	The Change Has Come	1982	2.50	5.00	10.00
PARKWAY					
P 7001 [M]	Twist with Chubby Checker	1960	10.00	20.00	40.00
—All-orange label					
P 7001 [M]	Twist with Chubby Checker	1962	7.50	15.00	30.00
—Orange and yellow label					
P 7002 [M]	For Twisters Only	1960	10.00	20.00	40.00
—All-orange label					
P 7002 [M]	For Twisters Only	1962	7.50	15.00	30.00
—Orange and yellow label					
P 7003 [M]	It's Pony Time	1961	10.00	20.00	40.00
—All-orange label					
P 7003 [M]	It's Pony Time	1962	7.50	15.00	30.00
—Orange and yellow label					
P 7004 [M]	Let's Twist Again	1961	10.00	20.00	40.00
—All-orange label					
P 7004 [M]	Let's Twist Again	1962	7.50	15.00	30.00
—Orange and yellow label					
P 7007 [M]	Your Twist Party	1961	10.00	20.00	40.00
—All-orange label					
P 7007 [M]	Your Twist Party	1962	7.50	15.00	30.00
—Orange and yellow label					
P 7008 [M]	Twistin' Round the World	1962	7.50	15.00	30.00
SP 7008 [B]	Twistin' Round the World	1962	10.00	20.00	40.00
P 7009 [M]	For Teen Twisters Only	1962	7.50	15.00	30.00
SP 7009 [S]	For Teen Twisters Only	1962	10.00	20.00	40.00
P 7014 [M]	All the Hits (For Your Dancin' Party)	1962	7.50	15.00	30.00
P 7020 [M]	Limbo Party	1962	7.50	15.00	30.00
SP 7020 [S]	Limbo Party	1962	10.00	20.00	40.00
P 7022 [M]	Chubby Checker's Biggest Hits	1962	7.50	15.00	30.00
SP 7022 [R]	Chubby Checker's Biggest Hits	1962	7.50	15.00	30.00
P 7026 [M]	Chubby Checker In Person	1963	7.50	15.00	30.00
SP 7026 [S]	Chubby Checker In Person	1963	10.00	20.00	40.00
—The above record is labeled "Twist It Up"					
P 7027 [M]	Let's Limbo Some More	1963	7.50	15.00	30.00
SP 7027 [S]	Let's Limbo Some More	1963	10.00	20.00	40.00
P 7030 [M]	Beach Party	1963	7.50	15.00	30.00
SP 7030 [S]	Beach Party	1963	10.00	20.00	40.00
P 7036 [M]	Chubby Checker With Sy Oliver and His Orchestra	1964	7.50	15.00	30.00
SP 7036 [S]	Chubby Checker With Sy Oliver and His Orchestra	1964	10.00	20.00	40.00
P 7040 [M]	Folk Album	1964	7.50	15.00	30.00
SP 7040 [S]	Folk Album	1964	10.00	20.00	40.00
P 7045 [M]	Discotheque	1965	7.50	15.00	30.00
SP 7045 [S]	Discotheque	1965	10.00	20.00	40.00
P 7048 [M]	Chubby Checker's Eighteen Golden Hits	1966	7.50	15.00	30.00
SP 7048 [P]	Chubby Checker's Eighteen Golden Hits	1966	10.00	20.00	40.00

CHECKERLADS, THE

45s

Number	Title (A Side/B Side)	Yr	VG	VG+	NM
RCA VICTOR					
47-8986	Shake Yourself Down/Baby Send for Me	1966	6.25	12.50	25.00

CHECKERS, THE (1)

45s

Number	Title (A Side/B Side)	Yr	VG	VG+	NM
FEDERAL					
12355	So Fine/Sentimental Heart	1959	12.50	25.00	50.00
12375	White Cliffs of Dover/Let Me Come Back	1960	12.50	25.00	50.00
KING					
4558	Flame in My Heart/Oh, Oh, Oh Baby	1952	250.00	500.00	1000.
4581	Night's Curtains/Let Me Come Back	1952	250.00	500.00	1000.
4596	My Prayer Tonight/Love Wasn't There	1953	250.00	500.00	1000.
4626	Ghost of My Baby/I Wanna Know	1953	200.00	400.00	800.00
4673	I Promise You/You Never Had It So Good	1953	125.00	250.00	500.00
4675	White Cliffs of Dover/Without a Song	1953	125.00	250.00	500.00
4710	House with No Windows/Don't Stop Dan	1954	125.00	250.00	500.00
4719	Over the Rainbow/You've Been Fooling Around	1954	100.00	200.00	400.00
4751	I Wasn't Thinking, I Was Drinking/Mama's Daughter	1954	125.00	250.00	500.00
4764	Trying to Hold My Girl/Can't Find My Sadie	1955	125.00	250.00	500.00
5156	Heaven Only Knows/Nine More Miles	1958	100.00	200.00	400.00
5592	Over the Rainbow/Love Wasn't There	1962	5.00	10.00	20.00
—As "The Original Checkers"					

CHECKERS, THE (2)

Different group than (1).

45s

Number	Title (A Side/B Side)	Yr	VG	VG+	NM
ARVEE					
5035	Skooby Doo (Part 1)/Skooby Doo (Part 2)	1961	5.00	10.00	20.00
5037	Swingin' Summer/Skooby Doo	1961	5.00	10.00	20.00

CHECKERS, THE (3)

Not the same group as (1) though on the same label. Also see THE FIVE WINGS.

45s

Number	Title (A Side/B Side)	Yr	VG	VG+	NM
KING					
5199	Teardrops Are Falling/Rock-A-Locka	1959	15.00	30.00	60.00
—Originally released as King 4781 by The Five Wings					

CHECKERS, THE (U)

Some of these may be the same group as (2), but not all of them.

45s

Number	Title (A Side/B Side)	Yr	VG	VG+	NM
DOTTIE					
1001	Big Car/Buzz	196?	5.00	10.00	20.00
JERDEN					
710	Black Cat/Soft Blue	1963	5.00	10.00	20.00
MERCURY					
72354	Red Ball Express/Come Back Home	1964	3.00	6.00	12.00
SKYLA					
1120	Blue Saturday/Cascade	1961	5.00	10.00	20.00

CHECKMATES, THE

Albums

Number	Title (A Side/B Side)	Yr	VG	VG+	NM
JUSTICE					
JLP-149	The Checkmates	1966	100.00	200.00	400.00

CHECKMATES LTD., THE

Also see SONNY CHARLES.

45s

Number	Title (A Side/B Side)	Yr	VG	VG+	NM
A&M					
1006	Spanish Harlem/Baby Don't You Get Crazy	1968	2.00	4.00	8.00
1040	Love Is All I Have to Give/Never Should Have Lied	1969	2.00	4.00	8.00
1053	Black Pearl/Lazy Susan	1969	2.50	5.00	10.00
—As "Sonny Charles and the Checkmates Ltd."					
1127	Spanish Harlem/Proud Mary	1969	2.00	4.00	8.00
—As "Sonny Charles and the Checkmates Ltd."					
1130	Proud Mary/Do You Love Your Baby	1969	2.00	4.00	8.00
—As "Sonny Charles and the Checkmates Ltd."					
CAPITOL					
5603	Do the Walk/Glad for You	1966	5.00	10.00	20.00
5753	I Can Hear the Rain/Kissin' Her and Cryin' for You	1966	7.50	15.00	30.00
5814	Please Don't Take My World Away/Mastered the Art of Love	1966	5.00	10.00	20.00
5922	Walk in the Sunlight/A & I	1967	5.00	10.00	20.00
FANTASY					
800	Let's Do It/Take All the Time You Need	1977	—	2.50	5.00
823	Greedy for Your Love/That's How It Feels (When Two People Fall in Love)	1978	—	2.50	5.00
GREEDY					
111	I'm Laying My Heart on the Line/Make Love to Your Mind	1977	—	2.50	5.00
POLYDOR					
14313	All Alone by the Telephone/Body Language	1976	—	2.50	5.00

Albums

Number	Title (A Side/B Side)	Yr	VG	VG+	NM
A&M					
SP-4183	Love Is All I Have to Give	1969	6.25	12.50	25.00
CAPITOL					
ST 2840 [S]	Live at Caesar's Palace	1968	5.00	10.00	20.00
T 2840 [M]	Live at Caesar's Palace	1968	7.50	15.00	30.00
FANTASY					
9541	We Got the Moves	1978	3.75	7.50	15.00

CHEECH AND CHONG

45s

Number	Title (A Side/B Side)	Yr	VG	VG+	NM
MCA					
52655	Born in East L.A./I'm a (Modern) Man	1985	—	—	3.00
52655 [PS]	Born in East L.A./I'm a (Modern) Man	1985	—	2.00	4.00
52732	I'm Not Home Right Now/Hot Saki	1985	—	—	3.00
ODE					
50471	Bloat On (Featuring the Bloaters)/Just Say "Right On"	1977	—	2.00	4.00
50471 [PS]	Bloat On (Featuring the Bloaters)/Just Say "Right On"	1977	—	3.00	6.00
50499	Santa Claus and His Old Lady/Rudolph the Red-Nosed Reindeer	1977	2.50	5.00	10.00
66021	Santa Claus and His Old Lady/Dave	1971	2.00	4.00	8.00
66021 [PS]	Santa Claus and His Old Lady/Dave	1971	3.00	6.00	12.00
66038	Basketball Jones/Don't Bug Me	1973	—	2.50	5.00
66038 [PS]	Basketball Jones/Don't Bug Me	1973	—	3.00	6.00
66041	Sister Mary Elephant/Wink Dinkerson	1974	—	2.50	5.00
66041 [PS]	Sister Mary Elephant/Wink Dinkerson	1974	—	3.00	6.00
66049	Earache My Eye (Featuring Alice Bowie)/Turn That Thing Down	1974	—	—	—
—Unreleased?					
66102	Earache My Eye (Featuring Alice Bowie)/Turn That Thing Down	1974	—	2.00	4.00
66102 [PS]	Earache My Eye (Featuring Alice Bowie)/Turn That Thing Down	1974	—	3.00	6.00
66104	Black Lassie (Featuring Johnny Stash)/Coming Attractions	1974	—	2.00	4.00
66104 [PS]	Black Lassie (Featuring Johnny Stash)/Coming Attractions	1974	—	3.00	6.00
66115	How I Spent My Summer Vacation, Or A Day at the Beach with Pedro and Man (Part 1/Part 2)	1975	—	2.00	4.00
66124	Framed/Pedro's Request	1976	—	2.00	4.00

Number	Title (A Side/B Side)	Yr	VG	VG+	NM
WARNER BROS.					
8666	Up in Smoke/Rock Fight	1978	—	2.50	5.00
Albums					
MCA					
5640	Get Out of My Room	1985	2.00	4.00	8.00
ODE					
PE 34947	Cheech and Chong	1977	2.50	5.00	10.00
—Reissue of 77010					
PE 34951	Los Cochinos	1977	2.50	5.00	10.00
—Reissue of 77019					
PE 34954	Cheech and Chong's Wedding Album	1977	2.50	5.00	10.00
—Reissue of 77025					
PE 34960	Sleeping Beauty	1977	2.50	5.00	10.00
—Reissue of 77040					
SP-77010	Cheech and Chong	1971	3.00	6.00	12.00
SP-77014	Big Bambu	1972	3.00	6.00	12.00
—Add 50% if rolling paper is still enclosed					
SP-77019	Los Cochinos	1973	3.00	6.00	12.00
SP-77025	Cheech and Chong's Wedding Album	1974	3.00	6.00	12.00
SP-77040	Sleeping Beauty	1976	3.00	6.00	12.00
WARNER BROS.					
BSK 3249	Up in Smoke	1978	2.50	5.00	10.00
BSK 3250	Cheech and Chong	1978	2.00	4.00	8.00
BSK 3251	Big Bambu	1978	2.00	4.00	8.00
BSK 3252	Los Cochinos	1978	2.00	4.00	8.00
BSK 3253	Cheech and Chong's Wedding Album	1978	2.00	4.00	8.00
BSK 3254	Sleeping Beauty	1978	2.00	4.00	8.00
HS 3391	Let's Make a New Dope Deal	1980	2.50	5.00	10.00
BSK 3614	Cheech and Chong's Greatest Hit	1982	2.00	4.00	8.00

CHEERIOS, THE

Number	Title (A Side/B Side)	Yr	VG	VG+	NM
45s					
GOLDEN OLDIES					
1	Ding Dong Honeymoon/Where Are You Tonight	196?	5.00	10.00	20.00
INFINITY					
011	Ding Dong Honeymoon/Where Are You Tonight	1961	100.00	200.00	400.00

CHEERS, THE

1970s game-show host Bert Convy was a member.

Number	Title (A Side/B Side)	Yr	VG	VG+	NM
45s					
CAPITOL					
F2921	Bazoom (I Need Your Lovin')/Arrividerci	1954	6.25	12.50	25.00
F3019	Whadaya Want/Bernie's Tune	1955	6.25	12.50	25.00
F3075	Can't We Be More Than Friends/Blueberries	1955	6.25	12.50	25.00
F3146	I Must Be Dreaming/Fancy Meeting You Here	1955	6.25	12.50	25.00
F3219	Black Denim Trousers and Motorcycle Boots/ Some Night in Alaska	1955	6.25	12.50	25.00
F3353	The Chicken/Don't Do Anything	1956	5.00	10.00	20.00
F3409	Heaven on Earth/Que Pasa Muchacha	1956	5.00	10.00	20.00
MERCURY					
71083	Chug Chug Toot Toot/Big Feet	1957	3.75	7.50	15.00
71100	Two Hearts/You Never Have the Time	1957	3.75	7.50	15.00
—As "Bert Convy and the Cheers"					
NRC					
5003	Hold That Line/Blue Serenade	1958	3.75	7.50	15.00

CHEETAHS, THE

Number	Title (A Side/B Side)	Yr	VG	VG+	NM
45s					
PHILIPS					
40239	Mecca/That Goodnight Kiss	1964	2.50	5.00	10.00

CHELSEA

Future Kiss member Peter Criss (as "Peter Cris") played drums on this LP.

Number	Title (A Side/B Side)	Yr	VG	VG+	NM
Albums					
DECCA					
DL 75262	The Chelsea Album	1972	37.50	75.00	150.00

CHER

Also see ALLMAN AND WOMAN; SONNY AND CHER.

Number	Title (A Side/B Side)	Yr	VG	VG+	NM
12-Inch Singles					
CASABLANCA					
20168 [DJ]	Take Me Home (7:30)/Wasn't It Good (7:03)	1979	5.00	10.00	20.00
GEFFEN					
PRO-A-3154 [DJ]	Skin Deep (4 versions)	1987	2.50	5.00	10.00
21657	Love and Understanding (5 versions)/Trail of Broken Hearts	1991	2.00	4.00	8.00
REPRISE					
43759 [(2)]	Paradise Is Here (8 versions)	1996	3.75	7.50	15.00
WARNER BROS.					
PRO-A-9719 [(2) DJ]	Strong Enough (8 versions)	1999	3.00	6.00	12.00
PRO-A-9926 [(2) DJ]	All or Nothing (5 versions)	1999	3.75	7.50	15.00
44576 [(2)]	Believe (8 versions)	1998	3.00	6.00	12.00
44774 [(2)]	All or Nothing (8 versions)	1999	2.00	4.00	8.00
45s					
ANNETTE					
1000	Ringo I Love You/Beatles Blues	1964	175.00	350.00	700.00
—As "Bonnie Jo Mason"; a Phil Spector production					
ATCO					
6658	Yours Until Tomorrow/Thought of Loving You	1969	—	3.00	6.00
6684	Chastity's Song/I Walk on Gilded Splinters	1969	—	3.00	6.00
6704	For What It's Worth/Hangin' On	1969	—	3.00	6.00
6713	You've Made Me So Very Happy/First Time	1969	—	3.00	6.00
6793	Superstar/First Time	1971	—	3.00	6.00
6868	Lay Baby Lay/(Just Enough to Keep Me) Hangin' On	1972	—	2.50	5.00
CASABLANCA					
965	Take Me Home/My Song (Too Far Gone)	1979	—	2.00	4.00
987	It's Too Late to Love Me Now/Wasn't It Good	1979	—	2.00	4.00
2208	Hell on Wheels/Git Down (Guitar Groupie)	1979	—	2.00	4.00
2228	Boys and Girls/Holdin' Out for Love	1979	—	2.00	4.00
COLUMBIA					
02850	Rudy/Do I Ever Cross Your Mind	1982	—	2.00	4.00
02850 [PS]	Rudy/Do I Ever Cross Your Mind	1982	—	2.50	5.00
03150	Walk With Me/I Paralyze	1982	—	2.00	4.00
GEFFEN					
19023	Love and Understanding/Trail of Broken Hearts	1991	—	2.00	4.00
19105	Save Up All Your Tears/A World Without Heroes	1991	—	—	3.00
19659	The Shoop Shoop Song (It's In His Kiss)/Love on a Rooftop	1990	—	—	3.00
19953	Heart of Stone/All Because of You	1990	—	—	3.00
22844	Just Like Jesse James/Starting Over	1989	—	—	3.00
22886	If I Could Turn Back Time/Some Guys	1989	—	—	3.00
22886 [PS]	If I Could Turn Back Time/Some Guys	1989	—	—	3.00
27529	After All (Love Theme from "Chances Are")/ Dangerous Times	1989	—	—	3.00
—With Peter Cetera					
27529 [PS]	After All (Love Theme from "Chances Are")/ Dangerous Times	1989	—	2.50	5.00
27742	Main Man/(It's Been Hard Enough) Gettin' Over You	1988	—	—	3.00
27742 [PS]	Main Man/(It's Been Hard Enough) Gettin' Over You	1988	—	—	3.00
27894	Skin Deep/Perfection	1988	—	—	3.00
27894 [PS]	Skin Deep/Perfection	1988	—	—	3.00
27986	We All Sleep Alone/Working Girl	1988	—	—	3.00
27986 [PS]	We All Sleep Alone/Working Girl	1988	—	—	3.00
28191	I Found Someone/Dangerous Times	1987	—	—	3.00
28191 [PS]	I Found Someone/Dangerous Times	1987	—	—	3.00
IMPERIAL					
66081	Dream Baby/Stan Quetzal	1964	10.00	20.00	40.00
—By "Cherilyn"					
66114	All I Really Want to Do/I'm Gonna Love You	1965	3.00	6.00	12.00
66136	See See Blues/Where Do You Go	1965	3.00	6.00	12.00
66160	Bang Bang (My Baby Shot Me Down)/Needles and Pins	1966	3.00	6.00	12.00
66160	Bang Bang (My Baby Shot Me Down)/Our Day Will Come	1966	3.00	6.00	12.00
66192	Alfie/She's No Better Than Me	1966	2.50	5.00	10.00
66217	Behind the Door/Magic in the Air	1966	2.50	5.00	10.00
66223	Dream Baby/Mama (When My Dollies Have Babies)	1966	2.50	5.00	10.00
66252	Hey Joe/Our Day Will Come	1967	2.50	5.00	10.00
66261	You Better Sit Down Kids/Elusive Butterfly	1967	3.00	6.00	12.00
66261	You Better Sit Down Kids/Mama (When My Dollies Have Babies)	1967	2.50	5.00	10.00
66282	But I Can't Love You More/Click Song Number One	1968	2.00	4.00	8.00
66307	Take Me for a Little While/A Song Called Children	1968	2.00	4.00	8.00
KAPP					
2134	Classified 1-A/Don't Put It on Me	1971	—	3.00	6.00
2146	Gypsys, Tramps and Thieves/He'll Never Know	1971	—	3.00	6.00
—Black label					
2146	Gypsys, Tramps and Thieves/He'll Never Know	1971	—	2.00	4.00
—Multi-color label					
2158	The Way of Love/Don't Put It on Me	1972	—	2.00	4.00
2171	Living in a House Divided/One Honest Man	1972	—	2.00	4.00
2184	Don't Hide Your Love/First Time	1972	—	2.00	4.00
MCA					
40039	Am I Blue/How Long Has This Been Going On	1973	—	2.00	4.00
40102	Half-Breed/Melody	1973	—	2.00	4.00
40161	Dark Lady/Two People Clinging to a Thread	1973	—	2.00	4.00
40245	Train of Thought/Dixie Girl	1974	—	2.00	4.00
40273	I Saw a Man and He Danced With His Wife/I Hate to Sleep Alone	1974	—	2.00	4.00
40324	Carousel Man/When You Find Out Where You're Going Let Me Know	1974	—	2.00	4.00
40375	Rescue Me/Dixie Girl	1975	—	2.00	4.00
REPRISE					
17695	One by One/I Wouldn't Treat a Dog (The Way You Treated Me)	1996	—	—	3.00
UNITED ARTISTS					
0106	All I Really Want to Do/Where Do You Go	1973	—	2.00	4.00
—"Silver Spotlight Series" reissue					
0107	Bang Bang (My Baby Shot Me Down)/You Better Sit Down Kids	1973	—	2.00	4.00
—"Silver Spotlight Series" reissue					
XW511	Sunny/Alfie	1974	—	2.00	4.00
50864	Reason to Believe/Will You Still Love Me Tomorrow	1971	—	2.00	4.00
50974	Old Man River/Our Day Will Come	1972	—	2.00	4.00
WARNER BROS.					
8096	Geronimo's Cadillac/These Days	1975	—	2.00	4.00
8263	Borrowed Time/Long Distance Love Affair	1976	—	2.00	4.00
8311	Pirate/Send the Man Over	1976	—	2.00	4.00
8366	War Paint and Soft Feathers/Sand the Man Over	1977	—	2.00	4.00
17119	Believe (Album Version)/Believe (Xenomania Mix)	1998	—	—	3.00
WARNER/SPECTOR					
0400	Baby, I Love You/A Woman's Story	1974	2.50	5.00	10.00
0402	Just Enough to Keep Me Hangin' On/A Love Like Yours	1975	2.50	5.00	10.00
—With Nilsson					
Albums					
ATCO					
33-298 [M]	3614 Jackson Highway	1969	7.50	15.00	30.00
—White label promo only (no stock copies issued in mono)					
SD 33-298 [S]	3614 Jackson Highway	1969	5.00	10.00	20.00
CASABLANCA					
NBLP-7133	Take Me Home	1979	2.50	5.00	10.00
NBPIX-7133 [PD]	Take Me Home	1979	12.50	25.00	50.00
NBLP-7184	Prisoner	1980	2.50	5.00	10.00
COLUMBIA					
FC 38096	I Paralyze	1982	2.50	5.00	10.00

Number	Title (A Side/B Side)	Yr	VG	VG+	NM
GEFFEN					
GHS 24164	Cher	1987	2.50	5.00	10.00
GHS 24239	Heart of Stone	1989	3.75	7.50	15.00
—Original cover with Cher in heart-shaped pose next to "skeleton rock"					
GHS 24239	Heart of Stone	1989	2.50	5.00	10.00
—Later cover with larger picture of Cher and no rock					
IMPERIAL					
LP-9292 [M]	All I Really Want to Do	1965	5.00	10.00	20.00
LP-9301 [M]	The Sonny Side of Cher	1966	5.00	10.00	20.00
LP-9320 [M]	Cher	1966	3.75	7.50	15.00
LP-9358 [M]	With Love — Cher	1967	3.75	7.50	15.00
LP-12292 [S]	All I Really Want to Do	1965	6.25	12.50	25.00
LP-12301 [S]	The Sonny Side of Cher	1966	6.25	12.50	25.00
LP-12320 [S]	Cher	1966	5.00	10.00	20.00
LP-12358 [S]	With Love — Cher	1967	5.00	10.00	20.00
LP-12373	Backstage	1968	5.00	10.00	20.00
LP-12406	Cher's Golden Greats	1968	5.00	10.00	20.00
KAPP					
KRS-3649	Cher	1971	5.00	10.00	20.00
—Original title of LP (renamed "Gypsys, Tramps & Thieves")					
KRS-3649	Gypsys, Tramps & Thieves	1971	3.75	7.50	15.00
—Retitled version of above LP					
KRS-5514	Foxy Lady	1972	3.75	7.50	15.00
LIBERTY					
LN-10110	The Very Best of Cher, Vol. 1	1981	2.00	4.00	8.00
LN-10111	The Very Best of Cher, Vol. 2	1981	2.00	4.00	8.00
MCA					
624	Cher	197?	2.50	5.00	10.00
2101	Bittersweet White Light	1973	3.00	6.00	12.00
2104	Half-Breed	1973	3.00	6.00	12.00
2113	Dark Lady	1974	3.00	6.00	12.00
2127	Greatest Hits	1974	3.00	6.00	12.00
37028	Greatest Hits	1981	2.00	4.00	8.00
—Reissue of MCA 2127					
SPRINGBOARD					
SPB-4028	Cher's Greatest Hits	197?	2.50	5.00	10.00
SPB-4029	Cher Sings the Hits	197?	2.50	5.00	10.00
SUNSET					
SUS-5276	This Is Cher	1970	3.75	7.50	15.00
UNITED ARTISTS					
UXS-88 [(2)]	Cher Superpak	1971	5.00	10.00	20.00
UXS-89 [(2)]	Cher Superpak, Vol. II	1972	5.00	10.00	20.00
—The above are reissues of Imperial recordings					
UA-LA237-G	The Very Best of Cher	1974	3.00	6.00	12.00
UA-LA377-E	The Very Best of Cher	1975	2.50	5.00	10.00
UA-LA435-E	The Very Best of Cher, Vol. 2	1975	3.00	6.00	12.00
WARNER BROS.					
BS 2850	Stars	1975	3.00	6.00	12.00
BS 2898	I'd Rather Believe in You	1976	3.00	6.00	12.00
BS 3046	Cherished	1977	3.00	6.00	12.00

CHEROKEE

45s

Number	Title (A Side/B Side)	Yr	VG	VG+	NM
ABC					
11295	Rosiana/All the Way Home	1971	2.00	4.00	8.00
11304	Girl, I've Got News for You/All the Way Home	1971	2.00	4.00	8.00

Albums

Number	Title (A Side/B Side)	Yr	VG	VG+	NM
ABC					
ABCS-719	Cherokee	1970	5.00	10.00	20.00

CHEROKEES, THE (1)

45s

Number	Title (A Side/B Side)	Yr	VG	VG+	NM
CHALLENGE					
9135	Cherokee Stomp/Uprisin'	1961	5.00	10.00	20.00

CHEROKEES, THE (2)

Male vocal group.

45s

Number	Title (A Side/B Side)	Yr	VG	VG+	NM
GRAND					
106	Rainbow of Love/I Had a Thrill	1954	250.00	500.00	1000.
110	Please Tell Me So/Remember When	1954	250.00	500.00	1000.
PEACOCK					
1656	Drip Drip/Is She Real	1955	50.00	100.00	200.00

CHEROKEES, THE (3)

45s

Number	Title (A Side/B Side)	Yr	VG	VG+	NM
GUYDEN					
2044	Cherokee/Harlem Nocturne	1960	3.75	7.50	15.00
2044 [PS]	Cherokee/Harlem Nocturne	1960	7.50	15.00	30.00

CHEROKEES, THE (4)

British band.

45s

Number	Title (A Side/B Side)	Yr	VG	VG+	NM
MGM					
13334	Seven Daffodils/Wondrous Place	1964	3.75	7.50	15.00
13433	Dig a Little Deeper/I Will Never Turn My Back on You	1965	5.00	10.00	20.00

CHEROKEES, THE (5)

FRED PARRIS of THE FIVE SATINS was a member.

45s

Number	Title (A Side/B Side)	Yr	VG	VG+	NM
UNITED ARTISTS					
367	My Heavenly Angel/Bed Bug	1961	25.00	50.00	100.00

CHERRY, DON

45s

Number	Title (A Side/B Side)	Yr	VG	VG+	NM
COLUMBIA					
40421	Tell It To Me Again/Clean Break	1955	3.00	6.00	12.00
40492	Be My Darling Once Again/You Still Mean the Same to Me	1955	3.00	6.00	12.00
40544	What Am I Trying to Forget/Fifty Million Salty Kisses	1955	3.00	6.00	12.00
40597	Band of Gold/Rumble Boogie	1955	3.75	7.50	15.00
40665	Wild Cherry/I'm Still a King to You	1956	2.50	5.00	10.00
40705	Ghost Town/I'll Be Around	1956	2.50	5.00	10.00
40746	Namely You/If I Had My Druthers	1956	2.50	5.00	10.00
40804	Give Me More/The Story of Sherry	1956	2.50	5.00	10.00
40828	The Last Dance/Don't You Worry Your Pretty Little Head	1957	2.50	5.00	10.00
40885	Mr. Teardrop/April Age	1957	2.50	5.00	10.00
40958	There's a Place Called Heaven/Fourteen Carat Gold	1957	2.50	5.00	10.00
41077	It'll Be Me/Love Me, If You Will	1957	2.50	5.00	10.00
41134	The Glide/Another Time, Another Place	1958	2.50	5.00	10.00
41259	Big Bad Wolf/I Look for a Love	1958	2.50	5.00	10.00
41351	Hasty Heart/The Golden Age	1959	2.50	5.00	10.00
DECCA					
27244	I'll Always Love You/Maybe on Sunday	1950	3.75	7.50	15.00
—With Eileen Wilson					
27245	I Need You So/Can't Seem to Laugh Anymore	1950	3.75	7.50	15.00
27435	Seven Wonders of the World/When You Return	1951	3.00	6.00	12.00
27475	Chapel of the Roses/Beautiful Madness	1951	3.00	6.00	12.00
27484	I Apologize/Bring Back the Thrill	1951	3.00	6.00	12.00
27535	Don't Cry/Don't Leave Me Now	1951	3.00	6.00	12.00
27618	Powder Blue/Vanity	1951	3.00	6.00	12.00
27626	My Life's Desire/I Can See You	1951	3.00	6.00	12.00
27633	Far, Far Away/Star of Hope	1951	3.00	6.00	12.00
—With Elieen Wilson					
27717	Belle, Belle, My Liberty Belle/Cara Cara Bella Bella	1951	3.00	6.00	12.00
27755	The Sweetest Waltz/I Will Never Change	1951	3.00	6.00	12.00
27807	The Lamp of Faith/Sin Ain't Nothing	1951	3.00	6.00	12.00
27836	I Can't Help It/Grievin' My Heart Out for You	1951	3.00	6.00	12.00
27904	Neither Am I/Take Me Back	1951	3.00	6.00	12.00
27944	I'll Sing to You/Your Sentimental Heart	1952	3.00	6.00	12.00
28050	It Doesn't Matter Where I Go/Sentimental Tears	1952	3.00	6.00	12.00
28153	Wonder/My Mother's Pearl	1952	3.00	6.00	12.00
28292	My Name Is Morgan, But It Ain't J.P./Pretty Girl	1952	3.00	6.00	12.00
28368	It's Been So Long, Darling/Silver Dew on the Blue Grass Tonight	1952	3.00	6.00	12.00
28452	I Don't Want to Set the World on Fire/From Your Lips Only	1952	3.00	6.00	12.00
28477	How Long/Second Star to the Right	1952	3.00	6.00	12.00
28548	Lover's Quarrel/Changeable	1953	3.00	6.00	12.00
28635	All By Myself/If They Should Ask Me	1953	3.00	6.00	12.00
28768	If You See Sally/I Got to Pass Your House to Get to My House	1953	3.00	6.00	12.00
28789	No Stone Unturned/Till the Moon Turns Green	1953	3.00	6.00	12.00
28844	Too Long/For Now and Always	1953	3.00	6.00	12.00
29005	I'm Through with Love/You Didn't Have to Tell Me	1954	2.50	5.00	10.00
29142	Lulu's Back in Town/Anyplace, Anytime, Anywhere	1954	2.50	5.00	10.00
29322	Where Can You Be/I'm Just a Country Boy	1954	2.50	5.00	10.00
29444	Home Again/Sip of Moonlight	1955	2.50	5.00	10.00
29807	The Thrill Is Gone/Wanted, Someone to Love Me	1956	2.50	5.00	10.00
MONUMENT					
880	More I Cannot Do/Sweet Sugar	1965	2.00	4.00	8.00
898	The Story of My Life/Things Called Sadness	1965	2.00	4.00	8.00
930	Don't Change/I Love You Drops	1966	2.00	4.00	8.00
947	Tip of My Fingers/After I'm Number One	1966	2.00	4.00	8.00
971	I Know Love/Married	1966	2.00	4.00	8.00
989	There Goes My Everything/I Don't Wanna Go Home	1966	2.00	4.00	8.00
1008	I Live to Love You/I Run to the Door	1967	—	3.00	6.00
1027	That Lucky Old Sun/No Hearts and Flowers	1967	—	3.00	6.00
1045	Theme from "Will Penny" (Lonely Rider)/Here Comes the Rain	1967	—	3.00	6.00
1062	Good Morning/Let Me Lead the Way	1968	—	3.00	6.00
1088	Take a Message to Mary/In My Youth	1968	—	3.00	6.00
1130	Whippoorwill/To Think You've Chosen Me	1969	—	3.00	6.00
1147	Days of Sand and Shovels/That Woman's Coming Home	1969	—	3.00	6.00
1156	I'll Catch the Sun/Ain't You Glad You're Living, Joe	1969	—	3.00	6.00
1185	Lilacs in Winter/Look for Me Tomorrow	1970	—	3.00	6.00
1201	Between Winston-Salem and Nashville, Tennessee/Just a Drop of Rain	1970	—	3.00	6.00
1222	Statue of a Fool/Ev'ry Body Else	1970	—	3.00	6.00
8530	Freedom Come, Freedom Go/Have You Ever Been to Georgia	1971	—	2.50	5.00
8542	For a Moment You Slipped My Mind/Is It Any Wonder	1972	—	2.50	5.00
8557	The Riddle Song/Wonder Where They're Going	1972	—	2.50	5.00
8578	When You Leave Amarillo, Turn Out the Lights/Cajun Fiddler	1973	—	2.50	5.00
8603	Going Away Party/The Old Rugged Cross	1974	—	2.50	5.00
8704	The Good Old Days Are Right Now/Pleasing You (As Long As I Live)	1976	—	2.50	5.00
45232	Come Sundown/Love Is Gone for Good	1977	—	2.50	5.00
45269	Six Weeks Every Summer, Christmas Every Day/Play Her Back to Yesterday	1978	—	2.50	5.00
STRAND					
25005	Vanity/Summer School Blues	1959	2.50	5.00	10.00
VERVE					
10270	Then You Can Tell Me Goodbye/When I Found I'd Lost	1962	2.50	5.00	10.00
WARWICK					
597	Hair of Gold/Somebody Cares for Me	1960	2.50	5.00	10.00

7-Inch Extended Plays

Number	Title (A Side/B Side)	Yr	VG	VG+	NM
COLUMBIA					
B-8931	When the Sun Comes Out/Love Is Just Around the Corner//For You/I'll String Along with You	195?	3.00	6.00	12.00
B-8931 [PS]	Swingin' for Two, Part 1	195?	3.00	6.00	12.00
B-8932	I Didn't Know About You/So Rare//I'm Yours/I'm Gonna Sit Right Down and Write Myself a Letter	195?	3.00	6.00	12.00

Number	Title (A Side/B Side)	Yr	VG	VG+	NM
B-8932 [PS]	Swingin' for Two, Part 2	195?	3.00	6.00	12.00
Albums					
ANTILLES					
7034	The Eternal Now	197?	3.00	6.00	12.00
ATLANTIC					
SD 18217	Hear and Now	197?	3.00	6.00	12.00
BASF					
20980	Eternal Rhythm	1972	5.00	10.00	20.00
BLACK SAINT					
BSR-0013	Old and New Dreams	198?	3.00	6.00	12.00
BLUE NOTE					
BLP-4226 [M]	Complete Communion	1966	6.25	12.50	25.00
BLP-4247 [M]	Symphony for Improvisers	1966	6.25	12.50	25.00
BST-84226 [S]	Complete Communion	1966	7.50	15.00	30.00
—"New York, USA" address on label					
BST-84226 [S]	Complete Communion	1968	3.75	7.50	15.00
—"A Division of Liberty Records" on label					
BST-84247 [S]	Symphony for Improvisers	1966	7.50	15.00	30.00
—"New York, USA" address on label					
BST-84247 [S]	Symphony for Improvisers	1968	3.75	7.50	15.00
—"A Division of Liberty Records" on label					
BST-84311	Where Is Brooklyn?	1969	6.25	12.50	25.00
—"A Division of Liberty Records" on label					
COLUMBIA					
CL 893 [M]	Swingin' for Two	1956	6.25	12.50	25.00
ECM					
1230	El Corazon	198?	3.00	6.00	12.00
—With Ed Blackwell					
HORIZON					
HP-717	Don Cherry	197?	3.00	6.00	12.00
INNER CITY					
IC 1009	Togetherness	197?	5.00	10.00	20.00
JCOA					
1006	Relativity Suite	1974	5.00	10.00	20.00
MONUMENT					
MLP-8049 [M]	Don Cherry Smashes	1966	3.00	6.00	12.00
MLP-8075 [M]	There Goes My Everything	1967	3.75	7.50	15.00
8601 [(2)]	The World of Don Cherry	197?	3.00	6.00	12.00
—Reissue of 32334					
SLP-18049 [S]	Don Cherry Smashes	1966	3.75	7.50	15.00
SLP-18075 [S]	There Goes My Everything	1967	3.00	6.00	12.00
SLP-18088	Let It Be Me	1968	3.00	6.00	12.00
SLP-18109	Take a Message to Mary	1969	3.00	6.00	12.00
SLP-18124	Don Cherry	1970	3.00	6.00	12.00
KZG 32334 [(2)]	The World of Don Cherry	1972	3.75	7.50	15.00
MOSAIC					
MQ3-145 [(3)]	The Complete Blue Note Recordings of Don Cherry	199?	10.00	20.00	40.00

CHERRY PEOPLE, THE

Number	Title (A Side/B Side)	Yr	VG	VG+	NM
Albums					
HERITAGE					
HTS 35000	The Cherry People	1968	5.00	10.00	20.00

CHERRY SLUSH

Number	Title (A Side/B Side)	Yr	VG	VG+	NM
45s					
U.S.A.					
895	I Cannot Stop You/Don't Walk Away	1968	5.00	10.00	20.00
904	Gotta Take It Easy/Day Don't Come	1968	5.00	10.00	20.00

CHESS, TUBBY, AND HIS CANDY STRIPE TWISTERS

Number	Title (A Side/B Side)	Yr	VG	VG+	NM
Albums					
GRAND PRIX					
K-187 [M]	Do the Twist	1962	3.75	7.50	15.00
KS-187 [S]	Do the Twist	1962	5.00	10.00	20.00

CHESTER, GARY

Number	Title (A Side/B Side)	Yr	VG	VG+	NM
Albums					
DCP					
DCL 3803 [M]	Yeah, Yeah, Yeah	1964	5.00	10.00	20.00
DCS 6803 [S]	Yeah, Yeah, Yeah	1964	6.25	12.50	25.00

CHESTERFIELDS, THE (1)

Number	Title (A Side/B Side)	Yr	VG	VG+	NM
45s					
A&M					
2041	That Is Rock and Roll/Why Do Fools Fall in Love	1978	—	2.50	5.00

CHESTERFIELDS, THE (2)

Number	Title (A Side/B Side)	Yr	VG	VG+	NM
45s					
CHESS					
1559	I'm in Heaven/All Messed Up	1954	100.00	200.00	400.00

CHESTERFIELDS, THE (3)

Number	Title (A Side/B Side)	Yr	VG	VG+	NM
45s					
CUB					
9008	I Got Fired/Meet Me at the Candy Store	1958	6.25	12.50	25.00

CHESTERFIELDS, THE (4)

Number	Title (A Side/B Side)	Yr	VG	VG+	NM
45s					
PHILIPS					
40060	A Dream Is But a Dream/You Walked Away	1962	50.00	100.00	200.00

CHESTERS, THE

See LITTLE ANTHONY AND THE IMPERIALS.

CHESTNUT, MORRIS

Number	Title (A Side/B Side)	Yr	VG	VG+	NM
45s					
AMY					
981	Too Darned Soulful/You Don't Love Me Anymore	1967	62.50	125.00	250.00

CHEVRONS, THE

Number	Title (A Side/B Side)	Yr	VG	VG+	NM
45s					
BRENT					
7000	That Comes With Love/Don't Be Heartless	1959	12.50	25.00	50.00
7007	Lullabye/The Day After Forever	1959	12.50	25.00	50.00
7015	Little Darlin'/Little Star	1960	12.50	25.00	50.00
TIME					
1	Come Go with Me/I'm in Love Again	1960	10.00	20.00	40.00
Albums					
TIME					
T-10008 [M]	Sing-a-Long Rock & Roll	1961	20.00	40.00	80.00

CHI-LITES, THE

Number	Title (A Side/B Side)	Yr	VG	VG+	NM
45s					
BLUE ROCK					
4007	I'm So Jealous/The Mix-Mix Song	1965	6.25	12.50	25.00
4020	Doing the Snatch/Bassology	1965	6.25	12.50	25.00
4037	Never No More/She's Mine	1965	12.50	25.00	50.00
BRUNSWICK					
55398	Give It Away/What Do I Wish For	1969	2.00	4.00	8.00
55414	Let Me Be the Man My Daddy Was/The Twelfth of Never	1969	2.00	4.00	8.00
55422	I'm Gonna Make You Love Me/To Change My Love	1969	2.00	4.00	8.00
55426	24 Hours of Sadness/You're No Longer Part of My Heart	1970	2.00	4.00	8.00
55438	I Like Your Lovin' (Do You Like Mine)/You're No Longer Part of My Heart	1970	2.00	4.00	8.00
55442	Are You My Woman (Tell Me So)/Troubles A-Comin'	1970	2.00	4.00	8.00
55450	(For God's Sake) Give More Power to the People/Troubles A-Comin'	1971	2.00	4.00	8.00
55455	We Are Neighbors/What Do I Wish For	1971	2.00	4.00	8.00
55458	I Want to Pay You back (For Loving Me)/Love Uprising	1971	2.00	4.00	8.00
55462	Have You Seen Her/Yes I'm Ready	1971	—	3.00	6.00
55471	Oh Girl/Being in Love	1972	—	3.00	6.00
55478	The Coldest Days of My Life (Part 1)/The Coldest Days of My Life (Part 2)	1972	—	3.00	6.00
55483	A Lonely Man/The Man and the Woman (The Boy and the Girl)	1972	—	3.00	6.00
55489	We Need Order/Living in the Footsteps of Another Man	1972	—	3.00	6.00
55491	A Letter to Myself/Sally	1973	—	3.00	6.00
55496	My Heart Just Keeps On Breakin'/Just Two Teenage Kids	1973	—	3.00	6.00
55500	Stoned Out of My Mind/Someone Else's Arms	1973	—	3.00	6.00
55502	I Found Someone/Marriage License	1973	—	3.00	6.00
55505	Homely Girl/Never Had It So Good and Felt So Bad	1974	—	3.00	6.00
55512	There Will Never Be Any Peace (Until God Is Seated at the Conference Table)/Too Good	1974	—	3.00	6.00
55514	You Got to Be the One/Happiness Is Your Middle Name	1974	—	3.00	6.00
55515	Toby/That's How Long	1974	—	3.00	6.00
55520	It's Time for Love/Here I Am	1975	—	3.00	6.00
55522	Don't Burn No Bridges/(Instrumental)	1975	—	3.00	6.00
—With Jackie Wilson					
55525	The Devil Is Doing His Work/I'm Not a Gambler	1976	—	3.00	6.00
55528	You Don't Have to Go/(Instrumental)	1976	—	3.00	6.00
55546	First Time/Marriage License	1978	—	2.50	5.00
CHI-SOUND					
2472	Heavenly Body/Strung Out	1980	—	2.00	4.00
2481	Have You Seen Her/Supermad (About You Baby)	1981	—	2.00	4.00
2495	All I Wanna Do Is Make Love to You/Round and Round	1981	—	2.00	4.00
2503	Me and You/Tell Me Where It Hurts	1981	—	2.00	4.00
2600	Hot on a Thing (Called Love)/Whole Lot of Good Lovin'	1982	—	2.00	4.00
2604	Try My Side (Of Love)/Get Down with Me	1982	—	2.00	4.00
DAKAR					
600	Baby It's Time/Price of Love	1968	3.00	6.00	12.00
—As "Marshall and the Chi-Lites"					
DARAN					
011	One by One/You Did That to Me	1964	25.00	50.00	100.00
—As "The Hi-Lites"					
0111	Pretty Girl/Love Bandit	1966	12.50	25.00	50.00
—As "Marshall and the Chi-Lites"					
222	I'm So Jealous/The Mix-Mix Song	1964	25.00	50.00	100.00
—As "The Hi-Lites"					
INPHASION					
7205	Stay a Little Longer/Higher	1979	—	2.50	5.00
7208	The Only One for Me (One in a Million)/You Won't Be Lonely Too Long	1979	—	2.50	5.00
JA-WES					
0888	You Did That to Me/I Won't Care About You	1966	3.75	7.50	15.00
LARC					
81015	Bottom's Up/Bottom's Up Groove	1983	—	2.00	4.00
81023	Bad Motor Scooter/I Just Wanna Hold You	1983	—	2.00	4.00
MERCURY					
73844	Happy Being Lonely/Love Can Be Dangerous	1976	—	2.50	5.00
73886	Vanishing Love/I Turn Away	1977	—	2.50	5.00
73934	My First Mistake/Stop Still	1977	—	2.50	5.00
73954	If I Had a Girl/I've Got Love on My Mind	1977	—	2.50	5.00
PRIVATE I					
04365	Stop What You're Doin'/Little Girl	1984	—	—	3.00
04484	Let Today Come Back Tomorrow/Gimme Whatcha Got	1984	—	—	3.00
REVUE					
11005	Love Is Gone/Love Me	1967	3.00	6.00	12.00
11018	(Um, Um) My Baby Loves Me/That's My Baby for You	1968	3.00	6.00	12.00

Albums

20TH CENTURY

Number	Title (A Side/B Side)	Yr	VG	VG+	NM
T-619	Heavenly Body	1980	3.75	7.50	15.00
T-635	Me and You	1982	3.75	7.50	15.00

BRUNSWICK

Number	Title (A Side/B Side)	Yr	VG	VG+	NM
BL 754152	Give It Away	1969	6.25	12.50	25.00
BL 754165	I Like Your Lovin', Do You Like Mine?	1970	6.25	12.50	25.00
BL 754170	(For God's Sake) Give More Power to the People	1971	6.25	12.50	25.00
BL 754179	A Lonely Man	1972	6.25	12.50	25.00
BL 754184	The Chi-Lites Greatest Hits	1972	6.25	12.50	25.00
BL 754188	A Letter to Myself	1973	6.25	12.50	25.00
BL 754197	Chi-Lites	1973	6.25	12.50	25.00
BL 754200	Toby	1974	6.25	12.50	25.00
BL 754204	Half a Love	1975	6.25	12.50	25.00
BL 754208	The Chi-Lites Greatest Hits, Volume 2	1976	6.25	12.50	25.00

EPIC

Number	Title (A Side/B Side)	Yr	VG	VG+	NM
PE 38627	Greatest Hits	1983	2.50	5.00	10.00

ICHIBAN

Number	Title (A Side/B Side)	Yr	VG	VG+	NM
ICH-1057	Just Say You Love Me	198?	2.50	5.00	10.00

LARC

Number	Title (A Side/B Side)	Yr	VG	VG+	NM
8103	Bottom's Up	1983	3.00	6.00	12.00

MERCURY

Number	Title (A Side/B Side)	Yr	VG	VG+	NM
SRM-1-1118	Happy Being Lonely	1976	3.75	7.50	15.00
SRM-1-1147	Fantastic	1977	3.75	7.50	15.00

PRIVATE I

Number	Title (A Side/B Side)	Yr	VG	VG+	NM
FZ 39316	Steppin' Out	1984	2.50	5.00	10.00
PZ 39316	Steppin' Out	1985	2.00	4.00	8.00
—Budget-line reissue					

CHIC-LETS, THE

45s

JOSIE

Number	Title (A Side/B Side)	Yr	VG	VG+	NM
919	I Want You to Be My Boyfriend/Don't Goof on Me	1964	3.75	7.50	15.00

CHICAGO

45s

COLUMBIA

Number	Title (A Side/B Side)	Yr	VG	VG+	NM
10049	Wishing You Were Here/Life Saver	1974	—	2.50	5.00
10092	Harry Truman/Till We Meet Again	1975	—	2.50	5.00
10092 [PS]	Harry Truman/Till We Meet Again	1975	—	3.00	6.00
10131	Old Days/Hideaway	1975	—	2.50	5.00
10200	Brand New Love Affair/Hideaway	1975	—	2.50	5.00
10360	Another Rainy Day in New York City/Hope for Love	1976	—	2.50	5.00
10390	If You Leave Me Now/Together Again	1976	—	2.50	5.00
10523	You Are On My Mind/Gently I'll Wake You	1977	—	2.50	5.00
10620	Baby, What a Big Surprise/Takin' It On Uptown	1977	—	2.50	5.00
10620 [PS]	Baby, What a Big Surprise/Takin' It On Uptown	1977	2.50	5.00	10.00
—Sleeve appears to be promo only					
10683	Little One/Till the End of Time	1978	—	2.50	5.00
10737	Take Me Back to Chicago/Policeman	1978	—	2.50	5.00
10845	Alive Again/Love Was New	1978	—	2.50	5.00
10879	No Tell Lover/Take a Chance	1979	—	2.50	5.00
10935	Gone Long Gone/The Greatest Love on Earth	1979	—	2.00	4.00
11061	Must Have Been Crazy/Closer to You	1979	—	2.00	4.00
11124	Street Player/Window Dreamin'	1979	—	2.00	4.00
11341	Song for You/I'd Rather Be Rich	1980	—	—	—
—Unreleased?					
11345	Thunder and Lightning/I'd Rather Be Rich	1980	—	2.00	4.00
11376	The American Dream/Song for You	1980	—	2.00	4.00
44909	Questions 67 and 68/Listen	1969	—	3.00	6.00
44909 [PS]	Questions 67 and 68/Listen	1969	2.50	5.00	10.00
45011	Beginnings/Poem 58	1969	—	3.00	6.00
45127	Make Me Smile/Colour My World	1970	—	2.50	5.00
45127 [PS]	Make Me Smile/Colour My World	1970	2.00	4.00	8.00
45194	25 or 6 to 4/Where Do We Go from Here	1970	—	2.50	5.00
45264	Does Anybody Really Know What Time It Is?/Listen	1970	—	2.50	5.00
45264 [PS]	Does Anybody Really Know What Time It Is?/Listen	1970	2.00	4.00	8.00
45331	Free/Free Country	1971	—	2.50	5.00
45331 [PS]	Free/Free Country	1971	2.00	4.00	8.00
45370	Lowdown/Loneliness Is Just a Word	1971	—	2.50	5.00
45370 [PS]	Lowdown/Loneliness Is Just a Word	1971	2.00	4.00	8.00
45417	Beginnings/Colour My World	1971	—	2.50	5.00
45417 [PS]	Beginnings/Colour My World	1971	2.00	4.00	8.00
45467	Questions 67 and 68/I'm a Man	1971	—	2.50	5.00
45657	Saturday in the Park/Alma Mater	1972	—	2.50	5.00
45717	Dialogue (Parts 1 and 2)/Now That You've Gone	1972	—	2.50	5.00
45717 [PS]	Dialogue (Parts 1 and 2)/Now That You've Gone	1972	—	3.00	6.00
45880	Feelin' Stronger Every Day/Jenny	1973	—	2.50	5.00
45933	Just You 'N' Me/Critic's Choice	1973	—	2.50	5.00
46020	(I've Been) Searchin' So Long/Byblos	1974	—	2.50	5.00
46062	Call On Me/Prelude to Aire	1974	—	2.50	5.00

FULL MOON

Number	Title (A Side/B Side)	Yr	VG	VG+	NM
29798	What You're Missing/Rescue You	1983	—	2.00	4.00
29911	Love Me Tomorrow/Bad Advice	1982	—	2.00	4.00
29979	Hard to Say I'm Sorry/Sonny Think Twice	1982	—	2.00	4.00

REPRISE

Number	Title (A Side/B Side)	Yr	VG	VG+	NM
19466	Chasin' the Wind/Only Time Can Heal the Wounded	1991	—	—	3.00
22741	What Kind of Man Would I Be?/25 or 6 to 4	1990	—	—	3.00
22741 [PS]	What Kind of Man Would I Be?/25 or 6 to 4	1990	—	2.50	5.00
22985	We Can Last Forever/One More Day	1989	—	—	3.00
27757	You're Not Alone/It's Alright	1988	—	—	3.00
27757 [PS]	You're Not Alone/It's Alright	1988	—	—	3.00
27766	Look Away/Come In from the Night	1988	—	—	3.00
27766 [PS]	Look Away/Come In from the Night	1988	—	—	3.00
27855	I Don't Wanna Live Without Your Love/I Stand Up	1988	—	—	3.00
27855 [PS]	I Don't Wanna Live Without Your Love/I Stand Up	1988	—	—	3.00

WARNER BROS.

Number	Title (A Side/B Side)	Yr	VG	VG+	NM
28283	Niagara Falls/I Believe	1987	—	—	3.00
28283 [PS]	Niagara Falls/I Believe	1987	—	2.50	5.00
28424	If She Would Have Been Faithful.../Forever	1987	—	—	3.00
28424 [PS]	If She Would Have Been Faithful.../Forever	1987	—	—	3.00
28512	Will You Still Love Me/25 or 6 to 4	1986	—	—	3.00
28628	25 or 6 to 4/One More Day	1986	—	—	3.00
28628 [PS]	25 or 6 to 4/One More Day	1986	—	—	3.00
29082	Along Comes a Woman/We Can't Stop the Hurtin'	1985	—	—	3.00
29126	You're the Inspiration/Once in a Lifetime	1984	—	—	3.00
29214	Hard Habit to Break/Remember the Feeling	1984	—	—	3.00
29214 [PS]	Hard Habit to Break/Remember the Feeling	1984	—	—	3.00
29306	Stay the Night/Only You	1984	—	—	3.00
29306 [PS]	Stay the Night/Only You	1984	—	—	3.00

Albums

ACCORD

Number	Title (A Side/B Side)	Yr	VG	VG+	NM
SN-7140	Toronto Rock 'n Roll Revival, Part I	1982	3.00	6.00	12.00
—Reissue of Magnum LP					

COLUMBIA

Number	Title (A Side/B Side)	Yr	VG	VG+	NM
(no #) [(17)]	Chicago	1976	62.50	125.00	250.00
—Promo-only set: The first 10 Chicago LPs with gold stamps on covers, box, side panel and wraparound					
GP 8 [(2)]	Chicago Transit Authority	1969	6.25	12.50	25.00
—Red labels with "360 Sound" at bottom					
GP 8 [(2)]	Chicago Transit Authority	1970	5.00	10.00	20.00
—Orange labels; most copies add a Roman numeral "I" to the title on spine					
KGP 24 [(2)]	Chicago	1970	10.00	20.00	40.00
—Red labels with "360 Sound" at bottom; label and spine call the album "Chicago"					
KGP 24 [(2)]	Chicago II	1970	5.00	10.00	20.00
—Orange labels					
KGP 24 [(2)]	Chicago II	1970	6.25	12.50	25.00
—Red labels with "360 Sound" at bottom; label and spine call the album "Chicago II"					
C2 30110 [(2)]	Chicago III	1971	5.00	10.00	20.00
C2Q 30110 [(2) Q]	Chicago III	1974	7.50	15.00	30.00
C2G 30863 [(2)]	Chicago at Carnegie Hall, Vol. 1 & 2	1971	5.00	10.00	20.00
—First half of the 4-LP box, possibly for Columbia Record Club only					
C2G 30864 [(2)]	Chicago at Carnegie Hall, Vol. 3 & 4	1971	5.00	10.00	20.00
—Second half of the 4-LP box, possibly for Columbia Record Club only					
C4Q 30865 [(4) Q]	Chicago at Carnegie Hall	1971	12.50	25.00	50.00
C4X 30865 [(4)]	Chicago at Carnegie Hall	1971	10.00	20.00	40.00
—With box, 4 posters and program. Deduct for missing items.					
CQ 31102 [Q]	Chicago V	1974	6.25	12.50	25.00
KC 31102	Chicago V	1972	5.00	10.00	20.00
CQ 32400 [Q]	Chicago VI	1974	6.25	12.50	25.00
KC 32400	Chicago VI	1973	3.75	7.50	15.00
C2 32810 [(2)]	Chicago VII	1974	5.00	10.00	20.00
C2Q 32810 [(2) Q]	Chicago VII	1974	7.50	15.00	30.00
PC 33100	Chicago VIII	1975	3.75	7.50	15.00
PCQ 33100 [Q]	Chicago VIII	1975	6.25	12.50	25.00
GQ 33255 [(2) Q]	Chicago Transit Authority	1975	6.25	12.50	25.00
GQ 33258 [(2) Q]	Chicago II	1975	6.25	12.50	25.00
PC 33900	Chicago IX — Chicago's Greatest Hits	1975	3.75	7.50	15.00
PCQ 33900 [Q]	Chicago IX — Chicago's Greatest Hits	1975	6.25	12.50	25.00
PC 34200	Chicago X	1976	3.75	7.50	15.00
PCQ 34200 [Q]	Chicago X	1976	6.25	12.50	25.00
JC 34860	Chicago XI	1977	3.75	7.50	15.00
FC 35512	Hot Streets	1978	3.75	7.50	15.00
FC 36105	Chicago 13	1979	3.75	7.50	15.00
FC 36517	Chicago XIV	1980	3.75	7.50	15.00
FC 37682	Chicago — Greatest Hits, Volume II	1981	3.75	7.50	15.00
PC 38590	If You Leave Me Now	1982	3.00	6.00	12.00
PC 39579	Take Me Back to Chicago	1983	3.00	6.00	12.00
HC 43900	Chicago IX — Chicago's Greatest Hits	1982	7.50	15.00	30.00
—Half-speed mastered edition					
HC 44200	Chicago X	1982	10.00	20.00	40.00
—Half-speed mastered edition					

FULL MOON

Number	Title (A Side/B Side)	Yr	VG	VG+	NM
23689	Chicago 16	1982	2.50	5.00	10.00

MAGNUM

Number	Title (A Side/B Side)	Yr	VG	VG+	NM
MR 604	Chicago Transit Authority Live in Concert	1978	5.00	10.00	20.00
—Taken from their 1969 Toronto Rock 'n Roll Revival performance					

MOBILE FIDELITY

Number	Title (A Side/B Side)	Yr	VG	VG+	NM
2-128 [(2)]	Chicago Transit Authority	1983	20.00	40.00	80.00
—Audiophile vinyl					

REPRISE

Number	Title (A Side/B Side)	Yr	VG	VG+	NM
25714	Chicago 19	1988	2.50	5.00	10.00
26080	Greatest Hits 1982-1989	1989	2.50	5.00	10.00
R 110533	Twenty 1	1991	5.00	10.00	20.00
—BMG Direct Marketing version					

WARNER BROS.

Number	Title (A Side/B Side)	Yr	VG	VG+	NM
25060	Chicago 17	1984	2.50	5.00	10.00
25060 [DJ]	Chicago 17	1984	5.00	10.00	20.00
—Promo pressing on Quiex II vinyl					
25509	Chicago 18	1986	2.50	5.00	10.00

CHICKEN SHACK

Also see CHRISTINE McVIE.

45s

BLUE HORIZON

Number	Title (A Side/B Side)	Yr	VG	VG+	NM
100	Tears in the Wind/The Things You Put Me Through	1970	—	3.00	6.00
302	Maudie/Diary of Your Life	1972	—	3.00	6.00

DERAM

Number	Title (A Side/B Side)	Yr	VG	VG+	NM
7537	As Time Goes Passing By/(B-side unknown)	1972	—	2.50	5.00

EPIC

Number	Title (A Side/B Side)	Yr	VG	VG+	NM
10414	Six Nights in Seven/Worried About My Woman	1968	2.50	5.00	10.00

Albums

BLUE HORIZON

Number	Title (A Side/B Side)	Yr	VG	VG+	NM
BH 4809	Accept Chicken Shack	1970	6.25	12.50	25.00
BH 7705	O.K. Ken?	1969	6.25	12.50	25.00
BH 7706	100-Ton Chicken	1969	6.25	12.50	25.00

DERAM

Number	Title (A Side/B Side)	Yr	VG	VG+	NM
DES 18063	Imagination Lady	1972	5.00	10.00	20.00

EPIC

Number	Title (A Side/B Side)	Yr	VG	VG+	NM
LN 24414 [M]	Forty Blue Fingers, Freshly Packed and Ready to Serve	1968	25.00	50.00	100.00
BN 26414 [S]	Forty Blue Fingers, Freshly Packed and Ready to Serve	1968	7.50	15.00	30.00

Number	Title (A Side/B Side)	Yr	VG	VG+	NM
LONDON					
XPS 632	Unlucky Boy	1973	5.00	10.00	20.00

CHIEFTAINS, THE

45s

Number	Title (A Side/B Side)	Yr	VG	VG+	NM
ISLAND					
048	Theme from "Barry Lyndon"/Timpan Reel	1976	—	2.50	5.00

Albums

Number	Title (A Side/B Side)	Yr	VG	VG+	NM
COLUMBIA					
JC 35612	The Chieftains 7	1979	3.00	6.00	12.00
PC 35612	The Chieftains 7	198?	2.00	4.00	8.00
—Budget-line reissue					
JC 35726	The Chieftains 8	1980	3.00	6.00	12.00
JC 36401	Boil the Breakfast Early	1981	3.00	6.00	12.00
PC 36401	Boil the Breakfast Early	198?	2.00	4.00	8.00
—Budget-line reissue					
ISLAND					
ILPS 9334	The Chieftains 5	1975	3.00	6.00	12.00
—Black label original					
ILPS 9364	The Chieftains 1	1976	3.00	6.00	12.00
—Black label original; first US issue					
ILPS 9365	The Chieftains 2	1976	3.00	6.00	12.00
—Black label original; first US issue					
ILPS 9379	The Chieftains 3	1976	3.00	6.00	12.00
—Black label original; first US issue					
ILPS 9380	The Chieftains 4	1976	3.00	6.00	12.00
—Black label original; first US issue					
ILPS 9432	Bonaparte's Retreat	1977	3.00	6.00	12.00
ILPS 9501	The Chieftains Live	1978	3.00	6.00	12.00
RCA					
6358-1-R	Celtic Wedding	1987	2.50	5.00	10.00
7858-1-R	A Chieftains Celebration	1989	3.00	6.00	12.00
SHANACHIE					
79019	Cotton-Eyed Joe	198?	2.50	5.00	10.00
79021	The Chieftains 1	198?	2.50	5.00	10.00
—Reissue of Island 9364					
79022	The Chieftains 2	198?	2.50	5.00	10.00
—Reissue of Island 9365					
79023	The Chieftains 3	198?	2.50	5.00	10.00
—Reissue of Island 9379					
79024	The Chieftains 4	198?	2.50	5.00	10.00
—Reissue of Island 9380					
79025	The Chieftains 5	198?	2.50	5.00	10.00
—Reissue of Island 9334					
79026	Bonaparte's Retreat	198?	2.50	5.00	10.00
—Reissue of Island 9432					
79050	The Chieftains in China	198?	2.50	5.00	10.00
79051	The Ballad of Iron Horse	198?	2.50	5.00	10.00

CHIFFONS, THE

45s

Number	Title (A Side/B Side)	Yr	VG	VG+	NM
BIG DEAL					
6003	Tonight's the Night/Do You Know	1960	20.00	40.00	80.00
BUDDAH					
171	So Much in Love/Strange, Strange Feeling	1970	2.50	5.00	10.00
B.T. PUPPY					
558	Secret Love/Strange, Strange Feeling	1970	2.50	5.00	10.00
LAURIE					
3152	He's So Fine/Oh My Lover	1963	5.00	10.00	20.00
3166	Lucky Me/Why Am I So Shy?	1963	3.75	7.50	15.00
3179	One Fine Day/Why Am I So Shy	1963	5.00	10.00	20.00
3195	A Love So Fine/Only My Friend	1963	3.00	6.00	12.00
3212	I Have a Boyfriend/I'm Gonna Dry My Eyes	1963	3.00	6.00	12.00
3224	Tonight I Met an Angel/Easy to Love	1964	3.00	6.00	12.00
3262	Sailor Boy/When the Summer Is Through	1964	3.00	6.00	12.00
3275	What Am I Gonna Do with You/Strange, Strange Feeling	1964	3.00	6.00	12.00
3301	Nobody Knows What's Going On (In My Mind But Me)/Did You Ever Go Steady	1965	3.00	6.00	12.00
3301	Nobody Knows What's Going On (In My Mind But Me)/The Real Thing	1965	3.00	6.00	12.00
3318	Tonight I'm Gonna Dream/Heavenly Place	1965	3.00	6.00	12.00
3340	Sweet Talkin' Guy/Did You Ever Go Steady	1966	3.75	7.50	15.00
3350	Out of This World/Just a Boy	1966	2.50	5.00	10.00
3357	Stop, Look, Listen/March	1966	2.50	5.00	10.00
3364	My Boyfriend's Back/I Got Plenty of Nuttin'	1966	2.50	5.00	10.00
3377	If I Knew Then/Keep the Boy Happy	1967	2.50	5.00	10.00
3423	Just for Tonight/Teach Me How	1968	2.50	5.00	10.00
3423	Just for Tonight/Keep the Boy Happy	1968	2.50	5.00	10.00
3460	Up on the Bridge/March	1968	2.50	5.00	10.00
3497	Love Me Like You're Gonna Lose Me/Three Dips of Ice Cream	1969	2.50	5.00	10.00
3630	My Sweet Lord/Main Nerve	1975	2.50	5.00	10.00
3648	Dream, Dream, Dream/Oh My Lover	1976	2.50	5.00	10.00
REPRISE					
20103	After Last Night/Doctor of Hearts	1962	5.00	10.00	20.00
RUST					
5070	When the Boy's Happy (The Girl's Happy Too)/Hockaday, Part 1	1963	6.25	12.50	25.00
—As "The Four Pennies"					
5071	Dry Your Eyes/My Block	1963	6.25	12.50	25.00
—As "The Four Pennies"					
WILDCAT					
601	Never Never/No More Tomorrows	1961	6.25	12.50	25.00

Albums

Number	Title (A Side/B Side)	Yr	VG	VG+	NM
B.T. PUPPY					
S-1011	My Secret Love	1970	100.00	200.00	400.00
COLLECTABLES					
COL-5042	Golden Classics	198?	3.00	6.00	12.00
LAURIE					
LLP-2018 [M]	He's So Fine	1963	30.00	60.00	120.00
LLP-2020 [M]	One Fine Day	1963	50.00	100.00	200.00
LLP-2036 [M]	Sweet Talkin' Guy	1966	25.00	50.00	100.00
SLP-2036 [S]	Sweet Talkin' Guy	1966	37.50	75.00	150.00
4001	Everything You Always Wanted to Hear by the Chiffons	1975	5.00	10.00	20.00
DT-90075 [R]	He's So Fine	1965	50.00	100.00	200.00
—Capitol Record Club edition					
ST-90779 [S]	Sweet Talkin' Guy	1966	50.00	100.00	200.00
—Capitol Record Club edition					

CHILDREN, THE

45s

Number	Title (A Side/B Side)	Yr	VG	VG+	NM
ATCO					
6633	Maypole/I'll Be Your Sunshine	1968	5.00	10.00	20.00
CINEMA					
025	Pills/(B-side unknown)	1968	7.50	15.00	30.00
LARAMIE					
666	Picture Me/(B-side unknown)	1967	10.00	20.00	40.00
MAP CITY					
304	What If I/Evil Woman	1970	3.00	6.00	12.00
ODE					
66005	From the Very Start/Such a Fine Night	1970	5.00	10.00	20.00
66013	Fire King/Hand of a Lady	1971	5.00	10.00	20.00

Albums

Number	Title (A Side/B Side)	Yr	VG	VG+	NM
ATCO					
SD 33-271	Rebirth	1968	6.25	12.50	25.00
CINEMA					
CLP-1	Rebirth	1968	37.50	75.00	150.00

CHILLIWACK

Also see THE COLLECTORS.

12-Inch Singles

Number	Title (A Side/B Side)	Yr	VG	VG+	NM
MILLENNIUM					
JD-13110 [DJ]	Whatcha Gonna Do (same on both sides)	1982	2.50	5.00	10.00
YD-13118	Secret Information/I Really Don't Mind	1982	2.00	4.00	8.00

45s

Number	Title (A Side/B Side)	Yr	VG	VG+	NM
A&M					
1310	Lonesome Mary/Ridin'	1971	—	3.00	6.00
1395	Ground Hog/Nothin' to Do	1972	—	3.00	6.00
MILLENNIUM					
YB-11813	My Girl (Gone, Gone, Gone)/Sign Here	1981	—	2.00	4.00
YB-13102	I Believe/Living in Stereo	1981	—	2.00	4.00
YB-13110	Whatcha Gonna Do/I Really Don't Mind	1982	—	2.00	4.00
YB-13117	Secret Information/I Really Don't Mind	1982	—	2.00	4.00
YB-13123	Lean On Me/Night Time	1983	—	—	—
—Canceled					
MUSHROOM					
7022	California Girl/Reach	1976	—	2.50	5.00
7024	Fly By Night/Mary Lo & Me	1977	—	2.50	5.00
7025	Something Better/Rain-O	1977	—	2.50	5.00
7028	Baby Blue/Something Better	1977	—	2.50	5.00
7033	Arms of Mary/I Wanna Be the One	1978	—	2.50	5.00
7038	Never Be the Same/I Wanna Be the One	1978	—	2.50	5.00
7046	Communication Breakdown/Are You With Me	1979	—	2.50	5.00
PARROT					
350	I Must Have Been Blind/Chain Train	1970	2.00	4.00	8.00
357	Everyday/Sundown	1970	2.00	4.00	8.00
SIRE					
716	Crazy Talk/In and Out	1974	—	2.50	5.00
718	Come On Over/Time Don't Mean a Thing to You	1975	—	2.50	5.00
720	If You Want My Love/Train's a-Comin' Back	1975	—	2.50	5.00
723	Last Day of December/Magnolia	1976	—	2.50	5.00

Albums

Number	Title (A Side/B Side)	Yr	VG	VG+	NM
A&M					
SP-3509 [(2)]	Chilliwack	1971	5.00	10.00	20.00
SP-4375	All Over You	1972	3.75	7.50	15.00
MILLENNIUM					
BXL1-7759	Wanna Be a Star	1981	2.50	5.00	10.00
BXL1-7766	Opus X	1982	2.50	5.00	10.00
MUSHROOM					
MRS-5006	Dreams, Dreams, Dreams	1977	3.00	6.00	12.00
MRS-5011	Lights from the Valley	1978	3.00	6.00	12.00
PARROT					
PAS 71040	Chilliwack	1970	5.00	10.00	20.00
SIRE					
SASD-7506	Chilliwack	1975	3.75	7.50	15.00
SASD-7511	Rockerbox	1976	3.75	7.50	15.00

CHIMES, THE (1)

45s

Number	Title (A Side/B Side)	Yr	VG	VG+	NM
LAURIE					
3211	Whose Heart Are You Breaking Now/Baby's Coming Home	1963	3.75	7.50	15.00
METRO					
1	Whose Heart Are You Breaking Now/Baby's Coming Home	1963	10.00	20.00	40.00
TAG					
444	Once in Awhile/Summer Night	1960	10.00	20.00	40.00
—Maroon label					
444	Once in Awhile/Summer Night	1960	10.00	20.00	40.00
—Light blue label					
444	Once in Awhile/Oh, How I Love You So	1960	12.50	25.00	50.00
—B-side is actually by a group called the Bi-Tones, though credited to the Chimes					
445	I'm in the Mood for Love/Only Love	1961	7.50	15.00	30.00
447	Let's Fall in Love/Dream Girl	1961	6.25	12.50	25.00
450	Paradise/My Love	1961	7.50	15.00	30.00

CHIMES, THE (2)

On the Arrow label, see FREDDIE SCOTT.

CHIMES, THE (3)

On the Flair label, see THE FLAIRS.

CHIMES, THE (U)

Some of these may be group (1).

45s

Number	Title (A Side/B Side)	Yr	VG	VG+	NM
HOUSE OF BEAUTY					
3	Tears from An Angel's Eyes/(B-side unknown)	1959	20.00	40.00	80.00
LIMELIGHT					
3000	Cry, Baby, Cry/Angel Child	1963	6.25	12.50	25.00
3002	Du Wap/Stop, Look and Listen	1963	6.25	12.50	25.00
RESERVE					
120	When School Starts Again/Nervous Heart	1957	10.00	20.00	40.00
ROYAL ROOST					
577	Dearest Darling/A Fool Was I	1955	175.00	350.00	700.00
SPECIALTY					
555	Tears on My Pillow/Cindy Lou	1955	15.00	30.00	60.00
574	Chop Chop/Pretty Little Girl	1956	15.00	30.00	60.00

CHIPMUNKS, THE, DAVID SEVILLE AND

Listings only include the "original" group, which made recordings from 1958-68. Also see ROSS BAGDASARIAN; DAVID SEVILLE.

45s

Number	Title (A Side/B Side)	Yr	VG	VG+	NM
DOT					
16997	Apple Picker/Sorry About That, Herb	1967	3.00	6.00	12.00
EMI					
S7-17645	The Chipmunk Song/Frosty the Snowman	1993	—	2.00	4.00
—Green vinyl					
LIBERTY					
55168	The Chipmunk Song/Almost Good	1958	6.25	12.50	25.00
—Blue-green label					
55168	The Chipmunk Song/Almost Good	1958	7.50	15.00	30.00
—Black label					
55179	Alvin's Harmonica/Mediocre	1959	5.00	10.00	20.00
55200	Ragtime Cowboy Joe/Flip Side	1959	5.00	10.00	20.00
55200 [PS]	Ragtime Cowboy Joe/Flip Side	1959	10.00	20.00	40.00
55233	Alvin's Orchestra/Copyright 1960	1960	3.75	7.50	15.00
55233 [PS]	Alvin's Orchestra/Copyright 1960	1960	10.00	20.00	40.00
55246	Coming 'Round the Mountain/Sing a Goofy Song	1960	3.75	7.50	15.00
55246 [PS]	Coming 'Round the Mountain/Sing a Goofy Song	1960	10.00	20.00	40.00
55250	The Chipmunk Song/Alvin's Harmonica	1959	3.75	7.50	15.00
—Blue-green label, no horizontal lines					
55250	The Chipmunk Song/Alvin's Harmonica	1961	3.00	6.00	12.00
—Blue-green label with horizontal lines					
55250 [PS]	The Chipmunk Song/Alvin's Harmonica	1959	10.00	20.00	40.00
—Sleeve has Chipmunks depicted somewhat like real chipmunks					
55250 [PS]	The Chipmunk Song/Alvin's Harmonica	1961	7.50	15.00	30.00
—Sleeve has Chipmunks depicted as the familiar cartoon characters					
55277	Alvin for President/Sack Time	1960	3.75	7.50	15.00
55277 [PS]	Alvin for President/Sack Time	1960	10.00	20.00	40.00
55289	Rudolph, the Red-Nosed Reindeer/Spain	1960	3.75	7.50	15.00
55289 [PS]	Rudolph, the Red-Nosed Reindeer/Spain	1960	10.00	20.00	40.00
55424	The Alvin Twist/I Wish I Could Speak French	1962	3.75	7.50	15.00
55452	America the Beautiful/My Wild Irish Rose	1962	3.75	7.50	15.00
55544	Alvin's All Star Chipmunk Band/Old MacDonald Cha Cha Cha	1963	3.75	7.50	15.00
55544 [PS]	Alvin's All Star Chipmunk Band/Old MacDonald Cha Cha Cha	1963	10.00	20.00	40.00
55632	Eefin' Alvin/Flip Side	1963	3.75	7.50	15.00
55635	The Night Before Christmas/Wonderful Day	1963	3.75	7.50	15.00
55635 [PS]	The Night Before Christmas/Wonderful Day	1963	7.50	15.00	30.00
55734	All My Lovin'/Do You Want to Know a Secret	1964	3.75	7.50	15.00
55773	Do-Re-Mi/Supercalifragilisticexpialidocious	1965	3.00	6.00	12.00
55832	I'm Henry VIII, I Am/What's New Pussycat	1965	3.00	6.00	12.00
56079	The Chipmunk Song/Christmas Blues	1968	4.00	8.00	16.00
—With Canned Heat					
SUNSET					
61002	Talk to the Animals/My Friend the Doctor	1968	2.50	5.00	10.00
61002 [PS]	Talk to the Animals/My Friend the Doctor	1968	3.75	7.50	15.00
61003	Chitty Chitty Bang Bang/Hushabye Mountain	1968	2.50	5.00	10.00
61003 [PS]	Chitty Chitty Bang Bang/Hushabye Mountain	1968	3.75	7.50	15.00
UNITED ARTISTS					
0056	The Chipmunk Song/Ragtime Cowboy Joe	1973	2.00	4.00	8.00
—"Silver Spotlight Series" reissue					
0057	Alvin's Harmonica/Rudolph, the Red-Nosed Reindeer	1973	2.00	4.00	8.00
—"Silver Spotlight Series" reissue					
XW576	The Chipmunk Song/Rudolph, the Red-Nosed Reindeer	1974	—	3.00	6.00

7-Inch Extended Plays

Number	Title (A Side/B Side)	Yr	VG	VG+	NM
LIBERTY					
LSX-1007	The Chipmunk Song/Ragtime Cowboy Joe//Alvin's Harmonica/If You Love Me	1960	7.50	15.00	30.00
LSX-1007 [PS]	Let's All Sing with the Chipmunks	1960	12.50	25.00	50.00
LSX-1017	Wonderful Day/Christmas Time//Deck The Halls/The Night Before Christmas	1963	5.00	10.00	20.00
LSX-1017 [PS]	Christmas with the Chipmunks, Volume 2	1963	12.50	25.00	50.00

Albums

Number	Title (A Side/B Side)	Yr	VG	VG+	NM
LIBERTY					
LM-1070	Christmas with the Chipmunks	1980	2.00	4.00	8.00
—Reissue with two tracks omitted					
LRP-3132 [M]	Let's All Sing with the Chipmunks	1959	15.00	30.00	60.00
—Red vinyl					
LRP-3132 [M]	Let's All Sing with the Chipmunks	1959	7.50	15.00	30.00
—Black vinyl; original cover features "realistic" chipmunks and no reference to "The Alvin Show"					
LRP-3132 [M]	Let's All Sing with the Chipmunks	1961	5.00	10.00	20.00
—Second cover features the "cartoon" Chipmunks and a reference to "The Alvin Show"					
LRP-3159 [M]	Sing Again with the Chipmunks	1960	10.00	20.00	40.00
—Original cover features "realistic" chipmunks					
LRP-3159 [M]	Sing Again with the Chipmunks	1961	5.00	10.00	20.00
—Second cover features the "cartoon" Chipmunks					
LRP-3170 [M]	Around the World with the Chipmunks	1960	10.00	20.00	40.00
—Original cover features "realistic" chipmunks on and near a plane					
LRP-3170 [M]	Around the World with the Chipmunks	1961	5.00	10.00	20.00
—Second cover features the "cartoon" Chipmunks on and near a camel					
LRP-3209 [M]	The Alvin Show	1961	6.25	12.50	25.00
LRP-3229 [M]	The Chipmunks Songbook	1962	6.25	12.50	25.00
LRP-3256 [M]	Christmas with the Chipmunks	1962	6.25	12.50	25.00
LRP-3334 [M]	Christmas with the Chipmunks, Vol. 2	1963	6.25	12.50	25.00
LRP-3388 [M]	The Chipmunks Sing the Beatles Hits	1964	7.50	15.00	30.00
LRP-3405 [M]	The Chipmunks Sing with Children	1965	5.00	10.00	20.00
LRP-3424 [M]	The Chipmunks A-Go-Go	1965	5.00	10.00	20.00
LST-7132 [S]	Let's All Sing with the Chipmunks	1959	20.00	40.00	80.00
—Red vinyl					
LST-7132 [S]	Let's All Sing with the Chipmunks	1959	10.00	20.00	40.00
—Black vinyl; original cover features "realistic" chipmunks and no reference to "The Alvin Show"					
LST-7132 [S]	Let's All Sing with the Chipmunks	1961	6.25	12.50	25.00
—Second cover features the "cartoon" Chipmunks and a reference to "The Alvin Show"					
LST-7159 [S]	Sing Again with the Chipmunks	1960	12.50	25.00	50.00
—Original cover features "realistic" chipmunks					
LST-7159 [S]	Sing Again with the Chipmunks	1961	6.25	12.50	25.00
—Second cover features the "cartoon" Chipmunks					
LST-7170 [S]	Around the World with the Chipmunks	1960	12.50	25.00	50.00
—Original covers have "realistic" chipmunks on and near a plane.					
LST-7170 [S]	Around the World with the Chipmunks	1960	6.25	12.50	25.00
—Second cover features the "cartoon" Chipmunks on and near a camel					
LST-7209 [S]	The Alvin Show	1961	7.50	15.00	30.00
LST-7229 [S]	The Chipmunks Songbook	1962	7.50	15.00	30.00
LST-7256 [S]	Christmas with the Chipmunks	1962	7.50	15.00	30.00
LST-7334 [S]	Christmas with the Chipmunks, Vol. 2	1963	7.50	15.00	30.00
LST-7388 [S]	The Chipmunks Sing the Beatles Hits	1964	10.00	20.00	40.00
LST-7405 [S]	The Chipmunks Sing with Children	1965	6.25	12.50	25.00
LST-7424 [S]	The Chipmunks A-Go-Go	1965	6.25	12.50	25.00
MISTLETOE					
MLP-1216	Christmas with the Chipmunks	197?	2.00	4.00	8.00
—Reissue of Liberty LST-7256					
MLP-1217	Christmas with the Chipmunks, Vol. 2	197?	2.00	4.00	8.00
—Reissue of Liberty LST-7334					
PICKWICK					
SPC-1034	Christmas with the Chipmunks	1980	2.50	5.00	10.00
SPC-1035	The Twelve Days of Christmas with The Chipmunks	1980	2.50	5.00	10.00
—Reissue of "Christmas with the Chipmunks, Vol. 2"					
SUNSET					
LST-7334 [S]	Christmas with the Chipmunks, Vol. 2	1968	5.00	10.00	20.00
—Budget-line reissue of Liberty LST-7334					
LST-7424 [S]	The Chipmunks A-Go-Go	196?	3.75	7.50	15.00
—Same cover as Liberty 7424, but with "SUNSET" sticker at upper right					
UNITED ARTISTS					
UA-LA352-E2 [(2)]	Christmas with the Chipmunks	1974	5.00	10.00	20.00
—Entire contents of both original Liberty LPs					

CHIPS, THE (1)

Male vocal group.

45s

Number	Title (A Side/B Side)	Yr	VG	VG+	NM
JOSIE					
803	Rubber Biscuit/Oh My Darlin'	1956	25.00	50.00	100.00

CHIPS, THE (2)

45s

Number	Title (A Side/B Side)	Yr	VG	VG+	NM
PHILIPS					
40520	Mixed Up Shook Up Girl/Break It Gently	1968	2.50	5.00	10.00

CHIPS, THE (3)

Memphis group.

45s

Number	Title (A Side/B Side)	Yr	VG	VG+	NM
SATELLITE					
105	As You can See/You Make Me Feel So Good	1961	30.00	60.00	120.00

CHIPS, THE (4)

45s

Number	Title (A Side/B Side)	Yr	VG	VG+	NM
STRAND					
25027	Darling (I Need Your Love)/You're On My Side	1961	10.00	20.00	40.00
VENICE					
101	Darling (I Need Your Love)/You're On My Side	1961	30.00	60.00	120.00

CHIPS, THE (5)

Lead singer: JOE SOUTH.

45s

Number	Title (A Side/B Side)	Yr	VG	VG+	NM
TOLLIE					
9042	Party People/Long Lonely Winter	1965	2.50	5.00	10.00

CHIPS, THE (U)

45s

Number	Title (A Side/B Side)	Yr	VG	VG+	NM
EMBER					
1077	What a Lie/Bye, Bye, My Love	1961	5.00	10.00	20.00

CHOCO AND HIS MALIMBA DRUM RHYTHMS

Albums

Number	Title (A Side/B Side)	Yr	VG	VG+	NM
AUDIO FIDELITY					
AFLP-2102 [M]	African Latin Voodoo Drums	1962	5.00	10.00	20.00
AFSD-6102 [S]	African Latin Voodoo Drums	1962	7.50	15.00	30.00

CHOCOLATE WATCH BAND, THE

45s

Number	Title (A Side/B Side)	Yr	VG	VG+	NM
TOWER					
373	Are You Gonna Be There (At the Love-In)/No Way Out	1967	12.50	25.00	50.00
UPTOWN					
740	Baby Blue/Sweet Young Thing	1967	75.00	150.00	300.00
749	Misty Lane/She Weaves a Tender Trap	1967	12.50	25.00	50.00

Albums

Number	Title (A Side/B Side)	Yr	VG	VG+	NM
RHINO					
RNLP-108	The Best of the Chocolate Watch Band	1983	3.00	6.00	12.00
TOWER					
ST 5096 [S]	No Way Out	1967	100.00	200.00	400.00
T 5096 [M]	No Way Out	1967	75.00	150.00	300.00
ST 5106 [S]	The Inner Mystique	1968	75.00	150.00	300.00
T 5106 [M]	The Inner Mystique	1968	100.00	200.00	400.00
ST 5153	One Step Beyond	1969	75.00	150.00	300.00

CHOIR, THE

Two members went on to form the RASPBERRIES.

45s

Number	Title (A Side/B Side)	Yr	VG	VG+	NM
CANADIAN AMERICAN					
203	It's Cold Outside/I'm Goin' Home	1967	10.00	20.00	40.00
INTREPID					
75020	Gonna Have a Good Time Tonight/So Much Love	1970	5.00	10.00	20.00
ROULETTE					
4738	It's Cold Outside/I'm Goin' Home	1967	3.75	7.50	15.00
4760	No One Here to Play With/Don't You Feel a Little Sorry for Me	1967	3.75	7.50	15.00
7005	Changin' My Mind/When You Were With Me	1968	3.75	7.50	15.00

Albums

Number	Title (A Side/B Side)	Yr	VG	VG+	NM
SUNDAZED					
LP 5009	Choir Practice	1992	2.50	5.00	10.00

CHORDCATS, THE

See THE CHORDS.

CHORDETTES, THE

45s

Number	Title (A Side/B Side)	Yr	VG	VG+	NM
ATLANTIC					
89310	Lollipop/Never on Sunday	1986	—	—	3.00
89310 [PS]	Lollipop/Never on Sunday	1986	—	—	3.00
CADENCE					
1239	It's You, It's You I Love/True Love Goes On and On	1954	3.75	7.50	15.00
1247	Mr. Sandman/I Don't Wanna See You Cryin'	1954	3.75	7.50	15.00
1259	Lonely Lips/The Dudelsack Song	1955	3.00	6.00	12.00
1267	Hummingbird/I Told a Lie	1955	3.00	6.00	12.00
1273	The Wedding/I Don't Know, I Don't Care	1955	3.00	6.00	12.00
1284	Eddie My Love/Whispering Willie	1956	3.00	6.00	12.00
1291	Born to Be with You/Love Never Changes	1956	3.00	6.00	12.00
1299	Lay Down Your Arms/Teenage Goodnight	1956	3.00	6.00	12.00
1307	Come Home to My Arms/(Fifi's) Walking the Poodle	1957	3.00	6.00	12.00
1319	Echo of Love/Like a Baby	1957	3.00	6.00	12.00
1330	Just Between You and Me/Soft Sands	1957	3.00	6.00	12.00
1341	Photographs/Baby of Mine	1957	3.00	6.00	12.00
1345	Lollipop/Baby Come-a Back-a	1958	3.75	7.50	15.00
1349	Zorro/Love Is a Two-Way Street	1958	3.00	6.00	12.00
1349 [PS]	Zorro/Love Is a Two-Way Street	1958	6.25	12.50	25.00
1361	No Other Arms, No Other Lips/We Should Be Together	1959	2.50	5.00	10.00
1366	A Girl's Work Is Never Done/No Wheels	1959	2.50	5.00	10.00
1366 [PS]	A Girl's Work Is Never Done/No Wheels	1959	6.25	12.50	25.00
1367	Forever/Ho Hum	1959	2.50	5.00	10.00
1382	All My Sorrows/A Broken Vow	1960	2.50	5.00	10.00
1402	Never on Sunday/A Faraway Star	1961	2.50	5.00	10.00
1412	The Exodus Song/Theme from Goodbye Again (Say No More-It's Goodbye)	1961	2.50	5.00	10.00
1417	Adios/White Rose of Athens	1962	2.50	5.00	10.00
1425	In the Deep Blue Sea/All My Sorrows	1962	2.50	5.00	10.00
1442	True Love Goes On and On/All My Sorrows	1963	2.50	5.00	10.00
COLUMBIA					
38756	When You Were Sweet Sixteen/Moonlight Bay	1950	3.75	7.50	15.00
38757	Carry Me Back to Old Virginny/Ballin' the Jack	1950	3.75	7.50	15.00
38758	Tell Me Why/Shine On Harvest Moon	1950	3.75	7.50	15.00
38759	I'd Love to Live in Loveland (With a Love Like You)/When Day Is Done	1950	3.75	7.50	15.00
—The above four comprise box set B-201					
39251	Runnin' Wild/Alice Blue Gown	1951	3.75	7.50	15.00
39252	Love Me and the World Is Mine/Lonesome That's All	1951	3.75	7.50	15.00
39253	Moonlight on the Ganges/Let the Rest of the World Go By	1951	3.75	7.50	15.00
39254	The World Is Waiting for the Sunrise/Love's Old Sweet Song	1951	3.75	7.50	15.00
39793	Carolina Moon//The Anniversary Waltz/Sentimental Journey	1952	3.75	7.50	15.00
39794	A Little Street Where Old Friends Meet//Basin Street Blues + 1	1952	3.75	7.50	15.00
39795	Drifting and Dreaming + 1//I'm Drifting Back to Dreamland/Angry	1952	3.75	7.50	15.00
39796	S'posin'/The Sweetheart of Sigma Chi//Kentucky Babe/In the Sweet Long Ago	1952	3.75	7.50	15.00

7-Inch Extended Plays

Number	Title (A Side/B Side)	Yr	VG	VG+	NM
COLUMBIA					
B-401 [PS]	The Chordettes Sing Your Requests	195?	3.00	6.00	12.00
—Double-pocket sleeve for 1878 and 1879					
5-1878	Wait Till the Sun Shines Nellie/They Say It's Wonderful//Wonderful One/Darkness on the Delta	195?	3.00	6.00	12.00
5-1879	I Wonder Who's Kissing Her Now?/For Me and My Gal//I Believe/Down Among the Sheltering Pines	195?	3.00	6.00	12.00

Albums

Number	Title (A Side/B Side)	Yr	VG	VG+	NM
BARNABY					
BR-4003	All the Very Best of the Chordettes	1976	3.00	6.00	12.00
CADENCE					
CLP-1002 [10]	Close Harmony	1955	12.50	25.00	50.00
CLP-3001 [M]	The Chordettes	1957	10.00	20.00	40.00
CLP-3020 [M]	Barbershop Harmony	1958	10.00	20.00	40.00
CLP-3056 [M]	Never on Sunday	1962	5.00	10.00	20.00
CLP-25056 [S]	Never on Sunday	1962	7.50	15.00	30.00
COLUMBIA					
CL 956 [M]	Listen	1955	12.50	25.00	50.00
CL 2519 [10]	The Chordettes	1955	10.00	20.00	40.00
CL 6111 [10]	Harmony Time	1950	12.50	25.00	50.00
CL 6170 [10]	Harmony Time, Vol. 2	1951	12.50	25.00	50.00
CL 6218 [10]	Harmony Encores	1952	12.50	25.00	50.00
CL 6285 [10]	Your Requests	1953	12.50	25.00	50.00
HARMONY					
HL 7164 [M]	The Chordettes	196?	3.75	7.50	15.00
RHINO					
R1-70849	The Best of the Chordettes	1989	3.00	6.00	12.00

CHORDS, THE

45s

Number	Title (A Side/B Side)	Yr	VG	VG+	NM
ATCO					
6213	Sh-Boom/Little Maiden	1961	3.75	7.50	15.00
—As "The Sh-Booms"					
ATLANTIC					
2074	Blue Moon/Short Skirts	1960	5.00	10.00	20.00
—As "The Sh-Booms"					
CASINO					
451	Tears in Your Eyes/Don't Be a Jumpin' Jack	1958	7.50	15.00	30.00
CAT					
104	Sh-Boom/Cross Over the Bridge	1954	30.00	60.00	120.00
104	Sh-Boom/Little Maiden	1954	15.00	30.00	60.00
109	Zippety Zum (I'm in Love)/Bless You (For Being an Angel)	1954	10.00	20.00	40.00
112	A Girl to Love/Hold Me Baby	1955	10.00	20.00	40.00
—As "The Chordcats"					
117	Could It Be/Pretty Wild	1955	10.00	20.00	40.00
—As "The Sh-Dooms"					
METRO					
20015	Elephant Walk/Pretty Face	1959	5.00	10.00	20.00
VIK					
0295	I Don't Want to Set the World on Fire/Lu Lu	1957	7.50	15.00	30.00
—As "The Sh-Booms"					

CHOSEN FEW, THE

Many different groups.

45s

Number	Title (A Side/B Side)	Yr	VG	VG+	NM
AUTUMN					
17	Nobody But Me/I Think It's Time	1965	2.50	5.00	10.00
CANADIAN AMERICAN					
202	Cute Thing/One of Those Songs	1967	3.00	6.00	12.00
CANUSA					
504	Summer's Love/Hey Joe	1967	3.75	7.50	15.00
CANYON					
1000	Talking All the Love I Can/Birth of a Playboy	196?	2.50	5.00	10.00
CO-OP					
510	Why Can't I Love You/La La La La La	1966	3.00	6.00	12.00
511	Summer's Love/(Instrumental)	1967	3.00	6.00	12.00
CRYSTAL					
1107	You're a Big Girl Now/(B-side unknown)	196?	2.50	5.00	10.00
DART					
1080	Foolin' Around with Me/We Walk Together	1967	2.00	4.00	8.00
DENIM					
1092	Pink Clouds and Lemonade/Stop in the Name of Love	196?	2.00	4.00	8.00
LIBERTY					
55919	Synthetic Man/The Last Man Alive	1966	2.50	5.00	10.00
55962	Asian Chrome/Earth Above, Sky Below	1967	2.50	5.00	10.00
NORTH BEACH					
1003	Nobody But Me/I Think It's Time	1965	3.75	7.50	15.00
PLAYBOY					
106	I've Had It/Ask Me Baby	196?	2.50	5.00	10.00
POWER INTERNATIONAL					
872	Another Goodbye/Forget About the Past	1966	10.00	20.00	40.00
RCA VICTOR					
74-0217	Maybe the Rain Will Fall/Deeper In	1969	2.00	4.00	8.00
74-0254	I'll Never Change You/Talk with Me	1969	2.00	4.00	8.00
ROULETTE					
7015	Footsee/You Can Never Be Wrong	1968	2.00	4.00	8.00

Albums

Number	Title (A Side/B Side)	Yr	VG	VG+	NM
MAPLE					
6000	Takin' All the Love I Can	196?	5.00	10.00	20.00
RCA VICTOR					
LSP-4242	The Chosen Few	1969	5.00	10.00	20.00

CHRISTIAN, DIANE

45s

Number	Title (A Side/B Side)	Yr	VG	VG+	NM
BELL					
610	It Happened One Night/Wonderful Guy	1965	2.50	5.00	10.00
617	Little Boy/Why Don't the Boy Leave Me Alone	1965	2.50	5.00	10.00
SMASH					
1862	Has Anybody Seen My Boyfriend/There's So Much About My Baby	1963	2.50	5.00	10.00

CHRISTIAN, NEIL

45s

Number	Title (A Side/B Side)	Yr	VG	VG+	NM
MORNING STAR					
517	That's Nice/She's Got the Action	19??	2.00	4.00	8.00
RCA VICTOR					
47-8828	That's Nice/She's Got the Action	1966	2.00	4.00	8.00

CHRISTIAN, ROGER

45s

Number	Title (A Side/B Side)	Yr	VG	VG+	NM
RENDEZVOUS					
195	The Meaning of Merry Christmas/Little Mary Christmas	1962	6.25	12.50	25.00

CHRISTIE

45s

Number	Title (A Side/B Side)	Yr	VG	VG+	NM
EPIC					
10626	Yellow River/Down the Mississippi Line	1970	—	2.50	5.00
10695	San Bernadino/Here I Am	1971	—	2.00	4.00
10732	Man of Many Faces/Country Sam	1971	—	2.00	4.00

Albums

Number	Title (A Side/B Side)	Yr	VG	VG+	NM
EPIC					
E 30403	Yellow River	1970	3.75	7.50	15.00

CHRISTIE, LOU

Also see THE CLASSICS; THE CLAMS; THE CRITTERS.

45s

Number	Title (A Side/B Side)	Yr	VG	VG+	NM
ALCAR					
207	Close Your Eyes/Funny Thing	1963	6.25	12.50	25.00
208	You're With It/Tomorrow Will Come	1963	6.25	12.50	25.00
AMERICAN MUSIC MAKERS					
006	The Jury/Little Did I Know	1963	7.50	15.00	30.00
BUDDAH					
65	Genesis and the Third Verse/Rake Up the Leaves	1968	2.00	4.00	8.00
76	Canterbury Road/Saints of Aquarius	1969	2.00	4.00	8.00
116	I'm Gonna Make You Mine/I'm Gonna Get Married	1969	—	3.00	6.00
149	Are You Getting Any Sunshine/It'll Take Time	1970	—	2.50	5.00
163	Love Is Over/She Sold Me Magic	1970	—	2.50	5.00
192	Indian Lady/Glory River	1970	—	2.50	5.00
231 [DJ]	Waco (same on both sides)	1971	—	3.00	6.00
—Stock copy does not exist					
235	Waco/Lighthouse	1971	—	2.50	5.00
257	Mickey's Monkey/She Sold Me Magic	1971	6.25	12.50	25.00
285	Sing Me, Sing Me/Paper Song	1972	—	2.50	5.00
285 [PS]	Sing Me, Sing Me/Paper Song	1972	2.50	5.00	10.00
—Sleeve appears to be promo only					
312	Shuffle On Down to Pittsburgh/I'm Gonna Get Married	1972	5.00	10.00	20.00
CO & CE					
235	Outside the Gates of Heaven/All That Glitters Isn't Gold	1966	2.50	5.00	10.00
COLPIX					
735	Merry-Go-Round/Guitars and Bongos	1964	3.00	6.00	12.00
753	Pot of Gold/Have I Sinned	1964	3.00	6.00	12.00
770	Make Summer Last Forever/Why Did You Do It Baby	1965	3.00	6.00	12.00
778	A Teenager in Love/Back Track	1965	3.00	6.00	12.00
799	Cryin' on My Knees/Big Time	1966	3.00	6.00	12.00
799 [PS]	Cryin' on My Knees/Big Time	1966	6.25	12.50	25.00
COLUMBIA					
44062	Shake Hands and Walk Away Cryin'/Escape	1967	3.75	7.50	15.00
44177	Self Expression/Back to the Days of the Romans	1967	3.75	7.50	15.00
44240	(I Remember) Gina/Escape	1967	3.75	7.50	15.00
44338	Back to the Days of the Romans/Don't Stop Me	1967	3.75	7.50	15.00
C&C					
102	The Gypsy Cried/Red Sails in the Sunset	1962	50.00	100.00	200.00
EPIC					
50244	Summer in Malibu/Ridin' in My Van	1976	3.75	7.50	15.00
LIFESONG					
1775	Theme from "People" (Part 1)/Theme from "People" (Part 2)	1978	12.50	25.00	50.00
—As "Sacco"					
MGM					
13412	Lightnin' Strikes/Cryin' in the Streets	1965	3.75	7.50	15.00
13473	Rhapsody in the Rain/Trapeze	1966	5.00	10.00	20.00
—Original version of A-side had racy (by 1966 standards) lyrics: "We were makin' out in the rain/And in this car, our love went much too far." Matrix number in dead wax is "66-XY-308"					
13473	Rhapsody in the Rain/Trapeze	1966	3.75	7.50	15.00
—Revised A-side has altered lyrics: "We fell in love in the rain/And in this car, love came like a falling star." Matrix number in dead wax is "66-XY-308 D.J."					
13473 [PS]	Rhapsody in the Rain/Trapeze	1966	5.00	10.00	20.00
13533	Painter/Du Ronda	1966	2.50	5.00	10.00
13533 [PS]	Painter/Du Ronda	1966	5.00	10.00	20.00
13576	If My Car Could Only Talk/Song of Lita	1966	2.50	5.00	10.00
13623	Since I Don't Have You/Wild Life's in Season	1966	2.50	5.00	10.00
MIDLAND INT'L.					
MB-10848	You're Gonna Make Love to Me/Fantasies	1976	3.75	7.50	15.00
MB-10959	Spanish Wine/Dancing in the Sand	1977	3.75	7.50	15.00
MIDSONG INT'L.					
72013	Don't Knock My Love (Short)/Don't Knock My Love (Long)	1980	2.50	5.00	10.00
—With Pia Zadora					
PLATEAU					
4551	Guardian Angels/(B-side unknown)	1981	10.00	20.00	40.00
RHINO					
90105	O Holy Night (same on both sides)	1991	—	3.00	6.00
—With the University of Pittsburgh Men's Glee Club					
ROULETTE					
4457	The Gypsy Cried/Red Sails in the Sunset	1963	5.00	10.00	20.00
—White label with spokes					
4457	The Gypsy Cried/Red Sails in the Sunset	1963	3.75	7.50	15.00
—Pink label					
4457	The Gypsy Cried/Red Sails in the Sunset	1964	2.50	5.00	10.00
—Orange and yellow label					
4481	Two Faces Have I/All That Glitters Isn't Gold	1963	3.75	7.50	15.00
4504	How Many Teardrops/You and I (Have a Right to Cry)	1963	3.00	6.00	12.00
4527	Shy Boy/It Can Happen	1963	3.00	6.00	12.00
4545	Stay/There They Go	1964	3.75	7.50	15.00
4554	When You Dance/Maybe You'll Be There	1964	6.25	12.50	25.00
SLIPPED DISC					
45270	Summer Days/The One and Only Original Sunshine Kid	1976	3.75	7.50	15.00
THREE BROTHERS					
400	Blue Canadian Rocky Dream/Wilma Lee and Stoney	1973	2.00	4.00	8.00
402	Beyond the Blue Horizon/Saddle the Wind	1974	—	2.50	5.00
403	You Were the One/Good Morning	1974	2.00	4.00	8.00
405	Hey You Cajun/Sunbeam	1974	2.50	5.00	10.00
WORLD					
1002	The Jury/Little Did I Know	1963	7.50	15.00	30.00

Albums

Number	Title (A Side/B Side)	Yr	VG	VG+	NM
51 WEST					
P 18260	Lou Christie Does Detroit	1983	3.75	7.50	15.00
BUDDAH					
BDS-5052	I'm Gonna Make You Mine	1969	3.75	7.50	15.00
BDS-5073	Paint America Love	1971	3.75	7.50	15.00
CO & CE					
LP-1231 [M]	Lou Christie Strikes Back	1966	10.00	20.00	40.00
LPS-1231 [S]	Lou Christie Strikes Back	1966	15.00	30.00	60.00
COLPIX					
CP-4001 [M]	Lou Christie Strikes Again	1966	7.50	5.00	30.00
SCP-4001 [S]	Lou Christie Strikes Again	1966	12.50	25.00	50.00
MGM					
E-4360 [M]	Lightnin' Strikes	1966	3.75	7.50	15.00
SE-4360 [S]	Lightnin' Strikes	1966	5.00	10.00	20.00
E-4394 [M]	Painter of Hits	1966	3.75	7.50	15.00
SE-4394 [S]	Painter of Hits	1966	5.00	10.00	20.00
RHINO					
R1-70246	EnLightnin'Ment: The Best of Lou Christie	1988	3.00	6.00	12.00
ROULETTE					
R 25208 [M]	Lou Christie	1963	12.50	25.00	50.00
—Blue background on front cover					
R 25208 [M]	Lou Christie	1963	10.00	20.00	40.00
—White wall in background on front cover					
SR 25208 [S]	Lou Christie	1963	20.00	40.00	80.00
—Blue background on front cover					
SR 25208 [S]	Lou Christie	1963	15.00	30.00	60.00
—White wall in background on front cover					
R 25332 [M]	Lou Christie Strikes Again	1966	6.25	12.50	25.00
SR 25332 [S]	Lou Christie Strikes Again	1966	7.50	15.00	30.00
SPIN-O-RAMA					
M-173 [M]	Starring Lou Christie and the Classics	1966	5.00	10.00	20.00
S-173 [R]	Starring Lou Christie and the Classics	1966	3.00	6.00	12.00
—The above LP also includes other artists					
THREE BROTHERS					
THB-2000	Lou Christie	1973	5.00	10.00	20.00

CHRISTIE, SUSAN

45s

Number	Title (A Side/B Side)	Yr	VG	VG+	NM
COLUMBIA					
43595	I Love Onions/Take Me As You Find Me	1966	2.50	5.00	10.00
44117	Tonight You Belong to Me/Toy Balloon	1967	—	3.00	6.00
44327	All I Have to Do Is Dream/Anywhere You Are	1967	—	3.00	6.00

CHRISTMAS SPIRIT, THE (1)

William B. Williams, narrator.

45s

Number	Title (A Side/B Side)	Yr	VG	VG+	NM
DUEL					
503	It's Christmas/A World to Grow Up In	1961	3.00	6.00	12.00

CHRISTMAS SPIRIT, THE (2)

Members of THE TURTLES with LINDA RONSTADT.

45s

Number	Title (A Side/B Side)	Yr	VG	VG+	NM
WHITE WHALE					
290	Christmas Is My Time of Year/Will You Still Believe	1968	20.00	40.00	80.00

CHRISTOPHER (1)

45s

Number	Title (A Side/B Side)	Yr	VG	VG+	NM
BELL					
679	Hey Girl/Every Boy in the World	1967	3.75	7.50	15.00
DATE					
1664	Santa Ana Winds/Spring	1970	3.00	6.00	12.00

Albums

Number	Title (A Side/B Side)	Yr	VG	VG+	NM
BELL					
1203	R.P.M.	1970	5.00	10.00	20.00

CHRISTOPHER (2)

Albums

Number	Title (A Side/B Side)	Yr	VG	VG+	NM
CHRIS-TEE					
12411	What'cha Gonna Do	1970	1500.	2250.	3000.
—100 copies were pressed					

CHRISTOPHER (3)

Albums

Number	Title (A Side/B Side)	Yr	VG	VG+	NM
METROMEDIA					
1024	Christopher	1970	75.00	150.00	300.00

CHRISTOPHER (U)

45s

Number	Title (A Side/B Side)	Yr	VG	VG+	NM
DOT					
17133	Valerie/Sunday Life	1968	3.75	7.50	15.00

CHRISTY, DON
See SONNY.

CHRISTY, JUNE
45s

CAPITOL

Number	Title (A Side/B Side)	Yr	VG	VG+	NM
F-2163	Live Oak Tree/The Man I Love	1952	3.75	7.50	15.00
F-2199	Bei Mir Bist Du Schoen/Some Folks Do	1952	3.75	7.50	15.00
F-2308	My Heart Belongs to Only You/I Was a Fool	1952	3.75	7.50	15.00
F-2384	I've Got a Letter/Let Me Share Your Name	1953	3.75	7.50	15.00
F-2432	Great Scot/I Lived When I Met You	1953	3.75	7.50	15.00
F-2590	Not I/Whee Baby	1953	3.75	7.50	15.00
F-2765	First Thing You Know/Magazines Are Magic	1954	3.75	7.50	15.00
F-3213	Pete Kelly's Blues/Kicks	1955	3.00	6.00	12.00
F-3375	I Never Wanna Look Into Those Eyes Again/Look Out Up There	1956	3.00	6.00	12.00
F-3471	Intrigue/You Took Advantage of Me	1956	3.00	6.00	12.00
4864	One Note Samba/Bossa Nova	1963	2.00	4.00	8.00

7-Inch Extended Plays

CAPITOL

Number	Title (A Side/B Side)	Yr	VG	VG+	NM
EAP 1-448	My Heart Belongs to Only You/Get Happy//The Man I Love/I Lived When I Met You	195?	5.00	10.00	20.00
EAP 1-448 [PS]	Get Happy with June Christy	195?	5.00	10.00	20.00

Albums

CAPITOL

Number	Title (A Side/B Side)	Yr	VG	VG+	NM
H 516 [10]	Something Cool	1954	20.00	40.00	80.00
SM-516 [R]	Something Cool	197?	2.50	5.00	10.00
T 516 [M]	Something Cool	1955	12.50	25.00	50.00
—Turquoise label					
T 516 [M]	Something Cool	1959	6.25	12.50	25.00
—Black label with colorband					
T 656 [M]	Duets	1955	10.00	20.00	40.00
—Turquoise label					
T 725 [M]	The Misty Miss Christy	1956	10.00	20.00	40.00
—Turquoise label					
T 833 [M]	June — Fair and Warmer!	1957	10.00	20.00	40.00
—Turquoise label					
T 902 [M]	Gone for the Day	1957	10.00	20.00	40.00
—Turquoise label					
T 1006 [M]	This Is June Christy!	1958	10.00	20.00	40.00
—Turquoise label					
ST 1076 [S]	June's Got Rhythm	1958	10.00	20.00	40.00
—Black label with colorband, Capitol logo at left					
T 1076 [M]	June's Got Rhythm	1958	7.50	15.00	30.00
—Black label with colorband, Capitol logo at left					
ST 1114 [S]	The Song Is June!	1959	10.00	20.00	40.00
—Black label with colorband, Capitol logo at left					
T 1114 [M]	The Song Is June!	1959	7.50	15.00	30.00
—Black label with colorband, Capitol logo at left					
ST 1202 [S]	June Christy Recalls Those Kenton Days	1959	10.00	20.00	40.00
—Black label with colorband, Capitol logo at left					
T 1202 [M]	June Christy Recalls Those Kenton Days	1959	7.50	15.00	30.00
—Black label with colorband, Capitol logo at left					
ST 1308 [S]	Ballads for Night People	1959	10.00	20.00	40.00
—Black label with colorband, Capitol logo at left					
T 1308 [M]	Ballads for Night People	1959	7.50	15.00	30.00
—Black label with colorband, Capitol logo at left					
STBO 1327 [(2) S]	Road Show	1960	10.00	20.00	40.00
—Black label with colorband, Capitol logo at left					
TBO 1327 [(2) M]	Road Show	1960	7.50	15.00	30.00
—Black label with colorband, Capitol logo at left					
ST 1398 [S]	The Cool School	1960	10.00	20.00	40.00
—Black label with colorband, Capitol logo at left					
T 1398 [M]	The Cool School	1960	7.50	15.00	30.00
—Black label with colorband, Capitol logo at left					
ST 1498 [S]	Off Beat	1961	12.50	25.00	50.00
—Black label with colorband, Capitol logo at left					
T 1498 [M]	Off Beat	1961	10.00	20.00	40.00
—Black label with colorband, Capitol logo at left					
ST 1586 [S]	Do-Re-Mi	1961	12.50	25.00	50.00
—Black label with colorband, Capitol logo at left					
T 1586 [M]	Do-Re-Mi	1961	10.00	20.00	40.00
—Black label with colorband, Capitol logo at left					
ST 1605 [S]	That Time of Year	1961	12.50	25.00	50.00
—Black label with colorband, Capitol logo at left					
T 1605 [M]	That Time of Year	1961	10.00	20.00	40.00
ST 1693 [S]	The Best of June Christy	1962	7.50	15.00	30.00
—Black logo with colorband					
T 1693 [M]	The Best of June Christy	1962	6.25	12.50	25.00
—Black label with colorband					
ST 1845 [S]	Big Band Specials	1962	6.25	12.50	25.00
T 1845 [M]	Big Band Specials	1962	5.00	10.00	20.00
ST 1953 [S]	The Intimate June Christy	1963	6.25	12.50	25.00
T 1953 [M]	The Intimate June Christy	1963	5.00	10.00	20.00
ST 2410 [S]	Something Broadway, Something Latin	1965	7.50	15.00	30.00
T 2410 [M]	Something Broadway, Something Latin	1965	6.25	12.50	25.00
SM-11961	The Best of June Christy	1979	2.50	5.00	10.00

DISCOVERY

Number	Title (A Side/B Side)	Yr	VG	VG+	NM
DS-836	Impromptu	1982	3.00	6.00	12.00
DS-911	Interlude	1986	2.50	5.00	10.00
DS-919	The Misty Miss Christy	1986	2.50	5.00	10.00

HINDSIGHT

Number	Title (A Side/B Side)	Yr	VG	VG+	NM
HSR-219	June Christy, Vol. 1	1986	2.50	5.00	10.00
HSR-235	June Christy, Vol. 2	1988	2.50	5.00	10.00

PAUSA

Number	Title (A Side/B Side)	Yr	VG	VG+	NM
9039	Big Band Specials	198?	2.50	5.00	10.00

CHRYSALIS
Albums

MGM

Number	Title (A Side/B Side)	Yr	VG	VG+	NM
SE-4547	Definition	1968	7.50	15.00	30.00

CHUBBY AND THE TURNPIKES
Some members later were in TAVARES.

45s

CAPITOL

Number	Title (A Side/B Side)	Yr	VG	VG+	NM
5840	I Didn't Try/I Know the Inside Story	1967	7.50	15.00	30.00

CHUCK-A-LUCKS, THE
45s

BOW

Number	Title (A Side/B Side)	Yr	VG	VG+	NM
305	Heaven Knows/Chuck-a-Luck	1957	12.50	25.00	50.00

CANDLELITE

Number	Title (A Side/B Side)	Yr	VG	VG+	NM
424	Heaven Knows/Chuck-a-Luck	196?	3.00	6.00	12.00

JUBILEE

Number	Title (A Side/B Side)	Yr	VG	VG+	NM
5415	Tarzan's Date/Unconditional Surrender	1961	5.00	10.00	20.00

LIN

Number	Title (A Side/B Side)	Yr	VG	VG+	NM
5010	Who Am I?/The Devil's Train	1958	6.25	12.50	25.00
5014	The Magic of First Love/Disc Jockey Fever	1958	12.50	25.00	50.00

MEL-O-DY

Number	Title (A Side/B Side)	Yr	VG	VG+	NM
106	Sugar Cane Curtain/Dingbat Diller	1963	6.25	12.50	25.00

WARNER BROS.

Number	Title (A Side/B Side)	Yr	VG	VG+	NM
5198	Long John/Pick Up and Deliver	1961	5.00	10.00	20.00
5234	Cotton Pickin' Love/I'm Hospitalized Over You	1961	5.00	10.00	20.00

CHUCKLES, THE
Also see THE THREE CHUCKLES.

45s

ABC-PARAMOUNT

Number	Title (A Side/B Side)	Yr	VG	VG+	NM
10276	Runaround/Lonely Traveler	1961	3.75	7.50	15.00

CHURCH, EUGENE
Also see THE CLIQUES.

45s

CLASS

Number	Title (A Side/B Side)	Yr	VG	VG+	NM
235	Pretty Girls Everywhere/For the Rest of My Life	1958	6.25	12.50	25.00
254	Miami/I Ain't Goin' for That	1959	3.00	6.00	12.00
261	Jack of All Trades/Without Soul	1959	3.00	6.00	12.00
266	The Struttin' Kind/That's What's Happenin'	1960	3.00	6.00	12.00

KING

Number	Title (A Side/B Side)	Yr	VG	VG+	NM
5545	Mind Your Own Business/You Got the Right Idea	1961	3.00	6.00	12.00
5589	That's All I Need/Geneva	1962	2.50	5.00	10.00
5610	Light of the Moon/I'm Your Taboo Man	1962	2.50	5.00	10.00
5659	The Right Girl, the Right Time/Pretty Baby Won't You Come On Home	1962	2.50	5.00	10.00
5715	Sixteen Tons/Time Has Brought About a Change	1963	2.50	5.00	10.00

RENDEZVOUS

Number	Title (A Side/B Side)	Yr	VG	VG+	NM
132	Good News/Polly	1960	3.00	6.00	12.00

SPECIALTY

Number	Title (A Side/B Side)	Yr	VG	VG+	NM
604	How Long/Open Up Your Heart	1957	5.00	10.00	20.00

WORLD PACIFIC

Number	Title (A Side/B Side)	Yr	VG	VG+	NM
77866	Dollar Bill/U Maka Hanna	1967	3.75	7.50	15.00

CHURCH STREET FIVE, THE
45s

LEGRAND

Number	Title (A Side/B Side)	Yr	VG	VG+	NM
1004	A Night with Daddy G (Part 1)/A Night with Daddy G (Part 2)	1961	6.25	12.50	25.00
—Purple label original					
1004	A Night with Daddy G (Part 1)/A Night with Daddy G (Part 2)	1961	3.75	7.50	15.00
—Red, gold and white "shield" label					
1010	Fallen Arches/Everybody's Happy	1961	5.00	10.00	20.00
1014	Church Street Walk/I'm Gonna Sue	1961	5.00	10.00	20.00
1021	Daddy G Rides Again/Hey Now	1962	5.00	10.00	20.00
1026	Moonlight in Vermont/Sing a Song Children	1963	5.00	10.00	20.00

CINDERELLAS, THE (1)
Female vocal group.

45s

COLUMBIA

Number	Title (A Side/B Side)	Yr	VG	VG+	NM
41540	The Trouble with Boys/Puppy Dog	1959	3.75	7.50	15.00

DECCA

Number	Title (A Side/B Side)	Yr	VG	VG+	NM
30830	Mr. Dee Jay/Yum Yum Yum	1959	6.25	12.50	25.00
30925	I Was Only 15/You Never Shoulda Gone Away	1959	6.25	12.50	25.00

CINDERELLAS, THE (2)
Another female vocal group.

45s

DIMENSION

Number	Title (A Side/B Side)	Yr	VG	VG+	NM
1026	Baby, Baby, I Still Love You/Please Don't Wake Me	1964	10.00	20.00	40.00

MERCURY

Number	Title (A Side/B Side)	Yr	VG	VG+	NM
72394	Fairy Tale/Mr. Happy Love	1965	2.50	5.00	10.00

CINDY AND LINDY
45s

ABC-PARAMOUNT

Number	Title (A Side/B Side)	Yr	VG	VG+	NM
9847	The Language of Love/Brigette's Song	1957	6.25	12.50	25.00
9886	Shakin'/Sittin' It Out	1958	6.25	12.50	25.00

CORAL

Number	Title (A Side/B Side)	Yr	VG	VG+	NM
62008	The Wonder That Is You/I'll String Along with You	1958	5.00	10.00	20.00
62072	Saturday Night in Tia-Juana/You Can't Mail an Elephant	1959	5.00	10.00	20.00
62119	Before and After/Big Bells and Bongo Drummers	1959	5.00	10.00	20.00
62165	Let's Go Steady/There Are Such Things	1960	5.00	10.00	20.00

PILGRIM

Number	Title (A Side/B Side)	Yr	VG	VG+	NM
702	Let's Go Steady/The Wedding Is Over	1956	3.75	7.50	15.00
705	Hungry Heart/Livin' and Bein' Loved	1956	3.75	7.50	15.00

CINNAMON ANGELS
May be the same group as THE CINNAMONS.

45s

B.T. PUPPY

Number	Title (A Side/B Side)	Yr	VG	VG+	NM
559	Calypso Girl/Let's Be Sweethearts	1970	2.00	4.00	8.00

CINNAMONS, THE

45s

B.T. PUPPY

Number	Title (A Side/B Side)	Yr	VG	VG+	NM
503	I'm Not Gonna Worry/Strange, Strange Feeling	1964	2.00	4.00	8.00
508	Mr. Cupid '65/Dance to the Music	1965	2.00	4.00	8.00

CIRCUS

45s

METROMEDIA

Number	Title (A Side/B Side)	Yr	VG	VG+	NM
68-0112	Feel So Right/Jonah's Fable	1973	—	2.50	5.00
265	Stop, Wait and Listen/I Need Your Love	1972	—	3.00	6.00

Albums

METROMEDIA

Number	Title (A Side/B Side)	Yr	VG	VG+	NM
7401	Circus	1973	7.50	15.00	30.00

CIRCUS MAXIMUS
Group features JERRY JEFF WALKER.

45s

VANGUARD

Number	Title (A Side/B Side)	Yr	VG	VG+	NM
35063	Lonely Man/Negative Dreamer Girl	1968	5.00	10.00	20.00

Albums

VANGUARD

Number	Title (A Side/B Side)	Yr	VG	VG+	NM
VRS-9260 [M]	Circus Maximus	1967	5.00	10.00	20.00
VSD-79260 [S]	Circus Maximus	1967	6.25	12.50	25.00
VSD-79274	Neverland Revisited	1968	6.25	12.50	25.00

CITATIONS, THE
More than one group.

45s

Number	Title (A Side/B Side)	Yr	VG	VG+	NM
BALLAD					
101	I Will Stand By You/To Win the Race	1967	25.00	50.00	100.00
CANADIAN AMERICAN					
136	Mystery of Love/Magic Eyes	1962	7.50	15.00	30.00
—As "Nicki North and the Citations"					
DON-EL					
113	It Hurts Me/Kiss in the Night	1961	10.00	20.00	40.00
EPIC					
9603	Moon Race/Slippin' and Slidin'	1963	6.25	12.50	25.00
FRATERNITY					
910	The Girl Next Door/Ten Miles from Nowhere	1963	5.00	10.00	20.00
992	The Girl Next Door/Ten Miles from Nowhere	1967	3.00	6.00	12.00
MERCURY					
72286	Chicago/The Stomp	1964	3.75	7.50	15.00
MGM					
13373	That Girl of Mine/Down Went the Curtain	1965	5.00	10.00	20.00
PRINCESS					
54	Carmen P./Everybody Philly	1965	7.50	15.00	30.00
ROULETTE					
4623	Carmen P./Everybody Philly	1965	3.75	7.50	15.00
SARA					
3301	Moon Race/Slippin' and Slidin'	1963	12.50	25.00	50.00
SWAN					
4062	Fiddlin' Around/Fire Ritual	1960	10.00	20.00	40.00
VANGEE					
301	The Girl Next Door/Ten Miles from Nowhere	1963	10.00	20.00	40.00

CITY, THE
CAROLE KING was a member.

45s

ODE

Number	Title (A Side/B Side)	Yr	VG	VG+	NM
113	Snow Queen/Paradise Alley	1968	3.00	6.00	12.00
—With Carole King					
117	That Old Sweet Rule/Why Are You Leaving	1968	3.00	6.00	12.00
119	(Hi-De-Ho) That Old Sweet Roll/Why Are You Leaving	1969	3.00	6.00	12.00

Albums

ODE

Number	Title (A Side/B Side)	Yr	VG	VG+	NM
Z12 44012	Now That Everything's Been Said	1968	20.00	40.00	80.00
—Color front cover					
Z12 44012	Now That Everything's Been Said	1971	3.00	6.00	12.00
—Black & white front cover					

CITY SURFERS, THE

45s

CAPITOL

Number	Title (A Side/B Side)	Yr	VG	VG+	NM
5002	Beach Ball/Sun Tan Baby	1963	6.25	12.50	25.00
5052	Powder Puff/Fifty Miles to Go	1963	6.25	12.50	25.00

CLAMS, THE

45s

THREE BROTHERS

Number	Title (A Side/B Side)	Yr	VG	VG+	NM
404	Close to You/First Time Ever I Saw Your Face	1974	2.50	5.00	10.00
—LOU CHRISTIE appears on this record					

CLANTON, JIMMY

45s

Number	Title (A Side/B Side)	Yr	VG	VG+	NM
ACE					
537	I Trusted You/That's You Baby	1958	5.00	10.00	20.00
546	Just a Dream/You Aim to Please	1958	5.00	10.00	20.00
551	A Letter to An Angel/A Part of Me	1958	5.00	10.00	20.00
560	My Love Is Strong/Ship on a Stormy Sea	1959	3.75	7.50	15.00
567 [M]	My Own True Love/Little Boy in Love	1959	3.75	7.50	15.00
567 [PS]	My Own True Love/Little Boy in Love	1959	7.50	15.00	30.00
567 [S]	My Own True Love/Little Boy in Love	1959	7.50	15.00	30.00
575	Go, Jimmy, Go/I Trusted You	1959	5.00	10.00	20.00
—Normal white label					
575	Go, Jimmy, Go/I Trusted You	1959	6.25	12.50	25.00
—Purple label					
575 [PS]	Go, Jimmy, Go/I Trusted You	1959	7.50	15.00	30.00
585	Another Sleepless Night/I'm Gonna Try	1960	3.75	7.50	15.00
585 [PS]	Another Sleepless Night/I'm Gonna Try	1960	7.50	15.00	30.00
600	Come Back/Wait	1960	3.75	7.50	15.00
600 [PS]	Come Back/Wait	1960	7.50	15.00	30.00
607	What Am I Gonna Do/If I	1961	3.75	7.50	15.00
607 [PS]	What Am I Gonna Do/If I	1961	7.50	15.00	30.00
616	Down the Aisle/No Longer Blue	1961	3.75	7.50	15.00
616 [PS]	Down the Aisle/No Longer Blue	1961	7.50	15.00	30.00
—With Mary Ann Mobley					
622	I Just Wanna Make Love/Don't Look at Me	1961	3.75	7.50	15.00
622 [PS]	I Just Wanna Make Love/Don't Look at Me	1961	7.50	15.00	30.00
634	Lucky in Love with You/Not Like a Brother	1961	3.75	7.50	15.00
634 [PS]	Lucky in Love with You/Not Like a Brother	1961	7.50	15.00	30.00
641	Twist On Little Girl/Wayward Love	1962	3.75	7.50	15.00
641 [PS]	Twist On Little Girl/Wayward Love	1962	7.50	15.00	30.00
642	Twist On Little Girl/Wayward Love//Green Light/Happy Times	1962	12.50	25.00	50.00
642 [PS]	Teenage Millionaire	1962	12.50	25.00	50.00
655	Just a Moment/Because I Do	1962	3.75	7.50	15.00
655 [PS]	Just a Moment/Because I Do	1962	7.50	15.00	30.00
664 [DJ]	Venus in Blue Jeans/Highway Bound	1962	6.25	12.50	25.00
—No stock copies exist with this catalog number					
668	Heart Hotel/Many Dreams	1963	3.00	6.00	12.00
8001	Venus in Blue Jeans/Highway Bound	1962	3.75	7.50	15.00
8005	Darkest Street in Town/Dreams of a Fool	1962	2.50	5.00	10.00
8006	Endless Nights/Another Day, Another Heartache	1963	2.50	5.00	10.00
8006 [PS]	Endless Nights/Another Day, Another Heartache	1963	5.00	10.00	20.00
8007	Cindy/I Care Enough (To Give the Very Best)	1963	2.50	5.00	10.00
IMPERIAL					
66242	Absence of Lisa/C'mon Jim	1967	2.00	4.00	8.00
66274	Calico Junction/I'll Be Loving You	1968	2.00	4.00	8.00
LAURIE					
3508	Curly/The Girl Who Cried Love (Once Too Often)	1969	2.00	4.00	8.00
3508	Curly/I'll Never Forget Your Love	1969	2.50	5.00	10.00
3534	Tell Me/I'll Never Forget Your Love	1969	2.00	4.00	8.00
MALA					
500	Hurting Each Other/Don't Keep Your Friends Away	1965	2.50	5.00	10.00
516	Everything I Touch Turns to Tears/That Special Way	1965	2.50	5.00	10.00
PHILIPS					
40161	Red Don't Go with Blue/All the Words in the World	1963	2.50	5.00	10.00
40181	I'll Step Aside/I Won't Cry Anymore	1964	2.50	5.00	10.00
40208	If I'm a Fool for Loving You/A Million Drums	1964	2.50	5.00	10.00
40219	Follow the Sun/Lock the Windows	1964	2.50	5.00	10.00
SPIRAL					
3406	The Coolest Hot Pants/(Instrumental)	1971	—	2.50	5.00
STARCREST					
078 [DJ]	Old Rock 'N Roller (mono/stereo)	1978	—	2.50	5.00
—May be promo only					
STARFIRE					
104	I Wanna Go Home/You Kissed a Fool Goodbye	1976	—	2.50	5.00
VIN					
1028	What Am I Living For/Wedding Blues	1962	2.50	5.00	10.00

7-Inch Extended Plays

ACE

Number	Title (A Side/B Side)	Yr	VG	VG+	NM
101	(contents unknown)	1959	25.00	50.00	100.00
101 [PS]	Jimmy Clanton	1959	25.00	50.00	100.00
102	(contents unknown)	1959	37.50	75.00	150.00
102 [PS]	Thinking of You	1959	37.50	75.00	150.00

Albums

Number	Title (A Side/B Side)	Yr	VG	VG+	NM
ACE					
DLP-100	Jimmy's Happy/Jimmy's Blue Poster	1960	20.00	40.00	80.00
DLP-100 [M]	Jimmy's Happy/Jimmy's Blue	1960	100.00	200.00	400.00
—The "Happy" album is red vinyl, the "Blue" album is blue					
DLP-100 [M]	Jimmy's Happy/Jimmy's Blue	1960	37.50	75.00	150.00
—Black vinyl; also released as two separate albums, 1007 and 1008					
1001 [M]	Just a Dream	1959	30.00	60.00	120.00
1007 [M]	Jimmy's Happy	1960	10.00	20.00	40.00
1008 [M]	Jimmy's Blue	1960	10.00	20.00	40.00
1011 [M]	My Best to You	1960	25.00	50.00	100.00
1014 [M]	Teenage Millionaire	1961	25.00	50.00	100.00
1026 [M]	Venus in Blue Jeans	1962	25.00	50.00	100.00
PHILIPS					
PHM 200154 [M]	The Best of Jimmy Clanton	1964	6.25	12.50	25.00
PHS 600154 [S]	The Best of Jimmy Clanton	1964	7.50	15.00	30.00

CLANTON, JIMMY/BRISTOW HOOPER

Albums

DESIGN

Number	Title (A Side/B Side)	Yr	VG	VG+	NM
DLP-176 [M]	Jimmy Clanton and Bristow Hooper	196?	3.75	7.50	15.00

CLANTON, JIMMY/BRISTOW HOOPER

Albums

DESIGN

Number	Title (A Side/B Side)	Yr	VG	VG+	NM
DLS-176 [R]	Jimmy Clanton and Bristow Hooper	196?	2.50	5.00	10.00

CLAP

Albums

NOVA SOL

Number	Title (A Side/B Side)	Yr	VG	VG+	NM
1001	Have You Reached Yet?	1970	250.00	500.00	1000.

CLAPTON, ERIC

Also see BLIND FAITH; CREAM; DEREK AND THE DOMINOS; GEORGE HARRISON AND FRIENDS; B.B. KING; JOHN MAYALL; THE YARDBIRDS.

Number	Title (A Side/B Side)	Yr	VG	VG+	NM
45s					
ATCO					
6784	After Midnight/Easy Now	1970	—	3.00	6.00
DUCK					
28279	Tearing Us Apart/Hold On	1987	—	—	3.00
—With Tina Turner					
28279 [PS]	Tearing Us Apart/Hold On	1987	—	—	3.00
—With Tina Turner					
28391	Behind the Sun/Grand Illusion	1987	—	—	3.00
28514	It's in the Way That You Use It/Grand Illusion	1986	—	—	3.00
28514 [PS]	It's in the Way That You Use It/Grand Illusion	1986	—	—	3.00
28986	See What Love Can Do/She's Waiting	1985	—	—	3.00
29081	Forever Man/Too Bad	1985	—	—	3.00
29081 [PS]	Forever Man/Too Bad	1985	—	—	3.00
29647	Pretty Girl/The Shape You're In	1983	—	2.00	4.00
29780	I've Got a Rock 'n' Roll Heart/Man in Love	1983	—	2.00	4.00
—Custom silver label with Duck logo					
POLYDOR					
15049	Let It Rain/Easy Now	1972	—	2.50	5.00
15056	Bell Bottom Blues/Little Wing	1973	—	2.50	5.00
—Reissue of Derek and the Dominos recordings, but under Clapton's name					
887403-7	After Midnight/I Can't Stand It	1988	—	—	3.00
887403-7 [PS]	After Midnight/I Can't Stand It	1988	—	—	3.00
REPRISE					
17621	Change the World/Danny Boy	1996	—	—	3.00
18044	Motherless Child/Driftin'	1994	—	—	3.00
18787	Layla/Signe	1992	—	—	3.00
19038	Tears in Heaven/Tracks and Lines	1992	—	—	3.00
22732	Pretending/Before You Accuse Me	1989	—	—	3.00
22732 [PS]	Pretending/Before You Accuse Me	1989	—	—	3.00
RSO					
409	I Shot the Sheriff/Give Me Strength	1974	—	2.50	5.00
500	I Shot the Sheriff/Give Me Strength	1974	—	2.00	4.00
503	Willie and the Hand Jive/Main Line Florida	1975	—	2.00	4.00
509	Swing Low Sweet Chariot/Pretty Blue Eyes	1975	—	2.00	4.00
513	Knockin' on Heaven's Door/Someone Like You	1975	—	2.00	4.00
861	Hello Old Friend/All Our Pastimes	1976	—	2.00	4.00
868	Carnival/Hungry	1976	—	2.00	4.00
886	Lay Down Sally/Next Time You See Her	1978	—	2.00	4.00
895	Wonderful Tonight/Peaches and Diesel	1978	—	2.00	4.00
910	Promises/Watch Out for Lucy	1978	—	2.00	4.00
928	Tulsa Time/Cocaine	1979	—	2.50	5.00
—Studio versions of the two songs					
1039	Tulsa Time/Cocaine	1980	—	2.00	4.00
—Live versions of the two songs					
1051	Early in the Morning/Blues Power	1980	—	2.00	4.00
1060	I Can't Stand It/Black Rose	1981	—	2.00	4.00
1064	Another Ticket/Rita Mae	1981	—	2.00	4.00
1064 [PS]	Another Ticket/Rita Mae	1981	—	2.50	5.00
WARNER BROS.					
29780	I've Got a Rock 'n' Roll Heart/Man in Love	1983	—	2.50	5.00
—Original pressing on white WB label					
Albums					
ATCO					
33-329 [DJ]	Eric Clapton	1970	25.00	50.00	100.00
—Mono pressing is promo only					
SD 33-329	Eric Clapton	1970	5.00	10.00	20.00
SD 33-329	Eric Clapton	1970	50.00	100.00	200.00
—Odd pressing with alternate takes of "After Midnight" and "Blues Power" plus remixes of other tracks. Look for "CTH" in trail-off area.					
SD 2-803 [(2)]	History of Eric Clapton	1972	5.00	10.00	20.00
—Contains tracks from the Yardbirds, John Mayall's Bluesbreakers, Cream, Blind Faith, and solo records					
DUCK					
23773	Money and Cigarettes	1983	2.50	5.00	10.00
25186	Behind the Sun	1985	2.50	5.00	10.00
25476	August	1986	2.50	5.00	10.00
26074	Journeyman	1989	3.00	6.00	12.00
W1-26420 [(2)]	24 Nights	1991	6.25	12.50	25.00
—Vinyl copies released only through Columbia House					
MOBILE FIDELITY					
1-030	Slowhand	1980	17.50	35.00	70.00
—Audiophile vinyl					
1-220	Eric Clapton	1995	6.25	12.50	25.00
—Audiophile vinyl					
NAUTILUS					
NR-32 [(2)]	Just One Night	1981	37.50	75.00	150.00
—Audiophile vinyl					
POLYDOR					
24-3503 [(2)]	Eric Clapton at His Best	1972	5.00	10.00	20.00
—Compiles tracks from his first solo album plus Derek and the Dominos					
24-5526	Clapton	1973	3.75	7.50	15.00
—Compiles tracks from his first solo album plus Derek and the Dominos					
835261-1 [(6)]	Crossroads	1988	12.50	25.00	50.00
—Box set; contains material from all phases of his career					
RSO					
035 [DJ]	Slowhand	1977	6.25	12.50	25.00
—White vinyl promo					
SO 877	Eric Clapton's Rainbow Concert	1973	3.75	7.50	15.00
1009 [DJ]	Limited Backless	1978	10.00	20.00	40.00
—White vinyl promo					
RS-1-3004	No Reason to Cry	1976	3.00	6.00	12.00
RS-1-3008	Eric Clapton	1977	3.00	6.00	12.00
—Reissue of Atco LP of the same name					
RS-1-3023	461 Ocean Boulevard	1977	3.00	6.00	12.00
—Reissue of RSO 4801					
RS-1-3030	Slowhand	1977	3.00	6.00	12.00
RS-1-3039	Backless	1978	3.00	6.00	12.00
RX-1-3095	Another Ticket	1981	2.50	5.00	10.00
RS-1-3099	Time Pieces/The Best of Eric Clapton	1982	2.50	5.00	10.00
RS-2-4202 [(2)]	Just One Night	1980	3.75	7.50	15.00
QD 4801 [Q]	461 Ocean Boulevard	1974	6.25	12.50	25.00
SO 4801	461 Ocean Boulevard	1974	3.75	7.50	15.00
—With "Give Me Strength"					
SO 4801	461 Ocean Boulevard	1974	3.00	6.00	12.00
—With "Better Make It Through the Day"					
QD 4806 [Q]	There's One in Every Crowd	1975	6.25	12.50	25.00
SO 4806	There's One in Every Crowd	1975	3.00	6.00	12.00
SO 4809	E.C. Was Here	1975	3.00	6.00	12.00
811697-1	461 Ocean Boulevard	198?	2.00	4.00	8.00
—Reissue of RSO 3023					
823276-1	Slowhand	1983	2.00	4.00	8.00
—Reissue of RSO 3030					
825093-1	Eric Clapton	1984	2.00	4.00	8.00
—Reissue of RSO 3008					
825382-1	Time Pieces/The Best of Eric Clapton	1984	2.00	4.00	8.00
—Reissue of RSO 3099					
825391-1 [(2)]	Just One Night	1984	2.50	5.00	10.00
—Reissue of RSO 4202					
827579-1	Another Ticket	1985	2.00	4.00	8.00
—Reissue of RSO 3095					

CLAREMONTS, THE

Number	Title (A Side/B Side)	Yr	VG	VG+	NM
45s					
APOLLO					
517	Why Keep Me Dreaming/Angel of Romance	1957	15.00	30.00	60.00
751	Why Keep Me Dreaming/Angel of Romance	1963	6.25	12.50	25.00

CLARK, CHRIS

Number	Title (A Side/B Side)	Yr	VG	VG+	NM
45s					
MOTOWN					
1114	From Head to Toe/The Beginning of the End	1967	3.75	7.50	15.00
1121	Whisper You Love Me Boy/The Beginning of the End	1968	3.75	7.50	15.00
V.I.P.					
25031	Do Right, Baby, Do Right/Don't Be Too Long	1965	3.75	7.50	15.00
25038	Love's Gone Mad/Put Yourself in My Place	1965	15.00	30.00	60.00
25038	Love's Gone Bad/Put Yourself in My Place	1965	5.00	10.00	20.00
—Same song as above A-side, but with corrected title					
25041	I Love You/I Want to Go Back There Again	1966	3.75	7.50	15.00
Albums					
MOTOWN					
M-664 [M]	Soul Sounds	1967	12.50	25.00	50.00
MS-664 [S]	Soul Sounds	1967	15.00	30.00	60.00
WEED					
801	C.C. Rides Again	1969	20.00	40.00	80.00

CLARK, CLAUDINE

Number	Title (A Side/B Side)	Yr	VG	VG+	NM
45s					
CHANCELLOR					
1113	Party Lights/Disappointed	1962	5.00	10.00	20.00
—exists on two different labels					
1124	Telephone Game/Walkin' Through a Cemetery	1962	3.00	6.00	12.00
1130	Walk Me Home/Who Will You Hurt	1963	3.00	6.00	12.00
HERALD					
523	Teenage Blues/Angel of Happiness	1958	10.00	20.00	40.00
JAMIE					
1279	Moon Madness/(The Strength) To Be Strong	1964	2.50	5.00	10.00
1291	Buttered Popcorn/A Sometimes Thing	1964	2.50	5.00	10.00
TCF HALL					
18	Foxy/Standin' on Tip Toes	196?	2.50	5.00	10.00
Albums					
CHANCELLOR					
CHL-5029 [M]	Party Lights	1962	62.50	125.00	250.00

CLARK, DAVE, FIVE

Number	Title (A Side/B Side)	Yr	VG	VG+	NM
45s					
CONGRESS					
212	I Knew It All the Time/That's What I Said	1964	5.00	10.00	20.00
212 [PS]	I Knew It All the Time/That's What I Said	1964	10.00	20.00	40.00
EPIC					
9656	Glad All Over/I Know You	1964	3.75	7.50	15.00
9656 [PS]	Glad All Over/I Know You	1964	5.00	10.00	20.00
9671	Bits and Pieces/All of the Time	1964	3.00	6.00	12.00
9678	Do You Love Me/Chaquita	1964	3.00	6.00	12.00
9692	Can't You See That She's Mine/No TIme to Lose	1964	3.00	6.00	12.00
9692 [PS]	Can't You See That She's Mine/No TIme to Lose	1964	5.00	10.00	20.00
9704	Because/Theme Without a Name	1964	3.00	6.00	12.00
9704 [PS]	Because/Theme Without a Name	1964	5.00	10.00	20.00
9722	Everybody Knows (I Still Love You)/Ol' Sol	1964	3.00	6.00	12.00
9722 [PS]	Everybody Knows (I Still Love You)/Ol' Sol	1964	5.00	10.00	20.00
9739	Any Way You Want It/Crying Over You	1964	3.00	6.00	12.00
9763	Come Home/Your Turn to Cry	1965	3.00	6.00	12.00
9763 [PS]	Come Home/Your Turn to Cry	1965	5.00	10.00	20.00
9786	Reelin' and Rockin'/I'm Thinking	1965	3.00	6.00	12.00
9811	I Like It Like That/Hurting Inside	1965	3.00	6.00	12.00
9811 [PS]	I Like It Like That/Hurting Inside	1965	5.00	10.00	20.00
9833	Catch Us If You Can/On the Move	1965	3.00	6.00	12.00
9833 [PS]	Catch Us If You Can/On the Move	1965	5.00	10.00	20.00
9863	Over and Over/I'll Be Yours (My Love)	1965	3.00	6.00	12.00
9863 [DJ]	Over and Over (same on both sides)	1965	10.00	20.00	40.00
—Promo only on red vinyl					
9863 [PS]	Over and Over/I'll Be Yours (My Love)	1965	5.00	10.00	20.00
9863 [PS]	Over and Over	1965	100.00	200.00	400.00
—Promo-only black and white sleeve					
9882	At the Scene/I Miss You	1966	3.00	6.00	12.00
9882 [PS]	At the Scene/I Miss You	1966	5.00	10.00	20.00
10004	Try Too Hard/All Night Long	1966	3.00	6.00	12.00
10004 [PS]	Try Too Hard/All Night Long	1966	5.00	10.00	20.00
10031	Please Tell Me Why/Look Before You Leap	1966	3.00	6.00	12.00
10031 [PS]	Please Tell Me Why/Look Before You Leap	1966	5.00	10.00	20.00
10053	Satisfied with You/Don't Let Me Down	1966	3.00	6.00	12.00
10053 [PS]	Satisfied with You/Don't Let Me Down	1966	5.00	10.00	20.00
10076	Nineteen Days/Sitting Here Baby	1966	3.00	6.00	12.00

Number	Title (A Side/B Side)	Yr	VG	VG+	NM
10076 [DJ]	Nineteen Days (same on both sides)	1966	10.00	20.00	40.00
—Promo only on red vinyl					
10076 [PS]	Nineteen Days/Sitting Here Baby	1966	5.00	10.00	20.00
10114	I've Got to Have a Reason/Good Time Woman	1966	3.00	6.00	12.00
10114 [PS]	I've Got to Have a Reason/Good Time Woman	1966	5.00	10.00	20.00
10144	You Got What It Takes/Doctor Rhythm	1967	3.00	6.00	12.00
10144 [PS]	You Got What It Takes/Doctor Rhythm	1967	5.00	10.00	20.00
10179	You Must Have Been a Beautiful Baby/Man in the Pin Stripe Suit	1967	3.00	6.00	12.00
10179 [PS]	You Must Have Been a Beautiful Baby/Man in the Pin Stripe Suit	1967	6.25	12.50	25.00
10209	A Little Bit Now/You Don't Play Me Around	1967	3.75	7.50	15.00
10209 [PS]	A Little Bit Now/You Don't Play Me Around	1967	5.00	10.00	20.00
10244	Red and Blue/Concentration Baby	1967	3.75	7.50	15.00
10244 [PS]	Red and Blue/Concentration Baby	1967	—	—	—
—Rumored to exist, but without conclusive evidence, we will delete this from future editions					
10265/60 [DJ]	Everybody Knows/Best of Both Worlds	1968	6.25	12.50	25.00
—B-side by Lulu; odd promo					
10265	Everybody Knows/Inside and Out	1967	3.75	7.50	15.00
10265 [PS]	Everybody Knows/Inside and Out	1967	7.50	15.00	30.00
10325	Please Stay/Forget	1968	3.75	7.50	15.00
10375	Red Balloon/Maze of Love	1968	3.75	7.50	15.00
10375 [PS]	Red Balloon/Maze of Love	1968	6.25	12.50	25.00
10476	Paradise (Is Half As Nice)/34-06	1969	3.75	7.50	15.00
10476 [PS]	Paradise (Is Half As Nice)/34-06	1969	7.50	15.00	30.00
10509	If Somebody Loves You/Best Day's Work	1969	3.75	7.50	15.00
10547	Bring It On Home to Me/Darling, I Love You	1969	3.75	7.50	15.00
10547 [PS]	Bring It On Home to Me/Darling, I Love You	1969	5.00	10.00	20.00
10635	Here Comes Summer/Five by Five	1970	3.75	7.50	15.00
10684	Good Old Rock and Roll (Medley)/One Night	1970	5.00	10.00	20.00
10684 [PS]	Good Old Rock and Roll (Medley)/One Night	1970	7.50	15.00	30.00
10704	Southern Man/If You Wanna See Me Cry	1971	10.00	20.00	40.00
10768	Won't You Be My Lady/Into Your Life	1971	5.00	10.00	20.00
10894	Rub It In/I'm Sorry Baby	1972	5.00	10.00	20.00
EPIC MEMORY LANE					
2225	Glad All Over/Bits and Pieces	1972	—	2.00	4.00
2230	Because/Do You Love Me	1972	—	2.00	4.00
2234	Any Way You Want It/Can't You See That She's Mine	1972	—	2.00	4.00
2239	I Like It Like That/Everybody Knows (I Still Love You)	1972	—	2.00	4.00
2248	Over and Over/Catch Us If You Can	1972	—	2.00	4.00
2294	Bring It On Home to Me/If Somebody Loves You	1972	—	2.00	4.00
2313	I Like It Like That/Can't You See That She's Mine	1972	—	2.00	4.00
2316	Come Home/You Got What It Takes	1972	—	2.00	4.00
HOLLYWOOD					
65909	Over and Over/You Got What It Takes	1993	—	2.00	4.00
65909 [PS]	Over and Over/You Got What It Takes	1993	—	3.00	6.00
65910	I Like It Like That/Reelin' and Rockin'	1993	—	2.00	4.00
65910 [PS]	I Like It Like That/Reelin' and Rockin'	1993	—	3.00	6.00
65911	Glad All Over/Bits and Pieces	1993	—	2.00	4.00
65911 [PS]	Glad All Over/Bits and Pieces	1993	—	3.00	6.00
65912	Do You Love Me/Can't You See That She's Mine	1993	—	2.00	4.00
65912 [PS]	Do You Love Me/Can't You See That She's Mine	1993	—	3.00	6.00
65913	Catch Us If You Can/Try Too Hard	1993	—	2.00	4.00
65913 [PS]	Catch Us If You Can/Try Too Hard	1993	—	3.00	6.00
65914	Because/Everybody Knows (I Still Love You)	1993	—	2.00	4.00
65914 [PS]	Because/Everybody Knows (I Still Love You)	1993	—	3.00	6.00
65915	Any Way You Want It/Come Home	1993	—	2.00	4.00
65915 [PS]	Any Way You Want It/Come Home	1993	—	3.00	6.00
JUBILEE					
5476	Chaquita/In Your Heart	1964	7.50	15.00	30.00
LAURIE					
3188	I Walk the Line/First Love	1963	12.50	25.00	50.00
RUST					
5078	I Walk the Line/First Love	1964	10.00	20.00	40.00
7-Inch Extended Plays					
EPIC					
E 26185 [PS]	The Dave Clark Five's Greatest Hits	1966	17.50	35.00	70.00
E 26185 [R]	Over and Over/Can't You See That She's Mine/I Like It Like That//Catch Us If You Can/Because/Glad All Over	1966	17.50	35.00	70.00
—33 1/3 rpm, small hole, jukebox edition					
E 26221 [PS]	More Greatest Hits	1966	17.50	35.00	70.00
E 26221 [R]	Try Too Hard/Please Tell Me Why/Reelin' and Rockin'//Satisfied with You/At the Scene/All Night Long	1966	17.50	35.00	70.00
—33 1/3 rpm, small hole, jukebox edition					
Albums					
CORTLEIGH					
C-1073 [M]	The Dave Clark Five with Ricky Astor	1964	7.50	15.00	30.00
—With two early DC5 tracks and assorted other stuff by other artists					
CS-1073 [R]	The Dave Clark Five with Ricky Astor	1964	3.75	7.50	15.00
—With two early DC5 tracks and assorted other stuff by other artists					
CROWN					
CST-400 [R]	The Dave Clark Five with the Playbacks	1964	3.75	7.50	15.00
—With two early DC5 tracks and assorted other stuff by other artists					
CST-473 [R]	Chaquita/In Your Heart	1964	3.75	7.50	15.00
—With two early DC5 tracks and assorted other stuff by other artists					
CLP-5400 [M]	The Dave Clark Five with the Playbacks	1964	7.50	15.00	30.00
—With two early DC5 tracks and assorted other stuff by other artists					
CLP-5473 [M]	Chaquita/In Your Heart	1964	7.50	15.00	30.00
—With two early DC5 tracks and assorted other stuff by other artists					
EPIC					
LN 24093 [M]	Glad All Over	1964	20.00	40.00	80.00
—Group photo, no instruments					
LN 24093 [M]	Glad All Over	1964	10.00	20.00	40.00
—Group photo with instruments					
LN 24104 [M]	The Dave Clark Five Return	1964	10.00	20.00	40.00
LN 24117 [M]	American Tour	1964	10.00	20.00	40.00
LN 24128 [M]	Coast to Coast	1965	10.00	20.00	40.00
LN 24139 [M]	Weekend in London	1965	10.00	20.00	40.00
LN 24162 [M]	Having a Wild Weekend	1965	10.00	20.00	40.00
LN 24178 [M]	I Like It Like That	1965	10.00	20.00	40.00
LN 24185 [M]	The Dave Clark Five's Greatest Hits	1966	6.25	12.50	25.00
LN 24198 [M]	Try Too Hard	1966	7.50	15.00	30.00
LN 24212 [M]	Satisfied with You	1966	7.50	15.00	30.00
LN 24221 [M]	More Greatest Hits	1966	6.25	12.50	25.00
LN 24236 [M]	5 by 5	1967	7.50	15.00	30.00
LN 24312 [M]	You Got What It Takes	1967	7.50	15.00	30.00
LN 24354 [M]	Everybody Knows	1968	7.50	15.00	30.00
BN 26093 [R]	Glad All Over	1964	12.50	25.00	50.00
—Group photo, no instruments					
BN 26093 [R]	Glad All Over	1964	7.50	15.00	30.00
—Group photo with instruments					
BN 26104 [R]	The Dave Clark Five Return	1964	7.50	15.00	30.00
BN 26117 [R]	American Tour	1964	7.50	15.00	30.00
BN 26128 [R]	Coast to Coast	1965	7.50	15.00	30.00
BN 26139 [R]	Weekend in London	1965	7.50	15.00	30.00
BN 26162 [R]	Having a Wild Weekend	1965	7.50	15.00	30.00
BN 26178 [R]	I Like It Like That	1965	7.50	15.00	30.00
BN 26185 [R]	The Dave Clark Five's Greatest Hits	1966	5.00	10.00	20.00
—Yellow label					
BN 26185 [R]	The Dave Clark Five's Greatest Hits	1973	10.00	20.00	40.00
—Orange label					
BN 26198 [R]	Try Too Hard	1966	6.25	12.50	25.00
BN 26212 [R]	Satisfied with You	1966	6.25	12.50	25.00
BN 26221 [R]	More Greatest Hits	1966	5.00	10.00	20.00
BN 26236 [S]	5 by 5	1967	10.00	20.00	40.00
BN 26312 [S]	You Got What It Takes	1967	10.00	20.00	40.00
BN 26354 [S]	Everybody Knows	1968	10.00	20.00	40.00
EG 30434 [(2) S]	The Dave Clark Five	1971	25.00	50.00	100.00
—Twenty hits and near-hits, all in true stereo! Yellow label.					
EG 30434 [(2) S]	The Dave Clark Five	1973	20.00	40.00	80.00
—Twenty hits and near-hits, all in true stereo! Orange label.					
KEG 33459 [(2) M]	Glad All Over Again	1975	12.50	25.00	50.00
XEM 77238/9 [DJ]	The Dave Clark Five Interview	1964	150.00	300.00	600.00

CLARK, DEE

Also see THE DELEGATES (3); KOOL GENTS.

Number	Title (A Side/B Side)	Yr	VG	VG+	NM
45s					
ABNER					
(no #) [DJ]	Blues Get Off My Shoulder (B-side blank)	1959	25.00	50.00	100.00
—White label; noted as "Special D.J. Release from Latest E.P."					
1019	Nobody But You/When I Call on You	1958	6.25	12.50	25.00
1026	Just Keep It Up/Whispering Grass	1959	6.25	12.50	25.00
1029	Hey Little Girl/If It Wasn't for Love	1959	6.25	12.50	25.00
1029 [PS]	Hey Little Girl/If It Wasn't for Love	1959	10.00	20.00	40.00
1032	How About That/Blues Get Off My Shoulder	1959	6.25	12.50	25.00
1037	At My Front Door/Cling-a-Ling	1960	6.25	12.50	25.00
CHELSEA					
3025	Ride a Wild Horse/(Instrumental)	1975	—	2.50	5.00
COLUMBIA					
44200	In These Very Tender Moments/Lost Girl	1967	2.00	4.00	8.00
CONSTELLATION					
108	Crossfire Time/I'm Going Home	1963	3.00	6.00	12.00
113	It's Raining/That's My Girl	1964	3.00	6.00	12.00
120	Come Closer/That's My Girl	1964	3.00	6.00	12.00
132	Warm Summer Breeze/Heartbreak	1964	3.00	6.00	12.00
142	Ain't Gonna Be Your Fool/In My Apartment	1964	3.00	6.00	12.00
147	T.C.B./It's Impossible	1965	3.00	6.00	12.00
155	I Can't Run Away/She's My Baby	1965	3.00	6.00	12.00
165	I Don't Need (Nobody Like You)/Hot Potatoe	1966	3.00	6.00	12.00
173	Old Fashion Love/I'm Goin' Home	1966	3.00	6.00	12.00
FALCON					
1002	Gloria/Kangaroo Hop	1957	7.50	15.00	30.00
1005	Seven Nights/24 Boy Friends	1957	10.00	20.00	40.00
1009	Oh Little Girl/Wondering	1958	10.00	20.00	40.00
LIBERTY					
56152	24 Hours of Loneliness/Where Did All the Good Times Go	1970	—	2.50	5.00
UNITED ARTISTS					
50759	You Can Make Me Feel So Good/Old Time Religion	1971	—	2.50	5.00
VEE JAY					
355	You're Looking Good/Gloria	1960	3.75	7.50	15.00
372	Your Friends/Because I Love You	1961	3.75	7.50	15.00
383	Raindrops/I Want to Love You	1961	5.00	10.00	20.00
394	Gotos Delluvia (Raindrops)/Livin' with Vivian	1961	3.75	7.50	15.00
—B-side by Al Smith					
409	Don't Walk Away from Me/You're Telling Our Secrets	1961	3.75	7.50	15.00
428	You Are Like the Wind/Drums in My Heart	1962	3.75	7.50	15.00
443	Dance On Little Girl/Fever	1962	3.75	7.50	15.00
462	I'm Going Back to School/Nobody But You	1962	3.75	7.50	15.00
487	I'm a Soldier Boy/Shook Up Over You	1963	3.75	7.50	15.00
532	How Is He Treating You/The Jones Boy	1963	3.75	7.50	15.00
548	Walking My Dog/Nobody But Me	1963	3.75	7.50	15.00
WAND					
1177	Nobody But You (Part 1)/Nobody But You (Part 2)	1968	2.00	4.00	8.00
WARNER BROS.					
7720	Raindrops '73/I'm a Happy Man	1973	—	2.50	5.00
7-Inch Extended Plays					
ABNER					
900	(contents unknown)	1959	30.00	60.00	120.00
900 [PS]	Dee Clark	1959	30.00	60.00	120.00
Albums					
ABNER					
LP-2000 [M]	Dee Clark	1959	30.00	60.00	120.00
SR-2000 [S]	Dee Clark	1959	87.50	175.00	350.00
LP-2002 [M]	How About That	1960	20.00	40.00	80.00
SR-2002 [S]	How About That	1960	30.00	60.00	120.00
SOLID SMOKE					
8026	His Best Recordings	1983	2.50	5.00	10.00
SUNSET					
SUS-5217	Wondering	1968	3.00	6.00	12.00

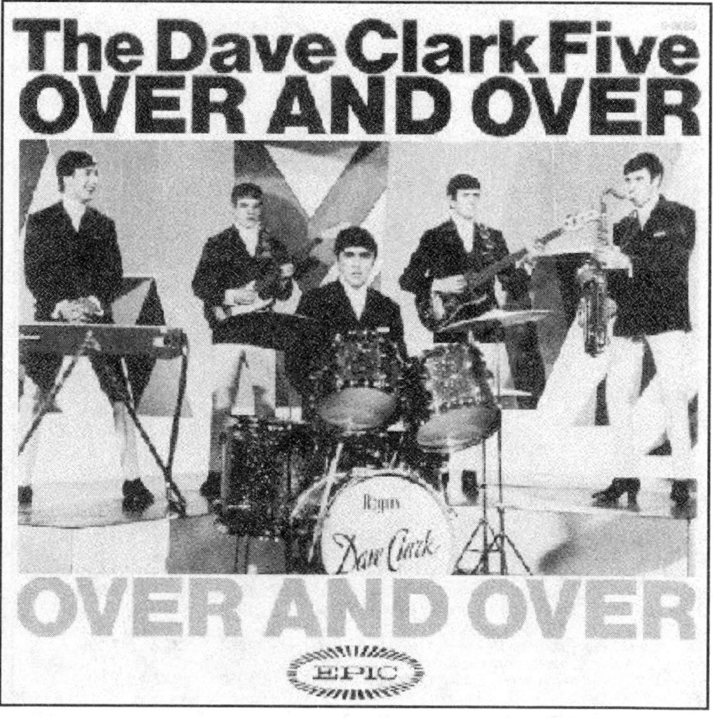

(Top left) At one time, it was believed that no stock copies existed of Captain Beefheart's *Trout Mask Replica* album on the Straight label. Here is a photo of a label that proves otherwise. (Top right) Four figures for a Carpenters record? You better believe it. The first single by Karen Carpenter, "I'll Be Yours," which was written by her brother Richard, has been known to fetch over $3,000 in top condition. (Bottom left) One of the most popular novelty records of all time is "The Chipmunk Song," which spent four weeks at Number One in *Billboard* in 1958. The picture sleeve didn't come out until 1959 when it was reissued with a new B-side. Even so, it's sought-after because the chipmunks are more animal-like than the 1961 "Alvin Show" version of the threesome. (Bottom right) Two different picture sleeves exist for "Over and Over" by the Dave Clark Five. This is the extremely rare-promo-only version that goes for hundreds.

Number	Title (A Side/B Side)	Yr	VG	VG+	NM
VEE JAY					
LP-1019 [M]	You're Looking Good	1960	12.50	25.00	50.00
LP-1037 [M]	Hold On, It's Dee Clark	1961	12.50	25.00	50.00
SR-1037 [S]	Hold On, It's Dee Clark	1961	25.00	50.00	100.00
LP-1047 [M]	The Best of Dee Clark	1964	12.50	25.00	50.00
SR-1047 [S]	The Best of Dee Clark	1964	25.00	50.00	100.00
VJLP-1047	The Best of Dee Clark	1986	3.00	6.00	12.00
—Authorized reissue					

CLARK, DICK
See VARIOUS ARTISTS COLLECTIONS.

CLARK, DOUG, AND THE HOT NUTS

Number	Title (A Side/B Side)	Yr	VG	VG+	NM
45s					
JUBILEE					
5536	Baby Let Me Bang Your Box Part 1/Baby Let Me Bang Your Box Part 2	1966	5.00	10.00	20.00
5546	Milk the Cow/Go, Doug, Go	1966	3.75	7.50	15.00
Albums					
GROSS					
101	Nuts to You	196?	7.50	15.00	30.00
102	On Campus	196?	7.50	15.00	30.00
103	Homecoming	196?	7.50	15.00	30.00
104	Rush Week	1967	7.50	15.00	30.00
105	Panty Raid	196?	7.50	15.00	30.00
106	Summer Session	196?	7.50	15.00	30.00
107	Hell Night	196?	7.50	15.00	30.00
108	Freak Out	196?	7.50	15.00	30.00
109	With a Hat On	196?	7.50	15.00	30.00

CLARK, GENE
Also see THE BYRDS.

Number	Title (A Side/B Side)	Yr	VG	VG+	NM
45s					
ASYLUM					
45222	Life's Greatest Fool/From a Silver Petal	1974	—	2.50	5.00
COLUMBIA					
43903	Echoes/I Found You	1966	3.75	7.50	15.00
43903 [PS]	Echoes/I Found You	1966	75.00	150.00	300.00
44088	Is Yours Mine/So You Say You Lost Your Baby	1967	3.75	7.50	15.00
RSO					
876	Home Run King/Lonely Saturday	1977	—	2.50	5.00
Albums					
ASYLUM					
7E-1016	No Other	1974	3.75	7.50	15.00
A&M					
SP-4292	White Light	1971	3.75	7.50	15.00
COLUMBIA					
CL 2618 [M]	Gene Clark with the Gosdin Brothers	1967	7.50	15.00	30.00
CS 9418 [S]	Gene Clark with the Gosdin Brothers	1967	12.50	25.00	50.00
KC 31123	Early L.A. Sessions	1972	3.75	7.50	15.00
RSO					
RS-1-3011	Two Sides to Every Story	1976	5.00	10.00	20.00
TAKOMA					
TAK-7112	Firebyrd	1984	2.50	5.00	10.00

CLARK, PETULA

Number	Title (A Side/B Side)	Yr	VG	VG+	NM
45s					
ABC DUNHILL					
15007	Never Been a Horse That Couldn't Be Rode/I'm the Woman You Need	1974	—	2.50	5.00
15019	Loving Arms/I'm the Woman You Need	1974	—	2.50	5.00
CORAL					
60971	Song of the Mermaid/Tell Me Truly	1953	6.25	12.50	25.00
61077	Where Did My Snowman Go/Three Little Kittens	1953	6.25	12.50	25.00
ESSEX					
(# unknown)	Majorca/Fascinating Rhythm	1955	—	—	—
—We have not been able to confirm this record's existence. Readers?					
IMPERIAL					
5582	The Little Blue Man/Baby Lover	1959	5.00	10.00	20.00
5600	Where Do I Go from Here/Mama's Talkin' Soft	1959	5.00	10.00	20.00
5655	Now That I Need You/I Love a Violin	1960	5.00	10.00	20.00
KING					
1371	The Little Shoemaker/Helpless	1954	6.25	12.50	25.00
LAURIE					
3143	Jumble Sale/The Road	1962	3.75	7.50	15.00
3156	I Will Follow Him/Darling Cheri	1963	3.75	7.50	15.00
3236	Elle Est Finie/J'ai Tout Oublie	1964	3.75	7.50	15.00
3259	In Love/The Road	1964	3.75	7.50	15.00
3316	In Love/Darling Cheri	1965	3.00	6.00	12.00
3573	Jumble Sale/The Road	1971	—	3.00	6.00
LONDON INT'L.					
10504	My Friend the Sea/With All My Love	1962	3.75	7.50	15.00
10510	I'm Counting on You/Some Other World	1962	3.75	7.50	15.00
10516	Tender Love/Whistlin' for the Moon	1962	3.75	7.50	15.00
MGM					
12049	The Pendulum Song/Romance in Rome	1955	6.25	12.50	25.00
14392	My Guy/Little Bit of Lovin'	1972	—	2.50	5.00
14431	Wedding Song (There Is Love)/Song Without End	1972	—	2.50	5.00
14511	Serenade of Love/I Can't Remember	1973	—	2.50	5.00
14577	Gratification/I Can't Remember	1973	—	2.50	5.00
14673	Silver Spoon/Fixing to Live	1973	—	2.50	5.00
14708	Come On Home/The Old Fashioned Way	1974	—	2.50	5.00
SCOTTI BROS.					
02676	Natural Love/Because I Love Him	1982	—	2.00	4.00
02979	Blue Eyes Crying in the Rain/Love Won't Always Pass You By	1982	—	2.00	4.00
03171	Dreamin' with My Eyes Wide Open/Afterglow	1982	—	2.00	4.00
WARNER BROS.					
5494	Downtown/You'd Better Love Me	1964	3.75	7.50	15.00
—Originals have red labels with arrows					
5494	Downtown/You'd Better Love Me	1964	2.50	5.00	10.00
—Later pressings have orange labels					
5612	I Know a Place/Jack and John	1965	2.50	5.00	10.00
5643	You'd Better Come Home/Heart	1965	2.50	5.00	10.00
5661	Round Every Corner/Two Rivers	1965	2.50	5.00	10.00
5684	My Love/Where Am I Going	1965	2.50	5.00	10.00
5802	A Sign of the Times/Time for Love	1966	2.50	5.00	10.00
5835	I Couldn't Live Without Your Love/Your Way of Life	1966	2.50	5.00	10.00
5863	Who Am I/Love Is a Long Journey	1966	2.50	5.00	10.00
5882	Color My World/Take Me Home Again	1966	2.50	5.00	10.00
7002	This Is My Song/High	1967	2.50	5.00	10.00
7049	Don't Sleep in the Subway/Here Comes the Morning	1967	2.50	5.00	10.00
7073	The Cat in the Window (The Bird in the Sky)/Fancy Dancin' Man	1967	2.50	5.00	10.00
7097	The Other Man's Grass Is Always Greener/At the Crossroads	1967	2.50	5.00	10.00
7170	Kiss Me Goodbye/I've Got Love Going for Me	1968	2.50	5.00	10.00
—Originals have orange labels					
7170	Kiss Me Goodbye/I've Got Love Going for Me	1968	2.00	4.00	8.00
—Later pressings have green labels with "W7" logo					
7216	Don't Give Up/Every Time I See a Rainbow	1968	2.00	4.00	8.00
7244	American Boys/Look to the Sky	1968	2.00	4.00	8.00
7275	Happy Heart/Love Is the Only Thing	1969	2.00	4.00	8.00
7310	Look at Mine/If Somebody Loves You	1969	2.00	4.00	8.00
7343	No One Better Than You/Things Bringht and Beautiful	1969	2.00	4.00	8.00
7422	Beautiful Sounds/The Song Is Love	1970	2.00	4.00	8.00
7467	The Song of My Life/Couldn't Sleep	1971	2.00	4.00	8.00
7484	I Don't Know How to Love Him (Superstar)/Maybe	1971	2.00	4.00	8.00
WARWICK					
652	Romeo/Isn't It a Lovely Day	1961	5.00	10.00	20.00
Albums					
COCA-COLA					
103 [DJ]	Petula Clark Swings the Jingle	1966	37.50	75.00	150.00
GNP CRESCENDO					
2069	Live at the Royal Albert Hall	1972	2.50	5.00	10.00
2170	The Greatest Hits of Petula Clark	1984	2.00	4.00	8.00
IMPERIAL					
LP-9079 [M]	Pet Clark	1959	12.50	25.00	50.00
LP-9281 [M]	Uptown with Petula Clark	1965	5.00	10.00	20.00
—Reissue of Imperial 9079					
LP-12079 [S]	Pet Clark	1959	20.00	40.00	80.00
LP-12281 [S]	Uptown with Petula Clark	1965	6.25	12.50	25.00
—Reissue of Imperial 12079					
JANGO					
779	Give It a Try	1986	2.50	5.00	10.00
LAURIE					
LLP-2032 [M]	In Love!	1965	3.75	7.50	15.00
SLP-2032 [S]	In Love!	1965	3.75	7.50	15.00
ST-90497 [S]	In Love!	1965	5.00	10.00	20.00
—Capitol Record Club edition					
MGM					
SE-4859	Pet Clark Now	1972	2.50	5.00	10.00
PREMIER					
PM-9016 [M]	The English Sound Starring Petula Clark	1965	3.00	6.00	12.00
PS-9016 [S]	The English Sound Starring Petula Clark	1965	3.75	7.50	15.00
ROULETTE					
1 [(3)]	Petula	1975	5.00	10.00	20.00
SUNSET					
SUM-1101 [M]	This Is Petula Clark	1965	3.00	6.00	12.00
SUS-5101 [S]	This Is Petula Clark	1965	3.75	7.50	15.00
WARNER BROS.					
W 1590 [M]	Downtown	1965	3.75	7.50	15.00
—Originals have gray labels					
W 1590 [M]	Downtown	1966	3.00	6.00	12.00
—Reissues have gold labels					
WS 1590 [S]	Downtown	1965	5.00	10.00	20.00
—Originals have gold labels					
W 1598 [M]	I Know a Place	1965	3.75	7.50	15.00
—Originals have gray labels					
W 1598 [M]	I Know a Place	1966	3.00	6.00	12.00
—Reissues have gold labels					
WS 1598 [S]	I Know a Place	1965	5.00	10.00	20.00
—Originals have gold labels					
W 1608 [M]	The World's Greatest International Hits	1965	3.75	7.50	15.00
—Originals have gray labels					
W 1608 [M]	The World's Greatest International Hits	1965	3.00	6.00	12.00
—Reissues have gold labels					
WS 1608 [S]	The World's Greatest International Hits	1965	5.00	10.00	20.00
—Originals have gold labels					
W 1630 [M]	My Love	1966	2.50	5.00	10.00
WS 1630 [S]	My Love	1966	3.00	6.00	12.00
W 1645 [M]	I Couldn't Live Without Your Love	1966	2.50	5.00	10.00
WS 1645 [S]	I Couldn't Live Without Your Love	1966	3.00	6.00	12.00
W 1673 [M]	Color My World/Who Am I	1967	2.50	5.00	10.00
WS 1673 [S]	Color My World/Who Am I	1967	3.00	6.00	12.00
W 1698 [M]	These Are My Songs	1967	2.50	5.00	10.00
WS 1698 [S]	These Are My Songs	1967	3.00	6.00	12.00
W 1719 [M]	The Other Man's Grass Is Always Greener	1968	3.00	6.00	12.00
WS 1719 [P]	The Other Man's Grass Is Always Greener	1968	3.00	6.00	12.00
—"The Other Man's Grass Is Always Greener" is rechanneled.					
W 1743 [M]	Petula	1968	3.00	6.00	12.00
WS 1743 [S]	Petula	1968	3.00	6.00	12.00
WS 1765	Greatest Hits, Volume I	1968	2.50	5.00	10.00
WS 1789	Portrait of Petula	1969	2.50	5.00	10.00
WS 1823	Just Pet	1969	2.50	5.00	10.00
WS 1862	Memphis	1970	2.50	5.00	10.00
WS 1865	Warm and Tender (The Song of My Life)	1971	2.50	5.00	10.00
ST-91598	Greatest Hits, Volume I	1968	3.75	7.50	15.00
—Capitol Record Club edition					
SQBO-93215 [(2) P]	Hits...My Way	1969	6.25	12.50	25.00
—Capitol Record Club exclusive; "The Other Man's Grass Is Always Greener" is rechanneled.					

CLARK, ROY

45s

ABC

Number	Title (A Side/B Side)	Yr	VG	VG+	NM
12328	Must You Throw Dirt in My Face/Lazy River	1978	—	2.00	4.00
12365	Where Have You Been All of My Life/Near You	1978	—	2.00	4.00
12402	The Happy Days/Shoulder to Shoulder (Arm and Arm)	1978	—	2.00	4.00
12437	Is It Hot in Here (Or Is It Me)/Jolly Ho (Happy Hour)	1978	—	2.00	4.00

—With Buck Trent

ABC DOT

Number	Title (A Side/B Side)	Yr	VG	VG+	NM
17530	Dear God/Take Good Care of Her	1974	—	2.00	4.00
17545	You're Gonna Love Yourself in the Morning/Banjoy	1975	—	2.00	4.00
17565	Heart to Heart/Someone Cares for You	1975	—	2.00	4.00
17605	If I Had to Do It All Over Again/It Sure Looks Good on You	1976	—	2.00	4.00
17626	Think Summer/Whatever Happened to Gauze	1976	—	2.00	4.00
17647	I Have a Dream, I Have a Love/Half a Love	1976	—	2.00	4.00
17712	We Can't Build a Fire in the Rain/I'm So Lonesome I Could Cry	1977	—	2.00	4.00

CAPITOL

Number	Title (A Side/B Side)	Yr	VG	VG+	NM
4595	Under the Double Eagle/Black Sapphire	1961	3.00	6.00	12.00
4670	Texas Twist/Wildwood Twist	1961	3.00	6.00	12.00
4794	Talk About a Party/As Long As I'm Movin'	1962	3.00	6.00	12.00
4956	Tips of My Fingers/Spooky Movies	1963	2.50	5.00	10.00
5047	Good Time Charlie/Application for Love	1963	2.50	5.00	10.00
5099	Through the Eyes of a Fool/Sweet Violets	1964	2.50	5.00	10.00
5163	Take Me As I Am/If You'll Pardon Me	1964	2.50	5.00	10.00
5233	It's My Way/I'm Forgetting Now	1964	2.50	5.00	10.00
5300	Alabama Jubilee/Down Yonder	1964	2.50	5.00	10.00
5350	When the Wind Blows In Chicago/Live Fast Love Hard	1965	2.50	5.00	10.00
5445	The Color of Her Love Is Blue/Too Pooped to Pop	1965	2.50	5.00	10.00
5512	So Much to Remember/Turn Around and Look Again	1965	2.50	5.00	10.00
5565	Malaguena/Overdue Blues	1965	2.50	5.00	10.00
5619	Rose Colored Glasses/Everybody Watches Me	1966	2.50	5.00	10.00
5664	Hey Sweet Thing/If You Want It, Come and Get It	1966	2.50	5.00	10.00

—With Mary Taylor

Number	Title (A Side/B Side)	Yr	VG	VG+	NM
5770	St. Louis Blues/Just a Closer Walk with Thee	1966	2.50	5.00	10.00

CHURCHILL

Number	Title (A Side/B Side)	Yr	VG	VG+	NM
52469	Another Lonely Night With You/(Instrumental)	1984	—	—	3.00
94002	Paradise Knife and Gun Club/I Don't Care	1982	—	—	3.00
94007	Tennessee Saturday Night/Tumbling Tumbleweeds	1982	—	—	3.00
94011	Here We Go Again/Early in the Morning	1982	—	—	3.00
94016	Christmas Wouldn't Be Christmas Without You/A Way Without Words	1982	—	2.00	4.00
94017	I'm a Booger/A Way Without Words	1983	—	—	3.00
94025	Wildwood Flower/Southern Nights	1983	—	—	3.00

DOT

Number	Title (A Side/B Side)	Yr	VG	VG+	NM
17117	Do You Believe This Town/It Just Happened That Way	1968	—	3.00	6.00
17187	Love Is Just a State of Mind/Look to the Sky	1968	—	3.00	6.00
17246	Yesterday, When I Was Young/Just Another Man	1969	—	2.50	5.00
17299	September Song/For the Life of Me	1969	—	2.50	5.00
17324	Right or Left at Oak Street/I Need to Be Needed	1969	—	2.50	5.00
17335	Then She's a Lover/Say Amen	1969	—	2.50	5.00
17349	I Never Picked Cotton/Lonesome Too Long	1970	—	2.50	5.00
17355	Thank God and Greyhound/Strangers	1970	—	2.50	5.00
17368	A Simple Thing As Love/I'd Fight the World	1971	—	2.50	5.00
17370	(Where Do I Begin) Love Story/Theme from "Love Story"	1971	—	2.50	5.00
17386	She Cried/Back in the Race	1971	—	2.50	5.00
17395	Magnificent Sanctuary Bird/Be Ready	1971	—	2.50	5.00
17413	I'll Take the Time/Ode to a Critter	1972	—	2.50	5.00
17426	The Lawrence Welk—Hee Haw Counter-Revolution Polka/When the Wind Blows	1972	—	2.50	5.00
17449	Come Live with Me/Darby's Castle	1973	—	2.50	5.00
17458	Riders in the Sky/Roy's Guitar Boogie	1973	—	2.50	5.00
17480	Somewhere Between Love and Tomorrow/I'll Paint You a Song	1973	—	2.50	5.00
17498	Honeymoon Feelin'/I Really Don't Want to Know	1974	—	2.50	5.00
17518	The Great Divide/Chomp'n	1974	—	2.50	5.00

HALLMARK

Number	Title (A Side/B Side)	Yr	VG	VG+	NM
0001	What a Wonderful World/(B-side unknown)	1989	—	2.00	4.00
0004	But, She Loves Me/(B-side unknown)	1989	—	2.00	4.00

MCA

Number	Title (A Side/B Side)	Yr	VG	VG+	NM
41122	Caldonia/Four O'Clock in the Morning	1979	—	2.00	4.00
41153	Chain Gang of Love/Why Don't We Go Somewhere and Love	1979	—	—	3.00
41208	If There Were Only Time for Love/Then I'll Be Over You	1980	—	—	3.00
41288	For Love's Own Sake/They'll Never Take Her Love from Me	1980	—	—	3.00
51031	I Ain't Got Nobody/Play Me a Little Traveling Music	1980	—	—	3.00
51079	She Can't Give It Away/(B-side unknown)	1981	—	—	3.00
51111	Love Takes Two/Come Sundown	1981	—	—	3.00

SILVER DOLLAR

Number	Title (A Side/B Side)	Yr	VG	VG+	NM
0001	Tobacco Road/(B-side unknown)	1986	—	2.00	4.00
0004	Juke Box Saturday Night/Night Life	1986	—	2.00	4.00

SONGBIRD

Number	Title (A Side/B Side)	Yr	VG	VG+	NM
51167	The Last Word in Jesus Is Us/Shinin' Face	1981	—	—	3.00

TOWER

Number	Title (A Side/B Side)	Yr	VG	VG+	NM
331	Orange Blossom Special/The Great Pretender	1967	2.00	4.00	8.00

Albums

ABC

Number	Title (A Side/B Side)	Yr	VG	VG+	NM
AB-1053	Labor of Love	1978	2.50	5.00	10.00
AY-1084	Banjo Bandits	1978	2.50	5.00	10.00

—With Buck Trent

ABC DOT

Number	Title (A Side/B Side)	Yr	VG	VG+	NM
2001	Roy Clark/The Entertainer	1974	2.50	5.00	10.00
2005	Roy Clark, Family & Friends	1974	2.50	5.00	10.00
2010	Classic Clark	1974	2.50	5.00	10.00
2015	A Pair of Fives (Banjos, That Is)	1975	2.50	5.00	10.00
2030	Roy Clark's Greatest Hits — Volume 1	1975	2.50	5.00	10.00
2041	Heart to Heart	1975	2.50	5.00	10.00
2054	Roy Clark In Concert	1976	2.50	5.00	10.00
2072 [(2)]	My Music and Me/Vocal & Instrumental	1977	3.00	6.00	12.00
2099	Hookin' It	1977	2.50	5.00	10.00

—Reissue of Record 2 of 2072

CAPITOL

Number	Title (A Side/B Side)	Yr	VG	VG+	NM
SKAO-369	The Greatest!	1969	3.00	6.00	12.00
SM-369	The Greatest!	197?	2.50	5.00	10.00

—Reissue with new prefix

Number	Title (A Side/B Side)	Yr	VG	VG+	NM
ST 1780 [S]	The Lightning Fingers of Roy Clark	1962	6.25	12.50	25.00
T 1780 [M]	The Lightning Fingers of Roy Clark	1962	5.00	10.00	20.00
ST 1972 [S]	The Tip of My Fingers	1963	6.25	12.50	25.00
T 1972 [M]	The Tip of My Fingers	1963	5.00	10.00	20.00
ST 2031 [S]	Happy to Be Unhappy	1964	6.25	12.50	25.00
T 2031 [M]	Happy to Be Unhappy	1964	5.00	10.00	20.00
SM-2425	The Roy Clark Guitar Spectacular	197?	2.50	5.00	10.00

—Reissue with new prefix

Number	Title (A Side/B Side)	Yr	VG	VG+	NM
ST 2425 [S]	The Roy Clark Guitar Spectacular	1965	6.25	12.50	25.00
T 2425 [M]	The Roy Clark Guitar Spectacular	1965	5.00	10.00	20.00
ST 2452 [S]	Roy Clark Sings Lonesome Love Ballads	1966	6.25	12.50	25.00
T 2452 [M]	Roy Clark Sings Lonesome Love Ballads	1966	5.00	10.00	20.00
ST 2535 [S]	Stringing Along with the Blues	1966	6.25	12.50	25.00
T 2535 [M]	Stringing Along with the Blues	1966	5.00	10.00	20.00
SABB-11264 [(2)]	The Entertainer of the Year	1974	3.75	7.50	15.00
SM-11412	So Much to Remember	1975	2.50	5.00	10.00
SM-12032	The Tip of My Fingers	1980	2.00	4.00	8.00
SN-16161	The Greatest!	198?	2.00	4.00	8.00
SN-16227	The Lightning Fingers of Roy Clark	198?	2.00	4.00	8.00

CHURCHILL

Number	Title (A Side/B Side)	Yr	VG	VG+	NM
9421	The Roy Clark Show Live from Austin City Limits	1982	2.50	5.00	10.00
9425	Turned Loose	1982	2.50	5.00	10.00

DOT

Number	Title (A Side/B Side)	Yr	VG	VG+	NM
DLP-25863	Urban, Suburban	1968	3.00	6.00	12.00
DLP-25895	Do You Believe This Roy Clark	1968	3.00	6.00	12.00
DLP-25953	Yesterday, When I Was Young	1969	3.00	6.00	12.00
DLP-25972	The Everlovin' Soul of Roy Clark	1969	3.00	6.00	12.00
DLP-25977	The Other Side of Roy Clark	1970	3.00	6.00	12.00
DLP-25980	I Never Picked Cotton	1970	3.00	6.00	12.00
DLP-25986	The Best of Roy Clark	1971	3.00	6.00	12.00
DLP-25990	The Incredible Roy Clark	1971	3.00	6.00	12.00
DLP-25993	The Magnificent Sanctuary Band	1971	3.00	6.00	12.00
DLP-25997	Roy Clark Country!	1972	3.00	6.00	12.00
DLP-26005	Roy Clark Live!	1972	3.00	6.00	12.00
DLP-26008	Roy Clark/Superpicker	1973	3.00	6.00	12.00
DLP-26010	Come Live with Me	1973	3.00	6.00	12.00
DLP-26018	Roy Clark's Family Album	1973	3.00	6.00	12.00

HILLTOP

Number	Title (A Side/B Side)	Yr	VG	VG+	NM
6046	Roy Clartk	196?	3.75	7.50	15.00
6080	Silver Threads and Golden Needles	1970	2.50	5.00	10.00
6094	He'll Have to Go	1970	2.50	5.00	10.00
6135	Take Me As I Am	197?	2.50	5.00	10.00
6154	Honky Tonk	197?	2.50	5.00	10.00

MCA

Number	Title (A Side/B Side)	Yr	VG	VG+	NM
675	Labor of Love	1980	2.00	4.00	8.00
676	Heart to Heart	1980	2.00	4.00	8.00
677	Hookin' It	1980	2.00	4.00	8.00
678	Yesterday, When I Was Young	198?	2.00	4.00	8.00
679	Roy Clark/Superpicker	198?	2.00	4.00	8.00
811	Back to the Country	198?	2.00	4.00	8.00
3161	Makin' Music	1980	2.50	5.00	10.00

—With Gatemouth Brown

Number	Title (A Side/B Side)	Yr	VG	VG+	NM
27015	The Best of Roy Clark	198?	2.00	4.00	8.00
27050	Roy Clark's Greatest Hits — Volume 1	198?	2.00	4.00	8.00
37130	Banjo Bandits	198?	2.00	4.00	8.00

—With Buck Trent

Number	Title (A Side/B Side)	Yr	VG	VG+	NM
37131	A Pair of Fives (Banjos, That Is)	198?	2.00	4.00	8.00
37132	Roy Clark In Concert	198?	2.00	4.00	8.00
37134	Roy Clark Live!	198?	2.00	4.00	8.00
37142	My Music	198?	2.00	4.00	8.00

PAIR

Number	Title (A Side/B Side)	Yr	VG	VG+	NM
PDL2-1088 [(2)]	Country Standard Time	1986	3.00	6.00	12.00

PICKWICK

Number	Title (A Side/B Side)	Yr	VG	VG+	NM
PTP-2043 [(2)]	Roy Clark	1973	3.00	6.00	12.00

SONGBIRD

Number	Title (A Side/B Side)	Yr	VG	VG+	NM
5260	The Last Word in Jesus Is Us	1981	2.50	5.00	10.00

TOWER

Number	Title (A Side/B Side)	Yr	VG	VG+	NM
ST 5055 [S]	Roy Clark Live	1967	5.00	10.00	20.00
T 5055 [M]	Roy Clark Live	1967	3.75	7.50	15.00
DT 5118 [R]	In the Mood	1968	3.75	7.50	15.00

WORD

Number	Title (A Side/B Side)	Yr	VG	VG+	NM
8654	Roy Clark Sings Gospel	1975	3.00	6.00	12.00

CLARK, SANFORD

45s

DOT

Number	Title (A Side/B Side)	Yr	VG	VG+	NM
15481	The Fool/Lonesome for a Letter	1956	12.50	25.00	50.00

—Originals have maroon labels

Number	Title (A Side/B Side)	Yr	VG	VG+	NM
15481	The Fool/Lonesome for a Letter	1956	6.25	12.50	25.00

—Second pressings have black labels

Number	Title (A Side/B Side)	Yr	VG	VG+	NM
15516	A Cheat/Usta Be My Baby	1956	6.25	12.50	25.00
15534	Oooo Baby/9 Lb. Hammer	1957	6.25	12.50	25.00
15556	The Glory of Love/Darling Dear	1957	6.25	12.50	25.00
15585	Love Charms/Loo-Be-Doo	1957	6.25	12.50	25.00
15646	Swanee River Rock/The Man Who Made an Angel Cry	1957	6.25	12.50	25.00
15738	Modern Romance/Travelin' Man	1958	37.50	75.00	150.00

JAMIE

Number	Title (A Side/B Side)	Yr	VG	VG+	NM
1107	Sing 'Em Some Blues/Still as the Night	1958	5.00	10.00	20.00
1120	Bad Luck/My Jealousy	1959	5.00	10.00	20.00
1129	Run Boy Run/New Kind of Fool	1959	5.00	10.00	20.00
1153	Go On Home/Pledging My Love	1960	5.00	10.00	20.00

Number	Title (A Side/B Side)	Yr	VG	VG+	NM
LHI					
1203	The Son of Hickory Holler's Tramp/Black Widow Spider	1968	2.00	4.00	8.00
1213	Love Me Till Then/Farm Labor Camp No. 2	1968	2.00	4.00	8.00
MCI					
1003	The Fool/Lonesome for a Letter	1956	50.00	100.00	200.00
RAMCO					
1972	The Fool '66/Step Aside	1966	3.75	7.50	15.00
1976	Shades/Once Upon a Time	1966	3.00	6.00	12.00
1979	They Call Me Country/Climbin' the Walls	1967	3.00	6.00	12.00
1987	It's Nothing to Me/Calling All Hearts	1967	3.00	6.00	12.00
1992	The Big Lie/Where's the Floor	1967	3.00	6.00	12.00
TREY					
3016	It Hurts Me Too/Guess It's Love	1961	5.00	10.00	20.00
WARNER BROS.					
5473	She Taught Me/Just Blessin'	1964	3.75	7.50	15.00
5624	Houston/Hard Feelings	1965	3.75	7.50	15.00
Albums					
LHI					
12003	Return of the Fool	1968	15.00	30.00	60.00

CLARKE, ALLAN
Also see THE HOLLIES.

Number	Title (A Side/B Side)	Yr	VG	VG+	NM
45s					
ASYLUM					
45313	Light a Light/If You Think You Know How to Love Me	1976	—	2.00	4.00
ATLANTIC					
3459	(I Will Be Your) Shadow in the Street/The Passenger	1978	—	2.00	4.00
3497	I Wasn't Born Yesterday/The Man Who Manufactured Daydreams	1978	—	2.00	4.00
3522	I'm Betting My Life on You/Who's Goin' Out the Back Door	1978	—	2.00	4.00
ELEKTRA					
46617	Slipstream/Imagination's Child	1979	—	2.00	4.00
47019	The Only Ones/Driving the Doomsday Cars	1980	—	2.00	4.00
EPIC					
10914	Baby It's Alright with Me/Ruby	1972	—	2.00	4.00
Albums					
ASYLUM					
7E-1056	I've Got Time	1976	2.50	5.00	10.00
ATLANTIC					
SD 19175	I Wasn't Born Yesterday	1978	2.50	5.00	10.00
ELEKTRA					
6E-267	Legendary Heroes	1980	2.50	5.00	10.00
EPIC					
KE 31757	My Real Name Is 'Arold	1972	3.75	7.50	15.00

CLARKE, STANLEY
Also see RETURN TO FOREVER.

Number	Title (A Side/B Side)	Yr	VG	VG+	NM
45s					
EPIC					
03038	Straight to the Top/The Force of Love	1982	—	—	3.00
03388	You Are the One for Me/Play the Bass	1982	—	—	3.00
04485	Heaven Sent You/Speedball	1984	—	—	3.00
04914	Born in the U.S.A./Camp Americano	1985	—	—	3.00
05584	What If I Should Fall in Love/Stereotypics	1985	—	—	3.00
50890	We Supply/Underestimation	1980	—	—	3.00
50924	Rocks, Pebbles and Sand/You're Together	1980	—	—	3.00
NEMPEROR					
001	Lopsy Lu/Vulcan Princess	1974	—	2.00	4.00
002	Silly Putty/Hello Jeff	1975	—	2.00	4.00
009	Hot Fun/Life Is Just a Game	1976	—	2.00	4.00
7518	Slow Dance/Rock 'n' Roll Jelly	1978	—	2.00	4.00
7521	Jamaican Boy/Rock 'n' Roll Jelly	1979	—	2.00	4.00
7522	Just a Feeling/The Streets of Philadelphia	1979	—	2.00	4.00
7523	Together Again (Part 1)/Together Again (Part 2)	1980	—	2.00	4.00
PORTRAIT					
08051	If This Bass Could Only Talk/Funny How Time Flies (When You're Having Fun)	1988	—	2.00	4.00
Albums					
EPIC					
JE 36506	Rocks, Pebbles and Sand	1980	2.50	5.00	10.00
PE 36973	Stanley Clarke	1981	2.00	4.00	8.00
—Reissue of Nemperor 431					
PE 36974	Journey to Love	1981	2.00	4.00	8.00
—Reissue of Nemperor 433					
PE 36975	School Days	1981	2.00	4.00	8.00
—Reissue of Nemperor 900					
FE 38386	Let Me Know You	1982	2.50	5.00	10.00
FE 38688	Time Exposure	1984	2.50	5.00	10.00
FE 40040	Find Out!	1985	2.50	5.00	10.00
FE 40275	Hideaway	1986	2.50	5.00	10.00
NEMPEROR					
SD 431	Stanley Clarke	1974	3.00	6.00	12.00
SD 433	Journey to Love	1975	3.00	6.00	12.00
SD 439	School Days	1976	3.00	6.00	12.00
SD 900	School Days	1978	2.50	5.00	10.00
—Reissue of 439					
JZ 35303	Modern Man	1978	2.50	5.00	10.00
PZ 35305	Modern Man	1985	2.00	4.00	8.00
—Reissue with new prefix					
KZ2 35680 [(2)]	I Wanna Play for You	1979	3.00	6.00	12.00
POLYDOR					
PD-5531	Children of Forever	1973	3.00	6.00	12.00
827559-1	Children of Forever	1985	2.00	4.00	8.00
—Reissue					
PORTRAIT					
OR 40923	If This Bass Could Only Talk	1988	2.50	5.00	10.00

CLASS-AIRES, THE

Number	Title (A Side/B Side)	Yr	VG	VG+	NM
45s					
HONEY BEE					
(# unknown)	Too Old to Cry/My Tears Start to Fall	195?	500.00	1000.	2000.
Albums					
HONEY BEE					
(# unknown)	Tears Start to Fall	195?	75.00	150.00	300.00

CLASS-NOTES, THE

Number	Title (A Side/B Side)	Yr	VG	VG+	NM
45s					
DOT					
15786	You Inspire Me/Goodness Gracious	1958	7.50	15.00	30.00
HAMILTON					
50011	Take It Back/Bessie's House	1959	15.00	30.00	60.00

CLASSIC IV, THE

Number	Title (A Side/B Side)	Yr	VG	VG+	NM
45s					
ALGONQUIN					
1650	Limbo Under The Christmas Tree/Early Christmas	1962	7.50	15.00	30.00
TWIST					
1001	Island of Paradise/Heavenly Bliss	1962	25.00	50.00	100.00

CLASSICS, THE (1)
Brooklyn vocal group led by Emil Stucchio.

Number	Title (A Side/B Side)	Yr	VG	VG+	NM
45s					
BED-STUY					
222	Again/The Way You Look Tonight	196?	2.50	5.00	10.00
DART					
1015	So in Love/Cinderella	1960	7.50	15.00	30.00
1024	Life Is But a Dream, Sweetheart/That's the Way	1961	50.00	100.00	200.00
1032	Angel Angela/Eenie Minie Mo	1961	12.50	25.00	50.00
MERCURY					
71829	Life Is But a Dream, Sweetheart/That's the Way	1961	6.25	12.50	25.00
MUSICNOTE					
118	P.S. I Love You/Wrap Your Troubles in Dreams	1963	6.25	12.50	25.00
1116	Till Then/Eenie Minie Mo	1963	6.25	12.50	25.00
—Black vinyl, blue label					
1116	Till Then/Eenie Minie Mo	1963	25.00	50.00	100.00
—Gold vinyl					
1116	Till Then/Eenie Minie Mo	1963	37.50	75.00	150.00
—Multi-color vinyl					
1116	Till Then/Eenie Minie Mo	1963	7.50	15.00	30.00
—Black vinyl, yellow label					
MUSICTONE					
1114	So in Love/Cinderella	1963	5.00	10.00	20.00
6131	Too Young/Who's Laughing, Who's Crying	1964	5.00	10.00	20.00
PICCOLO					
500	I Apologize/Love for Today	1965	6.25	12.50	25.00
STORK					
2	You'll Never Know/Dancing with You	1964	6.25	12.50	25.00
STREAM LINE					
1028	Life Is But a Dream, Sweetheart/Nuttin' in the Noggin	1961	6.25	12.50	25.00

CLASSICS, THE (2)
With LOU CHRISTIE.

Number	Title (A Side/B Side)	Yr	VG	VG+	NM
45s					
STARR					
508	Close Your Eyes/Funny Things	1960	50.00	100.00	200.00
—Reissued on Alcar with Lou Christie's name prominently mentioned					

CLASSICS, THE (3)
Canadian group.

Number	Title (A Side/B Side)	Yr	VG	VG+	NM
45s					
JERDEN					
742	Till I Met You/It Didn't Take Much	1964	7.50	15.00	30.00

CLASSICS, THE (U)
Some of these could be group (1); none of them are group (2); probably none of these are group (3).

Number	Title (A Side/B Side)	Yr	VG	VG+	NM
45s					
CLASS					
219	If Only the Sky Was a Mirror/Gosh, But This Is Love	1958	17.50	35.00	70.00
CREST					
1063	Let Me Dream/You're the Prettiest One	1959	20.00	40.00	80.00
MV					
1000	Christmas Is Here/(B-side unknown)	19??	2.50	5.00	10.00
PROMO					
1010	Blue Moon/Little Boy Lost	1961	7.50	15.00	30.00
—As "Herb Lance and the Classics"					
RO-ANN					
1002	Je Vous Aime/Burning Desire	1959	250.00	500.00	1000.
SHELTER					
7318	Mr. Fire Coal-Man/Flashing My Whip	1972	—	2.50	5.00
—B-side by Hugh Roy					
TOP RANK					
2061	You're Everything/Burning Love	1960	6.25	12.50	25.00

CLASSICS IV

Number	Title (A Side/B Side)	Yr	VG	VG+	NM
45s					
ARLEN					
746	Don't Make Me Wait/It's Too Late	1964	5.00	10.00	20.00
CAPITOL					
5710	Cry Baby/Pollyanna	1966	3.75	7.50	15.00
—As "The Classics"					
5816	Little Darlin'/Nothing to Lose	1966	3.75	7.50	15.00
IMPERIAL					
66259	Spooky/Poor People	1967	2.00	4.00	8.00
66293	Soul Train/Strange Changes	1968	2.00	4.00	8.00

Number	Title (A Side/B Side)	Yr	VG	VG+	NM
66304	Mama's and Papa's/Waves	1968	2.00	4.00	8.00
66328	Stormy/Ladies' Man	1968	5.00	10.00	20.00
66328	Stormy/24 Hours of Loneliness	1968	2.00	4.00	8.00
66352	Traces/Mary, Mary Row Your Boat	1969	2.00	4.00	8.00
66378	Everyday With You Girl/Sentimental Lady	1969	2.00	4.00	8.00
66393	Change of Heart/Rainy Day	1969	—	3.00	6.00
—Starting here, "Dennis Yost and the Classics IV"					
66424	Midnight/The Comic	1969	—	3.00	6.00
66439	The Funniest Thing/Nobody Loves You But Me	1970	—	3.00	6.00
LIBERTY					
56182	God Knows I Loved Her/We Miss You	1970	—	3.00	6.00
56200	Where Did All the Good Times Go/Ain't It the Truth	1970	—	3.00	6.00
MGM					
14785	My First Day Without You/Lovin' Each Other	1975	—	2.00	4.00
MGM SOUTH					
7002	What Am I Crying For/All in Your Mind	1972	—	2.50	5.00
7012	Rosanna/One Man Show	1973	—	2.50	5.00
7016	Save the Sunlight/Make Me Believe It	1973	—	2.50	5.00
7020	I Knew It Would Happen/Love Me or Leave Me Alone	1973	—	2.50	5.00
7027	It's Now Winter's Day/Losing My Mind	1974	—	2.50	5.00
UNITED ARTISTS					
0125	Stormy/Spooky	1973	—	2.00	4.00
—"Silver Spotlight Series" reissue					
0126	Traces/Everyday with You Girl	1973	—	2.00	4.00
—"Silver Spotlight Series" reissue					
50777	Most of All/It's Time for Love	1971	—	2.50	5.00
50805	Cherry Hill Park/Pick Up the Pieces	1971	—	2.50	5.00
Albums					
ACCORD					
SN-7107	Stormy	1981	2.50	5.00	10.00
IMPERIAL					
LP-12371	Spooky	1968	5.00	10.00	20.00
LP-12407	Mamas and Papas/Soul Train	1969	5.00	10.00	20.00
LP-12429	Traces	1969	5.00	10.00	20.00
LP-16000	Dennis Yost & the Classics IV/Golden Greats - Volume I	1969	5.00	10.00	20.00
LIBERTY					
LN-10109	The Very Best of the Classics IV	198?	2.00	4.00	8.00
LST-11003	Song	1970	3.75	7.50	15.00
MGM SOUTH					
702	Dennis Yost and the Classics IV	1973	3.75	7.50	15.00
UNITED ARTISTS					
UA-LA446-E	The Very Best of the Classics IV	1975	3.00	6.00	12.00

CLAY, CASSIUS

Number	Title (A Side/B Side)	Yr	VG	VG+	NM
45s					
COLUMBIA					
43007	Stand By Me/I Am the Greatest	1964	6.25	12.50	25.00
43007 [PS]	Stand By Me/I Am the Greatest	1964	12.50	25.00	50.00
ZSP 75717/77185	[DJ]The Prediction/Will the Real Sonny Liston Please Fall Down	1964	10.00	20.00	40.00
ZSP 75717/77185	[PS]The Prediction/Will the Real Sonny Liston Please Fall Down	1964	20.00	40.00	80.00
Albums					
COLUMBIA					
CL 2093 [M]	I Am the Greatest!	1963	10.00	20.00	40.00
CS 8893 [S]	I Am the Greatest!	1963	12.50	25.00	50.00

CLAY, CHRIS

Number	Title (A Side/B Side)	Yr	VG	VG+	NM
45s					
VELTONE					
111	Santa Under Analysis Part 1/Santa Under Analysis Part 2	1960	6.25	12.50	25.00

CLAY, JOE

Number	Title (A Side/B Side)	Yr	VG	VG+	NM
45s					
VIK					
0211	Duck Tail/Sixteen Chicks	1956	25.00	50.00	100.00
0218	Get On the Right Track/Cracker Jack	1956	25.00	50.00	100.00

CLAY, JUDY

Also see WILLIAM BELL, BILLY VERA.

Number	Title (A Side/B Side)	Yr	VG	VG+	NM
45s					
ATLANTIC					
2669	Get Together/Sister Pitiful	1969	—	3.00	6.00
2697	Greatest Love/Saving All for You	1969	—	3.00	6.00
EMBER					
1080	More Than You Know/I Thought I'd Gotten Over You	1961	3.00	6.00	12.00
1085	Stormy Weather/Do You Think That's Right	1962	3.00	6.00	12.00
SCEPTER					
1273	My Arms Aren't Strong Enough/That's All	1964	2.00	4.00	8.00
1281	Lonely People Do Foolish Things/I'm Comin' Home	1964	2.00	4.00	8.00
12135	The Way You Look Tonight/Haven't You Got What It Takes	1966	2.00	4.00	8.00
12157	He's the Kind of Guy/You Busted My Mind	1966	2.00	4.00	8.00
12218	I Want You/He's the Kind of Guy	1968	2.00	4.00	8.00
STAX					
0006	Bed of Roses/Remove the Clouds	1968	—	3.00	6.00
0026	It Ain't Long Enough/Give Love to Save Love	1969	—	3.00	6.00
230	You Can't Run Away from Your Heart/It Takes a Lot of Good Love	1967	2.00	4.00	8.00

CLAY, OTIS

Number	Title (A Side/B Side)	Yr	VG	VG+	NM
45s					
COTILLION					
44001	She's About a Mover/You Don't Miss Your Water	1968	2.00	4.00	8.00
44009	Do Right Woman, Do Right Man/That Kind of Lovin'	1968	—	3.50	7.00
44068	Pouring Water on a Drowning Man/Hard Working Women	1970	—	3.50	7.00
44101	Is It Over/I'm Qualified	1970	—	3.50	7.00
DAKAR					
610	Baby Jane/You Hurt Me for the Last Time	1969	—	3.50	7.00
ECHO					
2002	Check It Out/(B-side unknown)	1975	2.50	5.00	10.00
GLADES					
1736	All I Need Is You/Special Kind of Soul	1976	2.50	5.00	10.00
HI					
2206	Home Is Where the Heart Is/Brand New Thing	1972	—	3.00	6.00
2214	Precious Precious/Too Many Hands	1972	—	3.00	6.00
2226	Trying to Live My Life Without You/Let Me Be the One	1972	—	3.50	7.00
2239	I Can't Make It Alone/I Didn't Know the Meaning of Pain	1973	—	3.00	6.00
2252	If I Could Reach Out/I Die a Little Bit Each Day	1973	—	3.00	6.00
2266	Woman Don't Live Here No More/You Can't Escape the Hands of Love	1974	—	3.00	6.00
2270	You Did Something to Me/I Was Jealous	1974	—	3.00	6.00
KAYVETTE					
5130	All Because of Your Love/Today My World Fell	1977	—	2.50	5.00
5133	Let Me In/Sweet Woman's Love	1977	—	2.50	5.00
ONE-DERFUL!					
4834	Three Is a Crowd/Flame in Your Heart	1965	2.50	5.00	10.00
4837	I Paid the Price/Tired of Falling In (And Out of) Love	1966	2.50	5.00	10.00
4841	I Testify/I'm Satisfied	1966	2.50	5.00	10.00
4846	Flame in Your Heart/It's Easier Said, Than Done	1967	2.00	4.00	8.00
4848	That's How It Is (When You're in Love)/Show Place	1967	2.00	4.00	8.00
4850	A Lasting Love/Got to Find a Way	1967	2.00	4.00	8.00
4852	Don't Pass Me By/That'll Get You What You Want	1968	2.00	4.00	8.00
Albums					
HI					
6003	I Can't Take It	197?	3.00	6.00	12.00
SHL 32075	Trying to Live My Life Without You	1972	5.00	10.00	20.00
ROOSTER BLUES					
R-7609 [(2)]	Soul Man: Live in Japan	1985	3.75	7.50	15.00

CLAY, TOM

Number	Title (A Side/B Side)	Yr	VG	VG+	NM
45s					
BIG TOP					
3055	The Little Boy/That's All	1960	5.00	10.00	20.00
CHANT					
103	Marry Me/(B-side unknown)	1959	25.00	50.00	100.00
IBBB					
ZTSC 97436/7	Remember, We Don't Like Them, We Love Them: Official IBBB Interview	1964	37.50	75.00	150.00
—Interviews with the Beatles					
MOWEST					
5002	What the World Needs Now Is Love/Abraham, Martin and John//The Victors	1971	—	3.00	6.00
—Mostly orange label					
5002	What the World Needs Now Is Love/Abraham, Martin and John//The Victors	1971	—	2.50	5.00
—Blue and yellow label					
5007	Whatever Happened to Love/Baby I Need Your Loving	1971	—	2.00	4.00
Albums					
MOWEST					
103	What the World Needs Now Is Love	1971	3.75	7.50	15.00

CLAYTON, MERRY

Number	Title (A Side/B Side)	Yr	VG	VG+	NM
45s					
CAPITOL					
4984	It's In His Kiss/The Magic of Romance	1963	2.50	5.00	10.00
5100	Usher Boy/Nothing Left to Do But Cry	1963	2.50	5.00	10.00
5164	Beg Me/La La Jace Song	1964	2.50	5.00	10.00
5243	This Is My Dream/The Knocks on the Door	1964	2.50	5.00	10.00
MCA					
41195	Emotion/Let Me Make You Cry a Little Longer	1980	—	2.00	4.00
41266	You're Always There When I Need You/When the World Turns Blue	1980	—	2.00	4.00
ODE					
66003	Gimme Shelter/Good Girls	1970	—	2.50	5.00
66007	Country Road/Forget It, I Got It	1970	—	2.50	5.00
66011	Lift Every Voice and Sing/I Ain't Gonna Worry My Life Away	1970	—	2.50	5.00
66016	The Times They Are a-Changing/Wouldn't It Be Nice	1971	7.50	15.00	30.00
—B-side by the Beach Boys					
66018	After All This Time/Whatever	1971	—	2.00	4.00
66020	Steamroller/After All This Time	1971	—	2.00	4.00
66024	Southern Man/Oh No, Not My Baby	1972	—	2.00	4.00
66030	Oh No, Not My Baby/Suspicious Minds	1972	—	2.00	4.00
66108	The Acid Queen/Eyesight to the Blind	1975	—	2.00	4.00
—B-side by Richie Havens					
66110	Keep Your Eye on the Sparrow/Love Grows Up Slow	1975	—	2.00	4.00
66116	One More Ride/If I Lose	1976	—	2.00	4.00
RCA					
6989-7-R	Yes/In the Still of the Night	1988	—	—	3.00
—B-side by the Five Satins					
8917-7-R	Almost Paradise/Hungry Eyes	1989	—	—	3.00
—B-side with Eric Carmen					
Albums					
MCA					
3200	Emotion	1980	2.50	5.00	10.00
ODE					
PE 34948	Merry Clayton	1977	2.00	4.00	8.00
PE 34957	Keep Your Eye on the Sparrow	1977	2.00	4.00	8.00

Number	Title (A Side/B Side)	Yr	VG	VG+	NM
SP-77001	Gimme Shelter	1970	3.75	7.50	15.00
SP-77012	Merry Clayton	1971	3.00	6.00	12.00
SP-77030	Keep Your Eye on the Sparrow	1975	3.00	6.00	12.00

CLAYTON-THOMAS, DAVID

Also see BLOOD, SWEAT AND TEARS.

Number	Title (A Side/B Side)	Yr	VG	VG+	NM
45s					
ATCO					
6347	Hey Hey Hey Hey/Walk That Walk	1965	3.75	7.50	15.00
COLUMBIA					
45569	Sing a Song/We're All Meat from the Same Bone	1972	—	2.50	5.00
45603	North Beach Racetrack/Magnificent Sanctuary Band	1972	—	2.50	5.00
45675	Yesterday's Music/Falling by Degrees	1972	—	2.50	5.00
DECCA					
32556	Say Boss Man/Done Somebody Wrong	1969	2.50	5.00	10.00
EPIC					
03792	I Can't Blame a Broken Heart/Some Hearts Get All the Breaks	1983	—	2.00	4.00
RCA VICTOR					
APBO-0078	Workin' on the Railroad/Prof. Longhair	1973	—	2.00	4.00
APBO-0216	Yolanda/Workin' on the Railroad	1974	—	2.00	4.00
APBO-0296	Take the Money and Run/Anytime... Babe	1974	—	2.00	4.00
74-0966	Hernando's Hideaway/Harmony Junction	1973	—	2.00	4.00
ROULETTE					
7048	No, No, No/Monopoly	1969	2.50	5.00	10.00
TOWER					
206	Take Me Back/Out of the Sunshine	1966	3.00	6.00	12.00
263	Born with the Blues/Brainwashed	1966	3.00	6.00	12.00
Albums					
ABC					
AA-1104	Clayton	1978	2.50	5.00	10.00
COLUMBIA					
KC 31000	David Clayton-Thomas	1972	3.75	7.50	15.00
KC 31700	Tequila Sunrise	1972	3.75	7.50	15.00
DECCA					
DL 75146	David Clayton-Thomas!	1969	5.00	10.00	20.00
RCA VICTOR					
APD1-0173 [Q]	Harmony Junction	1973	5.00	10.00	20.00
APL1-0173	Harmony Junction	1973	3.00	6.00	12.00

CLEAN LIVING

Number	Title (A Side/B Side)	Yr	VG	VG+	NM
45s					
VANGUARD					
35162	In Heaven There Is No Beer/Backwoods Girl	1972	—	2.50	5.00
35170	Old Time Music/Jenny Regardless	1973	—	2.00	4.00
35171	Far North Again/Me and You	1973	—	2.00	4.00
Albums					
VANGUARD					
VSD-79318	Clean Living	1972	2.50	5.00	10.00
VSD-79334	Meadow Muffin	1973	2.50	5.00	10.00

CLEANLINESS AND GODLINESS SKIFFLE BAND, THE

Also see THE MASKED MARAUDERS.

Number	Title (A Side/B Side)	Yr	VG	VG+	NM
Albums					
VANGUARD					
VSD-79285	Greatest Hits	1968	6.25	12.50	25.00

CLEAR LIGHT

Also see CLIFF DeYOUNG.

Number	Title (A Side/B Side)	Yr	VG	VG+	NM
45s					
ELEKTRA					
45622	She's Ready to Be Free/Black Roses	1967	3.00	6.00	12.00
45626	They Who Have Nothing/Ballad of Freddie and Larry	1968	3.00	6.00	12.00
Albums					
ELEKTRA					
EKL-4011 [M]	Clear Light	1967	6.25	12.50	25.00
EKS-74011 [S]	Clear Light	1967	6.25	12.50	25.00

CLEARY, DON

Number	Title (A Side/B Side)	Yr	VG	VG+	NM
Albums					
PALOMINO					
302 [M]	Don Cleary Sings Traditional Cowboy Songs	1966	12.50	25.00	50.00

CLEAVER, ELDRIDGE

Number	Title (A Side/B Side)	Yr	VG	VG+	NM
Albums					
MORE					
4000 [M]	Soul On Wax	1968	6.25	12.50	25.00

CLEE-SHAYS, THE

Number	Title (A Side/B Side)	Yr	VG	VG+	NM
45s					
TRIUMPH					
65	The Man from U.N.C.L.E./Dynamite	1966	5.00	10.00	20.00

CLEFS OF LAVENDER HILL, THE

Number	Title (A Side/B Side)	Yr	VG	VG+	NM
45s					
DATE					
1510	Stop! — Get a Ticket/First Tell Me Why	1966	5.00	10.00	20.00
1530	One More Time/So I'll Try	1966	5.00	10.00	20.00
1533	Play with Fire/It Won't Be Long	1966	5.00	10.00	20.00
1567	Gimme One Good Reason/Oh, Say My Love	1967	5.00	10.00	20.00
THAMES					
100	Stop! — Get a Ticket/First Tell Me Why	1966	10.00	20.00	40.00

CLEFTONES, THE

Number	Title (A Side/B Side)	Yr	VG	VG+	NM
45s					
CLASSIC ARTISTS					
121	She's So Fine/Trudy	1990	—	2.00	4.00
GEE					
1000	You Baby You/I Was Dreaming	1955	15.00	30.00	60.00
1011	Little Girl of Mine/You're Driving Me Mad	1956	10.00	20.00	40.00
1016	Can't We Be Sweethearts/Niki-Hoeky	1956	10.00	20.00	40.00
1025	String Around My Heart/Happy Memories	1956	10.00	20.00	40.00
1031	Why Do You Do Me Like You Do/I Like Your Style of Making Love	1957	10.00	20.00	40.00
1038	See You Next Year/Ten Pairs of Shoes	1957	10.00	20.00	40.00
1041	Hey Babe/What Did I Do That Was Wrong	1957	10.00	20.00	40.00
1048	Lover Boy/Beginners in Love	1958	7.50	15.00	30.00
1064	Heart and Soul/How Do You Feel	1961	6.25	12.50	25.00
1067	(I Love You) For Sentimental Reasons/'Deed I Do	1961	5.00	10.00	20.00
1074	Earth Angel/Blues in the Night	1961	5.00	10.00	20.00
1077	Again/Do You	1961	5.00	10.00	20.00
1079	Lover Come Back to Me/There She Goes	1962	5.00	10.00	20.00
1080	How Deep Is the Ocean/Some Kinda Blue	1962	5.00	10.00	20.00
OLD TOWN					
1011	The Masquerade Is Over/My Dearest Darling	1955	125.00	250.00	500.00
ROULETTE					
4094	Trudy/She's So Fine	1958	6.25	12.50	25.00
4161	Mish Mash Baby/Cuzin Casanova	1959	6.25	12.50	25.00
4302	She's Gone/Shadows on the Very Last Row	1960	6.25	12.50	25.00
WARE					
6001	She's Forgotten You/Right from the Git Go	1964	3.75	7.50	15.00
Albums					
GEE					
GLP-705 [M]	Heart and Soul	1961	50.00	100.00	200.00
SGLP-705 [S]	Heart and Soul	1961	125.00	250.00	500.00
GLP-707 [M]	For Sentimental Reasons	1961	62.50	125.00	250.00
SGLP-707 [S]	For Sentimental Reasons	1961	300.00	600.00	1200.

CLEMENT, JACK

Number	Title (A Side/B Side)	Yr	VG	VG+	NM
45s					
ELEKTRA					
45474	We Must Believe in Magic/When I Dream	1978	—	2.00	4.00
45518	All I Want to Do in Life/It'll Be Her	1978	—	2.00	4.00
45547	Gone Girl/There She Goes	1978	—	2.00	4.00
RCA VICTOR					
47-7602	Whole Lotta Lookin'/Edge of Town	1959	3.75	7.50	15.00
SUN					
291	Ten Years/Your Lover Boy	1958	6.25	12.50	25.00
311	The Black Haired Man/Wrong	1958	6.25	12.50	25.00
Albums					
ELEKTRA					
6E-122	All I Want to Do in Life	1978	3.00	6.00	12.00

CLIBURN, VAN

Number	Title (A Side/B Side)	Yr	VG	VG+	NM
Albums					
RCA VICTOR RED SEAL					
LM-2252 [M]	Tchaikovsky: Piano Concerto No. 1	1958	6.25	12.50	25.00
LSC-2252 [S]	Tchaikovsky: Piano Concerto No. 1	1958	7.50	15.00	30.00
—"Shaded dog" pressing ("Living Stereo" on label)					
LSC-2252 [S]	Tchaikovsky: Piano Concerto No. 1	1965	5.00	10.00	20.00
—"White dog" pressing ("Stereo" on label)					
LSC-2252 [S]	Tchaikovsky: Piano Concerto No. 1	1969	3.00	6.00	12.00
—"No dog" pressing ("RCA" sideways at left)					
LSC-2252 [S]	Tchaikovsky: Piano Concerto No. 1	1976	2.00	4.00	8.00
—"Late dog" pressing (dog near top)					
LM-2355 [M]	Rachmaninoff: Piano Concerto No. 3	1959	6.25	12.50	25.00
LSC-2355 [S]	Rachmaninoff: Piano Concerto No. 3	1959	7.50	15.00	30.00
—"Shaded dog" pressing ("Living Stereo" on label)					
LSC-2355 [S]	Rachmaninoff: Piano Concerto No. 3	1965	5.00	10.00	20.00
—"White dog" pressing ("Stereo" on label)					
LSC-2355 [S]	Rachmaninoff: Piano Concerto No. 3	1969	3.00	6.00	12.00
—"No dog" pressing ("RCA" sideways at left)					
LM-2455 [M]	Schumann: Piano Concerto in A Minor	1960	3.75	7.50	15.00
LSC-2455 [S]	Schumann: Piano Concerto in A Minor	1960	7.50	15.00	30.00
—"Shaded dog" pressing ("Living Stereo" on label)					
LSC-2455 [S]	Schumann: Piano Concerto in A Minor	1965	5.00	10.00	20.00
—"White dog" pressing ("Stereo" on label)					
LSC-2455 [S]	Schumann: Piano Concerto in A Minor	1969	3.00	6.00	12.00
—"No dog" pressing ("RCA" sideways at left)					
LM-2507 [M]	Prokofiev: Piano Concerto No. 3; MacDowell: Piano Concerto No. 2	1961	3.75	7.50	15.00
LSC-2507 [S]	Prokofiev: Piano Concerto No. 3; MacDowell: Piano Concerto No. 2	1961	12.50	25.00	50.00
—"Shaded dog" pressing ("Living Stereo" on label)					
LSC-2507 [S]	Prokofiev: Piano Concerto No. 3; MacDowell: Piano Concerto No. 2	1965	5.00	10.00	20.00
—"White dog" pressing ("Stereo" on label)					
LSC-2507 [S]	Prokofiev: Piano Concerto No. 3; MacDowell: Piano Concerto No. 2	1969	3.00	6.00	12.00
—"No dog" pressing ("RCA" sideways at left)					
LM-2562 [M]	Beethoven: Piano Concerto No. 5 (Emperor Concerto)	1961	3.75	7.50	15.00
LSC-2562 [S]	Beethoven: Piano Concerto No. 5 (Emperor Concerto)	1961	5.00	10.00	20.00
—"Shaded dog" pressing ("Living Stereo" on label)					
LSC-2562 [S]	Beethoven: Piano Concerto No. 5 (Emperor Concerto)	1964	5.00	10.00	20.00
—"White dog" pressing ("Stereo" on label)					
LSC-2562 [S]	Beethoven: Piano Concerto No. 5 (Emperor Concerto)	1969	3.75	7.50	15.00
—"No dog" pressing ("RCA" sideways at left)					
LM-2576 [M]	My Favorite Chopin	1962	3.75	7.50	15.00
LSC-2576 [S]	My Favorite Chopin	1962	5.00	10.00	20.00
—"Shaded dog" pressing ("Living Stereo" on label)					
LSC-2576 [S]	My Favorite Chopin	1965	3.75	7.50	15.00
—"White dog" pressing ("Stereo" on label)					
LSC-2576 [S]	My Favorite Chopin	1969	3.00	6.00	12.00
—"No dog" pressing ("RCA" sideways at left)					
LSC-2576 [S]	My Favorite Chopin	1976	2.00	4.00	8.00
—"Late dog" pressing (dog near top)					
LM-2581 [M]	Brahms: Piano Concerto No. 2	1962	3.75	7.50	15.00

Number	Title (A Side/B Side)	Yr	VG	VG+	NM
LSC-2581 [S]	Brahms: Piano Concerto No. 2	1962	5.00	10.00	20.00
—"Shaded dog" pressing ("Living Stereo" on label)					
LSC-2581 [S]	Brahms: Piano Concerto No. 2	1965	3.75	7.50	15.00
—"White dog" pressing ("Stereo" on label)					
LSC-2581 [S]	Brahms: Piano Concerto No. 2	1969	3.00	6.00	12.00
—"No dog" pressing ("RCA" sideways at left)					
LSC-2581 [S]	Brahms: Piano Concerto No. 2	1976	2.00	4.00	8.00
—"Late dog" pressing (dog near top)					
LM-2601 [M]	Rachmaninoff: Piano Concerto No. 2	1962	3.75	7.50	15.00
LSC-2601 [S]	Rachmaninoff: Piano Concerto No. 2	1962	5.00	10.00	20.00
—"Shaded dog" pressing ("Living Stereo" on label)					
LSC-2601 [S]	Rachmaninoff: Piano Concerto No. 2	1962	3.75	7.50	15.00
—"White dog" pressing ("Stereo" on label)					
LSC-2601 [S]	Rachmaninoff: Piano Concerto No. 2	1962	3.00	6.00	12.00
—"No dog" pressing ("RCA" sideways at left)					
LM-2680 [M]	Beethoven: Piano Concerto No. 4	1963	3.00	6.00	12.00
LSC-2680 [S]	Beethoven: Piano Concerto No. 4	1963	3.75	7.50	15.00
—"Shaded dog" pressing ("Living Stereo" on label)					
LSC-2680 [S]	Beethoven: Piano Concerto No. 4	1965	3.00	6.00	12.00
—"White dog" pressing ("Stereo" on label)					
LSC-2680 [S]	Beethoven: Piano Concerto No. 4	1969	2.50	5.00	10.00
—"No dog" pressing ("RCA" sideways at left)					
ARP1-4441	Tchaikovsky: Piano Concerto No. 1	198?	3.00	6.00	12.00
—Half-speed mastered reissue					
ARP1-4688	Rachmaninoff: Piano Concerto No. 3	198?	3.00	6.00	12.00
—Half-speed mastered reissue					

CLICKETTES, THE

45s

Number	Title (A Side/B Side)	Yr	VG	VG+	NM
CHECKER					
1060	I Just Can't Help It/(Instrumental)	1963	5.00	10.00	20.00
DICE					
83/84	Jive Time Turkey/A Teenager's First Love	1959	37.50	75.00	150.00
92/93	To Be a Part of You/Because of My Best Friend	1959	30.00	60.00	120.00
94/95	Warm, Soft and Lovely/Why Oh Why	1959	30.00	60.00	120.00
96/97	Lover's Prayer/Grateful	1959	37.50	75.00	150.00
—With distribution by Memo Record Corp.					
96/97	Lover's Prayer/Grateful	1959	17.50	35.00	70.00
100	But Not for Me/I Love You I Swear	1960	30.00	60.00	120.00
GUYDEN					
2043	Where Is He/The Lone Lover	1960	7.50	15.00	30.00
TUFF					
373	I Just Can't Help It/(Instrumental)	1964	5.00	10.00	20.00

CLICKS, THE

45s

Number	Title (A Side/B Side)	Yr	VG	VG+	NM
JOSIE					
780	Come Back to Me/Peace and Commitment	1955	75.00	150.00	300.00

CLIFF, BENNY

45s

Number	Title (A Side/B Side)	Yr	VG	VG+	NM
DRIFT					
1441	Shake Um Um Rock/The Breaking Point	1959	1000.	2000.	3000.

CLIFF, JIMMY

12-Inch Singles

Number	Title (A Side/B Side)	Yr	VG	VG+	NM
COLUMBIA					
03045	Special/Peace Officer	1982	2.50	5.00	10.00
03507	Routes Radical/Treat the Youths Right	1983	2.50	5.00	10.00
04126	Reggae Night/(Instrumental)	1983	2.50	5.00	10.00

45s

Number	Title (A Side/B Side)	Yr	VG	VG+	NM
A&M					
1146	Wonderful World, Beautiful People/Waterfall	1969	2.00	4.00	8.00
1146 [PS]	Wonderful World, Beautiful People/Waterfall	1969	3.00	6.00	12.00
1167	Come Into My Life/Viet Nam	1970	2.00	4.00	8.00
1201	You Can Get It If You Really Want/Be Aware	1970	2.00	4.00	8.00
1270	Goodbye Yesterday/Let's Seize the Time	1971	2.00	4.00	8.00
COLUMBIA					
03216	Special/Peace Officer	1982	—	2.00	4.00
04141	Reggae Night/Love Heights	1983	—	2.00	4.00
04335	We All Are One/Roots Woman	1984	—	2.00	4.00
05396	Hot Shot/Modern World	1985	—	2.00	4.00
05716	American Sweet/Reggae Movement	1985	—	2.00	4.00
06235	Club Paradise/Third World People	1986	—	—	3.00
06235 [PS]	Club Paradise/Third World People	1986	—	—	3.00
07692	Love Me, Love Me/Sunshine in the Music	1988	—	—	3.00
MCA					
51043	I Am the Living/Love Again	1981	—	2.00	4.00
51094	Another Summer/It's the Beginning of the End	1981	—	2.00	4.00
51211	My Philosophy/Shelter of Your Love	1981	—	2.00	4.00
REPRISE					
1177	Black Queen/Born to Win	1973	—	3.00	6.00
1315	You Can't Be Wrong and Get Right/Music Maker	1974	—	3.00	6.00
1383	The Harder They Come/Viet Nam	1977	—	3.00	6.00
VEEP					
1265	Aim and Ambition/Give and Take	1967	3.75	7.50	15.00
1276	That's the Way Life Goes/Thank You	1968	3.75	7.50	15.00

Albums

Number	Title (A Side/B Side)	Yr	VG	VG+	NM
A&M					
SP-3189	Wonderful World, Beautiful People	198?	2.00	4.00	8.00
—Reissue of 4251					
SP-4251	Wonderful World, Beautiful People	1970	6.25	12.50	25.00
COLUMBIA					
FC 38099	Special	1982	2.50	5.00	10.00
PC 38099	Special	198?	2.00	4.00	8.00
—Budget-line reissue					
FC 38986	The Power and the Glory	1983	2.50	5.00	10.00
PC 38996	The Power and the Glory	1985	2.00	4.00	8.00
—Budget-line reissue					
FC 40002	Cliff Hanger	1985	2.50	5.00	10.00
FC 40845	Hanging Fire	1988	2.50	5.00	10.00
ISLAND					
SW-9343	Struggling Man	1973	5.00	10.00	20.00
MANGO					
ILPS 9235	Struggling Man	197?	3.00	6.00	12.00
—Reissue of Island SW-9343					
MCA					
813	I Am the Living	198?	2.00	4.00	8.00
—Reissue of 5153					
820	Give the People What They Want	198?	2.00	4.00	8.00
—Reissue of 5217					
5153	I Am the Living	1980	3.00	6.00	12.00
5217	Give the People What They Want	1981	3.00	6.00	12.00
REPRISE					
MS 2147	Unlimited	1973	3.75	7.50	15.00
MS 2188	Music Maker	1974	3.75	7.50	15.00
MS 2218	Follow My Mind	1975	3.75	7.50	15.00
MS 2256	In Concert: The Best of Jimmy Cliff	1976	3.75	7.50	15.00
VEEP					
VPS-16536	Can't Get Enough of It	1969	10.00	20.00	40.00
WARNER BROS.					
BSK 3240	Give Thankx	1978	3.00	6.00	12.00

CLIFFORD, BUZZ

45s

Number	Title (A Side/B Side)	Yr	VG	VG+	NM
A&M					
878	Just Can't Wait/On My Way	1967	2.50	5.00	10.00
CAPITOL					
5880	Bored to Tears/Swing in My Back Yard	1967	2.50	5.00	10.00
COLUMBIA					
41774	Hello, Mr. Moonlight/Blue Lagoon	1960	5.00	10.00	20.00
41876	Baby Sitter Boogie/Driftwood	1960	6.25	12.50	25.00
41876	Baby Sittin' Boogie/Driftwood	1960	5.00	10.00	20.00
41876 [PS]	Baby Sittin' Boogie/Driftwood	1960	12.50	25.00	50.00
41979	Three Little Fishes/Just Because	1961	5.00	10.00	20.00
41979 [PS]	Three Little Fishes/Just Because	1961	12.50	25.00	50.00
42019	I'll Never Forget/The Awakening	1961	12.50	25.00	50.00
42019 [PS]	I'll Never Forget/The Awakening	1961	20.00	40.00	80.00
42177	Moving Day/Loneliness	1961	5.00	10.00	20.00
42177 [PS]	Moving Day/Loneliness	1961	12.50	25.00	50.00
42290	Forever/Magic Circle	1962	6.25	12.50	25.00
42290 [PS]	Forever/Magic Circle	1962	12.50	25.00	50.00
DOT					
17329	(Baby I Could Be) So Good At Loving You/ Children Are Crying Aloud	1970	—	3.00	6.00
17344	Procter and Gunther/I Am the River	1971	—	3.00	6.00
RCA VICTOR					
47-8935	Until Then/Let Her Go (It's All Right)	1966	3.00	6.00	12.00
ROULETTE					
4451	No One Loves Me Like You Do/More Dead Than Alive	1962	3.75	7.50	15.00

Albums

Number	Title (A Side/B Side)	Yr	VG	VG+	NM
COLUMBIA					
CL 1616 [M]	Baby Sittin' with Buzz	1961	25.00	50.00	100.00
CS 8416 [S]	Baby Sittin' with Buzz	1961	37.50	75.00	150.00
DOT					
DLP-25965	See Your Way Clear	1969	7.50	15.00	30.00

CLIFFORD, DOUG

Of CREEDENCE CLEARWATER REVIVAL.

45s

Number	Title (A Side/B Side)	Yr	VG	VG+	NM
FANTASY					
686	Latin Music/Take a Train	1972	—	2.50	5.00
686 [PS]	Latin Music/Take a Train	1972	—	3.00	6.00

Albums

Number	Title (A Side/B Side)	Yr	VG	VG+	NM
FANTASY					
9411	Cosmo	1972	3.75	7.50	15.00

CLIFFORD, MIKE

45s

Number	Title (A Side/B Side)	Yr	VG	VG+	NM
AMERICAN INT'L.					
138	Broken Hearted Man/When Cindy When	1970	—	2.50	5.00
158	Do Your Own Thing/You Better Start Singing Soon	1971	—	2.50	5.00
171	You Say Love/It's a Dream Way	1970	—	2.00	4.00
CAMEO					
381	Before I Loved Her/Shirl Girl	1965	2.50	5.00	10.00
395	Out in the Country/Courtin'	1966	2.50	5.00	10.00
COLUMBIA					
41862	Stranger/Poor Little Girl	1960	3.00	6.00	12.00
41964	Look in Any Window/Uh Huh	1961	3.00	6.00	12.00
42029	Pretty Little Girl in the Yellow Dress/At Last	1961	3.00	6.00	12.00
42226	When We Marry/Bombay	1961	3.00	6.00	12.00
42226 [PS]	When We Marry/Bombay	1961	6.25	12.50	25.00
42335	Joanna/Mary, Mary	1962	3.00	6.00	12.00
LIBERTY					
55207	Should I/Whisper Whisper	1959	3.75	7.50	15.00
—With Patience and Prudence					
55219	I Don't Know Why/I'm Afraid to Say I Love You	1959	3.00	6.00	12.00
SIDEWALK					
917	Send Her Flowers/This Time, Time May Be Wrong	1967	2.00	4.00	8.00
939	Gas Hassle/Mary Jane	1968	2.00	4.00	8.00
UNITED ARTISTS					
489	Close to Cathy/She's Just Another Girl	1962	3.00	6.00	12.00
557	What to Do with Laurie/That's What They Said	1963	2.50	5.00	10.00
588	Danny's Dream/One Boy Too Late	1963	2.50	5.00	10.00
614	Gee, I Don't Remember/Cotton Dresses	1963	2.50	5.00	10.00
713	It Had Better Be Tonight/All the Colors of the Rainbow	1964	2.50	5.00	10.00
763	See You in September/One By One, The Roses Died	1964	2.50	5.00	10.00
794	Don't Make Her Cry/Barbara's Theme	1964	2.50	5.00	10.00

Number	Title (A Side/B Side)	Yr	VG	VG+	NM
823	How to Murder Your Wife/Here's To My Lover	1965	2.50	5.00	10.00

Albums

UNITED ARTISTS

Number	Title (A Side/B Side)	Yr	VG	VG+	NM
UAL-3409 [M]	For the Love of Mike	1965	5.00	10.00	20.00
UAS-6409 [S]	For the Love of Mike	1965	6.25	12.50	25.00

CLIMATES, THE

45s

HOLIDAY INN

Number	Title (A Side/B Side)	Yr	VG	VG+	NM
2206	Don't Be Cruel/Tell Him Tonite	1967	3.00	6.00	12.00

SUN

Number	Title (A Side/B Side)	Yr	VG	VG+	NM
404	No You for Me/Breaking Up Again	1967	6.25	12.50	25.00

CLIMAX

With Sonny Geraci, formerly of THE OUTSIDERS.

45s

CAROUSEL

Number	Title (A Side/B Side)	Yr	VG	VG+	NM
30050	Hard Rock Group/(B-side unknown)	1971	—	2.50	5.00
30055	Precious and Few/Park Preserve	1971	—	2.50	5.00

PARAMOUNT

Number	Title (A Side/B Side)	Yr	VG	VG+	NM
0023	You've Gotta Try/Friendship	1970	—	3.00	6.00

ROCKY ROAD

Number	Title (A Side/B Side)	Yr	VG	VG+	NM
30055	Precious and Few/Park Preserve	1972	—	2.00	4.00
—Reissue of Carousel 30055					
30061	Life and Breath/If It Feels Good, Do It	1972	—	2.00	4.00
30064	Caroline This Time/Rainbow Rides Are Free	1972	—	2.00	4.00
30072	Rock and Roll Heaven/Face the Music	1973	—	2.50	5.00
30074	Walking in the Georgia Rain/(B-side unknown)	1973	—	2.00	4.00
30077	It's Gonna Get Better/(B-side unknown)	1974	—	2.00	4.00

Albums

ROCKY ROAD

Number	Title (A Side/B Side)	Yr	VG	VG+	NM
3506	Climax	1972	3.75	7.50	15.00

CLIMAX BLUES BAND

Includes records as "Climax Chicago Blues Band."

45s

SIRE

Number	Title (A Side/B Side)	Yr	VG	VG+	NM
351	Reap What I've Sowed	1971	—	3.00	6.00
358	Hey Mama/That's All	1972	—	3.00	6.00
705	Shake Your Love/Mule on the Dole	1973	—	3.00	6.00
712	Goin' to New York/I Am Constant	1974	—	2.50	5.00
713	Sense of Direction/Losin' the Humbles	1974	—	2.50	5.00
715	Reaching Out/Milwaukee Truckin' Blues	1974	—	2.50	5.00
721	Running Out of Time/Using the Power	1975	—	2.50	5.00
736	Couldn't Get It Right/Sav'ry Gravy	1977	—	2.50	5.00
747	Berlin Blues/Together and Free	1977	—	2.00	4.00
1026	Makin' Love/Gospel Singer	1978	—	2.00	4.00
1031	Mistress Moonshine/Teardrops	1978	—	2.00	4.00
49012	Long Distance Love/Children of the Nightime	1979	—	2.00	4.00
49098	Money in Your Pocket/Summer Rain	1979	—	2.00	4.00

WARNER BROS.

Number	Title (A Side/B Side)	Yr	VG	VG+	NM
49605	One for Me and You/Gotta Have More Love	1980	—	2.00	4.00
49669	I Love You/Horizontalized	1981	—	2.50	5.00
49850	Darlin'/This Time You're the Singer	1981	—	2.00	4.00
50018	Breakdown/Shake It Lucy	1982	—	2.00	4.00

Albums

SIRE

Number	Title (A Side/B Side)	Yr	VG	VG+	NM
SRK 3334	Real to Reel	1979	2.50	5.00	10.00
SES-4901	#3	1971	3.75	7.50	15.00
SES-5903	Tightly Knit	1972	3.75	7.50	15.00
SR 6003	The Climax Chicago Blues Band	1978	2.50	5.00	10.00
SR 6004	Lot of Bottle	1977	2.50	5.00	10.00
SR 6008	Tightly Knit	1977	2.50	5.00	10.00
2XS 6013 [(2)]	FM/Live	1977	3.00	6.00	12.00
SR 6016	Stamp Album	1977	2.50	5.00	10.00
SR 6033	The Climax Chicago Blues Band Plays On	1978	2.50	5.00	10.00
SRK 6056	Shine On	1978	2.50	5.00	10.00
SES-7402	Rich Man	1972	3.75	7.50	15.00
SES-2-7411 [(2)]	FM/Live	1973	3.75	7.50	15.00
SASD-7501	Sense of Direction	1974	3.00	6.00	12.00
SASD-7507	Stamp Album	1975	3.00	6.00	12.00
SASD-7523	Gold Plated	1976	3.00	6.00	12.00
SES-97013	The Climax Chicago Blues Band	1969	3.75	7.50	15.00
SES-97023	The Climax Chicago Blues Band Plays On	1970	3.75	7.50	15.00

VIRGIN/EPIC

Number	Title (A Side/B Side)	Yr	VG	VG+	NM
FE 38631	Sample and Hold	1983	2.50	5.00	10.00

WARNER BROS.

Number	Title (A Side/B Side)	Yr	VG	VG+	NM
BSK 3493	Flying the Flag	1981	3.00	6.00	12.00
BSK 3623	Lucky for Some	1982	2.50	5.00	10.00

CLIMBERS, THE

45s

J&S

Number	Title (A Side/B Side)	Yr	VG	VG+	NM
1652/3	My Darlin' Dear/Angels in Heaven Know I Love You	1957	25.00	50.00	100.00
1658	I Love You/Train, Car, Boat or Plane	1957	200.00	400.00	800.00

CLINE, PATSY

45s

4 STAR

Number	Title (A Side/B Side)	Yr	VG	VG+	NM
1033	Life's Railway to Heaven/If I Could See the World	1978	—	2.50	5.00

CORAL

Number	Title (A Side/B Side)	Yr	VG	VG+	NM
61464	A Church, a Courtroom, Then Goodbye/Honky Tonk Merry-Go-Round	1955	7.50	15.00	30.00
61523	Turn the Cards Slowly/Hidin' Out	1955	7.50	15.00	30.00
61583	I Love You Honey/Come Right In	1956	6.25	12.50	25.00

DECCA

Number	Title (A Side/B Side)	Yr	VG	VG+	NM
29963	Stop, Look and Listen/I've Loved and Lost Again	1956	5.00	10.00	20.00
30221	Walkin' After Midnight/A Poor Man's Roses (Or a Rich Man's Gold)	1957	5.00	10.00	20.00
30339	Try Again/Today, Tomorrow and Forever	1957	3.75	7.50	15.00
30406	Three Cigarettes in an Ashtray/A Stranger in My Arms	1957	3.75	7.50	15.00
30504	I Don't Wanta/Then You'll Know	1957	3.75	7.50	15.00
30542	Stop the World/Walking Dream	1958	3.75	7.50	15.00
30659	Come On In/Let the Teardrops Fall	1958	3.75	7.50	15.00
30706	Never No More/I Can See an Angel	1958	3.75	7.50	15.00
30746	Just Out of Reach (Of My Two Open Arms)/If I Could See The World	1958	3.75	7.50	15.00
30794	Dear God/He Will Do for You	1958	3.75	7.50	15.00
30846	Yes, I Understand/Cry Not for Me	1959	3.75	7.50	15.00
30929	Got a Lot of Rhythm in My Soul/I'm Blue Again	1959	5.00	10.00	20.00
31061	Lovesick Blues/How Can I Face Tomorrow	1960	3.00	6.00	12.00
31128	There He Goes/Crazy Dream	1960	3.00	6.00	12.00
31205	I Fall to Pieces/Lovin' in Vain	1961	3.00	6.00	12.00
31317	Crazy/Who Can I Count On	1961	3.00	6.00	12.00
31354	She's Got You/Strange	1962	3.00	6.00	12.00
31377	When I Get Thru with You (You'll Love Me Too)/Imagine That	1962	3.00	6.00	12.00
31377 [PS]	When I Get Thru with You (You'll Love Me Too)/Imagine That	1962	6.25	12.50	25.00
31406	So Wrong/You're Stronger Than Me	1962	3.00	6.00	12.00
31429	Heartaches/Why Can't He Be You	1962	3.00	6.00	12.00
31455	Leavin' On Your Mind/Tra Le La Le La Triangle	1963	2.50	5.00	10.00
31455 [PS]	Leavin' On Your Mind/Tra Le La Le La Triangle	1963	6.25	12.50	25.00
31483	Sweet Dreams (Of You)/Back in Baby's Arms	1963	2.50	5.00	10.00
31522	Faded Love/Blue Moon of Kentucky	1963	2.50	5.00	10.00
31552	When You Need a Laugh/I'll Sail My Ship Alone	1963	2.50	5.00	10.00
31588	Your Kinda Love/Someday You'll Want Me to Love You	1964	2.50	5.00	10.00
31616	Love Letters in the Sand/That's How a Heartache Begins	1964	2.50	5.00	10.00
31671	He Called Me Baby/Bill Bailey Won't You Please Come Home	1964	2.50	5.00	10.00
31754	Your Cheatin' Heart/I Can't Help It (If I'm Still in Love with You)	1965	2.50	5.00	10.00
34130 [S]	Foolin' 'Round/The Wayward Wind	1962	5.00	10.00	20.00
34131 [S]	South of the Border (Down Mexico Way)/I Love You So Much It Hurts	1962	5.00	10.00	20.00
34132 [S]	Crazy/Seven Lonely Days	1962	6.25	12.50	25.00
34133 [S]	San Antonio Rose/True Love	1962	5.00	10.00	20.00
—The above four are 33 1/3, small hole jukebox singles					

EVEREST

Number	Title (A Side/B Side)	Yr	VG	VG+	NM
2011	Then You'll Know/Hungry for Love	1963	3.00	6.00	12.00
2020	Walking After Midnight/That Wonderful Someone	1963	3.00	6.00	12.00
2031	I Can See an Angel/Just Out of Reach	1963	3.00	6.00	12.00
2039	I've Loved and Lost Again/I Love You Honey	1964	2.50	5.00	10.00
2045	In Care of the Blues/If I Could See the World (Through the Eyes of a Child)	1964	2.50	5.00	10.00
2052	Got a Lot of Rhythm (In My Soul)/Love Me, Love Me, Honey Do	1964	2.50	5.00	10.00
2060	Crazy Dream/There He Goes	1965	2.50	5.00	10.00
20005	I Don't Wanta/I Can't Forget	1962	3.75	7.50	15.00

KAPP

Number	Title (A Side/B Side)	Yr	VG	VG+	NM
659	Just a Closer Walk with Thee	1965	3.75	7.50	15.00
—One-sided release, possibly promo only					

MCA

Number	Title (A Side/B Side)	Yr	VG	VG+	NM
41303	Always/I Sail My Ship Alone	1980	—	2.00	4.00
51038	I Fall to Pieces/True Love	1980	—	2.00	4.00
52052	So Wrong/I Fall to Pieces	1982	—	—	3.00
—A-side: With Jim Reeves (electronically created duet)					
52684	Sweet Dreams/Blue Moon of Kentucky	1985	—	—	3.00

RCA

Number	Title (A Side/B Side)	Yr	VG	VG+	NM
PB-12346	Have You Ever Been Lonely (Have You Ever Been Blue)/Welcome to My World	1981	—	—	3.00
—With Jim Reeves (electronically created duet)					

STARDAY

Number	Title (A Side/B Side)	Yr	VG	VG+	NM
7030	Walking After Midnight/Lovesick Blues	1965	2.50	5.00	10.00
8024	Walking After Midnight/Lovesick Blues	1971	—	3.00	6.00

7-Inch Extended Plays

CORAL

Number	Title (A Side/B Side)	Yr	VG	VG+	NM
EC 81159	(contents unknown)	1958	6.25	12.50	25.00
EC 81159 [PS]	Songs by Patsy Cline	1958	7.50	15.00	30.00

DECCA

Number	Title (A Side/B Side)	Yr	VG	VG+	NM
ED 2542	(contents unknown)	1958	5.00	10.00	20.00
ED 2542 [PS]	Patsy Cline	1958	5.00	10.00	20.00
ED 2703	(contents unknown)	1961	3.75	7.50	15.00
ED 2703 [PS]	Patsy Cline	1961	3.75	7.50	15.00
ED 2707	(contents unknown)	1961	3.75	7.50	15.00
ED 2707 [PS]	Patsy Cline	1961	3.75	7.50	15.00
ED 2719	(contents unknown)	1962	3.75	7.50	15.00
ED 2719 [PS]	Patsy Cline	1962	3.75	7.50	15.00
ED 2729	So Wrong/You're Stronger Than Me//Heartaches/Your Cheatin' Heart	1962	3.75	7.50	15.00
ED 2729 [PS]	Patsy Cline	1962	3.75	7.50	15.00
ED 2757	(contents unknown)	1963	3.75	7.50	15.00
ED 2757 [PS]	Patsy Cline	1963	3.75	7.50	15.00
ED 2759	Just a Closer Walk with Thee/Life's Railroad to Heaven//Dear God/He Will Do for You	1963	3.75	7.50	15.00
ED 2759 [PS]	Dear God	1963	3.75	7.50	15.00
ED 2768	I'm Blue Again/How Can I Face Tomorrow//I'm Moving Along/Love Love Love Me Honey Do	1964	3.75	7.50	15.00
ED 2768 [PS]	Patsy Cline	1964	3.75	7.50	15.00
ED 2770	Someday You'll Want Me to Want You/Faded Love//When You Need a Laugh/I'll Sail My Ship Alone	1964	3.75	7.50	15.00
ED 2770 [PS]	Someday You'll Want Me to Want You	1964	3.75	7.50	15.00
ED 2794	(contents unknown)	1965	3.75	7.50	15.00
ED 2794 [PS]	Portrait of Patsy Cline	1965	3.75	7.50	15.00
ED 2802	(contents unknown)	1965	3.75	7.50	15.00
ED 2802 [PS]	Love Letters in the Sand	1965	3.75	7.50	15.00

PATSY CLINE

Number	Title (A Side/B Side)	Yr	VG	VG+	NM
EPF-16	Try Again/Turn the Cards Slowly//Come On In/Stop Look and Listen	195?	10.00	20.00	40.00
EPF-16 [PS]	(title unknown)	195?	10.00	20.00	40.00

Number	Title (A Side/B Side)	Yr	VG	VG+	NM
EP-21	Three Cigarettes/Hungry for Love//Fingerprints/That Wonderful Someone	195?	10.00	20.00	40.00
EP-21 [PS]	(title unknown)	195?	10.00	20.00	40.00

Albums

ACCORD

Number	Title (A Side/B Side)	Yr	VG	VG+	NM
SN-7153	Let the Teardrops Fall	1981	2.50	5.00	10.00

ALLEGIANCE

Number	Title (A Side/B Side)	Yr	VG	VG+	NM
AV-5021	Stop, Look and Listen	198?	2.50	5.00	10.00

DECCA

Number	Title (A Side/B Side)	Yr	VG	VG+	NM
DXB 176 [(2) M]	The Patsy Cline Story	1963	10.00	20.00	40.00
DL 4202 [M]	Patsy Cline Showcase	1961	10.00	20.00	40.00
DL 4282 [M]	Sentimentally Yours	1962	7.50	15.00	30.00
DL 4508 [M]	A Portrait of Patsy Cline	1964	7.50	15.00	30.00
DL 4586 [M]	That's How a Heartache Begins	1964	7.50	15.00	30.00
DL 4854 [M]	Patsy Cline's Greatest Hits	1967	5.00	10.00	20.00
DXSB 7176 [(2) S]	The Patsy Cline Story	1963	12.50	25.00	50.00
DL 8611 [M]	Patsy Cline	1957	25.00	50.00	100.00
—Black label with silver print					
DL 8611 [M]	Patsy Cline	1960	12.50	25.00	50.00
—Black label with color bars					
DL 74202 [S]	Patsy Cline Showcase	1961	12.50	25.00	50.00
DL 74282 [S]	Sentimentally Yours	1962	10.00	20.00	40.00
DL 74508 [S]	A Portrait of Patsy Cline	1964	10.00	20.00	40.00
DL 74586 [S]	That's How a Heartache Begins	1964	10.00	20.00	40.00
DL 74854 [S]	Patsy Cline's Greatest Hits	1967	6.25	12.50	25.00

EVEREST

Number	Title (A Side/B Side)	Yr	VG	VG+	NM
1200 [R]	Golden Hits	1962	3.00	6.00	12.00
1204 [R]	Encores	1962	3.00	6.00	12.00
1217 [R]	In Memoriam	1963	3.00	6.00	12.00
1229 [R]	Reflections	1964	3.00	6.00	12.00
5200 [M]	Golden Hits	1962	5.00	10.00	20.00
5204 [M]	Encores	1962	5.00	10.00	20.00
5217 [M]	In Memoriam	1963	5.00	10.00	20.00
5223 [M]	Legend	1963	5.00	10.00	20.00
5229 [M]	Reflections	1964	5.00	10.00	20.00

HILLTOP

Number	Title (A Side/B Side)	Yr	VG	VG+	NM
6001 [M]	Today, Tomorrow, Forever	1965	3.00	6.00	12.00
S-6001 [R]	Today, Tomorrow, Forever	1965	2.50	5.00	10.00
6016 [M]	I Can't Forget You	1966	3.00	6.00	12.00
S-6016 [R]	I Can't Forget You	1966	2.50	5.00	10.00
S-6039	Stop the World	1968	2.50	5.00	10.00
S-6072	In Care of the Blues	1969	2.50	5.00	10.00
6148	Country Music Hall of Fame	197?	2.50	5.00	10.00

MCA

Number	Title (A Side/B Side)	Yr	VG	VG+	NM
12	Patsy Cline's Greatest Hits	1973	3.00	6.00	12.00
—Reissue of Decca 74854; black label with rainbow					
12	Patsy Cline's Greatest Hits	1977	2.50	5.00	10.00
—Tan label					
12	Patsy Cline's Greatest Hits	1980	2.00	4.00	8.00
—Blue label with rainbow					
87	Patsy Cline Showcase	1973	3.00	6.00	12.00
—Reissue of Decca 74202; black label with rainbow					
90	Sentimentally Yours	1973	3.00	6.00	12.00
—Reissue of Decca 74282; black label with rainbow					
224	A Portrait of Patsy Cline	1973	3.00	6.00	12.00
—Reissue of Decca 74508; black label with rainbow					
736	The Great Patsy Cline	198?	2.50	5.00	10.00
—Reissue of Vocalion 73872					
738	Here's Patsy Cline	198?	2.50	5.00	10.00
—Reissue of Vocalion 73753					
1440	Stop, Look and Listen	198?	2.00	4.00	8.00
1463	Today, Tomorrow and Forever	198?	2.00	4.00	8.00
3263	Always	1980	3.75	7.50	15.00
4038 [(2)]	The Patsy Cline Story	1974	3.75	7.50	15.00
—Reissue of Decca 7176;; black labels with rainbow					
6149	Sweet Dreams — The Life and Times of Patsy Cline	1985	2.50	5.00	10.00
27069	Always	198?	2.00	4.00	8.00
42142	Live at the Opry	1988	2.50	5.00	10.00
42284	Live Volume 2	1989	3.00	6.00	12.00

METRO

Number	Title (A Side/B Side)	Yr	VG	VG+	NM
M-540 [M]	Gotta Lot of Rhythm in My Soul	1965	3.00	6.00	12.00
MS-540 [R]	Gotta Lot of Rhythm in My Soul	1965	2.50	5.00	10.00

RHINO

Number	Title (A Side/B Side)	Yr	VG	VG+	NM
R1-70048	Her First Recordings, Vol. 1: Walkin' Dreams	1989	3.00	6.00	12.00
R1-70049	Her First Recordings, Vol. 2: Hungry for Love	1989	3.00	6.00	12.00
R1-70050	Her First Recordings, Vol. 3: The Rockin' Side	1989	3.00	6.00	12.00

SEARS

Number	Title (A Side/B Side)	Yr	VG	VG+	NM
SPS-127	In Care of the Blues	1968	6.25	12.50	25.00

VOCALION

Number	Title (A Side/B Side)	Yr	VG	VG+	NM
VL 3753 [M]	Here's Patsy Cline	1965	3.00	6.00	12.00
VL 73753 [R]	Here's Patsy Cline	1965	2.50	5.00	10.00
VL 73872	Country Great!	1969	2.50	5.00	10.00

CLINTON, GEORGE

Also see PARLIAMENT; FUNKADELIC; THE PARLIAMENTS.

45s

ABC

Number	Title (A Side/B Side)	Yr	VG	VG+	NM
12040	Hold On to Your Lady/Nothing in This Whole World	1974	—	3.00	6.00

CAPITOL

Number	Title (A Side/B Side)	Yr	VG	VG+	NM
B-5160	Loopzilla/Pot Sharing Tots	1982	—	2.00	4.00
B-5201	Atomic Dog/Atomic Dog (Instrumental)	1983	—	2.00	4.00
B-5201 [PS]	Atomic Dog/Atomic Dog (Instrumental)	1983	—	3.00	6.00
B-5222	Get Dressed/Free Alterations	1983	—	2.00	4.00
B-5222 [PS]	Get Dressed/Free Alterations	1983	—	2.00	4.00
B-5296	Nubian Nut/Free Alterations	1983	—	2.00	4.00
B-5296 [PS]	Nubian Nut/Free Alterations	1983	—	2.00	4.00
B-5324	Quickie/Last Dance	1984	—	2.00	4.00
B-5324 [PS]	Quickie/Last Dance	1984	—	2.00	4.00
B-5332	Last Dance/Get Dressed	1984	—	2.00	4.00
B-5332 [PS]	Last Dance/Get Dressed	1984	—	2.00	4.00
B-5473	Double Oh-Oh/Bangladesh	1985	—	2.00	4.00
B-5473 [PS]	Double Oh-Oh/Bangladesh	1985	—	2.00	4.00
B-5504	Bullet Proof/Silly Millimeter	1985	—	2.00	4.00
B-5558	Do Fries Go With That Shake/Pleasure of Exhaustion (Do It Till I Drop)	1986	—	2.00	4.00
B-5602	Hey Good Lookin' (Remix)/Hey Good Lookin' (Mirror Mix)	1986	—	2.00	4.00
B-5642	R&B Skeletons (In the Closet)/Nubian Nut	1986	—	2.00	4.00

PAISLEY PARK

Number	Title (A Side/B Side)	Yr	VG	VG+	NM
22790	Tweakin'/French Kiss	1989	—	—	3.00
27557	Why Should I Dog U Out?/(Instrumental)	1989	—	—	3.00
27557 [PS]	Why Should I Dog U Out?/(Instrumental)	1989	—	—	3.00

Albums

ABC

Number	Title (A Side/B Side)	Yr	VG	VG+	NM
D-831	The George Clinton Band Arrives	1974	3.75	7.50	15.00

CAPITOL

Number	Title (A Side/B Side)	Yr	VG	VG+	NM
ST-12246	Computer Games	1982	2.50	5.00	10.00
ST-12308	You Shouldn't-Nuf Bit Fish	1984	2.50	5.00	10.00
ST-12417	Some of My Best Jokes Are Friends	1985	2.50	5.00	10.00
ST-12481	R&B Skeletons in the Closet	1986	2.50	5.00	10.00
MLP-15021 [EP]	The Mothership Connection Live from Houston, Texas	1986	2.00	4.00	8.00
CJ-48424	The Best of George Clinton	1987	2.50	5.00	10.00

INVICTUS

Number	Title (A Side/B Side)	Yr	VG	VG+	NM
ST-9815	Black Vampire	1973	5.00	10.00	20.00

PAISLEY PARK

Number	Title (A Side/B Side)	Yr	VG	VG+	NM
25994	The Cinderella Theory	1989	3.00	6.00	12.00

WARNER BROS.

Number	Title (A Side/B Side)	Yr	VG	VG+	NM
25887	George Clinton Presents Our Gang Funky	1988	2.50	5.00	10.00
25991	Under a Nouveau Groove	1989	2.50	5.00	10.00

CLINTONIAN CUBS, THE

JIMMY CASTOR was a member.

45s

MY BROTHERS

Number	Title (A Side/B Side)	Yr	VG	VG+	NM
508	She's Just My Size/Confusion	1960	75.00	150.00	300.00

CLIQUE, THE (1)

Texas band.

45s

WHITE WHALE

Number	Title (A Side/B Side)	Yr	VG	VG+	NM
312	Superman/Shadow of Your Love	1969	3.00	6.00	12.00
323	Sugar on Sunday/Superman	1969	3.75	7.50	15.00
333	Soul Mate/I'll Hold Out My Hand	1969	2.50	5.00	10.00
338	I'm Alive/Sparkle and Shine	1970	2.50	5.00	10.00
361	Memphis/Southbound Wind	1970	2.50	5.00	10.00
367 [DJ]	Judy, Judy, Judy (same on both sides)	1970	3.00	6.00	12.00
—May be promo only					

Albums

WHITE WHALE

Number	Title (A Side/B Side)	Yr	VG	VG+	NM
WWS-7126	The Clique	1969	5.00	10.00	20.00

CLIQUE, THE (2)

British band.

45s

ABC-PARAMOUNT

Number	Title (A Side/B Side)	Yr	VG	VG+	NM
10655	She Ain't No Good/Time, Time, Time	1965	2.50	5.00	10.00

CLIQUE, THE (U)

Some of these may be early records by group (1) or later records by group (2).

45s

CINEMA

Number	Title (A Side/B Side)	Yr	VG	VG+	NM
001	Stay By Me/Splash One	1967	7.50	15.00	30.00

LAURIE

Number	Title (A Side/B Side)	Yr	VG	VG+	NM
3365	Sun Come Up/Drifter's Melody	1966	2.50	5.00	10.00

SCEPTER

Number	Title (A Side/B Side)	Yr	VG	VG+	NM
12202	Stay By Me/Splash One	1967	5.00	10.00	20.00
12212	Gotta Get Away/Love Ain't Easy	1967	5.00	10.00	20.00

CLIQUES, THE

Also see JESSE BELVIN; EUGENE CHURCH.

45s

MODERN

Number	Title (A Side/B Side)	Yr	VG	VG+	NM
987	Girl in My Dreams/I Wanna Know Why	1956	12.50	25.00	50.00
—Blue label					
987	Girl in My Dreams/I Wanna Know Why	1956	7.50	15.00	30.00
—Black label					
995	My Desire/I'm in Love with a Gal	1956	7.50	15.00	30.00

CLOONEY, ROSEMARY

45s

COLUMBIA

Number	Title (A Side/B Side)	Yr	VG	VG+	NM
4-123	Suzy Snowflake/Little Red Riding Hood's Christmas	1951	3.75	7.50	15.00
—Yellow-label Children's Series record; alternate number is 90137					
4-123 [PS]	Suzy Snowflake/Little Red Riding Hood's Christmas	1951	5.00	10.00	20.00
4-149	The Night Before Christmas Song/Look Out The Window (The Winter Song)	1952	3.75	7.50	15.00
—With Gene Autry; yellow-label Children's Series record; alternate number is 90170					
4-149 [PS]	The Night Before Christmas Song/Look Out The Window (The Winter Song)	1952	5.00	10.00	20.00
4-175	Winter Wonderland/Christmas Song	1954	3.75	7.50	15.00
—Yellow-label Children's Series record					
4-175 [PS]	Winter Wonderland/Christmas Song	1954	5.00	10.00	20.00
B-319 [PS]	Hollywood's Best	1952	3.00	6.00	12.00
—Box for records 39852-39855					
4-21423	Go On By/I Whsiper Your Name	1955	6.25	12.50	25.00
38988	C-H-R-I-S-T-M-A-S/Bless This House	1950	—	—	—
—Unconfirmed on 45 rpm					
39054	The Place Where I Worship/House of Singing Bamboo	1950	3.75	7.50	15.00
39141	Cherry Pies/Love Means Love	1951	3.75	7.50	15.00
39158	Sentimental Music/The Face	1951	3.75	7.50	15.00

Number	Title (A Side/B Side)	Yr	VG	VG+	NM
39185	I Still Feel the Same/When Apples Grow on Cherry Trees	1951	3.75	7.50	15.00
39212	Beautiful Brown Eyes/Shot Gun Boogie	1951	3.75	7.50	15.00
39333	Mixed Emotions/Kentucky Waltz	1951	3.75	7.50	15.00
39467	Come On-a My House/Rose of the Mountain	1951	3.75	7.50	15.00
39535	I'm Waiting Just for You/If Teardrops Were Pennies	1951	3.75	7.50	15.00
39536	I Wish I Wuz/Mixed Emotions	1951	3.75	7.50	15.00
39591	Find Me/I Only Saw Him Once	1951	3.75	7.50	15.00
39612	Suzy Snowflake/Little Red Riding Hood's Christmas	1951	3.75	7.50	15.00
39631	Be My Life's Companion/Why Don't You	1952	3.75	7.50	15.00
39648	Tenderly/Did Anyone Call	1952	3.75	7.50	15.00
39710	Half As Much/Poor Whippoorwill	1952	3.75	7.50	15.00
39730	Tenderly/Be Anything (But Be Mine)	1952	3.00	6.00	12.00
—B-side by Champ Butler; part of a various artists 4-record box set					
39767	Botch-a-Me (Ba-Ba-Baciami Piccina)/On the First Warm Day	1952	3.75	7.50	15.00
39812	Too Old to Cut the Mustard/Good for Nothing	1952	3.75	7.50	15.00
—A-side with Marlene Dietrich					
39813	Blues in the Night/Who Kissed Me Last Night	1952	3.75	7.50	15.00
39852	You'll Never Know/In the Cool, Cool, Cool of the Evening	1952	3.00	6.00	12.00
—Sides 1 and 8 of B-319					
39853	On the Atchison, Topeka and the Santa Fe/When You Wish Upon a Star	1952	3.00	6.00	12.00
—Sides 2 and 7 of B-319					
39854	It Might As Well Be Spring/The Continental	1952	3.00	6.00	12.00
—Sides 3 and 6 of B-319					
39855	Over the Rainbow/Sweet Leilani	1952	3.00	6.00	12.00
—Sides 4 and 5 of B-319					
39876	The Night Before Christmas Song/Look Out the Window (The Winter Song)	1952	3.75	7.50	15.00
—With Gene Autry					
39892	If I Had a Penny/You're After My Own Heart	1952	3.75	7.50	15.00
39905	You'll Never Know/The Continental	1952	3.75	7.50	15.00
39931	What Would You Do/I Laughed Until I Cried	1953	3.75	7.50	15.00
39943	Lovely Weather for Ducks/Haven't Got a Worry	1953	3.75	7.50	15.00
39980	Dot's Nice — Donna Fight/It's the Same	1953	3.75	7.50	15.00
—With Marlene Dietrich					
40003	When I See You/It Just Happened to Happen to Me	1953	3.75	7.50	15.00
40024	Stick with Me/Cheegah, Choonem	1953	3.75	7.50	15.00
40031	Blues in the Night/Tenderly	1953	3.00	6.00	12.00
40102	C-H-R-I-S-T-M-A-S/Happy Christmas, Little Friend	1953	3.75	7.50	15.00
40142	My Baby Rocks Me/When You Love Someone	1953	3.75	7.50	15.00
40144	Man (Uh-Huh)/Woman (Uh-Huh)	1953	3.75	7.50	15.00
—B-side by Jose Ferrer					
40158	Red Garters/A Man and a Woman	1954	3.00	6.00	12.00
40159	Bad News/A Dime and a Dollar	1954	3.00	6.00	12.00
—With Guy Mitchell					
40160	Brave Man/Meet a Happy Guy	1954	3.00	6.00	12.00
—With Guy Mitchell					
40161	This Is Greater Than I Thought/Good Intentions	1954	3.00	6.00	12.00
—With Joanne Gilbert					
40187	Brave Man/Tomorrow I'll Dream and Remember	1954	3.75	7.50	15.00
40266	Hey There/This Ole House	1954	3.75	7.50	15.00
40317	(Let's Give) A Christmas Present to Santa Claus/March of the Christmas Toys	1954	3.75	7.50	15.00
—With Jose Ferrer					
40355	White Christmas/Count Your Blessings	1954	3.00	6.00	12.00
40356	Mandy/The Best Things Happen While Dancing	1954	3.00	6.00	12.00
40357	Sisters/Snow	1954	3.00	6.00	12.00
—A-side with Betty Clooney					
40358	Love, You Didn't Do Right By Me/Gee, I Wish I Was Back in the Army	1954	3.00	6.00	12.00
40361	Mambo Italiano/We'll Be Together Again	1954	3.75	7.50	15.00
40370	Count Your Blessings Instead of Sheep/White Christmas	1954	3.75	7.50	15.00
40407	Mr. and Mrs./Marry the Man	1955	3.00	6.00	12.00
—With Jose Ferrer					
40434	Brahms' Lullaby/Where Will the Dimple Be	1955	3.00	6.00	12.00
40496	It Might As Well Be Spring/When You Wish Upon a Star	1955	3.00	6.00	12.00
40498	A Touch of the Blues/Love Among the Young	1955	3.00	6.00	12.00
40579	Pet Me, Poppa/Wake Me	1955	3.00	6.00	12.00
40616	Memories of You/It's Bad for Me	1955	3.00	6.00	12.00
—With Benny Goodman					
40619	The Key to My Heart/Little Girl at Heart	1955	3.00	6.00	12.00
40625	A Fine Romance/Goodbye	1955	3.00	6.00	12.00
—With Benny Goodman					
40676	I Could Have Danced All Night/I've Grown Accustomed to Your Face	1956	3.00	6.00	12.00
40701	Sophisticated Lady/Grievin'	1956	3.00	6.00	12.00
40723	Hello, Young Lovers/Peachy, Peachy	1956	3.00	6.00	12.00
40774	Come Rain or Come Shine/It's a Nuisance Having You Around	1956	3.00	6.00	12.00
40808	He'll Be Comin' Down the Chimney/Mommy Can I Keep the Kitten	1956	3.00	6.00	12.00
—With "Her Sister Gail"					
40812	(Don't That Take the) Rag Offen the Bush/Love Is a Feeling	1956	3.00	6.00	12.00
40835	Mangos/Independent (On My Own)	1957	3.00	6.00	12.00
40917	Sing Little Birdie Sing/Who Dot Mon, Mon	1957	3.00	6.00	12.00
40981	Colors/That's How It Is	1957	3.00	6.00	12.00
41053	Tonight/Love and Affection	1957	3.00	6.00	12.00
41107	You Don't Know Him/Surprise	1958	3.00	6.00	12.00
50007	Come On-a My House/(B-side unknown)	1954	2.50	5.00	10.00
—Early "Hall of Fame Series" issue					
CORAL					
62137	A Touch of the Blues/I Wish I Were in Love Again	1959	2.50	5.00	10.00
DOT					
17100	One Less Bell to Answer/Let Me Down Easy	1968	—	3.00	6.00

Number	Title (A Side/B Side)	Yr	VG	VG+	NM
GIBSON MUSICARDS					
100G 27104 [PS]	Happy Birthday, Dear Mother	1955	5.00	10.00	20.00
—7x7 card that comes with GIB-6... Others are likely to exist, but we haven't documented them yet.					
GIB-6	Happy Birthday, Dear Mother/(B-side blank)	1955	5.00	10.00	20.00
MGM					
12654	Morning Music of Montmartre/Give It All You Got	1958	2.50	5.00	10.00
—With Jose Ferrer					
12655	Hey, Madame/You're So Right for Me	1958	2.50	5.00	10.00
—With Jose Ferrer					
12705	It's a Boy/The Loudenboomer Bird	1958	2.50	5.00	10.00
12760	Love Eyes/Flattery	1959	2.50	5.00	10.00
12823	I Wonder/For You	1959	2.50	5.00	10.00
13349	I'm Glad It's You/Love and Learn	1965	—	3.00	6.00
RCA VICTOR					
47-7707	Watermelon Heart/Summertime Love	1960	2.50	5.00	10.00
—With Perez Prado					
47-7754	Many a Wonderful Moment/Vaya Vaya	1960	2.50	5.00	10.00
47-7754 [PS]	Many a Wonderful Moment/Vaya Vaya	1960	3.75	7.50	15.00
47-7806	Danke Schoen/Swing Me	1960	2.50	5.00	10.00
47-7819	Hey Look Me Over/What Takes My Fancy	1960	2.50	5.00	10.00
47-7887	Theme from Return to Peyton Place/Without Love	1961	2.50	5.00	10.00
47-7948	Give Myself a Party/If I Can Stay Away Long Enough	1961	2.50	5.00	10.00
REPRISE					
0327	A Spoonful of Sugar/Stay Awake	1964	2.00	4.00	8.00
20145	I Will Follow Him (Chariot)/The Rose and the Butterfly	1963	2.00	4.00	8.00
20173	Mixed Emotions/The Prisoner's Song	1963	2.00	4.00	8.00
20173	The Prisoner's Song/Mixed Emotions	1963	2.00	4.00	8.00
20222	Helo Faithless/A Hundred Years from Today	1963	2.00	4.00	8.00
7-Inch Extended Plays					
COLUMBIA					
B-1901	White Christmas/Mandy//Snow /Gee, I Wish I Was Back In The Army	195?	3.00	6.00	12.00
B-1901 [PS]	White Christmas Volume 2	195?	3.00	6.00	12.00
B-1932	Hey There/This Ole House//The Little Shoemaker (La Petit Cordonnier)/Love Is a Beautiful Stranger	195?	3.00	6.00	12.00
B-1932 [PS]	(title unknown)	195?	3.00	6.00	12.00
B-2524	*Come On-a My House/Mixed Emotions/Mambo Italiano/Tenderly	1957	3.00	6.00	12.00
B-2524 [PS]	Rosemary Clooney (Hall of Fame Series)	1957	3.00	6.00	12.00
B-2525	*Hey There/Botcha Me/Half as Much/This Ole House	1957	3.00	6.00	12.00
B-2525 [PS]	Rosemary Clooney (Hall of Fame Series)	1957	3.00	6.00	12.00
B-2550	*Be My Life's Companion/Blame It on My Youth/Blues in the Night/Why Fight the Feeling?	1958	3.00	6.00	12.00
B-2550 [PS]	Rosemary Clooney (Hall of Fame Series)	1958	3.00	6.00	12.00
B-10061	(contents unknown)	1957	3.00	6.00	12.00
B-10061 [PS]	Ring Around the Rosie, Vol. 1	1957	3.00	6.00	12.00
B-10062	(contents unknown)	1957	3.00	6.00	12.00
B-10062 [PS]	Ring Around the Rosie, Vol. 2	1957	3.00	6.00	12.00
B-10063	(contents unknown)	1957	3.00	6.00	12.00
B-10063 [PS]	Ring Around the Rosie, Vol. 3	1957	3.00	6.00	12.00
ZTV-60077/8	Tenderly/Hey There//Half As Much/I Could Have Danced All Night	195?	3.75	7.50	15.00
Albums					
COLUMBIA					
CL 585 [M]	Hollywood's Best	1955	12.50	25.00	50.00
CL 872 [M]	Blue Rose	1956	10.00	20.00	40.00
CL 969 [M]	Clooney Tunes	1957	20.00	40.00	80.00
CL 1006 [M]	Ring Around the Rosie	1957	10.00	20.00	40.00
—With the Hi-Lo's					
CL 1230 [M]	Rosie's Greatest Hits	1958	10.00	20.00	40.00
—Six "eye" logos on label					
CL 1230 [M]	Rosie's Greatest Hits	1962	6.25	12.50	25.00
—"Guaranteed High Fidelity" on label					
CL 1230 [M]	Rosie's Greatest Hits	1965	3.75	7.50	15.00
—"360 Sound Mono" on label					
CL 2525 [10]	Tenderly	1955	12.50	25.00	50.00
CL 2569 [10]	Children's Favorites	1955	12.50	25.00	50.00
CL 2572 [10]	A Date with the King	1956	12.50	25.00	50.00
CL 2581 [10]	On Stage	1956	12.50	25.00	50.00
CL 2597 [10]	My Fair Lady	1956	12.50	25.00	50.00
CL 6224 [10]	Hollywood's Best	1952	15.00	30.00	60.00
CL 6297 [10]	Rosemary Clooney (While We're Young)	1954	15.00	30.00	60.00
CL 6338 [10]	White Christmas	1954	15.00	30.00	60.00
COLUMBIA SPECIAL PRODUCTS					
P 13083	Hollywood's Best	197?	3.00	6.00	12.00
P 13085	Blue Rose	197?	3.00	6.00	12.00
P 14382	Come On-a My House	197?	3.00	6.00	12.00
CONCORD JAZZ					
CJ-47	Everything's Coming Up Rosie	1978	3.00	6.00	12.00
CJ-60	Rosie Sings Bing	1979	3.00	6.00	12.00
CJ-81	Here's to My Lady	1979	3.00	6.00	12.00
CJ-112	Rosemary Clooney Sings Ira Gershwin	1980	3.00	6.00	12.00
CJ-144	With Love	1981	3.00	6.00	12.00
CJ-185	Rosemary Clooney Sings Cole Porter	1982	3.00	6.00	12.00
CJ-210	Rosemary Clooney Sings Harold Arlen	1983	3.00	6.00	12.00
CJ-226	My Buddy	1984	3.00	6.00	12.00
—With Woody Herman					
CJ-255	Rosemary Clooney Sings the Music of Irving Berlin	1985	3.00	6.00	12.00
CJ-282	Rosemary Clooney Sings Ballads	1985	3.00	6.00	12.00
CJ-308	Rosemary Clooney Sings the Music of Jimmy Van Heusen	1987	3.00	6.00	12.00
CJ-333	Rosemary Clooney Sings the Lyrics of Johnny Mercer	1988	3.00	6.00	12.00
CJ-364	Show Tunes	1989	3.00	6.00	12.00
CORAL					
CRL 57266 [M]	Swing Around Rosie	1959	7.50	15.00	30.00
CRL 757266 [S]	Swing Around Rosie	1959	10.00	20.00	40.00

Number	Title (A Side/B Side)	Yr	VG	VG+	NM
HARMONY					
HL 7123 [M]	Rosemary Clooney in High Fidelity	195?	6.25	12.50	25.00
HL 7213 [M]	Hollywood Hits	195?	6.25	12.50	25.00
HL 7454 [M]	Mixed Emotions	1968	5.00	10.00	20.00
HL 9501 [M]	Rosemary Clooney Sings for Children	196?	5.00	10.00	20.00
HS 11254 [R]	Mixed Emotions	1968	3.00	6.00	12.00
HINDSIGHT					
HSR-234	Rosemary Clooney 1951-1952	1988	2.50	5.00	10.00
HOLIDAY					
1946	Christmas with Rosemary Clooney	1981	2.50	5.00	10.00
MGM					
E-3687 [M]	Oh, Captain!	1958	10.00	20.00	40.00
E-3782 [M]	Hymns from the Heart	1959	7.50	15.00	30.00
SE-3782 [S]	Hymns from the Heart	1959	10.00	20.00	40.00
E-3834 [M]	Rosie Clooney Swings Softly	1960	7.50	15.00	30.00
SE-3834 [S]	Rosie Clooney Swings Softly	1960	10.00	20.00	40.00
RCA VICTOR					
LPM-2133 [M]	A Touch of Tabasco	1960	5.00	10.00	20.00
LSP-2133 [S]	A Touch of Tabasco	1960	7.50	15.00	30.00
LPM-2212 [M]	Clap Hands, Here Comes Rosie	1960	5.00	10.00	20.00
LSP-2212 [S]	Clap Hands, Here Comes Rosie	1960	7.50	15.00	30.00
LPM-2265 [M]	Rosie Solves the Swingin' Riddle	1961	5.00	10.00	20.00
LSP-2265 [S]	Rosie Solves the Swingin' Riddle	1961	7.50	15.00	30.00
LPM-2565 [M]	Country Hits from the Heart	1963	5.00	10.00	20.00
LSP-2565 [S]	Country Hits from the Heart	1963	7.50	15.00	30.00
REPRISE					
R-6088 [M]	Love	1963	7.50	15.00	30.00
R9-6088 [S]	Love	1963	10.00	20.00	40.00
R-6108 [M]	Thanks for Nothing	1964	7.50	15.00	30.00
RS-6108 [S]	Thanks for Nothing	1964	10.00	20.00	40.00

CLOONEY, ROSEMARY, AND JIMMY BOYD

Also see each artist's individual listings.

45s

Number	Title (A Side/B Side)	Yr	VG	VG+	NM
COLUMBIA					
4-39988	Dennis the Menace/Little Josey	1953	5.00	10.00	20.00

CLOONEY, ROSEMARY, AND BING CROSBY

Albums

Number	Title (A Side/B Side)	Yr	VG	VG+	NM
CAPITOL					
ST 2300 [S]	That Travelin' Two-Beat	1965	7.50	15.00	30.00
T 2300 [M]	That Travelin' Two-Beat	1965	5.00	10.00	20.00
RCA CAMDEN					
CAS-2330	Rendezvous	1968	3.75	7.50	15.00
RCA VICTOR					
LPM-1854 [M]	Fancy Meeting You Here	1958	5.00	10.00	20.00
LSP-1854 [S]	Fancy Meeting You Here	1958	7.50	15.00	30.00

CLOONEY SISTERS, THE

Also see ROSEMARY CLOONEY.

Albums

Number	Title (A Side/B Side)	Yr	VG	VG+	NM
EPIC					
LN 3160 [M]	The Clooney Sisters with Tony Pastor	1956	15.00	30.00	60.00

CLOUD, CHRISTOPHER

See TOMMY BOYCE.

CLOVER, TIMOTHY

Albums

Number	Title (A Side/B Side)	Yr	VG	VG+	NM
TOWER					
ST 5114	A Harvard Square Affair	1968	5.00	10.00	20.00

CLOVERS, THE

45s

Number	Title (A Side/B Side)	Yr	VG	VG+	NM
ATLANTIC					
934	Don't You Know I Love You/Skylark	1951	250.00	500.00	1000.
944	Fool, Fool, Fool/Needless	1951	62.50	125.00	250.00
963	One Mint Julep/Middle of the Night	1952	25.00	50.00	100.00
969	Ting-A-Ling/Wonder Where My Baby's Gone	1952	25.00	50.00	100.00
977	I Played the Fool/Hey, Miss Fannie	1952	62.50	125.00	250.00
989	Yes, It's You/Crawlin'	1953	15.00	30.00	60.00
1000	Good Lovin'/Here Goes a Fool	1953	20.00	40.00	80.00
1010	Comin' On/The Feeling Is So Good	1953	37.50	75.00	150.00
1022	Lovey Dovey/Little Mama	1954	12.50	25.00	50.00
1035	Your Cash Ain't Nothin' But Trash/I've Got My Eyes on You	1954	12.50	25.00	50.00
1046	I Confess/Alrighty, Oh Sweetie	1954	12.50	25.00	50.00
1052	Blue Velvet/If You Love Me (Why Don't You Tell Me So)	1955	15.00	30.00	60.00
1060	Love Big/In the Morning Time	1955	12.50	25.00	50.00
1073	Nip Sip/If I Could Be Loved By You	1955	12.50	25.00	50.00
1083	Devil or Angel/Hey, Doll Baby	1956	50.00	100.00	200.00
—Yellow label, no spinner					
1083	Devil or Angel/Hey, Doll Baby	1956	10.00	20.00	40.00
—Red label, no spinner					
1083	Devil or Angel/Hey, Doll Baby	1956	2000.	3000.	4000.
—Red label, no spinner; red vinyl; value is conjecture					
1094	Love, Love, Love/Your Tender Lips	1956	10.00	20.00	40.00
1107	From the Bottom of My Heart/Bring Me Love	1956	7.50	15.00	30.00
1118	A Lonely Fool/Baby, Baby, Oh My Darling	1956	7.50	15.00	30.00
1129	Here Comes Romance/You Good-Looking Woman	1957	7.50	15.00	30.00
1139	I-I-I Love You/So Young	1957	7.50	15.00	30.00
1152	There's No Tomorrow/Down in the Alley	1957	7.50	15.00	30.00
1175	Wishing for Your Love/All About You	1958	7.50	15.00	30.00
2129	Drive It Home/The Bootie Green	1961	5.00	10.00	20.00
BRUNSWICK					
55249	Love! Love! Love!/The Kickapoo	1963	3.00	6.00	12.00
JOSIE					
992	For Days/Too Long Without Some Loving	1968	2.50	5.00	10.00
997	Try My Lovin' On You/Sweet Side of a Soulful Woman	1968	2.50	5.00	10.00
POPLAR					
110	The Gossip Wheel/Please Come On to Me	1958	6.25	12.50	25.00
111	The Good Old Summertime/Idaho	1958	6.25	12.50	25.00
PORT					
3004	Poor Baby/He Sure Could Hypnotize	1965	2.50	5.00	10.00
PORWIN					
1001/2	Stop Pretending/One More Time	1963	3.75	7.50	15.00
—As "Buddy Baliey and the Clovers"					
1004	It's All in the Game/That's What I Will Be	1963	3.75	7.50	15.00
—As "Buddy Baliey and the Clovers"					
STENTON					
7001	Please Mr. Sun/Gimme, Gimme, Gimme	1961	20.00	40.00	80.00
—As "Tippie and the Clovermen"					
TIGER					
201	Bossa Nova Baby/The Bossa Nova (My Heart Said)	1962	3.75	7.50	15.00
—As "Tippie and the Clovers"					
UNITED ARTISTS					
0133	Love Potion #9/Stay Awhile	1973	—	2.00	4.00
—"Silver Spotlight Series" reissue					
174	Rock and Roll Tango/That Old Black Magic	1959	6.25	12.50	25.00
180	Love Potion #9/Stay Awhile	1959	6.25	12.50	25.00
209	One Mint Julep/Lovey	1960	6.25	12.50	25.00
227	Easy Lovin'/I'm Confessin' That I Love You	1960	6.25	12.50	25.00
263	Yes It's You/Burning Fire	1960	6.25	12.50	25.00
307	The Honeydripper/Have Gun	1961	6.25	12.50	25.00
WINLEY					
255	Let Me Hold You/Wrapped Up in a Dream	1961	3.75	7.50	15.00
265	I Need You Now/Gotta Quit You	1962	3.75	7.50	15.00
265	They're Rockin' Down the Street/Be My Baby	1962	3.75	7.50	15.00
—As "The Fabulous Clovers"					

7-Inch Extended Plays

Number	Title (A Side/B Side)	Yr	VG	VG+	NM
ATLANTIC					
504	One Mint Julep/Fool, Fool, Fool//Hey, Miss Fannie/I Played the Fool	1953	50.00	100.00	200.00
504 [PS]	The Clovers Sing	1953	50.00	100.00	200.00
537	(contents unknown)	1954	37.50	75.00	150.00
537 [PS]	The Clovers Sing	1954	50.00	100.00	200.00
590	*Love, Love, Love/Devil or Angel/Blue Velvet/From the Bottom of My Heart	1955	37.50	75.00	150.00
590 [PS]	The Clovers	1955	50.00	100.00	200.00

Albums

Number	Title (A Side/B Side)	Yr	VG	VG+	NM
ATCO					
SD 33-374	Their Greatest Recordings/The Early Years	1971	3.00	6.00	12.00
ATLANTIC					
1248 [M]	The Clovers	1956	150.00	300.00	600.00
8009 [M]	The Clovers	1957	100.00	200.00	400.00
—Reissue of 1248 on the "pop" series; black label					
8009 [M]	The Clovers	1960	75.00	150.00	300.00
—White "bullseye" label					
8009 [M]	The Clovers	1961	50.00	100.00	200.00
—Red and white label					
8034 [M]	Dance Party	1959	100.00	200.00	400.00
—Black label					
8034 [M]	Dance Party	1960	75.00	150.00	300.00
—White "bullseye" label					
8034 [M]	Dance Party	1961	50.00	100.00	200.00
—Red and white label					
GRAND PRIX					
K-428 [M]	The Original Love Potion Number Nine	1964	7.50	15.00	30.00
KS-428 [R]	The Original Love Potion Number Nine	1964	3.00	6.00	12.00
POPLAR					
1001 [M]	The Clovers In Clover	1958	100.00	200.00	400.00
UNITED ARTISTS					
UAL-3033 [M]	The Clovers In Clover	1959	75.00	150.00	300.00
UAL-3099 [M]	Love Potion Number Nine	1959	62.50	125.00	250.00
UAS-6033 [R]	The Clovers In Clover	196?	50.00	100.00	200.00
UAS-6099 [S]	Love Potion Number Nine	1959	125.00	250.00	500.00

CLOWNEY, DAVID

See DAVE "BABY" CORTEZ.

CLUSTERS, THE

45s

Number	Title (A Side/B Side)	Yr	VG	VG+	NM
END					
1115	Pardon My Heart/Darling Can't You Tell	1962	10.00	20.00	40.00
EPIC					
9330	Forecast of Our Love/Long Legged Maggie	1959	20.00	40.00	80.00
TEE GEE					
102	Pardon My Heart/Darling Can't You Tell	1958	75.00	150.00	300.00
—No mention of Gone distribution					
102	Pardon My Heart/Darling Can't You Tell	1958	75.00	150.00	300.00
—With Gone distribution mentioned; publishing by Emkay Music					
102	Pardon My Heart/Darling Can't You Tell	1958	30.00	60.00	120.00
—With Gone distribution mentioned; publishing by Real Gone Music					

COASTERS, THE

Also see THE ROBINS.

45s

Number	Title (A Side/B Side)	Yr	VG	VG+	NM
AMERICAN INT'L.					
1122	If I Had a Hammer/If I Had a Hammer (Disco Version)	1976	—	2.50	5.00
—As "The World Famous Coasters"					
ATCO					
6064	Down in Mexico/Turtle Dovin'	1956	20.00	40.00	80.00
6073	One Kiss Led to Another/Brazil	1956	15.00	30.00	60.00
6087	Searchin'/Young Blood	1957	17.50	35.00	70.00
—Maroon label (first pressing)					
6087	Searchin'/Young Blood	1957	6.25	12.50	25.00
—White and yellow label					
6098	Idol with the Golden Head/(When She Wants Good Lovin') My Baby Comes to Me	1957	10.00	20.00	40.00

Number	Title (A Side/B Side)	Yr	VG	VG+	NM
6104	Sweet Georgia Brown/What Is the Secret of Your Success	1957	10.00	20.00	40.00
6111	Dance!/Gee, Golly	1958	10.00	20.00	40.00
6116	Yakety Yak/Zing Went the Strings of My Heart	1958	6.25	12.50	25.00
6126	The Shadow Knows/Sorry But I'm Gonna Have to Pass	1958	6.25	12.50	25.00
6132	Charlie Brown/Three Cool Cats	1959	6.25	12.50	25.00
6141	Along Came Jones/That Is Rock and Roll	1959	5.00	10.00	20.00
6146	Poison Ivy/I'm a Hog for You	1959	5.00	10.00	20.00
6153	Run Red Run/What About Us	1959	5.00	10.00	20.00
6163	Besame Mucho (Part 1)/Besame Mucho (Part 2)	1960	6.25	12.50	25.00
6168	Wake Me, Shake Me/Stewball	1960	6.25	12.50	25.00
6178	Shoppin' for Clothes/The Snake and the Book Worm	1960	6.25	12.50	25.00
6186	Thumbin' a Ride/Wait a Minute	1961	5.00	10.00	20.00
6192	Little Egypt (Ying-Yang)/Keep On Rolling	1961	5.00	10.00	20.00
6204	Girls, Girls, Girls (Part 1)/Girls, Girls, Girls (Part 2)	1961	5.00	10.00	20.00
6210	Bad Blood/(Ain't That) Just Like Me	1961	5.00	10.00	20.00
6219	Teach Me How to Shimmy/Ridin' Hood	1962	5.00	10.00	20.00
6234	The Climb/(Instrumental)	1962	5.00	10.00	20.00
6251	The P.T.A./Bull Tick Waltz	1962	5.00	10.00	20.00
6287	Speedo's Back in Town/T'Ain't Nothin' to Me	1964	3.75	7.50	15.00
6300	Lovey Dovey/Bad Detective	1964	3.75	7.50	15.00
6321	Wild One/I Must Be Dreaming	1964	3.75	7.50	15.00
6341	Hungry/Lady Like	1965	3.75	7.50	15.00
6356	Money Honey/Let's Go Get Stoned	1965	3.75	7.50	15.00
6379	Bell Bottom Slacks and a Chinese Kimono (She's My Little Spodee-O)/Crazy Baby	1965	6.25	12.50	25.00
6407	Saturday Night Fish Fry/She's a Yum Yum	1966	3.75	7.50	15.00
ATLANTIC					
89361	Yakety Yak/Stand By Me	1986	—	—	3.00
89361 [PS]	Yakety Yak/Stand By Me	1986	—	—	3.00
—B-side by Ben E. King. See listing of this record under "King, Ben E." for more information.					
CHELAN					
2000	Searchin' '75/Young BLood	1975	—	2.50	5.00
—As "The Coasters 2+2"					
DATE					
1552	Soul Pad/Down Home Girl	1967	5.00	10.00	20.00
1607	Everybody's Woman/She Can	1968	5.00	10.00	20.00
1617	D.W. Washburn/Everybody's Woman	1968	5.00	10.00	20.00
KING					
6385	Love Potion #9/D.W. Washburn	1972	—	3.00	6.00
6389	Cool Jerk/Talkin' 'Bout a Woman	1972	—	3.00	6.00
6404	Soul Pad/D.W. Washburn	1972	—	3.00	6.00
SAL WA					
1001	Take It Easy, Greasy/You Move Me	1975	—	2.50	5.00
TURNTABLE					
504	Act Right/The World Is Changing	1969	2.50	5.00	10.00

7-Inch Extended Plays

Number	Title (A Side/B Side)	Yr	VG	VG+	NM
ATCO					
4501	Searchin'/Young Blood//(When She Wants Good Lovin') My Baby Comes to Me/Idol with the Golden Head	1958	37.50	75.00	150.00
4501 [PS]	Rock and Roll	1958	50.00	100.00	200.00
4503	*Yakety Yak/Framed/Loop De Loop Mambo/Riot in Cell Block Number Nine	1959	50.00	100.00	200.00
4503 [PS]	Keep Rockin' with the Coasters	1959	50.00	100.00	200.00
4506	*Charlie Brown/Three Cool Cats/The Shadow Knows/Sorry But I'm Gonna Have to Pass	1959	37.50	75.00	150.00
4506 [PS]	The Coasters	1959	37.50	75.00	150.00
4507	Along Came Jones/That Is Rock & Roll//Dance!/Gee, Golly	1959	37.50	75.00	150.00
4507 [PS]	The Coasters' Top Hits	1959	37.50	75.00	150.00

Albums

Number	Title	Yr	VG	VG+	NM
ATCO					
33-101 [M]	The Coasters	1958	75.00	150.00	300.00
—Yellow "harp" label					
33-101 [M]	The Coasters	196?	15.00	30.00	60.00
—Gold and dark blue label					
33-111 [M]	The Coasters' Greatest Hits	1959	37.50	75.00	150.00
—Yellow "harp" label					
33-111 [M]	The Coasters' Greatest Hits	196?	15.00	30.00	60.00
—Gold and gray label					
33-123 [M]	One By One	1960	37.50	75.00	150.00
—Yellow "harp" label					
33-123 [M]	One By One	196?	15.00	30.00	60.00
—Gold and gray label					
SD 33-123 [S]	One By One	1960	100.00	200.00	400.00
—Yellow "harp" label					
SD 33-123 [S]	One By One	196?	37.50	75.00	150.00
—Purple and brown label					
33-135 [M]	Coast Along with the Coasters	1962	25.00	50.00	100.00
—Gold and gray label					
SD 33-135 [S]	Coast Along with the Coasters	1962	37.50	75.00	150.00
—Purple and brown label					
SD 33-371	Their Greatest Recordings/The Early Years	1971	5.00	10.00	20.00
CLARION					
605 [M]	That Is Rock and Roll	1965	10.00	20.00	40.00
SD 605 [S]	That Is Rock and Roll	1965	12.50	25.00	50.00
KING					
KS-1146	The Coasters On Broadway	1971	6.25	12.50	25.00
POWER PAK					
310	Greatest Hits	198?	2.50	5.00	10.00
TRIP					
8028	It Ain't Sanitary	197?	3.00	6.00	12.00

COBHAM, BILLY

45s

Number	Title (A Side/B Side)	Yr	VG	VG+	NM
ATLANTIC					
2998	Stratus (Part 1)/Stratus (Part 2)	1973	—	2.00	4.00
3014	Crosswinds/Le Lis	1974	—	2.00	4.00
3250	Bandit/Moon Germs	1975	—	2.00	4.00
COLUMBIA					
10858	Bolinas/Indigo	1978	—	2.00	4.00
11076	What Is Your Fantasy/Dana	1979	—	2.00	4.00
11142	Bring Up the House Lights/What Is Your Fantasy	1979	—	2.00	4.00

Albums

Number	Title	Yr	VG	VG+	NM
ATLANTIC					
SD 7268	Spectrum	1973	3.75	7.50	15.00
SD 7300	Crosswinds	1974	3.00	6.00	12.00
SD 18121	Total Eclipse	1974	3.00	6.00	12.00
SD 18139	Shabazz (Recorded Live in Europe)	1975	3.00	6.00	12.00
SD 18149	A Funky Thide of Sings	1975	2.50	5.00	10.00
SD 18166	Life & Times	1976	2.50	5.00	10.00
SD 19174	Inner Conflicts	1978	2.50	5.00	10.00
SD 19238	The Best of Billy Cobham	1979	2.50	5.00	10.00
COLUMBIA					
JC 34939	Magic	1977	2.50	5.00	10.00
JC 35457	Simplicity of Expression — Depth of Thought	1978	2.50	5.00	10.00
JC 35993	B.C.	1979	2.50	5.00	10.00
JC 36400	The Best of Billy Cobham	1980	2.50	5.00	10.00
ELEKTRA MUSICIAN					
60123	Observations &	1982	2.50	5.00	10.00
GRP					
GR-1020	Warning	1986	2.50	5.00	10.00
GR-1027	Power Play	1986	2.50	5.00	10.00
GR-1040	Picture This	1987	2.50	5.00	10.00
GR-9575	Billy's Best Hits	1988	2.50	5.00	10.00

COBHAM, BILLY, AND GEORGE DUKE

Albums

Number	Title	Yr	VG	VG+	NM
ATLANTIC					
SD 18194	Live On Tour in Europe	1976	2.50	5.00	10.00

COBRAS, THE (1)

Stevie Ray Vaughan was a member of this Cobras.

45s

Number	Title (A Side/B Side)	Yr	VG	VG+	NM
ARMADILLO					
79-1	Blow Joe Blow (Crazy 'Bout a Saxophone)/Sugaree	1980	25.00	50.00	100.00

COBRAS, THE (2)

45s

Number	Title (A Side/B Side)	Yr	VG	VG+	NM
CASINO					
1309	La La/Goodbye Molly	1963	20.00	40.00	80.00
SWAN					
4176	La La/Goodbye Molly	1964	6.25	12.50	25.00

COBRAS, THE (3)

45s

Number	Title (A Side/B Side)	Yr	VG	VG+	NM
MODERN					
964	Sindy/I Will Return	1955	75.00	150.00	300.00
—Original spelling of A-side					
964	Cindy/I Will Return	1955	37.50	75.00	150.00
—Revised spelling of A-side					

COBRAS, THE (U)

These may be by group (2), but we're not sure.

45s

Number	Title (A Side/B Side)	Yr	VG	VG+	NM
MONOGRAM					
519	Thumpin'/Don't Even Know Your Name	1964	3.00	6.00	12.00
STAX					
148	Shake Up/Restless	1964	3.75	7.50	15.00

COCHRAN, EDDIE

Also see COCHRAN BROTHERS; JEWEL AND EDDIE.

45s

Number	Title (A Side/B Side)	Yr	VG	VG+	NM
CAPEHART					
5003	Rough Stuff/Our Love	1960	6.25	12.50	25.00
5003 [PS]	Rough Stuff/Our Love	1960	50.00	100.00	200.00
CREST					
1026	Skinny Jim/Half Loved	1956	75.00	150.00	300.00
LIBERTY					
55056	Sittin' in the Balcony/Dark Lonely Street	1957	7.50	15.00	30.00
55070	Mean When I'm Mad/One Kiss	1957	7.50	15.00	30.00
55070 [PS]	Mean When I'm Mad/One Kiss	1957	500.00	1000.	1500.
55087	Drive In Show/Am I Blue	1957	7.50	15.00	30.00
55112	Twenty Flight Rock/Cradle Baby	1957	37.50	75.00	150.00
55123	Jeannie, Jeannie, Jeannie/Pocketful of Hearts	1958	7.50	15.00	30.00
55138	Pretty Girl/Theresa	1958	8.75	17.50	35.00
55144	Summertime Blues/Live Again	1958	7.50	15.00	30.00
55166	C'mon Everybody/Don't Ever Let Me Go	1958	7.50	15.00	30.00
55177	Teen Age Heaven/I Remember	1959	7.50	15.00	30.00
55177	Teenage Heaven/I Remember	1959	10.00	20.00	40.00
—Note difference in title					
55203	The Boll Weevil Song/Somethin' Else	1959	7.50	15.00	30.00
55217	Hallelujah I Love Her So/Little Angel	1959	7.50	15.00	30.00
55242	Three Steps to Heaven/Cut Across Shorty	1960	10.00	20.00	40.00
55278	Lonely/Sweetie Pie	1960	6.25	12.50	25.00
55389	Weekend/Lonely	1961	7.50	15.00	30.00
UNITED ARTISTS					
0014	Summertime Blues/Cut Across Shorty	1973	—	2.00	4.00
0015	C'mon Everybody/Twenty Flight Rock	1973	—	2.00	4.00
0016	Sittin' in the Balcony/Somethin' Else	1973	—	2.00	4.00
—0014, 0015, 0016 are "Silver Spotlight Series" reissues					

7-Inch Extended Plays

Number	Title (A Side/B Side)	Yr	VG	VG+	NM
LIBERTY					
3061-1	(contents unknown)	1958	50.00	100.00	200.00
3061-1 [PS]	Singin' to My Baby, Part 1	1958	50.00	100.00	200.00
3061-2	(contents unknown)	1958	50.00	100.00	200.00
3061-2 [PS]	Singin' to My Baby, Part 2	1958	50.00	100.00	200.00
3061-3	(contents unknown)	1958	50.00	100.00	200.00
3061-3 [PS]	Singin' to My Baby, Part 3	1958	50.00	100.00	200.00

Number	Title (A Side/B Side)	Yr	VG	VG+	NM
Albums					
LIBERTY					
LRP-3061 [M]	Singin' to My Baby	1957	200.00	400.00	800.00
—Green label					
LRP-3061 [M]	Singin' to My Baby	1960	75.00	150.00	300.00
—Black label					
LRP-3172 [M]	Eddie Cochran (12 of His Biggest Hits)	1960	30.00	60.00	120.00
LRP-3220 [M]	Never to Be Forgotten	1962	25.00	50.00	100.00
LN-10137	Singin' to My Baby	198?	3.00	6.00	12.00
—Budget-line reissue					
LN-10204	Great Hits	198?	2.00	4.00	8.00
SUNSET					
SUM-1123 [M]	Summertime Blues	1966	10.00	20.00	40.00
SUS-5123 [R]	Summertime Blues	1966	6.25	12.50	25.00
UNITED ARTISTS					
UA-LA428-E	The Very Best of Eddie Cochran	1975	3.00	6.00	12.00
UAS-9959 [(2)]	Legendary Masters Series #4	1972	6.25	12.50	25.00

COCHRAN, HANK

Also see COCHRAN BROTHERS.

Number	Title (A Side/B Side)	Yr	VG	VG+	NM
45s					
CAPITOL					
4585	Willie/Uphill All the Way	1978	—	2.00	4.00
DOT					
17361	One Night for Willie/Back to His	1970	—	3.00	6.00
ELEKTRA					
46596	Make the World Go Away/I Don't Do Windows	1980	—	2.00	4.00
47062	A Little Bitty Tear/He's Got You	1980	—	2.00	4.00
GAYLORD					
6431	A Good Country Song/(B-side unknown)	1963	3.00	6.00	12.00
LIBERTY					
55402	Lonely Little Mansion/Has Anybody Seen Me Lately	1962	3.00	6.00	12.00
55461	Sally Was a Good Old Girl/The Picture Behind the Picture	1962	3.00	6.00	12.00
55498	I'd Fight the World/Lucy, Let Your Lovelight Shine	1962	3.00	6.00	12.00
55520	I Remember/Private John Q	1963	2.50	5.00	10.00
55644	Tootsie's Orchid Lounge/Go On Home	1963	2.50	5.00	10.00
MONUMENT					
994	All of Me Belongs to You/I Just Burned a Dream	1967	—	3.00	6.00
1012	It Couldn't Happen to a Nicer Guy/Tootsie's Orchid Lounge	1967	—	3.00	6.00
1033	A Happy Goodbye/Speak Well of Me to the Kids	1967	—	3.00	6.00
1051	Has Anybody Seen Me Lately/I Woke Up	1968	—	3.00	6.00
RCA VICTOR					
47-8457	I Want to Go with You/Sad Songs and Waltzes	1964	2.50	5.00	10.00
47-8528	Somewhere in My Dreams/Going in Training	1965	2.50	5.00	10.00
47-8616	Who's Gonna/Let's Be Different	1965	2.50	5.00	10.00
47-8694	Hank Today and Him Tomorrow/I'm Alone	1965	2.50	5.00	10.00
47-8827	The Crying Section/Only You Can Make Me Well	1966	2.00	4.00	8.00
47-8955	That's What I'll Say/I Lie a Lot	1966	2.00	4.00	8.00
Albums					
CAPITOL					
ST-11807	With a Little Help from His Friends	1978	3.00	6.00	12.00
ELEKTRA					
6E-277	Make the World Go Away	1980	2.50	5.00	10.00
MONUMENT					
SLP-18089	The Heart of Hank	1968	5.00	10.00	20.00
RCA VICTOR					
LPM-3303 [M]	Hits from the Heart	1965	5.00	10.00	20.00
LSP-3303 [S]	Hits from the Heart	1965	6.25	12.50	25.00
LPM-3431 [M]	Going in Training	1965	5.00	10.00	20.00
LSP-3431 [S]	Going in Training	1965	6.25	12.50	25.00

COCHRAN, HANK, AND WILLIE NELSON

Also see each artist's individual listings.

Number	Title (A Side/B Side)	Yr	VG	VG+	NM
45s					
CAPITOL					
4635	Ain't Life Hell/I'm Going With You This Time	1978	—	2.50	5.00

COCHRAN, JACKIE LEE

Number	Title (A Side/B Side)	Yr	VG	VG+	NM
45s					
ABC-PARAMOUNT					
9930	Buy a Car/I Want You	1958	20.00	40.00	80.00
DECCA					
30206	Ruby Pearl/Mama Don't You Think I Know	1957	30.00	60.00	120.00
JAGUAR					
3031	Georgia Lee Brown/I Wanna See You	1959	30.00	60.00	120.00
SIMS					
107	Hip Shakin' Mama/Riverside Jump	1956	50.00	100.00	200.00
SPRY					
120	Pity Me/Endless Love	1959	62.50	125.00	250.00
VIV					
988	I Want You/Buy a Car	1958	37.50	75.00	150.00

COCHRAN, WAYNE

Number	Title (A Side/B Side)	Yr	VG	VG+	NM
45s					
BETHLEHEM					
3097	Hey Jude/Eleanor Rigby	1970	—	3.00	6.00
CHESS					
2020	When My Baby Cries/Some-a Your Sweet Lovin'	1967	2.00	4.00	8.00
2029	Get Ready/Hootchie Cootchie Man	1967	2.00	4.00	8.00
2054	You Can't Judge a Book By Its Cover/Up in My Mind	1968	2.00	4.00	8.00
EPIC					
10859	Do You Like the Sound of Music/Everybody's Been Cuttin' In on My Groove	1972	—	2.50	5.00
10893	Long, Long Day/Sleepless Nights	1972	—	2.50	5.00
KING					
5832	Little Orphan Annie/Monkey, Monkey	1963	3.00	6.00	12.00
5856	Last Kiss/I Dreamed, I Gambled, I Lost	1964	3.00	6.00	12.00
5874	Cindy Marie/The Coo	1964	3.00	6.00	12.00
5950	Mr. Lonely/Wrong Number, Wrong Gal	1964	3.00	6.00	12.00
5994	You Left the Water Running/Think	1965	3.00	6.00	12.00
6358	Let Me Come with You (Part 1)/Let Me Come with You (Part 2)	1971	—	3.00	6.00
MERCURY					
72507	Harlem Shuffle/Somebody Please	1965	2.50	5.00	10.00
72552	Got Down with It/No Rest for the Wicked	1966	2.50	5.00	10.00
72623	Goin' Back to Miami/I'm in Trouble	1966	2.50	5.00	10.00
SCOTTIE					
1303	My Little Girl/The Coo	1959	5.00	10.00	20.00
Albums					
BETHLEHEM					
10002	High and Ridin'	1970	3.75	7.50	15.00
CHESS					
LPS-1519	Wayne Cochran!	1968	10.00	20.00	40.00
EPIC					
KE 30889	Cochran	1972	3.75	7.50	15.00
KING					
KS-1116	Alive and Well	1970	5.00	10.00	20.00

COCHRAN BROTHERS

EDDIE COCHRAN and HANK COCHRAN, who are not brothers.

Number	Title (A Side/B Side)	Yr	VG	VG+	NM
45s					
EKKO					
1003	Mr. Fiddle/Two Blue Singing Stars	1955	62.50	125.00	250.00
1005	Guilty Conscience/Your Tomorrow Never Comes	1955	62.50	125.00	250.00
3001	Tired and Sleepy/Fool's Paradise	1956	75.00	150.00	300.00

COCKER, JOE

Number	Title (A Side/B Side)	Yr	VG	VG+	NM
45s					
ASYLUM					
45540	Fun Time/Watching the River Flow	1978	—	2.00	4.00
46001	Lady Put the Light Out/Wasted Years	1978	—	2.00	4.00
A&M					
928	Marjorine/New Age of the Lily	1968	2.50	5.00	10.00
991	With a Little Help from My Friends/Something's Coming On	1968	2.50	5.00	10.00
1063	Feeling Alright/Sandpaper Cadillac	1969	—	3.00	6.00
—Reissued in 1971 with the same number					
1112	Delta Lady/She's So Good to Me	1969	—	2.50	5.00
1147	She Came In Through the Bathroom Window/Change in Louise	1969	—	2.50	5.00
1147 [PS]	She Came In Through the Bathroom Window/Change in Louise	1969	—	3.00	6.00
1174	The Letter/Space Captain	1970	—	2.50	5.00
1174 [PS]	The Letter/Space Captain	1970	—	3.00	6.00
1200	Cry Me a River/Give Peace a Chance	1970	—	2.50	5.00
1200	Cry Me a River/Please Give Peace a Chance	1970	—	2.50	5.00
1200 [PS]	Cry Me a River/Give Peace a Chance	1970	—	3.00	6.00
1258	High Time We Went/Black-Eyed Blues	1971	—	2.00	4.00
1258 [PS]	High Time We Went/Black-Eyed Blues	1971	—	3.00	6.00
1370	Midnight Rider/Woman to Woman	1972	—	2.00	4.00
1370 [PS]	Midnight Rider/Woman to Woman	1972	—	3.00	6.00
1407	Pardon Me Sir/St. James Infirmary Blues	1973	—	2.00	4.00
1407 [PS]	Pardon Me Sir/St. James Infirmary Blues	1973	—	3.00	6.00
1539	Put Out the Light/If I Love You	1974	—	2.00	4.00
1539 [PS]	Put Out the Light/If I Love You	1974	—	3.00	6.00
1626	I Can Stand a Little Rain/I Get Mad	1974	—	2.00	4.00
1641	You Are So Beautiful/It's a Sin When You Love Somebody	1974	—	2.00	4.00
1749	I Think It's Going to Rain Today/Oh Mama	1975	—	2.00	4.00
1758	Jamaica Say You Will/It's All Over But the Shoutin'	1975	—	2.00	4.00
1805	The Man in Me (Part 1)/The Man in Me (Part 2)	1976	—	2.00	4.00
1830	Jealous Kind/You Came Along	1976	—	2.00	4.00
1855	I Broke Down/You Came Along	1976	—	2.00	4.00
2019	Feeling Alright/Cry Me a River	1978	—	2.00	4.00
CAPITOL					
B-5338	Civilized Man/A Girl Like You	1984	—	—	3.00
B-5338 [PS]	Civilized Man/A Girl Like You	1984	—	2.00	4.00
B-5390	Crazy in Love/Come On In	1984	—	—	3.00
B-5412	Edge of a Dream/Tempted	1984	—	—	3.00
B-5412 [PS]	Edge of a Dream/Tempted	1984	—	2.00	4.00
B-5557	Shelter Me/Tell Me There's a Way	1986	—	—	3.00
B-5589	You Can Leave Your Hat On/Long Drag of the Cigarette	1986	—	2.50	5.00
B-5589 [PS]	You Can Leave Your Hat On/Long Drag of the Cigarette	1986	—	3.00	6.00
B-5626	Don't Drink the Water/Don't You Love Me Anymore	1986	—	—	3.00
S7-18124	The Simple Things/Unchain My Heart (90's Version)	1994	—	—	3.00
—White vinyl					
B-44072	Unchain My Heart/Satisfied	1987	—	—	3.00
B-44072 [PS]	Unchain My Heart/Satisfied	1987	—	—	3.00
B-44101	Two Wrongs (Don't Make a Right)/Isolation	1987	—	—	3.00
B-44182	A Woman Loves a Man/La Vie En Rose	1988	—	—	3.00
—B-side by Edith Piaf					
B-44182 [PS]	A Woman Loves a Man/La Vie En Rose	1988	—	—	3.00
44590	Living in the Promiseland/She Came In Through the Bathroom Window (Live)	1990	—	2.00	4.00
NR-44590	Living in the Promiseland/She Came In Through the Bathroom Window (Live)	1990	—	2.00	4.00
S7-57988	Feels Like Forever/When the Night Comes	1992	—	—	3.00
7PRO-79025 [DJ]	What Are You Doing with a Fool Like Me (same on both sides)	1990	—	2.50	5.00
—Vinyl is promo only					
7PRO-79711 [DJ]	When the Night Comes (same on both sides)	1989	—	2.50	5.00
—Vinyl is promo only					
ISLAND					
99875	Throw It Away/Easy Rider	1983	—	2.00	4.00

Number	Title (A Side/B Side)	Yr	VG	VG+	NM
MCA					
51177	I'm So Glad I'm Standing Here Today/Standing Tall	1981	—	2.00	4.00
—With the Crusaders					
51222	This Old World's Too Funky for Me/Standing Tall	1981	—	2.00	4.00
—With the Crusaders					
53077	Love Lives On/On My Way to You	1987	—	2.00	4.00
53077 [PS]	Love Lives On/On My Way to You	1987	—	2.00	4.00
PHILIPS					
40255	I'll Cry Instead/Precious Words	1965	10.00	20.00	40.00
—Originally by "Vance Arnold and the Avengers"					
40255	I'll Cry Instead/Precious Words	1965	10.00	20.00	40.00
—Artist listed as "Joe Cocker"					
THE RIGHT STUFF					
S7-19857	Human Touch/One Step Up	1998	—	—	3.00
—B-side by Paul Cebar					
Albums					
ASYLUM					
6E-145	Luxury You Can Afford	1978	2.50	5.00	10.00
DP-400 [PD]	Luxury You Can Afford	1978	3.75	7.50	15.00
A&M					
SP-3106	With a Little Help from My Friends	1980	2.00	4.00	8.00
SP-3175	I Can Stand a Little Rain	1980	2.00	4.00	8.00
SP-3257	Joe Cocker's Greatest Hits	1982	2.00	4.00	8.00
SP-3633	I Can Stand a Little Rain	1974	2.50	5.00	10.00
SP-4182	With a Little Help from My Friends	1969	3.00	6.00	12.00
—Brown label					
SP-4182	With a Little Help from My Friends	1974	2.50	5.00	10.00
—Silver label					
SP-4224	Joe Cocker!	1969	3.00	6.00	12.00
—Brown label					
SP-4224	Joe Cocker!	1974	2.50	5.00	10.00
—Silver label					
SP-4368	Joe Cocker	1972	3.00	6.00	12.00
—Brown label					
SP-4368	Joe Cocker	1974	2.50	5.00	10.00
—Silver label					
SP-4529	Jamaica Say You Will	1975	2.50	5.00	10.00
SP-4574	Stingray	1976	2.50	5.00	10.00
SP-4670	Joe Cocker's Greatest Hits	1977	2.50	5.00	10.00
SP-6002 [(2)]	Mad Dogs and Englishmen	1970	3.75	7.50	15.00
—Brown labels					
SP-6002 [(2)]	Mad Dogs and Englishmen	1974	3.00	6.00	12.00
—Silver labels					
QU-54182 [Q]	With a Little Help from My Friends	1974	5.00	10.00	20.00
QU-54224 [Q]	Joe Cocker!	1974	5.00	10.00	20.00
CAPITOL					
ST-12335	Civilized Man	1984	2.50	5.00	10.00
ST-12394	Cocker	1986	2.50	5.00	10.00
CLT-48285	Unchain My Heart	1988	2.50	5.00	10.00
C1-92861	One Night of Sin	1989	3.00	6.00	12.00
ISLAND					
ILPS 9750	Sheffield Steel	1982	2.50	5.00	10.00
90096	One More Time	1983	2.50	5.00	10.00
MOBILE FIDELITY					
1-223	Sheffield Steel	1995	10.00	20.00	40.00
—Audiophile vinyl					

COCKER, JOE, AND JENNIFER WARNES

Also see JOE COCKER.

Number	Title (A Side/B Side)	Yr	VG	VG+	NM
45s					
ISLAND					
99996	Up Where We Belong/Sweet Li'l Woman	1982	—	2.00	4.00
99996 [PS]	Up Where We Belong/Sweet Li'l Woman	1982	—	2.00	4.00

COE, JAMIE

Number	Title (A Side/B Side)	Yr	VG	VG+	NM
45s					
ABC-PARAMOUNT					
10120	Goodbye, My Love, Goodbye/There's Never Been a Night	1960	5.00	10.00	20.00
10149	The Story of Jesse James/Say You	1960	5.00	10.00	20.00
10203	I'm Gettin' Married/Two Dozen and a Half	1961	5.00	10.00	20.00
10267	How Low Is Low/Little Darling, Little Darling	1961	5.00	10.00	20.00
ADDISON					
15001	Summertime Symphony/There's Gonna Be a Day	1959	5.00	10.00	20.00
15003	I'll Go On Loving You/School Day Blues	1959	5.00	10.00	20.00
BIG TOP					
3107	Cleopatra/But Yesterday	1962	5.00	10.00	20.00
3139	The Fool/I've Got That Feeling Again	1963	5.00	10.00	20.00
CAMEO					
424	Greenback Dollar/But Yesterday	1966	3.75	7.50	15.00
ENTERPRISE					
5005	The Dealer/Close Your Eyes	1964	3.00	6.00	12.00
5050	My Girl/I Cried on My Pillow	1964	3.00	6.00	12.00
5055	Good Enough for a King/I Was the One	1965	3.00	6.00	12.00
5070	The One Who Really Loves You/A Long Time Ago	1965	3.00	6.00	12.00
5080	Greenback Dollar/But Yesterday	1965	5.00	10.00	20.00
5095	First Girl/Very Few	1966	3.75	7.50	15.00
REPRISE					
295	Close Your Eyes/The Dealer	1964	3.00	6.00	12.00

COFFEE, RED

Number	Title (A Side/B Side)	Yr	VG	VG+	NM
45s					
WARNER BROS.					
5128	Ducky Christmas/Jolly Jingle Bells	1959	3.75	7.50	15.00

COFFEY, DENNIS

Number	Title (A Side/B Side)	Yr	VG	VG+	NM
45s					
SUSSEX					
208	Getting It On/Summertime Girl	1970	—	2.50	5.00
226	Scorpio/Sad Angel	1971	—	2.50	5.00
233	Taurus/Can You Feel It	1972	—	2.50	5.00
237	Ride, Sally, Ride/Getting It On	1972	—	2.50	5.00
251	Capricorn's Thing/Lonely Moon Child	1973	—	2.50	5.00
511	Theme from "Enter the Dragon"/Junction Flats	1973	—	2.50	5.00
631	Getting It On '75/Chicano	1974	—	2.50	5.00
WARNER BROS.					
7769	Theme from "Black Belt Jones"/Love Theme from "Black Belt Jones"	1974	—	2.50	5.00
WESTBOUND					
5020	Finger Lickin' Good/Wild Child	1975	—	2.00	4.00
5028	Honky Tonk/El Tigre	1976	—	2.00	4.00
55402	Our Love Goes On Forever/Back Home	1977	—	2.00	4.00
55414	Calling Planet Earth/A Sweet Taste of Sin	1978	—	2.00	4.00
Albums					
ORPHEUS					
D1-75617	Under the Moonlight	1989	3.00	6.00	12.00
SUSSEX					
SUX-7004	Evolution	1971	3.00	6.00	12.00
SUX-7010	Goin' for Myself	1972	3.00	6.00	12.00
SUX-7021	Electric Coffey	1972	3.00	6.00	12.00
SUX-8031	Instant Coffey	1974	3.00	6.00	12.00
WESTBOUND					
W-212	Finger Lickin' Good	1975	2.50	5.00	10.00
WD 300	Home	1977	2.50	5.00	10.00
6105	The Sweet Taste of Sin	1978	2.50	5.00	10.00

COGAN, ALMA

Number	Title (A Side/B Side)	Yr	VG	VG+	NM
45s					
AMERICAN ARTS					
4	I Love You Much Too Much/Tennessee Waltz	1964	2.50	5.00	10.00
CAPITOL					
F4170	Mama Says/Last Night on the Back Porch	1959	3.00	6.00	12.00
4547	Cowboy Jimmy Joe/Just Couldn't Resist Her with Her Pocket Transistor	1961	3.00	6.00	12.00
LAURIE					
TL 18	Snakes Snails and Puppy Dog Tails/How Many Days How Many Nights	1965	2.50	5.00	10.00
RCA VICTOR					
47-6063	Blue Again/Paper Kisses	1955	3.75	7.50	15.00
47-6236	Got N' Idea/Give a Fool a Chance	1955	3.75	7.50	15.00
47-6405	Twenty Tiny Fingers/Never Do a Tango with an Eskimo	1956	3.00	6.00	12.00
47-6573	Willie Can/Pickin' a Chicken	1956	3.00	6.00	12.00

COHEN, LEONARD

Number	Title (A Side/B Side)	Yr	VG	VG+	NM
45s					
COLUMBIA					
44439	Suzanne/Hey, That's No Way to Say Goodbye	1968	—	3.00	6.00
44827	Bird on the Wire/Seems So Long Ago (Nancy)	1969	—	3.00	6.00
45852	Nancy/Passing Thru	1973	—	2.50	5.00
Albums					
COLUMBIA					
CL 2733 [M]	Leonard Cohen	1967	6.25	12.50	25.00
CS 9533 [S]	Leonard Cohen	1967	3.00	6.00	12.00
—Red "360 Sound" label					
CS 9533 [S]	Leonard Cohen	1970	2.50	5.00	10.00
—Orange label					
PC 9533	Leonard Cohen	198?	2.00	4.00	8.00
—Reissue with new prefix					
CS 9767	Songs From a Room	1969	3.00	6.00	12.00
—Red "360 Sound" label					
CS 9767	Songs From a Room	1970	2.50	5.00	10.00
—Orange label					
PC 9767	Songs From a Room	198?	2.00	4.00	8.00
—Reissue with new prefix					
C 30103	Songs of Love and Hate	1971	3.00	6.00	12.00
PC 30103	Songs of Love and Hate	198?	2.00	4.00	8.00
—Budget-line reissue					
KC 31724	Leonard Cohen: Live Songs	1973	3.00	6.00	12.00
KC 33167	New Skin for the Old Ceremony	1974	3.00	6.00	12.00
PC 34077	The Best of Leonard Cohen	1975	2.50	5.00	10.00
—No bar code					
PC 34077	The Best of Leonard Cohen	198?	2.00	4.00	8.00
—Reissue with bar code					
JC 36264	Recent Songs	1979	2.50	5.00	10.00
PC 36264	Recent Songs	198?	2.00	4.00	8.00
—Budget-line reissue					
FC 44191	I'm Your Man	1988	2.50	5.00	10.00
PASSPORT					
PB-6045	Various Positions	1985	2.50	5.00	10.00
WARNER BROS.					
BSK 3125	Death of a Ladies' Man	1977	2.50	5.00	10.00

COHEN, MYRON

Number	Title (A Side/B Side)	Yr	VG	VG+	NM
45s					
CORAL					
61280	Mr. and Mrs./Soup and Fish	1954	3.00	6.00	12.00
Albums					
AUDIO FIDELITY					
701 [M]	Myron Cohen	196?	5.00	10.00	20.00
RCA VICTOR					
LPM-3534 [M]	Everybody Gotta Be Someplace	1966	3.00	6.00	12.00
LSP-3534 [S]	Everybody Gotta Be Someplace	1966	3.75	7.50	15.00
LPM-3791 [M]	It's Not a Question	1967	3.00	6.00	12.00
LSP-3791 [S]	It's Not a Question	1967	3.75	7.50	15.00
VPS-6052 [(2)]	This Is Myron Cohen	1972	3.75	7.50	15.00

COINS, THE

Number	Title (A Side/B Side)	Yr	VG	VG+	NM
45s					
GEE					
10	Cheatin' Baby/Blue, Can't Get No Place with You	1954	500.00	1000.	2000.
11	Look at Me Girl/S.R. Blues	1954	500.00	1000.	2000.

Number	Title (A Side/B Side)	Yr	VG	VG+	NM
1007	Look at Me Girl/Two Loves Have I	1956	150.00	300.00	600.00
—B-side by the Colonials					
MODEL					
2001	Loretta/Please	1955	500.00	1000.	2000.

COLD BLOOD

Number	Title (A Side/B Side)	Yr	VG	VG+	NM
45s					
ABC					
12173	I Get Off on You/We Came Down Here	1976	—	2.00	4.00
—As "Lydia Pense and Cold Blood"					
REPRISE					
1092	Down to the Bone/Valdes in the Country	1972	—	2.50	5.00
1157	Baby I Love You/Livin' Your Dream	1973	—	2.50	5.00
SAN FRANCISCO					
60	You Got Me Hummin'/If You Will	1970	—	3.00	6.00
61	I Wish I Knew How It Would Feel to Be Free/I'm a Good Woman	1970	—	3.00	6.00
62	Too Many People/I Can't Stay	1970	—	3.00	6.00
66	Understanding/Shop Talk	1971	—	3.00	6.00
Albums					
ABC					
D-917	Lydia Pense and Cold Blood	1976	2.50	5.00	10.00
REPRISE					
MS 2074	First Taste of Sin	1972	3.00	6.00	12.00
MS 2130	Thriller!	1973	3.00	6.00	12.00
SAN FRANCISCO					
200	Cold Blood	1969	5.00	10.00	20.00
205	Sisyphus	1970	5.00	10.00	20.00
WARNER BROS.					
BS 2806	Lydia	1974	2.50	5.00	10.00

COLDER, BEN

See SHEB WOOLEY.

COLE, ANN

Number	Title (A Side/B Side)	Yr	VG	VG+	NM
45s					
BATON					
218	Are You Satisfied?/Darling Don't Hurt Me	1955	5.00	10.00	20.00
224	Easy Easy Baby/New Love	1956	5.00	10.00	20.00
229	I'm Waiting for You/My Tearful Heart	1956	5.00	10.00	20.00
232	In the Chapel/Each Day	1956	6.25	12.50	25.00
237	Got My Mo-Jo Working/I've Got a Little Boy	1957	10.00	20.00	40.00
243	You're Mine/No Star Is Lost	1957	5.00	10.00	20.00
247	Give Me Love or Nothing/I've Got Nothing Working Now	1957	5.00	10.00	20.00
258	Love in My Heart/Summer Nights	1958	5.00	10.00	20.00
MGM					
12954	In the Chapel/Plain As the Nose on Your Face	1960	3.75	7.50	15.00
ROULETTE					
4452	Don't Stop the Wedding/Have Fun	1962	3.75	7.50	15.00
SIR					
272	Nobody But Me/That's Enough	1959	3.75	7.50	15.00
275	A Love of My Own/Brand New House	1960	3.75	7.50	15.00
TIMELY					
1006	Danny Boy/Smilin' Through	1954	6.25	12.50	25.00
1007	I'll Find a Way/Oh Love of Mine	1954	6.25	12.50	25.00
1010	So Proud of You/Down in the Valley	1955	6.25	12.50	25.00

COLE, COZY

Number	Title (A Side/B Side)	Yr	VG	VG+	NM
45s					
BETHLEHEM					
3067	Big Boss/Cozy and Bossa	1963	2.00	4.00	8.00
COLUMBIA					
43657	Whole Lotta Shakin' Goin' On/Watch It	1966	2.00	4.00	8.00
CORAL					
62339	Big Noise from Winnetka (Part 1)/Big Noise from Winnetka (Part 2)	1962	2.00	4.00	8.00
62379	Rockin' Drummer/Sing, Sing, Sing (With a Swing)	1963	2.00	4.00	8.00
—With Gary Chester					
62395	Ol' Man Moses/Christopher Columbus	1964	2.00	4.00	8.00
62417	Cozy Beat/Night Beach	1964	2.00	4.00	8.00
FELSTED					
8546	Caravan Part 1/Caravan Part 2	1959	2.50	5.00	10.00
GRAND AWARD					
1023	Caravan Part 1/Caravan Part 2	1959	3.00	6.00	12.00
KING					
5222	Blow-Up/Flop-Down	1959	2.50	5.00	10.00
5242	Strange/D Natural Rock	1959	2.50	5.00	10.00
5254	Melody of a Dreamer/Soft	1959	2.50	5.00	10.00
5265	Boy Meets Girl/Playtime Blues	1959	2.50	5.00	10.00
—With Lee Parker					
5287	Stain Glass/D'Mitri	1959	2.50	5.00	10.00
5303	Play, Cozy, Play/Cozy's Mambo	1960	2.50	5.00	10.00
5316	Blockhead/Teen-Age Ideas	1960	2.50	5.00	10.00
5337	Drum Fever/Bag of Tricks	1960	2.50	5.00	10.00
5363	Cozy's Corner/Red Ball	1960	2.50	5.00	10.00
5390	Ha Ha Cha-Cha/The Pogo Hop	1960	2.50	5.00	10.00
LOVE					
5003/4	Topsy I/Topsy II	1958	3.75	7.50	15.00
5014	Turvy I/Turvy II	1958	3.00	6.00	12.00
MERCURY					
71385	St. Louis Blues/Father Cooperates	1958	3.00	6.00	12.00
MGM					
11794	Hound Dog Special/Terrible Sight	1954	3.00	6.00	12.00
Albums					
AUDITION					
33-5943 [M]	Cozy Cole	1955	12.50	25.00	50.00
BETHLEHEM					
BCP-21 [M]	Jazz at the Metropole Café	1955	12.50	25.00	50.00
CHARLIE PARKER					
PLP-403S [S]	A Cozy Conaption of Carmen	1962	6.25	12.50	25.00
PLP-403 [M]	A Cozy Conaption of Carmen	1962	5.00	10.00	20.00
COLUMBIA					
CL 2553 [M]	It's a Rockin' Thing	1965	3.75	7.50	15.00
CS 9353 [S]	It's a Rockin' Thing	1965	5.00	10.00	20.00
CORAL					
CRL 57423 [M]	Drum Beat Dancing Feet	1962	3.75	7.50	15.00
CRL 57457 [M]	It's a Cozy World	1964	3.75	7.50	15.00
CRL 757423 [S]	Drum Beat Dancing Feet	1962	5.00	10.00	20.00
CRL 757457 [S]	It's a Cozy World	1964	5.00	10.00	20.00
FELSTED					
2002 [S]	Cozy's Caravan/Earl's Backroom	1958	10.00	20.00	40.00
7002 [M]	Cozy's Caravan/Earl's Backroom	1958	12.50	25.00	50.00
GRAND AWARD					
GA 33-334 [M]	After Hours	1956	10.00	20.00	40.00
KING					
673 [M]	Cozy Cole	1959	15.00	30.00	60.00
LOVE					
500 [M]	Topsy	1959	25.00	50.00	100.00
500 [S]	Topsy	1959	50.00	100.00	200.00
PARIS					
122 [M]	Cozy Cole and His All-Stars	1958	12.50	25.00	50.00
PLYMOUTH					
P 12-155 [M]	Cozy Cole and His All Stars	195?	7.50	15.00	30.00
SAVOY					
MG-12197 [M]	Concerto for Cozy	196?	5.00	10.00	20.00
WHO'S WHO IN JAZZ					
21003	Lionel Hampton Presents Cozy Cole & Marty Napoleon	1977	2.50	5.00	10.00

COLE, COZY/JIMMY MCPARTLAND

Number	Title (A Side/B Side)	Yr	VG	VG+	NM
Albums					
WALDORF MUSIC HALL					
MH 33-162 [10]	After Hours	195?	12.50	25.00	50.00

COLE, DON

Number	Title (A Side/B Side)	Yr	VG	VG+	NM
45s					
COED					
548	Free Flight/Squad Car	1961	5.00	10.00	20.00
GUYDEN					
2059	Lie Detector Machine/Born to Be with You	1961	25.00	50.00	100.00
KENT					
305	Saturday Night Party Time/Sweet Lovin' Honey	1958	20.00	40.00	80.00
RPM					
502	Snake Eyed Mama/Kiss of Love	1957	50.00	100.00	200.00
—With Al Casey					

COLE, JERRY

Number	Title (A Side/B Side)	Yr	VG	VG+	NM
45s					
CAPITOL					
5056	Midnight Mary/Land of Dreams	1963	3.00	6.00	12.00
5106	Pokey/One Color Blues	1964	2.50	5.00	10.00
5141	Night Rumble/Boss Dance	1964	2.50	5.00	10.00
5265	Meet Me on the Corner/Life Will Go On	1964	2.50	5.00	10.00
5394	Every Window in the City/Come On Over to My Place	1965	2.50	5.00	10.00
Albums					
CAPITOL					
ST 2044 [S]	Outer Limits	1963	20.00	40.00	80.00
T 2044 [M]	Outer Limits	1963	12.50	25.00	50.00
ST 2061 [S]	Hot Rod Dance Party	1964	25.00	50.00	100.00
T 2061 [M]	Hot Rod Dance Party	1964	20.00	40.00	80.00
(S)T 2061	Hot Rod Dance Party Bonus Photo	1964	6.25	12.50	25.00
ST 2112 [S]	Surf Age	1964	30.00	60.00	120.00
—With bonus single by Dick Dale, "Thunder Wave"/"Spanish Kiss"					
ST 2112 [S]	Surf Age	1964	25.00	50.00	100.00
—With bonus single missing					
T 2112 [M]	Surf Age	1964	25.00	50.00	100.00
—With bonus single by Dick Dale, "Thunder Wave"/"Spanish Kiss"					
T 2112 [M]	Surf Age	1964	20.00	40.00	80.00
—With bonus single missing					
LIBERTY					
LRP-3362 [M]	Sounds of the Big Irons	1964	12.50	25.00	50.00
LST-7362 [S]	Sounds of the Big Irons	1964	15.00	30.00	60.00

COLE, NAT KING

Includes reissues of material by the King Cole Trio.

Number	Title (A Side/B Side)	Yr	VG	VG+	NM
45s					
AMERICAN PIE					
9067	The Christmas Song/Ramblin' Rose	198?	—	2.50	5.00
—Reissue; B-side not a Christmas song					
CAPITOL					
54-530	Three Little Words/I'll Never Be the Same	1949	5.00	10.00	20.00
—Part of "CCF-156"					
F606	Lillian/Lush Life	1949	3.75	7.50	15.00
—Add 1/3 if "O.C." (optional center) is still in the center of the record					
F889	I Almost Lost My Mind/Baby Won't You Say You Love Me	1950	3.75	7.50	15.00
—Nat King Cole records on Capitol before F889 are unconfirmed on 45 rpm, except as listed					
F1010	Mona Lisa/The Greatest Inventor (Of Them All)	1950	3.75	7.50	15.00
F1030	I Don't Know Why/You're the Cream in My Coffee	1950	3.75	7.50	15.00
F1032	I'm in the Mood for Love/Don't Blame Me	1950	3.75	7.50	15.00
F1033	(I Love You) For Sentimental Reasons/I Can't See for Lookin'	1950	3.75	7.50	15.00
F1034	Little Girl/What Can I Say	1950	3.75	7.50	15.00
F1035	Portrait of Jenny/Lost April	1950	3.75	7.50	15.00
F1036	Exactly Like You/That's What	1950	3.75	7.50	15.00
F1037	Sweet Georgia Brown/I Know That You Know	1950	3.75	7.50	15.00
F1038	This Way Out/Rex Rhumba	1950	3.75	7.50	15.00
F1133	Home (When Shadows Fall)/Tunnel of Love	1950	3.75	7.50	15.00
F1176	Get Out and Get Under/Hey, Not Now	1950	3.75	7.50	15.00
F1184	Orange Colored Sky/Jambo	1950	3.75	7.50	15.00
F1203	Frosty the Snow Man/A Little Christmas Tree	1950	7.50	15.00	30.00

Number	Title (A Side/B Side)	Yr	VG	VG+	NM
F1270	Time Out for Tears/Get to Gettin'	1951	3.00	6.00	12.00
F1365	Jet/Magic Tree	1951	3.00	6.00	12.00
F1401	Always You/Destination Moon	1951	3.00	6.00	12.00
F1449	Too Young/That's My Girl	1951	3.00	6.00	12.00
F1468	Red Sails in the Sunset/Little Child	1951	3.00	6.00	12.00
F1501	Because of Rain/Song of Delilah	1951	3.00	6.00	12.00
F1565	Early American/My Brother	1951	3.00	6.00	12.00
F1613	Sweet Lorraine/Kee-Mo Ky-Mo	1951	3.00	6.00	12.00
F1627	Lost April/Calypso Blues	1951	3.00	6.00	12.00
F1650	Embraceable You/It's Only a Paper Moon	1951	2.50	5.00	10.00
—As "The King Cole Trio"					
F1663	Nature Boy/For All We Know	1951	2.50	5.00	10.00
F1669	Makin' Whoopee/This Is My Night to Dream	1951	2.50	5.00	10.00
F1672	Lush Life/I Miss You So	1951	2.50	5.00	10.00
F1673	Mona Lisa/No Moon at All	1951	2.50	5.00	10.00
F1674	Too Young/(I Love You) For Sentimental Reasons	1952	2.50	5.00	10.00
F1689	Pretend/Unforgettable	1954	2.50	5.00	10.00
—Most of the Capitol 1600 series were reissues, some of material from 78s					
F1747	Make Believe Land/I'll Always Remember You	1951	3.00	6.00	12.00
F1808	Unforgettable/My First, My Last Love	1951	3.00	6.00	12.00
F1815	I Still See Elisa/You're OK for TV	1951	3.00	6.00	12.00
F1863	Walkin'/I'm Hurtin'	1951	3.00	6.00	12.00
F1893	Here's to My Lady/Miss Me	1951	3.00	6.00	12.00
F1925	Wine, Women and Song/A Weaver of My Dreams	1952	3.00	6.00	12.00
F1968	You Weren't There/You Will Never Grow Old	1952	2.50	5.00	10.00
F1994	Easter Sunday Morning/Summer Is a Comin' On	1952	2.50	5.00	10.00
F2069	Somewhere Along the Way/What Does It Take to Make You Take Me	1952	2.50	5.00	10.00
2088	Thank You, Pretty Baby/Brazilian Love Song	1968	—	3.00	6.00
F2130	Walking My Baby Back Home/Funny (Not Much)	1952	2.50	5.00	10.00
F2212	Because You're Mine/I'm Never Satisfied	1952	2.50	5.00	10.00
F2230	Faith Can Move Mountains/The Ruby and the Pearl	1952	2.50	5.00	10.00
F2309	Strange/How (Do I Go About It)	1952	2.50	5.00	10.00
F2346	Pretend/Don't Let Your Eyes Go Shopping	1953	2.50	5.00	10.00
F2389	Can't I/Blue Gardenia	1953	2.50	5.00	10.00
2451	I'm Gonna Laugh You Right Out of My Life/People	1969	—	3.00	6.00
F2459	I Am in Love/My Flaming Heart	1953	2.50	5.00	10.00
F2498	Return to Paradise/Angel Eyes	1953	2.50	5.00	10.00
F2540	A Fool Was I/If Love Is Good to Me	1953	2.50	5.00	10.00
F2610	Lover Come Back to Me/That's All	1953	2.50	5.00	10.00
F2616	Mrs. Santa Claus/The Little Boy That Santa Claus Forgot	1953	5.00	10.00	20.00
F2687	Answer Me, My Love/Why	1953	2.50	5.00	10.00
F2734	It Happens to Be Me/Alone Too Long	1954	2.50	5.00	10.00
F2803	Make Her Mine/I Envy	1954	2.50	5.00	10.00
F2897	Smile/It's Crazy	1954	2.50	5.00	10.00
F2949	Hajji Baba (Persian Lament)/Unbelievable	1954	2.50	5.00	10.00
F2955	The Christmas Song (Merry Christmas to You)/ My Two Front Teeth (All I Want for Christmas)	1954	5.00	10.00	20.00
F2985	Open Up the Doghouse/Long, Long Ago	1954	3.75	7.50	15.00
—With Dean Martin					
F3027	Darling Je Vous Aime Beaucoup/The Sand and the Sea	1955	2.50	5.00	10.00
F3095	A Blossom Fell/If I May	1955	3.75	7.50	15.00
—B-side: With the Four Knights					
F3136	My One Sin/Blues from Kiss Me Deadly	1955	2.50	5.00	10.00
F3234	Forgive My Heart/Someone You Love	1955	2.50	5.00	10.00
F3305	Take Me Back to Toyland/I'm Gonna Laugh You Right Out of My Life	1955	5.00	10.00	20.00
F3328	Ask Me/Nothing Ever Changes My Love for You	1956	2.50	5.00	10.00
F3390	Too Young to Go Steady/Never Let Me Go	1956	2.50	5.00	10.00
F3456	That's All There Is to That/My Dream Sonata	1956	2.50	5.00	10.00
F3551	Night Lights/To the Ends of the Earth	1956	2.50	5.00	10.00
F3560	Mrs. Santa Claus/Take Me Back to Toyland	1956	3.75	7.50	15.00
3561	The Christmas Song (Merry Christmas to You)/ The Little Boy That Santa Claus Forgot	1960	2.00	4.00	8.00
—Purple label, Capitol logo on side					
3561	The Christmas Song (Merry Christmas to You)/ The Little Boy That Santa Claus Forgot	1962	—	3.00	6.00
—Orange and yellow swirl label					
3561	The Christmas Song (Merry Christmas to You)/ The Little Boy That Santa Claus Forgot	1973	—	2.00	4.00
—Orange label with "Capitol" at bottom					
F3561	The Christmas Song (Merry Christmas to You)/ The Little Boy That Santa Claus Forgot	1956	3.75	7.50	15.00
—Original with "F" prefix, Capitol logo on top					
F3619	Ballerina/You Are My First Love	1957	2.50	5.00	10.00
F3702	When Rock and Roll Come to Trinidad/China Gate	1957	3.75	7.50	15.00
F3737	Send for Me/My Personal Possession	1957	3.75	7.50	15.00
—B-side: With the Four Knights					
F3782	With You on My Mind/The Song of Raintree County	1957	2.50	5.00	10.00
F3860	Angel Smile/Back in My Arms	1957	2.50	5.00	10.00
F3939	Looking Back/Do I Like It	1958	2.50	5.00	10.00
F4004	Come Closer to Me/Nothing in the World	1958	2.50	5.00	10.00
F4056	Non Dimenticar (Don't Forget)/Bend a Little My Way	1958	2.50	5.00	10.00
F4125	Madrid/Give Me Your Love	1959	2.50	5.00	10.00
F4184	You Made Me Love You/I Must Be Dreaming	1959	2.50	5.00	10.00
F4248	Sweet Bird of Youth/Midnight Flyer	1959	2.50	5.00	10.00
F4248 [PS]	Sweet Bird of Youth/Midnight Flyer	1959	7.50	15.00	30.00
4301	The Happiest Christmas Tree/Buon Natale	1959	3.00	6.00	12.00
4325	What'cha Gonna Do/Time and the River	1960	2.00	4.00	8.00
4369	Is It Better to Have Loved and Lost/That's You	1960	2.00	4.00	8.00
4393	My Love/Steady	1960	2.00	4.00	8.00
4481	If I Knew/World in My Arms	1960	2.00	4.00	8.00
4519	Illusion/When It's Summer	1961	2.00	4.00	8.00
4555	Goodnight, Little Leaguer/The First Baseball Game	1961	2.00	4.00	8.00
4582	Take a Fool's Advice/Make It Last	1961	2.00	4.00	8.00
4623	Let True Love Begin/Cappuccina	1961	2.00	4.00	8.00
4672	Magic Moment/Step Right Up	1961	2.00	4.00	8.00
4714	Look No Further/The Right Thing to Say	1962	2.00	4.00	8.00
4804	Ramblin' Rose/Good Times	1962	3.00	6.00	12.00
4804 [PS]	Ramblin' Rose/Good Times	1962	5.00	10.00	20.00
4870	Dear Lonely Hearts/Who's Next in Line	1962	3.00	6.00	12.00
4870 [PS]	Dear Lonely Hearts/Who's Next in Line	1962	5.00	10.00	20.00
4919	All Over the World/Nothing Goes Up (Without Coming Down)	1963	2.00	4.00	8.00
4965	Those Lazy-Hazy-Crazy Days of Summer/In the Cool of Day	1963	3.00	6.00	12.00
4965 [PS]	Those Lazy-Hazy-Crazy Days of Summer/In the Cool of Day	1963	5.00	10.00	20.00
5027	That Sunday, That Summer/Mr. Wishing Well	1963	3.00	6.00	12.00
5125	My True Carrie, Love/A Rag a Bone, A Hank of Hair	1964	2.00	4.00	8.00
5155	I Don't Want to Be Hurt Anymore/People	1964	2.00	4.00	8.00
5219	Marnie/More and More of the Amore	1964	2.00	4.00	8.00
5261	L-O-V-E/I Don't Want to See Tomorrow	1964	2.00	4.00	8.00
5412	The Ballad of Cat Ballou/They Can't Make Her Cry	1965	2.00	4.00	8.00
—With Stubby Kay					
5412 [PS]	The Ballad of Cat Ballou/They Can't Make Her Cry	1965	3.75	7.50	15.00
5486	Wanderlust/You'll See	1965	2.00	4.00	8.00
5549	One Sun/Looking Back	1965	2.00	4.00	8.00
5683	Let Me Tell You, Babe/For the Want of a Kiss	1966	2.00	4.00	8.00
F15509	Straighten Up and Fly Right/Nature Boy	1950	3.75	7.50	15.00
—All the Capitol 15000 series on 45s are from multi-disc box sets					
F15510	You Call It Madness/The Frim Fram Sauce	1950	3.75	7.50	15.00
F15511	(Get Your Kicks on) Route 66/Gee Baby Ain't I Been Good to You	1950	3.75	7.50	15.00
F15552	Yes Sir That's My Baby/I Used to Love You	1950	3.75	7.50	15.00
F15553	For All We Know/'Tis Autumn	1950	3.75	7.50	15.00
F15554	Bop Kick/Laugh Cool Clown	1950	3.75	7.50	15.00
F15564	Sweet Lorraine/It's Only a Paper Moon	1950	3.75	7.50	15.00
F15565	The Man I Love/Body and Soul	1950	3.75	7.50	15.00
F15566	Embraceable You/What Is This Thing Called Love	1950	3.75	7.50	15.00
F15643	Jumpin' at Capitol/Love for Sale	1950	3.75	7.50	15.00
—B-side by Benny Carter Orchestra					
F15728	Makin' Whoopee/Honeysuckle Rose	1951	3.00	6.00	12.00
F15729	I'll String Along with You/Too Marvelous for Words	1951	3.00	6.00	12.00
F15730	This Is My Night to Dream/Rhumba Azul	1951	3.00	6.00	12.00
F15843	Return Trip/St. Louis Blues	1952	3.00	6.00	12.00
—B-side by Freddie Slack					
F15868	Penthouse Serenade/If I Should Lose You	1952	3.00	6.00	12.00
F15869	Somebody Loves Me/Down by the Old Mill Stream	1952	3.00	6.00	12.00
F15870	Laura/Polka Dots and Moonbeams	1952	3.00	6.00	12.00
F15922	Walkin' My Baby Back Home/Kay's Lament	1952	3.00	6.00	12.00
—B-side by Kay Starr					
S7-19764	Mrs. Santa Claus/Take Me Back to Toyland	1997	—	—	3.00
S7-57887	The Christmas Song/O Holy Night	1992	—	2.00	4.00
—Originals on black vinyl					
S7-57887	The Christmas Song/O Holy Night	1993	—	2.00	4.00
—Second pressing on red vinyl					
F-90036	(All I Want for Christmas Is) My Two Front Teeth/ The Christmas Song (Merry Christmas To You)	1949	5.00	10.00	20.00
—B-side is the original King Cole Trio hit version, possibly its only U.S. release on 45					

TAMPA

Number	Title (A Side/B Side)	Yr	VG	VG+	NM
134	Vom-Vim-Veedle/All for You	1957	3.00	6.00	12.00
134 [PS]	Vom-Vim-Veedle/All for You	1957	6.25	12.50	25.00

7-Inch Extended Plays

CAPITOL

Number	Title (A Side/B Side)	Yr	VG	VG+	NM
EAP 1-332	(contents unknown)	195?	3.00	6.00	12.00
EAP 1-332 [PS]	Penthouse Serenade, Part 1	195?	3.00	6.00	12.00
EAP 2-332	(contents unknown)	195?	3.00	6.00	12.00
EAP 2-332 [PS]	Penthouse Serenade, Part 2	195?	3.00	6.00	12.00
EAP 1-420	*Love Is Here to Stay/A Handful of Stars/Almost Like Being in Love/Tenderly	1954	3.00	6.00	12.00
EAP 1-420 [PS]	Two in Love, Part 1	1954	3.00	6.00	12.00
EAP 2-420	*A Little Street Where Old Friends Meet/This Can't Be Love/Dinner for One Please, James/ There Goes My Heart	1954	3.00	6.00	12.00
EAP 2-420 [PS]	Two in Love, Part 2	1954	3.00	6.00	12.00
EPA 1-500	*Lover Come Back/Pretend/A Fool Was I/I'm Hurtin'	1954	3.00	6.00	12.00
EPA 1-500 [PS]	Songs by Nat King Cole	1954	3.00	6.00	12.00
EAP 1-514	(contents unknown)	1954	3.00	6.00	12.00
EAP 1-514 [PS]	Tenth Anniversary Album, Part 1	1954	3.00	6.00	12.00
EAP 2-514	(contents unknown)	1954	3.00	6.00	12.00
EAP 2-514 [PS]	Tenth Anniversary Album, Part 2	1954	3.00	6.00	12.00
EAP 3-514	The Love Nest/But All I've Got Is Me//Lovelight/ Where Were You	1954	3.00	6.00	12.00
EAP 3-514 [PS]	Tenth Anniversary Album, Part 3	1954	3.00	6.00	12.00
EAP 4-514	Peaches/I Can't Be Bothered//Mother Nature and Father Time/Wish I Were Somebody Else	1954	3.00	6.00	12.00
EAP 4-514 [PS]	Tenth Anniversary Album, Part 4	1954	3.00	6.00	12.00
EBF 1-514 [PS]	Tenth Anniversary Album, Parts 1 and 2	1954	5.00	10.00	20.00
—Gatefold sleeve for some editions of EAP 1-514 and 2-514					
EBF 2-514 [PS]	Tenth Anniversary Album, Parts 3 and 4	1954	5.00	10.00	20.00
—Gatefold sleeve for some editions of EAP 3-514 and 4-514					
EAP 1-782	Sometimes I'm Happy//Just You, Just Me/When I Grow Too Old to Dream	1956	2.50	5.00	10.00
EAP 1-782 [PS]	After Midnight, Part 1	1956	2.50	5.00	10.00
EAP 2-782	Lonely One/I Know That You Know//Sweet Lorraine	1956	2.50	5.00	10.00
EAP 2-782 [PS]	After Midnight, Part 2	1956	2.50	5.00	10.00
EAP 3-782	(contents unknown)	1956	2.50	5.00	10.00
EAP 3-782 [PS]	After Midnight, Part 3	1956	2.50	5.00	10.00
EAP 4-782	(contents unknown)	1956	2.50	5.00	10.00
EAP 4-782 [PS]	After Midnight, Part 4	1956	2.50	5.00	10.00
EBF 1-782 [PS]	After Midnight, Parts 1 & 2	1956	5.00	10.00	20.00
—Gatefold sleeve for some editions of EAP 1-782 and 2-782					
EAP 1-813	*Around the World/Fascination/An Affair to Remember/There's a Gold Mine in the Sky	1957	3.00	6.00	12.00
EAP 1-813 [PS]	Around the World	1957	3.00	6.00	12.00

Number	Title (A Side/B Side)	Yr	VG	VG+	NM
EAP 1-824	*Love Is the Thing/Stay as Sweet as You Are/When I Fall in Love/Where Can I Go Without You?	1957	3.00	6.00	12.00
EAP 1-824 [PS]	Love Is the Thing, Part 1	1957	3.00	6.00	12.00
EAP 2-824	(contents unknown)	1957	3.00	6.00	12.00
EAP 2-824 [PS]	Love Is the Thing, Part 2	1957	3.00	6.00	12.00
EAP 3-824	(contents unknown)	1957	3.00	6.00	12.00
EAP 3-824 [PS]	Love Is the Thing, Part 3	1957	3.00	6.00	12.00
EAP 1-903	(contents unknown)	195?	3.00	6.00	12.00
EAP 1-903 [PS]	Just One of Those Things, Part 1	195?	3.00	6.00	12.00
EAP 2-903	Don't Get Around Much Anymore/The Party's Over//Once in a While/Just for the Fun of It	195?	3.00	6.00	12.00
EAP 2-903 [PS]	Just One of Those Things, Part 2	195?	3.00	6.00	12.00
EAP 3-903	(contents unknown)	195?	3.00	6.00	12.00
EAP 3-903 [PS]	Just One of Those Things, Part 3	195?	3.00	6.00	12.00
EAP-960	(contents unknown)	1958	2.50	5.00	10.00
EAP-960 [PS]	Looking Back	1958	2.50	5.00	10.00
EAP 1-993	*Overture (Introducing "Love Theme" and "Hesitating Blues")/Harlem Blues/Yellow Dog Blues/St. Louis Blues	1958	3.00	6.00	12.00
EAP 1-993 [PS]	St. Louis Blues, Part 1	1958	3.00	6.00	12.00
EAP 2-993	(contents unknown)	1958	3.00	6.00	12.00
EAP 2-993 [PS]	St. Louis Blues, Part 2	1958	3.00	6.00	12.00
EAP 3-993	(contents unknown)	1958	3.00	6.00	12.00
EAP 3-993 [PS]	St. Louis Blues, Part 3	1958	3.00	6.00	12.00
EAP 1-1031	*Cachito/Maria Elena/Las Mananitas/Quizas, Quizas, Quizas	1958	3.00	6.00	12.00
EAP 1-1031 [PS]	Cole Espanol, Part 1	1958	3.00	6.00	12.00
EAP 2-1031	(contents unknown)	1958	3.00	6.00	12.00
EAP 2-1031 [PS]	Cole Espanol, Part 2	1958	3.00	6.00	12.00
EAP 3-1031	(contents unknown)	1958	3.00	6.00	12.00
EAP 3-1031 [PS]	Cole Espanol, Part 3	1958	3.00	6.00	12.00
EAP 1-1084	Paradise/Cherchez La Femme//Impossible/Found A Million Dollar Baby (In A Five And Ten Cent Store)	195?	2.50	5.00	10.00
EAP 1-1084 [PS]	The Very Thought of You, Part 1	195?	2.50	5.00	10.00
EAP 2-1084	(contents unknown)	195?	2.50	5.00	10.00
EAP 2-1084 [PS]	The Very Thought of You, Part 2	195?	2.50	5.00	10.00
EAP-1138	(contents unknown)	195?	2.50	5.00	10.00
EAP-1138 [PS]	Non Dimenticar	195?	2.50	5.00	10.00
EAP 1346	(contents unknown)	195?	2.50	5.00	10.00
EAP 1346 [PS]	The Happiest Christmas Tree	195?	2.50	5.00	10.00
EAP-1500	(contents unknown)	196?	2.50	5.00	10.00
EAP-1500 [PS]	Songs by Nat King Cole	196?	2.50	5.00	10.00
EAP-1535	(contents unknown)	195?	2.50	5.00	10.00
EAP-1535 [PS]	By the Beautiful Sea	195?	2.50	5.00	10.00
EAP-1696	(contents unknown)	196?	2.50	5.00	10.00
EAP-1696 [PS]	Love Songs by Nat King Cole	196?	2.50	5.00	10.00
EAP-1709	(contents unknown)	196?	2.50	5.00	10.00
EAP-1709 [PS]	Strip for Action	196?	2.50	5.00	10.00
SXA-2195 [PS]	L-O-V-E	1965	2.50	5.00	10.00
SXA-2195 [S]	Your Love/My Kind of Girl/Three Little Words//L-O-V-E/Coquette/More	1965	2.50	5.00	10.00
—33 1/3 rpm, small hole					
EAP 1-9026	The Christmas Song/Mrs. Santa Claus//Frosty The Snowman/Little Christmas Tree	195?	3.00	6.00	12.00
EAP 1-9026 [PS]	The Christmas Song	195?	3.00	6.00	12.00
EAP 1-9120	If I Give My Heart To You/Hold My Hand//Pappa Loves Mambo/Teach Me Tonight	1954	3.00	6.00	12.00
EAP 1-9120 [PS]	Nat King Cole Sings	1954	3.00	6.00	12.00

Albums

ARCHIVE OF FOLK AND JAZZ

Number	Title (A Side/B Side)	Yr	VG	VG+	NM
290	Nature Boy	197?	2.50	5.00	10.00

CAMAY

Number	Title (A Side/B Side)	Yr	VG	VG+	NM
CA-3004	Nat King Cole	196?	3.00	6.00	12.00

CAPITOL

Number	Title (A Side/B Side)	Yr	VG	VG+	NM
H 8 [10]	The King Cole Trio	1950	25.00	50.00	100.00
H 29 [10]	The King Cole Trio, Volume 2	1950	25.00	50.00	100.00
H 59 [10]	The King Cole Trio, Volume 3	1950	25.00	50.00	100.00
H 156 [10]	Nat King Cole at the Piano	1950	25.00	50.00	100.00
H 177 [10]	The King Cole Trio, Volume 4	1950	17.50	35.00	70.00
H 213 [10]	Harvest of Hits	1950	17.50	35.00	70.00
H 220 [10]	The Nat King Cole Trio	1950	15.00	30.00	60.00
DWBB-252 [(2)]	Close-Up	1969	3.75	7.50	15.00
—Reissue of 680 and 1891					
ST-310	There! I've Said It Again	1969	3.00	6.00	12.00
H 332 [10]	Penthouse Serenade	1951	15.00	30.00	60.00
T 332 [M]	Penthouse Serenade	1955	10.00	20.00	40.00
DT 357 [R]	Unforgettable	1965	3.00	6.00	12.00
H 357 [10]	Unforgettable	1952	15.00	30.00	60.00
SM-357	Unforgettable	197?	2.00	4.00	8.00
—Reissue with new prefix					
T 357 [M]	Unforgettable	1955	10.00	20.00	40.00
—Turquoise label					
T 357 [M]	Unforgettable	1958	7.50	15.00	30.00
—Black label with colorband, "Capitol" at left					
T 357 [M]	Unforgettable	1962	5.00	10.00	20.00
—Black label with colorband, "Capitol" at top					
SKAO-373	Nat King Cole's Greatest	1969	3.00	6.00	12.00
DT 420 [R]	Nat King Cole Sings for Two in Love	1963	3.75	7.50	15.00
H 420 [10]	Nat King Cole Sings for Two in Love	1953	12.50	25.00	50.00
T 420 [M]	Nat King Cole Sings for Two in Love	1955	10.00	20.00	40.00
—Turquoise label					
T 420 [M]	Nat King Cole Sings for Two in Love	1958	7.50	15.00	30.00
—Black label with colorband, "Capitol" at left					
T 420 [M]	Nat King Cole Sings for Two in Love	1962	5.00	10.00	20.00
—Black label with colorband, "Capitol" at top					
STBB-503 [(2)]	Walkin' My Baby Back Home/A Blossom Fell	1970	3.75	7.50	15.00
H 514 [10]	Tenth Anniversary Album	1954	12.50	25.00	50.00
W 514 [M]	Tenth Anniversary Album	1955	10.00	20.00	40.00
T 591 [M]	Vocal Classics	1955	10.00	20.00	40.00
T 592 [M]	Instrumental Classics	1955	10.00	20.00	40.00
DT 680 [R]	Ballads of the Day	1963	3.75	7.50	15.00
—Black label with colorband					
T 680 [M]	Ballads of the Day	1956	10.00	20.00	40.00
—Turquoise label					
T 680 [M]	Ballads of the Day	1958	7.50	15.00	30.00
—Black label with colorband, "Capitol" at left					
T 680 [M]	Ballads of the Day	1962	5.00	10.00	20.00
—Black label with colorband, "Capitol" at top					
W 689 [M]	The Piano Style of Nat King Cole	1956	10.00	20.00	40.00
—Turquoise label					
W 689 [M]	The Piano Style of Nat King Cole	1958	7.50	15.00	30.00
—Black label with colorband, "Capitol" at left					
W 689 [M]	The Piano Style of Nat King Cole	1962	5.00	10.00	20.00
—Black label with colorband, "Capitol" at top					
W 782 [M]	After Midnight	1956	10.00	20.00	40.00
—Turquoise label					
W 782 [M]	After Midnight	1958	7.50	15.00	30.00
—Black label with colorband, "Capitol" at left					
W 782 [M]	After Midnight	1962	5.00	10.00	20.00
—Black label with colorband, "Capitol" at top					
SM-824	Love Is the Thing	197?	2.00	4.00	8.00
—Reissue with new prefix					
SW 824 [S]	Love Is the Thing	1959	7.50	15.00	30.00
—Black label with colorband, "Capitol" at left					
SW 824 [S]	Love Is the Thing	1962	5.00	10.00	20.00
—Black label with colorband, "Capitol" at top					
SW 824 [S]	Love Is the Thing	1969	3.00	6.00	12.00
—Lime green label					
W 824 [M]	Love Is the Thing	1957	10.00	20.00	40.00
—Turquoise or gray label					
W 824 [M]	Love Is the Thing	1958	7.50	15.00	30.00
—Black label with colorband, "Capitol" at left					
W 824 [M]	Love Is the Thing	1962	5.00	10.00	20.00
—Black label with colorband, "Capitol" at top					
DT 870 [R]	This Is Nat "King" Cole	1963	3.75	7.50	15.00
—Black label with colorband					
T 870 [M]	This Is Nat "King" Cole	1957	10.00	20.00	40.00
—Turquoise or gray label					
T 870 [M]	This Is Nat "King" Cole	1958	7.50	15.00	30.00
—Black label with colorband, "Capitol" at left					
T 870 [M]	This Is Nat "King" Cole	1962	5.00	10.00	20.00
—Black label with colorband, "Capitol" at top					
SW 903 [S]	Just One of Those Things	1959	7.50	15.00	30.00
—Black label with colorband, "Capitol" at left					
SW 903 [S]	Just One of Those Things	1962	5.00	10.00	20.00
—Black label with colorband, "Capitol" at top					
W 903 [M]	Just One of Those Things	1957	10.00	20.00	40.00
—Turquoise or gray label					
W 903 [M]	Just One of Those Things	1958	7.50	15.00	30.00
—Black label with colorband, "Capitol" at left					
W 903 [M]	Just One of Those Things	1962	5.00	10.00	20.00
—Black label with colorband, "Capitol" at top					
SW 993 [S]	St. Louis Blues	1959	12.50	25.00	50.00
—Black label with colorband, "Capitol" at left					
W 993 [M]	St. Louis Blues	1958	12.50	25.00	50.00
—Turquoise or gray label					
W 993 [M]	St. Louis Blues	1962	10.00	20.00	40.00
—Black label with colorband, "Capitol" at left					
DW 1031 [R]	Cole Espanol	196?	3.75	7.50	15.00
—Black label with colorband					
SM-1031	Cole Espanol	197?	2.00	4.00	8.00
—Reissue with new prefix					
W 1031 [M]	Cole Espanol	1958	7.50	15.00	30.00
—Black label with colorband, "Capitol" at left					
W 1031 [M]	Cole Espanol	1962	5.00	10.00	20.00
—Black label with colorband, "Capitol" at top					
SW 1084 [S]	The Very Thought of You	1959	7.50	15.00	30.00
—Black label with colorband, "Capitol" at left					
SW 1084 [S]	The Very Thought of You	1962	5.00	10.00	20.00
—Black label with colorband, "Capitol" at top					
W 1084 [M]	The Very Thought of You	1958	7.50	15.00	30.00
—Black label with colorband, "Capitol" at left					
W 1084 [M]	The Very Thought of You	1962	5.00	10.00	20.00
—Black label with colorband, "Capitol" at top					
SW 1120 [S]	Welcome to the Club	1959	10.00	20.00	40.00
—Black label with colorband, "Capitol" at left					
W 1120 [M]	Welcome to the Club	1959	7.50	15.00	30.00
—Black label with colorband, "Capitol" at left					
SW 1190 [S]	To Whom It May Concern	1959	10.00	20.00	40.00
—Black label with colorband, "Capitol" at left					
W 1190 [M]	To Whom It May Concern	1959	7.50	15.00	30.00
—Black label with colorband, "Capitol" at left					
SW 1220 [S]	A Mis Amigos	1959	10.00	20.00	40.00
—Black label with colorband, "Capitol" at left					
SW 1220 [S]	A Mis Amigos	1962	6.25	12.50	25.00
—Black label with colorband, "Capitol" at top					
W 1220 [M]	A Mis Amigos	1959	7.50	15.00	30.00
—Black label with colorband, "Capitol" at left					
W 1220 [M]	A Mis Amigos	1962	5.00	10.00	20.00
—Black label with colorband, "Capitol" at top					
SW 1249 [S]	Every Time I Feel the Spirit	1960	7.50	15.00	30.00
—Black label with colorband, "Capitol" at left					
W 1249 [M]	Every Time I Feel the Spirit	1960	6.25	12.50	25.00
—Black label with colorband, "Capitol" at left					
SW 1331 [S]	Tell Me About Yourself	1960	7.50	15.00	30.00
—Black label with colorband, "Capitol" at left					
W 1331 [M]	Tell Me About Yourself	1960	6.25	12.50	25.00
—Black label with colorband, "Capitol" at left					
SWAK 1392 [S]	Wild Is Love	1960	7.50	15.00	30.00
—Black label with colorband, "Capitol" at left					
WAK 1392 [M]	Wild Is Love	1960	6.25	12.50	25.00
—Black label with colorband, "Capitol" at left					
SW 1444 [S]	The Magic of Christmas	1960	5.00	10.00	20.00
W 1444 [M]	The Magic of Christmas	1960	5.00	10.00	20.00
SW 1574 [S]	The Touch of Your Lips	1961	6.25	12.50	25.00
—Black label with colorband, "Capitol" at left					
SW 1574 [S]	The Touch of Your Lips	1962	5.00	10.00	20.00
—Black label with colorband, "Capitol" at top					

Number	Title (A Side/B Side)	Yr	VG	VG+	NM
W 1574 [M]	The Touch of Your Lips	1961	5.00	10.00	20.00
—Black label with colorband, "Capitol" at left					
W 1574 [M]	The Touch of Your Lips	1962	3.75	7.50	15.00
—Black label with colorband, "Capitol" at top					
SWCL 1613 [(3) S]	The Nat King Cole Story	1961	7.50	15.00	30.00
WCL 1613 [(3) M]	The Nat King Cole Story	1961	6.25	12.50	25.00
SM-1675	Nat King Cole Sings/George Shearing Plays	197?	2.00	4.00	8.00
—Reissue with new prefix					
SW 1675 [S]	Nat King Cole Sings/George Shearing Plays	1962	7.50	15.00	30.00
—Black label with colorband, "Capitol" at left					
SW 1675 [S]	Nat King Cole Sings/George Shearing Plays	1963	5.00	10.00	20.00
—Black label with colorband, "Capitol" at top					
W 1675 [M]	Nat King Cole Sings/George Shearing Plays	1962	6.25	12.50	25.00
—Black label with colorband, "Capitol" at left					
W 1675 [M]	Nat King Cole Sings/George Shearing Plays	1963	3.75	7.50	15.00
—Black label with colorband, "Capitol" at top					
SW 1713 [S]	Nat King Cole Sings the Blues	1962	6.25	12.50	25.00
—Black label with colorband, "Capitol" at left					
W 1713 [M]	Nat King Cole Sings the Blues	1962	5.00	10.00	20.00
—Black label with colorband, "Capitol" at left					
SM-1749	More Cole Espanol	197?	2.00	4.00	8.00
—Reissue with new prefix					
SW 1749 [S]	More Cole Espanol	1962	7.50	15.00	30.00
—Black label with colorband, "Capitol" at left					
SW 1749 [S]	More Cole Espanol	1963	5.00	10.00	20.00
—Black label with colorband, "Capitol" at top					
W 1749 [M]	More Cole Espanol	1962	6.25	12.50	25.00
—Black label with colorband, "Capitol" at left					
W 1749 [M]	More Cole Espanol	1963	3.75	7.50	15.00
—Black label with colorband, "Capitol" at top					
ST 1793 [S]	Ramblin' Rose	1962	5.00	10.00	20.00
T 1793 [M]	Ramblin' Rose	1962	3.75	7.50	15.00
ST 1838 [S]	Dear Lonely Hearts	1962	5.00	10.00	20.00
T 1838 [M]	Dear Lonely Hearts	1962	3.75	7.50	15.00
SW 1859 [S]	Where Did Everyone Go?	1963	5.00	10.00	20.00
W 1859 [M]	Where Did Everyone Go?	1963	3.75	7.50	15.00
DT 1891 [R]	Nat King Cole's Top Pops	1963	3.00	6.00	12.00
T 1891 [M]	Nat King Cole's Top Pops	1963	3.75	7.50	15.00
SW 1926 [S]	The Nat King Cole Story, Volume 1	1962	3.75	7.50	15.00
W 1926 [M]	The Nat King Cole Story, Volume 1	1962	3.00	6.00	12.00
SW 1927 [S]	The Nat King Cole Story, Volume 2	1963	3.75	7.50	15.00
W 1927 [M]	The Nat King Cole Story, Volume 2	1963	3.00	6.00	12.00
SW 1928 [S]	The Nat King Cole Story, Volume 3	1963	3.75	7.50	15.00
W 1928 [M]	The Nat King Cole Story, Volume 3	1963	3.00	6.00	12.00
SW 1929 [S]	Nat King Cole Sings the Blues, Volume 2	1963	5.00	10.00	20.00
W 1929 [M]	Nat King Cole Sings the Blues, Volume 2	1963	3.75	7.50	15.00
ST 1932 [S]	Those Lazy-Hazy-Crazy Days of Summer	1963	5.00	10.00	20.00
T 1932 [M]	Those Lazy-Hazy-Crazy Days of Summer	1963	3.75	7.50	15.00
SM-1967 [S]	The Christmas Song	197?	2.00	4.00	8.00
—Budget-line reissue					
SW 1967 [S]	The Christmas Song	1962	3.75	7.50	15.00
—Black label with colorband					
SW 1967 [S]	The Christmas Song	1969	3.00	6.00	12.00
—Lime-green label					
SW 1967 [S]	The Christmas Song	1971	3.00	6.00	12.00
—Red label					
SW 1967 [S]	The Christmas Song	1973	2.50	5.00	10.00
—Orange label, "Capitol" at bottom					
W 1967 [M]	The Christmas Song	1962	3.75	7.50	15.00
—Reissue of W 1444 with title song added and another deleted					
SW 2008 [S]	Let's Face the Music	1963	5.00	10.00	20.00
W 2008 [M]	Let's Face the Music	1963	3.75	7.50	15.00
SM-2117	My Fair Lady	197?	2.00	4.00	8.00
—Reissue with new prefix					
SW 2117 [S]	My Fair Lady	1964	5.00	10.00	20.00
—Black label with colorband					
SW 2117 [S]	My Fair Lady	1969	3.00	6.00	12.00
—Lime green label					
W 2117 [M]	My Fair Lady	1964	3.75	7.50	15.00
ST 2118 [S]	I Don't Want to Be Hurt Anymore	1964	5.00	10.00	20.00
T 2118 [M]	I Don't Want to Be Hurt Anymore	1964	3.75	7.50	15.00
ST 2195 [S]	L-O-V-E	1965	5.00	10.00	20.00
T 2195 [M]	L-O-V-E	1965	3.75	7.50	15.00
T 2311 [M]	The Nat King Cole Trio	1965	3.00	6.00	12.00
ST 2340 [S]	Songs from "Cat Ballou" and Other Motion Pictures	1965	3.75	7.50	15.00
T 2340 [M]	Songs from "Cat Ballou" and Other Motion Pictures	1965	3.00	6.00	12.00
DT 2348 [R]	Nature Boy	1965	3.00	6.00	12.00
T 2348 [M]	Nature Boy	1965	3.75	7.50	15.00
ST 2361 [S]	Looking Back	1965	3.75	7.50	15.00
T 2361 [M]	Looking Back	1965	3.00	6.00	12.00
MAS 2434 [M]	Nat King Cole at the Sands	1966	3.00	6.00	12.00
SM-2434	Nat King Cole at the Sands	197?	2.00	4.00	8.00
—Reissue with new prefix					
SMAS 2434 [S]	Nat King Cole at the Sands	1966	3.75	7.50	15.00
ST 2454 [S]	Hymns and Spirituals	1966	3.75	7.50	15.00
T 2454 [M]	Hymns and Spirituals	1966	3.00	6.00	12.00
T 2529 [M]	The Vintage Years	1966	3.00	6.00	12.00
ST 2558 [S]	The Great Songs!	1966	3.75	7.50	15.00
T 2558 [M]	The Great Songs!	1966	3.00	6.00	12.00
ST 2680 [S]	Sincerely, Nat King Cole	1967	3.00	6.00	12.00
T 2680 [M]	Sincerely, Nat King Cole	1967	3.75	7.50	15.00
ST 2759 [S]	Thank You Pretty Baby	1967	3.00	6.00	12.00
T 2759 [M]	Thank You Pretty Baby	1967	3.75	7.50	15.00
ST 2820 [S]	Beautiful Ballads	1967	3.00	6.00	12.00
T 2820 [M]	Beautiful Ballads	1967	3.75	7.50	15.00
STCL 2873 [(3) P]	The Nat King Cole Deluxe Set	1968	6.25	12.50	25.00
TCL 2873 [(3) M]	The Nat King Cole Deluxe Set	1968	7.50	15.00	30.00
SKAO 2944	The Best of Nat King Cole	1968	3.00	6.00	12.00
H 9110 [10]	Eight Top Pops	1954	12.50	25.00	50.00
M-11033 [M]	Trio Days	1972	3.75	7.50	15.00
SWAK-11355	Love Is Here to Stay	1974	3.00	6.00	12.00
SM-11796	After Midnight	1978	2.50	5.00	10.00
SM-11804	Songs from "Cat Ballou" and Other Motion Pictures	1978	2.50	5.00	10.00
SM-11882	Looking Back	1979	2.50	5.00	10.00
ST-12219	16 Grandes Exitos	1982	2.50	5.00	10.00
SN-16032	Ramblin' Rose	1980	2.00	4.00	8.00
SN-16033	The Nat King Cole Story, Volume 1	1980	2.00	4.00	8.00
SN-16034	The Nat King Cole Story, Volume 2	1980	2.00	4.00	8.00
SN-16035	The Nat King Cole Story, Volume 3	1980	2.00	4.00	8.00
SN-16036	The Best of Nat King Cole	1980	2.00	4.00	8.00
SN-16037	Wild Is Love	1980	2.00	4.00	8.00
SN-16136	A Mis Amigos	1980	2.00	4.00	8.00
SN-16137	St. Louis Blues	1980	2.00	4.00	8.00
SN-16162	Unforgettable	1981	2.00	4.00	8.00
SN-16163	Love Is the Thing	1981	2.00	4.00	8.00
DN-16164	Walkin' My Baby Back Home	1981	2.00	4.00	8.00
DN-16165	A Blossom Fell	1981	2.00	4.00	8.00
N-16166	Cole Espanol	1981	2.00	4.00	8.00
SN-16167	More Cole Espanol	1981	2.00	4.00	8.00
N-16260	The Best of the King Cole Trio — Volume 1	1982	2.00	4.00	8.00
N-16281	The Best of the King Cole Trio — Volume 2	1982	2.00	4.00	8.00
SQBO 90938 [(2)]	The Velvet Moods of Nat King Cole	1967	6.25	12.50	25.00
—Capitol Record Club exclusive					
SQBO 91278 [(2)]	The Swingin' Moods of Nat King Cole	1967	6.25	12.50	25.00
—Capitol Record Club exclusive					

DCC COMPACT CLASSICS

Number	Title (A Side/B Side)	Yr	VG	VG+	NM
LPZ-2029	Love Is the Thing	1997	6.25	12.50	25.00
—Audiophile vinyl					
LPZ-2047	The Very Thought of You	1998	6.25	12.50	25.00
—Audiophile vinyl					
LPZ-2061 [(2)]	The Greatest Hits	1998	8.75	17.50	35.00
—Audiophile vinyl					

DECCA

Number	Title (A Side/B Side)	Yr	VG	VG+	NM
DL 8260 [M]	In the Beginning	1956	10.00	20.00	40.00
—Black label, silver print					
DL 8260 [M]	In the Beginning	1960	6.25	12.50	25.00
—Black label with color bars					

MARK 56

Number	Title (A Side/B Side)	Yr	VG	VG+	NM
739 [(2)]	Early 1940s	197?	3.75	7.50	15.00

MCA

Number	Title (A Side/B Side)	Yr	VG	VG+	NM
4020 [(2)]	From the Very Beginning	197?	3.00	6.00	12.00

MOBILE FIDELITY

Number	Title (A Side/B Side)	Yr	VG	VG+	NM
1-081	Nat King Cole Sings/George Shearing Plays	1981	10.00	20.00	40.00
—Audiophile vinyl					

MOSAIC

Number	Title (A Side/B Side)	Yr	VG	VG+	NM
MR27-138 [(27)]	The Complete Capitol Recordings of the Nat King Cole Trio	199?	150.00	300.00	600.00

PAIR

Number	Title (A Side/B Side)	Yr	VG	VG+	NM
PDL2-1025 [(2)]	Weaver of Dreams	1986	3.00	6.00	12.00
PDL2-1026 [(2)]	Love Moods	1986	3.00	6.00	12.00
PDL2-1128 [(2)]	Tenderly	1986	3.00	6.00	12.00

PICKWICK

Number	Title (A Side/B Side)	Yr	VG	VG+	NM
PTP-2058 [(2)]	Nature Boy	1973	3.00	6.00	12.00
SPC-3046	Love Is a Many Splendored Thing	196?	2.50	5.00	10.00
SPC-3071	When You're Smiling	196?	2.50	5.00	10.00
SPC-3105	Stay As Sweet As You Are	196?	2.50	5.00	10.00
SPC-3154	You're My Everything	197?	2.50	5.00	10.00
SPC-3249	Nature Boy	197?	2.50	5.00	10.00

SAVOY JAZZ

Number	Title (A Side/B Side)	Yr	VG	VG+	NM
SJL-1205	Nat King Cole & The King Cole Trio	1989	3.00	6.00	12.00

SCORE

Number	Title (A Side/B Side)	Yr	VG	VG+	NM
SLP-4019 [M]	The King Cole Trio and Lester Young	1957	20.00	40.00	80.00

TRIP

Number	Title (A Side/B Side)	Yr	VG	VG+	NM
7	The Nat "King" Cole Trio	197?	3.00	6.00	12.00

VERVE

Number	Title (A Side/B Side)	Yr	VG	VG+	NM
VSP-14 [M]	Nat Cole at JATP	1966	3.75	7.50	15.00
VSPS-14 [R]	Nat Cole at JATP	1966	3.00	6.00	12.00
VSP-25 [M]	Nat Cole at JATP 2	1966	3.75	7.50	15.00
VSPS-25 [R]	Nat Cole at JATP 2	1966	3.00	6.00	12.00

COLE, NATALIE

45s

CAPITOL

Number	Title (A Side/B Side)	Yr	VG	VG+	NM
4109	This Will Be/Joey	1975	—	2.50	5.00
4193	Inseparable/How Come You Won't Stay Here	1975	—	2.00	4.00
4259	Sophisticated Lady (She's a Different Lady)/Good Morning Heartache	1976	—	2.00	4.00
4328	Mr. Melody/Not Like Mine	1976	—	2.00	4.00
4360	I've Got Love on My Mind/Unpredictable You	1976	—	2.00	4.00
4439	Party Lights/Peaceful Living	1977	—	2.00	4.00
4509	Our Love/La Costa	1977	—	2.00	4.00
4572	Annie Mae/Just Can't Stay Away	1978	—	2.00	4.00
4623	Lucy in the Sky with Diamonds/Lovers	1978	—	2.00	4.00
4690	Stand By/Who Will Carry On	1979	—	2.00	4.00
4722	Sorry/You're So Good	1979	—	2.00	4.00
4767	Your Lonely Heart/The Winner	1979	—	2.00	4.00
4869	Someone That I Used to Love/Don't Look Back	1980	—	2.00	4.00
4924	Hold On/Paradise	1980	—	2.00	4.00
A-5021	You Were Right Girl/Across the Nation	1981	—	2.00	4.00
A-5045	Nothin' But a Fool/The Joke Is On You	1981	—	2.00	4.00

ELEKTRA

Number	Title (A Side/B Side)	Yr	VG	VG+	NM
64816	The Christmas Song (Chestnuts Roasting on an Open Fire)/Nature Boy	1991	—	2.00	4.00
64875	Unforgettable/Cottage for Sale	1991	—	2.00	4.00

EMI

Number	Title (A Side/B Side)	Yr	VG	VG+	NM
50185	Miss You Like Crazy/Good to Be Back	1989	—	—	3.00
50185 [PS]	Miss You Like Crazy/Good to Be Back	1989	—	2.50	5.00
50213	I Do/Miss You Like Crazy	1989	—	—	3.00
50231	As a Matter of Fact/(B-side unknown)	1989	—	—	3.00

EMI MANHATTAN

Number	Title (A Side/B Side)	Yr	VG	VG+	NM
50117	Pink Cadillac/I Wanna Be That Woman	1988	—	—	3.00
50138	When I Fall in Love/Pink Cadillac	1988	—	—	3.00
50138 [PS]	When I Fall in Love/Pink Cadillac	1988	—	2.00	4.00

EPIC

Number	Title (A Side/B Side)	Yr	VG	VG+	NM
04000	Too Much Mister/Where's Your Angel	1983	—	2.00	4.00
04147	Keep 'Em on the Outside/I Won't Deny You	1983	—	2.00	4.00

Number	Title (A Side/B Side)	Yr	VG	VG+	NM
GEFFEN					
28152	Over You/After Midnite	1987	—	—	3.00
—With Ray Parker Jr.					
MANHATTAN					
50073	Jump Start/More Than the Stars	1987	—	—	3.00
50073 [PS]	Jump Start/More Than the Stars	1987	—	2.00	4.00
50094	I Live for Your Love/More Than the Stars	1987	—	—	3.00
50094 [PS]	I Live for Your Love/More Than the Stars	1987	—	2.00	4.00
MODERN					
99589	Secrets/Nobody's Soldier	1985	—	—	3.00
99630	A Little Bit of Heaven/When I Need It Bad, You Got It Good	1985	—	—	3.00
99648	Dangerous/Love Is On the Way	1985	—	—	3.00
99648 [PS]	Dangerous/Love Is On the Way	1985	—	—	3.00
Albums					
CAPITOL					
ST-11429	Inseparable	1975	2.50	5.00	10.00
ST-11517	Natalie	1976	2.50	5.00	10.00
SO-11600	Unpredictable	1977	2.50	5.00	10.00
SW-11708	Thankful	1978	2.50	5.00	10.00
SKBL-11709 [(2)]	Natalie..Live!	1978	3.00	6.00	12.00
SO-11928	I Love You So	1979	2.50	5.00	10.00
ST-12079	Don't Look Back	1980	2.50	5.00	10.00
ST-12165	Happy Love	1981	2.50	5.00	10.00
ST-12242	A Collection	1982	2.50	5.00	10.00
SN-16038	Inseparable	198?	2.00	4.00	8.00
—Budget-line reissue					
SN-16310	A Collection	1985	2.00	4.00	8.00
—Budget-line reissue					
ELEKTRA					
61049 [(2)]	Unforgettable	1991	5.00	10.00	20.00
EMI					
E1-48902	Good to Be Back	1989	2.50	5.00	10.00
EPIC					
FE 38280	I'm Ready	1983	2.50	5.00	10.00
MANHATTAN					
53051	Everlasting	1987	2.50	5.00	10.00
MOBILE FIDELITY					
1-032	Thankful	1980	5.00	10.00	20.00
—Audiophile vinyl					
MODERN					
90270	Dangerous	1985	2.50	5.00	10.00

COLE, NATALIE, AND PEABO BRYSON

Number	Title (A Side/B Side)	Yr	VG	VG+	NM
45s					
CAPITOL					
4804	Gimme Some Time/Love Will Find You	1979	—	2.00	4.00
4826	What You Won't Do for Love/You're a Lonely Heart	1980	—	2.00	4.00
Albums					
CAPITOL					
SOO-12025	We're the Best of Friends	1979	2.50	5.00	10.00

COLEMAN, RAY

Number	Title (A Side/B Side)	Yr	VG	VG+	NM
45s					
ARCADE					
147	Jukebox Rock and Roll/Rock, Chicken Rock	1957	50.00	100.00	200.00

COLLECTORS, THE

Early incarnation of CHILLIWACK.

Number	Title (A Side/B Side)	Yr	VG	VG+	NM
45s					
VALIANT					
760	Old Man/Looking at a Baby	1967	7.50	15.00	30.00
WARNER BROS.					
7059	Listen to the Words/Fisherwoman	1967	5.00	10.00	20.00
7159	Make It Easy/Fat Bird	1968	5.00	10.00	20.00
7194	Lydia Purple/She (Will O' the Wind)	1968	3.75	7.50	15.00
7194	Lydia Purple/I Ain't No Rich Man	1968	3.00	6.00	12.00
7300	Early Morning/My Love Delights Me	1969	3.00	6.00	12.00
Albums					
WARNER BROS.					
WS 1746	The Collectors	1968	6.25	12.50	25.00
WS 1774	Grass and Wild Strawberries	1969	6.25	12.50	25.00

COLLEGIANS, THE (1)

Number	Title (A Side/B Side)	Yr	VG	VG+	NM
45s					
WINLEY					
224	Zoom, Zoom, Zoom/On Your Merry Way	1958	12.50	25.00	50.00
261	Oh I Need Your Love/Tonite, Oh Tonite	1962	7.50	15.00	30.00
263	Right Around the Corner/Teenie Weenie Little Bit	1962	7.50	15.00	30.00
X-TRA					
108	Let's Go for a Ride/Heavenly Night	1958	75.00	150.00	300.00
—Small print label (title and artist about 1/8-inch high)					
108	Let's Go for a Ride/Heavenly Night	1961	15.00	30.00	60.00
—Large print label (title and artist about 1/4-inch high)					
Albums					
WINLEY					
LP-6004 [M]	Sing Along with the Collegians	195?	100.00	200.00	400.00

COLLEGIANS, THE (U)

Some of these may be by group (1), but others are not.

Number	Title (A Side/B Side)	Yr	VG	VG+	NM
45s					
CAT					
110	Rickety Tickety Melody/The Sackbut, the Psaltery and the Dulcimer	1954	6.25	12.50	25.00
GROOVE					
0163	Blue Solitude/Please Let Me Be the One	1956	10.00	20.00	40.00
HILLTOP					
1866	Nomad/Fred's Boogie	1960	5.00	10.00	20.00
1867	The Saints (Part 1)/The Saints (Part 2)	1960	5.00	10.00	20.00
1868	Cookin'/Happy Parakeet	1961	5.00	10.00	20.00
HUDCO					
STAR-1/2	Ooh Poo Pah Doo/Silver Dollar	196?	3.00	6.00	12.00
POST					
10002	I'm Ready/Grandma Told Me So	1962	5.00	10.00	20.00

COLLINS, ALBERT

Number	Title (A Side/B Side)	Yr	VG	VG+	NM
45s					
20TH FOX					
6708	Cookin' Catfish/Taking My Time	1968	2.00	4.00	8.00
GREAT SCOTT					
007	Albert's Alley/Defrost	1963	7.50	15.00	30.00
HALLWAY					
1913	Albert's Alley/Defrost	1963	5.00	10.00	20.00
1920	Frosty/Tremble	1964	7.50	15.00	30.00
1925	Backstroke/Thaw Out	1964	5.00	10.00	20.00
IMPERIAL					
66351	Ain't Got Time/Got a Good Thing Goin'	1969	2.00	4.00	8.00
66391	Do the Sissy/Turnin' On	1969	2.00	4.00	8.00
66412	Conversation for Collins/And Then It Started Raining	1969	2.00	4.00	8.00
KANGAROO					
103	Freeze/(B-side unknown)	1958	15.00	30.00	60.00
104	Collins Shuffle/(B-side unknown)	1958	15.00	30.00	60.00
LIBERTY					
56184	Coon 'n Collards/Do What You Want to Do	1970	2.00	4.00	8.00
TCF HALL					
104	Sno Cone (Part 1)/Sno Cone (Part 2)	1965	2.50	5.00	10.00
116	Dyin' Flu/Hot 'N' Cold	1966	2.50	5.00	10.00
127	Frost Bite/Don't Lose Your Cool	1966	2.50	5.00	10.00
Albums					
ALLIGATOR					
AL-4713	Ice Pickin'	1978	2.50	5.00	10.00
AL-4719	Frostbite	1980	2.50	5.00	10.00
AL-4725	Frozen Alive!	1981	2.50	5.00	10.00
AL-4730	Don't Lose Your Cool	1983	2.50	5.00	10.00
AL-4733	Live in Japan	1984	2.50	5.00	10.00
AL-4743	Showdown!	1985	2.50	5.00	10.00
—With Robert Cray and Johnny Copeland					
AL-4752	Cold Snap	1986	2.50	5.00	10.00
BLUE THUMB					
BTS 8	Truckin' with Albert Collins	1969	6.25	12.50	25.00
—Reissue of TCF Hall LP					
IMPERIAL					
LP-12428	Love Can Be Found Anywhere	1968	7.50	15.00	30.00
LP-12438	Trash Talkin'	1969	7.50	15.00	30.00
LP-12449	The Compleat Albert Collins	1970	7.50	15.00	30.00
MOBILE FIDELITY					
1-217	Showdown!	1995	7.50	15.00	30.00
—With Robert Cray and Johnny Copeland; audiophile vinyl					
1-226	Cold Snap	1995	5.00	10.00	20.00
—Audiophile vinyl					
TCF HALL					
8002 [M]	The Cool Sound of Albert Collins	1965	75.00	150.00	300.00
TUMBLEWEED					
TWS-103	There's Gotta Be a Change	1971	3.75	7.50	15.00

COLLINS, BIG TOM

Number	Title (A Side/B Side)	Yr	VG	VG+	NM
45s					
KING					
4483	Heartache Blues/Real Good Feeling	1951	25.00	50.00	100.00
4568	Heart Breaking Woman/Watchin' My Stuff	1952	25.00	50.00	100.00

COLLINS, EDDIE

Number	Title (A Side/B Side)	Yr	VG	VG+	NM
45s					
FERNWOOD					
104	Patience Baby/Can't Face Life Alone	1958	25.00	50.00	100.00

COLLINS, GLENDA

Number	Title (A Side/B Side)	Yr	VG	VG+	NM
45s					
LAWN					
250	Lollipop/Everybody's Gotta Fall in Love	1965	2.50	5.00	10.00

COLLINS, JUDY

Number	Title (A Side/B Side)	Yr	VG	VG+	NM
45s					
ELEKTRA					
45008	Turn, Turn, Turn/Farewell	1963	2.50	5.00	10.00
45253	Send In the Clowns/Houses	1975	—	2.50	5.00
—Large print label (original)					
45253	Send In the Clowns/Houses	1977	—	2.00	4.00
—Small print label (reissue)					
45289	Angel, Spread Your Wings/The Moon Is a Harsh Mistress	1975	—	2.00	4.00
45355	Bread and Roses/Out of Control	1976	—	2.00	4.00
45372	Everything Must Change/Special Delivery	1976	—	2.00	4.00
45415	Born to the Breed/Special Delivery	1977	—	2.00	4.00
45601	I'll Keep It With Mine/Thirsty Boots	1965	2.00	4.00	8.00
45610	I Think It's Going to Rain Today/Hard Lovin' Losers	1966	2.00	4.00	8.00
45639	Both Sides Now/Who Knows Where the Time Goes	1968	2.00	4.00	8.00
—Red, white and black label					
45639	Both Sides Now/Who Knows Where the Time Goes	1968	—	3.00	6.00
—Yellow and black label					
45649	Someday Soon/My Father	1969	—	3.00	6.00
45657	Chelsea Morning/Pretty Polly	1969	—	3.00	6.00
45657 [PS]	Chelsea Morning/Pretty Polly	1969	3.75	7.50	15.00
45680	Pack Up Your Sorrows/Turn, Turn, Turn	1970	—	2.50	5.00
45709	Amazing Grace/Nightingale II	1971	—	2.50	5.00
45755	Open the Door/Innisfree	1971	—	2.50	5.00
45813	In My Life/Sunny Goodge Street	1972	—	2.00	4.00
45831	Cook with Honey/So Begins the Task	1973	—	2.00	4.00

Number	Title (A Side/B Side)	Yr	VG	VG+	NM
45849	The Hostage/Secret Gardens	1973	—	2.00	4.00
46020	Hard Times for Lovers/Happy End	1979	—	2.00	4.00
46020 [PS]	Hard Times for Lovers/Happy End	1979	—	3.00	6.00
46050	Where or When/Dorothy	1979	—	2.00	4.00
46623	Bright Morning Star/Almost Free	1980	—	2.00	4.00
46651	The Rainbow Connection/Running for My Life	1980	—	2.00	4.00
47243	Memory/The Life You Dream	1981	—	2.00	4.00
47434	It's Gonna Be One of Those Nights/Mama Mama	1982	—	2.00	4.00
69662	Only You/Dream On	1985	—	—	3.00
69697	Hello Again/Dream On	1984	—	—	3.00
—With T.G. Sheppard					
Albums					
DIRECT DISK					
SD-16607	Judith	1980	10.00	20.00	40.00
—Audiophile vinyl					
ELEKTRA					
6E-111	Judith	1977	2.00	4.00	8.00
—Reissue of 7E-1032					
6E-171	Hard Times for Lovers	1979	2.50	5.00	10.00
EKL-209 [M]	Maid of Constant Sorrow	1961	10.00	20.00	40.00
—"Guitar player" label					
EKL-209 [M]	Maid of Constant Sorrow	1966	5.00	10.00	20.00
—Gold/tan label					
EKL-222 [M]	Golden Apples of the Sun	1962	7.50	15.00	30.00
—"Guitar player" label					
EKL-222 [M]	Golden Apples of the Sun	1966	5.00	10.00	20.00
—Gold/tan label					
EKL-243 [M]	Judy Collins #3	1963	7.50	15.00	30.00
—"Guitar player" label					
EKL-243 [M]	Judy Collins #3	1966	5.00	10.00	20.00
—Gold/tan label					
6E-253	Running for My Life	1980	2.50	5.00	10.00
EKL-280 [M]	Judy Collins' Concert	1964	7.50	15.00	30.00
—"Guitar player" label					
EKL-280 [M]	Judy Collins' Concert	1966	5.00	10.00	20.00
—Gold/tan label					
EKL-300 [M]	Judy Collins' Fifth Album	1965	7.50	15.00	30.00
—"Guitar player" label					
EKL-300 [M]	Judy Collins' Fifth Album	1966	5.00	10.00	20.00
—Gold/tan label					
EKL-320 [M]	In My Life	1966	5.00	10.00	20.00
7E-1032	Judith	1975	3.00	6.00	12.00
EQ-1032 [Q]	Judith	1975	5.00	10.00	20.00
7E-1076	Bread and Roses	1976	2.50	5.00	10.00
EKL-4012 [M]	Wildflowers	1967	6.25	12.50	25.00
EQ-5030 [Q]	Colors of the Day/The Best of Judy Collins	1973	5.00	10.00	20.00
8E-6002 [(2)]	So Early in the Spring: The First 15 Years	1977	3.00	6.00	12.00
EKS-7209 [R]	Maid of Constant Sorrow	196?	3.00	6.00	12.00
—Gold/tan label or red label with large stylized "E"					
EKS-7209 [R]	Maid of Constant Sorrow	1971	2.50	5.00	10.00
—Butterfly label, no Warner Communications logo					
EKS-7209 [R]	Maid of Constant Sorrow	1975	2.00	4.00	8.00
—Any label with Warner Communications logo					
EKS-7222 [R]	Golden Apples of the Sun	196?	3.00	6.00	12.00
—Gold/tan label or red label with large stylized "E"					
EKS-7222 [R]	Golden Apples of the Sun	1971	2.50	5.00	10.00
—Butterfly label, no Warner Communications logo					
EKS-7222 [R]	Golden Apples of the Sun	1975	2.00	4.00	8.00
—Any label with Warner Communications logo					
EKS-7243 [S]	Judy Collins #3	1963	10.00	20.00	40.00
—"Guitar player" label					
EKS-7243 [S]	Judy Collins #3	1966	6.25	12.50	25.00
—Gold/tan label					
EKS-7243 [S]	Judy Collins #3	1969	3.75	7.50	15.00
—Red label with large stylized "E"					
EKS-7243 [S]	Judy Collins #3	1971	2.50	5.00	10.00
—Butterfly label, no Warner Communications logo					
EKS-7243 [S]	Judy Collins #3	1975	2.00	4.00	8.00
—Any label with Warner Communications logo					
EKS-7280 [S]	Judy Collins' Concert	1964	10.00	20.00	40.00
—"Guitar player" label					
EKS-7280 [S]	Judy Collins' Concert	1966	6.25	12.50	25.00
—Gold/tan label					
EKS-7280 [S]	Judy Collins' Concert	1969	3.75	7.50	15.00
—Red label with large stylized "E"					
EKS-7280 [S]	Judy Collins' Concert	1971	3.00	6.00	12.00
—Butterfly label, no Warner Communications logo					
EKS-7280 [S]	Judy Collins' Concert	1975	2.00	4.00	8.00
—Any label with Warner Communications logo					
EKS-7300 [S]	Judy Collins' Fifth Album	1965	10.00	20.00	40.00
—"Guitar player" label					
EKS-7300 [S]	Judy Collins' Fifth Album	1966	6.25	12.50	25.00
—Gold/tan label					
EKS-7300 [S]	Judy Collins' Fifth Album	1969	3.75	7.50	15.00
—Red label with large stylized "E"					
EKS-7300 [S]	Judy Collins' Fifth Album	1971	3.00	6.00	12.00
—Butterfly label, no Warner Communications logo					
EKS-7300 [S]	Judy Collins' Fifth Album	1975	2.00	4.00	8.00
—Any label with Warner Communications logo					
EKS-7320 [S]	In My Life	1966	6.25	12.50	25.00
60001	Times of Our Lives	1982	2.50	5.00	10.00
60304	Home Again	1985	2.50	5.00	10.00
EKS-74012 [S]	Wildflowers	1967	5.00	10.00	20.00
—Gold/tan label					
EKS-74012 [S]	Wildflowers	1969	3.75	7.50	15.00
—Red label with large stylized "E"					
EKS-74012 [S]	Wildflowers	1971	3.00	6.00	12.00
—Butterfly label, no Warner Communications logo					
EKS-74012 [S]	Wildflowers	1975	2.00	4.00	8.00
—Any label with Warner Communications logo					
EKS-74027	In My Life	1968	5.00	10.00	20.00
—Reissue of 7320; gold/tan label					
EKS-74027	In My Life	1969	3.75	7.50	15.00
—Red label with large stylized "E"					
EKS-74027	In My Life	1971	3.00	6.00	12.00
—Butterfly label, no Warner Communications logo					
EKS-74027	In My Life	1975	2.00	4.00	8.00
—Any label with Warner Communications logo					
EKS-74033	Who Knows Where the Time Goes	1968	5.00	10.00	20.00
—Gold/tan label					
EKS-74033	Who Knows Where the Time Goes	1969	3.75	7.50	15.00
—Red label with large stylized "E"					
EKS-74033	Who Knows Where the Time Goes	1971	3.00	6.00	12.00
—Butterfly label, no Warner Communications logo					
EKS-74033	Who Knows Where the Time Goes	1975	2.00	4.00	8.00
—Any label with Warner Communications logo					
EKS-74055	Recollections	1969	3.75	7.50	15.00
—Red label with large stylized "E"					
EKS-74055	Recollections	1971	3.00	6.00	12.00
—Butterfly label, no Warner Communications logo					
EKS-74055	Recollections	1975	2.00	4.00	8.00
—Any label with Warner Communications logo					
EKS-75010	Whales & Nightingales	1970	3.00	6.00	12.00
—Butterfly label, no Warner Communications logo					
EKS-75010	Whales & Nightingales	1975	2.00	4.00	8.00
—Any label with Warner Communications logo					
EKS-75014	Living	1971	3.00	6.00	12.00
—Butterfly label, no Warner Communications logo					
EKS-75014	Living	1975	2.00	4.00	8.00
—Any label with Warner Communications logo					
EKS-75030	Colors of the Day/The Best of Judy Collins	1972	3.00	6.00	12.00
—Butterfly label, no Warner Communications logo					
EKS-75030	Colors of the Day/The Best of Judy Collins	1975	2.00	4.00	8.00
—Any label with Warner Communications logo					
EKS-75053	True Stories and Other Dreams	1973	3.00	6.00	12.00
—Butterfly label					
EKS-75053	True Stories and Other Dreams	1980	2.00	4.00	8.00
—Red or red/black label					
GOLD CASTLE					
D1-71302	Trust Your Heart	1989	3.00	6.00	12.00
—Reissue of 171002					
D1-71318	Sanity and Grace	1989	3.00	6.00	12.00
171002	Trust Your Heart	1988	3.00	6.00	12.00
PAIR					
PDL2-1141 [(2)]	Her Finest Hour	1986	3.00	6.00	12.00

COLLINS, LYN

Also see JAMES BROWN.

Number	Title (A Side/B Side)	Yr	VG	VG+	NM
45s					
KING					
6373	Wheels of Life/Just Won't Do Right	1971	2.00	4.00	8.00
PEOPLE					
608	Think (About It)/Ain't No Sunshine	1972	2.50	5.00	10.00
615	Me and My Baby Got a Good Thing Goin'/I'll Never Let You Break My Heart Again	1972	—	3.00	6.00
618	Mama Feel Good/Fly Me to the Moon	1973	—	3.00	6.00
623	How Long Can I Keep It Up (Part 1)/How Long Can I Keep It Up (Part 2)	1973	—	3.00	6.00
626	Take Me As I Am/Make the World a Better Place	1973	—	3.00	6.00
630	We Wanted to Parrty, Parrty, Parrty/You Can't Beat Two People in Love	1973	—	3.00	6.00
633	Take Me Just As I Am/Don't Make Me Over	1973	—	3.00	6.00
636	Give It Up or Turnit A Loose/What the World Needs Now Is Love	1974	—	3.00	6.00
641	Wide Awake in a Dream/Rock Me Again & Again & Again & Again & Again & Again	1974	—	3.00	6.00
650	Rock Me Again & Again & Again & Again & Again & Again/You Can't Love Me If You Don't Respect Me	1974	—	3.00	6.00
657	Baby Don't Do It/How Long Can I Keep It Up	1975	—	3.00	6.00
659	If You Don't Know Me By Now/Baby Don't Do It	1975	—	3.00	6.00
662	Mr. Big Stuff/Rock Me Again & Again & Again & Again & Again & Again	1975	—	3.00	6.00
Albums					
PEOPLE					
PE-5602	Think (About It)	1972	15.00	30.00	60.00
PE-6605	Check Me Out	1975	12.50	25.00	50.00

COLOGNES, THE

Number	Title (A Side/B Side)	Yr	VG	VG+	NM
45s					
LUMMTONE					
102	A River Flows/A Bird and a Bee	1960	37.50	75.00	150.00

COLORADO

With members of THE FIREBALLS.

Number	Title (A Side/B Side)	Yr	VG	VG+	NM
45s					
UNI					
55280	My Babe/Country Comfort	1971	—	3.00	6.00
55302	Dogwood/Moonshine	1971	—	3.00	6.00

COLOSSEUM

Number	Title (A Side/B Side)	Yr	VG	VG+	NM
45s					
ABC DUNHILL					
4200	Those Who Are About to Die Salute You/Walking in the Park	1969	2.00	4.00	8.00
4211	Kettle/Plenty Hard Luck	1969	2.00	4.00	8.00
Albums					
ABC DUNHILL					
DS-50062	Those Who Are About to Die Salute You	1969	5.00	10.00	20.00
DS-50079	The Grass Is Green	1970	5.00	10.00	20.00
DSX-50101	Daughter of Time	1971	3.75	7.50	15.00
WARNER BROS.					
PRO 500 [DJ]	Colosseum Live	1972	3.75	7.50	15.00
—Highlights for radio					
2WS 1942 [(2)]	Colosseum Live	1972	3.75	7.50	15.00

COLOURS

45s

DOT

Number	Title (A Side/B Side)	Yr	VG	VG+	NM
17181	Hyannis Port Soul/Run Away from Here	1968	2.00	4.00	8.00

Albums

DOT

Number	Title (A Side/B Side)	Yr	VG	VG+	NM
DLP-25854	Colours	1968	6.25	12.50	25.00
DLP-25935	Atmosphere	1969	6.25	12.50	25.00

COLTER, JESSI

Also see DUANE AND MIRRIAM EDDY; WAYLON JENNINGS; WAYLON AND JESSI.

45s

Number	Title (A Side/B Side)	Yr	VG	VG+	NM
CAPITOL					
4009	I'm Not Lisa/For the First Time	1974	—	2.00	4.00
4087	What's Happened to Blue Eyes/You Ain't Never Been Loved (Like I'm Gonna Love You)	1975	—	2.00	4.00
4200	It's Morning (And I Still Love You)/Would You Walk with Me (To the Lilies)	1975	—	2.00	4.00
4252	Without You/All My Life I've Been Your Love	1976	—	2.00	4.00
4325	I Thought I Heard You Calling My Name/You Hung the Moon (Didn't You Waylon)	1976	—	2.00	4.00
4472	I Belong to Him/There Ain't No Rain	1977	—	2.00	4.00
4641	Maybe You Should've Been Listening/My Cowboy's Last Ride	1978	—	2.00	4.00
4696	Love Me Back to Sleep/Don't You Think I Felt It Too	1979	—	2.00	4.00
5073	Holdin' On/(B-side unknown)	1981	—	2.00	4.00
5113	Nobody Else But You/Ain't Makin' No Headlines	1982	—	2.00	4.00
JAMIE					
1193	I Cried Long Enough/Making Believe	1959	7.50	15.00	30.00
—As "Mirriam Johnson"					
RCA VICTOR					
PB-10309	He Called Me Baby/Take a Message to Laura	1975	—	2.50	5.00
47-9826	Cry Softly/If She's Where You Like Livin'	1970	—	2.50	5.00
74-0280	Take a Message to Laura/I Ain't the One	1969	—	2.50	5.00
74-0780	You Don't Need Me, Do You/I Don't Wanna Be a One-Night Stand	1972	—	2.50	5.00

Albums

Number	Title (A Side/B Side)	Yr	VG	VG+	NM
CAPITOL					
ST-11363	I'm Jessi Colter	1975	2.50	5.00	10.00
ST-11477	Jessi	1976	2.50	5.00	10.00
ST-11543	Diamond in the Rough	1976	2.50	5.00	10.00
ST-11583	Mirriam	1977	2.50	5.00	10.00
ST-11863	That's the Way a Cowboy Rocks and Rolls	1978	2.50	5.00	10.00
ST-12185	Ridin' Shotgun	1981	2.50	5.00	10.00
ST-511863	That's the Way a Cowboy Rocks and Rolls	1978	3.00	6.00	12.00
—Columbia House edition					
RCA VICTOR					
LSP-4333	Country Star	1970	5.00	10.00	20.00

COLTON, TONY

45s

Number	Title (A Side/B Side)	Yr	VG	VG+	NM
ABC-PARAMOUNT					
10705	I Stand Accused/Further On Down the Track	1965	3.75	7.50	15.00
10792	You're Wrong Baby/Have You Lost Your Mind	1966	3.75	7.50	15.00
ROULETTE					
4475	Tell the World/Goodbye Cindy, Goodbye	1963	3.75	7.50	15.00

COLTRANE, ALICE

Widow of JOHN COLTRANE. She played in his group for a time.

45s

ABC IMPULSE!

Number	Title (A Side/B Side)	Yr	VG	VG+	NM
279	Journey in Satchidananda (Part 1)/Journey in Satchidananda (Part 2)	1970	—	3.00	6.00

Albums

Number	Title (A Side/B Side)	Yr	VG	VG+	NM
ABC IMPULSE!					
AS-9156	The Monastic Trio	1968	3.00	6.00	12.00
AS-9185	Huntington Ashram Monastery	1969	3.00	6.00	12.00
AS-9196	Ptah the El Daoud	1969	3.00	6.00	12.00
AS-9203	Journey in Satchidananda	1970	3.00	6.00	12.00
AS-9210	Universal Consciousness	1971	2.50	5.00	10.00
AS-9218	World Galaxy	1972	2.50	5.00	10.00
AS-9224	Lord of Lords	1972	2.50	5.00	10.00
AS-9232 [(2)]	Reflection On Creation and Space	1973	3.00	6.00	12.00
GRP/IMPULSE!					
IMP-228	Journey in Satchidanada	1997	3.75	7.50	15.00
WARNER BROS.					
BS 2916	Eternity	1975	2.50	5.00	10.00
BS 2986	Radha Krsna	1976	2.50	5.00	10.00
BS 3077	Transcendence	1977	2.50	5.00	10.00
2WS 3218 [(2)]	Transfiguration	1978	3.00	6.00	12.00

COLTRANE, ALICE, AND CARLOS SANTANA

Also see ALICE COLTRANE; SANTANA.

Albums

COLUMBIA

Number	Title (A Side/B Side)	Yr	VG	VG+	NM
KC 32900	Illuminations	1974	2.50	5.00	10.00

COLTRANE, CHI

45s

Number	Title (A Side/B Side)	Yr	VG	VG+	NM
CLOUDS					
10	What's Happening to Me (It's a Spell)/Changes	1978	—	2.00	4.00
COLUMBIA					
45640	Thunder and Lightning/Time to Come In	1972	—	2.50	5.00
45749	It's Really Come to This/Go Like Elijah	1972	—	2.50	5.00
45802	Turn Me Around/You Are My Friend	1973	—	2.50	5.00
45960	Myself to You/Who Every Told You	1973	—	2.00	4.00

Albums

COLUMBIA

Number	Title (A Side/B Side)	Yr	VG	VG+	NM
KC 31275	Chi Coltrane	1972	3.00	6.00	12.00
KC 32463	Let It Ride	1973	3.00	6.00	12.00

COLTRANE, JOHN

Also see KENNY BURRELL; MILES DAVIS; THELONIOUS MONK.

45s

Number	Title (A Side/B Side)	Yr	VG	VG+	NM
ATLANTIC					
5003	Cousin Mary/Naimi	1960	2.50	5.00	10.00
5012	My Favorite Things (Part 1)/My Favorite Things (Part 2)	1961	3.00	6.00	12.00
BLUE NOTE					
1691	Blue Train (Part 1)/Blue Train (Part 2)	1957	3.75	7.50	15.00
IMPULSE!					
203	Easy to Remember/Greensleeves	1961	2.50	5.00	10.00
212	Nancy (With the Laughing Face)/Up 'Gainst the Wall	1962	2.50	5.00	10.00
218	Lush Life/My One and Only Love	1963	2.50	5.00	10.00
—With Johnny Hartman					
PRESTIGE					
107	Time Was (Part 1)/Time Was (Part 2)	195?	3.00	6.00	12.00
122	Things Ain't What They Used to Be (Part 1)/ Things Ain't What They Used to Be (Part 2)	195?	3.00	6.00	12.00
139	Good Bait (Part 1)/Good Bait (Part 2)	195?	3.00	6.00	12.00
249	Lush Life/I Love You	1960	3.00	6.00	12.00
267	Stardust/Love Thy Neighbor	1961	3.00	6.00	12.00
315	Dakar/The Believer	1963	2.50	5.00	10.00
394	By the Numbers (Part 1)/By the Numbers (Part 2)	196?	2.00	4.00	8.00
—With Red Garland					
415	Breathless/I Love You	196?	2.00	4.00	8.00

Albums

Number	Title (A Side/B Side)	Yr	VG	VG+	NM
ABC IMPULSE!					
AS-6 [S]	Africa/Brass	1968	3.75	7.50	15.00
AS-10 [S]	Live at the Village Vanguard	1968	3.75	7.50	15.00
AS-21 [S]	Coltrane	1968	3.75	7.50	15.00
AS-30 [S]	Duke Ellington and John Coltrane	1968	3.75	7.50	15.00
AS-32 [S]	Ballads	1968	3.75	7.50	15.00
AS-40 [S]	John Coltrane + Johnny Hartman	1968	3.75	7.50	15.00
AS-42 [S]	Impressions	1968	3.75	7.50	15.00
AS-50 [S]	Coltrane Live at Birdland	1968	3.75	7.50	15.00
AS-66 [S]	Crescent	1968	3.75	7.50	15.00
AS-77 [S]	A Love Supreme	1968	3.75	7.50	15.00
AS-85 [S]	The John Coltrane Quartet Plays	1968	3.75	7.50	15.00
AS-94 [S]	New Thing at Newport	1968	3.75	7.50	15.00
AS-95 [S]	Ascension	1968	3.75	7.50	15.00
—With "Edition II" in dead wax					
AS-9106 [S]	Kulu Se Mama	1968	3.75	7.50	15.00
AS-9110 [S]	Meditations	1968	3.75	7.50	15.00
AS-9120 [S]	Expression	1968	3.75	7.50	15.00
AS-9124 [S]	Live at the Village Vanguard Again!	1968	3.75	7.50	15.00
AS-9140 [S]	Om	1968	3.75	7.50	15.00
AS-9148	Cosmic Music	1969	5.00	10.00	20.00
—Reissue of Coltrane LP					
AS-9161	Selflessness	1969	5.00	10.00	20.00
AS-9165	Transition	1969	5.00	10.00	20.00
AS-9200 [(2)]	Greatest Years	1971	5.00	10.00	20.00
AS-9202 [(2)]	Live in Seattle	1971	5.00	10.00	20.00
AS-9211	Sun Ship	1971	5.00	10.00	20.00
AS-9223 [(2)]	Greatest Years, Volume 2	1973	3.75	7.50	15.00
AS-9225	Infinity	1973	3.00	6.00	12.00
IA-9246 [(2)]	Concert Japan	1973	3.75	7.50	15.00
IA-9273	Africa/Brass, Volume 2	1974	3.00	6.00	12.00
IA-9277	Interstellar Space	1974	3.00	6.00	12.00
IA-9278 [(2)]	Greatest Years, Volume 3	1974	3.75	7.50	15.00
IA-9306 [(2)]	The Gentle Side of John Coltrane	1976	3.75	7.50	15.00
IA-9325 [(2)]	The Other Village Vanguard Tapes	1977	3.75	7.50	15.00
IA-9332	First Meditations	1978	3.00	6.00	12.00
IZ-9345 [(2)]	The Mastery of John Coltrane Vol. 1: Feelin' Good	1978	3.00	6.00	12.00
IZ-9346 [(2)]	The Mastery of John Coltrane Vol. 2: Different Drum	1978	3.00	6.00	12.00
IA-9360	The Mastery of John Coltrane Vol. 3: Jupiter Variation	1978	3.00	6.00	12.00
IZ-9361 [(2)]	The Mastery of John Coltrane Vol. 4: Trane's Moods	1978	3.00	6.00	12.00
ATLANTIC					
SD 2-313 [(2)]	The Art of John Coltrane	1973	3.75	7.50	15.00
1311 [M]	Giant Steps	1959	12.50	25.00	50.00
—Black label					
1311 [M]	Giant Steps	1960	6.25	12.50	25.00
—Orange and purple label, white fan logo					
1311 [M]	Giant Steps	1962	3.75	7.50	15.00
—Orange and purple label, black fan logo					
SD 1311 [S]	Giant Steps	1959	15.00	30.00	60.00
—Green label					
SD 1311 [S]	Giant Steps	1960	6.25	12.50	25.00
—Green and blue label, white fan logo					
SD 1311 [S]	Giant Steps	1962	2.75	7.50	15.00
—Green and blue label, black fan logo					
SD 1311 [S]	Giant Steps	1969	3.00	6.00	12.00
—Red and green label					
1354 [M]	Coltrane Jazz	1960	7.50	15.00	30.00
—Orange and purple label, white fan logo					
1354 [M]	Coltrane Jazz	1962	3.75	7.50	15.00
—Orange and purple label, black fan logo					
SD 1354 [S]	Coltrane Jazz	1960	7.50	15.00	30.00
—Green and blue label, white fan logo					
SD 1354 [S]	Coltrane Jazz	1962	3.75	7.50	15.00
—Green and blue label, black fan logo					
SD 1354 [S]	Coltrane Jazz	1969	3.00	6.00	12.00
—Red and green label					
1361 [M]	My Favorite Things	1961	7.50	15.00	30.00
—Orange and purple label, white fan logo					
1361 [M]	My Favorite Things	1962	3.75	7.50	15.00
—Orange and purple label, black fan logo					
SD 1361 [S]	My Favorite Things	1961	7.50	15.00	30.00
—Green and blue label, white fan logo					
SD 1361 [S]	My Favorite Things	1962	3.75	7.50	15.00
—Green and blue label, black fan logo					

Number	Title (A Side/B Side)	Yr	VG	VG+	NM
SD 1361 [S]	My Favorite Things	1969	3.00	6.00	12.00
—Red and green label					
1373 [M]	Ole' Coltrane	1961	7.50	15.00	30.00
—Orange and purple label, white fan logo					
1373 [M]	Ole' Coltrane	1962	3.75	7.50	15.00
—Orange and purple label, black fan logo					
SD 1373 [S]	Ole' Coltrane	1961	7.50	15.00	30.00
—Green and blue label, white fan logo					
SD 1373 [S]	Ole' Coltrane	1962	3.75	7.50	15.00
—Green and blue label, black fan logo					
SD 1373 [S]	Ole' Coltrane	1969	3.00	6.00	12.00
—Red and green label					
1382 [M]	Coltrane Plays the Blues	1962	7.50	15.00	30.00
SD 1382 [S]	Coltrane Plays the Blues	1962	7.50	51.00	30.00
—Green and blue label, black fan logo					
SD 1382 [S]	Coltrane Plays the Blues	1969	3.00	6.00	12.00
—Red and green label					
1419 [M]	Coltrane's Sound	1964	6.25	12.50	25.00
SD 1419 [S]	Coltrane's Sound	1964	6.25	12.50	25.00
—Green and blue label, black fan logo					
SD 1419 [S]	Coltrane's Sound	1969	3.00	6.00	12.00
—Red and green label					
1451 [M]	The Avant Garde	1966	6.25	12.50	25.00
SD 1451 [S]	The Avant Garde	1966	6.25	12.50	25.00
—Green and blue label, black fan logo					
SD 1451 [S]	The Avant Garde	1969	3.00	6.00	12.00
—Red and green label					
SD 1541	The Best of John Coltrane	1969	3.00	6.00	12.00
SD 1553	The Coltrane Legacy	1971	3.00	6.00	12.00
90014	The Avant-Garde	1983	2.50	5.00	10.00
90462	Countdown	1986	2.50	5.00	10.00
ATLANTIC/RHINO					
R1-71984 [(12)]	The Heavyweight Champion: The Complete Atlantic Recordings	1995	50.00	100.00	200.00
BLUE NOTE					
BLP-1577 [M]	Blue Train	1957	37.50	75.00	150.00
—"Deep groove" version (deep indentation under label on both sides)					
BLP-1577 [M]	Blue Train	1957	25.00	50.00	100.00
—Regular version, W. 63rd St., NYC address on label					
BLP-1577 [M]	Blue Train	196?	7.50	15.00	30.00
—New York, USA address on label					
BST-1577 [S]	Blue Train	1959	30.00	60.00	120.00
—"Deep groove" version (deep indentation under label on both sides)					
BST-1577 [S]	Blue Train	1959	20.00	40.00	80.00
—Regular version, W. 63rd St., NYC address on label					
BST-1577 [S]	Blue Train	196?	6.25	12.50	25.00
—New York, USA address on label					
B1-46095	Blue Train	1997	3.75	7.50	15.00
B1-81577	Blue Train	1988	2.50	5.00	10.00
—Reissue with new prefix					
BST-81577	Blue Train	1967	3.75	7.50	15.00
—"A Division of Liberty Records" on label					
BST-81577	Blue Train	198?	2.50	5.00	10.00
—"The Finest in Jazz Since 1939" reissue					
COLTRANE					
AU-4950	Cosmic Music	1966	75.00	150.00	300.00
AU-5000	Cosmic Music	1966	50.00	100.00	200.00
DCC COMPACT CLASSICS					
LPZ-2032	Lush Life	1997	6.25	12.50	25.00
—Audiophile vinyl					
FANTASY					
OJC-020	Coltrane	198?	2.50	5.00	10.00
OJC-021	Soultrane	198?	2.50	5.00	10.00
OJC-078	Settin' the Pace	198?	2.50	5.00	10.00
OJC-127	Tenor Conclave	1991	3.00	6.00	12.00
OJC-131	Lush Life	198?	2.50	5.00	10.00
OJC-189	Traneing In	1986	2.50	5.00	10.00
OJC-246	Standard Coltrane	1987	2.50	5.00	10.00
OJC-292	Interplay for Two Trumpets and Two Tenors	1988	2.50	5.00	10.00
OJC-352	Black Pearls	1989	2.50	5.00	10.00
OJC-393	Dakar	1989	2.50	5.00	10.00
OJC-394	Last Trane	1989	2.50	5.00	10.00
OJC-415	Bahia	1990	3.00	6.00	12.00
OJC-460	Cattin' with Coltrane and Quinichette	1990	3.00	6.00	12.00
GRP/IMPULSE!					
GR-155	A Love Supreme	1995	3.75	7.50	15.00
GR-156	Ballads	1995	3.75	7.50	15.00
GR-157	John Coltrane + Johnny Hartman	1995	3.75	7.50	15.00
IMP-166	Duke Ellington and John Coltrane	1997	3.75	7.50	15.00
IMP-167	Sun Ship	1997	3.75	7.50	15.00
IMP-169	Stellar Regions	1995	3.75	7.50	15.00
IMP-198	Coltrane Live at Birdland	1997	3.75	7.50	15.00
IMP-200	Crescent	1997	3.75	7.50	15.00
IMP-213	Live at the Village Vanguard Again!	1997	3.75	7.50	15.00
IMP-214	The John Coltrane Quartet Plays	1997	3.75	7.50	15.00
IMP-215	Coltrane	1997	3.75	7.50	15.00
IMPULSE!					
A-6 [M]	Africa/Brass	1961	7.50	15.00	30.00
AS-6 [S]	Africa/Brass	1961	10.00	20.00	40.00
A-10 [M]	Live at the Village Vanguard	1962	7.50	15.00	30.00
AS-10 [S]	Live at the Village Vanguard	1962	10.00	20.00	40.00
A-21 [M]	Coltrane	1962	7.50	15.00	30.00
AS-21 [S]	Coltrane	1962	10.00	20.00	40.00
A-30 [M]	Duke Ellington and John Coltrane	1963	7.50	15.00	30.00
AS-30 [S]	Duke Ellington and John Coltrane	1963	10.00	20.00	40.00
A-32 [M]	Ballads	1963	7.50	15.00	30.00
AS-32 [S]	Ballads	1963	10.00	20.00	40.00
A-40 [M]	John Coltrane + Johnny Hartman	1963	10.00	20.00	40.00
AS-40 [S]	John Coltrane + Johnny Hartman	1963	12.50	25.00	50.00
A-42 [M]	Impressions	1963	6.25	12.50	25.00
AS-42 [S]	Impressions	1963	7.50	15.00	30.00
A-50 [M]	Coltrane Live at Birdland	1963	6.25	12.50	25.00
AS-50 [S]	Coltrane Live at Birdland	1963	7.50	15.00	30.00
A-66 [M]	Crescent	1964	6.25	12.50	25.00
AS-66 [S]	Crescent	1964	7.50	15.00	30.00

Number	Title (A Side/B Side)	Yr	VG	VG+	NM
A-77 [M]	A Love Supreme	1965	7.50	15.00	30.00
AS-77 [S]	A Love Supreme	1965	10.00	20.00	40.00
A-85 [M]	The John Coltrane Quartet Plays	1965	6.25	12.50	25.00
AS-85 [S]	The John Coltrane Quartet Plays	1965	7.50	15.00	30.00
A-94 [M]	New Thing at Newport	1965	6.25	12.50	25.00
AS-94 [S]	New Thing at Newport	1965	7.50	15.00	30.00
A-95 [M]	Ascension	1965	20.00	40.00	80.00
—Without "Edition II" in dead wax					
A-95 [M]	Ascension	1966	6.25	12.50	25.00
—With "Edition II" in dead wax					
AS-95 [S]	Ascension	1965	25.00	50.00	100.00
—Without "Edition II" in dead wax					
AS-95 [S]	Ascension	1966	7.50	15.00	30.00
—With "Edition II" in dead wax					
A-9106 [M]	Kulu Se Mama	1966	6.25	12.50	25.00
AS-9106 [S]	Kulu Se Mama	1966	7.50	15.00	30.00
A-9110 [M]	Meditations	1966	6.25	12.50	25.00
AS-9110 [S]	Meditations	1966	7.50	15.00	30.00
A-9120 [M]	Expression	1967	7.50	15.00	30.00
AS-9120 [S]	Expression	1967	6.25	12.50	25.00
A-9124 [M]	Live at the Village Vanguard Again!	1967	7.50	15.00	30.00
AS-9124 [S]	Live at the Village Vanguard Again!	1967	6.25	12.50	25.00
A-9140 [M]	Om	1967	7.50	15.00	30.00
AS-9140 [S]	Om	1967	6.25	12.50	25.00
MCA					
4131 [(2)]	Greatest Years	1981	2.50	5.00	10.00
4132 [(2)]	Greatest Years, Volume 2	1981	2.50	5.00	10.00
4133 [(2)]	Greatest Years, Volume 3	1981	2.50	5.00	10.00
4134 [(2)]	Live in Seattle	1981	2.50	5.00	10.00
4135 [(2)]	Concert Japan	1981	2.50	5.00	10.00
4136 [(2)]	The Gentle Side of John Coltrane	1981	2.50	5.00	10.00
4137 [(2)]	The Other Village Vanguard Tapes	1981	2.50	5.00	10.00
4138 [(2)]	The Mastery of John Coltrane Vol. 1: Feelin' Good	1981	2.50	5.00	10.00
4139 [(2)]	The Mastery of John Coltrane Vol. 2: Different Drum	1981	2.50	5.00	10.00
4140 [(2)]	The Mastery of John Coltrane Vol. 4: Trane's Moods	1981	2.50	5.00	10.00
29007	Africa/Brass	1981	2.00	4.00	8.00
29008	Africa/Brass, Volume 2	1981	2.00	4.00	8.00
29009	Live at the Village Vanguard	1981	2.00	4.00	8.00
29010	Live at the Village Vanguard Again!	1981	2.00	4.00	8.00
29011	Coltrane	1981	2.00	4.00	8.00
29012	Ballads	1981	2.00	4.00	8.00
29013	John Coltrane + Johnny Hartman	1981	2.00	4.00	8.00
29014	Impressions	1981	2.00	4.00	8.00
29015	Coltrane Live at Birdland	1981	2.00	4.00	8.00
29016	Crescent	1981	2.00	4.00	8.00
29017	A Love Supreme	1981	2.00	4.00	8.00
29018	The John Coltrane Quartet Plays	1981	2.00	4.00	8.00
29019	New Thing at Newport	1981	2.00	4.00	8.00
29020	Ascension	1981	2.00	4.00	8.00
29021	Kulu Se Mama	1981	2.00	4.00	8.00
29022	Meditations	1981	2.00	4.00	8.00
29023	Expression	1981	2.00	4.00	8.00
29024	Om	1981	2.00	4.00	8.00
29025	Cosmic Music	1981	2.00	4.00	8.00
29026	Selflessness	1981	2.00	4.00	8.00
29027	Transition	1981	2.00	4.00	8.00
29028	Sun Ship	1981	2.00	4.00	8.00
29029	Interstellar Space	1981	2.00	4.00	8.00
29030	First Meditations	1981	2.00	4.00	8.00
29031	The Mastery of John Coltrane Vol. 3: Jupiter Variation	1981	2.00	4.00	8.00
29032	Duke Ellington and John Coltrane	1981	2.00	4.00	8.00
MCA/IMPULSE!					
5660	A Love Supreme	1986	2.50	5.00	10.00
5661	John Coltrane + Johnny Hartman	1986	2.50	5.00	10.00
5883	Coltrane	1987	2.50	5.00	10.00
5885	Ballads	1987	2.50	5.00	10.00
5887	Impressions	1987	2.50	5.00	10.00
5889	Crescent	1987	2.50	5.00	10.00
33109	Coltrane Live at Birdland	198?	2.50	5.00	10.00
33110	The John Coltrane Quartet Plays	198?	2.50	5.00	10.00
39103	Duke Ellington and John Coltrane	1988	2.50	5.00	10.00
39118	Om	1988	2.50	5.00	10.00
39136	Live at the Village Vanguard	1988	2.50	5.00	10.00
42231	Africa/Brass	1988	2.50	5.00	10.00
42232	Africa/Brass, Volume 2	1988	2.50	5.00	10.00
PABLO					
2405417	The Best of John Coltrane	198?	2.50	5.00	10.00
PABLO LIVE					
2308217	The Paris Concert	1980	3.00	6.00	12.00
2308222	European Tour	1981	3.00	6.00	12.00
2308227	Bye Bye Blackbird	1981	3.00	6.00	12.00
2620101 [(2)]	Afro Blue Impressions	198?	3.00	6.00	12.00
PRESTIGE					
PRLP-7105 [M]	Coltrane	1957	25.00	50.00	100.00
—Yellow label					
PRLP-7105 [M]	Coltrane	1964	7.50	15.00	30.00
—Blue label with trident logo					
PRLP-7123 [M]	John Coltrane and the Red Garland Trio	1957	25.00	50.00	100.00
—Yellow label					
PRLP-7123 [M]	Traneing In	1964	7.50	15.00	30.00
—Blue label with trident logo; reissue with new title					
PRLP-7142 [M]	Soultrane	1958	20.00	40.00	80.00
—Yellow label					
PRLP-7142 [M]	Soultrane	1964	6.25	12.50	25.00
—Blue label with trident logo					
PRLP-7158 [M]	Cattin' with Coltrane and Quinichette	1959	20.00	40.00	80.00
—Yellow label					
PRLP-7158 [M]	Cattin' with Coltrane and Quinichette	1964	6.25	12.50	25.00
—Blue label with trident logo					
PRLP-7188 [M]	Lush Life	1960	20.00	40.00	80.00
—Yellow label					

Number	Title (A Side/B Side)	Yr	VG	VG+	NM
PRLP-7188 [M]	Lush Life	1964	6.25	12.50	25.00
—Blue label with trident logo					
PRLP-7213 [M]	Settin' the Pace	1961	20.00	40.00	80.00
—Yellow label					
PRLP-7213 [M]	Settin' the Pace	1964	6.25	12.50	25.00
—Blue label with trident logo					
PRLP-7243 [M]	Standard Coltrane	1962	10.00	20.00	40.00
—Yellow label					
PRLP-7243 [M]	Standard Coltrane	1964	6.25	12.50	25.00
—Blue label with trident logo					
PRST-7243 [S]	Standard Coltrane	1962	12.50	25.00	50.00
—Silver label					
PRST-7243 [S]	Standard Coltrane	1964	6.25	12.50	25.00
—Blue label with trident logo					
PRLP-7247 [M]	Mating Call	1962	10.00	20.00	40.00
—Yellow label					
PRLP-7247 [M]	Mating Call	1964	6.25	12.50	25.00
—Blue label with trident logo					
PRST-7247 [R]	Mating Call	1964	5.00	10.00	20.00
—Blue label with trident logo					
PRST-7247 [R]	Mating Call	196?	6.25	12.50	25.00
—Silver label					
PRLP-7249 [M]	Tenor Conclave	1962	10.00	20.00	40.00
—Yellow label					
PRLP-7249 [M]	Tenor Conclave	1964	6.25	12.50	25.00
—Blue label with trident logo					
PRST-7249 [R]	Tenor Conclave	1964	5.00	10.00	20.00
—Blue label with trident logo					
PRST-7249 [R]	Tenor Conclave	196?	6.25	12.50	25.00
—Silver label					
PRLP-7268 [M]	Stardust	1963	10.00	20.00	40.00
—Yellow label					
PRLP-7268 [M]	Stardust	1964	6.25	12.50	25.00
—Blue label with trident logo					
PRST-7268 [S]	Stardust	1963	10.00	20.00	40.00
—Silver label					
PRST-7268 [S]	Stardust	1964	6.25	12.50	25.00
—Blue label with trident logo					
PRLP-7280 [M]	Dakar	1963	10.00	20.00	40.00
—Yellow label					
PRLP-7280 [M]	Dakar	1964	6.25	12.50	25.00
—Blue label with trident logo					
PRST-7280 [S]	Dakar	1963	10.00	20.00	40.00
—Silver label					
PRST-7280 [S]	Dakar	1964	6.25	12.50	25.00
—Blue label with trident logo					
PRLP-7292 [M]	The Believer	1964	10.00	20.00	40.00
—Yellow label					
PRLP-7292 [M]	The Believer	1964	6.25	12.50	25.00
—Blue label with trident logo					
PRST-7292 [S]	The Believer	1964	10.00	20.00	40.00
—Silver label					
PRST-7292 [S]	The Believer	1964	6.25	12.50	25.00
—Blue label with trident logo					
PRLP-7316 [M]	Black Pearls	1964	10.00	20.00	40.00
—Yellow label					
PRLP-7316 [M]	Black Pearls	1964	6.25	12.50	25.00
—Blue label with trident logo					
PRST-7316 [S]	Black Pearls	1964	10.00	20.00	40.00
—Silver label					
PRST-7316 [S]	Black Pearls	1964	6.25	12.50	25.00
—Blue label with trident logo					
PRLP-7353 [M]	Bahia	1965	6.25	12.50	25.00
PRST-7353 [S]	Bahia	1965	6.25	12.50	25.00
PRLP-7378 [M]	The Last Trane	1965	6.25	12.50	25.00
PRST-7378 [S]	The Last Trane	1965	6.25	12.50	25.00
PRLP-7426 [M]	John Coltrane Plays for Lovers	1966	6.25	12.50	25.00
PRST-7426 [S]	John Coltrane Plays for Lovers	1966	6.25	12.50	25.00
PRLP-7531 [M]	Soultrane	1967	6.25	12.50	25.00
PRST-7531 [R]	Soultrane	1967	3.00	6.00	12.00
PRST-7581 [R]	Lush Life	1968	3.00	6.00	12.00
PRST-7609 [R]	The First Trane	1969	3.00	6.00	12.00
PRST-7651 [R]	Traneing In	1969	3.00	6.00	12.00
PRST-7670 [R]	Two Tenors	1969	3.00	6.00	12.00
PRST-7725	Mating Call	1970	3.00	6.00	12.00
PRST-7746	Trane's Reign	1970	3.00	6.00	12.00
PRST-7825	The Master	1971	3.00	6.00	12.00
24003 [(2)]	John Coltrane	1972	3.75	7.50	15.00
24014 [(2)]	More Lasting Than Bronze	1973	3.75	7.50	15.00
24037 [(2)]	Black Pearls	1974	3.75	7.50	15.00
24056 [(2)]	The Stardust Session	197?	3.75	7.50	15.00
24069 [(2)]	Wheelin'	197?	3.00	6.00	12.00
24084 [(2)]	On a Misty Night	198?	3.00	6.00	12.00
24094 [(2)]	Rain or Shine	198?	3.00	6.00	12.00
24104 [(2)]	Dakar	198?	3.00	6.00	12.00
24110 [(2)]	Bahia	198?	3.00	6.00	12.00
SOLID STATE					
SM-17025 [M]	Coltrane Time	1968	6.25	12.50	25.00
SS-18025 [S]	Coltrane Time	1968	3.75	7.50	15.00
TRIP					
5001 [(2)]	Trane Tracks	1974	3.75	7.50	15.00
UNITED ARTISTS					
UAS-5638	Coltrane Time	1972	3.00	6.00	12.00
—Reissue of 15001					
UAJ-14001 [M]	Coltrane Time	1962	10.00	20.00	40.00
UAJS-15001 [S]	Coltrane Time	1962	12.50	25.00	50.00

COLTS, THE

45s

Number	Title (A Side/B Side)	Yr	VG	VG+	NM
ANTLER					
4003	Never No More/The Shiek of Araby	1959	10.00	20.00	40.00
4007	Guiding Angel/The Shiek of Araby	1959	10.00	20.00	40.00
MAMBO					
112	Adorable/Lips Red as Wine	1955	100.00	200.00	400.00
PLAZA					
505	Hey, Pretty Baby/Sweet Sixteen	1962	5.00	10.00	20.00
VITA					
112	Adorable/Lips Red as Wine	1955	37.50	75.00	150.00
121	Honey Bun/Sweet Sixteen	1955	30.00	60.00	120.00
130	Never No More/Hey You Shoo-Bee-Ooh-Bee	1956	30.00	60.00	120.00

COLUMBUS PHARAOHS, THE

45s

Number	Title (A Side/B Side)	Yr	VG	VG+	NM
ESTA					
290	Give Me Your Love/China Girl	1958	250.00	500.00	1000.

COLWELL-WINFIELD BLUES BAND, THE

Number	Title (A Side/B Side)	Yr	VG	VG+	NM
45s					
VERVE FORECAST					
5098	Cold Wind Blues/Free Will Fantasy	1968	2.50	5.00	10.00
Albums					
VERVE FORECAST					
FTS-3056	Cold Wind Blues	1968	5.00	10.00	20.00
ZA-ZOO					
1	Live Bust	1971	7.50	15.00	30.00

COLYER, KEN

Number	Title (A Side/B Side)	Yr	VG	VG+	NM
45s					
LONDON					
1655	Down by the Riverside/Take This Hammer	1956	3.00	6.00	12.00
1674	Casey Jones/Streamline Train	1956	3.00	6.00	12.00
Albums					
GHB					
161	Live at the 100 Club	198?	2.50	5.00	10.00
LONDON					
PB 904 [10]	New Orleans to London	1954	12.50	25.00	50.00
LL 1340 [M]	Back to the Delta	1956	10.00	20.00	40.00
LL 1618 [M]	Club Session with Colyer	1957	10.00	20.00	40.00
STORYVILLE					
SLP-144	Ken's Early Days	197?	3.00	6.00	12.00

COMFORTABLE CHAIR, THE

Number	Title (A Side/B Side)	Yr	VG	VG+	NM
45s					
ODE					
109	Be Me/Some Soon, Some Day	1968	2.50	5.00	10.00
112	I'll See You/Now	1968	2.50	5.00	10.00
Albums					
ODE					
Z12 44005	The Comfortable Chair	1968	5.00	10.00	20.00

COMMANDER CODY AND HIS LOST PLANET AIRMEN

Includes records as "Commander Cody Band" and "Commander Cody."

Number	Title (A Side/B Side)	Yr	VG	VG+	NM
45s					
ARISTA					
0271	Seven-Eleven/You Snooze You Lose	1977	—	2.00	4.00
0344	Thank You Lone Ranger/My Day	1978	—	2.00	4.00
DOT					
17487	Daddy's Drinking Up Our Christmas/ Honeysuckle Honey	1973	—	3.00	6.00
17500	Diggy Liggy Lo/Outgoing Person	1974	—	2.50	5.00
PARAMOUNT					
0130	Lost in the Ozone/Midnight Shift	1971	—	3.00	6.00
0146	Hot Rod Lincoln/My Home in My Hand	1972	—	3.00	6.00
0169	Beat Me Daddy, Eight to the Bar/Daddy's Gonna Treat You Right	1972	—	3.00	6.00
0178	Truck Stop Rock/Mama Hated Diesels	1972	—	3.00	6.00
0193	Semi-Truck/Watch My .38	1973	—	3.00	6.00
0216	Smoke! Smoke! Smoke! (That Cigarette)/Rock That Boogie	1973	—	3.00	6.00
0278	Riot in Cell Block No. 9/Oh, Momma Momma	1974	—	3.00	6.00
WARNER BROS.					
8073	Don't Let Go/Keep On Lovin' Her	1975	—	2.00	4.00
8164	It's Gonna Be One of Those Nights/Roll Your Own	1975	—	2.00	4.00
Albums					
ARISTA					
AL 4125	Rock 'N' Roll Again	1977	2.50	5.00	10.00
AL 4183	Flying Dreams	1978	—	—	—
—Canceled?					
BLIND PIG					
BP-2086	Let's Rock	1986	2.50	5.00	10.00
MCA					
659	Live from Deep in the Heart of Texas	1980	2.00	4.00	8.00
—Reissue of Paramount 1017					
660	Country Casanova	1980	2.00	4.00	8.00
—Reissue of Paramount 6054					
661	Hot Licks, Cold Steel & Truckers Favorites	1980	2.00	4.00	8.00
—Reissue of Paramount 6031					
37101	Lost in the Ozone	1980	2.00	4.00	8.00
—Reissue of Paramount 6017					
PARAMOUNT					
PAS-1017	Live from Deep in the Heart of Texas	1974	3.00	6.00	12.00
PAS-6017	Lost in the Ozone	1971	3.75	7.50	15.00
PAS-6031	Hot Licks, Cold Steel & Truckers Favorites	1972	3.00	6.00	12.00
PAS-6054	Country Casanova	1973	3.00	6.00	12.00
WARNER BROS.					
BS 2847	Commander Cody and His Lost Planet Airmen	1975	2.50	5.00	10.00
BS 2883	Tales from the Ozone	1975	2.50	5.00	10.00
2LS 2939 [(2)]	We've Got a Live One Here!	1976	3.00	6.00	12.00

COMMODORES

Popular 1970s and 1980s soul group. Few, if any, of their records use the word "The" before "Commodores."

45s

MOTOWN

Number	Title (A Side/B Side)	Yr	VG	VG+	NM
1268	Are You Happy/There's a Song in My Heart	1973	—	3.00	6.00
1307	Machine Gun/There's a Song in My Heart	1974	—	2.50	5.00
1319	I Feel Sanctified/It Is As Good As You Make It	1974	—	2.50	5.00
1338	Slippery When Wet/The Bump	1975	—	2.50	5.00
1361	This Is Your Life/Look What You've Done to Me	1975	—	2.50	5.00
1366	Wide Open/(B-side unassigned)	1975	—	—	—
—Unreleased					
1381	Sweet Love/Better Never Than Forever	1976	—	2.00	4.00
1394	Come Inside/Time	1976	—	—	—
—Unreleased					
1399	High on Sunshine/Thumpin' Music	1976	—	—	—
—Unreleased					
1402	Just to Be Close to You/Thumpin' Music	1976	—	2.00	4.00
1408	Fancy Dancer/Cebu	1977	—	2.00	4.00
1418	Easy/Can't Let You Tease Me	1977	—	2.00	4.00
1425	Brick House/Captain Quickdraw	1977	—	2.00	4.00
1432	Too Hot Ta Trot/Funky Situation	1977	—	2.00	4.00
1443	Three Times a Lady/Look What You've Done to Me	1978	—	2.00	4.00
1452	Flying High/X-Rated Movie	1978	—	2.00	4.00
1457	Say Yeah/(B-side unassigned)	1978	—	—	—
—Unreleased					
1466	Sail On/Thumpin' Music	1979	—	2.00	4.00
1474	Still/Such a Woman	1979	—	2.00	4.00
1479	Wonderland/Lovin' You	1979	—	2.00	4.00
1489	Old Fashion Love/Sexy Lady	1980	—	2.00	4.00
1495	Heroes/Funky Situation	1980	—	2.00	4.00
1502	Jesus Is Love/Mighty Spirit	1980	—	3.00	6.00
1514	Lady (You Bring Me Up)/Gettin' It	1981	—	2.00	4.00
1527	Oh No/Lovin' You	1981	—	2.00	4.00
1604	Why You Wanna Try Me/X-Rated Movie	1982	—	2.00	4.00
1651	Painted Pictures/Reach High	1982	—	—	3.00
1661	Sexy Lady/Reach High	1983	—	—	3.00
1694	Only You/Cebu	1983	—	—	3.00
1719	Been Lovin' You/Turn Off the Lights	1984	—	—	3.00
1773	Nightshift/I Keep Running	1985	—	—	3.00
1773 [PS]	Nightshift/I Keep Running	1985	—	3.00	6.00
1788	Animal Instinct/Lightin' Up the Sky	1985	—	—	3.00
1802	Janet/I'm in Love	1985	—	—	3.00

MOWEST

Number	Title (A Side/B Side)	Yr	VG	VG+	NM
5009	I'm Looking for Love/At the Zoo	1972	2.00	4.00	8.00
5038	Determination/Don't You Be Worried	1973	2.00	4.00	8.00

POLYDOR

Number	Title (A Side/B Side)	Yr	VG	VG+	NM
871370-7	Ain't Giving Up/Grrip	1989	—	—	3.00
885358-7	Goin' to the Bank/Serious Love	1986	—	—	3.00
885358-7 [PS]	Goin' to the Bank/Serious Love	1986	—	—	3.00
885538-7	Take It from Me/I Wanna Rock You	1987	—	—	3.00
885538-7 [PS]	Take It from Me/I Wanna Rock You	1987	—	—	3.00
885760-7	United in Love/Talk to Me	1987	—	—	3.00
885760-7 [PS]	United in Love/Talk to Me	1987	—	—	3.00
887939-7	Solitaire/Stretchhh	1988	—	—	3.00
887939-7 [PS]	Solitaire/Stretchhh	1988	—	—	3.00

Albums

MOTOWN

Number	Title (A Side/B Side)	Yr	VG	VG+	NM
M5-121V1	Machine Gun	1981	2.50	5.00	10.00
—Reissue					
M5-179V1	Movin' On	1981	2.00	4.00	8.00
M5-222V1	Commodores	1982	2.00	4.00	8.00
M5-240V1	Caught in the Act	1982	2.00	4.00	8.00
M6-798	Machine Gun	1974	3.75	7.50	15.00
M6-820	Caught in the Act	1975	2.50	5.00	10.00
M6-848	Movin' On	1975	2.50	5.00	10.00
M6-867	Hot on the Tracks	1976	2.50	5.00	10.00
M7-884	Commodores	1977	2.50	5.00	10.00
M9-894 [(2)]	Commodores Live!	1977	3.00	6.00	12.00
M7-902	Natural High	1978	2.50	5.00	10.00
M7-912	Commodores' Greatest Hits	1978	2.50	5.00	10.00
M8-926	Midnight Magic	1979	2.50	5.00	10.00
M8-939	Heroes	1980	2.50	5.00	10.00
M8-955	In the Pocket	1981	2.50	5.00	10.00
5257 ML	Hot on the Tracks	1983	2.00	4.00	8.00
5293 ML	Natural High	1983	2.00	4.00	8.00
6028 ML	All the Great Hits	1982	2.50	5.00	10.00
6044 ML2 [(2)]	Anthology	1983	3.00	6.00	12.00
6054 ML	Commodores 13	1983	2.50	5.00	10.00
6124 ML	Nightshift	1985	2.50	5.00	10.00

POLYDOR

Number	Title (A Side/B Side)	Yr	VG	VG+	NM
831194-1	United	1986	2.50	5.00	10.00
835369-1	Rock Solid	1988	2.50	5.00	10.00

COMMODORES, THE

None of the below are the popular 1970s-1980s group, but they aren't all the same group, either.

45s

ATLANTIC

Number	Title (A Side/B Side)	Yr	VG	VG+	NM
2633	Keep On Dancing/Rise Up	1969	2.00	4.00	8.00

BRUNSWICK

Number	Title (A Side/B Side)	Yr	VG	VG+	NM
55126	Laughing with Tears/Who Dat	1959	5.00	10.00	20.00

CHALLENGE

Number	Title (A Side/B Side)	Yr	VG	VG+	NM
1004	Sweet Angel/Not a Day Goes By	1957	5.00	10.00	20.00
1007	Faith/I'll Be There	1957	5.00	10.00	20.00

DOT

Number	Title (A Side/B Side)	Yr	VG	VG+	NM
15372	Uranium/Riding on a Train	1955	6.25	12.50	25.00
15425	Cream Puff/Close to My Heart	1955	6.25	12.50	25.00
15439	Speedoo/Whole Lotta Shakin' Goin' On	1956	6.25	12.50	25.00
15461	Two Loves Have I/Who Said I Said That	1956	6.25	12.50	25.00

COMMON PEOPLE, THE

Albums

CAPITOL

Number	Title (A Side/B Side)	Yr	VG	VG+	NM
ST-266	Of the People/By the People/For the People/From the Common People	1969	25.00	50.00	100.00

COMO, PERRY

45s

RCA

Number	Title (A Side/B Side)	Yr	VG	VG+	NM
9096-7-R [DJ]	I May Never Pass This Way Again (same on both sides)	1989	—	2.50	5.00
—Promotional record for Christmas Seals					
PB-10122	Christmas Dream/Christ Is Born	1976	—	—	3.00
—Reissue; black label, dog near top					
PB-11185	Girl You Made It Happen/Where You're Concerned	1977	—	—	3.00
PB-11434	When I Wanted You/Forever	1978	—	—	3.00
PB-12028	Colors of My Life/Someone Is Waiting	1980	—	—	3.00
PB-12088	Not While I'm Around/When	1980	—	—	3.00
PB-12146	You Are My World/Regrets	1981	—	—	3.00
PB-13069	Goodbye for Now (Theme from "Reds")/Jason	1982	—	—	3.00
PB-13307	I Wish It Could Be Christmas Forever/Toyland	1982	—	2.00	4.00
PB-13453	So It Goes/Fancy Dancer	1983	—	—	3.00
PB-13613	As My Love for You/The Second Time	1983	—	—	3.00
PB-13690	The Best of Times/Son on the Sand	1983	—	—	3.00

RCA VICTOR

Number	Title (A Side/B Side)	Yr	VG	VG+	NM
APBO-0096	Love Don't Care/Walk Right Back	1973	—	2.00	4.00
SP-45-119 [DJ]	(There's No Place Like) Home For The Holidays/I'll Be Home For Christmas	1962	3.00	6.00	12.00
APBO-0225	Beyond Tomorrow/It All Seems to Fall Into Line	1974	—	2.00	4.00
APBO-0274	Weave Me the Sunshine/I Don't Know What He Told You	1974	—	2.00	4.00
E3VW 1339/F7OW 9047 [DJ]	Rudolph the Red-Nosed Reindeer/Rudolph the Red-Nosed Reindeer	1955	3.75	7.50	15.00
—B-side by the Three Suns					
K2NW 6096/7 [DJ]	(Intro) I May Never Pass This Way Again/(Alternate Intro) I May Never Pass This Way Again	1959	3.00	6.00	12.00
—Promotional record for Christmas Seals					
PB-10045	In These Crazy Times/Temptation	1974	—	—	3.00
PB-10122	Christmas Dream/Christ Is Born	1974	—	2.00	4.00
—Gray label					
GB-10174	Catch a Falling Star/Dream Along with Me	1975	—	—	3.00
—Gold Standard Series					
GB-10175	Hot Diggity (Dog Ziggity Boom)/Don't Let the Stars Get In Your Eyes	1975	—	—	3.00
—Gold Standard Series					
GB-10176	Prisoner of Love/Magic Moments	1975	—	—	3.00
—Gold Standard Series					
GB-10177	Round and Round/Wanted	1975	—	—	3.00
—Gold Standard Series					
PB-10257	Wonderful Baby/World of Dreams	1975	—	—	3.00
PB-10402	Love Put a Song in My Heart/Just Out of Reach	1975	—	—	3.00
GB-10471	And I Love You So/Love Looks So Good on You	1975	—	—	3.00
—Gold Standard Series					
PB-10604	Then You Can Tell Me Goodbye/The Grass Keeps Right On Growing	1976	—	—	3.00
47-2728	Because/If You Had All the World and All the Gold	1949	3.75	7.50	15.00
47-2747	What'll I Do?/Love Me or Leave Me	1949	3.75	7.50	15.00
47-2843	When Your Hair Has Turned to Silver/When Day Is Done	1949	3.75	7.50	15.00
47-2844	Carolina Moon/Body and Soul	1949	3.75	7.50	15.00
47-2845	I'm Always Chasing Rainbows/If We Can't Be the Same Old Sweethearts, We'll Just Be the Same Old Friends	1949	3.75	7.50	15.00
—The above three comprise box set WP 187, "A Sentimental Date with Perry"					
47-2886	Prisoner of Love/Temptation	1949	3.75	7.50	15.00
47-2887	Till the End of Time/Because	1949	3.75	7.50	15.00
47-2888	When You Were Sweet Sixteen/Song of Songs	1949	3.75	7.50	15.00
47-2892	Forever and Ever/I Don't See Me in Your Eyes Anymore	1949	3.75	7.50	15.00
47-2896	Bali Ha'i/Some Enchanted Evening	1949	3.75	7.50	15.00
47-2899	"A" You're Adorable/When Is Sometime?	1949	3.75	7.50	15.00
47-2919	Every Time I Meet You/Two Little, New Little, Blue Little Eyes	1949	3.75	7.50	15.00
47-2931	Let's Take an Old-Fashioned Walk/Just One Way to Say I Love You	1949	3.75	7.50	15.00
47-2969	That Christmas Feeling/Winter Wonderland	1949	5.00	10.00	20.00
47-2970	I'll Be Home for Christmas/Santa Claus Is Coming to Town	1949	5.00	10.00	20.00
47-2971	Silent Night/White Christmas	1949	5.00	10.00	20.00
47-2972	Jingle Bells/O Come All Ye Faithful	1949	5.00	10.00	20.00
47-2997	Give Me Your Hand/I Wish I Had a Record	1949	3.75	7.50	15.00
47-3036	A Dreamer's Holiday/The Meadows of Heaven	1949	3.75	7.50	15.00
47-3211	Please Believe Me/Did Anyone Ever Tell You, Mrs. Murphy	1949	3.75	7.50	15.00
47-3226	Easter Parade/Song of Songs	1949	3.75	7.50	15.00
47-3229	With a Song in My Heart/Blue Room	1949	3.75	7.50	15.00
47-3267	Far Away Places/Missouri Waltz	1949	3.75	7.50	15.00
47-3763	If You Were Only Mine/Let's Go to the Church	1950	3.00	6.00	12.00
47-3850	Bless This House/The Rosary	1950	3.00	6.00	12.00
47-3851	Mother Dear O Pray For Me/Hoy God, We Praise Thy Name	1950	3.00	6.00	12.00
47-3852	Rock of Ages/Prayer of Thanksgiving	1950	3.00	6.00	12.00
47-3905	Patricia/Watchin' the Trains Go By	1950	3.00	6.00	12.00
47-3922	The Best Thing for You/Marrying for Love	1950	3.00	6.00	12.00
47-3930	A Bushel and a Peck/She's a Lady	1950	3.00	6.00	12.00
—With Betty Hutton					
47-3931	Marchita/So Long Sally	1950	3.00	6.00	12.00
47-3933	The Christmas Symphony/There Is No Christmas Like a Home Christmas	1950	3.75	7.50	15.00
47-3997	If/Zing, Zing, Zoom, Zoom	1950	3.00	6.00	12.00
47-4033	Without a Song/More Than You Know	1951	3.00	6.00	12.00
47-4034	It's Only a Paper Moon/Me and My Shadow	1951	3.00	6.00	12.00

Number	Title (A Side/B Side)	Yr	VG	VG+	NM
47-4035	That Old Gang of Mine/I Found a Million Dollar Baby	1951	3.00	6.00	12.00
47-4081	Tumbling Tumbleweeds/You Don't Know What Lonesome Is	1951	3.00	6.00	12.00
—With the Sons of the Pioneers					
47-4112	Hello Young Lovers/We Kissed in a Shadow	1951	3.00	6.00	12.00
47-4158	There's No Boat Like a Rowboat/There's a Big Blue Cloud (Next to Heaven)	1951	3.00	6.00	12.00
47-4203	Surprising/Cara Cara Bella Bella	1951	3.00	6.00	12.00
47-4314	It's Beginning to Look Like Christmas/There Is No Christmas Like a Home Christmas	1951	3.75	7.50	15.00
47-4445	Garden in the Rain/Oh, How I Miss You Tonight	1952	3.00	6.00	12.00
47-4453	Please Mr. Sun/Tulips and Heather	1952	3.00	6.00	12.00
47-4527	You'll Never Walk Alone/Over the Rainbow	1952	3.00	6.00	12.00
47-4528	Black Moonlight/I Concentrate on You	1952	3.00	6.00	12.00
47-4529	My Heart Stood Still/If There's Someone	1952	3.00	6.00	12.00
47-4530	Summertime/While We're Young	1952	3.00	6.00	12.00
47-4631	One Little Candle/It's Easter Time	1952	3.00	6.00	12.00
47-4687	Why Did You Leave Me/Lonesome, That's All	1952	3.00	6.00	12.00
47-4707	Childhood Is a Meadow/One Little Candle	1952	3.00	6.00	12.00
47-4744	Maybe/Watermelon Weather	1952	3.00	6.00	12.00
—With Eddie Fisher					
47-4877	My Love and Devotion/Sweethearts' Holiday	1952	3.00	6.00	12.00
47-5064	Don't Let the Stars Get In Your Eyes/Lies	1952	3.00	6.00	12.00
47-5152	Wild Horses/I Confess	1953	3.00	6.00	12.00
47-5277	Say You're Mine Again/My One and Only Heart	1953	3.00	6.00	12.00
47-5317	No Other Love/Keep It Gay	1953	3.00	6.00	12.00
47-5317 [PS]	No Other Love/Keep It Gay	1953	5.00	10.00	20.00
47-5447	You Alone (Solo Tu)/Pa-Paya Mama	1953	3.00	6.00	12.00
47-5571	I Believe/Onward Christian Soldiers	1953	3.00	6.00	12.00
47-5572	Act of Contrition/Good Night Sweet Jesus	1953	3.00	6.00	12.00
47-5573	Abide with Me/Nearer, My God, To Thee	1953	3.00	6.00	12.00
47-5574	Eli, Eli/Kol Niore	1953	3.00	6.00	12.00
47-5647	Wanted/Look Out the Window	1954	3.00	6.00	12.00
47-5749	Hit and Run Affair/There Never Was a Night So Beautiful	1954	3.00	6.00	12.00
47-5857	Papa Loves Mambo/The Things I Didn't Do	1954	3.00	6.00	12.00
47-5950	(There's No Place Like) Home for the Holidays/Silk Stockings	1954	3.00	6.00	12.00
47-5994	Ko Ko Mo (I Love You So)/You'll Always Be My Lifetime Sweetheart	1955	2.50	5.00	10.00
47-6059	Door of Dreams/Nobody	1955	2.50	5.00	10.00
47-6137	Chee Chee O-Chee (Sang the Little Bird)/Two Lost Souls	1955	2.50	5.00	10.00
—With Jaye P. Morgan					
47-6192	Tina Marie/Fooled	1955	2.50	5.00	10.00
47-6294	All at Once You Love Her/The Rose Tattoo	1955	2.50	5.00	10.00
47-6321	Home for the Holidays/God Rest Ye Merry Gentlemen	1955	3.00	6.00	12.00
47-6427	Hot Diggity (Dog Ziggity Boom)/Juke Box Baby	1956	2.50	5.00	10.00
47-6554	More/Glendora	1956	2.50	5.00	10.00
47-6590	Somebody Up There Likes Me/Dream Along with Me	1956	2.50	5.00	10.00
47-6590 [PS]	Somebody Up There Likes Me/Dream Along with Me	1956	7.50	15.00	30.00
47-6670	Moonlight Love/Chincherinchee	1956	2.50	5.00	10.00
47-6815	Round and Round/Mi Casa, Su Casa (My House Is Your House)	1957	2.50	5.00	10.00
47-6904	The Girl with the Golden Braids/My Little Baby	1957	2.50	5.00	10.00
47-6991	Dancin'/Marchin' Along to the Blues	1957	2.50	5.00	10.00
47-7050	Just Born (To Be Your Baby)/Ivy Rose	1957	2.50	5.00	10.00
47-7128	Catch a Falling Star/Magic Moments	1957	3.00	6.00	12.00
47-7202	Kewpie Doll/Dance Only with Me	1958	2.50	5.00	10.00
47-7274	Moon Talk/Beats There a Heart So True	1958	2.50	5.00	10.00
47-7353	Love Makes the World Go 'Round/Mandolins in the Moonlight	1958	2.50	5.00	10.00
47-7464	Tomboy/Kiss Me and Kiss Me and Kiss Me	1959	2.50	5.00	10.00
47-7541	I Know/You Are in Love	1959	2.50	5.00	10.00
47-7541 [PS]	I Know/You Are in Love	1959	6.25	12.50	25.00
47-7628	I May Never Pass This Way Again/A Still Small Voice	1959	2.50	5.00	10.00
47-7650	Ave Maria/The Lord's Prayer	1959	2.50	5.00	10.00
47-7670	Delaware/I Know What God Is	1960	2.00	4.00	8.00
47-7812	Make Someone Happy/Gone Is My Love	1960	2.00	4.00	8.00
47-7962	You're Following Me/Especially for the Young	1961	2.00	4.00	8.00
47-8004	Caterina/The Island of Forgotten Lovers	1962	2.00	4.00	8.00
47-8004 [PS]	Caterina/The Island of Forgotten Lovers	1962	5.00	10.00	20.00
47-8186	(I Love You) Don't You Forget It/One More Mountain	1963	2.00	4.00	8.00
47-8186 [PS]	(I Love You) Don't You Forget It/One More Mountain	1963	5.00	10.00	20.00
47-8533	Dream On Little Dreamer/My Own Peculiar Way	1965	2.00	4.00	8.00
47-8533 [PS]	Dream On Little Dreamer/My Own Peculiar Way	1965	5.00	10.00	20.00
47-8636	Oowee, Oowee/Summer Wind	1965	2.00	4.00	8.00
47-8722	Meet Me at the Altar/Bye, Bye, Little Girl	1965	2.00	4.00	8.00
47-8823	Stay with Me/Coo Coo Roo Coo Coo Paloma	1966	2.00	4.00	8.00
47-8945	Forget Domani/One Day Is Like Another	1966	2.00	4.00	8.00
47-9165	Stop! And Think It Over/How Beautiful the World Can Be	1967	—	3.00	6.00
47-9262	I Looked Back/A World of Love (That I Found)	1967	—	3.00	6.00
47-9356	What Love Is Made Of/You Made It That Way	1967	—	3.00	6.00
47-9367	Christmas Bells/Love Is a Christmas Rose	1967	2.00	4.00	8.00
47-9367 [PS]	Christmas Bells/Love Is A Christmas Rose	1967	2.50	5.00	10.00
47-9448	The Father of Girls/Somebody Makes It So	1968	—	2.50	5.00
47-9533	Happy Man/Another Go-Round	1968	—	2.50	5.00
47-9683	There Is No Christmas Like a Home Christmas/Christmas Eve	1968	—	3.00	6.00
47-9722	Seattle/Sunshine Wine	1969	—	2.50	5.00
52-0071	Ave Maria/The Lord's Prayer	1949	6.25	12.50	25.00
—Blue vinyl original					
52-0071	Ave Maria/The Lord's Prayer	1949	3.00	6.00	12.00
—Black vinyl reissue					
74-0193	Happiness Comes, Happiness Goes/That's All This Old World Needs	1969	—	2.00	4.00
74-0356	Don't Leave Me/Love Is Spreading All Over the World	1970	—	2.00	4.00
74-0387	It's Impossible/Long Life, Lots of Happiness	1970	—	2.50	5.00
74-0436	Don't Leave Me/Love Is Spreading All Over the World	1971	—	2.00	4.00
74-0444	El Condor Pasa/I Think of You	1971	—	2.00	4.00
74-0518	My Days of Loving You/Yesterday I Heard the Rain	1971	—	2.00	4.00
74-0906	And I Love Her So/Love Looks So Good on You	1973	—	2.00	4.00
447-0110	Ave Maria/The Lord's Prayer	1955	3.00	6.00	12.00
447-0810	Silent Night/O Come, All Ye Faithful	196?	—	2.50	5.00
447-0811	That Christmas Feeling/I'll Be Home For Christmas	196?	—	2.50	5.00
447-0812	Home for the Holidays/God Rest Ye Merry Gentlemen	196?	—	2.50	5.00

USAF

Number	Title (A Side/B Side)	Yr	VG	VG+	NM
85/86 [DJ]	"Special Christmas Show" Home For The Holidays/Merry Merry Christmas To You	195?	3.75	7.50	15.00
—B-side by Art Mooney					

7-Inch Extended Plays

RCA CAMDEN

Number	Title (A Side/B Side)	Yr	VG	VG+	NM
CAE-410	Without a Song/More Than You Know//Me and My Shadow/Dream Along with Me	195?	2.00	4.00	8.00
CAE-410 [PS]	Dream Along with Me	195?	2.00	4.00	8.00

RCA VICTOR

Number	Title (A Side/B Side)	Yr	VG	VG+	NM
EYA-19	The Story of the First Christmas//Santa Claus Is Coming to Town/Jingle Bells	195?	3.75	7.50	15.00
—"Little Nipper" Children's Series issue					
SPD-27 [PS]	Perry Como	195?	3.75	7.50	15.00
—Box for 10-EP set plus booklet					
SPD-28	South of the Border/Because/Bless This House //Breezin' Along with the Breeze/Lies/You'll Never Walk Alone	1957	5.00	10.00	20.00
SPD-28 [PS]	Kleenex Presents Perry Como Highlighter	1957	5.00	10.00	20.00
547-0033	When Day Is Done/Carolina Moon//What'll I Do/If We Can't Be the Same Old Sweethearts We'll Just Be the Same Old Friends	1952	2.50	5.00	10.00
—Part of 2-EP set EPB 3035					
547-0034	I'm Always Chasing Rainbows/Love Me or Leave Me//Body and Soul/When Your Hair Has Turned to Silver (I Will Love You Just the Same)	1952	2.50	5.00	10.00
—Part of 2-EP set EPB 3035					
SP-45-55	Hot Diggity/Patricia/Lazy Bones//Dream Along with Me/Land of Dreams/Bewitched	1958	5.00	10.00	20.00
SP-45-55 [PS]	Kleenex Tissues Presents RCA Victor's '59 Highlighter: Perry Como and His Friends	1958	5.00	10.00	20.00
547-0059	Prisoner of Love/Because//When You Were Sweet Sixteen/Far Away Places	1952	2.50	5.00	10.00
—Part of 2-EP set EPB 3044					
EPA-293	(contents unknown)	195?	3.00	6.00	12.00
EPA-293 [PS]	Perry Como Sings His Favorite Songs of Worship	195?	3.00	6.00	12.00
EPA-409	(contents unknown)	195?	3.00	6.00	12.00
EPA-409 [PS]	Perry Como Sings the Hits from Broadway Shows	195?	3.00	6.00	12.00
EPA-410	(contents unknown)	195?	3.00	6.00	12.00
EPA-410 [PS]	Songs of Faith	195?	3.00	6.00	12.00
EPA-451	(contents unknown)	195?	3.00	6.00	12.00
EPA-451 [PS]	Perry Como Sings the Hits from Broadway Shows	195?	3.00	6.00	12.00
547-0454	(contents unknown)	1954	2.50	5.00	10.00
—Record 1 of 2-EP set EPB 3224					
547-0455	Temptation/Prisoner of Love//When You Were Sweet Sixteen/Because	1954	2.50	5.00	10.00
—Record 2 of 2-EP set EPB 3224					
EPA-496	The Night Before Christmas/God Rest Ye Merry, Gentlemen//The 12 Days of Christmas/C-H-R-I-S-T-M-A-S	195?	3.00	6.00	12.00
EPA-496 [PS]	Around The Christmas Tree	195?	3.00	6.00	12.00
EPA-497	(contents unknown)	195?	3.00	6.00	12.00
EPA-497 [PS]	Around the Christmas Tree	195?	3.00	6.00	12.00
EPA-563	(contents unknown)	1954	3.00	6.00	12.00
EPA-563 [PS]	Wanted	1954	3.00	6.00	12.00
EPA-642	For Me and My Gal/My Funny Valentine//It Happened in Monterey/It's the Talk of the Town	1955	3.00	6.00	12.00
EPA-642 [PS]	P.C.	1955	3.00	6.00	12.00
EPA-728	(contents unknown)	1955	3.00	6.00	12.00
EPA-728 [PS]	Perry Como Sings Hits from Broadway Shows	1955	3.00	6.00	12.00
EPA-738	(contents unknown)	1955	3.00	6.00	12.00
EPA-738 [PS]	Relaxing with Perry Como	1955	3.00	6.00	12.00
EPA-739	(contents unknown)	1955	3.00	6.00	12.00
EPA-739 [PS]	A Sentimental Date with Perry Como	1955	3.00	6.00	12.00
EPA-903	(contents unknown)	1956	3.00	6.00	12.00
EPA-903 [PS]	Perry Como Sings	1956	3.00	6.00	12.00
EPA-920	*Santa Claus Is Comin' to Town/Frosty the Snow Man/Winter Wonderland/Rudolph, the Red-Nosed Reindeer/Jingle Bells	1956	3.00	6.00	12.00
EPA-920 [PS]	Perry Como Sings Merry Christmas Music	1956	3.00	6.00	12.00
547-1049	Joy to the World/White Christmas//God Rest Ye Merry, Gentlemen/The Christmas Song	1955	2.50	5.00	10.00
—Part of 2-EP set EPB 1243					
EPB 1243 [PS]	Merry Christmas Music	1955	5.00	10.00	20.00
—Cover for 2-EP set					
EPA 1-1463	Swinging Down the Lane/South of the Border//Honey, Honey (Bless Your Heart)/Angry	1957	2.50	5.00	10.00
EPA 1-1463 [PS]	We Get Letters, Vol. 1	1957	2.50	5.00	10.00
EPB 3035 [PS]	A Sentimental Date with Perry	1952	2.50	5.00	10.00
—Double-pocket cover for 547-0033 and 547-0034					
EPB 3044 [PS]	Supper Club Favorites	1952	2.50	5.00	10.00
—Two-pocket jacket for two-EP set					
EPB 3224 [PS]	Como's Golden Records	1954	2.50	5.00	10.00
—Double-pocket cover for 547-0454 and 547-0455					
EPA-4285 [M]	Accentuate the Positive/Red Sails in the Sunset //Birth of the Blues/It Had to Be You	1958	2.50	5.00	10.00
EPA-4285 [PS]	(title unknown)	1958	2.50	5.00	10.00
ESP-4285 [PS]	(title unknown)	1958	5.00	10.00	20.00
ESP-4285 [S]	Accentuate the Positive/Red Sails in the Sunset //Birth of the Blues/It Had to Be You	1958	5.00	10.00	20.00

Number	Title (A Side/B Side)	Yr	VG	VG+	NM
EPA-4326	A Still Small Voice/I May Never Pass This Way Again//He's Got the Whole World in His Hands/When You Come to the End of the Day	1958	2.50	5.00	10.00
EPA-4326 [PS]	(title unknown)	1958	2.50	5.00	10.00
EPA-5012	*Don't Let the Stars Get In Your Eyes/Wanted/Papa Loves Mambo/Hot Diggity (Dog Ziggity Boom)	1958	2.50	5.00	10.00
EPA-5012 [PS]	Como's Golden Records	1958	2.50	5.00	10.00
EPA-5029	(contents unknown)	1958	2.50	5.00	10.00
EPA-5029 [PS]	Como's Golden Records, Volume 2	1958	2.50	5.00	10.00
EPA-5030	*Temptation/Mi Casa, Su Casa/Prisoner of Love/Because	1958	2.50	5.00	10.00
EPA-5030 [PS]	Como's Golden Records, Volume 3	1958	2.50	5.00	10.00
EPA-5109	Juke Box Baby/Catch a Falling Star//Tina Marie/Magic Moments	1959	2.50	5.00	10.00
EPA-5109 [PS]	(title unknown)	1959	2.50	5.00	10.00
599-9156	For Me and My Gal/As Time Goes By//I Believe/When Day Is Done	1957	2.00	4.00	8.00
—Side 1 and 20 of 10-EP set SPD-27					
599-9157	Far Away Places/Till the End of Time//Don't Let the Stars Get In Your Eyes/Bali Ha'l	1957	2.00	4.00	8.00
—Side 2 and 19 of 10-EP set SPD 27					
599-9158	It's a Good Day/My Funny Valentine//You'll Never Walk Alone/Hello Young Lovers	1957	2.00	4.00	8.00
—Side 3 and 18 of 10-EP set SPD 27					
599-9159	If There Is Someone Lovelier Than You/Over the Rainbow//Body and Soul/Lies	1957	2.00	4.00	8.00
—Side 4 and 17 of 10-EP set SPD 27					
599-9160	Temptation/Black Moonlight//All at Once You Love Her/Look Out the Window	1957	2.00	4.00	8.00
—Side 5 and 16 of 10-EP set SPD 27					
599-9161	If/When You Were Sweet Sixteen//I've Got the World on a String/You Do Something To Me	1957	2.00	4.00	8.00
—Side 6 and 15 of 10-EP set SPD 27					
599-9162	Prisoner of Love/Carolina Moon//One for My Baby/In the Still of the Night	1957	2.00	4.00	8.00
—Side 7 and 14 of 10-EP set SPD 27					
599-9163	What'll I Do/Blue Moon//Hot Diggity (Dog Ziggity Boom)/It Happened in Monterey	1957	2.00	4.00	8.00
—Side 8 and 13 of 10-EP set SPD 27					
599-9164	With a Song in My Heart/No Other Love//Breezin' Along with the Breeze/It's the Talk of the Town	1957	2.00	4.00	8.00
—Side 9 and 12 of 10-EP set SPD 27					
599-9165	Wanted/Love Me or Leave Me//Pa-Paya Mama/I Gotta Right to Sing the Blues	1957	2.00	4.00	8.00
—Side 10 and 11 of 10-EP set SPD 27					

Albums

PAIR

Number	Title	Yr	VG	VG+	NM
PDL2-1001 [(2)]	Easy Listening	1986	3.00	6.00	12.00
PDL2-1038 [(2)]	Love Moods	1986	3.00	6.00	12.00
PDL2-1112 [(2)]	Blue Skies	1986	3.00	6.00	12.00

PICKWICK

Number	Title	Yr	VG	VG+	NM
CAS-660 [R]	Perry Como Sings Merry Christmas Music	1977	2.00	4.00	8.00
—Reissue of RCA Camden CAS-660 with another new cover					

RCA

Number	Title	Yr	VG	VG+	NM
ANL1-1929	The Perry Como Christmas Album	1976	2.00	4.00	8.00
—Budget-line reissue of LSP-4016					
6368-1-R	Perry Como Today	1988	2.50	5.00	10.00

RCA CAMDEN

Number	Title	Yr	VG	VG+	NM
CAL-403 [M]	Dream Along with Me	1957	5.00	10.00	20.00
CAS-403(e) [R]	Dream Along with Me	1962	2.50	5.00	10.00
CAL-440 [M]	Perry Como Sings Just for You	1958	3.75	7.50	15.00
CAS-440(e) [R]	Perry Como Sings Just for You	1962	2.50	5.00	10.00
CAL-511 [M]	Como's Wednesday Night Music Hall	1959	5.00	10.00	20.00
CAL-582 [M]	Dreamer's Holiday	1960	3.75	7.50	15.00
CAL-660 [M]	Perry Como Sings Merry Christmas Music	1961	3.00	6.00	12.00
—Reissue of RCA Victor LPM-1243 with new cover					
CAS-660(e) [R]	Perry Como Sings Merry Christmas Music	1961	2.50	5.00	10.00
—Same as above, but in rechanneled stereo					
CAL-694 [M]	Make Someone Happy	1962	3.00	6.00	12.00
CAL-742 [M]	An Evening with Perry Como	196?	3.75	7.50	15.00
CAL-805 [M]	Love Makes the World Go 'Round	1964	3.00	6.00	12.00
CAS-805 [S]	Love Makes the World Go 'Round	1964	2.50	5.00	10.00
CAL-858 [M]	Somebody Loves Me	1965	3.00	6.00	12.00
CAS-858 [S]	Somebody Loves Me	1965	2.50	5.00	10.00
CAL-941 [M]	No Other Love	1966	3.00	6.00	12.00
CAS-941 [S]	No Other Love	1966	2.50	5.00	10.00
CAL-2122 [M]	Hello Young Lovers	1967	3.75	7.50	15.00
CAS-2122 [R]	Hello Young Lovers	1967	2.50	5.00	10.00
CAL-2201 [M]	You Are Never Far Away	1968	3.75	7.50	15.00
CAS-2201 [S]	You Are Never Far Away	1968	2.50	5.00	10.00
CAS-2299	The Lord's Prayer	1968	2.50	5.00	10.00
CAS-2482	Door of Dreams	1971	2.50	5.00	10.00
CAS-2547	The Shadow of Your Smile	1972	2.50	5.00	10.00
CAS-2609	Dream On Little Dreamer	1972	2.50	5.00	10.00
CXS-9002 [(2)]	Easy Listening	1972	3.00	6.00	12.00

RCA CUSTOM EDITION

Number	Title	Yr	VG	VG+	NM
DRL1-0010	Seattle	1973	3.00	6.00	12.00

RCA SPECIAL PRODUCTS

Number	Title	Yr	VG	VG+	NM
DPL1-0193	By Special Request	1974	3.00	6.00	12.00
—Sold only at Sylvania dealers					

RCA VICTOR

Number	Title	Yr	VG	VG+	NM
LPM-51 [10]	Merry Christmas	1951	10.00	20.00	40.00
APD1-0100 [Q]	And I Love You So	1974	3.75	7.50	15.00
APL1-0100	And I Love You So	1973	2.50	5.00	10.00
ACL1-0444	The Sweetest Sounds	1974	2.50	5.00	10.00
APD1-0585 [Q]	Perry	1974	3.75	7.50	15.00
CPL1-0585	Perry	1974	2.50	5.00	10.00
APD1-0863 [Q]	Just Out of Reach	1975	3.75	7.50	15.00
APL1-0863	Just Out of Reach	1975	2.50	5.00	10.00
ANL1-0972	Pure Gold	1975	2.50	5.00	10.00
LSPX-1001	Perry Como at the International Hotel, Las Vegas	1970	3.75	7.50	15.00
LOP-1004 [M]	Saturday Night with Mr. C.	1958	6.25	12.50	25.00
LOP-1007 [M]	Como's Golden Records	1958	6.25	12.50	25.00
LPM-1085 [M]	So Smooth	1955	7.50	15.00	30.00
LPM-1172 [M]	I Believe	1956	7.50	15.00	30.00
LSP-1172(e) [R]	I Believe	1962	3.00	6.00	12.00
LPM-1176 [M]	Relaxing with Perry Como	1956	7.50	15.00	30.00
LPM-1177 [M]	A Sentimental Date with Perry Como	1956	7.50	15.00	30.00
LPM-1191 [M]	Hits from Broadway Shows	1956	7.50	15.00	30.00
LPM-1243 [M]	Perry Como Sings Merry Christmas Music	1956	7.50	15.00	30.00
LPM-1463 [M]	We Get Letters	1957	6.25	12.50	25.00
CPL1-1752	A Legendary Performer	1976	2.50	5.00	10.00
LPM-1885 [M]	When You Come to the End of the Day	1958	5.00	10.00	20.00
LSP-1885 [S]	When You Come to the End of the Day	1958	7.50	15.00	30.00
LPM-1971 [M]	Saturday Night with Mr. C.	1959	5.00	10.00	20.00
—Reissue of LOP-1004					
LSP-1971(e) [R]	Saturday Night with Mr. C.	1962	3.00	6.00	12.00
AFL1-1981	Como's Golden Records	1977	2.50	5.00	10.00
—Reissue with new prefix					
LPM-1981 [M]	Como's Golden Records	1959	5.00	10.00	20.00
—Reissue of LOP-1007					
LSP-1981(e) [R]	Como's Golden Records	1962	3.00	6.00	12.00
LPM-2010 [M]	Como Swings	1959	5.00	10.00	20.00
LSP-2010 [S]	Como Swings	1959	6.25	12.50	25.00
LPM-2066 [M]	Season's Greetings from Perry Como	1959	6.25	12.50	25.00
—Original front covers have "LPM-2066" in lower left corner					
LPM-2066 [M]	Season's Greetings from Perry Como	1959	5.00	10.00	20.00
—Later front covers have "LPM-2066" in upper right, inside RCA Victor box					
LSP-2066 [S]	Season's Greetings from Perry Como	1959	6.25	12.50	25.00
LPM-2343 [M]	For the Young at Heart	1960	3.75	7.50	15.00
LSP-2343 [S]	For the Young at Heart	1960	5.00	10.00	20.00
LPM-2390 [M]	Sing to Me, Mr. C.	1961	3.75	7.50	15.00
LSP-2390 [S]	Sing to Me, Mr. C.	1961	5.00	10.00	20.00
ANL1-2485	Especially for You	1977	2.50	5.00	10.00
LPM-2567 [M]	By Request	1962	3.75	7.50	15.00
LSP-2567 [S]	By Request	1962	5.00	10.00	20.00
LPM-2630 [M]	The Best of Irving Berlin's Songs from "Mr. President"	1962	3.75	7.50	15.00
LSP-2630 [S]	The Best of Irving Berlin's Songs from "Mr. President"	1962	5.00	10.00	20.00
AFL1-2641	Where You're Concerned	1978	2.50	5.00	10.00
LPM-2708 [M]	The Songs I Love	1963	3.75	7.50	15.00
LSP-2708 [S]	The Songs I Love	1963	5.00	10.00	20.00
ANL1-2969(e)	Over the Rainbow	1976	2.50	5.00	10.00
LPM-3013 [10]	TV Favorites	1952	10.00	20.00	40.00
LPM-3035 [10]	A Sentimental Date with Perry Como	1952	10.00	20.00	40.00
LPM-3044 [10]	Supper Club Favorites	1952	10.00	20.00	40.00
LPM-3124 [10]	Hits from Broadway Shows	1953	10.00	20.00	40.00
LPM-3133 [10]	Around the Christmas Tree	1953	10.00	20.00	40.00
LPM-3188 [10]	I Believe	1954	10.00	20.00	40.00
LPM-3224 [10]	Como's Golden Records	1954	10.00	20.00	40.00
LPM-3396 [M]	The Scene Changes	1965	3.00	6.00	12.00
LSP-3396 [S]	The Scene Changes	1965	3.75	7.50	15.00
LPM-3552 [M]	Lightly Latin	1966	3.00	6.00	12.00
LSP-3552 [S]	Lightly Latin	1966	3.75	7.50	15.00
LPM-3608 [M]	Perry Como in Italy	1966	3.00	6.00	12.00
LSP-3608 [S]	Perry Como in Italy	1966	3.75	7.50	15.00
AFL1-3629	Perry Como	1980	2.50	5.00	10.00
AYL1-3672	And I Love You So	1980	2.00	4.00	8.00
—Reissue					
AYL1-3802	Como's Golden Records	1981	2.00	4.00	8.00
—Reissue					
AYL1-3803	Where You're Concerned	1981	2.00	4.00	8.00
—Reissue					
AYL1-3804	It's Impossible	1981	2.00	4.00	8.00
—Reissue					
LSP-4016	The Perry Como Christmas Album	1968	3.00	6.00	12.00
LSP-4052	Look to Your Heart	1968	3.75	7.50	15.00
LSP-4183	Seattle	1969	3.75	7.50	15.00
AFL1-4272	So It Goes	1983	2.50	5.00	10.00
AFL1-4473	It's Impossible	1977	2.50	5.00	10.00
—Reissue with new prefix					
LSP-4473	It's Impossible	1970	3.75	7.50	15.00
AYL1-4526	I Wish It Could Be Christmas Forever	1982	2.50	5.00	10.00
AFL1-4539	I Think of You	1977	2.50	5.00	10.00
—Reissue with new prefix					
LSP-4539	I Think of You	1971	3.75	7.50	15.00
VPS-6026 [(2)]	This Is Perry Como	1970	3.75	7.50	15.00
VPS-6067 [(2)]	This Is Perry Como, Volume 2	1972	3.75	7.50	15.00

READER'S DIGEST

Number	Title	Yr	VG	VG+	NM
RDA-144/D	Christmas with Perry Como	1983	2.50	5.00	10.00

COMO, PERRY, AND THE FONTANE SISTERS

Also see each artist's individual listings.

45s

RCA VICTOR

Number	Title (A Side/B Side)	Yr	VG	VG+	NM
47-3082	I Wanna Go Home (With You)/Hush Little Darlin'	1949	3.75	7.50	15.00
47-3113	Bibbidi-Bobbidi-Boo/A Dream Is a Wish Your Heart Makes	1949	3.75	7.50	15.00
47-3747	Hoop-Dee-Doo/On the Outgoing Tide	1950	3.00	6.00	12.00
47-3846	I Cross My Fingers/If You Were My Girl	1950	3.00	6.00	12.00
47-3945	You're Just in Love/It's a Lovely Day Today	1950	3.00	6.00	12.00
47-4269	Rollin' Stone/With All My Heart and Soul	1951	3.00	6.00	12.00
47-4344	Here's to My Lady/If Wishes Were Kisses	1951	3.00	6.00	12.00
47-4542	Noodlin' Rag/Play Me a Hurtin' Tune	1952	3.00	6.00	12.00
47-4959	To Know You (Is to Love You)/My Lady Loves to Dance	1952	3.00	6.00	12.00
47-5524	Silver Bells/Kissing Bridge	1953	3.00	6.00	12.00

COMPANIONS, THE

More than one group.

45s

AMY

Number	Title (A Side/B Side)	Yr	VG	VG+	NM
852	No Fool Am I/How Could You	1962	25.00	50.00	100.00

ARLEN

Number	Title (A Side/B Side)	Yr	VG	VG+	NM
722	These Foolish Things/It's Too Late	1963	20.00	40.00	80.00

BROOK'S

Number	Title (A Side/B Side)	Yr	VG	VG+	NM
100	Why, Oh Why Baby/I Didn't Know (You Got Married)	1959	15.00	30.00	60.00

Number	Title (A Side/B Side)	Yr	VG	VG+	NM
COLUMBIA					
42279	I'll Always Love You/A Little Bit of Blue	1962	7.50	15.00	30.00
DOVE					
240	Falling/Oh, What a Feeling!	1958	30.00	60.00	120.00
FEDERAL					
12397	Why, Oh Why Baby/I Didn't Know (You Got Married)	1960	7.50	15.00	30.00
GENERAL AMERICAN					
711	Be Yourself/Help a Lonely Guy	1962	5.00	10.00	20.00
GINA					
722	These Foolish Things/It's Too Late	1963	12.50	25.00	50.00

COMPETITORS, THE

45s

Number	Title (A Side/B Side)	Yr	VG	VG+	NM
DOT					
16560	Power Shift/Little Stick Nomad	1963	10.00	20.00	40.00

Albums

Number	Title (A Side/B Side)	Yr	VG	VG+	NM
DOT					
DLP-3542 [M]	Hits of the Street and Strip	1963	37.50	75.00	150.00
DLP-25542 [S]	Hits of the Street and Strip	1963	50.00	100.00	200.00

COMPLIMENTS, THE

45s

Number	Title (A Side/B Side)	Yr	VG	VG+	NM
CONGRESS					
243	Shake It Up, Shake It Down/You Are My Sunshine	1965	12.50	25.00	50.00
252	The Time of Her Life/Everybody Loves a Lover	1965	12.50	25.00	50.00
MIDAS					
304	Borrow 'Til Morning/Beware, Beware	1968	7.50	15.00	30.00

COMPOSERS, THE

45s

Number	Title (A Side/B Side)	Yr	VG	VG+	NM
AMPEN					
221	Woe Is Me/Elephant Drag	196?	75.00	150.00	300.00
ERA					
3118	I Had a Dream/You and Yours	1963	5.00	10.00	20.00

COMSTOCK, BOBBY

45s

Number	Title (A Side/B Side)	Yr	VG	VG+	NM
ASCOT					
2164	Right Hand Man/Always	1964	3.75	7.50	15.00
2175	I'm a Man/I'll Make You Glad	1965	3.00	6.00	12.00
2193	This Magic Moment/Shotgun Sally	1965	3.00	6.00	12.00
2216	Can't Judge a Book/Out of Sight	1966	3.00	6.00	12.00
ATLANTIC					
2051	Jambalaya/Let's Talk It Over	1960	5.00	10.00	20.00
BLAZE					
349	Tennessee Waltz/Sweet Talk	1959	6.25	12.50	25.00
FESTIVAL					
25000	Garden of Eden/Piece of Paper	1961	5.00	10.00	20.00
JUBILEE					
5392	Bony Maronie/Do That Little Thing	1960	5.00	10.00	20.00
5396	Jezebel/Your Big Brown Eyes	1961	5.00	10.00	20.00
LAWN					
202	Let's Stomp/I Want to Do It	1963	3.75	7.50	15.00
210	Susie Baby/Take a Walk	1963	3.75	7.50	15.00
217	The Chicken Back/Sunny	1963	3.75	7.50	15.00
219	Your Boyfriend's Back/This Little Love of Mine	1963	5.00	10.00	20.00
224	I Can't Help Myself/Run My Heart	1963	3.75	7.50	15.00
229	The Beatle Bounce/Since You Been Gone	1964	5.00	10.00	20.00
232	Can It Be True/Ain't That Just Like Me	1964	3.75	7.50	15.00
255	I Wanna Do It/This Little Love of Mine	1965	3.00	6.00	12.00
MOHAWK					
124	The Wayward Wind/Everyday Blues	1960	5.00	10.00	20.00
TRIUMPH					
602	Jealous Fool/Zig Zag	1959	6.25	12.50	25.00

Albums

Number	Title (A Side/B Side)	Yr	VG	VG+	NM
ASCOT					
AM-13026 [M]	Out of Sight	1966	6.25	12.50	25.00
AS-16026 [S]	Out of Sight	1966	7.50	15.00	30.00

CONCORDS, THE (1)

45s

Number	Title (A Side/B Side)	Yr	VG	VG+	NM
BOOM					
60021	Down the Aisle of Love/I Feel Love Comin'	1966	10.00	20.00	40.00
EPIC					
9697	Should I Cry/It's Our Wedding Day	1964	15.00	30.00	60.00
GRAMERCY					
304	Cross My Heart/Our Last Goodbye	1961	12.50	25.00	50.00
—No candy canes on label					
304	Cross My Heart/Our Last Goodbye	1961	50.00	100.00	200.00
—With candy canes on label					
305	My Dreams/Scarlet Ribbons	1961	10.00	20.00	40.00
HERALD					
576	Marlene/Our Love Wasn't Meant to Be	1962	6.25	12.50	25.00
578	Cold and Frosty Morning/Don't Go Now	1963	7.50	15.00	30.00
POLYDOR					
14036	Down the Aisle of Love/I Feel a Love Comin' On	1970	3.00	6.00	12.00
RCA VICTOR					
47-7911	Again/The Boy Most Likely	1961	7.50	15.00	30.00
RUST					
5048	One Step from Heaven/Away	1962	7.50	15.00	30.00

CONCORDS, THE (2)

45s

Number	Title (A Side/B Side)	Yr	VG	VG+	NM
EMBER					
1007	I'm Satisfied with Rock 'N' Roll/I'll Always Say Please	1956	15.00	30.00	60.00
HARLEM					
2328	Candlelight/Monticello	1954	150.00	300.00	600.00

CONDELLO

45s

Number	Title (A Side/B Side)	Yr	VG	VG+	NM
SCEPTER					
12233	Crystal Clear/See What Tomorrow Brings	1968	3.00	6.00	12.00

Albums

Number	Title (A Side/B Side)	Yr	VG	VG+	NM
SCEPTER					
SPS-542	Phase 1	1968	10.00	20.00	40.00

CONDORS, THE

45s

Number	Title (A Side/B Side)	Yr	VG	VG+	NM
HUNTER					
2503/4	Swetest Angel/Little Curly Top	1960	250.00	500.00	1000.

CONEY ISLAND KIDS, THE

45s

Number	Title (A Side/B Side)	Yr	VG	VG+	NM
JOSIE					
791	I Love It/Red Light, Green Light	1956	7.50	15.00	30.00
802	We Want a Rock & Roll President/Thwistle Rock and Thwistle Roll	1956	7.50	15.00	30.00
809	Popcorn and Candy/Not You, Pie Face	1957	7.50	15.00	30.00
JUBILEE					
5215	Moonlight Beach/Baby Baby You	1955	10.00	20.00	40.00

CONFESSIONS, THE

45s

Number	Title (A Side/B Side)	Yr	VG	VG+	NM
EPIC					
9474	Be-Bop Baby/Before You Change Your Mind	1961	6.25	12.50	25.00

CONLEY, ARTHUR

45s

Number	Title (A Side/B Side)	Yr	VG	VG+	NM
ATCO					
6463	Sweet Soul Music/Let's Go Steady	1967	2.50	5.00	10.00
6494	Shake, Rattle and Roll/You Don't Have to See Me	1967	2.00	4.00	8.00
6529	Whole Lot of Woman/Love Comes and Goes	1967	2.00	4.00	8.00
6563	Funky Street/Put Our Love Together	1968	2.00	4.00	8.00
6588	People Sure Act Funny/Burning Fire	1968	2.00	4.00	8.00
6622	Is That You Love/Aunt Dora's Love Soul Shack	1968	2.00	4.00	8.00
6640	Ob-La-Di, Ob-La-Da/Otis Sleep On	1968	2.00	4.00	8.00
6661	Speak Her Name/Run On	1969	—	3.00	6.00
6706	Star Review/Love Sure Is a Powerful Thing	1969	—	3.00	6.00
6733	Hurt/They Call the Wind Maria	1970	—	3.00	6.00
6747	God Bless/(Your Love Has Brought Me A) Mighty Long Way	1970	—	3.00	6.00
6790	Nobody's Fault But Mine/Day-O	1970	—	3.00	6.00
CAPRICORN					
0001	More Sweet Soul Music/Walking on Eggs	1972	2.50	5.00	10.00
0006	Rita/More Sweet Soul Music	1972	2.00	4.00	8.00
0047	Bless You/It's So Nice	1973	2.00	4.00	8.00
8017	I'm Living Good/I'm So Glad You're Here	1971	2.50	5.00	10.00
FAME					
1007	I Can't Stop/In the Same Old Way	1966	3.75	7.50	15.00
1009	Take Me (Just As I Am)/I'm Gonna Forget About You	1966	3.75	7.50	15.00
JOTIS					
470	I'm a Lonely Stranger/Where Lead Me	1965	5.00	10.00	20.00
472	Who's Fooling Who/There's a Place for Us	1966	5.00	10.00	20.00
PHILCO-FORD					
HP-15	Sweet Soul Music/You Don't Have to See Me	1968	3.75	7.50	15.00
—4-inch plastic "Hip Pocket Record" with color sleeve					

Albums

Number	Title (A Side/B Side)	Yr	VG	VG+	NM
ATCO					
33-215 [M]	Sweet Soul Music	1967	10.00	20.00	40.00
SD 33-215 [S]	Sweet Soul Music	1967	7.50	15.00	30.00
33-220 [M]	Shake, Rattle & Roll	1967	10.00	20.00	40.00
SD 33-220 [S]	Shake, Rattle & Roll	1967	7.50	15.00	30.00
SD 33-243	Soul Directions	1968	7.50	15.00	30.00
SD 33-276	More Sweet Soul	1969	7.50	15.00	30.00

CONNIFF, RAY

Includes the Ray Conniff Singers.

45s

Number	Title (A Side/B Side)	Yr	VG	VG+	NM
BRUNSWICK					
55020	Beamy Boy Boogie/Super Chief	1957	2.50	5.00	10.00
COLUMBIA					
10002	The Entertainer/I Understand Just How You Feel	1974	—	2.00	4.00
10097	Sing Along Song/Ecstasy	1975	—	2.00	4.00
10164	I Need You Baby/On the Run	1975	—	2.00	4.00
10294	Paloma Blanca/Lara's Theme from "Doctor Zhivago"	1976	—	2.00	4.00
10375	Moments to Remember/Vera's Theme	1976	—	2.00	4.00
10416	Song from "M*A*S*H"/Theme from "Love Story"	1976	—	2.00	4.00
30909 [S]	(titles unknown)	1960	2.50	5.00	10.00
30910 [S]	(titles unknown)	1960	2.50	5.00	10.00
30911 [S]	(titles unknown)	1960	2.50	5.00	10.00
30912 [S]	(titles unknown)	1960	2.50	5.00	10.00
30913 [S]	(titles unknown)	1960	2.50	5.00	10.00
31119 [S]	(titles unknown)	1961	2.50	5.00	10.00
31120 [S]	(titles unknown)	1961	2.50	5.00	10.00
31121 [S]	(titles unknown)	1961	2.50	5.00	10.00
31122 [S]	(titles unknown)	1961	2.50	5.00	10.00
31123 [S]	(titles unknown)	1961	2.50	5.00	10.00
31463 [S]	(titles unknown)	1962	2.50	5.00	10.00
31464 [S]	(titles unknown)	1962	2.50	5.00	10.00
31465 [S]	(titles unknown)	1962	2.50	5.00	10.00
31466 [S]	(titles unknown)	1962	2.50	5.00	10.00
31467 [S]	(titles unknown)	1962	2.50	5.00	10.00
31555 [S]	(titles unknown)	1962	2.50	5.00	10.00
31556 [S]	(titles unknown)	1962	2.50	5.00	10.00
31557 [S]	(titles unknown)	1962	2.50	5.00	10.00
31558 [S]	(titles unknown)	1962	2.50	5.00	10.00

Number	Title (A Side/B Side)	Yr	VG	VG+	NM
31559 [S]	(titles unknown)	1962	2.50	5.00	10.00
—Anyone who can fill in these gaps -- the above 20 all are Columbia "Stereo 7" singles -- please let us know.					
40827	'S Wonderful/Wagon Wheels	1957	2.50	5.00	10.00
40862	Three Way Love/Cuddle Up a Little Closer	1957	2.50	5.00	10.00
40991	Walkin' and Whistlin'/Melody for Two Guitars	1957	2.00	4.00	8.00
41040	Theme from Perry Mason/Symphony of Love	1957	3.00	6.00	12.00
41242	Tchaikovsky's First Piano Concerto/Schubert's Serenade	1958	2.00	4.00	8.00
41349	Oklahoma/On the Street Where You Live	1959	2.00	4.00	8.00
41404	They Tried to Tell Me/Early Evening	1959	2.00	4.00	8.00
41484	Christmas Bride/Silver Bells	1959	3.00	6.00	12.00
41582	None But the Lonely Heart (Improvisation)/ Warsaw Concerto	1960	2.00	4.00	8.00
41696	Theme from Perry Mason/Walkin; and Whistlin'	1960	2.00	4.00	8.00
41776	Besame Mucho/Brazil	1960	—	—	—
—Canceled					
41800	Midnight Lace — Part I/Midnight Lace — Part II	1960	2.00	4.00	8.00
42007	Golden Earrings/The Thrill Is Gone	1961	—	3.00	6.00
42695	Popsy/Scarlet	1963	2.00	4.00	8.00
42967	Blue Moon/Honeycomb	1964	—	3.00	6.00
42967 [DJ]	Blue Moon/Honeycomb	1964	3.00	6.00	12.00
—Blue vinyl promo; white label, blue print					
43061	Invisible Tears/Singing the Blues	1964	—	3.00	6.00
43168	Melodie D'Amour/If I Knew Then	1964	—	3.00	6.00
43352	Happiness Is/Miss You	1965	—	3.00	6.00
43448	The Real Meaning of Christmas/Go Tell It on the Mountain	1965	2.00	4.00	8.00
43503	Jamaica Farewell/The Sheik of Araby	1966	—	3.00	6.00
43626	Somewhere, My Love/Midsummer in Sweden	1966	—	3.00	6.00
43626 [DJ]	Somewhere, My Love (same on both sides)	1966	3.00	6.00	12.00
—Promo only on red vinyl					
43814	Lookin' for Love/It Takes Two	1966	—	3.00	6.00
43939	Mame/Wednesday's Child	1966	—	3.00	6.00
44055	The World Will Smile Again/"17"	1967	—	3.00	6.00
44192	Moonlight Brings Memories/Wonderful Season of Summer	1967	—	3.00	6.00
44298	The Hulilau Song/One Paddle Two Paddle	1967	—	3.00	6.00
44422	Winds of Change/We're a Home	1968	—	2.50	5.00
44536	A Certain Girl/Sounds of Silence	1968	—	2.50	5.00
44645	People/Look Homeward Angel	1968	—	2.50	5.00
44724	I've Got My Eyes on You/Dear World	1968	—	2.50	5.00
44872	I Love How You Love Me/Hold Me Tight	1969	—	2.50	5.00
44933	A Banda/La Felicidad	1969	—	2.50	5.00
45002	Love at First Sight/Love Made a Fool of Me	1969	—	2.50	5.00
45070	Jean/The Power of Love	1970	—	2.50	5.00
45137	Half and Half (A Song for Sarah)/Walk in the Spring Rain	1970	—	2.50	5.00
45187	Songs Are For Lovers/These Are My Flowers	1970	—	2.50	5.00
45267	Everybody Knows/Loss of Love	1970	—	2.50	5.00
45333	Love Story/Out of the Darkness	1971	—	2.00	4.00
45363	El Condor Pasa/Rosa	1971	—	2.00	4.00
45443	Tijuana Taxi/Happy Together	1971	—	2.00	4.00
45528	We Must Forget We Ever Met/Where Were You	1972	—	2.00	4.00
45543	Theme from "Summer of '42"/Imagine	1972	—	2.00	4.00
45595	With Every Beat of My Heart/Sleepy Shores	1972	—	2.00	4.00
45687	Where Is the Love/Because	1972	—	2.00	4.00
45782	Face on the Wind/A Man Without a Vision	1973	—	2.00	4.00
45823	Charlotte's Web/Someone	1973	—	2.00	4.00
45893	Harmony/Bah, Bah, Conniff Sprach	1973	—	2.00	4.00
45996	The Most Beautiful Girl/Beyond Tomorrow	1974	—	2.00	4.00
JZSP 111913/4 [DJ]	The Real Meaning of Christmas/Go Tell It on the Mountain	1965	2.50	5.00	10.00
—Black vinyl					
JZSP 111913/4 [DJ]	The Real Meaning of Christmas/Go Tell It on the Mountain	1965	3.00	6.00	12.00
—Green vinyl					

CORAL

Number	Title (A Side/B Side)	Yr	VG	VG+	NM
61371	Beamy Boy Boogie/Super Chief	1955	3.00	6.00	12.00

7-Inch Extended Plays

COLUMBIA

Number	Title (A Side/B Side)	Yr	VG	VG+	NM
B-2578	*'S Wonderful/I Get a Kick Out of You/Begin the Beguine/That Old Black Magic	1958	2.50	5.00	10.00
B-2578 [PS]	Ray Conniff (Hall of Fame Series)	1958	2.50	5.00	10.00
B-9251	*'S Wonderful/Dancing in the Dark/Speak Low/ Begin the Beguine	1956	2.50	5.00	10.00
B-9251 [PS]	'S Wonderful	1956	2.50	5.00	10.00
B-10043	Hand Around/Play a Gittar Solo//The Spinner/ Honky Tonk Rock-a-Round	1956	3.00	6.00	12.00
B-10043	(title unknown)	1956	3.00	6.00	12.00
B-11631	*Theme from Tchaikovsky's First Piano Concerto/Theme from Swan Lake Ballet/Theme from Rachmaninoff's Second Piano Concerto/ Theme from Tchaikovsky's Fifth Symphony	195?	2.50	5.00	10.00
B-11631 [PS]	Concert in Rhythm	195?	2.50	5.00	10.00

Albums

COLUMBIA

Number	Title (A Side/B Side)	Yr	VG	VG+	NM
GP 3 [(2)]	Here We Come a-Caroling/Ray Conniff's World of Hits	1968	3.75	7.50	15.00
CL 925 [M]	'S Wonderful!	1956	5.00	10.00	20.00
—Red and black label with six "eye" logos					
CL 1004 [M]	Dance the Bop	1957	7.50	15.00	30.00
—Red and black label with six "eye" logos; includes instruction booklet					
CS 1022	Bridge Over Troubled Water	1970	2.50	5.00	10.00
CL 1074 [M]	'S Marvelous	1957	3.75	7.50	15.00
CL 1137 [M]	'S Awful Nice	1958	3.75	7.50	15.00
CL 1163 [M]	Concert in Rhythm	1958	3.75	7.50	15.00
CL 1252 [M]	Broadway in Rhythm	1959	3.75	7.50	15.00
CL 1310 [M]	Hollywood in Rhythm	1959	3.75	7.50	15.00
CL 1334 [M]	It's the Talk of the Town	1959	3.00	6.00	12.00
CL 1346 [M]	Conniff Meets Butterfield	1959	5.00	10.00	20.00
—Red and black label with six "eye" logos					
CL 1390 [M]	Christmas with Conniff	1959	3.75	7.50	15.00
CL 1415 [M]	Concert in Rhythm — Volume II	1960	3.00	6.00	12.00
CL 1489 [M]	Young at Heart	1960	3.00	6.00	12.00
CL 1490 [M]	Say It With Music (A Touch of Latin)	1960	3.00	6.00	12.00
CL 1574 [M]	Memories Are Made of This	1961	3.00	6.00	12.00
CL 1642 [M]	Somebody Loves Me	1961	3.00	6.00	12.00
CL 1720 [M]	So Much in Love	1962	3.00	6.00	12.00
CL 1776 [M]	'S Continental	1962	3.00	6.00	12.00
CL 1878 [M]	Rhapsody in Rhythm	1962	3.00	6.00	12.00
CL 1892 [M]	We Wish You a Merry Christmas	1962	3.75	7.50	15.00
CL 1949 [M]	The Happy Beat	1963	3.00	6.00	12.00
CL 2022 [M]	Just Kiddin' Around	1963	3.00	6.00	12.00
CL 2118 [M]	You Make Me Feel So Young	1964	3.00	6.00	12.00
CL 2150 [M]	Speak to Me of Love	1964	2.50	5.00	10.00
CL 2210 [M]	Friendly Persuasion	1964	2.50	5.00	10.00
CL 2264 [M]	Invisible Tears	1964	2.50	5.00	10.00
CL 2352 [M]	Love Affair	1965	2.50	5.00	10.00
CL 2366 [M]	Music from Mary Poppins, The Sound of Music, My Fair Lady & Other Great Movie Themes	1965	2.50	5.00	10.00
CL 2406 [M]	Here We Come a-Caroling	1965	3.00	6.00	12.00
CL 2461 [M]	Happiness Is	1966	2.50	5.00	10.00
CL 2500 [M]	Ray Conniff's World of Hits	1966	3.00	6.00	12.00
CL 2519 [M]	Somewhere My Love	1966	3.00	6.00	12.00
CL 2608 [M]	En Espanol	1967	3.00	6.00	12.00
CL 2676 [M]	This Is My Song	1967	3.00	6.00	12.00
CL 2747 [M]	Hawaiian Album	1967	3.00	6.00	12.00
CL 2795 [M]	It Must Be Him	1968	3.75	7.50	15.00
CS 8001 [S]	'S Awful Nice	1958	5.00	10.00	20.00
—Red and black label with six "eye" logos					
CS 8022 [S]	Concert in Rhythm	1958	5.00	10.00	20.00
—Red and black label with six "eye" logos					
PC 8022	Concert in Rhythm	1988	—	3.00	6.00
—Reissue with new prefix					
CS 8037 [S]	'S Marvelous	1958	5.00	10.00	20.00
—Red and black label with six "eye" logos					
CS 8064 [S]	Broadway in Rhythm	1959	5.00	10.00	20.00
—Red and black label with six "eye" logos					
CS 8117 [S]	Hollywood in Rhythm	1959	5.00	10.00	20.00
—Red and black label with six "eye" logos					
CS 8143 [S]	It's the Talk of the Town	1959	3.75	7.50	15.00
CS 8155 [S]	Conniff Meets Butterfield	1959	6.25	12.50	25.00
—Red and black label with six "eye" logos					
CS 8185 [S]	Christmas with Conniff	1959	3.00	6.00	12.00
CS 8212 [S]	Concert in Rhythm — Volume II	1960	3.75	7.50	15.00
CS 8281 [S]	Young at Heart	1960	3.75	7.50	15.00
CS 8282 [S]	Say It With Music (A Touch of Latin)	1960	3.75	7.50	15.00
CS 8374 [S]	Memories Are Made of This	1961	3.75	7.50	15.00
CS 8442 [S]	Somebody Loves Me	1961	3.75	7.50	15.00
CS 8520 [S]	So Much in Love	1962	3.75	7.50	15.00
CS 8576 [S]	'S Continental	1962	3.75	7.50	15.00
CS 8678 [S]	Rhapsody in Rhythm	1962	3.75	7.50	15.00
CS 8692 [S]	We Wish You a Merry Christmas	1962	3.00	6.00	12.00
CS 8749 [S]	The Happy Beat	1963	3.75	7.50	15.00
CS 8822 [S]	Just Kiddin' Around	1963	3.75	7.50	15.00
CS 8918 [S]	You Make Me Feel So Young	1964	3.75	7.50	15.00
CS 8950 [S]	Speak to Me of Love	1964	3.00	6.00	12.00
CS 9064 [S]	Invisible Tears	1964	3.00	6.00	12.00
CS 9110 [S]	Friendly Persuasion	1964	3.00	6.00	12.00
CS 9152 [S]	Love Affair	1965	3.00	6.00	12.00
CS 9166 [S]	Music from Mary Poppins, The Sound of Music, My Fair Lady & Other Great Movie Themes	1965	3.00	6.00	12.00
CS 9206 [S]	Here We Come a-Caroling	1965	2.50	5.00	10.00
CS 9261 [S]	Happiness Is	1966	3.00	6.00	12.00
CS 9300 [S]	Ray Conniff's World of Hits	1966	2.50	5.00	10.00
CS 9319 [S]	Somewhere My Love	1966	2.50	5.00	10.00
PC 9319	Somewhere My Love	198?	—	3.00	6.00
—Reissue with new prefix					
CS 9408 [S]	En Espanol	1967	2.50	5.00	10.00
CS 9476 [S]	This Is My Song	1967	2.50	5.00	10.00
CS 9547 [S]	Hawaiian Album	1967	2.50	5.00	10.00
PC 9547	Hawaiian Album	198?	—	3.00	6.00
—Reissue with new prefix					
CS 9595 [S]	It Must Be Him	1968	2.50	5.00	10.00
CS 9661	Honey	1968	2.50	5.00	10.00
CS 9712	Turn Around Look at Me	1968	2.50	5.00	10.00
CS 9777	I Love How You Love Me	1969	2.50	5.00	10.00
CS 9839	Ray Conniff's Greatest Hits	1969	2.50	5.00	10.00
PC 9839	Ray Conniff's Greatest Hits	198?	—	3.00	6.00
—Reissue with new prefix					
CS 9920	Jean	1969	2.50	5.00	10.00
G 30122 [(2)]	Concert in Stereo/Live at the Sahara/Tahoe	1970	3.75	7.50	15.00
C 30410	We've Only Just Begun	1970	2.50	5.00	10.00
C 30498	Love Story	1971	2.50	5.00	10.00
CQ 30498 [Q]	Love Story	1972	3.75	7.50	15.00
C 30755	Great Contemporary Instrumental Hits	1971	2.50	5.00	10.00
KC 31220	I'd Like to Teach the World to Sing	1972	2.50	5.00	10.00
CQ 31473 [Q]	Love Theme from "The Godfather"	1972	3.75	7.50	15.00
KC 31473	Love Theme from "The Godfather"	1972	2.50	5.00	10.00
CQ 31629 [Q]	Alone Again (Naturally)	1972	3.75	7.50	15.00
KC 31629	Alone Again (Naturally)	1972	2.50	5.00	10.00
KC 32090	I Can See Clearly Now	1973	2.50	5.00	10.00
KC 32376	You Are the Sunshine of My Life	1973	2.50	5.00	10.00
C 32413	Charlotte's Web	1973	2.50	5.00	10.00
CQ 32553 [Q]	Harmony	1973	3.75	7.50	15.00
KC 32553	Harmony	1973	2.50	5.00	10.00
CQ 32802 [Q]	The Way We Were	1974	3.75	7.50	15.00
KC 32802	The Way We Were	1974	2.50	5.00	10.00
CQ 33139 [Q]	The Happy Sound	1974	3.75	7.50	15.00
KC 33139	The Happy Sound	1974	2.50	5.00	10.00
CQ 33564 [Q]	Another Somebody Done Somebody Wrong Song	1975	3.75	7.50	15.00
KC 33564	Another Somebody Done Somebody Wrong Song	1975	2.50	5.00	10.00
CG 33603 [(2)]	Somewhere My Love/Bridge Over Troubled Water	1975	3.00	6.00	12.00
CQ 33884 [Q]	Love Will Keep Us Together	1975	3.75	7.50	15.00
KC 33884	Love Will Keep Us Together	1975	2.50	5.00	10.00
CQ 34040 [Q]	I Write the Songs	1976	3.75	7.50	15.00
KC 34040	I Write the Songs	1976	2.50	5.00	10.00

Number	Title (A Side/B Side)	Yr	VG	VG+	NM
CQ 34170 [Q]	Send In the Clowns	1976	3.75	7.50	15.00
KC 34170	Send In the Clowns	1976	2.50	5.00	10.00
CQ 34312 [Q]	S.W.A.T.	1976	3.75	7.50	15.00
KC 34312	S.W.A.T.	1976	2.50	5.00	10.00
PC 34477	After the Lovin'	1977	2.50	5.00	10.00
JC 35659	Ray Conniff Plays the Bee Gees and Other Hits	1978	2.50	5.00	10.00
PC 36255	I Will Survive	1979	2.50	5.00	10.00
JC 36749	Perfect "10" Classics	1980	2.50	5.00	10.00
FC 38072	The Nashville Connection	1981	2.50	5.00	10.00
PC 38300	Christmas Album	1982	2.50	5.00	10.00
PC 39470	Christmas Caroling	1984	2.50	5.00	10.00
FC 40384	Say You, Say Me	1986	2.50	5.00	10.00
FC 44152	Always in My Heart	1988	2.50	5.00	10.00
HARMONY					
HS 11346	Love Is a Many-Splendored Thing	1969	2.50	5.00	10.00
KH 30134	The Impossible Dream	1970	2.50	5.00	10.00

CONNORS, CAROL

Also see THE CARMEL SISTERS; THE TEDDY BEARS.

45s

Number	Title (A Side/B Side)	Yr	VG	VG+	NM
CAPITOL					
5152	Never/Angel, My Angel	1964	6.25	12.50	25.00
COLUMBIA					
41976	You Are My Answer/My Diary	1961	6.25	12.50	25.00
42155	Listen to the Beat/My Special Boy	1961	6.25	12.50	25.00
42337	That's All It Takes/What Do You See in Him	1962	6.25	12.50	25.00
ERA					
3084	Two Rivers/Big, Big Love	1962	7.50	15.00	30.00
3096	Tommy Go Away/I Wanna Know	1962	7.50	15.00	30.00
MIRA					
219	Lonely Little Beach Girl/My Baby Looks, But He Don't Touch	1965	6.25	12.50	25.00
219 [PS]	Lonely Little Beach Girl/My Baby Looks, But He Don't Touch	1965	12.50	25.00	50.00
N.T.C.					
3131	Yum Yum Yamaha	1964	12.50	25.00	50.00
—One-sided single					
3131 [PS]	Yum Yum Yamaha	1964	25.00	50.00	100.00

CONNORS, NORMAN

45s

Number	Title (A Side/B Side)	Yr	VG	VG+	NM
ARISTA					
0343	This Is Your Life/Captain Connors	1978	—	2.00	4.00
0377	Wouldn't You Like to See/Listen	1978	—	2.00	4.00
0443	Your Love/Disco Land	1979	—	2.00	4.00
0460	Hand Me Gently/Be There In the Morning	1979	—	2.00	4.00
0548	Take It to the Limit/You Bring Me Joy	1980	—	2.00	4.00
0581	Melancholy Fire/You've Been On My Mind	1980	—	2.00	4.00
0632	She's Gone/(B-side unknown)	1981	—	2.00	4.00
BUDDAH					
499	Valentine Love/Aria	1975	—	2.50	5.00
534	We Both Need Each Other/You Are My Starship	1976	—	3.00	6.00
542	You Are My Starship/Bubbles	1976	—	2.50	5.00
554	Betcha By Golly Wow/Kwasi	1976	—	2.50	5.00
570	Once I've Been There/Romantic Journey	1977	—	2.50	5.00
580	For You Everything/Give the Drummer Some	1977	—	2.50	5.00
CAPITOL					
44110	I Am Your Melody/Samba for Maria	1988	—	—	3.00
44159	You're My One and Only Love/I Am Your Melody	1988	—	—	3.00
THE RIGHT STUFF					
58849	Didn't I (Blow Your Mind This Time)/River of Love	2000	—	—	3.00

Albums

Number	Title (A Side/B Side)	Yr	VG	VG+	NM
ACCORD					
SN-7210	Just Imagine	1982	2.00	4.00	8.00
ARISTA					
AB 4177	This Is Your Life	1978	2.50	5.00	10.00
AB 4216	Invitation	1979	2.50	5.00	10.00
AL 9534	Take It to the Limit	1980	2.50	5.00	10.00
AL 9575	Mr. C.	1981	2.50	5.00	10.00
BUDDAH					
BDS-5142	Love from the Sun	1973	3.00	6.00	12.00
BDS-5611	Slewfoot	1974	3.00	6.00	12.00
BDS-5643	Saturday Night Special	1975	2.50	5.00	10.00
BDS-5655	You Are My Starship	1976	2.50	5.00	10.00
BDS-5674	Dance of Magic	1977	2.50	5.00	10.00
—Reissue of Cobblestone 9024					
BDS-5675	Dark of Light	1977	2.50	5.00	10.00
—Reissue of Cobblestone 9035					
BDS-5682	Romantic Journey	1977	2.50	5.00	10.00
BDS-5716	The Best of Norman Connors & Friends	1978	2.50	5.00	10.00
CAPITOL					
C1-48515	Passion	1988	2.50	5.00	10.00
COBBLESTONE					
9024	Dance of Magic	1972	3.75	7.50	15.00
9035	Dark of Light	1973	3.75	7.50	15.00

CONRAD, JESS

45s

Number	Title (A Side/B Side)	Yr	VG	VG+	NM
LONDON					
1967	Mystery Girl/Just the Two of Us	1961	3.00	6.00	12.00
2005	Little Ship/Walk Away	1961	3.00	6.00	12.00

CONSORTS, THE

45s

Number	Title (A Side/B Side)	Yr	VG	VG+	NM
APT					
25066	Please Be Mine/Time After Time	1962	30.00	60.00	120.00
COUSINS					
1004	Please Be Mine/Time After Time	1961	100.00	200.00	400.00

CONTENDERS, THE

More than one group.

45s

Number	Title (A Side/B Side)	Yr	VG	VG+	NM
BETH					
1001	I'll Show You How to Love/(B-side unknown)	195?	5.00	10.00	20.00
BLUE SKY					
105	Mr. Dee Jay/Yes I Do	1959	150.00	300.00	600.00
CHATTAHOOCHIE					
644	The Dune Bugy/Go Ahead	1964	6.25	12.50	25.00
656	Johnny B. Goode/Rise 'N' Shine	1964	6.25	12.50	25.00
JACKPOT					
48002	Tequila Song/Wild Man	1959	10.00	20.00	40.00
JAVA					
101	The Clock/Look at Me	196?	25.00	50.00	100.00
—Gold label					
101	The Clock/Look at Me	196?	6.25	12.50	25.00
—Red label					

CONTINENTAL GEMS, THE

45s

Number	Title (A Side/B Side)	Yr	VG	VG+	NM
GUYDEN					
2091	My Love Will Follow You/Everywhere	1963	100.00	200.00	400.00

CONTINENTALS, THE (1)

45s

Number	Title (A Side/B Side)	Yr	VG	VG+	NM
ERA					
3003	Cool Penguin/Soap Sudz	1959	5.00	10.00	20.00
PENGUIN					
1002	Cool Penguin/Soap Sudz	1959	10.00	20.00	40.00

CONTINENTALS, THE (2)

45s

Number	Title (A Side/B Side)	Yr	VG	VG+	NM
PORT					
70018	Dear Lord/Fine Fine Frame	1960	7.50	15.00	30.00
70024	Picture of Love/Soft and Sweet	1961	7.50	15.00	30.00
WHIRLIN' DISC					
101	Dear Lord/Fine Fine Frame	1956	50.00	100.00	200.00
105	Picture of Love/Soft and Sweet	1957	50.00	100.00	200.00

CONTINENTALS, THE (3)

45s

Number	Title (A Side/B Side)	Yr	VG	VG+	NM
RAMA					
190	You Are An Angel/Giddy Up a Ding Dong	1956	375.00	750.00	1500.
—Blue label					
190	You Are An Angel/Giddy Up a Ding Dong	1956	37.50	75.00	150.00
—Red label					

CONTINENTALS, THE (U)

Some of these may be groups (1), (2) or (3); many are not.

45s

Number	Title (A Side/B Side)	Yr	VG	VG+	NM
AOK					
1025	Take Me/She Wants You	1966	6.25	12.50	25.00
BOLO					
720	I'm Coming Home/The Turnaround	1960	7.50	15.00	30.00
CUCA					
1063	Tic-Toc/Sue	1961	7.50	15.00	30.00
DAVIS					
466	Don't Do It, Baby/Tongue Twister	1959	10.00	20.00	40.00
HUNTER					
3503	It Doesn't Matter/Whisper It	1960	300.00	600.00	1200.
KEY					
517	Take a Gamble on Me/Meanwhile Back at the Ranch	1956	25.00	50.00	100.00
LIFETIME					
1019	Cathy's Clown/Maybe Baby	1966	2.50	5.00	10.00
VANDAN					
8067	No Money No Luck Blues/Pink Champagne	196?	5.00	10.00	20.00

CONTOURS, THE

45s

Number	Title (A Side/B Side)	Yr	VG	VG+	NM
GORDY					
7005	Do You Love Me/Move Mr. Man	1962	5.00	10.00	20.00
7012	Shake Sherry/You Better Get in Line	1963	3.75	7.50	15.00
7016	Don't Let Her Be Your Baby/It Must Be Love	1963	3.00	6.00	12.00
7019	Pa I Need a Car/You Get Ugly	1963	3.00	6.00	12.00
7029	Can You Do It/I'll Stand By You	1964	3.00	6.00	12.00
7037	Can You Jerk Like Me/That Day When She Needed Me	1964	3.00	6.00	12.00
7044	First I Look at the Purse/Searching for a Girl	1965	3.00	6.00	12.00
7052	Just a Little Misunderstanding/Determination	1966	3.00	6.00	12.00
7059	It's So Hard Being a Loser/Your Love Grows More Precious Every Day	1967	3.00	6.00	12.00
HOB					
116	I'm So Glad/Yours Is My Heart Alone	1961	30.00	60.00	120.00
MOTOWN					
1008	Whole Lotta Woman/Come On and Be Mine	1961	125.00	250.00	500.00
1012	The Stretch/Funny	1962	200.00	400.00	800.00
MOTOWN YESTERYEAR					
448	Do You Love Me/Shake Sherry	1972	—	2.00	4.00
448 [PS]	Do You Love Me/Shake Sherry	1988	—	2.50	5.00
—"Dirty Dancing" sleeve; without cut-out hole					
ROCKET					
41192	I'm a Winner/Makes Me Wanna Come Back	1980	—	2.00	4.00
TAMLA					
7012	Shake Sherry/You Better Get in Line	1963	37.50	75.00	150.00
—Tamla label used in error for a Gordy release					

Albums

Number	Title (A Side/B Side)	Yr	VG	VG+	NM
GORDY					
G 901 [M]	Do You Love Me?	1962	125.00	250.00	500.00

Number	Title (A Side/B Side)	Yr	VG	VG+	NM
MOTOWN					
M5-188V1	Do You Love Me?	1981	2.50	5.00	10.00

CONVINCERS, THE

Number	Title (A Side/B Side)	Yr	VG	VG+	NM
45s					
MOVIN'					
100	Rejected Love/Go Back Baby	1962	100.00	200.00	400.00

CONWAY, JULIE

Number	Title (A Side/B Side)	Yr	VG	VG+	NM
Albums					
HARMONY					
HL 7143 [M]	Good Housekeeping's Plan for Reducing Off-the-Record	1960	5.00	10.00	20.00

COODER, RY

Also see THE ROLLING STONES.

Number	Title (A Side/B Side)	Yr	VG	VG+	NM
45s					
MUSICOR					
1148	Life Game/1983	1966	2.50	5.00	10.00
REPRISE					
0910	Goin' to Brownsville/Available Space	1970	—	3.00	6.00
0940	Alimony/Pigmeat	1970	—	3.00	6.00
1009	Dark Is the Night/On a Monday	1971	—	3.00	6.00
1071	Billy the Kid/Money Honey	1972	—	3.00	6.00
1167	Billy the Kid/Boomer's Story	1973	—	3.00	6.00
WARNER BROS.					
8384	School Is Out/Jesus on the Mainline	1977	—	2.50	5.00
27945	Get Rhythm/Get Back to Okinawa	1988	—	2.00	4.00
28158	All Shook Up/Get Your Lies Straight	1987	—	2.00	4.00
28158 [PS]	All Shook Up/Get Your Lies Straight	1987	—	2.00	4.00
28723	Crossroads/Feel It (Bad Blues)	1986	—	2.00	4.00
28725	Tell Me Something Slick/Billy and Annie	1986	—	2.00	4.00
49055	Down in Hollywood/Little Sister	1979	—	2.50	5.00
49081	The Very Thing That Makes You Rich/Little Sister	1979	—	2.50	5.00
49677	Girls from Texas/Borderline	1981	—	2.00	4.00
49704	Crazy 'Bout an Automobile/Borderline	1981	—	2.00	4.00
Albums					
MOBILE FIDELITY					
1-085	Jazz	198?	100.00	200.00	400.00
—Audiophile vinyl					
REPRISE					
PRO 588 [DJ]	The Ry Cooder Radio Show	1976	25.00	50.00	100.00
MS 2052	Into the Purple Valley	1972	3.00	6.00	12.00
MS 2117	Boomer's Story	1973	3.00	6.00	12.00
MS 2179	Paradise and Lunch	1974	3.00	6.00	12.00
MS 2254	Chicken Skin Music	1976	3.00	6.00	12.00
RS-6402	Ry Cooder	1969	3.75	7.50	15.00
—Two-tone orange label with "r:" and "W7" logos					
RS-6402	Ry Cooder	1970	3.00	6.00	12.00
—No "W7" on label; one-tone orange (almost tan) label					
WARNER BROS.					
BS 3059	Show Time	1977	2.50	5.00	10.00
BSK 3197	Jazz	1978	2.50	5.00	10.00
BSK 3358	Bop Till You Drop	1979	2.50	5.00	10.00
HS 3448	The Long Riders	1980	2.50	5.00	10.00
BSK 3489	Borderline	1980	2.50	5.00	10.00
BSK 3651	The Slide Area	1982	2.50	5.00	10.00
25270	Paris, Texas	1984	2.50	5.00	10.00
25399	Crossroads	1986	2.50	5.00	10.00
25639	Get Rhythm	1987	2.50	5.00	10.00
25996	Johnny Handsome	1989	2.50	5.00	10.00

COOK, KEN

Number	Title (A Side/B Side)	Yr	VG	VG+	NM
45s					
PHILLIPS INT'L.					
3534	I Was a Fool/Crazy Baby	1959	12.50	25.00	50.00
—Roy Orbison appears on this record (uncredited)					

COOK, PETER, AND DUDLEY MOORE

Number	Title (A Side/B Side)	Yr	VG	VG+	NM
45s					
PARROT					
3016	Bedazzled/Love Me	1967	2.00	4.00	8.00

COOKE, SAM

Number	Title (A Side/B Side)	Yr	VG	VG+	NM
45s					
CHERIE					
4501	Darling I Need You Now/Win Your Love for Me	1971	2.00	4.00	8.00
KEEN					
2005	Stealing Kisses/All of My Life	1958	6.25	12.50	25.00
2006 [M]	Win Your Love for Me/Almost in Your Arms	1958	6.25	12.50	25.00
—Blue vinyl					
5-2006 [S]	Win Your Love for Me/Love Song from Houseboat	1959	25.00	50.00	100.00
—Blue vinyl					
3-2008	Love You Most of All/Blue Moon	1958	6.25	12.50	25.00
3-2018 [M]	Everybody Likes to Cha Cha Cha/Little Things You Do	1959	6.25	12.50	25.00
5-2018 [S]	Everybody Likes to Cha Cha Cha/Little Things You Do	1959	10.00	20.00	40.00
2022 [M]	Only Sixteen/Let's Go Steady Again	1959	6.25	12.50	25.00
5-2022 [S]	Only Sixteen/Let's Go Steady Again	1959	12.50	25.00	50.00
2101	Summertime/Summertime (Part 2)	1959	6.25	12.50	25.00
2105	There! I've Said It Again/One Hour Ahead of the Possee	1959	6.25	12.50	25.00
2111	'T'ain't Nobody's Bizness (If I Do)/No One	1960	6.25	12.50	25.00
2112	Wonderful World/Along the Navajo Trail	1960	5.00	10.00	20.00
2117	With You/I Thank God	1960	5.00	10.00	20.00
2118	Steal Away/So Glamorous	1960	5.00	10.00	20.00
2122	Mary, Mary Lou/Eee-Yi-Ee-Yi-Oh	1960	5.00	10.00	20.00
4002	(I Love You) For Sentimental Reasons/Desire Me	1958	6.25	12.50	25.00
4009	You Were Made for Me/Lonely Island	1958	6.25	12.50	25.00
34013	You Send Me/Summertime	1957	6.25	12.50	25.00
RCA					
PB-14146	Bring It On Home to Me/Nothing Can Change This Love	1985	2.00	4.00	8.00
RCA VICTOR					
37-7853	That's It-I Quit-I'm Movin' On/What Do You Say	1961	15.00	30.00	60.00
—"Compact Single 33" (small hole, plays at LP speed)					
47-7701	Teenage Sonata/If You Were the Only Girl	1960	5.00	10.00	20.00
47-7730	You Understand Me/I Belong to Your Heart	1960	3.75	7.50	15.00
47-7730 [PS]	You Understand Me/I Belong to Your Heart	1960	6.25	12.50	25.00
47-7783	Chain Gang/I Fall in Love Every Day	1960	3.75	7.50	15.00
47-7783 [PS]	Chain Gang/I Fall in Love Every Day	1960	6.25	12.50	25.00
47-7816	Sad Mood/Love Me	1960	3.75	7.50	15.00
47-7853	That's It-I Quit-I'm Movin' On/What Do You Say	1961	3.75	7.50	15.00
47-7883	Cupid/Farewell, My Darling	1961	3.75	7.50	15.00
47-7883 [PS]	Cupid/Farewell, My Darling	1961	6.25	12.50	25.00
47-7927	Feel It/It's All Right	1961	3.75	7.50	15.00
47-7927 [PS]	Feel It/It's All Right	1961	6.25	12.50	25.00
47-7983	Twistin' the Night Away/One More Time	1962	3.75	7.50	15.00
47-8036	Bring It On Home to Me/Having a Party	1962	3.75	7.50	15.00
47-8088	Nothing Can Change This Love/Somebody Have Mercy	1962	3.75	7.50	15.00
47-8088 [PS]	Nothing Can Change This Love/Somebody Have Mercy	1962	6.25	12.50	25.00
47-8129	Send Me Some Lovin'/Baby, Baby, Baby	1963	3.75	7.50	15.00
47-8129 [PS]	Send Me Some Lovin'/Baby, Baby, Baby	1963	6.25	12.50	25.00
47-8164	Another Saturday Night/Love Will Find a Way	1963	3.75	7.50	15.00
47-8164 [PS]	Another Saturday Night/Love Will Find a Way	1963	6.25	12.50	25.00
47-8215	Frankie and Johnny/Cool Train	1963	3.00	6.00	12.00
47-8215 [PS]	Frankie and Johnny/Cool Train	1963	6.25	12.50	25.00
47-8247	Little Red Rooster/You Gotta Move	1963	3.00	6.00	12.00
47-8247 [PS]	Little Red Rooster/You Gotta Move	1963	6.25	12.50	25.00
47-8299	Good News/Basin Street Blues	1963	3.00	6.00	12.00
47-8299	Ain't That Good News/Basin Street Blues	1963	5.00	10.00	20.00
—Original A-side title (or a scarce reissue)					
47-8368	Good Times/Tennessee Waltz	1964	3.00	6.00	12.00
47-8426	Cousin of Mine/That's Where It's At	1964	3.00	6.00	12.00
47-8486	Shake/A Change Is Gonna Come	1964	3.00	6.00	12.00
47-8539	It's Got the Whole World Shakin'/Ease My Troublin' Mind	1965	2.50	5.00	10.00
47-8586	When a Boy Falls in Love/The Piper	1965	2.50	5.00	10.00
47-8631	Sugar Dumpling/Bridge of Tears	1965	2.50	5.00	10.00
47-8631 [PS]	Sugar Dumpling/Bridge of Tears	1965	6.25	12.50	25.00
47-8751	Feel It/That's All	1965	2.50	5.00	10.00
47-8803	Let's Go Steady Again/Trouble Blues	1966	2.50	5.00	10.00
47-8934	Meet Me at Mary's Place/If I Had a Hammer	1966	2.50	5.00	10.00
SAR					
122 [DJ]	Just for You/Made for Me	1961	25.00	50.00	100.00
—Promo only ("Audition" on label); possibly made as leverage during contract renegotiation at RCA Victor, one source claims only five (5) copies were made					
SPECIALTY					
596	Forever/Lovable	1957	7.50	15.00	30.00
—As "Dale Cook"					
619	I'll Come Running Back to You/Forever	1957	7.50	15.00	30.00
627	That's All I Need to Know/I Don't Want to Cry	1958	7.50	15.00	30.00
667	Happy in Love/I Need You Now	1959	7.50	15.00	30.00
921	Must Jesus Bear the Cross Alone/The Last Mile of the Way	1970	2.50	5.00	10.00
—With the Soul Stirrers					
928	Just Another Day/Christ Is All	1973	2.50	5.00	10.00
—With the Soul Stirrers					
930	That's Heaven to Me/Lord, Remember Me	1974	2.50	5.00	10.00
—With the Soul Stirrers					
7-Inch Extended Plays					
KEEN					
B-2001	(contents unknown)	1958	20.00	40.00	80.00
B-2001 [PS]	Songs by Sam Cooke, Volume 1	1958	20.00	40.00	80.00
B-2002	*You Send Me/The Lonesome Road/That Lucky Old Sun/Canadian Sunset	1958	20.00	40.00	80.00
B-2002 [PS]	Songs by Sam Cooke, Volume 2	1958	20.00	40.00	80.00
B-2003	Summertime/Danny Boy//Around the World/Ol' Man River	1958	20.00	40.00	80.00
B-2003 [PS]	Songs by Sam Cooke, Volume 3	1958	20.00	40.00	80.00
B-2006	(contents unknown)	1958	20.00	40.00	80.00
B-2006 [PS]	Encore, Volume 1	1958	20.00	40.00	80.00
B-2007	*When I Fall in Love/I Cover the Waterfront/Running Wild/Today I Sing the Blues	1958	20.00	40.00	80.00
B-2007 [PS]	Encore, Volume 2	1958	20.00	40.00	80.00
B-2008	(contents unknown)	1958	20.00	40.00	80.00
B-2008 [PS]	Encore, Volume 3	1958	20.00	40.00	80.00
B-2010	Love Song from Houseboat/Lonely Island//Win Your Love for Me/All of My Life	1959	20.00	40.00	80.00
B-2010 [PS]	(title unknown)	1959	20.00	40.00	80.00
B-2012	Let's Call the Whole Thing Off/God Bless the Child//Comes Love/Lover Girl	1959	20.00	40.00	80.00
B-2012 [PS]	Tribute to the Lady, Volume 1	1959	20.00	40.00	80.00
B-2013	(contents unknown)	1959	20.00	40.00	80.00
B-2013 [PS]	Tribute to the Lady, Volume 2	1959	20.00	40.00	80.00
B-2014	(contents unknown)	1959	20.00	40.00	80.00
B-2014 [PS]	Tribute to the Lady, Volume 3	1959	20.00	40.00	80.00
RCA VICTOR					
LPC-126	Chain Gang/If You Were the Only Girl//Teenage Sonata/You Understand Me	1961	5.00	10.00	20.00
LPC-126 [PS]	Sam Cooke Sings	1961	5.00	10.00	20.00
EPA-4375	Another Saturday Night/You Send Me//Only Sixteen/Bring It On Home to Me	1963	5.00	10.00	20.00
EPA-4375 [PS]	Another Saturday Night	1963	5.00	10.00	20.00
Albums					
ABKCO					
1124-1	Sam Cooke's Night Beat	1995	3.00	6.00	12.00
—Reissue					
2970-1	Sam Cooke at the Copa	1988	3.00	6.00	12.00
—Reissue					
FAMOUS					
502	Sam's Songs	1969	10.00	20.00	40.00
505	Only Sixteen	1969	10.00	20.00	40.00

Number	Title (A Side/B Side)	Yr	VG	VG+	NM
508	So Wonderful	1969	10.00	20.00	40.00
509	You Send Me	1969	10.00	20.00	40.00
512	Cha-Cha-Cha	1969	10.00	20.00	40.00
KEEN					
A-2001 [M]	Sam Cooke	1958	50.00	100.00	200.00
A-2003 [M]	Encore	1958	50.00	100.00	200.00
A-2004 [M]	Tribute to the Lady	1959	37.50	75.00	150.00
AS-2004 [S]	Tribute to the Lady	1959	50.00	100.00	200.00
86101 [M]	Hit Kit	1959	62.50	125.00	250.00
86103 [M]	I Thank God	1960	100.00	200.00	400.00
86106 [M]	The Wonderful World of Sam Cooke	1960	87.50	1175.	350.00
PAIR					
PDL2-1006 [(2)]	You Send Me	1986	3.75	7.50	15.00
RCA CAMDEN					
ACS1-0445	You Send Me	1974	3.00	6.00	12.00
CAL-2264 [M]	The One and Only Sam Cooke	1967	5.00	10.00	20.00
CAS-2264 [R]	The One and Only Sam Cooke	1967	3.00	6.00	12.00
CAS-2433	Sam Cooke	1970	3.00	6.00	12.00
CAS-2610	The Unforgettable Sam Cooke	1972	3.00	6.00	12.00
RCA VICTOR					
LPM-2221 [M]	Cooke's Tour	1960	10.00	20.00	40.00
LSP-2221 [S]	Cooke's Tour	1960	12.50	25.00	50.00
LPM-2236 [M]	Hits of the 50's	1960	10.00	20.00	40.00
LSP-2236 [S]	Hits of the 50's	1960	12.50	25.00	50.00
LPM-2293 [M]	Swing Low	1960	10.00	20.00	40.00
LSP-2293 [S]	Swing Low	1960	12.50	25.00	50.00
LPM-2392 [M]	My Kind of Blues	1961	10.00	20.00	40.00
LSP-2392 [S]	My Kind of Blues	1961	12.50	25.00	50.00
LPM-2555 [M]	Twistin' the Night Away	1962	10.00	20.00	40.00
LSP-2555 [S]	Twistin' the Night Away	1962	12.50	25.00	50.00
AFL1-2625	The Best of Sam Cooke	1977	3.00	6.00	12.00
—Reissue with new prefix					
LPM-2625 [M]	The Best of Sam Cooke	1962	7.50	15.00	30.00
LSP-2625 [R]	The Best of Sam Cooke	1962	5.00	10.00	20.00
ANL1-2658	Sam Cooke at the Copa	1977	3.00	6.00	12.00
—Reissue of LSP-2970					
LPM-2673 [M]	Mr. Soul	1963	7.50	15.00	30.00
LSP-2673 [S]	Mr. Soul	1963	10.00	20.00	40.00
LPM-2709 [M]	Night Beat	1963	7.50	15.00	30.00
LSP-2709 [S]	Night Beat	1963	10.00	20.00	40.00
LPM-2899 [M]	Ain't That Good News	1964	7.50	15.00	30.00
LSP-2899 [S]	Ain't That Good News	1964	10.00	20.00	40.00
LPM-2970 [M]	Sam Cooke at the Copa	1964	7.50	15.00	30.00
LSP-2970 [S]	Sam Cooke at the Copa	1964	10.00	20.00	40.00
LPM-3367 [M]	Shake	1965	6.25	12.50	25.00
LSP-3367 [S]	Shake	1965	7.50	15.00	30.00
LPM-3373 [M]	The Best of Sam Cooke, Volume 2	1965	6.25	12.50	25.00
LSP-3373 [S]	The Best of Sam Cooke, Volume 2	1965	7.50	15.00	30.00
LPM-3435 [M]	Try a Little Love	1965	6.25	12.50	25.00
LSP-3435 [S]	Try a Little Love	1965	7.50	15.00	30.00
LPM-3517 [M]	The Unforgettable Sam Cooke	1966	5.00	10.00	20.00
LSP-3517 [S]	The Unforgettable Sam Cooke	1966	6.25	12.50	25.00
AYL1-3863	The Best of Sam Cooke	1981	2.00	4.00	8.00
—Budget-line reissue					
LPM-3991 [M]	The Man Who Invented Soul	1968	—	—	—
—Canceled?					
LSP-3991 [S]	The Man Who Invented Soul	1968	6.25	12.50	25.00
AFL1-5181	Live at the Harlem Square Club, 1963	1985	3.00	6.00	12.00
VPS-6027 [(2)]	This Is Sam Cooke	1970	5.00	10.00	20.00
CPL2-7127 [(2)]	The Man and His Music	1986	3.75	7.50	15.00
SPECIALTY					
SPS-2106	Sam Cooke and the Soul Stirrers	1970	3.75	7.50	15.00
SPS-2116	The Gospel Soul of Sam Cooke, Vol. 1	1970	3.75	7.50	15.00
SPS-2119	Two Sides of Sam Cooke	1970	3.75	7.50	15.00
SPS-2128	The Gospel Soul of Sam Cooke, Vol. 2	197?	3.75	7.50	15.00
SPS-2146	That's Heaven to Me	197?	3.75	7.50	15.00
TRIP					
8030 [(2)]	The Golden Sound of Sam Cooke	1972	3.75	7.50	15.00
UPFRONT					
160	The Billie Holiday Story	1973	3.75	7.50	15.00

COOKER, JOHN LEE

See JOHN LEE HOOKER.

COOKIE AND HIS CUPCAKES

45s

Number	Title (A Side/B Side)	Yr	VG	VG+	NM
CHESS					
1848	Got You On My Mind/I've Been So Lonely	1963	3.75	7.50	15.00
JUDD					
1002	Mathilda/Married Life	1958	12.50	25.00	50.00
—With "h" in A-side title					
1002	Matilda/Married Life	1958	7.50	15.00	30.00
—Without "h" in A-side title					
1015	Until Then/Close Up the Back Door	1959	10.00	20.00	40.00
KHOURY'S					
703	Mathilda/Married Life	1958	15.00	30.00	60.00
LYRIC					
1003	Mathilda/I'm Twisted	1963	5.00	10.00	20.00
1004	Got You On My Mind/I've Been So Lonely	1963	5.00	10.00	20.00
MERCURY					
71748	Matilda Has Finally Come Back/As Part of Everything	1961	5.00	10.00	20.00
PAULA					
221	Mathilda/I'm Twisted	1965	3.00	6.00	12.00
230	Belinda/Trouble in My Life	1965	2.50	5.00	10.00

COOKIES, THE

45s

Number	Title (A Side/B Side)	Yr	VG	VG+	NM
ATLANTIC					
1061	Precious Love/Later, Later	1955	7.50	15.00	30.00
1084	In Paradise/Passing Time	1956	7.50	15.00	30.00
1110	Down By the River/My Lover	1956	6.25	12.50	25.00
2079	Passing Time/In Paradise	1960	5.00	10.00	20.00
DIMENSION					
1002	Chains/Stranger in My Arms	1962	5.00	10.00	20.00
1008	Don't Say Nothin' Bad/Softly in the Night	1963	5.00	10.00	20.00
1008	Don't Say Nothin' Bad (About My Baby)/Softly in the Night	1963	3.75	7.50	15.00
1012	I Want a Boy for My Birthday/Will Power	1963	3.75	7.50	15.00
1020	Girls Grow Up Faster Than Boys/Only to Other People	1963	3.75	7.50	15.00
1032	I Never Dreamed/The Old Crowd	1964	3.75	7.50	15.00
JOSIE					
822	King of Hearts/Hippy-Dippy-Daddy	1957	7.50	15.00	30.00
LAMP					
8008	Don't Let Go/All Night Mambo	1954	10.00	20.00	40.00
WARNER BROS.					
7025	All My Trials/Wounded	1967	2.50	5.00	10.00
7047	Mr. Cupid (Don't You Call on Me)/Hang My Head and Cry	1967	2.50	5.00	10.00
—B-side by the Big Guys					

COOKIES, THE/LITTLE EVA/CAROLE KING

Albums

Number	Title (A Side/B Side)	Yr	VG	VG+	NM
DIMENSION					
DLP-6001 [M]	The Dimension Dolls, Vol. 1	1964	62.50	125.00	250.00

COOL, CALVIN, AND THE SURF KNOBS

45s

Number	Title (A Side/B Side)	Yr	VG	VG+	NM
CHARTER					
7	Beach Bash/El Tocolote	1963	10.00	20.00	40.00

Albums

Number	Title (A Side/B Side)	Yr	VG	VG+	NM
CHARTER					
CLP-103 [M]	The Surfer's Beat	1963	10.00	20.00	40.00
CLS-103 [S]	The Surfer's Beat	1963	12.50	25.00	50.00

COOL HEAT

See WIND.

COOL SOUNDS, THE

45s

Number	Title (A Side/B Side)	Yr	VG	VG+	NM
PULSAR					
2421	Comin' Home (Free)/Rag Doll	1969	12.50	25.00	50.00
WARNER BROS.					
7538	I'll Take You Back/Where Do We Go from Here	1971	7.50	15.00	30.00
7575	A Love Like Ours Could Last a Million Years or More/Who Can I Turn To	1972	7.50	15.00	30.00
7615	Boy Wonder/Free	1972	7.50	15.00	30.00

COOLBREEZERS, THE

45s

Number	Title (A Side/B Side)	Yr	VG	VG+	NM
ABC-PARAMOUNT					
9865	You Know I Go for You/My Brother	1957	25.00	50.00	100.00
BALE					
100/101	The Greatest Love of All/Eda Weda Bug	1958	15.00	30.00	60.00
102/103	Let Christmas Ring/Hello, Mister New Year	1958	50.00	100.00	200.00
EBONY					
1015	Won't You Come In/Pack Your Bags and Go	1956	125.00	250.00	500.00
—As "The Little Coolbreezers"					

COOLIDGE, RITA

Also see KRIS KRISTOFFERSON.

45s

Number	Title (A Side/B Side)	Yr	VG	VG+	NM
A&M					
1256	Crazy Love/Mountains	1971	—	2.50	5.00
1271	Mud Island/I Believe in You	1971	—	2.50	5.00
1324	Lay My Burden Down/Nice Feelin'	1972	—	2.00	4.00
1353	Most Likely You Go Your Way/Family Full of Soul	1972	—	2.00	4.00
1398	Fever/My Crew	1972	—	2.00	4.00
1398 [PS]	Fever/My Crew	1972	—	3.00	6.00
1414	Donut Man/Whiskey, Whiskey	1973	—	2.00	4.00
1545	Hold an Old Friend's Hand/Mama Lou	1974	—	2.00	4.00
1642	Love Has No Pride/Heaven's Dream	1974	—	2.00	4.00
1792	Am I Blue/Star	1976	—	2.00	4.00
1816	Late Again/Keep the Candle Burning	1976	—	2.00	4.00
1922	(Your Love Has Lifted Me) Higher and Higher/Who's to Bless and Who's to Blame	1977	—	2.00	4.00
1922 [PS]	(Your Love Has Lifted Me) Higher and Higher/Who's to Bless and Who's to Blame	1977	—	3.00	6.00
1965	We're All Alone/Southern Lady	1977	—	2.00	4.00
1965 [PS]	We're All Alone/Southern Lady	1977	—	2.00	4.00
2004	The Way You Do the Things You Do/I Feel the Burden (Being Lifted Off My Shoulders)	1977	—	2.00	4.00
2004 [PS]	The Way You Do the Things You Do/I Feel the Burden (Being Lifted Off My Shoulders)	1977	—	2.00	4.00
2058	You/Only You Know and I Know	1978	—	2.00	4.00
2058 [PS]	You/Only You Know and I Know	1978	—	2.00	4.00
2090	Love Me Again/Jealous Kind	1978	—	2.00	4.00
2169	One Fine Day/Sweet Emotions	1979	—	2.00	4.00
2199	I'd Rather Leave While I'm in Love/Sweet Emotions	1979	—	2.00	4.00
2281	Fool That I Am/Can She Keep You Satisfied	1980	—	2.00	4.00
2318	Words/Born Under a Bad Sign	1981	—	2.00	4.00
2361	The Closer You Get/Take It Home	1981	—	2.00	4.00
2385	Wishin' and Hopin'/I Did My Part	1981	—	2.00	4.00
2541	I'll Never Let You Go/Shadow in the Night	1983	—	—	3.00
2546 [DJ]	I Will Never Let You Go (same on both sides)	1983	—	2.00	4.00
—Stock copies do not exist					
2551	All Time High/(Instrumental)	1983	—	—	3.00
2551 [PS]	All Time High/(Instrumental)	1983	—	2.50	5.00
2586	Only You/Shadow in the Night	1983	—	—	3.00
2634	Something Said Love/Survivor	1984	—	—	3.00
PEPPER					
442	Rainbow Child/Secret Places, Hiding Faces	1969	2.00	4.00	8.00
443	Turn Around and Love You/Walking in the Morning	1969	2.00	4.00	8.00

Number	Title (A Side/B Side)	Yr	VG	VG+	NM
Albums					
A&M					
SP-3107	Rita Coolidge	198?	2.00	4.00	8.00
—Budget-line reissue					
SP-3130	Nice Feelin'	198?	2.00	4.00	8.00
—Budget-line reissue					
SP-3163	Anytime...Anywhere	198?	2.00	4.00	8.00
—Budget-line reissue					
SP-3238	Rita Coolidge/Greatest Hits	198?	2.00	4.00	8.00
—Budget-line reissue					
SP-3627	Fall Into Spring	1974	2.50	5.00	10.00
SP-3727	Heartbreak Radio	1981	2.50	5.00	10.00
SP-4291	Rita Coolidge	1971	2.50	5.00	10.00
SP-4325	Nice Feelin'	1971	2.50	5.00	10.00
AP-4370	The Lady's Not for Sale	1972	2.50	5.00	10.00
SP-4531	It's Only Love	1975	2.50	5.00	10.00
SP-4616	Anytime...Anywhere	1977	2.50	5.00	10.00
SP-4669	Love Me Again	1978	2.50	5.00	10.00
SP-4781	Satisfied	1979	2.50	5.00	10.00
SP-4836	Rita Coolidge/Greatest Hits	1981	2.50	5.00	10.00
SP-4914	Never Let You Gp	1983	2.50	5.00	10.00
SP-5003	Inside the Fire	1984	2.50	5.00	10.00
NAUTILUS					
NR-16	Anytime...Anywhere	1981	6.25	12.50	25.00
—Audiophile vinyl					

COOPER, ALICE

Also see NAZZ (2); THE SPIDERS (2).

Number	Title (A Side/B Side)	Yr	VG	VG+	NM
12-Inch Singles					
EPIC					
EAS 1347 [DJ]	I Got a Line on You (same on both sides)	1988	2.50	5.00	10.00
EAS 1663 [DJ]	Poison (same on both sides)	1989	2.50	5.00	10.00
EAS 1686 [DJ]	Trash (same on both sides)	1989	2.50	5.00	10.00
MCA					
L33-17177 [DJ]	He's Back (The Man Behind the Mask) (same on both sides)	1986	2.00	4.00	8.00
L33-17205 [DJ]	Give It Up (same on both sides)	1986	2.00	4.00	8.00
WARNER BROS.					
PRO-A-864 [DJ]	Clones (We're All)/Model Citizen	1980	3.75	7.50	15.00
PRO-A-1059 [DJ]	I Like Girls (same on both sides)	1981	3.00	6.00	12.00
45s					
ATLANTIC					
3254	Only Women/Cold Ethyl	1975	—	2.50	5.00
3280	Department of Youth/Some Folks	1975	—	2.50	5.00
3298	Welcome to My Nightmare/Cold Ethyl	1975	—	2.50	5.00
EPIC					
08114	I Got a Line on You/Livin' on the Edge	1988	—	—	3.00
—B-side by Britney Fox					
68958	Poison/Trash	1989	—	—	3.00
73085	House of Fire/Ballad of Dwight Fry	1989	—	—	3.00
73845	Hey Stoopid/It Rained All Night	1991	—	—	3.00
73983	Love's a Loaded Gun/Fire	1991	—	—	3.00
MCA					
52904	He's Back (The Man Behind the Mask)/Billion Dollar Baby	1986	—	—	3.00
52904 [PS]	He's Back (The Man Behind the Mask)/Billion Dollar Baby	1986	—	—	3.00
53212	Freedom/Time to Kill	1987	—	—	3.00
53212 [PS]	Freedom/Time to Kill	1987	—	—	3.00
STRAIGHT					
101	Reflected/Living	1969	75.00	150.00	300.00
—Promos worth about 10% of this value					
WARNER BROS.					
7141	Eighteen/Caught in a Dream	1972	—	2.00	4.00
—"Back to Back Hits" series (originals have green labels)					
7398	Shoe Salesman/Return of the Spiders	1970	5.00	10.00	20.00
7449	Eighteen/Body	1971	—	2.50	5.00
7490	Caught in a Dream/Hallowed Be My Name	1971	—	2.50	5.00
7529	Under My Wheels/Desperado	1971	—	2.50	5.00
7568	Be My Lover/Yeah, Yeah, Yeah	1972	—	2.50	5.00
7596	School's Out/Gutter Cat	1972	—	2.50	5.00
7596 [PS]	School's Out/Gutter Cat	1972	2.50	5.00	10.00
7631	Elected/Luney Tune	1972	—	2.50	5.00
7631 [PS]	Elected/Luney Tune	1972	2.50	5.00	10.00
7673	Hello Hurray/Generation Landslide	1972	—	2.50	5.00
7691	No More Mr. Nice Guy/Raped and Freezin'	1973	—	2.50	5.00
7724	Billion Dollar Babies/Mary Ann	1973	—	2.50	5.00
7762	Teenage Lament '74/Hard Hearted Alice	1973	—	2.50	5.00
7783	Muscle of Love/Crazy Little Child	1974	—	2.50	5.00
8023	I'm Eighteen/Muscle of Love	1974	—	2.50	5.00
8228	I Never Cry/Go to Hell	1976	—	2.00	4.00
8349	You and Me/It's Hot Tonight	1977	—	2.00	4.00
8349 [PS]	You and Me/It's Hot Tonight	1977	2.00	4.00	8.00
8448	(No More) Love at Your Convenience/I Never Wrote Those Songs	1977	—	2.50	5.00
8607	School's Out/Eighteen	1978	2.00	4.00	8.00
8695	How You Gonna See Me Now/No Tricks	1978	—	2.50	5.00
8760	From the Inside/Nurse Rosetta	1979	—	2.00	4.00
29828	I Am the Future/Tag, You're It	1982	—	2.00	4.00
29928	I Like Girls/Zorro's Ascent	1982	—	2.00	4.00
49204	Clones (We're All)/Model Citizen	1980	—	2.00	4.00
49204 [PS]	Clones (We're All)/Model Citizen	1980	—	2.50	5.00
49526	Dance Yourself to Death/Talk Talk	1980	—	2.00	4.00
49780	You Want It, You Got It/Who Do You Think We Are	1981	—	2.00	4.00
49848	Generation Landslide '81/Seven and Seven Is	1981	—	2.00	4.00
Albums					
ACCORD					
SN-7162	Toronto Rock 'n' Roll Revival 1969	1981	3.00	6.00	12.00
ATLANTIC					
SD 18130	Welcome to My Nightmare	1975	2.50	5.00	10.00
SD 19157	Welcome to My Nightmare	1978	2.00	4.00	8.00
EPIC					
OE 45137	Trash	1989	3.00	6.00	12.00
E 46786	Hey Stoopid	1991	3.75	7.50	15.00
MCA					
5761	Constrictor	1986	2.00	4.00	8.00
42091	Raise Your Fist and Yell	1987	2.00	4.00	8.00
MOBILE FIDELITY					
1-063	Welcome to My Nightmare	1980	12.50	25.00	50.00
—Audiophile vinyl					
PAIR					
PDL2-1163 [(2)]	A Man Called Alice	1987	3.75	7.50	15.00
STRAIGHT					
STS-1051	Pretties for You	1969	37.50	75.00	150.00
—Yellow label stock copy					
STS-1051 [DJ]	Pretties for You	1969	50.00	100.00	200.00
—White label promo					
WS 1840	Pretties for You	1970	15.00	30.00	60.00
—Pink label stock copy					
WS 1845	Easy Action	1970	12.50	25.00	50.00
—Pink label stock copy; "Alice Cooper" in black on cover					
WS 1845	Easy Action	1970	7.50	15.00	30.00
—Pink label stock copy; "Alice Cooper" in white on cover					
WS 1845 [DJ]	Easy Action	1970	25.00	50.00	100.00
—White label promo					
WS 1883	Love It to Death	1971	12.50	25.00	50.00
—Pink label stock copy					
WS 1883 [DJ]	Love It to Death	1971	25.00	50.00	100.00
—White label promo					
WARNER BROS.					
PRO 789 [DJ]	The Alice Cooper Radio Show	1978	6.25	12.50	25.00
WS 1883	Love It to Death	1971	7.50	15.00	30.00
—Version 1: Green "WB" label; cover has Alice's thumb sticking out in such a way that it appears to be another part of the body					
WS 1883	Love It to Death	1971	5.00	10.00	20.00
—Version 2: Green "WB" label; same as above, but has a white box reading "Contains the Hit 'I'm Eighteen' "					
WS 1883	Love It to Death	1971	5.00	10.00	20.00
—Version 3: Green "WB" label; cover has large white areas at top and bottom with lower half of the photo cropped out					
WS 1883	Love It to Death	1971	3.00	6.00	12.00
—Version 4: Green "WB" label; with "I'm Eighteen" box and Alice's protruding thumb airbrushed off the cover					
BS 2567	Killer	1971	7.50	15.00	30.00
—Early copies have an attached 1972 calendar/poster					
BS 2567	Killer	1972	3.00	6.00	12.00
—Later copies no longer have the calendar/poster					
BS 2623	School's Out	1972	10.00	20.00	40.00
—With paper panties intact; back cover does not list song titles					
BS 2623	School's Out	1972	5.00	10.00	20.00
—Back cover does not list song titles, but panties are missing					
BS 2623	School's Out	1972	7.50	15.00	30.00
—With paper panties intact; back cover lists song titles					
BS 2623	School's Out	1972	3.00	6.00	12.00
—No panties, with song titles listed					
BS 2685	Billion Dollar Babies	1973	3.00	6.00	12.00
—Green "WB" label					
BS4 2685 [Q]	Billion Dollar Babies	1974	6.25	12.50	25.00
BS 2748	Muscle of Love	1973	2.50	5.00	10.00
BS4 2748 [Q]	Muscle of Love	1974	6.25	12.50	25.00
BS4 2803 [Q]	Alice Cooper's Greatest Hits	1974	6.25	12.50	25.00
W 2803	Alice Cooper's Greatest Hits	1974	2.50	5.00	10.00
BS 2896	Alice Cooper Goes to Hell	1976	2.50	5.00	10.00
BSK 3027	Lace and Whiskey	1977	2.50	5.00	10.00
BSK 3107	Alice Cooper's Greatest Hits	1977	2.00	4.00	8.00
—Reissue of BS 2803					
BSK 3138	The Alice Cooper Show	1977	2.50	5.00	10.00
BSK 3263	From the Inside	1978	2.50	5.00	10.00
BSK 3436	Flush the Fashion	1980	2.50	5.00	10.00
BSK 3581	Special Forces	1981	2.50	5.00	10.00
23719	Zipper Catches Skin	1982	2.50	5.00	10.00
23969	Da Da	1983	2.50	5.00	10.00

COOPER, BO

See RON DANTE.

COOPER, CHRISTINE

Number	Title (A Side/B Side)	Yr	VG	VG+	NM
45s					
PARKWAY					
122	I Must Have You (Or No One)/Good Looks (They Don't Count)	1966	3.75	7.50	15.00
971	S.O.S./Say What You Feel	1966	6.25	12.50	25.00
983	(They Call Him) A Bad Boy/Heartaches Away My Boy	1966	10.00	20.00	40.00

COOPER, DOLLY

Number	Title (A Side/B Side)	Yr	VG	VG+	NM
45s					
DOT					
15495	Big Rock Inn/I'm Looking Through Your Window	1956	3.00	6.00	12.00
15535	The Confession of a Fool/Tell Me, Tell Me	1957	3.00	6.00	12.00
EBB					
109	Wild Love/Time Brings About a Change	1957	3.00	6.00	12.00
MODERN					
965	My Man/Ay La Bas	1955	10.00	20.00	40.00
977	Teenage Prayer/Down So Long	1956	12.50	25.00	50.00
986	Teenage Wedding Bells/Every Day and Every Night	1956	12.50	25.00	50.00
SAVOY					
1121	You Gotta Be Good to Yourself/Love Can't Be Blind	1954	5.00	10.00	20.00

COOPER, LES, AND THE SOUL ROCKERS

Also see THE EMPIRES (1).

Number	Title (A Side/B Side)	Yr	VG	VG+	NM
45s					
ARRAWAK					
1008	I Can Do the Soul Jerk/At the World's Fair	1965	3.00	6.00	12.00

Number	Title (A Side/B Side)	Yr	VG	VG+	NM
ATCO					
6644	Gonna Have a Lotta Fun/Thank God for You	1969	2.00	4.00	8.00
DIMENSION					
1023	Motor City/Swobblin'	1963	5.00	10.00	20.00
ENJOY					
2024	Owee Baby/Let's Do the Boston Monkey	1965	2.50	5.00	10.00
EVERLAST					
5016	Twistin'/Dig Yourself	1963	3.00	6.00	12.00
5019	Wiggle Wobble/Dig Yourself	1963	3.75	7.50	15.00
5023	Garbage Can/Bossa Nova Dance	1963	3.00	6.00	12.00
Albums					
EVERLAST					
ELP-202 [M]	Wiggle Wobble	1963	12.50	25.00	50.00

COOPER, PAT

Number	Title (A Side/B Side)	Yr	VG	VG+	NM
Albums					
UNITED ARTISTS					
UAL 3446 [M]	Our Hero...Pat Cooper	1966	3.00	6.00	12.00
UAL 3548 [M]	Spaghetti Sauce & Other Delights	1966	3.00	6.00	12.00
UAS 6446 [S]	Our Hero...Pat Cooper	1966	3.75	7.50	15.00
UAS 6548 [S]	Spaghetti Sauce & Other Delights	1966	3.75	7.50	15.00
UAS 6600	You Don't Have to Be Italian To Like Pat Cooper	1968	3.00	6.00	12.00
UAS 6690	More Saucy Stories from... Pat Cooper	1969	3.00	6.00	12.00

COOPERETTES, THE

Number	Title (A Side/B Side)	Yr	VG	VG+	NM
45s					
ABC					
11156	Peace Maker/Trouble	1968	3.00	6.00	12.00
11197	Spiral Road/Trouble	1969	3.00	6.00	12.00
BRUNSWICK					
55296	Goodbye School/Goodbye School (Part 2)	1966	3.75	7.50	15.00
55307	Don't Trust Him/Everything's Wrong	1966	3.75	7.50	15.00
55329	(Life Has) No Meaning Now/Shing-a-Ling	1967	6.25	12.50	25.00

COPASETICS, THE

Number	Title (A Side/B Side)	Yr	VG	VG+	NM
45s					
PREMIUM					
409	Believe in Me/Collegian	1956	50.00	100.00	200.00

COPELAND, KEN

Number	Title (A Side/B Side)	Yr	VG	VG+	NM
45s					
DOT					
15686	Where the Rio Rosa Flows/Locked in the Arms of Love	1958	3.75	7.50	15.00
IMPERIAL					
5432	Pledge of Love/Night Air	1957	5.00	10.00	20.00
—B-side by The Mints					
5453	Teenage/Bed of Lies	1957	5.00	10.00	20.00
5466	I Want to Go Steady/I Would Give My Heart	1957	5.00	10.00	20.00
LIN					
5007	Pledge of Love/Night Air	1957	10.00	20.00	40.00
—B-side by The Mints					
5017	Fanny Brown/Chaser of Hearts	1957	10.00	20.00	40.00

COPPER PLATED INTEGRATED CIRCUIT, THE

Number	Title (A Side/B Side)	Yr	VG	VG+	NM
Albums					
COMMAND					
RS-945 SD	Plugged In Pop	1969	6.25	12.50	25.00

COPS 'N ROBBERS

Number	Title (A Side/B Side)	Yr	VG	VG+	NM
45s					
CORAL					
62466	I Could Have Danced All Night/Just Keep Right On	1965	2.50	5.00	10.00
62473	It's All Over Now, Baby Blue/I Found Out	1965	2.50	5.00	10.00
PARROT					
9716	St. James Infirmary/There's Got to Be a Reason	1964	2.50	5.00	10.00

CORDEL, PAT

Also see THE ELEGANTS.

Number	Title (A Side/B Side)	Yr	VG	VG+	NM
45s					
CLUB					
1011	Darling, Come Back/My My Tears	1956	500.00	1000.	1500.
—And the Crescents					
MICHELLE					
503	Darling, Come Back/My My Tears	1959	37.50	75.00	150.00
—And the Elegants					
VICTORY					
1001	Darling, Come Back/My My Tears	1963	20.00	40.00	80.00
—And the Elegants					

CORDELLS, THE

Number	Title (A Side/B Side)	Yr	VG	VG+	NM
45s					
BARGAIN					
5004	The Beat of My Heart/Laid Off	1962	12.50	25.00	50.00
BULLSEYE					
1017	Believe in Me/Please Don't Go	1958	25.00	50.00	100.00

CORDET, LOUISE

Number	Title (A Side/B Side)	Yr	VG	VG+	NM
45s					
LONDON					
9560	I'm Just a Baby/In a Matter of Moments	1963	3.00	6.00	12.00

CORDIALS, THE

Several different groups.

Number	Title (A Side/B Side)	Yr	VG	VG+	NM
45s					
7 ARTS					
707	Dawn Is Almost Here/Keep An Eye	1961	25.00	50.00	100.00
BETHLEHEM					
3019	What's the Matter with Me/I'm Not Crying Anymore	1961	6.25	12.50	25.00
CORDIAL					
1001	I'm Ashamed/Sentimental Jorney	1960	25.00	50.00	100.00
FELSTED					
8653	Once in a Lifetime/What Kind of Fool Am I	1962	7.50	15.00	30.00
LIBERTY					
55784	Oh, How I Love Her/You Can't Believe in Love	1965	6.25	12.50	25.00
REVEILLE					
106	Eternal Love/The International Twist	1962	75.00	150.00	300.00
WHIP					
276	Listen My Heart/My Heart's Desire	1961	62.50	125.00	250.00
Albums					
CATAMOUNT					
902	Blue Eyed Soul	1967	6.25	12.50	25.00

CORDOVANS, THE

Number	Title (A Side/B Side)	Yr	VG	VG+	NM
45s					
JOHNSON					
731	Come On Baby/My Heart	1960	6.25	12.50	25.00

COREA, CHICK

Also see HERBIE HANCOCK; RETURN TO FOREVER.

Number	Title (A Side/B Side)	Yr	VG	VG+	NM
45s					
POLYDOR					
14538	Bagatelle #4/Central Park	1979	—	2.00	4.00
Albums					
ATLANTIC					
SD 2-305 [(2)]	Inner Space	1973	3.75	7.50	15.00
BLUE NOTE					
BN-LA395-H2 [(2)]	Chick Corea	1975	3.75	7.50	15.00
LWB-395 [(2)]	Chick Corea	1981	2.50	5.00	10.00
—Reissue with new prefix					
BN-LA472-H2 [(2)]	Circling In	1976	3.75	7.50	15.00
BN-LA882-J2 [(2)]	Circulus	1978	3.75	7.50	15.00
BST-84353	Song of Singing	1970	5.00	10.00	20.00
B1-90055	Now He Sings, Now He Sobs	1988	3.00	6.00	12.00
—Reissue					
ECM					
1009	A.R.C.	197?	3.00	6.00	12.00
1014	Piano Improvisations, Vol. 1	1974	3.00	6.00	12.00
1020	Piano Improvisations, Vol. 2	197?	3.00	6.00	12.00
1232 [(2)]	Trio Music	198?	3.00	6.00	12.00
23797	Lyric Suite for Sextet	1984	2.50	5.00	10.00
25005	Children's Songs	1985	2.50	5.00	10.00
25013	Voyage	1985	2.50	5.00	10.00
ELEKTRA/MUSICIAN					
60167	Again & Again	1984	2.50	5.00	10.00
GROOVE MERCHANT					
530	Sundance	1974	3.00	6.00	12.00
—Reissue of 2202					
2202	Sundance	1972	5.00	10.00	20.00
4406 [(2)]	Piano Giants	197?	3.75	7.50	15.00
GRP					
GR-1026	The Chick Corea Electric Band	1987	2.50	5.00	10.00
GR-1036	Light Years	1987	2.50	5.00	10.00
GR-1053	Eye of the Beholder	1988	2.50	5.00	10.00
GR-9582	The Chick Corea Akoustic Band	1989	3.00	6.00	12.00
GR-9601	Inside Out	1991	3.75	7.50	15.00
MUSE					
5011	Bliss!	1973	3.75	7.50	15.00
PACIFIC JAZZ					
LN-10057	Now He Sings, Now He Sobs	1981	2.50	5.00	10.00
—Reissue of Solid State 18039					
POLYDOR					
PD-6062	The Leprechaun	1976	2.50	5.00	10.00
PD-1-6130	The Mad Hatter	1978	2.50	5.00	10.00
PD-1-6160	Friends	1978	2.50	5.00	10.00
PD-1-6176	Secret Agent	1979	2.50	5.00	10.00
PD-1-6208	Delphi I	1979	2.50	5.00	10.00
PD-2-6334 [(2)]	Delphi II & III	1982	3.00	6.00	12.00
PD-2-9003 [(2)]	My Spanish Heart	1976	3.00	6.00	12.00
QUINTESSENCE					
25011	Before Forever	1978	3.00	6.00	12.00
SOLID STATE					
SS-18039	Now He Sings, Now He Sobs	1969	5.00	10.00	20.00
SS-18055	Chick Corea "Is"	1969	5.00	10.00	20.00
VORTEX					
2004	Tones	1971	5.00	10.00	20.00
WARNER BROS.					
BSK 3425	Tap Step	1980	2.50	5.00	10.00
BSK 3552	Three Quartets	1981	2.50	5.00	10.00
23699	Touchstone	1983	2.50	5.00	10.00

COREY, JOHN

Number	Title (A Side/B Side)	Yr	VG	VG+	NM
45s					
VEE JAY					
466	Pollyanna/I'll Forget	1962	7.50	15.00	30.00
—Backing group: The Four Seasons					
514	Hey Little Runaround/The Prettiest Girl I've Kissed Today	1963	2.50	5.00	10.00

CORNELIUS BROTHERS AND SISTER ROSE

Number	Title (A Side/B Side)	Yr	VG	VG+	NM
45s					
PLATINUM					
105/6	Treat Her Like a Lady/Over at My Place	1970	3.00	6.00	12.00
UNITED ARTISTS					
0131	Treat Her Like a Lady/Over at My Place	1973	—	2.00	4.00
—"Silver Spotlight Series" reissue					
XW208	Let Me Down Easy/Gonna Be Sweet for You	1973	—	2.50	5.00

Number	Title (A Side/B Side)	Yr	VG	VG+	NM
XW313	I Just Can't Stop Loving You/These Lonely Nights	1973	—	2.50	5.00
XW377	Big Time Lover/Wonderful Tune	1974	—	2.50	5.00
XW512	Too Late to Turn Back Now/Don't Ever Be Lonely (A Poor Little Fool Like Me)	1974	—	2.00	4.00
—Reissue					
XW533	Trouble Child/Got to Testify	1974	—	2.50	5.00
XW534	Since I Found My Baby/I Love Music	1974	—	2.50	5.00
50721	Treat Her Like a Lady/Over at My Place	1970	—	2.50	5.00
50910	Too Late to Turn Back Now/Lift Your Love Higher	1972	—	2.50	5.00
50954	Don't Ever Be Lonely (A Poor Little Fool Like Me)/I'm So Glad to Be Loved by You	1972	—	2.50	5.00
50996	I'm Never Gonna Be Alone Anymore/Let's Stay Together	1972	—	2.50	5.00
Albums					
UNITED ARTISTS					
UA-LA593-G	Greatest Hits	1976	3.00	6.00	12.00
UAS-5568	Cornelius Brothers and Sister Rose	1972	3.75	7.50	15.00

CORNELL, DON

Also see TERESA BREWER.

Number	Title (A Side/B Side)	Yr	VG	VG+	NM
45s					
20TH FOX					
515	If You Love Her Tell Her So/You Know You Don't Want Me	1964	2.00	4.00	8.00
ABC-PARAMOUNT					
10687	Italian Wedding Song/Please Lie to Me	1965	—	3.00	6.00
10740	Dingle Ling, Dingle Ling/Careless Hands	1965	—	3.00	6.00
CORAL					
60659	I'll Walk Alone/That's the Chance You Take	1952	3.00	6.00	12.00
60690	I'm Yours/My Mother's Pearls	1952	3.00	6.00	12.00
60748	This Is the Beginning of the End/I Can't Cry Anymore	1952	3.00	6.00	12.00
60859	Let's Have an Old Fashioned Christmas/I've Got the Christmas Spirit	1952	3.75	7.50	15.00
60860	I/Be Fair	1952	3.00	6.00	12.00
60900	For You/I Was Lucky	1953	2.50	5.00	10.00
60901	Stay As Sweet As You Are/We Three (My Echo, My Shadow and Me)	1953	2.50	5.00	10.00
60902	It Isn't Fair/Something to Remember You By	1953	2.50	5.00	10.00
60903	S'posin/If You Were Only Mine	1953	2.50	5.00	10.00
60968	There's No Escape/Many Are the Times	1953	3.00	6.00	12.00
61011	Who Loves Me/When the Hands of the Clock Pray at Midnight	1953	3.00	6.00	12.00
61030	Please Play Our Song (Mister Record Man)/If I Should Love Again	1953	3.00	6.00	12.00
61068	I'm Yearning/You're On Trial	1953	3.00	6.00	12.00
61125	Hold Me/Size 12	1954	3.00	6.00	12.00
61171	Believe in Me/Little Lucy	1954	3.00	6.00	12.00
61206	Hold My Hand/I'm Blessed	1954	3.00	6.00	12.00
61253	No Man Is an Island/All at Once	1954	3.00	6.00	12.00
61333	Athena/No Man Is an Island	1955	2.50	5.00	10.00
61367	When You Are in Love/Give Me Your Love	1955	2.50	5.00	10.00
61393	Most of All/The Door Is Still Open to My Heart	1955	2.50	5.00	10.00
61407	Unchained Melody/All of You	1955	2.50	5.00	10.00
61467	The Bible Tells Me So/Love Is a Many-Splendored Thing	1955	2.50	5.00	10.00
61521	Young Abe Lincoln/Dream World	1955	2.50	5.00	10.00
61549	Make a Wish/There Once Was a Beautiful...	1955	2.50	5.00	10.00
61584	Teenage Meeting (Gonna Rock It Up Right)/I Still Have a Prayer	1956	3.75	7.50	15.00
61613	Rock Island Line/Na-Ne-Na-Na	1956	2.50	5.00	10.00
61631	But Love Me/Fort Knox	1956	2.50	5.00	10.00
61659	Grazie/Could You	1956	2.50	5.00	10.00
61687	Heaven Only Knows/Life Is a Song	1956	2.50	5.00	10.00
61721	See-Saw/From the Bottom of My Heart	1956	2.50	5.00	10.00
61757	Let's Be Friends/Ma-Ma Pa-Pa Cha-Cha	1956	2.50	5.00	10.00
61790	Afternoon in Madrid/Let's Get Lost	1957	2.50	5.00	10.00
61811	Sittin' in the Balcony/My Faith, My Hope, My Love	1957	2.50	5.00	10.00
61817	Mama Guitar/A Face in the Crowd	1957	2.50	5.00	10.00
61854	Mailman, Bring Me No More Blues/No Matter What	1957	2.50	5.00	10.00
61905	Non Dimenticar/Before It's Time to Say Goodnight	1957	2.50	5.00	10.00
61993	You Go to My Head/Village in Capri	1958	2.50	5.00	10.00
62019	But Not Your Heart/Once More	1958	2.50	5.00	10.00
DOT					
15938	Heart of My Heart/This Earth Is Mine	1959	2.00	4.00	8.00
16044	I/Size 12	1960	2.00	4.00	8.00
JUBILEE					
5423	Night Train to Memphis/Bring Down the Curtain	1962	2.00	4.00	8.00
RCA VICTOR					
47-2914	Baby It's Cold Outside/Whispering Waters	1949	3.75	7.50	15.00
—With Laura Leslie					
47-3239	Come Back to Me/My Baby Is Blue	1949	3.75	7.50	15.00
47-3776	You Dreamer You/I Surrender Dear	1950	3.75	7.50	15.00
47-3839	You Wonderful You/Hawaii	1950	3.75	7.50	15.00
47-3884	I Need You So/It Couldn't Happen to a Sweeter Girl	1950	3.75	7.50	15.00
47-3909	Au Revoir Again/A Whistle and a Prayer	1950	3.75	7.50	15.00
47-3950	Take Me in Your Arms/The Breeze	1950	3.75	7.50	15.00
47-3991	Sue Me/Velvet Lips	1950	3.75	7.50	15.00
47-4042	Wedding Bells/Let a Smile Be Your Umbrella	1951	3.00	6.00	12.00
47-4043	Was That the Human Thing to Do/That Old Feeling	1951	3.00	6.00	12.00
47-4044	I'll Be Seeing You/When I Take My Sugar to Tea	1951	3.00	6.00	12.00
47-4083	My Inspiration/You Can't Tell a Lie to Your Heart	1951	3.75	7.50	15.00
47-4149	Why Don't You Tell Me So/If I Had Another Chance	1951	3.75	7.50	15.00
ROULETTE					
4355	The Flying Trapeze/Wish I Was	1961	2.00	4.00	8.00
SIGNATURE					
12002	Forever Couldn't Be Long Enough/Sempre Amore	1959	2.00	4.00	8.00
12020	Forever/There's Still Time Brother	1959	2.00	4.00	8.00
12027	Grateful/Only Time Will Tell	1960	2.00	4.00	8.00
12032	Your Kiss/I Have But One Heart	1960	2.00	4.00	8.00
7-Inch Extended Plays					
CORAL					
EC 81501	Hold My Hand/I'm Yours//It Isn't Fair/I'll Walk Alone	195?	3.00	6.00	12.00
EC 81501 [PS]	Don Cornell	195?	3.00	6.00	12.00
83010 [DJ]	Let's Have an Old Fashioned Christmas/I've Got the Christmas Spirit//Sing a Song Of Santa Claus/Winter's Here Again	195?	3.75	7.50	15.00
—B-side by the Ames Brothers					
RCA CAMDEN					
CAE-239	The Breeze (Bringin' My Honey Back to Me)/Are You Lonesome Tonight//Wedding Bells Are Breaking Up That Old Gang of Mine/Have You Ever Been Lonely	195?	2.50	5.00	10.00
CAE-239 [PS]	Don Cornell	195?	2.50	5.00	10.00
Albums					
ABC-PARAMOUNT					
ABC-537 [M]	Incomparable	1966	3.00	6.00	12.00
ABCS-537 [S]	Incomparable	1966	3.75	7.50	15.00
CORAL					
CRL 57055 [M]	Don	1955	7.50	15.00	30.00
CRL 57133 [M]	For Teenagers Only	1957	7.50	15.00	30.00
DOT					
DLP-3160 [M]	Don Cornell's Great Hits	1959	6.25	12.50	25.00
DLP-25160 [S]	Don Cornell's Great Hits	1959	7.50	15.00	30.00
MOVIETONE					
71013 [M]	I Wish You Love	1966	3.00	6.00	12.00
S-72013 [S]	I Wish You Love	1966	3.75	7.50	15.00
SIGNATURE					
SM-1001 [M]	Don Cornell Sings Love Songs	1960	5.00	10.00	20.00
SS-1001 [S]	Don Cornell Sings Love Songs	1960	6.25	12.50	25.00
VOCALION					
VL 3657 [M]	Don Cornell	196?	3.00	6.00	12.00

CORNELL, DON; JOHNNY DESMOND; ALAN DALE

Number	Title (A Side/B Side)	Yr	VG	VG+	NM
45s					
CORAL					
61076	The Gang That Sang "Heart of My Heart"/I Think I'll Fall in Love Today	1953	3.00	6.00	12.00

CORNELLS, THE

Number	Title (A Side/B Side)	Yr	VG	VG+	NM
45s					
GAREX					
100	Mama's Little Baby/Wak-A-Cha	1962	7.50	15.00	30.00
102	Malibu Surf/Agua Caliente	1963	7.50	15.00	30.00
201	Beach Bound/Lone Star Stomp	1963	7.50	15.00	30.00
206	Surf Fever/Do the Slauson	1963	7.50	15.00	30.00
Albums					
GAREX					
LPGA-100 [M]	Beach Bound	1963	125.00	250.00	500.00

CORNISH, GENE

Also see THE RASCALS.

Number	Title (A Side/B Side)	Yr	VG	VG+	NM
45s					
DAWN					
550	Let's Do the Capri/Lonely I Will Say	1964	7.50	15.00	30.00
551	I Wanna Be a Beatle/Oh Misery	1964	10.00	20.00	40.00
VASSAR					
319	Since I Lost You/Winner Take All	1962	5.00	10.00	20.00
—Later a member of the (Young) Rascals					
321	My Baby Ran Away from Me/(B-side unknown)	1962	6.25	12.50	25.00

CORONETS, THE

Number	Title (A Side/B Side)	Yr	VG	VG+	NM
45s					
CHESS					
1549	Nadine/I'm All Alone	1953	50.00	100.00	200.00
—Silver top label					
1549	Nadine/I'm All Alone	1958	3.00	6.00	12.00
—All-blue label					
1553	It Would Be Heavenly/Baby's Coming Home	1953	100.00	200.00	400.00
—Black vinyl					
1553	It Would Be Heavenly/Baby's Coming Home	1953	200.00	400.00	800.00
—Red vinyl					
GROOVE					
0114	I Love You More/Crime Doesn't Pay	1955	25.00	50.00	100.00
0116	The Bible Tells Me So/Hush	1955	37.50	75.00	150.00
STERLING					
903	Don't Deprive Me/Little Boy	1955	62.50	125.00	250.00

CORPORATION, THE

Number	Title (A Side/B Side)	Yr	VG	VG+	NM
45s					
CAPITOL					
2467	Highway/I Want to Get Out of My Grave	1969	3.75	7.50	15.00
CUCA					
1496	You Make Me Feel Good/Sitting by the Sea	1968	3.75	7.50	15.00
Albums					
AGE OF AQUARIUS					
4150	Get On Our Swing	1968	7.50	15.00	30.00
4250	Hassles in My Mind	1969	7.50	15.00	30.00
CAPITOL					
ST-175	The Corporation	1969	12.50	25.00	50.00

CORPUS

Number	Title (A Side/B Side)	Yr	VG	VG+	NM
Albums					
ACORN					
1001	Creation: A Child	1971	75.00	150.00	300.00

CORSAIRS, THE

45s

Number	Title (A Side/B Side)	Yr	VG	VG+	NM
HY-TONE					
110	Goodbye Darling/Rock Lilly Rock	1957	375.00	750.00	1500.
SMASH					
1715	Time Waits/It Won't Be a Sin	1961	3.75	7.50	15.00
TUFF					
375	Save a Little Monkey/(Instrumental)	1963	2.50	5.00	10.00
402	On the Spanish Side/The Change in You	1964	2.50	5.00	10.00
TUFF/CHESS					
1808	Smoky Places/Thinkin'	1961	6.25	12.50	25.00
1818	I'll Take You HJome/Sittin' on Your Doorstep	1962	3.00	6.00	12.00
1830	Dancing Shadows/While	1962	3.00	6.00	12.00
1840	At the Stroke of Midnight/Listen to My Little Heart	1962	3.00	6.00	12.00
1847	Stormy/It's Almost Sunday Morning	1963	3.00	6.00	12.00

CORT, BOB

45s

Number	Title (A Side/B Side)	Yr	VG	VG+	NM
LONDON					
1713	Don't You Rock Me Daddy-O/It Takes a Worried Man to Sing a Worried Blues	1957	3.75	7.50	15.00
1742	Freight Train/Roll Jen Jenkins	1957	3.00	6.00	12.00
1748	Maggie Mae/Jessamine	1957	3.00	6.00	12.00
—With Liz Winters					

CORTEZ, DAVE "BABY"

45s

Number	Title (A Side/B Side)	Yr	VG	VG+	NM
ALL PLATINUM					
2339	Funky Robot (Part 1)/Funky Robot (Part 2)	1972	—	2.50	5.00
2342	Unaddressed Letter/Funky Robot (Part 1)	1972	—	2.50	5.00
2343	Someone Has Taken Your Place/Born Funky	1973	—	2.50	5.00
2345	Hell Street Junction/(Instrumental)	1973	—	2.50	5.00
2347	Soul Walkin'/(B-side unknown)	1974	—	2.50	5.00
ARGO					
5462	Let It Be You/I'm Gonna Stay	1964	2.50	5.00	10.00
CHESS					
1829	Rinky Dink/Getting Right	1962	2.50	5.00	10.00
1834	Happy Weekend/Fiddle Sticks	1962	2.50	5.00	10.00
1842	Tweedle Dee/Gift of Love	1962	2.50	5.00	10.00
1850	Hot Cakes! 1st Serving/Hot Cakes! 2nd Serving	1963	2.00	4.00	8.00
1861	Organ Shout/Precious You	1963	2.00	4.00	8.00
1874	Happy Feet/Gettin' to the Point	1963	2.00	4.00	8.00
CLOCK					
1006	You're the Girl/Eeny Meeny Minie Mo	1958	5.00	10.00	20.00
1009	The Happy Organ/Love Me As I Love You	1959	5.00	10.00	20.00
1012	The Whistling Organ/I'm Happy	1959	3.00	6.00	12.00
1014	Piano Shuffle/It's a Sin to Tell a Lie	1959	3.00	6.00	12.00
1016	Dave's Special/Whispers	1959	3.00	6.00	12.00
1020	You're Just Right/Deep in the Heart of Texas	1960	3.00	6.00	12.00
1021	You're the Girl/I'm Happy	1960	3.00	6.00	12.00
1024	Cat Nip/Talk Is Cheap	1960	3.00	6.00	12.00
1031	Hurricane/The Shift	1960	3.00	6.00	12.00
1034	Summertime/Walking with You	1961	3.00	6.00	12.00
1036	Tootsie/Second Chance	1961	3.00	6.00	12.00
71824	Tootsie/Second Chance	1961	2.50	5.00	10.00
71851	The Happy Organ/Piano Shuffle	1961	2.50	5.00	10.00
71875	C'mon and Stomp/Calypso Love Song	1961	2.50	5.00	10.00
EMBER					
1011	Soft Lights/Movin' and Groovin'	1956	10.00	20.00	40.00
—As "David Clowney"					
EMIT					
301	Fiesta/(B-side unknown)	1962	2.50	5.00	10.00
EPIC					
9732	Poppin' Popcorn/The Question	1964	2.50	5.00	10.00
JULIA					
1829	Rinky Dink/Getting Right	1962	6.25	12.50	25.00
OKEH					
7102	You Give Me Heebie Jeebies/Honey Baby	1958	5.00	10.00	20.00
7208	Popping Popcorn/The Question (Do You Love Me)	1964	2.00	4.00	8.00
PARIS					
513	Shakin'/Hoot Owl	1958	7.50	15.00	30.00
—As "Dave Clowney"					
ROULETTE					
4628	Tweetie Pie/Things Ain't What They Used to Be	1965	2.00	4.00	8.00
4679	Count Down/Summertime	1966	2.00	4.00	8.00
4693	Sticks and Stones/Do Any Dance	1966	2.00	4.00	8.00
4717	Belly Rub (Part 1)/Belly Rub (Part 2)	1967	2.00	4.00	8.00
4759	Hula Hoop/Come Back	1967	2.00	4.00	8.00
4783	Hot Chocolate/Soul Groovin'	1967	2.00	4.00	8.00
T-NECK					
907	I Turned You On/I Know Who You Been Socking It To	1969	—	3.00	6.00
913	Save Me/My Little Girl	1969	—	3.00	6.00
WINLEY					
259	Jamin' (Part 1)/Jamin' (Part 2)	1961	2.50	5.00	10.00
262	Skins and Sounds/Little Paris Melody	1962	2.50	5.00	10.00
267	Scotty (Part 1)/Scotty (Part 2)	1962	2.50	5.00	10.00

7-Inch Extended Plays

Number	Title (A Side/B Side)	Yr	VG	VG+	NM
CLOCK					
EP 1-4039-C	The Happy Organ/The Whistling Organ//Catnip/Deep in the Heart of Texas	1959	6.25	12.50	25.00
EP 1-4039-C [PS]	Dave "Baby" Cortez and His Happy Organ	1959	6.25	12.50	25.00
RCA VICTOR					
EPA-4342 [M]	*The Happy Organ/Love Me As I Love You/Dave's Special/You're the Girl	1959	3.00	6.00	12.00
EPA-4342 [PS]	The Happy Organ	1959	3.00	6.00	12.00
ESP-4342 [PS]	The Happy Organ	1959	5.00	10.00	20.00
ESP-4342 [S]	(contents unknown)	1959	5.00	10.00	20.00

Albums

Number	Title (A Side/B Side)	Yr	VG	VG+	NM
CHESS					
LP-1473 [M]	Rinky Dink	1962	12.50	25.00	50.00
CLOCK					
C-331 [M]	Dave "Baby" Cortez	1960	10.00	20.00	40.00
CS-331 [S]	Dave "Baby" Cortez	1960	12.50	25.00	50.00
MGC-20647 [M]	Dave "Baby" Cortez	1961	7.50	15.00	30.00
SRC-60647 [S]	Dave "Baby" Cortez	1961	10.00	20.00	40.00
METRO					
M-550 [M]	The Fabulous Organ of Dave "Baby" Cortez	1965	3.75	7.50	15.00
MS-550 [R]	The Fabulous Organ of Dave "Baby" Cortez	1965	3.00	6.00	12.00
RCA VICTOR					
LPM-2099 [M]	The Happy Organ	1959	20.00	40.00	80.00
LSP-2099 [S]	The Happy Organ	1959	25.00	50.00	100.00
ROULETTE					
R-25298 [M]	Organ Shindig	1965	5.00	10.00	20.00
SR-25298 [S]	Organ Shindig	1965	6.25	12.50	25.00
R-25315 [M]	Tweety Pie	1966	5.00	10.00	20.00
SR-25315 [S]	Tweety Pie	1966	6.25	12.50	25.00
R-25328 [M]	In Orbit with Dave "Baby" Cortez	1966	5.00	10.00	20.00
SR-25328 [S]	In Orbit with Dave "Baby" Cortez	1966	6.25	12.50	25.00
T-NECK					
TNS-3005	The Isley Brothers Way	1970	5.00	10.00	20.00

CORVELLS, THE

45s

Number	Title (A Side/B Side)	Yr	VG	VG+	NM
ABC-PARAMOUNT					
10324	Take My Love/Daisy	1962	50.00	100.00	200.00
BLAST					
203	The Bells/Don't Forget	1961	37.50	75.00	150.00
CUB					
9122	One (Is Such a Lonely Number)/The Joke's On Me	1963	5.00	10.00	20.00
LIDO					
509	We Made a Vow/Miss Jones	1957	50.00	100.00	200.00
LUPINE					
104	He's So Fine/Baby Sitting	1962	6.25	12.50	25.00
TIP TOP					
509	We Made a Vow/Miss Jones	1957	75.00	150.00	300.00

COSBY, BILL

45s

Number	Title (A Side/B Side)	Yr	VG	VG+	NM
CAPITOL					
4258	Yes, Yes, Yes/Ben	1976	—	2.00	4.00
4299	I Luv Myself Better Than I Luv Myself/Do It To Me	1976	—	2.00	4.00
4501	Boogie on Your Face/What's in a Slang	1977	—	2.00	4.00
4523	Merry Christmas Mama (Vocal)/(Instrumental)	1977	5.00	10.00	20.00
TETRAGRAMMATON					
1539	Football/Golf	1969	—	3.00	6.00
UNI					
55184	Hikky Burr/Hikky Burr	1969	—	3.00	6.00
—A-side with the Bunions; B-side by the Bradford Band					
55223	Grover Henson Feels Forgotten/(Instrumental)	1970	—	3.00	6.00
55247	Hybish Skybish/Martin's Funeral	1970	—	2.50	5.00
—With Bad Foot Brown					
WARNER BROS.					
5499	Stand Still for My Lovin'/When I Marry	1965	2.50	5.00	10.00
7072	Little Ole Man (Uptight-Everything's Alright)/Don'cha Know	1967	2.00	4.00	8.00
7096	Hooray for the Salvation Army Band/Ursalena	1968	2.00	4.00	8.00
7126	Little Ole Man (Uptight-Everything's Alright)/Funky North Philly	1969	—	3.00	6.00
—Hall of Fame Hits (originals have green labels with "W7" logo)					
7171	Funky North Philly/Stop, Look and Listen	1968	2.00	4.00	8.00

Albums

Number	Title (A Side/B Side)	Yr	VG	VG+	NM
CAPITOL					
ST-11530	Bill Cosby Is Not Himself These Days, Rat Own, Rat Own, Rat Own	1976	2.50	5.00	10.00
ST-11590	My Father Confused Me…What Must I Do? What Must I Do?	1977	2.50	5.00	10.00
ST-11683	Let's Boogie (Disco Bill)	1977	2.50	5.00	10.00
ST-11731	Bill's Best Friend	1978	2.50	5.00	10.00
GEFFEN					
GHS 24104	Those of You With or Without Children, You'll Understand	1986	2.50	5.00	10.00
MCA					
169	When I Was a Kid	197?	2.00	4.00	8.00
—Reissue of Uni 73100					
333	Fat Albert	1973	2.50	5.00	10.00
553	For Adults Only	197?	2.00	4.00	8.00
—Reissue of Uni 73112					
554	Inside the Mind of Bill Cosby	197?	2.00	4.00	8.00
—Reissue of Uni 73139					
8005 [(2)]	Bill	197?	3.00	6.00	12.00
MOTOWN					
6026 ML	Bill Cosby "Himself"	1982	2.50	5.00	10.00
TETRAGRAMMATON					
T-5100 [(2)]	8:15 12:15	1969	5.00	10.00	20.00
UNI					
73066	Bill Cosby	1969	2.50	5.00	10.00
73082	"Live" Madison Square Garden Center	1970	2.50	5.00	10.00
73100	When I Was a Kid	1971	2.50	5.00	10.00
73112	For Adults Only	1971	2.50	5.00	10.00
73139	Inside the Mind of Bill Cosby	1972	2.50	5.00	10.00
WARNER BROS.					
PRO 249 [DJ]	Radio Sampler Album — The Best of Bill Cosby	1969	5.00	10.00	20.00
—Promo LP with edits of 12 tracks for radio use					
W 1518 [M]	Bill Cosby Is a Very Funny Fellow Right!	1964	3.75	7.50	15.00
W 1567 [M]	I Started Out as a Child	1964	3.75	7.50	15.00
W 1606 [M]	Why Is There Air?	1965	3.75	7.50	15.00
W 1634 [M]	Wonderfulness	1966	3.75	7.50	15.00
WS 1634 [S]	Wonderfulness	1966	3.75	7.50	15.00
—Gold label					
W 1691 [M]	Revenge	1967	3.75	7.50	15.00
W 1709 [M]	Bill Cosby Sings/Silver Throat	1967	3.75	7.50	15.00

Number	Title (A Side/B Side)	Yr	VG	VG+	NM
WS 1709 [S]	Bill Cosby Sings/Silver Throat	1967	3.00	6.00	12.00
W 1728 [M]	Bill Cosby Sings/Hooray for the Salvation Army Band	1968	3.75	7.50	15.00
WS 1728 [S]	Bill Cosby Sings/Hooray for the Salvation Army Band	1968	3.00	6.00	12.00
W 1734 [M]	To Russell, My Brother, Whom I Slept With	1968	3.75	7.50	15.00
WS 1734 [S]	To Russell, My Brother, Whom I Slept With	1968	3.00	6.00	12.00
WS 1757	200 M.P.H.	1968	3.00	6.00	12.00
WS 1770	It's True! It's True!	1969	3.00	6.00	12.00
WS 1798	The Best of Bill Cosby	1969	3.00	6.00	12.00
WS 1836	More of the Best of Bill Cosby	1970	3.00	6.00	12.00

COSMIC RAYS, THE

45s

SATURN

Number	Title (A Side/B Side)	Yr	VG	VG+	NM
222	Bye Bye/Someone's in Love	1960	750.00	1500.	3000.
401	Daddy's Gonna Tell You No Lies/Dreaming	1960	500.00	1000.	2000.

COTTON, GENE

45s

ABC

Number	Title (A Side/B Side)	Yr	VG	VG+	NM
12087	Country Spirit/Damn It All	1975	—	2.00	4.00
12137	Let Your Love Flow/Keepin' It on the Road	1975	—	2.00	4.00
12227	You've Got Me Runnin'/It's Over, Goodbye	1976	—	2.00	4.00
12250	Rain On/A Song for You	1977	—	2.00	4.00
12282	My Love Comes Alive/Sweet Destiny	1977	—	2.00	4.00

ARIOLA AMERICA

Number	Title (A Side/B Side)	Yr	VG	VG+	NM
7675	Before My Heart Finds Out/Like a Sunday in Salem	1977	—	2.50	5.00
7723	Like a Sunday in Salem (The Amos and Andy Song)/Shine On (You Got to Shine On)	1978	—	2.00	4.00
7778	Michael/Ocean of Love	1979	—	2.00	4.00

KNOLL

Number	Title (A Side/B Side)	Yr	VG	VG+	NM
5002	If I Could Get You (Into My Life)/(B-side unknown)	1982	—	2.00	4.00

MYRRH

Number	Title (A Side/B Side)	Yr	VG	VG+	NM
116	American Indian Blues/Lessons of History	1973	—	2.50	5.00
117	Lean On One Another/(B-side unknown)	1973	—	2.50	5.00
123	Great American Noel/Mrs. Oliver	1973	—	2.50	5.00
137	Sunshine Roses/Mrs. Oliver	1974	—	2.50	5.00

(NO LABEL)

Number	Title (A Side/B Side)	Yr	VG	VG+	NM
NR-16361 [DJ]	Child Of Peace (same on both sides)	1981	2.00	4.00	8.00

Albums

ABC

Number	Title (A Side/B Side)	Yr	VG	VG+	NM
D-933	For All the Young Writers	1975	2.50	5.00	10.00
D-983	Rain On	1977	2.50	5.00	10.00

ARIOLA AMERICA

Number	Title (A Side/B Side)	Yr	VG	VG+	NM
SW-50031	Save the Dancer	1978	2.50	5.00	10.00
SW-50070	No Strings Attached	1979	2.50	5.00	10.00

KNOLL

Number	Title (A Side/B Side)	Yr	VG	VG+	NM
1001	Eclipse of the Blue Moon	1981	2.50	5.00	10.00

MYRRH

Number	Title (A Side/B Side)	Yr	VG	VG+	NM
MSB-6517	In the Gray of the Morning	1973	3.00	6.00	12.00
MSB-6524	Liberty	1974	3.00	6.00	12.00

COTTON, GENE, AND KIM CARNES

Also see each artist's individual listings.

45s

ARIOLA AMERICA

Number	Title (A Side/B Side)	Yr	VG	VG+	NM
7704	You're a Part of Me/Shine On (You Got to Shine On)	1978	—	2.00	4.00

COTTON, JAMES

45s

BUDDAH

Number	Title (A Side/B Side)	Yr	VG	VG+	NM
461	Boogie Thing/Fever	1975	—	2.50	5.00
468	Rocket 88/One More Mile	1975	—	2.50	5.00

LOMA

Number	Title (A Side/B Side)	Yr	VG	VG+	NM
2042	Laying in the Weeds/Complete This Order	1966	3.00	6.00	12.00

SUN

Number	Title (A Side/B Side)	Yr	VG	VG+	NM
199	My Baby/Straighten Up, Baby	1954	375.00	750.00	1500.
206	Cotton Crop Blues/Hold Me in Your Arms	1954	450.00	900.00	1800.

VERVE FORECAST

Number	Title (A Side/B Side)	Yr	VG	VG+	NM
5053	Good Time Charlie/Off the Wall	1967	2.50	5.00	10.00
5066	Feelin' Good/Don't Start Me Talkin'	1967	2.50	5.00	10.00
5107	The Coach's Better Days/(B-side unknown)	1969	2.00	4.00	8.00

Albums

ALLIGATOR

Number	Title (A Side/B Side)	Yr	VG	VG+	NM
AL-4737	High Compression	1984	2.50	5.00	10.00
AL-4746	Live from Chicago	1986	2.50	5.00	10.00

ANTONE'S

Number	Title (A Side/B Side)	Yr	VG	VG+	NM
ANT-7	James Cotton Live	1988	3.00	6.00	12.00

BLIND PIG

Number	Title (A Side/B Side)	Yr	VG	VG+	NM
BP-2587	Take Me Back	1987	2.50	5.00	10.00

BUDDAH

Number	Title (A Side/B Side)	Yr	VG	VG+	NM
BDS-5620	100% Cotton	1974	3.00	6.00	12.00
BDS-5650	High Energy	1975	3.00	6.00	12.00
BDS-5661 [(2)]	Live & On the Move!	1976	3.75	7.50	15.00

CAPITOL

Number	Title (A Side/B Side)	Yr	VG	VG+	NM
SM-814	Taking Care of Business	197?	2.50	5.00	10.00
—Reissue with new prefix					
ST-814	Taking Care of Business	1971	3.75	7.50	15.00

INTERMEDIA

Number	Title (A Side/B Side)	Yr	VG	VG+	NM
QS-5006	Dealing with the Devil	198?	2.50	5.00	10.00
QS-5011	Two Sides of the Blues	198?	2.50	5.00	10.00

VANGUARD

Number	Title (A Side/B Side)	Yr	VG	VG+	NM
VSD-79283	Cut You Loose!	1969	3.75	7.50	15.00

VERVE FORECAST

Number	Title (A Side/B Side)	Yr	VG	VG+	NM
FT-3023 [M]	The James Cotton Blues Band	1967	6.25	12.50	25.00
FTS-3023 [S]	The James Cotton Blues Band	1967	5.00	10.00	20.00
FTS-3038	Pure Cotton	1968	5.00	10.00	20.00

COTTON PICKERS, THE

Albums

PHILIPS

Number	Title (A Side/B Side)	Yr	VG	VG+	NM
PHM 200025 [M]	Country Guitar	1962	5.00	10.00	20.00
PHS 600025 [S]	Country Guitar	1962	6.25	12.50	25.00

COUNT FIVE, THE

45s

DOUBLE SHOT

Number	Title (A Side/B Side)	Yr	VG	VG+	NM
104	Psychotic Reaction/They're Gonna Get You	1966	3.75	7.50	15.00
—First pressing, with label logo at top					
104	Psychotic Reaction/They're Gonna Get You	1966	3.00	6.00	12.00
—Later pressings, with label logo at side					
106	Peace of Mind/The Morning After	1966	3.00	6.00	12.00
110	You Must Believe Me/Teeny Bopper, Teeny Bopper	1967	3.00	6.00	12.00
115	Merry-Go-Round/Contrast	1967	3.00	6.00	12.00
125	Declaration of Independence/Revelation in Slow Motion	1968	3.00	6.00	12.00
141	Mailman/Pretty Big Mouth	1969	3.00	6.00	12.00

Albums

DOUBLE SHOT

Number	Title (A Side/B Side)	Yr	VG	VG+	NM
DSM-1001 [M]	Psychotic Reaction	1966	10.00	20.00	40.00
DSS-5001 [R]	Psychotic Reaction	1966	6.25	12.50	25.00

COUNT ROCKIN' SIDNEY

See ROCKIN' SIDNEY.

COUNT STEPHEN

See STEVE ALAIMO.

COUNTRY BOYS, THE

Also see DAVID GATES.

45s

DEL-FI

Number	Title (A Side/B Side)	Yr	VG	VG+	NM
4245	The Okie Surfer/Blue Surf	1964	10.00	20.00	40.00

COUNTRY HAMS, THE

See PAUL McCARTNEY.

COUNTRY JOE AND THE FISH

Includes releases by "Country Joe McDonald"

45s

FANTASY

Number	Title (A Side/B Side)	Yr	VG	VG+	NM
758	Breakfast for Two/Lost My Connection	1976	—	2.00	4.00
765	Save the Whales/Oh Jamaica	1976	—	2.00	4.00
780	Love Is a Fire/I Need You	1976	—	2.00	4.00
814	Southern Cross/Coyote	1978	—	2.00	4.00
822	Bring Back the Sixties, Man/Sunshine Through My Window	1978	—	2.00	4.00
876	Private Parts/Take Time Out	1979	—	2.00	4.00

PHILCO-FORD

Number	Title (A Side/B Side)	Yr	VG	VG+	NM
HP-35	Not So Sweet Martha Lorraine/Masked Marauder	1969	6.25	12.50	25.00
—4-inch plastic "Hip Pocket Record" with color sleeve					

VANGUARD

Number	Title (A Side/B Side)	Yr	VG	VG+	NM
35052	Not So Sweet Martha Lorraine/The Masked Marauder	1967	2.50	5.00	10.00
35059	Janis (Part 1)/Janis (Part 2)	1967	2.50	5.00	10.00
35061	Who Am I/Thursday	1968	2.50	5.00	10.00
35061 [PS]	Who Am I/Thursday	1968	5.00	10.00	20.00
35068	Rock and Soul (Part 1)/Rock and Soul (Part 2)	1968	2.50	5.00	10.00
35090	Here I Go Again/Baby, You're Driving Me Crazy	1969	2.00	4.00	8.00
35112	I-Feel-Like-I'm-Fixin'-to-Die Rag/Janis	1970	2.00	4.00	8.00
35133	Hold On, It's Coming/Playing with Fire	1971	—	2.50	5.00
—Starting here, as "Country Joe McDonald"					
35150	Hang On/Hand of Man	1972	—	2.50	5.00
35161	Fantasy/I Seen a Rocket	1972	—	2.50	5.00
35181	Doctor Hip/Satisfactorily	1973	—	2.00	4.00
35184	Chloe/Jesse James	1974	—	2.00	4.00

7-Inch Extended Plays

RAG BABY

Number	Title (A Side/B Side)	Yr	VG	VG+	NM
1001	(contents unknown)	1966	25.00	50.00	100.00
1001 [PS]	Rag Baby	1966	50.00	100.00	200.00
—Actually an envelope in which the record came					

Albums

CUSTOM FIDELITY

Number	Title (A Side/B Side)	Yr	VG	VG+	NM
CFS-2348	Joe McDonald	1968	500.00	750.00	1000.
—Recorded in 1964, 200 copies were pressed for Joe McDonald.					

FANTASY

Number	Title (A Side/B Side)	Yr	VG	VG+	NM
9495	Paradise with an Ocean View	1975	2.50	5.00	10.00
9511	Love Is a Fire	1976	2.50	5.00	10.00
9525	Goodbye Blues	1977	2.50	5.00	10.00
9530	Reunion	1977	3.00	6.00	12.00
9544	Rock and Roll Music From the Planet Earth	1978	2.50	5.00	10.00
9586	Leisure Suite	1980	2.50	5.00	10.00

FIRST AMERICAN

Number	Title (A Side/B Side)	Yr	VG	VG+	NM
PIC-3309	The Early Years	1979	2.50	5.00	10.00

MOBLIE FIDELITY

Number	Title (A Side/B Side)	Yr	VG	VG+	NM
1-056	Paradise with an Ocean View	1981	7.50	15.00	30.00
—Audiophile vinyl					

VANGUARD

Number	Title (A Side/B Side)	Yr	VG	VG+	NM
VSD-27/28 [(2)]	The Life and Times of Country Joe & the Fish From Haight-Ashbury to Woodstock	1971	5.00	10.00	20.00
VSD-85/86 [(2)]	The Essential Country Joe	1977	3.00	6.00	12.00
VSD-6545	Country Joe & The Fish/Greatest Hits	1969	5.00	10.00	20.00
VSD-6546	Thinking of Woody	1969	3.75	7.50	15.00
VSD-6555	C.J. Fish	1970	5.00	10.00	20.00
VSD-6557	Tonight I'm Singing Just for You	1970	3.75	7.50	15.00
VRS-9244 [M]	Electric Music for the Mind and Body	1967	25.00	50.00	100.00
—Black label					
VRS-9244 [M]	Electric Music for the Mind and Body	1967	5.00	10.00	20.00
—Gold label					

Number	Title (A Side/B Side)	Yr	VG	VG+	NM
9266/79266	I-Feel-Like-I'm-Fixin'-to-Die "Fish Game" Poster	1967	2.50	5.00	10.00
VRS-9266 [M]	I-Feel-Like-I'm-Fixin'-to-Die	1967	5.00	10.00	20.00
VSQ 40004/5 [(2) Q]	The Life and Times of Country Joe & the Fish From Haight-Ashbury to Woodstock	197?	10.00	20.00	40.00
VSD-79244 [S] *—Black label*	Electric Music for the Mind and Body	1967	12.50	25.00	50.00
VSD-79244 [S] *—Gold label*	Electric Music for the Mind and Body	1967	5.00	10.00	20.00
VSD-79266 [S]	I-Feel-Like-I'm-Fixin'-to-Die	1967	5.00	10.00	20.00
VSD-79277	Together	1968	5.00	10.00	20.00
VSD-79299	Here We Are Again	1969	5.00	10.00	20.00
VSD-79304	Hold On It's Coming	1971	3.75	7.50	15.00
VSD-79315	War, War, War	1971	3.75	7.50	15.00
VSD-79316	Incredible! Live!	1972	3.00	6.00	12.00
VSD-79328	Paris Sessions	1973	3.00	6.00	12.00
VSD-79348	Country Joe	1974	3.00	6.00	12.00

COUNTS, THE (1)

Male vocal group from Indianapolis.

45s

Number	Title (A Side/B Side)	Yr	VG	VG+	NM
DOT					
1188	Darling Dear/I Need You Always	1954	15.00	30.00	60.00
1199	Hot Tamales/Baby Don't You Know	1954	12.50	25.00	50.00
1210	My Dear, My Darling/She Won't Say Yes	1954	10.00	20.00	40.00
1226	Baby I Want You/Waitin' Around for You	1954	10.00	20.00	40.00
1235	Wailin' Little Mama/Let Me Go	1955	7.50	15.00	30.00
1243	From This Day On/Love and Understanding	1955	7.50	15.00	30.00
1265	I Need You Tonight/Sally Walker	1955	7.50	15.00	30.00
1275	To Our Love/Heartbreaker	1956	6.25	12.50	25.00
16105	Darling Dear/I Need You Always	1960	5.00	10.00	20.00
NOTE					
20000	Sweet Names/I Guess I Brought It All on Myself	1956	50.00	100.00	200.00

COUNTS, THE (2)

Detroit-based funk group.

45s

Number	Title (A Side/B Side)	Yr	VG	VG+	NM
AWARE					
038	Funk/Too Bad	1974	—	2.50	5.00
046	Sacrifice/Funk Pump	1974	—	2.50	5.00
049	All the Fair/On the Music	1975	—	2.50	5.00
054	Magic Ride/Short Cut	1975	—	2.50	5.00
WESTBOUND					
191	Thinking Single/Why Not Start All Over Again	1972	—	2.50	5.00

Albums

Number	Title (A Side/B Side)	Yr	VG	VG+	NM
AWARE					
2002	Love Sign	1973	6.25	12.50	25.00
2006	Funk Pump	1975	5.00	10.00	20.00
WESTBOUND					
2011	What's Up Front That Counts	1972	7.50	15.00	30.00

COUNTS, THE (U)

It appears as if none of these are by group (1) or (2), and they aren't all by the same group.

45s

Number	Title (A Side/B Side)	Yr	VG	VG+	NM
COUNT					
5	The Beat/After Beat	196?	5.00	10.00	20.00
MANCO					
1060	Surfer's Paradise/Chug-a-Lug	1964	10.00	20.00	40.00
MERCURY					
71318	Shake the Town/Teenage Guy and Girl	1958	3.75	7.50	15.00
PANORAMA					
9	Chitlins, Etc./Clyde, Clyde, The Cow's Outside	1965	2.50	5.00	10.00
33	Come Now/Since I Fell for You	1966	2.50	5.00	10.00
SEA CREST					
6003	Turn On Song/Enchanted Sea	1964	5.00	10.00	20.00
6004	Doggin'/And Then I Cried	1964	3.75	7.50	15.00
SMASH					
1821	Stormy Weather/True Love's Gone	1963	2.50	5.00	10.00

COURTNEY, LOU

45s

Number	Title (A Side/B Side)	Yr	VG	VG+	NM
BUDDAH					
121	Let Me Turn You On/Tryin' to Find My Woman	1969	2.00	4.00	8.00
EPIC					
11062	What Do You Want Me to Do/Beware	1973	—	2.50	5.00
11088	I Don't Need Nobody Else/Why	1974	—	2.50	5.00
50046	The Best Thing a Man Can Do for His Woman/I'm Serious About Lovin' You	1974	—	2.50	5.00
50070	Just to Let Him Break Your Heart/Somebody New Is Lovin' You	1975	—	2.50	5.00
IMPERIAL					
66006	Come On Home/The Man with the Cigar	1963	3.00	6.00	12.00
66043	Little Old Love Maker/Professional Lover	1964	3.00	6.00	12.00
PHILIPS					
40287	I Watched You Slowly Slip Away/I'll Cry If I Want To	1965	25.00	50.00	100.00
POP-SIDE					
4594	Hey Joyce/I'm Mad About You	1967	2.50	5.00	10.00
4596	If the Shoe Fits/It's Love Now	1968	2.50	5.00	10.00
RIVERSIDE					
4588	Skate Now/I Can Always Tell	1966	2.50	5.00	10.00
4589	Do the Thing/Man Is Lonely	1967	2.50	5.00	10.00
4591	You Ain't Ready/I've Got Just the Thing	1967	2.50	5.00	10.00
VERVE					
10602	Do the Horse/Rubber Neckin'	1968	2.00	4.00	8.00
10631	Please Stay/You Can Give Your Love to Me	1968	2.00	4.00	8.00

Albums

Number	Title (A Side/B Side)	Yr	VG	VG+	NM
EPIC					
KE 33011	I'm in Need of Love	1974	3.00	6.00	12.00
RCA VICTOR					
APL1-1969	Buffalo Smoke	1976	3.00	6.00	12.00

Number	Title (A Side/B Side)	Yr	VG	VG+	NM
RIVERSIDE					
92000	Skate Now (Shing-a-Ling)	1967	6.25	12.50	25.00

COURTSHIP, THE

45s

Number	Title (A Side/B Side)	Yr	VG	VG+	NM
TAMLA					
54217	It's the Same Old Love/Last Row, First Balcony	1972	—	2.50	5.00
54227	Oops, It Just Slipped Out/Love Ain't Love	1973	—	2.50	5.00

COURVALE, KEITH

45s

Number	Title (A Side/B Side)	Yr	VG	VG+	NM
DOT					
15844	Trapped Love/Steelworker Blues	1958	25.00	50.00	100.00

COUSINS, THE (1)

45s

Number	Title (A Side/B Side)	Yr	VG	VG+	NM
DECCA					
30609	I'm in Love with You/Be Nice to Me	1958	5.00	10.00	20.00
FIDELITY					
3010	Love Is Blind/How We'll Love	1959	7.50	15.00	30.00

COUSINS, THE (2)

45s

Number	Title (A Side/B Side)	Yr	VG	VG+	NM
PARKWAY					
823	St. Louis Blues/No One Knows	1961	3.75	7.50	15.00
848	When My Baby Smiles at Me/Some of These Days	1962	3.00	6.00	12.00
870	Sweet Georgia Brown/Outside the Wall	1963	3.00	6.00	12.00

Albums

Number	Title (A Side/B Side)	Yr	VG	VG+	NM
PARKWAY					
P-7005 [M]	Music of the Strip	1961	5.00	10.00	20.00
SP-7005 [S]	Music of the Strip	1961	6.25	12.50	25.00

COUSINS, THE (U)

Neither group (1) nor group (2).

45s

Number	Title (A Side/B Side)	Yr	VG	VG+	NM
VERSATILE					
105	Down That Lonely Road/(B-side unknown)	1960	20.00	40.00	80.00
WYNNE					
132	Guilty/(B-side unknown)	1959	125.00	250.00	500.00

COVAY, DON

Also see THE SOLDIER BOYS.

45s

Number	Title (A Side/B Side)	Yr	VG	VG+	NM
ARNOLD					
1002 *—As "The Goodtimers"*	Pony Time/Love Boat	1961	6.25	12.50	25.00
1002 *—As "Don Covay and the Goodtimers"*	Pony Time/Love Boat	1961	3.00	6.00	12.00
ATLANTIC					
1147 *—As "Pretty Boy"*	Bip Bop Bip/Silver Dollar	1957	20.00	40.00	80.00
2280	The Boomerang/Daddy Loves Baby	1965	2.50	5.00	10.00
2286	Please Do Something/A Woman's Love	1965	2.50	5.00	10.00
2301	See Saw/I Never Get Enough of Your Love	1965	2.50	5.00	10.00
2323	Sookie Sookie/Watching the Late Late Shoe	1966	2.50	5.00	10.00
2340	You Put Something On Me/Iron Out the Rough Spots	1966	2.50	5.00	10.00
2357	Somebody's Got to Love You/Temptation Was Too Strong	1966	2.50	5.00	10.00
2375	Shing-Aling '67/I Was There	1967	2.50	5.00	10.00
2407	40 Days — 40 Nights/The Usual Place	1967	2.50	5.00	10.00
2440	You've Got Me on the Critical List/Never Had No Love	1967	2.50	5.00	10.00
2481	Chain of Fools/Prove It	1968	2.50	5.00	10.00
2494	Don't Let Go/It's In the Wind	1968	2.50	5.00	10.00
2521	Gonna Send You Back to Your Mama/House on the Corner	1968	2.50	5.00	10.00
2565	I Stole Some Love/Snake in the Grass	1968	2.50	5.00	10.00
2609	Sweet Pea/C.C. Rider Blues	1969	2.50	5.00	10.00
2666	Ice Cream Man (The Gimmie Game)/Black Woman	1969	2.50	5.00	10.00
2725	Everything I Do Goin' Be Funky/Key to the Kighway	1970	2.00	4.00	8.00
2742	Soul Stirrer/Sookie Sookie	1970	2.00	4.00	8.00
BIG					
617 *—As "Pretty Boy"*	Switchin' in the Kitchen/Rockin' the Mule	1958	20.00	40.00	80.00
BIG TOP					
3060	Hey There/I'm Coming Down with the Blues	1960	3.75	7.50	15.00
BLAZE					
350	Standing in the Doorway/(B-side unknown)	1958	7.50	15.00	30.00
CAMEO					
239	The Popeye Waddle/One Little Bot Had Money	1962	3.00	6.00	12.00
251	Wiggle Wobble/Do the Bug	1963	3.00	6.00	12.00
COLUMBIA					
41981	Shake Wid the Snake/Every Which-a Way	1961	5.00	10.00	20.00
42058	Hand Jive Workout/See About Me	1961	5.00	10.00	20.00
42197	Now That I Need You/Teen Life Swag	1961	25.00	50.00	100.00
EPIC					
9484 *—As "The Goodtimers"*	It's Twistin' Time/Twistin' Train	1961	3.75	7.50	15.00
JANUS					
164	Sweet Thang/Standing in the Grits Line	1971	—	3.00	6.00
181	Daddy Please Don't Go Out/Shoes Under My Bed	1972	—	3.00	6.00
LANDA					
704	You're Good for Me/Truth of the Lite	1965	2.50	5.00	10.00
MERCURY					
71385	I Was Checkin' Out She Was Checkin' In/Money	1973	—	3.00	6.00
71430	Somebody's Been Enjoying My Home/Bad Mouthing	1973	—	3.00	6.00

Number	Title (A Side/B Side)	Yr	VG	VG+	NM
71469	It's Better to Have (And Don't Need)/Leave Him (Part 1)	1974	—	3.00	6.00
73311	Overtime Man/Dungeon #3	1972	—	3.00	6.00
73648	Rumble in the Jungle/We Can't Make It No More	1975	—	3.00	6.00
NEWMAN					
500	Badd Boy/(Instrumental)	1980	—	2.50	5.00
PARKWAY					
894	Ain't That Silly/Turn It On	1964	3.00	6.00	12.00
910	The Froog/One Little Boy Had Money	1964	3.00	6.00	12.00
PHILADELPHIA INT'L.					
3594	Right Time for Love/No Tell Motel	1976	—	2.50	5.00
3602	Travelin' in Heavy Traffic/Once You Have It	1976	—	2.50	5.00
ROSEMART					
801	Mercy Mercy/Can't Stay Away	1964	3.75	7.50	15.00
802	Take This Hurt Off Me/Please Don't Let Me Know	1964	3.00	6.00	12.00
SUE					
709	Betty Jean/Believe It or Not	1958	7.50	15.00	30.00
U-VON					
102	Back to the Roots (Part 1)/Back to the Roots (Part 2)	1977	—	2.50	5.00
Albums					
ATLANTIC					
8104 [M]	Mercy	1965	10.00	20.00	40.00
SD 8104 [S]	Mercy	1965	12.50	25.00	50.00
8120 [M]	See Saw	1966	10.00	20.00	40.00
SD 8120 [S]	See Saw	1966	12.50	25.00	50.00
SD 8237	The House of Blue Lights	1969	6.25	12.50	25.00
JANUS					
3038	Different Strokes for Different Folks	1972	3.75	7.50	15.00
MERCURY					
SRM-1-653	Super Dude I	1973	3.00	6.00	12.00
SRM-1-1020	Hot Blood	1974	3.00	6.00	12.00
835030-1	Checkin' In with Don Covay	1988	2.50	5.00	10.00
PHILADELPHIA INT'L.					
PZ 33958	Travelin' In Heavy Traffic	1977	2.50	5.00	10.00

COVEN

Number	Title (A Side/B Side)	Yr	VG	VG+	NM
45s					
ABC					
11377	One Tin Soldier (The Legend of Billy Jack)/I Think You Always Knew	1973	—	3.00	6.00
BUDDAH					
440	I Need a Hundred of You/(B-side unknown)	1974	—	2.00	4.00
LION					
192	Nightingale/Jailhouse Rock	1972	—	2.00	4.00
MERCURY					
72973	Wicked Woman/White Witch of Rose Hall	1969	—	3.00	6.00
MGM					
14308	One Tin Soldier/I Guess It's a Beautiful Day Today	1971	—	2.50	5.00
14348	Nightingale/Jailhouse Rock	1972	—	2.00	4.00
SGC					
003	I Shall Be Released/I've Come Too Far	1968	—	3.00	6.00
WARNER BROS.					
BJS 0101	One Tin Soldier, The Legend of Billy Jack/Johnnie	1973	—	2.00	4.00
—B-side by Teresa Kelly					
7509	One Tin Soldier, The Legend of Billy Jack/Say Goodbye, 'Cause You're Leavin'	1971	—	2.50	5.00
Albums					
BUDDAH					
BDS-5614	Blood on the Snow	1974	3.00	6.00	12.00
MERCURY					
SR 61239	Witchcraft Destroys Minds and Reaps Souls	1969	3.75	7.50	15.00
MGM					
SE-4801	Coven	1971	3.00	6.00	12.00

COWSILL, BILL

Also see THE COWSILLS.

Number	Title (A Side/B Side)	Yr	VG	VG+	NM
45s					
MGM					
14166	When Everybody's Here/I Wish I Could Say the Same About You	1970	—	3.00	6.00
Albums					
MGM					
SE-4706	Nervous Breakthrough	1970	3.75	7.50	15.00

COWSILL, JOHN

Also see THE COWSILLS.

Number	Title (A Side/B Side)	Yr	VG	VG+	NM
45s					
MGM					
14003	Path of Love/Captain Sad and His Ship of Fools	1968	2.00	4.00	8.00

COWSILL, SUSAN

Also see THE COWSILLS.

Number	Title (A Side/B Side)	Yr	VG	VG+	NM
45s					
WARNER BROS.					
8232	It Might As Well Rain Until September/Mohammad's Radio	1976	—	2.50	5.00
8333	The Next Time That I See You/I Think of You	1977	—	2.50	5.00

COWSILLS, THE

Also see BILL COWSILL; JOHN COWSILL; SUSAN COWSILL.

Number	Title (A Side/B Side)	Yr	VG	VG+	NM
45s					
GASATANKA/ROCKVILLE					
6139	Christmastime (Song for Marissa)/Some Good Years	1993	—	—	3.00
—Green vinyl					
6139	Christmastime (Song For Marisa)/Some Good Years	1993	—	2.00	4.00
—Clear vinyl					
6139 [PS]	Christmastime (Song for Marissa)/Some Good Years	1993	—	—	3.00
JODA					
103	All I Really Wanta Be Is Me/And the Next Day, Too	1965	7.50	15.00	30.00
LONDON					
149	On My Side/There Is No Child	1971	2.00	4.00	8.00
153	You/Crystal Claps	1971	2.00	4.00	8.00
170	Blue Road/Covered Wagon	1972	2.00	4.00	8.00
MGM					
13810	The Rain, the Park and Other Things/River Blue	1967	2.50	5.00	10.00
13810 [PS]	The Rain, the Park and Other Things/River Blue	1967	3.00	6.00	12.00
13886	We Can Fly/A Time for Remembrance	1967	2.00	4.00	8.00
13886 [PS]	We Can Fly/A Time for Remembrance	1967	3.00	6.00	12.00
13909	In Need of a Friend/Mister Flynn	1968	2.00	4.00	8.00
13909 [PS]	In Need of a Friend/Mister Flynn	1968	3.00	6.00	12.00
13944	Indian Lake/Newspaper Blanket	1968	2.50	5.00	10.00
—First pressings have black labels					
13944	Indian Lake/Newspaper Blanket	1968	2.00	4.00	8.00
—Second pressings have blue and gold labels					
13944 [PS]	Indian Lake/Newspaper Blanket	1968	3.00	6.00	12.00
13981	Poor Baby/Meet Me at the Wishing Well	1968	2.00	4.00	8.00
14011	The Impossible Years/Candy Kid	1968	2.00	4.00	8.00
14026	Hair/What Is Happy	1969	3.00	6.00	12.00
14063	The Prophecy of Daniel and John the Divine (Six-Six-Six)/Gotta Get Away from It All	1969	2.00	4.00	8.00
14084	Silver Threads and Golden Needles/Love, American Style	1969	2.50	5.00	10.00
14084 [PS]	Silver Threads and Golden Needles/Love, American Style	1969	3.00	6.00	12.00
14106	Start to Love/Two by Two	1970	2.00	4.00	8.00
PHILIPS					
40382	Most of All/Siamese Cat	1966	2.50	5.00	10.00
40382 [PS]	Most of All/Siamese Cat	1966	3.75	7.50	15.00
40406	Party Girl/What's It Gonna Be Like	1966	2.50	5.00	10.00
40437	A Most Peculiar Man/Could It Be, Let Me Know	1967	2.50	5.00	10.00
Albums					
LONDON					
PS 587	On My Side	1971	7.50	15.00	30.00
MGM					
GAS-103	The Cowsills (Golden Archive Series)	1970	3.75	7.50	15.00
E-4498 [M]	The Cowsills	1967	5.00	10.00	20.00
SE-4498 [S]	The Cowsills	1967	3.75	7.50	15.00
SE-4534	We Can Fly	1968	3.75	7.50	15.00
SE-4554	Captain Sad and His Ship of Fools	1968	3.75	7.50	15.00
SE-4597	The Best of the Cowsills	1968	3.75	7.50	15.00
SE-4619	The Cowsills in Concert	1969	3.75	7.50	15.00
SE-4639	II X II	1969	5.00	10.00	20.00
WING					
SRW-16354	The Cowsills Plus the Lincoln Park Zoo	1968	3.00	6.00	12.00

COXON'S ARMY

Pat Benatar was in this group.

Number	Title (A Side/B Side)	Yr	VG	VG+	NM
Albums					
TRACE					
(# unknown)	Coxon's Army	1975	100.00	200.00	400.00

CRABBY APPLETON

Number	Title (A Side/B Side)	Yr	VG	VG+	NM
45s					
ELEKTRA					
45687	Go Back/Try	1970	—	3.00	6.00
45702	Lucy/Some Madness	1970	—	2.50	5.00
45716	Grab On/Can't Live My Life	1971	—	2.50	5.00
45754	It's So Hard/Tomorrow Is a New Day	1971	—	2.50	5.00
45781	Love Can Change Everything/Smokin' in the Mornin'	1972	—	2.50	5.00
Albums					
ELEKTRA					
EKS-74067	Crabby Appleton	1970	3.75	7.50	15.00
EKS-74106	Rotten to the Core!	1971	3.75	7.50	15.00

CRACK THE SKY

Number	Title (A Side/B Side)	Yr	VG	VG+	NM
45s					
LIFESONG					
1763	Give Myself to You/A Night on the Town (With Snow White)	1978	—	2.00	4.00
1764	Long Nights/Give Myself to You	1978	—	2.00	4.00
1782	I Am the Walrus/Lighten Up McGraw	1979	—	2.00	4.00
45003	She's a Dancer/Robots for Ronnie	1976	—	2.00	4.00
45016	We Want Mine (We Don't Want Your Money)/Invaders from Mars	1976	—	2.00	4.00
45081	Techni-Generation/Suspicion	1980	—	2.00	4.00
Albums					
GRUDGE					
4500-1-F	From the Greenhouse	1989	2.50	5.00	10.00
LIFESONG					
LS 6000	Crack the Sky	1975	3.75	7.50	15.00
LS 6005	Animal Notes	1976	3.75	7.50	15.00
LS 6015	Safety in Numbers	1978	3.75	7.50	15.00
LS 8133	Photoflamingo	1981	2.50	5.00	10.00
PZ 34994	Crack the Sky	1977	2.50	5.00	10.00
—Reissue of 6000					
PZ 34998	Animal Notes	1977	2.50	5.00	10.00
—Reissue of 6004					
PZ 35041	Safety in Numbers	1978	2.50	5.00	10.00
—Reissue of 6015					
PZ 35620	Live Sky	1978	3.00	6.00	12.00

CRADDOCK, BILLY "CRASH"

Also recorded as "Bill Craddock" and "Crash Craddock," both included below.

45s

Number	Title (A Side/B Side)	Yr	VG	VG+	NM
ABC					
11342	Afraid I'll Want to Love Her One More Time/Treat Her Right	1972	—	2.00	4.00
11349	Don't Be Angry/I'm a White Boy	1973	—	2.00	4.00
11364	Slippin' and Slidin'/Living Example	1973	—	2.00	4.00
11379	'Till the Water Stops Runnin'/What Does a Loser Say	1973	—	2.00	4.00
11412	Sweet Magnolia Blossom/Home Is Such a Lonely Place to Go	1973	—	2.00	4.00
11437	Rub It In/It's Hard to Love a Hungry, Worried Man	1974	—	2.50	5.00
12013	Rub It In/It's Hard to Love a Hungry, Worried Man	1974	—	2.00	4.00
12036	Ruby, Baby/Walk When Love Walks	1974	—	2.00	4.00
12068	Still Thinkin' 'Bout You/Stay a Little Longer in Your Bed	1975	—	2.00	4.00
12104	I Love the Blues and the Boogie Woogie/No Deposit, No Return	1975	—	2.00	4.00
12335	Another Woman/The Words Still Rhyme	1978	—	2.00	4.00
12357	Think I'll Go Somewhere (And Cry Myself to Sleep)/It All Came Back	1978	—	2.00	4.00
12384	Don Juan/Things Are Mostly Fine	1978	—	2.00	4.00
ABC DOT					
17584	Easy As Pie/She's Mine	1975	—	2.00	4.00
17619	Walk Softly/She's About a Mover	1976	—	2.00	4.00
17635	You Rubbed It In All Wrong/I Need Somebody to Love Me	1976	—	2.00	4.00
17659	Broken Down in Tiny Pieces/Shake It Easy	1976	—	2.00	4.00
17682	Just a Little Thing/The First Time	1977	—	2.00	4.00
17701	A Tear Fell/A Piece of the Rock	1977	—	2.00	4.00
17723	The First Time/Walk When Love Walks	1977	—	2.00	4.00
ATLANTIC					
88851	Just Another Miserable Day (Here in Paradise)/Softly Diana	1989	—	—	3.00
CAPITOL					
4545	I Cheated on a Good Woman's Love/Not a Day Goes By	1978	—	2.00	4.00
4575	I've Been Too Long Lonely Baby/Jailhouse Rock	1978	—	2.00	4.00
4624	Hubba Hubba/Let's Go Back to the Beginning	1978	—	2.00	4.00
4672	If I Could Write a Song As Beautiful As You/Never Ending	1978	—	2.00	4.00
4707	My Mama Never Heard Me Sing/As Long As I Live	1979	—	2.00	4.00
4753	Robinhood/We Never Made It to Chicago	1979	—	2.00	4.00
4792	Till I Stop Shaking/Sneak Out of Love with You	1979	—	2.00	4.00
4838	I Just Had You on My Mind/You Just Wanta Be Mine	1980	—	2.00	4.00
4875	Sea Cruise/She's Got Legs	1980	—	2.00	4.00
4935	A Real Cowboy (You Say You're)/One Dream Coming, One Dream Going	1980	—	2.00	4.00
4972	It Was You/Betty Ruth	1981	—	2.00	4.00
5011	I Just Need You For Tonight/Leave Your Love A-Smokin'	1981	—	2.00	4.00
5051	Now That the Feeling's Gone/She's Good to Me	1981	—	2.00	4.00
5139	Love Busted/Darlin' Take Care of Yourself	1982	—	2.00	4.00
5170	The New Will Never Wear Off on You/Hold Me Tight	1982	—	2.00	4.00
CARTWHEEL					
193	Knock Three Times/The Best I Ever Had	1971	—	2.50	5.00
196	Dream Lover/I Ran Out of Time	1971	—	2.50	5.00
201	You Better Move On/Confidence and Common Sense	1971	—	2.50	5.00
210	Ain't Nothin' Shakin' (But the Leaves on the Trees)/She's My Angel	1972	—	2.50	5.00
216	I'm Gonna Knock on Your Door/What He Don't Know	1972	—	2.50	5.00
222	Afraid I'll Want to Love Her One More Time/Treat Her Right	1972	2.00	4.00	8.00
CEE CEE					
5400	Tell Me When I'm Hot/(B-side unknown)	1983	—	—	3.00
CHART					
1004	Go On Home Girl/Learning to Live Without You	1967	—	3.00	6.00
1025	Your Love Is What Is/Anything That's Part of You	1968	—	3.00	6.00
1415	There Ought to Be a Law/Two Arms Full of Lonely	1966	2.00	4.00	8.00
1450	Whipping Boy/The Love We Live Without	1967	2.00	4.00	8.00
5126	Go On Home Girl/Whipping Boy	1971	—	2.50	5.00
5154	Your Love Is What Is/Whipping Boy	1972	—	2.50	5.00
COLONIAL					
721	Bird Doggin'/Millionaire	1958	10.00	20.00	40.00
COLUMBIA					
41316	Am I to Be the One/I Miss You So Much	1959	6.25	12.50	25.00
41367	Sweetie Pie/Blabbermouth	1959	7.50	15.00	30.00
41470	Don't Destroy Me/Boom Boom Baby	1959	6.25	12.50	25.00
41470 [PS]	Don't Destroy Me/Boom Boom Baby	1959	12.50	25.00	50.00
41536	I Want That/Since She Turned Seventeen	1960	7.50	15.00	30.00
41619	All I Want Is You/Letter of Love	1960	6.25	12.50	25.00
41619 [PS]	All I Want Is You/Letter of Love	1960	12.50	25.00	50.00
41677	One Last Kiss/Is It True or False	1960	5.00	10.00	20.00
41822	Heavenly Love/Good Time Billy	1961	5.00	10.00	20.00
DATE					
1007	Lulu Lee/Ah, Poor Little Baby	1958	10.00	20.00	40.00
KING					
5912	Betty, Betty/Right Around the Corner	1964	6.25	12.50	25.00
5924	My Baby's Got Flat Feet/One Heartache Too Many	1964	6.25	12.50	25.00
5964	Teardrops on Your Letter/Love You More Everyday	1964	5.00	10.00	20.00
MERCURY					
71811	Truly True/How Lonely He Must Be	1961	5.00	10.00	20.00
71862	A Diamond Is Forever/Old King Cole	1962	6.25	12.50	25.00

Albums

Number	Title (A Side/B Side)	Yr	VG	VG+	NM
ABC					
X-777	Afraid I'll Want to Love Her One More Time	1973	6.25	12.50	25.00
X-777	Two Sides of "Crash"	1973	3.75	7.50	15.00
—Retitled version of above					
X-788	Mr. Country Rock	1973	3.75	7.50	15.00
X-817	Rub It In	1974	3.75	7.50	15.00
—Black label					
X-817	Rub It In	1974	3.00	6.00	12.00
—Multicolor label					
X-850	Greatest Hits — Volume One	1975	3.00	6.00	12.00
X-875	Still Thinkin' Bout You	1975	3.00	6.00	12.00
AB-1078	Billy "Crash" Craddock Sings His Greatest Hits	1978	2.50	5.00	10.00
ABC DOT					
2040	Easy as Pie	1976	3.00	6.00	12.00
2063	Crash	1976	3.00	6.00	12.00
2082	Live!	1977	3.00	6.00	12.00
ATLANTIC					
82012	Back on Track	1989	3.00	6.00	12.00
CAPITOL					
ST-11758	Billy "Crash" Craddock	1978	2.50	5.00	10.00
SW-11853	Turning Up and Turning On	1978	2.50	5.00	10.00
ST-11946	Laughing and Crying, Living and Dying	1979	2.50	5.00	10.00
ST-12054	Changes	1980	2.50	5.00	10.00
ST-12249	The New Will Never Wear Off	1981	2.50	5.00	10.00
ST-12304	Greatest Hits	1983	2.50	5.00	10.00
CARTWHEEL					
193	Knock Three Times	1971	5.00	10.00	20.00
05001	You Better Move On	1972	5.00	10.00	20.00
CHART					
1053	The Best of Billy Crash Craddock	1973	3.75	7.50	15.00
HARMONY					
KH 32186	Billy "Crash" Craddock	1973	3.00	6.00	12.00
KING					
912 [M]	I'm Tore Up	1964	25.00	50.00	100.00
MCA					
662	Greatest Hits — Volume One	1981	2.00	4.00	8.00
—Reissue of ABC 850					
663	Billy "Crash" Craddock Sings His Greatest Hits	1981	2.00	4.00	8.00
—Reissue of ABC 1078					
664	Easy as Pie	1981	2.00	4.00	8.00
—Reissue of ABC Dot 2040					
665	Live!	1981	2.00	4.00	8.00
—Reissue of ABC Dot 2082					
666	The First Time	1981	2.00	4.00	8.00
4165 [(2)]	The Best of Billy "Crash" Craddock	198?	3.00	6.00	12.00
MCA DOT					
39054	Crash Craddock	1986	2.50	5.00	10.00
STARDAY					
3005	16 Favorite Hits	1978	2.50	5.00	10.00

CRAIG, JIMMY

45s

Number	Title (A Side/B Side)	Yr	VG	VG+	NM
BRILL					
1	All for You/Gonna Love My Baby	1959	20.00	40.00	80.00
IMPERIAL					
5592	Walking in Darkness/Oh Little Girl	1959	3.75	7.50	15.00
WARWICK					
542	Drifter/Let Me Stay	1960	3.75	7.50	15.00

CRAIG, THE

45s

Number	Title (A Side/B Side)	Yr	VG	VG+	NM
FONTANA					
1579	I Must Be Mad/Suspense	1967	6.25	12.50	25.00

CRAMER, FLOYD

45s

Number	Title (A Side/B Side)	Yr	VG	VG+	NM
ABBOTT					
142	Little Brown Jug/Dancin' Diane	1953	3.75	7.50	15.00
146	Fancy Pants/Five Foot Two, Eyes of Blue	1953	3.75	7.50	15.00
—Black vinyl					
146	Fancy Pants/Five Foot Two, Eyes of Blue	1953	5.00	10.00	20.00
—Red vinyl					
159	Jolly Cholly/Oh! Suzanna	1954	3.75	7.50	15.00
181	Rag-a-tag/Aunt Dinah's Quilting Party	1955	3.75	7.50	15.00
MGM					
11990	Sweet Adeline/Howdy Ma'm	1955	3.00	6.00	12.00
12059	Piano Rag/Jealous, Cold, Cheatin' Heart	1955	3.00	6.00	12.00
12161	Battle Hymn of the Republic/Dixie	1955	3.00	6.00	12.00
12242	Succotash/Tennessee Central (#9)	1956	3.00	6.00	12.00
12306	Pretty Blue Jeans/Good Time Cakewalk	1956	3.00	6.00	12.00
12442	Rio Grande Valley/Slap Happy	1957	3.00	6.00	12.00
12520	Waltz with Cramer/Funny Face	1957	3.00	6.00	12.00
12619	Herman's Theme/Country Gentleman	1958	3.00	6.00	12.00
RCA					
PB-10761	I'm Thinking Tonight of My Blue Eyes/Hang On Sloopy	1976	—	2.00	4.00
PB-10901	La Chicana/Four in the Morning	1977	—	2.00	4.00
—With Chet Atkins and Danny Davis					
PB-10908	Prelude to Love/Rhythm of the Rain	1977	—	2.00	4.00
PB-11065	Coming Home/The Hurt	1977	—	2.00	4.00
PB-11163	Looking for Mr. Goodbar/Father Time	1977	—	2.00	4.00
PB-11284	Root Beer Rag/Morning Dew	1978	—	2.00	4.00
PB-11394	The Main Street Electrical Parade/Singing in the Country Rain	1978	—	2.00	4.00
PB-11432	Our Winter Love/For Lovers' Sake	1978	—	2.00	4.00
PB-11576	Georgia on My Mind/Boogie Woogie	1979	—	2.00	4.00
PB-11715	A Never Ending Love/Last Date	1979	—	2.00	4.00
PB-11916	Dallas/Lover's Minuet	1980	—	—	3.00
PB-12195	Sleepy Shores/Help Me Make It Through the Night	1981	—	—	3.00
PB-12272	High Noon/Lone Ranger	1981	—	—	3.00
RCA VICTOR					
APBO-0012	Lonely Street/The Battle of New Orleans	1973	—	2.00	4.00
APBO-0214	Theme from "The Young and the Restless"/Boogie, Boogie, Boogie	1974	—	2.00	4.00

Number	Title (A Side/B Side)	Yr	VG	VG+	NM
PB-10076	Forever/Flip, Flop and Fly	1974	—	2.00	4.00
PB-10336	The Last Farewell/My Melody of Love	1975	—	2.00	4.00
PB-10533	Eres Tu (Touch the Wind)/Faded Love	1975	—	2.00	4.00
PB-10597	Tonight's the Night/Candy Pants	1976	—	2.00	4.00
47-7156	Flip, Flop and Fly/Sophisticated Swing	1958	2.50	5.00	10.00
47-7250	Mumble Jumble/Cryin'	1958	2.50	5.00	10.00
47-7388	Rumpus/The Big Chihuahua	1958	2.50	5.00	10.00
47-7775	Last Date/Sweetie Baby	1960	3.00	6.00	12.00
47-7840	On the Rebound/Mood Indigo	1961	3.00	6.00	12.00
47-7840 [PS]	On the Rebound/Mood Indigo	1961	5.00	10.00	20.00
47-7893	San Antonio Rose/I Just Can't Imagine	1961	2.50	5.00	10.00
47-7907	Your Last Goodbye/Hang On	1961	2.50	5.00	10.00
47-7907 [PS]	Your Last Goodbye/Hang On	1961	5.00	10.00	20.00
47-7978	Chattanooga Choo Choo/Let's Go	1962	2.00	4.00	8.00
47-8013	Lovesick Blues/The First Hurt	1962	2.00	4.00	8.00
47-8041	Hot Pepper/For Those That Cry	1962	2.00	4.00	8.00
47-8084	Swing Low/Losers Weepers	1962	2.00	4.00	8.00
47-8116	Java/Melissa	1962	2.00	4.00	8.00
47-8171	(These Are) The Young Years/Kaapsedri	1963	2.00	4.00	8.00
47-8217	How High the Moon/Satan's Doll	1963	2.00	4.00	8.00
47-8265	The Hucklebuck/Heartless Heart	1963	2.00	4.00	8.00
47-8325	Want Me/Naomi	1964	2.00	4.00	8.00
47-8414	Tomorrow's Gone/Shrum	1964	2.00	4.00	8.00
47-8541	Town Square/Long Walk Home	1965	2.00	4.00	8.00
47-8899	Strangers in the Night/You've Lost That Lovin' Feelin'	1966	—	3.00	6.00
47-9065	Stood Up/Good Vibrations	1967	—	3.00	6.00
47-9157	I Wanna Be Free/Papa Gene's Blues	1967	—	3.00	6.00
47-9237	Theme for Sam/For No One	1967	—	3.00	6.00
47-9396	Gentle on My Mind/By the Time I Get to Phoenix	1967	—	3.00	6.00
47-9841	Theme from Room 222/Leaving on a Jet Plane	1970	—	2.00	4.00
47-9874	Fancy Free/Is This Tomorrow	1970	—	2.00	4.00
47-9940	For the Good Times/Everything Is Beautiful	1971	—	2.00	4.00
47-9978	Makin' Up/Theme from "Flight of the Doves"	1971	—	2.00	4.00
74-0152	Games People Play/Ob-La-Di, Ob-La-Da	1969	—	2.50	5.00
74-0209	Seattle/Lovin' Season	1969	—	2.50	5.00
74-0621	Corn Crib Symphony/Your Last Goodbye	1971	—	2.00	4.00
74-0674	Hony Tonk (Part 2)/Detour	1972	—	2.00	4.00
74-0821	Quiet Girl/Smile	1972	—	2.00	4.00
74-0869	Tonight's the Night/Crystal Chandelier	1973	—	2.00	4.00
SIMS					
121	Fancy Pants/Five Foot Two, Eyes of Blue	1961	2.00	4.00	8.00
STEP ONE					
454	Christmas Medley//We Wish You A Merry Christmas/I'll Be Home For Christmas	1992	—	2.50	5.00
—Red vinyl					

7-Inch Extended Plays

Number	Title (A Side/B Side)	Yr	VG	VG+	NM
RCA VICTOR					
DJEO-0272 [DJ]	Behind Closed Doors/The Most Beautiful Girl//Star Spangled Banner/Top of the World	1974	2.50	5.00	10.00
EPA-4377	Last Date/San Antonio Rose//Flip, Flop and Bop/Chattanooga Choo Choo	1961	2.50	5.00	10.00
EPA-4377 [PS]	Last Date	1961	2.50	5.00	10.00

Albums

Number	Title (A Side/B Side)	Yr	VG	VG+	NM
MGM					
E-3502 [M]	That Honky-Tonk Piano	1957	10.00	20.00	40.00
E-4223 [M]	Floyd Cramer Goes Honky Tonkin'	1964	3.75	7.50	15.00
SE-4223 [R]	Floyd Cramer Goes Honky Tonkin'	1964	3.00	6.00	12.00
SE-4666	Floyd Cramer Goes Honky Tonkin'	1970	3.00	6.00	12.00
—Reissue of 4223					
PAIR					
PDL2-1049 [(2)]	Country Classics	1986	3.00	6.00	12.00
RCA					
5621-1-R	Our Class Reunion	1987	2.50	5.00	10.00
RCA CAMDEN					
ACL2-0128 [(2)]	Floyd Cramer Plays the Big Hits	1973	3.00	6.00	12.00
ACL1-0563	Spotlight On Floyd Cramer	1974	2.50	5.00	10.00
CAL-874 [M]	The Magic Touch	1965	3.00	6.00	12.00
CAS-874 [S]	The Magic Touch	1965	3.00	6.00	12.00
CAL-2104 [M]	Distinctive Piano Styling	196?	3.00	6.00	12.00
CAS-2104 [S]	Distinctive Piano Styling	196?	3.00	6.00	12.00
CAL-2152 [M]	Night Train	1967	3.00	6.00	12.00
CAS-2152 [S]	Night Train	1967	3.00	6.00	12.00
CAS-2508	Almost Persuaded	1971	3.00	6.00	12.00
CXS-9016 [(2)]	A Date with Floyd Cramer	1972	3.75	7.50	15.00
RCA VICTOR					
APD1-0155 [Q]	Super Country Hits	1973	3.75	7.50	15.00
APL1-0155	Super Country Hits	1973	3.00	6.00	12.00
APD1-0299 [Q]	Class of '73	1973	3.75	7.50	15.00
APL1-0299	Class of '73	1973	3.00	6.00	12.00
APD1-0469 [Q]	The Young and the Restless	1974	3.75	7.50	15.00
APL1-0469	The Young and the Restless	1974	3.00	6.00	12.00
APL1-0661	Floyd Cramer In Concert	1974	3.00	6.00	12.00
APD1-0893 [Q]	Piano Masterpieces (1900-75)	1975	3.75	7.50	15.00
APL1-0893	Piano Masterpieces (1900-75)	1975	2.50	5.00	10.00
APD1-1191 [Q]	Class of '74 and '75	1975	3.75	7.50	15.00
APL1-1191	Class of '74 and '75	1975	2.50	5.00	10.00
APD1-1541 [Q]	Floyd Cramer Country	1976	3.75	7.50	15.00
APL1-1541	Floyd Cramer Country	1976	2.50	5.00	10.00
LPM-2151 [M]	Hello Blues	1960	3.75	7.50	15.00
LSP-2151 [S]	Hello Blues	1960	5.00	10.00	20.00
APL1-2278	Floyd Cramer & the Keyboard Kick Band	1977	2.50	5.00	10.00
ANL1-2344	Hits from Country Hall	1977	2.50	5.00	10.00
LPM-2350 [M]	Last Date	1961	5.00	10.00	20.00
LSP-2350 [S]	Last Date	1961	6.25	12.50	25.00
LPM-2359 [M]	On the Rebound	1961	3.75	7.50	15.00
LSP-2359 [S]	On the Rebound	1961	5.00	10.00	20.00
LPM-2428 [M]	Floyd Cramer Gets Organ-ized	1962	3.75	7.50	15.00
LSP-2428 [S]	Floyd Cramer Gets Organ-ized	1962	5.00	10.00	20.00
LPM-2466 [M]	America's Biggest Selling Pianist	1962	3.75	7.50	15.00
LSP-2466 [S]	America's Biggest Selling Pianist	1962	5.00	10.00	20.00
LPM-2544 [M]	I Remember Hank Williams	1962	3.75	7.50	15.00
LSP-2544 [S]	I Remember Hank Williams	1962	5.00	10.00	20.00
LPM-2642 [M]	Swing Along	1963	3.75	7.50	15.00
LSP-2642 [S]	Swing Along	1963	5.00	10.00	20.00
AHL1-2644	Looking for Mr. Goodbar	1978	2.50	5.00	10.00
LPM-2701 [M]	Comin' On	1963	3.75	7.50	15.00
LSP-2701 [S]	Comin' On	1963	5.00	10.00	20.00
LPM-2800 [M]	Country Piano — City Strings	1964	3.75	7.50	15.00
LSP-2800 [S]	Country Piano — City Strings	1964	5.00	10.00	20.00
LPM-2883 [M]	Cramer at the Console	1964	3.75	7.50	15.00
LSP-2883 [S]	Cramer at the Console	1964	5.00	10.00	20.00
LPM-2888 [M]	The Best of Floyd Cramer	1964	3.00	6.00	12.00
LSP-2888 [S]	The Best of Floyd Cramer	1964	3.75	7.50	15.00
AHL1-3209	Super Hits	1979	2.50	5.00	10.00
LPM-3318 [M]	Hits from the Country Hall of Fame	1965	3.75	7.50	15.00
LSP-3318 [S]	Hits from the Country Hall of Fame	1965	5.00	10.00	20.00
LPM-3405 [M]	Class of '65	1965	3.00	6.00	12.00
LSP-3405 [S]	Class of '65	1965	3.75	7.50	15.00
ANL1-3469	Floyd Cramer In Concert	1979	2.00	4.00	8.00
AHL1-3487	Last Date	1979	2.50	5.00	10.00
LPM-3533 [M]	The Big Ones	1966	3.00	6.00	12.00
LSP-3533 [S]	The Big Ones	1966	3.75	7.50	15.00
AHL1-3613	Dallas	1980	2.50	5.00	10.00
LPM-3650 [M]	Class of '66	1966	3.00	6.00	12.00
LSP-3650 [S]	Class of '66	1966	3.75	7.50	15.00
AYL1-3745	Piano Masterpieces (1900-75)	1980	2.00	4.00	8.00
LPM-3746 [M]	Here's What's Happening!	1967	3.75	7.50	15.00
LSP-3746 [S]	Here's What's Happening!	1967	3.75	7.50	15.00
LPM-3811 [M]	Floyd Cramer Plays the Monkees	1967	3.75	7.50	15.00
LSP-3811 [S]	Floyd Cramer Plays the Monkees	1967	3.75	7.50	15.00
LPM-3827 [M]	Class of '67	1967	3.75	7.50	15.00
LSP-3827 [S]	Class of '67	1967	3.75	7.50	15.00
LPM-3828 [M]	We Wish You a Merry Christmas	1967	7.50	15.00	30.00
LSP-3828 [S]	We Wish You a Merry Christmas	1967	3.00	6.00	12.00
AYL1-3900	The Best of Floyd Cramer	1981	2.00	4.00	8.00
LPM-3925 [M]	Floyd Cramer Plays Country Classics	1968	5.00	10.00	20.00
LSP-3925 [S]	Floyd Cramer Plays Country Classics	1968	3.75	7.50	15.00
AYL1-4008	Great Country Hits	1981	2.00	4.00	8.00
LPM-4025 [M]	Class of '68	1968	—	—	—
—Canceled?					
LSP-4025 [S]	Class of '68	1968	3.75	7.50	15.00
LSP-4070	MacArthur Park	1968	3.75	7.50	15.00
LSP-4091	The Best of Floyd Cramer, Volume 2	1969	3.75	7.50	15.00
AHL1-4119	Best of the West	1982	2.50	5.00	10.00
LSP-4162	Class of '69	1969	3.75	7.50	15.00
LSP-4220	Floyd Cramer Plays More Country Classics	1969	3.75	7.50	15.00
LSP-4312	The Big Ones, Volume II	1970	3.75	7.50	15.00
LSP-4367	Floyd Cramer with the Music City Pops	1970	3.75	7.50	15.00
LSP-4437	Class of '70	1970	3.75	7.50	15.00
LSP-4500	Sounds of Sunday	1971	3.75	7.50	15.00
LSP-4590	Class of '71	1971	3.75	7.50	15.00
LSP-4676	Detours	1972	3.75	7.50	15.00
LSP-4772	Class of '72	1972	3.75	7.50	15.00
LSP-4821	Best of the Class of...	1973	3.75	7.50	15.00
AHL1-5452	Collector's Series	1985	2.50	5.00	10.00
VPS-6031 [(2)]	This Is Floyd Cramer	1970	5.00	10.00	20.00

CRANE, BOB

45s

Number	Title (A Side/B Side)	Yr	VG	VG+	NM
EPIC					
10038	Theme from Get Smart/Happy Feet	1966	3.00	6.00	12.00
10108	Theme from Hogan's Heroes/Theme from "F" Troop	1966	3.00	6.00	12.00

Albums

Number	Title (A Side/B Side)	Yr	VG	VG+	NM
EPIC					
LN 24224 [M]	The Funny Side of TV	1966	6.25	12.50	25.00
BN 26224 [S]	The Funny Side of TV	1966	7.50	15.00	30.00

CRANE, LES

45s

Number	Title (A Side/B Side)	Yr	VG	VG+	NM
WARNER BROS.					
7520	Desiderata/A Different Drummer	1971	—	2.50	5.00
7520 [PS]	Desiderata/A Different Drummer	1971	—	3.00	6.00
7548	Desiderata (Spanish)/Desiderata (English)	1972	—	3.00	6.00
7582	Children Learn What They Live/The Wilderness	1972	—	2.00	4.00

Albums

Number	Title (A Side/B Side)	Yr	VG	VG+	NM
WARNER BROS.					
BS 2570	Desiderata	1970	2.50	5.00	10.00

CRANE, SHERRY

45s

Number	Title (A Side/B Side)	Yr	VG	VG+	NM
SUN					
328	Willie Willie/Winnie the Parakeet	1959	6.25	12.50	25.00

CRAWFORD, BOBBY

Also see THE CRAWFORD BROTHERS.

45s

Number	Title (A Side/B Side)	Yr	VG	VG+	NM
DEL-FI					
4211	Mrs. Smith, Please Wake Up/That Little Old Lovemaker Me	1963	3.75	7.50	15.00
4236	I Want to Be a Good Guy/(B-side unknown)	1964	3.75	7.50	15.00

CRAWFORD, CAROLYN

45s

Number	Title (A Side/B Side)	Yr	VG	VG+	NM
MERCURY					
74036	Coming On Strong/Love Song for You	1978	—	2.50	5.00
—Mercury titles as "Caroline Crawford"					
74054	You'll Wait/Breakdown	1979	—	2.50	5.00
76013	The Strut/I'll Be Here for You	1979	—	2.50	5.00
MOTOWN					
1050	Forget About Me/Devil in His Heart	1963	10.00	20.00	40.00
1064	My Smile Is Just a Frown Turned Upside Down/I'll Come Running	1964	12.50	25.00	50.00
—Original version of A-side title					

Number	Title (A Side/B Side)	Yr	VG	VG+	NM
1064	My Smile Is Just a Frown (Turned Upside Down)/I'll Come Running	1964	5.00	10.00	20.00
—Revised version of A-side title					
1070	My Heart/When Someone's Good to You	1964	10.00	20.00	40.00
PHILADELPHIA INT'L.					
3553	Just Got to Be More Careful/Saving All the Love I Got for You	1974	—	2.50	5.00
3570	It Takes Two to Make One/No Matter How Bad Things Are, I Still Love You	1975	—	2.50	5.00
3580	Good & Plenty/If You Move, You Lose	1975	—	2.50	5.00

CRAWFORD, HANK

Number	Title (A Side/B Side)	Yr	VG	VG+	NM
45s					
ATLANTIC					
5013	Misty (Part 1)/Misty (Part 2)	1961	2.50	5.00	10.00
5016	Easy Living/Playmates	1961	2.50	5.00	10.00
5022	Don't Cry Baby/The Peeper	1962	2.50	5.00	10.00
5030	Blueberry Hill/Any Time	1963	2.50	5.00	10.00
5033	Skunky Green/Whispering Grass	1963	2.50	5.00	10.00
5039	Shake a-Plenty/Mellow Down	1964	2.50	5.00	10.00
5042	Merry Christmas Baby/Read 'Em and Weep	1964	2.50	5.00	10.00
5049	Don't Get Around Much Anymore/Bluff City Blues	1966	2.00	4.00	8.00
5066	Soul Shoutin'/Who Can I Turn To When Nobody Needs Me	1968	2.00	4.00	8.00
5079	Smoky City/Hush Puppies	1969	2.00	4.00	8.00
KUDU					
905	Brian's Song/In the Wee Small Hours of the Morning	1972	—	2.50	5.00
908	Help Me Make It Through the Night/Uncle Funky	1972	—	2.50	5.00
911	The Christmas Song/Winter Wonderland	1974	—	2.50	5.00
923	Sho Is Funky/(B-side unknown)	1975	—	2.50	5.00
944	Daytime Friends/I Don't Want No Happy Songs	1978	—	2.50	5.00
Albums					
ATLANTIC					
SD 2-315 [(2)]	The Art of Hank Crawford	1973	3.75	7.50	15.00
1356 [M]	More Soul	1960	5.00	10.00	20.00
—Purple and red label, white fan logo					
1356 [M]	More Soul	1962	3.00	6.00	12.00
—Purple and red label, black fan logo					
SD 1356 [S]	More Soul	1960	6.25	12.50	25.00
—Green and blue label, white fan logo					
SD 1356 [S]	More Soul	1962	3.75	7.50	15.00
—Green and blue label, black fan logo					
1372 [M]	The Soul Clinic	1961	5.00	10.00	20.00
—Purple and red label, white fan logo					
1372 [M]	The Soul Clinic	1962	3.00	6.00	12.00
—Purple and red label, black fan logo					
SD 1372 [S]	The Soul Clinic	1961	6.25	12.50	25.00
—Green and blue label, white fan logo					
SD 1372 [S]	The Soul Clinic	1962	3.75	7.50	15.00
—Green and blue label, black fan logo					
1387 [M]	From the Heart	1962	3.75	7.50	15.00
SD 1387 [S]	From the Heart	1962	5.00	10.00	20.00
1405 [M]	Soul of the Ballad	1963	3.75	7.50	15.00
SD 1405 [S]	Soul of the Ballad	1963	5.00	10.00	20.00
1423 [M]	True Blue	1964	3.75	7.50	15.00
SD 1423 [S]	True Blue	1964	5.00	10.00	20.00
1436 [M]	Dig These Blues	1965	3.75	7.50	15.00
SD 1436 [S]	Dig These Blues	1965	5.00	10.00	20.00
1455 [M]	After Hours	1966	3.75	7.50	15.00
SD 1455 [S]	After Hours	1966	5.00	10.00	20.00
1470 [M]	Mr. Blues	1967	5.00	10.00	20.00
SD 1470 [S]	Mr. Blues	1967	3.75	7.50	15.00
SD 1503	Double Cross	1968	3.75	7.50	15.00
SD 1523	Mr. Blues Plays Lady Soul	1969	3.75	7.50	15.00
SD 1557	The Best of Hank Crawford	1970	3.75	7.50	15.00
COTILLION					
SD 18003	It's a Funny Thing to Do	1971	3.00	6.00	12.00
KUDU					
06	Help Me Make It	1972	3.00	6.00	12.00
08	We've Got a Good Thing	1973	3.00	6.00	12.00
15	Wildflower	1974	3.00	6.00	12.00
19	Don't You Worry 'Bout a Thing	1975	3.00	6.00	12.00
26	I Hear a Symphony	1976	3.00	6.00	12.00
33	Hank Crawford's Back	1977	3.00	6.00	12.00
35	Tico Rico	1977	3.00	6.00	12.00
39	Cajun Sunrise	1979	3.00	6.00	12.00
MILESTONE					
9112	Midnight Ramble	1983	2.50	5.00	10.00
9119	Indigo Blue	1984	2.50	5.00	10.00
9129	Down on the Deuce	1985	2.50	5.00	10.00
9140	Roadhouse Symphony	1986	2.50	5.00	10.00
9149	Mr. Chips	1987	2.50	5.00	10.00
9168	Night Beat	1988	2.50	5.00	10.00
9182	Groove Master	1990	3.00	6.00	12.00
MOBILE FIDELITY					
1-224	Soul of the Ballad	1995	6.25	12.50	25.00
—Audiophile vinyl					

CRAWFORD, HANK, AND JIMMY MCGRIFF

Also see each artist's individual listings.

Number	Title (A Side/B Side)	Yr	VG	VG+	NM
Albums					
MILESTONE					
9142	Soul Survivors	1986	2.50	5.00	10.00
9153	Steppin' Up	1988	2.50	5.00	10.00
9177	On the Blue Side	1990	3.00	6.00	12.00

CRAWFORD, JOHNNY

Also see THE CRAWFORD BROTHERS.

Number	Title (A Side/B Side)	Yr	VG	VG+	NM
45s					
DEL-FI					
4162	Daydreams/So Goes the Story	1961	3.75	7.50	15.00
4162 [PS]	Daydreams/So Goes the Story	1961	6.25	12.50	25.00
4165	Your Love Is Growing Cold/Treasure	1961	3.75	7.50	15.00
4165 [PS]	Your Love Is Growing Cold/Treasure	1961	6.25	12.50	25.00
4172	Patti Ann/Donna	1962	3.75	7.50	15.00
4178	Cindy's Birthday/Something Special	1962	3.75	7.50	15.00
4178 [PS]	Cindy's Birthday/Something Special	1962	6.25	12.50	25.00
4181	Your Nose Is Gonna Grow/Mr. Blue	1962	3.75	7.50	15.00
4181 [PS]	Your Nose Is Gonna Grow/Mr. Blue	1962	6.25	12.50	25.00
4188	Rumors/No One Really Loves a Clown	1962	3.75	7.50	15.00
4188 [PS]	Rumors/No One Really Loves a Clown	1962	6.25	12.50	25.00
4193	Proud/Lonesome Town	1963	3.75	7.50	15.00
4203	Cry on My Shoulder/When I Fall in Love	1963	3.75	7.50	15.00
4215	What Happened to Janie/Petite Chanson	1963	3.75	7.50	15.00
4221	Cindy's Gonna Cry/Debbie	1963	3.75	7.50	15.00
4229	Sandy/Ol' Shorty	1963	3.75	7.50	15.00
4231	Judy Loves Me/Living in the Past	1963	3.75	7.50	15.00
4242	The Girl Next Door (Once Upon a Time)/Sittin' and Watchin'	1964	3.75	7.50	15.00
4305	Am I Too Young/Janie Please Believe It	1965	3.75	7.50	15.00
SIDEWALK					
932	Angelica/Everybody Has Their Day	1968	3.00	6.00	12.00
941	Good Guys Finish Last/Everyone Should Own a Dream	1968	3.00	6.00	12.00
WYNNE					
124	Dance with the Dolly (With the Hole in Her Stocking)/Ask	1958	5.00	10.00	20.00
Albums					
DEL-FI					
DFLP-1220 [M]	The Captivating Johnny Crawford	1962	10.00	20.00	40.00
DFLP-1223 [M]	A Young Man's Fancy	1962	7.50	15.00	30.00
DFST-1223 [S]	A Young Man's Fancy	1962	10.00	20.00	40.00
DFLP-1224 [M]	Rumors	1963	7.50	15.00	30.00
DFST-1224 [S]	Rumors	1963	10.00	20.00	40.00
DFLP-1229 [M]	His Greatest Hits	1963	7.50	15.00	30.00
DFST-1229 [S]	His Greatest Hits	1963	10.00	20.00	40.00
DFLP-1248 [M]	Greatest Hits, Volume 2	1964	5.00	10.00	20.00
DFST-1248 [S]	Greatest Hits, Volume 2	1964	6.25	12.50	25.00
GUEST STAR					
GS-1470 [M]	Johnny Crawford	196?	5.00	10.00	20.00
GSS-1470 [S]	Johnny Crawford	196?	6.25	12.50	25.00
RHINO					
RNDF-202	The Best of Johnny Crawford	1982	3.00	6.00	12.00
SUPREME					
M-110 [M]	Songs from "The Restless Ones"	1965	5.00	10.00	20.00
MS-210 [S]	Songs from "The Restless Ones"	1965	6.25	12.50	25.00

CRAWFORD BROTHERS, THE

Also see BOBBY CRAWFORD; JOHNNY CRAWFORD.

Number	Title (A Side/B Side)	Yr	VG	VG+	NM
45s					
DEL-FI					
4191	Good Buddies/You Gotta Wear Shoes	1963	3.75	7.50	15.00
4191 [PS]	Good Buddies/You Gotta Wear Shoes	1963	6.25	12.50	25.00

CRAWLER

CRAYNE, LESLIE 'UGGAMS'

See LESLIE UGGAMS.

CRAYONS, THE

Number	Title (A Side/B Side)	Yr	VG	VG+	NM
45s					
COUNSEL					
122	Love at First Sight/I Saw You	1963	7.50	15.00	30.00

CRAYTON, PEE WEE

Number	Title (A Side/B Side)	Yr	VG	VG+	NM
45s					
ALADDIN					
3112	When It Rains It Pours/Daybreak	1952	25.00	50.00	100.00
3112	When It Rains It Pours/Daybreak	1952	500.00	1000.	1500.
—Green vinyl					
EDCO					
1009	Ev'ry Night About This Time/(B-side unknown)	196?	6.25	12.50	25.00
1010	Money Tree/When Darkness Falls	196?	6.25	12.50	25.00
FOX					
10069	Give Me One More Chance/(B-side unknown)	196?	7.50	15.00	30.00
GUYDEN					
2048	I'm Still in Love with You/Time on My Hands	1961	3.75	7.50	15.00
IMPERIAL					
5288	Do Unto Others/Every Dog Has a Day	1954	50.00	100.00	200.00
5297	Wine-O/Hurry Hurry	1954	125.00	250.00	500.00
5321	I Need Your Love/You Know — Yeah	1955	12.50	25.00	50.00
5338	My Idea About You/I Got News for You	1955	12.50	25.00	50.00
5345	Eyes Full of Tears/Runnin' Wild	1955	12.50	25.00	50.00
5353	Yours Truly/Be Faithful	1955	12.50	25.00	50.00
JAMIE					
1190	'Tain't Nobody's Business If I Do/Little Bitty Things	1961	3.75	7.50	15.00
MODERN					
892	Cool Evening/Have You Lost Your Love for Me	1951	25.00	50.00	100.00
POST					
2007	Don't Go/I Must Go On	1955	10.00	20.00	40.00
2007	I Must Go On/(B-side unknown)	1955	7.50	15.00	30.00
RECORDED IN HOLLYWOOD					
408	Pappy's Blues/Crying and Walking	1954	25.00	50.00	100.00
426	Baby Pat the Floor/I'm Your Prisoner	1954	25.00	50.00	100.00
SMASH					
1774	Sabre Twist/Hillbilly Blues	1962	3.00	6.00	12.00
VEE JAY					
214	A Frosty Night/The Telephone Is Ringing	1956	10.00	20.00	40.00
252	I Don't Care/I Found My Peace of Mind	1957	10.00	20.00	40.00
266	Fiddle Dee Dee/Is This the Price I Pay	1957	10.00	20.00	40.00

Number	Title (A Side/B Side)	Yr	VG	VG+	NM
Albums					
CROWN					
CLP-5175 [M]	Pee Wee Crayton	1959	25.00	50.00	100.00
—Black label					
CLP-5175 [M]	Pee Wee Crayton	196?	5.00	10.00	20.00
—Gray label					
VANGUARD					
VSD-6566	The Things I Used to Do	1971	3.75	7.50	15.00

CRAZY ELEPHANT

Number	Title (A Side/B Side)	Yr	VG	VG+	NM
45s					
BELL					
763	Gimme Gimme Good Lovin'/Dark Part of My Mind	1969	2.00	4.00	8.00
804	Pam/Sunshine, Red Wine	1969	—	3.00	6.00
817	Gimme Some More/My Babe (Honey Pie)	1969	—	3.00	6.00
846	There's a Better Day a-Comin' (Na, Na, Na, Na)/ Space Buggy	1969	—	3.00	6.00
875	Land Rover/There Ain't No Umbopo	1970	—	3.00	6.00
Albums					
BELL					
6034	Crazy Elephant	1969	5.00	10.00	20.00

CRAZY HORSE

Also see NEIL YOUNG.

Number	Title (A Side/B Side)	Yr	VG	VG+	NM
45s					
EPIC					
10925	Rock and Roll Band/Outside Lookin' In	1972	—	2.50	5.00
M.O.C.					
671	Love/High on Lovin'	1967	3.00	6.00	12.00
REPRISE					
1007	Downtown/Crow Jane Lady	1971	—	2.50	5.00
1025	Dance, Dance, Dance/Carolay	1971	—	2.50	5.00
1046	Beggars Day/Dirty, Dirty	1971	—	2.50	5.00
1075	All Alone Now/One Thing I Love	1972	—	2.50	5.00
Albums					
EPIC					
KE 31710	Crazy Horse at Crooked Lane	1972	3.75	7.50	15.00
RCA VICTOR					
AFL1-3054	Crazy Moon	1978	3.00	6.00	12.00
REPRISE					
MS 2059	Loose	1972	3.75	7.50	15.00
RS 6438	Crazy Horse	1971	3.75	7.50	15.00

CRAZY OTTO

Number	Title (A Side/B Side)	Yr	VG	VG+	NM
45s					
DECCA					
29403	Glad Rag Doll/Smiles	1955	5.00	10.00	20.00
—Original pressings credited to "Happy Otto"					
29403	Glad Rag Doll/Smiles	1955	3.00	6.00	12.00
—Later pressings credited to "Crazy Otto"					
29449	My Melancholy Baby/In the Mood	1955	2.50	5.00	10.00
29503	Crazy Otto Rag/Twelfth Street Rag	1955	2.50	5.00	10.00
29571	Oh Johnny, Oh Johnny, Oh!/Palestine	1955	2.50	5.00	10.00
29658	The Marching Otto Medley (Part 1)/The Marching Otto Medley (Part 2)	1955	3.00	6.00	12.00
—As "Marching Otto"					
29673	If You Knew Susie/Somebody Else Is Taking My Place	1955	2.50	5.00	10.00
29753	Tin Pan Alley Medley/Gaslight Medley	1955	2.50	5.00	10.00
29980	Alabamy Bound/Das Ist Musik	1956	2.00	4.00	8.00
30093	Derby Hat Medley/Swingin' Door Medley	1956	2.00	4.00	8.00
30377	Happy Piano Medley/Good Evening Friends Medley	1957	2.00	4.00	8.00
30608	Zippy Medley/Bouncy Medley	1958	2.00	4.00	8.00
30818	Chopin's Polonaise/Sunrise Serenade	1959	2.00	4.00	8.00
31185	Medley: Sleigh Ride-Winter Wonderland-White Christmas/Medley: Rudolph The Red-Nosed Reindeer-I Saw Mommy Kissing Santa Claus-Jingle Bells	1960	3.00	6.00	12.00
31235	Piccadilly/Spanish Holiday	1961	2.00	4.00	8.00
MGM					
13101	Alley Cat/Cheerio Choo Choo	1962	2.00	4.00	8.00
7-Inch Extended Plays					
DECCA					
ED 2201	(contents unknown)	1955	2.50	5.00	10.00
ED 2201 [PS]	Crazy Otto, Volume 1	1955	2.50	5.00	10.00
ED 2202	(contents unknown)	1955	2.50	5.00	10.00
ED 2202 [PS]	Crazy Otto, Volume 2	1955	2.50	5.00	10.00
ED 2260	(contents unknown)	1956	2.50	5.00	10.00
ED 2260 [PS]	Crazy Otto Rides Again, Volume 1	1956	2.50	5.00	10.00
ED 2261	(contents unknown)	1956	2.50	5.00	10.00
ED 2261 [PS]	Crazy Otto Rides Again, Volume 2	1956	2.50	5.00	10.00
ED 2263	(contents unknown)	1956	2.50	5.00	10.00
ED 2263 [PS]	Crazy Otto Rides Again, Volume 3	1956	2.50	5.00	10.00
ED 2569	(contents unknown)	1957	2.00	4.00	8.00
ED 2569 [PS]	Crazy Otto's Back in Town	1957	2.00	4.00	8.00
ED 2600	(contents unknown)	1958	2.00	4.00	8.00
ED 2600 [PS]	Honky Tonk Piano	1958	2.00	4.00	8.00
Albums					
DECCA					
DL 4157 [M]	Have Piano, Will Travel	1961	3.75	7.50	15.00
DL 8113 [M]	Crazy Otto	1955	5.00	10.00	20.00
—Black label, silver print					
DL 8113 [M]	Crazy Otto	1960	3.00	6.00	12.00
—Black label with color bars					
DL 8163 [M]	Crazy Otto Rides Again	1956	5.00	10.00	20.00
DL 8627 [M]	Crazy Otto's Back in Town	1957	3.75	7.50	15.00
DL 8737 [M]	Honky Tonk Piano	1958	3.75	7.50	15.00
DL 8919 [M]	Golden Award Songs	1960	3.75	7.50	15.00
DL 74157 [S]	Have Piano, Will Travel	1961	5.00	10.00	20.00
DL 78919 [S]	Golden Award Songs	1960	5.00	10.00	20.00
MGM					
E-4150 [M]	Crazy Otto Plays Crazy Tunes	1963	3.00	6.00	12.00
SE-4150 [S]	Crazy Otto Plays Crazy Tunes	1963	3.75	7.50	15.00
VOCALION					
VL 3663 [M]	Crazy Otto Goes Sentimental	196?	3.00	6.00	12.00

CREACH, PAPA JOHN

Also see HOT TUNA; JEFFERSON AIRPLANE; JEFFERSON STARSHIP.

Number	Title (A Side/B Side)	Yr	VG	VG+	NM
45s					
BUDDAH					
509	I'm the Fiddle Man/Joyce	1975	—	2.00	4.00
DJM					
1102	All the World Loves a Winner/Southern Strut	1979	—	2.00	4.00
GRUNT					
65-0501	Over the Rainbow/The Janitor Drives a Cadillac	1971	—	2.50	5.00
65-0505	Papa John's Down Home Blues/String Jet Rock	1971	—	2.50	5.00
65-0508	Filthy Funky (Part 1)/Filthy Funky (Part 2)	1972	—	2.50	5.00
Albums					
BUDDAH					
BDS-5649	I'm the Fiddle Man	1975	3.00	6.00	12.00
BDS-5660	Rock Father	1977	3.00	6.00	12.00
DJM					
11	Cat & Fiddle	1977	3.00	6.00	12.00
18	Inphasion	1978	3.00	6.00	12.00
GRUNT					
BFL1-0418	Playing My Fiddle for You	1974	3.75	7.50	15.00
BXL1-1003	Papa John Creach	197?	3.00	6.00	12.00
—Reissue with new prefix					
FTS-1003	Papa John Creach	1971	3.75	7.50	15.00
BXL1-1009	Filthy!	197?	3.00	6.00	12.00
—Reissue with new prefix					
FTS-1009	Filthy!	1972	3.75	7.50	15.00

CREAM

Also see GINGER BAKER'S AIR FORCE; JACK BRUCE; ERIC CLAPTON.

Number	Title (A Side/B Side)	Yr	VG	VG+	NM
45s					
ATCO					
6462	I Feel Free/N.S.U.	1967	3.75	7.50	15.00
6488	Strange Brew/Tales of Brave Ulysses	1967	3.75	7.50	15.00
6522	Spoonful/Spoonful (Part 2)	1967	3.75	7.50	15.00
6544	Sunshine of Your Love/SWLABR	1968	2.00	4.00	8.00
6575	Anyone for Tennis/Pressed Rat and Warthog	1968	2.00	4.00	8.00
6617	White Room/Those Were the Days	1968	2.00	4.00	8.00
6646	Crossroads/Passing the Time	1969	2.00	4.00	8.00
6668	Badge/What a Bringdown	1969	2.00	4.00	8.00
6708	Sweet Wine/Lawdy Mama	1969	2.50	5.00	10.00
Albums					
ATCO					
33-206 [M]	Fresh Cream	1967	12.50	25.00	50.00
SD 33-206 [S]	Fresh Cream	1967	7.50	15.00	30.00
—Purple and brown labels					
SD 33-206 [S]	Fresh Cream	1969	3.75	7.50	15.00
—Yellow labels					
33-232 [M]	Disraeli Gears	1967	12.50	25.00	50.00
SD 33-232 [S]	Disraeli Gears	1967	7.50	15.00	30.00
—Purple and brown labels					
SD 33-232 [S]	Disraeli Gears	1969	3.75	7.50	15.00
—Yellow labels					
SD 33-291	Best of Cream	1969	6.25	12.50	25.00
SD 33-328	Live Cream	1970	6.25	12.50	25.00
2-700 [(2) M]	Wheels of Fire	1968	50.00	100.00	200.00
—White label promo; no stock copies are mono					
SD 2-700 [(2) S]	Wheels of Fire	1968	12.50	25.00	50.00
—Purple and brown labels; foil-like cover					
SD 2-700 [(2) S]	Wheels of Fire	1969	5.00	10.00	20.00
—Yellow labels; dull gray cover					
SD 7001	Goodbye	1969	7.50	15.00	30.00
—Purple and brown labels; deduct 33% if poster is missing					
SD 7001	Goodbye	1969	3.75	7.50	15.00
—Yellow labels					
SD 7005	Live Cream — Volume II	1972	6.25	12.50	25.00
DCC COMPACT CLASSICS					
LPZ-2015	Fresh Cream	1996	7.50	15.00	30.00
—Audiophile vinyl					
MOBILE FIDELITY					
2-066 [(2)]	Wheels of Fire	1980	22.50	45.00	90.00
—Audiophile vinyl					
1-264	Goodbye	1996	—	—	—
—Audiophile vinyl; canceled					
POLYDOR					
24-3502 [(2)]	Heavy Cream	1972	3.75	7.50	15.00
24-5529	Off the Top	1973	3.75	7.50	15.00
RSO					
015 [(2) DJ]	Classic Cuts	1978	10.00	20.00	40.00
—Promo-only compilation					
RS-1-3009	Fresh Cream	1977	3.00	6.00	12.00
RS-1-3010	Disraeli Gears	1977	3.00	6.00	12.00
RS-1-3012	Best of Cream	1977	3.00	6.00	12.00
RS-1-3013	Goodbye	1977	3.00	6.00	12.00
RS-1-3014	Live Cream	1977	3.00	6.00	12.00
RS-1-3015	Live Cream — Volume 2	1977	3.00	6.00	12.00
RS-2-3802 [(2)]	Wheels of Fire	1977	3.75	7.50	15.00
SPRINGBOARD					
SPB 4037	Early Cream	1972	3.75	7.50	15.00

CREATION, THE

Number	Title (A Side/B Side)	Yr	VG	VG+	NM
45s					
DECCA					
32155	If I Stay Too Long/Nightmares	1967	3.00	6.00	12.00
32227	How Does It Feel to Feel/Life Is Just Beginning	1967	3.00	6.00	12.00
PLANET					
116	Making Time/Try and Stop Me	1966	3.75	7.50	15.00

Number	Title (A Side/B Side)	Yr	VG	VG+	NM
119	Painter Man/Biff Bang Pow	1966	3.75	7.50	15.00

CREATION OF SUNLIGHT

Albums

WINDI

Number	Title (A Side/B Side)	Yr	VG	VG+	NM
1001	Creation of Sunlight	1968	150.00	300.00	600.00

CREATIONS, THE

Many different groups.

45s

Number	Title (A Side/B Side)	Yr	VG	VG+	NM
GLOBE					
102	Just Remember Me/Times Are Changing	1967	5.00	10.00	20.00
103	I've Got to Find Her/Times Are Changing	1967	5.00	10.00	20.00
1000	Oh Baby/Plenty of Love	1967	5.00	10.00	20.00
JAMIE					
1197	The Bells/Shang Shang	1961	6.25	12.50	25.00
LIDO					
501	You Are My Darling/There Goes the Girl I Love	1956	75.00	150.00	300.00
MEL-O-DY					
101	This Is Our Night/You're My Inspiration	1962	—	—	—
MERIDIAN					
7550	The Wedding/I've Got a Feeling	1962	25.00	50.00	100.00
PATTI-JO					
1703	Seventeen/You'll Always Be Mine	1962	50.00	100.00	200.00
PENNY					
9022	Lady Luck/We're in Love	1962	15.00	30.00	60.00
PINE CREST					
101	Woke Up in the Morning/Strolling Through the Park	1961	100.00	200.00	400.00
RADIANT					
103	Don't Listen to What Others Say/Don't Listen to What Others Say, Part 2	1964	6.25	12.50	25.00
TAKE TEN					
1501	Lady Luck/We're in Love	1963	7.50	15.00	30.00
TIP TOP					
400	Every Night I Pray/Mommy and Daddy	1956	50.00	100.00	200.00
501	You Are My Darling/There Goes the Girl I Love	1956	50.00	100.00	200.00
—At least one source claims this is a bootleg.					
TOP HAT					
1003	Crash/Chickie Darling	1964	10.00	20.00	40.00
1003 [PS]	Crash/Chickie Darling	1964	20.00	40.00	80.00
1004	Don't Be Mean/(B-side unknown)	1965	12.50	235.00	50.00
1004 [PS]	Don't Be Mean/(B-side unknown)	1965	25.00	50.00	100.00
VIRTUE					
2517	I'm So in Love with You/Save the People	1971	—	3.00	6.00
2518	Don't Let Me Down/The Price I Have to Pay	1971	—	3.00	6.00
2520	Nothing Too Good for You/You Mean So Much	1972	—	3.00	6.00
2521	You Make Me Feel So Good/That's How Strong My Love Is	1972	—	3.00	6.00
2522	How Sweetly Simple/Lovin' Simple	1973	—	3.00	6.00
ZODIAC					
1005	A Dream/Foot Steps	1967	2.00	4.00	8.00

CREATIVE SOURCE

45s

Number	Title (A Side/B Side)	Yr	VG	VG+	NM
POLYDOR					
14291	Pass the Feelin' On/Turn On to Music	1975	—	2.50	5.00
14334	I'll Find You Anywhere/Singin' Funky Music	1976	—	—	—
—Canceled					
SUSSEX					
501	You Can't Hide Love/Lovesville	1973	—	2.50	5.00
508	You're Too Good to Be True/Oh Love	1973	—	2.50	5.00
509	Who Is He and What Is He to You (Part 1)/Who Is He and What Is He to You (Part 2)	1974	—	2.50	5.00
622	Keep On Movin'/I Just Can't See Myself Without You	1974	—	2.50	5.00
632	Migration/I Just Can't See Myself Without You	1974	—	2.50	5.00

Albums

Number	Title (A Side/B Side)	Yr	VG	VG+	NM
POLYDOR					
PD-1-6052	Pass the Feelin' On	1975	3.00	6.00	12.00
PD-1-6065	Consider the Source	1976	3.00	6.00	12.00
SUSSEX					
SUS-8027	Creative Source	1973	3.75	7.50	15.00
SUS-8035	Migration	1974	3.75	7.50	15.00

CREATORS, THE (1)

45s

Number	Title (A Side/B Side)	Yr	VG	VG+	NM
DOOTO					
463	I've Had You/Drafted, Volunteered, Enlisted	1961	6.25	12.50	25.00
DORE					
635	Too Far to Turn Around/Hello There, Mister Grave Digger	1962	15.00	30.00	60.00

CREATORS, THE (2)

45s

Number	Title (A Side/B Side)	Yr	VG	VG+	NM
EPIC					
9605	Crazy Love/Cross Fire	1963	3.75	7.50	15.00
HI-Q					
5021	Wear My Ring/Booga Bear	1961	20.00	40.00	80.00
—Normal print label					
5021	Wear My Ring/Booga Bear	1961	6.25	12.50	25.00
—Bold print label					
TIME					
1038	Do You Remember/There's Going to Be an Angel	1961	6.25	12.50	25.00

CREATORS, THE (3)

45s

Number	Title (A Side/B Side)	Yr	VG	VG+	NM
PHILIPS					
40058	Boy, He's Got It/Yeah, He's Got It	1962	6.25	12.50	25.00
40083	I'll Stay Home (New Year's Eve)/Shoom Ba Boom	1962	75.00	150.00	300.00

Number	Title (A Side/B Side)	Yr	VG	VG+	NM
T-KAY					
110	I'll Never, Never Do It Again/Boy, He's Got It!	1962	20.00	40.00	80.00

CREATURES, THE

45s

Number	Title (A Side/B Side)	Yr	VG	VG+	NM
COLUMBIA					
43689	Night Is Warm/String Along	1966	2.50	5.00	10.00
43894	Looking at Tomorrow/Someone Needs You	1967	2.00	4.00	8.00

CREEDENCE CLEARWATER REVIVAL

Also see DOUG CLIFFORD; JOHN FOGERTY; TOM FOGERTY; TOMMY FOGERTY AND THE BLUE VELVETS; THE GOLLIWOGS.

12-Inch Singles

Number	Title (A Side/B Side)	Yr	VG	VG+	NM
FANTASY					
759-D-LP [DJ]	I Heard It Through the Grapevine (11:05) (same on both sides)	1976	5.00	10.00	20.00

45s

Number	Title (A Side/B Side)	Yr	VG	VG+	NM
FANTASY					
616	Suzie Q (Part One)/Suzie Q (Part Two)	1968	—	3.00	6.00
617	I Put a Spell on You/Walk on the Water	1968	2.00	4.00	8.00
619	Proud Mary/Born on the Bayou	1969	—	3.00	6.00
622	Bad Moon Rising/Lodi	1969	—	3.00	6.00
625	Green River/Commotion	1969	—	3.00	6.00
634	Down on the Corner/Fortunate Son	1969	—	3.00	6.00
634 [PS]	Down on the Corner/Fortunate Son	1969	3.00	6.00	12.00
637	Travelin' Band/Who'll Stop the Rain	1970	—	3.00	6.00
637 [PS]	Travelin' Band/Who'll Stop the Rain	1970	3.00	6.00	12.00
641	Up Around the Bend/Run Through the Jungle	1970	—	3.00	6.00
641 [PS]	Up Around the Bend/Run Through the Jungle	1970	3.00	6.00	12.00
645	Lookin' Out My Back Door/Long As I Can See the Light	1970	—	3.00	6.00
645 [PS]	Lookin' Out My Back Door/Long As I Can See the Light	1970	3.00	6.00	12.00
655	Have You Ever Seen the Rain/Hey Tonight	1971	—	3.00	6.00
665	Sweet Hitch-Hiker/Door to Door	1971	—	3.00	6.00
665 [PS]	Sweet Hitch-Hiker/Door to Door	1971	3.00	6.00	12.00
676	Someday Never Comes/Tearin' Up the Country	1972	—	3.00	6.00
759	I Heard It Through the Grapevine/Good Golly Miss Molly	1976	—	2.00	4.00
759 [PS]	I Heard It Through the Grapevine/Good Golly Miss Molly	1976	—	2.50	5.00
908	Tombstone Shadow/Commotion	1981	—	2.00	4.00
917	Medley U.S.A./Bad Moon Rising	1981	—	2.00	4.00
920	Cotton Fields/Lodi	1981	—	2.00	4.00
957	Medley (from "I Heard It Through the Grapevine" to "Up Around the Bend")/Medley (from "Proud Mary" to "Lodi")	1985	2.50	5.00	10.00
2832/3 [DJ]	45 Revolutions Per Minute (Part 1)/45 Revolutions Per Minute (Part 2)	1970	10.00	20.00	40.00
2832/3 [PS]	45 Revolutions Per Minute (Part 1)/45 Revolutions Per Minute (Part 2)	1970	15.00	30.00	60.00
SCORPIO					
412	Porterville/Call It Pretending	1968	20.00	40.00	80.00

Albums

Number	Title (A Side/B Side)	Yr	VG	VG+	NM
DCC COMPACT CLASSICS					
LPZ-2019	Willie and the Poor Boys	1996	5.00	10.00	20.00
—Audiophile vinyl					
FANTASY					
CCR-1 [(2)]	Live in Europe	1973	3.00	6.00	12.00
CCR-2 [(2)]	Chronicle (The 20 Greatest Hits)	1976	3.75	7.50	15.00
—Brown labels					
CCR-2 [(2)]	Chronicle (The 20 Greatest Hits)	1979	3.00	6.00	12.00
—Whitish or light blue labels					
CCR-3 [(2)]	Chronicle, Volume 2	1987	3.75	7.50	15.00
CCR-68 [(2)]	Creedence Clearwater Revival 1968/69	1981	3.00	6.00	12.00
—Compilation of 8382 and 8387					
CCR-69 [(2)]	Creedence Clearwater Revival 1969	1981	3.00	6.00	12.00
—Compilation of 8393 and 8397					
CCR-70 [(2)]	Creedence Clearwater Revival 1970	1981	3.00	6.00	12.00
—Compilation of 8402 and 8410					
FPM-4001 [Q]	Creedence Gold	197?	12.50	25.00	50.00
MPF-4501	The Royal Albert Hall Concert	1980	3.75	7.50	15.00
—Album withdrawn and changed when it was discovered this didn't come from the Royal Albert Hall					
MPF-4501	The Concert	1981	2.50	5.00	10.00
—Retitled version					
MPF-4509	Creedence Country	1981	2.50	5.00	10.00
ORC-4512	Creedence Clearwater Revival	1981	2.00	4.00	8.00
—Reissue of 8382					
ORC-4513	Bayou Country	1981	2.00	4.00	8.00
—Reissue of 8387					
ORC-4514	Green River	1981	2.00	4.00	8.00
—Reissue of 8393					
ORC-4515	Willy and the Poor Boys	1981	2.00	4.00	8.00
—Reissue of 8397					
ORC-4516	Cosmo's Factory	1981	2.00	4.00	8.00
—Reissue of 8402					
ORC-4517	Pendulum	1981	2.00	4.00	8.00
—Reissue of 8410					
ORC-4518	Mardi Gras	1981	2.00	4.00	8.00
—Reissue of 9404					
MPF-4522	The Movie Album	1985	2.00	4.00	8.00
ORC-4526 [(2)]	Live in Europe	1986	2.50	5.00	10.00
F-8382	Creedence Clearwater Revival	1968	6.25	12.50	25.00
—With no reference to "Susie Q" on the front cover					
F-8382	Creedence Clearwater Revival	1968	3.75	7.50	15.00
—With "Susie Q" mentioned on the front cover; dark blue label					
F-8382	Creedence Clearwater Revival	1973	2.50	5.00	10.00
—Brown label					
F-8382 [DJ]	Creedence Clearwater Revival	1968	20.00	40.00	80.00
—White label promo					
F-8387	Bayou Country	1969	3.75	7.50	15.00
—Dark blue label					
F-8387	Bayou Country	1973	2.50	5.00	10.00
—Brown label					

Number	Title (A Side/B Side)	Yr	VG	VG+	NM
F-8387 [DJ]	Bayou Country	1969	20.00	40.00	80.00
—White label promo					
F-8393	Green River	1969	3.75	7.50	15.00
—Dark blue label					
F-8393	Green River	1973	2.50	5.00	10.00
—Brown label					
F-8393 [DJ]	Green River	1969	20.00	40.00	80.00
—White label promo					
F-8397	Willy and the Poor Boys	1969	3.75	7.50	15.00
—Dark blue label					
F-8397	Willy and the Poor Boys	1973	2.50	5.00	10.00
—Brown label					
F-8397 [DJ]	Willy and the Poor Boys	1969	20.00	40.00	80.00
—White label promo					
F-8402	Cosmo's Factory	1970	3.75	7.50	15.00
—Dark blue label					
F-8402	Cosmo's Factory	1973	2.50	5.00	10.00
—Brown label					
F-8402 [DJ]	Cosmo's Factory	1970	20.00	40.00	80.00
—White label promo					
F-8410	Pendulum	1970	3.75	7.50	15.00
—Dark blue label					
F-8410	Pendulum	1973	2.50	5.00	10.00
—Brown label					
F-9404	Mardi Gras	1972	3.75	7.50	15.00
—Dark blue label					
F-9404	Mardi Gras	1973	2.50	5.00	10.00
—Brown label					
F-9418	Creedence Gold	1972	2.50	5.00	10.00
F-9430	More Creedence Gold	1973	2.50	5.00	10.00
F-9621	Chooglin'	1982	2.00	4.00	8.00
HEARTLAND					
HR 2039 [(3)]	Creedence Clearwater Revival	1990	3.75	7.50	15.00
K-TEL					
NU 9360	The Best of Creedence Clearwater Revival — 20 Super Hits	1978	3.75	7.50	15.00
MOBILE FIDELITY					
1-037	Cosmo's Factory	1979	17.50	35.00	70.00
—Audiophile vinyl					
TIME-LIFE					
SCLR-18 [(2)]	Creedence Clearwater Revival	1989	3.75	7.50	15.00
—Part of Time-Life's "Classic Rock" series					

CRESCENDOS, THE (1)

Nashville-based vocal group.

Number	Title (A Side/B Side)	Yr	VG	VG+	NM
45s					
NASCO					
6005	Oh Julie/My Little Girl	1957	6.25	12.50	25.00
6009	School Girl/Crazy Hop	1958	6.25	12.50	25.00
6009 [PS]	School Girl/Crazy Hop	1958	12.50	25.00	50.00
6021	Rainy Sunday/Young and In Love	1958	6.25	12.50	25.00
6021 [PS]	Rainy Sunday/Young and In Love	1958	12.50	25.00	50.00
TAP					
7027	Oh Julie/Angel Face	1962	3.75	7.50	15.00
7027 [PS]	Oh Julie/Angel Face	1962	6.25	12.50	25.00
Albums					
GUEST STAR					
G-1453 [M]	Oh Julie	1962	12.50	25.00	50.00
GS-1453 [R]	Oh Julie	1962	5.00	10.00	20.00

CRESCENDOS, THE (2)

Number	Title (A Side/B Side)	Yr	VG	VG+	NM
45s					
ATLANTIC					
1109	Sweet Dreams/Finders Keepers	1956	7.50	15.00	30.00
2014	I'll Be Seeing You/Sweet Dreams	1959	3.75	7.50	15.00

CRESCENDOS, THE (U)

Some of these may be group (1); it's unlikely that any are group (2).

Number	Title (A Side/B Side)	Yr	VG	VG+	NM
45s					
DOMAIN					
1025	A Fellow Needs a Girl/Black Cat	1964	3.75	7.50	15.00
IMPRO					
5006	Tidal Wave/Crescendo Special	1962	10.00	20.00	40.00
NU SOUND					
1007	Count Down/Hawk Walk	1961	7.50	15.00	30.00
1014	Sweet Talk/Movin' Wild	1961	7.50	15.00	30.00
SCARLET					
4007	Strange Love/Let's Take a Walk	1960	7.50	15.00	30.00
4009	Angel Face/I'm So Ashamed	1961	12.50	25.00	50.00

CRESCHENDOS, THE

Number	Title (A Side/B Side)	Yr	VG	VG+	NM
45s					
GONE					
5100	My Heart's Desire/Take My Heart	1961	7.50	15.00	30.00
MUSIC CITY					
831	My Heart's Desire/Take My Heart	1960	100.00	200.00	400.00
—Green label					
831	My Heart's Desire/Take My Heart	1960	50.00	100.00	200.00
—Maroon label					
831	My Heart's Desire/Take My Heart	1961	12.50	25.00	50.00
—Black label					
839	Teenage Prayer/I Don't Mind	1961	62.50	125.00	250.00
SATURN					
404	Surfing Strip/Hanging Ten	1963	12.50	25.00	50.00

CRESENTS, THE

Number	Title (A Side/B Side)	Yr	VG	VG+	NM
45s					
JOYCE					
102	Everybody Knew But Me/Rosemarie	1957	62.50	125.00	250.00

CRESTONES, THE

Number	Title (A Side/B Side)	Yr	VG	VG+	NM
45s					
MARKIE					
117	She's a Bad Motorcycle/Grasshopper Dance	1963	12.50	25.00	50.00
U.S.A.					
835	My Girl/The Chopper	1965	3.00	6.00	12.00

CRESTS, THE

Also see JOHNNY MAESTRO.

Number	Title (A Side/B Side)	Yr	VG	VG+	NM
45s					
COED					
501	Pretty Little Angel/I Thank the Moon	1958	37.50	75.00	150.00
—"Coed" in red print					
501	Pretty Little Angel/I Thank the Moon	1958	10.00	20.00	40.00
—"Coed" in red and black print					
506	16 Candles/Beside You	1958	7.50	15.00	30.00
509	Six Nights a Week/I Do	1959	6.25	12.50	25.00
511	Flower of Love/Molly Mae	1959	6.25	12.50	25.00
515	The Angels Listened In/I Thank the Moon	1959	7.56	15.00	30.00
521	A Year Ago Tonight/Paper Clown	1959	6.25	12.50	25.00
525	Step by Step/Gee (But I'd Give the World)	1960	6.25	12.50	25.00
531	Trouble in Paradise/Always You	1960	6.25	12.50	25.00
535	Journey of Love/If My Heart Could Write a Letter	1960	5.00	10.00	20.00
537	Isn't It Amazing/Molly Mae	1960	5.00	10.00	20.00
543	I Remember (In the Still of the Night)/Good Golly Miss Molly	1961	6.25	12.50	25.00
561	Little Miracles/Baby I Gotta Know	1962	7.50	15.00	30.00
CORAL					
62403	You Blew Out the Candles/A Love to Last a Lifetime	1964	7.50	15.00	30.00
HARVEY					
5002	Sixteen Candles/My Juanita	1981	2.50	5.00	10.00
—Red vinyl					
JOYCE					
103	My Juanita/Sweetest One	1957	75.00	150.00	300.00
—Label name: "JoYce"					
103	My Juanita/Sweetest One	1959	12.50	25.00	50.00
—Label name: "Joyce"					
105	No One to Love/Wish She Was Mine	1957	75.00	150.00	300.00
KING TUT					
172	Earth Angel/Tweedlee Dee	197?	2.00	4.00	8.00
LANA					
101	16 Candles/(B-side unknown)	196?	2.00	4.00	8.00
—Oldies reissue					
102	Trouble in Paradise/I Thank the Moon	196?	2.00	4.00	8.00
—Oldies reissue					
103	Step by Step/Gee (But I'd Give the World)	196?	2.00	4.00	8.00
—Oldies reissue					
MUSICTONE					
1106	My Juanita/Sweetest One	1961	5.00	10.00	20.00
SCEPTER					
12112	I'm Stepping Out of the Picture/Afraid of Love	1965	3.75	7.50	15.00
SELMA					
311	Guilty/Number One with Me	1962	18.75	37.50	75.00
—A-side has spoken intro					
311	Guilty/Number One with Me	1962	6.25	12.50	25.00
—A-side does not have spoken intro					
4000	Did I Remember/Tears Will Fall	1963	7.50	15.00	30.00
TIMES SQUARE					
2	No One to Love/Wish She Was Mine	1962	5.00	10.00	20.00
—Red vinyl					
6	Baby/I Love You So	1964	3.75	7.50	15.00
97	Baby/I Love You So	1964	3.00	6.00	12.00
TRANS ATLAS					
696	The Actor/Three Tears in a Bucket	1962	7.50	15.00	30.00
7-Inch Extended Plays					
COED					
101	(contents unknown)	1960	100.00	200.00	400.00
101 [PS]	The Angels Listened In	1960	100.00	200.00	400.00
Albums					
COED					
LPC-901 [M]	The Crests Sing All Biggies	1960	100.00	200.00	400.00
—Yellow label, black print					
LPC-901 [M]	The Crests Sing All Biggies	1960	50.00	100.00	200.00
—Red label					
LPC-904 [M]	The Best of the Crests	1961	100.00	200.00	400.00
COLLECTABLES					
COL-5009	Greatest Hits	1982	3.00	6.00	12.00
POST					
3000	The Crests Sing	196?	10.00	20.00	40.00
RHINO					
R1-70948	The Best of the Crests	1989	3.00	6.00	12.00

CREW CUTS, THE

Number	Title (A Side/B Side)	Yr	VG	VG+	NM
45s					
4 CORNERS OF THE WORLD					
120	Don't Be Angry/Earth Angel	1962	2.50	5.00	10.00
ABC-PARAMOUNT					
10450	Hip-Huggers/You're a Star, Donna, Donna	1963	3.00	6.00	12.00
CHESS					
1892	Ain't That Nice/Yeah, Yeah, She Wants Me	1964	2.50	5.00	10.00
FIREBIRD					
1805	My Heart Belongs to Only You/You've Been In	1970	—	2.50	5.00
MERCURY					
70341	Crazy 'Bout You Baby/Angela Mia	1954	5.00	10.00	20.00
70404	Sh-Boom/I Spoke Too Soon	1954	6.25	12.50	25.00
70404	Sh-Boom/I Spoke Too Soon	1954	12.50	25.00	50.00
—7-inch 78 rpm on vinyl					
70404 [PS]	Sh-Boom/I Spoke Too Soon	1954	25.00	50.00	100.00
—Sleeve accompanying the 78: "PopSi Hit Record of the Month"					
70443	Oop-Shoop/Do Me Good Baby	1954	3.75	7.50	15.00

Number	Title (A Side/B Side)	Yr	VG	VG+	NM
70490	All I Wanna Do/The Barking Dog	1954	3.75	7.50	15.00
70491	Dance, Mr. Snowman, Dance/Twinkle Toes	1954	3.75	7.50	15.00
70494	The Whippenpoof Song/Varsity Drag	1954	3.75	7.50	15.00
70529	Ko Ko Mo (I Love You So)/Earth Angel	1955	3.75	7.50	15.00
70597	Don't Be Angry/Chop Chop Boom	1955	3.75	7.50	15.00
70598	Unchained Melody/Two Hearts, Two Kisses	1955	3.75	7.50	15.00
70634	A Story Untold/Carmen's Boogie	1955	3.75	7.50	15.00
70668	Gum Drop/Present Arms	1955	3.75	7.50	15.00
70710	Slam! Bam!/Are You Having Any Fun	1955	3.75	7.50	15.00
70741	Angels in the Sky/Mostly Martha	1955	3.75	7.50	15.00
70782	Seven Days/That's Your Mistake	1956	3.75	7.50	15.00
70840	Out of the Picture/Honey Hair, Sugar Lips, Eyes of Blue	1956	3.75	7.50	15.00
70890	Tell Me Why/Rebel in Town	1956	3.75	7.50	15.00
70922	Bei Mir Bist Du Schoen/Thirteen Going on Fourteen	1956	3.75	7.50	15.00
70977	Love in a Home/Keeper of the Flame	1956	3.75	7.50	15.00
70988	The Varsity Drag/Halls of Ivy	1956	3.75	7.50	15.00
71022	Young Love/Little by Little	1956	3.75	7.50	15.00
71076	The Angels/Whatever, Whenever. Whoever	1957	3.75	7.50	15.00
71125	Suzie Q/Such a Shame	1957	3.75	7.50	15.00
71168	I Sit in My Window/Hey, You Face	1957	3.75	7.50	15.00
71223	I Like It Like That/Be My Only Love	1957	3.75	7.50	15.00

RCA VICTOR

Number	Title (A Side/B Side)	Yr	VG	VG+	NM
47-7320	Forever My Darling/Hey Stella	1958	3.00	6.00	12.00
47-7359	That's My Desire/Baby Be Mine	1958	3.00	6.00	12.00
47-7446	Fraternity Pin/Can You Hear Me	1959	3.00	6.00	12.00
47-7509	Gone, Gone, Gone/Someone in Heaven	1959	3.00	6.00	12.00
47-7577	Bermuda/Kin-Ni-Ki-Nic	1959	3.00	6.00	12.00
47-7667	It Is No Secret/No, No, Nevermore	1960	3.00	6.00	12.00
47-7734	American Beauty Rose/The Shrine on Top of the Hill	1960	3.00	6.00	12.00
47-7759	Aura Lee/Going to Church on Sunday	1960	3.00	6.00	12.00

VEE JAY

Number	Title (A Side/B Side)	Yr	VG	VG+	NM
569	The Three Bells/Spanish Is the Loving Tongue	1963	3.00	6.00	12.00

WARWICK

Number	Title (A Side/B Side)	Yr	VG	VG+	NM
558	Over the Mountain/Searchin'	1960	3.00	6.00	12.00
585	You and the Angels/I Care for You	1960	3.00	6.00	12.00
595	Malaguena/Why Not	1960	3.00	6.00	12.00
623	The Legend of Gunga Din/Number One with Me	1961	3.00	6.00	12.00

WHALE

Number	Title (A Side/B Side)	Yr	VG	VG+	NM
507	Twistin' All the World/Electric Chair	1962	3.00	6.00	12.00
508	Laura Love/Little Donkey	1962	3.00	6.00	12.00
509	Hush Little Baby/Ti-Pi-Tum	1962	3.00	6.00	12.00

7-Inch Extended Plays

MERCURY

Number	Title (A Side/B Side)	Yr	VG	VG+	NM
EP-1-3274	Down the Old Ox Road/The Whiffenpoof Song// We're Working Our Way Through College/ Varsity Drag	1956	3.00	6.00	12.00
EP-1-3274 [PS]	The Crew Cuts On Campus	1956	3.00	6.00	12.00

Albums

CAMAY

Number	Title (A Side/B Side)	Yr	VG	VG+	NM
CA-1002 [M]	The Crew Cuts Sing Folk	196?	5.00	10.00	20.00
CA-3002 [S]	The Crew Cuts Sing Folk	196?	6.25	12.50	25.00

MERCURY

Number	Title (A Side/B Side)	Yr	VG	VG+	NM
MG-20067 [M]	The Crew Cuts Go Longhair	1955	12.50	25.00	50.00
MG-20140 [M]	The Crew Cuts On Campus	1956	12.50	25.00	50.00
MG-20143 [M]	Crew Cut Capers	1956	12.50	25.00	50.00
MG-20144 [M]	Rock and Roll Bash	1956	20.00	40.00	80.00
MG-20199 [M]	Music A La Carte	1957	12.50	25.00	50.00
MG-25200 [10]	The Crew Cuts On Campus	1956	20.00	40.00	80.00

RCA VICTOR

Number	Title (A Side/B Side)	Yr	VG	VG+	NM
PR-102 [M]	The Crew Cuts Sing Out!	1960	6.25	12.50	25.00
PR-129 [M]	The Crew Cuts Have a Ball	1960	6.25	12.50	25.00

—Produced for Ebonite bowling balls; Side 2 has "Bowling Tips by Top Stars"

Number	Title (A Side/B Side)	Yr	VG	VG+	NM
LPM-1933 [M]	Surprise Package	1958	7.50	15.00	30.00
LSP-1933 [S]	Surprise Package	1959	10.00	20.00	40.00
LPM-2037 [M]	The Crew Cuts Sing	1959	7.50	15.00	30.00
LSP-2037 [S]	The Crew Cuts Sing	1959	10.00	20.00	40.00
LPM-2067 [M]	You Must Have Been a Beautiful Baby	1960	7.50	15.00	30.00
LSP-2067 [S]	You Must Have Been a Beautiful Baby	1960	10.00	20.00	40.00

WING

Number	Title (A Side/B Side)	Yr	VG	VG+	NM
MGW-12125 [M]	Rock and Roll Bash	196?	6.25	12.50	25.00
MGW-12145 [M]	The Crew Cuts On Campus	196?	5.00	10.00	20.00
MGW-12177 [M]	The Crew Cuts	196?	5.00	10.00	20.00
MGW-12180 [M]	High School Favorites	196?	5.00	10.00	20.00
MGW-12195 [M]	The Crew Cuts Sing the Masters	196?	5.00	10.00	20.00

CREWE, BOB

Includes records as "The Bob Crewe Generation" and similar names.

45s

20TH CENTURY

Number	Title (A Side/B Side)	Yr	VG	VG+	NM
2271	Street Talk/Street Talk (Part 2)	1976	—	2.00	4.00

ABC-PARAMOUNT

Number	Title (A Side/B Side)	Yr	VG	VG+	NM
10204	Swingin' Family Tree/La La Loretta	1961	3.00	6.00	12.00
10246	One More Lie/I'm Goin' Home (On My Way)	1961	3.00	6.00	12.00
10273	Another Day/Come to Me	1961	3.00	6.00	12.00

BRUNSWICK

Number	Title (A Side/B Side)	Yr	VG	VG+	NM
55021	I Can't Shake the Blues/Torn and Tattered Heart	1957	3.75	7.50	15.00

CORAL

Number	Title (A Side/B Side)	Yr	VG	VG+	NM
61688	Melody for Lovers/Can't Get Away from It	1956	3.75	7.50	15.00

CREWE

Number	Title (A Side/B Side)	Yr	VG	VG+	NM
605	Dandylion/Day By Day & Prepare Ye	1971	—	2.50	5.00

DYNO VOICE

Number	Title (A Side/B Side)	Yr	VG	VG+	NM
229	Music to Watch Girls By/Girls on the Rocks	1966	2.00	4.00	8.00
231	After the Ball/One More Year	1967	—	3.00	6.00
233	Miniskirts/Theme for a Lazy Girl	1967	—	3.00	6.00
237	A Lover's Concerto/You Only Live Twice	1967	—	3.00	6.00
902	Birds of Britain/I Will Wait for You	1968	—	3.00	6.00
906	Winter Warm/Song from Moulin Rouge	1968	—	3.00	6.00
915	To Give (The Reason I Live)/Battle Hymn of the Republic	1968	—	3.00	6.00
928	Angel Is Love/Black Queen's Beads	1968	—	3.00	6.00

ELEKTRA

Number	Title (A Side/B Side)	Yr	VG	VG+	NM
45346	Time for You and Me/Free (Medley)	1976	—	2.00	4.00
45380	Menage a Trois/I Am Free-Keep Walkin'	1976	—	2.00	4.00
45404	It Took a Long Time (For the First Time in My Life)/In Another Life	1977	—	2.00	4.00
45425	Marriage Made in Heaven/In Another Life	1977	—	2.00	4.00

JUBILEE

Number	Title (A Side/B Side)	Yr	VG	VG+	NM
5148	Cash Register Heart/Change of Heart	1954	5.00	10.00	20.00
5164	Punch/It's All Over	1954	5.00	10.00	20.00

MELBA

Number	Title (A Side/B Side)	Yr	VG	VG+	NM
119	Guessin' Games/Don't Call Me Chicken	1957	3.75	7.50	15.00

METROMEDIA

Number	Title (A Side/B Side)	Yr	VG	VG+	NM
229	Mammy Blue/Better Be Gone	1972	—	2.50	5.00
243	Takin' Care of Each Other/(B-side unknown)	1972	—	2.50	5.00

PHILIPS

Number	Title (A Side/B Side)	Yr	VG	VG+	NM
40241	Rag Doll/Ronnie	1964	2.00	4.00	8.00
40241 [PS]	Rag Doll/Ronnie	1964	3.75	7.50	15.00

—Has photo of the Four Seasons on it; the sleeve even looks as if it belongs to a Four Seasons record until you read a bit more closely!

SPOTLIGHT

Number	Title (A Side/B Side)	Yr	VG	VG+	NM
393	Penny Nickel Dime Quarter (On a Teenage Date)/ How Long	1956	5.00	10.00	20.00

VIK

Number	Title (A Side/B Side)	Yr	VG	VG+	NM
0307	Charm Bracelet/Do Be Do Be Do	1957	6.25	12.50	25.00
0333	Of Sun, the Sea and the Sand/Sweet Talk	1958	5.00	10.00	20.00

WARWICK

Number	Title (A Side/B Side)	Yr	VG	VG+	NM
519	The Whippenpoof Song/Let's Pretend	1959	3.00	6.00	12.00
534	Cool Time/Quite a Picture	1960	3.00	6.00	12.00
553	Silhouettes/Let's Get Serious	1960	3.00	6.00	12.00
579	Little Girl of Mine/To Ev'ry Girl, To Ev'ry Boy	1960	3.00	6.00	12.00
601	Oh, How I Miss You Tonight/Ev'rytime	1960	3.00	6.00	12.00
616	She's Only Wonderful/On the Street Where You Live	1961	3.00	6.00	12.00

Albums

CGC

Number	Title (A Side/B Side)	Yr	VG	VG+	NM
1000	Let Me Touch You	1970	3.00	6.00	12.00

DYNO VOICE

Number	Title (A Side/B Side)	Yr	VG	VG+	NM
DV-1902 [M]	Music to Watch Birds By	1967	3.75	7.50	15.00
DV-1906 [M]	The Bob Crewe Generation In Classic Form	1968	3.75	7.50	15.00
DV-9003 [M]	Music to Watch Girls By	1967	3.75	7.50	15.00
DVS-9003 [S]	Music to Watch Girls By	1967	3.00	6.00	12.00
DV-31902 [S]	Music to Watch Birds By	1967	3.00	6.00	12.00
DV-31906 [S]	The Bob Crewe Generation In Classic Form	1968	3.00	6.00	12.00

ELEKTRA

Number	Title (A Side/B Side)	Yr	VG	VG+	NM
7E-1083	Street Talk	1976	3.00	6.00	12.00
7E-1103	Motivation	1977	3.00	6.00	12.00

PHILIPS

Number	Title (A Side/B Side)	Yr	VG	VG+	NM
PHM 200150 [M]	All the Song Hits of the Four Seasons	1964	6.25	12.50	25.00
PHM 200238 [M]	Bob Crewe Plays the Four Seasons' Hits	1967	5.00	10.00	20.00
PHS 600150 [S]	All the Song Hits of the Four Seasons	1964	7.50	15.00	30.00
PHS 600238 [S]	Bob Crewe Plays the Four Seasons' Hits	1967	3.75	7.50	15.00

WARWICK

Number	Title (A Side/B Side)	Yr	VG	VG+	NM
W-2009 [M]	Kicks	1960	6.25	12.50	25.00
WST-2009 [S]	Kicks	1960	12.50	25.00	50.00
W-2034 [M]	Crazy in the Heart	1961	6.25	12.50	25.00
WST-2034 [S]	Crazy in the Heart	1961	12.50	25.00	50.00

CRIBBINS, BERNARD

45s

CAPITOL

Number	Title (A Side/B Side)	Yr	VG	VG+	NM
5933	When I'm Sixty-Four/Oh My Word	1967	2.50	5.00	10.00

UNITED ARTISTS

Number	Title (A Side/B Side)	Yr	VG	VG+	NM
907	Right Said Fred/Quietly Bonkers	1965	2.50	5.00	10.00

CRICKETS, THE (1)

BUDDY HOLLY's group. Includes records credited to "The Crickets" both during and after Holly's life. Also see SONNY CURTIS; IVAN; NIKI SULLIVAN.

45s

BARNABY

Number	Title (A Side/B Side)	Yr	VG	VG+	NM
2061	Rockin' 50's Rock 'N' Roll/True Love Ways	1972	5.00	10.00	20.00

BRUNSWICK

Number	Title (A Side/B Side)	Yr	VG	VG+	NM
55009	That'll Be the Day/I'm Lookin' for Someone to Love	1957	12.50	25.00	50.00
55035	Oh, Boy!/Not Fade Away	1957	12.50	25.00	50.00
55053	Maybe Baby/Tell Me How	1958	12.50	25.00	50.00
55072	Think It Over/Fool's Paradise	1958	12.50	25.00	50.00
55094	It's So Easy/Lonesome Tears	1958	12.50	25.00	50.00
55124	Love's Made a Fool of You/Someone, Someone	1959	10.00	20.00	40.00
55153	When You Ask About Love/Deborah	1959	10.00	20.00	40.00

CORAL

Number	Title (A Side/B Side)	Yr	VG	VG+	NM
62198	More Than I Can Say/Baby, My Heart	1960	10.00	20.00	40.00
62238	Peggy Sue Got Married/Don't Cha Know	1960	10.00	20.00	40.00
62407	Maybe Baby/Not Fade Away	1964	7.50	15.00	30.00

EPIC

Number	Title (A Side/B Side)	Yr	VG	VG+	NM
34-08028	T-Shirt/Hollywould	1988	—	2.50	5.00
34-08028 [PS]	T-Shirt/Hollywould	1988	—	2.50	5.00

LIBERTY

Number	Title (A Side/B Side)	Yr	VG	VG+	NM
55392	He's Old Enough to Know Better/I'm Feeling Better	1961	6.25	12.50	25.00
55441	Don't Ever Change/I'm Not a Bad Boy	1962	6.25	12.50	25.00
55492	I Believe in You/Parisian Girl	1962	6.25	12.50	25.00
55495	Little Hollywood Girl/Parisian Girl	1962	6.25	12.50	25.00
55540	My Little Girl/Teardrops Fall Like Rain	1963	6.25	12.50	25.00
55603	Don't Say You Love Me/April Avenue	1963	6.25	12.50	25.00
55660	Lonely Avenue/You Can't Be In-Between	1964	6.25	12.50	25.00
55668	Please, Please Me/From Me to You	1964	12.50	25.00	50.00
55696	(They Call Her) La Bomba/All Over You	1964	6.25	12.50	25.00
55742	We Gotta Get Together/I Think I've Caught the Blues	1964	6.25	12.50	25.00
55767	Everybody's Got a Little Problem/Now Hear This	1965	6.25	12.50	25.00

MGM

Number	Title (A Side/B Side)	Yr	VG	VG+	NM
14541	Hayride/Wasn't It Nice	1973	3.75	7.50	15.00

Number	Title (A Side/B Side)	Yr	VG	VG+	NM
MUSIC FACTORY					
415	Million Dollar Movie/A Million Miles Apart	1968	5.00	10.00	20.00
7-Inch Extended Plays					
BRUNSWICK					
EB 71036	*I'm Looking for Someone to Love/That'll Be the Day/Not Fade Away/Oh! Boy	1957	75.00	150.00	300.00
EB 71036 [PS]	The Chirping Crickets	1957	75.00	150.00	300.00
EB 71038	*Maybe Baby/Rock Me My Baby/Send Me Some Lovin'/Tell Me How	1958	62.50	125.00	250.00
EB 71038 [PS]	The Sound of the Crickets	1958	62.50	125.00	250.00
Albums					
BARNABY					
Z 30268	Rockin' 50's Rock 'N' Roll	1970	6.25	12.50	25.00
BRUNSWICK					
BL 54038 [M]	The "Chirping" Crickets	1957	200.00	400.00	800.00
—Textured cover					
BL 54038 [M]	The "Chirping" Crickets	1958	150.00	300.00	600.00
—Regular cover					
CORAL					
CRL 57230 [M]	In Style with the Crickets	1960	50.00	100.00	200.00
CRL 757230 [S]	In Style with the Crickets	1960	100.00	200.00	400.00
EPIC					
FE 44446	T-Shirt	1988	3.75	7.50	15.00
LIBERTY					
LRP-3272 [M]	Something Old, Something New, Something Blue, Somethin' Else	1962	37.50	75.00	150.00
LRP-3351 [M]	California Sun/She Loves You	1964	25.00	50.00	100.00
LST-7272 [S]	Something Old, Something New, Something Blue, Somethin' Else	1962	50.00	100.00	200.00
LST-7351 [S]	California Sun/She Loves You	1964	37.50	75.00	150.00
VERTIGO					
VEL-1020	Remnants	1973	5.00	10.00	20.00

CRICKETS, THE (2)

Black vocal group featuring Dean Barlow.

Number	Title (A Side/B Side)	Yr	VG	VG+	NM
45s					
DAVIS					
459	I'm Going to Live My Life Alone/Man from the Moon	1958	15.00	30.00	60.00
JAY DEE					
777	Dreams and Wishes/When I Met You	1953	50.00	100.00	200.00
781	Fine As Wine/I'm Not the Same One You Love	1953	50.00	100.00	200.00
785	Changing Partners/Your Love	1954	37.50	75.00	150.00
786	Just You/My Little Baby's Shoes	1954	37.50	75.00	150.00
789	Are You Looking for a Sweetheart/Never Give Up Hope	1954	37.50	75.00	150.00
795	I'm Going to Live My Life Alone/Man from the Moon	1954	37.50	75.00	150.00
MGM					
11428	You're Mine/Milk and Gin	1953	62.50	125.00	250.00
11507	I'll Cry No More/For You I Have Eyes	1953	50.00	100.00	200.00
Albums					
RELIC					
LP-5040	The Crickets Featuring Dean Barlow	1987	2.50	5.00	10.00

CRISS, GARY

Number	Title (A Side/B Side)	Yr	VG	VG+	NM
12-Inch Singles					
SALSOUL					
2059	Rio De Janeiro/My Rio Lady	1978	3.00	6.00	12.00
45s					
DIAMOND					
114	Welcome Home to My Heart/Our Favorite Melodies	1962	3.00	6.00	12.00
122	My Heavenly Angel/The Girl I Told You About	1962	3.00	6.00	12.00
127	Long Lonely Nights/I Still Miss You So	1963	2.50	5.00	10.00
145	Little Joe/Sweet, Warm and Soft	1963	2.50	5.00	10.00
182	Hands of My Baby/If This Is Goodbye	1965	2.00	4.00	8.00
190	My Baby Left Me/This Love of Mine	1965	2.00	4.00	8.00
228	Welcome Home to My Heart/Hands Off Buddy	1967	5.00	10.00	20.00
SALSOUL					
2082	Amazon Queen/Brazilian Nights	1979	—	2.50	5.00
STRAND					
25044	Good Golly Miss Molly/I'll Love Only You	1961	7.50	15.00	30.00

CRITTERS, THE

Number	Title (A Side/B Side)	Yr	VG	VG+	NM
45s					
KAPP					
727	He'll Make You Cry/Children & Flowers	1965	2.50	5.00	10.00
752	Younger Girl/Gone for a While	1966	3.00	6.00	12.00
769	Mr. Dieingly Sad/It Won't Be That Way	1966	3.00	6.00	12.00
769 [PS]	Mr. Dieingly Sad/It Won't Be That Way	1966	5.00	10.00	20.00
793	Bad Misunderstanding/Forever or No More	1966	2.50	5.00	10.00
805	Marryin' Kind of Love/New York Bound	1967	2.50	5.00	10.00
838	Don't Let the Rain Fall Down on Me/Walk Like a Man Again	1967	2.50	5.00	10.00
858	Little Girl/Dancing in the Streets	1967	2.50	5.00	10.00
MUSICOR					
1044	I'm Gonna Give/Georgianna	1964	5.00	10.00	20.00
PRANCER					
6001	No One But You/I'm Telling Everyone	1969	2.00	4.00	8.00
PROJECT 3					
1326	Good Morning Sunshine/A Moment of Being with You	1968	2.00	4.00	8.00
1332	Touch 'N' Go/Younger Generation	1968	2.00	4.00	8.00
1349	Cool Sunday Morning/Lisa, But Not the Same	1969	2.00	4.00	8.00
1363	She Said She Loved Him/I Just Want to Sit Right Here and Look at You	1969	2.00	4.00	8.00
Albums					
KAPP					
KL-1485 [M]	Younger Girl	1966	7.50	15.00	30.00
KS-3485 [S]	Younger Girl	1966	10.00	20.00	40.00
PROJECT 3					
PR 4001SD	Touch 'n Go with the Critters	1968	7.50	15.00	30.00
PR 4002SD	The Critters	1969	7.50	15.00	30.00

CRITTERS, THE /THE YOUNG RASCALS/LOU CHRISTIE

Number	Title (A Side/B Side)	Yr	VG	VG+	NM
Albums					
BOUTIQUE					
CA-1079 [M]	A Taste of the Critters & The Young Rascals & Lou Christie	1966	10.00	20.00	40.00

CROCE, JIM

Number	Title (A Side/B Side)	Yr	VG	VG+	NM
45s					
21 RECORDS					
94969	Workin' at the Car Wash Blues/Rapid Roy (The Stock Car Boy)	1987	—	—	3.00
94970	It Doesn't Have to Be That Way/Time in a Bottle	1987	—	—	3.00
94971	I'll Have to Say I Love You in a Song/I Got a Name	1987	—	—	3.00
94972	You Don't Mess Around with Jim/Photographs and Memories	1987	—	—	3.00
94973	Bad, Bad Leroy Brown/Operator (That's Not the Way It Feels)	1987	—	—	3.00
ABC					
11328	You Don't Mess Around with Jim/Photographs and Memories	1972	—	2.00	4.00
11335	Operator (That's Not the Way It Feels)/Rapid Roy (The Stock Car Boy)	1972	—	2.00	4.00
11346	One Less Set of Footsteps/It Doesn't Have to Be That Way	1973	—	2.00	4.00
11359	Bad, Bad Leroy Brown/A Good Time Man Like Me Ain't Got No Business (Singin' the Blues)	1973	—	2.50	5.00
—ABC logo in children's building blocks					
11359	Bad, Bad Leroy Brown/A Good Time Man Like Me Ain't Got No Business (Singin' the Blues)	1973	—	2.00	4.00
—Regular ABC logo					
11389	I Got a Name/Alabama Rain	1973	—	2.00	4.00
11405	Time in a Bottle/Hard Time Losin' Man	1973	—	2.00	4.00
11413	It Doesn't Have to Be That Way/Roller Derby Queen	1973	—	2.00	4.00
11413 [PS]	It Doesn't Have to Be That Way/Roller Derby Queen	1973	—	2.50	5.00
11424	I'll Have to Say I Love You in a Song/Salon and Saloon	1974	—	2.00	4.00
11447	Workin' at the Car Wash Blues/Thursday	1974	—	2.00	4.00
12015	Workin' at the Car Wash Blues/Thursday	1974	—	2.50	5.00
LIFESONG					
45001	Chain Gang Medley/Stone Walls	1975	—	2.00	4.00
45005	Maybe Tomorrow/Mississippi Lady	1976	—	2.00	4.00
45018 [DJ]	It Doesn't Have to Be That Way (mono/stereo)	1976	—	2.50	5.00
—Promo-only release; Lifesong sleeve has custom sticker (add $4)					
Albums					
21 RECORDS					
90467	Photographs & Memories/His Greatest Hits	1985	2.00	4.00	8.00
90468	Time in a Bottle — Jim Croce's Greatest Love Songs	1985	2.00	4.00	8.00
90469	Down the Highway	1985	2.50	5.00	10.00
ABC					
ABCX-756	You Don't Mess Around with Jim	1972	5.00	10.00	20.00
—Original covers have no green box advertising "Time in a Bottle"					
ABCX-756	You Don't Mess Around with Jim	1973	3.75	7.50	15.00
—Posthumous covers have a green box advertising "Time in a Bottle"					
ABCX-769	Life and Times	1973	3.75	7.50	15.00
ABCX-797	I Got a Name	1973	3.75	7.50	15.00
ABCD-835	Photographs & Memories/His Greatest Hits	1974	3.75	7.50	15.00
CAPITOL					
SMAS-315	Jim and Ingrid Croce	1970	7.50	15.00	30.00
COMMAND					
QD-40006 [Q]	You Don't Mess Around with Jim	1974	6.25	12.50	25.00
QD-40007 [Q]	Life and Times	1974	6.25	12.50	25.00
QD-40008 [Q]	I Got a Name	1974	6.25	12.50	25.00
QD-40020 [Q]	Photographs & Memories/His Greatest Hits	1974	6.25	12.50	25.00
CROCE					
101	Facets	1966	75.00	150.00	300.00
DCC COMPACT CLASSICS					
LPZ-2054	His Greatest Recordings	1998	5.00	10.00	20.00
—Audiophile vinyl					
LIFESONG					
LS 900 [(2)]	The Faces I've Been	1975	3.75	7.50	15.00
LS 6007	Time in a Bottle — Jim Croce's Greatest Love Songs	1976	3.00	6.00	12.00
JZ 34993	You Don't Mess Around with Jim	1978	2.50	5.00	10.00
JZ 35000	Time in a Bottle — Jim Croce's Greatest Love Songs	1978	2.50	5.00	10.00
JZ 35008	Life and Times	1978	2.50	5.00	10.00
JZ 35009	I Got a Name	1978	2.50	5.00	10.00
JZ 35010	Photographs & Memories/His Greatest Hits	1978	2.50	5.00	10.00
JZ 35571	Bad, Bad Leroy Brown: Jim Croce's Greatest Character Songs	1978	2.50	5.00	10.00
MOBILE FIDELITY					
1-079	You Don't Mess Around with Jim	1981	10.00	20.00	40.00
—Audiophile vinyl					
PICKWICK					
SPC-3332	Another Day, Another Town	1973	2.50	5.00	10.00
—Reissue of Capitol LP					

CROCKETT, HOWARD

Number	Title (A Side/B Side)	Yr	VG	VG+	NM
45s					
DOT					
15593	If You'll Let Me/You've Got Me Lyin'	1957	12.50	25.00	50.00
15701	The Night Rider/Branded	1958	10.00	20.00	40.00
17457	The House Where Momma Lived/Last Will and Testament (Of a Drinking Man)	1973	—	3.00	6.00
17482	I Feel More Like Myself Than I Did a While Ago/I'd Like to Be Everybody for Just One Day	1973	—	3.00	6.00

Number	Title (A Side/B Side)	Yr	VG	VG+	NM
17509	The Calling/Pictures and Memories	1974	—	3.00	6.00
MANCO					
1002	Sluefoot the Bear/Polly Ann	1960	12.50	25.00	50.00
1012	That Old Juke Box/Steamboat Bill	1961	7.50	15.00	30.00
1023	Just a Poor Man/I've Got You Worried Too	1961	7.50	15.00	30.00
MEL-O-DY					
109	The Big Wheel/That Silver-Haired Daddy of Mine	1963	6.25	12.50	25.00
111	Bringing In the Gold/I've Been a Long Time Leaving	1963	6.25	12.50	25.00
115	My Lil's Run Off/Spanish Lace and Memories	1964	6.25	12.50	25.00
119	Put Me in Your Pocket/The Miles	1964	6.25	12.50	25.00
121	All the Good Times Are Gone/The Great Titanic	1965	6.25	12.50	25.00
SMASH					
1721	Deep Elm Dave/Going Down to Soldiers	1961	10.00	20.00	40.00
1750	Break Away Billy Boy/Out of Bounds Again	1962	10.00	20.00	40.00
1782	Jessie and the Glendale Train/Trail of Tears	1962	20.00	40.00	80.00
STOP					
136	The Big Cat/You're Messin' Up My Mind	1968	2.00	4.00	8.00
172	The Big Day/You Can't Get to All of 'Em Jack	1968	2.00	4.00	8.00
210	Soap and Water/A Man with No Face	1969	2.00	4.00	8.00
238	Where Were You/The Story of Bango	1969	2.00	4.00	8.00
250	The Law Says/Ask Little Brother	1969	2.00	4.00	8.00

CROME SYRCUS, THE

45s

Number	Title (A Side/B Side)	Yr	VG	VG+	NM
COMMAND					
4111	Cover Up/Take It Like a Man	1968	2.50	5.00	10.00
JERDEN					
921	Elevator Operator/Lord in Black	196?	3.00	6.00	12.00
PICCADILLY					
256	Lord in Black/Long Hard Road	196?	3.00	6.00	12.00

Albums

Number	Title (A Side/B Side)	Yr	VG	VG+	NM
COMMAND					
RS 925 SD	The Love Cycle	1968	10.00	20.00	40.00

CROPPER, STEVE

Also see BOOKER T. AND THE MG's; MAR-KEYS.

45s

Number	Title (A Side/B Side)	Yr	VG	VG+	NM
MCA					
51078	Playin' My Thang/Why Do You Say You Love Me	1981	—	2.00	4.00
51115	Fly/Sandy Beaches	1981	—	2.00	4.00
52103	634-5789/Night After Night	1982	—	2.00	4.00

Albums

Number	Title (A Side/B Side)	Yr	VG	VG+	NM
MCA					
5171	Playin' My Thang	1980	2.50	5.00	10.00
VOLT					
VOS-6006	With a Little Help from My Friends	1970	3.75	7.50	15.00

CROSBY, BING

Includes most of his duets with other performers. Crosby was past his peak of popularity when 45s and LPs were introduced; while much of his material showed up on these formats, many of his 1930s and 1940s releases did not. The list below is exhaustive as to the availability of Bing's music on vinyl, but probably not complete; it's likely that other singles in the 23000, 24000 and 25000 series exist on 45s, as well as other EPs. Also see DAVID BOWIE; FRANK SINATRA.

45s

Number	Title (A Side/B Side)	Yr	VG	VG+	NM
AMOS					
111	Hey Jude/Lonely Street	1969	—	3.00	6.00
116	It's All in the Game/More and More	1969	—	2.50	5.00
BING CROSBY					
(no #) [DJ]	How Lovely Is Christmas/Never Be Afraid	195?	5.00	10.00	20.00
—Crowley's Milk promotional item					
CAPITOL					
F-3695	Man on Fire/Seven Nights a Week	1957	3.00	6.00	12.00
4548	Simple Love Affair/That's How I Met Your Mother	1978	—	2.00	4.00
5088	Do You Hear What I Hear/Christmas Dinner Country Style	1963	2.00	4.00	8.00
S7-19766	Do You Hear What I Hear?/I Wish You a Merry Christmas	1997	—	—	3.00
COLUMBIA					
41104	Straight Down the Middle/Tomorrow's My Lucky Day	1958	3.00	6.00	12.00
41387	Say One for Me/I Couldn't Care Less	1959	3.00	6.00	12.00
41496	The Secret of Christmas/Just What I Wanted for Christmas	1959	3.75	7.50	15.00
DAYBREAK					
1001	A Time to Be Jolly/And the Bells Rang	1971	—	3.00	6.00
—Black label					
1001	A Time to Be Jolly/And the Bells Rang	1971	—	2.50	5.00
—Yellow label					
1001 [PS]	A Time to Be Jolly/And the Bells Rang	1971	—	2.50	5.00
DECCA					
1-256 [PS]	Jingle Bells/Santa's Coming	19??	3.75	7.50	15.00
—With the Andrews Sisters; alternate number is 23281					
23281	Jingle Bells/Santa Claus Is Comin' to Town	1950	3.00	6.00	12.00
—With the Andrews Sisters; lines label; Sides 1 and 2 of "Album No. 9-65"					
23495	McNamara's Band/Dear Old Donegal	1950	3.00	6.00	12.00
—Reissue of 78; part of "Album No. 9-31"					
23777	Silent Night/Adeste Fideles (O Come All Ye Faithful)	1950	3.00	6.00	12.00
—Lines label; Sides 3 and 4 of "Album No. 9-65"					
23777	Silent Night/Adeste Fideles (O Come All Ye Faithful)	1955	2.50	5.00	10.00
—Star on label					
23777	Silent Night/Adeste Fideles (O Come All Ye Faithful)	1960	2.00	4.00	8.00
—Color bars on label					
23777 [PS]	Silent Night/Adeste Fideles (O Come All Ye Faithful)	1960	3.75	7.50	15.00
—Sleeve came with early 1960s pressings					
23778	White Christmas/God Rest Ye Merry Gentlemen	1950	3.00	6.00	12.00
—Lines label; Sides 5 and 6 of "Album No. 9-65"					
23778	White Christmas/God Rest Ye Merry Gentlemen	1955	2.50	5.00	10.00
—Star on label					
23778	White Christmas/God Rest Ye Merry Gentlemen	1960	2.00	4.00	8.00
—Color bars on label					
23778 [PS]	White Christmas/God Rest Ye Merry Gentlemen	1960	3.75	7.50	15.00
—Sleeve came with early 1960s pressings					
23779	I'll Be Home for Christmas (If Only in My Dreams)/Faith of Our Fathers	1950	3.00	6.00	12.00
—Lines label; Sides 7 and 8 of "Album No. 9-65"					
23786	Who Threw the Overalls in Mrs. Murphy's Chowder?/It's the Same Old Overalls	1950	3.00	6.00	12.00
—Reissue of 78; part of "Album No. 9-31"					
23787	Did Your Mother Come from Ireland?/Where the River Shannon Flows	1950	3.00	6.00	12.00
—Reissue of 78; part of "Album No. 9-31"					
23789	Too-Ra-Loo-Ra-Loo-Ral/I'll Take You Home Again Kathleen	1950	3.00	6.00	12.00
—Reissue of 78; part of "Album No. 9-31"					
25003	Take Me Back to My Boots and Saddle/My Little Buckaroo	1950	3.00	6.00	12.00
—Reissue of 78; part of "Album No. 9-145"					
25020	Clementine/The Old Oaken Bucket	1950	3.00	6.00	12.00
—Reissue of 78; part of "Album No. 9-145"					
25497	Sierra Sue/Along the Santa Fe Trail	1950	3.00	6.00	12.00
—Reissue of 78; part of "Album No. 9-145"					
25520	Memories Are Made of This/My Blue Heaven	1961	—	3.00	6.00
25540	Moments to Remember/Vaya Con Dios	1961	—	3.00	6.00
25643	Avalon/On the Alamo	1964	—	3.00	6.00
25661	Chinatown, My Chinatown/I'm Confessin' (That I Love You)	1965	—	3.00	6.00
25665	Between the Devil and the Deep Blue Sea/Georgia on My Mind	1965	—	3.00	6.00
27013	Jamboree Jones/Dixieland Band	1950	3.00	6.00	12.00
27018	I Didn't Slip, I Wasn't Pushed, I Fell/So Tall a Tree	1950	3.00	6.00	12.00
27019	Home Cookin'/When the Sun Goes Down	1950	3.00	6.00	12.00
27111	La Vie En Rose/I Cross My Fingers	1950	3.00	6.00	12.00
27112	Play a Simple Melody/Sam's Song	1950	3.00	6.00	12.00
—By "Gary Crosby and Friend" (guess who the friend is)					
27117	All My Love/The Friendly Islands	1950	3.00	6.00	12.00
27143	This Could Be Forever/Helpless	1950	3.00	6.00	12.00
—With Louanne Hogan					
27158	Ave Maria/Home Sweet Home	1950	3.00	6.00	12.00
27159/30126 [DJ]	Rudolph The Red-Nosed Reindeer/I Heard the Bells on Christmas Day	1956	5.00	10.00	20.00
—Green label promo with two different numbers on the record!					
27159	Rudolph, the Red-Nosed Reindeer/The Teddy Bear's Picnic	1950	3.00	6.00	12.00
27173	Life Is So Peculiar/High on the List	1950	3.00	6.00	12.00
—With the Andrews Sisters					
27219	Harbor Lights/Beyond the Reef	1950	3.00	6.00	12.00
27228	Mele Kalikimaka/Poppa Santa Claus	1950	3.00	6.00	12.00
—With the Andrews Sisters					
27229	Silver Bells/That Christmas Feeling	1950	3.00	6.00	12.00
—A-side with Carol Richards					
27230	A Marshmallow World/Looks Like a Cold, Cold Winter	1950	3.00	6.00	12.00
27231	Autumn Leaves/This Is the Time	1950	3.00	6.00	12.00
27232	If I Were a Bell/I've Never Been in Love Before	1950	3.00	6.00	12.00
—A-side with Patti Andrews					
27241	And You'll Be Mine/Accidents Will Happen	1950	3.00	6.00	12.00
27249	A Crosby Christmas (Part 1)/A Crosby Christmas (Part 2)	1950	—	—	—
—As "Gary, Phillip, Dennis, Lindsay and Bing Crosby"; unreleased on this number?					
27250	The Best Thing for You/Marrying for Love	1950	3.00	6.00	12.00
27263	Wouldn't It Be Funny/One More for the Blue and White	1950	3.00	6.00	12.00
27264	Accidents Will Happen/Milady	1950	3.00	6.00	12.00
—With Dorothy Kirsten					
27275	Oh! What a Beautiful Morning/People Will Say We're in Love	1950	2.50	5.00	10.00
27276	If I Loved You/Close As Pages in a Book	1950	2.50	5.00	10.00
27277	They Say It's Wonderful/I Love You	1950	2.50	5.00	10.00
27278	Evalina/The Eagle and Me	1950	2.50	5.00	10.00
27404	May the Good Lord Bless and Keep You/A Perfect Day	1951	2.50	5.00	10.00
27441	An Early American/My Own Bit of Land	1951	2.50	5.00	10.00
27443	The Meadows of Heaven/The Last Mile Home	1951	2.50	5.00	10.00
27461	Then You've Never Been Blue/You Gotta Show Me	1951	2.50	5.00	10.00
27477	Sparrow in the Tree Top/Forsaking All Others	1951	2.50	5.00	10.00
—With the Andrews Sisters					
27478	St. Patrick's Day Parade/With My Shillelagh Under My Arm	1951	2.50	5.00	10.00
27483	Sentimental Music/Any Town Is Paris When You're Young	1951	2.50	5.00	10.00
27500	Feudin' and Fightin'/Goodbye, My Lovers, Goodbye	1951	2.50	5.00	10.00
27505	When My Dreamboat Comes Home/Walking the Floor Over You	1951	2.50	5.00	10.00
27508	Silver Moon/More I Cannot Wish You	1951	2.50	5.00	10.00
27536	Maria Bonita/Quizas, Quizas, Quizas	1951	2.50	5.00	10.00
27549	Yours Is My Heart Alone/Beautiful Love	1951	2.50	5.00	10.00
27550	I Kiss Your Hand, Madame/The Kiss in Your Eyes	1951	2.50	5.00	10.00
27551	Girl of My Dreams/I'll Remember April	1951	2.50	5.00	10.00
27553	Country Style/Home Cookin'	1951	2.50	5.00	10.00
27554	I Only Want a Buddy — Not a Sweetheart/When the White Azaleas Start Blooming	1951	2.50	5.00	10.00
27555	Weddin' Day/(B-side unknown)	1951	2.50	5.00	10.00
—With the Andrews Sisters					
27577	Moonlight Bay/When You and I Were Young Maggie Blues	1951	2.50	5.00	10.00
—As "Gary and Bing Crosby"					
27588	Hello Young Lovers/Something Wonderful	1951	2.50	5.00	10.00
27589	Getting to Know You/I Whistle a Happy Tune	1951	2.50	5.00	10.00
27595	With This Ring I Thee Wed/Here Ends the Rainbow	1951	2.50	5.00	10.00

Number	Title (A Side/B Side)	Yr	VG	VG+	NM
27605	Going My Way/Swinging on a Star	1951	2.50	5.00	10.00
27606	Old Soldiers Never Die/My Own Bit of Land	1951	2.50	5.00	10.00
27631	Black Ball Ferry Line/The Yodeling Ghost	1951	2.50	5.00	10.00
—With the Andrews Sisters					
27643	I Might Be Your Once in a While/Indian Summer	1951	2.50	5.00	10.00
27653	(Why Did I Twll You I Was Going to) Shanghai/ I've Got to Fall in Love Again	1951	2.50	5.00	10.00
27667	Row, Row, Row/Love Me or Leave Me	1951	2.50	5.00	10.00
27678	In the Cool, Cool, Cool of the Evening/Misto Christophe Columbo	1951	2.50	5.00	10.00
—With Jane Wyman					
27679	Your Own Little House/Bonne Nuit	1951	2.50	5.00	10.00
27768	I Will Remember You/The Loneliness of Evening	1951	2.50	5.00	10.00
27830	Domino/When the World Was Young	1951	2.50	5.00	10.00
27831	Christmas in Killarney/It's Beginning to Look Like Christmas	1951	3.75	7.50	15.00
27852	A Weaver of Dreams/I Still See Alisa	1951	2.50	5.00	10.00
27934	At Last, At Last!/The Isle of Innisfree	1952	2.50	5.00	10.00
27951	Copacabana/Granada	1952	2.50	5.00	10.00
28048	2 Shillelagh O'Sullivan/That Tumbledown Shack in Athlone	1952	2.50	5.00	10.00
28061	Don't Ever Be Afraid to Go Home/Rosaleen	1952	2.50	5.00	10.00
28195	Galway Bay/The Isle of Innisfree	1952	2.50	5.00	10.00
28210	Mine/You've Got Me Where You Want Me	1952	3.00	6.00	12.00
—With Judy Garland					
28217	Just for You/A Flight of Fancy	1952	2.50	5.00	10.00
28254	On the 10:10 from Ten-Ten-Tennessee/Just for You	1952	2.50	5.00	10.00
28255	Zing a Little Zong/The Maiden of Guadaloupe	1952	2.50	5.00	10.00
—With Jane Wyman					
28256	The Live Oak Tree/I'll Si-Si You in Bahia	1952	2.50	5.00	10.00
—With the Andrews Sisters					
28261	The Bells of St. Mary's/Kathleen	1952	2.50	5.00	10.00
28265	Till the End of the World/Just a Little Lovin'	1952	2.50	5.00	10.00
—With Grady Martin					
28303	Poinciana/Symphony	1952	2.50	5.00	10.00
28319	Deep in the Heart of Texas/Do You Care	1952	2.50	5.00	10.00
28419	Cool Water/South Rampart Street Parade	1952	2.50	5.00	10.00
—With the Andrews Sisters					
28463	Sleigh Ride/Little Jack Frost Get Lost	1952	3.75	7.50	15.00
28470	Open Up Your Heart/You Don't Know What Lonesome Is	1952	2.50	5.00	10.00
28511	Sleigh Bell Serenade/Keep It a Secret	1952	3.75	7.50	15.00
28513	The Road to Bali/Chicago Style	1952	2.50	5.00	10.00
—With Bob Hope					
28514	Merry Go Run Around/Hoot Mon	1952	2.50	5.00	10.00
—With Peggy Lee and Bob Hope					
28515	To See You/Moonflowers	1952	2.50	5.00	10.00
—B-side by Peggy Lee					
28581	Hush-a-Bye/Mother Darlin'	1953	2.50	5.00	10.00
28610	A Quiet Girl/Ohio	1953	2.50	5.00	10.00
28683	I Love My Baby (My Baby Loves Me)/There's Music in You	1953	2.50	5.00	10.00
28733	Tenderfoot/Walk Me By the River	1953	2.50	5.00	10.00
28743	It Had to Be You/Granada	1953	2.50	5.00	10.00
28805	Magic Window/Cela Mi Est Egal	1953	2.50	5.00	10.00
28814	Mademoiselle de Paris/Embrasse — Moi Bien	1953	2.50	5.00	10.00
28955	Down By the Riverside/What a Little Moonlight Can Do	1953	2.50	5.00	10.00
—As "Bing and Gary Crosby"					
28963	Ida! Sweet as Apple Cider/I Can't Believe ThatYou're in Love	1953	2.50	5.00	10.00
28969	Y'All Come/Changing Partners	1954	2.50	5.00	10.00
29024	Secret Love/My Love, My Love	1954	2.50	5.00	10.00
29054	Young at Heart/I Get So Lonely	1954	2.50	5.00	10.00
29144	If You Love Me (Really Love Me)/Liebchen	1954	2.50	5.00	10.00
29147	Call of the South/Cornbelt Symphony	1954	2.50	5.00	10.00
—As "Bing and Gary Crosby"					
29212	In the Good Old Summertime/Oh Tell Me Why (The Stars Do Shine)	1954	2.50	5.00	10.00
29251	Count Your Blessings Instead of Sheep/What Can You Do with a General	1954	2.50	5.00	10.00
29341	Old Man-Mandy/Gee, I Wish I Was Back in the Army	1954	2.50	5.00	10.00
29342	White Christmas/Snow	1954	3.75	7.50	15.00
—A-side with Danny Kaye; B-side by Peggy Lee and Trudi Stevens					
29357	The Song from Desiree/Who Gave You the Roses	1954	2.50	5.00	10.00
29376	River/Tobermory Bay	1954	2.50	5.00	10.00
29409	Dissertation on State of Bliss/It's Mine, It's Yours	1955	2.50	5.00	10.00
29410	The Land Around Us/The Search Is Through	1955	2.50	5.00	10.00
29483	Farewell/Jim, Johnny & Jonah	1955	2.50	5.00	10.00
29493	Silver Moon/Nobody	1955	2.50	5.00	10.00
29568	She Is the Sunshine of Virginia/(All She'd Say Was) Uh-Huh	1955	2.50	5.00	10.00
29634	You Are My Sunshine/Nobody's Darling But Mine	1955	2.50	5.00	10.00
29636	Angel Bells/Let's Harmonize	1955	2.50	5.00	10.00
29777	The First Snowfall/The Next Time It Happens	1956	2.00	4.00	8.00
29790	Christmas Is A-Comin'/Is Christmas Only a Tree	1955	3.00	6.00	12.00
29817	John Barleycorn/When You're in Love	1956	2.00	4.00	8.00
29850	In a Little Spanish Town ('Twas On a Night Like This)/Ol' Man River	1956	2.00	4.00	8.00
29981	Honeysucle Rose/Swanee	1956	2.00	4.00	8.00
30023	When My Baby Smiles at Me/April Showers	1956	2.00	4.00	8.00
30082	Now Is the Hour/Tumbling Tumbleweeds	1956	2.00	4.00	8.00
30120	Around the World/Love in a Home	1956	2.50	5.00	10.00
30126	I Heard the Bells on Christmas Day/Christmas Is a-Comin'	1956	3.00	6.00	12.00
30126 [DJ]	I Heard the Bells on Christmas Day/Christmas Is a-Comin'	1956	3.00	6.00	12.00
—Pink label, black type					
30262	Around the World/Around the World	1957	2.00	4.00	8.00
—B-side by Victor Young					
30262 [PS]	Around the World/Around the World	1957	3.75	7.50	15.00
30488	Chinatown My Chinatown/Alabamy Bound	1957	2.00	4.00	8.00
30555	Gigi/Trust Your Destiny to Your Star	1958	2.00	4.00	8.00
30828	Rain/Church Bells	1959	2.00	4.00	8.00

Number	Title (A Side/B Side)	Yr	VG	VG+	NM
38031 [DJ]	Around the World/Mississippi Mud	1957	2.50	5.00	10.00
—Green label					
38031 [PS]	Around the World/Mississippi Mud	1957	5.00	10.00	20.00
40181	A Crosby Christmas (Part 1)/A Crosby Christmas (Part 2)	1950	7.50	15.00	30.00
—As "Gary, Phillip, Dennis, Lindsay and Bing Crosby"					
KAPP					
196	How Lovely Is Christmas/My Own Individual Star	1957	3.00	6.00	12.00
196 [PS]	How Lovely Is Christmas/My Own Individual Star	1957	5.00	10.00	20.00
LITTLE GOLDEN					
EP407	Boy At A Window/How Lovely Is Christmas	195?	2.50	5.00	10.00
EP407 [PS]	Boy At A Window/How Lovely Is Christmas	195?	3.00	6.00	12.00
LONDON					
20095	There's Nothing I Haven't Sung About/The Way We Were	1977	—	2.00	4.00
MCA					
38056	Rudolph The Red-Nosed Reindeer/I Heard The Bells On Christmas Day	198?	—	2.00	4.00
40830	White Christmas/When the Blue of the Night Meets the Gold of the Day	1977	—	2.50	5.00
40830 [PS]	White Christmas/When the Blue of the Night Meets the Gold of the Day	1977	—	2.50	5.00
65019	Jingle Bells/Santa Claus Is Comin' to Town	1973	—	2.00	4.00
—With the Andrews Sisters; black label with rainbow					
65019	Jingle Bells/Santa Claus Is Comin' to Town	1980	—	—	3.00
—With the Andrews Sisters; blue label with rainbow					
65021	Silent Night/Adeste Fideles (O Come All Ye Faithful)	1973	—	2.00	4.00
—Black label with rainbow					
65021	Silent Night/Adeste Fideles (O Come All Ye Faithful)	1980	—	—	3.00
—Blue label with rainbow					
65022	White Christmas/God Rest Ye Merry Gentlemen	1973	—	2.00	4.00
—Black label with rainbow					
65022	White Christmas/God Rest Ye Merry Gentlemen	1980	—	—	3.00
—Blue label with rainbow					
MGM					
12946	The Second Time Around/Incurably Romantic	1960	2.00	4.00	8.00
POLYDOR					
14452	Yesterday, When I Was Young/June in January	1978	—	2.00	4.00
P.I.P.					
8903	Where the Rainbow Ends/What's More American	197?	—	2.50	5.00
RCA VICTOR					
47-7695	It's a Good Day/The Music of Home	1960	2.00	4.00	8.00
REPRISE					
0283	Don't Be a Do-Badder/The Hukilau Song	1964	—	3.00	6.00
0315	It's Christmas Time Again/Christmas Candles	1964	3.00	6.00	12.00
—With Fred Waring and the Pennsylvanians					
0315 [PS]	It's Christmas Time Again/Christmas Candles	1964	3.75	7.50	15.00
0424	The White World of Winter/The Secret of Christmas	1965	2.00	4.00	8.00
0478	How Green Was My Valley/Far from Home	1966	—	2.50	5.00
0645	Step to the Rear/What Do We Do with the World	1967	—	2.50	5.00
UNITED ARTISTS					
XW700	Send In the Clowns/That's What Life Is All About	1975	—	2.00	4.00
VERVE					
2025	I've Got Five Dollars/Mountain Greenery	1956	2.50	5.00	10.00
WARNER BROS.					
PRO 146 [DJ]	I Wish You a Merry Christmas/Winter Wonderland//The Littlest Angel	1962	5.00	10.00	20.00

7-Inch Extended Plays

Number	Title (A Side/B Side)	Yr	VG	VG+	NM
DECCA					
9-65 [(4)]	Merry Christmas	1950	12.50	25.00	50.00
—Includes records 23281, 23777, 23778 and 23779 (also priced separately) and box					
9-66 [(4)]	Christmas Greetings	1950	12.50	25.00	50.00
—Includes records and box					
ED 547 [PS]	Merry Christmas	195?	6.25	12.50	25.00
—Cover for 2-EP set					
ED 581 [PS]	Stardust	195?	5.00	10.00	20.00
—Cover for 2-EP set					
ED 662 [PS]	Down Memory Lane	195?	5.00	10.00	20.00
—Cover for 2-EP set					
ED 2000	Red Sails in the Sunset/Far Away Places//Harbor Lights/On Treasure Island	195?	3.00	6.00	12.00
ED 2000 [PS]	Bing Crosby, Vol. 1	195?	3.00	6.00	12.00
ED 2107	Do You Ever Think of Me/I Never Knew// Somebody Loves Me/After You've Gone	195?	3.00	6.00	12.00
ED 2107 [PS]	Some Fine Old Chestnuts, Vol. 1	195?	3.00	6.00	12.00
ED 2427	Prisoner of Love/Ain't Misbehavin'//Paper Doll/ This Love of Mine	1956	3.75	7.50	15.00
ED 2427 [PS]	Song I Wish I Had Sung the First Time Around... Part 2	1956	3.75	7.50	15.00
ED 2547	(contents unknown)	195?	3.00	6.00	12.00
ED 2547 [PS]	Christmas Time	195?	3.00	6.00	12.00
ED 2659	Silver Bells/The Christmas Song//Christmas Carols/God Rest Ye Merry Gentlemen	195?	3.00	6.00	12.00
ED 2659 [PS]	Christmas Songs	195?	3.00	6.00	12.00
7-38274	The First Nowell/Medley: Deck The Hall-Away In A Manger-I Saw Three Ships//God Rest Ye Merry, Gentlemen/Jingle Bells	196?	3.00	6.00	12.00
7-38274 [PS]	General Electric Wishes You a Merry Christmas	196?	3.00	6.00	12.00
91123	Silent Night/Adeste Fideles//White Christmas/ God Rest Ye Merry Gentlemen	195?	3.00	6.00	12.00
—Part of 2-EP set ED 547					
91124	I'll Be Home for Christmas/Faith of Our Fathers/ /Jingle Bells/Santa Claus Is Comin' to Town	195?	3.00	6.00	12.00
—Part of 2-EP set ED 547					
91168	I Cried for You/My Melancholy Baby//Star Dust/ Deep Purple	195?	3.00	6.00	12.00
—Part of 2-EP set ED 581					
91169	The One Rose/Moonlight and Shadows//A Blue Serenade/S'posin'	195?	3.00	6.00	12.00
—Part of 2-EP set ED 581					

Number	Title (A Side/B Side)	Yr	VG	VG+	NM
91289	Please/I Found a Million Dollar Baby//I Wonder What's Become of Sally/Mary's a Grand Old Name	195?	3.00	6.00	12.00
—Part of 2-EP set ED 662					
91290	I'm Waiting for Ships That Never Come In/When Day Is Done//I Don't Want to Walk Without You/Moonlight Cocktail	195?	3.00	6.00	12.00
—Part of 2-EP set ED 662					
RCA VICTOR					
EPA 3-1473	Mack the Knife/Tell Me//Down Among the Sheltering Palms/Mama Loved Papa	1957	2.00	4.00	8.00
EPA 3-1473 [PS]	Bing with a Beat	1957	2.50	5.00	10.00
Albums					
20TH CENTURY					
T-551	A Holiday Toast	1977	3.00	6.00	12.00
AMOS					
AAS-7001	Hey Jude/Hey Bing!	1969	3.00	6.00	12.00
BIOGRAPH					
M-1	When the Blue of the Night Meets the Gold of the Day	197?	2.50	5.00	10.00
C-13	Bing Crosby 1929-33	1973	3.00	6.00	12.00
BRUNSWICK					
BL 54005 [M]	The Voice of Bing in the 1930s	1957	6.25	12.50	25.00
BL 58000 [10]	Bing Crosby, Volume 1	1950	12.50	25.00	50.00
BL 58001 [10]	Bing Crosby, Volume 2	1950	12.50	25.00	50.00
CAPITOL					
ST 2300 [S]	That Travelin' Two-Beat	1965	5.00	10.00	20.00
T 2300 [M]	That Travelin' Two-Beat	1965	3.75	7.50	15.00
ST 2346 [S]	Great Country Hits	1965	5.00	10.00	20.00
T 2346 [M]	Great Country Hits	1965	3.75	7.50	15.00
SM-11732	Bing Crosby's Christmas Classics	1977	2.50	5.00	10.00
—"A Capitol Re-Issue"; same recordings as on Warner Bros. 1484					
SM-11736	That Travelin' Two-Beat	1977	2.50	5.00	10.00
SM-11737	Great Country Hits	1977	2.50	5.00	10.00
SM-11738	Bing Crosby Classics, Vol. 1	1977	2.50	5.00	10.00
SM-11739	Bing Crosby Classics, Vol. 2	1977	2.50	5.00	10.00
SM-11740	Bing Crosby Classics, Vol. 3	1977	2.50	5.00	10.00
COLUMBIA					
C2L 43 [(2)]	Bing in Hollywood 1930-1934	196?	3.75	7.50	15.00
—Red "360 Sound" labels					
C2L 43 [(2)]	Bing in Hollywood 1930-1934	1971	3.00	6.00	12.00
—Orange labels					
CL 2502 [10]	Der Bingle	1955	10.00	20.00	40.00
CL 6027 [10]	Crosby Classics	1949	12.50	25.00	50.00
CL 6105 [10]	Crosby Classics, Volume 2	1950	12.50	25.00	50.00
C 35093	Bing Crosby Collection, Vol. 1	1977	2.50	5.00	10.00
C 35094	Bing Crosby Collection, Vol. 2	1977	2.50	5.00	10.00
C4X 44229 [(4)]	The Crooner: The Columbia Years	1988	10.00	20.00	40.00
COLUMBIA SPECIAL PRODUCTS					
P 14369	Bing	197?	2.50	5.00	10.00
DAYBREAK					
2006	A Time to Be Jolly	1971	3.00	6.00	12.00
2014	Bing and Basie	1972	3.00	6.00	12.00
DECCA					
DX 151 [(5) M]	Bing: A Musical Autobiography	195?	37.50	75.00	150.00
DX 152 [(3) M]	Old Masters	195?	37.50	75.00	150.00
DXB 184 [(2) M]	The Best of Bing	1965	6.25	12.50	25.00
DL 4086 [M]	My Golden Favorites	1961	6.25	12.50	25.00
DL 4250 [M]	Bing's Hollywood: Easy to Remember	1962	6.25	12.50	25.00
DL 4251 [M]	Bing's Hollywood: Pennies from Heaven	1962	6.25	12.50	25.00
DL 4252 [M]	Bing's Hollywood: Pocket Full of Dreams	1962	6.25	12.50	25.00
DL 4253 [M]	Bing's Hollywood: East Side of Heaven	1962	6.25	12.50	25.00
DL 4254 [M]	Bing's Hollywood: The Road Begins	1962	6.25	12.50	25.00
DL 4255 [M]	Bing's Hollywood: Only Forever	1962	6.25	12.50	25.00
DL 4256 [M]	Bing's Hollywood: Holiday Inn	1962	6.25	12.50	25.00
DL 4257 [M]	Bing's Hollywood: Swinging on a Star	1962	6.25	12.50	25.00
DL 4258 [M]	Bing's Hollywood: Accentuate the Positive	1962	6.25	12.50	25.00
DL 4259 [M]	Bing's Hollywood: Blue Skies	1962	6.25	12.50	25.00
DL 4260 [M]	Bing's Hollywood: But Beautiful	1962	6.25	12.50	25.00
DL 4261 [M]	Bing's Hollywood: Sunshine Cake	1962	6.25	12.50	25.00
DL 4262 [M]	Bing's Hollywood: Cool of the Evening	1962	6.25	12.50	25.00
DL 4263 [M]	Bing's Hollywood: Zing a Little Zong	1962	6.25	12.50	25.00
DL 4264 [M]	Bing's Hollywood: Anything Goes	1962	6.25	12.50	25.00
DL 4281 [M]	Holiday in Europe	1962	6.25	12.50	25.00
DL 4283	Two Favorite Stories by Bing Crosby	1962	6.25	12.50	25.00
DL 4415 [M]	Songs Everybody Knows	1964	6.25	12.50	25.00
DLP 5000 [10]	Hits from Musical Comedies	1949	12.50	25.00	50.00
DLP 5001 [10]	Jerome Kern Songs	1949	12.50	25.00	50.00
DLP 5010 [10]	Stephen Foster Songs	1949	12.50	25.00	50.00
DLP 5011 [10]	El Bingo	1949	12.50	25.00	50.00
DLP 5019 [10]	Merry Christmas	1949	15.00	30.00	60.00
DLP 5020 [10]	Christmas Greetings	1949	15.00	30.00	60.00
DL 5028 [10]	Auld Lang Syne	1950	12.50	25.00	50.00
DL 5037 [10]	St. Patrick's Day	1950	12.50	25.00	50.00
DL 5039 [10]	St. Valentine's Day	1950	12.50	25.00	50.00
DL 5042 [10]	Blue Skies	1950	12.50	25.00	50.00
DL 5052 [10]	Going My Way/The Bells of St. Mary's	1950	15.00	30.00	60.00
DL 5063 [10]	Don't Fence Me In	1950	12.50	25.00	50.00
DL 5064 [10]	Cole Porter Songs	1950	12.50	25.00	50.00
DL 5081 [10]	Songs by Gershwin	1950	12.50	25.00	50.00
DL 5102 [10]	Blue of the Night	1950	12.50	25.00	50.00
DL 5107 [10]	Cowboy Songs	1950	12.50	25.00	50.00
DL 5119 [10]	Drifting and Dreaming	1950	12.50	25.00	50.00
DL 5122 [10]	Hawaiian Songs	1950	12.50	25.00	50.00
DL 5126 [10]	Stardust	1950	12.50	25.00	50.00
DL 5129 [10]	Cowboy Songs, Volume 2	1950	12.50	25.00	50.00
DL 5220 [10]	Bing Sings Hits	1950	12.50	25.00	50.00
DL 5272 [10]	Top o' the Morning/The Emperor Waltz	1950	12.50	25.00	50.00
DL 5284 [10]	Mr. Music	1950	12.50	25.00	50.00
DL 5298 [10]	Hits from Broadway Shows	1951	12.50	25.00	50.00
DL 5299 [10]	Favorite Hawaiian Songs	1951	12.50	25.00	50.00
DL 5302 [10]	Go West, Young Man	1951	12.50	25.00	50.00
DL 5310 [10]	Way Back Home	1951	12.50	25.00	50.00
DL 5323 [10]	Bing and the Dixieland Bands	1951	12.50	25.00	50.00

Number	Title (A Side/B Side)	Yr	VG	VG+	NM
DL 5326 [10]	Yours Is My Heart Alone	1951	12.50	25.00	50.00
DL 5331 [10]	Country Style	1951	12.50	25.00	50.00
DL 5340 [10]	Down Memory Lane	1951	12.50	25.00	50.00
DL 5343 [10]	Down Memory Lane, Volume 2	1951	12.50	25.00	50.00
DL 5351 [10]	Beloved Hymns	1951	12.50	25.00	50.00
DL 5355 [10]	Bing Sings Victor Herbert	1951	12.50	25.00	50.00
DL 5390 [10]	Bing and Connee	1953	12.50	25.00	50.00
—With Connee Boswell					
DL 5403 [10]	When Irish Eyes Are Smiling	1952	12.50	25.00	50.00
DL 5417 [10]	Just for You	1952	12.50	25.00	50.00
DL 5444 [10]	The Road to Bali	1952	15.00	30.00	60.00
DL 5499 [10]	Song Hits of Paris/Le Bing	1953	12.50	25.00	50.00
DL 5508 [10]	Some Fine Old Chestnuts	1953	12.50	25.00	50.00
DL 5520 [10]	Bing Sings the Hits	1954	12.50	25.00	50.00
DL 5556 [10]	Country Girl/Little Boy Lost/Anything Goes	1954	12.50	25.00	50.00
DL 6000 [10]	Two Favorite Stories by Bing Crosby	1950	15.00	30.00	60.00
DL 6001 [10]	Ichabod/Rip Van Winkle	1950	12.50	25.00	50.00
DL 6008 [10]	Collector's Classics: Mississippi/Here Is My Heart	1951	15.00	30.00	60.00
DL 6009 [10]	Collector's Classics: Anything Goes/Two for Tonight	1951	15.00	30.00	60.00
DL 6010 [10]	Collector's Classics: Rhythm on the Range/Pennies from Heaven	1951	15.00	30.00	60.00
DL 6011 [10]	Collector's Classics: Waikiki Wedding	1951	15.00	30.00	60.00
DL 6012 [10]	Collector's Classics: Paris Honeymoon	1951	15.00	30.00	60.00
DL 6013 [10]	Collector's Classics: The Star Maker/Doctor Rhythm	1951	15.00	30.00	60.00
DL 6014 [10]	Collector's Classics: Big Broadcast of 1936	1951	15.00	30.00	60.00
DL 6015 [10]	Collector's Classics: The Road to Singapore/If I Had My Way	1951	15.00	30.00	60.00
DXSB 7184 [(2) R]	The Best of Bing	1965	3.75	7.50	15.00
DL 8020 [M]	The Man Without a Country/What So Proudly We Hail	1950	10.00	20.00	40.00
DL 8110 [M]	Lullaby Time	1955	10.00	20.00	40.00
DL 8128 [M]	Merry Christmas	1955	10.00	20.00	40.00
—Expanded version of 10-inch LP; all-black label					
DL 8128 [M]	Merry Christmas	1960	6.25	12.50	25.00
—Reissue on black label with color bars					
DL 8178 [M]	Merry Christmas	196?	15.00	30.00	60.00
—Black label with color bars; at least one copy is known to exist on red vinyl					
DL 8207 [M]	Shillelaghs and Shamrocks	1956	10.00	20.00	40.00
DL 8210 [M]	Home on the Range	1956	10.00	20.00	40.00
DL 8262 [M]	When Irish Eyes Are Smiling	1956	10.00	20.00	40.00
DL 8268 [M]	Drifting and Dreaming	1956	10.00	20.00	40.00
DL 8269 [M]	Blue Hawaii	1956	10.00	20.00	40.00
DL 8272 [M]	High Tor	1956	100.00	200.00	400.00
DL 8318 [M]	Anything Goes	1956	12.50	25.00	50.00
DL 8352 [M]	Song I Wish I Had Sung…The First Time Around	1956	10.00	20.00	40.00
DL 8365 [M]	Twilight on the Trail	1957	10.00	20.00	40.00
DL 8374 [M]	Some Fine Old Chestnuts	1957	10.00	20.00	40.00
DL 8419 [M]	A Christmas Sing with Bing Around the World	1957	10.00	20.00	40.00
DL 8493 [M]	Bing and the Dixieland Bands	1957	10.00	20.00	40.00
DL 8575 [M]	New Tricks	1957	10.00	20.00	40.00
DL 8687 [M]	Around the World	1958	10.00	20.00	40.00
DL 8780 [M]	Bing in Paris	1958	10.00	20.00	40.00
DL 8781 [M]	That Christmas Feeling	1958	7.50	15.00	30.00
—Expanded version of DL 5020; all-black label, textured cover					
DL 8781 [M]	That Christmas Feeling	1960	5.00	10.00	20.00
—Reissue on black label with color bars, smooth cover					
DL 8846 [M]	In a Little Spanish Town	1959	7.50	15.00	30.00
DL 9054 [M]	Bing: A Musical Autobiography 1927-1934	1961	10.00	20.00	40.00
DL 9064 [M]	Bing: A Musical Autobiography 1934-1941	1961	10.00	20.00	40.00
DL 9067 [M]	Bing: A Musical Autobiography 1941-44	1961	10.00	20.00	40.00
DL 9077 [M]	Bing: A Musical Autobiography 1944-47	1961	10.00	20.00	40.00
DL 9078 [M]	Bing: A Musical Autobiography 1947-1953	1961	10.00	20.00	40.00
DL 9106 [M]	Ichabod/Rip Van Winkle	1962	6.25	12.50	25.00
DL 34522	Favorite Songs of Christmas	1968	3.75	7.50	15.00
—Decca Records Custom Division pressing					
DL 74281 [R]	Holiday in Europe	1962	3.75	7.50	15.00
DL 74283 [R]	The Small One	1962	2.50	5.00	10.00
DL 74415 [R]	Songs Everybody Knows	1964	3.75	7.50	15.00
DL 78128 [R]	Merry Christmas	196?	2.50	5.00	10.00
DL 78207 [R]	Shillelaghs and Shamrocks	196?	2.50	5.00	10.00
DL 78262 [R]	When Irish Eyes Are Smiling	196?	2.50	5.00	10.00
DL 78352 [R]	Songs I Wish I Had Sung…The First Time Around	196?	2.50	5.00	10.00
DL 78419 [R]	A Christmas Sing with Bing Around the World	196?	2.50	5.00	10.00
DL 78781 [R]	That Christmas Feeling	196?	2.50	5.00	10.00
DL 79106 [R]	Ichabod/Rip Van Winkle	1962	2.50	5.00	10.00
ENCORE					
E2E-201 [(2)]	The Bing Crosby Story, Volume 1	1968	3.75	7.50	15.00
E2E-202 [(2)]	The Bing Crosby Story, Volume 2	1968	3.75	7.50	15.00
FOX AMERICAN					
SMF 210	Bing Crosby Sings Christmas	1978	2.50	5.00	10.00
—Side 1 from radio show Dec. 19, 1951; Side 2 from radio show Dec. 14, 1949					
GNP CRESCENDO					
GNP-9044	The Radio Years, Vol. 1	1985	2.00	4.00	8.00
GNP-9046	The Radio Years, Vol. 2	1986	2.00	4.00	8.00
GNP-9047	The Radio Years, Vol. 3	1986	2.00	4.00	8.00
GNP-9048	The Radio Years, Vol. 4	1986	2.00	4.00	8.00
GOLDEN					
A298:20 [M]	Ali Baba and the 40 Thieves	1957	6.25	12.50	25.00
A298:21 [M]	How Lovely Is Christmas/A Christmas Story	195?	6.25	12.50	25.00
HARMONY					
HL 7094 [M]	Crosby Classics	1958	3.75	7.50	15.00
HS 11313 [R]	Crosby Classics	196?	2.50	5.00	10.00
LONDON					
PS 679	Feels Good	1977	3.00	6.00	12.00
MARK 56					
762	Original Radio Broadcasts	197?	2.50	5.00	10.00
MCA					
177	Shillelaghs and Shamrocks	1973	2.50	5.00	10.00
519	When Irish Eyes Are Smiling	197?	2.50	5.00	10.00
915	Hey Bing!	198?	2.50	5.00	10.00
1502	Rare 1930-31 Brunswick Recordings	198?	2.50	5.00	10.00
3031	Bing Crosby's Greatest Hits	1977	2.50	5.00	10.00
3031	Bing Crosby's Greatest Hits	1977	2.50	5.00	10.00

Number	Title (A Side/B Side)	Yr	VG	VG+	NM
4045 [(2)]	The Best of Bing	197?	3.00	6.00	12.00
15017	Two Favorite Stories by Bing Crosby	197?	2.50	5.00	10.00
—Reissue of Decca DL 4283					
15018 [R]	A Christmas Sing with Bing Around the World	197?	2.00	4.00	8.00
—Reissue of Decca DL7-8419					
15019 [R]	That Christmas Feeling	1973	2.00	4.00	8.00
—Reissue of Decca DL7-8781					
15024 [R]	Merry Christmas	197?	2.00	4.00	8.00
—Reissue of Decca DL7-8128					
37076	Bing Crosby's Greatest Hits	198?	2.00	4.00	8.00
METRO					
M-523 [M]	Bing Crosby	1965	3.00	6.00	12.00
MS-523 [S]	Bing Crosby	1965	3.75	7.50	15.00
MGM					
E-3890 [M]	Senor Bing	1961	3.75	7.50	15.00
SE-3890 [S]	Senor Bing	1961	5.00	10.00	20.00
E-4129 [M]	The Great Standards	1963	3.75	7.50	15.00
SE-4129 [S]	The Great Standards	1963	5.00	10.00	20.00
E-4203 [M]	The Very Best of Bing Crosby	1964	3.75	7.50	15.00
SE-4203 [S]	The Very Best of Bing Crosby	1964	5.00	10.00	20.00
MOBILE FIDELITY					
1-260	Bing Sings Whilst Bregman Swings	1996	5.00	10.00	20.00
—Audiophile vinyl					
MURRAY HILL					
894637 [(4)]	Bing Crosby and His Friends	197?	6.25	12.50	25.00
PHILCO					
LP 436 [10]	Crosby Classics	195?	10.00	20.00	40.00
—Custom item for Philco (front cover has "Philco: Famous for Quality the World Over")					
PICKWICK					
SPC-3583	Thoroughly Modern Bing	1978	2.00	4.00	8.00
POLYDOR					
PD-1-6128	Seasons: The Closing Chapter	1978	3.00	6.00	12.00
P.I.P.					
6802	Thoroughly Modern Bing	1971	3.00	6.00	12.00
RCA VICTOR					
LPM-1473 [M]	Bing with a Beat	1957	6.25	12.50	25.00
AFL1-1854	Fancy Meeting You Here	1977	2.50	5.00	10.00
LPM-1854 [M]	Fancy Meeting You Here	1958	5.00	10.00	20.00
LSP-1854 [S]	Fancy Meeting You Here	1958	7.50	15.00	30.00
LPM-2071 [M]	Young Bing Crosby	1959	5.00	10.00	20.00
CPL1-2086	A Legendary Performer	1976	2.50	5.00	10.00
READER'S DIGEST					
RDA-175	Christmas with Bing	1980	2.50	5.00	10.00
—Repackage of Warner Bros.and Capitol recordings					
REPRISE					
R-6106 [M]	Return to Paradise Islands	1964	3.75	7.50	15.00
R9-6106 [S]	Return to Paradise Islands	1964	5.00	10.00	20.00
SPOKANE					
1	Bing Crosby On the Air, 1934 and 1938	197?	2.50	5.00	10.00
5	Der Bingle, Vol. 1	197?	2.50	5.00	10.00
10	Der Bingle, Vol. 2	197?	2.50	5.00	10.00
12	Bing in the 30's	197?	2.50	5.00	10.00
14	Bing in the 30s, Vol. 2	197?	2.50	5.00	10.00
15	Holiday Inn/The Bells of St. Mary's	197?	2.50	5.00	10.00
16	Kraft Music Hall Highlights	197?	2.50	5.00	10.00
19	Kraft Music Hall Highlights, Vol. 2	197?	2.50	5.00	10.00
20	Der Bingle, Vol. 3	197?	2.50	5.00	10.00
21	Bing Crosby & the Music Maids	197?	2.50	5.00	10.00
24	Bing in the 30s, Vol. 3	1986	2.00	4.00	8.00
25	Bing in the 30s, Vol. 4	1986	2.00	4.00	8.00
26	Bing in the 30s, Vol. 5	1986	2.00	4.00	8.00
27	Bing in the 30s, Vol. 6	1986	2.00	4.00	8.00
SUNBEAM					
502	Distinctively Bing, Vol. 1	197?	2.50	5.00	10.00
504	Distinctively Bing, Vol. 2	197?	2.50	5.00	10.00
UNITED ARTISTS					
UA-LA554-G	That's What Life Is All About	1976	3.00	6.00	12.00
VERVE					
MGV 2020 [M]	Bing Sings Whilst Bregman Swings	1956	12.50	25.00	50.00
V-2020 [M]	Bing Sings Whilst Bregman Swings	1961	6.25	12.50	25.00
VOCALION					
VL 3603 [M]	Bing Crosby Sings	195?	3.75	7.50	15.00
VL 73603 [R]	Bing Crosby Sings	196?	2.50	5.00	10.00
WARNER BROS.					
W 1363 [M]	Join with Bing and Sing Along	1960	3.75	7.50	15.00
WS 1363 [S]	Join with Bing and Sing Along	1960	5.00	10.00	20.00
2W 1401 [(2) M]	101 Gang Songs	1961	5.00	10.00	20.00
2WS 1401 [(2) S]	101 Gang Songs	1961	6.25	12.50	25.00
W 1422 [M]	Join Bing in a Gang Song Sing-Along	1961	3.75	7.50	15.00
WS 1422 [S]	Join Bing in a Gang Song Sing-Along	1961	5.00	10.00	20.00
W 1435 [M]	Join Bing and Sing Along	1962	3.75	7.50	15.00
WS 1435 [S]	Join Bing and Sing Along	1962	5.00	10.00	20.00
W 1482 [M]	On the Happy Side	1962	3.75	7.50	15.00
WS 1482 [S]	On the Happy Side	1962	5.00	10.00	20.00
W 1484 [M]	I Wish You a Merry Christmas	1962	3.75	7.50	15.00
WS 1484 [S]	I Wish You a Merry Christmas	1962	5.00	10.00	20.00
"X"					
XLVA-4250 [M]	Young Bing Crosby	1955	12.50	25.00	50.00

CROSBY, BING, AND LOUIS ARMSTRONG

Also see each artist's individual listings.

Number	Title (A Side/B Side)	Yr	VG	VG+	NM
45s					
DECCA					
27623	Gone Fishin'/We All Have a Song in My Heart	1951	3.75	7.50	15.00
MGM					
SB 26 [S]	Muskrat Ramble/Way Down in New Orleans	1960	3.75	7.50	15.00
SB 27 [S]	Dardanella/Brother Bill	1960	3.75	7.50	15.00
SB 28 [S]	Preacher/Little Ol' Tune	1960	3.75	7.50	15.00
SB 29 [S]	Let's Sing Like a Dixieland Band/At the Jazz Band Ball	1960	3.75	7.50	15.00
SB 30 [S]	Rocky Mountain Moon/Bye Bye Blues	1960	3.75	7.50	15.00
—The above five are 33 1/3 rpm jukebox singles					
12961	Dardanella/Muskrat Ramble	1960	2.50	5.00	10.00
Albums					
CAPITOL					
SM-11735	Bing Crosby and Louis Armstrong	1977	2.50	5.00	10.00
MGM					
E-3882 [M]	Bing and Satchmo	1960	3.75	7.50	15.00
SE-3882 [S]	Bing and Satchmo	1960	5.00	10.00	20.00

CROSBY, BING, AND FRED ASTAIRE

Number	Title (A Side/B Side)	Yr	VG	VG+	NM
Albums					
UNITED ARTISTS					
UA-LA588-G	A Couple of Song and Dance Men	1976	3.00	6.00	12.00

CROSBY, BING, AND PEGGY LEE

Also see each artist's individual listings.

Number	Title (A Side/B Side)	Yr	VG	VG+	NM
45s					
DECCA					
28238	Watermelon Weather/The Moon Came Up with a Great Idea Last Night	1952	3.00	6.00	12.00

CROSBY, DAVID

Also see THE BYRDS; CROSBY, STILLS AND NASH; CROSBY, STILLS, NASH AND YOUNG; GRAHAM NASH AND DAVID CROSBY.

Number	Title (A Side/B Side)	Yr	VG	VG+	NM
45s					
ATLANTIC					
2792	Laughing/Music Is Love	1971	—	2.50	5.00
2809	Orleans/Traction in the Rain	1971	—	2.50	5.00
87360	Hero/Coverage	1993	—	—	3.00
—A-side: David Crosby and Phil Collins					
Albums					
ATLANTIC					
SD 8229	If I Could Only Remember My Name...	1971	3.75	7.50	15.00
A&M					
SP-5232	Oh Yes I Can	1989	2.50	5.00	10.00

CROSBY, DAVID, AND GRAHAM NASH

See GRAHAM NASH AND DAVID CROSBY.

CROSBY, STILLS AND NASH

Number	Title (A Side/B Side)	Yr	VG	VG+	NM
45s					
ATLANTIC					
2652	Marrakesh Express/Helplessly Hoping	1969	—	3.00	6.00
2676	Suite: Judy Blue Eyes/Long Time Gone	1969	—	3.00	6.00
3401	Just a Song Before I Go/Dark Star	1977	—	2.00	4.00
3401 [PS]	Just a Song Before I Go/Dark Star	1977	—	2.50	5.00
3432	Fair Game/Anything at All	1977	—	2.00	4.00
3453	I Give You Give Blind/Carried Away	1978	—	2.00	4.00
3784	Carry On/Shadow Captain	1980	—	2.50	5.00
4058	Wasted on the Way/Delta	1982	—	—	3.00
4058 [PS]	Wasted on the Way/Delta	1982	—	2.00	4.00
87909	Live It Up/Chuck's Lament	1990	—	2.00	4.00
89775	Raise a Voice/For What It's Worth	1983	—	—	3.00
89812	War Games/Shadow Captain	1983	—	—	3.00
89812 [PS]	War Games/Shadow Captain	1983	—	2.00	4.00
89888	Too Much Love to Hide/Song for Susan	1983	—	—	3.00
89969	Southern Cross/Into the Darkness	1982	—	—	3.00
89969 [PS]	Southern Cross/Into the Darkness	1982	—	2.00	4.00
Albums					
ATLANTIC					
SD 8229	Crosby, Stills & Nash	1969	5.00	10.00	20.00
SD 16026	Replay	1980	3.00	6.00	12.00
—Also has solo cuts by Stephen Stills					
SD 19104	CSN	1977	3.00	6.00	12.00
SD 19117	Crosby, Stills & Nash	1977	2.50	5.00	10.00
—Reissue of 8229					
SD 19360	Daylight Again	1982	3.00	6.00	12.00
80075	Allies	1983	3.00	6.00	12.00
82107	Live It Up	1990	3.75	7.50	15.00
NAUTILUS					
NR-48	Crosby, Stills and Nash	1982	37.50	75.00	150.00
—Audiophile vinyl					

CROSBY, STILLS, NASH & YOUNG

Number	Title (A Side/B Side)	Yr	VG	VG+	NM
45s					
ATLANTIC					
2723	Woodstock/Helpless	1970	—	3.00	6.00
2735	Teach Your Children/Carry On	1970	—	3.00	6.00
2740	Ohio/Find the Cost of Freedom	1970	—	3.00	6.00
2740 [PS]	Ohio/Find the Cost of Freedom	1970	3.00	6.00	12.00
2760	Our House/Deja Vu	1970	—	3.00	6.00
88967	Got It Made/This Old House	1989	—	—	3.00
88967 [PS]	Got It Made/This Old House	1989	—	—	3.00
89003	American Dream/Compass	1988	—	—	3.00
89003 [PS]	American Dream/Compass	1988	—	—	3.00
Albums					
ATLANTIC					
PR 165 [M-DJ]	Celebration/CSNY Month	1974	25.00	50.00	100.00
—Promo-only LP in mono					
PR 165 [S-DJ]	Celebration/CSNY Month	1974	12.50	25.00	50.00
—Promo-only LP in stereo					
2-902 [(2) M]	4 Way Street	1971	25.00	50.00	100.00
—White label promo; no stock copies are mono					
SD 2-902 [(2)]	4 Way Street	1971	5.00	10.00	20.00
SD 2-902 [(2) DJ]	4 Way Street	1971	12.50	25.00	50.00
—White label stereo promo					
7200 [M]	Deja Vu	1970	37.50	75.00	150.00
—White label promo; no stock copies are mono					
SD 7200	Deja Vu	1970	3.75	7.50	15.00
—Pasted-on front cover photo must still be intact					
SD 7200 [DJ]	Deja Vu	1970	15.00	30.00	60.00
—White label stereo promo					
SD 18100	So Far	1974	3.00	6.00	12.00

Number	Title (A Side/B Side)	Yr	VG	VG+	NM
PR 18102 [DJ]	A Rap with C, S, N & Y	1974	12.50	25.00	50.00
—Promo-only interview album					
SD 19118	Deja Vu	1977	2.50	5.00	10.00
—Reissue of 7200					
SD 19119	So Far	1977	2.50	5.00	10.00
—Reissue of 18100					
81888	American Dream	1988	2.50	5.00	10.00
MOBILE FIDELITY					
1-088	Deja Vu	198?	50.00	100.00	200.00
—Audiophile vinyl					

CROSS, JIMMY

45s

Number	Title (A Side/B Side)	Yr	VG	VG+	NM
CHICKEN					
101	Hey Little Girl/Hey Little Girl (Part 2)	1966	3.00	6.00	12.00
RECORDO					
502	Pretty Girls Everywhere/Suntan Sally	1961	3.75	7.50	15.00
RED BIRD					
10-042	Hey Little Girl/Super Duper Man	1965	3.75	7.50	15.00
TOLLIE					
9039	I Want My Baby Back/Play the Other Side	1965	5.00	10.00	20.00
9044	The Ballad of James Bong/Play the Other Side Again	1965	3.75	7.50	15.00

CROSS COUNTRY

Includes three members of THE TOKENS.

45s

Number	Title (A Side/B Side)	Yr	VG	VG+	NM
ATCO					
6932	Rock and Roll Music/Just a Thought	1973	2.00	4.00	8.00
6934	In the Midnight Hour/The Smile Song	1973	2.00	4.00	8.00
6947	Tastes So Good to Me/A Ball Song	1973	2.00	4.00	8.00

Albums

Number	Title (A Side/B Side)	Yr	VG	VG+	NM
ATCO					
SD 7024	Cross Country	1973	3.75	7.50	15.00

CROSSFIRES, THE (1)

Group evolved into THE TURTLES.

45s

Number	Title (A Side/B Side)	Yr	VG	VG+	NM
CAPCO					
104	Fiberglass Jungle/Dr. Jekyll and Mr. Hyde	1963	20.00	40.00	80.00
LUCKY TOKEN					
112	One Potato, Two Potato/That'll Be the Day	1965	12.50	25.00	50.00

Albums

Number	Title (A Side/B Side)	Yr	VG	VG+	NM
RHINO					
RNLP-019	Out of Control	1981	2.50	5.00	10.00

CROSSFIRES, THE (2)

45s

Number	Title (A Side/B Side)	Yr	VG	VG+	NM
CUCA					
1027	Young Love/When My Blue Moon Turns to Gold Again	1961	3.00	6.00	12.00

CROSSFIRES, THE (3)

Albums

Number	Title (A Side/B Side)	Yr	VG	VG+	NM
STRAND					
SL-1083 [M]	Limbo Rock	1963	5.00	10.00	20.00
SLS-1083 [S]	Limbo Rock	1963	6.25	12.50	25.00

CROSSFIRES, THE (4)

45s

Number	Title (A Side/B Side)	Yr	VG	VG+	NM
TOWER					
278	Who'll Be the Next One/Making Love Is Fun	1966	5.00	10.00	20.00

CROW

45s

Number	Title (A Side/B Side)	Yr	VG	VG+	NM
AMARET					
106	Busy Day/Time to Make a Turn	1969	—	3.00	6.00
112	Evil Woman Don't Play Your Games with Me/Gonna Leave a Mark	1969	2.00	4.00	8.00
119	Cottage Cheese/Slow Down	1970	—	3.00	6.00
119	Cottage Cheese/Busy Day	1970	—	3.00	6.00
125	Don't Try to Lay No Boogie-Woogie on the "King of Rock 'n' Roll"/Satisfied	1970	—	3.00	6.00
129	Watching Can Waste Up the Time/Yellow Dawg	1971	—	2.50	5.00
133	Something in Your Blood/Yellow Dawg	1971	—	2.50	5.00
145	Everything Has Got to Be Free/Mobile Blues	1972	—	2.50	5.00
148	If It Feels Good, Do It/Cado Queen	1972	—	2.50	5.00

Albums

Number	Title (A Side/B Side)	Yr	VG	VG+	NM
AMARET					
ST-5002	Crow Music	1969	5.00	10.00	20.00
ST-5006	Crow By Crow	1970	5.00	10.00	20.00
ST-5009	Mosaic	1971	5.00	10.00	20.00
AST-5012	Best of Crow	1972	3.75	7.50	15.00
ST-5013	David Crow d/b/a Crow	1973	3.75	7.50	15.00

CROWN, BOBBY

45s

Number	Title (A Side/B Side)	Yr	VG	VG+	NM
FELCO					
102	One Way Ticket/Your Conscience	1960	200.00	400.00	800.00
MANCO					
1005	I've Never Had a Broken Heart/Wait a Minute	1960	10.00	20.00	40.00

CROWN HEIGHTS AFFAIR

45s

Number	Title (A Side/B Side)	Yr	VG	VG+	NM
DE-LITE					
803	You Gave Me Love/Tell Me You Love Me	1980	—	2.00	4.00
805	Sure Shot/I See the Light	1980	—	2.00	4.00
821	Somebody Tell Me What to Do/You Gave Me Love	1982	—	2.00	4.00
823	Let Me Ride on the Wave of Your Love/Wine and Dine You	1982	—	2.00	4.00
908	Say a Prayer for Two/Galaxy of Love	1978	—	2.00	4.00
911	I Love You/Dream World	1978	—	2.00	4.00
912	Dance Lady Dance/Come Fly with Me	1979	—	2.00	4.00
915	Empty Soul of Mine/Rock Is Hot	1979	—	2.00	4.00
1570	Dreaming a Dream/Dreaming a Dream (Part 2)	1975	—	2.00	4.00
1575	Every Beat of My Heart/Every Beat of My Heart (Disco Version)	1975	—	2.00	4.00
1581	Foxy Lady/Picture Show	1976	—	2.00	4.00
1588	Dancin'/Love Me	1976	—	2.00	4.00
1592	Do It the French Way/Sexy Ways	1977	—	2.00	4.00
1592 [PS]	Do It the French Way/Sexy Ways	1977	—	3.00	6.00
RCA VICTOR					
APBO-0023	Super Rod (Part 1)/Super Rod (Part 2)	1973	—	2.50	5.00
APBO-0243	Leave the Kids Alone/Rip-Off	1974	—	2.50	5.00
PB-10018	Special Kind of Woman/Streaking	1974	—	2.50	5.00

Albums

Number	Title (A Side/B Side)	Yr	VG	VG+	NM
DE-LITE					
2017	Dreaming a Dream	1975	2.50	5.00	10.00
2021	Foxy Lady	1976	2.50	5.00	10.00
2022	Do It	1977	2.50	5.00	10.00
8504	Think Positive	1982	2.50	5.00	10.00
9506	Dream World	1978	2.50	5.00	10.00
9512	Dance Lady Dance	1979	2.50	5.00	10.00
9517	Sure Shot	1980	2.50	5.00	10.00
RCA VICTOR					
APL1-0492	Crown Heights Affair	1974	3.00	6.00	12.00
ANL1-2660	Crown Heights Affair	1977	2.00	4.00	8.00
—Reissue of above LP					

CROWNS, THE (1)

45s

Number	Title (A Side/B Side)	Yr	VG	VG+	NM
CHORDETTE					
1001	Party Time/Amazon Basin Pop	1962	5.00	10.00	20.00

CROWNS, THE (2)

45s

Number	Title (A Side/B Side)	Yr	VG	VG+	NM
OLD TOWN					
1171	Possibility/Watch Out	1964	10.00	20.00	40.00
—Old light blue Old Town label					
1171	Possibility/Watch Out	1964	3.75	7.50	15.00
—Black label with moon					

CROWNS, THE (3)

Four members of THE FIVE CROWNS plus Benjamin Nelson (BEN E. KING). Also see THE DRIFTERS.

45s

Number	Title (A Side/B Side)	Yr	VG	VG+	NM
R&B					
6901	Kiss and Make Up/I'll Forget About You	1958	20.00	40.00	80.00

CROWNS, THE (4)

45s

Number	Title (A Side/B Side)	Yr	VG	VG+	NM
VEE JAY					
546	Better Luck Next Time/You Make Me Blue	1963	3.75	7.50	15.00

CROWS, THE

45s

Number	Title (A Side/B Side)	Yr	VG	VG+	NM
RAMA					
3	Seven Lonely Days/No Help Wanted	1953	125.00	250.00	500.00
5	Gee/I Love You So	1953	17.50	35.00	70.00
—Blue label, black vinyl					
5	Gee/I Love You So	1953	100.00	200.00	400.00
—Blue label, red vinyl					
5	Gee/I Love You So	1955	7.50	15.00	30.00
—Red label, black vinyl					
10	Heartbreaker/Call a Doctor	1953	100.00	200.00	400.00
—Black vinyl					
10	Heartbreaker/Call a Doctor	1953	200.00	400.00	800.00
—Red vinyl					
10	Heartbreaker/Call a Doctor	1953	150.00	300.00	600.00
—Black vinyl, label says "The Jewels"					
10	Heartbreaker/Call a Doctor	1953	150.00	300.00	600.00
—Black vinyl, label says "The Jewels" on one side, "The Crows" on the other					
10	Heartbreaker/Call a Doctor	1953	400.00	800.00	1200.
—Red vinyl; label says "The Jewels"					
29	Baby/Untrue	1954	50.00	100.00	200.00
30	Miss You/I Really, Really Love You So	1954	100.00	200.00	400.00
—Black vinyl					
30	Miss You/I Really, Really Love You So	1954	250.00	500.00	1000.
—Red vinyl					
50	Baby Doll/Sweet Sue (It's You)	1954	100.00	200.00	400.00
TICO					
1082	Mambo Shevitz/Mambo #5	1955	50.00	100.00	200.00
—B-side by Melino and Orchestra; black vinyl					
1082	Mambo Shevitz/Mambo #5	1955	75.00	150.00	300.00
—B-side by Melino and Orchestra; red vinyl					

CROWS, THE / THE HARPTONES

Albums

Number	Title (A Side/B Side)	Yr	VG	VG+	NM
ROULETTE					
RE-114 [(2)]	Echoes of a Rock Era: The Groups	1973	5.00	10.00	20.00

CRUDUP, ARTHUR

45s

Number	Title (A Side/B Side)	Yr	VG	VG+	NM
ACE					
503	I Wonder/My Baby Boogies All the Time	1955	50.00	100.00	200.00
FIRE					
1501	Rock Me Mama/Mean Ole Frisco	1962	3.75	7.50	15.00
1502	Katie Mae/Dig Myself a Hole	1962	3.75	7.50	15.00
GROOVE					
0011	I Love My Baby/Fall on Your Knees and Pray	1954	10.00	20.00	40.00

Number	Title (A Side/B Side)	Yr	VG	VG+	NM
0026	She's Got No Hair/If You Ever Been to Georgia	1954	10.00	20.00	40.00
RCA VICTOR					
47-4367	Love Me Mama/Where Did You Stay Last Night	1951	25.00	50.00	100.00
47-4572	Goin' Back to Georgia/Mr. So and So	1952	20.00	40.00	80.00
47-4753	Worried 'Bout You Baby/Late in the Evening	1952	20.00	40.00	80.00
47-4933	Second Man Blues/Do It If You Want	1952	20.00	40.00	80.00
47-5070	Lookin' for My Baby/Pearly Lee	1952	20.00	40.00	80.00
47-5167	Keep On Drinkin'/Nelvina	1953	20.00	40.00	80.00
47-5563	War Is Over/My Wife and Woman	1953	20.00	40.00	80.00
50-0000	That's All Right/Crudup's After Hours	1949	100.00	200.00	400.00
—Gray label, orange vinyl; the first R&B 45 rpm record!					
50-0001	Boy Friend Blues/Katie May	1949	25.00	50.00	100.00
—Gray label, orange vinyl					
50-0013	Shout Sister Shout/Crudup's Vicksburg Blues	1949	25.00	50.00	100.00
—Gray label, orange vinyl					
50-0032	Hoodoo Lady Blues/Tired of Worry	1949	25.00	50.00	100.00
—Gray label, orange vinyl					
50-0046	Come Back Baby/Mercy Blues	1949	25.00	50.00	100.00
—Gray label, orange vinyl					
50-0074	Dust My Broom/You Know That I Love You	1950	25.00	50.00	100.00
—Gray label, orange vinyl					
50-0092	Mean Old Santa Fe/Oo Wee Baby	1950	25.00	50.00	100.00
—Gray label, orange vinyl					
50-0100	Lonesome World to Me/Hand Me Down My Walking Cane	1950	25.00	50.00	100.00
—Gray label, orange vinyl					
50-0105	She's Just Like Caldonia/(B-side unknown)	1951	25.00	50.00	100.00
—Gray label, orange vinyl					
50-0109	My Baby Left Me/Anytime Is the Right Time	1951	37.50	75.00	150.00
—Gray label, orange vinyl					
50-0117	Nobody Wants Me/Star Bootlegger	1951	25.00	50.00	100.00
—Gray label, black vinyl					
50-0126	Roberta Blues/Behind Closed Doors	1951	25.00	50.00	100.00
—Gray label, black vinyl					
50-0141	I'm Gonna Dig Myself a Hole/Too Much Competition	1951	25.00	50.00	100.00
—Gray label, black vinyl					
Albums					
COLLECTABLES					
COL-5130	Mean Ol' Frisco	1988	2.50	5.00	10.00
DELMARK					
DS-614	Look on Yonder's Wall	1969	10.00	20.00	40.00
DS-621	Crudup's Mood	1969	10.00	20.00	40.00
FIRE					
103 [M]	Mean Ol' Frisco	1960	300.00	600.00	900.00
RCA VICTOR					
LVP-573	Father of Rock and Roll	1971	5.00	10.00	20.00
TRIP					
7501	Mean Ol' Frisco	1975	3.75	7.50	15.00

CRUM, SIMON

See FERLIN HUSKY.

CRUSADERS, THE (1)

Jazz and soul band. Originally recorded as "The Jazz Crusaders"; all releases on Pacfic Jazz and World Pacific use that name.

Number	Title (A Side/B Side)	Yr	VG	VG+	NM
45s					
ABC BLUE THUMB					
261	Stomp and Buck Dance/A Ballad for Joe (Louis)	1975	—	2.50	5.00
267	Creole/I Feel the Love	1975	—	2.50	5.00
269	Keep That Same Old Feeling/'Til the Sun Shines	1976	—	2.50	5.00
270	And Then There Was the Blues/Feeling Funky	1976	—	2.50	5.00
272	Feel It/The Way We Was	1977	—	2.50	5.00
273	Free as the Wind/The Way We Was	1977	—	2.50	5.00
278	Bayou Bottoms/Covert Action	1978	—	2.50	5.00
BLUE THUMB					
208	Put It Where You Want It/Mosadi	1972	—	2.50	5.00
217	So Far Away/That's How I Feel	1972	—	2.50	5.00
225	Don't Let It Get You Down/Journey from Within	1973	—	2.50	5.00
232	Take It or Leave It/That's How I Feel	1973	—	2.50	5.00
245	Lay It On the Line/Let's Boogie	1974	—	2.50	5.00
249	Scratch/Way Back Home	1974	—	2.50	5.00
CHISA					
8010	Way Back Home/Jackson	1970	—	3.00	6.00
—As "Jazz Crusaders"					
8013	Pass the Plate/Greasy Spoon	1971	—	3.00	6.00
MCA					
41054	Street Life/Hustler	1979	—	2.00	4.00
41295	Sweet Gentle Love/Soul Shadows	1980	—	2.00	4.00
51029	Last Call/Honky Tonk Struttin'	1980	—	2.00	4.00
51177	I'm So Glad I'm Standing Here Today/Standing Tall	1981	—	2.00	4.00
—A-side with Joe Cocker					
51222	This Old World's Too Funky for Me/Standing Tall	1981	—	2.00	4.00
—A-side with Joe Cocker					
52098	Street Life/Overture	1982	—	2.00	4.00
—With B.B. King and the London Symphony Orchestra					
52365	New Move/Mr. Cool	1984	—	2.00	4.00
52398	Dream Street/Dead End	1984	—	2.00	4.00
52454	Gotta Lotta Shakalada/Zalal 'E Mini	1984	—	2.00	4.00
52966	The Way It Goes/Good Times	1986	—	2.00	4.00
53330	A.C. (Alternating Currents)/Mulholland Nights	1988	—	—	3.00
MOWEST					
5028	Spanish Harlem/Papa Hooper's Barrelhouse Groove	1972	—	3.00	6.00
PACIFIC JAZZ					
340	Sinnin' Sam/Tonight	1962	3.00	6.00	12.00
342	Young Rabbits/(B-side unknown)	1962	3.00	6.00	12.00
371	No Name Samba/Tough Talk	1963	2.50	5.00	10.00
88125	Uptight (Everything's Alright)/Scratch	1966	2.00	4.00	8.00
88144	Eleanor Rigby/Ooga Boogaloo	1968	—	3.00	6.00
88146	Hey Jude/Love and Peace	1969	—	3.00	6.00
88153	Get Back/Willie and Laura Mae Jones	1969	—	3.00	6.00
WORLD PACIFIC					
388	Boopie/Turkish Black	1963	2.50	5.00	10.00
—As "Jazz Crusaders"					
401	Heat Wave/On Broadway	1964	2.50	5.00	10.00
412	I Remember Tomorrow/Long John	1964	2.50	5.00	10.00
77800	The Thing/Tough Talk	1965	2.00	4.00	8.00
77806	Aqua Dulce/Soul Bourgeoise	1966	2.00	4.00	8.00
Albums					
ABC BLUE THUMB					
6022	Chain Reaction	1975	2.50	5.00	10.00
6024	Those Southern Knights	1976	2.50	5.00	10.00
6027 [(2)]	The Best of the Crusaders	1976	3.00	6.00	12.00
6029	Free As the Wind	1977	2.50	5.00	10.00
6030	Images	1978	2.50	5.00	10.00
9002 [(2)]	Southern Comfort	1974	3.00	6.00	12.00
BLUE NOTE					
BN-LA170-G [(2)]	Tough Talk	1974	3.00	6.00	12.00
BN-LA530-H2 [(2)]	Young Rabbits	1977	3.00	6.00	12.00
LWB-530 [(2)]	Young Rabbits	1981	2.50	5.00	10.00
—Reissue of BN-LA530-H2					
LT-1046	Live Sides	1980	2.50	5.00	10.00
BLUE THUMB					
BT-6001 [(2)]	Crusaders 1	1972	3.75	7.50	15.00
BT-6007	Unsung Heroes	1973	3.00	6.00	12.00
BT-6010	Scratch	1974	3.00	6.00	12.00
BT-7000 [(2)]	The 2nd Crusade	1973	3.75	7.50	15.00
CHISA					
804	Old Socks, New Shoes...New Socks, Old Shoes	1970	3.00	6.00	12.00
—As "Jazz Crusaders"					
807	Pass the Plate	1971	3.00	6.00	12.00
CRUSADERS					
16000	Street Life	1982	6.25	12.50	25.00
—Audiophile vinyl					
16002	Ongaku-Kai: Live in Japan	1982	6.25	12.50	25.00
—Audiophile vinyl					
LIBERTY					
LST-11005	Give Peace a Chance	1970	3.75	7.50	15.00
—As "Jazz Crusaders"					
MCA					
3094	Street Life	1979	2.50	5.00	10.00
5124	Rhapsody and Blues	1980	2.50	5.00	10.00
5254	Standing Tall	1981	2.50	5.00	10.00
5429	Ghetto Blaster	1984	2.50	5.00	10.00
5781	The Good and Bad Times	1987	2.50	5.00	10.00
6006 [(2)]	The Best of the Crusaders	1980	2.50	5.00	10.00
—Reissue of Blue Thumb 6027					
6014 [(2)]	Crusaders 1	198?	2.50	5.00	10.00
—Reissue of Blue Thumb 6001					
6015 [(2)]	2nd Crusade	198?	2.50	5.00	10.00
—Reissue of Blue Thumb 7000					
6016 [(2)]	Southern Comfort	198?	2.50	5.00	10.00
—Reissue of Blue Thumb 9002					
8017 [(2)]	Royal Jam	1982	3.00	6.00	12.00
37072	Scratch	198?	2.00	4.00	8.00
—Reissue of Blue Thumb 6010					
37073	Free As the Wind	198?	2.00	4.00	8.00
—Reissue of Blue Thumb 6029					
37074	Images	198?	2.00	4.00	8.00
—Reissue of Blue Thumb 6030					
37146	Chain Reaction	198?	2.00	4.00	8.00
—Reissue of Blue Thumb 6022					
37147	Those Southern Knights	198?	2.00	4.00	8.00
—Reissue of Blue Thumb 6024					
37174	Rhapsody and Blues	198?	2.00	4.00	8.00
—Reissue of 5124					
37240	Standing Tall	1985	2.00	4.00	8.00
—Reissue of 5254					
42087	The Vocal Album	1988	2.50	5.00	10.00
42168	Life in the Modern World	1988	2.50	5.00	10.00
MOBILE FIDELITY					
1-010	Chain Reaction	1979	5.00	10.00	20.00
—Audiophile vinyl					
MOTOWN					
M5-195V1	The Crusaders At Their Best	1981	2.50	5.00	10.00
M 796	The Crusaders At Their Best	1973	3.00	6.00	12.00
MOWEST					
118	Hollywood	1972	3.00	6.00	12.00
PACIFIC JAZZ					
PJ-27 [M]	Freedom Sound	1961	6.25	12.50	25.00
ST-27 [S]	Freedom Sound	1961	7.50	15.00	30.00
PJ-43 [M]	Lookin' Ahead	1962	6.25	12.50	25.00
ST-43 [S]	Lookin' Ahead	1962	7.50	15.00	30.00
—Black vinyl					
ST-43 [S]	Lookin' Ahead	1962	15.00	30.00	60.00
—Yellow vinyl					
PJ-57 [M]	The Jazz Crusaders at the Lighthouse	1962	6.25	12.50	25.00
ST-57 [S]	The Jazz Crusaders at the Lighthouse	1962	7.50	15.00	30.00
PJ-68 [M]	Tough Talk	1963	6.25	12.50	25.00
ST-68 [S]	Tough Talk	1963	7.50	15.00	30.00
PJ-76 [M]	Heat Wave	1963	6.25	12.50	25.00
ST-76 [S]	Heat Wave	1963	7.50	15.00	30.00
PJ-83 [M]	Stretchin' Out	1964	6.25	12.50	25.00
ST-83 [S]	Stretchin' Out	1964	7.50	15.00	30.00
PJ-87 [M]	The Thing	1964	6.25	12.50	25.00
ST-87 [S]	The Thing	1964	7.50	15.00	30.00
PJ-10092 [M]	Chili Con Soul	1965	5.00	10.00	20.00
PJ-10098 [M]	The Jazz Crusaders at the Lighthouse '66	1966	5.00	10.00	20.00
PJ-10106 [M]	Talk That Talk	1966	5.00	10.00	20.00
PJ-10115 [M]	The Festival Album	1967	6.25	12.50	25.00
PJ-10124	Uh Huh	1967	6.25	12.50	25.00
ST-20092 [S]	Chili Con Soul	1965	6.25	12.50	25.00
ST-20098 [S]	The Jazz Crusaders at the Lighthouse '66	1966	6.25	12.50	25.00
ST-20106 [S]	Talk That Talk	1966	6.25	12.50	25.00
ST-20115 [S]	The Festival Album	1967	5.00	10.00	20.00

Number	Title (A Side/B Side)	Yr	VG	VG+	NM
ST-20124	Uh Huh	1967	5.00	10.00	20.00
ST-20131	The Jazz Crusaders at the Lighthouse '68	1968	5.00	10.00	20.00
ST-20136	Powerhouse	1968	5.00	10.00	20.00
ST-20165	The Jazz Crusaders at the Lighthouse '69	1969	5.00	10.00	20.00
ST-20175	The Best of the Jazz Crusaders	1969	5.00	10.00	20.00
PAUSA					
9005	The Best of the Jazz Crusaders	1979	2.50	5.00	10.00
—As "Jazz Crusaders"					

CRUSADERS, THE (U)

None of these are by group (1).

45s

Number	Title (A Side/B Side)	Yr	VG	VG+	NM
CAMEO					
285	Boogie Woogie/At the Club	1963	3.00	6.00	12.00
DKR					
(no #)	Seminole/Busted Surfboard	1962	10.00	20.00	40.00
DOOTO					
472	Swinging Week-End/I Found Someone	1963	3.75	7.50	15.00
TOWER					
286	The Little Drummer Boy/Battle Hymn of the Republic	1966	2.50	5.00	10.00
328	Make a Joyful Noise/Praise We the Lord	1967	2.50	5.00	10.00

CRYAN' SHAMES, THE

45s

Number	Title (A Side/B Side)	Yr	VG	VG+	NM
COLUMBIA					
43836	I Wanna Meet You/We Could Be Happy	1966	2.50	5.00	10.00
44037	Mr. Unreliable/Georgia	1967	2.50	5.00	10.00
44191	It Could Be We're in Love/I Was Lonely When	1967	2.50	5.00	10.00
44191 [PS]	It Could Be We're in Love/I Was Lonely When	1967	5.00	10.00	20.00
44457	Up On the Roof/The Sailing Ship	1968	2.50	5.00	10.00
44545	Young Birds Fly/Sunshine Psalm	1968	2.00	4.00	8.00
44638	Greenburg, Blickstein, Charles, David Smith & Jones/The Warm	1968	2.00	4.00	8.00
44759	First Train to California/A Master's Fool	1969	2.00	4.00	8.00
45027	Rainmaker/Bits and Pieces	1969	2.00	4.00	8.00
DESTINATION					
624	Sugar and Spice/Ben Franklin's Almanac	1966	3.75	7.50	15.00

Albums

Number	Title (A Side/B Side)	Yr	VG	VG+	NM
COLUMBIA					
CL 2589 [M]	Sugar & Spice	1967	5.00	10.00	20.00
CL 2786 [M]	A Scratch in the Sky	1967	6.25	12.50	25.00
CS 9389 [S]	Sugar & Spice	1967	6.25	12.50	25.00
CS 9586 [S]	A Scratch in the Sky	1967	5.00	10.00	20.00
CS 9719	Synthesis	1969	5.00	10.00	20.00

CRYIN' SHAMES, THE

Not the same group as THE CRYAN' SHAMES.

45s

Number	Title (A Side/B Side)	Yr	VG	VG+	NM
LONDON					
1001	What's New Pussycat/Please Stay (Don't Go)	1966	2.50	5.00	10.00

CRYSTALS, THE (1)

Well-known girl group.

45s

Number	Title (A Side/B Side)	Yr	VG	VG+	NM
GUSTO					
2090	Da Doo Ron Ron/Then He Kissed Me	1979	—	2.00	4.00
—Re-recordings					
MICHELLE					
4113	Ring-a-Ting-a-Ling/Should I Keep On Waiting	1967	2.50	5.00	10.00
PAVILLION					
03333	Rudolph the Red-Nosed Reindeer/I Saw Mommy Kissing Santa Claus	1982	—	2.50	5.00
—B-side by The Ronettes					
PHILLES					
100	There's No Other (Like My Baby)/Oh Yeah, Maybe Baby	1961	10.00	20.00	40.00
102	Uptown/What a Nice Way to Turn Seventeen	1962	10.00	20.00	40.00
105	He Hit Me (And It Felt Like a Kiss)/No One Ever Tells You	1962	25.00	50.00	100.00
106	He's a Rebel/I Love You Eddie	1962	15.00	30.00	60.00
—Orange label					
106	He's a Rebel/I Love You Eddie	1962	10.00	20.00	40.00
—Light blue label					
106	He's a Rebel/I Love You Eddie	1964	6.25	12.50	25.00
—Yellow and red label					
109	He's Sure the Boy I Love/Walkin' Along (La-La-La)	1962	7.50	15.00	30.00
111 [DJ]	(Let's Dance) The Screw — Part 1/(Let's Dance) The Screw — Part 2	1963	2000.	3000.	4000.
—White label					
111 [DJ]	(Let's Dance) The Screw — Part 1/(Let's Dance) The Screw — Part 2	1963	3000.	4500.	6000.
—Light blue label. Matrix numbers are stamped in dead wax. Counterfeits have numbers hand-etched.					
112	Da Do Ron Ron (When He Walked Me Home)/Git' It	1963	7.50	15.00	30.00
115	Then He Kissed Me/Brother Julius	1963	10.00	20.00	40.00
—Light blue label					
115	Then He Kissed Me/Brother Julius	1963	6.25	12.50	25.00
—Yellow and red label					
119X	Little Boy/Harry (From West Virginia) and Milt	1964	5.00	10.00	20.00
119	Little Boy/Harry (From West Virginia) and Milt	1964	6.25	12.50	25.00
122	All Grown Up/Irving (Jaggered Sixteenths)	1964	6.25	12.50	25.00
—Possible Rolling Stones involvement on instrumental B-side; "Jaggered" refers to Mick					
PHILLES/COLLECTABLES					
3200	He's a Rebel/He Hit Me (And It Felt Like a Kiss)	1985	—	3.00	6.00
—Red vinyl; part of box set "Phil Spector Wall of Sound Series Vol. 2"					
3200	He's a Rebel/He Hit Me (And It Felt Like a Kiss)	1986	—	2.50	5.00
—Black vinyl					
3201	Then He Kissed Me/Puddin' and Tain	1985	—	3.00	6.00
—Red vinyl; part of box set "Phil Spector Wall of Sound Series Vol. 2"; B-side by the Alley Cats					
3201	Then He Kissed Me/Puddin' and Tain	1986	—	2.50	5.00
—Black vinyl					
3202	Uptown/He's Sure the Boy I Love	1985	—	3.00	6.00
—Red vinyl; part of box set "Phil Spector Wall of Sound Series Vol. 2"					
3202	Uptown/He's Sure the Boy I Love	1986	—	2.50	5.00
—Black vinyl					
3204	There's No Other (Like My Baby)/Not Too Young to Get Married	1985	—	3.00	6.00
—Gold vinyl; part of box set "Phil Spector Wall of Sound Series Vol. 1"; B-side by Bob B. Soxx and the Blue Jeans					
3204	There's No Other (Like My Baby)/Not Too Young to Get Married	1986	—	2.50	5.00
—Black vinyl; B-side by Bob B. Soxx and the Blue Jeans					
3206	Da Doo Ron Ron/All Grown Up	1985	—	3.00	6.00
—Gold vinyl; part of box set "Phil Spector Wall of Sound Series Vol. 1"					
3206	Da Doo Ron Ron/All Grown Up	1986	—	2.50	5.00
—Black vinyl					
UNITED ARTISTS					
927	You Can't Tie a Good Girl Down/My Place	1965	3.75	7.50	15.00
994	I Got a Man/Are You Trying to Get Rid of Me, Baby	1966	3.75	7.50	15.00

Albums

Number	Title (A Side/B Side)	Yr	VG	VG+	NM
PHILLES					
PHLP-4000 [M]	Twist Uptown	1962	150.00	300.00	600.00
PHLP-4001 [M]	He's a Rebel	1963	150.00	300.00	600.00
PHLP-4003 [M]	The Crystals Sing the Greatest Hits, Vol. 1	1963	150.00	300.00	600.00
DT-90722 [R]	Twist Uptown	1965	300.00	600.00	1200.
—Capitol Record Club edition					
T-90722 [M]	Twist Uptown	1965	150.00	300.00	600.00
—Capitol Record Club edition					

CRYSTALS, THE (2)

45s

Number	Title (A Side/B Side)	Yr	VG	VG+	NM
ALADDIN					
3355	I Love My Baby/I Do Believe	1957	15.00	30.00	60.00

CRYSTALS, THE (3)

45s

Number	Title (A Side/B Side)	Yr	VG	VG+	NM
BRENT					
7011	Malaguena/Gypsy Ribbon	1960	3.75	7.50	15.00
CUB					
9064	Oh My You/Watching You	1960	3.75	7.50	15.00
INDIGO					
114	Dreams and Wishes/Mr. Brush	1961	5.00	10.00	20.00
METRO					
20026	Better Come Back to Me/That's Where I Belong	1960	3.75	7.50	15.00
REGALIA					
17	Pony in Dixie/Espresso	1961	3.75	7.50	15.00

CRYSTALS, THE (4)

45s

Number	Title (A Side/B Side)	Yr	VG	VG+	NM
DELUXE					
6013	Four Women/My Dear	1953	500.00	1000.	2000.
6037	Have Faith in Me/My Love	1954	500.00	1000.	2000.
6077	God Only Knows/My Girl	1955	50.00	100.00	200.00
LUNA					
100	Squeeze Me Baby/Come to Me, Darling	1954	100.00	200.00	400.00
5001	Squeeze Me Baby/Come to Me, Darling	1954	50.00	100.00	200.00
ROCKIN'					
518	My Girl/Don't You Go	1953	62.50	125.00	250.00

CRYSTALS, THE (5)

45s

Number	Title (A Side/B Side)	Yr	VG	VG+	NM
FELSTED					
8566	Mary Ellen/Blind Date	1959	5.00	10.00	20.00
MERCURY					
71381	Vampire/Tropical Illusion	1958	3.75	7.50	15.00
SPECIALTY					
657	In the Deep/Love You So	1959	3.75	7.50	15.00

CUBY AND THE BLIZZARDS

45s

Number	Title (A Side/B Side)	Yr	VG	VG+	NM
PHILIPS					
40685	Thursday Night/Going Home	1970	2.00	4.00	8.00

Albums

Number	Title (A Side/B Side)	Yr	VG	VG+	NM
PHILIPS					
PHS 600307	Cuby and the Blizzards Live	1969	5.00	10.00	20.00
PHS 600331	King of the World	1970	5.00	10.00	20.00

CUES, THE

45s

Number	Title (A Side/B Side)	Yr	VG	VG+	NM
CAPITOL					
F3245	Burn That Candle/Oh My Darling	1955	5.00	10.00	20.00
F3310	Charlie Brown/You're On My Mind	1956	5.00	10.00	20.00
F3400	Destination 2100 and 65/Don't Make Believe	1956	5.00	10.00	20.00
F3483	The Girl I Love/Crackerjack	1956	5.00	10.00	20.00
F3582	Why/Prince or Pauper	1956	5.00	10.00	20.00
JUBILEE					
5201	Only You/I Feel for Your Loving	1955	5.00	10.00	20.00
LAMP					
8007	Forty 'Leven Dozen Ways/Scoochie Scoochie	1954	5.00	10.00	20.00
PREP					
104	I Pretend/Crazy, Crazy Party	1957	5.00	10.00	20.00

CUFF LINKS, THE (1)

Studio band with RON DANTE as lead singer.

45s

Number	Title (A Side/B Side)	Yr	VG	VG+	NM
ATCO					
6867	Sandi/The Oke-Fen-Okee Electric Harmonica Band	1972	—	2.50	5.00
DECCA					
32533	Tracy/Where Do You Go	1969	—	3.00	6.00

Number	Title (A Side/B Side)	Yr	VG	VG+	NM
32592	When Julie Comes Around/Sally Ann	1969	—	2.50	5.00
32639	Run, Sally, Run/I Remember	1970	—	2.50	5.00
32687	Lay a Little Love on Me/Robin's World	1970	—	2.50	5.00
32732	Thank You Pretty Baby/Kiss	1970	—	2.50	5.00
32791	All Because of You/Wake Up Judy	1971	—	2.50	5.00
Albums					
DECCA					
DL 75160	Tracy	1969	5.00	10.00	20.00
DL 75235	The Cuff Links	1970	5.00	10.00	20.00

CUFF LINKS, THE (2)

Black vocal group.

Number	Title (A Side/B Side)	Yr	VG	VG+	NM
45s					
DOOTO					
409	Guided Missiles/My Heart	1957	20.00	40.00	80.00
413	How You Lied/The Winner	1957	10.00	20.00	40.00
414	Twinkle/One Day Blues	1957	10.00	20.00	40.00
422	It's Too Late Now/Saxophone Rag	1957	12.50	25.00	50.00
474	Changing My Love/I Don't Want Nobody	1963	6.25	12.50	25.00
DOOTONE					
409	Guided Missiles/My Heart	1956	50.00	100.00	200.00

CULLEY, FRANK "FLOORSHOW"

Number	Title (A Side/B Side)	Yr	VG	VG+	NM
45s					
BATON					
226	After Hours Express/(B-side unknown)	1956	10.00	20.00	40.00
Albums					
BATON					
BL 1201 [M]	Rock 'n Roll: Instrumentals for Dancing the Lindy Hop	1955	150.00	300.00	600.00
—B-side tracks by Buddy Tate Orchestra					

CULMER, LITTLE IRIS, AND THE MAJESTICS

Also see THE MAJESTICS.

Number	Title (A Side/B Side)	Yr	VG	VG+	NM
45s					
MARLIN					
803	Frankie, My Eyes Are On You/(B-side unknown)	1957	1000.	1500.	2500.

CUNNINGHAM, BUDDY

Number	Title (A Side/B Side)	Yr	VG	VG+	NM
45s					
SUN					
208	Right or Wrong/Why Do I Care	1954	500.00	1000.	1500.

CUPIDS, THE (1)

Number	Title (A Side/B Side)	Yr	VG	VG+	NM
45s					
AANKO					
1002	Brenda/For You	1963	25.00	50.00	100.00
KC					
115	Brenda/For You	1963	12.50	25.00	50.00

CUPIDS, THE (2)

Number	Title (A Side/B Side)	Yr	VG	VG+	NM
45s					
ALADDIN					
3404	Now You Tell Me/Lillie Mae	1957	15.00	30.00	60.00
—Maroon label					
3404	Now You Tell Me/Lillie Mae	1958	6.25	12.50	25.00
—Black label					

CUPIDS, THE (3)

Number	Title (A Side/B Side)	Yr	VG	VG+	NM
45s					
DECCA					
30279	The Answer to Your Prayer/My Dog Likes Your Dog	1957	10.00	20.00	40.00

CUPIDS, THE (U)

Some of these may be groups (1), (2) or (3), but more likely they aren't. It's also likely they aren't all the same.

Number	Title (A Side/B Side)	Yr	VG	VG+	NM
45s					
CHAN					
107	I Don't Know/Troubles Not At End	1956	20.00	40.00	80.00
MUSICNOTE					
119	Lorraine/Little Girl of Mine	1963	3.75	7.50	15.00
TIMES SQUARE					
1	Pretty Baby/Let's Rock	1964	3.75	7.50	15.00
UWR					
4241/2	True Love, True Love/Let's Twist	1962	10.00	20.00	40.00

CURB, MIKE

Includes the Mike Curb Congregation.

Number	Title (A Side/B Side)	Yr	VG	VG+	NM
45s					
BUENA VISTA					
492	Robin Hood March/Oo-De-Lally	1973	—	2.50	5.00
494	Winnie the Pooh/Zip-a-Dee-Doo-Dah	1973	—	2.50	5.00
499	Mickey Mouse March/Mickey Mouse Alma Mater	1974	—	2.50	5.00
—B-side by Jimmy Dodd and the Mouseketeers					
CAPITOL					
4054	Po'r Folk/You Were On My Mind	1975	—	2.00	4.00
4102	Mickey Mouse March/You Were On My Mind	1975	—	2.00	4.00
4166	Fools Rush In (Where Angels Fear to Tread)/Do You Wanna Dance	1975	—	2.00	4.00
FORWARD					
214	Bandstand Theme/(B-side unknown)	1970	—	2.50	5.00
MGM					
14110	Long Haired Lover from Liverpool/Sweet Gingerbread Man	1970	—	2.00	4.00
14151	Burning Bridges/We'll Sing in the Sunshine	1970	—	2.00	4.00
14243	I Was Born in Love with You/Sweet Gingerbread Man	1971	—	2.00	4.00
14265	Sweet Gingerbread Man/Fly Me a Place for the Summer	1971	—	2.00	4.00
14336	Softly Whispering I Love You/Forty Days and Forty Nights	1971	—	2.00	4.00
14366	I Saw the Light/Take Up the Hammer of Hope	1972	—	2.00	4.00
14391	The Very Same Time Next Year/See You in September	1972	—	2.00	4.00
14442	This Land Is Your Land/I Understand	1972	—	2.00	4.00
14494	It's a Small, Small World/Shinin' on Me	1973	—	2.00	4.00
REPRISE					
0287	Hot Dawg/Velocita	1964	5.00	10.00	20.00
SMASH					
1938	The Rebel (Without a Cause)/Carole's Rebel	1964	3.00	6.00	12.00
TOWER					
202	Sunshine/Suzie Darling	1966	2.50	5.00	10.00
480	Let's Go/Eight Young Me (The Devil's Theme)	1969	2.00	4.00	8.00
WARNER BROS.					
8463	Cotton Fields/Dance On, Maria	1977	—	2.00	4.00
Albums					
COBURT					
CO 1002	Come Together	1970	2.50	5.00	10.00
CO 1003	Sweet Gingerbread Man	1970	2.50	5.00	10.00
MGM					
SE-4761	Burning Bridges and Other Great Motion Picture Themes	1971	2.50	5.00	10.00
SE-4785	Put Your Hand in the Hand	1971	2.50	5.00	10.00
SE-4804	The Mike Curb Congregation Sing Their Hits from the Glen Campbell Show	1971	2.50	5.00	10.00
SE-4821	Softly Whispering I Love You	1972	2.50	5.00	10.00
SE-4844	Song for a Young Love	1972	2.50	5.00	10.00
WARNER BROS.					
BS 3129	The Mike Curb Congregation	1977	2.50	5.00	10.00

CURLEY AND THE JADES

Number	Title (A Side/B Side)	Yr	VG	VG+	NM
45s					
MUSIC MAKERS					
109	Bullfighter/Boom Stix	1962	15.00	30.00	60.00
REPRISE					
20046	Bullfighter/Boom Stix	1962	7.50	15.00	30.00

CURRENTS, THE

Number	Title (A Side/B Side)	Yr	VG	VG+	NM
45s					
LAURIE					
3205	Night Run/Riff Raff	1963	7.50	15.00	30.00

CURTIS, MAC

Number	Title (A Side/B Side)	Yr	VG	VG+	NM
45s					
DOT					
16315	You're the One/Dance Her By Me (One More Time)	1962	2.50	5.00	10.00
EPIC					
10257	Too Close to Home/Too Good to Be True	1967	—	3.00	6.00
10324	The Quiet Kind/Love's Been Good to Me	1968	—	2.50	5.00
10385	The Sunshine Man/It's My Way	1968	—	2.50	5.00
10438	Almost Persuaded/The Friendly City	1969	—	2.50	5.00
10468	Happiness Lives in This House/Little Ole Wine Drinker Me	1969	—	2.50	5.00
10530	Don't Make Love/Us	1969	—	2.50	5.00
10574	Honey Don't/Today's Teardrops	1970	—	2.50	5.00
FELSTED					
8592	Come Back Baby/No, Never Alone	1959	5.00	10.00	20.00
GRT					
26	Early in the Morning/When the Hurt Moves In	1970	—	2.00	4.00
41	Gulf Stream Line/I'd Run a Mile	1971	—	2.00	4.00
KING					
4927	If I Had Me a Woman/Just So You Call Me	1956	37.50	75.00	150.00
4949	Grandaddy's Rockin'/Half Hearted Love	1956	37.50	75.00	150.00
4965	You Ain't Treatin' Me Right/The Low Road	1956	37.50	75.00	150.00
4995	That Ain't Nothin' But Right/Don't You Love Me	1956	37.50	75.00	150.00
5007	What You Want/To Protect the Innocent	1957	25.00	50.00	100.00
5059	Say So/I'll Be Gentle	1957	10.00	20.00	40.00
5107	What You Want/You Are My Special Baby	1958	15.00	30.00	60.00
5121	Missy Ann/Little Miss Linda	1958	15.00	30.00	60.00
TOWER					
319	Ties That Bind/Stepping Out on You	1967	—	3.00	6.00
Albums					
EPIC					
BN 26419	The Sunshine Man	1969	5.00	10.00	20.00
HMG/HIGHTONE					
HT 6601	Rockabilly Uprising: The Best of Mac Curtis	1997	2.50	5.00	10.00
ROLLIN' ROCK					
LP-002	Ruffabilly	197?	2.50	5.00	10.00
LP-007	Good Rockin' Tomorrow	197?	2.50	5.00	10.00

CURTIS, SONNY

Also see THE CRICKETS.

Number	Title (A Side/B Side)	Yr	VG	VG+	NM
45s					
'STEEM					
110185	Now I've Got a Heart of Gold/(B-side unknown)	1985	—	2.00	4.00
A&M					
1359	Lights of L.A./Sunny Mornin'	1972	7.50	15.00	30.00
1408	Love Is All Around/Last Days of Childhood	1973	—	—	—
—Unreleased?					
CAPITOL					
4158	Lovesick Blues/It's Only a Question of Time	1975	3.00	6.00	12.00
4227	It's Only a Question of Time/When It's Just You and Me	1976	3.00	6.00	12.00
4240	Where's Patricia Now/When It's Just You and Me	1976	3.00	6.00	12.00
CORAL					
60954	Someday You're Gonna Be Sorry/Forever Yours	1953	6.25	12.50	25.00
61023	No More Tears/The Best Way to Hold a Girl	1953	6.25	12.50	25.00
62207	Red Headed Stranger/Talk About My Baby	1960	10.00	20.00	40.00

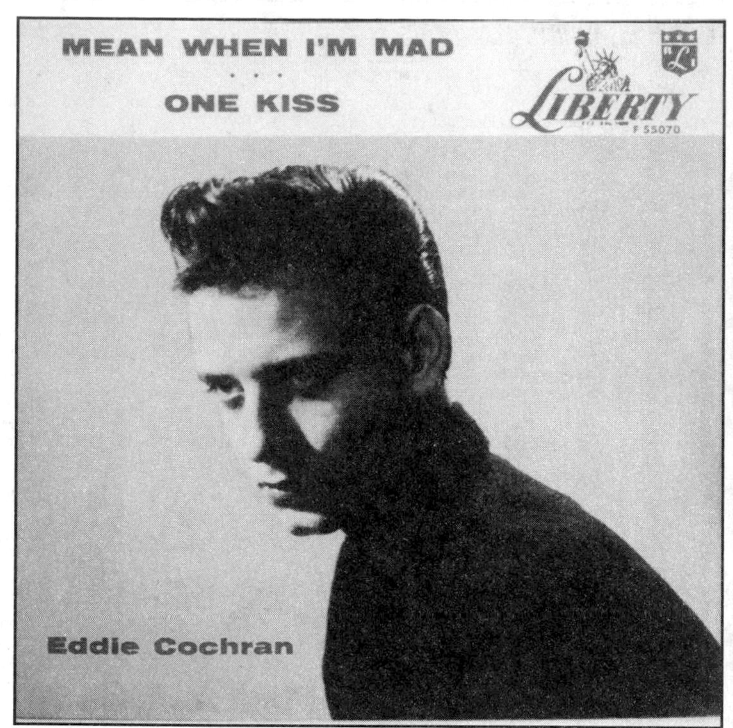

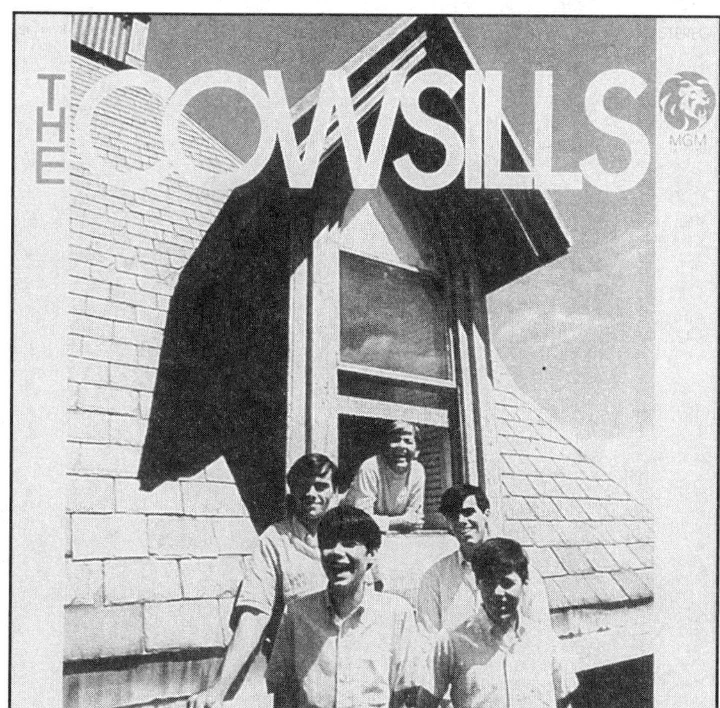

(Top left) Only one record issued by Eddie Cochran while he was alive had a picture sleeve. "Mean When I'm Mad" is one of the world's most sought-after covers. (Top right) The best American imitation of the Yardbirds was the classic "Psychotic Reaction" by Count Five. This is the first pressing of the 45 with the Double-Shot record logo at the top. (Bottom left) The Cowsills were the real-life basis for the Partridge Family. Whereas the Partridges' records have gone from junk-store staples to collectibles over the past decade or so, the Cowsills' own records have not kept pace. (Bottom right) One of the rarest of picture sleeves is for one of the most popular of songs. For some reason, The Cyrkle's "Red Rubber Ball" sleeve is almost impossible to find, and it's worth at least $400 in near-mint condition. A sleeve by the Beatles with comparable rarity would fetch in the thousands.

Number	Title (A Side/B Side)	Yr	VG	VG+	NM
DIMENSION					
1017	So Used to Loving You/The Last Song I'm Ever Gonna Sing	1963	5.00	10.00	20.00
1024	A Beatle I Want to Be/So Used to Loving You	1964	6.25	12.50	25.00
DOT					
15754	Wrong Again/Laughing Stock	1958	10.00	20.00	40.00
15799	A Pretty Girl/Willa May Jones	1958	7.50	15.00	30.00
ELEKTRA					
46526	The Cowboy Singer/Cheatin' Clouds	1979	—	2.50	5.00
46568	Do You Remember Roll Over Beethoven/Walk Right Back	1979	—	2.50	5.00
46616	The Real Buddy Holly Story/Ain't Nobody Honest	1980	—	3.00	6.00
46643	Love Is All Around/The Clone Song	1980	—	2.50	5.00
47048	You Made My Life a Song/50 Ways to Leave Your Lover	1980	—	2.50	5.00
47129	Good Ol' Girls/So Used to Loving You	1981	—	2.50	5.00
47176	Married Woman/I Live Your Music	1981	—	2.50	5.00
47231 [DJ]	The Christmas Song/Little Drummer Boy	1981	2.00	4.00	8.00
—B-side by Hank Williams, Jr.					
69942	Together Alone/Dream Well All of You Children	1982	—	2.50	5.00
LIBERTY					
55710	Bo Diddley Bach/I Pledge My Love to You	1964	5.00	10.00	20.00
MERCURY					
73438	Rock and Rol (I Gave You the Best Years of My Life)/My Mama Sure Left Me Some Good Old Days	1973	3.75	7.50	15.00
OVATION					
1006	Love Is All Around/Here, There and Everywhere	1970	5.00	10.00	20.00
1023	Unsaintly Judy/You Don't Belong in This Place	1970	3.75	7.50	15.00
VIVA					
602	My Way of Life/Last Call	1966	3.75	7.50	15.00
607	The Collection/Destiny's Child	1966	3.75	7.50	15.00
617	I'm a Gypsy Man/I Wanna Go Bummin' Around	1967	3.75	7.50	15.00
626	Day Drinker/Atlanta, Georgia Stray	1968	3.75	7.50	15.00
630	The Straight Life/How Little Men Care	1968	3.75	7.50	15.00
634	Holiday for Clowns/Day Gig	1969	3.75	7.50	15.00
636	Girl of the North/Hung Up in Your Eyes	1969	3.75	7.50	15.00
Albums					
ELEKTRA					
6E-227	Sonny Curtis	1979	2.50	5.00	10.00
6E-283	Love Is All Around	1980	2.50	5.00	10.00
6E-349	Rollin'	1981	2.50	5.00	10.00
IMPERIAL					
LP-9276 [M]	Beatle Hits Flamenco Style	1964	10.00	20.00	40.00
LP-12276 [S]	Beatle Hits Flamenco Style	1964	12.50	25.00	50.00
VIVA					
V-36012	The First of Sonny Curtis	1968	6.25	12.50	25.00
V-36021	The Sonny Curtis Style	1969	6.25	12.50	25.00

CUSTER AND THE SURVIVORS

Number	Title (A Side/B Side)	Yr	VG	VG+	NM
45s					
ASCOT					
2207	I Saw Her Walking/Flapjacks	1965	4.00	8.00	16.00
GOLDEN STATE					
1657	I Saw Her Walking/Flapjacks	1965	3.00	6.00	12.00
VARDAN					
202	I Saw Her Walking/Flapjacks	1965	5.00	10.00	20.00

CUTE-TEENS, THE

Number	Title (A Side/B Side)	Yr	VG	VG+	NM
45s					
ALADDIN					
3458	When My Teenage Days Are Over/From This Day Forward	1959	62.50	125.00	250.00

CYCLONE III

Number	Title (A Side/B Side)	Yr	VG	VG+	NM
45s					
PHILIPS					
40258	You've Got a Bomb/Surfnanny	1965	10.00	20.00	40.00

CYKLE, THE

Number	Title (A Side/B Side)	Yr	VG	VG+	NM
45s					
LABEL					
101	If You Can/(B-side unknown)	1969	7.50	15.00	30.00
101 [PS]	If You Can/(B-side unknown)	1969	15.00	30.00	60.00
Albums					
LABEL					
9-261	The Cykle	1969	125.00	250.00	500.00

CYMANDE

Number	Title (A Side/B Side)	Yr	VG	VG+	NM
45s					
JANUS					
203	The Message/Zion I	1972	—	2.50	5.00
215	Bra/Ras Tafarian Folk Song	1973	—	2.50	5.00
225	Anthracite/Fug	1973	—	2.50	5.00
Albums					
JANUS					
3044	Cymande	1972	2.50	5.00	10.00
3054	Second Time Round	1973	2.50	5.00	10.00

CYMARRON

Number	Title (A Side/B Side)	Yr	VG	VG+	NM
45s					
ENTRANCE					
7500	Rings/Like Children	1971	—	2.50	5.00
7502	Valerie/Across the Kansas Sky	1971	—	2.00	4.00
7506	Right Can Be Wrong/What's a Little Dirt	1972	—	2.00	4.00
7514	Keep Me Warm/Start Again	1972	—	2.00	4.00
Albums					
ENTRANCE					
Z 30962	Rings	1971	3.00	6.00	12.00

CYMBAL, JOHNNY

Includes releases as "Derek" on the Bang label. Also see CYMBAL AND CLINGER.

Number	Title (A Side/B Side)	Yr	VG	VG+	NM
45s					
AMARET					
110	Big River/Girl from Willow County	1969	2.00	4.00	8.00
111	Ode to Bubblegum/Save All Your Lovin' (Hold It for Me)	1969	2.00	4.00	8.00
BANG					
558	Cinnamon/This Is My Story	1968	2.00	4.00	8.00
566	Back Door Man/Tell Your Soul	1969	—	3.00	6.00
571	Inside Out-Outside In/Sell Your Soul	1969	—	3.00	6.00
COLUMBIA					
43842	Good Morning Blues/Jessica	1966	2.00	4.00	8.00
DCP					
1135	Go, VW, Go/Sorrow and Pain	1965	7.50	15.00	30.00
1146	My Last Day/Summertime's Here at Last	1965	3.75	7.50	15.00
KAPP					
503	Mr. Bass Man/Sacred Lovers' Vow	1963	5.00	10.00	20.00
524	Teenage Heaven/Cinderella Baby	1963	3.75	7.50	15.00
539	Surfin' at Tiajuana/Dum Dum Dee Dum	1963	3.75	7.50	15.00
556	Marshmallow/Hurdy Gurdy Man	1963	3.75	7.50	15.00
576	There Goes a Bad Girl/Refreshment Time	1964	3.75	7.50	15.00
594	Robinson Crusoe on Mars/Mitsu	1964	3.75	7.50	15.00
614	Connie/Little Miss Lonely	1964	3.75	7.50	15.00
634	Cheat, Cheat/16 Shades of Blue	1964	3.75	7.50	15.00
KEDLEN					
2001	Bachelor Man/Growing Up with You	1962	5.00	10.00	20.00
MGM					
12935	It'll Be Me/Always, Always	1960	5.00	10.00	20.00
12978	The Water Was Red/The Bunny	1961	5.00	10.00	20.00
MUSICOR					
1261	It Looks Like Love/May I Get to Know You	1967	3.00	6.00	12.00
1272	Breaking Your Balloon/The Marriage of Charlotte Brown	1967	3.00	6.00	12.00
VEE JAY					
495	Bachelor Man/Growing Up with You	1963	3.75	7.50	15.00
Albums					
KAPP					
KL-1324 [M]	Mr. Bass Man	1963	12.50	25.00	50.00
KS-3324 [S]	Mr. Bass Man	1963	17.50	35.00	70.00

CYMBAL & CLINGER

Also see JOHNNY CYMBAL.

Number	Title (A Side/B Side)	Yr	VG	VG+	NM
45s					
CHELSEA					
78-0106	God Bless You Rock & Roll/Forever and Forever	1972	—	2.50	5.00
78-0112	Dying River/Little Bit No, Little Bit Yes	1973	—	2.50	5.00
MARINA					
502	Pool Shooter/Mookie Mookie Man	1971	—	3.00	6.00
MGM					
14256	Pool Shooter/Mookie Mookie Man	1971	—	2.50	5.00
Albums					
CHELSEA					
1002	Cymbal & Clinger	1972	3.00	6.00	12.00

CYPRESS, BUDDY

Number	Title (A Side/B Side)	Yr	VG	VG+	NM
45s					
FLASH					
118	I'm in Love with You/Don't Forsake Me	1957	12.50	25.00	50.00

CYRKLE, THE

Number	Title (A Side/B Side)	Yr	VG	VG+	NM
45s					
COLUMBIA					
CSM-466	Camaro/SS 396	1967	6.25	12.50	25.00
—B-side by Paul Revere and the Raiders					
CSM-466 [PS]	Camaro/SS 396	1967	12.50	25.00	50.00
—B-side by Paul Revere and the Raiders					
43589	Red Rubber Ball/How Can I Leave Her	1966	3.00	6.00	12.00
43589 [DJ]	Red Rubber Ball (same on both sides)	1966	10.00	20.00	40.00
—Promo only on red vinyl					
43589 [PS]	Red Rubber Ball/How Can I Leave Her	1966	100.00	200.00	400.00
43729	Turn-Down Day/Big, Little Woman	1966	2.50	5.00	10.00
43729 [PS]	Turn-Down Day/Big, Little Woman	1966	3.75	7.50	15.00
43871	Please Don't Ever Leave Me/Money to Burn	1966	2.00	4.00	8.00
43965	I Wish You Could Be Here/The Visit (She Was Here)	1967	2.00	4.00	8.00
43965 [PS]	I Wish You Could Be Here/The Visit (She Was Here)	1967	3.00	6.00	12.00
44108	We Had a Good Thing Goin'/Two Rooms	1967	2.00	4.00	8.00
44224	Penny Arcade/The Words	1967	2.00	4.00	8.00
44366	Turn of the Century/Don't Cry, No Fears, No Tears Comin'	1967	2.00	4.00	8.00
44426	Friends/Reading Her Papers	1968	2.00	4.00	8.00
44491	Red Chair Fade Away/Where Are You Going	1968	2.00	4.00	8.00
Albums					
COLUMBIA					
CL 2544 [M]	Red Rubber Ball	1966	5.00	10.00	20.00
CL 2632 [M]	Neon	1967	3.75	7.50	15.00
CS 9344 [S]	Red Rubber Ball	1966	7.50	15.00	30.00
CS 9432 [S]	Neon	1967	5.00	10.00	20.00

CYRUS ERIE

Early ERIC CARMEN.

Number	Title (A Side/B Side)	Yr	VG	VG+	NM
45s					
EPIC					
10451	Sparrow/Get the Message	1969	3.00	6.00	12.00

D

D'ABO, MIKE

Lead singer of MANFRED MANN in the "Mighty Quinn" era.

45s

Number	Title (A Side/B Side)	Yr	VG	VG+	NM
A&M					
1374	Little Miss Understood/Belinda	1972	—	2.50	5.00
1628	Fuel to Burn/Hold On Sweet Darling	1974	—	2.00	4.00
BELL					
956	Miss Me in the Morning/Arabella Cinderella	1971	—	3.00	6.00

Albums

Number	Title (A Side/B Side)	Yr	VG	VG+	NM
A&M					
SP-3634	Broken Rainbows	1974	3.00	6.00	12.00
SP-4346	Down at Rachel's Place	1972	3.00	6.00	12.00

D-MEN, THE

Early incarnation of THE FIFTH ESTATE.

45s

Number	Title (A Side/B Side)	Yr	VG	VG+	NM
KAPP					
691	So Little Time/Every Moment of Every Day	1965	3.00	6.00	12.00
VEEP					
1206	Don't You Know/No Hope for Me	1965	3.75	7.50	15.00
1209	Just Don't Care/Mousin' Around	1965	3.75	7.50	15.00

DA-PREES, THE

45s

Number	Title (A Side/B Side)	Yr	VG	VG+	NM
TWIST					
70913	Pay Day/Sometimes	1963	37.50	75.00	150.00

DACHE, BERTELL

TONY ORLANDO with CAROLE KING on backing vocals.

45s

Number	Title (A Side/B Side)	Yr	VG	VG+	NM
DIAMOND					
201	Don't Stop the World for Me/Anchors Awaeigh Girl	1966	3.75	7.50	15.00
UNITED ARTISTS					
260	All the World Loves a Lover/You Gotta Have Chicks	1960	6.25	12.50	25.00
290	Not Just Tomorrow, But Today/Love Eyes	1961	6.25	12.50	25.00

DADDY COOL

45s

Number	Title (A Side/B Side)	Yr	VG	VG+	NM
REPRISE					
1038	Eagle Rock/Bom Bom	1971	—	3.00	6.00
1064	Hi Honey Ho/Come Back Again	1972	—	3.00	6.00
1087	Teenage Blues/Donna Forgive Me	1972	—	3.00	6.00
1090	I'll Never Smile Again/Daddy Rocks Off	1972	—	3.00	6.00

Albums

Number	Title (A Side/B Side)	Yr	VG	VG+	NM
REPRISE					
MS 2088	Teenage Heaven	1972	5.00	10.00	20.00
RS 6471	Daddy Who? Daddy Cool!	1971	3.75	7.50	15.00

DADDY DEWDROP

45s

Number	Title (A Side/B Side)	Yr	VG	VG+	NM
CAPITOL					
4066	Dynamite Dyna/Goddaughter	1975	—	2.00	4.00
INPHASION					
7201	Nanu, Nanu (I Wanna Funky with You)/The Real Thing	1978	—	2.00	4.00
7203	The Real Thing/(Instrumental)	1978	—	2.00	4.00
7206	If You Wanna Wanna/(B-side unknown)	1979	—	2.00	4.00
SUNFLOWER					
105	Chick-a-Boom (Don't Ya Jes' Love It)/John Jacob Jingleheimer Smith	1971	—	2.50	5.00
111	Fox Huntin' (On a Weekend)/March of the White Corpuscles	1971	—	2.00	4.00
119	Chantilly Lace/Migraine Headaches	1972	—	2.00	4.00

Albums

Number	Title (A Side/B Side)	Yr	VG	VG+	NM
SUNFLOWER					
SNF-5006	Daddy Dewdrop	1971	5.00	10.00	20.00

DAILEY, DON

Albums

Number	Title (A Side/B Side)	Yr	VG	VG+	NM
CROWN					
CST-314 [R]	Surf Stompin'	1963	3.75	7.50	15.00
CLP-5314 [M]	Surf Stompin'	1963	7.50	15.00	30.00

DAILY FLASH, THE

45s

Number	Title (A Side/B Side)	Yr	VG	VG+	NM
PARROT					
308	Jack of Diamonds/Queen Jane Approximately	1966	3.00	6.00	12.00
UNI					
55001	French Girl/Green Rocky Road	1967	3.00	6.00	12.00

DAISIES, THE

45s

Number	Title (A Side/B Side)	Yr	VG	VG+	NM
CAPITOL					
5667	Cold Wave/Put Your Arms Around Me	1966	6.25	12.50	25.00
ROULETTE					
4571	I Wanna Swim with Him/You Just Said You Loved Me	1964	3.00	6.00	12.00

DAKIL, FLOYD

45s

Number	Title (A Side/B Side)	Yr	VG	VG+	NM
EARTH					
402	Bad Boy/Stoppin' Traffic	1965	10.00	20.00	40.00
403	Kitty Kitty/It Takes a Lot to Hurt	1965	7.50	15.00	30.00
404	Stronger Than Dirt/You're the Kind of Girl	1965	7.50	15.00	30.00
GUYDEN					
2111	Dance, Franny, Dance/Look What You've Gone and Done	1964	7.50	15.00	30.00
JETSTAR					
103	Dance, Franny, Dance/Look What You've Gone and Done	1964	25.00	50.00	100.00
POMPEII					
66687	Merry Christmas, Baby/One Girl	1968	6.25	12.50	25.00

DAKOTAS, THE

Also see BILLY J. KRAMER AND THE DAKOTAS.

45s

Number	Title (A Side/B Side)	Yr	VG	VG+	NM
LIBERTY					
55618	The Cruel Surf/The Millionaire	1963	10.00	20.00	40.00

DALE, DICK, AND THE DEL-TONES

45s

Number	Title (A Side/B Side)	Yr	VG	VG+	NM
ACCENT					
1243	Eyes of a Child/Just a-Waitin'	1968	2.00	4.00	8.00
CAPITOL					
4963	King of the Surf Guitar/Havah Nagilah	1963	5.00	10.00	20.00
4963 [PS]	King of the Surf Guitar/Havah Nagilah	1963	20.00	40.00	80.00
5010	Secret Surfin' Spot/Surfin' and a-Swingin'	1963	5.00	10.00	20.00
5048	Wild Ideas/Scavenger	1963	5.00	10.00	20.00
5098	The Wedge/Night Rider	1963	5.00	10.00	20.00
5140	The Victor/Mr. Eliminator	1964	3.75	7.50	15.00
5187	Wild, Wild Mustang/Grunge Run	1964	3.75	7.50	15.00
5225	Never on Sunday/Glory Wave	1964	3.75	7.50	15.00
5290	Oh Marie/Who Can It Be	1964	3.75	7.50	15.00
5389	Let's Go Trippin' '65/Watusi Jo	1965	3.75	7.50	15.00
COLUMBIA					
07340	Pipeline/Love Struck Baby	1987	—	2.00	4.00
—B-side by Stevie Ray Vaughan					
07340 [PS]	Pipeline/Love Struck Baby	1987	—	3.00	6.00
CONCERT ROOM					
371	We'll Never Hear the End of It/Fairest of Them All	1963	6.25	12.50	25.00
COUGAR					
711	Ramblin' Man/You're Hurtin' Now	1967	3.75	7.50	15.00
712	Taco Wagon/Spanish Kiss	1967	3.75	7.50	15.00
CUPID					
106	We'll Never Hear the End of It/Fairest of Them All	1960	7.50	15.00	30.00
—Black vinyl					
106	We'll Never Hear the End of It/Fairest of Them All	1960	20.00	40.00	80.00
—Gold vinyl					
DELTONE					
4939	Misirlou/Eight Till Midnight	1963	5.00	10.00	20.00
4940	Surf Beat/Peppermint Man	1963	5.00	10.00	20.00
—Deltone 4939 and 4940 were part of the Capitol numbering system					
5012	Oh Whee Marie/Breaking Heart	1959	15.00	30.00	60.00
5013	Stop Teasin'/Without Your Love	1959	15.00	30.00	60.00
5014	Jessie Pearl/St. Louis Blues	1960	25.00	50.00	100.00
5017	Let's Go Trippin'/Del-Tone Rock	1961	7.50	15.00	30.00
5018	Shake and Stomp/Jungle Fever	1962	10.00	20.00	40.00
5019	Misirlou/Eight Till Midnight	1962	6.25	12.50	25.00
5020	Peppermint Man/Surf Beat	1962	6.25	12.50	25.00
5028	Run for Your Life/Lovin' on My Brain	1963	7.50	15.00	30.00
GNP CRESCENDO					
804	Let's Go Trippin'/Those Memories of You	1975	—	3.00	6.00
RENDEZVOUS					
204	Reincarnation (Part 1)/Reincarnation (Part 2)	1963	5.00	10.00	20.00
SATURN					
401	We'll Never Hear the End of It/Fairest of Them All	1963	7.50	15.00	30.00
U.S. ARMY					
1301 [DJ]	The Enlistment Twist/Dream Girl Waltz	1962	7.50	15.00	30.00
—B-side by Craig Adams and His Country Cousins; blue vinyl					
1301 [PS]	The Enlistment Twist/Dream Girl Waltz	1962	7.50	15.00	30.00
YES					
7014	We'll Never Hear the End of It/Fairest of Them All	1963	7.50	15.00	30.00
7014 [PS]	We'll Never Hear the End of It/Fairest of Them All	1963	10.00	20.00	40.00

Albums

Number	Title (A Side/B Side)	Yr	VG	VG+	NM
CAPITOL					
ST 1930 [S]	King of the Surf Guitar	1963	25.00	50.00	100.00
T 1930 [M]	King of the Surf Guitar	1963	15.00	30.00	60.00
ST 2002 [S]	Checkered Flag	1963	20.00	40.00	80.00
T 2002 [M]	Checkered Flag	1963	12.50	25.00	50.00
ST 2053 [S]	Mr. Eliminator	1964	20.00	40.00	80.00
T 2053 [M]	Mr. Eliminator	1964	12.50	25.00	50.00
ST 2111 [S]	Summer Surf	1964	30.00	60.00	120.00
—With bonus single by Jerry Cole, "Racing Waves"/"Movin' Surf," in front cover pocket					
ST 2111 [S]	Summer Surf	1964	17.50	35.00	70.00
—Without bonus single					
T 2111 [M]	Summer Surf	1964	25.00	50.00	100.00
—With bonus single by Jerry Cole, "Racing Waves"/"Movin' Surf," in front cover pocket					
T 2111 [M]	Summer Surf	1964	12.50	25.00	50.00
—Without bonus single					
ST 2293 [S]	Rock Out — Live at Ciro's	1965	37.50	75.00	150.00
T 2293 [M]	Rock Out — Live at Ciro's	1965	25.00	50.00	100.00
CLOISTER					
CLP-6301 [M]	Silver Sounds of the Surf	1963	50.00	100.00	200.00
—With tracks by the Stompers					
DELTONE					
LPM-1001 [M]	Surfer's Choice	1962	37.50	75.00	150.00
DT 1886 [R]	Surfer's Choice	1962	10.00	20.00	40.00
T 1886 [M]	Surfer's Choice	1962	15.00	30.00	60.00
DUB TONE					
LP-1246 [M]	The Surf Family	1964	7.50	15.00	30.00
—With tracks by the Hollywood Surfers					
GNP CRESCENDO					
GNPS-2095	Greatest Hits	1975	3.00	6.00	12.00

Number	Title (A Side/B Side)	Yr	VG	VG+	NM
RHINO					
RNLP-70074	King of the Surf Guitar: The Best of Dick Dale and the Del-Tones, 1961-1964	1986	3.00	6.00	12.00

DALE AND GRACE

45s

Number	Title (A Side/B Side)	Yr	VG	VG+	NM
GUYDEN					
6002	What's Happening to Me/Darling It's Wonderful	1972	—	2.50	5.00
HANNA-BARBERA					
472	Let Them Talk/I'd Rather Be Free	1966	2.00	4.00	8.00
MICHELLE					
921	I'm Leaving It Up to You/That's What I Like	1963	6.25	12.50	25.00
923	Stop and Think It Over/Bad Luck	1963	3.75	7.50	15.00
928	The Loneliest Night/I'm Not Free	1964	3.75	7.50	15.00
930	Darling It's Wonderful/What's Happening to Me	1964	3.75	7.50	15.00
936	Cool Water/Rules of Love	1964	3.75	7.50	15.00
MONTEL					
921	I'm Leaving It Up to You/That's What I Like About You	1963	3.00	6.00	12.00
922	Stop and Think It Over/Bad Luck	1963	3.00	6.00	12.00
928	The Loneliest Night/I'm Not Free	1964	3.00	6.00	12.00
930	Darling It's Wonderful/What's Happening to Me	1964	3.00	6.00	12.00
936	Cool Water/Rules of Love	1964	3.00	6.00	12.00
958	Make the World Go Away/Stranger	1965	3.00	6.00	12.00
989	It Keeps Right On a-Hurtin'/So Fine	1967	3.00	6.00	12.00
MONTEL/MICHELLE					
942	Something Special/What Am I Living For	1964	3.00	6.00	12.00

Albums

Number	Title (A Side/B Side)	Yr	VG	VG+	NM
MICHELLE					
100 [M]	I'm Leaving It Up to You	1964	37.50	75.00	150.00
MONTEL					
100 [M]	I'm Leaving It Up to You	1964	37.50	75.00	150.00

DALEY, JIMMY, AND THE DING-A-LINGS

45s

Number	Title (A Side/B Side)	Yr	VG	VG+	NM
DECCA					
30163	Rock, Pretty Baby/Can I Steal a Little Love	1956	10.00	20.00	40.00
30358	Red Lips and Green Eyes/How's About a Little Kiss?	1957	10.00	20.00	40.00
30532	Hole in the Wall/Bongo Rock	1957	10.00	20.00	40.00

7-Inch Extended Plays

Number	Title (A Side/B Side)	Yr	VG	VG+	NM
DECCA					
ED 2481	Rockabye Lullaby Blues/Teen Age Bop/The Most//(B-side unknown)	195?	12.50	25.00	50.00
ED 2481 [PS]	(title unknown)	195?	12.50	25.00	50.00
ED 2482	Happy Is a Boy Named Me/Hot Rod/Big Band Rock and Roll//(B-side unknown)	195?	12.50	25.00	50.00
ED 2482 [PS]	(title unknown)	195?	12.50	25.00	50.00

DALTON, KATHY

45s

Number	Title (A Side/B Side)	Yr	VG	VG+	NM
DISCREET					
1191	At the Tropicana/Long Gone Charlie Hit & Run	1974	—	2.50	5.00
1210	Boogie Bands and One Night Stands/Pour Your Wine All Over Me	1974	—	2.50	5.00
1313	Midnight Creeper/Justine	1974	—	2.50	5.00

Albums

Number	Title (A Side/B Side)	Yr	VG	VG+	NM
DISCREET					
MS 2168	Amazing	1973	4.50	9.00	18.00
DS 2208	Boogie Bands and One Night Stands	1974	3.00	6.00	12.00

DALTON BOYS, THE

45s

Number	Title (A Side/B Side)	Yr	VG	VG+	NM
SKYLA					
1124	I'm Thinkin'/It's Much More Stronger	1962	7.50	15.00	30.00
TEEN					
505	Who's Gonna Hold Your Hand/Walkin'	1959	12.50	25.00	50.00
V.I.P.					
25025	I've Been Cheated/Something's Bothering You	1965	12.50	25.00	50.00
25025	I've Been Cheated/Take My Hand	1965	50.00	100.00	200.00

DALTREY, ROGER

Also see THE WHO.

45s

Number	Title (A Side/B Side)	Yr	VG	VG+	NM
ATLANTIC					
89419	Under a Raging Moon/The Pride You Hide	1986	—	—	3.00
89457	Quicksilver Lightning/Love Me Like You Do	1986	—	—	3.00
89457 [PS]	Quicksilver Lightning/Love Me Like You Do	1986	—	2.50	5.00
89471	Let Me Down Easy/Fallen Angel	1985	—	—	3.00
89471 [PS]	Let Me Down Easy/Fallen Angel	1985	—	—	3.00
89491	After the Fire/Don't Satisfy Me	1985	—	—	3.00
89491 [PS]	After the Fire/Don't Satisfy Me	1985	—	—	3.00
89667	Parting Would Be Painless/Is There Anyone Out There?	1984	—	—	3.00
89704	Walking in My Sleep/Somebody Told Me	1984	—	—	3.00
89704 [PS]	Walking in My Sleep/Somebody Told Me	1984	—	—	3.00
A&M					
1779	Love's Dream/Orpheus Song	1975	—	2.50	5.00
—With Rick Wakeman					
MCA					
40453	Come and Get Your Love/Heart's Right	1975	—	2.50	5.00
40512	Oceans Away/Feeling	1976	—	2.50	5.00
40761	One of the Boys/Doing It All Again	1977	—	2.50	5.00
40765	Satin and Lace/Say It Ain't So, Joe	1977	—	2.00	4.00
40800	Avenging Annie/The Prisoner	1977	—	2.00	4.00
40862	Leon/The Prisoner	1978	—	2.00	4.00
52051	Martyrs and Madmen/Avenging Annie	1982	—	2.00	4.00
ODE					
66040	I'm Free/Underture	1973	—	2.50	5.00
POLYDOR					
2105	Free Me/McVicar	1980	—	2.00	4.00
2105 [PS]	Free Me/McVicar	1980	—	2.00	4.00
2121	Without Your Love/Escape (Part 1)	1980	—	2.00	4.00
2153	Waiting for a Friend/Bitter and Twisted	1981	—	2.00	4.00
2153 [DJ]	Waiting for a Friend (same on both sides)	1981	—	3.00	6.00
—One label has name misspelled as "Rodger Daltrey"					
15098	See Me, Feel Me-Listening to You/Overture from Tommy	1975	—	2.50	5.00
—B-side by Pete Townshend					
15098 [PS]	See Me, Feel Me-Listening to You/Overture from Tommy	1975	—	2.50	5.00
TRACK					
40053	Giving It All Away/Way of the World	1973	—	3.00	6.00
—B-side by Bryan Daly & the London Festival Orchestra					
40084	Thinking/There Is Love	1973	2.00	4.00	8.00

Albums

Number	Title (A Side/B Side)	Yr	VG	VG+	NM
ATLANTIC					
80128	Parting Should Be Painless	1984	2.50	5.00	10.00
81269	Under a Raging Moon	1985	2.50	5.00	10.00
MCA					
2147	Ride a Rock Horse	1975	3.00	6.00	12.00
2271	One of the Boys	1977	3.00	6.00	12.00
2349	Daltrey	1977	2.50	5.00	10.00
—Reissue of Track 328					
5301	Best Bits	1982	2.50	5.00	10.00
37030	Ride a Rock Horse	1980	2.00	4.00	8.00
—Budget-line reissue					
37031	One of the Boys	1980	2.00	4.00	8.00
—Budget-line reissue					
37032	Daltrey	1980	2.00	4.00	8.00
—Budget-line reissue					
POLYDOR					
PD-1-6284	McVicar	1980	2.50	5.00	10.00
TRACK					
328	Daltrey	1973	3.00	6.00	12.00

DAMIN EIH, A.L.K. AND BROTHER CLARK

Albums

Number	Title (A Side/B Side)	Yr	VG	VG+	NM
DEMELOT					
7310	Never Mind	1973	37.50	75.00	150.00

DAMITA JO

Also see BROOK BENTON AND DAMITA JO.

45s

Number	Title (A Side/B Side)	Yr	VG	VG+	NM
ABC-PARAMOUNT					
9822	How Will I Know/I'll Never Cry	1957	3.75	7.50	15.00
9849	My Heart Is Home/Disillusioned Lovers	1957	3.75	7.50	15.00
10176	How Will I Know/Disillusioned Lovers	1961	2.50	5.00	10.00
EPIC					
9766	Tomorrow Night/Silver Dollar	1965	2.00	4.00	8.00
9797	Gotta Travel On/Something You Got	1965	2.00	4.00	8.00
9821	Nobody Knows You When You're Down and Out/Whispering Grass (Don't Tell the Trees)	1965	2.00	4.00	8.00
9860	Sweet Pussycat/Who Could Ask for More	1965	2.00	4.00	8.00
9887	That Special Way/Tossin' and Turnin'	1966	2.00	4.00	8.00
10061	If You Go Away/When the Fog Rolls In to San Francisco	1966	2.00	4.00	8.00
10176	No Guilty Feelings/Yellow Days	1967	2.00	4.00	8.00
10235	Dinner For One/Please, James	1967	2.00	4.00	8.00
MERCURY					
71493	The Dance Was Over/Look at Yourself	1959	3.00	6.00	12.00
71568	What Would You Do/Widow Talk	1960	3.00	6.00	12.00
71608	Little Things Mean a Lot/I Burned Your Letter	1960	3.00	6.00	12.00
71690	I'll Save the Last Dance for You/Forgive	1960	3.75	7.50	15.00
71760	Keep Your Hands Off of Him/Hush, Somebody's Calling My Name	1961	3.00	6.00	12.00
71793	Sweet Georgia Brown/Do What You Want	1961	3.00	6.00	12.00
71840	I'll Be There/Love Laid Its Hands on Me	1962	3.75	7.50	15.00
71840 [PS]	I'll Be There/Love Laid Its Hands on Me	1962	6.25	12.50	25.00
71871	Dance with a Dolly (With a Hole in Her Stocking)/You're Nobody 'Til Somebody Loves You	1962	3.00	6.00	12.00
71929	I Didn't Know I Was Crying/I Built My World Around a Dream	1962	3.00	6.00	12.00
71946	Joey/You're Nobody 'Til Somebody Loves You	1962	3.00	6.00	12.00
71984	Another Dancing Partner/Please Send Me Someone to Love	1962	3.00	6.00	12.00
72019	The Window Up Above/Tennessee Waltz	1962	3.00	6.00	12.00
72056	Dance Him By Me/Las Vegas	1962	3.00	6.00	12.00
72086	Little Things/Mr. Blue	1963	2.50	5.00	10.00
72121	Drama of Love/Hobo Flats	1963	2.50	5.00	10.00
72162	In the Dark/Melancholy Baby	1963	2.50	5.00	10.00
RANWOOD					
820	Loving You/Reason to Believe	1968	—	3.00	6.00
826	Grown-Up Games/Lonely Letters	1968	—	3.00	6.00
844	Brother Love's Traveling Salvation Show/I'll Save the Last Dance for You	1969	—	3.00	6.00
857	Lonely Teardrops/Ain't Misbehavin'	1969	—	3.00	6.00
869	Paint Me Loving You/Tomorrow Is the First Day of the Rest of My Life	1970	—	3.00	6.00
884	Mrs. Robinson/Two Worlds	1970	—	2.50	5.00
894	Hallelujah Baby/Two Worlds	1971	—	2.50	5.00
RCA VICTOR					
47-4685	Lonesome and Blue/I Need You	1952	3.75	7.50	15.00
—By John Greer, vocals by Damita Jo					
47-5022	I'd Do It Again/I Don't Care	1952	3.75	7.50	15.00
47-5120	Go 'Way From My Window/Let Me Share Your Name	1953	3.75	7.50	15.00
47-5253	Missing/The Widow Walk	1953	3.75	7.50	15.00
47-5328	Do Me a Favor/Don't You Care	1953	3.75	7.50	15.00
47-5570	Face to Face/Sadie Thompson's Song	1953	3.75	7.50	15.00
47-5987	Win or Lose/My Tzatskele	1955	3.75	7.50	15.00
47-6096	Feelin' Kinda Happy/Nuff of That Stuff	1955	3.75	7.50	15.00
—B-side by Steve Gibson and His Red Caps					
47-6185	In My Heart/Abracadabra	1955	3.75	7.50	15.00
47-6281	Always/Freehearted	1955	3.75	7.50	15.00

Number	Title (A Side/B Side)	Yr	VG	VG+	NM
VEE JAY					
661	I'm Waiting for Ships That Never Come In/Hurt a Fool	1965	2.00	4.00	8.00
Albums					
ABC-PARAMOUNT					
378 [M]	The Big Fifteen	1961	20.00	40.00	80.00
S-378 [S]	The Big Fifteen	1961	25.00	50.00	100.00
EPIC					
LN 24131 [M]	This Is Damita Jo	1965	3.75	7.50	15.00
LN 24164 [M]	One More Time with Feeling	1965	3.75	7.50	15.00
LN 24202 [M]	Midnight Session	1966	3.75	7.50	15.00
LN 24244 [M]	If You Go Away	1967	5.00	10.00	20.00
BN 26131 [S]	This Is Damita Jo	1965	5.00	10.00	20.00
BN 26164 [S]	One More Time with Feeling	1965	5.00	10.00	20.00
BN 26202 [S]	Midnight Session	1966	5.00	10.00	20.00
BN 26244 [S]	If You Go Away	1967	3.75	7.50	15.00
MERCURY					
MG-20642 [M]	I'll Save the Last Dance for You	1961	7.50	15.00	30.00
MG-20703 [M]	Damita Jo at the Diplomat	1962	6.25	12.50	25.00
MG-20734 [M]	Sing a Country Song	1962	6.25	12.50	25.00
MG-20818 [M]	This One's for Me	1963	5.00	10.00	20.00
SR-60642 [S]	I'll Save the Last Dance for You	1961	10.00	20.00	40.00
SR-60703 [S]	Damita Jo at the Diplomat	1962	7.50	15.00	30.00
SR-60734 [S]	Sing a Country Song	1962	7.50	15.00	30.00
SR-60818 [S]	This One's for Me	1963	6.25	12.50	25.00
RANWOOD					
8037	Miss Damita Jo	1968	3.75	7.50	15.00
RCA CAMDEN					
CAL-900 [M]	Go Go with Damita Jo	196?	3.00	6.00	12.00
CAS-900 [S]	Go Go with Damita Jo	196?	3.00	6.00	12.00
SUNSET					
SUS-5198	The Irresistible Damita Jo	1968	3.00	6.00	12.00
VEE JAY					
LP-1137 [M]	Damita Jo Sings	1965	6.25	12.50	25.00
LPS-1137 [S]	Damita Jo Sings	1965	12.50	25.00	50.00

DAMNATION OF ADAM BLESSING, THE

Number	Title (A Side/B Side)	Yr	VG	VG+	NM
45s					
UNITED ARTISTS					
50609	Morning Dew/Cookbook	1969	2.00	4.00	8.00
50666	Last Train to Clarksville/Lonely	1970	2.00	4.00	8.00
50726	Back to the River/The Driver	1970	2.00	4.00	8.00
50819	Fingers on a Windmill/Leaving It Up to You	1971	—	3.00	6.00
50912	Cookbook/Leaving It Up to You	1972	—	3.00	6.00
Albums					
UNITED ARTISTS					
UAS-5533	Which Is the Justice, Which Is the Thief	1971	5.00	10.00	20.00
UAS-6738	The Damnation of Adam Blessing	1970	5.00	10.00	20.00
UAS-6773	The Second Damnation	1970	5.00	10.00	20.00

DAMON

Number	Title (A Side/B Side)	Yr	VG	VG+	NM
Albums					
ANKH					
968	Song of a Gypsy	1970	1500.	2250.	3000.
—Gatefold cover					
968	Song of a Gypsy	1970	500.00	1000.	1500.
—Regular cover					

DAMON, LIZ, 'S ORIENT EXPRESS

Number	Title (A Side/B Side)	Yr	VG	VG+	NM
45s					
ANTHEM					
51005	Loneliness Remembers/Quiet Sound	1971	2.50	5.00	10.00
51006	All in All/Walking Backwards Down the Road	1971	2.50	5.00	10.00
MAKAHA					
503	1900 Yesterday/You're Falling in Love	1970	3.00	6.00	12.00
WHITE WHALE					
368	1900 Yesterday/You're Falling in Love	1970	—	3.00	6.00
370	But For Love/You Make Me Feel Like Someone	1970	—	3.00	6.00
Albums					
WHITE WHALE					
WWS 5003	Liz Damon's Orient Express	1971	3.00	6.00	12.00

DAMONE, VIC

Also see JO STAFFORD AND VIC DAMONE.

Number	Title (A Side/B Side)	Yr	VG	VG+	NM
45s					
CAPITOL					
4645	Something You Never Had Before/Tender Is the Night	1961	2.00	4.00	8.00
4718	No Strings/Once Upon a Time	1962	2.00	4.00	8.00
4756	Ebb Tide/My Heart Will Tell You So	1962	2.00	4.00	8.00
4799	Vieni, Vieni/Cathy	1962	2.00	4.00	8.00
4827	What Kind of Fool Am I/Charmaine	1962	2.00	4.00	8.00
4947	One Hand, One Heart/You're Just Another Pretty Face	1963	2.00	4.00	8.00
5039	Wives and Lovers/Oooh Looka There Ain't She Pretty	1963	2.00	4.00	8.00
5092	Again/Sweet Someone	1963	2.00	4.00	8.00
5138	Breaking Point/Who Are You Now	1964	2.00	4.00	8.00
5191	I'm Gonna Miss You/Where Did the Magic Go	1964	2.00	4.00	8.00
5252	On the Street Where You Live/Maria	1964	2.00	4.00	8.00
COLUMBIA					
40630	Help Me/Sure	1956	2.50	5.00	10.00
40654	On the Street Where You Live/We All Need Love	1956	2.50	5.00	10.00
40682	I Cried for You/To Love Again	1956	2.50	5.00	10.00
40733	War and Peace/Speak, My Love	1956	2.50	5.00	10.00
40783	When My Love Smiles/One Little Boy	1956	2.50	5.00	10.00
40858	Do I Love You (Because You're Beautiful)/The Legend of the Bells	1957	2.50	5.00	10.00
40945	An Affair to Remember (Our Love Affair)/In the Eyes of the World	1957	2.50	5.00	10.00
41057	Junior Miss/I Can't Close the Book	1957	2.50	5.00	10.00
41122	Gigi/On the Street Where You Live	1958	2.50	5.00	10.00
41185	A Toujours/The Only Man on the Island	1958	2.50	5.00	10.00
41245	Forever New/Oooh, My Love	1958	2.50	5.00	10.00
41287	We Kiss in a Shadow/Separate Tables	1958	2.50	5.00	10.00
41333	Save a Kiss/Penny Serenade	1959	2.50	5.00	10.00
41407	My Heart Has Many Dreams/New Romance in Old Roma	1959	2.50	5.00	10.00
41510	The Night Has a Thousand Eyes/On a Sunday Afternoon	1959	2.50	5.00	10.00
41577	Your Smile/Very Warm	1959	2.50	5.00	10.00
41649	Christine/Never Will I Marry	1960	2.00	4.00	8.00
41783	Never Like This/What Fools We Mortals Be	1960	2.00	4.00	8.00
41915	If Ever I Would Love You/I'll Be Your Lover	1961	2.00	4.00	8.00
42006	Adrift on a Star/The Pleasure of Her Company	1961	2.00	4.00	8.00
42041	Theme from "By Love Possessed"/If It's the Last Thing I Do	1961	2.00	4.00	8.00
MERCURY					
5374	God's Country/Where I Belong	1950	3.75	7.50	15.00
—Mercury singles before 5374 are unconfirmed on 45					
5391	Don't Say Goodbye/This Is the Night	1950	3.75	7.50	15.00
5402	Where Can I Go/If We Could Be A-L-O-N-E	1950	3.75	7.50	15.00
5429	Vagabond Shoes/I Hadn't Anyone Till You	1950	3.75	7.50	15.00
5444	Mama/Operetta	1950	3.75	7.50	15.00
5454	Tzena, Tzena, Tzena/I Love That Girl	1950	3.75	7.50	15.00
5474	Just Say I Love Her/Can Anyone Explain (No! No! No!)	1950	3.75	7.50	15.00
5477	Cincinnati Dancing Pig/Forbidden Love	1950	3.75	7.50	15.00
5486	Take Me in Your Arms/Beloved, Be Faithful	1950	3.75	7.50	15.00
5496	A Marshmallow World/When the Lights Are Low	1950	3.75	7.50	15.00
5515	Silent Night/White Christmas	1950	3.75	7.50	15.00
5535	Ave Maria/Our Lady of Fatima	1950	3.75	7.50	15.00
5555	Possibilities/Use Your Imagination	1950	3.75	7.50	15.00
5563	My Heart Cries for You/Music by the Angels	1950	3.75	7.50	15.00
5565	If/You and Your Beautiful Eyes	1951	3.75	7.50	15.00
5566	Just For Tonight/The Night Is Young	1951	3.75	7.50	15.00
5572	Tell Me You Love Me/Little Café Paree	1951	3.75	7.50	15.00
5638	Someday/You Gotta Show Me	1951	3.75	7.50	15.00
5646	My Truly, Truly Fair/My Life's Desire	1951	3.75	7.50	15.00
5655	Longing for You/The Son of a Sailor	1951	3.75	7.50	15.00
5669	Wonder Why/I Can See You	1951	3.75	7.50	15.00
5670	In the Cool, Cool, Cool of the Evening/How D'Ya Like Your Eggs	1951	3.75	7.50	15.00
5698	Calla Calla/It's a Long Way	1951	3.75	7.50	15.00
5744	Don't Blame Me/I Remember You, Love	1951	3.75	7.50	15.00
5785	Jump Through the Ring/My Funny Valentine	1952	3.75	7.50	15.00
5831	Goodbye for Awhile/Good Morning, Morning Glory	1952	3.75	7.50	15.00
5855	Diane/Tenderly	1952	3.75	7.50	15.00
5858	Here in My Heart/Tomorrow Never Comes	1952	3.75	7.50	15.00
5865	A Message from Vic Damone to the Army Boys (Parts 1 & 2)	1952	6.25	12.50	25.00
5877	Roseanne/Take My Heart	1952	3.75	7.50	15.00
5878	Come Hell or High Water/Girls Are Marching	1952	3.75	7.50	15.00
5907	Nina Never Knew/Johnny with the Bandy Legs	1952	3.75	7.50	15.00
5909	Al-Lee-O! Al-Lee-Ay!/Roseanne	1952	3.75	7.50	15.00
70022	April in Paris/My Love Song	1953	3.00	6.00	12.00
70031	Greyhound/I Don't Care	1953	3.00	6.00	12.00
70054	Sugar/Amor	1953	3.00	6.00	12.00
70108	Afraid/Love Light	1953	3.00	6.00	12.00
70128	April in Portugal/I'm Walking Behind You	1953	3.00	6.00	12.00
70179	That Old Feeling/Serenade in Blue	1953	3.00	6.00	12.00
70186	Eternally (The Song from Limelight)/Simonetta	1953	3.00	6.00	12.00
70216	Ebb Tide/If I Could Make You Mine	1953	3.00	6.00	12.00
70257	Lover, Come Back to Me/I Just Love You	1953	3.00	6.00	12.00
70287	The Breeze and I/To Love You	1954	3.00	6.00	12.00
70326	Until You Came to Me/A Sparrow Sings	1954	3.00	6.00	12.00
70384	Sleeping Beauty/Don't Take Your Lips Away	1954	3.00	6.00	12.00
70436	Once and Only Once/In My Own Quiet Way	1954	3.00	6.00	12.00
70480	Wind Song/Silk Stockings	1954	3.00	6.00	12.00
70507	Ave Maria/Our Lady of Fatima	1954	3.00	6.00	12.00
—With Kitty Kallen					
70545	Foolishly/Hello, Mrs. Jones, Is Mary There	1955	3.00	6.00	12.00
70577	My Symphony/Meet Me Halfway	1955	3.00	6.00	12.00
70624	Don't Keep It a Secret/A Man Doesn't Know	1955	3.00	6.00	12.00
70699	Por Favor/Born to Sing the Blues	1955	3.00	6.00	12.00
MGM					
14398	Tomorrow Belongs to the Children/Come Live Your Life with Me	1972	—	2.00	4.00
14498	Love Me As I Love You/This Time	1973	—	2.00	4.00
14576	Beautiful Land/Tell Her You Love Her	1973	—	2.00	4.00
RCA VICTOR					
47-8836	You Don't Have to Say You Love Me/Stay	1966	—	3.00	6.00
47-8982	Ciao Compare/What Is a Woman	1966	—	3.00	6.00
47-9046	Love Me Longer/Pretty Butterfly	1966	—	3.00	6.00
47-9145	A Quiet Tear/On the South Side of Chicago	1967	—	3.00	6.00
47-9250	I'll Sleep Tonight/It Makes No Difference	1967	—	3.00	6.00
47-9399	The Glory of Love/Come Live with Me	1967	—	3.00	6.00
47-9488	Goin' Out of My Head/Nothing to Lose	1968	—	2.50	5.00
47-9626	When You Laughed All Your Laughter/Why Can't I Walk Away	1968	—	2.50	5.00
74-0139	To Make a Big Man Cry/Take Me Walking in Your Mind	1969	—	2.50	5.00
REBECCA					
714	The Christmas Song/Silver Bells	1977	—	2.00	4.00
715	Christmas In San Francisco/(B-side unknown)	1977	—	2.00	4.00
WARNER BROS.					
5609	Bellisima/For Mama	1965	—	3.00	6.00
5616	You Were Only Fooling (While I Was Falling in Love)/Please Help Me, I'm Falling	1965	—	3.00	6.00
5644	The Thrill of Lovin' You/Why Don't You Believe Me	1965	—	3.00	6.00
5653	Lost and Found/Turn Around	1965	—	3.00	6.00
5668	Tears/Turn Around	1965	—	3.00	6.00
5801	Two of a Kind/Wonder	1966	—	3.00	6.00

Number	Title (A Side/B Side)	Yr	VG	VG+	NM
7-Inch Extended Plays					
COLUMBIA					
B-2565	*On the Street Where You Live/Smoke Gets In Your Eyes/An Affair to Remember/You Stepped Out of a Dream	1959	3.00	6.00	12.00
B-2565 [PS]	Vic Damone (Hall of Fame Series)	1959	3.00	6.00	12.00
Albums					
APPLAUSE					
1018	Over the Rainbow	197?	2.50	5.00	10.00
CAPITOL					
ST 1646 [S]	Linger Awhile with Vic Damone	1962	3.75	7.50	15.00
T 1646 [M]	Linger Awhile with Vic Damone	1962	3.00	6.00	12.00
ST 1691 [S]	Strange Enchantment	1962	3.75	7.50	15.00
T 1691 [M]	Strange Enchantment	1962	3.00	6.00	12.00
ST 1748 [S]	The Lively Ones	1962	3.75	7.50	15.00
T 1748 [M]	The Lively Ones	1962	3.00	6.00	12.00
ST 1811 [S]	My Baby Loves to Swing	1963	3.75	7.50	15.00
T 1811 [M]	My Baby Loves to Swing	1963	3.00	6.00	12.00
ST 1944 [S]	The Liveliest	1963	3.75	7.50	15.00
T 1944 [M]	The Liveliest	1963	3.00	6.00	12.00
ST 2123 [S]	On the Street Where You Live	1964	3.75	7.50	15.00
T 2123 [M]	On the Street Where You Live	1964	3.00	6.00	12.00
COLUMBIA					
CL 900 [M]	That Towering Feeling!	1956	6.25	12.50	25.00
CL 1088 [M]	Angela Mia	1957	5.00	10.00	20.00
CL 1573 [M]	On the Swingin' Side	1961	3.75	7.50	15.00
CS 8019 [S]	Closer Than a Kiss	1959	7.50	15.00	30.00
CS 8046 [S]	Angela Mia	1959	7.50	15.00	30.00
CS 8169 [S]	This Game of Love	1960	5.00	10.00	20.00
CS 8373 [S]	On the Swingin' Side	1961	5.00	10.00	20.00
CL (# unknown) [M]	Closer Than a Kiss	195?	5.00	10.00	20.00
CL (# unknown) [M]	This Game of Love	1960	3.75	7.50	15.00
HARMONY					
HL 7328 [M]	The Best of Vic Damone	196?	3.00	6.00	12.00
HL 7431 [M]	Vic Damone Sings	196?	3.00	6.00	12.00
HS 11128 [S]	The Best of Vic Damone	196?	3.00	6.00	12.00
HS 11231 [S]	Vic Damone Sings	196?	3.00	6.00	12.00
HOLIDAY					
HDY 1936	Christmas with Vic Damone	1981	2.50	5.00	10.00
MERCURY					
MG-20163 [M]	Yours for a Song	1957	6.25	12.50	25.00
MG-20193 [M]	My Favorites	1957	6.25	12.50	25.00
MG-25028 [10]	Vic Damone	1950	10.00	20.00	40.00
MG-25029 [10]	Vic Damone	1950	10.00	20.00	40.00
MG-25045 [10]	Vic Damone	1950	10.00	20.00	40.00
MG-25054 [10]	Song Hits	1950	10.00	20.00	40.00
MG-25092 [10]	Christmas Favorites	1951	10.00	20.00	40.00
MG-25100 [10]	Vic Damone and Others	1952	10.00	20.00	40.00
MG-25131 [10]	The Night Has a Thousand Eyes	1952	10.00	20.00	40.00
MG-25132 [10]	Vocals by Vic	1952	10.00	20.00	40.00
MG-25133 [10]	April in Paris	1952	10.00	20.00	40.00
MG-25156 [10]	Vic Damone	1952	10.00	20.00	40.00
RANWOOD					
8204	The Best of Vic Damone — Live	198?	2.50	5.00	10.00
RCA VICTOR					
ANL1-2462	The Best of Vic Damone	1977	2.50	5.00	10.00
LPM-3671 [M]	Stay with Me	1966	3.00	6.00	12.00
LSP-3671 [S]	Stay with Me	1966	3.75	7.50	15.00
LPM-3765 [M]	On the South Side of Chicago	1967	3.00	6.00	12.00
LSP-3765 [S]	On the South Side of Chicago	1967	3.75	7.50	15.00
LPM-3916 [M]	A Damone Type of Thing	1968	3.75	7.50	15.00
LSP-3916 [S]	A Damone Type of Thing	1968	3.75	7.50	15.00
LSP-3984	Why Can't I Walk Away	1968	3.75	7.50	15.00
REBECCA					
100 [(2)]	Let's Fall in Love Again	1981	3.00	6.00	12.00
1212	Feelings	1976	2.50	5.00	10.00
1212	Feelings	197?	2.50	5.00	10.00
1213	Inspiration	19??	2.50	5.00	10.00
UNITED TALENT					
4501	Don't Let Me Go	1969	3.00	6.00	12.00
WARNER BROS.					
W 1602 [M]	You Were Only Fooling	1965	3.00	6.00	12.00
WS 1602 [S]	You Were Only Fooling	1965	3.75	7.50	15.00
W 1607 [M]	Country Love Songs	1965	3.00	6.00	12.00
WS 1607 [S]	Country Love Songs	1965	3.75	7.50	15.00
WING					
MGW 12113 [M]	I'll Sing for You	196?	3.00	6.00	12.00
MGW 12157 [M]	Tenderly	196?	3.00	6.00	12.00
MGW 12182 [M]	Yours for a Song	196?	3.00	6.00	12.00
SRW 16113 [R]	I'll Sing for You	196?	3.00	6.00	12.00
SRW 16157 [R]	Tenderly	196?	3.00	6.00	12.00
SRW 16182 [R]	Yours for a Song	196?	3.00	6.00	12.00

DAN AND DALE

Number	Title (A Side/B Side)	Yr	VG	VG+	NM
45s					
TIFTON					
125	Batman Theme/(B-side unknown)	1966	2.50	5.00	10.00
125 [PS]	Batman Theme/(B-side unknown)	1966	5.00	10.00	20.00
Albums					
DIPLOMAT					
D-2390 [M]	The Nearness of You	196?	2.50	5.00	10.00
DS-2390 [S]	The Nearness of You	196?	3.00	6.00	12.00
TIFTON					
M-8002 [M]	Batman and Robin	1966	7.50	15.00	30.00
S-78002 [S]	Batman and Robin	1966	10.00	20.00	40.00

DANA, BILL

See JOSE JIMENEZ.

DANA, VIC

Number	Title (A Side/B Side)	Yr	VG	VG+	NM
45s					
CASINO					
093	Lay Me Down (Roll Me Out to Sea)/You Never Really Know	1976	—	2.00	4.00
COLUMBIA					
45261	You Gave Me a Reason (To Believe)/It Won't Hurt to Try It	1970	—	2.50	5.00
45342	If You Think I Love You Now (I;ve Just Started)/Angel She Was Love	1971	—	2.50	5.00
45439	Child of Mine/The Love in Your Eyes	1971	—	2.50	5.00
DOLTON					
34	The Girl of My Dreams/Someone New	1961	2.00	4.00	8.00
42	Golden Boy/The Story Behind My Tears	1961	2.00	4.00	8.00
48	Little Altar Boy/Hello Roomate	1961	2.00	4.00	8.00
51	I Will/Proud	1962	2.00	4.00	8.00
51 [PS]	I Will/Proud	1962	3.75	7.50	15.00
58	To Love and Be Loved/Time Can Change	1962	2.00	4.00	8.00
64	A Very Good Year for Girls/I Wanna Be There	1962	2.00	4.00	8.00
64	A Very Good Year for Girls/Looking for Me	1962	2.00	4.00	8.00
73	Danger/Heart, Hand and Teardrop	1963	2.00	4.00	8.00
73 [PS]	Danger/Heart, Hand and Teardrop	1963	3.75	7.50	15.00
81	More/That's Why I'm Sorry	1963	2.00	4.00	8.00
87	The Prisoner's Song/Voice in the Wind	1963	2.00	4.00	8.00
89	So Wide the World/Close Your Eyes	1964	2.00	4.00	8.00
92	Shangri-La/Warm and Tender	1964	2.00	4.00	8.00
95	Love Is All We Need/I Need You Now	1964	2.00	4.00	8.00
95 [PS]	Love Is All We Need/I Need You Now	1964	3.75	7.50	15.00
99	Garden in the Rain/Stairway to the Stars	1964	2.00	4.00	8.00
99 [PS]	Garden in the Rain/Stairway to the Stars	1964	3.75	7.50	15.00
301	Frenchy/It Was Night	1964	2.00	4.00	8.00
304	Red Roses for a Blue Lady/Blue Ribbons	1965	2.00	4.00	8.00
305	Bring a Little Sunshine (To My Heart)/That's All	1965	2.00	4.00	8.00
305 [PS]	Bring a Little Sunshine (To My Heart)/That's All	1965	3.00	6.00	12.00
309	Moonlight and Roses (Bring Mem'ries of You)/What'll I Do	1965	2.00	4.00	8.00
313	Crystal Chandelier/What Now My Love	1965	2.00	4.00	8.00
317	Lovely Kravezit/Hello Roomate	1966	2.00	4.00	8.00
319	I Love You Drops/Sunny Skies	1966	2.00	4.00	8.00
322	A Million and One/My Baby Wouldn't Leave Me	1966	2.00	4.00	8.00
324	Distant Drums/Love Me With All of Your Heart	1966	2.00	4.00	8.00
326	Grown Up Games/So What's New	1966	2.00	4.00	8.00
LIBERTY					
55950	Fraulein/A Little Bit Later on Down the Line	1967	—	3.00	6.00
55998	A Lifetime Lovin' You/Guess Who, You	1967	—	3.00	6.00
56023	Glory of Love/Let the Good Times In	1968	—	2.50	5.00
56050	Didn't We/Them	1968	—	2.50	5.00
56071	Little Arrows/Roses Are Red	1968	—	2.50	5.00
56098	You Are My Destiny/Where Has All the Love Gone	1969	—	2.50	5.00
56109	Loneliness (Is Messin' Up My Mind)/Look of Leavin'	1969	—	2.50	5.00
56137	Aren't We the Lucky Ones/I Tried to Love You Today	1969	—	3.00	6.00
56150	If I Never Knew Your Name/Sad Day Song	1969	—	3.00	6.00
56163	Red Red Wine/Another Dream Shot Down	1970	—	2.50	5.00
MGM					
14795	The Best I Ever Had/Memories Can't Make Love to Me	1975	—	2.00	4.00
UNITED ARTISTS					
0095	Red Roses for a Blue Lady/More	1973	—	2.00	4.00
—"Silver Spotlight Series" reissue					
Albums					
DOLTON					
BLP-2013 [M]	This Is Bill Dana	1961	5.00	10.00	20.00
BLP-2015 [M]	Warm and Wild	1962	3.75	7.50	15.00
BLP-2026 [M]	More	1963	3.75	7.50	15.00
BLP-2028 [M]	Shangri-La	1964	3.75	7.50	15.00
BLP-2032 [M]	Now	1964	3.75	7.50	15.00
BLP-2034 [M]	Red Roses for a Blue Lady	1965	3.75	7.50	15.00
BLP-2036 [M]	Moonlight and Roses	1965	3.75	7.50	15.00
BLP-2041 [M]	Crystal Chandelier	1966	3.75	7.50	15.00
BLP-2046 [M]	Town and Country	1966	3.75	7.50	15.00
BLP-2048 [M]	Golden Greats	1966	3.75	7.50	15.00
BLP-2049 [M]	Little Altar Boy and Other Christmas Songs	1966	3.75	7.50	15.00
BST-8013 [S]	This Is Bill Dana	1961	7.50	15.00	30.00
BST-8015 [S]	Warm and Wild	1962	5.00	10.00	20.00
BST-8026 [S]	More	1963	5.00	10.00	20.00
BST-8028 [S]	Shangri-La	1964	5.00	10.00	20.00
BST-8032 [S]	Now	1964	5.00	10.00	20.00
BST-8034 [S]	Red Roses for a Blue Lady	1965	5.00	10.00	20.00
BST-8036 [S]	Moonlight and Roses	1965	5.00	10.00	20.00
BST-8041 [S]	Crystal Chandelier	1966	5.00	10.00	20.00
BST-8046 [S]	Town and Country	1966	5.00	10.00	20.00
BST-8048 [S]	Golden Greats	1966	5.00	10.00	20.00
BST-8049 [S]	Little Altar Boy and Other Christmas Songs	1966	5.00	10.00	20.00
LIBERTY					
BST-8049 [S]	Little Altar Boy and Other Christmas Songs	1967	3.00	6.00	12.00
—Liberty record in Dolton cover					
LST-8063	If I Never Knew	1969	3.00	6.00	12.00
SUNSET					
SUM-1130 [M]	Warm and Wonderful	196?	2.50	5.00	10.00
SUM-1182 [M]	On the Country Side	1967	2.50	5.00	10.00
SUS-5130 [S]	Warm and Wonderful	196?	3.00	6.00	12.00
SUS-5182 [S]	On the Country Side	1967	3.00	6.00	12.00

DANCER, PRANCER, AND NERVOUS

Number	Title (A Side/B Side)	Yr	VG	VG+	NM
45s					
CAPITOL					
4300	The Happy Reindeer/Dancer's Waltz	1959	3.00	6.00	12.00

Number	Title (A Side/B Side)	Yr	VG	VG+	NM
4300 [PS]	The Happy Reindeer/Dancer's Waltz	1959	6.25	12.50	25.00
4353	I Wanta Be an Easter Bunny/The Happy Birthday Song	1960	3.00	6.00	12.00
—As "The Singing Reindeer"					

DANDERLIERS, THE

45s

Number	Title (A Side/B Side)	Yr	VG	VG+	NM
B&F					
150	Shu-Wop/My Loving Partner	1960	6.25	12.50	25.00
160	My Love/She's Mine	1960	6.25	12.50	25.00
1344	Chop Chop Boom/My Autumn Love	1961	5.00	10.00	20.00
MIDAS					
9004	All the Way/Walk On with Your Nose Up	196?	5.00	10.00	20.00
STATES					
147	Chop Chop Boom/My Autumn Love	1955	100.00	200.00	400.00
—Black vinyl					
147	Chop Chop Boom/My Autumn Love	1955	300.00	600.00	1200.
—Red vinyl					
150	Shu-Wop/My Loving Partner	1955	50.00	100.00	200.00
152	May God Be With You/Little Man	1956	50.00	100.00	200.00
160	My Love/She's Mine	1956	62.50	125.00	250.00

DANDLEERS, THE

See THE DANLEERS.

DANETTA AND THE STARLETS

45s

Number	Title (A Side/B Side)	Yr	VG	VG+	NM
OKEH					
7155	You Belong to Me (We're Going Steady)/Impression	1962	25.00	50.00	100.00

DANIELS, CHARLIE, BAND

45s

Number	Title (A Side/B Side)	Yr	VG	VG+	NM
EPIC					
02154	In America/The Legend of Wooley Swamp	1981	—	—	3.00
—Reissue					
02185	Sweet Home Alabama/Falling in Love for the Night	1981	—	2.00	4.00
02828	Still in Saigon/Blowing Along with the Wind	1982	—	2.00	4.00
02995	Ragin' Cajun/Universal Hand	1982	—	2.00	4.00
03251	We Had It All One Time/Makes You Want to Go Home	1982	—	2.00	4.00
03918	Stroker's Theme/(B-side unknown)	1983	—	2.00	4.00
05638	American Farmer/Runnin' with That Crowd	1985	—	—	3.00
05699	Still Hurtin' Me/American Rock and Roll	1985	—	—	3.00
05835	Drinkin' My Baby Goodbye/Ever Changing Lady	1986	—	—	3.00
08002	Boogie Woogie Fiddle Country Blues/Working Man You Got It All	1988	—	—	3.00
50243	Wichita Jail/It's My Life	1976	—	2.00	4.00
50278	Sweet Louisiana/Sweetwater, Texas	1976	—	2.00	4.00
50322	Billy the Kid/Slow Song	1976	—	2.00	4.00
50456	Heaven Can Be Anywhere (Twin Pines Theme)/Good Ole Boy	1977	—	2.00	4.00
50516	Sugar Hill Saturday Night/Maria Teresa	1977	—	2.00	4.00
50637	Sweet Lousiana/Trudy	1978	—	2.00	4.00
50700	The Devil Went Down to Georgia/Rainbow Ride	1979	—	2.00	4.00
50768	Mississippi/Passing Lane	1979	—	2.00	4.00
50806	Behind Your Eyes/Blue Star	1979	—	2.00	4.00
50845	Long Haired Country Boy/Sweet Lousiana	1980	—	2.00	4.00
50888	In America/Blue Star	1980	—	2.00	4.00
50921	The Legend of Wooley Swamp/Money	1980	—	2.00	4.00
50955	Carolina (I Remember You)/South Sea Song	1980	—	2.00	4.00
68542	Cowboy Hat in Dallas/Easy Rider	1988	—	—	3.00
68738	Midnight Train/Back to Dixie	1989	—	—	3.00
73030	Simple Man/Ill Wind	1989	—	—	3.00
73236	Mister DJ/It's My Life	1990	—	—	3.00
73426	(What This World Needs Is) A Few More Rednecks/It's My Life	1990	—	—	3.00
73577	Oh Atlanta/What Is 26	1990	—	—	3.00
73768	Honky Tonk Life/Willie Jones	1991	—	—	3.00
74061	Little Folks/Let Freedom Ring	1991	—	—	3.00
HANOVER					
4541	Robot Bomp/Rover Had a Party	1959	7.50	15.00	30.00
KAMA SUTRA					
553	Great Big Bunches of Love/(B-side unknown)	1972	—	3.00	6.00
576	Uneasy Rider/Funky Junky	1973	—	3.00	6.00
590	Whiskey/(B-side unknown)	1974	—	2.50	5.00
593	Way Down Yonder/I've Been Down	1974	—	2.50	5.00
595	Land of Opportunity/(B-side unknown)	1974	—	2.50	5.00
598	The South's Gonna Do It/King Size Rosewood Bed	1974	—	2.50	5.00
601	Long Haired Country Boy/I've Been Down	1975	—	2.50	5.00
606	Birmingham Blues/Damn Good Cowboy	1975	—	2.50	5.00
607	Texas/Everything Is Kinda Alright	1975	—	2.50	5.00
LIBERTY					
S7-17398	All Night Long/America, I Believe in You	1993	—	2.50	5.00
PAULA					
246	The Middle of a Heartache/Skip It	1966	3.75	7.50	15.00
418	The Middle of a Heartache/Skip It	1976	—	2.00	4.00

Albums

Number	Title (A Side/B Side)	Yr	VG	VG+	NM
CAPITOL					
ST-11414	Charlie Daniels	1975	3.00	6.00	12.00
SN-16039	Charlie Daniels	1979	2.00	4.00	8.00
—Budget-line reissue					
EPIC					
AS 586 [DJ]	Interchords	1979	3.75	7.50	15.00
—Music and interviews; promo only					
EAS 1780 [DJ]	The Charlie Daniels Story	1990	3.75	7.50	15.00
—Promo-only interview/radio show					
PE 34150	Saddle Tramp	1976	2.50	5.00	10.00
—Orange label, no bar code on cover					
PE 34150	Saddle Tramp	198?	2.00	4.00	8.00
—With bar code on cover					
JE 34365	Fire on the Mountain	1976	2.50	5.00	10.00
—Reissue of Kama Sutra 2603 without bonus EP; orange label, no bar code on cover					
PE 34365	Fire on the Mountain	198?	2.00	4.00	8.00
—Budget-line reissue					
JE 34369	Uneasy Rider	1976	2.50	5.00	10.00
—Reissue of Kama Sutra 2071 with new name; orange label, no bar code on cover					
PE 34369	Uneasy Rider	198?	2.00	4.00	8.00
—Budget-line reissue					
JE 34377	High Lonesome	1976	2.50	5.00	10.00
—Orange label, no bar code on cover					
PE 34377	High Lonesome	198?	2.00	4.00	8.00
—Budget-line reissue					
JE 34402	Nightrider	1977	2.50	5.00	10.00
—Reissue of Kama Sutra 2607; orange label, no bar code on cover					
PE 34402	Nightrider	198?	2.00	4.00	8.00
—Budget-line reissue					
JE 34664	Whiskey	1977	2.50	5.00	10.00
—Reissue of Kama Sutra 2076 with new name; orange label, no bar code on cover					
PE 34664	Whiskey	198?	2.00	4.00	8.00
—Budget-line reissue					
JE 34665	Te John, Grease and Wolfman	1977	2.50	5.00	10.00
—Reissue of Kama Sutra 2060; orange label, no bar code on cover					
PE 34665	Te John, Grease and Wolfman	198?	2.00	4.00	8.00
—Budget-line reissue					
JE 34970	Midnight Wind	1977	2.50	5.00	10.00
—Orange label, no bar code on cover					
PE 34970	Midnight Wind	198?	2.00	4.00	8.00
—Budget-line reissue					
JE 35751	Million Mile Reflections	1979	2.50	5.00	10.00
PE 35751	Million Mile Reflections	198?	2.00	4.00	8.00
—Budget-line reissue					
FE 36571	Full Moon	1980	2.50	5.00	10.00
PE 36571	Full Moon	198?	2.00	4.00	8.00
—Budget-line reissue					
FE 37694	Windows	1982	2.50	5.00	10.00
PE 37694	Windows	198?	2.00	4.00	8.00
—Budget-line reissue					
FE 38795	A Decade of Hits	1983	2.50	5.00	10.00
FE 39878	Me and the Boys	1985	2.50	5.00	10.00
PE 39878	Me and the Boys	198?	2.00	4.00	8.00
—Budget-line reissue					
FE 40760	Powder Keg	1987	2.00	4.00	8.00
FE 44324	Homesick Man	1988	2.00	4.00	8.00
HE 44365	Fire on the Mountain	1982	10.00	20.00	40.00
—Half-speed mastered edition					
FE 45316	Simple Man	1989	3.00	6.00	12.00
HE 45751	Million Mile Reflections	1982	10.00	20.00	40.00
—Half-speed mastered edition					
KAMA SUTRA					
KSBS 2060	Te John, Grease and Wolfman	1972	3.75	7.50	15.00
KSBS 2071	Honey in the Rock	1973	3.75	7.50	15.00
KSBS 2076	Way Down Yonder	1974	3.75	7.50	15.00
KSBS 2603	Fire on the Mountain	1974	3.75	7.50	15.00
—Includes bonus EP, "Volunteer Jam" (deduct 20% if missing)					
KSBS 2607	Nightrider	1975	3.75	7.50	15.00
MOBILE FIDELITY					
1-176	Million Mile Reflections	1984	7.50	15.00	30.00
—Audiophile vinyl					

DANIELS, JEFF

45s

Number	Title (A Side/B Side)	Yr	VG	VG+	NM
ASTRO					
108	Foxy Dan/Someday You'll Remember	1960	25.00	50.00	100.00
BIG HOWDY					
777	Switch Blade Sam/You're Still on My Mind	1959	25.00	50.00	100.00
8120	Uh-Huh/Table for Two	196?	25.00	50.00	100.00
8121	Foxy Dan/Someday You'll Remember	1961	25.00	50.00	100.00
MELADEE					
117	Daddy-O Rock/Hey Woman	1958	100.00	200.00	400.00

DANLEERS, THE

45s

Number	Title (A Side/B Side)	Yr	VG	VG+	NM
AMP 3					
2115	One Summer Night/Wheelin' and Dealin'	1958	50.00	100.00	200.00
—By "Dandleers"					
2115	One Summer Night/Wheelin' and Dealin'	1958	10.00	20.00	40.00
—Corrected group name on label					
EPIC					
9367	I Live Half a Block from an Angel/If You Don't Care	1960	7.50	15.00	30.00
9421	I'll Always Be in Love with You/Little Lover	1960	7.50	15.00	30.00
EVEREST					
19412	Foolish/I'm Looking Around	1961	7.50	15.00	30.00
LEMANS					
004	The Truth Hurts/Baby You've Got It	1963	2.50	5.00	10.00
008	I'm Sorry/This Thing Called Love	1963	2.50	5.00	10.00
MERCURY					
71322	One Summer Night/Wheelin' and Dealin'	1958	5.00	10.00	20.00
71356	I Really Love You/My Flaming Heart	1958	5.00	10.00	20.00
71401	A Picture of You/Prelude to Love	1959	5.00	10.00	20.00
71441	I Can't Sleep/Your Love	1959	5.00	10.00	20.00
SMASH					
1872	Were You There/If	1964	3.00	6.00	12.00
1895	Where Is Love/The Angels Sent You	1964	3.00	6.00	12.00

DANNY AND JERRY

"Danny" is Danny Rapp of DANNY AND THE JUNIORS.

45s

Number	Title (A Side/B Side)	Yr	VG	VG+	NM
RONN					
5	We've Got a Groovy Thing Goin'/You Must Be Fooling	1966	3.00	6.00	12.00
12	I've Got Pride/Connection	1967	3.00	6.00	12.00
24	I Can't See Nobody/Mo'Reen	1967	3.00	6.00	12.00

DANNY AND THE JUNIORS

45s

Number	Title (A Side/B Side)	Yr	VG	VG+	NM
ABC-PARAMOUNT					
9871	At the Hop/Sometimes (When I'm All Alone)	1957	7.50	15.00	30.00
9888	Rock and Roll Is Here to Stay/School Boy Romance	1958	7.50	15.00	30.00
9926	Dottie/In the Meantime	1958	6.25	12.50	25.00
9953	A Thief/Crazy Cave	1958	6.25	12.50	25.00
9978	Sassy Fran/I Feel So Lonely	1958	12.50	25.00	50.00
10004	Do You Love Me/Somehow I Can't Forget	1959	6.25	12.50	25.00
10052	Playing Hard to Get/Of Love	1959	6.25	12.50	25.00
CRUNCH					
018001	At the Hop/Let the Good Times Roll	1973	—	2.50	5.00
GUYDEN					
2076	Oo-La-La-Limbo/Now and Then	1962	5.00	10.00	20.00
LUV					
252	Rock and Roll Is Here to Stay/Sometimes (When I'm All Alone)	1968	2.50	5.00	10.00
MERCURY					
72240	Sad Girl/Let's Go Ski-ing	1964	5.00	10.00	20.00
SINGULAR					
711	At the Hop/Sometimes	1957	250.00	500.00	1000.
—Blue label, machine-stamped in dead wax, no mention of Artie Singer on label					
711	At the Hop/Sometimes	1957	250.00	500.00	1000.
—Blue label, machine-stamped in dead wax, with "Orchestra Directed by Artie Singer" credit. Both versions have a "count-in" before the song starts. Singular records on black labels or without the count-in are probably reproductions.					
SWAN					
4060	Twistin' U.S.A./A Thousand Miles Away	1960	5.00	10.00	20.00
4064	Candy Cane. Sugary Plum/Oh Holy Night	1960	6.25	12.50	25.00
4064 [PS]	Candy Cane. Sugary Plum/Oh Holy Night	1960	62.50	125.00	250.00
4068	Daydreamer/Pony Express	1961	5.00	10.00	20.00
4072	Cha Cha Go Go (Chicago Cha-Cha)/Mister Whisper	1961	5.00	10.00	20.00
4082	Back to the Hop/The Charleston Fish	1961	5.00	10.00	20.00
4082 [PS]	Back to the Hop/The Charleston Fish	1961	25.00	50.00	100.00
4084	Just Because/You Hair's Too Long	1961	—	—	—
—Unreleased?					
4092	Twistin' All Night Long/Some Kind of Nut	1962	5.00	10.00	20.00
4100	(Do the) Mashed Potatoes/Doin' the Continental Walk	1962	5.00	10.00	20.00
4113	We Got Soul/Funny	1962	5.00	10.00	20.00

7-Inch Extended Plays

Number	Title (A Side/B Side)	Yr	VG	VG+	NM
ABC-PARAMOUNT					
EP-11	At The Hop/School Boy Romance//Rock And Roll Is Here To Stay/Sometimes (When I'm All Alone)	1958	150.00	300.00	600.00
EP-11 [PS]	At the Hop	1958	225.00	450.00	900.00

Albums

Number	Title (A Side/B Side)	Yr	VG	VG+	NM
MCA					
1555	Rockin' with Danny and the Juniors	1987	2.50	5.00	10.00

DANNY AND THE MEMORIES

"Danny" is Danny Whitten, later of CRAZY HORSE.

45s

Number	Title (A Side/B Side)	Yr	VG	VG+	NM
VALIANT					
705	Can't Help Lovin' That Girl of Mine/Don't Go	1965	6.25	12.50	25.00
6049	Can't Help Lovin' That Girl of Mine/Don't Go	1964	6.25	12.50	25.00

DANNY AND THE OTHER GUYS

45s

Number	Title (A Side/B Side)	Yr	VG	VG+	NM
CP					
(# unknown)	Hard Times/(B-side unknown)	196?	200.00	400.00	800.00

DANTE

45s

Number	Title (A Side/B Side)	Yr	VG	VG+	NM
A&M					
788	Speedoo/Sweet Lover	1966	2.50	5.00	10.00
DARROW					
515	How Much I Care/Baby Baby	1960	10.00	20.00	40.00
DECCA					
31178	If You Don't Know/Leave Your Tears Behind You	1960	3.75	7.50	15.00
31268	Bye Bye Baby/That's Why	1961	3.75	7.50	15.00
31319	Ring or Write or Call/Say It to Me	1961	3.75	7.50	15.00
IMPERIAL					
5798	Something Happens/Are You Just My Friend	1961	3.75	7.50	15.00
5827	Miss America/Now I've Got You	1962	3.75	7.50	15.00
5867	Magic Ring/Am I the One	1962	3.75	7.50	15.00
—Imperial titles as "Dante and His Friends"					
MADISON					
130	Alley Oop/The Right Time	1960	5.00	10.00	20.00
—As "Dante and the Evergreens"					
135	Time Machine/Dream Land	1960	3.75	7.50	15.00
143	What Are You Doing New Year's Eve/Yeah Baby	1960	3.75	7.50	15.00
—As "Dante and the Evergreens"					
154	Think Sweet Thoughts/Da Doo	1961	3.75	7.50	15.00
MERCURY					
71621	How Much I Care/Baby Baby	1960	5.00	10.00	20.00
TIDE					
003	My Lament/Aching Heart	1960	5.00	10.00	20.00

Albums

Number	Title (A Side/B Side)	Yr	VG	VG+	NM
MADISON					
MA-1002 [M]	Dante and the Evergreens	1961	125.00	250.00	500.00

DANTE, RON

Also see THE ARCHIES; THE CUFF LINKS (1); THE DETERGENTS.

45s

Number	Title (A Side/B Side)	Yr	VG	VG+	NM
ALMONT					
307	Little Lollypop/Funny	1963	3.75	7.50	15.00
BELL					
45460	Christine/Don't Call It Love	1974	—	2.50	5.00
—As "Bo Cooper"					
45610	Charmer/Yesterday Dreamin'	1974	—	2.00	4.00
45619	Midnight Show/The Christian	1974	—	2.00	4.00
COLUMBIA					
43720	Think/221 East Maple	1966	2.50	5.00	10.00
43862	I Give You Things/Janie, Janie	1966	2.50	5.00	10.00
DOT					
17023	Absence of Lisa/Gypsy Be Mine	1967	2.50	5.00	10.00
HANDSHAKE					
02107	Show and Tell/God Bless Rock and Roll	1981	—	2.00	4.00
02552	Letter from Zowie/God Bless Rock and Roll	1981	—	2.00	4.00
INFINITY					
50008	Ain't Misbehavin' (One Never Knows, Do One?)/'Round About Midnight	1979	—	2.50	5.00
50018	Fire Island/They're Playing Our Song	1979	—	2.50	5.00
50038	Brand New Key/They're Playing Our Song	1979	—	2.50	5.00
—Infinity sides as "Dante's Inferno"					
KIRSHNER					
63-1010	How Do You Know/Let Me Bring You Up	1970	—	3.00	6.00
63-1010 [PS]	How Do You Know/Let Me Bring You Up	1970	2.50	5.00	10.00
63-5007	Sweet Taste of Love/C'mon Girl	1970	—	3.00	6.00
MERCURY					
72812	Follow a Dream/He's Raining in My Sunshine	1968	2.50	5.00	10.00
MUSIC VOICE					
503	If You Love Me, Laurie/Don't Stand Up in a Canoe	1964	3.75	7.50	15.00
MUSICOR					
1058	Look at Me/There's Love	1965	3.00	6.00	12.00
1090	In the Rain/Poor Boys	1965	3.00	6.00	12.00
1105	If You Love Me, Laurie/Don't Stand Up in a Canoe	1965	3.00	6.00	12.00
1134	Hey Mom, Hey Pop/(Heart) Stop Calling Her Name	1965	3.00	6.00	12.00
RCA					
PB-10898	How Am I to Know/Sky Rider	1977	—	2.00	4.00
RCA VICTOR					
PB-10340	Sugar, Sugar/Sugar, Sugar (Disco)	1975	—	2.50	5.00
SCEPTER					
12333 [DJ]	That's What Life Is All About (mono/stereo)	1971	—	3.00	6.00
—Stock copy may not exist					

Albums

Number	Title (A Side/B Side)	Yr	VG	VG+	NM
HANDSHAKE					
JW 37341	Street Angel	1981	3.00	6.00	12.00
KIRSHNER					
KES-106	Ron Dante Brings You Up	1970	5.00	10.00	20.00

DAPPERS, THE

45s

Number	Title (A Side/B Side)	Yr	VG	VG+	NM
EPIC					
9423	My Love Is Real/Baby You Know You're Wrong	1960	6.25	12.50	25.00
FOXIE					
7005	Chicken Twist/Lonely Street	1961	10.00	20.00	40.00
GROOVE					
0156	Unwanted Love/That's All, That's All, That's All	1956	50.00	100.00	200.00
PEACOCK					
1651	Come Back to Me/Mambo Oongh	1955	37.50	75.00	150.00
RAINBOW					
373	Bop Bop Bu/How I Need You Baby	1956	10.00	20.00	40.00
STAR-X					
505	We're in Love/Spellbound	1958	62.50	125.00	250.00

DAPPERS QUINTET, THE

45s

Number	Title (A Side/B Side)	Yr	VG	VG+	NM
FLAYR					
500	Look What I've Found/(B-side unknown)	1955	500.00	1000.	1500.

DAPS, THE

45s

Number	Title (A Side/B Side)	Yr	VG	VG+	NM
MARTERRY					
5429	When You're Alone/Down and Out	1956	15.00	30.00	60.00

DARBISHIRE, STEVE

45s

Number	Title (A Side/B Side)	Yr	VG	VG+	NM
LONDON					
1011	Trains Trains/Yum Yum	1966	2.00	4.00	8.00

DARCEL, DENISE

Albums

Number	Title (A Side/B Side)	Yr	VG	VG+	NM
CAMEO					
C-1002 [M]	Banned in Boston	1958	10.00	20.00	40.00

DARIN, BOBBY

45s

Number	Title (A Side/B Side)	Yr	VG	VG+	NM
ATCO					
(no #) [DJ]	She's Tanfastic!/Moments of Love	1960	10.00	20.00	40.00
—Ferrion Inc. "Special Premium Record"					
6092	Million Dollar Baby/Talk to Me	1957	7.50	15.00	30.00
6103	Don't Call My Name/Pretty Betty	1957	7.50	15.00	30.00
6109	Just in Case You Change Your Mind/So Mean	1958	7.50	15.00	30.00
6117	Splish Splash/Judy, Don't Be Moody	1958	5.00	10.00	20.00
6121	Early in the Morning/Now We're One	1958	5.00	10.00	20.00
6121	Early in the Morning/Now We're One	1958	10.00	20.00	40.00
—As "The Rinky Dinks"					
6127	Queen of the Hop/Lost Love	1958	5.00	10.00	20.00
6128	Mighty Mighty Man/You're Gone	1958	5.00	10.00	20.00
6128	Mighty Mighty Man/You're Gone	1958	10.00	20.00	40.00
—As "The Rinky Dinks"					
6133 [M]	Plain Jane/While I'm Gone	1959	5.00	10.00	20.00
6133 [PS]	Plain Jane/While I'm Gone	1959	12.50	25.00	50.00
SD-45-6133 [S]	Plain Jane/While I'm Gone	1959	10.00	20.00	40.00
6140	Dream Lover/Bullmoose	1959	5.00	10.00	20.00
6140 [PS]	Dream Lover/Bullmoose	1959	12.50	25.00	50.00
6147	Mack the Knife/Was There a Call for Me	1959	5.00	10.00	20.00
6147 [PS]	Mack the Knife/Was There a Call for Me	1959	10.00	20.00	40.00

Number	Title (A Side/B Side)	Yr	VG	VG+	NM
6158	Beyond the Sea/That's the Way Love Is	1960	5.00	10.00	20.00
6158 [PS]	Beyond the Sea/That's the Way Love Is	1960	10.00	20.00	40.00
6161	Clementine/Tall Story	1960	5.00	10.00	20.00
6161 [PS]	Clementine/Tall Story	1960	10.00	20.00	40.00
6167	Won't You Come Home Bill Bailey/I'll Be There	1960	5.00	10.00	20.00
6167 [PS]	Won't You Come Home Bill Bailey/I'll Be There	1960	7.50	15.00	30.00
6173	Beachcomber/Autumn Blues	1960	5.00	10.00	20.00
6173 [PS]	Beachcomber/Autumn Blues	1960	7.50	15.00	30.00
6179	Artificial Flowers/Somebody to Love	1960	5.00	10.00	20.00
6179 [PS]	Artificial Flowers/Somebody to Love	1960	7.50	15.00	30.00
6183	Christmas Auld Lang Syne/Child of God	1960	6.25	12.50	25.00
6183 [PS]	Christmas Auld Lang Syne/Child of God	1960	10.00	20.00	40.00
6188	Lazy River/Oo-Ee Train	1961	3.00	6.00	12.00
6188 [PS]	Lazy River/Oo-Ee Train	1961	5.00	10.00	20.00
6196	Nature Boy/Look for My True Love	1961	3.00	6.00	12.00
6196 [PS]	Nature Boy/Look for My True Love	1961	5.00	10.00	20.00
6200	Come September/Walk Back to Me	1961	3.75	7.50	15.00
6200 [PS]	Come September/Walk Back to Me	1961	12.50	25.00	50.00
6206	You Must Have Been a Beautiful Baby/Sorrow Tomorrow	1961	3.00	6.00	12.00
6206 [PS]	You Must Have Been a Beautiful Baby/Sorrow Tomorrow	1961	5.00	10.00	20.00
6211	Ave Maria/O Come All Ye Faithful	1961	3.00	6.00	12.00
6211 [PS]	Ave Maria/O Come All Ye Faithful	1961	40.00	80.00	160.00
6214	Irresistible You/Multiplication	1961	3.00	6.00	12.00
6214 [PS]	Irresistible You/Multiplication	1961	5.00	10.00	20.00
6221	What'd I Say (Part 1)/What'd I Say (Part 2)	1962	3.00	6.00	12.00
6221 [PS]	What'd I Say (Part 1)/What'd I Say (Part 2)	1962	5.00	10.00	20.00
6229	Things/Jalier Bring Me Water	1962	3.00	6.00	12.00
6236	Baby Face/You Know How	1962	3.00	6.00	12.00
6244	I Found a New Baby/Keep a-Walkin'	1962	3.00	6.00	12.00
6297	Milord/Golden Earrings	1964	2.50	5.00	10.00
6316	Swing Low Sweet Chariot/Similau	1964	2.50	5.00	10.00
6334	Minnie the Moocher/Hard Hearted Hannah	1965	2.50	5.00	10.00
ATLANTIC					
2305	Funny What Love Can Do/We Didn't Ask to Be Brought Here	1965	2.00	4.00	8.00
2317	Silver Dollar/The Breaking Point	1966	2.00	4.00	8.00
2329	Mame/Walking in the Shadow of Love	1966	2.00	4.00	8.00
2341	Who's Afraid of Virginia Woolf?/Merci, Cheri	1966	2.00	4.00	8.00
2350	If I Were a Carpenter/Rainin'	1966	2.50	5.00	10.00
2367	The Girl That Stood Beside Me/Reason to Believe	1966	2.00	4.00	8.00
2376	Lovin' You/Amy	1967	2.00	4.00	8.00
2395	The Lady Came from Baltimore/I Am	1967	2.00	4.00	8.00
2420	Darlin' Be Home Soon/Hello, Sunshine	1967	2.00	4.00	8.00
2433	Talk to the Animals/After Today	1967	2.00	4.00	8.00
2433	Talk to the Animals/She Knows	1967	2.00	4.00	8.00
89166	Beyond the Sea/Mack the Knife	1987	—	—	3.00
89166 [PS]	Beyond the Sea/Mack the Knife	1987	—	—	3.00
—From the movie "Big Town"					
BRUNSWICK					
55073	Early in the Morning/Now We're One	1958	20.00	40.00	80.00
—As "The Ding Dongs"; also see Atco 6121					
CAPITOL					
4837	If a Man Answers/True, True Love	1962	2.50	5.00	10.00
4837 [PS]	If a Man Answers/True, True Love	1962	3.75	7.50	15.00
4897	You're the Reason I'm Living/Now You're Gone	1962	2.50	5.00	10.00
4897 [PS]	You're the Reason I'm Living/Now You're Gone	1962	3.75	7.50	15.00
4970	18 Yellow Roses/Not for Me	1963	2.50	5.00	10.00
4970 [PS]	18 Yellow Roses/Not for Me	1963	3.75	7.50	15.00
5019	Treat My Baby Good/Down So Long	1963	2.50	5.00	10.00
5079	Be Mad Little Girl/Since You've Been Gone	1963	2.50	5.00	10.00
5126	I Wonder Who's Kissing Her Now/As Long As I'm Singing	1964	2.50	5.00	10.00
5257	The Things in This House/Wait by the Water	1964	2.50	5.00	10.00
5359	Hello, Dolly!/Golden Earrings	1965	2.50	5.00	10.00
5399	A World Without You/Venice Blue	1965	2.50	5.00	10.00
5443	When I Get Home/Lonely Road	1965	2.50	5.00	10.00
5443 [PS]	When I Get Home/Lonely Road	1965	6.25	12.50	25.00
5481	Gyp the Cat/That Funny Feeling	1965	2.50	5.00	10.00
DECCA					
29883	Rock Island Line/Timber	1956	10.00	20.00	40.00
29922	Silly Willy/Blue Eyed Mermaid	1956	12.50	25.00	50.00
30031	The Greatest Builder (Of Them All)/Hear Them Bells	1956	10.00	20.00	40.00
30225	Dealer in Dreams/Help Me	1957	10.00	20.00	40.00
30737	Silly Willy/Dealer in Dreams	1958	7.50	15.00	30.00
DIRECTION					
350	Long Line Rider/Change	1968	2.00	4.00	8.00
351	Song for a Dollar/Mr. and Mrs. Hohner	1969	2.00	4.00	8.00
352	Distractions (Part 1)/Jive	1969	2.00	4.00	8.00
4000	Sugar Man/(9 to 5) Jive's Alive	1970	2.00	4.00	8.00
4001	Baby May/Sweet Reason	1970	2.00	4.00	8.00
4002	Maybe We Can Get It Together/Rx Pyro (Prescription: Fire)	1970	2.00	4.00	8.00
MOTOWN					
1183	Melodie/Someday We'll Be Together	1971	—	3.00	6.00
1193	Simple Song of Freedom/I'll Be Your Baby Tonight	1971	—	3.00	6.00
1203	Sail Away/Something in Her Love	1972	—	3.00	6.00
1212	Average People/Something in Her Love	1972	—	3.00	6.00
1217	Happy/Something in Her Love	1973	—	3.00	6.00

7-Inch Extended Plays

Number	Title (A Side/B Side)	Yr	VG	VG+	NM
ATCO					
4502	*Splish Splash/Judy, Don't Be Moody/I Found a Million Dollar Baby/(Since You're Gone) I Can't Go On	1959	12.50	25.00	50.00
4502 [PS]	Bobby Darin	1959	12.50	25.00	50.00
4504	Mack the Knife/That's the Way Love Is//Beyond the Sea/That's All	1959	12.50	25.00	50.00
4504 [PS]	That's All	1959	12.50	25.00	50.00
4505	Queen of the Hop/Lost Love//Plain Jane/While I'm Gone	1960	12.50	25.00	50.00
4505 [PS]	Bobby Darin	1960	12.50	25.00	50.00
4508	Clementine/My Gal Sal//Guys and Dolls/Down with Love	1960	12.50	25.00	50.00
4508 [PS]	This Is Darin	1960	12.50	25.00	50.00
4512	I Got A Woman/You'd Be So Nice To Come Home To//Medley: By Myself-When Your Lover Has Gone/Love For Sale	1960	12.50	25.00	50.00
4512 [PS]	Darin at the Copa	1960	12.50	25.00	50.00
CAPITOL CUSTOM					
TB-2262/3	18 Yellow Roses/Not for Me/The Things in This House//You're the Reason I'm Living/Treat My Baby Good/Wait by the Water, Lillian	1963	7.50	15.00	30.00
—Small hole, plays at 33 1/3 rpm					
TB-2262/3 [PS]	Bobby Darin Presents	1963	10.00	20.00	40.00
—"Manufactured by Capitol Records, Inc., Custom Services Department for Artistic Records"					
MB-2849/50	If a Man Answers/True, True Love//Sermon of Samson/All By Myself	1962	5.00	10.00	20.00
MB-2849/50 [PS]	Scripto Inc. Presents Bobby Darin	1962	7.50	15.00	30.00
—Value is for sleeve alone; the pen that came with the package is very rare					
DECCA					
ED 2676	(contents unknown)	1957	25.00	50.00	100.00
ED 2676 [PS]	Hear Them Bells	1957	25.00	50.00	100.00
MOTOWN					
PR-4 [DJ]	If I Were a Carpenter/Moritat (Mack the Knife)//Blue Monday/Happy	1973	3.75	7.50	15.00
PR-4 [PS]	(title unknown)	1973	5.00	10.00	20.00

Albums

Number	Title	Yr	VG	VG+	NM
ATCO					
33-102 [M]	Bobby Darin	1958	25.00	50.00	100.00
—Yellow "harp" label					
33-102 [M]	Bobby Darin	1962	7.50	15.00	30.00
—Gold and dark blue label					
33-104 [M]	That's All	1959	10.00	20.00	40.00
—Yellow "harp" label					
33-104 [M]	That's All	1962	5.00	10.00	20.00
—Gold and dark blue label					
SD 33-104 [S]	That's All	1959	25.00	50.00	100.00
—Yellow "harp" label					
SD 33-104 [S]	That's All	1962	6.25	12.50	25.00
—Purple and brown label					
33-115 [M]	This Is Darin	1960	10.00	20.00	40.00
—Yellow "harp" label					
33-115 [M]	This Is Darin	1962	5.00	10.00	20.00
—Gold and dark blue label					
SD 33-115 [S]	This Is Darin	1960	20.00	40.00	80.00
—Yellow "harp" label					
SD 33-115 [S]	This Is Darin	1962	6.25	12.50	25.00
—Purple and brown label					
33-122 [M]	Darin at the Copa	1960	10.00	20.00	40.00
—Yellow "harp" label					
33-122 [M]	Darin at the Copa	1962	5.00	10.00	20.00
—Gold and dark blue label					
SD 33-122 [S]	Darin at the Copa	1960	20.00	40.00	80.00
—Yellow "harp" label					
SD 33-122 [S]	Darin at the Copa	1962	6.25	12.50	25.00
—Purple and brown label					
33-124 [M]	It's You or No One	1960	10.00	20.00	40.00
—Yellow "harp" label					
33-124 [M]	It's You or No One	1962	5.00	10.00	20.00
—Gold and dark blue label					
SD 33-124 [S]	It's You or No One	1960	20.00	40.00	80.00
—Yellow "harp" label					
SD 33-124 [S]	It's You or No One	1962	6.25	12.50	25.00
—Purple and brown label					
33-125 [M]	The 25th Day of December	1960	12.50	25.00	50.00
—Yellow "harp" label					
33-125 [M]	The 25th Day of December	1962	5.00	10.00	20.00
—Gold and dark blue label					
SD 33-125 [S]	The 25th Day of December	1960	15.00	30.00	60.00
—Yellow "harp" label					
SD 33-125 [S]	The 25th Day of December	1962	6.25	12.50	25.00
—Gold and dark blue label					
33-126 [M]	Two of a Kind	1961	10.00	20.00	40.00
—Yellow "harp" label					
33-126 [M]	Two of a Kind	1962	5.00	10.00	20.00
—Gold and dark blue label					
SD 33-126 [S]	Two of a Kind	1961	12.50	25.00	50.00
—Yellow "harp" label					
SD 33-126 [S]	Two of a Kind	1962	6.25	12.50	25.00
—Purple and brown label					
33-131 [M]	The Bobby Darin Story	1961	10.00	20.00	40.00
—Yellow "harp" label; white cover					
33-131 [M]	The Bobby Darin Story	1962	5.00	10.00	20.00
—Gold and dark blue label; black cover					
SD 33-131	The Bobby Darin Story	1969	3.00	6.00	12.00
—Yellow label, "Atco" on left					
SD 33-131	The Bobby Darin Story	1978	2.00	4.00	8.00
—Any later Atco label					
SD 33-131 [S]	The Bobby Darin Story	1961	12.50	25.00	50.00
—Yellow "harp" label; white cover					
SD 33-131 [S]	The Bobby Darin Story	1962	6.25	12.50	25.00
—Purple and brown label; black cover					
33-134 [M]	Love Swings	1961	10.00	20.00	40.00
—Yellow "harp" label					
33-134 [M]	Love Swings	1962	5.00	10.00	20.00
—Gold and dark blue label					
SD 33-134 [S]	Love Swings	1961	12.50	25.00	50.00
—Yellow "harp" label					
SD 33-134 [S]	Love Swings	1962	6.25	12.50	25.00
—Purple and brown label					
33-138 [M]	Twist with Bobby Darin	1961	10.00	20.00	40.00
—Yellow "harp" label					
33-138 [M]	Twist with Bobby Darin	1962	5.00	10.00	20.00
—Gold and dark blue label					
SD 33-138 [S]	Twist with Bobby Darin	1961	12.50	25.00	50.00
—Yellow "harp" label					

Number	Title (A Side/B Side)	Yr	VG	VG+	NM
SD 33-138 [S]	Twist with Bobby Darin	1962	6.25	12.50	25.00
—Purple and brown label					
33-140 [M]	Bobby Darin Sings Ray Charles	1962	6.25	12.50	25.00
SD 33-140 [S]	Bobby Darin Sings Ray Charles	1962	7.50	15.00	30.00
33-146 [M]	Things & Other Things	1962	6.25	12.50	25.00
SD 33-146 [S]	Things & Other Things	1962	7.50	15.00	30.00
33-167 [M]	Winners	1964	6.25	12.50	25.00
SD 33-167 [S]	Winners	1964	7.50	15.00	30.00
SP 1001 [M]	For Teenagers Only	1960	37.50	75.00	150.00
—Gatefold with fold-open poster and paper insert					
SP 1001 [M]	For Teenagers Only	1960	18.75	37.50	75.00
—With extras missing					
90484	Two of a Kind	1986	2.50	5.00	10.00
ATLANTIC					
8121 [M]	The Shadow of Your Smile	1966	3.75	7.50	15.00
SD 8121 [S]	The Shadow of Your Smile	1966	5.00	10.00	20.00
8126 [M]	In a Broadway Bag	1966	3.75	7.50	15.00
SD 8126 [S]	In a Broadway Bag	1966	5.00	10.00	20.00
8135 [M]	If I Were a Carpenter	1967	3.75	7.50	15.00
SD 8135 [S]	If I Were a Carpenter	1967	12.50	25.00	50.00
—Inexplicably rare in stereo					
8142 [M]	Inside Out	1967	3.75	7.50	15.00
SD 8142 [S]	Inside Out	1967	7.50	15.00	30.00
8154 [M]	Bobby Darin Sings Doctor Dolittle	1967	3.75	7.50	15.00
SD 8154 [S]	Bobby Darin Sings Doctor Dolittle	1967	3.75	7.50	15.00
BAINBRIDGE					
6220	Bobby Darin at the Copa	1981	2.50	5.00	10.00
CAPITOL					
ST 1791 [S]	Oh! Look at Me Now	1962	5.00	10.00	20.00
SW 1791 [S]	Oh! Look at Me Now	1962	6.25	12.50	25.00
T 1791 [M]	Oh! Look at Me Now	1962	3.75	7.50	15.00
W 1791 [M]	Oh! Look at Me Now	1962	5.00	10.00	20.00
ST 1826 [S]	Earthy	1963	5.00	10.00	20.00
T 1826 [M]	Earthy	1963	3.75	7.50	15.00
ST 1866 [S]	You're the Reason I'm Living	1963	5.00	10.00	20.00
T 1866 [M]	You're the Reason I'm Living	1963	3.75	7.50	15.00
ST 1942 [S]	18 Yellow Roses	1963	5.00	10.00	20.00
T 1942 [M]	18 Yellow Roses	1963	3.75	7.50	15.00
ST 2007 [S]	Golden Folk Hits	1963	5.00	10.00	20.00
T 2007 [M]	Golden Folk Hits	1963	3.75	7.50	15.00
ST 2194 [S]	From Hello Dolly to Goodbye Charlie	1964	5.00	10.00	20.00
T 2194 [M]	From Hello Dolly to Goodbye Charlie	1964	3.75	7.50	15.00
ST 2322 [S]	Venice Blue	1965	5.00	10.00	20.00
T 2322 [M]	Venice Blue	1965	3.75	7.50	15.00
ST 2571 [S]	The Best of Bobby Darin	1966	3.75	7.50	15.00
T 2571 [M]	The Best of Bobby Darin	1966	3.75	7.50	15.00
CLARION					
603 [M]	Clementine	1966	5.00	10.00	20.00
SD 603 [S]	Clementine	1966	6.25	12.50	25.00
DIRECTION					
1936	Born Walden Robert Cassotto	1968	6.25	12.50	25.00
1937	Committment	1969	6.25	12.50	25.00
MOTOWN					
M5-185V1	Darin 1936-1973	1981	3.00	6.00	12.00
—Reissue					
MS-739	Finally	1972	125.00	250.00	500.00
—Unreleased; value is for RCA test pressing					
M 753L	Bobby Darin	1972	5.00	10.00	20.00
M6-813L	Darin 1936-1973	1974	3.75	7.50	15.00

DARIUS

Albums

Number	Title (A Side/B Side)	Yr	VG	VG+	NM
CHARTMAKER					
1102	Darius	1969	62.50	125.00	250.00

DARLING, JOHNNY

45s

Number	Title (A Side/B Side)	Yr	VG	VG+	NM
DELUXE					
6167	I Don't Want to Wind Up in Love/Baseball Baby	1956	37.50	75.00	150.00

DARNELL, LARRY

45s

Number	Title (A Side/B Side)	Yr	VG	VG+	NM
ANNA					
1109	With Tears in My Eyes/I'll Get Along Somehow	1960	100.00	200.00	400.00
ARGO					
5372	With Tears in My Eyes/I'll Get Along Somehow	1960	6.25	12.50	25.00
DELUXE					
6123	Ramblin' Man/I Care	1957	7.50	15.00	30.00
6136	If You Go/Fing Fang Foy	1957	7.50	15.00	30.00
6141	Just Tell Me When/It Must Be Love	1957	7.50	15.00	30.00
OKEH					
6848	Work Baby Work/Left My Baby	1952	6.25	12.50	25.00
6869	Darlin'/Boogie-Oogie	1952	6.25	12.50	25.00
6902	What's On Your Mind/Better Be on My Way	1952	6.25	12.50	25.00
6916	No Time at All/Singin' My Blues	1952	6.25	12.50	25.00
6919	I'll Get Along Somehow (Part 1)/I'll Get Along Somehow (Part 2)	1952	6.25	12.50	25.00
6926	Christmas Blues/I Am the Sparrow	1952	6.25	12.50	25.00
6954	I'll Be Sittin', I'll Be Rockin'/Crazy She Calls Me	1953	6.25	12.50	25.00
7024	I'll Carry On/What More Do You Want Me to Do	1954	5.00	10.00	20.00
7039	I'm Gonna Change/Thank You, Darlin'	1954	5.00	10.00	20.00
7056	My Love for You/Feelin' Mighty Sad and Low	1955	5.00	10.00	20.00
REGAL					
3328	Do You Love Me Baby/Sad and Lonesome	1951	6.25	12.50	25.00
—Larry Darnell records on Regal before 3328 are unconfirmed on 45 rpm					
SAVOY					
1151	That's All I Want from You/Who Showed My Baby How to Love Me	1955	7.50	15.00	30.00
WARWICK					
506	If I Had You/Thankful	1959	5.00	10.00	20.00

7-Inch Extended Plays

Number	Title (A Side/B Side)	Yr	VG	VG+	NM
EPIC					
7072	(contents unknown)	1961	5.00	10.00	20.00
7072 [PS]	For You My Love	1961	5.00	10.00	20.00

DARNELLS, THE

See THE MARVELETTES.

DARRELL, JOHNNY

45s

Number	Title (A Side/B Side)	Yr	VG	VG+	NM
CAPRICORN					
0207	Orange Blossom Special/Glendale, Arizona	1974	—	2.00	4.00
0223	Pieces of My Life/Glendale, Arizona	1975	—	2.00	4.00
0234	Rose Colored Gin/Glendale, Arizona	1975	—	2.00	4.00
CARTWHEEL					
203	Don't It Seem to Rain a Lot/I'll Never Get Up This Slow	1971	—	2.50	5.00
209	Mr. Tambourine Man/Let Me Stay Awhile	1972	—	2.50	5.00
GUSTO					
9001	Hard to Be Friends/These Days	1978	—	2.00	4.00
9011	Was Yesterday That Long Ago/Spanish Song	1978	—	2.00	4.00
MONUMENT					
8570	Crazy Daddy/Uncle Veneer	1973	—	2.50	5.00
8579	Dakota the Dancing Bear/Just a Memory	1973	—	2.50	5.00
UNITED ARTISTS					
943	As Long As the Wind Blows/Beggars Can't Be Choosers	1965	2.00	4.00	8.00
50008	Johnny Lose It All/For Old Times' Sake	1966	2.00	4.00	8.00
50047	She's Mighty Gone/Baby Sitter	1966	2.00	4.00	8.00
50126	Ruby, Don't Take Your Love to Town/Little Things I Love	1967	2.00	4.00	8.00
50183	My Elusive Dreams/Pickin' with Gold	1967	2.00	4.00	8.00
50207	Come See What's Left of Your Man/Passin' Through	1967	2.00	4.00	8.00
50235	The Son of Hickory Holler's Tramp/But That's Alright	1967	2.00	4.00	8.00
50292	With Pen in Hand/Poetry of Love	1968	—	3.00	6.00
50442	I Ain't Buying/Little Things	1968	—	3.00	6.00
50481	Woman Without Love/I Fought the Law	1968	—	3.00	6.00
50503	The Coming of the Roads/The Other Side of the Coin	1969	—	3.00	6.00
—With Anita Carter					
50518	Why You Been Gone So Long/You're Always the One	1969	—	3.00	6.00
50572	River Bottom/Ain't That Living	1969	—	3.00	6.00
50610	She's Headed for the Country/Trouble Maker	1969	—	3.00	6.00
50629	Mama Come'n Get Your Baby Boy/These Days	1970	—	3.00	6.00
50675	Brother River/Bed of Roses	1970	—	3.00	6.00
50716	They'll Never Take Her Love from Me/One Love, Two Hearts, Three Lives	1970	—	3.00	6.00
50739	Look Out Cleveland/Winter's Comin' On	1971	—	3.00	6.00

Albums

Number	Title (A Side/B Side)	Yr	VG	VG+	NM
CAPRICORN					
CP 0154	Water Glass Full of Whiskey	1975	2.50	5.00	10.00
SUNSET					
SUS-5232	The Johnny Darrell Sound	1969	2.50	5.00	10.00
UNITED ARTISTS					
UAL 3594 [M]	Ruby, Don't Take Your Love to Town	1967	6.25	12.50	25.00
UAS 6594 [S]	Ruby, Don't Take Your Love to Town	1967	5.00	10.00	20.00
UAS 6634	The Son of Hickory Holler's Tramp	1968	5.00	10.00	20.00
UAS 6660	With Pen in Hand	1968	5.00	10.00	20.00
UAS 6707	Why You Been Gone So Long	1969	5.00	10.00	20.00
UAS 6752	California Stop-Over	1970	5.00	10.00	20.00
UAS 6759	The Best of Johnny Darrell, Volume 1	1970	3.75	7.50	15.00

DARRELL AND THE OXFORDS

See THE TOKENS.

DARREN, JAMES

45s

Number	Title (A Side/B Side)	Yr	VG	VG+	NM
BUDDAH					
177	That's My World/Wheeling, West Virginia	1970	—	2.50	5.00
COLPIX					
102	There's No Such Thing/Mighty Pretty Territory	1959	3.75	7.50	15.00
102 [PS]	There's No Such Thing/Mighty Pretty Territory	1959	7.50	15.00	30.00
113	Gidget/You	1959	3.75	7.50	15.00
119 [M]	Angel Face/I Don't Wanna Lose Ya	1959	3.75	7.50	15.00
119 [PS]	Angel Face/I Don't Wanna Lose Ya	1959	7.50	15.00	30.00
SCP-119 [S]	Angel Face/I Don't Wanna Lose Ya	1959	10.00	20.00	40.00
128	I Ain't Sharin' Sharon/Love Among the Young	1959	3.75	7.50	15.00
130	Teenage Tears/Let There Be Love	1959	3.75	7.50	15.00
138	You Are My Dream/Your Smile	1960	3.75	7.50	15.00
142	Because They're Young/Tears in My Eyes	1960	3.75	7.50	15.00
142 [PS]	Because They're Young/Tears in My Eyes	1960	7.50	15.00	30.00
145	P.S. I Love You/Traveling Down a Lonesome Road	1960	3.75	7.50	15.00
155	How Sweet You Are/All the Young Men	1960	3.75	7.50	15.00
168	Man About Town/Come On My Love	1960	3.75	7.50	15.00
181	Walking My Baby Back Home/Goodbye My Lady	1960	3.75	7.50	15.00
—Colpix 102-181 by "Jimmy Darren"					
185	Fool's Paradise/Gotta Have Love	1961	3.75	7.50	15.00
189	Gidget Goes Hawaiian/Wild About the Girl	1961	3.75	7.50	15.00
194	Hand in Hand/You Are My Dream	1961	3.75	7.50	15.00
609	Goodbye Cruel World/Valerie	1961	3.75	7.50	15.00
609 [PS]	Goodbye Cruel World/Valerie	1961	6.25	12.50	25.00
622	Her Royal Majesty/If I Could Only Tell You	1962	3.00	6.00	12.00
630	Conscience/Dream Big	1962	3.00	6.00	12.00
644	Mary's Little Lamb/The Life of the Party	1962	3.00	6.00	12.00
655	Hail to the Conquering Hero/Too Young to Go Steady	1962	3.00	6.00	12.00
664	Hear What I Want to Hear/I'll Be Loving You	1962	3.00	6.00	12.00
672	Pin a Medal on Joey/Diamond Head	1963	3.00	6.00	12.00
685	They Should Have Given You the Oscar/Blame It on My Youth	1963	3.00	6.00	12.00
696	Gegetta/Grande Luna, Italiana	1963	3.00	6.00	12.00
708	Under the Yum Yum Tree/Backstage	1963	3.00	6.00	12.00

Number	Title (A Side/B Side)	Yr	VG	VG+	NM
758	Punch and Judy/Just Think of Tonight	1964	5.00	10.00	20.00
765	A Married Man/Baby, Talk to Me	1964	2.50	5.00	10.00
KIRSHNER					
63-1012	I Think Somebody Loves Me/Ain't Been Home in a Long Time	1970	—	2.50	5.00
63-5013	Bring Me Down Slow/More and More	1971	—	2.50	5.00
63-5015	Mammy Blue/As Long As You Love Me	1971	—	2.50	5.00
63-5025	Brian's Song/Thnak Heaven for Little Girls	1973	—	2.50	5.00
MGM					
14558	Let the Heartaches Begin/Sad Song	1973	—	2.00	4.00
14667	Sad-Eyed Romany Woman/Stay	1973	—	2.00	4.00
PRIVATE STOCK					
45050	Love on the Screen/Losing You	1975	—	2.00	4.00
45064	One Has My Name, The Other Has My Heart/ Sleepin' in a Bed of Lies	1975	—	2.00	4.00
45136	You Take My Heart Away/You Take My Heart Away (Disco)	1977	—	2.00	4.00
45152 [DJ]	Only a Dream Away (mono/stereo)	1977	—	2.50	5.00
—Stock copies may not exist					
RCA					
PB-11316	Let Me Take You in My Arms Again/California	1978	—	2.00	4.00
PB-11419	Next Time/Something Like Nothing Before	1978	—	2.00	4.00
WARNER BROS.					
5648	Because You're Mine/Millions of Roses	1965	2.00	4.00	8.00
5689	I Want to Be Lonely/Tom Hawk	1966	2.00	4.00	8.00
5812	Where Did We Go Wrong/Counting the Cracks	1966	2.00	4.00	8.00
5838	Crazy Me/They Don't Know	1966	2.00	4.00	8.00
5856	Love Is Where You Find It/(Let's Worry About) Tomorrow Tomorrow	1966	2.00	4.00	8.00
5874	All/Misty Morning Eyes	1966	2.00	4.00	8.00
7013	I Miss You So/Since I Don't Have You	1967	2.00	4.00	8.00
7053	Didn't We/Counting the Cracks	1967	2.00	4.00	8.00
7071	The House Song/They Don't Know	1967	2.00	4.00	8.00
7152	Cherie/Wait Until Dark	1967	2.00	4.00	8.00
7206	A Little Bit of Heaven/Each and Every Part of Me	1968	2.00	4.00	8.00
Albums					
COLPIX					
CLP-406 [M]	James Darren (Album No. 1)	1960	10.00	20.00	40.00
CLP-406 [M]	James Darren (Album No. 1)	1960	37.50	75.00	150.00
—Green vinyl					
CLP-418 [M]	Gidget Goes Hawaiian (James Darren Sings the Movies)	1961	7.50	15.00	30.00
SCP-418 [S]	Gidget Goes Hawaiian (James Darren Sings the Movies)	1961	10.00	20.00	40.00
CLP-424 [M]	James Darren Sings for All Sizes	1962	7.50	15.00	30.00
SCP-424 [S]	James Darren Sings for All Sizes	1962	10.00	20.00	40.00
CLP-428 [M]	Love Among the Young	1962	7.50	15.00	30.00
SCP-428 [S]	Love Among the Young	1962	10.00	20.00	40.00
KIRSHNER					
KES-115	Mammy Blue	1971	3.75	7.50	15.00
KES-116	Love Songs from the Movies	1972	3.75	7.50	15.00
WARNER BROS.					
W 1668 [M]	James Darren/All	1967	3.75	7.50	15.00
WS 1668 [S]	James Darren/All	1967	5.00	10.00	20.00

DARREN, JAMES/ SHELLEY FABARES/PAUL PETERSEN

Number	Title (A Side/B Side)	Yr	VG	VG+	NM
Albums					
COLPIX					
CP-444 [M]	Teenage Triangle	1963	10.00	20.00	40.00
SCP-444 [R]	Teenage Triangle	1963	10.00	20.00	40.00
CP-468 [M]	More Teenage Triangle	1964	10.00	20.00	40.00
SCP-468 [P]	More Teenage Triangle	1964	15.00	30.00	60.00

DARTELLS, THE

Number	Title (A Side/B Side)	Yr	VG	VG+	NM
45s					
ARLEN					
509	Hot Pastrami/Dartell Stomp	1963	6.25	12.50	25.00
513	Dance, Everybody, Dance/The Scoobie Song	1963	6.25	12.50	25.00
DOT					
16453	Hot Pastrami/Dartell Stomp	1963	5.00	10.00	20.00
16502	Dance, Everybody, Dance/The Scoobie Song	1963	5.00	10.00	20.00
16551	Convicted/Sweet Pea	1963	3.75	7.50	15.00
16646	Swiss Cheese/Dartell Stomp	1964	3.75	7.50	15.00
HANNA-BARBERA					
457	Clap Your Hands/Where Do We Stand	1965	3.75	7.50	15.00
SANDE					
103	The Girl Can't Help It/Stranger on the Shore	1964	7.50	15.00	30.00
Albums					
DOT					
DLP-3522 [M]	Hot Pastrami	1963	7.50	15.00	30.00
DLP-25522 [S]	Hot Pastrami	1963	10.00	20.00	40.00

DARTS, THE

Number	Title (A Side/B Side)	Yr	VG	VG+	NM
Albums					
DEL-FI					
DFLP-1244 [M]	Hollywood Drag	1963	10.00	20.00	40.00
DFST-1244 [S]	Hollywood Drag	1963	12.50	25.00	50.00

DARVELL, BARRY

Number	Title (A Side/B Side)	Yr	VG	VG+	NM
45s					
ATLANTIC					
2128	Lost Love/Silver Dollar	1961	5.00	10.00	20.00
2138	Adam and Eve/A King for Tonight	1962	5.00	10.00	20.00
COLT 45					
104	Teenage Love/(B-side unknown)	1959	5.00	10.00	20.00
107	Geronimo Stomp/How Will It End	1959	15.00	30.00	60.00
110	Butterfly Baby/Send Me Some Loving	1960	6.25	12.50	25.00
301	Run Little Billy/All I Need Is You	1961	5.00	10.00	20.00
COLUMBIA					
44197	My World of Make Believe/Beggar's Paradise	1967	2.00	4.00	8.00
CUB					
9088	Little Angel Lost/Fountain of Love	1961	5.00	10.00	20.00
PROVIDENCE					
404	When You're Alone/It's Rainin', It's Pourin'	1964	3.00	6.00	12.00
WORLD ARTISTS					
1042	I'll Remember/Where Is the Love for Me	1965	3.00	6.00	12.00
1058	I Found a Daisy (in the City)/Kissable Lips	1965	3.00	6.00	12.00

DASH, JULIAN, ORCHESTRA

Number	Title (A Side/B Side)	Yr	VG	VG+	NM
45s					
VEE JAY					
144	Zero/Rhythm Punch	1955	12.50	25.00	50.00

DASHIEL, BUD, AND THE KINSMEN

Number	Title (A Side/B Side)	Yr	VG	VG+	NM
45s					
WARNER BROS.					
5231	Pom Pa Lum/I Talk to the Trees	1961	2.50	5.00	10.00
5276	In Tarrytown/Big Manuel	1962	2.50	5.00	10.00
Albums					
WARNER BROS.					
W 1429 [M]	Folk Music in a Contemporary Manner	1961	6.25	12.50	25.00
WS 1429 [S]	Folk Music in a Contemporary Manner	1961	7.50	15.00	30.00
W 1432 [M]	Live Concert Extraordinaire — Bud Dashiel and the Kinsmen Sing Everybody's Hits	1961	6.25	12.50	25.00
WS 1432 [S]	Live Concert Extraordinaire — Bud Dashiel and the Kinsmen Sing Everybody's Hits	1961	7.50	15.00	30.00

DATE WITH SOUL, A

See HALE AND THE HUSHABYES.

DAUGHTERS OF ALBION, THE

Number	Title (A Side/B Side)	Yr	VG	VG+	NM
45s					
FONTANA					
1619	Well Wired/The Story of Sad	1968	2.50	5.00	10.00
Albums					
FONTANA					
SRF-67586	The Daughters of Albion	1968	5.00	10.00	20.00

DAVE AND THE CARDIGANS

Number	Title (A Side/B Side)	Yr	VG	VG+	NM
45s					
BAY					
216	My Falling Star/Cha Cha Baby	1963	50.00	100.00	200.00

DAVE AND THE MARKSMEN

With Dave Marks, former member of THE BEACH BOYS.

Number	Title (A Side/B Side)	Yr	VG	VG+	NM
45s					
A&M					
730	Cruisin'/Kustom Kar Show	1964	12.50	25.00	50.00
WARNER BROS.					
5485	I Wanna Cry/I Could Make You Mine	1964	7.50	15.00	30.00
WESTCO					
10	Down the Tubes/Ooh Poo Pa Doo	1963	12.50	25.00	50.00
—Black vinyl					
10	Down the Tubes/Ooh Poo Pa Doo	1963	25.00	50.00	100.00
—Yellow vinyl					

DAVE DEE, DOZY, BEAKY, MICK & TICH

Number	Title (A Side/B Side)	Yr	VG	VG+	NM
45s					
ATLANTIC					
89757 [DJ]	Staying With It (same on both sides)	1983	—	2.50	5.00
—May be promo only					
BELL					
905	Kelly/Annabella	1970	—	3.00	6.00
—As "Dave Dee"					
942	Frisco Annie/Hey! Mr. President	1970	—	3.00	6.00
—As "D.B.M. & T."					
COTILLION					
44061	Bad News/Tonight-Today	1970	—	3.00	6.00
—As "Dozy, Beaky, Mick & Tich"					
44061 [PS]	Bad News/Tonight-Today	1970	2.50	5.00	10.00
—As "Dozy, Beaky, Mick & Tich"					
FONTANA					
1537	You Make It Move/No Time	1965	2.50	5.00	10.00
1545	Hold Tight/You Know What I Want	1966	2.50	5.00	10.00
1553	Hideaway/Here's a Heart	1966	2.50	5.00	10.00
1559	Bend It/She's So Good	1966	3.00	6.00	12.00
—With "clean" lyrics that refer to a dance; matrix number of "Bend It" is 38890					
1559	Bend It/She's So Good	1966	3.00	6.00	12.00
—With "dirty" lyrics that don't mention a dance; matrix number of "Bend It" is 39024					
1569	Save Me/Shame	1967	2.50	5.00	10.00
1591	Okay/Master Llewellyn	1967	2.50	5.00	10.00
IMPERIAL					
66270	Zabadak/The Sun Goes Down	1968	2.50	5.00	10.00
66287	Legend of Xanadu/Please	1968	2.00	4.00	8.00
66309	Break Out/Mrs. Thursday	1968	2.00	4.00	8.00
66325	Break Out/Mrs. Thursday	1968	2.00	4.00	8.00
66339	Wreck of the Antoinette/Margarita Linman	1968	2.00	4.00	8.00
Albums					
FONTANA					
MGF-27567 [M]	Greatest Hits	1967	7.50	15.00	30.00
SRF-67567 [P]	Greatest Hits	1967	10.00	20.00	40.00
—"Bend It" and "Hold Tight" are rechanneled.					
IMPERIAL					
LP-12402 [P]	Time to Take Off	1968	10.00	20.00	40.00
—"Zabadak" is rechanneled.					

DAVENPORT SISTERS, THE

Number	Title (A Side/B Side)	Yr	VG	VG+	NM
45s					
TRI-PHI					
1008	You've Got Me Crying Again/Hoy Hoy	1962	15.00	30.00	60.00

DAVEY AND THE BADMEN

Albums

Number	Title (A Side/B Side)	Yr	VG	VG+	NM
GOTHIC					
KRW-054	Wanted	1963	50.00	100.00	200.00

DAVI

45s

Number	Title (A Side/B Side)	Yr	VG	VG+	NM
SPARK					
110	Reason for Love/Go, Charley, Go	1962	75.00	150.00	300.00

DAVID, THE

45s

Number	Title (A Side/B Side)	Yr	VG	VG+	NM
20TH CENTURY FOX					
6663	40 Miles/Bus Token	1966	7.50	15.00	30.00
V.M.C.					
716	I'm Not Alone/(B-side unknown)	1968	6.25	12.50	25.00

Albums

Number	Title (A Side/B Side)	Yr	VG	VG+	NM
V.M.C.					
124	Another Day, Another Lifetime	1968	25.00	50.00	100.00

DAVID AND JONATHAN

45s

Number	Title (A Side/B Side)	Yr	VG	VG+	NM
20TH FOX					
6641	Modesty/Willie Waltz	1966	2.00	4.00	8.00
AMY					
11012	Softly Whispering I Love You/Something's Gotten Hold of My Heart	1968	—	3.00	6.00
CAPITOL					
5563	Michelle/How Bitter the Taste of Love	1965	2.50	5.00	10.00
5625	I Know/Speak Her Name	1966	2.00	4.00	8.00
5700	On My Word/Lovers of the World, Unite	1966	2.00	4.00	8.00
5777	The Magic Book/Time	1966	2.00	4.00	8.00
5870	Ten Stories High/Looking for My Life	1967	2.00	4.00	8.00
5934	She's Leaving Home/One Born Every Minute	1967	2.00	4.00	8.00

Albums

Number	Title (A Side/B Side)	Yr	VG	VG+	NM
CAPITOL					
ST 2473 [S]	Michelle	1966	5.00	10.00	20.00
T 2473 [M]	Michelle	1966	3.75	7.50	15.00

DAVIDSON, JOHN

45s

Number	Title (A Side/B Side)	Yr	VG	VG+	NM
20TH CENTURY					
2063	We Had It All/I Want to Spend My Life with You	1973	—	2.00	4.00
2121	Have a Nice Day/Less Than the Sun	1974	—	2.00	4.00
2175	The Other Woman/What Will I Tell the Kids	1975	—	2.00	4.00
2293	Love in the Shadows/Everytime I See a Love Song	1976	—	2.00	4.00
2313	I Let You Walk Away/Steal Her Away	1976	—	2.00	4.00
2326	Patch It Up/Save the Last Dance for Me	1976	—	2.00	4.00
COLUMBIA					
43531	I Can't Help This Feeling I Feel/I Still Send Her Flowers	1966	—	3.00	6.00
43635	Summer Love/I'll Try Lovin' You Less	1966	—	3.00	6.00
44005	Daydream/I'll Always Remember	1967	—	3.00	6.00
44210	In the Sunshine Days/If You Can Put That in a Bottle	1967	—	3.00	6.00
44334	What Is a Woman/How Come You Love Me Like You Do	1967	—	3.00	6.00
44478	Visions of Sugarplums/Flame	1968	—	3.00	6.00
44770	Words/The Wonder of You	1969	—	3.00	6.00
44896	California Blood Lines/I Am Now	1969	—	3.00	6.00
45034	It's Such a Lovely Time of Year/What Makes a Woman Run	1969	—	3.00	6.00
45155	Five O'Clock Shadow/A Promise and a Lie	1970	—	2.50	5.00
45196	I Got Love/Politician	1970	—	2.50	5.00
45254	Let's Get Lost In Now/What You're Doing to Me	1970	—	2.50	5.00
45423	Say It Again/Just Magic	1971	—	2.50	5.00
45486	Good Times/A Clown Never Cries	1971	—	2.50	5.00
MERCURY					
73362	As Lonely As You/What She Left of Me	1973	—	2.50	5.00

Albums

Number	Title (A Side/B Side)	Yr	VG	VG+	NM
20TH CENTURY					
T-429	Touch Me	1974	2.50	5.00	10.00
T-512	Every Time I Sing	1976	2.50	5.00	10.00
ACCORD					
SN-7202	Closeup	1981	2.00	4.00	8.00
COLUMBIA					
CL 2580 [M]	The Time of My Life	1966	2.50	5.00	10.00
CL 2648 [M]	My Best to You	1967	2.50	5.00	10.00
CL 2734 [M]	A Kind of Hush	1967	2.50	5.00	10.00
CS 9380 [S]	The Time of My Life	1966	3.00	6.00	12.00
CS 9448 [S]	My Best to You	1967	3.00	6.00	12.00
CS 9534 [S]	A Kind of Hush	1967	3.00	6.00	12.00
CS 9654	Goin' Places	1968	2.50	5.00	10.00
CS 9795	John Davidson	1969	2.50	5.00	10.00
CS 9859	My Cherie Amour	1969	2.50	5.00	10.00
CS 9864	My Christmas Favorites	1969	3.00	6.00	12.00
C 30098	Everything Is Beautiful	1970	2.50	5.00	10.00
PC 36956	Incredible	1981	2.00	4.00	8.00
MERCURY					
SRM-1-658	Well, Here I Am	1973	2.50	5.00	10.00

DAVIE, HUTCH

45s

Number	Title (A Side/B Side)	Yr	VG	VG+	NM
ATCO					
6110	Woodchopper's Ball/Honky Tonk Train	1958	3.00	6.00	12.00
6123	In the Mood/Gwendolyn and the Werewolf	1958	3.00	6.00	12.00
6136	Begin the Beguine/The Dipsy Doodle	1959	3.00	6.00	12.00
6149	Sweet Georgia Brown/Heartaches	1959	3.00	6.00	12.00
CANADIAN-AMERICAN					
126	The Glow Worm/Down Home	1961	2.50	5.00	10.00
CLARIDGE					
311	East Is East (Part 1)/East Is East (Part 2)	1966	2.00	4.00	8.00
CONGRESS					
102	But I Do/Time Was	1962	2.50	5.00	10.00
DYNO VOICE					
904	Never My Love/A Lover's Concerto	1968	—	3.00	6.00

Albums

Number	Title (A Side/B Side)	Yr	VG	VG+	NM
ATCO					
33-105 [M]	Much Hutch	1958	12.50	25.00	50.00

DAVIES, CYRIL

45s

Number	Title (A Side/B Side)	Yr	VG	VG+	NM
DOT					
16515	Chicago Calling/Country Line Special	1963	3.00	6.00	12.00

DAVIES, DAVE

Also see THE KINKS.

45s

Number	Title (A Side/B Side)	Yr	VG	VG+	NM
RCA					
PB-12089	Imagination's Real/Wild Man	1980	2.50	5.00	10.00
PB-12089 [PS]	Imagination's Real/Wild Man	1980	3.75	7.50	15.00
PB-12147	Doing the Best for You/Got No More to Lose	1981	2.50	5.00	10.00
REPRISE					
0614	Death of a Clown/Love Me Till the Sun Shines	1967	10.00	20.00	40.00
0660	Suzannah's Still Alive/Funny Face	1968	10.00	20.00	40.00
WARNER BROS.					
29425	Mean Disposition/Cold Winter	1983	—	—	—
—Unreleased?					
29425 [DJ]	Mean Disposition (same on both sides)	1983	2.50	5.00	10.00
29509	Love Gets You/One Night with You	1983	12.50	25.00	50.00
29509 [DJ]	Love Gets You (same on both sides)	1983	2.50	5.00	10.00

Albums

Number	Title (A Side/B Side)	Yr	VG	VG+	NM
RCA VICTOR					
AFL1-3603	AFL1-3603	1980	2.50	5.00	10.00
AFL1-4036	Glamour	1981	2.50	5.00	10.00
WARNER BROS.					
23917	Chosen People	1983	2.50	5.00	10.00

DAVIS, ANDREA

See MINNIE RIPERTON.

DAVIS, BILLIE

45s

Number	Title (A Side/B Side)	Yr	VG	VG+	NM
JERDEN					
758	Last One to Be Loved/You Don't Know	1965	2.50	5.00	10.00
772	No Other Baby/Hands Off	1965	2.50	5.00	10.00
LONDON					
20041	I Want You to Be My Baby/Suffer	1968	—	3.00	6.00
20049	I Can Remember/I'll Come Home	1968	—	3.00	6.00
20062	There Must Be a Reason/Love	1971	—	2.50	5.00

DAVIS, BILLY

Also see THE FIFTH DIMENSION.

45s

Number	Title (A Side/B Side)	Yr	VG	VG+	NM
ABC					
12106	Three Steps from True Love/Light a Candle	1975	—	2.50	5.00
COBBLESTONE					
731	Stanky (Get Funky)/I've Tried	1969	—	3.00	6.00
HI					
2146	It's All Over/Once in a Lifetime	1968	—	3.00	6.00

DAVIS, BO

45s

Number	Title (A Side/B Side)	Yr	VG	VG+	NM
CREST					
1027	Let's Coast Awhile/Drownin' All My Sorrows	1956	37.50	75.00	150.00
—Eddie Cochran plays guitar on this record.					

DAVIS, DANNY, AND THE NASHVILLE BRASS

Also includes Danny Davis credited alone.

45s

Number	Title (A Side/B Side)	Yr	VG	VG+	NM
HICKORY					
1005	Can't You Feel It in Your Heart/Second Hand Dreams for Sale	1954	3.00	6.00	12.00
JAROCO					
8742	Green Eyes (Cryin' Those Blue Tears)/(B-side unknown)	1987	—	2.00	4.00
LIBERTY					
55213	Beauty and the Beast/Glory Bugle	1959	2.50	5.00	10.00
MGM					
11103	Crazy Heart/I'm Not Alone	1951	3.75	7.50	15.00
11175	Please Bring Back the Sunshine/Deep Water	1952	3.75	7.50	15.00
11244	Always/Do You Ever Think of Me	1952	3.75	7.50	15.00
11286	Forget/Love Came Out of the Night	1952	3.75	7.50	15.00
11443	I Don't Want Your Kisses/Come to the Wedding	1953	3.75	7.50	15.00
13077	Pots 'N' Pans/Travelin' Trumpets	1962	2.00	4.00	8.00
13106	Little Bandits of Juarez/Theme from "Kill Or Cure"	1962	2.00	4.00	8.00
13270	Circus World/There Goes My Heart	1964	—	3.00	6.00
13295	Night Train from Jamaica/Ska Dee Wah	1964	—	3.00	6.00
—With Byron Lee					
13368	Ballad of Cat Ballou/Theme from "The Saint"	1965	—	3.00	6.00
RCA					
PB-10871	Country Disco/Disco Dante	1977	—	2.00	4.00
PB-11278	Old Fashioned Love Song/Falsely Accused	1978	—	2.00	4.00
PB-11466	Sugarfoot Rag/Let Your Lovelight Shine	1979	—	2.00	4.00
PB-11612	Ain't Misbehavin'/I'm Gonna Sit Right Down and Write Myself a Letter	1979	—	2.00	4.00
PB-12070	Cotton Eyed Joe/Colinda	1980	—	2.00	4.00
RCA VICTOR					
APBO-0019	Superstar/Come See Us	1973	—	2.00	4.00

Number	Title (A Side/B Side)	Yr	VG	VG+	NM
APBO-0301	Ruby, Are You Mad at Your Man/Rollin' in My Sweet Baby's Arms	1974	—	2.00	4.00
PB-10232	Singing the Blues/Stay a Little Longer	1975	—	2.00	4.00
PB-10255	Branigan/Peppy Time Tune	1975	—	2.00	4.00
PB-10375	Running Bear/Nashville Brass Hoedown	1975	—	2.00	4.00
PB-10570	Paloma Blanca/Nashville Express	1976	—	2.00	4.00
PB-10814	Why Don't You Love Me/He'll Have to Go	1976	—	2.00	4.00
PB-11073	How I Love Them Old Songs/Tara Jeanne	1977	—	2.00	4.00
47-9785	Wabash Cannon Ball/Sweet Dreams	1969	—	2.00	4.00
47-9847	Columbus Stockade Blues/Wings of a Dove	1970	—	2.00	4.00
47-9905	Down Yonder/May the Circle Be Unbroken	1970	—	2.00	4.00
47-9936	Jingling Brass/Silent Night	1970	—	3.00	6.00
47-9936 [DJ]	Silent Night/Jingling Brass	1970	—	3.00	6.00
—Promos available on either yellow or green labels					
74-0439	I Can't Stop Loving You/Rose Garden	1971	—	2.00	4.00
74-0506	Highland Brass/Ruby, Don't Take Your Love to Town	1971	—	2.00	4.00
74-0560	Wait for the Light to Shine/Blue Bayou	1971	—	2.00	4.00
74-0649	Java/Flowers on the Wall	1972	—	2.00	4.00
74-0760	From Dixie with Love/Under the Double Eagle	1972	—	2.00	4.00
74-0847	I'll Fly Away/Woman	1972	—	2.00	4.00
74-0858	White Christmas/Winter Wonderland	1972	—	2.50	5.00
VERVE					
10233	Theme from "Carnival"/Stardust	1961	2.50	5.00	10.00
WARTRACE					
730	I Dropped Your Name/(B-side unknown)	1985	—	2.00	4.00
Albums					
PICKWICK					
ACL1-7034	Down Yonder	197?	2.00	4.00	8.00
RCA SPECIAL PRODUCTS					
DPL1-0176	America 200 Years Young	1976	3.75	7.50	15.00
—Available only at Amana dealers					
RCA VICTOR					
APD1-0034 [Q]	Travelin'	1973	3.00	6.00	12.00
APL1-0232	Cairbbean Cruise	1973	2.50	5.00	10.00
APL1-0425	The Best of Danny Davis and the Nashville Brass	1973	2.50	5.00	10.00
APL1-0565	Bluegrass Country	1974	2.50	5.00	10.00
APL1-0774	The Latest and Greatest	1974	2.50	5.00	10.00
ANL1-0902	Orange Blossom Special	1974	2.50	5.00	10.00
APD1-1043 [Q]	Dream Country	1975	3.00	6.00	12.00
APL1-1043	Dream Country	1975	2.50	5.00	10.00
APD1-1240 [Q]	Gold	1975	3.00	6.00	12.00
APL1-1240	Gold	1975	2.50	5.00	10.00
APD1-1578 [Q]	Texas	1976	3.00	6.00	12.00
APL1-1578	Texas	1976	2.50	5.00	10.00
ANL1-1930	Christmas with Danny Davis and the Nashville Brass	1976	2.00	4.00	8.00
—Reissue of LSP-4377					
APL1-1986	Super	1976	2.50	5.00	10.00
APL1-2310	Live Vegas	1977	2.50	5.00	10.00
APL1-2721	How I Love Them Ol' Songs	1977	2.50	5.00	10.00
APL1-2980	Cookin' Country	1978	2.50	5.00	10.00
AHL1-3405	Great Songs of the Big Band Era	1979	2.50	5.00	10.00
AHL1-4022	Cotton Eyed Joe	1981	2.50	5.00	10.00
LSP-4059	The Nashville Sound	1969	2.50	5.00	10.00
LSP-4176	More Nashville Sounds	1969	2.50	5.00	10.00
LSP-4232	Movin' On	1969	2.50	5.00	10.00
LSP-4334	You Ain't Heard Nothin' Yet	1970	2.50	5.00	10.00
LSP-4377	Christmas with Danny Davis and the Nashville Brass	1970	2.50	5.00	10.00
LSP-4424	Down Homers	1970	2.50	5.00	10.00
LSP-4475	Somethin' Else	1971	2.50	5.00	10.00
LSP-4571	Super Country	1971	2.50	5.00	10.00
LSP-4627	Turns to Gold	1972	2.50	5.00	10.00
LSP-4720	Live — In Person	1972	2.50	5.00	10.00
LSP-4803	Turn On Some Happy!	1972	2.50	5.00	10.00

DAVIS, DANNY, AND WILLIE NELSON

Also see each artist's individual listings.

Number	Title (A Side/B Side)	Yr	VG	VG+	NM
45s					
RCA VICTOR					
PB-11893	Night Life/December Day	1980	—	2.00	4.00
PB-11999	Funny How Time Slips Away/The Local Memory	1980	—	2.00	4.00

DAVIS, EUNICE

Number	Title (A Side/B Side)	Yr	VG	VG+	NM
45s					
ATLANTIC					
992	Go to Work Pretty Daddy/My Beat Is 125th Street	1953	15.00	30.00	60.00
CORAL					
65075	Work Daddy Work/What Do You Want	1952	5.00	10.00	20.00
DELUXE					
6068	Get Your Enjoys/24 Hours a Day	1954	7.50	15.00	30.00
DERBY					
760	Evening Train/I'm a Wild West Woman	1951	7.50	15.00	30.00
768	Good News for You Baby/Tell Me I'm the Baby	1951	7.50	15.00	30.00
GRAND					
130	Let's Have a Party/Every Time Your Lips Meet Mine	1955	5.00	10.00	20.00

DAVIS, HAL

Number	Title (A Side/B Side)	Yr	VG	VG+	NM
45s					
ALDEN					
1301	My Young Heart/(B-side unknown)	1959	10.00	20.00	40.00
1303	King of Lovers/(B-side unknown)	1959	10.00	20.00	40.00
DEL-FI					
4146	You're Playing with Me/Read the Book of Love	1960	7.50	15.00	30.00
DYNAMITE					
1010	I Don't Want Nobody/(B-side unknown)	195?	50.00	100.00	200.00
FEDERAL					
12429	My Only Flower/You're the Girl	1961	3.00	6.00	12.00
GARDENA					
125	One More Chance/Show Me	1962	7.50	15.00	30.00
GSP					
2	I Don't Know/(B-side unknown)	1963	7.50	15.00	30.00
KELLEY					
105	Way to My Heart/(B-side unknown)	196?	25.00	50.00	100.00
—Red vinyl					
MINASA					
6714	It's You/(B-side unknown)	196?	7.50	15.00	30.00
MJC					
104	You'll Find Love/(B-side unknown)	196?	7.50	15.00	30.00
VEE JAY					
387	Merchant of Love/What Do You Mean to Me	1961	5.00	10.00	20.00
WIZARD					
101	Merchant of Love/What Do You Mean to Me	1961	17.50	35.00	70.00
102	I Need Someone/(B-side unknown)	1961	7.50	15.00	30.00

DAVIS, JAN

Number	Title (A Side/B Side)	Yr	VG	VG+	NM
45s					
ALJO					
104	The Surfin' Matador/Scramble	1964	7.50	15.00	30.00
A&M					
733	Boss Machine/The Fugitive	1964	3.75	7.50	15.00
744	Guitar Star/The Unwanted	1964	3.75	7.50	15.00
BEAR					
1000	Hornet's Nest/Flamenco Funk (Mosaic)	1969	—	3.00	6.00
BIG BIRD					
128	International Love Process (Part 1)/International Love Process (Part 2)	1967	3.75	7.50	15.00
COLUMBIA					
43224	More (Theme from Mondo Cane)/Mystique	1965	3.75	7.50	15.00
DIRECT HIT					
1002	Raunchy 1970/Dark Blue	1970	—	3.00	6.00
HOLIDAY					
1213	Pooky/Watuci Zombie	1964	3.75	7.50	15.00
QUAD-ETT					
10039	Hot Sauce/Soul Mate	1974	—	2.50	5.00
RANWOOD					
1015	Hot Sauce/Soulmate	1974	—	2.50	5.00
1023	Gypsy Fox/Child of June (Danny's Theme)	1974	—	2.50	5.00
1035	El Lobo/Maiden Spain	1975	—	2.50	5.00
RCA VICTOR					
47-9018	Time Tunnel/Walkin' Back	1966	3.00	6.00	12.00
47-9923	Raunchy 1970/Dark Blue	1970	—	2.50	5.00
RENDEZVOUS					
131	Sleepless/Damascus	1960	5.00	10.00	20.00
—With the Ricco-Shays					
149	Sabre Dance/Hop, Skip and Jump	1961	5.00	10.00	20.00
205	Malaguena/Hop, Skip and Jump	1963	5.00	10.00	20.00
214	You're Not Welcome (Anymore)/Don't Walk Away	1963	7.50	15.00	30.00
218	Delicado/Sahara	1963	5.00	10.00	20.00
SHAMLEY					
44016	Hornet's Nest/Flamenco Funk (Mosaic)	1969	—	2.50	5.00
SMASH					
1863	The Snow Surfin' Matador/Scramble	1963	6.25	12.50	25.00
UNI					
55029	International Love Process (Part 1)/International Love Process (Part 2)	1967	2.00	4.00	8.00
55197	Walk Don't Run/Flamenco Funk	1970	—	2.50	5.00
WHITE WHALE					
226	Lost in Space/Run for Your Life	1966	3.00	6.00	12.00

DAVIS, JESSE ED

Number	Title (A Side/B Side)	Yr	VG	VG+	NM
45s					
ATCO					
6807	Every Night Is Saturday Night/Golden Sun Goddess	1971	—	2.50	5.00
6825	Reno Street Incident/Washita Love Child	1971	—	2.50	5.00
6873	Sue Me, Sue You Blues/My Captain	1972	2.00	4.00	8.00
6889	Ululu/Alcatraz	1972	—	2.50	5.00
EPIC					
11021	She's a Pain/Natural Anthem	1973	—	2.00	4.00
Albums					
ATCO					
SD 33-346	Jesse Ed Davis	1970	3.75	7.50	15.00
SD 33-382	Ululu	1972	3.75	7.50	15.00
EPIC					
KE 32133	Keep On Comin'	1973	3.00	6.00	12.00

DAVIS, MAC

Number	Title (A Side/B Side)	Yr	VG	VG+	NM
45s					
CAPITOL					
5554	Bad Scene/I Protest	1965	2.00	4.00	8.00
CASABLANCA					
2244	It's Hard to Be Humble/Greatest Gift of All	1980	—	2.00	4.00
2286	Let's Keep It That Way/I Know You're Out There Somewhere	1980	—	—	3.00
2305	Texas in My Rear View Mirror/Sad Songs	1980	—	—	3.00
2327	Hooked On Music/Me and Fat Boy	1981	—	—	3.00
2336	Secrets/Remember When Beverly	1981	—	—	3.00
2341	You're My Bestest Friend/You Are So Lovely	1981	—	—	3.00
2346	Midnight Crazy/I Got the Hots for You	1981	—	—	3.00
2350	Rodeo Clown/Dammit Girl	1982	—	—	3.00
2355	The Beer Drinkin' Song/You Are So Lovely	1982	—	—	3.00
2363	Lying Here Lying/Quiet Times	1982	—	—	3.00
818168-7	Most of All/Springtime Down in Dixie	1984	—	—	3.00
818929-7	Caroline's Still in Georgia/I've Got a Dream	1984	—	—	3.00
COLUMBIA					
10018	Stop and Smell the Roses/Poor Boy Boogie	1974	—	2.00	4.00
10070	Rock 'n' Roll (I Gave You the Best Years of My Life)/Emily Suzanne	1974	—	2.00	4.00
10111	(If You Add) All the Love in the World/Smiley	1975	—	2.00	4.00
10148	Burnin' Thing/A Special Place in Heaven	1975	—	2.00	4.00

Number	Title (A Side/B Side)	Yr	VG	VG+	NM
10187	I Still Love You (You Still Love Me)/The Hits Just Keep On Comin'	1975	—	2.00	4.00
10304	Forever Lovers/The Love Lamp	1976	—	2.00	4.00
10535	Picking Up the Pieces of My Life/Do It (With Someone You Love)	1977	—	2.00	4.00
10745	Music in My Life/You Are	1978	—	2.00	4.00
45117	Whoever Finds This, I Love You/Half and Half	1970	—	2.50	5.00
45192	I'll Paint You a Song/The Closest I Ever Came	1970	—	2.50	5.00
45245	I Believe in Music/Poor Man's Gold	1970	—	2.50	5.00
45302	Beginning to Feel the Pain/Butterfly Girl	1971	—	2.50	5.00
45355	Lucas Was a Red-Neck/Fall in Love with Your Wife	1971	—	2.50	5.00
45404	Sweet Dreams and Sarah/Poem for My Little Lady	1971	—	2.50	5.00
45456	I Believe in Music/Hollywood Humpty Dumpty	1971	—	2.50	5.00
45576	Beginning to Feel the Pain/Butterfly Girl	1972	—	2.00	4.00
45618	Baby Don't Get Hooked on Me/Poem for My Little Lady	1972	—	2.00	4.00
45727	Everybody Loves a Love Song/Friend, Lover, Woman, Wife	1972	—	2.00	4.00
45773	Dream Me Home/Spread Your Love on Me	1973	—	2.00	4.00
45839	Your Side of the Bed/(Hope You Didn't) Chop No Wood	1973	—	2.00	4.00
45911	Kiss It and Make It Better/Sunshine	1973	—	2.00	4.00
46004	One Hell of a Woman/A Poor Man's Gold	1974	—	2.00	4.00
JAMIE					
1227	I'm a Poor Loser/Let Him Try	1962	2.50	5.00	10.00
MCA					
52573	I Never Made Love (Till I Made Love to You)/I Think I'm Gonna Rain	1985	—	—	3.00
52669	I Feel the Country Callin' Me/Rainy Day Lovin'	1985	—	—	3.00
52765	Sexy Young Girl/Special Place in Heaven	1986	—	—	3.00
52826	Somewhere in America/I Need a Hug	1986	—	—	3.00
VEE JAY					
492	A Little Dutch Town/Looking at Linda	1963	2.50	5.00	10.00
Albums					
ACCORD					
SN-7165	Little Touch of Love	1981	2.00	4.00	8.00
SN-7189	With Love	1981	2.00	4.00	8.00
ALLEGIANCE					
AV-5019	Volume XC	198?	2.00	4.00	8.00
AV-5031	Losers	198?	2.00	4.00	8.00
CASABLANCA					
NBLP 7207	It's Hard to Be Humble	1980	2.00	4.00	8.00
NBLP 7239	Texas in My Rear View Mirror	1980	2.00	4.00	8.00
NBLP 7257	Midnight Crazy	1981	2.00	4.00	8.00
822638-1	The Very Best and More	1984	2.00	4.00	8.00
COLUMBIA					
CS 9969	Song Painter	1970	3.75	7.50	15.00
—Red "360 Sound" label					
CS 9969	Song Painter	1974	2.50	5.00	10.00
—Orange label					
C 30926	I Believe in Music	1971	2.50	5.00	10.00
CQ 31770 [Q]	Baby Don't Get Hooked on Me	1972	3.75	7.50	15.00
KC 31770	Baby Don't Get Hooked on Me	1972	2.50	5.00	10.00
KC 32206	Mac Davis	1973	2.50	5.00	10.00
KC 32582	Stop and Smell the Roses	1974	2.50	5.00	10.00
PC 32582	Stop and Smell the Roses	1986	—	3.00	6.00
—Budget-line reissue					
PC 32927	All the Love in the World	1975	2.50	5.00	10.00
PCQ 32927 [Q]	All the Love in the World	1975	3.75	7.50	15.00
PC 33551	Burnin' Thing	1975	2.50	5.00	10.00
PC 34105	Forever Lovers	1976	2.50	5.00	10.00
PCQ 34105 [Q]	Forever Lovers	1976	3.75	7.50	15.00
PC 34313	Thunder in the Afternoon	1976	2.50	5.00	10.00
PCQ 34313 [Q]	Thunder in the Afternoon	1976	3.75	7.50	15.00
JC 35284	Fantasy	1978	2.50	5.00	10.00
JC 36317	Greatest Hits	1979	2.50	5.00	10.00
PC 36317	Greatest Hits	198?	—	3.00	6.00
—Budget-line reissue					
FC 38950	Who's Lovin' You	1983	2.00	4.00	8.00
PC 38950	Who's Lovin' You	198?	—	3.00	6.00
—Budget-line reissue					
MCA					
5590	Till I Made It with You	1985	2.00	4.00	8.00
5718	Somewhere in America	1986	2.00	4.00	8.00
SPRINGBOARD					
SPB-4024	Mac Davis	197?	2.00	4.00	8.00
TRIP					
9502	Mac Davis	1973	2.00	4.00	8.00

DAVIS, MAXWELL

Number	Title (A Side/B Side)	Yr	VG	VG+	NM
Albums					
ALADDIN					
LP-709 [10]	Maxwell Davis	1955	100.00	200.00	400.00
LP-804 [M]	Maxwell Davis	1956	50.00	100.00	200.00
SCORE					
SLP-4106 [M]	Blue Tango	1957	50.00	100.00	200.00

DAVIS, MILES

Number	Title (A Side/B Side)	Yr	VG	VG+	NM
45s					
BLUE NOTE					
1595	Dear Old Stockholm/Wouldn't You	195?	3.75	7.50	15.00
1596	Chance It/Yesterdays	195?	3.75	7.50	15.00
1597	Donna/The Squirrel 2nd Master	195?	3.75	7.50	15.00
1618	Enigma/Tempus Fugit	195?	3.75	7.50	15.00
1619	Ray's Idea/I Waited for You	195?	3.75	7.50	15.00
1620	Kelo/C.T.A.	195?	3.75	7.50	15.00
1633	Donna/Well You Needn't	195?	3.75	7.50	15.00
1649	Lazy Susan/Tempus Fugit	195?	3.75	7.50	15.00
1650	The Leap/Weirdo	195?	3.75	7.50	15.00
COLUMBIA					
02467	Shout/Fat Time	1981	—	2.50	5.00
10110	Red China Blues/Maiysha	1975	—	3.00	6.00
30735 [S]	(contents unknown)	1960	3.75	7.50	15.00
30736 [S]	(contents unknown)	1960	3.75	7.50	15.00
30737 [S]	(contents unknown)	1960	3.75	7.50	15.00
30738 [S]	(contents unknown)	1960	3.75	7.50	15.00
30739 [S]	(contents unknown)	1960	3.75	7.50	15.00
31094 [S]	De Buzzard Song/Gone	1961	3.75	7.50	15.00
31095 [S]	Gone, Gone, Gone/Summertime	1961	3.75	7.50	15.00
31096 [S]	Bess, Oh Where's My Bess/Fisherman, Strawberries and Deviled Crab	1961	3.75	7.50	15.00
31097 [S]	It Ain't Necessarily So/Here Comes the Honeyman	1961	3.75	7.50	15.00
31098 [S]	I Loves You Porgy/There's a Boat That's Leaving Soon for New York	1961	3.75	7.50	15.00
31377 [S]	(contents unknown)	1962	3.75	7.50	15.00
31378 [S]	(contents unknown)	1962	3.75	7.50	15.00
31379 [S]	(contents unknown)	1962	3.75	7.50	15.00
31380 [S]	(contents unknown)	1962	3.75	7.50	15.00
31381 [S]	(contents unknown)	1962	3.75	7.50	15.00
—Anyone who can fill in these gaps -- the above 15 all are Columbia "Stereo 7" singles -- please let us know.					
42057	It Ain't Necessarily So/All Blues	1961	3.00	6.00	12.00
42069	I Loves You, Porgy/It Ain't Necessarily So	1961	3.00	6.00	12.00
42583	Slow Samba/New Rhumba	1962	3.00	6.00	12.00
42853	Seven Steps to Heaven/Devil May Care	1963	3.00	6.00	12.00
44652	Girls of Kilimanjaro/(B-side unknown)	1969	2.00	4.00	8.00
45090	Great Expectations/Little Blue Frog	1970	2.00	4.00	8.00
45171	Miles Runs the Voodoo Down/Spanish Key	1970	2.00	4.00	8.00
45327	Friday Miles/Saturday Miles	1971	2.00	4.00	8.00
45709	Molester/(B-side unknown)	1972	2.00	4.00	8.00
45822	Vote for Miles (Part 1)/Vote for Miles (Part 2)	1973	2.00	4.00	8.00
45946	Big Fun/Holly-Wood	1973	2.00	4.00	8.00
46074	Great Expectations/Go Ahead John	1974	2.00	4.00	8.00
PRESTIGE					
103	Green Haze (Part 1)/Green Haze (Part 2)	195?	3.75	7.50	15.00
114	A Night in Tunisia (Part 1)/A Night in Tunisia (Part 2)	195?	3.75	7.50	15.00
123	If I Were a Bell (Part 1)/If I Were a Bell (Part 2)	195?	3.75	7.50	15.00
157	Walkin' (Part 1)/Walkin' (Part 2)	1957	3.75	7.50	15.00
165	It Never Entered My Mind (Part 1)/It Never Entered My Mind (Part 2)	1957	3.75	7.50	15.00
195	When I Fall in Love (Part 1)/When I Fall in Love (Part 2)	195?	3.75	7.50	15.00
248	Surrey with the Fringe on Top/Diane	196?	3.75	7.50	15.00
268	S'posin'/Just Squeeze Me	196?	3.00	6.00	12.00
321	It's Only a Paper Moon/Dig	1964	3.00	6.00	12.00
353	Smooch/Valentine	196?	3.00	6.00	12.00
376	You Don't Know/That Old Devil Moon	196?	3.00	6.00	12.00
413	'Round Midnight/Airegin	196?	3.00	6.00	12.00
734	Morpheus/Blue Room	1952	5.00	10.00	20.00
742	Down/Whispering	195?	5.00	10.00	20.00
766	My Old Flame (Part 1)/My Old Flame (Part 2)	195?	5.00	10.00	20.00
777	Dig (Part 1)/Dig (Part 2)	1956	5.00	10.00	20.00
817	It's Only a Paper Moon (Part 1)/It's Only a Paper Moon (Part 2)	195?	5.00	10.00	20.00
846	Bluing (Part 1)/Bluing (Part 2)	195?	5.00	10.00	20.00
868	Conception/Bluing 3	195?	5.00	10.00	20.00
876	Out of the Blue (Part 1)/Out of the Blue (Part 2)	195?	5.00	10.00	20.00
884	Tasty Pudding (Part 1)/Tasty Pudding (Part 2)	195?	5.00	10.00	20.00
893	Blue Haze (Part 1)/Blue Haze (Part 2)	1956	5.00	10.00	20.00
898	That Old Devil Moon/Four	195?	5.00	10.00	20.00
902	Miles Ahead/When Lights Are Low	195?	5.00	10.00	20.00
915	But Not for Me (Part 1)/But Not for Me (Part 2)	195?	5.00	10.00	20.00
Albums					
ARCHIVE OF FOLK AND JAZZ					
283	Miles Davis	197?	2.50	5.00	10.00
BLUE NOTE					
BLP-1501 [M]	Miles Davis, Volume 1	1955	50.00	100.00	200.00
—"Deep groove" version (deep indentation under label on both sides)					
BLP-1501 [M]	Miles Davis, Volume 1	1955	37.50	75.00	150.00
—Regular version with Lexington Ave. address on label					
BLP-1501 [M]	Miles Davis, Volume 1	1958	12.50	25.00	50.00
—Regular version with W. 63rd St. address on label					
BLP-1501 [M]	Miles Davis, Volume 1	1963	6.25	12.50	25.00
—With New York, USA address on label					
BLP-1501 [M]	Miles Davis, Volume 1	1966	3.75	7.50	15.00
—With "A Division of Liberty Records" on label					
BLP-1502 [M]	Miles Davis, Volume 2	1955	50.00	100.00	200.00
—"Deep groove" version (deep indentation under label on both sides)					
BLP-1502 [M]	Miles Davis, Volume 2	1955	37.50	75.00	150.00
—Regular version with Lexington Ave. address on label					
BLP-1502 [M]	Miles Davis, Volume 2	1958	12.50	25.00	50.00
—Regular version with W. 63rd St. address on label					
BLP-1502 [M]	Miles Davis, Volume 2	1963	6.25	12.50	25.00
—With New York, USA address on label					
BLP-1502 [M]	Miles Davis, Volume 2	1966	3.75	7.50	15.00
—With "A Division of Liberty Records" on label					
BLP-5013 [10]	Miles Davis (Young Man with a Horn)	1952	75.00	150.00	300.00
BLP-5022 [10]	Miles Davis, Vol. 2	1953	75.00	150.00	300.00
BLP-5040 [10]	Miles Davis, Vol. 3	1954	75.00	150.00	300.00
BLP-81501	Miles Davis, Volume 1	1968	3.00	6.00	12.00
—Rechanneled stereo version of 1501					
BST-81501	Miles Davis, Volume 1	1985	2.50	5.00	10.00
—"The Finest in Jazz Since 1939" reissue label					
BLP-81502	Miles Davis, Volume 2	1968	3.00	6.00	12.00
—Rechanneled stereo version of 1502					
BST-81502	Miles Davis, Volume 2	1985	2.50	5.00	10.00
—"The Finest in Jazz Since 1939" reissue label					
CAPITOL					
H 459 [10]	Jeru	1954	62.50	125.00	250.00
—First 33 1/3 rpm issue of some of the "Birth of the Cool" sessions					
T 762 [M]	Birth of the Cool	1956	37.50	75.00	150.00
DT 1974 [R]	Birth of the Cool	196?	3.00	6.00	12.00
T 1974 [M]	Birth of the Cool	1963	7.50	15.00	30.00
—Reissue of 762					

Number	Title (A Side/B Side)	Yr	VG	VG+	NM
M-11026 [M]	The Complete Birth of the Cool	1972	3.00	6.00	12.00
N-16168 [M]	Birth of the Cool	198?	2.00	4.00	8.00
—Budget-line reissue					
COLUMBIA					
J 1	Facets	1973	3.00	6.00	12.00
J 17	Miles Davis at Newport	1973	3.00	6.00	12.00
C2L 20 [(2) M]	Miles Davis in Person (Friday & Saturday Nights at the Blackhawk, San Francisco)	1961	12.50	25.00	50.00
—Six "eye" logos on label					
C2L 20 [(2) M]	Miles Davis in Person (Friday & Saturday Nights at the Blackhawk, San Francisco)	1963	7.50	15.00	30.00
—"Guaranteed High Fidelity" on label					
C2L 20 [(2) M]	Miles Davis in Person (Friday & Saturday Nights at the Blackhawk, San Francisco)	1965	6.25	12.50	25.00
—"Mono" on label					
GP 26 [(2)]	Bitches Brew	1970	10.00	20.00	40.00
—"360 Sound Stereo" on red labels					
GP 26 [(2)]	Bitches Brew	1970	3.75	7.50	15.00
—Orange labels					
PG 26 [(2)]	Bitches Brew	1977	3.00	6.00	12.00
—Orange labels, new prefix					
C2S 820 [(2)]	Miles Davis in Person (Friday & Saturday Nights at the Blackhawk, San Francisco)	1971	3.75	7.50	15.00
—Orange labels					
C2S 820 [(2) S]	Miles Davis in Person (Friday & Saturday Nights at the Blackhawk, San Francisco)	1961	12.50	25.00	50.00
—Six "eye" logos on label					
C2S 820 [(2) S]	Miles Davis in Person (Friday & Saturday Nights at the Blackhawk, San Francisco)	1963	7.50	15.00	30.00
—"360 Sound Stereo" in black on label					
C2S 820 [(2) S]	Miles Davis in Person (Friday & Saturday Nights at the Blackhawk, San Francisco)	1965	6.25	12.50	25.00
—"360 Sound Stereo" in white on label					
CL 949 [M]	'Round About Midnight	1957	12.50	25.00	50.00
—Six "eye" logos on label					
CL 949 [M]	'Round About Midnight	1963	6.25	12.50	25.00
—"Guaranteed High Fidelity" on label					
CL 949 [M]	'Round About Midnight	1965	5.00	10.00	20.00
—"Mono" on label					
CL 1041 [M]	Miles Ahead	1957	20.00	40.00	80.00
—Six "eye" logos on label; cover has a while woman and her child on a sailboat					
CL 1041 [M]	Miles Ahead	1957	12.50	25.00	50.00
—Six "eye" logos on label; cover has Miles Davis blowing his trumpet					
CL 1041 [M]	Miles Ahead	1963	6.25	12.50	25.00
—"Guaranteed High Fidelity" on label					
CL 1041 [M]	Miles Ahead	1965	5.00	10.00	20.00
—"Mono" on label					
CL 1193 [M]	Milestones	1958	12.50	25.00	50.00
—Six "eye" logos on label					
CL 1193 [M]	Milestones	1963	6.25	12.50	25.00
—"Guaranteed High Fidelity" on label					
CL 1193 [M]	Milestones	1965	5.00	10.00	20.00
—"Mono" on label					
CL 1268 [M]	Jazz Track	1958	20.00	40.00	80.00
—Six "eye" logos on label; with abstract drawing on cover					
CL 1268 [M]	Jazz Track	1958	12.50	25.00	50.00
—Six "eye" logos on label; with Miles and a woman on cover					
CL 1274 [M]	Porgy and Bess	1958	12.50	25.00	50.00
—Six "eye" logos on label					
CL 1274 [M]	Porgy and Bess	1963	6.25	12.50	25.00
—"Guaranteed High Fidelity" on label					
CL 1274 [M]	Porgy and Bess	1965	5.00	10.00	20.00
—"Mono" on label					
CL 1355 [M]	Kind of Blue	1959	15.00	30.00	60.00
—Six "eye" logos on label					
CL 1355 [M]	Kind of Blue	1963	6.25	12.50	25.00
—"Guaranteed High Fidelity" on label					
CL 1355 [M]	Kind of Blue	1965	5.00	10.00	20.00
—"Mono" on label					
CL 1480 [M]	Sketches of Spain	1960	12.50	25.00	50.00
—Six "eye" logos on label					
CL 1480 [M]	Sketches of Spain	1963	6.25	12.50	25.00
—"Guaranteed High Fidelity" on label					
CL 1480 [M]	Sketches of Spain	1965	5.00	10.00	20.00
—"Mono" on label					
CL 1656 [M]	Someday My Prince Will Come	1961	10.00	20.00	40.00
—Six "eye" logos on label					
CL 1656 [M]	Someday My Prince Will Come	1963	6.25	12.50	25.00
—"Guaranteed High Fidelity" on label					
CL 1656 [M]	Someday My Prince Will Come	1965	5.00	10.00	20.00
—"Mono" on label					
CL 1669 [M]	Miles Davis in Person, Vol. 1 (Friday Nights at the Blackhawk, San Francisco)	1961	7.50	15.00	30.00
—Six "eye" logos on label; later pressings may exist					
CL 1670 [M]	Miles Davis in Person, Vol. 2 (Saturday Nights at the Blackhawk, San Francisco)	1961	7.50	15.00	30.00
—Six "eye" logos on label; later pressings may exist					
CL 1812 [M]	Miles Davis at Carnegie Hall	1962	12.50	25.00	50.00
—Six "eye" logos on label					
CL 1812 [M]	Miles Davis at Carnegie Hall	1963	6.25	12.50	25.00
—"Guaranteed High Fidelity" on label					
CL 1812 [M]	Miles Davis at Carnegie Hall	1965	5.00	10.00	20.00
—"Mono" on label					
CL 2051 [M]	Seven Steps to Heaven	1963	6.25	12.50	25.00
—"Guaranteed High Fidelity" on label					
CL 2051 [M]	Seven Steps to Heaven	1965	5.00	10.00	20.00
—"Mono" on label					
CL 2106 [M]	Quiet Nights	1964	6.25	12.50	25.00
—"Guaranteed High Fidelity" on label					
CL 2106 [M]	Quiet Nights	1965	5.00	10.00	20.00
—"Mono" on label					
CL 2183 [M]	Miles Davis in Europe	1964	6.25	12.50	25.00
—"Guaranteed High Fidelity" on label					
CL 2183 [M]	Miles Davis in Europe	1965	5.00	10.00	20.00
—"Mono" on label					

Number	Title (A Side/B Side)	Yr	VG	VG+	NM
CL 2306 [M]	My Funny Valentine	1965	6.25	12.50	25.00
—"Guaranteed High Fidelity" on label					
CL 2306 [M]	My Funny Valentine	1965	5.00	10.00	20.00
—"Mono" on label					
CL 2350 [M]	E.S.P.	1965	6.25	12.50	25.00
—"Guaranteed High Fidelity" on label					
CL 2350 [M]	E.S.P.	1965	5.00	10.00	20.00
—"Mono" on label					
CL 2453 [M]	"Four" & More — Recorded Live in Concert	1966	5.00	10.00	20.00
CL 2601 [M]	Miles Smiles	1966	5.00	10.00	20.00
CL 2628 [M]	Milestones	1967	7.50	15.00	30.00
—Reissue of 1193?					
CL 2732 [M]	Sorcerer	1967	7.50	15.00	30.00
CL 2794 [M]	Nefertiti	1968	12.50	25.00	50.00
CL 2828 [M]	Miles in the Sky	1968	20.00	40.00	80.00
CS 8021 [S]	Milestones	1959	12.50	25.00	50.00
—Six "eye" logos on label					
CS 8021 [S]	Milestones	1963	6.25	12.50	25.00
—"360 Sound Stereo" in black on label					
CS 8021 [S]	Milestones	1965	5.00	10.00	20.00
—"360 Sound Stereo" in white on label					
CS 8085	Porgy and Bess	1971	3.00	6.00	12.00
—Orange label					
CS 8085 [S]	Porgy and Bess	1959	12.50	25.00	50.00
—Six "eye" logos on label					
CS 8085 [S]	Porgy and Bess	1963	6.25	12.50	25.00
—"360 Sound Stereo" in black on label					
CS 8085 [S]	Porgy and Bess	1965	5.00	10.00	20.00
—"360 Sound Stereo" in white on label					
KCS 8085	Porgy and Bess	1974	2.50	5.00	10.00
—Orange label, new prefix					
PC 8085	Porgy and Bess	1977	2.00	4.00	8.00
—Orange label, new prefix					
CS 8163	Kind of Blue	1971	3.00	6.00	12.00
—Orange label					
CS 8163 [S]	Kind of Blue	1959	30.00	60.00	120.00
—Six "eye" logos on label					
CS 8163 [S]	Kind of Blue	1963	6.25	12.50	25.00
—"360 Sound Stereo" in black on label					
CS 8163 [S]	Kind of Blue	1965	5.00	10.00	20.00
—"360 Sound Stereo" in white on label					
CS 8163 [(2)]	Kind of Blue	1997	10.00	20.00	40.00
—Reissue; contains both the original Side 1, which was mastered slightly fast, and the "correct" Side 1 (as Side 3); distributed by Classic Records					
KCS 8163	Kind of Blue	1974	2.50	5.00	10.00
—Orange label, new prefix					
PC 8163	Kind of Blue	1977	2.00	4.00	8.00
—Orange label, new prefix					
CS 8271	Sketches of Spain	1971	3.00	6.00	12.00
—Orange label					
CS 8271 [S]	Sketches of Spain	1960	20.00	40.00	80.00
—Six "eye" logos on label					
CS 8271 [S]	Sketches of Spain	1963	6.25	12.50	25.00
—"360 Sound Stereo" in black on label					
CS 8271 [S]	Sketches of Spain	1965	5.00	10.00	20.00
—"360 Sound Stereo" in white on label					
CS 8271 [S]	Sketckes of Spain	1999	6.25	12.50	25.00
—Audiophile reissue; distributed by Classic Records					
KCS 8271	Sketches of Spain	1974	2.50	5.00	10.00
—Orange label, new prefix					
PC 8271	Sketches of Spain	1977	2.00	4.00	8.00
—Orange label, new prefix					
CS 8456	Someday My Prince Will Come	1971	3.00	6.00	12.00
—Orange label					
CS 8456 [S]	Someday My Prince Will Come	1961	10.00	20.00	40.00
—Six "eye" logos on label					
CS 8456 [S]	Someday My Prince Will Come	1963	6.25	12.50	25.00
—"360 Sound Stereo" in black on label					
CS 8456 [S]	Someday My Prince Will Come	1965	5.00	10.00	20.00
—"360 Sound Stereo" in white on label					
KCS 8456	Someday My Prince Will Come	1974	2.50	5.00	10.00
—Orange label, new prefix					
PC 8456	Someday My Prince Will Come	1977	2.00	4.00	8.00
—Orange label, new prefix					
CS 8469 [S]	Miles Davis in Person, Vol. 1 (Friday Nights at the Blackhawk, San Francisco)	1961	7.50	15.00	30.00
—Six "eye" logos on label; later pressings may exist					
CS 8470 [S]	Miles Davis in Person, Vol. 2 (Saturday Nights at the Blackhawk, San Francisco)	1961	7.50	15.00	30.00
—Six "eye" logos on label; later pressings may exist					
CS 8612 [S]	Miles Davis at Carnegie Hall	1962	12.50	25.00	50.00
—Six "eye" logos on label					
CS 8612 [S]	Miles Davis at Carnegie Hall	1962	6.25	12.50	25.00
—"360 Sound Stereo" in black on label					
CS 8612 [S]	Miles Davis at Carnegie Hall	1965	5.00	10.00	20.00
—"360 Sound Stereo" in white on label					
KCS 8612	Miles Davis at Carnegie Hall	1974	2.50	5.00	10.00
—Orange label, new prefix					
PC 8612	Miles Davis at Carnegie Hall	1977	2.00	4.00	8.00
—Orange label, new prefix					
CS 8633	Miles Ahead	1971	3.00	6.00	12.00
—Orange label					
CS 8633 [R]	Miles Ahead	1963	3.00	6.00	12.00
—Rechanneled stereo version of 1041					
KCS 8633	Miles Ahead	1974	2.50	5.00	10.00
—Orange label, new prefix					
PC 8633	Miles Ahead	1977	2.00	4.00	8.00
—Orange label, new prefix					
CS 8649	'Round About Midnight	1971	3.00	6.00	12.00
—Orange label					
CS 8649 [R]	'Round About Midnight	1963	3.00	6.00	12.00
—Rechanneled stereo version of 949					
KCS 8649	'Round About Midnight	1974	2.50	5.00	10.00
—Orange label, new prefix					
PC 8649	'Round About Midnight	1977	2.00	4.00	8.00
—Orange label, new prefix					

Number	Title (A Side/B Side)	Yr	VG	VG+	NM
CS 8851	Seven Steps to Heaven	1971	3.00	6.00	12.00
—Orange label					
CS 8851 [S]	Seven Steps to Heaven	1963	6.25	12.50	25.00
—"360 Sound Stereo" in black on label					
CS 8851 [S]	Seven Steps to Heaven	1965	5.00	10.00	20.00
—"360 Sound Stereo" in white on label					
KCS 8851	Seven Steps to Heaven	1974	2.50	5.00	10.00
—Orange label, new prefix					
PC 8851	Seven Steps to Heaven	1977	2.00	4.00	8.00
—Orange label, new prefix					
CS 8906	Quiet Nights	1971	3.00	6.00	12.00
—Orange label					
CS 8906 [S]	Quiet Nights	1964	6.25	12.50	25.00
—"360 Sound Stereo" in black on label					
CS 8906 [S]	Quiet Nights	1965	5.00	10.00	20.00
—"360 Sound Stereo" in white on label					
KCS 8906	Quiet Nights	1974	2.50	5.00	10.00
—Orange label, new prefix					
PC 8906	Quiet Nights	1977	2.00	4.00	8.00
—Orange label, new prefix					
CS 8983	Miles Davis in Europe	1971	3.00	6.00	12.00
—Orange label					
CS 8983 [S]	Miles Davis in Europe	1964	6.25	12.50	25.00
—"360 Sound Stereo" in black on label					
CS 8983 [S]	Miles Davis in Europe	1965	5.00	10.00	20.00
—"360 Sound Stereo" in white on label					
KCS 8983	Miles Davis in Europe	1974	2.50	5.00	10.00
—Orange label, new prefix					
PC 8983	Miles Davis in Europe	1977	2.00	4.00	8.00
—Orange label, new prefix					
CS 9106	My Funny Valentine	1971	3.00	6.00	12.00
—Orange label					
CS 9106 [S]	My Funny Valentine	1965	6.25	12.50	25.00
—"360 Sound Stereo" in black on label					
CS 9106 [S]	My Funny Valentine	1965	5.00	10.00	20.00
—"360 Sound Stereo" in white on label					
KCS 9106	My Funny Valentine	1974	2.50	5.00	10.00
—Orange label, new prefix					
PC 9106	My Funny Valentine	1977	2.00	4.00	8.00
—Orange label, new prefix					
CS 9150	E.S.P.	1971	3.00	6.00	12.00
—Orange label					
CS 9150 [S]	E.S.P.	1965	6.25	12.50	25.00
—"360 Sound Stereo" in black on label					
CS 9150 [S]	E.S.P.	1965	5.00	10.00	20.00
—"360 Sound Stereo" in white on label					
KCS 9150	E.S.P.	1974	2.50	5.00	10.00
—Orange label, new prefix					
PC 9150	E.S.P.	1977	2.00	4.00	8.00
—Orange label, new prefix					
CS 9253	"Four" and More — Recorded Live in Concert	1971	3.00	6.00	12.00
—Orange label					
CS 9253 [S]	"Four" & More — Recorded Live in Concert	1966	5.00	10.00	20.00
—"360 Sound Stereo" on red label					
KCS 9253	"Four" and More — Recorded Live in Concert	1974	2.50	5.00	10.00
—Orange label, new prefix					
PC 9253	"Four" and More — Recorded Live in Concert	1977	2.00	4.00	8.00
—Orange label, new prefix					
CS 9401	Miles Smiles	1971	3.00	6.00	12.00
—Orange label					
CS 9401 [S]	Miles Smiles	1966	5.00	10.00	20.00
—"360 Sound Stereo" on red label					
KCS 9401	Miles Smiles	1974	2.50	5.00	10.00
—Orange label, new prefix					
PC 9401	Miles Smiles	1977	2.00	4.00	8.00
—Orange label, new prefix					
CS 9428 [S]	Milestones	1967	5.00	10.00	20.00
—"360 Sound Stereo" on red label; reissue of 8021?					
KCS 9428	Milestones	1974	2.50	5.00	10.00
—Orange label, new prefix					
PC 9428	Milestones	1977	2.00	4.00	8.00
—Orange label, new prefix					
CS 9532	Sorcerer	1971	3.00	6.00	12.00
—Orange label					
CS 9532 [S]	Sorcerer	1967	5.00	10.00	20.00
—"360 Sound Stereo" on red label					
KCS 9532	Sorcerer	1974	2.50	5.00	10.00
—Orange label, new prefix					
PC 9532	Sorcerer	1977	2.00	4.00	8.00
—Orange label, new prefix					
CS 9594	Nefertiti	1971	3.00	6.00	12.00
—Orange label					
CS 9594 [S]	Nefertiti	1968	5.00	10.00	20.00
—"360 Sound Stereo" on red label					
KCS 9594	Nefertiti	1974	2.50	5.00	10.00
—Orange label, new prefix					
PC 9594	Nefertiti	1977	2.00	4.00	8.00
—Orange label, new prefix					
CS 9612	Miles Davis at Carnegie Hall	1971	3.00	6.00	12.00
—Orange label					
CS 9628	Miles in the Sky	1971	3.00	6.00	12.00
—Orange label					
CS 9628 [S]	Miles in the Sky	1968	5.00	10.00	20.00
—"360 Sound Stereo" on red label					
KCS 9628	Miles in the Sky	1974	2.50	5.00	10.00
—Orange label, new prefix					
PC 9628	Miles in the Sky	1977	2.00	4.00	8.00
—Orange label, new prefix					
CS 9750	Filles de Kilimanjaro	1969	5.00	10.00	20.00
—"360 Sound Stereo" on red label					
CS 9750	Filles de Kilimanjaro	1971	3.00	6.00	12.00
—Orange label					
KCS 9750	Filles de Kilimanjaro	1974	2.50	5.00	10.00
—Orange label, new prefix					
PC 9750	Filles de Kilimanjaro	1977	2.00	4.00	8.00
—Orange label, new prefix					
CS 9808	Miles Davis' Greatest Hits	1969	5.00	10.00	20.00
—"360 Sound Stereo" on red label					
CS 9808	Miles Davis' Greatest Hits	1971	3.00	6.00	12.00
—Orange label					
KCS 9808	Miles Davis' Greatest Hits	1974	2.50	5.00	10.00
—Orange label, new prefix					
PC 9808	Miles Davis' Greatest Hits	1977	2.00	4.00	8.00
—Orange label, new prefix					
CS 9875	In a Silent Way	1969	5.00	10.00	20.00
—"360 Sound Stereo" on red label					
CS 9875	In a Silent Way	1971	3.00	6.00	12.00
—Orange label					
KCS 9875	In a Silent Way	1974	2.50	5.00	10.00
—Orange label, new prefix					
PC 9875	In a Silent Way	1977	2.00	4.00	8.00
—Orange label, new prefix					
CG 30038 [(2)]	Miles Davis at Fillmore	1970	3.75	7.50	15.00
KC 30455	A Tribute to Jack Johnson	1971	3.00	6.00	12.00
PC 30455	A Tribute to Jack Johnson	1977	2.00	4.00	8.00
—Orange label, new prefix					
CG 30954 [(2)]	Live-Evil	1971	3.75	7.50	15.00
GQ 30954 [(2) Q]	Live-Evil	1973	7.50	15.00	30.00
GQ 30997 [(2) Q]	Bitches Brew	1972	10.00	20.00	40.00
KC 31906	On the Corner	1972	3.00	6.00	12.00
PC 31906	On the Corner	1977	2.00	4.00	8.00
—Orange label, new prefix					
KC 32025	Basic Miles — The Classic Performances of Miles Davis	1973	3.00	6.00	12.00
PC 32025	Basic Miles — The Classic Performances of Miles Davis	198?	2.00	4.00	8.00
—Budget-line reissue					
KG 32092 [(2)]	In Concert	1973	3.75	7.50	15.00
PG 32092 [(2)]	In Concert	1977	2.50	5.00	10.00
—Orange labels, new prefix					
C 32470	Jazz at the Plaza, Vol. 1	1973	3.00	6.00	12.00
CG 32866 [(2)]	Big Fun	1974	3.75	7.50	15.00
PG 32866 [(2)]	Big Fun	1977	3.00	6.00	12.00
—Orange labels, new prefix					
KG 33236 [(2)]	Get Up With It	1974	3.75	7.50	15.00
PG 33236 [(2)]	Get Up With It	1977	2.50	5.00	10.00
—Orange labels, new prefix					
PG 33967 [(2)]	Agharta	1976	3.75	7.50	15.00
PC 34396	Water Babies	1977	3.00	6.00	12.00
—Original has no bar code					
PC 34396	Water Babies	198?	2.00	4.00	8.00
—Reissue with bar code					
KC2 36278 [(2)]	Circle in the Round	1980	3.75	7.50	15.00
KC2 36472 [(2)]	Directions	1981	3.75	7.50	15.00
FC 36790	The Man with the Horn	1981	2.50	5.00	10.00
PC 36790	The Man with the Horn	198?	2.00	4.00	8.00
—Budget-line reissue					
C6X 36976 [(6)]	The Miles Davis Collection Vol. 1: 12 Sides of Miles	1980	12.50	25.00	50.00
C2 38005 [(2)]	We Want Miles	1982	3.00	6.00	12.00
C2 38266 [(2)]	Live at the Plugged Nickel	1982	3.00	6.00	12.00
C2 38506 [(2)]	Heard 'Round the World	1983	3.00	6.00	12.00
FC 38657	Star People	1983	2.50	5.00	10.00
FC 38991	Decoy	1984	2.50	5.00	10.00
FC 40023	You're Under Arrest	1985	2.50	5.00	10.00
C2X 45332	Aura	1989	3.75	7.50	15.00
HC 46790	The Man with the Horn	1982	10.00	20.00	40.00
—Half-speed mastered edition					
COLUMBIA JAZZ MASTERPIECES					
CJ2 40577 [(2)]	Bitches Brew	1987	3.00	6.00	12.00
CJ 40578	Sketches of Spain	1987	2.50	5.00	10.00
CJ 40579	Kind of Blue	1987	2.50	5.00	10.00
CJ 40580	In a Silent Way	1987	2.50	5.00	10.00
CJ 40609	Live Miles: More Music from the Legendary Carnegie Hall Concert	1987	2.50	5.00	10.00
CJ 40610	'Round About Midnight	1987	2.50	5.00	10.00
CJ 40645	Cookin' at the Plugged Nickel	1987	2.50	5.00	10.00
CJ 40647	Porgy and Bess	1987	2.50	5.00	10.00
CJ 40784	Miles Ahead	1987	2.50	5.00	10.00
CJ 40837	Milestones	1987	2.50	5.00	10.00
CJ 40947	Someday My Prince Will Come	1987	2.50	5.00	10.00
CJ 44052	Miles and Coltrane	1988	2.50	5.00	10.00
CJ 44151	Ballads	1988	2.50	5.00	10.00
CJ 44257	Miles Davis in Person, Vol. 1 (Friday Nights at the Blackhawk, San Francisco)	1988	2.50	5.00	10.00
CJ 44425	Miles Davis in Person, Vol. 2 (Saturday Nights at the Blackhawk, San Francisco)	1989	2.50	5.00	10.00
COLUMBIA SPECIAL PRODUCTS					
P 13811	Facets	1977	2.50	5.00	10.00
CONTEMPORARY					
7645	Miles Davis and the Lighthouse All-Stars At Last!	1985	3.00	6.00	12.00
DEBUT					
DEB 120 [M]	Blue Moods	1955	62.50	125.00	250.00
FANTASY					
OJC-004	The Musings of Miles	198?	2.50	5.00	10.00
—Reissue of Prestige 7007					
OJC-005	Dig Miles Davis/Sonny Rollins	198?	2.50	5.00	10.00
—Reissue of Prestige 7012					
OJC-006	Miles — The New Miles Davis Quintet	198?	2.50	5.00	10.00
—Reissue of Prestige 7014					
OJC-012	Miles Davis and the Milt Jackson Quintet/Sextet	198?	2.50	5.00	10.00
—Reissue of Prestige 7034					
OJC-043	Blue Moods	198?	2.50	5.00	10.00
—Reissue of Fantasy 6001					
OJC-053	Miles Davis and Horns	198?	2.50	5.00	10.00
—Reissue of Prestige 7025					
OJC-071	Collector's Item	198?	2.50	5.00	10.00
—Reissue of Prestige 7044					
OJC-093	Blue Haze	198?	2.50	5.00	10.00
—Reissue of Prestige 7054					

Number	Title (A Side/B Side)	Yr	VG	VG+	NM
OJC-128	Cookin' with the Miles Davis Quintet	198?	2.50	5.00	10.00
—Reissue of Prestige 7094					
OJC-190	Relaxin' with the Miles Davis Quintet	1985	2.50	5.00	10.00
—Reissue of Prestige 7129					
OJC-213	Walkin'	1987	2.50	5.00	10.00
—Reissue of Prestige 7076					
OJC-245	Bags Groove	1987	2.50	5.00	10.00
—Reissue of Prestige 7109					
OJC-296	Workin' with the Miles Davis Quintet	1987	2.50	5.00	10.00
—Reissue of Prestige 7166					
OJC-347	Miles Davis and the Modern Jazz Giants	198?	2.50	5.00	10.00
—Reissue of Prestige 7150					
OJC-391	Steamin' with the Miles Davis Quintet	1989	2.50	5.00	10.00
—Reissue of Prestige 7200					
OJC-480	Miles Davis and the Lighthouse All-Stars At Last!	1991	2.50	5.00	10.00
—Reissue of Contemporary 7645					
6001 [M]	Blue Moods	1962	12.50	25.00	50.00
—Reissue of Debut album; red vinyl					
6001 [M]	Blue Moods	1963	7.50	15.00	30.00
—Black vinyl, red label					
86001 [R]	Blue Moods	1962	7.50	15.00	30.00
—Blue vinyl					
86001 [R]	Blue Moods	1963	3.75	7.50	15.00
—Black vinyl, blue label					
MOBILE FIDELITY					
1-177	Someday My Prince Will Come	1985	20.00	40.00	80.00
—Audiophile vinyl					
MOSAIC					
MQ10-158 [(10)]	The Complete Plugged Nickel Sessions	199?	37.50	75.00	150.00
MQ11-164 [(11)]	Miles Davis & Gil Evans: The Complete Columbia Studio Recordings	199?	50.00	100.00	200.00
MQ10-177 [(10)]	The Complete Studio Recordings of the Miles Davis Quintet 1965-June 1968	1998	37.50	75.00	150.00
MQ6-183 [(6)]	The Complete Bitches Brew Sessions	1999	25.00	50.00	100.00
PAIR					
PDL2-1095 [(2)]	Best of Miles Davis	1986	3.00	6.00	12.00
PHILIPS					
836305-1	Elevator to the Scaffold (L'Ancenseur Pour L'Echafaud)	198?	3.00	6.00	12.00
—Reissue of Columbia 1268					
PRESTIGE					
P-12 [(12)]	Chronicle: The Complete Prestige Recordings	198?	25.00	50.00	100.00
PRLP-124 [10]	The New Sounds of Miles Davis	1952	62.50	125.00	250.00
PRLP-140 [10]	Blue Period	1953	62.50	125.00	250.00
PRLP-154 [10]	Miles Davis Plays Al Cohn Compositions	1953	62.50	125.00	250.00
PRLP-161 [10]	Miles Davis Featuring Sonny Rollins	1953	62.50	125.00	250.00
PRLP-182 [10]	Miles Davis Sextet	1954	62.50	125.00	250.00
PRLP-185 [10]	Miles Davis Quintet	1954	62.50	125.00	250.00
PRLP-187 [10]	Miles Davis Quintet Featuring Sonny Rollins	1954	62.50	125.00	250.00
PRLP-196 [10]	Miles Davis All Stars, Volume 1	1955	62.50	125.00	250.00
PRLP-200 [10]	Miles Davis All Stars, Volume 2	1955	62.50	125.00	250.00
PRLP-7007 [M]	The Musings of Miles	1955	37.50	75.00	150.00
PRLP-7012 [M]	Dig Miles Davis/Sonny Rollins	1956	37.50	75.00	150.00
—Gray cover					
PRLP-7012 [M]	Dig Miles Davis/Sonny Rollins	1957	30.00	60.00	120.00
—Color cover					
PRLP-7014 [M]	Miles — The New Miles Davis Quintet	1956	37.50	75.00	150.00
PRLP-7025 [M]	Miles Davis and Horns	1956	37.50	75.00	150.00
PRLP-7034 [M]	Miles Davis and the Milt Jackson Quintet/Sextet	1956	37.50	75.00	150.00
—With W. 50th St. address on yellow label					
PRLP-7034 [M]	Miles Davis and the Milt Jackson Quintet/Sextet	196?	7.50	15.00	30.00
—With trident on blue label					
PRLP-7044 [M]	Collectors' Item	1956	30.00	60.00	120.00
—With W. 50th St. address on yellow label					
PRLP-7044 [M]	Collectors' Item	196?	7.50	15.00	30.00
—With trident on blue label					
PRLP-7054 [M]	Blue Haze	1956	30.00	60.00	120.00
—With W. 50th St. address on yellow label					
PRLP-7054 [M]	Blue Haze	196?	7.50	15.00	30.00
—With trident on blue label					
PRLP-7076 [M]	Walkin'	1957	25.00	50.00	100.00
—With W. 50th St. address on yellow label					
PRLP-7076 [M]	Walkin'	196?	7.50	15.00	30.00
—With trident on blue label					
PRLP-7094 [M]	Cookin' with the Miles Davis Quintet	1957	25.00	50.00	100.00
—With W. 50th St. address on yellow label					
PRLP-7094 [M]	Cookin' with the Miles Davis Quintet	195?	15.00	30.00	60.00
—With Bergenfield, N.J. address on yellow label					
PRLP-7094 [M]	Cookin' with the Miles Davis Quintet	196?	7.50	15.00	30.00
—With trident on blue label					
PRLP-7109 [M]	Bags Groove	1957	25.00	50.00	100.00
—With W. 50th St. address on yellow label					
PRLP-7109 [M]	Bags Groove	196?	7.50	15.00	30.00
—With trident on blue label					
PRLP-7129 [M]	Relaxin' with the Miles Davis Quintet	1957	25.00	50.00	100.00
—With W. 50th St. address on yellow label					
PRLP-7129 [M]	Relaxin' with the Miles Davis Quintet	1957	15.00	30.00	60.00
—With Bergenfield, NJ address on yellow label					
PRLP-7129 [M]	Relaxin' with the Miles Davis Quintet	196?	7.50	15.00	30.00
—With trident on blue label					
PRLP-7150 [M]	Miles Davis and the Modern Jazz Giants	1958	20.00	40.00	80.00
—With Bergenfield, NJ address on yellow label					
PRLP-7150 [M]	Miles Davis and the Modern Jazz Giants	196?	7.50	15.00	30.00
—With trident on blue label					
PRLP-7166 [M]	Workin' with the Miles Davis Quintet	1959	20.00	40.00	80.00
—With Bergenfield, NJ address on yellow label					
PRLP-7166 [M]	Workin' with the Miles Davis Quintet	196?	7.50	15.00	30.00
—With trident on blue label					
PRLP-7168 [M]	Early Miles	1959	20.00	40.00	80.00
—Reissue of 7025; with Bergenfield, NJ address on yellow label					
PRLP-7168 [M]	Early Miles	196?	7.50	15.00	30.00
—With trident on blue label					
PRLP-7200 [M]	Steamin' with the Miles Davis Quintet	1961	20.00	40.00	80.00
—With Bergenfield, NJ address on yellow label					
PRLP-7200 [M]	Steamin' with the Miles Davis Quintet	196?	7.50	15.00	30.00
—With trident on blue label					
PRLP-7221 [M]	The Beginning	1962	12.50	25.00	50.00
—Reissue of 7007; with Bergenfield, NJ address on yellow label					
PRLP-7221 [M]	The Beginning	196?	7.50	15.00	30.00
—With trident on blue label					
PRLP-7254 [M]	The Original Quintet	1963	12.50	25.00	50.00
—Reissue of 7014; with Bergenfield, NJ address on yellow label					
PRLP-7254 [M]	The Original Quintet	196?	7.50	15.00	30.00
—With trident on blue label					
PRST-7254 [R]	The Original Quintet	1963	5.00	10.00	20.00
PRLP-7281 [M]	Diggin'	1963	12.50	25.00	50.00
—Reissue of 7012; with Bergenfield, NJ address on yellow label					
PRLP-7281 [M]	Diggin'	196?	7.50	15.00	30.00
—With trident on blue label					
PRST-7281 [R]	Diggin'	1963	5.00	10.00	20.00
PRLP-7322 [M]	Miles Davis Plays Richard Rodgers	1964	7.50	15.00	30.00
PRST-7322 [R]	Miles Davis Plays Richard Rodgers	1964	5.00	10.00	20.00
PRLP-7352 [M]	Miles Davis Plays for Lovers	1965	7.50	15.00	30.00
PRST-7352 [R]	Miles Davis Plays for Lovers	1965	5.00	10.00	20.00
PRLP-7373 [M]	Jazz Classics	1965	7.50	15.00	30.00
PRST-7373 [R]	Jazz Classics	1965	5.00	10.00	20.00
PRLP-7457 [M]	Miles Davis' Greatest Hits	1967	5.00	10.00	20.00
PRST-7457 [R]	Miles Davis' Greatest Hits	1967	3.00	6.00	12.00
PRST-7540 [R]	Odyssey	1968	3.00	6.00	12.00
—Reissue of 7034					
PRST-7580 [R]	Steamin'	1968	3.00	6.00	12.00
—Reissue of 7200					
PRST-7608 [R]	Walkin'	1969	3.00	6.00	12.00
—Reissue of 7076					
PRST-7650 [R]	Miles Davis and the Modern Jazz Giants	1969	3.00	6.00	12.00
—Reissue of 7150					
PRST-7674 [R]	Early Miles	1969	3.00	6.00	12.00
—Reissue of 7168					
PRST-7744 [R]	Conception	1970	3.00	6.00	12.00
PRST-7822 [R]	Miles Ahead!	1971	3.00	6.00	12.00
PRST-7847	Oleo	1972	3.00	6.00	12.00
24001 [(2)]	Miles Davis	1972	3.75	7.50	15.00
24012 [(2)]	The Tallest Trees	1972	3.75	7.50	15.00
24022 [(2)]	Collector's Items	1973	3.75	7.50	15.00
24034 [(2)]	Workin' and Steamin'	1973	3.75	7.50	15.00
24054 [(2)]	Dig	197?	3.00	6.00	12.00
24064 [(2)]	Green Haze	197?	3.00	6.00	12.00
24077 [(2)]	Tune Up	197?	3.00	6.00	12.00
SAVOY JAZZ					
SJL-1196	First Miles	1989	2.50	5.00	10.00
TRIP					
5015	Miles of Jazz	1974	2.50	5.00	10.00
UNITED ARTISTS					
UAS-9952 [(2)]	Miles Davis	1972	3.75	7.50	15.00
—Reissue of Blue Note material					
WARNER BROS.					
25490	Tutu	1986	2.50	5.00	10.00
25873	Amandla	1989	3.00	6.00	12.00
26938	Doo-Bop	1992	3.75	7.50	15.00

DAVIS, MILES, AND JOHN COLTRANE

Also see each artist's individual listings.

Albums

Number	Title (A Side/B Side)	Yr	VG	VG+	NM
MOODSVILLE					
MVLP-32 [M]	Miles Davis and John Coltrane Play Richard Rodgers	1963	12.50	25.00	50.00
—Green label					
MVLP-32 [M]	Miles Davis and John Coltrane Play Richard Rodgers	1965	6.25	12.50	25.00
—Blue label, trident logo at right					
PRESTIGE					
PRLP-7322 [M]	Miles Davis and John Coltrane Play Rodgers and Hart	1964	10.00	20.00	40.00
PRST-7322 [R]	Miles Davis and John Coltrane Play Rodgers and Hart	1964	5.00	10.00	20.00

DAVIS, MILES, AND TADD DAMERON

Albums

Number	Title (A Side/B Side)	Yr	VG	VG+	NM
COLUMBIA					
JC 34804	Paris Festival International, May 1949	1978	2.50	5.00	10.00

DAVIS, MILES, AND THELONIOUS MONK

Also see each artist's individual listings.

Albums

Number	Title (A Side/B Side)	Yr	VG	VG+	NM
COLUMBIA					
CL 2178 [M]	Miles and Monk at Newport	1964	6.25	12.50	25.00
—"Guaranteed High Fidelity" on label					
CL 2178 [M]	Miles and Monk at Newport	1965	5.00	10.00	20.00
—"Mono" on label					
CS 8978 [S]	Miles and Monk at Newport	1964	6.25	12.50	25.00
—"360 Sound Stereo" in black on label					
CS 8978 [S]	Miles and Monk at Newport	1965	5.00	10.00	20.00
—"360 Sound Stereo" in white on label					
KCS 8978	Miles and Monk at Newport	1974	2.50	5.00	10.00
—Orange label, new prefix					
PC 8978	Miles and Monk at Newport	1977	2.00	4.00	8.00
—Orange label, new prefix					

DAVIS, PAUL

Also see GRACIOUS.

45s

Number	Title (A Side/B Side)	Yr	VG	VG+	NM
ARISTA					
0645	Cool Night/One More Time for the Lonely	1981	—	2.00	4.00
0661	'65 Love Affair/We're Still Together	1982	—	2.00	4.00
0697	Love or Let Me Be Lonely/Oriental Eyes	1982	—	2.00	4.00
BANG					
568	If I Wuz a Magician/Mississippi River	1969	—	3.00	6.00

Number	Title (A Side/B Side)	Yr	VG	VG+	NM
576	A Little Bit of Soap/Three Little Words	1970	—	3.00	6.00
579	I Just Wanna Keep It Together/Pollyanna	1970	2.00	4.00	8.00
581	Can't You/Gonna Keep On Loving You	1970	—	3.00	6.00
587	I Feel Better/When My Little Girl Is Smiling	1971	—	3.00	6.00
590	Got to Find My Way Back/I Can't Get Her Off My Mind	1971	—	3.00	6.00
593	Come On Honey/Livin' On Your Love	1972	—	2.50	5.00
597	Simple Man/What Would We Do Without Music	1972	—	2.50	5.00
599	Boogie Woogie Man/Johnny Poverty	1972	—	2.50	5.00
702	Broken Hearted and Free/Mississippi River	1973	—	2.50	5.00
705	Daydreamer/Love Don't Come Easy	1973	—	2.50	5.00
712	Ride 'Em Cowboy/I'm the Only Sinner (In Salt Lake City)	1974	—	2.50	5.00
717	Make Her My Baby/Can't Get Back to Alabama	1975	—	2.00	4.00
718	Keep Our Love Alive/I Got a Yearning	1975	—	2.00	4.00
724	Thinking of You/Karma Baby	1976	—	2.00	4.00
726	Superstar/Magnolia Blues	1976	—	2.00	4.00
729	Medicine Woman/Hallelujah, Thank You, Jesus	1976	—	2.00	4.00
733	I Go Crazy/Reggae Kinda Way	1977	—	2.00	4.00
736	Darlin'/You're Not Just a Rose	1978	—	2.00	4.00
738	Sweet Life/Bad Dream	1978	—	2.00	4.00
4808	Do Right/He Sang Our Love Songs	1980	—	2.00	4.00
4811	Cry Just a Little/Do You Believe in Love	1980	—	2.00	4.00
CAPITOL					
B-5613	You're Still New to Me/New Love	1986	—	—	3.00
—With Marie Osmond					
B-44100	I Won't Take Less Than Your Love/Heartbreaker	1986	—	—	3.00
—With Tanya Tucker and Paul Overstreet					
B-44215	Sweet Life/My Home Town Boy	1988	—	—	3.00
—With Marie Osmond; B-side is Marie Osmond solo					
Albums					
ARISTA					
AL 8376	Cool Night	198?	2.00	4.00	8.00
—Reissue of 9578					
AL 9578	Cool Night	1981	2.50	5.00	10.00
BANG					
BLPS-223	A Little Bit of Paul Davis	1970	10.00	20.00	40.00
401	Ride 'Em Cowboy	1974	3.00	6.00	12.00
405	Southern Tracks and Fantasies	1976	3.00	6.00	12.00
410	Singer of Songs — Teller of Tales	1977	3.00	6.00	12.00
JZ 36094	Paul Davis	1980	2.50	5.00	10.00
PZ 37973	The Best of Paul Davis	1982	2.50	5.00	10.00

DAVIS, SAMMY, JR.

45s

Number	Title (A Side/B Side)	Yr	VG	VG+	NM
20TH CENTURY					
2236	Snap Your Fingers/Song and Dance Man	1975	—	2.00	4.00
2282	Chico and the Man (Main Theme)/(I'd Be) A Legend in My Time	1976	—	2.50	5.00
—May be promo only					
2292	Baretta's Theme (Keep Your Eye on the Sparrow)/I Heard a Song	1976	—	2.00	4.00
APPLAUSE					
100	Smoke, Smoke, Smoke (That Cigarette)/We Could Have Been the Closest of Friends	1982	—	2.00	4.00
DDR					
101/2	Who Needs Spring/(B-side unknown)	197?	2.00	4.00	8.00
—Red vinyl					
DECCA					
29199	Hey There/And This Is My Beloved	1954	3.00	6.00	12.00
29200	Because of You (Part 1)/Because of You (Part 2)	1954	3.00	6.00	12.00
29310	Glad to Be Unhappy/Red Grapes	1954	3.00	6.00	12.00
29393	The Birth of the Blues/Love	1954	3.00	6.00	12.00
29402	All of You/Six Bridges to Cross	1955	3.00	6.00	12.00
29484	Love Me or Leave Me/Something's Gotta Give	1955	3.00	6.00	12.00
29541	That Old Black Magic/A Man with a Dream	1955	3.00	6.00	12.00
29620	I Go for You/A Fine Romance	1955	3.00	6.00	12.00
—With Carmen McRae					
29649	Back Track/It's Bigger Than You and Me	1955	3.00	6.00	12.00
29672	I'll Know/Adelaide	1955	3.00	6.00	12.00
29737	Ac-Cent-Tchu-Ate the Positive/Beat Me, Daddy, Eight to the Bar	1955	3.00	6.00	12.00
—With Gary Crosby					
29759	The Man with the Golden Arm/In a Persian Blanket	1955	3.00	6.00	12.00
29795	Frankie and Johnny/Circus	1956	3.00	6.00	12.00
29861	Too Close for Comfort/Jacques d'Iraque	1956	3.00	6.00	12.00
29929	Without You I'm Nothing/Get Out of the Car	1956	3.00	6.00	12.00
29976	Five/You're Sensational	1956	3.00	6.00	12.00
30035	Earthbound/Just One of Those Things	1956	3.00	6.00	12.00
30111	New York's My Home/Never Like This	1956	3.00	6.00	12.00
30158	All About Love/Dangerous	1956	3.00	6.00	12.00
30189	The Golden Key/Long Before I Knew You	1957	2.50	5.00	10.00
30300	Good Bye, So Long, I'm Gone/French Friend Potatoes and Ketchup	1957	2.50	5.00	10.00
30371	Doncha Go 'Way Mad/'Specially for Little Girls	1957	2.50	5.00	10.00
30400	Baby It's Cold Outside/Happy to Make Your Acquaintance	1957	2.50	5.00	10.00
30441	Mad Ball/Cool Credo	1957	2.50	5.00	10.00
30479	All Dressed Up and No Place to Go/Moment of Madness	1957	2.50	5.00	10.00
30536	Hallelujah I Love Her So/I'm Comin' Home	1958	2.50	5.00	10.00
30611	No Fool Like an Old Fool/Unspoken	1958	2.50	5.00	10.00
30679	Song and Dance Man/I Ain't Gonna Change	1958	2.50	5.00	10.00
30769	That's Anna/I Never Got Out of Paris	1958	2.50	5.00	10.00
30898	Fair Warning/You'll Never Get Away from Me	1959	2.50	5.00	10.00
30915	I Got Plenty of Nothin'/There's a Boat Dat's Leaving Soon for New York	1959	2.50	5.00	10.00
31136	I Got a Woman/Mess Around	1960	2.50	5.00	10.00
31177	This Little Girl of Mine/Face to Face	1960	2.50	5.00	10.00
32470	Rhythm of Life/(B-side unknown)	1969	—	3.00	6.00
MGM					
14320	The Candy Man/I Want to Be Happy	1971	—	3.00	6.00
14426	Mr. Bojangles/The People Tree	1972	—	2.50	5.00
14513	(I'd Be) A Legend in My Time/I'm Not Anyone	1973	—	2.50	5.00
14685	Singin' in the Rain/Chattanooga Choo Choo	1973	—	2.50	5.00
14736	That's Entertainment/Singin' in the Rain	1974	—	2.00	4.00
14759	Sing/This Is the House of the People	1974	—	2.00	4.00
MOTOWN					
1738	Hello Detroit (Part 1)/Hello Detroit (Part 2)	1984	—	2.00	4.00
REPRISE					
(no #) [DJ]	Here's a Kiss for Christmas (The Christmas Seal Song)/What Kind of Fool Am I	1963	3.75	7.50	15.00
OE-DJ-2 [DJ]	Open End Disc Jockey Interview	196?	10.00	20.00	40.00
—Small hole, plays at 33 1/3 rpm					
0248	What Kind of Fool Am I/Gonna Buila a Mountain	1963	2.00	4.00	8.00
0278	Choose/Bee Bom	1964	2.00	4.00	8.00
0289	Not for Me/Night Song	1964	2.00	4.00	8.00
0321	Hello, Dolly!/Take the Moment	1964	3.75	7.50	15.00
—Possibly released only outside the U.S.					
0322	Don't Shut Me Out/Disorderly Orderly	1964	2.00	4.00	8.00
0345	If I Ruled the World/Flash, Bang, Wallop	1965	2.00	4.00	8.00
0361	Hello, Dolly!/Take the Moment	1965	2.00	4.00	8.00
0370	Unforgettable/No One Can Live Forever	1965	2.00	4.00	8.00
0399	Love, At Last You Have Found Me/Courage	1965	2.00	4.00	8.00
0416	Yes I Can/Courage	1965	2.00	4.00	8.00
0425	If You Want This Love of Mine/Second-Best Secret Agent in the Whole Wide World	1965	2.00	4.00	8.00
0437	Lonely Weekends/More Than One Way	1965	2.00	4.00	8.00
0502	All That Jazz/Ev'ry Time We Say Goodbye	1966	—	3.00	6.00
0521	The Good Life/We'll Be Together Again	1966	—	3.00	6.00
0549	The Birth of the Blues/With a Song in My Heart	1967	—	3.00	6.00
0566	Don't Blame the Children/She Believes in Me	1967	—	3.00	6.00
0621	Talk to the Animals/Something in Your Smile	1967	—	3.00	6.00
0673	Lonely Is the Name/Flash, Bang, Wallop	1968	—	3.00	6.00
0720	What Kind of Fool Am I/Gonna Build a Mountain	1968	—	2.00	4.00
—"Back to Back Hits" series					
0733	I've Gotta Be Me/Lonely Is the Name	1970	—	2.00	4.00
—"Back to Back Hits" series					
0757	Break My Mind/Children, Children	1968	—	3.00	6.00
0779	I've Gotta Be Me/Bein' Natural Bein' Me	1968	2.00	4.00	8.00
0827	I Have But One Life to Live/The Goin's Great	1969	—	3.00	6.00
0989	She Is Today/Runaround	1971	—	2.50	5.00
20003	I'm a Fool to Want You/Back in Your Own Back Yard	1961	2.50	5.00	10.00
20018	One More Time (A Tribute to Ray Charles)/There Was a Tavern in the Town	1961	2.50	5.00	10.00
20048	What Kind of Fool Am I/Gonna Build a Mountain	1962	2.50	5.00	10.00
20079	The Fool I Used to Be/Everybody Calls Me Joe	1962	2.50	5.00	10.00
20087	Once in a Lifetime/Someone Nice Like You	1962	2.50	5.00	10.00
20128	Me and My Shadow/Sam's Song	1962	3.75	7.50	15.00
—A-side: With Frank Sinatra; B-side: With Dean Martin					
20128 [PS]	Me and My Shadow/Sam's Song	1962	7.50	15.00	30.00
20138	As Long As She Needs Me/Two for the Seesaw	1963	2.50	5.00	10.00
20212	We Kiss in a Shadow/Bye, Bye Blackbird	1963	2.50	5.00	10.00
20216	The Shelter of Your Arms/This Was My Love	1963	2.50	5.00	10.00
20227	The Shelter of Your Arms/Falling in Love with Love	1963	5.00	10.00	20.00
—Released only in England					
UNITED ARTISTS					
50334	Salt and Pepper/I Like the Way You Dance	1968	—	3.00	6.00
VERVE					
10219	Ain't That a Kick in the Head/Eee-O Eleven	1960	2.00	4.00	8.00
WARNER BROS.					
49047	Showtime/That Old Black Magic	1979	—	2.00	4.00
7-Inch Extended Plays					
DECCA					
ED 2214	Hey There/Glad to Be Unhappy//And This Is My Beloved/Easy to Love	195?	3.00	6.00	12.00
ED 2214 [PS]	Starring Sammy Davis, Jr.	195?	3.00	6.00	12.00
Albums					
DECCA					
DXB 192 [(2) M]	The Best of Sammy Davis, Jr.	1966	3.75	7.50	15.00
DL 4153 [M]	Mr. Entertainment	1961	3.75	7.50	15.00
DL 4381 [M]	Forget-Me-Nots for First Nighters	1963	3.75	7.50	15.00
DL 4582 [M]	Try a Little Tenderness	1965	3.00	6.00	12.00
DXSB 7192 [(2) S]	The Best of Sammy Davis, Jr.	1966	5.00	10.00	20.00
DL 8118 [M]	Starring Sammy Davis, Jr.	1955	7.50	15.00	30.00
DL 8170 [M]	Just for Lovers	1955	7.50	15.00	30.00
DL 8351 [M]	Here's Looking at You	1956	6.25	12.50	25.00
DL 8486 [M]	Sammy Swings	1957	6.25	12.50	25.00
DL 8641 [M]	It's All Over But the Swingin'	1957	6.25	12.50	25.00
DL 8676 [M]	Mood to Be Wooed	1958	6.25	12.50	25.00
DL 8779 [M]	All the Way And Then Some	1958	6.25	12.50	25.00
DL 8841 [M]	Sammy Davis, Jr., at Town Hall	1959	5.00	10.00	20.00
DL 8854 [M]	Porgy and Bess	1959	5.00	10.00	20.00
DL 8921 [M]	The Sammy Awards	1960	5.00	10.00	20.00
DL 8981 [M]	I Got a Right to Swing	1960	5.00	10.00	20.00
DL 74153 [S]	Mr. Entertainment	1961	5.00	10.00	20.00
DL 74381 [S]	Forget-Me-Nots for First Nighters	1963	5.00	10.00	20.00
DL 74582 [S]	Try a Little Tenderness	1965	3.75	7.50	15.00
DL 78841 [S]	Sammy Davis, Jr., at Town Hall	1959	6.25	12.50	25.00
DL 78854 [S]	Porgy and Bess	1959	6.25	12.50	25.00
DL 78921 [S]	The Sammy Awards	1960	6.25	12.50	25.00
DL 78981 [S]	I Got a Right to Swing	1960	6.25	12.50	25.00
HARMONY					
HS 11299	The Great Sammy Davis, Jr.	196?	3.00	6.00	12.00
HS 11365	Let There Be Love	1970	2.50	5.00	10.00
H 30568	What Kind of Fool Am I	1971	2.50	5.00	10.00
MCA					
4109 [(2)]	Sammy Davis Jr. At His Greatest	1975	3.00	6.00	12.00
MGM					
SE-4832	Sammy Davis Jr. Now	1972	2.50	5.00	10.00
SE-4852	Portrait of Sammy Davis, Jr.	1972	2.50	5.00	10.00
M3G-4965	That's Entertainment!	1974	2.50	5.00	10.00
MOTOWN					
MS 710	Something for Everyone	1970	3.00	6.00	12.00
4519 ML	Hello Detroit!	1984	2.50	5.00	10.00

Number	Title (A Side/B Side)	Yr	VG	VG+	NM
PICKWICK					
SPC-3002	The Many Faces of Sammy Davis, Jr.	196?	2.50	5.00	10.00
REPRISE					
R-2003 [M]	The Wham of Sam	1961	3.75	7.50	15.00
R9-2003 [S]	The Wham of Sam	1961	5.00	10.00	20.00
R-2010 [M]	Sammy Davis, Jr., Belts the Best of Broadway	1962	3.75	7.50	15.00
R9-2010 [S]	Sammy Davis, Jr., Belts the Best of Broadway	1962	5.00	10.00	20.00
R-6033 [M]	All Star Spectacular	1962	3.75	7.50	15.00
R9-6033 [S]	All Star Spectacular	1962	5.00	10.00	20.00
R-6051 [M]	What Kind of Fool Am I and Other Show-Stoppers	1962	3.75	7.50	15.00
R9-6051 [S]	What Kind of Fool Am I and Other Show-Stoppers	1962	5.00	10.00	20.00
R-6063 [(2) M]	Sammy Davis Jr. at the Cocoanut Grove	1963	5.00	10.00	20.00
R9-6063 [(2) S]	Sammy Davis Jr. at the Cocoanut Grove	1963	6.25	12.50	25.00
R-6082 [M]	As Long As She Needs Me	1963	3.75	7.50	15.00
R9-6082 [S]	As Long As She Needs Me	1963	5.00	10.00	20.00
R-6095 [M]	Sammy Davis Jr. Salutes the Stars of the London Palladium	1964	3.75	7.50	15.00
R9-6095 [S]	Sammy Davis Jr. Salutes the Stars of the London Palladium	1964	5.00	10.00	20.00
R-6096 [M]	Treasury of Golden Hits	1964	3.75	7.50	15.00
R9-6096 [S]	Treasury of Golden Hits	1964	5.00	10.00	20.00
R-6114 [M]	The Shelter of Your Arms	1964	3.75	7.50	15.00
R9-6114 [S]	The Shelter of Your Arms	1964	5.00	10.00	20.00
R-6126 [M]	California Suite	1964	3.75	7.50	15.00
R9-6126 [S]	California Suite	1964	5.00	10.00	20.00
R-6131 [M]	Sammy Davis Jr. Sings the Big Ones for Young Lovers	1964	3.00	6.00	12.00
RS-6131 [S]	Sammy Davis Jr. Sings the Big Ones for Young Lovers	1964	3.75	7.50	15.00
R-6144 [M]	When the Feeling Hits You	1965	3.00	6.00	12.00
RS-6144 [S]	When the Feeling Hits You	1965	3.75	7.50	15.00
R-6159 [M]	If I Ruled the World	1965	3.00	6.00	12.00
RS-6159 [S]	If I Ruled the World	1965	3.75	7.50	15.00
R-6164 [M]	The Nat Cole Song Book	1965	3.00	6.00	12.00
RS-6164 [S]	The Nat Cole Song Book	1965	3.75	7.50	15.00
R-6169 [M]	Sammy's Back on Broadway	1965	3.00	6.00	12.00
RS-6169 [S]	Sammy's Back on Broadway	1965	3.75	7.50	15.00
R-6188 [M]	The Sammy Davis, Jr., Show	1965	3.00	6.00	12.00
RS-6188 [S]	The Sammy Davis, Jr., Show	1965	3.75	7.50	15.00
R-6214 [M]	The Sounds of '66	1966	3.00	6.00	12.00
RS-6214 [S]	The Sounds of '66	1966	3.75	7.50	15.00
R-6236 [M]	Sammy Davis. Jr., Sings/Laurindo Almeida Plays	1966	3.00	6.00	12.00
RS-6236 [S]	Sammy Davis. Jr., Sings/Laurindo Almeida Plays	1966	3.75	7.50	15.00
R-6237 [(2) M]	That's All	1967	3.75	7.50	15.00
RS-6237 [(2) S]	That's All	1967	5.00	10.00	20.00
RS-6291	Sammy Davis, Jr.'s Greatest Hits	1968	3.00	6.00	12.00
RS-6308	Lonely Is the Name	1968	3.00	6.00	12.00
RS-6324	I've Gotta Be Me	1969	3.00	6.00	12.00
RS-6339	The Goin's Great	1969	3.00	6.00	12.00
RS-6410	Sammy Davis, Jr., Steps Out	1970	3.00	6.00	12.00
WARNER BROS.					
BSK 3128	Live Performance	1977	2.50	5.00	10.00

DAVIS, SAMMY, JR., AND COUNT BASIE

Also see each artist's individual listings.

Albums

Number	Title (A Side/B Side)	Yr	VG	VG+	NM
MGM					
SE-4825	Sammy Davis Jr. and Count Basie	1972	2.50	5.00	10.00
—Reissue of Verve LP?					
VERVE					
V-8605 [M]	Our Shining Hour	1965	3.00	6.00	12.00
V6-8605 [S]	Our Shining Hour	1965	3.75	7.50	15.00

DAVIS, SAMMY, JR., AND CARMEN MCRAE

Albums

Number	Title (A Side/B Side)	Yr	VG	VG+	NM
DECCA					
DL 8490 [M]	Boy Meets Girl	1957	7.50	15.00	30.00

DAVIS, SKEETER

Also see THE DAVIS SISTERS.

45s

Number	Title (A Side/B Side)	Yr	VG	VG+	NM
MERCURY					
73818	I Love Us/It Feels So Good	1976	—	2.00	4.00
73898	If You Loved Me Now/It's Love That I Feel	1977	—	2.00	4.00
RCA VICTOR					
APBO-0188	Don't Forget to Remember/Baby Get That Leavin' Off Your Mind	1973	—	2.00	4.00
APBO-0277	One More Time/Stay Awhile with Me	1974	—	2.00	4.00
PB-10048	Come Mornin'/Lovin' Touch	1974	—	2.00	4.00
47-7034	He Left His Heart for Me/Don't Let Your Lips Say Yes	1957	3.75	7.50	15.00
47-7084	Lost to a Geisha Girl/I'm Going Steady with a Heartache	1957	3.75	7.50	15.00
47-7189	Walk Softly Darling/I Need You All the Time	1958	3.75	7.50	15.00
47-7293	Wave Bye Bye/I Forgot More Than You'll Ever Know	1958	3.75	7.50	15.00
47-7401	I Ain't A-Talkin'/Slave	1958	3.75	7.50	15.00
47-7471	Set Him Free/The Devil's Doll	1959	3.00	6.00	12.00
47-7570	Homebreaker/Give Me Death	1959	3.00	6.00	12.00
47-7671	Am I That Easy to Forget/Wishful Thinking	1960	3.00	6.00	12.00
47-7767	(I Can't Help You) I'm Falling Too/No, Never	1960	3.00	6.00	12.00
47-7825	My Last Date (With You)/Someone I'd Like to Forget	1960	3.00	6.00	12.00
47-7863	The Hand You're Holding Now/Someday Someday	1961	3.00	6.00	12.00
47-7928	Optimistic/Blueberry Hill	1961	3.00	6.00	12.00
47-7979	Where I Ought to Be/Something Precious	1962	2.50	5.00	10.00
47-8055	The Little Music Box/The Final Stop	1962	2.50	5.00	10.00
47-8098	The End of the World/Somebody Loves You	1962	3.00	6.00	12.00
47-8176	I'm Saving My Love/Somebody Else on Your Mind	1963	2.50	5.00	10.00
47-8219	I Can't Stay Mad at You/It Was Only a Heart	1963	2.50	5.00	10.00
47-8219 [PS]	I Can't Stay Mad at You/It Was Only a Heart	1963	5.00	10.00	20.00
47-8288	He Says the Same Things to Me/How Much Can a Lonely Heart Stand	1963	2.50	5.00	10.00
47-8347	Gonna Get Along Without You Now/Now You're Gone	1964	2.50	5.00	10.00
47-8397	Let Me Get Close to You/Face of a Clown	1964	2.50	5.00	10.00
47-8450	What Am I Going to Do with You/Don't Let Me Stand in Your Way	1964	2.50	5.00	10.00
47-8496	A Dear John Letter/Too Used to Being with You	1965	2.50	5.00	10.00
—With Bobby Bare					
47-8543	You Taught Me Everything I Know/I Can't Help It	1965	2.00	4.00	8.00
47-8642	Sun Glasses/He Loved Me Too Little	1965	2.00	4.00	8.00
47-8765	I Can't See Me Without You/Don't Anybody Need My Love	1965	2.00	4.00	8.00
47-8837	If I Ever Get to Heaven/If I Had Wheels	1966	2.00	4.00	8.00
47-8932	Goin' Down the Road/I Can't Stand the Sight of You	1966	2.00	4.00	8.00
47-9058	Fuel to the Flame/You Call This Love	1966	2.00	4.00	8.00
47-9242	What Does It Take (To Keep a Man Satisfied)/What I Go Through	1967	—	3.00	6.00
47-9371	Set Him Free/Is It Worth It to You	1967	—	3.00	6.00
47-9415	Baby, It's Cold Outside/For Loving You	1967	—	3.00	6.00
—With Don Bowman					
47-9459	How in the World/Instinct for Survival	1968	—	3.00	6.00
47-9543	There's a Fool Born Every Minute/I Can't See Past the Tears	1968	—	3.00	6.00
47-9625	I Look Up (And See You on My Mind)/Timothy	1968	—	3.00	6.00
47-9695	The Closest Thing to Love/Mama Your Big Girl's About to Cry	1968	—	3.00	6.00
47-9789	Your Husband, My Wife/Before the Sunshine	1969	—	3.00	6.00
—With Bobby Bare					
47-9818	It's Hard to Be a Woman/What a Little Girl Don't Know	1969	—	3.00	6.00
47-9871	We Need a Lot More Jesus/When You Gonna Bring Our Soldiers Home	1970	—	2.50	5.00
47-0803	Let's Get Together/Everything Is Beautiful	1970	—	3.00	6.00
—With George Hamilton IV					
47-9896	Bridge Over Troubled Water/How in the World Do You Kill a Memory	1970	—	2.50	5.00
47-9961	Bus Fare to Kentucky/From Her Arms Into Mine	1971	—	2.50	5.00
47-9997	Love Takes a Lot of Time/Love, Love, Love	1971	—	2.50	5.00
74-0148	Baby Sweet Baby/Keep Baltimore Beautiful	1969	—	3.00	6.00
74-0203	Teach Me to Love You/Bobby Blows a Blue Note	1969	—	3.00	6.00
74-0292	I Didn't Cry Today/I'm a Lover (Not a Fighter)	1969	—	3.00	6.00
74-0608	One Tin Soldier/Rachel	1971	—	2.50	5.00
74-0681	Sad Situation/All I Ever Wanted Was Love	1972	—	2.00	4.00
74-0827	Hillbilly Song/Once	1972	—	2.00	4.00
74-0968	I Can't Believe That It's All Over/Try Jesus	1973	—	2.00	4.00

Albums

Number	Title (A Side/B Side)	Yr	VG	VG+	NM
GUSTO					
0014	Best of the Best	1978	2.50	5.00	10.00
RCA CAMDEN					
ACL1-0622	He Wakes Me with a Kiss	1974	2.50	5.00	10.00
CAL-818 [M]	I Forgot More Than You'll Ever Know	196?	3.00	6.00	12.00
CAS-818 [S]	I Forgot More Than You'll Ever Know	196?	3.75	7.50	15.00
CAL-899 [M]	Blueberry Hill and Other Favorites	1965	3.00	6.00	12.00
CAS-899 [S]	Blueberry Hill and Other Favorites	1965	3.75	7.50	15.00
CAS-2367	Easy to Love	1970	3.00	6.00	12.00
CAS-2517	Foggy Mountain Top	1971	3.00	6.00	12.00
CAS-2607	The End of the World	1972	2.50	5.00	10.00
RCA VICTOR					
APL1-0190	The Best of Skeeter Davis, Volume 2	1973	3.00	6.00	12.00
APL1-0322	I Can't Believe It's All Over	1974	3.00	6.00	12.00
LPM-2197 [M]	I'll Sing You a Song and Harmonize, Too	1960	6.25	12.50	25.00
LSP-2197 [S]	I'll Sing You a Song and Harmonize, Too	1960	7.50	15.00	30.00
LPM-2327 [M]	Here's the Answer	1961	6.25	12.50	25.00
LSP-2327 [S]	Here's the Answer	1961	7.50	15.00	30.00
LPM-2699 [M]	The End of the World	1963	6.25	12.50	25.00
LSP-2699 [S]	The End of the World	1963	7.50	15.00	30.00
LPM-2736 [M]	Cloudy, With Occasional Tears	1963	6.25	12.50	25.00
LSP-2736 [S]	Cloudy, With Occasional Tears	1963	7.50	15.00	30.00
LPM-2980 [M]	Let Me Get Close to You	1964	5.00	10.00	20.00
LSP-2980 [S]	Let Me Get Close to You	1964	6.25	12.50	25.00
LPM-3374 [M]	The Best of Skeeter Davis	1965	5.00	10.00	20.00
LSP-3374 [S]	The Best of Skeeter Davis	1965	6.25	12.50	25.00
LPM-3382 [M]	Written by the Stars	1965	5.00	10.00	20.00
LSP-3382 [S]	Written by the Stars	1965	6.25	12.50	25.00
LPM-3463 [M]	Skeeter Sings Standards	1965	5.00	10.00	20.00
LSP-3463 [S]	Skeeter Sings Standards	1965	6.25	12.50	25.00
LPM-3567 [M]	Singin' in the Summer Sun	1966	5.00	10.00	20.00
LSP-3567 [S]	Singin' in the Summer Sun	1966	6.25	12.50	25.00
LPM-3667 [M]	My Heart's in the Country	1966	5.00	10.00	20.00
LSP-3667 [S]	My Heart's in the Country	1966	6.25	12.50	25.00
LSP-3667 [S]	Hand in Hand with Jesus	1967	5.00	10.00	20.00
LPM-3763 [M]	Hand in Hand with Jesus	1967	7.50	15.00	30.00
LPM-3790 [M]	Skeeter Davis Sings Buddy Holly	1967	12.50	25.00	50.00
LSP-3790 [S]	Skeeter Davis Sings Buddy Holly	1967	10.00	20.00	40.00
LPM-3876 [M]	What Does It Take (To Keep a Man Like You Satisfied)	1967	7.50	15.00	30.00
LSP-3876 [S]	What Does It Take (To Keep a Man Like You Satisfied)	1967	5.00	10.00	20.00
LPM-3960 [M]	Why So Lonely?	1968	12.50	25.00	50.00
LSP-3960 [S]	Why So Lonely?	1968	5.00	10.00	20.00
LSP-4055	I Love Flatt & Scruggs	1968	5.00	10.00	20.00
LSP-4124	The Closest Thing to Love	1969	5.00	10.00	20.00
LSP-4200	Maryfrances	1969	5.00	10.00	20.00
LSP-4310	A Place in the Country	1970	3.75	7.50	15.00
LSP-4382	It's Hard to Be a Woman	1970	3.75	7.50	15.00
LSP-4486	Skeeter	1971	3.75	7.50	15.00
LSP-4557	Love Takes a Lot	1971	3.75	7.50	15.00
LSP-4642	Bring It on Home	1972	3.75	7.50	15.00
LSP-4732	Skeeter Sings Dolly	1972	3.75	7.50	15.00
LSP-4818	Hillbilly Singer	1972	3.75	7.50	15.00

DAVIS, SKEETER, AND NRBQ

Also see each artist's individual listings.

Albums

ROUNDER

Number	Title (A Side/B Side)	Yr	VG	VG+	NM
3092	She Sings, They Play	1986	3.00	6.00	12.00

DAVIS, SPENCER, GROUP

Includes Spencer Davis solo. Also see STEVE WINWOOD.

45s

ATCO

Number	Title (A Side/B Side)	Yr	VG	VG+	NM
6400	Keep On Running/High Time Baby	1966	3.75	7.50	15.00
6416	Somebody Help Me/Stevie's Blues	1966	3.75	7.50	15.00

FONTANA

Number	Title (A Side/B Side)	Yr	VG	VG+	NM
1960	I Can't Stand It/Midnight Train	1964	3.75	7.50	15.00

UNITED ARTISTS

Number	Title (A Side/B Side)	Yr	VG	VG+	NM
SP 78 [DJ]	Voter Registration Spots	1972	3.75	7.50	15.00
—Two ads, 30 and 60 seconds in length					
0115	Gimme Some Lovin'/Keep On Running	1973	—	2.00	4.00
—"Silver Spotlight Series" reissue					
0116	I'm a Man/Somebody Help Me	1973	—	2.00	4.00
—"Silver Spotlight Series" reissue					
50108	Gimme Some Lovin'/Blues in F	1966	3.00	6.00	12.00
50144	I'm a Man/Can't Get Enough of It	1967	3.00	6.00	12.00
50162	Somebody Help Me/On the Green Light	1967	2.50	5.00	10.00
50202	Time Seller/Don't Want You No More	1967	2.50	5.00	10.00
50202 [PS]	Time Seller/Don't Want You No More	1967	5.00	10.00	20.00
50286	Looking Back/After Tea	1968	2.50	5.00	10.00
50922	Listen to the Rhythm/Sunday Walk in the Rain	1972	—	3.00	6.00
—Spencer Davis solo					
50993	Rainy Season/Tumble-Down Tenement Row	1972	—	3.00	6.00
—Spencer Davis solo					

VERTIGO

Number	Title (A Side/B Side)	Yr	VG	VG+	NM
110	Don't You Let It Bring You Down/Today Gluggo, Tomorrow the World	1973	—	2.50	5.00
112	Living in a Back Street/Need a Helping Hand	1974	—	2.50	5.00

Albums

ALLEGIANCE

Number	Title (A Side/B Side)	Yr	VG	VG+	NM
AV-442	Crossfire	1983	2.50	5.00	10.00

MEDIARTS

Number	Title (A Side/B Side)	Yr	VG	VG+	NM
41-11	It's Been So Long	1971	3.00	6.00	12.00

RHINO

Number	Title (A Side/B Side)	Yr	VG	VG+	NM
RNLP 117	The Best of the Spencer Davis Group	1983	2.00	4.00	8.00
RNLP 70172	The Best of the Spencer Davis Group (Golden Archive Series)	1987	3.00	6.00	12.00

UNITED ARTISTS

Number	Title (A Side/B Side)	Yr	VG	VG+	NM
UA-LA433-E	The Very Best of the Spencer Davis Group	1975	2.50	5.00	10.00
UAL 3578 [M]	Gimme Some Lovin'	1967	12.50	25.00	50.00
UAL 3589 [M]	I'm a Man	1967	10.00	20.00	40.00
UAS 6578 [R]	Gimme Some Lovin'	1967	10.00	20.00	40.00
UAS 6589 [P]	I'm a Man	1967	12.50	25.00	50.00
UAS 6641 [P]	The Spencer Davis Group's Greatest Hits	1968	6.25	12.50	25.00
UAS 6652	With Their New Face On	1968	5.00	10.00	20.00
UAS 6691	Heavies	1969	5.00	10.00	20.00

VERTIGO

Number	Title (A Side/B Side)	Yr	VG	VG+	NM
VEL-1015	Gluggo	1973	3.00	6.00	12.00
VEL-1021	Living in a Back Street	1974	3.00	6.00	12.00

DAVIS, TYRONE

45s

ABC

Number	Title (A Side/B Side)	Yr	VG	VG+	NM
11030	Bet You Win/What If a Man	1967	3.00	6.00	12.00

COLUMBIA

Number	Title (A Side/B Side)	Yr	VG	VG+	NM
02269	Just My Luck/Let's Be Closer Together	1981	—	2.00	4.00
02634	Leave Well Enough Alone/I Won't Let Go	1981	—	2.00	4.00
10388	Give It Up (Turn It Loose)/You're Too Much	1976	—	2.50	5.00
10457	Close to You/Wrong Doers	1976	—	2.50	5.00
10528	This I Swear/Givin' Myself to You	1977	—	2.50	5.00
10604	All You Got/I Got Carried Away	1977	—	2.50	5.00
10684	Get It Up (Disco)/It's You, It's You	1978	—	2.50	5.00
10773	Can't Help But Say/Bunky	1978	—	2.00	4.00
10904	In the Mood/I Can't Wait	1979	—	2.00	4.00
11035	Ain't Nothing I Can Do/The Love I Need	1979	—	2.00	4.00
11128	Be With Me/Love You Forever	1979	—	2.00	4.00
11199	Can't You Tell It's Me/I Don't Think You Heard Me	1980	—	2.00	4.00
11246	Keep On Dancin'/Heart Failure	1980	—	2.00	4.00
11344	How Sweet It Is (To Be Loved By You)/I Can't Wait	1980	—	2.00	4.00
11415	I Just Can't Keep On Going/We Don't Need No Music	1980	—	2.00	4.00

DAKAR

Number	Title (A Side/B Side)	Yr	VG	VG+	NM
602	Can I Change My Mind/A Woman Needs to Be Loved	1968	2.50	5.00	10.00
605	Is It Something You've Got/Undying Love	1969	2.00	4.00	8.00
609	All the Waiting Is Not in Vain/Need Your Lovin' Everybody	1969	2.00	4.00	8.00
611	If It's Love That You're After/When I'm Not Around	1969	2.00	4.00	8.00
615	If I Didn't Love You/You Can't Keep a Good Man Down	1969	2.00	4.00	8.00
616	Turn Back the Hands of Time/I Keep Coming Back	1970	2.00	4.00	8.00
618	I'll Be Right Here/Just Because of You	1970	—	3.00	6.00
621	Let Me Back In/Love Bones	1970	—	3.00	6.00
623	Could I Forget You/Just My Way of Loving You	1971	—	3.00	6.00
624	One-Way Ticket/We Got a Love	1971	—	3.00	6.00
626	You Keep Me Holding On/We Got a Love No One Can Deny	1971	—	3.00	6.00
1452	Can I Change My Mind/A Woman Needs to Be Loved	1968	3.00	6.00	12.00
4501	I Had It All the Time/You Wouldn't Believe	1972	—	2.50	5.00
4507	Was I Just a Fool/After All This Time	1972	—	2.50	5.00
4510	Come and Get This Ring/After All This Time	1972	—	2.50	5.00
4513	If You Had a Change in Mind/Was It Just a Feelin'	1972	—	2.50	5.00
4519	Without You in My Life/How Could I Forget You	1973	—	2.50	5.00
4523	There It Is/You Wouldn't Believe	1973	—	2.50	5.00
4526	Wrapped Up in Your Warm and Tender Love/True Love Is Hard to Find	1973	—	2.50	5.00
4529	I Wish It Was Me/You Don't Have to Beg Me to Stay	1974	—	2.50	5.00
4532	What Goes Up (Must Come Down)/There's Got to Be an Answer	1974	—	2.50	5.00
4536	Happiness Is Being with You/Where Lovers Meet	1974	—	2.50	5.00
4538	I Can't Make It Without You/You Wouldn't Believe	1974	—	2.50	5.00
4541	Homewreckers/This Time	1975	—	2.50	5.00
4545	A Woman Needs to Be Loved/Just Because of You (I Can See My Way Through)	1975	—	2.50	5.00
4550	Turning Point/Don't Let It Be Too Late	1975	—	2.50	5.00
4553	So Good (To Be Home with You)/I Can't Bump	1976	—	2.50	5.00
4558	I Can't Bump, Part 2/Saving My Love for You	1976	—	2.50	5.00
4561	Ever Lovin' Girl/Forever	1976	—	2.50	5.00
4563	Where Lovers Meet (At the Dark End of the Street)/It's All in the Game	1977	—	2.50	5.00

FUTURE

Number	Title (A Side/B Side)	Yr	VG	VG+	NM
101	Sexy Thing/Save Me	1987	—	2.50	5.00
102	I'm in Love Again/Serious Love	1987	—	2.00	4.00
103	Do You Feel It/(Instrumental)	1988	—	2.00	4.00
104	It's a Miracle/Wrong Doers	1988	—	2.00	4.00
204	Flashin' Back/Flashin' Back (LP Version)	1988	—	2.00	4.00

HIGHRISE

Number	Title (A Side/B Side)	Yr	VG	VG+	NM
2005	Are You Serious/Overdrive	1982	—	2.00	4.00
2009	A Little Bit of Loving (Goes a Long Way)/Where Did We Lose	1983	—	2.00	4.00

ICHIBAN

Number	Title (A Side/B Side)	Yr	VG	VG+	NM
139	Can I Change My Mind/Hey There Lonely Girl	1989	—	2.00	4.00
—B-side by Eddie Holman					
226	I'll Always Love You/Can I Change My Mind	1991	—	—	3.00
237	Mom's Apple Pie/Do U Still Love Me	1991	—	—	3.00
255	Something's Mighty Wrong/Let Me Love You	1992	—	—	3.00
261	Running In and Out of My Life/I've Gotta Get Over You	1992	—	—	3.00
273	Don't Make Me Choose/Ain't Gonna Get It	1992	—	—	3.00
285	It's a Miracle/Do You Feel It	1993	—	—	3.00
292	I Found Myself When I Lost You/Something About a Woman	1993	—	—	3.00

OCEAN-FRONT

Number	Title (A Side/B Side)	Yr	VG	VG+	NM
2001	I Found Myself When I Lost You/(Instrumental)	1983	—	2.00	4.00
2004	Let Me Be Your Pacifier/Turning Point	1984	—	2.00	4.00

Albums

COLUMBIA

Number	Title (A Side/B Side)	Yr	VG	VG+	NM
PC 34268	Love and Touch	1976	3.00	6.00	12.00
PC 34654	Let's Be Closer Together	1977	3.00	6.00	12.00
JC 35305	I Can't Go On This Way	1978	3.00	6.00	12.00
JC 35723	In the Mood with Tyrone Davis	1979	3.00	6.00	12.00
JC 36230	Can't You Tell It's Me	1979	3.00	6.00	12.00
JC 36598	I Just Can't Keep On Going	1980	3.00	6.00	12.00
FC 37366	Everything in Place	1981	3.00	6.00	12.00
PC 37979	The Best of Tyrone Davis	1982	2.50	5.00	10.00

DAKAR

Number	Title (A Side/B Side)	Yr	VG	VG+	NM
DK-9005	Can I Change My Mind	1969	7.50	15.00	30.00
DK-9027	Turn Back the Hands of Time	1970	7.50	15.00	30.00
DK-76901	I Had It All the Time	1972	7.50	15.00	30.00
DK-76902	Tyrone Davis' Greatest Hits	1972	6.25	12.50	25.00
DK-76904	Without You in My Life	1973	6.25	12.50	25.00
DK-76909	It's All in the Game	1974	5.00	10.00	20.00
DK-76915	Homewrecker	1975	5.00	10.00	20.00
DK-76918	Turning Point	1976	5.00	10.00	20.00

EPIC

Number	Title (A Side/B Side)	Yr	VG	VG+	NM
PE 38626	Tyrone Davis' Greatest Hits	1983	2.00	4.00	8.00

HIGHRISE

Number	Title (A Side/B Side)	Yr	VG	VG+	NM
103	Tyrone Davis	1982	2.50	5.00	10.00

ICHIBAN

Number	Title (A Side/B Side)	Yr	VG	VG+	NM
ICH 1103	I'll Always Love You	1991	3.00	6.00	12.00

DAVIS SISTERS, THE

SKEETER DAVIS and Betty Davis (replaced by Georgia Davis).

45s

FORTUNE

Number	Title (A Side/B Side)	Yr	VG	VG+	NM
170	Jealous Love/Going Down the Road	1952	10.00	20.00	40.00
—B-side by Roy Hall					
174	Kaw-Liga/Sorrow and Pain	1952	5.00	10.00	20.00
175	Heartbreak Ahead/Steelwood	1952	5.00	10.00	20.00

RCA VICTOR

Number	Title (A Side/B Side)	Yr	VG	VG+	NM
47-5345	I Forgot More Than You'll Ever Know/Rock-a-Bye Boogie	1953	5.00	10.00	20.00
47-5460	You're Gone/Sorrow and Pain	1953	3.75	7.50	15.00
47-5607	Takin' Time Out for Tears/Gotta Get a-Goin'	1954	3.75	7.50	15.00
47-5701	You Weren't Ashamed to Kiss Me Last Night/Foggy Mountain Top	1954	3.75	7.50	15.00
47-5843	Show Me/Just Like Me	1954	3.75	7.50	15.00
47-5906	The Christmas Boogie/Tomorrow I'll Cry	1954	3.75	7.50	15.00
47-5966	Everlovin'/Tomorrow's Just Another Day to Cry	1954	3.75	7.50	15.00
47-6086	Fiddle Diddle Diddle/Come Back to Me	1955	3.75	7.50	15.00
47-6187	I'll Get Him Back/I've Closed the Door	1955	3.75	7.50	15.00
47-6291	Baby Be Mine/It's the Girl Who Gets the Blame	1955	3.75	7.50	15.00
47-6409	Don't Take HIm for Granted/Blues for Company	1956	3.75	7.50	15.00
47-6490	Lonely and Blue/Lying Brown Eyes	1956	3.75	7.50	15.00

DAWE, TIM

Also see IRON BUTTERFLY.

Albums

STRAIGHT

Number	Title (A Side/B Side)	Yr	VG	VG+	NM
STS-1058	Penrod	1969	7.50	15.00	30.00

WARNER BROS.

Number	Title (A Side/B Side)	Yr	VG	VG+	NM
WS 1841	Penrod	1970	3.75	7.50	15.00

DAWN (1)

One-man, two-woman vocal group featuring TONY ORLANDO. Includes records issued as "Dawn Featuring Tony Orlando" and "Tony Orlando and Dawn."

45s

Number	Title (A Side/B Side)	Yr	VG	VG+	NM
ARISTA					
0105	Gimme a Good Old Mammy Song/Little Heads in Bunk Beds	1975	—	2.00	4.00
0156	Skybird/That's the Way a Wallflower Grows	1975	—	2.00	4.00
0301	Tie a Yellow Ribbon Round the Ole Oak Tree/Say, Has Anybody Seen My Sweet Gypsy Rose	1978	—	2.00	4.00
BELL					
903	Candida/Look At...	1970	—	3.00	6.00
938	Knock Three Times/Home	1970	—	3.00	6.00
970	I Play and Sing/Get Out from Where We Are	1971	—	2.50	5.00
45107	Summer Sand/The Sweet Soft Sounds of Love	1971	—	2.50	5.00
45141	What Are You Doing Sunday/The Sweet Soft Sounds of Love	1971	—	2.50	5.00
45175	Runaway-Happy Together/Don't Act Like a Baby	1972	—	2.50	5.00
45225	Vaya Con Dios/I Can't Believe How Much I Love You	1972	—	2.50	5.00
45285	You're a Lady/In the Park	1972	—	2.00	4.00
45318	Tie a Yellow Ribbon Round the Ole Oak Tree/I Can't Believe How Much I Love You	1973	—	2.50	5.00
45375	Say, Has Anybody Seen My Sweet Gypsy Rose/The Spark of Love Is Kindlin'	1973	—	2.00	4.00
45424	Who's in the Strawberry Patch with Sally/Ukulele Man	1973	—	2.00	4.00
45450	It Only Hurts When I Try to Smile/Sweet Summer Days of My Life	1974	—	2.00	4.00
45601	Steppin' Out (Gonna Boogie Tonight)/She Can't Hold a Candle to You	1974	—	2.00	4.00
45620	Look in My Eyes Pretty Woman/My Love Has No Pride	1974	—	2.00	4.00
ELEKTRA					
45240	He Don't Love You (Like I Love You)/Pick It Up	1975	—	2.00	4.00
45260	Mornin' Beautiful/Dance, Rosalie, Dance	1975	—	2.00	4.00
45275	You're All I Need to Get By/Know You Like a Book	1975	—	2.00	4.00
45302	Cupid/You're Growin' on Me	1976	—	2.00	4.00
45319	Midnight Love Affair/The Selfish Ones	1976	—	2.00	4.00
45387	Sing/Sweet on Candy	1977	—	2.00	4.00
45432	Growin' on Me/You're All I Need to Get By	1977	—	2.00	4.00
45501	Bring It On Home to Me/Don't Let Go	1978	—	2.00	4.00
45542	I Count the Tears/A Lover's Question	1978	—	2.00	4.00
45542	I Count the Tears/This Is Rock and Roll	1978	—	2.00	4.00

Albums

Number	Title	Yr	VG	VG+	NM
ARISTA					
AL 4045	Greatest Hits	1975	2.50	5.00	10.00
AQ 4045 [Q]	Greatest Hits	1975	3.75	7.50	15.00
AL 4059	Skybird	1975	2.50	5.00	10.00
A2L 9006 [(2)]	The World of Tony Orlando and Dawn	1977	3.00	6.00	12.00
BELL					
1112	Tuneweaving	1973	2.50	5.00	10.00
1130	Dawn's New Ragtime Follies	1973	2.50	5.00	10.00
1317	Prime Time	1974	2.50	5.00	10.00
1320	Candida & Knock Three Times	1974	2.50	5.00	10.00
—Reissue of 6052					
1322	Tony Orlando & Dawn II	1974	2.50	5.00	10.00
—Reissue of 6069					
6052	Candida	1970	3.00	6.00	12.00
6069	Dawn Featuring Tony Orlando	1971	3.00	6.00	12.00
ELEKTRA					
7E-1034	He Don't Love You (Like I Love You)	1975	2.50	5.00	10.00
EQ-1034 [Q]	He Don't Love You (Like I Love You)	1975	3.75	7.50	15.00
7E-1049	To Be with You	1976	2.50	5.00	10.00
EQ-1049 [Q]	To Be with You	1976	3.75	7.50	15.00

DAWN (2)

Girl group.

45s

Number	Title (A Side/B Side)	Yr	VG	VG+	NM
ABC-PARAMOUNT					
10791	Baby's Gone Away/Gotta Get Away	1966	2.00	4.00	8.00
APT					
25088	Can't Get Him Off My Mind/Two of a Kind	1965	3.75	7.50	15.00

DAWN (3)

Said to be THE FIVE DISCS in disguise.

45s

Number	Title (A Side/B Side)	Yr	VG	VG+	NM
LAURIE					
3388	I'm Afraid They're All Talking About Me/Lovers' Melody	1967	3.00	6.00	12.00
3417	Sandy/For the Love of Money	1968	3.00	6.00	12.00
RUST					
5128	Baby I Love You/Bring It On Home	1968	3.00	6.00	12.00

DAWN (U)

Definitely not groups (1) or (3), these may be by group (2), but we're not sure.

45s

Number	Title (A Side/B Side)	Yr	VG	VG+	NM
CADET					
5644	The Fifth Day of June/Ballad of Gene	1969	—	3.00	6.00
UNITED ARTISTS					
50096	Love Is a Magic Word/How Can I Get Off This Merry-Go-Round	1966	3.00	6.00	12.00

DAY, BING

45s

Number	Title (A Side/B Side)	Yr	VG	VG+	NM
FEDERAL					
12320	Pony Tail Partner/Since You Left Me	1958	17.50	35.00	70.00
MERCURY					
71446	I Can't Help It/Mama's Place	1959	15.00	30.00	60.00
71494	How Do I Do It/Mary's Place	1959	5.00	10.00	20.00

DAY, BOBBY

45s

Number	Title (A Side/B Side)	Yr	VG	VG+	NM
CASH					
1031	The Truth Hurts/Let's Live Together As One	1956	25.00	50.00	100.00
—As "Bobby Byrd and the Birds"					
CLASS					
207	Come Seven/So Long Baby	1957	5.00	10.00	20.00
211	Little Bitty Pretty One/When the Swallows Come Back to Capistrano	1957	6.25	12.50	25.00
215	Beep-Beep-Beep/Darling, If I Had You	1957	5.00	10.00	20.00
225	Little Turtle Dove/Saving My Life for You	1958	5.00	10.00	20.00
229	Rock-N Robin/Over and Over	1958	7.50	15.00	30.00
241	The Bluebird, the Buzzard, and the Oriole/Alone Too Long	1959	5.00	10.00	20.00
245	That's All I Want/Say Yes	1959	3.75	7.50	15.00
252	Mr. and Mrs. Rock & Roll/Gotta New Girl	1959	3.75	7.50	15.00
255	Ain't Gonna Cry No More/Love Is a One-Time Affair	1959	3.75	7.50	15.00
257	Unchained Melody/Three Young Rebs from Georgia	1959	3.75	7.50	15.00
263	My Blue Heaven/I Don't Want To	1960	3.75	7.50	15.00
705	Don't Leave Me Hangin' on a String/When I Started Dancin'	1965	3.00	6.00	12.00
CORVET					
1017	Why/Gotta Girl	1958	15.00	30.00	60.00
—As "Bobby Byrd and the Impalas"					
JAMIE					
1039	Bippin' and Boppin' Over You/Strawberry Stomp	1957	7.50	15.00	30.00
—As "Robert Byrd and His Birdies"					
RCA VICTOR					
47-8133	Another Country, Another World/Know-It-All	1963	2.50	5.00	10.00
47-8196	Buzz Buzz Buzz/Pretty Little Girl Next Door	1963	2.50	5.00	10.00
47-8230	Down on My Knees/Jole Blon, Little Darling	1963	2.50	5.00	10.00
47-8316	When I See My Baby Smile/On the Street Where You Live	1964	2.50	5.00	10.00
RENDEZVOUS					
130	Teenage Philosopher/Undecided	1960	3.00	6.00	12.00
133	Rockin' Robin/Over and Over	1960	3.00	6.00	12.00
136	Gee Whiz/Over and Over	1960	3.00	6.00	12.00
146	I Need Help/Life Can Be Beautiful	1961	3.00	6.00	12.00
158	King's Highway/What Fools We Mortals Be	1961	3.00	6.00	12.00
167	Don't Worry 'Bout Me/Oop-E-Du-Pers Ball	1962	3.00	6.00	12.00
175	Undecided/Slow Pokey Joe	1962	3.00	6.00	12.00
SAGE AND SAND					
203	Please Don't Hurt Me/Delicious Are Your Kisses	1955	10.00	20.00	40.00
—As "Bobby Byrd"					
SPARK					
501	Bippin' and Boppin' Over You/Strawberry Stomp	1957	12.50	25.00	50.00
—As "Robert Byrd and His Birdies"					
SURE SHOT					
5036	So Lonely/Spicks and Specks	1967	2.00	4.00	8.00
ZEPHYR					
70-018	If We Should Meet Again/Looby Loo	1957	7.50	15.00	30.00
—As "Bobby Byrd"					

Albums

Number	Title	Yr	VG	VG+	NM
CLASS					
LP-5002 [M]	Rockin' with Robin	1959	100.00	200.00	400.00
COLLECTABLES					
COL-5074	Golden Classics	198?	2.50	5.00	10.00
RENDEZVOUS					
M-1312 [M]	Rockin' with Robin	196?	20.00	40.00	80.00
RHINO					
RNDF-208	The Best of Bobby Day	1984	3.00	6.00	12.00

DAY, DARLENE

45s

Number	Title (A Side/B Side)	Yr	VG	VG+	NM
MUSIC MAKERS					
106	I Love You So/Will	1961	25.00	50.00	100.00

DAY, DAVE DIDDLE

45s

Number	Title (A Side/B Side)	Yr	VG	VG+	NM
FEE BEE					
212	Blue Moon Baby/Suzanne My Love	1958	6.25	12.50	25.00
215	Jelly Belly/Deep in My Heart	1958	6.25	12.50	25.00
219	Motorcycle Mike/Tired of Waiting	1958	3.75	7.50	15.00
MERCURY					
71114	Blue Moon Baby/Suzanne My Love	1957	37.50	75.00	150.00

DAY, DORIS

45s

Number	Title (A Side/B Side)	Yr	VG	VG+	NM
COLUMBIA					
1-108 (?)	If You Will Marry Me/You Was	1949	10.00	20.00	40.00
—Microgroove 7-inch, 33 1/3 rpm single					
1-113	Powder Your Face with Sunshine (Smile! Smile! Smile!)/I'll String Along with You	1949	10.00	20.00	40.00
—Microgroove 7-inch, 33 1/3 rpm single					
1-125 (?)	Beginning to Miss You/Don't Gamble with Romance	1949	10.00	20.00	40.00
—Microgroove 7-inch, 33 1/3 rpm single					
1-185 (?)	How It Lies, How It Lies/If I Could Be with You	1949	10.00	20.00	40.00
—Microgroove 7-inch, 33 1/3 rpm single					
1-211	Again/Everywhere You Go	1949	10.00	20.00	40.00
—Microgroove 7-inch, 33 1/3 rpm single					
1-251	(Where Are You) Now That I Need You/Blame My Absent-Minded Heart	1949	10.00	20.00	40.00
—Microgroove 7-inch, 33 1/3 rpm single					
1-266 (?)	At the Café Rendezvous/It's a Great Feeling	1949	10.00	20.00	40.00
—Microgroove 7-inch, 33 1/3 rpm single					
1-353	Canadian Capers (Cuttin' Capers)/Better To Conceal Than Reveal	1949	10.00	20.00	40.00
—Microgroove 7-inch, 33 1/3 rpm single					

Number	Title (A Side/B Side)	Yr	VG	VG+	NM
1-376	(There's a) Bluebird on Your Windowsill/The River Seine	1949	10.00	20.00	40.00
—Microgroove 7-inch, 33 1/3 rpm single					
1-381 (?)	The Three Rivers/Festival of Roses	1949	10.00	20.00	40.00
—Microgroove 7-inch, 33 1/3 rpm single					
1-406 (?)	The Game of Broken Hearts/I'll Never Slip Around Again	1949	10.00	20.00	40.00
—Microgroove 7-inch, 33 1/3 rpm single					
1-407	Quicksilver/Crocodile Tears	1949	10.00	20.00	40.00
—Microgroove 7-inch, 33 1/3 rpm single					
1-454 (?)	Mama, What'll I Do/Save a Little Sunbeam	1950	10.00	20.00	40.00
—Microgroove 7-inch, 33 1/3 rpm single					
1-457 (?)	I Don't Wanna Be Kissed/With You Anywhere You Are	1950	10.00	20.00	40.00
—Microgroove 7-inch, 33 1/3 rpm single					
1-480	Bewitched/Imagination	1950	10.00	20.00	40.00
—Microgroove 7-inch, 33 1/3 rpm single					
1-497	I Said My Pajamas (And Put On My Prayers)/ Enjoy Yourself (It's Later Than You Think)	1950	10.00	20.00	40.00
—Microgroove 7-inch, 33 1/3 rpm single					
1-591	Hoop-Dee-Doo/Marriage Ties	1950	10.00	20.00	40.00
—Microgroove 7-inch, 33 1/3 rpm single					
1-637	I Didn't Slip — I Wasn't Pushed — I Fell/Before I Loved You	1950	10.00	20.00	40.00
—Microgroove 7-inch, 33 1/3 rpm single					
1-708	Darn That Dream/I've Forgotten You	1950	10.00	20.00	40.00
—Microgroove 7-inch, 33 1/3 rpm single					
6-708	Darn That Dream/I've Forgotten You	1950	7.50	15.00	30.00
1-838 (?)	A Bushel and a Peck/The Best Thing for You	1950	10.00	20.00	40.00
—Microgroove 7-inch, 33 1/3 rpm single					
6-838 (?)	A Bushel and a Peck/The Best Thing for You	1950	7.50	15.00	30.00
1-859 (?)	If I Were a Bell/I've Never Been in Love Before	1950	10.00	20.00	40.00
—Microgroove 7-inch, 33 1/3 rpm single					
6-859 (?)	If I Were a Bell/I've Never Been in Love Before	1950	7.50	15.00	30.00
1-908 (?)	Nobody's Chasing Me/It's a Lovely Day Today	1950	10.00	20.00	40.00
—Microgroove 7-inch, 33 1/3 rpm single					
6-908 (?)	Nobody's Chasing Me/It's a Lovely Day Today	1950	7.50	15.00	30.00
31084 [S]	(contents unknown)	1961	2.50	5.00	10.00
31085 [S]	(contents unknown)	1961	2.50	5.00	10.00
31086 [S]	(contents unknown)	1961	2.50	5.00	10.00
31087 [S]	(contents unknown)	1961	2.50	5.00	10.00
31088 [S]	(contents unknown)	1961	2.50	5.00	10.00
—Anyone who can fill in these gaps -- the above 5 all are Columbia "Stereo 7" singles -- please let us know.					
4-38542	You're My Thrill/That Old Feeling	1950	3.75	7.50	15.00
—Alternate numbers are "B 189-1" and "B 189-2"					
4-38543	Bewitched/When Your Lover Has Gone	1950	3.75	7.50	15.00
—Alternate numbers are "B 189-3" and "B 189-4"					
4-38544	I'm Confessin'/I Didn't Know What Time It Was	1950	3.75	7.50	15.00
—Alternate numbers are "B 189-5" and "B 189-6"					
4-38545	You Go to My Head/Sometimes I'm Happy	1950	3.75	7.50	15.00
—Alternate numbers are "B 189-7" and "B 189-8"; the above four comprise box set B 189					
39008	A Bushel and a Peck/The Best Thing for You	1950	5.00	10.00	20.00
39031	If I Were a Bell/I've Never Been in Love Before	1950	5.00	10.00	20.00
39032	Christmas Story/Silver Bells	1950	3.00	6.00	12.00
39055	Nobody's Chasing Me/It's a Lovely Day Today	1950	5.00	10.00	20.00
39143	You Are My Sunshine/Comb and Paper Polka	1951	3.75	7.50	15.00
3-39143	You Are My Sunshine/Comb and Paper Polka	1951	7.50	15.00	30.00
—Microgroove 7-inch, 33 1/3 rpm single					
39159	Would I Love You (Love You, Love You)/Lullaby of Broadway	1951	3.75	7.50	15.00
3-39159	Would I Love You (Love You, Love You)/Lullaby of Broadway	1951	7.50	15.00	30.00
—Microgroove 7-inch, 33 1/3 rpm single					
39191	I'll Be Around/I Love the Way You Say Goodnight	1951	3.75	7.50	15.00
39197	Lullaby of Broadway/Please Don't Talk About Me When I'm Gone	1951	3.00	6.00	12.00
39198	Fine and Dandy/I Love the Way You Say Goodnight	1951	3.00	6.00	12.00
39199	In a Shanty in Old Shanty Town/You're Getting to Be a Habit with Me	1951	3.00	6.00	12.00
39200	Somebody Loves Me/Just One of Those Things	1951	3.00	6.00	12.00
—The above four comprise a box set					
39255	I Can't Get Over Pumpernickel/You Are My Sunshine	1951	3.75	7.50	15.00
39293	We Kissed in a Shadow/Something Wonderful	1951	3.75	7.50	15.00
39295	It's So Laughable/Very Good Advice	1951	3.75	7.50	15.00
39423	(Why Did I Tell You I Was Going to) Shanghai/ My Life's Desire	1951	3.75	7.50	15.00
39450	Moonlight Bay/Tell Me (Tell Me Why)	1951	3.00	6.00	12.00
39451	Till We Meet Again/Every Little Movement	1951	3.00	6.00	12.00
39452	Love You/Cuddle Up a Little Closer	1951	3.00	6.00	12.00
39453	Christmas Story/I'm Forever Blowing Bubbles	1951	3.00	6.00	12.00
—The above four comprise a box set					
39490	Ask Me/Lonesome and Sorry	1951	3.75	7.50	15.00
39534	Kiss Me Goodbye/Got Him Offa My Hands	1951	3.75	7.50	15.00
39596	Domino/If That Doesn't Do It	1951	3.75	7.50	15.00
39622	I'll See You in My Dreams/Ain't We Got Fun	1951	3.00	6.00	12.00
39623	The One I Love/Makin' Whoopee	1951	3.00	6.00	12.00
39624	My Buddy/I Wish I Had a Girl	1951	3.00	6.00	12.00
39625	It Had to Be You/Nobody's Sweetheart	1951	3.00	6.00	12.00
—The above four comprise a box set					
39637	Oops/Baby Doll	1952	3.00	6.00	12.00
39673	A Guy Is a Guy/Who, Who, Who	1952	3.00	6.00	12.00
39693	Sugarbush/When I Look Into Your Eyes	1952	3.00	6.00	12.00
—A-side with Frankie Laine					
39714	Gentle Johnny/Little Kiss Goodnight	1952	3.00	6.00	12.00
39729	A Guy Is a Guy/What's the Use?	1952	2.50	5.00	10.00
—B-side by Johnnie Ray					
39738	It's Magic/Too Fat Polka	1952	2.50	5.00	10.00
—B-side by Arthur Godfrey					
39786	When I Fall in Love/Take Me in Your Arms	1952	3.00	6.00	12.00
39817	Make It Soon/My Love and Devotion	1952	3.00	6.00	12.00
39863	No Two People/You Can't Lose Me	1952	3.00	6.00	12.00
—A-side with Donald O'Connor					
39881	April in Paris/Cherries	1952	3.00	6.00	12.00
39906	Mister Tap Toe/Your Mother and Mine	1952	3.00	6.00	12.00
39913	You Have My Symphony/Second Star to the Right	1953	3.00	6.00	12.00
39970	When the Red, Red Robin Comes Bob, Bob, Bobbin' Along/Beautiful Music to Love By	1953	2.00	4.00	8.00
39971	Little Silvery Moon/King Chant	1953	2.00	4.00	8.00
39972	Your Eyes Have Told Me So/I'll Forget You	1953	2.00	4.00	8.00
39973	Just One Girl/Be Bumble Bee	1953	2.00	4.00	8.00
39974	Ain't We Got Fun?/If You Were the Only Girl	1953	2.00	4.00	8.00
—The above five comprise a box set					
40020	Kiss Me Again Stranger/A Purple Cow	1953	2.50	5.00	10.00
40063	Chho Choo Train (Ch-Ch-Foo)/This Too Shall Pass Away	1953	2.50	5.00	10.00
40094	The Deadwood Stage (Whip Crack Away!)/I Can Do Without You	1953	2.00	4.00	8.00
40095	The Black Hills of Dakota/Just Blew In from the Windy City	1953	2.00	4.00	8.00
40096	A Woman's Touch/Higher Than the Hawk	1953	2.00	4.00	8.00
40097	Secret Love/'Tis Harry I'm Planning to Marry	1953	2.00	4.00	8.00
—The above four comprise a box set					
40108	Secret Love/The Deadwood Stage (Whip Crack Away!)	1953	2.50	5.00	10.00
40168	Lost in Loveliness/What Every Girl Should Know	1954	2.50	5.00	10.00
40210	I Speak to the Stars/The Blue Belles of Broadway	1954	2.50	5.00	10.00
40234	Someone Else's Roses/Kay-Muleta	1954	2.50	5.00	10.00
40300	If I Give My Heart to You/Anyone Can Fall in Love	1954	2.50	5.00	10.00
40371	Ready, Willing and Able/Hold Me In Your Arms	1954	2.50	5.00	10.00
40372	Till My Love Comes to Me/Ready and Able	1954	2.00	4.00	8.00
40373	Ready, Willing and Able/One for My Baby	1954	2.00	4.00	8.00
40374	Hold Me in Your Arms/There's a Rising Moon	1954	2.00	4.00	8.00
40375	Someone to Watch Over Me/Just One of Those Things	1954	2.00	4.00	8.00
—The above four comprise a box set					
40408	There's a Rising Moon/Till Your Love Comes to Me	1954	2.50	5.00	10.00
40483	Two Hearts, Two Kisses/Foolishly Yours	1955	2.50	5.00	10.00
40505	I'll Never Stop Loving You/Never Look Back	1955	2.50	5.00	10.00
40581	Ooh Bang Jiggily Bang/Jimmy Unknown	1955	2.50	5.00	10.00
40618	Let It Ring/Love's Little Island	1955	2.50	5.00	10.00
40673	We'll Love Again/Somebody Somewhere	1956	2.50	5.00	10.00
40704	Whatever Will Be, Will Me (Que Sera, Sera)/I've Gotta Sing Away the Blues	1956	2.50	5.00	10.00
40758	Julie/Love in a Home	1956	2.50	5.00	10.00
40798	The Party's Over/What'ya Put in That Kiss	1956	2.50	5.00	10.00
40870	Twelve O'Clock Tonight/Today Will Be Yesterday Tomorrow	1957	2.50	5.00	10.00
40952	Nothing in the World/Through the Eyes of Love	1957	2.50	5.00	10.00
41015	Rickety-Rackety Rendezvous/The Man Who Invented Love	1957	2.00	4.00	8.00
41071	Walk a Chalk Line/Soft As the Starlight	1957	2.00	4.00	8.00
41123	Teacher's Pet/A Very Precious Love	1958	2.00	4.00	8.00
41195	Everybody Loves a Lover/Instant Love	1958	2.00	4.00	8.00
41195 [PS]	Everybody Loves a Lover/Instant Love	1958	3.75	7.50	15.00
41252	Tunnel of Love/Run Away Skidaddle Skidoo	1958	2.00	4.00	8.00
41252 [PS]	Tunnel of Love/Run Away Skidaddle Skidoo	1958	3.75	7.50	15.00
41307	I Enjoy Being a Girl/Kissin' My Honey	1958	2.00	4.00	8.00
41354	Love Me in the Daytime/He's So Married	1959	2.00	4.00	8.00
41391	Be Prepared/It Happened to Jane	1959	2.00	4.00	8.00
41450	Roly Poly/Possess Me	1959	2.00	4.00	8.00
41463	Pillow Talk/Inspiration	1959	2.00	4.00	8.00
41463 [PS]	Pillow Talk/Inspiration	1959	3.75	7.50	15.00
41542	The Sound of Music/Heart Full of Love	1959	2.00	4.00	8.00
41569	Anyway the Wind Blows/Soft As the Starlight	1960	2.00	4.00	8.00
41630	Please Don't Eat the Daisies/Here We Go Again	1960	2.00	4.00	8.00
41703	The Blue Train/A Perfect Understanding	1960	2.00	4.00	8.00
41791	What Does a Woman Do/Daffa Down Dilly	1960	2.00	4.00	8.00
41944	Make Someone Happy/Bright and Shiny	1961	2.00	4.00	8.00
41993	Twinkle and Shine/Gotta Feelin'	1961	2.00	4.00	8.00
42260	Should I Surrender/Who Knows What Might Have Been	1962	2.00	4.00	8.00
42295	Lover Come Back/Falling	1962	2.00	4.00	8.00
42912	Move Over Darling/Twinkle Lullaby	1963	2.00	4.00	8.00
43153	Send Me No Flowers/Rainbow's End	1964	2.00	4.00	8.00
43174	Christmas Present/Be a Child at Christmas Time	1964	2.00	4.00	8.00
43278	How Insensitive/Meditation	1965	2.00	4.00	8.00
43314	Summer Has Gone/Catch the Bouquet	1965	2.00	4.00	8.00
43440	Another Go-Round/Not Only Should You Love Him	1965	2.00	4.00	8.00
43459	Au Revoir Is Goodbye with a Smile/Do Not Disturb	1965	2.00	4.00	8.00
43606	Every Now and Then/There They Are	1966	—	3.50	7.00
43688	Glass Bottom Boat/Soft As the Starlight	1966	—	3.50	7.00
44150	Caprice/Sorry	1967	—	3.50	7.00
JZSP 55070/1 [DJ]	Let No Walls Divide/God Rest Ye Merry, Gentlemen	1961	3.00	6.00	12.00
—B-side by Andre Previn					
JZSP 79171/2 [DJ]	Silver Bells/Winter Wonderland	1963	2.50	5.00	10.00
—"Special Album Excerpt" promo					

7-Inch Extended Plays

COLUMBIA

Number	Title (A Side/B Side)	Yr	VG	VG+	NM
B-2585	*A Bushel and a Peck/Hoop-Dee-Doo/If I Were a Bell/Lullaby of Broadway	1959	3.75	7.50	15.00
B-2585 [PS]	Doris Day (Hall of Fame Series)	1959	3.75	7.50	15.00

Albums

COLUMBIA

Number	Title (A Side/B Side)	Yr	VG	VG+	NM
DD 1 [M]	Listen to Day	1960	5.00	10.00	20.00
DDS 1 [S]	Listen to Day	1960	6.25	12.50	25.00
C2L 5 [(2) M]	Hooray for Hollywood	1959	10.00	20.00	40.00
CL 582 [M]	Young Man with a Horn	1954	10.00	20.00	40.00
—Reissue of 6106; red label, gold print					
CL 624 [M]	Day Dreams	1955	10.00	20.00	40.00
—Red label, gold print					
CL 624 [M]	Day Dreams	1956	6.25	12.50	25.00
—Six "eye" logos on label					
CL 710 [M]	Love Me or Leave Me	1955	12.50	25.00	50.00
—Red label, gold print					

Number	Title (A Side/B Side)	Yr	VG	VG+	NM
CL 710 [M]	Love Me or Leave Me	1956	6.25	12.50	25.00
—Six "eye" logos on label					
CL 710 [M]	Love Me or Leave Me	1962	3.75	7.50	15.00
—"Guaranteed High Fidelity" or "Mono" on label					
CL 749 [M]	Day in Hollywood	1956	7.50	15.00	30.00
C2S 805 [(2) S]	Hooray for Hollywood	1959	12.50	25.00	50.00
CL 942 [M]	Day By Day	1957	7.50	15.00	30.00
CL 1053 [M]	Day By Night	1958	5.00	10.00	20.00
CL 1210 [M]	Doris Day's Greatest Hits	1958	7.50	15.00	30.00
—Six "eye" logos on label					
CL 1210 [M]	Doris Day's Greatest Hits	1962	3.00	6.00	12.00
—"Guaranteed High Fidelity" or "Mono" on label					
CL 1232 [M]	Cuttin' Capers	1959	5.00	10.00	20.00
CL 1366 [M]	Hooray for Hollywood, Volume 1	1959	5.00	10.00	20.00
CL 1438 [M]	What Every Girl Should Know	1960	5.00	10.00	20.00
CL 1461 [M]	Show Time	1960	5.00	10.00	20.00
CL 1660 [M]	I Have Dreamed	1961	5.00	10.00	20.00
CL 1752 [M]	Duet	1962	5.00	10.00	20.00
—With Andre Previn					
CL 1904 [M]	You'll Never Walk Alone	1962	3.75	7.50	15.00
CL 2131 [M]	Love Him!	1964	3.75	7.50	15.00
CL 2226 [M]	The Doris Day Christmas Album	1964	3.00	6.00	12.00
CL 2266 [M]	With a Smile and a Song	1965	3.00	6.00	12.00
CL 2310 [M]	Latin for Lovers	1965	3.00	6.00	12.00
CL 2360 [M]	Sentimental Journey	1965	3.00	6.00	12.00
CL 2518 [10]	Lights, Camera, Action	1955	12.50	25.00	50.00
CL 6071 [10]	You're My Thrill	1949	15.00	30.00	60.00
CL 6106 [10]	Young Man with a Horn	1950	25.00	50.00	100.00
CL 6149 [10]	Tea for Two	1950	15.00	30.00	60.00
CL 6168 [10]	Lullaby of Broadway	1951	15.00	30.00	60.00
CL 6186 [10]	On Moonlight Bay	1951	15.00	30.00	60.00
CL 6198 [10]	I'll See You in My Dreams	1951	15.00	30.00	60.00
CL 6248 [10]	By the Light of the Silvery Moon	1953	15.00	30.00	60.00
CL 6273 [10]	Calamity Jane	1953	15.00	30.00	60.00
CL 6339 [10]	Young at Heart	1954	15.00	30.00	60.00
—Six songs by Doris Day, two by Frank Sinatra					
CS 8066 [S]	Hooray for Hollywood, Volume 1	1959	6.25	12.50	25.00
CS 8067 [S]	Hooray for Hollywood, Volume 2	1959	6.25	12.50	25.00
CS 8078 [S]	Cuttin' Capers	1959	6.25	12.50	25.00
CS 8089 [S]	Day By Night	1959	6.25	12.50	25.00
CS 8234 [S]	What Every Girl Should Know	1960	6.25	12.50	25.00
CS 8261 [S]	Show Time	1960	5.00	10.00	20.00
CS 8460 [S]	I Have Dreamed	1961	6.25	12.50	25.00
CS 8552 [S]	Duet	1962	6.25	12.50	25.00
—With Andre Previn					
CS 8635 [P]	Doris Day's Greatest Hits	1962	3.75	7.50	15.00
—"360 Sound Stereo" in black at bottom					
PC 8635	Doris Day's Greatest Hits	198?	2.00	4.00	8.00
—Budget-line reissue					
CS 8704 [S]	You'll Never Walk Alone	1962	5.00	10.00	20.00
CS 8773 [R]	Love Me or Leave Me	1963	3.00	6.00	12.00
CS 8931 [S]	Love Him!	1964	5.00	10.00	20.00
CS 9026 [S]	The Doris Day Christmas Album	1964	3.75	7.50	15.00
CS 9066 [S]	With a Smile and a Song	1965	3.75	7.50	15.00
CS 9110 [S]	Latin for Lovers	1965	3.75	7.50	15.00
CS 9160 [S]	Sentimental Journey	1965	3.75	7.50	15.00
CL (# unknown) [M]	Hooray for Hollywood, Volume 2	1959	5.00	10.00	20.00

COLUMBIA SPECIAL PRODUCTS

Number	Title (A Side/B Side)	Yr	VG	VG+	NM
C 10988	The Doris Day Christmas Album	197?	2.50	5.00	10.00
—Reissue of CS 9026					
P 13346	The Doris Day Christmas Album	197?	2.50	5.00	10.00
—Reissue of CS 9026					
XTV 82021/2 [M]	Wonderful Day	1961	10.00	20.00	40.00

HARMONY

Number	Title (A Side/B Side)	Yr	VG	VG+	NM
HL 7392 [M]	Great Movie Hits	1966	3.00	6.00	12.00
HL 9559 [M]	Do Re Mi (And Other Children's Favorites)	196?	3.00	6.00	12.00
HS 11192 [R]	Great Movie Hits	1966	3.00	6.00	12.00
HS 11282	Whatever Will Be, Will Be (Que Sera, Sera)	1968	3.00	6.00	12.00
HS 11382	It's Magic	1970	3.00	6.00	12.00
HS 14559 [S]	Do Re Mi (And Other Children's Favorites)	196?	3.00	6.00	12.00
KH 31498	Softly, As I Leave You	1972	2.50	5.00	10.00

HINDSIGHT

Number	Title (A Side/B Side)	Yr	VG	VG+	NM
HSR-200	Doris Day with Van Alexander's Orchestra	198?	2.50	5.00	10.00

DAY, DORIS/JOHNNIE RAY

Also see each artist's individual listings.

45s

COLUMBIA

Number	Title (A Side/B Side)	Yr	VG	VG+	NM
39898	A Full Time Job/Ma Says, Pa Says	1952	3.00	6.00	12.00
40001	Candy Lips/Let's Walk That-A-Way	1953	2.50	5.00	10.00

DAY, LITTLE SUNNY, AND THE CLOUDS

45s

TANDEM

Number	Title (A Side/B Side)	Yr	VG	VG+	NM
7001	Lou Ann/Baby Doll	1961	100.00	200.00	400.00

DAY, TERRY

See TERRY MELCHER.

DAY BLINDNESS

Albums

STUDIO 10

Number	Title (A Side/B Side)	Yr	VG	VG+	NM
DBX-101	Day Blindness	1969	15.00	30.00	60.00

DAYBREAKERS, THE (1)

45s

ALADDIN

Number	Title (A Side/B Side)	Yr	VG	VG+	NM
3434	I Wonder Why/Up, Up and Away	1958	10.00	20.00	40.00

LAMP

Number	Title (A Side/B Side)	Yr	VG	VG+	NM
2016	I Wonder Why/Up, Up and Away	1958	15.00	30.00	60.00

DAYBREAKERS, THE (2)

45s

DIAL

Number	Title (A Side/B Side)	Yr	VG	VG+	NM
4066	Psychedelic Siren/Afterthoughts	1967	7.50	15.00	30.00

DAYTONAS, THE

Also see RONNY AND THE DATYONAS.

45s

AMY

Number	Title (A Side/B Side)	Yr	VG	VG+	NM
961	Hey Little Girl/Please Go Away	1966	5.00	10.00	20.00

DAYTONES, THE

45s

JUBILEE

Number	Title (A Side/B Side)	Yr	VG	VG+	NM
5452	Krambuli/Bless My Love	1963	5.00	10.00	20.00

DAYTONS, THE

45s

NORGOLDE

Number	Title (A Side/B Side)	Yr	VG	VG+	NM
101	King of Broken Hearts/Friday Better Come	1959	50.00	100.00	200.00

DE BONAIRS

45s

PING

Number	Title (A Side/B Side)	Yr	VG	VG+	NM
1000	Lanky Linda/Mother's Son	1956	75.00	150.00	300.00
1001	Say a Prayer for Me/Cracker-Jack Daddy	1956	100.00	200.00	400.00

DE-FENDERS, THE

45s

DEL-FI

Number	Title (A Side/B Side)	Yr	VG	VG+	NM
4226	Little Deuce Coupe/Hayburner	1963	7.50	15.00	30.00
—B side by the Deuce Coupes					

WORLD PACIFIC

Number	Title (A Side/B Side)	Yr	VG	VG+	NM
382	(Dance to the) Yakety Sax/Wild One	1963	10.00	20.00	40.00

Albums

DEL-FI

Number	Title (A Side/B Side)	Yr	VG	VG+	NM
DFLP-1242 [M]	Drag Beat	1963	12.50	25.00	50.00
DFST-1242 [S]	Drag Beat	1963	15.00	30.00	60.00

WORLD PACIFIC

Number	Title (A Side/B Side)	Yr	VG	VG+	NM
ST-1810 [S]	The De-Fenders Play the Big Ones	1963	37.50	75.00	150.00
—Red vinyl					
ST-1810 [S]	The De-Fenders Play the Big Ones	1963	37.50	75.00	150.00
—Green vinyl					
ST-1810 [S]	The De-Fenders Play the Big Ones	1963	17.50	35.00	70.00
—Black vinyl					
WP-1810 [M]	The De-Fenders Play the Big Ones	1963	12.50	25.00	50.00

DEACON AND THE ROCK 'N' ROLLERS

45s

NAU-VOO

Number	Title (A Side/B Side)	Yr	VG	VG+	NM
804	Rockin' on the Moon/I Don't Wanna Leave	1959	500.00	1000.	1500.

DEADLY ONES, THE

Albums

VEE JAY

Number	Title (A Side/B Side)	Yr	VG	VG+	NM
LP-1090 [M]	It's Monster Surfing Time	1964	25.00	50.00	100.00
LPS-1090 [S]	It's Monster Surfing Time	1964	30.00	60.00	120.00

DEAL, BILL, AND THE RHONDELS

45s

BUDDAH

Number	Title (A Side/B Side)	Yr	VG	VG+	NM
318	It's Too Late/So What If It Rains	1972	—	3.00	6.00
330	Everybody's Got Something to Hide/I Live in the Night	1972	—	3.00	6.00

GIG/WAY

Number	Title (A Side/B Side)	Yr	VG	VG+	NM
902006	Freak 'N' Freeze/(Instrumental)	1978	—	2.50	5.00

HERITAGE

Number	Title (A Side/B Side)	Yr	VG	VG+	NM
803	May I/Day By Day My Love Grows	1968	2.00	4.00	8.00
812	I've Been Hurt/I've Got My Seeds	1969	2.00	4.00	8.00
812 [PS]	I've Been Hurt/I've Got My Seeds	1969	3.75	7.50	15.00
817	What Kind of Fool Do You Think I Am/Are You Ready for This	1969	2.00	4.00	8.00
818	Swingin' Tight/Tuck's Theme	1969	2.00	4.00	8.00
818 [PS]	Swingin' Tight/Tuck's Theme	1969	3.75	7.50	15.00
821	Nothing Succeeds Like Success/Swingin' Tight	1969	2.00	4.00	8.00
824	I'm Gonna Make You Love Me/Hey Bulldog	1970	—	3.00	6.00

MALA

Number	Title (A Side/B Side)	Yr	VG	VG+	NM
502	Big Toe in the Wind/Don't Put Me Down	1965	7.50	15.00	30.00
—As "Bill Deal and the Big Deals"					

POLYDOR

Number	Title (A Side/B Side)	Yr	VG	VG+	NM
14042	Do I Love You/Won't You Set Me Free	1970	—	3.00	6.00
14061	19 Years (Everything I Do Is Wrong)/Sea of Life	1971	—	3.00	6.00
14103	Sea of Life/You Can Make It	1971	—	3.00	6.00

Albums

HERITAGE

Number	Title (A Side/B Side)	Yr	VG	VG+	NM
HTS 35003	Vintage Rock	1969	7.50	15.00	30.00
HTS 35006	The Best of Bill Deal and the Rhondels	1970	7.50	15.00	30.00

RHINO

Number	Title (A Side/B Side)	Yr	VG	VG+	NM
RNLP-70129	The Best of Bill Deal and the Rhondels (1969-1970)	1986	2.50	5.00	10.00

DEAN, BOBBY

45s

CHESS

Number	Title (A Side/B Side)	Yr	VG	VG+	NM
1673	Just Go Wild Over Rock and Roll/Dime Store Pony Tail	1958	7.50	15.00	30.00
1710	I'm Ready/Go Mr. Dillon	1959	7.50	15.00	30.00

PROFILE

Number	Title (A Side/B Side)	Yr	VG	VG+	NM
4006	Just Between Tears/It's a Fad	1959	10.00	20.00	40.00

DEAN, CHARLES

45s

Number	Title (A Side/B Side)	Yr	VG	VG+	NM
BENTON					
103	Itchy/(B-side unknown)	1958	62.50	125.00	250.00

DEAN, DEBBIE

45s

Number	Title (A Side/B Side)	Yr	VG	VG+	NM
MOTOWN					
1007	Don't Let Him Shop Around/A New Girl	1961	10.00	20.00	40.00
1014	Itty, Bitty, Pity Love/But I'm Afraid	1961	7.50	15.00	30.00
1025	Everybody's Talking About My Baby/I Cried All Night	1962	10.00	20.00	40.00
1025 [PS]	Everybody's Talking About My Baby/I Cried All Night	1962	20.00	40.00	80.00
V.I.P.					
25044	Why Am I Lovin' You/Stay My Love	1967	75.00	150.00	300.00

DEAN, JIMMY

45s

Number	Title (A Side/B Side)	Yr	VG	VG+	NM
4 STAR					
1613	Bumming Around/Picking Sweethearts	1953	5.00	10.00	20.00
1640	Queen of Hearts/I'm Feeling For You	1953	5.00	10.00	20.00
1654	Release Me/Sweet Darling	1954	5.00	10.00	20.00
1732	Bumming Around/Release Me	1959	3.00	6.00	12.00
CASINO					
052	I.O.U./Let's Pick Up the Pieces	1976	—	2.00	4.00
074	To a Sleeping Beauty/I Didn't Have Time	1976	—	2.00	4.00
108	Where Is That Man/(B-side unknown)	1976	—	2.00	4.00
CHURCHILL					
94024	I.O.U./To a Sleeping Beauty	1983	—	2.00	4.00
COLUMBIA					
31550 [S]	Basin Street Blues/Please Pass the Biscuits	1962	5.00	10.00	20.00
31551 [S]	Have You Ever Been Lonely/Nobody	1962	5.00	10.00	20.00
31552 [S]	I Was Just Walking Out the Door/The Dark Town Poker Club	1962	5.00	10.00	20.00
31553 [S]	You're Nobody Until Somebody Loves You/ Kentucky Means Paradise	1962	5.00	10.00	20.00
31554 [S]	Little Black Book/Old Pappy's New Banjo	1962	5.00	10.00	20.00
—The above five are "Stereo Seven" 33 1/3 rpm jukebox singles from set "JS 7-63"					
40995	Deep Blue Sea/Love Me So I'll Know	1957	3.00	6.00	12.00
41025	Little Sandy Sleighfoot/When They Ring the Golden Bells	1957	3.75	7.50	15.00
41025 [PS]	Little Sandy Sleighfoot/When They Ring the Golden Bells	1957	6.25	12.50	25.00
41118	Starlight, Starbright/Makin' My Mind Up	1958	3.00	6.00	12.00
41196	School of Love/You Should See Tennessee, Mam'selle	1958	3.00	6.00	12.00
41265	My Heart Is An Open Book/Shark in the Bathtub	1958	3.00	6.00	12.00
41395	Sing Along/Weekend Blues	1959	3.00	6.00	12.00
41453	Stay a Little Longer/Counting Tears	1959	3.00	6.00	12.00
41543	Thanks for the Dream/There's Still Time, Brother	1959	3.00	6.00	12.00
41710	Little Boy Lost/There'll Be No Teardrops Tonight	1960	3.00	6.00	12.00
41956	Give Me Back My Heart/It's Been a Long, Long Time	1961	2.50	5.00	10.00
42175	Big John/I Won't Go Huntin' with You Jake (But I'll Go Chasin' Wimmin)	1961	5.00	10.00	20.00
—Lyrics say: "At the bottom of this mine lies one hell of a man."					
42175	Big Bad John/I Won't Go Huntin' with You Jake (But I'll Go Chasin' Wimmin)	1961	2.50	5.00	10.00
—Lyrics say: "At the bottom of this mine lies a big, big man." We think the song title was changed with the lyric, but we're not 100 percent sure. In other words, this title may exist with the "hell of a man" lyrics.					
42175 [PS]	Big Bad John/I Won't Go Huntin' with You Jake (But I'll Go Chasin' Wimmin)	1961	3.75	7.50	15.00
42248	Oklahoma Bill/To a Sleeping Beauty	1961	2.50	5.00	10.00
42259	Dear Ivan/Smoke, Smoke, Smoke That Cigarette	1962	2.50	5.00	10.00
42259 [PS]	Dear Ivan/Smoke, Smoke, Smoke That Cigarette	1962	3.75	7.50	15.00
42282	To a Sleeping Beauty/The Cajun Queen	1962	2.50	5.00	10.00
42282 [PS]	To a Sleeping Beauty/The Cajun Queen	1962	3.75	7.50	15.00
42338	P.T. 109/Walk On, Boy	1962	2.50	5.00	10.00
42338 [PS]	P.T. 109/Walk On, Boy	1962	3.75	7.50	15.00
42483	Steel Men/Little Bitty Big John	1962	2.50	5.00	10.00
42483 [PS]	Steel Men/Little Bitty Big John	1962	3.75	7.50	15.00
42529	Little Black Book/Please Pass the Biscuits	1962	2.50	5.00	10.00
42529 [PS]	Little Black Book/Please Pass the Biscuits	1962	3.75	7.50	15.00
42600	Gonna Raise a Rukus Tonight/A Day That Changed the World	1962	2.50	5.00	10.00
42600 [PS]	Gonna Raise a Rukus Tonight/A Day That Changed the World	1962	3.75	7.50	15.00
42738	Mile Long Train/This Ole House	1963	2.00	4.00	8.00
42861	The Funniest Thing I Ever Heard/Thumb Pick Pete	1963	2.00	4.00	8.00
42934	Mind Your Own Business/I Really Don't Want to Know	1963	2.00	4.00	8.00
43021	Shenandoah/Waitin' for the Wagon	1964	2.00	4.00	8.00
43159	Sam Hill/When I Grow Too Old to Dream	1964	2.00	4.00	8.00
43172	Yes, Patricia, There Is a Santa Claus/Little Sandy Sleighfoot	1964	2.50	5.00	10.00
43263	The First Thing Ev'ry Morning (And the Last Thing Ev'ry Night)/Awkward Situation	1965	—	3.00	6.00
43382	Harvest of Sunshine/Under the Sun	1965	—	3.00	6.00
43457	Blue Christmas/Yes, Patricia, There Is a Santa Claus	1965	2.00	4.00	8.00
43540	Things Have Gone to Pieces/Striker Bill	1966	—	3.00	6.00
43754	Once a Day/Let's Pretend	1966	—	3.00	6.00
45922	Your Sweet Love (Keeps Me Homeward Bound)/ I'm Gonna Be Gone	1973	—	2.50	5.00
45981	Who's Gonna Love Me Tomorrow/The Days When Jim Liked Jimmy	1973	—	2.50	5.00
46039	I've Been Down Some Road/Your Sweet Love	1974	—	2.50	5.00
JZSP 111915/6 [DJ]	Blue Christmas/Yes, Patricia, There Is a Santa Claus	1965	5.00	10.00	20.00
—Promo only on green vinyl					
KING					
5862	There Stands the Glass/Bumming Around	1964	2.00	4.00	8.00
MERCURY					
70691	False Pride/Big Blue Diamonds	1955	3.75	7.50	15.00
70745	Find 'Em, Fool 'Em, and Leave 'Em Alone/My World Is You	1955	3.75	7.50	15.00
70786	Freight Train Blues/Glad Rags	1956	3.75	7.50	15.00
70855	Hello Mr. Blues/I Found Out	1956	3.75	7.50	15.00
71120	Losing Game/Happy Child	1957	3.75	7.50	15.00
71172	Look on the Good Side/Do You Love Me	1957	3.75	7.50	15.00
71240	Bumming Around/Nothing Can Stop My Love	1957	3.75	7.50	15.00
71313	What This Old World Needs/A Fool in Love	1958	3.75	7.50	15.00
RCA VICTOR					
47-8971	Stand Beside Me/A Tiny Drop of Sadness	1966	2.00	4.00	8.00
47-9091	Sweet Misery/When Someone Mentions Your Name	1967	2.00	4.00	8.00
47-9241	Ninety Days/In the Same Old Way	1967	2.00	4.00	8.00
47-9350	I'm a Swinger/Your Country Boy	1967	2.00	4.00	8.00
47-9454	A Thing Called Love/One Last Time	1968	2.00	4.00	8.00
47-9567	Born to Be By Your Side/Read 'Em and Weep	1968	2.00	4.00	8.00
47-9652	A Hammer and Nails/I Taught Her Everything She Knows	1968	2.00	4.00	8.00
47-9800	When Judy Smiled/My Hometown Sweetheart	1969	—	3.00	6.00
47-9859	Down Comes the Rain/Us	1970	—	3.00	6.00
47-9915	Weakness in a Man/Aunt Maudie's Fun Garden	1970	—	3.00	6.00
47-9947	Slowly/Sweet Thang	1971	—	3.00	6.00
—With Dottie West					
47-9966	Everybody Knows/Ain't Life Sweet	1971	—	3.00	6.00
74-0122	A Rose Is a Rose Is a Rose/She's Mine	1969	—	3.00	6.00
74-0600	And I'm Still Missing You/The One You Say Good Mornin' To	1971	—	3.00	6.00

Albums

Number	Title	Yr	VG	VG+	NM
COLUMBIA					
CL 1025 [M]	Jimmy Dean's Hour of Prayer	1957	10.00	20.00	40.00
CL 1735 [M]	Big Bad John and Other Fabulous Songs and Tales	1961	5.00	10.00	20.00
—It's possible that two different editions exist, one with the "hell of a man" lyrics of "Big Bad John" and the other with the "big, big man" lyrics, but this has not been confirmed.					
CL 1894 [M]	Portrait of Jimmy Dean	1962	5.00	10.00	20.00
CL 2027 [M]	Everybody's Favorite	1963	3.75	7.50	15.00
CL 2188 [M]	Songs We All Love Best	1964	3.75	7.50	15.00
CL 2401 [M]	The First Thing Every Morning	1965	3.75	7.50	15.00
CL 2404 [M]	Jimmy Dean's Christmas Card	1965	3.75	7.50	15.00
CL 2485 [M]	Jimmy Dean's Greatest Hits	1966	3.75	7.50	15.00
CL 2538 [M]	The Big Ones	1966	3.75	7.50	15.00
CS 8535 [S]	Big Bad John and Other Fabulous Songs and Tales	1961	6.25	12.50	25.00
—It's possible that two different editions exist, one with the "hell of a man" lyrics of "Big Bad John" and the other with the "big, big man" lyrics, but this has not been confirmed.					
CS 8694 [S]	Portrait of Jimmy Dean	1962	6.25	12.50	25.00
CS 8827 [S]	Everybody's Favorite	1963	5.00	10.00	20.00
CS 8988 [S]	Songs We All Love Best	1964	5.00	10.00	20.00
CS 9201 [S]	The First Thing Every Morning	1965	5.00	10.00	20.00
CS 9204 [S]	Jimmy Dean's Christmas Card	1965	3.00	6.00	12.00
CS 9285 [S]	Jimmy Dean's Greatest Hits	1966	3.75	7.50	15.00
PC 9285	Jimmy Dean's Greatest Hits	198?	2.00	4.00	8.00
—Budget-line reissue					
CS 9338 [S]	The Big Ones	1966	3.75	7.50	15.00
CS 9424 [R]	Jimmy Dean's Hour of Prayer	1966	3.00	6.00	12.00
CS 9677	Dean's List	1968	3.75	7.50	15.00
CROWN					
291	Jimmy Dean and the Western Gentlemen	196?	3.00	6.00	12.00
GRT					
8014	I.O.U.	1977	2.50	5.00	10.00
HARMONY					
HL 7268 [M]	Hymns	1960	3.75	7.50	15.00
HL 7408 [M]	Mr. Country Music	1967	3.00	6.00	12.00
HS 11042 [R]	Hymns	1960	3.00	6.00	12.00
HS 11208 [S]	Mr. Country Music	1967	3.00	6.00	12.00
HS 11270	The Country's Favorite Son	1968	3.00	6.00	12.00
HILLTOP					
6004	Golden Favorites	196?	3.00	6.00	12.00
KING					
686 [M]	Favorites of Jimmy Dean	1961	15.00	30.00	60.00
MERCURY					
MG-20319 [M]	Jimmy Dean Sings His Television Favorites	1957	10.00	20.00	40.00
RCA VICTOR					
LPM-3727 [M]	Jimmy Dean Is Here	1967	3.75	7.50	15.00
LSP-3727 [S]	Jimmy Dean Is Here	1967	3.75	7.50	15.00
LPM-3824 [M]	Most Richly Blesed	1967	5.00	10.00	20.00
LSP-3824 [S]	Most Richly Blesed	1967	3.75	7.50	15.00
LPM-3890 [M]	The Jimmy Dean Show	1967	5.00	10.00	20.00
LSP-3890 [S]	The Jimmy Dean Show	1967	3.75	7.50	15.00
LPM-3999 [M]	A Thing Called Love	1968	7.50	15.00	30.00
LSP-3999 [S]	A Thing Called Love	1968	3.75	7.50	15.00
LSP-4035	Speaker of the House	1968	3.75	7.50	15.00
LSP-4323	Dean of Country	1970	3.75	7.50	15.00
LSP-4434	Country Boy and Country Girl	1970	3.75	7.50	15.00
LSP-4511	Everybody Knows	1971	3.75	7.50	15.00
LSP-4618	These Hands	1972	3.75	7.50	15.00
SEARS					
105	Jimmy Dean's Golden Favorites	196?	3.75	7.50	15.00
SPIN-O-RAMA					
108	Featuring the Coutnry Singing of Jimmy Dean	196?	3.00	6.00	12.00
137	Coutnry Round-Up Featuring Jimmy Dean	196?	3.00	6.00	12.00
WING					
MGW-12292 [M]	Jimmy Dean Sings His Television Favorites	196?	3.75	7.50	15.00
SRW-16292 [R]	Jimmy Dean Sings His Television Favorites	196?	3.00	6.00	12.00
WYNCOTE					
9032	Country Favorites	196?	3.00	6.00	12.00

Number	Title (A Side/B Side)	Yr	VG	VG+	NM
DEAN, JIMMY / JOHNNY HORTON					
Albums					
LA BREA					
L 8014 [M]	Bummin' Around with Jimmy Dean and Johnny Horton	1961	20.00	40.00	80.00
STARDAY					
SLP-325 [M]	Bummin' Around with Jimmy Dean and Johnny Horton	1965	7.50	15.00	30.00
DEAN, JIMMY / MARVIN RAINWATER					
Albums					
PREMIER					
9054	Nashville Showtime	196?	3.00	6.00	12.00
DEAN, LENNY					
See THE ROCKIN' CHAIRS.					
DEAN AND JEAN					
45s					
EMBER					
1048	We're Gonna Get Married/Too Young to Know	1958	3.00	6.00	12.00
1054	Turn It Off/Never Let Your Love Fade Away	1959	3.00	6.00	12.00
RUST					
TR 1	Seven Day Wonder/The Man Who Will Never Grow Old	196?	3.00	6.00	12.00
5044	Come Take a Walk with Me/Dance the Roach	1962	2.50	5.00	10.00
5046	Mack the Knife/You Can't Be Happy by Yourself	1962	2.50	5.00	10.00
5067	Tra La La La Suzy/I Love the Summertime	1963	2.50	5.00	10.00
5075	Hey Jean, Hey Dean/Please Don't Tell Me Now	1964	3.75	7.50	15.00
5081	I Wanna Be Loved/Thread Your Needle	1964	2.50	5.00	10.00
5085	Goddess of Love/The Man Who Will Never Grow Old	1964	2.50	5.00	10.00
5089	Sticks and Stones/In My Way	1964	2.50	5.00	10.00
5100	Lovingly Yours/Goddess of Love	1965	2.50	5.00	10.00
5107	She's Too Respectable/I Love the Summertime	1965	2.50	5.00	10.00
DEAN AND MARC					
Also see THE NEWBEATS.					
45s					
BULLSEYE					
1025	Tell Him No/Change of Heart	1959	12.50	25.00	50.00
1026	Cry/The Beginning of Love	1959	6.25	12.50	25.00
CHECKMATE					
1008	Boogie Woogie Twist (Parts 1 & 2)	1962	3.75	7.50	15.00
HICKORY					
1227	With Tears in My Eyes/Kissin' Game	1963	2.50	5.00	10.00
—Hickory titles as "Dean and Mark" unless noted					
1249	When I Stop Dreaming/There Oughta Be a Law	1964	2.50	5.00	10.00
1294	Just a Step Away/A Falling Star	1965	2.50	5.00	10.00
1353	In the Middle of the Night/You'll Never Really Know	1965	2.50	5.00	10.00
1414	When I Stop Dreaming/With Tears in My Eyes	1966	2.50	5.00	10.00
—As "The Mathis Brothers"					
MAY					
135	Somebody's Smiling (While I'm Crying)/Pins and Needles (In My Heart)	1963	3.00	6.00	12.00
—As "Dean and Mark"					
DEANS, THE					
45s					
LAURIE					
3114	I Don't Want to Wait/Little White Gardenia	1961	5.00	10.00	20.00
MOHAWK					
114	My Heart Is Low/I'll Love You Forever	1960	6.25	12.50	25.00
119	Humpty Dumpty/La Chiam	1960	6.25	12.50	25.00
126	It's You/I Don't Wanna Wait	1960	10.00	20.00	40.00
STAR MAKER					
1928	Oh Little Star/You Got Me Baby	1961	25.00	50.00	100.00
1931	Chills, Chills, Chills/(Lady of the) Caravan	1962	15.00	30.00	60.00
DEAUVILLE, RONNIE					
45s					
ERA					
1055	I Concentrate on You/As Children Go	1957	5.00	10.00	20.00
1056	Laura/It Wasn't Much of a Town	1957	5.00	10.00	20.00
1056 [PS]	Laura/It Wasn't Much of a Town	1957	15.00	30.00	60.00
1066	Hong Kong Affair/Crazy, Wonderful	1957	5.00	10.00	20.00
IMPERIAL					
5559	King of Fools/Blame Your Eyes	1959	3.75	7.50	15.00
Albums					
ERA					
20002 [M]	Smoke Dreams	1957	10.00	20.00	40.00
IMPERIAL					
LP-9060 [M]	Romance	1959	6.25	12.50	25.00
LP-12009 [S]	Romance	1959	7.50	15.00	30.00
DEBBIE AND THE TEEN DREAMS					
45s					
VERNON					
101	Santa, Teach Me How To Dance/The Time	1962	6.25	12.50	25.00
DEBERRY, JIMMY					
45s					
SUN					
185	Take a Little Chance/Time Has Made a Change	1953	750.00	1500.	3000.
DEBONAIRES, THE (1)					
45s					
DORE					
526	Every Once in a While/Mama Don't Care	1959	20.00	40.00	80.00
—As "The Debonairs"					
592	Every Once in a While/Gert's Skirt	1961	7.50	15.00	30.00
654	Hold Back the Dawn/Mama Don't Care	1962	6.25	12.50	25.00
702	Every Once in a While/Gert's Skirt	1964	5.00	10.00	20.00
712	Everybody's Movin'/Mama Don't Care	1964	5.00	10.00	20.00
GEE					
1008	Won't You Tell Me/I'm Gone	1956	20.00	40.00	80.00
1054	We'll Wait/Make Believe Lover	1960	6.25	12.50	25.00
HERALD					
509	Darlin'/Whispering Blues	1957	15.00	30.00	60.00
509	Darlin'/Whispering Blues	1957	50.00	100.00	200.00
—As "The Five Debonaires"					
DEBONAIRES, THE (2)					
45s					
ELMONT					
1004	This Must Be Paradise/I Need You Darling	1958	50.00	100.00	200.00
DEBONAIRES, THE (3)					
45s					
GOLDEN WORLD					
17	A Little Too Long/Please Don't Say We're Through	1964	5.00	10.00	20.00
26	Eenie Meenie Gypsaleenie/Please Don't Say We're Through	1965	5.00	10.00	20.00
38	Big Time Fun/How's Your New Love Treating You	1966	5.00	10.00	20.00
44	C.O.D./How's Your New Love Treating You	1966	5.00	10.00	20.00
DEBONAIRES, THE (U)					
This may be one of groups (1), (2) or (3), or it may be a completely different group.					
45s					
MASKE					
804	Every Other Day/Jivin' Guy	1959	10.00	20.00	40.00
DEBS, THE					
More than one group.					
45s					
BRUCE					
129	Shoo-Doo-De-Doo/Whadaya Want	1955	15.00	30.00	60.00
CROWN					
153	If You Were Here Tonight/Look What You're Doin' to Me	1955	10.00	20.00	40.00
DOUBLE L					
727	Danger Ahead/Just Another Fool	1964	3.00	6.00	12.00
KEEN					
34003	Johnny Darling/Doom-a-Roca	1957	6.25	12.50	25.00
MERCURY					
72458	Give Him My Love/Goodbye Boy	1965	5.00	10.00	20.00
72566	My Best Friend/The Life and Soul of the Party	1966	3.75	7.50	15.00
DEBUTANTES, THE (1)					
45s					
KAYO					
928	Going Steady/Memories	1958	62.50	125.00	250.00
DEBUTANTES, THE (2)					
45s					
LUCKY ELEVEN					
237	Love Is Strange/A New Love Today	196?	3.75	7.50	15.00
DEBUTANTES, THE (3)					
45s					
SAVOY					
1191	Just Leave It to Me/Is It Too Soon	1956	7.50	15.00	30.00
DECARLO, YVONNE					
45s					
IMPERIAL					
5532	Rockin' in Orbit/I Would Give My Heart	1958	20.00	40.00	80.00
Albums					
MASTERSEAL					
33-1869/70 [M]	Yvonne DeCarlo Sings	1957	20.00	40.00	80.00
DECARO, NICK					
45s					
A&M					
838	Amy's Theme/Spanish Flea	1967	—	3.00	6.00
1037	Happy Heart/Love Is All	1969	—	3.00	6.00
1109	I'm Gonna Make You Love Me/Amy's Theme	1969	—	3.00	6.00
Albums					
A&M					
SP-4176	Happy Heart	1969	2.50	5.00	10.00
DECASTRO SISTERS, THE					
45s					
ABBOTT					
3001	Teach Me Tonight/It's Love	1954	3.75	7.50	15.00
3002	I'm Bewildered/To Say You're Mine	1955	3.00	6.00	12.00
3003	Boom Boom Boomerang/Let Your Love Walk In	1955	3.00	6.00	12.00
3004	Cuckoo in the Clock/If I Ever Fall in Love	1955	3.00	6.00	12.00
3007	Cuban Love Song/I Can't Escape from You	1955	3.00	6.00	12.00
3008	Wedding Song/I'm Bewildered	1955	3.00	6.00	12.00
3011	Too Late Now/Give Me Time	1955	3.00	6.00	12.00
3012	Snowbound for Christmas/Christmas Is a-Comin'	1955	3.75	7.50	15.00
3014	Rockin' and Rollin' in Hawaii/Cry Baby Blues	1956	3.00	6.00	12.00

Number	Title (A Side/B Side)	Yr	VG	VG+	NM
3019	No One to Blame But You/Cowboys Don't Cry	1956	3.00	6.00	12.00
ABC-PARAMOUNT					
9932	Who Are They to Say/When You Look at Me	1958	2.50	5.00	10.00
9988	Teach Me Tonight Cha Cha/The Things I Tell My Pillow	1958	2.50	5.00	10.00
10007	Close to You/With My Eyes Wide Open	1959	2.50	5.00	10.00
BOHA					
1001	Feliz Navidad/Santa Claus Is Coming To Town	197?	—	2.00	4.00
CAPITOL					
4537	The Bells/Red Sails in the Sunset	1961	2.00	4.00	8.00
RCA VICTOR					
47-6661	Don't Call Me Sweetie/It's Yours	1956	2.50	5.00	10.00
47-6774	I Never Meant to Hurt You/I Hear a Melody	1956	2.50	5.00	10.00
47-6862	Flowers on a Hillside/I Know Plenty	1957	2.50	5.00	10.00
47-7028	Where Have You Been All My Life/That Little Word Called Love	1957	2.50	5.00	10.00
47-7108	Old Timers' Tune/Blue and Broken Hearted	1957	2.50	5.00	10.00
47-7177	You Take Care of Me/What a Relief	1958	2.50	5.00	10.00
ZODIAC					
1016	Before the Next Teardrop Falls/Teach Me Tonight	1977	—	2.00	4.00

Albums

Number	Title	Yr	VG	VG+	NM
ABBOTT					
5002 [M]	The DeCastro Sisters	1956	15.00	30.00	60.00
CAPITOL					
ST 1402 [S]	The DeCastros Sing	1960	7.50	15.00	30.00
T 1402 [M]	The DeCastros Sing	1960	6.25	12.50	25.00
ST 1501 [S]	The Rockin' Beat	1961	7.50	15.00	30.00
T 1501 [M]	The Rockin' Beat	1961	6.25	12.50	25.00

DECEMBER'S CHILDREN

45s

Number	Title	Yr	VG	VG+	NM
CAPITOL					
5883	A Girl Like You/Makin' Music	1967	3.00	6.00	12.00
LIBERTY					
56195	You're My Girl/Dirty City	1970	2.50	5.00	10.00
MAINSTREAM					
728	Sweet Talking Woman/(B-side unknown)	1970	3.75	7.50	15.00
WORLD PACIFIC					
77887	Backwards and Forwards/Kissin' Time	1968	2.50	5.00	10.00
77895	Lovin' Things/Extraordinary Man	1968	2.50	5.00	10.00
77910	I've Been Hurt/Good Time Boy	1969	2.50	5.00	10.00

Albums

Number	Title	Yr	VG	VG+	NM
MAINSTREAM					
S-6128	December's Children	1970	12.50	25.00	50.00

DEE, DONNA

45s

Number	Title	Yr	VG	VG+	NM
ABC-PARAMOUNT					
10296	Television/Nobody's Gonna Hurt You	1962	5.00	10.00	20.00

DEE, FRANKIE

45s

Number	Title	Yr	VG	VG+	NM
20TH FOX					
146	Swingin' in a Hammock/I Had the Craziest Dream	1959	7.50	15.00	30.00
ABCO					
1002	Walking in the Rain/Everybody's Doin' It	195?	5.00	10.00	20.00
RCA VICTOR					
47-7276	Shake It Up Baby/After Graduation	1958	15.00	30.00	60.00

DEE, JACKIE

See JACKIE DeSHANNON.

DEE, JIMMY

45s

Number	Title	Yr	VG	VG+	NM
DOT					
15664	Henrietta/Don't Cry No More	1957	10.00	20.00	40.00
15721	Here I Come/You're Late, Miss Kate	1958	10.00	20.00	40.00
TNT					
148	Henrietta/Don't Cry No More	1957	20.00	40.00	80.00
152	Here I Come/You're Late, Miss Kate	1958	20.00	40.00	80.00
161	Feel Like Rockin'/Rock-Tick-Rock	1958	15.00	30.00	60.00

DEE, JOEY, AND THE STARLITERS

45s

Number	Title	Yr	VG	VG+	NM
BONUS					
7009	Lorraine/The Girl I Walk to School	1963	12.50	25.00	50.00
7009 [PS]	Lorraine/The Girl I Walk to School	1963	20.00	40.00	80.00
JUBILEE					
5532	Feel Good About It Part 1/Feel Good About It Part 2	1966	3.75	7.50	15.00
5539	Dancing on the Beach/Good Little You	1966	3.75	7.50	15.00
5554	She's So Exceptional/It's Got You	1966	3.75	7.50	15.00
5566	Can't Sit Down/Put Your Heart In It	1967	3.75	7.50	15.00
—Stock copy may not exist					
LITTLE					
813/4	Lorraine/The Girl I Walk to School	1958	100.00	200.00	400.00
MONUMENT					
(# unknown) [DJ]	Ya Ya Twist/Runaround Sue	1962	6.25	12.50	25.00
—B-side by Dion					
ROULETTE					
4401	Peppermint Twist — Part 1/Peppermint Twist — Part 2	1961	4.00	8.00	16.00
4408	Hey, Let's Twist/Roly Poly	1962	3.75	7.50	15.00
4408 [PS]	Hey, Let's Twist/Roly Poly	1962	6.25	12.50	25.00
4416	Shout — Part 1/Shout — Part 2	1962	3.75	7.50	15.00
4416 [PS]	Shout — Part 1/Shout — Part 2	1962	6.25	12.50	25.00
4431	Every Time (I Think About You) Part 1/Every Time (I Think About You) Part 2	1962	3.00	6.00	12.00
4438	What Kind of Love Is This/Wing Ding	1962	3.00	6.00	12.00
4438 [PS]	What Kind of Love Is This/Wing Ding	1962	6.25	12.50	25.00
4456	I Lost My Baby/Keep Your Mind on What You're Doing	1962	3.00	6.00	12.00
4456 [PS]	I Lost My Baby/Keep Your Mind on What You're Doing	1962	6.25	12.50	25.00
4467	Baby You're Driving Me Crazy/Help Me Pick Up the Pieces	1963	3.00	6.00	12.00
4488	Hot Pastrami with Mashed Potatoes — Part 1/Hot Pastrami with Mashed Potatoes — Part 2	1963	3.00	6.00	12.00
4503	Dance, Dance, Dance/Let's Have a Party	1963	3.00	6.00	12.00
4523	Ya Ya/Fanny Mae	1963	3.00	6.00	12.00
4539	Down by the Riverside/Getting Nearer	1963	5.00	10.00	20.00
4617	Cry a Little Sometime/Wing Ding	1965	3.00	6.00	12.00
SCEPTER					
1210	Face of An Angel/Shimmy Baby	1960	7.50	15.00	30.00
—Originals have "Scepter" at top of label and are credited as "Joey Dee and the Starlights"					
1210	Face of An Angel/Shimmy Baby	1961	5.00	10.00	20.00
—Reissues have "Scepter Records" at side of label and are credited as listed					
1225	Three Memories/(Bad) Bulldog	1961	7.50	15.00	30.00
VASELINE HAIR TONIC					
(no #)	Learn to Dance the Authentic Peppermint Twist (Parts 1 & 2)	1962	3.75	7.50	15.00
(no #) [PS]	Learn to Dance the Authentic Peppermint Twist (Parts 1 & 2)	1962	3.75	7.50	15.00

Albums

Number	Title	Yr	VG	VG+	NM
FORUM					
FC 9099 [M]	Joey Dee and the Starliters	1963	3.00	6.00	12.00
FCS 9099 [S]	Joey Dee and the Starliters	1963	3.00	6.00	12.00
JUBILEE					
JLP-8000 [M]	Hitsville	1966	5.00	10.00	20.00
JLS-8000 [S]	Hitsville	1966	6.25	12.50	25.00
ROULETTE					
R-25166 [M]	Doin' the Twist at the Peppermint Lounge	1961	10.00	20.00	40.00
SR-25166 [S]	Doin' the Twist at the Peppermint Lounge	1961	12.50	25.00	50.00
R-25171 [M]	All the World Is Twistin'	1962	7.50	15.00	30.00
SR-25171 [S]	All the World Is Twistin'	1962	10.00	20.00	40.00
R-25173 [M]	Back at the Peppermint Lounge — Twistin'	1962	7.50	15.00	30.00
SR-25173 [S]	Back at the Peppermint Lounge — Twistin'	1962	10.00	20.00	40.00
R-25197 [M]	Joey Dee	1963	6.25	12.50	25.00
SR-25197 [S]	Joey Dee	1963	7.50	15.00	30.00
R-25221 [M]	Dance, Dance, Dance	1963	6.25	12.50	25.00
SR-25221 [S]	Dance, Dance, Dance	1963	7.50	15.00	30.00
SCEPTER					
S 503 [M]	The Peppermint Twisters	1962	6.25	12.50	25.00
SS 503 [S]	The Peppermint Twisters	1962	7.50	15.00	30.00

DEE, JOHNNY

See JOHN D. LOUDERMILK.

DEE, KIKI

Also see ELTON JOHN AND KIKI DEE.

45s

Number	Title	Yr	VG	VG+	NM
FONTANA					
1649	On a Magic Carpet Ride/Now the Flowers Die	1969	—	2.50	5.00
LIBERTY					
55994	Stop and Think/I	1967	—	3.00	6.00
56030	I'm Going Out/Patterns	1968	—	3.00	6.00
56089	On a Magic Carpet Ride/Now the Flowers Die	1969	—	3.00	6.00
POSSE					
5008	Nothing Can Stop Us Now/(B-side unknown)	1981	—	2.00	4.00
RARE EARTH					
5025	Love Makes the World Go Round/Jimmy	1970	—	2.50	5.00
RCA					
PB-12347	Star/There's a Need	1981	—	2.00	4.00
PB-13043	Loving You Is Sweeter Than Ever/Twenty-Four Hours	1982	—	—	—
—Unreleased					
ROCKET					
YB-11413	One Step/Dark Side of Your Soul	1978	—	2.00	4.00
YB-11490	Don't Stop Loving Me/One Step Ahead of the Storm	1979	—	2.00	4.00
40095	The Last Good Man in My Life/Lonnie and Josie	1973	—	2.00	4.00
40157	Amoureuse/Rest My Head	1973	—	2.00	4.00
40256	Super Cool/Loving and Free	1974	—	2.00	4.00
40293	I've Got the Music in Me/Simple Melody	1974	—	2.50	5.00
40355	Step by Step/Amoureuse	1975	—	2.00	4.00
40401	How Glad I Am/Peter	1975	—	2.00	4.00
40506	Once a Fool/Someone to Me	1976	—	2.00	4.00
40730	Chicago/Bad Day Child	1977	—	2.00	4.00
TAMLA					
54193	The Day Will Come Between Sunday and Monday/My Whole World Ended (The Moment You Left Me)	1970	—	2.50	5.00
WORLD PACIFIC					
77820	I Dig You Baby/Small Town	1966	2.00	4.00	8.00

Albums

Number	Title	Yr	VG	VG+	NM
LIBERTY					
LST-7613	Patterns	1969	3.75	7.50	15.00
LN-10148	Patterns	1981	2.00	4.00	8.00
—Budget-line reissue					
RCA VICTOR					
AFL1-4180	Perfect Timing	1981	2.50	5.00	10.00
ROCKET					
PIG-395	Loving and Free	1973	2.50	5.00	10.00
PIG-458	I've Got the Music In Me	1974	3.00	6.00	12.00
BXL1-2257	Kiki Dee	1977	2.50	5.00	10.00
BXL1-3011	Stay with Me	1979	2.50	5.00	10.00
TAMLA					
TS 303	Great Expectations	1970	3.75	7.50	15.00

DEE, LENNY

45s

DECCA

Number	Title (A Side/B Side)	Yr	VG	VG+	NM
25531	Parade of the Wooden Soldiers/Twilight Time	1961	—	3.00	6.00
25563	Ain't She Sweet/Alabamy Bound	1962	—	3.00	6.00
25578	Baubles, Bangles and Beads/Blues in the Night	1962	—	3.00	6.00
25592	Moon Over Miami/Atlanta G.A.	1963	—	3.00	6.00
25613	Wagon Wheels/Hominy Grits	1963	—	3.00	6.00
25633	Devil Woman/San Antonio Rose	1964	—	3.00	6.00
25678	The Gang That Sang Heart of My Heart/Down by the Old Mill Stream	1965	—	3.00	6.00
25696	Yakety Organ/A Walk in the Black Forest	1966	—	3.00	6.00
25702	Kerry Dancers/One of Those Songs	1966	—	3.00	6.00
25717	Cute/Daydream	1967	—	2.50	5.00
25725	There's a Kind of Hush/Exodus	1967	—	2.50	5.00
25735	Gentle on My Mind/Rossana's Theme	1968	—	2.50	5.00
25745	Folsom Prison Blues/Turn Around, Look at Me	1969	—	2.50	5.00
25750	Help Yourself/Try a Little Tenderness	1969	—	2.50	5.00
25755	Yesterday, When I Was Young/Ruby, Don't Take Your Love to Town	1970	—	2.50	5.00
28500	Midnight/Bye Bye Blues	1952	2.50	5.00	10.00
28639	Oh Johnny Oh/Them There Eyes	1953	2.50	5.00	10.00
29360	Plantation Boogie/The Birth of the Blues	1954	2.50	5.00	10.00
29579	Crazy Organ Rag/Punxsutawney Boogie	1955	2.50	5.00	10.00
29596	Little Brown Jug/The World Is Waiting for the Sunrise	1955	2.50	5.00	10.00
29689	Honeydripper/Flea Hop Boogie	1955	2.50	5.00	10.00
30032	Honky Tonk Train Blues/Yodelin' Organ	1956	2.00	4.00	8.00
30201	Stormy Weather/Goodnight Sweet Love	1957	2.00	4.00	8.00
30296	High Tide Boogie/Tara Lara	1957	2.00	4.00	8.00
30429	Big Boogie Dee/Cecelia	1957	2.00	4.00	8.00
30718	June Night/After You've Gone	1958	2.00	4.00	8.00
30801	Night Train/Chicken in the Rough	1959	2.00	4.00	8.00
31332	Mr. Santa/Auld Lang Syne	1961	2.50	5.00	10.00
32691	Rock Me Back to Little Rock/Sweet and Sassy	1970	—	2.50	5.00
32804	Help Me Make It Through the Night/Remember Me	1971	—	2.00	4.00
33026	All I Ever Need Is You/Vaya Con Dios	1972	—	2.00	4.00

7-Inch Extended Plays

DECCA

Number	Title (A Side/B Side)	Yr	VG	VG+	NM
ED 2266	(contents unknown)	195?	2.50	5.00	10.00
ED 2266 [PS]	Dee-Lirious, Part 1	195?	2.50	5.00	10.00
ED 2267	(contents unknown)	195?	2.50	5.00	10.00
ED 2267 [PS]	Dee-Lirious, Part 2	195?	2.50	5.00	10.00
ED 2552	(contents unknown)	195?	2.50	5.00	10.00
ED 2552 [PS]	Mr. Dee Goes to Town	195?	2.50	5.00	10.00
ED 2613	(contents unknown)	195?	2.50	5.00	10.00
ED 2613 [PS]	Dee-Day	195?	2.50	5.00	10.00
ED 2628 [M]	(contents unknown)	1959	2.50	5.00	10.00
ED 2628 [PS]	Mellow-Dee	1959	2.50	5.00	10.00
ED 7-2628 [PS]	Mellow-Dee	1959	3.75	7.50	15.00
ED 7-2628 [S]	(contents unknown)	1959	3.75	7.50	15.00
ED 2645	(contents unknown)	195?	2.50	5.00	10.00
ED 2645 [PS]	Lenny Dee Plays the Hits	195?	2.50	5.00	10.00

Albums

DECCA

Number	Title (A Side/B Side)	Yr	VG	VG+	NM
DL 4112 [M]	Golden Organ Favorites	1961	2.50	5.00	10.00
DL 4146 [M]	Happy Holi-Dee	1961	2.50	5.00	10.00
DL 4315 [M]	Lenny Dee In Hollywood	1962	2.50	5.00	10.00
DL 4365 [M]	Lenny Dee Down South	1963	2.50	5.00	10.00
DL 4429 [M]	By Popular Dee-Mand	1963	2.50	5.00	10.00
DL 4498 [M]	Something Special	1964	2.50	5.00	10.00
DL 4572 [M]	Most Requested	1964	2.50	5.00	10.00
DL 4632 [M]	Sweethearts on Parade	1965	2.50	5.00	10.00
DL 4654 [M]	The Lenny Dee Tour	1965	2.50	5.00	10.00
DL 4706 [M]	My Favorite Things	1966	2.50	5.00	10.00
DL 4818 [M]	In the Mood	1967	2.50	5.00	10.00
DL 4880 [M]	Moving On	1967	3.00	6.00	12.00
DL 4946 [M]	Relaxin'	1968	3.00	6.00	12.00
DL 4994 [M]	Gentle on My Mind	1968	3.00	6.00	12.00
DXS 7199 [(2)]	The Best of Lenny Dee	1968	3.00	6.00	12.00
DL 8114 [M]	Dee-Lightful	1955	3.75	7.50	15.00
DL 8165 [M]	Dee-Lirious	1956	3.00	6.00	12.00
DL 8275 [M]	Dee-Licious	1956	3.00	6.00	12.00
DL 8308 [M]	Dee-Most	1956	3.00	6.00	12.00
DL 8406 [M]	Hi-Dee-Fi	1957	3.00	6.00	12.00
DL 8497 [M]	Mr. Dee Goes to Town	1957	3.00	6.00	12.00
DL 8628 [M]	Dee-Day	1957	3.00	6.00	12.00
DL 8718 [M]	Dee-Latin Hi-Fi Organ	1958	3.00	6.00	12.00
DL 8796 [M]	Mellow-Dee	1959	3.00	6.00	12.00
DL 8857 [M]	Lenny Dee Plays the Hits	1959	3.00	6.00	12.00
DL 8913 [M]	The Lenny Dee Show	1960	2.50	5.00	10.00
DL 8978 [M]	Songs Everybody Knows	1960	2.50	5.00	10.00
DL 74112 [S]	Golden Organ Favorites	1961	3.00	6.00	12.00
DL 74146 [S]	Happy Holi-Dee	1961	3.00	6.00	12.00
DL 74315 [S]	Lenny Dee In Hollywood	1962	3.00	6.00	12.00
DL 74365 [S]	Lenny Dee Down South	1963	3.00	6.00	12.00
DL 74429 [S]	By Popular Dee-Mand	1963	3.00	6.00	12.00
DL 74498 [S]	Something Special	1964	3.00	6.00	12.00
DL 74572 [S]	Most Requested	1964	3.00	6.00	12.00
DL 74632 [S]	Sweethearts on Parade	1965	3.00	6.00	12.00
DL 74654 [S]	The Lenny Dee Tour	1965	3.00	6.00	12.00
DL 74706 [S]	My Favorite Things	1966	3.00	6.00	12.00
DL 74818 [S]	In the Mood	1967	3.00	6.00	12.00
DL 74946 [S]	Relaxin'	1968	2.50	5.00	10.00
DL 74994 [S]	Gentle on My Mind	1968	2.50	5.00	10.00
DL 75073	Turn Around, Look at Me	1969	2.50	5.00	10.00
DL 75112	Little Green Apples	1969	2.50	5.00	10.00
DL 75152	Spinning Wheel	1969	2.50	5.00	10.00
DL 75196	Easy Come, Easy Go	1970	2.50	5.00	10.00
DL 75255	Remember Me	1971	2.50	5.00	10.00
DL 75320	Easy Lovin'	1972	2.50	5.00	10.00
DL 75366	Where Is the Love	1972	2.50	5.00	10.00
DL 78796 [S]	Mellow-Dee	1959	3.75	7.50	15.00
DL 78857 [S]	Lenny Dee Plays the Hits	1959	3.75	7.50	15.00
DL 78880 [S]	Moving On	1967	2.50	5.00	10.00
DL 78913 [S]	The Lenny Dee Show	1960	3.00	6.00	12.00
DL 78978 [S]	Songs Everybody Knows	1960	3.00	6.00	12.00

MCA

Number	Title (A Side/B Side)	Yr	VG	VG+	NM
26	Remember Me	1971	2.00	4.00	8.00
—Reissue of Decca 75255					
172	In the Mood	1973	2.00	4.00	8.00
—Reissue of Decca 74818					
182	Golden Organ Favorites	1973	2.00	4.00	8.00
—Reissue of Decca 74112					
221	Something Special	1973	2.00	4.00	8.00
—Reissue of Decca 74498					
231	Most Requested	1973	2.00	4.00	8.00
—Reissue of Decca 74572					
241	My Favorite Things	1973	2.00	4.00	8.00
—Reissue of Decca 74706					
271	Gentle on My Mind	1973	2.00	4.00	8.00
—Reissue of Decca 74994					
279	Little Green Apples	1973	2.00	4.00	8.00
—Reissue of Decca 75112					
290	Easy Come, Easy Go	1973	2.00	4.00	8.00
—Reissue of Decca 75196					
297	Easy Lovin'	1973	2.00	4.00	8.00
—Reissue of Decca 75320					
334	Lenny Dee	1973	2.00	4.00	8.00
334	"Sing" and Others	1973	2.00	4.00	8.00
379	"Lenny"	1973	2.00	4.00	8.00
455	Steppin' Out with Lenny Dee	1974	2.00	4.00	8.00
476	City Lights	1974	2.00	4.00	8.00
504	Where Is the Love	1974	2.00	4.00	8.00
—Reissue of Decca 75366					
533	Songs Everybody Knows	1975	2.00	4.00	8.00
—Reissue of Decca 78978					
2162	I'll Play for You	1975	2.00	4.00	8.00
2200	Take It to the Limit	1976	2.00	4.00	8.00
2236	Misty Blue	1976	2.00	4.00	8.00
2301	Organ Magic	1977	2.00	4.00	8.00
2370	Organ Celebration	1978	2.00	4.00	8.00
4042 [(2)]	The Best of Lenny Dee	197?	2.50	5.00	10.00
—Reissue of Decca 7179					
4084 [(2)]	The Best of Lenny Dee, Volume II	1977	2.50	5.00	10.00

VOCALION

Number	Title (A Side/B Side)	Yr	VG	VG+	NM
VL 3782 [M]	Here's Lenny Dee at the Organ	1967	2.50	5.00	10.00
VL 73782 [S]	Here's Lenny Dee at the Organ	1967	2.50	5.00	10.00
VL 73817	Organ Special	1968	2.50	5.00	10.00
VL 73819	Varieties	1969	2.50	5.00	10.00

DEE, TOMMY

45s

CHALLENGE

Number	Title (A Side/B Side)	Yr	VG	VG+	NM
59083	The Hobo and the Puppy/There's a Star Spangled Banner Waving Somewhere	1960	5.00	10.00	20.00
59087	Ballad of a Drag Race/The Story of Susie	1960	5.00	10.00	20.00

CREST

Number	Title (A Side/B Side)	Yr	VG	VG+	NM
1057 [M]	Three Stars/I'll Never Change	1959	7.50	15.00	30.00
—With backing group and B-side credited to "The Teen Tones and Orchestra"					
1057 [M]	Three Stars/I'll Never Change	1959	6.25	12.50	25.00
—With backing group and B-side credited to "Carol Kay and the Teen-Aires"					
1057 [S]	Three Stars/I'll Never Change	1959	12.50	25.00	50.00
—With backing group and B-side credited to "Carol Kay and the Teen-Aires"					
1061	The Chair/Hello Lonesome	1959	5.00	10.00	20.00
1067	Merry Christmas, Mary/Angel of Love	1959	6.25	12.50	25.00
—With Carol Kay					

PIKE

Number	Title (A Side/B Side)	Yr	VG	VG+	NM
5906	Loving You (On Someone Else's Time)/Halfway to Hell	1961	5.00	10.00	20.00
5909	A Little Dog Cried/Look Homeward, Dear Angel	1961	5.00	10.00	20.00
5917	Missing on a Mountain/Look Homeward, Dear Angel	1962	5.00	10.00	20.00

SIMS

Number	Title (A Side/B Side)	Yr	VG	VG+	NM
260	Missing While Surfing/Goodbye High School	1966	5.00	10.00	20.00
308	How's Your Mama Em/Goodbye High School	1966	3.75	7.50	15.00

DEE, WILLIE

45s

TUMBLEWEED

Number	Title (A Side/B Side)	Yr	VG	VG+	NM
100	Tear Filled Eyes/My Daddy's Not a Young Man Anymore	1968	5.00	10.00	20.00

DEEP, THE

Albums

PARKWAY

Number	Title (A Side/B Side)	Yr	VG	VG+	NM
P 7051 [M]	Psychedelic Moods	1966	62.50	125.00	250.00
SP 7051 [S]	Psychedelic Moods	1966	125.00	250.00	500.00

DEEP PURPLE

45s

MERCURY

Number	Title (A Side/B Side)	Yr	VG	VG+	NM
880477-7	Knocking at Your Back Door/Wasted Sunset	1984	—	2.00	4.00
880477-7 [PS]	Knocking at Your Back Door/Wasted Sunset	1984	—	2.50	5.00
885617-7	Call of the Wild/Dead or Alive	1987	—	—	3.00
885617-7 [PS]	Call of the Wild/Dead or Alive	1987	—	—	3.00
885820-7	Bad Attitude/Black and White	1987	—	—	3.00

TETRAGRAMMATON

Number	Title (A Side/B Side)	Yr	VG	VG+	NM
1503	Hush/One More Rainy Day	1968	3.00	6.00	12.00
1503 [PS]	Hush/One More Rainy Day	1968	7.50	15.00	30.00
1508	Kentucky Woman/Hard Road	1968	3.00	6.00	12.00
1508 [PS]	Kentucky Woman/Hard Road	1968	3.75	7.50	15.00
1514	River Deep, Mountain High/Listen, Learn, Read On	1969	2.50	5.00	10.00
1519	The Bird Has Flown/Emmaretta	1969	2.50	5.00	10.00
1537	Hallelujah (I Am the Preacher)/April Part 1	1969	2.50	5.00	10.00

Number	Title (A Side/B Side)	Yr	VG	VG+	NM
WARNER BROS.					
7405	Black Night/Into the Fire	1970	2.00	4.00	8.00
7493	Strange Kind of Woman/I'm Alone	1971	2.00	4.00	8.00
7528	Fire Ball/I'm Alone	1971	2.00	4.00	8.00
7572	Never Before/When a Blind Man Cries	1972	—	3.00	6.00
7595	Lazy/When a Blind Man Cries	1972	—	3.00	6.00
7634	Highway Star (Part 1)/Highway Star (Part 2)	1972	—	3.00	6.00
7654	Hush/Kentucky Woman	1972	—	3.00	6.00
7672	Woman from Tokyo/Super Trouper	1972	—	3.00	6.00
7710	Smoke on the Water (Edited Version) Studio/ Smoke on the Water (Edited Version) Live	1973	—	2.50	5.00
7737	Woman from Tokyo/Super Trouper	1973	—	2.50	5.00
7784	Might Just Take Your Life/Coronorias Regid	1974	—	2.50	5.00
7784 [DJ]	Might Just Take Your Life (Mono 3:35/Stereo 4:36)	1974	2.00	4.00	8.00
7809	Burn/Coronarias Regid	1974	—	2.50	5.00
8049	High Ball Shooter/You Can't Do It Right	1974	—	2.50	5.00
8069	Stormbringer/Love Don't Mean a Thing	1975	—	2.50	5.00
8182	Gettin' Tighter/Love Child	1976	—	2.50	5.00
Albums					
DCC COMPACT CLASSICS					
LPZ-2052 [(2)]	Made in Japan	1998	10.00	20.00	40.00
—Audiophile vinyl					
MERCURY					
824003-1	Perfect Strangers	1984	2.50	5.00	10.00
835897-1	Nobody's Perfect	1988	2.50	5.00	10.00
RCA					
2421-1-R	Slaves and Masters	1990	3.75	7.50	15.00
SCEPTER					
CTN-18010	The Best of Deep Purple	1972	2.50	5.00	10.00
TETRAGRAMMATON					
T-102	Shades of Deep Purple	1968	7.50	15.00	30.00
T-107	The Book of Taliesyn	1968	7.50	15.00	30.00
T-119	Deep Purple	1969	7.50	15.00	30.00
T-131	Concerto for Group and Orchestra	1970	75.00	150.00	300.00
WARNER BROS.					
WS 1860	Concerto for Group and Orchestra	1970	3.00	6.00	12.00
WS 1877	Deep Purple in Rock	1970	3.00	6.00	12.00
BS 2564	Fireball	1971	3.00	6.00	12.00
BS 2607	Machine Head	1972	3.00	6.00	12.00
—Original copies have green "WB" labels					
BS 2607	Machine Head	1973	2.50	5.00	10.00
—"Burbank" labels					
BS4 2607 [Q]	Machine Head	1974	6.25	12.50	25.00
2LS 2644 [(2)]	(Purple Passages)	1972	3.75	7.50	15.00
BS 2678	Who Do We Think We Are!	1973	3.00	6.00	12.00
—Original copies have green "WB" labels					
BS 2678	Who Do We Think We Are!	1973	2.50	5.00	10.00
—"Burbank" labels					
2WS 2701 [(2)]	Made in Japan	1973	3.75	7.50	15.00
2WS 2701 [(2)]	Made in Japan	1979	2.00	6.00	12.00
—White labels					
BS 2766	Burn	1974	2.50	5.00	10.00
BSK 3100	Machine Head	1976	2.00	4.00	8.00
WARNER BROS./PURPLE					
PR4 2832 [Q]	Stormbringer	1974	6.25	12.50	25.00
PRK 2832	Stormbringer	1974	2.50	5.00	10.00
PRK 2895	Come Taste the Band	1975	2.50	5.00	10.00
PRK 2995	Made in Europe	1976	2.50	5.00	10.00
PRK 3223	When We Rock, We Rock, and When We Roll, We Roll	1978	2.50	5.00	10.00
PRK 3486	Deepest Purple: The Best of Deep Purple	1980	2.50	5.00	10.00

DEEP SIX, THE

Number	Title (A Side/B Side)	Yr	VG	VG+	NM
45s					
LIBERTY					
55838	Rising Sun/Strolling Blues	1965	2.00	4.00	8.00
55858	I Wanna Shout/Things We Say	1966	2.00	4.00	8.00
55882	When Morning Breaks/Counting	1966	2.00	4.00	8.00
55901	Why Say Goodbye/What Would You Wish from the Golden Fish	1966	2.00	4.00	8.00
55926	Image of a Girl/C'mon Baby	1966	2.00	4.00	8.00
Albums					
LIBERTY					
LRP-3475 [M]	The Deep Six	1966	3.75	7.50	15.00
LST-7475 [S]	The Deep Six	1966	5.00	10.00	20.00

DEERFIELD

Number	Title (A Side/B Side)	Yr	VG	VG+	NM
Albums					
FLAT ROCK					
FRS-1	Nil Desperandum	1971	30.00	60.00	120.00

DEFENDERS, THE

Number	Title (A Side/B Side)	Yr	VG	VG+	NM
45s					
PARKWAY					
926	Island of Love/I Laughed So Hard	1964	2.50	5.00	10.00

DEFRANCO FAMILY, THE

Number	Title (A Side/B Side)	Yr	VG	VG+	NM
45s					
20TH CENTURY					
2030	Heartbeat — It's a Lovebeat/Sweet, Sweet Loretta	1973	—	2.00	4.00
2030 [PS]	Heartbeat — It's a Lovebeat/Sweet, Sweet Loretta	1973	—	3.00	6.00
2070	Abra-Ca-Dabra/Some Kind a' Love	1973	—	2.00	4.00
2070 [PS]	Abra-Ca-Dabra/Some Kind a' Love	1973	—	3.00	6.00
2088	Save the Last Dance for Me/Because We Both Are Young	1974	—	2.00	4.00
2088 [PS]	Save the Last Dance for Me/Because We Both Are Young	1974	—	3.00	6.00
2128	Baby Blue/Write Me a Letter	1974	—	2.00	4.00
2214	We Belong Together/Time Enough for Love	1975	2.00	4.00	8.00
Albums					
20TH CENTURY					
T-422	Heartbeat, It's a Lovebeat	1973	2.50	5.00	10.00
T-441	Save the Last Dance for Me	1974	2.50	5.00	10.00

DEJOHN SISTERS, THE

Number	Title (A Side/B Side)	Yr	VG	VG+	NM
45s					
COLUMBIA					
40799	Mah Little Baby/Mu-Cha-Cha	1956	3.75	7.50	15.00
40843	Don't Promise Me (The Can Can Song)/He's Got Time	1957	3.00	6.00	12.00
EPIC					
9009	Should I Run/All Present But One	1953	3.75	7.50	15.00
9031	I Took Him from You/Juke-Box Polka	1954	3.75	7.50	15.00
9055	A Kiss and a Rose/Crazy Song of India	1954	3.75	7.50	15.00
9080	Lover's Slang/Mandolino	1954	3.75	7.50	15.00
9085	(My Baby Don't Love Me) No More/Theresa	1954	3.75	7.50	15.00
9097	D'Ja Hear What I Say/A Present for Bob	1955	3.00	6.00	12.00
9108	He Loves Me/Pass the Plate of Happiness Around	1955	3.00	6.00	12.00
9124	(Love Is) The Tender Trap/I'm Learning the Charleston	1955	—	—	—
—Canceled					
9131	C'est La Vie/Uninvited Love	1955	3.00	6.00	12.00
9133	The Only Thing I Want for Christmas/That's How Santa Claus Will Look This Year	1955	3.75	7.50	15.00
9145	Hotta Chocolotta/The Man with the Blue Guitar	1956	3.00	6.00	12.00
9172	Big D/In My Innocence	1956	3.00	6.00	12.00
MERCURY					
71131	Where Would I Be/Who Am I	1957	2.50	5.00	10.00
71203	Absence Makes the Heart Grow Fonder/That's My Weakness Now	1957	2.50	5.00	10.00
OKEH					
6989	The Angel Passed By/Never Since Then	1953	5.00	10.00	20.00
SUNBEAM					
106	Straighten Up and Fly Right/Wrong Guy	1958	2.50	5.00	10.00
116	Do-Die/Wedding Postponed	1958	2.50	5.00	10.00
124	Watermelon Heart/Sorry for Myself	1959	2.50	5.00	10.00
126	Hoppity Moe Joe/Don't Forget to Remember	1959	2.50	5.00	10.00
UNITED ARTISTS					
213	Be Anything (But Be Mine)/Yes Indeed	1960	2.00	4.00	8.00
Albums					
EPIC					
LN 1116 [M]	The DeJohn Sisters	195?	7.50	15.00	30.00
UNITED ARTISTS					
UAL-3103 [M]	Yes Indeed	1960	5.00	10.00	20.00
UAS-6103 [S]	Yes Indeed	1960	6.25	12.50	25.00

DEKKER, DESMOND, AND THE ACES

Number	Title (A Side/B Side)	Yr	VG	VG+	NM
45s					
UNI					
55129	Israelites/My Precious World	1969	—	3.00	6.00
55150	It Mek/Problems	1969	—	3.00	6.00
55261	You Can Get It If You Really Want It/ Perseverance	1970	—	3.00	6.00
Albums					
BULLDOG					
1037	The Israelites	198?	2.50	5.00	10.00
UNI					
73059	Israelites	1969	7.50	15.00	30.00

DEL-AIRES, THE

Number	Title (A Side/B Side)	Yr	VG	VG+	NM
45s					
CORAL					
62370	Elaine/Just Wigglin' and a-Wobblin'	1963	10.00	20.00	40.00
62404	The Drag/My Funny Valentine	1964	10.00	20.00	40.00
—As "Ronnie and the Del-Aires"					
62419	Arlene/I'm Yours Baby	1964	17.50	35.00	70.00

DEL AND THE ESCORTS

Number	Title (A Side/B Side)	Yr	VG	VG+	NM
45s					
ROME					
103	Baby Doll/Someone to Watch Over Me	1961	12.50	25.00	50.00
SYMBOL					
913	You Don't Love Me/Skokiian	1960	—	—	—
—Unreleased?					
TAURUS					
350/1	Happy/You're for Me (And I'm for You)	1961	7.50	15.00	30.00

DEL-PHIS, THE

Early incarnation of MARTHA AND THE VANDELLAS.

Number	Title (A Side/B Side)	Yr	VG	VG+	NM
45s					
CHECKMATE					
1005	I'll Let You Know/It Takes Two	1961	50.00	100.00	200.00

DEL RAYS, THE

Number	Title (A Side/B Side)	Yr	VG	VG+	NM
45s					
CORD					
1001	Our Love Is True/One Kiss, One Smile and a Dream	1958	1000.	2000.	4000.
MOON					
110	Have a Heart/Around the Corner	1959	75.00	150.00	300.00
WARNER BROS.					
5022	My Darling/The One I Adore	1958	20.00	40.00	80.00

DEL-RHYTHMETTES

Number	Title (A Side/B Side)	Yr	VG	VG+	NM
45s					
JVB					
5000	Chic-a-Boomer/I Need Your Love	1959	15.00	30.00	60.00

DEL RIOS, THE

Probably more than one group.

45s

Number	Title (A Side/B Side)	Yr	VG	VG+	NM
BET-T					
7001	Heavenly Angel/Dangerous Lover	1962	300.00	600.00	1200.
METEOR					
5038	Lizzie/Alone on a Rainy Night	1956	200.00	400.00	800.00
NEPTUNE					
108	Wait Wait Wait/I'm Crying	1959	15.00	30.00	60.00
RUST					
5066	Valerie/Mystery	1963	15.00	30.00	60.00
STAX					
125	There's a Love/Just Across the Street	1962	12.50	25.00	50.00

DEL SATINS

45s

Number	Title (A Side/B Side)	Yr	VG	VG+	NM
B.T. PUPPY					
506	Hang Around/Candy Apple 'Vette	1965	3.75	7.50	15.00
509	Sweets for My Sweet/A Girl Named Arlene	1965	7.50	15.00	30.00
514	Relief/Throwaway Song	1966	3.75	7.50	15.00
563	I'll Do My Crying Tomorrow/A Girl Named Arlene	1970	3.00	6.00	12.00
COLUMBIA					
42802	Feelin' No Pain/Who Cares	1963	6.25	12.50	25.00
42802 [PS]	Feelin' No Pain/Who Cares	1963	25.00	50.00	100.00
DIAMOND					
216	A Little Rain Must Fall/Love, Hate, Revenge (If I Want You to Cry)	1967	3.75	7.50	15.00
END					
1096	I'll Pray for You/I Remember the Night	1961	50.00	100.00	200.00
LAURIE					
3132	Teardrops Follow Me/Best Wishes, Good Luck, Goodbye	1962	6.25	12.50	25.00
3149	Ballad of a Deejay/Does My Love Stand a Chance	1962	6.25	12.50	25.00
MALA					
475	Believe in Me/Two Broken Hearts	1964	5.00	10.00	20.00
WIN					
702	Counting Teardrops/Remember	1961	40.00	80.00	120.00
—Black label					
702	Counting Teardrops/Remember	1961	15.00	30.00	60.00
—Orange label					

Albums

Number	Title (A Side/B Side)	Yr	VG	VG+	NM
B.T. PUPPY					
BTS-1019	Out to Lunch	1972	75.00	150.00	300.00

DEL-VETTS, THE

45s

Number	Title (A Side/B Side)	Yr	VG	VG+	NM
DUNWICH					
125	Last Time Around/Everytime	1966	5.00	10.00	20.00
142	I Call My Baby STP/That's the Way It Is	1966	5.00	10.00	20.00
142 [PS]	I Call My Baby STP/That's the Way It Is	1966	7.50	15.00	30.00
—Some sleeves contain an STP decal.					
SEEBERG					
3018 [M]	Ram Charger/Little Latin Lupe Lu	1965	7.50	15.00	30.00
3018 [S]	Ram Charger/Little Latin Lupe Lu	1965	10.00	20.00	40.00
—Some copies were pressed in stereo. We don't know if it's marked on the label or trail-off wax or if it must be played to identify.					

7-Inch Extended Plays

Number	Title (A Side/B Side)	Yr	VG	VG+	NM
SUNDAZED					
SEP 124	Last Time Around/Everytime//I Call My Baby STP/That's the Way It Is	1997	—	—	3.00
—Gold vinyl					
SEP 124 [PS]	The Del-Vetts	1997	—	—	3.00

DEL VIKINGS, THE

Usually considered to be one group, but actually three: Two of them splintered from the original group, one featuring Kripp Johnson, the other featuring Gus Backus. For convenience's sake, all are listed together.

45s

Number	Title (A Side/B Side)	Yr	VG	VG+	NM
ABC-PARAMOUNT					
10208	I'll Never Stop Crying/Bring Back Your Heart	1961	6.25	12.50	25.00
10248	I Hear Bells (Wedding Bells)/Don't Get Slick on Me	1961	12.50	25.00	50.00
10278	Kiss Me/Face the Music	1961	6.25	12.50	25.00
10304	Big Silence/One More River to Cross	1962	6.25	12.50	25.00
10341	Confession of Love/Kilimanjaro	1962	6.25	12.50	25.00
10385	An Angel Up in Heaven/Fishing Chant	1962	12.50	25.00	50.00
10425	Too Many Miles/Sorcerer's Apprentice	1963	6.25	12.50	25.00
ALPINE					
66	Pistol Packin' Mama/The Sun	1960	20.00	40.00	80.00
66 [PS]	Pistol Packin' Mama/The Sun	1960	25.00	50.00	100.00
BIM BAM BOOM					
111	Cold Feet/A Little Man Cried	1972	—	2.50	5.00
113	Watching the Moon/You Say You Love Me	1972	—	2.50	5.00
115	I'm Spinning/Girl Girl	1972	—	2.50	5.00
DOT					
15538	Come Go with Me/How Can I Find True Love	1957	7.50	15.00	30.00
15571	What Made Maggie Run/Little Billy Boy	1957	7.50	15.00	30.00
15592	Whispering Bells/Don't Be a Fool	1957	7.50	15.00	30.00
15636	I'm Spinning/When I Come Home	1957	7.50	15.00	30.00
—As "Kripp Johnson with the Dell-Vikings"					
16092	Come Go with Me/How Can I Find True Love	1960	5.00	10.00	20.00
16236	Come Go with Me/Whispering Bells	1961	5.00	10.00	20.00
16248	I Hear Bells (Wedding Bells)/Don't Get Slick on Me	1961	5.00	10.00	20.00
DRC					
101	Can't You See/Oh I	196?	10.00	20.00	40.00
FEE BEE					
173	Welfare Blues/Hollywood and Vine	1977	—	2.50	5.00
205	Come Go with Me/How Can I Find True Love	1957	125.00	250.00	500.00
—Orange label, bee on top					
205	Come Go with Me/How Can I Find True Love	1957	62.50	125.00	250.00
—Orange label, one side has bee, the other side doesn't					
205	Come Go with Me/How Can I Find True Love	1961	7.50	15.00	30.00
—Orange label, no bee					
205	Come Go with Me/Whispering Bells	1964	5.00	10.00	20.00
206	Down in Bermuda/Maggie	1964	20.00	40.00	80.00
210	What Made Maggie Run/Uh Uh Baby	1957	20.00	40.00	80.00
210	What Made Maggie Run/When I Come Home	1957	40.00	80.00	120.00
210	What Made Maggie Run/Down by the Stream	1964	7.50	15.00	30.00
214	Whispering Bells/Don't Be a Fool	1957	100.00	200.00	400.00
218	I'm Spinning/You Say You Love Me	1957	30.00	60.00	120.00
—Bee on label					
218	I'm Spinning/You Say You Love Me	1964	7.50	15.00	30.00
—No bee on label					
221	Willette/Woke Up This Morning	1958	25.00	50.00	100.00
221	Willette/I Want to Marry You	1958	20.00	40.00	80.00
227	Tell Me/Finger Poppin' Woman	1959	20.00	40.00	80.00
902	True Love/Baby, Let Me Know	1964	7.50	15.00	30.00
—As "The Original Dell Vikings"					
GATEWAY					
743	We Three/I've Got to Know	1964	7.50	15.00	30.00
JOJO					
108	Keep On Walkin'/My Body, Your Shadow	1976	—	2.50	5.00
LUNIVERSE					
106	Somewhere Over the Rainbow/Hey, Senorita	1957	25.00	50.00	100.00
110	Yours/Heaven and Paradise	1958	5.00	10.00	20.00
113	In the Still of the Night/The White Cliffs of Dover	1958	5.00	10.00	20.00
114	There I Go/Girl Girl	1958	5.00	10.00	20.00
—The above three Luniverse 45s are bootlegs, but they perversely do have collector's value!					
MERCURY					
71132	Cool Shake/Jitterbug Mary	1957	7.50	15.00	30.00
71180	Come Along with Me/Whatcha Gonna Lose	1957	7.50	15.00	30.00
71198	I'm Spinning/When I Come Home	1957	7.50	15.00	30.00
71241	Snowbound/Your Book of Life	1957	7.50	15.00	30.00
71266	The Voodoo Man/Can't Wait	1958	7.50	15.00	30.00
71345	You Cheated/Pretty Little Things Called Girls	1958	7.50	15.00	30.00
—Black label					
71345	You Cheated/Pretty Little Things Called Girls	1958	10.00	20.00	40.00
—Blue label					
71390	How Could You/Flat Tire	1958	7.50	15.00	30.00
SCEPTER					
12367	Come Go with Me/When You're Asleep	1973	—	2.50	5.00
SHIP					
214	Sunday Kind of Love/Over the Rainbow	197?	—	2.00	4.00

7-Inch Extended Plays

Number	Title (A Side/B Side)	Yr	VG	VG+	NM
DOT					
DEP-1058	(contents unknown)	1957	25.00	50.00	100.00
DEP-1058 [PS]	Come Go with Us	1957	50.00	100.00	200.00
MERCURY					
EP 1-3359	Come Along with Me/A Sunday Kind of Love//(There'll Be Blue Birds Over) The White Cliffs of Dover/Now Is the Hour	1957	25.00	50.00	100.00
EP 1-3359 [PS]	They Sing — They Swing, Vol. 1	1957	37.50	75.00	150.00
EP 1-3362	(contents unknown)	1957	25.00	50.00	100.00
EP 1-3362 [PS]	They Sing — They Swing, Vol. 2	1957	37.50	75.00	150.00
EP 1-3363	(contents unknown)	1957	25.00	50.00	100.00
EP 1-3363 [PS]	They Sing — They Swing, Vol. 3	1957	37.50	75.00	150.00

Albums

Number	Title (A Side/B Side)	Yr	VG	VG+	NM
COLLECTABLES					
COL-5010	The Best of the Dell-Vikings	198?	3.00	6.00	12.00
DOT					
DLP-3685 [M]	Come Go with Me	1966	50.00	100.00	200.00
DLP-25685 [R]	Come Go with Me	1966	37.50	75.00	150.00
LUNIVERSE					
LP-1000 [M]	Come Go with the Del Vikings	1957	125.00	250.00	500.00
—Eight tracks, cover is composed of slicks. Counterfeits have more tracks and a preprinted cover (not slicks)					
MERCURY					
MG-20314 [M]	They Sing — They Swing	1957	75.00	150.00	300.00
MG-20353 [M]	A Swinging, Singing Record Session	1958	50.00	100.00	200.00

DEL VIKINGS, THE / THE SONNETS

Albums

Number	Title (A Side/B Side)	Yr	VG	VG+	NM
CROWN					
CLP-5368 [M]	The Del Vikings and the Sonnets	1963	10.00	20.00	40.00

DEL-VUES, THE

45s

Number	Title (A Side/B Side)	Yr	VG	VG+	NM
U-TOWN					
8008	After New Year's/My Confession	195?	150.00	300.00	600.00

DELACARDOS, THE (1)

45s

Number	Title (A Side/B Side)	Yr	VG	VG+	NM
ELGEY					
1001	A Letter to a School Girl/I'll Never Let You Down	1959	12.50	25.00	50.00
SHELL					
308	Dream Girl/I Just Want to Know	1961	5.00	10.00	20.00
311	Love Is the Greatest Thing/Girl-Girl	1962	5.00	10.00	20.00
UNITED ARTISTS					
276	I Got It/Thing-A-Ma-Jig	1960	3.75	7.50	15.00
310	Hold Back the Tears/Mr. Dillon	1961	5.00	10.00	20.00

DELACARDOS, THE (2)

45s

Number	Title (A Side/B Side)	Yr	VG	VG+	NM
ATLANTIC					
2368	Got No One/She's the One I Love	1966	2.50	5.00	10.00
2389	I Know I'm Not Much/You Don't Have to See Me	1967	2.50	5.00	10.00
2419	They Put a Spell on You/A Fool for You	1967	2.50	5.00	10.00

DELACARDOS, THE (U)

These may be group (1) or (2), or they may be a completely different group or groups.

45s

Number	Title (A Side/B Side)	Yr	VG	VG+	NM
DIMENSION					
1040	Forget About the Guy/Dance, Gypsy, Dance	1964	5.00	10.00	20.00
IMPERIAL					
5992	On the Beach/Everybody's Rockin'	1963	3.75	7.50	15.00

DELANCEYS, THE

45s

Number	Title (A Side/B Side)	Yr	VG	VG+	NM
ABC-PARAMOUNT					
10353	High Voltage/The Scratch	1962	6.25	12.50	25.00

DELANEY AND BONNIE

Also see BONNIE BRAMLETT; DELANEY BRAMLETT.

45s

Number	Title (A Side/B Side)	Yr	VG	VG+	NM
ATCO					
6725	Groupie (Superstar)/Comin' Home	1969	2.00	4.00	8.00
6756	Soul Shake/Free the People	1970	2.00	4.00	8.00
6788	Miss Ann/They Call It Rock and Roll Music	1970	2.00	4.00	8.00
6804	Never Ending Song of Love/Don't Deceive Me	1971	2.00	4.00	8.00
6838	Only You Know and I Know/God Knows I Love You	1971	—	3.00	6.00
6866	Sing My Way Home/Move 'Em Out	1972	—	2.50	5.00
6883	Where There's a Will There's a Way/Lonesome and a Long Way from Home	1972	—	2.50	5.00
6904	Sing My Way Home/Will the Circle Be Unbroken	1972	—	2.50	5.00
COLUMBIA					
45608	Country Life/Walk in the River Jordan	1972	—	2.50	5.00
ELEKTRA					
45660	Soldiers of the Cross/Get Ourselves Together	1969	2.50	5.00	10.00
45662	When the Battle Is Over/Get Ourselves Together	1969	2.50	5.00	10.00
GARPAX					
44184	Cherry Pie/Hey Mr. Weatherman	1964	3.75	7.50	15.00
—As "Lani & Boni"					
INDEPENDENCE					
78	You've Lost That Lovin' Feelin'/Don't Let It (Be the Last Time)	1967	3.00	6.00	12.00
STAX					
0003	It's Been a Long Time Coming/We've Just Been Feeling Bad	1968	2.50	5.00	10.00
0057	Hard to Say Goodbye/Just Plain Beautiful	1969	2.50	5.00	10.00

Albums

Number	Title (A Side/B Side)	Yr	VG	VG+	NM
ATCO					
SD 33-326	Delaney & Bonnie & Friends On Tour with Eric Clapton	1970	6.25	12.50	25.00
—Yellow label original					
SD 33-326	Delaney & Bonnie & Friends On Tour with Eric Clapton	197?	2.50	5.00	10.00
—Later pressings on other labels					
33-341 [M]	To Bonnie from Delaney	1970	10.00	20.00	40.00
—White label promo; no stock copies were issued in mono					
SD 33-341 [S]	To Bonnie from Delaney	1970	6.25	12.50	25.00
SD 33-358	Motel Shot	1971	6.25	12.50	25.00
SD 33-383	Country Life	1972	5.00	10.00	20.00
SD 7014	The Best of Delaney and Bonnie	1972	5.00	10.00	20.00
COLUMBIA					
KC 31377	D&B Together	1972	5.00	10.00	20.00
ELEKTRA					
EKS-74039	Accept No Substitute — The Original Delaney & Bonnie & Friends	1969	7.50	15.00	30.00
GNP CRESCENDO					
GNPS-2054	Genesis	1970	5.00	10.00	20.00
STAX					
STS-2026	Home	1969	7.50	15.00	30.00

DELEGATES, THE (1)

Novelty group.

45s

Number	Title (A Side/B Side)	Yr	VG	VG+	NM
MAINSTREAM					
5525	Convention '72/Funky Butt	1972	2.50	5.00	10.00
5525	Convention '72 (same on both sides)	1972	2.00	4.00	8.00
—Stock copy; "Funky Butt" deleted because of retailers' protests to the title					
5530	Richard M. Nixon Faces the Issues (same on both sides)	1972	2.00	4.00	8.00
5530	Richard M. Nixon Faces the Issues/Touzie's Blues	1972	2.50	5.00	10.00

Albums

Number	Title (A Side/B Side)	Yr	VG	VG+	NM
MAINSTREAM					
100	The Delegates	1973	5.00	10.00	20.00

DELEGATES, THE (2)

Jazz group.

DELEGATES, THE (3)

DEE CLARK was a member.

45s

Number	Title (A Side/B Side)	Yr	VG	VG+	NM
VEE JAY					
212	The Convention/Jay's Rock	1956	15.00	30.00	60.00
—B-side by Big Jay McNeely					
243	Mother's Son/I'm Gonna Be Glad	1957	15.00	30.00	60.00

DELFONICS, THE

Also see MAJOR HARRIS.

45s

Number	Title (A Side/B Side)	Yr	VG	VG+	NM
ARISTA					
0308	Don't Throw It All Away/I Don't Care What People Say	1978	—	2.00	4.00
CAMEO					
472	You've Been Untrue/I Was There	1967	3.75	7.50	15.00
MOON SHOT					
6703	He Don't Really Love You/Without You	1967	3.75	7.50	15.00
PHILLY GROOVE					
150	La-La Means I Love You/Can't Get Over Losing You	1968	2.50	5.00	10.00
151	I'm Sorry/You're Gone	1968	2.50	5.00	10.00
152	Break Your Promise/Alfie	1968	2.50	5.00	10.00
154	Ready Or Not Here I Come (Can't Hide from Love)/Somebody Loves You	1968	2.50	5.00	10.00
156	Funny Feeling/My New Love	1969	2.50	5.00	10.00
157	You Got Yours and I'll Get Mine/Loving Him	1969	2.50	5.00	10.00
161	Didn't I (Blow Your Mind This Time)/Down Is Up, Up Is Down	1970	2.50	5.00	10.00
162	Trying to Make a Fool of Me/Baby I Love You	1970	2.50	5.00	10.00
163	When You Get Right Down To It/I Gave to You	1970	2.50	5.00	10.00
166	Over and Over/Hey! Love	1971	2.00	4.00	8.00
169	Walk Right Up to the Sun/Round and Round	1971	2.00	4.00	8.00
172	Tell Me This Is a Dream/I'm a Man	1972	2.00	4.00	8.00
174	Think It Over/I'm a Man	1972	2.00	4.00	8.00
176	I Don't Want to Make You Wait/Baby I Miss You	1973	2.00	4.00	8.00
177	Alfie/Start All Over Again	1973	2.00	4.00	8.00
182	I Told You So/Seventeen and In Love	1973	2.00	4.00	8.00
184	Lying to Myself/Hey Baby	1974	2.00	4.00	8.00

Albums

Number	Title (A Side/B Side)	Yr	VG	VG+	NM
ARISTA					
AL 8333	The Best of the Delfonics	198?	2.50	5.00	10.00
COLLECTABLES					
COL-5109	Golden Classics	198?	2.50	5.00	10.00
KORY					
1002	The Best of the Delfonics	1977	3.00	6.00	12.00
PHILLY GROOVE					
1150	La La Means I Love You	1968	20.00	40.00	80.00
1151	The Sexy Sound of Soul	1969	20.00	40.00	80.00
1152	The Delfonics Super Hits	1969	12.50	25.00	50.00
1153	The Delfonics	1970	12.50	25.00	50.00
1154	Tell Me This Is a Dream	1972	12.50	25.00	50.00
1501	Alive & Kicking	1974	12.50	25.00	50.00
POOGIE					
121680	The Delfonics Return	1981	3.00	6.00	12.00

DELICATES, THE

More than one group?

45s

Number	Title (A Side/B Side)	Yr	VG	VG+	NM
CELESTE					
676	My Pillow/I Played 1,2,3,4	1961	7.50	15.00	30.00
CHALLENGE					
59232	I've Been Hurt/Come On Everybody	1964	3.75	7.50	15.00
59267	I Want to Get Married/Home from Camp	1965	3.75	7.50	15.00
59304	Stop Shovin' Me Around/Comin' Down with Love	1965	3.75	7.50	15.00
DEE DEE					
677	My Pillow/I Played 1,2,3,4	1961	7.50	15.00	30.00
ROULETTE					
4321	Little Ship/Not Tomorrow	1961	5.00	10.00	20.00
4360	Little Boy of Mine/Dickie Went and Did It	1961	5.00	10.00	20.00
4387	I Don't Know Why (I Just Do)/Strange Love	1961	5.00	10.00	20.00
UNART					
2017	Black and White Thunderbird/Ronnie Is My Lover	1959	6.25	12.50	25.00
2024	Ringa Ding/Meusurry	1959	6.25	12.50	25.00
UNITED ARTISTS					
210	Flip Flip/Your Happiest Years	1960	5.00	10.00	20.00
228	The Kiss/Too Young to Date	1960	5.00	10.00	20.00

DELL, DICKEY, AND THE BING BONGS

45s

Number	Title (A Side/B Side)	Yr	VG	VG+	NM
DRAGON					
10205	Ding-a-Ling-a-Ling-Ding-Dong/The Cling	1958	37.50	75.00	150.00

DELL, EVELYN, AND THE VIBRATIONS

45s

Number	Title (A Side/B Side)	Yr	VG	VG+	NM
ABC-PARAMOUNT					
10218	Sincerely/Please Tell Me Why	1961	6.25	12.50	25.00

DELL, LENNY, AND THE DEMENSIONS

See THE DEMENSIONS.

DELL, RICHIE

45s

Number	Title (A Side/B Side)	Yr	VG	VG+	NM
KING					
5888	Come On Let's Sing/King Lover	1964	5.00	10.00	20.00

DELL, TONY

45s

Number	Title (A Side/B Side)	Yr	VG	VG+	NM
KING					
5766	My Girl/Magic Wand	1963	12.50	25.00	50.00

DELL-COEDS, THE

45s

Number	Title (A Side/B Side)	Yr	VG	VG+	NM
DOT					
16314	Hey Mr. Banjo/Love in Return	1962	3.00	6.00	12.00

DELL VIKINGS, THE

See THE DEL-VIKINGS.

DELLS, THE

45s

Number	Title (A Side/B Side)	Yr	VG	VG+	NM
20TH CENTURY					
2463	I Touched a Dream/All About the Paper	1980	—	2.00	4.00
2475	Passionate Breezes/Your Song	1980	—	2.00	4.00
2504	Happy Song/Look at Us Now	1981	—	2.00	4.00
2602	Ain't It a Shame/Stay in My Corner	1982	—	2.00	4.00

Number	Title (A Side/B Side)	Yr	VG	VG+	NM
ABC					
12386	Super Woman/My Life Is So Wonderful	1978	—	2.50	5.00
12422	(I Wanna) Testify/Don't Save Me	1978	—	2.50	5.00
12422	(I Wanna) Testify/Drowning for Your Love	1978	—	2.50	5.00
12440	(You Bring Out) The Best in Me/Wrapped Up Tight	1978	—	2.50	5.00
ARGO					
5415	God Bless the Child/I'm Going Home	1962	3.00	6.00	12.00
5428	The (Bossa Nova) Bird/Eternally	1962	3.00	6.00	12.00
5442	Hi Diddle Dee Dum Dum (It's a Good Feelin')/If It Ain't One Thing, It's Another	1963	3.00	6.00	12.00
5456	After You/Goodbye Mary Ann	1963	3.00	6.00	12.00
CADET					
5538	Thinkin' About You/The Change We Go Thru (For Love)	1966	—	3.00	6.00
5551	Over Again/Run for Cover	1967	—	3.00	6.00
5563	You Belong to Someone Else/Inspiration	1967	—	3.00	6.00
5574	O-O, I Love You/There Is	1967	—	3.00	6.00
5590	There Is/Show Me	1968	2.00	4.00	8.00
5599	Wear it On Our Face/Please Don't Change Me Now	1968	—	3.00	6.00
5612	Stay in My Corner/Love Is So Simple	1969	—	3.00	6.00
5621	Always Together/I Want My Mama	1968	—	3.00	6.00
5631	Does Anybody Know I'm Here/Make Sure (You Have Somebody to Love You)	1968	—	3.00	6.00
5636	I Can't Do Enough/Hallways of My Mind	1969	—	3.00	6.00
5641	I Can Sing a Rainbow-Love Is Blue/Hallelujah Baby	1969	—	3.00	6.00
5649	Oh What a Night/Believe Me	1969	—	3.00	6.00
5658	On the Dock of the Bay/When I'm in Your Arms	1969	—	3.00	6.00
5663	Oh What a Day/The Change We Go Thru (For Love)	1970	—	3.00	6.00
5667	Open Up My Heart/Nadine	1970	—	3.00	6.00
5672	Long Lonely Nights/A Little Understanding	1970	—	3.00	6.00
5679	The Glory of Love/A Whiter Shade of Pale	1970	—	3.00	6.00
5683	The Love We Had (Stays on My Mind)/Freedom Means	1971	—	3.00	6.00
5689	It's All Up to You/Oh, My Dear	1972	—	3.00	6.00
5691	Walk On By/This Guy's in Love with You	1972	—	3.00	6.00
5694	Just As Long As We're in Love/I'd Rather Be with You	1972	—	3.00	6.00
5696	Give Your Baby a Standing Ovation/Closer	1973	—	3.00	6.00
5698	My Pretending Days Are Over/Let's Make It Last	1973	—	3.00	6.00
5700	I Miss You/Don't Make Me a Storyteller	1973	—	3.00	6.00
5702	I Wish It Was Me You Loved/Two Together Is Better Than One	1974	—	3.00	6.00
5703	Bring Back the Love of Yesterday/Learning to Love You Was Easy (It's So Hard Trying to Get Over You)	1974	—	3.00	6.00
5703	Sweeter as the Days Go By/Learning to Love You Was Easy (It's So Hard Trying to Get Over You)	1974	—	3.00	6.00
—A-side is the same song with a new title					
5707	The Glory of Love/You're the Greatest	1975	—	3.00	6.00
5711	We Got to Get Our Thing Together/The Power of Love	1975	2.00	4.00	8.00
CHECKER					
794	Darling I Know/Christine	1954	400.00	800.00	1200.
—As "The El Rays"					
MCA					
41051	Plastic People/What I Could	1979	—	2.50	5.00
MERCURY					
73723	We Got to Get Our Thing Together/Reminiscing	1975	—	2.50	5.00
73759	The Power of Love/Gotta Get Home to My Baby	1976	—	2.50	5.00
73807	Slow Motion/Ain't No Black and White in Music	1976	—	2.50	5.00
73842	No Way Back/Too Late for Love	1976	—	2.50	5.00
73901	Betcha Never Been Loved (Like This Before)/Get On Down	1977	—	2.50	5.00
73909	Our Love/Could It Be	1977	—	2.50	5.00
73977	Private Property/Teaser	1977	—	2.50	5.00
PHILCO-FORD					
HP-32	There Is/Show Me	1968	5.00	10.00	20.00
—4-inch plastic "Hip Pocket Record" with color sleeve					
PRIVATE I					
04343	Don't Want Nobody/You Can't Just Walk Away	1984	—	2.00	4.00
04448	One Step Closer/Come On Back to Me	1984	—	2.00	4.00
04540	Love On/Don't Want Nobody	1984	—	2.00	4.00
SKYLARK					
558	I Can't Help Myself/She's Just an Angel	198?	—	2.00	4.00
581	Someone to Call Me Darling/Now I Pray	198?	—	2.00	4.00
VEE JAY					
134	Tell the World/Blues at Three	1955	2500.	3750.	5000.
—Red vinyl					
134	Tell the World/Blues at Three	1955	500.00	1000.	2000.
166	Dreams of Contentment/Zing, Zing, Zing	1955	50.00	100.00	200.00
204	Oh What a Nite/Jo-Jo	1956	30.00	60.00	120.00
230	Movin' On/I Wanna Go Home	1956	10.00	20.00	40.00
236	Why Do You Have to Go/Dance, Dance, Dance	1957	10.00	20.00	40.00
251	A Distant Love/O-Bop She-Bop	1957	10.00	20.00	40.00
258	Pain in My Heart/Time Makes You Change	1957	10.00	20.00	40.00
274	The Springer/What You Say Baby	1958	7.50	15.00	30.00
292	I'm Calling/Jeepers Creepers	1958	7.50	15.00	30.00
300	Wedding Day/My Best Girl	1958	25.00	50.00	100.00
324	Dry Your Eyes/Baby Open Up Your Heart	1959	10.00	20.00	40.00
338	Oh What a Nite/I Wanna Go Home	1960	5.00	10.00	20.00
376	Hold On to What You've Got/Swingin' Teens	1961	5.00	10.00	20.00
595	Shy Girl/What Do We Prove	1964	3.00	6.00	12.00
615	Wait Till Tomorrow/Oh What a Good Night	1964	3.00	6.00	12.00
674	Stay in My Corner/It's Not Unusual	1965	3.00	6.00	12.00
712	Poor Little Boy/Hey Sugar (Don't Get Serious)	1966	3.00	6.00	12.00
VETERAN					
7-101	Thought of You Just a Little Too Much/(B-side unknown)	1989	—	2.50	5.00

Albums

Number	Title (A Side/B Side)	Yr	VG	VG+	NM
20TH CENTURY					
T-618	I Touched a Dream	1980	3.00	6.00	12.00
T-633	Whatever Turns You On	1981	3.00	6.00	12.00
ABC					
AA-1100	New Beginnings	1978	3.00	6.00	12.00
AA-1113	Face to Face	1978	3.00	6.00	12.00
BUDDAH					
BDS-5053	The Dells	1969	3.75	7.50	15.00
CADET					
LPS-804	There Is	1968	12.50	25.00	50.00
LPS-822	The Dells Musical Menu/Always Together	1969	12.50	25.00	50.00
LPS-824	The Dells Greatest Hits	1969	12.50	25.00	50.00
LPS-829	Love Is Blue	1969	12.50	25.00	50.00
LPS-837	Like It Is, Like It Was	1970	12.50	25.00	50.00
50004	Freedom Means	1971	6.25	12.50	25.00
50017	The Dells Sing Dionne Warwicke's Greatest Hits	1972	6.25	12.50	25.00
50021	Sweet As Funk Can Be	1972	6.25	12.50	25.00
50037	Give Your Baby a Standing Ovation	1973	6.25	12.50	25.00
50046	The Dells	1973	6.25	12.50	25.00
60030	The Mighty Mighty Dells	1974	6.25	12.50	25.00
60036	The Dells' Greatest Hits, Vol. 2	1975	5.00	10.00	20.00
CHESS					
CH-9103	The Dells	198?	2.50	5.00	10.00
—Reissue					
CH-9288	There Is	1989	2.50	5.00	10.00
—Reissue of Cadet 804					
LOST-NITE					
LLP-21 [10]	The Dells	1981	3.75	7.50	15.00
—Red vinyl, generic red cover					
MERCURY					
SRM-1-1059	We Got to Get Our Thing Together	1975	3.75	7.50	15.00
SRM-1-1084	No Way Back	1976	3.75	7.50	15.00
SRM-1-1145	They Said It Couldn't Be Done	1977	3.75	7.50	15.00
SRM-1-3711	Love Connection	1977	3.75	7.50	15.00
PRIVATE I					
BFZ 39309	One Step Closer	1984	2.50	5.00	10.00
SOLID SMOKE					
8029	Breezy Ballads and Tender Tunes: The Best of the Early Years (1955-65)	1984	2.50	5.00	10.00
UPFRONT					
UPF-105	Stay In My Corner	1968	3.75	7.50	15.00
URGENT					
URG-4108	The Second Time	1991	3.00	6.00	12.00
VEE JAY					
LP 1010 [M]	Oh What a Nite	1959	200.00	400.00	800.00
—Maroon label					
LP 1010 [M]	Oh What a Nite	1961	75.00	150.00	300.00
—Black label with colorband					
VJLP-1010	Oh What a Nite	198?	2.50	5.00	10.00
—Late-80s reissue on reactivated Vee Jay label. "Trade Mark Reg." on label.					
LP 1141 [M]	It's Not Unusual	1965	25.00	50.00	100.00
LPS 1141 [S]	It's Not Unusual	1965	37.50	75.00	150.00
VJ INTERNATIONAL					
7305	The Dells In Concert	197?	3.00	6.00	12.00
ZOO					
11023	I Salute You	1992	3.75	7.50	15.00

DELLS, THE, AND THE DRAMATICS

Also see each artist's individual listings.

45s

Number	Title (A Side/B Side)	Yr	VG	VG+	NM
CADET					
5710	Love Is Missing from Our Lives/I'm in Love	1975	—	3.00	6.00

Albums

Number	Title (A Side/B Side)	Yr	VG	VG+	NM
CADET					
60027	The Dells Vs. the Dramatics	1974	6.25	12.50	25.00

DELLTONES, THE

45s

Number	Title (A Side/B Side)	Yr	VG	VG+	NM
BATON					
212	Don't Be Long/Baby Say You Love Me	1955	7.50	15.00	30.00
223	My Special Love/Believe It	1956	7.50	15.00	30.00
BRUNSWICK					
84015	My Heart's on Fire/Yours Alone	1953	50.00	100.00	200.00
RAINBOW					
244	I'm Not in Love with You/Little Short Daddy	1954	25.00	50.00	100.00

DELMIRAS, THE

45s

Number	Title (A Side/B Side)	Yr	VG	VG+	NM
DADE					
1821	Dry Your Eyes/The Big Sound	1961	75.00	150.00	300.00

DELMONICOS, THE

45s

Number	Title (A Side/B Side)	Yr	VG	VG+	NM
MUSICTONE					
6122	World's Biggest Fool/Until You	1963	7.50	15.00	30.00

DELRONS, THE

See REPARATA AND THE DELRONS.

DELROYS, THE

45s

Number	Title (A Side/B Side)	Yr	VG	VG+	NM
APOLLO					
514	Bermuda Shorts/Time	1957	6.25	12.50	25.00

DELTAIRS, THE

45s

Number	Title (A Side/B Side)	Yr	VG	VG+	NM
FELSTED					
8525	Who Would Have Thought It/You Won't Be Satisfied	1959	7.50	15.00	30.00

Number	Title (A Side/B Side)	Yr	VG	VG+	NM
IVY					
101	Lullaby of the Bells/It's Only You Dear	1957	37.50	75.00	150.00
—Yellow label					
101	Lullaby of the Bells/It's Only You Dear	1958	7.50	15.00	30.00
105	Standing at the Altar/I Might Like It	1958	7.50	15.00	30.00

DELTAS, THE

More than one group?

Number	Title (A Side/B Side)	Yr	VG	VG+	NM
45s					
CAMBRIDGE					
124	Goodnight My Love/Give My Love a Chance	1962	10.00	20.00	40.00
GONE					
5010	Let Me Share Your Dream/Lamplight	1957	750.00	1500.	3000.
—Black label					
5010	Let Me Share Your Dream/Lamplight	1957	20.00	40.00	80.00
—Multi-color label					
PHILIPS					
40023	My Own True Love/Work Song	1962	5.00	10.00	20.00
40023	My Own True Love/Hold Me, Thrill Me, Kiss Me	1962	3.75	7.50	15.00

DELTONES, THE

Number	Title (A Side/B Side)	Yr	VG	VG+	NM
45s					
JUBILEE					
5374	La La La/Bow-Legged Annie	1959	6.25	12.50	25.00
VEE JAY					
288	I'm Coming Home/Early Morning Rock	1958	10.00	20.00	40.00
303	A Lover's Prayer/First Man to the Moon	1958	10.00	20.00	40.00

DELVETTS, THE

Number	Title (A Side/B Side)	Yr	VG	VG+	NM
45s					
END					
1106	I Want a Boy for Christmas/Repeat After Me	1961	7.50	15.00	30.00
1107	Will You Love Me in Heaven/Repeat After Me	1962	5.00	10.00	20.00

DEMARCO, RALPH

Number	Title (A Side/B Side)	Yr	VG	VG+	NM
45s					
20TH FOX					
309	Keep On Walkin'/Lonely for a Girl	1962	5.00	10.00	20.00
GUARANTEED					
202	More Than Riches/Old Shep	1959	5.00	10.00	20.00
202 [PS]	More Than Riches/Old Shep	1959	10.00	20.00	40.00
SHELLEY					
1011	Donna/For All We Know	1960	10.00	20.00	40.00

DEMENS, THE

Number	Title (A Side/B Side)	Yr	VG	VG+	NM
45s					
TEENAGE					
1006	Take Me As I Am/You Broke My Heart	1958	50.00	100.00	200.00
1007	I'm Not in Love with You/Short Daddy	1958	50.00	100.00	200.00
1008	The Greatest of Them All/Hey Young Girl	1958	50.00	100.00	200.00

DEMENSIONS, THE

Number	Title (A Side/B Side)	Yr	VG	VG+	NM
45s					
CORAL					
62277	Again/Count Your Blessings Instead of Sheep	1961	6.25	12.50	25.00
62293	As Time Goes By/Seven Days a Week	1961	6.25	12.50	25.00
62323	Young at Heart/Your Cheatin' Heart	1962	5.00	10.00	20.00
62344	My Foolish Heart/Just One More Chance	1963	7.50	15.00	30.00
62359	Fly Me to the Moon/You'll Never Know	1963	6.25	12.50	25.00
62382	Just a Shoulder to Cry On/Don't Worry About Bobby	1963	6.25	12.50	25.00
62392	A Little White Gardenia/Don't Cry Pretty Baby	1964	5.00	10.00	20.00
62432	This Time Next Year/My Old Girlfriend	1964	5.00	10.00	20.00
—As "Lenny Dell and the Demensions"					
62444	Once a Day/Ting Along Ting Toy	1965	5.00	10.00	20.00
—As "Lenny Dell and the Demensions"					
65559	Over the Rainbow/Zing Went the Strings of My Heart	1962	5.00	10.00	20.00
65611	As Time Goes By/My Foolish Heart	1967	3.75	7.50	15.00
MOHAWK					
116	Over the Rainbow/Nursery Rhyme Rock	1960	12.50	25.00	50.00
—Maroon label					
116	Over the Rainbow/Nursery Rhyme Rock	1960	7.50	15.00	30.00
—Brown label					
116	Over the Rainbow/Nursery Rhyme Rock	1960	6.25	12.50	25.00
—Red label					
120	Zing Went the Strings of My Heart/Don't Take Your Love from Me	1960	6.25	12.50	25.00
—As "The Dimensions"					
121	God's Christmas/Ave Maria	1960	15.00	30.00	60.00
123	A Tear Fell/Theresa	1961	15.00	30.00	60.00
Albums					
CORAL					
CRL 57430 [M]	My Foolish Heart	1963	37.50	75.00	150.00
CRL 757430 [S]	My Foolish Heart	1963	75.00	150.00	300.00

DEMIAN

Includes members of THE BUBBLE PUPPY.

Number	Title (A Side/B Side)	Yr	VG	VG+	NM
45s					
ABC					
11297	Face the Crowd/Love People	1970	5.00	10.00	20.00
Albums					
ABC					
ABCS-718	Demian	1970	15.00	30.00	60.00

DEMILLES, THE

Number	Title (A Side/B Side)	Yr	VG	VG+	NM
45s					
LAURIE					
3230	Donna Lee/Um Ba Pa	1964	7.50	15.00	30.00
3247	Lazy Love/Cry and Be On Your Way	1964	12.50	25.00	50.00

DEMOLYRS, THE

Number	Title (A Side/B Side)	Yr	VG	VG+	NM
45s					
JASON SCOTT					
7	Rain/Hey Little Rosie	1978	—	3.00	6.00
U.W.R.					
900	Rain/Hey Little Rosie	1964	125.00	250.00	500.00

DEMOTRONS, THE

Number	Title (A Side/B Side)	Yr	VG	VG+	NM
45s					
ATLANTIC					
2589	I Want a Home in the Country/I Don't Want to Play No More	1969	2.50	5.00	10.00
CAMEO					
456	Beg, Borrow and Steal/Midnight in New York	1967	2.50	5.00	10.00
DORSET					
5010	Frisky/Steel Driving Man	196?	5.00	10.00	20.00
ENRICA					
1003	Rock-A-Way Special/Bugle Boy	1959	7.50	15.00	30.00
RADAR					
2615	Hombre/Swinging Soiree	1962	5.00	10.00	20.00
2616	Pretzel Twist/Meet Mister Callaghan	1962	5.00	10.00	20.00
2621	Sticks and Stones/Theme from "Adventures in Paradise"	1962	5.00	10.00	20.00
RUST					
5025	Rockin' with Mother Goose/Home on the Pad	1960	5.00	10.00	20.00
SCEPTER					
12148	Take This Love I Have/Sleep, Sleep, Sleep	1966	3.00	6.00	12.00
12174	Brother Where Are You/Take This Love I Have	1966	3.00	6.00	12.00

DEMURES, THE

Number	Title (A Side/B Side)	Yr	VG	VG+	NM
45s					
BRUNSWICK					
55284	Raining Teardrops/He's Got Your Number	1965	25.00	50.00	100.00

DENBY, JUNIOR

Number	Title (A Side/B Side)	Yr	VG	VG+	NM
45s					
KING					
4717	With This Ring/I'm Still Lonesome	1954	15.00	30.00	60.00
4725	This Fool Has Learned/If You Only Have Faith in Me	1954	15.00	30.00	60.00
5217	With This Ring/I'm Still Lonesome	1959	7.50	15.00	30.00

DENE, TERRY

Number	Title (A Side/B Side)	Yr	VG	VG+	NM
45s					
LONDON					
1802	Stairway of Love/Lover, Lover	1958	3.00	6.00	12.00

DENNIS AND THE EXPLORERS

See THE EXPLORERS.

DENNY, MARTIN

Number	Title (A Side/B Side)	Yr	VG	VG+	NM
45s					
LIBERTY					
55089	Hong Kong Blues/Ah Me Furi	1957	2.50	5.00	10.00
55162	Quiet Village/Llama Serenade	1958	3.00	6.00	12.00
55199	Martinique/Sake Rock	1959	2.50	5.00	10.00
55212	The Enchanted Sea/Stranger in Paradise	1959	2.50	5.00	10.00
55230	Beyond the Reef/Forever	1959	2.50	5.00	10.00
55236	Frankie and Johnny/Banana Choo Choo	1960	2.50	5.00	10.00
55283	Volcano/Sugar Train	1960	2.50	5.00	10.00
55301	My Tane (My Man)/Volcano	1961	2.00	4.00	8.00
55331	Scimitar/My First Romance	1961	2.00	4.00	8.00
55384	Fandango/Bonsoir Dame	1961	2.00	4.00	8.00
55426	Paradise Cove/Secu Secu	1962	2.00	4.00	8.00
55470	A Taste of Honey/Brighter Side	1962	2.00	4.00	8.00
55514	Cast Your Fate to the Wind/Pay Off	1962	2.00	4.00	8.00
55536	Blue Carousel/Anniversary Song	1963	2.00	4.00	8.00
55561	Quiet Village Bossa Nova/Strawberry Tree	1963	2.00	4.00	8.00
55571	More (Theme from Mondo Cane)/O Barquinho (Little Boat)	1963	2.00	4.00	8.00
55622	Theme from The V.I.P.'s/Cousin Ray	1963	2.00	4.00	8.00
55629	Something Latin/Once Is Enough	1963	2.00	4.00	8.00
55655	Sugar Cane/Everything Beautiful Happens	1963	2.00	4.00	8.00
55717	Latin Village/Angelito	1964	2.00	4.00	8.00
55754	Hawaii Tattoo/White Silver Sands	1964	2.00	4.00	8.00
55819	Hawaiian Village/Aloha Oe	1965	2.00	4.00	8.00
55851	Call Me/La Paloma	1965	2.00	4.00	8.00
55928	Tiny Bubbles/Hawaii	1967	—	3.00	6.00
56126	Midnight Cowboy/Quiet Village	1969	—	2.50	5.00
UNITED ARTISTS					
0069	Quiet Village/The Enchanted Sea	1973	—	2.00	4.00
—"Silver Spotlight Series" reissue					
7-Inch Extended Plays					
LIBERTY					
LEP-1-3034	*Quiet Village/Return to Paradise/Stone God/Jungle Fever	1959	2.50	5.00	10.00
LEP-1-3034 [PS]	Exotica Part One	1959	2.50	5.00	10.00
LEP-2-3034	(contents unknown)	1959	2.50	5.00	10.00
LEP-2-3034 [PS]	Exotica Part Two	1959	2.50	5.00	10.00
LEP-3-3034	(contents unknown)	1959	2.50	5.00	10.00
LEP-3-3034 [PS]	Exotica Part Three	1959	2.50	5.00	10.00
Albums					
FIRST AMERICAN					
7743	From Hawaii With Love	1981	2.50	5.00	10.00
LIBERTY					
LM-1009	Exotica Vol. 1	1982	2.00	4.00	8.00
—Reissue of United Artists 1009					
LRP-3034 [M]	Exotica	1957	10.00	20.00	40.00
—Turquoise label					
LRP-3034 [M]	Exotica	1960	6.25	12.50	25.00
—Black rainbow label					

Number	Title (A Side/B Side)	Yr	VG	VG+	NM
LRP-3077 [M]	Exotica, Volume II	1957	7.50	15.00	30.00
—Turquoise label					
LRP-3077 [M]	Exotica, Volume II	1960	5.00	10.00	20.00
—Black rainbow label					
LRP-3081 [M]	Forbidden Island	1958	7.50	15.00	30.00
—Turquoise label; woman in jungle on cover					
LRP-3081 [M]	Forbidden Island	1960	5.00	10.00	20.00
—Black rainbow label; white foil on cover					
LRP-3087 [M]	Primitiva	1958	7.50	15.00	30.00
—Turquoise label					
LRP-3087 [M]	Primitiva	1960	5.00	10.00	20.00
—Black rainbow label					
LRP-3102 [M]	Hypnotique	1958	7.50	15.00	30.00
—Turquoise label					
LRP-3102 [M]	Hypnotique	1960	5.00	10.00	20.00
—Black rainbow label					
LRP-3111 [M]	Afro-Desia	1959	7.50	15.00	30.00
—Turquoise label					
LRP-3111 [M]	Afro-Desia	1960	5.00	10.00	20.00
—Black rainbow label					
LRP-3116 [M]	Exotica, Vol. III	1959	7.50	15.00	30.00
—Turquoise label					
LRP-3116 [M]	Exotica, Vol. III	1960	5.00	10.00	20.00
—Black rainbow label					
LRP-3122 [M]	Quiet Village	1959	7.50	15.00	30.00
—Turquoise label					
LRP-3122 [M]	Quiet Village	1960	5.00	10.00	20.00
—Black rainbow label					
LRP-3141 [M]	The Enchanted Sea	1959	7.50	15.00	30.00
—Turquoise label					
LRP-3141 [M]	The Enchanted Sea	1960	5.00	10.00	20.00
—Black rainbow label					
LRP-3158 [M]	Exotic Sounds from the Silver Screen	1960	5.00	10.00	20.00
LRP-3163 [M]	Exotic Sounds Visit Broadway	1960	5.00	10.00	20.00
LRP-3168 [M]	Exotic Percussion	1961	6.00	10.00	20.00
LRP-3224 [M]	The Exotic Sounds of Martin Denny In Person	1962	3.75	7.50	15.00
LRP-3237 [M]	A Taste of Honey	1962	3.75	7.50	15.00
LRP-3277 [M]	Another Taste of Honey	1963	3.75	7.50	15.00
LRP-3307 [M]	The Versatile Martin Denny	1963	3.75	7.50	15.00
LRP-3328 [M]	A Taste of Hits	1964	3.00	6.00	12.00
LRP-3378 [M]	Latin Village	1964	3.00	6.00	12.00
LRP-3394 [M]	Hawaii Tattoo	1964	3.00	6.00	12.00
LRP-3415 [M]	20 Golden Hawaiian Hits	1965	3.00	6.00	12.00
LRP-3438 [M]	Martin Denny	1965	3.00	6.00	12.00
LRP-3445 [M]	Hawaiian A-Go-Go	1966	3.00	6.00	12.00
LRP-3467 [M]	Golden Greats	1966	3.00	6.00	12.00
LRP-3488 [M]	Hawaii	1967	3.00	6.00	12.00
LRP-3513 [M]	Exotica Classica	1967	3.00	6.00	12.00
LST-7001 [S]	Forbidden Island	1958	10.00	20.00	40.00
—All-black label; woman in jungle on cover					
LST-7001 [S]	Forbidden Island	1960	6.25	12.50	25.00
—Black rainbow label; white foil on cover					
LST-7006 [S]	Exotica, Volume II	1958	10.00	20.00	40.00
—All-black label					
LST-7006 [S]	Exotica, Volume II	1960	6.25	12.50	25.00
—Black rainbow label					
LST-7023 [S]	Primitiva	1958	10.00	20.00	40.00
—All-black label					
LST-7023 [S]	Primitiva	1960	6.25	12.50	25.00
—Black rainbow label					
LST-7034 [R]	Exotica	1958	6.25	12.50	25.00
—All-black label					
LST-7034 [R]	Exotica	1960	5.00	10.00	20.00
—Black rainbow label					
LST-7102 [S]	Hypnotique	1958	10.00	20.00	40.00
—All-black label					
LST-7102 [S]	Hypnotique	1960	6.25	12.50	25.00
—Black rainbow label					
LST-7111 [S]	Afro-Desia	1959	10.00	20.00	40.00
—All-black label					
LST-7111 [S]	Afro-Desia	1960	6.25	12.50	25.00
—Black rainbow label					
LST-7116 [S]	Exotica, Vol. III	1959	10.00	20.00	40.00
—All-black label					
LST-7116 [S]	Exotica, Vol. III	1960	6.25	12.50	25.00
—Black rainbow label					
LST-7122 [S]	Quiet Village	1959	10.00	20.00	40.00
—All-black label					
LST-7122 [S]	Quiet Village	1960	6.25	12.50	25.00
—Black rainbow label					
LST-7141 [S]	The Enchanted Sea	1959	10.00	20.00	40.00
—All-black label					
LST-7141 [S]	The Enchanted Sea	1960	6.25	12.50	25.00
—Black rainbow label					
LST-7158 [S]	Exotic Sounds from the Silver Screen	1960	6.25	12.50	25.00
LST-7163 [S]	Exotic Sounds Visit Broadway	1960	6.25	12.50	25.00
LST-7168 [S]	Exotic Percussion	1961	6.25	12.50	25.00
LST-7224 [S]	The Exotic Sounds of Martin Denny In Person	1962	5.00	10.00	20.00
LST-7237 [S]	A Taste of Honey	1962	5.00	10.00	20.00
LST-7277 [S]	Another Taste of Honey	1963	5.00	10.00	20.00
LST-7307 [S]	The Versatile Martin Denny	1963	5.00	10.00	20.00
LST-7328 [S]	A Taste of Hits	1964	3.75	7.50	15.00
LST-7378 [S]	Latin Village	1964	3.75	7.50	15.00
LST-7394 [S]	Hawaii Tattoo	1964	3.75	7.50	15.00
LST-7415 [S]	20 Golden Hawaiian Hits	1965	3.75	7.50	15.00
LST-7438 [S]	Martin Denny	1965	3.75	7.50	15.00
LST-7445 [S]	Hawaiian A-Go-Go	1966	3.75	7.50	15.00
LST-7467 [S]	Golden Greats	1966	3.75	7.50	15.00
LST-7488 [S]	Hawaii	1967	3.75	7.50	15.00
LST-7513 [S]	Exotica Classica	1967	3.75	7.50	15.00
LST-7621	Exotic Moog	1969	10.00	20.00	40.00
SUNSET					
SUM-1102 [M]	Paradise Moods	196?	3.00	6.00	12.00
SUM-1169 [M]	Sayonara	1967	3.00	6.00	12.00
SUS-5102 [S]	Paradise Moods	196?	3.00	6.00	12.00
SUS-5169 [S]	Sayonara	1967	3.00	6.00	12.00
SUS-5199	Exotic Night	1969	3.00	6.00	12.00
UNITED ARTISTS					
UA-LA234-G	The Very Best of Martin Denny	1974	2.50	5.00	10.00
LM-1009	Exotica Vol. 1	1980	2.50	5.00	10.00
—Reissue of Liberty 7034					

DENNY, SANDY

Also see FAIRPORT CONVENTION.

Number	Title (A Side/B Side)	Yr	VG	VG+	NM
45s					
A&M					
1331	Crazy Lady Blues/Let's Jump the Broomstick	1972	—	3.00	6.00
1410	Tomorrow Is a Long Time/Listen Listen	1973	—	3.00	6.00
Albums					
A&M					
SP-4317	The Northstar Grassman and the Ravens	1971	3.75	7.50	15.00
SP-4371	Sandy	1972	3.75	7.50	15.00
CARTHAGE					
CGLP-4423	Rendezvous	1985	2.50	5.00	10.00
—Reissue of Island 9433					
CGLP-4425	Like an Old Fashioned Waltz	1985	2.50	5.00	10.00
—Reissue of Island 9340					
CGLP-4429	The Northstar Grassman and the Ravens	1985	2.50	5.00	10.00
—Reissue of A&M 4317					
HANNIBAL					
HNBX-5301 [(3)]	Who Knows Where the Time Goes	198?	5.00	10.00	20.00
ISLAND					
SW-9340	Like an Old Fashioned Waltz	1974	3.75	7.50	15.00
ILPS 9433	Rendezvous	1977	3.75	7.50	15.00

DENSON, LEE

Number	Title (A Side/B Side)	Yr	VG	VG+	NM
45s					
ENTERPRISE					
9086	A Mom and Dad for Christmas/The Miracle of the Rosary	1973	—	2.50	5.00
KENT					
306	High School Hop/Devil Doll	1958	15.00	30.00	60.00
VIK					
0251	Heart of a Fool/The Pied Piper	1957	10.00	20.00	40.00
0281	New Shoes/Climb Love Mountain	1957	20.00	40.00	80.00
—With Eddie Cochran on guitar					

DENTON, BOB

Number	Title (A Side/B Side)	Yr	VG	VG+	NM
45s					
CHANCELLOR					
1112	I Guess I'm Still in Love with You/Wrong Side of the Door	1962	3.00	6.00	12.00
DOT					
15622	Love Me, So I'll Know/I'm Sending You This Record	1957	5.00	10.00	20.00
15833	Playboy/Twenty-Four Hour Night	1958	5.00	10.00	20.00
JUDD					
1001	Sweet and Innocent/Back to School Again	1958	3.75	7.50	15.00
1013	I'll Always Be Yours/A Lover's Prayer	1959	3.75	7.50	15.00

DENTON, MICKEY

Number	Title (A Side/B Side)	Yr	VG	VG+	NM
45s					
AMY					
902	Top Ten/Now I'm Mr. Blue	1964	3.00	6.00	12.00
BIG TOP					
3078	Steady Kind/Now You Can't Give Them Away	1961	6.25	12.50	25.00
3094	Nature Boy/Ain't Nobody	1962	5.00	10.00	20.00
3114	Tell Her/How Mighty Hath Fallen	1962	5.00	10.00	20.00
3142	Dance With Me Mary/The Other Side of Betty	1963	5.00	10.00	20.00
IMPACT					
1002	Ain't Love Grand/Mi Amore	1965	5.00	10.00	20.00
1011	Heartache Is My Name/King Lonely the Blue	1966	5.00	10.00	20.00
WORLD ARTISTS					
1043	One More Time/Don't Throw My Toys Away	1965	3.00	6.00	12.00

DENVER, JOHN

Also see DENVER, BOISE & JOHNSON; THE MITCHELL TRIO.

Number	Title (A Side/B Side)	Yr	VG	VG+	NM
12-Inch Singles					
RCA VICTOR					
JD-11189 [DJ]	Bet On the Blues (same on both sides)	1977	3.00	6.00	12.00
45s					
CHERRY MOUNTAIN					
01/02	Let Us Begin (What Are We Making Weapons For)/Flying for Me	1986	—	2.00	4.00
COLUMBIA					
02679	Perhaps Love/Annie's Song	1982	—	2.00	4.00
—With Placido Domingo					
03148	Perhaps Love/Annie's Song	1982	—	—	3.00
—With Placido Domingo; reissue					
LEGACY					
77993	For You/Rocky Mountain High (Live)	1995	—	—	2.00
77993 [PS]	For You/Rocky Mountain High (Live)	1995	—	—	3.00
RCA					
5086-7-R	Love Again/Let Us Begin (What Are We Making Weapons For)	1987	—	—	3.00
PB-10774	Like a Sad Song/Pegasus	1976	—	2.00	4.00
PB-10854	Baby, You Look Good to Me Tonight/Wrangle Mountain Song	1976	—	2.00	4.00
PB-10911	My Sweet Lady/Welcome to My Morning	1977	—	2.00	4.00
GB-10940	I'm Sorry/Fly Away	1977	—	—	3.00
—Gold Standard Series					
PB-11036	How Can I Leave You Again/To the Wild Country	1977	—	2.00	4.00
PB-11214	It Amazes Me/Druthers	1978	—	2.00	4.00
PB-11267	I Want to Live/Tradewinds	1978	—	2.00	4.00
GB-11327	My Sweet Lady/Like a Sad Song	1978	—	—	3.00
—Gold Standard Series					
PB-11479	Downhill Stuff/Life Is So Good	1979	—	2.00	4.00

Number	Title (A Side/B Side)	Yr	VG	VG+	NM
PB-11535	Sweet Melinda/What's On Your Mind	1979	—	2.00	4.00
PB-11637	Garden Song/Berkeley Woman	1979	—	2.00	4.00
PB-11915	Autograph/The Mountain Song	1980	—	2.00	4.00
PB-11915 [PS]	Autograph/The Mountain Song	1980	—	2.00	4.00
PB-12017	Dancing with the Mountains/American Child	1980	—	2.00	4.00
PB-12246	Some Days Are Diamonds (Some Days Are Stone)/Country Love	1981	—	2.00	4.00
PB-12345	The Cowboy and the Lady/Till You Opened My Eyes	1981	—	2.00	4.00
PB-13071	Shanghai Breezes/What One Man Can Do	1982	—	2.00	4.00
PB-13270	Seasons of the Heart/Islands	1982	—	2.00	4.00
PB-13371	Opposite Tables/Relatively Speaking	1982	—	2.00	4.00
PB-13562	Wild Montana Skies/I Remember Romance	1983	—	2.00	4.00
—With Emmylou Harris					
PB-13642	Flight (The Higher We Fly)/Hold On Tightly	1983	—	2.00	4.00
PB-13740	World Games/It's About Time	1984	—	—	3.00
PB-13782	The Way I Am/The Gold and Beyond	1984	—	—	3.00
PB-13931	Love Again/It's About Time	1984	—	—	3.00
—A-side: With Sylvie Vartan					
GB-14075	Calypso/Some Days Are Diamonds (Some Days Are Stone)	1985	—	—	3.00
—Gold Standard Series					
PB-14115	Don't Close Your Eyes Tonight/A Wild Heart Looking for Home	1985	—	—	3.00
PB-14227	Dreamland Express/African Sunrise	1985	—	—	3.00
PB-14227 [PS]	Dreamland Express/African Sunrise	1985	—	2.00	4.00
PB-14366 [DJ]	Flying for Me (same on both sides)	1986	—	2.00	4.00
—No stock copies were issued					
PB-14406	Along for the Ride ('56 T-Bird)/Let Us Begin (What Are We Making Weapons For)	1986	—	—	3.00

RCA VICTOR

Number	Title (A Side/B Side)	Yr	VG	VG+	NM
APBO-0067	Farewell Andromeda (Welcome to My Morning)/Whiskey Basin Blues	1973	—	2.00	4.00
APBO-0182	Please, Daddy (Don't Get Drunk This Christmas)/Rocky Mountain High	1973	—	2.50	5.00
APBO-0213	Sunshine on My Shoulders/Around and Around	1974	—	2.00	4.00
APBO-0295	Annie's Song/Cool An' Green An' Shady	1974	—	2.00	4.00
PB-10065	Back Home Again/It's Up to You	1974	—	2.00	4.00
PB-10148	Sweet Surrender/Summer	1974	—	2.00	4.00
PB-10239	Thank God I'm a Country Boy/My Sweet Lady	1975	—	2.00	4.00
PB-10353	I'm Sorry/Calypso	1975	—	2.00	4.00
PB-10464	Christmas for Cowboys/Silent Night, Holy Night	1975	—	2.00	4.00
GB-10472	Annie's Song/Cool An' Green An' Shady	1975	—	—	3.00
—Gold Standard Series					
GB-10473	Back Home Again/It's Up to You	1975	—	—	3.00
—Gold Standard Series					
GB-10474	Sunshine on My Shoulders/Around and Around	1975	—	—	3.00
—Gold Standard Series					
GB-10475	Farewell Andromeda (Welcome to My Morning)/Whiskey Basin Blues	1975	—	—	3.00
—Gold Standard Series					
GB-10476	Thank God I'm a Country Boy/My Sweet Lady	1975	—	—	3.00
—Gold Standard Series					
GB-10477	Rocky Mountain High/Spring	1975	—	—	3.00
—Gold Standard Series					
GB-10478	Sweet Surrender/Summer	1975	—	—	3.00
—Gold Standard Series					
PB-10517	Fly Away/Two Shots	1975	—	2.00	4.00
PB-10586	Looking for Space/Windsong	1976	—	2.00	4.00
PB-10687	It Makes Me Giggle/Spirit	1976	—	2.00	4.00
74-0275	Daydream/I Wish I Knew How It Would Feel to Be Free	1969	2.50	5.00	10.00
74-0305	Anthem (Revelation)/Sticky Summer Weather	1970	2.50	5.00	10.00
74-0332	Follow Me/Isabel	1970	2.50	5.00	10.00
74-0376	Sail Away Home/I Wish I Could Have Been There	1970	2.50	5.00	10.00
74-0391	Whose Garden Is This/Mr. Bojangles	1970	2.50	5.00	10.00
74-0445	Take Me Home, Country Roads/Poems, Prayers and Promises	1971	2.00	4.00	8.00
—With Fat City					
74-0567	Friends with You/Starwood in Aspen	1971	—	3.00	6.00
74-0647	Everyday/City of New Orleans	1972	—	3.00	6.00
74-0737	Goodbye Again/The Eagle and the Hawk	1972	—	3.00	6.00
74-0801	Late Winter, Early Spring/Hard Life Hard Times	1972	—	3.00	6.00
74-0829	Rocky Mountain High/Spring	1972	—	2.50	5.00
74-0955	I'd Rather Be a Cowboy/Sunshine on My Shoulders	1973	—	2.00	4.00

WINDSTAR

Number	Title (A Side/B Side)	Yr	VG	VG+	NM
75720	Country Girl in Paris/Bread and Roses	1988	—	—	3.00

Albums

HJD

Number	Title	Yr	VG	VG+	NM
66	John Denver Sings	1966	125.00	250.00	500.00
—Private issue of 300 or so, made by JD as Christmas gifts to friends.					

MERCURY

Number	Title	Yr	VG	VG+	NM
SRM-1-704	Beginnings	1972	5.00	10.00	20.00
—With illustration on cover					
SRM-1-704	Beginnings	1974	3.00	6.00	12.00
—With mountain scene on cover					

RCA

Number	Title	Yr	VG	VG+	NM
7624-1-R	Back Home Again	1988	2.50	5.00	10.00
—Last vinyl reissue					
7631-1-R	Poems, Prayers and Promises	1988	2.50	5.00	10.00
—Last vinyl reissue					
7632-1-R	Rocky Mountain High	1988	2.50	5.00	10.00
—Last vinyl reissue					

RCA VICTOR

Number	Title	Yr	VG	VG+	NM
DJL1-0075 [DJ]	The John Denver Radio Show	1973	7.50	15.00	30.00
APL1-0101	Farewell Andromeda	1973	3.00	6.00	12.00
—Orange label					
APL1-0101	Farewell Andromeda	1975	2.50	5.00	10.00
—Tan label or black label, dog near top					
APL1-0374	John Denver's Greatest Hits	197?	2.00	4.00	8.00
—Reissue					
AQL1-0374	John Denver's Greatest Hits	197?	2.00	4.00	8.00
—Later reissue					
CPL1-0374	John Denver's Greatest Hits	1974	2.50	5.00	10.00
—Orange label					
CPL1-0374	John Denver's Greatest Hits	1975	2.00	4.00	8.00
—Tan label or black label, dog near top					
AFL1-0548	Back Home Again	197?	2.00	4.00	8.00
—Reissue					
AQL1-0548	Back Home Again	197?	2.00	4.00	8.00
—Later reissue					
CPL1-0548	Back Home Again	1974	2.50	5.00	10.00
—Orange or tan label					
CPL1-0548	Back Home Again	1976	2.00	4.00	8.00
—Black label, dog near top					
DJL1-0683 [DJ]	The Second John Denver Radio Show	1974	7.50	15.00	30.00
CPL2-0764 [(2)]	An Evening with John Denver	1975	3.00	6.00	12.00
—Orange or tan labels					
CPL2-0764 [(2)]	An Evening with John Denver	1976	2.50	5.00	10.00
—Black label, dog near top					
AFL1-1183	Windsong	197?	2.00	4.00	8.00
—Reissue					
APL1-1183	Windsong	1975	2.50	5.00	10.00
—Tan label					
APL1-1183	Windsong	1976	2.00	4.00	8.00
—Black label, dog near top					
AQL1-1183	Windsong	197?	2.00	4.00	8.00
—Later reissue					
AFL1-1201	Rocky Mountain Christmas	197?	2.00	4.00	8.00
—Reissue					
APL1-1201	Rocky Mountain Christmas	1975	2.50	5.00	10.00
—Tan label					
APL1-1201	Rocky Mountain Christmas	1976	2.00	4.00	8.00
—Black label, dog near top					
APL2-1263 [(2)]	The John Denver Gift Pak	1974	7.50	15.00	30.00
—Contains "Rocky Mountain Christmas" and "Windsong" in a special Christmas sleeve.					
AFL1-1694	Spirit	197?	2.00	4.00	8.00
—Reissue					
APL1-1694	Spirit	1976	2.50	5.00	10.00
—Originals are black label, dog near top					
AQL1-2195	John Denver's Greatest Hits, Volume 2	197?	2.00	4.00	8.00
—Reissue					
CPL1-2195	John Denver's Greatest Hits, Volume 2	1977	2.50	5.00	10.00
AFL1-2521	I Want to Live	1977	2.00	4.00	8.00
AQL1-3075	John Denver	1979	2.00	4.00	8.00
AQL1-3449	Autograph	1980	2.00	4.00	8.00
AFL1-4055	Some Days Are Diamonds	1981	2.00	4.00	8.00
LSP-4207	Rhymes & Reasons	1969	3.75	7.50	15.00
—Orange label, non-flexible vinyl					
AFL1-4256	Seasons of the Heart	1982	2.00	4.00	8.00
LSP-4278	Take Me to Tomorrow	1970	3.75	7.50	15.00
—Orange label, non-flexible vinyl					
AFL1-4499	Poems, Prayers and Promises	197?	2.00	4.00	8.00
—Reissue					
LSP-4499	Poems, Prayers and Promises	1971	3.00	6.00	12.00
—Orange label					
LSP-4499	Poems, Prayers and Promises	1975	2.50	5.00	10.00
—Tan label or black label, dog near top					
AFL1-4607	Aerie	197?	2.00	4.00	8.00
—Reissue					
LSP-4607	Aerie	1971	3.00	6.00	12.00
—Orange label					
LSP-4607	Aerie	1975	2.50	5.00	10.00
—Tan label or black label, dog near top					
AFL1-4683	It's About Time	1983	2.00	4.00	8.00
AFL1-4731	Rocky Mountain High	197?	2.00	4.00	8.00
—Reissue					
AQL1-4731	Rocky Mountain High	197?	2.00	4.00	8.00
—Later reissue					
LSP-4731	Rocky Mountain High	1972	3.00	6.00	12.00
—Orange label					
LSP-4731	Rocky Mountain High	1975	2.50	5.00	10.00
—Tan label or black label, dog near top					
AYL1-5189	Poems, Prayers and Promises	198?	—	3.00	6.00
—"Best Buy Series" reissue					
AYL1-5190	Rocky Mountain High	198?	—	3.00	6.00
—"Best Buy Series" reissue					
AYL1-5191	Windsong	198?	—	3.00	6.00
—"Best Buy Series" reissue					
AYL1-5192	I Want to Live	198?	—	3.00	6.00
—"Best Buy Series" reissue					
AYL1-5193	Back Home Again	198?	—	3.00	6.00
—"Best Buy Series" reissue					
AYL1-5194	Spirit	198?	—	3.00	6.00
—"Best Buy Series" reissue					
AYL1-5195	Farewell Andromeda	198?	—	3.00	6.00
—"Best Buy Series" reissue					
AJL1-5313	John Denver's Greatest Hits, Volume 3	1984	2.00	4.00	8.00
DJL1-5398 [DJ]	The John Denver Holiday Radio Show	1984	5.00	10.00	20.00
AFL1-5458	Dreamland Express	1985	2.00	4.00	8.00
AFL1-5811	One World	1986	2.00	4.00	8.00

DENVER, JOHN, AND THE MUPPETS

45s

RCA

Number	Title (A Side/B Side)	Yr	VG	VG+	NM
PB-11767	Have Yourself a Merry Little Christmas//We Wish You a Merry Christmas/A Baby Just Like You	1979	—	2.50	5.00
PB-11767 [PS]	Have Yourself a Merry Little Christmas//We Wish You a Merry Christmas/A Baby Just Like You	1979	—	2.50	5.00

Albums

RCA

Number	Title	Yr	VG	VG+	NM
AFL1-3451	A Christmas Together	1979	3.00	6.00	12.00

DENVER, JOHN, AND THE NITTY GRITTY DIRT BAND

45s

UNIVERSAL

Number	Title (A Side/B Side)	Yr	VG	VG+	NM
UVL-66008	And So It Goes/Amazing Grace	1989	—	2.00	4.00

Number	Title (A Side/B Side)	Yr	VG	VG+	NM

DENVER, KARL
45s
LONDON

Number	Title (A Side/B Side)	Yr	VG	VG+	NM
2020	Marcheta/Joe Sweeney	1961	3.75	7.50	15.00
9521	Wimoweh/Sleepy Lagoon	1962	3.00	6.00	12.00
9534	Zimba/Uska Dara	1962	3.00	6.00	12.00
9576	Blue Weekend/Pastures of Plenty	1963	3.00	6.00	12.00

DENVER, BOISE, & JOHNSON
Also see JOHN DENVER.
45s
REPRISE

Number	Title (A Side/B Side)	Yr	VG	VG+	NM
0695	Take Me to Tomorrow/'68 Nixon (This Year's Model)	1968	3.00	6.00	12.00

DEODATO
45s
CTI

Number	Title (A Side/B Side)	Yr	VG	VG+	NM
12	Also Sprach Zarathustra (2001)/Spirit of Summer	1972	—	2.50	5.00
16	Rhapsody in Blue/Superstrut	1973	—	2.00	4.00
16 [PS]	Rhapsody in Blue/Superstrut	1973	—	3.00	6.00
42	Also Sprach Zarathustra (2001)/Spirit of Summer	1977	—	2.00	4.00
MCA					
40252	Havana Strut/Moonlight Serenade	1974	—	2.00	4.00
40469	Caravan/Watusi Street	1975	—	2.00	4.00
40631	Peter Gunn/Amani	1976	—	2.00	4.00
WARNER BROS.					
8588	Pina Colada/Love Island	1978	—	2.00	4.00
8606	Whistle Bump/Love Island	1978	—	2.00	4.00
29984	Happy Hour/Sweet Magic	1982	—	—	3.00

Albums
ATLANTIC

Number	Title (A Side/B Side)	Yr	VG	VG+	NM
82048	Somewhere Out There	1989	2.50	5.00	10.00
CTI					
CTS-6021	Prelude	1972	3.00	6.00	12.00
CTSQ-6021 [Q]	Prelude	1973	4.50	9.00	18.00
CTS-6029	Deodato 2	1973	3.00	6.00	12.00
CTSQ-6029 [Q]	Deodato 2	1973	4.50	9.00	18.00
7081	2001	1977	2.50	5.00	10.00
8021	Prelude	198?	2.00	4.00	8.00
—Reissue of 6021					
MCA					
410	Whirlwinds	1974	2.50	5.00	10.00
457	Artistry	1974	2.50	5.00	10.00
491	First Cuckoo	1975	2.50	5.00	10.00
697	Very Together	198?	2.00	4.00	8.00
—Reissue of 2219					
2219	Very Together	1976	2.50	5.00	10.00
WARNER BROS.					
BSK 3132	Love Island	1978	2.50	5.00	10.00
BSK 3321	Knights of Fantasy	1979	2.50	5.00	10.00
BSK 3467	Night Cruiser	1980	2.50	5.00	10.00
BSK 3649	Happy Hour	1981	2.50	5.00	10.00
25175	Motion	1984	2.00	4.00	8.00

DEODATO/AIRTO
45s
CTI

Number	Title (A Side/B Side)	Yr	VG	VG+	NM
18	Do It Again/Branches (O Galho Da Roseira)	1974	—	2.00	4.00

Albums
CTI

Number	Title (A Side/B Side)	Yr	VG	VG+	NM
CTS-6041	In Concert	1974	3.00	6.00	12.00

DEPENDABLES, THE
Albums
UNITED ARTISTS

Number	Title (A Side/B Side)	Yr	VG	VG+	NM
UAS-6799	Klaatu Berrada Niktu	1971	5.00	10.00	20.00

DERBY-HATVILLE
45s
SEA ELL

Number	Title (A Side/B Side)	Yr	VG	VG+	NM
102	You'll Forget Me/(B-side unknown)	1967	10.00	20.00	40.00
104	Instant Replay/(B-side unknown)	1967	10.00	20.00	40.00

DEREK
See JOHNNY CYMBAL.

DEREK AND THE DOMINOS
Also see ERIC CLAPTON.
45s
ATCO

Number	Title (A Side/B Side)	Yr	VG	VG+	NM
6780	Tell the Truth/Roll It Over	1970	6.25	12.50	25.00
—Produced by Phil Spector; withdrawn shortly after release					
6803	Bell Bottom Blues/Keep On Growing	1971	2.50	5.00	10.00
6809	Layla (2:43)/I Am Yours	1971	2.50	5.00	10.00
6809	Layla (7:10)/I Am Yours	1972	—	3.00	6.00
POLYDOR					
15040	Layla/I Am Yours	1972	—	—	—
—Unreleased?					
RSO					
400	Presence of the Lord/Why Does Love Got to Be So Sad	1973	—	3.00	6.00

Albums
ATCO

Number	Title (A Side/B Side)	Yr	VG	VG+	NM
2-704 [(2) M]	Layla and Other Assorted Love Songs	1970	75.00	150.00	300.00
—White label promo only					
SD 2-704 [(2) DJ]	Layla and Other Assorted Love Songs	1970	50.00	100.00	200.00
—White label promo					
SD 2-704 [(2) S]	Layla and Other Assorted Love Songs	1970	7.50	15.00	30.00
DIRECT DISK					
SD-16629 [(2)]	Layla and Other Assorted Love Songs	1981	37.50	75.00	150.00
—Audiophile vinyl					
MOBILE FIDELITY					
2-239 [(2)]	Derek and the Dominos In Concert	1996	12.50	25.00	50.00
—Audiophile vinyl					
POLYDOR					
PD2-3501 [(2)]	Layla and Other Assorted Love Songs	1972	5.00	10.00	20.00
RSO					
RS-2-3801 [(2)]	Layla and Other Assorted Love Songs	1977	3.75	7.50	15.00
SO 2-8800 [(2)]	Derek and the Dominos in Concert	1973	5.00	10.00	20.00
823277-1 [(2)]	Layla and Other Assorted Love Songs	1985	3.00	6.00	12.00

DERRINGER, RICK
Also see THE McCOYS.
45s
BLUE SKY

Number	Title (A Side/B Side)	Yr	VG	VG+	NM
2751	Rock and Roll Hoochie Koo/Time Warp	1974	—	2.50	5.00
2752	Teenage Love Affair/Slide Over Slinky	1974	—	2.00	4.00
2753	It's Raining/Cheqap Tequila	1974	—	2.00	4.00
2755	Hang On Sloopy/Skyscraper Blues	1975	—	2.00	4.00
2757	Don't Ever Say Goodbye/Gimme More	1975	—	2.00	4.00
2765	Let Me In/You Can Have Me	1976	—	2.00	4.00
—As "Derringer"					
2767	Don't Stop Loving Me/Let's Make It	1977	—	2.00	4.00
—As "Derringer"					
2770	Lawyers, Guns and Money/Sleepless	1977	—	2.00	4.00
—As "Derringer"					
2774	Midnight Road/Rocka-Rolla	1978	—	2.00	4.00
—As "Derringer"					
2783	Need a Little Girl (Just Like You)/Something Warm	1979	—	2.00	4.00
2788	Don't Ever Say Godbye/Timeless	1980	—	2.00	4.00
2793	Runaway/Teenage Love Affair	1980	—	2.00	4.00
2794	Let the Music Play/You'll Get Yours	1980	—	2.00	4.00
EPIC					
05830	The Real America/Grab Them Cakes	1986	—	—	3.00
—As "Derringer"					

Albums
BLUE SKY

Number	Title (A Side/B Side)	Yr	VG	VG+	NM
KZ 32481	All American Boy	1973	3.75	7.50	15.00
PZ 32481	All American Boy	197?	2.00	4.00	8.00
—Reissue with new prefix					
ZQ 32481 [Q]	All American Boy	1974	5.00	10.00	20.00
PZ 33423	Spring Fever	1975	3.00	6.00	12.00
PZ 34181	Derringer	1976	3.00	6.00	12.00
PZ 34470	Sweet Evil	1977	3.00	6.00	12.00
PZ 34848	Derringer Live	1977	3.00	6.00	12.00
—Without bar code					
PZ 34848	Derringer Live	198?	2.00	4.00	8.00
—Reissue with bar code					
JZ 35075	If I Weren't So Romantic I'd Shoot You	1978	2.50	5.00	10.00
JZ 36092	Guitars and Women	1979	2.50	5.00	10.00
JZ 36551	Face to Face	1980	2.50	5.00	10.00
PASSPORT					
PB-6025	Good Dirty Fun	1983	2.50	5.00	10.00

DESHANNON, JACKIE
45s
AMHERST

Number	Title (A Side/B Side)	Yr	VG	VG+	NM
725	I Don't Think I Can Wait/Don't Let the Flame Burn Out	1978	3.00	6.00	12.00
728	To Love Somebody/Just to Feel This Love from You	1978	3.00	6.00	12.00
733	You're the Only Dancer/Tonight You're Doin' It Right	1979	3.00	6.00	12.00
737	Things We Said Today/Way Above the Angels	1979	3.00	6.00	12.00
ATLANTIC					
2871	Only Love Can Break Your Heart/Vanilla Olay	1972	2.50	5.00	10.00
2895	I Wanna Roo You/Paradise	1972	2.50	5.00	10.00
2919	Sweet Sixteen/Speak Out to Me	1972	2.50	5.00	10.00
2924	Chains on My Soul/Peaceful in My Soul	1972	2.50	5.00	10.00
2994	Your Baby Is a Lady/(If You Never Have a Big Hit Record) You're Still Gonna Be My Star	1973	2.50	5.00	10.00
3041	You've Changed/Jimmie, Just Sing Me One More Song	1974	2.50	5.00	10.00
CAPITOL					
3130	Salinas/Keep Me Warm	1971	2.50	5.00	10.00
3185	Stone Cold Soul/West Virginia Mine	1971	2.50	5.00	10.00
COLUMBIA					
10221	Boat to Sail/Let the Sailors Dance	1975	3.75	7.50	15.00
—With Brian Wilson on backing vocal					
10340	Fire in the City/All Night Desire	1976	2.50	5.00	10.00
DOT					
15928	Cajun Blues/Just Another Lie	1959	6.25	12.50	25.00
—As "Jackie Shannon"					
15980	Trouble/Lies	1959	6.25	12.50	25.00
—As "Jackie Shannon"					
EDISON INTERNATIONAL					
416	I Wanna Go Home/So Warm	1960	25.00	50.00	100.00
418	Put My Baby Down/The Foolish One	1960	25.00	50.00	100.00
GONE					
5008	How Wrong I Was/I'll Be True	1957	7.50	15.00	30.00
—As "Jackie Dee"					
IMPERIAL					
66110	What the World Needs Now Is Love/I Remember the Boy	1965	2.00	4.00	8.00
66132	A Lifetime of Loneliness/Don't Turn Your Back on Me	1965	—	3.00	6.00
66171	Come and Get Me/Splendor in the Grass	1966	—	3.00	6.00
66194	Will You Love Me Tomorrow/Are You Ready for This	1966	—	3.00	6.00
66196	So Long Johnny/Windows and Doors	1966	—	3.00	6.00

Number	Title (A Side/B Side)	Yr	VG	VG+	NM
66202	I Can Make It with You/To Be Myself	1966	—	3.00	6.00
66224	Come On Down/Find Me Love	1967	—	3.00	6.00
66236	Where Does the Sun Go/Wishing Doll	1967	—	3.00	6.00
66251	It's All in the Game/Changin' My Mind	1967	—	3.00	6.00
66281	Me About You/I Keep Wanting You	1968	—	3.00	6.00
66301	Nobody's Home to Go Home To/Nicole	1968	—	3.00	6.00
66312	Didn't Want to Have to Do It/Splendor in the Grass	1968	—	3.00	6.00
66313	The Weight/Splendor in the Grass	1968	—	3.00	6.00
66342	Holly Would/My Heart's Been Marching	1968	—	3.00	6.00
66370	What Is This/Trust Me	1969	—	2.50	5.00
66385	Put a Little Love in Your Heart/Always Be Together	1969	—	3.00	6.00
66419	Love Will Find a Way/I Let Go Completely	1969	—	2.50	5.00
66430	One Christmas/Do You Know How Christmas Trees Are Grown	1969	—	3.00	6.00
66438	Brighton Hill/You Can Come to Me	1970	—	2.50	5.00
66452	You Keep Me Hangin' On-Hurt So Bad/What Was Your Day Like	1970	—	2.50	5.00
LIBERTY					
55148	Buddy/Strolypso Dance	1958	6.25	12.50	25.00
—As "Jackie Dee"					
55288	Lonely Girl/Teach Me	1960	3.75	7.50	15.00
55342	Think About You/Heaven Is Being with You	1961	3.75	7.50	15.00
55358	I Won't Turn You Down/Wish I Could Find a Boy	1961	3.75	7.50	15.00
55387	Baby (When You Kiss Me)/Ain't That Love	1961	3.75	7.50	15.00
55425	The Prince/I'll Drown in My Own Tears	1962	3.75	7.50	15.00
55425	The Prince/That's What Boys Are Made Of	1962	3.75	7.50	15.00
55484	Guess Who/Just Like in the Movies	1962	3.75	7.50	15.00
55497	You Won't Forget Me/I Don't Think So Much of Myself	1962	3.75	7.50	15.00
55526	Faded Love/Dancing Silhouettes	1962	3.75	7.50	15.00
55526 [PS]	Faded Love/Dancing Silhouettes	1962	10.00	20.00	40.00
55563	Needles and Pins/Did He Call Today, Mama?	1963	3.75	7.50	15.00
55602	Little Yellow Roses/Oh Sweet Chariot	1963	3.75	7.50	15.00
55602	Little Yellow Roses/500 Miles	1963	3.75	7.50	15.00
55602 [DJ]	Little Yellow Roses	1963	20.00	40.00	80.00
—Yellow vinyl promo					
55645	When You Walk in the Room/Til You Say You're Mine	1963	3.75	7.50	15.00
55673	I'm Gonna Be Strong/Should I Cry	1964	3.75	7.50	15.00
55678	Oh Boy/I'm Looking for Someone to Love	1964	3.75	7.50	15.00
55705	Hold Your Head High/She Don't Understand Him Like I Do	1964	3.75	7.50	15.00
55730	He's Got the Whole World in His Hands/It's Love Baby	1964	3.75	7.50	15.00
55735	When You Walk in the Room/Over You	1964	3.00	6.00	12.00
55787	What the World Needs Now Is Love/A Lifetime of Loneliness	1965	—	—	—
—Unreleased					
56187	Mediterranean Sky/It's So Nice	1970	—	3.00	6.00
PJ					
101	Trouble/Lies	1959	10.00	20.00	40.00
—As "Jackie Shannon"					
RCA					
PB-11902	I Don't Need You Anymore/Find Love	1980	—	2.50	5.00
SAGE AND SAND					
290	Just Another Lie/Cajun Blues	1960	6.25	12.50	25.00
330	Trouble/Lies	1960	6.25	12.50	25.00
UNITED ARTISTS					
0033	What the World Needs Now Is Love/Needles and Pins	1973	—	3.00	6.00
—"Silver Spotlight Series" reissue					
0034	Put a Little Love in Your Heart/When You Walk in the Room	1973	—	3.00	6.00
—"Silver Spotlight Series" reissue					
Albums					
AMHERST					
AMH 1010	You're the Only Dancer	1977	3.00	6.00	12.00
AMH 1016	Quick Touches	1978	3.00	6.00	12.00
ATLANTIC					
SD 7231	Jackie	1972	3.00	6.00	12.00
SD 7303	Your Baby Is a Lady	1974	3.00	6.00	12.00
CAPITOL					
ST-772	Songs	1971	3.00	6.00	12.00
COLUMBIA					
PC 33500	New Arrangement	1975	3.00	6.00	12.00
IMPERIAL					
LP-9286 [M]	This Is Jackie DeShannon	1965	5.00	10.00	20.00
—Black and pink label					
LP-9286 [M]	This Is Jackie DeShannon	1966	3.75	7.50	15.00
—Black and green label					
LP-9294 [M]	You Won't Forget Me	1965	5.00	10.00	20.00
—Black and pink label					
LP-9294 [M]	You Won't Forget Me	1966	3.75	7.50	15.00
—Black and green label					
LP-9296 [M]	In the Wind	1965	5.00	10.00	20.00
—Black and pink label					
LP-9296 [M]	In the Wind	1966	3.75	7.50	15.00
—Black and green label					
LP-9328 [M]	Are You Ready for This?	1966	3.75	7.50	15.00
LP-9344 [M]	New Image	1967	3.75	7.50	15.00
LP-9352 [M]	For You	1967	3.75	7.50	15.00
LP-12286 [S]	This Is Jackie DeShannon	1965	6.25	12.50	25.00
—Black and pink label					
LP-12286 [S]	This Is Jackie DeShannon	1966	5.00	10.00	20.00
—Black and green label					
LP-12294 [S]	You Won't Forget Me	1965	6.25	12.50	25.00
—Black and pink label					
LP-12294 [S]	You Won't Forget Me	1966	5.00	10.00	20.00
—Black and green label					
LP-12296 [S]	In the Wind	1965	6.25	12.50	25.00
—Black and pink label					
LP-12296 [S]	In the Wind	1966	5.00	10.00	20.00
—Black and green label					

Number	Title (A Side/B Side)	Yr	VG	VG+	NM
LP-12328 [S]	Are You Ready for This?	1966	5.00	10.00	20.00
LP-12344 [S]	New Image	1967	5.00	10.00	20.00
LP-12352 [S]	For You	1967	5.00	10.00	20.00
LP-12386	Me About You	1968	3.75	7.50	15.00
LP-12404	What the World Needs Now Is Love	1968	3.75	7.50	15.00
LP-12415	Laurel Canyon	1969	3.75	7.50	15.00
LP-12442	Put a Little Love in Your Heart	1969	3.75	7.50	15.00
LP-12453	To Be Free	1970	3.75	7.50	15.00
LIBERTY					
LRP-3320 [M]	Jackie DeShannon	1963	10.00	20.00	40.00
LRP-3390 [M]	Breakin' It Up on the Beatles Tour!	1964	10.00	20.00	40.00
LST-7320 [S]	Jackie DeShannon	1963	12.50	25.00	50.00
LST-7390 [S]	Breakin' It Up on the Beatles Tour!	1964	12.50	25.00	50.00
LN-10179	The Very Best of Jackie DeShannon	1983	2.00	4.00	8.00
—Reissue of United Artists 434					
LN-10265	Jackie DeShannon	1985	2.00	4.00	8.00
SUNSET					
SUS-5225	Lonely Girl	1968	3.00	6.00	12.00
SUS-5322	Jackie DeShannon	1970	3.00	6.00	12.00
UNITED ARTISTS					
UA-LA434-E	The Very Best of Jackie DeShannon	1975	3.00	6.00	12.00

DESIRES, THE

More than one group.

Number	Title (A Side/B Side)	Yr	VG	VG+	NM
45s					
20TH FOX					
195	I Don't Know Why/Longing	1960	6.25	12.50	25.00
DASA					
102	Phyllis Beloved/The Girl for Me	1962	7.50	15.00	30.00
HERALD					
532	Bobby You/Cold Lonely Heart	1958	6.25	12.50	25.00
HULL					
730	Hey Lena/Let It Please Be You	1959	20.00	40.00	80.00
733	Set Me Free/Rendezvous with You	1960	20.00	40.00	80.00
SEVILLE					
118	The Story of Love/I Ask You	1962	7.50	15.00	30.00
SMASH					
1763	There I Go Again/I Never Loved Like This	1962	6.25	12.50	25.00

DESMOND, JOHNNY

Also see DON CORNELL/JOHNNY DESMOND/ALAN DALE.

Number	Title (A Side/B Side)	Yr	VG	VG+	NM
45s					
20TH CENTURY FOX					
546	Fate Is the Hunter/Rio Conchos	1964	2.00	4.00	8.00
ARTISTS OF AMERICA					
119	Moonlight Serenade/(Instrumental)	1976	—	2.00	4.00
COLUMBIA					
41343	Goodbye, My Love, Goodbye/Bye-Bye Barbara	1959	2.00	4.00	8.00
41414	Dancin' Man/Hey Little Dolly	1959	2.00	4.00	8.00
41525	Maria/Please	1959	2.00	4.00	8.00
41631	Eighth Wonder of the World/Never Meant to Fall in Love	1960	2.00	4.00	8.00
41661	Hawk/Playing the Field	1960	2.00	4.00	8.00
41788	Lover Come Back to Me/I Got a Right to Sing the Blues	1960	—	—	—
—Canceled					
41803	Lover Come Back to Me/No One Ever Tells You	1960	2.00	4.00	8.00
CORAL					
60629	Oh My Darlin'/Until	1952	3.00	6.00	12.00
60670	Festival/Confetti, I Stood and Threw	1952	3.00	6.00	12.00
60736	Battle Hymn of the Republic/How Much Will I Miss You	1952	3.00	6.00	12.00
60798	One Way Heart/It's Meant to Be That Way	1952	3.00	6.00	12.00
60823	Trying/Wild Guitars	1952	3.00	6.00	12.00
60848	Nina Never Knew/Stay Where You Are	1952	3.00	6.00	12.00
60862	Christmas in the Air/Christmas Is a Time	1952	3.75	7.50	15.00
60929	The Gay Caballero/Thanks for Letting Me Know	1953	3.00	6.00	12.00
60978	The Japanese Sandman/Danger	1953	3.00	6.00	12.00
61031	It's So Nice to Be Your Neighbor/I'm a Love You	1953	3.00	6.00	12.00
61069	Woman/By the River Seine	1953	3.00	6.00	12.00
61153	Would You Let Me Hold Your Heart/The Zoo	1954	3.00	6.00	12.00
61198	Backward, Turn Backward/Forever Love	1954	3.75	7.50	15.00
—With Jane Russell					
61204	The High and the Mighty/In God We Trust	1954	3.00	6.00	12.00
61227	A Husband/A Wife	1954	3.00	6.00	12.00
—B-side by Eileen Barton					
61232	The High and the Mighty/Got No Time	1954	3.00	6.00	12.00
61255	Here I Go Walkin' Down the Road/Brooklyn Bridge	1954	3.00	6.00	12.00
61301	My Own True Love/The Song from Desiree	1954	3.00	6.00	12.00
61379	Play Me Hearts and Flowers (I Wanna Cry)/I'm So Ashamed	1955	2.50	5.00	10.00
61410	Togetherness/A Straw Hat and a Cane	1955	2.50	5.00	10.00
61436	It's a Sin to Tell a Lie/Learnin' the Blues	1955	2.50	5.00	10.00
61447	Land of the Pharaohs/This Too Shall Pass	1955	2.50	5.00	10.00
61476	The Yellow Rose of Texas/You're in Love with Someone	1955	2.50	5.00	10.00
61505	Miss America/Gentlemen Marry Brunettes	1955	2.50	5.00	10.00
61529	Sixteen Tons/Ballo Italiano	1955	2.50	5.00	10.00
61543	Santo Natale/Happy Holidays to You	1955	3.00	6.00	12.00
61569	In My Diary/I'll Cry Tomorrow	1956	2.50	5.00	10.00
61570	Now Is the Time/Never Again	1956	2.50	5.00	10.00
61608	The Most Happy Fella/Without You	1956	2.50	5.00	10.00
61632	A Little Love Can Go a Long, Long Way/Please Don't Forget Me Dear	1956	2.50	5.00	10.00
61663	The Proud Ones/I Only Know I Love You	1956	2.50	5.00	10.00
61729	A Girl Named Mary/Bueno	1956	2.50	5.00	10.00
61747	Old Fashioned Christmas/Birthday Party of the King	1956	3.00	6.00	12.00
61768	Down Where the River Meets the Sea/18th Century Music Box	1957	2.00	4.00	8.00
61797	I Just Want You to Want Me/That's Where I Shine	1957	2.00	4.00	8.00

Number	Title (A Side/B Side)	Yr	VG	VG+	NM
61835	A White Sport Coat (And a Pink Carnation)/Just Lookin'	1957	2.00	4.00	8.00
61846	Shenandoah Rose/Consideration	1957	2.00	4.00	8.00
61880	Be Patient with Me/Missing	1957	2.00	4.00	8.00
61896	Rich Man, Poor Man/I Would Love You Still	1957	2.00	4.00	8.00
61910	Keep Me in Mind/Lonely Lament	1957	2.00	4.00	8.00
61934	Farewell to Naples/Temperamental You	1958	2.00	4.00	8.00
61952	The Sands of Time/The Jealous Boyfriend	1958	2.00	4.00	8.00
61968	Anniversary Song/First, Last and Always	1958	2.00	4.00	8.00
DIAMOND					
108	Twistin' Rose of Texas/Hello Honey	1962	2.00	4.00	8.00
MGM					
10524	If Every Day Would Be Christmas/You're All I Want for Christmas	1949	—	—	—
—Unconfirmed on 45 rpm					
10703	The Picnic Song/I've Got a Heart	1950	3.75	7.50	15.00
—Earlier Johnny Desmond singles on MGM are unconfirned on 45 rpm					
10736	Pagalle/Stars	1950	3.75	7.50	15.00
10758	Just Say I Love Her/If Anyone Desires	1950	3.75	7.50	15.00
10800	A Bushel and a Peck/So Long Sally	1950	3.75	7.50	15.00
10827	Sleigh Ride/Marshmallow World	1950	3.75	7.50	15.00
10850	C'est La Vie/You're for Me	1950	3.75	7.50	15.00
10920	Too Young/I Fell	1951	3.75	7.50	15.00
10930	The Chapel of the Roses/Forever and Always	1951	3.75	7.50	15.00
10939	Mama/My Yiddishe Momme	1951	3.75	7.50	15.00
10947	Because of You/Andiano	1951	3.75	7.50	15.00
10974	Mister and Mississippi/I Fall in Love	1951	3.75	7.50	15.00
10992	Out o' Breath/I'm Glad I Gave It Up for You	1951	3.75	7.50	15.00
11005	America's Prayer/I See God	1951	3.75	7.50	15.00
11027	I Want to Be Near You/I Will Never Change	1951	3.75	7.50	15.00
11049	So/More Love	1951	3.75	7.50	15.00
11078	True Love/Simple, Simple, Simple	1951	3.75	7.50	15.00
11122	My Lost Love/Hands Across the Table	1951	3.75	7.50	15.00
RCA VICTOR					
47-8233	I Can't Help Falling in Love/I Still Look at You That Way	1963	—	3.00	6.00
VIGOR					
710	Untouchable/Red Lips	1973	—	2.00	4.00
7-Inch Extended Plays					
CORAL					
83011	Christmas in the Air/Christmas Is a Time//The Little Match Girl/The Night Before Christmas	195?	3.75	7.50	15.00
—B-side by Eileen Barton					
RCA CAMDEN					
CAE-260	Guilty/I'll Close My Eyes//Just Plain Love/If It's True	1955	3.00	6.00	12.00
CAE-260 [PS]	Johnny Desmond Sings	1955	3.00	6.00	12.00
Albums					
COLUMBIA					
CS 8194 [S]	Once Upon a Time	1959	6.25	12.50	25.00
CL (# unknown) [M]	Once Upon a Time	1959	5.00	10.00	20.00
MOVIETONE					
71011 [M]	Johnny Desmond On Location	1966	3.00	6.00	12.00
S-72011 [S]	Johnny Desmond On Location	1966	3.75	7.50	15.00
VOCALION					
VL 3773 [M]	Johnny Desmond	1966	3.00	6.00	12.00
VL 73773 [R]	Johnny Desmond	1966	2.50	5.00	10.00

DESMOND, JOHNNY/JOHNNY KAY

Number	Title (A Side/B Side)	Yr	VG	VG+	NM
Albums					
CORONET					
CX-193 [M]	Johnny Desmond Sings	196?	3.00	6.00	12.00
CXS-193 [R]	Johnny Desmond Sings	196?	2.50	5.00	10.00

DESMOND, PAUL

Also see DAVE BRUBECK (Desmond was the saxophone player on many of his LPs).

Number	Title (A Side/B Side)	Yr	VG	VG+	NM
45s					
RCA VICTOR					
47-8035	Advise and Consent/Desmond Blue	1962	2.50	5.00	10.00
47-8264	Take Ten/Embarcadero	1963	2.50	5.00	10.00
Albums					
ARTISTS HOUSE					
2	Paul Desmond	1979	2.50	5.00	10.00
A&M					
SP-3015	Summertime	1969	3.00	6.00	12.00
SP-3024	From the Hot Afternoon	1969	3.00	6.00	12.00
SP-3032	Bridge Over Troubled Water	1970	3.00	6.00	12.00
CTI					
CTS-6039	Skylark	1974	2.50	5.00	10.00
CTS-6059	Pure Desmond	1975	2.50	5.00	10.00
CTI/CBS ASSOCIATED					
FZ 40806	Pure Desmond	1987	2.50	5.00	10.00
—Reissue of CTI 6059					
FZ 44170	Skylark	1988	2.50	5.00	10.00
—Reissue of CTI 6039					
DISCOVERY					
840	East of the Sun	198?	2.50	5.00	10.00
FANTASY					
3-21 [10]	Paul Desmond	1955	25.00	50.00	100.00
OJC-119	Paul Desmond Quartet Featuring Don Elliott	198?	2.50	5.00	10.00
—Reissue of Fantasy 3235					
3235 [M]	Paul Desmond Quartet Featuring Don Elliott	1956	20.00	40.00	80.00
—Red vinyl					
3235 [M]	Paul Desmond Quartet Featuring Don Elliott	1957	10.00	20.00	40.00
—Black vinyl, red label, non-flexible vinyl					
3235 [M]	Paul Desmond Quartet Featuring Don Elliott	1962	5.00	10.00	20.00
—Black vinyl, red label, flexible vinyl					
FINESSE					
FW 37487	Paul Desmond and the Modern Jazz Quartet	1981	2.50	5.00	10.00
HORIZON					
850 [(2)]	Paul Desmond Live	1976	3.75	7.50	15.00
MOSAIC					
M6-120 [(6)]	The Complete Recordings of the Paul Desmond Quartet with Jim Hall	199?	17.50	35.00	70.00
RCA CAMDEN					
ACL1-0201	Samba de Orfeo	1973	2.50	5.00	10.00
RCA VICTOR					
LPM-2438 [M]	Desmond Blue	1961	7.50	15.00	30.00
LSP-2438 [S]	Desmond Blue	1961	7.50	15.00	30.00
LPM-2569 [M]	Take Ten	1962	6.25	12.50	25.00
LSP-2569 [S]	Take Ten	1962	7.50	15.00	30.00
LPM-2654 [M]	Two of a Mind	1963	6.25	12.50	25.00
LSP-2654 [S]	Two of a Mind	1963	7.50	15.00	30.00
ANL1-2807	Pure Gold	1978	2.50	5.00	10.00
LPM-3320 [M]	Boss Antigua	1965	5.00	10.00	20.00
LSP-3320 [S]	Boss Antigua	1965	6.25	12.50	25.00
LPM-3407 [M]	Glad to Be Unhappy	1965	5.00	10.00	20.00
LSP-3407 [S]	Glad to Be Unhappy	1965	6.25	12.50	25.00
LPM-3480 [M]	Easy Living	1965	5.00	10.00	20.00
LSP-3480 [S]	Easy Living	1965	6.25	12.50	25.00
WARNER BROS.					
W 1356 [M]	First Place Again	1960	7.50	15.00	30.00
WS 1356 [S]	First Place Again	1960	7.50	15.00	30.00

DETERGENTS, THE

Also see RON DANTE.

Number	Title (A Side/B Side)	Yr	VG	VG+	NM
45s					
KAPP					
735	I Can Never Eat Home Anymore/Igor's Cellar	1966	3.75	7.50	15.00
753	Pushin' the Panic Button/Some Sunday Morning	1966	3.75	7.50	15.00
ROULETTE					
4590	Leader of the Laundromat/Ulcers	1964	5.00	10.00	20.00
4590 [PS]	Leader of the Laundromat/Ulcers	1964	10.00	20.00	40.00
4603	Double-O-Seven/The Blue Kangaroo	1965	3.75	7.50	15.00
4616	Tea and Trumpets/Mrs. Jones (How "Bout It)	1965	3.75	7.50	15.00
4626	Little Dum-Dum/Soldier Girl	1965	3.75	7.50	15.00
4642	Bad Girl/Here She Comes	1965	3.75	7.50	15.00
Albums					
ROULETTE					
R 25308 [M]	The Many Faces of the Detergents	1965	30.00	60.00	120.00
SR 25308 [R]	The Many Faces of the Detergents	1965	25.00	50.00	100.00

DETOURS, THE

Number	Title (A Side/B Side)	Yr	VG	VG+	NM
45s					
ATCO					
6448	Who Do You Love/Peace of Mind	1966	6.25	12.50	25.00
MCSHERRY					
1285	Bring Back My Beatles to Me/Money	1964	6.25	12.50	25.00
1285	Bring Back My Beatles/Money	1964	6.25	12.50	25.00

DETROIT

Mitch Ryder's post-Detroit Wheels band.

Number	Title (A Side/B Side)	Yr	VG	VG+	NM
45s					
PARAMOUNT					
0094	It Ain't Easy/Long Neck Goose	1971	—	3.00	6.00
0133	Rock 'N Roll/Box of Old Roses	1971	—	3.00	6.00
0158	Gimmie Shelter/Oh Oh La La La Dee Da Doo	1972	—	3.00	6.00
Albums					
PARAMOUNT					
PAS-6010	Detroit	1971	3.75	7.50	15.00

DETROIT CITY LIMITS, THE

Number	Title (A Side/B Side)	Yr	VG	VG+	NM
45s					
OKEH					
7308	98c + Tax/Honey Chile	1968	2.00	4.00	8.00
Albums					
OKEH					
OKS 14127	98c + Tax	1968	7.50	15.00	30.00

DETROIT EMERALDS

Number	Title (A Side/B Side)	Yr	VG	VG+	NM
45s					
RIC TIC					
135	Show Time/(Instrumental)	1968	3.00	6.00	12.00
138	Shades Down/Ode to Billie Joe	1968	3.00	6.00	12.00
141	Take Me the Way I Am/I'll Keep On Coming Back	1968	3.00	6.00	12.00
WESTBOUND					
147	Holding On/Things Are Looking Up	1969	2.00	4.00	8.00
156	If I Lose Your Love/I Bet You Get the One	1969	2.00	4.00	8.00
161	I Can't See Myself Doing Without You/Just Now and Then	1970	2.00	4.00	8.00
172	Do Me Right/Just Now and Then	1970	2.00	4.00	8.00
181	Wear This Ring (With Love)/Bet You Got the One Who Loves You	1971	—	3.00	6.00
192	You Want It, You Got It/Till You Decide to Come Home	1971	—	3.00	6.00
203	Baby Let Me Take You (In My Arms)/I'll Never Sail the Sea Again	1972	—	3.00	6.00
209	Feel the Need in Me/There's a Love for Me Somewhere	1972	—	3.00	6.00
213	You're Gettin' a Little Too Smart/Heaven Couldn't Be Like This	1973	—	3.00	6.00
220	Lee/Whatcha Gonna Wear Tomorrow	1973	—	3.00	6.00
226	I'm Qualified/Set It Out	1974	—	3.00	6.00
5005	Yes I Know I'm in Love/Rosetta Stone	1974	—	3.00	6.00
55401	Feel the Need/Love Has Come to Me	1977	—	2.50	5.00
55404	Set It Out (Part 1)/Set It Out (Part 2)	1977	—	2.50	5.00
55410	Turn On Lady/Just Don't Know About This Girl of Mine	1977	—	2.50	5.00
Albums					
WESTBOUND					
302	Feel the Need	1977	3.75	7.50	15.00
2006	Do Me Right	1971	10.00	20.00	40.00

Number	Title (A Side/B Side)	Yr	VG	VG+	NM
2013	You Want It, You Got It	1972	10.00	20.00	40.00
2018	I'm in Love with You	1973	10.00	20.00	40.00
6101	Let's Get Together	1978	3.75	7.50	15.00

DETROIT WHEELS, THE

Mitch Ryder's band after he went solo.

45s

INFERNO

Number	Title (A Side/B Side)	Yr	VG	VG+	NM
5002	Linda Sue Dixon/Tally Ho	1968	5.00	10.00	20.00
5003	Think (Part 1)/Think (Part 2)	1968	5.00	10.00	20.00

DEUCE COUPES, THE

Albums

CROWN

Number	Title (A Side/B Side)	Yr	VG	VG+	NM
CST-393 [S]	The Shut Downs	1963	6.25	12.50	25.00
CLP-5393 [M]	The Shut Downs	1963	5.00	10.00	20.00

DEL-FI

Number	Title (A Side/B Side)	Yr	VG	VG+	NM
DFLP-1243 [M]	Hotrodder's Choice	1963	12.50	25.00	50.00
DFST-1243 [S]	Hotrodder's Choice	1963	15.00	30.00	60.00

DEUCES OF RHYTHM AND THE TEMPO TOPPERS, THE

Also see LITTLE RICHARD.

45s

PEACOCK

Number	Title (A Side/B Side)	Yr	VG	VG+	NM
1616	Ain't That Good News/A Fool at the Wheel	1953	20.00	40.00	80.00
1628	Always/Rice, Red Beans and Turnip Greens	1954	20.00	40.00	80.00

DEVAUGHN, WILLIAM

45s

ROXBURY

Number	Title (A Side/B Side)	Yr	VG	VG+	NM
BRBO-0236	Be Thankful for What You Got-Pt. 1/Be Thankful for What You Got-Pt. 2	1974	—	2.50	5.00
2001	Blood Is Thicker Than Water/Blood Is Thicker Than Water (Part 2)	1974	—	2.50	5.00
2005	Give the Little Man a Great Big Hand/Something Being Done	1974	—	2.50	5.00
2018	Kiss and Make Up/(B-side unknown)	1975	—	2.50	5.00

TEC

Number	Title (A Side/B Side)	Yr	VG	VG+	NM
767	Figures Can't Calculate/(B-side unknown)	1980	—	2.00	4.00

Albums

ROXBURY

Number	Title (A Side/B Side)	Yr	VG	VG+	NM
RLX-100	Be Thankful For What You Got	1974	3.00	6.00	12.00

DEVAURS, THE

45s

D-TONE

Number	Title (A Side/B Side)	Yr	VG	VG+	NM
3	Baby Doll/Teenager	1958	62.50	125.00	250.00

MOON

Number	Title (A Side/B Side)	Yr	VG	VG+	NM
105	Where Are You/Boy in Mexico	1959	50.00	100.00	200.00

RED FOX

Number	Title (A Side/B Side)	Yr	VG	VG+	NM
104	Where Are You/Boy in Mexico	1965	10.00	20.00	40.00

DEVIANTS, THE

Albums

SIRE

Number	Title (A Side/B Side)	Yr	VG	VG+	NM
SES-97001	Ptoof!	1968	15.00	30.00	60.00
SES-97005	Disposable	1969	15.00	30.00	60.00
SES-97016	No. 3	1969	15.00	30.00	60.00

DEVIL'S ANVIL, THE

Albums

COLUMBIA

Number	Title (A Side/B Side)	Yr	VG	VG+	NM
CL 2664 [M]	Hard Rock from the Middle East	1967	6.25	12.50	25.00
CS 9464 [S]	Hard Rock from the Middle East	1967	7.50	15.00	30.00

DEVILED HAM

Albums

SUPER K

Number	Title (A Side/B Side)	Yr	VG	VG+	NM
SKS-6003	I Had Too Much to Dream Last Night	1968	6.25	12.50	25.00

DEVOL, FRANK

45s

ABC-PARAMOUNT

Number	Title (A Side/B Side)	Yr	VG	VG+	NM
10608	Theme from "Peyton Place"/Hush, Hush, Sweet Charlotte	1964	2.00	4.00	8.00
10628	Combat/General Hospital	1965	2.50	5.00	10.00

CAPITOL

Number	Title (A Side/B Side)	Yr	VG	VG+	NM
F835	Sing a Happy Song/Lady Play Your Mandolin	1950	3.75	7.50	15.00
F1143	Dream a While/Powder and Paint	1950	3.75	7.50	15.00
F1178	Love Letters in the Sand/This Year's Kisses	1950	3.75	7.50	15.00
F1247	Jing-a-Ling/Sweethearts on Parade	1950	3.75	7.50	15.00
F1297	One Finger Melody/You Can Marry Me	1950	3.75	7.50	15.00
F1340	Teardrops/It's a Lonely Town	1950	3.75	7.50	15.00
F1359	Lullaby of Broadway/Seven Wonders of the World	1951	3.00	6.00	12.00
F1411	Ciribiribin on Mandolin/Chapel of Roses	1951	3.00	6.00	12.00
F1460	Theme John & Marsha/Playball	1951	3.00	6.00	12.00
F1503	Dear John/Lonely Acres	1951	3.00	6.00	12.00
F1560	Hopalong Cassidy March/Circus Days	1951	3.00	6.00	12.00
F3457	Toy Tiger/Three Fishermen	1956	2.50	5.00	10.00

COLGEMS

Number	Title (A Side/B Side)	Yr	VG	VG+	NM
66-1015	Guess Who's Coming to Dinner/The Glory of Love	1968	—	3.00	6.00

COLUMBIA

Number	Title (A Side/B Side)	Yr	VG	VG+	NM
40953	Love in the Afternoon/Venice	1957	2.50	5.00	10.00
41285	My Heart's in Portugal/How Can You Forget	1958	2.00	4.00	8.00
41366	House on Haunted Hill/Hadies	1959	2.00	4.00	8.00
41620	La Montana (If She Should Come to You)/"The Key" Theme	1960	2.00	4.00	8.00
41620 [PS]	La Montana (If She Should Come to You)/"The Key" Theme	1960	3.75	7.50	15.00
41702	Do You Think of Me/Same Old Summer	1960	2.00	4.00	8.00
41724	Same Old Summer/Do You Think of Me	1960	2.00	4.00	8.00
41987	David's Dream/Columbia	1961	2.00	4.00	8.00
42620	Whatever Happened to Baby Jane/I've Written a Letter to Daddy	1962	2.00	4.00	8.00

Albums

ABC-PARAMOUNT

Number	Title (A Side/B Side)	Yr	VG	VG+	NM
513 [M]	Theme from "Peyton Place" and 11 Other Great Themes	1965	3.00	6.00	12.00
S-513 [S]	Theme from "Peyton Place" and 11 Other Great Themes	1965	3.75	7.50	15.00
534 [M]	Italian Romance American Style	1966	3.00	6.00	12.00
S-534 [S]	Italian Romance American Style	1966	3.75	7.50	15.00

COLUMBIA

Number	Title (A Side/B Side)	Yr	VG	VG+	NM
C2L 12 [(2) M]	The Columbia Album of Irving Berlin	1958	7.50	15.00	30.00
C2S 812 [(2) S]	The Columbia Album of Irving Berlin	1958	10.00	20.00	40.00
CL 1108 [M]	Portraits	1957	3.75	7.50	15.00
CL 1260 [M]	The Columbia Album of Irving Berlin, Volume 1	1958	3.75	7.50	15.00
CL 1261 [M]	The Columbia Album of Irving Berlin, Volume 2	1958	3.75	7.50	15.00
CL 1371 [M]	Fabulous Hollywood	1959	3.75	7.50	15.00
CL 1413 [M]	The Old Sweet Songs	1960	3.75	7.50	15.00
CL 1451 [M]	Four Seasons of Love	1960	3.75	7.50	15.00
CL 1482 [M]	More Old Sweet Songs	1960	3.75	7.50	15.00
CL 1543 [M]	The Old Sweet Songs of Christmas	1960	3.75	7.50	15.00
CS 8172 [S]	Fabulous Hollywood	1959	5.00	10.00	20.00
CS 8209 [S]	The Old Sweet Songs	1960	5.00	10.00	20.00
CS 8273 [S]	More Old Sweet Songs	1960	5.00	10.00	20.00
CS 8343 [S]	The Old Sweet Songs of Christmas	1960	3.75	7.50	15.00
CS (# unknown) [S]	Four Seasons of Love	1960	5.00	10.00	20.00

COLUMBIA SPECIAL PRODUCTS

Number	Title (A Side/B Side)	Yr	VG	VG+	NM
EN2 16437 [(2)]	The Columbia Album of Irving Berlin	1983	3.00	6.00	12.00

HARMONY

Number	Title (A Side/B Side)	Yr	VG	VG+	NM
HL 7356 [M]	The Old Sweet Songs of Christmas	196?	3.00	6.00	12.00
HS 11156 [S]	The Old Sweet Songs of Christmas	196?	3.75	7.50	15.00

DEVONS, THE (1)

45s

DECCA

Number	Title (A Side/B Side)	Yr	VG	VG+	NM
31777	Honda Bike/Free Fall	1965	20.00	40.00	80.00
31822	Are You Really Real/It's All Over Now, Baby Blue	1965	10.00	20.00	40.00
31899	Come On/A Little Extra Effort	1966	10.00	20.00	40.00

DEVONS, THE (2)

45s

KING

Number	Title (A Side/B Side)	Yr	VG	VG+	NM
6226	Someone to Treat Me (The Way You Used To)/Soul Party	1969	2.00	4.00	8.00

DEVONS, THE (3)

Also recorded as SIR DOUGLAS QUINTET.

45s

PIC ONE

Number	Title (A Side/B Side)	Yr	VG	VG+	NM
111	Wine, Wine, Wine/Joey's Guitar	1965	20.00	40.00	80.00

DEVONS, THE (U)

May be group (2), but we're not sure.

45s

MR. G

Number	Title (A Side/B Side)	Yr	VG	VG+	NM
825	Groovin' with My Thing/Wise Up	1968	3.00	6.00	12.00

DEVORZON, BARRY

Also see BARRY AND THE TAMERLANES.

45s

A&M

Number	Title (A Side/B Side)	Yr	VG	VG+	NM
2129	Theme from "The Warriors"/Baseball Furies' Chase	1979	—	2.00	4.00

COLUMBIA

Number	Title (A Side/B Side)	Yr	VG	VG+	NM
41464	Betty, Betty/Across the Street from Your House	1959	7.50	15.00	30.00
41612	Hey Little Darlin'/Rosemary	1960	6.25	12.50	25.00
41663	Love You Baby/Can-Can Ladies	1960	6.25	12.50	25.00
42031	Penny Moved Away/Lindy Lou	1961	6.25	12.50	25.00
3-42031	Penny Moved Away/Lindy Lou	1961	10.00	20.00	40.00
—"Compact 33" single with small hole					

RCA VICTOR

Number	Title (A Side/B Side)	Yr	VG	VG+	NM
47-7124	Barbara Jean/Baby Doll	1957	7.50	15.00	30.00
47-7226	False Love/Raindrops at My Window	1958	7.50	15.00	30.00
47-7406	Honey Bunny/Too Soon	1958	7.50	15.00	30.00
47-7510	Cora Lee/Blue, Green and Gold	1959	7.50	15.00	30.00

Albums

ARISTA

Number	Title (A Side/B Side)	Yr	VG	VG+	NM
AL 4104	Nadia's Theme	1976	2.50	5.00	10.00

DEVORZON, BARRY, AND PERRY BOTKIN, JR.

Also see each artist's individual listings.

45s

A&M

Number	Title (A Side/B Side)	Yr	VG	VG+	NM
1856	Nadia's Theme (The Young and the Restless)/Down the Line	1976	—	2.00	4.00
—Reissue; the original is listed under PERRY BOTKIN, JR.					
1856 [PS]	Nadia's Theme (The Young and the Restless)/Down the Line	1976	—	2.00	4.00
—Green sleeve					
1856 [PS]	Nadia's Theme (The Young and the Restless)/Down the Line	1976	—	3.00	6.00
—Blue sleeve					
1856 [PS]	Nadia's Theme (The Young and the Restless)/Down the Line	1976	—	3.00	6.00
—Black sleeve					
1890	Bless the Beasts and Children/Down the Line	1976	—	2.00	4.00

Number	Title (A Side/B Side)	Yr	VG	VG+	NM

DEVOTIONS, THE
45s
DELTA

1001	Rip Van Winkle/I Love You for Sentimental Reasons	1961	37.50	75.00	150.00
KAPE					
701	(How Do You Speak) To An Angel/Teardrops Follow Me	1966	3.00	6.00	12.00
ROULETTE					
4406	Rip Van Winkle/I Love You for Sentimental Reasons	1962	10.00	20.00	40.00
4541	Rip Van Winkle/I Love You for Sentimental Reasons	1964	5.00	10.00	20.00
4556	A Sunday Kind of Love/Tears from a Broken Heart	1964	7.50	5.00	30.00
4580	Snow White/Zindy Lou	1964	7.50	5.00	30.00

DEWEY, GEORGE AND JACK
45s
RAVEN

700	The Flying Saucers Have Landed/The Flying Saucers Have Landed (Part 2)	195?	7.50	15.00	30.00

DEWITT, GEORGE
Albums
EPIC

BN 531 [S]	George DeWitt Sings That Tune	1959	7.50	15.00	30.00
LN 3562 [M]	George DeWitt Sings That Tune	1959	5.00	10.00	20.00

DEY, TRACEY
Also see DEY AND KNIGHT.
45s
AMY

894	Teddy's the Boy I Love/Here Comes the Boy	1963	3.75	7.50	15.00
901	Gonna Get Along Without You Now/Go Away	1964	3.75	7.50	15.00
908	Hangin' On to My Baby/Ska-Doo-Dee-Yah	1964	3.75	7.50	15.00
912	I Won't Tell/Any Kind of Love	1964	3.75	7.50	15.00
917	Blue Turns to Grey/Didn't Ya	1964	5.00	10.00	20.00
928	Hanky Panky/Shakin' the Blues Away	1965	3.75	7.50	15.00
LIBERTY					
55604	Teenage Cleopatra/Who's That	1963	3.75	7.50	15.00
VEE JAY					
467	Jerry (I'm Your Sherry)/Once in a Blue Moon	1962	6.25	12.50	25.00
506	Jealous Eyes/Long Time, No See	1963	5.00	10.00	20.00

DEY AND KNIGHT
Also see TRACEY DEY.
45s
COLUMBIA

43466	Young Love/I'm Gonna Love You Tomorrow	1965	3.00	6.00	12.00
43693	Sayin' Somethin'/Ooh Da La Da Lay	1966	3.00	6.00	12.00

DEYOUNG, CLIFF
Also see CLEAR LIGHT.
45s
MCA

40156	My Sweet Lady/Sunshine on My Shoulders	1973	—	2.00	4.00
40156 [PS]	My Sweet Lady/Sunshine on My Shoulders	1973	—	2.50	5.00
40239	Escaping Reality/She Bent Me Straight Again	1974	—	2.00	4.00
40294	It Hurts a Little Even Now/Lives	1974	—	2.00	4.00
40388	If I Could Put You in My Song/You Will Never Know	1975	—	2.00	4.00
Albums					
MCA					
387	Sunshine	1973	3.75	7.50	15.00
432	Cliff DeYoung	1974	2.50	5.00	10.00

DIABLOS, THE (1)
See NOLAN STRONG AND THE DIABLOS.

DIABLOS, THE (2)
45s
JUBILEE

5553	Hombre/El Bandito	1966	5.00	10.00	20.00

DIABLOS, THE (3)
45s
PYRAMID

159	White Christmas/Danny Boy	19??	5.00	10.00	20.00

DIALOGUE
Albums
COLD

(no #)	Dialogue	1968	75.00	150.00	300.00
—White cover with insert					
(no #)	Dialogue	1968	25.00	50.00	100.00
—Orange cover with insert					

DIALS, THE
45s
HILLTOP

219	No Hard Feelings/Win Yourself a Lover	1961	12.50	25.00	50.00
2009	Wondering About Your Love/Sorrento	1960	37.50	75.00	150.00
2010	School Bells Are Ringing/Ring Ting-a-Ling	1960	75.00	150.00	300.00
NORGOLDE					
105	Ring Ting-a Ling/All Kinds of Twistin'	1961	20.00	40.00	80.00
PHILIPS					
40040	These Foolish Things/At the Start of a New Romance	1962	10.00	20.00	40.00
TIME					
1068	Monkey Dance/Monkey Walk	1963	5.00	10.00	20.00
Albums					
TIME					
S-2100 [S]	It's Monkey Time	1964	7.50	15.00	30.00
52100 [M]	It's Monkey Time	1964	6.25	12.50	25.00

DIALTONES, THE (1)
45s
DIAL

4054	Don't Let the Sun Shine on Me/You Don't Know, You Just Don't Know	1967	5.00	10.00	20.00

DIALTONES, THE (2)
45s
GOLDISC

3005	Till I Heard It from You/Johnny	1960	7.50	15.00	30.00
3020	Till I Heard It from You/Johnny	1961	5.00	10.00	20.00

DIALTONES, THE (U)
Probably neither (1) nor (2), but we're not sure.
45s
LAWN

203	So Young/Chicago Bird	1963	6.25	12.50	25.00

DIAMOND, BRIAN, AND THE CUTTERS
45s
HICKORY

1321	Big Bad Wolf/See If I Care	1965	2.50	5.00	10.00

DIAMOND, LARRY
45s
ARGO

5330	Bye Bye Doll/True Love, Come My Way	1959	3.00	6.00	12.00

DIAMOND, LEO
45s
AMBASSADOR

1004	Off Shore/(B-side unknown)	1953	3.75	7.50	15.00
1006	On the Mall/(B-side unknown)	195?	3.75	7.50	15.00
RCA VICTOR					
47-5765	China Nights/Hold On to Your Dreams	1954	3.00	6.00	12.00
47-5834	The High and the Mighty/Lisbon	1954	3.00	6.00	12.00
47-5973	Melody of Love/Phantom Gaucho	1955	3.00	6.00	12.00
47-6090	The One Rose/Land of the Pharaohs	1955	3.00	6.00	12.00
47-6194	Theme from "Female on the Beach"/Destiny	1955	3.00	6.00	12.00
47-6307	Mister X/Fantasia Mexicana	1955	3.00	6.00	12.00
47-6406	Lisbon Antigua/Music Box Tango	1956	3.00	6.00	12.00
47-6513	Polynesian/Du Bist Schoen Wie Musik	1956	3.00	6.00	12.00
47-6600	Go See Tony/Le Refifi	1956	3.00	6.00	12.00
47-6710	Sixth Finger Tune/I Remember When	1956	3.00	6.00	12.00
REPRISE					
20004	Bridge of Sighs/Choo Choo to Chihuahua	1961	—	—	—
—Canceled					
20016	Sweet and Lovely/Dream of Olwen	1961	2.00	4.00	8.00
20036	The 400 BLows/La Dolce Vita	1961	2.00	4.00	8.00
20074	Harbor Lights/Theme for a New Love	1962	2.00	4.00	8.00
20126	Born to Be With You/Miramor	1962	2.00	4.00	8.00
ROULETTE					
4025	Till/Sunrise in Texas	1957	2.50	5.00	10.00
4047	Flunky/Te Amo	1957	2.50	5.00	10.00
Albums					
RCA VICTOR					
LPM-1165 [M]	Skin Diver Suite and Other Selections	1955	15.00	30.00	60.00
REPRISE					
R-6002 [M]	Exciting Sounds of the South Seas	1961	6.25	12.50	25.00
R9-6002 [S]	Exciting Sounds of the South Seas	1961	7.50	15.00	30.00
R-6009 [M]	Themes from Great Foreign Films	1961	6.25	12.50	25.00
R9-6009 [S]	Themes from Great Foreign Films	1961	7.50	15.00	30.00
R-6024 [M]	Off Shore	1962	6.25	12.50	25.00
R9-6024 [S]	Off Shore	1962	7.50	15.00	30.00

DIAMOND, NEIL
Also see BARBRA AND NEIL; NEIL AND JACK; TEN BROKEN HEARTS.
12-Inch Singles
CONTINUUM II

001	We Wrote a Song Together/Beautiful Noise	1976	500.00	1000.	2000.

—Private pressing done for the grade school class of Jesse Diamond, Neil's son. All were autographed by Neil; the version of "Beautiful Noise" is an alternate take. Supposedly, between 30 and 40 copies were made.

45s
BANG

105	Cherry, Cherry/Girl, You'll Be a Woman Soon	1973	—	2.00	4.00
—Reissue					
108	Solitary Man/I'm a Believer	1973	—	2.00	4.00
—Reissue					
519	Solitary Man/Do It	1966	3.75	7.50	15.00
528	Cherry, Cherry/I'll Come Running	1966	3.00	6.00	12.00
536	I Got the Feelin' (Oh No No)/The Boat That I Row	1966	3.00	6.00	12.00
540	You Got to Me/Someday Baby	1967	3.00	6.00	12.00
542	Girl, You'll Be a Woman Soon/You'll Forget	1967	3.00	6.00	12.00
547	I Thank the Lord for the Night Time/The Long Way Home	1967	3.75	7.50	15.00
547	Thank the Lord for the Night Time/The Long Way Home	1967	2.50	5.00	10.00
—Title altered on second pressing					
551	Kentucky Woman/The Time Is Now	1967	2.50	5.00	10.00
554	New Orleans/Hanky Panky	1968	2.50	5.00	10.00
556	Red Red Wine/Red Rubber Ball	1968	2.00	4.00	8.00
561	Shilo/La Bamba	1968	2.00	4.00	8.00
575	Shilo/La Bamba	1970	—	3.00	6.00
578	Solitary Man/The Time Is Now	1970	—	3.00	6.00
580	Do It/Hanky Panky	1970	—	3.00	6.00

Number	Title (A Side/B Side)	Yr	VG	VG+	NM
586	I'm a Believer/Crooked Street	1971	—	3.00	6.00
586	I'm a Believer/Crooked Street	1971	3.75	7.50	15.00
—Rare pressing with both sides in stereo					
703	The Long Way Home/Monday, Monday	1973	—	2.50	5.00
CAPITOL					
4939	Love on the Rocks/Acapulco	1980	—	2.00	4.00
4939 [PS]	Love on the Rocks/Acapulco	1980	—	2.00	4.00
4960	Hello Again/Amazed and Confused	1981	—	2.00	4.00
4960 [PS]	Hello Again/Amazed and Confused	1981	—	2.00	4.00
4994	America/Songs of Life	1981	—	2.00	4.00
4994 [PS]	America/Songs of Life	1981	—	2.00	4.00
COLUMBIA					
AE7 1115 [DJ]	Song Sung Blue (mono/stereo)	1977	3.75	7.50	15.00
—Live version from "Love at the Greek"					
02604	Yesterday's Songs/Guitar Heaven	1981	—	—	3.00
02604 [PS]	Yesterday's Songs/Guitar Heaven	1981	—	—	3.00
02712	On the Way to the Sky/Save Me	1982	—	—	3.00
02712 [PS]	On the Way to the Sky/Save Me	1982	—	—	3.00
02928	Be Mine Tonight/Right By You	1982	—	—	3.00
03219	Heartlight/You Don't Know Me	1982	—	—	3.00
03219 [PS]	Heartlight/You Don't Know Me	1982	—	2.00	4.00
CNR-03345	Heartlight	1982	—	2.50	5.00
—One-sided budget release					
03503	I'm Alive/Lost Among the Stars	1983	—	—	3.00
CNR-03572	I'm Alive	1983	—	2.50	5.00
—One-sided budget release					
03801	Front Page Story/I'm Guilty	1983	—	—	3.00
03801 [PS]	Front Page Story/I'm Guilty	1983	—	—	3.00
04541	Turn Around/Brooklyn on a Saturday Night	1984	—	—	3.00
04541 [PS]	Turn Around/Brooklyn on a Saturday Night	1984	—	—	3.00
04646	Sleep with Me Tonight/One by One	1984	—	—	3.00
04719	You Make It Feel Like Christmas/Crazy	1984	2.00	4.00	8.00
05889	Headed for the Future/Angel	1986	—	—	3.00
05889 [PS]	Headed for the Future/Angel	1986	—	—	3.00
06136	The Story of My Life/Love Doesn't Live Here Anymore	1986	—	—	3.00
06136 [PS]	The Story of My Life/Love Doesn't Live Here Anymore	1986	—	—	3.00
07614	I Dreamed a Dream/Sweet Caroline	1987	—	—	3.00
07614 [PS]	I Dreamed a Dream/Sweet Caroline	1987	—	—	3.00
07751	Cherry, Cherry/America	1988	—	—	3.00
08514	This Time/If I Couldn't See You Again	1988	—	—	3.00
10043	Longfellow Serenade/Rosemary's Wine	1974	—	2.50	5.00
10084	I've Been This Way Before/Reggae Strut	1975	—	2.50	5.00
10138	The Last Picasso/The Gift of Song	1975	—	2.50	5.00
10366	If You Know What I Mean/Street Life	1976	—	2.50	5.00
10405	Don't Think...Feel/Home Is a Wounded Heart	1976	—	2.50	5.00
10452	Beautiful Noise/Signs	1976	—	2.50	5.00
10657	Desiree/Once in a While	1977	—	2.50	5.00
10897	Forever in Blue Jeans/Remember Me	1979	—	2.00	4.00
10945	Say Maybe/Diamond Girls	1979	—	2.00	4.00
11175	September Morn/I'm a Believer	1980	—	2.00	4.00
11232	The Good Lord Loves You/Jazz Time	1980	—	2.00	4.00
42809	Clown Town/At Night	1963	125.00	250.00	500.00
42809 [DJ]	Clown Town/At Night	1963	62.50	125.00	250.00
45942	Be/Flight of the Gull	1973	—	2.50	5.00
45998	Skybird/Lonely Looking Sky	1974	—	2.50	5.00
68741	The Best Years of Our Lives/Carmelita's Eyes	1989	—	—	3.00
78242	One Good Love/Kentucky Woman	1996	—	—	3.00
—A-side: Duet with Waylon Jennings					
MCA					
40017	Cherry, Cherry from Hot August Night/ Morningside	1973	—	2.50	5.00
40092	The Last Thing on My Mind/Canta Libra	1973	—	2.50	5.00
PHILCO-FORD					
HP-5	Girl, You'll Be a Woman Soon/Cherry, Cherry	1967	3.75	7.50	15.00
—4-inch plastic "Hip Pocket Record" with color sleeve					
HP-17	Solitary Man/You Got to Me	1967	3.75	7.50	15.00
—4-inch plastic "Hip Pocket Record" with color sleeve					
UNI					
55065	Brooklyn Roads/Holiday Inn Blues	1968	2.00	4.00	8.00
55075	Two-Bit Manchild/Broad Old Woman	1968	2.00	4.00	8.00
55075 [DJ]	Two-Bit Manchild (same on both sides)	1968	20.00	40.00	80.00
—Red vinyl					
55075 [PS]	Two-Bit Manchild/Broad Old Woman	1968	6.25	12.50	25.00
55084	Sunday Sun/Honey-Drippin' Times	1968	2.00	4.00	8.00
55109	Brother Love's Travelling Salvation Show/A Modern-Day Version of Love	1969	—	3.00	6.00
55136	Sweet Caroline (Good Times Never Seemed So Good)/Dig In	1969	—	3.00	6.00
55175	Holly Holy/Hurtin' You Don't Come Easy	1969	—	3.00	6.00
55204	Until It's Time for You to Go/And the Singer Sings His Song	1970	—	3.00	6.00
55224	Soolaimon (African Trilogy II)/And the Grass Won't Pay No Mind	1970	—	3.00	6.00
55224 [PS]	Soolaimon (African Trilogy II)/And the Grass Won't Pay No Mind	1970	3.75	7.50	15.00
55250	Cracklin' Rosie/Lordy	1970	—	3.00	6.00
55264	He Ain't Heavy...He's My Brother/Free Life	1970	—	3.00	6.00
55278	I Am...I Said/Done Too Soon	1971	—	2.50	5.00
55310	Stones/Crunchy Granola Suite	1971	—	2.50	5.00
55326	Song Sung Blue/Gitchy Goomy	1972	—	2.50	5.00
55346	Play Me/Porcupine Pie	1972	—	2.50	5.00
55352	Walk on Water/High Rolling Man	1972	—	2.50	5.00

Albums

Number	Title	Yr	VG	VG+	NM
BANG					
BLP 214 [M]	The Feel of Neil Diamond	1966	15.00	30.00	60.00
—All tracks play mono					
BLP 214 [P]	The Feel of Neil Diamond	1966	20.00	40.00	80.00
—Album is labeled mono, but plays in stereo					
BLPS 214	The Feel of Neil Diamond	1974	3.00	6.00	12.00
—Later pressing on blue "clouds" label					
BLPS 214 [P]	The Feel of Neil Diamond	1966	25.00	50.00	100.00
—Album is labeled stereo and plays in stereo (except "Solitary Man," "Do It," "I'll Come Running" are rechanneled)					
BLP 217 [M]	Just For You	1967	10.00	20.00	40.00
—With blurb for "Thank the Lord for the Night Time" on cover					
BLPS 217	Just For You	1974	3.00	6.00	12.00
—Later pressing on blue "clouds" label					
BLPS 217 [P]	Just For You	1967	12.50	25.00	50.00
—With blurb for "Thank the Lord for the Night Time" on cover					
BLPS 217 [P]	Just For You	1968	10.00	20.00	40.00
—With blurb for "Shilo" pasted over "Thank the Lord for the Night Time" blurb					
BLPS 217 [P]	Just For You	1970	5.00	10.00	20.00
—With blurb for "Shilo" imprinted on cover					
BLPS 219	Neil Diamond's Greatest Hits	1974	3.00	6.00	12.00
—Later pressing on blue "clouds" label					
BLPS 219 [P]	Neil Diamond's Greatest Hits	1968	10.00	20.00	40.00
—First editions have the single version of "Solitary Man" in rechanneled stereo					
BLPS 219 [P]	Neil Diamond's Greatest Hits	196?	5.00	10.00	20.00
—Later editions have an alternate take of "Solitary Man" in true stereo					
BLPS 221	Shilo	1974	3.00	6.00	12.00
—Later pressing on blue "clouds" label					
BLPS 221 [S]	Shilo	1970	10.00	20.00	40.00
BLPS 224	Do It!	1974	3.00	6.00	12.00
—Later pressing on blue "clouds" label					
BLPS 224 [P]	Do It!	1971	7.50	15.00	30.00
BLPS-227 [(2) S]	Double Gold	1973	10.00	20.00	40.00
BLPS 227 [(2)]	Double Gold	1974	3.75	7.50	15.00
—Later pressing on blue "clouds" label					
CAPITOL					
SWAV-12120	The Jazz Singer	1980	2.50	5.00	10.00
COLUMBIA					
AS 99-1586 [DJ]	Heartlight	1982	5.00	10.00	20.00
—Promo-only picture disc					
KC 32550	Jonathan Livingston Seagull	1973	3.00	6.00	12.00
—With booklet					
PC 32919	Serenade	1974	3.00	6.00	12.00
PCQ 32919 [Q]	Serenade	1974	6.25	12.50	25.00
PC 33965	Beautiful Noise	1976	3.00	6.00	12.00
—Originals have no bar code					
KC2 34404 [(2)]	Love at the Greek	1977	3.75	7.50	15.00
JC 34990	I'm Glad You're Here with Me Tonight	1977	3.00	6.00	12.00
FC 35625	You Don't Bring Me Flowers	1978	3.00	6.00	12.00
FC 36121	September Morn	1979	3.00	6.00	12.00
TC 37628	On the Way to the Sky	1981	2.50	5.00	10.00
TC 38068	12 Greatest Hits, Vol. II	1982	2.50	5.00	10.00
TC 38359	Heartlight	1982	2.50	5.00	10.00
PC 38792	Classics — The Early Years	1983	2.50	5.00	10.00
—Possibly a reissue of Frog King 1					
QC 39199	Primitive	1984	2.50	5.00	10.00
9C9 39915 [PD]	Primitive	1984	5.00	10.00	20.00
OC 40368	Headed for the Future	1986	2.00	4.00	8.00
CG2 40990 [(2)]	Hot August Night II	1987	3.00	6.00	12.00
HC 42550	Jonathan Livingston Seagull	1982	12.50	25.00	50.00
—Half-speed mastered edition					
OC 45025	The Best Years of Our Lives	1988	2.00	4.00	8.00
HC 45625	You Don't Bring Me Flowers	1982	10.00	20.00	40.00
—Half-speed mastered edition					
HC 47628	On the Way to the Sky	1982	7.50	15.00	30.00
—Half-speed mastered edition					
HC 48068	12 Greatest Hits, Vol. II	1982	25.00	50.00	100.00
—Half-speed mastered edition					
HC 48359	Heartlight	1982	10.00	20.00	40.00
—Half-speed mastered edition					
C 48610	Lovescape	1991	3.75	7.50	15.00
DIRECT DISK					
SD 16612	His 12 Greatest Hits	1982	12.50	25.00	50.00
—Audiophile vinyl					
FROG KING					
AAR-1	Early Classics	1972	10.00	20.00	40.00
—Compilation of Bang material for Columbia Record Club; includes songbook (deduct 25% if missing)					
MCA					
1489	Neil Diamond/His 12 Greatest Hits	1987	2.00	4.00	8.00
—Reissue of MCA 5219					
2005	Moods	1973	2.50	5.00	10.00
2006	Touching You Touching Me	1973	2.50	5.00	10.00
2007	Neil Diamond/Gold	1973	2.50	5.00	10.00
2008	Stones	1973	2.50	5.00	10.00
2011	Sweet Caroline (Brother Love's Travelling Salvation Show)	1973	2.50	5.00	10.00
2013	Tap Root Manuscript	1973	2.50	5.00	10.00
2103	Rainbow	1973	3.75	7.50	15.00
—Compilation of Uni tracks					
2106	Neil Diamond/His 12 Greatest Hits	1974	3.75	7.50	15.00
2227	And the Singer Sings His Song	1976	3.75	7.50	15.00
5219	Neil Diamond/His 12 Greatest Hits	1981	2.50	5.00	10.00
—Reissue of MCA 2106					
5239	Love Songs	1981	2.50	5.00	10.00
6896 [(2)]	Hot August Night	1980	3.00	6.00	12.00
—Reissue of MCA 2-8000					
8000 [(2)]	Hot August Night	1972	5.00	10.00	20.00
37056	Velvet Gloves and Spit	1980	2.00	4.00	8.00
37057	Sweet Caroline/Brother Love's Travelling Salvation Show	1980	2.00	4.00	8.00
37058	Touching You Touching Me	1980	2.00	4.00	8.00
37059	Rainbow	1980	2.00	4.00	8.00
37060	And the Singer Sings His Song	1980	2.00	4.00	8.00
37194	Moods	1981	2.00	4.00	8.00
37195	Stones	1981	2.00	4.00	8.00
37196	Tap Root Manuscript	1981	2.00	4.00	8.00
37209	Gold	1981	2.00	4.00	8.00
MOBILE FIDELITY					
2-024 [(2)]	Hot August Night	1979	10.00	20.00	40.00
—Audiophile vinyl					
1-071	The Jazz Singer	1981	7.50	15.00	30.00
—Audiophile vinyl					
UNI					
ND-11 [DJ]	Neil Diamond DJ Sampler	1970	50.00	100.00	200.00

Number	Title (A Side/B Side)	Yr	VG	VG+	NM
1913 [DJ]	Open-End Interview with Neil Diamond	1971	75.00	150.00	300.00
73030	Velvet Gloves and Spit	1968	7.50	15.00	30.00
—First editions do not include "Shilo"					
73030	Velvet Gloves and Spit	1970	5.00	10.00	20.00
—Later editions add a new recording of "Shilo"					
73047	Brother Love's Travelling Salvation Show	1969	7.50	15.00	30.00
—First editions do not include "Sweet Caroline"					
73047	Brother Love's Travelling Salvation Show	1969	5.00	10.00	20.00
—Later editions add "Sweet Caroline"					
73071	Touching You Touching Me	1969	5.00	10.00	20.00
73084	Neil Diamond/Gold	1970	5.00	10.00	20.00
73092	Tap Root Manuscript	1970	5.00	10.00	20.00
93106	Stones	1971	5.00	10.00	20.00
93136	Moods	1972	5.00	10.00	20.00
ST-93501	Tap Root Manuscript	1970	6.25	12.50	25.00
—Capitol Record Club issue					

DIAMONDS, THE (1)

45s

CORAL

Number	Title (A Side/B Side)	Yr	VG	VG+	NM
61502	Black Denim Trousers and Motorcycle Boots/Nip Sip	1955	5.00	10.00	20.00
61577	Be My Lovin' Baby/Smooch Me	1956	5.00	10.00	20.00
GUSTO					
2019	Little Darlin'/The Stroll	1979	—	2.00	4.00
—Re-recordings					
MERCURY					
70790	Why Do Fools Fall in Love/You Baby You	1956	5.00	10.00	20.00
70835	The Church Bells May Ring/Little Girl of Mine	1956	5.00	10.00	20.00
70889	Love, Love, Love/Every Night About This Time	1956	5.00	10.00	20.00
70934	Ka-Ding-Dong/Soft Summer Breeze	1956	5.00	10.00	20.00
70983	My Judge and My Jury/Put Your House in Order	1956	5.00	10.00	20.00
71021	A Thousand Miles Away/Ev'ry Minute of the Day	1956	5.00	10.00	20.00
71060	Little Darlin'/Faithful and True	1957	10.00	20.00	40.00
—The only "cover version" generally considered a significant improvement over the original (by The Gladiolas)					
71128	Words of Love/Don't Say Goodbye	1957	5.00	10.00	20.00
71165	Zip Zip/Oh How I Wish	1957	5.00	10.00	20.00
71197	Silhouettes/Daddy Cool	1957	5.00	10.00	20.00
71242	The Stroll/Land of Beauty	1957	7.50	15.00	30.00
71291	High Sign/Chick-Lets (Don't Let Me Down)	1958	3.75	7.50	15.00
71291 [PS]	High Sign/Chick-Lets (Don't Let Me Down)	1958	25.00	50.00	100.00
71330	Kathy-O/Happy Years	1958	3.75	7.50	15.00
71366	Walking Along/Eternal Lovers	1958	3.75	7.50	15.00
71404	She Say (Oom Dooby Doom)/From the Bottom of My Heart	1959	5.00	10.00	20.00
71449	A Mother's Love/Gretchen	1959	3.75	7.50	15.00
71468	Sneaky Alligator/Holding Your Hand	1959	3.75	7.50	15.00
71505	Young in Years/The Twenty-Second Day	1959	3.75	7.50	15.00
71534	Walking the Stroll/Batman, Wolfman, Frankenstein or Dracula	1959	5.00	10.00	20.00
71586	Real True Love/Tell the Truth	1960	3.75	7.50	15.00
71633	The Pencil Song/Slave Girl	1960	3.75	7.50	15.00
71734	The Crumble/You'd Be Mine	1960	3.75	7.50	15.00
71782	You Sure Changed Me/I Sure Lawd Will	1961	3.75	7.50	15.00
71818	The Munch/Woomai Ling	1961	3.75	7.50	15.00
71831	One Summer Night/It's a Doggone Shame	1961	3.75	7.50	15.00
71956	The Vanishing American/The Horizontal Lieutenant	1962	3.75	7.50	15.00

7-Inch Extended Plays

BRUNSWICK

Number	Title (A Side/B Side)	Yr	VG	VG+	NM
EB 71031	(contents unknown)	1957	37.50	75.00	150.00
EB 71031 [PS]	The Diamonds	1957	37.50	75.00	150.00
MERCURY					
EP 1-3356	(contents unknown)	1957	10.00	20.00	40.00
EP 1-3356 [PS]	The Diamonds	1957	10.00	20.00	40.00
EP 1-3357	(contents unknown)	1957	10.00	20.00	40.00
EP 1-3357 [PS]	The Diamonds	1957	10.00	20.00	40.00
EP 1-3358	Till My Baby Comes Home/Girl of Mine//One and Only/Honey	1957	10.00	20.00	40.00
EP 1-3358 [PS]	The Diamonds: America's Number One Singing Stylists	1957	10.00	20.00	40.00
EP 1-3367	Silhouettes/Daddy Cool//Passion Flower/Sweet Wild Honey	1957	10.00	20.00	40.00
EP 1-3367 [PS]	The Diamonds	1957	10.00	20.00	40.00
EP 1-3390	(contents unknown)	1958	10.00	20.00	40.00
EP 1-3390 [PS]	The Stroll	1958	10.00	20.00	40.00

Albums

MERCURY

Number	Title (A Side/B Side)	Yr	VG	VG+	NM
MG-20213 [M]	Collection of Golden Hits	1956	30.00	60.00	120.00
MG-20309 [M]	The Diamonds	1957	30.00	60.00	120.00
MG-20368 [M]	The Diamonds Meet Pete Rugolo	1958	20.00	40.00	80.00
MG-20480 [M]	Songs from the Old West	1959	20.00	40.00	80.00
SR-60076 [S]	The Diamonds Meet Pete Rugolo	1959	30.00	60.00	120.00
SR-60159 [S]	Songs from the Old West	1959	30.00	60.00	120.00
RHINO					
RNDF-209	The Best of the Diamonds	1984	3.00	6.00	12.00
WING					
MGW-12114 [M]	The Diamonds: America's Famous Song Stylists	1959	7.50	15.00	30.00
MGW-12178 [M]	Pop Hits by the Diamonds	1962	7.50	15.00	30.00

DIAMONDS, THE (2)

Black vocal group.

45s

ATLANTIC

Number	Title (A Side/B Side)	Yr	VG	VG+	NM
981	A Beggar for Your Kisses/Call, Baby, Call	1952	375.00	750.00	1500.
1003	I'll Live Again/Two Loves Have I	1953	150.00	300.00	600.00
1017	Romance in the Dark/Cherry	1954	150.00	300.00	600.00

DIANE AND THE DARLETTES

45s

DUNES

Number	Title (A Side/B Side)	Yr	VG	VG+	NM
2016	Just You/The Wobble	1962	6.25	12.50	25.00
2026	Here She Comes/Just You	1963	3.75	7.50	15.00
—As "The Darlettes"					

DIBANGO, MANU

12-Inch Singles

CELLULOID

Number	Title (A Side/B Side)	Yr	VG	VG+	NM
CEL 171	Abele Dance/Abele Dance Dub	1984	2.00	4.00	8.00
CEL 182	Makossa Rock (2 versions)/Gammatron	1985	2.00	4.00	8.00
ISLAND					
8680 [DJ]	Big Blow/Aloko Party	1976	2.00	4.00	8.00

45s

ATLANTIC

Number	Title (A Side/B Side)	Yr	VG	VG+	NM
2971	Soul Makossa/Lily	1973	—	2.50	5.00
2983	Dangwa/Obaso	1973	—	2.50	5.00
3000	Weya/Moni	1974	—	2.00	4.00
3263	Super Kimba/Wasa N'Doto	1975	—	2.00	4.00
WARNER BROS.					
8680	Aloko Party/Big Blow	1978	—	2.00	4.00

Albums

ATLANTIC

Number	Title (A Side/B Side)	Yr	VG	VG+	NM
SD 7267	Soul Makossa	1973	2.50	5.00	10.00
SD 7276	Makossa Man	1974	2.50	5.00	10.00
ISLAND					
ILPS 9526	Afrovision	1976	3.00	6.00	12.00

DICK AND DEEDEE

Also see DICK ST. JOHN.

45s

DOT

Number	Title (A Side/B Side)	Yr	VG	VG+	NM
17145	Escape Suite/I'm Not Gonna Get Hung-Up About It	1968	3.75	7.50	15.00
17261	We'll Sing in the Sunshine/In the Season of Our Love	1969	2.50	5.00	10.00
17305	Do I Love You/You Came Back to Haunt Me	1970	2.50	5.00	10.00
LAMA					
7778	The Mountain's High/I Want Someone	1961	5.00	10.00	20.00
7780	Goodbye to Love/Swing Low	1961	4.00	8.00	16.00
7783	Tell Me/Will You Always Love Me	1961	4.00	8.00	16.00
LIBERTY					
55350	The Mountain's High/I Want Someone	1961	3.75	7.50	15.00
55382	Goodbye to Love/Swing Low	1961	3.00	6.00	12.00
55412	Tell Me/Will You Always Love Me	1962	3.00	6.00	12.00
55478	All I Want/Life's Just a Play	1962	3.00	6.00	12.00
UNITED ARTISTS					
0036	The Mountain's High/Tell Me	1973	—	2.50	5.00
—"Silver Spotlight Series" reissue					
WARNER BROS.					
5320	The River Took My Baby/My Lonely Self	1962	2.50	5.00	10.00
5320 [PS]	The River Took My Baby/My Lonely Self	1962	6.25	12.50	25.00
5342	Young and In Love/Say to Me	1963	3.00	6.00	12.00
5364	Love Is a Once in a Lifetime Thing/Chug-a Chug-a Choo Choo	1963	2.50	5.00	10.00
5383	Where Did the Good Times Go/Guess Our Love Must Show	1963	2.50	5.00	10.00
5396	Turn Around/Don't Leave Me	1963	2.50	5.00	10.00
5411	All My Trials/Don't Think Twice, It's All Right	1964	2.50	5.00	10.00
5426	Not Fade Away/The Gift	1964	2.50	5.00	10.00
5451	You Were Mine/Remember Then	1964	2.50	5.00	10.00
5470	The Riddle Song/Without Your Love	1964	2.50	5.00	10.00
5482	Thou Shalt Not Steal/Just 'Round the River Bend	1964	3.75	7.50	15.00
—Red label with arrows					
5482	Thou Shalt Not Steal/Just 'Round the River Bend	1964	2.50	5.00	10.00
—Orange label					
5482 [PS]	Thou Shalt Not Steal/Just 'Round the River Bend	1964	6.25	12.50	25.00
5608	Be My Baby/Room 404	1965	2.50	5.00	10.00
5627	Blue Turns to Grey/Some Things Just Stick in Your Mind	1965	5.00	10.00	20.00
—Both sides are Mick Jagger-Keith Richards songs produced by Andrew Loog Oldham					
5652	The World Is Waiting/Vini, Vini	1965	2.50	5.00	10.00
5671	P.S. 1402 (Your Local Charm School)/Use What You've Got	1965	2.50	5.00	10.00
5680	New Orleans/Use What You've Got	1965	2.50	5.00	10.00
5699	Till/Sha-Ta	1966	2.50	5.00	10.00
5830	She Didn't Even Say Goodbye/So Many Things We Didn't Know	1966	2.50	5.00	10.00
5860	Make Up Before We Break Up/Can't Get Enough of Your Love	1966	2.50	5.00	10.00
7017	Long Lonely Nights/I'll Always Be Around	1967	2.50	5.00	10.00
7069	One in a Million/Baby, I Need You	1967	2.50	5.00	10.00
7109	Young and In Love/Thou Shalt Not Steal	1968	2.00	4.00	8.00
—"Back to Back Hits" series; originals have green labels with "W7" logo					

Albums

LIBERTY

Number	Title (A Side/B Side)	Yr	VG	VG+	NM
LRP-3236 [M]	Tell Me/The Mountain's High	1962	12.50	25.00	50.00
LST-7236 [R]	Tell Me/The Mountain's High	1962	10.00	20.00	40.00
WARNER BROS.					
W 1500 [M]	Young and In Love	1963	6.25	12.50	25.00
WS 1500 [S]	Young and In Love	1963	7.50	15.00	30.00
W 1538 [M]	Turn Around	1964	6.25	12.50	25.00
WS 1538 [S]	Turn Around	1964	7.50	15.00	30.00
W 1586 [M]	Thou Shalt Not Steal	1965	6.25	12.50	25.00
WS 1586 [S]	Thou Shalt Not Steal	1965	7.50	15.00	30.00
W 1623 [M]	Song We've Sung on "Shindig"	1966	6.25	12.50	25.00
WS 1623 [S]	Song We've Sung on "Shindig"	1966	7.50	15.00	30.00

DICKENS, THE
See NRBQ.

DICKIE G. AND THE DON'TS
See DICKIE GOODMAN.

DICKY DOO AND THE DON'TS

Number	Title (A Side/B Side)	Yr	VG	VG+	NM
45s					
ASCOT					
2178	Click Clack '65/Don't Count Me Out	1965	2.50	5.00	10.00
CASINO					
106	Click Clack/Lonely Hours Lady	196?	3.00	6.00	12.00
107	Flip Top Box/That's Life (That's Tough)	196?	3.00	6.00	12.00
DANNA					
4001	The Judge/Doo Plus Two	1967	2.50	5.00	10.00
SWAN					
4001	Click Clack/Did You Cry	1958	5.00	10.00	20.00
4006	Ne Ne Na Na Na Na Nu Nu/Flip Top Box	1959	6.25	12.50	25.00
4014	Leave Me Alone (Let Me Cry)/Wild Party	1959	5.00	10.00	20.00
4025	Teardrops Will Fall/Come with Us	1959	5.00	10.00	20.00
4033	Ballad of a Train/Dear Heart, Don't Cry	1959	5.00	10.00	20.00
4046	Wabash Cannonball/The Drums of Richard A. Doo	1960	5.00	10.00	20.00
UNITED ARTISTS					
238	Teen Scene/Pity, Pity	1960	5.00	10.00	20.00
362	The Judge/The Little Dog Cried	1961	5.00	10.00	20.00
Albums					
UNITED ARTISTS					
UAL-3094 [M]	The Madison and Other Dances	1959	10.00	20.00	40.00
UAL-3097 [M]	Teen Scene	1959	10.00	20.00	40.00
UAS-6094 [S]	The Madison and Other Dances	1959	12.50	25.00	50.00
UAS-6097 [S]	Teen Scene	1959	12.50	25.00	50.00

DIDDLEY, BO

Number	Title (A Side/B Side)	Yr	VG	VG+	NM
45s					
CHECKER					
814	Bo Diddley/I'm a Man	1955	12.50	25.00	50.00
819	Diddley Daddy/She's Fine, She's Mine	1955	15.00	30.00	60.00
—A-side backing vocals: The Moonglows					
827	Pretty Thing/Bring It to Jerome	1955	12.50	25.00	50.00
832	Diddy Wah Diddy/I Am Looking for a Woman	1956	12.50	25.00	50.00
842	Who Do You Love?/In Bad	1956	15.00	30.00	60.00
842	Who Do You Love?/I'm Bad	1956	10.00	20.00	40.00
—Note altered B-side title					
850	Cops and Robbers/Down Home Special	1956	10.00	20.00	40.00
860	Hey! Bo Diddley/Mona	1957	12.50	25.00	50.00
—Originals of Checker 816-860 have "Checker" over a checkerboard on top of label					
878	Say! Boss Man/Before You Accuse Me	1957	6.25	12.50	25.00
896	Dearest Darling/Hush Your Mouth	1958	6.25	12.50	25.00
907	Bo Meets the Monster/Willie and Lillie	1958	7.50	15.00	30.00
914	I'm Sorry/Oh Yeah	1959	6.25	12.50	25.00
924	Crackin' Up/The Great Grandfather	1959	6.25	12.50	25.00
931	Say Man/Clock Strikes Twelve	1959	7.50	15.00	30.00
931 [PS]	Say Man/Clock Strikes Twelve	1959	100.00	200.00	400.00
936	Say Man, Back Again/She's Alright	1959	6.25	12.50	25.00
942	Road Runner/My Story	1960	5.00	10.00	20.00
951	Walkin' and Talkin'/Crawdad	1960	5.00	10.00	20.00
965	Gun Slinger/Signifying	1960	5.00	10.00	20.00
976	No Guilty/Aztec	1961	5.00	10.00	20.00
985	Pills/Call Me	1961	7.50	15.00	30.00
997	Bo Diddley/I'm a Man	1961	5.00	10.00	20.00
1019	You Can't Judge a Book By Its Cover/I Can Tell	1962	6.25	12.50	25.00
1045	Surfers' Love Call/Greatest Lover in the World	1963	5.00	10.00	20.00
1058	Memphis/Monkey Diddle	1963	5.00	10.00	20.00
1083	Jo Ann/Mama, Keep Your Big Mouth Shut	1964	5.00	10.00	20.00
1089	Bo's Beat/Chuck's Beat	1964	5.00	10.00	20.00
—B-side by Chuck Berry					
1098	Hey, Good Lookin'/You Ain't Bad	1965	3.75	7.50	15.00
1123	500% More Man/Let the Kids Dance	1965	3.75	7.50	15.00
1142	We're Gonna Get Married/Do the Frog	1966	3.75	7.50	15.00
1158	Ooh Baby/Back to School	1966	3.75	7.50	15.00
1168	Bo-Ga-Loo Before You Go/Wrecking My Love Life	1967	3.75	7.50	15.00
1200	Another Sugardaddy/I'm High Again	1968	3.75	7.50	15.00
1213	Bo Diddley 1969/Soul Train	1969	3.00	6.00	12.00
1238	The Shape I'm In/Pollution	1970	3.00	6.00	12.00
CHESS					
2117	I Love You More Than You'll Ever Know/I Said Shut Up Woman	1971	2.50	5.00	10.00
2129	Bo Diddley-Itis/Infatuation	1972	2.50	5.00	10.00
2134	Bo-Jam/Husband-in-Law	1972	2.50	5.00	10.00
2142	I Don't Want No Lyin' Woman/Make a Hit Record	1973	2.50	5.00	10.00
PHILCO-FORD					
HP-33	I'm a Man/Song of Bo Diddley	1968	7.50	15.00	30.00
—4-inch plastic "Hip Pocket Record" with color sleeve					
RCA VICTOR					
PB-10618	Not Fade Away/Drag On	1976	2.50	5.00	10.00
7-Inch Extended Plays					
CHECKER					
5125	(contents unknown)	1958	30.00	60.00	120.00
5125 [PS]	Bo Diddley	1958	45.00	90.00	180.00
Albums					
ACCORD					
SN-7182	Toronto Rock and Roll Revival, Vol. 5	1982	5.00	10.00	20.00
CHECKER					
LP 1431 [M]	Bo Diddley	1958	37.50	75.00	150.00
LP 1436 [M]	Go Bo Diddley	1959	37.50	75.00	150.00
LP 2974 [M]	Have Guitar, Will Travel	1960	37.50	75.00	150.00
LP 2976 [M]	Spotlight on Bo Diddley	1960	37.50	75.00	150.00
LP 2977 [M]	Bo Diddley Is a Gunslinger	1961	37.50	75.00	150.00
LP 2980 [M]	Bo Diddley Is a Lover	1961	37.50	75.00	150.00
LP 2982 [M]	Bo Diddley's a Twister	1962	25.00	50.00	100.00
LP 2982 [M]	Road Runner	1967	20.00	40.00	80.00
—Reissue of "Bo Diddley's a Twister"					
LP 2984 [M]	Bo Diddley	1962	25.00	50.00	100.00
LP 2985 [M]	Bo Diddley and Company	1963	40.00	80.00	120.00
LP 2987 [M]	Surfin' with Bo Diddley	1964	40.00	80.00	120.00
LPS 2987 [R]	Surfin' with Bo Diddley	1964	7.50	15.00	30.00
LP 2988 [M]	Bo Diddley's Beach Party	1963	25.00	50.00	100.00
LP 2989 [M]	16 All Time Greatest Hits	1964	12.50	25.00	50.00
LPS 2989 [R]	16 All Time Greatest Hits	1964	7.50	15.00	30.00
LP 2992 [M]	Hey! Good Lookin'	1965	15.00	30.00	60.00
LPS 2992 [R]	Hey! Good Lookin'	1965	7.50	15.00	30.00
LP 2996 [M]	500% More Man	1965	15.00	30.00	60.00
LPS 2996 [R]	500% More Man	1965	7.50	15.00	30.00
LP 3001 [M]	The Originator	1966	7.50	15.00	30.00
LPS 3001 [S]	The Originator	1966	10.00	20.00	40.00
LP 3006 [M]	Go Bo Diddley	1967	12.50	25.00	50.00
—Reissue of 1436					
LPS 3006 [R]	Go Bo Diddley	1967	10.00	20.00	40.00
LP 3007 [M]	Boss Man	1967	20.00	40.00	80.00
—Reissue of Chess 1431					
LPS 3007 [R]	Boss Man	1967	12.50	25.00	50.00
LPS 3013	The Black Gladiator	1968	7.50	15.00	30.00
CHESS					
LP 1431 [M]	Bo Diddley	1958	50.00	100.00	200.00
CH-9106	His Greatest Sides, Vol. 1	1984	2.50	5.00	10.00
CH-9187	Have Guitar, Will Travel	1985	2.50	5.00	10.00
—Reissue of Checker 2974					
CH-9194	Bo Diddley	1986	2.50	5.00	10.00
—Reissue of 1431					
CH-9196	Go Bo Diddley	1986	2.50	5.00	10.00
—Reissue of Checker 1436					
CH-9264	Spotlight on Bo Diddley	1987	2.50	5.00	10.00
—Reissue of Checker 2976					
CH-9285	Bo Diddley Is a Gunslinger	1989	2.50	5.00	10.00
—Reissue of Checker 2977					
CH-9296	The London Bo Diddley Sessions	1989	2.50	5.00	10.00
—Reissue of 50029					
CH3-19502 [(3)]	The Chess Box	1990	10.00	20.00	40.00
CH 50001	Another Dimension	1971	10.00	20.00	40.00
CH 50016	Where It All Began	1972	10.00	20.00	40.00
CH 50029	The London Bo Diddley Sessions	1973	6.25	12.50	25.00
CH 50047	Big Bad Bo	1974	6.25	12.50	25.00
2CH 60005 [(2)]	Got My Own Bag of Tricks	1972	6.25	12.50	25.00
RCA VICTOR					
APL1-1229	The 20th Anniversary of Rock and Roll	1976	5.00	10.00	20.00

DIDDLEY, BO/CHUCK BERRY
Also see each artist's individual listings.

Number	Title (A Side/B Side)	Yr	VG	VG+	NM
Albums					
CHECKER					
LP 2991 [M]	Two Great Guitars	1964	15.00	30.00	60.00
LPS 2991 [R]	Two Great Guitars	1964	10.00	20.00	40.00
CHESS					
CH-9170	Two Great Guitars	1985	2.50	5.00	10.00
—Reissue of Checker 2991					

DIDDLEY, BO/MUDDY WATERS/HOWLIN' WOLF
Also see each artist's individual listings.

Number	Title (A Side/B Side)	Yr	VG	VG+	NM
Albums					
CHECKER					
LP 3010 [M]	Super, Super Blues Band	1968	12.50	25.00	50.00
LPS 3010 [S]	Super, Super Blues Band	1968	10.00	20.00	40.00
CHESS					
CH-9169	Super, Super Blues Band	1985	2.50	5.00	10.00
—Reissue of Checker 3010					

DIDDLEY, BO/MUDDY WATERS/LITTLE WALTER
Also see each artist's individual listings.

Number	Title (A Side/B Side)	Yr	VG	VG+	NM
Albums					
CHECKER					
LP 3008 [M]	Super Blues Band	1968	12.50	25.00	50.00
LPS 3008 [S]	Super Blues Band	1968	10.00	20.00	40.00
CHESS					
CH-9168	Super Blues Band	1985	2.50	5.00	10.00
—Reissue of Checker 3008					

DIFFERENT SHADES OF BROWN

Number	Title (A Side/B Side)	Yr	VG	VG+	NM
45s					
TAMLA					
54219	Label Me Love/Life's a Ball	1972	—	2.50	5.00

DILL, DANNY

Number	Title (A Side/B Side)	Yr	VG	VG+	NM
45s					
ABC-PARAMOUNT					
9681	My Girl and His Girl/Geisha Sweetheart	1956	7.50	15.00	30.00
9734	I'm Hungry for Your Lovin'/The Stranger of Abilene	1956	12.50	25.00	50.00
CUB					
9045	He's Biding His Time/He Ain't Gonna Study War	1959	5.00	10.00	20.00

DILLARD, DOUG

Number	Title (A Side/B Side)	Yr	VG	VG+	NM
Albums					
TOGETHER					
STT-1003	The Banjo Album	1970	20.00	40.00	80.00

DILLARD, VARETTA

Number	Title (A Side/B Side)	Yr	VG	VG+	NM
45s					
CUB					
9073	Teaser/I Know I'm Good for You	1960	3.00	6.00	12.00
9083	Little Bitty Tear/Mercy Mr. Percy	1961	3.00	6.00	12.00
9091	You Better Come Home/I Don't Know What It Is, But I Like It	1961	3.00	6.00	12.00

Number	Title (A Side/B Side)	Yr	VG	VG+	NM
GROOVE					
0139	Darling, Listen to the Words of This Song/Mama Don't Want (What Poppa Don't Want)	1956	10.00	20.00	40.00
0152	Gonna Tell My Daddy/Cherry Blossom	1956	6.25	12.50	25.00
0159	Got You On My Mind/Skinny Jimmy	1956	6.25	12.50	25.00
0167	I Miss You Jimmy/If You Want to Be My Baby	1956	6.25	12.50	25.00
0177	One More Time/I Can't Help Myself	1956	6.25	12.50	25.00
RCA VICTOR					
47-6869	Pray for Me Mother/Leave a Happy Fool Alone	1957	5.00	10.00	20.00
47-6936	Time Was/I Got a Lot of Love	1957	5.00	10.00	20.00
47-7057	Undecided/That's Why I Cry	1957	5.00	10.00	20.00
47-7144	Star of Fortune/The Blues of Love	1958	5.00	10.00	20.00
47-7285	What'll I Do/Just Multiply	1958	5.00	10.00	20.00
SAVOY					
822	Love and Wine/Please Come Back to Me	1951	12.50	25.00	50.00
839	Hurry Up/Please Tell Me Why	1952	10.00	20.00	40.00
847	Easy, Easy Baby/A Letter in Blue	1952	10.00	20.00	40.00
851	I'm Yours/Here in My Heart	1952	10.00	20.00	40.00
871	I Cried and Cried/Double Crossing Daddy	1952	10.00	20.00	40.00
884	Three Lies/Getting Ready for My Daddy	1953	10.00	20.00	40.00
897	Mercy, Mr. Percy/No Kinda Good No How	1953	10.00	20.00	40.00
1118	I Ain't Gonna Tell/(That's the Way) My Mind Is Working	1953	7.50	15.00	30.00
1137	Send Me Some Money/Love	1954	7.50	15.00	30.00
1153	Johnny Has Gone/So Many Ways	1955	7.50	15.00	30.00
1160	You're the Answer to My Prayer/Promise Mr. Thomas	1955	7.50	15.00	30.00
1166	I'll Never Forget You/I Can't Stop Now	1955	7.50	15.00	30.00
TRIUMPH					
608	Good Gravy Baby/Scorched	1959	3.75	7.50	15.00
Albums					
SAVOY JAZZ					
SJL-1203	Mercy, Mr. Percy, Volume 1	1989	3.00	6.00	12.00

DILLARD AND CLARK

Number	Title (A Side/B Side)	Yr	VG	VG+	NM
Albums					
A&M					
SP-4158	The Fantastic Expedition of Dillard and Clark	1968	5.00	10.00	20.00
—Brown label					

DILLARDS, THE

Number	Title (A Side/B Side)	Yr	VG	VG+	NM
45s					
ANTHEM					
101	It's About Time/One A.M.	1971	—	2.50	5.00
51014	Billy Jack/America	1971	—	2.50	5.00
CAPITOL					
5494	Nobody Knows/Ebo Walker	1965	2.00	4.00	8.00
5524	Lemon Chimes/The Last Thing on My Mind	1965	2.00	4.00	8.00
ELEKTRA					
45003	Dooley/Dong's Love	1964	2.50	5.00	10.00
45006	Hootin' Banjo/Polly Vaughn	1964	2.50	5.00	10.00
45641	Reason to Believe/Nobody Knows	1968	2.00	4.00	8.00
45661	Listen to the Sound/The Biggest Whatever	1969	2.00	4.00	8.00
45679	Rain Maker/West Montana Hanna	1970	2.00	4.00	8.00
45681	Close the Door Lightly/Touch Her If You Can	1970	2.00	4.00	8.00
UNITED ARTISTS					
XW382	Hot Rod Banjo/Love Has Gone Away	1974	—	2.50	5.00
WHITE WHALE					
351	One Too Many Mornings/Turn It Around	1970	—	3.00	6.00
359	Comin' Home Again	1970	—	3.00	6.00
Albums					
ANTHEM					
ANS-5901	Roots and Branches	1972	3.75	7.50	15.00
CRYSTAL CLEAR					
CCS-5007	Mountain Rock	1979	6.25	12.50	25.00
—Direct-to-disc recording					
ELEKTRA					
EKL-232 [M]	Back Porch Bluegrass	1963	6.25	12.50	25.00
EKL-265 [M]	The Dillards, Live!!! Almost!!!	1964	5.00	10.00	20.00
EKL-285 [M]	Pickin' and Fiddlin'	1965	5.00	10.00	20.00
EKS-7232 [S]	Back Porch Bluegrass	1963	7.50	5.00	30.00
—Mandolin-player label					
EKS-7265 [S]	The Dillards, Live!!! Almost!!!	1964	6.25	12.50	25.00
—Mandolin-player label					
EKS-7285 [S]	Pickin' and Fiddlin'	1965	6.25	12.50	25.00
—Mandolin-player label					
EKS-74035	Wheatstraw Suite	1968	5.00	10.00	20.00
—Tan label with large stylized "E" on top					
EKS-74054	Copperfields	1969	5.00	10.00	20.00
—Red label with large stylized "E" on top					
FLYING FISH					
FF 040	The Dillards Vs. the Incredible L.A. Time Machine	1977	3.00	6.00	12.00
FF 082	Decade Waltz	1979	3.00	6.00	12.00
FF 215	Homecoming and Family Reunion	1979	3.00	6.00	12.00
POPPY					
PP-LA175-F	Tribute to the American Duck	1973	3.75	7.50	15.00

DING DONGS, THE

See BOBBY DARIN.

DINNING, MARK

Number	Title (A Side/B Side)	Yr	VG	VG+	NM
45s					
CAMEO					
299	January/Joey	1964	2.50	5.00	10.00
313	Should We Do It/Call Her Your Sweetheart	1964	2.50	5.00	10.00
HICKORY					
1293	Dial AL1-4883/I'm Glad We Fell in Love	1965	2.00	4.00	8.00
1368	Last Rose/There Stands a Lady	1966	2.00	4.00	8.00
1404	Run, Opie, Run/He Reminds Me of Me	1966	2.00	4.00	8.00
MGM					
12447	A Million Years Ago/Shameful Ways	1957	6.25	12.50	25.00
12553	School Fool/When You're Tired of Breaking Hearts	1957	6.25	12.50	25.00
12691	You Thrill Me/Do You Know	1958	6.25	12.50	25.00
12732	Blackeyed Gypsy/Secretly in Love with You	1958	6.25	12.50	25.00
12775	Cutie, Cutie/A Life of Love	1959	6.25	12.50	25.00
12845	Teen Angel/Bye Now Baby	1959	6.25	12.50	25.00
12888	A Star Is Born (A Love Has Died)/You Win Again	1960	5.00	10.00	20.00
12888 [PS]	A Star Is Born (A Love Has Died)/You Win Again	1960	6.25	12.50	25.00
12929	The Lovin' Touch/Come Back to Me (My Love)	1960	5.00	10.00	20.00
12929 [PS]	The Lovin' Touch/Come Back to Me (My Love)	1960	6.25	12.50	25.00
12958	She Cried On My Shoulder (When She Talked About You)/(Where Can You Hide Away) The World Is Getting Smaller	1960	5.00	10.00	20.00
12980	Top Forty, News, Weather and Sports/Suddenly (There's Only You)	1961	3.75	7.50	15.00
13007	Another Lonely Girl/Can't Forget	1961	3.75	7.50	15.00
13024	Lonely Island/Turn Me On	1961	3.75	7.50	15.00
13048	What Will My Mary Say/In a Matter of Moments	1961	3.75	7.50	15.00
13061	The Pickup/All of This for Sally	1962	3.75	7.50	15.00
13091	She's Changed/I Catch Myself Crying	1962	3.00	6.00	12.00
13150	The Twelfth of Never/Somebody Catch Me Kissin' Mary	1963	3.00	6.00	12.00
UNITED ARTISTS					
50169	It's Such a Pretty World Today/Atlanta, Georgia Stray	1967	2.00	4.00	8.00
50225	Hangin' On/Maggie (I Wish We'd Never Met)	1967	2.00	4.00	8.00
50305	Throw a Little Love My Way/Dissatisfied Man	1968	2.00	4.00	8.00
50540	How Little Men Care/Lemon Yellow	1969	2.00	4.00	8.00
Albums					
MGM					
E-3828 [M]	Teen Angel	1960	20.00	40.00	80.00
SE-3828 [S]	Teen Angel	1960	37.50	75.00	150.00
E-3855 [M]	Wanderin'	1960	20.00	40.00	80.00
SE-3855 [S]	Wanderin'	1960	30.00	60.00	120.00

DINO, KENNY

Number	Title (A Side/B Side)	Yr	VG	VG+	NM
45s					
COLUMBIA					
43062	Betty Jean/Show Me	1964	5.00	10.00	20.00
DOT					
16207	Just Wait and See/A Little Bit	1961	3.00	6.00	12.00
MUSICOR					
1013	You Ma Said You Cried in Your Sleep Last Night/Dream a Girl	1962	5.00	10.00	20.00
1015	Rosie, Why Do You Wear My Ring/What Did I Do	1962	3.75	7.50	15.00
1021	What Good Are Dreams/What Did I Do	1962	3.75	7.50	15.00
1027	Remembering Helps Me to Forget/Heartless Moon	1962	3.75	7.50	15.00
SMASH					
1827	Time Will Tell/I Wanna Know	1963	3.00	6.00	12.00
1861	You Had Your Chance/Danhoff's Theme	1963	3.00	6.00	12.00

DINO AND THE DIPLOMATS

Number	Title (A Side/B Side)	Yr	VG	VG+	NM
45s					
LAURIE					
3103	I Can't Believe/My Dream	1961	7.50	15.00	30.00
VIDA					
100/101	Hushabye My Love/Homework	1961	7.50	15.00	30.00
102/103	Soft Wind/Such a Fool for You	1961	7.50	15.00	30.00

DINO, DESI AND BILLY

Number	Title (A Side/B Side)	Yr	VG	VG+	NM
45s					
COLUMBIA					
4-44975	Hawley/Let's Talk It Over	1969	3.00	6.00	12.00
REPRISE					
0324	We Know/Since You Broke My Heart	1964	3.75	7.50	15.00
0367	I'm a Fool/So Many Ways	1965	3.00	6.00	12.00
0367 [PS]	I'm a Fool/So Many Ways	1965	5.00	10.00	20.00
0401	Not the Lovin' Kind/Chimes of Freedom	1965	2.50	5.00	10.00
0401 [PS]	Not the Lovin' Kind/Chimes of Freedom	1965	5.00	10.00	20.00
0426	Please Don't Fight It/The Rebel Kind	1965	2.50	5.00	10.00
0426 [PS]	Please Don't Fight It/The Rebel Kind	1965	5.00	10.00	20.00
0444	Superman/I Can't Get Her Out of My Mind	1966	2.00	4.00	8.00
0462	It's Just the Way You Are/Tie Me Down	1966	2.00	4.00	8.00
0496	Look Out Girls/She's So Far Out She's In	1966	2.00	4.00	8.00
0529	I Hope She's There Tonight/Josephine	1966	2.00	4.00	8.00
0544	If You're Thinkin' What I'm Thinkin'/Pretty Flamingo	1966	2.00	4.00	8.00
0579	Two in the Afternoon/Good Luck, Best Wishes to You	1967	2.50	5.00	10.00
0619	Kitty Doyle/Without Hurtin' Some	1967	2.50	5.00	10.00
0653	My What a Shame/The Inside Outside Caspar Milquetoast Eskimo Flash	1967	3.00	6.00	12.00
0653 [PS]	My What a Shame/The Inside Outside Caspar Milquetoast Eskimo Flash	1967	5.00	10.00	20.00
0698	Tell Someone You Love Them/General Outline	1968	3.00	6.00	12.00
0716	I'm a Fool/Not the Lovin' Kind	1968	2.00	4.00	8.00
—"Back to Back Hits" series; originals have both "W7" and "r:" logos					
0965	Lady Love/A Certain Sound	1970	7.50	15.00	30.00
—A-side is a Brian Wilson composition					
UNI					
55127	Someday/Thru Spray Colored Glasses	1969	3.00	6.00	12.00
Albums					
REPRISE					
R 6176 [M]	I'm a Fool	1965	5.00	10.00	20.00
RS 6176 [S]	I'm a Fool	1965	6.25	12.50	25.00
R 6194 [M]	Our Time's Coming	1966	5.00	10.00	20.00
RS 6194 [S]	Our Time's Coming	1966	6.25	12.50	25.00
R 6198 [M]	Memories Are Made of This	1966	5.00	10.00	20.00
RS 6198 [S]	Memories Are Made of This	1966	6.25	12.50	25.00
R 6224 [M]	Souvenir	1966	5.00	10.00	20.00
RS 6224 [S]	Souvenir	1966	6.25	12.50	25.00
R/RS 6224	Souvenir Bonus Photo Sheet	1966	—	2.50	5.00

DIO, ANDY

45s

Number	Title (A Side/B Side)	Yr	VG	VG+	NM
CRUSADE					
1023	Bonnie Jean/Rough and Bold	1961	10.00	20.00	40.00
GONE					
5038	Daisy Belle/Hey Little Bluebird	1958	12.50	25.00	50.00
JOHNSON					
114	You Are My Sunshine/Satellite	1962	5.00	10.00	20.00
JOY					
283	Daisy Belle/Some of These Days	1964	10.00	20.00	40.00
MUSICOR					
1118	Sass-Afrass/Shout	1965	2.50	5.00	10.00
1162	Dancing Bull/Sorrento	1966	2.50	5.00	10.00

DIO, RONNIE

45s

Number	Title (A Side/B Side)	Yr	VG	VG+	NM
ATLANTIC					
2145	Love Pains/Ooh-Poo-Pah-Do	1962	5.00	10.00	20.00
KAPP					
697	Say You're Mine Again/Where You Gonna Run To, Girl	1965	3.75	7.50	15.00
725	Dear Darlin' (I Won't Be Comin' Home)/Smiling by Day	1965	3.75	7.50	15.00
770	The Way of Love/Walking Alone	1966	3.75	7.50	15.00
LAWN					
218	Gonna Make It Alone/Swingin' Street	1963	6.25	12.50	25.00
PARKWAY					
143	Walking in Different Circles/Ten Days with Brenda	1967	5.00	10.00	20.00
SWAN					
4165	Mr. Misery/Our Year	1963	5.00	10.00	20.00

DION

Also see DION AND THE BELMONTS.

45s

Number	Title (A Side/B Side)	Yr	VG	VG+	NM
ARISTA					
9797	And the Night Stood Still/Tower of Love	1989	—	2.00	4.00
9797 [PS]	And the Night Stood Still/Tower of Love	1989	—	2.00	4.00
BIG TREE/SPECTOR					
16063	Born to Be with You/Running Close Behind You	1976	3.75	7.50	15.00
—Produced by Phil Spector					
COLUMBIA					
(no #) [PS]	"Dion Is Now on Columbia Records"	1962	12.50	25.00	50.00
—Promo-only sleeve issued with promos of Columbia 42662					
42662	Ruby Baby/He'll Only Hurt You	1962	5.00	10.00	20.00
42662 [PS]	Ruby Baby/He'll Only Hurt You	1962	10.00	20.00	40.00
42776	This Little Girl/The Loneliest Man in the World	1963	3.75	7.50	15.00
42810	Be Careful of Stones That You Throw/I Can't Believe (That You Don't Love Me Anymore)	1963	3.75	7.50	15.00
42810 [DJ]	Be Careful of Stones That You Throw (same on both sides)	1963	25.00	50.00	100.00
—Colored vinyl (some sources say blue, others red)					
42852	Donna the Prima Donna/You're Mine	1963	5.00	10.00	20.00
42852 [DJ]	Donna the Prima Donna (same on both sides)	1963	20.00	40.00	80.00
—Promo only on red vinyl					
42917	Drip Drop/No One's Waiting for Me	1963	3.75	7.50	15.00
42977	I'm the Hoochie Coochie Man/The Road I'm On	1964	3.75	7.50	15.00
42977 [PS]	I'm the Hoochie Coochie Man/The Road I'm On	1964	10.00	20.00	40.00
43096	Johnny B. Goode/Chicago Blues	1964	3.75	7.50	15.00
43213	Sweet Sweet Baby/Unloved, Unwanted Me	1965	3.75	7.50	15.00
43293	Spoonful/Kickin' Child	1965	3.75	7.50	15.00
43423	Tomorrow Won't Bring the Rain/You Move Me Babe	1965	3.75	7.50	15.00
43423 [PS]	Tomorrow Won't Bring the Rain/You Move Me Babe	1965	37.50	75.00	150.00
43483	Time in My Heart for You/Wake Up Baby	1965	3.75	7.50	15.00
43692	So Much Younger/Two-Ton Feather	1966	3.75	7.50	15.00
44719	I Can't Help But Wonder Where I'm Bound/Southern Train	1968	2.50	5.00	10.00
DAYSPRING					
622 [DJ]	The Best (mono/stereo)	197?	—	2.50	5.00
LAURIE					
3070	Lonely Teenager/Little Miss Blue	1960	5.00	10.00	20.00
3070 [PS]	Lonely Teenager/Little Miss Blue	1960	12.50	25.00	50.00
3081	Havin' Fun/Northeast End of the Corner	1961	5.00	10.00	20.00
3081 [PS]	Havin' Fun/Northeast End of the Corner	1961	12.50	25.00	50.00
3090	Kissin Game/Heaven Help Me	1961	5.00	10.00	20.00
3090 [PS]	Kissin Game/Heaven Help Me	1961	12.50	25.00	50.00
3101	Somebody Nobody Wants/Could Somebody Take My Place Tonight	1961	5.00	10.00	20.00
3110 [M]	Runaround Sue/Runaway Girl	1961	6.25	12.50	25.00
3110 [PS]	Runaround Sue/Runaway Girl	1961	10.00	20.00	40.00
3110 [S]	Runaround Sue/Runaway Girl	1961	12.50	25.00	50.00
—"Stereo" in white area at right of label					
3115 [M]	The Wanderer/The Majestic	1961	6.25	12.50	25.00
3115 [M]	The Wanderer/The Majestic	1979	2.50	5.00	10.00
—Reissue on regular Laurie label with "From the Orion Motion Picture 'The Wanderers'" on label					
3115 [PS]	The Wanderer/The Majestic	1961	10.00	20.00	40.00
3115 [S]	The Wanderer/The Majestic	1961	12.50	25.00	50.00
—"Stereo" in white area at right of label					
3123	Lovers Who Wander/(I Was) Born to Cry	1962	5.00	10.00	20.00
3123 [PS]	Lovers Who Wander/(I Was) Born to Cry	1962	10.00	20.00	40.00
3134	Little Diane/Lost for Sure	1962	5.00	10.00	20.00
3134 [PS]	Little Diane/Lost for Sure	1962	10.00	20.00	40.00
3145	Love Came to Me/Little Girl	1962	5.00	10.00	20.00
3153	Sandy/Faith	1963	5.00	10.00	20.00
3171	Come Go with Me/King Without a Queen	1963	5.00	10.00	20.00
3187	Lonely World/Tag Along	1963	5.00	10.00	20.00
3225	After the Dance/Then I'll Be Tired of You	1964	5.00	10.00	20.00
3240	Shout/Little Girl	1964	5.00	10.00	20.00
3303	I Got the Blues/(I Was) Born to Cry	1965	5.00	10.00	20.00
3464	Abraham, Martin, and John/Daddy Rollin' (In Your Arms)	1968	3.00	6.00	12.00
3478	Purple Haze/The Dolphins	1969	3.00	6.00	12.00
3495	From Both Sides Now/Sun Fun Song	1969	3.00	6.00	12.00
3504	Loving You Is Sweeter Than Ever/He Looks a Lot Like Me	1969	3.00	6.00	12.00
LAURIE DOUBLE GOLD					
100	Runaround Sue/I Wonder Why	197?	—	2.00	4.00
—B-side by Dion and the Belmonts					
101	The Wanderer/No One Knows	197?	—	2.00	4.00
—B-side by Dion and the Belmonts					
103	Lonely Teenager/Little Diane	197?	—	2.00	4.00
104	Lovers Who Wander/Where or When	197?	—	2.00	4.00
—B-side by Dion and the Belmonts					
105	Love Came to Me/Sandy	197?	—	2.00	4.00
118	Abraham, Martin and John/From Both Sides Now	197?	—	2.00	4.00
LIFESONG					
1765	Heart of Saturday Night/You've Awakened Something in Me	1978	—	3.00	6.00
1770	Midtown American Main Street Gang/Guitar Queen	1978	—	3.00	6.00
1785	(I Used to Be a) Brooklyn Dodger/Streetheart Theme	1979	—	3.00	6.00
45082	Fire in the Night/Street Mama	1980	6.25	12.50	25.00
MONUMENT					
(# unknown) [DJ]	Runaround Sue/Ya Ya Twist	1962	6.25	12.50	25.00
—B-side by Joey Dee and the Starliters					
THE RIGHT STUFF					
S7-17651	Christmas (Baby Please Come Home)/Jingle Bell Rock	1993	—	2.50	5.00
—Red vinyl					
S7-19769	Please Come Home for Christmas/Wintertime	1997	—	2.00	4.00
—B-side by the Belmonts on United Artists					
WARNER BROS.					
PRO-537 [DJ]	Seagull/Soft Parade	1972	3.75	7.50	15.00
PRO-814 [DJ]	The Wanderer (same on both sides)	1979	3.75	7.50	15.00
7356	Natural Man/If We Only Have Love	1969	2.50	5.00	10.00
7401	Your Own Back Yard/Sit Down Old Friend	1970	2.50	5.00	10.00
7469	Let It Be/Close to It All	1970	2.50	5.00	10.00
7491	Josie/Sunniland	1970	2.50	5.00	10.00
7537	Sanctuary/Brand New Morning	1971	2.50	5.00	10.00
7537 [PS]	Sanctuary/Brand New Morning	1971	5.00	10.00	20.00
7663	Seagull/Running Close Behind You	1972	2.50	5.00	10.00
7704	Doctor Rock and Roll/Sunshine Lady	1973	2.50	5.00	10.00
7793	New York City Song/Richer Than a Rich Man	1974	2.50	5.00	10.00
8234	Hey My Love/Lover Boy Supreme	1976	—	3.00	6.00
8258	The Way You Do the Things You Do/Lover Boy Supreme	1976	—	3.00	6.00
8293	Oh the Night/Queen of '59	1976	—	3.00	6.00
8406	Young Virgin Eyes (I'm All Wrapped Up)/Oh the Night	1977	—	3.00	6.00
WARNER/SPECTOR					
0403	Make the Woman Love Me/Running Close Behind You	1975	3.75	7.50	15.00
—Produced by Phil Spector					

Albums

Number	Title	Yr	VG	VG+	NM
ARISTA					
AL 8549	Yo Frankie	1989	2.50	5.00	10.00
COLLECTABLES					
5027	Runaround Sue	198?	2.50	5.00	10.00
COLUMBIA					
CL 2010 [M]	Ruby Baby	1963	7.50	15.00	30.00
CL 2107 [M]	Donna the Prima Donna	1963	7.50	15.00	30.00
CS 8810 [S]	Ruby Baby	1963	10.00	20.00	40.00
CS 8907 [S]	Donna the Prima Donna	1963	10.00	20.00	40.00
CS 9773	Wonder Where I'm Bound	1969	5.00	10.00	20.00
KC 31942	Dion's Greatest Hits	1973	5.00	10.00	20.00
PC 31942	Dion's Greatest Hits	198?	2.00	4.00	8.00
—Budget-line reissue					
DAYSPRING					
DST-4022	Inside Job	1980	3.00	6.00	12.00
DST-4027	Only Jesus	198?	3.00	6.00	12.00
WR-8111	I Put Away My Idols	198?	3.00	6.00	12.00
WR-8112	Seasons (The Best of Dion)	198?	3.00	6.00	12.00
LAURIE					
LLP 2004 [M]	Alone with Dion	1960	50.00	100.00	200.00
—With four wallet-size photos on inside strip (deduct 50% if missing)					
LLP 2009 [M]	Runaround Sue	1961	200.00	400.00	800.00
—Colored vinyl (gold, green or blue)					
LLP 2009 [M]	Runaround Sue	1961	25.00	50.00	100.00
—Black vinyl					
LLP 2009 [M]	Runaround Sue	1962	20.00	40.00	80.00
—Black vinyl; with sticker on front cover: "Includes the Hit Singles 'The Majestic'/'The Wanderer'"					
LLP 2012 [M]	Lovers Who Wander	1962	17.50	35.00	70.00
LLP 2013 [M]	Dion Sings His Greatest Hits	1962	17.50	35.00	70.00
SLP 2013 [R]	Dion Sings His Greatest Hits	196?	12.50	25.00	50.00
LLP 2015 [M]	Love Came to Me	1963	17.50	35.00	70.00
LLP 2017 [M]	Dion Sings to Sandy (And All His Other Girls)	1963	12.50	25.00	50.00
LLP 2019 [M]	Dion Sings the 15 Million Sellers	1963	12.50	25.00	50.00
SLP 2019 [R]	Dion Sings the 15 Million Sellers	196?	7.50	15.00	30.00
LLP 2022 [M]	More of Dion's Greatest Hits	1964	12.50	25.00	50.00
SLP 2022 [R]	More of Dion's Greatest Hits	196?	7.50	15.00	30.00
SLP 2047	Dion	1968	5.00	10.00	20.00
DT-90386 [R]	Dion Sings His Greatest Hits	1965	30.00	60.00	120.00
—Capitol Record Club edition					
T-90386 [M]	Dion Sings His Greatest Hits	1965	30.00	60.00	120.00
—Capitol Record Club edition					
DT-91027 [R]	Runaround Sue	196?	30.00	60.00	120.00
—Capitol Record Club edition					
T-91027 [M]	Runaround Sue	196?	30.00	60.00	120.00
—Capitol Record Club edition					
DT-91128 [R]	More of Dion's Greatest Hits	196?	30.00	60.00	120.00
—Capitol Record Club edition					
T-91128 [M]	More of Dion's Greatest Hits	196?	30.00	60.00	120.00
—Capitol Record Club edition					

Number	Title (A Side/B Side)	Yr	VG	VG+	NM
ST-91577	Dion	1968	6.25	12.50	25.00
—Capitol Record Club edition					
LIFESONG					
JZ 35356	Return of the Wanderer	1978	3.00	6.00	12.00
WARNER BROS.					
WS 1826	Sit Down, Old Friend	1969	5.00	10.00	20.00
WS 1872	You're Not Alone	1971	3.75	7.50	15.00
WS 1945	Sanctuary	1971	3.75	7.50	15.00
BS 2642	Suite for Late Summer	1972	3.75	7.50	15.00
BS 2954	Streetheart	1976	3.75	7.50	15.00
WORD					
WR-8285	Kingdom in the Streets	1985	3.00	6.00	12.00

DION AND THE BELMONTS

Also see THE BELMONTS; CARLO; DION.

45s

Number	Title (A Side/B Side)	Yr	VG	VG+	NM
ABC					
10868	My Girl the Month of May/Berimbau	1966	3.00	6.00	12.00
10896	For Bobbie/Movin' Man	1967	3.00	6.00	12.00
LAURIE					
ST-607 [S]	In the Still of the Night/All the Things You Are	196?	20.00	40.00	80.00
—Small hole, plays at 33 1/3 rpm					
ST-608 [S]	Swinging on a Star/In Other Words	196?	20.00	40.00	80.00
—Small hole, plays at 33 1/3 rpm					
ST-610 [S]	I've Cried Before/September Song	196?	20.00	40.00	80.00
—Small hole, plays at 33 1/3 rpm					
3013	I Wonder Why/Teen Angel	1958	15.00	30.00	60.00
—Gray label					
3013	I Wonder Why/Teen Angel	1958	7.50	15.00	30.00
—Light blue label					
3013	I Wonder Why/Teen Angel	1958	5.00	10.00	20.00
—Black, red and white label					
3015	No One Knows/I Can't Go On (Rosalie)	1958	12.50	25.00	50.00
—Gray label					
3015	No One Knows/I Can't Go On (Rosalie)	1958	7.50	15.00	30.00
—Light blue label					
3015	No One Knows/I Can't Go On (Rosalie)	1958	5.00	10.00	20.00
—Black, red and white label					
3021	Don't Pity Me/Just You	1958	6.25	12.50	25.00
3027 [M]	A Teenager in Love/I've Cried Before	1959	6.25	12.50	25.00
S-3027 [S]	A Teenager in Love/I've Cried Before	1959	12.50	25.00	50.00
3035	Every Little Thing I Do/A Lover's Prayer	1959	6.25	12.50	25.00
3035 [PS]	Every Little Thing I Do/A Lover's Prayer	1959	12.50	25.00	50.00
3044	Where or When/That's My Desire	1959	6.25	12.50	25.00
3044 [PS]	Where or When/That's My Desire	1959	12.50	25.00	50.00
3052	When You Wish Upon a Star/Wonderful Girl	1960	6.25	12.50	25.00
3052 [PS]	When You Wish Upon a Star/Wonderful Girl	1960	12.50	25.00	50.00
3059	In the Still of the Night/A Funny Feeling	1960	6.25	12.50	25.00
3059 [PS]	In the Still of the Night/A Funny Feeling	1960	12.50	25.00	50.00
LAURIE DOUBLE GOLD					
100	I Wonder Why/Runaround Sue	197?	—	2.00	4.00
—B-side by Dion					
101	No One Knows/The Wanderer	197?	—	2.00	4.00
—B-side by Dion					
102	A Teenager in Love/A Lover's Prayer	197?	—	2.00	4.00
104	Where or When/Lovers Who Wander	197?	—	2.00	4.00
—B-side by Dion					
MOHAWK					
106	Teenage Clementine/Santa Margarita	1957	15.00	30.00	60.00
—May be listed as "The Belmonts"					
107	Tag Along/We Went Away	1957	15.00	30.00	60.00

7-Inch Extended Plays

Number	Title (A Side/B Side)	Yr	VG	VG+	NM
LAURIE					
301	(contents unknown)	1958	30.00	60.00	120.00
301 [PS]	Dion and the Belmonts: Their Hits	1958	45.00	90.00	180.00
302	(contents unknown)	1959	25.00	50.00	100.00
302 [PS]	Where or When	1959	37.50	75.00	150.00

Albums

Number	Title (A Side/B Side)	Yr	VG	VG+	NM
ABC					
599 [M]	Together Again	1967	7.50	15.00	30.00
S-599 [S]	Together Again	1967	10.00	20.00	40.00
ARISTA					
A2L 8206 [(2)]	24 Original Classics	1984	3.00	6.00	12.00
COLLECTABLES					
5025	Presenting Dion & The Belmonts	198?	2.50	5.00	10.00
5026	Wish Upon a Star	198?	2.50	5.00	10.00
5041	20 Golden Classics	198?	2.50	5.00	10.00
LAURIE					
LLP 1002 [M]	Presenting Dion & The Belmonts	1959	62.50	125.00	250.00
LLP 2002 [M]	Presenting Dion & The Belmonts	1960	37.50	75.00	150.00
SLP 2002 [R]	Presenting Dion & The Belmonts	196?	300.00	600.00	900.00
—Despite its rechanneled stereo sound, this record is collectible because of its utter rarity					
LLP 2006 [M]	Wish Upon a Star	1960	37.50	75.00	150.00
LLP 2016 [M]	"Together" On Records — By Special Request	1963	12.50	25.00	50.00
LES 4002	Everything You Always Wanted to Hear by Dion and the Belmonts	197?	3.75	7.50	15.00
SLP 6000 [(3)]	60 Greatest Hits	197?	7.50	15.00	30.00
—In box					
SLP 6000 [(3)]	60 Greatest Hits	197?	5.00	10.00	20.00
—In regular cover					
PAIR					
PDL2-1142 [(2)]	The Best of Dion and the Belmonts	1986	3.00	6.00	12.00
PICKWICK					
SPC-3521	Doo Wop	1975	2.50	5.00	10.00
—Reissue of ABC tracks					
RHINO					
RNLP 70228	Reunion — Live at Madison Square Garden — 1972	1987	2.50	5.00	10.00
—Reissue of ABC tracks					
WARNER BROS.					
BS 2664	Reunion — Live at Madison Square Garden — 1972	1973	3.75	7.50	15.00

DION AND THE TIMBERLANES

Early version of DION AND THE BELMONTS.

45s

Number	Title (A Side/B Side)	Yr	VG	VG+	NM
JUBILEE					
5294	The Chosen Few/Out in Colorado	1957	7.50	15.00	30.00
MOHAWK					
105	The Chosen Few/Out in Colorado	1957	15.00	30.00	60.00

DIPPERS QUINTET, THE

45s

Number	Title (A Side/B Side)	Yr	VG	VG+	NM
FLAYR					
500	It's Almost Christmas/Look What I've Found	1955	2000.	3000.	4000.

DIRKSEN, SENATOR EVERETT MCKINLEY

45s

Number	Title (A Side/B Side)	Yr	VG	VG+	NM
CAPITOL					
2034	The First Time the Christmas Story Was Told/I Heard the Bells on Christmas Day	1967	2.00	4.00	8.00
5805	Gallant Men/The New Colossus	1966	—	3.00	6.00
5805 [PS]	Gallant Men/The New Colossus	1966	2.00	4.00	8.00
5912	Man Is Not Alone/The Shepherd and His Flock	1967	—	2.50	5.00

Albums

Number	Title (A Side/B Side)	Yr	VG	VG+	NM
CAPITOL					
ST 2643 [S]	Gallant Men	1966	3.75	7.50	15.00
T 2643 [M]	Gallant Men	1966	3.75	7.50	15.00
ST 2754 [S]	Man Is Not Alone	1967	3.75	7.50	15.00
T 2754 [M]	Man Is Not Alone	1967	5.00	10.00	20.00
ST 2792 [S]	Everett McKinley Dirksen at Christmas Time	1967	5.00	10.00	20.00

DIRT BAND, THE

See NITTY GRITTY DIRT BAND.

DIRTY BLUES BAND, THE

45s

Number	Title (A Side/B Side)	Yr	VG	VG+	NM
BLUESWAY					
61016	Hound Dog/New Orleans Woman	1968	2.00	4.00	8.00

Albums

Number	Title (A Side/B Side)	Yr	VG	VG+	NM
BLUESWAY					
BLS-6010	The Dirty Blues Band	1968	5.00	10.00	20.00
BLS-6020	Stone Dirt	1968	5.00	10.00	20.00

DISCO-TEX AND THE SEX-O-LETTES

45s

Number	Title (A Side/B Side)	Yr	VG	VG+	NM
CHELSEA					
3004	Get Dancin' (Part I)/Get Dancin' (Part II)	1974	—	2.00	4.00
3015	I Wanna Dance Wit'choo (Part I)/I Wanna Dance Wit'choo (Part II)	1975	—	2.00	4.00
3026	Jam Band/Jam Band Reprise	1975	—	2.00	4.00
3040	Hot Lava/Hot Lava 2	1976	—	2.00	4.00
3045	Dancin' Kid (Part I)/Dancin' Kid (Part II)	1976	—	2.00	4.00
3054	Strollin'/We're Havin' a Party (It's Gonna Be Alright)	1976	—	2.00	4.00
3070	Wooly Bully/On Broadway	1977	—	2.00	4.00

Albums

Number	Title (A Side/B Side)	Yr	VG	VG+	NM
CHELSEA					
CHL 505	Disco-Tex and His Sex-O-Lettes	1975	2.50	5.00	10.00
CHL 516	Manhattan Millionaire	1976	2.50	5.00	10.00
CHL 555	A Piece of the Rock	1977	2.50	5.00	10.00

DISENTRI, TURNER

Actually Bob Gaudio of THE ROYAL TEENS and THE FOUR SEASONS.

45s

Number	Title (A Side/B Side)	Yr	VG	VG+	NM
TOPIX					
6001	10,000,000 Tears/Spanish Lace	1961	25.00	50.00	100.00

DISTANTS, THE

45s

Number	Title (A Side/B Side)	Yr	VG	VG+	NM
NORTHERN					
3732	Come On/Always	1960	150.00	300.00	600.00
WARWICK					
546	Come On/Always	1960	25.00	50.00	100.00
577	Always/Open Up Your Heart	1960	25.00	50.00	100.00

DIXIE CUPS, THE

45s

Number	Title (A Side/B Side)	Yr	VG	VG+	NM
ABC					
10855	Love Ain't So Bad (After All)/Daddy Said No	1966	3.00	6.00	12.00
ABC-PARAMOUNT					
10692	That's Where It's At/Two-Way-Poc-A-Way	1965	3.00	6.00	12.00
10715	I'm Not the Kind of Girl (To Marry)/What Goes Up Must Go Down	1965	3.00	6.00	12.00
10755	A-B-C Song/That's What the Kids Said	1965	3.00	6.00	12.00
ANTILLES					
707	Iko Iko/Hey Hey (Indian's Coming)	1987	—	2.00	4.00
—B-side by The Wild Tchoupitoulas					
707 [PS]	Iko Iko/Hey Hey (Indian's Coming)	1987	—	2.00	4.00
RED BIRD					
10-001	Chapel of Love/Ain't That Nice	1964	7.50	15.00	30.00
10-006	People Say/Girls Can Tell	1964	5.00	10.00	20.00
10-012	You Should Have Seen the Way He Looked at Me/No True Love	1964	5.00	10.00	20.00
10-017	Little Bell/Another Boy Like Me	1964	5.00	10.00	20.00
10-024	Iko Iko/Gee, Baby, Gee	1965	5.00	10.00	20.00
10-024	Iko Iko/I'm Gonna Get You Yet	1965	5.00	10.00	20.00
10-032	Gee, the Moon Is Shining Bright/I'm Gonna Get You Yet	1965	5.00	10.00	20.00

Albums

Number	Title (A Side/B Side)	Yr	VG	VG+	NM
ABC-PARAMOUNT					
525 [M]	Riding High	1965	15.00	30.00	60.00
S-525 [S]	Riding High	1965	20.00	40.00	80.00

Number	Title (A Side/B Side)	Yr	VG	VG+	NM
RED BIRD					
RB 20-100 [M]	Chapel of Love	1964	15.00	30.00	60.00
RBS 20-100 [S]	Chapel of Love	1964	20.00	40.00	80.00
RB 20-103 [M]	Iko Iko	1965	37.50	75.00	150.00

DIXIEBELLES, THE

45s

Number	Title (A Side/B Side)	Yr	VG	VG+	NM
SOUND STAGE 7					
2507	(Down at) Papa Joe's/Rock, Rock, Rock	1963	2.50	5.00	10.00
2517	Southtown U.S.A./Why Don't You Set Me Free	1964	2.50	5.00	10.00
2521	New York Town/The Beale Street Dog	1964	2.50	5.00	10.00

Albums

Number	Title (A Side/B Side)	Yr	VG	VG+	NM
SOUND STAGE 7					
SSM-5000 [M]	Down at Papa Joe's	1963	10.00	20.00	40.00
SSS-15000 [R]	Down at Papa Joe's	1963	7.50	15.00	30.00

DIXIES, THE

45s

Number	Title (A Side/B Side)	Yr	VG	VG+	NM
AUTUMN					
12	He's Got You/Geisha Girl	1965	3.75	7.50	15.00

DIXON, BILLY, AND THE TOPICS

See THE FOUR SEASONS.

DIXON, FLOYD

45s

Number	Title (A Side/B Side)	Yr	VG	VG+	NM
ALADDIN					
3101	Do I Love You/Time and Place	1951	50.00	100.00	200.00
—Earlier Floyd Dixon 45s on Aladdin may exist					
3111	Too Much Jelly Roll/Baby, Let's Go to the Woods	1952	50.00	100.00	200.00
3121	Blues for Cuba/Bad Neighborhood	1952	50.00	100.00	200.00
3135	Wine, Wine, Wine/Call Operator 210	1952	50.00	100.00	200.00
3144	Red Cherries/The River	1952	75.00	150.00	300.00
—Black vinyl					
3144	Red Cherries/The River	1952	175.00	350.00	700.00
—Red vinyl					
3151	Tired, Broke and Busted/Come Back Baby	1952	37.50	75.00	150.00
3166	You Played Me for a Fool/Broken Hearted Traveler	1953	37.50	75.00	150.00
3196	Lovin'/Married Woman	1953	37.50	75.00	150.00
3230	You Need Me Now/A Long Time Ago	1954	25.00	50.00	100.00
CASH					
1057	Oh Baby/Never Can Tell	1957	12.50	25.00	50.00
CAT					
106	Moonshine/Roll Baby Roll	1954	15.00	30.00	60.00
114	Hey Bartender/It Is True	1955	15.00	30.00	60.00
CHATTAHOOCHIE					
652	Tell Me, Tell Me/There Goes My Heart	1964	2.50	5.00	10.00
CHECKER					
857	Alarm Clock Blues/I'm Ashamed of Myself	1957	7.50	15.00	30.00
DODGE					
807	Opportunity Blues/Daisy	1961	3.75	7.50	15.00
EBB					
105	What Is Life Without a Home/Oh-Ee Little Girl	1957	7.50	15.00	30.00
IMPERIAL					
5849	Tired, Broke and Busted/Call Operator 210	1962	3.00	6.00	12.00
KENT					
311	Change Your Mind/Dance the Thing	1958	5.00	10.00	20.00
SPECIALTY					
468	Hard Living Alone/Please Don't Go	1953	20.00	40.00	80.00
—Black vinyl					
468	Hard Living Alone/Please Don't Go	1953	50.00	100.00	200.00
—Red vinyl					
477	Hole in the Wall/Old Memories	1953	20.00	40.00	80.00
486	Ooh-Eee Ooh-Eee/Nose Job	1954	20.00	40.00	80.00
SWINGIN'					
626	Tight Skirts/Wake Up and Live	1960	5.00	10.00	20.00

DOBKINS, CARL, JR.

45s

Number	Title (A Side/B Side)	Yr	VG	VG+	NM
ATCO					
6283	If Teardrops Were Diamonds/I'm So Sorry Little Girl	1964	3.00	6.00	12.00
CHALET					
1053	Days of Sand and Shovel/Linda the Motel Maid	1969	2.50	5.00	10.00
1056	My Heart Is an Open Book/Pictures	1969	2.50	5.00	10.00
COLPIX					
762	His Loss Is My Gain/A Little Bit Later On Down the Line	1965	3.00	6.00	12.00
DECCA					
30656	Love Is Everything/If You Don't Want My Lovin'	1958	5.00	10.00	20.00
30803	My Heart Is an Open Book/My Pledge to You	1959	6.25	12.50	25.00
31020	Lucky Devil/In My Heart	1959	5.00	10.00	20.00
31020 [PS]	Lucky Devil/In My Heart	1959	7.50	15.00	30.00
31088	Exclusively Yours/One Little Girl	1960	3.75	7.50	15.00
31088 [PS]	Exclusively Yours/One Little Girl	1960	7.50	15.00	30.00
31143	Different Kind of Love/Genie	1960	3.75	7.50	15.00
31182	Lovelight/Take Time Out	1960	3.75	7.50	15.00
31260	Pretty Little Girl in the Yellow Dress/That's What I Call True Love	1961	3.75	7.50	15.00
31301	Sawdust Dolly/A Chance to Belong	1961	3.75	7.50	15.00
31353	Ask Me No Questions/Promise Me	1962	3.75	7.50	15.00
FRATERNITY					
794	That's Why I'm Asking/Take Hold of My Hand	1958	7.50	15.00	30.00

7-Inch Extended Plays

Number	Title (A Side/B Side)	Yr	VG	VG+	NM
DECCA					
ED 2664	My Heart Is An Open Book/My Pledge to You//Love Is Everything/If You Don't Want My Lovin'	1959	10.00	20.00	40.00
ED 2664 [PS]	My Heart Is An Open Book	1959	10.00	20.00	40.00

DOBRO, JIMMY

See JAMES BURTON.

DOBRO, LON

45s

Number	Title (A Side/B Side)	Yr	VG	VG+	NM
4 STAR					
1754	I Just Like You/All the Time	1961	15.00	30.00	60.00
TROY					
1003	Undercurrent/Mid-Night Surf	1963	12.50	25.00	50.00

DOC HOLLIDAY

45s

Number	Title (A Side/B Side)	Yr	VG	VG+	NM
METROMEDIA					
68-0114	Whiskey Lady/Magga Blue	1973	2.00	4.00	8.00

Albums

Number	Title (A Side/B Side)	Yr	VG	VG+	NM
METROMEDIA					
1017	Doc Holliday	1973	5.00	10.00	20.00

DR. FEELGOOD AND THE INTERNS

Also see PIANO RED.

45s

Number	Title (A Side/B Side)	Yr	VG	VG+	NM
COLUMBIA					
43372	Doctor of Love/Let the House Rock On	1965	2.00	4.00	8.00
43615	Where Did You Go/Don't Tell Me No Dirty	1966	2.00	4.00	8.00
OKEH					
7144	Mr. Moonlight/Dr. Feel-Good	1962	3.00	6.00	12.00
7153	Bald Headed Lena/What's Up Doc	1962	3.00	6.00	12.00
7156	The Right String But the Wrong Yo-Yo/What's Up Doc	1962	3.00	6.00	12.00
7161	Let's Have a Good Time Tonight/The Same Old Things Keep Happening	1962	3.00	6.00	12.00
7167	My Gal Jo/Bald Headed Lena	1963	3.00	6.00	12.00
7185	The Doctor's Boogie/Blang Dong	1963	3.00	6.00	12.00

Albums

Number	Title (A Side/B Side)	Yr	VG	VG+	NM
OKEH					
OKM 12101 [M]	Dr. Feelgood and the Interns	1962	25.00	50.00	100.00
OKS 14101 [S]	Dr. Feelgood and the Interns	1962	50.00	100.00	200.00

DR. HOOK

Includes records as "Dr. Hook and the Medicine Show." Also see RAY SAWYER.

45s

Number	Title (A Side/B Side)	Yr	VG	VG+	NM
CAPITOL					
4081	Levitate/Cooky and Lila	1975	—	2.00	4.00
4104	The Millionaire/Cooky and Lila	1975	—	2.00	4.00
4171	Only Sixteen/Let Me Be Your Lover	1975	—	2.50	5.00
4280	A Little Bit More/A Couple More Years	1976	—	2.50	5.00
4364	If Not You/Bad Eye Bill	1976	—	2.00	4.00
4423	Walk Right In/Sexy Energy	1977	—	2.00	4.00
4534	Making Love and Music/Who Dat	1978	—	2.00	4.00
4615	I Don't Want to Be Alone Tonight/You Make My Pants Want to Get Up and Dance	1978	—	2.00	4.00
4621	Sharing the Night Together/You Make My Pants Want to Get Up and Dance	1978	—	2.00	4.00
4677	All the Time in the World/Dooley Jones	1979	—	2.00	4.00
4705	When You're in Love with a Beautiful Woman/Knowing She's There	1979	—	2.00	4.00
4785	Better Love Next Time/Mountain Mary	1979	—	2.00	4.00
4831	Sexy Eyes/Help Me Mama	1980	—	2.00	4.00
4885	Years from Now/I Don't Feel Much Like Smilin'	1980	—	2.00	4.00
4885 [PS]	Years from Now/I Don't Feel Much Like Smilin'	1980	—	2.50	5.00
CASABLANCA					
2314	Girls Can Get It/Doin' It	1980	—	2.00	4.00
2325	S.O.S. For Love/99 and Me	1981	—	2.00	4.00
2347	Baby Makes Her Blue Jeans Talk/The Turn On	1981	—	2.00	4.00
2347 [PS]	Baby Makes Her Blue Jeans Talk/The Turn On	1981	—	2.50	5.00
2351	Loveline/Pity the Fool	1981	—	2.00	4.00
COLUMBIA					
3-10032	Make It Easy/Ballad of Lucy Jordan	1974	—	3.00	6.00
—All as "Dr. Hook and the Medicine Show"					
4-45392	Last Morning/One More Ride (Lucille and Bunky)	1971	—	3.00	6.00
4-45562	Sylvia's Mother/Makin' It Natural	1972	—	3.00	6.00
—Orange label with "Columbia" background print					
4-45562	Sylvia's Mother/Makin' It Natural	1972	—	2.50	5.00
—Gray label					
4-45667	Carry Me, Carrie/Call That True Love	1972	—	2.50	5.00
4-45667 [PS]	Carry Me, Carrie/Call That True Love	1972	—	3.00	6.00
45732	The Cover of "Rolling Stone"/Queen of the Silver Dollar	1972	—	2.50	5.00
—Orange label					
4-45732	The Cover of "Rolling Stone"/Queen of the Silver Dollar	1972	—	3.00	6.00
—Gray label					
45878	Roland the Roadie and Gertrude the Groupie/Put a Little Bit on Me	1973	—	2.50	5.00
4-45925	Life Ain't Easy/Wonderful Stone Soup	1973	—	2.50	5.00
4-46026	Monterey Jack/Cops and Robbers	1974	—	2.50	5.00

Albums

Number	Title (A Side/B Side)	Yr	VG	VG+	NM
CAPITOL					
ST-11397	Bankrupt	1975	2.50	5.00	10.00
ST-11522	A Little Bit More	1976	2.50	5.00	10.00
ST-11632	Makin' Love and Music	1977	2.50	5.00	10.00
SW-11859	Pleasure and Pain	1978	2.50	5.00	10.00
SOO-12018	Sometimes You Win...	1979	2.50	5.00	10.00
ST-12114	Live	1981	2.50	5.00	10.00
SOO-12122	Dr. Hook/Greatest Hits	1980	2.50	5.00	10.00
ST-12325	The Best of Dr. Hook	1984	2.00	4.00	8.00
SN-16179	Bankrupt	198?	2.00	4.00	8.00
—Budget-line reissue					
SN-16180	A Little Bit More	198?	2.00	4.00	8.00
—Budget-line reissue					
SN-16181	Pleasure and Pain	198?	2.00	4.00	8.00
—Budget-line reissue					

Number	Title (A Side/B Side)	Yr	VG	VG+	NM
SN-16228	Makin' Love and Music	198?	2.00	4.00	8.00
—Budget-line reissue					
SN-16229	Sometimes You Win...	198?	2.00	4.00	8.00
—Budget-line reissue					
SN-16325	Dr. Hook/Greatest Hits	198?	2.00	4.00	8.00
—Budget-line reissue					
CASABLANCA					
NBLP-7251	Rising	1980	2.50	5.00	10.00
NBLP-7264	Players in the Dark	1982	2.50	5.00	10.00
COLUMBIA					
KC 30898	Dr. Hook & The Medicine Show	1972	3.75	7.50	15.00
PC 30898	Dr. Hook & The Medicine Show	198?	2.00	4.00	8.00
—Budget-line reissue					
KC 31622	Sloppy Seconds	1972	3.75	7.50	15.00
PC 31622	Sloppy Seconds	198?	2.00	4.00	8.00
—Budget-line reissue					
KC 32270	Belly Up!	1973	3.75	7.50	15.00
C 34147	Dr. Hook and the Medicine Show Revisited	1976	2.50	5.00	10.00
PC 34147	Dr. Hook and the Medicine Show Revisited	198?	2.00	4.00	8.00
—Budget-line reissue					
MERCURY					
800054-1	Players in the Dark	1983	2.00	4.00	8.00
—Reissue of Casablanca 7264					

DR. HOOK AND THE MEDICINE SHOW

See DR. HOOK.

DR. JOHN

Also see MIKE BLOOMFIELD/JOHN PAUL HAMMOND/DR. JOHN; HUEY "PIANO" SMITH.

Number	Title (A Side/B Side)	Yr	VG	VG+	NM
45s					
ACE					
611	Good Times/Sahara	1961	6.25	12.50	25.00
—As "Mac Rebennack"					
ATCO					
6607	I Walk on Gilded Splinters (Part 1)/I Walk on Gilded Splinters (Part 2)	1968	3.00	6.00	12.00
6635	Jump Sturdy/Mama Roox	1968	3.00	6.00	12.00
6697	Patriotic Flag Waver (Long)/Patriotic Flag Waver (Short)	1969	2.00	4.00	8.00
6755	Wash, Mama, Wash/Loup Gardo	1970	3.00	6.00	12.00
6882	Iko Iko/The Huey Smith Medley	1972	2.50	5.00	10.00
6898	Wang Dang Doodle/Big Chief	1972	—	3.00	6.00
6900	Let the Good Times Roll/Stack-A-Lee	1972	—	3.00	6.00
6914	Right Place Wrong Time/I Been Hoodood	1973	—	3.00	6.00
6937	Such a Night/Cold, Cold, Cold	1973	—	3.00	6.00
6957	(Everybody Wanna Get Rich) Rite Away/Mos'Scocious	1974	—	3.00	6.00
6971	Let's Make a Better World/Me Minus You Equals Loneliness	1974	—	3.00	6.00
A.F.O.					
309	The Point/One Naughty Flat	1962	6.25	12.50	25.00
—As "Mac Rebenack"					
HORIZON					
117	Wild Honey/Dance the Night Away with You	1979	—	2.00	4.00
125	Keep That Music Simple/I Thought I Heard New Orleans	1979	—	2.00	4.00
RCA					
PB-11285	Take Me Higher/Sweet Rider	1978	—	2.00	4.00
REX					
1008	Storm Warning/Foolish Little Girl	1959	12.50	25.00	50.00
—As "Mac Rebennack"					
SCEPTER					
12393	One Night Late/She's Just a Square	1974	—	2.50	5.00
WARNER BROS.					
22976	Makin' Whoopee!/More Than You Know	1989	—	—	3.00
22976 [PS]	Makin' Whoopee!/More Than You Know	1989	—	—	3.00
49703	The Sailor and the Mermaid/One Good Turn	1981	—	2.00	4.00
—A-side with Libby Titus; B-side by Al Jarreau					
Albums					
ACCORD					
SN-7118	Love Potion	1982	2.50	5.00	10.00
ALLIGATOR					
AL-3901	Dr. John's Gumbo	1986	2.50	5.00	10.00
—Reissue of Atco 7006					
AL-3904	Gris-Gris	1987	2.50	5.00	10.00
—Reissue of Atco 33-234					
ATCO					
SD 33-234	Gris-Gris	1968	7.50	15.00	30.00
—Purple and brown label					
SD 33-234	Gris-Gris	1968	3.75	7.50	15.00
—Yellow label					
SD 33-270	Babylon	1969	3.75	7.50	15.00
SD 33-316	Remedies	1970	3.75	7.50	15.00
SD 33-362	Dr. John, The Night Tripper (The Sun, Moon & Herbs)	1971	3.75	7.50	15.00
SD 7006	Dr. John's Gumbo	1972	3.00	6.00	12.00
SD 7018	In the Right Place	1973	3.00	6.00	12.00
SD 7043	Desitively Bonaroo	1974	3.00	6.00	12.00
CLEAN CUTS					
705	Dr. John Plays Mac Rebennack	1982	2.50	5.00	10.00
707	The Brightest Smile in Town	1984	2.50	5.00	10.00
HORIZON					
SP-732	City Lights	1978	2.50	5.00	10.00
SP-740	Tango Palace	1979	2.50	5.00	10.00
KARATE					
5404	One Night Late	1978	2.50	5.00	10.00
TRIP					
TLX-350 [(2)]	Superpak	1975	3.00	6.00	12.00
UNITED ARTISTS					
UA-LA552-G	Hollywood Be Thy Name	1975	3.00	6.00	12.00
WARNER BROS.					
25889	In a Sentimental Mood	1989	3.00	6.00	12.00

DR. JOHN AND CHRIS BARBER

Also see each artist's individual listings.

Number	Title (A Side/B Side)	Yr	VG	VG+	NM
Albums					
GREAT SOUTHERN					
GS-11024	On a Mardi Gras Day	1991	3.00	6.00	12.00

DOCTOR ROSS

Number	Title (A Side/B Side)	Yr	VG	VG+	NM
45s					
HI-Q					
5027	Cannonball/Numbers Blues	1963	5.00	10.00	20.00
5033	Call the Doctor/New York Breakdown	1963	5.00	10.00	20.00
SUN					
193	Chicago Breakdown/Come Back Baby	1954	200.00	400.00	600.00
212	The Boogie Disease/Juke Box Boogie	1954	500.00	1000.	2000.
Albums					
FORTUNE					
F-3011 [M]	Doctor Ross, The Harmonica Boss	1962	12.50	25.00	50.00
FS-3011 [S]	Doctor Ross, The Harmonica Boss	1962	25.00	50.00	100.00
TESTAMENT					
2206 [M]	Doctor Ross	196?	5.00	10.00	20.00

DR. WEST'S MEDICINE SHOW AND JUG BAND

Also see NORMAN GREENBAUM.

Number	Title (A Side/B Side)	Yr	VG	VG+	NM
45s					
GO GO					
100	The Eggplant That Ate Chicago/You Can't Fight City Hall Blues	1966	3.00	6.00	12.00
102	Gondoliers, Shakespeares, Overseers, Playboys and Bums/Daddy, I Know	1967	2.50	5.00	10.00
102 [PS]	Gondoliers, Shakespeares, Overseers, Playboys and Bums/Daddy, I Know	1967	5.00	10.00	20.00
104	You Can Fly/The Circus Left Town Today	1967	2.50	5.00	10.00
GREGAR					
71-0100	Gondoliers, Shakespeares, Overseers, Playboys and Bums/Daddy, I Know	1969	2.50	5.00	10.00
106	Bullets Laverne/Jigsaw	1968	2.50	5.00	10.00
Albums					
GO GO					
22-17-002	The Eggplant That Ate Chicago	1967	6.25	12.50	25.00
GREGAR					
GG-101	Norman Greenbaum with Dr. West's Medicine Show and Jug Band	1970	5.00	10.00	20.00

DODD, DICK

Also see THE STANDELLS.

Number	Title (A Side/B Side)	Yr	VG	VG+	NM
45s					
ATTARACK					
102	Guilty/Requiem 820	1970	2.50	5.00	10.00
TOWER					
447	Lonely Weekends/Little Star	1968	3.00	6.00	12.00
447 [PS]	Lonely Weekends/Little Star	1968	7.50	15.00	30.00
490	Fanny/Don't Be Ashamed to Call My Name	1969	3.00	6.00	12.00

DODD, JIMMIE

Number	Title (A Side/B Side)	Yr	VG	VG+	NM
45s					
ABC-PARAMOUNT					
9665	Mouseketeer Theme/Hi to You	1956	5.00	10.00	20.00
9680	Mickey Mouse Mambo/Humphrey Hop-Pussy Cat	1956	5.00	10.00	20.00
9691	Zip-A-Dee-Doo-Dah/Song of the South	1956	5.00	10.00	20.00
—B-side by Jeanne Gayle					
Albums					
DISNEYLAND					
WDL-1014 [M]	Jimmie Dodd Sings His Favorite Hymns	1959	6.25	12.50	25.00
—Reissue of 3014 with new number					
DQ-1235 [M]	Sing Along with Jimmie Dodd	1963	7.50	15.00	30.00
DQ-1302 [M]	Favorite Hymns for Family Singing	1967	3.75	7.50	15.00
—Reissue of 1014					
WDL-3014 [M]	Jimmie Dodd Sings His Favorite Hymns	1958	6.25	12.50	25.00
IMPERIAL					
LP-9089 [M]	Lonely Guitar	1959	10.00	20.00	40.00
LP-9121 [M]	Swing-A-Spell	1960	10.00	20.00	40.00
LP-12058 [S]	Swing-A-Spell	1960	12.50	25.00	50.00

DODD, KEN

Number	Title (A Side/B Side)	Yr	VG	VG+	NM
45s					
LIBERTY					
55733	All of My Life/Happiness	1964	3.00	6.00	12.00
55835	Tears (For Souvenirs)/You and I	1965	2.50	5.00	10.00
55859	The River/My Thanks to You	1966	2.50	5.00	10.00
55893	Promises/Thank You for Being You	1966	2.50	5.00	10.00
LONDON					
1942	Love Is Like a Violin/Treasure in My Heart	1960	3.00	6.00	12.00
Albums					
LIBERTY					
LRP-3442 [M]	Tears and The River	1966	3.75	7.50	15.00
LST-7442 [S]	Tears and The River	1966	5.00	10.00	20.00

DODDS, MALCOLM

Number	Title (A Side/B Side)	Yr	VG	VG+	NM
45s					
AMY					
861	A Rendezvous with a Broken Heart/All My Wildest Dreams	1962	2.00	4.00	8.00
AURORA					
3250	Ich Bin Verry Happy (Merry, Merry Christmas)/Perfect Strangers	1962	2.50	5.00	10.00
DECCA					
30653	The Swingin' Platoon/Your Voice	1958	3.00	6.00	12.00
30766	I'll Always Be with You/This Is Real (This Is Love)	1958	3.00	6.00	12.00
30857	Deep Inside/Tremble	1959	3.00	6.00	12.00

Number	Title (A Side/B Side)	Yr	VG	VG+	NM
30922	I've Waited So Long/Somehow	1959	3.00	6.00	12.00
30970	I Feel Peculiar/Only for You	1959	3.00	6.00	12.00
END					
1000	It Took a Long Time/Beauty and the Beast	1957	15.00	30.00	60.00
1004	Fools Rush In/Can't See You	1957	20.00	40.00	80.00
1010	Tonight/Unspoken Love	1958	15.00	30.00	60.00
MGM					
12975	All for the Love of a Woman/Come, Oh Come	1961	2.50	5.00	10.00
13029	Without a Song/Laugh My Heart	1961	2.50	5.00	10.00
PROJECT 3					
1319	Hey World/I Don't Want to Cry	196?	—	3.00	6.00
1338	I Love, I Live, I Love/Mr. Broadloom	196?	—	3.00	6.00

Albums

Number	Title	Yr	VG	VG+	NM
RCA CAMDEN					
CAL-873 [M]	Happiness Is a Thing Called Love	196?	3.75	7.50	15.00
CAS-873 [S]	Happiness Is a Thing Called Love	196?	3.00	6.00	12.00

DODDS, NELLA

45s

Number	Title (A Side/B Side)	Yr	VG	VG+	NM
WAND					
167	Come See About Me/You Don't Love Me Anymore	1964	3.75	7.50	15.00
171	Finders Keepers Losers Weepers/A Girl's Life	1964	3.00	6.00	12.00
178	Your Love Back/P's and Q's	1965	3.00	6.00	12.00
187	Come Back Baby/Dream Boy	1965	3.00	6.00	12.00
1111	Gee Whiz/Maybe Baby	1966	3.75	7.50	15.00
1136	Honey Boy/I Just Gotta Have You	1966	20.00	40.00	80.00

DODO, JOE, AND THE GROOVERS

45s

Number	Title (A Side/B Side)	Yr	VG	VG+	NM
RCA VICTOR					
47-7207	Groovy/Goin' Steady	1958	6.25	12.50	25.00

DOGGETT, BILL

Also see EARL BOSTIC.

45s

Number	Title (A Side/B Side)	Yr	VG	VG+	NM
ABC-PARAMOUNT					
10611	Mudcat/The Kicker	1965	—	3.00	6.00
CHUMLEY					
90001	Blue Point of View/Funky Feet	1974	—	2.00	4.00
COLUMBIA					
42384	Buster/Ladies Choice	1962	2.50	5.00	10.00
42531	Oops/Choo Choo	1962	2.50	5.00	10.00
42689	Soda Pop/Ham Fat	1963	2.50	5.00	10.00
42792	The Worm/Hot Fudge	1963	2.50	5.00	10.00
CORAL					
61739	A Pretty Girl Is Like a Melody/If I Should Lose You	1956	3.00	6.00	12.00
KING					
4548	Please Don't Ever Let Me Go/Glo' Glug	1952	5.00	10.00	20.00
4702	It's a Dream/The Song Is Ended	1954	5.00	10.00	20.00
4711	There's No You/Easy	1954	5.00	10.00	20.00
4720	Sweet Lorraine/Tailor Made	1954	5.00	10.00	20.00
4732	Sweet Slumber/High Heels	1954	5.00	10.00	20.00
4738	The Nearness of You/Honey	1954	5.00	10.00	20.00
4742	The Christmas Song/Winter Wonderland	1954	5.00	10.00	20.00
4759	Tara's Theme/Gumbo	1955	3.75	7.50	15.00
4769	My Reverie/King Bee	1955	3.75	7.50	15.00
4784	Wild Oats/I'll Be Around	1955	3.75	7.50	15.00
4795	Oof/Street Scene	1955	3.75	7.50	15.00
4808	Quaker City/True Blue	1955	3.75	7.50	15.00
4825	You Don't Know What Love Is/Shove Off	1955	3.75	7.50	15.00
4838	Honey Boy/Misty Moon	1955	3.75	7.50	15.00
4888	In a Sentimental Mood/Who's Who	1956	3.75	7.50	15.00
4917	Squashy/We Found Love	1956	3.75	7.50	15.00
4936	What a Difference a Day Makes/Stella by Starlight	1956	3.75	7.50	15.00
4950	Honky Tonk (Part 1)/Honky Tonk (Part 2)	1956	5.00	10.00	20.00
5000	Slow Walk/Hand in Hand	1956	3.75	7.50	15.00
5001	Honky Tonk (Vocal)/Peacock Alley	1956	3.75	7.50	15.00
—Vocal by Tommy Brown					
5020	Ram-Bunk-Shush/Blue Largo	1957	3.00	6.00	12.00
5044	Chloe/Number Three	1957	3.00	6.00	12.00
5058	Ding Dong/Cling to Me	1957	3.00	6.00	12.00
5070	Hammer Head/Shindig	1957	3.00	6.00	12.00
5080	Hot Ginger/Soft	1957	3.00	6.00	12.00
5096	Hippy Dippy/Flying Home	1957	3.00	6.00	12.00
5101	Leaps and Bounds (Part 1)/Leaps and Bounds (Part 2)	1958	3.00	6.00	12.00
5125	Boo Da Ba/Pimento	1958	3.00	6.00	12.00
5130	How Could You/Blues for Handy	1958	3.00	6.00	12.00
5138	Tanya/Blip Bop	1958	3.00	6.00	12.00
5149	Birdie/Hold It	1958	3.00	6.00	12.00
5159	Rainbow Riot (Part 1)/Rainbow Riot (Part 2)	1958	3.00	6.00	12.00
5176	Monster Party/Scott's Bluff	1959	3.00	6.00	12.00
5204	The Madison/Ocean Liner	1959	3.00	6.00	12.00
5227	After Hours/Big City Drag	1959	3.00	6.00	12.00
5256	Yucky Dock (Part 1)/Yucky Dock (Part 2)	1959	3.00	6.00	12.00
5281	The Goofy Organ/Zee	1959	3.00	6.00	12.00
5310	Smokie Part 2/Evening Dreams	1960	2.50	5.00	10.00
5319	Back Woods/Raw Turkey	1960	2.50	5.00	10.00
5339	Big Boy/Smoochie	1960	2.50	5.00	10.00
5364	Buttered Popcorn/The Slush	1960	2.50	5.00	10.00
5387	A Lover's Dream/Trav'lin' Light	1960	2.50	5.00	10.00
5419	Slidin'/Afternoon Jump	1960	2.50	5.00	10.00
5444	Honky Tonk (Part 2)/Floyd's Guitar Blues	1961	2.50	5.00	10.00
5482	Bugle Nose/The Doodle	1961	2.50	5.00	10.00
5561	High and Wide/In the Wee Hours	1961	2.50	5.00	10.00
5599	The Doodle Twist/Gene's Dream	1962	2.00	4.00	8.00
5642	George Washington Twist/Eleven O'Clock Twist	1962	2.00	4.00	8.00
5665	Teardrops/Moon Dust	1962	2.00	4.00	8.00
5684	Hometown Shout/For All We Know	1962	2.00	4.00	8.00
5718	Honky Tonk Bossa Nova (Part 2)/Ocean Liner Bossa Nova	1963	2.00	4.00	8.00
5740	Down Home Bossa Nova/Si Si Nova	1963	2.00	4.00	8.00
5788	The Fog/Groovy Movie	1963	2.00	4.00	8.00
5873	The Rail/Hey Big Boy, Hey Hey	1964	2.00	4.00	8.00
5878	Night Train (Part 1)/Night Train (Part 2)	1964	2.00	4.00	8.00
5948	Crackers/That's Enough, Lock 'Em Up	1964	2.00	4.00	8.00
5957	Snuff Box/Blood Pressure	1964	2.00	4.00	8.00
6019	Teardrops/Slidin'	1966	—	3.00	6.00
6217	Take Your Shot/Mad	1969	—	2.50	5.00
6225	Twenty-Five Miles/For Once in My Life	1969	—	2.50	5.00
6239	Honky Tonk Popcorn/Honky Tonk	1969	—	2.50	5.00
6312	The Nearness of You/Moon Dust	1970	—	2.00	4.00
6350	High Heels/Soft	1971	—	2.00	4.00
6356	In a Sentimental Mood/Eventide	1971	—	2.00	4.00
ROULETTE					
4732	Sapphire/Ko-Ko	1967	—	3.00	6.00
4749	Lovin' Mood/The Funky Wrestler	1967	—	3.00	6.00
SUE					
10-002	Fat Back/Si Si Cisco	1968	—	2.50	5.00
WARNER BROS.					
5181	Jack Rabbit/Let's Do the Hully Gully Twist	1960	3.00	6.00	12.00
5209	Let's Do the Continental/Pony Walk	1961	3.00	6.00	12.00
5223	You Can't Sit Down (Part 1)/You Can't Sit Down (Part 2)	1961	3.00	6.00	12.00

7-Inch Extended Plays

Number	Title	Yr	VG	VG+	NM
KING					
EP-259	*Early Bird/Percy Speaks/Ready Mix/Moon Dust	1954	6.25	12.50	25.00
EP-259 [PS]	Bill Doggett	1954	6.25	12.50	25.00
EP-325	*The Song Is Ended/Eventide/And the Angels Sing/Tailor Made	1955	6.25	12.50	25.00
EP-325 [PS]	Bill Doggett, Vol. 2	1955	6.25	12.50	25.00
EP-334	*Honey/It's a Dream/High Heels/Real Gone Mambo	1955	6.25	12.50	25.00
EP-334 [PS]	Bill Doggett, His Organ and Combo, Vol. 4	1955	6.25	12.50	25.00
EP-352	*Sweet Slumber/The Nearness of You/Gumbo/ Tara's Theme	1955	6.25	12.50	25.00
EP-352 [PS]	Bill Doggett, His Organ and Combo, Vol. 5	1955	6.25	12.50	25.00
EP-382	*I'll Be Around/Street Scene/You Don't Know What Love Is/Misty Moon	1956	6.25	12.50	25.00
EP-382 [PS]	Doggett Dreams	1956	6.25	12.50	25.00
EP-388	*Quaker City/Oof!/Wild Oats/Shove Off	1956	6.25	12.50	25.00
EP-388 [PS]	Doggett Jumps	1956	6.25	12.50	25.00
EP-390	*Honky Tonk (Part 1)/Honky Tonk (Part 2)/ Squashy/Who's Who	1956	7.50	15.00	30.00
EP-390 [PS]	Honky Tonk	1956	7.50	15.00	30.00
EP-391	*Leaps and Bounds/On the Sunny Side of the Street/True Blue	1956	5.00	10.00	20.00
EP-391 [PS]	Bill Doggett, Vol. 1	1956	5.00	10.00	20.00
EP-392	*Honky Tonk Number Three/When Your Lover Has Gone/Big Boy/Nothin' Yet	1956	5.00	10.00	20.00
EP-392 [PS]	Bill Doggett, Vol. 2	1956	5.00	10.00	20.00
EP-393	*Slow Walk/Afternoon Jump/Peacock Alley/ Honey Boy	1956	5.00	10.00	20.00
EP-393 [PS]	Bill Doggett, Vol. 3	1956	5.00	10.00	20.00
EP-394	*I Hadn't Anyone Till You/Yesterdays/A Cottage for Sale/As You Desire Me	1957	5.00	10.00	20.00
EP-394 [PS]	As You Desire Me, Vol. 1	1957	5.00	10.00	20.00
EP-395	*Alone/As Time Goes By/Dedicated to You/ Sweet and Lovely	1957	5.00	10.00	20.00
EP-395 [PS]	As You Desire Me, Vol. 2	1957	5.00	10.00	20.00
EP-396	*Dream/Don't Blame Me/This Love of Mine/Fools Rush In	1957	5.00	10.00	20.00
EP-396 [PS]	As You Desire Me, Vol. 3	1957	5.00	10.00	20.00

Albums

Number	Title	Yr	VG	VG+	NM
ABC-PARAMOUNT					
507 [M]	Wow!	1965	5.00	10.00	20.00
S-507 [S]	Wow!	1965	6.25	12.50	25.00
AFTER HOURS					
AFT-4112	The Right Choice	1991	3.75	7.50	15.00
COLUMBIA					
CL 1814 [M]	Oops!	1962	5.00	10.00	20.00
CL 1942 [M]	Prelude to the Blues	1963	5.00	10.00	20.00
CL 2082 [M]	Fingertips	1963	5.00	10.00	20.00
CS 8614 [S]	Oops!	1962	6.25	12.50	25.00
CS 8742 [S]	Prelude to the Blues	1963	6.25	12.50	25.00
CS 8882 [S]	Fingertips	1963	6.25	12.50	25.00
KING					
295-82 [10]	Bill Doggett — His Organ and Combo	1955	37.50	75.00	150.00
295-83 [10]	Bill Doggett — His Organ and Combo, Volume 2	1955	37.50	75.00	150.00
295-89 [10]	All-Time Christmas Favorites	1955	50.00	100.00	200.00
295-102 [10]	Sentimentally Yours	1956	37.50	75.00	150.00
395-502 [M]	Moondust	1957	15.00	30.00	60.00
395-514 [M]	Hot Doggett	1957	15.00	30.00	60.00
395-523 [M]	As You Desire	1957	15.00	30.00	60.00
KLP-523 [M]	As You Desire	1987	2.50	5.00	10.00
—Reissue with "Highland Records" on label					
395-531 [M]	Everybody Dance to the Honky Tonk	1958	15.00	30.00	60.00
395-532 [M]	Dame Dreaming	1958	15.00	30.00	60.00
KLP-532 [M]	Dame Dreaming	1987	2.50	5.00	10.00
—Reissue with "Highland Records" on label					
395-533 [M]	A Salute to Ellington	1958	15.00	30.00	60.00
395-557 [M]	The Doggett Beat for Dancing Feet	1958	15.00	30.00	60.00
KLP-557 [M]	The Doggett Beat for Dancing Feet	1987	2.50	5.00	10.00
—Reissue with "Highland Records" on label					
395-563 [M]	Candle Glow	1958	15.00	30.00	60.00
395-582 [M]	Swingin' Easy	1959	15.00	30.00	60.00
395-585 [M]	Dance Awhile	1959	15.00	30.00	60.00
KLP-585 [M]	Dance Awhile	1987	2.50	5.00	10.00
—Reissue with "Highland Records" on label					
395-600 [M]	A Bill Doggett Christmas	1959	10.00	20.00	40.00
395-609 [M]	Hold It	1959	15.00	30.00	60.00
633 [M]	High and Wide	1959	12.50	25.00	50.00
641 [M]	Big City Dance Party	1959	12.50	25.00	50.00
667 [M]	Bill Doggett On Tour	1959	12.50	25.00	50.00
706 [M]	For Reminiscent Lovers, Romantic Songs	1960	12.50	25.00	50.00
723 [M]	Back Again with More	1960	12.50	25.00	50.00

Number	Title (A Side/B Side)	Yr	VG	VG+	NM
759 [M]	Bonanza of 24 Songs	1960	12.50	25.00	50.00
778 [M]	The Many Moods of Bill Doggett	1960	12.50	25.00	50.00
KLP-778 [M]	The Many Moods of Bill Doggett	1987	2.50	5.00	10.00
—Reissue with "Highland Records" on label					
830 [M]	American Songs in the Bossa Nova Style	1963	10.00	20.00	40.00
868 [M]	Impressions	1964	10.00	20.00	40.00
908 [M]	The Best of Bill Doggett	1964	10.00	20.00	40.00
959 [M]	Bonanza of 24 Hit Songs	1966	7.50	15.00	30.00
KS-1078	Honky Tonk Popcorn	1969	12.50	25.00	50.00
KS-1097	The Nearness of You	1970	6.25	12.50	25.00
KS-1101	Ram-Bunk-Shush	1970	6.25	12.50	25.00
KS-1104	Sentimental Journey	1970	6.25	12.50	25.00
KS-1108	Soft	1970	6.25	12.50	25.00
K-5009	14 Original Greatest Hits	1977	2.50	5.00	10.00
POWER PAK					
269	Hold It!	197?	2.50	5.00	10.00
ROULETTE					
R 25330 [M]	Honky Tonk A La Mod	1966	5.00	10.00	20.00
SR 25330 [S]	Honky Tonk A La Mod	1966	6.25	12.50	25.00
STARDAY					
3023	16 Bandstand Favorites	197?	2.50	5.00	10.00
WARNER BROS.					
W 1404 [M]	3,046 People Danced 'Til 4 AM	1960	5.00	10.00	20.00
WS 1404 [S]	3,046 People Danced 'Til 4 AM	1960	6.25	12.50	25.00
W 1421 [M]	The Band with the Beat	1961	5.00	10.00	20.00
WS 1421 [S]	The Band with the Beat	1961	6.25	12.50	25.00
W 1452 [M]	Bill Doggett Swings	1962	5.00	10.00	20.00
WS 1452 [S]	Bill Doggett Swings	1962	6.25	12.50	25.00
WHO'S WHO IN JAZZ					
21002	Lionel Hampton Presents Bill Doggett	1977	3.00	6.00	12.00

DOHERTY, DENNY

Also see THE MAMAS AND THE PAPAS.

Number	Title (A Side/B Side)	Yr	VG	VG+	NM
45s					
ABC					
11318	To Claudia on Thursday/Tuesday Morning	1972	—	3.00	6.00
COLUMBIA					
45779	Baby Catch the Moon/Indian Girl	1973	—	2.50	5.00
45866	My Song/Indian Girl	1973	—	2.50	5.00
PARAMOUNT					
0286	Good Night and Good Morning/You'll Never Know	1974	—	2.50	5.00
PLAYBOY					
6066	Simone (mono/stereo)	1976	—	2.50	5.00
—May be promo only					
Albums					
ABC DUNHILL					
DS-50096	Watcha' Gonna Do?	1970	3.75	7.50	15.00
EMBER					
EMS-1036	Waiting for a Song	1975	3.00	6.00	12.00

DOJO

Number	Title (A Side/B Side)	Yr	VG	VG+	NM
Albums					
ECLIPSE					
ES-7309	Down for the Last Time	1971	6.25	12.50	25.00

DOLENZ, MICKEY

Also see DOLENZ, JONES & TORK; DOLENZ, JONES, BOYCE & HART; THE MONKEES.

Number	Title (A Side/B Side)	Yr	VG	VG+	NM
45s					
BELL					
986	Do It in the Name of Love/Lady Jane	1971	12.50	25.00	50.00
—With Davy Jones; value is for stock copy (promos worth about 50% of this)					
CHALLENGE					
59353	Don't Do It/Plastic Symphony III	1967	5.00	10.00	20.00
59353 [PS]	Don't Do It/Plastic Symphony III	1967	15.00	30.00	60.00
59372	Huff Puff/(The Obvious) Fate	1967	5.00	10.00	20.00
59372 [PS]	Huff Puff/(The Obvious) Fate	1967	15.00	30.00	60.00
CHRYSALIS					
2297	Alicia/Love Light	1979	—	3.00	6.00
MGM					
14309	Easy on You/Oh Someone	1971	5.00	10.00	20.00
14395	A Lover's Prayer/Unattended in the Dungeon	1972	5.00	10.00	20.00
ROMAR					
710	Daybreak/Love War	1973	5.00	10.00	20.00
715	Buddy Holly Tribute/Ooh, Se's So Young	1974	5.00	10.00	20.00

DOLENZ, MICKEY, AND PETER TORK (OF THE MONKEES)

See THE MONKEES.

DOLENZ, JONES & TORK

Also see MICKEY DOLENZ; DAVY JONES; THE MONKEES.

Number	Title (A Side/B Side)	Yr	VG	VG+	NM
45s					
CHRISTMAS					
700	Christmas Is My Time of Year/White Christmas	1976	5.00	10.00	20.00
700 [PS]	Christmas Is My Time of Year/White Christmas	1976	10.00	20.00	40.00

DOLENZ, JONES, BOYCE & HART

Also see TOMMY BOYCE; TOMMY BOYCE AND BOBBY HART; MICKEY DOLENZ; BOBBY HART; DAVY JONES; THE MONKEES.

Number	Title (A Side/B Side)	Yr	VG	VG+	NM
45s					
CAPITOL					
4180	You and I/I Remember the Feeling	1975	2.50	5.00	10.00
4271	Savin' My Love for You/I Love You (And I'm Glad I Said It)	1976	2.50	5.00	10.00
Albums					
CAPITOL					
ST-11513	Dolenz, Jones, Boyce & Hart	1976	3.75	7.50	15.00

DOLLS, THE

Number	Title (A Side/B Side)	Yr	VG	VG+	NM
45s					
LOMA					
2036	The Reason Why/And That Reminds Me	1966	3.75	7.50	15.00
OKEH					
7122	In Love/Please Come Home	1959	3.00	6.00	12.00
TEENAGE					
1010	Just Before You Leave/I Love	1958	250.00	500.00	1000.

DOMINO, FATS

Number	Title (A Side/B Side)	Yr	VG	VG+	NM
45s					
ABC					
10902	I Don't Want to Set the World on Fire/I'm Living Right	1967	2.50	5.00	10.00
ABC-PARAMOUNT					
10444	There Goes (My Heart Again)/Can't Go On Without You	1963	2.50	5.00	10.00
10475	When I'm Walking (Let Me Walk)/I've Got a Right to Cry	1963	2.50	5.00	10.00
10484	Red Sails in the Sunset/Song for Rosemary	1963	3.00	6.00	12.00
10512	Who Cares/Just a Lonely Man	1963	2.50	5.00	10.00
10531	Lazy Lady/I Don't Want to Set the World on Fire	1964	2.50	5.00	10.00
10545	If You Don't Know What Love Is/Something You Got, Baby	1964	2.50	5.00	10.00
10567	Mary, Oh Mary/Packin' Up	1964	2.50	5.00	10.00
10584	Sally Was a Good Old Girl/For You	1964	2.50	5.00	10.00
10596	Heartbreak Hill/Kansas City	1964	2.50	5.00	10.00
10631	Why Don't You Do Right/Wigs	1965	2.50	5.00	10.00
10644	Let Me Call You Sweetheart/Goodnight Sweetheart	1965	2.50	5.00	10.00
BROADMOOR					
104	The Lady in Black/Work My Way Up Steady	1967	3.75	7.50	15.00
105	Big Mouth/Wait 'Til It Happens to You	1968	5.00	10.00	20.00
IMPERIAL					
5058	The Fat Man/Detroit City Blues	1950	500.00	1000.	2000.
—Blue-label "script" logo; pressed in 1952 or so; counterfeits exist					
5099	Korea Blues/Every Night About This Time	1950	200.00	400.00	800.00
—Blue-label "script" logo; pressed in 1952 or so					
5167	You Know I Miss You/I'll Be Gone	1952	125.00	250.00	500.00
—Fats Domino records on Imperial before 5167 are unconfirmed on 45 rpm, except those listed above.					
5180	Goin' Home/Reeling and Rocking	1952	75.00	150.00	300.00
5197	Poor Poor Me/Trust in Me	1952	50.00	100.00	200.00
5209	How Long/Dreaming	1952	20.00	40.00	80.00
—Black vinyl					
5209	How Long/Dreaming	1952	75.00	150.00	300.00
—Red vinyl					
5220	Nobody Loves Me/Cheatin'	1953	20.00	40.00	80.00
—Black vinyl					
5220	Nobody Loves Me/Cheatin'	1953	75.00	150.00	300.00
—Red vinyl					
5231	Going to the River/Mardi Gras in New Orleans	1953	25.00	50.00	100.00
—Black vinyl					
5231	Going to the River/Mardi Gras in New Orleans	1953	125.00	250.00	500.00
—Red vinyl					
5240	Please Don't Leave Me/The Girl I Love	1953	15.00	30.00	60.00
—Black vinyl					
5240	Please Don't Leave Me/The Girl I Love	1953	75.00	150.00	300.00
—Red vinyl					
5251	You Said You Loved Me/Rose Mary	1953	15.00	30.00	60.00
5262	Something's Wrong/Don't Leave Me This Way	1954	12.50	25.00	50.00
—Black vinyl					
5262	Something's Wrong/Don't Leave Me This Way	1954	62.50	125.00	250.00
—Red vinyl					
5272	Little School Girl/You Done Me Wrong	1954	15.00	30.00	60.00
5283	Baby, Please/Where Did You Stay	1954	15.00	30.00	60.00
5301	You Can Pack Your Suitcase/I Lived My Life	1954	10.00	20.00	40.00
5313	Love Me/Don't You Hear Me Calling You	1954	10.00	20.00	40.00
5323	I Know/Thinking of You	1955	12.50	25.00	50.00
—Black vinyl					
5323	I Know/Thinking of You	1955	125.00	250.00	500.00
—Red vinyl					
5340	Don't You Know/Helping Hand	1955	10.00	20.00	40.00
5348	Ain't It a Shame/La La	1955	10.00	20.00	40.00
5357	All By Myself/Troubles of My Own	1955	20.00	40.00	80.00
—Red label, script logo					
5357	All By Myself/Troubles of My Own	1955	6.25	12.50	25.00
—Red or maroon label, block logo					
5369	Poor Me/I Can't Go On	1955	6.25	12.50	25.00
5375	Bo Weevil/Don't Blame It on Me	1956	6.25	12.50	25.00
5386	I'm in Love Again/My Blue Heaven	1956	6.25	12.50	25.00
5396	When My Dreamboat Comes Home/So-Long	1956	6.25	12.50	25.00
5407	Blueberry Hill/Honey Chile	1956	6.25	12.50	25.00
—Black vinyl, red label					
5407	Blueberry Hill/Honey Chile	1956	37.50	75.00	150.00
—Red vinyl					
5407	Blueberry Hill/Honey Chile	1957	3.75	7.50	15.00
—Black vinyl, black label					
5417	Blue Monday/What's the Reason I'm Not Pleasing You	1957	6.25	12.50	25.00
5428	I'm Walkin'/I'm in the Mood for Love	1957	6.25	12.50	25.00
5428 [PS]	I'm Walkin'/I'm in the Mood for Love	1957	12.50	25.00	50.00
5442	Valley of Tears/It's You I Love	1957	6.25	12.50	25.00
5454	When I See You/How Will I Tell My Heart	1957	6.25	12.50	25.00
5467	Wait and See/I Still Love You	1957	6.25	12.50	25.00
5477	The Big Beat/I Want You to Know	1957	6.25	12.50	25.00
5477 [PS]	The Big Beat/I Want You to Know	1957	15.00	30.00	60.00
5492	Yes, My Darling/Don't You Know I Love You	1958	6.25	12.50	25.00
—Black vinyl					
5492	Yes, My Darling/Don't You Know I Love You	1958	37.50	75.00	150.00
—Red vinyl					
5515	Sick and Tired/No, No	1958	6.25	12.50	25.00
5526	Little Mary/The Prisoner's Song	1958	6.25	12.50	25.00
5537	Young School Girl/It Must Be Love	1958	6.25	12.50	25.00

Number	Title (A Side/B Side)	Yr	VG	VG+	NM
5553	Whole Lotta Loving/Coquette	1958	7.50	15.00	30.00
—Red label					
5553	Whole Lotta Loving/Coquette	1958	6.25	12.50	25.00
—Black label					
5553	Whole Lotta Loving/Coquette	1958	37.50	75.00	150.00
—Red vinyl (translucent)					
5569	Telling Lies/When the Saints Go Marching In	1959	3.75	7.50	15.00
5585	I'm Ready/Margie	1959	3.75	7.50	15.00
5606	I Want to Walk You Home/I'm Gonna Be a Wheel Some Day	1959	5.00	10.00	20.00
5606 [PS]	I Want to Walk You Home/I'm Gonna Be a Wheel Some Day	1959	—	—	—
—Rumored to exist, but without conclusive evidence, we will delete this from future editions					
5629	Be My Guest/I've Been Around	1959	3.75	7.50	15.00
5629 [PS]	Be My Guest/I've Been Around	1959	12.50	25.00	50.00
5645	Country Boy/If You Need Me	1960	3.75	7.50	15.00
5660	Tell Me That You Love Me/Before I Grow Too Old	1960	3.75	7.50	15.00
5675	Walking to New Orleans/Don't Come Knockin'	1960	5.00	10.00	20.00
5687	Three Nights a Week/Put Your Arms Around Me Honey	1960	3.75	7.50	15.00
5704	My Girl Josephine/Natural Born Lover	1960	5.00	10.00	20.00
5723	What a Price/Ain't That Just Like a Woman	1961	3.75	7.50	15.00
5734	Shu Rah/Fell in Love on Monday	1961	3.75	7.50	15.00
5753	It Keeps Rainin'/I Just Cry	1961	3.75	7.50	15.00
5764	Let the Four Winds Blow/Good Hearted Man	1961	3.75	7.50	15.00
5779	What a Party/Rockin' Bicycle	1961	3.75	7.50	15.00
5796	Jambalaya (On the Bayou)/I Hear You Knocking	1961	3.75	7.50	15.00
5816	You Win Again/Ida Jane	1962	3.75	7.50	15.00
5833	My Real Name/My Heart Is Bleeding	1962	3.75	7.50	15.00
5863	Nothing New (Same Old Thing)/Dance with Mr. Domino	1962	3.75	7.50	15.00
5875	Did You Ever See a Dream Walking/Stop the Clock	1962	3.75	7.50	15.00
5895	Won't You Come On Back/Hands Across the Table	1962	3.75	7.50	15.00
5895	Won't You Come On Back/Your Cheatin' Heart	1962	3.75	7.50	15.00
5909	Hum Diddy Doo/Those Eyes	1963	3.75	7.50	15.00
5937	You Always Hurt the One You Love/Trouble Blues	1963	3.75	7.50	15.00
5959	Isle of Capri/True Confession	1963	3.75	7.50	15.00
5980	One Night/I Can't Go On This Way	1963	3.75	7.50	15.00
5999	Your Cheatin' Heart/Goin' Home	1963	3.75	7.50	15.00
66005	I Can't Give You Anything But Love/Goin' Home	1963	3.00	6.00	12.00
66016	When I Was Young/Your Cheatin' Heart	1964	3.00	6.00	12.00
MERCURY					
72463	I Left My Heart in San Francisco/I Done Got Over You	1965	2.50	5.00	10.00
72485	It's Never Too Late/What's That You Got	1965	2.50	5.00	10.00
72485 [PS]	It's Never Too Late/What's That You Got	1965	5.00	10.00	20.00
REPRISE					
0696	One for the Highway/Honest Papas Love Their Mamas Better	1968	3.75	7.50	15.00
0763	Lady Madonna/One for the Highway	1968	3.75	7.50	15.00
0775	Lovely Rita/Wait Till It Happens to You	1968	3.75	7.50	15.00
0810	Everybody's Got Someting to Hide (Except Me and My Monkey)/So Swell When You're Well	1969	3.75	7.50	15.00
0891	Have You Seen My Baby?/Make Me Belong to You	1970	3.75	7.50	15.00
0944	New Orleans Ain't the Same/Sweet Patootie	1970	3.75	7.50	15.00
THE RIGHT STUFF					
S7-18216	Christmas Is a Special Day/Please Come Home for Christmas (Christmas Once Again)	1994	—	2.00	4.00
—Red vinyl					
S7-19768	Frosty the Snowman/Every Heart Is Home at Christmas	1997	—	2.50	5.00
—B-side by the Five Keys on Aladdin					
TOOT TOOT					
001	My Toot Toot/My Toot Toot (Rock)	1985	—	2.50	5.00
—With Doug Kershaw					
002	Don't Mess with My Popeye's/My Toot Toot	1985	—	2.50	5.00
—With Doug Kershaw					
UNITED ARTISTS					
0001	Ain't That a Shame/Goin' Home	1973	—	2.00	4.00
0002	Blue Monday/I'm Gonna Be a Wheel Someday	1973	—	2.00	4.00
0003	I'm in Love Again/Whole Lotta Lovin'	1973	—	2.00	4.00
0004	Blueberry Hill/Bo Weevil	1973	—	2.00	4.00
0005	I'm Walkin'/One Night	1973	—	2.00	4.00
0006	I Hear You Knockin'/My Blue Heaven	1973	—	2.00	4.00
0007	Walkin' to New Orleans/Country Boy	1973	—	2.00	4.00
0008	I Want to Walk You Home/It's You I Love	1973	—	2.00	4.00
0009	I'm Ready/Wait and See	1973	—	2.00	4.00
0010	My Girl Josephine/When My Dreamboat Comes Home	1973	—	2.00	4.00
0011	Three Nights a Week/Let the Four Winds Blow	1973	—	2.00	4.00
—0001 through 0011 are "Silver Spotlight Series" reissues					
XW 514	The Fat Man/Valley of Tears	1974	—	2.50	5.00
—Reissue					
WARNER BROS.					
49610	Whiskey Heaven/Beers to You	1980	—	2.00	4.00
—B-side by Texas Opera Company					

7-Inch Extended Plays

Number	Title (A Side/B Side)	Yr	VG	VG+	NM
IMPERIAL					
IMP 127	(contents unknown)	1955	37.50	75.00	150.00
—"Script" label					
IMP 127	(contents unknown)	1955	25.00	50.00	100.00
—Maroon label, block-letter logo					
IMP 127	(contents unknown)	1958	6.25	12.50	25.00
—Black label					
IMP 127 [PS]	Fats Domino	1955	12.50	25.00	50.00
IMP 138	(contents unknown)	1956	25.00	50.00	100.00
—Maroon label, block-letter logo					
IMP 138	(contents unknown)	1958	6.25	12.50	25.00
—Black label					
IMP 138 [PS]	Rock and Rollin' with Fats Domino	1956	12.50	25.00	50.00
IMP 139	Rosemary/All By Myself//Tired of Crying/You Said You Loved Me	1956	25.00	50.00	100.00
—Maroon label, block-letter logo					
IMP 139	Rosemary/All By Myself//Tired of Crying/You Said You Loved Me	1958	6.25	12.50	25.00
—Black label					
IMP 139 [PS]	Rock and Rollin' with Fats Domino	1956	12.50	25.00	50.00
IMP 140	Ain't It a Shame/Poor Me//Bo Weevil/Don't Blame It on Me	1956	25.00	50.00	100.00
—Maroon label, block-letter logo					
IMP 140	Ain't It a Shame/Poor Me//Bo Weevil/Don't Blame It on Me	1958	6.25	12.50	25.00
—Black label					
IMP 140 [PS]	Rock and Rollin' with Fats Domino	1956	12.50	25.00	50.00
IMP 141	(contents unknown)	1956	25.00	50.00	100.00
—Maroon label, block-letter logo					
IMP 141	(contents unknown)	1958	6.25	12.50	25.00
—Black label					
IMP 141 [PS]	Rock and Rollin'	1956	12.50	25.00	50.00
IMP 142	Careless Love/I Love Her//I'm in Love Again/When My Dreamboat Comes Home	1956	25.00	50.00	100.00
—Maroon label, block-letter logo					
IMP 142	Careless Love/I Love Her//I'm in Love Again/When My Dreamboat Comes Home	1958	6.25	12.50	25.00
—Black label					
IMP 142 [PS]	Rock and Rollin'	1956	12.50	25.00	50.00
IMP 143	Are Your Going My Way/If You Need Me//My Heart Is In Your Hands/Fats Frenzy	1956	25.00	50.00	100.00
—Maroon label, block-letter logo					
IMP 143	Are Your Going My Way/If You Need Me//My Heart Is In Your Hands/Fats Frenzy	1958	6.25	12.50	25.00
—Black label					
IMP 143 [PS]	Rock and Rollin'	1956	12.50	25.00	50.00
IMP 144	Blueberry Hill/Honey Chile//Troubles of My Own/You Done Me Wrong	1956	25.00	50.00	100.00
—Maroon label, block-letter logo					
IMP 144	Blueberry Hill/Honey Chile//Troubles of My Own/You Done Me Wrong	1958	6.25	12.50	25.00
—Black label					
IMP 144 [PS]	This Is Fats Domino	1956	12.50	25.00	50.00
IMP 145	What's the Reason I'm Not Pleasing You/Blue Monday//Reeling and Rocking/The Fat Man's Hop	1956	25.00	50.00	100.00
—Maroon label, block-letter logo					
IMP 145	What's the Reason I'm Not Pleasing You/Blue Monday//Reeling and Rocking/The Fat Man's Hop	1958	6.25	12.50	25.00
—Black label					
IMP 145 [PS]	This Is Fats Domino	1956	12.50	25.00	50.00
IMP 146	(contents unknown)	1956	25.00	50.00	100.00
—Maroon label, block-letter logo					
IMP 146	(contents unknown)	1958	6.25	12.50	25.00
—Black label					
IMP 146 [PS]	This Is Fats Domino	1956	12.50	25.00	50.00
IMP 147	The Rooster Song/My Happiness//As Time Goes By/Hey La Bas	1956	25.00	50.00	100.00
—Maroon label, block-letter logo					
IMP 147	The Rooster Song/My Happiness//As Time Goes By/Hey La Bas	1958	6.25	12.50	25.00
—Black label					
IMP 147 [PS]	Here Comes Fats	1956	12.50	25.00	50.00
IMP 148	Detroit City Blues/Hide Away Blues//She's My Baby/New Baby	1957	25.00	50.00	100.00
—Maroon label, block-letter logo					
IMP 148	Detroit City Blues/Hide Away Blues//She's My Baby/New Baby	1958	6.25	12.50	25.00
—Black label					
IMP 148 [PS]	Here Stands Fats Domino	1957	12.50	25.00	50.00
IMP 149	I'm Walkin'/Cheatin'//Little Bee/Every Night About This Time	1957	25.00	50.00	100.00
—Maroon label, block-letter logo					
IMP 149	I'm Walkin'/Cheatin'//Little Bee/Every Night About This Time	1958	6.25	12.50	25.00
—Black label					
IMP 149 [PS]	Here Stands Fats Domino	1957	12.50	25.00	50.00
IMP 150	I'm in the Mood for Love/You Can Pack Your Suitcase//Hey! Fat Man/I'll Be Gone	1957	25.00	50.00	100.00
—Maroon label, block-letter logo					
IMP 150	I'm in the Mood for Love/You Can Pack Your Suitcase//Hey! Fat Man/I'll Be Gone	1958	6.25	12.50	25.00
—Black label					
IMP 150 [PS]	Here Stands Fats Domino	1957	12.50	25.00	50.00
IMP 151	Love Me/Don't You Hear Me Calling You//It's You I Love/Valley of Tears	1957	25.00	50.00	100.00
—Maroon label, block-letter logo					
IMP 151	Love Me/Don't You Hear Me Calling You//It's You I Love/Valley of Tears	1958	6.25	12.50	25.00
—Black label					
IMP 151 [PS]	Cookin' with Fats	1957	12.50	25.00	50.00
IMP 152	Thinking of You/You Know I Miss You//Where Did You Stay/Baby Please	1957	25.00	50.00	100.00
—Maroon label, block-letter logo					
IMP 152	Thinking of You/You Know I Miss You//Where Did You Stay/Baby Please	1958	6.25	12.50	25.00
—Black label					
IMP 152 [PS]	Rockin' with Fats	1957	12.50	25.00	50.00

Albums

Number	Title (A Side/B Side)	Yr	VG	VG+	NM
ABC-PARAMOUNT					
455 [M]	Here Comes... Fats Domino	1963	5.00	10.00	20.00
S-455 [S]	Here Comes... Fats Domino	1963	6.25	12.50	25.00
479 [M]	Fats in the Fire	1964	5.00	10.00	20.00
S-479 [S]	Fats in the Fire	1964	6.25	12.50	25.00
510 [M]	Get Away with Fats Domino	1965	5.00	10.00	20.00
S-510 [S]	Get Away with Fats Domino	1965	6.25	12.50	25.00
ST-90167 [S]	Get Away with Fats Domino	1965	7.50	15.00	30.00
—Capitol Record Club edition					

Number	Title (A Side/B Side)	Yr	VG	VG+	NM
T-90167 [M]	Get Away with Fats Domino	1965	6.25	12.50	25.00
—Capitol Record Club edition					
ARCHIVE OF FOLK AND JAZZ					
280	Fats Domino	1974	2.50	5.00	10.00
330	Fats Domino, Vol. II	1975	2.50	5.00	10.00
ATLANTIC					
81751	Live in Montreux	1987	3.00	6.00	12.00
COLUMBIA					
C 35996	When I'm Walking	1979	2.50	5.00	10.00
—Reissue of Harmony LP					
PC 35996	When I'm Walking	1986	2.00	4.00	8.00
—Budget-line reissue					
COLUMBIA SPECIAL PRODUCTS					
P2 13197 [(2)]	The Legendary Music Man	1976	3.75	7.50	15.00
—Candelite Music TV offer					
GRAND AWARD					
267 [M]	Fats Domino	196?	5.00	10.00	20.00
S-267 [R]	Fats Domino	196?	2.50	5.00	10.00
HARLEM HIT PARADE					
5005	Fats' Hits	197?	2.50	5.00	10.00
HARMONY					
HS 11343	When I'm Walking	1969	3.00	6.00	12.00
IMPERIAL					
LP-9004 [M]	Rock and Rollin' with Fats Domino	1956	37.50	75.00	150.00
—Maroon label					
LP-9004 [M]	Rock and Rollin' with Fats Domino	1958	20.00	40.00	80.00
—Black label with stars on top					
LP-9004 [M]	Rock and Rollin' with Fats Domino	1964	6.25	12.50	25.00
—Black and pink label					
LP-9004 [M]	Rock and Rollin' with Fats Domino	1967	5.00	10.00	20.00
—Black and green label					
LP-9009 [M]	Fats Domino Rock and Rollin'	1956	37.50	75.00	150.00
—Maroon labol					
LP-9009 [M]	Fats Domino Rock and Rollin'	1958	20.00	40.00	80.00
—Black label with stars on top					
LP-9009 [M]	Fats Domino Rock and Rollin'	1964	6.25	12.50	25.00
—Black and pink label					
LP-9009 [M]	Fats Domino Rock and Rollin'	1967	5.00	10.00	20.00
—Black and green label					
LP-9028 [M]	This Is Fats Domino!	1957	37.50	75.00	150.00
—Maroon label					
LP-9028 [M]	This Is Fats Domino!	1958	20.00	40.00	80.00
—Black label with stars on top					
LP-9028 [M]	This Is Fats Domino!	1964	6.25	12.50	25.00
—Black and pink label					
LP-9028 [M]	This Is Fats Domino!	1967	5.00	10.00	20.00
—Black and green label					
LP-9038 [M]	Here Stands Fats Domino	1957	37.50	75.00	150.00
—Maroon label					
LP-9038 [M]	Here Stands Fats Domino	1958	20.00	40.00	80.00
—Black label with stars on top					
LP-9038 [M]	Here Stands Fats Domino	1964	6.25	12.50	25.00
—Black and pink label					
LP-9038 [M]	Here Stands Fats Domino	1967	5.00	10.00	20.00
—Black and green label					
LP-9040 [M]	This Is Fats	1957	37.50	75.00	150.00
—Maroon label					
LP-9040 [M]	This Is Fats	1958	20.00	40.00	80.00
—Black label with stars on top					
LP-9040 [M]	This Is Fats	1964	6.25	12.50	25.00
—Black and pink label					
LP-9040 [M]	This Is Fats	1967	5.00	10.00	20.00
—Black and green label					
LP-9055 [M]	The Fabulous Mr. D.	1958	25.00	50.00	100.00
—Black label with stars on top					
LP-9055 [M]	The Fabulous Mr. D.	1964	7.50	15.00	30.00
—Black and pink label					
LP-9055 [M]	The Fabulous Mr. D.	1967	5.00	10.00	20.00
—Black and green label					
LP-9062 [M]	Fats Domino Swings	1959	25.00	50.00	100.00
—Black label with stars on top					
LP-9062 [M]	Fats Domino Swings	1964	7.50	15.00	30.00
—Black and pink label					
LP-9062 [M]	Fats Domino Swings	1967	5.00	10.00	20.00
—Black and green label					
LP-9065 [M]	Let's Play Fats Domino	1959	25.00	50.00	100.00
—Black label with stars on top					
LP-9065 [M]	Let's Play Fats Domino	1964	7.50	15.00	30.00
—Black and pink label					
LP-9065 [M]	Let's Play Fats Domino	1967	5.00	10.00	20.00
—Black and green label					
LP-9103 [M]	Million Record Hits	1960	25.00	50.00	100.00
—Black label with stars on top					
LP-9103 [M]	Million Record Hits	1964	7.50	15.00	30.00
—Black and pink label					
LP-9103 [M]	Million Record Hits	1967	5.00	10.00	20.00
—Black and green label					
LP-9127 [M]	A Lot of Dominos	1960	25.00	50.00	100.00
—Black label with stars on top					
LP-9127 [M]	A Lot of Dominos	1964	7.50	15.00	30.00
—Black and pink label					
LP-9127 [M]	A Lot of Dominos	1967	5.00	10.00	20.00
—Black and green label					
LP-9138 [M]	I Miss You So	1961	25.00	50.00	100.00
—Black label with stars on top					
LP-9138 [M]	I Miss You So	1964	7.50	15.00	30.00
—Black and pink label					
LP-9138 [M]	I Miss You So	1967	5.00	10.00	20.00
—Black and green label					
LP-9153 [M]	Let the Four Winds Blow	1961	25.00	50.00	100.00
—Black label with stars on top					
LP-9153 [M]	Let the Four Winds Blow	1964	7.50	15.00	30.00
—Black and pink label					
LP-9153 [M]	Let the Four Winds Blow	1967	5.00	10.00	20.00
—Black and green label					
LP-9164 [M]	What a Party	1962	15.00	30.00	60.00
—Black label with stars on top					
LP-9164 [M]	What a Party	1964	7.50	15.00	30.00
—Black and pink label					
LP-9164 [M]	What a Party	1967	5.00	10.00	20.00
—Black and green label					
LP-9170 [M]	Twistin' the Stomp	1962	15.00	30.00	60.00
—Black label with stars on top					
LP-9170 [M]	Twistin' the Stomp	1964	7.50	15.00	30.00
—Black and pink label					
LP-9170 [M]	Twistin' the Stomp	1967	5.00	10.00	20.00
—Black and green label					
LP-9195 [M]	Million Sellers by Fats	1962	12.50	25.00	50.00
—Black label with stars on top					
LP-9195 [M]	Million Sellers by Fats	1964	7.50	15.00	30.00
—Black and pink label					
LP-9195 [M]	Million Sellers by Fats	1967	5.00	10.00	20.00
—Black and green label					
LP-9208 [M]	Just Domino	1962	12.50	25.00	50.00
—Black label with stars on top					
LP-9208 [M]	Just Domino	1964	7.50	15.00	30.00
—Black and pink label					
LP-9208 [M]	Just Domino	1967	5.00	10.00	20.00
—Black and green label					
LP-9227 [M]	Walking to New Orleans	1963	12.50	25.00	50.00
—Black label with stars on top					
LP-9227 [M]	Walking to New Orleans	1964	7.50	15.00	30.00
—Black and pink label					
LP-9227 [M]	Walking to New Orleans	1967	5.00	10.00	20.00
—Black and green label					
LP-9239 [M]	Let's Dance with Domino	1963	12.50	25.00	50.00
—Black label with stars on top					
LP-9239 [M]	Let's Dance with Domino	1964	7.50	15.00	30.00
—Black and pink labol					
LP-9239 [M]	Let's Dance with Domino	1967	5.00	10.00	20.00
—Black and green label					
LP-9248 [M]	Here He Comes Again	1963	12.50	25.00	50.00
—Black label with stars on top					
LP-9248 [M]	Here He Comes Again	1964	7.50	15.00	30.00
—Black and pink label					
LP-9248 [M]	Here He Comes Again	1967	5.00	10.00	20.00
—Black and green label					
LP-12066 [S]	A Lot of Dominos	1961	37.50	75.00	150.00
—Black label with silver top					
LP-12066 [S]	A Lot of Dominos	1964	10.00	20.00	40.00
—Black and pink label					
LP-12066 [S]	A Lot of Dominos	1967	6.25	12.50	25.00
—Black and green label					
LP-12073 [S]	Let the Four Winds Blow	1961	37.50	75.00	150.00
—Black label with silver top					
LP-12073 [S]	Let the Four Winds Blow	1964	10.00	20.00	40.00
—Black and pink label					
LP-12073 [S]	Let the Four Winds Blow	1967	6.25	12.50	25.00
—Black and green label					
LP-12091 [R]	Fats Domino Swings	1964	5.00	10.00	20.00
—Black and pink label					
LP-12091 [R]	Fats Domino Swings	1967	3.75	7.50	15.00
—Black and green label					
LP-12103 [R]	Million Record Hits	1964	5.00	10.00	20.00
—Black and pink label					
LP-12103 [R]	Million Record Hits	1967	3.75	7.50	15.00
—Black and green label					
LP-12195 [R]	Million Sellers by Fats	1964	5.00	10.00	20.00
—Black and pink label					
LP-12195 [R]	Million Sellers by Fats	1967	3.75	7.50	15.00
—Black and green label					
LP-12227 [R]	Walking to New Orleans	1964	5.00	10.00	20.00
—Black and pink label					
LP-12227 [R]	Walking to New Orleans	1967	3.75	7.50	15.00
—Black and green label					
LP-12248 [R]	Here He Comes Again	1964	5.00	10.00	20.00
—Black and pink label					
LP-12248 [R]	Here He Comes Again	1967	3.75	7.50	15.00
—Black and green label					
LP-12387 [R]	Rock and Rollin' with Fats Domino	1968	3.00	6.00	12.00
—Rechanneled reissue of 9004					
LP-12388 [R]	Fats Domino Rock and Rollin'	1968	3.00	6.00	12.00
—Rechanneled reissue of 9009					
LP-12389 [R]	This Is Fats Domino!	1968	3.00	6.00	12.00
—Rechanneled reissue of 9028					
LP-12390 [R]	Here Stands Fats Domino	1968	3.00	6.00	12.00
—Rechanneled reissue of 9038					
LP-12391 [R]	This Is Fats	1968	3.00	6.00	12.00
—Rechanneled reissue of 9040					
LP-12394 [R]	The Fabulous Mr. D.	1968	3.00	6.00	12.00
—Rechanneled reissue of 9055					
LP-12395 [R]	Let's Play Fats Domino	1968	3.00	6.00	12.00
—Rechanneled reissue of 9065					
LP-12398 [R]	I Miss You So	1968	3.00	6.00	12.00
—Rechanneled reissue of 9138					
LIBERTY					
LWB-122 [(2)]	Cookin' with Fats (Superpak)	1981	3.00	6.00	12.00
—Budget-line reissue of UA 122					
LM-1027	Million Sellers by Fats	1981	2.00	4.00	8.00
—Budget-line reissue of UA 1027					
LWB-9958 [(2)]	Legendary Masters	1981	2.50	5.00	10.00
—Budget-line reissue of UA 9958					
LN-10135	Let's Play Fats Domino	1981	2.00	4.00	8.00
—Budget-line reissue					
LN-10136	The Fabulous Mr. D.	1981	2.00	4.00	8.00
—Budget-line reissue					
MCA/SILVER EAGLE					
6170	Greatest Hits	198?	2.50	5.00	10.00
MERCURY					
MG-21039 [M]	Fats Domino '65	1965	6.25	12.50	25.00

Number	Title (A Side/B Side)	Yr	VG	VG+	NM
21065/61065	Southland U.S.A,	1966	—	—	—
—*Canceled*					
SR-61039 [S]	Fats Domino '65	1965	10.00	20.00	40.00
PICKWICK					
SPC-3111	Blueberry Hill	197?	2.50	5.00	10.00
SPC-3165	When My Dreamboat Comes Home	197?	2.50	5.00	10.00
SPC-3295	My Blue Heaven	1971	2.50	5.00	10.00
QUICKSILVER					
QS-1016	Live Hits	198?	2.50	5.00	10.00
REPRISE					
RS 6304	Fats Is Back	1968	7.50	15.00	30.00
RS 6439	Fats	1970	125.00	250.00	500.00
—*Officially unreleased, test pressings and coverless stock copies are known to exist*					
SEARS					
SPS-473	Blueberry Hill!	1970	6.25	12.50	25.00
SUNSET					
SUM-1103 [M]	Fats Domino	1966	3.00	6.00	12.00
SUM-1158 [M]	Stompin' Fats Domino	1967	3.00	6.00	12.00
SUS-5103 [R]	Fats Domino	1966	3.00	6.00	12.00
SUS-5158 [R]	Stompin' Fats Domino	1967	3.00	6.00	12.00
SUS-5200 [P]	Trouble in Mind	1968	5.00	10.00	20.00
SUS-5299 [R]	Ain't That a Shame	1970	3.00	6.00	12.00
UNITED ARTISTS					
UAMG-104 [DJ]	The Fats Domino Sound	1973	10.00	20.00	40.00
—*Promo compilation of 30 excerpts of Fats hits*					
UA-LA122-F2 [(2)]	Cookin' with Fats (Superpak)	1974	7.50	15.00	30.00
UA-LA122-F2 [(2) DJ]	Cookin' with Fats (Superpak)	1974	75.00	150.00	300.00
—*Promo with one black vinyl record and one colored vinyl record*					
UA-LA233-G	The Very Best of Fats Domino	1974	3.00	6.00	12.00
LM-1027	Million Sellers by Fats	1980	2.50	5.00	10.00
UAS-9958 [(2)]	Legendary Masters	1972	3.75	7.50	15.00

DOMINOES, THE

See BILLY WARD AND THE DOMINOES.

DON AND DEWEY

45s

Number	Title (A Side/B Side)	Yr	VG	VG+	NM
FIDELITY					
3017	Jump Awhile/H.B. Boogie	1960	3.75	7.50	15.00
3018	Kill Me/Little Sally Walker	1960	3.75	7.50	15.00
SHADE					
100	Miss Sue/My Heart Is Aching	195?	37.50	75.00	150.00
SPECIALTY					
599	Jungle Hop/A Little Love	1957	6.25	12.50	25.00
610	Leavin' It All Up to You/Jelly Bean	1957	7.50	15.00	30.00
617	Just a Little Lovin'/When the Sun Has Begun to Shine	1957	6.25	12.50	25.00
631	Justine/Bim Bam	1958	6.25	12.50	25.00
639	The Letter/Koko Joe	1958	6.25	12.50	25.00
659	Farmer John/Big Boy Pete	1959	6.25	12.50	25.00
691	Annie Lee/Get Your Hat	196?	3.00	6.00	12.00

Albums

Number	Title (A Side/B Side)	Yr	VG	VG+	NM
SPECIALTY					
SPS-2131	They're Rockin' Til Midnight, Rollin' Til Dawn	1970	7.50	15.00	30.00
—*Original labels are black and gold*					

DON AND HIS ROSES

45s

Number	Title (A Side/B Side)	Yr	VG	VG+	NM
DOT					
15755	Since You Went Away to School/Right Now	1958	12.50	25.00	50.00
15874	Leave Those Cats Alone/Don't Try to Change Me	1958	37.50	75.00	150.00

DON AND JUAN

45s

Number	Title (A Side/B Side)	Yr	VG	VG+	NM
BIG TOP					
3079	What's Your Name/Chicken Necks	1961	6.25	12.50	25.00
3106	Two Fools Are We/Pot Luck	1962	5.00	10.00	20.00
3121	Magic Wand/What I Really Meant to Say	1962	10.00	20.00	40.00
3145	True Love Never Runs Smooth/Is It All Right If I Love You	1963	12.50	25.00	50.00
LANA					
150	What's Your Name/Chicken Necks	196?	—	3.00	6.00
—*Early reissue*					
MALA					
469	Lonely Man/Could This Be Love	1963	3.00	6.00	12.00
479	Pledging My Love/Molinda	1964	3.00	6.00	12.00
484	Sincerely/Maryana Cherie	1964	3.00	6.00	12.00
494	I Can't Help Myself/All That's Missing Is You	1964	3.00	6.00	12.00
509	The Heartbreaking Truth/Thank Goodness	1965	7.50	15.00	30.00
TWIRL					
2021	Because I Love You/Are You Putting Me on the Shelf	1966	7.50	15.00	30.00

DON AND THE CHEVELLS

"Don" is Don Ciccone, later of THE CRITTERS and THE FOUR SEASONS.

45s

Number	Title (A Side/B Side)	Yr	VG	VG+	NM
SPEEDWAY					
1000	Inner Limits/The Only Girl	1964	20.00	40.00	80.00

DON AND THE GOODTIMES

45s

Number	Title (A Side/B Side)	Yr	VG	VG+	NM
BURDETTE					
3	Colors of Life/You Did It Before	196?	5.00	10.00	20.00
DUNHILL					
4008	Little Green Thing/Little Sally Tease	1965	2.50	5.00	10.00
4015	I'll Be Down Forever/Big Big Knight (On a Big White Horse)	1965	2.50	5.00	10.00
4022	Sweets for My Sweet/Hey There Mary Mae	1966	2.50	5.00	10.00
EPIC					
10145	I Could Be So Good to You/And It's So Good	1967	2.50	5.00	10.00
10145 [PS]	I Could Be So Good to You/And It's So Good	1967	3.75	7.50	15.00
10199	If You Love Her, Cherish Her and Such/Happy and Me	1967	2.50	5.00	10.00
10241	Bambi/Sally (Studio A at 6 O'Clock in the Morning)	1967	2.50	5.00	10.00
10280	Ball of Fire/May My Heart Be Cast Into Stone	1968	2.50	5.00	10.00
JERDEN					
762	You'll Never Walk Away/Little Sally Tease	1965	3.00	6.00	12.00
WAND					
165	Turn On/Make It	1964	2.50	5.00	10.00
184	Straight Scepter/There's Something on Your Mind	1965	2.50	5.00	10.00

Albums

Number	Title (A Side/B Side)	Yr	VG	VG+	NM
BURDETTE					
300 [M]	Don and the Goodtimes' Greatest Hits	1966	37.50	75.00	150.00
300S [R]	Don and the Goodtimes' Greatest Hits	1966	25.00	50.00	100.00
—*LP plays rechanneled stereo*					
300S [S]	Don and the Goodtimes' Greatest Hits	1966	75.00	150.00	300.00
—*LP plays true stereo*					
EPIC					
LN 24311 [M]	So Good	1967	5.00	10.00	20.00
BN 26311 [S]	So Good	1967	5.00	10.00	20.00
PICCADILLY					
3394	Goodtime Rock 'n' Roll	1980	6.25	12.50	25.00
WAND					
WDS-679	Where the Action Is	1969	7.50	15.00	30.00

DON, DICK & JIMMY

45s

Number	Title (A Side/B Side)	Yr	VG	VG+	NM
CROWN					
113	The Old Gray Mare/It Shall Come to Pass	195?	3.75	7.50	15.00
116	Ol' Man River/Hawaiian War Chant	1954	3.75	7.50	15.00
125	That's What I Like/You Can't Have Your Cake and Eat It, Too	1954	3.75	7.50	15.00
131	The Touch of Your Lips/I Go to You	1954	3.75	7.50	15.00
138	Make Yourself Comfortable/Songs from Desiree	1955	3.75	7.50	15.00
147	Baby, You!/Nobody Likes to Cry	1955	3.75	7.50	15.00
152	This Little Piggie/Make Me a Present	1955	3.75	7.50	15.00
158	Love Is a Many-Splendored Thing/In Madrid	1955	3.75	7.50	15.00
162	Stolen Love/Adios My Madonna	1956	3.75	7.50	15.00
DOT					
15768	Too Young to Bop/This Was My Sin	1958	3.00	6.00	12.00
VERVE					
2020	That's the Way I Feel/Two Voices in the Night	1956	3.00	6.00	12.00
10043	A Man's Gotta Do/My Faith, My Hope, My Love	1957	3.00	6.00	12.00
10062	Be Sweet to Me/Building a Paradise	1957	3.00	6.00	12.00

Albums

Number	Title (A Side/B Side)	Yr	VG	VG+	NM
CROWN					
CLP-5005 [M]	Spring Fever	1958	10.00	20.00	40.00
DOT					
DLP-3152 [M]	Don, Dick & Jimmy	1959	7.50	15.00	30.00
MODERN					
MLP-1205 [M]	Spring Fever	1957	30.00	60.00	120.00
VERVE					
MGV-2084 [M]	Medium Rare	1958	10.00	20.00	40.00
MGV-2107 [M]	Songs for the Hearth	1959	10.00	20.00	40.00

DON JUANS, THE

45s

Number	Title (A Side/B Side)	Yr	VG	VG+	NM
ONEZY					
101	The Girl of My Dreams/Dolores	1959	500.00	1000.	2000.

DONALDSON, BO, AND THE HEYWOODS

45s

Number	Title (A Side/B Side)	Yr	VG	VG+	NM
ABC					
11402	Deeper and Deeper/Drive Me Crazy	1973	—	2.00	4.00
11435	Billy, Don't Be a Hero/Don't Ever Look Back	1974	—	2.00	4.00
12006	Who Do You Think You Are/Fool's Way of Lovin'	1974	—	2.00	4.00
12011	Billy, Don't Be a Hero/Don't Ever Look Back	1974	—	2.50	5.00
12039	The Heartbreak Kid/Girl Don't Make Me Wait	1974	—	2.00	4.00
12072	Make the Most of This World/House on Telegraph Hill	1975	—	2.00	4.00
12108	Our Last Song Together/Make the Most of This World	1975	—	2.00	4.00
CAPITOL					
4237	Oh Boy/Tie Me Down	1976	—	2.00	4.00
4282	Teenage Rampage/Tie Me Down	1976	—	2.00	4.00
FAMILY PRODUCTIONS					
0917	Thank You Girl/You Don't Own Me	1972	—	2.50	5.00
0918	All Over the World/Just for You	1972	—	2.50	5.00
0923	Da Doo Ron Ron/Just Because	1973	—	2.50	5.00
PLAYBOY					
5820	Are You Cuckoo/Gimmie Some Time	1977	—	2.00	4.00

Albums

Number	Title (A Side/B Side)	Yr	VG	VG+	NM
ABC					
D-824	Bo Donaldson and the Heywoods	1974	2.50	5.00	10.00
FAMILY PRODUCTIONS					
FPS-2711	Special Someone	1972	3.75	7.50	15.00

DONALDSON, LOU

45s

Number	Title (A Side/B Side)	Yr	VG	VG+	NM
ARGO					
5449	Signifyin'/Time After Time	1963	2.00	4.00	8.00
5478	Possum Head/Laura	1964	2.00	4.00	8.00
5494	Soul Gumbo/Cole Slaw	1965	2.00	4.00	8.00
BLUE NOTE					
XW189	You Are the Sunshine of My Life/Long Goodbye	1973	—	2.50	5.00
XW287	Pillow Talk/Sassy Soul Strut	1973	—	2.50	5.00
XW381	Sanford and Son/Good Morning Heartache	1974	—	2.50	5.00
1598	Roccus/Cheek to Cheek	195?	3.75	7.50	15.00
1599	The Things We Did Last Summer/Lou's Blues	195?	3.75	7.50	15.00
1609	The Best Things in Life/Sweet Juice	195?	3.75	7.50	15.00
1610	If I Love Again/Down Home	195?	3.75	7.50	15.00

Number	Title (A Side/B Side)	Yr	VG	VG+	NM
1622	You Go to My Head/Brownie Speak	1954	5.00	10.00	20.00
—With Clifford Brown					
1623	Cookin'/Bellarosa	1954	3.75	7.50	15.00
1624	Dedah/Carving the Rock	1954	3.75	7.50	15.00
1662	Caravan/Old Folks	1955	3.75	7.50	15.00
1663	That Good Old Feeling/L.D. Blues	1955	3.75	7.50	15.00
1680	Dorothy/Peck Time	195?	3.75	7.50	15.00
1681	Grits and Gravy/Herman's Mambo	195?	3.75	7.50	15.00
1713	Sputnik (Part 1)/Sputnik (Part 2)	1957	3.75	7.50	15.00
1720	The Masquerade Is Over/Blue Walk	195?	3.75	7.50	15.00
1721	Autumn Nocturne/Play Ray	195?	3.75	7.50	15.00
1752	Mack the Knife/The Nearness of You	1959	3.75	7.50	15.00
1753	Be My Love/Lou's Blues	1959	3.75	7.50	15.00
1772	Blue Moon/Smooth Groove	196?	3.00	6.00	12.00
1773	Goose Grease/The Truth	196?	3.00	6.00	12.00
1774	Politely/Blues for J.P.	196?	3.00	6.00	12.00
1806	Hog Maw/Day Dreams	196?	3.00	6.00	12.00
1807	Here 'Tis (Part 1)/Here 'Tis (Part 2)	196?	3.00	6.00	12.00
1808	Watusi Jump (Part 1)/Watusi Jump (Part 2)	196?	3.00	6.00	12.00
1830	Gravy Train (Part 1)/Gravy Train (Part 2)	196?	2.50	5.00	10.00
1831	Polka Dots and Moonbeams/South of the Border	196?	2.50	5.00	10.00
1832	Glory of Love/Avalon	196?	2.50	5.00	10.00
1868	Funky Mama (Part 1)/Funky Mama (Part 2)	196?	2.50	5.00	10.00
1869	That's All (Part 1)/That's All (Part 2)	196?	2.50	5.00	10.00
1934	Alligator Boogaloo/Reverend Moses	1967	2.00	4.00	8.00
1936	Say It Loud/Snake Bone	1968	2.00	4.00	8.00
1949	Hot Dog/Who's Making Love	1969	2.00	4.00	8.00
1956	Everything I Do Gohn Be Funky/Minor Bash	1970	—	3.00	6.00
1970	Caterpillar/Make It with You	1971	—	3.00	6.00

CADET

Number	Title (A Side/B Side)	Yr	VG	VG+	NM
5521	Musty Rusty (Part 1)/Musty Rusty (Part 2)	1966	—	3.00	6.00

Albums

ARGO

Number	Title (A Side/B Side)	Yr	VG	VG+	NM
LP-724 [M]	Signifyin'	1963	6.25	12.50	25.00
LPS-724 [S]	Signifyin'	1963	6.25	12.50	25.00
LP-734 [M]	Possum Head	1964	6.25	12.50	25.00
LPS-734 [S]	Possum Head	1964	6.25	12.50	25.00
LP-747 [M]	Cole Slaw	1965	6.25	12.50	25.00
LPS-747 [S]	Cole Slaw	1965	6.25	12.50	25.00

BLUE NOTE

Number	Title (A Side/B Side)	Yr	VG	VG+	NM
BN-LA024-F	Sophisticated Lou	1972	3.75	7.50	15.00
BN-LA109-F	Sassy Soul Strut	1973	3.75	7.50	15.00
BN-LA259-G	Sweet Lou	1974	3.75	7.50	15.00
LT-1028	Midnight Sun	1980	2.50	5.00	10.00
BLP-1537 [M]	Lou Donaldson Quartet/Quintet/Sextet	1957	50.00	100.00	200.00
—"Deep groove" version (deep indentation under label on both sides)					
BLP-1537 [M]	Lou Donaldson Quartet/Quintet/Sextet	1957	37.50	75.00	150.00
—Regular version with Lexington Ave. address on label					
BLP-1537 [M]	Lou Donaldson Quartet/Quintet/Sextet	1957	10.00	20.00	40.00
—Regular version with W. 63rd St. address on label					
BLP-1537 [M]	Lou Donaldson Quartet/Quintet/Sextet	1963	6.25	12.50	25.00
—With New York, USA address on label					
BLP-1545 [M]	Wailing with Lou	1957	30.00	60.00	120.00
—"Deep groove" version (deep indentation under label on both sides)					
BLP-1545 [M]	Wailing with Lou	1957	20.00	40.00	80.00
—Regular version with W. 63rd St. address on label					
BLP-1545 [M]	Wailing with Lou	1963	6.25	12.50	25.00
—With New York, USA address on label					
BLP-1566 [M]	Swing and Soul	1957	30.00	60.00	120.00
—"Deep groove" version (deep indentation under label on both sides)					
BLP-1566 [M]	Swing and Soul	1957	20.00	40.00	80.00
—Regular version with W. 63rd St. address on label					
BLP-1566 [M]	Swing and Soul	1963	6.25	12.50	25.00
—With New York, USA address on label					
BST-1566 [S]	Swing and Soul	1959	20.00	40.00	80.00
—"Deep groove" version (deep indentation under label on both sides)					
BST-1566 [S]	Swing and Soul	1959	12.50	25.00	50.00
—Regular version with W. 63rd St. address on label					
BST-1566 [S]	Swing and Soul	1963	5.00	10.00	20.00
—With New York, USA address on label					
BLP-1591 [M]	Lou Takes Off	1958	30.00	60.00	120.00
—"Deep groove" version (deep indentation under label on both sides)					
BLP-1591 [M]	Lou Takes Off	1958	20.00	40.00	80.00
—Regular version with W. 63rd St. address on label					
BLP-1591 [M]	Lou Takes Off	1963	6.25	12.50	25.00
—With New York, USA address on label					
BST-1591 [S]	Lou Takes Off	1959	20.00	40.00	80.00
—"Deep groove" version (deep indentation under label on both sides)					
BST-1591 [S]	Lou Takes Off	1959	12.50	25.00	50.00
—Regular version with W. 63rd St. address on label					
BST-1591 [S]	Lou Takes Off	1963	5.00	10.00	20.00
—With New York, USA address on label					
BLP-1593 [M]	Blues Walk	1958	30.00	60.00	120.00
—"Deep groove" version (deep indentation under label on both sides)					
BLP-1593 [M]	Blues Walk	1958	20.00	40.00	80.00
—Regular version with W. 63rd St. address on label					
BLP-1593 [M]	Blues Walk	1963	6.25	12.50	25.00
—With New York, USA address on label					
BST-1593 [S]	Blues Walk	1959	20.00	40.00	80.00
—"Deep groove" version (deep indentation under label on both sides)					
BST-1593 [S]	Blues Walk	1959	12.50	25.00	50.00
—Regular version with W. 63rd St. address on label					
BST-1593 [S]	Blues Walk	1963	5.00	10.00	20.00
—With New York, USA address on label					
BLP-4012 [M]	LD + 3	1959	30.00	60.00	120.00
—"Deep groove" version (deep indentation under label on both sides)					
BLP-4012 [M]	LD + 3	1959	20.00	40.00	80.00
—Regular version with W. 63rd St. address on label					
BLP-4012 [M]	LD + 3	1963	6.25	12.50	25.00
—With New York, USA address on label					
BST-4012 [S]	LD + 3	1960	20.00	40.00	80.00
—"Deep groove" version (deep indentation under label on both sides)					
BST-4012 [S]	LD + 3	1960	12.50	25.00	50.00
—Regular version with W. 63rd St. address on label					
BST-4012 [S]	LD + 3	1963	5.00	10.00	20.00
—With New York, USA address on label					
BLP-4025 [M]	The Time Is Right	1960	30.00	60.00	120.00
—"Deep groove" version (deep indentation under label on both sides)					
BLP-4025 [M]	The Time Is Right	1960	20.00	40.00	80.00
—Regular version with W. 63rd St. address on label					
BLP-4025 [M]	The Time Is Right	1963	6.25	12.50	25.00
—With New York, USA address on label					
BLP-4036 [M]	Sunny Side Up	1960	30.00	60.00	120.00
—"Deep groove" version (deep indentation under label on both sides)					
BLP-4036 [M]	Sunny Side Up	1960	20.00	40.00	80.00
—Regular version with W. 63rd St. address on label					
BLP-4036 [M]	Sunny Side Up	1963	6.25	12.50	25.00
—With New York, USA address on label					
BLP-4053 [M]	Light Foot	1960	20.00	40.00	80.00
—With W. 63rd St. address on label					
BLP-4053 [M]	Light Foot	1963	6.25	12.50	25.00
—With New York, USA address on label					
BLP-4066 [M]	Here 'Tis	1961	20.00	40.00	80.00
—With W. 63rd St. address on label					
BLP-4066 [M]	Here 'Tis	1963	6.25	12.50	25.00
—With New York, USA address on label					
BLP-4079 [M]	Gravy Train	1962	20.00	40.00	80.00
—With 61st St. address on label					
BLP-4079 [M]	Gravy Train	1963	6.25	12.50	25.00
—With New York, USA address on label					
BLP-4108 [M]	The Natural Soul	1963	6.25	12.50	25.00
BLP-4125 [M]	Good Gracious	1963	6.25	12.50	25.00
4254/84254	Sweet Slumber	1967	—	—	—
—Canceled					
BLP-4263 [M]	Alligator Boogaloo	1967	7.50	15.00	30.00
BLP-4271 [M]	Mr. Shing-a-Ling	1968	7.50	15.00	30.00
BLP-5021 [10]	Lou Donaldson Quintet/Quartet	1953	50.00	100.00	200.00
BLP 5030 [10]	Lou Donaldson Clifford Brown	1054	50.00	100.00	200.00
BLP-5055 [10]	Lou Donaldson Sextet, Volume 2	1955	50.00	100.00	200.00
B1-28267	Hot Dog	1994	3.75	7.50	15.00
—Reissue of 84318					
B1-31248	Everything I Play Is Funky	1995	3.75	7.50	15.00
—Reissue of 84337					
B1-31876	The Scorpion: Live at the Cadillac Club	1995	3.75	7.50	15.00
B1-32095	Sunny Side Up	1995	3.75	7.50	15.00
—Reissue of 84036					
B1-81537	Lou Donaldson Quartet/Quintet/Sextet	1989	2.50	5.00	10.00
—Reissue of 1537					
BST-81591 [S]	Lou Takes Off	1966	3.00	6.00	12.00
—With "A Division of Liberty Records" on label					
BST-81593	Blues Walk	1985	2.50	5.00	10.00
—"The Finest in Jazz Since 1939" reissue					
BST-81593 [S]	Blues Walk	1967	3.00	6.00	12.00
—With "A Division of Liberty Records" on label					
BST-84025 [S]	The Time Is Right	1960	12.50	25.00	50.00
—With W. 63rd St. address on label					
BST-84025 [S]	The Time Is Right	1963	5.00	10.00	20.00
—With New York, USA address on label					
BST-84036 [S]	Sunny Side Up	1960	12.50	25.00	50.00
—With W. 63rd St. address on label					
BST-84036 [S]	Sunny Side Up	1963	5.00	10.00	20.00
—With New York, USA address on label					
BST-84053 [S]	Light Foot	1960	12.50	25.00	50.00
—With W. 63rd St. address on label					
BST-84053 [S]	Light Foot	1963	5.00	10.00	20.00
—With New York, USA address on label					
BST-84066 [S]	Here 'Tis	1961	12.50	25.00	50.00
—With W. 63rd St. address on label					
BST-84066 [S]	Here 'Tis	1963	5.00	10.00	20.00
—With New York, USA address on label					
BST-84066 [S]	Here 'Tis	1967	3.00	6.00	12.00
—With "A Division of Liberty Records" on label					
BST-84079 [S]	Gravy Train	1962	12.50	25.00	50.00
—With 61st St. address on label					
BST-84079 [S]	Gravy Train	1963	5.00	10.00	20.00
—With New York, USA address on label					
BST-84079 [S]	Gravy Train	1967	3.00	6.00	12.00
—With "A Division of Liberty Records" on label					
BST-84108	The Natural Soul	1987	2.50	5.00	10.00
—"The Finest in Jazz Since 1939" reissue					
BST-84108 [S]	The Natural Soul	1963	6.25	12.50	25.00
BST-84108 [S]	The Natural Soul	1967	3.00	6.00	12.00
—With "A Division of Liberty Records" on label					
BST-84125 [S]	Good Gracious	1963	6.25	12.50	25.00
BST-84125 [S]	Good Gracious	1967	3.00	6.00	12.00
—With "A Division of Liberty Records" on label					
BST-84254	Lush Life	1986	2.50	5.00	10.00
—"The Finest in Jazz Since 1939" label; first issue of this LP					
BST-84263 [S]	Alligator Boogaloo	1967	5.00	10.00	20.00
BST-84271 [S]	Mr. Shing-a-Ling	1968	5.00	10.00	20.00
BST-84280	Midnight Creeper	1968	5.00	10.00	20.00
BST-84299	Say It Loud!	1969	5.00	10.00	20.00
BST-84318	Hot Dog	1969	5.00	10.00	20.00
BST-84337	Everything I Play Is Funky	1970	3.75	7.50	15.00
BST-84359	Pretty Things	1970	3.75	7.50	15.00
BST-84370	Cosmos	1971	3.75	7.50	15.00
B1-89794	Pretty Thing	1993	3.75	7.50	15.00
—Reissue of 84359					

CADET

Number	Title (A Side/B Side)	Yr	VG	VG+	NM
LP-724 [M]	Signifyin'	1966	5.00	10.00	20.00
—Reissue of Argo 724					
LPS-724 [S]	Signifyin'	1966	3.75	7.50	15.00
—Reissue of Argo 724					
LP-734 [M]	Possum Head	1966	5.00	10.00	20.00
—Reissue of Argo 734					
LPS-734 [S]	Possum Head	1966	3.75	7.50	15.00
—Reissue of Argo 734					
LP-747 [M]	Cole Slaw	1966	5.00	10.00	20.00
—Reissue of Argo 747					

Number	Title (A Side/B Side)	Yr	VG	VG+	NM
LPS-747 [S]	Cole Slaw	1966	3.75	7.50	15.00
—Reissue of Argo 747					
LP-759 [M]	Musty Rusty	1966	6.25	12.50	25.00
LPS-759 [S]	Musty Rusty	1966	6.25	12.50	25.00
LP-768 [M]	Rough House Blues	1966	6.25	12.50	25.00
LPS-768 [S]	Rough House Blues	1966	6.25	12.50	25.00
LP-789 [M]	Blowin' in the Wind	1967	6.25	12.50	25.00
LPS-789 [S]	Blowin' in the Wind	1967	5.00	10.00	20.00
LPS-815	Lou Donaldson At His Best	1969	5.00	10.00	20.00
LPS-842	Fried Buzzard — Lou Donaldson Live	1970	5.00	10.00	20.00
CHESS					
2CA 60007	Ha' Mercy	1972	3.00	6.00	12.00
COTILLION					
SD 9905	A Different Scene	1976	3.00	6.00	12.00
SD 9915	Color As a Way of Life	1977	3.00	6.00	12.00
MUSE					
5247	Sweet Poppa Lou	1982	3.00	6.00	12.00
5292	Back Street	1983	3.00	6.00	12.00
SUNSET					
SUS-5258	Down Home	1969	3.00	6.00	12.00
SUS-5318	I Won't Cry Anymore	1970	3.00	6.00	12.00
TIMELESS					
SJP-153	Forgotten Man	198?	2.50	5.00	10.00

DONAYS, THE

45s

Number	Title (A Side/B Side)	Yr	VG	VG+	NM
BRENT					
7033	Devil in His Heart/Bad Boy	1962	10.00	20.00	40.00
—The Beatles re-made the A-side as "Devil in Her Heart"					

DONEGAN, LONNIE

45s

Number	Title (A Side/B Side)	Yr	VG	VG+	NM
APT					
25067	Pick a Bale of Cotton/Ramblin' Round	1962	2.50	5.00	10.00
ATLANTIC					
2058	My Old Man's a Dustman/The Golden Vanity	1960	3.00	6.00	12.00
2063	Take This Hammer/Nobody Understands Me	1960	3.00	6.00	12.00
2081	Lorelei/Junco Partner	1960	3.00	6.00	12.00
2108	Have a Drink On Me/Beyond the Sunset	1961	3.00	6.00	12.00
2123	Wreck of the John B/Sorry, But I'm Gonna Have to Pass	1961	3.00	6.00	12.00
DOT					
15792	The Grand Coulee Dam/Nobody Loves Like an Irishman	1958	5.00	10.00	20.00
15873	Sally Don't You Grieve/Times Are Getting Hard, Boys	1958	5.00	10.00	20.00
15911	Does Your Chewing Gum Lose Its Flavor (On the Bedpost Overnight)/Aunt Rhody	1959	5.00	10.00	20.00
—Reissued in 1961 with the same number					
15953	Fort Worth Jail/Whoa, Back, Back	1959	5.00	10.00	20.00
16263	Whoa, Back, Back/Light from the Lighthouse	1961	3.75	7.50	15.00
FELSTED					
8630	Rock Island Line/John Henry	1961	3.00	6.00	12.00
HICKORY					
1247	Lemon Tree/A Very Good Year	1964	2.50	5.00	10.00
1267	Fisherman's Luck/There's a Big Wheel	1964	2.50	5.00	10.00
1274	Bad News/Interstate 40	1964	2.50	5.00	10.00
1299	Louisiana Man/Lovey Told Me Goodbye	1965	2.50	5.00	10.00
1345	Cajun Jo (Bully of the Bayou)/Nothing to Gain	1965	2.50	5.00	10.00
LONDON					
1650	Rock Island Line/John Henry	1956	7.50	15.00	30.00
20055	Juanita/Who Knows Where the Time Goes	1969	—	3.00	6.00
MERCURY					
70872	Lost John/Stewball	1956	6.25	12.50	25.00
70949	Bring a Little Water, Sylvie/Dead or Alive	1956	6.25	12.50	25.00
71026	Don't You Rock Me Daddy-O/How Long, How Long Blues	1957	6.25	12.50	25.00
71094	Cumberland Gap/Wabash Cannonball	1957	6.25	12.50	25.00
71181	Puttin' On the Style/Gamblin' Man	1957	6.25	12.50	25.00
71248	My Dixie Darling/I'm Just a Rolling Stone	1957	6.25	12.50	25.00

Albums

Number	Title (A Side/B Side)	Yr	VG	VG+	NM
ABC-PARAMOUNT					
433 [M]	Sing Hallelujah	1963	5.00	10.00	20.00
S-433 [S]	Sing Hallelujah	1963	6.25	12.50	25.00
ATLANTIC					
8038 [M]	Skiffle Folk Songs	1960	10.00	20.00	40.00
SD 8038 [S]	Skiffle Folk Songs	1960	12.50	25.00	50.00
DOT					
DLP-3159 [M]	Lonnie Donegan	1959	10.00	20.00	40.00
MERCURY					
MG-20229 [M]	An Englishman Sings American Folk Songs	1957	12.50	25.00	50.00
UNITED ARTISTS					
UA-LA827-?	Puttin' On the Style	1977	2.50	5.00	10.00

DONLEY, JIMMY

45s

Number	Title (A Side/B Side)	Yr	VG	VG+	NM
CHESS					
1843	Santa, Don't Pass Me By/Think It Over	1962	3.00	6.00	12.00
CRAZY CAJUN					
9001	Santa, Don't Pass Me By/Think It Over	197?	—	2.50	5.00
9002	Forever Lillie Mae/I Still Care	197?	—	3.00	6.00
9003	Love Bug/I Still Care	197?	—	3.00	6.00
9004	I Really Got the Blues/Just a Game	197?	—	3.00	6.00
9005	You're Why I'm So Lonely/Let Me Hold You	197?	—	3.00	6.00
9006	Baby, Heaven Sent Me You/Door to My Heart	197?	—	3.00	6.00
9007	A Woman's Gotta Have Her Way/Hello, Remember Me	197?	—	3.00	6.00
9008	Please Mr. Sandman/Honey Stop	197?	—	3.00	6.00
9009	Lovin' Cajun Style/(B-side unknown)	197?	—	3.00	6.00
9010	Born to Be a Loser/Now I Know	197?	—	3.00	6.00
DECCA					
30308	Kickin' My Hound Around/Come Along	1957	20.00	40.00	80.00
30392	South of the Border/The Trail of the Lonesome Pine	1957	6.25	12.50	25.00
30519	Baby How Long/I Gotta Go	1957	6.25	12.50	25.00
30574	Please Baby Come Home/Born to Be a Loser	1958	6.25	12.50	25.00
30738	Radio, Jukebox and TV/I'm Alone	1958	6.25	12.50	25.00
30887	What Must I Do/The Shape You Left Me In	1959	6.25	12.50	25.00
31005	Now I Know/I Can't Love You	1959	6.25	12.50	25.00
31116	My Baby's Gone/Our Love	1960	10.00	20.00	40.00
TEARDROP					
3005	Honey Stop Twistin'/Hello, Remember Me	1962	3.75	7.50	15.00
3007	Santa, Don't Pass Me By/Forever Lillie Mae	1962	3.00	6.00	12.00
3007	Think It Over/Forever Lillie Mae	1962	3.00	6.00	12.00
3009	Baby, Heaven Sent Me You/Loving Cajun Style	1963	3.00	6.00	12.00
3017	You're Why I'm So Lonely/Let Me Hold You	1963	3.00	6.00	12.00
3021	Santa, Don't Pass Me By/Santa's Alley	1963	3.00	6.00	12.00
3026	I Really Got the Blues/Just a Game	1964	2.50	5.00	10.00
3034	I'm So Lonesome Without the Blues/Forget the Past	1964	2.50	5.00	10.00
3051	Love Bug/I'm to Blame	196?	2.50	5.00	10.00
3119	My Forbidden Love/Strange, Strange Feeling	196?	2.00	4.00	8.00

DONNER, RAL

45s

Number	Title (A Side/B Side)	Yr	VG	VG+	NM
CHICAGO FIRE					
7402	The Wedding Song/Godfather Per Me	1974	2.00	4.00	8.00
END					
GG-19	You Don't Know What You've Got (Until You Lose It)/She's Everything (I Wanted You to Be)	1963	7.50	15.00	30.00
—An early, and sought-after, reissue					
FONTANA					
1502	Poison Ivy League/You Finally Said Something Good	1965	6.25	12.50	25.00
1502	Poison Ivy League/A Tear in My Eye	1965	6.25	12.50	25.00
1515	Good Lovin'/The Other Side of Me	1965	6.25	12.50	25.00
GONE					
5102	Girl of My Best Friend/It's Been a Long, Long Time	1961	10.00	20.00	40.00
—Black label					
5102	Girl of My Best Friend/It's Been a Long, Long Time	1961	6.25	12.50	25.00
—Multi-color label					
5108	You Don't Know What You've Got (Until You Lose It)/So Close to Heaven	1961	7.50	15.00	30.00
5108	To Love/And Then	1961	10.00	20.00	40.00
—Deleted shortly after release					
5114	Please Don't Go/I Didn't Figure on Him	1961	6.25	12.50	25.00
5119	School of Heartbreakers/Because We're Young	1961	10.00	20.00	40.00
5121	She's Everything (I Wanted You to Be)/Because We're Young	1961	6.25	12.50	25.00
5121	She's Everything (I Wanted You to Be)/Will You Love Me in Heaven	1961	7.50	15.00	30.00
—B-side sung by a girl group, not Ral Donner.					
5125	To Love Someone/Will You Love Me in Heaven	1962	6.25	12.50	25.00
—B-side sung by Ral Donner as advertised					
5129	Loveless Life/Bells of Love	1962	6.25	12.50	25.00
5133	To Love/Sweetheart	1962	6.25	12.50	25.00
MID-EAGLE					
101	(If I Had My) Life to Live Over/Lost	1968	2.50	5.00	10.00
275	The Wedding Song/So Much Lovin'	1976	—	3.00	6.00
MJ					
222	(All of a Sudden) My Heart Sings/Lovin' Place	1970	—	3.00	6.00
222 [PS]	(All of a Sudden) My Heart Sings/Lovin' Place	1970	—	3.00	6.00
RED BIRD					
10-057	Love Isn't Like That/It Will Only Make You Love	1966	37.50	75.00	150.00
REPRISE					
20135	(These Are the Things That Make Up) Christmas Day/Second Miracle (Of Christmas)	1962	10.00	20.00	40.00
20141	I Got Burned/A Tear in My Eye	1963	10.00	20.00	40.00
20141 [PS]	I Got Burned/A Tear in My Eye	1963	45.00	90.00	180.00
20176	I Wish This Night Would Never End/Don't Put Your Heart in His Hand	1963	12.50	25.00	50.00
20192	Beyond the Heartbreak/Run Little Linda	1963	15.00	30.00	60.00
RISING SONS					
714	Just a Little Sunshine (In the Rain)/If I Promise	1968	2.50	5.00	10.00
SCOTTIE					
1310	Tell Me Why/That's All Right with Me	1959	62.50	125.00	250.00
SMASH					
34774/5 [DJ]	Good Lovin'/The Other Side of Me	1964	10.00	20.00	40.00
—A Fontana promo using Smash labels in error and omitting the Fontana number?					
STARFIRE					
100	Don't Let It Slip Away/Wait a Minute Now	1978	2.50	5.00	10.00
—Black vinyl					
100	Don't Let It Slip Away/Wait a Minute Now	1978	2.50	5.00	10.00
—White vinyl					
100 [PS]	Don't Let It Slip Away/Wait a Minute Now	1978	2.50	5.00	10.00
103	(Things That Make Up) Christmas Day/Second Miracle (Of Christmas)	1978	2.50	5.00	10.00
—Green vinyl					
103 [PS]	(Things That Make Up) Christmas Day/Second Miracle (Of Christmas)	1978	2.50	5.00	10.00
114	Rip It Up/Don't Leave Me Now	1979	2.50	5.00	10.00
114	Rip It Up/Don't Leave Me Now	1979	6.25	12.50	25.00
—Picture disc					
114 [PS]	Rip It Up/Don't Leave Me Now	1979	2.50	5.00	10.00
SUNLIGHT					
1006	Don't Let It Slip Away/Wait a Minute Now	1972	3.00	6.00	12.00
TAU					
105	Loneliness of a Star/And Then	1963	12.50	25.00	50.00
—Blue label					
105	Loneliness of a Star/And Then	1963	7.50	15.00	30.00
—Yellow label					
THUNDER					
7801	The Day the Beat Stopped/Rock on Me	1978	—	3.00	6.00

Number	Title (A Side/B Side)	Yr	VG	VG+	NM
Albums					
GONE					
LP-5012 [M]	Takin' Care of Business	1961	75.00	150.00	300.00
STARFIRE					
1004	An Evening with Ral Donner	1982	3.75	7.50	15.00
—All copies on multi-color vinyl					

DONNER, RAL/RAY SMITH/BOBBY DALE

Number	Title (A Side/B Side)	Yr	VG	VG+	NM
Albums					
CROWN					
CST-335 [R]	Ral Donner, Ray Smith and Bobby Dale	1963	5.00	10.00	20.00
CLP-5335 [M]	Ral Donner, Ray Smith and Bobby Dale	1963	10.00	20.00	40.00

DONNIE AND THE DARLINGTONS

Number	Title (A Side/B Side)	Yr	VG	VG+	NM
45s					
ABC-PARAMOUNT					
10633	Poppin' My Clutch/Since Grandpa Got a Rail Job	1965	6.25	12.50	25.00

DONNIE AND THE DELCHORDS

Number	Title (A Side/B Side)	Yr	VG	VG+	NM
45s					
EPIC					
9495	So Lonely/When You're Alone	1962	6.25	12.50	25.00
TAURUS					
352	So Lonely/When You're Alone	1962	10.00	20.00	40.00
357	I Don't Care/I'll Be With You in Apple Blossom Time	1963	6.25	12.50	25.00
361	Transylvania Mist/That Old Feeling	1963	6.25	12.50	25.00
363	Be with You/I Found Heaven	1963	6.25	12.50	25.00
364	I'm in the Mood for Love/I've Got a Woman	1964	6.25	12.50	25.00
Albums					
TAURUS					
1000	Sing with Triple Stereo	1967	75.00	150.00	300.00

DONNIE AND THE DREAMERS

Number	Title (A Side/B Side)	Yr	VG	VG+	NM
45s					
DECCA					
31312	Carole/Ruby My Love	1961	12.50	25.00	50.00
WHALE					
500	Dorothy/Count Every Star	1961	6.25	12.50	25.00
505	Teenage Love/My Memories of You	1961	10.00	20.00	40.00

DONNYBROOKS, THE

Number	Title (A Side/B Side)	Yr	VG	VG+	NM
45s					
CALICO					
108	Every Time We Kiss/Break the Glass	1959	5.00	10.00	20.00
112	Coming Home from School/Mandolins of Love	1959	5.00	10.00	20.00

DONOVAN

Number	Title (A Side/B Side)	Yr	VG	VG+	NM
45s					
ALLEGIANCE					
3910	Lady of the Stars/(B-side unknown)	1983	—	2.00	4.00
ARISTA					
0280	Dare to Be Different/International Man	1977	—	2.00	4.00
EPIC					
10045	Sunshine Superman/The Trip	1966	2.50	5.00	10.00
10045 [DJ]	Sunshine Superman/The Trip	1966	10.00	20.00	40.00
—Promo only on red vinyl					
10045 [PS]	Sunshine Superman/The Trip	1966	3.75	7.50	15.00
10098	Mellow Yellow/Sunny South Kensington	1966	2.50	5.00	10.00
10098 [PS]	Mellow Yellow/Sunny South Kensington	1966	3.75	7.50	15.00
10127	Epistle to Dippy/Preachin' Love	1967	2.00	4.00	8.00
10127 [PS]	Epistle to Dippy/Preachin' Love	1967	3.00	6.00	12.00
10212	There Is a Mountain/Sand and Foam	1967	2.00	4.00	8.00
10253	Wear Your Love Like Heaven/Oh Gosh	1967	2.00	4.00	8.00
10253 [PS]	Wear Your Love Like Heaven/Oh Gosh	1967	3.00	6.00	12.00
10300	Jennifer Juniper/Poor Cow	1968	2.00	4.00	8.00
10300 [PS]	Jennifer Juniper/Poor Cow	1968	3.00	6.00	12.00
10345	Hurdy Gurdy Man/Teen Angel	1968	2.00	4.00	8.00
—Features John Paul Jones, Jimmy Page, and possibly John Bonham, all later of Led Zeppelin					
10345 [PS]	Hurdy Gurdy Man/Teen Angel	1968	3.00	6.00	12.00
10393	Lalena/Aye My Love	1968	2.00	4.00	8.00
10393 [PS]	Lalena/Aye My Love	1968	3.00	6.00	12.00
10434	Atlantis/To Susan on the West Coast Waiting	1969	2.00	4.00	8.00
10434 [PS]	Atlantis/To Susan on the West Coast Waiting	1969	3.00	6.00	12.00
10510	Goo Goo Barabajagal (Love Is Hot)/Trust	1969	2.00	4.00	8.00
10510 [PS]	Goo Goo Barabajagal (Love Is Hot)/Trust	1969	3.00	6.00	12.00
—With the Jeff Beck Group					
10649	Riki Tiki Tavi/Roots of Oak	1970	2.00	4.00	8.00
10649 [PS]	Riki Tiki Tavi/Roots of Oak	1970	3.00	6.00	12.00
10694	Celia of the Seals/Song of the Wandering Aengus	1971	2.00	4.00	8.00
10694 [PS]	Celia of the Seals/Song of the Wandering Aengus	1971	3.00	6.00	12.00
10983	I Like You/Earth Sign Man	1973	—	2.50	5.00
11023	Maria Magenta/Intergalactic Laxative	1973	—	2.50	5.00
11108	Yellow Star/Sailing Homeward	1974	—	2.50	5.00
50016	Rock and Roll with Me/Divine Daze of Deathless Delight	1974	—	2.50	5.00
50077	Rock and Roll Souljer/How Silly	1975	—	2.50	5.00
50237	Dark Eyed Blue Jean Angel/Well Known Has-Been	1976	—	2.50	5.00
HICKORY					
1309	Catch the Wind/Why Do You Treat Me Like You Do	1965	3.75	7.50	15.00
1324	Colours/Josie	1965	3.00	6.00	12.00
1338	Universal Soldier/Do You Hear Me Now	1965	3.00	6.00	12.00
1375	You're Gonna Need Somebody on Your Mind/Little Tin Soldier	1966	3.00	6.00	12.00
1402	Turquoise/To Try for the Sun	1966	3.00	6.00	12.00
1417	Hey Gyp/The War Drags On	1966	3.00	6.00	12.00
1470	Sunny Goodge Street/Summer Day Reflection Song	1967	2.50	5.00	10.00
1492	Do You Hear Me Now/Why Do You Treat Me Like You Do	1968	2.50	5.00	10.00
JANUS					
138	Keep On Truckin'/Hey Gyp	1971	2.00	4.00	8.00
Albums					
ALLEGIANCE					
AV-437	Lady of the Stars	1983	2.50	5.00	10.00
ARISTA					
AB 4143	Donovan	1980	2.50	5.00	10.00
BELL					
1135	Early Treasures	1973	2.50	5.00	10.00
EPIC					
B2N 171 [(2) S]	A Gift from a Flower to a Garden	1967	6.25	12.50	25.00
—Boxed set of two LPs with portfolio of lyrics and drawings. The two records also were issued separately as Epic 26349 and 26350.					
E2 171 [(2)]	A Gift from a Flower to a Garden	1979	3.75	7.50	15.00
—Blue label					
L2N 6071 [(2) M]	A Gift from a Flower to a Garden	1967	12.50	25.00	50.00
—Boxed set of two LPs with portfolio of lyrics and drawings. The two records also were issued separately as Epic 24349 and 24350.					
LN 24217 [M]	Sunshine Superman	1966	7.50	15.00	30.00
—Contains the single version of "Sunshine Superman"					
LN 24239 [M]	Mellow Yellow	1967	7.50	15.00	30.00
LN 24349 [M]	Wear Your Love Like Heaven	1967	3.00	6.00	12.00
—Part of Epic 6071, issued simultaneously					
LN 24350 [M]	For Little Ones	1967	3.00	6.00	12.00
—Part of Epic 6071, issued simultaneously					
BN 26217 [R]	Sunshine Superman	1966	3.75	7.50	15.00
—Contains the single version of "Sunshine Superman" (rechanneled)					
BN 26239 [R]	Mellow Yellow	1967	3.75	7.50	15.00
BN 26349 [S]	Wear Your Love Like Heaven	1967	3.75	7.50	15.00
—Part of Epic 171, issued simultaneously					
BN 26350 [S]	For Little Ones	1967	3.75	7.50	15.00
—Part of Epic 171, issued simultaneously					
BN 26386	Donovan in Concert	1968	3.00	6.00	12.00
BN 26420	Hurdy Gurdy Man	1968	3.00	6.00	12.00
PE 26420	Hurdy Gurdy Man	1986	2.00	4.00	8.00
—Blue label, new prefix					
BXN 26439 [P]	Donovan's Greatest Hits	1969	3.00	6.00	12.00
—Yellow label; "Mellow Yellow" is rechanneled; "Sunshine Superman" is the full-length version in stereo; "Catch the Wind" and "Colours" were re-recorded					
BXN 26439 [P]	Donovan's Greatest Hits	1973	2.50	5.00	10.00
—Orange label					
PE 26439	Donovan's Greatest Hits	1979	2.00	4.00	8.00
—Blue label					
BN 26481	Barabajagal	1969	3.00	6.00	12.00
PE 26481	Barabajagal	1987	2.00	4.00	8.00
—Blue label, new prefix					
E 30125	Open Road	1970	3.00	6.00	12.00
KEG 31210 [(2)]	The World of Donovan	1972	3.00	6.00	12.00
KE 32156	Cosmic Wheels	1973	3.75	7.50	15.00
KE 32800	Essence to Essence	1974	3.00	6.00	12.00
PE 33245	7-Tease	1974	3.00	6.00	12.00
EG 33731 [(2)]	Hurdy Gurdy Man/Barabajagal	1975	3.75	7.50	15.00
EG 33734 [(2)]	Donovan in Concert/Sunshine Superman	1975	3.75	7.50	15.00
PE 33945	Slow Down World	1976	3.00	6.00	12.00
HICKORY					
LPM-123 [M]	Catch the Wind	1965	6.25	12.50	25.00
LPS-123 [R]	Catch the Wind	1965	6.25	12.50	25.00
LPM-127 [M]	Fairy Tale	1965	5.00	10.00	20.00
LPS-127 [P]	Fairy Tale	1965	6.25	12.50	25.00
—"Colours" is rechanneled					
LPM-135 [M]	The Real Donovan	1966	5.00	10.00	20.00
LPS-135 [P]	The Real Donovan	1966	6.25	12.50	25.00
—Half stereo, including "Colours," the rest rechanneled.					
LPS-143 [P]	Like It Is, Was and Evermore Shall Be	1968	5.00	10.00	20.00
LPS-149 [P]	The Best of Donovan	1969	5.00	10.00	20.00
JANUS					
3022	Donovan P. Leitch	1970	2.50	5.00	10.00
3025	Hear Me Now	1971	2.50	5.00	10.00
KORY					
3012	Early Treasures	1977	2.00	4.00	8.00
PYE					
502	Donovan	1975	2.50	5.00	10.00

DONTELS, THE

Number	Title (A Side/B Side)	Yr	VG	VG+	NM
45s					
BELTONE					
2040	Lover's Reunion/Make a Chance	1963	62.50	125.00	250.00

DOOBIE BROTHERS, THE

Also see MICHAEL McDONALD.

Number	Title (A Side/B Side)	Yr	VG	VG+	NM
45s					
ASYLUM					
46630	Power/Cape Fear River	1980	—	2.50	5.00
—A-side: With John Hall and James Taylor; B-side by Sweet Honey in the Rock					
CAPITOL					
B-44376	The Doctor/Too High a Price	1989	—	—	3.00
B-44376 [PS]	The Doctor/Too High a Price	1989	—	—	3.00
7PRO-79723 [DJ]	Need a Little Taste of Love (same on both sides)	1989	—	3.00	6.00
—Vinyl is promo only					
SESAME STREET					
49642	Wynken, Blynken and Nod/In Harmony	1980	—	2.50	5.00
—B-side by Kate Taylor and the Simon-Taylor Family					
49642 [PS]	Wynken, Blynken and Nod/In Harmony	1980	—	2.50	5.00
WARNER BROS.					
7495	Nobody/Slippery St. Paul	1971	—	3.00	6.00
7527	Travelin' Man/Feelin' Down Partner	1971	—	3.00	6.00
7544	Beehive State/Closer Every Day	1971	—	3.00	6.00
7619	Listen to the Music/Toulouse Street	1972	—	2.50	5.00
7661	Jesus Is Just Alright/Rockin' Down the Highway	1972	—	2.50	5.00
7698	Long Train Runnin'/Without You	1973	—	2.00	4.00
7728	China Grove/Evil Woman	1973	—	2.00	4.00
7795	Another Park, Another Sunday/Black Water	1974	—	2.50	5.00
7832	Eyes of Silver/You Just Can't Stop It	1974	—	2.50	5.00

Number	Title (A Side/B Side)	Yr	VG	VG+	NM
8011	Eyes of Silver/You Just Can't Stop It	1974	—	2.00	4.00
8041	Nobody/Flying Cloud	1974	—	2.00	4.00
8062	Black Water/Song to See You Through	1974	—	2.00	4.00
8092	Take Me in Your Arms (Rock Me)/Slat Key Soquel Rag	1975	—	2.00	4.00
8126	Sweet Maxine/Double Dealin' Four Flusher	1975	—	2.00	4.00
8161	I Cheat the Hangman/Music Man	1975	—	2.00	4.00
8196	Takin' It to the Streets/For Someone Special	1976	—	2.00	4.00
8233	Wheels of Fortune/Slat Key Soquel Rag	1976	—	2.00	4.00
8282	It Keeps You Runnin'/Turn It Loose	1976	—	2.00	4.00
8408	Little Darling (I Need You)/Losin' End	1977	—	2.00	4.00
8471	Echoes of Love/There's a Light	1977	—	2.00	4.00
8500	Livin' on the Fault Line/Nothin' but a Heartache	1977	—	2.00	4.00
8725	What a Fool Believes/Don't Stop to Watch the Wheels	1978	—	2.00	4.00
8725 [PS]	What a Fool Believes/Don't Stop to Watch the Wheels	1978	—	2.50	5.00
8828	Minute by Minute/Sweet Feelin'	1979	—	2.00	4.00
29552	You Belong to Me/South City Midnight Lady	1983	—	2.00	4.00
29552 [PS]	You Belong to Me/South City Midnight Lady	1983	—	2.50	5.00
49029	Dependin' on You/How Do the Fools Survive	1979	—	2.00	4.00
49503	Real Love/Thank You Love	1980	—	2.00	4.00
49503 [PS]	Real Love/Thank You Love	1980	—	2.50	5.00
49622	One Step Closer/South Bay Street	1980	—	2.00	4.00
49670	Keep This Train A-Rollin'/Just in Time	1981	—	2.00	4.00
50001	Here to Love You/Wynken, Bliinken and Nod	1982	—	2.00	4.00

7-Inch Extended Plays

WARNER BROS.

Number	Title (A Side/B Side)	Yr	VG	VG+	NM
S 2750 [DJ]	Eyes of Silver/Pursuit on 53rd St./Spirit//Road Angel/Tell Me What You Want	1974	2.00	4.00	8.00
—Jukebox issue, small hole, plays at 33 1/3 rpm					
S 2750 [PS]	What Were Once Vices Are Now Habits	1974	2.50	5.00	10.00
—Part of Little LP series (LLP #247)					

Albums

Number	Title (A Side/B Side)	Yr	VG	VG+	NM
CAPITOL					
C1-90371	Cycles	1989	3.00	6.00	12.00
DCC COMPACT CLASSICS					
LPZ-2053	Best of the Doobies	1998	6.25	12.50	25.00
—Audiophile vinyl					
MOBILE FIDELITY					
1-122	Takin' It to the Streets	1983	10.00	20.00	40.00
—Audiophile vinyl					
NAUTILUS					
NR-5	The Captain and Me	1980	10.00	20.00	40.00
—Audiophile vinyl					
NR-18	Minute by Minute	1981	7.50	15.00	30.00
—Audiophile vinyl					
PICKWICK					
SPC-3721	Introducing the Doobie Brothers	1980	5.00	10.00	20.00
—Pre-Warner Bros. recordings; withdrawn shortly after release					
WARNER BROS.					
WS 1919	The Doobie Brothers	1971	3.75	7.50	15.00
—Green label original					
WS 1919	The Doobie Brothers	1973	2.50	5.00	10.00
—"Burbank" label					
BS 2634	Toulouse Street	1972	3.75	7.50	15.00
—Green label original					
BS 2634	Toulouse Street	1973	2.50	5.00	10.00
—"Burbank" label					
BS 2634	The Captain and Me	1973	3.00	6.00	12.00
—"Burbank" label					
BS 2634	The Captain and Me	1979	2.00	4.00	8.00
—Cream label					
BS4 2634 [Q]	The Captain and Me	1974	5.00	10.00	20.00
BS 2750	What Were Once Vices Are Now Habits	1974	2.50	5.00	10.00
—"Burbank" label					
BS 2750	What Were Once Vices Are Now Habits	1979	2.00	4.00	8.00
—Cream label					
BS4 2750 [Q]	What Were Once Vices Are Now Habits	1974	5.00	10.00	20.00
BS 2835	Stampede	1975	2.50	5.00	10.00
—"Burbank" label					
BS 2835	Stampede	1979	2.00	4.00	8.00
—Cream label					
BS4 2835 [Q]	Stampede	1975	5.00	10.00	20.00
BS 2899	Takin' It to the Streets	1976	2.50	5.00	10.00
—"Burbank" label					
BS 2899	Takin' It to the Streets	1979	2.00	4.00	8.00
—Cream label					
BS 2978	Best of the Doobies	1976	3.00	6.00	12.00
BSK 3045	Livin' on the Fault Line	1977	2.50	5.00	10.00
—"Burbank" label					
BSK 3045	Livin' on the Fault Line	1977	2.00	4.00	8.00
—Cream label					
BSK 3112	Best of the Doobies	1978	2.50	5.00	10.00
—"Burbank" label					
BSK 3112	Best of the Doobies	1979	2.00	4.00	8.00
—Cream label					
BSK 3193	Minute by Minute	1978	2.50	5.00	10.00
HS 3452	One Step Closer	1980	2.50	5.00	10.00
BSK 3612	Best of the Doobies, Volume 2	1981	2.50	5.00	10.00
23772 [(2)]	Farewell Tour	1983	3.75	7.50	15.00

DOONICAN, VAL

45s

Number	Title (A Side/B Side)	Yr	VG	VG+	NM
DECCA					
32252	I'd Rather Think of You/If the Whole World Stopped Lovin'	1968	—	2.50	5.00
32337	The Sun Always Shines When You're Young/Now	1968	—	2.50	5.00
LONDON					
1014	Two Streets/It Must Be You	1967	—	3.00	6.00
9717	Walk Talll/Only the Heartaches	1964	2.50	5.00	10.00
9735	The Special Years/Traveling Home	1965	2.50	5.00	10.00
9753	I'm Gonna Get There Somehow/How Can I Find Her	1965	2.50	5.00	10.00
PRESS					
5008	Gentle Mary/What Would I Be	1967	—	3.00	6.00

Albums

Number	Title (A Side/B Side)	Yr	VG	VG+	NM
DECCA					
DL 4962 [M]	If the Whole World Stopped Lovin'	1968	3.75	7.50	15.00
DL 74962 [S]	If the Whole World Stopped Lovin'	1968	3.00	6.00	12.00
LONDON					
PS 515 [S]	The Many Shades of Val Doonican	1967	3.75	7.50	15.00
LL 3515 [M]	The Many Shades of Val Doonican	1967	3.00	6.00	12.00

DOORS, THE

Also see BUTTS BAND; RAY MANZAREK.

12-Inch Singles

Number	Title (A Side/B Side)	Yr	VG	VG+	NM
ELEKTRA					
ED 4942 [DJ]	Gloria (clean edit)/Gloria (dirty LP)	1983	5.00	10.00	20.00
ED 4955 [DJ]	Love Me Two Times/Moonlight Drive	1983	3.75	7.50	15.00
ED 5245 [DJ]	Light My Fire (edit)/Light My Fire (live edit)	1987	3.75	7.50	15.00

45s

Number	Title (A Side/B Side)	Yr	VG	VG+	NM
ELEKTRA					
45051	Light My Fire/Love Me Two Times	1972	—	3.00	6.00
—"Spun Gold" series; originals have a very dark gold label					
45051	Light My Fire/Love Me Two Times	1975	—	2.00	4.00
—"Spun Gold" series; reissues have a lighter gold label					
45052	Touch Me/Hello, I Love You	1972	—	3.00	6.00
—"Spun Gold" series; originals have a very dark gold label					
45052	Touch Me/Hello, I Love You	1975	—	2.00	4.00
—"Spun Gold" series; reissues have a lighter gold label					
45059	Riders on the Storm/Love Her Madly	1973	—	3.00	6.00
—"Spun Gold" series; originals have a very dark gold label					
45059	Riders on the Storm/Love Her Madly	1975	—	2.00	4.00
—"Spun Gold" series; reissues have a lighter gold label					
45122	L.A. Woman/Roadhouse Blues	1983	—	2.00	4.00
—"Spun Gold" series; lighter gold label					
45123	People Are Strange/Break On Through	1983	—	2.00	4.00
—"Spun Gold" series; lighter gold label					
45611	Break On Through (To the Other Side)/End of the Night	1966	7.50	15.00	30.00
—Originals have a yellow and black label					
45611	Break On Through (To the Other Side)/End of the Night	1967	5.00	10.00	20.00
—Second pressings have a red, black and white label					
45611 [PS]	Break On Through (To the Other Side)/End of the Night	1966	30.00	60.00	120.00
45615	Light My Fire/The Crystal Ship	1967	7.50	15.00	30.00
—Originals have a yellow and black label					
45615	Light My Fire/The Crystal Ship	1967	3.00	6.00	12.00
—Second pressings have a red, black and white label					
45621	People Are Strange/Unhappy Girl	1967	3.00	6.00	12.00
45621 [PS]	People Are Strange/Unhappy Girl	1967	10.00	20.00	40.00
45624	Love Me Two Times/Moonlight Drive	1967	3.00	6.00	12.00
45628	The Unknown Soldier/We Could Be So Good Together	1968	3.00	6.00	12.00
45628 [PS]	The Unknown Soldier/We Could Be So Good Together	1968	7.50	15.00	30.00
45635	Hello, I Love You, Won't You Tell Me Your Name?/Love Street	1968	5.00	10.00	20.00
—Original pressings have longer title					
45635	Hello, I Love You/Love Street	1968	3.00	6.00	12.00
45646	Touch Me/Wild Child	1968	3.00	6.00	12.00
45656	Wishful Sinful/Who Scared You?	1969	2.50	5.00	10.00
45663	Tell All the People/Easy Ride	1969	2.50	5.00	10.00
45663 [PS]	Tell All the People/Easy Ride	1969	6.25	12.50	25.00
45675	Runnin' Blue/Do It	1969	2.50	5.00	10.00
45685	You Make Me Real/Roadhouse Blues	1970	2.50	5.00	10.00
45726	Love Her Madly/(You Need Meat) Don't Go No Further	1971	2.00	4.00	8.00
45738	Riders on the Storm/Changeling	1971	2.00	4.00	8.00
45757	Tightrope Ride/Variety Is the Spice of Life	1971	2.00	4.00	8.00
45768	Ships w/ Sails/In the Eye of the Sun	1972	2.00	4.00	8.00
45793	Get Up and Dance/Treetrunk	1972	2.00	4.00	8.00
45807	The Mosquito/It Slipped My Mind	1972	2.00	4.00	8.00
45825	The Piano Bird/Good Rockin'	1972	2.00	4.00	8.00
46005	Roadhouse Blues (Live)/Albinoni/Adagio	1979	—	2.50	5.00
47097	People Are Strange/Not to Touch the Earth	1980	—	2.00	4.00
47097 [PS]	People Are Strange/Not to Touch the Earth	1980	2.00	4.00	8.00
—Also has an insert with photos of Doors albums					
69770	Gloria/Moonlight Drive	1983	—	2.00	4.00
—Contrary to prior reports, this was not issued with a picture sleeve					
PHILCO-FORD					
HP-9	Light My Fire/Break On Through	1968	10.00	20.00	40.00
—4-inch plastic "Hip Pocket Record" with color sleeve					

Albums

Number	Title (A Side/B Side)	Yr	VG	VG+	NM
DCC COMPACT CLASSICS					
LPZ-2045	Strange Days	1997	6.25	12.50	25.00
—Audiophile vinyl					
LPZ-2046	The Doors	1997	6.25	12.50	25.00
—Audiophile vinyl					
LPZ-2049	Waiting for the Sun	1998	6.25	12.50	25.00
—Audiophile vinyl					
LPZ-2050	L.A. Woman	1998	6.25	12.50	25.00
—Audiophile vinyl					
ELEKTRA					
5E-502	An American Prayer	1978	3.00	6.00	12.00
—Butterfly labels					
5E-502	An American Prayer	1980	2.50	5.00	10.00
—Red labels with Warner Communications logo in lower right					
5E-502	An American Prayer	1983	2.00	4.00	8.00
—Red and black labels					
5E-515	Greatest Hits	1980	2.50	5.00	10.00
—Red labels with Warner Communications logo in lower right					
5E-515	Greatest Hits	1983	2.00	4.00	8.00
—Red and black labels					
EKL-4007 [M]	The Doors	1967	50.00	100.00	200.00

Number	Title (A Side/B Side)	Yr	VG	VG+	NM
EKL-4014 [M]	Strange Days	1967	150.00	300.00	600.00
—Value assumes the record is mono. Possibly, the only place where the jacket identifies this as mono is on the spine; both mono and stereo covers have the stereo number on front and back.					
EKL-4024 [M]	Waiting for the Sun	1968	250.00	500.00	1000.
EQ-5035 [Q]	Best of the Doors	1973	5.00	10.00	20.00
—Butterfly labels					
EQ-5035 [Q]	Best of the Doors	1980	3.00	6.00	12.00
—Red labels with Warner Communications logo in lower right					
EQ-5035 [Q]	Best of the Doors	1983	2.50	5.00	10.00
—Red and black labels					
8E-6001 [(2)]	Weird Scenes Inside the Gold Mine	1972	5.00	10.00	20.00
—Butterfly labels					
8E-6001 [(2)]	Weird Scenes Inside the Gold Mine	1980	3.00	6.00	12.00
—Red labels with Warner Communications logo in lower right					
8E-6001 [(2)]	Weird Scenes Inside the Gold Mine	1983	2.50	5.00	10.00
—Red and black labels					
EKS-9002 [(2)]	Absolutely Live	1970	6.25	12.50	25.00
—Butterfly labels					
EKS-9002 [(2)]	Absolutely Live	1980	3.75	7.50	15.00
—Red labels with Warner Communications logo in lower right					
EKS-9002 [(2)]	Absolutely Live	1983	3.00	6.00	12.00
—Red and black labels					
EKS-9002 [(2) DJ]	Absolutely Live	1970	20.00	40.00	80.00
—White label promo					
60269	Alive, She Cried	1984	3.00	6.00	12.00
60345 [(2)]	The Best of the Doors	1985	3.75	7.50	15.00
60345 [(2)]	The Best of the Doors	1985	10.00	20.00	40.00
—White label promo on audiophile vinyl					
60417	Classics	1986	3.00	6.00	12.00
60741 [EP]	Live at the Hollywood Bowl	1988	3.00	6.00	12.00
E1-61047	The Doors	1991	5.00	10.00	20.00
—Soundtrack from the movie; only available on US vinyl from Columbia House					
61812	An American Prayer	1995	3.75	7.50	15.00
—Remastered and lengthened version of 5E-502					
EKS-74007 [S]	The Doors	1967	12.50	25.00	50.00
—Brown labels					
EKS-74007 [S]	The Doors	1969	3.75	7.50	15.00
—Red labels with large stylized "E"					
EKS-74007 [S]	The Doors	1971	3.00	6.00	12.00
—Butterfly labels					
EKS-74007 [S]	The Doors	1980	2.50	5.00	10.00
—Red labels with Warner Communications logo in lower right					
EKS-74007 [S]	The Doors	1983	2.00	4.00	8.00
—Red and black labels					
EKS-74014 [S]	Strange Days	1967	10.00	20.00	40.00
—Brown labels					
EKS-74014 [S]	Strange Days	1969	3.75	7.50	15.00
—Red labels with large stylized "E"					
EKS-74014 [S]	Strange Days	1971	3.00	6.00	12.00
—Butterfly labels					
EKS-74014 [S]	Strange Days	1980	2.50	5.00	10.00
—Red labels with Warner Communications logo in lower right					
EKS-74014 [S]	Strange Days	1983	2.00	4.00	8.00
—Red and black labels					
EKS-74024 [S]	Waiting for the Sun	1968	7.50	15.00	30.00
—Brown labels					
EKS-74024 [S]	Waiting for the Sun	1969	3.75	7.50	15.00
—Red labels with large stylized "E"					
EKS-74024 [S]	Waiting for the Sun	1971	3.00	6.00	12.00
—Butterfly labels					
EKS-74024 [S]	Waiting for the Sun	1980	2.50	5.00	10.00
—Red labels with Warner Communications logo in lower right					
EKS-74024 [S]	Waiting for the Sun	1983	2.00	4.00	8.00
—Red and black labels					
EKS-74024 [S-DJ]	Waiting for the Sun	1968	37.50	75.00	150.00
—White label promo					
EKS-74079	13	1970	3.75	7.50	15.00
—Butterfly labels					
EKS-74079	13	1980	2.50	5.00	10.00
—Red labels with Warner Communications logo in lower right					
EKS-74079	13	1983	2.00	4.00	8.00
—Red and black labels					
EKS-74079 [DJ]	13	1970	10.00	20.00	40.00
—White label promo					
EKS-75005	The Soft Parade	1969	12.50	25.00	50.00
—Brown labels					
EKS-75005	The Soft Parade	1969	5.00	10.00	20.00
—Red labels with large stylized "E"					
EKS-75005	The Soft Parade	1971	3.00	6.00	12.00
—Butterfly labels					
EKS-75005	The Soft Parade	1980	2.50	5.00	10.00
—Red labels with Warner Communications logo in lower right					
EKS-75005	The Soft Parade	1983	2.00	4.00	8.00
—Red and black labels					
EKS-75007	Morrison Hotel/Hard Rock Café	1970	6.25	12.50	25.00
—Red labels with large stylized "E"					
EKS-75007	Morrison Hotel/Hard Rock Café	1971	3.00	6.00	12.00
—Butterfly labels					
EKS-75007	Morrison Hotel/Hard Rock Café	1980	2.50	5.00	10.00
—Red labels with Warner Communications logo in lower right					
EKS-75007	Morrison Hotel/Hard Rock Café	1983	2.00	4.00	8.00
—Red and black labels					
EKS-75007 [DJ]	Morrison Hotel/Hard Rock Café	1970	25.00	50.00	100.00
—White label promo					
EKS-75011	L.A. Woman	1971	12.50	25.00	50.00
—With see-through window on cover and yellow innersleeve with photo of Jim Morrison on a cross					
EKS-75011	L.A. Woman	197?	3.00	6.00	12.00
—Butterfly label, standard cover					
EKS-75011	L.A. Woman	1980	2.50	5.00	10.00
—Red labels with Warner Communications logo in lower right					
EKS-75011	L.A. Woman	1983	2.00	4.00	8.00
—Red and black labels					
EKS-75011 [DJ]	L.A. Woman	1971	25.00	50.00	100.00
—White label promo					
EKS-75017	Other Voices	1971	3.75	7.50	15.00
EKS-75038	Full Circle	1972	3.75	7.50	15.00
MOBILE FIDELITY					
1-051	The Doors	1980	15.00	30.00	60.00
—Audiophile vinyl					

DOOTONES, THE

45s

Number	Title (A Side/B Side)	Yr	VG	VG+	NM
DOOTONE					
366	Teller of Fortune/Ay Si Si	1955	50.00	100.00	200.00
470	Strange Love Affair/The Day You Said Goodbye	1962	7.50	15.00	30.00
471	Sailor Boy/Down the Road	1962	7.50	15.00	30.00

DORELLS, THE

45s

Number	Title (A Side/B Side)	Yr	VG	VG+	NM
ATLANTIC					
2244	Beating of My Heart/Maybe Baby	1964	3.75	7.50	15.00
GEI					
4401	Beating of My Heart/Maybe Baby	1963	7.50	15.00	30.00

DORMAN, HAROLD

45s

Number	Title (A Side/B Side)	Yr	VG	VG+	NM
RITA					
1003	Mountain of Love/To Be with You	1960	6.25	12.50	25.00
1008	I'll Come Running/River of Tears	1960	5.00	10.00	20.00
1012	Moved to Kansas City/Take a Chance on Me	1960	5.00	10.00	20.00
SANTO					
9005	In an Instant/There on Yonder Hill	1962	3.75	7.50	15.00
9051	Ain't Gonna Change/What Comes Next	1962	3.75	7.50	15.00
SUN					
362	I'll Stick By You/There They Go	1961	5.00	10.00	20.00
370	Just One Step/Uncle Jonah's Place	1961	5.00	10.00	20.00
377	Wait 'Til Saturday Night/In the Beginning	1962	5.00	10.00	20.00

DORN, JERRY

45s

Number	Title (A Side/B Side)	Yr	VG	VG+	NM
ARWIN					
122	Brother, Can You Spare a Dime/Disappointed Lover	1959	3.00	6.00	12.00
FLING					
711	Rocking Chair Rock/Prayer of Love	1959	12.50	25.00	50.00
KING					
4932	Wishing Well/Sentimental Heaven	1956	20.00	40.00	80.00
4968	I'm So in Love with You/Nightmare	1956	3.75	7.50	15.00
5029	Quicksand/The Key	1957	3.75	7.50	15.00

DORRELLES, THE

45s

Number	Title (A Side/B Side)	Yr	VG	VG+	NM
RSVP					
1108	You Are/Good Luck to the Lucky Girl	1965	3.00	6.00	12.00

DORSAM, TOM

45s

Number	Title (A Side/B Side)	Yr	VG	VG+	NM
LOREN					
5001	Baby of Mine/(B-side unknown)	1964	125.00	250.00	500.00

DORSEY, GERRY

See ENGELBERT HUMPERDINCK.

DORSEY, JACK

45s

Number	Title (A Side/B Side)	Yr	VG	VG+	NM
PARKWAY					
938	Ringo's Dog/March of the Gonks	1965	3.00	6.00	12.00

DORSEY, LEE

45s

Number	Title (A Side/B Side)	Yr	VG	VG+	NM
ABC					
12326	Night People/Can I Be the One	1978	—	2.00	4.00
12361	God Must Have Blessed America/Say It Again	1978	—	2.00	4.00
ABC-PARAMOUNT					
10192	Lottie Mo/Lover of Love	1961	3.75	7.50	15.00
ACE					
640	Lonely Evening/Rock	1961	3.75	7.50	15.00
AMY					
927	Ride Your Pony/The Kitty Cat Song	1965	2.00	4.00	8.00
939	Can You Hear Me/Work, Work, Work	1965	2.00	4.00	8.00
945	Get Out of My Life, Woman/So Long	1965	2.00	4.00	8.00
952	Confusion/The Neighbors' Daughter	1966	2.00	4.00	8.00
958	Workin' in the Coal Mine/Mexico	1966	2.50	5.00	10.00
965	Holy Cow/Operation Heartache	1966	2.00	4.00	8.00
974	Gotta Find a Job/Rain, Rain, Rain, Go Away	1967	—	3.00	6.00
987	My Old Car/Why Wait Until Tomorrow	1967	—	3.00	6.00
994	Can't Get Away/Vista Vista	1967	—	3.00	6.00
998	Go-Go Girl/I Can Hear You Callin'	1967	—	3.00	6.00
11010	I Can't Get Away/Cynthia	1968	—	3.00	6.00
11020	Wonder Woman/A Little Dab A Do Ya	1968	—	3.00	6.00
11031	Four Corners (Part 1)/Four Corners (Part 2)	1968	—	3.00	6.00
11048	I'm Gonna Sit Right Down/Little Ba-By	1968	—	3.00	6.00
11052	What Now My Love/A Lover Was Born	1969	—	3.00	6.00
11055	Everything I Do Gonna be Funky (From Now On)/There Should Be a Book	1969	—	3.00	6.00
11057	Give It Up/Candy Man	1969	—	3.00	6.00
BELL					
908	I Can Hear You Callin'/What You Want	1970	—	2.50	5.00
CONSTELLATION					
115	Organ Grinder's Swing/I Gotta Find a New Love	1964	5.00	10.00	20.00
135	You're Breaking Me Up/Messed Around and Fell in Love	1964	5.00	10.00	20.00
FURY					
1053	Ya Ya/Give Me You	1961	3.75	7.50	15.00
1056	Do-Re-Mi/People Gonna' Talk	1961	3.00	6.00	12.00
1061	Eenie Meenie Miny Moe/Behind the 8-Ball	1962	3.00	6.00	12.00
1066	You Are My Sunshine/Give Me Your Love	1962	3.00	6.00	12.00

Number	Title (A Side/B Side)	Yr	VG	VG+	NM
1074	Hoodlum Joe/When I Met My Baby	1963	3.00	6.00	12.00
POLYDOR					
14038	Yes We Can — Part 1/O Me O, My O	1970	—	2.50	5.00
14055	Sneakin' Sally Through the Alley/Tears, Tears and More Tears	1971	—	2.50	5.00
14106	Freedom for the Stallion/If She Won't (Find Someone Who Will)	1971	—	2.50	5.00
14147	When Can I Come Home/Gator Tail	1972	—	2.50	5.00
14181	On Your Way Down/Freedom for the Stallion	1973	—	2.50	5.00
REX					
1005	Rock/Lonely Evening	1959	6.25	12.50	25.00
SANSU					
474	Love Lots of Lovin'/Take Care of Our Love	1967	3.00	6.00	12.00
—With Betty Harris					
SMASH					
1842	Hello Good Looking/Someday	1963	2.50	5.00	10.00
SPRING					
114	Occapella/Tears, Tears and More Tears	1971	—	2.50	5.00
VALIANT					
1001	Lottie Mo/Lover of Love	1958	10.00	20.00	40.00

Albums

Number	Title (A Side/B Side)	Yr	VG	VG+	NM
AMY					
8010 [M]	Ride Your Pony	1966	7.50	15.00	30.00
S-8010 [S]	Ride Your Pony	1966	10.00	20.00	40.00
8011 [M]	The New Lee Dorsey	1966	6.25	12.50	25.00
S-8011 [S]	The New Lee Dorsey	1966	7.50	15.00	30.00
ARISTA					
AL 8387	Holy Cow! The Best of Lee Dorsey	1985	2.50	5.00	10.00
FURY					
1002 [M]	Ya Ya	1962	75.00	150.00	300.00
POLYDOR					
24-4024	Yes We Can	1970	3.00	6.00	12.00
SPHERE SOUND					
SR-7003 [M]	Ya Ya	196?	25.00	50.00	100.00
—Reissue of Fury 1002					
SSR-7003 [R]	Ya Ya	196?	12.50	25.00	50.00
—Rechanneled reissue of Fury 1002					

DORSEY, TOMMY

On albums with asterisks (*) after them, some of the tracks feature FRANK SINATRA as lead vocalist.

45s

Number	Title (A Side/B Side)	Yr	VG	VG+	NM
DECCA					
27247	Music Maestro, Please/Strangers	1950	3.75	7.50	15.00
27248	Goofus/Ev'rybody Wants to Go to Heaven	1950	3.75	7.50	15.00
27396	As Time Goes By/Lullaby of Broadway	1951	3.00	6.00	12.00
27429	Alone Together/Dancing in the Dark	1951	3.00	6.00	12.00
27430	Louisiana Hayride/Something to Remember You By	1951	3.00	6.00	12.00
27431	I Guess I'll Have to Change My Ways/I See Your Face Before Me	1951	3.00	6.00	12.00
27539	Sweet Adeline/Diane	1951	3.00	6.00	12.00
27690	My Magic Heart/If You Turn Me Down	1951	3.00	6.00	12.00
27691	I Fall in Love with You/Everything I Have Is Yours	1951	3.00	6.00	12.00
27709	September in the Rain/Black Strap Molasses	1951	3.00	6.00	12.00
27723	You Blew Out the Flame in My Heart/The Hula Hula Boo Boogie	1951	3.00	6.00	12.00
27733	Show Me You Love Me/Oh! Look at Me Now	1951	3.00	6.00	12.00
27759	My Love/Flower of Dawn	1951	3.00	6.00	12.00
27843	Solitaire/With All My Heart and Soul	1951	3.00	6.00	12.00
27973	May I/One Morning in May	1952	3.00	6.00	12.00
28035	There Are Such Things/What Is Time	1952	3.00	6.00	12.00
28057	Hambone/Come What May	1952	3.00	6.00	12.00
28064	Trouble in Mind/The Dirty Dozens	1952	3.00	6.00	12.00
28077	Keel Row/Love, Where Are You Now	1952	3.00	6.00	12.00
28152	Homing Pigeon/I Got Big Eyes	1952	3.00	6.00	12.00
28257	Your Daddy's Got the Gleeks/Deep in the Blue	1952	3.00	6.00	12.00
28328	They Didn't Believe Me/Nobody Knows the Trouble I've Seen	1952	3.00	6.00	12.00
28366	This Is the Beginning of the End/You Could Make Me Smile Again	1952	3.00	6.00	12.00
28425	Sentimental Serenade/I'm Going Home	1952	3.00	6.00	12.00
28451	This Love of Mine/Yours Is My Heart Alone	1952	3.00	6.00	12.00
28684	Sentimental Me and Romantic You/I'm Getting Sentimental Over You	1953	3.00	6.00	12.00
28766	The Most Beautiful Girl in the World/One Kiss	1953	3.00	6.00	12.00
28978	Island Queen/You're the Cause of It All	1953	3.00	6.00	12.00
29057	Liza Jane/Blue Moon	1954	2.50	5.00	10.00
RCA VICTOR					
47-2874	Royal Garden Blues/After You've Gone	1949	3.75	7.50	15.00
47-2875	Opus No. 1/On the Sunny Side of the Street	1949	3.75	7.50	15.00
47-2876	Marie/Song of India	1949	3.75	7.50	15.00
—The above three comprise a box set					
47-2900	Enjoy Yourself (It's Later Than You Think)/She's a Home Girl	1949	5.00	10.00	20.00
47-2917	The Continental/Ain'tcha Glad I Love Youq	1949	5.00	10.00	20.00
47-2958	Dream of You/Pussy Willow	1949	5.00	10.00	20.00
47-3002	Summertime/Dry Bones	1949	5.00	10.00	20.00
47-3028	The Huckle-Buck/Again	1949	5.00	10.00	20.00
47-3037	The Knock Song/Twilight	1949	5.00	10.00	20.00
47-3087	Shake That Tree/Hollywood Hat	1949	5.00	10.00	20.00
47-3132	Puddle Wump/Nice to Know You Care	1949	5.00	10.00	20.00
47-3159	Love for Sale/Just One of Those Things	1949	3.75	7.50	15.00
47-3160	You Do Something to Me/Why Shouldn't I	1949	3.75	7.50	15.00
47-3161	It's Delovely/I Get a Kick Out of You	1949	3.75	7.50	15.00
—The above three comprise a box set					
47-3210	When/Just for Old Times	1949	5.00	10.00	20.00
47-3712	I Oughta Know More About You/C'est Si Bon	1950	3.75	7.50	15.00
47-3715	Washboard Blues/Panama	1950	3.75	7.50	15.00
47-3716	Davenport Blues/Down Home Rag	1950	3.75	7.50	15.00
47-3717	Milenberg Joys (Part 1)/Milenberg Joys (Part 2)	1950	3.75	7.50	15.00
—The above three comprise a box set					
47-3791	Tiger Rag/Way Down Yonder in New Orleans	1950	3.75	7.50	15.00
47-3840	Happy Feet/Birmingham Bounce	1950	3.75	7.50	15.00
47-3869	I've Forgotten You/No Other Love	1950	3.75	7.50	15.00
47-3910	It All Begins and Ends with You/Lullaby in Boogie	1950	3.75	7.50	15.00
47-3932	Nevada/Weary Blues	1950	3.75	7.50	15.00
447-0116	I'll Never Smile Again/I'll Be Seeing You	195?	2.50	5.00	10.00
—Black label, dog on top					
447-0117	Mississippi Mud/I'm Getting Sentimental Over You	195?	2.50	5.00	10.00
—Black label, dog on top					
447-0118	Marie/Song of India	195?	2.50	5.00	10.00
—Black label, dog on top					
447-0119	Opus #1/Boogie Woogie	195?	2.50	5.00	10.00
—Black label, dog on top					
447-0120	We'll Get It/Summertime	195?	2.50	5.00	10.00
—Black label, dog on top					
447-0121	On the Sunny Side of the Street/Who?	195?	2.50	5.00	10.00
—Black label, dog on top					
447-0122	The Huckle-Buck/Dry Bones	195?	2.50	5.00	10.00
—Black label, dog on top					
447-0123	There Are Such Things/Star Dust	195?	2.50	5.00	10.00
—Black label, dog on top					
447-0124	Chicago/Hawaiian War Chant	195?	2.50	5.00	10.00
—Black label, dog on top					
447-0445	Street of Dreams/East of the Sun	195?	2.50	5.00	10.00
—Black label, dog on top					

7-Inch Extended Plays

Number	Title (A Side/B Side)	Yr	VG	VG+	NM
DECCA					
ED 2016	*Diane/Opus Two/Marcheta/T.D.'s Boogie Woogie	195?	2.50	5.00	10.00
ED 2016 [PS]	Tommy Dorsey, Vol. 1	195?	2.50	5.00	10.00

Albums

Number	Title (A Side/B Side)	Yr	VG	VG+	NM
20TH CENTURY FOX					
TCF 101/102 [(2) M]	Tommy Dorsey's Greatest Band	1959	7.50	15.00	30.00
TFM-3157 [M]	This Is Tommy Dorsey and His Greatest Band, Vol. 1	196?	5.00	10.00	20.00
TFM-3158 [M]	This Is Tommy Dorsey and His Greatest Band, Vol. 2	196?	5.00	10.00	20.00
TFS-4157 [R]	This Is Tommy Dorsey and His Greatest Band, Vol. 1	196?	3.00	6.00	12.00
TFS-4158 [R]	This Is Tommy Dorsey and His Greatest Band, Vol. 2	196?	3.00	6.00	12.00
BLUEBIRD					
AXM2-5521 [(2)]	The Complete Tommy Dorsey, Volume 1	197?	3.75	7.50	15.00
AXM2-5549 [(2)]	The Complete Tommy Dorsey, Volume 2	197?	3.75	7.50	15.00
AXM2-5560 [(2)]	The Complete Tommy Dorsey, Volume 3	197?	3.75	7.50	15.00
AXM2-5564 [(2)]	The Complete Tommy Dorsey, Volume 4	197?	3.75	7.50	15.00
AXM2-5573 [(2)]	The Complete Tommy Dorsey, Volume 5	197?	3.75	7.50	15.00
AXM2-5578 [(2)]	The Complete Tommy Dorsey, Volume 6	197?	3.75	7.50	15.00
AXM2-5582 [(2)]	The Complete Tommy Dorsey, Volume 7	197?	3.75	7.50	15.00
AXM2-5586 [(2)]	The Complete Tommy Dorsey, Volume 8	197?	3.75	7.50	15.00
9987-1-RB	Yes, Indeed!	1990	3.75	7.50	15.00
DECCA					
DL 5317 [10]	Tommy Dorsey Plays Howard Dietz	1951	12.50	25.00	50.00
DL 5448 [10]	In a Sentimental Mood	1952	12.50	25.00	50.00
DL 5449 [10]	Tenderly	1952	12.50	25.00	50.00
DL 5452 [10]	Your Invitation to Dance	1952	12.50	25.00	50.00
HARMONY					
HL 7324 [M]	On the Sentimental Side	196?	3.75	7.50	15.00
KH 32014	The Beat of the Big Bands	1972	2.50	5.00	10.00
MCA					
732	Sentimental	198?	2.00	4.00	8.00
4074 [(2)]	The Best of Tommy Dorsey	197?	3.00	6.00	12.00
MOVIETONE					
MTM-1004 [M]	Tommy Dorsey's Hullaballoo	196?	3.75	7.50	15.00
MTM-1019 [M]	The Tommy Dorsey Years	1967	3.75	7.50	15.00
MTS-72004 [R]	Tommy Dorsey's Hullaballoo	196?	3.00	6.00	12.00
MTS-72019 [R]	The Tommy Dorsey Years	1967	3.00	6.00	12.00
PICKWICK					
PTP-2035 [(2)]	I'm Getting Sentimental*	197?	3.00	6.00	12.00
RCA CAMDEN					
ADL2-0178 [(2)]	I'll See You in My Dreams*	1973	3.75	7.50	15.00
CAL-650 [M]	The One and Only Tommy Dorsey*	1961	3.75	7.50	15.00
CAS-650(e) [R]	The One and Only Tommy Dorsey*	196?	2.50	5.00	10.00
CAL-800 [M]	Dedicated to You*	1964	3.75	7.50	15.00
CAS-800(e) [R]	Dedicated to You*	1964	2.50	5.00	10.00
CXS-9027 [(2)]	I'm Getting Sentimental*	1972	3.75	7.50	15.00
RCA VICTOR					
LPT-10 [M]	Getting Sentimental with Tommy Dorsey*	1951	20.00	40.00	80.00
ALPT-15 [M]	All Time Hits*	1951	20.00	40.00	80.00
LPM-22 [10]	Tommy Dorsey Plays Cole Porter for Dancing	1951	12.50	25.00	50.00
ANL1-1087	The Best of Tommy Dorsey	1976	2.50	5.00	10.00
LPM-1229 [M]	Yes Indeed*	1956	12.50	25.00	50.00
LPM-1425 [M]	Tommy Dorsey Plays Cole Porter and Jerome Kern	1956	6.25	12.50	25.00
LPM-1432 [M]	Tribute to Dorsey, Volume 1*	1956	10.00	20.00	40.00
LPM-1433 [M]	Tribute to Dorsey, Volume 2*	1956	10.00	20.00	40.00
ANL1-1586	Pure Gold*	1976	2.50	5.00	10.00
LPM-1643 [M]	Having a Wonderful Time*	1958	10.00	20.00	40.00
ANL1-2162(e)	On the Sunny Side of the Street	1977	2.50	5.00	10.00
LPT-3005 [M]	This Is Tommy Dorsey*	1952	20.00	40.00	80.00
LPT-3018 [10]	This Is Tommy Dorsey	1952	12.50	25.00	50.00
LPM-3674 [M]	The Best of Tommy Dorsey*	1966	5.00	10.00	20.00
LSP-3674 [R]	The Best of Tommy Dorsey*	1966	3.00	6.00	12.00
LPM-6003 [(2) M]	That Sentimental Gentleman*	1957	20.00	40.00	80.00
—Box set					
VPM-6038 [(2)]	This Is Tommy Dorsey*	197?	6.25	12.50	25.00
VPM-6064 [(2)]	This Is Tommy Dorsey, Volume 2*	197?	6.25	12.50	25.00
VPM-6087 [(2)]	Tommy Dorsey with the Clambake Seven	197?	5.00	10.00	20.00
SUNBEAM					
201	Tommy Dorsey and His Orchestra 1935-39	197?	2.50	5.00	10.00
220	Tommy Dorsey and His Orchestra 1944-46	197?	2.50	5.00	10.00
TIME-LIFE					
STBB-02 [(2)]	Tommy Dorsey*	1983	5.00	10.00	20.00
VOCALION					
VL 3613 [M]	Dance Party	196?	3.75	7.50	15.00
VL 73613 [R]	Dance Party	196?	2.50	5.00	10.00

DOTS, THE

45s

CADDY

Number	Title (A Side/B Side)	Yr	VG	VG+	NM
101	I Confess/I Wish I Could Meet You	1956	20.00	40.00	80.00
107	I Lost You/Johnny	1957	20.00	40.00	80.00
111	Good Luck to You/Heartsick and Lonely	1957	20.00	40.00	80.00

REV

Number	Title (A Side/B Side)	Yr	VG	VG+	NM
3512	Ring Chimes/Wolf Call	1958	375.00	750.00	1500.

DOUBLE SIX OF PARIS, THE

45s

CAPITOL

Number	Title (A Side/B Side)	Yr	VG	VG+	NM
4394	French Rat Race/Meet Benny Bailey	1960	3.75	7.50	15.00

PHILIPS

Number	Title (A Side/B Side)	Yr	VG	VG+	NM
40192	One Mint Julep/Hallelujah I Love Her So	1964	6.25	12.50	25.00
40220	Lonely Avenue/Sherri	1964	6.25	12.50	25.00

Albums

CAPITOL

Number	Title (A Side/B Side)	Yr	VG	VG+	NM
ST 10259 [S]	The Double Six of Paris	1961	6.25	12.50	25.00
T 10259 [M]	The Double Six of Paris	1961	5.00	10.00	20.00

PHILIPS

Number	Title (A Side/B Side)	Yr	VG	VG+	NM
PHM 200026 [M]	Swingin' Singin'	1962	5.00	10.00	20.00
PHM 200141 [M]	The Double Six of Paris Sings Ray Charles	1964	5.00	10.00	20.00
PHS 600026 [S]	Swingin' Singin'	1962	6.25	12.50	25.00
PHS 600141 [S]	The Double Six of Paris Sings Ray Charles	1964	6.25	12.50	25.00

DOUGLAS, CARL

45s

20TH CENTURY

Number	Title (A Side/B Side)	Yr	VG	VG+	NM
2140	Kung Fu Fighting/Gamblin' Man	1974	—	2.00	4.00
2168	Dance the Kung Fu/Changing Times	1975	—	2.00	4.00
2179	Blue Eyed Soul (Part 1)/Blue Eyed Soul (Part 2)	1975	—	2.00	4.00
2192	Witchfinder General/Never Had This Dream Before	1975	—	2.00	4.00

OKEH

Number	Title (A Side/B Side)	Yr	VG	VG+	NM
7268	Crazy Feeling/Keep It to Myself	1966	3.00	6.00	12.00
7287	Let the Birds Sing/Something for Nothing	1967	3.00	6.00	12.00

Albums

20TH CENTURY

Number	Title (A Side/B Side)	Yr	VG	VG+	NM
T-464	Kung Fu Fighting and Other Great Love Songs	1974	3.00	6.00	12.00

DOUGLAS, CAROL

12-Inch Singles

MIDSONG INT'L.

Number	Title (A Side/B Side)	Yr	VG	VG+	NM
L33-1975 [DJ]	Night Fever (6:20) (same on both sides)	1978	2.50	5.00	10.00
13905	Night Fever/Let You Come Into My Life	1978	3.00	6.00	12.00

45s

20TH CENTURY

Number	Title (A Side/B Side)	Yr	VG	VG+	NM
2484	Slip Into Something Comfortable/My Simple Heart	1981	—	—	3.00

MIDLAND INT'L.

Number	Title (A Side/B Side)	Yr	VG	VG+	NM
MB-10113	Doctor's Orders/Baby, Don't Let This Good Love Die	1974	—	2.00	4.00
MB-10229	Hurricane Is Coming Tonight/I Fell in Love with You	1975	—	2.00	4.00
MB-10304	Will We Make It Tonight/Take Me (Make Me Lose Control)	1975	—	2.00	4.00
MB-10372	Headline News/Boy, YouKnow Just What I'm After	1975	—	2.00	4.00
MB-10753	Midnight Love Affair/Midnight Love Affair (Long Version)	1976	—	2.00	4.00
MB-10870	Dancing Queen/In the Morning	1976	—	2.00	4.00
MB-10979	We Do It/Lie to Me	1977	—	2.00	4.00

MIDSONG INT'L.

Number	Title (A Side/B Side)	Yr	VG	VG+	NM
1008	I Got the Answer/We're Gonna Make It	1979	—	2.00	4.00
40860	Night Fever/Let You Come Into My Life	1978	—	2.00	4.00
—A-side appeared in the movie Saturday Night Fever, but not on the soundtrack LP					
40912	So You Win Again/Let You Come Into My Life	1978	—	2.00	4.00
40945	Let's Get Down to Doin' It Tonight/Burnin'	1978	—	2.00	4.00

RCA VICTOR

Number	Title (A Side/B Side)	Yr	VG	VG+	NM
GB-10479	Doctor's Orders/Baby, Don't Let This Good Love Die	1975	—	—	3.00
—Gold Standard Series					

Albums

MIDLAND INT'L.

Number	Title (A Side/B Side)	Yr	VG	VG+	NM
BKL1-0931	The Carol Douglas Album	1975	2.50	5.00	10.00
BKL1-1798	Midnight Love Affair	1976	2.50	5.00	10.00
BKL1-2222	Full Bloom	1977	2.50	5.00	10.00

MIDSONG INT'L.

Number	Title (A Side/B Side)	Yr	VG	VG+	NM
3048	Burnin'	1978	2.50	5.00	10.00
W 36852	The Best of Carol Douglas	1980	2.50	5.00	10.00

DOUGLAS, CRAIG

45s

BETHLEHEM

Number	Title (A Side/B Side)	Yr	VG	VG+	NM
3057	When My Little Girl Is Smiling/Ring-a-Ding	1963	3.00	6.00	12.00

EMBASSY

Number	Title (A Side/B Side)	Yr	VG	VG+	NM
202	No Greater Love/We'll Have a Lot to Tell	1962	3.00	6.00	12.00

JARO

Number	Title (A Side/B Side)	Yr	VG	VG+	NM
77016	My First Love Affair/What Do You Want	1960	3.00	6.00	12.00
77030	Heart of a Teenage Girl/New Boy	1960	3.00	6.00	12.00

LONDON

Number	Title (A Side/B Side)	Yr	VG	VG+	NM
9611	Danke Schoen/Love Her While She's Young	1963	3.00	6.00	12.00

TCF HALL

Number	Title (A Side/B Side)	Yr	VG	VG+	NM
107	Around the Corner/Find the Girl	1965	2.50	5.00	10.00

DOUGLAS, KELLIE

45s

RCA VICTOR

Number	Title (A Side/B Side)	Yr	VG	VG+	NM
47-8005	My Mama Don't Like Him/Big Hunky Baby	1962	3.00	6.00	12.00

DOUGLAS, KIRK

45s

DECCA

Number	Title (A Side/B Side)	Yr	VG	VG+	NM
29355	A Whale of a Tale/The Moon Grew Brighter and Brighter	1954	6.25	12.50	25.00

DOUGLAS, LEW

45s

CARLTON

Number	Title (A Side/B Side)	Yr	VG	VG+	NM
533	Theme from "The Angel Wore Red"/"From the Terrace" Love Theme	1960	2.50	5.00	10.00

Albums

CARLTON

Number	Title (A Side/B Side)	Yr	VG	VG+	NM
LP 12-126 [M]	Themes from Motion Pictures and TV	1960	6.25	12.50	25.00

DOUGLAS, MIKE

45s

ATLANTIC

Number	Title (A Side/B Side)	Yr	VG	VG+	NM
3328	Philadelphia/Smile, Smile, Smile	1976	—	2.00	4.00
3344	Loneliness/Dancin' Again	1976	—	2.00	4.00

BLUE RIVER

Number	Title (A Side/B Side)	Yr	VG	VG+	NM
220	Tonight/High on a Hill	196?	2.00	4.00	8.00

DECCA

Number	Title (A Side/B Side)	Yr	VG	VG+	NM
32495	The Day After Forever/Someday You'll Be Sorry	1969	—	2.50	5.00
32567	Jean/Rainbow of Love	1969	—	2.50	5.00
32618	That's a Woman/Tell Me Why, Why Don't You Cry	1970	—	2.50	5.00

EPIC

Number	Title (A Side/B Side)	Yr	VG	VG+	NM
9876	The Men in My Little Girl's Life/Stranger on the Shore	1965	—	3.00	6.00
10002	Here's to My Jenny/While We're Young	1966	—	3.00	6.00
10041	Parents of the Kids in Love/Real Love	1966	—	3.00	6.00
10078	Cabaret/House of Love	1966	—	3.00	6.00
10089	Touch Hands on Christmas Morning/(The Story Of) The First Christmas Carol	1966	3.00	6.00	12.00
10126	What Is a Square/That's How Love Goes	1967	—	3.00	6.00
10132	Galway/A Little Town in Old County Down	1967	—	3.00	6.00
10170	Here Comes My Baby Back Again/Someone Took the Sweetness Out of Sweetheart	1967	—	3.00	6.00
10223	Father of the Bride/Hold Me	1967	—	3.00	6.00
JZSP 135100/1 [DJ]	Silver Bells (mono/stereo)	1967	2.50	5.00	10.00

MGM

Number	Title (A Side/B Side)	Yr	VG	VG+	NM
14337	For a Little While/Heaven Everyday	1971	—	2.00	4.00
14453	Ole Buttermilk Sky/Wonderful World	1972	—	2.00	4.00
14508	High Hopes/Song for Erik	1973	—	2.00	4.00

PROJECT 3

Number	Title (A Side/B Side)	Yr	VG	VG+	NM
1335	Do Unto Others/Young at Heart	1968	—	3.00	6.00
—With Pearl Bailey					

STAX

Number	Title (A Side/B Side)	Yr	VG	VG+	NM
0211	Birthday Song/Mother's Day	1974	—	2.00	4.00

Albums

ATLANTIC

Number	Title (A Side/B Side)	Yr	VG	VG+	NM
SD 18168	Mike Douglas Sings It All	1976	2.50	5.00	10.00

EPIC

Number	Title (A Side/B Side)	Yr	VG	VG+	NM
LN 24169 [M]	It's Time for Mike Douglas	1965	3.00	6.00	12.00
LN 24179 [M]	You Don't Have to Be Irish	1965	3.00	6.00	12.00
LN 24186 [M]	The Men in My Little Girl's Life	1966	3.00	6.00	12.00
LN 24205 [M]	Dear Mike, Please Sing	1966	3.00	6.00	12.00
LN 24322 [M]	My Kind of Christmas	1967	3.00	6.00	12.00
BN 26169 [S]	It's Time for Mike Douglas	1965	3.75	7.50	15.00
BN 26179 [S]	You Don't Have to Be Irish	1965	3.75	7.50	15.00
BN 26186 [S]	The Men in My Little Girl's Life	1966	3.75	7.50	15.00
BN 26205 [S]	Dear Mike, Please Sing	1966	3.75	7.50	15.00
BN 26322 [S]	My Kind of Christmas	1967	3.00	6.00	12.00

HARMONY

Number	Title (A Side/B Side)	Yr	VG	VG+	NM
HS 11263	Young at Heart	1968	3.00	6.00	12.00

WORD

Number	Title (A Side/B Side)	Yr	VG	VG+	NM
WR-8791	I'll Sing This Song for You	197?	2.50	5.00	10.00
8815	Christmas Album	198?	2.50	5.00	10.00

DOUGLAS, SCOTT, AND THE VENTURE QUINTET

See THE VENTURES.

DOUGLAS, STEVE

45s

CAPITOL

Number	Title (A Side/B Side)	Yr	VG	VG+	NM
5527	Yesterday (Part 1)/Yesterday (Part 2)	1965	3.00	6.00	12.00

GRAPEVINE

Number	Title (A Side/B Side)	Yr	VG	VG+	NM
601	Rockin' Green Sleeves/(B-side unknown)	1961	5.00	10.00	20.00

MGM

Number	Title (A Side/B Side)	Yr	VG	VG+	NM
13218	Snowplows Schussing (Part 1)/Snowplows Schussing (Part 2)	1964	3.00	6.00	12.00

PHILLES

Number	Title (A Side/B Side)	Yr	VG	VG+	NM
104	Yes Sir, That's My Baby/Lt. Col. Bogey's Parade	1962	6.25	12.50	25.00

TANDEM

Number	Title (A Side/B Side)	Yr	VG	VG+	NM
7000	Magic Sound/There You Go	1961	5.00	10.00	20.00

TEXAS OPRY

Number	Title (A Side/B Side)	Yr	VG	VG+	NM
588	Tyke (The Christmas Elf)/(Instrumental)	19??	—	2.00	4.00
—May not be the same artist as the others.					

Albums

CROWN

Number	Title (A Side/B Side)	Yr	VG	VG+	NM
CLP-5251 [M]	Twist with Steve Douglas and the Rebel Rousers	1962	5.00	10.00	20.00

MERCURY

Number	Title (A Side/B Side)	Yr	VG	VG+	NM
SR-61217	Reflections in a Golden Horn	1969	6.25	12.50	25.00

DOUGLAS, WAYNE
See DOUG SAHM.

DOVAL, JIM, AND THE GAUCHOS
45s

Number	Title (A Side/B Side)	Yr	VG	VG+	NM
ABC-PARAMOUNT					
10621	Annie Ya Ya/Out of Sight	1965	2.50	5.00	10.00
10637	I Know You're Fooling Around/Uptown Caballero	1965	2.50	5.00	10.00
DIPLOMACY					
3	Donna/The Scrub	1964	5.00	10.00	20.00
5	Stranded in the Pool/Right Now	1964	5.00	10.00	20.00
6	Beatles Rule/Pink Elephant	1964	6.25	12.50	25.00
7	She's a Very Nice Girl/Bony Moronie	1964	25.00	50.00	100.00
8	The Good and the Bad/Fireballed	1965	5.00	10.00	20.00
17	She's So Fine/Mama, Keep Your Big Mouth Shut	1965	5.00	10.00	20.00
1000	Love Me One More Time (Part 1)/Love Me One More Time (Part 2)	1963	5.00	10.00	20.00
—As "Jim SanDoval and the Gauchos"					
DOT					
16468	Fire Ball/Good and Bad	1963	3.75	7.50	15.00
16548	Love Me One More Time (Part 1)/Love Me One More Time (Part 2)	1963	3.75	7.50	15.00
16571	Barracuda/The Scrub	1964	3.75	7.50	15.00

Albums

Number	Title (A Side/B Side)	Yr	VG	VG+	NM
ABC-PARAMOUNT					
ABC-506 [M]	The Gauchos Featuring Jim Doval	1965	7.50	15.00	30.00
ABCS-506 [S]	The Gauchos Featuring Jim Doval	1965	10.00	20.00	40.00

DOVE, RONNIE
45s

Number	Title (A Side/B Side)	Yr	VG	VG+	NM
DECCA					
31288	Yes Darling, I'll Be Around/Party Doll	1961	5.00	10.00	20.00
32853	Just the Other Side of Nowhere/If I Cried	1971	—	3.00	6.00
32919	Kiss the Hurt Away/He Cries Like a Baby	1972	—	3.00	6.00
32997	It's No Sin/My World of Memories	1972	—	3.00	6.00
33038	Lilacs in Winter/Is It Wrong	1972	—	3.00	6.00
DIAMOND					
163	Sweeter Than Sugar/I Believe in You	1964	2.50	5.00	10.00
167	Say You/Let Me Stay Today	1964	2.50	5.00	10.00
173	Right or Wrong/Baby Put Your Arms Around Me	1964	2.00	4.00	8.00
176	Hello Pretty Girl/Keep It a Secret	1965	2.00	4.00	8.00
179	One Kiss for Old Times' Sake/No Greater Love	1965	2.00	4.00	8.00
179	One Kiss for Old Times' Sake/Bluebird	1965	2.00	4.00	8.00
184	A Little Bit of Heaven/If I Live to Be a Hundred	1965	2.00	4.00	8.00
188	I'll Make All Your Dreams Come True/I Had to Lose You	1965	2.00	4.00	8.00
191	Kiss Away/Where in the World	1965	2.00	4.00	8.00
195	When Liking Turns to Loving/I'm Learning How to Smile Again	1965	2.00	4.00	8.00
198	Let's Start All Over Again/That Empty Feeling	1966	2.00	4.00	8.00
205	Happy Summer Days/Long After	1966	2.00	4.00	8.00
205 [PS]	Happy Summer Days/Long After	1966	3.75	7.50	15.00
208	I Really Don't Want to Know/Years of Tears	1966	2.00	4.00	8.00
214	Cry/Autumn Rhapsody	1966	2.00	4.00	8.00
217	One More Mountain to Climb/All	1967	2.00	4.00	8.00
221	My Babe/Put My Mind at Ease	1967	2.50	5.00	10.00
—A-side written and produced by Neil Diamond					
227	I Want to Love You for What You Are/I Thank You for Your Love	1967	2.00	4.00	8.00
233	Dancin' Out of My Heart/Back from Baltimore	1967	5.00	10.00	20.00
—B-side written and produced by Neil Diamond, who also supplies backing vocals					
240	In Some Time/Livin' for Your Lovin'	1968	2.00	4.00	8.00
244	Mountain of Love/Never Gonna Cry	1968	2.00	4.00	8.00
249	Tomboy/Tell Me Tomorrow	1968	2.00	4.00	8.00
256	What's Wrong with My World/That Empty Feeling	1969	—	3.00	6.00
260	I Need You Now/Bluebird	1969	—	3.00	6.00
271	Chains of Love/If I Live to Be a Hundred	1970	—	3.00	6.00
378	Heart/(B-side unknown)	1987	—	2.50	5.00
378 [PS]	Heart/(B-side unknown)	1987	—	2.50	5.00
379	Rise and Shine/(B-side unknown)	1987	—	2.50	5.00
DOVE					
1021	Lover Boy/(B-side unknown)	1955	250.00	500.00	1000.
HITSVILLE					
6038	Tragedy/Songs We Sang As Children	1976	—	2.50	5.00
6045	The Morning After the Night Before/Why Daddy	1976	—	2.50	5.00
JALO					
1406	No Greater Love/Saddest Hour	1962	6.25	12.50	25.00
MCA					
40106	So Long Dixie/Take My Love	1973	—	2.50	5.00
MELODYLAND					
6004	Please Come to Nashville/Pictures on Paper	1975	—	2.50	5.00
6011	Things/Here We Go Again	1975	—	2.50	5.00
6021	Drina (Take Your Lady Off for Me)/Your Sweet Love	1975	—	2.50	5.00
6030	Right or Wrong/Guns	1976	—	2.50	5.00
M.C.					
5013	The Angel in Your Eyes (Brings Out the Devil in Me)/Songs We Sang As Children	1978	—	3.00	6.00

Albums

Number	Title (A Side/B Side)	Yr	VG	VG+	NM
DIAMOND					
D 5002 [M]	Right Or Wrong	1964	5.00	10.00	20.00
DS 5002 [S]	Right Or Wrong	1964	6.25	12.50	25.00
D 5003 [M]	One Kiss for Old Times' Sake	1965	5.00	10.00	20.00
DS 5003 [S]	One Kiss for Old Times' Sake	1965	6.25	12.50	25.00
D 5004 [M]	I'll Make All Your Dreams Come True	1965	5.00	10.00	20.00
DS 5004 [S]	I'll Make All Your Dreams Come True	1965	6.25	12.50	25.00
D 5005 [M]	The Best of Ronnie Dove	1966	3.75	7.50	15.00
DS 5005 [S]	The Best of Ronnie Dove	1966	5.00	10.00	20.00
D 5006 [M]	Ronnie Dove Sings the Hits for You	1966	3.75	7.50	15.00
DS 5006 [S]	Ronnie Dove Sings the Hits for You	1966	5.00	10.00	20.00
D 5007 [M]	Cry	1967	3.75	7.50	15.00
DS 5007 [S]	Cry	1967	5.00	10.00	20.00
D-5008 [M]	Ronne Dove's Greatest Hits, Vol. 2	1968	7.50	15.00	30.00
DS-5008 [S]	Ronne Dove's Greatest Hits, Vol. 2	1968	3.75	7.50	15.00
POWER PAK					
286	Greatest Hits	1975	3.00	6.00	12.00

DOVELLS, THE
Also see LEN BARRY.

45s

Number	Title (A Side/B Side)	Yr	VG	VG+	NM
ABKCO					
4011	Bristol Stomp/You Can't Sit Down	1972	—	2.00	4.00
4029	Baby Workout/Hully Gully Baby	1973	2.50	5.00	10.00
4032	Bristol Twistin' Annie/Betty in Bermudas	1973	—	2.00	4.00
EVENT					
216	Dancing in the Street/Back on the Road Again	1974	—	2.50	5.00
3310	Roll Over Beethoven/Something About You Boy	1970	—	2.50	5.00
JAMIE					
1369	Our Winter Love/Blue	1969	2.50	5.00	10.00
MGM					
13628	There's a Girl/Love Is Everywhere	1966	2.50	5.00	10.00
14568	Don't Vote for Luke McCabe/Mary's Magic Show	1973	—	2.50	5.00
PARAMOUNT					
0134	L-O-V-E Love/We're All In This Together	1971	—	2.50	5.00
PARKWAY					
819	No, No, No/Letters of Love	1961	5.00	10.00	20.00
827	Bristol Stomp/Out in the Cold Again	1961	7.50	15.00	30.00
827	Bristol Stomp/Letters of Love	1961	3.75	7.50	15.00
833	Do the New Continental/Mope-Itty Mope Stomp	1962	3.75	7.50	15.00
833 [PS]	Do the New Continental/Mope-Itty Mope Stomp	1962	7.50	15.00	30.00
838	Bristol Twistin' Annie/The Actor	1962	3.75	7.50	15.00
838 [PS]	Bristol Twistin' Annie/The Actor	1962	7.50	15.00	30.00
845	Hully Gully Baby/Your Last Chance	1962	3.75	7.50	15.00
845 [PS]	Hully Gully Baby/Your Last Chance	1962	7.50	15.00	30.00
855	The Jitterbug/Kissin' in the Kitchen	1962	3.75	7.50	15.00
855 [PS]	The Jitterbug/Kissin' in the Kitchen	1962	7.50	15.00	30.00
861	Save Me Baby/You Can't Run Away from Yourself	1963	5.00	10.00	20.00
861 [PS]	Save Me Baby/You Can't Run Away from Yourself	1963	7.50	15.00	30.00
867	You Can't Sit Down/Stompin' Everywhere	1963	3.00	6.00	12.00
867	You Can't Sit Down/Wildwood Days	1963	3.75	7.50	15.00
867 [PS]	You Can't Sit Down/Stompin' Everywhere	1963	10.00	20.00	40.00
867 [PS]	You Can't Sit Down/Wildwood Days	1963	10.00	20.00	40.00
882	Betty in Bermudas/Dance the Froog	1963	3.00	6.00	12.00
882 [PS]	Betty in Bermudas/Dance the Froog	1963	7.50	15.00	30.00
889	Stop Monkeyin' Aroun'/No, No, No	1963	3.00	6.00	12.00
889 [PS]	Stop Monkeyin' Aroun'/No, No, No	1963	7.50	15.00	30.00
901	Be My Girl/Dragster on the Prowl	1964	5.00	10.00	20.00
911	One Potato/Happy Birthday Just the Same	1964	3.75	7.50	15.00
925	Watusi with Lucy/What in the World's Come Over You	1964	3.00	6.00	12.00
925 [PS]	Watusi with Lucy/What in the World's Come Over You	1964	7.50	15.00	30.00
SWAN					
4231	Happy/(Hey, Hey, Hey) Alright	1965	5.00	10.00	20.00
VERVE					
10701	Far Away/Sometimes	1973	—	2.50	5.00

Albums

Number	Title (A Side/B Side)	Yr	VG	VG+	NM
CAMEO					
C-1082 [M]	Len Barry Sings with the Dovells	1965	7.50	15.00	30.00
SC-1082 [S]	Len Barry Sings with the Dovells	1965	12.50	25.00	50.00
PARKWAY					
P 7006 [M]	The Bristol Stomp	1961	20.00	40.00	80.00
—Light orange label					
P 7006 [M]	The Bristol Stomp	1962	12.50	25.00	50.00
—Dark orange and yellow label					
P 7010 [M]	All the Hits of the Teen Groups	1962	12.50	25.00	50.00
P 7021 [M]	For Your Hully Gully Party	1962	12.50	25.00	50.00
P 7025 [M]	You Can't Sit Down	1963	12.50	25.00	50.00
WYNCOTE					
SW 9052 [R]	Discotheque	1965	3.75	7.50	15.00
W 9052 [M]	Discotheque	1965	5.00	10.00	20.00
SW 9114 [R]	The Dovells' Biggest Hits	1965	3.75	7.50	15.00
W 9114 [M]	The Dovells' Biggest Hits	1965	5.00	10.00	20.00

DOWD, LARRY
45s

Number	Title (A Side/B Side)	Yr	VG	VG+	NM
SPINNING					
6004	Why, Oh Why/Forbidden Love	1958	6.25	12.50	25.00
6009	Blue Swinging Mama/Pink Cadillac	1959	37.50	75.00	150.00

DOWELL, JOE
45s

Number	Title (A Side/B Side)	Yr	VG	VG+	NM
JOURNEY					
1238 [DJ]	Homeward on the Wind (mono/stereo)	1973	—	3.00	6.00
—Stock copy not known to exist					
1238 [PS]	Homeward on the Wind (mono/stereo)	1973	—	3.00	6.00
MONUMENT					
952	If I Could Find Out What Is Wrong/Indian Summer Days	1966	2.00	4.00	8.00
SMASH					
1708	Wooden Heart/Little Bo Peep	1961	3.75	7.50	15.00
1708 [PS]	Wooden Heart/Little Bo Peep	1961	6.25	12.50	25.00
1717	The Bridge of Love/Just Love Me	1961	3.00	6.00	12.00
1717 [PS]	The Bridge of Love/Just Love Me	1961	4.00	8.00	16.00
1728	(I Wonder) Who's Spending Christmas with You/A Kiss for Christmas	1961	3.75	7.50	15.00
1730	The Sound of Sadness/The Thorn on the Rose	1962	3.00	6.00	12.00
1759	Little Red Rented Rowboat/The One I Left for You	1962	3.00	6.00	12.00
1759 [PS]	Little Red Rented Rowboat/The One I Left for You	1962	3.00	6.00	12.00
1786	Poor Little Cupid/No Secrets	1962	3.00	6.00	12.00
1786 [PS]	Poor Little Cupid/No Secrets	1962	4.00	8.00	16.00
1799	Our School Days/Bringa-Branga-Brought	1963	3.00	6.00	12.00
1799 [PS]	Our School Days/Bringa-Branga-Brought	1963	4.00	8.00	16.00

Number	Title (A Side/B Side)	Yr	VG	VG+	NM
1816	Bobby Blue Loves Linda Lou/My Darling Wears White Today	1963	3.00	6.00	12.00
1816 [PS]	Bobby Blue Loves Linda Lou/My Darling Wears White Today	1963	4.00	8.00	16.00
Albums					
SMASH					
MGS-27000 [M]	Wooden Heart	1961	10.00	20.00	40.00
MGS-27011 [M]	German American Hits	1962	6.25	12.50	25.00
SRS-67000 [S]	Wooden Heart	1961	12.50	25.00	50.00
SRS-67011 [S]	German American Hits	1962	7.50	15.00	30.00
WING					
MGW-12328 [M]	Wooden Heart	196?	5.00	10.00	20.00
SRW-16328 [S]	Wooden Heart	196?	5.00	10.00	20.00

DOWLANDS, THE

Number	Title (A Side/B Side)	Yr	VG	VG+	NM
45s					
TOLLIE					
9002	All My Loving/Hey Sally	1964	3.75	7.50	15.00

DOWNBEATS, THE (1)

Number	Title (A Side/B Side)	Yr	VG	VG+	NM
45s					
GEE					
1019	My Girl/China Girl	1956	200.00	400.00	800.00
—Red label					
1019	My Girl/China Girl	1958	7.50	15.00	30.00
—Gray label					
PEACOCK					
1689	You're So Fine/Someday She'll Come Along	1958	6.25	12.50	25.00

DOWNBEATS, THE (2)

Number	Title (A Side/B Side)	Yr	VG	VG+	NM
45s					
SARG					
168	Darling of Mine/Come On Over	1959	10.00	20.00	40.00
173	Run to Me Baby/I Need Your Love	1959	10.00	20.00	40.00
197	Falling Stars/I Just Can't Understand	1960	10.00	20.00	40.00
—As "O.S. Grant and the Downbeats"					
200	You Did Me Wrong/This Woman I Love	1960	10.00	20.00	40.00
223	Greyhound (Part 1)/Greyhound (Part 2)	196?	5.00	10.00	20.00
228	Grant's Soul Blues/Sock It Uptight	196?	5.00	10.00	20.00
233	Soul Bag/Darling Dear	196?	5.00	10.00	20.00
—As "O.S. Grant and the Downbeats"					

DOWNBEATS, THE (3)

If the record in question is on the TAMLA or V.I.P. label, see THE ELGINS.

DOWNBEATS, THE (4)

Number	Title (A Side/B Side)	Yr	VG	VG+	NM
45s					
WILCO					
9	Alfalfa/Red X	1960	5.00	10.00	20.00
16	Playin' Possum/One at a Time	1960	5.00	10.00	20.00

DOWNEY, MORTON, JR.

Number	Title (A Side/B Side)	Yr	VG	VG+	NM
45s					
ARTISTS OF AMERICA					
109	He Played a Yo-Yo in Nashville/You'll Never Have to Ask Me If I Love You	1976	—	2.50	5.00
—As "Sean Morton Downey"					
123	He Played a Yo-Yo in Nashville/You'll Never Have to Ask Me If I Love You	1976	—	2.00	4.00
—As "Sean Morton Downey"					
124	You Made Me Love You/As Time Goes By	1976	—	2.00	4.00
—As "Sean Morton Downey"					
BULLDOG					
105	A Tear Fell in the Chapel/Tender Years	1959	3.75	7.50	15.00
—As "Sean Downey"					
CADENCE					
1407	The Ballad of Billy Brown/Flattery	1961	2.50	5.00	10.00
CONTENDER					
1317	Love Bug/Rags to Riches	1959	3.75	7.50	15.00
CUB					
9004	You Let Go/Hearts Are Wild	1958	3.00	6.00	12.00
—As "Sean Downey"					
ESO					
932	Green Eyed Girl/(B-side unknown)	1981	2.00	4.00	8.00
—As "Sean Morton Downey"					
IMPERIAL					
5556	Boulevard of Broken Dreams/Proud Possession	1958	2.50	5.00	10.00
LAKE ERIE					
(# unknown)	Cleveland's Coming Back Again/(B-side unknown)	197?	2.00	4.00	8.00
MAGIC LAMP					
517	The Ballad of Billy Brown/Flattery	1964	2.00	4.00	8.00
NRLC					
1977	Got a Right to Live/Theme for Life	197?	—	3.00	6.00
PERSONALITY					
3506	Little Miss U.S.A./Football Freddy	1959	3.00	6.00	12.00
PRIVATE STOCK					
45168	Family Tree/Spanish Harlem	1977	—	2.00	4.00
SCEPTER					
12316	Love Theme from Christine/Christine's a Lady	1971	—	3.00	6.00
—As "Sean Morton Downey, Jr."					
12360	Break the Habit of Hate/Second Chance Lord	1972	—	3.00	6.00
—As "Sean Downey"					
STAX					
0195	I Believe in America/My Last Day on Earth	1974	—	2.00	4.00
—As "Sean Downey"					
WYE					
1010	I Beg Your Pardon/Three Steps to the Phone	1961	3.00	6.00	12.00
Albums					
ARTISTS OF AMERICA					
AOA-5005	You'll Never Ask Me If I Love You	1976	3.00	6.00	12.00
COMPOSE					
9901	Morton Downey Jr. Sings!	1989	3.75	7.50	15.00

DOWNEY, PAUL

Number	Title (A Side/B Side)	Yr	VG	VG+	NM
45s					
HICKORY					
1632	Camp Meeting, U.S.A./Love	1972	—	3.50	7.00

DOWNEY, SEAN; DOWNEY, SEAN MORTON

See MORTON DOWNEY, JR.

DOWNING, BIG AL

Number	Title (A Side/B Side)	Yr	VG	VG+	NM
45s					
CARLTON					
489	Miss Lucy/Just Around the Corner	1959	12.50	25.00	50.00
507	It Must Be Love/When My Blue Moon Turns to Gold Again	1959	10.00	20.00	40.00
CHALLENGE					
59006	Down on the Farm/Oh Babe	1958	12.50	25.00	50.00
CHESS					
1817	The Story of My Life/I'd Love to Be Loved	1962	3.00	6.00	12.00
2158	I'll Be Holding On/Baby Let's Talk It Over	1974	—	2.50	5.00
COLUMBIA					
43028	I'm Just Nobody/All I Want Is You	1964	2.50	5.00	10.00
43185	I Feel Good/Georgia Slop	1964	2.50	5.00	10.00
DOOR KNOB					
328	I Guess By Now/(B-side unknown)	1989	—	2.00	4.00
340	Bound for Baltimore/(B-side unknown)	1989	—	2.00	4.00
345	Father #1/(B-side unknown)	1989	—	2.00	4.00
JANUS					
211	Thank You Baby/(B-side unknown)	1974	—	3.00	6.00
234	I'll Be Holding On/Hands	1974	—	3.00	6.00
LENOX					
5565	You Never Miss Your Water (Till the Well Runs Dry)/If You Want It (I Got It)	1963	3.00	6.00	12.00
—As "Little Esther Phillips and Big Al Downing"					
5572	Mr. Hurt Walked In/If I Had Our Love to Live Over	1963	3.00	6.00	12.00
POLYDOR					
14311	I Love to Love/I'm Just Nobody	1976	—	2.00	4.00
SILVER FOX					
3	Cornbreak Row/The Saints	1969	2.00	4.00	8.00
11	Medley of Soul/These Arms You Push Away	1969	2.00	4.00	8.00
TEAM					
1001	I'll Be Loving You/Don't Mess with an Angel	1982	—	2.00	4.00
1002	Darlene/(B-side unknown)	1982	—	2.00	4.00
1003	Let's Sing About Love/We Can Only Say Goodbye	1983	—	2.00	4.00
1004	It Takes Love/If You're Leaving	1983	—	2.00	4.00
1007	The Best of Families/Fool of the Year	1983	—	2.00	4.00
1008	There'll Never Be a Better Night for Bein' Wrong/(B-side unknown)	1984	—	2.00	4.00
V-TONE					
215	Yes, I'm Loving You/Please Come Home	1960	3.00	6.00	12.00
220	If I Had Our Love to Live Over/Words of Love	1961	3.00	6.00	12.00
230	So Many Memories/There'll Come a Time	1961	3.00	6.00	12.00
VINE ST.					
103	How Beautiful You Are (To Me)/The Only Thing Missing Is You	1986	—	2.00	4.00
105	Just One Night Won't Do/How Beautiful You Are (To Me)	1987	—	2.00	4.00
106	How Ya Gonna Do It/The Only Thing Missing Is You	1987	—	2.00	4.00
WARNER BROS.					
8716	Mr. Jones/I Don't Cry (The Onion Song)	1978	—	2.00	4.00
8787	Touch Me (I'll Be Your Fool Once More)/I Ain't No Fool	1979	—	2.00	4.00
49034	Midnight Lace/Counting Highway Signs	1979	—	2.00	4.00
49141	I Ain't No Fool/Mr. Jones	1979	—	2.00	4.00
49161	The Story Behind the Story/Daddy Played the Banjo	1980	—	2.00	4.00
49270	Bring It On Home/Beer Drinking People	1980	—	2.00	4.00
WHITE ROCK					
1111	Down on the Farm/Oh Babe	1958	37.50	75.00	150.00
1113	Miss Lucy/Just Around the Corner	1958	37.50	75.00	150.00
Albums					
TEAM					
2001	Big Al Downing	1982	3.00	6.00	12.00

DOWNLINERS SECT, THE

Number	Title (A Side/B Side)	Yr	VG	VG+	NM
45s					
SMASH					
1954	Little Egypt/I Feel Good	1965	3.00	6.00	12.00

DOWNS, HUGH

Number	Title (A Side/B Side)	Yr	VG	VG+	NM
Albums					
EPIC					
BN 541 [S]	An Evening with Hugh Downs	1961	7.50	15.00	30.00
LN 3597 [M]	An Evening with Hugh Downs	1961	6.25	12.50	25.00

DOYLE, BOBBY, THREE

KENNY ROGERS was in this group.

Number	Title (A Side/B Side)	Yr	VG	VG+	NM
Albums					
COLUMBIA					
CL 1858 [M]	In a Most Unusual Way	1962	10.00	20.00	40.00
CS 8658 [S]	In a Most Unusual Way	1962	12.50	25.00	50.00

DOYLE, MIKE

Number	Title (A Side/B Side)	Yr	VG	VG+	NM
Albums					
FLEETWOOD					
FLP-3018 [M]	The Secrets of Surfing	1963	30.00	60.00	120.00

DOZIER, GENE, AND THE BROTHERHOOD

45s

MINIT

Number	Title (A Side/B Side)	Yr	VG	VG+	NM
32026	House of Funk/One for Bess	1967	2.50	5.00	10.00
32031	I Wanna Testify/Mustang Sally	1967	2.50	5.00	10.00
32041	Funky Broadway/Soul Stroll	1968	2.50	5.00	10.00

Albums

MINIT

Number	Title (A Side/B Side)	Yr	VG	VG+	NM
24010 [S]	Blues Power	1967	6.25	12.50	25.00
40010 [M]	Blues Power	1967	6.25	12.50	25.00

DOZIER, LAMONT

Also see HOLLAND-DOZIER.

12-Inch Singles

WARNER BROS.

Number	Title (A Side/B Side)	Yr	VG	VG+	NM
8802	Boogie Business/True Love Is Bittersweet	1979	2.50	5.00	10.00

45s

ABC

Number	Title (A Side/B Side)	Yr	VG	VG+	NM
11407	Trying to Hold On to My Woman/We Don't Want Nobody to Come Between Us	1973	—	2.00	4.00
—Also see "Holland-Dozier"					
11438	Fish Ain't Bitin'/Breaking Out All Over	1974	—	2.00	4.00
12012	Fish Ain't Bitin'/Breaking Out All Over	1974	—	2.00	4.00
12044	Let Me Start Tonite/I Wanna Be with You	1974	—	2.00	4.00
12076	All Cried Out/Rose	1975	—	2.00	4.00
12234	Out Here on My Own/Take Off Your Make-Up	1976	—	2.00	4.00

ANNA

Number	Title (A Side/B Side)	Yr	VG	VG+	NM
1125	Let's Talk It Over/Benny the Skinny Man	1960	6.25	12.50	25.00
—As "Lamont Anthony"					
1125	Let's Talk It Over/Popeye	1960	62.50	125.00	250.00
—As "Lamont Anthony"					

CHECKMATE

Number	Title (A Side/B Side)	Yr	VG	VG+	NM
1001	Just to Be Loved/I Didn't Know	1961	62.50	125.00	250.00
—As "Lamont Anthony"					

COLUMBIA

Number	Title (A Side/B Side)	Yr	VG	VG+	NM
02035	Cool Me Out/Starting Over (We've Made the Necessary Changes)	1981	—	2.00	4.00
02238	Too Little Too Long/Chained (To Your Love)	1981	—	2.00	4.00

MEL-O-DY

Number	Title (A Side/B Side)	Yr	VG	VG+	NM
102	Dearest One/Fortune Teller Please Tell Me	1962	25.00	50.00	100.00

M&M

Number	Title (A Side/B Side)	Yr	VG	VG+	NM
502	Shout About It/(Instrumental)	1982	—	2.50	5.00

WARNER BROS.

Number	Title (A Side/B Side)	Yr	VG	VG+	NM
8432	Sight for Sore Eyes/Tear Down the Walls	1977	—	2.00	4.00
8792	Boogie Business/True Love Is Bittersweet	1979	—	2.00	4.00

Albums

ABC

Number	Title (A Side/B Side)	Yr	VG	VG+	NM
D-804	Out Here on My Own	1973	2.50	5.00	10.00
D-839	Black Bach	1974	2.50	5.00	10.00

INVICTUS

Number	Title (A Side/B Side)	Yr	VG	VG+	NM
KZ 33134	Love and Beauty	1974	3.00	6.00	12.00

WARNER BROS.

Number	Title (A Side/B Side)	Yr	VG	VG+	NM
BS 2929	Right There	1976	2.50	5.00	10.00
BS 3039	Peddlin'	1977	2.50	5.00	10.00
BSK 3282	Bittersweet	1979	2.50	5.00	10.00

DOZY, BEAKY, MICK & TICH

See DAVE DEE, DOZY, BEAKY, MICK & TICH.

DRAG KINGS, THE

45s

UNITED ARTISTS

Number	Title (A Side/B Side)	Yr	VG	VG+	NM
676	Bearing Burners/Nitro	1963	7.50	15.00	30.00

DRAGONFLY

Albums

MEGAPHONE

Number	Title (A Side/B Side)	Yr	VG	VG+	NM
MS-1202	Dragonfly	1968	50.00	100.00	200.00

DRAGONS, THE

With Daryl Dragon, later of THE CAPTAIN AND TENNILLE.

45s

CAPITOL

Number	Title (A Side/B Side)	Yr	VG	VG+	NM
5278	Elephant Stomp/Troll	1964	5.00	10.00	20.00

DRAGSTERS, THE

Albums

WING

Number	Title (A Side/B Side)	Yr	VG	VG+	NM
MGW-12269 [M]	Hey Little Cobra/Drag City	1964	20.00	40.00	80.00
SRW-16269 [S]	Hey Little Cobra/Drag City	1964	25.00	50.00	100.00

DRAKE, CHARLIE

45s

UNITED ARTISTS

Number	Title (A Side/B Side)	Yr	VG	VG+	NM
398	My Boomerang Won't Come Back/She's My Girl	1961	7.50	15.00	30.00
—With A-side lyric "Practiced 'til I was black in the face."					
398	My Boomerang Won't Come Back/She's My Girl	1961	3.75	7.50	15.00
—With A-side lyric "Practiced 'til I was blue in the face."					
437	Tanglefoot/Drake's Progress	1962	3.00	6.00	12.00
477	Sweet Freddie Green/Zulu Drake	1962	3.00	6.00	12.00

DRAKE, NICK

Albums

ANTILLES

Number	Title (A Side/B Side)	Yr	VG	VG+	NM
AN-7010	Five Leaves Left	197?	3.75	7.50	15.00
—Released in England in 1969					
AN-7028	Bryter Layter	1977	3.75	7.50	15.00
—Released in England in 1970					

HANNIBAL

Number	Title (A Side/B Side)	Yr	VG	VG+	NM
NHBL-1318	Time of No Reply	198?	3.00	6.00	12.00
HNBX-5302 [(3)]	Fruit Tree	198?	6.25	12.50	25.00

ISLAND

Number	Title (A Side/B Side)	Yr	VG	VG+	NM
SMAS-9307	Nick Drake	1971	6.25	12.50	25.00
SMAS-9318	Pink Moon	1972	6.25	12.50	25.00

DRAKE, PETE

45s

SMASH

Number	Title (A Side/B Side)	Yr	VG	VG+	NM
1867	Forever/Sleepwalk	1964	2.00	4.00	8.00
1888	Midnight in Amarillo/Forever	1964	2.00	4.00	8.00
1910	I'm Sorry/I'm Just a Guitar (Everybody Picks On Me)	1964	2.00	4.00	8.00
1935	I'm Walkin'/Are You Sincere	1964	2.00	4.00	8.00
1978	Dream/Am I That Easy to Forget	1965	2.00	4.00	8.00
2046	I'm a Fool to Care/Mystic Dream	1966	2.00	4.00	8.00

STARDAY

Number	Title (A Side/B Side)	Yr	VG	VG+	NM
751	My Abilene/Y'All Come	1966	2.00	4.00	8.00

STOP

Number	Title (A Side/B Side)	Yr	VG	VG+	NM
222	Joggin'/Mama's Talkin' Guitar	1968	—	3.00	6.00
349	Lay Lady Lay/For Pete's Sake	1970	—	3.00	6.00

Albums

CANAAN

Number	Title (A Side/B Side)	Yr	VG	VG+	NM
4640 [M]	Steel Away	1967	3.75	7.50	15.00
9640 [S]	Steel Away	1967	5.00	10.00	20.00

CUMBERLAND

Number	Title (A Side/B Side)	Yr	VG	VG+	NM
MGC-29053 [M]	Country Steel Guitar	1963	5.00	10.00	20.00
SRC-69053 [S]	Country Steel Guitar	1963	6.25	12.50	25.00

HILLTOP

Number	Title (A Side/B Side)	Yr	VG	VG+	NM
6052 [M]	Are You Sincere	1967	3.00	6.00	12.00
S-6052 [S]	Are You Sincere	1967	3.00	6.00	12.00

SMASH

Number	Title (A Side/B Side)	Yr	VG	VG+	NM
MGS-27053 [M]	Forever	1964	3.75	7.50	15.00
MGS-27060 [M]	Talking Steel Guitar	1965	3.75	7.50	15.00
MGS-27064 [M]	Talking Steel and Singing Strings	1965	3.75	7.50	15.00
SRS-67053 [S]	Forever	1964	5.00	10.00	20.00
SRS-67060 [S]	Talking Steel Guitar	1965	5.00	10.00	20.00
SRS-67064 [S]	Talking Steel and Singing Strings	1965	5.00	10.00	20.00

STARDAY

Number	Title (A Side/B Side)	Yr	VG	VG+	NM
SLP-180 [M]	The Fabulous Steel Guitar of Pete Drake	1962	10.00	20.00	40.00
SLP-319 [M]	The Amazing Incredible Pete Drake	1964	7.50	15.00	30.00

STOP

Number	Title (A Side/B Side)	Yr	VG	VG+	NM
1011	The Pete Drake Show	1970	3.00	6.00	12.00

DRAKES, THE

45s

CONQUEST

Number	Title (A Side/B Side)	Yr	VG	VG+	NM
1001	Oo Wee So Good/Kitty	1958	150.00	300.00	600.00

OLIMPIC

Number	Title (A Side/B Side)	Yr	VG	VG+	NM
252	I Made a Wish/Ole King Cole	1965	30.00	60.00	120.00

DRAMATICS, THE

Probably all the same group. Also see THE DELLS AND THE DRAMATICS.

45s

ABC

Number	Title (A Side/B Side)	Yr	VG	VG+	NM
12090	Mr. and Mrs. Jones/I Cried All the Way Home	1975	—	2.50	5.00
12125	(I'm Going By) The Stars in Your Eyes/Trying to Get Over You	1975	—	2.50	5.00
12150	You're Fooling You/I'll Make It So Good	1975	—	2.50	5.00
12180	Treat Me Like a Man/I Was the Life of the Party	1976	—	2.50	5.00
12220	Finger Fever/Say the Word	1976	—	2.50	5.00
12235	Be My Girl/The Nicest Man Alive	1976	—	2.50	5.00
12258	I Can't Get Over You/Sundown Is Coming (Hold Back the Night)	1977	—	2.50	5.00
12299	Shake It Well/That Heaven Kind of Feeling	1977	—	2.50	5.00
12331	Ocean of Thoughts and Dreams/Come Inside	1978	—	2.50	5.00
12372	Stop Your Weeping/California Sunrise	1978	—	2.50	5.00
12400	Do What You Want to Do/Jane	1978	—	2.50	5.00
12429	Why Do You Wanna Do Me Wrong/Yo' Love (Can Only Bring Me Happiness)	1978	—	2.50	5.00
12460	I Just Wanna Dance with You/I've Got a Schoolboy Crush on You	1979	—	2.50	5.00

CADET

Number	Title (A Side/B Side)	Yr	VG	VG+	NM
5704	Door to Your Heart/Choosing Up on You	1974	—	3.00	6.00
5706	Don't Make Me No Promises/Tune Up	1974	—	3.00	6.00
5710	Love Is Missing from Our Lives/I'm in Love	1975	—	3.00	6.00
—With the Dells					

CAPITOL

Number	Title (A Side/B Side)	Yr	VG	VG+	NM
B-5103	Live It Up/She's My Kind of Girl	1982	—	2.00	4.00
B-5140	Treat Me Right/Night Life	1982	—	2.00	4.00

CRACKERJACK

Number	Title (A Side/B Side)	Yr	VG	VG+	NM
4015	Toy Soldier/Hello Summer	1968	15.00	30.00	60.00

FANTASY

Number	Title (A Side/B Side)	Yr	VG	VG+	NM
966	Luv's Calling/Dream Lady	1985	—	—	3.00
967	One Love Ago/Dream Lady	1986	—	—	3.00

MAINSTREAM

Number	Title (A Side/B Side)	Yr	VG	VG+	NM
5571	No Rebate on Love/Feel It	1976	—	2.50	5.00

MCA

Number	Title (A Side/B Side)	Yr	VG	VG+	NM
12460	I Just Wanna Dance with You/I've Got a Schoolboy Crush on You	1979	—	2.00	4.00
41017	I Just Wanta Dance With You/I've Got a Schoolboy Crush on You	1979	—	2.00	4.00
41056	That's My Favorite Song/Bottom Line Woman	1979	—	2.00	4.00
41178	Welcome Back Home/Marriage on Paper Only	1980	—	2.00	4.00
41241	Be With the One You Love/If You Feel Like You Wanna Dance, Dance	1980	—	2.00	4.00
51004	Share Your Love with Me/Get It	1980	—	2.00	4.00
51041	(We Need More) Lovin' Time/You're the Best Thing in My Life	1980	—	2.00	4.00

SPORT

Number	Title (A Side/B Side)	Yr	VG	VG+	NM
101	All Because of You/If You Haven't Got Love	1967	15.00	30.00	60.00

VOLT

Number	Title (A Side/B Side)	Yr	VG	VG+	NM
302	Bridge Over Troubled Water/(B-side unknown)	1989	—	2.00	4.00

Number	Title (A Side/B Side)	Yr	VG	VG+	NM
4029	Since I've Been in Love/Your Love Was Strange	1969	2.00	4.00	8.00
4058	Whatcha See Is Whatcha Get/Thankful for Your Love	1971	2.00	4.00	8.00
4071	Get Up and Get Down/Fall in Love, Lady Love	1971	2.00	4.00	8.00
4075	In the Rain/Good Soul Music	1972	2.00	4.00	8.00
4082	Toast to the Fool/Your Love Was Strange	1972	2.00	4.00	8.00
4090	Hey You! Get Off My Mountain/The Devil Is Dope	1973	2.00	4.00	8.00
4099	Fell for You/Now You Got Me Loving You	1973	2.00	4.00	8.00
4105	And I Panicked/Beware of the Man	1974	2.00	4.00	8.00
4108	I Made Myself Lonely/Highway to Heaven	1974	2.00	4.00	8.00
WINGATE					
18	Somewhere/Bingo!	1966	12.50	25.00	50.00
—As "The Dynamics"					
22	Baby I Need You/Inky Dinky Wang Dang Doo	1966	12.50	25.00	50.00
—As "The Dynamics"					
Albums					
ABC					
D-867	The Dramatic Jackpot	1975	3.75	7.50	15.00
D-916	Drama V	1975	3.75	7.50	15.00
D-955	Joy Ride	1976	3.75	7.50	15.00
AB-1010	Shake It Well	1977	3.75	7.50	15.00
AA-1072	Do What You Wanna Do	1978	3.75	7.50	15.00
AA-1125	Anytime, Anyplace	1979	3.75	7.50	15.00
CAPITOL					
ST-12205	New Dimension	1982	2.50	5.00	10.00
FANTASY					
9642	Somewhere in Time: A Dramatic Reunion	1986	3.00	6.00	12.00
MCA					
761	Dramatic Way	198?	2.00	4.00	8.00
—Reissue of 5149					
762	10 1/2	198?	2.00	4.00	8.00
—Reissue of 3196					
AA-1125	Anytime, Anyplace	1979	3.00	6.00	12.00
—Reissue of ABC 1125					
3196	10 1/2	1980	2.50	5.00	10.00
5149	Dramatic Way	1981	2.50	5.00	10.00
STAX					
STX-4111	Whatcha See Is Whatcha Get	1978	3.00	6.00	12.00
—Reissue of Volt 6018					
STX-4131	A Dramatic Experience	1979	3.00	6.00	12.00
—Reissue of Volt 6019					
MPS-8523	Dramatically Yours	198?	2.00	4.00	8.00
—Reissue of Volt 9501					
MPS-8526	The Best of the Dramatics	198?	2.50	5.00	10.00
MPS-8545	The Dramatics Live	1988	2.50	5.00	10.00
VOLT					
V-3402	Positive State of Mind	1989	2.50	5.00	10.00
V-3407	Stone Cold	1990	2.50	5.00	10.00
VOS-6018	Whatcha See Is Whatcha Get	1972	6.25	12.50	25.00
VOS-6019	A Dramatic Experience	1973	6.25	12.50	25.00
VOS-9501	Dramatically Yours	1974	6.25	12.50	25.00

DRAPER, RUSTY

Also see PATTI PAGE.

Number	Title (A Side/B Side)	Yr	VG	VG+	NM
45s					
KL					
001	Harbor Lights/(B-side unknown)	1979	—	2.00	4.00
MERCURY					
5820	Just Because/How Could You (Blue Eyes)	1952	3.75	7.50	15.00
5851	Devil of a Woman/Bouncing on the Bayou	1952	3.75	7.50	15.00
5894	Sing Baby Sing/I Gotta Have My Baby Back	1952	3.75	7.50	15.00
70004	Angry/Blue Tears	1952	3.00	6.00	12.00
70077	No Help Wanted/Texarkana Baby	1953	3.00	6.00	12.00
70167	Gambler's Guitar/Free Home Demonstration	1953	3.00	6.00	12.00
70178	Lazy River/Bummin' Around	1953	3.00	6.00	12.00
70256	Native Dancer/Lonesome Song	1953	3.00	6.00	12.00
70300	Peter Rabbit/Easter Morning	1954	3.00	6.00	12.00
70327	The Train with a Rhumba Beat/Melancholy Baby	1954	3.00	6.00	12.00
70365	It Ain't Me Baby/Knock on Wood	1954	3.00	6.00	12.00
70415	Please, Please/Workshop of the Lord	1954	3.00	6.00	12.00
70446	Muskrat Ramble/The Magic Circle	1954	3.00	6.00	12.00
70526	Lookin' Back to See/Shame on You	1955	3.00	6.00	12.00
70555	The Ballad of Davy Crockett/I've Been Thinkin'	1955	3.75	7.50	15.00
70619	Eating Goober Peas/That's All I Need	1955	3.00	6.00	12.00
70651	Seventeen/Can't Live Without Them Anymore	1955	3.00	6.00	12.00
70696	The Shifting, Whispering Sands/Time	1955	2.50	5.00	10.00
70757	Are You Satisfied/Wabash Cannonball	1955	2.50	5.00	10.00
70818	Held for Questioning/Forty-Two	1956	2.50	5.00	10.00
70853	Sometimes You Win, Sometimes You Lose/The Gun of Billy the Kid	1956	2.50	5.00	10.00
70879	Rock and Roll Baby/House of Cards	1956	3.75	7.50	15.00
70921	In the Middle of the House/Pink Cadillac	1956	2.50	5.00	10.00
70938	Giant/Old Buttermilk Sky	1956	3.75	7.50	15.00
71039	Let's Go Calypso/Should I Ever Love Again	1957	2.50	5.00	10.00
71102	Freight Train/Seven Come Eleven	1957	2.50	5.00	10.00
71162	No Hu Hu/Good Golly	1957	2.50	5.00	10.00
71221	Buzz Buzz Buzz/I Get the Blues When It Rains	1957	2.50	5.00	10.00
71298	Gamblin' Gal/That's My Doll	1958	2.50	5.00	10.00
71336	June, July and August/Chicken-Pluckin' Hawk	1958	2.50	5.00	10.00
71351	Hip Monkey/Can You Depend on Me	1958	2.50	5.00	10.00
71388	With This Ring/Shopping Around	1958	2.50	5.00	10.00
71418	Hey Li Lee Li Lee Li/The Sun Will Always Shine	1959	2.50	5.00	10.00
71463	Next Stop Paradise/Don't Forget Your Shoes	1959	2.50	5.00	10.00
71545	I Get So Jealous/But For the Flow of Flo	1959	2.50	5.00	10.00
71564	Two of a Kind/If My Mother'd Only Let Me Cross the Street	1960	2.00	4.00	8.00
71581	That Lucky Old Sun/Any Time	1960	2.00	4.00	8.00
71634	Please Help Me, I'm Falling/Mule Skinner Blues	1960	2.00	4.00	8.00
71664	It's a Little More Like Heaven/Luck of the Irish	1960	2.00	4.00	8.00
71706	Jealous Heart/Ten Thousand Years Ago	1960	2.00	4.00	8.00
71784	Another/The Meadow	1961	2.00	4.00	8.00
71854	Signed, Sealed and Delivered/Scared to Go Home	1961	2.00	4.00	8.00
71914	Well I've Learned/Tongue Tied Over You	1961	2.00	4.00	8.00
71976	Beggar to a King/Deep Roots	1962	2.00	4.00	8.00
MONUMENT					
823	Night Life/That's Why I Love You Like I Do	1963	—	3.50	7.00
832	It Should Be Easier Now/Lady of the House	1964	—	3.50	7.00
843	The Puppeteer/My Baby's Not Here (In Town Tonight)	1964	—	3.50	7.00
858	I'm Worried About Me/When I've Learned	1964	—	3.50	7.00
871	I Got What I Wanted/Love Don't Grow on Trees	1965	—	3.50	7.00
894	Folsom Prison Blues/You Can't Be True, Dear	1965	—	3.50	7.00
944	Mystery Train/The Shifting, Whispering Sands	1966	—	3.00	6.00
969	Love Is Gone for Good/You Call Everybody Darling	1966	—	3.00	6.00
1019	My Elusive Dreams/Memory Lane	1967	—	3.00	6.00
1044	California Sunshine/The Gypsy	1968	—	3.00	6.00
1074	Buffalo Nickel/Make Believe I'm Him	1968	—	3.00	6.00
1116	Love Is Just a Game/Something Old, Something New	1968	—	3.00	6.00
1137	Don't Build No Fences for Me/Am I That Easy to Forget	1969	—	3.00	6.00
1157	I Walk Alone/Sunshine Man	1969	—	3.00	6.00
1188	Two Little Boys/It Don't Mean a Thing to Me	1970	—	2.50	5.00
1202	Every Man Has a Prison/Tie Me to Your Apron Strings Again	1970	—	2.50	5.00
1223	There She Goes/Travelling Song	1970	—	2.50	5.00
8628	Walking on New Grass/You Were Right	1974	—	2.00	4.00
Albums					
GOLDEN CREST					
31029	The Rusty Draper Show	1973	3.00	6.00	12.00
31030	Tour the USA	1973	3.00	6.00	12.00
MERCURY					
MG-20068 [M]	Music for a Rainy Night	1956	7.50	15.00	30.00
MG-20117 [M]	Encores	1957	7.50	15.00	30.00
MG-20118 [M]	Rusty Draper Sings	1957	7.50	15.00	30.00
MG-20173 [M]	Rusty Meets Hoagy	1957	7.50	15.00	30.00
MG-20499 [M]	Hits That Sold a Million	1960	7.50	15.00	30.00
MG-20657 [M]	Country and Western Golden Greats	1961	7.50	15.00	30.00
SR-60176 [S]	Hits That Sold a Million	1960	10.00	20.00	40.00
SR-60657 [S]	Country and Western Golden Greats	1961	10.00	20.00	40.00
MONUMENT					
6638	Greatest Hits	1977	3.00	6.00	12.00
MLP-8005 [M]	Greatest Hits	1964	3.75	7.50	15.00
MLP-8018 [M]	Night Life	1964	3.75	7.50	15.00
MLP-8026 [M]	Rusty Draper Plays Guitar	1965	3.75	7.50	15.00
SLP-18005 [S]	Greatest Hits	1964	5.00	10.00	20.00
SLP-18018 [S]	Night Life	1964	5.00	10.00	20.00
SLP-18026 [S]	Rusty Draper Plays Guitar	1965	5.00	10.00	20.00
SLP-18105	Something Old, Something New	1969	3.75	7.50	15.00
ZG 33870 [(2)]	Swingin' Country/Something Old, Something New	1976	3.75	7.50	15.00
WING					
MGW-12243 [M]	Hits That Sold a Million	196?	3.75	7.50	15.00
MGW-12274 [M]	Country Classics	196?	3.75	7.50	15.00
SRW-16243 [S]	Hits That Sold a Million	196?	3.75	7.50	15.00
SRW-16274 [S]	Country Classics	196?	3.75	7.50	15.00

DREAM GIRLS, THE

Number	Title (A Side/B Side)	Yr	VG	VG+	NM
45s					
BIG TOP					
3059	Don't Break My Heart/I Could Write a Book	1960	5.00	10.00	20.00
3085	Wanted/Mr. Fine	1961	5.00	10.00	20.00
—The rest of the Big Top singles as "Bobbie Smith and the Dream Girls"					
3100	Duchess of Earl/Mine All Mine	1962	5.00	10.00	20.00
3111	Here Comes Baby/I Got a Feeling My Love	1962	5.00	10.00	20.00
3129	Your Lovey Dovey Ways/Now He's Gone	1962	5.00	10.00	20.00
CAMEO					
165	Don't Break My Heart/Oh This Is Why	1959	6.25	12.50	25.00
METRO					
20029	I'm in Love with You/Cryin' in the Night	1960	7.50	15.00	30.00
20034	Heartaches/Love Hen	1961	6.25	12.50	25.00
TWIRL					
1002	Don't Break My Heart/Oh This Is Why	1959	12.50	25.00	50.00

DREAM KINGS, THE

Number	Title (A Side/B Side)	Yr	VG	VG+	NM
45s					
CHECKER					
858	M.T.Y.L.T.T./Oh What a Baby	1957	37.50	75.00	150.00

DREAM TEAM, THE

Number	Title (A Side/B Side)	Yr	VG	VG+	NM
45s					
EPIC					
9701	I'm Not Afraid/Inka Dinka Doo	1964	3.00	6.00	12.00

DREAM WEAVERS, THE

Number	Title (A Side/B Side)	Yr	VG	VG+	NM
45s					
DECCA					
29683	It's Almost Tomorrow/You've Got Me Wondering	1955	3.75	7.50	15.00
29818	You're Mine/Into the Night	1956	3.00	6.00	12.00
29905	A Little Love Can Go a Long, Long Way/Is There Somebody Else	1956	3.00	6.00	12.00
29990	Give Us This Day/Why I Chose You	1956	3.00	6.00	12.00
30156	Till We Meet Again/All This Is Home	1956	3.00	6.00	12.00
30276	Fool's Gold/I'll Try, I'll Try	1957	3.00	6.00	12.00

DREAMERS, THE

Several different groups.

Number	Title (A Side/B Side)	Yr	VG	VG+	NM
45s					
ABC-PARAMOUNT					
9746	The Girl Down the Street/The Right Time for Love	1956	5.00	10.00	20.00
ALADDIN					
3303	My Plea/Charles My Darling	1955	37.50	75.00	150.00
APT					
25053	Mary's Little Lamb/I Sing This Song	1960	6.25	12.50	25.00

Number	Title (A Side/B Side)	Yr	VG	VG+	NM
BLUE STAR					
8001	I Really Love You/You Made Me Darling	1960	6.25	12.50	25.00
COUSINS					
1005	Because of You/Little Girl	1961	25.00	50.00	100.00
EVENT					
4270	Rock 'N Roll Baby/Ding Dong	1958	7.50	15.00	30.00
FAIRMOUNT					
612	Daydreamin' of You/The Promise	1963	5.00	10.00	20.00
FLIP					
319	Since You've Been Gone/Do Not Forget	1956	10.00	20.00	40.00
354	Since You've Been Gone/Do Not Forget	1961	5.00	10.00	20.00
GOLDISC					
3015	Teenage Vows of Love/Natalie	1961	7.50	15.00	30.00
GRAND					
131	Tears in My Eyes/535	1955	75.00	150.00	300.00
GUARANTEED					
219	Mary, Mary/Canadian Sunset	1961	3.75	7.50	15.00
JUBILEE					
5053	These Things I Miss/Can't Get You Off My Mind	1951	75.00	150.00	300.00
MANHATTAN					
503	Lips Were Meant for Kissing/No Obligation	1956	25.00	50.00	100.00
MAY					
133	Because of You/Little Girl	1963	10.00	20.00	40.00
MERCURY					
5843	I'm Gonna Hate Myself in the Morning/Ain't Gonna Worry No More	1952	37.50	75.00	150.00
70019	Please Don't Leave Me/Walkin' My Blues	1953	37.50	75.00	150.00
NUGGET					
1000	Don't Cry/It's Gonna Be Alright	1959	7.50	15.00	30.00
ROLLIN'					
1001	No Man Is an Island/Melba	1954	81.25	162.50	325.00
UNITED ARTISTS					
841	Henry, Henry, Henry/Love, Love, Love	1965	3.00	6.00	12.00

DREAMETTES, THE

45s

Number	Title (A Side/B Side)	Yr	VG	VG+	NM
UNITED ARTISTS					
921	Gonna Make That Little Boy Mine/Run, Steven, Run	1965	5.00	10.00	20.00

DREAMLOVERS, THE

45s

Number	Title (A Side/B Side)	Yr	VG	VG+	NM
CAMEO					
326	These Will Be the Good Old Days/Oh Baby Mine (I Get So Lonely)	1964	3.75	7.50	15.00
—The Cameo, Casino, Mercury, Swan and Warner Bros. are all the same group.					
CASINO					
1308	Amazons and Coyotes/Together	1963	3.75	7.50	15.00
COLUMBIA					
42698	Sad, Sad Boy/If I Were a Magician	1963	5.00	10.00	20.00
42752	Sad, Sad Boy/Black Bottom	1963	3.00	6.00	12.00
42842	Pretty Little Girl/I'm Through with You	1963	12.50	25.00	50.00
END					
1114	If I Should Lose You/I Miss You	1962	5.00	10.00	20.00
HERITAGE					
102	When We Get Married/Just Because	1961	5.00	10.00	20.00
104	Welcome Home/Let Them Love (And Be Loved)	1961	3.75	7.50	15.00
107	Zoom, Zoom, Zoom/While We Were Dancing	1962	3.75	7.50	15.00
LEN					
1006	Take It from a Fool/For the First Time	1958	50.00	100.00	200.00
MERCURY					
72595	Bless Your Soul/Bad Time Make the Good Times	1966	2.50	5.00	10.00
72630	Calling Jo-Ann/You Gave Me Someone to Love	1966	2.50	5.00	10.00
SWAN					
4167	Amazons and Coyotes/Together	1963	5.00	10.00	20.00
—White label					
4167	Amazons and Coyotes/Together	1963	3.00	6.00	12.00
—Black label					
V-TONE					
211	Annabelle Lee/Home Is Where the Heart Is	1960	5.00	10.00	20.00
229	May I Kiss the Bride/Time	1961	5.00	10.00	20.00
WARNER BROS.					
5619	You Gave Me Someone to Love/Doin' Things Together with You	1965	6.25	12.50	25.00

Albums

Number	Title (A Side/B Side)	Yr	VG	VG+	NM
COLLECTABLES					
COL-5004	The Best of the Dreamlovers	198?	3.00	6.00	12.00
COL-5005	The Best of the Dreamlovers, Volume Two	198?	3.00	6.00	12.00
COLUMBIA					
CL 2020 [M]	The Bird and Other Golden Dancing Grooves	1963	10.00	20.00	40.00
CS 8820 [S]	The Bird and Other Golden Dancing Grooves	1963	12.50	25.00	50.00

DREAMS

45s

Number	Title (A Side/B Side)	Yr	VG	VG+	NM
COLUMBIA					
45300	Devil Lady/Maryanne	1971	—	2.50	5.00
45369	Try Me/15 Miles to Provo	1971	—	2.50	5.00
45524	Medicated Goo/New York	1972	—	2.50	5.00

Albums

Number	Title (A Side/B Side)	Yr	VG	VG+	NM
COLUMBIA					
C 30225	Dreams	1970	3.75	7.50	15.00
C 30960	Imagine My Surprise	1971	3.75	7.50	15.00

DREAMS, THE

45s

Number	Title (A Side/B Side)	Yr	VG	VG+	NM
SAVOY					
1130	Darlene/A Letter to My Girl	1954	50.00	100.00	200.00
1140	Under the Willow/I'm Losing My Mind	1954	30.00	60.00	120.00
—A copy on gold vinyl with a blue Savoy label has shown up; its authenticity is unknown					
1157	I'll Be Faithful/My Little Honeybun	1955	25.00	50.00	100.00

DREAMS AND ILLUSIONS

Albums

Number	Title (A Side/B Side)	Yr	VG	VG+	NM
VERVE FORECAST					
FTS-3040	Dreams and Illusions	1968	5.00	10.00	20.00

DREW, PATTI

Also see THE DREW-VELS.

45s

Number	Title (A Side/B Side)	Yr	VG	VG+	NM
CAPITOL					
2042	Where Is Daddy/Sufferer	1967	2.00	4.00	8.00
2121	Keep On Movin'/There'll Never Be Another	1968	2.00	4.00	8.00
2197	Workin' on a Groovy Thing/Without a Doubt	1968	2.00	4.00	8.00
2339	Hard to Handle/Just Can't Forget About You	1968	2.00	4.00	8.00
2389	I've Been Here All the Time/Welcome Back	1969	2.00	4.00	8.00
2473	The Love That a Woman Should Give to a Man/Save the Last Dance for Me	1969	2.00	4.00	8.00
2575	He's the One/Which One Should I Choose	1969	2.00	4.00	8.00
2712	Wild Is Love/World of No Return	1969	2.00	4.00	8.00
—B-side by John Stewart					
2713	The Pick-Up/Hundreds and Thousands of Guys	1970	2.00	4.00	8.00
5861	Tell Him/Turn Away from Me	1967	2.00	4.00	8.00
5969	Stop and Listen/Tired of Falling In and Out of Love	1967	2.00	4.00	8.00
QUILL					
101	Where Is Daddy/Sufferer	1966	2.50	5.00	10.00

Albums

Number	Title (A Side/B Side)	Yr	VG	VG+	NM
CAPITOL					
ST-156	I've Been Here All the Time	1969	5.00	10.00	20.00
ST-408	Wild Is Love	1970	5.00	10.00	20.00
ST 2804 [S]	Tell Him	1968	7.50	15.00	30.00
T 2804 [M]	Tell Him	1968	7.50	15.00	30.00

DREW-VELS, THE

Also see PATTI DREW.

45s

Number	Title (A Side/B Side)	Yr	VG	VG+	NM
CAPITOL					
5055	Tell Him/Just Because	1963	3.00	6.00	12.00
5145	It's My Time/Everybody Knows	1964	2.50	5.00	10.00
5244	Creepin'/I've Known	1964	2.50	5.00	10.00
QUILL					
100	True Enough/Chilly Kisses	1966	2.50	5.00	10.00

DRIFTERS, THE

Several different groups with a common heritage, thus we list them together. Also see BEN E. KING; RUDY LEWIS; CLYDE McPHATTER; BILL PINKNEY.

45s

Number	Title (A Side/B Side)	Yr	VG	VG+	NM
ATLANTIC					
1006	Money Honey/The Way I Feel	1953	20.00	40.00	80.00
1019	Such a Night/Lucille	1954	17.50	35.00	70.00
1029	Honey Love/Warm Your Heart	1954	12.50	25.00	50.00
1043	Bip Bam/Someday You'll Want Me to Want You	1954	10.00	20.00	40.00
1048	White Christmas/The Bells of St. Mary's	1954	15.00	30.00	60.00
—Yellow label, no spinner (original)					
1048	White Christmas/The Bells of St. Mary's	1956	6.25	12.50	25.00
—Red label, no "fan" logo at lower left					
1048	White Christmas/The Bells of St. Mary's	1962	2.00	4.00	8.00
—Red label with "fan" logo at lower left					
1048	White Christmas/The Bells of St. Mary's	197?	—	2.50	5.00
—Glossy yellow label with "fan" logo					
1048 [DJ]	White Christmas/The Bells of St. Mary's	196?	6.25	12.50	25.00
—White/red label promo, no "fan" logo, with holly leaves encircling "45 R.P.M."					
1055	What'Cha Gonna Do/Gone	1955	12.50	25.00	50.00
1078	Adorable/Steamboat	1955	10.00	20.00	40.00
1089	Ruby Baby/Your Promise to Be Mine	1956	7.50	15.00	30.00
1101	Soldier of Fortune/I Got to Get Myself a Woman	1956	7.50	15.00	30.00
1123	Fools Fall in Love/It Was a Tear	1957	7.50	15.00	30.00
1141	Hypnotized/Drifting Away from You	1957	7.50	15.00	30.00
1161	I Know/Yodee Yakee	1957	7.50	15.00	30.00
1187	Drip Drop/Moonlight Bay	1958	7.50	15.00	30.00
—Last record by the "old" Drifters. The below Atlantic 45s are by a completely different group, although personnel changes resulted in at least one "old" Drifter (Johnny Moore) spending time with the "new" Drifters.					
2025	There Goes My Baby/Oh My Love	1959	6.25	12.50	25.00
2040	Dance with Me/(If You Cry) True Love, True Love	1959	5.00	10.00	20.00
2050	This Magic Moment/Baltimore	1960	5.00	10.00	20.00
2062	Lonely Winds/Hey Senorita	1960	5.00	10.00	20.00
2071	Save the Last Dance for Me/Nobody But Me	1960	5.00	10.00	20.00
2087	I Count the Tears/Suddenly There's a Valley	1960	3.75	7.50	15.00
2096	Some Kind of Wonderful/Honey Bee	1961	3.75	7.50	15.00
2105	Please Stay/No Sweet Lovin'	1961	3.75	7.50	15.00
2117	Sweets for My Sweet/Loneliness or Happiness	1961	3.75	7.50	15.00
2127	Room Full of Tears/Somebody New Dancin' with You	1961	3.75	7.50	15.00
2134	When My Little Girl Is Smiling/Mexican Divorce	1962	3.75	7.50	15.00
2143	Stranger on the Shore/What to Do	1962	3.75	7.50	15.00
2151	Sometimes I Wonder/Jackpot	1962	3.75	7.50	15.00
2162	Up On the Roof/Another Night with the Boys	1962	5.00	10.00	20.00
2182	On Broadway/Let the Music Play	1963	3.75	7.50	15.00
2191	Rat Race/If You Don't Come Back	1963	3.75	7.50	15.00
2201	I'll Take You Home/I Feel Good All Over	1963	3.75	7.50	15.00
2216	Vaya Con Dios/In the Land of Make Believe	1964	3.75	7.50	15.00
2225	One Way Love/Didn't It	1964	3.75	7.50	15.00
2237	Under the Boardwalk/I Don't Want to Go On Without You	1964	3.75	7.50	15.00
2253	I've Got Sand in My Shoes/He's Just a Playboy	1964	3.00	6.00	12.00
2260	Saturday Night at the Movies/Spanish Lace	1964	3.00	6.00	12.00
2260 [PS]	Saturday Night at the Movies/Spanish Lace	1964	10.00	20.00	40.00
2261	The Christmas Song/I Remember Christmas	1964	3.00	6.00	12.00
2261 [PS]	The Christmas Song/I Remember Christmas	1964	7.50	15.00	30.00
2268	At the Club/Answer the Phone	1965	2.50	5.00	10.00
2285	Come On Over to My Place/Chains of Love	1965	2.50	5.00	10.00
2292	Follow Me/The Outside World	1965	2.50	5.00	10.00
2298	I'll Take You Where the Music's Playing/Far from the Maddening Crowd	1965	2.50	5.00	10.00

Number	Title (A Side/B Side)	Yr	VG	VG+	NM
2310	Nylon Stockings/We Gotta Sing	1965	2.50	5.00	10.00
2325	Memories Are Made of This/My Islands in the Sun	1966	2.00	4.00	8.00
2336	Up in the Streets of Harlem/You Can't Love Them All	1966	2.00	4.00	8.00
2366	Aretha/Baby What I Mean	1966	2.00	4.00	8.00
2426	Up Jumped the Devil/Ain't It the Truth	1967	2.00	4.00	8.00
2471	I Need You Now/Still Burning in My Heart	1968	2.00	4.00	8.00
2624	Your Best Friend/Steal Away	1969	2.00	4.00	8.00
2746	You Got to Pay Your Dues/Black Silk	1970	2.50	5.00	10.00
2786	A Rose By Any Other Name/Be My Lady	1971	2.50	5.00	10.00
89189	Ruby Baby/Fever	1987	—	2.00	4.00
—B-side by Little Willie John					
89189 [PS]	Ruby Baby/Fever	1987	—	2.00	4.00
—From the movie "Big Town"					
BELL					
45320	You've Got Your Troubles/I'm Feelin' Sad	1973	—	2.50	5.00
45387	The Songs We Used to Sing/Like Sister and Brother	1973	—	2.50	5.00
45600	Kissin' in the Back Row of the Movies/I'm Feelin' Sad	1974	—	2.50	5.00
CROWN					
108	The World Is Changing/Sacroiliac Swing	1954	50.00	100.00	200.00
EMI-CAPITOL MUSIC					
S7-19351	Christmas Time Is Here/I'll Be Home for Christmas	1996	—	—	3.00
—As "The Drifters Featuring Rick Sheppard"					
MUSICOR					
1498	Midsummer Night in Harlem/Lonely Drifter, Don't Cry	1974	—	2.50	5.00
—As "Charlie Thomas and the Drifters"					
S&J					
800826	(More Than a Number in My) Little Red Book/I Count the Tears	196?	2.50	5.00	10.00
—As "Bill Pinkney and the Original Drifters"					
7-Inch Extended Plays					
ATLANTIC					
534	(contents unknown)	1954	50.00	100.00	200.00
534 [PS]	Clyde McPhatter and the Drifters	1954	75.00	150.00	300.00
592	Fools Fall in Love/Adorable//Steamboat/Ruby Baby	1957	25.00	50.00	100.00
592 [PS]	The Drifters	1957	50.00	100.00	200.00
Albums					
ARISTA					
AB 4140	Every Night Is Saturday Night	1976	3.00	6.00	12.00
ATCO					
SD 33-375 [R]	Their Greatest Recordings — The Early Years	1971	3.00	6.00	12.00
ATLANTIC					
8003 [M]	Clyde McPhatter and the Drifters	1956	125.00	250.00	500.00
—Black label					
8003 [M]	Clyde McPhatter and the Drifters	1959	15.00	30.00	60.00
—Mostly red label					
8022 [M]	Rockin' and Driftin'	1958	150.00	300.00	600.00
—Black label					
8022 [M]	Rockin' and Driftin'	1958	125.00	250.00	500.00
—White "bullseye" label					
8022 [M]	Rockin' and Driftin'	1959	15.00	30.00	60.00
—Mostly red label					
8041 [M]	The Drifters' Greatest Hits	1960	150.00	300.00	600.00
—Black label					
8041 [M]	The Drifters' Greatest Hits	1960	25.00	50.00	100.00
—Mostly red label, white "fan" logo					
8059 [M]	Save the Last Dance for Me	1962	30.00	60.00	120.00
—Mostly red label, white "fan" logo					
SD 8059 [S]	Save the Last Dance for Me	1962	50.00	100.00	200.00
—Mostly red label, white "fan" logo					
8073 [M]	Up on the Roof — The Best of the Drifters	1963	25.00	50.00	100.00
—Mostly red label, black "fan" logo					
SD 8073 [S]	Up on the Roof — The Best of the Drifters	1963	37.50	75.00	150.00
—Mostly red label, black "fan" logo					
8093 [M]	Our Biggest Hits	1964	15.00	30.00	60.00
—Mostly red label, black "fan" logo					
SD 8093 [S]	Our Biggest Hits	1964	20.00	40.00	80.00
—Mostly red label, black "fan" logo					
8099 [M]	Under the Boardwalk	1964	20.00	40.00	80.00
—Black and white photo of group on cover					
8099 [M]	Under the Boardwalk	1964	12.50	25.00	50.00
—Color photo of group on cover					
SD 8099 [S]	Under the Boardwalk	1964	30.00	60.00	120.00
—Black and white photo of group on cover					
SD 8099 [S]	Under the Boardwalk	1964	15.00	30.00	60.00
—Color photo of group on cover					
8103 [M]	The Good Life with the Drifters	1965	10.00	20.00	40.00
SD 8103 [S]	The Good Life with the Drifters	1965	12.50	25.00	50.00
8113 [M]	I'll Take You Where the Music's Playing	1965	10.00	20.00	40.00
SD 8113 [S]	I'll Take You Where the Music's Playing	1965	12.50	25.00	50.00
8153 [M]	The Drifters' Golden Hits	1968	7.50	15.00	30.00
SD 8153 [P]	The Drifters' Golden Hits	1968	7.50	15.00	30.00
—Green and blue label					
SD 8153 [P]	The Drifters' Golden Hits	1969	3.75	7.50	15.00
—Red and green label					
81927 [(2)]	Let the Boogie-Woogie Roll: Greatest Hits 1953-1958	1989	3.75	7.50	15.00
81931 [(2)]	All-Time Greatest Hits and More: 1959-1965	1989	3.75	7.50	15.00
CLARION					
608 [M]	The Drifters	1964	5.00	10.00	20.00
SD 608 [P]	The Drifters	1964	7.50	15.00	30.00
GUSTO					
63	Greatest Hits — The Drifters	1980	2.50	5.00	10.00
TRIP					
TOP-16-6	16 Greatest Hits — The Drifters	1976	2.50	5.00	10.00

DRIFTERS, THE (2)

Instrumental group from England, and backing band for CLIFF RICHARD. They had one record in the US on Capitol; see THE SHADOWS, the name they adopted after the R&B Drifters became popular.

DRIFTERS, THE (3)

Number	Title (A Side/B Side)	Yr	VG	VG+	NM
45s					
CORAL					
65037	Wine Head Woman/I'm the Caring Kind	1950	75.00	150.00	300.00
65040	And I Shook/I Had to Find Out for Myself	1951	75.00	150.00	300.00

DRIFTERS, THE (4)

Number	Title (A Side/B Side)	Yr	VG	VG+	NM
45s					
RAMA					
22	Besame Mucho/Summertime	1953	50.00	100.00	200.00

DRIFTERS, THE (U)

Definitely not group (2), (3) or (4), though it could be one of the many variants of group (1).

Number	Title (A Side/B Side)	Yr	VG	VG+	NM
45s					
STEELTOWN					
671	Peace of Mind/The Struggler	1973	—	2.50	5.00

DRIFTIN' SLIM

Number	Title (A Side/B Side)	Yr	VG	VG+	NM
Albums					
MILESTONE					
MLS-93004 [(2)]	Driftin' Slim and His Blues Band	1968	6.25	12.50	25.00

DRIVERS, THE

More than one group.

Number	Title (A Side/B Side)	Yr	VG	VG+	NM
45s					
COMET					
2142	High Gear/Low Gear	1961	6.25	12.50	25.00
DELUXE					
6094	Women/Smooth, Slow and Easy	1956	25.00	50.00	100.00
6104	My Lonely Prayer/Midnight Hours	1957	50.00	100.00	200.00
6117	Dangerous Lips/Oh Miss Nellie	1957	20.00	40.00	80.00
KING					
5645	Mr. Astronaut/Dry Bones Twist	1962	3.00	6.00	12.00
LIN					
1002	A Man's Glory/Teeter Totter	1954	100.00	200.00	400.00
RCA VICTOR					
47-7023	Blue Moon/I Get Weak	1957	15.00	30.00	60.00

DRONGOS, THE

Number	Title (A Side/B Side)	Yr	VG	VG+	NM
45s					
WHITE WHALE					
235	Under My Thumb/If You Wanna Know	1966	5.00	10.00	20.00

DRUIDS OF STONEHENGE, THE

Number	Title (A Side/B Side)	Yr	VG	VG+	NM
45s					
UNI					
55021	A Garden Where Nothing Grows/Painted Woman	1967	5.00	10.00	20.00
Albums					
UNI					
3004 [M]	Creation	1967	15.00	30.00	60.00
73004 [S]	Creation	1967	20.00	40.00	80.00

DRY CITY SCAT BAND, THE

Number	Title (A Side/B Side)	Yr	VG	VG+	NM
Albums					
ELEKTRA					
EKL-292 [M]	The Dry City Scat Band	1965	6.25	12.50	25.00
EKS-7292 [S]	The Dry City Scat Band	1965	7.50	15.00	30.00

DRYSDALE, DON

Number	Title (A Side/B Side)	Yr	VG	VG+	NM
45s					
REPRISE					
20162	Give Her Love/Our Love	1963	2.50	5.00	10.00
20162 [PS]	Give Her Love/Our Love	1963	5.00	10.00	20.00

DU DROPPERS, THE

Number	Title (A Side/B Side)	Yr	VG	VG+	NM
45s					
GROOVE					
0001	Speed King/Dead Broke	1954	20.00	40.00	80.00
0013	Just Whisper/How Much Longer	1954	25.00	50.00	100.00
0036	Boot 'Em Up/Let Nature Take Its Course	1955	12.50	25.00	50.00
0104	Talk That Talk/Give Me Some Consideration	1955	12.50	25.00	50.00
0120	I Wanna Love You/You're Mine Already	1955	12.50	25.00	50.00
RCA VICTOR					
47-5229	I Wanna Know/Laughing Blues	1953	10.00	20.00	40.00
47-5321	I Found Out/Little Girl, Little Girl	1953	10.00	20.00	40.00
47-5425	Whatever You're Doin'/Somebody Work on My Baby's Mind	1953	10.00	20.00	40.00
47-5504	Don't Pass Me By/Get Lost	1953	10.00	20.00	40.00
47-5543	The Note in the Bottle/Mama's Gone Goodbye	1953	10.00	20.00	40.00
RED ROBIN					
108	Can't Do Sixty No More/Chain Me Baby (Blues of Desire)	1952	125.00	250.00	500.00
—Red vinyl					
108	Can't Do Sixty No More/Chain Me Baby (Blues of Desire)	1952	50.00	100.00	200.00
116	Come On and Love Me Baby/Go Back	1953	37.50	75.00	150.00
7-Inch Extended Plays					
GROOVE					
2	(contents unknown)	1955	50.00	100.00	200.00
2 [PS]	Talk That Talk	1955	50.00	100.00	200.00
5	(contents unknown)	1955	50.00	100.00	200.00
5 [PS]	Tops in Rhythm and Blues	1955	50.00	100.00	200.00

DUALS, THE

45s

Number	Title (A Side/B Side)	Yr	VG	VG+	NM
ARC					
4446	Nearest to My Heart/Bye Bye	1959	5.00	10.00	20.00
FURY					
1013	Wait Up Baby/Forever and Ever	1958	10.00	20.00	40.00
INFINITY					
032	Oozy Groove/The Big Race	1964	6.25	12.50	25.00
JUGGY					
321	Oozy Groove/The Big Race	1964	12.50	25.00	50.00
STAR REVUE					
1031	Stick Shift/Cruising	1961	200.00	400.00	800.00
SUE					
745	Stick Shift/Cruising	1961	7.50	15.00	30.00
758	Travelin' Guitar/Cha Cha Guitar	1962	6.25	12.50	25.00
UNITED ARTISTS					
0128	Stick Shift/Keem-O-Sabe	1973	—	2.00	4.00
—"Silver Spotlight Series" reissue; B-side by The Electric Indian					

Albums

Number	Title (A Side/B Side)	Yr	VG	VG+	NM
SUE					
LP-2002 [M]	Stick Shift	1961	100.00	200.00	400.00
—Cartoon cover					
LP-2002 [M]	Stick Shift	1964	50.00	100.00	200.00
—Photo cover					

DU'AMBRA, JOEY

45s

Number	Title (A Side/B Side)	Yr	VG	VG+	NM
ABC-PARAMOUNT					
9917	Baby Sue/Come Back-A Little Mama	1958	7.50	15.00	30.00

DUANE, DICK

45s

Number	Title (A Side/B Side)	Yr	VG	VG+	NM
ABC-PARAMOUNT					
9656	Sobony/Now	1955	7.50	15.00	30.00
9677	To Make a Mistake/Blue Prelude	1956	7.50	15.00	30.00
9709	Fame and Fortune/Mean Don't Cry	1956	7.50	15.00	30.00

DUBS, THE

45s

Number	Title (A Side/B Side)	Yr	VG	VG+	NM
ABC-PARAMOUNT					
10056	No One/Early in the Evening	1959	6.25	12.50	25.00
10100	Don't Laugh at Me/You Never Belong to Me	1960	12.50	25.00	50.00
10150	For the First Time/Ain't That So	1960	6.25	12.50	25.00
10198	If I Only Had Magic/Joogie Boogie	1961	7.50	15.00	30.00
10269	Lullaby/Down, Down, Down I Go	1961	7.50	15.00	30.00
CLIFTON					
2	Where Do We Go from Here/I Only Have Eyes for You	1973	—	3.00	6.00
END					
1108	Now That We Broke Up/This to Me Is Love	1962	12.50	25.00	50.00
GONE					
5002	Don't Ask Me (To Be Lonely)/Darling	1957	25.00	50.00	100.00
—Black label, "shadow" logo					
5002	Don't Ask Me (To Be Lonely)/Darling	1957	15.00	30.00	60.00
—Black label, clown-face logo					
5002	Don't Ask Me (To Be Lonely)/Darling	1957	6.25	12.50	25.00
—Multi-color label					
5011	Could This Be Magic/Such Lovin'	1957	12.50	25.00	50.00
—Black label					
5011	Could This Be Magic/Such Lovin'	1957	6.25	12.50	25.00
—Multi-color label					
5020	Beside My Love/Gonna Make a Change	1957	15.00	30.00	60.00
5034	Song in My Heart/Be Sure (My Love)	1958	15.00	30.00	60.00
5046	Chapel of Dreams/Is There a Love for Me	1958	15.00	30.00	60.00
5069	Chapel of Dreams/Is There a Love for Me	1959	12.50	25.00	50.00
5138	You're Free to Go/Is There a Love for Me	1962	12.50	25.00	50.00
JOHNSON					
097	Connie/Home Under My Hat	1973	—	3.00	6.00
098	Somebody Goofed/I Won't Have You Breaking My Heart	1973	—	3.00	6.00
102	Don't Ask Me (To Be Lonely)/Darling	1957	500.00	1000.	1500.
JOSIE					
911	Wisdom of a Fool/This I Swear	1963	5.00	10.00	20.00
LANA					
115	Could This Be Magic/Blue Velvet	1964	2.00	4.00	8.00
—A-side is an alternate take of the hit version					
116	Don't Ask Me (To Be Lonely)/Your Very First Love	1964	2.00	4.00	8.00
—A-side is an alternate take of the hit version					
MARK-X					
8008	Be Sure My Love/Song in My Heart	1960	5.00	10.00	20.00
VICKIE					
229	I'm Downtown/Lost in the Wilderness	1971	2.50	5.00	10.00
—As "Richard Blandon and the Dubs"					
WILSHIRE					
201	Just You/Your Very First Love	1963	10.00	20.00	40.00

Albums

Number	Title (A Side/B Side)	Yr	VG	VG+	NM
CANDELITE					
1003	You've Got to Be Good to Make It in New York City	197?	3.00	6.00	12.00
1004	The Best of the Dubs	197?	3.00	6.00	12.00

DUBS, THE / THE SHELLS

Albums

Number	Title (A Side/B Side)	Yr	VG	VG+	NM
JOSIE					
JM-4001 [M]	The Dubs Meet the Shells	1962	75.00	150.00	300.00
JSS-4001 [S]	The Dubs Meet the Shells	1962	150.00	300.00	600.00

DUCKS DELUXE

45s

Number	Title (A Side/B Side)	Yr	VG	VG+	NM
RCA VICTOR					
APBO-0297	Daddy Put the Bomp/Please, Please, Please	1974	2.00	4.00	8.00

Albums

Number	Title (A Side/B Side)	Yr	VG	VG+	NM
RCA VICTOR					
AFL1-3025	Don't Mind Rockin' Tonight	1978	2.50	5.00	10.00
LPL1-5008	Ducks Deluxe	1973	3.75	7.50	15.00

DUFFILL, TAM

45s

Number	Title (A Side/B Side)	Yr	VG	VG+	NM
GROOVE					
58-0004	Cooly Dooly/You Put the Hurt on Me	1963	15.00	30.00	60.00

DUKAYS, THE

Also see GENE CHANDLER.

45s

Number	Title (A Side/B Side)	Yr	VG	VG+	NM
NAT					
4001	The Big Lie/The Girl's a Devil	1961	5.00	10.00	20.00
4002	Nite Owl/Festival of Love	1961	5.00	10.00	20.00
VEE JAY					
430	Nite Owl/Festival of Love	1962	3.75	7.50	15.00
442	I'm Gonna Love You So/Please Help	1962	3.75	7.50	15.00
460	I Feel Good All Over/I Never Knew	1962	3.75	7.50	15.00
491	Combination/Every Step	1963	3.75	7.50	15.00

DUKE, DENVER, AND JEFFERY NULL

45s

Number	Title (A Side/B Side)	Yr	VG	VG+	NM
BLUE HEN					
127	A Babe, A Star, A Manger/Christ, Who Came To Bethlehem	19??	3.00	6.00	12.00
MERCURY					
70970	Hank Williams Isn't Dead/Rock and Roll Blues	1956	15.00	30.00	60.00

DUKE, GEORGE

12-Inch Singles

Number	Title (A Side/B Side)	Yr	VG	VG+	NM
ELEKTRA					
ED 5162 [DJ]	Broken Glass (4 versions)	1986	2.00	4.00	8.00
EPIC					
AE 595 [DJ]	Straight from the Heart/Pluck	1979	2.50	5.00	10.00
—Red vinyl					
05052	Celebrate (Extended)/(Instrumental)	1983	2.00	4.00	8.00
WARNER BROS.					
PRO-A-6463 [DJ]	6 O'Clock (4 versions)	1993	2.00	4.00	8.00

45s

Number	Title (A Side/B Side)	Yr	VG	VG+	NM
ELEKTRA					
69296	Love Ballad/560SL	1989	—	—	3.00
69315	Guilty/(Instrumental)	1989	—	—	3.00
69504	Good Friend/African Violet	1986	—	—	3.00
69504 [PS]	Good Friend/African Violet	1986	—	—	3.00
69524	Broken Glass/Island Girl	1986	—	—	3.00
69649	Thief in the Night/La La	1985	—	—	3.00
EPIC					
02701	Shine On/Positive Energy	1982	—	2.00	4.00
02932	Ride On Love/Let Your Love Shine	1982	—	2.00	4.00
03760	Reach Out (Part 1)/Reach Out (Part 2)	1983	—	2.00	4.00
50463	Reach For It/Just for You	1977	—	2.00	4.00
50531	Dukey Stick (Part One)/Dukey Stick(Part Two)	1978	—	2.00	4.00
50593	Movin' On/The Way I Feel	1978	—	2.00	4.00
50660	Say That You Will/I Am for Real (May the Funk Be With You)	1979	—	2.00	4.00
50719	Straight from the Heart/Pluck	1979	—	2.00	4.00
50792	I Want You for Myself/Party Down	1979	—	2.00	4.00
50853	Every Little Step I Take/Games	1980	—	2.00	4.00

Albums

Number	Title (A Side/B Side)	Yr	VG	VG+	NM
ELEKTRA					
60398	Thief in the Night	1985	2.50	5.00	10.00
60778	Night After Night	1989	2.50	5.00	10.00
EPIC					
PE 34469	From Me to You	1977	2.50	5.00	10.00
—Originals have no bar code					
PE 34469	From Me to You	198?	2.00	4.00	8.00
—Budget-line reissue with bar code					
JE 34883	Reach For It	1977	2.50	5.00	10.00
PE 34883	Reach For It	198?	2.00	4.00	8.00
—Budget-line reissue					
JE 35366	Don't Let Go	1978	2.50	5.00	10.00
PE 35366	Don't Let Go	198?	2.00	4.00	8.00
—Budget-line reissue					
JE 35701	Follow the Rainbow	1979	2.50	5.00	10.00
JE 36263	Master of the Game	1979	2.50	5.00	10.00
PE 36263	Master of the Game	198?	2.00	4.00	8.00
—Budget-line reissue					
FE 36483	A Brazilian Love Affair	1980	2.50	5.00	10.00
FE 37532	Dream On	1982	2.50	5.00	10.00
FE 38208	1976 Solo Album	1983	2.50	5.00	10.00
FE 39262	Rendezvous	1984	2.50	5.00	10.00
MPS/BASF					
22018	Faces in Reflection	1974	3.00	6.00	12.00
22835	Liberated Fantasies	1976	2.50	5.00	10.00
25355	Feel	1974	2.50	5.00	10.00
25613	The Aura Will Prevail	1975	2.50	5.00	10.00
25671	I Love the Blues, She Heard My Cry	1975	2.50	5.00	10.00
PACIFIC JAZZ					
PJ-LA891-H	George Duke	1978	2.50	5.00	10.00
LN-10127	Save the Country	198?	2.00	4.00	8.00
PAUSA					
7042	The Aura Will Prevail	198?	2.00	4.00	8.00
—Reissue of MPS/BASF 25613					
7070	I Love the Blues	1980	2.00	4.00	8.00
PICKWICK					
SPC-3588	Save the Country	1978	2.00	4.00	8.00
VERVE/MPS					
821665-1	Feel	1984	2.00	4.00	8.00
—Reissue of MPS/BASF 25355					

Number	Title (A Side/B Side)	Yr	VG	VG+	NM
821837-1	The Aura Will Prevail	1984	2.00	4.00	8.00
—Reissue of Pausa 7042					

DUKE, PATTY

45s

UNITED ARTISTS

Number	Title (A Side/B Side)	Yr	VG	VG+	NM
0127	Don't Just Stand There/Say Something Funny	1973	—	2.00	4.00
—"Silver Spotlight Series" reissue					
875	Don't Just Stand There/Everything But Love	1965	2.50	5.00	10.00
875 [PS]	Don't Just Stand There/Everything But Love	1965	5.00	10.00	20.00
915	Funny Little Butterflies/Say Something Funny	1965	2.00	4.00	8.00
915 [PS]	Funny Little Butterflies/Say Something Funny	1965	5.00	10.00	20.00
958	Why Don't They Understand/Ribbons and Roses	1965	—	—	—
—Unreleased					
978	Whenever She Holds You/Nothing But Me	1966	2.00	4.00	8.00
50034	Little Things Mean a Lot/The World Is Watching Us	1966	2.00	4.00	8.00
50057	The Wall Came Tumbling Down/What Makes You Special	1966	2.00	4.00	8.00
50073	Why Don't They Understand/Danke Schoen	1966	2.00	4.00	8.00
50216	Come Live with Me/My Own Little Place	1967	—	3.00	6.00
50299	Dona, Dona/And We Were Strangers	1968	—	3.00	6.00

Albums

UNART

Number	Title (A Side/B Side)	Yr	VG	VG+	NM
20005 [M]	TV's Teen Star	1967	3.00	6.00	12.00
S 20005 [S]	TV's Teen Star	1967	3.75	7.50	15.00

UNITED ARTISTS

Number	Title (A Side/B Side)	Yr	VG	VG+	NM
UAL-3452 [M]	Don't Just Stand There	1965	5.00	10.00	20.00
UAL-3492 [M]	Patty	1966	5.00	10.00	20.00
UAL-3535 [M]	Patty Duke's Greatest Hits	1966	3.75	7.50	15.00
UAS-6452 [S]	Don't Just Stand There	1965	7.50	15.00	30.00
UAS-6492 [S]	Patty	1966	7.50	15.00	30.00
UAS-6535 [S]	Patty Duke's Greatest Hits	1966	6.25	12.50	25.00
UAS-6632	Songs from the Valley of the Dolls	1968	6.25	12.50	25.00

DUKE, PATTY, WITH NORMAN VINCENT PEALE

Albums

GUIDEPOSTS

Number	Title (A Side/B Side)	Yr	VG	VG+	NM
GP-101 [M]	Guideposts for Christmas	1963	20.00	40.00	80.00

DUKE OF EARL, THE

See GENE CHANDLER.

DUKES, THE

Possibly more than one group.

45s

FLIP

Number	Title (A Side/B Side)	Yr	VG	VG+	NM
343	Looking for You/Groceries Sir	1959	7.50	15.00	30.00
345	I Love You/Leap Year Cha Cha	1959	10.00	20.00	40.00

IMPERIAL

Number	Title (A Side/B Side)	Yr	VG	VG+	NM
5401	Teardrop Eyes/Shimmies and Shakes	1956	62.50	125.00	250.00
5415	Wini Brown/Cotton Pickin' Hands	1956	30.00	60.00	120.00

SPECIALTY

Number	Title (A Side/B Side)	Yr	VG	VG+	NM
543	Ooh Bop She Bop/Oh-Kay	1954	18.75	37.50	75.00

DUKES OF DIXIELAND, THE

45s

COLUMBIA

Number	Title (A Side/B Side)	Yr	VG	VG+	NM
OP 50 [DJ]	If I Were a Bell/(B-side unknown)	195?	3.00	6.00	12.00
—"Special Coin-Operator Release"					
31356 [S]	(contents unknown)	1962	2.00	4.00	8.00
31357 [S]	(contents unknown)	1962	2.00	4.00	8.00
31358 [S]	(contents unknown)	1962	2.00	4.00	8.00
31359 [S]	(contents unknown)	1962	2.00	4.00	8.00
31360 [S]	(contents unknown)	1962	2.00	4.00	8.00
31575 [S]	(contents unknown)	1962	2.00	4.00	8.00
31576 [S]	(contents unknown)	1962	2.00	4.00	8.00
31577 [S]	(contents unknown)	1962	2.00	4.00	8.00
31578 [S]	(contents unknown)	1962	2.00	4.00	8.00
31579 [S]	(contents unknown)	1962	2.00	4.00	8.00
—Anyone who can fill in these gaps -- the above 10 all are Columbia "Stereo 7" singles -- please let us know.					
42416	What's the Time?/Too Bad	1962	2.00	4.00	8.00
42599	Bye and Bye/Deep River	1962	2.00	4.00	8.00
43013	Fair Is Fair/Big Parade	1964	2.00	4.00	8.00

DECCA

Number	Title (A Side/B Side)	Yr	VG	VG+	NM
25693	Everybody Loves My Baby/Yvette	1966	—	2.50	5.00
25715	Baby Face/Rose of Washington Square	1967	—	2.50	5.00
25729	Smile/More and More	1968	—	2.50	5.00
31798	I Will Wait for You/Exactly Like You	1966	—	3.00	6.00

Albums

AUDIO FIDELITY

Number	Title (A Side/B Side)	Yr	VG	VG+	NM
AFLP-1823 [M]	You Have to Hear It to Believe It — The Dukes of Dixieland, Vol. 1	1956	3.75	7.50	15.00
AFLP-1840 [M]	You Have to Hear It to Believe It — The Dukes of Dixieland, Vol. 2	1957	3.75	7.50	15.00
AFLP-1851 [M]	Marching Along with the Dukes of Dixieland, Vol. 3	1957	3.75	7.50	15.00
AFLP-1860 [M]	The Dukes of Dixieland On Bourbon Street, Vol. 4	1958	3.75	7.50	15.00
AFLP-1862 [M]	Mardi Gras Time	1958	3.75	7.50	15.00
AFLP-1891 [M]	The Dukes of Dixieland On Campus	1959	3.75	7.50	15.00
AFLP-1892 [M]	Up the Mississippi	1959	3.75	7.50	15.00
AFLP-1918 [M]	Carnegie Hall Concert	1959	3.75	7.50	15.00
AFLP-1924 [M]	Louie and the Dukes	196?	3.75	7.50	15.00
AFLP-1928 [M]	Piano Ragtime (Vol. 11)	196?	3.75	7.50	15.00
AFLP-1956 [M]	The Best of the Dukes of Dixieland	1961	3.75	7.50	15.00
AFLP-1976 [M]	More of the Best of the Dukes of Dixieland	1962	3.75	7.50	15.00
AFSD-5823 [S]	You Have to Hear It to Believe It — The Dukes of Dixieland, Vol. 1	196?	5.00	10.00	20.00
AFSD-5840 [S]	You Have to Hear It to Believe It — The Dukes of Dixieland, Vol. 2	196?	5.00	10.00	20.00
AFSD-5851 [S]	Marching Along with the Dukes of Dixieland, Vol. 3	1958	5.00	10.00	20.00
AFSD-5860 [S]	The Dukes of Dixieland On Bourbon Street, Vol. 4	1958	5.00	10.00	20.00
AFSD-5862 [S]	Mardi Gras Time	1958	5.00	10.00	20.00
AFSD-5891 [S]	The Dukes of Dixieland On Campus	1959	5.00	10.00	20.00
AFSD-5892 [S]	Up the Mississippi	1959	5.00	10.00	20.00
AFSD-5918 [S]	Carnegie Hall Concert	1959	3.75	7.50	15.00
AFSD-5924 [S]	Louie and the Dukes	196?	3.75	7.50	15.00
AFSD-5928 [S]	Piano Ragtime (Vol. 11)	196?	3.75	7.50	15.00
AFSD-5956 [S]	The Best of the Dukes of Dixieland	1961	3.75	7.50	15.00
AFSD-5976 [S]	More of the Best of the Dukes of Dixieland	1962	3.75	7.50	15.00
AFSD-6172	Tailgating	1967	3.00	6.00	12.00
AFSD-6174	The Dukes of Dixieland On Parade	1967	3.00	6.00	12.00

COLUMBIA

Number	Title (A Side/B Side)	Yr	VG	VG+	NM
CL 1728 [M]	Breakin' It Up on Broadway	1962	3.00	6.00	12.00
CL 2194 [M]	Struttin' at the World's Fair	1964	3.00	6.00	12.00
CS 8528 [S]	Breakin' It Up on Broadway	1962	3.75	7.50	15.00
CS 8994 [S]	Struttin' at the World's Fair	1964	3.75	7.50	15.00

DECCA

Number	Title (A Side/B Side)	Yr	VG	VG+	NM
DL 4653 [M]	"Live" At Bourbon Street, Chicago	1965	3.00	6.00	12.00
DL 4708 [M]	Come On and Hear	1966	3.00	6.00	12.00
DL 4807 [M]	Sunrise, Sunset	1966	3.00	6.00	12.00
DL 4863 [M]	Come to the Cabaret	1967	3.75	7.50	15.00
DL 4864 [M]	Thoroughly Modern Millie	1967	3.75	7.50	15.00
DL 74653 [S]	"Live" At Bourbon Street, Chicago	1965	3.75	7.50	15.00
DL 74708 [S]	Come On and Hear	1966	3.75	7.50	15.00
DL 74807 [S]	Sunrise, Sunset	1966	3.75	7.50	15.00
DL 74863 [S]	Come to the Cabaret	1967	3.00	6.00	12.00
DL 74864 [S]	Thoroughly Modern Millie	1967	3.00	6.00	12.00
DL 74975	Dixieland's Greatest Hits	1968	3.00	6.00	12.00

HARMONY

Number	Title (A Side/B Side)	Yr	VG	VG+	NM
HL 7349 [M]	Best of the Dukes of Dixieland	1965	3.00	6.00	12.00
HS 11149 [S]	Best of the Dukes of Dixieland	1965	3.00	6.00	12.00

MCA

Number	Title (A Side/B Side)	Yr	VG	VG+	NM
268	Dixieland's Greatest Hits	1973	2.50	5.00	10.00
—Reissue of Decca 74975					

RCA VICTOR

Number	Title (A Side/B Side)	Yr	VG	VG+	NM
LPM-2097 [M]	The Dukes of Dixieland at the Jazz Band Ball	1960	3.00	6.00	12.00
LSP-2097(e) [R]	The Dukes of Dixieland at the Jazz Band Ball	1960	3.75	7.50	15.00

ROULETTE

Number	Title (A Side/B Side)	Yr	VG	VG+	NM
R-25029 [M]	Curtain Going Up	1958	5.00	10.00	20.00

VIK

Number	Title (A Side/B Side)	Yr	VG	VG+	NM
LX-1025 [M]	The Dukes of Dixieland at the Jazz Band Ball	1956	7.50	15.00	30.00

VOCALION

Number	Title (A Side/B Side)	Yr	VG	VG+	NM
VL 73846	Hello, Dolly!	1968	2.50	5.00	10.00

DUMAURIERS, THE

45s

FURY

Number	Title (A Side/B Side)	Yr	VG	VG+	NM
1011	Baby I Love You/All Night Long	1957	25.00	50.00	100.00

DUNAVAN, TERRY

45s

FANFARE

Number	Title (A Side/B Side)	Yr	VG	VG+	NM
727	Rock It on Mars/(B-side unknown)	195?	100.00	200.00	400.00

DUNBAR, AYNSLEY

Also see JEFFERSON AIRPLANE; JOURNEY; JOHN MAYALL.

Albums

BLUE THUMB

Number	Title (A Side/B Side)	Yr	VG	VG+	NM
BTS-4	The Aynsley Dunbar Retaliation	1968	6.25	12.50	25.00
BTS-6	Doctor Dunbar's Prescription	1969	6.25	12.50	25.00
BTS-16	To Mum From Aynsley and the Boys	1970	6.25	12.50	25.00

DUNCAN, HERBIE

45s

GLENN

Number	Title (A Side/B Side)	Yr	VG	VG+	NM
1400	Hot Lips Baby/Little Angel	1961	100.00	200.00	400.00
1401	Roll Along/Escape	1961	30.00	60.00	120.00
1402	That's All/End of the Rainbow	1961	20.00	40.00	80.00

MAR-VEL

Number	Title (A Side/B Side)	Yr	VG	VG+	NM
1400	Hot Lips Baby/Little Angel	1960	25.00	50.00	100.00

DUNDEE, CARLYLE, AND THE DUNDEES

45s

SPACE

Number	Title (A Side/B Side)	Yr	VG	VG+	NM
201	Never/Evil One	1954	100.00	200.00	400.00

DUNGAREE DARLINGS, THE

45s

KAREN

Number	Title (A Side/B Side)	Yr	VG	VG+	NM
1005	Boy of My Dreams/Little Wallflower	1959	25.00	50.00	100.00

REGO

Number	Title (A Side/B Side)	Yr	VG	VG+	NM
1003	Boy of My Dreams/Little Wallflower	1958	62.50	125.00	250.00
—As "The Dungaree Dolls"					

DUNGAREE DOLLS, THE

See THE DUNGAREE DARLINGS.

DUPONTS, THE

Little Anthony's group before joining the Imperials. They are NOT the same group as the Imperials.

45s

ROULETTE

Number	Title (A Side/B Side)	Yr	VG	VG+	NM
4060	Half Past Nothing/A Screamin' Ball (At Dracula Hall)	1958	6.25	12.50	25.00

ROYAL ROOST

Number	Title (A Side/B Side)	Yr	VG	VG+	NM
627	Somebody/Prove It Tonight	1957	12.50	25.00	50.00

SAVOY

Number	Title (A Side/B Side)	Yr	VG	VG+	NM
1552	Must Be Falling in Love/You	1958	6.25	12.50	25.00
—As "Little Anthony Guardine and the Duponts"					

WINLEY

Number	Title (A Side/B Side)	Yr	VG	VG+	NM
212	Must Be Falling in Love/You	1957	20.00	40.00	80.00

DUPREE, CHAMPION JACK

45s

Number	Title (A Side/B Side)	Yr	VG	VG+	NM
ATLANTIC					
2032	Frankie and Johnny/Strollin'	1959	3.00	6.00	12.00
—As "Champion Jack"					
2095	My Mother-in-Law/Evil Woman	1961	2.50	5.00	10.00
EVERLAST					
5025	Shake Baby Shake/Walking Down the Highway	1963	2.50	5.00	10.00
5032	Highway Blues/Shake Baby Shake	1964	2.00	4.00	8.00
FEDERAL					
12408	Two Below Zero/Sharp Harp	1961	3.00	6.00	12.00
GROOVE					
0171	Lonely Road Blues/When I Get Married	1956	10.00	20.00	40.00
—With Mr. Bear					
KING					
4695	Hard Feeling/Walking Upside Your Head	1954	7.50	15.00	30.00
4706	Camille/Rub a Little Boogie	1954	7.50	15.00	30.00
4779	Blues for Everybody/Two Below Zero	1955	7.50	15.00	30.00
4797	Let the Doorbell Ring/Harelip Blues	1955	7.50	15.00	30.00
4812	Walking the Blues/Daybreak Rock	1955	7.50	15.00	30.00
—B-side by Mr. Bear and the Bearcats					
4827	That's My Pa/Stumbling Block	1955	7.50	15.00	30.00
4859	Silent Partner/She Cooks Me Cabbage	1955	7.50	15.00	30.00
4876	Me and My Mule/Failing Health Blues	1956	7.50	15.00	30.00
4906	So Sorry, So Sorry/Overhead	1956	7.50	15.00	30.00
4938	Big Leg Woman/Mail Order Woman	1956	7.50	15.00	30.00
6299	Blues for Everybody/Tongue-Tied Blues	1970	—	3.00	6.00
RED ROBIN					
109	Stumblin' Block Blues/Number Nine Blues	1952	100.00	200.00	400.00
112	Shake Baby Shake/Highway Blues	1952	50.00	100.00	200.00
130	Drunk Again/Shim Sham Shimmy	1954	50.00	100.00	200.00
VIK					
0260	Just Like a Woman/Dirty Woman	1957	10.00	20.00	40.00
0279	Old Time Rock and Roll/Rocky Mountain	1957	10.00	20.00	40.00
0304	Shake Baby Shake/Lollipop Baby	1957	10.00	20.00	40.00

Albums

Number	Title (A Side/B Side)	Yr	VG	VG+	NM
ARCHIVE OF FOLK AND JAZZ					
217	Champion Jack Dupree	197?	2.50	5.00	10.00
ATLANTIC					
8019 [M]	Blues from the Gutter	1959	37.50	75.00	150.00
—Black label					
8019 [M]	Blues from the Gutter	1960	12.50	25.00	50.00
—White "fan" logo at right of label					
8019 [M]	Blues from the Gutter	1963	5.00	10.00	20.00
—Black "fan" logo at right of label					
SD 8019 [S]	Blues from the Gutter	1959	50.00	100.00	200.00
—Green label					
SD 8019 [S]	Blues from the Gutter	1960	15.00	30.00	60.00
—Green and blue label, white "fan' logo at right of label					
SD 8019 [S]	Blues from the Gutter	1963	6.25	12.50	25.00
—Green and blue label, black "fan' logo at right of label					
8045 [M]	Natural and Soulful Blues	1961	12.50	25.00	50.00
—White "fan' logo at right of label					
8045 [M]	Natural and Soulful Blues	1963	5.00	10.00	20.00
—Black "fan" logo at right of label					
SD 8045 [S]	Natural and Soulful Blues	1961	15.00	30.00	60.00
—Green and blue label, white "fan' logo at right of label					
SD 8045 [S]	Natural and Soulful Blues	1963	6.25	12.50	25.00
—Green and blue label, black "fan' logo at right of label					
8056 [M]	Champion of the Blues	1961	12.50	25.00	50.00
—White "fan' logo at right of label					
8056 [M]	Champion of the Blues	1963	5.00	10.00	20.00
—Black "fan" logo at right of label					
SD 8056 [R]	Champion of the Blues	196?	3.75	7.50	15.00
SD 8255	Blues from the Gutter	1970	3.75	7.50	15.00
BLUE HORIZON					
7702	When You Feel the Feeling	1969	6.25	12.50	25.00
BULLSEYE					
BB-9502	Back Home In New Orleans	1990	3.00	6.00	12.00
CONTINENTAL					
CLP-16002 [M]	Low Down Blues	1961	62.50	125.00	250.00
FOLKWAYS					
FS-3825 [M]	Women Blues of Champion Jack Dupree	1961	6.25	12.50	25.00
GNP CRESCENDO					
GNPS-10001	Tricks	1974	3.00	6.00	12.00
GNPS-10005	Happy to Be Free	1974	3.00	6.00	12.00
GNPS-10013	Legacy of Blues 3	197?	3.00	6.00	12.00
JAZZ MAN					
BLZ-5501	Champion Jack Dupree	1982	2.50	5.00	10.00
KING					
735 [M]	Champion Jack Dupree Sings the Blues	1961	75.00	150.00	300.00
KS-1084	Walking the Blues	1970	3.75	7.50	15.00
LONDON					
PS 553	From New Orleans to Chicago	1969	5.00	10.00	20.00
OKEH					
OKM 12103 [M]	Cabbage Greens	1963	7.50	15.00	30.00
STORYVILLE					
4010	Best of the Blues	1982	2.50	5.00	10.00
4040	I'm Growing Older Every Day	198?	2.50	5.00	10.00

DUPREE, CHAMPION JACK, AND MICKEY BAKER

Albums

Number	Title (A Side/B Side)	Yr	VG	VG+	NM
SIRE					
SES-97010	In Heavy Blues	1969	7.50	15.00	30.00

DUPREE, CHAMPION JACK, AND JIMMY RUSHING

Albums

Number	Title (A Side/B Side)	Yr	VG	VG+	NM
AUDIO LAB					
AL-1512 [M]	Two Shades of Blue	1958	50.00	100.00	200.00

DUPREE, DAVE

See DAVE BURGESS.

DUPREE, SIMON, AND THE BIG SOUND

45s

Number	Title (A Side/B Side)	Yr	VG	VG+	NM
TOWER					
427	Daytime, Night Time/I've Seen It All Before	1968	2.00	4.00	8.00

Albums

Number	Title (A Side/B Side)	Yr	VG	VG+	NM
TOWER					
ST-5097	Without Reservations	1968	10.00	20.00	40.00

DUPREES, THE

45s

Number	Title (A Side/B Side)	Yr	VG	VG+	NM
COED					
569	You Belong to Me/Take Me As I Am	1962	5.00	10.00	20.00
571	My Own True Love/Ginny	1962	5.00	10.00	20.00
574	I'd Rather Be Here in Your Arms/I Wish You Could Believe Me	1963	3.75	7.50	15.00
576	Gone with the Wind/Let's Make Love Again	1963	3.75	7.50	15.00
580	I Gotta Tell Her Now/Take Me As I Am	1963	3.75	7.50	15.00
584	Why Don't You Believe Me/The Things I Love	1963	7.50	15.00	30.00
584	Why Don't You Believe Me/My Dearest One	1963	3.75	7.50	15.00
585	Have You Heard/Love Eyes	1963	3.75	7.50	15.00
587	(It's No) Sin/The Sand and the Sea	1964	3.75	7.50	15.00
591	Please Let Her Know/Where Are You	1964	3.75	7.50	15.00
593	Unbelievable/So Many Have Told Me	1964	3.75	7.50	15.00
595	So Little Time/It Isn't Fair	1964	3.75	7.50	15.00
596	I'm Yours/Wishing Ring	1964	3.75	7.50	15.00
COLOSSUS					
110	Check Yourself/The Sky's the Limit	1970	—	3.00	6.00
—As "The Italian Asphalt and Pavement Company" or "The I.A.P. Co." for short					
110 [PS]	Check Yourself/The Sky's the Limit	1970	—	3.00	6.00
—As "The Italian Asphalt and Pavement Company" or "The I.A.P. Co." for short					
COLUMBIA					
43336	Around the Corner/They Said It Couldn't Be Done	1965	3.00	6.00	12.00
43464	Norma Jean/She Waits for Him	1965	3.00	6.00	12.00
43577	The Exodus Song/Let Them Talk	1966	3.00	6.00	12.00
43802	It's Not Time Now/Don't Want to Have to Do It	1966	2.50	5.00	10.00
44078	Be My Love/I Understand	1967	2.50	5.00	10.00
HERITAGE					
804	My Special Angel/Ring of Love	1968	2.50	5.00	10.00
805	Goodnight My Love/Ring of Love	1968	2.50	5.00	10.00
805 [PS]	Goodnight My Love/Ring of Love	1968	5.00	10.00	20.00
808	My Love, My Love/The Sky's the Limit	1968	2.50	5.00	10.00
808 [PS]	My Love, My Love/The Sky's the Limit	1968	5.00	10.00	20.00
811	Two Different Worlds/Hope	1969	2.50	5.00	10.00
811 [PS]	Two Different Worlds/Hope	1969	5.00	10.00	20.00
826	Have You Heard/My Love, My Love	1970	2.50	5.00	10.00
RCA VICTOR					
PB-10407	The Sky's the Limit/Delicious	1975	2.50	5.00	10.00

Albums

Number	Title (A Side/B Side)	Yr	VG	VG+	NM
COED					
LPC-905 [M]	You Belong to Me	1962	75.00	150.00	300.00
LPC-906 [M]	Have You Heard	1963	50.00	100.00	200.00
COLLECTABLES					
COL-5008	The Best of the Duprees	198?	3.00	6.00	12.00
COLOSSUS					
5000	Duprees Gold	1970	7.50	15.00	30.00
—As "The Italian Asphalt & Pavement Co."					
HERITAGE					
HTS-35002	Total Recall	1968	7.50	15.00	30.00
POST					
1000	The Duprees Sing	196?	7.50	15.00	30.00

DURANTE, JIMMY

45s

Number	Title (A Side/B Side)	Yr	VG	VG+	NM
MGM					
30257	Frosty The Snowman/Christmas Comes But Once A Year	1950	3.75	7.50	15.00
WARNER BROS.					
5382	September Song/Young at Heart	1963	2.00	4.00	8.00
5410	Hello Young Lovers/This Is All I Ask	1964	2.00	4.00	8.00
5456	This Train/When Love Flies Out the Window	1964	2.00	4.00	8.00
5483	Old Man Time/I Came Here to Swim	1964	2.00	4.00	8.00
5686	(I Wonder) What Became of Life/One of Those Songs	1965	2.00	4.00	8.00
5823	Mame/We're Going UFO'ing	1966	3.00	6.00	12.00
5843	Bill Bailey (Won't You Please Come Home)/ Margie	1966	2.00	4.00	8.00
7024	Hellzapoppin'/M.F. O'Brien	1967	—	3.00	6.00
7253	He Touched Me/Amen	1968	—	3.00	6.00
7367	He Ain't Heavy, He's My Brother/Look Ahead Little Girl	1970	—	3.00	6.00

Albums

Number	Title (A Side/B Side)	Yr	VG	VG+	NM
DECCA					
DL 5116 [10]	Jimmy Durante	195?	12.50	25.00	50.00
DL 8884 [M]	Jimmy Durante at the Piano	1959	3.75	7.50	15.00
DL 9049 [M]	Club Durant	195?	6.25	12.50	25.00
DL 78884 [S]	Jimmy Durante at the Piano	1959	5.00	10.00	20.00
LION					
L-70053 [M]	Jimmy Durante in Person	195?	7.50	15.00	30.00
MGM					
E-3242 [M]	Jimmy Durante in Person	1955	7.50	15.00	30.00
E-4207 [M]	The Very Best of Jimmy Durante	1964	3.00	6.00	12.00
SE-4207 [S]	The Very Best of Jimmy Durante	1964	3.75	7.50	15.00
ROULETTE					
R-25123 [M]	Jimmy Durante at the Copacabana	1961	5.00	10.00	20.00
SR-25123 [S]	Jimmy Durante at the Copacabana	1961	6.25	12.50	25.00
WARNER BROS.					
W 1506 [M]	September Song	1963	3.75	7.50	15.00
WS 1506 [S]	September Song	1963	5.00	10.00	20.00

Number	Title (A Side/B Side)	Yr	VG	VG+	NM
W 1531 [M]	Hello Young Lovers	1964	3.75	7.50	15.00
WS 1531 [S]	Hello Young Lovers	1964	5.00	10.00	20.00
W 1577 [M]	Jimmy Durante's Way of Life	1965	3.75	7.50	15.00
WS 1577 [S]	Jimmy Durante's Way of Life	1965	5.00	10.00	20.00
W 1655 [M]	One of Those Songs	1966	3.75	7.50	15.00
WS 1655 [S]	One of Those Songs	1966	5.00	10.00	20.00
W 1713 [M]	Songs for Sunday	1967	3.75	7.50	15.00
WS 1713 [S]	Songs for Sunday	1967	5.00	10.00	20.00

DUSK

With Peggy Santaglia of THE ANGELS.

45s

BELL

Number	Title (A Side/B Side)	Yr	VG	VG+	NM
961	Angel Baby/If We Just Leave Today	1971	—	3.00	6.00
961	Angel Baby/Reach Out and Speak My Name	1971	—	3.00	6.00
990	I Hear Those Church Bells Ringing/I Cannot See to See You	1971	—	3.00	6.00
45148	Suburbia U.S.A./Treat Me Like a Good Piece of Candy	1971	—	3.00	6.00
45207	Point of No Return/(B-side unknown)	1972	—	3.00	6.00

DUST

45s

KAMA SUTRA

Number	Title (A Side/B Side)	Yr	VG	VG+	NM
534	Stone Woman/(B-side unknown)	1971	—	3.00	6.00
541	Love Me Hard/(B-side unknown)	1972	—	3.00	6.00

Albums

KAMA SUTRA

Number	Title (A Side/B Side)	Yr	VG	VG+	NM
KSBS-2041	Dust	1971	6.25	12.50	25.00
—Pink label					
KSBS-2059	Hard Attack	1972	6.25	12.50	25.00
—Pink label					

DUSTERS, THE (1)

45s

ABC-PARAMOUNT

Number	Title (A Side/B Side)	Yr	VG	VG+	NM
9887	Pretty Girl/Coolation	1958	7.50	15.00	30.00

CUPID

Number	Title (A Side/B Side)	Yr	VG	VG+	NM
5003	Rock at the Hop/She's Mine	1958	17.50	35.00	70.00

GLORY

Number	Title (A Side/B Side)	Yr	VG	VG+	NM
287	Darling Love/Teen-Age Jamboree	1958	12.50	25.00	50.00

DUSTERS, THE (2)

TOMMY TUCKER was a member of this group.

45s

ARC

Number	Title (A Side/B Side)	Yr	VG	VG+	NM
3000	Give Me Time/Sallie Mae	1956	75.00	150.00	300.00

DUVALL, HUELYN

45s

CHALLENGE

Number	Title (A Side/B Side)	Yr	VG	VG+	NM
1012	Teen Queen/Comin' or Goin'	1957	25.00	50.00	100.00
—Blue label					
1012	Teen Queen/Comin' or Goin'	1957	7.50	15.00	30.00
—Maroon label					
59002	Hum-Dinger/You Knock Me Out	1958	7.50	15.00	30.00
59014	Little Boy Blue/Three Months to Kill	1958	10.00	20.00	40.00
59025	Friday Night on a Dollar Bill/Juliette	1958	7.50	15.00	30.00
59069	Pucker Paint/Boom Boom Baby	1960	7.50	15.00	30.00

DYKE AND THE BLAZERS

45s

ORIGINAL SOUND

Number	Title (A Side/B Side)	Yr	VG	VG+	NM
64	Funky Broadway — Part 1/Funky Broadway — Part 2	1966	2.50	5.00	10.00
69	So Sharp/Don't Bug Me	1967	2.00	4.00	8.00
79	Funky Walk Part 1 — East/Funky Walk Part 2 — West	1967	2.00	4.00	8.00
83	Funky Bull — Part 1/Funky Bull — Part 2	1968	2.00	4.00	8.00
86	We Got More Soul/Shotgun Slim	1969	2.00	4.00	8.00
89	Let a Woman Be a Woman — Let a Man Be a Man/Uhh	1969	2.00	4.00	8.00
90	You Are My Sunshine/City Dump	1969	2.00	4.00	8.00
91	Uhh/My Sister's and My Brother's Day Is Coming	1970	2.00	4.00	8.00
96	Runaway People/I'm So All Alone	1970	2.00	4.00	8.00

Albums

ORIGINAL SOUND

Number	Title (A Side/B Side)	Yr	VG	VG+	NM
LP 8876 [M]	The Funky Broadway	1967	12.50	25.00	50.00
LPS 8876 [S]	The Funky Broadway	1967	18.75	37.50	75.00
LPS 8877	Dyke's Greatest Hits	1968	18.75	37.50	75.00

DYLAN, BOB

Also see HARRY BELAFONTE; GEORGE HARRISON AND FRIENDS; CAROLYN HESTER.

12-Inch Singles

COLUMBIA

Number	Title (A Side/B Side)	Yr	VG	VG+	NM
CAS 2169 [DJ]	When the Night Comes Falling from the Sky (Edit) (same on both sides)	1985	2.50	5.00	10.00

45s

ASYLUM

Number	Title (A Side/B Side)	Yr	VG	VG+	NM
11033	On a Night Like This/You Angel You	1974	—	3.00	6.00
11035	Something There Is About You/Going, Going, Gone	1974	—	3.00	6.00
11043	Most Likely You Go Your Way (And I'll Go Mine)/Stage Fright	1974	—	3.00	6.00
—With The Band					
45212	All Along the Watchtower/It Ain't Me Babe	1974	3.00	6.00	12.00

COLUMBIA

Number	Title (A Side/B Side)	Yr	VG	VG+	NM
AE 25 [DJ]	All the Tired Horses (mono/stereo)	1970	10.00	20.00	40.00
AE7 1039 [DJ]	If Not for You/Tomorrow Is a Long Time	1971	10.00	20.00	40.00
02510	Heart of Mine/The Groom's Still Waiting at the Altar	1981	—	2.00	4.00
02510 [PS]	Heart of Mine/The Groom's Still Waiting at the Altar	1981	—	2.50	5.00
04301	Sweetheart Like You/Union Sundown	1983	—	2.00	4.00
04301 [PS]	Sweetheart Like You/Union Sundown	1983	—	2.50	5.00
04425	Jokerman/Isis	1984	—	2.50	5.00
04933	Tight Connection to My Heart (Has Anybody Seen My Love)/We Better Talk This Over	1985	—	2.00	4.00
04933 [PS]	Tight Connection to My Heart (Has Anybody Seen My Love)/We Better Talk This Over	1985	—	2.00	4.00
05697	Emotionaly Yours/When the Night Comes Falling from the Sky	1985	—	2.00	4.00
07970	Silvio/Too Far from Home	1988	—	2.50	5.00
10106	Tangled Up in Blue/If You See Her Say Hello	1975	—	3.00	6.00
10217	Million Dollar Bash/Tears of Rage	1975	2.50	5.00	10.00
10245	Hurricane (Part 1)/Hurricane (Part 2)	1975	—	3.00	6.00
10245 [DJ]	Hurricane (mono/stereo)	1975	5.00	10.00	20.00
—Plays at 33 1/3 rpm; does not have "Special Rush Reservice" on label					
10245 [DJ]	Hurricane (mono/stereo)	1975	3.75	7.50	15.00
—Plays at 33 1/3 rpm; has "Special Rush Reservice" on label					
10245 [PS]	Hurricane (mono/stereo)	1975	3.75	7.50	15.00
—Special sleeve for above record					
10245 [PS]	Hurricane (Part 1)/Hurricane (Part 2)	1975	3.00	6.00	12.00
10298	Mozambique/Oh, Sister	1976	—	3.00	6.00
10454	Stuck Inside of Mobile with the Memphis Blues Again/Rita Mae	1976	—	2.50	5.00
10454 [PS]	Stuck Inside of Mobile with the Memphis Blues Again/Rita Mae	1976	—	3.00	6.00
10805	Baby Stop Crying/New Pony	1978	—	2.50	5.00
10851	Changing of the Guards/Senor (Tales of Yankee Power)	1978	—	2.00	4.00
11072	Gotta Serve Somebody/Trouble in Mind	1979	—	2.00	4.00
11168	Man Gave Names to All the Animals/When You Gonna Wake Up	1979	—	2.00	4.00
11235	Slow Train/Do Right to Me Baby (Do Unto Others)	1980	—	2.00	4.00
11235 [PS]	Slow Train/Do Right to Me Baby (Do Unto Others)	1980	—	2.50	5.00
11318	Solid Rock/Covenant Woman	1980	—	2.00	4.00
11370	Saved/Are You Ready	1980	6.25	12.50	25.00
—Scarce on stock copy (promos worth about 20%)					
42656	Mixed-Up Confusion/Corrina, Corrina	1962	500.00	1000.	1500.
—Orange label					
42656 [DJ]	Mixed-Up Confusion/Corrina, Corrina	1962	125.00	250.00	500.00
—White label					
42856	Blowin' in the Wind/Don't Think Twice, It's All Right	1963	125.00	250.00	500.00
42856 [DJ]	Blowin' in the Wind/Don't Think Twice, It's All Right	1963	75.00	150.00	300.00
—Regular promo					
42856 [PS]	Blowin' in the Wind/Don't Think Twice, It's All Right	1963	200.00	400.00	800.00
—"Rebel with a Cause" promotional flyer					
43242	Subterranean Homesick Blues/She Belongs to Me	1965	5.00	10.00	20.00
43242	Subterranean Homesick Blues/She Belongs to Me	1972	7.50	15.00	30.00
—Briefly issued on gray label, which was used for about six months in 1972					
43242 [DJ]	Subterranean Homesick Blues (same on both sides)	1965	62.50	125.00	250.00
—Promo only on red vinyl					
43242 [PS]	Subterranean Homesick Blues/She Belongs to Me	1965	500.00	1000.	1500.
—Only issued with some promos					
43346	Like a Rolling Stone/Gates of Eden	1965	5.00	10.00	20.00
43346 [DJ]	Like a Rolling Stone (same on both sides)	1965	50.00	100.00	200.00
—Promo only on red vinyl					
43389	Positively 4th Street/From a Buick 6	1965	5.00	10.00	20.00
—Standard version					
43389	Positively 4th Street/From a Buick 6	1965	37.50	75.00	150.00
—A-side contains alternate version of "Can You Please Crawl Out Your Window." Evidently must be heard to identify.					
43389	Positively 4th Street/From a Buick 6	1965	7.50	15.00	30.00
—Odd version, possibly pressed for export, that plays at 45 but has a small center hole					
43389	Positively 4th Street/From a Buick 6	1972	6.25	12.50	25.00
—Briefly issued on gray label, which was used for about six months in 1972					
43389 [DJ]	Positively 4th Street/From a Buick 6	1965	30.00	60.00	120.00
—A-side contains alternate version of "Can You Please Crawl Out Your Window." Evidently must be heard to identify.					
43389 [DJ]	Positively 4th Street (same on both sides)	1965	37.50	75.00	150.00
—Promo only on red vinyl					
43389 [PS]	Positively 4th Street/From a Buick 6	1965	17.50	35.00	70.00
43477	Can You Please Crawl Out Your Window?/Highway 61 Revisited	1965	5.00	10.00	20.00
43541	Queen Jane Approximately/One of Us Must Know (Sooner or Later)	1966	5.00	10.00	20.00
43592	Rainy Day Women #12 and 35/Pledging My Time	1966	3.75	7.50	15.00
43592 [DJ]	Rainy Day Women #12 and 35 (same on both sides)	1966	37.50	75.00	150.00
—Promo only on red vinyl					
43683	I Want You/Just Like Tom Thumb's Blues (Live)	1966	3.75	7.50	15.00
43683 [DJ]	I Want You (same on both sides)	1966	37.50	75.00	150.00
—Promo only on red vinyl					
43683 [PS]	I Want You/Just Like Tom Thumb's Blues (Live)	1966	20.00	40.00	80.00
43792	Just Like a Woman/Obviously 5 Believers	1966	3.75	7.50	15.00
44069	Leopard-Skin Pill-Box Hat/Most Likely You'll Go Your Way and I'll Go Mine	1967	5.00	10.00	20.00
44826	I Threw It All Away/Drifter's Escape	1969	2.00	4.00	8.00
44926	Lay Lady Lay/Peggy Day	1969	2.00	4.00	8.00
45004	Tonight I'll Be Staying Here with You/Country Pie	1969	2.50	5.00	10.00
45199	Wigwam/Copper Kettle (The Pale Moonlight)	1970	—	3.00	6.00
—Red label, black print					
45199	Wigwam/Copper Kettle (The Pale Moonlight)	1970	—	3.00	6.00
—Red label, "Columbia" repeated around outside of label					
45199	Wigwam/Copper Kettle (The Pale Moonlight)	1970	—	3.00	6.00
—Orange label with "Columbia" background print					
45409	Watching the River Flow/Spanish Is the Loving Tongue	1971	—	3.00	6.00

Number	Title (A Side/B Side)	Yr	VG	VG+	NM
45516	George Jackson (Acoustic Version)/George Jackson (Big Band Version)	1971	2.50	5.00	10.00
45913	Knockin' on Heaven's Door/Turkey Chase	1973	—	2.50	5.00
45982	A Fool Such As I/Lily of the West	1973	—	3.00	6.00
73042	Everything Is Broken/Dead Man, Dead Man	1989	2.00	4.00	8.00
JZSP 75606/7 [DJ]	Blowin' in the Wind/Don't Think Twice, It's All Right	1963	75.00	150.00	300.00
—"Special Album Excerpt" promo					
JZSP 110939/40 [DJ]	Like a Rolling Stone (Part 1)/Like a Rolling Stone (Part 2)	1965	15.00	30.00	60.00
JZSP 113096/147 [DJ]	One Of Us Must Know (Sooner or Later) (4:49)/(3:07)	1966	25.00	50.00	100.00
—Promo only, long and short versions					
MCA					
52811	Band of the Hand/Theme from Joe's Death	1986	—	—	3.00
—By "Bob Dylan and the Heartbreakers"					
52811 [PS]	Band of the Hand/Theme from Joe's Death	1986	—	—	3.00
Albums					
ASYLUM					
AB-201 [(2)]	Before the Flood	1974	5.00	10.00	20.00
AB-201 [(2) DJ]	Before the Flood	1974	12.50	25.00	50.00
—White label promo					
7E-1003	Planet Waves	1974	3.75	7.50	15.00
—Without wraparound (olive green) second cover					
7E-1003	Planet Waves	1974	5.00	10.00	20.00
—With wraparound (olive green) second cover					
7E-1003 [DJ]	Planet Waves	1974	12.50	25.00	50.00
—White label promo					
7E-1003 [DJ]	Ceremonies of the Horsemen	1974	1500.	2250.	3000.
—Original title of "Planet Waves"; no records were pressed with this title, but never-glued covers exist, of which 3 or 4 are known. Value is for one of these covers.					
EQ-1003 [Q]	Planet Waves	1974	12.50	25.00	50.00
COLUMBIA					
C2L 41 [(2) M]	Blonde on Blonde	1966	250.00	500.00	1000.
—White label promo					
C2L 41 [(2) M]	Blonde on Blonde	1966	25.00	50.00	100.00
—"Female photos" inner gatefold with two women pictured					
C2L 41 [(2) M]	Blonde on Blonde	1968	75.00	150.00	300.00
—No photos of women inside gatefold					
AS 422 [DJ]	Renaldo and Clara	1976	12.50	25.00	50.00
—Promo-only sampler from the movie. Authentic copies have a sticker on a white cover; counterfeits have the title printed on the cover					
AS 798 [DJ]	Saved	1980	6.25	12.50	25.00
—Promo sampler from LP					
C2S 841 [(2) S]	Blonde on Blonde	1966	15.00	30.00	60.00
—"Female photos" inner gatefold with two women pictured					
C2S 841 [(2) S]	Blonde on Blonde	1968	7.50	15.00	30.00
—No photos of women inside gatefold; "360 Sound Stereo" on label					
C2S 841 [(2) S]	Blonde on Blonde	1970	3.75	7.50	15.00
—Orange label					
CG 841 [(2) S]	Blonde on Blonde	198?	3.00	6.00	12.00
AS 1259 [DJ]	The Dylan London Interview, July 1981	1981	6.25	12.50	25.00
AS 1471 [DJ]	Electric Lunch	1982	6.25	12.50	25.00
—Promo-only sampler					
AS 1770 [DJ]	Infidels	1983	5.00	10.00	20.00
—Promo-only sampler					
CL 1779 [M]	Bob Dylan	1962	125.00	250.00	500.00
—Six "eye" logos on label; "A New Star on Columbia" sticker on cover and promo stamp on label					
CL 1779 [M]	Bob Dylan	1962	62.50	125.00	250.00
—Six "eye" logos on label; stock copy					
CL 1779 [M]	Bob Dylan	1963	10.00	20.00	40.00
—"Guaranteed High Fidelity" on label					
CL 1779 [M]	Bob Dylan	1966	7.50	15.00	30.00
—"Mono" on label					
CL 1986 [M]	The Freewheelin' Bob Dylan	1963	4000.	8000.	12000.
—"Guaranteed High Fidelity" on label; plays "Let Me Die in My Footsteps," "Rocks and Gravel," "Talkin' John Birch Blues" and "Gamblin' Willie's Dead Man's Hand." Label does NOT list these. In dead wax, matrix number ends in "--1" followed by a letter					
CL 1986 [M]	The Freewheelin' Bob Dylan	1963	1000.	2000.	3000.
—White label promo; label and timing strip list the deleted tracks but record plays the "correct" tracks					
CL 1986 [M]	The Freewheelin' Bob Dylan	1963	500.00	1000.	2000.
—White label promo; label lists deleted tracks; timing strip lists, and record plays, "correct" tracks					
CL 1986 [M]	The Freewheelin' Bob Dylan	1963	200.00	400.00	800.00
—White label promo; timing strip lists deleted tracks; label lists, and record plays, "correct" tracks					
CL 1986 [M]	The Freewheelin' Bob Dylan	1963	125.00	250.00	500.00
—White label promo; label AND timing strip list, and record plays, "correct" tracks					
CL 1986 [M]	The Freewheelin' Bob Dylan	1963	10.00	20.00	40.00
—"Guaranteed High Fidelity" on label; corrected version (record plays what label says)					
CL 1986 [M]	The Freewheelin' Bob Dylan	1966	7.50	15.00	30.00
—"Mono" on label					
CL 2105 [M]	The Times They Are a-Changin'	1964	100.00	200.00	400.00
—White label promo					
CL 2105 [M]	The Times They Are a-Changin'	1964	10.00	20.00	40.00
—"Guaranteed High Fidelity" on label					
CL 2105 [M]	The Times They Are a-Changin'	1965	7.50	15.00	30.00
—"Mono" on label					
CL 2193 [M]	Another Side of Bob Dylan	1964	100.00	200.00	400.00
—White label promo					
CL 2193 [M]	Another Side of Bob Dylan	1964	10.00	20.00	40.00
—"Guaranteed High Fidelity" on label					
CL 2193 [M]	Another Side of Bob Dylan	1965	7.50	15.00	30.00
—"Mono" on label					
CAS 2222 [DJ]	Time Passes Slowly	1985	6.25	12.50	25.00
—Promo-only sampler from Biograph box set					
CL 2302/CS 9102	Bob Dylan In Concert	1965	2000.	3000.	4000.
—Never pressed; value is for a cover slick, some of which were printed					
CL 2328 [M]	Bringing It All Back Home	1965	75.00	150.00	300.00
—White label promo					
CL 2328 [M]	Bringing It All Back Home	1965	12.50	25.00	50.00
—"Guaranteed High Fidelity" on label					
CL 2328 [M]	Bringing It All Back Home	1965	7.50	15.00	30.00
—"Mono" on label					
CL 2389 [M]	Highway 61 Revisited	1965	100.00	200.00	400.00
—White label promo					
CL 2389 [M]	Highway 61 Revisited	1965	20.00	40.00	80.00

Number	Title (A Side/B Side)	Yr	VG	VG+	NM
2663/9463	Bob Dylan's Greatest Hits Poster	1967	—	2.00	4.00
—Almost every copy into the late 1970s came with a poster					
KCL 2663 [M]	Bob Dylan's Greatest Hits	1967	12.50	25.00	50.00
CL 2804 [M]	John Wesley Harding	1968	37.50	75.00	150.00
CS 8579 [S]	Bob Dylan	1962	150.00	300.00	600.00
—Six "eye" logos on label; "A New Star on Columbia" sticker on cover and promo stamp on label					
CS 8579 [S]	Bob Dylan	1962	100.00	200.00	400.00
—Red and black label with six white "eye" logos, three together at the left, three together at the right; stock copy					
CS 8579 [S]	Bob Dylan	1963	10.00	20.00	40.00
—"360 Sound Stereo" in black on label					
CS 8579 [S]	Bob Dylan	1965	6.25	12.50	25.00
—"360 Sound Stereo" in white on label					
CS 8579 [S]	Bob Dylan	1970	3.00	6.00	12.00
—Orange label					
JC 8579 [S]	Bob Dylan	197?	2.00	4.00	8.00
—Some copies of this pressing of the above album may have the song "You're No Good" listed on the label as "She's No Good." No extra premium has been attached to this error as yet.					
KCS 8579 [S]	Bob Dylan	197?	2.50	5.00	10.00
PC 8579 [S]	Bob Dylan	198?	2.00	4.00	8.00
—Budget-line reissue					
CS 8786 [S]	The Freewheelin' Bob Dylan	1963	15000.	22500.	30000.
—"360 Sound Stereo" in black on label (no arrows); record plays, and label lists, "Let Me Die in My Footsteps," "Rocks and Gravel," "Talkin' John Birch Blues" and "Gamblin' Willie's Dead Man's Hand." No known stereo copies play these without listing them.					
CS 8786 [S]	The Freewheelin' Bob Dylan	1963	12.50	25.00	50.00
—"360 Sound Stereo" in black on label (no arrows)					
CS 8786 [S]	The Freewheelin' Bob Dylan	1963	100.00	200.00	400.00
—Canadian pressing with the deleted tracks listed on the front cover. The label lists, and the record plays, the "correct" tracks.					
CS 8786 [S]	The Freewheelin' Bob Dylan	1964	10.00	20.00	40.00
—"360 Sound Stereo" in black on label (with arrows)					
CS 8786 [S]	The Freewheelin' Bob Dylan	1965	6.25	12.50	25.00
—"360 Sound Stereo" in white on label					
CS 8786 [S]	The Freewheelin' Bob Dylan	1970	3.00	6.00	12.00
—Orange label					
CS 8786 [S]	The Freewheelin' Bob Dylan	197?	250.00	500.00	1000.
—Orange label; unauthorized red vinyl pressing					
KCS 8786 [S]	The Freewheelin' Bob Dylan	197?	2.50	5.00	10.00
PC 8786 [S]	The Freewheelin' Bob Dylan	198?	2.00	4.00	8.00
—Budget-line reissue					
CS 8905 [S]	The Times They Are a-Changin'	1964	10.00	20.00	40.00
—"360 Sound Stereo" in black on label					
CS 8905 [S]	The Times They Are a-Changin'	1965	6.25	12.50	25.00
—"360 Sound Stereo" in white on label					
CS 8905 [S]	The Times They Are a-Changin'	1970	3.00	6.00	12.00
—Orange label					
KCS 8905 [S]	The Times They Are a-Changin'	197?	2.50	5.00	10.00
PC 8905 [S]	The Times They Are a-Changin'	198?	2.00	4.00	8.00
—Budget-line reissue					
CS 8993 [S]	Another Side of Bob Dylan	1964	10.00	20.00	40.00
—"360 Sound Stereo" in black on label					
CS 8993 [S]	Another Side of Bob Dylan	1965	6.25	12.50	25.00
—"360 Sound Stereo" in white on label					
CS 8993 [S]	Another Side of Bob Dylan	1970	3.00	6.00	12.00
—Orange label					
KCS 8993 [S]	Another Side of Bob Dylan	197?	2.50	5.00	10.00
PC 8993 [S]	Another Side of Bob Dylan	198?	2.00	4.00	8.00
—Budget-line reissue					
CS 9128 [S]	Bringing It All Back Home	1965	10.00	20.00	40.00
—"360 Sound Stereo" in black on label					
CS 9128 [S]	Bringing It All Back Home	1965	6.25	12.50	25.00
—"360 Sound Stereo" in white on label					
CS 9128 [S]	Bringing It All Back Home	1970	3.00	6.00	12.00
—Orange label					
JC 9128 [S]	Bringing It All Back Home	197?	2.50	5.00	10.00
KCS 9128 [S]	Bringing It All Back Home	197?	2.50	5.00	10.00
PC 9128 [S]	Bringing It All Back Home	198?	2.00	4.00	8.00
—Budget-line reissue					
CS 9189 [S]	Highway 61 Revisited	1965	62.50	125.00	250.00
—With alterrnate take of "From a Buick 6." Matrix number on Side 1 will end in "--1" plus a letter					
CS 9189 [S]	Highway 61 Revisited	1965	7.50	15.00	30.00
—With "regular" take of "From a Buick 6." Matrix number on Side 1 will end in "--2" or higher, plus a letter; "360 Sound Stereo" on label					
CS 9189 [S]	Highway 61 Revisited	1970	3.00	6.00	12.00
—Orange label					
JC 9189 [S]	Highway 61 Revisited	197?	2.50	5.00	10.00
KCS 9189 [S]	Highway 61 Revisited	197?	2.50	5.00	10.00
PC 9189 [S]	Highway 61 Revisited	198?	2.00	4.00	8.00
—Budget-line reissue					
JC 9463 [S]	Bob Dylan's Greatest Hits	197?	2.50	5.00	10.00
KCS 9463 [S]	Bob Dylan's Greatest Hits	1967	3.75	7.50	15.00
—"360 Sound Stereo" label					
KCS 9463 [S]	Bob Dylan's Greatest Hits	1970	3.00	6.00	12.00
—Orange label					
CS 9604 [S]	John Wesley Harding	1968	5.00	10.00	20.00
—"360 Sound Stereo" label					
CS 9604 [S]	John Wesley Harding	1970	3.00	6.00	12.00
—Orange label					
JC 9604 [S]	John Wesley Harding	197?	2.50	5.00	10.00
KCS 9604 [S]	John Wesley Harding	197?	2.50	5.00	10.00
PC 9604 [S]	John Wesley Harding	198?	2.00	4.00	8.00
—Budget-line reissue					
JC 9825	Nashville Skyline	197?	2.50	5.00	10.00
KCS 9825	Nashville Skyline	1969	7.50	15.00	30.00
—"360 Sound Stereo" label					
KCS 9825	Nashville Skyline	1970	3.00	6.00	12.00
—Orange label					
PC 9825	Nashville Skyline	198?	2.00	4.00	8.00
—Budget-line reissue					
C2X 30050 [(2)]	Self Portrait	1970	37.50	75.00	150.00
—"360 Sound Stereo" labels					
C2X 30050 [(2)]	Self Portrait	1970	5.00	10.00	20.00
—Orange labels					
CG 30050 [(2)]	Self Portrait	198?	3.00	6.00	12.00
P2X 30050 [(2)]	Self Portrait	197?	3.75	7.50	15.00

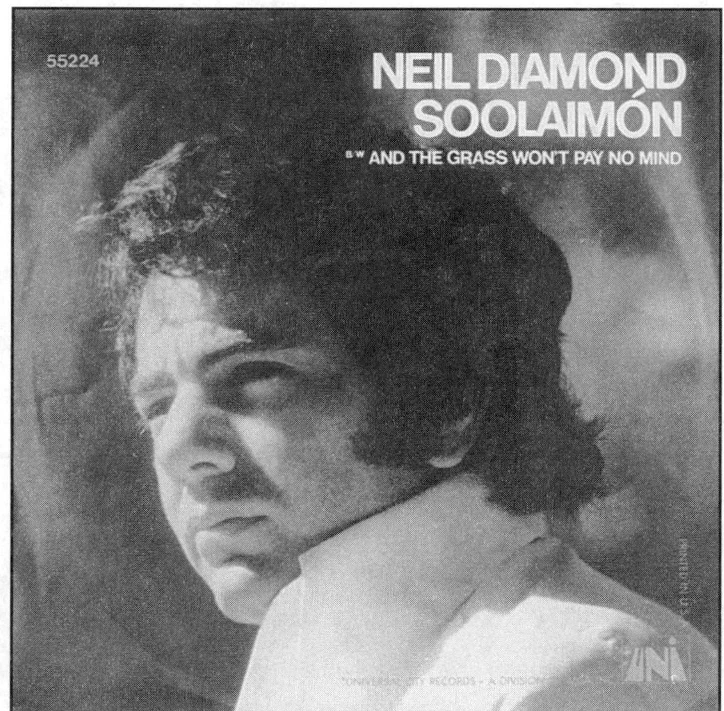

(Top left) Here's the second, and even rarer, edition of the Singular 45 of "At the Hop" by Danny and the Juniors. This version gives a credit to Artie Singer at the bottom of the label; earlier pressings do not. Both editions predate the hit single on ABC-Paramount. (Top right) Before his success on the Atco label, Bobby Darin recorded for Decca with no success. Here's one of those scarce 45s. (Bottom left) Most Neil Diamond material is pretty common. But his two picture sleeves on the Uni label are not. Here's one of the two, for the 1970 hit "Soolaimon." (Bottom right) Bob Dylan has his share of rarities. This promotional picture sleeve for "Subterranean Homesick Blues" is among the rarest; it can bring $1,500 in near-mint condition.

Number	Title (A Side/B Side)	Yr	VG	VG+	NM
KC 30290	New Morning	1970	3.75	7.50	15.00
PC 30290	New Morning	197?	2.00	4.00	8.00
CG 31120 [(2)]	Bob Dylan's Greatest Hits, Vol. II	198?	2.50	5.00	10.00
KG 31120 [(2)]	Bob Dylan's Greatest Hits, Vol. II	1971	3.75	7.50	15.00
PG 31120 [(2)]	Bob Dylan's Greatest Hits, Vol. II	197?	3.00	6.00	12.00
KC 32460	Pat Garrett and Billy the Kid	1973	3.75	7.50	15.00
PC 32460	Pat Garrett and Billy the Kid	197?	2.00	4.00	8.00
PC 32747	Dylan	1973	3.75	7.50	15.00
—No bar code on cover					
PC 32747	Dylan	1979	2.00	4.00	8.00
—With bar code on back cover					
KCQ 32825 [Q]	Nashville Skyline	1973	7.50	15.00	30.00
PC 33235	Blood on the Tracks	1975	3.00	6.00	12.00
—With liner notes on back cover. Original pressings have them, then they were deleted, then restored after they won a Grammy Award! No bar code on cover.					
PC 33235	Blood on the Tracks	1975	3.75	7.50	15.00
—With drawing on back cover and no liner notes. Actually a second pressing, but available only for a short time					
PC 33235	Blood on the Tracks	1979	2.00	4.00	8.00
—With bar code on back cover					
PC 33235 [DJ]	Blood on the Tracks	1975	2500.	3750.	5000.
—Test pressing with radically different versions of five songs including "Idiot Wind" and "Tangled Up in Blue"					
PC 33235 [DJ]	Blood on the Tracks	1975	7.50	15.00	30.00
—Regular white label promo					
CG 33682 [(2)]	The Basement Tapes	198?	3.00	6.00	12.00
PC2 33682 [(2)]	The Basement Tapes	1975	5.00	10.00	20.00
PC2 33682 [(2) DJ]	The Basement Tapes	1975	10.00	20.00	40.00
—White label promo					
JC 33893	Desire	1977	2.50	5.00	10.00
—No bar code on back cover					
JC 33893	Desire	1979	2.00	4.00	8.00
—With bar code on back cover					
PC 33893	Desire	1976	3.00	6.00	12.00
PC 33893 [DJ]	Desire	1976	7.50	15.00	30.00
—White label promo					
PCQ 33893 [Q]	Desire	1976	7.50	15.00	30.00
JC 34349	Hard Rain	1977	2.50	5.00	10.00
PC 34349	Hard Rain	1976	3.00	6.00	12.00
—No bar code on back cover					
PC 34349	Hard Rain	198?	2.00	4.00	8.00
—With bar code on back cover					
PC 34349 [DJ]	Hard Rain	1976	7.50	15.00	30.00
—White label promo					
JC 35453	Street Legal	1978	3.00	6.00	12.00
JC 35453 [DJ]	Street Legal	1978	6.25	12.50	25.00
—White label promo					
PC 35453	Street Legal	198?	2.00	4.00	8.00
CG 36067 [(2)]	Bob Dylan at Budokan	198?	3.00	6.00	12.00
PC2 36067 [(2)]	Bob Dylan at Budokan	1979	3.75	7.50	15.00
PC2 36067 [(2) DJ]	Bob Dylan at Budokan	1979	7.50	15.00	30.00
—White label promo					
FC 36120	Slow Train Coming	1979	2.50	5.00	10.00
FC 36120 [DJ]	Slow Train Coming	1979	6.25	12.50	25.00
—White label promo					
PC 36120	Slow Train Coming	198?	2.00	4.00	8.00
—Budget-line reissue					
FC 36553	Saved	1980	2.50	5.00	10.00
PC 36553	Saved	198?	2.00	4.00	8.00
—Budget-line reissue with new cover					
PC 37496	Shot of Love	198?	2.00	4.00	8.00
—Budget-line reissue					
TC 37496	Shot of Love	1981	2.50	5.00	10.00
PC 37637	Planet Waves	1981	2.50	5.00	10.00
—Reissue of Asylum 7E-1003					
CG 37661 [(2)]	Before the Flood	1983	3.00	6.00	12.00
—Reissue of Asylum AB-201					
PC 38819	Infidels	1986	2.00	4.00	8.00
—Budget-line reissue					
QC 38819	Infidels	1983	2.50	5.00	10.00
C5X 38830 [(5)]	Biograph	1985	7.50	15.00	30.00
FC 39944	Real Live	1984	2.50	5.00	10.00
FC 40110	Empire Burlesque	1985	2.50	5.00	10.00
OC 40439	Knocked Out Loaded	1986	2.50	5.00	10.00
OC 40957	Down in the Groove	1988	2.50	5.00	10.00
HC 43235	Blood on the Tracks	198?	12.50	25.00	50.00
—Half-speed mastered edition					
OC 45056	Dylan and the Dead	1989	3.00	6.00	12.00
—With backing by The Grateful Dead					
OC 45281	Oh Mercy	1989	3.00	6.00	12.00
C 46794	Under the Red Sky	1990	3.00	6.00	12.00
HC 49825	Nashville Skyline	198?	15.00	30.00	60.00
—Half-speed mastered edition					
C 53200	Good As I Been to You	1992	5.00	10.00	20.00
CK2-65759-1 [(2)]	The Bootleg Series Vol. 4: Bob Dylan Live 1966, The "Royal Albert Hall" Concert	1999	12.50	25.00	50.00
—Classic Records box set with 12x12 booklet and two records individually packaged in cardboard jackets and sleeves					
C2 67000 [(2)]	MTV Unplugged	1995	3.75	7.50	15.00
C2 68556 [(2)]	Time Out of Mind	1998	3.75	7.50	15.00
474000 [(3)]	Bob Dylan — The 30th Anniversary Concert Celebration	1993	7.50	15.00	30.00
—Albums pressed in US for export to Europe; some stayed here					
ISLAND					
AB-201 [(2)]	Before the Flood	1974	10.00	20.00	40.00
—Error pressing with wrong labels (should be Asylum)					
MOBILE FIDELITY					
1-114	The Times They Are a-Changin'	1982	12.50	25.00	50.00
—Audiophile vinyl					
WARNER/7 ARTS					
221567 [DJ]	Bob Dylan	1967	375.00	750.00	1500.
—Publisher's demo with 12 Dylan performances of then-unreleased songs from the "Basement Tapes" era					

DYLAN, BOB, AND ALAN J. WEBERMAN

Albums

Number	Title (A Side/B Side)	Yr	VG	VG+	NM
FOLKWAYS					
FB-5322 [M]	Bob Dylan Vs. A.J. Weberman	1977	75.00	150.00	300.00
—No music, but a tape-recorded phone conversation; quickly withdrawn from the market					

DYNA-SORES, THE

45s

Number	Title (A Side/B Side)	Yr	VG	VG+	NM
RENDEZVOUS					
120	Alley-Oop/Jungle Walk	1960	6.25	12.50	25.00

DYNAMIC SUPERIORS

45s

Number	Title (A Side/B Side)	Yr	VG	VG+	NM
MOTOWN					
1324	Shoe Shoe Shine/Release Me	1974	—	3.00	6.00
1342	Leave It Alone/One-Nighter	1975	—	3.00	6.00
1357	Romeo/I Got Away	1975	—	—	—
—Canceled?					
1359	Nobody's Gonna Change Me/I Got Away	1975	—	3.00	6.00
1365	Deception/One Nighter	1975	—	3.00	6.00
1413	Can't Stay Away (From the One I Love)/Supersensuosensation (Try Some Love)	1977	—	3.00	6.00
1419	Nowhere to Run, Pt. 1/Nowhere to Run, Pt. 2	1977	—	3.00	6.00
1428	You're What I Need/Here Comes That Feeling	1977	—	3.00	6.00

Albums

Number	Title (A Side/B Side)	Yr	VG	VG+	NM
MOTOWN					
M6-822	Dynamic Superiors	1974	3.00	6.00	12.00
M6-841	Pure Pleasure	1975	3.00	6.00	12.00
M6-875	You Name It	1976	3.00	6.00	12.00
M6-879	Give and Take	1977	3.00	6.00	12.00

DYNAMICS, THE (1)

Detroit R&B group with several charted hits.

45s

Number	Title (A Side/B Side)	Yr	VG	VG+	NM
BIG TOP					
516	And That's a Natural Fact/I Wanna Know	1964	3.75	7.50	15.00
3161	Misery/I'm the Man	1963	3.75	7.50	15.00
BLACK GOLD					
8	What a Shame/Shucks, I Love You	1973	—	3.00	6.00
9	Funkey Key/Count Your Chips	1973	—	3.00	6.00
11	She's for Real (Bless You)/(B-side unknown)	1974	—	3.00	6.00
COTILLION					
44004	Ain't No Sun/Murder in the First Degree	1968	2.50	5.00	10.00
44021	Ice Cream Song/The Love That I Need	1969	2.50	5.00	10.00
44038	What Would I Do/Ain't No Love at All	1969	2.50	5.00	10.00
44045	Dum-De-Dum/I Want to Thank You	1969	2.50	5.00	10.00

Albums

Number	Title (A Side/B Side)	Yr	VG	VG+	NM
BLACK GOLD					
5001	What a Shame	1973	3.00	6.00	12.00
COTILLION					
SD 9009	First Landing	1969	3.75	7.50	15.00

DYNAMICS, THE (2)

Mostly an instrumental group.

45s

Number	Title (A Side/B Side)	Yr	VG	VG+	NM
BOLO					
730	At the Mardi Gras/J.A.J.	1962	2.50	5.00	10.00
735	Wild Child/Spongy	1962	2.50	5.00	10.00
740	Tennessee Boy/Tough Talk	1963	2.50	5.00	10.00
751	Knee Poppin'/Who's Afraid of Virginia Woolf?	1964	2.50	5.00	10.00
GUARANTEED					
201	Aces Up/Baby	1959	5.00	10.00	20.00
PENGUIN					
1006	Aces Up/Baby	1959	12.50	25.00	50.00
SEAFAIR					
100	Onion Salad/Lonesome Llama	1960	5.00	10.00	20.00
107	At the Mardi Gras/J.A.J.	1961	5.00	10.00	20.00

Albums

Number	Title (A Side/B Side)	Yr	VG	VG+	NM
BOLO					
BLP-8001 [M]	The Dynamics with Jimmy Hanna	1964	12.50	25.00	50.00

DYNAMICS, THE (3)

Early version of ANTHONY AND THE SOPHOMORES.

45s

Number	Title (A Side/B Side)	Yr	VG	VG+	NM
HERALD					
569	Forever/Betty My Own	1962	125.00	250.00	500.00

DYNAMICS, THE (4)

Band from Chicago (probably).

45s

Number	Title (A Side/B Side)	Yr	VG	VG+	NM
U.S.A.					
769	Summertime in the U.S.A./Coast to Coast	1964	6.25	12.50	25.00

DYNAMICS, THE (5)

For records on Wingate, see THE DRAMATICS.

DYNAMICS, THE (U)

Some of these may be groups (1) or (2). We're pretty sure that none of these are groups (3), (4) or (5). It's possible that five more groups, if not more, are represented below. Any help in grouping these correctly will be appreciated.

45s

Number	Title (A Side/B Side)	Yr	VG	VG+	NM
ARC					
4450	Enchanted Love/Happiness and Love	1959	10.00	20.00	40.00
CAPRI					
104	No One but You/Always, I Have Loved You	1959	100.00	200.00	400.00
CINDY					
3005	When the Saints Come Marching In/Gone Is My Love	1957	20.00	40.00	80.00
COLUMBIA					
3-10666	We Found Love/You Can Make It If You Try	1978	—	2.50	5.00

Number	Title (A Side/B Side)	Yr	VG	VG+	NM
DECCA					
31046	How Should I Feel/Seems Like Only Yesterday	1960	7.50	15.00	30.00
31129	At the End of Each Day/Girl by the Gate	1960	7.50	15.00	30.00
31450	How Should I Feel/Seems Like Only Yesterday	1962	3.75	7.50	15.00
DELTA					
1002	Blue Moon/Pigeon-Toed	1959	7.50	15.00	30.00
DO-KAY-LO					
101	I Guess You Don't Love Me (No More)/Oh Night of Nights	1963	7.50	15.00	30.00
DOUGLAS					
200	I Love to Be Loved/You Don't Seem to Realize	1961	7.50	15.00	30.00
DYNAMIC					
109	Don't Be Late/Eenie Meenie	1959	10.00	20.00	40.00
504	The Girl I Met Last Night/Nobody's Going Out with Me	1959	10.00	20.00	40.00
578/9	Christmas Plea/Dream Girl	1962	17.50	35.00	70.00
1001	Don't Leave Me/Wasted	1959	12.50	25.00	50.00
1002	So Fine/Delsinia	1963	10.00	20.00	40.00
1008	If She Should Call/Dream Girl	1961	10.00	20.00	40.00
FARRALL					
964	Later On/Departure	196?	7.50	15.00	30.00
IMPALA					
501	Moonlight/Someone	1959	30.00	60.00	120.00
JERDEN					
800	I'll Be Standing There/All She Said	1966	2.50	5.00	10.00
LAVERE					
186	Wrap Your Troubles in Dreams/I Can't Give You Anything But Love	1961	6.25	12.50	25.00
LIBAN					
1006	If I Give My Heart to You/Blind Date	1962	20.00	40.00	80.00
LIBERTY					
55628	Chapel on a Hill/Conquistador	1963	10.00	20.00	40.00
PANORAMA					
51	Stop and Take a Look Around/(B-side unknown)	1967	2.50	5.00	10.00
RCA VICTOR					
47-9084	Love Me/I Need Your Love	1967	10.00	20.00	40.00
47-9278	Lights Out/You Make Me Feel So Good	1967	15.00	30.00	60.00
—As "Zerben R. Hicks and the Dynamics"					
REPRISE					
20183	So Fine/Delsinia	1963	3.75	7.50	15.00
SEECO					
6008	Moonlight/Someone	1959	10.00	20.00	40.00
TOP TEN					
100	Yes I Love You Baby/Soul Sloopy	1965	20.00	40.00	80.00
927	Love to a Guy/Whenever I'm Without You	196?	15.00	30.00	60.00
WARNER					
1016	A Hundred Million Les/Ka Joom	1957	20.00	40.00	80.00
DYNAMO, SKINNY					
45s					
EXCELLO					
2097	So Long, So Long/Jingle Bell	1956	7.50	15.00	30.00

Number	Title (A Side/B Side)	Yr	VG	VG+	NM
DYNATONES, THE					
45s					
HANNA-BARBERA					
494	The Fife Piper/And I Always Will	1966	2.50	5.00	10.00
ST. CLAIR					
117	The Fife Piper/And I Always Will	1966	7.50	5.00	30.00
Albums					
HANNA-BARBERA					
HLP-8509 [M]	The Fife Piper	1966	5.00	10.00	20.00
HST-8509 [S]	The Fife Piper	1966	6.25	12.50	25.00
DYSON, RONNIE					
45s					
COLUMBIA					
10071	Captain of Your Soul/Life and Breath	1974	—	2.50	5.00
10211	Lady in Red/Cup (Runneth Over)	1975	—	2.50	5.00
10356	The More You Do It (The More I Like It Done to Me)/You and Me	1976	—	2.50	5.00
10441	(I Like Being) Close to You/Lovin' Feelin'	1976	—	2.50	5.00
10599	Don't Be Afraid/I Just Want to Be There	1977	—	2.50	5.00
10667	Ain't Nothing Wrong/Just As You Are	1978	—	2.50	5.00
10716	Sara Smile/No Way	1978	—	2.00	4.00
45110	(If You Let Me Make Love to You Then) Why Can't I Touch You?	1970	—	2.50	5.00
45240	I Don't Wanna Cry/She's Gone	1970	—	2.50	5.00
45387	When You Get Right Down To It.../Sleeping Sun	1971	—	2.50	5.00
45599	Jesus Is Just Alright/Love Is Slipping Away	1972	—	3.00	6.00
45776	One Man Band (Plays All Alone)/I Think I'll Tell Her	1973	—	2.50	5.00
45776 [PS]	One Man Band (Plays All Alone)/I Think I'll Tell Her	1973	2.00	4.00	8.00
45867	Just Don't Want to Be Lonely/Point of No Return	1973	—	2.50	5.00
45974	Wednesday in Your Garden/I Think I'll Tell Her	1973	—	3.00	6.00
46021	We Can Make It Last Forever/Just a Little Love from Me	1974	—	2.50	5.00
COTILLION					
47005	Heart to Heart/Bring It On Home	1982	—	—	3.00
99811	You Better Be Fierce/(B-side unknown)	1983	—	2.00	4.00
99841	All Over Your Face/Don't Need You Now	1983	—	—	3.00
RCA VICTOR					
GB-10658	Aquarius/Hair	1976	—	2.50	5.00
—"Gold Standard Series" reissue					
74-0128	Aquarius/Hair	1969	2.50	5.00	10.00
—By "Ronald Dyson & Co."					
Albums					
COLUMBIA					
C 30223	(If You Let Me Make Love to You Then) Why Can't I Touch You?	1970	3.00	6.00	12.00
KC 31305	Back Home	1972	3.00	6.00	12.00
KC 32211	One Man Band	1973	3.00	6.00	12.00
PC 34350	The More You Do	1976	2.50	5.00	10.00
PC 34866	Love in All Flavors	1977	2.50	5.00	10.00
COTILLION					
90119	Brand New Day	1982	2.50	5.00	10.00

E

E-TYPES, THE

45s

Number	Title (A Side/B Side)	Yr	VG	VG+	NM
DOT					
16864	I Can't Do It/Long Before	1966	3.00	6.00	12.00
LINK					
1	I Can't Do It/Long Before	1966	7.50	15.00	30.00
1 [PS]	I Can't Do It/Long Before	1966	7.50	15.00	30.00
SUNBURST					
001	Love of the Loved/She Moves Me	1966	6.25	12.50	25.00
TOWER					
325	Put the Clock Back On the Wall/14th Street	1967	6.25	12.50	25.00
UPTOWN					
754	Big City/Back to Me	1967	6.25	12.50	25.00

EADY, ERNESTINE

45s

Number	Title (A Side/B Side)	Yr	VG	VG+	NM
JUNIOR					
1007	The Change/That's the Way It Goes	1963	7.50	15.00	30.00
SCEPTER					
12102	The Change/That's the Way It Goes	1965	3.00	6.00	12.00

EAGER, BRENDA LEE

Also see JERRY BUTLER.

45s

Number	Title (A Side/B Side)	Yr	VG	VG+	NM
MERCURY					
73292	I'm a Lonely Woman/In My World	1972	—	3.00	6.00
73450	Let Me Be/When I'm With You	1974	—	2.50	5.00
73607	Ah, Sweet Mystery of Life/There Ain't No Way	1974	—	2.50	5.00
73627	You Gave Me Everything/When I'm With You	1974	—	2.50	5.00
PLAYBOY					
6047	Good Old Fashioned Lovin'/I'll Get By	1975	—	2.50	5.00
PRIVATE I					
04621	Watch My Body Talk/(Instrumental)	1984	—	2.00	4.00

EAGER, JIMMY

45s

Number	Title (A Side/B Side)	Yr	VG	VG+	NM
SABRE					
100	Please Mr. Doctor/I Should Have Loved Her More	1953	50.00	100.00	200.00

EAGER, VINCE

45s

Number	Title (A Side/B Side)	Yr	VG	VG+	NM
LONDON INT'L.					
10527	It's Only Make Believe/I Shall Not Be Moved	1964	3.00	6.00	12.00

EAGLE

Also see THE BEACON STREET UNION.

45s

Number	Title (A Side/B Side)	Yr	VG	VG+	NM
JANUS					
113	Kickin' It Back to You/Come In, It's All for Free	1970	2.00	4.00	8.00
135	Brown Hair/Working Man	1970	2.00	4.00	8.00

Albums

Number	Title (A Side/B Side)	Yr	VG	VG+	NM
JANUS					
JLS-3011	Come Under Nancy's Tent	1970	5.00	10.00	20.00

EAGLES

Popular 1970s California band. Few of its records used the article "The" before the name. Its members had previously been in THE JAMES GANG; LONGBRANCH PENNYWHISTLE; POCO; and SHILOH, among others. Also see JOE WALSH.

12-Inch Singles

Number	Title (A Side/B Side)	Yr	VG	VG+	NM
ASYLUM					
11402 [DJ]	Please Come Home for Christmas/Funky New Year (both mono)//Please Come Home for Christmas/Funky New Year (both stereo)	1978	5.00	10.00	20.00

45s

Number	Title (A Side/B Side)	Yr	VG	VG+	NM
ASYLUM					
11005	Take It Easy/Get You in the Mood	1972	—	2.50	5.00
11008	Witchy Woman/Early Bird	1972	—	2.00	4.00
11013	Peaceful Easy Feeling/Trying	1973	—	2.00	4.00
11013	Tequila Sunrise/21	1973	—	2.00	4.00
11025	Outlaw Man/Certain Kind of Fool	1973	—	2.00	4.00
11036	Already Gone/Is It True	1974	—	2.00	4.00
45202	James Dean/Good Day in Hell	1974	—	2.00	4.00
45218	Best of My Love/Ol' 55	1974	—	2.00	4.00
45257	One of These Nights/Visions	1975	—	2.00	4.00
45279	Lyin' Eyes/Too Many People	1975	—	2.00	4.00
45293	Take It to the Limit/After the Thrill Is Gone	1975	—	2.00	4.00
45373	New Kid in Town/Victim of Love	1976	—	2.00	4.00
45386	Hotel California/Pretty Maids All in a Row	1977	—	2.00	4.00
45403	Life in the Fast Lane/The Last Resort	1977	—	2.00	4.00
45555	Please Come Home for Christmas/Funky New Year	1978	—	2.00	4.00
—Original with "clouds" label					
45555	Please Come Home for Christmas/Funky New Year	1984	—	—	3.00
—Reissue with black and yellow label					
45555 [PS]	Please Come Home for Christmas/Funky New Year	1978	—	2.00	4.00
—Sleeve was available with both original and reissue					
46545	Heartache Tonight/Teenage Jail	1979	—	2.00	4.00
46569	The Long Run/The Disco Strangler	1979	—	2.00	4.00
46608	I Can't Tell You Why/The Greeks Don't Want No Freaks	1980	—	2.00	4.00
47100	Seven Bridges Road/The Long Run	1980	—	2.00	4.00
FULL MOON					
49654	I Can't Tell You Why/Outside	1981	—	2.50	5.00
—B-side by Ambrosia					
FULL MOON/ASYLUM					
47004	Lyin' Eyes/Looking for Love	1980	—	2.00	4.00
—B-side by Johnnie Lee; contains the full-length version of "Lyin' Eyes"					
47004 [PS]	Lyin' Eyes/Looking for Love	1980	—	2.50	5.00
47073	Lyin' Eyes/Hello Texas	1980	—	2.50	5.00
—B-side by Jimmy Buffett					
GEFFEN					
19376	Get Over It/Get Over It (Live)	1994	—	2.50	5.00

Albums

Number	Title (A Side/B Side)	Yr	VG	VG+	NM
ASYLUM					
6E-103	Hotel California	1977	2.00	4.00	8.00
6E-105	Eagles — Their Greatest Hits 1971-1975	1977	2.00	4.00	8.00
5E-508	The Long Run	1979	2.00	4.00	8.00
BB-705 [(2)]	Eagles Live	1980	3.00	6.00	12.00
7E-1004	On the Border	1974	3.00	6.00	12.00
—Clouds label					
EQ 1004 [Q]	On the Border	1974	5.00	10.00	20.00
7E-1039	One of These Nights	1975	2.50	5.00	10.00
—Clouds label					
EQ 1039 [Q]	One of These Nights	1975	5.00	10.00	20.00
7E-1052	Eagles — Their Greatest Hits 1971-1975	1976	2.50	5.00	10.00
7E-1084	Hotel California	1976	2.50	5.00	10.00
SD 5054	Eagles	1972	3.75	7.50	15.00
—Gatefold cover; white label with door-in-a-circle logo at top					
SD 5054	Eagles	1973	3.00	6.00	12.00
—Regular cover; clouds label					
SD 5068	Desperado	1973	3.00	6.00	12.00
—Clouds label					
60205	Eagles Greatest Hits, Volume 2	1982	2.50	5.00	10.00
DCC COMPACT CLASSICS					
LPZ-2043	Hotel California	1997	6.25	12.50	25.00
—Audiophile vinyl					
LPZ-2051	Eagles — Their Greatest Hits 1971-1975	1998	6.25	12.50	25.00
—Audiophile vinyl					
ELEKTRA					
60422	Anthology of the Eagles	1985	—	—	—
—Canceled					
MOBILE FIDELITY					
1-126	Hotel California	1984	25.00	50.00	100.00
—Audiophile vinyl					

EAGLES, THE (2)

45s

Number	Title (A Side/B Side)	Yr	VG	VG+	NM
MERCURY					
70391	Tryin' to Get to You/Please, Please	1954	7.50	15.00	30.00
70464	Such a Fool/Don't You Wanna Be Mine	1954	7.50	15.00	30.00
70524	I Told Myself/What a Crazy Feeling	1955	7.50	15.00	30.00

EAGLES, THE (3)

British group.

45s

Number	Title (A Side/B Side)	Yr	VG	VG+	NM
SMASH					
1837	Christine/Stalactite	1963	3.00	6.00	12.00

EAGLES, THE (U)

The record on Prep may be group (2); the record on Warner Bros. may be group (3). Then again, maybe not.

45s

Number	Title (A Side/B Side)	Yr	VG	VG+	NM
PREP					
18	Kiss Them for Me/Ladies in the Sky	1957	5.00	10.00	20.00
WARNER BROS.					
5654	Ballad to a Lady/Eagle	1965	3.00	6.00	12.00

EAGLIN, SNOOKS

Albums

Number	Title (A Side/B Side)	Yr	VG	VG+	NM
ARHOOLIE					
2014	Possum Up a Simmon Tree	198?	2.50	5.00	10.00
BLACK TOP					
BT-1037	Baby, You Can Get Your Gun	1987	2.50	5.00	10.00
BT-1046	Out of Nowhere	198?	2.50	5.00	10.00
BLUESVILLE					
BVLP-1046 [M]	That's All Right	1962	15.00	30.00	60.00
—Blue label, silver print					
BVLP-1046 [M]	That's All Right	1964	6.25	12.50	25.00
—Blue label, trident logo at right					
FOLKWAYS					
FA-2476 [M]	New Orleans Street Singer	1959	10.00	20.00	40.00
GNP CRECENDO					
10023	Down Yonder	1979	2.50	5.00	10.00

EARL-JEAN

45s

Number	Title (A Side/B Side)	Yr	VG	VG+	NM
COLPIX					
729	I'm Into Somethin' Good/We Love and Learn	1964	3.00	6.00	12.00
748	Randy/They're Jealous of Me	1964	2.50	5.00	10.00

EARLAND, CHARLES

45s

Number	Title (A Side/B Side)	Yr	VG	VG+	NM
COLUMBIA					
02710	The Only One/Never Knew Love Like This Before	1982	—	—	3.00
02881	Animal/Guilty	1982	—	—	3.00
11427	Coming to You (Live)/(B-side unknown)	1981	—	—	3.00
MERCURY					
73793	From My Heart to Yours/Intergalactic Love Song	1976	—	2.00	4.00
73869	Ahead of Your Time/Driftin'	1976	—	2.00	4.00
PRESTIGE					
731	Black Talk (Part 1)/Black Talk (Part 2)	1970	—	2.50	5.00
732	More Today Than Yesterday/Mighty Burner	197?	—	2.50	5.00
736	Raindrops Keep Falling on My Head/Sing a Simple Song	197?	—	2.50	5.00

Number	Title (A Side/B Side)	Yr	VG	VG+	NM
741	Westbound No. 9 (Part 1)/Westbound No. 9 (Part 2)	197?	—	2.50	5.00
746	One for Scotty/I Was Made to Love Her	197?	—	2.50	5.00
755	Will You Still Love Me Tomorrow/'Cause I Love Her	197?	—	2.50	5.00
761	Charles III/Girl You Need a Change of Mind	197?	—	2.50	5.00
763	Brown Eyes/Leaving This Planet	197?	—	2.50	5.00
Albums					
COLUMBIA					
JC 36449	Coming to You Live	1980	2.50	5.00	10.00
FC 37573	Earland's Jam	1982	2.50	5.00	10.00
FC 38547	Earland's Street Themes	1983	2.50	5.00	10.00
FANTASY					
OJC-335	Black Talk!	1988	2.50	5.00	10.00
—Reissue of Prestige 7758					
MERCURY					
SRM-1-1049	Odyssey	1976	2.50	5.00	10.00
SRM-1-1139	The Great Pyramid	1976	2.50	5.00	10.00
SRM-1-1149	Revelation	1977	2.50	5.00	10.00
SRM-1-3720	Perception	1978	2.50	5.00	10.00
MILESTONE					
M-9165	Front Burner	1988	2.50	5.00	10.00
M-9175	Third Degree Burn	1989	2.50	5.00	10.00
MUSE					
MR-5126	Smokin'	1978	2.50	5.00	10.00
MR-5156	Mama Roots	1979	2.50	5.00	10.00
MR-5181	Infant Eyes	1980	2.50	5.00	10.00
MR-5201	Pleasant Afternoon	1981	2.50	5.00	10.00
MR-5240	In the Pocket	1984	2.50	5.00	10.00
PRESTIGE					
2501	Burners	1982	2.50	5.00	10.00
PRST-7758	Black Talk!	1970	5.00	10.00	20.00
PRST-7815	Black Drops	1970	3.75	7.50	15.00
10009	Living Black!	1971	3.00	6.00	12.00
10018	Soul Story	1971	3.00	6.00	12.00
10024	Black Talk!	1971	2.50	5.00	10.00
—Reissue of 7758					
10029	Black Drops	1971	2.50	5.00	10.00
—Reissue of 7815					
10041	Intensity	1972	3.00	6.00	12.00
10051	Live at the Lighthouse	1972	3.00	6.00	12.00
10061	Charles III	1973	3.00	6.00	12.00
10095	Kharma	1975	3.00	6.00	12.00
66002 [(2)]	Leaving This Planet	1974	3.75	7.50	15.00
TRIP					
5004	Charles Earland	1974	2.50	5.00	10.00

EARLS, JACK, AND THE JIMBOS

Number	Title (A Side/B Side)	Yr	VG	VG+	NM
45s					
SUN					
240	Slow Down/A Fool for Loving You	1956	15.00	30.00	60.00

EARLS, THE (1)

All of the below are by the same group or closely related.

Number	Title (A Side/B Side)	Yr	VG	VG+	NM
45s					
ABC					
11109	It's Been a Long Time Coming/My Lonely, Lonely Room	1968	3.75	7.50	15.00
BARRY					
1021	I Believe/Don't Forget	1963	10.00	20.00	40.00
CLIFTON					
39	Lookin' for My Baby/Cross My Heart	1974	—	2.50	5.00
43	Lost Love/My Heart's Desire	1974	—	2.50	5.00
47	Dreams Come True/My Heart's Desire	1974	—	2.50	5.00
COLUMBIA					
3-10225	Goin' Uptown/Mrs. Woman	1975	2.00	4.00	8.00
GONE					
5117	I'll Never Cry/My Heart's Desire	1961	15.00	30.00	60.00
HARVEY					
100	A Sunday Kind of Love/Teenage Dreams	1975	2.00	4.00	8.00
MR. G					
801	If I Could Do It Over Again/Papa	1967	3.75	7.50	15.00
OLD TOWN					
1130	Remember Then/Let's Waddle	1963	12.50	25.00	50.00
—Blue label					
1130	Remember Then/Let's Waddle	1963	6.25	12.50	25.00
—Mostly black label with moon					
1133	Never/I Keep a-Telling You	1963	10.00	20.00	40.00
—Blue label					
1133	Never/I Keep a-Telling You	1963	5.00	10.00	20.00
—Mostly black label with moon					
1141	Eyes/Look My Way	1963	5.00	10.00	20.00
1145	Cry, Cry, Cry/Kissin'	1963	5.00	10.00	20.00
1149	I Believe/Don't Forget	1963	10.00	20.00	40.00
—Blue label					
1149	I Believe/Don't Forget	1963	5.00	10.00	20.00
—Mostly black label with moon					
1169	Oh What a Time/Ask Anybody	1964	7.50	15.00	30.00
1181 [DJ]	Remember Me Baby/Amor	1965	12.50	25.00	50.00
—Assigned 1181 in error, as another record had been released with the number					
1182	Remember Me Baby/Amor	1965	5.00	10.00	20.00
—Error was corrected on stock copies					
POWER MARTIN					
1005	Stormy Weather/Could This Be Magic	1975	—	2.50	5.00
—B-side by the Pretenders					
ROME					
101	Life Is But a Dream/It's You	1961	30.00	60.00	120.00
101	Life Is But a Dream/Without You	1961	10.00	20.00	40.00
102	Lookin' for My Baby/Cross My Heart	1961	10.00	20.00	40.00
111	Stormy Weather/Could This Be Magic	1976	—	2.50	5.00
—B-side by the Pretenders					
112/3	Little Boy and Girl/Lost Love	1976	—	2.00	4.00
114/5	All Through Our Teens/Whoever You Are	1976	2.00	4.00	8.00
—Black vinyl					
114/5	All Through Our Teens/Whoever You Are	1976	3.00	6.00	12.00
—Colored vinyl					
WOODBURY					
101	Tonight (Could Be the Night)/Meditation	1977	2.00	4.00	8.00
Albums					
CHANCE					
1001	The Earls Today	1983	3.00	6.00	12.00
OLD TOWN					
LP-104 [M]	Remember Me Baby	1963	125.00	250.00	500.00
—Counterfeit identification: Counterfeits have more than 1-inch trailoffs or as little as 1/2 inch trailoffs; legitimate copies have 5/8- to 3/4-inch trailoff					
WOODBURY					
104	Remember Me Baby	1976	3.75	7.50	15.00

EARLS, THE (2)

Number	Title (A Side/B Side)	Yr	VG	VG+	NM
45s					
GEM					
221	Believe Me My Love/Spinnin'	1954	100.00	200.00	400.00
227	My Marie/Out of This World	197?	2.00	4.00	8.00
—There are differences of opinion on this record. Some claim that it was released in 1954 not long after Gem 221; others claim that it's a 1970s reproduction on a number that Gem never used. As no 78s are known to exist of this title, we lean toward the latter, but would appreciate positive evidence one way or the other.					

EARLY, SAM

Number	Title (A Side/B Side)	Yr	VG	VG+	NM
45s					
APT					
25041	Do You Love Me/You Are the Greatest of Them All	1960	6.25	12.50	25.00

EARTH AND FIRE

Produced by members of GOLDEN EARRING.

Number	Title (A Side/B Side)	Yr	VG	VG+	NM
45s					
ATCO					
6744	Seasons/Hazy Paradise	1970	2.50	5.00	10.00
Albums					
RED BULLET					
RBLP-3000	Earth and Fire	197?	3.75	7.50	15.00

EARTH ISLAND

Number	Title (A Side/B Side)	Yr	VG	VG+	NM
45s					
PHILIPS					
40673	Doomsday Afternoon/Tuesday Afternoon	1970	2.00	4.00	8.00
Albums					
PHILIPS					
PHS 600340	We Must Survive	1970	6.25	12.50	25.00

EARTH OPERA

Number	Title (A Side/B Side)	Yr	VG	VG+	NM
45s					
ELEKTRA					
45636	American Eagle Tragedy/When You Were Full of Wonder	1968	2.00	4.00	8.00
45650	Home to You/Alfie Finney	1969	2.00	4.00	8.00
Albums					
ELEKTRA					
EKS-74016	Earth Opera	1968	5.00	10.00	20.00
EKS-74038	The Great American Eagle Tragedy	1969	5.00	10.00	20.00

EARTH QUAKE

Number	Title (A Side/B Side)	Yr	VG	VG+	NM
45s					
A&M					
1301	Tickler/Guarding You	1971	2.00	4.00	8.00
1338	I Get the Sweetest Feeling/Live and Let Live	1972	2.00	4.00	8.00
1365	Bright Lights/Live and Let Live	1972	2.00	4.00	8.00
BESERKLEY					
5701	Friday on My Mind/Roadrunner	1975	2.50	5.00	10.00
—B-side by Jonathan Richman and the Modern Lovers					
5701 [PS]	Friday on My Mind/Roadrunner	1975	2.50	5.00	10.00
5734/5	Mr. Security/Madness	1975	—	2.50	5.00
5736/7	Friday on My Mind/Tall Order for a Short Guy	1975	—	2.50	5.00
5742	Hit the Floor/Don't Want to Go Back	1976	—	2.50	5.00
5747	Kicks/Trainride	1977	—	2.50	5.00
Albums					
A&M					
SP-4308	Earth Quake	1971	3.75	7.50	15.00
SP-4337	Why Don't You Try Me?	1972	3.75	7.50	15.00
BESERKLEY					
0045	Rockin' the World	1975	3.00	6.00	12.00
0047	8.5	1976	3.00	6.00	12.00
0054	Leveled	1977	3.00	6.00	12.00
BZ-10065	Two Years in a Padded Cell	1979	2.50	5.00	10.00
PZ 34752	Rockin' the World	1977	2.50	5.00	10.00
—Reissue of 0045					
PZ 34754	8.5	1977	2.50	5.00	10.00
—Reissue of 0047					
PZ 34801	Leveled	1977	2.50	5.00	10.00
—Reissue of 0054					

EARTH, WIND, AND FIRE

Also see WADE FLEMONS.

Number	Title (A Side/B Side)	Yr	VG	VG+	NM
12-Inch Singles					
ARC					
AS 853 [DJ]	Let Me Talk (Remix)/(Instrumental)	1980	2.50	5.00	10.00
AS 924 [DJ]	And Love Goes On (Single Version)/(LP Version)	1980	2.50	5.00	10.00
COLUMBIA					
AS 1648 [DJ]	Side by Side/Something Special	1983	2.00	4.00	8.00
AS 1842 [DJ]	Moonwalk/We're Living in Our Own Time	1983	2.00	4.00	8.00
44-04008	Spread Your Love/Freedom of Choice	1983	—	3.00	6.00
44-04211	Magnetic (Extended Dance Remix)/(Instrumental)	1983	—	3.00	6.00

Number	Title (A Side/B Side)	Yr	VG	VG+	NM
44-04211	Magnetic (Extended Dance Remix)/(Album Version)	1983	—	3.00	6.00
07475	System of Survival (4 versions)	1987	—	3.00	6.00
07562	Evil Roy (4 versions)	1987	—	3.00	6.00
08140	Turn On (The Beat Box) (4 versions)	1988	—	3.00	6.00
10512	Saturday Nite/On Your Face	1977	3.75	7.50	15.00
10786	Got to Get You Into My Life/I'll Write a Song for You	1978	2.50	5.00	10.00
73157	Heritage (Extended)/Heritage (Edit)	1990	—	3.00	6.00
73193	For the Love of You (6 versions)	1990	2.00	4.00	8.00

45s

ARC

Number	Title (A Side/B Side)	Yr	VG	VG+	NM
02536	Let's Groove/(Instrumental)	1981	—	2.00	4.00
02688	Wanna Be with You/Kalimba Tree	1982	—	2.00	4.00
10854	September/Love's Holiday	1978	—	2.50	5.00
11033	After the Love Has Gone/Rock That!	1979	—	2.50	5.00
11093	In the Stone/You and I	1979	—	2.00	4.00
11165	Star/You and I	1979	—	2.00	4.00
11366	Let Me Talk/(Instrumental)	1980	—	2.00	4.00
11366 [PS]	Let Me Talk/(Instrumental)	1980	—	2.50	5.00
11407	You/Share Your Love	1980	—	2.00	4.00
11434	And Love Goes On/Win or Lose	1981	—	2.00	4.00

COLUMBIA

Number	Title (A Side/B Side)	Yr	VG	VG+	NM
13-03136	Let's Groove/Sing a Song	1982	—	—	3.00
—Reissue					
38-03375	Fall in Love with Me/(Instrumental)	1982	—	2.00	4.00
38-03375 [PS]	Fall in Love with Me/(Instrumental)	1982	—	2.00	4.00
CNR-03566	Fall in Love with Me	1983	—	3.00	6.00
—One-sided budget release					
38-03814	Side by Side/Something Special	1983	—	2.00	4.00
38-04002	Spread Your Love/Freedom of Choice	1983	—	2.00	4.00
38-04210	Magnetic/Speed of Love	1983	—	2.00	4.00
38-04210 [PS]	Magnetic/Speed of Love	1983	—	2.00	4.00
38-04329	Touch/Sweet Sassy Lady	1984	—	2.00	4.00
38-04329 [PS]	Touch/Sweet Sassy Lady	1984	—	2.00	4.00
38-04427	Moonwalk/We're Living in Our Own Time	1984	—	2.00	4.00
38-07608	System of Survival/Writing on the Wall	1987	—	—	3.00
38-07608 [PS]	System of Survival/Writing on the Wall	1987	—	—	3.00
38-07678	You and I/Musical Interlude: New Horizons	1988	—	—	3.00
38-07687	Evil Roy/(Instrumental)	1988	—	—	3.00
38-07695	Thinking of You/Money Tight	1988	—	—	3.00
38-07695 [PS]	Thinking of You/Money Tight	1988	—	—	3.00
38-08107	Turn On (The Beat Box)/(Instrumental)	1988	—	—	3.00
3-10026	Devotion/Fair But So Uncool	1974	—	3.00	6.00
3-10056	Hot Dawgit/R.L. Tambura	1974	—	2.50	5.00
—With Ramsey Lewis					
3-10090	Shining Star/Yearnin', Learnin'	1975	—	2.50	5.00
3-10090 [PS]	Shining Star/Yearnin', Learnin'	1975	2.50	5.00	10.00
3-10103	Sun Goddess/Jungle Strut	1975	—	2.50	5.00
—With Ramsey Lewis					
3-10172	That's the Way of the World/Africano	1975	—	2.50	5.00
3-10251	Singasong/(Instrumental)	1975	—	3.00	6.00
—Original pressings have title as one word					
3-10251	Sing a Song/(Instrumental)	1975	—	2.50	5.00
—Later pressings have title as three words					
3-10309	Can't Hide Love/Gratitude	1976	—	2.50	5.00
3-10373	Getaway/(Instrumental)	1976	—	2.50	5.00
3-10373 [PS]	Getaway/(Instrumental)	1976	2.50	5.00	10.00
3-10439	Saturday Nite/Departure	1976	—	2.50	5.00
3-10492	On Your Face/Biyo	1977	—	2.50	5.00
3-10625	Serpentine Fire/(Instrumental)	1977	—	2.50	5.00
3-10688	Fantasy/Runnin'	1978	—	2.50	5.00
3-10796	Got to Get You Into My Life/I'll Write a Song for You	1978	—	2.50	5.00
4-45747	Power/M-O-M	1972	—	3.00	6.00
4-45800	Tims Is On Your Side/Where Have All the Flowers Gone	1973	—	3.00	6.00
4-45888	Evil/Clover	1973	—	2.50	5.00
4-45888 [PS]	Evil/Clover	1973	2.50	5.00	10.00
4-45953	Keep Your Head to the Sky/Build Your Nest	1973	—	2.50	5.00
4-46007	Mighty Mighty/Drum Song	1974	—	2.50	5.00
4-46007 [PS]	Mighty Mighty/Drum Song	1974	2.50	5.00	10.00
4-46070	Kalimba Story/Tee Nine Chee Bit	1974	—	2.50	5.00
73205	Heritage/Gotta Find Out	1990	—	2.50	5.00

WARNER BROS.

Number	Title (A Side/B Side)	Yr	VG	VG+	NM
7480	Fan the Fire/This World Today	1971	—	3.00	6.00
7492	Love Is Life/This World Today	1971	—	3.00	6.00
7549	I Think About Lovin' You/C'mon Children	1972	—	3.00	6.00

Albums

ARC

Number	Title (A Side/B Side)	Yr	VG	VG+	NM
FC 35647	The Best of Earth, Wind & Fire, Vol. 1	1978	2.50	5.00	10.00
FC 35730	I Am	1979	2.50	5.00	10.00
PC 35730	I Am	1984	2.00	4.00	8.00
—Budget-line reissue					
KC2 36795 [(2)]	Faces	1980	3.00	6.00	12.00
PC 37548	Raise!	1984	2.00	4.00	8.00
—Budget-line reissue					
TC 37548	Raise!	1981	2.50	5.00	10.00
HC 45647	The Best of Earth, Wind & Fire, Vol. 1	1981	7.50	15.00	30.00
—Half-speed mastered edition					
HC 45730	I Am	1981	7.50	15.00	30.00
—Half-speed mastered edition					
HC 47548	Raise!	1982	7.50	15.00	30.00
—Half-speed mastered edition					

COLUMBIA

Number	Title (A Side/B Side)	Yr	VG	VG+	NM
KC 31702	Last Days and Time	1972	3.75	7.50	15.00
PC 31702	Last Days and Time	197?	2.00	4.00	8.00
—Reissue					
CQ 32194 [Q]	Head to the Sky	1973	5.00	10.00	20.00
KC 32194	Head to the Sky	1973	3.00	6.00	12.00
PC 32194	Head to the Sky	197?	2.00	4.00	8.00
—Reissue					
CQ 32712 [Q]	Open Our Eyes	1974	5.00	10.00	20.00
KC 32712	Open Our Eyes	1974	3.00	6.00	12.00
PC 32712	Open Our Eyes	197?	2.00	4.00	8.00
—Reissue					
PC 33280	That's the Way of the World	1975	3.00	6.00	12.00
—No bar code					
PC 33280	That's the Way of the World	198?	2.00	4.00	8.00
—Budget-line reissue with bar code					
PG 33694 [(2)]	Gratitude	1975	3.75	7.50	15.00
—No bar code					
PG 33694 [(2)]	Gratitude	198?	2.50	5.00	10.00
—Budget-line reissue with bar code					
PC 34241	Spirit	1976	3.00	6.00	12.00
—No bar code					
PC 34241	Spirit	198?	2.00	4.00	8.00
—Budget-line reissue with bar code					
PCQ 34241 [Q]	Spirit	1976	6.25	12.50	25.00
JC 34905	All 'N All	1977	3.00	6.00	12.00
PC 34905	All 'N All	198?	2.00	4.00	8.00
—Budget-line reissue					
PC 38367	Powerlight	1984	2.00	4.00	8.00
—Budget-line reissue					
TC 38367	Powerlight	1983	2.50	5.00	10.00
QC 38980	Electric Universe	1983	2.50	5.00	10.00
FC 40596	Touch the World	1987	2.50	5.00	10.00
OC 45013	The Best of Earth, Wind & Fire, Vol. II	1988	2.50	5.00	10.00
C 45268	Heritage	1990	3.75	7.50	15.00
HC 48367	Powerlight	1983	10.00	20.00	40.00
—Half-speed mastered edition					

MOBILE FIDELITY

Number	Title (A Side/B Side)	Yr	VG	VG+	NM
1-159	That's the Way of the World	198?	7.50	15.00	30.00
—Audiophile vinyl					

PAIR

Number	Title (A Side/B Side)	Yr	VG	VG+	NM
PDL2-1064 [(2)]	Beat It to Life	1986	3.00	6.00	12.00

WARNER BROS.

Number	Title (A Side/B Side)	Yr	VG	VG+	NM
WS 1905	Earth, Wind, and Fire	1971	5.00	10.00	20.00
—Green label					
WS 1958	The Need of Love	1971	5.00	10.00	20.00
—Green label					
2WS 2798 [(2)]	Another Time	1974	5.00	10.00	20.00
—"Burbank" palm trees labels					

EARTH, WIND, AND FIRE WITH THE EMOTIONS

12-Inch Singles

ARC

Number	Title (A Side/B Side)	Yr	VG	VG+	NM
10950	Boogie Wonderland/(Instrumental)	1979	2.00	4.00	8.00

45s

ARC

Number	Title (A Side/B Side)	Yr	VG	VG+	NM
10956	Boogie Wonderland/(Instrumental)	1979	—	2.50	5.00

EAST

45s

CAPITOL

Number	Title (A Side/B Side)	Yr	VG	VG+	NM
3321	Some Sweet Day/Chanson D'Amour	1972	—	3.00	6.00
3400	Beautiful Morning/Black Hearted Woman	1972	—	3.00	6.00

Albums

CAPITOL

Number	Title (A Side/B Side)	Yr	VG	VG+	NM
ST-11083	East	1972	6.25	12.50	25.00

EAST OF EDEN

45s

DERAM

Number	Title (A Side/B Side)	Yr	VG	VG+	NM
85042	Southern Hemisphere/Communion	1969	2.00	4.00	8.00
85075	Jig-a-Jig/Marcus Junior	1971	2.00	4.00	8.00

Albums

DERAM

Number	Title (A Side/B Side)	Yr	VG	VG+	NM
DES 18023	Mercator Projected	1969	5.00	10.00	20.00
DES 18043	Snafu	1970	5.00	10.00	20.00

HARVEST

Number	Title (A Side/B Side)	Yr	VG	VG+	NM
SW-806	East of Eden	1971	5.00	10.00	20.00

EASY RIDERS, THE

See TERRY GILKYSON.

EASYBEATS, THE

45s

ASCOT

Number	Title (A Side/B Side)	Yr	VG	VG+	NM
2214	In My Book/Make You Feel Alright (Women)	1966	3.75	7.50	15.00
2214 [PS]	In My Book/Make You Feel Alright (Women)	1966	10.00	20.00	40.00

RARE EARTH

Number	Title (A Side/B Side)	Yr	VG	VG+	NM
5009	St. Louis/Can't Find Love	1969	3.75	7.50	15.00

UNITED ARTISTS

Number	Title (A Side/B Side)	Yr	VG	VG+	NM
0114	Friday on My Mind/Gonna Have a Good Time	1973	—	2.00	4.00
—"Silver Spotlight Series" reissue					
50106	Friday on My Mind/Made My Bed; Gonna Lie in It	1966	3.75	7.50	15.00
50187	Pretty Girl/Heaven and Hell	1967	2.50	5.00	10.00
50206	Falling Off the Edge of the World/Remember Sam	1967	2.50	5.00	10.00
50289	Come In, You'll Get Pneumonia/Hello, How Are You	1968	2.50	5.00	10.00
50488	Gonna Have a Good Time/Lay Me Down and Die	1969	2.50	5.00	10.00

Albums

RARE EARTH

Number	Title (A Side/B Side)	Yr	VG	VG+	NM
517	Easy Ridin'	1970	—	—	—
—Canceled					

RHINO

Number	Title (A Side/B Side)	Yr	VG	VG+	NM
RNLP-124	The Best of the Easybeats	1985	2.00	4.00	8.00

UNITED ARTISTS

Number	Title (A Side/B Side)	Yr	VG	VG+	NM
UAL 3588 [M]	Friday on My Mind	1967	10.00	20.00	40.00
UAS 6588 [P]	Friday on My Mind	1967	12.50	25.00	50.00
—"Make You Feel Alright" is rechanneled.					
UAS 6667 [P]	Falling Off the Edge of the World	1968	10.00	20.00	40.00
—"Women" is rechanneled.					

Number	Title (A Side/B Side)	Yr	VG	VG+	NM

EBB TIDES, THE
See NINO AND THE EBB TIDES.

EBBTIDES, THE
May be four different groups!

45s

Number	Title (A Side/B Side)	Yr	VG	VG+	NM
DUANE					
1022	Star of Love/First Love	1964	2000.	3000.	4000.
JAN-LAR					
101	Love Doctor/Lonesome	1959	75.00	150.00	300.00
MONUMENTAL					
520	Come On and Cry/Straightaway	1960	10.00	20.00	40.00
TEEN					
121	What Is Your Name Dear/Only Be Mine	1957	2000.	3000.	4000.

EBBTONES, THE

45s

Number	Title (A Side/B Side)	Yr	VG	VG+	NM
EBB					
100	I've Got a Feeling/Danny's Blues	1957	37.50	75.00	150.00
PORT					
70026	Rockin' on the Range/Ram Induction	1961	6.25	12.50	25.00

EBON-KNIGHTS, THE

45s

Number	Title (A Side/B Side)	Yr	VG	VG+	NM
STEPHENY					
1817	Poor Butterfly/The Way the Ball Bounces	1958	6.25	12.50	25.00
1822	First Date/Only Only You	1958	6.25	12.50	25.00

Albums

Number	Title (A Side/B Side)	Yr	VG	VG+	NM
STEPHENY					
4001 [M]	First Date	1959	375.00	750.00	1500.

EBONAIRES, THE

45s

Number	Title (A Side/B Side)	Yr	VG	VG+	NM
ALADDIN					
3211	3 O'Clock in the Morning/Baby, You're the One	1953	125.00	250.00	500.00
3212	You're Nobody 'Til Somebody Loves You/Lawd, Lawd, Lawd	1954	125.00	250.00	500.00
COLONIAL					
117	We're in Love/Thinkin' and Thinkin'	1959	30.00	60.00	120.00
HOLLYWOOD					
1046	Love For Christmas/Jingle Bell Hop	1955	100.00	200.00	400.00
1062	Let's Kiss and Say Hello Again/Jivarama Hop	1956	100.00	200.00	400.00
LENA					
101	Love Call/Somewhere in My Heart	1959	50.00	100.00	200.00
MONEY					
220	The Very Best Luck in the World/Hey Baby Stop	1956	20.00	40.00	80.00

EBONYS, THE

45s

Number	Title (A Side/B Side)	Yr	VG	VG+	NM
BUDDAH					
537	Makin' Love Ain't No Fun (Without the One You Love) Part 1/Part 2	1976	—	3.00	6.00
PHILADELPHIA INT'L.					
3503	You're the Reason Why/Sexy Ways	1971	2.00	4.00	8.00
3510	Determination/Do It	1971	2.00	4.00	8.00
3513 [DJ]	(Christmas Ain't Christmas, New Year's Ain't New Year's) Without The One You Love (mono/stereo)	1971	2.00	4.00	8.00
3514	Do You Like the Way I Love/I'm So Glad I'm Me	1972	2.00	4.00	8.00
3529	It's Forever/Sexy Ways	1973	—	3.50	7.00
3541	I Believe/Nation Time	1974	—	3.50	7.00
3548	Life in the Country/Hook Up and Get Down	1974	—	3.50	7.00
SOUL CLOCK					
108	Don't Knock Me/Can't Get Enough	1969	3.75	7.50	15.00

Albums

Number	Title (A Side/B Side)	Yr	VG	VG+	NM
PHILADELPHIA INT'L.					
KZ 32419	The Ebonys	1973	3.00	6.00	12.00

ECHO VALLEY BOYS, THE

45s

Number	Title (A Side/B Side)	Yr	VG	VG+	NM
ISLAND					
1/2	Ramblin' Man/Wash Machine Boogie	195?	75.00	150.00	300.00

ECHOES, THE (1)

45s

Number	Title (A Side/B Side)	Yr	VG	VG+	NM
SEG-WAY					
103	Baby Blue/Boomerang	1961	6.25	12.50	25.00
106	Sad Eyes (Don't You Cry)/It's Raining	1961	6.25	12.50	25.00
1002	Angel of My Heart/Gee Oh Gee	1962	10.00	20.00	40.00
SMASH					
1766	Bluebirds Over the Mountain/A Chicken Ain't Nothin' But a Bird	1962	3.75	7.50	15.00
1807	Keep an Eye on Her/A Million Miles from Nowhere	1963	3.75	7.50	15.00
1850	Annabelle Lee/If Love Is	1963	3.75	7.50	15.00
SRG					
101	Baby Blue/Boomerang	1960	50.00	100.00	200.00

ECHOES, THE (2)
Early version of THE INNOCENTS.

45s

Number	Title (A Side/B Side)	Yr	VG	VG+	NM
ANDEX					
22102	Time/Dee Dee Di Oh	1958	7.50	15.00	30.00

ECHOES, THE (3)

45s

Number	Title (A Side/B Side)	Yr	VG	VG+	NM
COMBO					
128	My Little Honey/Aye Senorita	1957	10.00	20.00	40.00

ECHOES, THE (4)
BONNIE GUITAR was in this group.

45s

Number	Title (A Side/B Side)	Yr	VG	VG+	NM
DOLTON					
18	Born to Be With You/My Guiding Light	1960	5.00	10.00	20.00

ECHOES, THE (5)

45s

Number	Title (A Side/B Side)	Yr	VG	VG+	NM
ROCKIN'					
523	All That Wine Is Gone/Please Say You're Mine	1953	100.00	200.00	400.00

ECHOES, THE (U)
Some of these may belong with the above groups. The record on Felsted is a reissue of the Hi Tide release.

45s

Number	Title (A Side/B Side)	Yr	VG	VG+	NM
ASCOT					
2188	I Love Candy/Paper Roses	1965	12.50	25.00	50.00
COLUMBIA					
4-41549	Bye-Bye My Baby/Do I Love You?	1960	3.75	7.50	15.00
4-41709	Loving and Losing/Ecstasy	1960	3.75	7.50	15.00
FELSTED					
8614	Angel of Love/Twistin' Town	1961	12.50	25.00	50.00
GEE					
1028	Ding Dong/My Heart Beats for You	1957	15.00	30.00	60.00
HI TIDE					
106 —*Black vinyl*	Angel of Love/Twistin' Town	1961	50.00	100.00	200.00
106 —*Colored vinyl*	Angel of Love/Twistin' Town	1961	100.00	200.00	400.00
SPECIALTY					
601	Over the Rainbow/Someone	1957	7.50	15.00	30.00
SWAN					
4013	Scratch My Back/The Little Green Man	1959	3.00	6.00	12.00

ECKSTINE, BILLY
Also see SARAH VAUGHAN.

45s

Number	Title (A Side/B Side)	Yr	VG	VG+	NM
A&M					
1858	The Best Thing/Love Theme from "The Getaway"	1976	—	2.00	4.00
1858 [PS]	The Best Thing/Love Theme from "The Getaway"	1976	—	3.00	6.00
ENTERPRISE					
9009	Stormy/When You Look in the Mirror	1970	—	3.00	6.00
9025	I Wanna Be Your Baby/The Name of My Sorrow	1970	—	3.00	6.00
9046	When Something Is Wrong with My Baby/Today Was Tomorrow Yesterday	1972	—	3.00	6.00
9076	I Didn't Mean to Love You/I Wanna Be Your Man	1973	—	2.50	5.00
9093	If She Walked Into My Life/Remembering	1974	—	2.50	5.00
MERCURY					
71161	All of My Life/Poor Little Heart	1957	2.50	5.00	10.00
71217	Boulevard of Broken Dreams/If I Can Help Somebody	1957	2.50	5.00	10.00
71250	Gigi/Trust in Me	1957	2.50	5.00	10.00
71325	Vertigo/In the Rain	1958	2.50	5.00	10.00
71372	Prisoner of Love/Funny	1958	2.50	5.00	10.00
71861	Theme from Exodus/It Isn't Fair	1961	2.00	4.00	8.00
71907	Jeannie/Alright, Okay, You Win	1961	2.00	4.00	8.00
71967	Guilty/I Want to Talk About You	1962	2.00	4.00	8.00
72022	What Kind of Fool Am I/Till There Was You	1962	2.00	4.00	8.00
72050	You've Changed/The Beauty of True Love	1962	2.00	4.00	8.00
72128	Everything I Have Is Yours/Darling, Why Did You	1963	2.00	4.00	8.00
72264	People/Sweet Georgia Brown	1963	2.00	4.00	8.00
72302	Wanted/What Are You Afraid Of	1964	2.00	4.00	8.00
MGM					
10525	O Come, All Ye Faithful/O, Holy Night	1949	3.75	7.50	15.00
10623	My Foolish Heart/Sure Thing	1950	5.00	10.00	20.00
10643	Free/Baby Won't You Say You Love Me	1950	5.00	10.00	20.00
10684	My Destiny/Roses	1950	5.00	10.00	20.00
10690	You're All I Need/Dedicated to You	1950	5.00	10.00	20.00
10716	I Wanna Be Loved/Stardust	1950	5.00	10.00	20.00
10778	The Show Must Go On/You've Got Me Cryin' Again	1950	5.00	10.00	20.00
10796	Blue Christmas/The Lonely Shepherd	1950	5.00	10.00	20.00
10799	Be My Love/Only a Moment Ago	1950	5.00	10.00	20.00
10825	I'll Know/I've Never Been in Love Before	1951	3.75	7.50	15.00
10856	I'm So Crazy for Love/Guess I'll Have to Dream	1951	3.75	7.50	15.00
10896	If/When You Return	1951	3.75	7.50	15.00
10903	I Apologize/Bring Back the Thrill	1951	3.75	7.50	15.00
10916	I Left My Hat/Here Come the Blues	1951	3.75	7.50	15.00
10944	I'm Yours to Command/What Will I Tell My Heart	1951	3.75	7.50	15.00
10982	I'm a Fool/Lose Me	1951	3.75	7.50	15.00
10996	Pandora/Wonder Why	1951	3.75	7.50	15.00
11028	Enchanted Land/I've Got My Mind on You	1951	3.75	7.50	15.00
11073	Once/Out in the Cold	1951	3.75	7.50	15.00
11101	Taking a Chance/You're Driving Me Crazy	1951	3.75	7.50	15.00
11111	Jalousie/Strange Interlude	1951	3.75	7.50	15.00
11125	Take Me Back/Weaver of Dreams	1952	3.75	7.50	15.00
11144	Every Day/I Love You	1952	3.75	7.50	15.00
11177	Carnival/Room with a View	1952	3.75	7.50	15.00
11217	If They Ask Me/Hold Me Close to You	1952	3.75	7.50	15.00
11225	Kiss of Fire/Never Like This	1952	3.75	7.50	15.00
11291	Have a Good Time/Strange Sensation	1952	3.75	7.50	15.00
11301	Early Autumn/Because You're Mine	1952	3.75	7.50	15.00
11351	Be Fair/Come to the Mardi Gras	1952	3.75	7.50	15.00
11396	Until Eternity/Everything Depends on You	1953	3.75	7.50	15.00
11439	A Fool in Love/Until Today	1953	3.75	7.50	15.00
11511	Send My Baby Back to Me/Laugh to Keep From Crying	1953	3.75	7.50	15.00
11550	It Can't Be Wrong/I Can Read Between the Lines	1953	3.75	7.50	15.00
11573	St. Louis Blues (Part 1)/St. Louis Blues (Part 2)	1953	3.75	7.50	15.00
11587	I'm Saving Dreams/Fortune Telling Cards	1953	3.75	7.50	15.00
11623	What Are You Doing New Year's Eve/Christmas Eve	1953	5.00	10.00	20.00
11655	Rendezvous/I'm In a Mood	1954	3.75	7.50	15.00

Number	Title (A Side/B Side)	Yr	VG	VG+	NM
11694	Don't Get Around Much Anymore/Lost in Loveliness	1954	3.75	7.50	15.00
11712	No One But You/Seabreeze	1954	3.75	7.50	15.00
11744	Beloved/Temporarily Blue	1954	3.75	7.50	15.00
11803	Olay, Olay/You Leave Me Breathless	1954	3.75	7.50	15.00
11845	Mood Indigo/Do Nothing 'Till You Hear from Me	1954	3.75	7.50	15.00
11855	Love Me/One Sweet Kiss	1954	3.75	7.50	15.00
11915	What More Is There to Say/Touching Shoulders	1955	3.00	6.00	12.00
11948	Give Me Another Chance/More Than You'll Ever Know	1955	3.00	6.00	12.00
11984	Love Me or Leave Me/Only You	1955	3.00	6.00	12.00
11998	Careless Lips/A Man Doesn't Know	1955	3.00	6.00	12.00
12055	September Song/Pass the Word Around	1955	3.00	6.00	12.00
12105	La De Do De Do (The Honey Bug Song)/Farewell to Romance	1955	3.00	6.00	12.00
12160	You'll Get Yours/Lonely Avenue	1955	3.00	6.00	12.00
12180	Good-Bye/The Show Must Go On	1956	3.00	6.00	12.00
12237	Out of My Mind/My Fickle Heart	1956	3.00	6.00	12.00
MOTOWN					
1077	Had You Been Around/Down to Earth	1965	3.00	6.00	12.00
1091	Wish You Were Here/Slender Thread	1966	3.00	6.00	12.00
1100	A Warmer World/And There You Were	1966	3.00	6.00	12.00
1105	I Wonder Why (Nobody Loves Me)/I've Been Blessed	1967	3.00	6.00	12.00
1120	Is Anyone Here Going My Way/Thank You Love	1968	2.50	5.00	10.00
1131	For Love of Ivy/A Woman	1968	2.50	5.00	10.00
1143	My Cup Runneth Over/Ask the Lonely	1969	2.50	5.00	10.00
RCA VICTOR					
47-6436	The Bitter with the Sweet/Grapevine	1956	3.00	6.00	12.00
47-6488	My Heart Says No/Joey, Joey, Joey	1956	3.00	6.00	12.00
47-6524	Tennessee Rock 'n' Roll/Condemned for Life	1956	5.00	10.00	20.00
47-6691	The Chosen Few/Just Call Me Crazy	1956	3.00	6.00	12.00
47-6827	Blue Illusion/Oh My Pretty Pretty	1957	3.00	6.00	12.00
ROULETTE					
4199	Anything You Wanna Do/Like Wow	1959	3.00	6.00	12.00
4239	I Love You/I Apologize	1960	3.00	6.00	12.00
7-Inch Extended Plays					
EMARCY					
16041	(contents unknown)	195?	5.00	10.00	20.00
16041 [PS]	Billy's Blues	195?	5.00	10.00	20.00
MGM					
X-1002	(contents unknown)	195?	5.00	10.00	20.00
X-1002 [PS]	Dedicated to You	195?	5.00	10.00	20.00
X-1011	(contents unknown)	195?	5.00	10.00	20.00
X-1011 [PS]	My Foolish Heart	195?	5.00	10.00	20.00
X-1015	(contents unknown)	195?	3.75	7.50	15.00
X-1015 [PS]	I Apologize	195?	3.75	7.50	15.00
X-1041	(contents unknown)	195?	5.00	10.00	20.00
X-1041 [PS]	Songs by Billy Eckstine	195?	5.00	10.00	20.00
X-1052	(contents unknown)	195?	3.75	7.50	15.00
X-1052 [PS]	Tenderly	195?	3.75	7.50	15.00
X-1053	(contents unknown)	195?	3.75	7.50	15.00
X-1053 [PS]	Smoke Gets In Your Eyes	195?	3.75	7.50	15.00
X-1078	(contents unknown)	195?	3.75	7.50	15.00
X-1078 [PS]	Billy Eckstine	195?	3.75	7.50	15.00
X-1084	(contents unknown)	195?	3.75	7.50	15.00
X-1084 [PS]	A Fool in Love	195?	3.75	7.50	15.00
X-1099	(contents unknown)	195?	3.75	7.50	15.00
X-1099 [PS]	Love Songs, Vol. 1	195?	3.75	7.50	15.00
X-1100	(contents unknown)	195?	3.75	7.50	15.00
X-1100 [PS]	Love Songs, Vol. 2	195?	3.75	7.50	15.00
X-1103	(contents unknown)	195?	3.75	7.50	15.00
X-1103 [PS]	Billy Eckstine Favorites, Vol. 1	195?	3.75	7.50	15.00
X-1104	(contents unknown)	195?	3.75	7.50	15.00
X-1104 [PS]	Billy Eckstine Favorites, Vol. 2	195?	3.75	7.50	15.00
X-1110	(contents unknown)	1955	3.75	7.50	15.00
X-1110 [PS]	I Let a Song Go Out of My Heart, Vol. 1	1955	3.75	7.50	15.00
X-1111	(contents unknown)	1955	3.75	7.50	15.00
X-1111 [PS]	I Let a Song Go Out of My Heart, Vol. 2	1955	3.75	7.50	15.00
X-1152	(contents unknown)	195?	3.00	6.00	12.00
X-1152 [PS]	Early Autumn	195?	3.00	6.00	12.00
Albums					
AUDIO LAB					
AL-1549 [M]	Mr. B	1960	30.00	60.00	120.00
DELUXE					
FA-2010 [M]	Billy Eckstine and His Orchestra	195?	20.00	40.00	80.00
EMARCY					
MG-26025 [10]	Blues for Sale	1954	30.00	60.00	120.00
MG-26027 [10]	The Love Songs of Mr. B	1954	30.00	60.00	120.00
MG-36010 [M]	I Surrender, Dear	1955	20.00	40.00	80.00
MG-36029 [M]	Blues for Sale	1955	20.00	40.00	80.00
MG-36030 [M]	The Love Songs of Mr. B	1955	20.00	40.00	80.00
MG-36129 [M]	Billy Eckstine's Imagination	1958	15.00	30.00	60.00
ENTERPRISE					
ENS-1013	Stormy	1971	3.75	7.50	15.00
ENS-1017	Feel the Warm	1971	3.75	7.50	15.00
ENS-5004	Senior Soul	1972	3.75	7.50	15.00
FORUM					
F-9027 [M]	Once More with Feeling	196?	3.75	7.50	15.00
SF-9027 [S]	Once More with Feeling	196?	3.75	7.50	15.00
KING					
295-12 [10]	The Great Mr. B	1953	75.00	150.00	300.00
LION					
L-70057 [M]	The Best of Billy Eckstine	1958	6.25	12.50	25.00
MERCURY					
MG-20333 [M]	Billy's Best	1958	10.00	20.00	40.00
MG-20637 [M]	Broadway, Bongos and Mr. B	1961	6.25	12.50	25.00
MG-20674 [M]	Billy Eckstine and Quincy Jones at Basin St. East	1962	6.25	12.50	25.00
MG-20736 [M]	Don't Worry 'Bout Me	1962	6.25	12.50	25.00
MG-20796 [M]	The Golden Hits of Billy Eckstine	1963	3.75	7.50	15.00
SR-60086 [S]	Billy's Best	1958	12.50	25.00	50.00
SR-60637 [S]	Broadway, Bongos and Mr. B	1961	7.50	15.00	30.00
SR-60674 [S]	Billy Eckstine and Quincy Jones at Basin St. East	1962	7.50	15.00	30.00
SR-60736 [S]	Don't Worry 'Bout Me	1962	7.50	15.00	30.00
SR-60796 [S]	The Golden Hits of Billy Eckstine	1963	5.00	10.00	20.00
METRO					
M-537 [M]	Everything I Have Is Yours	1965	3.75	7.50	15.00
MS-537 [R]	Everything I Have Is Yours	1965	3.00	6.00	12.00
MGM					
E-153 [10]	Billy Eckstine Sings Rodgers & Hammerstein	1952	37.50	75.00	150.00
E-219 [10]	Tenderly	1953	37.50	75.00	150.00
E-257 [10]	I Let a Song Go Out of My Heart	1954	37.50	75.00	150.00
E-523 [10]	Songs by Billy Eckstine	1951	40.00	80.00	160.00
E-548 [10]	Favorites	1951	40.00	80.00	160.00
E-3176 [M]	Mr. B with a Beat	1955	12.50	25.00	50.00
E-3209 [M]	Rendezvous	1955	12.50	25.00	50.00
E-3275 [M]	That Old Feeling	1956	12.50	25.00	50.00
MOTOWN					
M 632 [M]	Prime of My Life	1965	5.00	10.00	20.00
MS 632 [S]	Prime of My Life	1965	6.25	12.50	25.00
M 646 [M]	My Way	1966	5.00	10.00	20.00
MS 646 [S]	My Way	1966	6.25	12.50	25.00
MS 677	For Love of Ivy	1969	6.25	12.50	25.00
NATIONAL					
NLP-2001 [10]	Billy Eckstine Sings	1949	50.00	100.00	200.00
REGENT					
MG-6052 [M]	Prisoner of Love	1957	12.50	25.00	50.00
MG-6053 [M]	The Duke, the Blues and Me	1957	12.50	25.00	50.00
MG-6054 [M]	My Deep Blue Dream	1957	12.50	25.00	50.00
MG-6058 [M]	You Call It Madness	1957	12.50	25.00	50.00
ROULETTE					
R-25052 [M]	No Cover, No Minimum	1961	6.25	12.50	25.00
SR-25052 [S]	No Cover, No Minimum	1961	7.50	15.00	30.00
R-25104 [M]	Once More with Feeling	1962	6.25	12.50	25.00
SR-25104 [S]	Once More with Feeling	1962	7.50	15.00	30.00
SAVOY					
1127	Billy Eckstine Sings	1979	3.00	6.00	12.00
SJL-2214 [(2)]	Mr. B and the Band/The Savoy Sessions	1976	3.75	7.50	15.00
TRIP					
5567	The Modern Sound of Mr. B	197?	2.50	5.00	10.00
VERVE					
819442-1 [(2)]	Everything I Have Is Yours: The MGM Years	1986	3.75	7.50	15.00
XANADU					
207	I Want to Talk About You	1987	2.50	5.00	10.00

ECKSTINE, BILLY, AND SARAH VAUGHAN

See SARAH VAUGHAN AND BILLY ECKSTINE.

ECLECTION

Number	Title (A Side/B Side)	Yr	VG	VG+	NM
Albums					
ELEKTRA					
EKS-74023	Eclection	1968	3.75	7.50	15.00

ECSTASIES, THE

Number	Title (A Side/B Side)	Yr	VG	VG+	NM
45s					
AMY					
853	That Lucky Old Sun/Time for Love	1962	12.50	25.00	50.00
CLIFTON					
40	White Christmas/Silent Night	19??	3.75	7.50	15.00

EDDIE AND THE EVERGREENS

See SHA NA NA.

EDDIE AND THE SHOWMEN

Number	Title (A Side/B Side)	Yr	VG	VG+	NM
45s					
LIBERTY					
55566	Toes on the Nose/Border Town	1963	7.50	15.00	30.00
55608	Squad Car/Scratch	1963	7.50	15.00	30.00
55659	Movin'/Mr. Rebel	1963	7.50	15.00	30.00
55695	Faw Away Places/Lanky Bones	1964	7.50	15.00	30.00
55720	We Are the Young/Young and Lonely	1964	7.50	15.00	30.00

EDDIE AND THE STARLITES

Number	Title (A Side/B Side)	Yr	VG	VG+	NM
45s					
ALJON					
1260	Come On Home/(B-side unknown)	1963	7.50	15.00	30.00
SCEPTER					
1202	To Make a Long Story Short/Pretty Little Girl	1958	15.00	30.00	60.00
—White label					
1202	To Make a Long Story Short/Pretty Little Girl	1958	7.50	15.00	30.00
—Red label					

EDDY, DUANE

Also see AL CASEY; DUANE AND MIRRIAM EDDY.

Number	Title (A Side/B Side)	Yr	VG	VG+	NM
45s					
BIG TREE					
157	Renegade/Nightly News	1972	2.00	4.00	8.00
CAPITOL					
B-44018	Spies/Rockabilly Holiday	1987	—	2.50	5.00
B-44018 [PS]	Spies/Rockabilly Holiday	1987	—	2.50	5.00
CHINA					
42986	Peter Gunn/Something Always Happens	1986	—	—	3.00
—With Art of Noise; B-side does not feature Eddy					
42986 [PS]	Peter Gunn/Something Always Happens	1986	—	—	3.00
COLPIX					
779	Trash/South Phoenix	1965	3.75	7.50	15.00
788	Don't Think Twice, It's All Right/House of the Rising Sun	1965	3.75	7.50	15.00
788 [PS]	Don't Think Twice, It's All Right/House of the Rising Sun	1965	12.50	25.00	50.00
795	El Rancho Grande/Poppa's Movin' On	1966	3.75	7.50	15.00
CONGRESS					
6010	Freight Train/Put a Little Love in Your Heart	1970	3.75	7.50	15.00
ELEKTRA					
45359	You Are My Sunshine/From 8 to 7	1977	—	2.50	5.00

Number	Title (A Side/B Side)	Yr	VG	VG+	NM
FORD					
500	Ramrod/Caravan	1957	500.00	1000.	1500.
—As "Duane Eddy and His Rock-A-Billies"					
GREGMARK					
5	Caravan (Part 1)/Caravan (Part 2)	1961	3.75	7.50	15.00
—Credited to Duane Eddy, but is actually Al Casey					
GUSTO					
2047	Rebel Rouser/40 Miles of Bad Road	1979	—	2.00	4.00
—Re-recordings					
JAMIE					
JLP-71 [S]	Lonesome Road/I Almost Lost My Mind	1960	6.25	12.50	25.00
JLP-72 [S]	Loving You/Anything	1960	6.25	12.50	25.00
JLP-73 [S]	Peter Gunn/Along the Navaho Trail	1960	6.25	12.50	25.00
JLP-74 [S]	Hard Times/Along Came Linda	1960	6.25	12.50	25.00
JLP-75 [S]	The Battle/You Are My Sunshine	1960	6.25	12.50	25.00
—The above five are 33 1/3 rpm singles with small holes					
1101	Moovin N' Groovin'/Up and Down	1958	12.50	25.00	50.00
—Originals have pink labels					
1101	Moovin N' Groovin'/Up and Down	1958	6.25	12.50	25.00
—All-yellow label, "Jamie" at top					
1104	Rebel-'Rouser/Stalkin'	1958	6.25	12.50	25.00
1109	Ramrod/The Walker	1958	6.25	12.50	25.00
1111	Cannonball/Mason Dixon Line	1958	5.00	10.00	20.00
1117 [M]	The Lonely One/Detour	1959	5.00	10.00	20.00
1117 [S]	The Lonely One/Detour	1959	12.50	25.00	50.00
1122	Yep!/Three-30-Blues	1959	5.00	10.00	20.00
1122 [PS]	Yep!/Three-30-Blues	1959	12.50	25.00	50.00
1126 [M]	Forty Miles of Bad Road/The Quiet Three	1959	5.00	10.00	20.00
1126 [PS]	Forty Miles of Bad Road/The Quiet Three	1959	12.50	25.00	50.00
1126 [S]	Forty Miles of Bad Road/The Quiet Three	1959	12.50	25.00	50.00
1130 [M]	Some Kind-a Earthquake/First Love, First Tears	1959	5.00	10.00	20.00
1130 [PS]	Some Kind-a Earthquake/First Love, First Tears	1959	10.00	20.00	40.00
1130 [S]	Some Kind-a Earthquake/First Love, First Tears	1959	12.50	25.00	50.00
1144	Bonnie Came Back/Lost Island	1959	5.00	10.00	20.00
1144 [PS]	Bonnie Came Back/Lost Island	1959	10.00	20.00	40.00
1151	Shazam!/The Secret Seven	1960	3.75	7.50	15.00
1151 [PS]	Shazam!/The Secret Seven	1960	7.50	15.00	30.00
1156	Because They're Young/Rebel Walk	1960	3.75	7.50	15.00
1156 [PS]	Because They're Young/Rebel Walk	1960	7.50	15.00	30.00
1163	Kommotion/Theme from Moon Children	1960	3.75	7.50	15.00
1163 [PS]	Kommotion/Theme from Moon Children	1960	7.50	15.00	30.00
1168	Peter Gunn/Along the Navaho Trail	1960	3.75	7.50	15.00
1168 [PS]	Peter Gunn/Along the Navaho Trail	1960	7.50	15.00	30.00
1175	"Pepe"/Lost Friend	1960	3.75	7.50	15.00
1175 [PS]	"Pepe"/Lost Friend	1960	10.00	20.00	40.00
—Red sleeve					
1175 [PS]	"Pepe"/Lost Friend	1960	7.50	15.00	30.00
—Yellow sleeve					
1183	Theme from Dixie/Gidget Goes Hawaiian	1961	3.75	7.50	15.00
1183 [PS]	Theme from Dixie/Gidget Goes Hawaiian	1961	7.50	15.00	30.00
1187	Ring of Fire/Bobbie	1961	3.75	7.50	15.00
1187 [PS]	Ring of Fire/Bobbie	1961	7.50	15.00	30.00
1195	Drivin' Home/Tammy	1961	3.75	7.50	15.00
1195 [PS]	Drivin' Home/Tammy	1961	7.50	15.00	30.00
1200	My Blue Heaven/Along Came Linda	1961	3.75	7.50	15.00
1200 [PS]	My Blue Heaven/Along Came Linda	1961	7.50	15.00	30.00
1206	The Avenger/Londonderry Air	1961	3.75	7.50	15.00
1209	The Battle/Trambone	1962	3.75	7.50	15.00
1224	Runaway Pony/Just Because	1962	3.75	7.50	15.00
1303	Rebel Rouser/Movin' N' Groovin'	1965	3.00	6.00	12.00
RCA VICTOR					
47-7999	Deep in the Heart of Texas/Saints and Sinners	1962	3.00	6.00	12.00
47-7999 [PS]	Deep in the Heart of Texas/Saints and Sinners	1962	6.25	12.50	25.00
47-8047	The Ballad of Paladin/The WIld Westerner	1962	3.00	6.00	12.00
47-8047 [PS]	The Ballad of Paladin/The WIld Westerner	1962	6.25	12.50	25.00
47-8087	(Dance with the) Guitar Man/Stretchin' Out	1962	3.75	7.50	15.00
47-8087 [PS]	(Dance with the) Guitar Man/Stretchin' Out	1962	7.50	15.00	30.00
47-8131	Boss Guitar/Desert Rat	1963	3.00	6.00	12.00
47-8131 [PS]	Boss Guitar/Desert Rat	1963	6.25	12.50	25.00
47-8180	Lonely Boy, Lonely Guitar/Joshin'	1963	3.00	6.00	12.00
47-8180 [PS]	Lonely Boy, Lonely Guitar/Joshin'	1963	6.25	12.50	25.00
47-8214	Your Baby's Gone Surfin'/Shuckin'	1963	3.75	7.50	15.00
47-8214 [PS]	Your Baby's Gone Surfin'/Shuckin'	1963	7.50	15.00	30.00
47-8276	The Son of Rebel Rouser/The Story of Three Loves	1963	3.00	6.00	12.00
47-8276 [PS]	The Son of Rebel Rouser/The Story of Three Loves	1963	6.25	12.50	25.00
47-8335	Guitar Child/Jerky Jalopy	1964	3.00	6.00	12.00
47-8376	Water Skiing/Theme from A Summer Place	1964	3.00	6.00	12.00
47-8442	Guitar Star/The Iguana	1964	3.00	6.00	12.00
47-8507	Moonshot/Roughneck	1965	3.00	6.00	12.00
REPRISE					
0504	Daydream/This Guitar Was Made for Twangin'	1966	2.50	5.00	10.00
0557	Roarin'/Monsoon	1967	2.50	5.00	10.00
0662	There Is a Mountain/This Town	1968	2.50	5.00	10.00
0690	Niki-Hoeky/Velvet Nights	1968	2.50	5.00	10.00
UNI					
55237	The Five-Seventeen/Something	1970	3.75	7.50	15.00
7-Inch Extended Plays					
JAMIE					
JEP-100	Cannonball/Moovin' N' Groovin'//Mason-Dixon Lion/The Lonely One	1958	12.50	25.00	50.00
JEP-100 [PS]	Duane Eddy	1958	12.50	25.00	50.00
JEP-301	Lonesome Road/I Almost Lost My Mind//Detour/Loving You	1959	12.50	25.00	50.00
JEP-301 [PS]	Detour	1959	12.50	25.00	50.00
JEP-302	Yep/Three-30 Blues//Anytime/Stalkin'	1959	12.50	25.00	50.00
JEP-302 [PS]	Yep!	1959	12.50	25.00	50.00
JEP-303	Shazam/Tiger Love//My Blue Heaven/Night Train To Memphis	1960	12.50	25.00	50.00
JEP-303 [PS]	Shazam!	1960	12.50	25.00	50.00
JEP-304	Because They're Young/Easy//Rebel Walk/The Battle	1960	12.50	25.00	50.00
JEP-304 [PS]	Because They're Young	1960	12.50	25.00	50.00

Number	Title (A Side/B Side)	Yr	VG	VG+	NM
Albums					
CAPITOL					
ST-12567	Duane Eddy	1987	3.00	6.00	12.00
COLPIX					
CP-490 [M]	Duane A-Go-Go	1965	7.50	15.00	30.00
CPS-490 [S]	Duane A-Go-Go	1965	10.00	20.00	40.00
CP-494 [M]	Duane Eddy Does Bob Dylan	1965	7.50	15.00	30.00
CPS-494 [S]	Duane Eddy Does Bob Dylan	1965	10.00	20.00	40.00
JAMIE					
JLP-3000 [M]	Have "Twangy" Guitar — Will Travel	1958	30.00	60.00	120.00
—Duane sitting with guitar case, title on cover in white (1st)					
JLP-3000 [M]	Have "Twangy" Guitar — Will Travel	1959	25.00	50.00	100.00
—Duane sitting with guitar case, title on cover in green and red (2nd)					
JLP-3000 [M]	Have "Twangy" Guitar — Will Travel	1959	12.50	25.00	50.00
—Duane standing with guitar (3rd)					
JLPS-3000 [R]	Have "Twangy" Guitar — Will Travel	196?	12.50	25.00	50.00
—Duane standing with guitar (3rd), album plays fake stereo					
JLPS-3000 [S]	Have "Twangy" Guitar — Will Travel	1958	100.00	200.00	400.00
—Duane sitting with guitar case, title on cover in white (1st)					
JLPS-3000 [S]	Have "Twangy" Guitar — Will Travel	1959	75.00	150.00	300.00
—Duane sitting with guitar case, title on cover in green and red (2nd)					
JLPS-3000 [S]	Have "Twangy" Guitar — Will Travel	1959	25.00	50.00	100.00
—Duane standing with guitar (3rd), album plays true stereo					
JLPM-3006 [M]	Especially for You...	1959	10.00	20.00	40.00
JLPS-3006 [S]	Especially for You...	1959	15.00	30.00	60.00
JLPM-3009 [M]	The "Twangs" The "Thang"	1959	10.00	20.00	40.00
JLPS-3009 [S]	The "Twangs" The "Thang"	1959	15.00	30.00	60.00
JLPM-3011 [M]	Songs of Our Heritage	1960	20.00	40.00	80.00
—Gatefold cover					
JLPM-3011 [M]	Songs of Our Heritage	196?	7.50	15.00	30.00
—Regular cover					
JLPS-3011 [S]	Songs of Our Heritage	1960	25.00	50.00	100.00
—Gatefold cover					
JLPS-3011 [S]	Songs of Our Heritage	1960	125.00	250.00	500.00
—Gatefold cover, red vinyl					
JLPS-3011 [S]	Songs of Our Heritage	1960	125.00	250.00	500.00
—Gatefold cover, blue vinyl					
JLPS-3011 [S]	Songs of Our Heritage	196?	10.00	20.00	40.00
—Regular cover					
JLPM-3014 [M]	$1,000,000.00 Worth of Twang	1960	10.00	20.00	40.00
JLPS-3014 [S]	$1,000,000.00 Worth of Twang	1960	17.50	35.00	70.00
—All but one song -- "Up and Down" -- is in true stereo					
JLPM-3019 [M]	Girls! Girls! Girls!	1961	10.00	20.00	40.00
JLPS-3019 [R]	Girls! Girls! Girls!	1961	7.50	15.00	30.00
JLPM-3021 [M]	$1,000,000.00 Worth of Twang, Volume 2	1962	10.00	20.00	40.00
JLPS-3021 [R]	$1,000,000.00 Worth of Twang, Volume 2	1962	7.50	15.00	30.00
JLPM-3022 [M]	Twistin' with Duane Eddy	1962	10.00	20.00	40.00
JLPS-3022 [P]	Twistin' with Duane Eddy	1962	10.00	20.00	40.00
JLPM-3024 [M]	Surfin'	1963	12.50	25.00	50.00
JLPS-3024 [S]	Surfin'	1963	20.00	40.00	80.00
JLPM-3025 [M]	Duane Eddy & The Rebels — In Person	1963	7.50	15.00	30.00
JLPS-3025 [S]	Duane Eddy & The Rebels — In Person	1963	10.00	20.00	40.00
JLPM-3026 [M]	16 Greatest Hits	1964	10.00	20.00	40.00
JLPS-3026 [R]	16 Greatest Hits	1964	7.50	15.00	30.00
ST-90663 [S]	Duane Eddy & The Rebels — In Person	1965	12.50	25.00	50.00
—Capitol Record Club edition					
T-90663 [M]	Duane Eddy & The Rebels — In Person	1965	10.00	20.00	40.00
—Capitol Record Club edition					
ST-90682 [S]	Have "Twangy" Guitar — Will Travel	1965	20.00	40.00	80.00
—Capitol Record Club edition					
T-90682 [M]	Have "Twangy" Guitar — Will Travel	1965	15.00	30.00	60.00
—Capitol Record Club edition					
ST-91301 [S]	The "Twangs" The "Thang"	1966	15.00	30.00	60.00
—Capitol Record Club edition					
T-91301 [M]	The "Twangs" The "Thang"	1966	15.00	30.00	60.00
—Capitol Record Club edition					
RCA VICTOR					
LPM-2525 [M]	Twistin' 'N' Twangin'	1962	6.25	12.50	25.00
LSP-2525 [S]	Twistin' 'N' Twangin'	1962	10.00	20.00	40.00
LPM-2576 [M]	Twangy Guitar — Silky Strings	1962	6.25	12.50	25.00
LSP-2576 [S]	Twangy Guitar — Silky Strings	1962	10.00	20.00	40.00
LPM-2648 [M]	Dance with the Guitar Man	1962	6.25	12.50	25.00
LSP-2648 [S]	Dance with the Guitar Man	1962	10.00	20.00	40.00
ANL1-2671	Pure Gold	1978	2.50	5.00	10.00
LPM-2681 [M]	Twang a Country Song	1963	6.25	12.50	25.00
LSP-2681 [S]	Twang a Country Song	1963	10.00	20.00	40.00
LPM-2700 [M]	"Twangin' " Up a Storm!	1963	6.25	12.50	25.00
LSP-2700 [S]	"Twangin' " Up a Storm!	1963	10.00	20.00	40.00
LPM-2798 [M]	Lonely Guitar	1964	5.00	10.00	20.00
LSP-2798 [S]	Lonely Guitar	1964	7.50	15.00	30.00
LPM-2918 [M]	Water Skiing	1964	5.00	10.00	20.00
LSP-2918 [S]	Water Skiing	1964	7.50	15.00	30.00
LPM-2993 [M]	Twangin' the Golden Hits	1965	5.00	10.00	20.00
LSP-2993 [S]	Twangin' the Golden Hits	1965	7.50	15.00	30.00
LPM-3432 [M]	Twangsville	1965	5.00	10.00	20.00
LSP-3432 [S]	Twangsville	1965	7.50	15.00	30.00
LPM-3477 [M]	The Best of Duane Eddy	1965	5.00	10.00	20.00
LSP-3477 [P]	The Best of Duane Eddy	1965	6.25	12.50	25.00
—Black "Stereo" label					
LSP-3477 [P]	The Best of Duane Eddy	1969	3.75	7.50	15.00
—Orange label					
REPRISE					
R-6218 [M]	The Biggest Twang of Them All	1966	7.50	15.00	30.00
RS-6218 [S]	The Biggest Twang of Them All	1966	10.00	20.00	40.00
R-6240 [M]	The Roaring Twangies	1967	7.50	15.00	30.00
RS-6240 [S]	The Roaring Twangies	1967	10.00	20.00	40.00
SIRE					
SASH-3702 [(2)]	The Vintage Years	1975	6.25	12.50	25.00

EDDY, DUANE AND MIRRIAM

Also see JESSI COLTER, DUANE EDDY.

Number	Title (A Side/B Side)	Yr	VG	VG+	NM
45s					
REPRISE					
0622	Guitar on My Mind/Wicked Women from Wickenborg	1967	2.50	5.00	10.00

EDEN, BARBARA

Number	Title (A Side/B Side)	Yr	VG	VG+	NM
45s					
DOT					
16999	Bend It/I Wouldn't Be a Fool	1967	2.00	4.00	8.00
17022	Rebel/Heartaches	1967	2.00	4.00	8.00
17032	Pledge of Love/I'm a Fool to Care	1967	2.00	4.00	8.00
PLANTATION					
178	Widow Jones/We Tried	1978	—	2.50	5.00
Albums					
DOT					
DLP-3795 [M]	Miss Barbara Eden	1967	10.00	20.00	40.00
DLP-25795 [S]	Miss Barbara Eden	1967	12.50	25.00	50.00

EDEN'S CHILDREN

Number	Title (A Side/B Side)	Yr	VG	VG+	NM
45s					
ABC					
11053	Goodbye Girl/Just Let Go	1968	3.00	6.00	12.00
Albums					
ABC					
624 [M]	Eden's Children	1968	10.00	20.00	40.00
S-624 [S]	Eden's Children	1968	6.25	12.50	25.00
S-652	Sure Looks Real	1968	5.00	10.00	20.00

EDGE, GRAEME

Of THE MOODY BLUES.

Number	Title (A Side/B Side)	Yr	VG	VG+	NM
45s					
LONDON					
1071	Everybody Needs Somebody/Be My Eyes	1977	—	2.50	5.00
—With Adrian Gurvitz					
THRESHOLD					
67018	We Like to Do It/Shotgun	1974	—	2.50	5.00
67022	The Tunnel/Bareback Rider	1975	—	2.50	5.00
Albums					
LONDON					
PS 686	Paradise Ballroom	1977	3.00	6.00	12.00
THRESHOLD					
THS 15	Kick Off Your Muddy Boots	1975	3.75	7.50	15.00

EDGE, THE

Number	Title (A Side/B Side)	Yr	VG	VG+	NM
Albums					
NOSE					
NRS-48003	The Edge	1970	10.00	20.00	40.00

EDISON LIGHTHOUSE

Number	Title (A Side/B Side)	Yr	VG	VG+	NM
45s					
BELL					
858	Love Grows (Where My Rosemary Goes)/Every Lonely Day	1970	—	3.00	6.00
907	She Works in a Woman's Way/It's Gonna Be a Lonely Summer	1970	—	2.50	5.00
960	It's Up to You Petula/Let's Make It Up	1971	—	2.50	5.00
989	Take a Little Time/What's Happening	1971	—	2.50	5.00

EDMUNDS, DAVE

Also see LOVE SCULPTURE.

Number	Title (A Side/B Side)	Yr	VG	VG+	NM
12-Inch Singles					
COLUMBIA					
AS 1660 [DJ]	Slipping Away (same on both sides)	1982	2.00	4.00	8.00
AS99-1725 [DJ]	Information	1983	6.25	12.50	25.00
—Promo-only picture disc					
AS 1911 [DJ]	Something About You (same on both sides)	1984	—	3.00	6.00
CAS 2077 [DJ]	Do You Want to Dance (same on both sides)	1985	—	3.00	6.00
CAS 02598 [DJ]	The Wanderer/Dave Edmunds Mega-Mix	1986	—	3.00	6.00
45s					
CAPITOL					
7PRO-79973 [DJ]	Closer to the Flame (same on both sides)	1990	2.50	5.00	10.00
COLUMBIA					
02960	From Small Things (Big Things One Day Come)/Warmed Over Kisses (Left Over Love)	1982	—	2.00	4.00
—A-side is a Bruce Springsteen composition.					
03428	Run Rudolph Run/Deep in the Heart of Texas	1982	—	2.00	4.00
03428 [PS]	Run Rudolph Run/Deep in the Heart of Texas	1982	2.00	4.00	8.00
03877	Slipping Away/Don't Call Me Tonight	1983	—	—	3.00
04080	Information/What Have I Got to Do to Win	1983	—	—	3.00
04585	Something About You/You Can't Get Enough	1984	—	—	3.00
04700	Breaking Out/How Could I Be So Wrong	1984	—	—	3.00
04762	High School Nights/Porky's Revenge	1985	—	—	2.50
04762 [PS]	High School Nights/Porky's Revenge	1985	—	—	2.50
04887	Queen of the Hop/I Don't Want to Do It	1985	5.00	10.00	20.00
—B-side by George Harrison, thus accounting for this 45's value					
04923	Do You Want to Dance/Don't Call Me Tonight	1985	—	—	3.00
05487	Run Rudolph Run/From Small Things (Big Things One Day Come)	198?	—	—	3.00
—"Golden Oldies" reissue					
06599	The Wanderer/Information	1987	—	—	3.00
07040	Paralyzed/Here Comes the Weekend	1987	—	—	3.00
MAM					
3601	I Hear You Knocking/Black Bill	1970	2.00	4.00	8.00
3608	I'm Coming Home/Country Roll	1971	—	3.00	6.00
3611	Blue Monday/I'll Get Along	1971	—	3.00	6.00
MCA					
53256	Gonna Move/Red River Rock	1988	—	—	2.50
—B-side by Silicon Teens					
53256 [PS]	Gonna Move/Red River Rock	1988	—	—	2.50
—B-side by Silicon Teens					
RCA VICTOR					
LPBO-5000	Born to Be with You/Pick Axe Rag	1973	—	3.00	6.00
PB-10118	Let It Be Me/Need a Shot of Rhythm and Blues	1974	—	2.50	5.00
74-0882	Baby I Love You/Maybe	1973	—	3.00	6.00
SWAN SONG					
70113	I Knew the Bride/Little Darlin'	1978	—	2.00	4.00
70116	Get Out of Denver/Work Out Suits	1978	—	2.00	4.00
70118	Trouble Boys/What Looks Best on You	1978	—	2.00	4.00
71001	Girls Talk/Creature from the Black Lagoon	1979	—	2.50	5.00
71002	Crawling from the Wreckage/Queen of Hearts	1979	—	2.50	5.00
72000	Almost Saturday Night/You'll Never Get Me Up	1981	—	—	3.00
72000 [PS]	Almost Saturday Night/You'll Never Get Me Up	1981	—	—	3.00
72003	The Race Is On/Singin' the Blues	1981	—	2.50	5.00
—Backing group: Stray Cats					
Albums					
ATLANTIC					
PR 320 [DJ]	College Network	1978	12.50	25.00	50.00
—Promo-only interview album					
CAPITOL					
C1-90372	Closer to the Flame	1990	3.75	7.50	15.00
COLUMBIA					
FC 37930	D.E. 7th	1982	3.00	6.00	12.00
PC 37930	D.E. 7th	198?	2.00	4.00	8.00
—Budget-line reissue ("02" added to bar code on back cover)					
FC 38651	Information	1983	3.00	6.00	12.00
PC 38651	Information	198?	2.00	4.00	8.00
—Budget-line reissue ("02" added to bar code on back cover)					
FC 39273	Riff Raff	1984	2.50	5.00	10.00
FC 40603	I Hear You Rockin'	1987	2.50	5.00	10.00
PC 40603	I Hear You Rockin'	198?	2.00	4.00	8.00
—Budget-line reissue ("02" added to bar code on back cover)					
MAM					
3	Rockpile	1972	10.00	20.00	40.00
RCA VICTOR					
AYL1-4238	Subtle as a Flying Mallet	1982	2.50	5.00	10.00
—Reissue (black label, dog near top)					
LPL1-5003	Subtle as a Flying Mallet	1975	3.00	6.00	12.00
SWAN SONG					
SS 8418	Get It	1977	3.75	7.50	15.00
SS 8505	Trax on Wax 4	1978	3.75	7.50	15.00
SS 8507	Repeat When Necessary	1979	3.75	7.50	15.00
SS 8510	The Best of Dave Edmunds	1981	3.00	6.00	12.00
SD 16034	Twangin'	1981	3.00	6.00	12.00

EDMUNDS, DAVE, AND NICK LOWE

Number	Title (A Side/B Side)	Yr	VG	VG+	NM
45s					
COLUMBIA					
AE7-1219	Take a Message to Mary/Crying in the Rain//Poor Jenny/When Will I Be Loved	1980	—	3.00	6.00
—Bonus EP included in the Rockpile LP "Seconds of Pleasure"					
AE7-1219 [PS]	Nick Lowe and Dave Edmunds Sing The Everly Brothers	1980	—	3.00	6.00

EDSELS, THE

Number	Title (A Side/B Side)	Yr	VG	VG+	NM
45s					
CAPITOL					
4588	Bone Shaker Joe/My Jealous One	1961	5.00	10.00	20.00
4675	If Your Pillow Could Talk/Shake Shake Sherry	1961	5.00	10.00	20.00
4836	Shaddy Daddy Dip Dip/Don't You Feel	1962	5.00	10.00	20.00
DOT					
16311	My Whispering Heart/Could It Be	1962	6.25	12.50	25.00
DUB					
2843	Lama Rama Ding Dong/Bells	1958	17.50	35.00	70.00
—Originals have the wrong title and the same recording as on Twin 700					
2843	Rama Lama Ding Dong/Bells	1958	12.50	25.00	50.00
—Repress with corrected title and the same recording as on Twin 700					
2843	Rama Lama Ding Dong/Bells	197?	—	2.50	5.00
—Reproduction with an alternate take of the A-side; this has confused many who believe that the original Dub and Twin records are different.					
EMBER					
1078	Three Precious Words/Let's Go	1961	6.25	12.50	25.00
MUSICTONE					
1144	Rama Lama Ding Dong/Bells	1961	3.00	6.00	12.00
ROULETTE					
4151	Do You Love Me/Rink-a-Dink-a-Doo	1959	6.25	12.50	25.00
TAMMY					
1010	What Brought Us Together/Don't Know What to Do	1960	12.50	25.00	50.00
1014	Three Precious Words/Let's Go	1960	12.50	25.00	50.00
1023	The Girl I Love/Got to FInd Out About Love	1961	10.00	20.00	40.00
1027	Count the Tears/Twenty-Four Hours	1961	10.00	20.00	40.00
TWIN					
700	Rama Lama Ding Dong/Bells	1961	6.25	12.50	25.00

EDWARD BEAR

Number	Title (A Side/B Side)	Yr	VG	VG+	NM
45s					
CAPITOL					
2801	You, Me and Mexico/Sinking Ship	1970	—	3.00	6.00
2955	You Can't Deny It/Toe Jam	1970	—	3.00	6.00
3351	Masquerade/The Pirate King	1972	—	2.00	4.00
3452	Last Song/Best Friend	1972	—	2.50	5.00
3452 [PS]	Last Song/Best Friend	1972	2.00	4.00	8.00
3581	Close Your Eyes/Cachet County	1973	—	2.00	4.00
3683	I Love Her (You Love Me)/Walking On Back	1973	—	2.00	4.00
3780	Coming Home Christmas/Does Your Mother Know	1973	2.00	4.00	8.00
3804	Same Old Feeling/Fool	1973	—	2.00	4.00
3869	I Had Dreams/You, Me and Mexico	1974	—	2.00	4.00
3978	Freedom for the Stallion/Why Don't You Marry Me	1974	—	2.00	4.00
Albums					
CAPITOL					
SKAO-426	Bearings	1970	3.75	7.50	15.00
ST-580	Eclipse	1971	3.75	7.50	15.00
ST-11157	Edward Bear	1972	2.50	5.00	10.00
ST-11192	Close Your Eyes	1973	2.50	5.00	10.00

EDWARDS, BOBBY

45s

Number	Title (A Side/B Side)	Yr	VG	VG+	NM
CAPITOL					
4674	What's the Reason/Walk Away Slowly	1961	2.00	4.00	8.00
4726	Singing the Blues/What'll I Do Without You	1962	2.00	4.00	8.00
4789	Someone New/Here's My Heart	1962	2.00	4.00	8.00
4874	Remember Who Brought You Here/The Way I Am	1962	2.00	4.00	8.00
5006	Don't Pretend/Help Me	1963	2.00	4.00	8.00
CHART					
1020	I'm Sorry to See You Go/Once a Fool (Always a Fool)	1968	—	2.50	5.00
1045	Each Time You Cross My Mind/Just Ain't My Day	1968	—	2.50	5.00
5016	Bring My Baby Home/Loving You Is Killing Me	1969	—	2.50	5.00
5061	You're the Reason/Don't Pretend	1970	—	2.50	5.00
CREST					
1075	You're the Reason/I'm a Fool for Loving You	1961	2.50	5.00	10.00
MANCO					
1026	Jealous Heart/I've Lost Everything But the Memories	1962	2.00	4.00	8.00
MUSICOR					
1101	A Little Less Heartache/Within Your Arms	1965	—	3.00	6.00

EDWARDS, J.D.

45s

Number	Title (A Side/B Side)	Yr	VG	VG+	NM
IMPERIAL					
5245	Crying/Hobo	1953	30.00	60.00	120.00

EDWARDS, JIMMY

45s

Number	Title (A Side/B Side)	Yr	VG	VG+	NM
MERCURY					
71209	Love Bug Crawl/Honey Lovin'	1957	7.50	15.00	30.00
71272	My Honey/Golden Ruby Blue	1958	7.50	15.00	30.00
71348	Do That Again/Wedding Band	1958	7.50	15.00	30.00
RCA VICTOR					
47-7597	A Favor for a Friend/Your Love Is a Good Love	1959	6.25	12.50	25.00
47-7717	Rosie Lee/Live and Let Live	1960	5.00	10.00	20.00
47-7773	Silver Slippers/What Do You Want from Me	1960	5.00	10.00	20.00

EDWARDS, JOHNNY, AND THE WHITE CAPS

45s

Number	Title (A Side/B Side)	Yr	VG	VG+	NM
NORTHLAND					
90-7002	Rock 'n Roll Saddles/Why'd You Leave Me?	1957	50.00	100.00	200.00

EDWARDS, JONATHAN

45s

Number	Title (A Side/B Side)	Yr	VG	VG+	NM
ATCO					
6881	Train of Glory/Everybody Knows Her	1972	—	2.50	5.00
6911	That's What Our Life Is/Stop and Start It All Again	1972	—	2.50	5.00
6920	Honky-Tonk Stardust Cowboy/(B-side unknown)	1973	—	2.50	5.00
6952	Rollin' Alone/The Place I've Been	1974	—	2.50	5.00
CAPRICORN					
8021	Sunshine/Emma	1971	—	2.50	5.00
MCA CURB					
53390	We Need to Be Locked Away/Back Up Grinnin'	1988	—	—	3.00
53467	Look What We Made (When We Made Love)/ Fewer Threads Than These	1988	—	—	3.00
53613	My Baby's a Country Song/It's a Natural Thing	1989	—	—	3.00
REPRISE					
1358	White Line/Favorite Song	1976	—	2.00	4.00
WARNER BROS.					
8364	Carolina Caroline/Never Together (But Close Sometimes)	1977	—	2.00	4.00

Albums

Number	Title (A Side/B Side)	Yr	VG	VG+	NM
ATCO					
SD 36-104	Lucky Day	1974	3.00	6.00	12.00
SD 7015	Honky-Tonk Stardust Cowboy	1972	3.00	6.00	12.00
SD 7036	Have a Good Time for Me	1973	3.00	6.00	12.00
CAPRICORN					
SD 862	Jonathan Edwards	1971	3.00	6.00	12.00
—Original has green label					
SD 862	Jonathan Edwards	198?	2.00	4.00	8.00
—Reissue with tan label					
CHRONIC					
1001	Live!	1982	3.00	6.00	12.00
MCA CURB					
42256	The Natural Thing	1989	2.50	5.00	10.00
REPRISE					
MS 2238	Rockin' Chair	1976	2.50	5.00	10.00
SUGAR HILL					
SH-3747	Blue Ridge	1985	2.50	5.00	10.00
—With the Seldom Scene					
WARNER BROS.					
BS 3020	Sailboat	1977	2.50	5.00	10.00

EDWARDS, JONATHAN AND DARLENE

Actually JO STAFFORD and PAUL WESTON as a comedy team.

45s

Number	Title (A Side/B Side)	Yr	VG	VG+	NM
DOT					
17012	Carioca/Who	1967	2.00	4.00	8.00

Albums

Number	Title (A Side/B Side)	Yr	VG	VG+	NM
COLUMBIA					
CL 1024 [M]	The Piano Artistry of Jonathan Edwards	1955	12.50	25.00	50.00
CL 1513 [M]	Jonathan and Darlene Edwards In Paris	1960	6.25	12.50	25.00
CS 8313 [S]	Jonathan and Darlene Edwards In Paris	1960	7.50	15.00	30.00
CORINTHIAN					
103	Jonathan and Darlene Edwards In Paris	198?	2.50	5.00	10.00
104	The Original Piano Artistry of Jonathan Edwards	198?	2.50	5.00	10.00
120	Sing Along with Jonathan and Darlene	198?	2.50	5.00	10.00
122	Songs for Sheiks and Flappers	1986	2.50	5.00	10.00
DOT					
DLP-3792 [M]	Songs for Sheiks and Flappers	1967	3.75	7.50	15.00
DLP-25792 [S]	Songs for Sheiks and Flappers	1967	5.00	10.00	20.00
RCA VICTOR					
LPM-2495 [M]	Sing Along with Jonathan and Darlene	1962	5.00	10.00	20.00
LSP-2495 [S]	Sing Along with Jonathan and Darlene	1962	6.25	12.50	25.00

EDWARDS, TOM

45s

Number	Title (A Side/B Side)	Yr	VG	VG+	NM
CORAL					
61773	What Is a Teen Age Boy/What Is a Teen Age Girl	1957	3.00	6.00	12.00
61826	The Story of Elvis Presley/What Is Rock 'n' Roll	1957	5.00	10.00	20.00
61938	Goodnight Rock 'n' Roll/The Spirit of Seventeen	1958	2.50	5.00	10.00
DOT					
15811	What Is a Boyfriend/All About Girls and Women	1958	2.50	5.00	10.00

EDWARDS, TOMMY

45s

Number	Title (A Side/B Side)	Yr	VG	VG+	NM
MGM					
10884	Once There Lived a Fool/A Friend of Johnny's	1951	5.00	10.00	20.00
10921	Gypsy Heart/Operetta	1951	5.00	10.00	20.00
10973	I'll Never Know Why/A Beggar in Love	1951	5.00	10.00	20.00
10989	The Morning Side of the Mountain/For Instance	1951	6.25	12.50	25.00
11035	It's All in the Game/All Over Again	1951	6.25	12.50	25.00
11077	Solitaire/My Concerto	1951	5.00	10.00	20.00
11097	Christmas Is for Children/Kris Kringle	1951	5.00	10.00	20.00
11134	Please Mr. Sun/I May Live with You	1952	6.25	12.50	25.00
11170	Forgive Me/The Bridge	1952	5.00	10.00	20.00
11209	My Girl/Piano, Bass and Drums	1952	5.00	10.00	20.00
11268	Easy to Say/The Greatest Sinner of Them All	1952	5.00	10.00	20.00
11326	You Win Again/Sinner and Saint	1952	5.00	10.00	20.00
11395	(Now and Then, There's) A Fool Such As I/I Can't Love Another	1953	5.00	10.00	20.00
11465	Au Revoir/I Lived When I Met You	1953	5.00	10.00	20.00
11485	Take These Chains from My Heart/Paging Mr. Jackson	1953	5.00	10.00	20.00
11541	Lover's Waltz/Baby, Baby, Baby	1953	5.00	10.00	20.00
11582	So Little Time/Blue Bird	1953	5.00	10.00	20.00
11604	That's All/Secret Love	1953	5.00	10.00	20.00
11624	Every Day Is Christmas/It's Christmas Once Again	1953	5.00	10.00	20.00
11668	There Was a Time/Wall of Ice	1954	5.00	10.00	20.00
11718	The Joker (In the Card Game of Life)/Within My Heart	1954	5.00	10.00	20.00
11763	Linger in My Arms/If You Would Love Me Again	1954	5.00	10.00	20.00
11821	You Walk By/I Have That Kind of Heart	1954	5.00	10.00	20.00
11932	Serenade to a Fool/It Could Have Been Me	1955	5.00	10.00	20.00
11993	Welcome to My Heart/Spring Never Came Around This Year	1955	5.00	10.00	20.00
12054	Teardrop on a Rose/To Those Who Wait	1955	5.00	10.00	20.00
12095	Baby, Let Me Take You Dreaming/My Sweetheart	1955	5.00	10.00	20.00
12248	Love Is a Child/There Must Be a Way to Your Heart	1956	5.00	10.00	20.00
12342	The Day That I Lost You/My Ship	1956	5.00	10.00	20.00
12514	We're Not Children Anymore/Any Place, Any Time	1957	5.00	10.00	20.00
12688	It's All in the Game/Please Love Me Forever	1958	3.75	7.50	15.00
12722	Love Is All We Need/Mr. Music Man	1958	3.75	7.50	15.00
12757	Please Mr. Sun/The Morning Side of the Mountain	1959	3.75	7.50	15.00
12794	My Melancholy Baby/It's Only the Good Times	1959	3.75	7.50	15.00
12814	I've Been There/I Looked at Heaven	1959	3.75	7.50	15.00
12837	Honestly and Truly/(New In) The Ways of Love	1959	3.75	7.50	15.00
12871	Don't Fence Me In/I'm Building Castles Again	1960	3.00	6.00	12.00
12890	I Really Don't Want to Know/Unloved	1960	3.00	6.00	12.00
12890 [PS]	I Really Don't Want to Know/Unloved	1960	7.50	15.00	30.00
12916	It's Not the End of Everything/Blue Heartaches	1960	3.00	6.00	12.00
12959	Suzie Wong/As You Desire Me	1960	3.00	6.00	12.00
12981	Vaya Con Dios/One and Twenty	1961	3.00	6.00	12.00
13002	The Golden Chain/That's the Way with Love	1961	3.00	6.00	12.00
13032	I'm So Lonesome I Could Cry/My Heart Would Know	1961	3.00	6.00	12.00
13057	I'll Cry You Out of My Heart/Tables Are Turning	1962	3.00	6.00	12.00
13100	Please Don't Tell Me/Tonight I Won't Be There	1962	3.00	6.00	12.00
13128	May I/Sometimes You Win, Sometimes You Lose	1963	2.50	5.00	10.00
13172	Country Boy/Love Is Best of All	1963	2.50	5.00	10.00
13317	Take These Chains from My Heart/You Win Again	1965	2.50	5.00	10.00
MUSICOR					
1046	Left-Over Dreams/9 Chances Out of 10	1964	2.50	5.00	10.00
1159	I Must Be Doing Something Wrong/I Cried, I Cried	1966	2.50	5.00	10.00

7-Inch Extended Plays

Number	Title (A Side/B Side)	Yr	VG	VG+	NM
MGM					
X-1003	(contents unknown)	1952	10.00	20.00	40.00
X-1003 [PS]	It's All in the Game	1952	10.00	20.00	40.00
X-1614	*It's All in the Game/My Sugar, My Sweet/I'll Always Be with You/That's All	1958	5.00	10.00	20.00
X-1614 [PS]	It's All in the Game, Vol. 1	1958	5.00	10.00	20.00
SX-1666 [PS]	For Young Lovers, Vol. 1	1959	6.25	12.50	25.00
SX-1666 [S]	(contents unknown)	1959	6.25	12.50	25.00
X-1666 [M]	(contents unknown)	1959	5.00	10.00	20.00
X-1666 [PS]	For Young Lovers, Vol. 1	1959	5.00	10.00	20.00
SX-1667 [PS]	For Young Lovers, Vol. 2	1959	6.25	12.50	25.00
SX-1667 [S]	(contents unknown)	1959	6.25	12.50	25.00
X-1667 [M]	(contents unknown)	1959	5.00	10.00	20.00
X-1667 [PS]	For Young Lovers, Vol. 2	1959	5.00	10.00	20.00
SX-1668 [PS]	For Young Lovers, Vol. 3	1959	6.25	12.50	25.00
SX-1668 [S]	(contents unknown)	1959	6.25	12.50	25.00
X-1668 [M]	(contents unknown)	1959	5.00	10.00	20.00
X-1668 [PS]	For Young Lovers, Vol. 3	1959	5.00	10.00	20.00

Albums

Number	Title (A Side/B Side)	Yr	VG	VG+	NM
LION					
L-70120 [M]	Tommy Edwards	1959	7.50	15.00	30.00
METRO					
M-511 [M]	Tommy Edwards	1965	3.00	6.00	12.00

Number	Title (A Side/B Side)	Yr	VG	VG+	NM
MS-511 [S]	Tommy Edwards	1965	3.75	7.50	15.00
MGM					
E-3732 [M]	It's All in the Game	1958	7.50	15.00	30.00
—Yellow label					
E-3732 [M]	It's All in the Game	1960	5.00	10.00	20.00
—Black label					
SE-3732 [S]	It's All in the Game	1959	10.00	20.00	40.00
—Yellow label					
SE-3732 [S]	It's All in the Game	1960	6.25	12.50	25.00
—Black label					
E-3760 [M]	For Young Lovers	1959	7.50	15.00	30.00
—Yellow label					
E-3760 [M]	For Young Lovers	1960	5.00	10.00	20.00
—Black label					
SE-3760 [S]	For Young Lovers	1959	10.00	20.00	40.00
—Yellow label					
SE-3760 [S]	For Young Lovers	1960	6.25	12.50	25.00
—Black label					
E-3805 [M]	You Started Me Dreaming	1960	5.00	10.00	20.00
SE-3805 [S]	You Started Me Dreaming	1960	6.25	12.50	25.00
E-3822 [M]	Step Out Singing	1960	5.00	10.00	20.00
SE-3822 [S]	Step Out Singing	1960	6.25	12.50	25.00
E-3838 [M]	Tommy Edwards in Hawaii	1960	5.00	10.00	20.00
SE-3838 [S]	Tommy Edwards in Hawaii	1960	6.25	12.50	25.00
E-3884 [M]	Tommy Edwards' Greatest Hits	1961	5.00	10.00	20.00
SE-3884 [S]	Tommy Edwards' Greatest Hits	1961	6.25	12.50	25.00
E-3959 [M]	Golden Coutnry Hits	1961	5.00	10.00	20.00
SE-3959 [S]	Golden Coutnry Hits	1961	6.25	12.50	25.00
E-4020 [M]	Stardust	1962	5.00	10.00	20.00
SE-4020 [S]	Stardust	1962	6.25	12.50	25.00
E-4060 [M]	Soft Strings and Two Guitars	1962	5.00	10.00	20.00
SE-4060 [S]	Soft Strings and Two Guitars	1962	6.25	12.50	25.00
E-4141 [M]	The Very Best of Tommy Edwards	1963	3.75	7.50	15.00
SE-4141 [S]	The Very Best of Tommy Edwards	1963	5.00	10.00	20.00
REGENT					
MG-6096 [M]	Tommy Edwards Sings	1958	15.00	30.00	60.00

EDWARDS, VERN

45s

Number	Title (A Side/B Side)	Yr	VG	VG+	NM
PROBE					
100	Cool Baby, Cool/Glenda	1959	50.00	100.00	200.00

EDWARDS, VINCENT

45s

Number	Title (A Side/B Side)	Yr	VG	VG+	NM
CAPITOL					
4819	Lollipop/As You Desire Me	1962	2.50	5.00	10.00
COLPIX					
771	No, Not Much/See That Girl	1965	2.00	4.00	8.00
771 [PS]	No, Not Much/See That Girl	1965	2.50	5.00	10.00
DECCA					
31413	Don't Worry 'Bout Me/And Now	1962	2.00	4.00	8.00
31426	I Got It Bad (And That Ain't Good)/Say It Isn't So	1962	2.00	4.00	8.00
31426 [PS]	I Got It Bad (And That Ain't Good)/Say It Isn't So	1962	3.00	6.00	12.00
31460	To Kill a Mockingbird/You'll Still Have Me	1963	2.00	4.00	8.00
31534	This Train/Looking for Someone	1963	2.00	4.00	8.00
31563	Does Goodnight Mean Goodbye/Per Te Per Me	1963	2.00	4.00	8.00
KAMA SUTRA					
221	Nylon Stockings/To Be with You	1967	—	3.00	6.00
221 [PS]	Nylon Stockings/To Be with You	1967	2.50	5.00	10.00
MAGIC LAMP					
701	I'm Not the Marrying Kind/What Colors Are You	1964	2.00	4.00	8.00
RUSS-FI					
1	Oh Babe/Squealin' Parrot Twist	196?	3.00	6.00	12.00
7001	Why Did You Leave Me/Squealin' Parrot Twist	1962	2.50	5.00	10.00

Albums

Number	Title (A Side/B Side)	Yr	VG	VG+	NM
DECCA					
DL 4311 [M]	Vincent Edwards Sings	1962	5.00	10.00	20.00
DL 4336 [M]	Sometimes I'm Happy...Sometimes I'm Blue	1962	5.00	10.00	20.00
DL 4399 [M]	In Person at the Riviera	1963	5.00	10.00	20.00
DL 74311 [S]	Vincent Edwards Sings	1962	6.25	12.50	25.00
DL 74336 [S]	Sometimes I'm Happy...Sometimes I'm Blue	1962	6.25	12.50	25.00
DL 74399 [S]	In Person at the Riviera	1963	6.25	12.50	25.00
VOCALION					
VL 3852 [M]	Here's Vincent Edwards	1967	3.00	6.00	12.00
VL 73852 [S]	Here's Vincent Edwards	1967	3.00	6.00	12.00

EELY, JACK

Sang lead on THE KINGSMEN's version of "Louie Louie."

45s

Number	Title (A Side/B Side)	Yr	VG	VG+	NM
BANG					
520	Louie Louie '66/David's Mood	1966	3.75	7.50	15.00
534	Louie Go Home/Ride Ride Baby	1966	3.75	7.50	15.00

EHRET, BOB

45s

Number	Title (A Side/B Side)	Yr	VG	VG+	NM
ALADDIN					
3377	Stop the Clock/So Lonely	1957	37.50	75.00	150.00

8TH DAY, THE

Probably all the same group.

45s

Number	Title (A Side/B Side)	Yr	VG	VG+	NM
A&M					
2539	Call Me Up/I've Got My Heart in the Right Place	1983	—	2.00	4.00
2595 [DJ]	In the Valley (same on both sides)	1983	—	2.00	4.00
CRIB					
101	Let's Share the Miracle/It's Christmas Day	19??	—	2.00	4.00
INVICTUS					
9087	She's Not Just Another Woman/I Can't Fool Myself	1971	—	2.50	5.00
9098	You've Got to Crawl (Before You Walk)/It's Instrumental to Be Free	1971	—	2.50	5.00
9107	If I Could See the Light/If I Could See the Light (Part 2)	1971	—	2.50	5.00
9117	Eeny-Meeny-Miny-Mo (Three's a Crowd)/Rocks in My Head	1972	—	2.50	5.00
9124	Good Book/I Gotta Get Home	1972	—	2.50	5.00
KAPP					
862	Hey Boy (The Girl's in Love with You)/Million Lights	1967	2.00	4.00	8.00
894	Raining Sunshine/That Good Old Fashioned Way	1968	2.00	4.00	8.00
916	Glory/Building with a Steeple	1968	2.00	4.00	8.00

Albums

Number	Title (A Side/B Side)	Yr	VG	VG+	NM
A&M					
SP-4942	The 8th Day	1983	2.50	5.00	10.00
INVICTUS					
ST-7306	The 8th Day	1971	3.00	6.00	12.00
ST-9809	I Gotta Get Home	1973	3.00	6.00	12.00
KAPP					
KS 3554	On the Eighth Day	1968	3.75	7.50	15.00

EIRE APPARENT, THE

Produced by JIMI HENDRIX.

45s

Number	Title (A Side/B Side)	Yr	VG	VG+	NM
BUDDAH					
67	Yes I Need Someone/Let Me Stay	1968	3.75	7.50	15.00

Albums

Number	Title (A Side/B Side)	Yr	VG	VG+	NM
BUDDAH					
BDS-5031	Sunrise	1969	10.00	20.00	40.00

EL CAPRIS

45s

Number	Title (A Side/B Side)	Yr	VG	VG+	NM
ARGYLE					
1010	Ooh But She Did/(Shimmy, Shimmy) Ko Ko Wop	1961	7.50	15.00	30.00
BULLSEYE					
102	Ooh But She Did/(Shimmy Shimmy) Ko Ko Wop	1956	50.00	100.00	200.00
102	Oh But She Did/(Shimmy Shimmy) Ko Ko Wop	1956	37.50	75.00	150.00
—Note slight difference in A-side title					
FEE BEE					
216	Your Star/To Live Again	1957	10.00	20.00	40.00
HI-Q					
5006	Girl of Mine/These Lonely Nights	1958	25.00	50.00	100.00
—Blue label					
5006	Girl of Mine/These Lonely Nights	1958	10.00	20.00	40.00
—Yellow label					
PARIS					
525	They're Always Laughing at Me/Ivy League Clean	1958	10.00	20.00	40.00
RING-O					
308	Safari/Quit Pulling My Woman	1960	7.50	15.00	30.00

EL CHICANO

45s

Number	Title (A Side/B Side)	Yr	VG	VG+	NM
GORDO					
703	Viva Tirado — Part I/Viva Tirado — Part II	1970	2.50	5.00	10.00
KAPP					
2085	Viva Tirado — Part I/Viva Tirado — Part II	1970	—	2.50	5.00
2129	Cuban Chant/Viva La Raza	1971	—	2.50	5.00
2150	Sugar, Sugar/Don't Put Me Down	1971	—	2.50	5.00
2173	Brown Eyed Girl/Mas Zacate	1972	—	2.50	5.00
2182	Senor Blues/Satisfy Me Woman	1972	—	2.50	5.00
MCA					
40021	Last Tango in Paris/In a Silent Way	1973	—	2.00	4.00
40104	Chachita/Tell Her She's Lonely	1973	—	2.00	4.00
40240	El Cayuco/You've Been Wrong So Long	1974	—	2.00	4.00
40359	Follow the Apollo/You Can Have the Best of Everything	1975	—	2.00	4.00
40391	Put On a Show/Might As Well	1975	—	2.00	4.00
40422	Baretta's Theme (Keep Your Eyes on the Sparrow)/One More Night	1975	—	2.00	4.00
40457	Michael's Theme/When You Got a Heartache	1975	—	2.00	4.00
40520	All I Can Remember/Lake Aquabi	1976	—	2.00	4.00

Albums

Number	Title (A Side/B Side)	Yr	VG	VG+	NM
KAPP					
KS-3632	Viva Tirado	1970	3.00	6.00	12.00
KS-3640	Revolucion	1971	3.00	6.00	12.00
KS-3663	Celebration	1972	3.00	6.00	12.00
MCA					
69	Revolucion	1973	2.50	5.00	10.00
—Reissue of Kapp 3640					
312	El Chicano	1973	2.50	5.00	10.00
401	Cinco	1974	2.50	5.00	10.00
437	The Best of Everything	1975	2.50	5.00	10.00
548	Viva Tirado	197?	2.50	5.00	10.00
—Reissue of Kapp 3632					
2150	Pyramid of Love	1975	2.50	5.00	10.00
SHADYBROOK					
SB 33-005	This Is El Chicano	1977	3.75	7.50	15.00

EL CLOD

45s

Number	Title (A Side/B Side)	Yr	VG	VG+	NM
CHALLENGE					
9159	Tijuana Border (Wolverton Mountain)/Pedro's Piano Roll Twist	1962	5.00	10.00	20.00
MERCURY					
72082	He's Not a Rebel/Holiday in Havana	1963	3.75	7.50	15.00
VEE JAY					
647	Tijuana Watusi/Gringo	1965	3.75	7.50	15.00

EL DOMINGOS

45s

Number	Title (A Side/B Side)	Yr	VG	VG+	NM
CANDLELITE					
418	Made in Heaven/Lucky Me, I'm in Love	1963	6.25	12.50	25.00

Number	Title (A Side/B Side)	Yr	VG	VG+	NM
CHELSEA					
1009	Made in Heaven/Lucky Me, I'm in Love	1962	50.00	100.00	200.00
KARMIN					
1001	Are You Ready to Say "I Do"/I Want to Know	1964	75.00	150.00	300.00

EL DORADOS

45s

Number	Title (A Side/B Side)	Yr	VG	VG+	NM
PAULA					
347	Looking In from the Outside/Since You Came Into My Life	1971	2.50	5.00	10.00
369	Loose Booty (Part 1)/Loose Booty (Part 2)	1971	2.50	5.00	10.00
TORRID					
100	In Over My Head/You Make My Heart Sing	1970	3.75	7.50	15.00
VEE JAY					
115	Baby I Need You/My Loving Baby	1954	100.00	200.00	400.00
—Red vinyl					
115	Baby I Need You/My Loving Baby	1954	20.00	40.00	80.00
118	Annie's Answer/Living with Vivian	1954	75.00	150.00	300.00
—Red vinyl					
118	Annie's Answer/Living with Vivian	1954	20.00	40.00	80.00
127	One More Chance/Little Miss Love	1954	50.00	100.00	200.00
147	At My Front Door/What's Buggin' You Baby	1955	17.50	35.00	70.00
165	I'll Be Forever Lovin' You/I Began to Realize	1955	15.00	30.00	60.00
180	Now That You've Gone/Rock 'N' Roll's for Me	1956	12.50	25.00	50.00
197	Fallen Tear/Chop Ling Soon	1956	12.50	25.00	50.00
211	Bim Bam Boom/There in the Night	1956	20.00	40.00	80.00
250	Tears on My Pillow/A Rose for My Darling	1957	7.50	15.00	30.00
263	Three Reasons Why/Boom Diddle Boom	1958	37.50	75.00	150.00
302	Oh What a Girl/The Lights Are Low	1958	37.50	75.00	150.00

Albums

Number	Title (A Side/B Side)	Yr	VG	VG+	NM
LOST-NITE					
LLP-20 [10]	The El Dorados	1981	3.00	6.00	12.00
—Red vinyl					
SOLID SMOKE					
8025	Low Mileage/High Octane	1984	2.50	5.00	10.00
VEE JAY					
LP-1001 [M]	Crazy Little Mama	1959	200.00	400.00	800.00
—Maroon label, thick silver band					
LP-1001 [M]	Crazy Little Mama	1960	100.00	200.00	400.00
—Maroon label, thin silver band					
LP-1001 [M]	Crazy Little Mama	1962	62.50	125.00	250.00
—Black label with colorband					
VJLP-1001 [M]	Crazy Little Mama	198?	2.50	5.00	10.00
—Authorized reissue					

EL RAYS, THE

See THE DELLS.

EL VENOS, THE

45s

Number	Title (A Side/B Side)	Yr	VG	VG+	NM
GROOVE					
0170	Now We're Together/Geraldine	1956	20.00	40.00	80.00
RCA VICTOR					
47-8303	My Heart Beats Faster/You Won't Be There	1963	6.25	12.50	25.00
VIK					
0305	My Heart Beats Faster/You Must Be True	1957	20.00	40.00	80.00

ELBERT, DONNIE

45s

Number	Title (A Side/B Side)	Yr	VG	VG+	NM
ALL PLATINUM					
2330	Where Did Our Love Go/That's If You Love Me	1971	—	3.00	6.00
2333	Sweet Baby/Can't Get Over Losing You	1971	—	3.00	6.00
2336	If I Can't Have You/Can't Get Over Losing You	1972	—	3.00	6.00
2337	Little Piece of Leather/Sweet Baby	1972	—	3.00	6.00
2338	That's If You Love Me/Can't Get Over Losing You	1972	—	3.00	6.00
2346	This Feeling of Losing You/Can't Stand These Lonely Nights	1973	—	3.00	6.00
2351	Love Is Strange/(Instrumental)	1973	—	3.00	6.00
2367	What Do You Do/Will You Love Me Tomorrow	1974	—	2.50	5.00
2374	You Should Be Dancing/What Do You Do	1974	—	2.50	5.00
ATCO					
6550	Too Far Gone/In Between the Heartaches	1968	2.00	4.00	8.00
AVCO					
4587	I Can't Help Myself/Love Is Here and Now You're Gone	1972	—	3.00	6.00
4598	Ooh, Baby Baby/Tell Her for Me	1972	—	3.00	6.00
CUB					
9125	Don't Cry My Love/Love Stew	1963	3.00	6.00	12.00
DELUXE					
6125	What Can I Do/Hear My Plea	1957	5.00	10.00	20.00
6143	Believe It or Not/Tell Me So	1957	5.00	10.00	20.00
6148	Leona/Have I Sinned	1957	5.00	10.00	20.00
6156	Wild Child/Let's Do the Stroll	1958	5.00	10.00	20.00
6161	My Confession of Love/Peek-a-Boo	1958	5.00	10.00	20.00
6168	I Want to Be Near You/Come On Sugar	1958	5.00	10.00	20.00
6175	Just a Little Bit of Lovin'/When You're Near Me	1958	5.00	10.00	20.00
DERAM					
7526	Without You/Baby Please Come Home	1969	2.00	4.00	8.00
PARKWAY					
844	Set My Heart at Ease/Baby Cares	1962	3.75	7.50	15.00
RARE BULLET					
101	Can't Get Over Losing You/Got to Get Myself Together	1970	—	3.00	6.00
VEE JAY					
336	Hey Baby/Will You Ever Be Mine	1960	3.75	7.50	15.00
353	Baby Let Me Love You Tonight/Half as Old	1960	3.75	7.50	15.00
370	I've Loved You Baby/I Beg of You	1960	3.75	7.50	15.00

Albums

Number	Title (A Side/B Side)	Yr	VG	VG+	NM
ALL PLATINUM					
3007	Where Did Our Love Go	1971	6.25	12.50	25.00
3019	Dancin' the Night Away	1977	6.25	12.50	25.00
DELUXE					
12003	Have I Sinned	1971	6.25	12.50	25.00
KING					
629 [M]	The Sensational Donnie Elbert Sings	1959	100.00	200.00	400.00
SUGAR HILL					
256	From the Git Go	1981	3.00	6.00	12.00
TRIP					
9514	Donnie Elbert Sings	197?	3.75	7.50	15.00
9524	Stop in the Name of Love	197?	3.75	7.50	15.00

ELCHORDS, THE

45s

Number	Title (A Side/B Side)	Yr	VG	VG+	NM
GOOD					
544	Peppermint Stick/Gee, I'm in Love	1958	20.00	40.00	80.00
—Straight lines on label					
544	Peppermint Stick/Gee, I'm in Love	1962	15.00	30.00	60.00
—Red vinyl					
544	Peppermint Stick/Gee, I'm in Love	1962	5.00	10.00	20.00
—Sawtooth lines on label					
544	Peppermint Stick/Gee, I'm in Love	1962	3.75	7.50	15.00
—No lines on label					

ELECTRIC FLAG, THE

45s

Number	Title (A Side/B Side)	Yr	VG	VG+	NM
ATLANTIC					
3222	Sweet Soul Music/Every Now and Then	1974	—	2.00	4.00
3237	Doctor Oh Doctor/The Band Kept Playing	1975	—	2.00	4.00
COLUMBIA					
44307	Groovin' Is Easy/Over-Lovin' You	1967	2.00	4.00	8.00
44307 [PS]	Groovin' Is Easy/Over-Lovin' You	1967	5.00	10.00	20.00
44376	Soul Searchin'/Sunny	1967	2.00	4.00	8.00
44765	Soul Searchin'/Sunny	1969	—	3.00	6.00
SIDEWALK					
929	Green and Gold/Peter's Trip	1967	3.75	7.50	15.00

Albums

Number	Title (A Side/B Side)	Yr	VG	VG+	NM
ATLANTIC					
SD 18112	The Band Kept Playing	1974	2.50	5.00	10.00
COLUMBIA					
CS 9597	A Long Time Comin'	1968	3.75	7.50	15.00
—"360 Sound" label					
CS 9597	A Long Time Comin'	1970	2.50	5.00	10.00
—Orange label					
PC 9597	A Long Time Comin'	198?	2.00	4.00	8.00
—Budget-line reissue					
CS 9714	The Electric Flag	1968	3.75	7.50	15.00
—"360 Sound" label					
CS 9714	The Electric Flag	1970	2.50	5.00	10.00
—Orange label					
C 30422	The Best of the Electric Flag	1971	2.50	5.00	10.00

ELECTRIC INDIAN, THE

45s

Number	Title (A Side/B Side)	Yr	VG	VG+	NM
MARMADUKE					
4001	Keem-O-Sabe/Broad Street	1969	5.00	10.00	20.00
UNITED ARTISTS					
0128	Keem-O-Sabe/Stick Shift	1973	—	2.00	4.00
—"Silver Spotlight Series" reissue; B-side by The Duals					
50563	Keem-O-Sabe/Broad Street	1969	—	3.00	6.00
50613	Geronimo/Land of 1,000 Dances	1969	—	2.50	5.00
50647	Rain Dance/Storm Warning	1970	—	2.50	5.00
50701	Apotchee/Chicago Hawk	1970	—	2.50	5.00
50744	Geronimo/My Cherie Amour	1971	—	2.50	5.00

Albums

Number	Title (A Side/B Side)	Yr	VG	VG+	NM
UNITED ARTISTS					
UAS 6728	Keem-O-Sabe	1969	3.75	7.50	15.00

ELECTRIC LIGHT ORCHESTRA

45s

Number	Title (A Side/B Side)	Yr	VG	VG+	NM
CBS ASSOCIATED					
05766	Calling America/Caught in a Trap	1986	—	—	3.00
05766 [PS]	Calling America/Caught in a Trap	1986	—	—	3.00
05892	So Serious/Endless Lies	1986	—	—	3.00
05892 [PS]	So Serious/Endless Lies	1986	—	—	3.00
JET					
XW 1099	Turn to Stone/Mister Kingdom	1977	—	2.00	4.00
XW 1099 [PS]	Turn to Stone/Mister Kingdom	1977	2.00	4.00	8.00
XW 1145	Sweet Talkin' Woman/Fire on High	1978	—	2.50	5.00
—Purple vinyl					
XW 1145	Sweet Talkin' Woman/Fire on High	1978	—	2.00	4.00
XW 1145 [PS]	Sweet Talkin' Woman/Fire on High	1978	—	2.50	5.00
02408	Hold On Tight/When Time Stood Still	1981	—	2.00	4.00
02559	Twilight/Julie Don't Live Here	1981	—	2.00	4.00
02693	Rain Is Falling/Another Heart Broke	1982	—	2.00	4.00
03086	Hold On Tight/Mr. Blue Sky	1982	—	—	3.00
—Reissue					
03964	Rock and Roll Is King/After All	1983	—	2.00	4.00
04130	Four Little Diamonds/Letter from Spain	1983	—	2.00	4.00
04208	Stranger/Train of Gold	1983	—	2.00	4.00
5050	Mr. Blue Sky/One Summer Dream	1978	—	2.00	4.00
5052	It's Over/The Whale	1978	—	2.00	4.00
5057	Shine a Little Love/Jungle	1979	—	2.00	4.00
5057 [PS]	Shine a Little Love/Jungle	1979	2.00	4.00	8.00
5060	Don't Bring Me Down/Dreaming of 4000	1979	—	2.00	4.00
5064	Confusion/Poker	1979	—	2.00	4.00
5067	Last Train to London/Down Home Town	1979	—	2.00	4.00
MCA					
41246	I'm Alive/Drum Dreams	1980	—	2.00	4.00
41246 [PS]	I'm Alive/Drum Dreams	1980	—	2.50	5.00
41285	Xanadu/Whenever You're Away from Me	1980	—	2.00	4.00
—A-side: Olivia Newton-John/Electric Light Orchestra					
41289	All Over the World/Drum Dreams	1980	—	2.00	4.00
41289 [PS]	All Over the World/Drum Dreams	1980	—	2.50	5.00

Number	Title (A Side/B Side)	Yr	VG	VG+	NM
UNITED ARTISTS					
XW 173	Roll Over Beethoven/Queen of the Hours	1973	—	3.00	6.00
XW 337	Showdown/In Old England Town	1973	—	3.00	6.00
XW 405	Daybreaker/Ma-Ma-Ma-Belle	1974	—	3.00	6.00
XW 513	Roll Over Beethoven/Showdown	1974	—	2.00	4.00
—Reissue					
XW 573	Can't Get It Out of My Head/Illusions in G Major	1974	—	2.00	4.00
XW 573 [PS]	Can't Get It Out of My Head/Illusions in G Major	1974	—	3.00	6.00
XW 634	Boy Blue/Eldorado	1975	—	2.50	5.00
XW 729	Evil Woman/10538 Overture (Live)	1975	—	2.00	4.00
XW 770	Strange Magic/New World Rising	1976	—	2.00	4.00
XW 770 [PS]	Strange Magic/New World Rising	1976	—	3.00	6.00
XW 842	Showdown/Daybreaker (Live)	1976	—	2.50	5.00
XW 888	Livin' Thing/Ma-Ma-Ma-Belle	1976	—	2.00	4.00
XW 939	Do Ya/Nightrider	1977	—	2.00	4.00
XW 1000	Telephone Line/Poorboy (The Greenwood)	1977	—	2.50	5.00
—Green vinyl					
XW 1000	Telephone Line/Poorboy (The Greenwood)	1977	—	2.00	4.00
XW 1000 [PS]	Telephone Line/Poorboy (The Greenwood)	1977	—	2.50	5.00
—Picture sleeves were not issued with black vinyl versions					
XW 1176	Can't Get It Out of My Head/Strange Magic	1978	—	2.00	4.00
XW 1177	Evil Woman/Livin' Thing	1978	—	2.00	4.00
XW 1178	Do Ya/Nightrider	1978	—	2.00	4.00
XW 1179	Boy Blue/Telephone Line	1978	—	2.00	4.00
XW 1180	Ma-Ma-Ma-Belle/10538 Overture	1978	—	2.00	4.00
—1176 through 1180 were available for a very short time just before ELO's rights transfered from UA to CBS.					
50914	10538 Overture/(Battle of) Marston Moor	1972	2.00	4.00	8.00
Albums					
CBS ASSOCIATED					
FZ 40048	Balance of Power	1986	2.50	5.00	10.00
JET					
JT-LA823-L2 [(2)]	Out of the Blue	1977	3.75	7.50	15.00
—Originals include poster and die-cut cardboard "spaceship"					
JT-LA823-L2 [(2) DJ]	Out of the Blue	1977	6.25	12.50	25.00
—Promo only on blue vinyl					
JZ 35524	No Answer	1978	2.50	5.00	10.00
PZ 35524	No Answer	1981	2.00	4.00	8.00
JZ 35525	On the Third Day	1978	2.50	5.00	10.00
PZ 35525	On the Third Day	1981	2.00	4.00	8.00
JZ 35526	Eldorado	1978	2.50	5.00	10.00
PZ 35526	Eldorado	198?	2.00	4.00	8.00
JZ 35527	Face the Music	1978	2.50	5.00	10.00
PZ 35527	Face the Music	1981	2.00	4.00	8.00
JZ 35528	Ole Elo	1978	2.50	5.00	10.00
PZ 35528	Ole Elo	1981	2.00	4.00	8.00
JZ 35529	A New World Record	1978	2.50	5.00	10.00
PZ 35529	A New World Record	1981	2.00	4.00	8.00
KZ2 35530 [(2)]	Out of the Blue	1978	3.00	6.00	12.00
JZ 35533	Electric Light Orchestra II	1978	2.50	5.00	10.00
PZ 35533	Electric Light Orchestra II	1981	2.00	4.00	8.00
FZ 35769	Discovery	1979	2.50	5.00	10.00
PZ 35769	Discovery	1987	2.00	4.00	8.00
FZ 36310	ELO's Greatest Hits	1979	2.50	5.00	10.00
HZ 36310	ELO's Greatest Hits	1981	10.00	20.00	40.00
—Half-speed mastered edition					
PZ 36310	ELO's Greatest Hits	1987	2.00	4.00	8.00
Z4X 36966 [(4)]	A Box of Their Best	1980	6.25	12.50	25.00
FZ 37371	Time	1981	2.50	5.00	10.00
PZ 37371	Time	1987	2.00	4.00	8.00
PZ 38490	Secret Messages	1987	2.00	4.00	8.00
QZ 38490	Secret Messages	1983	2.50	5.00	10.00
HZ 45789	Discovery	1980	6.25	12.50	25.00
—Half-speed mastered edition					
HZ 47371	Time	1982	6.25	12.50	25.00
—Half-speed mastered edition					
HZ 48490	Secret Messages	1983	7.50	15.00	30.00
—Half-speed mastered edition					
UNITED ARTISTS					
UA-LA040-F	Electric Light Orchestra II	1973	3.75	7.50	15.00
—Tan label					
UA-LA040-F	Electric Light Orchestra II	1978	2.50	5.00	10.00
—Sunrise label					
SP-123 [DJ]	Ole Elo	1976	25.00	50.00	100.00
—Gold vinyl, cover similar to the released version except for the single line "Ole Elo" (no "Electric Light Orchestra" underneath) at the top of the front cover					
SP-123 [DJ]	Ole Elo	1976	20.00	40.00	80.00
—Red, blue or white vinyl promos with generic cover					
SP-123 [DJ]	Ole Elo	1976	12.50	25.00	50.00
—Gold vinyl promo with generic cover					
UA-LA188-F	On the Third Day	1973	3.75	7.50	15.00
—Tan label					
UA-LA188-F	On the Third Day	1978	2.50	5.00	10.00
—Sunrise label					
UA-LA318-F	The Night the Light Went On in Long Beach	1974	—	—	—
—Canceled					
UA-LA339-G	Eldorado	1974	3.00	6.00	12.00
—Tan label					
UA-LA339-G	Eldorado	1977	2.50	5.00	10.00
—Sunrise label					
UA-LA546-DJ [DJ]	Face the Music	1975	6.25	12.50	25.00
—Promo only, banded for airplay					
UA-LA546-G	Face the Music	1975	3.00	6.00	12.00
—Tan label					
UA-LA546-G	Face the Music	1978	2.50	5.00	10.00
—Sunrise label					
UA-LA630-G	Ole Elo	1976	3.00	6.00	12.00
—Tan label					
UA-LA630-G	Ole Elo	1978	2.50	5.00	10.00
—Sunrise label					
UA-LA679-G	A New World Record	1976	3.00	6.00	12.00
—All copies have custom labels					
UAS-5573	No Answer	1972	3.75	7.50	15.00
—Tan label					
UAS-5573	No Answer	1978	2.50	5.00	10.00
—Sunrise label					

ELECTRIC PRUNES, THE

Number	Title (A Side/B Side)	Yr	VG	VG+	NM
45s					
REPRISE					
PRO 277 [DJ]	Sanctus/Credo	1968	12.50	25.00	50.00
PRO 305 [DJ]	Help Us (Our Father, Our King)/The Adoration	1968	10.00	20.00	40.00
0473	Ain't It Hard/Little Olive	1966	10.00	20.00	40.00
0532	I Had Too Much to Dream (Last Night)/Lovin	1966	5.00	10.00	20.00
0564	Get Me to the World on Time/Are You Lovin' Me	1967	6.25	12.50	25.00
0594	Hideaway/Dr. Do-Good	1967	6.25	12.50	25.00
0607	The Great Banana Hoax/Wind-Up Toys	1967	6.25	12.50	25.00
0652	You Never Had It So Good/Everybody Knows You're Not in Love	1967	10.00	20.00	40.00
0704	I Had Too Much to Dream (Last Night)/Get Me to the World On Time	1968	—	2.50	5.00
—"Back to Back Hits" series -- originals have "W7" and "r:" logos					
0805	Hey, Mr. President/Flowing Smoothly	1969	6.25	12.50	25.00
0833	Violent Rose/Sell	1969	10.00	20.00	40.00
0858	Love Grows/Finders Keepers, Losers Weepers	1969	6.25	12.50	25.00
Albums					
REPRISE					
R-6248 [M]	The Electric Prunes	1967	12.50	25.00	50.00
RS-6248 [S]	The Electric Prunes	1967	10.00	20.00	40.00
R-6262 [M]	Underground	1967	12.50	25.00	50.00
RS-6262 [S]	Underground	1967	10.00	20.00	40.00
R-6275 [M]	Mass in F Minor	1967	10.00	20.00	40.00
RS-6275 [S]	Mass in F Minor	1967	7.50	15.00	30.00
RS-6316	Release of an Oath	1968	7.50	15.00	30.00
RS-6342	Just Good Rock 'n Roll	1969	7.50	15.00	30.00

ELECTRIC TOILET, THE

Number	Title (A Side/B Side)	Yr	VG	VG+	NM
Albums					
NASCO					
9004	In the Hands of Karma	1970	50.00	100.00	200.00

ELECTRIC UNDERGROUND, THE

Number	Title (A Side/B Side)	Yr	VG	VG+	NM
Albums					
PREMIER					
P-9060 [M]	Guitar Explosion	1967	12.50	25.00	50.00
PS-9060 [S]	Guitar Explosion	1967	12.50	25.00	50.00

ELECTRONIC CONCEPT ORCHESTRA

Number	Title (A Side/B Side)	Yr	VG	VG+	NM
45s					
LIMELIGHT					
3090	Aquarius/Grazing in the Grass	1969	—	3.00	6.00
Albums					
LIMELIGHT					
86070	Moog Groove	1969	2.50	5.00	10.00
86072	Electric Love	1969	2.50	5.00	10.00
MERCURY					
SR-61279	Cinemoog	1970	2.50	5.00	10.00

ELECTROSONICS, THE

Number	Title (A Side/B Side)	Yr	VG	VG+	NM
Albums					
PHILIPS					
PHM 200047 [M]	Electronic Music	1962	17.50	35.00	70.00
PHS 600047 [S]	Electronic Music	1962	22.50	45.00	90.00

ELEGANTS, THE

Also see PAT CORDEL.

Number	Title (A Side/B Side)	Yr	VG	VG+	NM
45s					
ABC-PARAMOUNT					
10219	I've Seen Everything/Tiny Cloud	1961	10.00	20.00	40.00
APT					
25005	Little Star/Getting Dizzy	1958	12.50	25.00	50.00
—All-black label					
25005	Little Star/Getting Dizzy	1958	10.00	20.00	40.00
—Black label with rainbow					
25017	Goodnight/Please Believe Me	1958	7.50	15.00	30.00
25029	Pay Day/True Love Affair	1959	7.50	15.00	30.00
BANGAR					
613	Minor Chaos/Lost Souls	1964	7.50	15.00	30.00
BIM BAM BOOM					
121	It's Just a Matter of Time/Lonesome Weekends	1974	—	3.00	6.00
—Colored vinyl					
121	It's Just a Matter of Time/Lonesome Weekends	1974	—	2.00	4.00
—Black vinyl					
CRYSTAL BALL					
139	Maybe/Woo Woo Train	197?	—	2.50	5.00
HULL					
732	Little Boy Blue/Get Well Soon	1960	25.00	50.00	100.00
LAURIE					
3283	A Letter from Viet Nam/Barbara Beware	1965	7.50	15.00	30.00
3298	Wake Up/Bring Back Wendy	1965	12.50	25.00	50.00
3324	Belinda/Lazy Love	1965	6.25	12.50	25.00
—As "Vito and the Elegants"					
PHOTO					
2662	Dressin' Up/A Dream Can Come True	1963	12.50	25.00	50.00
2662 [PS]	Dressin' Up/A Dream Can Come True	1963	37.50	75.00	150.00
UNITED ARTISTS					
230	Speak Low/Let My Prayers Be With You	1960	10.00	20.00	40.00
295	Happiness/Spiritual	1961	12.50	25.00	50.00
Albums					
MURRAY HILL					
210	Little Star	1986	2.50	5.00	10.00

Number	Title (A Side/B Side)	Yr	VG	VG+	NM

ELENA

45s

Number	Title (A Side/B Side)	Yr	VG	VG+	NM
ROULETTE					
4605	Evening Time/Road of Love	1965	3.75	7.50	15.00

ELEPHANTS MEMORY

45s

Number	Title (A Side/B Side)	Yr	VG	VG+	NM
APPLE					
1854	Liberation Special/Madness	1972	2.00	4.00	8.00
1854	Liberation Special/Power Boogie	1972	100.00	200.00	400.00
1854 [PS]	Liberation Special/Madness	1972	2.50	5.00	10.00
ATLANTIC					
3257	Shakedown/Brother Can You Spare Me a Dime	1975	—	2.50	5.00
BUDDAH					
98	Cross Roads of the Stepping Stones/Jungle Gym at the Zoo	1969	2.00	4.00	8.00
209	Don't Put Me on Trial No More/Hot Dog	1971	2.00	4.00	8.00
METROMEDIA					
182	Mongoose/I Couldn't Dream	1970	—	3.00	6.00
182 [PS]	Mongoose/I Couldn't Dream	1970	—	3.00	6.00
210	Skyscraper Commando/Power	1971	—	3.00	6.00
RCA VICTOR					
APBO-0268	Rock and Roll Streaker/Angels Forever	1974	—	2.50	5.00

Albums

Number	Title (A Side/B Side)	Yr	VG	VG+	NM
APPLE					
SMAS-3389	Elephants Memory	1972	6.25	12.50	25.00
BUDDAH					
BDS-5033	Elephants Memory	1969	3.75	7.50	15.00
BDS-5038	Songs from Midnight Cowboy	1970	3.75	7.50	15.00
METROMEDIA					
MD-1035	Take It to the Streets	1970	5.00	10.00	20.00
RCA VICTOR					
APL1-0569	Angela Forever	1974	3.75	7.50	15.00

ELEVENTH HOUSE, THE (WITH LARRY CORYELL)

45s

Number	Title (A Side/B Side)	Yr	VG	VG+	NM
ARISTA					
0154	Some Greasy Stuff/(B-side unknown)	1975	—	2.00	4.00
VANGUARD					
35176	The Funky Waltz/Low-Lee-Tah	1974	—	2.50	5.00

Albums

Number	Title (A Side/B Side)	Yr	VG	VG+	NM
ARISTA					
AL 4052	Level One	1975	2.50	5.00	10.00
AL 4077	Aspects	1976	2.50	5.00	10.00
VANGUARD					
VSQ-40036 [Q]	Introducing the Eleventh House with Larry Coryell	1974	6.25	12.50	25.00
VSD-79342	Introducing the Eleventh House with Larry Coryell	1974	3.00	6.00	12.00

ELF

45s

Number	Title (A Side/B Side)	Yr	VG	VG+	NM
EPIC					
5-10933	Hoochie Koochie Lady/First Avenue	1972	—	3.00	6.00

Albums

Number	Title (A Side/B Side)	Yr	VG	VG+	NM
EPIC					
KE 31789	Elf	1972	5.00	10.00	20.00

ELGINS, THE (1)

Detroit R&B group.

45s

Number	Title (A Side/B Side)	Yr	VG	VG+	NM
LUMMTONE					
113	Your Lovely Ways/Finding a Sweetheart	1963	6.25	12.50	25.00
TAMLA					
54056	Request of a Fool/Your Baby's Back	1962	75.00	150.00	300.00
—As "The Downbeats"; with "Tamla" circling globe at top of label					
54056	Request of a Fool/Your Baby's Back	1962	7.50	15.00	30.00
—As "The Downbeats"; with "Tamla" in globe at top of label					
V.I.P.					
25029	Darling Baby/Put Yourself in My Place	1965	50.00	100.00	200.00
—First pressings credited "The Downbeats"					
25029	Darling Baby/Put Yourself in My Place	1965	5.00	10.00	20.00
25037	Heaven Must Have Sent You/Stay in My Lonely Arms	1965	5.00	10.00	20.00
25043	It's Been a Long, Long Time/I Understand My Man	1966	5.00	10.00	20.00
25065	Heaven Must Have Sent You/Stay in My Lonely Arms	1970	2.50	5.00	10.00

Albums

Number	Title (A Side/B Side)	Yr	VG	VG+	NM
V.I.P.					
400 [M]	Darling Baby	1966	17.50	35.00	70.00
S-400 [S]	Darling Baby	1966	25.00	50.00	100.00

ELGINS, THE (2)

45s

Number	Title (A Side/B Side)	Yr	VG	VG+	NM
A.B.S.					
113	Pretending/Lonesome	1961	100.00	200.00	400.00

ELGINS, THE (3)

45s

Number	Title (A Side/B Side)	Yr	VG	VG+	NM
CONGRESS					
214	The Times We've Wasted/Ritha Mae	1964	6.25	12.50	25.00
225	Here in Your Arms/We're Gonna Have a Good Time	1964	7.50	15.00	30.00

ELGINS, THE (4)

45s

Number	Title (A Side/B Side)	Yr	VG	VG+	NM
LUMMTONE					
109	A Winner Never Quits/Johnny I'm Sorry	1962	6.25	12.50	25.00
110	You Got Your Magnet on Me Baby/Johnny I'm Sorry	1962	6.25	12.50	25.00
112	Finally/I Lost My Love in the Big City	1963	6.25	12.50	25.00

ELGINS, THE (U)

Some of these may be by group (3) or (4), but not all.

45s

Number	Title (A Side/B Side)	Yr	VG	VG+	NM
DOT					
16563	Cheryl/Tell Gina	1963	15.00	30.00	60.00
FLIP					
353	Uncle Sam's Man/Casey Cop	1961	7.50	15.00	30.00
JOED					
716	Once Upon a Time/The Huddle	1964	175.00	350.00	700.00
MGM					
12670	A Picture of You/Mademoiselle	1958	15.00	30.00	60.00
TITAN					
1724	My Illness/Extra, Extra	1962	62.50	125.00	250.00
1724	My Illness/Heartache Heartbreak	1962	50.00	100.00	200.00
VALIANT					
712	Street Scene/You Found Yourself Another Fool	1965	5.00	10.00	20.00

ELIGIBLES, THE

45s

Number	Title (A Side/B Side)	Yr	VG	VG+	NM
CAPITOL					
4203	Car Trouble/I Wrote a Song	1959	3.00	6.00	12.00
4265	Faker, Faker/24 Hours	1959	3.00	6.00	12.00
4304	My First Christmas with You/Little Engine	1959	3.75	7.50	15.00
4409	East of West Berlin/Young Is My Lover	1960	3.00	6.00	12.00
MERCURY					
72000	That Carmen Twist/Come Back, Music	1962	2.50	5.00	10.00
WARNER BROS.					
5344	Gabie/See What You Can Do For Me	1963	2.50	5.00	10.00

Albums

Number	Title (A Side/B Side)	Yr	VG	VG+	NM
CAPITOL					
ST 1310 [S]	Along the Trail	1960	7.50	15.00	30.00
T 1310 [M]	Along the Trail	1060	6.25	12.50	25.00
ST 1411 [S]	Love Is a Gamble	1960	7.50	15.00	30.00
T 1411 [M]	Love Is a Gamble	1960	6.25	12.50	25.00

ELIMINATORS, THE

Albums

Number	Title (A Side/B Side)	Yr	VG	VG+	NM
LIBERTY					
LRP-3365 [M]	Liverpool! Dragsters! Cycles! Surfing!	1964	20.00	40.00	80.00
LST-7365 [S]	Liverpool! Dragsters! Cycles! Surfing!	1964	25.00	50.00	100.00

ELIZABETH

45s

Number	Title (A Side/B Side)	Yr	VG	VG+	NM
VANGUARD					
35070	Mary Anne/The World's For Free	1968	3.75	7.50	15.00

Albums

Number	Title (A Side/B Side)	Yr	VG	VG+	NM
VANGUARD					
VSD-6501	Elizabeth	1968	15.00	30.00	60.00

ELLEDGE, JIMMY

45s

Number	Title (A Side/B Side)	Yr	VG	VG+	NM
4 STAR					
1003	One By One/After You	1975	—	2.00	4.00
1015	Lady Lover/(B-side unknown)	1976	—	2.00	4.00
HICKORY					
1313	Follow Every Rainbow/I Just Walked In (Your Heart Last Night)	1965	2.00	4.00	8.00
1341	A Good Woman's Love (Not Easy to Find)/World of Lavender Lace	1965	2.00	4.00	8.00
1363	A Legend in My Time/Pink Dally Rue	1966	2.00	4.00	8.00
1393	Time Is a Thief/I Just Walked In (Your Heart Last Night)	1966	2.00	4.00	8.00
1420	Let Me Love You a Little (So I Can Love You a Lot)/She Should Save Some Loving (For a Rainy Day)	1966	2.00	4.00	8.00
1452	The Darkest Part of Night (Is Dawn)/She Should Save Some Loving (For a Rainy Day)	1967	2.00	4.00	8.00
LITTLE DARLIN'					
0047	Florence Jean/No One Ever Lost More	1968	—	3.00	6.00
RCA VICTOR					
47-7910	Send Me a Letter/Swanee River Rocket	1961	3.00	6.00	12.00
47-7946	Funny How Time Slips Away/Hey Jimmy Joe John Jim Jack	1961	2.50	5.00	10.00
47-8012	Can't You See It in My Eyes/What a Laugh	1962	5.00	10.00	20.00
47-8042	Bo Diddley/Diamonds	1962	2.00	4.00	8.00
47-8081	A Golden Tear/I'll Get By (Don't Worry)	1962	2.00	4.00	8.00
47-8136	You Can Have Her/I Miss Her Already	1963	2.00	4.00	8.00
47-8191	Please Love Me Forever/A Penny's Worth of Happiness	1963	2.00	4.00	8.00
47-8241	I Had to Run Away/There's Nothing There for Me	1963	2.00	4.00	8.00
47-8355	Dream of the Year/Gonna Turn My Voodoo On	1964	2.00	4.00	8.00
SIMS					
204	I Gotta Live Here/Hold My Heart for Awhile	1964	2.00	4.00	8.00

ELLEN, IVY, & FAMILY

45s

Number	Title (A Side/B Side)	Yr	VG	VG+	NM
FELSTED					
8609	Go Tell Santa/(Instrumental)	1960	3.75	7.50	15.00
—B-side by the Reindeers					
8609 [PS]	Go Tell Santa/(Instrumental)	1960	5.00	10.00	20.00

ELLIE POP

45s

Number	Title (A Side/B Side)	Yr	VG	VG+	NM
MAINSTREAM					
686	Can't Be Love/Seven North Frederick	1968	5.00	10.00	20.00

Albums

Number	Title (A Side/B Side)	Yr	VG	VG+	NM
MAINSTREAM					
S-6115	Ellie Pop	1968	10.00	20.00	40.00

ELLIMAN, YVONNE

45s

Number	Title (A Side/B Side)	Yr	VG	VG+	NM
DECCA					
32785	I Don't Know How to Love Him/Overture	1971	—	2.50	5.00
32870	Everything's Alright/Heaven on Their Minds	1971	—	2.50	5.00
32949	Can't Find My Way Home/I Would Have Had a Good Time	1972	—	2.00	4.00
32987	Nothing Rhymed/Speak Your Mind	1972	—	2.00	4.00
33018	Could We Start Again, Please/Heaven on Their Minds	1972	—	2.50	5.00
—B-side by Ben Vereen					
MCA					
40121	Hawaii/I Can't Explain	1973	—	2.00	4.00
40235	Casserole Me Over/Come On Back Where You Belong	1974	—	2.00	4.00
RSO					
514	Somewhere in the Night/Who's Gonna Save the World	1975	—	2.00	4.00
517	Walk Right In/Small Town Talk	1975	—	2.00	4.00
858	Love Me/I Keep Hangin' On (I Don't Know Why)	1976	—	2.00	4.00
871	Hello Stranger/She'll Be the Home	1977	—	2.00	4.00
877	I Knew/I Can't Get You Out of My Mind	1977	—	2.00	4.00
882	If I Can't Have You/Good Sign	1977	—	2.00	4.00
905	Savannah/Up to the Man in You	1978	—	2.00	4.00
915	Moment by Moment/Sailing Ships	1978	—	2.00	4.00
915 [PS]	Moment by Moment/Sailing Ships	1978	—	2.00	4.00
1007	Love Pains/Rock Me Slowly	1979	—	2.00	4.00

Albums

Number	Title (A Side/B Side)	Yr	VG	VG+	NM
DECCA					
DL 75341	Yvonne Elliman	1972	3.75	7.50	15.00
MCA					
356	Food of Love	1973	3.00	6.00	12.00
RSO					
RS-1-3018	Love Me	1977	2.50	5.00	10.00
RS-1-3031	Night Flight	1978	2.50	5.00	10.00
RS-1-3038	Yvonne	1979	2.50	5.00	10.00

ELLINGTON, DUKE

Also see LOUIS ARMSTRONG.

45s

Number	Title (A Side/B Side)	Yr	VG	VG+	NM
BETHLEHEM					
11007	Indian Summer/The Jeep Is Jumpin'	1958	2.50	5.00	10.00
11016	The Blues (Part 1)/The Blues (Part 2)	1959	2.50	5.00	10.00
11066	In a Mellow Tone/Jack the Bear	1960	2.50	5.00	10.00
CAPITOL					
F2458	Satin Doll/Without a Song	1953	3.00	6.00	12.00
F2546	Blue Jean Beguine/Warm Vallen	1953	3.00	6.00	12.00
F2598	Boo-Dar/Doe Me the Right	1953	3.00	6.00	12.00
F2723	Blue Moon/Ultra Deluxe	1954	3.00	6.00	12.00
F2817	Isle of Capri/Band Call	1954	3.00	6.00	12.00
F2875	Bunny Hop Mambo/Is It a Sin	1954	3.00	6.00	12.00
F2930	Smile/If I Give My Heart to You	1954	3.00	6.00	12.00
F2980	12th Street Rag Mambo/Chile Bowl	1954	3.00	6.00	12.00
F3049	Echo Tango/All Day Long	1955	3.00	6.00	12.00
COLUMBIA					
31099 [S]	Three J's Blues/Smada	1961	3.00	6.00	12.00
31100 [S]	Pie Eye's Blues/Sweet and Pungent	1961	3.00	6.00	12.00
31101 [S]	(titles unknown)	1961	3.00	6.00	12.00
31102 [S]	(titles unknown)	1961	3.00	6.00	12.00
31103 [S]	(titles unknown)	1961	3.00	6.00	12.00
31433 [S]	(titles unknown)	1962	3.00	6.00	12.00
31434 [S]	(titles unknown)	1962	3.00	6.00	12.00
31435 [S]	(titles unknown)	1962	3.00	6.00	12.00
31436 [S]	(titles unknown)	1962	3.00	6.00	12.00
31437 [S]	(titles unknown)	1962	3.00	6.00	12.00
31478 [S]	(titles unknown)	1962	3.00	6.00	12.00
31479 [S]	(titles unknown)	1962	3.00	6.00	12.00
31480 [S]	(titles unknown)	1962	3.00	6.00	12.00
31481 [S]	(titles unknown)	1962	3.00	6.00	12.00
31482 [S]	(titles unknown)	1962	3.00	6.00	12.00
—The above 15 all are Columbia "Stereo 7" singles. Any of the gaps you can fill in, please let us know.					
39110	Build That Railroad/Love You Madly	1950	3.75	7.50	15.00
39496	Monologue/8th Veil	1951	3.75	7.50	15.00
39545	Deep Night/Please Be Kind	1951	3.75	7.50	15.00
39670	Jam with Sam/V.I.P.'s Boogie	1952	3.75	7.50	15.00
39712	Blues at Sundown/Bensonality	1952	3.75	7.50	15.00
39942	Rock Skippin' at the Blue Note/The Vulture Song	1953	3.75	7.50	15.00
40903	Cop-Out/Rock City Rock	1957	2.50	5.00	10.00
41098	My Heart, My Mind, My Everything/Together	1958	2.50	5.00	10.00
41180	Duke's Place/Jones	1958	2.50	5.00	10.00
41362	Spank No. 1/Spank No. 2	1959	2.50	5.00	10.00
41401	Walkin' and Singin' the Blues/Hand Me Down Love	1959	2.50	5.00	10.00
41421	Anatomy of a Murder/Flirtbird	1959	2.50	5.00	10.00
41689	Blues in Orbit/Villes, Ville Is the Place, Man	1960	2.50	5.00	10.00
42144	Asphalt Jungle Theme (Part 1)/Asphalt Jungle Theme (Part 2)	1961	2.50	5.00	10.00
42237	Paris Blues (Part 1)/Paris Blues (Part 2)	1962	2.50	5.00	10.00
IMPULSE!					
210	Limbo Jazz (Part 1)/Limbo Jazz (Part 2)	196?	2.00	4.00	8.00
RCA VICTOR					
47-2955	The Sidewalks of New York/Don't Get Around Much Anymore	1949	5.00	10.00	20.00
47-3033	Frankie & Johnny/Royal Garden Blues	1949	3.00	6.00	12.00
47-3034	Drawing Room Blues/St. Louis Blues	1949	3.00	6.00	12.00
47-3035	Beale Street Blues/Pretty Woman	1949	3.00	6.00	12.00
47-4281	Jumping Room Only/A Gathering in a Clearing	1951	3.75	7.50	15.00
47-4711	Balcony Serenade/Strange Feeling	1952	3.75	7.50	15.00
47-4712	Dancers in Love/Coloratura	1952	3.75	7.50	15.00
REPRISE					
0545	Satin Doll/Don't Get Around Much Anymore	1967	—	3.00	6.00

7-Inch Extended Plays

Number	Title (A Side/B Side)	Yr	VG	VG+	NM
RCA VICTOR					
EPA-5054	Caravan/Sophisticated Lady//Perdido/Mood Indigo	1958	3.75	7.50	15.00
EPA-5054 [PS]	(title unknown)	1958	3.75	7.50	15.00

Albums

Number	Title (A Side/B Side)	Yr	VG	VG+	NM
AAMCO					
ALP-301 [M]	The Royal Concert of Duke Ellington, Vol. 1	196?	7.50	15.00	30.00
—Reissue of Bethlehem material					
ALP-313 [M]	The Royal Concert of Duke Ellington, Vol. 2	196?	7.50	15.00	30.00
—Reissue of Bethlehem material					
ABC IMPULSE!					
9256 [(2)]	Ellingtonia: Reevaluations, The Impulse Years	1973	3.75	7.50	15.00
9285 [(2)]	Ellingtonia, Volume 2	1974	3.75	7.50	15.00
IA-9350 [(2)]	Great Tenor Encounters	1978	3.75	7.50	15.00
AIRCHECK					
4	Duke on the Air	197?	2.50	5.00	10.00
29	Duke on the Air, Vol. 2	198?	2.50	5.00	10.00
ALLEGRO					
1591 [M]	Duke Ellington and His Orchestra Play	1955	12.50	25.00	50.00
3082 [M]	Duke Ellington	1953	12.50	25.00	50.00
4014 [10]	Duke Ellington and His Orchestra Play	1954	25.00	50.00	100.00
4038 [10]	Duke Ellington and His Orchestra Play	1954	25.00	50.00	100.00
ARCHIVE OF FOLK AND JAZZ					
221	Early Duke Ellington	1968	3.00	6.00	12.00
249	Early Duke Ellington Vol. 2	1970	3.00	6.00	12.00
266	Early Duke Ellington Vol. 3	1972	3.00	6.00	12.00
327	Duke Ellington at Carnegie Hall	197?	3.00	6.00	12.00
ATLANTIC					
SD 2-304 [(2)]	The Great Paris Concert	1972	3.75	7.50	15.00
QD 1580 [Q]	New Orleans Suite	1974	6.25	12.50	25.00
SD 1580	New Orleans Suite	1971	3.00	6.00	12.00
SD 1665	Recollections of the Big Band Era	1974	3.00	6.00	12.00
SD 1688	Jazz Violin Session	1976	3.00	6.00	12.00
90043	Recollections of the Big Band Era	1982	2.50	5.00	10.00
BASF					
21704	Collages	1973	3.00	6.00	12.00
BETHLEHEM					
BCP-60 [M]	Historically Speaking, The Duke	1956	15.00	30.00	60.00
BCP-6005 [M]	Duke Ellington Presents	1956	15.00	30.00	60.00
6013	The Bethlehem Years, Vol. 1	197?	2.50	5.00	10.00
BIOGRAPH					
M-2	Band Shorts (1929-1935)	1978	2.50	5.00	10.00
BLUE NOTE					
BT-85129	Money Jungle	1986	2.50	5.00	10.00
—Reissue of United Artists 15017					
BLUEBIRD					
5659-1-RB [(4)]	Duke Ellington: The Blanton-Webster Band	1986	6.25	12.50	25.00
6287-1-RB	And His Mother Called Him Bill	1987	2.00	4.00	8.00
—Reissue of RCA Victor 3906					
6641-1-RB [(4)]	Black, Brown and Beige	1988	6.25	12.50	25.00
6852-1-RB	Early Ellington	1989	2.50	5.00	10.00
BRIGHT ORANGE					
709	The Stereophonic Sound of Duke Ellington	1973	3.00	6.00	12.00
BRUNSWICK					
BL 54007 [M]	Early Ellington	1954	12.50	25.00	50.00
BL 58002 [10]	Ellingtonia, Volume 1	1950	25.00	50.00	100.00
BL 58012 [10]	Ellingtonia, Volume 2	1950	25.00	50.00	100.00
BULLDOG					
BDL-2021	20 Golden Pieces of Duke Ellington	198?	2.50	5.00	10.00
CAPITOL					
H 440 [10]	Premiered by Ellington	1953	25.00	50.00	100.00
H 477 [10]	The Duke Plays Ellington	1954	25.00	50.00	100.00
T 477 [M]	The Duke Plays Ellington	1954	10.00	20.00	40.00
—Turquoise label					
T 477 [M]	The Duke Plays Ellington	1958	5.00	10.00	20.00
—Black label with colorband, logo at left					
T 521 [M]	Ellington '55	1955	10.00	20.00	40.00
—Turquoise label					
T 521 [M]	Ellington '55	1958	5.00	10.00	20.00
—Black label with colorband, logo at left					
T 637 [M]	Dance to the Duke	1955	10.00	20.00	40.00
—Turquoise label					
T 637 [M]	Dance to the Duke	1958	5.00	10.00	20.00
—Black label with colorband, logo at left					
T 679 [M]	Ellington Showcase	1956	10.00	20.00	40.00
—Turquoise label					
T 679 [M]	Ellington Showcase	1958	5.00	10.00	20.00
—Black label with colorband, logo at left					
DT 1602 [R]	The Best of Duke Ellington	1961	3.00	6.00	12.00
SM-1602	The Best of Duke Ellington	197?	2.50	5.00	10.00
—Reissue with new prefix					
T 1602 [M]	The Best of Duke Ellington	1961	5.00	10.00	20.00
M-11058	Piano Reflections	1972	3.00	6.00	12.00
M-11674	Ellington '55	1977	2.50	5.00	10.00
N-16172	The Best of Duke Ellington	198?	2.00	4.00	8.00
—Budget-line reissue					
CIRCLE					
CLP-101	Duke Ellington World Broadcasting Series, Vol. 1	1986	2.50	5.00	10.00
CLP-102	Duke Ellington World Broadcasting Series, Vol. 2	1986	2.50	5.00	10.00
CLP-103	Duke Ellington World Broadcasting Series, Vol. 3	1986	2.50	5.00	10.00
CLP-104	Duke Ellington World Broadcasting Series, Vol. 4	199?	2.50	5.00	10.00
CLP-105	Duke Ellington World Broadcasting Series, Vol. 5 (1943)	199?	2.50	5.00	10.00
CLP-106	Duke Ellington World Broadcasting Series, Vol. 6 (1945)	1988	2.50	5.00	10.00
CLP-108	Duke Ellington World Broadcasting Series, Vol. 8 (1945)	1988	2.50	5.00	10.00
CLP-109	Duke Ellington World Broadcasting Series, Vol. 9 (1945)	1988	2.50	5.00	10.00
COLUMBIA					
C3L 27 [M (3)]	The Ellington Era, Vol. 1	1963	10.00	20.00	40.00
C3L 39 [M (3)]	The Ellington Era, Vol. 2	1964	10.00	20.00	40.00

Number	Title (A Side/B Side)	Yr	VG	VG+	NM
CL 558 [M]	The Music of Duke Ellington	1954	12.50	25.00	50.00
—Maroon label with gold print					
CL 558 [M]	The Music of Duke Ellington	1956	10.00	20.00	40.00
—Red and black label with six "eye" logos					
CL 558 [M]	The Music of Duke Ellington	1963	3.75	7.50	15.00
—Red label with "Guaranteed High Fidelity" or "360 Sound Mono"					
CL 663 [M]	Blue Light	1955	10.00	20.00	40.00
CL 825 [M]	Masterpieces by Ellington	1956	10.00	20.00	40.00
—Reissue of Columbia Masterworks 4418					
CL 825 [M]	Masterpieces by Ellington	1963	3.75	7.50	15.00
—Red label with "Guaranteed High Fidelity" or "360 Sound Mono"					
CL 830 [M]	Hi-Fi Ellington Uptown	1956	10.00	20.00	40.00
CL 830 [M]	Hi-Fi Ellington Uptown	1963	3.75	7.50	15.00
—Red label with "Guaranteed High Fidelity" or "360 Sound Mono"					
CL 848 [M]	Liberian Suite	1956	10.00	20.00	40.00
—Reissue of Columbia 6073					
CL 934 [M]	Ellington at Newport '56	1957	10.00	20.00	40.00
—Red and black label with six "eye" logos					
CL 934 [M]	Ellington at Newport '56	1963	3.75	7.50	15.00
—Red label with "Guaranteed High Fidelity" or "360 Sound Mono"					
CL 951 [M]	A Drum Is a Woman	1957	10.00	20.00	40.00
CL 1033 [M]	Such Sweet Thunder	1957	10.00	20.00	40.00
CL 1085 [M]	Ellington Indigos	1958	6.25	12.50	25.00
CL 1085 [M]	Ellington Indigos	1963	3.75	7.50	15.00
—Red label with "Guaranteed High Fidelity" or "360 Sound Mono"					
CL 1162 [M]	Brown, Black and Beige	1958	6.25	12.50	25.00
CL 1198 [M]	The Cosmic Scene	1959	20.00	40.00	80.00
CL 1245 [M]	Newport 1958	1959	6.25	12.50	25.00
CL 1282 [M]	Duke Ellington at the Bal Masque	1959	6.25	12.50	25.00
CL 1323 [M]	Duke Ellington Jazz Party	1959	6.25	12.50	25.00
CL 1400 [M]	Festival Session	1960	6.25	12.50	25.00
CL 1445 [M]	Blues in Orbit	1960	6.25	12.50	25.00
CL 1541 [M]	The Nutcracker Suite	1960	7.50	15.00	30.00
CL 1546 [M]	Piano in the Background	1960	7.50	15.00	30.00
CL 1546 [M]	Piano in the Background	1963	3.75	7.60	15.00
—Red label with "Guaranteed High Fidelity" or "360 Sound Mono"					
CL 1597 [M]	Peer Gynt Suite/Suite Thursday	1961	6.25	12.50	25.00
CL 1715 [M]	First Time	1962	6.25	12.50	25.00
CL 1790 [M]	All American	1962	5.00	10.00	20.00
CL 1907 [M]	Midnight in Paris	1963	5.00	10.00	20.00
CL 2522 [10]	Duke's Mixture	1955	20.00	40.00	80.00
CL 2562 [10]	Here's the Duke	1955	20.00	40.00	80.00
CL 2593 [10]	Al Hibbler with the Duke	1956	20.00	40.00	80.00
CL 6024 [10]	Mood Ellington	1949	25.00	50.00	100.00
CL 6073 [10]	Liberian Suite	1949	25.00	50.00	100.00
CS 8015 [S]	Brown, Black and Beige	1958	7.50	15.00	30.00
CS 8053 [S]	Ellington Indigos	1958	7.50	15.00	30.00
CS 8053 [S]	Ellington Indigos	1963	3.75	7.50	15.00
—Red label with "360 Sound Stereo"					
PC 8053	Ellington Indigos	198?	2.00	4.00	8.00
—Budget-line reissue					
CS 8072 [S]	Newport 1958	1959	7.50	15.00	30.00
CS 8098 [S]	Duke Ellington at the Bal Masque	1959	7.50	15.00	30.00
CS 8127 [S]	Duke Ellington Jazz Party	1959	7.50	15.00	30.00
CS 8241 [S]	Blues in Orbit	1960	7.50	15.00	30.00
CS 8341 [S]	The Nutcracker Suite	1960	10.00	20.00	40.00
CS 8346 [S]	Piano in the Background	1960	10.00	20.00	40.00
CS 8346 [S]	Piano in the Background	1963	3.75	7.50	15.00
—Red label with "360 Sound Stereo"					
CS 8397 [S]	Peer Gynt Suite/Suite Thursday	1961	7.50	15.00	30.00
CS 8515 [S]	First Time	1962	7.50	15.00	30.00
CS 8590 [S]	All American	1962	6.25	12.50	25.00
CS 8648 [R]	Ellington at Newport	1963	3.00	6.00	12.00
PC 8648	Ellington at Newport	198?	2.00	4.00	8.00
—Budget-line reissue					
CS 8829 [S]	Midnight in Paris	1963	6.25	12.50	25.00
CS 9629	Duke Ellington's Greatest Hits	1969	3.75	7.50	15.00
KG 32064 [(2)]	Duke Ellington Presents Ivie Anderson	1973	3.75	7.50	15.00
C 32471	Jazz at the Plaza — Vol. II	1973	3.00	6.00	12.00
G 32564 [(2)]	The World of Duke Ellington	1974	3.75	7.50	15.00
KG 33341 [(2)]	The World of Duke Ellington, Volume 2	1975	3.75	7.50	15.00
CG 33961 [(2)]	The World of Duke Ellington, Volume 3	1975	3.75	7.50	15.00
PC 37340	It Don't Mean a Thing	1981	2.00	4.00	8.00
—Reissue					
FC 38028	The Girl's Suite & Perfume Suite	1982	2.50	5.00	10.00
COLUMBIA JAZZ MASTERPIECES					
CJ 40586	First Time	1987	2.50	5.00	10.00
—Reissue of Columbia 8515					
CJ 40587	Ellington at Newport	1987	2.50	5.00	10.00
—Reissue of Columbia 934					
CJ 40712	Duke Ellington Jazz Party	1987	2.50	5.00	10.00
—Reissue of Columbia 8127					
CJ 40836	Uptown	1987	2.50	5.00	10.00
CJ 44051	Blues in Orbit	1988	2.50	5.00	10.00
—Reissue of Columbia 8241					
CJ 44444	Ellington Indigos	1989	2.50	5.00	10.00
—Reissue of Columbia 8053					
COLUMBIA JAZZ ODYSSEY					
PC 36979	The Festival Session	1981	2.50	5.00	10.00
COLUMBIA MASTERWORKS					
ML 4418 [M]	Masterpieces by Ellington	1951	25.00	50.00	100.00
ML 4639 [M]	Ellington Uptown	1951	25.00	50.00	100.00
—Blue or green label, gold print					
ML 4639 [M]	Ellington Uptown	195?	12.50	25.00	50.00
—Oddly, this exists as a reissue on the red and black "6 eye" label					
COLUMBIA SPECIAL PRODUCTS					
P 14359	Suite Thursday/Controversial Suite/Harlem Suite	198?	2.50	5.00	10.00
DAYBREAK					
DR 2017	The Symphonic Ellington	1973	3.00	6.00	12.00
DECCA					
DL 9224 [M]	Duke Ellington, Volume 1 — In the Beginning	1958	10.00	20.00	40.00
—Black label, silver print					
DL 9224 [M]	Duke Ellington, Volume 1 — In the Beginning	1961	6.25	12.50	25.00
—Black label with color bars					

Number	Title (A Side/B Side)	Yr	VG	VG+	NM
DL 9241 [M]	Duke Ellington, Volume 2 — Hot in Harlem	1959	10.00	20.00	40.00
—Black label, silver print					
DL 9241 [M]	Duke Ellington, Volume 2 — Hot in Harlem	1961	6.25	12.50	25.00
—Black label with color bars					
DL 9247 [M]	Duke Ellington, Volume 3 — Rockin' in Rhythm	1959	10.00	20.00	40.00
—Black label, silver print					
DL 9247 [M]	Duke Ellington, Volume 3 — Rockin' in Rhythm	1961	6.25	12.50	25.00
—Black label with color bars					
DL 75069	Duke Ellington in Canada	1969	3.75	7.50	15.00
DL 79224 [R]	Duke Ellington, Volume 1 — In the Beginning	1958	6.25	12.50	25.00
—Black label, silver print					
DL 79224 [R]	Duke Ellington, Volume 1 — In the Beginning	1961	3.75	7.50	15.00
—Black label with color bars					
DL 79241 [R]	Duke Ellington, Volume 2 — Hot in Harlem	1959	6.25	12.50	25.00
—Black label, silver print					
DL 79241 [R]	Duke Ellington, Volume 2 — Hot in Harlem	1961	3.75	7.50	15.00
—Black label with color bars					
DL 79247 [R]	Duke Ellington, Volume 3 — Rockin' in Rhythm	1959	6.25	12.50	25.00
—Black label, silver print					
DL 79247 [R]	Duke Ellington, Volume 3 — Rockin' in Rhythm	1961	3.75	7.50	15.00
—Black label with color bars					
DISCOVERY					
841	Concert in the Virgin Islands	198?	2.50	5.00	10.00
—Reissue of Reprise 6185					
871	Afro Bossa	198?	2.50	5.00	10.00
—Reissue of Reprise 6069					
DO YOU LIKE JAZZ					
P 13293	Monologue	1973	3.00	6.00	12.00
DOCTOR JAZZ					
W2X 39137 [(2)]	All-Star Road Band	1984	3.00	6.00	12.00
W2X 40012 [(2)]	All-Star Road Band, Vol. 2	1985	3.00	6.00	12.00
FW 40030	Happy Reunion	1985	2.50	5.00	10.00
FW 40359	New Mood Indigo	1986	2.50	5.00	10.00
FANTASY					
OJC-108	Great Times!	198?	2.50	5.00	10.00
—Reissue of Riverside 9475					
OJC-446	The Ellington Suites	1990	2.50	5.00	10.00
—Reissue of Pablo 2310 762					
OJC-469	Latin American Suite	1990	2.50	5.00	10.00
—Reissue of 8419					
OJC-623	Duke Ellington Featuring Paul Gonsalves	1991	3.00	6.00	12.00
—Reissue of 9636					
OJC-624	The Intimacy of the Blues	1991	3.00	6.00	12.00
—Reissue of 9640					
OJC-633	Up in Duke's Workshop	1991	3.00	6.00	12.00
—Reissue of Pablo 2310 815					
OJC-645	The Afro-Eurasian Eclipse	1991	3.00	6.00	12.00
—Reissue of 9498					
F-8407/8 [(2)]	Duke Ellington's Second Sacred Concert	1971	3.75	7.50	15.00
F-8419	Latin American Suite	1971	3.00	6.00	12.00
F-9433	Yale Concert	1974	3.00	6.00	12.00
F-9462	The Pianist	1974	3.00	6.00	12.00
F-9498	Afro-American Eclipse	1976	3.00	6.00	12.00
F-9636	Duke Ellington Featuring Paul Gonsalves	198?	2.50	5.00	10.00
F-9640	The Intimacy of the Blues	1986	2.50	5.00	10.00
FLYING DUTCHMAN					
BXL1-2832	It Don't Mean a Thing	1978	2.50	5.00	10.00
—Reissue					
10112	My People	1969	3.75	7.50	15.00
10166	It Don't Mean a Thing	1973	3.00	6.00	12.00
FOLKWAYS					
FJ-2968	First Annual Tourn of the Pacific Northwest, Spring, 1952	198?	2.50	5.00	10.00
GALAXY					
4807	Duke Ellington and His Famous Orchestra and Soloists	197?	3.75	7.50	15.00
GNP CRESCENDO					
GNP-9045	The 1953 Pasadena Concert	1986	2.50	5.00	10.00
GNP-9049	The 1954 Los Angeles Concert	1987	2.50	5.00	10.00
HALL OF FAME					
625/6/7 [(3)]	The Immortal Duke Ellington	197?	5.00	10.00	20.00
HARMONY					
HL 7436 [M]	Fantasies	1967	3.75	7.50	15.00
HS 11236 [R]	Fantasies	1967	3.00	6.00	12.00
HS 11323	In My Solitude	1969	3.00	6.00	12.00
H 30566	Duke Ellington's Greatest Hits Live	1971	3.00	6.00	12.00
HINDSIGHT					
HSR-125	Duke Ellington 1946	198?	2.50	5.00	10.00
HSR-126	Duke Ellington 1946, Volume 2	198?	2.50	5.00	10.00
HSR-127	Duke Ellington 1946, Volume 3	198?	2.50	5.00	10.00
HSR-128	Duke Ellington 1947	198?	2.50	5.00	10.00
HSR-129	Duke Ellington 1947, Volume 2	198?	2.50	5.00	10.00
IAJRC					
LP-45	Fairfield, Connecticut Jazz Fest 1956	198?	2.00	4.00	8.00
INTERMEDIA					
QS-5002	Sophisticated Duke	198?	2.50	5.00	10.00
QS-5020	Lullaby of Birdland	198?	2.50	5.00	10.00
QS-5021	Do Nothin' Till You Hear from Me	198?	2.50	5.00	10.00
QS-5063	Satin Doll	198?	2.50	5.00	10.00
JAZZ ODYSSEY					
32160252	Nutcracker and Peer Gynt Suites	196?	3.00	6.00	12.00
JAZZ PANORAMA					
1802 [10]	Duke Ellington — Vol. 1	1951	25.00	50.00	100.00
1811 [10]	Duke Ellington — Vol. 2	1951	25.00	50.00	100.00
1816 [10]	Duke Ellington — Vol. 3	1951	25.00	50.00	100.00
JAZZBIRD					
2009	Meadowbrook to Manhattan	1980	2.50	5.00	10.00
LONDON					
AL-3551 [10]	The Duke — 1926	195?	25.00	50.00	100.00
MCA					
1358	Duke Ellington, Volume 1 — In the Beginning	198?	2.00	4.00	8.00
—Reissue of 2075					

Number	Title (A Side/B Side)	Yr	VG	VG+	NM
1359	Duke Ellington, Volume 2 — Hot in Harlem	198?	2.00	4.00	8.00
—Reissue of 2076					
1360	Duke Ellington, Volume 3 — Rockin' in Rhythm	198?	2.00	4.00	8.00
—Reissue of 2077					
2075	Duke Ellington, Volume 1 — In the Beginning	197?	2.50	5.00	10.00
—Reissue of Decca 79224					
2076	Duke Ellington, Volume 2 — Hot in Harlem	197?	2.50	5.00	10.00
—Reissue of Decca 79241					
2077	Duke Ellington, Volume 3 — Rockin' in Rhythm	197?	2.50	5.00	10.00
—Reissue of Decca 79247					
4142 [(2)]	Great Tenor Encounters	198?	3.00	6.00	12.00
—Reissue of Impulse! 9350					
42325	The Brunswick Era, Vol. 1	1990	3.00	6.00	12.00
MOBILE FIDELITY					
1-214	Anatomy of a Murder	1995	10.00	20.00	40.00
—Audiophile vinyl					
MOSAIC					
MQ8-160 [(8)]	The Complete Capitol Recordings of Duke Ellington	199?	37.50	75.00	150.00
MUSICRAFT					
2002	Carnegie Hall Concert	1986	2.50	5.00	10.00
PABLO					
2310703	Duke's Big 4	1974	3.00	6.00	12.00
2310721	This One's for Blanton	197?	3.00	6.00	12.00
2310762	The Ellington Suites	197?	3.00	6.00	12.00
2310787	Intimate	197?	3.00	6.00	12.00
2310815	Up in Duke's Workshop	1980	2.50	5.00	10.00
2405401	The Best of Duke Ellington	198?	2.50	5.00	10.00
PABLO LIVE					
2308245	Harlem	198?	2.50	5.00	10.00
2308247	In the Uncommon Market	198?	2.50	5.00	10.00
PAIR					
PDL2-1011 [(2)]	Original Recordings by Duke Ellington	1986	3.00	6.00	12.00
PICCADILLY					
3524	Classic Ellington	198?	2.50	5.00	10.00
PICKWICK					
SPC-3390	We Love You Madly	197?	2.50	5.00	10.00
PRESTIGE					
24029 [(2)]	The Golden Duke	1973	3.75	7.50	15.00
24045 [(2)]	Duke Ellington's Second Sacred Concert	1974	3.00	6.00	12.00
—Reissue of Fantasy 8407/8					
24073 [(2)]	The Carnegie Hall Concerts: December 1944	197?	3.75	7.50	15.00
24074 [(2)]	The Carnegie Hall Concerts: January 1946	197?	3.75	7.50	15.00
24075 [(2)]	The Carnegie Hall Concerts: December 1947	197?	3.75	7.50	15.00
34003 [(3)]	The Carnegie Hall Concerts: January 1943	197?	5.00	10.00	20.00
RCA CAMDEN					
ACL2-0152 [(2)]	Mood Indigo	1973	3.75	7.50	15.00
CAL-394 [M]	Duke Ellington at Tanglewood	1958	5.00	10.00	20.00
CAL-459 [M]	Duke Ellington at the Cotton Club	1959	5.00	10.00	20.00
ACL-7052	The Duke at Tanglewood	197?	2.50	5.00	10.00
—Reissue of RCA Red Seal LSC-2857					
RCA VICTOR					
WPT-11 [10]	Duke Ellington	1951	25.00	50.00	100.00
LPV-506 [M]	Daybreak Express	1964	5.00	10.00	20.00
LPV-517 [M]	Jumpin' Punkins	1965	5.00	10.00	20.00
LPV-541 [M]	Johnny Come Lately	1967	5.00	10.00	20.00
LPV-553 [M]	Pretty Woman	1968	5.00	10.00	20.00
LPV-568 [M]	Flaming Youth	1969	5.00	10.00	20.00
LJM-1002 [M]	Seattle Concert	1954	12.50	25.00	50.00
LPT-1004 [M]	Ellington's Greatest	1954	10.00	20.00	40.00
APL1-1023	Eastbourne Performance	1974	3.00	6.00	12.00
LPM-1092 [M]	Duke and His Men	1955	10.00	20.00	40.00
LPM-1364 [M]	In a Mellotone	1957	10.00	20.00	40.00
LPM-1715 [M]	Duke Ellington at His Very Best	1958	10.00	20.00	40.00
ANL1-2811	Pure Gold	1978	2.50	5.00	10.00
LPT-3017 [10]	This Is Duke Ellington and His Orchestra	1952	25.00	50.00	100.00
LPT-3067 [10]	Duke Ellington Plays the Blues	1952	25.00	50.00	100.00
LPM-3576 [M]	The Popular Duke Ellington	1966	3.75	7.50	15.00
LSP-3576 [S]	The Popular Duke Ellington	1966	5.00	10.00	20.00
LPM-3582 [M]	Concert of Sacred Music	1966	3.75	7.50	15.00
LSP-3582 [S]	Concert of Sacred Music	1966	5.00	10.00	20.00
LPM-3782 [M]	Far East Suite	1967	6.25	12.50	25.00
LSP-3782 [S]	Far East Suite	1967	3.75	7.50	15.00
LPM-3906 [M]	And His Mother Called Him Bill	1968	12.50	25.00	50.00
LSP-3906 [S]	And His Mother Called Him Bill	1968	3.75	7.50	15.00
CPL2-4098 [(2)]	Sophisticated Ellington	1983	3.00	6.00	12.00
LPM-6009 [(2) M]	The Indispensible Duke Ellington	1961	12.50	25.00	50.00
VPM-6042 [(2)]	This Is Duke Ellington	1972	3.75	7.50	15.00
RCA VICTOR RED SEAL					
LM-2857 [M]	The Duke at Tanglewood	1966	3.75	7.50	15.00
LSC-2857 [S]	The Duke at Tanglewood	1966	5.00	10.00	20.00
REPRISE					
R-6069 [M]	Afro-Bossa	1962	5.00	10.00	20.00
R9-6069 [S]	Afro-Bossa	1962	5.00	10.00	20.00
R-6097 [M]	The Symphonic Ellington	1963	5.00	10.00	20.00
R9-6097 [S]	The Symphonic Ellington	1963	5.00	10.00	20.00
R-6122 [M]	Ellington '65: Hits of the '60s/This Time by Ellington	1964	5.00	10.00	20.00
RS-6122 [S]	Ellington '65: Hits of the '60s/This Time by Ellington	1964	5.00	10.00	20.00
R-6141 [M]	Mary Poppins	1964	5.00	10.00	20.00
RS-6141 [S]	Mary Poppins	1964	5.00	10.00	20.00
R-6154 [M]	Ellington '66	1965	5.00	10.00	20.00
RS-6154 [S]	Ellington '66	1965	3.75	7.50	15.00
R-6168 [M]	Will Big Bands Ever Come Back?	1965	5.00	10.00	20.00
RS-6168 [S]	Will Big Bands Ever Come Back?	1965	3.75	7.50	15.00
R-6185 [M]	Concert in the Virgin Islands	1965	5.00	10.00	20.00
RS-6185 [S]	Concert in the Virgin Islands	1965	3.75	7.50	15.00
R-6234 [M]	Duke Ellington's Greatest Hits	1967	5.00	10.00	20.00
RS-6234 [S]	Duke Ellington's Greatest Hits	1967	3.75	7.50	15.00
RIVERSIDE					
RLP 12-129 [M]	Birth of Big Band Jazz	1956	15.00	30.00	60.00
—White label, blue print					
RLP 12-129 [M]	Birth of Big Band Jazz	195?	7.50	15.00	30.00
—Blue label with mike logo					
RLP-475 [M]	Great Times!	1963	6.25	12.50	25.00
RS-9475 [S]	Great Times!	1963	6.25	12.50	25.00
RONDO-LETTE					
A-7 [M]	Duke Ellington and Orchestra	1958	7.50	15.00	30.00
ROULETTE					
108 [(2)]	Echoes of An Era	1971	3.75	7.50	15.00
ROYALE					
18143 [10]	Duke Ellington and His Orchestra	195?	12.50	25.00	50.00
18152 [10]	Duke Ellington Plays Ellington	195?	12.50	25.00	50.00
SOLID STATE					
SM-18022	Money Jungle	1968	3.75	7.50	15.00
—Reissue of United Artists 15017					
SS-19000 [(2)]	75th Birthday	1970	5.00	10.00	20.00
STANYAN					
10105	For Always	197?	3.00	6.00	12.00
STORYVILLE					
SLP-4003	Duke Ellington and His Orchestra	198?	2.50	5.00	10.00
SUPER MAJESTIC					
2000	Duke Ellington	197?	3.00	6.00	12.00
SUTTON					
SU-276 [M]	Duke Meets Leonard Feather	196?	3.00	6.00	12.00
TREND					
529	The Symphonic Ellington	1982	5.00	10.00	20.00
2004	Carnegie Hall Concert	198?	2.50	5.00	10.00
UNITED ARTISTS					
UXS-92 [(2)]	Togo Bravo Suite	1972	3.75	7.50	15.00
UAS-5632	Money Jungle	1972	3.00	6.00	12.00
—Reissue					
UAJ-14017 [M]	Money Jungle	1962	10.00	20.00	40.00
UAJS-15017 [S]	Money Jungle	1962	10.00	20.00	40.00
VEE JAY					
VJS-3061	Love You Madly	198?	2.50	5.00	10.00
VERVE					
V-8701 [M]	Soul Call	1967	3.75	7.50	15.00
V6-8701 [S]	Soul Call	1967	3.00	6.00	12.00
"X"					
LVA-3037 [10]	Duke Ellington Plays	1955	25.00	50.00	100.00

ELLINGTON, HARVEY

Albums

Number	Title (A Side/B Side)	Yr	VG	VG+	NM
STEPHENY					
MF-4010 [M]	I Can't Hide the Blues	1959	20.00	40.00	80.00

ELLIOT, CASS

Also see THE BIG THREE; THE MAMAS AND THE PAPAS; DAVE MASON; THE MUGWUMPS.

45s

Number	Title (A Side/B Side)	Yr	VG	VG+	NM
ABC DUNHILL					
4145	Dream a Little Dream of Me/Midnight Voyage	1968	2.00	4.00	8.00
—Label credit: "Featuring Mama Cass with the Mamas and the Papas"					
4166	California Earthquake/Talkin' to Your Toothbrush	1968	—	3.00	6.00
4184	Move In a Little Closer, Baby/All for Me	1969	—	3.00	6.00
4195	It's Getting Better/Who's to Blame	1969	—	3.00	6.00
—The above three as "Mama Cass"					
4214	Make Your Own Kind of Music/Ladylove	1969	—	3.00	6.00
4225	New World Coming/Blow Me a Kiss	1970	—	3.00	6.00
4244	A Song That Never Comes/I Can Dream, Can't I?	1970	—	3.00	6.00
4253	Good Times Are Coming/Welcome to the World	1970	—	3.00	6.00
4264	Don't Let the Good Times Pass You By/A Song That Never Comes	1971	—	3.00	6.00
—The above five as "Mama Cass Elliott"					
DUNHILL					
4145	Dream a Little Dream of Me/Midnight Voyage	1968	6.25	12.50	25.00
—Label credit: "Featuring Mama Cass with the Mamas and the Papas"; no "ABC" at top of label					
RCA VICTOR					
74-0644	Baby, I'm Yours/Cherries Jubilee	1972	—	3.00	6.00
74-0693	That Song/When It Doesn't Work Out	1972	—	3.00	6.00
74-0764	Disney Girls/Break Another Heart	1972	—	3.00	6.00
74-0830	The Road Is No Place for a Lady/Does Anybody Love You	1972	—	3.00	6.00
74-0957	I Think a Lot About You/Listen to the World	1973	—	3.00	6.00

Albums

Number	Title (A Side/B Side)	Yr	VG	VG+	NM
ABC DUNHILL					
DS-50040	Dream a Little Dream	1968	5.00	10.00	20.00
DS-50055	Bubble Gum, Lemonade &...Something for Mama	1969	5.00	10.00	20.00
DS-50071	Make Your Own Kind of Music	1969	3.75	7.50	15.00
—Reissue of 50055 with new title and one added song					
DS-50093	Mama's Big Ones	1970	3.75	7.50	15.00
MCA					
719	Mama's Big Ones	1980	2.00	4.00	8.00
RCA VICTOR					
APL1-0303	Don't Call Me Mama Anymore	1973	3.75	7.50	15.00
LSP-4619	Cass Elliot	1971	3.75	7.50	15.00
LSP-4753	The Road Is No Place for a Lady	1972	3.75	7.50	15.00

ELLIOTT, BERN, AND THE FENMEN

45s

Number	Title (A Side/B Side)	Yr	VG	VG+	NM
LONDON					
9670	New Orleans/Everybody Needs a Little Love	1964	3.00	6.00	12.00
9733	Money/Nobody But Me	1965	3.00	6.00	12.00

ELLIOTT, BILL, AND THE ELASTIC OZ BAND

Also see JOHN LENNON; YOKO ONO.

45s

Number	Title (A Side/B Side)	Yr	VG	VG+	NM
APPLE					
1835	God Save Us/Do the Oz	1971	2.00	4.00	8.00
1835 [PS]	God Save Us/Do the Oz	1971	2.50	5.00	10.00
P-1835 [DJ]	God Save Us/Do the Oz	1971	6.25	12.50	25.00
—Has black star on A-side and unsliced apple on both sides					

ELLIOTT, RON

Also see THE BEAU BRUMMELS.

Albums

Number	Title (A Side/B Side)	Yr	VG	VG+	NM
WARNER BROS.					
WS 1833	Candlestickmaker	1969	3.75	7.50	15.00

ELLIS, JIMMY

Also see ORION.

45s

Number	Title (A Side/B Side)	Yr	VG	VG+	NM
ATLANTIC					
2572	I Don't Mind/Take the Lord With You	1968	2.00	4.00	8.00
BOBLO					
526	Tupelo Woman/The Closer He Gets	1976	—	2.00	4.00
531	There You Go/Here Comes That Wonderful Feeling	1977	—	2.00	4.00
532	Movin' On/My Baby's Out of Sight	1977	—	2.00	4.00
536	I'm Not Trying to Be Like Elvis/Games You've Been Playing	1978	—	2.00	4.00
536 [PS]	I'm Not Trying to Be Like Elvis/Games You've Been Playing	1978	2.50	5.00	10.00
DRADCO					
1892	Don't Count Your Chickens/Love Is But Love	1964	3.75	7.50	15.00
GOLDBAND					
1191	Woman in the Picture/What Swinging Doors Did to Me	196?	2.50	5.00	10.00
KRIS					
8115	Outskirts of Town (Part 1)/Outskirts of Town (Part 2)	196?	2.00	4.00	8.00
MCA					
40060	There Ya Go/Here Comes That Feeling Again	1973	—	2.00	4.00
RIDE					
146	Baby I Love You/Kiddio	196?	2.00	4.00	8.00
As "Jimmie Ellis"; may not be the same performer as the others					
SOUTHERN TRACKS					
1069	I Make the Livin' (You Make the Livin' Worthwhile)/Thank God for America	1986	—	2.00	4.00
1080	Sunday Fathers/Thank God for America	1987	—	2.00	4.00
SUN					
1129	That's All Right/Blue Moon of Kentucky	1973	—	2.50	5.00
—Originals have no artist on label in an attempt to make people believe these were lost Elvis Presley outtakes					
1129	That's All Right/Blue Moon of Kentucky	1973	—	2.00	4.00
—Second pressings credit Jimmy Ellis					
1131	I Use Her to Remind Me of You/Changing	1974	—	2.00	4.00
1136	D.O.A./Misty/That's All Right/Blue Moon of Kentucky	1977	—	2.00	4.00

Albums

Number	Title (A Side/B Side)	Yr	VG	VG+	NM
BOBLO					
78-829	By Request Jimmy Sings Elvis	1978	25.00	50.00	100.00

ELLIS, LORRAINE

45s

Number	Title (A Side/B Side)	Yr	VG	VG+	NM
BULLSEYE					
100	Perfidia/Piano Player Play a Tune	1955	15.00	30.00	60.00
GEE					
1	Perfidia/Piano Player Play a Tune	1953	75.00	150.00	300.00

ELLIS, SHIRLEY

45s

Number	Title (A Side/B Side)	Yr	VG	VG+	NM
COLUMBIA					
43829	Truly, Truly, Truly/Birds, Bees, Cupids and Bows	1966	2.00	4.00	8.00
44021	Soul Time/Waitin'	1967	2.00	4.00	8.00
44137	Sugar Let's Shing-a-Ling/How Lonely Is Lonely	1967	2.00	4.00	8.00
CONGRESS					
202	The Nitty Gritty/Give Me a List	1963	3.75	7.50	15.00
208	(That's) What the Nitty Gritty Is/Get Out	1964	2.50	5.00	10.00
210	Shy One/Takin' Care of Business	1964	2.50	5.00	10.00
221	Such a Night/Bring It On Home to Me	1964	2.50	5.00	10.00
230	The Name Game/Whisper to the Wind	1964	3.00	6.00	12.00
230 [PS]	The Name Game/Whisper to the Wind	1964	5.00	10.00	20.00
234	The Clapping Song (Clap Pat Clap Slap)/This Is Beautiful	1965	2.50	5.00	10.00
234 [PS]	The Clapping Song (Clap Pat Clap Slap)/This Is Beautiful	1965	5.00	10.00	20.00
238	The Puzzle Song (A Puzzle in Song)/I See It, I Like It, I Want It	1965	2.50	5.00	10.00
246	I Never Will Forget/I Told You So	1965	2.50	5.00	10.00
251	One Sour Note/You Better Be Good, World	1965	2.50	5.00	10.00
260	Ever See a Diver Kiss His Wife While the Bubbles Bounce About Above the Water/Stardust	1965	2.50	5.00	10.00

Albums

Number	Title (A Side/B Side)	Yr	VG	VG+	NM
COLUMBIA					
CL 2679 [M]	Sugar, Let's Shing-a-Ling	1967	5.00	10.00	20.00
CS 9479 [S]	Sugar, Let's Shing-a-Ling	1967	6.25	12.50	25.00
CONGRESS					
CGL-3002 [M]	Shirley Ellis In Action	1964	6.25	12.50	25.00
CGS-3002 [S]	Shirley Ellis In Action	1964	7.50	15.00	30.00
CGL-3003 [M]	The Name Game	1965	6.25	12.50	25.00
CGS-3003 [S]	The Name Game	1965	7.50	15.00	30.00

ELLIS, STEVE, AND THE STARFIRES

Albums

Number	Title (A Side/B Side)	Yr	VG	VG+	NM
I.G.L.					
105	The Steve Ellis Songbook	1967	125.00	250.00	500.00

ELMER GANTRY'S VELVET OPERA

Albums

Number	Title (A Side/B Side)	Yr	VG	VG+	NM
EPIC					
BN 26415	Elmer Gantry's Velvet Opera	1968	12.50	25.00	50.00

EMANONS, THE

45s

Number	Title (A Side/B Side)	Yr	VG	VG+	NM
ABC-PARAMOUNT					
9913	Dear One/We Teenagers (Know What We Want)	1958	5.00	10.00	20.00
GEE					
1005	Change of Time/Hindu Baby	1956	30.00	60.00	120.00
JOSIE					
801	Blue Moon/Wish I Had My Baby	1956	25.00	50.00	100.00
WINLEY					
226	Dear One/We Teenagers (Know What We Want)	1958	10.00	20.00	40.00

EMBERS, THE

Several different groups.

45s

Number	Title (A Side/B Side)	Yr	VG	VG+	NM
ATLANTIC					
2627	Where Did I Go Wrong/You Got What You Want	1969	2.50	5.00	10.00
BELL					
664	It Ain't No Big Thing/It Ain't Necessary	1967	5.00	10.00	20.00
COLUMBIA					
40287	Sweet Lips/There'll Be No One Else But You	1954	10.00	20.00	40.00
DOT					
16101	Wait for Me/Couldn't Wait Any Longer	1960	3.75	7.50	15.00
16162	Please Mr. Sun/My Dearest Darling	1960	3.75	7.50	15.00
EMBER					
101	Sound of Love/Paradise Hill	1953	200.00	400.00	800.00
EMPRESS					
101	Solitaire/I'm Feeling All Right Again	1961	7.50	15.00	30.00
104	I Won't Cry Anymore/I Was Too Careful	1961	7.50	15.00	30.00
107	Abigail/I Was Too Careful	1962	7.50	15.00	30.00
108	What a Surprise/I Was Too Careful	1962	10.00	20.00	40.00
HERALD					
410	Sound of Love/Paradise Hill	1953	50.00	100.00	200.00
—Black label					
410	Sound of Love/Paradise Hill	1953	20.00	40.00	80.00
—Yellow label					
410	Sound of Love/Paradise Hill	1953	37.50	75.00	150.00
—Red vinyl					
JCP					
1008	In My Lonely Room/Good Good Lovin'	1964	15.00	30.00	60.00
LIBERTY					
55944	Evelyn/And Now I'm Blue	1967	2.50	5.00	10.00
MGM					
14167	Watch Out Girl/Far Away Places	1970	7.50	15.00	30.00
WYNNE					
101	Peter Gunn Cha Cha/Chinny Chin Cha Cha	1958	3.75	7.50	15.00

Albums

Number	Title (A Side/B Side)	Yr	VG	VG+	NM
JCP					
2006 [M]	The Embers Roll Eleven	1965	50.00	100.00	200.00
2009 [M]	Just for the Birds	1966	37.50	75.00	150.00

EMBRY, TED

45s

Number	Title (A Side/B Side)	Yr	VG	VG+	NM
ACCENT					
1057	New Shoes/Teen Age Confession	1958	15.00	30.00	60.00

EMERALDS, THE

Several different groups.

45s

Number	Title (A Side/B Side)	Yr	VG	VG+	NM
ABC-PARAMOUNT					
9889	You Belong to My Heart/The One I Adore	1958	6.25	12.50	25.00
9948	I'm Dreaming/Confess	1958	6.25	12.50	25.00
ALLIED					
10002	Sally Lou/Why Must I Wonder	1958	10.00	20.00	40.00
BOBBIN					
107	That's the Way It's Got to Be/Maria's Cha-Cha	1959	12.50	25.00	50.00
121	Lover's Cry/Rumblin' Tumblin' Baby	1960	10.00	20.00	40.00
JUBILEE					
5474	Dancing Alone/Wanna Make Him Mine	1964	3.00	6.00	12.00
5489	Did You Ever Love a Guy/I'm Gonna Ask That Boy to Dance	1964	3.00	6.00	12.00
KICKS					
3	Sally Lou/Why Must I Wonder	1954	175.00	350.00	700.00
KING					
6078	Baby You've Got Me/Promises	1967	6.25	12.50	25.00
MOONGLOW					
230	Ooh Poo Pah Doo/Sally's Snake	1964	7.50	15.00	30.00
232	Moonlight Surf/Little D Special	1964	7.50	15.00	30.00
—Black vinyl					
232	Moonlight Surf/Little D Special	1964	20.00	40.00	80.00
—Green vinyl					
REX					
1004	All the Time/Gotta Be on Time	1959	7.50	15.00	30.00
1013	I Kneel at Your Throne/Custer's Last Stand	1960	7.50	15.00	30.00
TOY					
7734	Silver/Roadrunner	1961	5.00	10.00	20.00
VENUS					
1002	Mademoiselle/The Lover	1959	25.00	50.00	100.00
1003	Marsha/You're Driving Me Crazy	1959	37.50	75.00	150.00
YALE					
232	The Web/Trapped	1960	5.00	10.00	20.00

EMERALS, THE

45s

Number	Title (A Side/B Side)	Yr	VG	VG+	NM
TRIPLE X					
100/101	Please Don't Crush My Dreams/Jukebox Rock	1960	150.00	300.00	600.00

EMERSON, BILLY

45s

Number	Title (A Side/B Side)	Yr	VG	VG+	NM
CHESS					
1711	Give Me a Little Love/Woodchuck	1959	5.00	10.00	20.00
1728	Holy Mackerel Baby/Believe Me	1959	5.00	10.00	20.00
1740	Uh Huh, My Baby/I'll Get to You	1959	5.00	10.00	20.00
CONSTELLATION					
148	Aunt Molly (Part 1)/Aunt Molly (Part 2)	1965	3.75	7.50	15.00
SUN					
195	No Teasin' Around/If Lovin' Is Believin'	1954	100.00	200.00	400.00
203	I'm Not Going Home/The Woodchuck	1954	200.00	400.00	600.00
214	Move, Baby, Move/When It Rains, It Pours	1955	12.50	25.00	50.00
219	Red Hot/No Greater Love	1955	25.00	50.00	100.00
233	Something for Nothing/Little Fine Healthy Thing	1956	12.50	25.00	50.00
VEE JAY					
219	Every Woman I Know/Tomorrow Never Comes	1956	7.50	15.00	30.00
247	Somebody Show Me/The Pleasure Is All Mine	1957	7.50	15.00	30.00
261	You Never Miss the Water/Do Yourself a Favor Billy	1957	7.50	15.00	30.00

EMERSON, LAKE AND PALMER

45s

Number	Title (A Side/B Side)	Yr	VG	VG+	NM
ATLANTIC					
3398	Fanfare for the Common Man/Brain Salad Surgery	1977	—	2.50	5.00
3555	All I Want Is You/Tiger in a Spotlight	1979	—	2.50	5.00
3641	Peter Gunn Theme/Tiger in a Spotlight	1980	—	2.50	5.00
COTILLION					
44106	Lucky Man/Knife's Edge	1971	—	3.00	6.00
44131	A Time and a Place/Stone of Years	1971	—	2.50	5.00
44151	Nutrocker/The Great Gates of Kiev	1972	—	2.50	5.00
44158	From the Beginning/Living Sin	1972	—	2.50	5.00
MANTICORE					
2003	Still...You Turn Me On/Brain Salad Surgery	1973	—	2.50	5.00
2003 [PS]	Still...You Turn Me On/Brain Salad Surgery	1973	2.50	5.00	10.00

Albums

Number	Title	Yr	VG	VG+	NM
ATLANTIC					
PR 277 [DJ]	Works Volume 1	1977	3.75	7.50	15.00
—Promo-only sampler					
PR 281 [DJ]	On Tour with Emerson, Lake and Palmer	1977	10.00	20.00	40.00
SD 7000 [(2)]	Works Volume 1	1977	3.75	7.50	15.00
SD 19120	Emerson, Lake and Palmer	1977	2.00	4.00	8.00
SD 19121	Tarkus	1977	2.00	4.00	8.00
SD 19122	Pictures at an Exhibition	1977	2.00	4.00	8.00
SD 19123	Trilogy	1977	2.00	4.00	8.00
SD 19124	Brain Salad Surgery	1977	2.00	4.00	8.00
SD 19147	Works Volume 2	1977	2.50	5.00	10.00
SD 19211	Love Beach	1978	2.50	5.00	10.00
SD 19255	Emerson, Lake and Palmer In Concert	1979	2.50	5.00	10.00
SD 19283	The Best of Emerson, Lake and Palmer	1980	2.50	5.00	10.00
COTILLION					
SD 9040	Emerson, Lake and Palmer	1971	3.00	6.00	12.00
SD 9900	Tarkus	1971	3.00	6.00	12.00
SD 9903	Trilogy	1972	3.00	6.00	12.00
ELP 66666	Pictures at an Exhibition	1971	3.00	6.00	12.00
SMAS-94773	Trilogy	1972	3.75	7.50	15.00
—Capitol Record Club edition					
MANTICORE					
SD 3-200 [(3)]	Welcome Back, My Friends, to the Show That Never Ends, Ladies and Gentlemen	1974	5.00	10.00	20.00
ELP 66669	Brain Salad Surgery	1973	3.00	6.00	12.00
MOBILE FIDELITY					
1-031	Pictures at an Exhibition	1980	7.50	15.00	30.00
—Audiophile vinyl					
1-203	Tarkus	1994	6.25	12.50	25.00
—Audiophile vinyl					
1-218	Trilogy	1994	10.00	20.00	40.00
—Audiophile vinyl					

EMERSON'S OLD-TIMEY CUSTARD-SUCKIN' BAND

Albums

Number	Title	Yr	VG	VG+	NM
ESP-DISK'					
2006	Emerson's Old-Timey Custard-Suckin' Band	1970	7.50	15.00	30.00

EMOTIONS, THE (1)

Female R&B vocal group.
Also see EARTH, WIND AND FIRE WITH THE EMOTIONS.

45s

Number	Title (A Side/B Side)	Yr	VG	VG+	NM
ARC					
18-02239	Turn It Out/When You Gonna Wake Up	1981	—	2.00	4.00
18-02535	Now That I Know/Here You Come Again	1981	—	2.00	4.00
11134	What's the Name of Your Love?/Layed Back	1979	—	2.50	5.00
11205	Where Is Your Love?/Layed Back	1980	—	2.50	5.00
COLUMBIA					
3-10347	Flowers/I Don't Wanna Lose Your Love	1976	—	2.50	5.00
3-10544	Best of My Love/A Feeling Is	1977	—	2.50	5.00
3-10622	Don't Ask My Neighbors/Love's What's Happenin'	1977	—	2.50	5.00
3-10791	Smile/Changes	1978	—	2.50	5.00
3-10828	Whole Lotta Shakin'/Time Is Passing By	1978	—	2.50	5.00
3-10874	Walking the Line/Ain't No Doubt About It	1978	—	2.50	5.00
MOTOWN					
1784	I Can't Wait to Make You Mine/I'm Gonna Miss Your Love	1985	—	2.00	4.00
1792	If I Only Knew Then (What I Know Now)/Eternally	1985	—	2.00	4.00
RED LABEL					
001-1	You're the One/I Can Do Anything	1984	—	2.50	5.00
001-2	You're the Best/(B-side unknown)	1984	—	2.50	5.00
001-3	Are You Through with My Heart/(B-side unknown)	1984	—	2.50	5.00
STAX					
1056	What Do The Lonely Do At Christmas?/Santa Claus Wants Some Lovin'	197?	—	3.00	6.00
—B-side by Albert King; reissue					
3200	Shouting Out Love/Baby, I'm Through	1977	—	2.50	5.00
3205	Baby, I'm Through/Any Way You Look at It	1978	—	2.50	5.00
3215	What Do the Lonely Do at Christmas/(Instrumental)	1978	—	2.50	5.00
TWIN STACKS					
126	Somebody New/Brushfire	1968	2.50	5.00	10.00
130	I Love You But I'll Leave You/Brushfire	1968	2.50	5.00	10.00
VOLT					
4010	So I Can Love You/Got to Be the Man	1969	2.00	4.00	8.00
4021	The Best Part of a Love Affair/I Like It	1969	2.00	4.00	8.00
4031	Stealing Love/When Tomorrow Comes	1970	2.00	4.00	8.00
4045	Heart Association/The Touch of Your Lips	1970	2.00	4.00	8.00
4053	Black Christmas/(Instrumental)	1970	2.50	5.00	10.00
4054	You Make Me Want to Love You/What You See Is What You Get	1971	—	3.50	7.00
4062	If You Think It/Love Ain't Easy One-Sided	1971	—	3.50	7.00
4066	Show Me How/Boss Love Maker	1971	—	3.50	7.00
4077	My Honey and Me/Blind Alley	1972	—	3.50	7.00
4083	I Could Never Be Happy/I've Fallen in Love	1972	—	3.50	7.00
4088	From Toys to Boys/I Call This Loving You	1972	—	3.50	7.00
4095	Runnin' Back (And Forth)/I Wanna Come Back	1973	—	3.50	7.00
4100	Peace Be Still/Runnin' Back (And Forth)	1973	—	3.50	7.00
4104	What Do the Lonely Do at Christmas/(Instrumental)	1973	2.00	4.00	8.00
4106	Put a Little Love Away/I Call This Loving You	1974	—	3.50	7.00
4110	Baby I'm Through/I Wanna Come Back	1974	—	3.50	7.00
4113	Any Way You Look At It/There Are More Questions Than Answers	1974	—	3.50	7.00

Albums

Number	Title	Yr	VG	VG+	NM
ARC					
JC 36149	Come Into Our World	1979	2.50	5.00	10.00
FC 37456	New Affair	1981	2.50	5.00	10.00
COLUMBIA					
PC 34163	Flowers	1976	2.50	5.00	10.00
—No bar code on cover					
PC 34163	Flowers	198?	2.00	4.00	8.00
—With bar code on cover					
PC 34762	Rejoice	1977	2.50	5.00	10.00
—No bar code on cover					
PC 34762	Rejoice	198?	2.00	4.00	8.00
—With bar code on cover					
JC 35385	Sunbeam	1978	2.50	5.00	10.00
MOTOWN					
6136 ML	If I Only Knew	1985	2.00	4.00	8.00
STAX					
STX-4100	Sunshine	1977	2.50	5.00	10.00
STX-4110	So I Can Love You	1978	2.50	5.00	10.00
—Reissue of Volt 6008					
STX-4112	Untouched	1978	2.50	5.00	10.00
—Reissue of Volt 6015					
STX-4121	Chronicle	1979	2.50	5.00	10.00
VOLT					
VOS-6008	So I Can Love You	1971	6.25	12.50	25.00
VOS-6015	Untouched	1972	6.25	12.50	25.00

EMOTIONS, THE (2)

Brooklyn-based male vocal group.

45s

Number	Title (A Side/B Side)	Yr	VG	VG+	NM
20TH FOX					
430	A Story Untold/One Life. One Love, One You	1963	5.00	10.00	20.00
452	Rainbow/Little Miss Blue	1963	5.00	10.00	20.00
478	Boomerang/I Love You Madly	1964	5.00	10.00	20.00
6623	Heart Strings/Every Time	1966	3.75	7.50	15.00
CALLA					
122	Baby I Need Your Lovin'/She's My Baby (I Just Can't Let Her Go)	1966	3.75	7.50	15.00
KAPP					
490	Echo/Come Dance Baby	1962	6.25	12.50	25.00
513	L-O-V-E/A Million Reasons	1963	6.25	12.50	25.00

EMOTIONS, THE (U)

It's unlikely than any of these are group (1). Some of these may be group (2). Others are different.

45s

Number	Title (A Side/B Side)	Yr	VG	VG+	NM
BRAINSTORM					
125	Can't Stand No More Heartaches/You'd Better Get Used to It	1968	2.00	4.00	8.00
129	Never Let Me Go/I Can't Control These Emotions	1968	2.00	4.00	8.00
CARD					
600	(By the Light of the) Silvery Moon/Do You Love Me	1962	37.50	75.00	150.00
FLIP					
356	I Ran to You/Keep Lookin' Your Way	1961	7.50	15.00	30.00
FURY					
1010	Candlelight/It's Love	1958	10.00	20.00	40.00
KARATE					
506	Hey Baby/I Wonder	1964	5.00	10.00	20.00
LAURIE					
3167	Fool's Paradise/Starlit Night	1963	5.00	10.00	20.00
VARDAN					
201	Love of a Girl/Do This for Me	1965	5.00	10.00	20.00

EMPERORS, THE (1)

Band from Harrisburg, Pa.

45s

Number	Title (A Side/B Side)	Yr	VG	VG+	NM
BRUNSWICK					
55333	Karate Boogaloo/Mumble Shing-a-Ling	1967	2.50	5.00	10.00
MALA					
543	Karate/I've Got to Have Her	1966	3.75	7.50	15.00

Number	Title (A Side/B Side)	Yr	VG	VG+	NM
554	My Baby Likes to Doogaloo/You Got Me Where You Want Me	1967	3.00	6.00	12.00
561	Searchin'/Lookin' for My Baby	1967	3.00	6.00	12.00

EMPERORS, THE (2)

Sometimes called "The Emperors with Rhythm."

45s

Number	Title (A Side/B Side)	Yr	VG	VG+	NM
HAVEN					
511	I May Be Wrong/Come Back, Come Back	1954	2000.	3000.	4000.

EMPERORS, THE (3)

45s

Number	Title (A Side/B Side)	Yr	VG	VG+	NM
OLIMPIC					
245	Darlin' in the Moonlight/Steve Allen	1964	10.00	20.00	40.00

EMPERORS, THE (4)

45s

Number	Title (A Side/B Side)	Yr	VG	VG+	NM
SABRA					
5555	I Want My Woman/(B-side unknown)	196?	10.00	20.00	40.00

EMPIRES, THE (1)

LES COOPER was a member of this group.

45s

Number	Title (A Side/B Side)	Yr	VG	VG+	NM
AMP 3					
132	If I'm a Fool/Zippety Zip	1957	25.00	50.00	100.00
HARLEM					
2325	Corn Whiskey/My Baby, My Baby	1954	100.00	200.00	400.00
2333	Magic Mirror/Make Me or Break Me	1955	100.00	200.00	400.00
WHIRLIN' DISC					
104	Linda/Whispering Heart	1957	17.50	35.00	70.00
WING					
90023	I Want to Know/Shirley	1955	12.50	25.00	50.00
90050	By the Riverside/Tell Me Pretty Baby	1956	10.00	20.00	40.00
90080	Don't Touch My Gal/My First Discovery	1956	10.00	20.00	40.00

EMPIRES, THE (2)

45s

Number	Title (A Side/B Side)	Yr	VG	VG+	NM
CALICO					
121	Definition of Love/Only in My Dreams	1960	5.00	10.00	20.00
CANDI					
1026	Love You So Bad/Come Back Girl	1962	6.25	12.50	25.00
1033	You're on Top, Girl/Slide On By	1963	10.00	20.00	40.00
CHAVIS					
1026	Love You So Bad/Come Back Girl	1962	3.75	7.50	15.00
COLPIX					
680	Everyone Knew But Me/Three Little Fishes	1963	5.00	10.00	20.00
DCP					
1116	Have Mercy/Love Is Strange	1964	3.00	6.00	12.00
LAKE					
711	Over the Summer Vacation/You're So Popular	1961	5.00	10.00	20.00

EMPIRES, THE (3)

Featuring David Blatt, later known as JAY BLACK of JAY AND THE AMERICANS.

45s

Number	Title (A Side/B Side)	Yr	VG	VG+	NM
EPIC					
5-9527	A Time and a Place/Punch Your Nose	1962	10.00	20.00	40.00

ENALOUISE AND THE HEARTS

45s

Number	Title (A Side/B Side)	Yr	VG	VG+	NM
ARGYLE					
1635	From a Cap and a Gown/A Prisoner to You	1959	12.50	25.00	50.00

ENCHANTERS, THE (1)

45s

Number	Title (A Side/B Side)	Yr	VG	VG+	NM
BALD EAGLE					
3001	Come On Baby, Let's Do the Stroll/Rock Around	1958	7.50	15.00	30.00
BAMBOO					
513	Touch of Love/Cafe Bohemian	1961	6.25	12.50	25.00
CANDELITE					
432	Oh Rose Marie/Bewildered	1964	3.00	6.00	12.00
EP-SOM					
103	I Need Your Love/Goddess of Love	1962	100.00	200.00	400.00
J.J. & M.					
1562	Oh Rose Marie/Bewildered	1962	50.00	100.00	200.00
MUSITRON					
1072	I Lied to My Heart/Talk While You Walk	1961	10.00	20.00	40.00
ORBIT					
532	Touch of Love/Cafe Bohemian	1959	12.50	25.00	50.00
SHARP					
105	We Make Mistakes/The Decision	1960	6.25	12.50	25.00
STARDUST					
102	Spellbound by the Moon/Know It All	1956	375.00	750.00	1500.

ENCHANTERS, THE (2)

Also see GARNET MIMMS AND THE ENCHANTERS.

45s

Number	Title (A Side/B Side)	Yr	VG	VG+	NM
LOMA					
2012	I Want to Be Loved/I Paid for the Party	1965	2.50	5.00	10.00
2035	You Were Meant to Be My Baby/God Bless the Girl, and Me	1966	2.50	5.00	10.00
2054	We Got Love/I've Lost All Communications	1966	2.50	5.00	10.00
WARNER BROS.					
5460	I Wanna Thank You/I'm a Good Man	1964	3.75	7.50	15.00

ENCHANTERS, THE (3)

45s

Number	Title (A Side/B Side)	Yr	VG	VG+	NM
CORAL					
61756	True Love Gone/Wait a Minute Baby	1956	15.00	30.00	60.00
61832	There Goes (A Pretty Girl)/Fan Me Baby	1957	20.00	40.00	80.00
	—Full-length version of A-side; matrix number is "100,974"				
61832	There Goes (A Pretty Girl)/Fan Me Baby	1957	6.25	12.50	25.00
	—Edited version of A-side; matrix number is "102,966"				
61916	Mambo Santa Mambo/Bottle Up and Go	1957	10.00	20.00	40.00
62373	True Love Gone/The Day	1963	5.00	10.00	20.00
65610	True Love Gone/Today Is Your Birthday	1963	3.00	6.00	12.00
MERCER					
992	True Love Gone/Wait a Minute Baby	1956	500.00	1000.	2000.

ENCHANTERS, THE (4)

45s

Number	Title (A Side/B Side)	Yr	VG	VG+	NM
JUBILEE					
5072	Today Is Your Birthday/How Could You	1952	62.50	125.00	250.00
5080	I've Lost/Housewife Blues	1952	50.00	100.00	200.00

ENCHANTERS, THE (U)

May be group (1); may be a fifth different group also.

45s

Number	Title (A Side/B Side)	Yr	VG	VG+	NM
TOM TOM					
301	Surf Blast/Tom Tiki	1963	12.50	25.00	50.00

ENCHANTMENTS, THE

45s

Number	Title (A Side/B Side)	Yr	VG	VG+	NM
FARO					
620	I'm in Love with Your Daughter/(B-side unknown)	1964	25.00	50.00	100.00
GONE					
5130	(I Love You) Sherry/Come On Home	1962	7.50	15.00	30.00
RITZ					
17003	I Love You Baby/Pains in My Heart	1963	25.00	50.00	100.00

ENCHORDS, THE

45s

Number	Title (A Side/B Side)	Yr	VG	VG+	NM
LAURIE					
3089	Zoom Zoom Zoom/I Need You Baby	1961	12.50	25.00	50.00

ENCORES, THE

More than one group.

45s

Number	Title (A Side/B Side)	Yr	VG	VG+	NM
BOW					
302	Barbara/Thank You	1958	25.00	50.00	100.00
CHECKER					
760	When I Look at You/Young Girls, Young Girls	1952	2000.	3000.	4000.
HOLLYWOOD					
1034	Time Is Moving On/Ha-Chi-Bi-Ri-Bi-Ri	1955	20.00	40.00	80.00
LOOK					
105	Time Is Moving On/Ha-Chi-Bi-Ri-Bi-Ri	1955	100.00	200.00	400.00
MGM					
11947	Chloe/Wa Va Ga Dot	1955	3.00	6.00	12.00

ENCOUNTERS, THE

45s

Number	Title (A Side/B Side)	Yr	VG	VG+	NM
SWAN					
4206	Don't Stop Now/Place in Your Heart	1964	37.50	75.00	150.00

END, THE

45s

Number	Title (A Side/B Side)	Yr	VG	VG+	NM
LONDON					
1016	Shades of Orange/Loving, Sacred Loving	1968	5.00	10.00	20.00
PHILIPS					
40323	Hey Little Girl/I Can't Get Any Joy	1965	2.50	5.00	10.00

Albums

Number	Title (A Side/B Side)	Yr	VG	VG+	NM
LONDON					
PS 560	Introspection	1969	12.50	25.00	50.00

ENDEAVORS, THE (1)

45s

Number	Title (A Side/B Side)	Yr	VG	VG+	NM
J&S					
254	Suffering with My Heart/I Got the Feeling	1960	300.00	600.00	1200.

ENDEAVORS, THE (2)

Country group.

45s

Number	Title (A Side/B Side)	Yr	VG	VG+	NM
STOP					
372	Shattered Dreams/I Know You Don't Want Me	1971	2.50	5.00	10.00

ENDORSERS, THE

45s

Number	Title (A Side/B Side)	Yr	VG	VG+	NM
MOON					
109	Crying/Hold My Hand	1959	500.00	1000.	2000.

ENEMYS, THE

With Cory Wells, later of THREE DOG NIGHT.

45s

Number	Title (A Side/B Side)	Yr	VG	VG+	NM
MGM					
13485	Glitter and Gold/Too Much Monkey Business	1966	3.75	7.50	15.00
13525	Hey Joe/My Dues Have Been Paid	1966	3.75	7.50	15.00
13573	Mo-Jo Woman/My Dues Have Been Paid	1966	3.75	7.50	15.00
VALIANT					
714	Say Goodbye to Donna/Sinner Man	1965	6.25	12.50	25.00
	—As "Corey Wells and the Enemys"				

ENGEL, SCOTT

Also see THE WALKER BROTHERS.

45s

Number	Title (A Side/B Side)	Yr	VG	VG+	NM
CHALLENGE					
9206	Devil Surfer/Your Guess	1963	5.00	10.00	20.00
LIBERTY					
55312	Mr. Jones/Anything Will Do	1961	5.00	10.00	20.00

Number	Title (A Side/B Side)	Yr	VG	VG+	NM
55428	Anything Will Do/Forever More	1962	5.00	10.00	20.00
MARTAY					
2004	Devil Surfer/Your Guess	1963	10.00	20.00	40.00
ORBIT					
506	The Livin' End/Good for Nothin'	1958	5.00	10.00	20.00
506 [PS]	The Livin' End/Good for Nothin'	1958	12.50	25.00	50.00
511	Charley Bop/All I Do Is Dream	1958	7.50	15.00	30.00
511 [PS]	Charley Bop/All I Do Is Dream	1958	15.00	30.00	60.00
512	Blue Bell/Paper Doll	1958	5.00	10.00	20.00
512 [PS]	Blue Bell/Paper Doll	1958	12.50	25.00	50.00
537	The Golden Rule/Sunday	1959	5.00	10.00	20.00
537 [PS]	The Golden Rule/Sunday	1959	12.50	25.00	50.00
545	Comin' Home/I Don't Wanna Know	1959	5.00	10.00	20.00
RKO UNIQUE					
386	Steady As a Rock/When Is a Boy a Man	1957	6.25	12.50	25.00

ENGEL, SCOTT, AND JOHN STEWART

See THE WALKER BROTHERS.

ENGLAND, BENNY

Number	Title (A Side/B Side)	Yr	VG	VG+	NM
45s					
SNAP					
400	Eloping/Some How	1958	75.00	150.00	300.00

ENGLAND DAN AND JOHN FORD COLEY

Also see SOUTHWEST F.O.B.

Number	Title (A Side/B Side)	Yr	VG	VG+	NM
45s					
A&M					
1278	New Jersey/Tell Her Hello	1971	—	3.00	6.00
1354	Casey/Simone	1972	—	2.50	5.00
1369	Carolina/Free the People	1972	—	2.50	5.00
1465	I Hear the Music/Miss You Song	1973	—	2.50	5.00
1871	I Hear the Music/Simone	1976	—	2.00	4.00
BIG TREE					
16069	I'd Really Love to See You Tonight/It's Not the Same	1976	—	2.00	4.00
16079	Nights Are Forever Without You/Showboat Gambler	1976	—	2.00	4.00
16088	It's Sad to Belong/The Time Has Come	1977	—	2.00	4.00
16102	Gone Too Far/Where Do I Go from Here	1977	—	2.00	4.00
16110	We'll Never Have to Say Goodbye Again/Calling for You Again	1978	—	2.00	4.00
16117	You Can't Dance/Wantin' You Desperately	1978	—	2.00	4.00
16125	If the World Ran Out of Love Tonight/Lovin' Somebody on a Rainy Night	1978	—	2.00	4.00
16130	Westward Wind/Some Things Don't Come Easy	1979	—	2.00	4.00
16131	Love Is the Answer/Running After You	1979	—	2.00	4.00
16135	Hollywood Heckle and Jive/Rolling Fever	1979	—	2.00	4.00
17000	What Can I Do with My Broken Heart/Caught Up in the Middle	1979	—	2.00	4.00
17002	In It for Love/Who's Lonely Now	1980	—	2.00	4.00
MCA					
51027	Part of Me, Part of You/Just Tell Me You Love Me	1980	—	2.00	4.00
Albums					
A&M					
SP-4305	England Dan and John Ford Coley	1971	3.75	7.50	15.00
SP-4350	Fables	1972	3.75	7.50	15.00
SP-4613	I Hear Music	1976	3.00	6.00	12.00
BIG TREE					
BT 76000	Dowdy Ferry Road	1977	2.50	5.00	10.00
BT 76006	Some Things Don't Come Easy	1978	2.50	5.00	10.00
BT 76015	Dr. Heckle & Mr. Jive	1979	2.50	5.00	10.00
BT 76018	Best of England Dan & John Ford Coley	1980	2.50	5.00	10.00
BT 89517	Nights Are Forever	1976	2.50	5.00	10.00

ENGLER, JERRY, AND THE FOUR EKKOS

Number	Title (A Side/B Side)	Yr	VG	VG+	NM
45s					
BRUNSWICK					
55037	Sputnik (Satellite Girl)/Unfaithful One	1957	20.00	40.00	80.00
—BUDDY HOLLY appears on this record					

ENGLISH, BARBARA

Also includes records as "Barbara Jean English." Also see THE FASHIONS (1).

Number	Title (A Side/B Side)	Yr	VG	VG+	NM
45s					
ALITHIA					
6040	I'm Living a Lie/All This	1972	—	3.00	6.00
6041	So Many Ways to Die/(B-side unknown)	1972	—	3.00	6.00
6042	I'm Sorry/Lil' Baby	1972	—	3.00	6.00
6046	Baby I'm-a Want You/Don't Make Me Over	1973	—	3.00	6.00
6053	You're Gonna Need Somebody to Love (While You're Looking for Someone to Love)/All This	1973	—	3.00	6.00
6059	Comin' or Goin'/Love's Arrangement	1973	—	3.00	6.00
6064	Breakin' Up a Happy Home/Guess Who	1974	—	3.00	6.00
AURORA					
155	Standin' on Tip-Toe/(You Got Me) Sittin' in the Corner	1965	20.00	40.00	80.00
MALA					
488	Easy Come, Easy Go/I Don't Deserve a Boy Like You	1964	6.25	12.50	25.00
REPRISE					
0290	I've Gotta Date/Shoo Fly	1964	6.25	12.50	25.00
0349	Small Town Girl/Tell It Like It Is	1965	6.25	12.50	25.00
ROULETTE					
4428	We Need Them/La-Ta-Tee-Ta-Ta	1962	7.50	15.00	30.00
4450	Fever/Bad News	1962	7.50	15.00	30.00
WARNER BROS.					
5685	All Because I Love Somebody/All the Good Times Are Gone	1965	5.00	10.00	20.00

ENGLISH, SCOTT

Number	Title (A Side/B Side)	Yr	VG	VG+	NM
45s					
DOT					
16099	White Cliffs of Dover/4000 Miles Away	1960	7.50	15.00	30.00
JANUS					
171	Brandy/Lead Me Back	1971	3.00	6.00	12.00
—A-side later recorded by Barry Manilow as "Mandy"					
192	Woman in My Life/Ballad of the Unloved	1972	—	2.50	5.00
JOKER					
777	Ugly Pills (You're Takin')/When	1962	12.50	25.00	50.00
SPOKANE					
4003	High on a Hill/When	1964	6.25	12.50	25.00
4007	Here Comes the Pain/All I Want Is You	1964	10.00	20.00	40.00
SULTAN					
1003	High on a Hill/When	1963	12.50	25.00	50.00

ENJOYABLES, THE

Number	Title (A Side/B Side)	Yr	VG	VG+	NM
45s					
CAPITOL					
5321	Push a Little Harder/We'll Make Our Way	1964	3.00	6.00	12.00
SHRINE					
118	Shame/(B-side unknown)	1966	100.00	200.00	400.00

ENNIS, ETHEL

Number	Title (A Side/B Side)	Yr	VG	VG+	NM
45s					
JUBILEE					
5236	I've Got You Under My Skin/You Better Go Now	1956	3.00	6.00	12.00
RCA VICTOR					
47-8379	The Boy from Ipanema/When Will the Hurt Be Over	1964	2.00	4.00	8.00
47-8448	Matchmaker, Matchmaker/Now I Have Everything	1964	2.00	4.00	8.00
47-8491	For a Short While/San Juan	1964	2.00	4.00	8.00
Albums					
BASF					
25121	10 Sides of Ethel Ennis	1973	3.75	7.50	15.00
CAPITOL					
T 941	Change of Scenery	1957	10.00	20.00	40.00
JUBILEE					
JLP-1021 [M]	Lullabies for Losers	1956	12.50	25.00	50.00
JLP-5024 [M]	Ethel Ennis Sings	1963	5.00	10.00	20.00
SJLP-5024 [S]	Ethel Ennis Sings	1963	6.25	12.50	25.00
RCA CAMDEN					
ACL1-0157	God Bless the Child	1973	2.50	5.00	10.00
RCA VICTOR					
LPM-2786 [M]	This Is Ethel Ennis	1964	5.00	10.00	20.00
LSP-2786 [S]	This Is Ethel Ennis	1964	6.25	12.50	25.00
LPM-2984 [M]	Eyes for You	1964	5.00	10.00	20.00
LSP-2984 [S]	Eyes for You	1964	6.25	12.50	25.00

ENO, BRIAN

Also see ROXY MUSIC.

Number	Title (A Side/B Side)	Yr	VG	VG+	NM
12-Inch Singles					
OPAL					
40539	Fractal Zoom (6 versions)/The Roll, The Choke	1992	2.00	4.00	8.00
45s					
ISLAND					
036	The Lion Sleeps Tonight/I'll Come Running (To Tie Your Shoes)	1975	6.25	12.50	25.00
036 [DJ]	The Lion Sleeps Tonight (mono/stereo)	1975	3.75	7.50	15.00
Albums					
ANTILLES					
AN-7001	No Pussyfooting	1973	3.75	7.50	15.00
—By Robert Fripp and Eno					
AN-7018	Evening Star	1975	3.00	6.00	12.00
—By Robert Fripp and Eno					
AN-7030	Discreet Music	1975	3.00	6.00	12.00
AN-7070	Music for Films	1978	3.75	7.50	15.00
EDITIONS EG					
ENO-1	Here Come the Warm Jets	1982	2.50	5.00	10.00
—Reissue					
EGBS-2 [(11)]	Working Backwards: 1983-1973	1984	15.00	30.00	60.00
—Boxed set of nine albums plus Music For Films II and Rarities 12"					
ENO-2	Taking Tiger Mountain (By Strategy)	1982	2.50	5.00	10.00
—Reissue					
ENO-3	Another Green World	1982	2.50	5.00	10.00
—Reissue					
ENO-4	Before and After Science	1982	2.50	5.00	10.00
—Reissue					
ENO-5	Apollo: Atmospheres and Soundtracks	1983	2.50	5.00	10.00
EGED-20	Ambient 4 — On Land	1982	2.50	5.00	10.00
EGED-37	The Pearl	1984	3.00	6.00	12.00
—By Harold Budd and Brian Eno					
EGS-102	No Pussyfooting	1982	2.50	5.00	10.00
—By Robert Fripp and Eno; reissue					
EGS-103	Evening Star	1982	2.50	5.00	10.00
—By Robert Fripp and Eno; reissue					
EGS-105	Music for Films	1982	2.50	5.00	10.00
—Reissue					
EGS-107	Fourth World Volume 1: Possible Musics	1980	3.00	6.00	12.00
—With Jon Hassell					
EGS-201	Ambient #1 — Music for Airports	1982	3.00	6.00	12.00
—Reissue					
EGS-202	Ambient 2 — The Plateaux of Mirrors	1982	3.00	6.00	12.00
—By Harold Budd and Brian Eno					
EGS-301	Pavilion of Dreams	1982	3.00	6.00	12.00
—By Harold Budd and Brian Eno					
EGS-303	Discreet Music	1983	3.00	6.00	12.00
—Reissue					
ISLAND					
ILPS 9268	Here Come the Warm Jets	1973	3.00	6.00	12.00

Number	Title (A Side/B Side)	Yr	VG	VG+	NM
ILPS 9309	Taking Tiger Mountain (By Strategy)	1974	3.00	6.00	12.00
ILPS 9351	Another Green World	1975	3.00	6.00	12.00
ILPS 9478	Before and After Science	1977	3.00	6.00	12.00
—Double the value if four lithographs are included with the package.					
JEM					
ENO DJ [DJ]	Music for Airplay	1981	12.50	25.00	50.00
—Promo-only 10-track sampler					
OPAL/WARNER BROS.					
25769	Music for Films, Vol. III	1988	2.50	5.00	10.00
26421	Wrong Way Up	1990	2.50	5.00	10.00
—With John Cale					
PVC					
7908	Ambient #1 — Music for Airports	1979	3.00	6.00	12.00

ENTWISTLE, JOHN

Also see THE WHO.

Number	Title (A Side/B Side)	Yr	VG	VG+	NM
45s					
ATCO					
7337	Too Late the Hero/Dancin' Master	1981	—	2.00	4.00
7344	Talk Dirty/Try Me	1982	—	2.00	4.00
DECCA					
32896	I Believe in Everything/My Size	1971	—	3.00	6.00
33052	I Wonder/Who Cares	1973	—	3.00	6.00
TRACK					
40066	Made in Japan/Roller Skate Kate	1973	—	2.50	5.00
Albums					
ATCO					
SD 38-142	Too Late the Hero	1981	2.50	5.00	10.00
DECCA					
DL 79183	Smash Your Head Against the Wall	1971	6.25	12.50	25.00
MCA					
2024	Smash Your Head Against the Wall	1973	3.00	6.00	12.00
—Reissue of Decca 79183					
TRACK					
MCA-321	Rigor Mortis Sets In	1973	3.75	7.50	15.00
L33-1926 [DJ]	Who's Ox	1975	12.50	25.00	50.00
—Promo-only sampler					
MCA-2129	Mad Dog	1975	3.75	7.50	15.00
DL 79190	Whistle Rymes	1972	6.25	12.50	25.00

EPISODE SIX

Number	Title (A Side/B Side)	Yr	VG	VG+	NM
45s					
CHAPTER ONE					
2902	Lucky Sunday/Mr. Universe	1968	3.00	6.00	12.00
COMPASS					
7007	Morning Dew/Sunshine Girl	1967	3.75	7.50	15.00
ELEKTRA					
45617	Baby, Baby, Baby/Love-Hate-Revenge	1967	3.75	7.50	15.00
WARNER BROS.					
5851	Here, There and Everywhere/Mighty Morris Ten	1966	3.75	7.50	15.00

EPISODES, THE

Number	Title (A Side/B Side)	Yr	VG	VG+	NM
45s					
FOUR SEASONS					
1014	The Christmas Tree/Where Is My Love	1965	37.50	75.00	150.00

EPPS, PRESTON

Number	Title (A Side/B Side)	Yr	VG	VG+	NM
45s					
ADMIRAL					
901	Bongo Express/Flamenco Bongo	1963	3.75	7.50	15.00
DONNA					
1367	Mister Bongo/B'Wana Bongo	1962	3.75	7.50	15.00
EMBASSY					
203	Rockin' in the Congo/Sing Donna Go	1961	3.75	7.50	15.00
JO JO					
106	Afro Mania/Love Is the Only Good Thing	1969	—	3.00	6.00
MAJESTY					
1300	Bongo Boogie/Flamenco Bongo	1962	3.75	7.50	15.00
ORIGINAL SOUND					
4 [M]	Bongo Rock/Bongo Party	1959	5.00	10.00	20.00
4 [S]	Bongo Rock/Bongo Party	1959	12.50	25.00	50.00
9	Bongo, Bongo, Bongo/Hully Gully Bongo	1960	5.00	10.00	20.00
14	Bongo Shuffle/Bongo in the Congo	1960	3.75	7.50	15.00
17	Bongo Rocket/Jungle Drums	1961	3.75	7.50	15.00
POLO					
218	Bongo Rock 1965/Bongo Waltz	1965	3.00	6.00	12.00
TOP RANK					
2067	Blue Bongo/Bongola	1960	3.75	7.50	15.00
2091	Bongo Hop/Caravan	1960	3.75	7.50	15.00
7-Inch Extended Plays					
ORIGINAL SOUND					
EP 1001	Bongo Rock/Doin' the Cha Cha Cha//Bongos in Pastel/Bongo Party	1959	10.00	20.00	40.00
EP 1001 [PS]	Bongo Rock	1959	10.00	20.00	40.00
Albums					
ORIGINAL SOUND					
LPM-5002 [M]	Bongo, Bongo, Bongo	1960	12.50	25.00	50.00
LPM-5009 [M]	Surfin' Bongos	1963	10.00	20.00	40.00
LPS-8851 [S]	Bongo, Bongo, Bongo	1960	20.00	40.00	80.00
LPS-8872 [S]	Surfin' Bongos	1963	12.50	25.00	50.00
TOP RANK					
RM-349 [M]	Bongola	1961	10.00	20.00	40.00
RS-349 [S]	Bongola	1961	12.50	25.00	50.00

EQUADORS, THE

Number	Title (A Side/B Side)	Yr	VG	VG+	NM
45s					
ARGO					
5353	Say You'll Be Mine/Let Me Sleep, Woman	1959	15.00	30.00	60.00
MIRACLE					
7	You're My Desire/Someone to Call My Own	1961	37.50	75.00	150.00

EQUALLOS, THE

Number	Title (A Side/B Side)	Yr	VG	VG+	NM
45s					
M&M					
1296	Beneath the Sun/In Between Tears	1962	375.00	750.00	1500.

EQUALS, THE

Number	Title (A Side/B Side)	Yr	VG	VG+	NM
45s					
BANG					
582	Ain't Got Nothing to Give You/Black Skin, Blue Eyed Boys	1971	2.50	5.00	10.00
PRESIDENT					
103	Fire/I Won't Be There	1967	3.00	6.00	12.00
105	My Life Ain't Easy/You Got Too Many Boyfriends	1967	3.00	6.00	12.00
108	Giddy Up a Ding-Dong/I Get So Excited	1968	3.00	6.00	12.00
109	Lovely Rita/Softly, Softly	1968	3.00	6.00	12.00
110	Honey Gun/Michael and the Slipper Tree	1968	3.00	6.00	12.00
111	I Can't Let You Go/Viva Bobby Joe	1969	3.00	6.00	12.00
RCA VICTOR					
47-9186	Baby Come Back/Hold Me Closer	1967	3.75	7.50	15.00
47-9583	Baby Come Back/Hold Me Closer	1968	2.50	5.00	10.00
SHOUT					
247	Ain't Got Nothing to Give You/Black Skin, Blue Eyed Boys	1970	3.00	6.00	12.00
Albums					
LAURIE					
LLP-2045 [M]	Unequalled	1967	6.25	12.50	25.00
SLP-2045 [S]	Unequalled	1967	7.50	15.00	30.00
PRESIDENT					
PTL-1015	Equal Sensation	1968	6.25	12.50	25.00
PTL-1020	The Sensational Equals	1968	6.25	12.50	25.00
PTL-1025	Equals Supreme	1968	6.25	12.50	25.00
PTL-1030	Strikeback	1969	6.25	12.50	25.00
RCA VICTOR					
LSP-4078	Baby Come Back	1968	6.25	12.50	25.00

EQUIPE 84

Number	Title (A Side/B Side)	Yr	VG	VG+	NM
45s					
IMPERIAL					
66266	The Twenty-Ninth of September/Auschwitz	1967	5.00	10.00	20.00

ERICA

Number	Title (A Side/B Side)	Yr	VG	VG+	NM
Albums					
ESP-DISK'					
1099	You Used to Think	1968	15.00	30.00	60.00

ERLENE AND HER GIRLFRIENDS

Number	Title (A Side/B Side)	Yr	VG	VG+	NM
45s					
OLD TOWN					
1150	A Guy Is a Guy/My Dada Say	1963	5.00	10.00	20.00
1152	Because of You/Casanova	1963	5.00	10.00	20.00

ERMINES, THE

See CORNEL GUNTER.

ERNIE AND THE EMPERORS

Number	Title (A Side/B Side)	Yr	VG	VG+	NM
45s					
REPRISE					
0414	Got a Lot I Want to Say/Meet Me at the Corner	1965	7.50	15.00	30.00

ERVIN, SENATOR SAM

Number	Title (A Side/B Side)	Yr	VG	VG+	NM
45s					
COLUMBIA					
4-45956	Bridge Over Troubled Water/Zeke and the Snake	1973	—	3.00	6.00
Albums					
COLUMBIA					
KC 32756	Senator Sam at Home	1973	6.25	12.50	25.00

ERVIN SISTERS, THE

Number	Title (A Side/B Side)	Yr	VG	VG+	NM
45s					
TRI PHI					
1014	Changing Baby/Do It Right	1962	15.00	30.00	60.00
1022	Every Day's a Holiday/Why I Love Him	1963	20.00	40.00	80.00

ERWIN, DEE

See BIG DEE IRWIN.

ESCORTS, THE (1)

Group from Rahway State Prison in New Jersey.

Number	Title (A Side/B Side)	Yr	VG	VG+	NM
45s					
ALITHIA					
6048	All We Need (Is Another Chance) (Short)/All We Need (Is Another Chance) (Long)	1973	—	3.00	6.00
6052	Look Over Your Shoulder/By the Time I Get to Phoenix	1973	—	2.50	5.00
6055	I'll Be Sweeter Tomorrow/I'm So Glad I Found You	1973	—	2.50	5.00
6062	Disrespect Can Wreck/All We Need	1974	—	2.50	5.00
6066	Let's Make Love (At Home Sometime)/Within Without	1974	—	2.50	5.00
Albums					
ALITHIA					
9104	All We Need Is One More Chance	1973	3.75	7.50	15.00
9106	Three Down and Four to Go	1974	3.75	7.50	15.00

ESCORTS, THE (2)

Number	Title (A Side/B Side)	Yr	VG	VG+	NM
45s					
CORAL					
62302	Gloria/Seven Wonders of the World	1961	10.00	20.00	40.00
62317	As I Love You/Gaudeamus	1962	10.00	20.00	40.00

Number	Title (A Side/B Side)	Yr	VG	VG+	NM
62336	Somewhere/Submarine Race Watching	1962	6.25	12.50	25.00
62349	One Hand. One Heart/I Can't Be Free	1963	6.25	12.50	25.00
62372	Back Home Again/Something Has Changed Him	1963	6.25	12.50	25.00
—As "Goldie and the Escorts"					
62385	Give Me Tomorrow/My Heart Cries for You	1963	6.25	12.50	25.00

ESCORTS, THE (3)

British group.

45s

Number	Title (A Side/B Side)	Yr	VG	VG+	NM
FONTANA					
1512	Come On Home Baby/She Gets No Loving	1965	3.75	7.50	15.00
1912	Dizzy Miss Lizzy/All I Want Is You	1964	3.75	7.50	15.00

ESCORTS, THE (4)

Albums

Number	Title (A Side/B Side)	Yr	VG	VG+	NM
TEO					
LPM-5000 [M]	The Escorts Bring Down the House	1966	30.00	60.00	120.00

ESCORTS, THE (U)

None of these are group (1) or (3). Some could be group (2) or (4). More likely, they are more than one other group.

45s

Number	Title (A Side/B Side)	Yr	VG	VG+	NM
BOOMERANG					
621	Little Big Horn/Wiped Out	1962	10.00	20.00	40.00
JUDD					
1014	My First Year/Clap Happy	1959	3.75	7.50	15.00
RCA VICTOR					
47-6834	Bad Boy/Tore Up Over You	1957	3.75	7.50	15.00
47-6963	So Hard to Laugh, So Easy to Cry/Lonely Man	1957	3.75	7.50	15.00
47-8228	You Can't Even Be My Friend/Itchy Coo	1963	3.00	6.00	12.00
47-8327	The Hurt/No City Folks Allowed	1964	3.00	6.00	12.00
SCARLET					
4005	I Will Be Home Again/Leaky Heart and His Red Go-Kart	1960	15.00	30.00	60.00
SCEPTER					
1201	Why Why Why/Ugly Duckling	1958	10.00	20.00	40.00
—With Don Crawford					
SOMA					
1144	Main Drag/Judy or Jo Ann	1961	6.25	12.50	25.00

ESQUERITA

45s

Number	Title (A Side/B Side)	Yr	VG	VG+	NM
CAPITOL					
F4007	Please Come On Home/Oh Baby	1958	7.50	15.00	30.00
F4058	Rockin' the Joint/Esquerita and the Voola	1958	7.50	15.00	30.00
F4145	Laid Off/Just Another Lie	1959	7.50	15.00	30.00

Albums

Number	Title (A Side/B Side)	Yr	VG	VG+	NM
CAPITOL					
T 1186 [M]	Esquerita	1959	250.00	500.00	1000.

ESQUIRES, THE (1)

Milwaukee-based R&B group.

45s

Number	Title (A Side/B Side)	Yr	VG	VG+	NM
BUNKY					
7750	Get On Up/Listen to Me	1967	2.50	5.00	10.00
7752	And Get Away/Everybody's Laughin'	1967	2.50	5.00	10.00
7753	You Say/State Fair	1968	2.50	5.00	10.00
7755	Why Can't I Stop/The Feeling's Gone	1968	2.50	5.00	10.00
7756	How Could It Be/I Know I Can	1968	2.50	5.00	10.00
CAPITOL					
2650	Reach Out/Listen to Me	1969	2.00	4.00	8.00
CIGAR MAN					
79880	The Show Ain't Over/What Good Is Music?	1980	—	3.00	6.00
JU-PAR					
104	Get On Up '76/Feeling's Gone (Also Known As Disco Dancing)	1976	—	3.00	6.00
LAMARR					
1001	Girls in the City/Ain't Gonna Give It Up	1971	2.00	4.00	8.00
SCEPTER					
12232	You've Got the Power/No Doubt About It	1968	—	—	—
—Unreleased? (Possibly reassigned to Wand?)					
WAND					
1193	You've Got the Power/No Doubt About It	1968	2.00	4.00	8.00
1195	I Don't Know/Part Angel	1969	2.00	4.00	8.00
11201	Whip It On Me/It Was Yesterday	1969	2.00	4.00	8.00

Albums

Number	Title (A Side/B Side)	Yr	VG	VG+	NM
BUNKY					
300	Get On Up and Get Away	1968	8.75	17.50	35.00

ESQUIRES, THE (2)

45s

Number	Title (A Side/B Side)	Yr	VG	VG+	NM
ARGO					
5435	Boat of Love/With a Feeling	1963	5.00	10.00	20.00

ESQUIRES, THE (3)

45s

Number	Title (A Side/B Side)	Yr	VG	VG+	NM
EPIC					
5-9024	If You Only Knew What a Three-Cent Stamp Can Do/Now, Now, Now	1954	375.00	750.00	1500.
—This may not exist on 45, though it certainly should.					
HI-PO					
1003	Only the Angels Know/One Word for This	1955	500.00	1000.	2000.

ESQUIRES, THE (U)

None of these are groups (1) or (3), but they may not all be the same group, either.

45s

Number	Title (A Side/B Side)	Yr	VG	VG+	NM
COLUMBIA					
4-43815	It's a Dirty Shame/Love Hides a Multitude of Sins	1966	5.00	10.00	20.00
DOT					
16954	Misfortune/She's My Woman	1966	3.75	7.50	15.00
DURCO					
1001	Flashin' Red/What a Burn	1964	10.00	20.00	40.00
TOWER					
174	Love's Made a Fool of You/Summertime	1965	3.75	7.50	15.00

ESQUIVEL

45s

Number	Title (A Side/B Side)	Yr	VG	VG+	NM
RCA VICTOR					
47-5969	Beasme Mucho/Vereda Tropical	1954	5.00	10.00	20.00
—As "Juan Garcia Esquivel"					
47-6008	Nocturnal/Amor	1955	5.00	10.00	20.00
47-6496	Nightingale/Jungle Drums	1956	3.75	7.50	15.00
47-6514	Port Au Prince/To Love Again	1956	3.75	7.50	15.00
47-7316	That Old Black Magic/Cielito Lindo	1958	3.75	7.50	15.00
47-7360	It Had to Be You/Begin the Beguine	1958	3.75	7.50	15.00
47-7361	Night and Day/Ballerina	1958	3.75	7.50	15.00
47-7462	I Feel Merely Marvelous/Whatchamacallit	1959	3.75	7.50	15.00

Albums

Number	Title (A Side/B Side)	Yr	VG	VG+	NM
BAR NONE					
LP-043	Space Age Bachelor Pad Music	1994	3.00	6.00	12.00
LP-056	Music for a Sparkling Planet	1995	3.00	6.00	12.00
RCA VICTOR					
LPM-1345 [M]	To Love Again	1957	12.50	25.00	50.00
LPM-1749 [M]	Four Corners of the World	1958	6.25	12.50	25.00
LSP-1749 [S]	Four Corners of the World	1958	12.50	25.00	50.00
LPM-1753 [M]	Other Worlds, Other Sounds	1959	6.25	12.50	25.00
LSP-1753 [S]	Other Worlds, Other Sounds	1959	12.50	25.00	50.00
LPM-1978 [M]	Exploring New Sounds in Hi-Fi	1959	7.50	15.00	30.00
LSP-1978 [S]	Exploring New Sounds in Hi-Fi	1959	15.00	30.00	60.00
LPM-1988 [M]	Strings Aflame	1959	6.25	12.50	25.00
LSP-1988 [S]	Strings Aflame	1959	12.50	25.00	50.00
LPM-2225 [M]	Infinity in Sound	1960	7.50	15.00	30.00
LSP-2225 [S]	Infinity in Sound	1960	15.00	30.00	60.00
LPM-2296 [M]	Infinity in Sound, Vol. 2	1961	7.50	15.00	30.00
LSP-2296 [S]	Infinity in Sound, Vol. 2	1961	15.00	30.00	60.00
LPM-2418 [M]	Latin-esque	1962	5.00	10.00	20.00
LSP-2418 [S]	Latin-esque	1962	15.00	30.00	60.00
—Die-cut cover that reveals inner sleeve					
LSP-2418 [S]	Latin-esque	1962	10.00	20.00	40.00
—Standard cover					
LPM-3502 [M]	The Best of Esquivel	1966	5.00	10.00	20.00
LSP-3502 [S]	The Best of Esquivel	1966	7.50	15.00	30.00
LPM-3697 [M]	The Genius of Esquivel	1967	5.00	10.00	20.00
LSP-3697 [S]	The Genius of Esquivel	1967	7.50	15.00	30.00
REPRISE					
P9-6046 [S]	More of Other World, Other Sounds	1962	7.50	15.00	30.00
R-6046 [M]	More of Other World, Other Sounds	1962	6.25	12.50	25.00

ESSEX, DAVID

45s

Number	Title (A Side/B Side)	Yr	VG	VG+	NM
COLUMBIA					
10005	America/Dance Little Girl	1974	—	2.50	5.00
10005 [PS]	America/Dance Little Girl	1974	2.00	4.00	8.00
10039	Gonna Make You a Star/Window	1974	—	2.50	5.00
10183	Rolling Stone/Coconut Ice	1975	—	2.50	5.00
10183 [PS]	Rolling Stone/Coconut Ice	1975	2.00	4.00	8.00
10256	Good Ol' Rock 'N' Roll/Hold Me Close	1975	—	2.50	5.00
45940	Rock On/On and On	1973	—	2.50	5.00
45940 [PS]	Rock On/On and On	1973	2.50	5.00	10.00
46041	Lamplight/We're All Insane	1974	—	2.50	5.00
46041 [PS]	Lamplight/We're All Insane	1974	2.50	5.00	10.00
RSO					
1006	Oh What a Circus (From Evita)/Ships That Pass in the Night	1979	—	2.00	4.00
UNI					
55020	She's Leaving Home/He's a Better Man Than Me	1967	2.50	5.00	10.00

Albums

Number	Title (A Side/B Side)	Yr	VG	VG+	NM
COLUMBIA					
CQ 32560 [Q]	Rock On	1974	7.50	15.00	30.00
KC 32560	Rock On	1974	5.00	10.00	20.00
KC 33289	David Essex	1974	3.75	7.50	15.00
PC 33813	All the Fun of the Fair	1975	3.75	7.50	15.00
MERCURY					
812936-1	David Essex	1983	3.75	7.50	15.00

ESSEX, THE

Also see ANITA HUMES.

45s

Number	Title (A Side/B Side)	Yr	VG	VG+	NM
BANG					
537	The Eagle/Moonlight, Music, and You	1966	2.00	4.00	8.00
ROULETTE					
4494	Easier Said Than Done/Are You Going My Way	1963	3.75	7.50	15.00
4515	A Walkin' Miracle/What I Don't Know Won't Hurt Me	1963	3.75	7.50	15.00
4530	She's Got Everything/Out of Sight, Out of Mind	1964	2.50	5.00	10.00
4542	What Did I Do/Curfew Lover	1964	2.50	5.00	10.00

Albums

Number	Title (A Side/B Side)	Yr	VG	VG+	NM
ROULETTE					
R-25234 [M]	Easier Said Than Done	1963	10.00	20.00	40.00
SR-25234 [S]	Easier Said Than Done	1963	12.50	25.00	50.00
R-25235 [M]	A Walkin' Miracle	1963	10.00	20.00	40.00
SR-25235 [S]	A Walkin' Miracle	1963	12.50	25.00	50.00
R-25246 [M]	Young and Lively	1964	10.00	20.00	40.00
SR-25246 [S]	Young and Lively	1964	12.50	25.00	50.00

ESTABLISHMENT, THE

45s

Number	Title (A Side/B Side)	Yr	VG	VG+	NM
KING					
6320	In My Heart I Am a Free Man/Stop Fightin' Start Lovin'	1970	—	3.00	6.00
6349	House of Jack/Why Is She All I See	1971	—	3.00	6.00

Number	Title (A Side/B Side)	Yr	VG	VG+	NM
Albums					
KING					
KS-1123	The Establishment	1971	3.00	6.00	12.00

ESTELLE

Estelle Bennett, formerly of THE RONETTES.

Number	Title (A Side/B Side)	Yr	VG	VG+	NM
45s					
LAURIE					
3449	The Year 2000/The Naked Boy	1968	25.00	50.00	100.00

ESTRADA, ROY, AND THE ROCKETEERS

Number	Title (A Side/B Side)	Yr	VG	VG+	NM
45s					
KING					
5368	Jungle Dream (Part 1)/Jungle Dream (Part 2)	1960	12.50	25.00	50.00

ETERNALS, THE (1)

Number	Title (A Side/B Side)	Yr	VG	VG+	NM
45s					
HOLLYWOOD					
68	Rockin' in the Jungle/Rock and Roll Cha Cha	1959	15.00	30.00	60.00
—White label					
68	Rockin' in the Jungle/Rock and Roll Cha Cha	1959	10.00	20.00	40.00
—Blue label					
68	Rockin' in the Jungle/Rock and Roll Cha Cha	1959	5.00	10.00	20.00
—Yellow label					
70	Babalu's Wedding Day/My Girl	1959	12.50	25.00	50.00
—Red label					
70	Babalu's Wedding Day/My Girl	1959	6.25	12.50	25.00
—Blue label					
WARWICK					
611	Blind Date/Today	1961	5.00	10.00	20.00

ETERNALS, THE (2)

Number	Title (A Side/B Side)	Yr	VG	VG+	NM
45s					
QUALITY					
1902	Falling Tears/Sticks and Stones	1968	5.00	10.00	20.00

ETERNITY'S CHILDREN

Number	Title (A Side/B Side)	Yr	VG	VG+	NM
45s					
A&M					
866	Rumors/Wait and See	1967	2.50	5.00	10.00
LIBERTY					
56162	Alone Again/From You Unto Us	1970	2.00	4.00	8.00
TOWER					
416	Mrs. Bluebird/Little Boy	1968	2.50	5.00	10.00
416 [PS]	Mrs. Bluebird/Little Boy	1968	6.25	12.50	25.00
439	Rupert White/Sunshine Among Us	1968	2.50	5.00	10.00
449	Till I Hear from You/I Wanna Be with You	1968	2.50	5.00	10.00
476	Sidewalks of the Ghetto/Look Away	1969	2.50	5.00	10.00
498	Blue Horizon/Lifetime Day	1969	2.50	5.00	10.00
Albums					
TOWER					
ST-5123	Eternity's Children	1968	6.25	12.50	25.00
ST-5144	Timeless	1969	7.50	15.00	30.00

ETTA AND HARVEY

Also see HARVEY; ETTA JAMES.

Number	Title (A Side/B Side)	Yr	VG	VG+	NM
45s					
CHESS					
1760	If I Can't Have You/My Heart Cries	1960	6.25	12.50	25.00
1771	Spoonful/It's a Crying Shame	1960	6.25	12.50	25.00

ETZEL, ROY

Number	Title (A Side/B Side)	Yr	VG	VG+	NM
45s					
HICKORY					
1197	I Can't Stop Loving You/I Hate to Love You	1963	2.00	4.00	8.00
MGM					
13381	Melancholy/The Silence	1965	2.00	4.00	8.00
13801	Mexican Holiday/Vaya Con Dios	1967	2.00	4.00	8.00
PRESIDENT					
820	Tell Laura I Love Her/Reach for the Stars	1961	2.50	5.00	10.00
TIME					
1029	Jenny Oh Jenny/Apache Blues	1961	2.50	5.00	10.00

EUPHONIOUS WAIL

Number	Title (A Side/B Side)	Yr	VG	VG+	NM
Albums					
KAPP					
KS-3668	Euphonious Wail	1973	10.00	20.00	40.00

EUPHORIA (1)

Number	Title (A Side/B Side)	Yr	VG	VG+	NM
45s					
BAND BOX					
393	Somebody Listen/Dedication of Sally and Cher	196?	7.50	15.00	30.00
MAINSTREAM					
655	Hungry Women/No Me Tomorrow	1967	5.00	10.00	20.00

EUPHORIA (2)

Number	Title (A Side/B Side)	Yr	VG	VG+	NM
45s					
HERITAGE					
831	You Must Forget/(B-side unknown)	1971	3.00	6.00	12.00
Albums					
HERITAGE					
HTS 35005	Euphoria	1971	7.50	15.00	30.00

EUPHORIA (3)

Number	Title (A Side/B Side)	Yr	VG	VG+	NM
Albums					
CAPITOL					
SKAO-363	A Gift from Euphoria	1969	30.00	60.00	120.00

EUPHORIA (4)

Number	Title (A Side/B Side)	Yr	VG	VG+	NM
Albums					
RAINBOW					
1003	Lost in a Trance	1973	75.00	150.00	300.00

EVANS, BARBARA

Number	Title (A Side/B Side)	Yr	VG	VG+	NM
45s					
RCA VICTOR					
47-7519	Souvenirs/Play for Me, Mother	1959	5.00	10.00	20.00
47-7576	Oo La La La La/The Little Girl Cried	1959	5.00	10.00	20.00
47-7634	Beatnik Daddy/A Game of Poker	1959	5.00	10.00	20.00

EVANS, MAUREEN

Number	Title (A Side/B Side)	Yr	VG	VG+	NM
45s					
COLUMBIA					
43189	Get Away/I've Often Wondered	1964	2.50	5.00	10.00
43354	Never Let Me Go/Poco Sole	1965	2.50	5.00	10.00
DOT					
16678	Time and Time Again/Tomorrow Is Another Day	1964	2.50	5.00	10.00
LITTLE DARLIN'					
0019	Touch My Heart/(B-side unknown)	1967	2.50	5.00	10.00
LONDON INT'L.					
10407	Like I Do/Starlight, Starbright	1963	3.00	6.00	12.00
10409	Melancholy Me/Pick the Petals	1963	3.00	6.00	12.00

EVANS, PAUL

Number	Title (A Side/B Side)	Yr	VG	VG+	NM
45s					
ATCO					
6138	At My Party/Beat Generation	1959	3.75	7.50	15.00
6170	Long Gone/Mickey, My Love	1960	3.75	7.50	15.00
BIG TREE					
16050	Happy Birthday, America/You Made Me Over	1975	—	2.50	5.00
CARLTON					
539	Show Folk/I Love to Make Love to You	1961	3.75	7.50	15.00
543	After the Hurricane/Not Me	1961	3.75	7.50	15.00
554	Just Because I Love You/This Pullover	1961	3.75	7.50	15.00
558	Over the Mountain, Across the Sea/Sisal Twine	1961	3.75	7.50	15.00
COLUMBIA					
44472	One Red Rose/Bound to Silence	1968	—	3.00	6.00
DECCA					
30680	I Think About You All the Time/Oh No	1958	5.00	10.00	20.00
DOT					
17463	That's What Loving You Is All About/Do You Remember	1973	—	2.50	5.00
EPIC					
9726	Bewitched/I Think I'm Gonna Kill Myself	1964	2.50	5.00	10.00
—By Paul & Mimi Evans					
9751	Little Miss Tease/Gina Marina Petunia	1964	2.50	5.00	10.00
9842	I Wonder What to Do/Always Thinking of the Roses	1965	2.50	5.00	10.00
GUARANTEED					
200	Seven Little Girls Sitting in the Back Seat/Worshipping an Idol	1959	5.00	10.00	20.00
205	Midnite Special/Since I Met You Baby	1960	3.75	7.50	15.00
208	Happy-Go-Lucky Me/Fish in the Ocean	1960	3.75	7.50	15.00
210	The Brigade of Broken Hearts/Twins	1960	3.75	7.50	15.00
213	Hushabye Little Guitar/Blind Boy	1960	3.75	7.50	15.00
KAPP					
473	A Picture of You/Feelin' No Pain	1962	3.00	6.00	12.00
486	D-Darling/Gonna Build a Mountain	1962	3.00	6.00	12.00
499	The Bell That Couldn't Jingle/Gilding the Lily	1962	3.00	6.00	12.00
520	(Mama and Papa) We've Got Something On You/What Are the Lips of Janet	1963	3.00	6.00	12.00
527	Ten Thousand Years/Evan Tan	1963	3.00	6.00	12.00
LAURIE					
3571	Think Summer/For Old Times Sake	1971	—	3.00	6.00
3581	The Man in a Row Boat/Here We Go Around Again	1971	—	3.00	6.00
MERCURY					
73499	But I Was Born in New York City/Just As Long As You Are There	1974	—	2.50	5.00
73650	All My Children/Move In with Me	1975	—	2.50	5.00
MUSICOR					
6305	Roses Are Red Medley/If I Had My Life to Live Over	1977	—	2.00	4.00
RANWOOD					
928	Try It, You'll Like It/We Liked It	1972	—	3.00	6.00
RCA VICTOR					
47-6806	What Do You Know/Dorothy	1957	5.00	10.00	20.00
47-6924	Looking for a Sweetie/Any Little Thing	1957	5.00	10.00	20.00
47-6992	Caught/Poor Broken Heart	1957	5.00	10.00	20.00
SPRING					
183	Hello, This Is Joanie (The Telephone Answering Machine Song)/Lullabye Tissue Paper Company	1978	—	2.00	4.00
187	Down at the Bluebird/I'm Givin' Up My Baby	1978	—	2.00	4.00
193	Disneyland Daddy/Build An Ark	1979	—	2.00	4.00
Albums					
CARLTON					
STLP-129 [S]	Hear Paul Evans in Your Home Tonight	1961	15.00	30.00	60.00
TLP-129 [M]	Hear Paul Evans in Your Home Tonight	1961	10.00	20.00	40.00
STLP-130 [S]	Folk Songs of Many Lands	1961	15.00	30.00	60.00
TLP-130 [M]	Folk Songs of Many Lands	1961	10.00	20.00	40.00
GUARANTEED					
GUL-1000 [M]	Fabulous Teens	1960	17.50	35.00	70.00
GUS-1000 [S]	Fabulous Teens	1960	20.00	40.00	80.00
KAPP					
KL-1346 [M]	21 Years in a Tennessee Jail	1964	6.25	12.50	25.00
KL-1475 [M]	Another Town, Another Jail	1966	6.25	12.50	25.00
KS-3346 [S]	21 Years in a Tennessee Jail	1964	10.00	20.00	40.00
KS-3475 [S]	Another Town, Another Jail	1966	7.50	15.00	30.00

EVELS, THE

45s

Number	Title (A Side/B Side)	Yr	VG	VG+	NM
TRA-X					
14	The Magic of Love/Wonderful Guy	1960	15.00	30.00	60.00

EVER-READY SINGERS, THE

45s

Number	Title (A Side/B Side)	Yr	VG	VG+	NM
CAPITOL					
F2763	I'm a Pilgrim and a Stranger/One Day While I Was Walking	1954	7.50	15.00	30.00
F2867	This Heart of Mine/Two Wings	1954	7.50	15.00	30.00
F2984	I Don't Care What the World May Do/Oh Mary Don't You Weep	1954	10.00	20.00	40.00

EVERETT, BETTY

45s

Number	Title (A Side/B Side)	Yr	VG	VG+	NM
ABC					
10829	In Your Arms/Nothing I Wouldn't Do	1966	2.00	4.00	8.00
10861	Bye, Bye Baby/Your Love Is Important to Me	1966	2.00	4.00	8.00
10919	Love Comes Tumbling Down/People Around Me	1967	2.00	4.00	8.00
10978	I Can't Say/My Baby Loving My Best Friend	1967	2.00	4.00	8.00
CJ					
611	Why Did You Have to Go/Please Come Back	1961	5.00	10.00	20.00
—As "Bettie Everett & Daylighters"					
619	Your Lovin' Arms/Happy I Long to Be	1961	5.00	10.00	20.00
674	Days Gone By/Her New Love	1964	3.75	7.50	15.00
COBRA					
5019	My Love/My Life Depends on You	1957	7.50	15.00	30.00
5024	Ain't Gonna Cry/Killer Diller	1958	6.25	12.50	25.00
5031	Weep No More/Tell Me Darling	1959	6.25	12.50	25.00
FANTASY					
652	I Got to Tell Somebody/Why Are You Leaving Me	1970	—	2.50	5.00
658	Ain't Nothing Gonna Change Me/What Is It?	1971	—	2.50	5.00
667	I'm a Woman/Prove It	1971	—	2.50	5.00
687	Black Girl/Innocent Bystanders	1972	—	2.50	5.00
687	Black Girl/What Is It?	1972	—	2.50	5.00
696	Danger/Just a Matter of Time Till You're Gone	1973	—	2.50	5.00
714	Sweet Dan/Who Will Your Next Fool Be	1973	—	2.50	5.00
725	Try It, You'll Like It/Wondering	1974	—	2.50	5.00
738	Happy Endings/Keep It Up	1974	—	2.50	5.00
ONE-DERFUL					
4806	I've Got a Claim on You/Your Love Is Important to Me	1962	3.75	7.50	15.00
4823	I'll Be There/Please Love Me	1964	3.00	6.00	12.00
UNI					
55100	Take Me/There'll Come a Time	1968	—	3.00	6.00
55122	I Can't Say No to You/Better Tomorrow Than Today	1969	—	3.00	6.00
55141	1900 Yesterday/Maybe	1969	—	3.00	6.00
55174	Just a Man's Way/Been a Long Time	1969	—	3.00	6.00
55189	Sugar/Just Another Winter	1969	—	3.00	6.00
55219	Unlucky Girl/Better Tomorrow Than Today	1970	—	3.00	6.00
UNITED ARTISTS					
XW1200	True Love (You Took My Heart)/You Can Do It	1978	—	2.00	4.00
VEE JAY					
513	By My Side/Prince of Players	1963	3.75	7.50	15.00
566	You're No Good/Chained to Your Love	1963	5.00	10.00	20.00
585	The Shoop Shoop Song (It's In His Kiss)/Hands Off	1964	5.00	10.00	20.00
599	I Can't Hear You/Can I Get to Know You	1964	3.75	7.50	15.00
610	It Hurts to Be in Love/Until You Were Gone	1964	3.75	7.50	15.00
628	Getting Mighty Crowded/Chained to a Memory	1964	3.75	7.50	15.00
683	The Real Thing/Gonna Be Ready	1965	3.75	7.50	15.00
699	I Don't Hurt Anymore/Too Hot to Hold	1965	3.75	7.50	15.00
716	Trouble Over the Weekend/My Shoe Won't Fly	1966	3.75	7.50	15.00

Albums

Number	Title	Yr	VG	VG+	NM
FANTASY					
9447	Love Rhymes	1974	3.00	6.00	12.00
9480	Happy Endings	1975	3.00	6.00	12.00
SUNSET					
SUS-5220	I Need You So	1968	3.75	7.50	15.00
UNI					
73048	There'll Come a Time	1969	6.25	12.50	25.00
VEE JAY					
LP 1077 [M]	You're No Good	1964	10.00	20.00	40.00
LP 1077 [M]	It's In His Kiss	1964	7.50	15.00	30.00
SR 1077 [S]	You're No Good	1964	17.50	35.00	70.00
SR 1077 [S]	It's In His Kiss	1964	12.50	25.00	50.00
LP 1122 [M]	The Very Best of Betty Everett	1965	10.00	20.00	40.00
VJLP 1122	The Very Best of Betty Everett	198?	2.50	5.00	10.00
—Authorized reissue					
VJS 1122 [S]	The Very Best of Betty Everett	1965	12.50	25.00	50.00

EVERETT, BETTY, AND JERRY BUTLER

Also see each artist's individual listings.

45s

Number	Title (A Side/B Side)	Yr	VG	VG+	NM
VEE JAY					
613	Let It Be Me/Ain't That Loving You Baby	1964	3.00	6.00	12.00
633	Smile/Love Is Strange	1964	3.00	6.00	12.00
676	Since I Don't Have You/Just Be True	1965	3.00	6.00	12.00
691	Fever/The Way You Do the Things You Do	1965	3.00	6.00	12.00

Albums

Number	Title	Yr	VG	VG+	NM
BUDDAH					
BDS-7505	Together	1969	3.75	7.50	15.00
BDS-7505	Together	1969	3.75	7.50	15.00
TRADITION					
2073	Starring Betty Everett with Jerry Butler	197?	3.00	6.00	12.00
VEE JAY					
LP-1099 [M]	Delicious Together	1964	5.00	10.00	20.00
LP 1099 [M]	Delicious Together	1964	5.00	10.00	20.00
VJLP-1099	Delicious Together	198?	2.50	5.00	10.00
—Reissue of original 1099; has softer vinyl					
VJLP 1099	Delicious Together	198?	3.00	6.00	12.00
—Authorized reissue					
VJS-1099 [S]	Delicious Together	1964	6.25	12.50	25.00
VJS 1099 [S]	Delicious Together	1964	6.25	12.50	25.00

EVERETT, VINCE

45s

Number	Title (A Side/B Side)	Yr	VG	VG+	NM
ABC-PARAMOUNT					
10313	Such a Night/Don't Go	1962	15.00	30.00	60.00
10360	I Ain't Gonna Be Your Low Down Dog No More/Sugaree	1962	12.50	25.00	50.00
10472	Baby, Let's Play House/Livin' High	1963	20.00	40.00	80.00
10538	Sweet Flavors/Box Candy	1964	10.00	20.00	40.00
10624	Big Brother/To Have, to Hold and Let Go	1965	10.00	20.00	40.00
TOWN					
1964	Buttercup/Land of No Return	1960	10.00	20.00	40.00

EVERGREEN BLUES, THE

45s

Number	Title (A Side/B Side)	Yr	VG	VG+	NM
ABC					
11198	Funky Woman/Don't Mess Up My Mind	1969	—	3.00	6.00
11216	The Moon Is High/Girl I Got Wise	1969	—	3.00	6.00
MERCURY					
72756	Midnight Confessions/That's My Baby (Yes)	1967	2.50	5.00	10.00
72756 [PS]	Midnight Confessions/That's My Baby (Yes)	1967	5.00	10.00	20.00
72780	Yesterday's Coming/Laura (Keep Hangin' On)	1968	2.50	5.00	10.00
72826	Feelin' Your Love/Three's a Crowd	1968	2.50	5.00	10.00

Albums

Number	Title	Yr	VG	VG+	NM
ABC					
S-669	Comin' On	1969	3.75	7.50	15.00
MERCURY					
SR-61157	7 Do 11	1968	5.00	10.00	20.00

EVERGREENS, THE

45s

Number	Title (A Side/B Side)	Yr	VG	VG+	NM
CHART					
605	Very Truly Yours/Guitar Player	1955	37.50	75.00	150.00

EVERLY, DON

Also see THE EVERLY BROTHERS.

45s

Number	Title (A Side/B Side)	Yr	VG	VG+	NM
ABC HICKORY					
54002	Love at Last Sight/Oh I'd Like to Go Away	1976	—	3.00	6.00
54005	Deep Water/Since You Broke My Heart	1977	—	3.00	6.00
54012	Brother Juke-Box/Oh, What a Feeling	1977	—	3.00	6.00
HICKORY/MGM					
368	Never Like This/Yesterday Just Passed My Way Again	1976	—	3.00	6.00
ODE					
66009	Only Me/Tumbling Tumbleweeds	1970	2.00	4.00	8.00
66046	Warming Up the Band/Evelyn Swing	1974	2.00	4.00	8.00

Albums

Number	Title	Yr	VG	VG+	NM
ABC HICKORY					
AH-44003	Brother Juke-Box	1977	3.00	6.00	12.00
ODE					
SP-77005	Don Everly	1970	3.75	7.50	15.00
SP-77023	Sunset Towers	1974	3.75	7.50	15.00

EVERLY, PHIL

Also see THE EVERLY BROTHERS.

45s

Number	Title (A Side/B Side)	Yr	VG	VG+	NM
CAPITOL					
B-5197	One Way Love/Who's Gonna Keep Me Warm	1983	2.50	5.00	10.00
CURB					
02116	Sweet Southern Love/In Your Eyes	1981	2.50	5.00	10.00
5401	Dare to Dream Again/Lonely Days, Lonely Nights	1980	2.50	5.00	10.00
ELEKTRA					
46007	Don't Say You Don't Love Me No More/I Seek the Night	1979	—	2.50	5.00
—A-side: With Sondra Locke; B-side: Sondra Locke solo					
46519	Living Alone/I Just Don't Feel Like Dancing	1979	—	2.50	5.00
46556	Buy Me a Beer/You Broke It	1979	—	2.50	5.00
PYE					
71014	Old Kentucky River/Summershine	1975	2.00	4.00	8.00
71036	New Old Song/Better Than Now	1975	2.00	4.00	8.00
71050	You and I Are a Song/Better Than Now	1975	2.00	4.00	8.00
71055	Words in Your Eyes/Back When the Bands Played in Rag Time	1976	2.00	4.00	8.00
71056	God Bless Older Ladies/Sweet Grass Country	1976	—	3.00	6.00
RCA VICTOR					
APBO-0064	God Bless Older Ladies/Sweet Grass Country	1973	2.00	4.00	8.00

Albums

Number	Title	Yr	VG	VG+	NM
ELEKTRA					
6E-213	Living Alone	1979	2.50	5.00	10.00
PYE					
12104	Phil's Diner	1975	3.00	6.00	12.00
12121	Mystic Line	1976	3.00	6.00	12.00
RCA VICTOR					
APL1-0092	Star Spangled Springer	1973	3.75	7.50	15.00

EVERLY BROTHERS, THE

Also see DON EVERLY; PHIL EVERLY.

45s

Number	Title (A Side/B Side)	Yr	VG	VG+	NM
BARNABY					
500	('Til) I Kissed You/Oh, What a Feeling	197?	—	2.50	5.00
501	Wake Up Little Susie/Maybe Tomorrow	197?	—	2.50	5.00
502	Bye, Bye Love/I Wonder If I Care As Much	197?	—	2.50	5.00
503	This Little Girl of Mine/Should We Tell Him?	197?	—	2.50	5.00

Number	Title (A Side/B Side)	Yr	VG	VG+	NM
504	Problems/Love of My Life	197?	—	2.50	5.00
505	Take a Message to Mary/Poor Jenny	197?	—	2.50	5.00
506	Let It Be Me/Since You Broke My Heart	197?	—	2.50	5.00
507	When Will I Be Loved/Be Bop A-Lula	197?	—	2.50	5.00
508	Like Strangers/Brand New Heartache	197?	—	2.50	5.00
509	All I Have to Do Is Dream/Claudette	197?	—	2.50	5.00
510	Bird Dog/Devoted to You	197?	—	2.50	5.00
511	I'm Here to Get My Baby Out of Jail/Lightning Express	197?	—	2.50	5.00
—All Barnaby records are reissues of original Cadence recordings					
CADENCE					
1315	Bye, Bye Love/I Wonder If I Care As Much	1957	6.25	12.50	25.00
1337	Wake Up Little Susie/Maybe Tomorrow	1957	7.50	15.00	30.00
1337 [PS]	Wake Up Little Susie/Maybe Tomorrow	1957	62.50	125.00	250.00
1342	This Little Girl of Mine/Should We Tell Him?	1958	6.25	12.50	25.00
1348	All I Have to Do Is Dream/Claudette	1958	6.25	12.50	25.00
1348	All I Have to Do Is Dream/Claudette	1961	5.00	10.00	20.00
—Reissue with red and black label; scarcer than original					
1350	Bird Dog/Devoted to You	1958	6.25	12.50	25.00
1355	Problems/Love of My Life	1958	6.25	12.50	25.00
1355 [PS]	Problems/Love of My Life	1958	12.50	25.00	50.00
1364	Take a Message to Mary/Poor Jenny	1959	6.25	12.50	25.00
1369	('Til) I Kissed You/Oh, What a Feeling	1959	6.25	12.50	25.00
1369 [PS]	('Til) I Kissed You/Oh, What a Feeling	1959	12.50	25.00	50.00
1376	Let It Be Me/Since You Broke My Heart	1959	6.25	12.50	25.00
1376 [PS]	Let It Be Me/Since You Broke My Heart	1959	12.50	25.00	50.00
1380	When Will I Be Loved/Be Bop A-Lula	1960	6.25	12.50	25.00
1388	Like Strangers/Brand New Heartache	1960	6.25	12.50	25.00
1429	I'm Here to Get My Baby Out of Jail/Lightning Express	1962	5.00	10.00	20.00
1429 [PS]	I'm Here to Get My Baby Out of Jail/Lightning Express	1962	10.00	20.00	40.00
CAPITOL					
B-44297	Don't Worry Baby/Tequila Dreams	1989	—	2.00	4.00
—A-side: With the Beach Boys; B-side by Dave Grusin					
B-44297 [PS]	Don't Worry Baby/Tequila Dreams	1989	2.50	5.00	10.00
COLUMBIA					
4-21496	Keep A Lovin' Me/The Sun Keeps Shining	1956	150.00	300.00	600.00
—Maroon label					
4-21496 [DJ]	Keep A Lovin' Me/The Sun Keeps Shining	1956	62.50	125.00	250.00
—White label					
MERCURY					
872098-7	Ride the Wind/Don't Worry Baby	1988	—	—	3.00
872420-7	Ballad of a Teenage Queen/Get Rhythm	1988	—	—	3.00
—With Johnny Cash and Roseanne Cash					
880213-7	On the Wings of a Nightingale/Asleep	1984	—	2.50	5.00
—A-side written and produced by Paul McCartney					
880423-7	The Story of Me/First in Line	1984	—	2.00	4.00
884428-7	Don't Say Goodnight/Born Yesterday	1986	—	2.00	4.00
884694-7	I Know Love/These Shoes	1986	—	2.00	4.00
884694-7 [PS]	I Know Love/These Shoes	1986	—	2.00	4.00
RCA VICTOR					
SP-45-409 [DJ]	Pass the Chicken and Listen	1971	7.50	15.00	30.00
—Promo-only interview record					
74-0717	Stories We Could Tell/Ridin' High	1972	2.50	5.00	10.00
74-0849	Lay It Down/Paradise	1972	2.50	5.00	10.00
74-0901	Not Fade Away/Ladies Love Outlaws	1973	2.50	5.00	10.00
WARNER BROS.					
GWB 0311	That's Old Fashioned/Bowling Green	197?	—	2.00	4.00
—"Back to Back Hits" series; originals have palm-tree labels					
GWB 0314	Ebony Eyes/Walk Right Back	197?	—	2.00	4.00
—"Back to Back Hits" series; originals have palm-tree labels					
5151 [DJ]	Cathy's Clown/Always It's You	1960	25.00	50.00	100.00
—Promo-only gold vinyl pressing					
5151 [M]	Cathy's Clown/Always It's You	1960	5.00	10.00	20.00
—Original stock copies have pink labels					
5151 [M]	Cathy's Clown/Always It's You	1960	3.75	7.50	15.00
—Second-pressing stock copies have red labels with arrows					
5151 [PS]	Cathy's Clown/Always It's You	1960	12.50	25.00	50.00
S-5151 [S]	Cathy's Clown/Always It's You	1960	12.50	25.00	50.00
5163	So Sad (To Watch Good Love Go Bad)/Lucille	1960	3.75	7.50	15.00
5163 [DJ]	So Sad (To Watch Good Love Go Bad)/Lucille	1960	25.00	50.00	100.00
—Promo-only gold vinyl pressing					
5163 [PS]	So Sad (To Watch Good Love Go Bad)/Lucille	1960	12.50	25.00	50.00
5199	Ebony Eyes/Walk Right Back	1961	3.75	7.50	15.00
5199 [DJ]	Ebony Eyes/Walk Right Back	1961	25.00	50.00	100.00
—Promo-only gold vinyl pressing					
5199 [PS]	Ebony Eyes/Walk Right Back	1961	6.25	12.50	25.00
5220	Temptation/Stick With Me, Baby	1961	3.75	7.50	15.00
5220 [PS]	Temptation/Stick With Me, Baby	1961	7.50	15.00	30.00
5250	Crying in the Rain/I'm Not Angry	1961	3.75	7.50	15.00
5250 [PS]	Crying in the Rain/I'm Not Angry	1961	5.00	10.00	20.00
5273	That's Old Fashioned (That's the Way Love Should Be)/How Can I Meet Her?	1962	3.75	7.50	15.00
5273 [PS]	That's Old Fashioned (That's the Way Love Should Be)/How Can I Meet Her?	1962	7.50	15.00	30.00
5297	Don't Ask Me to Be Friends/No One Can Make My Sunshine Smile	1962	5.00	10.00	20.00
5297 [PS]	Don't Ask Me to Be Friends/No One Can Make My Sunshine Smile	1962	7.50	15.00	30.00
5346	(So It Was...So It Is...) So It Always Will Be/Nancy's Minuet	1963	3.75	7.50	15.00
5362	I'm Afraid/It's Been Nice	1963	3.75	7.50	15.00
5389	Love Her/The Girl Sang the Blues	1963	3.75	7.50	15.00
5422	Hello, Amy/Ain't That Loving You, Baby	1964	3.75	7.50	15.00
5441	The Ferris Wheel/Don't Forget to Cry	1964	3.75	7.50	15.00
5466	You're the One I Love/Ring Around My Rosie	1964	3.75	7.50	15.00
5478	Gone, Gone, Gone/Torture	1964	3.75	7.50	15.00
5501	Don't Blame Me/Walk Right Back//Muskrat/Lucille	1961	5.00	10.00	20.00
5501 [PS]	Don't Blame Me/Walk Right Back//Muskrat/Lucille	1961	10.00	20.00	40.00
—Part of Warner Bros. "+2" series, with two new songs and excerpts of two prior hits					
5600	You're My Girl/Don't Let the World Know	1965	3.00	6.00	12.00
5611	That'll Be the Day/Give Me a Sweetheart	1965	3.00	6.00	12.00
5628	The Price of Love/It Only Costs a Dime	1965	3.00	6.00	12.00
5639	I'll Never Get Over You/Follow Me	1965	3.00	6.00	12.00
5649	Love Is Strange/A Man with Money	1965	3.00	6.00	12.00
5649 [PS]	Love Is Strange/A Man with Money	1965	7.50	15.00	30.00
5682	It's All Over/I Used to Love You	1965	3.00	6.00	12.00
5698	The Doll House Is Empty/Lovey Kravezit	1966	3.00	6.00	12.00
5808	The Power of Love/Leave My Girl Alone	1966	3.00	6.00	12.00
5833	Somebody Help Me/Hard, Hard Year	1966	3.00	6.00	12.00
5857	Fifi the Flea/Like Every Time Before	1966	5.00	10.00	20.00
—A-side listed as "Don Everly Brother," B-side as "Phil Everly Brother"					
5901	She Never Smiles Anymore/Devil Child	1967	3.00	6.00	12.00
7020	Bowling Green/I Don't Want to Love You	1967	3.00	6.00	12.00
7062	Mary Jane/Talking to the Flowers	1967	3.00	6.00	12.00
7088	Love of the Common People/The Voice Within	1967	3.00	6.00	12.00
7110	Cathy's Clown/So Sad	1968	2.00	4.00	8.00
—"Back to Back Hits" series; originals have green "W7" label					
7111	Crying in the Rain/Lucille	1968	2.00	4.00	8.00
—"Back to Back Hits" series; originals have green "W7" label					
7120	Wake Up Little Susie/Bird Dog	1969	2.00	4.00	8.00
—"Back to Back Hits" series; originals have green "W7" label; re-recordings					
7121	Bye Bye Love/All I Have to Do Is Dream	1969	2.00	4.00	8.00
—"Back to Back Hits" series; originals have green "W7" label; re-recordings					
7192	Empty Boxes/It's My Time	1968	3.00	6.00	12.00
7226	Lord of the Manor/Milk Train	1968	3.00	6.00	12.00
7262	T for Texas/I Wonder If I Care As Much	1969	3.00	6.00	12.00
7290	I'm On My Way Home Again/Cuckoo Bird	1969	3.00	6.00	12.00
7326	Carolina on My Mind/My Little Yellow Bird	1969	3.75	7.50	15.00
7425	Yves/The Human Race	1970	3.75	7.50	15.00

7-Inch Extended Plays

Number	Title (A Side/B Side)	Yr	VG	VG+	NM
CADENCE					
CEP-104	Wake Up Little Susie/Maybe Tomorrow//Bye Bye Love/I Wonder If I Care As Much	1957	12.50	25.00	50.00
CEP-104 [PS]	The Everly Brothers	1957	12.50	25.00	50.00
CEP-105	This Little Girl of Mine/Leave My Woman Alone//Should We Tell Him/Be-Bop-a-Lula	1957	12.50	25.00	50.00
CEP-105 [PS]	The Everly Brothers	1957	12.50	25.00	50.00
CEP-107	Brand New Heartache/Keep a Knockin'//Rip It Up/Hey Doll Baby	1957	12.50	25.00	50.00
CEP-107 [PS]	The Everly Brothers	1957	12.50	25.00	50.00
CEP-108	Roving Gambler/Oh So Many Years//Put My Little Shoes Away/That Silver Haired Daddy Of Mine	1958	12.50	25.00	50.00
CEP-108 [PS]	Songs Our Daddy Taught Us, Vol. 1	1958	12.50	25.00	50.00
CEP-109	Barbara Allen/Long Time Gone//Lightning Express/Who's Gonna Shoe Your Pretty Little Feet	1958	12.50	25.00	50.00
CEP-109 [PS]	Songs Our Daddy Taught Us, Vol. 2	1958	12.50	25.00	50.00
CEP-110	*Down in the Willow Garden/Kentucky/I'm Here to Get My Baby Out of Jail/Rockin' Alone in My Old Rockin' Chair	1958	12.50	25.00	50.00
CEP-110 [PS]	Songs Our Daddy Taught Us, Vol. 3	1958	12.50	25.00	50.00
CEP-111	Bird Dog/Devoted to You//All I Have to Do Is Dream/Claudette	1959	12.50	25.00	50.00
CEP-111 [PS]	The Everly Brothers	1959	12.50	25.00	50.00
CEP-118	(contents unknown)	1959	12.50	25.00	50.00
CEP-118 [PS]	The Everly Brothers	1959	12.50	25.00	50.00
CEP-121	(contents unknown)	1960	6.25	12.50	25.00
CEP-121 [PS]	The Very Best of the Everly Brothers	1960	6.25	12.50	25.00
WARNER BROS.					
EA 1381	So Sad (To Watch Good Love Go Bad)/You Thrill Me (Through and Through)//Memories Are Made of This/Oh, True Love	1960	10.00	20.00	40.00
EA 1381 [PS]	Foreverly Yours	1960	10.00	20.00	40.00
EB 1381	Sleepless Nights/Carol Jane//Nashville Blues/That's What You Do to Me	1960	10.00	20.00	40.00
EB 1381 [PS]	Especially for You	1960	10.00	20.00	40.00

Albums

Number	Title	Yr	VG	VG+	NM
ARISTA					
AL9-8207 [(2)]	24 Original Classics	1985	3.75	7.50	15.00
BARNABY					
BGP-350 [(2)]	The Everly Brothers' Original Golden Hits	1970	5.00	10.00	20.00
4004	Greatest Hits, Vol. 1	1977	2.50	5.00	10.00
4005	Greatest Hits, Vol. 2	1977	2.50	5.00	10.00
4006	Greatest Hits, Vol. 3	1977	2.50	5.00	10.00
BR-6006 [(2)]	The Everly Brothers' Greatest Hits	1974	3.75	7.50	15.00
BR-15008 [(2)]	History of the Everly Brothers	1973	3.75	7.50	15.00
ZG 30260 [(2)]	End of an Era	1971	3.75	7.50	15.00
CADENCE					
CLP-3003 [M]	The Everly Brothers	1958	25.00	50.00	100.00
—Maroon label with metronome logo					
CLP-3003 [M]	The Everly Brothers	1962	15.00	30.00	60.00
—Red label with black border					
CLP-3016 [M]	Songs Our Daddy Taught Us	1958	25.00	50.00	100.00
—Maroon label with metronome logo					
CLP-3016 [M]	Songs Our Daddy Taught Us	1962	15.00	30.00	60.00
—Red label with black border					
CLP-3025 [M]	The Everly Brothers' Best	1959	22.50	45.00	90.00
—Maroon label with metronome logo					
CLP-3025 [M]	The Everly Brothers' Best	1962	15.00	30.00	60.00
—Red label with black border					
CLP-3040 [M]	The Fabulous Style of the Everly Brothers	1960	20.00	40.00	80.00
—Maroon label with metronome logo					
CLP-3040 [M]	The Fabulous Style of the Everly Brothers	1962	12.50	25.00	50.00
—Red label with black border					
CLP-3059 [M]	Folk Songs of the Everly Brothers	1963	12.50	25.00	50.00
—Reissue of 3016					
CLP-3062 [M]	15 Everly Hits 15	1963	10.00	20.00	40.00
CLP-25040 [P]	The Fabulous Style of the Everly Brothers	1960	30.00	60.00	120.00
—Maroon label with metronome logo					
CLP-25040 [P]	The Fabulous Style of the Everly Brothers	1962	15.00	30.00	60.00
—Red label with black border					
CLP-25059 [R]	Folk Songs of the Everly Brothers	1963	10.00	20.00	40.00
CLP-25062 [P]	15 Everly Hits 15	1963	12.50	25.00	50.00
HARMONY					
HS 11304	Wake Up Little Susie	1969	3.00	6.00	12.00

Number	Title (A Side/B Side)	Yr	VG	VG+	NM
HS 11350	Christmas with the Everly Brothers and the Boys Town Choir	1969	5.00	10.00	20.00
KH 11388	Chained to a Memory	1970	3.00	6.00	12.00
MERCURY					
822431-1	EB 84	1984	2.50	5.00	10.00
826142-1	Born Yesterday	1986	2.50	5.00	10.00
832520-1	Some Hearts	1989	3.00	6.00	12.00
PAIR					
PDL1-1063 [(2)]	Living Legends	1986	3.00	6.00	12.00
PASSPORT					
11001 [(2)]	The Everly Brothers Reunion Concert	1984	3.75	7.50	15.00
RCA VICTOR					
LSP-4620	Stories We Could Tell	1972	3.75	7.50	15.00
LSP-4781	Pass the Chicken and Listen	1972	3.75	7.50	15.00
AFL1-5401	Home Again	1985	2.50	5.00	10.00
RHINO					
RNLP-211	The Everly Brothers	1985	2.50	5.00	10.00
RNLP-212	Songs Our Daddy Taught Us	1985	2.50	5.00	10.00
RNLP-213	The Fabulous Style of the Everly Brothers	1985	2.50	5.00	10.00
RNLP-214	All They Had to Do Was Dream	1985	2.50	5.00	10.00
RNDF-258 [PD]	Heartaches and Harmonies	1985	5.00	10.00	20.00
RNLP-70173	The Best of the Everly Brothers (Golden Archive Series)	1987	2.50	5.00	10.00
TIME-LIFE					
SRNR-09 [(2)]	The Everly Brothers: 1957-1962	1986	5.00	10.00	20.00
—Part of "The Rock 'n' Roll Era" series; box set with insert					
WARNER BROS.					
PRO 134 [10]	It's Everly Time!	1960	150.00	300.00	600.00
—Promo "souvenir sampler" from their debut on WB					
W 1381 [M]	It's Everly Time!	1960	7.50	15.00	30.00
WS 1381 [S]	It's Everly Time!	1960	10.00	20.00	40.00
W 1395 [M]	A Date with the Everly Brothers	1960	12.50	25.00	50.00
—Gatefold edition with poster and wallet-size photos					
W 1395 [M]	A Date with the Everly Brothers	1960	10.00	20.00	40.00
—Gatefold edition without poster or photos					
W 1395 [M]	A Date with the Everly Brothers	1961	7.50	15.00	30.00
—Regular edition					
WS 1395 [S]	A Date with the Everly Brothers	1960	18.75	37.50	75.00
—Gatefold edition with poster and wallet-size photos					
WS 1395 [S]	A Date with the Everly Brothers	1960	12.50	25.00	50.00
—Gatefold edition without poster or photos					
WS 1395 [S]	A Date with the Everly Brothers	1961	10.00	20.00	40.00
—Regular edition					
W 1418 [M]	Both Sides of an Evening	1961	7.50	15.00	30.00
WS 1418 [S]	Both Sides of an Evening	1961	10.00	20.00	40.00
W 1430 [M]	Instant Party!	1962	7.50	15.00	30.00
WS 1430 [S]	Instant Party!	1962	10.00	20.00	40.00
W 1471 [M]	The Golden Hits of the Everly Brothers	1962	7.50	15.00	30.00
WS 1471	The Golden Hits of the Everly Brothers	1967	5.00	10.00	20.00
—Green "W7" label					
WS 1471	The Golden Hits of the Everly Brothers	1970	3.75	7.50	15.00
—Green "WB" label					
WS 1471	The Golden Hits of the Everly Brothers	1973	3.00	6.00	12.00
—"Burbank" palm-tree label					
WS 1471	The Golden Hits of the Everly Brothers	1979	2.50	5.00	10.00
—White or tan label					
WS 1471 [S]	The Golden Hits of the Everly Brothers	1962	10.00	20.00	40.00
—Gold label					
W 1483 [M]	Christmas with the Everly Brothers and the Boys Town Choir	1962	10.00	20.00	40.00
WS 1483 [S]	Christmas with the Everly Brothers and the Boys Town Choir	1962	12.50	25.00	50.00
W 1513 [M]	Great Country Hits	1963	10.00	20.00	40.00
WS 1513 [S]	Great Country Hits	1963	12.50	25.00	50.00
W 1554 [M]	The Very Best of the Everly Brothers	1964	7.50	15.00	30.00
—Originals have yellow covers					
W 1554 [M]	The Very Best of the Everly Brothers	1965	5.00	10.00	20.00
—Later pressings have white covers					
WS 1554	The Very Best of the Everly Brothers	1967	5.00	10.00	20.00
—Green "W7" label					
WS 1554	The Very Best of the Everly Brothers	1970	3.75	7.50	15.00
—Green "WB" label					
WS 1554	The Very Best of the Everly Brothers	1973	3.00	6.00	12.00
—"Burbank" palm-tree label					
WS 1554	The Very Best of the Everly Brothers	1979	2.50	5.00	10.00
—White or tan label					
WS 1554 [S]	The Very Best of the Everly Brothers	1964	10.00	20.00	40.00
—Originals have yellow covers					
WS 1554 [S]	The Very Best of the Everly Brothers	1965	6.25	12.50	25.00
—White cover; gold label					
W 1578 [M]	Rock & Soul	1964	10.00	20.00	40.00
WS 1578 [S]	Rock & Soul	1964	12.50	25.00	50.00
W 1585 [M]	Gone, Gone, Gone	1965	10.00	20.00	40.00
WS 1585 [S]	Gone, Gone, Gone	1965	12.50	25.00	50.00
W 1605 [M]	Beat & Soul	1965	10.00	20.00	40.00
WS 1605 [S]	Beat & Soul	1965	12.50	25.00	50.00
W 1620 [M]	In Our Image	1966	10.00	20.00	40.00
WS 1620 [S]	In Our Image	1966	12.50	25.00	50.00
W 1646 [M]	Two Yanks in London	1966	10.00	20.00	40.00
WS 1646 [S]	Two Yanks in London	1966	12.50	25.00	50.00
W 1676 [M]	The Hit Sound of the Everly Brothers	1967	12.50	25.00	50.00
WS 1676 [S]	The Hit Sound of the Everly Brothers	1967	10.00	20.00	40.00
W 1708 [M]	The Everly Brothers Sing	1967	12.50	25.00	50.00
WS 1708 [S]	The Everly Brothers Sing	1967	10.00	20.00	40.00
WS 1752	Roots	1968	10.00	20.00	40.00
WS 1858	The Everly Brothers Show	1970	7.50	15.00	30.00
ST-91343 [S]	The Very Best of the Everly Brothers	1967	10.00	20.00	40.00
–Capitol Record Club edition					
-91601	Roots	1968	12.50	25.00	50.00
pitol Record Club edition					
93286	The Everly Brothers Show	1970	10.00	20.00	40.00
l Record Club edition					

EVERPRESENT FULLNESS, THE

Number	Title (A Side/B Side)	Yr	VG	VG+	NM
45s					
WHITE WHALE					
233	Wild About My Lovin'/Doin' a Number	1966	3.75	7.50	15.00
233	Wild About My Lovin'/Fine and Dandy	1966	3.75	7.50	15.00
248	Darlin' You Can Count On Me/Yeah	1967	3.75	7.50	15.00
Albums					
WHITE WHALE					
7132	The Everpresent Fullness	1970	6.25	12.50	25.00

EVERY FATHER'S TEENAGE SON

Number	Title (A Side/B Side)	Yr	VG	VG+	NM
45s					
BUDDAH					
25	A Letter to Dad/Josephine's Song	1968	2.00	4.00	8.00

EVERY MOTHER'S SON

Number	Title (A Side/B Side)	Yr	VG	VG+	NM
45s					
MGM					
13733	Come On Down to My Boat/I Believe in You	1967	2.50	5.00	10.00
13788	Put Your Mind at Ease/Proper Four Leaf Clover	1967	2.00	4.00	8.00
13788 [PS]	Put Your Mind at Ease/Proper Four Leaf Clover	1967	3.00	6.00	12.00
13844	Pony with the Golden Mane/Dolls in the Clock	1967	2.00	4.00	8.00
13887	No One Knows/What Became of Mary	1968	2.00	4.00	8.00
13987	Rainflowers/For Brandy	1968	2.00	4.00	8.00
Albums					
MGM					
E-4471 [M]	Every Mother's Son	1967	5.00	10.00	20.00
SE-4471 [S]	Every Mother's Son	1967	5.00	10.00	20.00
E-4504 [M]	Every Mother's Son's Back	1967	5.00	10.00	20.00
SE-4504 [S]	Every Mother's Son's Back	1967	5.00	10.00	20.00

EVERYTHING IS EVERYTHING

Number	Title (A Side/B Side)	Yr	VG	VG+	NM
45s					
VANGUARD APOSTOLIC					
35082	Witchi Tai To/Ooh Baby	1969	2.00	4.00	8.00
35097	Ya Hay Ho/You Don't Need No Music	1969	2.00	4.00	8.00
Albums					
VANGUARD					
VSD-6512	Everything Is Everything	1969	6.25	12.50	25.00

EVIL, THE

Number	Title (A Side/B Side)	Yr	VG	VG+	NM
45s					
CAPITOL					
2038	Whatcha Gonna Do About It/Always Runnin' Around	1967	5.00	10.00	20.00
LIVING LEGEND					
108	Whatcha Gonna Do About It/Always Runnin' Around	1967	10.00	20.00	40.00

EVIL ENCORPORATED

Number	Title (A Side/B Side)	Yr	VG	VG+	NM
45s					
SCENE					
101	Hey You/The Thing Is...	1967	7.50	15.00	30.00
102	Baby It's You/All I Really Want to Do	1967	7.50	15.00	30.00

EXCALIBURS, THE

Number	Title (A Side/B Side)	Yr	VG	VG+	NM
45s					
TRENT TOWN					
1017	Christmas Dreaming/Peace On Earth	19??	25.00	50.00	100.00

EXCELLENTS, THE

Number	Title (A Side/B Side)	Yr	VG	VG+	NM
45s					
BLAST					
205	Coney Island Baby/You Baby You	1962	7.50	15.00	30.00
—All-red label					
205	Coney Island Baby/You Baby You	1962	5.00	10.00	20.00
—Red and white label					
205	Coney Island Baby/You Baby You	1965	6.25	12.50	25.00
—Purple label					
207	I Hear a Rhapsody/Why Did You Laugh	1963	15.00	30.00	60.00
MERMAID					
106	Love No One But You/Red Red Robin	1961	50.00	100.00	200.00
—With mermaid on label					
106	Love No One But You/Red Red Robin	1961	12.50	25.00	50.00
—No mermaid on label					

EXCELS, THE (1)

Number	Title (A Side/B Side)	Yr	VG	VG+	NM
45s					
GONE					
5094	My Foolish Heart/Just You and I Together	1960	6.25	12.50	25.00
RSVP					
111	Can't Help Lovin' That Girl of Mine/Till You	1961	12.50	25.00	50.00

EXCELS, THE (2)

Number	Title (A Side/B Side)	Yr	VG	VG+	NM
45s					
CARLA					
1901	Little Innocent Girl/Some Kind of Fun	1968	5.00	10.00	20.00
2529	Gonna Make You Mine Girl/Goodbye Poor Boy	1966	5.00	10.00	20.00
2534	I Wanna Be Free/Too Much Too Soon	1967	5.00	10.00	20.00
2536	California on My Mind/Arrival of Mary	1967	5.00	10.00	20.00

EXCELS, THE (3)

Number	Title (A Side/B Side)	Yr	VG	VG+	NM
45s					
CENTRAL					
2601	You're Mine Forever/Baby Doll	1957	12.50	25.00	50.00
RELIC					
1007	You're Mine Forever/Baby Doll	1965	2.50	5.00	10.00

EXCEPTION, THE

Peter Cetera (later of CHICAGO) was a member of this group.

45s

Number	Title (A Side/B Side)	Yr	VG	VG+	NM
CAPITOL					
2046	Business As Usual/My Mind Goes Traveling	1967	3.00	6.00	12.00
2120	You Always Hurt Me/You Don't Know Like I Know	1968	3.00	6.00	12.00
5982	The Girl from New York City/As Far As I Can See	1967	3.00	6.00	12.00

EXCITERS, THE

45s

Number	Title (A Side/B Side)	Yr	VG	VG+	NM
BANG					
515	A Little Bit of Soap/I'm Gonna Get Him Someday	1966	3.00	6.00	12.00
518	You Better Come Home/Weddings Make Me Cry	1966	7.50	15.00	30.00
FARGO					
1400	Alone Again, Naturally/(B-side unknown)	1972	2.00	4.00	8.00
RCA VICTOR					
47-9633	Take One Step (I'll Take Two)/If You Want My Love	1968	7.50	15.00	30.00
47-9723	You Don't Know What You're Missing ('Til It's Gone!)/Blowing Up My Mind	1969	7.50	15.00	30.00
48-1035	You Don't Know What You're Missing ('Til It's Gone!)/Blowing Up My Mind	1972	3.75	7.50	15.00
ROULETTE					
4591	I Want You to Be My Boy/Tonight, Tonight	1965	3.00	6.00	12.00
4591 [PS]	I Want You to Be My Boy/Tonight, Tonight	1965	12.50	25.00	50.00
4594	Are You Satisfied/Just Not Ready	1965	3.00	6.00	12.00
4614	My Father/Run Mascara	1965	3.00	6.00	12.00
4632	I Knew You Would/There They Go	1965	3.00	6.00	12.00
SHOUT					
205	Number One/You Got Love	1966	2.50	5.00	10.00
214	Soulmotion/You Know It Ain't Right	1967	2.50	5.00	10.00
TODAY					
1002	Learning How to Fly/Life, Love and Peace	1970	2.00	4.00	8.00
UNITED ARTISTS					
0029	Tell Him/Do Wah Diddy	1973	—	2.00	4.00
—"Silver Spotlight Series" reissue					
544	Tell Him/Hard Way to Go	1963	3.75	7.50	15.00
572	Drama of Love/He's Got the Power	1963	3.00	6.00	12.00
604	Get Him/It's So Exciting	1963	3.00	6.00	12.00
662	Do-Wah-Diddy/If Love Came Your Way	1963	3.00	6.00	12.00
721	Having My Fun/We Were Lovers (When the Party Began)	1964	3.00	6.00	12.00
830	Having My Fun/We Were Lovers (When the Party Began)	1965	2.50	5.00	10.00

Albums

Number	Title	Yr	VG	VG+	NM
ROULETTE					
R 25326 [M]	The Exciters	1966	7.50	15.00	30.00
SR 25326 [S]	The Exciters	1966	10.00	20.00	40.00
TODAY					
1001	Black Beauty	1971	5.00	10.00	20.00
UNITED ARTISTS					
UAL-3264 [M]	Tell Him	1963	17.50	35.00	70.00
UAS-6264 [S]	Tell Him	1963	37.50	75.00	150.00

EXODUS

45s

Number	Title (A Side/B Side)	Yr	VG	VG+	NM
JAMIE					
1442	Four Seasons Medley (mono/stereo)	1981	—	2.50	5.00
—As "Exodus II"					
WAND					
11248	M&M/Silhouettes-You Cheated	1972	25.00	50.00	100.00
—Black and white label					
11248	M&M/Silhouettes-You Cheated	1972	7.50	15.00	30.00
—Multi-colored label					

EXOTIC GUITARS

AL CASEY was guitarist for this studio group.

45s

Number	Title (A Side/B Side)	Yr	VG	VG+	NM
RANWOOD					
804	Spanish Eyes/C'est Si Bon	1968	—	2.50	5.00
811	I Will Wait for You/Blueberry Hill	1968	—	2.50	5.00
830	I Walk Alone/Twilight Time	1969	—	2.50	5.00
843	Indian Love Call/Trying	1969	—	2.50	5.00
856	To Rome with Love/Peg o' My Heart	1969	—	2.50	5.00
863	I Was Kaiser Bill's Batman/Now Is the Hour	1970	—	2.50	5.00
871	Holly Holy/High Noon	1970	—	2.50	5.00
882	Orange Blossom Special/San Antonio Rose	1970	—	2.50	5.00
898	Till Love Touches Your Life/I Can't Stop Loving You	1971	—	2.00	4.00
914	Memphis/Maria Elena	1971	—	2.00	4.00
936	Crusing Down the River/You Can't Be True Dear	1971	—	2.00	4.00

Albums

Number	Title	Yr	VG	VG+	NM
RANWOOD					
8002	The Exotic Guitars	1968	3.00	6.00	12.00
8040	Those Were the Days	1968	3.00	6.00	12.00
8051	Indian Love Call	1969	3.00	6.00	12.00
8061	Everybody's Talkin'	1970	2.50	5.00	10.00
8073	Holly Holy	1970	2.50	5.00	10.00
8080	Country Music	1970	2.50	5.00	10.00
8085	I Can't Stop Loving You	1971	2.50	5.00	10.00
8090	All the Guitar Hits	1971	2.50	5.00	10.00
8171	300 Watt Music Box	1975	2.50	5.00	10.00

EXOTICS, THE

More than one group.

45s

Number	Title (A Side/B Side)	Yr	VG	VG+	NM
BOLO					
722	Oasis/Chattanooga Choo Choo	1962	3.00	6.00	12.00
CORAL					
62268	That's My Desire/Darking, I Want to Get Married	1961	5.00	10.00	20.00
62289	The Gang That Sang (Heart of My Heart)/Hotcha Mighty Knows	1961	5.00	10.00	20.00
62310	Fortune Hunter/Manpower	1962	5.00	10.00	20.00
62343	My Life's Desire (Part 1)/My Life's Desire (Part 2)	1963	3.75	7.50	15.00
62399	Let's Get Together/Sad, Sad Song	1964	3.75	7.50	15.00
62439	Like You Hurt Me/Big Time Charlie	1964	5.00	10.00	20.00
EXCELLO					
2284	Boogaloo Investigator/I Won't Ever Stop Loving You	1967	2.00	4.00	8.00
2292	Let Me Be a Part of You/Let's Try to Build a Love Affair	1968	2.00	4.00	8.00
JERDEN					
106	Four Banger/Cat Hairs	1960	3.75	7.50	15.00
MONUMENT					
984	Fire Engine Red/Morning Sun	1966	3.00	6.00	12.00
SEAFAIR					
108	Ginger Snap/(B-side unknown)	1962	2.50	5.00	10.00
113	Jerk Time/For the Winds	1965	2.50	5.00	10.00
SPRINGBOARD					
101	Gee/Lorraine	1963	5.00	10.00	20.00
101 [PS]	Gee/Lorraine	1963	10.00	20.00	40.00

EXPLORERS, THE

45s

Number	Title (A Side/B Side)	Yr	VG	VG+	NM
CORAL					
62147	Vision of Love/On a Clear Night	1959	15.00	30.00	60.00
62175	Don't Be a Fool/In the Wee Small Hours of the Morning	1960	25.00	50.00	100.00
62295	Remember/Every Road (I Walk Along)	1961	15.00	30.00	60.00
—As "Dennis and the Explorers"					
65575	Don't Be a Fool/Vision of Love	196?	7.50	15.00	30.00
—Was listed in the last edition under "The Visions"					

EXPORTS, THE

45s

Number	Title (A Side/B Side)	Yr	VG	VG+	NM
KING					
5917	Car Hop/Seat Belts Please	1964	6.25	12.50	25.00
5985	Mustang '65/Always It's You	1965	6.25	12.50	25.00

EXPRESSIONS, THE

45s

Number	Title (A Side/B Side)	Yr	VG	VG+	NM
ARLISS					
1012	My Love, My Love/The Sign of Happiness	1962	12.50	25.00	50.00
FEDERAL					
12533	You Better Know It/Out of My Life	1964	2.50	5.00	10.00
GUYDEN					
2122	Be-Bop-a-Lula/Skinnie Minnie	1965	3.75	7.50	15.00
—As "J-D and the Expressions"					
PARKWAY					
892	On the Corner/To Cry	1963	3.75	7.50	15.00
REPRISE					
0360	Playboy/One Plus One	1965	5.00	10.00	20.00
SMASH					
1848	Karen/Thrill	1963	3.75	7.50	15.00
TEEN					
101	Now That You've Gone/Crazy	1957	50.00	100.00	200.00

EXTERMINATORS, THE

45s

Number	Title (A Side/B Side)	Yr	VG	VG+	NM
CHANCELLOR					
1143	The Beetle Bomb/Stomp 'Em Out	1963	6.25	12.50	25.00
1148	Beatle Stomp/Stomp 'Em Out	1964	3.75	7.50	15.00
—A-sides are the same song with different titles					
GOLDEN WEST					
1002	Beatle Stomp/Stomp 'Em Out	1964	5.00	10.00	20.00

EXTREMES, THE

45s

Number	Title (A Side/B Side)	Yr	VG	VG+	NM
EVERLAST					
5013	Come Next Spring/Let's Elope	1958	37.50	75.00	150.00
PARO					
733	The Bells/That's All I Want	1962	75.00	150.00	300.00

EYES OF BLUE

45s

Number	Title (A Side/B Side)	Yr	VG	VG+	NM
DERAM					
85001	Heart Trouble/Up and Down	1967	2.00	4.00	8.00
85003	Don't Ask Me to Mend Your Broken Heart/Supermarket Full of Cans	1967	2.00	4.00	8.00
MERCURY					
72911	Apache '69/QIII	1969	2.00	4.00	8.00

Albums

Number	Title	Yr	VG	VG+	NM
MERCURY					
SR-61184	Crossroads of Time	1968	7.50	15.00	30.00
SR-61220	In Fields of Ardath	1969	7.50	15.00	30.00

F

FABARES, SHELLEY

45s

Number	Title (A Side/B Side)	Yr	VG	VG+	NM
COLPIX					
621	Johnny Angel/Where's It Gonna Get Me	1962	5.00	10.00	20.00
621 [PS]	Johnny Angel/Where's It Gonna Get Me	1962	125.00	250.00	500.00
631	What Did They Do Before Rock and Roll/Very Unlikely	1962	5.00	10.00	20.00
—With Paul Petersen					
631 [PS]	What Did They Do Before Rock and Roll/Very Unlikely	1962	100.00	200.00	400.00
636	Johnny Loves Me/I'm Growing Up	1962	5.00	10.00	20.00
636 [PS]	Johnny Loves Me/I'm Growing Up	1962	30.00	60.00	120.00
654	The Things We Did Last Summer/Breaking Up Is Hard to Do	1962	5.00	10.00	20.00
667	Big Star/Telephone (Don't You Ring)	1962	5.00	10.00	20.00
682	Ronnie, Call Me When You Get a Chance/I Left a Note to Say Goodbye	1963	5.00	10.00	20.00
705	Welcome Home/Billy Boy	1963	5.00	10.00	20.00
721	Football Season's Over/He Don't Love Me	1963	25.00	50.00	100.00
—Produced by Jan Berry of Jan and Dean					
DUNHILL					
4001	My Prayer/Pretty Please	1965	7.50	15.00	30.00
4041	See Ya 'Round on the Rebound/Pretty Please	1966	7.50	15.00	30.00
VEE JAY					
632	I Know You'll Be There/Lost Summer Love	1964	10.00	20.00	40.00

Albums

Number	Title (A Side/B Side)	Yr	VG	VG+	NM
COLPIX					
CLP-426 [M]	Shelley!	1962	37.50	75.00	150.00
CST-426 [S]	Shelley!	1962	150.00	300.00	600.00
CLP-431 [M]	The Things We Did Last Summer	1962	25.00	50.00	100.00
CST-431 [S]	The Things We Did Last Summer	1962	100.00	200.00	400.00

FABIAN

45s

Number	Title (A Side/B Side)	Yr	VG	VG+	NM
CHANCELLOR					
1020	I'm in Love/Shivers	1958	6.25	12.50	25.00
1024	Be My Steady Date/Lilly Lou	1958	6.25	12.50	25.00
1029 [M]	I'm a Man/Hypnotized	1959	5.00	10.00	20.00
1029 [PS]	I'm a Man/Hypnotized	1959	10.00	20.00	40.00
1029 [PS]	I Am a Man/Hypnotized	1959	12.50	25.00	50.00
—Incorrect title on A-side of sleeve					
S-1029 [S]	I'm a Man/Hypnotized	1959	12.50	25.00	50.00
1033 [M]	Turn Me Loose/Stop Thief!	1959	5.00	10.00	20.00
1033 [PS]	Turn Me Loose/Stop Thief!	1959	10.00	20.00	40.00
S-1033 [S]	Turn Me Loose/Stop Thief!	1959	12.50	25.00	50.00
1037 [M]	Tiger/Mighty Cold (To a Warm, Warm Heart)	1959	5.00	10.00	20.00
1037 [PS]	Tiger/Mighty Cold (To a Warm, Warm Heart)	1959	10.00	20.00	40.00
S-1037 [S]	Tiger/Mighty Cold (To a Warm, Warm Heart)	1959	12.50	25.00	50.00
1041 [M]	Come On and Get Me/Got the Feeling	1959	5.00	10.00	20.00
1041 [PS]	Come On and Get Me/Got the Feeling	1959	10.00	20.00	40.00
S-1041 [S]	Come On and Get Me/Got the Feeling	1959	12.50	25.00	50.00
1044	Hound Dog Man/Friendly World	1959	6.25	12.50	25.00
1044 [M]	Hound Dog Man/This Friendly World	1959	5.00	10.00	20.00
—Note difference in B-side title					
1044 [PS]	Hound Dog Man/This Friendly World	1959	10.00	20.00	40.00
S-1044 [S]	Hound Dog Man/This Friendly World	1959	12.50	25.00	50.00
1047 [M]	About This Thing Called Love/String Along	1960	3.00	6.00	12.00
1047 [PS]	About This Thing Called Love/String Along	1960	7.50	15.00	30.00
S-1047 [S]	About This Thing Called Love/String Along	1960	12.50	25.00	50.00
1051	I'm Gonna Sit Right Down and Write Myself a Letter/Strollin' in the Springtime	1960	3.00	6.00	12.00
1051 [PS]	I'm Gonna Sit Right Down and Write Myself a Letter/Strollin' in the Springtime	1960	7.50	15.00	30.00
1055	Tomorrow/King of Love	1960	3.00	6.00	12.00
1055 [PS]	Tomorrow/King of Love	1960	7.50	15.00	30.00
1061	Kissin' and Twistin'/Long Before	1960	3.00	6.00	12.00
1061 [PS]	Kissin' and Twistin'/Long Before	1960	7.50	15.00	30.00
1067	You Know You Belong to Someone Else/Hold On	1961	3.00	6.00	12.00
1067 [PS]	You Know You Belong to Someone Else/Hold On	1961	7.50	15.00	30.00
1072	Grapevine/David and Goliath	1961	3.00	6.00	12.00
1079	The Love That I'm Giving to You/You're Only Young Once	1961	3.75	7.50	15.00
1079 [PS]	The Love That I'm Giving to You/You're Only Young Once	1961	10.00	20.00	40.00
1084	A Girl Like You/Dream Factory	1961	3.00	6.00	12.00
1084 [PS]	A Girl Like You/Dream Factory	1961	7.50	15.00	30.00
1086	Tongue-Tied/Kansas City	1961	5.00	10.00	20.00
1092	Wild Party/Made You	1961	5.00	10.00	20.00
1092	Wild Party/The Gospel Truth	1961	6.25	12.50	25.00
1092 [PS]	Wild Party/Made You	1961	10.00	20.00	40.00
CREAM					
7717	Ease On (Into My Life)/The American East	1977	—	2.50	5.00
7717 [PS]	Ease On (Into My Life)/The American East	1977	—	2.50	5.00
DOT					
16413	Break Down and Cry/She's Staying Inside with Me	1963	2.50	5.00	10.00

7-Inch Extended Plays

Number	Title (A Side/B Side)	Yr	VG	VG+	NM
CHANCELLOR					
A-301	*Hound Dog Man/This Friendly World/Pretty Little Girl/I'm Growin' Up/Single	1960	12.50	25.00	50.00
A-301 [PS]	5 Songs from Hound Dog Man	1960	12.50	25.00	50.00
A-5003	*Hold Me (In Your Arms)/Just One More Time/Please Don't Stop/Ooh, What You Do!	1959	15.00	30.00	60.00
A-5003 [PS]	Hold That Tiger! Volume 1	1959	15.00	30.00	60.00
B-5003	(contents unknown)	1959	15.00	30.00	60.00
B-5003 [PS]	Hold That Tiger! Volume 2	1959	15.00	30.00	60.00
C-5003	(contents unknown)	1959	15.00	30.00	60.00
C-5003 [PS]	Hold That Tiger! Volume 3	1959	15.00	30.00	60.00
A-5005	Remember Me/I'm Sincere//Everything Is Just Right/You'll Never Tame Me	1959	15.00	30.00	60.00
A-5005 [PS]	The Fabulous Fabian, Volume 1	1959	15.00	30.00	60.00
B-5005	(contents unknown)	1959	15.00	30.00	60.00
B-5005 [PS]	The Fabulous Fabian, Volume 2	1959	15.00	30.00	60.00
C-5005	(contents unknown)	1959	15.00	30.00	60.00
C-5005 [PS]	The Fabulous Fabian, Volume 3	1959	15.00	30.00	60.00
A-9802	Young and Wonderful/Think of Me//Take Me/Exactly Like You	1960	12.50	25.00	50.00
A-9802 [PS]	Young and Wonderful	1960	12.50	25.00	50.00

Albums

Number	Title (A Side/B Side)	Yr	VG	VG+	NM
ABC					
X-806	16 Greatest Hits	1973	3.00	6.00	12.00
CHANCELLOR					
CHL-5003 [M]	Hold That Tiger!	1959	25.00	50.00	100.00
—Pink label					
CHL-5003 [M]	Hold That Tiger!	1959	12.50	25.00	50.00
—Black label					
CHLS-5003 [S]	Hold That Tiger!	1959	37.50	75.00	150.00
—Pink label					
CHLS-5003 [S]	Hold That Tiger!	1959	18.75	37.50	75.00
—Black label					
CHL-5005 [M]	Fabulous Fabian	1959	12.50	25.00	50.00
CHLS-5005 [S]	Fabulous Fabian	1959	18.75	37.50	75.00
CHL-5012 [M]	The Good Old Summertime	1960	12.50	25.00	50.00
CHLS-5012 [S]	The Good Old Summertime	1960	18.75	37.50	75.00
CHL-5019 [M]	Rockin' Hot	1961	18.75	37.50	75.00
CHL-5024 [M]	Fabian's 16 Fabulous Hits	1962	18.75	37.50	75.00
CHL-69802 [M]	The Fabian Facade: Young and Wonderful	1960	20.00	40.00	80.00
—Felt gatefold cover with die-cut window					
MCA					
27095	The Best of Fabian	1985	2.00	4.00	8.00
UNITED ARTISTS					
UA-LA449-E	The Very Best of Fabian	1975	3.00	6.00	12.00

FABIAN / FRANKIE AVALON

Albums

Number	Title (A Side/B Side)	Yr	VG	VG+	NM
CHANCELLOR					
CHL-5009 [M]	The Hit Makers	1960	25.00	50.00	100.00

FABRIC, BENT

Also see ACKER BILK.

45s

Number	Title (A Side/B Side)	Yr	VG	VG+	NM
ATCO					
6226	Alley Cat/Marking Time	1962	2.00	4.00	8.00
6226 [PS]	Alley Cat/Marking Time	1962	—	—	—
—Rumored to exist, but without conclusive evidence, we will delete this from future editions					
6245	Chicken Feed/That Certain Party	1962	2.00	4.00	8.00
6271	The Happy Puppy/Sermonette	1963	2.00	4.00	8.00
6304	The Organ Grinder's Swing/Goofus	1964	2.00	4.00	8.00
6333	The Old Piano Roll Blues/Titena	1964	2.00	4.00	8.00
6363	The Drunken Penguin/Alley Cat	1965	2.00	4.00	8.00
6401	Sweet Charity Theme/Can't You See	1966	2.00	4.00	8.00

Albums

Number	Title (A Side/B Side)	Yr	VG	VG+	NM
ATCO					
33-148 [M]	Alley Cat	1962	3.75	7.50	15.00
SD 33-148 [S]	Alley Cat	1962	5.00	10.00	20.00
33-155 [M]	The Happy Puppy	1963	3.00	6.00	12.00
SD 33-155 [S]	The Happy Puppy	1963	3.75	7.50	15.00
33-164 [M]	Organ Grinder's Swing	1964	3.00	6.00	12.00
SD 33-164 [S]	Organ Grinder's Swing	1964	3.75	7.50	15.00
33-173 [M]	The Drunken Penguin	1965	3.00	6.00	12.00
SD 33-173 [S]	The Drunken Penguin	1965	3.75	7.50	15.00
33-185 [M]	Never Tease Tigers	1966	3.00	6.00	12.00
SD 33-185 [S]	Never Tease Tigers	1966	3.75	7.50	15.00
33-202 [M]	Operation Lovebirds	1967	3.00	6.00	12.00
SD 33-202 [S]	Operation Lovebirds	1967	3.75	7.50	15.00
33-221 [M]	Relax	1967	3.75	7.50	15.00
SD 33-221 [S]	Relax	1967	3.00	6.00	12.00

FABS, THE

45s

Number	Title (A Side/B Side)	Yr	VG	VG+	NM
COTTON BALL					
1005	That's the Bag I'm In/Dinah Wants Religion	1966	37.50	75.00	150.00

FABULAIRES, THE

45s

Number	Title (A Side/B Side)	Yr	VG	VG+	NM
EASTWEST					
103	While Walking/No No	1957	75.00	150.00	300.00
MAIN LINE					
103	While Walking/No No	1958	50.00	100.00	200.00

FABULONS, THE (1)

45s

Number	Title (A Side/B Side)	Yr	VG	VG+	NM
EMBER					
1069	Smoke From Your Cigarette/Give Me Back My Ring	1960	12.50	25.00	50.00
—White label					
1069	Smoke From Your Cigarette/Give Me Back My Ring	1960	6.25	12.50	25.00
—Black label					

FABULONS, THE (2)

Also see THE TIKIS AND THE FABULONS.

45s

Number	Title (A Side/B Side)	Yr	VG	VG+	NM
TOWER					
259	Since You've Been Gone/Don't Ask Me	1966	3.75	7.50	15.00

FABULOUS FARQUAHR

See FARQUAHR.

FABULOUS FIVE, THE

45s

Number	Title (A Side/B Side)	Yr	VG	VG+	NM
KING					
5220	Janie Made a Monster/Gettin' Old	1959	3.75	7.50	15.00

FABULOUS FLAMES, THE (1)

45s

Number	Title (A Side/B Side)	Yr	VG	VG+	NM
BAY-TONE					
102	Do You Remember/Get to Stepping	1961	10.00	20.00	40.00
105	Lover/I'm So All Alone	1961	12.50	25.00	50.00
REX					
3000	Josephine/My Joan	1958	30.00	60.00	120.00

FABULOUS FLAMES, THE (2)

For records on Harlem, see THE FLAMES.

FABULOUS FOUR, THE

45s

Number	Title (A Side/B Side)	Yr	VG	VG+	NM
BRASS					
311	Now You Cry/Got to Get Her Back	1964	5.00	10.00	20.00
314	Who Could It Be/Happy	1964	5.00	10.00	20.00
316	I'm Always Doing Something Wrong/Young Blood	1964	5.00	10.00	20.00
CHANCELLOR					
1062	In the Chapel in the Moonlight/Mr. Twist	1960	6.25	12.50	25.00
1068	Let's Try Again/Precious Moments	1961	6.25	12.50	25.00
1078	Why Do Fools Fall in Love/Sounds of Summer	1961	10.00	20.00	40.00
1085	Prisoner of Love/Betty Ann	1961	20.00	40.00	80.00
1090	Everybody Knows/I'm Coming Home	1961	5.00	10.00	20.00
1098	Mr. Twist/Everybody Knows	1961	5.00	10.00	20.00
1102	Forever/(It's No) Sin	1962	6.25	12.50	25.00
CORAL					
62479	Now You Cry/Got to Get Her Back	1966	3.75	7.50	15.00
MELIC					
4114	Welcome Me Home/Oop Shoobee Doop	1962	12.50	25.00	50.00

FABULOUS JOKERS, THE

Albums

Number	Title (A Side/B Side)	Yr	VG	VG+	NM
MONUMENT					
MLP-8059 [M]	Guitars Extraordinaire	1966	25.00	50.00	100.00
SLP-18059 [S]	Guitars Extraordinaire	1966	37.50	75.00	150.00

FABULOUS PACK, THE

See TERRY KNIGHT AND THE PACK.

FABULOUS PEARL DEVINES, THE

45s

Number	Title (A Side/B Side)	Yr	VG	VG+	NM
ALCO					
101	You've Been Gone/So Lonely	1963	100.00	200.00	400.00

FABULOUS PEPS, THE

45s

Number	Title (A Side/B Side)	Yr	VG	VG+	NM
D-TOWN					
1049	You Never Had It So Good/Detroit, Michigan	1965	10.00	20.00	40.00
—As "The Peps"					
1060	Thinking About You/This I Pray	1965	10.00	20.00	40.00
—As "The Peps"					
1065	My Love Looks Good on You/Speak Your Peace	1966	12.50	25.00	50.00
GE GE					
503	This Love I Have for You/She's Going to Leave You	1965	10.00	20.00	40.00
PREMIUM STUFF					
1	Why Are You Blowing My Mind/I Can't Get Right	1967	10.00	20.00	40.00
3	So Fine/I'll Never Be the Same Again	1967	10.00	20.00	40.00
7	Gypsy Woman/Why Are You Blowing My Mind	1967	10.00	20.00	40.00
WEE-3					
233	With These Eyes/I've Been Trying	1967	7.50	15.00	30.00
WHEELSVILLE					
109	With These Eyes/Light of My Life	1968	3.00	6.00	12.00

FABULOUS RHINESTONES, THE

45s

Number	Title (A Side/B Side)	Yr	VG	VG+	NM
JUST SUNSHINE					
500	What a Wonderful Thing We Have/Nothing New	1972	—	2.50	5.00
500 [PS]	What a Wonderful Thing We Have/Nothing New	1972	—	3.00	6.00
501	Free/Live It Out to the End	1972	—	2.50	5.00
509	Freewheelin'/Whitecaps	1973	—	2.50	5.00

Albums

Number	Title (A Side/B Side)	Yr	VG	VG+	NM
JUST SUNSHINE					
1	The Fabulous Rhinestones	1972	3.00	6.00	12.00
9	Freewheelin'	1973	3.00	6.00	12.00

FABULOUS UPTONES, THE

45s

Number	Title (A Side/B Side)	Yr	VG	VG+	NM
TULIP					
100	New Love I've Found/Turtle	1962	75.00	150.00	300.00

FABULOUS VALIENTS, THE

45s

Number	Title (A Side/B Side)	Yr	VG	VG+	NM
HOLIDAY					
61005	Your Golden Teardrops/Carmelita	1962	62.50	125.00	250.00

FACENDA, JOHN (NARRATOR)

Albums

Number	Title (A Side/B Side)	Yr	VG	VG+	NM
RCA VICTOR					
LOP-1504 [M]	The Nativity	1958	7.50	15.00	30.00
—Gatefold with 12-page booklet					

FACENDA, TOMMY

45s

Number	Title (A Side/B Side)	Yr	VG	VG+	NM
ATLANTIC					
45-51	High School U.S.A.-Virginia/Plea of Love	1959	10.00	20.00	40.00
45-52	High School U.S.A.-New York City/Plea of Love	1959	10.00	20.00	40.00
45-53	High School U.S.A.-North & South Carolina/Plea of Love	1959	10.00	20.00	40.00
45-54	High School U.S.A.-Washington, D.C./Plea of Love	1959	10.00	20.00	40.00
45-55	High School U.S.A.-Philadelphia/Plea of Love	1959	10.00	20.00	40.00
45-56	High School U.S.A.-Detroit/Plea of Love	1959	10.00	20.00	40.00
45-57	High School U.S.A.-Pittsburgh/Plea of Love	1959	10.00	20.00	40.00
45-58	High School U.S.A.-Minneapolis-St. Paul/Plea of Love	1959	10.00	20.00	40.00
45-59	High School U.S.A.-Florida/Plea of Love	1959	10.00	20.00	40.00
45-60	High School U.S.A.-Newark, N.J./Plea of Love	1959	10.00	20.00	40.00
45-61	High School U.S.A.-Boston/Plea of Love	1959	10.00	20.00	40.00
45-62	High School U.S.A.-Cleveland/Plea of Love	1959	10.00	20.00	40.00
45-63	High School U.S.A.-Buffalo/Plea of Love	1959	10.00	20.00	40.00
45-64	High School U.S.A.-Hartford, Conn./Plea of Love	1959	10.00	20.00	40.00
45-65	High School U.S.A.-Nashville/Plea of Love	1959	10.00	20.00	40.00
45-66	High School U.S.A.-Indianapolis/Plea of Love	1959	10.00	20.00	40.00
45-67	High School U.S.A.-Chicago/Plea of Love	1959	10.00	20.00	40.00
45-68	High School U.S.A.-New Orleans/Plea of Love	1959	10.00	20.00	40.00
45-69	High School U.S.A.-St. Louis & Kansas City/Plea of Love	1959	10.00	20.00	40.00
45-70	High School U.S.A.-Georgia, Alabama/Plea of Love	1959	10.00	20.00	40.00
45-71	High School U.S.A.-Cincinnati/Plea of Love	1959	10.00	20.00	40.00
45-72	High School U.S.A.-Memphis/Plea of Love	1959	10.00	20.00	40.00
45-73	High School U.S.A.-Los Angeles/Plea of Love	1959	10.00	20.00	40.00
45-74	High School U.S.A.-San Francisco/Plea of Love	1959	10.00	20.00	40.00
45-75	High School U.S.A.-Texas/Plea of Love	1959	10.00	20.00	40.00
45-76	High School U.S.A.-Seattle, Portland/Plea of Love	1959	10.00	20.00	40.00
45-77	High School U.S.A.-Denver/Plea of Love	1959	10.00	20.00	40.00
45-78	High School U.S.A.-Oklahoma/Plea of Love	1959	10.00	20.00	40.00
2057	Bubba Ditty/I Don't Know	1960	5.00	10.00	20.00
LEGRAND					
1001	High School U.S.A./Give Me Another Chance	1959	6.25	12.50	25.00
—Original pressings have purple labels					
NASCO					
6018	Little Baby/You Are My Everything	1958	6.25	12.50	25.00

FACES

Also see SMALL FACES; ROD STEWART; RONNIE WOOD.

45s

Number	Title (A Side/B Side)	Yr	VG	VG+	NM
WARNER BROS.					
7393	Around the Phynth/Wicked Messenger	1970	2.50	5.00	10.00
—As "Small Faces"					
7442	Real Good Time/Real Wheel Skid	1970	2.50	5.00	10.00
7483	Maybe I'm Amazed/Oh Lord I'm Browned Off	1971	2.00	4.00	8.00
7545	Stay with Me/You're So Rude	1971	—	3.00	6.00
7681	Cindy Incidentally/Skewiff (Mend the Fuse)	1973	—	2.50	5.00
7681 [PS]	Cindy Incidentally/Skewiff (Mend the Fuse)	1973	—	3.00	6.00
7711	Ooh-La-La/Borstal Boys	1973	—	2.50	5.00

Albums

Number	Title (A Side/B Side)	Yr	VG	VG+	NM
WARNER BROS.					
WS 1851	First Step	1970	5.00	10.00	20.00
—First pressings have "small faces." on front cover					
WS 1851	First Step	197?	3.00	6.00	12.00
—Later pressings have "faces." on front cover					
WS 1892	Long Player	1971	3.75	7.50	15.00
BS 2574	A Nod Is As Good As a Wink...To a Blind Horse	1971	3.75	7.50	15.00
—Green label					
BS 2574	A Nod Is As Good As a Wink...To a Blind Horse	1973	3.00	6.00	12.00
—"Burbank" palm trees label					
BS 2665	Ooh La La	1973	3.75	7.50	15.00
—Green label					
BS 2665	Ooh La La	1973	3.00	6.00	12.00
—"Burbank" palm trees label					
BS 2897	Snakes and Ladders: The Best of Faces	1976	3.00	6.00	12.00

FACES, THE

45s

Number	Title (A Side/B Side)	Yr	VG	VG+	NM
IGUANA					
601	Christmas/New Year's Resolution	1965	25.00	50.00	100.00
REGINA					
326	Skier Jones/What Is This Dream (I Have)	1965	6.25	12.50	25.00
328	I'll Walk Alone/I Didn't Want Her	1965	6.25	12.50	25.00

FACTORY, THE

Lowell George was in this group before LITTLE FEAT.

45s

Number	Title (A Side/B Side)	Yr	VG	VG+	NM
UNI					
55005	Smile, Let Your Life Begin/When I Was An Apple	1967	3.00	6.00	12.00

FAHEY, JOHN

45s

Number	Title (A Side/B Side)	Yr	VG	VG+	NM
VANGUARD					
35076	A March for Martin Luther King/Singing Bridge	1968	3.00	6.00	12.00

Albums

Number	Title (A Side/B Side)	Yr	VG	VG+	NM
REPRISE					
MS 2089	Of Rivers and Religions	1972	5.00	10.00	20.00
MS 2145	After the Ball	1973	5.00	10.00	20.00
RIVERBOAT					
1 [M]	The Transfiguration of Blind Joe Death	1965	25.00	50.00	100.00
—With booklet					
SHANACHIE					
97006	God, Time and Causality	1990	3.75	7.50	15.00
TAKOMA					
C-1002	Blind Joe Death	196?	10.00	20.00	40.00

Number	Title (A Side/B Side)	Yr	VG	VG+	NM
C-1003	Death Chants, Breakdowns and Military Waltzes	196?	10.00	20.00	40.00
C-1004	Dance of Death and Other Plantation Favorites	196?	10.00	20.00	40.00
C-1008	The Great San Bernardino Birthday Party	196?	7.50	15.00	30.00
C-1014	Days Have Gone By	196?	7.50	15.00	30.00
C-1019	The Voice of the Turtle	1971	7.50	15.00	30.00
—With gatefold jacket and booklet					
C-1019	The Voice of the Turtle	197?	3.75	7.50	15.00
—Later pressings with no gatefold					
C-1020	The New Possibility: John Fahey's Guitar Soli Christmas Album	1971	6.25	12.50	25.00
—Originals with gatefold and booklet					
C-1020	The New Possibility: John Fahey's Guitar Soli Christmas Album	197?	3.75	7.50	15.00
—Later pressings with no gatefold					
C-1030	America	1972	6.25	12.50	25.00
—With gatefold jacket and booklet					
C-1030	America	197?	3.75	7.50	15.00
—Later pressings with no gatefold					
C-1035	Fare Forward Voyagers	1973	5.00	10.00	20.00
C-1043	Old Fashioned Love	1975	3.75	7.50	15.00
C-1045	Christmas with John Fahey, Vol. 2	1975	3.75	7.50	15.00
C-1058	The Best of John Fahey 1959-1977	1977	3.75	7.50	15.00
TAK-7002	Blind Joe Death	1979	3.00	6.00	12.00
—Reissue of 1002					
TAK-7003	Death Chants, Breakdowns and Military Waltzes	198?	3.00	6.00	12.00
—Reissue of 1003					
TAK-7004	Dance of Death and Other Plantation Favorites	198?	3.00	6.00	12.00
—Reissue of 1004					
TAK-7020	The New Possibility: John Fahey's Guitar Soli Christmas Album	198?	3.00	6.00	12.00
—Reissue of 1020					
TAK-7035	Fare Forward Voyagers	198?	3.00	6.00	12.00
—Reissue of 1035					
TAK-7043	Old Fashioned Love	198?	3.00	6.00	12.00
—Reissue of 1043					
TAK-7045	Christmas with John Fahey, Vol. 2	198?	3.00	6.00	12.00
—Reissue of 1045					
TAK-7058	The Best of John Fahey 1959-1977	198?	3.00	6.00	12.00
—Reissue of 1058					
TAK-7069	John Fahey Visits Washington, D.C.	1979	3.00	6.00	12.00
TAK-7085	Yes! Jesus Loves Me	1980	3.00	6.00	12.00
TAK-7089	Live in Tasmania	198?	3.00	6.00	12.00
TAK-7102	Railroads I	1981	3.00	6.00	12.00
TERRA					
T-2	Requia	1985	2.50	5.00	10.00
—Reissue of Vanguard 79259					
VANGUARD					
VSD 55/56 [(2)]	Essential John Fahey	1974	5.00	10.00	20.00
VRS-9259 [M]	Requia	1968	6.25	12.50	25.00
VSD-79259 [S]	Requia	1968	5.00	10.00	20.00
VSD-79293	The Yellow Princess	1969	5.00	10.00	20.00
VARRICK					
VR-002	John Fahey Christmas Guitar, Volume 1	1982	3.75	7.50	15.00
VR-008	Let Go	1983	3.75	7.50	15.00
VR-012	Popular Songs of Christmas and New Year's	1983	3.75	7.50	15.00
VR-019	Rain Forests, Oceans & Other Themes	1985	3.00	6.00	12.00
VR-028	I Remember Blind Joe Death	1987	3.00	6.00	12.00

FAIR, YVONNE

Number	Title (A Side/B Side)	Yr	VG	VG+	NM
45s					
DADE					
1851	Straighten Up/Say Yeah Yeah	1963	3.00	6.00	12.00
5006	Straighten Up/Say Yeah Yeah	1963	5.00	10.00	20.00
KING					
5594	I Found You/If I Knew	1962	3.75	7.50	15.00
—With the James Brown Band					
5654	Tell Me Why/Say So Long	1962	3.75	7.50	15.00
—With James Brown					
5687	It Hurts to Be in Love/You Can Make It If You Try	1962	3.75	7.50	15.00
—With James Brown					
6017	Tell Me Why/You Can Make It If You Try	1966	2.00	4.00	8.00
MOTOWN					
1306	Funky Music Sho Nuff Turns Me On/Let Your Hair Down	1974	—	2.50	5.00
1323	Walk Out the Door If You Wanna/It Should Have Been Me	1974	—	2.50	5.00
1344	You Can't Judge a Book By Its Cover/It's Bad for Me to See You	1975	—	2.50	5.00
1354	Love Ain't No Toy/It's Bad for Me to See You	1975	—	2.50	5.00
1384	It Should Have Been Me/Tell Me Something Good	1976	—	2.50	5.00
SMASH					
2030	Just As Sure (As You Play, You Must Pay)/Baby, Baby, Baby	1966	2.50	5.00	10.00
SOUL					
35075	Stay a Little Longer/We Should Never Be Lonely My Love	1970	—	3.00	6.00

FAIRLANES, THE

Number	Title (A Side/B Side)	Yr	VG	VG+	NM
45s					
ARGO					
5357	Little Girl, Little Girl/Comin' After You	1960	7.50	15.00	30.00
CONTINENTAL					
1001	Writing This Letter/Playboy	1961	75.00	150.00	300.00
DART					
109	Just for Me/Bullseye	1959	20.00	40.00	80.00
LUCKY SEVEN					
102	Seventeen Steps/Johnny Rhythm	1959	15.00	30.00	60.00
MINARET					
103	The Dagwood/I'm Not the Kind of Guy	1962	5.00	10.00	20.00
RADIANT					
101	Baby Baby/Tell Me	1964	62.50	125.00	250.00
REPRISE					
20213	Surf Train/Lonely Weekends	1963	7.50	15.00	30.00

FAIRPORT CONVENTION

Also see SANDY DENNY; RICHARD THOMPSON.

Number	Title (A Side/B Side)	Yr	VG	VG+	NM
45s					
A&M					
1108	Fotheringay/I'll Keep It with Mine	1969	3.00	6.00	12.00
1155	Genesis Hall/Si Tu Dois Partie	1969	3.00	6.00	12.00
1333	Journeyman's Grace/The World Has Surely Lost Its Head	1972	2.00	4.00	8.00
1348	John Lee/The Time Is Near	1972	2.00	4.00	8.00
Albums					
ANTILLES					
7054	Gottle O' Geer	1976	3.00	6.00	12.00
A&M					
SP-3530 [(2)]	The Fairport Chronicles	1976	3.75	7.50	15.00
SP-3603	Fairport Nine	1974	3.00	6.00	12.00
—Early reissue of 4407					
SP-4185	Fairport Convention	1969	3.75	7.50	15.00
—Not a reissue of Cotillion LP, but the US issue of the second UK LP "What We Did On Our Holidays"					
SP-4206	Unhalfbricking	1969	3.75	7.50	15.00
SP-4257	Liege and Lief	1970	3.75	7.50	15.00
SP-4265	Full House	1970	3.75	7.50	15.00
SP-4316	Angel Delight	1971	3.75	7.50	15.00
SP-4333	"Babbacombe" Lee	1972	3.75	7.50	15.00
SP-4383	Rosie	1973	3.75	7.50	15.00
SP-4407	Fairport Nine	1973	3.75	7.50	15.00
SP-6016 [(2)]	The Fairport Chronicles	198?	3.00	6.00	12.00
—Reissue of 3530					
CARTHAGE					
CGLP-4417	Full House	198?	2.50	5.00	10.00
—Reissue of A&M 4265					
CGLP-4418	Unhalfbricking	198?	2.50	5.00	10.00
—Reissue of A&M 4206					
CGLP-4430	What We Did on Our Holidays	198?	2.50	5.00	10.00
—Reissue of A&M 4185 with UK title restored					
COTILLION					
SD 9024	Fairport Convention	1968	7.50	15.00	30.00
HANNIBAL					
HNBL-1319	House Full	1986	2.50	5.00	10.00
HNBL-1329	Heyday	1987	2.50	5.00	10.00
ISLAND					
ILPS-9285	Fairport Live/A Movable Feast	1974	3.00	6.00	12.00
ILPS-9313	Rising for the Moon	1975	3.00	6.00	12.00
90678	In Real Time — Live '87	1987	2.50	5.00	10.00
VARRICK					
VR-023	Gladys' Leap	1986	2.50	5.00	10.00
VR-029	Expletive Delighted!	1987	2.50	5.00	10.00

FAITH, ADAM

Number	Title (A Side/B Side)	Yr	VG	VG+	NM
45s					
AMY					
895	The First Time/So Long Baby	1964	3.75	7.50	15.00
899	We Are in Love/What Now	1964	3.75	7.50	15.00
913	It's Alright/I Just Don't Know	1964	3.75	7.50	15.00
922	Talk About Love/Stop Feeling Sorry for Yourself	1965	3.75	7.50	15.00
936	Don't You Know/Someone's Taken Marie Away	1965	3.75	7.50	15.00
CAPITOL					
5543	I'm Used to Losing You/I Don't Need That Kind of Lovin'	1965	2.50	5.00	10.00
5699	To Make a Big Man Cry/Here's Another Day	1966	2.50	5.00	10.00
CUB					
9061	What Do You Want/From Now Until September	1960	5.00	10.00	20.00
9068	Poor Me/The Reason	1960	5.00	10.00	20.00
9074	I Did What You Told Me/When Johnny Comes Marching Home	1960	5.00	10.00	20.00
DOT					
16405	Don't That Beat All/Mix Me a Person	1962	3.75	7.50	15.00
LAURIE					
3455	Daddy, What'll Happen to Me/Cowman, Milk Your Cow	1968	2.00	4.00	8.00
Albums					
AMY					
8005 [M]	Adam Faith	1965	6.25	12.50	25.00
S-8005 [S]	Adam Faith	1965	0.50	15.00	30.00
MGM					
E-3951 [M]	England's Top Singer	1961	10.00	20.00	40.00
SE-3951 [S]	England's Top Singer	1961	12.50	25.00	50.00

FAITH, PERCY

Number	Title (A Side/B Side)	Yr	VG	VG+	NM
45s					
COLUMBIA					
1-607	I Cross My Fingers/Valencia	1950	5.00	10.00	20.00
—Microgroove 33 1/3 rpm 7-inch single					
1-619 (?)	Violins from Nowhere/Tzin-Tzun-Tzan	1950	5.00	10.00	20.00
—Microgroove 33 1/3 rpm 7-inch single					
1-681 (?)	They Can't Take That Away from Me/If I Had a Magic Carpet	1950	5.00	10.00	20.00
—Microgroove 33 1/3 rpm 7-inch single					
1-699 (?)	I Was Dancing with Someone/Friendly Star	1950	5.00	10.00	20.00
—Microgroove 33 1/3 rpm 7-inch single					
1-752	All My Love/This Is the Time	1950	4.50	9.00	18.00
—Microgroove 33 1/3 rpm 7-inch single					
6-752	All My Love/This Is the Time	1950	3.75	7.50	15.00
1-812 (?)	Brazilian Sleighride/What Is This Thing Called Love	1950	5.00	10.00	20.00
—Microgroove 33 1/3 rpm 7-inch single					
6-812 (?)	Brazilian Sleighride/What Is This Thing Called Love	1950	3.75	7.50	15.00
1-830 (?)	Green Grass/I'm in the Middle of a Riddle	1950	4.50	9.00	18.00
—Microgroove 33 1/3 rpm 7-inch single					
6-830 (?)	Green Grass/I'm in the Middle of a Riddle	1950	3.75	7.50	15.00
1-841 (?)	Christmas in My Heart/Sleigh Ride	1950	5.00	10.00	20.00
—Microgroove 33 1/3 rpm 7-inch single					

Number	Title (A Side/B Side)	Yr	VG	VG+	NM
6-841 (?)	Christmas in My Heart/Sleigh Ride	1950	3.75	7.50	15.00
1-899	Christmas In Killarney/Norah	1950	5.00	10.00	20.00
—Microgroove 33 1/3 rpm 7-inch single					
6-899	Christmas in Killarney/Norah	1950	3.75	7.50	15.00
10010	Theme from "Chinatown"/Tubular Bells	1974	—	2.00	4.00
10098	Orange Blossom Special/1,2,3,4	1975	—	2.00	4.00
10165	El Bimbo/Cherry Cherry	1975	—	2.00	4.00
10233	Summer Place '76/Chompin'	1975	—	2.00	4.00
10301	Emmanuelle-The Joys of a Woman/Ding Dong	1976	—	2.00	4.00
31500 [S]	Non Dimenticar/Tropical Merengue	1962	2.00	4.00	8.00
31501 [S]	The Syncopated Clock/Delicado	1962	2.00	4.00	8.00
31502 [S]	The Rain in Spain/Till	1962	2.00	4.00	8.00
31503 [S]	Jamaican Rhumba/They Can't Take That Away from Me	1962	2.00	4.00	8.00
31504 [S]	Swedish Rhapsody/All My Love	1962	2.00	4.00	8.00
31536 [S]	(contents unknown)	1962	2.00	4.00	8.00
31537 [S]	(contents unknown)	1962	2.00	4.00	8.00
31538 [S]	(contents unknown)	1962	2.00	4.00	8.00
31539 [S]	Maxine/The Minute Samba	1962	2.00	4.00	8.00
31540 [S]	(contents unknown)	1962	2.00	4.00	8.00
—The above 10 are Columbia "Stereo 7" singles					
39155	Zing Zing/Kiss and Promise	1951	3.75	7.50	15.00
39192	The Loveliest Night of the Year/You Are the One	1951	3.75	7.50	15.00
39257	No One But You/Goodbye John	1951	3.75	7.50	15.00
39329	Nervous Gavotte/Hot Canary	1951	3.75	7.50	15.00
39356	Carousel Waltz/When I'm Not Near the Girl I Love	1951	3.00	6.00	12.00
39357	While We're Young/The Girl That I Marry	1951	3.00	6.00	12.00
39358	A Kiss in the Dark/Valse Huguette	1951	3.00	6.00	12.00
39359	Waltz in Swingtown/I'll Take Romance	1951	3.00	6.00	12.00
—The above four comprise a box set					
39426	Black Ball Perry Line/Wondrous Word	1951	3.75	7.50	15.00
39491	Fiddle Derby/March of the Siamese Children	1951	3.75	7.50	15.00
39528	When the Saints Go Marching In/I Want to Be Near You	1951	3.75	7.50	15.00
39559	Sleigh Ride/Christmas in Killarney	1951	3.75	7.50	15.00
39613	If I Loved You/Dizzy Fingers	1951	3.75	7.50	15.00
39638	Would You/I Talk to the Trees	1952	3.00	6.00	12.00
39640	Flight 33 1/3/Ba-Tu-Ca-Da	1952	2.50	5.00	10.00
39641	One Night of Love/My Shawl	1952	2.50	5.00	10.00
39642	Brazilian Sleighride/What Is This Thing Called Love	1952	2.50	5.00	10.00
39643	Beautiful Love/Nightingale	1952	2.50	5.00	10.00
—The above four comprise a box set					
39664	Carefree/Invitation	1952	3.00	6.00	12.00
39708	Delicado/Festival	1952	3.00	6.00	12.00
39732	Delicado/The Gandy Dancers' Ball	1952	2.50	5.00	10.00
—B-side by Frankie Laine; this is part of a various-artists box set					
39781	Enlloro/Jungle Fantasy	1952	2.50	5.00	10.00
39782	Caribbean Night/Cu-Tu-Gu-Ru	1952	2.50	5.00	10.00
39783	Minute Samba/The Girl with the Spanish Drawl	1952	2.50	5.00	10.00
39784	Oye Negra/Jamaican Rhumba	1952	2.50	5.00	10.00
—The above four comprise a box set					
39790	Jamaican Rhumba/Dadu	1952	3.00	6.00	12.00
39874	Amorada/Funny Fellow	1952	3.00	6.00	12.00
39907	Over the Mountain/Caress	1952	3.00	6.00	12.00
39944	The Song from Moulin Rouge (Where Is Your Heart)/Swedish Rhapsody	1953	2.50	5.00	10.00
—Vocal on A-side by Felicia Sanders					
39998	Return to Paradise (Part 1)/Return to Paradise (Part 2)	1953	2.50	5.00	10.00
40029	Tropic Holiday/Gaviotta	1953	2.50	5.00	10.00
40076	Many Times/In Love	1953	2.50	5.00	10.00
40115	Ev'rybody Loves Saturday Night/True or False	1953	2.50	5.00	10.00
40155	Non Dimenticar (Don't Forget)/They Can't Take That Away from Me	1954	2.50	5.00	10.00
40174	Baubles, Bangles and Beads/And This Is My Beloved	1954	2.50	5.00	10.00
40185	Eleanora/Dream, Dream, Dream	1954	2.50	5.00	10.00
40323	Rainfall/The Bandit	1954	2.50	5.00	10.00
40390	Ching-Ching-a-Ling/Petite	1954	2.50	5.00	10.00
40428	If Hearts Could Talk/Blue Mirage	1955	2.50	5.00	10.00
40482	Land of the Pharaohs/The World Is Mine	1955	2.50	5.00	10.00
40512	The Fiddling Bullfighter/Not As a Stranger	1955	2.50	5.00	10.00
40543	Tropical Merengue/We Won't Say Goodbye	1955	2.50	5.00	10.00
40588	The Rose Tattoo/Tambora	1955	2.50	5.00	10.00
40633	Valley Valparaiso/Bluebell	1956	2.50	5.00	10.00
40644	We All Need Love/Carmelita	1956	2.50	5.00	10.00
40696	With a Little Bit of Luck/The Rain in Spain	1956	2.50	5.00	10.00
40719	Wouldn't It Be Loverly/Sierra Madre	1956	2.50	5.00	10.00
40764	Baby Doll/Vagabond Waltz King	1956	2.50	5.00	10.00
40826	Till/The Last Dance	1957	2.50	5.00	10.00
40900	Italiano!/Bahama Lullaby	1957	2.50	5.00	10.00
40949	Hey Jose/What's It Like in Paree?	1957	2.50	5.00	10.00
41024	Never Till Now/Katsumi Love Theme	1957	2.50	5.00	10.00
41095	Maria/The Stars	1958	2.00	4.00	8.00
41126	The Impala Theme/Pizzicato Polka	1958	2.00	4.00	8.00
41181	Same Old Moon/Indiscreet	1958	2.00	4.00	8.00
41271	The Pyramid Dance/Quia Quia	1958	2.00	4.00	8.00
41328	Goin' Home Train/Isle of Paradise	1959	2.00	4.00	8.00
41490	Theme from "A Summer Place"/Go-Go-Po-Go	1959	2.00	4.00	8.00
41490 [PS]	Theme from "A Summer Place"/Go-Go-Po-Go	1959	3.75	7.50	15.00
41655	Theme for Young Lovers/Bimini Goombay	1960	2.00	4.00	8.00
41731	Sons and Lovers/Hawaiian Lullaby	1960	2.00	4.00	8.00
41796	Theme from "The Dark at the Top of the Stairs"/Our Language of Love	1960	2.00	4.00	8.00
41978	The Bilbao Song/Lover's Prelude	1961	2.00	4.00	8.00
42011	At Last-Angel Face/Tammy Tell Me True	1961	2.00	4.00	8.00
42239	Brass Ring/I Just Can't Wait	1961	2.00	4.00	8.00
42333	Love Theme from "The Four Horsemen of the Apocalypse"/Theme from "Light in the Piazza"	1962	—	3.00	6.00
42423	Advise and Consent/Jacqueline's Journey	1962	—	3.00	6.00
42844	The Sound of Surf/Our Love	1963	—	3.00	6.00
42979	The Virginian/Melody from "Mahogany"	1964	—	3.00	6.00
42991	Sloop John B/This Train	1964	—	3.00	6.00
43116	Judy/Love Goddess	1964	—	3.00	6.00
43208	Kahlua/Insensatez	1965	—	3.00	6.00
43326	Love Me/We're Gonna Be Alright	1965	—	3.00	6.00
43555	Song from "The Oscar"/Glass Mountain	1966	—	3.00	6.00
43642	Cheryl/Swingin' Village	1966	—	3.00	6.00
43746	Tropic Holiday/Reza	1966	—	3.00	6.00
43846	Christmas Is.../Silver Bells	1966	—	3.00	6.00
44086	A Man and a Woman/This Hotel	1967	—	2.50	5.00
44166	Kahlua/Yellow Days	1967	—	2.50	5.00
44319	Can't Take My Eyes Off You/Windy	1967	—	2.50	5.00
44412	Theme from "The Dark at the Top of the Stairs"/Tara's Theme (From "Gone with the Wind")	1967	—	2.50	5.00
44446	For Those in Love/There Was a Time	1968	—	2.50	5.00
44585	MacArthur Park/Elvira Madigan Theme	1968	—	2.50	5.00
44734	Zorba/A Quiet Day	1969	—	2.50	5.00
44876	The Windmills of Your Mind/Theme from "The Fox"	1969	—	2.00	4.00
44932	Theme from "A Summer Place"/Hello Tomorrow	1969	—	2.50	5.00
44987	Spinning Wheel/April Fools	1969	—	2.00	4.00
45051	Peppermint Hill and Strawberry Lane/The Time for Love Is Anytime	1969	—	2.00	4.00
45114	Airport Love Theme/Theme for Young Lovers	1970	—	2.00	4.00
45297	I Don't Know How to Love Him/Everything's Alright	1971	—	2.00	4.00
45374	Anytime of the Year/I Can Hear the Music	1971	—	2.00	4.00
45401	Theme from "Summer of '42"/Tres	1971	—	2.00	4.00
45525	Diamonds Are Forever/Love Theme from "Mary Queen of Scots"	1972	—	2.00	4.00
45563	Love Theme from "The Godfather"/Godfather Waltz	1972	—	2.50	5.00
45619	Theme from "Kotch"/Back's Lunch	1972	—	2.00	4.00
45868	Viva Vivaldi/We Were Having Some Fun at the Conservatory, When ...	1973	—	2.00	4.00
45945	Corazon/Crunchy Granola Suite	1973	—	2.00	4.00
46013	Euterpe/Hill Where the Lord Hides	1974	—	2.00	4.00
JZSP 111903/4 [DJ]	Away In A Manger/We Three Kings Of Orient Are	1965	3.00	6.00	12.00
—Promo only on green vinyl					
JZSP 119961/2 [DJ]	Christmas Is . . ./Happy Holiday	1966	2.50	5.00	10.00
—Yellow label					
JZSP 119961/2 [DJ]	Christmas Is . . ./Happy Holiday	1967	2.50	5.00	10.00
—White label					
JZSP 119961/2 [PS]	Christmas Is . . ./Happy Holiday	1967	3.75	7.50	15.00
—Sleeve announces this as the 1967 Christmas Seals Record					

DECCA

Number	Title (A Side/B Side)	Yr	VG	VG+	NM
27542	I Love You/Long Ago (and Far Away)	1951	3.00	6.00	12.00
27543	I'll Close My Eyes/There's No Holding Me	1951	3.00	6.00	12.00
—With Hildegarde					
27544	Amor/Spring Will Be a Little Late This Year	1951	3.00	6.00	12.00

RCA VICTOR

Number	Title (A Side/B Side)	Yr	VG	VG+	NM
47-3004	Deep Purple/Oodles of Noodles	1949	3.75	7.50	15.00
47-3063	Whirlwind/My Dream Concerto	1949	3.75	7.50	15.00
47-4001	Perpetual Motion/Solitude	1950	3.75	7.50	15.00
47-4002	Body and Soul/Cumana	1950	3.75	7.50	15.00
47-4003	Beyond the Sea/El Cumbanchero	1950	3.75	7.50	15.00

7-Inch Extended Plays

COLUMBIA

Number	Title (A Side/B Side)	Yr	VG	VG+	NM
B-1610	Would You/I Talk to the Trees//If I Loved You/Easy to Love	195?	2.50	5.00	10.00
B-1610 [PS]	(title unknown)	195?	2.50	5.00	10.00
B-2529	*The Song from Moulin Rouge/Swedish Rhapsody/Delicado/Invitation	1958	2.50	5.00	10.00
B-2529 [PS]	Percy Faith (Hall of Fame Series)	1958	2.50	5.00	10.00
B-2623	Mademoiselle De Paree/Under the Bridges of Paris//Non Dimenticar/April in Portugal	195?	2.50	5.00	10.00
B-2623 [PS]	(title unknown)	195?	2.50	5.00	10.00

Albums

COLUMBIA

Number	Title (A Side/B Side)	Yr	VG	VG+	NM
GP 1 [(2)]	Forever Young	1968	3.75	7.50	15.00
C2L 15 [(2) M]	The Columbia Album of Christmas Music	1958	7.50	15.00	30.00
—Combines CL 588 and CL 1187 into one gatefold package					
CL 525 [M]	Continental Music	1955	5.00	10.00	20.00
CL 550 [M]	Kismet	1955	5.00	10.00	20.00
CL 577 [M]	Music from Hollywood	1955	5.00	10.00	20.00
CL 588 [M]	Music of Christmas	1955	6.25	12.50	25.00
CL 640 [M]	House of Flowers	1956	5.00	10.00	20.00
CL 681 [M]	Delicado	1956	5.00	10.00	20.00
CL 705 [M]	Music for Her	1956	5.00	10.00	20.00
CL 880 [M]	Passport to Romance	1956	5.00	10.00	20.00
CL 895 [M]	My Fair Lady	1957	5.00	10.00	20.00
CL 955 [M]	L'il Abner	1957	5.00	10.00	20.00
CL 1010 [M]	Adventure in the Sun	1957	5.00	10.00	20.00
CS 1019	Held Over! Today's Great Movie Themes	1970	3.00	6.00	12.00
CL 1075 [M]	Viva!	1957	5.00	10.00	20.00
CL 1105 [M]	South Pacific	1957	3.75	7.50	15.00
CL 1182 [M]	Touchdown!	1957	5.00	10.00	20.00
CL 1187 [M]	Hallelujah!	1957	5.00	10.00	20.00
CL 1188 [M]	Jubliation!	1957	5.00	10.00	20.00
CL 1267 [M]	Malaguena	1958	5.00	10.00	20.00
CL 1298 [M]	Porgy and Bess	1958	3.75	7.50	15.00
CL 1302 [M]	A Night with Sigmund Romberg	1959	3.75	7.50	15.00
CL 1322 [M]	Bouquet	1959	3.75	7.50	15.00
CL 1381 [M]	Music of Christmas	1959	5.00	10.00	20.00
—Re-recorded version of CL 588 with same track order					
CL 1386 [M]	A Night with Jerome Kern	1959	3.75	7.50	15.00
CL 1417 [M]	Bon Voyage!	1960	3.75	7.50	15.00
CL 1418 [M]	The Sound of Music	1960	3.75	7.50	15.00
CL 1493 [M]	Percy Faith's Greatest Hits	1960	3.75	7.50	15.00
CL 1501 [M]	Jealousy	1960	3.00	6.00	12.00
CL 1570 [M]	Camelot	1960	3.00	6.00	12.00
CL 1627 [M]	Tara's Theme from "Gone with the Wind" and Other Themes	1961	3.00	6.00	12.00
CL 1639 [M]	Mucho Gusto! More Music of Brazil	1961	3.00	6.00	12.00
CL 1681 [M]	Bouquet of Love	1962	3.00	6.00	12.00
CL 1783 [M]	Hollywood's Great Themes	1962	3.00	6.00	12.00
CL 1822 [M]	The Music of Brazil!	1962	3.00	6.00	12.00
CL 1902 [M]	Exotic Strings	1963	3.00	6.00	12.00

Number	Title (A Side/B Side)	Yr	VG	VG+	NM
CL 1957 [M]	American Serenade	1963	3.00	6.00	12.00
CL 2023 [M]	Themes for Young Lovers	1963	3.00	6.00	12.00
CL 2024 [M]	Shangri-La!	1963	3.00	6.00	12.00
CL 2108 [M]	Great Folk Themes	1964	3.00	6.00	12.00
CL 2167 [M]	More Themes for Young Lovers	1964	3.00	6.00	12.00
CL 2209 [M]	Love Goddess	1966	3.00	6.00	12.00
CL 2279 [M]	Latin Themes for Young Lovers	1966	3.00	6.00	12.00
CL 2317 [M]	Do I Hear a Waltz	1965	3.00	6.00	12.00
CL 2356 [M]	Broadway Bouquet	1965	3.00	6.00	12.00
CL 2405 [M]	Music of Christmas, Volume 2	1965	3.00	6.00	12.00
CL 2441 [M]	Themes for the "In" Crowd	1966	3.00	6.00	12.00
CL 2529 [M]	Bim Bam Boom	1966	3.00	6.00	12.00
CL 2577 [M]	Christmas Is...	1966	3.00	6.00	12.00
CL 2650 [M]	The Academy Award Winner and Other Great Movie Themes	1967	3.75	7.50	15.00
CL 2704 [M]	Today's Themes for Young Lovers	1967	3.75	7.50	15.00
CL 2810 [M]	For Those in Love	1968	5.00	10.00	20.00
CS 8005 [S]	South Pacific	1958	6.25	12.50	25.00
CS 8033 [S]	Hallelujah!	1958	6.25	12.50	25.00
CS 8038 [S]	Viva!	1958	6.25	12.50	25.00
CS 8081 [S]	Malaguena	1958	6.25	12.50	25.00
CS 8105 [S]	Porgy and Bess	1959	5.00	10.00	20.00
CS 8108 [S]	A Night with Sigmund Romberg	1959	5.00	10.00	20.00
CS 8124 [S]	Bouquet	1959	3.75	7.50	15.00
CS 8176 [S]	Music of Christmas	1959	3.75	7.50	15.00
CS 8181 [S]	A Night with Jerome Kern	1959	5.00	10.00	20.00
CS 8214 [S]	Bon Voyage!	1960	3.75	7.50	15.00
CS 8215 [S]	The Sound of Music	1960	3.75	7.50	15.00
CS 8292 [S]	Jealousy	1960	3.75	7.50	15.00
CS 8370 [S]	Camelot	1960	3.75	7.50	15.00
CS 8427 [S]	Tara's Theme from "Gone with the Wind" and Other Themes	1961	3.75	7.50	15.00
CS 8439 [S]	Mucho Gusto! More Music of Brazil	1961	3.75	7.50	15.00
CS 8481 [S]	Bouquet of Love	1962	3.75	7.50	15.00
CS 8583 [S]	Hollywood's Great Themes	1962	3.75	7.50	15.00
CS 8622 [S]	The Music of Brazil!	1962	3.75	7.50	15.00
CS 8637 [R]	Percy Faith's Greatest Hits	1963	2.50	5.00	10.00
PC 8637 [R]	Percy Faith's Greatest Hits	198?	2.00	4.00	8.00
—Budget-line reissue					
CS 8642 [R]	Kismet	1963	2.50	5.00	10.00
CS 8702 [S]	Exotic Strings	1963	3.00	6.00	12.00
CS 8757 [S]	American Serenade	1963	3.00	6.00	12.00
CS 8823 [S]	Themes for Young Lovers	1963	3.00	6.00	12.00
CS 8824 [S]	Shangri-La!	1963	3.00	6.00	12.00
CS 8908 [S]	Great Folk Themes	1964	3.00	6.00	12.00
CS 8967 [S]	More Themes for Young Lovers	1964	3.00	6.00	12.00
CS 9004 [R]	My Fair Lady	1964	3.00	6.00	12.00
CS 9009 [S]	Love Goddess	1964	3.00	6.00	12.00
CS 9079 [S]	Latin Themes for Young Lovers	1965	3.00	6.00	12.00
CS 9117 [S]	Do I Hear a Waltz	1965	3.00	6.00	12.00
CS 9156 [S]	Broadway Bouquet	1965	3.00	6.00	12.00
CS 9205 [S]	Music of Christmas, Volume 2	1965	3.00	6.00	12.00
CS 9241 [S]	Themes for the "In" Crowd	1966	3.00	6.00	12.00
CS 9329 [S]	Bim Bam Boom	1966	3.00	6.00	12.00
3C 9377	Christmas Is...	198?	2.00	4.00	8.00
—Budget-line reissue					
CS 9377 [S]	Christmas Is...	1966	3.00	6.00	12.00
CS 9450 [S]	The Academy Award Winner and Other Great Movie Themes	1967	3.00	6.00	12.00
CS 9504 [S]	Today's Themes for Young Lovers	1967	3.00	6.00	12.00
CS 9610 [S]	For Those in Love	1968	3.00	6.00	12.00
CS 9706	Angel of the Morning (Hit Themes for Young Lovers)	1968	3.00	6.00	12.00
CS 9762	Those Were the Days	1969	3.00	6.00	12.00
CS 9835	Windmills of Your Mind	1969	3.00	6.00	12.00
CS 9906	Love Theme from "Romeo & Juliet"	1969	3.00	6.00	12.00
CS 9983	Leaving on a Jet Plane	1970	3.00	6.00	12.00
LE 10082	Music of Christmas	197?	2.50	5.00	10.00
—Brown label "Limited Edition" series; same contents as CS 8176					
C 30097	The Beatles Album	1970	3.00	6.00	12.00
G 30330 [(2)]	A Time for Love	1971	3.75	7.50	15.00
C 30502	I Think I Love You	1971	2.50	5.00	10.00
C 30800	Black Magic Woman	1971	2.50	5.00	10.00
CQ 31004 [Q]	Love Theme from "Romeo & Juliet"	1971	3.75	7.50	15.00
C 31042	Jesus Christ Superstar	1971	2.50	5.00	10.00
C 31301	Joy	1972	2.50	5.00	10.00
KG 31588 [(2)]	All-Time Greatest Hits	1972	3.00	6.00	12.00
PG 31588 [(2)]	All-Time Greatest Hits	198?	2.50	5.00	10.00
—Budget-line reissue					
KC 31627	Day by Day	1972	2.50	5.00	10.00
CQ 32164 [Q]	Clair	1973	3.75	7.50	15.00
KC 32164	Clair	1973	2.50	5.00	10.00
KC 32380	My Love	1973	2.50	5.00	10.00
C 32585	Remembering the Hits of the 60's	1973	2.50	5.00	10.00
KC 32714	Corazon	1974	2.50	5.00	10.00
KC 32803	A New Thing	1974	2.50	5.00	10.00
KC 33142	Country Bouquet	1975	2.50	5.00	10.00
CQ 33244 [Q]	Chinatown (Featuring "The Entertainer")	1974	3.75	7.50	15.00
KC 33244	Chinatown (Featuring "The Entertainer")	1974	2.50	5.00	10.00
KC 33549	Disco Party	1975	2.50	5.00	10.00
CG 33606 [(2)]	Viva!/Mucho Gusto!	1975	3.00	6.00	12.00
CG 33895 [(2)]	Great Moments of Percy Faith	1976	3.00	6.00	12.00
KC 33915	Summer of '76	1976	2.50	5.00	10.00
PC 38302	Music of Christmas	1983	2.00	4.00	8.00
PC 39471	Christmas Melodies	1984	2.00	4.00	8.00
—Repackage of previously released material					
COLUMBIA SPECIAL PRODUCTS					
P 13091	Broadway Bouquet	197?	2.00	4.00	8.00
P2 13719 [(2)]	The Columbia Album of George Gershwin	197?	3.00	6.00	12.00
P 13827	American Serenade	197?	2.00	4.00	8.00
HARMONY					
HS 11348	Sounds of Music	1969	2.50	5.00	10.00
H 30020	Younger Than Springtime	1970	2.50	5.00	10.00
KH 30607	A Summer Place	1971	2.50	5.00	10.00
KH 30977	Raindrops Keep Fallin'	1971	2.50	5.00	10.00
KH 31777	Every Night at the Movies	1972	2.50	5.00	10.00

Number	Title (A Side/B Side)	Yr	VG	VG+	NM
VOCALION					
VL 3600 [M]	North and South of the Border	1958	3.75	7.50	15.00

FAITH HOPE & CHARITY

45s

Number	Title (A Side/B Side)	Yr	VG	VG+	NM
20TH CENTURY					
2370	Don't Pity Me/Find What You Need	1978	—	2.00	4.00
2391	How Can I Help But Love You/Keep Me Baby	1978	—	2.00	4.00
MAXWELL					
805	So Much Love/Let's Try It Over	1970	—	3.00	6.00
808	Baby Don't Take Your Love/Make Love to Me	1970	—	3.00	6.00
RCA					
PB-10749	You're My Peace of Mind/Rescue Me	1976	—	2.50	5.00
PB-10865	Life Goes On/You've Gotta Tell Her	1976	—	2.50	5.00
RCA VICTOR					
PB-10343	To Each His Own/Find a Way	1975	—	2.50	5.00
PB-10542	Don't Go Looking for Love/Disco Dan	1976	—	2.50	5.00
SUSSEX					
216	Come Back and Finish What You Started/I Worship the Very Ground You Walk On	1971	—	2.50	5.00
224	No Trespassing/Ghosts Keep Haunting Me	1971	—	2.50	5.00
231	We Can Change the World/God Bless the World	1972	—	2.50	5.00
243	I Was There/Who Could Love You More Than I	1972	—	2.50	5.00
252	Who Made You Go/Heavy Love	1973	—	2.50	5.00

Albums

Number	Title (A Side/B Side)	Yr	VG	VG+	NM
RCA VICTOR					
APL1-1100	Faith, Hope & Charity	1975	3.00	6.00	12.00
APL1-1827	Life Goes	1976	3.00	6.00	12.00
SUSSEX					
SXSB-7019	Heavy Love	1972	3.75	7.50	15.00

FAITHFULL, MARIANNE

12-Inch Singles

Number	Title (A Side/B Side)	Yr	VG	VG+	NM
ANTILLES					
AN 801	Broken English (5:59)/Why D'Ya Do It	1979	2.50	5.00	10.00
ISLAND					
DMD 627 [DJ]	Blue Millionaire (Long)/Blue Millionaire (Short)	1983	2.00	4.00	8.00

45s

Number	Title (A Side/B Side)	Yr	VG	VG+	NM
COLLECTABLES					
2605	Broken English/Why D'Ya Do It	199?	—	—	3.00
—Reissue					
4238	As Tears Go By/Gloria	199?	—	—	3.00
—Reissue; B-side by Them					
ISLAND					
49121	Broken English/Brain Drain	1979	—	2.50	5.00
49873	Sweetheart/For Beauty's Sake	1981	—	2.00	4.00
94997	Broken English/Why D'Ya Do It?	198?	2.50	5.00	10.00
—Gold label "Revival of the Fittest" series					
99888	Running for Our Lives/(B-side unknown)	1983	—	2.00	4.00
LONDON					
1022	Sister Morphine/Something Better	1969	25.00	50.00	100.00
—Promo worth about 50% of these values.					
9697	As Tears Go By/Greensleeves	1964	3.00	6.00	12.00
9731	Come and Stay with Me/What Have I Done Wrong Come and Stay with Me/What Have I Done Wrong	1965	2.50	5.00	10.00
9759	This Little Bird/Morning Sun	1965	2.50	5.00	10.00
9780	Summer Nights/The Sha-La-La Song	1965	2.50	5.00	10.00
9802	Go Away from My World/Oh Look Around You	1965	2.50	5.00	10.00
9802 [PS]	Go Away from My World/Oh Look Around You	1965	5.00	10.00	20.00
20012	Counting/Tomorrow's Calling	1966	2.50	5.00	10.00
20012 [PS]	Counting/Tomorrow's Calling	1966	5.00	10.00	20.00
20020	Is This What I Get for Loving You/Tomorrow's Calling	1966	2.50	5.00	10.00

Albums

Number	Title (A Side/B Side)	Yr	VG	VG+	NM
ABKCO					
75471	Greatest Hits	1988	2.50	5.00	10.00
—Reissue of London PS 547					
ISLAND					
PRO 794 [EP]	Blazing Away Sampler	1990	5.00	10.00	20.00
—Promo-only sampler for radio					
ILPS 9570	Broken English	1979	2.50	5.00	10.00
ILPS 9648	Dangerous Acquaintances	1981	2.50	5.00	10.00
90039	Broken English	1983	2.00	4.00	8.00
—Reissue					
90066	A Child's Adventure	1983	2.50	5.00	10.00
90066 [DJ]	A Child's Adventure	1983	3.75	7.50	15.00
—Promo-only Quiex II audiophile pressing					
90613	Strange Weather	1987	2.50	5.00	10.00
LONDON					
PS 423 [R]	Marianne Faithfull	1965	3.75	7.50	15.00
PS 452 [S]	Go Away from My World	1965	5.00	10.00	20.00
PS 482 [S]	Faithfull Forever	1966	5.00	10.00	20.00
PS 547	Greatest Hits	1969	3.75	7.50	15.00
LL 3423 [M]	Marianne Faithfull	1965	5.00	10.00	20.00
LL 3452 [M]	Go Away from My World	1965	3.75	7.50	15.00
LL 3482 [M]	Faithfull Forever	1966	3.75	7.50	15.00
MOBILE FIDELITY					
1-235	Broken English	1995	6.25	12.50	25.00
—Audiophile vinyl					

FALCONS, THE (1)

Detroit R&B group. Also see EDDIE FLOYD; WILSON PICKETT.

45s

Number	Title (A Side/B Side)	Yr	VG	VG+	NM
ANNA					
1110	Just for Your Love/This Heart of Mine	1959	25.00	50.00	100.00
ATLANTIC					
2153	Darling/Lah-Tee-Lah-Tah	1962	5.00	10.00	20.00
2179	Let's Kiss and Make Up/Take This Love I've Got	1963	5.00	10.00	20.00
2207	Oh Baby/Fine, Fine, Fine	1963	5.00	10.00	20.00
BIG WHEEL					
321	I Must Love You/Love, Love, Love	1966	5.00	10.00	20.00
323/4	I Can't Help It/Standing on Guard	1966	5.00	10.00	20.00

Number	Title (A Side/B Side)	Yr	VG	VG+	NM
1967	Standing On Guard/I Can't Help It	1966	5.00	10.00	20.00
1972	Good Good Feeling/You Like You Never Been Loved	1966	5.00	10.00	20.00
CHESS					
1743	Just for Your Love/This Heart of Mine	1959	6.25	12.50	25.00
FALCON					
1006	Now That It's Over/My Only Love	1957	50.00	100.00	200.00
FLICK					
001	You're So Fine/Goddess of Angels	1959	100.00	200.00	400.00
008	You Must Know I Love You/That's What I Aim to Do	1960	30.00	60.00	120.00
KUDO					
661	This Heart of Mine/Romanita	1958	100.00	200.00	400.00
LUPINE					
103	I Found a Love/Swim	1962	12.50	25.00	50.00
124	Lonely Nights/Has It Happened to You	1962	25.00	50.00	100.00
1003	I Found a Love/Swim	1962	12.50	25.00	50.00
1024	Lonely Nights/Has It Happened to You	1962	10.00	20.00	40.00
UNART					
2013 [M]	You're So Fine/Goddess of Angels	1959	7.50	15.00	30.00
2013-S [S]	You're So Fine/Goddess of Angels	1959	25.00	50.00	100.00
—Though labeled as stereo, this seems to be rechanneled					
2022	You're Mine/Country Shack	1959	6.25	12.50	25.00
UNITED ARTISTS					
0108	You're So Fine/Showtime	1973	—	2.00	4.00
—"Silver Spotlight Series" reissue					
229	The Teacher/Waiting for You	1960	5.00	10.00	20.00
255	I Plus Love Plus You/Wonderful Love	1960	5.00	10.00	20.00
289	Pow! You're in Love/Workin' Man's Song	1961	5.00	10.00	20.00
420	You're So Fine/Goddess of Angels	1962	5.00	10.00	20.00
1624	You're So Fine/Goddess of Angels	196?	2.00	4.00	8.00
—"Silver Spotlight Series" issue					
7-Inch Extended Plays					
UNITED ARTISTS					
10010	(contents unknown)	1960	75.00	150.00	300.00
10010 [PS]	The Falcons	1960	75.00	150.00	300.00
Albums					
RELIC					
8005	You're So Fine (The Falcons' Story Part One: 1956-1959)	1987	3.00	6.00	12.00
8006	I Found a Love (The Falcons' Story Part Two: 1960-1964)	1987	3.00	6.00	12.00

FALCONS, THE (2)

Number	Title (A Side/B Side)	Yr	VG	VG+	NM
45s					
CASH					
1002	Tell Me Why/I Miss You Darling	1955	125.00	250.00	500.00
FLIP					
301	Stay Mine/Du-Bi-A-Do	1954	50.00	100.00	200.00
302	You Are the Only One/Mambo Baby Tonight	1954	50.00	100.00	200.00

FALCONS, THE (U)

These may be by group (1) or by group (2) or by neither.

Number	Title (A Side/B Side)	Yr	VG	VG+	NM
45s					
MERCURY					
70940	Baby That's It/This Day	1956	15.00	30.00	60.00
SILHOUETTE					
522	Can This Be Christmas/Sent Up	1957	75.00	150.00	300.00

FALLEN ANGELS, THE

Number	Title (A Side/B Side)	Yr	VG	VG+	NM
45s					
LAURIE					
3343	Eveytime I Fall in Love/I Have Found	1966	6.25	12.50	25.00
3369	Have You Ever Lost a Love/A Little Love from You Will Do	1966	6.25	12.50	25.00
PHILCO-FORD					
HP-23	Room at the Top/Most Children Do	1968	5.00	10.00	20.00
—4-inch plastic "Hip Pocket Record" with color sleeve					
ROULETTE					
4770	Room at the Top/Your Friends Here in Dunderville	1967	5.00	10.00	20.00
4785	Most Children Do/Hello Girl	1967	5.00	10.00	20.00
TOLLIE					
9049	Up on the Mountain/So Young, So Fine	1965	6.25	12.50	25.00
Albums					
ROULETTE					
R 25358 [M]	The Fallen Angels	1967	7.50	15.00	30.00
SR 25358 [S]	The Fallen Angels	1967	10.00	20.00	40.00
SR 42011	It's a Long Way Down	1968	25.00	50.00	100.00

FALLENROCK

Number	Title (A Side/B Side)	Yr	VG	VG+	NM
45s					
CAPRICORN					
0211	Sayin' It's So Don't Make It So/She's a Mystery	1974	—	2.50	5.00
0227	Mary Anne/My World Begins and Ends with You	1975	—	2.50	5.00
Albums					
CAPRICORN					
CP 0143	Watch for Fallenrock	1974	2.50	5.00	10.00

FALLING PEBBLES, THE

Early version of THE BUCKINGHAMS.

Number	Title (A Side/B Side)	Yr	VG	VG+	NM
45s					
ALLEY CAT					
201	Lawdy Miss Clawdy/Virginia Wolf	1964	6.25	12.50	25.00

FALLOWS, SCOTT, AND THE EBBTONES

Number	Title (A Side/B Side)	Yr	VG	VG+	NM
45s					
DOT					
16577	Surfing Boop-Boop-A-Do/King of Lovers	1964	5.00	10.00	20.00

FAME, GEORGIE

Number	Title (A Side/B Side)	Yr	VG	VG+	NM
45s					
EPIC					
10166	Because I Love You/Bidin' My Time ('Cos I Love You)	1967	2.00	4.00	8.00
10283	The Ballad of Bonnie and Clyde/Beware of the Dog	1968	2.50	5.00	10.00
10347	Hideaway/Runaway Child	1968	—	3.00	6.00
10402	Someone to Watch Over Me/For Your Pleasure	1968	—	3.00	6.00
10477	I'll Be Your Baby Tonight/Down Along the Cove	1969	—	3.00	6.00
10546	Peaceful/Hideaway	1969	—	3.00	6.00
10640	Fire and Rain/The Movie Star Song	1970	—	3.00	6.00
IMPERIAL					
66086	Yeh, Yeh/Preach and Teach	1965	3.00	6.00	12.00
66104	Let the Sunshine In/In the Meantime	1965	2.50	5.00	10.00
66125	Blue Monday/Like We Used to Be	1965	2.50	5.00	10.00
66189	El Bandido/Get Away	1966	2.50	5.00	10.00
66220	Last Night/Sitting in the Park	1966	2.50	5.00	10.00
66299	Funny How Time Slips Away/Last Night	1968	2.00	4.00	8.00
ISLAND					
035	Everlovin' Woman/Ozone	1975	—	2.50	5.00
Albums					
EPIC					
BN 26368	The Ballad of Bonnie and Clyde	1968	6.25	12.50	25.00
IMPERIAL					
LP-9282 [M]	Yeh, Yeh	1965	6.25	12.50	25.00
LP-9331 [M]	Get Away	1966	6.25	12.50	25.00
LP-12282 [P]	Yeh, Yeh	1965	7.50	15.00	30.00
—Entire album is stereo except "Yeh, Yeh" (rechanneled)					
LP-12331 [R]	Get Away	1966	5.00	10.00	20.00
ISLAND					
ILPS 9293	Georgie Fame	1975	2.50	5.00	10.00

FAME, GEORGIE, AND ANNIE ROSS

Number	Title (A Side/B Side)	Yr	VG	VG+	NM
Albums					
DRG					
5197	Georgie Fame and Annie Ross in Hoagland	198?	3.00	6.00	12.00

FAME & PRICE — PRICE & FAME TOGETHER

GEORGIE FAME and ALAN PRICE.

Number	Title (A Side/B Side)	Yr	VG	VG+	NM
45s					
REPRISE					
1014	John and Mary/Rosetta	1971	—	2.50	5.00

FAMILY

Number	Title (A Side/B Side)	Yr	VG	VG+	NM
45s					
REPRISE					
0786	Hey Mr. Policeman/Old Songs, New Songs	1968	2.00	4.00	8.00
0809	Second Generation Woman/Hometown	1969	2.00	4.00	8.00
0881	Good Friend of Mine/No Mule Fool	1969	2.00	4.00	8.00
UNITED ARTISTS					
XW171	My Friend the Sun/Glove	1973	—	2.50	5.00
XW416	Suspicion/It's Only a Movie	1974	—	2.50	5.00
50832	Seasons/In My Own Time	1971	—	3.00	6.00
50882	Between Blue and Me/Laff and Sing	1972	—	2.50	5.00
Albums					
REPRISE					
RS-6313	Music in a Doll's House	1968	5.00	10.00	20.00
RS-6340	Family Entertainment	1969	3.75	7.50	15.00
RS-6384	A Song for Me	1970	3.75	7.50	15.00
UNITED ARTISTS					
UA-LA181-F	It's Only a Movie	1974	3.00	6.00	12.00
UAS-5527	Anyway	1971	3.75	7.50	15.00
UAS-5562	Fearless	1972	3.75	7.50	15.00
UAS-5644	Bandstand	1972	3.75	7.50	15.00

FAMILY DOGG

Number	Title (A Side/B Side)	Yr	VG	VG+	NM
45s					
BELL					
848	Arizona/The House and the Heather	1969	—	3.00	6.00
863	Moonshine Mary/Sympathy	1970	—	3.00	6.00
885	This Unhappy Heart of Mine/When Tomorrow Becomes Tomorrow	1970	—	3.00	6.00
939	This Unhappy Heart of Mine/(B-side unknown)	1970	—	2.50	5.00
Albums					
BUDDAH					
BDS-5100	The View from Rowland's Head	1972	6.25	12.50	25.00

FAMILY TREE, THE

Number	Title (A Side/B Side)	Yr	VG	VG+	NM
45s					
MIRA					
228	Prince of Dreams/Live Your Own Life	1966	2.50	5.00	10.00
PAULA					
329	Electric Kangaroo/Terry Tommy	1970	—	3.00	6.00
RCA VICTOR					
47-9184	Do You Have the Time/Keepin' a Secret	1967	2.00	4.00	8.00
Albums					
RCA VICTOR					
LSP-3955	Miss Butters	1968	3.75	7.50	15.00

FAMOUS FLAMES, THE

Backing group for JAMES BROWN.

Number	Title (A Side/B Side)	Yr	VG	VG+	NM
45s					
KING					
6341	Nobody Knows But My Baby and Me/Who Am I	1970	2.00	4.00	8.00

FANADOS, THE

45s

Number	Title (A Side/B Side)	Yr	VG	VG+	NM
CARTER					
2050	The One I Love/She Must Be from a Different Planet	195?	200.00	400.00	800.00

FANNY

45s

Number	Title (A Side/B Side)	Yr	VG	VG+	NM
CASABLANCA					
0009	I've Had It/First Time	1974	—	2.50	5.00
814	Butter Boy/Beggar Man	1974	—	2.50	5.00
REPRISE					
901	Ladies' Choice/New Day	1970	—	3.00	6.00
938	One Step at a Time/Nowhere to Run	1970	—	3.00	6.00
963	Changing Horses/Conversation with a Copy	1970	—	3.00	6.00
1033	Charity Ball/Place in the Country	1971	—	3.00	6.00
1080	Ain't That Peculiar/Think About the Children	1972	—	3.00	6.00
1097	Rock Bottom Blues/Wonderful Feeling	1972	—	3.00	6.00
1119	Knock on My Door/Young and Dumb	1972	—	3.00	6.00
1148	All Mine/I Need You Need Me	1972	—	3.00	6.00
1162	Last Night I Had a Dream/Beside Myself	1973	—	3.00	6.00

Albums

Number	Title (A Side/B Side)	Yr	VG	VG+	NM
CASABLANCA					
NBLP 7007	Rock & Roll Survivors	1974	3.00	6.00	12.00
REPRISE					
MS-2058	Fanny Hill	1972	3.75	7.50	15.00
MS-2137	Mother's Pride	1973	3.75	7.50	15.00
RS-6416	Fanny	1970	3.75	7.50	15.00
RS-6456	Charity Ball	1971	3.75	7.50	15.00

FANS, THE

45s

Number	Title (A Side/B Side)	Yr	VG	VG+	NM
DOT					
16688	I Want a Beatle for Christmas/How Far Should I Let My Heart Go Tonight	1964	3.75	7.50	15.00

FANTASTIC BAGGYS, THE

Also see STEVE BARRI; P.F. SLOAN.

45s

Number	Title (A Side/B Side)	Yr	VG	VG+	NM
IMPERIAL					
66047	Tell 'Em I'm Surfin'/Surfer Boy's Dream	1964	17.50	35.00	70.00
66072	Anywhere the Girls Are/Debbie Be True	1964	12.50	25.00	50.00
66092	Alone on the Beach/It Was I	1965	12.50	25.00	50.00

Albums

Number	Title (A Side/B Side)	Yr	VG	VG+	NM
IMPERIAL					
LP-9270 [M]	Tell 'Em I'm Surfin'	1964	37.50	75.00	150.00
LP-12270 [S]	Tell 'Em I'm Surfin'	1964	75.00	150.00	300.00
LIBERTY					
LN-10192	Tell 'Em I'm Surfin'	1982	2.50	5.00	10.00

FANTASTIC DEE JAYS, THE

Albums

Number	Title (A Side/B Side)	Yr	VG	VG+	NM
STONE					
SLP-4003	The Fantastic Dee Jays	1966	250.00	500.00	1000.

FANTASTIC FOUR, THE

45s

Number	Title (A Side/B Side)	Yr	VG	VG+	NM
EASTBOUND					
609	I Had the Whole World to Choose From/If You Need Me	1973	—	3.00	6.00
620	I'm Falling in Love (I Feel Good All Over)/I Believe in Miracles	1974	—	3.00	6.00
RIC-TIC					
113	Can't Stop Looking for My Baby/Can't Stop Looking for My Baby (Part 2)	1966	50.00	100.00	200.00
119	Girl Have Pity/Live Up to What She Thinks	1967	3.75	7.50	15.00
121	Can't Stop Looking for My Baby/Just the Lonely	1967	25.00	50.00	100.00
122	The Whole World Is a Stage/Ain't Love Wonderful	1967	3.75	7.50	15.00
128	You Gave Me Something (And Everything's Alright)/I Don't Wanna Live Without You	1967	3.75	7.50	15.00
130	To Share Your Love/As Long As I Live (I Live for You)	1967	3.75	7.50	15.00
134	Goddess of Love/As Long As the Feeling Is There	1968	3.75	7.50	15.00
136	Love Is a Many-Splendored Thing/Goddess of Love	1968	3.75	7.50	15.00
137	No Love Like Your Love/A Man in Love	1968	3.75	7.50	15.00
139	I've Got to Have You/Win or Lose	1968	3.75	7.50	15.00
144	I Love You Madly/(Instrumental)	1968	5.00	10.00	20.00
SOUL					
35052	I Love You Madly/(Instrumental)	1968	3.00	6.00	12.00
35058	I Feel Like I'm Falling in Love/Pin Point It Out	1969	3.75	7.50	15.00
35065	Just Another Lonely Night/I Don't Care Why You Want Me	1969	3.75	7.50	15.00
35072	On the Brighter Side of a Blue World/I'm Gonna Hurry On	1970	3.00	6.00	12.00
WESTBOUND					
5009	Alvin Stone (The Birth & Death of a Gangster)/I Believe in Miracles, I Believe in You	1975	—	2.50	5.00
5017	Have a Little Mercy/County Line	1975	—	2.50	5.00
5030	Don't Risk Your Happiness On Foolish Things/They Took the Show on the Road	1976	—	2.50	5.00
5032	Hideaway/They Took the Show on the Road	1976	—	2.50	5.00
55403	I Got to Have Your Love/Ain't I Been Good to You	1977	—	2.50	5.00
55408	Mixed Up Moods and Attitudes/Disco Fool Blues	1978	—	2.50	5.00
55417	Sexy Lady/If This Is Love	1979	—	2.50	5.00
55419	B.Y.O.F. (Bring Your Own Funk)/If This Is Love	1979	—	2.50	5.00

Albums

Number	Title (A Side/B Side)	Yr	VG	VG+	NM
SOUL					
SS-717	The Best of the Fantastic Four	1969	10.00	20.00	40.00
SS-722	How Sweet He Is	1970	—	—	—
—Canceled					
WESTBOUND					
201	Alvin Stone (The Birth and Death of a Gangster)	1975	3.75	7.50	15.00
226	Night People	1976	3.75	7.50	15.00
SD 306	Got to Have Your Love	1977	3.75	7.50	15.00
SD 6108	BYOF (Bring Your Own Funk)	1978	3.75	7.50	15.00

FANTASTIC JOHNNY C, THE

45s

Number	Title (A Side/B Side)	Yr	VG	VG+	NM
KAMA SUTRA					
511	Let's Do It Together/Peace Treaty	1970	—	2.50	5.00
515	Good Love/You Got Your Hooks in Me	1970	—	2.50	5.00
PHILCO-FORD					
HP-39	Boogaloo Down Broadway/Got What You Need	1969	5.00	10.00	20.00
—4-inch plastic "Hip Pocket Record" with color sleeve					
PHIL.-LA OF SOUL					
305	Boogaloo Down Broadway/Look What Love Can Make You Do	1967	2.00	4.00	8.00
309	Got What You Need/New Love	1968	—	3.00	6.00
315	Hitch It to the Horse/Cool Broadway	1968	—	3.00	6.00
320	Baby I Need You/Some Kind of Wonderful	1968	—	3.00	6.00
327	Is There Anything Better Than Making Love/New Love	1969	—	3.00	6.00
361	Don't Depend on Me/Waitin' for the Rain	1973	—	2.00	4.00
363	Just Say the Word/I'm a Man	1973	—	2.00	4.00

Albums

Number	Title (A Side/B Side)	Yr	VG	VG+	NM
PHIL-LA OF SOUL					
4000	Boogaloo Down Broadway	1968	20.00	40.00	80.00

FANTASTICS, THE (1)

Male R&B group.

45s

Number	Title (A Side/B Side)	Yr	VG	VG+	NM
BELL					
977	Something Old, Something New/High and Dry	1971	5.00	10.00	20.00
45157	(Love Me) Love the Life I Lead/Old Rags and Tatters	1971	3.75	7.50	15.00
DERAM					
7528	Face to Face with Heartache/This Must Be My Rainy Day	1970	3.75	7.50	15.00

FANTASTICS, THE (2)

45s

Number	Title (A Side/B Side)	Yr	VG	VG+	NM
RCA VICTOR					
47-7572	There Goes My Love/Millionaire Hobo	1959	10.00	20.00	40.00
—Black label, dog on top					
47-7572	There Goes My Love/I Wanna Be a Millionaire Hobo	1965	3.75	7.50	15.00
—Evidenly, a reissue with the same number, but the dog on side of label rather than on top, exists					
47-7664	This Is My Wedding Day/I Got a Zero	1960	10.00	20.00	40.00
UNITED ARTISTS					
309	Dancing Doll/I Told You Once	1961	12.50	25.00	50.00

FANTASTICS, THE (U)

Neither group (1) nor group (2), but are they both the same?

45s

Number	Title (A Side/B Side)	Yr	VG	VG+	NM
SCORPIO					
407	Malaguena/Dance for an Unnamed Gypsy Queen	1966	6.25	12.50	25.00
SOUND STAGE 7					
2565	Have a Little You/Me and You	1966	3.00	6.00	12.00

FANTASY

45s

Number	Title (A Side/B Side)	Yr	VG	VG+	NM
IMPERIAL					
66394	Painted Horse/I Got the Fever	1969	2.50	5.00	10.00
LIBERTY					
56190	Stoned Cowboy/Understand	1970	2.00	4.00	8.00

Albums

Number	Title (A Side/B Side)	Yr	VG	VG+	NM
LIBERTY					
LSP-7643	Fantasy	1970	5.00	10.00	20.00

FAPARDOKLY

Albums

Number	Title (A Side/B Side)	Yr	VG	VG+	NM
U.I.P.					
2250	Fapardokly	1967	250.00	500.00	1000.

FAR CRY

45s

Number	Title (A Side/B Side)	Yr	VG	VG+	NM
VANGUARD					
35085	Shapes/Hellhound	1969	2.50	5.00	10.00

Albums

Number	Title (A Side/B Side)	Yr	VG	VG+	NM
VANGUARD					
VSD-6510	Far Cry	1969	6.25	12.50	25.00

FARDON, DON

45s

Number	Title (A Side/B Side)	Yr	VG	VG+	NM
CAPITOL					
3929	St. Matthew, St. Mark, St. Luke and St. John/Lola	1974	—	2.50	5.00
CHELSEA					
78-0115	Delta Queen/Home Town Baby	1973	—	3.00	6.00
DECCA					
32696	Belfast Boy/Echoes of the Cheers	1970	—	3.00	6.00
GNP CRESCENDO					
405	(The Lament of the Cherokee) Indian Reservation/Dreaming Room	1968	2.00	4.00	8.00
418	Take a Heart/How Do You Break a Broken Heart	1968	—	3.00	6.00
421	Sally Goes 'Round the Moon/How Do You Break a Broken Heart	1969	—	3.00	6.00
424	Running Bear/Ruby's Picture	1969	—	3.00	6.00
ROXBURY					
BRBO-0159	Louisiana/Lady Zelda	1973	—	2.50	5.00

Albums

Number	Title (A Side/B Side)	Yr	VG	VG+	NM
DECCA					
DL 75225	I've Paid My Dues	1970	3.75	7.50	15.00
GNP CRESCENDO					
GNPS-2044	Indian Reservation	1968	5.00	10.00	20.00

FARGO, DONNA

45s

Number	Title (A Side/B Side)	Yr	VG	VG+	NM
ABC/DOT					
17523	U.S. of A./A Woman's Prayer	1974	—	2.50	5.00
17541	If Do Feel Good/Only the Strong	1974	—	2.50	5.00
17557	Hello Little Bluebird/2 Sweet 2 Be 4 Gotten	1975	—	2.50	5.00
17579	Whatever I Say/Rain Song	1975	—	2.50	5.00
17586	What Will the New Year Bring/A Woman's Prayer	1975	—	2.50	5.00
17609	You're Not Charlie Brown (And I'm Not Raggedy Ann)/Sing, Sing, Sing	1976	—	2.00	4.00
17660	Don't Be Angry/You Don't Mess Around with Jim	1976	—	2.00	4.00
17692	I'd Love You to Want Me/How Close You Came (To Being Gone)	1977	—	2.00	4.00
CHALLENGE					
59387	Daddy/Sticks and Stones	1968	2.50	5.00	10.00
59391	Wishful Thinking/All That's Keeping Me Alive	1968	2.50	5.00	10.00
CLEVELAND INTERNATIONAL					
1	My Heart Will Always Belong to You/Reasons to Be	1984	—	2.00	4.00
10	Soldier Boy/Stand Tall	1991	—	2.50	5.00
COLUMBIA					
04097	The Sign of the Times/Reasons to Be	1983	—	2.00	4.00
COUNTRY HEARTS					
CH-001 [DJ]	My Side of the Bed/Country Singer's Wife	1970	7.50	15.00	30.00
—Promo-only release					
DECCA					
33001	Daddy/Sticks and Stones	1972	2.00	4.00	8.00
DOT					
17409	The Happiest Girl in the Whole U.S.A./The Awareness of Nothing	1972	—	3.00	6.00
17429	Funny Face/How Close You Came (To Being Gone)	1972	—	3.00	6.00
17444	Superman/Forever Is As Far As I Could Go	1973	—	2.50	5.00
17460	You Were Always There/He Can Have All He Wants	1973	—	2.50	5.00
17476	Little Girl Gone/Just Call Me	1973	—	2.50	5.00
17491	I'll Try a Little Bit Harder/All About a Feeling	1973	—	2.50	5.00
17506	You Can't Be a Beacon (If Your Light Don't Shine)/Just a Friend of Mine	1974	—	2.50	5.00
MCA					
51209	Say "I Do"/All About a Feeling	1981	—	2.00	4.00
MERCURY					
884712-7	Woman of the 80's/You Were Always There	1986	—	—	3.00
888043-7	Winners/I've Laid Too Many Eggs	1986	—	—	3.00
888093-7	Me and You/I've Laid Too Many Eggs	1986	—	—	3.00
888680-7	Members Only/Funny Face	1987	—	—	3.00
—A-side: With Billy Joe Royal					
RAMCO					
1982	You Make Me Feel Like a Woman/Would You Believe a Lifetime	1967	3.75	7.50	15.00
1988	Who's Been Playin' House/You Reach for the Bottle	1967	3.75	7.50	15.00
1991	Kind of Glad I'm Me/Then You Haven't Lied	1967	3.75	7.50	15.00
RCA					
PB-13264	It's Hard to Be the Dreamer/I Just Saw My Reflection in You	1982	—	2.00	4.00
PB-13329	Did We Have to Go This Far (To Say Goodbye)/All I Need to Know	1982	—	2.00	4.00
WARNER BROS.					
8186	Mr. Doodles/If You Can't Love All of Me	1976	—	2.50	5.00
8227	I've Loved You All the Way/One of God's Children	1976	—	2.50	5.00
8305	Mockingbird Hill/Second Chance	1976	—	2.50	5.00
8375	That Was Yesterday/Cricket Song	1977	—	2.50	5.00
8431	Shame on Me/Hey, Mister Music Man	1977	—	2.50	5.00
8509	Do I Love You (Yes in Every Way)/Dee Dee	1977	—	2.50	5.00
8578	Ragamuffin Girl/Everybody's Girl	1978	—	2.00	4.00
8643	Another Goodbye/Changes in My Life	1978	—	2.00	4.00
8722	Somebody Special/Changes in My Life	1978	—	2.00	4.00
8867	Daddy/For the Rest of My Life	1979	—	2.00	4.00
49093	Preacher Berry/I Don't Know What to Do	1979	—	2.00	4.00
49183	Walk On By/I Wrote This Song Just for You	1980	—	2.00	4.00
49514	Land of Cotton/I Still Believe in You	1980	—	2.00	4.00
49575	Seeing Is Believing/Look What You've Done	1980	—	2.00	4.00
49757	Lonestar Cowboy/Utah Song	1981	—	2.00	4.00
49852	Jacamo/Song to Celebrate Life	1981	—	2.00	4.00

Albums

Number	Title (A Side/B Side)	Yr	VG	VG+	NM
ABC/DOT					
DOSD-2002	Miss Donna Fargo	1974	3.00	6.00	12.00
DOSD-2029	Whatever I Say Means I Love You	1975	3.00	6.00	12.00
DO-2075	The Best of Donna Fargo	1977	3.00	6.00	12.00
DOT					
DLP-26000	The Happiest Girl in the Whole U.S.A.	1972	3.00	6.00	12.00
DLP-26006	My Second Album	1973	3.00	6.00	12.00
DLP-26019	All About a Feeling	1973	3.00	6.00	12.00
MCA					
667	The Happiest Girl in the Whole U.S.A.	198?	2.00	4.00	8.00
—Budget-line reissue					
37108	The Best of Donna Fargo	198?	2.00	4.00	8.00
—Budget-line reissue					
MERCURY					
830236-1	Winners	1986	3.00	6.00	12.00
832507-1	Winners	1987	2.00	4.00	8.00
—Reissue with two songs deleted and one added from above					
PICKWICK					
6187	Superman	197?	2.00	4.00	8.00
SONGBIRD					
5203	Brotherly Love	1982	2.50	5.00	10.00
WARNER BROS.					
BS 2926	On the Move	1976	2.50	5.00	10.00
BS 2996	Donna Fargo Country	1977	2.50	5.00	10.00
BS 3099	Shame on Me	1977	2.50	5.00	10.00
BS 3191	Dark Eyed Lady	1978	2.50	5.00	10.00
BSK 3377	Just for You	1979	2.50	5.00	10.00
BSK 3470	Fargo	1980	2.50	5.00	10.00

FARLOWE, CHRIS

45s

Number	Title (A Side/B Side)	Yr	VG	VG+	NM
GENERAL AMERICAN					
718	What You Gonna Do/Just a Dream	1964	3.75	7.50	15.00
IMMEDIATE					
5002	Paint It Black/You're So Good to Me	1967	2.50	5.00	10.00
5005	Handbags and Gladrags/Everyone Makes a Mistake	1968	2.50	5.00	10.00
5011	What Have I Been Doing/Paint It Black	1968	2.50	5.00	10.00
MGM					
13567	Out of Time/Baby Make It Soon	1966	5.00	10.00	20.00
—A-side is a Mick Jagger-Keith Richards composition only later recorded by the Rolling Stones.					
POLYDOR					
14008	Circles 'Round the Sun/Save Your Tears	1969	2.00	4.00	8.00
14013	Medicated Goo/Betty Lou	1970	2.00	4.00	8.00

Albums

Number	Title (A Side/B Side)	Yr	VG	VG+	NM
COLUMBIA					
CL 2593 [M]	The Fabulous Chris Farlowe	1966	10.00	20.00	40.00
CS 9393 [R]	The Fabulous Chris Farlowe	1966	6.25	12.50	25.00
IMMEDIATE					
Z12 52010	Paint It Farlowe	1968	5.00	10.00	20.00
POLYDOR					
24-4041	From Here to Mama Rosa with the Hill	1970	3.00	6.00	12.00

FARM BAND, THE

Albums

Number	Title (A Side/B Side)	Yr	VG	VG+	NM
MANTRA					
777 [(2)]	The Farm Band	1972	7.50	15.00	30.00
—With poster					

FARNER, MARK

Of GRAND FUNK RAILROAD.

45s

Number	Title (A Side/B Side)	Yr	VG	VG+	NM
ATLANTIC					
3448	You and Me Baby/Second Chance to Dance	1977	—	2.00	4.00
3510	When a Man Loves a Woman/If It Took All Day	1978	—	2.00	4.00
3529	Just One Look/Crystal Eyes	1978	—	2.00	4.00
LUCKY ELEVEN					
352	Down in the Valley/I Got News for You	1968	2.50	5.00	10.00

Albums

Number	Title (A Side/B Side)	Yr	VG	VG+	NM
ATLANTIC					
SD 18232	Mark Farner	1977	2.50	5.00	10.00
SD 19196	No Frills	1978	2.50	5.00	10.00

FARNER, MARK, AND DON BREWER

Both later of GRAND FUNK RAILROAD.

45s

Number	Title (A Side/B Side)	Yr	VG	VG+	NM
LUCKY ELEVEN					
366	Does It Matter to You Girl/We Gotta Have Love	1968	3.00	6.00	12.00

Albums

Number	Title (A Side/B Side)	Yr	VG	VG+	NM
QUADICO					
7401	Monumental Funk	1977	2.50	5.00	10.00
7401 [PD]	Monumental Funk	1977	5.00	10.00	20.00
—Picture disc					

FARON'S FLAMINGOS

45s

Number	Title (A Side/B Side)	Yr	VG	VG+	NM
COLUMBIA					
43018	Let's Stomp/I Can Tell	1964	6.25	12.50	25.00
—B-side by Rory Storm and the Hurricanes					

FARQUAHR

45s

Number	Title (A Side/B Side)	Yr	VG	VG+	NM
ELEKTRA					
45735	Holy Moses/My Island	1971	—	3.00	6.00
VERVE FORECAST					
5077	My Eggs Don't Taste the Same Without You/Sister Theresa's East River Orphanage	1968	2.00	4.00	8.00
5085	Teddy Bear Days/My Island	1968	2.00	4.00	8.00
WARNER BROS.					
7354	Kiss the Wind Goodbye/Neither Here Nor There	1969	—	3.00	6.00

Albums

Number	Title (A Side/B Side)	Yr	VG	VG+	NM
ELEKTRA					
EKS-74083	Farquahr	1970	3.00	6.00	12.00
VERVE FORECAST					
FTS-3053	Fabulous Farquahr	1969	3.00	6.00	12.00

FARR, GARY, AND THE T-BONES

45s

Number	Title (A Side/B Side)	Yr	VG	VG+	NM
EPIC					
9832	Don't Stop and Stare/Give All She's Got	1965	3.00	6.00	12.00

FARR, LITTLE JOEY

45s

Number	Title (A Side/B Side)	Yr	VG	VG+	NM
BAND BOX					
286	Rock & Roll Santa/Big White Cadillac	196?	12.50	25.00	50.00

FARRELL AND THE FLAMES

45s

Number	Title (A Side/B Side)	Yr	VG	VG+	NM
FRANSIL					
14	Dreams and Memories/You'll Be Sorry	1961	100.00	200.00	400.00

FASCINATIONS, THE (1)

Female vocal group.

45s

Number	Title (A Side/B Side)	Yr	VG	VG+	NM
ABC-PARAMOUNT					
10387	Mama Didn't Lie/Someone Like You	1962	5.00	10.00	20.00
—Some of the ABC-Paramount pressings are misspelled "Fasinations"					
10443	Tears In My Eyes/You're Gonna Be Sorry	1963	6.25	12.50	25.00
MAYFIELD					
7711	(Say It Isn't So) Say You'd Never Go/(B-side unknown)	1966	2.50	5.00	10.00
7714	Girls Are Out to Get You/You'll Be Sorry	1966	2.50	5.00	10.00
7716	I Can't Stay Away from You/(B-side unknown)	1967	2.50	5.00	10.00

FASCINATIONS, THE (2)

45s

Number	Title (A Side/B Side)	Yr	VG	VG+	NM
DORE					
593	If I Had Your Love/Why	1961	12.50	25.00	50.00
PAXLEY					
750	If I Had Your Love/Why	1960	37.50	75.00	150.00

FASCINATIONS, THE (U)

It's doubtful that any of these are group (1), but they could be group (2).

45s

Number	Title (A Side/B Side)	Yr	VG	VG+	NM
A&G					
101	I'm Gonna Cry/Since You Went Away	1972	5.00	10.00	20.00
SURE					
106	It's Midnight/Boom Bada Boom	1960	20.00	40.00	80.00
106	Midnight/Boom Bada Boom	1960	30.00	60.00	120.00

FASCINATORS, THE (1)

45s

Number	Title (A Side/B Side)	Yr	VG	VG+	NM
BIM BAM BOOM					
110	Oh, Rose Marie/Forgive Me, My Darling	1974	2.50	5.00	10.00
CAPITOL					
F-4053	Chapel Bells/I Wonder Who	1958	37.50	75.00	150.00
F-4137	Come to Paradise/Who Do You Think You Are	1959	50.00	100.00	200.00
F-4247	Oh Rose Marie/Fried Chicken and Macaroni	1959	50.00	100.00	200.00
4544	Chapel Bells/I Wonder Who	1961	20.00	40.00	80.00

FASCINATORS, THE (2)

45s

Number	Title (A Side/B Side)	Yr	VG	VG+	NM
BLUE LAKE					
112	Can't Stop/Don't Give My Love Away	1953	500.00	1000.	2000.

FASCINATORS, THE (3)

45s

Number	Title (A Side/B Side)	Yr	VG	VG+	NM
BURN					
845	I'll Be Gone/Can't You See I'm Lonely	1965	5.00	10.00	20.00

FASCINATORS, THE (4)

45s

Number	Title (A Side/B Side)	Yr	VG	VG+	NM
DOOTO					
441	Teardrop Eyes/Shivers and Shakes	1958	15.00	30.00	60.00

FASCINATORS, THE (5)

45s

Number	Title (A Side/B Side)	Yr	VG	VG+	NM
YOUR COPY					
1135	The Bells of My Heart/Sweet Baby	1954	250.00	500.00	1000.
—Black vinyl					
1135	The Bells of My Heart/Sweet Baby	1954	500.00	1000.	2000.
—Red vinyl					
1136	My Beauty, My Own/Don't Give It Away	1954	250.00	500.00	1000.

FASCINATORS, THE (U)

If these are not completely different groups, these are most likely by group (3) or (4).

45s

Number	Title (A Side/B Side)	Yr	VG	VG+	NM
KING					
5119	Cuddle Up with Carolyn/Tee Hee	1958	12.50	25.00	50.00
TRANS ATLAS					
688	You're to Blame/Revived	196?	7.50	15.00	30.00

FASHIONS, THE (1)

BARBARA ENGLISH was a member of this group.

45s

Number	Title (A Side/B Side)	Yr	VG	VG+	NM
CAMEO					
331	Baby That's Me/Nick and Joe Callin'	1964	2.50	5.00	10.00
ELMOR					
301	Please Let It Be Me/Fairy Tales	1961	6.25	12.50	25.00
EMBER					
1084	I Just Got a Letter/Try My Love	1962	3.00	6.00	12.00
V-TONE					
202	I'm Dreaming of You/Lonesome Road	1959	12.50	25.00	50.00
202	I'm Dreaming of You/I Love You So	1959	7.50	15.00	30.00
—Orange label					
202	I'm Dreaming of You/I Love You So	1959	5.00	10.00	20.00
—Blue label					
WARWICK					
646	All I Want/Dearest One	1961	5.00	10.00	20.00

FASHIONS, THE (2)

45s

Number	Title (A Side/B Side)	Yr	VG	VG+	NM
FELSTED					
8689	Surfer's Memories/Surfin' Back to School	1964	7.50	15.00	30.00

FASHIONS, THE (3)

45s

Number	Title (A Side/B Side)	Yr	VG	VG+	NM
PHIL-L.A. OF SOUL					
354	I Don't Mind Doin' It/What Goes Up (Must Come Down)	1972	—	3.00	6.00

FASHIONS, THE (4)

45s

Number	Title (A Side/B Side)	Yr	VG	VG+	NM
20TH CENTURY FOX					
6710	Lover's Stand/Only Those in Love	1968	2.00	4.00	8.00

FASTEST GROUP ALIVE, THE

45s

Number	Title (A Side/B Side)	Yr	VG	VG+	NM
TEEN					
100	The Bears/Beside	1966	7.50	15.00	30.00
VALIANT					
754	The Bears/Beside	1966	5.00	10.00	20.00
759	Lullabye/5:15 Sports	1967	5.00	10.00	20.00

FAT CITY

Also see JOHN DENVER.

45s

Number	Title (A Side/B Side)	Yr	VG	VG+	NM
ABC PROBE					
469	Wall Street/City Cat	1969	—	3.00	6.00
PARAMOUNT					
0162	I Guess He'd Rather Be in Colorado/Morning Go Away	1972	—	3.00	6.00
0176	Workingman's Day/Hey, Loretta	1972	—	2.50	5.00

Albums

Number	Title (A Side/B Side)	Yr	VG	VG+	NM
ABC PROBE					
4508	Reincarnation	1969	5.00	10.00	20.00
PARAMOUNT					
PAS-6028	Welcome to Fat City	1972	3.75	7.50	15.00

FAT MATTRESS

Albums

Number	Title (A Side/B Side)	Yr	VG	VG+	NM
ATCO					
SD 33-309	Fat Mattress	1969	5.00	10.00	20.00
SD 33-347	Fat Mattress II	1970	3.75	7.50	15.00

FATBACK

Includes records as "Fatback Band."

12-Inch Singles

Number	Title (A Side/B Side)	Yr	VG	VG+	NM
COTILLION					
PR 763 [DJ]	You've Got That Magic (6:43)/You've Got That Magic (3:55)	1984	2.00	4.00	8.00
SPRING					
PRO 184 [DJ]	On the Floor (same on both sides)	1982	2.00	4.00	8.00
402	King Tim III (Personalty Jock)/You're My Candy Sweet	1979	2.50	5.00	10.00
409	The Girl Is Fine (So Fine)/(B-side unknown)	1983	2.00	4.00	8.00
414	Spread Love/(B-side unknown)	1984	—	3.00	6.00

45s

Number	Title (A Side/B Side)	Yr	VG	VG+	NM
COTILLION					
99642	Lover Undercover/(B-side unknown)	1985	—	—	3.00
99665	Girls on My Mind/Osiris (There's a Party Goin' On)	1985	—	—	3.00
99730	You've Got That Magic/(B-side unknown)	1984	—	—	3.00
99749	Call Out My Name/I Love You So	1984	—	—	3.00
EVENT					
217	Keep On Steppin'/Breakin' Up Is Hard to Do	1974	—	2.50	5.00
219	Wicki-Wacky/Can't Fight the Flame	1974	—	2.50	5.00
224	(Hey I) Feel Real Good (Part 1)/(Hey I) Feel Real Good (Part 2)	1975	—	2.50	5.00
226	Yum Yum (Gimme Some)/Let the Drums Speak	1975	—	2.50	5.00
227	(Are You Ready) Do the Bus Stop/Gotta Learn to Dance	1975	—	2.50	5.00
229	Spanish Hustle/Put Your Love (In My Tender Care)	1976	—	2.50	5.00
PERCEPTION					
520	Soul March/To Be with You	1973	—	2.50	5.00
526	Street Dance/Goin' to See My Baby	1973	—	2.50	5.00
540	Nija (Nija) Walk (Street Walk)/Soul Man	1973	—	2.50	5.00
SPRING					
165	Party Time/Groovy Kind of Day	1976	—	2.50	5.00
168	The Booty/If That's the Way You Want It	1976	—	2.50	5.00
171	Double Dutch/Spank the Baby	1977	—	2.50	5.00
174	NYCNY USA (Nik-Ne-Yoo-Sa)/Soulfinger	1977	—	2.50	5.00
177	Master Booty/Zodiac Man	1977	—	2.50	5.00
180	Mile High/Midnight Freak	1978	—	2.50	5.00
181	I Like Girls/Get Out on the Dance Floor	1978	—	2.50	5.00
188	Boogie Freak/I'm Fired Up	1978	—	2.50	5.00
191	Freak the Freak the Funk (Rock)/Wild Dreams	1979	—	2.50	5.00
195	(Do the) Boogie Woogie/Hesitation	1979	—	2.50	5.00
199	King Tim III (Personality Jock)/You're My Candy Sweet	1979	—	3.00	6.00
3005	Love in Perfect Harmony/Disco Bass	1979	—	2.00	4.00
3008	Gotta Get My Hands on Some (Money)/Street Band	1980	—	2.00	4.00
3012	Backstrokin'/Love Spell	1980	—	2.00	4.00
3015	Let's Do It Again/Come and Get the Love	1980	—	2.00	4.00
3016	Angel/Concrete Jungle	1981	—	2.00	4.00
3018	Take It Any Way You Want It/Lady Groove	1981	—	2.00	4.00
3020	Kool Whip/Keep Your Fingers Out of the Jam	1981	—	2.00	4.00
3022	Rockin' to the Beat/Wanna Dance	1981	—	2.00	4.00
3023	Na Na Hey Hey Kiss Her Goodbye/I'm So in Love	1982	—	2.00	4.00
3025	On the Floor/Chillin' Out	1982	—	2.00	4.00
3026	She's My Shining Star/UFO (Unidentified Funk Object)	1982	—	2.00	4.00
3030	The Girl Is Fine (So Fine)/(B-side unknown)	1983	—	2.00	4.00
3032	Is This the Future/Double Love Affair	1983	—	2.00	4.00
3033	Up Against the Wall/With Love	1983	—	2.00	4.00
3037	I Wanna Be Your Lover/(B-side unknown)	1984	—	2.00	4.00

Albums

Number	Title (A Side/B Side)	Yr	VG	VG+	NM
COTILLION					
90168	Phoenix	1984	2.00	4.00	8.00
90253	So Delicious	1985	2.00	4.00	8.00

Number	Title (A Side/B Side)	Yr	VG	VG+	NM
EVENT					
6902	Keep On Steppin'	1974	3.75	7.50	15.00
—As "The Fatback Band"					
6904	Yum Yum	1975	3.75	7.50	15.00
—As "The Fatback Band"					
6905	Raising Hell	1976	3.75	7.50	15.00
—As "The Fatback Band"					
SPRING					
6711	Night Fever	1976	3.00	6.00	12.00
—As "The Fatback Band"					
6714	NYCNYUSA	1977	3.00	6.00	12.00
—As "The Fatback Band"					
6717	Man with a Plan	1978	3.00	6.00	12.00
—As "The Fatback Band"					
6718	Fired Up 'N' Kickin'	1978	2.50	5.00	10.00
6721	Bright Lites, Big City	1979	2.50	5.00	10.00
6723	Fatback XII	1979	2.50	5.00	10.00
6726	Hot Box	1980	2.50	5.00	10.00
6729	14 Karat	1980	2.50	5.00	10.00
6731	Tasty Jam	1981	2.50	5.00	10.00
6734	Gigolo	1981	2.50	5.00	10.00
6736	On the Floor	1982	2.50	5.00	10.00

FATBACK BAND, THE
See FATBACK.

FATHER YOD AND THE SPIRIT OF '76
See YA HO WA 13.

FAUN
45s

Number	Title (A Side/B Side)	Yr	VG	VG+	NM
GREGAR					
7000	Better Dig What You Find/I Asked My Mother	1969	5.00	10.00	20.00
7001	Son of a Literate Man/Yes I'm Really Lonely	1969	5.00	10.00	20.00

Albums

Number	Title (A Side/B Side)	Yr	VG	VG+	NM
GREGAR					
7000	Faun	1969	12.50	25.00	50.00

FAWNS, THE
45s

Number	Title (A Side/B Side)	Yr	VG	VG+	NM
APT					
25015	Come On/Until I Die	1958	6.25	12.50	25.00

FEAR ITSELF
45s

Number	Title (A Side/B Side)	Yr	VG	VG+	NM
DOT					
17278	The Letter/Born Under a Bad Sign	1969	2.00	4.00	8.00

Albums

Number	Title (A Side/B Side)	Yr	VG	VG+	NM
DOT					
DLP-25942	Fear Itself	1969	5.00	10.00	20.00

FEATHERBED
Early BARRY MANILOW.

45s

Number	Title (A Side/B Side)	Yr	VG	VG+	NM
BELL					
971	Amy/Morning	1971	15.00	30.00	60.00
—Stock copies are much scarcer than promo copies					
45133 [DJ]	Could It Be Magic (mono/stereo)	1971	25.00	50.00	100.00
—Stock copy may not exist					

FEATHERS, CHARLIE
45s

Number	Title (A Side/B Side)	Yr	VG	VG+	NM
FLIP					
503	I've Been Deceived/Peeping Eyes	1955	125.00	250.00	500.00
HOLIDAY INN					
114	Deep Elm Blues/Nobody's Darling	1962	50.00	100.00	200.00
KAY					
1001	Jungle Fever/Why Don't You	1960	50.00	100.00	200.00
KING					
4971	Can't Hardly Stand It/Everybody's Lovin' My Baby	1956	150.00	300.00	600.00
4997	One Hand Loose/Bottle to the Baby	1956	125.00	250.00	500.00
5022	Nobody's Woman/When You Decide	1957	100.00	200.00	400.00
5043	When You Come Around/Too Much Alike	1957	100.00	200.00	400.00
MEMPHIS					
103	Wild, Wild Party/Today and Tomorrow	1961	25.00	50.00	100.00
METEOR					
5032	Tongue-Tied Jill/Get With It	1956	500.00	1000.	1500.
—Maroon label					
5032	Tongue-Tied Jill/Get With It	1956	100.00	200.00	400.00
—Blue label					
PHILWOOD					
223	Tear It Up/Stutterin' Cindy	197?	2.00	4.00	8.00
POMPADOUR					
231	Uh-Huh Honey/A Wedding Gown of White	1974	2.00	4.00	8.00
ROLLIN' ROCK					
45-025	That Certain Female/She Set Me Free	1978	2.00	4.00	8.00
SUN					
231	Defrost Your Heart/Wedding Gown of White	1956	200.00	400.00	600.00
503	I've Been Deceived/Peeping Eyes	1956	200.00	400.00	600.00
WAL-MAY					
101	Dinky John/South of Chicago	1960	50.00	100.00	200.00

FEATHERS, THE (1)
45s

Number	Title (A Side/B Side)	Yr	VG	VG+	NM
ALADDIN					
3267	Johnny Darling/Shake 'Em Up	1954	50.00	100.00	200.00
3277	I Need a Girl/Standing Right There	1955	50.00	100.00	200.00
HOLLYWOOD					
1051	Dear One/Lonesome Tonight	1956	1000.	2000.	3000.
SHOW TIME					
1104	Nona/Johnny Darling	1954	75.00	150.00	300.00
1105	Why Don't You Write Me/Busy as a Bee	1954	50.00	100.00	200.00
1105	Why Don't You Write Me/Where Did Caledonia Go	1954	37.50	75.00	150.00
1106	Love Only You/Crashing the Party	1955	50.00	100.00	200.00

FEATHERS, THE (2)
45s

Number	Title (A Side/B Side)	Yr	VG	VG+	NM
KAPP					
887	Give Him Love/To Be Loved by You	1968	2.00	4.00	8.00

FEATHERS, THE (U)
May or may not be by group (2).

45s

Number	Title (A Side/B Side)	Yr	VG	VG+	NM
VEEP					
1200	The Dummy/Them Onions	1964	2.00	4.00	8.00

FEDERALS, THE (1)
British group.

45s

Number	Title (A Side/B Side)	Yr	VG	VG+	NM
CAPITOL					
5526	Bucketful of Love/Leah	1965	2.50	5.00	10.00

FEDERALS, THE (2)
45s

Number	Title (A Side/B Side)	Yr	VG	VG+	NM
DELUXE					
6112	Come Go with Me/Cold Cash	1957	20.00	40.00	80.00
FURY					
1005	While Our Hearts Are Young/You're the One I Love	1957	25.00	50.00	100.00
1009	Dear Lorraine/She's My Girl	1958	25.00	50.00	100.00

FELDERS ORIOLES
45s

Number	Title (A Side/B Side)	Yr	VG	VG+	NM
MERCURY					
72480	Down Home Girl/Misty	1965	2.50	5.00	10.00

FELICIANO, JOSE
45s

Number	Title (A Side/B Side)	Yr	VG	VG+	NM
EMI LATIN					
S7-18214	Feliz Navidad/Blue Christmas	1994	—	2.00	4.00
—B-side on Liberty by Glen Campbell; red vinyl					
MOTOWN					
1517	The Drought Is Over/Everybody Loves Me	1981	—	2.00	4.00
1524	I Second That Emotion/Let's Make Love Over the Telephone	1981	—	2.00	4.00
1530	I Wanna Be Where You Are/Let's Make Love Over the Telephone	1981	—	2.00	4.00
1618	Free Me from My Freedom/I Second That Emotion	1982	—	2.00	4.00
1647	Samba Pa Ti (Long)/Samba Pa Ti (Short)	1982	—	2.00	4.00
1673 [DJ]	Balada Del Pianista (same on both sides)	1983	—	2.00	4.00
—May be promo only					
1674	Let's Find Each Other Tonight/Cuidado	1983	—	2.00	4.00
1679	Lonely Teardrops/Cuidado	1983	—	2.00	4.00
PRIVATE STOCK					
45062	Angela/Willful Strut	1975	—	2.00	4.00
45085	Angela (Spanish)/(B-side unknown)	1976	—	2.00	4.00
45103	Why/(B-side unknown)	1976	—	2.00	4.00
45143	Marguerita/(B-side unknown)	1977	—	2.00	4.00
45151	The Air That I Breathe/I Love Making Love to You	1977	—	2.00	4.00
RCA					
447-0936	Feliz Navidad/The Little Drummer Boy	197?	—	—	3.00
—Black label, dog near top					
RCA VICTOR					
APBO-0051	Yes We Can Can/I'm Leavin'	1973	—	2.50	5.00
APBO-0140	I Want to Learn a Love Song/Find Somebody	1973	—	2.50	5.00
APBO-0206	The Gypsy/I Like What You Give	1974	—	2.00	4.00
PB-10094	Golden Lady/Virgo	1974	—	2.00	4.00
PB-10145	Chico and the Man/Hard Times in El Barrio	1974	—	2.00	4.00
PB-10306	Twilight Time/Stay with Me	1975	—	2.00	4.00
47-8425	Everybody Do the Click/Ginny's Garden	1964	2.00	4.00	8.00
47-8683	Where I'm Goin'/A Woman, a Lover, a Friend	1965	2.00	4.00	8.00
47-8884	(I Love You) For Sentimental Reasons/Quit While You're Ahead	1966	2.00	4.00	8.00
47-9085	A Man and a Woman/And We Were Lovers (Theme from The Sand Pebbles)	1967	2.00	4.00	8.00
47-9550	Light My Fire/California Dreamin'	1968	2.00	4.00	8.00
47-9641	Hi-Heel Sneakers/Hitchcock Railway	1968	—	3.00	6.00
47-9665	The Star Spangled Banner/And I Love Her	1968	2.50	5.00	10.00
47-9714	Hey Baby/My World Is Empty Without You	1969	—	3.00	6.00
47-9739	Marley Purt Drive/The Old Turkey Buzzard	1969	—	3.00	6.00
47-9757	Rain/She's a Woman	1969	—	3.00	6.00
47-9807	Wichita Lineman/Point of View	1969	—	3.00	6.00
47-9912	Pegao/Life Is That Way	1970	—	3.00	6.00
74-0290	So Long, Paul/Here Comes Werbley	1969	2.50	5.00	10.00
—As "Werbley Finster"					
74-0341	Girl (You'll Never Get Away from Me)/Younger Generation	1970	—	3.00	6.00
74-0358	Susie Q/Destiny	1970	—	3.00	6.00
74-0404	Feliz Navidad/The Little Drummer Boy	1970	2.50	5.00	10.00
74-0451	Que Sera/There's No One About	1971	—	2.50	5.00
74-0452	Shake a Hand/There's No One About	1971	—	2.50	5.00
74-0476	I Only Want to Say/Watch It With My Heart	1971	—	2.50	5.00
74-0545	Come Down Jesus/Only Once	1971	—	2.50	5.00
74-0586	Daytime Dreams/Fireworks	1971	—	2.50	5.00
74-0768	Magnolia/It Doesn't Matter Anyhow	1972	—	2.50	5.00
74-0841	Where Is My Woman/One More Mile	1972	—	2.50	5.00
74-0975	Hey Look at the Sun/Compartments	1973	—	2.50	5.00
447-0936	Feliz Navidad/The Little Drummer Boy	197?	—	2.00	4.00
—Red label reissue					

Albums

Number	Title (A Side/B Side)	Yr	VG	VG+	NM
MOTOWN					
M8-953	Jose Feliciano	1981	2.50	5.00	10.00

Number	Title (A Side/B Side)	Yr	VG	VG+	NM
6018 ML	Escenas de Amor	1982	2.50	5.00	10.00
6035 ML	Romance in the Night	1983	2.50	5.00	10.00
PAIR					
PDL2-1091 [(2)]	His Hits and Other Classics	1986	3.00	6.00	12.00
PRIVATE STOCK					
PS-2010	Angela	1976	2.50	5.00	10.00
PS-2022	Sweet Soul	1977	2.50	5.00	10.00
RCA CAMDEN					
CAS-2563	Jose Feliciano Sings	1972	2.50	5.00	10.00
RCA VICTOR					
APD1-0141 [Q]	Compartments	1973	3.75	7.50	15.00
APL1-0141	Compartments	1973	2.50	5.00	10.00
FSP-253	Fantastico	1970	4.50	9.00	18.00
AFL1-0266	For My Love...Mother Music	1977	2.00	4.00	8.00
—Reissue with new prefix					
APL1-0266	For My Love...Mother Music	1974	2.50	5.00	10.00
FSP-277	En Mi Soldead	1971	4.50	9.00	18.00
AFL1-0407	And the Feeling's Good	1977	2.00	4.00	8.00
—Reissue with new prefix					
CPL1-0407	And the Feeling's Good	1974	2.50	5.00	10.00
AFL1-1005	Just Wanna Rock 'n' Roll	1977	2.00	4.00	8.00
—Reissue with new prefix					
APL1-1005	Just Wanna Rock 'n' Roll	1975	2.50	5.00	10.00
LSPX-1005	Encore! Jose Feliciano's Finest Performances	1971	3.00	6.00	12.00
AFL1-2824	Encore! Jose Feliciano's Finest Performances	1978	2.50	5.00	10.00
—Reissue of LSPX-1005					
LPM-3358 [M]	The Voice and Guitar of Jose Feliciano	1965	3.75	7.50	15.00
LSP-3358 [S]	The Voice and Guitar of Jose Feliciano	1965	5.00	10.00	20.00
LPM-3503 [M]	Bag Full of Soul (Folk, Rock and Blues)	1966	3.75	7.50	15.00
LSP-3503 [S]	Bag Full of Soul (Folk, Rock and Blues)	1966	5.00	10.00	20.00
LPM-3581 [M]	Fantastic Feliciano	1966	3.75	7.50	15.00
LSP-3581 [S]	Fantastic Feliciano	1966	5.00	10.00	20.00
AFL1-3957	Feliciano!	1977	2.00	4.00	8.00
—Reissue with new prefix					
LPM-3957 [M]	Feliciano!	1968	6.25	12.50	25.00
LSP-3957 [S]	Feliciano!	1968	3.75	7.50	15.00
LSP-4045	Souled	1968	3.75	7.50	15.00
AFL1-4185	Feliciano/10 to 23	1977	2.00	4.00	8.00
—Reissue with new prefix					
LSP-4185	Feliciano/10 to 23	1969	3.75	7.50	15.00
AFL1-4370	Fireworks	1977	2.00	4.00	8.00
—Reissue with new prefix					
LSP-4370	Fireworks	1970	3.00	6.00	12.00
LSP-4421	Jose Feliciano	1970	3.75	7.50	15.00
LSP-4573	That the Spirit Needs	1971	3.00	6.00	12.00
LSP-4656	Memphis Menu	1972	3.00	6.00	12.00
LSP-6021 [(2)]	Alive Alive-O!	1969	3.75	7.50	15.00

FELICITY

Either Don Henley or Glenn Frey was a member of this group (sources conflict).

45s

Number	Title (A Side/B Side)	Yr	VG	VG+	NM
WILSON					
101	Hurtin'/I'll Try It	1965	7.50	15.00	30.00

FELIX AND THE ESCORTS

An early version of THE (YOUNG) RASCALS. "Felix" is FELIX CAVALIERE.

45s

Number	Title (A Side/B Side)	Yr	VG	VG+	NM
JAG					
685	The Syracuse/Save	1964	37.50	75.00	150.00

FELT

Albums

Number	Title (A Side/B Side)	Yr	VG	VG+	NM
NASCO					
9006	Felt	1971	50.00	100.00	200.00

FEMALE BEATLES, THE

45s

Number	Title (A Side/B Side)	Yr	VG	VG+	NM
20TH FOX					
531	I Don't Want to Cry/I Want You	1964	5.00	10.00	20.00

FEMININE COMPLEX, THE

45s

Number	Title (A Side/B Side)	Yr	VG	VG+	NM
ATHENA					
5003	Six O'Clock in the Morning/I've Been Workin' on You	1969	3.00	6.00	12.00
5006	I Won't Run/Forgetting	1969	3.00	6.00	12.00
5008	Are You Lonesome Like Me/Run That Through Your Mind	1969	3.00	6.00	12.00

Albums

Number	Title (A Side/B Side)	Yr	VG	VG+	NM
ATHENA					
600	The Feminine Complex	1969	7.50	15.00	30.00

FENDER, FREDDY

45s

Number	Title (A Side/B Side)	Yr	VG	VG+	NM
ABC					
12339	Louisiana Woman/If You're Looking for a Fool	1978	—	2.00	4.00
12370	Talk to Me/Please Mr. Sun	1978	—	2.00	4.00
12415	I'm Leaving It All Up to You/Whe It Rains It Really Pours	1978	—	2.00	4.00
12453	Sweet Summer Day/Walking Piece of Heaven	1979	—	2.00	4.00
ABC/DOT					
17540	Before the Next Teardrop Falls/Waiting for Your Love	1974	—	2.50	5.00
17558	Wasted Days and Wasted Nights/I Love My Rancho Grande	1975	—	2.50	5.00
17585	Secret Love/Loving Cajun Style	1975	—	2.00	4.00
17607	You'll Lose a Good Thing/I'm to Blame	1976	—	2.00	4.00
17627	Vaya Con Dios/My Happiness	1976	—	2.00	4.00
17652	Living It Down/Take Her a Message, I'm Lonely	1976	—	2.00	4.00
17686	The Rains Came/Sugar Coated Love	1977	—	2.00	4.00
17713	If You Don't Love Me (Why Don't You Just Leave Me Alone)/Thank You, My Love	1977	—	2.00	4.00
17730	Think About Me/If That's the Way You Want It	1977	—	2.00	4.00
17734	Christmas Time in the Valley/Please Come Home for Christmas	1977	—	2.50	5.00
ARGO					
5375	A Man Can Cry/You're Something Else for Me	1960	3.75	7.50	15.00
ARV INTERNATIONAL					
5083	Crazy Arms/She Thinks I Still Care	196?	2.50	5.00	10.00
5102	Un Dia de Sol/La Costumbre	196?	2.50	5.00	10.00
5146	El Rock de la Carcel/No Seasa Cruel	196?	2.50	5.00	10.00
5216	Crazy Arms/She Thinks I Still Care	198?	—	2.50	5.00
CRAZY CAJUN					
2002	Before the Next Teardrop Falls/Waiting for Your Love	198?	—	2.50	5.00
2002	Before the Next Teardrop Falls/Crazy, Crazy Baby	198?	—	2.50	5.00
2006	Esta Noche Mia Sera/(B-side unknown)	198?	—	2.50	5.00
2014	No Toquen Ya/I Love My Rancho Grande	198?	—	2.50	5.00
2019	Vaya Con Dios/No Say El Mismo	198?	—	2.50	5.00
2037	Fannie Mae/Going Out with the Tide	198?	—	2.50	5.00
—With Tommy McLain					
2060	My Confession/Goin' Honky Tonkin'	198?	—	2.00	4.00
DUNCAN					
1000	Mean Woman/Holy One	1959	10.00	20.00	40.00
1001	Wasted Days and Wasted Nights/San Antonio Walk	1959	6.25	12.50	25.00
1002	Wild Side of Life/Crazy Baby	1959	6.25	12.50	25.00
1004	Since I Met You Baby/Little Mama	1959	6.25	12.50	25.00
GOLDBAND					
1214	My Tears of Love/Carmelia	1969	2.50	5.00	10.00
1264	Bye, Bye, Little Angel/Oh My Love	1975	—	2.50	5.00
1272	Three Wishes/Me and My Bottle of Rum	1975	—	2.50	5.00
GRT					
031	Since I Met You Baby/Little Mama	1975	—	2.50	5.00
039	Wild Side of Life/Go On Baby	1975	—	2.50	5.00
IMPERIAL					
5659	Mean Woman/Holy One	1960	5.00	10.00	20.00
5670	Wasted Days and Wasted Nights/I Can't Remember When I Didn't Love You	1960	5.00	10.00	20.00
INSTANT					
3332	Some People Say/Today's Your Wedding Day	1972	2.00	4.00	8.00
MCA					
12453	Sweet Summer Day/Walking Piece of Heaven	1979	—	2.00	4.00
52003	Across the Borderline/Before the Next Teardrop Falls	1982	—	2.00	4.00
NORCO					
100	Love's Light Is an Ember/The New Stroll	1963	2.50	5.00	10.00
102	You Made Me Cry/Never Trust a Cheating Woman	1963	2.50	5.00	10.00
103	Coming Home Soon/Going Out with the Tide	1964	2.50	5.00	10.00
104	Just a Little Bit/You Made Me a Fool	1964	2.50	5.00	10.00
106	Ooh Poo Pah Doo/Three Wishes	1964	2.50	5.00	10.00
107	Magic of Love/Bony Moronie	1965	2.50	5.00	10.00
—With Noel Vill					
108	In the Still of the Night/You Don't Have to Go	1965	2.50	5.00	10.00
111	Donna/Lover's Quarrel	1965	2.50	5.00	10.00
PA GO GO					
115	Cool Mary Lou/You Are My Sunshine	1967	2.50	5.00	10.00
PACEMAKER					
1973	Wasted Days and Wasted Nights/Bidin' My Time	197?	—	2.50	5.00
REPRISE					
19143	It's All in the Game/Before the Next Teardrop Falls	1992	—	—	3.00
STARFLITE					
4900	Yours/Rock Down in My Shoe	1979	—	2.00	4.00
4904	Squeeze Box/Turn Around	1979	—	2.00	4.00
4906	My Special Prayer/(B-side unknown)	1979	—	2.00	4.00
4908	Please Talk to My Heart/(B-side unknown)	1980	—	2.00	4.00
WARNER BROS.					
29794	Chokin' Kind/I Might As Well Forget You	1983	—	2.00	4.00

Albums

Number	Title (A Side/B Side)	Yr	VG	VG+	NM
ABC					
AA-1062	Swamp Gold	1978	2.50	5.00	10.00
AA-1132	Tex-Mex	1979	3.00	6.00	12.00
ABC/DOT					
DOSD-2020	Before the Next Teardrop Falls	1975	3.00	6.00	12.00
DOSD-2044	Are You Ready for Freddy	1975	3.00	6.00	12.00
DOSD-2050	Rock 'n Country	1976	3.00	6.00	12.00
DOSD-2061	If You're Ever in Texas	1976	3.00	6.00	12.00
DO-2079	The Best of Freddy Fender	1977	3.00	6.00	12.00
DP-2090	If You Don't Love Me	1977	3.00	6.00	12.00
DO-2101	Merry Christmas — Feliz Navidad	1977	3.00	6.00	12.00
ACCORD					
SN-7121	Since I Met You Baby	1981	2.50	5.00	10.00
GRT					
8005	Since I Met You Baby	1975	3.00	6.00	12.00
INTERMEDIA					
QS-5035	Before the Next Teardrop Falls	198?	2.00	4.00	8.00
MCA					
639	Are You Ready for Freddy	1980	2.00	4.00	8.00
—Reissue of ABC/Dot 2044					
668	Swamp Gold	1980	2.00	4.00	8.00
—Reissue of ABC 1062					
669	If You Don't Love Me	1980	2.00	4.00	8.00
—Reissue of ABC/Dot 2090					
835	The Best of Freddy Fender	198?	2.00	4.00	8.00
—Reissue of MCA 3285					
AA-1132	Tex-Mex	1979	2.50	5.00	10.00
—Reissue of ABC 1132					
3285	The Best of Freddy Fender	1979	2.50	5.00	10.00
—Reissue of ABC/Dot 2079					
15025	Merry Christmas	198?	2.00	4.00	8.00
15037	Christmas Time in the Valley	198?	2.50	5.00	10.00
37109	Tex-Mex	1980	2.00	4.00	8.00
—Reissue of MCA 1132					

(Top left) One of the most popular instrumental artists of the early 1960's, Duane Eddy had many singles with picture sleeves. His version of "Peter Gunn" is just one of them. (Top right) Esquerita (sometimes known as "Eskew Reeder") was a wild man on the piano, just as Little Richard was. His one Capitol LP is extremely hard to find. (Bottom left) Among the singers who passed through the Falcons were Eddie Floyd and Wilson Pickett. One of the rarest Falcons pieces is their Unart 7-inch EP from 1959. (Bottom right) Charlie Feathers is one of the most collectible rockabilly artists, though he's relatively unknown outside the record-collecting field. One of his multi-hundred-dollar items is this King single.

Number	Title (A Side/B Side)	Yr	VG	VG+	NM
37110	Before the Next Teardrop Falls	1980	2.00	4.00	8.00
—Reissue of ABC/Dot 2020					
PICCADILLY					
3589	Enter My Heart	1981	2.50	5.00	10.00
PICKWICK					
JS-6178	Freddy Fender	1975	2.50	5.00	10.00
POWER PAK					
PO-280	Recorded Inside Louisiana State Prison	1975	2.50	5.00	10.00
STARFLITE					
JZ 36073	Balladeer	1980	2.50	5.00	10.00
JZ 36284	Together We Drifted Apart	1980	2.50	5.00	10.00

FENDER IV

45s

Number	Title (A Side/B Side)	Yr	VG	VG+	NM
IMPERIAL					
66061	Mar-Gaya/You Better Tell Me Now	1964	12.50	25.00	50.00
66098	Malibu Run/Everybody Up	1965	12.50	25.00	50.00

FENDERMEN, THE

45s

Number	Title (A Side/B Side)	Yr	VG	VG+	NM
CUCA					
1003	Mule Skinner Blues/Torture	1960	50.00	100.00	200.00
SOMA					
1137	Mule Skinner Blues/Torture	1960	6.25	12.50	25.00
1142	Don't You Just Know It/Beach Party	1960	5.00	10.00	20.00
1155	Heartbreakin' Special/Can't You Wait	1960	5.00	10.00	20.00

Albums

Number	Title (A Side/B Side)	Yr	VG	VG+	NM
SOMA					
MG-1240 [M]	Mule Skinner Blues	1960	2000.	3000.	4000.
—Blue vinyl					
MG-1240 [M]	Mule Skinner Blues	1960	300.00	600.00	1200.
—Black vinyl					

FENTON, SHANE, AND THE FENTONES

45s

Number	Title (A Side/B Side)	Yr	VG	VG+	NM
20TH FOX					
439	Don't Do That/I'll Know	1963	3.75	7.50	15.00
LAURIE					
3287	Don't Do That/I'll Know	1965	2.50	5.00	10.00

FERG, JOHNNY

May be the same person as JOHNNY FERGUSON.

45s

Number	Title (A Side/B Side)	Yr	VG	VG+	NM
DECCA					
30572	Candy Love/Sad, Sad Day	1958	7.50	15.00	30.00

FERGUSON, JOHNNY

Also see JOHNNY FERG.

45s

Number	Title (A Side/B Side)	Yr	VG	VG+	NM
DECCA					
30731	Last Date/'Til School Starts Again	1959	5.00	10.00	20.00
MGM					
12789	Afterglow/Waitin' for the Sandman	1959	7.50	15.00	30.00
12855	Angela Jones/Blue Serge and White Lace	1959	5.00	10.00	20.00
12905	I Understand Just How You Feel/Flutter Flutter	1960	7.50	15.00	30.00
12960	No One Can Love You (Like I Do)/Valley of Love	1960	3.75	7.50	15.00

FERGUSON, MAYNARD

12-Inch Singles

Number	Title (A Side/B Side)	Yr	VG	VG+	NM
COLUMBIA					
10546	Gonna Fly Now (Theme from "Rocky")/The Fly	1977	2.50	5.00	10.00
11039	Rocky II Disco/Gabriel	1979	2.50	5.00	10.00

45s

Number	Title (A Side/B Side)	Yr	VG	VG+	NM
CAMEO					
261	Antony & Cleopatr/Theme from Naked City	1963	2.00	4.00	8.00
275	Blues for a Four-String Guitar/Groove	1963	2.00	4.00	8.00
CAPITOL					
F1269	Love Locked Out/Band Ain't Draggin'	1950	3.75	7.50	15.00
F1713	Hot Canary/What's New	1951	3.75	7.50	15.00
COLUMBIA					
10468	Gonna Fly Now (Theme from "Rocky")/The Fly	1977	—	2.00	4.00
10595	Main Title (From the 20th Century Fox Film Star Wars)/Oasis	1977	—	2.00	4.00
10678	Maria/Oasis	1978	—	2.00	4.00
10823	Theme from "Battlestar Galactica"/M.F. Carnival	1978	—	2.00	4.00
11037	Rocky II Disco/Gabriel	1979	—	2.00	4.00
11151	Theme from Star Trek/Topa-Topa Woman	1979	—	2.00	4.00
11183	Main Theme from Star Trek The Motion Picture/Naima	1980	—	2.00	4.00
11411	An Offering of Love Pt. 1/Dance to Your Heart	1980	—	2.00	4.00
45352	Eli's Coming/MacArthur Park	1971	—	2.50	5.00
MAINSTREAM					
603	People/Marcarena	1965	2.00	4.00	8.00
604	Marcarena (Part 1)/Marcarena (Part 2)	1965	2.00	4.00	8.00
MERCURY					
70355	The Way You Look Tonight/Lonely Town	1954	3.00	6.00	12.00
70686	Autumn Leaves/Finger-Snappin'	1955	3.00	6.00	12.00
ROULETTE					
4207	Hey There/Let's Fall in Love	1959	2.50	5.00	10.00
4250	Doin' the Madison (Part 1)/Doin' the Madison (Part 2)	1960	2.50	5.00	10.00
4317	Christmas for Moderns (Part 1)/Christmas for Moderns (Part 2)	1960	3.00	6.00	12.00
4421	Hip Twist/Maria	1962	2.50	5.00	10.00

7-Inch Extended Plays

Number	Title (A Side/B Side)	Yr	VG	VG+	NM
ROULETTE					
SEPR-1-333	Send for Me/When the Sun Comes Out/Can't Get Out of This Mood//(B-side unknown)	196?	5.00	10.00	20.00
SEPR-1-333 [PS]	(title unknown)	196?	5.00	10.00	20.00
—With Chris Connor					

Albums

Number	Title (A Side/B Side)	Yr	VG	VG+	NM
BASF					
20662	Trumpet Rhapsody	1973	3.00	6.00	12.00
BLACK HAWK					
BKH-50101	Body and Soul	1986	2.50	5.00	10.00
BLUEBIRD					
6455-1-RB	The Bluebird Dreamband	1987	2.50	5.00	10.00
CAMEO					
C-1046 [M]	The New Sounds of Maynard Ferguson	1963	5.00	10.00	20.00
SC-1046 [S]	The New Sounds of Maynard Ferguson	1963	6.25	12.50	25.00
C-1066 [M]	Come Blow Your Horn	1964	5.00	10.00	20.00
SC-1066 [S]	Come Blow Your Horn	1964	6.25	12.50	25.00
COLUMBIA					
C 30466	M.F. Horn	1971	3.00	6.00	12.00
PC 30466	M.F. Horn	198?	2.00	4.00	8.00
—Budget-line reissue					
C 31117	Alive and Well in London	1972	3.00	6.00	12.00
PC 31117	Alive and Well in London	198?	2.00	4.00	8.00
—Budget-line reissue					
KC 31709	M.F. Horn Two	1972	3.00	6.00	12.00
PC 31709	M.F. Horn Two	198?	2.00	4.00	8.00
—Budget-line reissue					
KC 32403	M.F. Horn/3	1973	3.00	6.00	12.00
PC 32403	M.F. Horn/3	198?	2.00	4.00	8.00
—Budget-line reissue					
KG 32732 [(2)]	M.F. Horn 4 & 5/Live at Jimmy's	1973	3.75	7.50	15.00
PG 32732 [(2)]	M.F. Horn 4 & 5/Live at Jimmy's	198?	2.50	5.00	10.00
—Budget-line reissue					
KC 33007	Chameleon	1974	3.00	6.00	12.00
PC 33007	Chameleon	1975	2.50	5.00	10.00
—Early reissue of KC 33007; no bar code					
PC 33007	Chameleon	1980	2.00	4.00	8.00
—Budget-line reissue with bar code					
CG 33660 [(2)]	M.F. Horn/M.F. Horn Two	1975	3.75	7.50	15.00
PC 33953	Primal Scream	1976	2.50	5.00	10.00
—No bar code					
PC 34457	Conquistador	1977	2.50	5.00	10.00
—No bar code					
PC 34457	Conquistador	1980	2.00	4.00	8.00
—Budget-line reissue with bar code					
PCQ 34457 [Q]	Conquistador	1977	5.00	10.00	20.00
JC 34971	New Vintage	1977	2.50	5.00	10.00
JC 35480	Carnival	1978	2.50	5.00	10.00
PC 35480	Carnival	1980	2.00	4.00	8.00
—Budget-line reissue					
JC 36124	Hot	1979	2.50	5.00	10.00
JC 36361	The Best of Maynard Ferguson	1980	2.50	5.00	10.00
PC 36361	The Best of Maynard Ferguson	1986	2.00	4.00	8.00
—Budget-line reissue					
JC 36766	It's My Time	1980	2.50	5.00	10.00
PC 36978	Maynard Ferguson	1981	2.50	5.00	10.00
FC 37713	Hollywood	1982	2.50	5.00	10.00
HC 44457	Conquistador	1982	12.50	25.00	50.00
—Half-speed mastered edition					
EMARCY					
EMS-2-406 [(2)]	Stratospheric	1976	3.00	6.00	12.00
MG-26017 [10]	Maynard Ferguson's Hollywood Party	1954	25.00	50.00	100.00
MG-26024 [10]	Dimensions	1954	25.00	50.00	100.00
MG-36009 [M]	Jam Session Featuring Maynard Ferguson	1955	12.50	25.00	50.00
MG-36021 [M]	Maynard Ferguson Octet	1955	15.00	30.00	60.00
MG-36044 [M]	Dimensions	1956	12.50	25.00	50.00
MG-36046 [M]	Maynard Ferguson's Hollywood Party	1956	12.50	25.00	50.00
MG-36076 [M]	Around the Horn with Maynard Ferguson	1956	12.50	25.00	50.00
MG-36114 [M]	Boy with Lots of Brass	1957	12.50	25.00	50.00
ENTERPRISE					
S-13-101	Ridin' High	1968	3.75	7.50	15.00
FORUM					
F-9035 [M]	Jazz for Dancing	196?	3.00	6.00	12.00
SF-9035 [S]	Jazz for Dancing	196?	3.75	7.50	15.00
INTIMA					
SJ-73279	High Voltage	1987	3.00	6.00	12.00
D1-73390	Big Bop Nouveau	1990	3.00	6.00	12.00
MAINSTREAM					
MRL-316	Screamin' Blue	1971	3.00	6.00	12.00
MRL-359	Dues	1972	3.00	6.00	12.00
MRL-372	6 By 6	1973	3.00	6.00	12.00
805 [(2)]	Big "F"	1974	3.75	7.50	15.00
S-6031 [S]	Color Him Wild	1965	5.00	10.00	20.00
S-6045 [S]	The Blues Roar	1965	5.00	10.00	20.00
S-6060 [S]	Maynard Ferguson Sextet	1966	5.00	10.00	20.00
56031 [M]	Color Him Wild	1965	3.75	7.50	15.00
56045 [M]	The Blues Roar	1965	3.75	7.50	15.00
56060 [M]	Maynard Ferguson Sextet	1966	3.75	7.50	15.00
MERCURY					
MG-20556 [M]	Boy with Lots of Brass	1960	7.50	15.00	30.00
SR-60124 [S]	Boy with Lots of Brass	1960	7.50	15.00	30.00
MOSAIC					
MQ14-156 [(14)]	The Complete Roulette Recordings of the Maynard Ferguson Orchestra	199?	62.50	125.00	250.00
NAUTILUS					
NR-57	Storm	1983	10.00	20.00	40.00
—Audiophile vinyl					
PALO ALTO					
PA-8052	Storm	1983	2.50	5.00	10.00
PA-8077	Live from San Francisco	1985	2.50	5.00	10.00
PAUSA					
7037	Trumpet Rhapsody	1980	2.50	5.00	10.00
—Reissue of BASF LP					
PRESTIGE					
PRLP-7636	Maynard Ferguson 1969	1969	3.75	7.50	15.00
ROULETTE					
SK-101 [(2)]	The Ferguson Years	197?	3.75	7.50	15.00
RE-116 [(2)]	A Message from Newport/Newport Suite	1972	3.75	7.50	15.00
—Reissue of 52012 and 52047 in one package					

Number	Title (A Side/B Side)	Yr	VG	VG+	NM
RE-122 [(2)]	Maynard '61/Si! Si! M.F.	1973	3.75	7.50	15.00
—Reissue of 52064 and 52084 in one package					
R 52012 [M]	A Message from Newport	1958	6.25	12.50	25.00
SR 52012 [S]	A Message from Newport	1958	6.25	12.50	25.00
R 52027 [M]	A Message from Birdland	1959	6.25	12.50	25.00
SR 52027 [S]	A Message from Birdland	1959	6.25	12.50	25.00
R 52038 [M]	Maynard Ferguson Plays Jazz for Dancing	1959	6.25	12.50	25.00
SR 52038 [S]	Maynard Ferguson Plays Jazz for Dancing	1959	6.25	12.50	25.00
R 52047 [M]	Newport Suite	1960	6.25	12.50	25.00
SR 52047 [S]	Newport Suite	1960	6.25	12.50	25.00
R 52055 [M]	Let's Face the Music and Dance	1960	6.25	12.50	25.00
SR 52055 [S]	Let's Face the Music and Dance	1960	6.25	12.50	25.00
R 52058 [M]	Swingin' My Way Through College	1960	6.25	12.50	25.00
SR 52058 [S]	Swingin' My Way Through College	1960	6.25	12.50	25.00
R 52064 [M]	Maynard '61	1961	6.25	12.50	25.00
SR 52064 [S]	Maynard '61	1961	6.25	12.50	25.00
R 52083 [M]	Maynard '62	1962	3.75	7.50	15.00
SR 52083 [S]	Maynard '62	1962	5.00	10.00	20.00
R 52084 [M]	Si! Si! M.F.	1962	3.75	7.50	15.00
SR 52084 [S]	Si! Si! M.F.	1962	5.00	10.00	20.00
R 52097 [M]	Maynard '63	1963	3.75	7.50	15.00
SR 52097 [S]	Maynard '63	1963	5.00	10.00	20.00
R 52107 [M]	Maynard '64	1964	3.75	7.50	15.00
SR 52107 [S]	Maynard '64	1964	5.00	10.00	20.00
R 52110 [M]	The World of Maynard Ferguson	1964	3.75	7.50	15.00
SR 52110 [S]	The World of Maynard Ferguson	1964	5.00	10.00	20.00
TRIP					
5507	Dimensions	197?	2.00	4.00	8.00
5525	Jam Session Featuring Maynard Ferguson	197?	2.00	4.00	8.00
5558	Around the Horn with Maynard Ferguson	197?	2.00	4.00	8.00

FERGUSON, SHEILA

45s

Number	Title (A Side/B Side)	Yr	VG	VG+	NM
LANDA					
706	How Did That Happen/Little Red Riding Hood	1965	7.50	15.00	30.00
SWAN					
4217	I Weep for You/Don't (Leave Me Lover)	1965	10.00	20.00	40.00
4225	And In Return/Are You Satisfied	1965	7.50	15.00	30.00
4234	Signs of Love/Heartbroken Memories	1965	10.00	20.00	40.00

FERLINGHETTI, LAWRENCE

Albums

Number	Title (A Side/B Side)	Yr	VG	VG+	NM
FANTASY					
7004 [M]	The Impeachment of Eisenhower	1958	50.00	100.00	200.00
—Red vinyl					
7004 [M]	The Impeachment of Eisenhower	1958	25.00	50.00	100.00
—Black vinyl					

FERRANTE AND TEICHER

45s

Number	Title (A Side/B Side)	Yr	VG	VG+	NM
ABC-PARAMOUNT					
9957	Che Si Dice/How High the Moon	1958	3.00	6.00	12.00
9975	Aflame/How High the Moon	1958	3.00	6.00	12.00
10017	Prairie Blues/Side Saddle	1959	3.00	6.00	12.00
10165	Take Me Along/Lida Rose	1960	3.00	6.00	12.00
10347	Till There Was You/Lida Rose	1962	3.00	6.00	12.00
COLUMBIA					
40088	Taboo/Semper Fideles	1953	3.75	7.50	15.00
UNITED ARTISTS					
0111	Exodus/Tonight	1973	—	2.00	4.00
0112	Midnight Cowboy/Theme from "The Apartment"	1973	—	2.00	4.00
0113	Rudolph, the Red-Nosed Reindeer/Silent Night	1973	—	2.00	4.00
—0111, 0112 and 0113 are "Silver Spotlight Series" reissues					
XW168	Song Sung Blue/American Pie	1973	—	2.00	4.00
196	Lover's Symphony/Dream Concerto	1960	2.50	5.00	10.00
XW205 [DJ]	Last Tango in Paris (mono/stereo)	1973	—	2.00	4.00
231	Theme from "The Apartment"/Lonely Room	1960	2.50	5.00	10.00
231 [PS]	Theme from "The Apartment"/Lonely Room	1960	3.75	7.50	15.00
274	Exodus/Twilight	1960	3.00	6.00	12.00
274 [PS]	Exodus/Twilight	1960	3.75	7.50	15.00
XW295	Love Theme from "Lady Sings the Blues"/ Summer Is Coming	1973	—	2.00	4.00
300	Love Theme from One-Eyed Jacks/Tara's Theme	1961	2.50	5.00	10.00
300 [PS]	Love Theme from One-Eyed Jacks/Tara's Theme	1961	3.75	7.50	15.00
319	Theme from "Goodbye Again"/Possessed	1961	2.50	5.00	10.00
XW367	When Heaven Smiles/I Want to Spend My Life with You	1973	—	2.00	4.00
373	Tonight/Dream of Love	1961	2.50	5.00	10.00
431	Smile/Streets of Paris	1962	2.50	5.00	10.00
XW433	Freedom/Early Morning	1974	—	2.00	4.00
XW448	I'm Stone in Love with You/Cristo Redentor	1974	—	2.00	4.00
470	Lisa/Negligee	1962	2.50	5.00	10.00
537	Theme from "The Eleventh Hour"/Wishing Star	1963	2.00	4.00	8.00
563	Lawrence of Arabia/Paris Joy Ride	1963	2.00	4.00	8.00
607	(Love Theme from) Cleopatra/Caesar and Cleopatra Theme	1963	2.00	4.00	8.00
631	Sands of Time/Devotion	1963	2.00	4.00	8.00
654	Japanese Garden/April in Portugal	1963	2.00	4.00	8.00
660	Crystal Fingers/Greensleeves	1963	2.00	4.00	8.00
700	It's Alright/Corn Pone	1964	2.00	4.00	8.00
735	You're Too Much/Seventh Dawn	1964	2.00	4.00	8.00
XW759	Theme from "Breakheart Pass"/Mandy	1976	—	2.00	4.00
770	What More Can I Say/I've Grown Accustomed to Her Face	1964	2.00	4.00	8.00
XW779	Theme from "Mahogany"/Theme from "Breakheart Pass"	1976	—	2.00	4.00
816	The Greatest Story Ever Told/To Spring	1965	—	3.00	6.00
XW821	Theme from "The Missouri Breaks"/Serendipity	1976	—	2.00	4.00
903	Country Boy/The Knack	1965	—	3.00	6.00
XW915	Gonna Fly Now (Theme from "Rocky")/You Take My Heart Away	1976	—	2.00	4.00
925	Race to Live/Debutante Waltz	1965	—	3.00	6.00
977	Ol' Man River/Judith	1966	—	3.00	6.00
XW1034	A Bridge Too Far/Theme from "New York, New York"	1977	—	2.00	4.00
XW1173	Theme from "Star Trek"/Swinging on a Star	1978	—	2.00	4.00
XW1224	Theme from "The Last Waltz"/Finger Painting	1978	—	2.00	4.00
XW1272	Can You Read My Mind/Ski Fever	1979	—	2.00	4.00
50038	Firebird/Theme from "Khartoum"	1966	—	3.00	6.00
50084	Theme from "The Bible"/Three Over Four	1966	—	3.00	6.00
50101	A Man and a Woman/Dark Eyes	1966	—	3.00	6.00
50188	Rage to Live/Exodus	1967	—	3.00	6.00
50228	Live for Life/Pavanne	1967	—	3.00	6.00
50257	In the Heat of the Night/You Only Live Twice	1968	—	2.50	5.00
50259	Rock-a-Bye Baby/Here Is Where I Belong	1968	—	2.50	5.00
50468	Prelude to Love/A Boy and a Girl	1969	—	2.50	5.00
50501	Chitty Chitty Bang Bang/Buona Sera, Mrs. Campbell	1969	—	2.50	5.00
50512	Joanna/Andrea	1969	—	2.50	5.00
50554	Midnight Cowboy/Rock-a-Bye Baby	1969	—	2.50	5.00
50646	Lay Lady Lay/Theme from "Z"	1970	—	2.00	4.00
50711	Pieces of Dreams/Magical Connection	1970	—	2.00	4.00
50747	Music Lovers/Love Is Now	1971	—	2.00	4.00
50869	Diamonds Are Forever/There's a New Day Coming	1971	—	2.00	4.00
50895	Love Theme from "The Godfather"/There's a New Day Coming	1972	—	2.00	4.00
50963	Everything You Always Wanted to Know But Were Afraid to Ask/Tranquillo	1972	—	2.00	4.00

Albums

Number	Title (A Side/B Side)	Yr	VG	VG+	NM
ABC					
553 [M]	World's Greatest Semi-Classical Favorites	1966	2.50	5.00	10.00
S-553 [S]	World's Greatest Semi-Classical Favorites	1966	3.00	6.00	12.00
554 [M]	Memories	1966	2.50	5.00	10.00
S-554 [S]	Memories	1966	3.00	6.00	12.00
555 [M]	Heaven Sounds	1966	2.50	5.00	10.00
S-555 [S]	Heaven Sounds	1966	3.00	6.00	12.00
556 [M]	We've Got Rhythm	1966	2.50	5.00	10.00
S-556 [S]	We've Got Rhythm	1966	3.00	6.00	12.00
557 [M]	Twin Piano Magic, Vol. 1	1966	2.50	5.00	10.00
S-557 [S]	Twin Piano Magic, Vol. 1	1966	3.00	6.00	12.00
558 [M]	Autumn Leaves	1966	2.50	5.00	10.00
S-558 [S]	Autumn Leaves	1966	3.00	6.00	12.00
559 [M]	Twin Piano Magic, Vol. 2	1966	2.50	5.00	10.00
S-559 [S]	Twin Piano Magic, Vol. 2	1966	3.00	6.00	12.00
560 [M]	Bolero	1966	2.50	5.00	10.00
S-560 [S]	Bolero	1966	3.00	6.00	12.00
561 [M]	Temptation	1966	2.50	5.00	10.00
S-561 [S]	Temptation	1966	3.00	6.00	12.00
ABC-PARAMOUNT					
221 [M]	Heavenly Sounds in Hi-Fi	1958	3.75	7.50	15.00
S-221 [S]	Heavenly Sounds in Hi-Fi	1958	5.00	10.00	20.00
248 [M]	Ferrante and Teicher with Percussion	1958	3.75	7.50	15.00
S-248 [S]	Ferrante and Teicher with Percussion	1958	5.00	10.00	20.00
285 [M]	Ferrante and Teicher Blast Off	1959	3.75	7.50	15.00
S-285 [S]	Ferrante and Teicher Blast Off	1959	5.00	10.00	20.00
313 [M]	Ferrante and Teicher Play Light Classics	1960	3.75	7.50	15.00
S-313 [S]	Ferrante and Teicher Play Light Classics	1960	5.00	10.00	20.00
336 [M]	Themes from Broadway Shows	1960	3.75	7.50	15.00
S-336 [S]	Themes from Broadway Shows	1960	5.00	10.00	20.00
430 [M]	Postcards from Paris	1962	3.00	6.00	12.00
S-430 [S]	Postcards from Paris	1962	3.75	7.50	15.00
437 [M]	Popular Classics	1962	3.00	6.00	12.00
S-437 [S]	Popular Classics	1962	3.75	7.50	15.00
454 [M]	The Artistry of Ferrante and Teicher	1963	3.00	6.00	12.00
S-454 [S]	The Artistry of Ferrante and Teicher	1963	3.75	7.50	15.00
BAINBRIDGE					
BT-6263	A Few of Our Favorites on Stage	1986	2.50	5.00	10.00
BT-6266	American Fantasy	1987	2.50	5.00	10.00
COLUMBIA					
CL 573 [M]	Hi-Fire Works	1955	6.25	12.50	25.00
GRAND AWARD					
GA-263	Themes from Broadway Shows	1962	3.00	6.00	12.00
HARMONY					
HL 7325 [M]	Twin Piano Magic	1965	3.00	6.00	12.00
HL 7427 [M]	Fireworks	1967	3.00	6.00	12.00
HS 11125 [R]	Twin Piano Magic	1965	2.50	5.00	10.00
HS 11227 [R]	Fireworks	1967	2.50	5.00	10.00
HS 11411	Encore	1970	2.50	5.00	10.00
LIBERTY					
LWB-70 [(2)]	10th Anniversary — Golden Piano Hits	198?	2.50	5.00	10.00
—Reissue of United Artists 70					
LWB-73 [(2)]	The Best of Ferrante and Teicher	198?	2.50	5.00	10.00
—Reissue of United Artists 73					
LW-662	Feelings	198?	2.00	4.00	8.00
—Reissue of United Artists 662					
LT-782	Rocky and Other Knockouts	198?	2.00	4.00	8.00
—Reissue of United Artists 782					
LKDL-831 [(4)]	For You with Love	198?	4.50	9.00	18.00
—Reissue of United Artists 831					
LT-908	You Light Up My Life	198?	2.00	4.00	8.00
—Reissue of United Artists 908					
LT-980	Classical Disco	198?	2.00	4.00	8.00
—Reissue of United Artists 980					
LM-1016	Midnight Cowboy	1981	2.00	4.00	8.00
—Reissue of United Artists 1016					
LN-10112	Supermen	198?	2.00	4.00	8.00
—Reissue of United Artists 941					
LN-10113	Star Wars	198?	2.00	4.00	8.00
—Reissue of United Artists 855					
LN-10141	The People's Choice	1981	2.00	4.00	8.00
—Budget-line reissue of United Artists 6385					
LN-10142	Snowbound	1981	2.00	4.00	8.00
—Budget-line reissue of United Artists 6233					
LN-10158	Concert for Lovers	1981	2.00	4.00	8.00
—Budget-line reissue of United Artists 6315					
LN-10175	Showstoppers	1983	2.00	4.00	8.00
LN-10176	The Movie Theme Team	1983	2.00	4.00	8.00

Number	Title (A Side/B Side)	Yr	VG	VG+	NM
LN-10198	Classic Lites	1983	2.00	4.00	8.00
LN-10210	The Movie Theme Team II	1984	2.00	4.00	8.00
LN-10242 [(2)]	Ferrante and Teicher Superpak	1984	2.50	5.00	10.00
PICKWICK					
PC-3003 [M]	Excitement	196?	2.50	5.00	10.00
SPC-3003 [S]	Excitement	196?	2.50	5.00	10.00
PC-3077 [M]	In Love	196?	2.50	5.00	10.00
SPC-3077 [S]	In Love	196?	2.50	5.00	10.00
SPC-3397	How High the Moon	197?	2.00	4.00	8.00
SPC-3586	Getting Together	1978	2.00	4.00	8.00
SPC-3612	Fabulous Favorites	197?	2.00	4.00	8.00
SUNSET					
SUS-5235	Incomparable Piano	1969	2.00	4.00	8.00
SUS-5277	Midnight Memories	1970	2.00	4.00	8.00
SUS-5313	Love Is a Rainbow	1971	2.00	4.00	8.00
UNITED ARTISTS					
UA-LA018-F	Hear & Now	1972	2.50	5.00	10.00
UXS-70 [(2)]	10th Anniversary — Golden Piano Hits	1969	3.00	6.00	12.00
UA-LA072-G	The Roaring 20's	1973	2.50	5.00	10.00
UXS-73 [(2)]	The Best of Ferrante and Teicher	1971	3.00	6.00	12.00
UXS-77 [(2)]	Ferrante and Teicher Superpak	1972	3.00	6.00	12.00
UA-LA101-G2 [(2)]	Greatest Love Themes of the Twentieth Century	1973	3.00	6.00	12.00
UA-LA118-G	Killing Me Softly	1973	2.50	5.00	10.00
UA-LA195-G	Dial M for Music	1974	2.50	5.00	10.00
UA-LA227-G	In a Soulful Mood	1974	2.50	5.00	10.00
UA-LA236-G	The Very Best of Ferrante and Teicher	1974	2.50	5.00	10.00
UA-LA490-G	The Carpenters Songbook	1975	2.50	5.00	10.00
UA-LA573-G	Spirit of 1976	1975	2.50	5.00	10.00
UA-LA585-G	Piano Portraits	1976	2.50	5.00	10.00
UA-LA662-G	Feelings	1976	2.50	5.00	10.00
UA-LA681-G	Around	1977	2.50	5.00	10.00
UA-LA782-G	Rocky and Other Knockouts	1977	2.50	5.00	10.00
UA-LA831-P [(4)]	For You with Love	1978	5.00	10.00	20.00
UA-LA855-G	Star Wars	1978	3.00	6.00	12.00
UA-LA908-H	You Light Up My Life	1978	2.50	5.00	10.00
UA-LA941-H	Supermen	1979	2.50	5.00	10.00
LT-980	Classical Disco	1979	2.50	5.00	10.00
LM-1016	Midnight Cowboy	1980	2.00	4.00	8.00
—Reissue of 6725					
UAL 3121 [M]	The World's Greatest Themes	1960	3.00	6.00	12.00
UAL 3135 [M]	Latin Pianos	1960	3.00	6.00	12.00
UAL 3166 [M]	West Side Story & Other Motion Picture & Broadway Hits	1961	3.00	6.00	12.00
UAL 3171 [M]	Tonight	1962	3.00	6.00	12.00
UAL 3210 [M]	Golden Themes from Motion Pictures	1962	3.00	6.00	12.00
UAL 3211 [M]	The Many Moods of Ferrante & Teicher	1962	3.00	6.00	12.00
UAL 3230 [M]	Pianos in Paradise	1962	3.00	6.00	12.00
UAL 3233 [M]	Snowbound	1962	3.00	6.00	12.00
UAL 3247 [M]	Keys to Her Apartment	1963	3.00	6.00	12.00
UAL 3269 [M]	Golden Piano Hits	1963	2.50	5.00	10.00
—Reissue of 7505					
UAL 3282 [M]	Love Themes	1963	2.50	5.00	10.00
—Reissue of 7514					
UAL 3284 [M]	Keyboard Kapers	1963	2.50	5.00	10.00
UAL 3290 [M]	Love Themes from Cleopatra	1963	3.00	6.00	12.00
UAL 3298 [M]	Holiday for Pianos	1963	2.50	5.00	10.00
UAL 3315 [M]	Concert for Lovers	1964	3.00	6.00	12.00
UAL 3340 [M]	Exotic Love Themes	1964	3.00	6.00	12.00
UAL 3343 [M]	50 Fabulous Piano Favorites	1964	3.00	6.00	12.00
UAL 3361 [M]	My Fair Lady	1964	2.50	5.00	10.00
UAL 3375 [M]	The Enchanted World of Ferrante and Teicher	1964	3.00	6.00	12.00
UAL 3385 [M]	The People's Choice	1964	2.50	5.00	10.00
UAL 3406 [M]	Springtime	1965	2.50	5.00	10.00
UAL 3416 [M]	By Popular Demand	1965	2.50	5.00	10.00
UAL 3434 [M]	Only the Best	1965	2.50	5.00	10.00
UAL 3444 [M]	The Ferrante and Teicher Concert	1965	2.50	5.00	10.00
UAL 3475 [M]	The Ferrante and Teicher Concert, Part 2	1966	2.50	5.00	10.00
UAL 3483 [M]	For Lovers of All Ages	1966	2.50	5.00	10.00
UAL 3526 [M]	You Asked For It!	1966	2.50	5.00	10.00
UAL 3536 [M]	We Wish You a Merry Christmas	1966	3.75	7.50	15.00
UAL 3556 [M]	Our Golden Favorites	1967	3.00	6.00	12.00
UAL 3572 [M]	A Man and a Woman & Other Motion Picture Themes	1967	2.50	5.00	10.00
UAS 5501	Getting Together	1970	2.50	5.00	10.00
UAS 5531	It's Too Late	1971	2.50	5.00	10.00
UAS 5552	Fiddler on the Roof	1971	2.50	5.00	10.00
UAS 5588	Ferrante and Teicher Play Hit Themes	1972	2.50	5.00	10.00
UAS 5645	Ferrante and Teicher Salute Nashville	1972	2.50	5.00	10.00
UAS 6121 [S]	The World's Greatest Themes	1960	3.75	7.50	15.00
UAS 6135 [S]	Latin Pianos	1960	3.75	7.50	15.00
UAS 6166 [S]	West Side Story & Other Motion Picture & Broadway Hits	1961	3.75	7.50	15.00
UAS 6171 [S]	Tonight	1962	3.75	7.50	15.00
UAS 6210 [S]	Golden Themes from Motion Pictures	1962	3.75	7.50	15.00
UAS 6211 [S]	The Many Moods of Ferrante & Teicher	1962	3.75	7.50	15.00
UAS 6230 [S]	Pianos in Paradise	1962	3.75	7.50	15.00
UAS 6233 [S]	Snowbound	1962	3.75	7.50	15.00
UAS 6247 [S]	Keys to Her Apartment	1963	3.75	7.50	15.00
UAS 6269 [S]	Golden Piano Hits	1963	3.00	6.00	12.00
—Reissue of 8505					
UAS 6282 [S]	Love Themes	1963	3.00	6.00	12.00
—Reissue of 8514					
UAS 6284 [S]	Keyboard Kapers	1963	3.00	6.00	12.00
UAS 6290 [S]	Love Themes from Cleopatra	1963	3.75	7.50	15.00
UAS 6298 [S]	Holiday for Pianos	1963	3.00	6.00	12.00
UAS 6315 [S]	Concert for Lovers	1964	3.75	7.50	15.00
UAS 6340 [S]	Exotic Love Themes	1964	3.75	7.50	15.00
UAS 6343 [S]	50 Fabulous Piano Favorites	1964	3.75	7.50	15.00
UAS 6361 [S]	My Fair Lady	1964	3.00	6.00	12.00
UAS 6375 [S]	The Enchanted World of Ferrante and Teicher	1964	3.75	7.50	15.00
UAS 6385 [S]	The People's Choice	1964	3.00	6.00	12.00
UAS 6406 [S]	Springtime	1965	3.00	6.00	12.00
UAS 6416 [S]	By Popular Demand	1965	3.00	6.00	12.00
UAS 6434 [S]	Only the Best	1965	3.00	6.00	12.00
UAS 6444 [S]	The Ferrante and Teicher Concert	1965	3.00	6.00	12.00
UAS 6475 [S]	The Ferrante and Teicher Concert, Part 2	1966	3.00	6.00	12.00
UAS 6483 [S]	For Lovers of All Ages	1966	3.00	6.00	12.00
UAS 6526 [S]	You Asked For It!	1966	3.00	6.00	12.00
UAS 6536 [S]	We Wish You a Merry Christmas	1966	3.00	6.00	12.00
—Same as above, but in stereo					
UAS 6536 [S]	We Wish You a Merry Christmas	1972	2.00	4.00	8.00
—Tan label (may also exist on late-1960s UA labels)					
UAS 6556 [S]	Our Golden Favorites	1967	2.50	5.00	10.00
UAS 6572 [S]	A Man and a Woman & Other Motion Picture Themes	1967	3.00	6.00	12.00
UAS 6659	A Bouquet of Hits	1968	2.50	5.00	10.00
UAS 6701	Listen to the Movies	1969	2.50	5.00	10.00
UAS 6725	Midnight Cowboy	1969	2.50	5.00	10.00
UAS 6771	Love Is a Soft Touch	1970	2.50	5.00	10.00
UAS 6792	The Music Lovers	1971	2.50	5.00	10.00
UAL 7505 [M]	Golden Piano Hits	1961	3.00	6.00	12.00
UAL 7514 [M]	Love Themes	1961	3.00	6.00	12.00
UAS 8505 [S]	Golden Piano Hits	1961	3.75	7.50	15.00
UAS 8514 [S]	Love Themes	1961	3.75	7.50	15.00
URANIA					
8011	Rhapsody	196?	3.00	6.00	12.00
WESTMINSTER					
SW 1045 [S]	Soundproof	195?	6.25	12.50	25.00
SW 1048 [S]	Latin American Adventure	195?	6.25	12.50	25.00
WL 3044 [M]	Christmas Hi-Fi Favorites	195?	5.00	10.00	20.00
WP 6001 [M]	Postcards from Paris	195?	5.00	10.00	20.00
WP 6021 [M]	Adventure in Carols	195?	5.00	10.00	20.00

FERRIER, GARRY

45s

Number	Title (A Side/B Side)	Yr	VG	VG+	NM
ACADEMY					
112	Ringo-Deer/Just My Luck	1964	5.00	10.00	20.00

FERRIS AND THE WHEELS

45s

Number	Title (A Side/B Side)	Yr	VG	VG+	NM
BAMBI					
801	I Want to Dance (Every Night)/Chop Chop	1961	6.25	12.50	25.00
UNITED ARTISTS					
458	Moments Like This/He Was a Fortune Teller	1962	25.00	50.00	100.00

FERRY, BRYAN

Also see ROXY MUSIC.

12-Inch Singles

Number	Title (A Side/B Side)	Yr	VG	VG+	NM
MCA					
23620	Is Your Love Strong Enough (2 versions)/Windswept	1986	2.00	4.00	8.00
REPRISE					
PRO-A-2852 [DJ]	The Right Stuff (same on both sides)	1987	—	3.00	6.00
20799	The Right Stuff (3 mixes)	1987	—	3.00	6.00
20841	Kiss and Tell (3 versions)/Zamba	1988	2.50	5.00	10.00
—With picture cover; deduct 40% if cover is missing					
20846	Limbo (2 versions)/Bete Noire	1989	2.50	5.00	10.00
WARNER BROS.					
PRO-A-2304 [DJ]	Slave to Love (Long)/Slave to Love (Short)	1985	2.00	4.00	8.00
PRO-A-2352 [DJ]	Don't Stop the Dance/Don't Stop the Dance (Edit)	1985	2.00	4.00	8.00
PRO-A-2577 [DJ]	Help Me (same on both sides)	1986	3.00	6.00	12.00
20385	Don't Stop the Dance/Slave to Love	1985	—	3.00	6.00

45s

Number	Title (A Side/B Side)	Yr	VG	VG+	NM
ATLANTIC					
3017	A Hard Rain's Gonna Fall/2 HB	1974	—	2.50	5.00
3351	Let's Stick Together (Let's Work Together)/Sea Breezes	1976	—	2.00	4.00
3364	Heart on My Sleeve/Re-Make, Re-Model	1976	—	2.00	4.00
3399	Tokyo Joe/As the World Turns	1977	—	2.00	4.00
3539	Sign of the Times/Can't Let Go	1978	—	2.00	4.00
MCA					
52788	Is Your Love Strong Enough/Windswept	1986	—	—	3.00
52788 [PS]	Is Your Love Strong Enough/Windswept	1986	—	—	3.00
REPRISE					
28116	Limbo (Brooklyn Version)/Limbo (Latin Version)	1988	—	—	3.00
28116 [PS]	Limbo (Brooklyn Version)/Limbo (Latin Version)	1988	—	—	3.00
28117	Kiss and Tell/Zamba	1988	—	—	3.00
28117 [PS]	Kiss and Tell/Zamba	1988	—	—	3.00
28172	The Right Stuff/The Right Stuff (Brooklyn Mix)	1987	—	—	3.00
VIRGIN					
S7-18133	Mamouna/Don't Stop the Dance (Live)	1994	—	2.00	4.00
38684	As Time Goes By/Falling in Love Again	1999	—	—	3.00
WARNER BROS.					
28582	Help Me/Broken Wings	1986	—	—	3.00
28582 [PS]	Help Me/Broken Wings	1986	—	—	3.00
28887	Don't Stop the Dance/Nocturne	1985	—	—	3.00
28887 [PS]	Don't Stop the Dance/Nocturne	1985	—	—	3.00
28990	Slave to Love/Valentine	1985	—	—	3.00
28990 [PS]	Slave to Love/Valentine	1985	—	—	3.00

Albums

Number	Title (A Side/B Side)	Yr	VG	VG+	NM
ATLANTIC					
SD 7304	These Foolish Things	1973	3.75	7.50	15.00
SD 18113	Another Time, Another Place	1974	3.75	7.50	15.00
SD 18187	Let's Stick Together	1976	3.00	6.00	12.00
SD 18216	In Your Mind	1977	3.00	6.00	12.00
SD 19205	The Bride Stripped Bare	1978	3.00	6.00	12.00
REPRISE					
25598	Bete Noire	1988	3.00	6.00	12.00
WARNER BROS.					
25082	Boys and Girls	1985	3.00	6.00	12.00

FESTIVALS, THE

45s

Number	Title (A Side/B Side)	Yr	VG	VG+	NM
BLUE ROCK					
4076	Hey Girl/Checkin' Out	1969	2.00	4.00	8.00
COLOSSUS					
122	You're Gonna Make It/So in Love	1970	—	3.50	7.00
136	Baby Show It/Take Your Time	1971	—	3.50	7.00

Number	Title (A Side/B Side)	Yr	VG	VG+	NM
146	Gee Baby/Give Her Up	1971	—	3.50	7.00
GORDY					
7120	Green Grows the Lilacs/So in Love	1972	—	3.00	6.00
SMASH					
2056	I'll Always Love You/Music	1966	2.00	4.00	8.00
2196	Hey Girl/Not Gonna Let Her	1968	2.00	4.00	8.00

FEVER TREE

Number	Title (A Side/B Side)	Yr	VG	VG+	NM
45s					
AMPEX					
11013	She Comes in Colors/You're Not the Same Baby	1970	3.75	7.50	15.00
11028	I Put a Spell on You/Hey Joe, Where You Gonna Go	1970	3.75	7.50	15.00
MAINSTREAM					
661	Hey Mister/I Can Beat Your Drum	1967	3.00	6.00	12.00
665	Girl, Oh Girl (Don't Push Me)/Steve Lenore	1967	3.00	6.00	12.00
UNI					
55060	San Fransisco Girls (Return of the Native)/Come with Me	1968	3.00	6.00	12.00
55060 [DJ]	San Fransisco Girls (Return of the Native) (same on both sides)	1968	10.00	20.00	40.00
—Promo only on blue vinyl					
55095	What Time Did You Say It Is in Salt Lake City/Where Do You Go	1968	3.75	7.50	15.00
55146	Love Makes the Sun Rise/Filigree and Shadow	1969	3.75	7.50	15.00
55172	The Sun Also Rises/Clancey	1969	3.75	7.50	15.00
55202	Catcher in the Rye/What Time Did You Say It Is in Salt Lake City?	1970	5.00	10.00	20.00
55228	I Am/Grand Candy Young Sweet	1970	5.00	10.00	20.00
Albums					
AMPEX					
A-10113	For Sale	1970	6.25	12.50	25.00
MCA					
551	Fever Tree	197?	2.50	5.00	10.00
UNI					
73024	Fever Tree	1968	6.25	12.50	25.00
73040	Another Time, Another Place	1968	6.25	12.50	25.00
73067	Creation	1970	6.25	12.50	25.00

FI-DELLS, THE

Number	Title (A Side/B Side)	Yr	VG	VG+	NM
45s					
IMPERIAL					
5780	What Is Love/Don't Let Me Love You	1961	6.25	12.50	25.00
WARNER					
1014	No Other Love/Come Back to Me	1957	5.00	10.00	20.00

FI-TONES, THE

Number	Title (A Side/B Side)	Yr	VG	VG+	NM
45s					
ANGLE TONE					
525	You'll Be the Last/Wake Up	1958	25.00	50.00	100.00
530	It Wasn't a Lie/What Am I Goin' to Do	1958	20.00	40.00	80.00
536	Deep In My Heart/Minnie	1959	15.00	30.00	60.00
ATLAS					
1050	Foolish Dreams/Let's Fall in Love	1955	100.00	200.00	400.00
—Originals identify label as "Atlas Record Company" and have Atlas logo at far upper left					
1050	Foolish Dreams/Let's Fall in Love	1955	25.00	50.00	100.00
—Second pressings identify label as "Atlas Records" and have Atlas logo at left side					
1051	It Wasn't a Lie/Lots and Lots of Love	1955	25.00	50.00	100.00
1052	I Call to You/Love You Baby	1955	25.00	50.00	100.00
1055	I Belong to You/Silly and Happy	1956	25.00	50.00	100.00
1056	Waiting for Your Call/My Tired Feet	1956	25.00	50.00	100.00
OLD TOWN					
1042	My Faith/My Heart	1957	100.00	200.00	400.00

FIDELITY'S, THE

BUDDY MILES was in this group.

Number	Title (A Side/B Side)	Yr	VG	VG+	NM
45s					
BATON					
252	The Things I Love/Hold On to Whatcha Got	1958	6.25	12.50	25.00
256	Memories of You/Can't You Come Out	1958	6.25	12.50	25.00
261	Captain of My Ship/My Greatest Thrill	1958	6.25	12.50	25.00
SIR					
271	Marie/The Invitation	1959	5.00	10.00	20.00
274	Walk with the Wind/Only to You	1959	5.00	10.00	20.00
276	Where in the World/This Girl of Mine	1960	5.00	10.00	20.00
277	Wishing Star/Broken Love	1960	7.50	15.00	30.00

FIELD, JERRY, AND THE LAWYERS

Number	Title (A Side/B Side)	Yr	VG	VG+	NM
45s					
PARKWAY					
801	The Trial/Easy Steppin'	1958	7.50	15.00	30.00
—Blue label					
801	The Trial/Easy Steppin'	1958	5.00	10.00	20.00
—White label. This is actually a cover of a break-in record (for the original, see HERB B. LOU AND THE LEGAL EAGLES).					

FIELD, SALLY

Number	Title (A Side/B Side)	Yr	VG	VG+	NM
45s					
COLGEMS					
66-1008	Felicidad/Find Yourself a Rainbow	1967	2.50	5.00	10.00
66-1008 [PS]	Felicidad/Find Yourself a Rainbow	1967	3.75	7.50	15.00
66-1014	Golden Days/You're a Grand Old Flag	1967	2.00	4.00	8.00
Albums					
COLGEMS					
COM-106 [M]	The Flying Nun	1967	7.50	15.00	30.00
COS-106 [S]	The Flying Nun	1967	6.25	12.50	25.00

FIELDS, BOBBY

Number	Title (A Side/B Side)	Yr	VG	VG+	NM
45s					
ACE					
504	Pity Poor Me/Give Me a Helping Hand	1955	15.00	30.00	60.00

FIELDS, ERNIE

Number	Title (A Side/B Side)	Yr	VG	VG+	NM
45s					
CAPITOL					
5161	St. Louis Blues/Lilies of the Field	1964	2.00	4.00	8.00
5326	Swanne River/Chloe	1964	2.00	4.00	8.00
RENDEZVOUS					
110	In the Mood/Christopher Columbus	1959	3.00	6.00	12.00
117	Chattanooga Choo Choo/Workin' Out	1960	2.50	5.00	10.00
122	Begin the Beguine/Things Ain't What They Used to Be	1960	2.50	5.00	10.00
129	Teen Flip/Sweet Slumber	1960	2.50	5.00	10.00
138	The Honeydripper/(B-side unknown)	1960	2.50	5.00	10.00
142	The Happy Whistler/Monkey	1961	2.50	5.00	10.00
148	Be Anything (But Be Mine)/Fallin'	1961	2.50	5.00	10.00
150	The Charleston/12th Street Rag	1961	2.50	5.00	10.00
161	A String of Pearls/Castle Rock	1961	2.50	5.00	10.00
170	Hucklebuck (Twist)/Ernie's Tune	1962	2.00	4.00	8.00
181	Theme from Perry Mason/Me and My Shadow	1962	2.50	5.00	10.00
Albums					
RENDEZVOUS					
1309 [M]	In the Mood	1960	15.00	30.00	60.00

FIELDS, GRACIE

Number	Title (A Side/B Side)	Yr	VG	VG+	NM
Albums					
LIBERTY					
LRP-3059 [M]	Our Gracie	1957	10.00	20.00	40.00

FIELDS, THE

Number	Title (A Side/B Side)	Yr	VG	VG+	NM
45s					
UNI					
55106	Bide My Time/Take You Home	1969	2.50	5.00	10.00
Albums					
UNI					
73050	Fields	1969	12.50	25.00	50.00

FIESTAS, THE

Number	Title (A Side/B Side)	Yr	VG	VG+	NM
45s					
CHIMNEYVILLE					
10216	Tina, the Disco Queen/I'm No Better Than You	1977	3.00	6.00	12.00
10221	Is That Long Enough for You/I'm Gonna Make Myself	1977	3.00	6.00	12.00
COTILLION					
44117	So Fine/Broken Heart	1971	6.25	12.50	25.00
OLD TOWN					
1062	So Fine/Last Night I Dreamed	1958	12.50	25.00	50.00
—Versions pressed by Columbia have a piano intro not available elsewhere. Look for "ZTSP" on label					
1062	So Fine/Last Night I Dreamed	1958	7.50	15.00	30.00
—Standard version; no "ZTSP" on label					
1067	Grandma Gave a Party/I'm Your Slave	1959	6.25	12.50	25.00
1069	Our Anniversary/I'm Your Slave	1959	6.25	12.50	25.00
1074	Good News/That Was Me	1959	6.25	12.50	25.00
1080	Dollar Bill/It Don't Make Sense	1960	6.25	12.50	25.00
1090	So Nice/You Could Be My Girlfriend	1960	6.25	12.50	25.00
1104	Look at That Girl/Mr. Dillon, Mr. Dillon	1961	6.25	12.50	25.00
1111	Hobo's Prayer/She's Mine	1961	10.00	20.00	40.00
1122	Broken Heart/Railroad Song	1962	5.00	10.00	20.00
1127	I Feel Good All Over/Look at That Girl	1962	5.00	10.00	20.00
1134	The Gypsy Said/Mama Put the Law Down	1963	5.00	10.00	20.00
1140	The Party's Over/Try It One More Time	1963	5.00	10.00	20.00
1148	Foolish Dreamer/Rock-a-By Baby	1963	5.00	10.00	20.00
1166	All That's Good/Rock-a-By Baby	1964	5.00	10.00	20.00
1178	Think Smart/Anna	1965	20.00	40.00	80.00
1187	Love Is Strange/Love Is Good to Me	1965	3.75	7.50	15.00
1189	Ain't She Sweet/I Gotta Have Your Lovin'	1965	3.75	7.50	15.00
RESPECT					
2509	I Can't Shake Your Love (Can't Shake You Loose)/A Sometimes Storm	1972	2.00	4.00	8.00
STRAND					
25046	Come On Everybody/Julia	1961	10.00	20.00	40.00
VIGOR					
712	So Fine/Darling You've Changed	1974	2.00	4.00	8.00

FIFTH DIMENSION, THE

Also see BILLY DAVIS.

Number	Title (A Side/B Side)	Yr	VG	VG+	NM
45s					
ABC					
12136	Magic in My Life/Lean On Me Always	1975	—	2.00	4.00
12168	Walk Your Feet in the Sunshine/Speaking with My Heart	1976	—	2.00	4.00
12181	Love Hangover/Will You Be There	1976	—	2.00	4.00
ARISTA					
0101	No Love in the Room/I Don't Know How to Look for Love	1975	—	2.00	4.00
BELL					
860	Medley: A Change Is Gonna Come & People Gotta Be Free/The Declaration	1970	—	2.50	5.00
880	Puppet Man/A Love Like Ours	1970	—	2.50	5.00
895	Save the Country/Dimension 5	1970	—	2.50	5.00
913	On the Beach (In the Summertime)/This Is Your Life	1970	—	2.50	5.00
940	One Less Bell to Answer/Feelin' Alright?	1970	—	2.50	5.00
965	Love's Lines, Angles and Rhymes/The Singer	1971	—	2.50	5.00
999	Light Sings/Viva Tirado	1971	—	2.50	5.00
45134	Never My Love/A Love Like Ours	1971	—	2.50	5.00
45170	Together Let's Find Love/I Just Wanta Be Your Friend	1972	—	2.50	5.00
45195	(Last Night) I Didn't Get to Sleep at All/The River Witch	1972	—	2.50	5.00
45261	If I Could Reach You/Tomorrow Belongs to the Children	1972	—	2.50	5.00
45310	Living Together, Growing Together/What Do I Need to Be Me	1973	—	2.00	4.00

Number	Title (A Side/B Side)	Yr	VG	VG+	NM
45338	Everything's Been Changed/There Never Was a Day	1973	—	2.00	4.00
45380	Ashes to Ashes/The Singer	1973	—	2.00	4.00
45425	Flashback/Diggin' for a Livin'	1973	—	2.00	4.00
45612	Harlem/My Song	1974	—	2.00	4.00
MOTOWN					
1437	You Are the Reason (I Feel Like Dancing)/ Slipping Into Something New	1978	—	2.00	4.00
1453	Everybody's Got to Give It Up/You're My Star	1978	—	2.00	4.00
SOUL CITY					
752	I'll Be Loving You Forever/Train, Keep On Moving	1966	15.00	30.00	60.00
753	Go Where You Wanna Go/Too Poor to Die	1967	2.00	4.00	8.00
753 [PS]	Go Where You Wanna Go/Too Poor to Die	1967	5.00	10.00	20.00
755	Another Day, Another Heartache/Rosecrans Blvd.	1967	2.50	5.00	10.00
755 [PS]	Another Day, Another Heartache/Rosecrans Blvd.	1967	5.00	10.00	20.00
756	Up-Up and Away/Which Way to Nowhere	1967	2.00	4.00	8.00
760	Paper Cup/Poor Side of Town	1967	2.00	4.00	8.00
762	Carpet Man/Magic Garden	1968	2.00	4.00	8.00
766	Stoned Soul Picnic/The Saliboat Song	1968	2.00	4.00	8.00
766 [PS]	Stoned Soul Picnic/The Saliboat Song	1968	3.75	7.50	15.00
768	Sweet Blindness/Bobby's Blues	1968	2.00	4.00	8.00
768 [PS]	Sweet Blindness/Bobby's Blues	1968	3.75	7.50	15.00
770	California Soul/It'll Never Be the Same	1968	2.00	4.00	8.00
772	Aquarius/Let the Sunshine In (The Flesh Failures)//Don'tcha Hear Me Callin' To Ya	1969	2.00	4.00	8.00
772 [PS]	Aquarius/Let the Sunshine In (The Flesh Failures)//Don'tcha Hear Me Callin' To Ya	1969	3.75	7.50	15.00
776	Workin' on a Groovy Thing/Broken Wing Bird	1969	2.00	4.00	8.00
779	Wedding Bell Blues/Lovin' Stew	1969	2.00	4.00	8.00
780	Blowing Away/Skinny Man	1970	—	3.00	6.00
781	The Girls' Song/It'll Never Be the Same Again	1970	—	3.00	6.00
SUTRA					
122	Surrender/Fantasy	1983	—	2.00	4.00

Albums

Number	Title (A Side/B Side)	Yr	VG	VG+	NM
ABC					
D-897	Earthbound	1975	2.50	5.00	10.00
ARISTA					
ABM-1106	Greatest Hits on Earth	1975	2.00	4.00	8.00
—Reissue of Bell 1106					
AL 8335	Greatest Hits on Earth	198?	2.00	4.00	8.00
—Reissue of Arista 1106					
BELL					
1106	Greatest Hits on Earth	1972	2.50	5.00	10.00
1116	Living Together, Growing Together	1973	2.50	5.00	10.00
1315	Soul and Inspiration	1974	2.50	5.00	10.00
6045	Portrait	1970	3.00	6.00	12.00
6060	Love's Lines, Angles and Rhymes	1971	3.00	6.00	12.00
6065	Reflections	1971	2.50	5.00	10.00
6073	Individually & Collectively	1972	2.50	5.00	10.00
9000 [(2)]	The 5th Dimension/Live!!	1971	3.00	6.00	12.00
MOTOWN					
M7-896	Star	1978	2.50	5.00	10.00
PAIR					
PDL2-1108 [(2)]	The Glory Days	1986	3.00	6.00	12.00
RHINO					
RNDA-71104 [(2)]	The 5th Dimension Anthology	1986	3.00	6.00	12.00
SOUL CITY					
SCS-33900	The 5th Dimension/Greatest Hits	1970	3.00	6.00	12.00
SCS-33901	The July 5th Album	1970	3.00	6.00	12.00
SCM-91000 [M]	Up, Up and Away	1967	5.00	10.00	20.00
SCM-91001 [M]	The Magic Garden	1967	5.00	10.00	20.00
SCS-92000 [S]	Up, Up and Away	1967	3.75	7.50	15.00
SCS-92001 [S]	The Magic Garden	1967	3.75	7.50	15.00
SCS-92002	Stoned Soul Picnic	1968	3.75	7.50	15.00
SCS-92005	The Age of Aquarius	1969	3.75	7.50	15.00

FIFTH ESTATE, THE

Also see THE D-MEN.

45s

Number	Title (A Side/B Side)	Yr	VG	VG+	NM
JUBILEE					
5573	Ding! Dong! The Witch Is Dead/The Rub-a-Dub	1967	3.00	6.00	12.00
5588	Lost Generation/The Goofin' Song	1967	2.00	4.00	8.00
5595	Heigh-Ho/It's Waiting There for You	1967	2.00	4.00	8.00
5607	Morning, Morning/Tomorrow Is My Turn	1967	2.00	4.00	8.00
5617	Do Drop Inn/That's Love	1968	2.00	4.00	8.00
5627	Coney Island Sally/Tomorrow Is My Turn	1968	2.00	4.00	8.00
5655	Mickey Mouse Club March/I Knew You Before I Met You	1969	2.00	4.00	8.00
5683 [DJ]	Parade of the Wooden Soldiers (mono/stereo)	1969	2.50	5.00	10.00
—Stock copies may not exist ("I Knew You Before I Met You" was listed as B-side)					
RED BIRD					
10-064	Love Is All a Game/Like I Love You	1966	3.75	7.50	15.00

Albums

Number	Title (A Side/B Side)	Yr	VG	VG+	NM
JUBILEE					
JGM-8005 [M]	Ding Dong! The Witch Is Dead	1967	6.25	12.50	25.00
JGS-8005 [S]	Ding Dong! The Witch Is Dead	1967	7.50	15.00	30.00

FIFTY FOOT HOSE

Albums

Number	Title (A Side/B Side)	Yr	VG	VG+	NM
LIMELIGHT					
86062	Cauldron	1968	25.00	50.00	100.00

FILETS OF SOUL

45s

Number	Title (A Side/B Side)	Yr	VG	VG+	NM
SAVOY					
1630	Since I Fell for You/C'mon Let's Dance	1968	6.25	12.50	25.00

Albums

Number	Title (A Side/B Side)	Yr	VG	VG+	NM
SQUID					
4857	Freedom	1968	25.00	50.00	100.00

FINCHLEY BOYS, THE

Albums

Number	Title (A Side/B Side)	Yr	VG	VG+	NM
GOLDEN THROAT					
200-19	Everlasting Tribute	1971	50.00	100.00	200.00

FINDERS KEEPERS

45s

Number	Title (A Side/B Side)	Yr	VG	VG+	NM
CHALLENGE					
59338	Lavender Blue/Raggedy Ann	1966	3.75	7.50	15.00
59364	Don't Give In to Him/I've Done All I Can	1967	3.75	7.50	15.00
FONTANA					
1609	Friday Kind of Monday/On the Beach	1968	3.00	6.00	12.00

FINN, MICKY

45s

Number	Title (A Side/B Side)	Yr	VG	VG+	NM
CHATTAHOOCHIE					
663	I Still Want You/Reelin' and Rockin'	1965	3.00	6.00	12.00
WORLD ARTISTS					
1048	Night Comes Down/This Sporting Life	1965	3.00	6.00	12.00

FINNEGAN, LARRY

45s

Number	Title (A Side/B Side)	Yr	VG	VG+	NM
CORAL					
62313	I'll Be Back, Jack/There Ain't Nothin' in This World	1962	2.50	5.00	10.00
OLD TOWN					
1113	Dear One/Candy Lips	1961	3.00	6.00	12.00
1120	Pretty Susie Sunshine/It's Walkin' Talkin' Time	1962	2.50	5.00	10.00
1136	A Kiss and a Dozen Roses/Pick Up the Pieces	1963	2.50	5.00	10.00
RIC					
146	The Other Ringo (A Tribute to Ringo Starr)/When My Love Passes By	1964	3.75	7.50	15.00

FINNEGAN, MIKE, AND THE SERFS

45s

Number	Title (A Side/B Side)	Yr	VG	VG+	NM
PARKWAY					
113	Help Me Somebody/Bread and Water	1966	5.00	10.00	20.00

FINSTER, WERBLEY

See JOSE FELICIANO.

FIRE

Albums

Number	Title (A Side/B Side)	Yr	VG	VG+	NM
ABC					
ABCS-661	Fire	1969	5.00	10.00	20.00

FIRE ESCAPE, THE

45s

Number	Title (A Side/B Side)	Yr	VG	VG+	NM
GNP CRESCENDO					
384	Blood Beat/Love Special Delivery	1967	3.00	6.00	12.00

Albums

Number	Title (A Side/B Side)	Yr	VG	VG+	NM
GNP CRESCENDO					
GNP-2034 [M]	Psychotic Reaction	1967	10.00	20.00	40.00
GNPS-2034 [S]	Psychotic Reaction	1967	7.50	15.00	30.00

FIRE & ICE LTD.

45s

Number	Title (A Side/B Side)	Yr	VG	VG+	NM
CAPITOL					
2587	Music Man/For the Money	1969	2.00	4.00	8.00
—As "Fire & Ice"					

Albums

Number	Title (A Side/B Side)	Yr	VG	VG+	NM
CAPITOL					
ST 2577 [S]	The Happening	1966	10.00	20.00	40.00
T 2577 [M]	The Happening	1966	7.50	15.00	30.00

FIREBALLET

45s

Number	Title (A Side/B Side)	Yr	VG	VG+	NM
PASSPORT					
7908	Desiree/Carrollon	1975	—	2.50	5.00

Albums

Number	Title (A Side/B Side)	Yr	VG	VG+	NM
PASSPORT					
98010	Night on Bald Mountain	1975	3.00	6.00	12.00
98016	Two, Too...	1976	3.00	6.00	12.00

FIREBALLS, THE

Includes records credited to "Jimmy Gilmer and the Fireballs." Also see JIMMY GILMER.

45s

Number	Title (A Side/B Side)	Yr	VG	VG+	NM
7 ARTS					
714	Callin' the Sheriff/Don't Stop	1961	—	—	—
—Evidently, record was never released, though its picture sleeve exists					
714 [PS]	Callin' the Sheriff/Don't Stop	1961	12.50	25.00	50.00
ASTRA					
1021	Torquay/Sweet Walk	1966	2.50	5.00	10.00
ATCO					
6491	Bottle of Wine/Can't You See I'm Tryin'	1967	2.50	5.00	10.00
6569	Goin' Away/Groovy Motions	1968	2.00	4.00	8.00
6595	Chicken Little/Three Minutes' Time	1968	2.00	4.00	8.00
6614	Come On, React!/Woman Help Me	1968	2.00	4.00	8.00
6651	Long Green/Light in the Window	1969	2.00	4.00	8.00
6678	Watch Her Walk/Good Morning Shame	1969	2.00	4.00	8.00
DOT					
16487	Sugar Shack/My Heart Is Free	1963	3.75	7.50	15.00
—Jimmy Gilmer and the Fireballs					
16493	Torquay Two/Peg Leg	1963	3.75	7.50	15.00
16539	Daisy Petal Pickin'/When My Tears Have Dried	1963	3.00	6.00	12.00
—Jimmy Gilmer and the Fireballs					
16583	Ain't Gonna Tell Anybody/Young Am I	1964	3.00	6.00	12.00
—Jimmy Gilmer and the Fireballs					
16591	Daytona Drag/Gently, Gently	1964	3.75	7.50	15.00
16609	I'll Send for You/Look at Me	1964	2.50	5.00	10.00
—Jimmy Gilmer and the Fireballs					

Number	Title (A Side/B Side)	Yr	VG	VG+	NM
16642	Wishing/What Kinda Love	1964	2.50	5.00	10.00
—Jimmy Gilmer and the Fireballs					
16661	Dumbo/Mr. Reed	1964	3.75	7.50	15.00
16666	Cry Baby/Thunder 'N' Lightnin'	1964	2.50	5.00	10.00
—Jimmy Gilmer and the Fireballs					
16687	Break His Heart for Me/Cinnamon Cindy	1965	2.50	5.00	10.00
—Jimmy Gilmer and the Fireballs					
16692	Yummie Yama Papa/Baby, What's Wrong	1965	3.75	7.50	15.00
16714	Born to Be with You/Lonesome Tears	1965	2.50	5.00	10.00
—Jimmy Gilmer and the Fireballs					
16715	More Than I Can Say/Beating of My Heart	1965	3.75	7.50	15.00
16743	The Fool/Somebody Stole My Watermelon	1965	2.50	5.00	10.00
—Jimmy Gilmer and the Fireballs					
16745	Ahhh, Soul/Campusology	1965	3.75	7.50	15.00
16768	Codine/Come to Me	1965	2.50	5.00	10.00
—Jimmy Gilmer and the Fireballs					
16786	She Belongs to Me/Rambler's Blues	1965	2.50	5.00	10.00
—Jimmy Gilmer and the Fireballs					
16833	Hungry, Hungry, Hungry/Wild Roses	1966	2.50	5.00	10.00
—Jimmy Gilmer and the Fireballs					
16834	Jada/What I Am	1966	3.75	7.50	15.00
16881	All I Do Is Dream of You/Ain't That Rain	1966	2.50	5.00	10.00
—Jimmy Gilmer and the Fireballs					
16918	Torquay Two/Say I Am	1966	3.75	7.50	15.00
16979	Sugar Shack/Daisy Petal Pickin'	1966	2.50	5.00	10.00
—Jimmy Gilmer and the Fireballs					
16992	Shy Girl/I Think I'll Catch a Bus	1967	2.50	5.00	10.00
—Jimmy Gilmer and the Fireballs					
HAMILTON					
50036	Blacksmith Blues/Tuff-a-Nuff	1960	5.00	10.00	20.00
JARO					
77029	Long, Long Ponytail/Let There Be Love	1960	20.00	40.00	80.00
—Chuck Tharp and the Fireballs					
KAPP					
248	Fireball/I Don't Know	1958	25.00	50.00	100.00
—Chuck Tharp and the Fireballs					
TOP RANK					
2008	Torquay/Cry Baby	1959	5.00	10.00	20.00
2026ST [S]	Bulldog/Nearly Sunrise	1959	12.50	25.00	50.00
2026 [M]	Bulldog/Nearly Sunrise	1959	5.00	10.00	20.00
2038ST [S]	Foot Patter/Kissin'	1959	12.50	25.00	50.00
2038 [M]	Foot Patter/Kissin'	1959	5.00	10.00	20.00
2054	Vaquero/Chief Whoopin'-Koff	1960	5.00	10.00	20.00
2081	Almost Paradise/Sweet Talk	1960	5.00	10.00	20.00
3003	Rick-a-Tic/Tacky Doo	1961	5.00	10.00	20.00
WARWICK					
630	Rik-A-Tik/Yackey-Doo	1961	4.00	8.00	16.00
644	Quite a Party/Gunshot	1961	4.00	8.00	16.00
7-Inch Extended Plays					
TOP RANK					
REX 1000	Bulldog/Torquay//Kissin'/Foot Patter	196?	37.50	75.00	150.00
REX 1000 [PS]	The Fireballs	196?	37.50	75.00	150.00
Albums					
ATCO					
33-239 [M]	Bottle of Wine	1968	10.00	20.00	40.00
SD 33-239 [S]	Bottle of Wine	1968	6.25	12.50	25.00
SD 33-275	Come On, React!	1969	6.25	12.50	25.00
CROWN					
CST-376 [R]	Jimmy Gilmer and the Fireballs & The Sugar Shackers	1963	6.25	12.50	25.00
CST-387 [R]	The Sensational Jimmy Gilmer & The Fireballs	1964	6.25	12.50	25.00
CLP-5376 [M]	Jimmy Gilmer and the Fireballs & The Sugar Shackers	1963	6.25	12.50	25.00
CLP-5387 [M]	The Sensational Jimmy Gilmer & The Fireballs	1964	6.25	12.50	25.00
DOT					
DLP-3512 [M]	Torquay	1963	12.50	25.00	50.00
DLP-3545 [M]	Sugar Shack	1963	10.00	20.00	40.00
—Jimmy Gilmer and the Fireballs					
DLP-3577 [M]	Buddy's Buddy	1964	12.50	25.00	50.00
—Jimmy Gilmer and the Fireballs					
DLP-3643 [M]	Lucky 'Leven	1965	7.50	15.00	30.00
DLP-3668 [M]	Folkbeat	1965	7.50	15.00	30.00
DLP-3709 [M]	Campusology	1966	7.50	15.00	30.00
DLP-25512 [S]	Torquay	1963	20.00	40.00	80.00
DLP-25545 [S]	Sugar Shack	1963	15.00	30.00	60.00
—Jimmy Gilmer and the Fireballs					
DLP-25577 [S]	Buddy's Buddy	1964	20.00	40.00	80.00
—Jimmy Gilmer and the Fireballs					
DLP-25643 [S]	Lucky 'Leven	1965	10.00	20.00	40.00
DLP-25668 [S]	Folkbeat	1965	10.00	20.00	40.00
DLP-25709 [S]	Campusology	1966	10.00	20.00	40.00
DLP-25856	Firewater	1968	6.25	12.50	25.00
SUNDAZED					
LP-5016	The Fireballs	1995	2.50	5.00	10.00
LP-5017	Torquay	1995	2.50	5.00	10.00
LP-5018	Gunshot!	1995	2.50	5.00	10.00
TOP RANK					
RM-324 [M]	The Fireballs	1960	37.50	75.00	150.00
RM-343 [M]	Vaquero	1960	37.50	75.00	150.00
RS-643 [S]	Vaquero	1960	50.00	100.00	200.00
WARWICK					
W-2042 [M]	Here Are the Fireballs	1961	37.50	75.00	150.00
WST-2042 [S]	Here Are the Fireballs	1961	62.50	125.00	250.00

FIREBIRDS, THE

Number	Title (A Side/B Side)	Yr	VG	VG+	NM
Albums					
CROWN					
CST-589	Light My Fire	1968	17.50	35.00	70.00

FIREFLIES, THE

Number	Title (A Side/B Side)	Yr	VG	VG+	NM
45s					
CANADIAN AMERICAN					
117	Marianne/Give All Your Love to Me	1960	5.00	10.00	20.00
RIBBON					
6901	You Were Mine/Stella Got a Fella	1959	6.25	12.50	25.00
—With "Ribbon" encased in a ribbon on label					
6901	You Were Mine/Stella Got a Fella	1959	7.50	15.00	30.00
—With "Ribbon" standing alone on label					
6904	I Can't Say Goodbye/What Did I Do Wrong	1959	5.00	10.00	20.00
6906	My Girl/Because of My Pride	1960	5.00	10.00	20.00
TAURUS					
355	One O'Clock Twist/You Were Mine for Awhile	1962	5.00	10.00	20.00
366	Good Friends/My Prayer for You	1964	5.00	10.00	20.00
376	Runaround/Could You Mean More	1965	5.00	10.00	20.00
380	Tonight/A Time for Us	1965	5.00	10.00	20.00
Albums					
TAURUS					
1002 [M]	You Were Mine	196?	25.00	50.00	100.00
S-1002 [S]	You Were Mine	196?	75.00	150.00	300.00

FIRESIGN THEATRE, THE

Number	Title (A Side/B Side)	Yr	VG	VG+	NM
45s					
COLUMBIA					
45052	Forward Into the Past/Station Break	1969	2.50	5.00	10.00
45052 [PS]	Forward Into the Past/Station Break	1969	10.00	20.00	40.00
Albums					
BUTTERFLY					
001	Jost Folks...A Firesign Chat	1977	2.50	5.00	10.00
COLUMBIA					
CL 2718 [M]	Waiting for the Electrician or Someone Like Him	1968	6.25	12.50	25.00
CS 9518 [S]	Waiting for the Electrician or Someone Like Him	1968	3.75	7.50	15.00
—"360 Sound" label					
CS 9884	How Can You Be in Two Places at Once When You're Not Anywhere at All	1969	3.75	7.50	15.00
—"360 Sound" label					
C 30102	Don't Crush That Dwarf, Hand Me the Pliers	1970	3.75	7.50	15.00
C 30737	I Think We're All Bozos on This Bus	1971	3.75	7.50	15.00
CQ 30737 [Q]	I Think We're All Bozos on This Bus	1972	5.00	10.00	20.00
KG 31099 [(2)]	Dear Friends	1972	5.00	10.00	20.00
KC 31585	Not Insane or Anything You Want To	1972	3.75	7.50	15.00
KC 32411	David Ossman's How Time Flys	1973	3.00	6.00	12.00
KC 32730	The Tale of the Giant Rat of Sumatra	1974	3.00	6.00	12.00
CQ 33141 [Q]	Everything You Know Is Wrong	1974	5.00	10.00	20.00
KC 33141	Everything You Know Is Wrong	1974	3.00	6.00	12.00
PC 33475	In the Next World You're On Your Own	1975	3.00	6.00	12.00
PG 34391 [(2)]	Forward Into the Past (An Anthology)	1977	3.75	7.50	15.00
MERCURY					
826452-1	Eat or Be Eaten	1985	2.50	5.00	10.00
RHINO					
RNLP-018	Fighting Clowns	1979	3.00	6.00	12.00
RNEP-506 [EP]	Nick Danger, Third Eye	1983	2.50	5.00	10.00
RNLP-806	Lawyer's Hospital	1981	3.00	6.00	12.00
RNLP-807	Shakespeare's Lost Comedie	1982	3.00	6.00	12.00
RNLP-812	Nick Danger In: The Three Faces of Al	1984	3.00	6.00	12.00
RNLP-904	Reagan/Carter	1980	3.00	6.00	12.00

FIRST CHOICE

Number	Title (A Side/B Side)	Yr	VG	VG+	NM
45s					
GOLD MIND					
4004	Doctor Love/I Love You More Than Before	1977	—	2.50	5.00
4009	Love Having You Around/Indian Giver	1977	—	2.50	5.00
4017	Hold Your Horses/Now I've Thrown It All Away	1979	—	2.50	5.00
4019	Double Cross/Game of Love	1979	—	2.50	5.00
4022	Love Thang/Great Expectations	1980	—	2.50	5.00
4023	Breakaway/House for Sale	1980	—	2.50	5.00
PHILLY GROOVE					
175	Armed and Extremely Dangerous/Gonna Keep On Lovin' Him	1973	—	2.50	5.00
179	Smarty Pants/One Step Away	1973	—	2.50	5.00
183	Newsy Neighbors/This Little Woman	1974	—	2.50	5.00
200	The Player — Part 1/The Player — Part 2	1974	—	2.50	5.00
202	Guilty/Wake Up to Me	1974	—	2.50	5.00
204	Love Freeze/A Boy Named Junior	1975	—	2.50	5.00
SCEPTER					
12347	One Step Away/This Is the House	1972	—	3.00	6.00
WARNER BROS.					
8214	Gotta Get Away (From You Baby)/Yes, Maybe Not	1976	—	2.50	5.00
8251	Let Him Go/First Choice Theme	1976	—	2.50	5.00
Albums					
GOLD MIND					
7501	Delusions	1977	3.00	6.00	12.00
9502	Hold Your Horses	1979	3.00	6.00	12.00
9505	Breakaway	1980	3.00	6.00	12.00
PHILLY GROOVE					
1400	Armed and Extremely Dangerous	1973	3.75	7.50	15.00
1502	The Player	1974	3.75	7.50	15.00
WARNER BROS.					
BS 2934	Let Us Entertain You	1976	3.75	7.50	15.00

FIRST CLASS (1)

British studio group featuring Tony Burrows on vocals.

Number	Title (A Side/B Side)	Yr	VG	VG+	NM
45s					
UK					
49022	Beach Baby/Both Sides of the Story	1974	—	2.50	5.00
—Most stock copies have the full-length (4:59) version of the A-side					
49022	Beach Baby/Both Sides of the Story	1974	—	3.00	6.00
—Some stock copies have a short version of the A-side					
49028	Dreams Are Ten a Penny/Lavender Man	1974	—	2.00	4.00
49033	Funny How Love Can Be/Surfer Queen	1975	—	2.00	4.00
Albums					
UK					
53108	The First Class	1974	3.75	7.50	15.00

FIRST CLASS (2)
U.S. R&B group.

45s
ALL PLATINUM

Number	Title (A Side/B Side)	Yr	VG	VG+	NM
2365	Me and My Gemini/Me and My Gemini (Part 2)	1976	—	2.50	5.00
2368	This Is It/Filled with Desire	1977	—	2.50	5.00
2372	Coming Back to You/This Is It	1977	—	2.50	5.00

EBONY SOUNDS

Number	Title (A Side/B Side)	Yr	VG	VG+	NM
187	The Beginning of My End/(B-side unknown)	1975	—	2.50	5.00

TODAY

Number	Title (A Side/B Side)	Yr	VG	VG+	NM
1528	What About Me/Outside Your World	1974	—	2.50	5.00

FIRST CLASS (U)
This is either group (1) or group (2).

45s
PRIVATE STOCK

Number	Title (A Side/B Side)	Yr	VG	VG+	NM
45093	Ain't No Love/Long Time Gone	1976	—	2.00	4.00

FIRST EDITION, THE
Includes "Kenny Rogers and the First Edition." Also see KENNY ROGERS.

45s
JOLLY ROGERS

Number	Title (A Side/B Side)	Yr	VG	VG+	NM
1001	Lady, Play Your Symphony/There's An Old Man in Our Town	1973	—	2.50	5.00
1003	(Do You Remember) The First Time/Indian Joe	1973	—	2.50	5.00
1004	Today I Started Loving You Again/She Thinks I Still Care	1973	—	2.50	5.00
1006	Whatcha Gonna Do/Something About Your Song	1973	—	2.50	5.00
1007	A Stranger in My Place/Makin' Music for Money	1974	—	2.50	5.00

—All of the above as "Kenny Rogers and the First Edition"

REPRISE

Number	Title (A Side/B Side)	Yr	VG	VG+	NM
0628	Ticket to Nowhere/I Found a Reason	1967	2.00	4.00	8.00
0655	Just Dropped In (To See What Condition My Condition Was In)/Shadow in the Corner of Your Mind	1967	3.00	6.00	12.00
—Original pressing has orange and brown label					
0655	Just Dropped In (To See What Condition My Condition Was In)/Shadow in the Corner of Your Mind	1967	2.50	5.00	10.00
—Second pressing has lighter orange "steamboat" Reprise/W7 label					
0683	Dream On/Only Me	1968	—	3.00	6.00
0693	Look Around, I'll Be There/Charlie the Fer-De-Lance	1968	—	3.00	6.00
0737	Just Dropped In (To See What Condition My Condition Was In)/But You Know I Love You	1971	—	2.00	4.00
—As "Kenny Rogers and the First Edition"; "Back to Back Hits" series					
0738	Ruby, Don't Take Your Love to Town/Reuben James	1971	—	2.00	4.00
—As "Kenny Rogers and the First Edition"; "Back to Back Hits" series					
0747	Something's Burning/Someone Who Cares	1972	—	2.00	4.00
—As "Kenny Rogers and the First Edition"; "Back to Back Hits" series					
0748	Tell It All Brother/Heed the Call	1972	—	2.00	4.00
—As "Kenny Rogers and the First Edition"; "Back to Back Hits" series					
0773	If I Could Only Change Your Mind/Are My Thoughts With You	1968	—	3.00	6.00
0799	But You Know I Love You/Homemade Lies	1968	—	3.00	6.00
0822	Good Time Liberator/Once Again She's All Alone	1969	—	2.50	5.00
—Starting above, by "Kenny Rogers and the First Edition"					
0829	Ruby, Don't Take Your Love to Town/Girl Get a Hold of Yourself	1969	—	2.50	5.00
0854	Ruben James/Sunshine	1969	—	2.50	5.00
0854	Reuben James/Sunshine	1969	—	2.50	5.00
0888	Something's Burning/Mama's Waiting	1970	—	2.50	5.00
0923	Tell It All Brother/Just Remember You're My Sunshine	1970	—	2.50	5.00
0953	Heed the Call/A Stranger in My Place	1970	—	2.50	5.00
0999	Someone Who Cares/Mission of San Mohera	1971	—	2.50	5.00
1018	Take My Hand/All God's Lonely Children	1971	—	2.50	5.00
1053	Where Does Rosie Go/What Am I Gonna Do	1971	—	2.50	5.00
1069	School Teacher/Trigger Happy Kid	1972	—	2.50	5.00

Albums
JOLLY ROGERS

Number	Title (A Side/B Side)	Yr	VG	VG+	NM
5001	Backroads	1973	3.75	7.50	15.00
5003	Rollin'	1974	3.75	7.50	15.00
5004	Monumental	1974	3.75	7.50	15.00

—All the above as "Kenny Rogers and the First Edition"

MCA

Number	Title (A Side/B Side)	Yr	VG	VG+	NM
913	Country Songs	1984	2.00	4.00	8.00
942	Hits and Pieces	1985	2.00	4.00	8.00
943	The 60's Revisited	1985	2.00	4.00	8.00
944	Pieces of Calico Silver	1985	2.00	4.00	8.00
1460	Greatest Hits	1985	2.00	4.00	8.00

—Reissue of Reprise 6437

REPRISE

Number	Title (A Side/B Side)	Yr	VG	VG+	NM
MS 2039	Transition	1971	5.00	10.00	20.00
—As "Kenny Rogers and the First Edition"					
R-6276 [M]	The First Edition	1967	7.50	15.00	30.00
RS-6276 [S]	The First Edition	1967	6.25	12.50	25.00
RS-6302	The First Edition's Second	1968	6.25	12.50	25.00
RS-6328	The First Edition '69	1969	6.25	12.50	25.00
RS-6352	Ruby, Don't Take Your Love to Town	1969	5.00	10.00	20.00
—Starting above, as "Kenny Rogers and the First Edition"					
RS-6385	Something's Burning	1970	5.00	10.00	20.00
RS-6412	Tell It All Brother	1970	5.00	10.00	20.00
RS-6437	Greatest Hits	1971	5.00	10.00	20.00
2SX 6476 [(2)]	The Ballad of Calico	1972	6.25	12.50	25.00

FISCHER, WILD MAN

45s
REPRISE

Number	Title (A Side/B Side)	Yr	VG	VG+	NM
0781	Merry-Go-Round/The Circle	1968	5.00	10.00	20.00

Albums
REPRISE

Number	Title (A Side/B Side)	Yr	VG	VG+	NM
2XS 6332 [(2)]	An Evening with Wild Man Fischer	1969	12.50	25.00	50.00

RHINO

Number	Title (A Side/B Side)	Yr	VG	VG+	NM
RNLP-001	Wildmania	1978	3.75	7.50	15.00
RNLP-021	Pronounced Normal	1981	2.50	5.00	10.00
RNLP-022	Nothing Scary	1981	2.50	5.00	10.00

FISCHER, WILLIAM S.

Albums
EMBRYO

Number	Title (A Side/B Side)	Yr	VG	VG+	NM
529	Circles	1970	3.75	7.50	15.00

FISHER, EDDIE

45s
7 ARTS

Number	Title (A Side/B Side)	Yr	VG	VG+	NM
719	Tonight/Breezin' Along with the Breeze	1961	2.00	4.00	8.00

ABC-PARAMOUNT

Number	Title (A Side/B Side)	Yr	VG	VG+	NM
10264	Milk and Honey/Shalom	1961	2.00	4.00	8.00
10326	Arrividerci Roma/A Camminane	1962	2.00	4.00	8.00
10371	Back in Your Back Yard/The Sweetest Sounds	1962	2.00	4.00	8.00

DOT

Number	Title (A Side/B Side)	Yr	VG	VG+	NM
16732	Sunrise, Sunset/Walking in the Footsteps of a Fool	1965	—	3.00	6.00
16753	Any Time/When I Was Wrong	1965	—	3.00	6.00
16779	I Don't Care If the Sun Don't Shine/Young and Foolish	1965	—	3.00	6.00
16792	White Christmas/Mary Christmas	1965	5.00	10.00	20.00
16824	They Call the Wind Maria/Great Day	1966	—	3.00	6.00

MUSICOR

Number	Title (A Side/B Side)	Yr	VG	VG+	NM
1354	I'll Pick a Rose for My Rose/Lady Mae	1969	—	2.50	5.00

RAMROD

Number	Title (A Side/B Side)	Yr	VG	VG+	NM
(# unknown)	Scent of Mystery/The Chase	1960	2.00	4.00	8.00
(# unknown) [PS]	Scent of Mystery/The Chase	1960	2.50	5.00	10.00

RCA VICTOR

Number	Title (A Side/B Side)	Yr	VG	VG+	NM
AMAO-0121	Dungaree Doll/Anytime	1973	—	2.00	4.00
—Gold Standard Series					
47-3764	Where in the World/A Little Bit Independent	1950	5.00	10.00	20.00
47-3792	Nightwind/Warm Kisses in the Cool of Night	1950	5.00	10.00	20.00
47-3829	Just Say I Love Her/Give a Broken Heart a Chance to Cry	1950	5.00	10.00	20.00
47-3901	Thinking of You/If You Should Leave Me	1950	3.75	7.50	15.00
47-3955	When You Kiss a Stranger/You Love Me	1950	3.75	7.50	15.00
47-4016	Bring Back the Thrill/If It Hadn't Been for You	1951	3.75	7.50	15.00
47-4036	My Mammy/My Blue Heaven	1951	3.75	7.50	15.00
47-4037	What Can I Say After I Say I'm Sorry/My Mom	1951	3.75	7.50	15.00
47-4038	My Buddy/At Sundown	1951	3.75	7.50	15.00
—The above three comprise a box set					
47-4100	Goodbye, G.I. Al/Get Your Paper	1951	3.75	7.50	15.00
47-4120	Unless/I Have No Heart	1951	3.75	7.50	15.00
47-4191	I'll Hold You in My Heart ('Til I Can Hold You in My Arms)/I Heard a Song	1951	3.75	7.50	15.00
47-4257	Turn Back the Hands of Time/I Can't Go On Without You	1951	3.75	7.50	15.00
47-4359	Any Time/Never Before	1951	3.75	7.50	15.00
47-4444	Tell Me Why/Trust in Me	1951	3.75	7.50	15.00
47-4574	Forgive Me/That's the Chance You Take	1952	3.75	7.50	15.00
47-4616	Just Say I Love Her/Sorry	1952	3.00	6.00	12.00
47-4617	A Little Bit Independent/If You Should Love Me	1952	3.00	6.00	12.00
47-4618	I Remember When/Am I Wasting My Time on You	1952	3.00	6.00	12.00
47-4619	I Love You Because/Thinking of You	1952	3.00	6.00	12.00
—The above four comprise a box set					
47-4680	I'm Yours/Just a Little Lovin' (Will Go a Long Way)	1952	3.75	7.50	15.00
47-4744	Maybe/Watermelon Weather	1952	3.00	6.00	12.00
—With Perry Como					
47-4830	Wish You Were Here/The Hand of Fate	1952	3.00	6.00	12.00
47-4840	I'm in the Mood for Love/You'll Never Know	1952	3.00	6.00	12.00
47-4841	Hold Me/Everything I Have Is Yours	1952	3.00	6.00	12.00
47-4842	That Old Feeling/Full Moon and Empty Arms	1952	3.00	6.00	12.00
47-4843	Paradise/I've Got You Under My Skin	1952	3.00	6.00	12.00
—The above four comprise a box set					
47-4910	Silent Night/White Christmas	1952	3.75	7.50	15.00
47-4911	Christmas Baby/You're All I Want for Christmas	1952	3.75	7.50	15.00
47-4912	Here Comes Santa/Christmas Means	1952	3.75	7.50	15.00
47-4913	Jingle Bells/O Come All Ye Faithful	1952	3.75	7.50	15.00
—The above four comprise a box set					
47-4953	Lady of Spain/Outside of Heaven	1952	3.00	6.00	12.00
47-5038	Christmas Day/That's What Christmas Means to Me	1952	3.75	7.50	15.00
47-5106	Even Now/I Wish It Were Up to Me	1952	3.00	6.00	12.00
47-5106 [PS]	Even Now/I Wish It Were Up to Me	1952	6.25	12.50	25.00
47-5137	Downhearted/How Do You Speak to an Angel	1953	3.00	6.00	12.00
47-5293	I'm Walking Behind You/Just Another Polka	1953	3.00	6.00	12.00
47-5365	With These Hands/When I Was Young	1953	3.00	6.00	12.00
47-5365 [PS]	With These Hands/When I Was Young	1953	6.25	12.50	25.00
47-5453	Many Times/Just to Be with You	1953	3.00	6.00	12.00
47-5552	Oh! My Pa-Pa (O Mein Papa)/Until You Said Goodbye	1953	3.00	6.00	12.00
47-5552	Oh My Papa (O Mein Papa)/Until You Said Goodbye	1953	3.00	6.00	12.00
—The above exists with both punctuated and unpuctuated A-side					
47-5552 [PS]	Oh My Papa (O Mein Papa)/Until You Said Goodbye	1953	6.25	12.50	25.00
47-5675	A Girl, A Girl (Zoom-Ba Di Alli Nella)/Anema E Core (With All My Heart and Soul)	1954	3.00	6.00	12.00
47-5748	Green Years/My Friend	1954	3.00	6.00	12.00
47-5830	I Need You Now/Heaven Was Never Like This	1954	3.00	6.00	12.00
47-5871	Count Your Blessings (Instead of Sheep)/Fanny	1954	3.75	7.50	15.00
47-5871	Count Your Blessings/Fanny	1954	3.75	7.50	15.00
—Some pressings do not list the subtitle					
47-6015	A Man Chases a Girl (Until She Catches Him)/(I'm Always Hearing) Wedding Bells	1955	3.00	6.00	12.00

Number	Title (A Side/B Side)	Yr	VG	VG+	NM
47-6015 [PS]	A Man Chases a Girl (Until She Catches Him)/ (I'm Always Hearing) Wedding Bells	1955	6.25	12.50	25.00
—"This Is His Life" picture sleeve (possibly promo only)					
47-6071	Just One More Time/Take My Love	1955	3.00	6.00	12.00
47-6097	Heart/Near to You	1955	3.00	6.00	12.00
47-6196	Song of the Dreamer/Don't Stay Away Too Long	1955	3.00	6.00	12.00
47-6264	Magic Fingers/I Wanna Go Where You Go, Do What You Do (Then I'll Be Happy)	1955	3.00	6.00	12.00
47-6337	Dungaree Doll/Everybody's Got a Home But Me	1955	2.50	5.00	10.00
47-6470	Without You/No Other One	1956	2.50	5.00	10.00
47-6470 [PS]	Without You/No Other One	1956	—	—	—
—Rumored to exist, but without conclusive evidence, we will delete this from future editions					
47-6529	On the Street Where You Live/Sweet Heartaches	1956	2.50	5.00	10.00
47-6615	Oh My Maria/If I'm Elected	1956	2.50	5.00	10.00
47-6677	Cindy, Oh Cindy/Around the World	1956	2.50	5.00	10.00
47-6746	Some Day Soon/All About Love	1956	2.50	5.00	10.00
47-6849	Tonight My Heart Will Be Crying/Blues for Me	1957	2.50	5.00	10.00
47-6913	Sunshine Girl/Did You Close Your Eyes	1957	2.50	5.00	10.00
47-6947	Around the World/Slow Burning Love	1957	2.50	5.00	10.00
47-7051	Sayonara/That's the Way It Goes	1957	2.50	5.00	10.00
47-7135	I Don't Hurt Anymore/What's the Use of Cryin'	1958	2.50	5.00	10.00
47-7230	Pick a Partner/Kari Waits for Me	1958	2.50	5.00	10.00
47-7352	Take Me/The Best Thing for You	1958	2.50	5.00	10.00
47-8956	Games That Lovers Play/Name	1966	—	3.00	6.00
47-9070	People Like You/Come Love	1967	—	3.00	6.00
47-9204	Now I Know/I Haven't Got Anything Better to Do	1967	—	3.00	6.00
47-9311	Jerusalem, Jerusalem/There's a World Full of Girls	1967	—	3.00	6.00
47-9430	Fool on the Hill/Sunny	1968	—	3.00	6.00
47-9574	Rain in My Heart/Eyes of a Child	1968	—	3.00	6.00
7-Inch Extended Plays					
DOT					
DLP 631 [PS]	Eddie Fisher Today!	196?	2.50	5.00	10.00
DLP 631 [S]	Red Roses for a Blue Lady/Who Can I Turn To/ Hello, Dolly!//Once Upon a Time/Downtown/ Dear Heart	196?	2.50	5.00	10.00
—33 1/3 rpm, small hole					
RCA VICTOR					
547-0009	I'm in the Mood for Love/You'll Never Know//Hold Me/Everything I Have Is Yours	1952	3.75	7.50	15.00
—Part of 2-EP set EPB 3058					
EPA-448	(contents unknown)	195?	3.75	7.50	15.00
EPA-448 [PS]	Berlin Favorites	195?	3.75	7.50	15.00
EPA-561	(contents unknown)	195?	3.75	7.50	15.00
EPA-561 [PS]	Broadway Classics	195?	3.75	7.50	15.00
EPA-710	(contents unknown)	1956	3.75	7.50	15.00
EPA-710 [PS]	Dungaree Doll	1956	3.75	7.50	15.00
EPA-742	(contents unknown)	1956	3.75	7.50	15.00
EPA-742 [PS]	I'm In the Mood for Love	1956	3.75	7.50	15.00
EPB-3058 [PS]	I'm in the Mood for Love	1952	3.75	7.50	15.00
—Two-pocket jacket for two-EP set					
EPA-4018	(contents unknown)	1957	3.75	7.50	15.00
EPA-4018 [PS]	Bundle of Joy	1957	3.75	7.50	15.00
CEP-6144X	Wish You Were Here/I'll Hold You in My Heart (Till I Can Hold You in My Arms)/Lady of Spain //I'm Walking Behind You/Downhearted/Outside of Heaven	1956	3.00	6.00	12.00
—Coca-Cola logo on label					
CEP-6144X [PS]	Souvenir Record from Coke Time with Eddie Fisher	1956	5.00	10.00	20.00
Albums					
DOT					
DLP-3631 [M]	Eddie Fisher Today!	1965	3.00	6.00	12.00
DLP-3648 [M]	When I Was Young	1965	3.00	6.00	12.00
DLP-3658 [M]	Mary Christmas	1965	3.75	7.50	15.00
DLP-3670 [M]	Young and Foolish	1966	3.00	6.00	12.00
DLP-3785 [M]	His Greatest Hits	1967	3.00	6.00	12.00
DLP-25361 [S]	Eddie Fisher Today!	1965	3.75	7.50	15.00
DLP-25648 [S]	When I Was Young	1965	3.75	7.50	15.00
DLP-25658 [S]	Mary Christmas	1965	5.00	10.00	20.00
DLP-25670 [S]	Young and Foolish	1966	3.75	7.50	15.00
DLP-25785 [S]	His Greatest Hits	1967	3.75	7.50	15.00
MCA					
1549	The Best of Eddie Fisher	1983	2.00	4.00	8.00
RAMROD					
RR-1 [(2) M]	Eddie Fisher at the Winter Garden	1963	3.75	7.50	15.00
RRS-1 [(2) S]	Eddie Fisher at the Winter Garden	1963	5.00	10.00	20.00
RCA CAMDEN					
CAL-789 [M]	Bring Back the Thrill	196?	3.00	6.00	12.00
CAS-789 [R]	Bring Back the Thrill	196?	2.50	5.00	10.00
RCA VICTOR					
LOC-1024 [M]	Academy Award Winners	1955	10.00	20.00	40.00
LPM-1097 [M]	I Love You	1955	7.50	15.00	30.00
ANL1-1138	Eddie Fisher's Greatest Hits	1975	2.00	4.00	8.00
LPM-1180 [M]	I'm in the Mood for Love	1955	7.50	15.00	30.00
LPM-1181 [M]	May I Sing to You?	1955	7.50	15.00	30.00
LPM-1399 [M]	Bundle of Joy	1957	7.50	15.00	30.00
LPM-1548 [M]	Thinking of You	1957	7.50	15.00	30.00
LPM-1647 [M]	As Long As There's Music	1958	7.50	15.00	30.00
LSP-1647 [S]	As Long As There's Music	1958	12.50	25.00	50.00
LPM-2504 [M]	Eddie Fisher's Greatest Hits	1962	3.75	7.50	15.00
LSP-2504 [S]	Eddie Fisher's Greatest Hits	1962	5.00	10.00	20.00
LPM-3025 [10]	Fisher Sings	1952	12.50	25.00	50.00
LPM-3058 [10]	I'm in the Mood for Love	1952	12.50	25.00	50.00
LPM-3065 [10]	Christmas with Fisher	1952	12.50	25.00	50.00
LPM-3122 [10]	Irving Berlin Favorites	1953	12.50	25.00	50.00
LPM-3185 [10]	May I Sing to You?	1953	12.50	25.00	50.00
LPM-3375 [M]	The Best of Eddie Fisher	1965	3.75	7.50	15.00
LSP-3375 [R]	The Best of Eddie Fisher	1965	3.00	6.00	12.00
LPM-3726 [M]	Games That Lovers Play	1966	3.75	7.50	15.00
LSP-3726 [S]	Games That Lovers Play	1966	3.75	7.50	15.00
LPM-3820 [M]	People Like You	1967	5.00	10.00	20.00
LSP-3820 [S]	People Like You	1967	3.00	6.00	12.00
LSP-3914	You Ain't Heard Nothin' Yet	1968	3.00	6.00	12.00

Number	Title (A Side/B Side)	Yr	VG	VG+	NM
FISHER, EDDIE, AND DEBBIE REYNOLDS					
45s					
RCA VICTOR					
47-6820	Lullaby in Love/I Never Felt This Way Before	1957	2.50	5.00	10.00
FISHER, TONI					
45s					
BIG TOP					
3097	West of the Wall/What Did I Do	1962	3.00	6.00	12.00
3124	The Music from the House Next Door/Quickly My Love	1962	3.00	6.00	12.00
CAPITOL					
5901	Train of Love/A Million Heartbeats from Now	1967	2.00	4.00	8.00
COLUMBIA					
42066	If I Loved You/Love Big	1961	3.00	6.00	12.00
SIGNET					
275	The Big Hurt/Memphis Belle	1959	3.75	7.50	15.00
276	How Deep Is the Ocean/Blue, Blue, Blue	1960	3.00	6.00	12.00
279	Everlasting Love/The Red Sea of Mars	1960	3.00	6.00	12.00
364	You Never Told Me/Toot Toot Amore	1964	2.00	4.00	8.00
400	A Man That's Steady/You Never Told Me	196?	2.00	4.00	8.00
664	Springtime of Love/Train of Love	1964	2.00	4.00	8.00
SMASH					
1797	Hold Me/Laugh or Cry	1963	2.50	5.00	10.00
1820	Cry a Little for Me/365 Disappointments	1963	2.50	5.00	10.00
1832	Lovers, Dreamers, Fools/You Won't Forget Me	1963	2.50	5.00	10.00
1847	Your Royal Majesty/Billy, Marry Me	1963	2.50	5.00	10.00
Albums					
SIGNET					
WP-509 [S]	The Big Hurt	1960	12.50	25.00	50.00
—Issued in "Stereomonic"					
FITZGERALD, ELLA					
45s					
CAPITOL					
2099	Born to Lose/I Taught Him Everything He Knows	1968	2.00	4.00	8.00
2212	Brighten the Corner/It's Up to Me and You	1968	2.00	4.00	8.00
2267	Hawaiian War Chant/It's Only Love	1968	2.00	4.00	8.00
5946	Just a Closer Walk with Thee/I Shall Not Be Moved	1967	2.00	4.00	8.00
DECCA					
27061	Mississippi/I Don't Want the World (With a Fence Around It)	1950	5.00	10.00	20.00
27120	I've Got the World on a String/Peas and Rice	1950	5.00	10.00	20.00
27200	Ain't Nobody's Business If I Do/I'll Never Be Free	1950	5.00	10.00	20.00
—With Louis Jordan					
27255	Santa Claus Got Stuck (In My Chimney)/ Molasses, Molasses (It's Icky Sticky Goo)	1950	5.00	10.00	20.00
27368	My One and Only/Someone to Watch Over Me	1951	3.75	7.50	15.00
27369	But Not for Me/Looking for a Boy	1951	3.75	7.50	15.00
27370	I've Got a Crush on You/How Long Has This Been Going On	1951	3.75	7.50	15.00
27371	Soon/Maybe	1951	3.75	7.50	15.00
—The above four comprise a box set					
27419	Little Small Town/I Still Feel the Same About You	1951	5.00	10.00	20.00
—With the Ink Spots					
27453	The Beanbag Song/Lonesome Gal	1951	5.00	10.00	20.00
27578	The Hot Canary/Two Little Men	1951	5.00	10.00	20.00
27602	The Chesapeke and Ohio/Because of Rain	1951	5.00	10.00	20.00
27634	Do You Really Love Me/Even As You and I	1951	5.00	10.00	20.00
27680	Come On-a My House/Mixed Emotions	1951	5.00	10.00	20.00
27693	Smooth Sailing/Love You Madly	1951	5.00	10.00	20.00
27724	Give a Little — Get a Little/There Never Was a Baby (Like My Baby)	1951	5.00	10.00	20.00
27900	Baby Doll/Lady Bug	1951	5.00	10.00	20.00
27901	Oops!/Necessary Evil	1951	5.00	10.00	20.00
27948	I Don't Want to Take a Chance/Rough Ridin'	1952	3.75	7.50	15.00
28034	Lazy Day/What Does It Take	1952	3.75	7.50	15.00
28049	A Guy Is a Guy/That Old Feeling	1952	3.75	7.50	15.00
28126	Goody Goody/Air Mail Special	1952	3.75	7.50	15.00
28181	I Hadn't Anyone Till You/Gee, But I'm Glad to Know You Love Me	1952	3.75	7.50	15.00
28321	Ding-Dong Boogie/Preview	1952	3.75	7.50	15.00
28375	Trying/My Bonnie Lies Over the Ocean	1952	3.75	7.50	15.00
28433	My Favorite Song/Walkin' by the River	1952	3.75	7.50	15.00
28589	I Can't Lie to Myself/Don't Wake Me Up	1953	3.75	7.50	15.00
28671	Careless/Blue Lou	1953	3.75	7.50	15.00
28707	Angel Eyes/Nowhere Guy	1953	3.75	7.50	15.00
28762	Crying in the Chapel/When the Hands of the Clock Pray at Midnite	1953	3.75	7.50	15.00
28774	You'll Have to Swing It (Part 1)/You'll Have to Swing It (Part 2)	1953	3.75	7.50	15.00
28930	The Greatest There Is/I Wonder What Kind of Guy You'd Be	1953	3.75	7.50	15.00
28993	A Sunday Kind of Love/That's My Desire	1954	3.75	7.50	15.00
29008	Somebody Bad Stole De Wedding Bell/ Melancholy Me	1954	3.75	7.50	15.00
29108	Baby/I Need	1954	3.75	7.50	15.00
29136	(I Love You) For Sentimental Reasons/It's Only a Paper Moon	1954	3.75	7.50	15.00
—With the Delta Rhythm Boys					
29137	Who's Afraid/I Wished on the Moon	1954	3.75	7.50	15.00
29198	Lullaby of Birdland/Later	1954	3.75	7.50	15.00
29259	Empty Ballroom/If You Don't, I Know Who Will	1954	3.75	7.50	15.00
29475	Moanin' Low/Take a Chance on Love	1955	3.00	6.00	12.00
29580	Old Devil Moon/Lover, Come Back to Me	1955	3.00	6.00	12.00
29609	Pete Kelly's Blues/Hard Hearted Hannah	1955	3.00	6.00	12.00
29648	Soldier Boy/A Satisfied Mind	1955	3.00	6.00	12.00
29665	The Impatient Years/But Not Like Mine	1955	3.00	6.00	12.00
29746	(Love Is) The Tender Trap/My One and Only Love	1955	3.00	6.00	12.00
29810	Early Autumn/Ella's Contribution to the Blues	1956	3.00	6.00	12.00
30222	Stone Cold Dead in the Market/Peas and Rice	1957	3.00	6.00	12.00
30405	Goody Goody/It's Too Soon to Know	1957	6.25	12.50	25.00
—Reissued to compete with Frankie Lymon's remake, this is scarcer than the original on 28126					

Number	Title (A Side/B Side)	Yr	VG	VG+	NM
31142	How High the Moon/Smooth Sailing	1960	2.50	5.00	10.00
PRESTIGE					
715	Hey Jude/Sunshine of Your Love	1969	2.00	4.00	8.00
REPRISE					
0850	Get Ready/Open Your Window	1969	—	3.00	6.00
0875	I'll Never Fall in Love Again/Savoy Truffle	1969	—	3.00	6.00
0922	Yellow Man/Try a Little Bit	1970	—	3.00	6.00
0995	I Wonder Why/Ooo Baby Baby	1971	—	3.00	6.00
VERVE					
2002	It's Only a Man/Too Young for the Blues	1956	3.00	6.00	12.00
2012	A Beautiful Friendship/Stay There	1956	3.00	6.00	12.00
2021	The Silent Treatment/The Sun Forgot to Shine This Morning	1956	3.00	6.00	12.00
10031	Hotta Chocolatta/Hear My Heart	1957	3.00	6.00	12.00
10050	Let's Do It (Let's Fall in Love)/Manhattan	1957	3.00	6.00	12.00
10077	All of Me/It's All Right with Me	1957	3.00	6.00	12.00
10111	What Will I Tell My Heart/Midnight Sun	1958	2.50	5.00	10.00
10130	Beale Street Blues/St. Louis Blues	1958	2.50	5.00	10.00
10132	Swingin' Shepherd Blues/Teach Me How to Cry	1958	2.50	5.00	10.00
10143	Trav'lin' Light/Your Red Wagon	1958	2.50	5.00	10.00
10158	Oh What a Night for Love/Dreams Are Made for Children	1959	2.50	5.00	10.00
10166	Teardrops from My Eyes/A Little Jazz	1959	2.50	5.00	10.00
10171	Stairway to the Stars/I'm Through with Love	1959	2.50	5.00	10.00
10180	But Not for Me/You Make Me Feel So Young	1959	2.50	5.00	10.00
10186	The Christmas Song/The Secret of Christmas	1959	3.75	7.50	15.00
10189	Like Young/Beat Me Daddy, Eight to the Bar	1959	2.50	5.00	10.00
10209	Mack the Knife/Lorelei	1960	2.50	5.00	10.00
10220	How High the Moon (Part 1)/How High the Moon (Part 2)	1960	2.50	5.00	10.00
10222	I Can't Give You Anything But Love/Reach for Tomorrow	1960	2.50	5.00	10.00
10224	Jingle Bells/Good Morning Blues	1960	3.75	7.50	15.00
10237	Mr. Paganini (You'll Have to Swing It)/You're Driving Me Crazy	1961	2.50	5.00	10.00
10241	Clap Hands, Here Come Charley/Cry Me a River	1961	2.50	5.00	10.00
10248	What Is This Thing Called Love/Call Me Darling	1962	2.00	4.00	8.00
10274	Desafinado (Slightly Out of Tune)/Stardust Bossa Nova	1962	2.00	4.00	8.00
10288	Bill Bailey, Won't You Please Come Home/Ol' Man Mose	1963	2.00	4.00	8.00
10305	Shiny Stockings/Into Each Love Some Rain Must Fall	1963	2.00	4.00	8.00
10319	See See Rider/Trouble in Mind	1964	2.00	4.00	8.00
10324	Can't Buy Me Love/Hello, Dolly!	1964	2.50	5.00	10.00
10337	I've Grown Accustomed to Your Face/I Could Have Danced All Night	1964	2.00	4.00	8.00
10340	Ringo Beat/I'm Falling in Love	1964	3.75	7.50	15.00
10341	All the Livelong Day/(B-side unknown)	1965	2.00	4.00	8.00
10359	Mae (She's Just a Quiet Girl)/We Three	1965	2.00	4.00	8.00
10368	A Hard Day's Night/And the Angels Sing	1965	2.50	5.00	10.00
10379	Imagine My Frustration (Part 1)/Imagine My Frustration (Part 2)	1966	2.00	4.00	8.00
10408	Love Theme from "The Sandpiper"/Duke's Place	1966	2.00	4.00	8.00
7-Inch Extended Plays					
DECCA					
ED 2014	It's Only a Paper Moon/(I Love You) For Sentimental Reasons//Guilty/Stairway to the Stars	195?	5.00	10.00	20.00
ED 2014 [PS]	Ella Fitzgerald Sings — Volume 1	195?	5.00	10.00	20.00
ED 2028	Smooth Sailing/Flying Home//Oh, Lady Be Good/How High the Moon	195?	5.00	10.00	20.00
ED 2028 [PS]	Smooth Sailing	195?	5.00	10.00	20.00
ED 2049	(contents unknown)	195?	5.00	10.00	20.00
ED 2049 [PS]	Ella Fitzgerald Sings — Volume 2	195?	5.00	10.00	20.00
ED 2269	(contents unknown)	1955	5.00	10.00	20.00
ED 2269 [PS]	Pete Kelly's Blues	1955	5.00	10.00	20.00
34244 [PS]	Early Ella	196?	3.00	6.00	12.00
34244 [S]	Mixed Emotions/It's Too Soon to Know/Walkin' by the River//Baby Doll/I Hadn't Anyone Till You/So Long	196?	3.00	6.00	12.00
—33 1/3 rpm, small hole					
Albums					
AMERICAN RECORDING SOCIETY					
G-433 [M]	Ella Fitzgerald At Newport	195?	10.00	20.00	40.00
ARCHIVE OF FOLK AND JAZZ					
276	Ella Fitzgerald	1973	3.00	6.00	12.00
ATLANTIC					
SD 1631	Ella Loves Cole	1972	3.00	6.00	12.00
BAINBRIDGE					
6223	Things Ain't What They Used to Be	1982	2.50	5.00	10.00
—Reissue of Reprise 6432					
BASF					
20712	Watch What Happens	1972	3.00	6.00	12.00
CAPITOL					
ST 2685 [S]	Brighten the Corner	1967	3.75	7.50	15.00
T 2685 [M]	Brighten the Corner	1967	5.00	10.00	20.00
ST 2805 [S]	Ella Fitzgerald's Christmas	1967	3.00	6.00	12.00
—Same as above, but in stereo					
T 2805 [M]	Ella Fitzgerald's Christmas	1967	5.00	10.00	20.00
ST 2888	Misty Blue	1968	3.75	7.50	15.00
ST 2960	Thirty by Ella	1968	3.75	7.50	15.00
SM-11793	Brighten the Corner	1978	2.50	5.00	10.00
SN-16276	Thirty by Ella	1983	2.50	5.00	10.00
—Budget-line reissue					
COLUMBIA					
KG 32557 [(2)]	Carnegie Hall & Newport Jazz Festival 1973	1973	3.75	7.50	15.00
DECCA					
DXB 156 [(2) M]	The Best of Ella	1959	10.00	20.00	40.00
—Black labels, silver print					
DXB 156 [(2) M]	The Best of Ella	1961	6.25	12.50	25.00
—Black labels with color bars					
DL 4129 [M]	Golden Favorites	1961	5.00	10.00	20.00
DL 4446 [M]	Stairway to the Stars	1964	3.75	7.50	15.00

Number	Title (A Side/B Side)	Yr	VG	VG+	NM
DL 4447 [M]	Early Ella	1964	3.75	7.50	15.00
DL 4451 [M]	Ella Sings Gershwin	1964	3.75	7.50	15.00
DL 4887 [M]	Smooth Sailing	1967	3.75	7.50	15.00
DL 5084 [10]	Souvenir Album	1950	30.00	60.00	120.00
DL 5300 [10]	Ella Fitzgerald Sings Gershwin Songs	1951	30.00	60.00	120.00
DXSB 7156 [(2) R]	The Best of Ella	196?	5.00	10.00	20.00
DL 8068 [M]	Songs in a Mellow Mood	1954	12.50	25.00	50.00
DL 8149 [M]	Lullabies of Birdland	1955	12.50	25.00	50.00
DL 8155 [M]	Sweet and Hot	1955	12.50	25.00	50.00
DL 8378 [M]	Ella Sings Gershwin	1957	10.00	20.00	40.00
DL 8477 [M]	Ella and Her Fellas	1957	10.00	20.00	40.00
DL 8695 [M]	The First Lady of Song	1958	10.00	20.00	40.00
DL 8696 [M]	Miss Ella Fitzgerald and Mr. Nelson Riddle Invite You to Listen and Relax	1958	10.00	20.00	40.00
DL 8832 [M]	For Sentimental Reasons	1958	10.00	20.00	40.00
DL 74129 [R]	Golden Favorites	1961	3.00	6.00	12.00
DL 74446 [R]	Stairway to the Stars	1964	3.00	6.00	12.00
DL 74447 [R]	Early Ella	1964	3.00	6.00	12.00
DL 74451 [R]	Ella Sings Gershwin	1964	3.00	6.00	12.00
DL 74887 [R]	Smooth Sailing	1967	3.00	6.00	12.00
FANTASY					
OJC-376	Montreux '77	1989	3.00	6.00	12.00
—Reissue of Pablo Live 2308 206					
OJC-442	Ella & Nice	1990	3.00	6.00	12.00
—Reissue of Pablo Live 2308 234					
INTERMEDIA					
QS-5049	Ella by Starlight	198?	2.50	5.00	10.00
MCA					
215	Ella Sings Gershwin	1973	2.50	5.00	10.00
734	Memories	198?	2.50	5.00	10.00
4016 [(2)]	The Best of Ella, Vol. 2	1973	3.75	7.50	15.00
4047 [(2)]	The Best of Ella	197?	3.75	7.50	15.00
METRO					
M-500 [M]	Ella Fitzgerald	1965	3.00	6.00	12.00
MS-500 [S]	Ella Fitzgerald	1965	3.00	6.00	12.00
M-567 [M]	The World of Ella Fitzgerald	1966	3.00	6.00	12.00
MS-567 [S]	The World of Ella Fitzgerald	1966	3.00	6.00	12.00
MGM					
GAS-130	Ella Fitzgerald (Golden Archive Series)	1970	3.75	7.50	15.00
PABLO					
2310702	Take Love Easy	1974	3.00	6.00	12.00
2310711	Ella in London	1974	3.00	6.00	12.00
2310751	Montreux '75	1976	3.00	6.00	12.00
2310759	Ella and Oscar	1976	3.00	6.00	12.00
2310772	Again	1977	3.00	6.00	12.00
2310814	Dream Dancing	1978	3.00	6.00	12.00
2310825	Lady Time	1978	3.00	6.00	12.00
2310829	Fine and Mellow	1979	3.00	6.00	12.00
2310888	Speak Love	1983	2.50	5.00	10.00
2310921	Easy Living	1987	2.50	5.00	10.00
2310938	All That Jazz	1990	3.00	6.00	12.00
2405421	The Best of Ella Fitzgerald	198?	2.50	5.00	10.00
2630201 [(2)]	Ella Embraces Jobim	1981	3.75	7.50	15.00
PABLO LIVE					
2308206	Montreux '77	1978	3.00	6.00	12.00
2308234	Ella & Nice	197?	3.75	7.50	15.00
2308242	Stockholm Concert 1966	198?	2.50	5.00	10.00
PABLO TODAY					
2312110	A Perfect Match	1980	3.00	6.00	12.00
2312132	A Classy Pair	1983	2.50	5.00	10.00
2312138	The Best Is Yet to Come	1982	2.50	5.00	10.00
2312140	Nice Work If You Can Get It	198?	2.50	5.00	10.00
PAUSA					
7130	Love You Madly	198?	2.50	5.00	10.00
PICKWICK					
SPC-3259	Misty Blues	1974	2.50	5.00	10.00
PRESTIGE					
PRLP-7685	Sunshine of Your Love	1970	3.75	7.50	15.00
REPRISE					
RS-6354	Ella	1969	3.75	7.50	15.00
RS-6432	Things Ain't What They Used to Be	1971	3.00	6.00	12.00
SUNBEAM					
205	Ella Fitzgerald and Her Orchestra, 1940	197?	2.50	5.00	10.00
VERVE					
V-10-4 [(4) M]	Ella Fitzgerald Sings the Duke Ellington Song Book	196?	12.50	25.00	50.00
V-29-5 [(5) M]	Ella Fitzgerald Sings the George and Ira Gershwin Song Book	196?	25.00	50.00	100.00
—Reissue of MGV-4029					
V6-29-5 [(5) S]	Ella Fitzgerald Sings the George and Ira Gershwin Song Book	196?	25.00	50.00	100.00
—Reissue of MGVS-6082					
VE-2-2511 [(2)]	The Cole Porter Song Book	197?	3.75	7.50	15.00
VE-2-2519 [(2)]	The Rodgers and Hart Song Book	197?	3.75	7.50	15.00
VE-2-2525 [(2)]	The George Gershwin Song Book	1978	3.75	7.50	15.00
VE-2-2535 [(2)]	The Duke Ellington Song Book	1979	3.75	7.50	15.00
VE-1-2539	Ella Wishes You a Swinging Christmas	198?	3.00	6.00	12.00
—Reissue					
VE-2-2540 [(2)]	The Duke Ellington Song Book, Vol. 2	1982	3.75	7.50	15.00
MGV-4001-2 [(2) M]	Ella Fitzgerald Sings the Cole Porter Song Book	1956	20.00	40.00	80.00
V-4001-2 [(2) M]	Ella Fitzgerald Sings the Cole Porter Song Book	1961	6.25	12.50	25.00
MGV-4002-2 [(2) M]	Ella Fitzgerald Sings the Rodgers & Hart Song Book	1956	20.00	40.00	80.00
V-4002-2 [(2) M]	Ella Fitzgerald Sings the Rodgers and Hart Song Book	1961	6.25	12.50	25.00
MGV-4004 [M]	Like Someone in Love	1957	12.50	25.00	50.00
V-4004 [M]	Like Someone in Love	1961	5.00	10.00	20.00
V6-4004 [S]	Like Someone in Love	1961	5.00	10.00	20.00
MGV-4008-2 [(2) M]	Ella Fitzgerald Sings the Duke Ellington Song Book, Vol. 1	1957	20.00	40.00	80.00
V-4008-2 [(2) M]	Ella Fitzgerald Sings the Duke Ellington Song Book, Vol. 1	1961	6.25	12.50	25.00

Number	Title (A Side/B Side)	Yr	VG	VG+	NM
MGV-4009-2 [(2) M]	Ella Fitzgerald Sings the Duke Ellington Song Book, Vol. 2	1957	20.00	40.00	80.00
V-4009-2 [(2) M]	Ella Fitzgerald Sings the Duke Ellington Song Book, Vol. 2	1961	6.25	12.50	25.00
MGV-4010-4 [(4) M]	Ella Fitzgerald Sings the Duke Ellington Song Book	1957	37.50	75.00	150.00
—Combines 4008 and 4009 into one package					
MGV-4013 [M]	Ella Fitzgerald Sings the Gershwin Song Book	1957	12.50	25.00	50.00
MGV-4019-2 [(2) M]	Ella Fitzgerald Sings the Irving Berlin Song Book	1958	20.00	40.00	80.00
V-4019-2 [(2) M]	Ella Fitzgerald Sings the Irving Berlin Song Book	1961	6.25	12.50	25.00
V6-4019-2 [(2) S]	Ella Fitzgerald Sings the Irving Berlin Song Book	1961	6.25	12.50	25.00
MGV-4021 [M]	Ella Swings Lightly	1958	12.50	25.00	50.00
V-4021 [M]	Ella Swings Lightly	1961	5.00	10.00	20.00
V6-4021 [S]	Ella Swings Lightly	1961	5.00	10.00	20.00
MGV-4022 [M]	Ella Fitzgerald Sings the Rodgers & Hart Song Book, Vol. 1	1959	12.50	25.00	50.00
V-4022 [M]	Ella Fitzgerald Sings the Rodgers & Hart Song Book, Vol. 1	1961	5.00	10.00	20.00
V6-4022 [S]	Ella Fitzgerald Sings the Rodgers & Hart Song Book, Vol. 1	1961	5.00	10.00	20.00
MGV-4023 [M]	Ella Fitzgerald Sings the Rodgers & Hart Song Book, Vol. 2	1959	12.50	25.00	50.00
V-4023 [M]	Ella Fitzgerald Sings the Rodgers & Hart Song Book, Vol. 2	1961	5.00	10.00	20.00
V6-4023 [S]	Ella Fitzgerald Sings the Rodgers & Hart Song Book, Vol. 2	1961	5.00	10.00	20.00
MGV-4024 [M]	Ella Fitzgerald Sings the George and Ira Gershwin Song Book, Vol. 1	1959	12.50	25.00	50.00
V-4024 [M]	Ella Fitzgerald Sings the George and Ira Gershwin Song Book, Vol. 1	1961	5.00	10.00	20.00
V6-4024 [S]	Ella Fitzgerald Sings the George and Ira Gershwin Song Book, Vol. 1	1961	5.00	10.00	20.00
MGV-4025 [M]	Ella Fitzgerald Sings the George and Ira Gershwin Song Book, Vol. 2	1959	12.50	25.00	50.00
V-4025 [M]	Ella Fitzgerald Sings the George and Ira Gershwin Song Book, Vol. 2	1961	5.00	10.00	20.00
V6-4025 [S]	Ella Fitzgerald Sings the George and Ira Gershwin Song Book, Vol. 2	1961	5.00	10.00	20.00
MGV-4026 [M]	Ella Fitzgerald Sings the George and Ira Gershwin Song Book, Vol. 3	1959	12.50	25.00	50.00
V-4026 [M]	Ella Fitzgerald Sings the George and Ira Gershwin Song Book, Vol. 3	1961	5.00	10.00	20.00
V6-4026 [S]	Ella Fitzgerald Sings the George and Ira Gershwin Song Book, Vol. 3	1961	5.00	10.00	20.00
MGV-4027 [M]	Ella Fitzgerald Sings the George and Ira Gershwin Song Book, Vol. 4	1959	12.50	25.00	50.00
V-4027 [M]	Ella Fitzgerald Sings the George and Ira Gershwin Song Book, Vol. 4	1961	5.00	10.00	20.00
V6-4027 [S]	Ella Fitzgerald Sings the George and Ira Gershwin Song Book, Vol. 4	1961	5.00	10.00	20.00
MGV-4028 [M]	Ella Fitzgerald Sings the George and Ira Gershwin Song Book, Vol. 5	1959	12.50	25.00	50.00
V-4028 [M]	Ella Fitzgerald Sings the George and Ira Gershwin Song Book, Vol. 5	1961	5.00	10.00	20.00
V6-4028 [S]	Ella Fitzgerald Sings the George and Ira Gershwin Song Book, Vol. 5	1961	5.00	10.00	20.00
MGV-4029-5 [(5) M]	Ella Fitzgerald Sings the George and Ira Gershwin Song Book	1959	62.50	125.00	250.00
—Box set with 4024 through 4028 plus bonus 10-inch LP					
MGV-4029-5 [(5) M]	Ella Fitzgerald Sings the George and Ira Gershwin Song Book	1959	125.00	250.00	500.00
—Box set with 4024 through 4028 plus bonus 10-inch LP, all in walnut box with leather pockets					
MGV-4030 [M]	Ella Fitzgerald Sings the Irving Berlin Song Book, Vol. 1	1959	12.50	25.00	50.00
V-4030 [M]	Ella Fitzgerald Sings the Irving Berlin Song Book, Vol. 1	1961	5.00	10.00	20.00
V6-4030 [S]	Ella Fitzgerald Sings the Irving Berlin Song Book, Vol. 1	1961	5.00	10.00	20.00
MGV-4031 [M]	Ella Fitzgerald Sings the Irving Berlin Song Book, Vol. 2	1959	12.50	25.00	50.00
V-4031 [M]	Ella Fitzgerald Sings the Irving Berlin Song Book, Vol. 2	1961	5.00	10.00	20.00
V6-4031 [S]	Ella Fitzgerald Sings the Irving Berlin Song Book, Vol. 2	1961	5.00	10.00	20.00
MGV-4032 [M]	Sweet Songs for Swingers	1959	12.50	25.00	50.00
V-4032 [M]	Sweet Songs for Swingers	1961	5.00	10.00	20.00
V6-4032 [S]	Sweet Songs for Swingers	1961	5.00	10.00	20.00
MGV-4034 [M]	Hello, Love	1959	12.50	25.00	50.00
V-4034 [M]	Hello, Love	1961	5.00	10.00	20.00
V6-4034 [S]	Hello, Love	1961	5.00	10.00	20.00
MGV-4036 [M]	Get Happy!	1960	10.00	20.00	40.00
V-4036 [M]	Get Happy!	1961	5.00	10.00	20.00
V6-4036 [S]	Get Happy!	1961	5.00	10.00	20.00
MGV-4041 [M]	Mack the Knife — Ella in Berlin	1960	10.00	20.00	40.00
V-4041 [M]	Mack the Knife — Ella in Berlin	1961	5.00	10.00	20.00
V6-4041 [S]	Mack the Knife — Ella in Berlin	1961	5.00	10.00	20.00
MGV-4042 [M]	Ella Wishes You a Swinging Christmas	1960	12.50	25.00	50.00
V-4042 [M]	Ella Wishes You a Swinging Christmas	1961	10.00	20.00	40.00
V6-4042 [S]	Ella Wishes You a Swinging Christmas	1961	12.50	25.00	50.00
MGV-4043 [M]	Let No Man Write My Epitaph	1961	10.00	20.00	40.00
V-4043 [M]	Let No Man Write My Epitaph	1961	5.00	10.00	20.00
V6-4043 [S]	Let No Man Write My Epitaph	1961	5.00	10.00	20.00
MGV-4046-2 [(2) M]	Ella Fitzgerald Sings the Harold Arlen Song Book	1961	15.00	30.00	60.00
MGV-4049 [M]	Ella Fitzgerald Sings Cole Porter	1961	10.00	20.00	40.00
V-4049 [M]	Ella Fitzgerald Sings Cole Porter	1961	5.00	10.00	20.00
MGV-4050 [M]	Ella Fitzgerald Sings More Cole Porter	1961	10.00	20.00	40.00
V-4050 [M]	Ella Fitzgerald Sings More Cole Porter	1961	5.00	10.00	20.00
MGV-4052 [M]	Ella in Hollywood	1961	10.00	20.00	40.00
V-4052 [M]	Ella in Hollywood	1961	5.00	10.00	20.00
V-4053 [M]	Clap Hands, Here Comes Charley	1962	10.00	20.00	40.00
V6-4053 [S]	Clap Hands, Here Comes Charley	1962	37.50	75.00	150.00
V-4054 [M]	Ella Swings Brightly with Nelson	1962	7.50	15.00	30.00
V6-4054 [S]	Ella Swings Brightly with Nelson	1962	7.50	15.00	30.00
V-4055 [M]	Ella Swings Gently with Nelson	1962	7.50	15.00	30.00
V6-4055 [S]	Ella Swings Gently with Nelson	1962	7.50	15.00	30.00
V-4056 [M]	Rhythm Is My Business	1962	7.50	15.00	30.00
V6-4056 [S]	Rhythm Is My Business	1962	7.50	15.00	30.00
V-4057 [M]	Ella Fitzgerald Sings the Harold Arlen Song Book, Vol. 1	1962	7.50	15.00	30.00
V6-4057 [S]	Ella Fitzgerald Sings the Harold Arlen Song Book, Vol. 1	1962	7.50	15.00	30.00
V-4058 [M]	Ella Fitzgerald Sings the Harold Arlen Song Book, Vol. 2	1962	7.50	15.00	30.00
V6-4058 [S]	Ella Fitzgerald Sings the Harold Arlen Song Book, Vol. 2	1962	7.50	15.00	30.00
V-4059 [M]	Ella Sings Broadway	1963	6.25	12.50	25.00
V6-4059 [S]	Ella Sings Broadway	1963	6.25	12.50	25.00
V-4060 [M]	Ella Fitzgerald Sings the Jerome Kern Song Book	1963	6.25	12.50	25.00
V6-4060 [S]	Ella Fitzgerald Sings the Jerome Kern Song Book	1963	6.25	12.50	25.00
V-4061 [M]	Ella and Basie!	1963	6.25	12.50	25.00
V6-4061 [S]	Ella and Basie!	1963	6.25	12.50	25.00
V-4062 [M]	These Are the Blues	1963	6.25	12.50	25.00
V6-4062 [S]	These Are the Blues	1963	6.25	12.50	25.00
V-4063 [M]	The Best of Ella Fitzgerald	1964	3.75	7.50	15.00
V6-4063 [S]	The Best of Ella Fitzgerald	1964	3.75	7.50	15.00
V-4064 [M]	Hello, Dolly!	1964	6.25	12.50	25.00
V6-4064 [S]	Hello, Dolly!	1964	6.25	12.50	25.00
V-4065 [M]	Ella at Juan Les Pins	1964	6.25	12.50	25.00
V6-4065 [S]	Ella at Juan Les Pins	1964	6.25	12.50	25.00
V-4066 [M]	A Tribute to Cole Porter	1964	6.25	12.50	25.00
V6-4066 [S]	A Tribute to Cole Porter	1964	6.25	12.50	25.00
V-4067 [M]	Ella Fitzgerald Sings the Johnny Mercer Song Book	1965	5.00	10.00	20.00
V6-4067 [S]	Ella Fitzgerald Sings the Johnny Mercer Song Book	1965	5.00	10.00	20.00
V-4068 [M]	Porgy & Bess	1965	5.00	10.00	20.00
V6-4068 [S]	Porgy & Bess	1965	5.00	10.00	20.00
V-4069 [M]	Ella in Hamburg	1966	5.00	10.00	20.00
V6-4069 [S]	Ella in Hamburg	1966	5.00	10.00	20.00
V-4070 [M]	Ella at Duke's Place	1966	5.00	10.00	20.00
V6-4070 [S]	Ella at Duke's Place	1966	5.00	10.00	20.00
V-4071 [M]	Whisper Not	1966	5.00	10.00	20.00
V6-4071 [S]	Whisper Not	1966	5.00	10.00	20.00
V-4072 [M]	Ella & Duke at Cote d'Azur	1967	6.25	12.50	25.00
V6-4072 [S]	Ella & Duke at Cote d'Azur	1967	3.75	7.50	15.00
MGVS-6000 [S]	Like Someone in Love	1960	10.00	20.00	40.00
MGVS-6005-2 [(2) S]	Ella Fitzgerald Sings the Irving Berlin Song Book	1960	15.00	30.00	60.00
MGVS-6009 [S]	Ella Fitzgerald Sings the Rodgers & Hart Song Book, Vol. 1	1960	10.00	20.00	40.00
MGVS-6010 [S]	Ella Fitzgerald Sings the Rodgers & Hart Song Book, Vol. 2	1960	10.00	20.00	40.00
MGVS-6019 [S]	Ella Swings Lightly	1960	10.00	20.00	40.00
MGVS-6026 [S]	Ella Fitzgerald at the Opera House	1960	10.00	20.00	40.00
MGVS-6052 [S]	Ella Fitzgerald Sings the Irving Berlin Song Book, Vol. 1	1960	10.00	20.00	40.00
MGVS-6053 [S]	Ella Fitzgerald Sings the Irving Berlin Song Book, Vol. 2	1960	10.00	20.00	40.00
MGVS-6072 [S]	Sweet Songs for Swingers	1960	10.00	20.00	40.00
MGVS-6077 [S]	Ella Fitzgerald Sings the George and Ira Gershwin Song Book, Vol. 1	1960	10.00	20.00	40.00
MGVS-6078 [S]	Ella Fitzgerald Sings the George and Ira Gershwin Song Book, Vol. 2	1960	10.00	20.00	40.00
MGVS-6079 [S]	Ella Fitzgerald Sings the George and Ira Gershwin Song Book, Vol. 3	1960	10.00	20.00	40.00
MGVS-6080 [S]	Ella Fitzgerald Sings the George and Ira Gershwin Song Book, Vol. 4	1960	10.00	20.00	40.00
MGVS-6081 [S]	Ella Fitzgerald Sings the George and Ira Gershwin Song Book, Vol. 5	1960	10.00	20.00	40.00
MGVS-6082-5 [(5) S]	Ella Fitzgerald Sings the George and Ira Gershwin Song Book	1960	50.00	100.00	200.00
—Box set with 6077 through 6081 plus bonus 10-inch LP					
MGVS-6100 [S]	Hello, Love	1960	10.00	20.00	40.00
MGVS-6102 [S]	Get Happy!	1960	10.00	20.00	40.00
MGVS-6163 [S]	Mack the Knife — Ella in Berlin	1960	10.00	20.00	40.00
MGVS-7000 [S]	Ella Fitzgerald Sings the Gershwin Song Book	1959	12.50	25.00	50.00
MGV-8264 [M]	Ella Fitzgerald at the Opera House	1958	12.50	25.00	50.00
V-8264 [M]	Ella Fitzgerald at the Opera House	1961	5.00	10.00	20.00
V6-8264 [S]	Ella Fitzgerald at the Opera House	1961	5.00	10.00	20.00
MGV-8288 [M]	One O'Clock Jump	1958	12.50	25.00	50.00
V-8288 [M]	One O'Clock Jump	1961	5.00	10.00	20.00
V-8670 [M]	Ella Fitzgerald Sings the Jerome Kern Song Book	1967	—	—	—
—Canceled reissue					
V-8720 [M]	The Best of Ella Fitzgerald	1967	3.75	7.50	15.00
V6-8720 [S]	The Best of Ella Fitzgerald	1967	3.00	6.00	12.00
V-8745 [M]	Ella "Live"	1968	7.50	15.00	30.00
V6-8745 [S]	Ella "Live"	1968	3.75	7.50	15.00
V6-8795	The Best of Ella Fitzgerald, Vol. 2	1969	3.00	6.00	12.00
V6-8817 [(2)]	History	1973	3.75	7.50	15.00
MGVS-64042 [S]	Ella Wishes You a Swinging Christmas	1960	15.00	30.00	60.00
ST-90028 [S]	Ella and Basie!	1964	7.50	15.00	30.00
—Capitol Record Club edition					
T-90028 [M]	Ella and Basie!	1964	7.50	15.00	30.00
—Capitol Record Club edition					
817526-1 [(2)]	The Harold Arlen Song Book	1984	3.75	7.50	15.00
821693-1 [(2)]	The Rodgers and Hart Song Book	198?	3.00	6.00	12.00
823247-1	The Johnny Mercer Song Book	1985	2.50	5.00	10.00
823278-1 [(2)]	The Cole Porter Song Book	198?	3.00	6.00	12.00
823279-1 [(2)]	The George and Ira Gershwin Songbook (Highlights)	198?	3.00	6.00	12.00
825024-1 [(5)]	The George and Ira Gershwin Songbook (Complete)	198?	6.25	12.50	25.00
825098-1	Lady Be Good	1985	2.50	5.00	10.00
825669-1	The Jerome Kern Song Book	1985	2.50	5.00	10.00
825670-1	Mack the Knife — Ella in Berlin	1985	2.50	5.00	10.00
827150-1	Ella Wishes You a Swinging Christmas	198?	2.50	5.00	10.00
827163-1 [(2)]	The Duke Ellington Song Book, Vol. 1	198?	3.00	6.00	12.00
827169-1 [(2)]	The Duke Ellington Song Book, Vol. 2	198?	3.00	6.00	12.00
829533-1 [(2)]	The Irving Berlin Song Book	1988	3.00	6.00	12.00
835454-1	Ella in Rome: The Birthday Concert	1988	2.50	5.00	10.00

Number	Title (A Side/B Side)	Yr	VG	VG+	NM
VOCALION					
VL 3797 [M]	Ella Fitzgerald	1967	3.00	6.00	12.00
VL 73797 [R]	Ella Fitzgerald	1967	3.00	6.00	12.00

FITZGERALD, ELLA, AND LOUIS ARMSTRONG

Also see each artist's individual listings.

45s

Number	Title (A Side/B Side)	Yr	VG	VG+	NM
DECCA					
27209	Can Anyone Explain? (No, No, No)/Dream a Little Dream of Me	1950	5.00	10.00	20.00
28552	Who Walks In When I Walk Out/Would You Like to Take a Walk	1953	3.75	7.50	15.00
VERVE					
2023	Stars Fell on Alabama/Can't We Be Friends	1956	3.00	6.00	12.00
10079	Goody Goody/A-Tisket, A-Tasket	1957	5.00	10.00	20.00

7-Inch Extended Plays

Number	Title (A Side/B Side)	Yr	VG	VG+	NM
DECCA					
ED 2027	You Won't Be Satisfied/Dream a Little Dream of Me//Would You Like to Take a Walk/The Frim-Fram Sauce	195?	3.75	7.50	15.00
ED 2027 [PS]	Ella Fitzgerald and Louis Armstrong, Vol. 1	195?	3.75	7.50	15.00

Albums

Number	Title (A Side/B Side)	Yr	VG	VG+	NM
METRO					
M-601 [M]	Louis and Ella	1967	3.00	6.00	12.00
MS-601 [S]	Louis and Ella	1967	3.00	6.00	12.00
MOBILE FIDELITY					
2-248 [(2)]	Ella and Louis Again	1996	37.50	75.00	150.00
—Audiophile vinyl					
VERVE					
VE-1-2507	Porgy and Bess	197?	2.50	5.00	10.00
MGV-4003 [M]	Ella and Louis	1956	12.50	25.00	50.00
V-4003 [M]	Ella and Louis	1961	5.00	10.00	20.00
MGV-4006-2 [(2) M]	Ella and Louis Again	1956	20.00	40.00	80.00
V-4006-2 [(2) M]	Ella and Louis Again	1961	6.25	12.50	25.00
MGV-4011-2 [(2) M]	Porgy and Bess	1957	20.00	40.00	80.00
V-4011-2 [(2) M]	Porgy and Bess	1961	6.25	12.50	25.00
V6-4011-2 [(2) S]	Porgy and Bess	1961	6.25	12.50	25.00
MGV-4017 [M]	Ella and Louis Again, Vol. 1	1958	12.50	25.00	50.00
V-4017 [M]	Ella and Louis Again, Vol. 1	1961	5.00	10.00	20.00
MGV-4018 [M]	Ella and Louis Again, Vol. 2	1958	12.50	25.00	50.00
V-4018 [M]	Ella and Louis Again, Vol. 2	1961	5.00	10.00	20.00
MGVS-6040-2 [(2) S]	Porgy and Bess	1960	15.00	30.00	60.00
V6-8811 [(2)]	Ella and Louis	1972	3.75	7.50	15.00
827475-1 [(2)]	Porgy and Bess	198?	3.00	6.00	12.00

FITZGERALD, ELLA, AND BILLIE HOLIDAY

Also see each artist's individual listings.

Albums

Number	Title (A Side/B Side)	Yr	VG	VG+	NM
AMERICAN RECORDING SOCIETY					
G-433 [M]	Ella Fitzgerald and Billie Holiday at Newport	1957	10.00	20.00	40.00
VERVE					
MGVS-6022 [S]	Ella Fitzgerald and Billie Holiday at Newport	1960	10.00	20.00	40.00
MGV-8234 [M]	Ella Fitzgerald and Billie Holiday at Newport	1958	12.50	25.00	50.00
V-8234 [M]	Ella Fitzgerald and Billie Holiday at Newport	1961	5.00	10.00	20.00
V6-8234 [S]	Ella Fitzgerald and Billie Holiday at Newport	1961	5.00	10.00	20.00
V-8826	Newport Years	1973	3.00	6.00	12.00

FIVE AMERICANS, THE

45s

Number	Title (A Side/B Side)	Yr	VG	VG+	NM
ABC-PARAMOUNT					
10686	Show Me/Love, Love, Love	1965	—	—	—
ABNAK					
106	Say That You Love Me/Without You	1965	2.50	5.00	10.00
106 [DJ]	Say That You Love Me/Without You	1965	6.25	12.50	25.00
—Promo only on yellow vinyl					
109	I See the Light/The Outcast	1965	5.00	10.00	20.00
109 [DJ]	I See the Light/The Outcast	1965	6.25	12.50	25.00
—Promo only on yellow vinyl					
114	Reality/Sympathy	1966	2.50	5.00	10.00
114 [DJ]	Reality/Sympathy	1966	6.25	12.50	25.00
—Promo only on yellow vinyl					
116	If I Could/Now That It's Over	1966	2.50	5.00	10.00
116 [DJ]	If I Could/Now That It's Over	1966	6.25	12.50	25.00
—Promo only on yellow vinyl					
118	Western Union/Now That It's Over	1967	3.00	6.00	12.00
118 [DJ]	Western Union/Now That It's Over	1967	6.25	12.50	25.00
—Promo only on yellow vinyl					
120	Sound of Love/Sympathy	1967	2.00	4.00	8.00
120 [DJ]	Sound of Love/Sympathy	1967	6.25	12.50	25.00
—Promo only on yellow vinyl					
123	Zip Code/Sweet Bird of Youth	1967	2.00	4.00	8.00
123 [DJ]	Zip Code/Sweet Bird of Youth	1967	6.25	12.50	25.00
—Promo only on yellow vinyl					
125	Stop Light/Tell Ann I Love Her	1967	2.00	4.00	8.00
125 [DJ]	Stop Light/Tell Ann I Love Her	1967	6.25	12.50	25.00
—Promo only on yellow vinyl					
125 [PS]	Stop Light/Tell Ann I Love Her	1967	3.75	7.50	15.00
126	7:30 Guided Tour/See Saw Baby	1967	2.00	4.00	8.00
126 [DJ]	7:30 Guided Tour/See Saw Baby	1967	6.25	12.50	25.00
—Promo only on yellow vinyl					
126 [PS]	7:30 Guided Tour/See Saw Baby	1967	3.75	7.50	15.00
128	The Rain Maker/No Communication	1968	2.00	4.00	8.00
128 [DJ]	The Rain Maker/No Communication	1968	6.25	12.50	25.00
—Promo only on yellow vinyl					
131	Con Man/Lovin' Is Lovin'	1968	2.00	4.00	8.00
131 [DJ]	Con Man/Lovin' Is Lovin'	1968	6.25	12.50	25.00
—Promo only on yellow vinyl					
132	Generation Gap/The Source	1968	2.00	4.00	8.00
132 [DJ]	Generation Gap/The Source	1968	6.25	12.50	25.00
—Promo only on yellow vinyl					
134	Virginia Girl/Call on Me	1969	2.00	4.00	8.00
134 [DJ]	Virginia Girl/Call on Me	1969	6.25	12.50	25.00
—Promo only on yellow vinyl					
137	Scrooge/Ignert Woman	1969	2.00	4.00	8.00
137 [DJ]	Scrooge/Ignert Woman	1969	6.25	12.50	25.00
—Promo only on yellow vinyl					
139	I See the Light '69/Red Cape	1969	2.00	4.00	8.00
—As "Michael Rabon and the Five Americans"					
139 [DJ]	I See the Light '69/Red Cape	1969	6.25	12.50	25.00
—As "Michael Rabon and the Five Americans"; promo only on yellow vinyl					
142	She's Too Good to Me/Molly Black	1969	2.00	4.00	8.00
142 [DJ]	She's Too Good to Me/Molly Black	1969	6.25	12.50	25.00
—Promo only on yellow vinyl					
HANNA-BARBERA					
454	I See the Light/The Outcast	1965	3.00	6.00	12.00
468	Evol-Not Love/Don't Blame Me	1966	3.00	6.00	12.00
468 [PS]	Evol-Not Love/Don't Blame Me	1966	3.75	7.50	15.00
483	Good Times/The Losing Game	1966	3.00	6.00	12.00
JETSTAR					
104	It's You Girl/I'm Gonna Leave You	1966	6.25	12.50	25.00
105	I'm Feeling OK/Slippin' and Slidin'	1966	7.50	15.00	30.00
PHILCO-FORD					
HP-10	Western Union/Sounds of Love	1968	5.00	10.00	20.00
—4-inch plastic "Hip Pocket Record" with color sleeve					

Albums

Number	Title (A Side/B Side)	Yr	VG	VG+	NM
ABNAK					
AB-1967 [M]	Western Union/Sound of Love	1967	5.00	10.00	20.00
AB-1969 [M]	Progressions	1967	5.00	10.00	20.00
ABST-2067 [S]	Western Union/Sound of Love	1967	7.50	15.00	30.00
ABST-2069 [S]	Progressions	1967	7.50	15.00	30.00
ABST-2071 [(2)]	Now and Then	1968	6.25	12.50	25.00
HANNA-BARBERA					
HLP-8505 [M]	I See the Light	1966	10.00	20.00	40.00
HST-9505 [S]	I See the Light	1966	15.00	30.00	60.00

FIVE BARS, THE

45s

Number	Title (A Side/B Side)	Yr	VG	VG+	NM
MONEY					
224	Stormy Weather/Somebody Else's Fool	1957	15.00	30.00	60.00

FIVE BELLS, THE

45s

Number	Title (A Side/B Side)	Yr	VG	VG+	NM
BRUNSWICK					
84002	Till I Waltz Again with You/Can't Wait for Tomorrow	1952	125.00	250.00	500.00
84004	Till Dawn and Tomorrow/Waiting, Waiting	1952	125.00	250.00	500.00

FIVE BLOBS, THE

45s

Number	Title (A Side/B Side)	Yr	VG	VG+	NM
COLUMBIA					
41250	The Blob/Saturday Night in Tijuana	1958	6.25	12.50	25.00
JOY					
226	Rockin' Pow Wow/From the Top of Your Guggle	1959	5.00	10.00	20.00
230	Juliet/Young and Wild	1959	5.00	10.00	20.00

FIVE BLUE FLAMES, THE

See CHRIS POWELL AND THE FIVE BLUE FLAMES.

FIVE BLUE NOTES, THE

45s

Number	Title (A Side/B Side)	Yr	VG	VG+	NM
SABRE					
103	My Gal Is Gone/Ooh Baby	1953	250.00	500.00	1000.
108	The Beat of Our Hearts/You Gotta Go Baby	1954	625.00	1250.	2500.

FIVE BUDDS, THE

45s

Number	Title (A Side/B Side)	Yr	VG	VG+	NM
RAMA					
1	I Was Such a Fool (To Fall in Love with You)/Midnight	1953	125.00	250.00	500.00
2	I Guess It's All Over Now/I Want Her Back	1953	125.00	250.00	500.00

FIVE BY FIVE

45s

Number	Title (A Side/B Side)	Yr	VG	VG+	NM
PAULA					
261	Shake a Tail Feather/Tell Me What to Do	1967	3.00	6.00	12.00
283	Harlem Shuffle/You Really Got a Hold on Me	1967	3.00	6.00	12.00
302	Fire/Hang Up	1968	3.75	7.50	15.00
311	Ain't Gonna Be Your Fool No More/She Digs My Love	1968	3.00	6.00	12.00
319	Apple Cider/Fruitstand Man	1970	2.50	5.00	10.00
322	Too Much Tomorrow/Ain't Gonna Be Your Fool No More	1970	2.50	5.00	10.00
326	15 Going on 20/Penthouse Pauper	1970	2.50	5.00	10.00
328	Never/Good Connection	1970	2.50	5.00	10.00

FIVE CAMPBELLS, THE

45s

Number	Title (A Side/B Side)	Yr	VG	VG+	NM
MUSIC CITY					
794	Hey Baby/Morrine	1956	125.00	250.00	500.00

FIVE CARD STUD

45s

Number	Title (A Side/B Side)	Yr	VG	VG+	NM
RED BIRD					
10-082	Be-Bop-A-Lula/Everybody Needs Somebody	1967	3.75	7.50	15.00
SMASH					
2080	Bag Me/Once	1967	3.75	7.50	15.00

FIVE CATS, THE

45s

Number	Title (A Side/B Side)	Yr	VG	VG+	NM
RCA VICTOR					
47-5885	He Follows She/Santa Lucia	1954	6.25	12.50	25.00
47-6012	Rockin' Chair/Mine, Mine, Mine	1955	7.50	15.00	30.00
47-6181	I Was So Wrong/Someone's Gonna Cry	1955	10.00	20.00	40.00

FIVE CHANCES, THE

Number	Title (A Side/B Side)	Yr	VG	VG+	NM
45s					
ATOMIC					
2494	Make Love to Me/California	1977	3.00	6.00	12.00
BLUE LAKE					
115	All I Want/Shake-a-Link	1955	200.00	400.00	800.00
CHANCE					
1157	I May Be Small/Nagasaki	1954	250.00	500.00	1000.
FEDERAL					
12303	My Days Are Blue/Tell Me Why	1957	125.00	250.00	500.00
P.S.					
1510	Is This Love/Need Your Love	1960	75.00	150.00	300.00
STATES					
156	Gloria/Sugar Lips	1956	200.00	400.00	800.00
—Black vinyl					
156	Gloria/Sugar Lips	1956	300.00	600.00	1200.
—Red vinyl					

FIVE DEBONAIRES, THE

See THE DEBONAIRES.

FIVE DELIGHTS, THE

Number	Title (A Side/B Side)	Yr	VG	VG+	NM
45s					
ABEL					
228	The Thought of Losing You/That Love Affair	1959	75.00	150.00	300.00
NEWPORT					
7002	There'll Be No Goodbye/Okey Dokey Mama	1958	37.50	75.00	150.00
UNART					
2003	There'll Be No Goodbye/Okey Dokey Mama	1958	7.50	15.00	30.00

FIVE DISCS, THE

Evidently these are all the same group or closely related. Also see DAWN (3).

Number	Title (A Side/B Side)	Yr	VG	VG+	NM
45s					
CALO					
202	Adios/My Baby Loves Me	1961	37.50	75.00	150.00
—Green label					
202	Adios/My Baby Loves Me	1962	25.00	50.00	100.00
—White label					
CHEER					
1000	Never Let You Go/That Was the Time	1962	25.00	50.00	100.00
—Black label					
1000	Never Let You Go/That Was the Time	1962	12.50	25.00	50.00
—Red label					
1000 [DJ]	Never Let You Go/That Was the Time	1962	75.00	150.00	300.00
—White label, promo only					
CRYSTAL BALL					
114	Mirror Mirror/Most of All I Wonder Why	1978	2.50	5.00	10.00
120	Unchained Melody/The Shrine of St. Cecelia	1978	2.50	5.00	10.00
136	Playing a Game of Love/Bells	1979	2.00	4.00	8.00
141	This Love of Ours/To the Fair	1979	2.00	4.00	8.00
DWAIN					
803	My Chinese Girl/Roses	1959	50.00	100.00	200.00
—As "Mario and the Five Discs"					
803	My Chinese Girl/Roses	1959	37.50	75.00	150.00
6072	My Chinese Girl/Roses	1959	500.00	1000.	2000.
EMGE					
1004	I Remember/The World Is a Beautiful Place	1958	100.00	200.00	400.00
LAURIE					
3601	Rock and Roll Revival/Gypsy Women	1973	3.75	7.50	15.00
MELLO MOOD					
1002	My Chinese Girl/Roses	1964	3.75	7.50	15.00
PYRAMID					
166	Let's Fall in Love/That Was the Time	197?	—	3.00	6.00
RUST					
5027	I Remember/The World Is a Beautiful Place	1961	6.25	12.50	25.00
VIK					
0327	I Remember/The World Is a Beautiful Place	1958	20.00	40.00	80.00
YALE					
240	When Love Comes Knocking/Go-Go	1961	100.00	200.00	400.00
243/4	Come On Baby/I Don't Know What to Do	1961	100.00	200.00	400.00
Albums					
CRYSTAL BALL					
119	Unchained	1978	3.75	7.50	15.00
MAGIC CARPET					
1002	The Five Discs Sing Again	1991	5.00	10.00	20.00
—Dark blue cover					

FIVE DOLLARS, THE

Number	Title (A Side/B Side)	Yr	VG	VG+	NM
45s					
FORTUNE					
821	Harmony of Love/Doctor Baby	1955	25.00	50.00	100.00
826	So Strange/You Know I Can't Refuse	1956	25.00	50.00	100.00
830	I Will Wait/Hard Working Mama	1956	25.00	50.00	100.00
833	You Fool/How Do You Do the Bacon Fat	1957	20.00	40.00	80.00
854	That's the Way It Goes/My Baby-O	1960	12.50	25.00	50.00
FRATERNITY					
821	Harmony of Love/Doctor Baby	1958	10.00	20.00	40.00

FIVE ECHOES, THE

Number	Title (A Side/B Side)	Yr	VG	VG+	NM
45s					
SABRE					
102	Baby Come Back to Me/Lonely Mood	1953	150.00	300.00	600.00
—Black vinyl					
102	Baby Come Back to Me/Lonely Mood	1953	750.00	1125.	1500.
—Red vinyl					
105	So Lonesome/Broke	1954	150.00	300.00	600.00
—Black vinyl					
105	So Lonesome/Broke	1954	750.00	1125.	1500.
—Red vinyl					
VEE JAY					
129	I Really Do/Tell Me Baby	1954	75.00	150.00	300.00
156	Fool's Prayer/Tastee Freeze	1955	250.00	500.00	1000.
190	Soldier Boy/Pledging to You	1956	50.00	100.00	200.00

FIVE EMBERS, THE

Number	Title (A Side/B Side)	Yr	VG	VG+	NM
45s					
GEM					
224	Please Come Home/(B-side unknown)	1954	200.00	400.00	800.00

FIVE EMERALDS, THE

Number	Title (A Side/B Side)	Yr	VG	VG+	NM
45s					
S.R.C.					
106	I'll Beg/Let Me Take You Out Tonight	1953	250.00	500.00	1000.
—Label uses numeral "5" in group name, and "S.R.C." has periods in it					
106	I'll Beg/Let Me Take You Out Tonight	1953	250.00	500.00	1000.
—Label spells out "Five" in group name, and "S-R-C" has hyphens in it					
107	Darling/Pleasure Me	1954	300.00	600.00	1200.

FIVE EMPREES, THE

Number	Title (A Side/B Side)	Yr	VG	VG+	NM
45s					
FREEPORT					
1001	Little Miss Sad/Hey Lover	1965	3.00	6.00	12.00
1001	Little Miss Sad/Hey Lover	1965	6.25	12.50	25.00
—Originally released as "The Five Empressions"					
1002	Hey Baby/Why	1965	3.00	6.00	12.00
1007	Little Miss Happiness/Over the Mountain	1966	3.00	6.00	12.00
1009	Pretty Face (Part 1)/Pretty Face (Part 2)	1966	3.00	6.00	12.00
1010	Johnny B. Goode/Hey Lover	1966	3.00	6.00	12.00
SMASH					
2065	Gone from My Mind/Hey Diddle Diddle	1966	2.50	5.00	10.00
Albums					
FREEPORT					
3001 [M]	The Five Emprees	1965	12.50	25.00	50.00
3001 [M]	Little Miss Sad	1966	7.50	15.00	30.00
—Same LP, new title					
4001 [S]	The Five Emprees	1965	15.00	30.00	60.00
4001 [S]	Little Miss Sad	1966	10.00	20.00	40.00
—Same LP, new title					

FIVE FORTUNES, THE

Number	Title (A Side/B Side)	Yr	VG	VG+	NM
45s					
RANSOM					
103	You Are My Only Love/Time Out for Love	1958	250.00	500.00	1000.

FIVE JETS, THE

Number	Title (A Side/B Side)	Yr	VG	VG+	NM
45s					
DELUXE					
6018	I Am in Love/Not a Hand to Shake	1953	37.50	75.00	150.00
6053	I'm Stuck/I Want a Woman	1954	37.50	75.00	150.00
6058	Tell Me You're Mine/Give In	1954	50.00	100.00	200.00
6064	Crazy Chicken/Everybody Do the Chicken	1954	15.00	30.00	60.00
6071	Down Slow/Please Love Me Baby	1955	20.00	60.00	120.00
KING					
6058	Tell Me You're Mine/Give In	1966	5.00	10.00	20.00

FIVE KEYS, THE

Number	Title (A Side/B Side)	Yr	VG	VG+	NM
45s					
ALADDIN					
3085	With a Broken Heart/Too Late	1951	—	—	—
—Unconfirmed on 45 rpm					
3099	The Glory of Love/Hucklebuck with Jimmy	1951	250.00	500.00	1000.
3113	It's Christmas Time/Old Mac Donald	1951	250.00	500.00	1000.
3118	Yes Sir That's My Baby/Old Mac Donald	1952	250.00	500.00	1000.
3119	Darling/Goin' Downtown	1952	250.00	500.00	1000.
3127	Red Sails in the Sunset/Be Anything, But Be Mine	1952	3000.	4500.	6000.
3131	How Long/Mistakes	1952	300.00	600.00	1200.
3136	Hold Me/I Hadn't Anyone Till You	1952	200.00	400.00	800.00
3158	I Cried for You/Serve Another Round	1953	225.00	450.00	900.00
3167	Can't Keep From Crying/Come Go My Bail, Louise	1953	200.00	400.00	800.00
3175	There Ought to Be a Law/Mama (Your Daughter Told a Lie on Me)	1953	200.00	400.00	800.00
3182	I'll Always Be in Love with You/Rocking and Crying Blues	1953	200.00	400.00	800.00
3190	These Foolish Things/Lonesome Old Story	1953	1000.	2000.	4000.
3204	Teardrops in Your Eyes/I'm So High	1953	200.00	400.00	800.00
3214	My Saddest Hour/Oh! Babe!	1953	200.00	400.00	800.00
3228	Someday Sweetheart/Love My Loving	1954	200.00	400.00	800.00
3245	Deep in My Heart/How Do You Expect Me to Get It	1954	200.00	400.00	800.00
3263	My Love/Why, Oh Why	1954	75.00	150.00	300.00
3312	Story of Love/Serve Another Round	1956	75.00	150.00	300.00
S7-19768	Every Heart Is Home at Christmas/Frosty the Snowman	1997	—	2.50	5.00
—B-side by Fats Domino on The Right Stuff					
BANGAR					
661	Run-Around/I Tell My Heart	1965	3.75	7.50	15.00
CAPITOL					
F-2945	Ling, Ting, Tong/I'm Alone	1954	10.00	20.00	40.00
F-3032	Close Your Eyes/Doggone It, You Did It	1955	10.00	20.00	40.00
F-3127	The Verdict/Me Make Um Pow Wow	1955	10.00	20.00	40.00
F-3185	Don't You Know I Love You/I Wish I'd Never Learned to Read	1955	10.00	20.00	40.00
F-3267	'Cause You're My Lover/Gee Whittakers	1955	10.00	20.00	40.00
F-3318	You Broke the Rules of Love/What Goes On	1956	10.00	20.00	40.00
F-3392	She's the Most/I Dreamt I Dwelt in Heaven	1956	10.00	20.00	40.00
—Regular large hole					
F-3392	She's the Most/I Dreamt I Dwelt in Heaven	1956	17.50	35.00	70.00
—Small hole					
F-3455	My Pigeon's Gone/Peace and Love	1956	10.00	20.00	40.00
F-3502	Out of Sight, Out of Mind/That's Right	1956	7.50	15.00	30.00
F-3597	Wisdom of a Fool/Now Don't That Prove I Love You	1956	7.50	15.00	30.00
F-3660	Tiger Lily/Let There Be You	1957	6.25	12.50	25.00
F-3710	Four Walls/It's a Groove	1957	6.25	12.50	25.00

Number	Title (A Side/B Side)	Yr	VG	VG+	NM
F-3738	This I Promise You/The Blues Don't Care	1957	6.25	12.50	25.00
F-3786	Boom Boom/Face of An Angel	1957	6.25	12.50	25.00
F-3830	Do Anything/It's a Cryin' Shame	1957	6.25	12.50	25.00
F-3861	From Me to You/Whippety Whirl	1957	6.25	12.50	25.00
F-3948	You're for Me/With All My Love	1958	6.25	12.50	25.00
F-4009	Emily Please/Handy Andy	1958	6.25	12.50	25.00
F-4092	One Great Love/Really-O, Truly-O	1958	6.25	12.50	25.00
4828	Out of Sight, Out of Mind/From the Bottom of My Heart	1962	5.00	10.00	20.00
CLASSIC ARTISTS					
115	I Want You For Christmas/Express Yourself Back Home	1989	—	2.50	5.00
—As "Rudy West and the Five Keys"					
GROOVE					
0031	I'll Follow You/Lawdy Miss Mary	1954	2000.	3000.	4000.
—There is some debate about whether this record actually exists.					
INFERNO					
4500	Hey Girl/No Matter	1967	5.00	10.00	20.00
KING					
5251	I Took Your Love for a Toy/Ziggus	1959	7.50	15.00	30.00
5273	Dancing Senorita/Dream On	1959	5.00	10.00	20.00
5302	How Can I Forget You/I Burned Your Letter	1960	5.00	10.00	20.00
5330	Gonna Be Too Late/Rosetta	1960	5.00	10.00	20.00
5358	I Didn't Know/No, Says My Heart	1960	5.00	10.00	20.00
5398	Bimbo/Valley of Love	1960	5.00	10.00	20.00
5446	You Broke the Only Heart/That's What You're Doing to Me	1961	5.00	10.00	20.00
5496	Do Something for Me/Stop Your Crying	1961	5.00	10.00	20.00
5877	I'll Never Stop Loving You/I Can't Escape from You	1964	3.00	6.00	12.00
LIBERTY					
1394	It's Christmas Time/It's Christmas	1980	2.00	4.00	8.00
—B-side by Marvin and Johnny					
OWL					
321	A Dreamer/Your Teeth and Your Tongue	1973	2.00	4.00	8.00
SEG-WAY					
1008	Out of Sight, Out of Mind/You're the One	1962	3.75	7.50	15.00
UNITED ARTISTS					
0150	The Glory of Love/My Saddest Hour	1973	—	2.00	4.00
—"Silver Spotlight Series" reissue					

7-Inch Extended Plays

Number	Title (A Side/B Side)	Yr	VG	VG+	NM
CAPITOL					
EAP 572	(contents unknown)	1955	25.00	50.00	100.00
EAP 572 [PS]	The Five Keys	1955	25.00	50.00	100.00
EAP 1-828	(contents unknown)	1957	25.00	50.00	100.00
EAP 1-828 [PS]	The Five Keys On Stage! Volume 1	1957	37.50	75.00	150.00
—On cover, the far left singer has his thumb sticking out (inadvertently?) in a phallic way					
EAP 1-828 [PS]	The Five Keys On Stage! Volume 1	1957	25.00	50.00	100.00
—On cover, the far left singer's "offending" thumb is airbrushed out					
EAP 2-828	(contents unknown)	1957	25.00	50.00	100.00
EAP 2-828 [PS]	The Five Keys On Stage! Volume 2	1957	37.50	75.00	150.00
—On cover, the far left singer has his thumb sticking out (inadvertently?) in a phallic way					
EAP 2-828 [PS]	The Five Keys On Stage! Volume 2	1957	25.00	50.00	100.00
—On cover, the far left singer's "offending" thumb is airbrushed out					

Albums

Number	Title (A Side/B Side)	Yr	VG	VG+	NM
ALADDIN					
LP-806 [M]	The Best of the Five Keys	1956	1000.	1500.	2000.
—Copies of Aladdin 806 entitled "On the Town" are bootlegs.					
CAPITOL					
T 828 [M]	The Five Keys On Stage!	1957	75.00	150.00	300.00
—On cover, the far left singer has his thumb sticking out (inadvertently?) in a phallic way					
T 828 [M]	The Five Keys On Stage!	1957	125.00	250.00	500.00
—On cover, the far left singer's "offending" thumb is airbrushed out					
M-1769	The Fantastic Five Keys	1977	5.00	10.00	20.00
—Reissue with new prefix					
T 1769 [M]	The Fantastic Five Keys	1962	75.00	150.00	300.00
HARLEM HIT PARADE					
5004	The Five Keys	1972	3.75	7.50	15.00
KING					
688 [M]	The Five Keys	1960	200.00	400.00	800.00
692 [M]	Rhythm and Blues Hits, Past and Present	1960	150.00	300.00	600.00
5013	14 Hits	197?	3.00	6.00	12.00
SCORE					
LP-4003 [M]	The Five Keys On the Town	1957	200.00	400.00	800.00
—Reissue of Aladdin 806.					

FIVE KIDS, THE

45s

Number	Title (A Side/B Side)	Yr	VG	VG+	NM
MAXWELL					
101	Carolyn/Oh Baby	1955	1000.	2000.	3000.

FIVE LYRICS, THE

45s

Number	Title (A Side/B Side)	Yr	VG	VG+	NM
MUSIC CITY					
799	I'm Traveling Light/My Honeysweet Pea	1956	375.00	750.00	1500.

FIVE MAN ELECTRICAL BAND

45s

Number	Title (A Side/B Side)	Yr	VG	VG+	NM
CAPITOL					
2368	It Never Rains on Maple Lane/Private Train	1968	—	3.00	6.00
2517	Baby/Lovin' Look	1969	—	3.00	6.00
2562	Sunrise to Sunset/Little Bit of Love	1969	—	3.00	6.00
2628	Riverboat/Good	1969	—	3.00	6.00
LION					
112	Coming of Age/The Devil and Miss Lucy	1972	—	2.50	5.00
127	Money Back Guarantee/Find the One	1972	—	2.50	5.00
149	I'm a Stranger Here/Doin' The Best We Can Rag	1973	—	2.50	5.00
160	Sweet Paradise/Baby Wanna Boogie	1973	—	2.50	5.00
LIONEL					
3213	Signs/Hello Melinda Goodbye	1971	2.00	4.00	8.00
—Lists "Hello Melinda Goodbye" as the A-side and contains the full-length version of "Signs"					
3213	Signs/Hello Melinda Goodbye	1971	—	3.00	6.00
—Lists no A and B sides and contains an edited version (3:20) of "Signs"					
3220	Absolutely Right/Butterfly	1971	—	2.50	5.00
3224	Friends and Family/Julianna	1971	—	2.50	5.00
MGM					
14149	Moonshine/Forever Together	1970	—	3.00	6.00
14182 [DJ]	Hello Melinda Goodbye/Signs	1970	2.50	5.00	10.00
—Evidently only exists as a promo					
POLYDOR					
14221	Werewolf/Country Angel	1974	—	2.00	4.00
14263	Johnnie Get a Gun/And the World Goes Round	1974	—	3.00	6.00

Albums

Number	Title (A Side/B Side)	Yr	VG	VG+	NM
CAPITOL					
ST-165	Five Man Electrical Band	1969	5.00	10.00	20.00
LION					
LN-1009	Sweet Paradise	1973	5.00	10.00	20.00
LIONEL					
LRS-1100	Good-Byes & Butterflies	1970	7.50	15.00	30.00
LRS-1101	Coming of Age	1971	5.00	10.00	20.00
MGM					
SE-4725	Good-Byes & Butterflies	1970	12.50	25.00	50.00
—The existence of this LP has been confirmed					
PICKWICK					
SPC-3289	Five Man Electrical Band	1973	2.50	5.00	10.00
—Reissue of Capitol material					

FIVE NOTES, THE

45s

Number	Title (A Side/B Side)	Yr	VG	VG+	NM
CHESS					
1614	Show Me the Way/Park Your Lover	1955	37.50	75.00	150.00
JEN D					
4185	You Are So Beautiful/Broken Hearted Baby	1955	125.00	250.00	500.00
JOSIE					
784	You Are So Beautiful/Broken Hearted Baby	1955	20.00	40.00	80.00

FIVE PLAYBOYS, THE

45s

Number	Title (A Side/B Side)	Yr	VG	VG+	NM
DOT					
15605	When We Were Young/Pages of My Scrapbook	1957	6.25	12.50	25.00
FEE BEE					
213	When We Were Young/Pages of My Scrapbook	1958	12.50	25.00	50.00
232	Angel Mine/She's My Baby	1959	25.00	50.00	100.00
MERCURY					
71269	Time Will Allow/Why Be a Fool	1958	6.25	12.50	25.00
PETITE					
504	She's My Baby/Mr. Echo	1959	10.00	20.00	40.00

FIVE ROVERS, THE

45s

Number	Title (A Side/B Side)	Yr	VG	VG+	NM
MUSIC CITY					
798	Down to the Sea/Change Your Mind	1956	30.00	60.00	120.00

FIVE ROYALES, THE

Also includes "The Five Royals" and "The '5' Royales."

45s

Number	Title (A Side/B Side)	Yr	VG	VG+	NM
ABC-PARAMOUNT					
10348	Catch That Teardrop/Goof Ball	1962	2.50	5.00	10.00
10368	What's In Your Heart/I Want It Like That	1962	2.50	5.00	10.00
APOLLO					
441	Courage to Love/You Know I Know	1952	25.00	50.00	100.00
—Black vinyl					
441	Courage to Love/You Know I Know	1952	100.00	200.00	400.00
—Red vinyl					
443	Baby Don't Do It/Take All of Me	1952	25.00	50.00	100.00
—Black vinyl					
443	Baby Don't Do It/Take All of Me	1952	100.00	200.00	400.00
—Red vinyl					
446	Help Me, Somebody/Crazy, Crazy, Crazy	1953	25.00	50.00	100.00
448	Too Much Lovin' (Much Too Much)/Laundromat Blues	1953	30.00	60.00	120.00
449	I Want to Thank You/All Righty	1953	20.00	40.00	80.00
452	I Do/Good Things	1954	20.00	40.00	80.00
454	Cry Some More/I Like It Like That	1954	20.00	40.00	80.00
458	What's That/Let Me Come Back Home	1954	17.50	35.00	70.00
467	With All Your Heart/6 O'Clock in the Morning	1955	17.50	35.00	70.00
HOME OF THE BLUES					
112	Please, Please, Please/I Got to Know	1960	3.75	7.50	15.00
218	If You Don't Need Me/I'm Gonna Tell Them	1961	3.75	7.50	15.00
232	Take Me With You Baby/Not Going to Cry	1961	3.75	7.50	15.00
234	Nuch in Need/They Don't Know	1962	3.75	7.50	15.00
243	Catch That Teardrop/Goof Ball	1962	3.75	7.50	15.00
KING					
4740	I'm Gonna Run It Down/Behave Yourself	1954	20.00	40.00	80.00
4744	Monkey Hips and Rice/Devil with the Rest	1954	20.00	40.00	80.00
4762	School Girl/One Mistake	1955	20.00	40.00	80.00
4770	Every Dog Has His Day/You Didn't Learn It at Home	1955	20.00	40.00	80.00
4785	How I Wonder/Mohawk Squaw	1955	20.00	40.00	80.00
4806	I Need Your Lovin'/When I Get Like This	1955	12.50	25.00	50.00
4819	Women About to Make Me Go Crazy/Do Unto You	1955	12.50	25.00	50.00
4830	I Ain't Gettin' Caught/Someone Made You for Me	1955	12.50	25.00	50.00
4869	When You Walked Through the Door/Right Around the Corner	1956	12.50	25.00	50.00
4901	I Could Love You/My Wants for Love	1956	12.50	25.00	50.00
4952	Get Something Out of It/Come On and Save Me	1956	12.50	25.00	50.00
4973	Just As I Am/Mine Forevermore	1956	12.50	25.00	50.00
5032	Tears of Joy/Thirty Second Lover	1957	10.00	20.00	40.00
5053	Think/I'd Better Make a Move	1957	10.00	20.00	40.00
5082	Messin' Up/Say It	1957	10.00	20.00	40.00
5098	Dedicated to the One I Love/Don't Be Ashamed	1958	10.00	20.00	40.00
5131	Do the Cha Cha Cherry/The Feeling Is Real	1958	6.25	12.50	25.00
5141	Tell the Truth/Double or Nothing	1958	6.25	12.50	25.00
5153	The Slummer the Slum/Don't Let It Be in Vain	1958	6.25	12.50	25.00

Number	Title (A Side/B Side)	Yr	VG	VG+	NM
5162	Your Only Love/The Real Thing	1958	6.25	12.50	25.00
5191	Miracle of Love/I Know It's Hard, But It's Fair	1959	6.25	12.50	25.00
5237	Tell Me You Care/Wonder Where Your Love Has Gone	1959	6.25	12.50	25.00
5266	My Sugar Sugar/It Hurts Inside	1959	6.25	12.50	25.00
5329	Don't Give No More Than You Can Take/I'm with You	1960	6.25	12.50	25.00
5357	Why/Within My Heart	1960	6.25	12.50	25.00
5453	Dedicated to the One I Love/Miracle of Love	1961	3.75	7.50	15.00
5756	Dedicated to the One I Love/Tears of Joy	1963	3.75	7.50	15.00
5892	I Wonder Where Your Love Has Gone/I Need Your Lovin' Baby	1964	3.75	7.50	15.00
—The Five Royals					
SMASH					
1936	Baby Don't Do It/I Like It Like That	1964	2.50	5.00	10.00
1963	Never Turn Your Back/Faith	1965	2.50	5.00	10.00
TODD					
1086	I'm Standing in the Shadows/Doin' Everything	1963	2.50	5.00	10.00
1088	Baby Don't Do It/There's Somebody Over There	1963	2.50	5.00	10.00
VEE JAY					
412	Much in Need/They Don't Know	1961	3.75	7.50	15.00
431	Help Me Somebody/Talk About My Woman	1962	3.75	7.50	15.00
Albums					
APOLLO					
LP-488 [M]	The Rockin' 5 Royales	1956	2000.	3000.	4000.
—Purple label					
LP-488 [M]	The Rockin' 5 Royales	1956	1000.	1500.	2000.
—Green label					
LP-488 [M]	The Rockin' 5 Royales	1956	250.00	500.00	1000.
—Yellow label					
KING					
580 [M]	Dedicated to You	1957	125.00	250.00	500.00
616 [M]	The 5 Royales Sing for You	1959	100.00	200.00	400.00
678 [M]	The Five Royales	1960	62.50	125.00	250.00
955 [M]	24 All Time Hits	1966	25.00	50.00	100.00
5014	17 Hits	197?	3.00	6.00	12.00

FIVE SATINS, THE

Also see FRED PARRIS; THE WILDWOODS.

45s

Number	Title (A Side/B Side)	Yr	VG	VG+	NM
BUDDAH					
477	Everybody Stand and Clap Your Hands/Hey There Pretty Lady	1975	—	2.50	5.00
—As "Black Satin"					
CANDELITE					
411	She's Gone (With the Wind)/Somewhere a Voice Is Calling	1974	—	3.00	6.00
CHANCELLOR					
1110	The Masquerade Is Over/Raining in My Heart	1962	5.00	10.00	20.00
1121	Do You Remember/Downtown	1962	5.00	10.00	20.00
CUB					
9071	Your Memory/I Didn't Know	1960	6.25	12.50	25.00
9077	These Foolish Things/A Beggar with a Dream	1960	6.25	12.50	25.00
9090	Golden Earrings/Can I Come Over Tonight	1961	6.25	12.50	25.00
ELEKTRA					
47411	Memories of Days Gone By Medley/Loving You (Would Be the Sweetest Thing)	1982	5.00	10.00	20.00
—As "Fred Parris and the Five Satins"					
69888	Didn't I (Blow Your Mind)/Loving You (Would Be the Sweetest Thing)	1982	—	2.50	5.00
69938	Breaking Up/Loving You (Would Be the Sweetest Thing)	1982	—	2.50	5.00
69984	I'll Be Seeing You/Loving You (Would Be the Sweetest Thing)	1982	—	2.50	5.00
EMBER					
1005	In the Still of the Nite/The Jones Girl	1956	50.00	100.00	200.00
—Red label; has "6106A" in the trail-off vinyl					
1005	In the Still of the Nite/The Jones Girl	1956	12.50	25.00	50.00
—Red label; has "E-2105-45" in the trail-off vinyl					
1005	In the Still of the Nite/The Jones Girl	1956	7.50	15.00	30.00
—Red label; has "E-1005" in the trail-off vinyl					
1005	I'll Remember (In the Still of the Nite)/The Jones Girl	1956	7.50	15.00	30.00
—Red label					
1005	I'll Remember (In the Still of the Nite)/The Jones Girl	1959	12.50	25.00	50.00
—Multi-color "logs" label; reads "Special Demand Release"					
1005	I'll Remember (In the Still of the Nite)/The Jones Girl	1959	7.50	15.00	30.00
—Multi-color "logs" label; no "Special Demand Release"					
1005	In the Still of the Nite/The Jones Girl	1959	10.00	20.00	40.00
—Multi-color "logs" label with original A-side title					
1005	I'll Remember (In the Still of the Nite)/The Jones Girl	1961	7.50	15.00	30.00
—Black label					
1008	Weeping Willow/Wonderful Girl	1956	10.00	20.00	40.00
1014	Our Love Is Forever/Oh Happy Day	1957	10.00	20.00	40.00
1019	To the Aisle/Wish I Had My Baby	1957	10.00	20.00	40.00
—Red label					
1019	To the Aisle/Wish I Had My Baby	1960	7.50	15.00	30.00
—Multi-color "logs" label					
1019	To the Aisle/Wish I Had My Baby	1961	5.00	10.00	20.00
—Black label					
1025	Our Anniversary/Pretty Baby	1957	10.00	20.00	40.00
—Red label					
1025	Our Anniversary/Pretty Baby	1957	5.00	10.00	20.00
—Black label					
1028	A Million to One/Love with No Love in Return	1957	10.00	20.00	40.00
1038	A Night to Remember/Senorita Lolita	1958	7.50	15.00	30.00
—As "Fred Parris and the Satins"					
1056	Shadows/Toni My Love	1959	7.50	15.00	30.00
1061	I'll Be Seeing You/A Night Like This	1960	7.50	15.00	30.00
1066	Candlelight/The Time	1960	6.25	12.50	25.00
1070	Wishing Ring/Tell Me Dear	1961	6.25	12.50	25.00
FIRST					
104	When Your Love Comes Along/Skippity Doo	1959	10.00	20.00	40.00
—Orange label					
104	When Your Love Comes Along/Skippity Doo	1959	6.25	12.50	25.00
—Green label					
KIRSHNER					
4251	Very Precious Oldies/You Are Love	1974	2.50	5.00	10.00
4252	Two Different Worlds/Love Is Such a Beautiful Thing	1974	2.50	5.00	10.00
KLIK					
1020	I Love You So/Story to You	1973	2.50	5.00	10.00
MAMA SADIE					
1001	In the Still of the Night "67"/Heck No (Instrumental)	1967	3.00	6.00	12.00
MUSICTONE					
1108	To the Aisle/Just to Be Near You	1961	6.25	12.50	25.00
NIGHTRAIN					
901	All Mine/The Voice	1970	2.50	5.00	10.00
RCA					
6989-7-R	In the Still of the Night/Yes	1988	—	—	3.00
—B-side by Merry Clayton					
RCA VICTOR					
74-0478	Summer in New York/Dark at the Top of My Heart	1971	2.50	5.00	10.00
ROULETTE					
4563	Ain't Gonna Cry/You Can Count on Me	1964	2.50	5.00	10.00
SAMMY					
103	No One Knows/Musical Chairs	196?	7.50	15.00	30.00
SIGNATURE					
001	Everybody's Got a Home But Me/Heartache	1990	—	2.50	5.00
STANDORD					
100	All Mine/Rose Mary	1956	175.00	2350.	700.00
—Red label					
100	All Mine/Rose Mary	1962	50.00	100.00	200.00
—Maroon label					
200	In the Still of the Nite/The Jones Girl	1956	300.00	600.00	900.00
200	In the Still of the Nite/The Jones Girl	1956	1000.	1500.	2000.
—With "Produced by Martin Kuegell" credit					
TIME MACHINE					
570	Wonder Why/No One Knows	1962	2.00	4.00	8.00
571	The Masquerade Is Over/Lonely Hearts	1962	2.00	4.00	8.00
TIMES SQUARE					
4	All Mine/Rose Mary	1962	5.00	10.00	20.00
—Blue vinyl					
21	Paradise on Earth/Monkey Business	1963	5.00	10.00	20.00
94	Paradise on Earth/Monkey Business	1964	3.75	7.50	15.00
UNITED ARTISTS					
368	On a Lover's Island/Till the End	1961	6.25	12.50	25.00
WARNER BROS.					
5367	Remember Me/Kangaroo	1963	3.00	6.00	12.00
X-BAT					
1000	When the Swallows Come Back to Capistrano/Dance Girl Dance	1995	—	2.50	5.00
—Red vinyl					
1000 [PS]	When the Swallows Come Back to Capistrano/Dance Girl Dance	1995	—	2.50	5.00

7-Inch Extended Plays

Number	Title (A Side/B Side)	Yr	VG	VG+	NM
EMBER					
EEP-100	I'll Remember/The Jones Girl//Wonderful Girl/Pretty Baby	1957	50.00	100.00	200.00
EEP-100 [PS]	The Five Satins Sing (Vol. 1)	1957	50.00	100.00	200.00
EEP-101	To the Aisle/Sugar//Our Love Is Forever/Weeping Willow	1957	50.00	100.00	200.00
EEP-101 [PS]	The Five Satins Sing (Vol. 2)	1957	50.00	100.00	200.00
EEP-102	(contents unknown)	1957	50.00	100.00	200.00
EEP-102 [PS]	The Five Satins Sing (Vol. 3)	1957	50.00	100.00	200.00

Albums

Number	Title (A Side/B Side)	Yr	VG	VG+	NM
BUDDAH					
BDS-5654	Black Satin	1976	3.75	7.50	15.00
—As "Black Satin"					
CELEBRITY SHOWCASE					
JB-7671	The Best of the Five Satins	1970	5.00	10.00	20.00
COLLECTABLES					
COL-5017	The Five Satins Sing Their Greatest Hits	198?	2.50	5.00	10.00
EMBER					
ELP-100 [M]	The Five Satins Sing	1957	1000.	1500.	2000.
—Red label; group pictured on front cover; blue vinyl					
ELP-100 [M]	The Five Satins Sing	1957	150.00	300.00	600.00
—Red label; group pictured on front cover; black vinyl					
ELP-100 [M]	The Five Satins Sing	1959	75.00	150.00	300.00
—Mostly white "logs" label; group pictured on front cover					
ELP-100 [M]	The Five Satins Sing	1959	50.00	100.00	200.00
—Mostly white "logs" label; no picture on cover					
ELP-100 [M]	The Five Satins Sing	1961	25.00	50.00	100.00
—Black label; no picture on cover					
ELP-401 [M]	The Five Satins Encore	1960	50.00	100.00	200.00
—Mostly white "logs" label					
ELP-401 [M]	The Five Satins Encore	1961	25.00	50.00	100.00
—Black label					
LOST-NITE					
LLP-8 [10]	The Five Satins	1981	2.50	5.00	10.00
—Red vinyl					
LLP-9 [10]	The Five Satins	1981	2.50	5.00	10.00
—Red vinyl					
MOUNT VERNON					
108	The Five Satins Sing	196?	7.50	15.00	30.00
RELIC					
5008	The Five Satins' Greatest Hits (1956-1959), Volume 1	198?	2.50	5.00	10.00
5013	The Five Satins' Greatest Hits (1956-1959), Volume 2	198?	2.50	5.00	10.00
5024	The Five Satins' Greatest Hits (1956-1959), Volume 3	198?	2.50	5.00	10.00

FIVE SCALDERS, THE

45s

Number	Title (A Side/B Side)	Yr	VG	VG+	NM
DRUMMOND					
3000	If Only You Were Mine/There Will Come a Time	1956	250.00	500.00	1000.
3001	Girl Friend/Willow Blues	1956	500.00	1000.	1500.
—Blue label					
3001	Girl Friend/Willow Blues	1956	250.00	500.00	1000.
—Maroon label					
SUGAR HILL					
3000	If Only You Were Mine/There Will Come a Time	1956	500.00	1000.	2000.

FIVE SECRETS, THE

45s

Number	Title (A Side/B Side)	Yr	VG	VG+	NM
DECCA					
30350	See You Next Year/Queen Bee	1957	20.00	40.00	80.00
30350	See You Next Year/Queen Bee	1957	10.00	20.00	40.00
—As "The Secrets"					

FIVE SHARKS, THE

45s

Number	Title (A Side/B Side)	Yr	VG	VG+	NM
AMBER					
852	The Lion Sleeps Tonight/Land of 1000 Dances	1966	2.50	5.00	10.00
OLD TIMER					
604	Gloria/Flames	1964	5.00	10.00	20.00
605	Stand By Me/I'll Never Let You Go	1964	5.00	10.00	20.00
—Gold vinyl					
605	Stand By Me/I'll Never Let You Go	1964	4.00	8.00	16.00
—Blue vinyl					
611	Gloria/Flames	1965	5.00	10.00	20.00
—Red vinyl					
611	Gloria/Flames	1965	3.75	7.50	15.00
—Black vinyl					
RELIC					
525	Stormy Weather (2:45)/If You Love Me	1965	2.50	5.00	10.00
SIAMESE					
404	Gloria/Flames	1965	3.00	6.00	12.00
TIMES SQUARE					
35	Stormy Weather (3:45)/If You Love Me	1964	15.00	30.00	60.00
—Blue vinyl					
35	Stormy Weather (3:45)/If You Love Me	1964	10.00	20.00	40.00
—Black vinyl					
35	Stormy Weather (2:45)/If You Love Me	1964	7.50	15.00	30.00

FIVE SHARPS, THE (1)

45s

Number	Title (A Side/B Side)	Yr	VG	VG+	NM
BIM BAM BOOM					
103	Stormy Weather/Sleepy Cowboy	1972	2.00	4.00	8.00
—Reissue mastered off the cracked Jubilee 78 (see below); the original master has long since disappeared					
JUBILEE					
5104	Stormy Weather/Sleepy Cowboy	1952	—	—	—
—Unknown on 45 RPM (3 known copies, one of which is cracked, exist on 78); all known 45s are counterfeits. Known counterfeits do not match the proper typeface of the era for the label, and the blue labels are too bright compared to authentic Jubilee 45s of the early 1950s. Even the cracked 78 would likely sell for $10,000; if a legitimate 45 would be confirmed, it could sell for more than any record ever made!					

FIVE SHARPS, THE (2)

A completely different group than (1), they were assembled by Jubilee to record a new version of "Stormy Weather" in the midst of the hubbub about the first Five Sharps version. (For the full story, see The Complete Book of Doo-Wop by Gribin and Schiff, Krause Publications, 2000.)

45s

Number	Title (A Side/B Side)	Yr	VG	VG+	NM
JUBILEE					
5478	Stormy Weather/Mammy Jammy	1964	3.00	6.00	12.00

FIVE STAIRSTEPS, THE

Includes records by "Five Stairsteps and Cubie" and "Stairsteps."

45s

Number	Title (A Side/B Side)	Yr	VG	VG+	NM
BUDDAH					
20	Something's Missing/Tell Me Who	1967	2.00	4.00	8.00
—As "Five Stairsteps and Cubie"					
20 [PS]	Something's Missing/Tell Me Who	1967	3.75	7.50	15.00
26	A Million to One/You Make Me So Mad	1968	2.00	4.00	8.00
—As "Five Stairsteps and Cubie"					
26 [PS]	A Million to One/You Make Me So Mad	1968	3.75	7.50	15.00
35	The Shadow of Your Love/Bad News	1968	2.00	4.00	8.00
165	Dear Prudence/O-o-h Child	1970	2.00	4.00	8.00
165	O-o-h Child/Who Do You Belong To	1970	—	3.00	6.00
188	Because I Love You/America Standing	1970	—	2.50	5.00
213	Didn't It Look So Easy/Peace Is Gonna Come	1971	—	2.50	5.00
—Starting with the above, as "Stairsteps"					
222	Snow/Look Out	1971	—	2.50	5.00
277	I Love You-Stop/I Feel a Song (In My Heart Again)	1972	—	2.50	5.00
291	Hush Child/The Easy Way	1972	—	2.50	5.00
320	Every Single Way/Two Weeks' Notice	1972	—	2.50	5.00
CURTOM					
1931	Don't Change Your Love/New Dance Craze	1968	—	3.00	6.00
—Curtom releases as "Five Stairsteps and Cubie"					
1933	I Made a Mistake/Stay Close to Me	1968	—	3.00	6.00
1936	Baby Make Me Feel So Good/Little Young Lover	1969	—	3.00	6.00
1944	Madame Mary/Little Boy Blue	1969	—	3.00	6.00
1945	We Must Be in Love/Little Young Lover	1969	—	3.00	6.00
DARK HORSE					
10005	From Us to You/Time	1975	—	2.50	5.00
10005 [PS]	From Us to You/Time	1975	—	3.00	6.00
10009	Tell Me Why/Salaam	1976	—	2.50	5.00
WINDY "C"					
601	You Waited Too Long/Don't Waste Your Time	1966	2.50	5.00	10.00
602	World of Fantasy/Playgirl's Love	1966	2.50	5.00	10.00
603	Come Back/You Don't Love Me	1966	2.50	5.00	10.00
604	Danger, She's a Stranger/Behind Curtains	1967	2.50	5.00	10.00
605	Ain't Gonna Rest (Till I Get You)/You Can't See	1967	2.50	5.00	10.00
607	Oooh, Baby Baby/The Girl I Love	1967	2.50	5.00	10.00
608	The Touch of You/Change of Face	1967	2.50	5.00	10.00

Albums

Number	Title (A Side/B Side)	Yr	VG	VG+	NM
BUDDAH					
BDS-5008	Our Family Portrait	1967	5.00	10.00	20.00
BDS-5061	Stairsteps	1970	3.75	7.50	15.00
—As "Stairsteps"					
BDS-5068	Step by Step by Step	1970	3.75	7.50	15.00
—As "Stairsteps"					
COLLECTABLES					
COL-5023	Greatest Hits	1985	2.50	5.00	10.00
CURTOM					
8002	Love's Happening	1969	5.00	10.00	20.00
WINDY C					
6000 [M]	The Five Stairsteps	1967	6.25	12.50	25.00
S-6000 [S]	The Five Stairsteps	1967	6.25	12.50	25.00

FIVE STARS, THE (1)

45s

Number	Title (A Side/B Side)	Yr	VG	VG+	NM
ABC-PARAMOUNT					
9911	Pickin' on the Wrong Chicken/Dreaming	1958	6.25	12.50	25.00
HUNT					
318	Pickin' on the Wrong Chicken/Dreaming	1959	5.00	10.00	20.00
NOTE					
10011	Pickin' on the Wrong Chicken/Dreaming	1958	7.50	15.00	30.00
10016	My Paradise/Friction	1958	10.00	20.00	40.00
10031	Am I Wasting My Time/Gamblin' Man	1959	7.50	15.00	30.00

FIVE STARS, THE (2)

45s

Number	Title (A Side/B Side)	Yr	VG	VG+	NM
SHOW TIME					
1102	Where Did Caledonia Go?/Walkin' An' Talkin'	1954	62.50	125.00	250.00

FIVE STARS, THE (U)

Many of these are probably group (1); the Treat release may be group (2).

45s

Number	Title (A Side/B Side)	Yr	VG	VG+	NM
ATCO					
6065	Take Five/Humpty Dump	1956	7.50	15.00	30.00
BLUES BOYS KINGDOM					
106	So Lonely, Baby/Hey Juanita	1957	50.00	100.00	200.00
COLUMBIA					
4-42056	Baby Baby/Blabber Mouth	1961	15.00	30.00	60.00
END					
1028	Baby Baby/Blabber Mouth	1958	20.00	40.00	80.00
KERNEL					
3195	Atom Bomb Baby/You Sweet Little Thing	1957	25.00	50.00	100.00
MARK-X					
7006	Dead Wrong/Ooh Shucks	1957	25.00	50.00	100.00
TREAT					
505	Let's Fall in Love/We Danced in the Moonlight	1955	500.00	1000.	2000.

FIVE SUPERIORS, THE

45s

Number	Title (A Side/B Side)	Yr	VG	VG+	NM
GARPAX					
44170	There's a Fool Born Every Day/Big Shot	1962	37.50	75.00	150.00

FIVE SWANS, THE

45s

Number	Title (A Side/B Side)	Yr	VG	VG+	NM
MUSIC CITY					
795	Little Girl of My Dreams/Little Tipa Tins	1956	75.00	150.00	300.00

FIVE THRILLS, THE

45s

Number	Title (A Side/B Side)	Yr	VG	VG+	NM
PARROT					
796	My Baby's Gone/Feel So Good	1954	200.00	400.00	800.00
800	Gloria/Wee Wee Baby	1954	1000.	1500.	2000.
—Black vinyl					
800	Gloria/Wee Wee Baby	1954	2000.	3000.	4000.
—Red vinyl					

FIVE TINOS, THE

45s

Number	Title (A Side/B Side)	Yr	VG	VG+	NM
SUN					
222	Sitting By My Window/Don't Do That	1955	300.00	600.00	1200.

FIVE TRUMPETS, THE

45s

Number	Title (A Side/B Side)	Yr	VG	VG+	NM
GOTHAM					
681	Stand By Me/Jesus Is Here Today	1951	15.00	30.00	60.00
693	My Chains Fell Off/The Lord Knows What I Need	1952	15.00	30.00	60.00
696	No Not One/A Hand I Can See	1952	15.00	30.00	60.00
RCA VICTOR					
50-0014	Oh Lord/Don't Let Nobody Turn You Around	1949	17.50	35.00	70.00
—Orange vinyl					
50-0034	Swing Low Sweet Chariot/Sign of the Judgment	1949	17.50	35.00	70.00
—Orange vinyl					
50-0080	When the Saints Go Marching In/Preach My Word	1950	17.50	35.00	70.00
—Orange vinyl					
SAVOY					
4060	Amazing Grace/Lord I Want to Be a Christian	1955	6.25	12.50	25.00
4072	I've Got Jesus/I Shall Not Be Moved	1956	6.25	12.50	25.00

FIVE WHISPERS, THE

45s

Number	Title (A Side/B Side)	Yr	VG	VG+	NM
DOLTON					
61	Awake or Asleep/Especially for You	1962	3.75	7.50	15.00
69	Awake of Asleep/Especially for You	1963	3.75	7.50	15.00
90	Can't Face the Crowd/Sleep Walker	1964	3.75	7.50	15.00

FIVE WILLOWS, THE

45s

Number	Title (A Side/B Side)	Yr	VG	VG+	NM
ALLEN					
1000	My Dear, Dearest Darling/Rock, Little Francis	1953	75.00	150.00	300.00
1002	Delores/All Night Long	1953	150.00	300.00	600.00
1003	The White Cliffs of Dover/With These Hands	1953	175.00	350.00	700.00
HERALD					
433	Baby Come a Little Closer/Lay Your Head on My Shoulder	1954	75.00	150.00	300.00
442	Look Me in the Eyes/So Help Me	1954	100.00	200.00	400.00
LOST-NITE					
174	My Dear, Dearest Darling/Rock, Little Francis	196?	—	3.00	6.00
183	Delores/All Night Long	196?	—	3.00	6.00
187	The White Cliffs of Dover/With These Hands	196?	—	3.00	6.00
—Lost-Nite records are reissues					
192	Love Bells/Please Baby	196?	—	3.00	6.00
PEE DEE					
290	Love Bells/Please, Baby	1953	375.00	750.00	1500.

FIVE WINGS, THE

45s

Number	Title (A Side/B Side)	Yr	VG	VG+	NM
KING					
4778	Johnny Has Gone/Johnny's Still Singing	1955	50.00	100.00	200.00
4781	Teardrops Are Falling/Rock-A-Locka	1955	100.00	200.00	400.00
—Later released on King 5199 as The Checkers.					

FLACK, ROBERTA

45s

Number	Title (A Side/B Side)	Yr	VG	VG+	NM
ANGEL					
S7-19773	The Christmas Song (Chestnuts Roasting on an Open Fire)/25th of Last December	1997	—	2.00	4.00
ATLANTIC					
2665	Compared to What/That's No Way to Say Goodbye	1969	2.00	4.00	8.00
2730	How Many Broken Wings/Baby Baby	1970	—	3.00	6.00
—With Les McCann					
2758	Reverend Lee/Business Goes On As Usual	1970	—	3.00	6.00
2785	Let It Be Me/Do What Cha Gotta Do	1971	—	3.00	6.00
2851	Will You Still Love Me Tomorrow/Go Up Moses	1972	—	2.50	5.00
2864	The First Time Ever I Saw Your Face/Trade Winds	1972	—	2.50	5.00
2940	Killing Me Softly with His Song/Just Like a Woman	1973	—	2.50	5.00
2982	Jesse/No Tears	1973	—	2.50	5.00
3025	Feel Like Makin' Love/When You Smile	1974	—	2.50	5.00
3203	Feel Like Makin' Love/When You Smile	1974	—	2.00	4.00
3271	Feelin' That Glow/Some Gospel According to Matthew	1975	—	2.00	4.00
3441	The 25th of Last December/Move In with Me	1977	—	2.00	4.00
3483	If Ever I See You Again/I'd Like to Be a Baby to You	1978	—	2.00	4.00
3521	When It's Over/Come Share My Love	1978	—	2.00	4.00
3560	You Are Everything/Knowing That We're Made for Each Other	1979	—	2.00	4.00
3627	You Are My Heaven/I'll Love You Forever and Ever	1979	—	2.00	4.00
3753	Don't Make Me Wait Too Long/Only Heaven Can Wait (For Love)	1980	—	2.00	4.00
4005	Making Love/Jesse	1982	—	2.00	4.00
4005 [PS]	Making Love/Jesse	1982	—	3.00	6.00
4068	I'm the One/'Til the Morning Comes	1982	—	2.00	4.00
87607	Set the Night to Music/Natural Thing	1991	—	2.00	4.00
—A-side: With Maxi Priest					
88898	Shock to My System/You Know What It's Like	1989	—	—	3.00
88941	Uh-Uh Ooh-Ooh Look Out (Here It Comes)/You Know What It's Like	1989	—	—	3.00
88941 [PS]	Uh-Uh Ooh-Ooh Look Out (Here It Comes)/You Know What It's Like	1989	—	—	3.00
88996	Oasis/You Know What It's Like	1988	—	—	3.00
88996 [PS]	Oasis/You Know What It's Like	1988	—	—	3.00
89295	We Shall Overcome/We Shall Overcome	1987	—	—	3.00
89440	Let Me Be a Light to Shine/We Shall Overcome	1986	—	—	3.00
—With Howard Hewett					
89931	Our Love Will Stop the World/Only Heaven Can Wait (For Love)	1982	—	2.00	4.00
—A-side: With Eric Mercury					
89932	In the Name of Love/Happiness	1982	—	2.00	4.00
COLUMBIA					
44050	Si, Si, Senor/This Year	1967	2.50	5.00	10.00
44448	Cold, Cold Winter/If You Ever Leave Me Now	1968	2.50	5.00	10.00
MCA					
51126	You Stopped Loving Me/Qual E Maundrinio	1981	—	2.00	4.00
51173	Lovin' You/Hittin' Me Where It Hurts	1981	—	2.00	4.00
VIVA					
29401	This Side of Forever/Robbery Suspects	1983	—	2.00	4.00
—B-side by The Enforcers					

Albums

Number	Title	Yr	VG	VG+	NM
ATLANTIC					
SD 1569	Chapter Two	1970	2.50	5.00	10.00
SD 1594	Quiet Fire	1971	2.50	5.00	10.00
SD 7271	Killing Me Softly	1973	2.50	5.00	10.00
SD 8230	First Take	1969	2.50	5.00	10.00
SD 16013	Roberta Flack Featuring Donny Hathaway	1980	2.50	5.00	10.00
—Only two tracks feature Mr. Hathaway					
SD 18131	Feel Like Makin' Love	1974	2.50	5.00	10.00
SD 19149	Blue Lights in the Basement	1977	2.50	5.00	10.00
SD 19154	Killing Me Softly	1978	2.00	4.00	8.00
—Reissue of 7271					
SD 19186	Roberta Flack	1978	2.50	5.00	10.00
SD 19317	The Best of Roberta Flack	1981	2.50	5.00	10.00
SD 19354	I'm the One	1982	2.50	5.00	10.00
81916	Oasis	1988	2.50	5.00	10.00
MCA					
5141	Bustin' Loose	1981	2.50	5.00	10.00

FLACK, ROBERTA, AND DONNY HATHAWAY

Also see each artist's individual listings.

45s

Number	Title (A Side/B Side)	Yr	VG	VG+	NM
ATLANTIC					
2808	You've Got a Friend/Gone Away	1971	—	2.50	5.00
2837	You've Lost That Lovin' Feeling/Be Real Black for Me	1971	—	2.50	5.00
2879	Where Is the Love/Mood	1972	—	2.50	5.00
3463	The Closer I Get to You/Love Is the Healing	1978	—	2.00	4.00
3661	Back Together Again/God Don't Like Ugly	1980	—	2.00	4.00

Albums

Number	Title	Yr	VG	VG+	NM
ATLANTIC					
SD 7216	Roberta Flack and Donny Hathaway	1972	2.50	5.00	10.00

FLAGG, BILL

45s

Number	Title (A Side/B Side)	Yr	VG	VG+	NM
MGM					
12637	Doin' My Time/I Will Always Love You	1958	25.00	50.00	100.00
TETRA					
4445	Go Cat, Go/A Good Woman's Leaving	1956	37.50	75.00	150.00
4448	Guitar Rock/(B-side unknown)	1957	37.50	75.00	150.00

FLAGG, FANNIE

Albums

Number	Title	Yr	VG	VG+	NM
RCA VICTOR					
LPM-3856 [M]	Rally 'Round the Flagg	1967	5.00	10.00	20.00
LSP-3856 [S]	Rally 'Round the Flagg	1967	3.75	7.50	15.00

FLAIRS, THE (1)

Also see CORNEL GUNTER; SHIRLEY GUNTER.

45s

Number	Title (A Side/B Side)	Yr	VG	VG+	NM
ABC-PARAMOUNT					
9740	Aladdin's Lamp/Steppin' Out	1956	10.00	20.00	40.00
FLAIR					
1012	I Had a Love/She Wants to Rock	1953	100.00	200.00	400.00
1019	Tell Me You Love Me/You Should Care for Me	1953	100.00	200.00	400.00
1028	Love Me Girl/Gettin' High	1954	100.00	200.00	400.00
1041	Baby Wants/You Were Untrue	1954	100.00	200.00	400.00
1044	This Is the Night for Love/Let's Make with Some Love	1954	100.00	200.00	400.00
1051	Love Me, Love Me, Love Me/My Heart's Crying for You	1954	100.00	200.00	400.00
—As "The Chimes"					
1056	I'll Never Let You Go/Hold Me, Thrill Me, Chill Me	1955	100.00	200.00	400.00
1067	She Loves to Dance/My Darling, My Sweet	1955	100.00	200.00	400.00

Albums

Number	Title	Yr	VG	VG+	NM
CROWN					
CLP-5356 [M]	The Flairs	1963	20.00	40.00	80.00

FLAIRS, THE (2)

For records on Epic, see THE REDWOODS.

FLAIRS, THE (3)

45s

Number	Title (A Side/B Side)	Yr	VG	VG+	NM
PALMS					
726	Roll Over Beethoven/Brazil	1961	12.50	25.00	50.00
—Reissued on Jamie under the name "The Velaires"					

FLAME, THE

With Rikki Fataar and Blondie Chaplin, who later spent time in THE BEACH BOYS. (Fataar also was with The Rutles in the studio.)

45s

Number	Title (A Side/B Side)	Yr	VG	VG+	NM
BROTHER					
3501	See the Light/Got Your Mind Made Up	1970	3.75	7.50	15.00
3502	Another Day Like Heaven/I'm So Happy	1970	3.75	7.50	15.00

Albums

Number	Title	Yr	VG	VG+	NM
BROTHER					
BR-2500	The Flame	1970	7.50	15.00	30.00
—Deduct 1/3 if poster is missing					

FLAMES, THE

More than one group. Also see THE HOLLYWOOD FLAMES.

45s

Number	Title (A Side/B Side)	Yr	VG	VG+	NM
HARLEM					
114	So Long My Darling/I'm Going to Try to Live My Life All Over	1960	1500.	2250.	3000.
—As "The Fabulous Flames"					
114	So Long My Darling/I'm Going to Try to Live My Life All Over	1960	200.00	400.00	800.00
—As "The Flames"					

FLAMIN' GROOVIES, THE

45s

Number	Title (A Side/B Side)	Yr	VG	VG+	NM
BOMP!					
101	You Tore Me Down/Him or Me (What's It Gonna Be?)	1975	2.00	4.00	8.00
EPIC					
10507	Rockin' Pneumonia & The Boogie Woogie Flu/The First One's Free	1969	2.50	5.00	10.00
10564	Somethin' Else/Laurie Did It	1969	2.50	5.00	10.00
KAMA SUTRA					
527	Have You Seen My Baby/Yesterday's Numbers	1971	2.50	5.00	10.00
RCA					
PB-11266	Too Many Cooks/Watch Me Run	1978	—	3.00	6.00
SIRE					
731	I Can't Hide/Teenage Confidential	1976	—	3.00	6.00

Albums

Number	Title	Yr	VG	VG+	NM
BUDDAH					
BDS-5683	Shill Shakin'	1977	3.75	7.50	15.00

Number	Title (A Side/B Side)	Yr	VG	VG+	NM
EPIC					
BN 26487	Supersnazz	1969	12.50	25.00	50.00
KAMA SUTRA					
KSBS-2021	Flamingo	1970	7.50	15.00	30.00
—Pink label					
KSBS-2021	Flamingo	1972	3.75	7.50	15.00
—Blue label					
KSBS-2031	Teenage Head	1971	7.50	15.00	30.00
—Pink label					
KSBS-2031	Teenage Head	1972	3.75	7.50	15.00
—Blue label					
SIRE					
SRK 6059	The Flamin' Groovies Now	1978	3.75	7.50	15.00
—Originals have 12 tracks					
SRK 6059	The Flamin' Groovies Now	1978	3.00	6.00	12.00
—Reissues have 14 tracks					
SRK 6067	Jumpin' in the Night	1979	3.00	6.00	12.00
SASD-7521	Shake Some Action	1976	3.75	7.50	15.00
SNAZZ					
R-2371 [10]	Sneekers	1969	25.00	50.00	100.00
—This album has been counterfeited					

FLAMING EMBER, THE

45s

Number	Title (A Side/B Side)	Yr	VG	VG+	NM
FORTUNE					
869	Gone, Gone, Gone/You Can Count on Me	1965	15.00	30.00	60.00
HOT WAX					
6902	Mind, Body and Soul/Filet de Soul	1969	—	3.00	6.00
6907	Shades of Green/Don't You Wanna Wanna	1969	—	3.00	6.00
7003	Westbound #9/Why Don't You Stay	1970	—	3.00	6.00
7006	I'm Not My Brothers Keeper/Deserted Village	1970	—	3.00	6.00
7010	Stop the World and Let Me Off/Robot in a Robot's World	1970	—	3.00	6.00
7103	Sunshine/1200 Miles	1971	—	3.00	6.00
7109	If It's Good to You (Part 1)/If It's Good to You (Part 2)	1971	—	3.00	6.00
RIC-TIC					
129	Let's Have a Love-In (Vocal)/Let's Have a Love-In (Instrumental)	1967	5.00	10.00	20.00
—B-side credited to Wingate's Love-In Strings					
131	She's a Real Live Wire/Let's Have a Love-In (Instrumental)	1967	5.00	10.00	20.00
—B-side credited to Wingate's Love-In Strings					
132	Hey Mama/Let's Have a Love-In	1967	5.00	10.00	20.00
140	Bless You (My Love) (Instrumental)/Bless You (My Love) (Vocal)	1968	3.75	7.50	15.00
—B-side by Al Kent					
143	Children (Vocal)/Children (Instrumental)	1968	3.75	7.50	15.00
145	Tell It Like It Is/Just Like Children	1968	3.75	7.50	15.00

Albums

Number	Title (A Side/B Side)	Yr	VG	VG+	NM
HOT WAX					
HA-702	Westbound #9	1970	3.75	7.50	15.00
HA-705	Sunshine	1971	3.75	7.50	15.00

FLAMING YOUTH

Phil Collins was in this group.

Albums

Number	Title (A Side/B Side)	Yr	VG	VG+	NM
UNI					
73075	Ark 2	1969	10.00	20.00	40.00

FLAMINGOS, THE

45s

Number	Title (A Side/B Side)	Yr	VG	VG+	NM
CHANCE					
1133	If I Can't Have You/Someday, Somehow	1953	200.00	400.00	800.00
—Black vinyl					
1133	If I Can't Have You/Someday, Somehow	1953	1000.	1500.	2000.
—Red vinyl					
1140	That's My Desire/Hurry Home Baby	1953	150.00	300.00	600.00
—Black vinyl					
1140	That's My Desire/Hurry Home Baby	1953	375.00	750.00	1500.
—Red vinyl					
1145	Golden Teardrops/Carried Away	1953	250.00	500.00	1000.
—Black vinyl					
1145	Golden Teardrops/Carried Away	1953	750.00	1500.	3000.
—Red vinyl					
1149	Plan for Love/You Ain't Ready	1953	500.00	1000.	2000.
—Yellow and black label					
1149	Plan for Love/You Ain't Ready	1953	200.00	400.00	800.00
—Blue and silver label					
1154	Cross Over the Bridge/Listen to My Plea	1954	250.00	500.00	1000.
1162	Jump Children/Blues in the Letter	1954	150.00	300.00	600.00
CHECKER					
815	That's My Baby (Chick-a-Boom)/When	1955	20.00	40.00	80.00
821	I Want to Love You/Please Come Back Home	1955	20.00	40.00	80.00
830	I'll Be Home/Need Your Love	1956	20.00	40.00	80.00
837	A Kiss from Your Lips/Get With It	1956	20.00	40.00	80.00
846	The Vow/Shilly Dilly	1956	20.00	40.00	80.00
853	Just for a Kick/Would I Be Crying	1957	20.00	40.00	80.00
—Originals of above Checker singles are maroon with a checkerboard at top of label					
915	Whispering Stars/Dream of a Lifetime	1959	12.50	25.00	50.00
1084	Lover Come Back to Me/Your Little Guy	1964	3.75	7.50	15.00
1091	Goodnight Sweetheart/Does It Really Matter	1964	3.75	7.50	15.00
DECCA					
30335	The Ladder of Love/Let's Make Up	1957	7.50	15.00	30.00
30454	Helpless/My Faith in You	1957	7.50	15.00	30.00
30687	Rock and Roll March/Where Mary Go	1958	7.50	15.00	30.00
30880	Kiss-A Me/Ever Since I Met Lucy	1959	7.50	15.00	30.00
30948	Jerri-Lee/Hey Now	1959	7.50	15.00	30.00
END					
1035	Please Wait for Me/That Love Is You	1958	15.00	30.00	60.00
1035	Lovers Never Say Goodbye/That Love Is You	1958	10.00	20.00	40.00
—A-sides of End 1035 are the same song, the titles were changed					
1040	I Shed a Tear at Your Wedding/But Not for Me	1959	7.50	15.00	30.00
1044	At the Prom/Love Walked In	1959	10.00	20.00	40.00
1046 [M]	I Only Have Eyes for You/Goodnight Sweetheart	1959	7.50	15.00	30.00
1046 [M]	I Only Have Eyes for You/At the Prom	1959	6.25	12.50	25.00
1046 [M]	I Only Have Eyes for You/Love Walked In	1959	6.25	12.50	25.00
1046 [S]	I Only Have Eyes for You/At the Prom	1959	12.50	25.00	50.00
—This B-side has been confirmed for the stereo version; others are not yet known					
1055 [M]	Yours/Love Walked In	1959	6.25	12.50	25.00
1055 [S]	Yours/Love Walked In	1959	12.50	25.00	50.00
1062	I Was Such a Fool/Heavenly Angel	1959	6.25	12.50	25.00
1065	Mio Amore/You, Me and the Sea	1960	6.25	12.50	25.00
1068	Nobody Loves Me Like You/Besame Mucho	1960	7.50	15.00	30.00
1068	Nobody Loves Me Like You/You, Me and the Sea	1960	6.25	12.50	25.00
1070	Besame Mucho/You, Me and the Sea	1960	6.25	12.50	25.00
1073	Mio Amore/At Night	1960	5.00	10.00	20.00
1079	Beside You/When I Fall in Love	1960	5.00	10.00	20.00
1081	Your Other Love/Lovers Gotta Cry	1960	5.00	10.00	20.00
1085	Thatr's Why I Love You/Ko Ko Mo	1961	5.00	10.00	20.00
1092	Time Was/Dream Girl	1961	5.00	10.00	20.00
1099	My Memories of You/I Want to Love You	1961	5.00	10.00	20.00
1111	It Must Be Love/I'm No Fool Anymore	1962	5.00	10.00	20.00
1116	For All We Know/Near You	1962	5.00	10.00	20.00
1121	I Know Better/Flame of Love	1963	5.00	10.00	20.00
1124	(Talk About) True Love/Come to My Party	1963	5.00	10.00	20.00
JULMAR					
506	Dealin' (Groovin' with Feelin')/Dealin' All the Way	1969	2.50	5.00	10.00
MERCURY					
72455	Temptation/Call Her on the Phone	1965	—	—	—
—Cancelled					
PARROT					
808	Dream of a Lifetime/On My Merry Way	1954	200.00	400.00	800.00
—Black vinyl					
808	Dream of a Lifetime/On My Merry Way	1954	400.00	800.00	1600.
—Red vinyl					
811	I Really Don't Want to Know/Get With It	1955	4000.	6000.	8000.
—Red vinyl					
811	I Really Don't Want to Know/Get With It	1955	2500.	2750.	5000.
—Black vinyl					
812	I'm Yours/Ko Ko Mo	1955	200.00	400.00	800.00
—Black vinyl					
812	I'm Yours/Ko Ko Mo	1955	400.00	800.00	1600.
—Red vinyl					
PHILIPS					
40308	Temptation/Call Her on the Phone	1965	3.75	7.50	15.00
40347	The Boogaloo Party/The Nearness of You	1965	3.75	7.50	15.00
40378	Brooklyn Boogaloo/Since My Baby Put Me Down	1966	3.75	7.50	15.00
40413	Itty Bitty Baby/She Shook My World	1966	3.75	7.50	15.00
40452	Koo Koo/It Keeps the Doctor Away	1967	3.75	7.50	15.00
40496	Oh Mary Don't You Worry/Do It, Do It	1967	3.75	7.50	15.00
POLYDOR					
14019	Buffalo Soldier (Long)/Buffalo Soldier (Short)	1970	2.50	5.00	10.00
14044	Straighten It Up (Get It Together)/Lover Come Back to Me	1970	2.50	5.00	10.00
RONZE					
111	Welcome Home/Gotta Have All Your Lovin'	1971	—	2.50	5.00
115	Someone to Watch Over Me/Heavy Hips	1972	—	2.50	5.00
116	Love Keeps the Doctor Away (Long)/Love Keeps the Doctor Away (Short)	1972	—	2.50	5.00
ROULETTE					
4524	Ol' Man River (Part 1)/Ol' Man River (Part 2)	1963	5.00	10.00	20.00
SKYLARK					
541	If I Could Love You/I Found a New Baby	197?	—	2.50	5.00
TIMES SQUARE					
102	A Lovely Way to Spend an Evening/Walking My Baby Back Home	1964	3.75	7.50	15.00
VEE JAY					
384	Golden Teardrops/Carried Away	1961	6.25	12.50	25.00
WORLDS					
103	Think About Me/(Instrumental)	1974	—	2.50	5.00

7-Inch Extended Plays

Number	Title (A Side/B Side)	Yr	VG	VG+	NM
END					
205	(contents unknown)	1959	50.00	100.00	200.00
205 [PS]	The Flamingos	1959	50.00	100.00	200.00

Albums

Number	Title (A Side/B Side)	Yr	VG	VG+	NM
CHECKER					
LP-1433 [M]	The Flamingos	1959	100.00	200.00	400.00
—Black label					
LP-1433 [M]	The Flamingos	196?	37.50	75.00	150.00
—Blue label					
LPS-3005 [R]	The Flamingos	1966	6.25	12.50	25.00
—Rechanneled reissue of 1433					
CONSTELLATION					
CS-3 [M]	Collectors Showcase: The Flamingos	1964	25.00	50.00	100.00
—With hot pink lettering on cover					
CS-3 [M]	Collectors Showcase: The Flamingos	1964	12.50	25.00	50.00
—With more restrained pink lettering on cover					
END					
LP-304 [M]	Flamingo Serenade	1959	50.00	100.00	200.00
—Gray label with dog					
LP-304 [M]	Flamingo Serenade	1959	100.00	200.00	400.00
—Black label with shadow print logo					
LPS-304 [S]	Flamingo Serenade	1959	125.00	250.00	500.00
—Cover says "Stereo"					
LPS-304 [S]	Flamingo Serenade	196?	50.00	100.00	200.00
—Cover says "Rechanneled Stereo" (only one track is)					
LP-307 [M]	Flamingo Favorites	1960	25.00	50.00	100.00
LPS-307 [R]	Flamingo Favorites	1960	17.50	35.00	70.00
LP-308 [M]	Requestfully Yours	1960	25.00	50.00	100.00
LPS-308 [R]	Requestfully Yours	1960	17.50	35.00	70.00
LP-316 [M]	The Sound of the Flamingos	1962	25.00	50.00	100.00
LPS-316 [R]	The Sound of the Flamingos	1962	17.50	35.00	70.00
LPS-316 [S]	The Sound of the Flamingos	1962	50.00	100.00	200.00
—"Stereo" at upper right corner of front cover					

Number	Title (A Side/B Side)	Yr	VG	VG+	NM
LOST-NITE					
LLP-7 [10]	The Flamingos	1981	2.50	5.00	10.00
—Red vinyl					
PHILIPS					
PHM 200206 [M]	Their Hits — Then and Now	1966	6.25	12.50	25.00
PHS 600206 [S]	Their Hits — Then and Now	1966	7.50	15.00	30.00
RONZE					
RLP-1001	The Flamingos Today	1972	3.75	7.50	15.00
SOLID SMOKE					
8018	Golden Teardrops	198?	2.50	5.00	10.00

FLAMINGOS, THE, AND THE MOONGLOWS

Number	Title (A Side/B Side)	Yr	VG	VG+	NM
Albums					
VEE JAY					
LP-1052 [M]	The Flamingos Meet the Moonglows on the Dusty Road of Hits	1962	37.50	75.00	150.00
VJLP-1052 [M]	The Flamingos Meet the Moonglows on the Dusty Road of Hits	198?	3.00	6.00	12.00
—Authorized reissue					

FLARES, THE

Number	Title (A Side/B Side)	Yr	VG	VG+	NM
45s					
FELSTED					
8604	Loving You/Hotcha Cha-Cha Brown	1960	5.00	10.00	20.00
8607	What Do You Want If You Don't Want Love/Jump and Hump	1960	5.00	10.00	20.00
8624	Foot Stomping — Part 1/Foot Stomping — Part 2	1961	5.00	10.00	20.00
PRESS					
2800	Rock and Roll Heaven — Part 1/Rock and Roll Heaven — Part 2	1962	3.75	7.50	15.00
2802	Doing the Hully Gully/Truck and Trailer	1962	3.75	7.50	15.00
2803	Madhouse/Make It Be Me	1962	3.75	7.50	15.00
2807	Do It with Me/Yon He Go	1963	3.75	7.50	15.00
2808	Hand Clappin'/Shimmy and Stomp	1963	3.75	7.50	15.00
2810	Monkey Walk/Do It If You Wanna	1963	3.75	7.50	15.00
2814	I Didn't Lose a Doggone Thing/Write a Song About Me	1964	3.75	7.50	15.00
Albums					
PRESS					
PR 73001 [M]	Encore of Foot Stompin' Hits	196?	20.00	40.00	80.00
PRS 83001 [S]	Encore of Foot Stompin' Hits	196?	30.00	60.00	120.00

FLASH

Number	Title (A Side/B Side)	Yr	VG	VG+	NM
45s					
CAPITOL					
3345	Small Beginnings/Morning Haze	1972	—	2.50	5.00
Albums					
SOVEREIGN/CAPITOL					
SMAS-11040	Flash	1972	3.00	6.00	12.00
SMAS-11115	Flash in the Can	1972	3.00	6.00	12.00
SMAS-11218	Out of Our Hands	1973	3.00	6.00	12.00

FLASH CADILLAC AND THE CONTINENTAL KIDS

Number	Title (A Side/B Side)	Yr	VG	VG+	NM
45s					
EPIC					
10930	Muleskinner Blues/Teenage Eyes	1972	—	2.50	5.00
11043	At the Hop/She's So Fine	1973	—	2.50	5.00
11102	The Way I Feel Tonight/Dancin'	1974	—	2.50	5.00
PRIVATE STOCK					
45006	Good Times, Rock and Roll/It's Hard	1974	—	2.00	4.00
45026	Hot Summer Girls/Time Will Tell	1975	—	2.00	4.00
45079	Did You Boogie (With Your Baby)/Maybe It's All in My Mind	1976	—	2.00	4.00
45134	See My Baby Jive/Brown Water	1977	—	2.00	4.00
Albums					
EPIC					
KE 31787	Flash Cadillac and the Continental Kids	1972	3.75	7.50	15.00
—Yellow label					
KE 31787	Flash Cadillac and the Continental Kids	1973	3.00	6.00	12.00
—Orange label					
KE 32488	There's No Face Like Chrome	1974	3.00	6.00	12.00
PRIVATE STOCK					
PS 2003	Sons of Beaches	1975	3.00	6.00	12.00

FLAT EARTH SOCIETY, THE

Number	Title (A Side/B Side)	Yr	VG	VG+	NM
Albums					
FLEETWOOD					
3027	Waleeco	1968	75.00	150.00	300.00

FLATT AND SCRUGGS

Also includes records credited to "Lester Flatt and Earl Scruggs."

Number	Title (A Side/B Side)	Yr	VG	VG+	NM
45s					
COLUMBIA					
20777	Come Back Darling/I'm Waiting to Hear You Call Me Darling	1951	5.00	10.00	20.00
20805	We Can't Be Darlings/I'm Head Over Heels in Love	1951	5.00	10.00	20.00
20830	Jimmy Brown the Newsboy/Somehow Tonight	1951	5.00	10.00	20.00
20854	Don't Get Above Your Raisin'/I've Lost You	1951	5.00	10.00	20.00
20886	'Tis Sweet to Be Remembered/Earl's Breakdown	1952	5.00	10.00	20.00
20915	Brother I'm Getting Ready to Go/Get in Line Brother	1952	5.00	10.00	20.00
20957	I'll Stay Around/Old Home Town	1952	5.00	10.00	20.00
21002	Over the Hills to the Poorhouse/My Darling's Last Goodbye	1952	5.00	10.00	20.00
21043	I'm Gonna Settle Down/I'm Lonesome and Blue	1952	5.00	10.00	20.00
21054	Dim Lights Thick Smoke/Flint Hill Special	1952	5.00	10.00	20.00
21091	Why Did You Wander/Thinking About You	1953	5.00	10.00	20.00
21125	Dear Old Dixie/If I Should Wander Back	1953	5.00	10.00	20.00
21147	I'm Workin' on a Road/He Took Your Place	1953	5.00	10.00	20.00
21179	Foggy Mountain Chimes/I'll Go Steppin' Too	1953	5.00	10.00	20.00
21209	Be Ready/Mother Prays Loud	1954	5.00	10.00	20.00
21248	Somebody Took My Place with You/I'd Rather Be Alone	1954	5.00	10.00	20.00
21295	Foggy Mountain Breakdown/You're Not a Drop in the Bucket	1954	5.00	10.00	20.00
21334	Till the End of the World Rolls Around/Don't This Road Look Rough	1954	5.00	10.00	20.00
21370	You Can Feel It in Your Soul/Old Fashioned Preacher	1955	3.75	7.50	15.00
21412	I'm Gonna Sleep with One Eye Open/Before I Met You	1955	3.75	7.50	15.00
21460	Gone Home/Bubbling in My Soul	1955	3.75	7.50	15.00
21501	Randy Lynn Rag/On My Mind	1956	3.75	7.50	15.00
21536	Joy Bells/Give Mother My Crown	1956	3.75	7.50	15.00
21561	No Doubt About It/What's Good for You	1956	3.75	7.50	15.00
30904 [S]	(contents unknown)	1960	3.75	7.50	15.00
30905 [S]	(contents unknown)	1960	3.75	7.50	15.00
30906 [S]	(contents unknown)	1960	3.75	7.50	15.00
30907 [S]	(contents unknown)	1960	3.75	7.50	15.00
30908 [S]	(contents unknown)	1960	3.75	7.50	15.00
—Anyone who can fill in these gaps -- the above five all are Columbia "Stereo 7" singles -- please let us know.					
40853	Shuckin' the Corn/Six White Horses	1957	3.75	7.50	15.00
40928	Give Me Flowers While I'm Living/Is There Room for Me?	1957	3.75	7.50	15.00
41064	A Hundred Years from Now/I Won't Be Hanging Around	1957	3.75	7.50	15.00
41125	Bog Black Train/Crying Alone	1958	3.00	6.00	12.00
41184	Building on Sand/Heaven	1958	3.00	6.00	12.00
41244	Mama's and Daddy's Little Girl/I Don't Care Anymore	1958	3.00	6.00	12.00
41336	A Million Years in Glory/Jesus Savior, Pilot Me	1959	3.00	6.00	12.00
41389	Cabin in the Hills/Someone You Have Forgotten	1959	3.00	6.00	12.00
41518	Crying My Heart Out Over You/Foggy Mountain Rock	1959	3.00	6.00	12.00
41708	The Great Historical Bum/All I Want Is You	1960	2.50	5.00	10.00
41786	Polka on a Banjo/Shuckin' the Corn	1960	2.50	5.00	10.00
41983	I Ain't Going to Work Tomorrow/I Should Wander Back Tonight	1961	2.50	5.00	10.00
42141	Go Home/Where Will I Shelter My Sheep	1961	2.50	5.00	10.00
42280	Just Ain't/Cold, Cold Loving	1962	2.50	5.00	10.00
42413	The Legend of the Johnson Boys/Hear the Whistle Blow a Hundred Miles	1962	2.50	5.00	10.00
42606	The Ballad of Jed Clampett/Coal Loadin' Johnny	1962	3.75	7.50	15.00
42606 [PS]	The Ballad of Jed Clampett/Coal Loadin' Johnny	1962	5.00	10.00	20.00
42755	Pearl Pearl Pearl/Hard Travelin'	1963	3.00	6.00	12.00
42755 [PS]	Pearl Pearl Pearl/Hard Travelin'	1963	3.75	7.50	15.00
42840	New York Town/Mama Don't Allow It	1963	2.00	4.00	8.00
42954	You Are My Flower/My Saro Jane	1964	2.00	4.00	8.00
42982	Petticoat Junction/Have You Seen My Dear Companion	1964	3.00	6.00	12.00
43080	Workin' It Out/Fireball	1964	2.00	4.00	8.00
43135	Sally Don't You Grieve/Little Birdie	1964	2.00	4.00	8.00
43204	I Still Miss Someone/Father's Table Grace	1964	2.00	4.00	8.00
43259	Rock Salt and Nails/Gonna Have Myself a Ball	1965	2.00	4.00	8.00
43412	Memphis/Foggy Mountain Breakdown	1965	2.00	4.00	8.00
43497	Green Acres/I Had a Dream	1965	3.00	6.00	12.00
—With June Carter					
43627	For Lovin' Me/Colours	1966	2.00	4.00	8.00
43803	The Last Thing on My Mind/Mama You Been on My Mind	1966	2.00	4.00	8.00
43973	It Was Only the Wind/Why Can't I Find Myself with You	1967	—	3.00	6.00
44040	Nashville Cats/Roust-A-Bout	1967	—	3.00	6.00
44194	California Up Tight Band/Last Train to Clarksville	1967	—	3.00	6.00
44194 [PS]	California Up Tight Band/Last Train to Clarksville	1967	2.50	5.00	10.00
44380	Foggy Mountain Breakdown/Down in the Flood	1967	2.00	4.00	8.00
44380 [PS]	Foggy Mountain Breakdown/Down in the Flood	1967	2.50	5.00	10.00
44623	Like a Rolling Stone/I'd Like to Say a Word About Texas	1968	—	3.00	6.00
45030	Maggie's Farm/Tonight We'll Be Fine	1969	—	3.00	6.00
MERCURY					
6161	God Loves His Children/I'm Going to Make Heaven My Home	1950	6.25	12.50	25.00
—Note: Earlier Mercury 45s by Flatt and Scruggs may exist					
6211	Down the Road/Why Don't You Tell Me So	1950	6.25	12.50	25.00
6268	Is It Too Late Now/So Happy I'll Be	1950	6.25	12.50	25.00
6287	I'll Never Love Another/My Little Girl in Tennessee	1950	6.25	12.50	25.00
6302	That Little Old Country Church House/Cora Is Gone	1951	5.00	10.00	20.00
6317	Pain in My Heart/Take Me in a Lifeboat	1951	5.00	10.00	20.00
6333	Doin' My Time/Farewell Blues	1951	5.00	10.00	20.00
6372	Roll in My Sweet Baby's Arms/I'll Just Pretend	1952	5.00	10.00	20.00
6396	Pike County Breakdown/Old Salty Dog Blues	1952	5.00	10.00	20.00
70016	Preachin', Prayin', Singin'/Will Roses Bloom	1952	5.00	10.00	20.00
70064	God Loves His Children/Back to the Cross	1953	5.00	10.00	20.00
72739	Foggy Mountain Breakdown (Theme from Bonnie & Clyde)/My Cabin in Caroline	1967	2.00	4.00	8.00
72739 [PS]	Foggy Mountain Breakdown (Theme from Bonnie & Clyde)/My Cabin in Caroline	1967	2.50	5.00	10.00
7-Inch Extended Plays					
COLUMBIA					
B-2823	Jimmy Brown, The Newsboy/Mother Prays Loud in Her Sleep//I'll Go Stepping Too/Randy Lynn Rag	195?	5.00	10.00	20.00
B-2823 [PS]	(title unknown)	195?	5.00	10.00	20.00
Albums					
ARCHIVE OF FOLK AND JAZZ					
259	Lester Flatt & Earl Scruggs	197?	2.50	5.00	10.00
COLUMBIA					
GP 30 [(2)]	20 All-Time Great Recordings	1970	5.00	10.00	20.00
CL 1019 [M]	Foggy Mountain Jamboree	1957	12.50	25.00	50.00
CL 1424 [M]	Songs of Glory	1960	5.00	10.00	20.00
CL 1564 [M]	Foggy Mountain Banjo	1961	5.00	10.00	20.00
CL 1664 [M]	Songs of the Famous Carter Family	1961	5.00	10.00	20.00

Number	Title (A Side/B Side)	Yr	VG	VG+	NM
CL 1830 [M]	Folk Songs of Our Land	1962	5.00	10.00	20.00
CL 1951 [M]	Hard Travelin' Featuring The Ballad of Jed Clampett	1963	5.00	10.00	20.00
CL 2045 [M]	Flatt and Scruggs at Carnegie Hall	1963	5.00	10.00	20.00
CL 2134 [M]	Recorded Live at Vanderbilt University	1964	5.00	10.00	20.00
CL 2255 [M]	The Fabulous Sound of Flatt & Scruggs	1964	5.00	10.00	20.00
CL 2354 [M]	Pickin' Strummin' and Singin'	1965	3.75	7.50	15.00
CL 2443 [M]	Town and Country	1966	3.75	7.50	15.00
CL 2513 [M]	When the Saints Go Marching In	1966	3.75	7.50	15.00
CL 2570 [M]	Flatt and Scruggs' Greatest Hits	1966	3.75	7.50	15.00
CL 2643 [M]	Strictly Instrumental	1967	5.00	10.00	20.00
CL 2686 [M]	Hear the Whistle Blow	1967	5.00	10.00	20.00
CS 8221 [S]	Songs of Glory	1960	6.25	12.50	25.00
CS 8364 [S]	Foggy Mountain Banjo	1961	6.25	12.50	25.00
CS 8464 [S]	Songs of the Famous Carter Family	1961	6.25	12.50	25.00
CS 8630 [S]	Folk Songs of Our Land	1962	6.25	12.50	25.00
CS 8751 [S]	Hard Travelin' Featuring The Ballad of Jed Clampett	1963	6.25	12.50	25.00
CS 8845 [S]	Flatt and Scruggs at Carnegie Hall	1963	6.25	12.50	25.00
PC 8845	Flatt and Scruggs at Carnegie Hall	198?	2.00	4.00	8.00
—Budget-line reissue					
CS 8934 [S]	Recorded Live at Vanderbilt University	1964	6.25	12.50	25.00
CS 9055 [S]	The Fabulous Sound of Flatt & Scruggs	1964	6.25	12.50	25.00
CS 9154 [S]	Pickin' Strummin' and Singin'	1965	5.00	10.00	20.00
CS 9243 [S]	Town and Country	1966	5.00	10.00	20.00
CS 9313 [S]	When the Saints Go Marching In	1966	5.00	10.00	20.00
CS 9370 [S]	Flatt and Scruggs' Greatest Hits	1966	5.00	10.00	20.00
PC 9370	Flatt and Scruggs' Greatest Hits	198?	2.00	4.00	8.00
—Budget-line reissue					
CS 9443 [S]	Strictly Instrumental	1967	5.00	10.00	20.00
CS 9486 [S]	Hear the Whistle Blow	1967	5.00	10.00	20.00
CS 9596	Changin' Times Featuring Foggy Mountain Breakdown	1968	5.00	10.00	20.00
CS 9649	The Story of Bonnie & Clyde	1968	5.00	10.00	20.00
CS 9741	Nashville Airplane	1969	5.00	10.00	20.00
CS 9945	Final Fling	1970	3.75	7.50	15.00
LE 10149	Breaking Out	197?	2.50	5.00	10.00
—Brown label "Limited Edition"					
C 30347	Breaking Out	1971	3.00	6.00	12.00
CG 31964 [(2)]	The World of Flatt and Scruggs	1972	3.75	7.50	15.00
C 32244	A Boy Named Sue	1973	3.00	6.00	12.00
FC 37469	Lester Flatt & Earl Scruggs	1981	2.50	5.00	10.00
COLUMBIA MUSICAL TREASURY					
DS 493	Detroit City	1969	3.75	7.50	15.00
COUNTY					
CCS-111	You Can Feel It in Your Soul	1988	2.50	5.00	10.00
HARMONY					
HL 7250 [M]	Lester Flatt & Earl Scruggs	1960	3.75	7.50	15.00
HL 7340 [M]	Great Original Recordings	1965	3.75	7.50	15.00
HL 7402 [M]	Sacred Songs	1967	3.75	7.50	15.00
HL 7465 [M]	Songs to Cherish	1968	3.75	7.50	15.00
HS 11202 [S]	Sacred Songs	1967	3.00	6.00	12.00
HS 11265 [S]	Songs to Cherish	1968	3.00	6.00	12.00
HS 11401	Foggy Mountain Chimes	1970	3.00	6.00	12.00
MERCURY					
MG-20358 [M]	Country Music	1958	10.00	20.00	40.00
MG-20542 [M]	Lester Flatt & Earl Scruggs	1959	10.00	20.00	40.00
MG-20773 [M]	The Original Sound of Flatt & Scruggs	1963	6.25	12.50	25.00
SR-60773 [R]	The Original Sound of Flatt & Scruggs	1963	3.75	7.50	15.00
SR-61162	Original Theme from Bonnie & Clyde	1968	5.00	10.00	20.00
NASHVILLE					
2087	The Best of Flatt and Scruggs	1970	3.00	6.00	12.00
PICKWICK					
6093	Foggy Mountain Breakdown	197?	3.00	6.00	12.00
6140	Blue Grass Banjos	197?	2.50	5.00	10.00
POWER PAK					
297	Golden Hits	197?	2.50	5.00	10.00
ROUNDER					
SS-5	The Golden Era	198?	2.50	5.00	10.00
SS-8	Don't Get Above Your Raisin'	198?	2.50	5.00	10.00
SS-18	The Mercury Sessions, Volume 1	1985	2.50	5.00	10.00
SS-19	The Mercury Sessions, Volume 2	1985	2.50	5.00	10.00
STARDAY					
SLP-365 [M]	Stars of the Grand Ol' Opry	1966	6.25	12.50	25.00
—With Jim and Jesse					
WING					
SRW-16376	The Original Foggy Mountain Breakdown	1968	3.00	6.00	12.00

FLEAS, THE

All-star studio group supposedly with DAVE BURGESS, GLEN CAMPBELL, JERRY FULLER and RICK NELSON!

45s

Number	Title (A Side/B Side)	Yr	VG	VG+	NM
CHALLENGE					
9115	Scratchin'/Tears	1961	10.00	20.00	40.00

FLEETWOOD MAC

Also see BUCKINGHAM NICKS; PETER GREEN; CHRISTINE McVIE; JEREMY SPENCER.

12-Inch Singles

Number	Title (A Side/B Side)	Yr	VG	VG+	NM
WARNER BROS.					
PRO-A-652 [DJ]	Go Your Own Way/Silver Springs	1977	3.75	7.50	15.00
PRO-A-831 [DJ]	Tusk/Never Make Me Cry	1979	3.00	6.00	12.00
PRO-A-845 [DJ]	Sara (Edit) (same on both sides)	1979	2.50	5.00	10.00
PRO-A-853 [DJ]	Think About Me (Remix)/Save Me a Place	1980	5.00	10.00	20.00
PRO-A-932 [DJ]	Fireflies (Remix Long Version)(Remix Edit)	1981	3.00	6.00	12.00
PRO-A-1040 [DJ]	Hold Me (same on both sides)	1982	2.50	5.00	10.00
PRO-A-2688 [DJ]	Big Love (same on both sides)	1987	—	3.00	6.00
PRO-A-2723 [DJ]	Big Love (Extended Remix)/(Remix Edit)	1987	2.50	5.00	10.00
PRO-A-2728 [DJ]	Tango in the Night (same on both sides)	1987	2.50	5.00	10.00
PRO-A-2773 [DJ]	Isn't It Midnight (same on both sides)	1987	2.50	5.00	10.00
PRO-A-2884 [DJ]	Everywhere (same on both sides)	1987	—	3.00	6.00
20683	Big Love (Extended Remix)/(House on the Hill Dub)//(Piano Dub)/You and I, Part I	1987	2.50	5.00	10.00
—Despite label, "You and I, Part I" is actually "You and I, Part II"					
20746	Seven Wonders (Extended Version)//(Dub)/Book of Miracles	1987	2.50	5.00	10.00
20761	Little Lies (Extended Version)//(Dub)/Ricky	1987	2.50	5.00	10.00
20842	Family Man (Extended Vocal Remix)/(I'm a Jazz Man Dub)//(Extended Guitar Remix)/Family Party (Bonus Beats)/Down Endless Street	1988	2.50	5.00	10.00

45s

Number	Title (A Side/B Side)	Yr	VG	VG+	NM
BLUE HORIZON					
304	Hungry Country Woman/Walkin'	1970	3.00	6.00	12.00
—A-side by Otis Spann with Fleetwood Mac; B-side by Otis Spann					
DJM					
1007	Man of the World/Best Girl in the World	1976	—	3.00	6.00
—B-side by Danny Kirwan					
EPIC					
10351	Black Magic Woman/Long Grey Mare	1968	3.75	7.50	15.00
10368	Stop Messin' Around/Need Your Love So Bad	1968	3.00	6.00	12.00
10436	Albatross/Jigsaw Puzzle Blues	1969	3.00	6.00	12.00
11029	Albatross/Black Magic Woman	1973	2.00	4.00	8.00
REPRISE					
GRE 0119	Rhiannon (Will You Ever Win)/Over My Head	1978	—	—	3.00
—"Back to Back Hits" series					
0860	Rattlesnake Shake/Coming Your Way	1969	5.00	10.00	20.00
0860 [DJ]	Rattlesnake Shake/Coming Your Way	1969	2.50	5.00	10.00
0883	Oh Well, Part 1/Oh Well, Part 2	1970	4.00	8.00	16.00
0883 [DJ]	Oh Well, Part 1/Oh Well, Part 2	1970	2.50	5.00	10.00
0925	The Green Manalishi (With the Two-Prong Crown)/World In Harmony	1970	4.00	8.00	16.00
0925 [DJ]	The Green Manalishi (With the Two-Prong Crown)/World In Harmony	1970	2.50	5.00	10.00
0984	Jewel-Eyed Judy/Station Man	1971	4.00	8.00	16.00
0984 [DJ]	Jewel-Eyed Judy/Station Man	1971	2.50	5.00	10.00
1057	Sands of Time/Lay It All Down	1971	2.00	4.00	8.00
1077	Oh Well, Part 1/The Green Manalishi (With the Two-Prong Crown)	1971	—	2.50	5.00
—"Back to Back Hits" reissue					
1093	Sentimental Lady/Sunny Side of Heaven	1972	2.00	4.00	8.00
1159	Remember Me/Dissatisfied	1973	—	3.00	6.00
1172	Did You Ever Love Me/Revelation	1973	—	3.00	6.00
1188	For Your Love/Hypnotized	1973	—	3.00	6.00
1188 [DJ]	For Your Love (Long)/For Your Love (Short)	1973	2.50	5.00	10.00
1317	Heroes Are Hard to Find/Born Enchanter	1974	—	3.00	6.00
1339	Over My Head/I'm So Afraid	1975	—	2.00	4.00
1345	Rhiannon (Will You Ever Win)/Sugar Daddy	1976	—	2.00	4.00
1356	Say You Love Me (Edited)/Monday Morning	1976	—	2.00	4.00
—The A-sides of Reprise 1339, 1345 and 1356 feature significantly different mixes than those on their parent album, "Fleetwood Mac."					
17300	Silver Springs/Go Your Own Way	1997	—	—	2.50
17300 [PS]	Silver Springs/Go Your Own Way	1997	—	—	2.50
WARNER BROS.					
GWB 0348	Go Your Own Way/Dreams	1979	—	—	3.00
—"Back to Back Hits" series					
GWB 0388	Tusk/Sara	1981	—	—	3.00
—"Back to Back Hits" series					
GWB 0439	Hold Me/Gypsy	1984	—	—	3.00
—"Back to Back Hits" series					
8304	Go Your Own Way/Silver Springs	1976	2.00	4.00	8.00
—Sought-after because of its non-LP B-side					
8371	Dreams/Songbird	1977	—	2.00	4.00
8413	Don't Stop/Never Going Back Again	1977	—	2.00	4.00
8413 [PS]	Don't Stop/Never Going Back Again	1977	—	2.50	5.00
8483	You Make Loving Fun/Gold Dust Woman	1977	—	2.00	4.00
18661	Paper Doll/The Chain	1993	—	2.00	4.00
19537	Hard Feelings/Freedom	1990	—	3.00	6.00
19866	Save Me/Another Woman	1990	—	2.00	4.00
19867	Skies the Limit/The Second Time	1990	—	2.00	4.00
21888	Little Lies/Everywhere	1989	—	—	3.00
—"Back to Back Hits" series					
21943	Big Love/Seven Wonders	1988	—	—	3.00
—"Back to Back Hits" series					
21990	Don't Stop/Silver Springs	1988	—	—	3.00
—"Back to Back Hits" series					
21991	You Make Loving Fun/Say You Love Me	1988	—	—	3.00
—"Back to Back Hits" series					
27644	As Long As You Follow/Oh Well (Live)	1988	—	—	3.00
27644 [PS]	As Long As You Follow/Oh Well (Live)	1988	—	—	3.00
28114	Family Man/Down Endless Street	1988	—	—	3.00
28114 [PS]	Family Man/Down Endless Street	1988	—	—	3.00
28143	Everywhere/When I See You Again	1987	—	—	3.00
28143 [PS]	Everywhere/When I See You Again	1987	—	—	3.00
28291	Little Lies/Ricky	1987	—	—	3.00
28291 [PS]	Little Lies/Ricky	1987	—	—	3.00
28317	Seven Wonders/Book of Miracles	1987	—	—	3.00
28317 [PS]	Seven Wonders/Book of Miracles	1987	—	—	3.00
28398	Big Love/You and I, Part 1	1987	—	—	3.00
28398 [PS]	Big Love/You and I, Part 1	1987	—	—	3.00
29698	Oh Diane/That's Alright	1983	—	—	3.00
29848	Love in Store/Can't Go Back	1983	—	—	3.00
29918	Gypsy/Cool Water	1982	—	—	3.00
29918 [PS]	Gypsy/Cool Water	1982	—	—	3.00
29966	Hold Me/Eyes of the World	1982	—	—	3.00
29966 [PS]	Hold Me/Eyes of the World	1982	—	—	3.00
49077	Tusk/Never Make Me Cry	1979	—	2.00	4.00
49077 [PS]	Tusk/Never Make Me Cry	1979	—	2.50	5.00
—Version 1: Brown print, small dog photo					
49077 [PS]	Tusk/Never Make Me Cry	1979	—	2.00	4.00
—Version 2: Black print, large dog photo					
49150	Sara/That's Enough for Me	1979	—	2.00	4.00
49150 [PS]	Sara/That's Enough for Me	1979	—	3.00	6.00
49196	Think About Me/Save Me a Place	1980	—	2.00	4.00
49196 [PS]	Think About Me/Save Me a Place	1980	—	3.00	6.00
49500	Sisters of the Moon/Walk a Thin Line	1980	2.50	5.00	10.00
—Scarce on stock copy; A-side is a different mix than the LP version					
49660	Fireflies/Over My Head (Live)	1981	—	2.00	4.00
49660 [PS]	Fireflies/Over My Head (Live)	1981	—	2.00	4.00
49700	The Farmer's Daughter/Monday Morning (Live)	1982	—	3.00	6.00

Number	Title (A Side/B Side)	Yr	VG	VG+	NM
49700 [PS]	The Farmer's Daughter/Monday Morning (Live)	1982	—	3.00	6.00
Albums					
BLUE HORIZON					
BH-3801 [(2)]	Fleetwood Mac in Chicago	1970	7.50	15.00	30.00
BH-4802	Blues Jam in Chicago, Vol. 1	1970	3.75	7.50	15.00
BH-4803	Blues Jam in Chicago, Vol. 2	1970	3.75	7.50	15.00
EPIC					
LN 24402 [M]	Fleetwood Mac	1968	25.00	50.00	100.00
—White label promo only					
LN 24446 [M]	English Rose	1969	25.00	50.00	100.00
—White label promo only					
BN 26402 [S]	Fleetwood Mac	1968	7.50	15.00	30.00
BN 26406 [S]	English Rose	1969	7.50	15.00	30.00
KE 30632 [(2)]	Black Magic Woman	1971	5.00	10.00	20.00
KE 33740 [(2)]	Fleetwood Mac/English Rose	1974	3.75	7.50	15.00
MOBILE FIDELITY					
1-012	Fleetwood Mac	1980	10.00	20.00	40.00
—Audiophile vinyl					
1-119	Mirage	1984	10.00	20.00	40.00
—Audiophile vinyl					
NAUTILUS					
NR-8	Rumours	1980	10.00	20.00	40.00
—Audiophile vinyl					
REPRISE					
MS 2080	Bare Trees	1972	3.75	7.50	15.00
MS 2138	Penguin	1973	3.75	7.50	15.00
MS 2158	Mystery to Me	1973	5.00	10.00	20.00
—With "Good Things Come to Those Who Wait"					
MS 2158	Mystery to Me	1973	3.00	6.00	12.00
—With the above track replaced by "For Your Love"					
MS 2196	Heroes Are Hard to Find	1974	3.00	6.00	12.00
MS 2225	Fleetwood Mac	1975	2.50	5.00	10.00
MSK 2278	Bare Trees	1977	2.00	4.00	8.00
MSK 2279	Mystery to Me	1977	2.00	4.00	8.00
MSK 2281	Fleetwood Mac	1977	2.00	4.00	8.00
RS 6368	Then Play On	1969	5.00	10.00	20.00
—First pressings have "When You Say" and "My Dream."					
RS 6368	Then Play On	1970	3.75	7.50	15.00
—Later pressings replace above two tracks with "Oh Well (Parts 1 and 2)."					
RS 6408	Kiln House	1970	3.75	7.50	15.00
RS 6465	Future Games	1971	6.25	12.50	25.00
—Originals have a pale yellow cover					
RS 6465	Future Games	1972	3.75	7.50	15.00
—Later pressings have a pale green cover					
SIRE					
SASH-3706 [(2)]	Vintage Years	1975	3.75	7.50	15.00
SASH-3715 [(2)]	Fleetwood Mac in Chicago	1975	3.75	7.50	15.00
—Reissue of Blue Horizon 3801					
2XS-6006 [(2)]	Vintage Years	1977	3.00	6.00	12.00
2XS-6009 [(2)]	Fleetwood Mac in Chicago	1977	3.00	6.00	12.00
2XS-6045 [(2)]	The Original Fleetwood Mac	1977	3.00	6.00	12.00
VARRICK					
VR-020	Jumping at Shadows	1985	3.00	6.00	12.00
WARNER BROS.					
PRO-A-866 [DJ]	Tusk Remix	1979	5.00	10.00	20.00
—Promo-only EP					
BSK 3010	Rumours	1977	2.50	5.00	10.00
—With short version (2:02) of "Never Going Back Again"					
BSK 3010	Rumours	1977	2.00	4.00	8.00
—With long version (2:16) of "Never Going Back Again"					
2HS 3350 [(2)]	Tusk	1979	3.75	7.50	15.00
2WB 3500 [(2)]	Fleetwood Mac Live	1980	3.00	6.00	12.00
23607	Mirage	1982	2.50	5.00	10.00
23607 [DJ]	Mirage	1982	5.00	10.00	20.00
—Promo on Quiex II vinyl					
25471	Tango in the Night	1987	2.50	5.00	10.00
25801	Greatest Hits	1989	2.50	5.00	10.00
26111	Behind the Mask	1990	3.75	7.50	15.00

FLEETWOODS, THE

Number	Title (A Side/B Side)	Yr	VG	VG+	NM
45s					
DOLPHIN					
1	Come Softly to Me/I Care So Much	1959	6.25	12.50	25.00
DOLTON					
3	Graduation's Here/Oh Lord, Let It Be	1959	5.00	10.00	20.00
S-3 [S]	Graduation's Here/Oh Lord, Let It Be	1959	12.50	25.00	50.00
5	Mr. Blue/You Mean Everything to Me	1959	5.00	10.00	20.00
15	Outside My Window/Magic Star	1960	5.00	10.00	20.00
22	Runaround/Truly Do	1960	5.00	10.00	20.00
22 [PS]	Runaround/Truly Do	1960	12.50	25.00	50.00
27	The Last One to Know/Dormilona	1960	3.75	7.50	15.00
30	Confidential/I Love You So	1960	3.75	7.50	15.00
40	Tragedy/Little Miss Sad One	1961	3.75	7.50	15.00
45	(He's) The Great Impostor/Poor Little Girl	1961	3.75	7.50	15.00
49	Billy Old Buddy/Trouble	1962	3.75	7.50	15.00
62	They Tell Me It's Summer/Lovers by Night, Strangers by Day	1962	3.75	7.50	15.00
74	You Should Have Been There/Sure Is Lonesome Downtown	1963	3.75	7.50	15.00
75	Goodnight My Love/Jimmy Beware	1963	3.75	7.50	15.00
86	Baby Bye-O/What'll I Do	1963	2.50	5.00	10.00
93	Lonesome Town/Ruby Red Baby Blue	1964	2.50	5.00	10.00
97	Ten Times Blue/Ska Light Ska Bright	1964	2.50	5.00	10.00
98	Mr. Sandman/This Is My Prayer	1964	2.50	5.00	10.00
302	Before and After (Losing You)/Lonely Is As Lonely Does	1964	2.50	5.00	10.00
307	Come Softly to Me/I'm Not Jimmy	1965	2.50	5.00	10.00
310	Rainbow/Just As I Need You	1965	2.50	5.00	10.00
315	For Lovin' Me/This Is Where I See Her	1965	2.50	5.00	10.00
LIBERTY					
62	They Tell Me It's Summer/Lovers by Night, Strangers by Day	1970	3.75	7.50	15.00
—Odd reissue keeping the Dolton number					
55188 [M]	Come Softly to Me/I Care So Much	1959	6.25	12.50	25.00
77188 [S]	Come Softly to Me/I Care So Much	1959	12.50	25.00	50.00
UNITED ARTISTS					
0038	Come Softly to Me/Runaround	1973	—	2.00	4.00
0039	Mr. Blue/Tragedy	1973	—	2.00	4.00
0040	He's the Great Impostor/Goodnight My Love	1973	—	2.00	4.00
—0038, 0039 and 0040 are "Silver Spotlight Series" reissues					
XW515	(He's) The Great Impostor/Goodnight My Love	1974	—	2.00	4.00
—Reissue					
7-Inch Extended Plays					
DOLTON					
BEP-502	Runaround/Mr. Blue//Outside My Window/Come Softly to Me	1960	15.00	30.00	60.00
BEP-502 [PS]	The Fleetwoods	1960	22.50	45.00	90.00
Albums					
DOLTON					
BLP-2001 [M]	Mr. Blue	1959	20.00	40.00	80.00
—Pale blue label with dolphins on top					
BLP-2001 [M]	Mr. Blue	1963	5.00	10.00	20.00
—Dark label, logo on left					
BLP-2002 [M]	The Fleetwoods	1960	12.50	25.00	50.00
—Pale blue label with dolphins on top					
BLP-2002 [M]	The Fleetwoods	1963	5.00	10.00	20.00
—Dark label, logo on left					
BLP-2005 [M]	Softly	1961	12.50	25.00	50.00
—Pale blue label with dolphins on top					
BLP-2005 [M]	Softly	1963	5.00	10.00	20.00
—Dark label, logo on left					
BLP-2007 [M]	Deep in a Dream	1961	10.00	20.00	40.00
—Pale blue label with dolphins on top					
BLP-2007 [M]	Deep in a Dream	1963	5.00	10.00	20.00
—Dark label, logo on left					
BLP-2011 [M]	The Best of the Oldies	1962	10.00	20.00	40.00
—Pale blue label with dolphins on top					
BLP-2011 [M]	The Best of the Oldies	1963	5.00	10.00	20.00
—Dark label, logo on left					
BLP-2018 [M]	The Fleetwoods' Greatest Hits	1962	6.25	12.50	25.00
BLP-2020 [M]	The Fleetwoods Sings for Lovers by Night	1963	7.50	15.00	30.00
BLP-2025 [M]	Goodnight My Love	1963	7.50	15.00	30.00
BLP-2030 [M]	Before and After	1965	7.50	15.00	30.00
BLP-2039 [M]	Folk Rock	1965	7.50	15.00	30.00
BST-8001 [S]	Mr. Blue	1959	25.00	50.00	100.00
—Pale blue label with dolphins on top					
BST-8001 [S]	Mr. Blue	1963	6.25	12.50	25.00
—Dark label, logo on left					
BST-8002 [S]	The Fleetwoods	1960	17.50	35.00	70.00
—Pale blue label with dolphins on top					
BST-8002 [S]	The Fleetwoods	1963	6.25	12.50	25.00
—Dark label, logo on left					
BST-8005 [S]	Softly	1961	17.50	35.00	70.00
—Pale blue label with dolphins on top					
BST-8005 [S]	Softly	1963	6.25	12.50	25.00
—Dark label, logo on left					
BST-8007 [S]	Deep in a Dream	1961	12.50	25.00	50.00
—Pale blue label with dolphins on top					
BST-8007 [S]	Deep in a Dream	1963	6.25	12.50	25.00
—Dark label, logo on left					
BST-8011 [S]	The Best of the Oldies	1962	12.50	25.00	50.00
—Pale blue label with dolphins on top					
BST-8011 [S]	The Best of the Oldies	1963	6.25	12.50	25.00
—Dark label, logo on left					
BST-8018 [S]	The Fleetwoods' Greatest Hits	1962	7.50	15.00	30.00
BST-8020 [S]	The Fleetwoods Sings for Lovers by Night	1963	10.00	20.00	40.00
BST-8025 [S]	Goodnight My Love	1963	10.00	20.00	40.00
BST-8030 [S]	Before and After	1965	10.00	20.00	40.00
BST-8039 [S]	Folk Rock	1965	10.00	20.00	40.00
LIBERTY					
LN-10159	The Fleetwoods' Greatest Hits	1982	2.00	4.00	8.00
LN-10160	The Best Goodies of the Oldies	1982	2.00	4.00	8.00
LN-10199	Buried Treasure	1983	2.00	4.00	8.00
SUNSET					
SUM-1131 [M]	In a Mellow Mood	1966	3.00	6.00	12.00
SUS-5131 [S]	In a Mellow Mood	1966	3.75	7.50	15.00
UNITED ARTISTS					
UA-LA334-E	The Very Best of the Fleetwoods	1975	3.00	6.00	12.00

FLEMONS, WADE

Also see EARTH, WIND AND FIRE.

Number	Title (A Side/B Side)	Yr	VG	VG+	NM
45s					
VEE JAY					
295	Here I Stand/My Baby Likes to Rock	1958	7.50	15.00	30.00
309	Hold Me Close/You'll Remain Forever	1959	7.50	15.00	30.00
321	Slow Motion/Wailing by the River	1959	7.50	15.00	30.00
335	Goodnite, It's Time To Go/What's Happening	1959	7.50	15.00	30.00
344	Easy Lovin'/Woops Now	1960	7.50	15.00	30.00
368	Ain't That Lovin' You Baby/I'll Come Runnin'	1960	5.00	10.00	20.00
377	At the Party/Devil in Your Soul	1961	5.00	10.00	20.00
389	Please Send Me Someone to Love/Keep On Loving Me	1961	5.00	10.00	20.00
427	Half a Love/Welcome Stranger	1962	5.00	10.00	20.00
471	Ain't These Tears/I Hope, I Think, I Wish	1962	5.00	10.00	20.00
533	That Time of the Year/I Came Running	1963	3.75	7.50	15.00
578	When It Rains, It Pours/Watch Over Her	1964	3.75	7.50	15.00
—The Four Seasons sing backup on this record					
614	I Knew You When/That Other Place	1964	3.75	7.50	15.00
668	Where Did You Go Last Night/Empty Balcony	1965	3.00	6.00	12.00
Albums					
VEE JAY					
LP-1011 [M]	Wade Flemons	1959	37.50	75.00	150.00
—Maroon label					
LP-1011 [M]	Wade Flemons	196?	20.00	40.00	80.00
—Black label					

FLESH GORDON AND THE NUDE HOLLYWOOD ARGYLES
Also see THE HOLLYWOOD ARGYLES.

Number	Title (A Side/B Side)	Yr	VG	VG+	NM
45s					
PARAMOUNT					
0289	Superstreaker/Naked	1974	3.00	6.00	12.00

FLINT, SHELBY

Number	Title (A Side/B Side)	Yr	VG	VG+	NM
45s					
CADENCE					
1352	Oh, I Miss Him So/I Will Love You	1958	3.75	7.50	15.00
VALIANT					
701	Angel on My Shoulder/I Will Love You	1965	2.00	4.00	8.00
716	Joy in the Morning/Lonely Cinderella	1965	2.00	4.00	8.00
743	Cast Your Fate to the Wind/The Lily	1966	2.00	4.00	8.00
6001	Angel on My Shoulder/Someday	1960	3.00	6.00	12.00
6010	I Will Love You/Every Night	1961	2.50	5.00	10.00
6014	A Broken Vow/Magic Wand	1961	2.50	5.00	10.00
6017	The Riddle Song/I Love a Wanderer	1962	2.50	5.00	10.00
6022	The Boy I Love/Ugly Duckling	1962	2.50	5.00	10.00
6031	Little Dancing Doll/It Really Doesn't Matter	1963	2.50	5.00	10.00
6052	Wonderland/Pipes of Keith	1964	2.50	5.00	10.00
6060	I've Grown Accustomed to Her (Your) Face/Our Town	1964	2.50	5.00	10.00
Albums					
MAD SATYR					
MSR-101	You've Been On My Mind	1982	6.25	12.50	25.00
VALIANT					
LP-401 [M]	Shelby Flint — The Quiet Girl	1961	10.00	20.00	40.00
LP-403 [M]	Shelby Flint Sings Folk	1962	10.00	20.00	40.00
LPS-403 [S]	Shelby Flint Sings Folk	1962	12.50	25.00	50.00
VL-5003 [M]	Cast Your Fate to the Wind	1966	6.25	12.50	25.00
VLS-25003 [S]	Cast Your Fate to the Wind	1966	7.50	15.00	30.00

FLINTSTONE, FRED

Number	Title (A Side/B Side)	Yr	VG	VG+	NM
45s					
EPIC					
9475	Bedrock Beat/Stone Age Roll	1961	5.00	10.00	20.00

FLIRTATIONS, THE (1)
Female vocal group.

Number	Title (A Side/B Side)	Yr	VG	VG+	NM
45s					
DERAM					
7531	Give Me Love, Love, Love/This Must Be the End	1970	2.00	4.00	8.00
85036	Christmas Time Is Here Again/Nothing But a Heartache	1968	2.00	4.00	8.00
85038	Nothing But a Heartache/How Can You Tell Me	1969	—	3.00	6.00
85048	Need Your Loving/South Caroline	1969	—	3.00	6.00
85057	I Wanna Be There/Keep On Searching	1970	—	3.00	6.00
85062	Can't Stop Lovin' You/Everybody Needs Somebody	1970	—	3.00	6.00
PARROT					
40028	Somewhere Out There/How Can You Tell Me	1968	3.00	6.00	12.00
Albums					
DERAM					
DES-18028	Nothing But a Heartache	1969	5.00	10.00	20.00

FLIRTATIONS, THE (2)
Male vocal group.

Number	Title (A Side/B Side)	Yr	VG	VG+	NM
45s					
FESTIVAL					
705	Stronger Than Her Love/Settle Down	1967	15.00	30.00	60.00

FLIRTATIONS, THE (U)
May be group (2), or perhaps a completely different group.

Number	Title (A Side/B Side)	Yr	VG	VG+	NM
45s					
JOSIE					
956	Natural Born Lover/Change My Darkness Into Light	1965	3.75	7.50	15.00

FLO AND EDDIE
Also see THE TURTLES.

Number	Title (A Side/B Side)	Yr	VG	VG+	NM
45s					
COLUMBIA					
10028	Come to My Rescue, Webelos/Let Me Make Love to You	1974	—	3.00	6.00
10204	Come to My Rescue, Webelos/Let Me Make Love to You	1975	—	2.50	5.00
10264	Illegal, Immoral and Fattening/Rebecca	1975	—	2.50	5.00
10425	Elenore/The Love You Gave Away	1976	—	2.50	5.00
10458	Keep It Warm/Hot	1976	—	2.50	5.00
REPRISE					
1113	Nikki Hoi/Godbye Surprise	1972	—	2.50	5.00
1142	Afterglow/Original Soundtract from "Carlos & De Bull"	1972	—	2.50	5.00
1160	If We Only Had the Time/You're a Lady	1973	—	2.50	5.00
Albums					
COLUMBIA					
PC 33554	Illegal, Immoral and Fattening	1975	3.00	6.00	12.00
PC 34262	Moving Targets	1976	3.00	6.00	12.00
EPIPHANY					
ELP-4010	Rock Steady with Flo & Eddie	1981	2.50	5.00	10.00
REPRISE					
MS 2099	The Phlorescent Leech and Eddie	1972	5.00	10.00	20.00
MS 2141	Flo and Eddie	1973	5.00	10.00	20.00
RHINO					
RNTA-1999 [(3)]	History of Flo & Eddie	198?	5.00	10.00	20.00

FLOATING BRIDGE, THE

Number	Title (A Side/B Side)	Yr	VG	VG+	NM
45s					
VAULT					
947	Watch Your Step/Brought Up Wrong	1969	2.50	5.00	10.00
953	Don't Mean a Thing/Mr. Jaybird	1969	2.50	5.00	10.00
Albums					
VAULT					
VS-124	The Floating Bridge	1969	7.50	15.00	30.00

FLOCK, THE

Number	Title (A Side/B Side)	Yr	VG	VG+	NM
45s					
COLUMBIA					
45021	Tired of Waiting/Store Bought Store Thought	1969	2.00	4.00	8.00
45295	Mermaid/Crabfoot	1971	2.00	4.00	8.00
DESTINATION					
628	Can't You See/Hold On to My Mind	1966	2.50	5.00	10.00
631	Are You the Kind/I Like You	1966	2.50	5.00	10.00
635	Take Me Back/Each Day Is a Lonely Night	1967	2.50	5.00	10.00
U.S.A.					
910	Magical Winds/What Would You Do If the Sun Died?	1968	2.00	4.00	8.00
Albums					
COLUMBIA					
CS 9911	The Flock	1969	5.00	10.00	20.00
—"360 Sound" label					
CS 9911	The Flock	1970	3.75	7.50	15.00
—Orange label					
C 30007	Dinosaur Swamps	1970	5.00	10.00	20.00
—"360 Sound" label					
C 30007	Dinosaur Swamps	1970	3.75	7.50	15.00
—Orange label					
MERCURY					
SRM-1-1035	Inside Out	1975	3.75	7.50	15.00

FLORIDIANS, THE

Number	Title (A Side/B Side)	Yr	VG	VG+	NM
45s					
ABC-PARAMOUNT					
10185	That Lucky Old Sun/I Love Marie	1961	12.50	25.00	50.00

FLOW

Number	Title (A Side/B Side)	Yr	VG	VG+	NM
45s					
CTI					
503	Mr. Invisible/Daddy	1970	—	3.00	6.00
Albums					
CTI					
1003	Flow	1970	5.00	10.00	20.00

FLOWERPOT MEN, THE

Number	Title (A Side/B Side)	Yr	VG	VG+	NM
45s					
DERAM					
7513	Let's Go to San Francisco/Let's Go to San Francisco, Part 2	1967	3.75	7.50	15.00
—As "The Flower Pots"					
7516	Am I Losing You/A Walk in the Sky	1968	3.75	7.50	15.00
85051	A Moment of Madness/Young Birds Fly	1969	3.00	6.00	12.00

FLOYD, EDDIE
Also see THE FALCONS.

Number	Title (A Side/B Side)	Yr	VG	VG+	NM
45s					
ATLANTIC					
2275	Hush Hush/Drive On	1965	3.00	6.00	12.00
LUPINE					
115	Set My Soul on Fire/Will I Be the One	1963	3.75	7.50	15.00
MALACO					
1032	Somebody Touch Me/Never Too Old	1976	—	2.50	5.00
1035	Chi-Town Hustler/In Paradise	1976	—	2.50	5.00
1039	Special Christmas Day/Mother, My Dear Mother	1976	—	2.50	5.00
1040	We Should Really Be in Love/I'll Never Be Loved	1977	—	2.50	5.00
—With Dorothy Moore					
1043	You're Gonna Walk Out on Me/Prove It to Me	1977	—	2.50	5.00
MERCURY					
73964	If You Really Love Me/It's Me	1977	—	2.00	4.00
74003	Disco Summer/Do It in the Water	1978	—	2.00	4.00
SAFICE					
336	Can This Be Christmas/I'll Be Home For Christmas	1964	3.00	6.00	12.00
STAX					
0002	I've Never Found a Girl (To Love Me Like You Do)/I'm Just the Kind of Fool	1968	—	3.00	6.00
0012	Bring It On Home to Me/The Sweet Things You Do	1968	—	3.00	6.00
0025	I've Got to Have Your Love/Girl I Love You	1969	—	3.00	6.00
0036	Don't Tell Your Mama (Where You've Been)/Consider Me	1969	—	3.00	6.00
0041	Never Never Let You Go/Ain't That Good	1969	—	3.00	6.00
—With Mavis Staples					
0051	Why Is the Wine Sweeter (On the Other Side)/People Get It Together	1969	—	3.00	6.00
0060	California Girl/The Woodman	1970	—	3.00	6.00
0072	My Girl/Laurie	1970	—	3.00	6.00
0077	The Best Years of My Life/My Little Girl	1970	—	3.00	6.00
0087	Oh How It Rained/When My Baby Said Goodbye	1971	—	3.00	6.00
0095	Blood Is Thicker Than Water/Have You Heard the Word	1971	—	3.00	6.00
0109	Yum Yum Yum (I Want Some)/Tears of Joy	1971	—	3.00	6.00
0134	You're Good Enough (To Be My Baby)/Spend All You Have on Love	1972	—	3.00	6.00
0158	Knock on Wood/Lay Your Loving on Me	1973	—	3.00	6.00
0171	Baby Lay Your Head Down (Gently on My Bed)/Check Me Out	1973	—	3.00	6.00
187	Things Get Better/Good Love, Bad Love	1966	3.00	6.00	12.00

Number	Title (A Side/B Side)	Yr	VG	VG+	NM
0188	I Wanna Do Things for You/We've Been Through Too Much Together	1973	—	3.00	6.00
194	Knock on Wood/Got to Make a Comeback	1966	3.75	7.50	15.00
208	Raise Your Hand/I've Just Been Feeling Bad	1967	2.50	5.00	10.00
0209	Guess Who/Something to Write Home About	1974	—	3.00	6.00
0216	Soul Street/Highway Man	1974	—	3.00	6.00
219	Don't Rock the Boat/This House	1967	2.50	5.00	10.00
223	Love Is a Doggone Good Thing/Hey Now	1967	2.50	5.00	10.00
0232	Stealing Love/I Got a Reason to Smile	1974	—	3.00	6.00
233	On a Saturday Night/Under My Nose	1967	2.50	5.00	10.00
0239	Talk to the Man/I Got a Reason to Smile	1975	—	3.00	6.00
246	Holding On with Both Hands/Big Bird	1968	2.50	5.00	10.00
0251	I'm So Glad I Met You/I'm So Grateful	1975	—	3.00	6.00

Albums

MALACO

Number	Title (A Side/B Side)	Yr	VG	VG+	NM
6352	Experience	1977	3.00	6.00	12.00

STAX

Number	Title (A Side/B Side)	Yr	VG	VG+	NM
714 [M]	Knock on Wood	1967	17.50	35.00	70.00
ST 714 [S]	Knock on Wood	1967	17.50	35.00	70.00
STS-2002	I've Never Found a Girl	1968	7.50	15.00	30.00
STS-2011	Rare Stamps	1969	6.25	12.50	25.00
STS-2017	You've Got to Have Eddie	1969	6.25	12.50	25.00
STS-2029	California Girl	1970	6.25	12.50	25.00
STS-2041	Down to Earth	1971	6.25	12.50	25.00
STS-3016	Baby Lay Your Head Down	1973	6.25	12.50	25.00
STX-4122	Chronicle	1979	3.00	6.00	12.00
STS-5512	Soul Street	1974	6.25	12.50	25.00
MPS-8527	Soul Street	198?	2.50	5.00	10.00

FLYERS, THE

45s

ATCO

Number	Title (A Side/B Side)	Yr	VG	VG+	NM
6088	On Bended Knee/My Only Desire	1957	10.00	20.00	40.00

FLYING BURRITO BROTHERS, THE

Also includes records as "Burrito Brothers." Also see GRAM PARSONS.

45s

A&M

Number	Title (A Side/B Side)	Yr	VG	VG+	NM
1067	Train Song/Hot Burrito #1	1969	2.00	4.00	8.00
1166	If You Gotta Go, Go Now/Cody, Cody	1970	2.00	4.00	8.00
1189	Down in the Churchyard/Older Guys	1970	2.00	4.00	8.00
1277	White Line Fever/Colorado	1971	2.00	4.00	8.00

COLUMBIA

Number	Title (A Side/B Side)	Yr	VG	VG+	NM
10229	Building Fires/Hot Burrito No. 3	1975	—	2.50	5.00
10287	Bon Soir Blues/Hot Burrito No. 3	1976	—	2.50	5.00
10389	Big Bayou/Waiting for Love to Begin	1976	—	2.50	5.00

CURB

Number	Title (A Side/B Side)	Yr	VG	VG+	NM
02243	She Belongs to Everyone But Me/Why Must the Ending Always Be So Sad	1981	—	2.00	4.00
—As "Burrito Brothers"					
02641	If Something Should Come Between Us/Damned If I'll Be Lonely Tonight	1981	—	2.00	4.00
—As "Burrito Brothers"					
02667	If Something Should Come Between Us	1982	—	2.00	4.00
—As "Burrito Brothers"					
02835	Closer to You/Coast to Coast	1982	—	2.00	4.00
—As "Burrito Brothers"					
03023	I'm Drinkin' Canada Dry/How'd We Ever Get This Way	1982	—	2.00	4.00
—As "Burrito Brothers"					
03314	Blue and Broken Hearted Me/Our Roots Are Country Music	1982	—	2.00	4.00
—As "Burrito Brothers"					
5402	She's a Friend of a Friend/(B-side unknown)	1981	—	2.00	4.00
—As "Burrito Brothers"					

MCA CURB

Number	Title (A Side/B Side)	Yr	VG	VG+	NM
52329	Almost Saturday Night/Juke Box Kind of Night	1983	—	—	3.00
—As "Burrito Brothers"					
52379	My Kind of Lady/Dream Chaser	1984	—	—	3.00
—As "Burrito Brothers"					

REGENCY

Number	Title (A Side/B Side)	Yr	VG	VG+	NM
45001	White Line Fever/(B-side unknown)	1980	—	2.50	5.00

Albums

A&M

Number	Title (A Side/B Side)	Yr	VG	VG+	NM
SP-3122	The Gilded Palace of Sin	198?	2.00	4.00	8.00
—Budget-line reissue					
SP-3631 [(2)]	Close Up the Honky-Tonks	1974	3.75	7.50	15.00
SP-4175	The Gilded Palace of Sin	1969	5.00	10.00	20.00
—Brown label					
SP-4175	The Gilded Palace of Sin	1974	3.00	6.00	12.00
—Silvery label					
SP-4258	Burrito Deluxe	1970	3.75	7.50	15.00
—Brown label					
SP-4258	Burrito Deluxe	1974	3.00	6.00	12.00
—Silvery label					
SP-4295	The Flying Burrito Bros.	1971	3.75	7.50	15.00
—Brown label					
SP-4295	The Flying Burrito Bros.	1974	3.00	6.00	12.00
—Silvery label					
SP-4343	Last of the Red Hot Burritos	1972	3.75	7.50	15.00
—Brown label					
SP-4343	Last of the Red Hot Burritos	1974	3.00	6.00	12.00
—Silvery label					
SP-4578	Sleepless Nights	1976	3.00	6.00	12.00
—As "Gram Parsons/The Flying Burrito Bros."					
SP-6510 [(2)]	Close Up the Honky-Tonks	198?	3.00	6.00	12.00
—Reissue of 3631					
SP-8070 [DJ]	Hot Burrito	1975	10.00	20.00	40.00
—Promo-only issue with poster					

COLUMBIA

Number	Title (A Side/B Side)	Yr	VG	VG+	NM
PC 33817	Flying Again	1975	3.00	6.00	12.00
PC 34222	Airborne	1976	3.00	6.00	12.00

CURB

Number	Title (A Side/B Side)	Yr	VG	VG+	NM
JZ 37004	Hearts on the Line	1981	2.50	5.00	10.00
—As "Burrito Brothers"					
FZ 37705	Sunset Sundown	1982	2.50	5.00	10.00
—As "Burrito Brothers"					

REGENCY

Number	Title (A Side/B Side)	Yr	VG	VG+	NM
REG-79001	Live from Tokyo	1980	2.50	5.00	10.00

FLYING MACHINE, THE

This is a British group, no relation to the American group that featured JAMES TAYLOR.

45s

CONGRESS

Number	Title (A Side/B Side)	Yr	VG	VG+	NM
6000	Smile a Little Smile for Me/Maybe We've Been Loving Too Long	1969	2.00	4.00	8.00
6012	There She Goes/Baby Make It Soon	1970	—	3.00	6.00

JANUS

Number	Title (A Side/B Side)	Yr	VG	VG+	NM
121	Hanging on the Edge of Sadness/My Baby's Coming Home	1970	—	3.00	6.00
137	Hey Little Girl/The Devil Has Possession of My Mind	1971	—	3.00	6.00

Albums

JANUS

Number	Title (A Side/B Side)	Yr	VG	VG+	NM
JLS-3007	The Flying Machine	1969	3.75	7.50	15.00

FOCUS

Also see JAN AKKERMAN.

45s

ATCO

Number	Title (A Side/B Side)	Yr	VG	VG+	NM
7002	Harem Scarem/Birth	1974	—	2.50	5.00

SIRE

Number	Title (A Side/B Side)	Yr	VG	VG+	NM
352	Black Beauty/House of the King	1971	—	2.50	5.00
704	Hocus Pocus/Hocus Pocus II	1973	—	3.00	6.00
708	Sylvia/Love Remembered	1973	—	2.50	5.00

Albums

ATCO

Number	Title (A Side/B Side)	Yr	VG	VG+	NM
SD 36-100	Hamburger Concerto	1974	3.00	6.00	12.00
SD 36-117	Mother Focus	1975	3.00	6.00	12.00

HARVEST

Number	Title (A Side/B Side)	Yr	VG	VG+	NM
ST-11721	Focus Con Proby	1978	3.00	6.00	12.00
—With P.J. Proby					

MERCURY

Number	Title (A Side/B Side)	Yr	VG	VG+	NM
824524-1	Focus	1986	2.50	5.00	10.00

SIRE

Number	Title (A Side/B Side)	Yr	VG	VG+	NM
SAS-3901 [(2)]	Focus 3	1973	3.75	7.50	15.00
SAS-7401	Moving Waves	1972	3.00	6.00	12.00
SAS-7404	In and Out of Focus	1973	3.00	6.00	12.00
—Reissue of 97027					
SAS-7408	Live at the Rainbow	1973	3.00	6.00	12.00
SASD-7505	Dutch Masters — A Selection of Their Finest Recordings 1969-1973	1975	3.00	6.00	12.00
SASD-7531	Ship of Memories	1977	3.00	6.00	12.00
SES-97027	In and Out of Focus	1970	5.00	10.00	20.00

FOGELBERG, DAN

45s

COLUMBIA

Number	Title (A Side/B Side)	Yr	VG	VG+	NM
45764	Anyway I Love You/Looking for a Lady	1973	—	3.00	6.00

FULL MOON/EPIC

Number	Title (A Side/B Side)	Yr	VG	VG+	NM
02488	Hard to Say/The Innocent Age	1981	—	2.00	4.00
02647	Leader of the Band/Times Like These	1981	—	2.00	4.00
02821	Run for the Roses/The Sand and the Foam	1982	—	2.00	4.00
03087	Same Old Lang Syne/Hard to Say	1982	—	—	3.00
—Reissue					
03289	Missing You/Hearts and Crafts	1982	—	2.00	4.00
03323	Missing You	1982	—	3.00	6.00
—One-sided budget release					
03525	Make Love Stay/Hearts and Crafts	1983	—	2.00	4.00
03570	Make Love Stay	1983	—	3.00	6.00
—One-sided budget release					
03843	Leader of the Band/Run for the Roses	1983	—	—	3.00
—Reissue					
04314	The Language of Love/Windows and Walls	1984	—	—	3.00
04314 [PS]	The Language of Love/Windows and Walls	1984	—	—	3.00
04447	Believe in Me/Windows and Walls	1984	—	—	3.00
04660	Sweet Magnolia and the Traveling Salesman/The Loving Cup	1984	—	—	3.00
04835	Go Down Easy/High Country Snows	1985	—	—	3.00
05446	Down the Road-Mountain Pass/High Country Snows	1985	—	—	3.00
07044	She Don't Look Back/It Doesn't Matter	1987	—	—	3.00
07044 [PS]	She Don't Look Back/It Doesn't Matter	1987	—	—	3.00
07275	Lonely in Love/Beyond the Edge	1987	—	—	3.00
07640	Hearts in Decline/Seeing You Again	1987	—	—	3.00
07756	The Way It Must Be/What You're Doing	1988	—	—	3.00
50055	Part of the Plan/Song from Half Mountain	1974	—	2.50	5.00
50108	Changing Horses/Morning Sky	1975	—	2.00	4.00
50165	Captured Angel/Next Time	1975	—	2.00	4.00
50189	Below the Surface/Comes and Goes	1976	—	2.00	4.00
50234	Old Tennessee/The Crow	1976	—	2.00	4.00
50412	Scarecrow's Dream/Love Gone By	1977	—	2.00	4.00
50462	Nether Lands/False Faces	1977	—	2.00	4.00
50536	Sketches/Promises Made	1978	—	2.00	4.00
50577	There's a Place in the World for a Gambler/Souvenirs	1978	—	2.50	5.00
50824	Longer/Along the Road	1980	—	2.00	4.00
50862	Heart Hotels/Beggar's Game	1980	—	2.00	4.00
50961	Same Old Lang Syne/Hearts and Crafts	1980	—	2.00	4.00
50961 [PS]	Same Old Lang Syne/Hearts and Crafts	1980	—	3.00	6.00
73513	Rhythm of the Rain-Rain/Ever On	1990	—	2.00	4.00

Albums

COLUMBIA

Number	Title (A Side/B Side)	Yr	VG	VG+	NM
KC 31751	Home Free	1972	3.00	6.00	12.00

Number	Title (A Side/B Side)	Yr	VG	VG+	NM
PC 31751	Home Free	197?	2.00	4.00	8.00
—Reissue with new prefix					
FULL MOON/EPIC					
A2S 1335 [(2) DJ]	Interchords	1982	6.25	12.50	25.00
—Promo-only release					
QE 28208	Dan Fogelberg/Greatest Hits	1982	2.50	5.00	10.00
KE 33137	Souvenirs	1974	3.00	6.00	12.00
—First pressings have orange Epic label with small Full Moon logo					
KE 33137	Souvenirs	1975	2.50	5.00	10.00
—Second pressings have dark blue/black Full Moon label					
PE 33137	Souvenirs	197?	2.00	4.00	8.00
—Reissue with new prefix					
PE 33499	Captured Angel	1975	2.50	5.00	10.00
—No bar code on cover					
PE 33499	Captured Angel	198?	2.00	4.00	8.00
—With bar code on cover					
PEQ 33499 [Q]	Captured Angel	1975	5.00	10.00	20.00
PE 34185	Nether Lands	1977	2.50	5.00	10.00
—No bar code on cover					
PE 34185	Nether Lands	198?	2.00	4.00	8.00
—With bar code on cover					
PE 35364	Phoenix	198?	2.00	4.00	8.00
—Budget-line reissue					
FE 35634	Phoenix	1979	2.50	5.00	10.00
KE2 37393 [(2)]	The Innocent Age	1981	3.00	6.00	12.00
QE 39004	Windows and Walls	1984	2.50	5.00	10.00
FE 39616	High Country Snows	1985	2.50	5.00	10.00
OE 40271	Exiles	1987	2.50	5.00	10.00
HE 45634	Phoenix	1981	7.50	15.00	30.00
—Half-speed mastered edition					
HE 48308	Dan Fogelberg/Greatest Hits	1983	7.50	15.00	30.00
—Half-speed mastered edition					

FOGELBERG, DAN, AND TIM WEISBERG

45s

Number	Title (A Side/B Side)	Yr	VG	VG+	NM
FULL MOON/EPIC					
50605	Tell Me to My Face/Hurtwood Alley	1978	—	2.50	5.00
50606	The Power of Gold/Lahaina Luna	1978	—	2.00	4.00

Albums

Number	Title (A Side/B Side)	Yr	VG	VG+	NM
FULL MOON/EPIC					
JE 35339	Twin Sons of Different Mothers	1978	2.50	5.00	10.00
PE 35339	Twin Sons of Different Mothers	198?	2.00	4.00	8.00
—Budget-line reissue					
HE 45339	Twin Sons of Different Mothers	198?	7.50	15.00	30.00
—Half-speed mastered edition					

FOGERTY, JOHN

Includes records as "The Blue Ridge Rangers." Also see CREEDENCE CLEARWATER REVIVAL; TOMMY FOGERTY AND THE BLUE VELVETS; THE GOLLIWOGS.

12-Inch Singles

Number	Title (A Side/B Side)	Yr	VG	VG+	NM
WARNER BROS.					
PRO-A-2234 [DJ]	The Old Man Down the Road (same on both sides)	1984	2.00	4.00	8.00
PRO-A-2267 [DJ]	Rock and Roll Girls/Centerfield	1985	2.00	4.00	8.00
PRO-A-2337 [DJ]	I Can't Help Myself (same on both sides)	1985	2.00	4.00	8.00
PRO-A-2362 [DJ]	Vanz Kant Danz (edit)/Vanz Kant Danz (LP)	1985	2.00	4.00	8.00
PRO-A-2514 [DJ]	Eye of the Zombie (same on both sides)	1986	2.00	4.00	8.00
PRO-A-2595 [DJ]	Change in the Weather (edit)/(LP)	1986	2.00	4.00	8.00
PRO-A-2637 [DJ]	Knockin' on Your Door (same on both sides)	1986	2.00	4.00	8.00

45s

Number	Title (A Side/B Side)	Yr	VG	VG+	NM
ASYLUM					
45274	Rockin' All Over the World/The Wall	1975	—	2.50	5.00
45293	Almost Saturday Night/Sea Cruise	1975	—	2.50	5.00
45309	You Got the Magic/Evil Thing	1976	—	2.50	5.00
ELEKTRA					
45309 [DJ]	You Got the Magic (stereo/mono)	1976	2.50	5.00	10.00
—Promo-only version with wrong label					
FANTASY					
683	Blue Ridge Mountain Blues/Have Thine Own Way, Lord	1972	—	2.50	5.00
—As "The Blue Ridge Rangers"					
683 [PS]	Blue Ridge Mountain Blues/Have Thine Own Way, Lord	1972	3.75	7.50	15.00
—As "The Blue Ridge Rangers"					
689	Jambalaya (On the Bayou)/Workin' on a Building	1972	—	3.00	6.00
—As "The Blue Ridge Rangers"; green, red and orange label					
689	Jambalaya (On the Bayou)/Workin' on a Building	1972	—	2.50	5.00
—As "The Blue Ridge Rangers"; brown label					
700	Hearts of Stone/Somewhere Listening	1973	—	2.50	5.00
—As "The Blue Ridge Rangers"					
710	Back in the Hills/You Don't Own Me	1973	—	2.50	5.00
—As "The Blue Ridge Rangers"					
717	Coming Down the Road/Ricochet	1973	—	2.50	5.00
REPRISE					
17191	Premonition/Born on the Bayou	1998	—	—	3.00
17192	Almost Saturday Night/Who'll Stop the Rain	1998	—	—	3.00
WARNER BROS.					
17283	Blueboy/Bad Bad Boy	1997	—	—	3.00
28535	Change in the Weather/My Toot Toot	1986	—	2.00	4.00
28535 [PS]	Change in the Weather/My Toot Toot	1986	—	2.00	4.00
28657	Eye of the Zombie/I Confess	1986	—	2.00	4.00
28657 [PS]	Eye of the Zombie/I Confess	1986	—	2.00	4.00
29053	Rock and Roll Girls/Centerfield	1985	—	2.00	4.00
29053 [PS]	Rock and Roll Girls/Centerfield	1985	—	2.00	4.00
29100	The Old Man Down the Road/Big Train (From Memphis)	1985	—	2.00	4.00
29100 [PS]	The Old Man Down the Road/Big Train (From Memphis)	1985	—	2.00	4.00

Albums

Number	Title (A Side/B Side)	Yr	VG	VG+	NM
ASYLUM					
7E-1046	John Fogerty	1975	3.00	6.00	12.00
7E-1081	Hoodoo	1976	—	—	—
—Canceled; poor quality bootleg cassettes exist					
FANTASY					
MPF-4502	John Fogerty: The Blue Ridge Rangers	1981	2.50	5.00	10.00
—Reissues prominently place John Fogerty's name on the cover					
F-9415	The Blue Ridge Rangers	1973	3.75	7.50	15.00
—As "The Blue Ridge Rangers"					
WARNER BROS.					
25203	Centerfield	1985	3.75	7.50	15.00
—Originals have the last song on side 2 as "Zanz Kant Danz"					
25203	Centerfield	1985	2.50	5.00	10.00
—Later editions have the last song on side 2 re-recorded and listed as "Vanz Kant Danz"					
25203 [DJ]	Centerfield	1985	5.00	10.00	20.00
—Promo versions on Quiex II audiophile vinyl					
25449	Eye of the Zombie	1986	2.50	5.00	10.00

FOGERTY, TOM

Also see CREEDENCE CLEARWATER REVIVAL; TOMMY FOGERTY AND THE BLUE VELVETS; THE GOLLIWOGS.

45s

Number	Title (A Side/B Side)	Yr	VG	VG+	NM
FANTASY					
661	Goodbye, Media Man/Goodbye, Media Man (Part 2)	1971	—	2.50	5.00
661 [PS]	Goodbye, Media Man/Goodbye, Media Man (Part 2)	1971	2.50	5.00	10.00
680	Cast the First Stone/Lady of Fatima	1972	—	2.50	5.00
691	Forty Years/Faces, Places, People	1972	—	2.50	5.00
702	Heartbeat/Joyful Resurrection	1973	—	2.50	5.00
715	Mystic Island Avalon/Reggie	1973	—	2.50	5.00
726	It's Been a Good Day/Money	1974	—	2.50	5.00
737	Sweet Things to Come/There Was a Time	1974	—	2.50	5.00

Albums

Number	Title (A Side/B Side)	Yr	VG	VG+	NM
FANTASY					
9407	Tom Fogerty	1972	3.75	7.50	15.00
9413	Excalibur	1972	3.75	7.50	15.00
9448	Zephyr National	1974	3.00	6.00	12.00
9469	Myopia	1974	3.00	6.00	12.00
9611	Deal It Out	1981	2.50	5.00	10.00

FOGERTY, TOMMY, AND THE BLUE VELVETS

Early version of THE GOLLIWOGS, which was an early version of CREEDENCE CLEARWATER REVIVAL.

45s

Number	Title (A Side/B Side)	Yr	VG	VG+	NM
ORCHESTRA					
1010	Have You Ever Been Lonely/Bonita	1961	20.00	40.00	80.00
6177	Come On Baby/Oh! My Love	1961	20.00	40.00	80.00
(# unknown)	Yes, You Did/Now You're Not Mine	1962	20.00	40.00	80.00

FOGHAT

45s

Number	Title (A Side/B Side)	Yr	VG	VG+	NM
BEARSVILLE					
0008	I Just Want to Make Love to You/Hole to Hide In	1973	—	2.50	5.00
0014	What a Shame/Helping Hand	1973	—	2.50	5.00
0019	That'll Be the Day/Wild Cherry	1974	—	2.50	5.00
0021	Maybelline/Step Outside	1974	—	2.50	5.00
0306	Slow Ride/Save Your Loving	1975	—	2.50	5.00
0307	Fool for the City/Take It or Leave It	1976	—	2.50	5.00
0313	Drivin' Wheel/Night Shift	1976	—	2.00	4.00
0315	I'll Be Standing By/Take Me to the River	1977	—	2.00	4.00
0319	I Just Want to Make Love to You (Live)/Fool for the City (Live)	1977	—	2.00	4.00
0325	Stone Blue/Chevrolet	1978	—	2.00	4.00
0329	High on Love/Sweet Home Chicago	1978	—	2.00	4.00
PRO-S-780 [DJ]	Run, Run, Rudolph (same on both sides)	1978	2.50	5.00	10.00
PRO-S-1002 [DJ]	All I Want For Christmas Is You (same on both sides)	1981	2.50	5.00	10.00
29612	Seven Day Weekend/That's What Love Can Do	1983	—	2.00	4.00
29860	Slipped, Tripped, Fell in Love/And I Do Just What I Want	1982	—	2.00	4.00
49125	Third Time Lucky (First Time I Was a Fool)/Love in Motion	1979	—	2.00	4.00
49125 [PS]	Third Time Lucky (First Time I Was a Fool)/Love in Motion	1979	—	2.50	5.00
49510	Stranger in My Home Town/Be My Woman	1980	—	2.00	4.00
49779	Wide Boy/Love Zone	1981	—	2.00	4.00
49779 [PS]	Wide Boy/Love Zone	1981	—	3.00	6.00
FOGHAT					
1069	Goin' Home For Christmas/Santa Claus Is Back In Town	1986	—	3.00	6.00
1069 [PS]	Goin' Home For Christmas/Santa Claus Is Back In Town	1986	—	3.00	6.00

Albums

Number	Title (A Side/B Side)	Yr	VG	VG+	NM
BEARSVILLE					
BR 2077	Foghat	1972	3.00	6.00	12.00
BR 2136	Foghat	1973	3.00	6.00	12.00
BSK 3578	Girls to Chat & Boys to Bounce	1981	2.50	5.00	10.00
BR 6950	Energized	1974	2.50	5.00	10.00
BR 6956	Rock and Roll Outlaws	1974	2.50	5.00	10.00
BR 6959	Fool for the City	1975	2.50	5.00	10.00
BR 6962	Night Shift	1976	2.50	5.00	10.00
BRK 6971	Foghat Live	1977	2.50	5.00	10.00
BRK 6977	Stone Blue	1978	2.50	5.00	10.00
BRK 6980	Fool for the City	1978	2.00	4.00	8.00
—Reissue of 6959					
BHS 6990	Boogie Motel	1979	2.50	5.00	10.00
HS 6999	Tight Shoes	1980	2.50	5.00	10.00
23747	In the Mood for Something Rude	1982	2.50	5.00	10.00
23888	Zig-Zag Walk	1983	2.50	5.00	10.00
RHINO					
R1-70088	The Best of Foghat	1989	2.50	5.00	10.00
RNLP-70881	Stone Blue	1987	2.00	4.00	8.00
—Reissue of Bearsville 6977					
RNLP-70882	Fool for the City	1987	2.00	4.00	8.00
—Reissue of Bearsville 6980					

Number	Title (A Side/B Side)	Yr	VG	VG+	NM
RNLP-70883	Energized	1988	2.00	4.00	8.00
—Reissue of Bearsville 6950					
RNLP-70884	Foghat Live	1988	2.00	4.00	8.00
—Reissue of Bearsville 6971					
RNLP-70887	Foghat	1988	2.00	4.00	8.00
—Reissue of Bearsville 2077					
RNLP-70888	Night Shift	1988	2.00	4.00	8.00
—Reissue of Bearsville 6962					
R1-70889	Rock and Roll Outlaws	1988	2.00	4.00	8.00
—Reissue of Bearsville 6956					
R1-70890	Foghat	1988	2.00	4.00	8.00
—Reissue of Bearsville 2136					

FOLKSWINGERS, THE

45s

WORLD PACIFIC

Number	Title (A Side/B Side)	Yr	VG	VG+	NM
391	This Train/Black Mountain Rag	1963	2.50	5.00	10.00
396	12 String Special/Amor A Todos	1963	2.50	5.00	10.00
77831	Norwegian Wood/Raga Rock	1966	2.00	4.00	8.00

Albums

WORLD PACIFIC

Number	Title (A Side/B Side)	Yr	VG	VG+	NM
ST-1812 [S]	12 String Guitar!	1963	7.50	15.00	30.00
—Black vinyl					
ST-1812 [S]	12 String Guitar!	1963	15.00	30.00	60.00
—Red vinyl					
WP-1812 [M]	12 String Guitar!	1963	6.25	12.50	25.00
ST-1814 [S]	12 String Guitar, Volume 2	1963	7.50	15.00	30.00
WP-1814 [M]	12 String Guitar, Volume 2	1963	6.25	12.50	25.00
ST-1846 [S]	Raga Rock	1966	7.50	15.00	30.00
WP-1846 [M]	Raga Rock	1966	6.25	12.50	25.00

FONTAINE, EDDIE

45s

Number	Title (A Side/B Side)	Yr	VG	VG+	NM
ARGO					
5309	Nothin' Shakin'/Don't Ya Know	1958	6.25	12.50	25.00
CHANCELLOR					
1018	Goodness, It's Gladys/Middle of the Road	1958	5.00	10.00	20.00
DECCA					
30042	Cool It Baby/Into Each Life Some Rain Must Fall	1956	6.25	12.50	25.00
30108	A Rose and a Baby Ruth/The Years Before	1956	6.25	12.50	25.00
30121	As Far As I'm Concerned/'Til Tonight	1956	6.25	12.50	25.00
—With Karen Chandler					
30202	I'll Be There/East of Mississippi	1957	6.25	12.50	25.00
30256	Money/Homesick Blues	1957	6.25	12.50	25.00
30338	Hey Marie, Rock with Me/The One and Only	1957	6.25	12.50	25.00
30446	Fun Lovin'/Honky Tonk Man	1957	6.25	12.50	25.00
JALO					
102	Where Is Da Woman/It Ain't Gonna Happen No More	1956	20.00	40.00	80.00
LIBERTY					
55776	Blue Roses/Way Down Home	1965	2.50	5.00	10.00
55823	I Need You/It Can Happen to You	1965	2.50	5.00	10.00
SUNBEAM					
105	Nothin' Shakin'/Oh, Wonderful Night	1958	10.00	20.00	40.00
112	Nobody Can Handle This Job/I'm Ready As I'll Ever Be	1958	6.25	12.50	25.00
—B-side by Gerry Granahan					
118	Love Eyes/Something Cha Cha	1958	6.25	12.50	25.00
VIK					
0184	Turn the Light On/Boom-De-De-Boom	1955	6.25	12.50	25.00
0193	Here 'Tis/I Look at You	1956	6.25	12.50	25.00
0203	Stand On That Rock/Baby You Did This to Me	1956	6.25	12.50	25.00
WARNER BROS.					
5313	My Heart Belongs to You/I'm Gonna Settle Down	1962	3.75	7.50	15.00
5345	(It's No) Sin/All I Want Is You	1963	3.75	7.50	15.00
"X"					
0096	Rock Love/All My Love Belongs to You	1955	7.50	15.00	30.00
0108	On Bended Knees/I Miss You So	1955	7.50	15.00	30.00
0128	Rollin' Stone/I'm Through Chasin' After You	1955	7.50	15.00	30.00
0151	Poor Little Monday/The Rain Song	1955	7.50	15.00	30.00
0184	Turn the Light On/Boom-De-De-Boom	1955	7.50	15.00	30.00
0193	Here 'Tis/I Look at You	1956	7.50	15.00	30.00
0203	Stand On That Rock/Baby You Did This to Me	1956	7.50	15.00	30.00

FONTAINE, FRANK

45s

Number	Title (A Side/B Side)	Yr	VG	VG+	NM
ABC-PARAMOUNT					
10384	When Your Hair Has Turned to Silver/Here in My Heart	1962	2.00	4.00	8.00
10384 [PS]	When Your Hair Has Turned to Silver/Here in My Heart	1962	3.00	6.00	12.00
10430	Easter Parade/Always	1963	2.00	4.00	8.00
10491	Daddy's Little Girl/Oh How I Miss You Tonight	1963	2.00	4.00	8.00
10517	RSVP/Alouette, Sweet Alouette	1964	2.00	4.00	8.00
10574	Any Man Who Loves His Mother/When Your Old Wedding Ring Was New	1964	2.00	4.00	8.00
10618	Mexicali Rose/I'm Counting on You	1965	2.00	4.00	8.00
10662	I Ain't Got Nobody/Someday	1965	2.00	4.00	8.00
CAPITOL					
4929	John L.C. Savoney The Sweepstakes Winner/The Maharajah	1963	2.00	4.00	8.00
—B-side by Lou Holtz					
4929 [PS]	John L.C. Savoney The Sweepstakes Winner/The Maharajah	1963	3.00	6.00	12.00
MGM					
12129	Everybody Rocks/Livin' It Up	1955	15.00	30.00	60.00

Albums

Number	Title (A Side/B Side)	Yr	VG	VG+	NM
ABC-PARAMOUNT					
442 [M]	Songs I Sing on the Jackie Gleason Show	1963	3.75	7.50	15.00
S-442 [S]	Songs I Sing on the Jackie Gleason Show	1963	5.00	10.00	20.00
460 [M]	Sings Like Crazy	1963	3.75	7.50	15.00
S-460 [S]	Sings Like Crazy	1963	5.00	10.00	20.00
470 [M]	How Sweet It Is	1964	3.75	7.50	15.00
S-470 [S]	How Sweet It Is	1964	5.00	10.00	20.00
490 [M]	More Songs I Sing on the Jackie Gleason Show	1964	3.75	7.50	15.00
S-490 [S]	More Songs I Sing on the Jackie Gleason Show	1964	5.00	10.00	20.00
514 [M]	I'm Counting on You	1965	3.75	7.50	15.00
S-514 [S]	I'm Counting on You	1965	5.00	10.00	20.00
541 [M]	All Time Great Hits	1966	3.75	7.50	15.00
S-541 [S]	All Time Great Hits	1966	5.00	10.00	20.00
MGM					
E-4470 [M]	Frank Fontaine's Ireland	1967	3.00	6.00	12.00
SE-4470 [S]	Frank Fontaine's Ireland	1967	3.75	7.50	15.00

FONTANA, WAYNE

Also see WAYNE FONTANA AND THE MINDBENDERS.

45s

Number	Title (A Side/B Side)	Yr	VG	VG+	NM
BRUT					
812	Sweet America/Interested	1973	—	2.50	5.00
METROMEDIA					
133	Say Goodbye to Yesterday/Dayton, Ohio	1969	—	3.00	6.00
MGM					
13456	It Was Easier to Hurt Her/You Made Me What I Am Today	1966	2.00	4.00	8.00
13516	Come On Home/My Eyes	1966	2.00	4.00	8.00
13661	Pamela, Pamela/Something Keeps Calling Me Back	1967	—	3.00	6.00
13762	From a Boy to a Girl/24 Sycamore	1967	—	3.00	6.00

Albums

MGM

Number	Title (A Side/B Side)	Yr	VG	VG+	NM
E-4459 [M]	Wayne Fontana	1967	5.00	10.00	20.00
SE-4459 [S]	Wayne Fontana	1967	6.25	12.50	25.00

FONTANA, WAYNE, AND THE MINDBENDERS

Also see WAYNE FONTANA; THE MINDBENDERS.

45s

Number	Title (A Side/B Side)	Yr	VG	VG+	NM
A&M					
3010	Game of Love/What a Wonderful World	1988	—	2.00	4.00
—B-side by Louis Armstrong					
3010 [PS]	Game of Love/What a Wonderful World	1988	—	2.00	4.00
—"Good Morning Vietnam" sleeve					
FONTANA					
1503	Game of Love/Since You've Been Gone	1965	3.75	7.50	15.00
1509	Game of Love/One More Time	1965	3.00	6.00	12.00
1514	It's Just a Little Bit Too Late/Long Time Comin'	1965	2.50	5.00	10.00
1524	She Needs Love/Like I Do	1965	2.50	5.00	10.00
1917	Stop, Look, Listen/Road Runner	1964	3.00	6.00	12.00
1945	Um, Um, Um, Um, Um, Um/First Taste of Love	1964	3.00	6.00	12.00

Albums

FONTANA

Number	Title (A Side/B Side)	Yr	VG	VG+	NM
MGF-27542 [M]	The Game of Love	1965	7.50	15.00	30.00
SRF-67542 [R]	The Game of Love	1965	6.25	12.50	25.00

FONTANE SISTERS, THE

Also see PERRY COMO.

45s

Number	Title (A Side/B Side)	Yr	VG	VG+	NM
DOT					
15171	Happy Days and Lonely Nights/If I Didn't Have You	1954	3.00	6.00	12.00
15248	Willow Weep for Me/A Love Like You	1954	3.00	6.00	12.00
15265	Hearts of Stone/Bless Your Heart	1954	3.75	7.50	15.00
15333	Rock Love/You're Mine	1955	3.00	6.00	12.00
15352	Most of All/Put Me in the Mood	1955	3.00	6.00	12.00
15370	Rollin' Stone/Playmates	1955	3.00	6.00	12.00
15386	Seventeen/If I Could Be with You	1955	3.00	6.00	12.00
15428	Daddy-O/Adorable	1955	3.00	6.00	12.00
15434	Nuttin' for Christmas/Silver Bells	1955	3.00	6.00	12.00
15450	Eddie My Love/Yum, Yum	1956	3.00	6.00	12.00
15462	I'm in Love Again/You Always Hurt the One You Love	1956	3.00	6.00	12.00
15480	Voices/Lonesome Lover Blues	1956	3.00	6.00	12.00
15501	Please Don't Leave Me/Still	1956	3.00	6.00	12.00
15527	The Banana Boat Song/Honolulu Moon	1957	2.50	5.00	10.00
15547	Dancing to the Rock and Roll/I'm the One Who Loves You	1957	2.50	5.00	10.00
15555	I'm Stickin' with You/Let the Rest of the World Go By	1957	2.50	5.00	10.00
15581	Fool Around/Which Way to Your Heart	1957	2.50	5.00	10.00
15682	Ain't It the Truth/Love Like a Fool	1957	2.50	5.00	10.00
15736	Chanson D'Amour/Coconut Grove	1958	2.50	5.00	10.00
15782	Buttermilk/Take a Step	1958	2.50	5.00	10.00
15853	Encore D'Amour/Jealous Heart	1958	2.50	5.00	10.00
15908	Billy Boy/Third Man Theme	1959	2.50	5.00	10.00
15943	You Are My Sunshine/A Lover's Hymn	1959	2.50	5.00	10.00
16014	Listen to Your Heart/Please Be Kind	1959	2.50	5.00	10.00
16027	Hearts of Stone/Seventeen	1960	2.00	4.00	8.00
16059	Theme from "A Summer Place"/Darling, It's Wonderful	1960	2.00	4.00	8.00
16086	Come Home Eddie/Lover's Leap	1960	2.00	4.00	8.00
16499	The Tip of My Fingers/Summertime Love	1963	—	3.00	6.00
RCA VICTOR					
47-2926	I'm a Little Cuckoo/Turtle Song	1949	3.00	6.00	12.00
—With the Cavanaugh Trio					
47-2976	The Bumpity Bus/24 Hours of Sunshine	1949	3.00	6.00	12.00
47-3127	Fairy Tales/The Cinderella Work Song	1949	3.00	6.00	12.00
47-3713	(If I Knew You Were Comin') I'd've Baked a Cake/Mississippi Mud	1950	3.00	6.00	12.00
47-3772	I Wanna Be Loved/I Didn't Know What Time It Was	1950	3.00	6.00	12.00
47-3814	Three Little Rings/Down Home Rag	1950	3.00	6.00	12.00
47-3940	Sleigh Bells/Jing-a-Ling, Jing-a-Ling	1950	3.00	6.00	12.00
—With Dick Contino					
47-3979	Tennessee Waltz/I Guess I'll Have to Dream the Rest	1950	3.00	6.00	12.00
47-4009	Bouncy Bouncy Bally/What Did I Do	1950	3.00	6.00	12.00

Number	Title (A Side/B Side)	Yr	VG	VG+	NM
47-4077	Let Me In/Hurry Home to Me	1951	3.75	7.50	15.00
—With Texas Jim Robertson					
47-4106	The Fortune Teller Song/The Fifth Wheel on the Wagon	1951	3.00	6.00	12.00
47-4168	Rhumba Boogie/Moon-June-Spoon	1951	3.00	6.00	12.00
47-4233	Castle Rock/Makin' Like a Train	1951	3.00	6.00	12.00
47-4274	Cold, Cold Heart/I Get the Blues When It Rains	1951	3.00	6.00	12.00
47-4322	A Howdy Doody Christmas/The Popcorn Song	1951	5.00	10.00	20.00
—With Howdy Doody					
47-4387	Alabama Jubilee/Grand Central Station	1951	3.00	6.00	12.00
47-4449	Snowflakes/River in Moonlight	1952	3.00	6.00	12.00
—With Merv Griffin and Freddie Martin					
47-4667	When I Dream/I Grabbed for the Ending	1952	3.00	6.00	12.00
47-4776	If You Would Only Be Mine/There's Doubt in My Mind	1952	3.00	6.00	12.00
47-5049	Winter's Here Again/Lonesome Road	1952	3.00	6.00	12.00
47-5162	Walkin' the Floor Over You/The Price I Paid for Loving You	1953	3.00	6.00	12.00
47-5266	Mexican Joe/He Who Has Love	1953	3.00	6.00	12.00
47-5383	Please Play Our Song/Falling	1953	3.00	6.00	12.00
47-5612	Till Then/Baion	1954	3.00	6.00	12.00
Albums					
DOT					
DLP-104 [10]	The Fontane Sisters	1955	12.50	25.00	50.00
DLP-3004 [M]	The Fontane Sisters	1956	10.00	20.00	40.00
—Maroon label					
DLP-3004 [M]	The Fontane Sisters	1957	6.25	12.50	25.00
—Black label					
DLP-3042 [M]	The Fontanes Sing	1957	7.50	15.00	30.00
DLP-3531 [M]	The Tips of My Fingers	1963	3.75	7.50	15.00
DLP-25531 [S]	The Tips of My Fingers	1963	5.00	10.00	20.00

FOOD

Number	Title (A Side/B Side)	Yr	VG	VG+	NM
Albums					
CAPITOL					
ST-304	Forever Is a Dream	1969	15.00	30.00	60.00

FOOL, THE

Number	Title (A Side/B Side)	Yr	VG	VG+	NM
45s					
MERCURY					
72896	Lay It Down/Rainbow Man	1969	2.00	4.00	8.00
72918	We Are One/Shining Light	1969	2.00	4.00	8.00
Albums					
MERCURY					
SR-61178	The Fool	1968	7.50	15.00	30.00

FOOTPRINTS

Number	Title (A Side/B Side)	Yr	VG	VG+	NM
45s					
CAPITOL					
2052	Never Say Die/Mama Rand's	1967	3.75	7.50	15.00

FORBES, GRAHAM

Number	Title (A Side/B Side)	Yr	VG	VG+	NM
Albums					
PHILLIPS INTERNATIONAL					
PLP-1955 [M]	The Martini Set	1959	200.00	400.00	800.00

FORCE FIVE, THE

Number	Title (A Side/B Side)	Yr	VG	VG+	NM
45s					
ASCOT					
2206	Gee Too Tiger/I Want You Babe	1966	12.50	25.00	50.00

FORD, BILLY

Of BILLY AND LILLIE.

Number	Title (A Side/B Side)	Yr	VG	VG+	NM
45s					
JOSIE					
775	String of Pearls/Stop Lyin' on Me	1955	10.00	20.00	40.00
REPRISE					
0265	This Is Worth Fighting For/My Girl	1964	3.00	6.00	12.00
UNITED					
142	Smooth Rocking/You Foxie Thing	1954	7.50	15.00	30.00
167	Confessing/Old Age	1955	7.50	15.00	30.00
VIK					
0263	How Can I Be Sure/Billy Boy Blow	1957	6.25	12.50	25.00

FORD, DEE DEE

Also see DON GARDNER AND DEE DEE FORD.

Number	Title (A Side/B Side)	Yr	VG	VG+	NM
45s					
ABC-PARAMOUNT					
10503	Just Like a Fool (I Keep Hopin')/Shoo-Fly Pie	1963	3.00	6.00	12.00
BRIAR					
142	Good Morning Blues/I Just Can't Believe	1962	3.00	6.00	12.00
TODD					
1049	Good Morning Blues/I Just Can't Believe	1959	3.75	7.50	15.00

FORD, EMILE, AND THE CHECKMATES

Number	Title (A Side/B Side)	Yr	VG	VG+	NM
45s					
ANDIE					
5018	Don't Tell Me Your Troubles/What Do You Want to Make Those Eyes at Me For	1960	3.75	7.50	15.00

FORD, FRANKIE

Number	Title (A Side/B Side)	Yr	VG	VG+	NM
45s					
ABC					
11431	All Alone Am I/Blue Monday	1974	—	2.50	5.00
ACE					
549	The Last One to Cry/Cheatin' Woman	1958	6.25	12.50	25.00
554	Sea Cruise/Roberta	1959	7.50	15.00	30.00
566	Alimony/Can't Tell My Heart (What to Do)	1959	6.25	12.50	25.00
580	Time After Time/Want to Be Your Man	1960	6.25	12.50	25.00
592	Chinatown/What's Goin' On	1960	6.25	12.50	25.00
592 [PS]	Chinatown/What's Goin' On	1960	12.50	25.00	50.00
8009	Ocean Full of Tears/Hour of Need	1963	3.75	7.50	15.00
BRIARMEADE					
7600	I've Found Someone of My Own/Battle Hymn of the Republic	1976	—	2.50	5.00
7701	Desperado/Mardi Gras in New Orleans	1977	—	2.50	5.00
7901	Halfway to Paradise/I'm Proud of What I Am	1979	—	2.50	5.00
CINNAMON					
752	When I Stop Dreamin'/I'm Proud of What I Am	1972	—	2.50	5.00
767	Talk to a Carpenter/When I Stop Dreamin'	1973	—	2.50	5.00
CONSTELLATION					
101	Chinatown/Ocean Full of Tears	1963	3.75	7.50	15.00
DOUBLOON					
101	Half a Crown/I Can't Face Tomorrow	1967	2.50	5.00	10.00
IMPERIAL					
5686	You Talk Too Much/If You've Got Troubles	1960	3.75	7.50	15.00
5706	My Southern Belle/The Groom	1960	3.75	7.50	15.00
5735	Seventenn/Doghouse	1961	3.75	7.50	15.00
5749	Saturday Night Fish Fry/Love Don't Love Nobody	1961	3.75	7.50	15.00
5776	Let 'Em Talk/What Happened to You	1961	3.75	7.50	15.00
5819	They Said It Couldn't Be Done/A Man Only Does	1962	3.75	7.50	15.00
PAULA					
351	Peace of Mind/I'm Proud of What I Am	1971	2.00	4.00	8.00
SYC					
1227	Growing Pains/Ups and Downs	1982	—	2.00	4.00
1228	My Prayer/Gospel Ship	1983	—	2.00	4.00
7-Inch Extended Plays					
ACE					
105	(contents unknown)	1959	37.50	75.00	150.00
105 [PS]	The Best of Frankie Ford	1959	37.50	75.00	150.00
Albums					
ACE					
LP 1005 [M]	Let's Take a Sea Cruise	1959	75.00	150.00	300.00
BRIARMEADE					
BR-5002	Frankie Ford	1976	3.00	6.00	12.00

FORD, ROCKY BILLY

Number	Title (A Side/B Side)	Yr	VG	VG+	NM
Albums					
AUDIO LAB					
AL-1561 [M]	A New Singing Star	1960	37.50	75.00	150.00

FORD, TENNESSEE ERNIE

Includes records issued as "Tennessee Ernie."

Number	Title (A Side/B Side)	Yr	VG	VG+	NM
45s					
CANADA DRY					
72-6596 [DJ]	The Real Story Of Christmas from St. Luke, Chapter 2	1972	—	2.50	5.00
—Special promo for his 1972 Christmas TV special					
72-6596 [PS]	The Real Story Of Christmas from St. Luke, Chapter 2	1972	—	2.50	5.00
—Special promo for his 1972 Christmas TV special					
CAPITOL					
F-985	I've Got to Feed 'Em in the Morning/My Hobby	1950	3.75	7.50	15.00
F-1124	I'll Never Be Free/Ain't Nobody's Business But My Own	1950	3.75	7.50	15.00
—With Kay Starr					
F-1174	Bright Lights/The Cincinnati Dancing Pig	1950	3.75	7.50	15.00
F-1205	Mama Goes Everywhere Papa Goes/Please Love Me	1950	3.75	7.50	15.00
—With Kay Starr					
F-1275	Bryant's Boogie/Little Juan Pedro	1950	5.00	10.00	20.00
F-1295	The Shot Gun Boogie/I Ain't Gonna Let It Happen No More	1950	5.00	10.00	20.00
F-1349	Tailor Made Woman/Stack-O-Lee	1951	3.75	7.50	15.00
F-1470	Kentucky Waltz/Strange Little Girl	1951	3.75	7.50	15.00
F-1521	Mr. and Mississippi/She's My Baby	1951	3.75	7.50	15.00
F-1567	Oceans of Tears/You're My Sugar	1951	3.75	7.50	15.00
—With Kay Starr					
F-1623	I'll Never Be Free/Ain't Nobody's Business But My Own	1951	3.00	6.00	12.00
—With Kay Starr; reissue					
F1626	The Shot Gun Boogie/Anticipation Blues	1951	3.00	6.00	12.00
F1695	Mule Train/The Cry of the Wild Goose	1951	3.00	6.00	12.00
F1775	Kissin' Bug Boogie/Woman Is a Five-Letter Word	1951	5.00	10.00	20.00
F1809	Hey, Good Lookin'/Cool, Cool Kisses	1951	3.75	7.50	15.00
F1830	A Rootin' Tootin' Santa Claus/Christmas Dinner	1951	3.75	7.50	15.00
F1911	Rock City Boogie/Streamline Cannonball	1951	5.00	10.00	20.00
—With the Dinning Sisters					
F2017	Hambone/Candy Dancers' Ball	1952	3.75	7.50	15.00
F2042	Put Your Arms Around Me/Everybody's Got a Girl But Me	1952	3.75	7.50	15.00
F2066	Snowshoe Thompson/Fatback Louisiana USA	1952	3.75	7.50	15.00
2145	Talk to the Animals/What a Wonderful World	1968	—	3.00	6.00
F2170	Blackberry Boogie/Tennessee Local	1952	5.00	10.00	20.00
F2179	Smokey Mountain Boogie/Country Junction	1952	5.00	10.00	20.00
F2215	I'm Hog Tied Over You/False Hearted Girl	1952	3.75	7.50	15.00
—With Ella Mae Morse					
2334	The Little Boy King/Bring a Torch, Jeanette, Isabella	1968	—	3.00	6.00
F2338	Sweet Temptation/I Don't Know	1953	3.75	7.50	15.00
F2443	Hey, Mr. Cotton Picker/Three Things (A Man Must Do)	1953	3.75	7.50	15.00
F2473	Don't Start Courtin' in a Hot Rod/We're a-Growin' Up	1953	5.00	10.00	20.00
—With Molly Bee					
2522	Honey-Eyed Girl (That's You That's You)/Good Morning, Dear	1969	—	3.00	6.00
F2602	Catfish Boogie/Kiss Me Big	1953	5.00	10.00	20.00
F2809	The Honeymoon's Over/This Must Be the Place	1954	3.00	6.00	12.00
—With Betty Hutton					
F2810	River of No Return/Give Me Your Word	1954	3.00	6.00	12.00
F2876	Losing You/Eins, Zwei, Drei	1954	3.00	6.00	12.00
2918	Rainy Night in Georgia/Let the Lovelight in Your Eyes Lead Me On	1970	—	2.50	5.00

Number	Title (A Side/B Side)	Yr	VG	VG+	NM
F2939	Somebody Bigger Than You and I/There Is Beauty in Everything	1954	3.00	6.00	12.00
F3058	Ballad of Davy Crockett/Farewell	1955	3.75	7.50	15.00
3079	Happy Songs of Love/Don't Let the Good Life Pass You By	1971	—	2.50	5.00
F3135	I Am a Pilgrim/His Hands	1955	3.00	6.00	12.00
F3262	Sixteen Tons/You Don't Have to Be a Baby to Cry	1955	3.75	7.50	15.00
F-3343	Bright Lights and Blonde Haired Women/That's All	1956	5.00	10.00	20.00
F3421	John Henry/Rovin' Gambler	1956	3.00	6.00	12.00
3422	Pea-Pickin' Cook/The Song	1972	—	2.50	5.00
F3474	Rock Roll Boogie/Call Me Darling, Call Me Sweetheart	1956	5.00	10.00	20.00
F3553	First Born/Have You Seen Her	1956	3.00	6.00	12.00
3556	Printers' Alley Stars/Baby	1973	—	2.00	4.00
3631	Farther Down the River (Where the Fishin's Good)/You've Still Got Love All Over You	1973	—	2.00	4.00
F3649	The Watermelon Song/One Suit	1957	3.00	6.00	12.00
F3700	Lonely Man/False Hearted Girl	1957	3.00	6.00	12.00
3704	Colorado Country Morning/Daddy Usta Say	1973	—	2.00	4.00
F3762	In the Middle of An Island/Ivy League	1957	3.00	6.00	12.00
3783	She Picked Up the Pieces/Sweet Child of Sunshine	1973	—	2.00	4.00
3848	I've Got Confidence/I'd Like to Be	1974	—	2.00	4.00
F3868	Bless Your Pea Pickin' Heart/Down Deep	1957	3.00	6.00	12.00
3916	Come On Down/Bits and Pieces of Life	1974	—	2.00	4.00
F3997	Love Makes the World Go Round/Sunday Barbecue	1958	2.50	5.00	10.00
4044	Baby/I'd Like to Be	1975	—	2.00	4.00
—With Andra Willis					
F4107	Sleepin' at the Foot of the Bed/Glad Rags	1958	2.50	5.00	10.00
4160	The Devil Ain't a Lonely Woman's Friend/Smokey Taverns, Bar Room Girls	1975	—	2.00	4.00
F4173	Code of the Mountains/Black-Eyed Susie	1959	2.50	5.00	10.00
4285	I Been to Georgia on a Fast Train/Baby's Home	1976	—	2.00	4.00
4302	Love Is the Only Thing/Sunny Side of Heaven	1959	2.00	4.00	8.00
4333	Sweet Feelin's/Dogs and Sheriff John	1976	—	2.00	4.00
4416	Joshua Fit De Battle/Oh Mary, Don't You Weep	1960	2.00	4.00	8.00
4446	Little Klinker/Jingle-O-The-Brownie	1960	3.00	6.00	12.00
4446 [PS]	Little Klinker/Jingle-O-The-Brownie	1960	5.00	10.00	20.00
4468	Bless This Land/Lord of All Creation	1960	2.00	4.00	8.00
4531	Dark As a Dungeon/His Love (Makes the World Go Round)	1961	2.00	4.00	8.00
4577	Little Red Rockin' Hood/I Gotta Have My Baby Back	1961	2.00	4.00	8.00
4734	Take Your Girlie to the Movies/There'll Be No New Tunes	1962	2.00	4.00	8.00
4793	The Work Song/Rags and Old Iron	1962	2.00	4.00	8.00
4838	How Great Thou Art/Eternal Life	1962	2.00	4.00	8.00
5425	Sixteen Tons/Hicktown	1965	—	3.00	6.00
5520	Girl Don't You Know/Now It's All Over	1965	—	3.00	6.00
5534	Sing We Now of Christmas/The Little Drummer Boy	1965	2.00	4.00	8.00
5757	God Lives/How Great Thou Art	1966	—	3.00	6.00
5900	Pearly Shells/Lahaina Luna	1967	—	3.00	6.00
5996	The Road/Hand Me Down Things	1967	—	3.00	6.00
F40280	The Cry of the Wild Goose/The Donkey Serenade	1950	5.00	10.00	20.00

7-Inch Extended Plays

CAPITOL

Number	Title (A Side/B Side)	Yr	VG	VG+	NM
EAP-413	(contents unknown)	1953	5.00	10.00	20.00
EAP-413 [PS]	Backwoods Boogie and Blues	1953	5.00	10.00	20.00
EAP 1-639	His Hands/Somebody Bigger Than You and I//I Am a Pilgrim/There Is Beauty in Everything	195?	3.75	7.50	15.00
EAP 1-639 [PS]	Tennessee Ernie Ford	195?	3.75	7.50	15.00
EAP-693	(contents unknown)	1956	3.75	7.50	15.00
EAP-693 [PS]	Sixteen Tons	1956	3.75	7.50	15.00
EAP 1-700	John Henry/Trouble in Mind//Gaily the Troubadour/The Lost Letter	1956	3.75	7.50	15.00
EAP 1-700 [PS]	This Lusty Land! Part 1	1956	3.75	7.50	15.00
EAP 2-700	Dark as a Dungeon/False Hearted Girl//I Gave My Love a Cherry/Nine Pound Hammer	1956	3.75	7.50	15.00
EAP 2-700 [PS]	This Lusty Land! Part 2	1956	3.75	7.50	15.00
EAP 3-700	Chicken Road/Who Will Shoe Your Pretty Little Foot//The Rovin' Gambler/In the Pines	1956	3.75	7.50	15.00
EAP 3-700 [PS]	This Lusty Land! Part 3	1956	3.75	7.50	15.00
EAP 1-756	The Ninety and Nine/Softly and Tenderly//Who at My Door Is Standing/Rock of Ages	1956	3.75	7.50	15.00
EAP 1-756 [PS]	Hymns, Part 1	1956	3.75	7.50	15.00
EAP 2-756	When They Ring the Golden Bells/In the Garden//Sweet Hour of Prayer/The Old Rugged Cross	1956	3.75	7.50	15.00
EAP 2-756 [PS]	Hymns, Part 2	1956	3.75	7.50	15.00
EAP 3-756	Let the Lower Lights Be Burning/Others//My Task/Ivory Palaces	1956	3.75	7.50	15.00
EAP 3-756 [PS]	Hymns, Part 3	1956	3.75	7.50	15.00
EAP 1-818	Just a Closer Walk with Thee/Peace in the Valley//Wayfaring Pilgrim/Were You There	195?	3.75	7.50	15.00
EAP 1-818 [PS]	Spirituals, Part 1	195?	3.75	7.50	15.00
EAP 2-818	He'll Understand and Say "Well Done"/I Know the Lord Laid His Hands on Me//Noah Found Grace in the Eyes of the Lord/I Want to Be Ready	195?	3.75	7.50	15.00
EAP 2-818 [PS]	Spirituals, Part 2	195?	3.75	7.50	15.00
EAP 3-818	Take My Hand, Precious Lord/Stand By Me//When God Dips His Love in My Heart/Get On Board, Little Children	195?	3.75	7.50	15.00
EAP 3-818 [PS]	Spirituals, Part 3	195?	3.75	7.50	15.00
EAP 1-888	(contents unknown)	1956	3.75	7.50	15.00
EAP 1-888 [PS]	Ol' Rockin' Ern, Part 1	1956	3.75	7.50	15.00
EAP 2-888	(contents unknown)	1956	3.75	7.50	15.00
EAP 2-888 [PS]	Ol' Rockin' Ern, Part 2	1956	3.75	7.50	15.00
EAP 3-888	(contents unknown)	1956	3.75	7.50	15.00
EAP 3-888 [PS]	Ol' Rockin' Ern, Part 3	1956	3.75	7.50	15.00
EAP 1-1005	*What a Friend We Have in Jesus/Jesus, Savior, Pilot Me/His Eye Is on the Sparrow/Beautiful Isle of Somewhere	1958	2.50	5.00	10.00
EAP 1-1005 [PS]	Nearer the Cross, Part 1	1958	2.50	5.00	10.00
EAP 2-1005	Now the Day Is Over/Nearer My God to Thee//Sweet Peace the Gift of God's Love/Whispering Hope	1958	2.50	5.00	10.00
EAP 2-1005 [PS]	Nearer the Cross, Part 2	1958	2.50	5.00	10.00
EAP 3-1005	(contents unknown)	1958	2.50	5.00	10.00
EAP 3-1005 [PS]	Nearer the Cross, Part 3	1958	2.50	5.00	10.00
EAP 1-1071	*Joy to the World/O Little Town of Bethlehem/The Star Carol/Hark! The Herald Angels Sing	1958	3.00	6.00	12.00
EAP 1-1071 [PS]	The Star Carol, Part 1	1958	3.00	6.00	12.00
EAP 2-1071	(contents unknown)	1958	3.00	6.00	12.00
EAP 2-1071 [PS]	The Star Carol, Part 2	1958	3.00	6.00	12.00
EAP 3-1071	(contents unknown)	1958	3.00	6.00	12.00
EAP 3-1071 [PS]	The Star Carol, Part 3	1958	3.00	6.00	12.00

GREEN GIANT

Number	Title (A Side/B Side)	Yr	VG	VG+	NM
PB-2565 [DJ]	Down in the Valley/Medley: The More We Get Together-Dear Evalina-Keep on the Sunny Side of Life-How Many Biscuits Can We Eat-For He's a Jolly Green Giant/How the Green Giant Found His Song (And Almost Lost His Ho-Ho-Ho)/Good Things from the Garden	1963	2.50	5.00	10.00
—Promotional item for the Green Giant Company/Le Sueur Peas					
PB-2565 [PS]	When Pea-Pickers Get Together	1963	2.50	5.00	10.00
—Promotional item for the Green Giant Company/Le Sueur Peas					

Albums

ARCHIVE OF FOLK AND JAZZ

Number	Title (A Side/B Side)	Yr	VG	VG+	NM
279	Tennessee Ernie Ford	197?	2.50	5.00	10.00

CAPITOL

Number	Title (A Side/B Side)	Yr	VG	VG+	NM
ST-127	Songs I Like to Sing	1969	3.00	6.00	12.00
ST-334	Holy, Holy, Holy	1969	3.00	6.00	12.00
SM-412	America the Beautiful	197?	2.00	4.00	8.00
—Reissue with new prefix					
STAO-412	America the Beautiful	1970	3.00	6.00	12.00
STBB-485 [(2)]	Christmas Special	1970	3.75	7.50	15.00
STBB-506 [(2)]	Sweet Hour of Prayer/Let Me Walk with Thee	1971	3.75	7.50	15.00
ST-583	Everything Is Beautiful	1971	3.00	6.00	12.00
DT 700 [R]	This Lusty Land!	196?	3.00	6.00	12.00
T 700 [M]	This Lusty Land	1956	6.25	12.50	25.00
—Turquoise or gray label					
T 700 [M]	This Lusty Land	1959	5.00	10.00	20.00
—Black label with colorband, logo at left					
T 700 [M]	This Lusty Land!	1963	3.75	7.50	15.00
—Black label with colorband, logo at top					
ST-730	Abide with Me	1971	3.00	6.00	12.00
ST 756 [S]	Hymns	196?	3.75	7.50	15.00
T 756 [M]	Hymns	1956	6.25	12.50	25.00
—Turquoise or gray label					
T 756 [M]	Hymns	1959	5.00	10.00	20.00
—Black label with colorband, logo at left					
T 756 [M]	Hymns	1962	3.75	7.50	15.00
—Black label with colorband, logo at top					
ST 818 [S]	Spirituals	195?	3.75	7.50	15.00
T 818 [M]	Spirituals	1957	6.25	12.50	25.00
—Turquoise or gray label					
T 818 [M]	Spirituals	1959	5.00	10.00	20.00
—Black label with colorband, logo at left					
T 818 [M]	Spirituals	1962	3.75	7.50	15.00
—Black label with colorband, logo at top					
ST-831 [S]	C-H-R-I-S-T-M-A-S	1971	3.00	6.00	12.00
ST-833	The Folk Album	1971	3.00	6.00	12.00
DT 841 [R]	Tennessee Ernie Ford Favorites	196?	3.00	6.00	12.00
T 841 [M]	Tennessee Ernie Ford Favorites	1958	5.00	10.00	20.00
—Black label with colorband, logo at left					
T 841 [M]	Tennessee Ernie Ford Favorites	1962	3.75	7.50	15.00
—Black label with colorband, logo at top					
T 888 [M]	Ol' Rockin' Ern	1957	12.50	25.00	50.00
—Turquoise or gray label					
ST 1005 [S]	Nearer the Cross	1959	6.25	12.50	25.00
—Black label with colorband, logo at left					
ST 1005 [S]	Nearer the Cross	1962	5.00	10.00	20.00
—Black label with colorband, logo at top					
T 1005 [M]	Nearer the Cross	1958	5.00	10.00	20.00
—Black label with colorband, logo at left					
T 1005 [M]	Nearer the Cross	1962	3.75	7.50	15.00
—Black label with colorband, logo at top					
ST 1071 [S]	The Star Carol	1958	7.50	15.00	30.00
—Same contents as above, but in stereo; originals have black labels with colorband and "Capitol" logo on left					
ST 1071 [S]	The Star Carol	1962	5.00	10.00	20.00
—Black label with colorband, "Capitol" logo on top. This was also likely reissued on later Capitol labels into the 1970s with values no more than half the above.					
T 1071 [M]	The Star Carol	1958	6.25	12.50	25.00
—Originals have black labels with colorband and "Capitol" logo on left					
T 1071 [M]	The Star Carol	1962	3.75	7.50	15.00
—Later pressings have black label with colorband, "Capitol" logo on top					
ST 1227 [S]	Gather 'Round	1959	5.00	10.00	20.00
T 1227 [M]	Gather 'Round	1959	3.75	7.50	15.00
ST 1272 [S]	A Friend We Have	1959	5.00	10.00	20.00
T 1272 [M]	A Friend We Have	1959	3.75	7.50	15.00
STAO 1332 [S]	Sing a Hymn with Me	1960	6.25	12.50	25.00
—With hymnal					
TAO 1332 [M]	Sing a Hymn with Me	1960	5.00	10.00	20.00
—With hymnal					
DT 1380 [R]	Sixteen Tons	196?	3.00	6.00	12.00
T 1380 [M]	Sixteen Tons	1960	3.75	7.50	15.00
ST 1539 [S]	Civil War Songs of the North	1961	5.00	10.00	20.00
T 1539 [M]	Civil War Songs of the North	1961	3.75	7.50	15.00
ST 1540 [S]	Civil War Songs of the South	1961	5.00	10.00	20.00
T 1540 [M]	Civil War Songs of the South	1961	3.75	7.50	15.00
ST 1679 [S]	Sing a Hymn with Me	1962	3.75	7.50	15.00
—Reissue of 1332 with standard cover?					
T 1679 [M]	Sing a Hymn with Me	1962	3.00	6.00	12.00
—Reissue of 1332 with standard cover?					
T 1680 [M]	Sing a Spiritual with Me	1962	3.00	6.00	12.00
ST 1684 [S]	Here Comes the Mississippi Showboat	1962	3.75	7.50	15.00
T 1684 [M]	Here Comes the Mississippi Showboat	1962	3.00	6.00	12.00
ST 1689 [S]	Sing a Spiritual with Me	1962	3.75	7.50	15.00

Number	Title (A Side/B Side)	Yr	VG	VG+	NM
ST 1694 [S]	Hymns at Home	1962	3.75	7.50	15.00
T 1694 [M]	Hymns at Home	1962	3.00	6.00	12.00
ST 1751 [S]	I Love to Tell the Story	1962	3.75	7.50	15.00
T 1751 [M]	I Love to Tell the Story	1962	3.00	6.00	12.00
ST 1794 [S]	Book of Favorite Hymns	1962	5.00	10.00	20.00
T 1794 [M]	Book of Favorite Hymns	1962	3.75	7.50	15.00
ST 1875 [S]	Long Long Ago	1963	3.75	7.50	15.00
T 1875 [M]	Long Long Ago	1963	3.00	6.00	12.00
ST 1937 [S]	We Gather Together	1963	3.75	7.50	15.00
T 1937 [M]	We Gather Together	1963	3.00	6.00	12.00
ST 1994 [S]	The Story of Christmas	1963	5.00	10.00	20.00
T 1994 [M]	The Story of Christmas	1963	3.75	7.50	15.00
—With the Roger Wagner Chorale					
SM-2026	Great Gospel Songs	197?	2.00	4.00	8.00
—Reissue with new prefix					
ST 2026 [S]	Great Gospel Songs	1964	3.75	7.50	15.00
T 2026 [M]	Great Gospel Songs	1964	3.00	6.00	12.00
SM-2097	Country Hits...Feelin' Blue	197?	2.00	4.00	8.00
—Reissue with new prefix					
ST 2097 [S]	Country Hits...Feelin' Blue	1964	3.75	7.50	15.00
T 2097 [M]	Country Hits...Feelin' Blue	1964	3.00	6.00	12.00
ST 2144 [S]	My Favorite Things	1966	3.75	7.50	15.00
STBL 2183 [(2) S]	The World's Best Loved Hymns	1964	6.25	12.50	25.00
TBL 2183 [(2) M]	The World's Best Loved Hymns	1964	5.00	10.00	20.00
ST 2296 [S]	Let Me Walk with Thee	1965	3.75	7.50	15.00
T 2296 [M]	Let Me Walk with Thee	1965	3.00	6.00	12.00
ST 2394 [S]	Sing We Now of Christmas	1965	3.75	7.50	15.00
—Same as above, but in stereo					
T 2394 [M]	Sing We Now of Christmas	1965	3.00	6.00	12.00
T 2444 [M]	My Favorite Things	1966	3.00	6.00	12.00
ST 2557 [S]	Wonderful Peace	1966	3.75	7.50	15.00
T 2557 [M]	Wonderful Peace	1966	3.00	6.00	12.00
ST 2618 [S]	God Lives	1966	3.75	7.50	15.00
T 2618 [M]	God Lives	1966	3.00	6.00	12.00
ST 2681 [S]	Aloha from Tennessee Ernie Ford	1967	3.00	6.00	12.00
T 2681 [M]	Aloha from Tennessee Ernie Ford	1967	3.75	7.50	15.00
SM-2761	Faith of Our Fathers	197?	2.00	4.00	8.00
—Reissue with new prefix					
ST 2761 [S]	Faith of Our Fathers	1967	3.00	6.00	12.00
T 2761 [M]	Faith of Our Fathers	1967	3.75	7.50	15.00
ST 2845 [S]	Our Garden of Hymns	1968	3.00	6.00	12.00
T 2845 [M]	Our Garden of Hymns	1968	5.00	10.00	20.00
ST 2896	The World of Pop and Country Hits	1968	3.00	6.00	12.00
STCL 2942 [(3)]	The Tennessee Ernie Ford Deluxe Set	1968	5.00	10.00	20.00
SKAO 2949	Best Hymns	1968	3.00	6.00	12.00
ST 2968	O Come All Ye Faithful	1968	3.00	6.00	12.00
ST-11001	Mr. Words and Music	1972	2.50	5.00	10.00
ST-11092	It's Tennessee Ernie Ford	1973	2.50	5.00	10.00
ST-11232	Tennessee Ernie Ford Sings About Jesus	1973	2.50	5.00	10.00
ST-11290	Make a Joyful Noise	1974	2.50	5.00	10.00
SVBB-11325 [(2)]	25th Anniversary/Yesterday and Today	1974	3.00	6.00	12.00
SVBB-11326 [(2)]	25th Anniversary/Hymns & Gospel	1974	3.00	6.00	12.00
SVBB-11382 [(2)]	Precious Memories	1975	3.00	6.00	12.00
ST-11495	Tennessee Ernie Ford Sings His Great Love Songs	1975	2.50	5.00	10.00
SM-12033	Book of Favorite Hymns	1980	2.50	5.00	10.00
SN-16040	Yesterday	1981	2.00	4.00	8.00
SN-16042	Gospel	1981	2.00	4.00	8.00
SN-16043	Hymns	1981	2.00	4.00	8.00
SN-16173	Hymns	1981	2.00	4.00	8.00
SN-16174	Spirituals	1981	2.00	4.00	8.00
SN-16289	The Star Carol	1982	2.00	4.00	8.00
—Budget-line reissue					
PICKWICK					
PTP-2016 [(2)]	Tennessee Ernie Ford	197?	3.00	6.00	12.00
PTP-2050 [(2)]	Hymns	197?	3.00	6.00	12.00
SPC-3047	Bless Your Pea-Pickin' Heart	196?	3.00	6.00	12.00
SPC-3066	I Love You So Much	196?	3.00	6.00	12.00
SPC-3222	The Need for Prayer	197?	2.50	5.00	10.00
SPC-3268	Sixteen Tons	197?	2.50	5.00	10.00
SPC-3273	Jesus Loves Me	197?	2.50	5.00	10.00
SPC-3308	Amazing Grace	197?	2.50	5.00	10.00
SPC-3353	Rock of Ages	197?	2.50	5.00	10.00
RANWOOD					
RLP-7026 [(2)]	Tennessee Ernie Ford Sings 22 Favorite Hymns	198?	3.00	6.00	12.00
WORD					
8764	He Touched Me	1978	2.50	5.00	10.00
8798	Swing Wide Your Golden Gate	198?	2.50	5.00	10.00
8841	Tell Me the Old Story	1979	2.50	5.00	10.00
8841	Tell Me the Old Story	198?	2.50	5.00	10.00
8858	There's a Song in My Heart	198?	2.50	5.00	10.00

FORD THEATRE, THE

Number	Title (A Side/B Side)	Yr	VG	VG+	NM
45s					
ABC					
11118	Theme for the Masses/I Can't Help It Baby	1968	2.50	5.00	10.00
11227	I've Got the Fever/Jefferson Airplane	1969	2.50	5.00	10.00
Albums					
ABC					
S-658	Trilogy	1968	6.25	12.50	25.00
S-681	Time Changes	1969	5.00	10.00	20.00

FOREST

Number	Title (A Side/B Side)	Yr	VG	VG+	NM
Albums					
HARVEST					
SKAO-419	Forest	1970	12.50	25.00	50.00

FOREVER MORE

Number	Title (A Side/B Side)	Yr	VG	VG+	NM
45s					
RCA VICTOR					
74-0277	Home Country Blues/Back in the States Again	1969	2.00	4.00	8.00
74-0335	Beautiful Afternoon/One O'Clock and All's Well	1970	2.00	4.00	8.00
Albums					
RCA VICTOR					
LSP-4272	Yours Forever More	1970	3.75	7.50	15.00
LSP-4425	Words on Black Plastic	1971	3.75	7.50	15.00

FORMATIONS, THE

Number	Title (A Side/B Side)	Yr	VG	VG+	NM
45s					
BANK					
1007	At the Top of the Stairs/Magic Melody	1968	7.50	15.00	30.00
MGM					
13899	At the Top of the Stairs/Magic Melody	1968	2.50	5.00	10.00
13963	Love's Not Only for the Heart/Lonely Voice of Love	1968	5.00	10.00	20.00
14009	Don't Get Close/There's No Room	1968	3.00	6.00	12.00

FORTUNE, JOHNNY

Number	Title (A Side/B Side)	Yr	VG	VG+	NM
45s					
ARENA					
102	I'm a Fool for You/Gee But I Miss You	1963	5.00	10.00	20.00
ARHAVEN					
1001	I'm a Fool for You/Gee But I Miss You	1962	6.25	12.50	25.00
BEAVER					
111	I'm Requesting a Love Song/Stay Just One More Day	1966	3.75	7.50	15.00
CRUSADER					
104	If You Love Me/Gee But I Miss You	1964	3.75	7.50	15.00
CURRENT					
101	Say You Will/Come On and Love Me	1965	3.75	7.50	15.00
104	Dan Stole My Girl/You Want Me to Be Your Baby	1965	3.75	7.50	15.00
105	I Am Lonely for You/I'll Never Let You Go	1965	3.75	7.50	15.00
EMMY					
1001	If You Love Me/Alone and Crying	1960	7.50	15.00	30.00
1002	I'm in Heaven (When You Kiss Me)/Gee But I Miss You	1960	7.50	15.00	30.00
PARK AVENUE					
104	Need You/One Less Angel	1963	3.75	7.50	15.00
110	Midnight Surf/Soul Surfer	1963	3.75	7.50	15.00
126	Surfer's Trip/Soul Traveler	1963	3.75	7.50	15.00
130	Dragster/Siboney	1963	3.75	7.50	15.00
4905	I'm Talkin' About You/My Wandering Love	1963	3.75	7.50	15.00
UNITED ARTISTS					
720	Juarez/It Ain't Necessarily So	1964	3.75	7.50	15.00
780	Don't You Lie to Me/Don't Stay Out After Midnight	1964	3.75	7.50	15.00
VAULT					
954	Your True Love/Tell me You Love Me	1969	2.50	5.00	10.00

FORTUNES, THE (1)

British band.

Number	Title (A Side/B Side)	Yr	VG	VG+	NM
45s					
CAPITOL					
3086	Here Comes That Rainy Day Feeling Again/I Gotta Dream	1971	—	3.00	6.00
3086	Here Comes That Rainy Day Feeling Again/Bad Side of Town	1971	2.50	5.00	10.00
3179	Freedom Comes, Freedom Goes/There's a Man	1971	—	2.50	5.00
3248	Storm in a Teacup/I'm Not Following You	1971	—	2.50	5.00
3445	Wait Until September/Don't Sing to Me	1972	—	2.50	5.00
3514	I Can't Remember When the Sun Went In/Secret Love	1973	—	2.50	5.00
3626	Give Me Some Room/Whenever It's a Sunday	1973	—	2.50	5.00
PRESS					
9773	You've Got Your Troubles/I've Gotta Go	1965	4.00	8.00	16.00
—White label stock copy					
9773	You've Got Your Troubles/I've Gotta Go	1965	3.00	6.00	12.00
—Purple label					
9798	Here It Comes Again/Things I Should Have Known	1965	3.75	7.50	15.00
—White label stock copy					
9798	Here It Comes Again/Things I Should Have Known	1965	2.50	5.00	10.00
—Purple label					
9811	This Golden Ring/Someone to Care	1966	2.50	5.00	10.00
60001	Gone from My Mind/Silent Street	1966	2.50	5.00	10.00
UNITED ARTISTS					
50211	The Idol/His Smile Was a Lie	1967	2.50	5.00	10.00
50280	Painting a Shadow/Fire Brigade	1968	2.50	5.00	10.00
WORLD PACIFIC					
77937	That Same Old Feeling/Lifetime of Love	1970	2.00	4.00	8.00
Albums					
CAPITOL					
ST-647	Freedom	1971	—	—	—
—Canceled					
ST-809	Here Comes That Rainy Day Feeling Again	1971	5.00	10.00	20.00
ST-11041	Storm in a Teacup	1972	3.75	7.50	15.00
—Contains the canceled "Freedom" LP with one track deleted, plus the title song added					
COCA-COLA					
(no #) [DJ]	It's the Real Thing	1969	15.00	30.00	60.00
PRESS					
PR 73002 [M]	The Fortunes	1965	8.75	17.50	35.00
PRS 83002 [S]	The Fortunes	1965	12.50	25.00	50.00
WORLD PACIFIC					
WPS-21904	That Same Old Feeling	1970	3.75	7.50	15.00

FORTUNES, THE (U)

None of these are by group (1), but exactly which ones are by the same group as others, we have not yet determined.

Number	Title (A Side/B Side)	Yr	VG	VG+	NM
45s					
ARGO					
5364	Congratulations/Look at Me, Look at You	1960	15.00	30.00	60.00
CHECKER					
818	Believe in Me/My Baby Is Fine	1955	15.00	30.00	60.00

Number	Title (A Side/B Side)	Yr	VG	VG+	NM
CUB					
9123	The Ghoul in School/You Don't Know (What I've Been Through)	1963	3.75	7.50	15.00
DECCA					
30541	Tarnished Angel/Who Cares?	1958	15.00	30.00	60.00
30688	How Clever of You/Trees	1958	12.50	25.00	50.00
DRA					
320	Tell Me/Running Away from Love	1962	75.00	150.00	300.00
LAKE					
704	St. John's Cha Cha/Runnin'	196?	3.75	7.50	15.00
QUEEN					
24010	Nothing Matters Anymore/Ugly Duckling	1962	6.25	12.50	25.00
TOP RANK					
2019	Steady Vows/In the Night	1959	10.00	20.00	40.00
YUCCA					
168	Laugh of the Train/Chi Wawa	1964	7.50	15.00	30.00
170	Lonely Teardrops/This Is Love	1964	10.00	20.00	40.00

49TH PARALLEL, THE

45s

Number	Title (A Side/B Side)	Yr	VG	VG+	NM
MAVERICK					
1004	Close the Barn Door/Twilight Woman	1968	5.00	10.00	20.00
1011	(Come On Little Child and) Talk to Me/Now That I'm a Man	1968	5.00	10.00	20.00

Albums

Number	Title (A Side/B Side)	Yr	VG	VG+	NM
MAVERICK					
MAS-7001	The 49th Parallel	1969	62.50	125.00	250.00

FORUM, THE

45s

Number	Title (A Side/B Side)	Yr	VG	VG+	NM
MIRA					
232	The River Is Wide/I Fall in Love	1967	3.00	6.00	12.00
243	Trip on Me/It's Sunday	1967	3.00	6.00	12.00
248	A Girl Without a Boy/Go Try to Put Out the Sun	1968	3.00	6.00	12.00
PENTHOUSE					
504	The River Is Wide/(B-side unknown)	1966	5.00	10.00	20.00

Albums

Number	Title (A Side/B Side)	Yr	VG	VG+	NM
MIRA					
MLP-301 [M]	The River Is Wide	1967	3.75	7.50	15.00
MLPS-301 [S]	The River Is Wide	1967	5.00	10.00	20.00

FOSTER, CELL, AND THE AUDIOS

45s

Number	Title (A Side/B Side)	Yr	VG	VG+	NM
ULTRA					
105	Honest I Do/I Prayed for You	1956	100.00	200.00	400.00
—Yellow label					
105	Honest I Do/I Prayed for You	1956	62.50	125.00	250.00
—Maroon label					

FOSTER, JOHN, AND SONS BLACK DYKE MILLS BAND

45s

Number	Title (A Side/B Side)	Yr	VG	VG+	NM
APPLE					
1800	Thingumybob/Yellow Submarine	1968	25.00	50.00	100.00
—With "Thingumybob" on uncut apple side					
1800	Thingumybob/Yellow Submarine	1968	25.00	50.00	100.00
—With "Yellow Submarine" on uncut apple side					
1800	Thingumybob/Yellow Submarine	1968	30.00	60.00	120.00
—With black star on uncut apple side					

FOTHERINGAY

Also see SANDY DENNY.

Albums

Number	Title (A Side/B Side)	Yr	VG	VG+	NM
A&M					
SP-4289	Faotheringay	1970	3.75	7.50	15.00

FOTO-FI FOUR, THE

Some sources say Harry NILSSON is on this recording.

45s

Number	Title (A Side/B Side)	Yr	VG	VG+	NM
FOTO-FI					
107	Stand Up and Holler!/Ismael	1964	6.25	12.50	25.00
107 [PS]	Stand Up and Holler!/Ismael	1964	12.50	25.00	50.00

—Sleeve states: "The Beatles arrive in America! Have fun running the film with this specially scored recording." Price does not include film.

FOUL DOGS, THE

Albums

Number	Title (A Side/B Side)	Yr	VG	VG+	NM
RHYTHM SOUND					
GA-481	No. 1	1968	75.00	150.00	300.00

FOUNDATIONS, THE

45s

Number	Title (A Side/B Side)	Yr	VG	VG+	NM
UNI					
55038	Baby, Now That I've Found You/Come On Back to Me	1967	2.00	4.00	8.00
55058	Back on My Feet Again/I Can Take or Leave Your Loving	1968	—	3.00	6.00
55073	We Are Happy People/Any Old Time	1968	—	3.00	6.00
55101	Build Me Up Buttercup/New Direction	1968	2.00	4.00	8.00
55117	In the Bad, Bad Old Days (Before You Loved Me)/Give Me Love	1969	—	3.00	6.00
55137	My Little Chickadee/Solomon Grundy	1969	—	3.00	6.00
55162	Why Did You Cry/Born to Live, Born to Die	1969	—	3.00	6.00
55210	Take a Girl Like You/I'm Gonna Be a Rich Man	1970	—	3.00	6.00
55315	I'll Give You Love/Stoney Ground	1972	—	3.00	6.00

Albums

Number	Title (A Side/B Side)	Yr	VG	VG+	NM
UNI					
73016	Baby Now That I've Found You	1968	7.50	15.00	30.00
73043	Build Me Up Buttercup	1969	7.50	15.00	30.00
73058	Digging the Foundations	1969	7.50	15.00	30.00

FOUNTAIN, PETE

45s

Number	Title (A Side/B Side)	Yr	VG	VG+	NM
CORAL					
62107	My Inspiration/Japansy	1959	2.00	4.00	8.00
62154	A Closer Walk/Do You Know What It Means to Miss New Orleans	1959	2.00	4.00	8.00
62211	Sentimental Journey/Columbus Stockade Blues	1960	2.00	4.00	8.00
62243	Alone Together/Forbidden Love	1961	2.00	4.00	8.00
62266	Oh, Didn't He Ramble/Allison's Theme from Parrish	1962	2.00	4.00	8.00
62350	The Grasshopper/Lonely Little Tune	1963	—	3.00	6.00
62365	Casablanca/Lost Love	1963	—	3.00	6.00
62376	China Nights/Theme from "Women of the World"	1963	—	3.00	6.00
62413	Licorice Stick/Estrellita	1964	—	3.00	6.00
62427	The Horny Wind Blows/Humbug	1964	—	3.00	6.00
62441	Mr. Stick Man/Amazon	1965	—	3.00	6.00
62446	Whipped Cream/Midnight Pete	1965	—	3.00	6.00
62454	Mae/Gotta Travel On	1965	—	3.00	6.00
62460	Rave On/The Whippenpoof Song	1965	—	3.00	6.00
62474	Juliet's Theme/Walking the Floor Over You	1965	—	3.00	6.00
62496	Mood Indigo/Sleepy Serenade	1966	—	2.50	5.00
62516	Thoroughly Modern Millie/Jimmy	1967	—	2.50	5.00
62527	Music to Turn You On/(Carol's Theme) The Eyes of Love	1967	—	2.50	5.00
62545	For Pete's Sake/Danke Schoen	1967	—	2.50	5.00
62557	Les Bicyclettes De Belsize/Puddin	1969	—	2.50	5.00
62561	Aquarius/The Flesh Failures	1969	—	2.50	5.00
62564	Sunday in the Country/Applause	1970	—	2.00	4.00
62565	Night Train to Memphis/San Antonio Rose	1970	—	2.00	4.00
65545	San Antonio Rose/Dixie	1961	2.00	4.00	8.00
65549	Yes Indeed/While We Danced at the Mardi Gras	1962	2.00	4.00	8.00
65563	Corrine, Corrina/Talkin' 'Bout You	196?	—	3.00	6.00
65566	Shine/Mighty Like the Blues	196?	—	3.00	6.00
65577	Sugar Bowl Parade/Marching 'Round the Mountain	196?	—	3.00	6.00
65579	Birth of the Blues/Begin the Beguine	196?	—	3.00	6.00
65586	Hello, Dolly!/Tippin' In	1964	—	3.00	6.00
65601	Born to Lose/I Love You So Much It Hurts	196?	—	2.50	5.00
65602	Tiger Rag/I Love You So Much It Hurts	196?	—	2.50	5.00
65605	The Christmas Song (Merry Christmas To You)/Santa Claus Medley	1966	2.00	4.00	8.00
65606	Fountain in the Rain/Over the Waves	196?	—	2.50	5.00
65612	My Blue Heaven/Tiger Rag	196?	—	2.50	5.00
65614	Swing Low, Sweet Chariot/Walking Through New Orleans	196?	—	2.50	5.00
65616	Maria Elena/Put On Your Old Grey Bonnet	196?	—	2.50	5.00
65617	When the Saints Go Marching In March/Mardi Gras Walking Club	196?	—	2.50	5.00
65619	Make Your Own Kind of Music/Early in the Morning	1970	—	2.00	4.00

7-Inch Extended Plays

Number	Title (A Side/B Side)	Yr	VG	VG+	NM
CORAL					
EC 81190	Yes Indeed/Dis Ol' Train//Nobody Knows the Trouble I've Seen/Sing You Sinners	195?	2.50	5.00	10.00
EC 81190 [PS]	Yes Indeed	195?	2.50	5.00	10.00

Albums

Number	Title (A Side/B Side)	Yr	VG	VG+	NM
ARCHIVE OF FOLK AND JAZZ					
257	New Orleans All-Stars	197?	2.50	5.00	10.00
CAPITOL					
SN-16224	Pete Fountain and Friends	1982	2.00	4.00	8.00
SN-16225	Way Down Yonder in New Orleans	1982	2.00	4.00	8.00
CORAL					
CXS-710 [(2)]	The Best of Pete Fountain	1969	3.75	7.50	15.00
CRL 57200 [M]	Lawrence Welk Presents Pete Fountain	1958	5.00	10.00	20.00
CRL 57282 [M]	Pete Fountain's New Orleans	1959	3.75	7.50	15.00
CRL 57284 [M]	The Blues	1959	3.75	7.50	15.00
CRL 57313 [M]	Pete Fountain Day	1960	3.75	7.50	15.00
CRL 57314 [M]	Pete Fountain at the Bateau Lounge	1960	3.75	7.50	15.00
CRL 57333 [M]	Pete Fountain Salutes the Great Clarinetists	1960	3.75	7.50	15.00
CRL 57357 [M]	Pete Fountain On Tour	1961	3.75	7.50	15.00
CRL 57359 [M]	Pete Fountain's French Quarter	1961	3.75	7.50	15.00
CRL 57378 [M]	I Love Paris	1961	3.75	7.50	15.00
CRL 57394 [M]	Swing Low Sweet Chariot	1962	3.75	7.50	15.00
CRL 57401 [M]	Pete Fountain's Music from Dixie	1962	3.75	7.50	15.00
CRL 57419 [M]	New Orleans Scene	1963	3.75	7.50	15.00
CRL 57424 [M]	Plenty of Pete	1963	3.00	6.00	12.00
CRL 57429 [M]	New Orleans at Midnight	1964	3.00	6.00	12.00
CRL 57440 [M]	South Rampart Street Parade	1963	3.00	6.00	12.00
CRL 57453 [M]	Pete's Place	1964	3.00	6.00	12.00
CRL 57460 [M]	Licorice Stick	1964	3.00	6.00	12.00
CRL 57473 [M]	Mr. Stick Man	1965	3.00	6.00	12.00
CRL 57474 [M]	Standing Room Only	1965	3.00	6.00	12.00
CRL 57484 [M]	Mood Indigo	1966	3.00	6.00	12.00
CRL 57486 [M]	A Taste of Honey	1966	3.00	6.00	12.00
CRL 57487 [M]	Candy Clarinet — Merry Christmas from Pete Fountain	1966	3.00	6.00	12.00
CRL 57488 [M]	I've Got You Under My Skin	1967	3.00	6.00	12.00
CRL 57496 [M]	Music to Turn You On	1967	3.75	7.50	15.00
CRL 57499 [M]	Pete Fountain Plays Bert Kaempfert	1968	3.75	7.50	15.00
CRL 757282 [S]	Pete Fountain's New Orleans	1959	5.00	10.00	20.00
CRL 757284 [S]	The Blues	1959	5.00	10.00	20.00
CRL 757313 [S]	Pete Fountain Day	1960	5.00	10.00	20.00
CRL 757314 [S]	Pete Fountain at the Bateau Lounge	1960	5.00	10.00	20.00
CRL 757333 [S]	Pete Fountain Salutes the Great Clarinetists	1960	5.00	10.00	20.00
CRL 757357 [S]	Pete Fountain On Tour	1961	5.00	10.00	20.00
CRL 757359 [S]	Pete Fountain's French Quarter	1961	5.00	10.00	20.00
CRL 757378 [S]	I Love Paris	1961	5.00	10.00	20.00
CRL 757394 [S]	Swing Low Sweet Chariot	1962	5.00	10.00	20.00
CRL 757401 [S]	Pete Fountain's Music from Dixie	1962	5.00	10.00	20.00
CRL 757419 [S]	New Orleans Scene	1963	5.00	10.00	20.00
CRL 757424 [S]	Plenty of Pete	1963	3.75	7.50	15.00
CRL 757429 [S]	New Orleans at Midnight	1964	3.75	7.50	15.00
CRL 757440 [S]	South Rampart Street Parade	1963	3.75	7.50	15.00
CRL 757453 [S]	Pete's Place	1964	3.75	7.50	15.00

Number	Title (A Side/B Side)	Yr	VG	VG+	NM
CRL 757460 [S]	Licorice Stick	1964	3.75	7.50	15.00
CRL 757473 [S]	Mr. Stick Man	1965	3.75	7.50	15.00
CRL 757474 [S]	Standing Room Only	1965	3.75	7.50	15.00
CRL 757484 [S]	Mood Indigo	1966	3.75	7.50	15.00
CRL 757486 [S]	A Taste of Honey	1966	3.75	7.50	15.00
CRL 757487 [S]	Candy Clarinet — Merry Christmas from Pete Fountain	1966	3.75	7.50	15.00
CRL 757488 [S]	I've Got You Under My Skin	1967	3.75	7.50	15.00
CRL 757496 [S]	Music to Turn You On	1967	3.00	6.00	12.00
CRL 757499 [S]	Pete Fountain Plays Bert Kaempfert	1968	3.00	6.00	12.00
CRL 757503	Walking Through New Orleans	1968	3.00	6.00	12.00
CRL 757505	Those Were the Days	1969	3.00	6.00	12.00
CRL 757507	Both Sides Now	1969	3.00	6.00	12.00
CRL 757510	Make Your Own Kind of Music	1970	3.00	6.00	12.00
CRL 757511	Golden Favorites	1970	3.00	6.00	12.00
CRL 757513	Dr. Fountain's Magical Licorice Stick	1971	3.00	6.00	12.00
CRL 757516	Something/Misty	1971	3.00	6.00	12.00
CRL 757517	New Orleans Tennessee	1971	3.00	6.00	12.00
DECCA					
DL 75374	Pete Fountain's New Orleans	1972	3.00	6.00	12.00
—Reissue of Coral 757282					
DL 75375	The Blues	1972	3.00	6.00	12.00
—Reissue of Coral 757284					
DL 75377	Mr. New Orleans	1972	3.00	6.00	12.00
DL 75378	Dr. Fountain's Magical Licorice Stick	1972	2.50	5.00	10.00
—Reissue of Coral 757513					
DL 75379	Something/Misty	1972	2.50	5.00	10.00
—Reissue of Coral 757516					
DL 75380	New Orleans Tennessee	1972	3.00	6.00	12.00
—Reissue of Coral 757517					
FIRST AMERICAN					
7706	New Orleans Jazz	1978	2.50	5.00	10.00
INTERMEDIA					
QS-5038	Down on Rampart Street	198?	2.00	4.00	8.00
MCA					
165	Mr. New Orleans	1973	2.50	5.00	10.00
—Reissue of Decca 75377					
176	Something/Misty	1973	2.50	5.00	10.00
—Reissue of Decca 75379					
336	Crescent City	1974	2.50	5.00	10.00
505	Pete Fountain's New Orleans	1974	2.50	5.00	10.00
—Reissue of Decca 75374					
506	The Blues	1974	2.50	5.00	10.00
—Reissue of Decca 75375					
507	Dr. Fountain's Magical Licorice Stick	1974	2.50	5.00	10.00
—Reissue of Decca 75378					
508	New Orleans Tennessee	1974	2.50	5.00	10.00
—Reissue of Decca 75380					
4032 [(2)]	The Best of Pete Fountain	197?	3.00	6.00	12.00
—Reissue of Coral 710					
4095 [(2)]	The Best of Pete Fountain, Vol. 2	197?	3.00	6.00	12.00
PICKWICK					
SPC-3024	Pete Fountain	196?	3.00	6.00	12.00
SPC-3201	High Society	1971	2.50	5.00	10.00
RCA CAMDEN					
CAL-727 [M]	Dixieland	1962	3.00	6.00	12.00
CAS-727 [S]	Dixieland	1962	3.00	6.00	12.00
RCA VICTOR					
LPM-2097 [M]	Pete Fountain at the Jazz Band Ball	1960	3.75	7.50	15.00
LSP-2097 [S]	Pete Fountain at the Jazz Band Ball	1960	5.00	10.00	20.00
VOCALION					
VL 3803 [M]	And the Angels Sing	1967	3.00	6.00	12.00
VL 73803 [S]	And the Angels Sing	1967	3.00	6.00	12.00

FOUNTAIN, PETE, AND AL HIRT

Also see each artist's individual listings.

45s

Number	Title (A Side/B Side)	Yr	VG	VG+	NM
CORAL					
65544	March of the Bob Cats/Farewell Blues	1962	2.00	4.00	8.00

Albums

Number	Title (A Side/B Side)	Yr	VG	VG+	NM
CORAL					
CRL 57389 [M]	Bourbon Street	1962	3.75	7.50	15.00
CRL 757389 [S]	Bourbon Street	1962	5.00	10.00	20.00
MONUMENT					
8602 [(2)]	Super I	1975	2.50	5.00	10.00

FOUNTAIN, PETE, AND "BIG" TINY LITTLE

45s

Number	Title (A Side/B Side)	Yr	VG	VG+	NM
CORAL					
65557	Ain't Misbehavin'/American Patrol	196?	—	3.00	6.00
65598	Honeysuckle Rose/Darktown Strutters' Ball	196?	—	2.50	5.00

Albums

Number	Title (A Side/B Side)	Yr	VG	VG+	NM
CORAL					
CRL 57334 [M]	Mr. New Orleans Meets Mr. Honky Tonk	1961	3.75	7.50	15.00
CRL 757334 [S]	Mr. New Orleans Meets Mr. Honky Tonk	1961	5.00	10.00	20.00

FOUNTAIN OF YOUTH

45s

Number	Title (A Side/B Side)	Yr	VG	VG+	NM
COLGEMS					
66-1020	Livin' Too Fast/(Angie, Love Me) Make the Hurt Go Away	1968	5.00	10.00	20.00
66-1024	Take a Giant Step/Don't Blame Me (For Trying)	1968	5.00	10.00	20.00
66-1032	The Day Don't Come/Sunshine on a Cold Morning	1969	3.75	7.50	15.00
66-5003	Liza Jane/Mistress People	1969	3.75	7.50	15.00

FOUR ACES

Also see AL ALBERTS.

45s

Number	Title (A Side/B Side)	Yr	VG	VG+	NM
ABC-PARAMOUNT					
10166	Searching/Dolce Par Niente	1960	2.50	5.00	10.00
10183	Me Without You/The Ballad of Patrick Henry	1961	2.50	5.00	10.00
DECCA					
27860	Tell Me Why/A Garden in the Rain	1951	5.00	10.00	20.00
27937	Perfidia/You Brought Me Love	1952	5.00	10.00	20.00
28073	My Hero/Spring Is a Wonderful Thing	1952	5.00	10.00	20.00
28162	I'm Yours/I Understand	1952	5.00	10.00	20.00
28323	Should I/There's Only Tonight	1952	5.00	10.00	20.00
28390	Heart and Soul/Just Squeeze Me	1952	5.00	10.00	20.00
28391	I'll Never Smile Again/My Devotion	1952	5.00	10.00	20.00
28392	Tip-Pi-Tin/Heaven Can Wait	1952	5.00	10.00	20.00
28393	La Rosita/Take Me in Your Arms	1952	5.00	10.00	20.00
28650	You Fooled Me/If You Take My Heart Away	1953	3.75	7.50	15.00
28691	Organ Grinder's Swing/Honey in the Horn	1953	3.75	7.50	15.00
28744	Don't Forget Me/False Love	1953	3.75	7.50	15.00
28843	Laughing on the Outside (Crying on the Inside)/I've Been Waiting a Lifetime	1953	3.75	7.50	15.00
28927	The Gang That Sang "Heart of My Heart"/Stranger in Paradise	1953	3.75	7.50	15.00
28979	Bandera (Texas Polka)/What More Is There	1954	3.75	7.50	15.00
29036	Amor/So Long	1954	3.75	7.50	15.00
29123	Three Coins in the Fountain/Wedding Bells (Are Breaking Up That Old Gang of Mine)	1954	3.75	7.50	15.00
29217	Dream/It Shall Come to Pass	1954	3.75	7.50	15.00
29269	It's a Woman's World/The Cuckoo Bird in the Pickle Tree	1954	3.75	7.50	15.00
29344	Mister Sandman/(I'll Be With You) In Apple Blossom Time	1954	3.75	7.50	15.00
29395	Melody of Love/There Is a Tavern in the Town	1954	3.75	7.50	15.00
29435	There Goes My Heart/You'll Always Be the One	1955	3.00	6.00	12.00
29476	Heart/Sluefoot	1955	3.00	6.00	12.00
29625	Love is a Many-Splendored Thing/Shine On Harvest Moon	1955	3.00	6.00	12.00
29702	The Christmas Song (Merry Christmas to You)/Jingle Bells	1955	3.00	6.00	12.00
29712	O Holy Night/Silent Night	1955	3.00	6.00	12.00
29725	A Woman in Love/Of This I'm Sure	1955	3.00	6.00	12.00
29809	If You Can Dream/The Gal with the Yaller Shoes	1956	3.00	6.00	12.00
29889	To Love Again/Charlie Was a Boxer	1956	3.00	6.00	12.00
29989	I Only Know I Love You/Dreamer	1956	3.00	6.00	12.00
30041	Friendly Persuasion (Thee I Love)/You Can't Run Away from It	1956	3.00	6.00	12.00
30123	Someone to Love/Written on the Wind	1956	3.00	6.00	12.00
30242	Bahama Mama/You're Mine	1957	3.00	6.00	12.00
30348	Three Sheets to the Wind/Yes Sir, That's My Baby	1957	3.00	6.00	12.00
30384	Half of My Heart/When My Sugar Walks Down the Street	1957	3.00	6.00	12.00
30466	How Do You Say Goodbye?/I Would Love You Still	1957	3.00	6.00	12.00
30575	Rock and Roll Rhapsody/I Wish I May, I Wish I Might	1958	3.00	6.00	12.00
30649	Saturday Swing-Out/Take My Heart	1958	3.00	6.00	12.00
30695	Two Arms, Two Lips, One Heart/Heartache in Costume	1958	3.00	6.00	12.00
30721	Roses of Rio/Hangin' Up a Horseshoe	1958	3.00	6.00	12.00
30764	The World Outside/How Can You Forget	1958	3.00	6.00	12.00
30775	Ol' Fatso/Christmas Tree	1958	3.00	6.00	12.00
30822	No Other Arms, No Other Lips/The Inn of the Sixth Happiness	1959	2.50	5.00	10.00
30874	Ciao, Ciao Bambino/Paradise Island	1959	2.50	5.00	10.00
30897	The Five Pennies/Anyone Would Love You	1959	2.50	5.00	10.00
30989	Waltzing Matilda/The Wonder of It All	1959	2.50	5.00	10.00
31027	I Love Paris/Till Tomorrow	1959	2.50	5.00	10.00
31081	Poor Butterfly/You Are Music	1960	2.50	5.00	10.00
FLASH					
103	Who's to Blame/Two Little Kisses	1950	7.50	15.00	30.00
JUBILEE					
5416	It's All Over But the Crying/Lonely Hill	1962	2.00	4.00	8.00
RADNOR					
301	Always Keep Me in Your Heart/Didn't We	1968	—	2.50	5.00
302	I Started a Joke/Summer Won't Be Summer	1969	—	2.50	5.00
VICTORIA					
101	Sin/Arizona Moon	1951	15.00	30.00	60.00
—Red vinyl					
101	Sin/Arizona Moon	1951	6.25	12.50	25.00
—Black vinyl					
102	There's a Christmas Tree in Heaven/There's a Small Hotel	1951	7.50	15.00	30.00

7-Inch Extended Plays

Number	Title (A Side/B Side)	Yr	VG	VG+	NM
DECCA					
ED 2004	Tell Me Why/Perfidia//I Understand/My Hero	195?	3.75	7.50	15.00
ED 2004 [PS]	The Four Aces, Vol. 1	195?	3.75	7.50	15.00
ED 2170	*I Don't Know Why/(I'll Be With You) In Apple Blossom Time/Dream/Among My Souvenirs	195?	3.75	7.50	15.00
ED 2170 [PS]	Dream	195?	3.75	7.50	15.00
ED 2211	I'm in the Mood for Love/What a Difference a Day Makes//Stars Fell on Alabama/Pennies from Heaven	195?	3.00	6.00	12.00
ED 2211 [PS]	Mood for Love, Volume 1	195?	3.00	6.00	12.00
ED 2212	(contents unknown)	195?	3.00	6.00	12.00
ED 2212 [PS]	Mood for Love, Volume 2	195?	3.00	6.00	12.00
ED 2213	(contents unknown)	195?	3.00	6.00	12.00
ED 2213 [PS]	Mood for Love, Volume 3	195?	3.00	6.00	12.00
ED 2309	White Christmas/The Christmas Song//Silent Night/O Little Town of Bethlehem/Joy to the World	1956	3.00	6.00	12.00
ED 2309 [PS]	A Merry Christmas with the Four Aces, Part 1	1956	3.00	6.00	12.00
ED 2310	(contents unknown)	1956	3.00	6.00	12.00
ED 2310 [PS]	A Merry Christmas with the Four Aces, Part 2	1956	3.00	6.00	12.00
ED 2311	(contents unknown)	1956	3.00	6.00	12.00
ED 2311 [PS]	A Merry Christmas with the Four Aces, Part 3	1956	3.00	6.00	12.00
ED 2324	Amor/I'm Yours//Organ Grinder's Swing/So Long	195?	3.00	6.00	12.00
ED 2324 [PS]	Amor	195?	3.00	6.00	12.00
ED 2529	(contents unknown)	195?	3.00	6.00	12.00
ED 2529 [PS]	Shufflin' Along, Volume 1	195?	3.00	6.00	12.00
ED 2565	(contents unknown)	195?	3.00	6.00	12.00
ED 2565 [PS]	Hits from Hollywood	195?	3.00	6.00	12.00

Number	Title (A Side/B Side)	Yr	VG	VG+	NM
ED 2675	(contents unknown)	1959	3.00	6.00	12.00
ED 2675 [PS]	Beyond the Blue Horizon	1959	3.00	6.00	12.00
Albums					
DECCA					
DL 4013 [M]	The Golden Hits of the Four Aces	1960	5.00	10.00	20.00
DL 5429 [10]	The Four Aces	1952	20.00	40.00	80.00
DL 8122 [M]	The Mood for Love	1955	12.50	25.00	50.00
—All-black label, silver print					
DL 8122 [M]	The Mood for Love	196?	5.00	10.00	20.00
—Black label with color bars					
DL 8191 [M]	Merry Christmas	1956	12.50	25.00	50.00
DL 8227 [M]	Sentimental Souvenirs	1956	12.50	25.00	50.00
—All-black label, silver print					
DL 8227 [M]	Sentimental Souvenirs	196?	5.00	10.00	20.00
—Black label with color bars					
DL 8228 [M]	Heart and Soul	1956	12.50	25.00	50.00
—All-black label, silver print					
DL 8228 [M]	Heart and Soul	196?	5.00	10.00	20.00
—Black label with color bars					
DL 8312 [M]	She Sees All the Hollywood Hits	1957	12.50	25.00	50.00
DL 8567 [M]	Shuffling Along	1957	12.50	25.00	50.00
—All-black label, silver print					
DL 8567 [M]	Shuffling Along	196?	5.00	10.00	20.00
—Black label with color bars					
DL 8693 [M]	Hits from Hollywood	1958	12.50	25.00	50.00
—All-black label, silver print					
DL 8693 [M]	Hits from Hollywood	196?	5.00	10.00	20.00
—Black label with color bars					
DL 8766 [M]	The Swingin' Aces	1958	10.00	20.00	40.00
—All-black label, silver print					
DL 8766 [M]	The Swingin' Aces	196?	5.00	10.00	20.00
—Black label with color bars					
DL 8855 [M]	Hits from Broadway	1959	10.00	20.00	40.00
—All-black label, silver print					
DL 8855 [M]	Hits from Broadway	196?	5.00	10.00	20.00
—Black label with color bars					
DL 8944 [M]	Beyond the Blue Horizon	1959	10.00	20.00	40.00
—All-black label, silver print					
DL 8944 [M]	Beyond the Blue Horizon	196?	5.00	10.00	20.00
—Black label with color bars					
DL 74013 [S]	The Golden Hits of the Four Aces	1960	6.25	12.50	25.00
DL 78766 [S]	The Swingin' Aces	1958	12.50	25.00	50.00
—All-black label, silver print					
DL 78766 [S]	The Swingin' Aces	196?	6.25	12.50	25.00
—Black label with color bars					
DL 78855 [S]	Hits from Broadway	1959	12.50	25.00	50.00
—All-black label, silver print					
DL 78855 [S]	Hits from Broadway	196?	6.25	12.50	25.00
—Black label with color bars					
DL 78944 [S]	Beyond the Blue Horizon	1959	12.50	25.00	50.00
—All-black label, silver print					
DL 78944 [S]	Beyond the Blue Horizon	196?	6.25	12.50	25.00
—Black label with color bars					
MCA					
4033 [(2)]	The Best of the Four Aces	197?	3.75	7.50	15.00
PICKWICK					
SPC-3527	Love Is a Many-Splendored Thing	197?	2.50	5.00	10.00
UNITED ARTISTS					
UAL-3337 [M]	Record Oldies	1963	5.00	10.00	20.00
UAS-6337 [S]	Record Oldies	1963	6.25	12.50	25.00
VOCALION					
VL 3604 [M]	The Four Aces Sing	196?	3.75	7.50	15.00
VL 73881	There Goes My Heart	1969	3.00	6.00	12.00
VL 73902	Written on the Wind	1970	3.00	6.00	12.00

FOUR AIMS, THE

See FOUR TOPS.

FOUR BARS, THE

Number	Title (A Side/B Side)	Yr	VG	VG+	NM
45s					
JOSIE					
762	Grief by Day, Grief by Night/Hey Baby	1954	75.00	150.00	300.00
768	If I Give My Heart to You/Stop It! Quit It!	1954	75.00	150.00	300.00
783	Let Me Live/Why Do You Treat Me This Way	1955	150.00	300.00	600.00
REPUBLIC					
7101	Memories of You/When Did You Leave Heaven	1954	150.00	300.00	600.00

FOUR BELLS, THE

Number	Title (A Side/B Side)	Yr	VG	VG+	NM
45s					
GEM					
207	Please Tell It to Me/Long Way to Go	1953	200.00	400.00	800.00
220	Only a Miracle/My Tree	1954	200.00	400.00	800.00

FOUR BROTHERS AND A COUSIN

Number	Title (A Side/B Side)	Yr	VG	VG+	NM
45s					
JAGUAR					
3003	Trust in Me/Whistle Stop Blues	1954	100.00	200.00	400.00
3005	Whispeing Wind/Can It Be	1954	125.00	250.00	500.00

FOUR BUDDIES, THE (1)

Vocal group from Baltimore.

Number	Title (A Side/B Side)	Yr	VG	VG+	NM
45s					
SAVOY					
769	I Will Wait/Just to See You Smile Again	1951	100.00	200.00	400.00
769	I Will Wait/Just to See You Smile Again	1951	125.00	250.00	500.00
—As "The Four Buds"					
779	Don't Leave Me Now/Sweet Slumber	1951	100.00	200.00	400.00
789	My Summer's Gone/Why at a Time Like This	1951	75.00	150.00	300.00
817	Heart and Soul/Sin	1951	75.00	150.00	300.00
823	Window Eyes/Simply Say Goodbye	1951	75.00	150.00	300.00
845	You're Part of Me/Story Blues	1952	75.00	150.00	300.00
866	What's the Matter with Me/Sweet Tooth for My Baby	1952	75.00	150.00	300.00
888	My Mother's Eyes/Ooh Ow	1953	75.00	150.00	300.00
891	I'd Climb the Highest Mountain/I Wanna Know	1953	75.00	150.00	300.00
—B-side by Dolly Cooper					

FOUR BUDDIES, THE (2)

Vocal group from Chicago.

Number	Title (A Side/B Side)	Yr	VG	VG+	NM
45s					
CLUB 51					
105	Delores/Look Out	1956	50.00	100.00	200.00
—Black vinyl					
105	Delores/Look Out	1956	1000.	2000.	4000.
—Red vinyl					

FOUR BUDDIES, THE (3)

Number	Title (A Side/B Side)	Yr	VG	VG+	NM
45s					
CORAL					
62217	Hurt/Moonglow & Theme from Picnic	1960	5.00	10.00	20.00
62325	The Light/Cin Cin (Che Bell)	1962	5.00	10.00	20.00
IMPERIAL					
66018	I Want to Be the Boy You Love/Just Enough of Your Love	1964	15.00	30.00	60.00
PHILIPS					
40122	Lonely Summer/Slow Locomotion	1963	5.00	10.00	20.00

FOUR CAL-QUETTES, THE

Number	Title (A Side/B Side)	Yr	VG	VG+	NM
45s					
CAPITOL					
4534	Sparkle and Shine/In This World	1961	7.50	15.00	30.00
—As "The Four Coquettes"					
4574	Billy, My Billy/Star Bright	1961	7.50	15.00	30.00
4657	Most of All/I'm Gonna Love Him Anyway	1961	7.50	15.00	30.00
4725	I'll Never Come Back (Silly Boy)/Again	1962	7.50	15.00	30.00
LIBERTY					
55549	I Cried/Movie Magazines	1963	3.75	7.50	15.00

FOUR CASTS, THE

Number	Title (A Side/B Side)	Yr	VG	VG+	NM
45s					
ATLANTIC					
2228	Stormy Weather/Workin' at the Factory	1964	3.00	6.00	12.00

FOUR CHEERS, THE

Number	Title (A Side/B Side)	Yr	VG	VG+	NM
45s					
END					
1034	Fatal Charms of Love/Periwinkle Blue	1958	50.00	100.00	200.00

FOUR CHEVELLES, THE

Number	Title (A Side/B Side)	Yr	VG	VG+	NM
45s					
BAND BOX					
357	This Is Our Wedding Day/Darling Forever	1957	5.00	10.00	20.00
358	I Can't Believe/I Know	1957	5.00	10.00	20.00
DELFT					
357	This Is Our Wedding Day/Darling Forever	1957	150.00	300.00	600.00

FOUR CHICADEES, THE

Number	Title (A Side/B Side)	Yr	VG	VG+	NM
45s					
CHECKER					
849	Ding Dong/Teenage Blues	1956	15.00	30.00	60.00

FOUR COINS, THE

Number	Title (A Side/B Side)	Yr	VG	VG+	NM
45s					
COLUMBIA					
44006	If You Love Me (Really Love Me)/Learning to Live Without Your Love	1967	—	3.00	6.00
EPIC					
9074	Once More/We'll Be Married...	1954	3.75	7.50	15.00
9082	I Love You Madly/Maybe	1954	3.75	7.50	15.00
9091	My Anxious Heart/Oh Mother Dear	1955	3.75	7.50	15.00
9104	Promises, Promises/That's the Way	1955	3.75	7.50	15.00
9107	A Story Untold/Magnolia	1955	3.75	7.50	15.00
9116	The Song That Brought Us Together/Need You	1955	3.75	7.50	15.00
9129	Memories of You/Tear Down the Fence	1955	3.75	7.50	15.00
9148	The Song That God Sings/The Old Professor	1956	3.00	6.00	12.00
9164	This I Offer You/One Kiss (Is Worth a Thousand Words)	1956	3.00	6.00	12.00
9183	Manhattan Serenade/Too Late	1956	3.00	6.00	12.00
9192	Destination Love/The Time of the Year	1956	3.00	6.00	12.00
9200	Falling Star/My Love Is a Little Kitten	1957	3.00	6.00	12.00
9213	Shangri-La/First in Line	1957	3.00	6.00	12.00
9229	My One Sin/This Life	1957	3.00	6.00	12.00
9253	Follow Your Heart/A Broken Promise	1957	3.00	6.00	12.00
9258	My Love Loves Me/New World	1957	3.00	6.00	12.00
9276	Dream World/One Life, One Love	1958	2.50	5.00	10.00
9286	Wendy, Wendy/Be Still My Heart	1958	2.50	5.00	10.00
9295	The World Outside/Roselle	1958	2.50	5.00	10.00
9306	Angel of Love/Who Are You	1959	2.50	5.00	10.00
9314	My First Love/One Love, One Heart	1959	2.50	5.00	10.00
9337	Angel in the Rain/First Signs of Love	1959	2.50	5.00	10.00
9348	Buon Natale/Serenade of the Bells	1959	2.50	5.00	10.00
9383	My Only Love/You're Breaking My Heart	1960	2.50	5.00	10.00
JOY					
287	Answer Me, My Love/Joanna	1964	2.00	4.00	8.00
JUBILEE					
5411	Gee, Officer Krupki/The Miracle of St. Marie	1961	2.00	4.00	8.00
5419	Come a Little Closer/Windows of Heaven	1962	2.00	4.00	8.00
5429	One Red Rose/I Wish You Were Here	1962	2.00	4.00	8.00
LAURIE					
3331	I'll Never Love Again/Try Your Luck	1966	—	3.00	6.00
3360	Shout Shout (Knock Yourself Out)/People Get Jealous	1966	—	3.00	6.00
MGM					
12951	Pledging My Love/I Want a Little Girl	1960	2.00	4.00	8.00

Number	Title (A Side/B Side)	Yr	VG	VG+	NM
12977	Love Is Where You Find It/Beat on Your Drum Little Susan	1961	2.00	4.00	8.00
13003	To Love/From Your Very Own Lips	1961	2.00	4.00	8.00
13031	Pretty Nina/Moon of Manakoora	1961	2.00	4.00	8.00
VEE JAY					
474	They Say/Jimmy San	1962	2.00	4.00	8.00
551	Take a Bow (Little Darlin')/Nina	1963	2.00	4.00	8.00
7-Inch Extended Plays					
EPIC					
EG-7121	(contents unknown)	195?	3.00	6.00	12.00
EG-7121 [PS]	The Four Coins	195?	3.00	6.00	12.00
EG-7186	(contents unknown)	195?	3.00	6.00	12.00
EG-7186 [PS]	The Four Coins in Shangri-La	195?	3.00	6.00	12.00
EG-7196	(contents unknown)	195?	2.50	5.00	10.00
EG-7196 [PS]	The Four Coins Sing	195?	2.50	5.00	10.00
EG-7197	(contents unknown)	195?	2.50	5.00	10.00
EG-7197 [PS]	The Four Coins Sing	195?	2.50	5.00	10.00
Albums					
EPIC					
LN 1104 [M]	The Four Coins	1955	12.50	25.00	50.00
LN 3445 [M]	The Four Coins in Shangri-La	1958	7.50	15.00	30.00
MGM					
E-3944 [M]	Greek Songs	1961	3.75	7.50	15.00
SE-3944 [S]	Greek Songs	1961	5.00	10.00	20.00
ROULETTE					
R-25288 [M]	Greek Songs Mama Never Taught Me	1965	3.75	7.50	15.00
SR-25288 [S]	Greek Songs Mama Never Taught Me	1965	5.00	10.00	20.00

FOUR COQUETTES, THE

See THE FOUR CAL-QUETTES.

FOUR DATES, THE

Number	Title (A Side/B Side)	Yr	VG	VG+	NM
45s					
CHANCELLOR					
1014	I'm Happy/Eloise	1958	5.00	10.00	20.00
1019	I say babe/Hey Roly Poly	1958	5.00	10.00	20.00
1027	Feel Good/Teenage Neighbor	1958	6.25	12.50	25.00

FOUR DEALS, THE

Number	Title (A Side/B Side)	Yr	VG	VG+	NM
45s					
CAPITOL					
F-1313	It's Too Late Now/There Ain't No Bears	1950	25.00	50.00	100.00

FOUR DEEP TONES, THE

Number	Title (A Side/B Side)	Yr	VG	VG+	NM
45s					
CORAL					
65061	Just in Case You Change Your Mind/Castle Rock	1951	50.00	100.00	200.00
65062	The Night You Said Goodbye/When the Saints Go Marching In	1951	50.00	100.00	200.00

FOUR DEUCES, THE

Number	Title (A Side/B Side)	Yr	VG	VG+	NM
45s					
EVEREST					
19311	Polly/Yella Shoes	1959	7.50	15.00	30.00
MUSIC CITY					
790	W-P-L-J/Here Lies My Love	1955	37.50	75.00	150.00
—Maroon label					
790	W-P-L-J/Here Lies My Love	1955	10.00	20.00	40.00
—Black label					
796	Down It Went/Goose Is Gone	1955	15.00	30.00	60.00

FOUR DIRECTIONS, THE

Number	Title (A Side/B Side)	Yr	VG	VG+	NM
45s					
CORAL					
62456	(Doin' the) Arthur/Tonight We Love	1965	7.50	15.00	30.00

FOUR DUKES, THE (1)

Number	Title (A Side/B Side)	Yr	VG	VG+	NM
45s					
DUKE					
116	Crying in the Chapel/I Done Done It	1953	200.00	400.00	800.00

FOUR DUKES, THE (2)

Number	Title (A Side/B Side)	Yr	VG	VG+	NM
45s					
IMPERIAL					
5653	Baby Won't You Please Come Home/John Henry	1960	7.50	15.00	30.00

FOUR EPICS, THE

Number	Title (A Side/B Side)	Yr	VG	VG+	NM
45s					
HERITAGE					
109	I'm On My Way to Love/When the Music Ends	1962	25.00	50.00	100.00
LAURIE					
3155	Again/I Love You Diane	1963	6.25	12.50	25.00
3183	How I Wish I Was Single Again/Dance Joanne	1963	6.25	12.50	25.00

FOUR ESQUIRES, THE

Number	Title (A Side/B Side)	Yr	VG	VG+	NM
45s					
CADENCE					
1260	Three Things/The Sphinx Won't Tell	1955	5.00	10.00	20.00
1277	Adorable/Thunderbolt	1955	5.00	10.00	20.00
LONDON					
1652	Look Homeward Angel/Santo Domingo	1956	6.25	12.50	25.00
PARIS					
501	Song of April/Everyone's Sweet on My Sugar	1957	5.00	10.00	20.00
505	The Chopstick Rock/Never Look for Love	1957	5.00	10.00	20.00
509	Love Me Forever/I Ain't Been Right Since You Left	1957	5.00	10.00	20.00
512	Always and Forever/I Walk Down the Street	1958	5.00	10.00	20.00
515	All Around the Clock/The Big Dance	1958	5.00	10.00	20.00
520	Hideaway/Repeat After Me	1958	5.00	10.00	20.00
—With Rosemary June					
526	Follow Me/The Land of You and Me	1958	5.00	10.00	20.00
531	Lucky Old Sun/Non E Cosi	1959	5.00	10.00	20.00
535	Act Your Age/So Ends the Night	1959	5.00	10.00	20.00
539	Wonderful One/Wouldn't It Be Wonderful	1959	5.00	10.00	20.00
544	Make Them Mine/Peg O' My Heart	1960	5.00	10.00	20.00
549	Sweet Sixteen She'll Never Be/The Chopstick Rock	1960	5.00	10.00	20.00
PILGRIM					
717	Follow Me/Summer Vacation	1956	6.25	12.50	25.00
TERRACE					
7502	Can't Help Falling in Love/Merry-Go-Round of Love	1961	3.75	7.50	15.00
7516	The James Bond Theme (Double-O-Seven)/ Summer Vacation	1963	6.25	12.50	25.00
—Betcha didn't know this had lyrics...					

FOUR-EVERS, THE

Number	Title (A Side/B Side)	Yr	VG	VG+	NM
45s					
CHATTAHOOCHIE					
630	Colors/Come Up in the World	1963	3.75	7.50	15.00
COLUMBIA					
42303	You Belong to Me/Such a Good Night for Dreaming	1962	15.00	30.00	60.00
43886	A Lovely Way to Spend An Evening/The Girl I Want	1966	5.00	10.00	20.00
CONSTELLATION					
151	Stormy/Out of the Crowd	1965	7.50	15.00	30.00
JAMIE					
1247	Everybody South Street/One More Time	1963	3.75	7.50	15.00
RED BIRD					
10-078	You Never Had It So Good/What a Scene	1966	6.25	12.50	25.00
SMASH					
1853	Lover Come Back to Me/It's Love	1963	3.75	7.50	15.00
1887	Please Be Mine/If I Were a Magician	1964	7.50	15.00	30.00
1887	Be My Girl/If I Were a Magician	1964	3.75	7.50	15.00
—Same A-side, different title					
1921	(Say I Love You) Do Be Dum/Everlasting	1964	3.75	7.50	15.00

FOUR EXCEPTIONS, THE

Number	Title (A Side/B Side)	Yr	VG	VG+	NM
45s					
PARKWAY					
986	You Got the Power/A Sad Goodbye	1966	12.50	25.00	50.00

FOUR FELLOWS, THE

Number	Title (A Side/B Side)	Yr	VG	VG+	NM
45s					
DERBY					
862	I Tried/Bend of the River	1954	100.00	200.00	400.00
GLORY					
231	I Wish I Didn't Know You/I Know Love	1955	20.00	40.00	80.00
234	Soldier Boy/Take Me Back Baby	1955	15.00	30.00	60.00
236	Angels Say/In the Rain	1955	15.00	30.00	60.00
238	Fallen Angel/Hold 'Em Joe	1956	15.00	30.00	60.00
242	Darling You/Please Don't Deprive Me of My Love	1956	20.00	40.00	80.00
244	I Sit in My Window/Please Play My Song	1956	15.00	30.00	60.00
248	You Don't Know Me/Sweet Girl	1956	15.00	30.00	60.00
250	Loving You, Darling/Give Me Back My Broken Heart	1957	15.00	30.00	60.00
NESTOR					
27	Remember/That Kiss You Gave Me	1958	75.00	150.00	300.00

FOUR FIFTHS, THE

Number	Title (A Side/B Side)	Yr	VG	VG+	NM
45s					
COLUMBIA					
43913	If You Still Want Me/Have You Ever Loved a Girl	1966	3.00	6.00	12.00
HUDSON					
8101	After Graduation/Come On Girl	1963	100.00	200.00	400.00
—Blue vinyl					
8101	After Graduation/Come On Girl	1963	37.50	75.00	150.00
—Black vinyl					

FOUR FRESHMEN, THE

Number	Title (A Side/B Side)	Yr	VG	VG+	NM
45s					
CAPITOL					
F1293	Mr. B's Blues/Then I'll Be Happy	1950	3.75	7.50	15.00
F1377	Now You Know/Pick Up Tears	1951	3.75	7.50	15.00
F2152	It's a Blue World/Tuxedo Junction	1952	3.00	6.00	12.00
F2286	Stormy Weather/The Day Isn't Long Enough	1952	3.00	6.00	12.00
F2398	Baltimore Oriole/Poinciana	1953	3.00	6.00	12.00
F2564	Holiday/It Happened Once Before	1953	3.00	6.00	12.00
F2745	Seems Like Old Times/Crazy Bones	1954	3.00	6.00	12.00
F2832	I'll Be Seeing You/Please Remember	1954	3.00	6.00	12.00
F2898	We'll Be Together Again/My Heart Stood Still	1954	3.00	6.00	12.00
F2961	Mood Indigo/Love Turns Winter to Spring	1954	3.00	6.00	12.00
F3070	It Never Occurred to Me/Malaya	1955	2.50	5.00	10.00
F3154	Day by Day/How Can I Tell Her	1955	2.50	5.00	10.00
F3292	Charmaine/In This Whole Wide World	1955	2.50	5.00	10.00
F3359	Angel Eyes/Love Is Just Around the Corner	1956	2.50	5.00	10.00
F3410	Graduation Day/Lonely Night in Paris	1956	3.75	7.50	15.00
F3532	You're So Far Above Me/He Who Loves and Runs Away	1956	2.50	5.00	10.00
F3652	That's the Way I Feel/What's It Gonna Be	1957	2.50	5.00	10.00
F3779	Julie Is Her Name/Sometimes I'm Happy	1957	2.50	5.00	10.00
F3832	Grenada/How Can I Begin to Tell	1957	2.50	5.00	10.00
F3930	Whistle Me Some Blues/Nights Are Longer	1958	2.50	5.00	10.00
4341	Candy/Route 66	1960	2.00	4.00	8.00
4749	Shangri-La/Teach Me Tonight	1962	2.00	4.00	8.00
4824	I'm Gonna Go Fishin'/Taps Miller	1962	2.00	4.00	8.00
5007	Summertime/Baby Won't You Please Come Home	1963	2.00	4.00	8.00
5083	Charade/Funny How Time Slips Away	1963	2.00	4.00	8.00
5151	Don't Make Me Sorry/My Baby's Gone	1964	2.00	4.00	8.00
5471	Those Magnificent Men in Their Flying Machines/ Old Cape Cod	1965	2.50	5.00	10.00
DECCA					
32070	Cry/Nowhere to Go	1966	—	3.00	6.00

Number	Title (A Side/B Side)	Yr	VG	VG+	NM
LIBERTY					
56047	Cherish-Windy/Come Fly with Me-Up Up and Away	1968	—	3.00	6.00
56099	By the Time I Get to Phoenix-My Special Angel/It's a Blue World	1969	—	3.00	6.00
7-Inch Extended Plays					
CAPITOL					
EAP 1-763	*After You've Gone/Ev'ry Time We Say Goodbye/Easy Street/Good Night Sweetheart	1957	2.50	5.00	10.00
EAP 1-763 [PS]	4 Freshmen and 5 Trumpets, Part 1	1957	2.50	5.00	10.00
EAP 2-763	(contents unknown)	1957	2.50	5.00	10.00
EAP 2-763 [PS]	4 Freshmen and 5 Trumpets, Part 2	1957	2.50	5.00	10.00
EAP 3-763	(contents unknown)	1957	2.50	5.00	10.00
EAP 3-763 [PS]	4 Freshmen and 5 Trumpets, Part 3	1957	2.50	5.00	10.00
EAP 1-844	*Liza/You've Got Me Cryin' Again/This Love of Mine/I Get Along Without You Very Well	1957	2.50	5.00	10.00
EAP 1-844 [PS]	Four Freshmen and Five Saxes, Part 1	1957	2.50	5.00	10.00
EAP 2-844	(contents unknown)	1957	2.50	5.00	10.00
EAP 2-844 [PS]	Four Freshmen and Five Saxes, Part 2	1957	2.50	5.00	10.00
EAP 3-844	(contents unknown)	1957	2.50	5.00	10.00
EAP 3-844 [PS]	Four Freshmen and Five Saxes, Part 3	1957	2.50	5.00	10.00
EAP 1-1255	(contents unknown)	1959	2.50	5.00	10.00
EAP 1-1255 [PS]	The Four Freshmen and Five Guitars, Part 1	1959	2.50	5.00	10.00
EAP 2-1255	(contents unknown)	1959	2.50	5.00	10.00
EAP 2-1255 [PS]	The Four Freshmen and Five Guitars, Part 2	1959	2.50	5.00	10.00
EAP 3-1255	(contents unknown)	1959	2.50	5.00	10.00
EAP 3-1255 [PS]	The Four Freshmen and Five Guitars, Part 3	1959	2.50	5.00	10.00
Albums					
CAPITOL					
H 522 [10]	Voices in Modern	1955	12.50	25.00	50.00
T 522 [M]	Voices in Modern	1955	10.00	20.00	40.00
T 683 [M]	Four Freshmen and Five Trombones	1956	10.00	20.00	40.00
DT 743 [R]	Freshmen Favorites	196?	3.00	6.00	12.00
SM-743	Freshmen Favorites	197?	2.50	5.00	10.00
T 743 [M]	Freshmen Favorites	1956	10.00	20.00	40.00
T 763 [M]	4 Freshmen and 5 Trumpets	1957	10.00	20.00	40.00
T 844 [M]	Four Freshmen and Five Saxes	1957	10.00	20.00	40.00
T 992 [M]	Voices in Latin	1958	7.50	15.00	30.00
ST 1008 [S]	The Four Freshmen In Person	1958	10.00	20.00	40.00
T 1008 [M]	The Four Freshmen In Person	1958	7.50	15.00	30.00
ST 1074 [S]	Voices in Love	1958	7.50	15.00	30.00
T 1074 [M]	Voices in Love	1958	5.00	10.00	20.00
ST 1103 [S]	Freshmen Favorites, Vol. 2	1959	7.50	15.00	30.00
T 1103 [M]	Freshmen Favorites, Vol. 2	1959	5.00	10.00	20.00
ST 1189 [S]	Love Lost	1959	7.50	15.00	30.00
T 1189 [M]	Love Lost	1959	5.00	10.00	20.00
ST 1255 [S]	The Four Freshmen and Five Guitars	1959	7.50	15.00	30.00
T 1255 [M]	The Four Freshmen and Five Guitars	1959	5.00	10.00	20.00
ST 1295 [S]	Voices and Brass	1960	7.50	15.00	30.00
T 1295 [M]	Voices and Brass	1960	5.00	10.00	20.00
ST 1378 [S]	First Affair	1960	7.50	15.00	30.00
T 1378 [M]	First Affair	1960	5.00	10.00	20.00
ST 1485 [S]	Freshmen Year	1961	6.25	12.50	25.00
T 1485 [M]	Freshmen Year	1961	5.00	10.00	20.00
ST 1543 [S]	Voices in Fun	1961	6.25	12.50	25.00
T 1543 [M]	Voices in Fun	1961	5.00	10.00	20.00
ST 1640 [S]	The Best of the Four Freshmen	1962	6.25	12.50	25.00
T 1640 [M]	The Best of the Four Freshmen	1962	5.00	10.00	20.00
ST 1682 [S]	Stars in Our Eyes	1962	6.25	12.50	25.00
T 1682 [M]	Stars in Our Eyes	1962	5.00	10.00	20.00
ST 1753 [S]	Swingers	1963	5.00	10.00	20.00
T 1753 [M]	Swingers	1963	3.75	7.50	15.00
ST 1860 [S]	The Four Freshmen In Person, Volume 2	1963	5.00	10.00	20.00
T 1860 [M]	The Four Freshmen In Person, Volume 2	1963	3.75	7.50	15.00
ST 1950 [S]	Got That Feelin'	1963	5.00	10.00	20.00
T 1950 [M]	Got That Feelin'	1963	3.75	7.50	15.00
ST 2067 [S]	Funny How Time Slips Away	1964	5.00	10.00	20.00
T 2067 [M]	Funny How Time Slips Away	1964	3.75	7.50	15.00
ST 2168 [S]	More Four Freshmen and Five Trombones	1964	5.00	10.00	20.00
T 2168 [M]	More Four Freshmen and Five Trombones	1964	3.75	7.50	15.00
SM-11639	Four Freshmen and Five Trombones	1977	2.50	5.00	10.00
SM-11965	Best of the Four Freshmen	1978	2.50	5.00	10.00
CREATIVE WORLD					
ST-1059 [(2)]	Stan Kenton and the Four Freshmen at Butler University	1972	5.00	10.00	20.00
LIBERTY					
LST-7563	Today Is Tomorrow	1968	3.75	7.50	15.00
LST-7590	In a Class By Themselves	1969	3.75	7.50	15.00
LST-7630	Different Strokes	1969	3.75	7.50	15.00
LN-10181	In a Class By Themselves	198?	2.00	4.00	8.00
PAUSA					
PR-7193	Fresh!	1986	2.50	5.00	10.00
PR-9029	The Four Freshmen and Five Guitars	198?	2.50	5.00	10.00
PR-9040	4 Freshmen and 5 Trumpets	1985	2.50	5.00	10.00
PICKWICK					
SPC-3080	The Fabulous Four Freshmen	196?	3.00	6.00	12.00
SPC-3563	A Taste of Honey	1977	2.50	5.00	10.00
SUNSET					
SUS-5289	My Special Angel	1970	3.00	6.00	12.00

FOUR GRADUATES, THE

Number	Title (A Side/B Side)	Yr	VG	VG+	NM
45s					
CRYSTAL BALL					
116	May I Have This Dance/Caught in a Lie	1978	—	2.00	4.00
119	Your Initials/Every Year About This Time	1978	—	2.00	4.00
RUST					
5062	Picture of An Angel/A Lovely Way to Spend An Evening	1963	25.00	50.00	100.00
5084	Candy Queen/A Girl in Love	1964	45.00	90.00	180.00

FOUR HAVEN KNIGHTS, THE

Number	Title (A Side/B Side)	Yr	VG	VG+	NM
45s					
ANGLETONE					
1066	In My Lonely Room/I'm Just a Dreamer	1958	12.50	25.00	50.00
1092	Just to Be in Love/Why Go On Pretending	1958	12.50	25.00	50.00
ATLAS					
1066	In My Lonely Room/I'm Just a Dreamer	1957	37.50	75.00	150.00
1092	Just to Be in Love/Why Go On Pretending	1957	37.50	75.00	150.00
JOSIE					
824	In My Lonely Room/I'm Just a Dreamer	1957	7.50	15.00	30.00

FOUR HOLIDAYS, THE

Number	Title (A Side/B Side)	Yr	VG	VG+	NM
45s					
UNITED ARTISTS					
163	Who Can Say/Nobody Loves You Like-a Me	1959	7.50	15.00	30.00
VERVE					
10204	I Don't Wanna Go to School/Love Ya' Baby	1960	3.75	7.50	15.00

FOUR HUES, THE

Number	Title (A Side/B Side)	Yr	VG	VG+	NM
45s					
CORAL					
61617	Ivory Tower/Sister Jenny	1956	7.50	15.00	30.00
CROWN					
159	Rock-a-Bye/Take Me Out of Your Heart	1955	10.00	20.00	40.00

FOUR IMPERIALS, THE

Number	Title (A Side/B Side)	Yr	VG	VG+	NM
45s					
CHANT					
10067	My Girl/Teen Age Fool	1958	12.50	25.00	50.00
DIAL					
101	Valley of Tears/Time Out	1959	37.50	75.00	150.00
DOT					
15737	Lazy Bonnie/Let's Make a Scene	1958	6.25	12.50	25.00
FOX					
102	Give Me One More Chance/Look Up and Live	1958	20.00	40.00	80.00
LORELEI					
4444	Lazy Bonnie/Let's Make a Scene	1958	25.00	50.00	100.00
TWIRL					
2005	Santa's Got a Coupe de Ville/Seven Lonely Days	1960	6.25	12.50	25.00

FOUR J'S, THE

Number	Title (A Side/B Side)	Yr	VG	VG+	NM
45s					
4-J					
506	Will You Be My Love/Nursery	1963	3.75	7.50	15.00
CONGRESS					
6003	Dreamin'/Love My Life	1969	2.50	5.00	10.00
HERALD					
528	Kissin' at the Drive-In/Dreams Are a Dime a Dozen	1958	7.50	15.00	30.00
JAMIE					
1267	Here I Am Broken-Hearted/She Said That She Loved Me	1964	6.25	12.50	25.00
1274	By Love Possessed/My Love, My Love	1964	6.25	12.50	25.00
UNITED ARTISTS					
125	Rock and Roll Age/Be Nice, Don't Fight	1958	10.00	20.00	40.00

FOUR J'S, THE, AND THE FABULOUS IMPERIALS

Number	Title (A Side/B Side)	Yr	VG	VG+	NM
45s					
MGM					
12687	Class Ring/Weird	1958	20.00	40.00	80.00

FOUR JACKS, THE

Number	Title (A Side/B Side)	Yr	VG	VG+	NM
45s					
FEDERAL					
12075	You Met a Fool/Goodbye Baby	1952	200.00	400.00	800.00
12087	The Last of the Good Rockin' Men/I'll Be Home Again	1952	125.00	250.00	500.00
MGM					
11179	You're in Love with Someone Else/Darling, Lonesome for You	1952	5.00	10.00	20.00

FOUR JACKS AND A JILL (1)

Number	Title (A Side/B Side)	Yr	VG	VG+	NM
45s					
RCA VICTOR					
47-9473	Master Jack/I Looked Back	1968	2.00	4.00	8.00
47-9572	Mister Nico/Hamba Liliwam	1968	—	3.00	6.00
47-9655	Hey Mister/Sad Little Pigeon	1968	—	3.00	6.00
47-9728	Stone in My Shoe/Grandfather Dugan	1969	—	3.00	6.00
Albums					
RCA VICTOR					
LSP-4019	Master Jack	1968	3.75	7.50	15.00
LSP-4103	Fables	1968	3.75	7.50	15.00

FOUR JACKS AND A JILL (2)

Number	Title (A Side/B Side)	Yr	VG	VG+	NM
45s					
FORTUNE					
507	Love's Not Love Without You/I'm in Love with Someone	1955	7.50	15.00	30.00

FOUR JACKS AND A JILL (U)

Number	Title (A Side/B Side)	Yr	VG	VG+	NM
45s					
HEART SONG					
103	It's Christmas Time Again/(B-side unknown)	19??	2.50	5.00	10.00

FOUR JETS, THE

See THE SHADOWS.

FOUR JEWELS, THE

Number	Title (A Side/B Side)	Yr	VG	VG+	NM
45s					
CHECKER					
1039	Dapper Dan/Loaded with Goodies	1963	5.00	10.00	20.00
1069	Time for Love/That's What They Put Erasers on Pencils For	1964	5.00	10.00	20.00

Number	Title (A Side/B Side)	Yr	VG	VG+	NM
START					
638	Loaded with Goodies/Fire	1963	10.00	20.00	40.00
638	Johnny Jealousy/Someone Special	1963	7.50	15.00	30.00
641	All That's Good/I Love Me Some You	1963	7.50	15.00	30.00
TEC					
3007	Baby It's You/She's Wrong for You Baby	1964	6.25	12.50	25.00

FOUR JOKERS, THE (1)

45s

Number	Title (A Side/B Side)	Yr	VG	VG+	NM
AMY					
832	She's a Flirt/Uggaboo	1961	5.00	10.00	20.00

FOUR JOKERS, THE (2)

45s

Number	Title (A Side/B Side)	Yr	VG	VG+	NM
CRYSTALLETTE					
730	Your Decision/We Met in Catalina	1959	3.75	7.50	15.00
733	Beyond the Reef/That's the Way	1959	3.75	7.50	15.00

FOUR JOKERS, THE (3)

Jimmy Drake, a.k.a. NERVOUS NORVUS, was in this group.

45s

Number	Title (A Side/B Side)	Yr	VG	VG+	NM
DIAMOND					
3004	Transfusion/You Dig	1956	7.50	15.00	30.00

FOUR JOKERS, THE (4)

45s

Number	Title (A Side/B Side)	Yr	VG	VG+	NM
MGM					
11815	Tell Me Now/Caring	1954	7.50	15.00	30.00

FOUR JOKERS, THE (5)

45s

Number	Title (A Side/B Side)	Yr	VG	VG+	NM
SUE					
703	Written in the Stars/The Run-Around	1958	15.00	30.00	60.00

FOUR JUST MEN

Also see FREDDIE AND THE DREAMERS.

45s

Number	Title (A Side/B Side)	Yr	VG	VG+	NM
TOWER					
118	That's My Baby/Things Will Never Be the Same	1965	3.00	6.00	12.00

FOUR KNIGHTS, THE

45s

Number	Title (A Side/B Side)	Yr	VG	VG+	NM
CAPITOL					
F1587	I Love the Sunshine of Your Smile/Sentimental Fool	1951	12.50	25.00	50.00
F1707	Walkin' Whistlin' Blues/Who Am I	1951	10.00	20.00	40.00
F1787	I Go Crazy/Get Her Off My Hands	1951	10.00	20.00	40.00
F1806	It's No Sin/The Glory of Love	1951	10.00	20.00	40.00
F1875	Cry/Charmaine	1951	10.00	20.00	40.00
F1914	Marshmallow Moon/Five Foot Two, Eyes of Blue	1951	7.50	15.00	30.00
F1930	The Way I Feel/I Wish I Had a Girl	1952	7.50	15.00	30.00
F1971	There Are Two Sides to Every Heartache/Walkin' in Sunshine	1952	7.50	15.00	30.00
F1998	The More I Go Out with Somebody Else/The Doll with the Sawdust Heart	1952	7.50	15.00	30.00
F2087	I'm the World's Biggest Fool/It's a Sin to Tell a Lie	1952	7.50	15.00	30.00
F2127	Win or Lose/Do-Wacka-Do	1952	7.50	15.00	30.00
F2195	Say No More/That's the Way It's Gonna Be	1952	7.50	15.00	30.00
F2234	Lies/One Way Kisses	1952	7.50	15.00	30.00
F2315	Oh Happy Day/A Million Tears	1953	6.25	12.50	25.00
F2403	Anniversary Song/A Few Kind Words	1953	6.25	12.50	25.00
F2517	Baby Doll/Tennessee Train	1953	6.25	12.50	25.00
F2654	Oh Baby Mine/I Couldn't Stay Away from You	1953	10.00	20.00	40.00
F2654	I Get So Lonely (When I Dream About You)/I Couldn't Stay Away from You	1953	5.00	10.00	20.00
F2782	I Was Meant for You/They Tell Me	1954	5.00	10.00	20.00
F2847	How Wrong Can You Be/Period	1954	5.00	10.00	20.00
F2894	In the Chapel in the Moonlight/Easy Street	1954	5.00	10.00	20.00
F2938	I Don't Wanna See You Cryin'/Saw Your Eyes	1954	5.00	10.00	20.00
F3024	Write Me Baby/Honey Bunch	1955	5.00	10.00	20.00
F3093	Foolishly Yours/Inside You	1955	5.00	10.00	20.00
F3155	Gratefully Yours/Me	1955	5.00	10.00	20.00
F3192	Don't Sit Under the Apple Tree/Believing You	1955	5.00	10.00	20.00
F3250	Perdido/After	1955	5.00	10.00	20.00
F3279	Guilty/You	1955	5.00	10.00	20.00
F3339	I Love You Still/Happy Birthday Baby	1956	3.75	7.50	15.00
F3386	Bottle Up the Moonlight/Mistaken	1956	3.75	7.50	15.00
F3494	Don't Depend on Me/You're a Honey	1956	3.75	7.50	15.00
F3689	It Doesn't Cost Money/How Can You Not Believe	1957	3.75	7.50	15.00
F3730	Walkin' and Whistlin' Blues/I Love That Song	1957	3.75	7.50	15.00
F15895	I Ain't Got Nobody/When My Baby Smiles at Me	1952	7.50	15.00	30.00
F15896	Easy Street/Ida, Sweet As Apple Cider	1952	7.50	15.00	30.00
F15897	Georgia on My Mind/Sentimental Journey	1952	7.50	15.00	30.00
CORAL					
61936	The Four Minute Mile/When Your Lover Has Gone	1958	3.00	6.00	12.00
61981	Yes I Do/If You Ever Change Your Mind	1958	3.00	6.00	12.00
62045	O Falling Star/Foolish Tears	1959	3.00	6.00	12.00
62110	Where Is the Love/Things to Do Today	1959	3.00	6.00	12.00
DECCA					
48018	He'll Understand and Say Well Done/Lead Me to That Rock	1952	25.00	50.00	100.00

—Reissue of original 78 from 1947. (Decca 48014 and 48026 are known to exist only on 78s.)

7-Inch Extended Plays

Number	Title (A Side/B Side)	Yr	VG	VG+	NM
CAPITOL					
EAP 414	(contents unknown)	1953	10.00	20.00	40.00
EAP 414 [PS]	The Four Knights Sing	1953	10.00	20.00	40.00
EAP 506	(contents unknown)	1954	10.00	20.00	40.00
EAP 506 [PS]	I Get So Lonely	1954	10.00	20.00	40.00
MONOGRAM					
2	Speaking of Angels/What Are You Doing New Year's Eve// + 2	19??	2.50	5.00	10.00

Albums

Number	Title (A Side/B Side)	Yr	VG	VG+	NM
CAPITOL					
H 346 [10]	Spotlight Songs	1953	50.00	100.00	200.00
T 346 [M]	Spotlight Songs	1956	37.50	75.00	150.00
CORAL					
CRL 57221 [M]	The Four Knights	1959	25.00	50.00	100.00
CRL 57309 [M]	Million Dollar Baby	1960	15.00	30.00	60.00
CRL 757309 [S]	Million Dollar Baby	1960	20.00	40.00	80.00

FOUR LADS, THE

45s

Number	Title (A Side/B Side)	Yr	VG	VG+	NM
COLUMBIA					
39865	Somebody Loves Me/Thanks to You	1952	3.75	7.50	15.00
39902	Blackberry Boogie/Girl on the Shore	1952	3.75	7.50	15.00
39958	He Who Has Love/I Wonder, I Wonder, I Wonder	1953	3.75	7.50	15.00
40005	Down By the Riverside/Take Me Back	1953	3.75	7.50	15.00
40082	Istanbul (Not Constantinople)/I Should Have Told You Long Ago	1953	3.75	7.50	15.00
40140	Harmony Brown/Gotta Go to the Fais Do Do	1953	3.75	7.50	15.00
40204	Long John/The Place Where I Worship	1954	3.75	7.50	15.00
40220	What Can I Lose by Letting You Know/Oh That'll Be Joyful	1954	3.75	7.50	15.00
40236	Gilly Gilly Ossenfeffer Katzenelle Bogen by the Sea/I Hear It Everywhere	1954	3.75	7.50	15.00
40306	Skokiaan (South African Song)/Why Should I Love You So	1954	3.75	7.50	15.00
40402	Two Ladies in De Shade of De Banana Tree/Dance Calinda	1954	3.75	7.50	15.00
40436	Pledging My Love/I've Been Thinking	1955	3.00	6.00	12.00
40490	Too Much! Baby, Baby/The Average Giraffe	1955	3.00	6.00	12.00
40539	Moments to Remember/Dream On, My Love, Dream On	1955	3.00	6.00	12.00
40629	No, Not Much!/I'll Never Know	1955	3.00	6.00	12.00
40674	Standing on the Corner/My Little Angel	1956	3.00	6.00	12.00
40736	The Bus Stop Song (A Paper of Pins)/A House with Love In It	1956	3.00	6.00	12.00
40788	Mary's Little Boy Child/The Stingiest Man in Town	1956	3.00	6.00	12.00
40811	Who Needs You/It's So Easy to Forget	1956	3.00	6.00	12.00
40811 [PS]	Who Needs You/It's So Easy to Forget	1956	5.00	10.00	20.00
40914	I Just Don't Know/Golly	1957	3.00	6.00	12.00
40974	The Eyes of God/His Invisible Hand	1957	3.00	6.00	12.00
41058	Put a Light in the Window/The Things We Did Last Summer	1957	2.50	5.00	10.00
41136	There's Only One of You/Blue Tattoo	1958	2.50	5.00	10.00
41194	Enchanted Island/Guess What the Neighbors'll Say	1958	2.50	5.00	10.00
41194 [PS]	Enchanted Island/Guess What the Neighbors'll Say	1958	3.75	7.50	15.00
41266	The Mocking Bird/I May Hate Myself in the Morning	1958	2.50	5.00	10.00
41310	The Girl on Page 44/Sunday	1958	2.50	5.00	10.00
41365	The Fountain of Youth/Meet Me Tonight in Dreamland	1959	2.50	5.00	10.00
41409	The Chosen Few/Together Wherever We Go	1959	2.50	5.00	10.00
41443	Got a Locket in My Pocket/Real Thing	1959	2.50	5.00	10.00
41497	Happy Anniversary/Who Do You Think You Are	1959	2.50	5.00	10.00
41497 [PS]	Happy Anniversary/Who Do You Think You Are	1959	3.75	7.50	15.00
41629	You're Nobody 'Til Somebody Loves You/Goona Goona	1960	2.50	5.00	10.00
41682	Our Lady of Fatima (Vocal)/Our Lady of Fatima (Recitation)	1960	2.50	5.00	10.00
41733	Two Other People/The Sheik of Chicago (Mustafa)	1960	2.50	5.00	10.00
DOT					
16328	Don't Fly Away, Flamingo/Winter Snow	1962	2.00	4.00	8.00
16373	The Exodus Song/Never on Sunday	1962	2.00	4.00	8.00
16390	That's What I Like/Sweet Mama Tree-Top Tall	1962	2.00	4.00	8.00
16412	Beyond My Heart/Not That I Care	1962	2.00	4.00	8.00
EPIC					
9150	The Mocking Bird/I May Hate Myself in the Morning	1956	3.00	6.00	12.00
FONA					
1000	You'll Never Know/(B-side unknown)	1977	—	2.00	4.00
1001	Moments to Remember/Skokiaan	1977	—	2.00	4.00
KAPP					
359	Just Young/Goodbye Mr. Love	1960	2.00	4.00	8.00
359 [PS]	Just Young/Goodbye Mr. Love	1960	2.50	5.00	10.00
404	555 Times/I Should Know Better	1961	2.00	4.00	8.00
412	Giuggigla/Oceans of Love	1961	2.00	4.00	8.00
OKEH					
6885	The Mocking Bird/I May Hate Myself in the Morning	1952	5.00	10.00	20.00
REPRISE					
20163	My Home Town/Cornflower Blue	1963	2.00	4.00	8.00
UNITED ARTISTS					
653	It's a Mad, Mad, Mad, Mad World/Stolen Hours	1963	—	3.00	6.00
702	Love Theme from "Tom Jones"/Theme from "Lilies of the Field"	1964	—	3.00	6.00
760	Memories of You/Always Thinking of the Roses	1964	—	3.00	6.00
852	Thanks, Mr. Florist/Barabanchik	1965	—	3.00	6.00
893	With My Eyes Wide Open/I'm Not a Run-Around	1965	—	3.00	6.00
962	Give Her My Love/All the Winds	1965	—	3.00	6.00
50006	No, Not Much/Standing on the Corner	1966	—	2.50	5.00
50339	Where Do I Go/A Woman	1968	—	2.50	5.00
50517	My Heart's Symphony/Pardon Me Kiss	1969	—	2.50	5.00
50585	Moments to Remember/Free Again	1969	—	2.50	5.00

7-Inch Extended Plays

Number	Title (A Side/B Side)	Yr	VG	VG+	NM
COLUMBIA					
B-2557	*Standing on the Corner/Take Me Back/ Skokiaan/Who Needs You	1958	3.75	7.50	15.00
B-2557 [PS]	The Four Lads (Hall of Fame Series)	1958	3.75	7.50	15.00

Number	Title (A Side/B Side)	Yr	VG	VG+	NM
Albums					
COLUMBIA					
CL 861 [M]	The Four Lads with Frankie Laine	1956	10.00	20.00	40.00
CL 912 [M]	On the Sunny Side	1956	10.00	20.00	40.00
CL 1045 [M]	The Four Lads Sing Frank Loesser	1957	10.00	20.00	40.00
CL 1111 [M]	Four on the Aisle	1958	6.25	12.50	25.00
CL 1223 [M]	Breezin' Along	1958	6.25	12.50	25.00
CL 1235 [M]	The Four Lads' Greatest Hits	1958	6.25	12.50	25.00
CL 1299 [M]	The Four Lads Swing Along	1959	6.25	12.50	25.00
CL 1407 [M]	High Spirits!	1959	6.25	12.50	25.00
CL 1502 [M]	Love Affair	1960	3.75	7.50	15.00
CL 1550 [M]	Everything Goes	1960	3.75	7.50	15.00
CL 2545 [10]	The Four Lads Sing Frank Loesser	1956	12.50	25.00	50.00
CL 2577 [10]	Stage Show	1956	12.50	25.00	50.00
CL 6329 [10]	Stage Show	1954	12.50	25.00	50.00
CS 8035 [S]	Breezin' Along	1958	7.50	15.00	30.00
CS 8047 [S]	Four on the Aisle	1958	7.50	15.00	30.00
CS 8106 [S]	The Four Lads Swing Along	1959	7.50	15.00	30.00
CS 8203 [S]	High Spirits!	1959	7.50	15.00	30.00
CS 8293 [S]	Love Affair	1960	5.00	10.00	20.00
CS 8350 [S]	Everything Goes	1960	5.00	10.00	20.00
DOT					
DLP-3438 [M]	Hits of the 60's	1962	3.75	7.50	15.00
DLP-3533 [M]	Oh Happy Day	1963	3.75	7.50	15.00
DLP-25438 [S]	Hits of the 60's	1962	5.00	10.00	20.00
DLP-25533 [S]	Oh Happy Day	1963	5.00	10.00	20.00
HARMONY					
HS 11369	Moments to Remember	1970	3.00	6.00	12.00
KAPP					
KL-1224 [M]	Twelve Hits	1961	3.75	7.50	15.00
KL-1254 [M]	Dixieland Doin's	1961	3.75	7.50	15.00
KS-3224 [S]	Twelve Hits	1961	5.00	10.00	20.00
KS-3254 [S]	Dixieland Doin's	1961	5.00	10.00	20.00
UNITED ARTISTS					
UAL-3356 [M]	This Year's Top Movie Hits	1964	3.75	7.50	15.00
UAL-3399 [M]	Songs of World War I	1964	3.75	7.50	15.00
UAS-6356 [S]	This Year's Top Movie Hits	1964	5.00	10.00	20.00
UAS-6399 [S]	Songs of World War I	1964	5.00	10.00	20.00

FOUR LARKS, THE

Number	Title (A Side/B Side)	Yr	VG	VG+	NM
45s					
TOWER					
364	Rain/Another Chance	1967	7.50	15.00	30.00
402	I Still Love You (From the Bottom of My Heart)/Groovin' at the Go-Go	1968	10.00	20.00	40.00
450	Can I Have Another Helping, Please/I've Got Plenty	1968	2.50	5.00	10.00
UPTOWN					
748	You and Me/That's All That Counts	1967	10.00	20.00	40.00

FOUR LOVERS, THE

Also see THE FOUR SEASONS; FRANKIE VALLI.

Number	Title (A Side/B Side)	Yr	VG	VG+	NM
45s					
EPIC					
9255	My Life for Your Love/Pucker Up	1957	500.00	1000.	2000.
RCA VICTOR					
47-6518	You're the Apple of My Eye/The Girl of My Dreams	1956	10.00	20.00	40.00
47-6519	Honey Love/Please Don't Leave Me	1956	10.00	20.00	40.00
47-6646	Be Lovey Dovey/Jambalaya	1956	7.50	15.00	30.00
47-6768	Happy Am I/Never Never	1956	7.50	15.00	30.00
47-6812	Shake a Hand/The Stranger	1957	10.00	20.00	40.00
47-6819	Night Train/The Stranger	1957	10.00	20.00	40.00
7-Inch Extended Plays					
RCA VICTOR					
EPA-869	Diddley Diddley Babe/Shake a Hand//The Stranger/Night Train	1956	37.50	75.00	150.00
EPA-869 [PS]	The Four Lovers	1956	37.50	75.00	150.00
EPA-871	I Want a Girl Just Like the Girl That Married Dear Old Dad/(I Love You) For Sentimental Reasons //This Is My Story/Memories of You	1956	37.50	75.00	150.00
EPA-871 [PS]	Joyride	1956	37.50	75.00	150.00
Albums					
RCA VICTOR					
LPM-1317 [M]	Joyride	1956	175.00	350.00	700.00

FOUR NATURALS, THE

Number	Title (A Side/B Side)	Yr	VG	VG+	NM
45s					
RED TOP					
113	How Strange/Blue Moon	1958	12.50	25.00	50.00
—As "The Naturals"					
119	I Hear a Rhapsody/When I'm In Your Arms	1959	12.50	25.00	50.00
125	The Thought of You Darling/Long Long Ago	1959	20.00	40.00	80.00

FOUR OF A KIND

More than one group.

Number	Title (A Side/B Side)	Yr	VG	VG+	NM
45s					
BOMARC					
302	It's Better That Way/I Care for You	1959	5.00	10.00	20.00
CAMEO					
154	You Were Made T'Love/Love Every Moment You Love	1958	5.00	10.00	20.00
LAURIE					
3309	Chippies' Playground/Prance Around	1965	2.50	5.00	10.00
MELBA					
110	I'm Gonna Rock My Heart/Our Song Dedicated to You	1957	6.25	12.50	25.00
117	Dreamy Eyes/Fools Fall in Love	1957	6.25	12.50	25.00

FOUR PEARLS, THE

Number	Title (A Side/B Side)	Yr	VG	VG+	NM
45s					
DOLTON					
26	Look at Me/It's Almost Tomorrow	1960	50.00	100.00	200.00

FOUR PENNIES, THE (1)

See THE CHIFFONS.

FOUR PENNIES, THE (2)

British group.

Number	Title (A Side/B Side)	Yr	VG	VG+	NM
45s					
PHILIPS					
40202	Juliet/Tell Me Girl, What Are You Gonna Do	1964	3.75	7.50	15.00
40333	Until It's Time for You to Go/Till Another Day	1965	3.75	7.50	15.00

FOUR PENNIES, THE (U)

May also be by group (2), but we're not sure.

Number	Title (A Side/B Side)	Yr	VG	VG+	NM
45s					
BRUNSWICK					
55304	You Have No Time to Lose/You're a Gas with Your Trash	1966	2.50	5.00	10.00
55324	Shake a Hand/'Tis the Season	1967	5.00	10.00	20.00

FOUR PREPS, THE

Number	Title (A Side/B Side)	Yr	VG	VG+	NM
45s					
CAPITOL					
F3576	Dreamy Eyes/Fools Will Be Fools	1956	5.00	10.00	20.00
F3621	Moonstruck in Madrid/I Cried a Million Tears	1957	5.00	10.00	20.00
F3699	Falling Star/Where Wuzz You	1957	5.00	10.00	20.00
F3761	Promise Me Baby/Again 'N Again 'N Again	1957	5.00	10.00	20.00
F3775	Band of Angels/How About That	1957	5.00	10.00	20.00
F3845	26 Miles (Santa Catalina)/It's You	1957	5.00	10.00	20.00
F3960	Big Man/Stop Baby	1958	5.00	10.00	20.00
F4023	Lazy Summer Night/Summertime Lies	1958	5.00	10.00	20.00
F4078	Cinderella/Gidget	1958	5.00	10.00	20.00
F4126	She Was Five and He Was Ten/Riddle of Love	1959	5.00	10.00	20.00
F4218	Big Surprise/Try My Arms	1959	5.00	10.00	20.00
F4256	I Ain't Never/Memories, Memories	1959	5.00	10.00	20.00
4312	Down by the Station/Listen Honey	1959	3.00	6.00	12.00
4362	Got a Girl/Wait Till You Hear It from Me	1960	3.00	6.00	12.00
4400	Sentimental Kid/Madelina	1960	3.00	6.00	12.00
4435	The Sand and the Sea/Kaw-Liga	1960	3.00	6.00	12.00
4478	Balboa/I've Already Started In	1960	3.00	6.00	12.00
4508	Calcutta/Gone Are the Days	1961	3.00	6.00	12.00
4568	Dream, Boy, Dream/Grounded	1961	7.50	15.00	30.00
4599	More Money for You and Me/Swing Down Chariot	1961	3.75	7.50	15.00
—With full-length version of A-side					
4599	More Money for You and Me/Swing Down Chariot	1961	3.00	6.00	12.00
—With edited version of A-side					
4599 [PS]	More Money for You and Me/Swing Down Chariot	1961	5.00	10.00	20.00
4641	Smoke Gets In Your Eyes/Swing Down Chariot	1961	3.00	6.00	12.00
4659	Once Around the Block/The Seine	1961	3.00	6.00	12.00
4716	The Big Draft/Suzy Cockroach	1962	2.50	5.00	10.00
4716 [PS]	The Big Draft/Suzy Cockroach	1962	2.50	5.00	10.00
4792	Alice/Goodnight Sweetheart	1962	2.50	5.00	10.00
4974	Charmaine/Hi-Ho Anybody Home	1963	2.50	5.00	10.00
5020	Oh Where, Oh Where/Demons and Witches	1963	2.50	5.00	10.00
5074	The Greatest Surfer Couple/I'm Falling in Love with a Girl	1963	2.50	5.00	10.00
5143	A Letter to the Beatles/College Cannonball	1964	6.25	12.50	25.00
5178	I've Known You All My Life/What Kind of Bird Is That	1964	2.00	4.00	8.00
5236	A Girl Without a Top/Two Wrongs Don't Make a Right	1964	2.00	4.00	8.00
5274	How to Succeed in Love/My Love, My Love	1964	2.00	4.00	8.00
5351	Everlasting/I'll Set My Love to Music	1965	2.00	4.00	8.00
5450	Now I'll Never Be the Same/Our First American Dance	1965	2.00	4.00	8.00
5609	Annie in Her Granny/Something to Remember You By	1966	2.00	4.00	8.00
5687	Let's Call It a Day, Girl/The Girl in the Shade of a Striped Umbrella	1966	2.00	4.00	8.00
5819	Love of the Common People/What I Don't Know Won't Hurt Me	1967	2.00	4.00	8.00
5921	Draft Dodger Rag/The Hitchhiker	1967	2.00	4.00	8.00
7-Inch Extended Plays					
CAPITOL					
EAP 1-1015	(contents unknown)	1958	6.25	12.50	25.00
EAP 1-1015 [PS]	Twenty-Six Miles	1958	6.25	12.50	25.00
EAP 1-1064	*Big Man/Too Young to Love/Stop, Baby/Humble Pie	1958	6.25	12.50	25.00
EAP 1-1064 [PS]	Big Man	1958	6.25	12.50	25.00
EAP 1-1090	(contents unknown)	1959	6.25	12.50	25.00
EAP 1-1090 [PS]	Things We Did Last Summer	1959	6.25	12.50	25.00
EAP 1-1139	(contents unknown)	1959	6.25	12.50	25.00
EAP 1-1139 [PS]	Lazy Summer Night	1959	6.25	12.50	25.00
Albums					
CAPITOL					
T 994 [M]	The Four Preps	1958	7.50	15.00	30.00
T 1090 [M]	The Things We Did Last Summer	1958	6.25	12.50	25.00
ST 1216 [S]	Dancing and Dreaming	1959	6.25	12.50	25.00
T 1216 [M]	Dancing and Dreaming	1959	5.00	10.00	20.00
DT 1291 [R]	Early in the Morning	1960	3.00	6.00	12.00
T 1291 [M]	Early in the Morning	1960	6.25	12.50	25.00
ST 1566 [S]	The Four Preps on Campus	1961	6.25	12.50	25.00
T 1566 [M]	The Four Preps on Campus	1961	5.00	10.00	20.00
ST 1647 [S]	Campus Encore	1962	6.25	12.50	25.00
T 1647 [M]	Campus Encore	1962	5.00	10.00	20.00
ST 1814 [S]	Campus Confidential	1963	5.00	10.00	20.00
T 1814 [M]	Campus Confidential	1963	3.75	7.50	15.00
ST 1976 [S]	Songs for a Campus Party	1963	5.00	10.00	20.00
T 1976 [M]	Songs for a Campus Party	1963	3.75	7.50	15.00
ST 2169 [S]	How to Succeed in Love	1964	5.00	10.00	20.00
T 2169 [M]	How to Succeed in Love	1964	3.75	7.50	15.00
ST 2708 [S]	The Best of the Four Preps	1967	3.00	6.00	12.00
T 2708 [M]	The Best of the Four Preps	1967	3.75	7.50	15.00

FOUR SEASONS, THE

Also see THE FOUR LOVERS; FRANKIE VALLI.

45s

Number	Title (A Side/B Side)	Yr	VG	VG+	NM
COLUMBIA					
(# unknown)	Big Man's World	1964	7.50	15.00	30.00
—One-sided cardboard soundsheet, a promo for the Columbia Record Club. Number has been reported as both 6675 and 6724.					
CREWE					
333	And That Reminds Me (My Heart Reminds Me)/The Singles Game	1969	2.00	4.00	8.00
333 [PS]	And That Reminds Me (My Heart Reminds Me)/The Singles Game	1969	2.50	5.00	10.00
—No shadow behind Frankie Valli's and Joe Long's heads					
333 [PS]	And That Reminds Me (My Heart Reminds Me)/The Singles Game	1969	3.00	6.00	12.00
—With shadow behind Frankie Valli's and Joe Long's heads					
FBI					
7701	East Meets West/Rhapsody	1986	5.00	10.00	20.00
—With the Beach Boys					
FOUR SEASONS					
0019	I Saw Mommy Kissing Santa Claus/Santa Claus Is Coming To Town	198?	—	2.00	4.00
GONE					
5122	Bermuda/Spanish Lace	1961	20.00	40.00	80.00
5122 [DJ]	Bermuda/Spanish Lace	1961	15.00	30.00	60.00
MCA/CURB					
52618	Streetfighter/Deep Inside Your Love	1985	—	2.00	4.00
52724	Moonlight Memories/What About Tomorrow	1985	—	2.00	4.00
52871	Book of Love/What About Tomorrow	1986	—	2.00	4.00
53440	Big Girls Don't Cry (Enhanced Original Mix)/Big Girls Don't Cry (Dirty Dancing Rap)	1988	—	2.00	4.00
MOTOWN					
1255	How Come/Life and Breath	1973	2.50	5.00	10.00
1288	Hickory/Charisma	1973	2.50	5.00	10.00
MOWEST					
5026	Walk On, Don't Look Back/Sun Country	1972	2.50	5.00	10.00
OLDIES 45					
#18	Sherry/I've Cried Before	1964	2.00	4.00	8.00
#47	Big Girls Don't Cry/Connie-O	1964	2.00	4.00	8.00
#60	Walk Like a Man/Lucky Ladybug	1964	2.00	4.00	8.00
#116	Candy Girl/Marlena	1964	2.00	4.00	8.00
#319	Stay/Goodnight My Love	1965	2.00	4.00	8.00
PHILIPS					
40166	Dawn (Go Away)/No Surfin' Today	1964	3.75	7.50	15.00
—Black label					
40166	Dawn (Go Away)/No Surfin' Today	1967	2.00	4.00	8.00
—Light blue label with "S" stamp					
40185	Ronnie/Born to Wander	1964	3.00	6.00	12.00
40185 [PS]	Ronnie/Born to Wander	1964	7.50	15.00	30.00
40211	Rag Doll/Silence Is Golden	1964	3.75	7.50	15.00
—Black label					
40211	Rag Doll/Silence Is Golden	1967	2.00	4.00	8.00
—Light blue label with "S" stamp					
40211 [PS]	Rag Doll/Silence Is Golden	1964	7.50	15.00	30.00
—Yellow sleeve					
40211 [PS]	Rag Doll/Silence Is Golden	1964	7.50	15.00	30.00
—Green sleeve					
40225	Save It for Me/Funny Face	1964	2.50	5.00	10.00
40238	Big Man in Town/Little Angel	1964	2.50	5.00	10.00
40238 [PS]	Big Man in Town/Little Angel	1964	6.25	12.50	25.00
40260	Bye, Bye Baby (Baby Goodbye)/Searching Wind	1965	2.50	5.00	10.00
40260 [PS]	Bye, Bye Baby (Baby Goodbye)/Searching Wind	1965	6.25	12.50	25.00
40278	Toy Soldier/Betrayed	1965	2.50	5.00	10.00
40278 [PS]	Toy Soldier/Betrayed	1965	6.25	12.50	25.00
40305	Girl Come Running/Cry Myself to Sleep	1965	2.50	5.00	10.00
40305 [PS]	Girl Come Running/Cry Myself to Sleep	1965	6.25	12.50	25.00
40317	Let's Hang On!/On Broadway Tonight	1965	2.50	5.00	10.00
—Black label					
40317	Let's Hang On!/On Broadway Tonight	1967	2.00	4.00	8.00
—Light blue label with "S" stamp					
40324	Don't Think Twice/Sassy	1965	2.50	5.00	10.00
40324 [PS]	Don't Think Twice/Sassy	1965	6.25	12.50	25.00
—Philips 40324 by "The Wonder Who?"					
40350	Working My Way Back to You/Too Many Memories	1966	2.50	5.00	10.00
40370	Opus 17 (Don't You Worry 'Bout Me)/Beggar's Paradise	1966	2.50	5.00	10.00
40370 [PS]	Opus 17 (Don't You Worry 'Bout Me)/Beggar's Paradise	1966	6.25	12.50	25.00
40380	On the Good Ship Lollipop/You're Nobody Until Somebody Loves You	1966	2.50	5.00	10.00
40380 [PS]	On the Good Ship Lollipop/You're Nobody Until Somebody Loves You	1966	6.25	12.50	25.00
—Philips 40380 by "The Wonder Who?"					
40393	I've Got You Under My Skin/Huggin' My Pillow	1966	2.50	5.00	10.00
40393 [PS]	I've Got You Under My Skin/Huggin' My Pillow	1966	6.25	12.50	25.00
40412	Tell It to the Rain/Show Girl	1966	2.50	5.00	10.00
40412 [PS]	Tell It to the Rain/Show Girl	1966	6.25	12.50	25.00
40433	Beggin'/Dody	1967	2.50	5.00	10.00
—Black label					
40433	Beggin'/Dody	1967	2.00	4.00	8.00
—Light blue label					
40433 [PS]	Beggin'/Dody	1967	6.25	12.50	25.00
40460	C'mon Marianne/Let's Ride Again	1967	2.50	5.00	10.00
—Black label					
40460	C'mon Marianne/Let's Ride Again	1967	3.00	6.00	12.00
—Blue label; contains a noticeably different, slowed-down mix of A-side					
40460 [PS]	C'mon Marianne/Let's Ride Again	1967	6.25	12.50	25.00
40471	Lonesome Road/Around and Around	1967	2.50	5.00	10.00
40471 [PS]	Lonesome Road/Around and Around	1967	6.25	12.50	25.00
—Philips 40471 by "The Wonder Who?"; B-side listed as The Four Seasons					
40490	Watch the Flowers Grow/Raven	1967	2.50	5.00	10.00
40490 [PS]	Watch the Flowers Grow/Raven	1967	6.25	12.50	25.00
40500	Donneybrook/Around and Around	1968	5.00	10.00	20.00
—Only released in Canada					
40523	Will You Love Me Tomorrow/Around and Around	1968	3.00	6.00	12.00
—Black label					
40523	Will You Love Me Tomorrow/Around and Around	1968	2.50	5.00	10.00
—Blue label					
40542	Saturday's Father/Good-Bye Girl	1968	—	3.00	6.00
40542 [PS]	Saturday's Father/Good-Bye Girl	1968	2.50	5.00	10.00
—Standard sleeve					
40542 [PS]	Saturday's Father/Good-Bye Girl	1968	3.75	7.50	15.00
—Fold-open sleeve					
40577	Electric Stories/Pity	1968	—	3.00	6.00
40597	Something's On Her Mind/Idaho	1969	—	3.00	6.00
40597 [PS]	Something's On Her Mind/Idaho	1969	2.50	5.00	10.00
40662	Patch of Blue/She Gives Me Light	1970	2.00	4.00	8.00
—As "Frankie Valli & THE 4 SEASONS"					
40662 [PS]	Patch of Blue/She Gives Me Light	1970	2.50	5.00	10.00
40688	Lay Me Down (Wake Me Up)/Heartaches and Rainbows	1970	6.25	12.50	25.00
40688 [DJ]	Lay Me Down (Wake Me Up) (mono/stereo)	1970	3.75	7.50	15.00
40694	Where Are My Dreams?/Any Day Now-Oh Happy Day	1971	6.25	12.50	25.00
40694 [DJ]	Where Are My Dreams? (mono/stereo)	1971	3.75	7.50	15.00
SEASONS 4-EVER					
777	Trance/I Am All Alone	1971	3.75	7.50	15.00
—As "Billy Dixon and the Topics"; blue vinyl					
777	Trance/I Am All Alone	1971	2.00	4.00	8.00
—As "Billy Dixon and the Topics"; green vinyl					
TOPIX					
6000	Too Young to Start/Red Lips	1960	37.50	75.00	150.00
—As "The Village Voices"; yellow and black label					
6000	Too Young to Start/Red Lips	1960	25.00	50.00	100.00
—As "The Village Voices"; yellow, black and white label					
6002	I Am All Alone/Trance	1961	37.50	75.00	150.00
—As "Billy Dixon and the Topics"					
6008	Lost Lullaby/Trance	1961	50.00	100.00	200.00
—As "Billy Dixon and the Topics"					
VEE JAY					
456	Sherry/I've Cried Before	1962	6.25	12.50	25.00
—First pressings have black rainbow labels with oval logo					
456	Sherry/I've Cried Before	1962	6.25	12.50	25.00
—A later pressing has an all-black label					
465	Big Girls Don't Cry/Connie-O	1962	5.00	10.00	20.00
—First pressings have black rainbow labels with oval logo					
465	Big Girls Don't Cry/Connie-O	1962	6.25	12.50	25.00
—A later pressing has an all-black label					
478	Santa Claus Is Coming to Town/Christmas Tears	1962	6.25	12.50	25.00
485	Walk Like a Man/Lucky Ladybug	1963	3.75	7.50	15.00
512	Ain't That a Shame!/Soon (I'll Be Home Again)	1963	5.00	10.00	20.00
539	Candy Girl/Marlena	1963	3.75	7.50	15.00
539 [PS]	Candy Girl/Marlena	1963	—	—	—
—Rumored to exist, but without conclusive evidence, we will delete this from future editions					
562	New Mexican Rose/That's the Only Way	1963	3.75	7.50	15.00
562 [DJ]	New Mexican Rose/That's the Way It Goes	1963	7.50	15.00	30.00
—Wrong title on B-side; evidently only exists on promos					
576	Peanuts/Stay	1963	25.00	50.00	100.00
576 [DJ]	Peanuts/Stay	1963	15.00	30.00	60.00
582	Stay/Goodnight My Love	1964	3.75	7.50	15.00
597	Alone/Long, Lonely Nights	1964	3.75	7.50	15.00
—Black rainbow label					
597	Alone/Long, Lonely Nights	1964	6.25	12.50	25.00
—Plain black label					
597	Alone/Long, Lonely Nights	1964	7.50	15.00	30.00
—Yellow label					
597 [PS]	Alone/Long, Lonely Nights	1964	12.50	25.00	50.00
608	Sincerely/One Song	1964	5.00	10.00	20.00
618	Happy, Happy Birthday Baby/You're the Apple of My Eye	1964	5.00	10.00	20.00
626	I Saw Mommy Kissing Santa Claus/Christmas Tears	1964	5.00	10.00	20.00
626 [PS]	I Saw Mommy Kissing Santa Claus/Christmas Tears	1964	12.50	25.00	50.00
639	Never on Sunday/Connie-O	1965	5.00	10.00	20.00
664	Since I Don't Have You/Tonite, Tonite	1965	7.50	15.00	30.00
713	Little Boy (In Grown Up Clothes)/Silver Wings	1965	5.00	10.00	20.00
—Maroon label					
713	Little Boy (In Grown Up Clothes)/Silver Wings	1965	7.50	15.00	30.00
—Black label					
717	Peanuts/My Sugar	1966	7.50	15.00	30.00
—As "The Wonder Who"					
719	My Mother's Eyes/Stay	1966	3.75	7.50	15.00
901 [DJ]	Peanuts	1963	25.00	50.00	100.00
—One-sided promo from EP 901					
WABC RADIO					
77	Cousin Brucie Go Go	1964	37.50	75.00	150.00
—One-sided yellow vinyl; theme song for Cousin Brucie's radio show					
WARNER BROS.					
8122	Who Loves You/Who Loves You (Disco Version)	1975	—	2.50	5.00
8168	December, 1963 (Oh, What a Night)/Slip Away	1975	—	2.50	5.00
8203	Silver Star/Mystic Mr. Sam	1976	—	2.50	5.00
8407	Down the Hall/I Believe in You	1977	2.00	4.00	8.00
49585	Heaven Must Have Sent You (Here in the Night)/Silver Star	1981	2.00	4.00	8.00
49597	Spend the Night in Love/Slip Away	1980	2.00	4.00	8.00
WIBBAGE					
WIBG-	Joey Reynolds Theme/Rats in My Room	1965	25.00	50.00	100.00
—Custom pressing for Philadelphia radio station; B-side by Joey and Danny					
WXYZ DETROIT					
121003	Joey Reynolds Theme/Rats in My Room	1965	25.00	50.00	100.00
—Custom pressing for Detroit radio station; B-side by Joey and Danny					

7-Inch Extended Plays

Number	Title (A Side/B Side)	Yr	VG	VG+	NM
VEE JAY					
EP 1-901	Never on Sunday/Peanuts//I Can't Give You Anything But Love/La Dee Dah	1962	6.25	12.50	25.00
EP 1-901 [PS]	The Four Seasons Sing	1962	6.25	12.50	25.00

Number	Title (A Side/B Side)	Yr	VG	VG+	NM
EP 1-902	Why Do Fools Fall in Love/Silhouettes//Since I Don't Have You/Alone	1963	6.25	12.50	25.00
EP 1-902 [PS]	The Four Seasons Sing	1963	6.25	12.50	25.00

Albums

MCA/CURB

Number	Title (A Side/B Side)	Yr	VG	VG+	NM
5632	Starfighter	1985	2.50	5.00	10.00

MOTOWN

Number	Title (A Side/B Side)	Yr	VG	VG+	NM
788	Inside Out	1973	—	—	—
—Canceled					

MOWEST

Number	Title (A Side/B Side)	Yr	VG	VG+	NM
MW 108L	Chameleon	1972	3.00	6.00	12.00

PHILIPS

Number	Title (A Side/B Side)	Yr	VG	VG+	NM
PHS-2-6501 [(2)]	Edizione d'Oro	1968	6.25	12.50	25.00
—Number "4" on cover is red on gold foil					
PHS-2-6501 [(2)]	Edizione d'Oro	1968	7.50	15.00	30.00
—Number "4" on cover is white on gold foil					
PHS-2-6501 [(2)]	Edizione d'Oro	1969	6.25	12.50	25.00
—Number "4" on cover is white on gold board					
PHM 200124 [M]	Dawn (Go Away) and 11 Other Great Songs	1964	5.00	10.00	20.00
PHM 200129 [M]	Born to Wander	1964	5.00	10.00	20.00
PHM 200146 [M]	Rag Doll	1964	5.00	10.00	20.00
—Without yellow seal noting presence of "Save It For Me"					
PHM 200146 [M]	Rag Doll	1964	5.00	10.00	20.00
—With yellow seal noting presence of "Save It For Me"					
PHM 200150 [M]	All the Song Hits of the Four Seasons	1964	5.00	10.00	20.00
PHM 200164 [M]	The 4 Seasons Entertain You	1965	5.00	10.00	20.00
—With orange seal noting presence of "Bye Bye Baby"					
PHM 200164 [M]	The 4 Seasons Entertain You	1965	5.00	10.00	20.00
—With orange seal noting presence of "Bye Bye Baby" and "Toy Soldier"					
PHM 200164 [M]	The 4 Seasons Entertain You	1965	3.75	7.50	15.00
—With blue seal noting presence of "Bye Bye Baby" and "Toy Soldier"					
PHM 200193 [M]	Big Hits by Burt Bacharach...Hal David...Bob Dylan	1965	5.00	10.00	20.00
—"Open book" cover					
PHM 200193 [M]	Big Hits by Burt Bacharach...Hal David...Bob Dylan	1966	7.50	15.00	30.00
—Group photos on cover					
PHM 200196 [M]	The 4 Seasons' Gold Vault of Hits	1965	5.00	10.00	20.00
—Title in red print with no border					
PHM 200196 [M]	The 4 Seasons' Gold Vault of Hits	1965	3.75	7.50	15.00
—Title in red print with black border					
PHM 200196 [M]	The 4 Seasons' Gold Vault of Hits	196?	3.00	6.00	12.00
—Title in all-black print					
PHM 200201 [M]	Working My Way Back to You	1966	5.00	10.00	20.00
PHM 200221 [M]	2nd Vault of Golden Hits	1966	3.75	7.50	15.00
PHM 200222 [M]	Lookin' Back	1966	5.00	10.00	20.00
PHM 200223 [M]	The Four Seasons' Christmas Album	1966	6.25	12.50	25.00
—Reissue of Vee Jay album (same contents and order) with new cover					
PHM 200243 [M]	New Gold Hits	1967	5.00	10.00	20.00
PHS 600124 [S]	Dawn (Go Away) and 11 Other Great Songs	1964	6.25	12.50	25.00
PHS 600129 [S]	Born to Wander	1964	6.25	12.50	25.00
PHS 600146 [S]	Rag Doll	1964	6.25	12.50	25.00
—Without yellow seal noting presence of "Save It For Me"					
PHS 600146 [S]	Rag Doll	1964	6.25	12.50	25.00
—With yellow seal noting presence of "Save It For Me"					
PHS 600150 [S]	All the Song Hits of the Four Seasons	1964	6.25	12.50	25.00
PHS 600164 [S]	The 4 Seasons Entertain You	1965	6.25	12.50	25.00
—With orange seal noting presence of "Bye Bye Baby"					
PHS 600164 [S]	The 4 Seasons Entertain You	1965	6.25	12.50	25.00
—With orange seal noting presence of "Bye Bye Baby" and "Toy Soldier"					
PHS 600164 [S]	The 4 Seasons Entertain You	1965	5.00	10.00	20.00
—With blue seal noting presence of "Bye Bye Baby" and "Toy Soldier"					
PHS 600193 [S]	Big Hits by Burt Bacharach...Hal David...Bob Dylan	1965	6.25	12.50	25.00
—"Open book" cover					
PHS 600193 [S]	Big Hits by Burt Bacharach...Hal David...Bob Dylan	1966	10.00	20.00	40.00
—Group photos on cover					
PHS 600196 [S]	The 4 Seasons' Gold Vault of Hits	1965	6.25	12.50	25.00
—Title in red print with no border					
PHS 600196 [S]	The 4 Seasons' Gold Vault of Hits	1965	5.00	10.00	20.00
—Title in red print with black border					
PHS 600196 [S]	The 4 Seasons' Gold Vault of Hits	196?	3.75	7.50	15.00
—Title in all-black print					
PHS 600201 [S]	Working My Way Back to You	1966	6.25	12.50	25.00
PHS 600221 [S]	2nd Vault of Golden Hits	1966	5.00	10.00	20.00
PHS 600222 [S]	Lookin' Back	1966	6.25	12.50	25.00
PHS 600223 [S]	The Four Seasons' Christmas Album	1966	7.50	15.00	30.00
PHS 600243 [S]	New Gold Hits	1967	6.25	12.50	25.00
PHS 600290	The Genuine Imitation Life Gazette	1969	6.25	12.50	25.00
—Yellow newspaper					
PHS 600290	The Genuine Imitation Life Gazette	1969	3.75	7.50	15.00
—White newspaper					
PHS 600341	Half & Half	1970	5.00	10.00	20.00

PICKWICK

Number	Title (A Side/B Side)	Yr	VG	VG+	NM
SPC-3223	Brotherhood of Man	1970	3.00	6.00	12.00
—Mass-market version of Sears 609					

PRIVATE STOCK

Number	Title (A Side/B Side)	Yr	VG	VG+	NM
PS-7000 [(2)]	The Four Seasons Story	1975	3.75	7.50	15.00

RHINO

Number	Title (A Side/B Side)	Yr	VG	VG+	NM
RNLP 70234	The Four Seasons' Christmas Album	1987	3.00	6.00	12.00
—Reissue of Philips album (same contents and order)					
R1-70247	Working My Way Back to You	1988	2.50	5.00	10.00
—Reissue of Philips 600-201					
R1-70249	The Genuine Imitation Life Gazette	1988	2.50	5.00	10.00
—Reissue of Philips 600-290					
R1-71248	Big Hits by Burt Bacharach...Hal David...Bob Dylan	1988	2.50	5.00	10.00
—Reissue of Philips 600-193					
R1-71490 [(2)]	Anthology	1988	3.00	6.00	12.00
RNRP-72998 [(4)]	25th Anniversary Collection	1987	6.25	12.50	25.00

SEARS

Number	Title (A Side/B Side)	Yr	VG	VG+	NM
SPS-609	Brotherhood of Man	1970	6.25	12.50	25.00

VEE JAY

Number	Title (A Side/B Side)	Yr	VG	VG+	NM
LP-1053 [M]	Sherry & 11 Others	1962	7.50	15.00	30.00
SR-1053 [S]	Sherry & 11 Others	1962	10.00	20.00	40.00
LP 1055 [M]	The Four Seasons Greetings	1962	7.50	15.00	30.00
SR 1055 [S]	The Four Seasons Greetings	1962	10.00	20.00	40.00
LP-1056 [M]	Big Girls Don't Cry and Twelve Others	1963	7.50	15.00	30.00
SR-1056 [S]	Big Girls Don't Cry and Twelve Others	1963	10.00	20.00	40.00
LP-1059 [M]	Ain't That a Shame and 11 Others	1963	7.50	15.00	30.00
SR-1059 [S]	Ain't That a Shame and 11 Others	1963	10.00	20.00	40.00
LP-1065 [M]	Golden Hits of the Four Seasons	1963	7.50	15.00	30.00
SR-1065 [S]	Golden Hits of the Four Seasons	1963	10.00	20.00	40.00
LP-1082 [M]	Folk-Nanny	1964	7.50	15.00	30.00
LP-1082 [M]	Stay & Other Great Hits	1964	6.25	12.50	25.00
—Retitled version of Folk-Nanny					
SR-1082 [S]	Folk-Nanny	1964	10.00	20.00	40.00
SR-1082 [S]	Stay & Other Great Hits	1964	7.50	15.00	30.00
—Retitled version of Folk-Nanny					
LP-1088 [M]	More Golden Hits by the Four Seasons	1964	7.50	15.00	30.00
—With "Long Lonely Nights" on record					
LP-1088 [M]	More Golden Hits by the Four Seasons	1964	5.00	10.00	20.00
—With "Apple of My Eye" on record					
SR-1088 [S]	More Golden Hits by the Four Seasons	1964	10.00	20.00	40.00
—With "Long Lonely Nights" on record					
SR-1088 [S]	More Golden Hits by the Four Seasons	1964	6.25	12.50	25.00
—With "Apple of My Eye" on record					
LP-1121 [M]	We Love Girls	1965	7.50	15.00	30.00
LPS-1121 [S]	We Love Girls	1965	10.00	20.00	40.00
LP-1154 [M]	Recorded Live on Stage	1965	7.50	15.00	30.00
LPS-1154 [S]	Recorded Live on Stage	1965	10.00	20.00	40.00

WARNER BROS.

Number	Title (A Side/B Side)	Yr	VG	VG+	NM
BS 2900	Who Loves You	1975	3.00	6.00	12.00
BS 3016	Helicon	1977	3.00	6.00	12.00
2WB 3497 [(2)]	Reunited Live	1980	3.75	7.50	15.00

FOUR SEASONS, THE (2)

Not the same as the better-known group.

45s

ALANNA

Number	Title (A Side/B Side)	Yr	VG	VG+	NM
555	Don't Sweat It Baby/That's the Way the Ball Bounces	1959	10.00	20.00	40.00
555	I'm Still in Love with You, Baby/That's the Way the Ball Bounces	1959	15.00	30.00	60.00
558	Love Knows No Season/Hot Water Bottle	1959	7.50	15.00	30.00

ROBBEE

Number	Title (A Side/B Side)	Yr	VG	VG+	NM
106	Mirage/Nancy's Trampoline	1960	37.50	75.00	150.00

FOUR SPARKS, THE

45s

ABC-PARAMOUNT

Number	Title (A Side/B Side)	Yr	VG	VG+	NM
9906	My Sweet Juanita/Out of This World	1958	5.00	10.00	20.00

FOUR SPEEDS, THE

45s

CHALLENGE

Number	Title (A Side/B Side)	Yr	VG	VG+	NM
9187	R.P.M./My Sting Ray	1963	10.00	20.00	40.00
9202	Four on the Floor/Cheater Slicks	1963	10.00	20.00	40.00

FEDERAL

Number	Title (A Side/B Side)	Yr	VG	VG+	NM
6070	I Need You Baby/The Girls Back Home	1954	20.00	40.00	80.00

FOUR STUDENTS, THE

45s

GROOVE

Number	Title (A Side/B Side)	Yr	VG	VG+	NM
0110	So Near and Yet So Far/Hot Rotten Soda Pop	1955	12.50	25.00	50.00

FOUR TEENS, THE

45s

CHALLENGE

Number	Title (A Side/B Side)	Yr	VG	VG+	NM
59021	Go Little Go Cat/Spark Plug	1958	15.00	30.00	60.00

FOUR TEMPTATIONS, THE

45s

ABC-PARAMOUNT

Number	Title (A Side/B Side)	Yr	VG	VG+	NM
9920	Cathy/Rock and Roll Baby	1958	7.50	15.00	30.00

FOUR TOPS, THE

Also see DELORES CARROLL AND THE FOUR TOPS.

45s

ABC

Number	Title (A Side/B Side)	Yr	VG	VG+	NM
12096	Seven Lonely Nights/I Can't Hold Out Much Longer	1975	—	2.00	4.00
12123	We All Gotta Stick Together/(It Would Almost) Drive Me Out of My Mind	1975	—	2.00	4.00
12155	I'm Glad You Walked Into My Life/Mama, You're All Right with Me	1975	—	2.00	4.00
12214	Catfish/Look at My Baby	1976	—	2.00	4.00
12223	Look at My Baby/Catfish	1976	—	2.00	4.00
12236	Feel Free/I Know You Like It	1976	—	2.00	4.00
12267	Strung Out for Your Love/You Can't Hold Back on Love	1977	—	2.00	4.00
12315	Runnin' From Your Love/The Show Must Go On	1977	—	2.00	4.00
12427	Inside a Brokenhearted Man/H.E.L.P.	1978	—	2.00	4.00
12457	Just in Time/This House	1978	—	2.00	4.00

ABC DUNHILL

Number	Title (A Side/B Side)	Yr	VG	VG+	NM
4330	Keeper of the Castle/Jubilee with Soul	1972	—	2.50	5.00
4334	Guardian De Tu Castle/Jubilee with Soul	1972	—	2.50	5.00
4339	Ain't No Woman (Like the One I've Got)/The Good Lord Knows	1973	—	2.50	5.00
4354	Are You Man Enough/Peace of Mind	1973	—	2.50	5.00
4366	Sweet Understanding Love/Main Street People	1973	—	2.50	5.00
4377	I Just Can't Get You Out of My Mind/Am I My Brother's Keeper?	1973	—	2.50	5.00
4386	One Chain Don't Make No Prison/Light of Your Love	1974	—	2.50	5.00
15005	Midnight Flower/All My Love	1974	—	2.50	5.00

Number	Title (A Side/B Side)	Yr	VG	VG+	NM
ARISTA					
9706	Indestructible/Are You With Me	1988	—	—	3.00
9706 [PS]	Indestructible/Are You With Me	1988	—	—	3.00
9766	If Ever a Love There Was/Let's Jam	1988	—	—	3.00
—A-side: With Aretha Franklin					
9766 [PS]	If Ever a Love There Was/Let's Jam	1988	—	—	3.00
9801	Change of Heart/Loco in Acapulco	1989	—	—	3.00
9850	If Ever a Love There Was/It Wasn't, It Isn't, It Ain't Never Gonna Be	1989	—	—	3.00
—A-side: With Aretha Franklin; B-side: Aretha Franklin and Whitney Houston					
9850 [PS]	If Ever a Love There Was/It Wasn't, It Isn't, It Ain't Never Gonna Be	1989	—	—	3.00
CASABLANCA					
2338	When She Was My Girl/Something to Remember	1981	—	2.00	4.00
2344	Let Me Set You Free/From a Distance	1981	—	2.00	4.00
2345	Tonight I'm Gonna Love You All Over/I'll Never Leave Again	1981	—	2.00	4.00
2353	Sad Hearts/I Believe in You and Me	1982	—	2.00	4.00
CHESS					
1623	Could It Be You?/Kiss Me, Baby	1956	50.00	100.00	200.00
COLUMBIA					
41755	Ain't That Love/Lonely Summer	1960	15.00	30.00	60.00
43356	Ain't That Love/Lonely Summer	1965	6.25	12.50	25.00
GRADY					
012	If Only I Had Known/(B-side unknown)	1956	150.00	300.00	600.00
—As "The Four Aims"					
MOTOWN					
1062	Baby I Need Your Loving/Call On Me	1964	3.75	7.50	15.00
1069	Without the One You Love (Life's Not Worth While)/Love Has Gone	1964	3.00	6.00	12.00
1073	Ask the Lonely/Where Did You Go	1965	3.75	7.50	15.00
1073 [PS]	Ask the Lonely/Where Did You Go	1965	20.00	40.00	80.00
1076	I Can't Help Myself/Sad Souvenirs	1965	3.75	7.50	15.00
1081	It's the Same Old Song/Your Love Is Amazing	1965	3.75	7.50	15.00
1084	Something About You/Darling, I Hum Our Song	1965	3.75	7.50	15.00
1090	Shake Me, Wake Me (When It's Over)/Just As Long As You Need Me	1966	3.75	7.50	15.00
1096	Loving You Is Sweeter Than Ever/I Like Everything About You	1966	3.75	7.50	15.00
1098	Reach Out I'll Be There/Until You Love Someone	1966	3.75	7.50	15.00
1098 [PS]	Reach Out I'll Be There/Until You Love Someone	1966	20.00	40.00	80.00
1102	Standing in the Shadows of Love/Since You've Been Gone	1966	3.75	7.50	15.00
1104	Bernadette/I Got a Feeling	1967	3.00	6.00	12.00
1110	7-Rooms of Gloom/I'll Turn to Stone	1967	3.00	6.00	12.00
1113	You Keep Running Away/If You Don't Want My Love	1967	3.00	6.00	12.00
1119	Walk Away Renee/Your Love Is Wonderful	1968	3.00	6.00	12.00
1124	If I Were a Carpenter/Wonderful Baby	1968	3.00	6.00	12.00
1127	Yesterday's Dreams/For Once in My Life	1968	2.00	4.00	8.00
1132	I'm in a Different World/Remember When	1968	2.00	4.00	8.00
1147	What Is a Man/Don't Bring Back Memories	1969	2.00	4.00	8.00
1159	Don't Let Him Take Your Love from Me/The Key	1969	2.00	4.00	8.00
1164	It's All in the Game/Love (Is the Answer)	1970	2.00	4.00	8.00
1164 [PS]	It's All in the Game/Love (Is the Answer)	1970	5.00	10.00	20.00
1170	Still Water (Love)/Still Water (Peace)	1970	—	3.00	6.00
1175	Just Seven Numbers (Can Straighten Out My Life)/I Wish I Were Your Mirror	1971	—	3.00	6.00
1175 [PS]	Just Seven Numbers (Can Straighten Out My Life)/I Wish I Were Your Mirror	1971	5.00	10.00	20.00
1185	In These Changing Times/Right Before My Eyes	1971	—	3.00	6.00
1189	MacArthur Park (Part 2)/MacArthur Park (Part 1)	1971	—	3.00	6.00
1196	A Simple Game/L.A. My Town	1972	—	3.00	6.00
1198	I Can't Quit Your Love/Happy (Is a Bumpy Road)	1972	—	3.00	6.00
1210	(It's the Way) Nature Planned It/I'll Never Change	1972	—	3.00	6.00
1254	Hey Man-We Gotta Get You a Woman/How Can I Forget You	1973	—	—	—
—Unreleased					
1706	I Just Can't Walk Away/Hang	1983	—	—	3.00
1718	Make Yourself Right at Home/Sing a Song of Yesterday	1984	—	—	3.00
1790	Sexy Ways/Body and Soul	1985	—	—	3.00
1811	Don't Tell Me That It's Over/I'm Ready for Love	1985	—	—	3.00
1854	Hot Nights/Again	1986	—	—	3.00
RELIANT					
1691	I'm Here Again/(Instrumental)	198?	—	2.00	4.00
RIVERSIDE					
4534	Pennies from Heaven/Where Are You?	1962	18.75	37.50	75.00
RSO					
1069	Back to School Again/Rock-a-Hula Luau	1982	—	—	3.00
1069 [PS]	Back to School Again/Rock-a-Hula Luau	1982	—	—	3.00
—B-side: by The Cast (from the movie Grease 2)					
TOPPS/MOTOWN					
5	I Can't Help Myself	1967	18.75	37.50	75.00
9	Baby I Need Your Loving	1967	18.75	37.50	75.00
—These are cardboard discs					
Albums					
ABC					
D-862	Night Lights Harmony	1975	3.00	6.00	12.00
D-968	Catfish	1976	3.00	6.00	12.00
D-1014	The Show Must Go On	1977	3.00	6.00	12.00
AA-1092	At the Top	1978	3.00	6.00	12.00
ABC DUNHILL					
DSX-50129	Keeper of the Castle	1972	3.00	6.00	12.00
DSX-50144	Main Street People	1973	3.00	6.00	12.00
DSX-50166	Meeting of the Minds	1974	3.00	6.00	12.00
DSX-50188	Live & In Concert	1974	3.00	6.00	12.00
ARISTA					
AL-8492	Indestructible	1988	2.00	4.00	8.00
CASABLANCA					
NBLP 7258	Tonight!	1981	2.50	5.00	10.00
NBLP 7266	One More Mountain	1982	2.50	5.00	10.00
COMMAND					
CQD-40011 [Q]	Keeper of the Castle	1974	5.00	10.00	20.00
CQD-40012 [Q]	Main Street People	1974	5.00	10.00	20.00
MCA					
27019	Greatest Hits	198?	2.50	5.00	10.00
MOTOWN					
M5-114V1	Superstar Series, Vol. 14	1981	2.50	5.00	10.00
M5-122V1	Four Tops	1981	2.00	4.00	8.00
—Reissue of 622					
M5-149V1	Four Tops Reach Out	1981	2.00	4.00	8.00
—Reissue of 660					
M5-209V1	The Four Tops' Greatest Hits	1981	2.00	4.00	8.00
—Reissue of 662					
622 [M]	Four Tops	1964	7.50	15.00	30.00
MS-622 [S]	Four Tops	1964	10.00	20.00	40.00
634 [M]	Four Tops Second Album	1965	6.25	12.50	25.00
MS-634 [S]	Four Tops Second Album	1965	7.50	15.00	30.00
647 [M]	4 Tops On Top	1966	6.25	12.50	25.00
MS-647 [S]	4 Tops On Top	1966	7.50	15.00	30.00
654 [M]	Four Tops Live!	1966	6.25	12.50	25.00
MS-654 [S]	Four Tops Live!	1966	7.50	15.00	30.00
657 [M]	4 Tops on Broadway	1967	6.25	12.50	25.00
MS-657 [S]	4 Tops on Broadway	1967	7.50	15.00	30.00
660 [M]	Four Tops Reach Out	1967	7.50	15.00	30.00
MS-660 [S]	Four Tops Reach Out	1967	6.25	12.50	25.00
662 [M]	The Four Tops Greatest Hits	1967	7.50	15.00	30.00
MS-662 [S]	The Four Tops Greatest Hits	1967	5.00	10.00	20.00
669 [M]	Yesterday's Dreams	1968	7.50	15.00	30.00
MS-669 [S]	Yesterday's Dreams	1968	5.00	10.00	20.00
MS-675	Four Tops Now!	1969	5.00	10.00	20.00
MS-695	Soul Spin	1969	5.00	10.00	20.00
MS-704	Still Waters Run Deep	1970	5.00	10.00	20.00
MS-721	Changing Times	1970	5.00	10.00	20.00
MS-740	Four Tops Greatest Hits, Vol. 2	1971	5.00	10.00	20.00
MS-748	Nature Planned It	1972	5.00	10.00	20.00
MS-764 [(2)]	The Best of the 4 Tops	1973	3.75	7.50	15.00
M9-809 [(3)]	Anthology	1974	5.00	10.00	20.00
5224 ML	Still Waters Run Deep	1982	2.00	4.00	8.00
—Reissue of 704					
5258 ML	Four Tops Live!	1983	2.00	4.00	8.00
—Reissue of 654					
6066 ML	Back Where I Belong	1983	2.50	5.00	10.00
6130 ML	Magic	1985	2.50	5.00	10.00
WORKSHOP JAZZ					
217 [M]	Breakin' Through	1962	—	—	—
—This album is pictured on some early Motown inner sleeves, but is not known to exist					

FOUR TUNES, THE

Number	Title (A Side/B Side)	Yr	VG	VG+	NM
45s					
JUBILEE					
5128	Marie/I Gambled with Love	1953	10.00	20.00	40.00
5132	I Understand Just How You Feel/Sugar Lump	1953	7.50	15.00	30.00
5135	My Wild Irish Rose/Do-Do-Do It Again	1954	7.50	15.00	30.00
5152	Lonesome/The Greatest Feeling in the World	1954	7.50	15.00	30.00
5165	Don't Cry Darling/L'Amour Toujours, L'Amour	1954	7.50	15.00	30.00
5174	I Sold My Heart to the Junkman/Let Me Go Lover	1954	7.50	15.00	30.00
5174	I Sold My Heart to the Junkman/Good News	1954	7.50	15.00	30.00
5183	I Hope/I Close My Eyes	1955	6.25	12.50	25.00
5200	Tired of Waitin'/Time Out for Texas	1955	6.25	12.50	25.00
5212	Brooklyn Bridge/Three Little Chickens	1955	6.25	12.50	25.00
5218	You Are My Love/At the Steamboat River Ball	1955	6.25	12.50	25.00
5232	Rock and Roll Call/Our Love	1956	5.00	10.00	20.00
5239	I Gotta Go/Hold Me Closer	1956	5.00	10.00	20.00
5245	Far Away Places/Dancing with Tears in My Eyes	1956	5.00	10.00	20.00
5255	The Ballad of James Dean/Japanses Farewell	1956	5.00	10.00	20.00
5276	Cool Water/A Little on the Lonely Side	1957	5.00	10.00	20.00
6000	I Understand/Marie	196?	2.50	5.00	10.00
KAY-RON					
1000	I Want to Be Loved/Savannah Sings the Blues	1953	10.00	20.00	40.00
1005	I Understand/Just in Case You Change Your Mind	1953	10.00	20.00	40.00
RCA VICTOR					
47-3881	Say When/Do I Worry?	1950	12.50	25.00	50.00
47-3967	How Can You Say That I Don't Care/Cool Water	1950	10.00	20.00	40.00
47-4102	Wishing You Were Here Tonight/The Last Roundup	1951	10.00	20.00	40.00
47-4198	Cool Water/Carry Me Back to the Lone Prairie	1951	10.00	20.00	40.00
47-4241	The Prisoner's Song/I Married An Angel	1951	7.50	15.00	30.00
47-4305	My Buddy/Early in the Morning	1951	7.50	15.00	30.00
47-4427	Tell Me Why/I'll See You in My Dreams	1951	10.00	20.00	40.00
47-4489	Greatest Song I Ever Heard/Come What May	1952	6.25	12.50	25.00
47-4663	I Wonder/Can I Say Any More?	1952	6.25	12.50	25.00
47-4828	They Don't Understand/Why Did You Do This	1952	6.25	12.50	25.00
47-4968	I Don't Want to Set the World On Fire/Let's Give Love Another Chance	1952	10.00	20.00	40.00
47-5532	Don't Get Around Much Anymore/Water Boy	1953	7.50	15.00	30.00
50-0008	You're Heartless/Careless Love	1949	50.00	100.00	200.00
—Gray label, orange vinyl					
50-0016	My Last Affair/I'm the Guy	1949	50.00	100.00	200.00
—Gray label, orange vinyl					
50-0042	I'm Just a Fool in Love/The Lonesome Road	1949	50.00	100.00	200.00
—Gray label, orange vinyl					
50-0072	There Goes My Heart/Am I Blue	1950	37.50	75.00	150.00
—Gray label, orange vinyl					
50-0085	Old Fashioned Love/Kentucky Babe	1950	37.50	75.00	150.00
—Gray label, orange vinyl					
50-0131	May That Day Never Come/Carry Me Back to the Lone Prairie	1951	37.50	75.00	150.00
—Gray label, orange vinyl					
7-Inch Extended Plays					
RCA VICTOR					
EPA-586	(contents unknown)	1954	10.00	20.00	40.00
EPA-586 [PS]	The Four Tunes	1954	10.00	20.00	40.00

FOUR UPSETTERS, THE

45s

Number	Title (A Side/B Side)	Yr	VG	VG+	NM
SUN					
381	Crazy Arms/Midnight Soiree	1962	5.00	10.00	20.00
386	Surfin' Calliope/Wabash Cannonball	1963	7.50	15.00	30.00

FOUR WINDS, THE (1)

Also see THE TOKENS, to which they are related.

45s

Number	Title (A Side/B Side)	Yr	VG	VG+	NM
B.T. PUPPY					
555	Let It Ride/One Face in the Crowd	1970	2.50	5.00	10.00
CRYSTAL BALL					
102	Come Softly to Me/Judy	1978	—	2.50	5.00
105	Arlene/Goodbye, Maureen	1978	2.50	5.00	10.00
—Red vinyl					
105	Arlene/Goodbye, Maureen	1978	—	2.50	5.00
—Black vinyl					
SWING					
100	Remember Last Summer/Strange, Strange Feeling	1964	5.00	10.00	20.00

FOUR WINDS, THE (U)

None of these are group (1), but they aren't all the same group, either.

45s

Number	Title (A Side/B Side)	Yr	VG	VG+	NM
CHATTAHOOCHIE					
655	Down and Out/To Love or Not to Love	1964	3.75	7.50	15.00
DECOR					
175	Short Shorts/Five Minutes More	1961	5.00	10.00	20.00
DERBY					
10022	Playgirl/Jennifer	1964	7.50	15.00	30.00
DIAL					
3006	Woe Is Me/Promised Land	1962	3.75	7.50	15.00
FELSTED					
8703	Playgirl/Jennifer	1964	5.00	10.00	20.00
HIDE-A-WAY					
101	Mission by the Sea/These Hearts Were Mine	1958	5.00	10.00	20.00
VIK					
0221	Colorado Moon/Find Someone New	1956	5.00	10.00	20.00
WARWICK					
633	Daddy's Home/Bull-Moose Stomp	1961	10.00	20.00	40.00

FOURMOST, THE

45s

Number	Title (A Side/B Side)	Yr	VG	VG+	NM
ATCO					
6280	Hello Little Girl/Just in Case	1963	5.00	10.00	20.00
6285	I'm in Love/Respectable	1964	3.75	7.50	15.00
6307	If You Cry/Little Bit of Loving	1964	3.75	7.50	15.00
6317	How Can I Tell Her/You Got That Way	1964	3.75	7.50	15.00
CAPITOL					
5591	Girls, Girls, Girls/Why Do Fools Fall in Love	1966	3.00	6.00	12.00
5738	Here, There and Everywhere/You've Changed	1966	5.00	10.00	20.00

FOURTH CEKCION, THE

Albums

Number	Title (A Side/B Side)	Yr	VG	VG+	NM
SOLAR					
110	The Fourth Cekcion	1970	15.00	30.00	60.00

FOURTH WAY, THE

45s

Number	Title (A Side/B Side)	Yr	VG	VG+	NM
CAPITOL					
2619	Bucklehuggin'/Clouds	1969	2.00	4.00	8.00
SOUL CITY					
765	Far Side of Your Moon/Pink Cloud	1968	2.00	4.00	8.00

Albums

Number	Title (A Side/B Side)	Yr	VG	VG+	NM
CAPITOL					
ST-317	The Fourth Way	1969	6.25	12.50	25.00
HARVEST					
SKAO-423	The Sun and Moon Have Come Together	1970	5.00	10.00	20.00
ST-666	Werewolf	1971	5.00	10.00	20.00

FOWLEY, KIM

45s

Number	Title (A Side/B Side)	Yr	VG	VG+	NM
CAPITOL					
3403	Forbidden Love/I'm Bad	1972	—	3.00	6.00
3534	International Heroes/E.S.P. Reader	1973	—	3.00	6.00
3662	A Born Dancer/Something New	1973	—	3.00	6.00
IMPERIAL					
66326	Born to Be Wild/Space Odyssey	1968	2.50	5.00	10.00
66349	Bubble Gum/Wildfire	1969	2.50	5.00	10.00
LIVING LEGEND					
721	Mr. Responsibility/My Foolish Heart	1965	3.75	7.50	15.00
725	Underground Lady/Pop Art '66	1966	3.75	7.50	15.00
LOMA					
2064	Lights/Something New and Different	1966	2.50	5.00	10.00
MIRA					
209	American Dream/The Statue	1965	2.50	5.00	10.00
ORIGINAL SOUND					
98	Thunder Road/Born to Make You Cry	1970	2.50	5.00	10.00
RCA VICTOR					
74-0511	Citizen Kane/The Sky Is On Fire	1971	—	—	—
—Canceled					
REPRISE					
0569	Don't Be Cruel/Strangers from the Sky	1967	2.50	5.00	10.00
TOWER					
342	Love Is Alive and Well/Reincarnation	1967	2.50	5.00	10.00

Albums

Number	Title (A Side/B Side)	Yr	VG	VG+	NM
ANTILLES					
AN-7075	Snake Document Masquerade	1979	3.00	6.00	12.00
CAPITOL					
ST-11075	I'm Bad	1972	5.00	10.00	20.00
ST-11159	International Heroes	1973	5.00	10.00	20.00
ST-11248	Automatic	1974	5.00	10.00	20.00
GNP CRESCENDO					
GNPS-2132	Hollywood Confidential	197?	3.00	6.00	12.00
IMPERIAL					
LP-12413	Born to Be Wild	1968	10.00	20.00	40.00
LP-12423	Outrageous	1969	10.00	20.00	40.00
LP-12443	Good Clean Fun	1969	10.00	20.00	40.00
PVC					
7906	Sunset Boulevard	1978	3.00	6.00	12.00
TOWER					
ST 5080 [S]	Love Is Alive and Well	1967	10.00	20.00	40.00
T 5080 [M]	Love Is Alive and Well	1967	7.50	15.00	30.00

FOX, NORMAN, AND THE ROB ROYS

45s

Number	Title (A Side/B Side)	Yr	VG	VG+	NM
BACK BEAT					
499	Lover Doll/Little Star	197?	—	2.00	4.00
—Bootleg					
501	Tell Me Why/Audrey	1957	20.00	40.00	80.00
—White label					
501	Tell Me Why/Audrey	1957	10.00	20.00	40.00
—Red label					
508	Dance Girl Dance/My Dearest One	1958	20.00	40.00	80.00
CAPITOL					
4128	Dream Girl/Pizza Pie	1959	175.00	350.00	700.00
HAMMER					
544	Dream Girl/Pizza Pie	1958	7.50	15.00	30.00

FOXX, INEZ (AND CHARLIE)

45s

Number	Title (A Side/B Side)	Yr	VG	VG+	NM
DYNAMO					
102	Baby Take It All/Tightrope	1967	2.00	4.00	8.00
104	I Stand Accused/Guilty	1967	2.00	4.00	8.00
109	You Are the Man/Hard to Get	1967	2.00	4.00	8.00
112	(1-2-3-4-5-6-7) Count the Days/A Stranger I Don't Know	1967	2.00	4.00	8.00
117	Undecided/I Ain't Goin' for That	1968	2.00	4.00	8.00
119	Vaya Con Dios/Fellows in Vietnam	1968	2.00	4.00	8.00
126	Come On In/Baby Drop a Dime	1968	2.00	4.00	8.00
127	Baby Give It to Me/You Fixed My Heartache	1968	2.00	4.00	8.00
134	We Got a Chance to Be Free/Speed Ticket	1969	2.00	4.00	8.00
138	North Carolina (South Carolina)/I Got It	1970	2.00	4.00	8.00
144	You Shouldn't Have Set My Soul on Fire/Live for Today	1970	2.00	4.00	8.00
MUSICOR					
1201	No Stranger to Love/Come By Here	1966	2.50	5.00	10.00
SYMBOL					
20-001	Hurt by Love/Confusion	1964	3.00	6.00	12.00
201	La De Da, I Love You/Yankee Doodle Dandy	1964	3.00	6.00	12.00
204	Don't Do It No More/I Fancy You	1964	3.00	6.00	12.00
206	I Feel Alright/My Mama Told Me	1965	3.00	6.00	12.00
208	I've Come to One Conclusion/Down by the Seashore	1965	3.00	6.00	12.00
213	Hummingbird/If I Need Anyone	1966	3.00	6.00	12.00
919	Mockingbird/Jaybirds	1963	6.25	12.50	25.00
922	Broken Hearted Fool/He's the One You Love	1963	3.75	7.50	15.00
924	Hi Diddle Diddle/Talk with Me	1963	3.75	7.50	15.00
926	Ask Me/I See You My Love	1963	3.75	7.50	15.00
UNITED ARTISTS					
XW516	Mockingbird/I Know (You Don't Love Me No More)	1974	—	2.00	4.00
—Reissue; B-side by Barbara George					
VOLT					
4087	Watch the Dog/You Hurt Me for the Last Time	1972	—	3.00	6.00
4093	One Woman's Man/The Time	1973	—	3.00	6.00
4096	Crossing Over That Bridge/You're Saving Me for a Rainy Day	1973	—	3.00	6.00
4101	I Had a Talk with My Man/The Lady, The Doctor and the Prescription	1973	—	3.00	6.00
4107	Circuit's Overloaded/There's a Hand That's Reading Out	1974	—	3.00	6.00

Albums

Number	Title (A Side/B Side)	Yr	VG	VG+	NM
DYNAMO					
D-7000 [M]	Come By Here	1967	7.50	15.00	30.00
D-7002 [M]	Inez and Charlie Foxx's Greatest Hits	1967	7.50	15.00	30.00
DS-8000 [S]	Come By Here	1967	10.00	20.00	40.00
DS-8002 [S]	Inez and Charlie Foxx's Greatest Hits	1967	10.00	20.00	40.00
DS-8003	Swingin' Mockin' Band	1968	7.50	15.00	30.00
SUE					
LP-1027 [M]	Mockingbird	1966	25.00	50.00	100.00
SYMBOL					
SYM-4400 [M]	Mockingbird	1963	37.50	75.00	150.00
VOLT					
6022	Inez Foxx at Memphis	1973	3.75	7.50	15.00

FRACTION

45s

Number	Title (A Side/B Side)	Yr	VG	VG+	NM
ANGELUS					
5005	Sanc Divided/(B-side unknown)	1971	25.00	50.00	100.00

Albums

Number	Title (A Side/B Side)	Yr	VG	VG+	NM
ANGELUS					
571	Moon Blood	1971	1000.	1500.	2000.

FRAMPTON, PETER

Also see THE HERD; HUMBLE PIE; THE TAGES.

45s

Number	Title (A Side/B Side)	Yr	VG	VG+	NM
ATLANTIC					
88820	Holding On to You/Give Me a Little Love That's Real	1990	—	—	3.00

Number	Title (A Side/B Side)	Yr	VG	VG+	NM
89395	Hiding from a Heartache/Into View	1986	—	—	3.00
89426	All Eyes on You/So Far Away	1986	—	—	3.00
89426 [PS]	All Eyes on You/So Far Away	1986	—	—	3.00
89463	Lying/Into View	1985	—	—	3.00
89463 [PS]	Lying/Into View	1985	—	—	3.00
A&M					
1379	Jumping Jack Flash/On for Another Day	1972	—	3.00	6.00
1456	Don't Fade Away/All Night Long	1973	—	2.50	5.00
—As "Frampton's Camel"					
1470	I Believe (When I Fall in Love It Will Be Forever)/ Which Way the Wind Blows	1973	—	2.50	5.00
—As "Frampton's Camel"					
1506	Somethin's Happening/I Wanna Go to the Sun	1974	—	2.50	5.00
1693	Show Me the Way/Crying Clown	1975	—	2.50	5.00
1738	Baby I Love Your Way/(I'll Give You) Money	1975	—	2.50	5.00
1763	Nowhere's Too Far (For My Baby)/(I'll Give You) Money	1975	—	2.50	5.00
1795	Show Me the Way/Shine On	1976	—	2.00	4.00
1795 [PS]	Show Me the Way/Shine On	1976	—	3.00	6.00
1832	Baby, I Love Your Way/It's a Plain Shame	1976	—	2.00	4.00
1832 [PS]	Baby, I Love Your Way/It's a Plain Shame	1976	—	3.00	6.00
1867	Do You Feel Like We Do/Penny for Your Thoughts	1976	—	2.00	4.00
1941	I'm in You/St. Thomas (Know How I Feel)	1977	—	2.50	5.00
1941	I'm in You/St. Thomas (Don't You Know How I Feel)	1977	—	2.00	4.00
1941 [PS]	I'm in You/St. Thomas (Know How I Feel)	1977	—	3.50	7.00
1941 [PS]	I'm in You/St. Thomas (Don't You Know How I Feel)	1977	—	3.00	6.00
1972	Signed, Sealed, Delivered (I'm Yours)/Rocky's Hot Club	1977	—	2.00	4.00
1972 [PS]	Signed, Sealed, Delivered (I'm Yours)/Rocky's Hot Club	1977	—	3.00	6.00
1988	Tried to Love/You Don't Have to Worry	1977	—	2.00	4.00
1988 [PS]	Tried to Love/You Don't Have to Worry	1977	—	3.00	6.00
2070	The Long and Winding Road/Tried to Love	1978	—	2.50	5.00
2148	I Can't Stand It No More/Where Should I Be	1979	—	2.00	4.00
2148 [PS]	I Can't Stand It No More/Where Should I Be	1979	—	2.50	5.00
2174	She Don't Reply/St. Thomas (Don't Cha Know How I Feel)	1979	—	2.00	4.00
2350	Breaking All the Rules/Night Town	1981	—	2.00	4.00
2362	Wasting the Night Away/You Kill Me	1981	—	2.00	4.00
2442	Sleepwalk/Theme from Nivram	1982	—	2.00	4.00
Albums					
ATLANTIC					
81290	Premonition	1986	2.00	4.00	8.00
82030	Where All the Pieces Fit	1989	2.00	4.00	8.00
A&M					
SP-3133	Wind of Change	198?	2.00	4.00	8.00
—Budget-line reissue					
SP-3619	Somethin's Happening	1974	3.00	6.00	12.00
SP-3703 [(2)]	Frampton Comes Alive!	1976	3.00	6.00	12.00
SP-3710	Where I Should Be	1979	2.50	5.00	10.00
SP-3722	Breaking All the Rules	1981	2.50	5.00	10.00
SP-4348	Wind of Change	1972	3.00	6.00	12.00
—Brown label					
SP-4348	Wind of Change	1974	2.50	5.00	10.00
—Silvery label					
SP-4389	Frampton's Camel	1973	3.00	6.00	12.00
—Brown label					
SP-4389	Frampton's Camel	1974	2.50	5.00	10.00
—Silvery label					
SP-4512	Frampton	1975	2.50	5.00	10.00
SP-4704	I'm In You	1977	2.50	5.00	10.00
SP-4905	The Art of Control	1982	2.50	5.00	10.00
SP-6505 [(2)]	Frampton Comes Alive!	198?	2.50	5.00	10.00
—Budget-line reissue					
MOBILE FIDELITY					
2-262 [(2)]	Frampton Comes Alive!	1996	10.00	20.00	40.00
—Audiophile vinyl					
SWEET THUNDER					
6 [(2)]	Frampton Comes Alive	198?	25.00	50.00	100.00
—Audiophile edition					

FRANCHI, SERGIO

Number	Title (A Side/B Side)	Yr	VG	VG+	NM
12-Inch Singles					
LAX					
L33-1836 [DJ]	Laugh You Silly Clown/More (Theme from Mondo Cane)	1979	2.50	5.00	10.00
45s					
LAX					
41164	Laugh You Silly Clown/(B-side unknown)	1979	—	2.00	4.00
METROMEDIA					
238	If/Somehow	1971	—	2.00	4.00
RCA VICTOR					
47-8103	I Mustn't Say I Love You/Once	1962	2.00	4.00	8.00
47-8149	The Good Life/Bella Nina	1963	2.00	4.00	8.00
47-8315	Cuando Caliente El Sol/Chicago	1964	—	3.00	6.00
47-8409	No Arms Can Ever Hold You/Seventh Dawn	1964	—	3.00	6.00
47-8552	Someone Like You/Take the Moment	1965	—	3.00	6.00
47-8686	Ciao, Ciao (So Long for Now)/Moon Over Naples	1965	—	3.00	6.00
47-9124	What Will Tomorrow Bring/Maybe It's Time for Me	1967	—	3.00	6.00
47-9277	I Should Care/No One Else	1967	—	3.00	6.00
47-9471	Time Alone Will Tell/I'm a Fool to Want You	1968	—	3.00	6.00
UNITED ARTISTS					
50612	Hold Me/Song of Santa Vittoria	1969	—	2.50	5.00
50630	Granada/Within Me	1970	—	2.50	5.00
50664	More Than Strangers/Buona Fortuna, Addio Bambino	1970	—	2.50	5.00
50681	Here We Go Again/Love Is All	1970	—	2.50	5.00
Albums					
4 CORNERS OF THE WORLD					
FCL-4221 [M]	La Bella Italia	196?	3.00	6.00	12.00
FCS-4221 [S]	La Bella Italia	196?	3.75	7.50	15.00
FCL 4223 [M]	Buon Natale	196?	3.00	6.00	12.00
FCS 4223 [S]	Buon Natale	196?	3.75	7.50	15.00
FCL-4228 [M]	Il Fantastico	196?	3.00	6.00	12.00
FCS-4228 [S]	Il Fantastico	196?	3.75	7.50	15.00
METROMEDIA					
MD 1047	Sergio Franchi	1971	2.50	5.00	10.00
RCA VICTOR					
ANL1-1070	The Best of Sergio Franchi	1975	2.50	5.00	10.00
APL1-2132	Volare	1976	2.50	5.00	10.00
ANL1-2643	Songs of Richard Rodgers	1977	2.00	4.00	8.00
—Reissue of LSP-3365					
LPM-2943 [M]	The Exciting Voice of Sergio Franchi	1964	3.00	6.00	12.00
LSP-2943 [S]	The Exciting Voice of Sergio Franchi	1964	3.75	7.50	15.00
LPM-3310 [M]	Live at the Cocoanut Grove	1965	2.50	5.00	10.00
LSP-3310 [S]	Live at the Cocoanut Grove	1965	3.00	6.00	12.00
LPM-3365 [M]	Songs of Richard Rodgers	1965	2.50	5.00	10.00
LSP-3365 [S]	Songs of Richard Rodgers	1965	3.00	6.00	12.00
LPM-3437 [M]	The Heart of Christmas (Cuor' di Natale)	1965	3.00	6.00	12.00
LSP-3437 [S]	The Heart of Christmas (Cuor' di Natale)	1965	3.75	7.50	15.00
LPM-3500 [M]	La Dolce Italy	1966	2.50	5.00	10.00
LSP-3500 [S]	La Dolce Italy	1966	3.00	6.00	12.00
LPM-3654 [M]	From Sergio — With Love	1966	2.50	5.00	10.00
LSP-3654 [S]	From Sergio — With Love	1966	3.00	6.00	12.00
LPM-3810 [M]	There Goes My Heart	1967	2.50	5.00	10.00
LSP-3810 [S]	There Goes My Heart	1967	3.00	6.00	12.00
LPM-3933 [M]	I'm a Fool to Want You	1968	3.75	7.50	15.00
LSP-3933 [S]	I'm a Fool to Want You	1968	3.00	6.00	12.00
AFL1-4018	Wine and Song	1977	2.00	4.00	8.00
—Reissue of LSP-4018					
LPM-4018 [M]	Wine and Song	1968	5.00	10.00	20.00
LSP-4018	Wine and Song	1968	3.00	6.00	12.00
VPS-6082 [(2)]	This Is Sergio Franchi	1972	3.00	6.00	12.00
RCA VICTOR RED SEAL					
LM-2640 [M]	Sergio Franchi	1962	3.00	6.00	12.00
LSC-2640 [S]	Sergio Franchi	1962	3.75	7.50	15.00
LM-2657 [M]	Our Man from Italy	1963	3.00	6.00	12.00
LSC-2657 [S]	Our Man from Italy	1963	3.75	7.50	15.00
LM-2674 [M]	Broadway...I Love You	1963	3.00	6.00	12.00
LSC-2674 [S]	Broadway...I Love You	1963	3.75	7.50	15.00
LM-2675 [M]	The Dream Duet	1963	3.00	6.00	12.00
—With Anna Moffo					
LSC-2675 [S]	The Dream Duet	1963	3.75	7.50	15.00
—With Anna Moffo					
LM-2696 [M]	The Women in My Life	1964	3.00	6.00	12.00
LSC-2696 [S]	The Women in My Life	1964	3.75	7.50	15.00
UNITED ARTISTS					
UAS-6727	Within Me	1970	2.50	5.00	10.00

FRANCIS, CONNIE

Number	Title (A Side/B Side)	Yr	VG	VG+	NM
45s					
GSF					
6901	The Answer (Should I Tie a Yellow Ribbon Round the Ole Oak Tree?)/Paint the Rain	1973	—	2.50	5.00
IVANHOE					
508	I Don't Wanna Walk Without You/Don't Turn Around	197?	—	2.50	5.00
MGM					
CS6-5	Celebrity Scene: Connie Francis	1967	15.00	30.00	60.00
—Box set of five singles (13708-13712). Price includes box, all 5 singles, jukebox title strips, bio. Records are sometimes found by themselves, so they are also listed separately.					
SB-9 [S]	Rock-A-Bye Your Baby with a Dixie Melody/Ciao Ciao Bambino	1960	12.50	25.00	50.00
SB-10 [S]	I Almost Lost My Mind/Come Back to Sorrento	1960	12.50	25.00	50.00
126	Stupid Cupid/I'm Sorry I Made You Cry	196?	2.00	4.00	8.00
—Reissue					
129	Who's Sorry Now/You Were Only Fooling	196?	2.00	4.00	8.00
—Reissue					
135	Mama/You're Gonna Miss Me	196?	2.00	4.00	8.00
—Reissue					
136	Among My Souvenirs/God Bless America	196?	2.00	4.00	8.00
—Reissue					
139	Lipstick on Your Collar/Frankie	196?	2.00	4.00	8.00
—Reissue					
141	My Happiness/If I Didn't Care	196?	2.00	4.00	8.00
—Reissue					
148	My Heart Has a Mind of Its Own/Malaguena	196?	2.00	4.00	8.00
—Reissue					
150	Where the Boys Are/No One	196?	2.00	4.00	8.00
—Reissue					
153	Breakin' In a Brand New Broken Heart/Somebody Else's Boy	196?	2.00	4.00	8.00
—Reissue					
155	Together/Too Many Rules	196?	2.00	4.00	8.00
—Reissue					
156	Many Tears Ago/Senza Mama E Numerata	196?	2.00	4.00	8.00
—Reissue					
157	Don't Break the Heart That Loves You/Second Hand Love	196?	2.00	4.00	8.00
—Reissue					
165	Everybody's Somebody's Fool/Al Di La	196?	2.00	4.00	8.00
—Reissue					
169	Jealous Heart/Forget Domani	196?	2.00	4.00	8.00
—Reissue					
511	Who's Sorry Now/Stupid Cupid	197?	—	2.50	5.00
—Reissue					
512	Lipstick on Your Collar/Mama	197?	—	2.50	5.00
—Reissue					
513	Everybody's Somebody's Fool/Al Di La	197?	—	2.50	5.00
—Reissue					
524	My Happiness/If I Didn't Care	197?	—	2.50	5.00
—Reissue					
12015	Freddy/Didn't I Love You Enough	1955	12.50	25.00	50.00
12056	Oh Please Make Him Jealous/Goody Goodbye	1955	12.50	25.00	50.00
12122	Are You Satisfied/My Treasure	1956	6.25	12.50	25.00
12191	My First Real Love/Believe in Me	1956	15.00	30.00	60.00

Number	Title (A Side/B Side)	Yr	VG	VG+	NM
12251	Send for My Baby/Forgetting	1956	6.25	12.50	25.00
12335	My Sailor Boy/Everyone Needs Someone	1956	6.25	12.50	25.00
12375	I Never Had a Sweetheart/Little Blue Wren	1957	6.25	12.50	25.00
12440	No Other One/I Leaned on a Man	1957	6.25	12.50	25.00
12490	Eighteen/Faded Orchid	1957	6.25	12.50	25.00
12555	You, My Darlin', You/The Majesty of Love	1957	6.25	12.50	25.00
—Connie Francis and Marvin Rainwater					
12588	Who's Sorry Now?/You Were Only Fooling	1958	5.00	10.00	20.00
12647	I'm Sorry I Made You Cry/Lock Up Your Heart	1958	5.00	10.00	20.00
12669	Heartaches/I Miss You So	1958	12.50	25.00	50.00
12683	Stupid Cupid/Carolina Moon	1958	5.00	10.00	20.00
12713	Fallin'/Happy Days and Lonely Nights	1958	5.00	10.00	20.00
12738 [M]	My Happiness/Never Before	1958	5.00	10.00	20.00
12738 [PS]	My Happiness/Never Before	1958	7.50	15.00	30.00
—Pink sleeve					
12738 [PS]	My Happiness/Never Before	1958	10.00	20.00	40.00
—White sleeve					
12769	If I Didn't Care/Toward the End of the Day	1959	5.00	10.00	20.00
12769 [PS]	If I Didn't Care/Toward the End of the Day	1959	7.50	15.00	30.00
12793 [M]	Lipstick on Your Collar/Frankie	1959	5.00	10.00	20.00
12824 [M]	You're Gonna Miss Me/Plenty Good Lovin'	1959	5.00	10.00	20.00
12841 [M]	Among My Souvenirs/God Bless America	1959	7.50	15.00	30.00
—First pressing has a yellow label					
12841 [M]	Among My Souvenirs/God Bless America	1959	5.00	10.00	20.00
—Second pressing has a black label					
12878	Mama/Teddy	1960	3.75	7.50	15.00
12899	Everybody's Somebody's Fool/Jealous of You	1960	3.75	7.50	15.00
12899 [PS]	Everybody's Somebody's Fool/Jealous of You	1960	5.00	10.00	20.00
12923	My Heart Has a Mind of Its Own/Malaguena	1960	3.75	7.50	15.00
12923 [PS]	My Heart Has a Mind of Its Own/Malaguena	1960	5.00	10.00	20.00
12964	Many Tears Ago/Senza Mama (With No One)	1960	3.75	7.50	15.00
12964 [PS]	Many Tears Ago/Senza Mama (With No One)	1960	5.00	10.00	20.00
12971	Where the Boys Are/No One	1961	3.75	7.50	15.00
12971 [PS]	Where the Boys Are/No One	1961	5.00	10.00	20.00
12995	Breakin' In a Brand New Broken Heart/Someone Else's Boy	1961	3.75	7.50	15.00
12995 [PS]	Breakin' In a Brand New Broken Heart/Someone Else's Boy	1961	5.00	10.00	20.00
13005	Atashi-No/Swanee	1961	7.50	15.00	30.00
13019	Together/Too Many Rules	1961	3.75	7.50	15.00
13019 [PS]	Together/Too Many Rules	1961	5.00	10.00	20.00
13039	(He's My) Dreamboat/Hollywood	1961	3.75	7.50	15.00
13039 [PS]	(He's My) Dreamboat/Hollywood	1961	5.00	10.00	20.00
13051	When the Boy in Your Arms (Is the Boy in Your Heart)/Baby's First Christmas	1961	3.75	7.50	15.00
13051 [PS]	When the Boy in Your Arms (Is the Boy in Your Heart)/Baby's First Christmas	1961	5.00	10.00	20.00
13059	Don't Break the Heart That Loves You/Drop It, Joe	1962	3.75	7.50	15.00
13059 [PS]	Don't Break the Heart That Loves You/Drop It, Joe	1962	5.00	10.00	20.00
13074	Second Hand Love/Gonna Git That Man	1962	5.00	10.00	20.00
—A-side: Produced by Phil Spector					
13074 [PS]	Second Hand Love/Gonna Git That Man	1962	6.25	12.50	25.00
13087	Vacation/The Biggest Sin of All	1962	3.75	7.50	15.00
13087 [PS]	Vacation/The Biggest Sin of All	1962	5.00	10.00	20.00
13096	I Was Such a Fool (To Fall in Love with You)/He Thinks I Still Care	1962	3.00	6.00	12.00
13096 [PS]	I Was Such a Fool (To Fall in Love with You)/He Thinks I Still Care	1962	4.00	8.00	16.00
13116	I'm Gonna' Be Warm This Winter/Al Di La	1962	3.00	6.00	12.00
13116 [PS]	I'm Gonna' Be Warm This Winter/Al Di La	1962	4.00	8.00	16.00
13127	Follow the Boys/Waiting for Billy	1962	3.00	6.00	12.00
13127 [PS]	Follow the Boys/Waiting for Billy	1962	4.00	8.00	16.00
13143	If My Pillow Could Talk/You're the Only One Can Hurt Me	1963	3.00	6.00	12.00
13143 [PS]	If My Pillow Could Talk/You're the Only One Can Hurt Me	1963	4.00	8.00	16.00
13160	Drownin' My Sorrows/Mala Femmena	1963	3.00	6.00	12.00
13160 [PS]	Drownin' My Sorrows/Mala Femmena	1963	4.00	8.00	16.00
13176	Your Other Love/Whatever Happened to Rosemarie?	1963	3.00	6.00	12.00
13176 [PS]	Your Other Love/Whatever Happened to Rosemarie?	1963	4.00	8.00	16.00
13203	In the Summer of His Years/My Buddy	1963	3.00	6.00	12.00
13203 [PS]	In the Summer of His Years/My Buddy	1963	4.00	8.00	16.00
13214	Blue Winter/You Know You Don't Want Me (So Why Don't You Leave Me Alone)	1964	3.00	6.00	12.00
13214 [PS]	Blue Winter/You Know You Don't Want Me (So Why Don't You Leave Me Alone)	1964	4.00	8.00	16.00
13237	Be Anything (But Be Mine)/Tommy	1964	3.00	6.00	12.00
13237 [PS]	Be Anything (But Be Mine)/Tommy	1964	4.00	8.00	16.00
13256	Looking for Love/This Is My Happiest Moment	1964	3.00	6.00	12.00
13256 [PS]	Looking for Love/This Is My Happiest Moment	1964	4.00	8.00	16.00
13287	Don't Ever Leave Me/We Have Something More (Than a Summer Love)	1964	3.00	6.00	12.00
13287 [PS]	Don't Ever Leave Me/We Have Something More (Than a Summer Love)	1964	4.00	8.00	16.00
13303	Whose Heart Are You Breaking Tonight/Come On Jerry	1965	2.50	5.00	10.00
13303 [PS]	Whose Heart Are You Breaking Tonight/Come On Jerry	1965	3.00	6.00	12.00
13325	For Mama (La Mamma)/She'll Be Coming 'Round the Mountain	1965	3.00	6.00	12.00
13331	Wishing It Was You/You're Mine (Just When You're Lonely)	1965	2.50	5.00	10.00
13331 [PS]	Wishing It Was You/You're Mine (Just When You're Lonely)	1965	3.00	6.00	12.00
13363	Forget Domani/No One Sends Me Roses	1965	2.50	5.00	10.00
13389	Roundabout/Bossa Nova Hand Dance	1965	2.50	5.00	10.00
13420	Jealous Heart/Can I Rely on You	1965	2.50	5.00	10.00
13470	Love Is Me, Love Is You/I'd Let You Break My Heart All Over Again	1966	2.50	5.00	10.00
13470 [PS]	Love Is Me, Love Is You/I'd Let You Break My Heart All Over Again	1966	3.00	6.00	12.00
13505	It's a Different World/Empty Chapel	1966	2.50	5.00	10.00
13505 [PS]	It's a Different World/Empty Chapel	1966	5.00	10.00	20.00

Number	Title (A Side/B Side)	Yr	VG	VG+	NM
13545	A Letter from a Soldier (Dear Mama)/Somewhere, My Love	1966	2.50	5.00	10.00
13550 [DJ]	A Nurse in the U.S. Army (same on both sides)	1966	7.50	15.00	30.00
—Promotional item for the U.S. Army					
13578	All the Love in the World/So Nice	1966	2.50	5.00	10.00
13610	Spanish Nights and You/Games That Lovers Play	1966	2.50	5.00	10.00
13610 [PS]	Spanish Nights and You/Games That Lovers Play	1966	5.00	10.00	20.00
13665	Another Page/Souvenir d'Italie	1967	2.50	5.00	10.00
13708	Mama/Never on Sunday	1967	2.50	5.00	10.00
—Part of Celebrity Series CS-5					
13709	My Happiness/Al Di La	1967	2.50	5.00	10.00
—Part of Celebrity Series CS-5					
13710	Malaguena/I Love You Much Too Much	1967	2.50	5.00	10.00
—Part of Celebrity Series CS-5					
13711	Once in a Lifetime/Oh Lonesome Me	1967	2.50	5.00	10.00
—Part of Celebrity Series CS-5					
13712	Jealous Heart/Will You Still Be Mine	1967	2.50	5.00	10.00
—Part of Celebrity Series CS-5					
13718	Time Alone Will Tell/Born Free	1967	2.50	5.00	10.00
13773	My Heart Cries for You/Someone Took the Sweetness Out of Sweetheart	1967	2.50	5.00	10.00
13773 [PS]	My Heart Cries for You/Someone Took the Sweetness Out of Sweetheart	1967	5.00	10.00	20.00
13814	Lonely Again/When You Care a Lot for Someone	1967	2.50	5.00	10.00
13876	My World Is Slipping Away/Till We're Together	1967	2.50	5.00	10.00
13923	Why Say Goodbye/Adios, Me Amore	1968	2.00	4.00	8.00
13948	Somebody Else Is Taking My Place/Brother, Can You Spare a Dime?	1968	2.00	4.00	8.00
14004	I Don't Wanna Play House/The Welfare Check	1968	2.00	4.00	8.00
14034	The Wedding Cake/Over Hill, Under Ground	1969	2.00	4.00	8.00
14058	Gone Like the Wind/Am I Blue?	1969	2.00	4.00	8.00
14058 [PS]	Gone Like the Wind/Am I Blue?	1969	5.00	10.00	20.00
14089	Invierno Trieste/Noches Espanolas Y Tu	1969	—	—	—
—Not known to exist					
14091	Mr. Love/Zingara	1969	2.00	4.00	8.00
14091 [PS]	Mr. Love/Zingara	1969	5.00	10.00	20.00
14853	I'm Me Again/Comme Si, Comme Sa	1976	—	3.00	6.00
SK-50117 [S]	My Happiness/Never Before	1958	12.50	25.00	50.00
SK-50121 [S]	Lipstick on Your Collar/Frankie	1959	15.00	30.00	60.00
SK-50129 [S]	You're Gonna Miss Me/Plenty Good Lovin'	1959	12.50	25.00	50.00
SK-50133 [S]	Among My Souvenirs/God Bless America	1959	12.50	25.00	50.00

POLYDOR

Number	Title (A Side/B Side)	Yr	VG	VG+	NM
2143	I'm Me Again/Comme Si, Comme Sa	1981	—	2.50	5.00
810087-7	There's Still a Few Good Love Songs Left in Me/Let's Make It Love Tonight	1983	—	2.50	5.00

7-Inch Extended Plays

MGM

Number	Title	Yr	VG	VG+	NM
HC5-6 [DJ]	Heart Circuit Interview	1959	25.00	50.00	100.00
X-1599	(contents unknown)	1958	10.00	20.00	40.00
X-1599 [PS]	Connie Francis	1958	10.00	20.00	40.00
X-1603	(contents unknown)	1958	10.00	20.00	40.00
X-1603 [PS]	Who's Sorry Now? (Part 1)	1958	10.00	20.00	40.00
X-1604	(contents unknown)	1958	10.00	20.00	40.00
X-1604 [PS]	Who's Sorry Now? (Part 2)	1958	10.00	20.00	40.00
X-1605	(contents unknown)	1958	10.00	20.00	40.00
X-1605 [PS]	Who's Sorry Now? (Part 3)	1958	10.00	20.00	40.00
X-1655	(contents unknown)	1958	10.00	20.00	40.00
X-1655 [PS]	My Happiness	1958	10.00	20.00	40.00
X-1662	(contents unknown)	1959	10.00	20.00	40.00
X-1662 [PS]	If I Didn't Care	1959	10.00	20.00	40.00
X-1663	(contents unknown)	1959	10.00	20.00	40.00
X-1663 [PS]	The Exciting Connie Francis (Part 1)	1959	10.00	20.00	40.00
X-1664	(contents unknown)	1959	10.00	20.00	40.00
X-1664 [PS]	The Exciting Connie Francis (Part 2)	1959	10.00	20.00	40.00
X-1665	(contents unknown)	1959	10.00	20.00	40.00
X-1665 [PS]	The Exciting Connie Francis (Part 3)	1959	10.00	20.00	40.00
X-1687	(contents unknown)	1960	7.50	15.00	30.00
X-1687 [PS]	Connie Francis	1960	7.50	15.00	30.00
X-1688	(contents unknown)	1960	7.50	15.00	30.00
X-1688 [PS]	Connie's Greatest Hits (Part 1)	1960	7.50	15.00	30.00
X-1689	(contents unknown)	1960	7.50	15.00	30.00
X-1689 [PS]	Connie's Greatest Hits (Part 2)	1960	7.50	15.00	30.00
X-1690	(contents unknown)	1960	7.50	15.00	30.00
X-1690 [PS]	Connie's Greatest Hits (Part 3)	1960	7.50	15.00	30.00
X-1691	(contents unknown)	1960	7.50	15.00	30.00
X-1691 [PS]	Rock 'N Roll Million Sellers (Part 1)	1960	7.50	15.00	30.00
X-1692	(contents unknown)	1960	7.50	15.00	30.00
X-1692 [PS]	Rock 'N Roll Million Sellers (Part 2)	1960	7.50	15.00	30.00
X-1693	(contents unknown)	1960	7.50	15.00	30.00
X-1693 [PS]	Rock 'N Roll Million Sellers (Part 3)	1960	7.50	15.00	30.00
X-1694	(contents unknown)	1960	7.50	15.00	30.00
X-1694 [PS]	Country & Western Golden Hits (Part 1)	1960	7.50	15.00	30.00
X-1695	(contents unknown)	1960	7.50	15.00	30.00
X-1695 [PS]	Country & Western Golden Hits (Part 2)	1960	7.50	15.00	30.00
X-1696	(contents unknown)	1960	7.50	15.00	30.00
X-1696 [PS]	Country & Western Golden Hits (Part 3)	1960	7.50	15.00	30.00
X-1703	(contents unknown)	1961	7.50	15.00	30.00
X-1703 [PS]	Connie Francis	1961	7.50	15.00	30.00
—Has paper sleeve rather than a cardboard sleeve					

Albums

LEO

Number	Title	Yr	VG	VG+	NM
LE-903 [M]	Connie Francis and the Kids Next Door	1967	12.50	25.00	50.00
LES-903 [S]	Connie Francis and the Kids Next Door	1967	15.00	30.00	60.00

MATI-MOR

Number	Title	Yr	VG	VG+	NM
8002 [M]	Sing Along wth Connie Francis	1961	10.00	20.00	40.00
—Made for Brylcreem					

METRO

Number	Title	Yr	VG	VG+	NM
M-519 [M]	Connie Francis	1964	5.00	10.00	20.00
MS-519 [S]	Connie Francis	1964	6.25	12.50	25.00
M-538 [M]	Folk Favorites	1965	5.00	10.00	20.00
MS-538 [S]	Folk Favorites	1965	6.25	12.50	25.00
M-571 [M]	Songs of Love	1966	5.00	10.00	20.00
MS-571 [S]	Songs of Love	1966	6.25	12.50	25.00
M-603 [M]	The Incomparable Connie Francis	1967	5.00	10.00	20.00
MS-603 [S]	The Incomparable Connie Francis	1967	6.25	12.50	25.00

Number	Title (A Side/B Side)	Yr	VG	VG+	NM
MGM					
GAS-109	Greatest Golden Groovie Goodies (Golden Archive Series)	1970	6.25	12.50	25.00
SE-3253 [S]	A New Kind of Connie	1964	7.50	15.00	30.00
SE-3298 [S]	All Time International Hits	1965	7.50	15.00	30.00
E-3686 [M]	Who's Sorry Now?	1958	25.00	50.00	100.00
—Yellow label					
E-3686 [M]	Who's Sorry Now?	1960	10.00	20.00	40.00
—Black label					
E-3761 [M]	The Exciting Connie Francis	1959	20.00	40.00	80.00
—Yellow label					
E-3761 [M]	The Exciting Connie Francis	1959	7.50	15.00	30.00
—Black label					
SE-3761 [S]	The Exciting Connie Francis	1959	25.00	50.00	100.00
—Yellow label					
SE-3761 [S]	The Exciting Connie Francis	1959	10.00	20.00	40.00
—Black label					
E-3776 [M]	My Thanks to You	1959	7.50	15.00	30.00
SE-3776 [S]	My Thanks to You	1959	10.00	20.00	40.00
E-3791 [M]	Italian Favorites	1959	7.50	15.00	30.00
SE-3791 [S]	Italian Favorites	1959	10.00	20.00	40.00
E-3792 [M]	Christmas in My Heart	1959	7.50	15.00	30.00
SE-3792 [S]	Christmas in My Heart	1959	10.00	20.00	40.00
—Same as above, but in stereo					
E-3793 [M]	Connie's Greatest Hits	1960	7.50	15.00	30.00
E-3794 [M]	Rock 'N' Roll Million Sellers	1960	7.50	15.00	30.00
SE-3794 [S]	Rock 'N' Roll Million Sellers	1960	10.00	20.00	40.00
E-3795 [M]	Country and Western Golden Hits	1960	7.50	15.00	30.00
SE-3795 [S]	Country and Western Golden Hits	1960	10.00	20.00	40.00
E-3853 [M]	Spanish and Latin American Favorites	1960	7.50	15.00	30.00
SE-3853 [S]	Spanish and Latin American Favorites	1960	10.00	20.00	40.00
E-3869 [M]	Jewish Favorites	1961	7.50	15.00	30.00
SE-3869 [S]	Jewish Favorites	1961	10.00	20.00	40.00
E-3871 [M]	More Italian Favorites	1960	7.50	15.00	30.00
SE-3871 [S]	More Italian Favorites	1960	10.00	20.00	40.00
E-3893 [M]	Songs to a Swinging Band	1961	7.50	15.00	30.00
SE-3893 [S]	Songs to a Swinging Band	1961	10.00	20.00	40.00
E-3913 [M]	Connie Francis at the Copa	1961	7.50	15.00	30.00
SE-3913 [S]	Connie Francis at the Copa	1961	10.00	20.00	40.00
E-3942 [M]	More Greatest Hits	1961	7.50	15.00	30.00
SE-3942 [S]	More Greatest Hits	1961	10.00	20.00	40.00
E-3965 [M]	Never on Sunday and Other Title Songs from Motion Pictures	1961	7.50	15.00	30.00
SE-3965 [S]	Never on Sunday and Other Title Songs from Motion Pictures	1961	10.00	20.00	40.00
E-3969 [M]	Folk Song Favorites	1961	7.50	15.00	30.00
SE-3969 [S]	Folk Song Favorites	1961	10.00	20.00	40.00
E-4013 [M]	Irish Favorites	1962	7.50	15.00	30.00
SE-4013 [S]	Irish Favorites	1962	10.00	20.00	40.00
E-4022 [M]	Do the Twist	1962	7.50	15.00	30.00
E-4022 [M]	Dance Party	196?	6.25	12.50	25.00
—Retitled version of "Do the Twist"					
SE-4022 [S]	Do the Twist	1962	10.00	20.00	40.00
SE-4022 [S]	Dance Party	196?	7.50	15.00	30.00
—Retitled version of "Do the Twist"					
E-4023 [M]	Fun Songs for Children	1962	12.50	25.00	50.00
E-4048 [M]	Award Winning Motion Picture Hits	1963	6.25	12.50	25.00
SE-4048 [S]	Award Winning Motion Picture Hits	1963	7.50	15.00	30.00
E-4049 [M]	Connie Francis Sings Second Hand Love and Other Hits	1962	6.25	12.50	25.00
SE-4049 [S]	Connie Francis Sings Second Hand Love and Other Hits	1962	7.50	15.00	30.00
E-4079 [M]	Country Music Connie Style	1962	6.25	12.50	25.00
SE-4079 [S]	Country Music Connie Style	1962	7.50	15.00	30.00
E-4102 [M]	Modern Italian Hits	1963	6.25	12.50	25.00
SE-4102 [S]	Modern Italian Hits	1963	7.50	15.00	30.00
E-4123 [M]	Follow the Boys	1963	6.25	12.50	25.00
SE-4123 [S]	Follow the Boys	1963	7.50	15.00	30.00
E-4124 [M]	German Favorites	1963	6.25	12.50	25.00
SE-4124 [S]	German Favorites	1963	7.50	15.00	30.00
E-4145 [M]	Greatest American Waltzes	1963	6.25	12.50	25.00
SE-4145 [S]	Greatest American Waltzes	1963	7.50	15.00	30.00
E-4161 [M]	Mala Femmena & Connie's Big Hits from Italy	1963	6.25	12.50	25.00
SE-4161 [S]	Mala Femmena & Connie's Big Hits from Italy	1963	7.50	15.00	30.00
E-4167 [M]	The Very Best of Connie Francis	1963	6.25	12.50	25.00
SE-4167 [S]	The Very Best of Connie Francis	1963	7.50	15.00	30.00
E-4210 [M]	In the Summer of His Years	1964	6.25	12.50	25.00
SE-4210 [S]	In the Summer of His Years	1964	7.50	15.00	30.00
E-4229 [M]	Looking for Love	1964	6.25	12.50	25.00
SE-4229 [S]	Looking for Love	1964	7.50	15.00	30.00
E-4253 [M]	A New Kind of Connie	1964	6.25	12.50	25.00
E-4294 [M]	Connie Francis Sings For Mama	1965	6.25	12.50	25.00
SE-4294 [S]	Connie Francis Sings For Mama	1965	7.50	15.00	30.00
E-4298 [M]	All Time International Hits	1965	6.25	12.50	25.00
E-4355 [M]	Jealous Heart	1966	6.25	12.50	25.00
SE-4355 [S]	Jealous Heart	1966	7.50	15.00	30.00
E-4382 [M]	Movie Greats of the 60's	1966	6.25	12.50	25.00
SE-4382 [S]	Movie Greats of the 60's	1966	7.50	15.00	30.00
E-4399 [M]	Connie's Christmas	1966	6.25	12.50	25.00
SE-4399 [S]	Connie's Christmas	1966	7.50	15.00	30.00
E-4411 [M]	Live at the Sahara in Las Vegas	1967	6.25	12.50	25.00
SE-4411 [S]	Live at the Sahara in Las Vegas	1967	7.50	15.00	30.00
E-4448 [M]	Love, Italian Style	1967	6.25	12.50	25.00
SE-4448 [S]	Love, Italian Style	1967	7.50	15.00	30.00
E-4472 [M]	Connie Francis On Broadway Today	1967	6.25	12.50	25.00
SE-4472 [S]	Connie Francis On Broadway Today	1967	7.50	15.00	30.00
E-4474 [M]	Grandes Exitos del Cine de los Anos 60	1967	6.25	12.50	25.00
SE-4474 [S]	Grandes Exitos del Cine de los Anos 60	1967	7.50	15.00	30.00
E-4487 [M]	My Heart Cries for You	1967	7.50	15.00	30.00
SE-4487 [S]	My Heart Cries for You	1967	6.25	12.50	25.00
E-4522 [M]	Hawaii: Connie	1968	25.00	50.00	100.00
SE-4522 [S]	Hawaii: Connie	1968	6.25	12.50	25.00
SE-4573	Connie & Clyde	1968	6.25	12.50	25.00
SE-4585	Connie Francis Sings Bacharach & David	1968	6.25	12.50	25.00
SE-4637	The Wedding Cake	1969	6.25	12.50	25.00
SE-4655	The Songs of Les Reed	1969	6.25	12.50	25.00

Number	Title (A Side/B Side)	Yr	VG	VG+	NM
MG-1-5406	I'm Me Again	198?	3.00	6.00	12.00
MG-1-5410	Greatest Hits	198?	3.00	6.00	12.00
MG-1-5411	Greatest Jewish Hits	198?	3.00	6.00	12.00
ST-90068 [S]	A New Kind of Connie	1964	8.75	17.50	35.00
—Capitol Record Club issue					
T-90068 [M]	A New Kind of Connie	1964	7.50	15.00	30.00
—Capitol Record Club issue					
ST 90510 [S]	The Very Best of Connie Francis	1965	10.00	20.00	40.00
—Capitol Record Club edition					
T 90510 [M]	The Very Best of Connie Francis	1965	10.00	20.00	40.00
—Capitol Record Club edition					
ST-91145	My Best to You	1968	7.50	15.00	30.00
—Capitol Record Club					
POLYDOR					
827569-1	The Very Best of Connie Francis	1985	2.50	5.00	10.00
827582-1	Greatest Hits	1985	2.50	5.00	10.00
827584-1	Greatest Jewish Hits	1985	2.50	5.00	10.00
839922-1	Lo Mejor De Su Repertorio	198?	2.50	5.00	10.00
839923-1	12 Exitos De Connie Francis	198?	2.50	5.00	10.00

FRANK, JOE, AND THE KNIGHTS

45s

Number	Title (A Side/B Side)	Yr	VG	VG+	NM
ABC-PARAMOUNT					
10782	Can't Find a Way/Won't You Come Home	1966	5.00	10.00	20.00

FRANK AND JACK

45s

Number	Title (A Side/B Side)	Yr	VG	VG+	NM
BERGEN					
100	'Twas The Night Before Christmas/Jingle Bells	1957	5.00	10.00	20.00
JOSIE					
827	Twas the Night Before Christmas (Breaking Thru the Sound Barrier)/Jingle Bells (From the Sound Track)	1957	3.75	7.50	15.00

FRANKIE AND THE C-NOTES

45s

Number	Title (A Side/B Side)	Yr	VG	VG+	NM
RICHIE					
2	Forever and Ever/Fade Out	1959	100.00	200.00	400.00

FRANKLIN, ALAN, EXPLOSION

Albums

Number	Title (A Side/B Side)	Yr	VG	VG+	NM
ALADDIN					
104049	Come Home Baby	1969	20.00	40.00	80.00
HORNE					
JC-888	The Blues Climax	1970	20.00	40.00	80.00

FRANKLIN, ARETHA

12-Inch Singles

Number	Title (A Side/B Side)	Yr	VG	VG+	NM
ARISTA					
SP-103 [DJ]	What a Fool Believes (Long)/What a Fool Believes (Short)	1980	2.00	4.00	8.00
SP-138 [DJ]	Jump To It (6:40) (3:58)/Just My Daydream	1982	2.00	4.00	8.00
2240	Everyday People (People Remix) (Bonus Beats)/(Everyday Remix) (People Dub)	1991	2.00	4.00	8.00
2651 [(3)]	A Deeper Love (9 mixes on 3 records)	1994	5.00	10.00	20.00
9043	Get It Right (Long Version)/(Instrumental)	1983	2.00	4.00	8.00
9355	Freeway of Love (Rock Mix)/(Radio Mix) (Extended Remix)	1985	2.00	4.00	8.00
9411	Who's Zoomin' Who (Dance Mix) (Dub Mix)/(Radio) (Acapella)	1985	2.00	4.00	8.00
9454	Another Night (Dance Mix) (Dub)/(Radio Mix) (7" Edit)	1985	2.00	4.00	8.00
9473	Ain't Nobody Ever Loved You (4 versions)	1986	2.00	4.00	8.00
9529	Jumpin' Jack Flash (LP Mix) (Street Mix)/(Street-Radio) (Master Dub) (Beat Dub)	1986	2.50	5.00	10.00
9547	Jimmy Lee (Extended) (Single) (Dub)/(Aretha Megamix)	1986	2.00	4.00	8.00
9560	I Knew You Were Waiting (For Me) (Edited Remix) (Percapella)/(LP) (Extended Remix)	1987	2.00	4.00	8.00
—With George Michael					
9575	Rock-a-Lott (Street Mix) (Radio Mix)/(Dub Mix) (A Capella)	1987	—	3.00	6.00
ADP 9682 [DJ]	Oh Happy Day/The Lord's Prayer//(B-side unknown)	1988	3.00	6.00	12.00
9851	It Wasn't, It Isn't, It Ain't Never Gonna Be (Extended Radio) (House Radio Mix)/(Hip Hop Radio) (New Jack Swing Dub)/Think '89	1989	—	3.00	6.00
—With Whitney Houston					
ADP 9877 [DJ]	It Wasn't, It Isn't, It Ain't Never Gonna Be (6:12) (6:20)/(7:35) (5:36)	1989	2.50	5.00	10.00
—With Whitney Houston					
9885	Gimme Your Love (Single Edit) (Extended Remix)/Think '89	1989	—	3.00	6.00
—With James Brown					
ADP 9906 [DJ]	Gimme Your Love (Single Edit) (Extended Remix)/Interview	1989	2.50	5.00	10.00
—With James Brown					

45s

Number	Title (A Side/B Side)	Yr	VG	VG+	NM
ARISTA					
0569	United Together/Take Me With You	1980	—	2.00	4.00
0591	What a Fool Believes/Love Me Forever	1980	—	2.00	4.00
0600	Come to Me/School Days	1981	—	2.00	4.00
0624	Love All the Hurt Away/Whole Lotta Me	1981	—	2.00	4.00
—Aretha Franklin and George Benson					
0646	It's My Turn/Kind of Man	1981	—	2.00	4.00
0665	Livin' in the Streets/There's a Star for Everyone	1982	—	2.00	4.00
0699	Jump To It/Just My Daydream	1982	—	2.00	4.00
1023	Love Me Right/(It's Just) Your Love	1982	—	2.00	4.00
1043	This Is for Real/I Just Want to Make It Up to You	1983	—	2.00	4.00
2239	Everyday People/You Can't Take Me for Granted	1991	—	2.50	5.00
9034	Get It Right/Giving In	1983	—	2.00	4.00
9095	Every Girl (Wants My Guy)/I Got Your Love	1983	—	2.00	4.00
9354	Freeway of Love/Until You Say You Love Me	1985	—	—	3.00
9354 [PS]	Freeway of Love/Until You Say You Love Me	1985	—	—	3.00

Number	Title (A Side/B Side)	Yr	VG	VG+	NM
9410	Who's Zoomin' Who/Bittersweet Love	1985	—	—	3.00
9410 [PS]	Who's Zoomin' Who/Bittersweet Love	1985	—	—	3.00
9453	Another Night/Kind of Man	1986	—	—	3.00
9474	Ain't Nobody Ever Loved You/Push	1986	—	—	3.00
—B-side with Peter Wolf					
9528	Jumpin' Jack Flash/Integrity	1986	—	2.50	5.00
—Original pressings on clear vinyl					
9528	Jumpin' Jack Flash/Integrity	1986	—	—	3.00
—Second pressing on black vinyl					
9528 [PS]	Jumpin' Jack Flash/Integrity	1986	—	2.50	5.00
—Picture sleeve with clear vinyl pressing lists catalog number as ALC-9528					
9528 [PS]	Jumpin' Jack Flash/Integrity	1986	—	—	3.00
—Picture sleeve with black vinyl pressing lists catalog number as AL-9528					
9541	Jumpin' Jack Flash/Jumpin' Jack Flash	1986	—	2.00	4.00
—Reissue with two different versions of the song					
9546	Jimmy Lee/If You Need My Love Tonight	1986	—	2.00	4.00
9546 [PS]	Jimmy Lee/If You Need My Love Tonight	1986	—	2.00	4.00
—B-side with Larry Graham					
9557	Jimmy Lee/An Angel Cries	1986	—	—	3.00
9557 [PS]	Jimmy Lee/An Angel Cries	1986	—	—	3.00
9559	I Knew You Were Waiting (For Me)/(Instrumental)	1987	—	—	3.00
—With George Michael					
9559 [PS]	I Knew You Were Waiting (For Me)/(Instrumental)	1987	—	—	3.00
—With George Michael					
9574	Rock-A-Lott/Look to the Rainbow	1987	—	—	3.00
9574 [PS]	Rock-A-Lott/Look to the Rainbow	1987	—	—	3.00
9623	If You Need My Love Tonight/He'll Come Along	1987	—	—	3.00
—A-side with Larry Graham					
9672	Oh Happy Day/The Lord's Prayer	1988	—	2.00	4.00
9766	If Ever a Love There Was/Let's Jam	1988	—	—	3.00
—A-side with the Four Tops; B-side: Four Tops solo					
9809	Through the Storm/Come to Me	1989	—	—	3.00
—A-side: Aretha Franklin and Elton John					
9809 [PS]	Through the Storm/Come to Me	1989	—	—	3.00
9850	It Isn't, It Wasn't, It Ain't Never Gonna Be/If Ever a Love There Was	1989	—	—	3.00
—A-side with Whitney Houston; B-side with the Four Tops					
9850 [PS]	It Isn't, It Wasn't, It Ain't Never Gonna Be/If Ever a Love There Was	1989	—	—	3.00
—A-side with Whitney Houston; B-side with the Four Tops					
9884	Gimme Your Love/Think	1989	—	—	3.00
—With James Brown					
9884 [PS]	Gimme Your Love/Think	1989	—	—	3.00
—With James Brown					
ATLANTIC					
2386	I Never Loved a Man (The Way I Love You)/Do Right Woman, Do Right Man	1967	2.50	5.00	10.00
2403	Respect/Dr. Feelgood	1967	2.50	5.00	10.00
2427	Baby I Love You/Going Down Now	1967	2.50	5.00	10.00
2441	(You Make Me Feel Like) A Natural Woman/Baby, Baby, Baby	1967	2.50	5.00	10.00
2464	Chain of Fools/Prove It	1967	2.50	5.00	10.00
2486	(Sweet Sweet Baby) Since You've Been Gone/Ain't No Way	1968	2.50	5.00	10.00
2518	Think/You Send Me	1968	2.50	5.00	10.00
2546	I Say a Little Prayer/The House That Jack Built	1968	2.50	5.00	10.00
2574	See Saw/My Song	1968	2.00	4.00	8.00
2603	The Weight/Tracks of My Tears	1969	2.00	4.00	8.00
2619	I Can't See Myself Leaving You/Gentle On My Mind	1969	2.00	4.00	8.00
2650	Share Your Love with Me/Pledging My Love-The Clock	1969	2.00	4.00	8.00
2683	Eleanor Rigby/It Ain't Fair	1969	2.00	4.00	8.00
2706	Call Me/Son of a Preacher Man	1970	2.00	4.00	8.00
2731	Spirit in the Dark/The Thrill Is Gone	1970	2.00	4.00	8.00
2751	Don't Play That Song/Let It Be	1970	2.00	4.00	8.00
2772	Border Song (Holy Moses)/You and Me	1970	2.00	4.00	8.00
2787	You're All I Need to Get By/Pullin'	1971	—	3.00	6.00
2796	Bridge Over Troubled Water/Brand New Me	1971	—	3.00	6.00
2817	Spanish Harlem/Lean On Me	1971	—	3.00	6.00
2838	Rock Steady/Oh Me Oh My (I'm a Fool for You Baby)	1971	—	3.00	6.00
2866	Day Dreaming/I've Been Loving You Too Long	1972	—	3.00	6.00
2883	All the King's Horses/April Fools	1972	—	3.00	6.00
2901	Wholy Holy/Give Yourself to Jesus	1972	—	3.00	6.00
2941	Master of Eyes (The Deepness of Your Eyes)/Moody's Mood for You	1973	—	3.00	6.00
2969	Angel/Hey Hey Now (Sister from Texas)	1973	—	3.00	6.00
2995	Until You Come Back to Me (That's What I'm Gonna Do)/If You Don't Think	1973	—	3.00	6.00
2999	I'm in Love/Oh Baby	1974	—	3.00	6.00
3200	Ain't Nothing Like the Real Thing/Eight Days a Week	1974	—	3.00	6.00
3224	Without Love/Don't Go Breaking My Heart	1974	—	3.00	6.00
3249	With Everything I Feel in Me/Sing It Again, Say It Again	1975	—	3.00	6.00
3289	Mr. D.J. (5 for the D.J.)/As Long As You Are There	1975	—	3.00	6.00
3311	You/Without You	1975	—	3.00	6.00
3326	Something He Can Feel/Loving You, Baby	1976	—	3.00	6.00
3358	Jump/Hooked on Your Love	1976	—	3.00	6.00
3373	Look Into Your Heart/Rock with Me	1977	—	3.00	6.00
3393	Break It To Me Gently/Meadows of Springtime	1977	—	3.00	6.00
3418	When I Think About You/Touch Me Up	1978	—	3.00	6.00
3468	Almighty Fire/I'm Your Speed	1978	—	3.00	6.00
3495	More Than Just a Joy/This You Can Believe	1979	—	3.00	6.00
CHECKER					
861	Never Grow Old/You Grow Closer	1957	5.00	10.00	20.00
941	Precious Lord, Part 1/Precious Lord, Part 2	1960	3.75	7.50	15.00
COLUMBIA					
31202 [S]	titles unknown	1961	3.00	6.00	12.00
31203 [S]	titles unknown	1961	3.00	6.00	12.00
31204 [S]	titles unknown	1961	3.00	6.00	12.00
31205 [S]	titles unknown	1961	3.00	6.00	12.00
31206 [S]	titles unknown	1961	3.00	6.00	12.00
—Anyone who can fill in these gaps -- the above five all are Columbia "Stereo 7" singles -- please let us know.					

Number	Title (A Side/B Side)	Yr	VG	VG+	NM
41793	Today I Sing the Blues/Love Is the Only Thing	1960	3.00	6.00	12.00
41923	Won't Be Long/Right Now	1961	3.00	6.00	12.00
41965	Are You Sure/Maybe I'm a Fool	1961	3.00	6.00	12.00
42157	Rock-A-Bye Your Baby with a Dixie Melody/Operation Heartbreak	1961	3.00	6.00	12.00
42266	I Surrender, Dear/Rough Lover	1962	2.50	5.00	10.00
42266 [PS]	I Surrender, Dear/Rough Lover	1962	7.50	15.00	30.00
42456	Don't Cry, Baby/Without the One You Love	1962	2.50	5.00	10.00
42456 [PS]	Don't Cry, Baby/Without the One You Love	1962	7.50	15.00	30.00
42520	Try a Little Tenderness/Just for a Thrill	1962	2.50	5.00	10.00
42625	Trouble in Mind/God Bless the Child	1962	2.50	5.00	10.00
42796	Here's Where I Came In/Say It Isn't So	1963	2.50	5.00	10.00
42796 [PS]	Here's Where I Came In/Say It Isn't So	1963	7.50	15.00	30.00
42874	Skylark/You've Got Her	1963	2.50	5.00	10.00
42933	Johnny/Kissin' by the Mistletoe	1963	2.50	5.00	10.00
43009	Soulville/Evil Gal Blues	1964	2.50	5.00	10.00
43113	Runnin' Out of Fools/It's Just a Matter of Time	1964	2.50	5.00	10.00
43177	Winter Wonderland/The Christmas Song (Chestnuts Roasting on an Open Fire)	1964	2.50	5.00	10.00
43203	Can't You Just See Me/Little Miss Raggedy Ann	1965	2.50	5.00	10.00
43241	One Step Ahead/I Can't Wait Until I See My Baby's Face	1965	2.50	5.00	10.00
43333	(No, No) I'm Losing You/Sweet Bitter Love	1965	2.50	5.00	10.00
43442	You Made Me Love You/There Is No Greater Love	1966	2.50	5.00	10.00
43515	Hands Off/Tighten Up Your Tie, Button Up Your Jacket	1966	2.50	5.00	10.00
43637	Until You Were Gone/Swanee	1966	2.50	5.00	10.00
43827	Cry Like a Baby/Swanee	1966	2.50	5.00	10.00
44181	Until You Were Gone/Lee Cross	1967	2.50	5.00	10.00
44270	Take a Look/Follow Your Heart	1967	2.50	5.00	10.00
44381	Mockingbird/A Mother's Love	1967	2.00	4.00	8.00
44441	Soulville/If Ever I Would Leave You	1968	2.00	4.00	8.00
44851	Friendly Persuasion/Jim	1969	2.00	4.00	8.00
44951	Today I Sing the Blues/People	1969	2.00	4.00	8.00
JVB					
47	Never Grow Old/You Grow Closer	1957	7.50	15.00	30.00
75	Precious Lord, Part 1/Precious Lord, Part 2	1959	7.50	15.00	30.00
PHILCO-FORD					
HP-24	Respect/Soul Serenade	1968	6.25	12.50	25.00
—4-inch plastic "Hip Pocket Record" with color sleeve					

Albums

Number	Title	Yr	VG	VG+	NM
ARISTA					
AL-8019	Get It Right	1983	2.50	5.00	10.00
AL-8286	Who's Zoomin' Who	1985	2.50	5.00	10.00
AL-8344	Jump To It	1985	2.00	4.00	8.00
—Budget-line reissue					
AL-8368	Love All the Hurt Away	1985	2.00	4.00	8.00
—Budget-line reissue					
AL-8442	Aretha	1986	2.50	5.00	10.00
—Different album than 9538					
AL-8572	Through the Storm	1989	2.50	5.00	10.00
AL-9538	Aretha	1980	2.50	5.00	10.00
AL-9552	Love All the Hurt Away	1981	2.50	5.00	10.00
AL-9602	Jump To It	1982	2.50	5.00	10.00
ATLANTIC					
SD 2-906 [(2)]	Amazing Grace	1972	5.00	10.00	20.00
SD 7205	Aretha Live at Fillmore West	1971	3.75	7.50	15.00
SD 7213	Yoing, Gifted & Black	1972	3.75	7.50	15.00
SD 7265	Hey Now Hey (The Other Side of the Sky)	1973	3.00	6.00	12.00
SD 7292	Let Me in Your Life	1974	3.00	6.00	12.00
8139 [M]	I Never Loved a Man the Way I Love You	1967	6.25	12.50	25.00
SD 8139	I Never Loved a Man the Way I Love You	1969	3.00	6.00	12.00
—Green and red label					
SD 8139 [S]	I Never Loved a Man the Way I Love You	1967	5.00	10.00	20.00
—Green and blue label					
8150 [M]	Aretha Arrives	1967	6.25	12.50	25.00
SD 8150	Aretha Arrives	1969	3.00	6.00	12.00
—Green and red label					
SD 8150 [S]	Aretha Arrives	1967	5.00	10.00	20.00
—Green and blue label					
8176 [M]	Aretha: Lady Soul	1968	7.50	15.00	30.00
SD 8176	Aretha: Lady Soul	1969	3.00	6.00	12.00
—Green and red label					
SD 8176 [S]	Aretha: Lady Soul	1968	5.00	10.00	20.00
—Green and blue label					
SD 8186	Aretha Now	1968	5.00	10.00	20.00
—Green and blue label					
SD 8186	Aretha Now	1969	3.00	6.00	12.00
—Green and red label					
SD 8207	Aretha in Paris	1968	3.75	7.50	15.00
SD 8212	Aretha Franklin: Soul '69	1969	3.75	7.50	15.00
SD 8227	Aretha's Gold	1969	3.75	7.50	15.00
SD 8248	This Girl's in Love with You	1970	3.75	7.50	15.00
SD 8265	Spirit in the Dark	1970	3.75	7.50	15.00
SD 8295	Aretha's Greatest Hits	1971	3.75	7.50	15.00
QD 8305 [Q]	The Best of Aretha Franklin	1974	5.00	10.00	20.00
SD 18116	With Everything I Feel in Me	1974	3.00	6.00	12.00
SD 18151	You	1975	3.00	6.00	12.00
SD 18176	Sparkle	1976	3.00	6.00	12.00
SD 18204	Ten Years of Gold	1976	3.00	6.00	12.00
SD 19102	Sweet Passion	1977	3.00	6.00	12.00
SD 19161	Almighty Fire	1978	3.00	6.00	12.00
SD 19248	La Diva	1979	3.00	6.00	12.00
81230	Aretha's Jazz	1984	2.50	5.00	10.00
81280	The Best of Aretha Franklin	1985	2.50	5.00	10.00
81668 [(2)]	20 Greatest Hits	1986	3.75	7.50	15.00
STAO-95151	Hey Now Hey (The Other Side of the Sky)	1973	3.75	7.50	15.00
—Capitol Record Club edition					
CHECKER					
10009 [M]	Songs of Faith	1965	125.00	250.00	500.00
—Original issue of this album; cover has Aretha sitting at a piano					
10009 [M]	Gospel Soul	1967	5.00	10.00	20.00
—Reissue with new title and cover					

COLUMBIA

Number	Title (A Side/B Side)	Yr	VG	VG+	NM
CL 1612 [M]	Aretha	1961	12.50	25.00	50.00
—Red and black label with six "eye" logos					
CL 1612 [M]	Aretha	1963	5.00	10.00	20.00
—"Guaranteed High Fidelity" on label					
CL 1612 [M]	Aretha	1965	3.75	7.50	15.00
—"360 Sound Mono" on label					
CL 1761 [M]	The Electrifying Aretha Franklin	1962	10.00	20.00	40.00
—Red and black label with six "eye" logos					
CL 1761 [M]	The Electrifying Aretha Franklin	1963	5.00	10.00	20.00
—"Guaranteed High Fidelity" on label					
CL 1761 [M]	The Electrifying Aretha Franklin	1965	3.75	7.50	15.00
—"360 Sound Mono" on label					
CL 1876 [M]	The Tender, The Moving, The Swinging Aretha Franklin	1962	10.00	20.00	40.00
—Red and black label with six "eye" logos					
CL 1876 [M]	The Tender, The Moving, The Swinging Aretha Franklin	1963	5.00	10.00	20.00
—"Guaranteed High Fidelity" on label					
CL 1876 [M]	The Tender, The Moving, The Swinging Aretha Franklin	1965	3.75	7.50	15.00
—"360 Sound Mono" on label					
CL 2079 [M]	Laughing on the Outside	1963	5.00	10.00	20.00
—"Guaranteed High Fidelity" on label					
CL 2079 [M]	Laughing on the Outside	1965	3.75	7.50	15.00
—"360 Sound Mono" on label					
CL 2163 [M]	Unforgettable	1964	5.00	10.00	20.00
—"Guaranteed High Fidelity" on label					
CL 2163 [M]	Unforgettable	1965	3.75	7.50	15.00
—"360 Sound Mono" on label					
CL 2281 [M]	Runnin' Out of Fools	1964	5.00	10.00	20.00
—"Guaranteed High Fidelity" on label					
CL 2281 [M]	Runnin' Out of Fools	1965	3.75	7.50	15.00
—"360 Sound Mono" on label					
CL 2351 [M]	Yeah!!!	1965	5.00	10.00	20.00
—"Guaranteed High Fidelity" on label					
CL 2351 [M]	Yeah!!!	1966	3.75	7.50	15.00
—"360 Sound Mono" on label					
CL 2521 [M]	Soul Sister	1966	5.00	10.00	20.00
CL 2629 [M]	Take It Like You Give It	1967	6.25	12.50	25.00
CL 2673 [M]	Aretha Franklin's Greatest Hits	1967	6.25	12.50	25.00
CL 2754 [M]	Take a Look	1967	7.50	15.00	30.00
CS 8412 [S]	Aretha	1961	20.00	40.00	80.00
—Red and black label with six "eye" logos					
CS 8412 [S]	Aretha	1963	6.25	12.50	25.00
—"360 Sound Stereo" on label					
CS 8561 [S]	The Electrifying Aretha Franklin	1962	12.50	25.00	50.00
—Red and black label with six "eye" logos					
CS 8561 [S]	The Electrifying Aretha Franklin	1963	6.25	12.50	25.00
—"360 Sound Stereo" on label					
CS 8676 [S]	The Tender, The Moving, The Swinging Aretha Franklin	1962	12.50	25.00	50.00
—Red and black label with six "eye" logos					
CS 8676 [S]	The Tender, The Moving, The Swinging Aretha Franklin	1963	6.25	12.50	25.00
—"360 Sound Stereo" on label					
CS 8879 [S]	Laughing on the Outside	1963	6.25	12.50	25.00
—"360 Sound Stereo" on label					
CS 8963 [S]	Unforgettable	1964	6.25	12.50	25.00
—"360 Sound Stereo" on label					
CS 9081 [S]	Runnin' Out of Fools	1964	6.25	12.50	25.00
—"360 Sound Stereo" on label					
CS 9151 [S]	Yeah!!!	1965	6.25	12.50	25.00
—"360 Sound Stereo" on label					
CS 9321 [S]	Soul Sister	1966	6.25	12.50	25.00
—"360 Sound Stereo" on label					
CS 9429 [S]	Take It Like You Give It	1967	5.00	10.00	20.00
—"360 Sound Stereo" on label					
CS 9473 [S]	Aretha Franklin's Greatest Hits	1967	5.00	10.00	20.00
—"360 Sound Stereo" on label					
CS 9554 [S]	Take a Look	1967	5.00	10.00	20.00
—"360 Sound Stereo" on label					
CS 9601	Aretha Franklin's Greatest Hits, Volume 2	1968	5.00	10.00	20.00
—"360 Sound Stereo" on label					
CS 9776	Soft and Beautiful	1969	5.00	10.00	20.00
—"360 Sound Stereo" on label					
CS 9956	Today I Sing the Blues	1970	3.75	7.50	15.00
—"360 Sound Stereo" on label					
KG 31355 [(2)]	In the Beginning/The World of Aretha Franklin 1960-1967	1972	5.00	10.00	20.00
KC 31953	The First 12 Sides	1973	3.00	6.00	12.00
C2 37377 [(2)]	The Legendary Queen of Soul	1981	3.00	6.00	12.00
PC 38042	Sweet Bitter Love	1982	2.50	5.00	10.00
FC 40105	Aretha Franklin Sings the Blues	1985	2.50	5.00	10.00
FC 40708	Aretha After Hours	1987	2.50	5.00	10.00

COLUMBIA SPECIAL PRODUCTS

Number	Title (A Side/B Side)	Yr	VG	VG+	NM
C 10589	Take a Look	1971	3.00	6.00	12.00

HARMONY

Number	Title (A Side/B Side)	Yr	VG	VG+	NM
HS 11349	Once in a Lifetime	1969	3.00	6.00	12.00
HS 11418	Two Sides of Love	1970	3.00	6.00	12.00
KH 30606	Greatest Hits 1960-1965	1971	3.00	6.00	12.00
KH 30606	Greatest Hits 1960-1966	1972	3.00	6.00	12.00

FRANKLIN, CAROLYN

45s

RCA VICTOR

Number	Title (A Side/B Side)	Yr	VG	VG+	NM
APBO-0022	You Are Everything/If You Want Me	1973	—	2.50	5.00
PB-10688	I Can't Help My Feeling So Blue/If You Want Me	1976	—	2.00	4.00
47-9734	The Boxer/I Don't Want to Lose You	1969	—	3.00	6.00
74-0188	Reality/It's True I'm Gonna Miss You	1969	—	3.00	6.00
74-0289	Ain't That Groovy/All I Want Is to Be Your Woman	1969	—	3.00	6.00
74-0314	Everybody's Talkin'/Chain Reaction	1970	—	2.50	5.00
74-0373	You Really Didn't Mean It/All I Want Is to Be Your Woman	1970	—	2.50	5.00
74-0783	As Long As You're There/I Want to Be With You	1972	—	2.50	5.00

Albums

RCA VICTOR

Number	Title (A Side/B Side)	Yr	VG	VG+	NM
LSP-4160	Baby Dynamite	1969	5.00	10.00	20.00
LSP-4317	Chain Reaction	1970	5.00	10.00	20.00
LSP-4411	I'd Rather Be Lonely	1973	5.00	10.00	20.00

FRANKLIN, ERMA

45s

BRUNSWICK

Number	Title (A Side/B Side)	Yr	VG	VG+	NM
55403	Change My Thoughts from You/Gotta Find Me a Lover	1969	2.00	4.00	8.00
55415	Saving My Love/You've Been Cancelled	1969	2.00	4.00	8.00
55424	I Just Don't Need You (At All)/It Could've Been Me	1969	2.00	4.00	8.00
55430	Whispers (Gettin' Louder)/(I Get the) Swetest Feeling	1970	2.00	4.00	8.00

EPIC

Number	Title (A Side/B Side)	Yr	VG	VG+	NM
9488	Hello Again/It's Over	1962	5.00	10.00	20.00
9511	Each Night I Cry/Time After Time	1962	5.00	10.00	20.00
9516	Dear Mama/Never Again	1962	5.00	10.00	20.00
9559	Don't Wait Too Long/Time After Time	1962	5.00	10.00	20.00
9594	Have You Ever Had the Blues/I Don't Want No Mama's Boy	1963	3.75	7.50	15.00
9610	Abracadabra/Love Is Blind	1963	3.75	7.50	15.00

SHOUT

Number	Title (A Side/B Side)	Yr	VG	VG+	NM
218	Big Boss Man/Didn't Catch the Dog's Bone	1967	2.50	5.00	10.00
221	Piece of My Heart/Baby What You Want Me to Do	1967	3.00	6.00	12.00
230	Open Up Your Soul/I'm Just Not Ready for Love	1967	2.50	5.00	10.00
234	Right to Cry/I'm Just Not Ready for Love	1968	2.50	5.00	10.00

Albums

BRUNSWICK

Number	Title (A Side/B Side)	Yr	VG	VG+	NM
BL 754147	Soul Sister	1969	5.00	10.00	20.00

EPIC

Number	Title (A Side/B Side)	Yr	VG	VG+	NM
BN 619 [S]	Her Name Is Erma	1962	10.00	20.00	40.00
LN 3824 [M]	Her Name Is Erma	1962	7.50	15.00	30.00

FRANTIC

45s

LIZARD

Number	Title (A Side/B Side)	Yr	VG	VG+	NM
20002	Shady Sam/(B-side unknown)	1970	3.75	7.50	15.00

Albums

LIZARD

Number	Title (A Side/B Side)	Yr	VG	VG+	NM
20103	Conception	1971	6.25	12.50	25.00

FRANTICS, THE

45s

BOLO

Number	Title (A Side/B Side)	Yr	VG	VG+	NM
728	Pony Moronie/Meet Me in Seattle Twist	1962	2.50	5.00	10.00
736	Oh Yeah/Let Our Love Roll On	1962	2.50	5.00	10.00

DOLTON

Number	Title (A Side/B Side)	Yr	VG	VG+	NM
2	Straight Flush/Young Blues	1959	5.00	10.00	20.00
6	Fog Cutter/Black Sapphire	1959	5.00	10.00	20.00
13	Checkerboard/Werewolf	1959	5.00	10.00	20.00
16	Werewolf/No Werewolf	1960	3.75	7.50	15.00
24	The Whip/Delilah	1960	3.75	7.50	15.00
31	Yankee Doodlin'/One Minute of Flamenco	1961	3.75	7.50	15.00
33	San Antonio Rose/Trees	1961	3.75	7.50	15.00

SEAFAIR

Number	Title (A Side/B Side)	Yr	VG	VG+	NM
111	San Francisco Swim/Blue Day	1964	2.50	5.00	10.00

FRATERNITY OF MAN, THE

45s

ABC

Number	Title (A Side/B Side)	Yr	VG	VG+	NM
11106	Don't Bogart Me/Wispy Paisley Skies	1968	2.00	4.00	8.00

Albums

ABC

Number	Title (A Side/B Side)	Yr	VG	VG+	NM
S-647	The Fraternity of Man	1968	7.50	15.00	30.00

DOT

Number	Title (A Side/B Side)	Yr	VG	VG+	NM
DLP-25955	Get It On	1969	6.25	12.50	25.00

FRAWLEY, WILLIAM

Albums

DOT

Number	Title (A Side/B Side)	Yr	VG	VG+	NM
DLP-3061 [M]	William Frawley Sings the Old Ones	1958	10.00	20.00	40.00

FREAK SCENE, THE

45s

COLUMBIA

Number	Title (A Side/B Side)	Yr	VG	VG+	NM
4-44056	A Million Grains of Sand/Behind the Mind	1967	6.25	12.50	25.00

Albums

COLUMBIA

Number	Title (A Side/B Side)	Yr	VG	VG+	NM
CL 2656 [M]	Psychedelic Psoul	1967	17.50	35.00	70.00
CS 9456 [S]	Psychedelic Psoul	1967	25.00	50.00	100.00

FREBERG, STAN

45s

CAPITOL

Number	Title (A Side/B Side)	Yr	VG	VG+	NM
F1356	John & Marsha/Ragtime Dan	1951	7.50	15.00	30.00
F1697	St. George and the Dragonet/Little Blue Riding Hood	1954	5.00	10.00	20.00
—Reissue (despite the lower number)					
F1711	That's My Boy/I've Got You Under My Skin	1951	7.50	15.00	30.00
F1962	Maggie/Tele-Vee-Shun	1951	7.50	15.00	30.00
F2029	Try/Pass the Udder Udder	1952	7.50	15.00	30.00
F2125	Abe Snake for President/Ba Ba Ball and Chain	1952	12.50	25.00	50.00
F2279	The World Is Waiting for the Sunrise/Boogie Woogie Banjo Man from Birmingham	1952	6.25	12.50	25.00
F2596	St. George and the Dragonet/Little Blue Riding Hood	1953	7.50	15.00	30.00
F2671	Christmas Dragnet Part 1/Christmas Dragnet Part 2	1953	7.50	15.00	30.00

Number	Title (A Side/B Side)	Yr	VG	VG+	NM
F2677	C'est Si Bon (It's So Good)/A Dear John & Marsha Letter	1953	6.25	12.50	25.00
F2838	Point of Order/Person to Pearson	1954	6.25	12.50	25.00
F2929	Sh-Boom/Widescreen Mama Blues	1954	6.25	12.50	25.00
F2986	Yulenet (Part 1)/Yulenet (Part 2)	1954	6.25	12.50	25.00
—Same recording as "Christmas Dragnet" (Capitol 2671)					
F3138	The Honey Earthers/The Lone Psychiatrist	1955	7.50	15.00	30.00
—With Daws Butler					
F3249	The Yellow Rose of Texas/Rock Around Stephen Foster	1955	6.25	12.50	25.00
F3280	Nuttin' for Christmas/The Night Before Christmas	1955	6.25	12.50	25.00
3355	Try/John and Marsha	1972	2.50	5.00	10.00
F3396	The Great Pretender/The Quest for Bridey Hammerschlaugen	1956	6.25	12.50	25.00
F3480	Heartbreak Hotel/Rock Island Line	1956	6.25	12.50	25.00
3503	Green Chritma (Part 1)/Green Chritma (Part 2)	1972	2.50	5.00	10.00
F3687	Banana Boat (Day-O)/Tele-Vee-Shun	1957	6.25	12.50	25.00
F3815	Wun'erful, Wun'erful! (Part uh-one)/Wun'erful, Wun'erful! (Part uh-two)	1957	6.25	12.50	25.00
F3892	Ya Got Trouble/Gary Indiana	1958	5.00	10.00	20.00
F4097	Green Chritma/The Meaning of Christmas	1958	5.00	10.00	20.00
F4097 [PS]	Green Chritma/The Meaning of Christmas	1958	7.50	15.00	30.00
4329	The Old Payola Roll Blues Part 1/The Old Payola Roll Blues Part 2	1960	5.00	10.00	20.00
4329 [PS]	The Old Payola Roll Blues Part 1/The Old Payola Roll Blues Part 2	1960	7.50	15.00	30.00
4433	Comments for Our Time Part 1/Comments for Our TIme Part 2	1960	5.00	10.00	20.00
5726	Flackman and Reagan Part 1/Flackman and Reagan Part 2	1966	5.00	10.00	20.00
5726 [PS]	Flackman and Reagan Part 1/Flackman and Reagan Part 2	1966	7.50	15.00	30.00
S7-19761	Green Chritma/The Meaning of Christmas	1997	—	—	3.00
S7-57891	Nuttin' for Christmas/I Yust Go Nuts at Christmas	1992	—	2.00	4.00
—B-side by Yogi Yorgesson					
7-Inch Extended Plays					
CAPITOL					
EAP 496	(contents unknown)	1954	7.50	15.00	30.00
EAP 496 [PS]	Any Requests?	1954	7.50	15.00	30.00
EAP 628	(contents unknown)	1955	7.50	15.00	30.00
EAP 628 [PS]	The Real St. George	1955	7.50	15.00	30.00
Albums					
CAPITOL					
T 777 [M]	A Child's Garden of Freberg	1957	12.50	25.00	50.00
—Turquoise label					
WBO 1035 [(2) M]	The Best of the Stan Freberg Shows	1958	15.00	30.00	60.00
SM-1242 [R]	Stan Freberg with the Original Cast	197?	2.50	5.00	10.00
T 1242 [M]	Stan Freberg with the Original Cast	1959	7.50	15.00	30.00
SW 1573 [S]	Stan Freberg Presents the United States of America	1961	7.50	15.00	30.00
W 1573 [M]	Stan Freberg Presents the United States of America	1961	6.25	12.50	25.00
T 1694 [M]	Face the Funnies	1962	6.25	12.50	25.00
T 1816 [M]	Madison Ave. Werewolf	1962	6.25	12.50	25.00
SM-2020 [R]	The Best of Stan Freberg	197?	2.50	5.00	10.00
T 2020 [M]	The Best of Stan Freberg	1964	6.25	12.50	25.00
SM-2551 [S]	The Stan Freberg Underground Show #1	197?	2.50	5.00	10.00
ST 2551 [S]	The Stan Freberg Underground Show #1	1966	6.25	12.50	25.00
T 2551 [M]	The Stan Freberg Underground Show #1	1966	5.00	10.00	20.00
SM-11765	The Best of the Stan Freberg Shows	197?	3.00	6.00	12.00

FRED, JOHN, AND HIS PLAYBOY BAND

Number	Title (A Side/B Side)	Yr	VG	VG+	NM
45s					
BELL					
45382	I'm in Love Again/In the Mood	1973	—	2.50	5.00
—As "John Fred and the Creepers"					
JEWEL					
730	The Fool/There'll Be No Teardrops Tonight	1964	2.50	5.00	10.00
736	Lenne/You're Mad at Me	1964	2.50	5.00	10.00
737	Boogie Children/My First Love	1964	2.50	5.00	10.00
—As "The Playboys"					
743	Wrong to Me/How Can I Prove	1965	2.50	5.00	10.00
MONTEL					
904	Down in New Orleans/I Love You	1959	3.75	7.50	15.00
1002	Shirley/My Love for You	1959	3.75	7.50	15.00
1007	Good Lovin'/You Know You Made Me Cry	1961	2.50	5.00	10.00
2000	Mirror Mirror (On the Wall)/To Have and to Hold	1962	2.50	5.00	10.00
N-JOY					
1005	Boogie Children/My First Love	1965	2.50	5.00	10.00
PAULA					
225	Fortune Teller/Making Love to You	1965	2.00	4.00	8.00
234	Can't I Get a Word In/Sun City	1966	2.00	4.00	8.00
244	Doin' the Best I Can/Leave Her Never	1966	2.00	4.00	8.00
247	Outta My Head/Love Comes in Time	1966	2.00	4.00	8.00
259	Up and Down/Wind-Up Doll	1967	2.00	4.00	8.00
273	Agnes English/Sad Story	1967	2.00	4.00	8.00
282	Judy in Disguise (With Glasses)/When the Lights Go Out	1967	3.00	6.00	12.00
—White label					
282	Judy in Disguise (With Glasses)/When the Lights Go Out	1967	2.50	5.00	10.00
—Yellow label					
282	Judy in Disguise (With Glasses)/When the Lights Go Out	1967	2.00	4.00	8.00
—Pink label					
294	Hey Hey Bunny/No Letter Today	1968	2.00	4.00	8.00
303	Lonely Are the Lonely/We Played Games	1968	2.00	4.00	8.00
310	Tissue Paper/Little Dum Dum	1968	2.00	4.00	8.00
315	What Is Happiness/Sometimes You Just Can't Win	1968	2.00	4.00	8.00
PHILCO-FORD					
HP-25	Judy in Disguise/No Letter Today	1968	5.00	10.00	20.00
—4-inch plastic "Hip Pocket Record" with color sleeve					
SUGARCANE					
1001	Keep It Hid/You Had to Be a Woman	1975	—	2.00	4.00
1002	Jukebox Shirley/Hey, Good Lookin'	1975	—	2.00	4.00
UNI					
55135	Back in the U.S.S.R./Silly Sarah Carter	1969	—	3.00	6.00
55160	Open Doors/Three Deep Is a Feeling	1969	—	3.00	6.00
55187	Love My Soul/Julia Julia	1969	—	3.00	6.00
55220	Come with Me/Where's Everybody Going	1970	—	3.00	6.00
Albums					
JIN					
9027	The Best of John Fred and His Playboys	198?	2.50	5.00	10.00
PAULA					
LP-2191 [M]	John Fred and His Playboys	1966	5.00	10.00	20.00
LPS-2191 [S]	John Fred and His Playboys	1966	6.25	12.50	25.00
LP-2193 [M]	34:40 of John Fred and His Playboys	1967	5.00	10.00	20.00
LPS-2193 [S]	34:40 of John Fred and His Playboys	1967	6.25	12.50	25.00
LP-2197 [M]	Agnes English	1967	6.25	12.50	25.00
LPS-2197 [S]	Agnes English	1967	5.00	10.00	20.00
LPS-2197 [S]	Judy in Disguise with Glasses	1968	5.00	10.00	20.00
—Retitled version of "Agnes English"					
LPS-2201	Permanently Stated	1969	5.00	10.00	20.00
UNI					
73077	Love in My Soul	1970	10.00	20.00	40.00

FREDDIE AND THE DREAMERS

Number	Title (A Side/B Side)	Yr	VG	VG+	NM
45s					
CAPITOL					
5053	I'm Telling You Now/What Have I Done to You	1963	5.00	10.00	20.00
5137	You Were Made for Me/Send a Letter to Me	1964	5.00	10.00	20.00
MERCURY					
72285	I Love You Baby/Don't Make Me Cry	1965	2.50	5.00	10.00
72285 [PS]	I Love You Baby/Don't Make Me Cry	1965	5.00	10.00	20.00
72327	Don't Do That to Me/Just for You	1965	2.50	5.00	10.00
72377	I Understand (Just How You Feel)/I Will	1965	2.50	5.00	10.00
72428	Do the Freddie/Tell Me When	1965	2.50	5.00	10.00
72428	Do the Freddie/A Love Like You	1965	3.00	6.00	12.00
72462	A Little You/Things I'd Like to Say	1965	2.50	5.00	10.00
72487	I Don't Know/Windmill in Old Amsterdam	1965	2.50	5.00	10.00
72487 [PS]	I Don't Know/Windmill in Old Amsterdam	1965	5.00	10.00	20.00
72548	When I'm Home with You/If You Got a Minute Baby	1966	2.50	5.00	10.00
72604	Some Day/Short Shorts	1966	2.50	5.00	10.00
SUPER K					
146	She Needs Me/Susan's Tuba	1970	2.00	4.00	8.00
TOWER					
125	I'm Telling You Now/What Have I Done to You	1964	3.75	7.50	15.00
127	You Were Made for Me/Send a Letter to Me	1965	5.00	10.00	20.00
127	You Were Made for Me/So Fine	1965	3.75	7.50	15.00
—B-side: "Introducing the Beat Merchants"					
163	Send a Letter to Me/There's Not One Thing	1965	3.75	7.50	15.00
—B-side by 4 Just Men					
UNITED ARTISTS					
50239	Come Back When You Grow Up/Oh What a Lovely Day	1967	—	—	—
—Unreleased					
7-Inch Extended Plays					
MERCURY					
SRC 661-C	Thou Shalt Not Steal/Funny Over You/He Got What He Wanted//I Fell in Love with Your Picture/I Think of You/Some Other Guy	1965	5.00	10.00	20.00
—Jukebox mini-LP					
SRC 661-C [PS]	Fun Lovin' Freddie	1965	5.00	10.00	20.00
Albums					
CAPITOL					
SM-11896 [B]	The Best of Freddie and the Dreamers	1976	2.50	5.00	10.00
—"I'm Telling You Now," "You Were Made for Me," "I Just Don't Understand," "A Little You" and "Over You" are in stereo, the rest are mono.					
MERCURY					
MG-21017 [M]	Freddie and the Dreamers	1965	6.25	12.50	25.00
MG-21026 [M]	Do the Freddie	1965	5.00	10.00	20.00
MG-21031 [M]	Seaside Swingers	1965	5.00	10.00	20.00
MG-21053 [M]	Frantic Freddie	1965	3.75	7.50	15.00
MG-21061 [M]	Fun Lovin' Freddie	1966	3.75	7.50	15.00
SR-61017 [R]	Freddie and the Dreamers	1965	5.00	10.00	20.00
SR-61026 [S]	Do the Freddie	1965	6.25	12.50	25.00
SR-61031 [S]	Seaside Swingers	1965	6.25	12.50	25.00
SR-61053 [S]	Frantic Freddie	1965	5.00	10.00	20.00
SR-61061 [S]	Fun Lovin' Freddie	1966	5.00	10.00	20.00
TOWER					
DT 5003 [R]	I'm Telling You Now	1965	5.00	10.00	20.00
—Contains only two Freddie and the Dreamers songs, but the group's picture is on the cover. Also includes Four Just Men (2), Heinz (2), Linda Laine and the Sinners (2), Mike Rabin and the Demons (2) and The Toggery Five (2)					
T 5003 [M]	I'm Telling You Now	1965	6.25	12.50	25.00
—Contains only two Freddie and the Dreamers songs, but the group's picture is on the cover. Also includes Four Just Men (2), Heinz (2), Linda Laine and the Sinners (2), Mike Rabin and the Demons (2) and The Toggery Five (2)					

FREDDIE AND THE PARLIAMENTS

Number	Title (A Side/B Side)	Yr	VG	VG+	NM
45s					
TWIRL					
1003	Darlene/That Girl	1959	25.00	50.00	100.00

FREDRIC

Number	Title (A Side/B Side)	Yr	VG	VG+	NM
45s					
EVOLUTION					
1001	Five O'Clock Traffic/Red Pier	1968	6.25	12.50	25.00
FORTE					
3001	Five O'Clock Traffic/Red Pier	1968	10.00	20.00	40.00
Albums					
FORTE					
80461	Phases and Faces	1968	200.00	400.00	800.00

FREE

Also see PAUL KOSSOFF.

45s

A&M

Number	Title (A Side/B Side)	Yr	VG	VG+	NM
1099	I'm a Mover/Worry	1969	—	2.00	4.00
1172	I'll Be Creepin'/Mouthful of Grass	1970	—	2.00	4.00
1206	All Right Now/Mouthful of Grass	1970	—	2.50	5.00
1230	Stealer/Broad Daylight	1970	—	2.00	4.00
1248	Highway Song/Love You So	1971	—	2.00	4.00
1266	Mr. Big/I'll Be Creepin'	1971	—	2.00	4.00
1276	My Brother Jake/Only My Soul	1971	—	2.00	4.00
1352	Little Bit of Love/Sail On	1972	—	2.00	4.00
1720	All Right Now/Stealer	1975	—	2.00	4.00

ISLAND

Number	Title (A Side/B Side)	Yr	VG	VG+	NM
1212	Wishing Well/Let Me Show You	1972	—	2.00	4.00

Albums

A&M

Number	Title (A Side/B Side)	Yr	VG	VG+	NM
SP-3126	Fire and Water	198?	2.00	4.00	8.00
—Budget-line reissue					
SP-3663	Best of Free	1975	3.00	6.00	12.00
SP-4198	Tons of Sobs	1969	3.75	7.50	15.00
SP-4204	Free	1969	3.75	7.50	15.00
SP-4268	Fire and Water	1970	3.75	7.50	15.00
SP-4287	Highway	1971	3.75	7.50	15.00
SP-4306	Free Live!	1971	3.75	7.50	15.00
SP-4349	Free at Last	1972	3.75	7.50	15.00

ISLAND

Number	Title (A Side/B Side)	Yr	VG	VG+	NM
ILSD 4 [(2)]	The Free Story	1975	3.75	7.50	15.00
ILPS 9217	Heartbreaker	1975	2.50	5.00	10.00
—U.S. reissue with same number as original U.K. issue					
SW-9324	Heartbreaker	1973	3.00	6.00	12.00
—Original U.S. number, distributed by Capitol					

FREE BAND, THE

Albums

VANGUARD

Number	Title (A Side/B Side)	Yr	VG	VG+	NM
VSD-6507	The Free Band	1969	5.00	10.00	20.00

FREE DESIGN, THE

45s

PROJECT 3

Number	Title (A Side/B Side)	Yr	VG	VG+	NM
1324	Kites Are Fun/Proper Ornaments	1967	2.00	4.00	8.00
1331	You Be You and I'll Be Me/Never Tell the World	1967	2.00	4.00	8.00
1336	I Found Love/Umbrellas	1968	2.00	4.00	8.00
1345	Eleanor Rigby/Make the Madness Stop	1968	2.00	4.00	8.00
1347 [DJ]	Close Your Mouth (It's Christmas)/Christmas Is The Day	1968	2.50	5.00	10.00
—Stock copy may not exist					
1350	You Could Be Born Again/A Leaf Has Veins	1968	2.00	4.00	8.00
1356	Where Do I Go/Girls Alone	1969	2.00	4.00	8.00
1358	Summertime/Dorian Benediction	1969	2.00	4.00	8.00
1360	If I Were a Carpenter/Now Is the Time	1969	2.00	4.00	8.00
1366	2002: A Hit Song/Hurry Sundown	1969	2.00	4.00	8.00
1370	Butterflies Are Free/(B-side unknown)	1970	2.00	4.00	8.00
1375	I'm a Yogi/Bubbles	1970	2.00	4.00	8.00
1383	Tomorrow Is the First Day of the Rest of My Life/Kije's Ouija	1970	2.00	4.00	8.00
1393	Felt So Good/You Are My Sunshine	1971	2.00	4.00	8.00
1404	Stay Off of Your Frown/Friendly Man	1971	2.00	4.00	8.00

Albums

AMBROTYPE

Number	Title (A Side/B Side)	Yr	VG	VG+	NM
1016	There Is a Song	1972	12.50	25.00	50.00

PROJECT 3

Number	Title (A Side/B Side)	Yr	VG	VG+	NM
PR 4006 SD	The Free Design Sing for Very Important People	1970	6.25	12.50	25.00
PR-5019 SD	Kites Are Fun	1967	6.25	12.50	25.00
PR-5031 SD	You Could Be Born Again	1968	6.25	12.50	25.00
PR-5037 SD	Heaven/Earth	1969	6.25	12.50	25.00
PR-5045 SD	Stars/Times/Bubbles/Love	1971	6.25	12.50	25.00
PR-5061 SD	One By One	1971	6.25	12.50	25.00

FREE MOVEMENT, THE

45s

COLUMBIA

Number	Title (A Side/B Side)	Yr	VG	VG+	NM
45512	The Harder I Try (The Bluer I Get)/Comin' Home	1972	—	2.50	5.00
45567	Could You Believe in a Dream/Love the One You're With	1972	—	2.50	5.00
45778	Every Step of the Way/I Can't Move No Mountains	1973	—	2.50	5.00

DECCA

Number	Title (A Side/B Side)	Yr	VG	VG+	NM
32818	I've Found Someone of My Own/I Can't Convince My Heart	1971	—	3.00	6.00

Albums

COLUMBIA

Number	Title (A Side/B Side)	Yr	VG	VG+	NM
KC 31136	I've Found Someone of My Own	1972	3.75	7.50	15.00

FREEBORNE

Albums

MONITOR

Number	Title (A Side/B Side)	Yr	VG	VG+	NM
MPS-607	Peak Impressions	1967	25.00	50.00	100.00

FREED, ALAN

Also see VARIOUS ARTISTS COLLECTIONS.

45s

CORAL

Number	Title (A Side/B Side)	Yr	VG	VG+	NM
61626	Right Now, Right Now/Tina's Cantine	1956	7.50	15.00	30.00
61660	THe Camel Rock/I Don't Need Lotsa Money	1956	7.50	15.00	30.00
61693	The Space Man/Jazzbo's Theory	1956	7.50	15.00	30.00
—With Al "Jazzbo" Collins and the Modernaires					
61749	Rock 'N' Roll Boogie/The Grey Bear	1956	10.00	20.00	40.00
61818	Sentimental Journey/Stop! Look! and Run!	1957	10.00	20.00	40.00

Albums

BRUNSWICK

Number	Title (A Side/B Side)	Yr	VG	VG+	NM
BL 54043 [M]	The Alan Freed Rock 'n' Roll Show	1959	37.50	75.00	150.00

CORAL

Number	Title (A Side/B Side)	Yr	VG	VG+	NM
CRL 57063 [M]	Alan Freed's Rock 'n' Roll Dance Party, Vol. 1	1956	37.50	75.00	150.00
CRL 57115 [M]	Alan Freed's Rock 'n' Roll Dance Party, Vol. 2	1957	37.50	75.00	150.00
CRL 57177 [M]	Go Go Go — Alan Freed's TV Record Hop	1957	37.50	75.00	150.00
CRL 57213 [M]	Rock Around the Block	1958	37.50	75.00	150.00
CRL 57216 [M]	Alan Freed Presents the King's Henchmen	1958	37.50	75.00	150.00

MGM

Number	Title (A Side/B Side)	Yr	VG	VG+	NM
E-293 [10]	The Big Beat	195?	50.00	100.00	200.00

FREEMAN, ART

45s

FAME

Number	Title (A Side/B Side)	Yr	VG	VG+	NM
1008	I Can't Get You Out of My Mind/Slippin' Around with You	1966	12.50	25.00	50.00
1012	A Piece of My Heart/Everybody's Got to Cry Sometime	1966	7.50	15.00	30.00

FREEMAN, ARTHUR

45s

EXCELLO

Number	Title (A Side/B Side)	Yr	VG	VG+	NM
2322	Here I Am/Played Out Play Girl	1971	5.00	10.00	20.00

FREEMAN, BOBBY

45s

AUTUMN

Number	Title (A Side/B Side)	Yr	VG	VG+	NM
1	Come to Me/Let's Surf Again	1964	5.00	10.00	20.00
2	C'mon and Swim/C'mon and Swim — Part 2	1964	3.00	6.00	12.00
—White label, red print					
2	C'mon and Swim/C'mon and Swim — Part 2	1964	2.50	5.00	10.00
—Tan label					
5	S-W-I-M/That Little Old Heartbreaker	1964	2.50	5.00	10.00
9	I'll Never Fall in Love Again/Friends	1965	2.50	5.00	10.00
25	Cross My Heart/The Duck	1965	2.50	5.00	10.00

DOUBLE SHOT

Number	Title (A Side/B Side)	Yr	VG	VG+	NM
139	There Oughta Be a Law/Everybody's Got a Hang-Up	1969	—	3.00	6.00
144	Susie Sunshine/Four Piece Funky Nitty Gritty Junky Band	1969	—	3.00	6.00
148	Can You Stand the Pressure/Put Another Dime in the Parking Meter	1970	—	3.00	6.00
152	Do You Wanna Dance 1970/Society for the Prevention of Cruelty to People	1970	—	3.00	6.00

JOSIE

Number	Title (A Side/B Side)	Yr	VG	VG+	NM
835	Do You Want to Dance/Big Fat Woman	1958	5.00	10.00	20.00
841	Betty Lou Got a New Pair of Shoes/Starlight	1958	5.00	10.00	20.00
844	Need Your Love/Shame On You, Miss Johnson	1958	3.75	7.50	15.00
855	A Love to Last a Lifetime/When You're Smiling	1959	3.75	7.50	15.00
863	Love Me/Mary Ann Thomas	1959	3.75	7.50	15.00
867	My Guardian Angel/Where Did My Baby Go	1959	3.75	7.50	15.00
872	Ebb Tide/Sinbad	1959	3.75	7.50	15.00
879	I Need Someone/First Day of Spring	1960	3.00	6.00	12.00
886	Miss You So/Baby What Would You Do	1961	3.00	6.00	12.00
887	The Mess Around/So Much to Do	1961	3.00	6.00	12.00
889	Put You Down/She Said She Wants to Dance	1961	3.00	6.00	12.00
896	Love Me/Little Girl Don't You Understand	1962	3.00	6.00	12.00
928	The Mess Around/Little Girl Don't You Understand	1965	2.50	5.00	10.00

KING

Number	Title (A Side/B Side)	Yr	VG	VG+	NM
5373	Shimmy Shimmy/You Don't Understand	1960	3.00	6.00	12.00
5953	Fever/What Can I Do	1964	2.50	5.00	10.00
5962	Somebody, Somewhere/Be My Little Chick-A-Dee	1964	2.50	5.00	10.00
5975	Come to Me/There's Gonna Be a Change	1965	2.50	5.00	10.00

LOMA

Number	Title (A Side/B Side)	Yr	VG	VG+	NM
2056	Shadow of Your Love/Soulful Sound of Music	1966	2.00	4.00	8.00
2080	I Got a Good Thing/Lies	1967	2.00	4.00	8.00

PARKWAY

Number	Title (A Side/B Side)	Yr	VG	VG+	NM
875	She's a Hippy/Whip It Up Baby	1963	3.00	6.00	12.00

Albums

AUTUMN

Number	Title (A Side/B Side)	Yr	VG	VG+	NM
LP 102 [M]	C'mon and S-W-I-M	1964	12.50	25.00	50.00

JOSIE

Number	Title (A Side/B Side)	Yr	VG	VG+	NM
JM-4007 [M]	Get In the Swim with Bobby Freeman	1965	7.50	15.00	30.00
JS-4007 [R]	Get In the Swim with Bobby Freeman	1965	6.25	12.50	25.00

JUBILEE

Number	Title (A Side/B Side)	Yr	VG	VG+	NM
JLP-1086 [M]	Do You Wanna Dance?	1959	35.00	70.00	140.00
JLPS-1086 [S]	Do You Wanna Dance?	1959	50.00	100.00	200.00
JGM-5010 [M]	Twist with Bobby Freeman	1962	25.00	50.00	100.00

KING

Number	Title (A Side/B Side)	Yr	VG	VG+	NM
930 [M]	The Lovable Style of Bobby Freeman	1965	62.50	125.00	250.00

FREEMAN, ERNIE

45s

AVA

Number	Title (A Side/B Side)	Yr	VG	VG+	NM
176	Raunchy '65/Jivin' Around	1965	2.00	4.00	8.00

CASH

Number	Title (A Side/B Side)	Yr	VG	VG+	NM
1017	Jivin' Around (Part 1)/Jivin' Around (Part 2)	1955	3.75	7.50	15.00

IMPERIAL

Number	Title (A Side/B Side)	Yr	VG	VG+	NM
5381	Rockin' Around/Lost Dreams	1956	3.75	7.50	15.00
5391	Rainy Day/Funny Face	1956	3.75	7.50	15.00
5403	Spring Fever/Walking the Beat	1956	3.75	7.50	15.00
5419	Return to Me/A Touch of the Blues	1957	3.75	7.50	15.00
5430	Without Love/Night Life	1957	3.75	7.50	15.00
5444	Swing It/River Boat	1957	3.75	7.50	15.00
5461	Dumplin's/Beautiful Weekend	1957	3.75	7.50	15.00
5474	Raunchy/Puddin'	1957	6.25	12.50	25.00
5486	The Tuttle/Leaps and Bounds	1958	3.00	6.00	12.00
5518	Indian Love Call/Summer Serenade	1958	3.00	6.00	12.00
5527	Rose Marie/After Sunset	1958	3.00	6.00	12.00

Number	Title (A Side/B Side)	Yr	VG	VG+	NM
5541	Jamboree/Junior Jive	1958	3.00	6.00	12.00
5551	School Room Rock/Blues After Hours	1958	3.00	6.00	12.00
5566	Live It Up/Whispering Hope (Freedom and Land)	1959	2.50	5.00	10.00
5574	Marshmallows, Popcorn & Soda Pop/Honey Dripper	1959	2.50	5.00	10.00
5612	A Summer Love/Always with You	1959	2.50	5.00	10.00
5621	Lost Dreams/One More Time Around	1959	2.50	5.00	10.00
5633	Big River/Night Sounds	1959	2.50	5.00	10.00
5656	Rockin' Red Wing/Dark Eyes	1960	2.00	4.00	8.00
5677	Autumn and Eve/Prayer	1960	2.00	4.00	8.00
5693	Theme from "The Dark at the Top of the Stairs"/ Come On Home	1960	2.00	4.00	8.00
5716	Hawaiian Eye/Heartbreak Hotel	1960	2.00	4.00	8.00
5732	Swamp Meeting/That's All	1961	2.00	4.00	8.00
5752	Theme from "Return to Peyton Place"/Warsaw Concerto	1961	2.00	4.00	8.00
5769	Conquest/Swingin' Preacher	1961	2.00	4.00	8.00
5793	The Twist/Shine On Harvest Moon	1961	2.00	4.00	8.00
5815	What Am I Living For/I Didn't Want to Do It	1962	2.00	4.00	8.00
5841	The Stripper/I Hear You Knocking	1962	2.00	4.00	8.00
5883	The Freeloader/Say It Isn't So	1962	2.00	4.00	8.00
LIBERTY					
55515	Half as Much/I'm Sorry for You My Friend	1962	2.00	4.00	8.00

Albums

Number	Title	Yr	VG	VG+	NM
DUNHILL					
D 50026 [M]	Hitmaker	1967	3.00	6.00	12.00
DS 50026 [S]	Hitmaker	1967	3.75	7.50	15.00
IMPERIAL					
LP-9022 [M]	Ernie Freeman Plays Irving Berlin	1957	12.50	25.00	50.00
LP-9030 [M]	Jivin' Around	1957	12.50	25.00	50.00
LP-9057 [M]	Ernie Freeman	1958	12.50	25.00	50.00
LP-9148 [M]	Raunchy	1960	12.50	25.00	50.00
LP-9157 [M]	Twistin' Time	1961	7.50	15.00	30.00
LP-9193 [M]	The Stripper	1962	5.00	10.00	20.00
LP-12067 [S]	Dark at the Top of the Stairs	1959	10.00	20.00	40.00
LP-12081 [S]	Twistin' Time	1961	10.00	20.00	40.00
LP-12193 [S]	The Stripper	1962	6.25	12.50	25.00
LP- [M]	Dark at the Top of the Stairs	1959	7.50	15.00	30.00
LIBERTY					
LRP-3283 [M]	Limbo Dance Party	1962	5.00	10.00	20.00
LRP-3331 [M]	Comin' Home Baby	1963	5.00	10.00	20.00
LST-7263 [S]	Limbo Dance Party	1962	6.25	12.50	25.00
LST-7331 [S]	Comin' Home Baby	1963	6.25	12.50	25.00

FREEMAN BROTHERS, THE

45s

Number	Title	Yr	VG	VG+	NM
MALA					
553	I'm Counting on You/Everyday It's You	1966	6.25	12.50	25.00
SOUL					
35011	My Baby/Beautiful Brown Eyes	1965	10.00	20.00	40.00

FREEPORT

45s

Number	Title	Yr	VG	VG+	NM
MAINSTREAM					
730	I Need Your Lovin'/(B-side unknown)	1970	2.50	5.00	10.00
732	Now That She's Gone/Misunderstood	1970	2.50	5.00	10.00

Albums

Number	Title	Yr	VG	VG+	NM
MAINSTREAM					
S-6130	Freeport	1970	12.50	25.00	50.00

FREEWHEELERS, THE

45s

Number	Title	Yr	VG	VG+	NM
EPIC					
9664	Walk, Walk/The Best of It	1964	5.00	10.00	20.00
9700	San Francisco Bay Blues/Susu	1964	5.00	10.00	20.00
9725	Beach Boy/Annie	1964	3.75	7.50	15.00

FRIAR TUCK

Curt Boetcher was in the group.

45s

Number	Title	Yr	VG	VG+	NM
BANSHEE					
100	The Return of Robin Hood/(B-side unknown)	196?	3.75	7.50	15.00
MERCURY					
72684	Alley-Oop/Sweet Pea	1967	2.50	5.00	10.00

Albums

Number	Title	Yr	VG	VG+	NM
MERCURY					
MG-21111 [M]	Friar Tuck and His Psychedelic Guitar	1967	10.00	20.00	40.00
SR-61111 [S]	Friar Tuck and His Psychedelic Guitar	1967	12.50	25.00	50.00

FRIEDMAN, KINKY

45s

Number	Title	Yr	VG	VG+	NM
ABC					
12073	Lover Please/Autograph	1975	—	2.50	5.00
12107	Wild Man from Borneo/Popeye the Sailor Man	1975	—	2.50	5.00
EPIC					
50299	Catfish/Dear Abby	1976	—	2.00	4.00
VANGUARD					
35173	Sold American/Western Union Wire	1973	—	3.00	6.00

Albums

Number	Title	Yr	VG	VG+	NM
ABC					
X-829	Kinky Friedman	1974	2.50	5.00	10.00
EPIC					
PE 34304	Lasso from El Paso	1976	2.50	5.00	10.00
VANGUARD					
VSD-79333	Sold American	1973	3.00	6.00	12.00

FRIEND AND LOVER

45s

Number	Title	Yr	VG	VG+	NM
ABC					
10910	Town Called Love/If Tomorrow	1967	3.00	6.00	12.00
CADET CONCEPT					
7019	Hard Lovin'/Colorado Exile	1970	—	3.00	6.00
7019 [PS]	Hard Lovin'/Colorado Exile	1970	3.75	7.50	15.00
VERVE FORECAST					
5069	Reach Out of the Darkness/Time on Your Side (You're Only 15 Years Old)	1967	2.50	5.00	10.00
5091	If Love Is In Your Heart/Zig Zag	1968	2.00	4.00	8.00
5100	I Want to Be Free/Circus	1968	2.00	4.00	8.00
5106	Ode to a Dandelion/A Wise Man Changes His Mind	1969	—	3.00	6.00

Albums

Number	Title	Yr	VG	VG+	NM
VERVE FORECAST					
FTS-3055	Reach Out of the Darkness	1968	5.00	10.00	20.00

FRIENDLY TORPEDOES, THE

45s

Number	Title	Yr	VG	VG+	NM
ORIGINAL SOUND					
95	Nothing's Too Good for My Car/So Long Ago	1970	6.25	12.50	25.00

FRIENDS OF DISTINCTION, THE

45s

Number	Title	Yr	VG	VG+	NM
RCA VICTOR					
PB-10197	Honey Baby Theme Part 1/Honey Baby Theme Part 2	1975	—	2.00	4.00
PB-10220	Love Shack Part 1/Love Shack Part 2	1975	—	2.00	4.00
74-0107	Grazing in the Grass/I Really Hope You Do	1969	—	3.00	6.00
74-0204	Going in Circles/Let Yourself Go	1969	—	3.00	6.00
74-0319	Love Or Let Me Be Lonely/This Generation	1970	—	3.00	6.00
74-0385	Time Waits for No One/Mother Nature	1970	—	2.50	5.00
74-0416	Check It Out/I Need You	1971	—	2.50	5.00
74-0516	It Don't Matter to Me/Down I Go	1971	—	2.50	5.00
74-0562	Let Me Be/Long Time Comin' My Way	1971	—	2.50	5.00
74-0679	Love Is the Way of Life/Jenny Wants to Know	1972	—	2.50	5.00
74-0787	Now Is the Time/Thumb Tripping	1972	—	2.50	5.00
74-0888	Ain't No Woman (Like the One I've Got)/Easy Evil	1973	—	2.50	5.00
74-0956	Check It Out/Love Can Make It Easier	1973	—	2.50	5.00

Albums

Number	Title	Yr	VG	VG+	NM
RCA VICTOR					
APD1-0276	Greatest Hits	1973	5.00	10.00	20.00
LSP-4149	Grazin'	1969	3.75	7.50	15.00
LSP-4212	Highly Distinct	1969	3.75	7.50	15.00
LSP-4313	Real Friends	1970	3.75	7.50	15.00
LSP-4408	Whatever	1970	3.75	7.50	15.00
LSP-4492	Friends & People	1971	3.75	7.50	15.00
LSP-4819	Greatest Hits	1972	3.00	6.00	12.00
LSP-4829	Love Can Make It Easier	1973	3.00	6.00	12.00

FRIJID PINK

45s

Number	Title	Yr	VG	VG+	NM
LION					
115	Earth Omen/Lazy Day	1972	2.00	4.00	8.00
136	Go Now/Lazy Day	1972	2.00	4.00	8.00
158	Big Betty/Shady Lady	1973	—	3.00	6.00
PARROT					
334	Tell Me Why/Cryin' Shame	1969	—	3.00	6.00
340	God Gave Me You/Drivin' Blues	1970	—	3.00	6.00
341	House of the Rising Sun/Drivin' Blues	1970	2.00	4.00	8.00
349	Sing a Song for Freedom/End of the Line	1970	—	3.00	6.00
352	Heartbreak Hotel/Bye Bye Blues	1970	—	3.00	6.00
355	Music for the People/Sloony	1971	—	3.00	6.00
358	We're Gonna Be There/Shorty Kline	1971	—	3.00	6.00
360	Lost Son/I Love Her	1971	—	3.00	6.00

Albums

Number	Title	Yr	VG	VG+	NM
FANTASY					
9464	All Pink Inside	1974	3.75	7.50	15.00
LION					
LN-1004	Earth Omen	1972	5.00	10.00	20.00
PARROT					
PAS 71033	Frijid Pink	1970	6.25	12.50	25.00
PAS 71041	Defrosted	1970	6.25	12.50	25.00

FROGGIE BEAVER

Albums

Number	Title	Yr	VG	VG+	NM
FROGGIE BEAVER					
7301	From the Pond	1973	12.50	25.00	50.00

FROGMEN, THE

45s

Number	Title	Yr	VG	VG+	NM
ASTRA					
1009	Underwater/The Mad Rush	196?	12.50	25.00	50.00
1010	Beware Below/Tioga	196?	12.50	25.00	50.00
—The above two are East Coast reissues					
CANDIX					
314	Underwater/The Mad Rush	1961	6.25	12.50	25.00
326	Beware Below/Tioga	1961	6.25	12.50	25.00
SCOTT					
101	Seahorse Flats/Tioga	1961	12.50	25.00	50.00
102	Underwater/Beware Below	1961	12.50	25.00	50.00
TEE JAY					
131	Sea Haunt/Diamond Back	1964	20.00	40.00	80.00
—Blue vinyl					

FROLK HEAVEN

Albums

Number	Title	Yr	VG	VG+	NM
LRS					
RF-6023	At the Apex of High	197?	100.00	200.00	400.00

FRONT PAGE NEWS

45s

Number	Title	Yr	VG	VG+	NM
DIAL					
4052	Thoughts/You Better Behave	1967	6.25	12.50	25.00

FROST, FRANK

45s

Number	Title (A Side/B Side)	Yr	VG	VG+	NM
JEWEL					
765	My Back Scratcher/Harp and Soul	1966	3.75	7.50	15.00
771	Things You Do/Harpin' On It	1966	3.75	7.50	15.00
778	Pocketful of Money/Ride with Your Daddy Tonight	1967	5.00	10.00	20.00
PHILLIPS INTERNATIONAL					
3578	Jelly Roll King/Crawlback	1962	5.00	10.00	20.00

Albums

Number	Title (A Side/B Side)	Yr	VG	VG+	NM
EARWIG					
4901	Rockin' the Juke Joint Down	1986	2.50	5.00	10.00
4914	Midnight Prowler	1990	2.50	5.00	10.00
JEWEL					
LPS-5013	Frank Frost	1973	3.75	7.50	15.00
PHILLIPS INTERNATIONAL					
PLP-1975 [M]	Hey Boss Man!	1961	1500.	2250.	3000.

FROST, MAX, AND THE TROOPERS

45s

Number	Title (A Side/B Side)	Yr	VG	VG+	NM
SIDEWALK					
938	There Is a Party Going On/Stomper's Ride	1968	3.75	7.50	15.00
TOWER					
419	Shape of Things to Come/Free Lovin'	1968	3.75	7.50	15.00
452	52%/Max Frost Theme	1968	3.75	7.50	15.00
452 [PS]	52%/Max Frost Theme	1968	5.00	10.00	20.00
478	Paxton Quigley's Had the Course/Sittin' in Circles	1969	3.75	7.50	15.00
478 [PS]	Paxton Quigley's Had the Course/Sittin' in Circles	1969	5.00	10.00	20.00

Albums

Number	Title (A Side/B Side)	Yr	VG	VG+	NM
TOWER					
ST-5147	Shape of Things to Come	1968	12.50	25.00	50.00

FROST, THE

45s

Number	Title (A Side/B Side)	Yr	VG	VG+	NM
DATE					
1577	Bad Girl/Rainy Day	1967	3.00	6.00	12.00
—As "Dick Wagner and the Frosts"					
1596	Little Girl/Sunshine	1968	3.00	6.00	12.00
—As "Dick Wagner and the Frosts"					
VANGUARD					
35099	Linda/Sweet Lady Love	1969	2.00	4.00	8.00
35111	Rock and Roll Music/Donny's Blues	1969	2.00	4.00	8.00
35115	A Long Way from Home/Black As Night	1970	2.00	4.00	8.00

Albums

Number	Title (A Side/B Side)	Yr	VG	VG+	NM
VANGUARD					
VSD-6520	Frost Music	1969	5.00	10.00	20.00
VSD-6541	Rock and Roll Music	1969	5.00	10.00	20.00
VSD-6556	Through the Eyes of Love	1970	5.00	10.00	20.00
VSD-79392	Early Frost	1978	3.75	7.50	15.00

FRUMIOUS BANDERSNATCH

7-Inch Extended Plays

Number	Title (A Side/B Side)	Yr	VG	VG+	NM
MUGGLES GRAMOPHONE WORKS					
(no #)	(contents unknown)	1967	62.50	125.00	250.00
—Legitimate copies show purple vinyl when held to a light. All others are bootlegs.					
(no #) [PS]	Frumious Bandersnatch	1967	62.50	125.00	250.00

FRUMMOX

45s

Number	Title (A Side/B Side)	Yr	VG	VG+	NM
PROBE					
470	Mary Martin/There You Go	1970	2.00	4.00	8.00

Albums

Number	Title (A Side/B Side)	Yr	VG	VG+	NM
PROBE					
4511	From Here to There	1970	3.75	7.50	15.00

FRUT

45s

Number	Title (A Side/B Side)	Yr	VG	VG+	NM
WESTBOUND					
189	Prison of Love/Send Me Down	1972	2.50	5.00	10.00

Albums

Number	Title (A Side/B Side)	Yr	VG	VG+	NM
TRASH					
(# unknown)	Keep On Truckin'	1971	20.00	40.00	80.00
—Originals on yellow vinyl					
WESTBOUND					
WB-2005	Keep On Truckin'	1971	7.50	15.00	30.00
—Reissue of Trash LP					
WB-2008	Spoiled Rotten	1972	7.50	15.00	30.00

FRYE, DAVID

45s

Number	Title (A Side/B Side)	Yr	VG	VG+	NM
BUDDAH					
378 [DJ]	Nixon Meets the Godfather (mono/stereo)	1973	2.50	5.00	10.00
—Promo only?					
ELEKTRA					
45722	My Way/Farm Report	1971	2.50	5.00	10.00

Albums

Number	Title (A Side/B Side)	Yr	VG	VG+	NM
BUDDAH					
1600	Richard Nixon: A Fantasy	1973	3.00	6.00	12.00
BDS-5097	Richard Nixon: Superstar	1971	3.00	6.00	12.00
ELEKTRA					
EKS-74085	Radio Free Nixon	1971	3.00	6.00	12.00
EKS-75006	I Am the President	1969	3.00	6.00	12.00
FRYE					
DFP-80	The Great Debate	1980	3.75	7.50	15.00

FUGS, THE

45s

Number	Title (A Side/B Side)	Yr	VG	VG+	NM
ESP-DISK'					
4507	Frenzy/I Want to Know	1966	3.75	7.50	15.00

Albums

Number	Title (A Side/B Side)	Yr	VG	VG+	NM
BROADSIDE					
304 [M]	The Village Fugs Sing Ballads of Contemporary Protest, Point of View, and General Dissatisfaction	1965	125.00	250.00	500.00
—With insert					
304 [M]	The Village Fugs Sing Ballads of Contemporary Protest, Point of View, and General Dissatisfaction	1965	100.00	200.00	400.00
—Without insert					
ESP-DISK					
1018 [M]	The Fugs First Album	1966	10.00	20.00	40.00
—"Reissue of Broadside 304" on cover					
1018 [M]	The Fugs First Album	1966	37.50	75.00	150.00
—Turquoise and black cover, different from all other versions					
1018 [M]	The Fugs First Album	1967	7.50	15.00	30.00
—No reference to reissue on cover					
1028 [S]	The Fugs	1966	12.50	25.00	50.00
—Black and white cover, back cover photos staggered					
1028 [S]	The Fugs	1966	7.50	5.00	30.00
—Black and white cover, back cover photos aligned					
1028 [S]	The Fugs	1966	20.00	40.00	80.00
—Psychedelic color shield on cover					
1038 [S]	Virgin Fugs	1967	25.00	50.00	100.00
—"For Adult Minds" sticker on cover; with poster, book and stickers					
1038 [S]	Virgin Fugs	1967	12.50	25.00	50.00
—"For Adult Minds" sticker, no inserts					
1038 [S]	Virgin Fugs	1967	12.50	25.00	50.00
—"For Adult Minds" stamped on cover					
1038 [S]	Virgin Fugs	1967	7.50	15.00	30.00
—"For Adult Minds" printed on cover					
2018	Fugs 4, Rounders Score	196?	20.00	40.00	80.00
PVC					
8914	Proto Punk: The Fugs Greatest Hits, Vol. 1	1982	3.75	7.50	15.00
REPRISE					
R-6280 [M]	Tenderness Junction	1968	10.00	20.00	40.00
RS-6280 [S]	Tenderness Junction	1968	7.50	15.00	30.00
RS-6305	It Crawled Into My Hand, Honest	1968	6.25	12.50	25.00
RS-6359	Belle of Avenue A	1969	6.25	12.50	25.00
RS-6396	Golden Fifth	1970	6.25	12.50	25.00

FULL MOON

Albums

Number	Title (A Side/B Side)	Yr	VG	VG+	NM
DOUGLAS					
KZ 31904	Full Moon	1972	3.75	7.50	15.00

FULLER, BOBBY, FOUR

45s

Number	Title (A Side/B Side)	Yr	VG	VG+	NM
CAPITOL					
3038	The Only God I Know/A Name Like Watermelon	1971	5.00	10.00	20.00
DONNA					
1403	Those Memories of You/Our Favorite Martian	1965	50.00	100.00	200.00
—As "Bobby Fuller and the Fantastics"					
EASTWOOD					
345	Not Fade Away/Nervous Breakdown	1962	25.00	50.00	100.00
EXETER					
122	King of the Beach/Wine, Wine, Wine	1964	50.00	100.00	200.00
124	I Fought the Law/She's My Girl	1964	87.50	175.00	350.00
126	Fool of Love/Shakedown	1964	30.00	60.00	120.00
LIBERTY					
55812	Let Her Dance/Another Sad and Lonely Night	1965	7.50	15.00	30.00
MUSTANG					
3004	She's My Girl/Take My Hand	1965	6.25	12.50	25.00
3006	Let Her Dance/Another Sad and Lonely Night	1965	3.75	7.50	15.00
3011	Never to Be Forgotten/You Kissed Me	1965	6.25	12.50	25.00
3012	Let Her Dance/Another Sad and Lonely Night	1965	3.75	7.50	15.00
3014	I Fought the Law/Little Annie Lou	1966	3.75	7.50	15.00
3016	Love's Made a Fool of You/Don't Ever Let Me Know	1966	3.75	7.50	15.00
3018	Magic Touch/My True Love	1966	3.00	6.00	12.00
TODD					
1090	Saturday Night/The Stinger	1963	25.00	50.00	100.00
YUCCA					
140	You're in Love/Guess We'll Fall in Love	1961	20.00	40.00	80.00
—Slow version					
140	You're in Love/Guess We'll Fall in Love	1961	10.00	20.00	40.00
—Fast version					
144	My Heart Jumped/Gently My Love	1961	20.00	40.00	80.00

Albums

Number	Title (A Side/B Side)	Yr	VG	VG+	NM
MUSTANG					
M-900 [M]	KRLA King of the Wheels	1965	37.50	75.00	150.00
MS-900 [S]	KRLA King of the Wheels	1965	50.00	100.00	200.00
M-901 [M]	The Bobby Fuller Four (I Fought the Law)	1966	20.00	40.00	80.00
MS-901 [S]	The Bobby Fuller Four (I Fought the Law)	1966	37.50	75.00	150.00
RHINO					
RNLP-057	The Bobby Fuller Tapes, Vol. 1	1983	2.50	5.00	10.00
RNDF-201	The Best of the Bobby Fuller Four	1981	3.00	6.00	12.00
RNLP 70174	The Best of the Bobby Fuller Four (Golden Archive Series)	1987	2.50	5.00	10.00
VOXX					
VXS 200028	The Bobby Fuller Tapes, Vol. 2	1984	2.50	5.00	10.00

FULLER, JERRY

Also see THE FLEAS; THE FULLER BROTHERS.

45s

Number	Title (A Side/B Side)	Yr	VG	VG+	NM
ABC					
12436	Salt on the Wound/No Time	1978	—	2.00	4.00
BELL					
45233	Rhyme/Thumb Tripping	1972	—	2.50	5.00
45295	Bookends/(B-side unknown)	1972	—	2.50	5.00
45349	Lazy Susan/How Do We Stand	1973	—	2.50	5.00
45433	Arianne/(B-side unknown)	1974	—	2.50	5.00

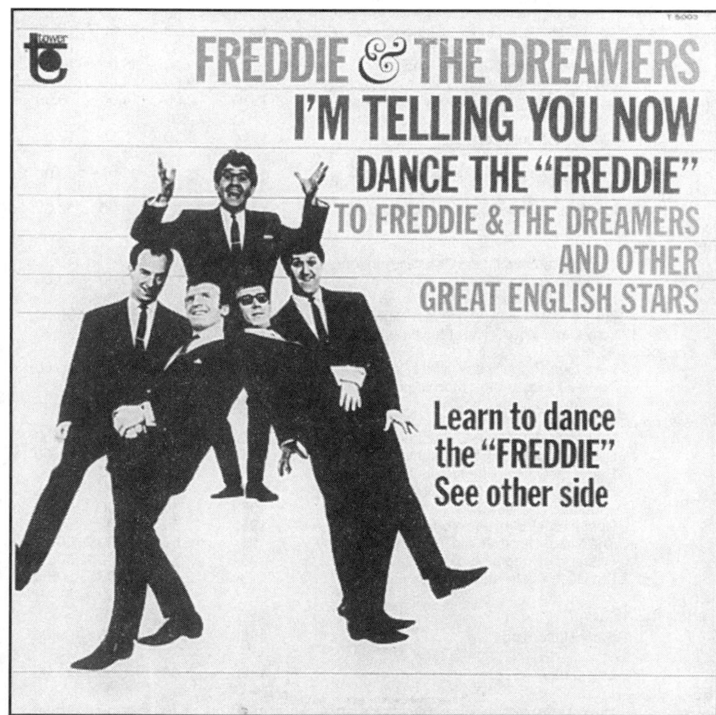

(Top left) The Fendermen, who took their name from the brand of guitars they played, had one hit record, after which this very rare album was named. In near-mint condition, editions on the Soma label go for over a grand, and a rare blue vinyl version for even more. (Top right) How about a rare vocal group record? One of the rarest is the Five Keys' remake of the standard "Red Sails in the Sunset." On the blue Aladdin label, the 45 goes for four figures in almost any condition. (Bottom left) By looking at the cover of this Tower LP, you'd think it was by Freddie and the Dreamers. But you would be only partially correct. It also contains tracks by less well-known British Invasion acts as Heinz, Linda Laine and the Sinners, and the Toggery Five, just to name three. (Bottom right) Long before the song became a hit on the Mustang label, Bobby Fuller recorded his classic "I Fought the Law" on the obscure Exeter label. It's a major collectible today.

Number	Title (A Side/B Side)	Yr	VG	VG+	NM
CHALLENGE					
9114	Guilty of Loving You/First Love Never Dies	1961	5.00	10.00	20.00
9128	The Place Where I Cry/Poor Little Heart	1961	5.00	10.00	20.00
9132	Wake Up Sleeping Beauty/Trust Me	1962	5.00	10.00	20.00
9148	Too Many People/Willingly, I'll Let You Go	1962	5.00	10.00	20.00
9161	Why Do They Say Goodbye/Let Me Be with You	1962	5.00	10.00	20.00
9184	Give My Love to Christy/Dear Teresa	1963	5.00	10.00	20.00
59052	Betty My Angel/Memories of You	1959	7.50	15.00	30.00
59057	Tennessee Waltz/Charlene	1959	5.00	10.00	20.00
59068	Two Loves Have I/I Dreamed About My Lover	1960	5.00	10.00	20.00
59074	Above and Beyond/One Heart	1960	5.00	10.00	20.00
—With Diane Maxwell					
59085	Gone for the Summer/Anna from Louisiana	1960	5.00	10.00	20.00
59104	Shy Away/Heavenly	1961	5.00	10.00	20.00
59217	I Only Came to Dance with You/Young Land	1963	5.00	10.00	20.00
59235	Footprints in the Snow/Hollywood Star	1964	3.75	7.50	15.00
59252	Don't Let Go/Roses Love Sunshine	1964	3.75	7.50	15.00
59269	The Killer/Mi Amora Mi Vidor	1965	3.75	7.50	15.00
59279	I Get Carried Away/Am I That Easy to Forget	1965	7.50	15.00	30.00
59307	Don't Look at Me Like That/What Happened to the Music	1965	3.75	7.50	15.00
59315	Man in Black/Master Plan	1965	3.75	7.50	15.00
59329	Double Life/Turn to Me	1966	6.25	12.50	25.00
COLUMBIA					
45131	Could It Be/I Know We Can Make It	1970	2.00	4.00	8.00
LIN					
5011	Blue Memories/I Found a New Love	1958	7.50	15.00	30.00
5012	Do You Love Me/Teenage Love	1958	7.50	15.00	30.00
5015	A Certain Smile/Angel from Above	1958	7.50	15.00	30.00
5016	The Door Is Open/Through Eternity	1958	7.50	15.00	30.00
5019	Lipstick and Rouge/Mother Goose at the Bandstand	1959	7.50	15.00	30.00
MCA					
41022	Lines/Over You	1979	—	2.00	4.00
41114	Don't Do Anything/Don't Tell Me	1979	—	2.00	4.00
Albums					
LIN					
100 [M]	Teenage Love	1960	62.50	125.00	250.00
MCA					
3170	My Turn Now	1979	3.00	6.00	12.00

FULLER, JOHNNY

45s

Number	Title (A Side/B Side)	Yr	VG	VG+	NM
ALADDIN					
3278	Johnny Ace's Last Letter/Fools Paradise	1955	20.00	40.00	80.00
3286	Cruel, Cruel World/My Heart Beats for You	1955	15.00	30.00	60.00
ART TONE					
828	No More/The Power	1962	5.00	10.00	20.00
CHECKER					
899	You Got Me Whistling/All Night Long	1958	6.25	12.50	25.00
FLAIR					
1054	Buddy/Hard Times	1955	37.50	75.00	150.00
HOLLYWOOD					
1043	Train Train Blues/Bad Luck Overtook Me	1955	20.00	40.00	80.00
1057	Mean Old World/How Long	1956	20.00	40.00	80.00
1063	Comin' Round the Corner/Roughest Place in Town	1956	20.00	40.00	80.00
1077	My Mama Told Me/Too Late to Change My Mind	1956	20.00	40.00	80.00
1084	Sunny Road/I Can't Succeed	1957	20.00	40.00	80.00
IMPERIAL					
5580	Heavenly Love/Whispering Wind	1959	5.00	10.00	20.00
5697	Miss You/Stop, Look and Listen	1960	5.00	10.00	20.00
IRMA					
106	Weeping and Mourning/Strange Land	1958	20.00	40.00	80.00
110	First Stage of the Blues/No More, No More	1958	20.00	40.00	80.00
112	You Got Me Whistling/All Night Long	1958	15.00	30.00	60.00
MONEY					
206	I Walk All Night/These Young Girls	1955	15.00	30.00	60.00
SPECIALTY					
655	Haunted House/The Mighty Hand	1959	5.00	10.00	20.00
671	Swingin' at the Creek/Many Rivers, Mighty Seas	1959	5.00	10.00	20.00

FULLER BROTHERS, THE

Also see JERRY FULLER.

45s

Number	Title (A Side/B Side)	Yr	VG	VG+	NM
CHALLENGE					
9119	Moon River/Framed, Convicted and Condemned	1961	5.00	10.00	20.00
9145	Ballad of the Midnight Special/The Gallows Tree	1962	5.00	10.00	20.00

FULSON, LOWELL

Also recorded as "Lowell Folsom" and "Lowell Fulsom," both included below.

45s

Number	Title (A Side/B Side)	Yr	VG	VG+	NM
ALADDIN					
3088	Double Trouble/Good Woman Blues	1951	37.50	75.00	150.00
3104	Night and Day/Stormin' and Rainin'	1951	25.00	50.00	100.00
—Black vinyl					
3104	Night and Day/Stormin' and Rainin'	1951	50.00	100.00	200.00
—Green vinyl					
3217	Don't Leave Me Baby/Check with the Boys	1954	20.00	40.00	80.00
3233	Blues Never Fail/You've Gotta Reap	1954	20.00	40.00	80.00
CASH					
1051	Love Society Blues/Blue Shadows	1957	10.00	20.00	40.00
CHECKER					
804	Reconsider Baby/I Believe I'll Give It Up	1954	10.00	20.00	40.00
812	Loving You (Is All I Crave)/Check Yourself	1955	10.00	20.00	40.00
820	Lonely Hours/Do Me Right	1955	7.50	15.00	30.00
829	Trouble, Trouble/I Still Love You Baby	1955	7.50	15.00	30.00
841	It's Your Fault, Baby/Tollin' Bells	1956	7.50	15.00	30.00
854	Blues Rhumba/Please Don't Go	1957	6.25	12.50	25.00
865	Don't Drive Me, Baby/You're Gonna Miss Me	1957	6.25	12.50	25.00
882	I Want to Make Love to You/Rock This Morning	1958	6.25	12.50	25.00
937	It Took a Long Time/That's Alright	1960	5.00	10.00	20.00
952	Comin' Home/Have You Changed Your Mind	1960	5.00	10.00	20.00
959	I'm Glad You Reconsidered/Blue Shadows	1960	5.00	10.00	20.00
972	I Want to Know (Part 1)/I Want to Know (Part 2)	1961	3.75	7.50	15.00
992	So Many Tears/Hung Down Head	1961	3.75	7.50	15.00
1027	Shed No Tears/Can She	1962	3.75	7.50	15.00
1046	Trouble with the Blues/Love Grows Cold	1963	3.75	7.50	15.00
GRANITE					
533	Do You Love Me/A Step at a Time	1975	—	2.50	5.00
538	The Old Blues Singer/Monday Morning Blues	1976	—	2.50	5.00
HOLLYWOOD					
567-242	The Original Lonesome Christmas Part 1/The Original Lonesome Christmas Part 2	196?	2.50	5.00	10.00
1022	The Original Lonesome Christmas Part 1/The Original Lonesome Christmas Part 2	1955	5.00	10.00	20.00
1029	Everyday I Have the Blues/Guitar Shuffle	1955	12.50	25.00	50.00
1103	Everyday I Have the Blues/Guitar Shuffle	1962	3.75	7.50	15.00
JEWEL					
801	Letter Home/Lady in the Rain	1969	2.00	4.00	8.00
802	Why Don't We Do It in the Road/Too Soon	1969	2.50	5.00	10.00
805	How Do You Want Your Man/Sleeper	1969	2.00	4.00	8.00
808	Don't Leave Me/Thug	1970	2.00	4.00	8.00
811	Do You Feel It/Don't Destroy Me	1970	2.00	4.00	8.00
813	Lonesome Christmas (Part 1)/Lonesome Christmas (Part 2)	1970	—	3.00	6.00
818	My Baby/Bluesway	1971	—	3.00	6.00
820	Teach Me/Man of Motion	1971	—	3.00	6.00
827	Change of Heart/Every Second a Fool Is Born	1972	—	3.00	6.00
832	Look at You Baby/Fed Up	1972	—	3.00	6.00
KENT					
395	Every Time It Rains/My Heart Belongs to You	1964	3.00	6.00	12.00
395	Every Time It Rains/Just One More Time	1964	3.00	6.00	12.00
401	Key to My Heart/Too Many Drivers	1964	3.00	6.00	12.00
410	Strange Feeling/What's Gonna Be	1965	3.00	6.00	12.00
422	No More (Part 1)/No More (Part 2)	1965	3.00	6.00	12.00
431	Black Nights/Little Angel	1965	2.50	5.00	10.00
440	Sittin' Here Thinkin'/Shattered Dreams	1966	2.50	5.00	10.00
443	Blues Around Midnight/Talkin' Woman	1966	2.50	5.00	10.00
448	Change Your Ways/My Aching Back	1966	2.50	5.00	10.00
452	The Trouble I'm In/Ask at Any Door in Town	1966	2.50	5.00	10.00
456	Tramp/Pico	1966	2.50	5.00	10.00
463	Make a Little Love/I'm Sinking	1967	2.50	5.00	10.00
463 [PS]	Make a Little Love/I'm Sinking	1967	5.00	10.00	20.00
466	Everyday I Have the Blues/No Hard Feelings	1967	2.50	5.00	10.00
471	I Cried/The Thing	1967	2.50	5.00	10.00
474	I'm a Drifter/Hobo Meetin'	1967	2.50	5.00	10.00
477	I Wanna Spend Christmas with You Part 1/I Wanna Spend Christmas with You Part 2	1967	3.00	6.00	12.00
479	Tomorrow/Push Me	1968	2.50	5.00	10.00
486	The Letter/Let's Go Get Stoned	1968	2.50	5.00	10.00
489	Blues Pain/Mellow Together	1968	2.50	5.00	10.00
497	Sweetest Thing/What the Heck	1968	2.50	5.00	10.00
505	Lovin' Touch/Price for Love	1969	2.50	5.00	10.00
4535	Let's Go Get Stoned/Funky Broadway	1970	2.00	4.00	8.00
MOVIN'					
128	Stop and Think/Baby	1964	3.00	6.00	12.00
PARROT					
787	I've Been Mistreated/Juke Box Shuffle	1953	25.00	50.00	100.00
—Black vinyl					
787	I've Been Mistreated/Juke Box Shuffle	1953	50.00	100.00	200.00
—Red vinyl					
SWING TIME					
242	Lonesome Christmas (Part 1)/Lonesome Christmas (Part 2)	1951	15.00	30.00	60.00
—78 released in 1950; 45 released in 1951					
243	I'm a Night Owl (Part 1)/I'm a Night Owl (Part 2)	1951	25.00	50.00	100.00
272	Why Can't You Cry for Me/Blues with a Feeling	1951	—	—	—
—Unreleased on 45 rpm?					
289	Let's Live Right/Best Wishes	1952	12.50	25.00	50.00
290	Three O'Clock in the Morning Blues/I'm Wild About You Baby	1952	—	—	—
—Unreleased on 45 rpm?					
295	Guitar Shuffle/Mean Old Lonesome Song	1952	12.50	25.00	50.00
308	Black Widow Spider/Midnight Showers of Rain	1953	12.50	25.00	50.00
315	Raggedy Daddy Blues/Goodbye	1953	12.50	25.00	50.00
320	Ride Until the Sun Goes Down/Good Party Shuffle	1953	12.50	25.00	50.00
325	Upstairs/Let Me Ride Your Automobile	1953	12.50	25.00	50.00
330	The Blues Come Rollin' In/I Love My Baby	1954	12.50	25.00	50.00
335	Cash Box Boogie/My Daily Prayer	1954	12.50	25.00	50.00
338	I've Been Mistreated/Juke Box Shuffle	1954	12.50	25.00	50.00
Albums					
ARHOOLIE					
R-2003	Early Recordings	1962	7.50	15.00	30.00
BIG TOWN					
1008	Lovemaker	1978	3.00	6.00	12.00
CHESS					
408	Hung Down Head	197?	3.75	7.50	15.00
GRANITE					
1006	Ol' Blues Singer	1976	3.75	7.50	15.00
JEWEL					
LPS-5003	In a Heavy Bag	1970	3.75	7.50	15.00
LPS-5009	I've Got the Blues	1973	3.75	7.50	15.00
KENT					
KST-516 [S]	Lowell Fulsom	1965	10.00	20.00	40.00
KST-520 [S]	Tramp	1967	10.00	20.00	40.00
KST-531	Lowell Fulsom Now	1969	7.50	15.00	30.00
KLP-5016 [M]	Lowell Fulsom	1965	7.50	15.00	30.00
KLP-5020 [M]	Tramp	1967	7.50	15.00	30.00
ROUNDER					
2088	It's a Good Day	198?	3.00	6.00	12.00

FUN AND GAMES

Number	Title (A Side/B Side)	Yr	VG	VG+	NM
45s					
UNI					
55086	Elephant Candy/The Way She Smiles	1968	3.00	6.00	12.00
55098	The Grooviest Girl in the World/It Must Have Been the Wind	1968	3.00	6.00	12.00
55128	Gotta Say Goodbye/We	1969	3.00	6.00	12.00
Albums					
UNI					
73042	Elephant Candy	1968	6.25	12.50	25.00

FUNK INC.

Number	Title (A Side/B Side)	Yr	VG	VG+	NM
45s					
PRESTIGE					
752	Whipper (Part 1)/Whipper (Part 2)	1972	—	3.00	6.00
754	The Thrill Is Gone/Bowlegs	1973	—	3.00	6.00
759	Dirty Red (Part 1)/Dirty Red (Part 2)	197?	—	3.00	6.00
762	Goodbye, So Long/Just Don't Mean a Thing	197?	—	3.00	6.00
Albums					
PRESTIGE					
10031	Funk Inc.	1971	3.75	7.50	15.00
10043	Chicken Lickin'	1972	3.75	7.50	15.00
10059	Hangin' Out	1973	3.75	7.50	15.00
10071	Superfunk	1973	3.75	7.50	15.00
10087	Priced to Sell	1974	3.75	7.50	15.00

FUNKADELIC

Also see GEORGE CLINTON; FUNKADELIC (2); PARLIAMENT; THE PARLIAMENTS.

Number	Title (A Side/B Side)	Yr	VG	VG+	NM
45s					
MCA					
53654	By Way of the Drum/(Instrumental)	1989	—	—	3.00
WARNER BROS.					
8618	One Nation Under a Groove (Part 1)/One Nation Under a Groove (Part 2)	1978	—	2.50	5.00
8618 [PS]	One Nation Under a Groove (Part 1)/One Nation Under a Groove (Part 2)	1978	—	2.50	5.00
8735	Cholly (Funk Getting Ready to Roll)/Into You	1979	—	2.50	5.00
49040	(Not Just) Knee Deep — Part 1/(Not Just) Knee Deep — Part 2	1979	—	2.50	5.00
49117	Uncle Jam (Part 1)/Uncle Jam (Part 2)	1979	—	2.50	5.00
49667	The Electric Spanking of War Babies/The Electric Spanking of War Babies (Part 2)	1981	—	2.00	4.00
49667 [PS]	The Electric Spanking of War Babies/The Electric Spanking of War Babies (Part 2)	1981	—	2.50	5.00
49807	Shockwaves/Bullino's Bounce	1981	—	2.00	4.00
WESTBOUND					
148	Music for My Mother/(Instrumental)	1969	2.50	5.00	10.00
150	I'll Bet You/Open Your Eyes	1969	2.50	5.00	10.00
158	I Got a Thing, You Got a Thing, Everybody's Got a Thing/Fish, Chips and Sweat	1970	2.50	5.00	10.00
167	I Wanna Know If It's Good to You?/I Wanna Know If It's Good to You? (Part 2)	1970	2.50	5.00	10.00
175	You and Your Folks, Me and My Folks/Funky Dollar Bill	1971	2.50	5.00	10.00
185	Can You Get to That/Back in Our Minds	1971	2.50	5.00	10.00
197	I Miss My Baby/Baby I Owe You Something Good	1972	2.50	5.00	10.00
—As "U.S. Music with Funkadelic"					
198	Hit It and Quit It/A Whole Lot of B.S.	1972	2.50	5.00	10.00
205	A Joyful Process/Loose Booty	1972	2.50	5.00	10.00
218	Cosmic Slop/If You Don't Like the Effects, Don't Produce the Cause	1973	2.50	5.00	10.00
224	Standing on the Verge of Getting It On/Jimmy's Got a Little Bit of Bitch in Him	1974	2.50	5.00	10.00
5000	Red Hot Momma/Vital Juices	1975	2.00	4.00	8.00
5014	Better by the Pound/Stuffs and Things	1975	2.00	4.00	8.00
5026	Let's Take It to the Stage/Bilogical Speculation	1976	2.00	4.00	8.00
5029	Undisco Kidd/How Do Yeau View You	1976	2.00	4.00	8.00
Albums					
SCARFACE/PRIORITY					
53872	One Nation Under a Groove	1993	3.75	7.50	15.00
—Limited-edition reissue of Warner Bros. 3209					
53873	Hardcore Jollies	1993	3.75	7.50	15.00
—Limited-edition reissue of Warner Bros. 2973					
53874	The Electric Spanking of War Babies	1993	3.75	7.50	15.00
—Limited-edition reissue of Warner Bros. 3482					
53875	Uncle Jam Wants You	1993	3.75	7.50	15.00
—Limited-edition reissue of Warner Bros. 3371					
WARNER BROS.					
BS 2973	Hardcore Jollies	1976	6.25	12.50	25.00
BS 3209	One Nation Under a Groove	1978	6.25	12.50	25.00
—Includes bonus 7-inch single with small hole (deduct 20% if missing)					
BSK 3371	Uncle Jam Wants You	1979	6.25	12.50	25.00
BSK 3482	The Electric Spanking of War Babies	1981	6.25	12.50	25.00
WESTBOUND					
208	Standing on the Verge of Getting It On	1975	6.25	12.50	25.00
—Reissue of Westbound 1001					
215	Let's Take It to the Stage	1975	12.50	25.00	50.00
215	Let's Take It to the Stage	1992	3.75	7.50	15.00
—Reissue with bar code					
216	Funkadelic	1975	7.50	15.00	30.00
—Reissue of Westbound 2000					
217	Free Your Mind...And Your Ass Will Follow	1975	6.25	12.50	25.00
—Reissue of Westbound 2001					
218	Maggot Brain	1975	6.25	12.50	25.00
—Reissue of Westbound 2007					
221 [(2)]	America Eats Its Young	1976	6.25	12.50	25.00
—Reissue of Westbound 2020					
223	Cosmic Slop	1976	6.25	12.50	25.00
—Reissue of Westbound 2022					
227	Tales of Kidd Funkadelic	1976	12.50	25.00	50.00
227	Tales of Kidd Funkadelic	1992	3.75	7.50	15.00
—Reissue with bar code					
303	Best of the Early Years	197?	10.00	20.00	40.00
1001	Standing on the Verge of Getting It On	1974	12.50	25.00	50.00
1001	Standing on the Verge of Getting It On	1991	3.75	7.50	15.00
—Reissue with bar code					
1004	Funkadelic's Greatest Hits	1975	12.50	25.00	50.00
2000	Funkadelic	1970	12.50	25.00	50.00
2000	Funkadelic	1990	3.75	7.50	15.00
—Reissue with bar code					
2001	Free Your Mind...And Your Ass Will Follow	1970	12.50	25.00	50.00
2001	Free Your Mind...And Your Ass Will Follow	1990	3.75	7.50	15.00
—Reissue with bar code					
2007	Maggot Brain	1971	12.50	25.00	50.00
2007	Maggot Brain	1990	3.75	7.50	15.00
—Reissue with bar code					
2020 [(2)]	America Eats Its Young	1972	15.00	30.00	60.00
2020 [(2)]	America Eats Its Young	1991	5.00	10.00	20.00
—Reissue with bar code					
2022	Cosmic Slop	1973	12.50	25.00	50.00
2022	Cosmic Slop	1991	3.75	7.50	15.00
—Reissue with bar code					

FUNKADELIC (2)

Splinter group from the original band, listed separately because GEORGE CLINTON is not involved.

Number	Title (A Side/B Side)	Yr	VG	VG+	NM
45s					
LAX					
70055	Connections and Disconnections/The Witch	1981	—	2.00	4.00
Albums					
LAX					
FW 37087	Connections and Disconnections	1981	2.50	5.00	10.00

FURY, BILLY

Number	Title (A Side/B Side)	Yr	VG	VG+	NM
45s					
LONDON					
1857	Maybe Tomorrow/Gonna Type a Letter	1959	5.00	10.00	20.00
1925	Colette/Baby How I Cried	1960	5.00	10.00	20.00
1991	Halfway to Paradise/Cross My Heart	1961	5.00	10.00	20.00
2004	Stick Around/Coming Up in the World	1961	5.00	10.00	20.00
9515	I'll Never Find Another You/Don't Jump	1962	3.75	7.50	15.00
9548	Once Upon a Dream/Running Around	1962	3.75	7.50	15.00
9594	Because of Love/Like I've Never Loved Before	1963	3.75	7.50	15.00
9615	Don't Walk Away/When Will I Say I Love You	1963	3.75	7.50	15.00
9662	Hippy Hippy Shake/Glad All Over	1964	3.75	7.50	15.00
9675	I Will/What Am I Living For	1964	3.75	7.50	15.00
9740	I'm Lost Without You/Go Ahead and Ask Her	1965	3.75	7.50	15.00
MALA					
569	Loving You/I'll Go Along With It	1967	2.50	5.00	10.00
583	Suzanne in the Mirror/It Just Don't Matter Now	1968	2.50	5.00	10.00
595	Beyond the Shadow of a Doubt/Baby Do You Love Me	1968	2.50	5.00	10.00
12018	Silly Boy Blue/One Minute Woman	1968	2.50	5.00	10.00
PARROT					
9692	Baby What You Want Me to Do/It's Only Make Believe	1964	3.75	7.50	15.00
UNITED ARTISTS					
968	In Thoughts of You/Away from You	1966	3.00	6.00	12.00
50061	She's So Far Out She's In/Give Me Your Word	1966	3.00	6.00	12.00

FUSE

Early version of Cheap Trick.

Number	Title (A Side/B Side)	Yr	VG	VG+	NM
45s					
EPIC					
10514	Cruisin' for Burgers/Hound Dog	1969	6.25	12.50	25.00
Albums					
EPIC					
BN 26502	Fuse	1970	20.00	40.00	80.00

FUT, THE

Maurice Gibb was in this group, whose single often was bootlegged as a "lost" Beatles track. It has no Beatles involvement whatsoever.

Number	Title (A Side/B Side)	Yr	VG	VG+	NM
45s					
BEACON					
160	Have You Heard the Word/Futting	1970	2.50	5.00	10.00
FUT					
160	Have You Heard the Word/Futting	1976	—	2.50	5.00

FUTURE, THE

Number	Title (A Side/B Side)	Yr	VG	VG+	NM
45s					
UNI					
55082	The Shape of Things to Come/52%	1968	2.00	4.00	8.00
Albums					
SHAMLEY					
703	Down the Country Road	1969	5.00	10.00	20.00

FUZZ, THE

Number	Title (A Side/B Side)	Yr	VG	VG+	NM
45s					
CALLA					
174	I Love You for All Seasons/I Love You for All Seasons (Part 2)	1970	—	3.00	6.00
177	Like an Open Door/Leave It All Behind Me	1971	—	3.00	6.00
179	I'm So Glad/All About Love	1971	—	3.00	6.00
183	Mr. Heartache and Miss Tears/Do Just What You Can	1971	—	3.00	6.00
Albums					
CALLA					
SD 2001	The Fuzz	1971	3.75	7.50	15.00

G

G-CLEFS, THE

45s

Number	Title (A Side/B Side)	Yr	VG	VG+	NM
LOMA					
2034	Party '66/Little Lonely Boy	1966	2.50	5.00	10.00
2048	I Can't Stand It/Whirlwind	1966	2.50	5.00	10.00
PARIS					
502	Symbol of Love/Love Her in the Mornin'	1957	7.50	15.00	30.00
506	Zing Zang Zoo/Is This the Way	1957	6.25	12.50	25.00
PILGRIM					
715	Ka-Ding-Dong/Darla My Darlin'	1956	7.50	15.00	30.00
—Purple label					
715	Ka-Ding-Dong/Darla My Darlin'	1956	5.00	10.00	20.00
—Red label					
720	'Cause You're Mine/Please Write While I'm Away	1956	7.50	15.00	30.00
REGINA					
1314	To the Winner Goes the Prize/I Believe in All I Feel	1964	3.75	7.50	15.00
1319	Angel Listen to Me/Nobody But Betty	1964	5.00	10.00	20.00
TERRACE					
7500	I Understand (Just How You Feel)/Little Girl I Love You	1961	5.00	10.00	20.00
7503	Girl Has to Know/Lad (There Never Was a Dog Like You)	1962	5.00	10.00	20.00
7507	Make Up Your Mind/They'll Call Me Away	1962	5.00	10.00	20.00
7510	A Lover's Prayer/Sitting in the Moonlight	1962	6.25	12.50	25.00
7514	All My Trials/Big Train	1963	6.25	12.50	25.00
VEEP					
1218	I Have/On the Other Side of Town	1965	3.75	7.50	15.00
1226	This Time/On the Other Side of Town	1965	3.75	7.50	15.00

G.T.O.'S, THE (1)

Also see JOEY AND THE CONTINENTALS.

45s

Number	Title (A Side/B Side)	Yr	VG	VG+	NM
CLARIDGE					
312	She Rides with Me/Rudy Vahoo	1966	5.00	10.00	20.00
—Reissue of Claridge 304 by "Joey and the Continentals"					
PARKWAY					
108	Girl from New York City/Missing Out on the Fun	1966	3.75	7.50	15.00

G.T.O.'S, THE (2)

Short for "Girls Together Outrageously."

Albums

Number	Title (A Side/B Side)	Yr	VG	VG+	NM
REPRISE					
RS 6390	Permanent Damage	1970	12.50	25.00	50.00
—Without booklet					
RS 6390	Permanent Damage	1970	17.50	35.00	70.00
—With booklet					
STRAIGHT					
STS-1059	Permanent Damage	1969	20.00	40.00	80.00
—Without booklet					
STS-1059	Permanent Damage	1969	25.00	50.00	100.00
—With booklet					

GABRIEL AND THE ANGELS

45s

Number	Title (A Side/B Side)	Yr	VG	VG+	NM
AMY					
802	Chumba/Hey	1960	5.00	10.00	20.00
823	Zing Went the Strings of My Heart/The Rooster	1961	10.00	20.00	40.00
APRIL					
1102	Chumba/Hey	1960	12.50	25.00	50.00
NORMAN					
506	I'm Gabriel/Ginza	1961	3.75	7.50	15.00
510	Gabriel, Blow Your Horn (Part 1)/Gabriel, Blow Your Horn (Part 2)	1961	3.75	7.50	15.00
514	Miss You So/See See Rider	1962	3.75	7.50	15.00
—As "Gabriel and His Trumpet"					
SWAN					
4118	That's Life (That's Tough)/Don't Wanna Twist No More	1962	3.00	6.00	12.00
4118	That's Life/Don't Wanna Twist No More	1962	3.75	7.50	15.00
—No subtitle on A-side					
4133	The Peanut Butter Song/All Work and No Play	1963	3.00	6.00	12.00

GABRIEL BONDAGE

Albums

Number	Title (A Side/B Side)	Yr	VG	VG+	NM
DHARMA					
D-804	Angel Dust	1975	12.50	25.00	50.00
D-808	Another Trip to Earth	1977	5.00	10.00	20.00
—Exists on white, red, or blue vinyl; each of similar value					

GADABOUTS, THE

45s

Number	Title (A Side/B Side)	Yr	VG	VG+	NM
JARO					
77022	Caress Me/Deep Are the Roots of a Happy Home	1960	3.75	7.50	15.00
MERCURY					
70495	By the Waters of the Minnetonka/Giuseppe Mandolino	1954	6.25	12.50	25.00
70581	Go Boom Boom/Oochi Pachi	1955	6.25	12.50	25.00
70823	Busy Body Rock/All My Love Belongs to You	1956	6.25	12.50	25.00
70898	Stranded in the Jungle/Blues Train	1956	6.25	12.50	25.00
70978	Too Much Monkey Business/To Be with You	1956	6.25	12.50	25.00
WING					
90008	Two Things I Love/Glass Heart	1955	6.25	12.50	25.00
90043	Teenage Rock/If You Only Had a Heart	1955	6.25	12.50	25.00
90062	Busy Body Rock/All My Love Belongs to You	1956	5.00	10.00	20.00

GADDY, BOB

45s

Number	Title (A Side/B Side)	Yr	VG	VG+	NM
DOT					
1185	Honey Stealin' Blues/Hold That Train, Conductor	1954	25.00	50.00	100.00
—As "Doctor Gaddy and His Orchestra"					
HARLEM					
2330	The Blues Has Walked in My Room/Slow Down Baby	1954	37.50	75.00	150.00
JAX					
308	No Help Wanted/Little Girls Boogie	1952	75.00	150.00	300.00
OLD TOWN					
1031	I Love My Baby/Operator	1956	6.25	12.50	25.00
1039	Paper Lady/Out of My Name	1957	6.25	12.50	25.00
1050	Woe, Woe Is Me/Rip and Run	1958	6.25	12.50	25.00
1057	You Are the One/Take My Advice	1958	6.25	12.50	25.00
1064	What Would I Do/Paper Lady	1959	5.00	10.00	20.00
1070	Till the Day I Die/I'll Go My Way	1959	5.00	10.00	20.00
1077	Early One Morning/What Wrong Did I Do	1960	5.00	10.00	20.00
1085	Don't Tell Her/Could I	1960	5.00	10.00	20.00
1162	I Love My Baby/Operator	1964	3.00	6.00	12.00

GADDY, DOCTOR

See BOB GADDY.

GADSON, MEL

45s

Number	Title (A Side/B Side)	Yr	VG	VG+	NM
BIG TOP					
3034	Comin' Down with Love/I'm Getting Sentimental Over You	1959	6.25	12.50	25.00

GAILTONES, THE

45s

Number	Title (A Side/B Side)	Yr	VG	VG+	NM
DECCA					
30726	Lover Boy/Please Don't Go	1958	10.00	20.00	40.00

GAINES, ROY

45s

Number	Title (A Side/B Side)	Yr	VG	VG+	NM
CHART					
606	Loud Mouth Lucy/I'm Setting You Free	1955	15.00	30.00	60.00
DEL-FI					
4169	What Is This Thing Called Love/Lizzie	1961	3.75	7.50	15.00
DELUXE					
6119	Isabella/Gainesville	1957	6.25	12.50	25.00
6132	You're Right, I'm Left/Stolen Moments	1957	6.25	12.50	25.00
6147	Annabelle/Night Beat	1957	6.25	12.50	25.00
GROOVE					
0146	Right Now Baby/De Dat De Dum Dum	1956	7.50	15.00	30.00
0161	Worried 'Bout You Baby/All My Life	1956	7.50	15.00	30.00
RCA VICTOR					
47-7243	Skippy Is a Sissy/Weeping Willow	1958	15.00	30.00	60.00

GALAHADS, THE

Albums

Number	Title (A Side/B Side)	Yr	VG	VG+	NM
LIBERTY					
LRP-3371 [M]	Hello, Galahads	1964	5.00	10.00	20.00
LST-7371 [S]	Hello, Galahads	1964	6.25	12.50	25.00

GALAXYS, THE

45s

Number	Title (A Side/B Side)	Yr	VG	VG+	NM
CARTHAY					
103	A Lover's Prayer/Jelly Bean	1959	375.00	750.00	1500.

GALE, BARBARA

45s

Number	Title (A Side/B Side)	Yr	VG	VG+	NM
LLOYDS					
107	Lonely Weather/So Long, Good-Bye Joe	1953	30.00	60.00	120.00
109	Once Again/Fool Fool Me	1953	30.00	60.00	120.00
111	When You're Near/Who Walks In	1954	75.00	150.00	300.00
—With the Larks					
115	Johnny Darlin'/You're Gonna Lose That Gal	1954	75.00	150.00	300.00
—With the Larks					

GALES, THE

45s

Number	Title (A Side/B Side)	Yr	VG	VG+	NM
DEBRA					
1002	Tommy/Around the Clock with You	1963	10.00	20.00	40.00
JVB					
34	His Eyes Keep Me in Trouble/Don't Let the Sun Catch You Cryin'	1955	1000.	2000.	3000.
35	Darling Patricia/All Is Well, All Is Well	1955	125.00	250.00	500.00
J.O.B.					
3001	Darling Patricia/All Is Well, All Is Well	1956	50.00	100.00	200.00
MEL-O					
111	Guiding Angel/Boy Come Home	1958	62.50	125.00	250.00
113	Josephine/If I Could Forget	1958	62.50	125.00	250.00
WINN					
916	I Love You/Squeeze Me	1960	125.00	250.00	500.00

GALLAGHER, JAMES

45s

Number	Title (A Side/B Side)	Yr	VG	VG+	NM
DECCA					
29984	Crazy Chicken/Just for You	1956	30.00	60.00	120.00

GALLAGHER, RORY

Albums

Number	Title (A Side/B Side)	Yr	VG	VG+	NM
ATCO					
SD 33-368	Rory Gallagher	1971	3.75	7.50	15.00
SD 7004	Deuce	1971	3.75	7.50	15.00
CHRYSALIS					
CHR 1098	Against the Grain	1975	2.50	5.00	10.00

Number	Title (A Side/B Side)	Yr	VG	VG+	NM
CHR 1124	Calling Card	1976	2.50	5.00	10.00
CHR 1170	Photo-Finish	1978	2.50	5.00	10.00
CHR 1235	Top Priority	1979	2.50	5.00	10.00
CHR 1280	Stage Struck	1980	2.50	5.00	10.00
MERCURY					
SRM-1-4051	Jinx	1982	2.50	5.00	10.00
POLYDOR					
PD-5513	Rory Gallagher/Live!	1972	3.00	6.00	12.00
PD-5522	Blueprint	1973	3.00	6.00	12.00
PD-5539	Tattoo	1973	3.00	6.00	12.00
PD-1-6510	Sinner...And Saint	1975	3.00	6.00	12.00
PD-1-6519	The Story So Far	1975	3.00	6.00	12.00
PD-9501 [(2)]	Irish Tour '74	1974	3.00	6.00	12.00
SPRINGBOARD					
4056	In the Beginning	1976	2.50	5.00	10.00

GALLAHADS, THE (1)

45s

Number	Title (A Side/B Side)	Yr	VG	VG+	NM
CAPITOL					
F-3060	Ooh Ah/Careless	1955	6.25	12.50	25.00
F-3175	Do You Believe Me/If It Wasn't for You	1955	6.25	12.50	25.00
JUBILEE					
5252	The Fool/The Morning Mail	1956	7.50	15.00	30.00
5259	Take My Love/I Give You My Word	1956	6.25	12.50	25.00
VIK					
0291	Take Back My Ring/One Love Alone	1957	6.25	12.50	25.00
0316	Best Wishes/Steady Man	1958	6.25	12.50	25.00
0332	Silently/Barracuda	1958	6.25	12.50	25.00

GALLAHADS, THE (2)

45s

Number	Title (A Side/B Side)	Yr	VG	VG+	NM
DEL-FI					
4137	Lonely Guy/Jo Jo the Big Wheel	1960	10.00	20.00	40.00
—Green label					
4137	Lonely Guy/Jo Jo the Big Wheel	1960	5.00	10.00	20.00
—Black label					
4148	Be Fair/I'm Without a Girl Friend	1960	10.00	20.00	40.00
—Green label					
4148	Be Fair/I'm Without a Girl Friend	1960	5.00	10.00	20.00
—Black label					
DONNA					
1322	Lonely Guy/Jo Jo the Big Wheel	1960	10.00	20.00	40.00
1361	This Letter to You/The Answer to Love	1962	12.50	25.00	50.00

GALLAHADS, THE (U)

It's unlikely any of these are group (1). Some of these are probably group (2). Others could be by different groups.

45s

Number	Title (A Side/B Side)	Yr	VG	VG+	NM
BEECHWOOD					
3001	Keeper of Dreams/Sad Girl	1960	30.00	60.00	120.00
—More than one group.					
NITE OWL					
20	Gone/So Long	1961	15.00	30.00	60.00
RENDEZVOUS					
153	Gone/Why Do Fools Fall in Love	1961	10.00	20.00	40.00
SEA CREST					
6005	Have Love, Will Travel/My Offering	1964	10.00	20.00	40.00
STARLA					
15	Keeper of Dreams/Sad Girl	1960	5.00	10.00	20.00

GALLANT, RONNIE

45s

Number	Title (A Side/B Side)	Yr	VG	VG+	NM
ATLANTIC					
2169	Shake Shake Baby/Shadows	1962	3.00	6.00	12.00
WARNER BROS.					
5251	Hole in the Wall/In the Night	1962	3.00	6.00	12.00

GALLERY

45s

Number	Title (A Side/B Side)	Yr	VG	VG+	NM
SUSSEX					
232	Nice to Be with You/Ginger Haired Man	1972	—	2.50	5.00
239	I Believe in Music/Someone	1972	—	2.50	5.00
239 [PS]	I Believe in Music/Someone	1972	2.00	4.00	8.00
248	Big City Miss Ruth Ann/Lover's Hideaway	1972	—	2.50	5.00
255	Rest in Peace/Riverboat Captain	1973	—	2.50	5.00
259	Maybe Baby/Lady Luck	1973	—	2.50	5.00
512	Friends/I Love Every Little Thing About You	1974	—	2.00	4.00
630	Living Next Door to Alice/Captain Sam	1975	—	2.00	4.00
639	Power to All Our Friends/(B-side unknown)	1975	—	2.00	4.00

Albums

Number	Title (A Side/B Side)	Yr	VG	VG+	NM
ECM					
1206	Gallery	1982	3.00	6.00	12.00
SUSSEX					
SUX-7017	Nice to Be with You	1972	3.00	6.00	12.00
SUX-7026	Jim Gold and Gallery	1973	3.00	6.00	12.00

GALLOP, FRANK

45s

Number	Title (A Side/B Side)	Yr	VG	VG+	NM
ABC-PARAMOUNT					
9931	Got a Match?/I Beg Your Pardon	1958	3.00	6.00	12.00
KAPP					
745	The Ballad of Irving/Would You Believe It	1966	2.50	5.00	10.00
—B-side by Phil Leeds					
MUSICOR					
1191	Son of Irving/One Love I'll Never Forget	1966	2.00	4.00	8.00
1191 [PS]	Son of Irving/One Love I'll Never Forget	1966	3.00	6.00	12.00

Albums

Number	Title (A Side/B Side)	Yr	VG	VG+	NM
MUSICOR					
(# unknown) [M]	Frank Gallop Sings	1966	3.75	7.50	15.00
(# unknown) [S]	Frank Gallop Sings	1966	5.00	10.00	20.00

GALS & PALS

Albums

Number	Title (A Side/B Side)	Yr	VG	VG+	NM
FONTANA					
MGF-27538 [M]	Gals & Pals (The Exciting Vocal Sounds of Europe's Newest "In" Group)	1965	3.75	7.50	15.00
MGF-27557 [M]	Gals & Pals Sing Something for Everybody	1966	3.75	7.50	15.00
SRF-67538 [S]	Gals & Pals (The Exciting Vocal Sounds of Europe's Newest "In" Group)	1965	5.00	10.00	20.00
SRF-67557 [S]	Gals & Pals Sing Something for Everybody	1966	5.00	10.00	20.00

GALT, JAMES

45s

Number	Title (A Side/B Side)	Yr	VG	VG+	NM
AURORA					
158	With My Baby/Most Unusual Feeling	1966	7.50	15.00	30.00

GAMBLE, DEE DEE SHARP

See DEE DEE SHARP.

GAMBLE, KENNY

45s

Number	Title (A Side/B Side)	Yr	VG	VG+	NM
ARCTIC					
107	Down by the Seashore (Part 1)/Down by the Seashore (Part 2)	1965	50.00	100.00	200.00
114	Ain't It Baby (Part 1)/Ain't It Baby (Part 2)	1965	50.00	100.00	200.00
123	The Joke's on You/Don't Stop Loving Me	1966	50.00	100.00	200.00
COLUMBIA					
43132	Our Love/You Don't Know What You Got Until You Lose It	1964	7.50	15.00	30.00
EPIC					
9636	Standing in the Shadows/No Mail on Monday	1963	7.50	15.00	30.00

GAMBLERS, THE (1)

BRUCE JOHNSTON and SANDY NELSON were in this group.

45s

Number	Title (A Side/B Side)	Yr	VG	VG+	NM
LAST CHANCE					
2	Teen Machine/Tonky	1961	10.00	20.00	40.00
108	Teen Machine/Tonky	1962	6.25	12.50	25.00
WORLD PACIFIC					
815	Moon Dawg/LSD-25	1960	15.00	30.00	60.00

GAMBLERS, THE (2)

British group.

45s

Number	Title (A Side/B Side)	Yr	VG	VG+	NM
CORAL					
62525	Cry Me a River/Who Will Buy	1967	2.00	4.00	8.00
PRESS					
9739	Now I'm All Alone/Find Out What's Happening	1965	3.00	6.00	12.00

GAME

45s

Number	Title (A Side/B Side)	Yr	VG	VG+	NM
EVOLUTION					
1042	Fat Mama/The Girl Next Door	1970	—	3.00	6.00
1053	Two Songs for the Senorita/(B-side unknown)	1971	—	3.00	6.00

Albums

Number	Title (A Side/B Side)	Yr	VG	VG+	NM
EVOLUTION					
2021	Game	1970	3.00	6.00	12.00
3008	Long Hot Summer	1971	3.00	6.00	12.00
FAITHFUL VIRTUE					
2003	Game	1969	5.00	10.00	20.00

GAMMA GOOCHEE

45s

Number	Title (A Side/B Side)	Yr	VG	VG+	NM
COLPIX					
786	I'm Gonna Buy Me a Dog/(You Got the) Gamma Goochee	1965	5.00	10.00	20.00
804	I'm So Glad/Sweet Violets	1966	3.75	7.50	15.00
MGM					
13874	Booga-Loo/Everybody's Somebody's Fool	1967	3.75	7.50	15.00

GANDALF

45s

Number	Title (A Side/B Side)	Yr	VG	VG+	NM
CAPITOL					
2400	Golden Earrings/Never Too Far	1969	6.25	12.50	25.00

Albums

Number	Title (A Side/B Side)	Yr	VG	VG+	NM
CAPITOL					
ST-121	Gandalf	1969	50.00	100.00	200.00

GANDALF THE GREY

Albums

Number	Title (A Side/B Side)	Yr	VG	VG+	NM
G.W.R.					
7	The Grey Wizard Am I	1972	75.00	150.00	300.00

GANEY, JERRY

45s

Number	Title (A Side/B Side)	Yr	VG	VG+	NM
MGM					
13697	Hi-Heel Sneakers/You Don't Love Me	1967	5.00	10.00	20.00
VERVE					
10454	Who Am I/Just a Fool	1966	25.00	50.00	100.00

GANT, CECIL

45s

Number	Title (A Side/B Side)	Yr	VG	VG+	NM
DECCA					
30320	I Wonder/Cecil's Boogie	1957	7.50	15.00	30.00
48171	Someday You'll Be Sorry (Part 1)/Someday You'll Be Sorry (Part 2)	1950	10.00	20.00	40.00
48185	It's Christmas Time Again/Hello Santa Claus	1950	10.00	20.00	40.00
48191	Train Time Blues No. 2/It Ain't Gonna Be Like That	1951	10.00	20.00	40.00
48200	Shot Gun Boogie/Rock Little Baby	1951	12.50	25.00	50.00
48212	Don't You Worry/My Little Baby	1951	10.00	20.00	40.00

Number	Title (A Side/B Side)	Yr	VG	VG+	NM
48231	Owl Stew/Playin' Myself the Blues	1951	10.00	20.00	40.00
48249	God Bless My Daddy/The Grass Is Gettin' Greener	1951	10.00	20.00	40.00
DOT					
1112	All By Myself/It Hurts Me Too	1952	10.00	20.00	40.00
—Earlier singles on Dot may not exist on 45s					
1121	Sloppy Joes/Train Time Blues	1952	10.00	20.00	40.00
GILT EDGE					
5090	I Wonder/Cecil's Boogie	1955	10.00	20.00	40.00
—Reissue of 78 first released in 1944					
Albums					
KING					
671 [M]	Cecil Gant	1960	20.00	40.00	80.00
RED MILL					
(no #) [M]	Cecil Gant	1956	125.00	250.00	500.00
—Red vinyl					
SOUND					
601 [M]	The Incomparable Cecil Gant	1958	25.00	50.00	100.00

GANTS, THE

Number	Title (A Side/B Side)	Yr	VG	VG+	NM
45s					
ALADDIN					
3387	My Unfaithful Love/Happening After School	1957	15.00	30.00	60.00
LIBERTY					
55829	Road Runner/My Baby Don't Care	1965	3.75	7.50	15.00
55853	Smoke Rings/Little Boy Sad	1966	2.50	5.00	10.00
55884	Dr. Feelgood/Crackin' Up	1966	2.50	5.00	10.00
55903	I Want Your Lovin'/A Spoonful of Sugar	1966	2.50	5.00	10.00
55940	Greener Days/I Wonder	1967	2.50	5.00	10.00
55965	Drifter's Sunrise/Just a Good Show	1967	2.50	5.00	10.00
STATUE					
605	Road Runner/My Baby Don't Care	1965	12.50	25.00	50.00
608	What's Happening/Careless Hands	1965	6.25	12.50	25.00
—B-side by the Niteliters					
Albums					
LIBERTY					
LRP-3432 [M]	Road Runner	1965	7.50	15.00	30.00
LRP-3455 [M]	The Gants Galore	1966	7.50	15.00	30.00
LRP-3473 [M]	The Gants Again	1966	7.50	15.00	30.00
LST-7432 [S]	Road Runner	1965	10.00	20.00	40.00
LST-7455 [S]	The Gants Galore	1966	10.00	20.00	40.00
LST-7473 [S]	The Gants Again	1966	10.00	20.00	40.00

GAP BAND, THE

Number	Title (A Side/B Side)	Yr	VG	VG+	NM
12-Inch Singles					
ARISTA					
9777	I'm Gonna Git Ya Sucka (5 versions)	1988	—	3.00	6.00
CAPITOL					
V-15493	All of My Love (6 versions)	1989	—	3.00	6.00
V-15534	Addicted to Your Love (6 versions)	1990	—	3.00	6.00
MERCURY					
MK 124 [DJ]	Steppin' (Out) (same on both sides)	1979	2.00	4.00	8.00
MK 175 [DJ]	Yearning for Your Love/Humpin'	1980	2.00	4.00	8.00
RAGING BULL					
8013	First Lover (4 versions)	1995	2.00	4.00	8.00
TOTAL EXPERIENCE					
707 [DJ]	I'm Ready (same on both sides)	1983	—	3.50	7.00
1003	Straight from the Heart (4 versions)	1988	—	3.00	6.00
2606	Beep a Freak (3 versions)	1984	—	3.50	7.00
2624	Desire (3 versions)	1985	—	3.50	7.00
2632	Going in Circles (3 versions)	1985	—	3.50	7.00
2636	Automatic Brain (4 versions)	1986	—	3.50	7.00
2701	Big Fun (5 versions)	1986	—	3.50	7.00
2705	Zibble Zibble (3 versions)	1986	—	3.50	7.00
45s					
ARISTA					
9788	I'm Gonna Git Ya Sucka/Clean Up Your Act	1988	—	—	3.00
—B-side by Jermaine Jackson					
9788 [PS]	I'm Gonna Git Ya Sucka/Clean Up Your Act	1988	—	—	3.00
A&M					
1788	Hard Time Charlie/This Place Called Heaven	1976	—	2.50	5.00
CAPITOL					
B-44418	All of My Love (7" Mix)/All of My Love (Radio Mix)	1989	—	—	3.00
7PRO-79045 [DJ]	We Can Make It Alright (same on both sides)	1990	—	3.00	6.00
—Vinyl is promo only					
MEGA					
4005	Not Guilty/(B-side unknown)	1984	—	2.50	5.00
MERCURY					
74053	Shake/Got to Get Away	1979	—	2.00	4.00
74080	Open Up Your Mind (Wide)/I Can Sing	1979	—	2.00	4.00
76021	Steppin' (Out)/You Are My High	1979	—	2.00	4.00
76037	I Don't Believe You Want to Get Up and Dance (Oops, Up Side Your Head)/Who Do You Call	1980	—	2.00	4.00
76062	Party Lights/The Boys Are Back in Town	1980	—	2.00	4.00
76091	Burn Rubber (Why You Wanna Hurt Me)/Nothin' Comes to a Sleeper	1980	—	2.00	4.00
76101	Yearning for Your Love/When I Look in Your Eyes	1981	—	2.00	4.00
76114	Humpin'/No Hiding Place	1981	—	2.00	4.00
RCA					
5035-7-R	Sweeter Than Candy (Penitentiary III)/(Instrumental)	1986	—	—	3.00
SHELTER					
40228	Backbone/Loving You Is Everything	1974	—	3.00	6.00
40295	I-Yike-It/Tommy's Groove	1974	—	3.00	6.00
TATTOO					
TB-10884	Out of the Blue (Can You Feel It)/Silly Grin	1977	—	2.50	5.00
TB-10990	Little Bit of Love/Knucklehead Sunckin'	1977	—	2.50	5.00
TOTAL EXPERIENCE					
101	Straight from the Heart/(Instrumental)	1988	—	—	3.00
101 [PS]	Straight from the Heart/(Instrumental)	1988	—	2.00	4.00
2405	Beep a Freak/Beep a Freak (Dub Version)	1984	—	—	3.00
2405 [PS]	Beep a Freak/Beep a Freak (Dub Version)	1984	—	2.00	4.00
2412	I Found My Baby/(Instrumental)	1985	—	—	3.00
2418	Disrespect/(Instrumental)	1985	—	—	3.00
2427	Desire/(Instrumental)	1985	—	—	3.00
2428	Automatic Brain/(Instrumental)	1986	—	2.00	4.00
2435	The Christmas Song (Chestnuts Roasting on an Open Fire)/Joy to the World	1985	—	2.00	4.00
—B-side by Oliver Scott					
2436	Going in Circles/I Believe	1986	—	—	3.00
2440	Automatic Brain/Automatic Brain (With Rap)	1986	—	—	3.00
2700	Big Fun/Big Fun (Ooh Ah Dub)	1986	—	—	3.00
2703	Zibble, Zibble (Get the Money) (aka: Get Loose, Get Funky)/(Instrumental)	1987	—	—	3.00
8201	Early in the Morning/I'm in Love	1982	—	2.00	4.00
8201 [PS]	Early in the Morning/I'm in Love	1982	—	2.50	5.00
8203	You Dropped a Bomb on Me/Lonely Like Me	1982	—	2.00	4.00
8205	Outstanding/The Blues Are Back in Town	1982	—	2.00	4.00
8209	Party Train/The Special Party Train Dance Mix	1983	—	2.00	4.00
8210	Jam the Motha'/Jam the Motha' (Munchkin People)	1983	—	2.00	4.00
8211	I'm Ready (If You're Ready)/Shake a Leg	1984	—	2.00	4.00
Albums					
CAPITOL					
C1-90799	Round Trip	1989	2.50	5.00	10.00
MERCURY					
SRM-1-3758	The Gap Band	1979	2.50	5.00	10.00
SRM-1-3804	The Gap Band II	1979	2.50	5.00	10.00
SRM-1-4003	The Gap Band III	1980	2.50	5.00	10.00
822788-1	The Gap Band III	198?	2.00	4.00	8.00
—Reissue					
826808-1	The 12" Collection	1986	2.00	4.00	8.00
PASSPORT					
PB-6026	Strike a Groove	1983	2.50	5.00	10.00
SHELTER					
2111	Magicians' Holiday	1974	3.75	7.50	15.00
TATTOO					
BJL1-2168	The Gap Band	1977	3.75	7.50	15.00
TOTAL EXPERIENCE					
2700-1-T	Gap Band VIII	1986	2.00	4.00	8.00
2710-1-T	Straight from the Heart	1987	2.00	4.00	8.00
TE-1-3001	Gap Band IV	1982	2.00	4.00	8.00
TE-1-3004	Gap Band V — Jammin'	1983	2.00	4.00	8.00
TEL8-5705	Gap Band VI	1984	2.00	4.00	8.00
TEL8-5714	Gap Band VII	1986	2.00	4.00	8.00
812186-1	Gap Band V — Jammin'	198?	—	3.00	6.00
—Reissue					
822794-1	Gap Band IV	198?	—	3.00	6.00
—Reissue					
824343-1	Gap Gold/Best of the Gap Band	1985	2.00	4.00	8.00

GARAGIOLA, JOE

Number	Title (A Side/B Side)	Yr	VG	VG+	NM
Albums					
UNITED ARTISTS					
UAL-3032 [M]	That Holler Guy!	1959	10.00	20.00	40.00
UAS-6032 [S]	That Holler Guy!	1959	12.50	25.00	50.00

GARCIA, JERRY

Also see THE GRATEFUL DEAD; NEW RIDERS OF THE PURPLE SAGE; OLD & IN THE WAY.

Number	Title (A Side/B Side)	Yr	VG	VG+	NM
45s					
ROUND					
4504	Let It Rock/Midnight Town	1974	—	3.00	6.00
WARNER BROS.					
7551	Deal/The Wheel	1972	—	3.00	6.00
7569	Deep Hour/Sugaree	1972	—	3.00	6.00
Albums					
ARISTA					
AB 4160	Cats Under the Stars	1978	3.00	6.00	12.00
AL 8364	Run for the Roses	198?	2.00	4.00	8.00
—Reissue of 9603					
AL 9603	Run for the Roses	1982	3.00	6.00	12.00
ROUND					
RX-102	Garcia	1974	6.25	12.50	25.00
RX-107	Reflections	1975	7.50	15.00	30.00
RN-LA565-G	Reflections	1976	5.00	10.00	20.00
—Reissue of Round 107 with United Artists distribution					
WARNER BROS.					
BS 2582	Garcia	1972	10.00	20.00	40.00
—Green label with "WB" logo					

GARDENIAS, THE (1)

Number	Title (A Side/B Side)	Yr	VG	VG+	NM
45s					
FEDERAL					
12284	Flaming Love/My Baby's Tops	1956	30.00	60.00	120.00

GARDENIAS, THE (2)

Number	Title (A Side/B Side)	Yr	VG	VG+	NM
45s					
FAIRLANE					
21019	Darling It's You, You, You/What's the Matter with Me	1962	6.25	12.50	25.00

GARDNER, BROTHER DAVE

Includes records as "Dave Gardner."

Number	Title (A Side/B Side)	Yr	VG	VG+	NM
45s					
DECCA					
30548	Hop Along Rock/All By Myself	1958	5.00	10.00	20.00
30627	Slick Slacks/Wild Streak	1958	10.00	20.00	40.00
OJ					
1002	White Silver Sands/Fat Charlie	1957	3.75	7.50	15.00
1006	Love Is My Business/Mad Witch	1958	3.75	7.50	15.00
RCA VICTOR					
47-7876	Coward at the Alamo/You Are My Love	1961	2.50	5.00	10.00

Number	Title (A Side/B Side)	Yr	VG	VG+	NM
Albums					
4 STAR					
4S 75003	Brother Dave Gardner's New Comedy Album	1976	5.00	10.00	20.00
CAPITOL					
ST 1867 [S]	It Don't Make No Difference	1963	6.25	12.50	25.00
T 1867 [M]	It Don't Make No Difference	1963	5.00	10.00	20.00
ST 2055 [S]	It's All in How You Look at It	1964	6.25	12.50	25.00
T 2055 [M]	It's All in How You Look at It	1964	5.00	10.00	20.00
RCA VICTOR					
LPM-2083 [M]	Rejoice, Dear Hearts!	1960	5.00	10.00	20.00
LSP-2083(e) [S]	Rejoice, Dear Hearts!	196?	6.25	12.50	25.00
LPM-2239 [M]	Kick Thy Own Self	1960	5.00	10.00	20.00
LSP-2239(e) [S]	Kick Thy Own Self	196?	6.25	12.50	25.00
LPM-2335 [M]	Ain't That Weird?	1961	5.00	10.00	20.00
LSP-2335 [S]	Ain't That Weird?	1961	6.25	12.50	25.00
LPM-2498 [M]	Did You Ever?	1962	5.00	10.00	20.00
LSP-2498 [S]	Did You Ever?	1962	6.25	12.50	25.00
LPM-2628 [M]	All Seriousness Aside	1963	5.00	10.00	20.00
LSP-2628 [S]	All Seriousness Aside	1963	6.25	12.50	25.00
LPM-2761 [M]	It's Bigger Than Both of Us	1963	5.00	10.00	20.00
LSP-2761 [S]	It's Bigger Than Both of Us	1963	6.25	12.50	25.00
LPM-2852 [M]	Best of Dave Gardner	1964	5.00	10.00	20.00
LSP-2852 [S]	Best of Dave Gardner	1964	6.25	12.50	25.00
TONKA					
TLP 713	Out Front	1969	5.00	10.00	20.00
TOWER					
ST 5050 [S]	Hip-ocracy	1966	5.00	10.00	20.00
T 5050 [M]	Hip-ocracy	1966	3.75	7.50	15.00
ST 5075 [S]	It Don't Make No Difference	1967	5.00	10.00	20.00
T 5075 [M]	It Don't Make No Difference	1967	3.75	7.50	15.00

GARDNER, DON

Also see DON GARDNER AND DEE DEE FORD.

Number	Title (A Side/B Side)	Yr	VG	VG+	NM
45s					
BRUCE					
105	How Do You Speak to an Angel/Sonotone Bounce	1954	15.00	30.00	60.00
108	I'll Walk Alone/Going Down Mary	1954	12.50	25.00	50.00
127	It's a Sin to Tell a Lie/I Hear a Rhapsody	1955	12.50	25.00	50.00
DELUXE					
6133	This Nearly Was Mine/A Dagger in My Chest	1957	6.25	12.50	25.00
6155	There! I've Said It Again/I Don't Want to Go Home	1958	6.25	12.50	25.00
JUBILEE					
5482	I Really Love You Baby/Talking About You	1964	2.50	5.00	10.00
5484	The Bitter with the Sweet/I Don't Know What I'm Gonna Do	1964	2.50	5.00	10.00
5493	Little Girl Blue/I'm In Such Misery	1964	2.50	5.00	10.00
MR. G					
824	Your Love Is Driving Me Crazy/There Ain't Gonna Be No Loving	1969	2.00	4.00	8.00

GARDNER, DON, AND DEE DEE FORD

Also see each artist's individual listings.

Number	Title (A Side/B Side)	Yr	VG	VG+	NM
45s					
FIRE					
508	I Need Your Loving/Tell Me	1962	5.00	10.00	20.00
—Red label					
508	I Need Your Loving/Tell Me	1962	3.75	7.50	15.00
—Multicolor label					
513	Don't You Worry/I'm Coming Home to Stay	1962	3.75	7.50	15.00
517	Lead Me On/TCB (Taking Care of Business)	1962	3.75	7.50	15.00
KC					
196	Glory of Love/'Deed I Do	1963	3.00	6.00	12.00
LUDIX					
104	You Upset My Soul/Son My Son	1963	3.00	6.00	12.00
Albums					
COLLECTABLES					
COL-5155	Golden Classics: Need Your Lovin'	198?	3.00	6.00	12.00
FIRE					
LP-105 [M]	Need Your Lovin'	1962	100.00	200.00	400.00
SUE					
LP-1044 [M]	Don Gardner and Dee Dee Ford In Sweden	1965	30.00	60.00	120.00

GARDNERS, THE

Number	Title (A Side/B Side)	Yr	VG	VG+	NM
Albums					
PRESTIGE INT'L.					
PRLP-13062 [M]	Folk Songs Far and Near	1962	7.50	15.00	30.00

GARFUNKEL, ART

Also see SIMON AND GARFUNKEL; TOM AND JERRY (1).

Number	Title (A Side/B Side)	Yr	VG	VG+	NM
45s					
COLUMBIA					
02307	A Heart in New York/Is This Love	1981	—	2.00	4.00
02307 [PS]	A Heart in New York/Is This Love	1981	—	2.00	4.00
02627	Bright Eyes/The Romance	1981	—	2.00	4.00
06590	Carol of the Birds/The Decree	1986	—	—	3.00
—With Amy Grant					
06590 [PS]	Carol of the Birds/The Decree	1986	—	—	3.00
07711	So Much in Love/King of Tonga	1988	—	—	3.00
07949	This Is the Moment/Slow Breakup	1988	—	—	3.00
08511	When a Man Loves a Woman/I Have a Love	1988	—	—	3.00
10020	Second Avenue/Woyaya	1974	—	2.50	5.00
—As "Garfunkel"					
10190	I Only Have Eyes for You/Looking for the Right One	1975	—	2.50	5.00
10274	Breakaway/Disney Girls	1975	—	2.50	5.00
10608	Crying in My Sleep/Mr. Shuck 'N' Jive	1977	—	2.50	5.00
10676	(What a) Wonderful World/Wooden Planes	1978	—	3.00	6.00
—A-side: Art Garfunkel with Paul Simon and James Taylor					
10933	In a Little While (I'll Be On My Way)/And I Know	1979	—	2.00	4.00
10999	Since I Don't Have You/When Someone Doesn't Want You	1979	—	2.00	4.00
11050	Bright Eyes/Sail on a Rainbow	1979	—	2.00	4.00
45926	All I Know/Mary Was An Only Child	1973	—	2.50	5.00
—As "Garfunkel"					
45926	All I Know/Mary Was An Only Child	1973	—	2.50	5.00
—As "Art Garfunkel"					
45926 [Q]	All I Know/Mary Was An Only Child	1973	2.50	5.00	10.00
—As "Garfunkel"; promo-only quadraphonic pressing					
45983	I Shall Sing/Feuilles-Oh: Do Space Men Pass Dead Souls on Their Way to the Moon	1973	—	2.50	5.00
—As "Garfunkel"					
46030	Traveling Boy/Old Men	1974	—	2.50	5.00
—As "Garfunkel"					
OCTAVIA					
8002	Forgive Me/Private World	1960	10.00	20.00	40.00
—As "Artie Garr"					
WARWICK					
515	Beat Love/Dream Alone	1959	10.00	20.00	40.00
—As "Artie Garr"					
Albums					
COLUMBIA					
CQ 31474 [Q]	Angel Clare	1973	5.00	10.00	20.00
KC 31474	Angel Clare	1973	3.00	6.00	12.00
PC 31474	Angel Clare	197?	2.00	4.00	8.00
—Reissue					
PC 33700	Breakaway	1975	3.00	6.00	12.00
—Originals have no bar code					
PC 33700	Breakaway	197?	2.00	4.00	8.00
—With bar code on cover					
PCQ 33700 [Q]	Breakaway	1975	5.00	10.00	20.00
JC 34975	Watermark	1978	25.00	50.00	100.00
—Stock copy with "Fingerpaint" on side 2					
JC 34975	Watermark	1978	3.00	6.00	12.00
—Stock copy with "(What a) Wonderful World" on side 2					
JC 34975 [DJ]	Watermark	1978	15.00	30.00	60.00
—Test pressing or white label promo with "Fingerpaint" on side 2					
PC 34975	Watermark	198?	2.00	4.00	8.00
—Reissue					
JC 35780	Fate for Breakfast	1979	3.00	6.00	12.00
—With six different covers, each illustrating Art Garfunkel at a different stage of eating breakfast. No difference in value.					
FC 37392	Scissors Cut	1981	2.50	5.00	10.00
FC 40212	The Animals' Christmas By Jimmy Webb	1986	2.50	5.00	10.00
—With Amy Grant					
FC 40942	Lefty	1988	2.00	4.00	8.00
OC 45008	Garfunkel	1989	2.50	5.00	10.00

GARLAND, JUDY

Number	Title (A Side/B Side)	Yr	VG	VG+	NM
45s					
ABC					
10973	I Feel a Song Coming On/What Now My Love	1967	2.00	4.00	8.00
CAPITOL					
4624	Rock-a-Bye Your Baby with a Dixie Melody/Zing Went the Strings of My Heart	1961	2.50	5.00	10.00
4656	Sweet Dancer/Comes Once in a Lifetime	1961	2.50	5.00	10.00
4938	Hello Bluebird/I Could Go On Singing	1963	2.50	5.00	10.00
CAPITOL STARLINE					
6125	San Francisco/Chicago	1968	2.00	4.00	8.00
—Originals have red and white "target" labels					
6126	The Man That Got Away/April Showers	1968	2.00	4.00	8.00
—Originals have red and white "target" labels					
6127	Rock-a-Bye Your Baby with a Dixie Melody/Come Rain or Come Shine	1968	2.00	4.00	8.00
—Originals have red and white "target" labels					
6128	Over the Rainbow/Maybe I'll Come Back	1968	2.00	4.00	8.00
—Originals have red and white "target" labels					
6129	That's Entertainment/Swanee	1968	2.00	4.00	8.00
—Originals have red and white "target" labels					
COLUMBIA					
40010	Send My Baby Back to Me/Without a Memory	1953	3.75	7.50	15.00
40023	Go Home Joe/Heartbroken	1953	3.75	7.50	15.00
40270	The Man That Got Away/Here's What I'm Here For	1954	3.75	7.50	15.00
DECCA					
23658	The Birthday of a King/The Star of the East	195?	3.75	7.50	15.00
29295	Have Yourself a Merry Little Christmas/You'll Never Walk Alone	1954	3.75	7.50	15.00
MGM					
166	Over the Rainbow/You Made Me Love You	196?	2.00	4.00	8.00
505	Over the Rainbow/You Made Me Love You	1969	2.00	4.00	8.00
WARNER BROS.					
5310	Little Drops of Rain/Paris Is a Lonely Town	1962	2.50	5.00	10.00
7-Inch Extended Plays					
DECCA					
ED 2050	Smilin' Through/You'll Never Walk Alone//The Boy Next Door/I'm Always Chasing Rainbows	195?	3.75	7.50	15.00
ED 2050 [PS]	Judy Garland Vol. 2	195?	3.75	7.50	15.00
Albums					
ABC					
620 [M]	Judy Garland At Home at the Palace — Opening Night	1967	5.00	10.00	20.00
S-620 [S]	Judy Garland At Home at the Palace — Opening Night	1967	6.25	12.50	25.00
AC-30007	The ABC Collection	1976	3.75	7.50	15.00
A.E.I.					
2108	Judy Garland Vol. 1: Born in a Trunk	198?	2.50	5.00	10.00
2109	Judy Garland Vol. 2: 1940-45	198?	2.50	5.00	10.00
2110	Judy Garland Vol. 3: Superstar 1945-50	198?	2.50	5.00	10.00
CAPITOL					
W 676 [M]	Miss Show Business	1955	10.00	20.00	40.00
DT 734 [R]	Judy	1963	3.75	7.50	15.00
T 734 [M]	Judy	1956	10.00	20.00	40.00
DT 835 [R]	Alone	1963	3.75	7.50	15.00
T 835 [M]	Alone	1957	10.00	20.00	40.00

Number	Title (A Side/B Side)	Yr	VG	VG+	NM
ST 1036 [S]	Judy in Love	1959	10.00	20.00	40.00
T 1036 [M]	Judy in Love	1958	6.25	12.50	25.00
ST 1118 [S]	Garland at the Grove	1959	10.00	20.00	40.00
T 1118 [M]	Garland at the Grove	1959	6.25	12.50	25.00
ST 1188 [S]	The Letter	1959	10.00	20.00	40.00
—Add 80% if letter is on cover					
T 1188 [M]	The Letter	1959	6.25	12.50	25.00
—Add 80% if letter is on cover					
ST 1467 [S]	Judy — That's Entertainment	1960	10.00	20.00	40.00
T 1467 [M]	Judy — That's Entertainment	1960	6.25	12.50	25.00
SWBO 1569 [(2) S]	Judy at Carnegie Hall	1961	12.50	25.00	50.00
WBO 1569 [(2) M]	Judy at Carnegie Hall	1961	10.00	20.00	40.00
SW 1710 [S]	The Garland Touch	1962	7.50	15.00	30.00
W 1710 [M]	The Garland Touch	1962	5.00	10.00	20.00
SW 1861 [S]	I Could Go On Singing	1963	15.00	30.00	60.00
W 1861 [M]	I Could Go On Singing	1963	10.00	20.00	40.00
ST 1941 [S]	Our Love Letter	1963	7.50	15.00	30.00
T 1941 [M]	Our Love Letter	1963	5.00	10.00	20.00
SM-1999	The Hits of Judy Garland	197?	2.50	5.00	10.00
—Reissue					
ST 1999 [S]	The Hits of Judy Garland	1964	7.50	15.00	30.00
T 1999 [M]	The Hits of Judy Garland	1964	5.00	10.00	20.00
DW 2062 [R]	Just for Openers	1964	3.75	7.50	15.00
W 2062 [M]	Just for Openers	1964	5.00	10.00	20.00
STCL 2988 [(3)]	The Judy Garland Deluxe Set	1968	10.00	20.00	40.00
SM-11763	Alone	1978	2.50	5.00	10.00
—Reissue of 835					
SM-11876	Judy — That's Entertainment	1978	2.50	5.00	10.00
—Reissue					
M-12034	Just for Openers	1979	2.50	5.00	10.00
SN-16175	The Hits of Judy Garland	198?	2.00	4.00	8.00
—Budget-line reissue					
DECCA					
DXB 172 [(2) M]	The Best of Judy Garland	1963	5.00	10.00	20.00
DL 4199 [M]	The Magic of Judy Garland	1961	7.50	15.00	30.00
DL 6020 [10]	Judy at the Palace	1952	25.00	50.00	100.00
DXSB 7172 [(2) R]	The Best of Judy Garland	1963	5.00	10.00	20.00
DL 8190 [M]	Judy Garland's Greatest Performances	1955	10.00	20.00	40.00
DL 75150 [R]	Judy Garland's Greatest Hits	1969	3.00	6.00	12.00
DRG					
SL-5179	The Wit and the Wonder	198?	2.50	5.00	10.00
SL-5187	The Beginning	198?	2.50	5.00	10.00
MARK 56					
632 [PD]	In Concert: San Francisco	1978	15.00	30.00	60.00
MCA					
907	From the Decca Vaults	198?	2.50	5.00	10.00
4003 [(2)]	The Best of Judy Garland	197?	3.00	6.00	12.00
4046 [(2)]	Collector's Items (1936-45)	197?	3.00	6.00	12.00
25165	The Best of Judy Garland from MGM Classic Films	1988	3.00	6.00	12.00
METRO					
M-506 [M]	Judy Garland	1965	3.75	7.50	15.00
MS-506 [S]	Judy Garland	1965	5.00	10.00	20.00
M-581 [M]	Judy Garland in Song	1966	3.75	7.50	15.00
MS-581 [S]	Judy Garland in Song	1966	5.00	10.00	20.00
MGM					
SDP-1 [(2)]	Golden Years at MGM	1969	7.50	15.00	30.00
E-82 [10]	Judy Garland Sings	1951	25.00	50.00	100.00
E-3149 [M]	If You Feel Like Singing, Sing	1955	15.00	30.00	60.00
E-3989 [M]	The Judy Garland Story Vol. 1: The Star Years	1961	7.50	15.00	30.00
E-4005 [M]	The Judy Garland Story Vol. 2: The Hollywood Years	1962	7.50	15.00	30.00
E-4204 [M]	The Very Best of Judy Garland	1964	7.50	15.00	30.00
SE-4204 [R]	The Very Best of Judy Garland	1964	3.75	7.50	15.00
PAIR					
PDL2-1030 [(2)]	Golden Memories	1986	3.00	6.00	12.00
PDL2-1127 [(2)]	The Legendary Judy Garland	1986	3.00	6.00	12.00
PICKWICK					
PTP-2010 [(2)]	Her Greatest Hits	197?	3.00	6.00	12.00
SPC-3053	I Feel a Song Coming On	197?	3.00	6.00	12.00
STANYAN					
POW-3001	More Than a Memory	198?	2.50	5.00	10.00
—Reissue of 10095					
10095	More Than a Memory	1974	2.50	5.00	10.00

GARLAND, JUDY, AND LIZA MINNELLI

Also see each artist's individual listings.

45s

Number	Title (A Side/B Side)	Yr	VG	VG+	NM
CAPITOL					
5497	Hello Dolly/He's Got the Whole World In His Hands	1965	2.00	4.00	8.00

Albums

Number	Title (A Side/B Side)	Yr	VG	VG+	NM
CAPITOL					
SWBO 2295 [(2) S]	"Live" at the London Palladium	1965	7.50	15.00	30.00
WBO 2295 [(2) M]	"Live" at the London Palladium	1965	6.25	12.50	25.00
ST-11191	"Live" at the London Palladium	1973	3.00	6.00	12.00
—Condensation of above 2-record set					
MOBILE FIDELITY					
1-048	"Live" at the London Palladium	1981	6.25	12.50	25.00
—Audiophile vinyl					

GARNER, ERROLL

45s

Number	Title (A Side/B Side)	Yr	VG	VG+	NM
ABC-PARAMOUNT					
10260	Dreamstreet/When You're Smiling	1961	2.00	4.00	8.00
10301	You Do Something to Me/Some of These Days	1962	2.00	4.00	8.00
COLUMBIA					
1-868 (?)	When Johnny Comes Marching Home/I Don't Know Why	1950	5.00	10.00	20.00
—Microgroove 33 1/3 rpm 7-inch single					
6-868 (?)	When Johnny Comes Marching Home/I Don't Know Why	1950	3.75	7.50	15.00
1-880 (?)	Petite Waltz Bounce/Petite Waltz	1950	5.00	10.00	20.00
—Microgroove 33 1/3 rpm 7-inch single					
6-880 (?)	Petite Waltz Bounce/Petite Waltz	1950	3.75	7.50	15.00
39100	People Will Say We're in Love/Lover	1950	3.75	7.50	15.00
39145	How High the Moon/Poor Butterfly	1951	3.75	7.50	15.00
39165	When Johnny Comes Marching Home/My Heart Stood Still	1951	3.00	6.00	12.00
39166	Poor Butterfly/Long Ago and Far Away	1951	3.00	6.00	12.00
39167	When You're Smiling/Spring Is Here	1951	3.00	6.00	12.00
39168	It Could Happen to You/I Don't Know Why	1951	3.00	6.00	12.00
—The above four comprise a box set					
39249	Honeysuckle Rose/My Heart Stood Still	1951	3.75	7.50	15.00
39273	I Cover the Waterfront/Laura	1951	3.00	6.00	12.00
39274	I'm in the Mood for Love/Body and Soul	1951	3.00	6.00	12.00
39275	The Way You Look Tonight/Indiana	1951	3.00	6.00	12.00
39276	Penthouse Serenade/Play, Piano, Play	1951	3.00	6.00	12.00
—The above four comprise a box set					
39580	It's the Talk of the Town/Robbins' Nest	1951	3.75	7.50	15.00
39615	Sophisticated Lady/Fine and Dandy	1951	3.75	7.50	15.00
39681	Ain't She Sweet/Please Don't Talk About Me When I'm Gone	1952	3.00	6.00	12.00
39713	Ja Da/Oh Lady Be Good	1952	3.00	6.00	12.00
39734	Out of Nowhere/Music, Maestro, Please	1952	3.00	6.00	12.00
39746	Cocktails for Two/Dancing in the Dark	1952	2.50	5.00	10.00
39747	Willow Weep for Me/I Don't Hear a Thing	1952	2.50	5.00	10.00
39748	Chopin Impressions/How Come You Do	1952	2.50	5.00	10.00
39749	With Every Breath I Take/Love Me or Leave Me	1952	2.50	5.00	10.00
—The above four comprise a box set					
39888	Summertime/What's New	1952	3.00	6.00	12.00
39918	Am I Blue/I Never Knew	1953	3.00	6.00	12.00
39996	Lullaby of Birdland/Easy to Love	1953	3.00	6.00	12.00
40043	St. Louis Blues/My Ideal	1953	3.00	6.00	12.00
40074	Frenesi/Mean to Me	1953	3.00	6.00	12.00
40172	You're Driving Me Crazy/Oh, What a Beautiful Morning	1954	3.00	6.00	12.00
40766	On the Street Where You Live/Dreamy	1956	2.50	5.00	10.00
40899	Way Back Blues (Part 1)/Way Back Blues (Part 2)	1957	2.50	5.00	10.00
41067	Misty/Moment's Delight	1957	3.00	6.00	12.00
41231	I Can't Get Started/Just Blues	1958	2.50	5.00	10.00
41482	Misty/Solitude	1959	2.50	5.00	10.00
MERCURY					
1001	Embraceable You/Lover Come Back to Me	195?	3.75	7.50	15.00
70442	Misty/Exactly Like You	1954	3.75	7.50	15.00
70487	Rosalie/There's a Small Hotel	1954	3.00	6.00	12.00
70649	That Old Black Magic/Night and Day	1955	3.00	6.00	12.00
72192	Mimi/Theme from "A New Kind of Love"	1963	2.00	4.00	8.00
73177	For Once in My Life/Mood Island	1971	—	2.00	4.00
MGM					
13471	As Time Goes By/You Made Me Love You	1966	—	3.00	6.00
13547	Affinidad/That's My Kick	1966	—	3.00	6.00
13677	It Ain't Necessarily So/More	1967	—	3.00	6.00
13834	Nervous Waltz/As Time Goes By	1967	—	3.00	6.00
13870	Blue Moon/Like It Is	1967	—	3.00	6.00
13916	Watermelon Man/Gaslight	1968	—	2.50	5.00
13988	Coffee Song/Up in Erroll's Room	1968	—	2.50	5.00
14043	Cheek to Cheek/It's the Talk of the Town	1969	—	2.50	5.00
OKEH					
6898	Laura/Penthouse Serenade	1952	5.00	10.00	20.00
RCA VICTOR					
47-4723	Stariway to the Stars/I Can't Escape from You	1952	3.75	7.50	15.00
REPRISE					
20179	Moritat/Sweet and Lovely	1963	2.00	4.00	8.00

7-Inch Extended Plays

Number	Title (A Side/B Side)	Yr	VG	VG+	NM
COLUMBIA					
B-2586	*Penthouse Serenade/The Way You Look Tonight/I'm in the Mood for Love/Indiana	1959	3.00	6.00	12.00
B-2586 [PS]	Erroll Garner (Hall of Fame Series)	1959	3.00	6.00	12.00

Albums

Number	Title (A Side/B Side)	Yr	VG	VG+	NM
ABC-PARAMOUNT					
365 [M]	Dreamstreet	1961	5.00	10.00	20.00
S-365 [S]	Dreamstreet	1961	6.25	12.50	25.00
395 [M]	Closeup in Swing	1961	5.00	10.00	20.00
S-395 [S]	Closeup in Swing	1961	6.25	12.50	25.00
ARCHIVE OF FOLK AND JAZZ					
245	Erroll Garner	1970	2.50	5.00	10.00
ATLANTIC					
ALR-109 [10]	Rhapsody	1950	20.00	40.00	80.00
ALR-112 [10]	Erroll Garner at the Piano	1951	20.00	40.00	80.00
ALR-128 [10]	Passport to Fame	1952	25.00	50.00	100.00
ALR-135 [10]	Piano Solos, Volume 2	1952	20.00	40.00	80.00
1227 [M]	The Greatest Garner	1956	10.00	20.00	40.00
—Black label					
1227 [M]	The Greatest Garner	1961	3.75	7.50	15.00
—Multi-color label with white "fan" logo					
1227 [M]	The Greatest Garner	196?	3.00	6.00	12.00
—Multi-color label with black "fan" logo					
1315 [M]	Perpetual Motion	1959	10.00	20.00	40.00
—Black label					
BARONET					
B-109 [M]	Informal Piano Improvisations	1962	3.00	6.00	12.00
BS-109 [R]	Informal Piano Improvisations	1962	2.50	5.00	10.00
BLUE NOTE					
BLP-5007 [10]	Overture to Dawn, Volume 1	1952	50.00	100.00	200.00
BLP-5008 [10]	Overture to Dawn, Volume 2	1952	50.00	100.00	200.00
BLP-5014 [10]	Overture to Dawn, Volume 3	1953	50.00	100.00	200.00
BLP-5015 [10]	Overture to Dawn, Volume 4	1953	50.00	100.00	200.00
BLP-5016 [10]	Overture to Dawn, Volume 5	1953	50.00	100.00	200.00
CLARION					
610 [M]	Serenade in Blue	1966	3.00	6.00	12.00
SD 610 [S]	Serenade in Blue	1966	3.00	6.00	12.00
COLUMBIA					
C2L 9 [(2) M]	Paris Impressions	1958	10.00	20.00	40.00
CL 535 [M]	Erroll Garner	1953	15.00	30.00	60.00
—Red label with gold print					

Number	Title (A Side/B Side)	Yr	VG	VG+	NM
CL 535 [M]	Erroll Garner	1956	7.50	15.00	30.00
—Red and black label with six "eye" logos					
CL 583 [M]	Gems	1954	15.00	30.00	60.00
—Red label with gold print					
CL 583 [M]	Gems	1956	7.50	15.00	30.00
—Red and black label with six "eye" logos					
CL 617 [M]	Gone Garner Gonest	1955	15.00	30.00	60.00
—Red label with gold print					
CL 617 [M]	Gone Garner Gonest	1956	7.50	15.00	30.00
—Red and black label with six "eye" logos					
CL 667 [M]	Erroll Garner Plays for Dancing	1956	7.50	15.00	30.00
CL 883 [M]	Concert by the Sea	1956	7.50	15.00	30.00
CL 939 [M]	The Most Happy Piano	1957	7.50	15.00	30.00
CL 1014 [M]	Other Voices	1957	7.50	15.00	30.00
CL 1060 [M]	Soliloquy	1957	7.50	15.00	30.00
CL 1141 [M]	Encores in Hi-Fi	1958	7.50	15.00	30.00
CL 1216 [M]	Paris Impressions, Volume 1	1958	5.00	10.00	20.00
CL 1217 [M]	Paris Impressions, Volume 2	1958	5.00	10.00	20.00
CL 1452 [M]	The One and Only Erroll Garner	1960	5.00	10.00	20.00
CL 1512 [M]	Swinging Solos	1960	5.00	10.00	20.00
CL 1587 [M]	The Provocative Erroll Garner	1961	5.00	10.00	20.00
CL 2540 [10]	Garnerland	1955	15.00	30.00	60.00
CL 2606 [10]	He's Here! He's Gone! He's Garner!	1956	15.00	30.00	60.00
CL 6139 [10]	Piano Moods	1950	20.00	40.00	80.00
CL 6173 [10]	Gems	1951	20.00	40.00	80.00
CL 6209 [10]	Solo Flight	1952	20.00	40.00	80.00
CL 6259 [10]	Erroll Garner Plays for Dancing	1953	20.00	40.00	80.00
CS 8252 [S]	The One and Only Erroll Garner	1960	6.25	12.50	25.00
CS 8312 [S]	Swinging Solos	1960	6.25	12.50	25.00
CS 8387 [S]	The Provocative Erroll Garner	1961	6.25	12.50	25.00
CS 9820 [R]	Other Voices	1970	3.00	6.00	12.00
CS 9821 [R]	Concert by the Sea	1970	3.00	6.00	12.00
PG 33424 [(2)]	Play It Again, Erroll!	1975	3.00	6.00	12.00
COLUMBIA JAZZ MASTERPIECES					
CJ 40863	Long Ago and Far Away	1987	3.00	6.00	12.00
COLUMBIA SPECIAL PRODUCTS					
P 14386	Dreamy	1978	2.50	5.00	10.00
DIAL					
LP-205 [10]	Erroll Garner, Volume 1	1950	50.00	100.00	200.00
LP-902 [M]	Free Piano Improvisations Recorded by Baron Timme Rosenkranz at One of His Famous Gaslight Jazz Sessions	1949	75.00	150.00	300.00
EMARCY					
MG-26016 [10]	Garnering	1954	20.00	40.00	80.00
MG-26042 [10]	Gone with Garner	1954	20.00	40.00	80.00
MG-36001 [M]	Contrasts	1955	7.50	15.00	30.00
MG-36026 [M]	Garnering	1955	7.50	15.00	30.00
MG-36069 [M]	Erroll!	1956	7.50	15.00	30.00
826224-1	Erroll Garner Plays Gershwin and Kern	1986	2.50	5.00	10.00
832994-1	The Erroll Garner Collection Vol. 1: Easy to Love	1988	2.50	5.00	10.00
834935-1	The Erroll Garner Collection Vol. 2: Dancing on the Ceiling	1989	2.50	5.00	10.00
HALL OF FAME					
610	Early Erroll	198?	2.50	5.00	10.00
HARMONY					
HS 11268	One More Time	1968	3.00	6.00	12.00
JAZZTONE					
J-1269 [M]	Early Erroll	1957	10.00	20.00	40.00
KING					
295-17 [10]	Piano Stylist	1952	20.00	40.00	80.00
395-540 [M]	Piano Variations	1958	12.50	25.00	50.00
LONDON					
XPS 617	Gemini	1972	3.00	6.00	12.00
APS 640	Magician	1973	3.00	6.00	12.00
MERCURY					
MG-20009 [M]	Erroll Garner at the Piano	1953	12.50	25.00	50.00
MG-20055 [M]	Mambo Moves Garner	1954	12.50	25.00	50.00
MG-20063 [M]	Solitaire	1954	12.50	25.00	50.00
MG-20090 [M]	Afternoon of an Elf	1955	12.50	25.00	50.00
MG-20662 [M]	Erroll Garner Plays Misty	1962	3.75	7.50	15.00
MG-20803 [M]	The Best of Erroll Garner	1963	3.75	7.50	15.00
MG-20859 [M]	New Kind of Love	1963	3.75	7.50	15.00
MG-21308 [M]	Feeling Is Believing	1964	3.75	7.50	15.00
MG-25117 [10]	Erroll Garner at the Piano	1951	20.00	40.00	80.00
MG-25157 [10]	Gone with Garner	1951	20.00	40.00	80.00
SR-60662 [S]	Erroll Garner Plays Misty	1962	5.00	10.00	20.00
SR-60803 [S]	The Best of Erroll Garner	1963	5.00	10.00	20.00
SR-60859 [S]	New Kind of Love	1963	5.00	10.00	20.00
SR-61308 [S]	Feeling Is Believing	1964	5.00	10.00	20.00
826457-1	Afternoon of an Elf	1986	2.50	5.00	10.00
—Reissue					
MGM					
E-4335 [M]	Now Playing: Erroll Garner	1966	3.00	6.00	12.00
SE-4335 [S]	Now Playing: Erroll Garner	1966	3.75	7.50	15.00
E-4361 [M]	Campus Concert	1966	3.00	6.00	12.00
SE-4361 [S]	Campus Concert	1966	3.75	7.50	15.00
E-4463 [M]	That's My Kick	1967	3.75	7.50	15.00
SE-4463 [S]	That's My Kick	1967	3.00	6.00	12.00
E-4520 [M]	Up in Erroll's Room	1967	3.75	7.50	15.00
SE-4520 [S]	Up in Erroll's Room	1967	3.00	6.00	12.00
PICKWICK					
SPC-3254	Deep Purple	197?	2.50	5.00	10.00
REPRISE					
R 6080 [DJ]	One World Concert	1963	10.00	20.00	40.00
—Six-song sampler -- three on each side -- on a 12-inch record that plays at 45 rpm. This comes in a different cover than the stock copy; this is clearly marked "Special 45 RPM Preview Record" on the top front.					
R 6080 [M]	One World Concert	1963	5.00	10.00	20.00
RS 6080 [S]	One World Concert	1963	6.25	12.50	25.00
RONDO-LETTE					
A-15 [M]	Erroll Garner	1958	6.25	12.50	25.00
SAVOY					
SJC-411	Penthouse Serenade	1985	2.50	5.00	10.00
SJL-1118	Yesterdays	198?	2.50	5.00	10.00
SJL-2207 [(2)]	Elf	198?	3.00	6.00	12.00
MG-12002 [M]	Penthouse Serenade	1955	7.50	15.00	30.00
MG-12003 [M]	Serenade to "Laura"	1955	7.50	15.00	30.00
MG-15000 [10]	Erroll Garner Plays Piano Solos	1950	20.00	40.00	80.00
MG-15001 [10]	Erroll Garner Plays Piano Solos, Volume 2	1950	20.00	40.00	80.00
MG-15002 [10]	Erroll Garner Plays Piano Solos, Volume 3	1950	20.00	40.00	80.00
MG-15003 [10]	Erroll Garner Plays Piano Solos, Volume 4	1950	20.00	40.00	80.00
MG-15026 [10]	Erroll Garner at the Piano	1953	20.00	40.00	80.00
TRIP					
5519	Garnering	197?	2.50	5.00	10.00
WING					
MGW 12134	Erroll Garner Moods	196?	3.00	6.00	12.00

GARNER, ERROLL/PETE JOHNSON

Albums

Number	Title (A Side/B Side)	Yr	VG	VG+	NM
GRAND AWARD					
GA 33-321 [M]	Jazz Piano	1956	20.00	40.00	80.00
—With removable David Stone Martin cover still attached					
GA 33-321 [M]	Jazz Piano	1956	6.25	12.50	25.00
—Without removable cover					

GARNER, ERROLL/OSCAR PETERSON/ART TATUM

Albums

Number	Title (A Side/B Side)	Yr	VG	VG+	NM
RCA CAMDEN					
CAL-882 [M]	Great Jazz Pianists of Our Time	196?	3.75	7.50	15.00
CAS-882 [R]	Great Jazz Pianists of Our Time	196?	3.00	6.00	12.00

GARNER, ERROLL/BILLY TAYLOR

Albums

Number	Title (A Side/B Side)	Yr	VG	VG+	NM
SAVOY					
MG-12008 [M]	Erroll Garner/Billy Taylor	1955	12.50	25.00	50.00

GARNER, JOHNNY

45s

Number	Title (A Side/B Side)	Yr	VG	VG+	NM
IMPERIAL					
5536	Kiss Me Sweet/Little Starry Eyes	1958	6.25	12.50	25.00
5548	Didi Didi/The Fool	1958	12.50	25.00	50.00

GARNETT, GALE

45s

Number	Title (A Side/B Side)	Yr	VG	VG+	NM
COLUMBIA					
44479	Breaking Through/Fall in Love Again	1968	—	2.50	5.00
RCA VICTOR					
47-8388	We'll Sing in the Sunshine/Prism Song	1964	2.50	5.00	10.00
47-8472	Lovin' Place/I Used to Live Here	1964	2.00	4.00	8.00
47-8472 [PS]	Lovin' Place/I Used to Live Here	1964	2.00	4.00	8.00
47-8549	I'll Cry Alone/Where Do You Go to Go Away	1965	2.00	4.00	8.00
47-8668	I'm Gonna Sit Right Down and Write Myself a Letter/Why Am I Standing in the Window	1965	2.00	4.00	8.00
47-8824	This Kind of Love/Oh There'll Be Laughter	1966	—	3.00	6.00
47-8961	It's Been a Lonely Summer/You've Got to Fall in Love Again	1966	—	3.00	6.00
47-9020	The Sun Is Gray/I Make Him Fly	1966	—	3.00	6.00
47-9196	Over the Rainbow/The Cats I Know	1967	—	3.00	6.00

Albums

Number	Title (A Side/B Side)	Yr	VG	VG+	NM
COLUMBIA					
CL 2825 [M]	An Audience with the King of Wands	1968	5.00	10.00	20.00
CS 9625 [S]	An Audience with the King of Wands	1968	3.75	7.50	15.00
CS 9760	Sausalito Heliport	1969	3.75	7.50	15.00
RCA VICTOR					
LPM-2833 [M]	My Kind of Folk Songs	1964	10.00	20.00	40.00
—Black and white/blueish cover					
LPM-2833 [M]	My Kind of Folk Songs	1965	3.75	7.50	15.00
—Color photo on cover					
LSP-2833 [S]	My Kind of Folk Songs	1964	12.50	25.00	50.00
—Black and white/blueish cover					
LSP-2833 [S]	My Kind of Folk Songs	1965	5.00	10.00	20.00
—Color photo on cover					
LPM-3305 [M]	Lovin' Place	1965	3.75	7.50	15.00
LSP-3305 [S]	Lovin' Place	1965	5.00	10.00	20.00
LPM-3325 [M]	The Many Faces of Gale Garnett	1965	3.75	7.50	15.00
LSP-3325 [S]	The Many Faces of Gale Garnett	1965	5.00	10.00	20.00
LPM-3498 [M]	Variety Is the Spice of Gale Garnett	1966	3.75	7.50	15.00
LSP-3498 [S]	Variety Is the Spice of Gale Garnett	1966	5.00	10.00	20.00
LPM-3586 [M]	New Adventures	1966	3.75	7.50	15.00
LSP-3586 [S]	New Adventures	1966	5.00	10.00	20.00
LPM-3747 [M]	Flying and Rainbows and Love	1967	6.25	12.50	25.00
LSP-3747 [S]	Flying and Rainbows and Love	1967	5.00	10.00	20.00

GARR, ARTIE

See ART GARFUNKEL.

GARRETT, SCOTT

45s

Number	Title (A Side/B Side)	Yr	VG	VG+	NM
LAURIE					
3023	House of Love/So Far So Good	1959	5.00	10.00	20.00
3029	Love Story/Graduation Souvenir	1959	12.50	25.00	50.00
—With vocal backing by the Mystics					
3034	Where Are You/Jumpin' Blue Blazes	1959	5.00	10.00	20.00
OKEH					
7104	In My Heart/The Day I Died	1960	5.00	10.00	20.00

GARRETT, TOMMY, 50 GUITARS OF

45s

Number	Title (A Side/B Side)	Yr	VG	VG+	NM
LIBERTY					
55731	Stranger from Durango/Juarez	1964	—	3.00	6.00
55797	Corcovado/La Violettra	1965	—	3.00	6.00
55868	Our Man Flint/Tender Moments	1966	—	3.00	6.00
55888	La Cucaracha/Spanish Lights	1966	—	3.00	6.00
55969	Theme for Someone in Love/Courtin'	1967	—	3.00	6.00
56046	Hang 'Em High/Spanish Pearls	1968	—	2.50	5.00
56129	Flamenco Funk/Mexican Standoff	1969	—	2.50	5.00

Number	Title (A Side/B Side)	Yr	VG	VG+	NM
Albums					
LIBERTY					
L-5507 [M]	Limited Edition	196?	3.00	6.00	12.00
S-6607 [S]	Limited Edition	196?	3.75	7.50	15.00
LMM-13005 [M]	50 Guitars Go South of the Border	1961	3.00	6.00	12.00
—Better known as "Snuff" Garrett, longtime producer					
LMM-13016 [M]	50 Guitars Go South of the Border, Volume 2	1962	3.00	6.00	12.00
LMM-13022 [M]	50 Guitars Visit Hawaii	1962	3.00	6.00	12.00
LMM-13025 [M]	50 Guitars Go Country	1963	3.00	6.00	12.00
LMM-13028 [M]	50 Guitars Go Italiano	1964	3.00	6.00	12.00
LMM-13030 [M]	Maria Elena	1963	3.00	6.00	12.00
LMM-13031 [M]	Bordertown Bandito	1964	3.00	6.00	12.00
LMM-13032 [M]	Espana	1964	3.00	6.00	12.00
LMM-13033 [M]	Return to Paradise	1965	3.00	6.00	12.00
LMM-13035 [M]	Love Songs from South of the Border	1965	3.00	6.00	12.00
LMM-13036 [M]	Viva Mexico	1966	3.00	6.00	12.00
LMM-13037 [M]	50 Guitars in Love	1966	3.00	6.00	12.00
LMM-13039 [M]	More 50 Guitars in Love	1967	3.00	6.00	12.00
LSS-14005 [S]	50 Guitars Go South of the Border	1961	3.75	7.50	15.00
LSS-14016 [S]	50 Guitars Go South of the Border, Volume 2	1962	3.75	7.50	15.00
LSS-14022 [S]	50 Guitars Visit Hawaii	1962	3.75	7.50	15.00
LSS-14025 [S]	50 Guitars Go Country	1963	3.75	7.50	15.00
LSS-14028 [S]	50 Guitars Go Italiano	1964	3.75	7.50	15.00
LSS-14030 [S]	Maria Elena	1963	3.75	7.50	15.00
LSS-14031 [S]	Bordertown Bandito	1964	3.75	7.50	15.00
LSS-14032 [S]	Espana	1964	3.75	7.50	15.00
LSS-14033 [S]	Return to Paradise	1965	3.75	7.50	15.00
LSS-14035 [S]	Love Songs from South of the Border	1965	3.75	7.50	15.00
LSS-14036 [S]	Viva Mexico	1966	3.75	7.50	15.00
LSS-14037 [S]	50 Guitars in Love	1966	3.75	7.50	15.00
LSS-14039 [S]	More 50 Guitars in Love	1967	3.00	6.00	12.00
LSS-14045	The Best of the 50 Guitars of Tommy Garrett	1969	3.00	6.00	12.00
LSS-14046	Mexican Leather	1969	3.00	6.00	12.00
LSS-14047	For Midnight Lovers	1970	3.00	6.00	12.00
LSS-35001 [(2)]	The Best of the 50 Guitars of Tommy Garrett, Volumes 2 & 3	1970	3.75	7.50	15.00
MUSICOR					
4606 [(2)]	The Best of the 50 Guitars of Tommy Garrett	1976	3.00	6.00	12.00
PICKWICK					
SPC-3585	In Love	197?	2.00	4.00	8.00
SPC-3615	Brazilian Mood	197?	2.00	4.00	8.00
SUNSET					
SUS-5282	The Fabulous 50 Guitars of Tommy Garrett	197?	2.50	5.00	10.00
UNITED ARTISTS					
UA-LA039-F	You're a Lady	1973	2.50	5.00	10.00
UXS-79 [(2)]	Tommy Garrett Superpak	1972	3.00	6.00	12.00
UAS-5528	50 Guitars Go South of the Border, Volume 3	1971	2.50	5.00	10.00
UAS-5569	The Way of Love	1972	2.50	5.00	10.00

GARRIGAN, EDDIE

Number	Title (A Side/B Side)	Yr	VG	VG+	NM
45s					
FONTANA					
1575	I Wish I Was/Mail Call	1966	10.00	20.00	40.00

GARRISON, GLEN

Number	Title (A Side/B Side)	Yr	VG	VG+	NM
45s					
CREST					
1047	Lovin' Lorene/You're My Darling	1958	15.00	30.00	60.00
IMPERIAL					
66191	Green to Blue/You Can't Win 'Em All	1966	2.50	5.00	10.00
66215	Where Do I Go from Here/Strong and Handsome, Sweet and Simple Side	1966	2.50	5.00	10.00
66230	Listen, They're Playing My Song/My New Creation	1967	2.50	5.00	10.00
66257	Goodbye Swingers/Hello Mama	1967	2.50	5.00	10.00
66279	Your Side of Me/If I Lived Here (I'd Be Home Now)	1968	2.00	4.00	8.00
66300	I'll Be Your Baby Tonight/You Know I Love You	1968	2.00	4.00	8.00
66333	That Lucky Old Sun/She Thinks I Still Care	1968	2.00	4.00	8.00
66401	Goodnight Irene/Change Me	1969	2.00	4.00	8.00
LODE					
106	Pony Tail Girl/Ballad of Hank Gordon	1959	15.00	30.00	60.00

GARROWAY, DAVE

Number	Title (A Side/B Side)	Yr	VG	VG+	NM
Albums					
CAMEO					
C-1001 [M]	An Adventure in Hi-Fi Music	1958	10.00	20.00	40.00
—Black label, brown print, cameo figure at top					

GARY, JOHN

Number	Title (A Side/B Side)	Yr	VG	VG+	NM
45s					
ACE					
861	First Lady Waltz/A River of Silver	1962	3.00	6.00	12.00
FRATERNITY					
844	Let Them Talk/Tell My Love	1959	3.75	7.50	15.00
858	Little Things Mean a Lot/Ever Since I Met Lucy	1959	3.75	7.50	15.00
860	Thank the Lord (For This Thanksgiving Day)/The Rest of My Days	1959	3.75	7.50	15.00
864	The Shrine of St. Cecelia/When I'm Alone	1960	3.00	6.00	12.00
870	The Bell Rings/Forget It	1960	3.00	6.00	12.00
958	Let Them Talk/Tell My Love	1966	—	3.00	6.00
RCA VICTOR					
47-8292	That's Life/Ciumanchella	1963	2.00	4.00	8.00
47-8386	Warm and Willing/Friend and Lover	1964	2.00	4.00	8.00
47-8413	Soon I'll Wed My Love/The Young Lovers	1964	2.00	4.00	8.00
47-8475	Do You Hear What I Hear/Little Snow Girl	1964	3.00	6.00	12.00
47-8479	Sunrise, Sunset/The Bell Rings	1964	2.00	4.00	8.00
47-8526	Color of Love/My First Love Song	1965	—	3.00	6.00
47-8617	Joy in the Morning/Linger Awhile	1965	—	3.00	6.00
47-8677	Don't Throw Those Roses Away/Give Me This Moment	1965	—	3.00	6.00
47-8731	Ashamed/She Wasn't You	1965	—	3.00	6.00
47-8806	You Don't Know Me/Don't Let the Music Play	1966	—	3.00	6.00
47-8890	Sunrise, Sunset/The Bell Rings	1966	—	3.00	6.00
47-8993	Mine/You've Never Kissed Her	1966	—	3.00	6.00
47-9119	Hang On to Me/Sleeping Beauty	1967	—	3.00	6.00
47-9213	Everybody Say Peace/Spanish Moonlight	1967	—	3.00	6.00
47-9361	Cold/Imagine	1967	—	3.00	6.00
47-9456	A Certain Girl/The End of Time	1968	—	2.50	5.00
47-9540	Let There Be Peace on Earth/Give Some Time to Be Happy	1968	—	2.50	5.00
47-9868	In the Morning/In the Wind	1970	—	2.50	5.00
74-0149	The Windmills of Your Mind/Then She's a Lover	1969	—	2.50	5.00
74-0218	Natalie/Summer Me, Winter Me	1969	—	2.50	5.00
Albums					
CHURCHILL					
67236	In a Class By Himself	1977	2.50	5.00	10.00
LA BREA					
8010 [M]	John Gary	1961	6.25	12.50	25.00
S-8010 [S]	John Gary	1961	7.50	15.00	30.00
METRO					
M-522 [M]	John Gary	1966	2.50	5.00	10.00
MS-522 [S]	John Gary	1966	3.00	6.00	12.00
PICKWICK					
SPC-3025	John Gary	197?	2.50	5.00	10.00
RCA CAMDEN					
CAL-983 [M]	The One and Only John Gary	1966	2.50	5.00	10.00
CAS-983 [S]	The One and Only John Gary	1966	3.00	6.00	12.00
RCA VICTOR					
LOC-1139 [M]	The John Gary Carnegie Hall Concert	1967	5.00	10.00	20.00
LSO-1139 [S]	The John Gary Carnegie Hall Concert	1967	3.00	6.00	12.00
ANL1-2342	Pure Gold	1977	2.50	5.00	10.00
ANL1-2672	A Little Bit of Heaven	1978	2.50	5.00	10.00
—Reissue of LSP-2994					
LPM-2745 [M]	Catch a Rising Star	1963	3.75	7.50	15.00
LSP-2745 [S]	Catch a Rising Star	1963	5.00	10.00	20.00
LPM-2804 [M]	Encore	1964	3.75	7.50	15.00
LSP-2804 [S]	Encore	1964	5.00	10.00	20.00
LPM-2922 [M]	So Tenderly	1964	3.75	7.50	15.00
LSP-2922 [S]	So Tenderly	1964	5.00	10.00	20.00
LPM-2940 [M]	The John Gary Christmas Album	1964	3.75	7.50	15.00
LSP-2940 [S]	The John Gary Christmas Album	1964	5.00	10.00	20.00
LPM-2994 [M]	A Little Bit of Heaven	1965	3.00	6.00	12.00
LSP-2994 [S]	A Little Bit of Heaven	1965	3.75	7.50	15.00
LPM-3349 [M]	The Nearness of You	1965	3.00	6.00	12.00
LSP-3349 [S]	The Nearness of You	1965	3.75	7.50	15.00
LPM-3411 [M]	Your All-Time Favorite Songs	1965	3.00	6.00	12.00
LSP-3411 [S]	Your All-Time Favorite Songs	1965	3.75	7.50	15.00
LPM-3501 [M]	Choice	1966	3.00	6.00	12.00
LSP-3501 [S]	Choice	1966	3.75	7.50	15.00
LPM-3570 [M]	Your All-Time Country Favorites	1966	3.00	6.00	12.00
LSP-3570 [S]	Your All-Time Country Favorites	1966	3.75	7.50	15.00
LPM-3666 [M]	A Heart Filled with Song	1966	3.00	6.00	12.00
LSP-3666 [S]	A Heart Filled with Song	1966	3.75	7.50	15.00
LPM-3695 [M]	Especially for You	1967	3.75	7.50	15.00
LSP-3695 [S]	Especially for You	1967	3.00	6.00	12.00
LPM-3730 [M]	The Best of John Gary	1967	3.75	7.50	15.00
LSP-3730 [S]	The Best of John Gary	1967	3.00	6.00	12.00
LPM-3785 [M]	Spanish Moonlight	1967	3.75	7.50	15.00
LSP-3785 [S]	Spanish Moonlight	1967	3.00	6.00	12.00
LPM-3928 [M]	John Gary On Broadway	1968	5.00	10.00	20.00
LSP-3928 [S]	John Gary On Broadway	1968	3.00	6.00	12.00
LPM-3992 [M]	John Gary Sings/John Gary Swings	1968	5.00	10.00	20.00
LSP-3992 [S]	John Gary Sings/John Gary Swings	1968	3.00	6.00	12.00
LSP-4075	Holding Your Mind	1968	3.00	6.00	12.00
LSP-4134	Love of a Gentle Woman	1969	3.00	6.00	12.00
VPS-6041 [(2)]	This Is John Gary	1971	3.75	7.50	15.00

GARY AND CLYDE

See SKIP AND FLIP.

GARY AND THE CASUALS

Number	Title (A Side/B Side)	Yr	VG	VG+	NM
45s					
VANDAN					
609	My Own Desire/Someone Like You	1959	15.00	30.00	60.00

GARY AND THE KNIGHT-LITES

Evolved into THE AMERICAN BREED.

Number	Title (A Side/B Side)	Yr	VG	VG+	NM
45s					
BELL					
643	Lonely Soldier's Pledge/So Far Away from Home	1966	3.75	7.50	15.00
NIKE					
1020	I'm Glad She's Mine/How Can I Forget Her	1963	10.00	20.00	40.00
PRIMA					
1016	I Can't Love You Anymore/Will You Go Steady	1963	25.00	50.00	100.00
SEEBURG					
3016	Sweet Little Sixteen/Take Me Back	1965	6.25	12.50	25.00
3017	Bony Moronie/Glad You're Mine	1965	6.25	12.50	25.00
U.S.A.					
833	Bid Bad Wolf/I Don't Need Your Help	1966	5.00	10.00	20.00

GAS AND FUNK FACTORY, THE

Number	Title (A Side/B Side)	Yr	VG	VG+	NM
45s					
BRUNSWICK					
55434	Goodnight Song/Everybody Get Some Love	1970	7.50	15.00	30.00

GAS MASK

Number	Title (A Side/B Side)	Yr	VG	VG+	NM
Albums					
TONSIL					
4001	Gas Mask	1970	5.00	10.00	20.00

GASCA, LUIS

Number	Title (A Side/B Side)	Yr	VG	VG+	NM
Albums					
ATLANTIC					
SD 1527	Little Giant	1970	3.75	7.50	15.00

Number	Title (A Side/B Side)	Yr	VG	VG+	NM
BLUE THUMB					
BTS-37	Luis Gasca	1972	3.00	6.00	12.00
BTS-37	Luis Gasca	1972	3.75	7.50	15.00
FANTASY					
9461	Born to Love You	1974	3.00	6.00	12.00
F-9461	Born to Love You	1974	3.75	7.50	15.00
9504	Collage	1975	3.00	6.00	12.00
F-9504	Collage	1975	3.75	7.50	15.00

GASSAWAY, SENATOR BOLLIVAR E.

45s

Number	Title (A Side/B Side)	Yr	VG	VG+	NM
RCA VICTOR					
47-7743	Senator Bollivar E. Gassaway for President/ Senator Bolivar E. Gassaway Visits Russia	1960	3.00	6.00	12.00
47-7743 [PS]	Senator Bollivar E. Gassaway for President/ Senator Bolivar E. Gassaway Visits Russia	1960	5.00	10.00	20.00

GATEMEN, THE

45s

Number	Title (A Side/B Side)	Yr	VG	VG+	NM
COLPIX					
671	Silent Night/White Christmas	1962	5.00	10.00	20.00
MAY					
141	Goodnight Irene/The Klan	1963	5.00	10.00	20.00

GATES, DAVID

Also see BREAD; THE MANCHESTERS.

45s

Number	Title (A Side/B Side)	Yr	VG	VG+	NM
ARISTA					
0615	Take Me Now/It's What You Say	1981	—	2.00	4.00
0653	Come Home for Christmas/Lady Valentine	1981	2.00	4.00	8.00
DEL-FI					
4206	No One Really Loves a Clown/You Had It Comin' To Ya	1963	6.25	12.50	25.00
EASTWEST					
123	Walkin' and Talkin'/Swingin' Baby Doll	1959	37.50	75.00	150.00
ELEKTRA					
45223	Never Let Her Go/Watch Out	1974	—	2.00	4.00
45245	Part-Time Love/Chain Me	1975	—	2.00	4.00
45450	Goodbye Girl/Sunday Rider	1977	—	2.00	4.00
45450 [PS]	Goodbye Girl/Sunday Rider	1977	—	2.50	5.00
—Version 1: Titles on both sides, no photo					
45450 [PS]	Goodbye Girl/Sunday Rider	1977	—	2.50	5.00
—Version 2: Titles on one side, photo on other side					
45500	Took the Last Train/Ann	1978	—	2.00	4.00
45857	Clouds/I Use the Soap	1973	—	2.00	4.00
45868	Sail Around the World/Help Is On the Way	1973	—	2.00	4.00
46588	Where Does the Lovin' Go/Starship Ride	1980	—	2.00	4.00
46646	Can I Call You/Chingo	1980	—	2.00	4.00
47011	Falling in Love Again/Sweet Desire	1980	—	2.00	4.00
MALA					
413	You'll Be My Baby/What's This I Hear	1960	12.50	25.00	50.00
418	The Happiest Man Alive/A Road That Leads to Love	1960	12.50	25.00	50.00
427	Jo-Baby/Teardrops in My Heart	1961	12.50	25.00	50.00
MANCHESTER					
101	There's a Heaven/She Don't Cry	196?	10.00	20.00	40.00
—As "Del Ashley"					
PERSPECTIVE					
(no #)	Jo-Baby/Lovin' at Night	1961	37.50	75.00	150.00
PLANETARY					
103	Little Miss Stuck-Up/The Brighter Side	1965	6.25	12.50	25.00
—As "Del Ashley"					
108	Let You Go/Once Upon a Time	1965	5.00	10.00	20.00
ROBBINS					
1008	Jo-Baby/Lovin' at Night	1961	25.00	50.00	100.00

Albums

Number	Title (A Side/B Side)	Yr	VG	VG+	NM
ARISTA					
AL 9563	Take Me Now	1981	2.50	5.00	10.00
ELEKTRA					
6E-148	Goodbye Girl	1978	3.00	6.00	12.00
6E-251	Falling in Love Again	1980	2.50	5.00	10.00
7E-1028	Never Let Her Go	1975	3.00	6.00	12.00
EQ-5066 [Q]	First	1973	5.00	10.00	20.00
EKS-75066	First	1973	3.00	6.00	12.00

GATES, HEN

Albums

Number	Title (A Side/B Side)	Yr	VG	VG+	NM
MASTERSEAL					
MLP-700 [M]	Let's All Dance to Rock and Roll	1956	25.00	50.00	100.00
PALACE					
P-700 [M]	Let's All Dance to Rock and Roll	1958	15.00	30.00	60.00
—Reissue of Masterseal 700					
PST-700 [S]	Let's All Dance to Rock and Roll	1958	20.00	40.00	80.00
—Labeled stereo, but plays in mono					
PARIS					
101 [M]	Rock and Roll Festival	1957	15.00	30.00	60.00
PLYMOUTH					
R12-144 [M]	Rock and Roll	1956	15.00	30.00	60.00
R12-149 [M]	Rock and Roll, No. 2	1957	15.00	30.00	60.00

GATEWAY SINGERS, THE

45s

Number	Title (A Side/B Side)	Yr	VG	VG+	NM
DECCA					
29972	The Midnight Special/Puttin' On the Style	1956	3.00	6.00	12.00
30088	Bury Me in My Overalls/Monaco	1956	3.00	6.00	12.00
30630	Hey Li Lee/Come to the Dance	1958	2.50	5.00	10.00
MGM					
12927	Billy Boy/Goin' Down the Road	1960	2.00	4.00	8.00
12939	Wait for the Wagon/Kingston Market	1960	2.00	4.00	8.00
WARNER BROS.					
5073	The M.T.A./Keep a-Movin'	1959	2.50	5.00	10.00

Albums

Number	Title (A Side/B Side)	Yr	VG	VG+	NM
DECCA					
DL 8413 [M]	Puttin' On the Style	1956	10.00	20.00	40.00
DL 8671 [M]	The Gateway Singers at the Hungry I	1958	7.50	15.00	30.00
DL 8742 [M]	The Gateway Singers in Hi-Fi	1958	7.50	15.00	30.00
MGM					
E-3905 [M]	Down in the Valley	1961	5.00	10.00	20.00
SE-3905 [S]	Down in the Valley	1961	6.25	12.50	25.00
E-4154 [M]	Hootenanny	1963	5.00	10.00	20.00
SE-4154 [S]	Hootenanny	1963	6.25	12.50	25.00
WARNER BROS.					
W 1295 [M]	The Gateway Singers on the Lot	1959	6.25	12.50	25.00
WS 1295 [S]	The Gateway Singers on the Lot	1959	7.50	15.00	30.00
W 1334 [M]	Wagons West	1960	6.25	12.50	25.00
WS 1334 [S]	Wagons West	1960	7.50	15.00	30.00

GATEWAY TRIO, THE

45s

Number	Title (A Side/B Side)	Yr	VG	VG+	NM
CAPITOL					
5045	Soldiers Who Want to Be Heroes/Poor Man's Travellin' Blues	1963	3.75	7.50	15.00
5286	Coney Island/All the Good Times	1964	3.75	7.50	15.00

Albums

Number	Title (A Side/B Side)	Yr	VG	VG+	NM
CAPITOL					
ST 1868 [S]	The Mad, Mad, Mad Gateway Trio	1963	5.00	10.00	20.00
T 1868 [M]	The Mad, Mad, Mad Gateway Trio	1963	3.75	7.50	15.00
ST 2184 [S]	The Gateway Trio	1964	5.00	10.00	20.00
T 2184 [M]	The Gateway Trio	1964	3.75	7.50	15.00

GATLIN, LARRY, AND THE GATLIN BROTHERS BAND

Includes records issued as "Larry Gatlin"; "Larry Gatlin with Family and Friends"; "The Gatlins: Larry, Steve, Rudy"; "The Gatlin Quartet."

45s

Number	Title (A Side/B Side)	Yr	VG	VG+	NM
CAPITOL					
7PRO-79053 [DJ]	Boogie and Beethoven (same on both sides)	1990	—	2.50	5.00
—Vinyl is promo only					
7PRO-79378 [DJ]	Country Girl Heart (same on both sides)	1991	—	2.50	5.00
—Vinyl is promo only					
COLUMBIA					
02123	Wind Is Bound to Change/Help Yourself to Me	1981	—	—	3.00
02522	What Are We Doin' Lonesome/You Wouldn't Know Love	1981	—	—	3.00
02698	In Like With Each Other/Hard Workin' Hands	1982	—	—	3.00
02910	She Used to Sing on Sunday/Can't Take It With You	1982	—	—	3.00
03159	Sure Feels Like Love/Home Is Where the Healin' Is	1982	—	—	3.00
03356	Steps/Sweet Baby Jesus	1982	—	2.00	4.00
CNR-03364	Sure Feels Like Love	1982	—	2.50	5.00
—One-sided budget release					
03517	Almost Called Her Baby By Mistake/Somethin' Like Each Other's Arms	1983	—	—	3.00
03885	Easy on the Eye/Anything But Leavin'	1983	—	—	3.00
04105	Houston (Means I'm One Day Closer to You)/The Whole Wide World Stood Still	1983	—	—	3.00
04395	Denver/A Dream That Got Out of Hand	1984	—	—	3.00
04533	The Lady Takes the Cowboy Everytime/It's Me	1984	—	—	3.00
05632	Runaway Go Home/Nothing But Your Love Matters	1985	—	—	3.00
05764	Nothing But Your Love Matters/When the Night Closes In	1985	—	—	3.00
06252	She Used to Be Somebody's Baby/Being Alone	1986	—	—	3.00
06592	Talkin' to the Moon/Give Me a Chance	1986	—	—	3.00
07088	From Time to Time (It Feels Like Love Again)/ Texas (Is What Life Is All About)	1987	—	—	3.00
—With Janie Frickie					
07320	Changin' Partners/Got a Lot of Women on His Hands	1987	—	—	3.00
07747	Love of a Lifetime/Don't Blame Me for Colorado	1988	—	—	3.00
07998	Alive and Well/One on One	1988	—	—	3.00
11066	All the Gold in California/How Much Is Man Supposed to Take	1979	—	2.00	4.00
11169	The Midnight Choir/Hold Me Closer	1980	—	2.00	4.00
11219	Taking Somebody With Me When I Fall/Piece by Piece	1980	—	2.00	4.00
11282	We're Number One/Can't Cry Anymore	1980	—	2.00	4.00
11369	Take Me to Your Lovin' Place/Straight to My Heart	1980	—	2.00	4.00
11438	It Don't Get No Better Than This/Straight to My Heart	1981	—	2.00	4.00
MONUMENT					
8569	My Mind's Gone to Memphis/Try to Win a Friend	1973	—	2.50	5.00
8584	Sweet Becky Walker/You've Been Handed Down to Me	1973	—	2.50	5.00
8602	Bitter They Are Harder They Fall/Silver Threads and Golden Needles	1974	—	2.50	5.00
8622	Delta Dirt/Those Also Love	1974	—	2.50	5.00
8643	Jannie/Penny Annie	1975	—	2.50	5.00
8657	Let's Turn the Lights On/Takin' a Chance on You	1975	—	2.50	5.00
8680	Broken Lady/Heart	1975	—	2.50	5.00
8696	Warm and Tender/The Heart Is Quicker Than the Eye	1976	—	2.50	5.00
45201	Statues Without Hearts/What Will I Do Now	1976	—	2.00	4.00
45212	Anything But Leavin'/Take Back "It's Over"	1977	—	2.00	4.00
45221	I Don't Wanna Cry/Mercy River	1977	—	2.00	4.00
45226	Love Is Just a Game/Everytime a Plane Flies Over Our House	1977	—	2.00	4.00
45234	I Just Wish You Were Someone I Love/Kiss It All Goodbye	1977	—	2.00	4.00
45249	Night Time Magic/It's Love at Last	1978	—	2.00	4.00
45259	Do It Again Tonight/Cold Day in Hell	1978	—	2.00	4.00
45270	I've Done Enough Dyin' Today/Nothin' You Do	1978	—	2.00	4.00
UNIVERSAL					
53501	When She Holds Me/Go or Stay	1989	—	—	3.00
UVL-66005	I Might Be What You're Looking For/Rain	1989	—	—	3.00

Number	Title (A Side/B Side)	Yr	VG	VG+	NM
UVL-66021	#1 Heartache Place/Your Door	1989	—	—	3.00
Albums					
COLUMBIA					
JC 36250	Straight Ahead	1979	2.50	5.00	10.00
JC 36488	Larry Gatlin's Greatest Hits, Volume 1	1980	2.00	4.00	8.00
—Reissue of Monument 7628					
PC 36541	The Pilgrim	1980	2.00	4.00	8.00
—Reissue of Monument 6632					
JC 36582	Help Yourself	1980	2.50	5.00	10.00
PC 36582	Help Yourself	198?	2.00	4.00	8.00
—Budget-line reissue					
PC 36582	Help Yourself	198?	2.00	4.00	8.00
—Budget-line reissue					
FC 37464	Not Guilty	1981	2.50	5.00	10.00
PC 37464	Not Guilty	198?	2.00	4.00	8.00
—Budget-line reissue					
FC 38135	Sure Feels Like Love	1982	2.50	5.00	10.00
PC 38135	Sure Feels Like Love	198?	2.00	4.00	8.00
—Budget-line reissue					
FC 38183	A Gatlin Family Christmas	1982	3.00	6.00	12.00
PC 38183	A Gatlin Family Christmas	198?	2.00	4.00	8.00
—Budget-line reissue					
PC 38336	Love Is Just a Game	1982	2.00	4.00	8.00
—Reissue of Monument 7616					
PC 38337	Larry Gatlin with Family and Friends	1982	2.00	4.00	8.00
—Reissue of Monument 6634					
PC 38338	High Time	1982	2.00	4.00	8.00
—Reissue of Monument 6644					
PC 38339	Rain-Rainbow	1982	2.00	4.00	8.00
—Reissue of Monumnet 6633					
PC 38340	Oh! Brother	1982	2.00	4.00	8.00
—Reissue of Monumnet 7626					
FC 38923	Larry Gatlin's Greatest Hits, Volume 2	1983	2.50	5.00	10.00
FC 39291	Houston to Denver	1984	2.50	5.00	10.00
FC 40068	Smile!	1985	2.50	5.00	10.00
FC 40431	Partners	1986	2.50	5.00	10.00
FC 40905	Alive and Well...Living in the Land of Dreams	1988	2.50	5.00	10.00
FC 44471	The Gatlin Brothers' Biggest Hits (1984-88)	1989	2.50	5.00	10.00
HC 48135	Sure Feels Like Love	1982	62.50	125.00	250.00
—Half-speed mastered edition					
MONUMENT					
6632	The Pilgrim	1976	3.00	6.00	12.00
—Reissue of KZ 32571					
6633	Rain-Rainbow	1976	3.00	6.00	12.00
—Reissue of KZ 33069					
6634	Larry Gatlin with Family and Friends	1976	3.00	6.00	12.00
6644	High Time	1977	3.00	6.00	12.00
7616	Love Is Just a Game	1978	3.00	6.00	12.00
7626	Oh! Brother	1978	3.00	6.00	12.00
7628	Larry Gatlin's Greatest Hits	1978	3.00	6.00	12.00
KZ 32571	The Pilgrim	1974	3.75	7.50	15.00
KZ 33069	Rain-Rainbow	1974	3.75	7.50	15.00
SWORD & SHIELD					
9009 [M]	The Old Country Church	1961	25.00	50.00	100.00
—As "The Gatlin Quartet" (wisth sister Donna joining Larry, Rudy and Steve)					

GATORCREEK

Number	Title (A Side/B Side)	Yr	VG	VG+	NM
Albums					
MERCURY					
SR-61311	Gatorcreek	1970	3.00	6.00	12.00

GAUCHOS, THE

See JIM DOVAL AND THE GAUCHOS.

GAUDET, JOHN, AND THE LAURELS

Number	Title (A Side/B Side)	Yr	VG	VG+	NM
45s					
MARY GLEN					
1001/2	Christmas Will Soon Be Here/Your Name Shall Be Remembered	1961	6.25	12.50	25.00

GAVIN, TONY

Number	Title (A Side/B Side)	Yr	VG	VG+	NM
45s					
20TH FOX					
228	Ever Lovin' Baby/I Just Don't Know	1960	10.00	20.00	40.00

GAY KNIGHTS, THE

Number	Title (A Side/B Side)	Yr	VG	VG+	NM
45s					
PET					
801	The Loudness of My Heart/Angel	1958	10.00	20.00	40.00

GAY NOTES, THE

Number	Title (A Side/B Side)	Yr	VG	VG+	NM
45s					
DREXEL					
905	For Only a Moment/Pu-Pu-Pa-Doo	1955	150.00	300.00	600.00
POST					
2006	Crossroads/Hear My Plea	1955	15.00	30.00	60.00
VIM					
501	Something Special/Cherie	1959	15.00	30.00	60.00

GAYE, ELLIE

May be ELLIE GREENWICH.

Number	Title (A Side/B Side)	Yr	VG	VG+	NM
45s					
RCA VICTOR					
47-7231	Silly Isn't It/Cha Cha Charming	1958	10.00	20.00	40.00

GAYE, MARVIN

Also see THE MARQUEES (5).

Number	Title (A Side/B Side)	Yr	VG	VG+	NM
12-Inch Singles					
COLUMBIA					
CAS 2124 [DJ]	Masochistic Beauty/(Instrumental)	1985	—	3.00	6.00
05188	Sanctified Lady/(Instrumental)	1985	—	3.00	6.00
MOTOWN					
00014	A Funky Space Reincarnation/(Instrumental)	1978	3.00	6.00	12.00
45s					
COLUMBIA					
03302	Sexual Healing/(Instrumental)	1982	—	2.00	4.00
CNR-03344	Sexual Healing	1982	—	3.00	6.00
—One-sided budget release					
03585	Sexual Healing/(Instrumental)	1983	—	—	3.00
—Reissue					
03589	'Til Tomorrow/Rockin' After Midnight	1983	—	2.00	4.00
03860	Joy/(Instrumental)	1983	—	2.00	4.00
03870	Star Spangled Banner/Turn On Some Music	1983	—	—	—
—Unreleased?					
03935	Joy/Turn On Some Music	1983	—	2.00	4.00
04861	Sanctified Lady/(Instrumental)	1985	—	2.00	4.00
05442	It's Madness/Ain't It Funny (How Things Turn Around)	1985	—	2.00	4.00
05791	Just Like/More	1986	—	2.00	4.00
DETROIT FREE PRESS					
(no #) [DJ]	The Teen Beat Song/Loraine Alterman Interviews Marvin Gaye	1966	37.50	75.00	150.00
TAMLA					
(no #) [DJ]	Masquerade (Is Over)/Witchcraft	1962	150.00	300.00	600.00
—As "Marvin Gay"; label states "Single Not Available extracted from Album (TM-221)"					
S4KM 0741/2 [DJ]	This Is the Life/My Way	1965	12.50	25.00	50.00
1836	This World Is Rated X/No Greater Love	1986	—	2.50	5.00
1836 [PS]	This World Is Rated X/No Greater Love	1986	—	2.50	5.00
54041	Let Your Conscience Be Your Guide/Never Let You Go	1961	100.00	200.00	400.00
54055	Sandman/I'm Yours, You're Mine	1962	15.00	30.00	60.00
54062	Masquerade (Is Over)/Witchcraft	1962	—	—	—
—Unreleased					
54063	Soldier's Plea/Taking My Time	1962	10.00	20.00	40.00
—With label credit "Marvin Gaye Love Tones"					
54063	Soldier's Plea/Taking My Time	1962	12.50	25.00	50.00
—With label credit "Marvin Gaye"					
54068	Stubborn Kind of Fellow/It Hurts Me Too	1962	7.50	15.00	30.00
54075	Hitch Hike/Hello There Angel	1963	5.00	10.00	20.00
54079	Pride and Joy/One of These Days	1963	5.00	10.00	20.00
54087	Can I Get a Witness/I'm Crazy 'Bout My Baby	1963	5.00	10.00	20.00
54093	You're a Wonderful One/When I'm Alone I Cry	1964	3.75	7.50	15.00
54095	Try It Baby/If My Heart Could Sing	1964	3.75	7.50	15.00
54095 [PS]	Try It Baby/If My Heart Could Sing	1964	15.00	30.00	60.00
54101	Baby Don't You Do It/Walk on the Wild Side	1964	3.75	7.50	15.00
54101 [PS]	Baby Don't You Do It/Walk on the Wild Side	1964	15.00	30.00	60.00
54107	How Sweet It Is To Be Loved By You/Forever	1964	3.75	7.50	15.00
54112	I'll Be Doggone/You've Been a Long Time Coming	1965	3.75	7.50	15.00
54117	Pretty Little Baby/Now That You've Won Me	1965	3.75	7.50	15.00
54122	Ain't That Peculiar/She's Got to Be Real	1965	3.75	7.50	15.00
54129	One More Heartache/When I Had Your Love	1966	3.00	6.00	12.00
54132	Take This Heart of Mine/Need Your Lovin' (Want You Back)	1966	3.00	6.00	12.00
54138	Little Darling, I Need You/Hey Diddle Diddle	1966	3.00	6.00	12.00
54153	Your Unchanging Love/I'll Take Care of You	1967	2.50	5.00	10.00
54160	You/Change What You Can	1967	2.50	5.00	10.00
54170	Chained/At Last I Found a Love	1968	2.50	5.00	10.00
54176	I Heard It Through the Grapevine/You're What's Happening (In the World Today)	1968	2.50	5.00	10.00
54181	Too Busy Thinking About My Baby/Wherever I Lay My Hat (That's My Home)	1969	2.00	4.00	8.00
54185	That's the Way Love Is/Gonna Keep On Tryin' Till I Win Your Love	1969	2.00	4.00	8.00
54190	Gonna Give Her All the Love I've Got/How Can I Forget You	1970	2.00	4.00	8.00
54195	The End of Our Road/Me and My Lonely Room	1970	2.00	4.00	8.00
54201	What's Going On/God Is Love	1971	—	3.00	6.00
54207	Mercy Mercy Me (The Ecology)/Sad Tomorrows	1971	—	3.00	6.00
54209	Inner City Blues (Make Me Wanna Holler)/Wholly Holy	1971	—	3.00	6.00
54221	You're the Man (Part 1)/You're the Man (Part 2)	1972	—	3.00	6.00
54228	Trouble Man/Don't Mess With Mister "T"	1972	—	3.00	6.00
54229	Christmas in the City/I Want to Come Home for Christmas	1972	—	—	—
—Canceled					
54234	Let's Get It On/I Wish It Would Rain	1973	—	2.00	4.00
54241	Come Get to This/Distant Lover	1973	—	2.00	4.00
54244	You Sure Love to Ball/Just to Keep You Satisfied	1974	—	2.00	4.00
54253	Distant Lover/Trouble Man	1974	—	2.00	4.00
54264	I Want You/I Want You (Instrumental)	1975	—	2.00	4.00
54273	After the Dance/Feel All My Love Inside	1976	—	2.00	4.00
54280	Got to Give It Up — Pt. 1/Got to Give It Up — Pt. 2	1977	—	2.00	4.00
54280 [PS]	Got to Give It Up — Pt. 1/Got to Give It Up — Pt. 2	1977	2.50	5.00	10.00
54298	Funky Space Reincarnation — Pt. 1/Funky Space Reincarnation — Pt. 2	1979	—	2.00	4.00
54300	Time to Get It Together/Anger	1979	2.50	5.00	10.00
—Only released in Canada					
54305	Ego Tripping Out/(Instrumental)	1979	—	2.00	4.00
54322	Funk Me/Praise	1981	—	2.00	4.00
54326	Heavy Love Affair/Far Cry	1981	—	2.00	4.00
TOPPS/MOTOWN					
6	How Sweet It Is	1967	18.75	37.50	75.00
—Cardboard record					
Albums					
COLUMBIA					
FC 38197	Midnight Love	1982	2.50	5.00	10.00
PC 38197	Midnight Love	1986	2.00	4.00	8.00
—Budget-line reissue					
FC 39916	Dream of a Lifetime	1985	2.50	5.00	10.00
9C9 40133 [PD]	Dream of a Lifetime	1985	5.00	10.00	20.00
FC 40208	Romantically Yours	1986	2.50	5.00	10.00
HC 48197	Midnight Love	1984	10.00	20.00	40.00
—Half-speed mastered edition					
MOTOWN					
M5-115V1	Motown Superstar Series, Vol. 15	1981	2.50	5.00	10.00

Number	Title (A Side/B Side)	Yr	VG	VG+	NM
M5-125V1	M.P.G.	1981	2.50	5.00	10.00
—Reissue of Tamla 292					
M5-181V1	Marvin Gaye Live!	1981	2.50	5.00	10.00
—Reissue of Tamla 333					
M5-191V1	Marvin Gaye's Greatest Hits	1981	2.50	5.00	10.00
—Reissue of Tamla 348					
M5-192V1	Let's Get It On	1981	2.50	5.00	10.00
—Reissue of Tamla 329					
M5-216V1	A Tribute to the Great Nat King Cole	1981	2.50	5.00	10.00
—Reissue of Tamla 261					
M5-218V1	That Stubborn Kinda' Fellow	1981	2.50	5.00	10.00
—Reissue of Tamla 239					
M9-791A3 [(3)]	Anthology	1974	5.00	10.00	20.00
37463 1296-1 [DJ]	The Master 1961-1984	1995	5.00	10.00	20.00
—Vinyl is promo only; 8-song sampler from box set					
5259 ML [(2)]	Marvin Gaye Live at the London Palladium	1983	3.00	6.00	12.00
—Reissue of Tamla 352					
5306 ML	Super Hits	198?	2.50	5.00	10.00
5339 ML	What's Going On	198?	2.50	5.00	10.00
—Reissue of Tamla 322					
6058 ML	Every Great Motown Hit of Marvin Gaye	1983	2.50	5.00	10.00
6255 ML [(2)]	A Musical Testament 1964-1984	1988	3.00	6.00	12.00
NATURAL RESOURCES					
NR 4007T1	The Soulful Moods of Marvin Gaye	1978	3.00	6.00	12.00
—Reissue of Tamla 221					
TAMLA					
T 221 [M]	The Soulful Moods of Marvin Gaye	1961	250.00	500.00	1000.
T 239 [M]	That Stubborn Kinda' Fella	1963	150.00	300.00	600.00
T 242 [M]	Recorded Live — Marvin Gaye on Stage	1963	75.00	150.00	300.00
T 251 [M]	When I'm Alone I Cry	1964	62.50	125.00	250.00
T 252 [M]	Marvin Gaye/Greatest Hits	1964	7.50	15.00	30.00
TS 252 [S]	Marvin Gaye/Greatest Hits	1964	10.00	20.00	40.00
T 258 [M]	How Sweet It Is to Be Loved by You	1965	10.00	20.00	40.00
TS 258 [S]	How Sweet It Is to Be Loved by You	1965	12.50	25.00	50.00
T 259 [M]	Hello Broadway, This Is Marvin	1965	10.00	20.00	40.00
TS 259 [S]	Hello Broadway, This Is Marvin	1965	12.50	25.00	50.00
T 261 [M]	A Tribute to the Great Nat King Cole	1965	10.00	20.00	40.00
TS 261 [S]	A Tribute to the Great Nat King Cole	1965	12.50	25.00	50.00
T 266 [M]	Moods of Marvin Gaye	1966	10.00	20.00	40.00
TS 266 [S]	Moods of Marvin Gaye	1966	12.50	25.00	50.00
T 278 [M]	Marvin Gaye/Greatest Hits, Vol. 2	1967	6.25	12.50	25.00
TS 278 [S]	Marvin Gaye/Greatest Hits, Vol. 2	1967	5.00	10.00	20.00
T 285 [M]	In the Groove	1968	12.50	25.00	50.00
TS 285 [S]	In the Groove	1968	6.25	12.50	25.00
TS 285 [S]	I Heard It Through the Grapevine	1969	5.00	10.00	20.00
—Retitled version of "In the Groove"					
TS 292	M.P.G.	1969	5.00	10.00	20.00
TS 293	Marvin Gaye and His Girls	1969	5.00	10.00	20.00
—Includes duets with Tammi Terrell, Mary Wells, Kim Weston					
TS 299	That's the Way Love Is	1969	5.00	10.00	20.00
TS 300	Marvin Gaye Super Hits	1970	5.00	10.00	20.00
T5-310	What's Going On	1971	3.75	7.50	15.00
T5-322	Trouble Man	1972	3.75	7.50	15.00
T6-329	Let's Get It On	1973	3.75	7.50	15.00
T6-333	Marvin Gaye Live!	1974	3.75	7.50	15.00
T6-342	I Want You	1976	3.75	7.50	15.00
T6-348	Marvin Gaye's Greatest Hits	1976	3.75	7.50	15.00
T7-352 [(2)]	Marvin Gaye Live at the London Palladium	1977	3.75	7.50	15.00
T13-364 [(2)]	Here, My Dear	1978	3.75	7.50	15.00
T8-374	In Our Lifetime	1981	2.50	5.00	10.00
6172	Motown Remembers Marvin Gaye	1986	2.50	5.00	10.00

GAYE, MARVIN, AND TAMMI TERRELL

Number	Title (A Side/B Side)	Yr	VG	VG+	NM
45s					
TAMLA					
54149	Ain't No Mountain High Enough/Give a Little Love	1967	2.00	4.00	8.00
54156	Your Precious Love/Hold Me Oh My Darling	1967	2.00	4.00	8.00
54161	If I Could Build My Whole World Around You/If This World Were Mine	1967	2.00	4.00	8.00
54163	Ain't Nothing Like the Real Thing/Little Ole Boy, Little Ole Girl	1968	2.00	4.00	8.00
54169	You're All I Need to Get By/Two Can Have a Party	1968	2.00	4.00	8.00
54173	You Ain't Livin' Till You're Lovin'/Keep On Lovin' Me Honey	1968	—	3.00	6.00
54179	Good Lovin' Ain't Easy to Come By/Satisfied Feelin'	1969	—	3.00	6.00
54179 [PS]	Good Lovin' Ain't Easy to Come By/Satisfied Feelin'	1969	5.00	10.00	20.00
54187	What You Gave Me/How You Gonna Keep It	1969	—	3.00	6.00
54192	The Onion Song/California Soul	1970	—	3.00	6.00
Albums					
MOTOWN					
M5-102V1	Motown Superstar Series, Vol. 2	1981	2.50	5.00	10.00
M5-142V1	You're All I Need	1981	2.50	5.00	10.00
—Reissue of Tamla 284					
M5-200V1	United	1981	2.50	5.00	10.00
—Reissue of Tamla 277					
TAMLA					
T 277 [M]	United	1967	7.50	15.00	30.00
TS 277 [S]	United	1967	6.25	12.50	25.00
T 284 [M]	You're All I Need	1968	12.50	25.00	50.00
TS 284 [S]	You're All I Need	1968	5.00	10.00	20.00
TS 294	Easy	1969	5.00	10.00	20.00
TS 302	Marvin Gaye & Tammi Terrell/Greatest Hits	1970	5.00	10.00	20.00

GAYE, MARVIN, AND MARY WELLS

Number	Title (A Side/B Side)	Yr	VG	VG+	NM
45s					
MOTOWN					
1057	Once Upon a Time/What's the Matter with You Baby	1964	3.75	7.50	15.00
1057 [PS]	Once Upon a Time/What's the Matter with You Baby	1964	15.00	30.00	60.00
Albums					
MOTOWN					
M 613 [M]	Together	1964	12.50	25.00	50.00
5260 ML	Together	1982	2.50	5.00	10.00

GAYE, MARVIN, AND KIM WESTON

Number	Title (A Side/B Side)	Yr	VG	VG+	NM
45s					
TAMLA					
54104	What Good Am I Without You/I Want You 'Round	1964	3.75	7.50	15.00
54141	It Takes Two/It's Got to Be a Miracle	1966	3.00	6.00	12.00
Albums					
TAMLA					
T/TS 260	Side by Side	1965	—	—	—
—Canceled					
T 270 [M]	Take Two	1966	7.50	15.00	30.00
TS 270 [S]	Take Two	1966	10.00	20.00	40.00

GAYLARKS, THE

Number	Title (A Side/B Side)	Yr	VG	VG+	NM
45s					
MUSIC CITY					
792	Tell Me Darling/Whole Lot of Love	1956	30.00	60.00	120.00
—B-side by the Rovers					
793	Romantic Memories/Li'l Dream Girl	1956	30.00	60.00	120.00
805	My Greatest Sin/Teenage Mambo	1957	25.00	50.00	100.00
809	Church on the Hill/Mr. Rock-n-Roll	1957	30.00	60.00	120.00
812	Just One More Chance/Somewhere in This World	1957	15.00	30.00	60.00
819	Ivy League Clothes/Rockin' Satellite	1958	12.50	25.00	50.00

GAYLE, CRYSTAL

Number	Title (A Side/B Side)	Yr	VG	VG+	NM
45s					
CAPITOL					
7PRO-79256	Never Ending Song of Love (same on both sides)	1990	—	2.50	5.00
—Vinyl is promo only					
COLUMBIA					
02078	Too Many Lovers/Help Yourself to Each Other	1981	—	2.00	4.00
02523	The Woman in Me/Crying in the Rain	1981	—	2.00	4.00
02718	You Never Gave Up on Me/Tennessee	1982	—	2.00	4.00
03048	Livin' in These Troubled Times/Ain't No Sunshine	1982	—	2.00	4.00
04093	Keepin' Power/Half the Way	1983	—	2.00	4.00
11087	Half the Way/Room for One More	1979	—	2.00	4.00
11198	It's Like We Never Said Goodbye/Don't Go My Love	1980	—	2.00	4.00
11270	The Blue Side/The Danger Zone	1980	—	2.00	4.00
11359	If You Ever Change Your Mind/I Just Can't Leave Your Love Alone	1980	—	2.00	4.00
11436	Take It Easy/Ain't No Love in the Heart of the City	1981	—	2.00	4.00
DECCA					
32721	I've Cried (The Blue Right Out of My Eyes)/Sparkling Look of Love	1970	2.00	4.00	8.00
32925	Everybody Oughta Cry/MRS Degree	1972	2.00	4.00	8.00
32969	I Hope You're Havin' Better Luck Than Me/Too Far	1972	2.00	4.00	8.00
ELEKTRA					
69893	'Til I Gain Control Again/Easier Said Than Done	1982	—	2.00	4.00
69893 [PS]	'Til I Gain Control Again/Easier Said Than Done	1982	—	2.00	4.00
69936	You and I/All My Life, All My Love	1982	—	2.00	4.00
—A-side: With Eddie Rabbitt; B-side by Eddie Rabbitt solo					
MCA					
40016	Clock on the Wall/Show Me How	1973	—	3.00	6.00
40837	I've Cried (The Blue Right Out of My Eyes)/Sparklin' Look of Love	1977	—	3.00	6.00
UNITED ARTISTS					
XW428	Restless/Layback Lover	1974	—	2.50	5.00
XW555	Wrong Road Again/They Come Out at Night	1974	—	2.50	5.00
XW600	Beyond You/Loving You So Long Now	1975	—	2.50	5.00
XW680	This Is My Year for Mexico/When I Dream	1975	—	2.50	5.00
XW740	Somebody Loves You/Coming Closer	1975	—	2.50	5.00
XW781	I'll Get Over You/High Time	1976	—	2.50	5.00
XW838	One More Time/Oh My Soul	1976	—	2.50	5.00
XW883	You Never Miss a Real Good Thing (Till He Says Goodbye)/Forgetting About You	1976	—	2.50	5.00
XW948	I'll Do It All Over Again/I'm Not So Far Away	1977	—	2.50	5.00
XW1016	Don't It Make My Brown Eyes Blue/It's All Right with Me	1977	—	2.00	4.00
XW1136	Ready for the Times to Get Better/Beyond You	1978	—	2.00	4.00
XW1146	I'll Get Over You/The Wrong Road Again	1978	—	2.00	4.00
—Reissue					
XW1147	Somebody Loves You/You Never Miss a Real Good Thing (Till He Says Goodbye)	1978	—	2.00	4.00
—Reissue					
XW1148	Don't It Make My Brown Eyes Blue/The Green Door	1978	—	2.00	4.00
—Reissue					
XW1149	I Wanna Come Back to You/One More Time	1978	—	2.00	4.00
—Reissue					
XW1150	I'll Do It All Over Again/This Is My Year for Mexico	1978	—	2.00	4.00
—Reissue					
XW1214	Talking in Your Sleep/Paintin' This Old Town Blue	1978	—	2.00	4.00
XW1259	Why Have You Left the One You Left Me For/Cry Me a River	1978	—	2.00	4.00
XW1288	When I Dream/Hello I Love You	1979	—	2.00	4.00
XW1306	Your Kisses Will/Time Will Prove I'm Right	1979	—	2.00	4.00
1329	Your Old Cold Shoulder/We Should Be Together	1979	—	2.00	4.00
1347	Come Home Daddy/River Road	1980	—	2.00	4.00
1362	Heart Mender/This Is My Year for Mexico	1980	—	2.00	4.00
WARNER BROS.					
27682	Tennessee Nights/When Love Is New	1988	—	—	3.00
27811	Nobody's Angel/When Love Is New	1988	—	—	3.00
28209	Only Love Can Save Me Now/Till I Gain Control Again	1987	—	—	3.00
28210	Oh Holy Night/I'll Be Home for Christmas	1987	—	2.00	4.00
28409	Nobody Should Have to Love You This Way/A Little Bit Closer	1987	—	—	3.00

Number	Title (A Side/B Side)	Yr	VG	VG+	NM
28499	I Still Hear the Music of Nashville/I Still Hear the Music of Nashville (Part 2)	1987	—	—	3.00
28518	Straight to the Heart/Do I Have to Say Goodbye	1986	—	—	3.00
28555	Have Yourself a Merry Little Christmas/Silver Bells	1986	—	2.00	4.00
28689	Cry/Crazy in the Heart	1986	—	—	3.00
28963	A Long and Lasting Love/Someone Like You	1985	—	—	3.00
29050	Nobody Wants to Be Alone/Coming to the Dance	1985	—	—	3.00
29151	Me Against the Night/You Made a Fool of Me	1984	—	2.00	4.00
29254	Turning Away/On Our Way to Love	1984	—	2.00	4.00
29356	I Don't Wanna Lose Your Love/Victim or a Fool	1984	—	2.00	4.00
29452	The Sound of Goodbye/Take Me Home	1983	—	2.00	4.00
29582	Baby, What About You/He Is Beautiful to Me	1983	—	2.00	4.00
29719	Our Love Is On the Faultline/Deeper in the Fire	1983	—	2.00	4.00
Albums					
COLUMBIA					
JC 36203	Miss the Mississippi	1979	2.50	5.00	10.00
PC 36203	Miss the Mississippi	198?	2.00	4.00	8.00
—Budget-line reissue					
JC 36512	These Days	1980	2.50	5.00	10.00
PC 36512	These Days	198?	2.00	4.00	8.00
—Budget-line reissue					
FC 37438	Hollywood, Tennessee	1981	2.50	5.00	10.00
PC 37438	Hollywood, Tennessee	198?	2.00	4.00	8.00
—Budget-line reissue					
FC 38803	Crystal Gayle's Greatest Hits	1983	2.50	5.00	10.00
ELEKTRA					
60200	True Love	1982	2.50	5.00	10.00
LIBERTY					
LMAS-858	When I Dream	1981	2.00	4.00	8.00
—Reissue of UA 858					
LOO-1034	Favorites	1981	2.00	4.00	8.00
—Reissue of UA 1034					
LOO-1080	A Woman's Heart	1981	2.50	5.00	10.00
LN-10002	Crystal Gayle	1981	2.00	4.00	8.00
LN-10003	Somebody Loves You	1981	2.00	4.00	8.00
—Budget-line reissue of UA 543					
LN-10004	Crystal	1981	2.00	4.00	8.00
—Budget-line reissue of UA 614					
LN-10005	We Must Believe in Magic	1981	2.00	4.00	8.00
—Budget-line reissue of UA 771					
LN-10006	We Should Be Together	1980	2.00	4.00	8.00
—Budget-line reissue					
LN-10150	Classic Crystal	1982	2.00	4.00	8.00
—Budget-line reissue of UA 982					
LN-10227	When I Dream	1984	2.00	4.00	8.00
—Budget-line reissue					
LN-10229	Favorites	1984	2.00	4.00	8.00
—Budget-line reissue					
MCA					
2334	I've Cried the Blue Right Out of My Eyes	1977	2.50	5.00	10.00
—Reissue of Decca material					
37077	I've Cried the Blue Right Out of My Eyes	198?	2.00	4.00	8.00
—Budget-line reissue					
MOBILE FIDELITY					
1-043	We Must Believe in Magic	1981	5.00	10.00	20.00
—Audiophile vinyl					
NAUTILUS					
NR-36	When I Dream	198?	7.50	15.00	30.00
—Audiophile vinyl					
PAIR					
PDL2-1083 [(2)]	Country Pure	1986	3.00	6.00	12.00
PDL2-1126 [(2)]	Musical Jewels	1986	3.00	6.00	12.00
UNITED ARTISTS					
UA-LA543-G	Somebody Loves You	1975	3.00	6.00	12.00
UA-LA614-G	Crystal	1976	3.00	6.00	12.00
UA-LA771-G	We Must Believe in Magic	1977	2.50	5.00	10.00
UA-LA858-H	When I Dream	1978	2.50	5.00	10.00
UA-LA969-H	We Should Be Together	1979	2.50	5.00	10.00
LOO-982	Classic Crystal	1979	2.50	5.00	10.00
LOO-1034	Favorites	1980	2.50	5.00	10.00
WARNER BROS.					
23958	Cage the Songbird	1983	2.50	5.00	10.00
25154	Nobody Wants to Be Alone	1984	2.50	5.00	10.00
25405	Straight to the Heart	1986	2.50	5.00	10.00
25508	A Crystal Christmas	1986	2.50	5.00	10.00
25622	The Best of Crystal Gayle	1987	2.50	5.00	10.00
25706	Nobody's Angel	1988	2.50	5.00	10.00
60200	True Love	1983	2.00	4.00	8.00
—Reissue of Elektra 60200					

GAYLE, CRYSTAL, AND GARY MORRIS

Number	Title (A Side/B Side)	Yr	VG	VG+	NM
45s					
WARNER BROS.					
28106	All of This And More/Makin' Up for Lost Time	1988	—	—	3.00
28373	Another World/Makin' Up for Lost Time	1987	—	—	3.00
28856	Makin' Up for Lost Time (The Dallas Lovers' Song)/A Few Good Men	1985	—	—	3.00
28856 [PS]	Makin' Up for Lost Time (The Dallas Lovers' Song)/A Few Good Men	1985	—	—	3.00
Albums					
WARNER BROS.					
25507	What If We Fell in Love?	1987	2.50	5.00	10.00

GAYLES, BILLY, WITH IKE TURNER'S RHYTHM ROCKERS

Number	Title (A Side/B Side)	Yr	VG	VG+	NM
45s					
FEDERAL					
12265	I'm Tore Up/If I Had Never Known You	1956	10.00	20.00	40.00
12272	Let's Call It a Day/Take Your Fine Frame Home	1956	10.00	20.00	40.00
12282	No Coming Back/Do Right Baby	1956	10.00	20.00	40.00
12287	Just One More Time/Sad as a Man Can Be	1957	10.00	20.00	40.00

GAYLES, THE

Number	Title (A Side/B Side)	Yr	VG	VG+	NM
45s					
ABC-PARAMOUNT					
9707	Shortnin' Bread Rock/You Fool	1956	6.25	12.50	25.00
KING					
4846	My Boy, Flat Top/I Get So Happy	1955	5.00	10.00	20.00
4860	I Had to Love You/Too Late I Learned	1955	5.00	10.00	20.00

GAYLORDS, THE

Number	Title (A Side/B Side)	Yr	VG	VG+	NM
45s					
MERCURY					
70030	Tell Me You're Mine/Cuban Love Song	1952	3.75	7.50	15.00
70067	Tell Me You're Mine/Aye Aye Aye	1952	3.00	6.00	12.00
70112	Ramona/Spinning a Web	1953	3.00	6.00	12.00
70170	Tell Me That You Love Me/Coquette	1953	3.00	6.00	12.00
70235	Wonderin'/Sweet Sue	1953	3.00	6.00	12.00
70286	Stolen Moments/Patzo for Pizza	1954	3.00	6.00	12.00
70296	From the Vine Came the Grape/Stolen Moments	1954	3.00	6.00	12.00
70308	From the Vine Came the Grape/Patzo for Pizza	1954	2.50	5.00	10.00
70350	Isle of Capri/Love I You	1954	3.00	6.00	12.00
70403	The Little Shoemaker/Masque, Masque	1954	3.00	6.00	12.00
70427	Veni, Vida, Vida/A Kiss to Call My Own	1954	3.00	6.00	12.00
70543	Chow Mein/Poppa Poppadopolis	1955	2.50	5.00	10.00
70586	The Woodpecker Song/My Babe	1955	2.50	5.00	10.00
70589	Mambo Rock/Plantation Boogie	1955	2.50	5.00	10.00
70630	Chee Chee O-Chee/Who's Got the Pain	1955	2.50	5.00	10.00
70660	Medley: Minnie the Mermaid; The Man Who Broke the Bank at Monte Carlo; Goodbye My Coney Island Baby; If You Knew Susie/Madalaina	1955	2.50	5.00	10.00
70706	No Arms Can Ever Hold You/Bring Me a Bluebird	1955	2.50	5.00	10.00
70778	Molly-O/Vino Vino	1956	2.50	5.00	10.00
70834	Bella Bambinella/Who's Gonna Take You to the Prom	1956	2.50	5.00	10.00
70979	A Little Love, A Little Kiss/The Mountain Climber	1956	2.50	5.00	10.00
71051	The Dum-De-Dum Song/Open the Letter	1957	2.50	5.00	10.00
71186	Satin Doll/Wandering Heart	1957	2.50	5.00	10.00
71236	O Mari/Magic Song	1957	2.50	5.00	10.00
71265	Love/Each Time I Love You More	1958	2.00	4.00	8.00
71337	Ma Ma Ma Marie/Buona Sera	1958	2.00	4.00	8.00
71369	Flamingo L'Amore/I'm Longing for Love	1958	2.00	4.00	8.00
71399	Again/How About Me	1959	2.00	4.00	8.00
71450	Sweeter Than You/Homin' Pigeon	1959	2.00	4.00	8.00
71503	Jesse James/The Shovel	1959	2.00	4.00	8.00
71569	She's Gone/Please Consider	1960	2.00	4.00	8.00
71601	Love Me Now and Forever/Whip of the Wind	1960	2.00	4.00	8.00
71625	Sensation/Carina	1960	2.00	4.00	8.00
71762	Daisy, You're Driving Me Crazy/Born to Be Loved	1961	2.00	4.00	8.00
71832	Oh Lonesome Me/Yakety Yak	1961	2.00	4.00	8.00
71902	It Hurts Me More (The Second Time Around)/American 100%	1961	2.00	4.00	8.00
71970	How About Me/Two-Ton Tessie	1962	2.00	4.00	8.00
Albums					
MERCURY					
MG-20186 [M]	Italia	1957	7.50	15.00	30.00
MG-20213 [M]	Collection of Golden Hits	1957	7.50	15.00	30.00
MG-20356 [M]	Let's Have a Pizza Party	1958	5.00	10.00	20.00
MG-20430 [M]	That's Amore	1959	5.00	10.00	20.00
MG-20620 [M]	American Hits in Italian	1961	5.00	10.00	20.00
MG-20695 [M]	The Gaylords at the Shamrock	1962	5.00	10.00	20.00
MG-20742 [M]	Party Style	1963	5.00	10.00	20.00
MG-25198 [10]	By Request	1955	12.50	25.00	50.00
SR-60075 [S]	Let's Have a Pizza Party	1959	7.50	15.00	30.00
SR-60102 [S]	That's Amore	1959	7.50	15.00	30.00
SR-60620 [S]	American Hits in Italian	1961	7.50	15.00	30.00
SR-60695 [S]	The Gaylords at the Shamrock	1962	6.25	12.50	25.00
SR-60742 [S]	Party Style	1963	6.25	12.50	25.00
TIME					
S-2109 [S]	Live at Lake Tahoe	196?	5.00	10.00	20.00
S-2127 [S]	Bella Italia	196?	5.00	10.00	20.00
52109 [M]	Live at Lake Tahoe	196?	3.75	7.50	15.00
52127 [M]	Bella Italia	196?	3.75	7.50	15.00
WING					
MGW-12139 [M]	Italiano Favorites	196?	3.00	6.00	12.00
MGW-12278 [M]	Let's Have a Pizza Party	196?	3.00	6.00	12.00
SRW-16139 [S]	Italiano Favorites	196?	3.00	6.00	12.00
SRW-16278 [S]	Let's Have a Pizza Party	196?	3.00	6.00	12.00

GAYNOR, GLORIA

Number	Title (A Side/B Side)	Yr	VG	VG+	NM
12-Inch Singles					
ATLANTIC					
369	Tease Me (2 versions)	1982	—	3.00	6.00
633	America/Runaround Love	1982	—	3.00	6.00
MCA					
L33-1847 [DJ]	Love Is a Heartbeat Away (2 versions)	1979	2.50	5.00	10.00
POLYDOR					
PRO 107 [DJ]	Most of All/As Time Goes By	1977	2.50	5.00	10.00
PRO 111 [DJ]	Let Me Know (I Have a Right) (2 versions)	1979	2.00	4.00	8.00
PD-D-504 [DJ]	Substitute (same on both sides)	1978	2.00	4.00	8.00
PD-D-507 [DJ]	Anybody Wanna Party (same on both sides)	1978	2.00	4.00	8.00
PD-D-517 [DJ]	Let's Mend What's Been Broken (same on both sides)	1981	2.00	4.00	8.00
SILVER BLUE					
220	I Am What I Am (From La Cage Aux Folles)/(Dub Mix)	198?	2.00	4.00	8.00
05018	Bullseye/Chain of Whispers	1984	—	3.00	6.00
45s					
ATLANTIC					
89824 [DJ]	America (same on both sides)	1983	—	2.00	4.00
—May be promo only					
89887	Stop in the Name of Love/For You, My Love	1982	—	2.00	4.00
89947	Tease Me/Mack Side	1982	—	2.00	4.00

Number	Title (A Side/B Side)	Yr	VG	VG+	NM
COLUMBIA					
45909	Honey Bee/All It Took, Boy, Was Losing You	1973	—	3.00	6.00
MGM					
14706	Honey Bee/Come Tonight	1974	—	2.50	5.00
14748	Never Can Say Goodbye/We Can Just Make It	1974	—	2.00	4.00
14790	Reach Out, I'll Be There/Searchin'	1975	—	2.00	4.00
14808	Walk On By/Real Good People	1975	—	2.00	4.00
14823	(If You Want It) Do It Yourself/I'm Still Yours	1975	—	2.00	4.00
14838	How High the Moon/My Man's Gone	1975	—	2.00	4.00
POLYDOR					
2021	Let Me Know (I Have a Right)/One Plus One	1979	—	2.00	4.00
2056	Midnight Rocker/Can't Fight This Feelin'	1980	—	2.00	4.00
2089	The Luckiest Girl in the World/Ain't No Bigger Fool	1980	—	2.00	4.00
2173	Let's Mend What's Been Broken/I Love You Because	1981	—	2.00	4.00
2179	I Kinda Like Me/Fingers in the Rain	1981	—	2.00	4.00
14342	Do It Right/Touch of Lightning	1976	—	2.00	4.00
14357	Let's Make a Deal/Let's Make Love	1976	—	2.00	4.00
14391	Most of All/So Much Love	1977	—	2.00	4.00
14443	After the Lovin'/You're All I Need to Get By	1977	—	2.00	4.00
14472	This Love Affair/For the First Time in My Life	1978	—	2.00	4.00
14508	I Will Survive/Substitute	1978	—	2.00	4.00
14558	Anybody Wanna Party?/Please Be There	1979	—	2.00	4.00
SILVER BLUE					
720	I Am What I Am/More Than Enough	1983	—	2.50	5.00
04294	I Am What I Am/More Than Enough	1983	—	2.00	4.00
04422	Strive/I've Been Watching You	1984	—	2.00	4.00
Albums					
ATLANTIC					
80033	Gloria Gaynor	1982	2.50	5.00	10.00
MGM					
M3G-4982	Never Can Say Goodbye	1975	2.50	5.00	10.00
M3G-4997	Experience Gloria Gaynor	1975	2.50	5.00	10.00
POLYDOR					
PD-1-6063	I've Got You	1976	2.50	5.00	10.00
PD-1-6095	Glorious	1977	2.50	5.00	10.00
PD-1-6184	Love Tracks	1978	2.50	5.00	10.00
PD-1-6231	I Have a Right	1979	2.50	5.00	10.00
PD-1-6274	Stories	1980	2.50	5.00	10.00

GAYTEN, PAUL

Also see THE TUNE WEAVERS.

Number	Title (A Side/B Side)	Yr	VG	VG+	NM
45s					
ANNA					
1106	The Hunch/Hot Cross Buns	1959	5.00	10.00	20.00
1112	Beatnick Beat/Scratch Back	1960	5.00	10.00	20.00
ARGO					
5257	The Music Goes Round and Round/Be My Baby	1956	6.25	12.50	25.00
5263	Driving Home Part 1/Driving Home Part 2	1957	6.25	12.50	25.00
5267	Old Buttermilk Sky/The Sweeper	1957	6.25	12.50	25.00
5277	Nervous Boogie/Flatfoot Sam	1957	6.25	12.50	25.00
—B-side by Oscar Wiles					
5300	Windy/Tickle Toe	1958	6.25	12.50	25.00
CHECKER					
801	I'm Tired/Get It	1954	6.25	12.50	25.00
836	You Better Believe It/Mother Roux	1956	6.25	12.50	25.00
OKEH					
6847	Lonesome for My Baby/All Alone and Lovely	1952	7.50	15.00	30.00
6870	Give Me Liberty or Give Me Death/Happy Days	1952	7.50	15.00	30.00
6908	True (You Don't Love Me)/They All Ask for You	1952	7.50	15.00	30.00
6934	Yes You Do, Yes You Do/Don't Worry Me	1953	7.50	15.00	30.00
6972	Time Is a-Passin'/Ain't Nothin' Happenin'	1953	7.50	15.00	30.00
6982	Cow Cow Blues/Ooh-Boo	1953	7.50	15.00	30.00
7003	Hurry Home/Sugar Baby	1953	7.50	15.00	30.00
7019	Mule Face/It's Over	1954	7.50	15.00	30.00
7068	True (You Don't Love Me)/Cow Cow Blues	1956	6.25	12.50	25.00

GAYTUNES, THE

Number	Title (A Side/B Side)	Yr	VG	VG+	NM
45s					
JOYCE					
101	I Love You/You Left Me	1957	50.00	100.00	200.00
106	Pen Pal/Plea in the Moonlight	199?	2.00	4.00	8.00
—Black vinyl					
106	Pen Pal/Plea in the Moonlight	199?	2.50	5.00	10.00
—Red vinyl					

GAZELLES, THE

Number	Title (A Side/B Side)	Yr	VG	VG+	NM
45s					
GOTHAM					
315	Honest/Pretty Baby, Baby	1956	75.00	150.00	300.00

GEDDES, DAVID

Number	Title (A Side/B Side)	Yr	VG	VG+	NM
45s					
ATCO					
7028	Run Joey Run/Honey Don't Blow It	1975	—	—	—
—Canceled?					
BIG TREE					
16044	Run Joey Run/Honey Don't Blow It	1975	—	2.00	4.00
16052	The Last Game of the Season (A Blind Man in the Bleachers)/Wake Up Girl	1975	—	2.00	4.00
16059	Stephanie/Changing Colours	1976	—	2.00	4.00
16067	Trouble/Wait for Me	1976	—	2.00	4.00
H&L					
4684	Rocky's Girl/Changing Colours	1977	—	2.00	4.00
ZODIAC					
1019	Rocky's Girl/Changing Colours	1977	—	2.00	4.00
Albums					
BIG TREE					
BT 89511	Run Joey Run	1975	3.00	6.00	12.00

GEE, ELLIE

See ELLIE GREENWICH.

GEE, JOEY

Number	Title (A Side/B Side)	Yr	VG	VG+	NM
45s					
ABC-PARAMOUNT					
10781	Don't Blow Your Cool/It's More Than I Deserve	1966	6.25	12.50	25.00
SARA					
2599	She's Mean/(B-side unknown)	1966	3.75	7.50	15.00

GEE CEES, THE

Also see THE KELLY FOUR.

Number	Title (A Side/B Side)	Yr	VG	VG+	NM
45s					
CREST					
1088	Buzz Saw/Annie Had a Party	1961	10.00	20.00	40.00
—Glen Campbell is on A-side; Eddie Cochran is on B-side					
1088	Buzz Saw Twist/Annie Had a Party	1962	7.50	5.00	30.00

GEILS, J., BAND

Number	Title (A Side/B Side)	Yr	VG	VG+	NM
45s					
ATLANTIC					
2784	First I Look at the Purse/Homework	1971	2.00	4.00	8.00
2802	Cruisin' for a Love/Wait	1971	—	3.00	6.00
2843	Dead Presidents/I Don't Need You No More	1971	—	3.00	6.00
2844	Looking for a Love/What's Your Whammer Jammer	1971	—	3.00	6.00
2929	Hard Drivin' Man/Whammer Jammer	1972	—	3.00	6.00
2953	Give It To Me/Hold Your Loving	1973	—	2.50	5.00
2974	Make Up Your Mind/Southside Shuffle	1973	—	2.50	5.00
2974 [PS]	Make Up Your Mind/Southside Shuffle	1973	2.50	5.00	10.00
3007	Did You No Wrong/That's Why I'm Thinking of You	1974	—	2.50	5.00
3214	Must of Got Lost/Funky Judge	1074	—	2.50	5.00
3251	Givin' It All Up/Gettin' Out	1975	—	2.50	5.00
3301	Think It Over/Love-Itis	1975	—	2.50	5.00
3320	Where Did Our Love Go/What's Your Hurry	1976	—	2.50	5.00
3350	(Ain't Nothing But a) House Party/Give It To Me	1976	—	2.50	5.00
3378	Peanut Buuter/Magic's Mood	1976	—	2.50	5.00
3411	You're the Only One/Wreckage	1977	—	2.50	5.00
—As "Geils"					
3438	Monkey Island (Part 1)/Surrender	1977	—	2.50	5.00
—As "Geils"					
3454	I Do/Trying to Live My Life Without You	1978	—	2.50	5.00
—As "Geils"					
3454 [PS]	I Do/Trying to Live My Life Without You	1978	2.00	4.00	8.00
—As "Geils"					
EMI AMERICA					
8007	One Last Kiss/Revenge	1978	—	2.00	4.00
8007 [PS]	One Last Kiss/Revenge	1978	—	3.00	6.00
8012	Take It Back/I Can't Believe You	1979	—	2.00	4.00
8016	Wild Man/Just Can't Stop Me	1979	—	2.00	4.00
8032	Come Back/Takin' You Down	1980	—	2.00	4.00
8032 [DJ]	Come Back (Long)/Come Back (Edit)	1980	—	2.50	5.00
8039	Love Stinks/Till the Walls Come Tumblin' Down	1980	—	2.00	4.00
8039 [PS]	Love Stinks/Till the Walls Come Tumblin' Down	1980	—	2.50	5.00
8047	Just Can't Wait/No Anchovies, Please	1980	—	2.00	4.00
8100	Angel in Blue/Rage in the Cage	1982	—	—	3.00
8100 [PS]	Angel in Blue/Rage in the Cage	1982	—	2.00	4.00
8102	Centerfold/Rage in the Cage	1981	—	2.50	5.00
—Regular gray EMI America label					
8102	Centerfold/Rage in the Cage	1981	—	—	3.00
—Custom pink label					
8102 [PS]	Centerfold/Rage in the Cage	1981	2.50	5.00	10.00
8108	Freeze-Frame/Flamethrower	1982	—	—	3.00
8108 [PS]	Freeze-Frame/Flamethrower	1982	—	3.00	6.00
8148	I Do/Sanctuary	1982	—	—	3.00
8148 [PS]	I Do/Sanctuary	1982	—	2.00	4.00
8156	Land of 1000 Dances/Jus' Can't Stop Me	1983	—	—	3.00
8242	Concealed Weapons/Tell 'Em Jonsey	1984	—	—	3.00
8242 [PS]	Concealed Weapons/Tell 'Em Jonsey	1984	—	2.00	4.00
8260	Eenie Meenie Miney Mo/I Will Carry You Home	1985	—	—	3.00
PRIVATE I					
05462	Fright Night/Boppin' Tonight	1985	—	—	3.00
—B-side by The Fabulous Fontaines					
05462 [PS]	Fright Night/Boppin' Tonight	1985	—	2.00	4.00
Albums					
ATLANTIC					
SD 2-507 [(2)]	Live — Blow Your Face Out	1976	3.75	7.50	15.00
SD 7241	"Live" — Full House	1972	3.00	6.00	12.00
QD 7260 [Q]	Bloodshot	1973	5.00	10.00	20.00
SD 7260	Bloodshot	1973	5.00	10.00	20.00
—Red vinyl					
SD 7260	Bloodshot	1973	3.00	6.00	12.00
—Black vinyl					
QD 7286 [Q]	Ladies Invited	1973	5.00	10.00	20.00
SD 7286	Ladies Invited	1973	3.00	6.00	12.00
SD 8275	The J. Geils Band	1970	3.75	7.50	15.00
SD 8297	The Morning After	1971	3.00	6.00	12.00
QD 18107 [Q]	Nightmares and Other Tales from the Vinyl Jungle	1974	5.00	10.00	20.00
SD 18107	Nightmares and Other Tales from the Vinyl Jungle	1974	3.00	6.00	12.00
SD 18147	Hotline	1975	3.00	6.00	12.00
SD 19103	Monkey Island	1977	3.00	6.00	12.00
—As "Geils"					
SD 19234	Best of the J. Geils Band	1979	2.50	5.00	10.00
SD 19284	Best of the J. Geils Band — 2	1980	2.50	5.00	10.00
EMI AMERICA					
SN-16316	Sanctuary	1985	2.00	4.00	8.00
—Reissue					
SN-16373	Showtime!	1986	2.00	4.00	8.00
—Reissue					
SN-16374	Freeze-Frame	1986	2.00	4.00	8.00
—Reissue					

Number	Title (A Side/B Side)	Yr	VG	VG+	NM
SN-16375	Love Stinks	1986	2.00	4.00	8.00
—Reissue					
SO-17006	Sanctuary	1978	2.50	5.00	10.00
SOO-17016	Love Stinks	1980	2.50	5.00	10.00
SOO-17062	Freeze-Frame	1981	2.50	5.00	10.00
SO-17087	Showtime!	1982	2.50	5.00	10.00
SJ-17137	You're Gettin' Even While I'm Gettin' Odd	1984	2.00	4.00	8.00
ST-17174	Flashback — The Best of the J. Geils Band	1985	2.00	4.00	8.00
NAUTILUS					
NR-25	Love Stinks	1982	5.00	10.00	20.00
—Audiophile vinyl					

GEMS, THE (1)

45s

Number	Title (A Side/B Side)	Yr	VG	VG+	NM
CHESS					
1863	One More Year/Let Your Hair Down	1963	3.00	6.00	12.00
1875	If It's the Last Thing I Do/A Girl's Impression	1963	3.00	6.00	12.00
1882	A Love of Mine/That's Why They Put Erasers On	1964	3.00	6.00	12.00
1908	I Can't Help Myself/Can't You Take a Hint	1964	3.00	6.00	12.00
1917	Love For Christmas/All Of It	1964	3.00	6.00	12.00
1930	He Makes Me Feel So Good/Happy New Love	1965	2.50	5.00	10.00
2104	Girls Can Do It/Ain't That Loving You	1971	—	3.00	6.00

GEMS, THE (2)

45s

Number	Title (A Side/B Side)	Yr	VG	VG+	NM
DREXEL					
901	Deed I Do/Talk About the Weather	1954	100.00	200.00	400.00
—Black vinyl					
901	Deed I Do/Talk About the Weather	1954	625.00	1250.	2500.
—Red vinyl					
903	I Thought You'd Care/Kitty from New York City	1954	75.00	150.00	300.00
—Black vinyl					
903	I Thought You'd Care/Kitty from New York City	1954	150.00	300.00	600.00
—Red vinyl					
904	You're Tired of Love/Ol' Man River	1954	75.00	150.00	300.00
—Black vinyl					
904	You're Tired of Love/Ol' Man River	1954	150.00	300.00	600.00
—Red vinyl					
909	One Woman Man/The Darkest Night	1955	100.00	200.00	400.00
915	Till the Day I Die/Monkey Face Baby	1956	100.00	200.00	400.00

GEMS, THE (U)

These probably are neither group (1) nor (2).

45s

Number	Title (A Side/B Side)	Yr	VG	VG+	NM
MERCURY					
71819	Crazy Chicken/Hippy Dippy	1961	2.50	5.00	10.00
PAT					
101	There's No One Like My Love/School Rock	1961	7.50	15.00	30.00
RECORTE					
407	Waiting/Please Change Your Mind	1959	12.50	25.00	50.00
RIVERSIDE					
4590	I'll Be There/I Miss Him	1967	7.50	15.00	30.00
WIN					
701	Nursery Rhymes/The Night Is Over	1958	75.00	150.00	300.00

GENE AND DEBBE

Also see GENE THOMAS.

45s

Number	Title (A Side/B Side)	Yr	VG	VG+	NM
HICKORY					
1643	Lovin' Season/Then You Can Tell Me Goodbye	1972	—	3.50	7.00
SAN					
1519	Go with Me/The Torch I Carry	1967	5.00	10.00	20.00
TRX					
5002	Go with Me/The Torch I Carry	1967	2.00	4.00	8.00
5006	Playboy/I'll Come Running	1967	2.50	5.00	10.00
5010	Lovin' Season/Love Will Give Us Wings	1968	2.00	4.00	8.00
5014	Rings of Gold/Make a Noise Like Love	1968	2.00	4.00	8.00
5017	Memories Are Made of This/The Sun Won't Shine Again	1969	2.00	4.00	8.00
5021	I'm Only Human/Loan Some	1969	2.00	4.00	8.00

Albums

Number	Title (A Side/B Side)	Yr	VG	VG+	NM
TRX					
1001	Here and Now	1968	6.25	12.50	25.00

GENE AND EUNICE

45s

Number	Title (A Side/B Side)	Yr	VG	VG+	NM
ALADDIN					
3276	Ko Ko Mo (I Need You So)/You and Me	1954	6.25	12.50	25.00
3282	This Is My Story/Move It Over Baby	1954	6.25	12.50	25.00
3292	Flim Flam/Can We Forget It	1954	6.25	12.50	25.00
3305	I Gotta Go Home/Have You Changed Your Mind	1954	6.25	12.50	25.00
3315	Hootchy Kootchy/I'll Never Believe in You	1955	5.00	10.00	20.00
3321	Let's Get Together/I'm So in Love with You	1955	5.00	10.00	20.00
3351	Bom Bom Lulu/Hi Diddle Diddle	1956	5.00	10.00	20.00
3374	The Vow/Strange World	1957	5.00	10.00	20.00
3376	Doodle Doodle Doo/Don't Treat Me This Way	1957	5.00	10.00	20.00
3414	I Mean Love/The Angels Gave You to Me	1958	5.00	10.00	20.00
CASE					
1001	Poco-Loco/Go-On Kokomo	1959	7.50	15.00	30.00
1002	Ah! Ah!/You Think I'm Not Thinking	1959	7.50	15.00	30.00
COMBO					
64	Ko Ko Mo (I Need You So)/You and Me	1954	7.50	15.00	30.00
LILLY					
512	Everlovin' Baby/Got a Right to Know	1962	3.75	7.50	15.00
UNITED ARTISTS					
0151	Ko Ko Mo (I Love You So)/This Is My Story	1973	—	2.00	4.00
—"Silver Spotlight Series" reissue					

GENE AND TOMMY

Real names: TERRY CASHMAN; TOMMY WEST.

45s

Number	Title (A Side/B Side)	Yr	VG	VG+	NM
ABC					
10981	Richard and Me/Can't Get to Stopping	1967	2.00	4.00	8.00

GENESIS

Popular British group with Phil Collins, Peter Gabriel, Tony Banks and Mike Rutherford, among others.

12-Inch Singles

Number	Title (A Side/B Side)	Yr	VG	VG+	NM
ATLANTIC					
PR 311 [DJ]	Go West Young Man (same on both sides)	1978	5.00	10.00	20.00
PR 404 [DJ]	No Reply at All (4:37) (4:00)	1981	2.50	5.00	10.00
PR 416 [DJ]	Abacab (same on both sides)	1981	2.50	5.00	10.00
PR 425 [DJ]	Man on the Corner (same on both sides)	1981	2.00	4.00	8.00
PR 535 [DJ]	Mama (same on both sides)	1983	2.00	4.00	8.00
PR 581 [DJ]	Illegal Alien//Home by the Sea/Second Home by the Sea	1983	2.00	4.00	8.00
PR 897 [DJ]	Invisible Touch (same on both sides)	1986	—	3.00	6.00
PR 924 [DJ]	Invisible Touch (Special Remix) (same on both sides)	1986	3.00	6.00	12.00
86722	Tonight, Tonight, Tonight (Remix) (12" Remix)// In the Glow of the Night/Paperlate	1987	—	3.00	6.00
86812	Invisible Touch (Special Remix)/The Last Domino	1986	—	3.00	6.00

45s

Number	Title (A Side/B Side)	Yr	VG	VG+	NM
ATCO					
7013	The Lamb Lies Down on Broadway/Counting Out Time	1975	5.00	10.00	20.00
7050	Entangled/Ripples	1976	2.50	5.00	10.00
7076	Your Own Special Way/In That Quiet Earth	1977	2.50	5.00	10.00
ATLANTIC					
3474	Follow You Follow Me/Inside and Out	1978	—	2.00	4.00
—A radically different mix than the LP version of A-side					
3511	Go West Young Man (In the Motherlode)/Scene from a Night's Dream	1978	—	2.00	4.00
3662	Misunderstanding/Behind the Lines	1980	—	2.00	4.00
3662 [PS]	Misunderstanding/Behind the Lines	1980	—	2.50	5.00
3751	Turn It On Again/Evidence of Autumn	1980	—	2.00	4.00
3858	No Reply At All/Heaven Love My Life	1981	—	2.00	4.00
3891	Abacab/Who Dunnit?	1982	—	2.00	4.00
3891 [PS]	Abacab/Who Dunnit?	1982	—	2.00	4.00
4025	Man on the Corner/Submarine	1982	—	2.00	4.00
4025 [PS]	Man on the Corner/Submarine	1982	—	2.00	4.00
4053	Paperlate/You Might Recall	1982	—	2.00	4.00
4053 [PS]	Paperlate/You Might Recall	1982	—	2.50	5.00
84043	Not About Us/Turn It On Again (Live)	1997	—	—	3.00
87481	Hold On My Heart/Way of the World	1992	—	2.00	4.00
87532	I Can't Dance/On the Shoreline	1992	—	2.00	4.00
87571	No Son of Mine/Living Forever	1991	—	2.00	4.00
89290	Tonight, Tonight, Tonight/In the Glow of the Night	1987	—	—	3.00
89290 [PS]	Tonight, Tonight, Tonight/In the Glow of the Night	1987	—	2.00	4.00
—Color sleeve					
89290 [PS]	Tonight, Tonight, Tonight/In the Glow of the Night	1987	—	2.50	5.00
—Black and white sleeve					
89316	In Too Deep/I'd Rather Be You	1987	—	—	3.00
89316 [PS]	In Too Deep/I'd Rather Be You	1987	—	2.00	4.00
89336	Land of Confusion/Feeding the Fire	1986	—	—	3.00
—Regular Atlantic red and black label					
89336	Land of Confusion/Feeding the Fire	1986	2.50	5.00	10.00
—Black label with different Atlantic logo					
89336 [PS]	Land of Confusion/Feeding the Fire	1986	2.50	5.00	10.00
—Sleeve came only with black-label versions					
89372	Throwing It All Away/Do the Neurotic	1986	—	—	3.00
89372 [PS]	Throwing It All Away/Do the Neurotic	1986	—	—	3.00
89407	Invisible Touch/The Last Domino	1986	—	—	3.00
89407 [PS]	Invisible Touch/The Last Domino	1986	—	—	3.00
89656	Taking It All Too Hard/Silver Rainbow	1984	—	—	3.00
89656 [PS]	Taking It All Too Hard/Silver Rainbow	1984	—	—	3.00
89698	Illegal Alien/Turn It On Again (Live in Philadelphia)	1984	—	—	3.00
89698 [PS]	Illegal Alien/Turn It On Again (Live in Philadelphia)	1984	—	—	3.00
89724	That's All/Second Home by the Sea	1983	—	—	3.00
89724 [PS]	That's All/Second Home by the Sea	1983	—	2.50	5.00
—Brown title sleeve with no center cut-out					
89724 [PS]	That's All/Second Home by the Sea	1983	—	2.00	4.00
—Brown title sleeve with center cut-out					
89770	Mama/It's Gonna Get Better	1983	—	—	3.00
89770 [PS]	Mama/It's Gonna Get Better	1983	—	2.00	4.00
CHARISMA					
103	Watcher of the Skies/Willow Farm	1973	12.50	25.00	50.00
26002	I Know What I Like/Twilight Ale House	1973	10.00	20.00	40.00
PARROT					
3018	Silent Sun/That's Me	1968	100.00	200.00	400.00
—Stock copy with black label and green and yellow bird. This has been proven to exist.					
3018 [DJ]	Silent Sun/That's Me	1968	25.00	50.00	100.00
—Promotional copy; orangeish label with black bird					

Albums

Number	Title (A Side/B Side)	Yr	VG	VG+	NM
ABC					
X-816	Trespass	1971	3.00	6.00	12.00
—Reissue of Impulse album					
ABC IMPULSE!					
ASD-9205	Trespass	1971	7.50	15.00	30.00
ATCO					
SD 38-100	Wind & Wuthering	1978	2.50	5.00	10.00
SD 38-101	A Trick of the Tail	1978	2.50	5.00	10.00
SD 36-129	A Trick of the Tail	1976	3.00	6.00	12.00
SD 36-144	Wind & Wuthering	1977	3.00	6.00	12.00
SD 2-401 [(2)]	The Lamb Lies Down on Broadway	1974	3.75	7.50	15.00
—Originals have yellow labels (other labels worth less)					
ATLANTIC					
SD 2-2000 [(2)]	Three Sides Live	1982	3.00	6.00	12.00
SD 2-9002 [(2)]	Seconds Out	1977	3.00	6.00	12.00

Number	Title (A Side/B Side)	Yr	VG	VG+	NM
SD 16014	Duke	1980	2.50	5.00	10.00
SD 19173	...And Then There Were Three	1978	2.50	5.00	10.00
SD 19277	Selling England by the Pound	1981	2.00	4.00	8.00
—Reissue of Charisma LP of same name					
SD 19313	Abacab	1981	2.50	5.00	10.00
—Released with four different covers, lettered "A" through "D" on spine; no difference in value					
80030	Nursery Cryme	1982	2.00	4.00	8.00
—Reissue of Charisma LP of same name					
80116	Genesis	1983	2.00	4.00	8.00
81641	Invisible Touch	1986	2.00	4.00	8.00
81848	Foxtrot	1988	2.50	5.00	10.00
—Reissue of Charisma LP of the same name					
81855	Genesis Live	1988	2.50	5.00	10.00
—Reissue of Charisma LP of the same name					
BUDDAH					
BDS-5659	The Best of Genesis	1976	3.75	7.50	15.00
CHARISMA					
CAS-1052	Nursery Cryme	1971	3.75	7.50	15.00
CAS-1058	Foxtrot	1972	3.75	7.50	15.00
CA-1666	Genesis Live	1974	3.75	7.50	15.00
CA-2701 [(2)]	Nursery Cryme/Foxtrot	1976	3.75	7.50	15.00
—Repackage of the individual albums of these names					
CAS-6060	Selling England by the Pound	1973	3.75	7.50	15.00
LONDON					
PS 643	From Genesis to Revelation	1974	5.00	10.00	20.00
—First US release of debut album					
LC-50006	In the Beginning	1977	3.00	6.00	12.00
820322-1	In the Beginning	198?	2.00	4.00	8.00
—Reissue of London 50006					
MCA					
816	Trespass	1979	2.50	5.00	10.00
—Reissue of ABC album					
37151	Trespass	198?	2.00	4.00	8.00
—Reissue of MCA 816					
MOBILE FIDELITY					
1-062	A Trick of the Tail	1981	12.50	25.00	50.00
—Audiophile vinyl					

GENESIS (2)

45s

Number	Title (A Side/B Side)	Yr	VG	VG+	NM
BUDDAH					
132	Journey to the Moon (Part 1)/Journey to the Moon (Part 2)	1969	2.50	5.00	10.00

GENESIS (3)

45s

Number	Title (A Side/B Side)	Yr	VG	VG+	NM
MERCURY					
72806	Angeline/Suzanne	1968	2.50	5.00	10.00
72869	Gloomy Sunday/What's It All About	1968	2.50	5.00	10.00

GENESIS (4)

45s

Number	Title (A Side/B Side)	Yr	VG	VG+	NM
RIPCHORD					
004	Window of Sand/Would You Like To	1967	6.25	12.50	25.00

GENESIS (5)

45s

Number	Title (A Side/B Side)	Yr	VG	VG+	NM
SCEPTER					
12341	Second Coming/Double Bubble	1972	—	2.50	5.00

GENIES, THE (1)

45s

Number	Title (A Side/B Side)	Yr	VG	VG+	NM
HOLLYWOOD					
69	No More Knockin'/On the Edge of Town	1959	5.00	10.00	20.00
SHAD					
5002	Who's That Knocking/The First Time	1959	6.25	12.50	25.00
—Pink label					
5002	Who's That Knocking/The First Time	1959	3.75	7.50	15.00
—Blue label					
WARWICK					
573	Crazy Love/There Goes That Rain	1960	3.75	7.50	15.00
607	Just Like the Bluebird/Twistin' Pneumonia	1960	3.75	7.50	15.00
643	Little Young Girl/Crazy Feeling	1961	3.75	7.50	15.00

GENIES, THE (2)

45s

Number	Title (A Side/B Side)	Yr	VG	VG+	NM
RONN					
50	Anybody Here Know How to Pray/Take Me There	1971	—	3.00	6.00
56	No News Is Good News/Sunday Morning People	1971	—	3.00	6.00
68	Know Whatr to Do When You Get It/Prove It	197?	—	3.00	6.00

GENTEELS, THE

45s

Number	Title (A Side/B Side)	Yr	VG	VG+	NM
CAPITOL					
4798	Take It Off/Hitchhiker	1962	6.25	12.50	25.00
STAG					
2930/1	Take It Off/Hitch Hiker	1962	12.50	25.00	50.00
4949/50	The Force of Gravity/Springboard	1962	12.50	25.00	50.00

GENTLE GIANT

45s

Number	Title (A Side/B Side)	Yr	VG	VG+	NM
CAPITOL					
4484	Cogs in Cogs/I'm Turning Around	1977	—	2.50	5.00
4652	Spooky Boogie/Words from the Wise	1978	—	2.50	5.00

Albums

Number	Title (A Side/B Side)	Yr	VG	VG+	NM
CAPITOL					
ST-11337	The Power and the Glory	1974	2.50	5.00	10.00
ST-11428	Free Hand	1975	2.50	5.00	10.00
ST-11532	Interview	1976	2.50	5.00	10.00
SKBB-11592 [(2)]	The Official "Live" Gentle Giant — Playing the Fool	1977	3.00	6.00	12.00
ST 11696	The Missing Piece	1977	2.50	5.00	10.00
SW-11813	Giant for a Day	1978	2.50	5.00	10.00
SN-16044	The Power and the Glory	1980	2.00	4.00	8.00
—Budget-line reissue					
SN-16045	Giant for a Day	1980	2.00	4.00	8.00
—Budget-line reissue					
SN-16046	The Missing Piece	1980	2.00	4.00	8.00
—Budget-line reissue					
SN-16047	Interview	1980	2.00	4.00	8.00
—Budget-line reissue					
SN-16048	Free Hand	1980	2.00	4.00	8.00
—Budget-line reissue					
COLUMBIA					
KC 31649	Three Friends	1972	3.00	6.00	12.00
PC 31649	Three Friends	197?	2.00	4.00	8.00
—Reissue					
KC 32022	Octopus	1973	3.00	6.00	12.00
PC 32022	Octopus	197?	2.00	4.00	8.00
—Reissue					
JC 36341	Civilian	1980	2.50	5.00	10.00
VERTIGO					
VE-1005	Acquiring the Taste	1971	3.75	7.50	15.00

GENTLE SOUL

45s

Number	Title (A Side/B Side)	Yr	VG	VG+	NM
EPIC					
10448	Reelin'/2:30 Train	1969	3.00	6.00	12.00

Albums

Number	Title (A Side/B Side)	Yr	VG	VG+	NM
EPIC					
BN 26374	Gentle Soul	1969	25.00	50.00	100.00

GENTLEMEN FOUR, THE

45s

Number	Title (A Side/B Side)	Yr	VG	VG+	NM
WAND					
1184	It Won't Hurt Baby/You Can't Keep a Good Man Down	1968	20.00	40.00	80.00

GENTRY, BOBBIE

45s

Number	Title (A Side/B Side)	Yr	VG	VG+	NM
BRUNSWICK					
55517	Another Place — Another Time/I Think I'll Cry Out Loud	1975	—	3.00	6.00
CAPITOL					
2044	Okolona River Bottom Band/Penduli Pendulum	1967	2.00	4.00	8.00
2044 [PS]	Okolona River Bottom Band/Penduli Pendulum	1967	3.75	7.50	15.00
2147	Louisiana Man/Courtyard	1968	2.00	4.00	8.00
2295	Hushabye Mountain/Sweet Peony	1968	2.00	4.00	8.00
2501	Touch 'Em With Love/Casket Vignette	1969	—	3.00	6.00
2675	Fancy/Courtyard	1969	—	3.00	6.00
2788	He Made a Woman Out of Me/Billy the Kid	1970	—	3.00	6.00
2849	Apartment 21/Seasons Come, Seasons Go	1970	—	3.00	6.00
3071	But I Can't Get Back/Marigolds and Tangerines	1971	—	3.00	6.00
3413	Girl from Cincinnati/You and Me Together	1972	—	3.00	6.00
4294	Ode to Billie Joe/Mississippi Delta	1976	—	2.50	5.00
5950	Ode to Billie Joe/Mississippi Delta	1967	2.50	5.00	10.00
5992	I Saw An Angel Die/Poppa, Won'tcha Let Me Go to Town with You	1967	2.00	4.00	8.00
TITAN					
1736	Requiem for Love/Stranger in the Mirror	1963	3.75	7.50	15.00
—With Jody Reynolds					
WARNER BROS.					
8210	Ode to Billie Joe/There'll Be a Time	1976	—	2.50	5.00
—B-side by Michel Legrand					
8210 [PS]	Ode to Billie Joe/There'll Be a Time	1976	2.50	5.00	10.00
8532	Steal Away/He Did Me Wrong But He Did It Right	1978	—	2.00	4.00

Albums

Number	Title (A Side/B Side)	Yr	VG	VG+	NM
CAPITOL					
ST-155	Touch 'Em with Love	1969	3.75	7.50	15.00
SKAO-381	Bobbie Gentry's Greatest!	1969	3.75	7.50	15.00
SM-381	Bobbie Gentry's Greatest!	197?	2.00	4.00	8.00
ST-428	Fancy	1970	3.75	7.50	15.00
ST-494	Patchwork	1970	3.75	7.50	15.00
STBB-704 [(2)]	Sittin' Pretty/Tobacco Road	1971	3.75	7.50	15.00
SM-2830	Ode to Billie Joe	197?	2.00	4.00	8.00
ST 2830 [S]	Ode to Billie Joe	1967	3.75	7.50	15.00
T 2830 [M]	Ode to Billie Joe	1967	5.00	10.00	20.00
ST 2842	The Delta Sweete	1968	3.75	7.50	15.00
ST 2964	The Local Gentry	1968	3.75	7.50	15.00

GENTRY, BOBBIE, AND GLEN CAMPBELL

See GLEN CAMPBELL AND BOBBIE GENTRY

GENTRY, RAY

45s

Number	Title (A Side/B Side)	Yr	VG	VG+	NM
MAVERICK					
614	Willie Was a Bad Boy/Do the Fly	1958	100.00	200.00	400.00

GENTRYS, THE

45s

Number	Title (A Side/B Side)	Yr	VG	VG+	NM
BELL					
720	You Better Come Home/I Can't Go Back to Denver	1968	—	3.00	6.00
740	Thinking Like a Child/Silky	1968	—	3.00	6.00
753	Midnight Train/You Tell Me You Care	1968	—	3.00	6.00
CAPITOL					
3459	Changin'/Let Me Put This Ring Upon Your Finger	1972	—	2.50	5.00
HIT					
229	Keep On Dancing/A Lover's Concerto	1965	5.00	10.00	20.00
—B-side by Alpha Zoe					
MGM					
13379	Keep On Dancing/Make Up Your Mind	1965	3.75	7.50	15.00
13432	Spread It On Thick/Brown Paper Bag	1965	3.00	6.00	12.00

Number	Title (A Side/B Side)	Yr	VG	VG+	NM
13432 [PS]	Spread It On Thick/Brown Paper Bag	1965	4.00	8.00	16.00
13495	Everyday I Have to Cry/Don't Let It Be (This Time)	1966	3.00	6.00	12.00
13561	There Are Two Sides to Every Story/Woman of the World	1966	3.00	6.00	12.00
13690	There's a Love/You Make Me Feel So Good	1967	6.25	12.50	25.00
13749	I Can See/90 Pound Weakling	1967	2.50	5.00	10.00
STAX					
0223	All Hung Up on You/Little Gold Band	1974	—	2.00	4.00
0242	High Flyer/Little Gold Band	1975	—	2.00	4.00
SUN					
1108	I Need Love/Why Should I Cry	1969	—	2.50	5.00
1114	Cinnamon Girl/I Just Got the News	1970	—	2.50	5.00
1114 [DJ]	Cinnamon Girl/I Just Got the News	1970	2.50	5.00	10.00
—Promo only on blue vinyl					
1118	I Hate to See You Go/He'll Never Love Me	1970	—	2.50	5.00
1120	Friends/Goddess of Love	1970	—	2.50	5.00
1122	Wild World/Sunshine	1971	—	2.50	5.00
1126	God Save Our Country/Love You All My Life	1971	—	2.50	5.00
YOUNGSTOWN					
600	Sometimes/Little Drops of Water	1965	6.25	12.50	25.00
601	Keep On Dancing/Make Up Your Mind	1965	7.50	15.00	30.00
Albums					
MGM					
GAS-127	The Gentrys (Golden Archive Series)	1970	5.00	10.00	20.00
E-4336 [M]	Keep On Dancing	1965	6.25	12.50	25.00
SE-4336 [P]	Keep On Dancing	1965	7.50	15.00	30.00
E-4346 [M]	Gentry Time	1966	5.00	10.00	20.00
SE-4346 [S]	Gentry Time	1966	6.25	12.50	25.00
SUN					
LP-117	The Gentrys	1970	7.50	15.00	30.00

GEORDIE

45s

MGM

Number	Title (A Side/B Side)	Yr	VG	VG+	NM
14539	Ain't It Just Like a Woman/All Because of You	1973	—	3.00	6.00
Albums					
MGM					
SE-4903	Hope You Like It	1973	7.50	15.00	30.00

GEORGE, BARBARA

45s

A.F.O.

Number	Title (A Side/B Side)	Yr	VG	VG+	NM
302	I Know (You Don't Love Me No More)/Love	1961	3.00	6.00	12.00
—Orange and black label					
302	I Know (You Don't Love Me No More)/Love	1961	3.75	7.50	15.00
—All-orange label					
304	You Talk About Love/Whip-O-Will	1962	2.50	5.00	10.00
SUE					
763	If You Think/If When You've Done the Best You Can	1962	2.00	4.00	8.00
766	Send for Me (If You Need Some Lovin')/Bless You	1962	2.00	4.00	8.00
773	Recipe (For Perfect Fools)/Try Again	1962	2.00	4.00	8.00
796	Something's Definitely Wrong/I Need Something Different	1963	2.50	5.00	10.00
UNITED ARTISTS					
XW516	I Know (You Don't Love Me No More)/ Mockingbird	1974	—	2.00	4.00
—Reissue; B-side by Charles and Inez Foxx					
Albums					
A.F.O.					
5001 [M]	I Know (You Don't Love Me No More)	1962	62.50	125.00	250.00

GEORGE, LLOYD

45s

IMPERIAL

Number	Title (A Side/B Side)	Yr	VG	VG+	NM
5837	Twistville/Young Date	1962	3.75	7.50	15.00
5896	Come On Train/Frog Hunt	1962	3.75	7.50	15.00

GEORGE AND EARL

45s

MERCURY

Number	Title (A Side/B Side)	Yr	VG	VG+	NM
70605	Got Anything Good/Can I?	1955	6.25	12.50	25.00
70632	Goin' Steady with the Blues/Sweet Little Miss Blue Eyes	1955	6.25	12.50	25.00
70683	Heartaches/Don't, Don't, Don't	1955	6.25	12.50	25.00
70773	Cry, Baby, Cry/Take a Look at My Darlin'	1956	6.25	12.50	25.00
70852	Done Gone/Better Stop, Look and Listen	1956	15.00	30.00	60.00
70935	Eleven Roses/Remember and Regret	1956	6.25	12.50	25.00

GEORGE AND GREER

45s

GOLDWAX

Number	Title (A Side/B Side)	Yr	VG	VG+	NM
313	You Don't Know It, But You Had Me/Good Times	1966	10.00	20.00	40.00
313	You Don't Know It, But You Had Me/Good Times	1966	7.50	15.00	30.00
—Reissue as "George Jackson and Dan Greer"					

GEORGE AND LOUIS

45s

SUN

Number	Title (A Side/B Side)	Yr	VG	VG+	NM
301	The Return of Jerry Lee/Lewis Boogie	1958	7.50	15.00	30.00
—B-side by Jerry Lee Lewis					
301	The Return of Jerry Lee/The Return of Jerry Lee, Part 2	1958	6.25	12.50	25.00

GERMZ, THE

45s

VERTIGO

Number	Title (A Side/B Side)	Yr	VG	VG+	NM
8001	Boy-Girl Love/No Easy Way Down	1967	3.75	7.50	15.00

GERONIMO BLACK

45s

UNI

Number	Title (A Side/B Side)	Yr	VG	VG+	NM
55339	Let Us Live/'59 Chevy	1972	2.50	5.00	10.00
Albums					
UNI					
73132	Geronimo Black	1972	6.25	12.50	25.00

GERRY AND THE PACEMAKERS

45s

LAURIE

Number	Title (A Side/B Side)	Yr	VG	VG+	NM
3162	How Do You Do It/Away From You	1963	5.00	10.00	20.00
3196	I Like It/It Happened to Me	1963	5.00	10.00	20.00
3218	You'll Never Walk Alone/It's All Right	1964	5.00	10.00	20.00
3233	I'm the One/You've Got What I Like	1964	5.00	10.00	20.00
3233	I'm the One/It's All Right	1964	3.75	7.50	15.00
3233	I'm the One/How Do You Do It	1964	3.75	7.50	15.00
3251	Don't Let the Sun Catch You Crying/Away from You	1964	3.75	7.50	15.00
3261	How Do You Do It/You'll Never Walk Alone	1964	3.00	6.00	12.00
3271	I Like It/Jambalaya	1964	3.00	6.00	12.00
3279	I'll Be There/You, You, You	1964	3.00	6.00	12.00
3284	Ferry Across the Mersey/Pretend	1965	3.00	6.00	12.00
3293	It's Gonna Be Alright/Skinny Minnie	1965	2.50	5.00	10.00
3302	You'll Never Walk Alone/Away from You	1965	2.50	5.00	10.00
3313	Give All Your Love to Me/You're the Reason	1965	2.50	5.00	10.00
3323	Dreams/Walk Hand in Hand	1965	2.50	5.00	10.00
3337	La La La/Without You	1966	2.50	5.00	10.00
3354	Girl on a Swing/The Way You Look Tonight	1966	2.50	5.00	10.00
3370	The Big Bright Green Pleasure Machine/Looking for My Life	1966	3.00	6.00	12.00
Albums					
CAPITOL					
SM-11898 [B]	The Best of Gerry and the Pacemakers	1979	2.00	4.00	8.00
—All stereo except "I Like It," "Away from You" and "I'm the One," which are mono.					
LAURIE					
LLP-2024 [M]	Don't Let the Sun Catch You Crying	1964	7.50	15.00	30.00
SLP-2024 [R]	Don't Let the Sun Catch You Crying	1964	6.25	12.50	25.00
LLP-2027 [M]	Gerry and the Pacemakers' Second Album	1964	7.50	15.00	30.00
SLP-2027 [R]	Gerry and the Pacemakers' Second Album	1964	6.25	12.50	25.00
LLP-2030 [M]	I'll Be There	1964	7.50	15.00	30.00
SLP-2030 [R]	I'll Be There	1964	6.25	12.50	25.00
LLP-2031 [M]	Greatest Hits	1965	6.25	12.50	25.00
SLP-2031 [R]	Greatest Hits	1965	3.75	7.50	15.00
LLP-2037 [M]	Girl on a Swing	1966	6.25	12.50	25.00
SLP-2037 [S]	Girl on a Swing	1966	5.00	10.00	20.00
DT 90384 [R]	Greatest Hits	1965	6.25	12.50	25.00
—Capitol Record Club edition					
T 90384 [M]	Greatest Hits	1965	6.25	12.50	25.00
—Capitol Record Club edition					
DT 90555 [R]	Don't Let the Sun Catch You Crying	1964	7.50	15.00	30.00
—Capitol Record Club edition					
T 90555 [M]	Don't Let the Sun Catch You Crying	1964	10.00	20.00	40.00
—Capitol Record Club edition					
UNITED ARTISTS					
UAL 3387 [M]	Ferry Cross the Mersey	1965	6.25	12.50	25.00
—Also contains incidental music by George Martin					
UAS 6387 [S]	Ferry Cross the Mersey	1965	10.00	20.00	40.00
ST 90812 [S]	Ferry Cross the Mersey	1965	12.50	25.00	50.00
—Capitol Record Club edition					
T 90812 [M]	Ferry Cross the Mersey	1965	10.00	20.00	40.00
—Capitol Record Club edition					

GETZ, STAN

Also see BILLIE HOLIDAY AND STAN GETZ; CAL TJADER AND STAN GETZ.

45s

CLEF

Number	Title (A Side/B Side)	Yr	VG	VG+	NM
89090	Rustie Hop/Cool Mix	1954	3.75	7.50	15.00
89193	Nature Boy/'Round Midnight	195?	3.75	7.50	15.00
COLUMBIA					
10132	La Fiesta/(B-side unknown)	1975	—	2.50	5.00
DAWN					
204	Pennies from Heaven/It's the Talk of the Town	1954	3.75	7.50	15.00
MERCURY					
89042	'Tis Autumn/Lover Come Back to Me	1953	3.75	7.50	15.00
89059	Erudition/Have You Met Miss Jones	1953	3.75	7.50	15.00
MGM					
13430	Once Upon a Time/Taste of Living	1965	—	3.00	6.00
PRESTIGE					
240	My Old Flame/The Lady in Red	1962	2.50	5.00	10.00
—Reissue of 712					
708	I've Got You Under My Skin/There's a Small Hotel	195?	3.75	7.50	15.00
710	Long Island Sound/Mar-Cia	195?	3.75	7.50	15.00
712	My Old Flame/The Lady in Red	195?	3.75	7.50	15.00
724	Wrap Your Troubles in Dreams/Battle of Saxes	195?	3.75	7.50	15.00
729	Too Marvelous for Words/Michelle	195?	3.75	7.50	15.00
—B-side by Terry Gibbs					
740	What's New/Indian Summer	195?	3.75	7.50	15.00
800	T & S/Terry's Tune	195?	3.00	6.00	12.00
802	Four and One More/Five Brothers	195?	3.00	6.00	12.00
811	Speedway/Crazy Chords	195?	3.00	6.00	12.00
818	Battleground/Preservation	195?	3.00	6.00	12.00
867	Into It/You Stepped Out of a Dream	195?	3.00	6.00	12.00
VERVE					
10251	I Remember When/I'm Late-I'm Late	1962	2.00	4.00	8.00
10279	Balanco No Samba/Mahna de Carnaval	1963	2.00	4.00	8.00
10291	O Morro/Sambalero	1963	2.00	4.00	8.00
10557	Midnight Samba/Once	1967	—	3.00	6.00
10571	My Own True Love/A Tribute to Stan	1967	—	3.00	6.00
10676	Communication '72/Back to Bach	1972	—	2.50	5.00

Number	Title (A Side/B Side)	Yr	VG	VG+	NM
Albums					
AMERICAN RECORDING SOCIETY					
G 407 [M]	Cool Jazz of Stan Getz	1956	10.00	20.00	40.00
G-428 [M]	Intimate Portrait	1957	10.00	20.00	40.00
G-443 [M]	Stan Getz '57	1957	10.00	20.00	40.00
A&M					
SP-5297	Apasionado	1990	3.75	7.50	15.00
BLACKHAWK					
BKH-51101	Voyage	1986	2.50	5.00	10.00
BLUE RIBBON					
BR-8012 [M]	Rhythms	1961	5.00	10.00	20.00
BS-8012 [R]	Rhythms	1961	2.50	5.00	10.00
CLEF					
MGC-137 [10]	Stan Getz Plays	1953	50.00	100.00	200.00
MGC-143 [10]	The Artistry of Stan Getz	1953	50.00	100.00	200.00
COLUMBIA					
PC 32706	Captain Marvel	1974	3.75	7.50	15.00
PC 33703	Best of Two Worlds	1975	3.75	7.50	15.00
JC 34873	The Peacocks	1977	3.00	6.00	12.00
JC 35992	Children of the World	1979	3.00	6.00	12.00
JC 36403	The Best of Stan Getz	1980	3.00	6.00	12.00
FC 38272	The Master	1983	2.50	5.00	10.00
CJ 44047	The Lyrical Stan Getz	1988	3.00	6.00	12.00
CONCORD JAZZ					
CJ-158	The Dolphin	198?	3.00	6.00	12.00
CJ-188	Pure Getz	1983	3.00	6.00	12.00
CROWN					
CLP-5002 [M]	Groovin' High	1957	10.00	20.00	40.00
—Reissue of Modern 1202					
CLP-5284 [M]	Groovin' High	196?	5.00	10.00	20.00
—Reissue of 5002					
DALE					
21 [10]	In Retrospect	1951	75.00	150.00	300.00
EMARCY					
838771-1	Billy Highstreet Samba	1990	3.00	6.00	12.00
FANTASY					
OJC-121	Stan Getz Quartets	198?	2.50	5.00	10.00
—Reissue of Prestige 7002					
HALL OF FAME					
606	Stan Getz and His Tenor Sax	197?	3.00	6.00	12.00
INNER CITY					
1040 [(2)]	Gold	1977	3.00	6.00	12.00
INTERMEDIA					
QS-5057	Stella by Starlight	198?	2.50	5.00	10.00
JAZZ MAN					
5014	Forrest Eyes	1982	3.00	6.00	12.00
JAZZTONE					
J-1230 [M]	Stan Getz	1956	10.00	20.00	40.00
J-1240 [M]	Stan Getz '57	1957	10.00	20.00	40.00
METRO					
M-501 [M]	The Melodic Stan Getz	1965	3.00	6.00	12.00
MS-501 [S]	The Melodic Stan Getz	1965	3.75	7.50	15.00
METRONOME					
BLP-6 [M]	The Sound	1956	12.50	25.00	50.00
MGM					
SE-4696	Marrakesh Express	1970	3.75	7.50	15.00
MODERN					
MLP-1202 [M]	Groovin' High	1956	37.50	75.00	150.00
MOSAIC					
M4-131 [(4)]	The Complete Recordings of the Stan Getz Quintet with Jimmy Raney	199?	12.50	25.00	50.00
NEW JAZZ					
NJLP-8214 [M]	Long Island Sound	1959	15.00	30.00	60.00
—Reissue of Prestige 7002; purple label					
NJLP-8214 [M]	Long Island Sound	1965	6.25	12.50	25.00
—Blue label with trident logo on right					
NORGRAN					
MGN-1000 [M]	Interpretations by the Stan Getz Quintet	1954	30.00	60.00	120.00
MGN-1008 [M]	Interpretations by the Stan Getz Quintet #2	1954	30.00	60.00	120.00
MGN-1029 [M]	Interpretations by the Stan Getz Quintet #3	1955	37.50	75.00	150.00
MGN-1032 [M]	West Coast Jazz	1955	37.50	75.00	150.00
MGN-1042 [M]	Stan Getz Plays	1955	25.00	50.00	100.00
—Reissue of Clef 137 and 143 on one 12-inch LP					
MGN-1087 [M]	Stan Getz '56	1956	25.00	50.00	100.00
MGN-1088 [M]	More West Coast Jazz with Stan Getz	1956	25.00	50.00	100.00
MGN-2000-2 [(2) M]	Stan Getz at the Shrine	1955	50.00	100.00	200.00
—Boxed set with booklet					
PICKWICK					
SPC-3031	Stan Getz In Concert	197?	2.50	5.00	10.00
PRESTIGE					
PRLP-102 [10]	Stan Getz and the Tenor Sax Stars	1951	50.00	100.00	200.00
PRLP-104 [10]	Stan Getz, Volume 2	1951	50.00	100.00	200.00
PRLP-108 [10]	Stan Getz-Lee Konitz	1951	50.00	100.00	200.00
PRLP-7002 [M]	Stan Getz Quartets	1955	25.00	50.00	100.00
PRLP-7255 [M]	Early Stan	1963	10.00	20.00	40.00
PRST-7255 [R]	Early Stan	1963	5.00	10.00	20.00
PRLP-7256 [M]	Stan Getz' Greatest Hits	1963	10.00	20.00	40.00
PRST-7256 [R]	Stan Getz' Greatest Hits	1963	5.00	10.00	20.00
PRLP-7337 [M]	Stan Getz' Greatest Hits	1967	6.25	12.50	25.00
—Reissue of PRLP 7256					
PRST-7337 [R]	Stan Getz' Greatest Hits	1967	3.75	7.50	15.00
—Reissue of PRST 7256					
PRLP-7434 [M]	Getz Plays Jazz Classics	1967	6.25	12.50	25.00
—Reissue of PRLP 7255					
PRST-7434 [R]	Getz Plays Jazz Classics	1967	3.75	7.50	15.00
—Reissue of PRST 7255					
PRLP-7516 [M]	Preservation	1967	6.25	12.50	25.00
PRST-7516 [R]	Preservation	1967	3.75	7.50	15.00
24019 [(2)]	Stan Getz	197?	3.75	7.50	15.00
24088 [(2)]	Early Getz	197?	3.00	6.00	12.00
ROOST					
RK-103 [(2) M]	The Stan Getz Years	1964	10.00	20.00	40.00

Number	Title (A Side/B Side)	Yr	VG	VG+	NM
RKS-103 [(2) R]	The Stan Getz Years	1964	6.25	12.50	25.00
R-402 [10]	Stan Getz	1950	50.00	100.00	200.00
R-404 [10]	Stan Getz and the Swedish All Stars	1951	50.00	100.00	200.00
R-407 [10]	Jazz at Storyville	1952	37.50	75.00	150.00
R-411 [10]	Jazz at Storyville, Volume 2	1952	37.50	75.00	150.00
R-417 [10]	Chamber Music	1953	37.50	75.00	150.00
R-420 [10]	Jazz at Storyville, Volume 3	1954	37.50	75.00	150.00
R-423 [10]	Split Kick	1954	37.50	75.00	150.00
LP-2207 [M]	The Sounds of Stan Getz	1956	20.00	40.00	80.00
—Reissue of R-402					
LP-2209 [M]	Storyville	1956	20.00	40.00	80.00
—Reissue of R-407 and half of R-411					
LP-2225 [M]	Storyville, Volume 2	1957	20.00	40.00	80.00
—Reissue of R-423 and the other half of R-411					
LP-2249 [M]	The Greatest of Stan Getz	1963	7.50	15.00	30.00
SLP-2249 [R]	The Greatest of Stan Getz	1963	3.75	7.50	15.00
LP-2251 [M]	Moonlight in Vermont	1963	7.50	15.00	30.00
SLP-2251 [R]	Moonlight in Vermont	1963	3.75	7.50	15.00
LP-2255 [M]	Modern World	1963	7.50	15.00	30.00
SLP-2255 [R]	Modern World	1963	3.75	7.50	15.00
LP-2258 [M]	Getz Age	1963	7.50	15.00	30.00
SLP-2258 [R]	Getz Age	1963	3.75	7.50	15.00
ROULETTE					
RE-119 [(2)]	The Best of Stan Getz	1972	3.75	7.50	15.00
RE-123 [(2)]	Stan Getz/Sonny Stitt	1973	3.75	7.50	15.00
SAVOY					
SJL-1105	Opus de Bop	197?	3.00	6.00	12.00
MG-9004 [10]	New Sounds in Modern Music	1951	75.00	150.00	300.00
STEEPLECHASE					
SCS-1073/4 [(2)]	Live at Montmartre	1986	3.00	6.00	12.00
VERVE					
VSP-2 [M]	Eloquence	1966	3.75	7.50	15.00
VSPS-2 [R]	Eloquence	1966	2.50	5.00	10.00
VSP-22 [M]	Another Time, Another Place	1966	3.75	7.50	15.00
VSPS-22 [R]	Another Time, Another Place	1966	2.50	5.00	10.00
VSP-31 [M]	Stan Getz Plays Blues	1966	3.75	7.50	15.00
VSPS-31 [R]	Stan Getz Plays Blues	1966	2.50	5.00	10.00
UMV-2071	Focus	198?	2.50	5.00	10.00
—Reissue					
UMV-2075	Getz Au Go Go	198?	2.50	5.00	10.00
—Reissue					
UMV-2100	Jazz Samba Encore	198?	2.50	5.00	10.00
—Reissue					
VE-2-2510 [(2)]	The Corea/Evans Sessions	1976	3.75	7.50	15.00
VR-1-2528	Focus	1977	2.50	5.00	10.00
—Reissue of 8412					
UMV-2614	Stan Getz in Stockholm	198?	2.50	5.00	10.00
—Reissue					
MGVS-6160 [S]	Cool Velvet — Stan Getz and Strings	1960	—	—	—
—Unreleased					
MGV-8028 [M]	West Coast Jazz	1957	12.50	25.00	50.00
—Reissue of Norgran 1032					
V-8028 [M]	West Coast Jazz	1961	5.00	10.00	20.00
—Reissue of MGV-8028					
V6-8028 [R]	West Coast Jazz	196?	3.00	6.00	12.00
MGV-8029 [M]	Stan Getz '57	1957	12.50	25.00	50.00
—Reissue of Norgran 1087 with revised title					
V-8029 [M]	Stan Getz '57	1961	5.00	10.00	20.00
—Reissue of MGV-8029					
MGV-8122 [M]	Interpretations by the Stan Getz Quintet #3	1957	12.50	25.00	50.00
—Reissue of Norgran 1029					
V-8122 [M]	Interpretations by the Stan Getz Quintet #3	1961	5.00	10.00	20.00
—Reissue of MGV-8122					
MGV-8133 [M]	Stan Getz Plays	1957	12.50	25.00	50.00
—Reissue of Norgran 1042					
V-8133 [M]	Stan Getz Plays	1961	5.00	10.00	20.00
—Reissue of MGV-8133					
V6-8133 [R]	Stan Getz Plays	196?	3.00	6.00	12.00
MGV-8177 [M]	More West Coast Jazz with Stan Getz	1957	12.50	25.00	50.00
—Reissue of Norgran 1088					
V-8177 [M]	More West Coast Jazz with Stan Getz	1961	5.00	10.00	20.00
—Reissue of MGV-8177					
V6-8177 [R]	More West Coast Jazz with Stan Getz	196?	3.00	6.00	12.00
MGV-8188-2 [M]	Stan Getz at the Shrine	1957	25.00	50.00	100.00
—Reissue of Norgran 2000-2					
V-8188-2 [(2) M]	Stan Getz at the Shrine	1961	6.25	12.50	25.00
—Reissue of MGV-8188-2					
V6-8188-2 [(2) R]	Stan Getz at the Shrine	196?	3.75	7.50	15.00
MGV-8200 [M]	Stan Getz and the Cool Sounds	1957	12.50	25.00	50.00
—Reissue of American Recording Society 407 with new name					
V-8200 [M]	Stan Getz and the Cool Sounds	1961	5.00	10.00	20.00
—Reissue of MGV-8200					
V6-8200 [R]	Stan Getz and the Cool Sounds	196?	3.00	6.00	12.00
MGV-8213 [M]	Stan Getz in Stockholm	1958	12.50	25.00	50.00
—Reissue of American Recording Society 428 with new name					
V-8213 [M]	Stan Getz in Stockholm	1961	5.00	10.00	20.00
—Reissue of MGV-8213					
V6-8213 [R]	Stan Getz in Stockholm	196?	3.00	6.00	12.00
MGV-8263 [M]	Stan Meets Chet	1958	15.00	30.00	60.00
—With Chet Baker					
V-8263 [M]	Stan Meets Chet	1961	5.00	10.00	20.00
—Reissue of MGV-8263					
V6-8263 [R]	Stan Meets Chet	196?	3.00	6.00	12.00
MGV-8294 [M]	The Steamer	1959	12.50	25.00	50.00
V-8294 [M]	The Steamer	1961	5.00	10.00	20.00
—Reissue of MGV-8294					
V6-8294 [R]	The Steamer	196?	3.00	6.00	12.00
MGV-8296 [M]	Award Winner	1959	12.50	25.00	50.00
V-8296 [M]	Award Winner	1961	5.00	10.00	20.00
—Reissue of MGV-8296					
V6-8296 [R]	Award Winner	196?	3.00	6.00	12.00
MGV-8321 [M]	The Soft Swing	1959	12.50	25.00	50.00
V-8321 [M]	The Soft Swing	1961	5.00	10.00	20.00
—Reissue of MGV-8321					
V6-8321 [R]	The Soft Swing	196?	3.00	6.00	12.00

Number	Title (A Side/B Side)	Yr	VG	VG+	NM
MGV-8331 [M]	Imported from Europe	1959	12.50	25.00	50.00
V-8331 [M]	Imported from Europe	1961	5.00	10.00	20.00
—Reissue of MGV-8331					
V6-8331 [R]	Imported from Europe	196?	3.00	6.00	12.00
MGV-8356 [M]	Stan Getz Quintet	1960	—	—	—
—Unreleased					
MGV-8379 [M]	Cool Velvet — Stan Getz and Strings	1960	12.50	25.00	50.00
V-8379 [M]	Cool Velvet — Stan Getz and Strings	1961	5.00	10.00	20.00
—Reissue of MGV-8379					
V6-8379 [S]	Cool Velvet — Stan Getz and Strings	1961	5.00	10.00	20.00
MGV-8393-2 [(2) M]	Stan Getz At Large	1960	15.00	30.00	60.00
V-8393-2 [(2) M]	Stan Getz At Large	1961	6.25	12.50	25.00
—Reissue of MGV-8393-2					
V6-8393-2 [(2) R]	Stan Getz At Large	1961	3.75	7.50	15.00
MGV-8401 [M]	Stan Getz At Large, Volume 1	1960	—	—	—
—Unreleased					
MGV-8402 [M]	Stan Getz At Large, Volume 2	1960	—	—	—
—Unreleased					
V-8412 [M]	Focus	1961	6.25	12.50	25.00
V6-8412 [S]	Focus	1961	5.00	10.00	20.00
V-8494 [M]	Big Band Bossa Nova	1962	5.00	10.00	20.00
V6-8494 [S]	Big Band Bossa Nova	1962	6.25	12.50	25.00
V-8523 [M]	Jazz Samba Encore!	1963	5.00	10.00	20.00
—With Luiz Bonfa					
V6-8523 [S]	Jazz Samba Encore!	1963	6.25	12.50	25.00
—With Luiz Bonfa					
V-8554 [M]	Reflections	1964	3.75	7.50	15.00
V6-8554 [S]	Reflections	1964	5.00	10.00	20.00
V-8600 [M]	Getz Au Go Go	1964	3.75	7.50	15.00
V6-8600 [S]	Getz Au Go Go	1964	5.00	10.00	20.00
V-8693 [M]	Sweet Rain	1967	6.25	12.50	25.00
V6-8693 [S]	Sweet Rain	1967	3.75	7.50	15.00
V-8707 [M]	Voices	1967	6.25	12.50	25.00
V6-8707 [S]	Voices	1967	3.75	7.50	15.00
V-8719 [M]	The Best of Stan Getz	1967	6.25	12.50	25.00
V6-8719 [S]	The Best of Stan Getz	1967	3.75	7.50	15.00
V-8752 [M]	What the World Needs Now — Stan Getz Plays Bacharach and David	1968	7.50	15.00	30.00
V6-8752 [S]	What the World Needs Now — Stan Getz Plays Bacharach and David	1968	3.75	7.50	15.00
V6-8780	Didn't We	1969	3.75	7.50	15.00
V6-8802-2 [(2)]	Dynasty	1971	5.00	10.00	20.00
V6-8807	Communications '72	1972	3.75	7.50	15.00
V6-8815-2 [(2)]	History of Stan Getz	1973	3.75	7.50	15.00
V3HB-8844 [(2)]	Return Engagement	1974	3.75	7.50	15.00
815239-1	Stan the Man	1983	2.50	5.00	10.00
821725-1	Getz Au Go Go	198?	2.50	5.00	10.00
—Reissue					
823242-1 [(2)]	The Corea/Evans Sessions	198?	3.00	6.00	12.00
—Reissue					
823611-1 [(5)]	The Girl from Ipamena: The Bossa Nova Years	1984	12.50	25.00	50.00
823613-1	Jazz Samba Encore	198?	2.50	5.00	10.00
—Reissue					

GETZ, STAN, AND LAURINDO ALMEIDA

45s

VERVE

Number	Title (A Side/B Side)	Yr	VG	VG+	NM
10468	Winter Moon/Menina Moca	1966	—	3.00	6.00

Albums

VERVE

Number	Title (A Side/B Side)	Yr	VG	VG+	NM
V-8665 [M]	Stan Getz with Guest Artist Laurindo Almeida	1965	3.75	7.50	15.00
V6-8665 [S]	Stan Getz with Guest Artist Laurindo Almeida	1965	5.00	10.00	20.00

GETZ, STAN, AND CHET BAKER

Albums

STORYVILLE

Number	Title (A Side/B Side)	Yr	VG	VG+	NM
4090	Line for Lyons	1984	2.50	5.00	10.00

GETZ, STAN, AND BOB BROOKMEYER

Albums

VERVE

Number	Title (A Side/B Side)	Yr	VG	VG+	NM
V-8418 [M]	Stan Getz and Bob Brookmeyer (Recorded Fall 1961)	1961	5.00	10.00	20.00
V6-8418 [S]	Stan Getz and Bob Brookmeyer (Recorded Fall 1961)	1961	5.00	10.00	20.00

GETZ, STAN, AND CHARLIE BYRD

45s

VERVE

Number	Title (A Side/B Side)	Yr	VG	VG+	NM
10260	Desafinado/Theme from Dr. Kildare	1962	2.00	4.00	8.00

Albums

DCC COMPACT CLASSICS

Number	Title (A Side/B Side)	Yr	VG	VG+	NM
LPZ-2011	Jazz Samba	1995	6.25	12.50	25.00
—Audiophile vinyl					

VERVE

Number	Title (A Side/B Side)	Yr	VG	VG+	NM
UMJ-3158	Jazz Samba	198?	2.50	5.00	10.00
V-8432 [M]	Jazz Samba	1962	5.00	10.00	20.00
V6-8432 [S]	Jazz Samba	1962	6.25	12.50	25.00
810061-1	Jazz Samba	198?	2.50	5.00	10.00
—Reissue					

GETZ, STAN, AND ALBERT DAILEY

Albums

ELEKTRA/MUSICIAN

Number	Title (A Side/B Side)	Yr	VG	VG+	NM
60370	Poetry	1985	2.50	5.00	10.00

GETZ, STAN, AND BILL EVANS

Albums

VERVE

Number	Title (A Side/B Side)	Yr	VG	VG+	NM
V3G-8833	Previously Unreleased Recordings	1974	3.00	6.00	12.00

GETZ, STAN, AND JOAO GILBERTO

45s

VERVE

Number	Title (A Side/B Side)	Yr	VG	VG+	NM
10321	Reflections/Blowin' in the Wind	1964	2.50	5.00	10.00
10322	The Girl from Ipanema/Corcovado	1964	2.50	5.00	10.00
10323	The Girl from Ipanema/Blowin' in the Wind	1964	2.00	4.00	8.00
10336	Only Trust Your Heart/Telephone Song	1964	2.00	4.00	8.00

Albums

MOBILE FIDELITY

Number	Title (A Side/B Side)	Yr	VG	VG+	NM
1-208	Getz/Gilberto	1994	12.50	25.00	50.00
—Audiophile vinyl					

VERVE

Number	Title (A Side/B Side)	Yr	VG	VG+	NM
UMV-2099	Getz/Gilberto	198?	2.50	5.00	10.00
—Reissue					
V-8545 [M]	Getz/Gilberto	1964	3.75	7.50	15.00
V6-8545 [S]	Getz/Gilberto	1964	5.00	10.00	20.00
V-8623 [M]	Getz/Gilberto #2	1965	3.75	7.50	15.00
V6-8623 [S]	Getz/Gilberto #2	1965	5.00	10.00	20.00
810048-1	Getz/Gilberto	198?	2.50	5.00	10.00
—Reissue					

GETZ, STAN; DIZZY GILLESPIE; SONNY STITT

Albums

VERVE

Number	Title (A Side/B Side)	Yr	VG	VG+	NM
MGV-8198 [M]	For Musicians Only	1958	20.00	40.00	80.00
V-8198 [M]	For Musicians Only	1961	6.25	12.50	25.00

GETZ, STAN, AND WARDELL GRAY

Albums

DAWN

Number	Title (A Side/B Side)	Yr	VG	VG+	NM
DLP-1126 [M]	Tenors Anyone?	1958	20.00	40.00	80.00

SEECO

Number	Title (A Side/B Side)	Yr	VG	VG+	NM
SLP-7 [10]	Highlights in Modern Jazz	1954	50.00	100.00	200.00

GETZ, STAN, AND J.J. JOHNSON

Albums

VERVE

Number	Title (A Side/B Side)	Yr	VG	VG+	NM
MGVS-6027 [S]	Stan Getz and J.J. Johnson at the Opera House	1960	10.00	20.00	40.00
MGV-8265 [M]	Stan Getz and J.J. Johnson at the Opera House	1958	12.50	25.00	50.00
V-8265 [M]	Stan Getz and J.J. Johnson at the Opera House	1961	5.00	10.00	20.00
V6-8265 [S]	Stan Getz and J.J. Johnson at the Opera House	1961	3.75	7.50	15.00
MGV-8405 [M]	Stan Getz and J.J. Johnson	1961	—	—	—
—Unreleased					

GETZ, STAN, AND GERRY MULLIGAN

Albums

MAINSTREAM

Number	Title (A Side/B Side)	Yr	VG	VG+	NM
MRL 364	Yesterday	1972	3.75	7.50	15.00

GETZ, STAN, AND OSCAR PETERSON

Albums

VERVE

Number	Title (A Side/B Side)	Yr	VG	VG+	NM
UMV-2665	Stan Getz and the Oscar Peterson Trio	198?	2.50	5.00	10.00
—Reissue					
MGV-8251 [M]	Stan Getz and the Oscar Peterson Trio	1958	12.50	25.00	50.00
V-8251 [M]	Stan Getz and the Oscar Peterson Trio	1961	5.00	10.00	20.00
—Reissue of MGV-8251					
V6-8251 [R]	Stan Getz and the Oscar Peterson Trio	196?	3.00	6.00	12.00
MGV-8348 [M]	Stan Getz with Gerry Mulligan and the Oscar Peterson Trio	1959	12.50	25.00	50.00
V-8348 [M]	Stan Getz with Gerry Mulligan and the Oscar Peterson Trio	1961	5.00	10.00	20.00
—Reissue of MGV-8348					
V6-8348 [R]	Stan Getz with Gerry Mulligan and the Oscar Peterson Trio	1961	3.00	6.00	12.00

GETZ, STAN, AND HORACE SILVER

Albums

BARONET

Number	Title (A Side/B Side)	Yr	VG	VG+	NM
B-102 [M]	A Pair of Kings	1962	3.75	7.50	15.00
BS-102 [R]	A Pair of Kings	196?	2.50	5.00	10.00

GETZ, STAN, AND ZOOT SIMS

Albums

FANTASY

Number	Title (A Side/B Side)	Yr	VG	VG+	NM
OJC-008	The Brothers	1982	2.50	5.00	10.00

PRESTIGE

Number	Title (A Side/B Side)	Yr	VG	VG+	NM
PRLP-7022 [M]	The Brothers	1956	37.50	75.00	150.00
PRLP-7252 [M]	The Brothers	1963	12.50	25.00	50.00

GHOULS, THE

Albums

CAPITOL

Number	Title (A Side/B Side)	Yr	VG	VG+	NM
ST 2215 [S]	Dracula's Deuce	1965	37.50	75.00	150.00
T 2215 [M]	Dracula's Deuce	1965	30.00	60.00	120.00

GIANT CRAB, THE

45s

UNI

Number	Title (A Side/B Side)	Yr	VG	VG+	NM
55094	Hi Ho Silver Lining/Hot Line Conversation	1968	2.00	4.00	8.00
55103	Believe It or Not/The Color Purple	1968	2.00	4.00	8.00
55134	Cool It/Intensify My Soul	1969	2.00	4.00	8.00
55155	ESP/Hot Line Conversation	1969	2.00	4.00	8.00

Albums

UNI

Number	Title (A Side/B Side)	Yr	VG	VG+	NM
73037	A Giant Crab Comes Forth	1968	6.25	12.50	25.00
73057	Cool It, Helios	1969	6.25	12.50	25.00

GIBB, BARRY

Also see BEE GEES; BARBRA STREISAND.

45s

Number	Title (A Side/B Side)	Yr	VG	VG+	NM
ATCO					
6786	One Bad Thing/The Day Your Eyes Met Mine	1970	2.00	4.00	8.00
MCA					
52443	Shine Shine/She Says	1984	—	—	3.00
52443 [PS]	Shine Shine/She Says	1984	—	—	3.00
52501	Stay Alone/Fine Line	1984	—	—	3.00

GIBB, MAURICE

Also see BEE GEES.

45s

Number	Title (A Side/B Side)	Yr	VG	VG+	NM
ATCO					
6757	Railroad/I've Come Back	1970	2.00	4.00	8.00

GIBB, ROBIN

Also see BEE GEES.

12-Inch Singles

Number	Title (A Side/B Side)	Yr	VG	VG+	NM
MIRAGE					
DMD 740 [DJ]	Boys Do Fall in Love (same on both sides?)	1984	2.50	5.00	10.00
PR 775 [DJ]	Secret Agent/Robot	1984	2.50	5.00	10.00

45s

Number	Title (A Side/B Side)	Yr	VG	VG+	NM
ATCO					
6698	Saved by the Bell/Mother and Jack	1969	2.00	4.00	8.00
6727	Weekend/One Million Years	1969	2.00	4.00	8.00
6737	Give Me a Smile/August October	1970	2.00	4.00	8.00
EMI AMERICA					
8291	Like a Fool/Possession	1985	—	—	3.00
8291 [PS]	Like a Fool/Possession	1985	—	2.00	4.00
8304	Toys/Do You Love Her	1986	—	—	3.00
8304 [PS]	Toys/Do You Love Her	1986	—	2.00	4.00
MIRAGE					
99688 [DJ]	In Your Diary (same on both sides)	1984	—	2.00	4.00
—Stock copy unknown					
99712	Secret Agent/Robot	1984	—	—	3.00
99743	Boys Do Fall in Love/Diamonds	1984	—	—	3.00
99743 [PS]	Boys Do Fall in Love/Diamonds	1984	—	—	3.00
POLYDOR					
810895-7	Juliet/Hearts on Fire	1983	—	—	3.00
810895-7 [PS]	Juliet/Hearts on Fire	1983	—	2.00	4.00
RSO					
907	Oh Darling/She's Leaving Home	1978	—	2.00	4.00
—B-side by The Bee Gees					
1047	Help Me/(Instrumental)	1980	—	2.00	4.00
—With Marcy Levy					
1047 [PS]	Help Me/(Instrumental)	1980	—	2.00	4.00
SESAME STREET					
99070	Sesame Street Fever/Trash	1978	—	2.50	5.00
99070 [PS]	Sesame Street Fever/Trash	1978	—	3.00	6.00

Albums

Number	Title (A Side/B Side)	Yr	VG	VG+	NM
ATCO					
SD 33-323	Robin's Reign	1969	5.00	10.00	20.00
MIRAGE					
90170	Secret Agent	1984	2.00	4.00	8.00
POLYDOR					
810896-1	How Old Are You?	1983	2.50	5.00	10.00

GIBBS, GEORGIA

45s

Number	Title (A Side/B Side)	Yr	VG	VG+	NM
BELL					
608	I Wouldn't Have It Any Other Way/You Can Never Get Away from Me	1965	—	3.00	6.00
615	Lert Me Cry on Your Shoulder/You Can Never Get Away from Me	1965	—	3.00	6.00
626	Call Me/Don't Cry Joe	1965	—	3.00	6.00
635	In Time/Let Me Dream	1965	—	3.00	6.00
641	Kiss of Fire/Blue Grass	1966	—	3.00	6.00
CORAL					
60210	I Don't Care If the Sun Don't Shine/I'll Get Myself a Choo-Choo Train (And Go Far, Far Away)	1950	3.75	7.50	15.00
60227	Simple Melody/A Little Bit Independent	1950	3.75	7.50	15.00
—With Bob Crosby					
60234	Red Hot Mama/Razz-A-Ma-Tazz	1950	3.75	7.50	15.00
60255	I Was Dancing with Someone/Then I'll Be Happy	1950	3.75	7.50	15.00
60310	If I Were a Bell/I'll Know	1950	3.75	7.50	15.00
60315	Ballin' the Jack/Looks Like a Cold Winter	1950	3.75	7.50	15.00
60353	I Still Feel the Same About You/Get Out Those Old Records	1951	3.75	7.50	15.00
60406	Shoo Shoo Baby/Once Upon a Nickel	1951	3.75	7.50	15.00
60462	Ballin' the Jack/Then I'll Be Happy	1951	3.75	7.50	15.00
60463	Get Out Those Old Records/I'll Get Myself a Choo-Choo Train (And Go Far, Far Away)	1951	3.75	7.50	15.00
61525	If I Were a Bell/I'll Know	1955	2.50	5.00	10.00
EPIC					
9573	Candy Kisses/Nobody's Asking Questions	1963	—	—	—
—Unreleased?					
9585	I Will Follow Him (You)/Candy Kisses	1963	2.00	4.00	8.00
9606	Tater Poon/Nine Girls Out of Ten Girls	1963	5.00	10.00	20.00
IMPERIAL					
5652	Seven Lonely Days/The Stroll That Stole My Heart	1960	2.50	5.00	10.00
5688	So in Love/Loch Lomond	1960	2.50	5.00	10.00
KAPP					
286	Pretend/Hamburgers, Frankfurters and Potato Chips	1959	2.50	5.00	10.00
MERCURY					
5644	Tom's Tune/I Wish, I Wish	1951	3.75	7.50	15.00
5662	Good Morning Mister Echo/Be Doggone Sure You Call	1951	3.75	7.50	15.00
5681	While You Danced, Danced, Danced/While We're Young	1951	3.75	7.50	15.00
5687	Got Him Offa My Hands/Cherry Pink	1951	3.75	7.50	15.00
5718	What You Do to Me/While We Danced	1951	3.75	7.50	15.00
5749	Cry/My Old Flame	1951	3.75	7.50	15.00
5758	Be My Life's Companion/The Oklahoma Polka	1951	3.75	7.50	15.00
5823	Kiss of Fire/A Lasting Thing	1952	3.00	6.00	12.00
5874	So Madly in Love/Make Me Love You	1952	3.00	6.00	12.00
5912	My Favorite Song/Sinner or Saint	1952	3.00	6.00	12.00
70034	A Moth and a Flame/Photograph on the Piano	1953	3.00	6.00	12.00
70057	What Does It Mean/Winter's Here Again	1953	3.00	6.00	12.00
70095	Seven Lonely Days/If I Take My Heart Away	1953	3.00	6.00	12.00
70172	For Me, For Me/Thunder and Lightning	1953	3.00	6.00	12.00
70218	Say It Isn't So/He's Funny That Way	1953	3.00	6.00	12.00
70238	Bridge of Sighs/Hard Lovin' Man	1953	3.00	6.00	12.00
70274	I Love Paris/Under Paris Skies	1953	3.00	6.00	12.00
70298	Somebody Bad Stole De Wedding Bell (Who's Got de Ding Dong)/Baubles, Bangles and Beads	1954	3.00	6.00	12.00
70339	My Sin/I'll Always Be Happy with You	1954	3.00	6.00	12.00
70386	Wait for Me Darling/Whistle and I'll Wait	1954	3.00	6.00	12.00
70430	The Man That Got Away/More Than Ever	1954	3.00	6.00	12.00
70473	Mambo Baby/Love Me	1954	3.00	6.00	12.00
70517	Tweedle Dee/You're Wrong, All Wrong	1954	3.75	7.50	15.00
70572	Dance with Me Henry (Wallflower)/Ballin' the Jack	1955	3.75	7.50	15.00
70647	Sweet and Gentle/Blueberries	1955	3.00	6.00	12.00
70685	I Want You to Be My Baby/Come Rain or Come Shine	1955	3.00	6.00	12.00
70743	Goodbye to Rome (Arrividerci Roma)/24 Hours a Day (365 a Year)	1955	3.00	6.00	12.00
70811	Rock Right/The Greatest Thing	1956	3.00	6.00	12.00
70850	Kiss Me Another/Fool of the Year	1956	3.00	6.00	12.00
70920	Happiness Street/Happiness Is a Thing Called Joe	1956	3.00	6.00	12.00
70998	Tra La La/Morning, Noon and Night	1956	3.00	6.00	12.00
71058	Silent Lips/Pretty Pretty	1957	3.00	6.00	12.00
71103	The Sheik of Araby/I Am a Heart, a Heart, a Heart	1957	3.00	6.00	12.00
RCA VICTOR					
47-6922	I'm Walking the Floor Over You/Sugar Candy	1957	3.00	6.00	12.00
47-7047	Fun Lovin' Baby/I Never Had the Blues	1957	3.00	6.00	12.00
47-7098	Great Balls of Fire/I Miss You	1957	3.00	6.00	12.00
47-7166	You're Doin' It/Way Way Down	1958	3.00	6.00	12.00
47-7239	Hello Happiness, Goodbye Blues/It's My Pleasure	1958	3.00	6.00	12.00
47-9173	Time Will Tell/Where's the Music Coming From	1967	—	3.00	6.00
ROULETTE					
4106	The Hula Hoop Song/Keep in Touch	1958	2.50	5.00	10.00
4126	Ther Hucklebuck/Better Loved You'll Never Be	1959	2.50	5.00	10.00

7-Inch Extended Plays

Number	Title (A Side/B Side)	Yr	VG	VG+	NM
MERCURY					
EP1-3061	Say It Isn't So/It Had to Be You//I'll Always Be in Love with You/How Long Has This Been Going On	195?	3.00	6.00	12.00
EP1-3061 [PS]	Georgia Sings Oldies	195?	3.00	6.00	12.00
EP1-3062	(contents unknown)	195?	3.00	6.00	12.00
EP1-3062 [PS]	Her Nibs, Miss Georgia Gibbs	195?	3.00	6.00	12.00
EP1-3082	(contents unknown)	195?	3.00	6.00	12.00
EP1-3082 [PS]	Encores	195?	3.00	6.00	12.00
EP1-3130	My Favorite Song/A Moth and a Flame//Seven Lonely Days/Sinner or Saint	195?	3.00	6.00	12.00
EP1-3130 [PS]	For Gentlemen Only	195?	3.00	6.00	12.00
EP1-3214	(contents unknown)	195?	3.00	6.00	12.00
EP1-3214 [PS]	Bridge of Sighs	195?	3.00	6.00	12.00
EP1-3226	(contents unknown)	195?	3.00	6.00	12.00
EP1-3226 [PS]	Somebody Bad Stole De Wedding Bell	195?	3.00	6.00	12.00
EP1-3241	(contents unknown)	195?	3.00	6.00	12.00
EP1-3241 [PS]	Thunder and Lightning	195?	3.00	6.00	12.00
EP1-3242	(contents unknown)	195?	3.00	6.00	12.00
EP1-3242 [PS]	Kiss of Fire	195?	3.00	6.00	12.00
EP1-3243	(contents unknown)	195?	3.00	6.00	12.00
EP1-3243 [PS]	So Madly in Love	195?	3.00	6.00	12.00
EP1-3266	(contents unknown)	195?	3.00	6.00	12.00
EP1-3266 [PS]	After You've Gone	195?	3.00	6.00	12.00
EP-1-4002	Tweedle Dee/You're Wrong, All Wrong//Melancholy Baby/Ballin' the Jack	195?	3.00	6.00	12.00
EP-1-4002 [PS]	Tops in Pops	195?	3.00	6.00	12.00
ROYALE					
EP 259	Ballin' the Jack/Old Man Mose//Wrap Your Troubles in Dreams/The One I Love	195?	5.00	10.00	20.00
—Red vinyl					
EP 259 [PS]	Georgia Gibbs Sings	195?	5.00	10.00	20.00

Albums

Number	Title (A Side/B Side)	Yr	VG	VG+	NM
BELL					
6000S [S]	Call Me Georgia Gibbs	1966	5.00	10.00	20.00
6000 [M]	Call Me Georgia Gibbs	1966	3.75	7.50	15.00
CORAL					
CRL 56037 [10]	Ballin' the Jack	1951	12.50	25.00	50.00
CRL 57183 [M]	Her Nibs	1957	10.00	20.00	40.00
EMARCY					
MG-36103 [M]	Swingin' with Gibbs	1957	7.50	15.00	30.00
EPIC					
LN 24059 [M]	Georgia Gibbs' Greatest Hits	1963	3.75	7.50	15.00
BN 26059 [S]	Georgia Gibbs' Greatest Hits	1963	5.00	10.00	20.00
IMPERIAL					
LP-9107 [M]	Something's Gotta Give	1960	5.00	10.00	20.00
LP-12064 [S]	Something's Gotta Give	1960	6.25	12.50	25.00
MERCURY					
MG-20071 [M]	Music and Memories	1955	10.00	20.00	40.00
MG-20114 [M]	Song Favorites	1956	10.00	20.00	40.00
MG-20170 [M]	Swingin' with Her Nibs	1956	10.00	20.00	40.00
MG-25175 [10]	Georgia Gibbs Sings Oldies	1953	12.50	25.00	50.00
MG-25199 [10]	The Man That Got Away	1954	12.50	25.00	50.00
ROYALE					
18126 [10]	Georgia Gibbs and Orchestra	195?	10.00	20.00	40.00

Number	Title (A Side/B Side)	Yr	VG	VG+	NM
SUNSET					
SUM-1113 [M]	Her Nibs, Miss Georgia Gibbs	196?	3.75	7.50	15.00
SUS-5113 [S]	Her Nibs, Miss Georgia Gibbs	196?	3.75	7.50	15.00

GIBSON, ALTHEA

Albums

Number	Title (A Side/B Side)	Yr	VG	VG+	NM
DOT					
DLP-3105 [M]	Althea Gibson Sings	1959	10.00	20.00	40.00
DLP-25105 [S]	Althea Gibson Sings	1959	12.50	25.00	50.00

GIBSON, BOBBY, AND THE VOYAGERS

45s

Number	Title (A Side/B Side)	Yr	VG	VG+	NM
GIBSON					
6003	B-52/Samoa	1959	12.50	25.00	50.00

GIBSON, DON

Also see DOTTIE WEST.

45s

Number	Title (A Side/B Side)	Yr	VG	VG+	NM
ABC HICKORY					
54001	I'm All Wrapped Up in You/We Live in Two Different Worlds	1976	—	2.50	5.00
54010	Fan the Flame, Feed the Fire/Bringin' In the Georgia Mail	1977	—	2.50	5.00
54014	If You Ever Get to Houston (Look Me Down)/It's All Over	1977	—	2.50	5.00
54019	When Do We Stop Starting Over/Love Is Not the Way (You Told Me)	1977	—	2.50	5.00
54024	Starting All Over Again/I'd Rather Die Young (Than Grow Old Without You)	1978	—	2.50	5.00
54029	The Fool/Every Song I Sang Would Be Blue	1978	—	2.50	5.00
54036	Oh, Such a Stranger/I Love You Because	1978	—	2.50	5.00
54039	Any Day Now/Baby's Not Home	1978	—	2.50	5.00
COLUMBIA					
20999	No Shoulder to Cry On/We're Stepping Out	1952	5.00	10.00	20.00
21060	Sample Kisses/Let Me Stay in Your Arms	1952	5.00	10.00	20.00
21109	Just Walkin' in the Moonlight/I Just Love the Way You Tell a Lie	1953	5.00	10.00	20.00
21156	You Cast Me Out/Waitin' Down the Road	1953	5.00	10.00	20.00
21231	Symptoms of Love/Many Times I've Waited	1954	5.00	10.00	20.00
21281	Selfish with Your Kisses/Ice Cold Heart	1954	5.00	10.00	20.00
HICKORY					
1559	Don't Take All Your Loving/Pretending Every Day	1970	—	2.50	5.00
1571	A Perfect Mountain/Would You Believe	1970	—	2.50	5.00
1579	Someway/Comfort for Your Mind	1970	—	2.50	5.00
1588	Guess Away the Blues/I Wanna Live	1970	—	2.50	5.00
1598	(I Heard That) Lonesome Whistle/Window Shopping	1971	2.00	4.00	8.00
1614	Country Green/Move It On Over	1971	2.00	4.00	8.00
1623	Far, Far Away/What's Happened to Me	1972	2.00	4.00	8.00
1638	Woman (Sensuous Woman)/If You Want Me To I'll Go	1972	2.00	4.00	8.00
1651	Is This the Best I'm Gonna Feel/Watching It Go	1972	2.00	4.00	8.00
1661	If You're Goin' Girl/Lonesome Number One	1973	2.00	4.00	8.00
1671	Touch the Morning/Too Much to Know	1973	2.00	4.00	8.00
HICKORY/MGM					
301	Touch the Morning/Too Much to Know	1973	—	3.00	6.00
306	That's What I'll Do/Sweet Dreams	1973	—	3.00	6.00
312	Snap Your Fingers/Love Is a Lonesome Thing	1973	—	3.00	6.00
318	One Day at a Time/Rainbow Love	1974	—	3.00	6.00
327	Bring Back Your Love to Me/Drinking Champagne	1974	—	3.00	6.00
338	I'll Sing for You/Pocatello	1974	—	3.00	6.00
345	(There She Goes) I Wish Her Well/Funny Familiar Forgotten Feelings	1975	—	3.00	6.00
353	Don't Stop Loving Me/Somebody's Words	1975	—	3.00	6.00
361	I Don't Think I'll Ever (Get Over You)/It Can't Last Always	1975	—	3.00	6.00
365	You've Got to Stop Hurting Me, Darling/Blues in My Mind	1976	—	3.00	6.00
372	Doing My Time/The World Is Waiting for the Sunrise	1976	—	3.00	6.00
MCA					
41031	Forever One Day at a Time/Look Who's Blue	1979	—	2.00	4.00
MGM					
12109	Run Boy/I Must Forget You	1955	7.50	15.00	30.00
12194	Sweet Dreams/The Road of Life Alone	1956	7.50	15.00	30.00
12290	I Ain't Gonna Waste My Time/Ah-Ha	1956	10.00	20.00	40.00
12331	I Believed in You/What a Fool I Was to Fall	1956	7.50	15.00	30.00
12494	I Ain't a-Studying You Baby/It's Hoppin'	1957	10.00	20.00	40.00
RCA VICTOR					
37-7841	What About Me/The World Is Waiting for the Sunrise	1961	5.00	10.00	20.00
—"Compact Single 33" (small hole, plays at LP speed)					
47-4364	Red Lips, White Lies and Blue Hours/Just Let Me Love You	1951	6.25	12.50	25.00
47-4473	Dark Future/Blue Million Tears	1952	6.25	12.50	25.00
47-6860	I Can't Leave/I Love You Still	1957	5.00	10.00	20.00
47-6942	Everything Turns Out for the Best/Sittin' Here Cryin'	1957	5.00	10.00	20.00
47-7010	Blue Blue Day/Too Soon to Know	1957	3.75	7.50	15.00
47-7133	Oh Lonesome Me/I Can't Stop Lovin' You	1958	3.75	7.50	15.00
47-7330	Give Myself a Party/Look Who's Blue	1958	3.75	7.50	15.00
47-7437	Who Cares/A Stranger to Me	1959	3.75	7.50	15.00
47-7505	Lonesome Old House/I Couldn't Care Less	1959	3.75	7.50	15.00
47-7566	Don't Tell Me Your Troubles/Heartbreak Avenue	1959	3.75	7.50	15.00
47-7629	I'm Movin' On/Big Hearted Man	1959	3.75	7.50	15.00
47-7690	Just One Time/I May Never Get to Heaven	1960	3.00	6.00	12.00
47-7762	Far, Far Away/A Legend in My Time	1960	3.00	6.00	12.00
47-7805	Sweet Dreams/The Same Street	1960	3.00	6.00	12.00
47-7841	What About Me/The World Is Waiting for the Sunrise	1961	3.00	6.00	12.00
47-7890	Sea of Heartbreak/I Think It's Best (To Forget Me)	1961	3.00	6.00	12.00
47-7959	Lonesome Number One/Same Old Trouble	1961	3.00	6.00	12.00
47-8017	I Can Mend Your Broken Heart/I Let Her Get Lonely	1962	2.50	5.00	10.00
47-8085	So How Come (No One Loves Me)/Baby We're Really in Love	1962	2.50	5.00	10.00
47-8085 [PS]	So How Come (No One Loves Me)/Baby We're Really in Love	1962	3.75	7.50	15.00
47-8144	Head Over Heels in Love with You/It Was Worth It All	1963	2.50	5.00	10.00
47-8144 [PS]	Head Over Heels in Love with You/It Was Worth It All	1963	3.75	7.50	15.00
47-8192	Anything New Gets Old (Except My Love for You)/After the Heartache	1963	2.50	5.00	10.00
47-8192 [PS]	Anything New Gets Old (Except My Love for You)/After the Heartache	1963	3.75	7.50	15.00
47-8367	Fireball Mail/Oh, Such a Stranger	1964	2.50	5.00	10.00
47-8456	Cause I Believe in You/A Love That Can't Be	1964	2.50	5.00	10.00
47-8589	Again/You're Going Away	1965	2.00	4.00	8.00
47-8678	Watch Where You're Going/There's a Big Wheel	1965	2.00	4.00	8.00
47-8732	A Born Loser/All the World Is Lonely Now	1965	2.00	4.00	8.00
47-8812	(Yes) I'm Hurting/My Whole World Is Hurt	1966	2.00	4.00	8.00
47-8975	Funny, Familiar, Forgotten, Feelings/Forget Me	1966	2.00	4.00	8.00
47-9177	Lost Highway/Around the Town	1967	2.00	4.00	8.00
47-9266	All My Love/No Doubt About It	1967	2.00	4.00	8.00
47-9395	Satisfied/Where No Man Stands Alone	1967	2.00	4.00	8.00
47-9460	Ashes of Love/Good Morning, Dear	1968	—	3.00	6.00
47-9563	It's a Long, Long Way to Georgia/Low and Lonely	1968	—	3.00	6.00
47-9663	Ever Changing Mind/Thoughts	1968	—	3.00	6.00
47-9906	Montego Bay/If My Heart Had Windows	1970	—	3.00	6.00
48-0424	I Love No One But You/Carolina Breakdown	1951	6.25	12.50	25.00
48-0460	Roses Are Red/Wiggle Wag	1951	6.25	12.50	25.00
61-7762 [S]	Far, Far Away/A Legend in My Time	1960	6.25	12.50	25.00
—"Living Stereo" (large hole, plays at 45 rpm)					
74-0143	Solitary/I Just Said Goodbye to My Dreams	1969	—	3.00	6.00
74-0219	I Will Always/Half As Much	1969	—	3.00	6.00
WARNER BROS.					
49193	Sweet Sensuous Sensations/Stranger to Me	1980	—	2.00	4.00
49504	I'd Be Crazy Over You/Somewhere Between Yesterday	1980	—	2.00	4.00
49602	Love Fires/Come Back and Love Me	1980	—	2.00	4.00

7-Inch Extended Plays

Number	Title (A Side/B Side)	Yr	VG	VG+	NM
COLUMBIA					
B-2146	(contents unknown)	1957	5.00	10.00	20.00
B-2146 [PS]	Don Gibson	1957	5.00	10.00	20.00
RCA VICTOR					
EPA-4323	(contents unknown)	1958	3.75	7.50	15.00
EPA-4323 [PS]	Blue, Blue Day	1958	3.75	7.50	15.00
EPA-4335	(contents unknown)	1958	3.75	7.50	15.00
EPA-4335 [PS]	That Lonesome Valley	1958	3.75	7.50	15.00
EPA-5114	Oh Lonesome Me/Look Who's Blue//Who Cares/Blue, Blue Day	1959	3.75	7.50	15.00
EPA-5114 [PS]	Blue and Lonesome	1959	3.75	7.50	15.00

Albums

Number	Title (A Side/B Side)	Yr	VG	VG+	NM
ABC HICKORY					
44001	All Wrapped Up in You	1976	3.00	6.00	12.00
44007	If You Ever	1977	3.00	6.00	12.00
44010	Starting All Over	1978	3.00	6.00	12.00
44014	Look Who's Blue	1978	3.00	6.00	12.00
HARMONY					
HL 7358 [M]	Don Gibson Sings	196?	3.00	6.00	12.00
HS 11158 [S]	Don Gibson Sings	196?	3.75	7.50	15.00
KH 31765	Sample Kisses	1972	2.50	5.00	10.00
HICKORY					
LPS-153	Hits, The Don Gibson Way	1970	3.75	7.50	15.00
LPS-155	Perfect Mountain	1971	3.75	7.50	15.00
LPS-157	Don Gibson Sings Hank Williams	1971	3.75	7.50	15.00
LPS-160	Country Green	1971	3.75	7.50	15.00
LPS-166	Woman (Sensuous Woman)	1972	3.75	7.50	15.00
HICKORY/MGM					
H3F-4501	Touch the Morning/That's What I'll Do	1973	3.75	7.50	15.00
H3F-4502	The Very Best of Don Gibson	1974	3.75	7.50	15.00
H3G-4509	Snap Your Fingers	1974	3.75	7.50	15.00
H3G-4516	Bring Back Your Love to Me	1974	3.00	6.00	12.00
H3G-4519	I'm the Loneliest Man	1975	3.00	6.00	12.00
LION					
L-70069 [M]	Songs by Don Gibson	1958	20.00	40.00	80.00
MGM					
GAS-138	Don Gibson (Golden Archive Series)	1970	3.75	7.50	15.00
RCA CAMDEN					
ACL1-0328	Just Call Me Lonesome	1973	2.50	5.00	10.00
ACL1-0758	Just One Time	1974	2.50	5.00	10.00
CAL-852 [M]	Blue Million Tears	196?	3.00	6.00	12.00
CAS-852 [S]	Blue Million Tears	196?	3.75	7.50	15.00
CAL-2101 [M]	Hurtin' Inside	1966	3.00	6.00	12.00
CAS-2101 [S]	Hurtin' Inside	1966	3.75	7.50	15.00
CAS-2246	I Love You So Much	1968	3.00	6.00	12.00
CAS-2317	My God Is Real	1969	3.00	6.00	12.00
CAS-2392	Lovin' Lies	1970	3.00	6.00	12.00
CAS-2502	I Walk Alone	1971	3.00	6.00	12.00
CAS-2592	Am I That Easy to Forget	1972	3.00	6.00	12.00
RCA VICTOR					
LPM-1743 [M]	Oh Lonesome Me	1958	12.50	25.00	50.00
LPM-1918 [M]	No One Stands Alone	1959	7.50	15.00	30.00
LSP-1918 [S]	No One Stands Alone	1959	10.00	20.00	40.00
LPM-2038 [M]	That Gibson Boy	1959	7.50	15.00	30.00
LSP-2038 [S]	That Gibson Boy	1959	10.00	20.00	40.00
LPM-2184 [M]	Look Who's Blue	1960	7.50	15.00	30.00
LSP-2184 [S]	Look Who's Blue	1960	10.00	20.00	40.00
LPM-2269 [M]	Sweet Dreams	1960	7.50	15.00	30.00
LSP-2269 [S]	Sweet Dreams	1960	10.00	20.00	40.00
LPM-2361 [M]	Girls, Guitars and Gibson	1961	7.50	15.00	30.00
LSP-2361 [S]	Girls, Guitars and Gibson	1961	10.00	20.00	40.00
LPM-2448 [M]	Some Favorites of Mine	1962	7.50	15.00	30.00
LSP-2448 [S]	Some Favorites of Mine	1962	10.00	20.00	40.00
LPM-2702 [M]	I Wrote a Song	1963	7.50	15.00	30.00

Number	Title (A Side/B Side)	Yr	VG	VG+	NM
LSP-2702 [S]	I Wrote a Song	1963	10.00	20.00	40.00
LPM-2878 [M]	God Walks These Hills	1964	5.00	10.00	20.00
LSP-2878 [S]	God Walks These Hills	1964	6.25	12.50	25.00
LPM-3376 [M]	The Best of Don Gibson	1965	5.00	10.00	20.00
LSP-3376 [S]	The Best of Don Gibson	1965	6.25	12.50	25.00
LPM-3470 [M]	Too Much Hurt	1965	5.00	10.00	20.00
LSP-3470 [S]	Too Much Hurt	1965	6.25	12.50	25.00
LPM-3594 [M]	Don Gibson with Spanish Guitars	1966	5.00	10.00	20.00
LSP-3594 [S]	Don Gibson with Spanish Guitars	1966	6.25	12.50	25.00
LPM-3680 [M]	Great Country Songs	1966	5.00	10.00	20.00
LSP-3680 [S]	Great Country Songs	1966	6.25	12.50	25.00
LPM-3843 [M]	All My Love	1967	5.00	10.00	20.00
LSP-3843 [S]	All My Love	1967	6.25	12.50	25.00
LPM-3974 [M]	The King of Country Soul	1968	12.50	25.00	50.00
LSP-3974 [S]	The King of Country Soul	1968	5.00	10.00	20.00
LSP-4053	More Country Soul	1968	5.00	10.00	20.00
LSP-4169	All-Time Country Gold	1969	3.75	7.50	15.00
LSP-4281	The Best of Don Gibson, Vol. 2	1970	3.75	7.50	15.00
CPL1-7052	Collector's Series	1985	2.50	5.00	10.00

GIBSON, DON (2)

Pianist; not to be confused with the country singer.

Albums

Number	Title (A Side/B Side)	Yr	VG	VG+	NM
JAZZOLOGY					
J-40	The Al Capone Memorial Jazz Band	197?	3.00	6.00	12.00

GIBSON, DON, AND SUE THOMPSON

Also see each artist's individual listings.

45s

Number	Title (A Side/B Side)	Yr	VG	VG+	NM
HICKORY					
1607	The Two of Us Together/Oh Yes, I Love You	1971	2.00	4.00	8.00
1629	Did You Ever Think/Love Garden	1972	2.00	4.00	8.00
1646	I Think They Call It Love/Over There's the Door	1972	2.00	4.00	8.00
1654	Cause I Love You/My Tears Don't Show	1972	2.00	4.00	0.00
1665	Go with Me/Two of Us Together	1973	2.00	4.00	8.00
HICKORY/MGM					
303	Warm Love/Fly the Friendly Skies with Jesus	1973	—	3.00	6.00
324	Good Old Fashioned Country Love/Ages and Ages Ago	1974	—	3.00	6.00
342	No One Will Ever Know/Put It Off Till Tomorrow	1975	—	3.00	6.00
350	Oh, How Love Changes/Sweet and Tender Times	1975	—	3.00	6.00
360	Maybe Tomorrow/I Can't Tell My Heart That	1975	—	3.00	6.00
367	Get Ready, Here I Come/Once More	1976	—	3.00	6.00
373	You've Still Got a Place in My Heart/Let's Get Together	1976	—	3.00	6.00

Albums

Number	Title (A Side/B Side)	Yr	VG	VG+	NM
HICKORY/MGM					
H3G-4520	Oh How Love Changes	1975	3.00	6.00	12.00

GIBSON, JILL

For a very brief time in late 1966, she was a member of THE MAMAS AND THE PAPAS.

45s

Number	Title (A Side/B Side)	Yr	VG	VG+	NM
IMPERIAL					
66068	It's as Easy as 1,2,3/Jilly's Flip Side	1964	15.00	30.00	60.00
—Produced by Jan Berry					

GIBSON, STEVE, AND THE RED CAPS

45s

Number	Title (A Side/B Side)	Yr	VG	VG+	NM
ABC-PARAMOUNT					
9702	Love Me Tenderly/Rock and Roll Stomp	1956	5.00	10.00	20.00
9750	Write to Me/Cuacho Serenade	1956	5.00	10.00	20.00
9796	You've Got Me Dizzy/You May Not Love Me	1957	5.00	10.00	20.00
9856	Silhouettes/Flamingo	1957	5.00	10.00	20.00
10105	I Went to Your Wedding/Together	1960	3.75	7.50	15.00
BAND BOX					
325	No More/Peppermint Baby	1962	3.00	6.00	12.00
HUNT					
326	Bless You/Cheryl Lee	1959	3.75	7.50	15.00
330	Where Are You/San Antonio Rose	1959	3.75	7.50	15.00
JAY DEE					
796	It Hurts Me But I Like It/Ouch!	1954	10.00	20.00	40.00
MERCURY					
5380	I'll Never Love Anyone Else/(B-side unknown)	1950	37.50	75.00	150.00
8146	Blueberry Hill/I Love You	1951	20.00	40.00	80.00
—78 released in 1949					
70389	Wedding Bells (Are Breaking Up That Old Gang of Mine)/Second Hand Romance	1954	12.50	25.00	50.00
RCA VICTOR					
47-3986	The Thing/Am I To Blame?	1950	15.00	30.00	60.00
47-4076	Did Ya Eat Yet, Joe/$3.98	1951	12.50	25.00	50.00
47-4294	Shame/Boogie Woogie on Saturday Night	1951	12.50	25.00	50.00
47-4670	Two Little Kisses/I May Hate Myself in the Morning	1952	10.00	20.00	40.00
47-4835	I Went to Your Wedding/Wait	1952	10.00	20.00	40.00
47-5013	Why Don't You Love Me/Truthfully	1952	10.00	20.00	40.00
47-5130	Big Game Hunter/Do I, Do I, Do I	1953	10.00	20.00	40.00
47-6096	Nuff of That Stuff/Feelin' Kinda Happy	1955	5.00	10.00	20.00
—B-side by Damita Jo					
47-6345	How I Cry/Bobbin'	1955	5.00	10.00	20.00
50-0127	I'm to Blame/Sidewalk Shuffle	1951	15.00	30.00	60.00
50-0138	Would I Mind/When You Come Back to Me	1951	15.00	30.00	60.00

7-Inch Extended Plays

Number	Title (A Side/B Side)	Yr	VG	VG+	NM
MERCURY					
EP1-3215	(contents unknown)	1952	50.00	100.00	200.00
EP1-3215 [PS]	Blueberry Hill	1952	50.00	100.00	200.00

Albums

Number	Title (A Side/B Side)	Yr	VG	VG+	NM
MERCURY					
MG-25115 [10]	You're Driving Me Crazy (Harmony Time)	1952	100.00	200.00	400.00
MG-25116 [10]	Blueberry Hill (Singing & Swinging)	1952	100.00	200.00	400.00

GIGOLOS, THE

45s

Number	Title (A Side/B Side)	Yr	VG	VG+	NM
BROADWAY					
1000	Movin' Out/Black and Blue	1961	7.50	15.00	30.00
CHESS					
1715	Luna Rock/La Companola	1959	7.50	15.00	30.00
DAYNITE					
1	Sqingin' Saints/Night Crawlers	1960	12.50	25.00	50.00
ENTERPRISE					
5000	Don't You Just Know It/Movin' Out	1965	3.75	7.50	15.00

GILBERTO, ASTRUD

Also see STAN GETZ AND JOAO GILBERTO.

45s

Number	Title (A Side/B Side)	Yr	VG	VG+	NM
PERCEPTION					
524	Make Love to Me/General Da Banda	1973	—	2.50	5.00
VERVE					
CS?-5	Celebrity Scene: Astrud Gilberto	1967	12.50	25.00	50.00
—Box set of five singles (10531-10535). Price includes box, all 5 singles, jukebox title strips, bio. Records are sometimes found by themselves, so they are also listed separately.					
10339	Who Can I Turn To/Funny World	1965	2.00	4.00	8.00
10347	Day by Day/Ecco Homo	1965	2.00	4.00	8.00
10358	The Shadow of Your Smile/O Gauso	1965	2.00	4.00	8.00
10414	Don't Go Breaking My Heart/Wish Me a Rainbow	1966	—	3.00	6.00
10457	Who Needs Forever/Main Theme "The Deadly Affair"	1966	—	3.00	6.00
10480	A Certain Smile/A Certain Sadness	1967	—	3.00	6.00
—With Walter Wanderley					
10531 [DJ]	Once Upon a Summertime/Once I Loved	1967	2.00	4.00	8.00
10532 [DJ]	Aruanda/Dindi	1967	2.00	4.00	8.00
10533 [DJ]	Manha De Carnival/Berimbau	1967	2.00	4.00	8.00
10534 [DJ]	Look to the Rainbow/Lugar Bonita	1967	2.00	4.00	8.00
10535 [DJ]	So Nice/Wish Me a Rainbow	1967	2.00	4.00	8.00
10548	Stay/I Had the Craziest Dream	1967	—	3.00	6.00
10554	A Banda/You Didn't Have to Be So Nice	1967	—	3.00	6.00
10580	Come Softly to Me-Hushabye/Lilies by Monet	1968	—	3.00	6.00
10638	I Haven't Got Anything Better to Do/The Sea Is My Soul	1969	—	2.50	5.00
10643	Love Theme from "Romeo and Juliet"/The Thought of Loving You	1969	—	2.50	5.00
10651	Holiday/Let's Have the Morning After	1970	—	2.50	5.00

Albums

Number	Title (A Side/B Side)	Yr	VG	VG+	NM
CTI					
CTS-6008	Astrud Gilberto with Stanley Turrentine	1970	3.00	6.00	12.00
ELEKTRA/MUSICIAN					
60760	Live in Montreux	1988	2.50	5.00	10.00
PERCEPTION					
29	Now	1973	2.50	5.00	10.00
VERVE					
V-8608 [M]	The Astrud Gilberto Album	1965	3.00	6.00	12.00
V6-8608 [S]	The Astrud Gilberto Album	1965	3.75	7.50	15.00
V-8629 [M]	The Shadow of Your Smile	1965	3.00	6.00	12.00
V6-8629 [S]	The Shadow of Your Smile	1965	3.75	7.50	15.00
V-8643 [M]	Look to the Rainbow	1966	3.00	6.00	12.00
V6-8643 [S]	Look to the Rainbow	1966	3.75	7.50	15.00
V-8673 [M]	A Certain Smile, A Certain Sadness	1966	3.00	6.00	12.00
V6-8673 [S]	A Certain Smile, A Certain Sadness	1966	3.75	7.50	15.00
V-8708 [M]	Beach Samba	1967	3.00	6.00	12.00
V6-8708 [S]	Beach Samba	1967	3.75	7.50	15.00
V6-8754	Windy	1968	3.00	6.00	12.00
V6-8776	I Haven't Got Anything Better to Do	1969	3.00	6.00	12.00
V6-8793	September 17, 1969	1969	3.00	6.00	12.00
821566-1	Look to the Rainbow	1986	2.50	5.00	10.00
—Reissue of V6-8643					

GILES, GILES & FRIPP

Albums

Number	Title (A Side/B Side)	Yr	VG	VG+	NM
DERAM					
DES 18019	The Cheerful Insanity of Giles, Giles & Fripp	1968	15.00	30.00	60.00

GILKYSON, TERRY

Also includes records credited to "The Easy Riders." Also see THE WEAVERS.

45s

Number	Title (A Side/B Side)	Yr	VG	VG+	NM
COLUMBIA					
40189	Tall Timber/Come Home Zelda	1954	3.00	6.00	12.00
40742	The Sky Is High/Yearmo's Nightmare and Yearmo's Red	1956	3.00	6.00	12.00
40817	Marianne/Goodbye Chiquita	1957	3.00	6.00	12.00
40817 [PS]	Marianne/Goodbye Chiquita	1957	3.75	7.50	15.00
40860	True Love and Tender Care/Don't Hurry Worry Me	1957	2.50	5.00	10.00
40910	Tina/Strollin' Blues	1957	2.50	5.00	10.00
41016	The Times/South Coast	1957	2.50	5.00	10.00
41088	Blue Mountain/Shorty Joe	1958	2.50	5.00	10.00
41147	Windjammer/Kari Waits for Me	1958	2.50	5.00	10.00
41284	Wanderin' Blues/Sweet Sugar Cane	1958	2.50	5.00	10.00
41347	John Henry/East Virginia	1959	2.50	5.00	10.00
DECCA					
27068	I Know Where I'm Going/Black Is the Color (Of My True Love's Hair)	1950	3.75	7.50	15.00
27069	Jennie Jenkins/Rovin' Gambler	1950	3.75	7.50	15.00
27070	The Story of the Creation//Cotton Eyed Joe/Billy Boy	1950	3.75	7.50	15.00
27071	Black Eyed Susie/Boll Weevil	1950	3.75	7.50	15.00
—The above four comprise a box set					
27337	A Solitary Singer/Runnin' Away	1950	3.75	7.50	15.00
27338	Fast Freight/The Secret	1950	3.75	7.50	15.00
27339	Nellie Lou/The Tick Tock Song	1950	3.75	7.50	15.00
27340	Mr. Buzzard/Everyone's Crazy 'Ceptin' Me	1950	3.75	7.50	15.00
—The above four comprise a box set					
27586	Hoofbeat Serenade/Fast Freight	1951	3.75	7.50	15.00
27708	The Girl in the Wood/Mr. Buzzard	1951	3.75	7.50	15.00
27793	Stay Awhile/Rollin' Stone	1951	3.75	7.50	15.00

Number	Title (A Side/B Side)	Yr	VG	VG+	NM
28258	Fond Affection/The Man You Don't Meet Everyday	1952	3.75	7.50	15.00
KAPP					
350	Saturday's Child/Young In Love	1960	2.00	4.00	8.00
355	Ballad of the Alamo/The Green Leaves of Summer	1960	2.00	4.00	8.00
Albums					
COLUMBIA					
CL 990 [M]	Marianne and Other Songs	1957	12.50	25.00	50.00
CL 1302 [M]	Wanderin' Folk Songs	1959	7.50	15.00	30.00
DECCA					
DL 5263 [10]	Folk Songs	1950	12.50	25.00	50.00
DL 5457 [10]	Golden Minutes of Folk Music	1952	12.50	25.00	50.00
KAPP					
KL 1196 [M]	Rollin'	1960	3.75	7.50	15.00
KL 1327 [M]	The Cry of the Wild Goose	1963	3.75	7.50	15.00
KS 3196 [S]	Rollin'	1960	5.00	10.00	20.00
KS 3327 [S]	The Cry of the Wild Goose	1963	5.00	10.00	20.00

GILLESPIE, DANA

Number	Title (A Side/B Side)	Yr	VG	VG+	NM
45s					
JERDEN					
764	Donna Donna/It's No Use Saying If	1965	3.00	6.00	12.00
Albums					
LONDON					
PS 540	Foolish Seasons	1968	5.00	10.00	20.00

GILLESPIE, DARLENE

Number	Title (A Side/B Side)	Yr	VG	VG+	NM
45s					
CORAL					
62178	I Loved, I Laughed, I Cried/Ring the Bell, Beat the Drum	1960	3.75	7.50	15.00
DISNEYLAND					
F-050	Sittin' in the Balcony/Too Much	1957	7.50	15.00	30.00
F-051	Butterfly/Seven Days	1957	7.50	15.00	30.00
F-052	I've Never Been in Love/Rock-a-Billy	1957	7.50	15.00	30.00
F-060	Together Time/Now to Sleep	1957	6.25	12.50	25.00
—A-side with Jimmie Dodd					
F-061	Break of Day/Perri	1957	6.25	12.50	25.00
—With Jimmie Dodd					
Albums					
DISNEYLAND					
WDL-1010 [M]	Top Tunes of the '50's — Darlene Gillespie Sings TV Favorites	1959	10.00	20.00	40.00
—Reissue of 3010					
DQ-1228 [M]	Sleeping Beauty	1962	5.00	10.00	20.00
—Cover is black and white; later pressings, which go for less, are shaded blue on the back					
WDL-3010 [M]	Darlene of the Teens	1957	20.00	40.00	80.00
WDL-3010 [M]	Top Tunes of the '50's — Darlene Gillespie Sings TV Favorites	1958	12.50	25.00	50.00
—Reissue with new title and cover					
MICKEY MOUSE CLUB					
MM-32 [M]	Sleeping Beauty	1959	10.00	20.00	40.00

GILLEY, MICKEY

Also see RAY CHARLES.

Number	Title (A Side/B Side)	Yr	VG	VG+	NM
45s					
ACT 1					
101	Say No More/Make Me Believe	1966	2.50	5.00	10.00
AIRBORNE					
10002	I'm Your Puppet/(B-side unknown)	1988	—	2.00	4.00
10008	She Reminded Me of You/(B-side unknown)	1988	—	2.00	4.00
10016	You Still Got a Way with My Heart/(B-side unknown)	1989	—	2.00	4.00
75740	There I've Said It Again/(B-side unknown)	1989	—	2.00	4.00
ASTRO					
102	Down the Line/Lonely Wine	196?	25.00	50.00	100.00
103	Is It Wrong/Turn Around	196?	6.25	12.50	25.00
104	Night After Night/Susie Q	196?	6.25	12.50	25.00
106	Lotta Lovin'/I Miss You So	196?	6.25	12.50	25.00
110	A Certain Smile/If I Didn't Have a Dime	196?	6.25	12.50	25.00
112	Little Egypt/If I Didn't Have a Dime	196?	6.25	12.50	25.00
5002	Everything Is Yours That Once Was Mine/Don't Throw a Good Love Away	1971	2.00	4.00	8.00
5003	You Touch My Life/Toast to Mary Ann	1971	2.00	4.00	8.00
10003	Room Full of Roses/She Called Me Baby	1973	2.50	5.00	10.00
DARYL					
101	What Have I Done/Three's a Crowd	1963	2.50	5.00	10.00
DOT					
15706	Call Me Shorty/Come On Baby	1958	50.00	100.00	200.00
EPIC					
AE7 1356 [DJ]	Mickey Gilley's Christmas Medley (2:51)/Mickey Gilley's Christmas Medley (3:34)	1981	2.50	5.00	10.00
AE7 1774	Home to Texas for Christmas/I'm Spending Christmas with You	1982	—	2.50	5.00
02172	You Don't Know Me/Juke Box Argument	1981	—	—	3.00
02578	Lonely Nights/We've Watched Another Evening Waste Away	1981	—	—	3.00
02774	Tears of the Lonely/Ladies Night	1982	—	—	3.00
03055	Put Your Dreams Away/If I Can't Hold Her on the Outside	1982	—	—	3.00
03326	Talk to Me/Honky Tonkin' (I Guess I Done Some)	1982	—	—	3.00
03332	Blue Christmas/Jingle Bell Rock	1982	—	2.00	4.00
03783	Fool for Your Love/Shakin' a Heartache	1983	—	—	3.00
04007	Paradise Tonight/Four Seasons of Love	1983	—	—	3.00
—With Charly McClain					
04018	Your Love Shines Through/Wish You Were Mine Again	1983	—	—	3.00
04269	You've Really Got a Hold on Me/Giving Up Getting Over You	1983	—	—	3.00
04368	Candy Man/The Phone Call	1984	—	—	3.00
—With Charly McClain					
04489	The Right Stuff/We Got a Love Thing	1984	—	—	3.00
—With Charly McClain					
04563	Too Good to Stop Now/A Shoulder to Cry On	1984	—	—	3.00
04746	I'm the One Mama Warned You About/You Can Lie to Me Tonight	1985	—	—	3.00
05460	You've Got Something on Your Mind/I Feel Good About Lovin' You	1985	—	—	3.00
05744	Your Memory Ain't What It Used to Be/Lonely Nights, Lonely Heartaches	1985	—	—	3.00
06184	Doo-Wah Days/After She's Gone	1986	—	—	3.00
07009	Full Grown Fool/To My One and Only	1987	—	—	3.00
50580	Here Comes the Hurt Again/I Hate It, But I Drink It Anyway	1978	—	2.00	4.00
50631	The Song We Made Love To/Memphis Memories	1978	—	2.00	4.00
50672	Just Long Enough to Say Goodbye/Tying One On	1979	—	2.00	4.00
50740	My Silver Lining/Picture of Our Love	1979	—	2.00	4.00
50801	A Little Getting Used To/Can't Nobody Love You	1979	—	2.00	4.00
50876	True Love Ways/The More I Turn the Bottle	1980	—	2.00	4.00
50940	That's All That Matters/The Blues Don't Care Who's Got 'Em	1980	—	2.00	4.00
50973	A Headache Tomorrow (Or a Heartache Tonight)/ Million Dollar Memories	1981	—	2.00	4.00
51003	Mamas Don't Let Your Babies Grow Up to Be Cowboys/Cotton-Eyed Joe	1981	—	2.00	4.00
—A-side with Johnny Lee; B-side by Bayou City Beats					
FULL MOON/ASYLUM					
46640	Stand By Me/Cotton Eyed Joe	1980	—	2.00	4.00
—B-side by the Unstrung Heroes					
46640 [PS]	Stand By Me/Cotton Eyed Joe	1980	—	2.50	5.00
—"Urban Cowboy" sleeve (John Travolta pictured)					
GOLDBAND					
1223	I Ain't Goin' Home/No Greater Love	1964	2.50	5.00	10.00
GRT					
27	I'm Nobody Today (But I Was Somebody Last Night)/She's Not Yours Anymore	1970	2.00	4.00	8.00
45	Time to Tell Another Lie/Because I Love You	1970	2.00	4.00	8.00
KHOURY'S					
712	Drive In Movie/Give Me a Chance	1959	75.00	150.00	300.00
LYNN					
503	Your Selfish Pride/Everything Turned to Love	1960	6.25	12.50	25.00
508	My Baby's Been Cheating Again/Turn Around	1960	6.25	12.50	25.00
512	Slippin' and Slidin'/End of the Line	1961	6.25	12.50	25.00
515	Long Lonely Nights/My Babe	1961	6.25	12.50	25.00
MINOR					
106	Oo-Ee Baby/Tell Me Why	1957	150.00	300.00	600.00
PAULA					
256	Make Me Believe/Say No to You	1966	2.50	5.00	10.00
269	A World of My Own/Love in the Want Ads	1967	2.00	4.00	8.00
280	Blame It on the Moon/Sounds Like Trouble	1967	2.00	4.00	8.00
281	One Way Street/Tears in My Eyes	1967	2.00	4.00	8.00
301	A New Way to Live/That Heart Belongs to Me	1968	2.00	4.00	8.00
402	Night After Night/I'm to Blame	1974	—	2.50	5.00
441	She Cheats on Me/You Can Count Me Missing	1983	—	2.00	4.00
1200	Now I Can Live Again/Without You	1968	2.00	4.00	8.00
1208	She's Still Got a Hold on You/There's No One Like You	1969	2.00	4.00	8.00
1215	Watching the Way/It's Just a Matter of Making Up My Mind	1969	2.00	4.00	8.00
PLAYBOY					
5807	Honky Tonk Memories/Five Foot Two, Eyes of Blue	1977	—	2.00	4.00
5818	Chains of Love/No. 1 Rock 'n Roll C & W Boogie Blues Man	1977	—	2.00	4.00
5826	The Power of Positive Drinkin'/Playing My Old Piano	1978	—	2.00	4.00
6004	I Overlooked an Orchid/Swinging Doors	1974	—	2.50	5.00
6015	City Lights/Fraulein	1974	—	2.50	5.00
6031	Window Up Above/I'm Movin' On	1975	—	2.50	5.00
6041	Bouquet of Roses/If You Were Mine to Lose	1975	—	2.50	5.00
6045	Roll You Like a Wheel/Let's Sing a Song Together	1975	—	2.50	5.00
—With Barbi Benton					
6045 [PS]	Roll You Like a Wheel/Let's Sing a Song Together	1975	—	3.00	6.00
—With Barbi Benton					
6055	Overnight Sensation/I'll Sail My Ship Alone	1975	—	2.50	5.00
6063	Don't All the Girls Get Prettier at Closing Time/ Where Do You Go to Lose a Heartache	1976	—	2.50	5.00
6075	Bring It On Home to Me/How's My Ex Treating You	1976	—	2.50	5.00
6089	Lawdy Miss Clawdy/What Is It	1976	—	2.50	5.00
6095	Pretty Paper/Lonely Christmas Call	1976	—	2.50	5.00
6100	She's Pulling Me Back Again/Sweet Mama Goodtime	1977	—	2.50	5.00
50056	Room Full of Roses/She Called Me Baby	1974	—	2.50	5.00
POTOMAC					
901	Is It Wrong/No Greater Love	1960	3.75	7.50	15.00
PRINCESS					
4004	Drive-In Movie/Your First Time	1962	10.00	20.00	40.00
4006	Wild Side of Life/Caught in the Middle	1962	10.00	20.00	40.00
4011	I'll Keep On Dancing/I'll Keep On Searching	196?	3.75	7.50	15.00
4015	A World of My Own/I Still Care	196?	3.75	7.50	15.00
RESCO					
617	You Touch My Life/Toast to Mary Ann	1974	—	3.00	6.00
622	She Gives Me Love/Quittin' Time	1974	—	3.00	6.00
REX					
1007	Grapevine/That's How It's Got to Be	1959	7.50	15.00	30.00
SABRA					
518	Valley of Tears/I Need Your Love	1961	5.00	10.00	20.00
SAN					
1513	I Ain't No Bo Diddley/I'm to Blame	1966	2.50	5.00	10.00
SUPREME					
101	Now That I Have You/Happy Birthday	1962	3.75	7.50	15.00
102	Everything Turned to Love/No One Will Ever Know	1962	3.75	7.50	15.00

Number	Title (A Side/B Side)	Yr	VG	VG+	NM
TCF HALL					
126	When Two Worlds Collide/Let's Hurt Together	1965	2.00	4.00	8.00
Albums					
ACCORD					
SN-7151	Suburban Cowboy	1981	2.50	5.00	10.00
ASTRO					
101 [M]	Lonely Wine	1964	75.00	150.00	300.00
COLUMBIA SPECIAL PRODUCTS					
P 16198	All My Best	1982	2.50	5.00	10.00
EPIC					
PE 34736	Room Full of Roses	198?	2.00	4.00	8.00
—Budget-line reissue					
PE 34749	Smokin'	198?	2.00	4.00	8.00
—Budget-line reissue					
PE 34776	First Class	198?	2.00	4.00	8.00
—Budget-line reissue					
KE 35174	Songs We Made Love To	1979	2.50	5.00	10.00
JE 36201	Mickey Gilley	1980	2.50	5.00	10.00
JE 36492	That's All That Matters to Me	1980	2.50	5.00	10.00
PE 36492	That's All That Matters to Me	198?	2.00	4.00	8.00
—Budget-line reissue					
JE 36851	Encore	1981	2.50	5.00	10.00
FE 37416	You Don't Know Me	1981	2.50	5.00	10.00
PE 37416	You Don't Know Me	198?	2.00	4.00	8.00
—Budget-line reissue					
PE 37595	Christmas at Gilley's	1981	2.50	5.00	10.00
—Some labels have "FE" prefix					
FE 38082	Put Your Dreams Away	1982	2.50	5.00	10.00
PE 38082	Put Your Dreams Away	198?	2.00	4.00	8.00
—Budget-line reissue					
FE 38320	Mickey Gilley's Biggest Hits	1982	2.50	5.00	10.00
FE 38583	Fool for Your Love	1983	2.50	5.00	10.00
PE 38583	Fool for Your Love	1985	2.00	4.00	8.00
—Budget-line reissue					
FE 39000	You've Really Got a Hold on Me	1983	2.50	5.00	10.00
FE 39324	Too Good to Stop Now	1983	2.50	5.00	10.00
KE2 39867 [(2)]	Ten Years of Hits	1984	3.00	6.00	12.00
FE 39900	Live at Gilley's	1984	2.50	5.00	10.00
FE 40115	I Feel Good (About Lovin' You)	1985	2.50	5.00	10.00
FE 40353	The One and Only	1986	2.50	5.00	10.00
INTERMEDIA					
QS-5024	With Love from Pasadena, Texas	198?	2.50	5.00	10.00
J.M.					
8127	Norwegian Wood	1981	3.00	6.00	12.00
PAIR					
PDL2-1072 [(2)]	The Best of Mickey Gilley	1986	3.00	6.00	12.00
PAULA					
LP-2195 [M]	Down the Line	1967	10.00	20.00	40.00
LPS-2195 [S]	Down the Line	1967	10.00	20.00	40.00
LPS-2224	Mickey Gilley at His Best	1974	3.75	7.50	15.00
LPS-2234	Mickey Gilley	1978	3.00	6.00	12.00
PICKWICK					
SPC-6180	Wild Side of Life	197?	2.50	5.00	10.00
PLAYBOY					
PB-128	Room Full of Roses	1974	5.00	10.00	20.00
PB-403	City Lights	1974	5.00	10.00	20.00
PB-405	Mickey's Movin' On	1975	3.75	7.50	15.00
PB-408	Overnight Sensation	1976	3.75	7.50	15.00
PB-409	Gilley's Greatest Hits Vol. 1	1976	3.75	7.50	15.00
PZ 34736	Room Full of Roses	1977	2.50	5.00	10.00
—Reissue of 128					
PZ 34742	Overnight Sensation	1977	2.50	5.00	10.00
—Reissue of 408					
PZ 34743	Gilley's Greatest Hits Vol. 1	1977	2.50	5.00	10.00
—Reissue of 409					
PZ 34749	Smokin'	1977	3.00	6.00	12.00
PZ 34776	First Class	1977	3.00	6.00	12.00
KZ 34881	Gilley's Greatest Hits, Vol. 2	1977	3.00	6.00	12.00
KZ 35099	Flyin' High	1978	3.00	6.00	12.00

GILMER, JIMMY

Also see THE FIREBALLS.

Number	Title (A Side/B Side)	Yr	VG	VG+	NM
45s					
ATCO					
6583	Three Squares (And a Place to Lay Your Head)/Baby	1968	2.00	4.00	8.00
6716	Sugar in the Woods/Model Child	1969	2.00	4.00	8.00
DECCA					
30942	Look Alive/Because I Need You	1959	6.25	12.50	25.00
HAMILTON					
50037	Won't Be Long/I'm Gonna Go Walkin'	1960	3.75	7.50	15.00
WARWICK					
592	Good Good Lovin'/Do You Think	1960	5.00	10.00	20.00

GILMER, JIMMY, AND THE FIREBALLS

See THE FIREBALLS.

GILSTRAP, JIM

Number	Title (A Side/B Side)	Yr	VG	VG+	NM
45s					
BELL					
45435	Airport/(B-side unknown)	1974	—	2.50	5.00
45474	When You Come Back Down/(B-side unknown)	1974	—	2.50	5.00
ROXBURY					
2006	Swing Your Daddy/Swing Your Daddy (Part 2)	1975	—	2.00	4.00
2013	House of Strangers/Take Your Daddy for a Ride	1975	—	2.00	4.00
2016	I'm on Fire/I'm on Fire (Part 2)	1975	—	2.00	4.00
2026	Move Me/Move Me (Part 2)	1976	—	2.00	4.00
2029	Love Talk/Love Talk (Part 2)	1976	—	2.00	4.00
2032	Hello It's Me/Never Stop Your Loving Me	1976	—	2.00	4.00
Albums					
ROXBURY					
102	Swing Your Daddy	1975	2.50	5.00	10.00
105	Love Talk	1976	2.50	5.00	10.00

GINGER

Also see GINGER AND THE SNAPS; THE HONEYS.

Number	Title (A Side/B Side)	Yr	VG	VG+	NM
45s					
TITAN					
1717	Dry Tears/Spare Time	1961	25.00	50.00	100.00

GINGER AND THE CHIFFONS

Number	Title (A Side/B Side)	Yr	VG	VG+	NM
45s					
GROOVE					
58-0003	She/Where Were You Last Night	1963	7.50	15.00	30.00

GINGER AND THE SNAPS

Also see GINGER.

Number	Title (A Side/B Side)	Yr	VG	VG+	NM
45s					
MGM					
13413	Growing Up Is Hard to Do/Seven Days in September	1965	37.50	75.00	150.00
TORE					
1008	Love Me the Way That I Love You/Truly	1961	18.75	37.50	75.00

GINGER-SNAPS, THE

Number	Title (A Side/B Side)	Yr	VG	VG+	NM
45s					
DUNHILL					
4003	The Sh-Down-Down Song/I've Got Faith in Him	1965	5.00	10.00	20.00

GINGOLEERS, THE

Number	Title (A Side/B Side)	Yr	VG	VG+	NM
45s					
BRUNSWICK					
55108	Jingle Bell Rock/Christmas Morn	1958	3.75	7.50	15.00

GINNY AND THE GALLIONS

Number	Title (A Side/B Side)	Yr	VG	VG+	NM
45s					
DOWNEY					
110	Hava Nagila/Hava Nagila Part 2	1963	3.00	6.00	12.00
112	Wheel of Fortune/Hava Nagila	1963	3.00	6.00	12.00
Albums					
DOWNEY					
D-1003 [M]	Two Sides of Ginny and the Gallions	1964	7.50	15.00	30.00
DS-1003 [S]	Two Sides of Ginny and the Gallions	1964	10.00	20.00	40.00

GINO AND THE DELLS

Number	Title (A Side/B Side)	Yr	VG	VG+	NM
45s					
GOLDEN CREST					
567	Altar of Dreams/Baby Don't Go Now	1962	75.00	150.00	300.00
576	We'll Make It Someday/I'm a Boy in Love	1963	10.00	20.00	40.00
581	It's Only a Paper Moon/Home Sweet Home	1963	10.00	20.00	40.00

GINSBERG, ALLEN

Number	Title (A Side/B Side)	Yr	VG	VG+	NM
Albums					
ATLANTIC					
4001 [M]	Allen Ginsburg Reads Kaddish	1966	7.50	15.00	30.00
FANTASY					
F-7006 [M]	Howl and Other Poems	1959	100.00	200.00	400.00
—Red vinyl					
F-7006 [M]	Howl and Other Poems	1959	50.00	100.00	200.00
—Black non-flexible vinyl					

GIORDANO, LOU

Number	Title (A Side/B Side)	Yr	VG	VG+	NM
45s					
BRUNSWICK					
55115	Stay Close to Me/Don'Cha Know	1959	400.00	800.00	1200.
—With Buddy Holly on guitar					

GIOVANNI, NIKKI

Number	Title (A Side/B Side)	Yr	VG	VG+	NM
Albums					
NIKTOM					
NK 4200	Like a Ripple on a Pond	1973	2.50	5.00	10.00
NK 4201	The Way I Feel	1975	2.50	5.00	10.00
RIGHT-ON					
5001	Truth Is On Its Way	1971	2.50	5.00	10.00

GIRLFRIENDS, THE

Number	Title (A Side/B Side)	Yr	VG	VG+	NM
45s					
COLPIX					
712	My One and Only Jimmy Boy/For My Sake	1963	5.00	10.00	20.00
744	Baby Don't Cry/I Don't Believe in You	1964	5.00	10.00	20.00
MELIC					
4125	No More Tears/I Want to Be Happy	1963	3.75	7.50	15.00
PIONEER					
71833	Four Shy Girls (In Their Itsy Bitsy Teeny Weeny Yellow Polka Dot Bikinis)/Jackie	1961	5.00	10.00	20.00

GIRLS, THE

Number	Title (A Side/B Side)	Yr	VG	VG+	NM
45s					
20TH CENTURY FOX					
6651	Way, Way Out/Modesty Blaise	1966	5.00	10.00	20.00
CAPITOL					
5528	My Baby/My Love	1965	5.00	10.00	20.00
5675	Chico's Girl/The Dumb Song	1966	5.00	10.00	20.00
SCEPTER					
12242	Perfect Love/Mr. Poster	1969	2.00	4.00	8.00

GLACIERS, THE

Number	Title (A Side/B Side)	Yr	VG	VG+	NM
Albums					
MERCURY					
MG-20895 [M]	From Sea to Ski	1964	12.50	25.00	50.00
SR-60895 [S]	From Sea to Ski	1964	15.00	30.00	60.00

Number	Title (A Side/B Side)	Yr	VG	VG+	NM

GLAD, THE

45s

ABC

Number	Title (A Side/B Side)	Yr	VG	VG+	NM
11163	Johnny Silver's Ride/Love Needs the World	1969	3.00	6.00	12.00

EQUINOX

Number	Title (A Side/B Side)	Yr	VG	VG+	NM
70004	See What You Mean/(B-side unknown)	1968	5.00	10.00	20.00
70006	A New Tomorrow/Pickin' Up the Pieces	1968	5.00	10.00	20.00

Albums

ABC

Number	Title (A Side/B Side)	Yr	VG	VG+	NM
S-655	Feelin' Glad	1969	6.25	12.50	25.00

GLADIATORS, THE

45s

DIG

Number	Title (A Side/B Side)	Yr	VG	VG+	NM
135	Girl of My Heart/My Baby Doll	1957	75.00	150.00	300.00

GLADIOLAS, THE

Evolved into MAURICE WILLIAMS AND THE ZODIACS.

45s

EXCELLO

Number	Title (A Side/B Side)	Yr	VG	VG+	NM
2101	Little Darlin'/Sweetheart, Please Don't Go	1957	18.75	37.50	75.00
2110	Run, Run, Little Joe/Comin' Home to You	1957	12.50	25.00	50.00
2120	Hey Little Girl/I Wanta Know	1957	12.50	25.00	50.00
2136	Shoop Shoop/Say You'll Be Mine	1958	12.50	25.00	50.00

GLADSTONE

45s

ABC

Number	Title (A Side/B Side)	Yr	VG	VG+	NM
11327	Livin' in the Country/Piece of Paper	1972	—	2.50	5.00
11340	Marietta Station/Lady Eyes	1972	—	2.50	5.00
11361	Natural Inclination/Texas Sparrow	1973	—	2.50	5.00

GLASS BOTTLE, THE

45s

AVCO

Number	Title (A Side/B Side)	Yr	VG	VG+	NM
4584	The Girl Who Loved Me When/Because She's Mine Again	1971	—	3.00	6.00
4592	Don't It Make You Feel So Good/(B-side unknown)	1972	—	2.50	5.00
4597	Pretty Thing/(B-side unknown)	1972	—	2.50	5.00

—Both of the above credit lead singer Gary Criss

AVCO EMBASSY

Number	Title (A Side/B Side)	Yr	VG	VG+	NM
4575	I Ain't Got Time Anymore/The First Time	1971	—	3.00	6.00

Albums

AVCO

Number	Title (A Side/B Side)	Yr	VG	VG+	NM
33012	The Glass Bottle	1971	3.75	7.50	15.00

GLASS HARP

Christian rock pioneer Phil Keaggy was in this group.

45s

DECCA

Number	Title (A Side/B Side)	Yr	VG	VG+	NM
32830	Children's Fantasy/Village Queen	1971	2.50	5.00	10.00
32915	The Answer/Just Always	1972	2.50	5.00	10.00
32995	La De Da/(B-side unknown)	1972	2.50	5.00	10.00

Albums

DECCA

Number	Title (A Side/B Side)	Yr	VG	VG+	NM
DL 75261	Glass Harp	1971	6.25	12.50	25.00
DL 75306	Synergy	1971	6.25	12.50	25.00
DL 75358	It Makes Me Glad	1972	6.25	12.50	25.00

MCA

Number	Title (A Side/B Side)	Yr	VG	VG+	NM
293	Glass Harp	1977	2.50	5.00	10.00

—Reissue of Decca 75261

GLASS HOUSE, THE

45s

INVICTUS

Number	Title (A Side/B Side)	Yr	VG	VG+	NM
9071	Crumbs Off the Table/Bad Bill of Goods	1969	—	3.00	6.00
9076	I Can't Be You (You Can't Be Me)/He's In My Life	1970	—	3.00	6.00
9082	Stealing Moments From Another Woman's Life/If It Ain't Love, It Don't Matter	1970	—	3.00	6.00
9090	Touch Me Jesus/If It Ain't Love, It Don't Matter	1971	—	3.00	6.00
9097	Look What We've Done to Love/Heaven's There to Guide Us	1971	—	3.00	6.00
9111	Let It Flow/Playing Games	1972	—	3.00	6.00
9129	Thanks I Needed That/I Don't See Me in Your Eyes Anymore	1972	—	3.00	6.00

Albums

INVICTUS

Number	Title (A Side/B Side)	Yr	VG	VG+	NM
ST-7305	Inside the Glass House	1971	3.00	6.00	12.00
ST-9810	Thanks I Needed That	1972	3.00	6.00	12.00

GLASS PRISM, THE

45s

RCA VICTOR

Number	Title (A Side/B Side)	Yr	VG	VG+	NM
74-0205	The Raven/El Dorado	1969	—	3.00	6.00

Albums

RCA VICTOR

Number	Title (A Side/B Side)	Yr	VG	VG+	NM
LSP-4201	Poe Through the Glass Prism	1969	3.75	7.50	15.00
LSP-4270	On Joy and Sorrow	1970	3.75	7.50	15.00

GLEASON, JACKIE

45s

CAPITOL

Number	Title (A Side/B Side)	Yr	VG	VG+	NM
F2361	Melancholy Serenade/You're Getting to Be a Habit	1953	3.75	7.50	15.00
F2437	Alone Together/Body & Soul	1953	2.50	5.00	10.00
F2438	My Funny Valentine/Love Is Here to Stay	1953	2.50	5.00	10.00
F2439	But Not for Me/Love	1953	2.50	5.00	10.00
F2440	I'm in the Mood for Love/I Only Have Eyes for You	1953	2.50	5.00	10.00

—The above four comprise a box set

Number	Title (A Side/B Side)	Yr	VG	VG+	NM
F2507	Terry's Theme from "Limelight"/Peg o' My Heart	1953	3.75	7.50	15.00
F2515	White House Serenade/The President's Lady	1953	3.75	7.50	15.00
F2659	Mystery Street/Golden Violins	1954	3.75	7.50	15.00
F3144	The Band Played On/In the Good Old Summertime	1955	3.00	6.00	12.00
F3223	Autumn Leaves/Oo! What You Do to Me	1955	3.00	6.00	12.00
F4062	Where Is She Now/Just One Yesterday	1958	2.50	5.00	10.00
4800	'Allo 'Allo 'Allo/Joi De Vivre	1962	2.00	4.00	8.00

DECCA

Number	Title (A Side/B Side)	Yr	VG	VG+	NM
27684	What Is a Girl?/What Is a Boy?	1951	3.75	7.50	15.00

7-Inch Extended Plays

CAPITOL

Number	Title (A Side/B Side)	Yr	VG	VG+	NM
EAP 1-352	Alone Together/My Funny Valentine//I Only Have Eyes for You/Body and Soul	195?	2.50	5.00	10.00
EAP 1-352 [PS]	Music for Lovers Only, Part 1	195?	2.50	5.00	10.00
EAP 2-352	But Not for Me/Love (Your Spell Is Everywhere)//I'm in the Mood for Love/Love Is Here to Stay	195?	2.50	5.00	10.00
EAP 2-352 [PS]	Music for Lovers Only, Part 2	195?	2.50	5.00	10.00
EBF-352 [PS]	Music for Lovers Only	195?	6.25	12.50	25.00

—Gatefold sleeve for some editions of EAP 1-352 and 2-352

Number	Title (A Side/B Side)	Yr	VG	VG+	NM
EAP 1-627	(contents unknown)	1955	2.50	5.00	10.00
EAP 1-627 [PS]	Lonesome Echo, Part 1	1955	3.00	6.00	12.00
EAP 2-627	(contents unknown)	1955	2.50	5.00	10.00
EAP 2-627 [PS]	Lonesome Echo, Part 2	1955	3.00	6.00	12.00
EAP 3-627	Deep Purple/I Still Get a Thrill//I Don't Know Why/A Garden in the Rain	1955	2.50	5.00	10.00
EAP 3-627 [PS]	Lonesome Echo, Part 3	1955	3.00	6.00	12.00
EAP 4-627	(contents unknown)	1955	2.50	5.00	10.00
EAP 4-627 [PS]	Lonesome Echo, Part 4	1955	3.00	6.00	12.00
EAP 1-674	Autumn Leaves/Can This Be Love//Oo! What You Do to Me/After My Laughter Came Tears	195?	2.50	5.00	10.00
EAP 1-674 [PS]	Autumn Leaves	195?	2.50	5.00	10.00
EAP 1-758	(contents unknown)	1956	2.50	5.00	10.00
EAP 1-758 [PS]	Merry Christmas	1956	3.00	6.00	12.00
EAP 1-859	You're Driving Me Crazy/Skyliner//Out of Nowhere/Chinatown, My Chinatown	195?	2.50	5.00	10.00
EAP 1-859 [PS]	Velvet Brass, Part 1	195?	2.50	5.00	10.00
EAP 1-871	To a Sleeping Beauty//Apology at Bedtime	1957	3.75	7.50	15.00
EAP 1-871 [PS]	To a Sleeping Beauty	1957	3.75	7.50	15.00

Albums

CAPITOL

Number	Title (A Side/B Side)	Yr	VG	VG+	NM
SW-106	Irving Berlin's Music	1968	3.00	6.00	12.00
SKAO-146	The Best of Jackie Gleason (Vol. 2)	1968	3.00	6.00	12.00
SWBB-256 [(2)]	Close-Up	1969	3.75	7.50	15.00

—Reissue of Capitol DW 352 and DW 509 in one package

Number	Title (A Side/B Side)	Yr	VG	VG+	NM
STBB-346 [(2)]	All I Want for Christmas	1969	3.75	7.50	15.00
DW 352 [R]	Music for Lovers Only	196?	2.50	5.00	10.00
H 352 [10]	Music for Lovers Only	1952	7.50	15.00	30.00
SM-352	Music for Lovers Only	197?	2.50	5.00	10.00

—Reissue

Number	Title (A Side/B Side)	Yr	VG	VG+	NM
W 352 [M]	Music for Lovers Only	1953	6.25	12.50	25.00
H 366 [10]	Lover's Rhapsody	1953	7.50	15.00	30.00
ST-398	Romeo and Juliet	1970	3.00	6.00	12.00
DW 455 [R]	Music to Make You Misty	196?	2.50	5.00	10.00
H 455 [10]	Music to Make You Misty	1954	7.50	15.00	30.00
SM-455	Music to Make You Misty	197?	2.50	5.00	10.00

—Reissue

Number	Title (A Side/B Side)	Yr	VG	VG+	NM
W 455 [M]	Music to Make You Misty	1954	6.25	12.50	25.00
L 471 [10]	Tawny	1954	7.50	15.00	30.00
W 471 [M]	Tawny	1954	6.25	12.50	25.00
WAO 475 [(2) M]	Music for Lovers Only/Music to Make You Misty	1954	10.00	20.00	40.00
ST-480	Come Saturday Morning	1970	3.00	6.00	12.00
DW 509 [R]	Music, Martini and Memories	196?	2.50	5.00	10.00
SM-509	Music, Martini and Memories	197?	2.50	5.00	10.00

—Reissue

Number	Title (A Side/B Side)	Yr	VG	VG+	NM
W 509 [M]	Music, Martini and Memories	1954	6.25	12.50	25.00
STBB-510 [(2)]	Tenderly/Laura	1971	3.75	7.50	15.00
H 511 [10]	And Awaaay We Go!	1954	20.00	40.00	80.00
W 511 [M]	And Awaaay We Go!	1955	10.00	20.00	40.00
W 568 [M]	Romantic Jazz	1955	6.25	12.50	25.00
DW 570 [R]	Music to Remember Her	196?	2.50	5.00	10.00
W 570 [M]	Music to Remember Her	1955	6.25	12.50	25.00
DW 627 [R]	Lonesome Echo	196?	2.50	5.00	10.00
H 627 [10]	Lonesome Echo	1955	7.50	15.00	30.00
W 627 [M]	Lonesome Echo	1955	6.25	12.50	25.00
DW 632 [R]	Music to Change Her Mind	196?	2.50	5.00	10.00
W 632 [M]	Music to Change Her Mind	1956	6.25	12.50	25.00
ST-693	Words of Love	1971	3.00	6.00	12.00
DW 717 [R]	Night Winds	196?	2.50	5.00	10.00
W 717 [M]	Night Winds	1956	6.25	12.50	25.00
DW 758 [R]	Merry Christmas	196?	2.50	5.00	10.00
W 758 [M]	Merry Christmas	1956	6.25	12.50	25.00
DW 816 [R]	Music for the Love Hours	196?	2.50	5.00	10.00
W 816 [M]	Music for the Love Hours	1957	6.25	12.50	25.00
SM-859	Velvet Brass	197?	2.50	5.00	10.00

—Reissue

Number	Title (A Side/B Side)	Yr	VG	VG+	NM
SW 859 [S]	Velvet Brass	1959	6.25	12.50	25.00

—We haven't confirmed if this is in true stereo or not.

Number	Title (A Side/B Side)	Yr	VG	VG+	NM
W 859 [M]	Velvet Brass	1957	6.25	12.50	25.00
SW 905 [S]	Jackie Gleason Presents "Oooo!"	1959	6.25	12.50	25.00

—We haven't confirmed if this is in true stereo or not.

Number	Title (A Side/B Side)	Yr	VG	VG+	NM
W 905 [M]	Jackie Gleason Presents "Oooo!"	1957	6.25	12.50	25.00
SW 961 [S]	The Torch with Blue Flame	1959	6.25	12.50	25.00
W 961 [M]	The Torch with Blue Flame	1958	5.00	10.00	20.00
SW 1020 [S]	Riff Jazz	1959	6.25	12.50	25.00
W 1020 [M]	Riff Jazz	1958	5.00	10.00	20.00
SW 1075 [S]	Rebound	1959	6.25	12.50	25.00
W 1075 [M]	Rebound	1959	5.00	10.00	20.00
SW 1147 [S]	That Moment	1959	6.25	12.50	25.00
W 1147 [M]	That Moment	1959	5.00	10.00	20.00
SW 1250 [S]	Aphrodisia	1960	6.25	12.50	25.00
W 1250 [M]	Aphrodisia	1960	5.00	10.00	20.00
SW 1315 [S]	Opiate D'Amour	1960	5.00	10.00	20.00
W 1315 [M]	Opiate D'Amour	1960	3.75	7.50	15.00
SW 1439 [S]	Lazy Lively Love	1961	6.25	12.50	25.00

Number	Title (A Side/B Side)	Yr	VG	VG+	NM
W 1439 [M]	Lazy Lively Love	1961	5.00	10.00	20.00
SW 1519 [S]	The Gentle Touch	1961	6.25	12.50	25.00
W 1519 [M]	The Gentle Touch	1961	5.00	10.00	20.00
SWBO 1619 [(2) S]	A Lover's Portfolio	1962	6.25	12.50	25.00
WBO 1619 [(2) M]	A Lover's Portfolio	1962	5.00	10.00	20.00
SW 1689 [S]	Love, Embers and Flame	1962	5.00	10.00	20.00
W 1689 [M]	Love, Embers and Flame	1962	3.75	7.50	15.00
SW 1830 [S]	Champagne, Candlelight & Kisses	1963	3.75	7.50	15.00
W 1830 [M]	Champagne, Candlelight & Kisses	1963	3.00	6.00	12.00
SW 1877 [S]	Movie Themes — For Lovers Only	1963	3.75	7.50	15.00
W 1877 [M]	Movie Themes — For Lovers Only	1963	3.00	6.00	12.00
SW 1978 [S]	Today's Romantic Hits/For Lovers Only	1963	3.75	7.50	15.00
W 1978 [M]	Today's Romantic Hits/For Lovers Only	1963	3.00	6.00	12.00
SW 1979 [S]	A Lover's Portfolio, Vol. 1 (Music for Sippin' and Dancin')	1963	3.75	7.50	15.00
W 1979 [M]	A Lover's Portfolio, Vol. 1 (Music for Sippin' and Dancin')	1963	3.00	6.00	12.00
SW 1980 [S]	A Lover's Portfolio, Vol. 2 (Music for Listenin' and Lovin')	1963	3.75	7.50	15.00
W 1980 [M]	A Lover's Portfolio, Vol. 2 (Music for Listenin' and Lovin')	1963	3.00	6.00	12.00
SW 2056 [S]	Today's Romantic Hits/For Lovers Only, Vol. 2	1964	3.75	7.50	15.00
W 2056 [M]	Today's Romantic Hits/For Lovers Only, Vol. 2	1964	3.00	6.00	12.00
SW 2144 [S]	Last Dance For Lovers Only	1964	3.75	7.50	15.00
W 2144 [M]	Last Dance For Lovers Only	1964	3.00	6.00	12.00
SW 2409 [S]	Silk 'N' Brass	1966	3.75	7.50	15.00
W 2409 [M]	Silk 'N' Brass	1966	3.00	6.00	12.00
SW 2471 [S]	Music Around the World — For Lovers Only	1966	3.75	7.50	15.00
W 2471 [M]	Music Around the World — For Lovers Only	1966	3.00	6.00	12.00
SW 2582 [S]	How Sweet It Is For Lovers	1966	3.75	7.50	15.00
W 2582 [M]	How Sweet It Is For Lovers	1966	3.00	6.00	12.00
SW 2684 [S]	A Taste of Brass For Lovers Only	1967	3.75	7.50	15.00
W 2684 [M]	A Taste of Brass For Lovers Only	1967	3.00	6.00	12.00
ST 2791 [S]	'Tis the Season	1967	3.75	7.50	15.00
T 2791 [M]	'Tis the Season	1967	5.00	10.00	20.00
SM-2796	The Best of Jackie Gleason	197?	2.50	5.00	10.00
—Reissue					
SW 2796 [S]	The Best of Jackie Gleason	1967	3.75	7.50	15.00
W 2796 [M]	The Best of Jackie Gleason	1967	3.75	7.50	15.00
STCL 2816 [(3) S]	The Jackie Gleason Deluxe Set	1968	6.25	12.50	25.00
—Reissue of three complete LPs (titles unknown)					
TCL 2816 [(3) M]	The Jackie Gleason Deluxe Set	1968	6.25	12.50	25.00

PAIR

Number	Title (A Side/B Side)	Yr	VG	VG+	NM
PDL2-1069 [(2)]	Lush Moods	1986	3.00	6.00	12.00

PICKWICK

Number	Title (A Side/B Side)	Yr	VG	VG+	NM
SPC-1008	White Christmas	197?	2.50	5.00	10.00
—Abridged version of Capitol ST 2791					
SPC-2004	Romantic Moods	197?	2.50	5.00	10.00
SPC-2029	The More I See You	197?	2.50	5.00	10.00
SPC-3064	Plays Pretty for the People	196?	2.50	5.00	10.00
SPC-3218	Shangri-La	197?	2.50	5.00	10.00

GLEEMS, THE

45s

PARKWAY

Number	Title (A Side/B Side)	Yr	VG	VG+	NM
893	Sandra Baby/You Are the One	1964	5.00	10.00	20.00

GLENN, GLEN

45s

DORE

Number	Title (A Side/B Side)	Yr	VG	VG+	NM
523	Goofin' Around/Susie Green from Abilene	1959	3.75	7.50	15.00

ERA

Number	Title (A Side/B Side)	Yr	VG	VG+	NM
1061	Everybody's Movin'/I'm Glad My Baby's Gone	1957	15.00	30.00	60.00
1074	One Cup of Coffee/Laurie Ann	1958	12.50	25.00	50.00

GLENN, LLOYD

45s

ALADDIN

Number	Title (A Side/B Side)	Yr	VG	VG+	NM
3268	Nite Flite/Still Waters	1954	6.25	12.50	25.00
3288	Footloose/Glen's Glide	1955	6.25	12.50	25.00
3307	Sunrise/Tiddly Winks	1955	6.25	12.50	25.00
3327	Southbound Special/Blue Ivories	1956	5.00	10.00	20.00
3346	After Hours (Part 1)/After Hours (Part 2)	1956	5.00	10.00	20.00
3353	Chica-Boo/Old Time Shuffle	1957	5.00	10.00	20.00
3378	The Vamp/Ballroom Shuffle	1957	5.00	10.00	20.00
3400	Hyde Park/Love for Sale	1957	5.00	10.00	20.00
3407	Cute-Tee/Black Fantasy	1958	5.00	10.00	20.00
3446	Petite Fleur/Honky Tonk Train	1959	3.75	7.50	15.00
3459	Long Gone (Part 1)/Long Gone (Part 2)	1959	3.75	7.50	15.00

HOLLYWOOD

Number	Title (A Side/B Side)	Yr	VG	VG+	NM
1021	Merry Christmas Baby/Sleigh Ride	1954	5.00	10.00	20.00
—B-side by Charles Brown; red label					
1021	Merry Christmas Baby/Sleigh Ride	196?	2.00	4.00	8.00
—B-side by Charles Brown; color label					
1021	Merry Christmas Baby/Sleigh Ride	197?	—	2.50	5.00
—B-side by Charles Brown; black label					
1028	Chica-Boo/Old Time Shuffle	1954	6.25	12.50	25.00
1033	Sleigh Ride/China Doll	1954	6.25	12.50	25.00

IMPERIAL

Number	Title (A Side/B Side)	Yr	VG	VG+	NM
5839	Twistville/Young Date	1962	3.00	6.00	12.00

SWING TIME

Number	Title (A Side/B Side)	Yr	VG	VG+	NM
254	Chica-Boo/Jungle Town Jubilee	1951	7.50	15.00	30.00
271	Sleigh Ride/Savage Boy	1951	7.50	15.00	30.00
277	Day Break Stomp/Jungle Twilight	1952	7.50	15.00	30.00
278	Cute-Tee/Rhumba	1952	7.50	15.00	30.00
292	After Hours/Yancey Special	1952	7.50	15.00	30.00
293	Honky Tonk Train/Pine Top Boogie Woogie	1952	7.50	15.00	30.00
296	Angora/Cuba Doll	1952	7.50	15.00	30.00
311	Boogie Woogie on St. Louis Blues/Ugh	1953	7.50	15.00	30.00
324	Night Time/It Moves Me	1953	7.50	15.00	30.00
336	Not the Girl for Me/Black Fantasy	1954	7.50	15.00	30.00

Albums

ALADDIN

Number	Title (A Side/B Side)	Yr	VG	VG+	NM
LP-808 [M]	Chica-Boo	1956	1000.	1500.	2000.
—Red vinyl					
LP-808 [M]	Chica-Boo	1956	250.00	500.00	1000.
—Black vinyl					

BLACK & BLUE

Number	Title (A Side/B Side)	Yr	VG	VG+	NM
33077	Old Time Shuffle	1977	3.00	6.00	12.00

IMPERIAL

Number	Title (A Side/B Side)	Yr	VG	VG+	NM
LP-9174 [M]	Chica-Boo	1962	37.50	75.00	150.00
LP-9175 [M]	After Hours	1962	37.50	75.00	150.00
LP-12174 [S]	Chica-Boo	1962	50.00	100.00	200.00
LP-12175 [S]	After Hours	1962	50.00	100.00	200.00

SCORE

Number	Title (A Side/B Side)	Yr	VG	VG+	NM
SLP-4006 [M]	Lloyd Glenn	1957	250.00	500.00	1000.
SLP-4020 [M]	After Hours	1958	250.00	500.00	1000.

SWING TIME

Number	Title (A Side/B Side)	Yr	VG	VG+	NM
1901 [10]	Lloyd Glenn	1954	1500.	2250.	3000.

GLITTER, GARY

45s

ARISTA

Number	Title (A Side/B Side)	Yr	VG	VG+	NM
0173	I Love You Love Me Love/Hands Up! It's a Stick-Up	1976	—	2.50	5.00

BELL

Number	Title (A Side/B Side)	Yr	VG	VG+	NM
45237	Rock and Roll, Part 2/Rock and Roll, Part 1	1972	—	3.00	6.00
45276	I Didn't Know I Loved You (Till I Saw You Rock and Roll)/Shakey Sue	1972	—	2.50	5.00
45326	Do You Wanna Touch Me (Oh Yeah)/I Would If I Could But I Can't	1973	—	2.50	5.00
45345	Baby Please Don't Go/I.O.U.	1973	—	2.50	5.00
45375	Come On, Come In/Happy Birthday	1973	—	2.50	5.00
45398	(I'm the) Leader of the Gang (I Am)/(B-side unknown)	1973	—	2.50	5.00
45438	I Love You Love Me Love/(B-side unknown)	1974	—	2.50	5.00

DECCA

Number	Title (A Side/B Side)	Yr	VG	VG+	NM
32714	Goodbye Seattle/Wait for Me	1970	3.75	7.50	15.00
—As "Paul Raven"					

TOMMY BOY

Number	Title (A Side/B Side)	Yr	VG	VG+	NM
639	Rock 'N' Roll Part 2...The Hey Song (same on both sides)	1995	—	—	3.00
—Original recording with overdubbed crowd sounds					

Albums

BELL

Number	Title (A Side/B Side)	Yr	VG	VG+	NM
1108	Glitter	1972	3.75	7.50	15.00
6082	Gary Glitter	1973	3.75	7.50	15.00

EPIC

Number	Title (A Side/B Side)	Yr	VG	VG+	NM
PE 39299	The Leader	1984	3.75	7.50	15.00

EPIC/NU-DISK

Number	Title (A Side/B Side)	Yr	VG	VG+	NM
3E 36848 [10]	Glitter & Gold	1981	3.00	6.00	12.00

GLITTERHOUSE

45s

DYNOVOICE

Number	Title (A Side/B Side)	Yr	VG	VG+	NM
925	I Lost Me a Friend/Tinkerbell's Mind	1968	2.50	5.00	10.00
927	Barbarella/Love Drags Me Down	1968	3.00	6.00	12.00

Albums

DYNOVOICE

Number	Title (A Side/B Side)	Yr	VG	VG+	NM
31905	Color Bland	1968	5.00	10.00	20.00

GLOBETROTTERS

45s

BUDDAH

Number	Title (A Side/B Side)	Yr	VG	VG+	NM
309	Don't Rock the Boat/Hatfield Small	1972	2.50	5.00	10.00

KIRSHNER

Number	Title (A Side/B Side)	Yr	VG	VG+	NM
63-5006	Cheer Me Up/Gravy	1970	3.00	6.00	12.00
63-5006 [PS]	Cheer Me Up/Gravy	1970	3.75	7.50	15.00
63-5008	Rainy Day Bells/Medowlark	1970	3.75	7.50	15.00
63-5012	Duke of Earl/Everybody's Got Hot Pants	1971	3.00	6.00	12.00
63-5016	Everybody Needs Love/ESP	1971	3.00	6.00	12.00

Albums

KIRSHNER

Number	Title (A Side/B Side)	Yr	VG	VG+	NM
KES-108	Globetrotters	1971	5.00	10.00	20.00

GLORIES, THE

45s

DATE

Number	Title (A Side/B Side)	Yr	VG	VG+	NM
1553	I Stand Accused (Of Loving You)/Wish They Could Write a Song	1967	2.50	5.00	10.00
1571	Give Me My Freedom/Security	1967	6.25	12.50	25.00
1579	Sing Me a Love Song/Ooh, That's Love, Baby	1967	6.25	12.50	25.00
1593	Stand By (I'm Coming Home)/My Sweet, Sweet Baby	1968	6.25	12.50	25.00
1615	I Worship You Baby/Don't Dial My Number	1968	12.50	25.00	50.00
1622	No News/Oh Baby That's Love	1968	6.25	12.50	25.00
1636	Try a Little Tenderness/There He Is	1969	6.25	12.50	25.00
1647	Don't Make the Good Girls Go Bad/The Dark End of the Street	1969	5.00	10.00	20.00

GLORY (1)

45s

AVALANCHE

Number	Title (A Side/B Side)	Yr	VG	VG+	NM
XW-289	Find Out Lover/Mrs. Walter	1973	—	3.00	6.00

Albums

AVALANCHE

Number	Title (A Side/B Side)	Yr	VG	VG+	NM
AV-LA148-F	Glory	1973	3.75	7.50	15.00

Number	Title (A Side/B Side)	Yr	VG	VG+	NM

GLORY (2)
Albums
TEXAS REVOLUTION

CFS-2531	A Meat Music Sampler	1969	25.00	50.00	100.00

GLORYTONES, THE
45s
EPIC

9243	You Only Came Back to Hurt Me/Was That the Right Thing to Do	1957	10.00	20.00	40.00

GLOWTONES, THE
45s
ATLANTIC

1156	The Girl I Love/Ping Pong	1957	—	—	—

—Only known on 78 rpm; 45 rpm release was on EastWest 101
EASTWEST

101	The Girl I Love/Ping Pong	1957	7.50	15.00	30.00

GO-GO'S, THE
No relation to the 1980s girl group.
45s
RCA VICTOR

47-8370	Lonely Girl/Chicken of the Sea	1964	3.75	7.50	15.00

—No relation to the 1980s girl group

47-8435	The Wild One/Saturday's Hero	1964	7.50	15.00	30.00

Albums
RCA VICTOR

LPM-2930 [M]	Swim with the Go-Go's	1964	6.25	12.50	25.00
LSP-2930 [S]	Swim with the Go-Go's	1964	7.50	15.00	30.00

GODCHAUX, KEITH AND DONNA
See KEITH AND DONNA.

GODDARD, GEOFF
45s
LAWN

235	Walk With My Angel/Sky Men	1964	3.00	6.00	12.00

GODSPELL
45s
BELL

45147	By My Side/Crucifixion, Resurrection	1971	—	2.50	5.00
45210	Day By Day/Bless the Lord	1972	—	2.00	4.00
45240	We Beseech Thee/On the Willows	1972	—	2.50	5.00
45275	By My Side/(B-side unknown)	1972	—	2.50	5.00
45351	Beautiful City/Bless the Lord	1973	—	2.50	5.00

GODZ, THE
No relation to the late-1970s punk/metal band of the same name.
45s
ESP-DISK'

4503	Lay in the Sun/I Want a Word with You	1966	2.50	5.00	10.00

Albums
ESP-DISK'

1037 [M]	Contact High with the Godz	1967	15.00	30.00	60.00
S-1037 [S]	Contact High with the Godz	1967	12.50	25.00	50.00
1047	Godz 2	1968	12.50	25.00	50.00
1077	Third Testament	1969	12.50	25.00	50.00
2017	Godzundheit	1970	12.50	25.00	50.00

GOGGLES, THE
45s
AUDIO FIDELITY

168	Don't Say You Don't Remember/We All Live on a Rainbow	1971	—	2.50	5.00

Albums
AUDIO FIDELITY

AFSD-6244	The Goggles	1971	3.75	7.50	15.00

GOINS, HERBIE, AND THE NIGHT-RIDERS
45s
CAPITOL

5978	Coming Home to You/The Incredible Miss Brown	1967	2.50	5.00	10.00

GOLD, ANDREW
Also see BRYNDLE.
45s
ASYLUM

45286	That's Why I Love You/A Note from You	1975	—	2.00	4.00
45339	Stay/Firefly	1976	—	2.00	4.00
45378	Angel Woman/Do Wah Diddy	1976	—	2.00	4.00
45384	Lonely Boy/Must Be Crazy	1977	—	2.00	4.00
45384 [PS]	Lonely Boy/Must Be Crazy	1977	—	2.50	5.00
45417	One of Them Is Me/Passing Thing	1977	—	2.00	4.00
45439	Go Back Home Again/Firefly	1977	—	2.00	4.00
45456	Thank You for Being a Friend/Still You Linger On	1978	—	2.00	4.00
45489	Never Let Her Slip Away/Genevieve	1978	—	2.00	4.00
45489 [PS]	Never Let Her Slip Away/Genevieve	1978	—	2.50	5.00
45521	Looking for My Love/How Can This Be Love	1978	—	2.00	4.00
45522	I'm On My Way/Always for You	1978	—	2.00	4.00
46626	Kiss This One Goodbye/Make Up Your Mind	1980	—	2.00	4.00

Albums
ASYLUM

6E-116	All This and Heaven Too	1978	2.50	5.00	10.00
6E-264	Whirlwind	1979	2.50	5.00	10.00
7E-1047	Andrew Gold	1975	2.50	5.00	10.00
7E-1086	What's Wrong with This Picture?	1977	2.50	5.00	10.00

GOLD, MARTY
45s
KAPP

244	Hey! Paesano Cha Cha Cha/I'm Not Afraid Anymore	1958	2.50	5.00	10.00

RCA VICTOR

47-7696	Lissabon/Music of Home	1960	2.00	4.00	8.00
47-7722	Lonely Guitar/Home from the Hill	1960	2.00	4.00	8.00
47-7822	The Breeze and I/Cry Like the Wind	1960	2.00	4.00	8.00
47-7856	Carnival in Rome/My Romance	1961	2.00	4.00	8.00

Albums
KAPP

KL-1125 [M]	By the Waters of the Minnetonka	1959	3.75	7.50	15.00

PICKWICK

ACL-9003	Songs from "How the Grinch Stole Christmas" and Other Children's Christmas Songs	197?	2.00	4.00	8.00

RCA VICTOR

LPM-2290 [M]	It's Magic	1961	3.00	6.00	12.00
LSP-2290 [S]	It's Magic	1961	3.75	7.50	15.00
LSP-2381 [S]	Stereo Action Goes Hollywood	1962	3.00	6.00	12.00
LPM-2620 [M]	Soundpower!	1963	3.00	6.00	12.00
LSP-2620 [S]	Soundpower!	1963	3.75	7.50	15.00
LSP-3599 [S]	Soundaroundus	1966	3.00	6.00	12.00

VIK

LX-1069 [M]	Organized for Hi-Fi	1957	3.75	7.50	15.00

GOLD BUGS, THE
45s
CORAL

62453	Stop That Wedding/It's So Nice	1965	10.00	20.00	40.00

GOLDBERG, BARRY
Also see GOLDBERG-MILLER BLUES BAND.
45s
BUDDAH

59	Sittin' in Circles/Hole in My Pocket	1968	2.50	5.00	10.00
103	Jimi the Fox/On the Road Again	1969	2.50	5.00	10.00

EPIC

10007	Blowing My Mind/Think	1966	3.75	7.50	15.00
10033	Ginger Man/Whole Lotta Shakin' Goin' On	1966	3.75	7.50	15.00

Albums
ATCO

SD 7040	Barry Goldberg	1974	3.00	6.00	12.00

BUDDAH

BDS-5012	The Barry Goldberg Reunion	1968	6.25	12.50	25.00
BDS-5029	Two Jews Blues	1969	6.25	12.50	25.00
BDS-5051	Street Man	1970	3.75	7.50	15.00
BDS-5081	Blast from My Past	1974	3.75	7.50	15.00

EPIC

LN 24199 [M]	Blowing My Mind	1966	7.50	15.00	30.00
BN 26199 [S]	Blowing My Mind	1966	10.00	20.00	40.00

RECORD MAN

CR 5015	Barry Goldberg and Friends	1972	3.75	7.50	15.00

GOLDBERG-MILLER BLUES BAND
Also see BARRY GOLDBERG; STEVE MILLER.
45s
EPIC

9865	More Soul Than Soulful/Mother Song	1965	3.75	7.50	15.00
9865 [DJ]	More Soul Than Soulful/Mother Song	1965	6.25	12.50	25.00

—Promo only on blue vinyl

9865 [PS]	More Soul Than Soulful/Mother Song	1965	12.50	25.00	50.00

—Promo only

GOLDDIGGERS, THE
DEAN MARTIN's girl group from his TV show.
45s
METROMEDIA

141	I Wanna Be Loved/It's Fun to Be Young	1969	—	2.50	5.00
156	We Need A Little Christmas/I Just Want You For Christmas	1969	—	3.00	6.00

RCA VICTOR

74-0670	A-Flat Cricket and B-Flat Frog/Nobody Else But You	1972	—	2.50	5.00

Albums
METROMEDIA

MD 1009	The Golddiggers	1969	3.00	6.00	12.00
MD 1012	We Need a Little Christmas	1969	3.75	7.50	15.00

RCA VICTOR

LSP-4643	The Golddiggers Today!	1972	3.00	6.00	12.00

GOLDEBRIARS, THE
Curt Boetcher was a member of this group.
45s
EPIC

9673	Pretty Girls and Rolling Stones/Shenandoah	1964	3.00	6.00	12.00
9719	The Castle in the Corner/I've Got to Love Somebody	1964	3.00	6.00	12.00
9806	Don't Want Your Love/Give Me Lovin'	1965	3.00	6.00	12.00

Albums
EPIC

LN 24087 [M]	The Goldebriars	1964	3.75	7.50	15.00
LN 24114 [M]	Straight Ahead	1964	3.75	7.50	15.00
BN 26087 [S]	The Goldebriars	1964	5.00	10.00	20.00
BN 26114 [S]	Straight Ahead	1964	5.00	10.00	20.00

GOLDEN DAWN
Albums
INTERNATIONAL ARTISTS

4	Power Plant	1968	25.00	50.00	100.00

Number	Title (A Side/B Side)	Yr	VG	VG+	NM
4	Power Plant	1979	3.75	7.50	15.00
—Reissue with "Masterfonics" in trail-off wax					

GOLDEN EARRING

45s

Number	Title (A Side/B Side)	Yr	VG	VG+	NM
21 RECORDS					
103	Twilight Zone/King Dark	1982	—	2.00	4.00
108	The Devil Made Me Do It/Chargin' Batteries	1983	—	2.00	4.00
112	When the Lady Smiles/Orwell's Ear	1984	—	—	3.00
112 [PS]	When the Lady Smiles/Orwell's Ear	1984	—	2.50	5.00
113	Fist in Glove/One Night Moonlight	1984	—	—	3.00
99515	Love in Motion/Why Do I	1986	—	—	3.00
99533	Quiet Eyes/Love in Motion	1986	—	—	3.00
881415-7	Something Heavy Going Down/Enough Is Enough	1984	—	—	3.00
ATLANTIC					
2710	Eight Miles High/One High Road	1970	—	3.00	6.00
DWARF					
2001	Back Home/As Long As the Wind Blows	1969	2.50	5.00	10.00
2001 [PS]	Back Home/As Long As the Wind Blows	1969	5.00	10.00	20.00
MCA					
40513	Babylon/Sleep Walkin'	1976	—	2.00	4.00
40802	Radar Love (Live)/Radar Love (Studio)	1977	—	2.00	4.00
POLYDOR					
2004	Weekend Love/Tiger Bay	1979	—	2.00	4.00
14001	It's Alright, But I Admit It Could Be Better/Song of a Devil's Servant	1969	2.50	5.00	10.00
14581	Weekend Love/Tiger Bay	1979	—	—	—
—Unreleased					
TRACK					
40202	Radar Love/Just Like Vince Taylor	1974	—	3.00	6.00
40309	Candy's Going Bad/She Flies on Strange Wings	1974	—	2.50	5.00
40369	Ce Soir/Lucky Numbers	1975	—	2.50	5.00
40412	The Switch/Lonesome D.J.	1975	—	2.50	5.00

Albums

Number	Title (A Side/B Side)	Yr	VG	VG+	NM
21 RECORDS					
T1-1-9004	Cut	1982	2.50	5.00	10.00
T1-1-9008	N.E.W.S.	1984	2.50	5.00	10.00
90514	The Hole	1986	2.50	5.00	10.00
817585-1	Cut	1985	2.00	4.00	8.00
—Reissue					
823717-1	Something Heavy Going Down — Live from the Twilight Zone	1984	2.50	5.00	10.00
ATLANTIC					
SD 8244	Eight Miles High	1970	6.25	12.50	25.00
CAPITOL					
ST-164	Miracle Mirror	1969	10.00	20.00	40.00
ST 2823 [S]	Winter Harvest	1967	6.25	12.50	25.00
T 2823 [M]	Winter Harvest	1967	12.50	25.00	50.00
ST-11315	The Golden Earring	1974	3.00	6.00	12.00
DWARF					
2000	Golden Earring	1971	6.25	12.50	25.00
MCA					
703	Grab It For a Second	198?	2.00	4.00	8.00
—Reissue of 3057					
827	Switch	198?	2.00	4.00	8.00
—Reissue of 2139					
2139	Switch	197?	2.50	5.00	10.00
—Reissue of Track 2139					
2183	To the Hilt	1976	3.00	6.00	12.00
2254	Mad Love	1977	3.00	6.00	12.00
2352	Moontan	1978	2.50	5.00	10.00
—Reissue of Track 396					
3057	Grab It For a Second	1978	3.00	6.00	12.00
6004 [(2)]	Golden Earring Live!	198?	2.50	5.00	10.00
—Reissue of 8009					
8009 [(2)]	Golden Earring Live!	1977	3.75	7.50	15.00
37172	Moontan	198?	2.00	4.00	8.00
—Reissue of 2352					
POLYDOR					
PD-1-6223	No Promises...No Debts	1979	3.00	6.00	12.00
PD-1-6303	Long Blond Animal	1980	3.00	6.00	12.00
TRACK					
396	Moontan	1974	6.25	12.50	25.00
—Original cover with nude dancer					
396	Moontan	1974	3.75	7.50	15.00
—Reissue cover with close-up of earring in ear					
2139	Switch	1975	3.75	7.50	15.00

GOLDEN GATE STRINGS, THE

Albums

Number	Title (A Side/B Side)	Yr	VG	VG+	NM
EPIC					
LN 24158 [M]	The Bob Dylan Song Book	1965	3.00	6.00	12.00
LN 24160 [M]	A String of Hits	1965	3.00	6.00	12.00
LN 24248 [M]	The Monkees Song Book	1967	3.00	6.00	12.00
BN 26158 [S]	The Bob Dylan Song Book	1965	3.75	7.50	15.00
BN 26160 [S]	A String of Hits	1965	3.75	7.50	15.00
BN 26248 [S]	The Monkees Song Book	1967	3.75	7.50	15.00

GOLDEN NUGGETS, THE

45s

Number	Title (A Side/B Side)	Yr	VG	VG+	NM
FUTURA					
1691	I Was a Fool/Teenage Josephine	1959	150.00	300.00	600.00
HAWK					
107/8	Surf Everybody/Everybody Bird	1963	10.00	20.00	40.00

GOLDENROD

Albums

Number	Title (A Side/B Side)	Yr	VG	VG+	NM
CHARTMAKER					
CSG-1101	Goldenrod	1968	50.00	100.00	200.00

GOLDENRODS, THE

45s

Number	Title (A Side/B Side)	Yr	VG	VG+	NM
VEE JAY					
307	Wish I Was Back in School/Color Cartoons	1959	62.50	125.00	250.00

GOLDIE, DAN

45s

Number	Title (A Side/B Side)	Yr	VG	VG+	NM
TEARDROP					
3070	Take Our Last Walk Tonight/Walking the Streets	1966	6.25	12.50	25.00
—The Sir Douglas Quintet is the backing band					

GOLDSBORO, BOBBY

45s

Number	Title (A Side/B Side)	Yr	VG	VG+	NM
BLUE SKY					
70052	Green-Eyed Woman, Nashville Blues/Alice Doesn't Love Here Anymore	1981	—	2.00	4.00
BUENA VISTA					
561	These Are the Best Times/(B-side unknown)	1979	—	2.50	5.00
CURB					
02117	Love Ain't Never Hurt Nobody/Wings of an Angel	1981	—	2.00	4.00
02583	The Round-Up Saloon/Green-Eyed Woman, Nashville Blues	1981	—	2.00	4.00
02726	Lucy and the Stranger/Outrun the Sun	1982	—	2.00	4.00
EPIC					
50342	I Love Music/Me and the Elephants	1977	—	2.00	4.00
50413	The Cowboy and the Lady/Me and Millie	1977	—	2.00	4.00
50480	He'll Have to Go/Too Hot to Handle	1977	—	2.00	4.00
50535	Life Gets Hard on Easy Street/Black Fool's Gold	1978	—	2.00	4.00
LAURIE					
3130	Lonely Traveler/You Better Go Home	1962	3.75	7.50	15.00
3148	Molly/Honey Baby	1962	3.75	7.50	15.00
3159	The Letter/The Runaround	1963	3.75	7.50	15.00
3168	Light the Candles/That's What Love Will Do	1963	3.75	7.50	15.00
UNITED ARTISTS					
0044	See the Funny Little Clown/Little Things	1973	—	2.00	4.00
0045	It's Too Late/Voodoo Woman	1973	—	2.00	4.00
0046	Honey/Autumn of My Life	1973	—	2.00	4.00
0047	Watching Scotty Grow/I'm a Drifter	1973	—	2.00	4.00
—0044 through 0047 are "Silver Spotlight Series" reissues					
XW251	Summer (The First Time)/Childhood 1949	1973	—	2.50	5.00
XW251 [PS]	Summer (The First Time)/Childhood 1949	1973	—	3.00	6.00
XW371	Marlena/Sing Me a Smile	1973	—	2.50	5.00
XW422	I Believe the South Is Gonna Rise Again/She	1974	—	2.00	4.00
XW451	And Then There Was Gina/Quicksand	1974	—	2.00	4.00
XW517	Summer (The First Time)/Marlena	1974	—	2.00	4.00
—Reissue					
XW529	Hello Summertime/And Then There Was Gina	1974	—	2.00	4.00
XW633	And Then There Was Gina/You Pull Me Down (Into Sweet, Sweet Love)	1975	—	2.00	4.00
672	See the Funny Little Clown/Hello Loser	1963	2.50	5.00	10.00
XW681	I Wrote a Song (Sing Along)/You Pull Me Down (Into Sweet, Sweet Love)	1975	—	2.00	4.00
710	Whenever He Holds You/If She Was Mine	1964	2.00	4.00	8.00
710 [PS]	Whenever He Holds You/If She Was Mine	1964	3.75	7.50	15.00
742	Me Japanese Boy, I Love You/Everyone But Me	1964	2.00	4.00	8.00
781	I Don't Know You Anymore/Little Drops of Water	1964	2.00	4.00	8.00
XW793	Another Night Long/A Butterfly for Bucky	1976	—	2.00	4.00
810	Little Things/I Can't Go On Pretending	1965	2.50	5.00	10.00
862	Voodoo Woman/It Breaks My Heart	1965	2.00	4.00	8.00
XW866	She Taught Me How to Live Again/Reunion	1976	—	2.00	4.00
908	If You Wait for Love/If You've Got a Heart	1965	2.00	4.00	8.00
952	Broomstick Cowboy/Ain't Got Time for Happy	1965	2.00	4.00	8.00
980	It's Too Late/I'm Goin' Home	1966	2.00	4.00	8.00
50018	I Know You Better Than That/When Your Love Has Gone	1966	2.00	4.00	8.00
50018 [PS]	I Know You Better Than That/When Your Love Has Gone	1966	3.75	7.50	15.00
50044	Longer Than Forever/Take Your Love	1966	2.00	2.00	8.00
50056	It Hurts Me/Pity the Fool	1966	2.00	2.00	8.00
50087	Blue Autumn/I Just Don't Love You Anymore	1966	2.00	2.00	8.00
50138	Love Is/Goodbye to All You Women	1967	2.00	2.00	8.00
50186	Three in the Morning/Trusty Little Herbert	1967	2.00	2.00	8.00
50224	Pledge of Love/Jo-Jo's Place	1967	2.00	2.00	8.00
50283	Honey/Danny	1968	2.50	5.00	10.00
—Black label					
50283	Honey/Danny	1968	2.00	4.00	8.00
—Orange and pink label					
50318	Autumn of My Life/She Chased Me	1968	—	3.00	6.00
50318 [PS]	Autumn of My Life/She Chased Me	1968	3.75	7.50	15.00
50321	Autumn of My Life/She Chased Me	1968	—	—	—
—Unreleased; these were edits of the versions on UA 50318					
50461	The Straight Life/Tomorrow Is Forgotten	1968	—	3.00	6.00
50470	A Christmas Wish/Look Around You (It's Christmas Time)	1968	2.50	5.00	10.00
50497	Glad She's a Woman/Letter to Emily	1969	—	3.00	6.00
50525	I'm a Drifter/Hobos and Kings	1969	—	3.00	6.00
50565	A Richer Man Than I/Muddy Mississippi Line	1969	—	3.00	6.00
50591	She Thinks I Still Care/Take a Little Good Will Home	1969	—	3.00	6.00
—With Del Reeves					
50614	Requiem/Mornin' Mornin'	1969	—	3.00	6.00
50650	Time Good, Time Bad/Can You Feel It	1970	—	2.50	5.00
50696	Down on the Bayou/It's Gonna Change	1970	—	2.50	5.00
50715	My God and I/The World Beyond	1970	—	2.50	5.00
50727	Watching Scotty Grow/Water Color Days	1970	—	2.50	5.00
50776	And I Love You So/Gentle of a Man	1971	—	2.50	5.00
50807	I'll Remember You/Come Back Home	1971	—	2.50	5.00
50846	Poem for the Little Lady/Danny Is a Mirror to Me	1971	—	2.50	5.00
50891	California Wine/To Be with You	1972	—	2.50	5.00
50938	With Pen in Hand/Southern Fried Singin' Sunday Mornin'	1972	—	2.50	5.00
51107	Country Feelin's/Brand New Kind of Love	1973	—	2.50	5.00

Albums

Number	Title (A Side/B Side)	Yr	VG	VG+	NM
CURB					
JZ 36822	Bobby Goldsboro	1980	3.00	6.00	12.00
FZ 37734	Round-Up Saloon	1982	2.50	5.00	10.00
EPIC					
PE 34703	Goldsboro	1977	3.00	6.00	12.00
LIBERTY					
LMAS-5502	Bobby Goldsboro's Greatest Hits	1981	2.00	4.00	8.00
—Reissue of United Artists 5502					
LN-10007	Bobby Goldsboro's 10th Anniversary Album, Volume 1	1981	2.00	4.00	8.00
LN-10047	Bobby Goldsboro's 10th Anniversary Album, Volume 2	1981	2.00	4.00	8.00
LN-10114	The Best of Bobby Goldsboro	1981	2.00	4.00	8.00
SUNSET					
SUS-5236	This Is Bobby Goldsboro	1969	3.00	6.00	12.00
SUS-5284	Pledge of Love	1970	3.00	6.00	12.00
SUS-5313	Autumn of My Life	1971	3.00	6.00	12.00
UNITED ARTISTS					
UA-LA019-F	Brand New Kind of Love	1972	3.75	7.50	15.00
SP-58 [DJ]	The Bobby Goldsboro Family Album	1971	12.50	25.00	50.00
—Promo-only compilation					
UA-LA124-F	Summer (The First Time)	1973	3.75	7.50	15.00
UA-LA311-H2 [(2)]	Bobby Goldsboro's 10th Anniversary Album	1974	5.00	10.00	20.00
UA-LA424-G	Through the Eyes of a Man	1975	3.00	6.00	12.00
UA-LA639-G	Butterfly for Bucky	1976	3.00	6.00	12.00
UAL 3358 [M]	The Bobby Goldsbob Album	1964	5.00	10.00	20.00
UAL 3381 [M]	I Can't Stop Loving You	1964	5.00	10.00	20.00
UAL 3425 [M]	Little Things	1965	5.00	10.00	20.00
UAL 3471 [M]	Broomstick Cowboy	1966	5.00	10.00	20.00
UAL 3486 [M]	It's Too Late	1966	5.00	10.00	20.00
UAL 3552 [M]	Blue Autumn	1967	5.00	10.00	20.00
UAL 3561 [M]	Sold Goldsboro/Bobby Goldsboro's Greatest Hits	1967	5.00	10.00	20.00
UAL 3599 [M]	Romantic, Soulful, Wacky	1967	5.00	10.00	20.00
UAS 5502	Bobby Goldsboro's Greatest Hits	1970	5.00	10.00	20.00
UAS 5516	Come Back Home	1971	3.75	7.50	15.00
UAS-5578	California Wine	1972	3.75	7.50	15.00
UAS 6358 [S]	The Bobby Goldsbob Album	1964	6.25	12.50	25.00
UAS 6358 [S]	I Can't Stop Loving You	1964	6.25	12.50	25.00
UAS 6425 [S]	Little Things	1965	6.25	12.50	25.00
UAS 6471 [S]	Broomstick Cowboy	1966	6.25	12.50	25.00
UAS 6486 [S]	It's Too Late	1966	6.25	12.50	25.00
UAS 6552 [S]	Blue Autumn	1967	6.25	12.50	25.00
UAS 6561 [S]	Sold Goldsboro/Bobby Goldsboro's Greatest Hits	1967	5.00	10.00	20.00
UAS 6599 [S]	Romantic, Soulful, Wacky	1967	5.00	10.00	20.00
UAS 6642	Honey	1968	5.00	10.00	20.00
UAS 6657	Word Pictures Featuring Autumn of My Life	1968	5.00	10.00	20.00
UAS 6704	Today	1969	5.00	10.00	20.00
UAS 6735	Muddy Mississippi Line	1969	5.00	10.00	20.00
UAS 6777	We Gotta Start Lovin'	1970	5.00	10.00	20.00
UAS 6777	Watching Scotty Grow	1971	3.75	7.50	15.00
—Retitled version of above					

GOLDSBORO, BOBBY, AND DEL REEVES

Albums

Number	Title (A Side/B Side)	Yr	VG	VG+	NM
UNITED ARTISTS					
UAL 3615 [M]	Our Way of Life	1967	5.00	10.00	20.00
UAS 6615 [S]	Our Way of Life	1967	5.00	10.00	20.00

GOLDTONES, THE

Two different groups?

45s

Number	Title (A Side/B Side)	Yr	VG	VG+	NM
A&R					
714	Strike/Gutterball	1963	7.50	15.00	30.00
714 [PS]	Strike/Gutterball	1963	12.50	25.00	50.00

Albums

Number	Title (A Side/B Side)	Yr	VG	VG+	NM
LABREA					
L-8011 [M]	The Goldtones	1961	10.00	20.00	40.00
LS-8011 [S]	The Goldtones	1961	12.50	25.00	50.00

GOLLIWOGS, THE

Early CREEDENCE CLEARWATER REVIVAL. Also see TOMMY FOGERTY AND THE BLUE VELVETS.

45s

Number	Title (A Side/B Side)	Yr	VG	VG+	NM
FANTASY					
590	Don't Tell Me No Lies/Little Girl, Does Your Mama Know	1964	15.00	30.00	60.00
597	Where You Been/You Came Walking	1965	15.00	30.00	60.00
599	You Got Nothin' on Me/You Can't Be True	1965	12.50	25.00	50.00
SCORPIO					
404	Brown Eyed Girl/You Better Be Careful	1967	12.50	25.00	50.00
405	Fragile Child/Fight Fire	1967	12.50	25.00	50.00
408	Walking on the Water/You Better Get It Before It Gets You	1967	12.50	25.00	50.00
412 [DJ]	Porterville/Call It Pretending	1968	15.00	30.00	60.00
—Only promos credit the Golliwogs; all known stock copies credit Creedence Clearwater Revival.					

Albums

Number	Title (A Side/B Side)	Yr	VG	VG+	NM
FANTASY					
F-9474	Pre-Creedence	1975	7.50	15.00	30.00
—Reissue of Fantasy and Scorpio sides					

GONE ALL STARS

45s

Number	Title (A Side/B Side)	Yr	VG	VG+	NM
GONE					
5016	7-11/Down Yonder Rock	1957	6.25	12.50	25.00

GONKS, THE

45s

Number	Title (A Side/B Side)	Yr	VG	VG+	NM
LONDON					
9696	The Gonk Song/Take Care	1964	3.00	6.00	12.00

GONN

45s

Number	Title (A Side/B Side)	Yr	VG	VG+	NM
EMIR					
9217	Blackout of Gretley/Pain in My Heart	1966	100.00	200.00	400.00
EMIR/MCCM					
88-9217	Blackout of Gretley/Pain in My Heart	1988	—	2.50	5.00
—Black vinyl					
88-9217	Blackout of Gretley/Pain in My Heart	1988	3.75	7.50	15.00
—Colored vinyl					
MERRY JAINE					
2318	You're Looking Fine/Come with Me	1967	25.00	50.00	100.00

GONZALES, FRANK

45s

Number	Title (A Side/B Side)	Yr	VG	VG+	NM
FESTIVAL					
1001	Let's Make Up/(B-side unknown)	1961	62.50	125.00	250.00

GONZALES, NITOY

Albums

Number	Title (A Side/B Side)	Yr	VG	VG+	NM
CAPITOL					
ST 10305 [S]	Christmas in the Philippines	196?	3.75	7.50	15.00
T 10305 [M]	Christmas in the Philippines	196?	3.00	6.00	12.00

GOOBERS, THE

45s

Number	Title (A Side/B Side)	Yr	VG	VG+	NM
SURF					
1001	Hawaiian Holiday/Buyer Beware	1963	12.50	25.00	50.00

GOOD, TOMMY

45s

Number	Title (A Side/B Side)	Yr	VG	VG+	NM
GORDY					
7034	Baby I Miss You/Leaving Here	1964	10.00	20.00	40.00

GOOD AND PLENTY

45s

Number	Title (A Side/B Side)	Yr	VG	VG+	NM
SENATE					
2105	Living in a World of Make Believe/I Played My Part Well	1967	2.50	5.00	10.00
2106	Sunny and Me/Children Dreamin'	1967	2.50	5.00	10.00

Albums

Number	Title (A Side/B Side)	Yr	VG	VG+	NM
SENATE					
LP-21001 [M]	The World of Good and Plenty	1967	7.50	15.00	30.00
LPS-21001 [S]	The World of Good and Plenty	1967	7.50	15.00	30.00

GOOD GUYS, THE

45s

Number	Title (A Side/B Side)	Yr	VG	VG+	NM
GNP CRESCENDO					
326	Asphalt Wipe Out/Scratch	1964	5.00	10.00	20.00

Albums

Number	Title (A Side/B Side)	Yr	VG	VG+	NM
GNP CRESCENDO					
GNP-2001 [M]	Sidewalk Surfing	1964	7.50	15.00	30.00
GNPS-2001 [S]	Sidewalk Surfing	1964	10.00	20.00	40.00
UNITED ARTISTS					
UAL-3370 [M]	The Good Guys Sing	1964	3.75	7.50	15.00
UAS-6370 [S]	The Good Guys Sing	1964	5.00	10.00	20.00

GOOD RATS, THE

45s

Number	Title (A Side/B Side)	Yr	VG	VG+	NM
KAPP					
946	The Hobo/Truth Is Gone	1968	3.00	6.00	12.00
PASSPORT					
7912	Just Found a Lady/Coo Coo Coo Blues	1978	—	2.50	5.00

Albums

Number	Title (A Side/B Side)	Yr	VG	VG+	NM
KAPP					
KS-3580	The Good Rats	1969	10.00	20.00	40.00
PASSPORT					
SP-20 [DJ]	Rats the Way You Like It (Live)	1978	15.00	30.00	60.00
PB-9825	From Rats to Riches	1978	3.00	6.00	12.00
PB-9830	Birth Comes to Us All	1978	3.00	6.00	12.00
RAT CITY					
998 [(2)]	Live at Last	1979	3.75	7.50	15.00
RCR-8001	Rat City in Blue	1975	5.00	10.00	20.00
RCR-8002	Tasty	1978	3.00	6.00	12.00
RCR-8003	Great American Music	1981	3.00	6.00	12.00
WARNER BROS.					
BS 2813	Tasty	1974	7.50	15.00	30.00

GOOD ROCKIN' SAM

45s

Number	Title (A Side/B Side)	Yr	VG	VG+	NM
EXCELLO					
2059	Baby I'm Fool Proof/Thing-a-Ma-Jig	1955	12.50	25.00	50.00

GOOD TIMES, THE

45s

Number	Title (A Side/B Side)	Yr	VG	VG+	NM
KAMA SUTRA					
215	That's When Your Heartaches Begin/Good Life	1966	2.00	4.00	8.00
247	You Got the Fever/Mr. & Mrs. Arthur Thompson Request (Your Presence at the Marriage of Their Daughter Lorna Beth)	1968	2.00	4.00	8.00

Albums

Number	Title (A Side/B Side)	Yr	VG	VG+	NM
KAMA SUTRA					
KLP-8052 [M]	The Good Times	1966	3.75	7.50	15.00
KSLP-8052 [S]	The Good Times	1966	5.00	10.00	20.00

GOODEES, THE

45s

Number	Title (A Side/B Side)	Yr	VG	VG+	NM
HIP					
109	For a Little While/Would You, Could You	1968	2.00	4.00	8.00
8005	Condition Red/Didn't Know Love Was So Good	1968	2.50	5.00	10.00

Number	Title (A Side/B Side)	Yr	VG	VG+	NM
8010	Jilted/Love Is Here	1969	2.00	4.00	8.00
8016	He's a Rebel/Goodies	1969	2.00	4.00	8.00
Albums					
HIP					
HIS-7002	Candy Coated Goodees	1969	6.25	12.50	25.00

GOODMAN, BENNY

Number	Title (A Side/B Side)	Yr	VG	VG+	NM
45s					
CAPITOL					
F828	Spin a Record/Little Girl Don't Cry	1950	5.00	10.00	20.00
F860	It Isn't Fair/You're Always There	1950	5.00	10.00	20.00
CHESS					
1742	Mission to Moscow/You Do Something to Me	1959	2.50	5.00	10.00
COLUMBIA					
1-889	Oh Babe/Walkin' with the Blues	1950	7.50	15.00	30.00
—Microgroove 33 1/3 rpm 7-inch small hole single					
6-889	Oh Babe/Walkin' with the Blues	1950	6.25	12.50	25.00
39121	Lullaby of the Leaves/Temptation Rag	1950	5.00	10.00	20.00
3-39121	Lullaby of the Leaves/Temptation Rag	1950	7.50	15.00	30.00
—Microgroove 7-inch, 33 1/3 rpm, small hole single					
39277	Don't Be That Way/The Man I Love	1951	3.00	6.00	12.00
39278	One O'Clock Jump/Avalon	1951	3.00	6.00	12.00
39279	One O'Clock Jump/Body and Soul	1951	3.00	6.00	12.00
39280	Dixieland One Step/Jam Session	1951	3.00	6.00	12.00
39281	Shine/Blue Reverie	1951	3.00	6.00	12.00
39282	Life Goes to a Party (Beginning)/Life Goes to a Party (Conclusion)	1951	3.00	6.00	12.00
39284	Blue Skies/Sing, Sing, Sing (Conclusion)	1951	3.00	6.00	12.00
39285	Loch Lomond/Sing, Sing, Sing (Beginning)	1951	3.00	6.00	12.00
39286	Swingtime in the Rockies/Dizzy Spells (Conclusion)	1951	3.00	6.00	12.00
39287	Bei Mir Bist Du Schoen/Stompin' at the Savoy (Conclusion)-Dizzy Spells (Beginning)	1951	3.00	6.00	12.00
39288	China Boy/Stompin' at the Savoy	1951	3.00	6.00	12.00
39304	Don't Be That Way/Sing, Sing, Sing (Conclusion)	1951	3.00	6.00	12.00
39305	One O'Clock Jump (Beginning)/Sing, Sing, Sing (Continuation)	1951	3.00	6.00	12.00
39306	One O'Clock Jump (Conclusion)/Sing, Sing, Sing (Beginning)	1951	3.00	6.00	12.00
39307	Dixieland One Step-I'm Coming Virginia-When My Baby Smiles at Me/Dizzy Spells (Conclusion)-Big John's Special	1951	3.00	6.00	12.00
39308	Shine-Blue Reverie/Stompin' at the Savoy (Conclusion)-Dizzy Spells (Beginning)	1951	3.00	6.00	12.00
39309	Life Goes to a Parrty/Stompin' at the Savoy (Beginning)	1951	3.00	6.00	12.00
39310	Jam Session (Beginning)/China Boy	1951	3.00	6.00	12.00
39311	Jam Session (Continuation)/Bei Mir Bist Du Schoen	1951	3.00	6.00	12.00
39312	Blue Moon/Swingtime in the Rockies	1951	3.00	6.00	12.00
39313	Body and Soul/Loch Lomond	1951	3.00	6.00	12.00
39314	Avalon/Blue Skies	1951	3.00	6.00	12.00
39315	The Man I Love/I Got Rhythm	1951	3.00	6.00	12.00
39416	South of the Border/Down South CampMeeting'	1951	3.75	7.50	15.00
39478	The Wang-Wang Blues/It Never Entered My Mind	1951	3.75	7.50	15.00
39564	Farewell Blues/King Porter Stomp	1951	3.75	7.50	15.00
39741	Jersey Bounce/You'll Never Walk Alone	1952	5.00	10.00	20.00
—B-side by Frank Sinatra					
39976	I'll Never Say "Never Again" Again/What a Little Moonlight Can Do	1952	3.75	7.50	15.00
40616	Memories of You/It's Bad for Me	1955	3.00	6.00	12.00
—With Rosemary Clooney					
40625	A Fine Romance/Goodbye	1955	3.00	6.00	12.00
—With Rosemary Clooney					
COMMAND					
4104	Peace/Hava Nagila	1967	—	3.00	6.00
4108	Mimi/Petite Fleur	1967	—	3.00	6.00
DECCA					
25548	Don't Be That Way/Jersey Bounce	1962	2.50	5.00	10.00
RCA VICTOR					
47-2953	Don't Be That Way/My Melancholy Baby	1949	3.75	7.50	15.00
47-2954	Tiger Rag/Alexander's Ragtime Band	1949	3.75	7.50	15.00
47-2973	Jingle Bells/Santa Claus Is Coming to Town	1949	5.00	10.00	20.00
7-Inch Extended Plays					
COLUMBIA					
B-2556	On the Sunny Side of the Street/Where or When//Blues in the Night/The Way You Look Tonight	195?	3.75	7.50	15.00
B-2556 [PS]	Benny Goodman Sextet with Peggy Lee	195?	3.75	7.50	15.00
B-2587	Why Don't You Do It Right/Flying Home// Someday Sweetheart/Down South Camp Meeting	195?	3.00	6.00	12.00
B-2587 [PS]	Benny Goodman (Hall of Fame Series)	195?	3.00	6.00	12.00
B-8201	Sing Sing Sing (With a Swing) (Beginning)/Sing Sing Sing (With a Swing) (Conclusion)	195?	3.75	7.50	15.00
Albums					
AIRCHECK					
16	Benny Goodman and His Orchestra	197?	3.00	6.00	12.00
16	Benny Goodman and His Orchestra On the Air, Vol. 1	1986	2.50	5.00	10.00
—Reissue of above with revised title					
32	Benny Goodman and His Orchestra On the Air, Vol. 2	1986	2.50	5.00	10.00
34	Benny Goodman and His Orchestra On the Air, Vol. 3	1986	2.50	5.00	10.00
ARCHIVE OF FOLK AND JAZZ					
277	Benny Goodman	1973	3.00	6.00	12.00
BIOGRAPH					
C-1	Great Soloist 1929-33	197?	2.50	5.00	10.00
BLUEBIRD					
AXM2-5505 [(2)]	The Complete Benny Goodman, Vol. 1 (1935)	197?	3.00	6.00	12.00
AXM2-5515 [(2)]	The Complete Benny Goodman, Vol. 2 (1935-36)	197?	3.00	6.00	12.00
AXM2-5532 [(2)]	The Complete Benny Goodman, Vol. 3 (1936)	197?	3.00	6.00	12.00
AXM2-5537 [(2)]	The Complete Benny Goodman, Vol. 4 (1936-37)	197?	3.00	6.00	12.00
AXM2-5557 [(2)]	The Complete Benny Goodman, Vol. 5 (1937-38)	197?	3.00	6.00	12.00
AXM2-5566 [(2)]	The Complete Benny Goodman, Vol. 6 (1938)	197?	3.00	6.00	12.00
AXM2-5567 [(2)]	The Complete Benny Goodman, Vol. 7 (1938-39)	197?	3.00	6.00	12.00
AXM2-5568 [(2)]	The Complete Benny Goodman, Vol. 8 (1936-39)	197?	3.00	6.00	12.00
BRUNSWICK					
BL 54010 [M]	Benny Goodman 1927-34	1954	7.50	15.00	30.00
BL 58015 [10]	Chicago Jazz Classics	1950	12.50	25.00	50.00
CAPITOL					
H 202 [10]	Session for Six	1950	12.50	25.00	50.00
H 295 [10]	Easy Does It	1952	12.50	25.00	50.00
H 343 [10]	The Benny Goodman Trio	1952	12.50	25.00	50.00
T 395 [M]	Session for Six	1953	10.00	20.00	40.00
—Turquoise label					
T 395 [M]	Session for Six	1958	5.00	10.00	20.00
—Black label with colorband, Capitol logo on left					
H 409 [10]	The Benny Goodman Band	1953	12.50	25.00	50.00
T 409 [M]	The Benny Goodman Band	1953	10.00	20.00	40.00
—Turquoise label					
T 409 [M]	The Benny Goodman Band	1958	5.00	10.00	20.00
—Black label with colorband, Capitol logo on left					
H 441 [10]	The Goodman Touch	1953	12.50	25.00	50.00
T 441 [M]	The Goodman Touch	1953	10.00	20.00	40.00
—Turquoise label					
T 441 [M]	The Goodman Touch	1958	5.00	10.00	20.00
—Black label with colorband, Capitol logo on left					
H 479 [10]	Small Combo 1947	1954	12.50	25.00	50.00
H1-565 [10]	B.G. in Hi-Fi (Volume 1)	1955	7.50	15.00	30.00
H2-565 [10]	B.G. in Hi-Fi (Volume 2)	1955	7.50	15.00	30.00
W 565 [M]	B.G. in Hi-Fi	1955	10.00	20.00	40.00
—Turquoise label					
W 565 [M]	B.G. in Hi-Fi	1958	5.00	10.00	20.00
—Black label with colorband, Capitol logo on left					
T 668 [M]	Mostly Sextets	1956	7.50	15.00	30.00
—Turquoise label					
T 668 [M]	Mostly Sextets	1958	5.00	10.00	20.00
—Black label with colorband, Capitol logo on left					
T 669 [M]	Benny Goodman Combos	1956	7.50	15.00	30.00
—Turquoise label					
T 669 [M]	Benny Goodman Combos	1958	5.00	10.00	20.00
—Black label with colorband, Capitol logo on left					
S 706 [M]	Selections Featured in "The Benny Goodman Story"	1956	7.50	15.00	30.00
—Turquoise label					
S 706 [M]	Selections Featured in "The Benny Goodman Story"	1958	5.00	10.00	20.00
—Black label with colorband, Capitol logo on left					
SM-706	Selections Featured in "The Benny Goodman Story"	197?	2.50	5.00	10.00
—Reissue of S 706					
DT 1514 [R]	The Hits of Benny Goodman	1961	3.00	6.00	12.00
SM-1514	The Hits of Benny Goodman	197?	2.50	5.00	10.00
—Reissue of DT 1514					
T 1514 [M]	The Hits of Benny Goodman	1961	5.00	10.00	20.00
—Black label with colorband, Capitol logo on left					
T 1514 [M]	The Hits of Benny Goodman	1963	3.75	7.50	15.00
—Black label with colorband, Capitol logo on top					
ST 2157 [S]	Hello Benny!	1964	3.75	7.50	15.00
T 2157 [M]	Hello Benny!	1964	3.00	6.00	12.00
ST 2282 [S]	Made in Japan	1965	3.75	7.50	15.00
T 2282 [M]	Made in Japan	1965	3.00	6.00	12.00
CENTURY					
1150	The King of Swing Direct to Disc	1979	7.50	15.00	30.00
—Direct-to-disc audiophile recording					
CHESS					
LP-1440 [DJ]	Benny Rides Again	1960	25.00	50.00	100.00
—Multi-color swirl vinyl					
LP-1440 [M]	Benny Rides Again	1960	12.50	25.00	50.00
LPS-1440 [S]	Benny Rides Again	1960	7.50	15.00	30.00
CLASSICS RECORD LIBRARY					
RL-7673 [(3) M]	An Album of Swing Classics	1967	12.50	25.00	50.00
RLS-7673 [(3) S]	An Album of Swing Classics	1967	10.00	20.00	40.00
—Above two were compiled for Book-of-the-Month Club					
COLUMBIA					
GL 102 [10]	Let's Hear the Melody	1950	15.00	30.00	60.00
CL 500 [M]	Combos	1952	10.00	20.00	40.00
—Maroon label with gold print					
CL 500 [M]	Combos	1955	7.50	15.00	30.00
—Red and black label with six "eye" logos					
GL 500 [M]	Combos	1951	12.50	25.00	50.00
—Black label, silver print					
CL 501 [M]	Bands	1952	10.00	20.00	40.00
—Maroon label with gold print					
CL 501 [M]	Bands	1955	7.50	15.00	30.00
—Red and black label with six "eye" logos					
GL 501 [M]	Bands	1951	12.50	25.00	50.00
—Black label, silver print					
CL 516 [M]	The Benny Goodman Trio Plays for the Fletcher Henderson Fund	1953	10.00	20.00	40.00
—Maroon label with gold print					
CL 516 [M]	The Benny Goodman Trio Plays for the Fletcher Henderson Fund	1955	7.50	15.00	30.00
—Red and black label with six "eye" logos					
GL 516 [M]	The Benny Goodman Trio Plays for the Fletcher Henderson Fund	1952	12.50	25.00	50.00
—Reissue of Martin Block 1000; black label, silver print					
CL 523 [M]	Benny Goodman Presents Eddie Sauter Arrangements	1953	10.00	20.00	40.00
—Maroon label with gold print					
CL 523 [M]	Benny Goodman Presents Eddie Sauter Arrangements	1955	7.50	15.00	30.00
—Red and black label with six "eye" logos					
GL 523 [M]	Benny Goodman Presents Eddie Sauter Arrangements	1953	12.50	25.00	50.00
—Black label, silver print					

Number	Title (A Side/B Side)	Yr	VG	VG+	NM
CL 524 [M]	Benny Goodman Presents Fletcher Henderson Arrangements	1953	7.50	15.00	30.00
—Red and black label with six "eye" logos					
CL 524 [M]	Benny Goodman Presents Fletcher Henderson Arrangements	1954	10.00	20.00	40.00
—Maroon label with gold print					
GL 524 [M]	Benny Goodman Presents Fletcher Henderson Arrangements	1953	12.50	25.00	50.00
—Black label, silver print					
CL 534 [M]	Benny Goodman and His Orchestra	1953	10.00	20.00	40.00
—Maroon label with gold print					
CL 534 [M]	Benny Goodman and His Orchestra	1955	7.50	15.00	30.00
—Red and black label with six "eye" logos					
CL 552 [M]	The New Benny Goodman Sextet	1954	10.00	20.00	40.00
—Maroon label with gold print					
CL 552 [M]	The New Benny Goodman Sextet	1955	7.50	15.00	30.00
—Red and black label with six "eye" logos					
CL 652 [M]	The Benny Goodman Sextet and Orchestra with Charlie Christian	1955	7.50	15.00	30.00
—Red and black label with six "eye" logos					
CL 652 [M]	The Benny Goodman Sextet and Orchestra with Charlie Christian	1963	5.00	10.00	20.00
—Red label with "Guaranteed High Fidelity" or "Mono" at bottom					
CL 814 [M]	Carnegie Hall Jazz Concert, Volume 1	1956	7.50	15.00	30.00
—Red and black label with six "eye" logos					
CL 814 [M]	Carnegie Hall Jazz Concert, Volume 1	1963	5.00	10.00	20.00
—Red label with "Guaranteed High Fidelity" or "Mono" at bottom					
CL 815 [M]	Carnegie Hall Jazz Concert, Volume 2	1956	7.50	15.00	30.00
—Red and black label with six "eye" logos					
CL 815 [M]	Carnegie Hall Jazz Concert, Volume 2	1963	5.00	10.00	20.00
—Red label with "Guaranteed High Fidelity" or "Mono" at bottom					
CL 816 [M]	Carnegie Hall Jazz Concert, Volume 3	1956	7.50	15.00	30.00
—Red and black label with six "eye" logos					
CL 816 [M]	Carnegie Hall Jazz Concert, Volume 3	1963	5.00	10.00	20.00
—Red label with "Guaranteed High Fidelity" or "Mono" at bottom					
CL 817 [M]	The King of Swing, Volume 1	1956	7.50	15.00	30.00
CL 818 [M]	The King of Swing, Volume 2	1956	7.50	15.00	30.00
CL 819 [M]	The King of Swing, Volume 3	1956	7.50	15.00	30.00
CL 820 [M]	The Great Benny Goodman	1956	7.50	15.00	30.00
—Red and black label with six "eye" logos					
CL 820 [M]	The Great Benny Goodman	1963	5.00	10.00	20.00
—Red label with "Guaranteed High Fidelity" or "Mono" at bottom					
CL 821 [M]	Vintage Goodman	1956	7.50	15.00	30.00
CL 1247 [M]	Benny Goodman in Brussels, Volume 1	1958	7.50	15.00	30.00
CL 1248 [M]	Benny Goodman in Brussels, Volume 2	1958	7.50	15.00	30.00
CL 1324 [M]	The Happy Session	1959	7.50	15.00	30.00
CL 1579 [M]	Benny Goodman Swings Again	1960	7.50	15.00	30.00
CL 2483 [M]	Benny Goodman's Greatest Hits	1966	3.75	7.50	15.00
CL 2533 [10]	Benny at the Ballroom	1955	10.00	20.00	40.00
—Retitled reissue of 6100					
CL 2564 [10]	The B.G. Six	1955	10.00	20.00	40.00
—Retitled reissue of 6052					
CL 6033 [10]	Benny Goodman and Peggy Lee	1949	20.00	40.00	80.00
CL 6048 [10]	Dance Parade	1949	12.50	25.00	50.00
CL 6052 [10]	Goodman Sextet Session	1949	12.50	25.00	50.00
CL 6100 [10]	Dance Parade, Volume 2	1950	12.50	25.00	50.00
CL 6302 [10]	Let's Hear the Melody	1951	12.50	25.00	50.00
—Reissue of GL 102					
CS 8075 [S]	Benny Goodman in Brussels, Volume ?	1959	10.00	20.00	40.00
CS 8129 [S]	The Happy Session	1959	6.25	12.50	25.00
CS 8379 [S]	Benny Goodman Swings Again	1960	6.25	12.50	25.00
CS 8643 [R]	The Great Benny Goodman	1962	3.00	6.00	12.00
PC 8643	The Great Benny Goodman	198?	2.00	4.00	8.00
—Reissue					
CS 9283 [S]	Benny Goodman's Greatest Hits	1966	3.00	6.00	12.00
—"360 Sound Stereo" on label					
PC 9283	Benny Goodman's Greatest Hits	198?	2.00	4.00	8.00
—Reissue					
XTV 28995/6 [M]	Swing Into Spring	1959	5.00	10.00	20.00
—Special item made for Texaco service stations					
KG 31547 [(2)]	The All-Time Greatest Hits of Benny Goodman	1972	3.75	7.50	15.00
PG 31547 [(2)]	The All-Time Greatest Hits of Benny Goodman	197?	3.00	6.00	12.00
—Reissue					
PG 33405 [(2)]	Solid Gold Instrumentals	1975	3.00	6.00	12.00
FC 38265	Seven Come Eleven	1983	2.50	5.00	10.00
COLUMBIA MASTERWORKS					
OSL 160 [(2) M]	Carnegie Hall Jazz Concert	1956	18.75	37.50	75.00
—Gray and black labels with six "eye" logos					
OSL 160 [(2) M]	Carnegie Hall Jazz Concert	1963	10.00	20.00	40.00
—Gray labels with "Columbia" at top					
SL 160 [(2) M]	Carnegie Hall Jazz Concert	1950	25.00	50.00	100.00
—Green labels					
SL 176 [(6) M]	King of Swing	1950	37.50	75.00	150.00
OSL 180 [(2) M]	The King of Swing	1956	18.75	37.50	75.00
—Gray and black labels with six "eye" logos					
OSL 180 [(2) M]	The King of Swing	1963	10.00	20.00	40.00
—Gray labels with "Columbia" at top					
SL 180 [(2) M]	1937-38 Jazz Concert No. 2	1950	18.75	37.50	75.00
ML 4358 [M]	Carnegie Hall Jazz Concert, Volume 1	1950	10.00	20.00	40.00
ML 4359 [M]	Carnegie Hall Jazz Concert, Volume 2	1950	10.00	20.00	40.00
ML 4590 [M]	1937-38 Jazz Concert No. 2, Volume 1	1950	10.00	20.00	40.00
ML 4591 [M]	1937-38 Jazz Concert No. 2, Volume 2	1950	10.00	20.00	40.00
ML 4613 [M]	King of Swing, Volume 1	1950	10.00	20.00	40.00
ML 4614 [M]	King of Swing, Volume 2	1950	10.00	20.00	40.00
ML 6205 [M]	Meeting at the Summit	1961	3.75	7.50	15.00
—With the Columbia Jazz Combo and the Columbia Orchestra					
MS 6805 [S]	Meeting at the Summit	1961	5.00	10.00	20.00
—With the Columbia Jazz Combo and the Columbia Orchestra					
COLUMBIA MUSICAL TREASURY					
P4M 5678 [(4)]	The Best of Benny Goodman	197?	7.50	15.00	30.00
—Issued by Columbia House					
COMMAND					
RS-921	Benny Goodman & Paris: Listen to the Magic	1967	3.75	7.50	15.00
DECCA					
DXB 188 [(2) M]	The Benny Goodman Story	1956	15.00	30.00	60.00
—Black label, silver print					
DXB 188 [(2) M]	The Benny Goodman Story	1961	10.00	20.00	40.00
—Black label with color bars					
DXSB 7188 [(2) R]	The Benny Goodman Story	196?	3.75	7.50	15.00
DL 8252 [M]	The Benny Goodman Story, Volume 1	1956	7.50	15.00	30.00
—Black label, silver print					
DL 8252 [M]	The Benny Goodman Story, Volume 1	1961	5.00	10.00	20.00
—Black label with color bars					
DL 8253 [M]	The Benny Goodman Story, Volume 2	1956	7.50	15.00	30.00
—Black label, silver print					
DL 8253 [M]	The Benny Goodman Story, Volume 2	1961	5.00	10.00	20.00
—Black label with color bars					
DL 78252 [R]	The Benny Goodman Story, Volume 1	1961	2.50	5.00	10.00
DL 78253 [R]	The Benny Goodman Story, Volume 2	1961	2.50	5.00	10.00
DOCTOR JAZZ					
W2X 40350 [(2)]	Airplay	1986	3.00	6.00	12.00
GIANTS OF JAZZ					
1030	The Benny Goodman Caravans — Big Band Broadcasts Vol. 1: Ciribiribin	1985	2.50	5.00	10.00
1033	The Benny Goodman Caravans — Big Band Broadcasts Vol. 2: Swingin' Down the Lane	1985	2.50	5.00	10.00
1034	The Benny Goodman Caravans — The Small Groups, Vol. 1	1985	2.50	5.00	10.00
1036	The Benny Goodman Caravans — Big Band Broadcasts Vol. 3: One O'Clock Jump	1985	2.50	5.00	10.00
1039	The Benny Goodman Caravans — Big Band Broadcasts Vol. 4: Sing, Sing, Sing	1985	2.50	5.00	10.00
HARMONY					
HL 7005 [M]	Peggy Lee Sings with Benny Goodman	1957	5.00	10.00	20.00
HL 7190 [M]	Swing with Benny Goodman in High Fidelity	196?	3.75	7.50	15.00
HL 7225 [M]	Swing Time	196?	3.75	7.50	15.00
HL 7278 [M]	Swingin' Benny Goodman Sextet	196?	3.75	7.50	15.00
HS 11090 [R]	Swing with Benny Goodman in High Fidelity	196?	2.50	5.00	10.00
HS 11271 [R]	Sing, Sing, Sing	1968	2.50	5.00	10.00
INTERMEDIA					
QS-5046	All the Cats Join In	198?	2.50	5.00	10.00
LONDON					
PS 918/9 [(2)]	Live at Carnegie Hall 1978	1979	3.75	7.50	15.00
LONDON PHASE 4					
SPB-21 [(2)]	Benny Goodman Today	1971	3.75	7.50	15.00
SP-44182/3 [(2)]	Benny Goodman On Stage	1972	3.75	7.50	15.00
MARTIN BLOCK					
MB-1000 [M]	The Benny Goodman Trio Plays for the Fletcher Henderson Fund	1951	15.00	30.00	60.00
MCA					
4018 [(2)]	Jazz Holiday	197?	3.00	6.00	12.00
MEGA					
606	Let's Dance Again	1974	2.50	5.00	10.00
—Reissue of 51-5002					
51-5002	Let's Dance Again	1971	3.00	6.00	12.00
MGM					
3E-9 [(3) M]	The Benny Goodman Treasure Chest	1959	37.50	75.00	150.00
E-3788 [M]	Performance Recordings, Volume 1	1959	6.25	12.50	25.00
E-3788 [M]	The Benny Goodman Treasure Chest, Volume 1	198?	2.00	4.00	8.00
—Reissue on blue and gold label					
E-3789 [M]	Performance Recordings, Volume 2	1959	6.25	12.50	25.00
E-3789 [M]	The Benny Goodman Treasure Chest, Volume 2	198?	2.00	4.00	8.00
—Reissue on blue and gold label					
E-3790 [M]	Performance Recordings, Volume 3	1959	6.25	12.50	25.00
E-3790 [M]	The Benny Goodman Treasure Chest, Volume 3	198?	2.00	4.00	8.00
—Reissue on blue and gold label					
E-3810 [M]	The Sound of Music	1960	5.00	10.00	20.00
SE-3810 [S]	The Sound of Music	1960	6.25	12.50	25.00
MOSAIC					
MQ6-148 [(6)]	The Complete Capitol Small Group Recordings of Benny Goodman 1944-1955	199?	25.00	50.00	100.00
MUSICMASTERS					
MM-20112 Z	Let's Dance	1986	2.50	5.00	10.00
—From the PBS TV special of 1985					
PAIR					
PDL2-1014 [(2)]	Original Recordings by Benny Goodman	1986	3.00	6.00	12.00
PDL2-1054 [(2)]	Original Recordings by Benny Goodman, Volume 2	1986	3.00	6.00	12.00
PDL2-1093 [(2)]	Original Recordings by Benny Goodman, Volume 3	1986	3.00	6.00	12.00
PAUSA					
9031	The Benny Goodman Trios (and One Duet)	198?	2.50	5.00	10.00
PICKWICK					
SPC-3270	Let's Dance	197?	2.50	5.00	10.00
SPC-3529	Francaise	197?	2.50	5.00	10.00
PRESTIGE					
PRST-7644	Benny Goodman and the Giants of Swing	1969	3.75	7.50	15.00
RCA CAMDEN					
CAL-624 [M]	Swing, Swing, Swing	1960	3.75	7.50	15.00
CAS-624(e) [R]	Swing, Swing, Swing	1960	2.50	5.00	10.00
CAL-872 [M]	Benny Goodman and His Orchestra Featuring Great Vocalists of Our Times	1965	3.75	7.50	15.00
CAS-872 [S]	Benny Goodman and His Orchestra Featuring Great Vocalists of Our Times	1965	3.00	6.00	12.00
RCA VICTOR					
WPT 12 [10]	Benny Goodman	1951	12.50	25.00	50.00
LPT-17 [10]	A Treasury of Immortal Performances	1951	12.50	25.00	50.00
WPT 26 [10]	Immortal Performances	1952	12.50	25.00	50.00
LPV-521 [M]	B.G. The Small Groups	1965	3.75	7.50	15.00
ANL1-0973	Pure Gold	1974	2.50	5.00	10.00
LPT-1005 [M]	Benny Goodman	1954	10.00	20.00	40.00
LPM-1099 [M]	The Golden Age of Benny Goodman	1955	10.00	20.00	40.00
LPM-1226 [M]	The Benny Goodman Trio/Quartet/Quintet	1956	10.00	20.00	40.00
LPM-1239 [M]	This Is Benny Goodman	1956	10.00	20.00	40.00
LPM-2247 [M]	The Kingdom of Swing	1960	5.00	10.00	20.00
LSP-2247 [S]	The Kingdom of Swing	1960	6.25	12.50	25.00
CPL1-2470	A Legendary Performer	1977	2.50	5.00	10.00
LPM-2968 [M]	Together Again	1964	3.75	7.50	15.00
LSP-2968 [S]	Together Again	1964	5.00	10.00	20.00

Number	Title (A Side/B Side)	Yr	VG	VG+	NM
LPT-3004 [10]	Benny Goodman Quartet	1952	12.50	25.00	50.00
LPT-3056 [10]	This Is Benny Goodman and His Orchestra	1954	12.50	25.00	50.00
AFL1-4005(e)	The Best of Benny Goodman	1977	2.50	5.00	10.00
—Reissue of LSP-4005					
LSP-4005	The Best of Benny Goodman	1968	3.75	7.50	15.00
LOC-6008 [(2) M]	Benny Goodman in Moscow	1962	5.00	10.00	20.00
LSO-6008 [(2) S]	Benny Goodman in Moscow	1962	6.25	12.50	25.00
VPM-6040 [(2)]	This Is Benny Goodman	1972	3.75	7.50	15.00
VPM-6063 [(2)]	This Is Benny Goodman, Vol. 2	1973	3.75	7.50	15.00
LPT-6703 [(5) M]	The Golden Age of Swing	1956	150.00	300.00	600.00
—Five-record set in white vinyl binder with bound-in booklet					
SUNBEAM					
100	The Let's Dance Broadcasts 1934-35, Volume 1	197?	2.50	5.00	10.00
104	The Let's Dance Broadcasts 1934-35, Volume 2	197?	2.50	5.00	10.00
105	Benny Goodman On the Air 1935-36, Volume 1	197?	2.50	5.00	10.00
106	Benny Goodman In a Mellotone Manner 1930-31	197?	2.50	5.00	10.00
107	Benny Goodman On the Side 1929-31	197?	2.50	5.00	10.00
111	Benny Goodman Accompanies Girls 1931-33	197?	2.50	5.00	10.00
112	Rare Benny Goodman 1927-29	197?	2.50	5.00	10.00
113	The Hotsy Totsy Gang 1928-29	197?	2.50	5.00	10.00
114	Whoopee Makers 1928-29	197?	2.50	5.00	10.00
116/27 [(12)]	Manhattan Room 1937	197?	15.00	30.00	60.00
128/32 [(5)]	From the Congress Hotel, Chicago, 1935-36	197?	6.25	12.50	25.00
133	Benny Goodman 1933	197?	2.50	5.00	10.00
135	Benny Goodman and the Modernists 1934-35	197?	2.50	5.00	10.00
138	Benny Goodman and His Orchestra 1931-33, Volume 1	197?	2.50	5.00	10.00
139	Benny Goodman and His Orchestra 1931-33, Volume 2	197?	2.50	5.00	10.00
140	Benny Goodman and His Orchestra 1931-33, Volume 3	197?	2.50	5.00	10.00
141	The Benny Goodman Boys 1928-29	197?	2.50	5.00	10.00
142	Benny Goodman On V-Disc 1939-48, Volume 1	197?	2.50	5.00	10.00
143	Benny Goodman On V-Disc 1939-48, Volume 2	197?	2.50	5.00	10.00
144	Benny Goodman On V-Disc 1939-48, Volume 3	197?	2.50	5.00	10.00
145	Fitch Bandwagon 1945	197?	2.50	5.00	10.00
146	Camel Caravan 1937, Volume 1	197?	2.50	5.00	10.00
147	Camel Caravan 1937, Volume 2	197?	2.50	5.00	10.00
148	Benny Goodman 1934	197?	2.50	5.00	10.00
149	Jam Session 1935-37	197?	2.50	5.00	10.00
150	The Let's Dance Broadcasts 1934-35, Volume 3	197?	2.50	5.00	10.00
151	The Benny Goodman Show 1946	197?	2.50	5.00	10.00
152 [(2)]	Benny Goodman and His Orchestra 1937-38	197?	3.00	6.00	12.00
153	Benny Goodman On the Air 1935-36, Volume 2	197?	2.50	5.00	10.00
154	Benny Goodman 1946	197?	2.50	5.00	10.00
156	Broadcasts from Hollywood 1946-47	197?	2.50	5.00	10.00
VERVE					
MGV-4013 [M]	The Superlative Goodman, Volume 1	1958	—	—	—
—Canceled					
MGV-4014 [M]	The Superlative Goodman, Volume 2	1958	—	—	—
—Canceled					
MGV-4015-2 [(2) M]	The Superlative Goodman	1958	—	—	—
—Canceled					
V-8582 [M]	The Essential Benny Goodman	1964	3.75	7.50	15.00
V6-8582 [S]	The Essential Benny Goodman	1964	3.75	7.50	15.00
WESTINGHOUSE					
(no #) [M]	Benny Goodman Plays World Favorites in High Fidelity	1958	7.50	15.00	30.00
(no #) [(5) M]	Benny in Brussels	1958	25.00	50.00	100.00

GOODMAN, BENNY/CHARLIE BARNET

Albums

Number	Title (A Side/B Side)	Yr	VG	VG+	NM
CAPITOL					
M-11061	BeBop Spoken Here	197?	3.00	6.00	12.00

GOODMAN, DICKIE

Also see BUCHANAN AND GOODMAN; JOHN AND ERNEST; SPENCER AND SPENCER.

45s

Number	Title (A Side/B Side)	Yr	VG	VG+	NM
20TH FOX					
443	Senate Hearing/Lock-Up	1963	3.75	7.50	15.00
ASI					
1013	Rocky and the Angel/Pug Rock	1977	—	3.00	6.00
—As "Dickie G. and the Don'ts"					
AUDIO SPECTRUM					
75	Presidential Interview (Flying Saucer '64)/Paul Revere	1964	10.00	20.00	40.00
CASH					
451	Mr. Jaws/Irv's Theme	1975	—	2.50	5.00
COTIQUE					
158	On Campus/Mombo Suzie	1969	—	3.00	6.00
—B-side by Johnny Colo					
173	Luna Trip/My Victrola	1969	—	3.00	6.00
—B-side by Joey Pastrana					
DAVY JONES					
663	White House Happening/President Johnson	1967	6.25	12.50	25.00
663 [PS]	White House Happening/President Johnson	1967	10.00	20.00	40.00
DIAMOND					
119	Ben Crazy/Flip Side	1962	3.75	7.50	15.00
EXTRAN					
601	Hey, E.T./Get a Job	1982	—	2.50	5.00
GOODNAME					
7100	Safe Sex Report/Safety First	1987	3.75	7.50	15.00
—His last record					
HOT LINE					
1017	Energy Crisis '79/Pain	1979	—	3.00	6.00
JANUS					
271	Star Warts/The Boys Tune	1977	—	2.50	5.00
J.M.D.					
001	Ben Crazy/Flip Side	1962	6.25	12.50	25.00
MARK-X					
8009	The Touchables/Martian Melody	1961	7.50	15.00	30.00
—Yellow label					
8009	The Touchables/Martian Melody	1961	5.00	10.00	20.00
—Black label					
8010	The Touchables in Brooklyn/Mystery	1961	5.00	10.00	20.00
MONTAGE					
1220	Hey, E.T./The Ride of Paul Revere	1982	3.75	7.50	15.00
1220 [DJ]	Hey, E.T. (same on both sides)	1982	—	2.50	5.00
M.D.					
101	Schmonanza/Backwards Theme	1961	5.00	10.00	20.00
ORON					
101	Washington Uptight/The Cat	1967	6.25	12.50	25.00
—As "The Pennsylvania Players"					
PRELUDE					
8018	Election '80 (same on both sides)	1980	—	2.50	5.00
RAINY WEDNESDAY					
202	Watergrate/Friends	1973	—	3.00	6.00
204	Purple People Eater/Ruthie's Theme	1973	—	3.00	6.00
205	The Constitution/The End	1973	—	3.00	6.00
206	Energy Crisis '74/The Mistake	1974	—	3.00	6.00
206	Energy Crisis '74/Ruthie's Theme	1974	2.00	4.00	8.00
207	Mr. President/Popularity	1974	—	3.00	6.00
208	Gerry Ford, A Special Report/Robert	1974	—	3.00	6.00
209	Inflation in the Nation/Jon and Jed's Theme	1975	—	3.00	6.00
RAMGO					
501	Speaking of Ecology/Dayton's Theme	1970	6.25	12.50	25.00
RED BIRD					
10-058	Batman & His Grandmother/Suspense	1966	5.00	10.00	20.00
RHINO					
019	Radio Russia/Washington Inside Out	1984	—	2.00	4.00
RORI					
601	Horror Movies/Whoa, Mule	1961	6.25	12.50	25.00
602	The Berlin Top Ten/Little Tiger	1961	6.25	12.50	25.00
701	Santa and the Touchables/North Pole Rock	1961	6.25	12.50	25.00
SCEPTER					
12339	Speaking of Ecology/Dayton's Theme	1971	3.00	6.00	12.00
SHARK					
1001	Mrs. Jaws/(B-side unknown)	1979	5.00	10.00	20.00
1002	Super Superman/Chomp Chomp	1979	3.75	7.50	15.00
SHELL					
711	Election '84/Herb's Theme	1984	—	2.00	4.00
SHOCK					
6	Kong/Ed's Tune	1977	—	2.50	5.00
TWIRL					
2015	James Bomb/Seventh Theme	1966	3.75	7.50	15.00
WACKO					
1001	Mr. President/Dancin' U.S.A.	1981	—	2.50	5.00
1002	Super-Duper Man/Robert's Tune	1981	—	2.50	5.00
1381	America '81/(B-side unknown)	1981	2.00	4.00	8.00
Z-100					
100 [DJ]	Attack of the Z Monster/Mystery	1984	2.50	5.00	10.00
—Promo item for New York radio station					

Albums

Number	Title (A Side/B Side)	Yr	VG	VG+	NM
CASH					
CR 6000	Mr. Jaws and Other Fables	1975	6.25	12.50	25.00
COMET					
69	My Son, the Joke	1963	10.00	20.00	40.00
IX CHAINS					
NCS 9000	The Original Flying Saucers	1973	10.00	20.00	40.00
RHINO					
RNLP-811	Dickie Goodman's Greatest Hits	1983	3.75	7.50	15.00
RORI					
3301	The Many Heads of Dickie Goodman	1962	20.00	40.00	80.00

GOODMAN, JERRY, AND JAN HAMMER

Albums

Number	Title (A Side/B Side)	Yr	VG	VG+	NM
NEMPEROR					
SD 430	Like Children	1975	2.50	5.00	10.00

GOODMAN, SHIRLEY

Of SHIRLEY AND LEE; also of SHIRLEY (AND COMPANY).

45s

Number	Title (A Side/B Side)	Yr	VG	VG+	NM
IMPERIAL					
5944	When a Boy Meets a Girl/Don't Marry Too Soon	1963	3.00	6.00	12.00

GOODMAN, STEVE

45s

Number	Title (A Side/B Side)	Yr	VG	VG+	NM
ASYLUM					
45284	Jessie's Jig (Rob's Romp, Beth's Bounce)/It's a Sin to Tell a Lie	1975	—	3.00	6.00
45331	Between the Lines/Can't Go Back	1976	—	3.00	6.00
45481	Video Tape/My Old Man	1978	—	3.00	6.00
46012	Men Who Love Women Who Love Men/The One That Got Away	1979	—	3.00	6.00
46522	Men Who Love Women Who Love Men/The One That Got Away	1979	—	2.50	5.00
47107	Bobby Don't Stop/Trust Me	1981	—	2.50	5.00
BUDDAH					
270	City of New Orleans/(B-side unknown)	1971	3.00	6.00	12.00
326	Election Year Rag/Someone Else's Troubles	1972	2.50	5.00	10.00
348	The Dutchman/Song for David	1973	2.50	5.00	10.00
RED PAJAMA					
1001	A Dying Cub Fan's Last Request/Take Me Out to the Ball Game	1981	2.50	5.00	10.00
WGN					
784	Go Cubs Go (WGN Radio Cubs Theme) (same on both sides)	1984	2.00	4.00	8.00

Albums

Number	Title (A Side/B Side)	Yr	VG	VG+	NM
ASYLUM					
6E-174	High and Outside	1979	3.00	6.00	12.00
6E-297	Hot Spot	1980	3.00	6.00	12.00
7E-1037	Jessie's Jig & Other Favorites	1975	3.00	6.00	12.00

Number	Title (A Side/B Side)	Yr	VG	VG+	NM
7E-1061	Words We Can Dance To	1976	3.00	6.00	12.00
7E-1118	Say It in Private	1977	3.00	6.00	12.00
BUDDAH					
BDS 5096	Steve Goodman	1971	3.75	7.50	15.00
BDS 5121	Somebody Else's Troubles	1972	3.75	7.50	15.00
BDS 5665 [(2)]	The Essential Steve Goodman	1976	3.75	7.50	15.00
RED PAJAMAS					
RPJ-001	Artistic Hair	1982	3.00	6.00	12.00
RPJ-002	Affordable Art	1983	3.00	6.00	12.00
RPJ-003	Santa Ana Winds	1984	3.00	6.00	12.00
RPJ-005	Unfinished Business	1985	3.00	6.00	12.00
RPJ-006	Best of the Asylum Years, Vol. 1	198?	3.00	6.00	12.00
RPJ-007	Best of the Asylum Years, Vol. 2	198?	3.00	6.00	12.00

GOODMAN, STEVE, AND PHOEBE SNOW

Also see each artist's individual listings.

Number	Title (A Side/B Side)	Yr	VG	VG+	NM
45s					
ASYLUM					
47069	Sometimes Love Forgets/Can't Find My Heart	1980	—	2.50	5.00

GOODTIMERS, THE

See DON COVAY.

GOONS, THE

Number	Title (A Side/B Side)	Yr	VG	VG+	NM
45s					
LONDON					
1684	I'm Walking Backwards for Christmas/Bluebottle Blues	1956	6.25	12.50	25.00

GOOSE CREEK SYMPHONY

Number	Title (A Side/B Side)	Yr	VG	VG+	NM
45s					
CAPITOL					
2729	Big Time Saturday Nite/Beautiful Bertha	1970	—	3.00	6.00
2853	Charlie's Tune/No News Is Good News	1970	—	3.00	6.00
3246	(Oh Lord Won't You Buy Me a) Mercedes Benz/Rich on Love	1971	—	2.50	5.00
3371	Guitars Pickin', Fiddles Playin'/Broken Creek Goose Down	1972	—	2.50	5.00
COLUMBIA					
10062	Hot Dog Daddy/Plans of the Lord	1974	—	2.50	5.00
Albums					
CAPITOL					
SM-444	Goose Creek Symphony	197?	2.50	5.00	10.00
—Reissue					
ST-444	Goose Creek Symphony	1970	3.75	7.50	15.00
ST-690	Welcome to Goose Creek	1971	3.75	7.50	15.00
ST-11044	Words of Earnest	1972	3.75	7.50	15.00
COLUMBIA					
KC 32918	Do Your Thing But Don't Touch Mine	1974	3.00	6.00	12.00

GORDIAN KNOT, THE

JIM WEATHERLY was in this group.

Number	Title (A Side/B Side)	Yr	VG	VG+	NM
45s					
VERVE					
10595	Year of the Sun/If Only I Could Cry	1968	2.50	5.00	10.00
10612	Broken Down Old Merry-Go-Round/We Must Be Doin' Something Right	1968	2.50	5.00	10.00
Albums					
VERVE					
V-5062 [M]	Tones	1968	7.50	15.00	30.00
—White label promo only (no stock copies were issued in mono)					
V6-5062 [S]	Tones	1968	3.75	7.50	15.00

GORDON, JUSTIN

Number	Title (A Side/B Side)	Yr	VG	VG+	NM
Albums					
DOT					
DLP-3214 [M]	Justin Gordon Swings	1959	10.00	20.00	40.00

GORDON, MIKE, AND THE AGATES

Number	Title (A Side/B Side)	Yr	VG	VG+	NM
45s					
DORE					
681	Rumble ant Newport Beach/Last Call for Dinner	1963	7.50	15.00	30.00
780	Curfew on the Strip/Last Call for Dinner	1966	3.75	7.50	15.00

GORDON, MIKE, AND THE EL TEMPOS

Number	Title (A Side/B Side)	Yr	VG	VG+	NM
45s					
CAT					
101	Why Don't You Do Right/You Got to Give	1954	12.50	25.00	50.00

GORDON, ROSCOE

Number	Title (A Side/B Side)	Yr	VG	VG+	NM
45s					
ABC-PARAMOUNT					
10351	A Girl to Love/As You Walk Away	1962	3.00	6.00	12.00
10407	A Little Bit of Magic/I Want Revenge	1963	3.00	6.00	12.00
10501	I Don't Stand a Chance/That's What You Did	1963	3.00	6.00	12.00
—As "Barbara & Roscoe Gordon"					
CALLA					
145	Just a Little Bit/I Really Love You	1968	2.00	4.00	8.00
CHESS					
1487	Booted/I Love You Till the Day I Die	1951	375.00	750.00	1500.
DUKE					
101	Tell Daddy/Hey Fat Girl	1952	25.00	50.00	100.00
106	T-Model Boogie/New Orleans Woman	1953	12.50	25.00	50.00
109	Too Many Women/Wise to You, Baby	1953	12.50	25.00	50.00
114	Ain't No Use/Roscoe's Mambo	1953	12.50	25.00	50.00
129	Three Can't Love/You Figure It Out	1954	12.50	25.00	50.00
165	Keep On Doggin'/Bad Dream	1957	7.50	15.00	30.00
173	I've Loved and Lost/Tummer Tee	1957	7.50	15.00	30.00
320	Dilly Bop/You'll Never Know	1960	3.75	7.50	15.00
FLIP					
227	Weeping Blues/Just Love Me, Baby	1956	75.00	150.00	300.00
237	The Chicken (Dance with You)/Love for You Baby	1956	12.50	25.00	50.00
OLD TOWN					
1167	Gotta Keep Rollin'/Just a Little at a Time	1964	2.50	5.00	10.00
1175	It Ain't Right/Could This Be Love	1965	2.50	5.00	10.00
—As "Roscoe and Barbara"					
RPM					
324	Saddled the Cow/Ouch, Pretty Baby	1951	100.00	200.00	400.00
336	Dime a Dozen/A New Remedy for Love	1951	62.50	125.00	250.00
344	Booted/Cold, Cold Winter	1952	50.00	100.00	200.00
350	No More Doggin'/Maria	1952	50.00	100.00	200.00
358	New Orleans Woman/I Remember Your Kisses	1952	25.00	50.00	100.00
365	What You Got on Your Mind/Two Kinds of Women	1952	25.00	50.00	100.00
369	Trying/Dream Baby	1952	15.00	30.00	60.00
373	Lucille/Blues for My Baby	1953	15.00	30.00	60.00
379	I'm in Love/Just In from Texas	1953	15.00	30.00	60.00
384	We're All Loaded/Tomorrow May Be Too Late	1953	15.00	30.00	60.00
SUN					
227	Weeping Blues/Just Love Me, Baby	1956	125.00	250.00	500.00
237	The Chicken (Dance with You)/Love for You Baby	1956	50.00	100.00	200.00
257	Shoobie Oobie/Cheese and Crackers	1956	12.50	25.00	50.00
305	Sally Jo/Torro	1958	6.25	12.50	25.00
VEE JAY					
316	A Fool in Love/No More Doggin'	1959	3.75	7.50	15.00
332	Just a Little Bit/Goin' Home	1959	3.75	7.50	15.00
348	Surely I Love You/What You Do to Me	1960	3.75	7.50	15.00
385	What I Wouldn't Do/Let 'Em Try	1961	3.00	6.00	12.00

GORDON 'N ROGERS' INTER-URBAN ELECTRIC A&E PIT CREW & RHYTHM BAND

Number	Title (A Side/B Side)	Yr	VG	VG+	NM
Albums					
CAPITOL					
STAO-276	Bug In!	1969	5.00	10.00	20.00

GORE, LESLEY

Number	Title (A Side/B Side)	Yr	VG	VG+	NM
45s					
A&M					
1710	Give It to Me, Sweet Thing/Immortality	1975	—	2.50	5.00
1710 [PS]	Give It to Me, Sweet Thing/Immortality	1975	—	3.00	6.00
1830	Sometimes/Give It To Me, Sweet Thing	1976	—	2.50	5.00
CREWE					
338	Why Doesn't Love Make Me Happy/Tomorrow's Children	1970	2.50	5.00	10.00
344	When Yesterday Was Tomorrow/Why Me, Why You	1970	2.50	5.00	10.00
601	Back Together/Quiet Love	1971	2.50	5.00	10.00
MANHATTAN					
50039	Since I Don't Have You-It's Only Make Believe/Our Love Was Meant to Be	1986	2.00	4.00	8.00
—With Lou Christie					
MERCURY					
72119	It's My Party/Danny	1963	3.75	7.50	15.00
72119 [PS]	It's My Party/Danny	1963	7.50	15.00	30.00
72143	Judy's Turn to Cry/Just Let Me Cry	1963	3.75	7.50	15.00
72143 [PS]	Judy's Turn to Cry/Just Let Me Cry	1963	6.25	12.50	25.00
72180	She's a Fool/The Old Crowd	1963	3.75	7.50	15.00
72180 [PS]	She's a Fool/The Old Crowd	1963	6.25	12.50	25.00
72206	You Don't Own Me/Run, Bobby, Run	1963	3.75	7.50	15.00
72206 [PS]	You Don't Own Me/Run, Bobby, Run	1963	10.00	20.00	40.00
—With insert (deduct 25% if missing)					
72245	Je Ne Sais Plus/Je N'ose Pas	1964	5.00	10.00	20.00
72259	That's the Way Boys Are/That's the Way the Ball Bounces	1964	2.50	5.00	10.00
72259 [PS]	That's the Way Boys Are/That's the Way the Ball Bounces	1964	5.00	10.00	20.00
72270	I Don't Wanna Be a Loser/It's Gotta Be You	1964	2.50	5.00	10.00
72270 [PS]	I Don't Wanna Be a Loser/It's Gotta Be You	1964	5.00	10.00	20.00
72309	Maybe I Know/Wonder Boy	1964	2.50	5.00	10.00
72309 [PS]	Maybe I Know/Wonder Boy	1964	5.00	10.00	20.00
72352	Hey Now/Sometimes I Wish I Were a Boy	1964	2.50	5.00	10.00
72352 [PS]	Hey Now/Sometimes I Wish I Were a Boy	1964	5.00	10.00	20.00
72372	Look of Love/Little Girl Gone Home	1964	2.50	5.00	10.00
72372 [PS]	Look of Love/Little Girl Gone Home	1964	5.00	10.00	20.00
72412	All of My Life/I Cannot Hope for Anything	1965	2.50	5.00	10.00
72412 [PS]	All of My Life/I Cannot Hope for Anything	1965	5.00	10.00	20.00
72433	Sunshine, Lollipops and Rainbows/You've Come Back	1965	2.50	5.00	10.00
72433 [PS]	Sunshine, Lollipops and Rainbows/You've Come Back	1965	5.00	10.00	20.00
72475	My Town, My Guy and Me/Girl in Love	1965	2.50	5.00	10.00
72475 [PS]	My Town, My Guy and Me/Girl in Love	1965	5.00	10.00	20.00
72513	I Won't Love You Anymore (Sorry)/No Matter What You Do	1966	2.50	5.00	10.00
72513 [PS]	I Won't Love You Anymore (Sorry)/No Matter What You Do	1966	5.00	10.00	20.00
72530	We Know We're in Love/That's What We'll Do	1966	2.50	5.00	10.00
72553	Young Love/I Just Don't Know If I Can	1966	2.50	5.00	10.00
72580	Off and Running/I Don't Care	1966	2.50	5.00	10.00
72611	Maybe Now/Treat Me Like a Lady	1966	2.50	5.00	10.00
72649	California Nights/I'm Goin' Out	1967	2.50	5.00	10.00
72649 [PS]	California Nights/I'm Goin' Out	1967	—	—	—
—Rumored to exist, but without conclusive evidence, we will delete this from future editions					
72683	Summer and Sandy/I'm Fallin' Down	1967	2.50	5.00	10.00
72683 [PS]	Summer and Sandy/I'm Fallin' Down	1967	5.00	10.00	20.00
72726	Brink of Disaster/On a Day Like This	1967	2.50	5.00	10.00
72759	It's a Happening/Magic Colors	1967	2.50	5.00	10.00
72787	Small Talk/Say What You See	1968	3.00	6.00	12.00
72819	He Gives Me Love (La, La, La)/Brand New Me	1968	3.00	6.00	12.00
72842	Where Can I Go/I Can't Make It Without You	1968	3.00	6.00	12.00
72867	Look the Other Way/I'll Be Standing By	1968	3.00	6.00	12.00
72892	Take Good Care (Of My Heart)/I Can't Make It Without You	1969	3.00	6.00	12.00

Number	Title (A Side/B Side)	Yr	VG	VG+	NM
72892	Take Good Care (Of My Heart)/You Sent Me Silver Bells	1969	3.00	6.00	12.00
72931	Summer Symphony/98.6-Lazy Day	1969	3.75	7.50	15.00
72969	Wedding Bell Blues/One by One	1969	3.75	7.50	15.00
MOWEST					
5029	The Road I Walk/She Said That	1972	2.50	5.00	10.00
5042	Give It to Me, Sweet Thing/Don't Want to Be One	1973	—	—	—
—Unreleased					
PHILCO-FORD					
HP-21	You Don't Own Me/That's the Way Boys Are	1968	3.75	7.50	15.00
—4-inch plastic "Hip Pocket Record" with color sleeve					
Albums					
A&M					
SP-4564	Love Me by Name	1975	3.75	7.50	15.00
MERCURY					
ML-8016	I'll Cry If I Want To	1980	2.50	5.00	10.00
—Reissue of 60805					
MG 20805 [M]	I'll Cry If I Want To	1963	7.50	15.00	30.00
—With no blurb for "It's My Party"					
MG 20805 [M]	I'll Cry If I Want To	1964	5.00	10.00	20.00
—With blurb for "It's My Party"					
MG 20849 [M]	Lesley Gore Sings of Mixed-Up Hearts	1963	7.50	15.00	30.00
MG 20901 [M]	Boys, Boys, Boys	1964	7.50	15.00	30.00
MG 20943 [M]	Girl Talk	1964	7.50	15.00	30.00
MG 21024 [M]	The Golden Hits of Lesley Gore	1965	7.50	15.00	30.00
MG 21042 [M]	My Town, My Guy & Me	1965	7.50	15.00	30.00
MG 21066 [M]	All About Love	1966	7.50	15.00	30.00
MG 21120 [M]	California Nights	1967	7.50	15.00	30.00
SR 60805 [S]	I'll Cry If I Want To	1963	10.00	20.00	40.00
—With no blurb for "It's My Party"					
SR 60805 [S]	I'll Cry If I Want To	1964	7.50	15.00	30.00
—With blurb for "It's My Party"					
SR 60849 [S]	Lesley Gore Sings of Mixed-Up Hearts	1963	10.00	20.00	40.00
SR 60901 [S]	Boys, Boys, Boys	1964	10.00	20.00	40.00
SR 60943 [S]	Girl Talk	1964	10.00	20.00	40.00
SR 61024 [S]	The Golden Hits of Lesley Gore	1965	10.00	20.00	40.00
—Originals have 12 tracks					
SR 61024 [S]	The Golden Hits of Lesley Gore	196?	3.75	7.50	15.00
—Reissues have 10 tracks					
SR 61042 [S]	My Town, My Guy & Me	1965	10.00	20.00	40.00
SR 61066 [S]	All About Love	1966	10.00	20.00	40.00
—Stereo version has a different cover and liner notes than the mono version					
SR 61120 [S]	California Nights	1967	10.00	20.00	40.00
SR 61185	The Golden Hits of Lesley Gore, Vol. 2	1968	10.00	20.00	40.00
810370-1	The Golden Hits of Lesley Gore	1983	2.50	5.00	10.00
—Reissue of 61024					
MOWEST					
MW 117L	Someplace Else Now	1972	3.75	7.50	15.00
RHINO					
RNFP-71496 [(2)]	The Lesley Gore Anthology (1963-1968)	1986	3.75	7.50	15.00
WING					
PRW-2-119 [(2)]	The Sound of Young Love	1969	5.00	10.00	20.00
SRW-16350	Girl Talk	1968	3.75	7.50	15.00
SRW-16382	Love, Love, Love	1968	3.75	7.50	15.00

GORMAN, FREDDIE

Number	Title (A Side/B Side)	Yr	VG	VG+	NM
45s					
MIRACLE					
11	The Day Will Come/(B-side unknown)	1962	17.50	35.00	70.00
RIC-TIC					
101	In a Bad Way/There Can Be Too Much	1964	7.50	15.00	30.00
102	Take Me Back/Can't Get It Out of My Mind	1965	7.50	15.00	30.00

GORME, EYDIE

Also see STEVE LAWRENCE AND EYDIE GORME.

Number	Title (A Side/B Side)	Yr	VG	VG+	NM
45s					
ABC-PARAMOUNT					
9655	Sincerely Yours/Come Home	1955	3.75	7.50	15.00
—The first 45 (numerically) on ABC-Paramount					
9684	Too Close for Comfort/That's How	1956	2.50	5.00	10.00
9722	Mama, Teach Me to Dance/You Bring Out the Lover in Me	1956	2.50	5.00	10.00
9758	Soda Pop Hop/I've Got a Right to Cry	1956	2.50	5.00	10.00
9780	I'll Take Romance/First Impression	1957	2.50	5.00	10.00
9817	Your Kisses Kill Me/Kiss in Your Eyes	1957	2.50	5.00	10.00
9852	When Your Lover Has Gone/Until They Sail	1957	2.50	5.00	10.00
9863	Love Me Forever/Let Me Be Loved	1957	2.50	5.00	10.00
9925	You Need Hands/Dormi, Dormi, Dormi	1958	2.50	5.00	10.00
9944	Gotta Have Rain/To You From Me	1958	2.50	5.00	10.00
9971	The Voice in My Heart/Separate Tables	1958	2.50	5.00	10.00
10006	I'm Yours/Don't Take Your Love from Me	1959	2.50	5.00	10.00
10041	Taking a Chance on Love/The Years Between	1959	2.50	5.00	10.00
10061	Happiness/Fool Around	1959	2.50	5.00	10.00
10111	The Dance Is Over/Too Young to Know	1960	2.50	5.00	10.00
10155	Be Sure My Love/I Will Follow You	1960	2.50	5.00	10.00
10383	Fly Me to the Moon/I'm Yours	1962	2.50	5.00	10.00
CALENDAR					
63-1002	He Needs Me/How Could I Be So Wrong	1968	—	2.50	5.00
63-1004	This Guy's (Girl's) in Love with You/It's You Again	1968	—	2.50	5.00
COLUMBIA					
42424	Yes My Darling Daughter/Sonny Boy	1962	2.00	4.00	8.00
42424 [PS]	Yes My Darling Daughter/Sonny Boy	1962	2.50	5.00	10.00
42607	Where Is Love/Before Your Time	1962	2.00	4.00	8.00
42661	Blame It on the Bossa Nova/Guess I Should Have Loved Him More	1963	2.00	4.00	8.00
42661 [PS]	Blame It on the Bossa Nova/Guess I Should Have Loved Him More	1963	2.50	5.00	10.00
42790	Don't Try to Fight It, Baby/Theme from Light Fantastic (My Secret World)	1963	—	3.00	6.00
42854	Everybody Go Home/The Message	1963	—	3.00	6.00
42953	The Friendliest Thing/Something to Live For	1963	—	3.00	6.00
43082	I Want You to Meet My Baby/Can't Get Over (The Bossa Nova)	1964	—	3.00	6.00
43191	The Moon and the Stars and a Little Bit of Wine/Piel Canela	1964	—	3.00	6.00
43225	Do I Hear a Waltz/After You've Gone	1965	—	3.00	6.00
43302	Just Dance On By/Where Are You Now	1965	—	3.00	6.00
43444	Don't Go to Strangers/Mas Amor (More Love)	1965	—	3.00	6.00
43542	What Did I Have That I Didn't Have/Tell Him I Said Hello	1966	—	3.00	6.00
43660	If He Walked Into My Life/Tell Him I Said Hello	1966	—	3.00	6.00
43856	Allegre Navidad/Navidad Y Ano Nuevo	1966	2.00	4.00	8.00
43906	Guess I Should Have Loved Him More/What Is a Woman	1966	—	3.00	6.00
43971	Softly, As I Leave You/What's Good About Goodbye	1967	—	3.00	6.00
44299	Life Is But a Moment/What Makes Me Love Him	1967	—	3.00	6.00
JZSP 116419/20 [DJ]	Alegre Navidad/Blanca Navidad	1966	2.50	5.00	10.00
—With Trio Los Panchos					
CORAL					
60879	That Night of Heaven/Tell Me More	1952	3.75	7.50	15.00
60921	Don't Tell Lies/Love Me Not Just a Little	1953	3.00	6.00	12.00
60977	Frenesi/All Night Long	1953	3.00	6.00	12.00
60999	Uska Dara/Coconuts	1953	3.00	6.00	12.00
61036	I Danced with My Darling/I'd Be Forgotten	1953	3.00	6.00	12.00
61093	Gimme Gimme John/Fini	1953	3.00	6.00	12.00
61138	Crocodile Tears/Fallen Apples	1954	3.00	6.00	12.00
61189	Tea for Two/Climb Up the Wall	1954	3.00	6.00	12.00
61347	Give a Fool a Chance/A Girl Can't Say	1955	3.00	6.00	12.00
61481	Soldier Boy/What Is the Secret to Success	1955	3.00	6.00	12.00
MGM					
14213	Mem'ries and Souvenirs/Rosy's Theme	1971	—	2.00	4.00
14276	Sal and Sally/Somebody Waiting	1971	—	2.00	4.00
14397	Mr. Number One/Butterfly	1972	—	2.00	4.00
14563	The Garden/Take One Stop	1973	—	2.00	4.00
14681	Touch the Wind (Eres Tu)/It Takes Too Long to Learn to Live Alone	1973	—	2.00	4.00
RCA VICTOR					
74-0206	Runaway/Girl with a Suitcase	1969	—	2.50	5.00
74-0250	Wild One/Tonight I'll Say a Prayer	1969	—	2.50	5.00
74-0360	Ladies Who Lunch/My World Keeps Getting Smaller Every Day	1970	—	2.50	5.00
UNITED ARTISTS					
283	Let Me Be the First to Wish You a Merry Christmas/I Love to Dance (But Never on Sunday)	1960	3.00	6.00	12.00
292	What Happened to Our Love/Yours Tonight	1961	2.00	4.00	8.00
325	Mem'ries and Souvenirs/My Heart	1961	2.00	4.00	8.00
414	Frenesi/Granada	1962	2.00	4.00	8.00
XW852	What I Did for Love/Can It Ever Be the Same	1976	—	2.00	4.00
7-Inch Extended Plays					
ABC-PARAMOUNT					
C-218	Chicago/Button Up Your Overcoat//Tip Toe Through the Tulips with Me/Back in Your Own Backyard	195?	2.50	5.00	10.00
C-218 [PS]	Eydie Gorme Vamps the Roaring 20's, Volume 3	195?	2.50	5.00	10.00
Albums					
ABC-PARAMOUNT					
150 [M]	Eydie Gorme	1957	7.50	15.00	30.00
192 [M]	Eydie Swings the Blues	1957	7.50	15.00	30.00
218 [M]	Eydie Gorme Vamps the Roaring 20's	1958	7.50	15.00	30.00
S-218 [S]	Eydie Gorme Vamps the Roaring 20's	196?	3.00	6.00	12.00
246 [M]	Eydie in Love	1958	7.50	15.00	30.00
S-246 [S]	Eydie in Love	196?	3.00	6.00	12.00
254 [M]	Show Stoppers	1959	6.25	12.50	25.00
S-254 [S]	Show Stoppers	1959	7.50	15.00	30.00
273 [M]	Love Is a Season	1959	6.25	12.50	25.00
S-273 [S]	Love Is a Season	1959	7.50	15.00	30.00
307 [M]	On Stage	1959	6.25	12.50	25.00
S-307 [S]	On Stage	1959	7.50	15.00	30.00
343 [M]	Eydie in Dixieland	1960	6.25	12.50	25.00
S-343 [S]	Eydie in Dixieland	1960	7.50	15.00	30.00
512 [M]	The Best of Romance, Ballads, Blues, Dixieland, Roaring 20's, Showstoppers	1965	3.75	7.50	15.00
S-512 [S]	The Best of Romance, Ballads, Blues, Dixieland, Roaring 20's, Showstoppers	1965	5.00	10.00	20.00
COLUMBIA					
CL 2012 [M]	Blame It on the Bossa Nova	1963	3.75	7.50	15.00
CL 2065 [M]	Let the Good Times Roll	1963	3.75	7.50	15.00
CL 2120 [M]	Gorme Country Style	1964	3.75	7.50	15.00
CL 2203 [M]	Amor	1964	3.75	7.50	15.00
CL 2300 [M]	The Sound of Music (And Other Broadway Hits)	1965	3.75	7.50	15.00
CL 2376 [M]	More Amor	1965	3.75	7.50	15.00
CL 2476 [M]	Don't Go to Strangers	1966	3.75	7.50	15.00
CL 2594 [M]	Softly, As I Leave You	1967	3.75	7.50	15.00
CL 2764 [M]	Eydie Gorme's Greatest Hits	1967	5.00	10.00	20.00
CS 8812 [S]	Blame It on the Bossa Nova	1963	5.00	10.00	20.00
CS 8865 [S]	Let the Good Times Roll	1963	5.00	10.00	20.00
CS 8920 [S]	Gorme Country Style	1964	5.00	10.00	20.00
CS 9003 [S]	Amor	1964	5.00	10.00	20.00
PC 9003	Amor	198?	2.00	4.00	8.00
—Budget-line reissue					
CS 9100 [S]	The Sound of Music (And Other Broadway Hits)	1965	5.00	10.00	20.00
CS 9176 [S]	More Amor	1965	5.00	10.00	20.00
CS 9276 [S]	Don't Go to Strangers	1966	5.00	10.00	20.00
CS 9394 [S]	Softly, As I Leave You	1967	5.00	10.00	20.00
CS 9564 [S]	Eydie Gorme's Greatest Hits	1967	3.75	7.50	15.00
PC 9564	Eydie Gorme's Greatest Hits	198?	2.00	4.00	8.00
—Budget-line reissue					
CORAL					
CRL 57109 [M]	Delight	1957	10.00	20.00	40.00
HARMONY					
HS 11361	Yes Indeed!	1970	2.50	5.00	10.00
KH 30319	If He Walked Into My Life	1971	2.50	5.00	10.00
MGM					
SE-4780	It Was a Good Time	1971	3.00	6.00	12.00

Number	Title (A Side/B Side)	Yr	VG	VG+	NM
RCA VICTOR					
LSP-4093	Eydie	1968	3.00	6.00	12.00
LSP-4303	Tonight I'll Say a Prayer	1970	3.00	6.00	12.00
UNITED ARTISTS					
UAL 3143 [M]	Come Sing with Me	1961	5.00	10.00	20.00
UAL 3152 [M]	I Feel So Spanish	1961	5.00	10.00	20.00
UAL 3189 [M]	The Very Best of Eydie	1962	5.00	10.00	20.00
UAS 6143 [S]	Come Sing with Me	1961	6.25	12.50	25.00
UAS 6152 [S]	I Feel So Spanish	1961	6.25	12.50	25.00
UAS 6189 [S]	The Very Best of Eydie	1962	6.25	12.50	25.00
VOCALION					
VL 3708 [M]	Here's Eydie Gorme	196?	3.75	7.50	15.00
VL 73708 [R]	Here's Eydie Gorme	196?	3.00	6.00	12.00

GOSPEL STARS, THE

45s

Number	Title (A Side/B Side)	Yr	VG	VG+	NM
TAMLA					
54037	He Lifted Me/Behold the Saints of God	1961	37.50	75.00	150.00
—Horizontal lines logo					
54037	He Lifted Me/Behold the Saints of God	1961	15.00	30.00	60.00
—Globe logo					

Albums

Number	Title (A Side/B Side)	Yr	VG	VG+	NM
TAMLA					
TM-222 [M]	The Great Gospel Stars	1961	1000.	2000.	3000.

GOTHAM CITY CRIME FIGHTERS, THE

45s

Number	Title (A Side/B Side)	Yr	VG	VG+	NM
BATWING					
1001	Who Stole the Batmobile/That's Life	1966	7.50	15.00	30.00

GOULDMAN, GRAHAM

Also see THE MOCKINGBIRDS; 10CC.

45s

Number	Title (A Side/B Side)	Yr	VG	VG+	NM
A&M					
2251	Away from It All/Bionic Boar	1980	—	2.00	4.00
RCA VICTOR					
47-9453	Impossible Years/No Milk Today	1968	3.00	6.00	12.00
47-9584	For Your Love/Pamela, Pamela	1968	3.00	6.00	12.00

Albums

Number	Title (A Side/B Side)	Yr	VG	VG+	NM
RCA VICTOR					
LPM-3954 [M]	The Graham Gouldman Thing	1968	12.50	25.00	50.00
LSP-3954 [S]	The Graham Gouldman Thing	1968	12.50	25.00	50.00

GOULET, ROBERT

45s

Number	Title (A Side/B Side)	Yr	VG	VG+	NM
ABC					
12049	The Little Prince: Title/Mack and Mable: I Won't Send Roses	1974	—	2.00	4.00
12049 [PS]	The Little Prince: Title/Mack and Mable: I Won't Send Roses	1974	—	2.50	5.00
ARTISTS OF AMERICA					
103	Someone to Give My Love To/Something to Believe In	1975	—	2.00	4.00
118	After All Is Said and Done/(B-side unknown)	1976	—	2.00	4.00
COLUMBIA					
42249	One Life/I'mJust Taking My Time	1961	2.00	4.00	8.00
42369	Too Soon/Two Different Worlds	1962	—	3.00	6.00
42369 [PS]	Too Soon/Two Different Worlds	1962	2.00	4.00	8.00
42519	What Kind of Fool Am I/Where Do I Go from Here	1962	—	3.00	6.00
42519 [PS]	What Kind of Fool Am I/Where Do I Go from Here	1962	2.00	4.00	8.00
42612	Young at Love/Don't Be Afraid of Romance	1962	—	3.00	6.00
42740	These Are the Closing Credits/Two of Us	1963	—	3.00	6.00
42740 [PS]	These Are the Closing Credits/Two of Us	1963	2.00	4.00	8.00
42835	Believe in Me/How Very Special You Are	1963	—	3.00	6.00
42885	Under the Yum Yum Tree/If You Go	1963	—	3.00	6.00
43029	The Name of the Game/Choose	1964	—	3.00	6.00
43131	My Love, Forgive Me (Amore, Scusami)/I'd Rather Be Rich	1964	—	3.00	6.00
43224	I Never Got to Paris/Begin to Love	1965	—	2.50	5.00
43301	Summer Sounds/The More I See of Mimi	1965	—	2.50	5.00
43394	On a Clear Day You Can See Forever/Come Back to Me, My Love	1965	—	2.50	5.00
43481	Crazy Heart of Love/Everlasting	1965	—	2.50	5.00
43558	Young Only Yesterday/Why Be Ashamed	1966	—	2.50	5.00
43668	Daydreamer/My Best Girl	1966	—	2.50	5.00
43760	Once I Had a Heart/I Heard a Different Drummer	1966	—	2.50	5.00
43865	There But for You Go I/Fortissimo	1966	—	2.50	5.00
44019	Ciao Compare/World of Clowns	1967	—	2.50	5.00
44100	One Life, One Dream/If There's a Way	1967	—	2.50	5.00
44186	The Sinner/How Can I Leave You	1967	—	2.50	5.00
44305	Mon Amour, Mon Amour/This Year	1967	—	2.50	5.00
44368	Follow Me/If Ever I Would Leave You	1967	—	2.50	5.00
44466	Happy Time/I Don't Remember You	1968	—	2.50	5.00
44548	What a Wonderful World/I Don't Want to Hurt You Anymore	1968	—	2.50	5.00
44618	Thirty Days Hath September/A Chance to Live in Camelot	1968	—	2.50	5.00
44710	Hurry Home for Christmas/Wonderful World of Christmas	1968	2.00	4.00	8.00
44754	Wait for Me/I'll Catch the Sun	1969	—	2.50	5.00
44847	Didn't We/Bon Soir Dame	1969	—	2.50	5.00
44935	One Life to Live/Only Yesterday	1969	—	2.50	5.00
45054	One Night/I Can't Live Without You	1969	—	2.50	5.00
45165	My Woman, My Woman, My Wife/Come Saturday	1970	—	2.50	5.00
45250	Heaing River/One at a Time	1970	—	2.50	5.00
JZSP 76415/6 [DJ]	December Time/Silver Bells	1963	2.50	5.00	10.00
JZSP 111805/6 [DJ]	This Christmas I Spend With You/White Christmas	1965	2.50	5.00	10.00
—Promotional record for Christmas Seals					
JZSP 111805/6 [PS]	This Christmas I Spend With You/White Christmas	1965	3.00	6.00	12.00
MGM					
14487	God Is at Work Within You/One Solitary Life	1973	—	2.00	4.00
PARAMOUNT					
0271	Pages of Life/Summer Green, Autumn Gold	1974	—	2.00	4.00

7-Inch Extended Plays

Number	Title (A Side/B Side)	Yr	VG	VG+	NM
COLUMBIA					
7-9096 [PS]	My Love, Forgive Me	1964	2.50	5.00	10.00
7-9096 [S]	My Love, Forgive Me/Softly, As I Leave You/What Kind of Fool Am I//Just Say I Love Her/Welcome Home Angelina/Too Good	1964	2.50	5.00	10.00
—33 1/3 rpm, small hole, "Special Coin Operator Release"					

Albums

Number	Title (A Side/B Side)	Yr	VG	VG+	NM
COLUMBIA					
C 1051	Today's Greatest Hits	1970	3.00	6.00	12.00
CS 1051	Today's Greatest Hits	1970	3.00	6.00	12.00
PC 1051	Today's Greatest Hits	198?	2.00	4.00	8.00
—Budget-line reissue					
CL 1676 [M]	Always You	1962	3.00	6.00	12.00
CL 1826 [M]	Two of Us	1962	3.00	6.00	12.00
CL 1931 [M]	Sincerely Yours	1962	3.00	6.00	12.00
CL 1993 [M]	The Wonderful World of Love	1963	3.00	6.00	12.00
CL 2076 [M]	This Christmas I Spend with You	1963	3.00	6.00	12.00
CL 2088 [M]	Robert Goulet in Person	1963	3.00	6.00	12.00
CL 2200 [M]	Without You	1964	3.00	6.00	12.00
CL 2296 [M]	My Love Forgive Me	1964	3.00	6.00	12.00
CL 2342 [M]	Begin to Love	1965	3.00	6.00	12.00
CL 2380 [M]	Summer Sounds	1965	3.00	6.00	12.00
CL 2418 [M]	Robert Goulet on Broadway	1965	3.00	6.00	12.00
CL 2482 [M]	I Remember You	1966	3.00	6.00	12.00
CL 2541 [M]	Traveling On	1966	3.00	6.00	12.00
CL 2586 [M]	Robert Goulet on Broadway, Volume 2	1967	3.00	6.00	12.00
CL 2727 [M]	Hollywood Mon Amour (Great Songs from the Movies)	1967	3.75	7.50	15.00
CS 8476 [S]	Always You	1962	3.75	7.50	15.00
CS 8626 [S]	Two of Us	1962	3.75	7.50	15.00
CS 8731 [S]	Sincerely Yours	1962	3.75	7.50	15.00
CS 8793 [S]	The Wonderful World of Love	1963	3.75	7.50	15.00
CS 8876 [S]	This Christmas I Spend with You	1963	3.75	7.50	15.00
CS 8888 [S]	Robert Goulet in Person	1963	3.75	7.50	15.00
CS 9000 [S]	Without You	1964	3.75	7.50	15.00
CS 9096 [S]	My Love Forgive Me	1964	3.75	7.50	15.00
CS 9142 [S]	Begin to Love	1965	3.75	7.50	15.00
CS 9180 [S]	Summer Sounds	1965	3.75	7.50	15.00
CS 9218 [S]	Robert Goulet on Broadway	1965	3.75	7.50	15.00
CS 9282 [S]	I Remember You	1966	3.75	7.50	15.00
CS 9341 [S]	Traveling On	1966	3.75	7.50	15.00
CS 9386 [S]	Robert Goulet on Broadway, Volume 2	1967	3.75	7.50	15.00
CS 9527 [S]	Hollywood Mon Amour (Great Songs from the Movies)	1967	3.00	6.00	12.00
CS 9695	Woman, Woman	1968	3.00	6.00	12.00
CS 9734	Robert Goulet's Wonderful World of Christmas	1968	3.00	6.00	12.00
CS 9763	Both Sides Now	1969	3.00	6.00	12.00
CS 9815	Robert Goulet's Greatest Hits	1969	3.00	6.00	12.00
PC 9815	Robert Goulet's Greatest Hits	197?	2.00	4.00	8.00
—Reissue with new prefix					
CS 9874	Souvenir d'Italie	1969	3.00	6.00	12.00
CG 30011 [(2)]	I Wish You Love	1970	3.75	7.50	15.00
COLUMBIA SPECIAL PRODUCTS					
P 13345	Robert Goulet's Wonderful World of Christmas	1976	3.00	6.00	12.00
—Same as CS 9734, but "Exclusively distributed by Sutton Distributors, Inc."					
HARMONY					
KH 30507	Raindrops Keep Fallin' on My Head	1971	2.50	5.00	10.00
KH 31107	Bridge Over Troubled Water	1972	2.50	5.00	10.00
MERLIN					
2001	I Never Did As I Was Told	1971	3.00	6.00	12.00

GOWENS, SAMMY

45s

Number	Title (A Side/B Side)	Yr	VG	VG+	NM
UNITED ARTISTS					
114	Kissin' at the Drive-In/Rockin' By Myself	1958	25.00	50.00	100.00

GRACIE, CHARLIE

45s

Number	Title (A Side/B Side)	Yr	VG	VG+	NM
20TH CENTURY					
5033	Head Home, Honey/My Baby Loves Me	1955	12.50	25.00	50.00
5035	Honey Honey/Wildwood Boogie	1955	15.00	30.00	60.00
CADILLAC					
141	Boogie Boogie Blues/I'm Gonna Sit Right Down and Write Myself a Letter	1953	37.50	75.00	150.00
144	Rockin' and Rollin'/(B-side unknown)	1954	37.50	75.00	150.00
CAMEO					
105	Butterfly/Ninety-Nine Ways	1957	6.25	12.50	25.00
107	Fabulous/Just Lookin'	1957	5.00	10.00	20.00
111	I Love You So Much It Hurts/Wandering Eyes	1957	5.00	10.00	20.00
118	Cool Baby/You've Got a Heart Like a Rock	1957	5.00	10.00	20.00
127	Crazy Girl/Dressin' Up	1958	5.00	10.00	20.00
141	Love Bird/Trying	1958	5.00	10.00	20.00
CORAL					
62073	Hurry Up Buttercup/Doodlebug	1959	3.75	7.50	15.00
62115	Angel of Love/I'm a Fool, That's Why	1959	3.75	7.50	15.00
62141	Oh-Well-a/Because I Love You So	1959	3.75	7.50	15.00
DIAMOND					
178	He'll Never Love You Like I Do/Keep My Love Next to Your Heart	1965	6.25	12.50	25.00
FELSTED					
8629	W-Wow/Makin' Whoopee	1961	3.75	7.50	15.00
PRESIDENT					
825	Pretty Baby/Night and Day U.S.A.	1962	3.75	7.50	15.00
828	Count to Three/Just Like Us	1963	3.75	7.50	15.00
ROULETTE					
4255	I Look for You/The Race	1960	3.75	7.50	15.00
4312	Sorry for You/Scenery	1960	3.75	7.50	15.00

Number	Title (A Side/B Side)	Yr	VG	VG+	NM

GRACIOUS

PAUL DAVIS was in this group.

Albums

CAPITOL

Number	Title (A Side/B Side)	Yr	VG	VG+	NM
ST-602	Gracious	1970	10.00	20.00	40.00

GRADS, THE

45s

Number	Title (A Side/B Side)	Yr	VG	VG+	NM
A&M					
797	Everything in the Garden/Stage Door	1966	2.50	5.00	10.00
MERCURY					
72346	Cool One/Wild One	1964	5.00	10.00	20.00
MGM					
13216	Their Hearts Were Full of Spring/It Happened Once Before	1964	2.50	5.00	10.00
VALIANT					
6023	Once Again/White Steeple	1962	3.75	7.50	15.00

GRADUATES, THE (1)

45s

Number	Title (A Side/B Side)	Yr	VG	VG+	NM
CORSICAN					
0058	What Good Is Graduation/Lonely	1959	10.00	20.00	40.00
LAWN					
208	Ballad of a Girl and Boy/Goodbye My Love	1963	5.00	10.00	20.00
SHAN-TODD					
0055	Ballad of a Girl and Boy/Care	1959	7.50	15.00	30.00

GRADUATES, THE (2)

45s

Number	Title (A Side/B Side)	Yr	VG	VG+	NM
GNP CRESCENDO					
404	(The Shape of) Things to Come/Listen to the Music	1968	2.50	5.00	10.00

GRADUATES, THE (U)

Definitely not group (1); might not be group (2), either.

45s

Number	Title (A Side/B Side)	Yr	VG	VG+	NM
RISING SONS					
712	If Ever I Get Out of This Mess I'm In/Seventh Generation Breakthrough	1968	7.50	15.00	30.00

GRAFFITI

45s

Number	Title (A Side/B Side)	Yr	VG	VG+	NM
ABC					
11123	He's Got the Knack/Love In Spite	1968	7.50	15.00	30.00

Albums

Number	Title (A Side/B Side)	Yr	VG	VG+	NM
ABC					
S-663	Graffiti	1968	15.00	30.00	60.00

GRAHAM, DAVY

Albums

Number	Title (A Side/B Side)	Yr	VG	VG+	NM
LONDON					
PS 552	Large As Life and Twice As Natural	1968	3.75	7.50	15.00

GRAHAM, LARRY

Also see GRAHAM CENTRAL STATION; SLY AND THE FAMILY STONE.

12-Inch Singles

Number	Title (A Side/B Side)	Yr	VG	VG+	NM
WARNER BROS.					
PRO-A-1027 [DJ]	Don't Stop When You're Hot (edit)/(LP version)	1982	2.00	4.00	8.00
PRO-A-1046 [DJ]	Sooner or Later/(Instrumental)	1982	2.00	4.00	8.00
PRO-A-2065 [DJ]	I'm Sick and Tired (same on both sides)	1983	2.00	4.00	8.00

45s

Number	Title (A Side/B Side)	Yr	VG	VG+	NM
WARNER BROS.					
29003	What We All Need Is More Love/Tearing Out My Heart	1985	—	—	3.00
29529	I'm Sick and Tired/I'd Rather Be Loving You	1983	—	2.00	4.00
29620	I Never Forgot Your Eyes/Movin' Inside Your Love	1983	—	2.00	4.00
29884	Let Me Come Into Your Life/What You Are Inside	1982	—	2.00	4.00
29956	Sooner or Later/I Feel Good	1982	—	2.00	4.00
29956 [PS]	Sooner or Later/I Feel Good	1982	—	2.50	5.00
49221	One in a Million You/The Entertainer	1980	—	2.00	4.00
49221 [PS]	One in a Million You/The Entertainer	1980	—	2.50	5.00
49581	When We Get Married/Tonight	1980	—	2.00	4.00
49744	Just Be My Lady/Feels Like Love	1981	—	2.00	4.00
49833	Guess Who/Sweetheart	1981	—	2.00	4.00
50068	Don't Stop When You're Hot/I Love Loving You	1982	—	2.00	4.00
50068 [PS]	Don't Stop When You're Hot/I Love Loving You	1982	—	2.50	5.00

Albums

Number	Title (A Side/B Side)	Yr	VG	VG+	NM
WARNER BROS.					
BSK 3447	One in a Million You	1980	2.00	4.00	8.00
BSK 3554	Just Be My Lady	1981	2.00	4.00	8.00
BSK 3668	Sooner or Later	1982	2.00	4.00	8.00
23878	Victory	1983	2.00	4.00	8.00
25307	Fired Up	1985	2.00	4.00	8.00

GRAHAM, LOU

45s

Number	Title (A Side/B Side)	Yr	VG	VG+	NM
CLYMAX					
318	Wee Willie Brown/You Were Mean Baby	1957	75.00	150.00	300.00
CORAL					
61931	Wee Willie Brown/You Were Mean Baby	1958	25.00	50.00	100.00

GRAHAM CENTRAL STATION

Also see LARRY GRAHAM.

12-Inch Singles

Number	Title (A Side/B Side)	Yr	VG	VG+	NM
WARNER BROS.					
PRO-A-639 [DJ]	Entrow (2 versions)	1976	3.75	7.50	15.00
PRO-A-673 [DJ]	Now Do U Wanta Dance (same on both sides)	1977	3.75	7.50	15.00

45s

Number	Title (A Side/B Side)	Yr	VG	VG+	NM
WARNER BROS.					
7782	Can You Handle It/Ghetto	1974	—	2.50	5.00
8025	Release Yourself/'Tis Your Kind of Music	1974	—	2.50	5.00
8061	Feel the Need/We Be's Gettin' Down	1974	—	2.50	5.00
8105	Your Love/I Believe in You	1975	—	2.00	4.00
8148	It's Alright/Luckiest People	1975	—	2.00	4.00
8175	The Jam/The Jam (Disco Version)	1975	—	2.00	4.00
8205	Love/Why	1976	—	2.00	4.00
8235	Entrow — Part 1/Entrow — Part 2	1976	—	2.00	4.00
8288	Do Yah/I Got a Reason	1976	—	2.00	4.00
8378	Now Do-U-Wanta Dance/(B-side unknown)	1977	—	2.00	4.00
8417	Stomped Beat-Up and Whooped/Ole Smokey	1977	—	2.00	4.00
8464	Crazy Chicken/Saving My Love for You	1977	—	2.00	4.00
8602	My Radio Sure Sounds Good to Me/Turn It Out	1978	—	2.00	4.00
8665	Is It Love?/Are You Happy?	1978	—	2.00	4.00
8816	(You're a) Foxy Lady/Tonight	1979	—	2.00	4.00
49011	Star Walk/Boogie Baby	1979	—	2.00	4.00
49067	Sneaky Freak/Boogie Baby	1979	—	2.00	4.00

Albums

Number	Title (A Side/B Side)	Yr	VG	VG+	NM
WARNER BROS.					
BS 2763	Graham Central Station	1974	2.50	5.00	10.00
BS4 2763 [Q]	Graham Central Station	1974	3.75	7.50	15.00
BS 2814	Release Yourself	1974	2.50	5.00	10.00
BS 2876	Ain't No 'Bout-a-Doubt It	1975	2.50	5.00	10.00
BS4 2876 [Q]	Ain't No 'Bout-a-Doubt It	1975	3.75	7.50	15.00
BS 2937	Mirror	1976	2.50	5.00	10.00
BS 3041	Now Do U Wanta Dance	1977	2.50	5.00	10.00
BSK 3175	My Radio Sure Sounds Good to Me	1978	2.50	5.00	10.00
—As "Larry Graham and Graham Central Station"					
BSK 3322	Star Walk	1979	2.50	5.00	10.00
—As "Larry Graham and Graham Central Station"					

GRAMMER, BILLY

45s

Number	Title (A Side/B Side)	Yr	VG	VG+	NM
DECCA					
31226	Columbus Stockade Blues/There's a Rainbow 'Round My Shoulder	1961	2.50	5.00	10.00
31274	Have a Drink on Me/Finger	1961	2.50	5.00	10.00
31321	Save Your Tears/I'd Like to Know You	1961	2.50	5.00	10.00
31396	He Ain't My Buddy No More/Blue Roller Rink	1962	2.50	5.00	10.00
31449	I Wanna Go Home (Detroit City)/Bottom of the Glass	1962	2.50	5.00	10.00
31514	Love Gets Better with Time/Lonesome Life	1963	2.50	5.00	10.00
31562	Old Foolish Me/I'll Leave the Porch Lights a-Burning	1963	2.50	5.00	10.00
31618	Don't Drop It/I Saw Your Face in the Moon	1964	2.00	4.00	8.00
31669	Wabash Cannonball/Gonna Lay Down My Old Guitar	1964	2.00	4.00	8.00
31757	Little Bit of Happiness/I'm Letting You Go (Goodbye)	1965	2.00	4.00	8.00
31892	Brown's Ferry Blues/Souvenirs of Sorrow	1966	2.00	4.00	8.00
EPIC					
10052	Bottles/Temporarily	1966	2.00	4.00	8.00
10103	Heaven Help This Heart of Mine/The Real Thing	1966	2.00	4.00	8.00
10169	I've Seen That Look on Me (A Thousand Times)/Written on a Jailhouse	1967	2.00	4.00	8.00
EVEREST					
19353	Unknown Soldier/Princess of Persia	1960	2.50	5.00	10.00
19384	Big Big Dream/River of Regret	1960	2.50	5.00	10.00
MERCURY					
72785	Money, Love and War/Last of My Future	1968	2.00	4.00	8.00
72836	The Ballad of John Dillinger/Do You Still Believe	1968	2.00	4.00	8.00
72893	The Hour of Separation/The Changing Scene	1969	—	3.00	6.00
MONUMENT					
400	Gotta Travel On/Chasing a Dream	1958	3.75	7.50	15.00
403	Bonaparte's Retreat/The Kissing Tree	1959	3.00	6.00	12.00
407	It Takes You/Willie, Quit Your Playing	1959	3.00	6.00	12.00
413	Loveland/On the Job Too Long	1960	3.00	6.00	12.00
8653	Family Man/What We Have in Common Is Love	1975	—	2.00	4.00
8665	Steppin' Out/Mom and Dad's Waltz	1975	—	2.00	4.00
8685	That's Life/Who's Gonna Buy You the Ribbons	1976	—	2.00	4.00
RICE					
5025	Mabel (You Have Been a Friend to Me)/Papa and Mama	1967	2.00	4.00	8.00
STOP					
321	Jesus Is a Soul Man/Peace on Earth Begins Today	1969	—	3.00	6.00

7-Inch Extended Plays

Number	Title (A Side/B Side)	Yr	VG	VG+	NM
DECCA					
ED 2767	Detroit City/Old Foolish Me//Love Gets Better with Time/Have a Drink on Me	196?	3.00	6.00	12.00
ED 2767 [PS]	Billy Grammer	196?	3.00	6.00	12.00

Albums

Number	Title (A Side/B Side)	Yr	VG	VG+	NM
DECCA					
DL 4212 [M]	Gospel Guitar	1962	3.75	7.50	15.00
DL 4460 [M]	Golden Gospel Favorites	1964	3.00	6.00	12.00
DL 4542 [M]	Gotta Travel On	1965	3.00	6.00	12.00
DL 4642 [M]	Country Guitar	1965	3.00	6.00	12.00
DL 74212 [S]	Gospel Guitar	1962	5.00	10.00	20.00
DL 74460 [S]	Golden Gospel Favorites	1964	3.75	7.50	15.00
DL 74542 [S]	Gotta Travel On	1965	3.75	7.50	15.00
DL 74642 [S]	Country Guitar	1965	3.75	7.50	15.00
EPIC					
LN 24233 [M]	Sunday Guitar	1967	3.75	7.50	15.00
BN 26233 [S]	Sunday Guitar	1967	3.75	7.50	15.00
MONUMENT					
MLP-4000 [M]	Travelin' On	1959	10.00	20.00	40.00
MLP-8039 [M]	Travelin' On	1965	6.25	12.50	25.00
SLP-18039 [P]	Travelin' On	1965	7.50	15.00	30.00
VOCALION					
VL 73826	Favorites	1968	3.00	6.00	12.00

GRANAHAN, GERRY

Also see JERRY GRANT.

45s

20TH CENTURY FOX

Number	Title (A Side/B Side)	Yr	VG	VG+	NM
425	Hang Up the Phone/Too Weak to Win	1963	3.75	7.50	15.00
541	Racing Fever: Title/Racing Fever: Mainstream	1964	3.75	7.50	15.00

—B-side by Arnold Goland and His Orchestra

ATCO

Number	Title (A Side/B Side)	Yr	VG	VG+	NM
6122	Sweet Affection/Confess It to Your Heart	1958	7.50	15.00	30.00

CANADIAN AMERICAN

Number	Title (A Side/B Side)	Yr	VG	VG+	NM
116	When Irish Eyes Are Smiling/In My Heart	1960	5.00	10.00	20.00
119	You'll Never Walk Alone/Where's the Girl	1960	5.00	10.00	20.00
121	Short Skirts/I'm Afraid You'll Never Know	1960	5.00	10.00	20.00

CAPRICE

Number	Title (A Side/B Side)	Yr	VG	VG+	NM
106	Unchained Melody/Dancing Man	1961	5.00	10.00	20.00
108	Too Big for Her Bikini/Dance, Girl, Dance	1961	25.00	50.00	100.00

—With backing by the Belmonts or the Five Satins (sources disagree)

GONE

Number	Title (A Side/B Side)	Yr	VG	VG+	NM
5065	Let the Rumors Fly/Put Me Anywhere	1959	5.00	10.00	20.00
5081	It Hurts/Look for Me	1959	5.00	10.00	20.00
5081 [PS]	It Hurts/Look for Me	1959	7.50	15.00	30.00

MARK

Number	Title (A Side/B Side)	Yr	VG	VG+	NM
121	Love's Young Dream/Oh Well-A Watch-A Gonna Do	1957	8.75	17.50	35.00

SUNBEAM

Number	Title (A Side/B Side)	Yr	VG	VG+	NM
102	No Chemise, Please/Girl of My Dreams	1958	7.50	15.00	30.00
108	Baby Wait/Completely	1958	6.25	12.50	25.00
112	I'm Ready As I'll Ever Be/Nobody Can Handle This Job	1958	6.25	12.50	25.00

—B-side by Eddie Fontaine

Number	Title (A Side/B Side)	Yr	VG	VG+	NM
122	King Size/I'm Afraid You'll Never Know	1958	6.25	12.50	25.00
127	A Ring, a Bracelet, a Heart/You're Adorable	1959	6.25	12.50	25.00

VEEP

Number	Title (A Side/B Side)	Yr	VG	VG+	NM
1205	All the Live-Long Day/Sophia	1965	3.00	6.00	12.00

GRAND FUNK RAILROAD

Includes records as "Grand Funk." Also see MARK FARNER; TERRY KNIGHT AND THE PACK.

45s

CAPITOL

Number	Title (A Side/B Side)	Yr	VG	VG+	NM
2567	Time Machine/High on a Horse	1969	—	3.00	6.00
2691	Mr. Limousine Driver/High Falootin' Woman	1969	—	3.00	6.00
2732	Heartbreaker/Please Don't Worry	1970	—	3.00	6.00
2816	Nothing Is the Same/Sin's a Good Man's Brother	1970	—	3.00	6.00
2877	Closer to Home/Aimless Lady	1970	—	3.00	6.00
2996	Mean Mistreater/Mark Says Alright	1970	—	3.00	6.00
3095	Feelin' Alright/I Want Freedom	1971	—	3.00	6.00
3160	Gimme Shelter/I Can Feel Him in the Morning	1971	—	3.00	6.00
3160 [PS]	Gimme Shelter/I Can Feel Him in the Morning	1971	2.50	5.00	10.00
3217	People, Let's Stop the War/Save the Land	1971	—	3.00	6.00
3255	Footstompin' Music/I Come Tumblin'	1972	—	3.00	6.00
3316	Upsetter/No Lies	1972	—	3.00	6.00
3363	Rock 'N Roll Soul/Flight of the Phoenix	1972	—	3.00	6.00
3660	We're An American Band/Creepin'	1973	—	3.00	6.00

—Originals on gold vinyl

Number	Title (A Side/B Side)	Yr	VG	VG+	NM
3660	We're An American Band/Creepin'	1973	—	2.00	4.00
3660 [PS]	We're An American Band/Creepin'	1973	—	2.50	5.00
3760	Walk Like a Man/The Railroad	1973	—	2.00	4.00
3760 [PS]	Walk Like a Man/The Railroad	1973	—	2.50	5.00
3840	The Loco-Motion/Destitute and Losin'	1974	—	2.00	4.00
3840 [PS]	The Loco-Motion/Destitute and Losin'	1974	—	2.50	5.00
3917	Shinin' On/Mr. Pretty Boy	1974	—	2.00	4.00
3917 [PS]	Shinin' On/Mr. Pretty Boy	1974	—	2.50	5.00
4002	Some Kind of Wonderful/Wild	1974	—	2.00	4.00
4002 [PS]	Some Kind of Wonderful/Wild	1974	—	2.50	5.00
4046	Bad Time/Good and Evil	1975	—	2.00	4.00
4199	Take Me/Genevieve	1975	—	2.00	4.00
4199 [PS]	Take Me/Genevieve	1975	—	2.50	5.00
4235	Sally/Love Is Dyin'	1976	—	2.00	4.00
4235 [PS]	Sally/Love Is Dyin'	1976	—	2.50	5.00

FULL MOON

Number	Title (A Side/B Side)	Yr	VG	VG+	NM
49823	Testify/Y.O.U.	1981	—	2.00	4.00
49866	No Reason Why/Stuck in the Middle	1981	—	2.00	4.00

MCA

Number	Title (A Side/B Side)	Yr	VG	VG+	NM
40590	Can You Do It/1976	1976	—	2.50	5.00
40590 [PS]	Can You Do It/1976	1976	—	3.00	6.00
40641	Out to Get You/Just Couldn't Wait	1976	—	2.50	5.00

—The MCA sides were produced by Frank Zappa

Albums

CAPITOL

Number	Title (A Side/B Side)	Yr	VG	VG+	NM
ST-307	On Time	1969	3.75	7.50	15.00
SKAO-406	Grand Funk	1970	3.75	7.50	15.00
SKAO-471	Closer to Home	1970	3.75	7.50	15.00
SWBB-633 [(2)]	Live Album	1970	3.75	7.50	15.00
SW-764	Survival	1971	3.75	7.50	15.00
SW-853	E Pluribus Funk	1971	3.75	7.50	15.00

—Round cover designed like a coin

Number	Title (A Side/B Side)	Yr	VG	VG+	NM
SABB-11042 [(2)]	Mark, Don and Mel 1969-71	1972	3.75	7.50	15.00
SMAS-11099	Phoenix	1972	3.00	6.00	12.00
SMAS-11207	We're An American Band	1973	7.50	15.00	30.00

—Gold vinyl with sheet of four stickers

Number	Title (A Side/B Side)	Yr	VG	VG+	NM
SMAS-11207	We're An American Band	1973	2.50	5.00	10.00

—Black vinyl

Number	Title (A Side/B Side)	Yr	VG	VG+	NM
SMAS-11207	We're An American Band	1973	5.00	10.00	20.00

—Gold vinyl without sheet of four stickers

Number	Title (A Side/B Side)	Yr	VG	VG+	NM
SWAE-11278	Shinin' On	1974	3.00	6.00	12.00

—With 3-D glasses attached to cover

Number	Title (A Side/B Side)	Yr	VG	VG+	NM
SWAE-11278	Shinin' On	1974	2.00	4.00	8.00

—With 3-D glasses missing

Number	Title (A Side/B Side)	Yr	VG	VG+	NM
SO-11356	All the Girls in the World Beware!!!	1974	3.75	7.50	15.00

—With poster (deduct 33% if missing)

Number	Title (A Side/B Side)	Yr	VG	VG+	NM
SABB-11445	Caught in the Act	1975	2.50	5.00	10.00
ST-11482	Born to Die	1976	2.50	5.00	10.00
ST-11579	Grand Funk Hits	1976	2.50	5.00	10.00
SN-16138	Grand Funk Hits	1981	2.00	4.00	8.00
SN-16176	Closer to Home	1981	2.00	4.00	8.00
SN-16177	Grand Funk	1981	2.00	4.00	8.00
SN-16178	On Time	1981	2.00	4.00	8.00
21692	We're An American Band	1999	6.25	12.50	25.00

—Limited-edition reissue on 180-gram gold vinyl with original 1973 packaging

FULL MOON

Number	Title (A Side/B Side)	Yr	VG	VG+	NM
HS 3625	Grand Funk Lives	1981	2.50	5.00	10.00
23750	What's Funk	1983	2.50	5.00	10.00

MCA

Number	Title (A Side/B Side)	Yr	VG	VG+	NM
2216	Good Singin' Good Playin'	1976	3.00	6.00	12.00

—Produced by Frank Zappa

GRANDMA'S ROCKERS

Albums

FREDLO

Number	Title (A Side/B Side)	Yr	VG	VG+	NM
6727	Homemade Apple Pie	1967	500.00	1000.	1500.

GRANT, CARY

45s

COLUMBIA

Number	Title (A Side/B Side)	Yr	VG	VG+	NM
44377	Christmas Lullaby/Here's to You	1967	7.50	15.00	30.00

GRANT, EARL

45s

DECCA

Number	Title (A Side/B Side)	Yr	VG	VG+	NM
25526	Ebb Tide/Deep Purple	1962	2.00	4.00	8.00
25560	Swingin' Gently/Beyond the Roof	1962	2.00	4.00	8.00
25574	Sweet Sixteen Bars/Learnin' the Blues	1962	2.00	4.00	8.00
25601	Caravan/I'll Build a Stariway to Paradise	1963	2.00	4.00	8.00
25607	More (Theme from "Mondo Cane")/Sukiyaki	1963	2.00	4.00	8.00
25626	Black Coffee/I'm Just a Lucky So-and-So	1964	2.00	4.00	8.00
25638	Satin Doll/Just One More Time	1964	2.00	4.00	8.00
25659	Without a Song/Meditation	1965	2.00	4.00	8.00
25674	Stand By Me/After Hours	1965	2.00	4.00	8.00
25683	Rudolph the Red-Nosed Reindeer/Santa Claus Is Comin' to Town	1965	2.00	4.00	8.00
25697	Blue Velvet/The Sweetest Sounds	1966	—	3.00	6.00
25703	Jingle Bells/Silver Bells	1966	—	3.00	6.00
25704	The Lonesome Road/When I Grow Too Old to Dream	1966	—	3.00	6.00
25713	Summertime/September in the Rain	1967	—	3.00	6.00
25721	Without a Song/I'm in the Mood for Love	1967	—	3.00	6.00
25730	I Miss You So/Stormy Weather	1967	—	3.00	6.00
25737	My Foolish Heart/One Note Samba	1968	—	3.00	6.00
25743	Bewitched/In Motion	1968	—	3.00	6.00
30150	Goodnight My Love, Pleasant Dreams/My Consolation	1956	3.75	7.50	15.00
30244	Thanks for You/Through the Eyes of a Boy and Girl	1956	3.75	7.50	15.00
30475	Fever/Malaguena	1957	3.75	7.50	15.00
30561	Honky Tonk/The Next Time You See Me	1958	3.00	6.00	12.00
30640	Ol' Man River/Kathy-O	1958	3.00	6.00	12.00
30719	The End/Hunky Dunky Doo	1958	3.75	7.50	15.00
30719	(At) The End (Of a Rainbow)/Hunky Dunky Doo	1958	3.00	6.00	12.00

—Same song, altered title on A-side

Number	Title (A Side/B Side)	Yr	VG	VG+	NM
30819	Evening Rain/Evening Rain (Instrumental)	1959	2.50	5.00	10.00
30856	Last Night/Imitation of Life	1959	2.50	5.00	10.00
30908	The Wish/Don't Point Your Finger at Anyone Else	1959	2.50	5.00	10.00
30983	All for the Best/Not One Minute More	1959	2.50	5.00	10.00
31022	Christmas Card/Swingin' Christmas	1959	2.50	5.00	10.00
31044	House of Bamboo/Two Loves Have I	1960	2.50	5.00	10.00
31110	Dreamy/Building Castles	1960	2.50	5.00	10.00
31203	You Thrill Me/Quando La Luna	1961	2.00	4.00	8.00
31222	Ebb Tide/Next Time	1961	2.00	4.00	8.00
31263	My Foolish Heart/Sermonette	1961	2.00	4.00	8.00
31328	Honey/Tender Is the Night	1961	2.00	4.00	8.00
31468	Steve's Theme (From "Forty Pounds of Trouble")/Yes Sirree	1963	2.00	4.00	8.00
31716	This Little Girl of Mine/Come to Me (Pretty Baby)	1964	2.00	4.00	8.00
31902	I'll Drown in My Own Tears/I Can't Stop Loving You	1966	—	3.00	6.00
32093	I Love You, Yes I Do/Hide Nor Hair	1967	—	3.00	6.00
32443	It Was a Very Good Year/If I Only Had Time	1969	—	2.50	5.00
32499	I Wonder/The Importance of the Rose	1969	—	2.50	5.00
32667	Grant's Pass/Elizabethan Reggae	1970	—	2.50	5.00

MCA

Number	Title (A Side/B Side)	Yr	VG	VG+	NM
65023	Silver Bells/Jingle Bells	1973	—	2.00	4.00

—Black label with rainbow

Number	Title (A Side/B Side)	Yr	VG	VG+	NM
65023	Silver Bells/Jingle Bells	1980	—	—	3.00

—Blue label with rainbow

PRINCE

Number	Title (A Side/B Side)	Yr	VG	VG+	NM
1201	One Way Street/(B-side unknown)	1956	3.75	7.50	15.00

—Black vinyl

Number	Title (A Side/B Side)	Yr	VG	VG+	NM
1201	One Way Street/(B-side unknown)	1956	6.25	12.50	25.00

—Colored vinyl

7-Inch Extended Plays

DECCA

Number	Title (A Side/B Side)	Yr	VG	VG+	NM
ED 2591	(contents unknown)	195?	2.50	5.00	10.00
ED 2591 [PS]	The Versatile Earl Grant	195?	2.50	5.00	10.00
ED 2634	(contents unknown)	195?	2.50	5.00	10.00
ED 2634 [PS]	The Versatile Earl Grant	195?	2.50	5.00	10.00
ED 2635	(contents unknown)	195?	2.50	5.00	10.00
ED 2635 [PS]	The Versatile Earl Grant	195?	2.50	5.00	10.00
ED 2639 [M]	(contents unknown)	1959	2.50	5.00	10.00
ED 2639 [PS]	The End	1959	2.50	5.00	10.00
ED 7-2639 [PS]	The End	1959	3.75	7.50	15.00
ED 7-2639 [S]	(contents unknown)	1959	3.75	7.50	15.00
ED 2705	Ebb Tide/My Foolish Heart//Exodus Theme/I'm in the Mood for Love	196?	2.50	5.00	10.00
ED 2705 [PS]	Earl Grant	196?	2.50	5.00	10.00
ED 2722	Swingin' Gently/Beyond the Reef//Yellow Bird/Make Someone Happy	196?	2.50	5.00	10.00
ED 2722 [PS]	Swingin' Gently	196?	2.50	5.00	10.00

Number	Title (A Side/B Side)	Yr	VG	VG+	NM
ED 2736	Sweet Sixteen Bars/Learnin' the Blues//Because of Rain/Too Close for Comfort	196?	2.50	5.00	10.00
ED 2736 [PS]	Earl Grant	196?	2.50	5.00	10.00
Albums					
DECCA					
DL 4044 [M]	The Magic of Earl Grant	1960	3.00	6.00	12.00
DL 4165 [M]	Ebb Tide	1961	3.00	6.00	12.00
DL 4188 [M]	Earl After Dark	1961	3.00	6.00	12.00
DL 4231 [M]	Beyond the Reef	1962	3.00	6.00	12.00
DL 4299 [M]	Earl Grant at Basin Street East	1962	3.00	6.00	12.00
DL 4338 [M]	Midnight Sun	1963	3.00	6.00	12.00
DL 4405 [M]	Yes Sirree	1963	3.00	6.00	12.00
DL 4454 [M]	Fly Me to the Moon	1963	3.00	6.00	12.00
DL 4506 [M]	Just for a Thrill	1964	3.00	6.00	12.00
DL 4576 [M]	Just One More Time	1964	3.00	6.00	12.00
DL 4623 [M]	Trade Winds	1965	3.00	6.00	12.00
DL 4624 [M]	Spotlight on Earl Grant	1965	3.00	6.00	12.00
DL 4677 [M]	Winter Wonderland	1965	3.00	6.00	12.00
DL 4729 [M]	Songs Made Famous by Nat Cole	1966	3.00	6.00	12.00
DL 4738 [M]	Stand By Me	1966	3.00	6.00	12.00
DL 4806 [M]	Bali Ha'I	1967	3.00	6.00	12.00
DL 4811 [M]	Just a Closer Walk with Thee	1967	3.75	7.50	15.00
DL 4813 [M]	Earl Grant's Greatest Hits	1967	3.75	7.50	15.00
DL 4937 [M]	Gently Swingin'	1968	5.00	10.00	20.00
DL 4974 [M]	Spanish Eyes	1968	6.25	12.50	25.00
DXS 7204 [(2)]	The Best of Earl Grant	1969	5.00	10.00	20.00
DL 8672 [M]	The Versatile Earl Grant	1958	5.00	10.00	20.00
DL 8830 [M]	The End	1959	3.75	7.50	15.00
DL 8905 [M]	Grant Takes Rhythm	1959	3.75	7.50	15.00
DL 8916 [M]	Nothing But the Blues	1960	3.75	7.50	15.00
DL 8935 [M]	Paris Is My Beat	1960	3.75	7.50	15.00
DL 74044 [S]	The Magic of Earl Grant	1960	3.75	7.50	15.00
DL 74165 [S]	Ebb Tide	1961	3.75	7.50	15.00
DL 74188 [S]	Earl After Dark	1961	3.75	7.50	15.00
DL 74231 [S]	Beyond the Heet	1962	3.75	7.50	15.00
DL 74299 [S]	Earl Grant at Basin Street East	1962	3.75	7.50	15.00
DL 74338 [S]	Midnight Sun	1963	3.75	7.50	15.00
DL 74405 [S]	Yes Sirree	1963	3.75	7.50	15.00
DL 74454 [S]	Fly Me to the Moon	1963	3.75	7.50	15.00
DL 74506 [S]	Just for a Thrill	1964	3.75	7.50	15.00
DL 74576 [S]	Just One More Time	1964	3.75	7.50	15.00
DL 74623 [S]	Trade Winds	1965	3.75	7.50	15.00
DL 74624 [S]	Spotlight on Earl Grant	1965	3.75	7.50	15.00
DL 74677 [S]	Winter Wonderland	1965	3.75	7.50	15.00
DL 74729 [S]	Songs Made Famous by Nat Cole	1966	3.75	7.50	15.00
DL 74738 [S]	Stand By Me	1966	3.75	7.50	15.00
DL 74806 [S]	Bali Ha'I	1967	3.75	7.50	15.00
DL 74811 [S]	Just a Closer Walk with Thee	1967	3.75	7.50	15.00
DL 74813 [S]	Earl Grant's Greatest Hits	1967	3.75	7.50	15.00
DL 74937 [S]	Gently Swingin'	1968	3.75	7.50	15.00
DL 74974 [S]	Spanish Eyes	1968	3.75	7.50	15.00
DL 75052	In Motion	1969	3.75	7.50	15.00
DL 75108	This Magic Moment	1970	3.75	7.50	15.00
DL 75158	A Time for Us	1970	3.00	6.00	12.00
DL 75223	Earl Grant	1970	3.00	6.00	12.00
DL 78830 [S]	The End	1959	5.00	10.00	20.00
DL 78905 [S]	Grant Takes Rhythm	1959	5.00	10.00	20.00
DL 78916 [S]	Nothing But the Blues	1960	5.00	10.00	20.00
DL 78935 [S]	Paris Is My Beat	1960	5.00	10.00	20.00
VOCALION					
VL 3793 [M]	It's So Good	1967	3.00	6.00	12.00
VL 73793 [S]	It's So Good	1967	3.00	6.00	12.00
VL 73860	Send for Me	1969	3.00	6.00	12.00
VL 73893	One for My Baby	1969	3.00	6.00	12.00

GRANT, GEORGE, AND THE CASTELLES

See THE CASTELLES.

GRANT, GOGI

Number	Title (A Side/B Side)	Yr	VG	VG+	NM
45s					
20TH FOX					
284	Johnny, I Hardly Knew Ye/The Second Time Around	1961	2.50	5.00	10.00
297	Magic Music/Tender Is the Night	1962	2.50	5.00	10.00
403	Magic Music/Tender Is the Night	1963	2.00	4.00	8.00
ERA					
1003	Suddenly There's a Valley/Love Is	1955	3.75	7.50	15.00
1008	Who Are We/We Believe in Love	1955	3.75	7.50	15.00
1013	The Wayward Wind/No More Than Forever	1956	4.00	8.00	16.00
1019	You're in Love/When the Tide Is High	1956	3.75	7.50	15.00
1053	The Golden Ladder/All of Me	1957	3.00	6.00	12.00
1062	I Gave You My Heart/I Don't Want to Walk Without You	1957	3.00	6.00	12.00
3046	The Wayward Wind/The Tide Is High	1961	2.00	4.00	8.00
3205	The Wayward Wind/Suddenly There's a Valley	1969	—	2.50	5.00
LIBERTY					
55214	If and When/I'll Never Smile Again	1959	2.50	5.00	10.00
55229	Goin' Home/All God's Children Got Shoes	1959	2.50	5.00	10.00
55252	I Never Meant to Fall in Love/Stay Here with Me	1960	2.50	5.00	10.00
55286	Two Lovers by the Sea/In a Sentimental Mood	1960	2.50	5.00	10.00
55316	That One Kiss/Adrift on a Star	1961	2.50	5.00	10.00
MONUMENT					
986	Don't Touch Me/Pathfinder	1966	—	3.00	6.00
1005	The Sea/How Much Will I Love You	1967	—	3.00	6.00
PETE					
701	Down Here on the Ground/The Magic of People	1968	—	2.50	5.00
708	Buy Me Penny Candy/Paradise	1968	—	2.50	5.00
717	Yesterday, When I Was Young/(B-side unknown)	1969	—	2.50	5.00
718	On the Mountain/Faure	1969	—	2.50	5.00
RCA VICTOR					
47-4994	Forget Me Not/Where There's Smoke, There's Fire	1952	5.00	10.00	20.00
47-5053	Mommy's Little Angel/My Tormented Heart	1952	5.00	10.00	20.00
—B-side by the Three Suns					
47-5436	Everyone Knows I Love You/Ricochet	1953	5.00	10.00	20.00
47-5512	Secret Love/Ricochet	1953	5.00	10.00	20.00
47-6996	That's the Life for Me/It's a Wonderful Thing to Be Loved	1957	2.50	5.00	10.00
47-7082	Johnny's Dream/What a Beautiful Combination	1957	2.50	5.00	10.00
47-7146	Georgia Nightingale/Bonjour Tristesse	1958	2.50	5.00	10.00
47-7215	My Secret Prayer/How Do We Know We're in Love	1958	2.50	5.00	10.00
47-7294	Strange Are the Ways of Love/Marjolaino	1958	2.50	5.00	10.00
47-7438	Two Dreams/(Kiss Me) Honey Honey (Kiss Me)	1959	2.50	5.00	10.00
47-7492	The Ride Back from Boot Hill/A Restless Pair	1959	2.50	5.00	10.00
Albums					
ERA					
EL-106 [M]	The Wayward Wind	196?	6.25	12.50	25.00
20001 [M]	Suddenly There's Gogi Grant	1956	25.00	50.00	100.00
—Red vinyl					
20001 [M]	Suddenly There's Gogi Grant	1956	15.00	30.00	60.00
—Black vinyl					
LIBERTY					
LRP-3144 [M]	If You Want to Get to Heaven, Shout	1960	7.50	15.00	30.00
LST-7144 [S]	If You Want to Get to Heaven, Shout	1960	10.00	20.00	40.00
PETE					
S-1101	Gogi Grant	1968	3.75	7.50	15.00
S-1111	The Way a Woman Feels	1970	3.75	7.50	15.00
RCA VICTOR					
LOC-1030 [M]	The Helen Morgan Story	1957	15.00	30.00	60.00
LPM-1717 [M]	Welcome to My Heart	1958	10.00	20.00	40.00
LPM-1940 [M]	Torch Time	1959	7.50	15.00	30.00
LSP-1940 [S]	Torch Time	1959	10.00	20.00	40.00
LPM-2000 [M]	Granted... It's Gogi	1960	7.50	15.00	30.00
LSP-2000 [S]	Granted... It's Gogi	1960	10.00	20.00	40.00

GRANT, JANIE

Number	Title (A Side/B Side)	Yr	VG	VG+	NM
45s					
CAPRICE					
104	Triangle/She's Going Steady with You	1961	3.75	7.50	15.00
109	Romeo/Roller Coaster	1961	3.75	7.50	15.00
111	I Wonder Who's Kissing You Now/Unhappy	1961	3.75	7.50	15.00
113	Oh Johnny/Oh My Love	1962	3.75	7.50	15.00
115	That Greasy Kid Stuff/Trying to Forget You	1962	3.75	7.50	15.00
119	Peggy Got Engaged/Two Is Company and Three's a Crowd	1962	3.75	7.50	15.00
PARKWAY					
982	My Heart, Your Heart/And That Reminds Me of You	1966	7.50	15.00	30.00
UNITED ARTISTS					
616	Tell Me Mama/Whose Heart Are You Breaking Now	1963	3.00	6.00	12.00
649	That Kind of Boy/Priceless Persuasion	1963	3.00	6.00	12.00
731	Ribbons and Roses/Too Young for Me	1964	3.00	6.00	12.00
775	After Last Night/All I Did Was Fall in Love	1964	3.00	6.00	12.00
843	I Shouldn't Care (If You're Using Me)/There Ain't No Party Tonight	1965	3.00	6.00	12.00

GRANT, JERRY

Probably the artist who later recorded as GERRY GRANAHAN.

Number	Title (A Side/B Side)	Yr	VG	VG+	NM
45s					
ATCO					
6100	Talkin' About Love/Some Day, Maybe Tonight	1957	10.00	20.00	40.00

GRANT, JULIE

Number	Title (A Side/B Side)	Yr	VG	VG+	NM
45s					
HICKORY					
1260	Every Day I Have to Cry/Watch What You Do with Your Baby	1964	3.00	6.00	12.00
1288	You're Nobody 'Til Somebody Loves You/Come to Me	1964	3.00	6.00	12.00

GRAPEFRUIT

Number	Title (A Side/B Side)	Yr	VG	VG+	NM
45s					
ABC DUNHILL					
4178	This Little Man/Round Going Round	1968	2.50	5.00	10.00
EQUINOX					
70000	Dead Boot/Dear Delilah	1967	3.00	6.00	12.00
70005	Elevator/Yes	1968	3.00	6.00	12.00
70008	C'mon Marianne/Ain't It Good	1968	3.00	6.00	12.00
RCA VICTOR					
74-0241	Thunder and Lightning/Blues in Your Head	1969	2.00	4.00	8.00
Albums					
ABC DUNHILL					
DS-50050	Around Grapefruit	1968	5.00	10.00	20.00
RCA VICTOR					
LSP-4215	Deep Water	1969	3.75	7.50	15.00

GRASS ROOTS, THE

Originally a studio group led by STEVE BARRI and P.F. SLOAN; the touring group, recruited after the success of "Where Were You When I Needed You," featured Rob Grill on vocals.

Number	Title (A Side/B Side)	Yr	VG	VG+	NM
45s					
ABC DUNHILL					
4144	Midnight Confessions/Who Will You Be Tomorrow	1968	2.00	4.00	8.00
4162	Della Linda/Hot Bright Blues	1968	3.00	6.00	12.00
—Some labels have A-side typographical error as shown					
4162	Bella Linda/Hot Bright Blues	1968	2.00	4.00	8.00
4180	Lovin' Things/You and Love Are the Same	1969	2.00	4.00	8.00
4187	The River Is Wide/(You Gotta) Live for Love	1969	2.00	4.00	8.00
4198	I'd Wait a Million Years/Fly Me to Havana	1969	—	3.00	6.00
4217	Heaven Knows/Don't Remind Me	1969	—	3.00	6.00
4227	Walking Through the Country/Truck Drivin' Man	1970	—	3.00	6.00
4237	Baby Hold On/Get It Together	1970	—	3.00	6.00
4237 [PS]	Baby Hold On/Get It Together	1970	2.50	5.00	10.00

Number	Title (A Side/B Side)	Yr	VG	VG+	NM
4249	Come On and Say It/Something's Comin' Over Me	1970	—	3.00	6.00
4249 [PS]	Come On and Say It/Something's Comin' Over Me	1970	2.50	5.00	10.00
4263	Temptation Eyes/Keepin' Me Down	1971	—	2.50	5.00
4279	Sooner or Later/I Can Turn Off the Rain	1971	—	2.50	5.00
4289	Two Divided by Love/Let It Go	1971	—	2.50	5.00
4302	Glory Bound/The Only One	1972	—	2.50	5.00
4316	The Runway/Move Along	1972	—	2.50	5.00
4325	Any Way the Wind Blows/Monday Love	1972	—	2.50	5.00
4335	Love Is What You Make It/Someone to Love	1973	—	3.00	6.00
4345	Where There's Smoke There's Fire/Look but Don't Touch	1973	2.50	5.00	10.00
4371	We Can't Dance to Your Music/Look but Don't Touch	1973	2.50	5.00	10.00
15006	Stealin' Love (In the Night)/We Almost Made It Together	1974	3.75	7.50	15.00
DUNHILL					
4013	Mr. Jones (A Ballad of a Thin Man)/You're a Lonely Girl	1965	5.00	10.00	20.00
4029	Where Were You When I Needed You/(These Are) Bad Times	1966	5.00	10.00	20.00
4043	Only When You're Lonely/This Is What I Was Made For	1966	5.00	10.00	20.00
4053	Tip of My Tongue/Look Out, Girl	1966	6.25	12.50	25.00
4084	Let's Live for Today/Depressed Feeling	1967	3.00	6.00	12.00
4094	Things I Should Have Said/Tip of My Tongue	1967	2.50	5.00	10.00
4094 [PS]	Things I Should Have Said/Tip of My Tongue	1967	3.75	7.50	15.00
4105	Wake Up, Wake Up/No Exit	1967	2.50	5.00	10.00
4122	A Melody for You/Hey Friend	1968	2.50	5.00	10.00
4129	Feelings/Here's Where You Belong	1968	2.50	5.00	10.00
4144	Midnight Confessions/Who Will You Be Tomorrow	1968	7.50	15.00	30.00
—Original label has no "ABC" logo next to "Dunhill"					
HAVEN					
802	Out in the Open/Optical Illusion	1976	2.00	4.00	8.00
7015	Mamacita/Last Time Around	1975	—	2.50	5.00
7021	Naked Man/Nothing Good Comes Easy	1975	—	2.50	5.00
MCA					
52058	Here Comes That Feeling Again/Temptation Eyes	1982	2.50	5.00	10.00
52104	She Don't Know Me/Keep On Burning	1982	2.50	5.00	10.00

Albums

Number	Title	Yr	VG	VG+	NM
ABC					
AC-30003	The ABC Collection	1976	3.75	7.50	15.00
ABC DUNHILL					
DS-50027	Feelings	1968	3.75	7.50	15.00
—Reissue with ABC logo					
DS-50047	Golden Grass	1968	5.00	10.00	20.00
DS-50052	Lovin' Things	1969	5.00	10.00	20.00
DS-50067	Leaving It All Behind	1969	5.00	10.00	20.00
DS-50087	More Golden Grass	1970	5.00	10.00	20.00
DSX-50107	Their 16 Greatest Hits	1971	5.00	10.00	20.00
DSX-50112	Move Along	1972	3.75	7.50	15.00
DSX-50137	A Lotta Mileage	1973	3.75	7.50	15.00
COMMAND					
QD-40013 [Q]	Their 16 Greatest Hits	1974	7.50	15.00	30.00
DUNHILL					
D-50011 [M]	Where Were You When I Needed You	1966	37.50	75.00	150.00
DS-50011 [S]	Where Were You When I Needed You	1966	25.00	50.00	100.00
D-50020 [M]	Let's Live for Today	1967	6.25	12.50	25.00
DS-50020 [S]	Let's Live for Today	1967	7.50	15.00	30.00
D-50027 [M]	Feelings	1968	7.50	15.00	30.00
DS-50027 [S]	Feelings	1968	5.00	10.00	20.00
HAVEN					
ST-9204	The Grass Roots	1975	3.75	7.50	15.00
MCA					
5331	Powers of the Night	1982	3.00	6.00	12.00
37154	Their 16 Greatest Hits	198?	2.00	4.00	8.00
—Budget-line reissue of ABC Dunhill 50107					

GRATEFUL DEAD, THE

Also see JERRY GARCIA; MICKEY HART; BOB WEIR.

12-Inch Singles

Number	Title (A Side/B Side)	Yr	VG	VG+	NM
ARISTA					
ADP 9757 [DJ]	Throwing Stones (Ashes Ashes) (LP version)/(Edit Remix)	1987	3.00	6.00	12.00

45s

Number	Title (A Side/B Side)	Yr	VG	VG+	NM
ARISTA					
0276	Dancin' in the Streets/Terrapin Station	1977	—	3.00	6.00
0291	Passenger/Terrapin Station	1977	—	3.00	6.00
0383	Good Lovin'/Stagger Lee	1978	—	3.00	6.00
0410	France/Shakedown Street	1979	—	3.00	6.00
0519	Alabama Getaway/Far from Me	1980	—	2.50	5.00
0519 [PS]	Alabama Getaway/Far from Me	1980	—	2.50	5.00
0546	Don't Ease Me In/Far from Me	1980	—	2.50	5.00
9606	Touch of Grey/My Brother Esau	1987	—	2.50	5.00
—Grey vinyl					
9606	Touch of Grey/My Brother Esau	1987	—	—	3.00
—Black vinyl (not issued with picture sleeve)					
9606 [PS]	Touch of Grey/My Brother Esau	1987	—	2.50	5.00
—Fold-open poster sleeve (add $2 for sticker attached to original shrink wrap)					
9643	Throwing Stones (Ashes Ashes) Edit/Throwing Stones (Ashes Ashes) LP Version	1987	—	—	3.00
9643 [PS]	Throwing Stones (Ashes Ashes) Edit/Throwing Stones (Ashes Ashes) LP Version	1987	—	—	3.00
9899	Foolish Heart/We Can Run	1989	—	2.00	4.00
9899 [PS]	Foolish Heart/We Can Run	1989	—	2.00	4.00
GRATEFUL DEAD					
01	Here Comes Sunshine/Let Me Sing Your Blues Away	1973	3.00	6.00	12.00
02	Eyes of the World/Weather Report (Part 1)	1974	3.00	6.00	12.00
03	U.S. Blues/Loose Lucy	1974	2.50	5.00	10.00
03 [PS]	U.S. Blues/Loose Lucy	1974	6.25	12.50	25.00
XW-718	The Music Never Stopped/Help on the Way	1975	3.75	7.50	15.00
XW-762	Franklin's Tower/Help on the Way	1976	6.25	12.50	25.00
SCORPIO					
201	Stealin'/Don't Ease Me In	1966	250.00	500.00	1000.
WARNER BROS.					
7016	The Golden Road (To Unlimited Devotion)/Cream Puff War	1967	6.25	12.50	25.00
7186	Dark Star/Born Cross-Eyed	1968	6.25	12.50	25.00
7186 [PS]	Dark Star/Born Cross-Eyed	1968	125.00	250.00	500.00
7324	Dupree's Diamond Blues/Cosmic Charlie	1969	6.25	12.50	25.00
7410	Uncle John's Band/New Speedway Boogie	1970	3.75	7.50	15.00
—A picture sleeve for this is rumored to exist					
7464	Truckin'/Ripple	1971	3.75	7.50	15.00
7627	Johnny B. Goode/So Fine	1972	5.00	10.00	20.00
—B-side by Elvin Bishop Group					
7653	Truckin'/Johnny B. Goode	1973	2.00	4.00	8.00
—"Back to Back Hits" series					
7667	Sugar Magnolia/Mr. Charlie	1972	3.75	7.50	15.00

7-Inch Extended Plays

Number	Title (A Side/B Side)	Yr	VG	VG+	NM
WARNER BROS.					
S 1893 [DJ]	Sugar Magnolia/Operator/Till the Morning Comes//Truckin'/Friend of the Devil	1973	5.00	10.00	20.00
—Jukebox issue, small hole, plays at 33 1/3 rpm					
S 1893 [PS]	American Beauty	1973	7.50	15.00	30.00
—Part of Little LP series (LLP #226)					

Albums

Number	Title	Yr	VG	VG+	NM
ARISTA					
SP-35 [DJ]	Grateful Dead Sampler	1978	7.50	15.00	30.00
AL 4198	Shakedown Street	1978	3.00	6.00	12.00
AL 7001	Terrapin Station	1977	3.75	7.50	15.00
AL 7001 [DJ]	Terrapin Station	1977	12.50	25.00	50.00
—Radio station promos are banded for airplay					
AL 8112 [(2)]	Dead Set	198?	2.50	5.00	10.00
—Budget-line reissue of 8606					
AL 8321	Shakedown Street	198?	2.00	4.00	8.00
—Budget-line reissue of 4198					
AL 8329	Terrapin Station	198?	2.00	4.00	8.00
—Budget-line reissue of 7001					
AL 8332	Go to Heaven	198?	2.00	4.00	8.00
—Budget-line reissue of 9508					
AL 8452	In the Dark	1987	2.50	5.00	10.00
AL 8575	Built to Last	1989	2.50	5.00	10.00
A2L 8604 [(2)]	Reckoning	1981	3.75	7.50	15.00
A2L 8606 [(2)]	Dead Set	1981	3.75	7.50	15.00
AL3 8634 [(3)]	Without a Net	1990	6.25	12.50	25.00
AL 9508	Go to Heaven	1980	3.00	6.00	12.00
DIRECT DISK					
SD-16619	Terrapin Station	1980	25.00	50.00	100.00
—Audiophile vinyl					
GRATEFUL DEAD					
GD-01	Wake of the Flood	1973	5.00	10.00	20.00
—With no contributing artists on back cover					
GD-01	Wake of the Flood	1975	3.75	7.50	15.00
—With contributing artists on back cover and United Artists distribution					
GD-01 [DJ]	Wake of the Flood	1973	100.00	200.00	400.00
—Green vinyl meant for fan-club members; ironically, most copies were damaged in a flood before distribution					
GD-102	Grateful Dead from the Mars Hotel	1974	5.00	10.00	20.00
—Without United Artists distribution					
GD-102	Grateful Dead from the Mars Hotel	1975	3.75	7.50	15.00
—With United Artists distribution					
GD-LA494-G	Blues for Allah	1975	5.00	10.00	20.00
GD-LA620-J2 [(2)]	Steal Your Face	1976	6.25	12.50	25.00
MOBILE FIDELITY					
1-014	American Beauty	1980	12.50	25.00	50.00
—Audiophile vinyl					
1-172	Grateful Dead from the Mars Hotel	1984	10.00	20.00	40.00
—Audiophile vinyl					
PAIR					
PDL2-1053 [(2)]	For the Faithful...	1986	3.00	6.00	12.00
SUNFLOWER					
SUN-5001	Vintage Dead	1970	10.00	20.00	40.00
—Album has been counterfeited, but bogus covers are 1/4" shorter than normal LP cover					
SNF-5004	Historic Dead	1971	10.00	20.00	40.00
WARNER BROS.					
W 1689 [M]	The Grateful Dead	1967	50.00	100.00	200.00
WS 1689 [S]	The Grateful Dead	1967	20.00	40.00	80.00
—Gold label					
WS 1689 [S]	The Grateful Dead	1968	6.25	12.50	25.00
—Green label with "W7" logo					
WS 1689 [S]	The Grateful Dead	1970	3.75	7.50	15.00
—Green label with "WB" logo					
WS 1689 [S]	The Grateful Dead	1973	3.00	6.00	12.00
—"Burbank" palm-trees label					
WS 1689 [S]	The Grateful Dead	1979	2.00	4.00	8.00
—White or tan label					
WS 1749	Anthem of the Sun	1968	7.50	15.00	30.00
—Green label with "W7" logo					
WS 1749	Anthem of the Sun	1970	3.75	7.50	15.00
—Green label with "WB" logo, purple cover					
WS 1749	Anthem of the Sun	1973	3.00	6.00	12.00
—"Burbank" palm-trees label					
WS 1749	Anthem of the Sun	1979	2.00	4.00	8.00
—White or tan label					
WS 1749	Anthem of the Sun	197?	12.50	25.00	50.00
—Green label with "WB" logo, white background on cover with radically remixed version of LP					
WS 1790	Aoxomoxoa	1969	7.50	15.00	30.00
—Green label with "W7" logo					
WS 1790	Aoxomoxoa	1970	3.75	7.50	15.00
—Green label with "WB" logo					
WS 1790	Aoxomoxoa	1973	3.00	6.00	12.00
—"Burbank" palm-trees label					

Number	Title (A Side/B Side)	Yr	VG	VG+	NM
WS 1790	Aoxomoxoa	1979	2.00	4.00	8.00
—White or tan label					
2WS 1830 [(2)]	Live/Dead	1969	10.00	20.00	40.00
—Green labels with "W7" logo					
2WS 1830 [(2)]	Live/Dead	1970	5.00	10.00	20.00
—Green labels with "WB" logo					
2WS 1830 [(2)]	Live/Dead	1973	3.75	7.50	15.00
—"Burbank" palm-trees labels					
2WS 1830 [(2)]	Live/Dead	1979	2.50	5.00	10.00
—White or tan labels					
WS 1869	Workingman's Dead	1970	6.25	12.50	25.00
—Green label with "WB" logo; textured cover with back cover slick upside down					
WS 1869	Workingman's Dead	1973	3.00	6.00	12.00
—"Burbank" palm-trees label; standard cover with back cover right side up					
WS 1869	Workingman's Dead	1979	2.00	4.00	8.00
—White or tan label					
WS 1893	American Beauty	1970	6.25	12.50	25.00
—Green label with "WB" logo					
WS 1893	American Beauty	1973	3.00	6.00	12.00
—"Burbank" palm-trees label					
WS 1893	American Beauty	1979	2.00	4.00	8.00
—White or tan label					
2WS 1935 [(2)]	Grateful Dead	1971	7.50	15.00	30.00
—Green labels with "WB" logo					
2WS 1935 [(2)]	Grateful Dead	1973	3.75	7.50	15.00
—"Burbank" palm-trees labels					
2WS 1935 [(2)]	Grateful Dead	1979	2.50	5.00	10.00
—White or tan labels					
3WX 2668 [(3)]	Europe '72	1972	10.00	20.00	40.00
—Green labels with "WB" logo					
3WX 2668 [(3)]	Europe '72	1973	5.00	10.00	20.00
—"Burbank" palm-trees labels					
3WX 2668 [(3)]	Europe '72	1979	3.00	6.00	12.00
—White or tan labels					
BS 2721	History of the Grateful Dead, Vol. 1 (Bear's Choice)	1973	5.00	10.00	20.00
—"Burbank" palm-trees labels					
BS 2721	History of the Grateful Dead, Vol. 1 (Bear's Choice)	1973	2.00	4.00	8.00
—White or tan labels					
BS 2764	The Best of/Skeleton's from the Closet	1974	5.00	10.00	20.00
—"Burbank" palm-trees labels					
BS 2764	The Best of/Skeleton's from the Closet	1979	2.00	4.00	8.00
—White or tan labels					
2WS 3091 [(2)]	What a Long Strange Trip It's Been: The Best of the Grateful Dead	1977	5.00	10.00	20.00
—"Burbank" palm-trees labels					
2WS 3091 [(2)]	What a Long Strange Trip It's Been: The Best of the Grateful Dead	1979	2.50	5.00	10.00
—White or tan labels					
ST-93416	American Beauty	1970	12.50	25.00	50.00
—Capitol Record Club edition; green label with "W7" logo					

GRAVENITES, NICK

Albums

COLUMBIA

Number	Title (A Side/B Side)	Yr	VG	VG+	NM
CS 9899	My Labors	1969	3.75	7.50	15.00

GRAVES, BILLY

45s

MONUMENT

Number	Title (A Side/B Side)	Yr	VG	VG+	NM
401	The Shag (Is Totally Cool)/Uncertain	1958	5.00	10.00	20.00
404	Long Journey Home/Midnight Bus	1959	3.75	7.50	15.00
418	Right or Wrong (I'll Be With You)/Mount Fujiyama	1960	3.00	6.00	12.00
992	The Lonesome Ape/I've Got a Feeling	1966	2.00	4.00	8.00

GRAVES, JOE

45s

PARKWAY

Number	Title (A Side/B Side)	Yr	VG	VG+	NM
103	Debbie/A Boy and a Girl Fall in Love	1966	3.75	7.50	15.00
964	See Saw/Beautiful Girl	1965	3.75	7.50	15.00

GRAVITY ADJUSTERS EXPANSION BAND

Albums

NOCTURNE

Number	Title (A Side/B Side)	Yr	VG	VG+	NM
NRS-302	One	1973	75.00	150.00	300.00

GRAY, BARRY, AND THE SPACEMAKERS

45s

ABC-PARAMOUNT

Number	Title (A Side/B Side)	Yr	VG	VG+	NM
10424	Fireball/XL 5	1963	3.00	6.00	12.00

GRAY, BILLY

45s

DECCA

Number	Title (A Side/B Side)	Yr	VG	VG+	NM
29489	Okie Blondie/I've Had At My Heart	1955	7.50	15.00	30.00
29678	Harbor of Love/Girls, Girls, Girls	1955	7.50	15.00	30.00
29800	Tennessee Toddy/It Could Have Been Me	1956	10.00	20.00	40.00

GRAY, DOBIE

12-Inch Singles

INFINITY

Number	Title (A Side/B Side)	Yr	VG	VG+	NM
INF-16001	You Can Do It/Thank You for Tonight	1979	3.00	6.00	12.00

45s

Number	Title (A Side/B Side)	Yr	VG	VG+	NM
ANTHEM					
200	Guess Who?/Bits and Pieces	1972	—	2.50	5.00
ARISTA					
1047	One Can Fake It/(B-side unknown)	1983	—	2.00	4.00
CAPITOL					
2241	We the People/Funny and Groovy	1968	2.50	5.00	10.00
B-5562	Gonna Be a Long Night/That's One to Grown On	1986	—	—	3.00
B-5596	The Dark Side of Life/A Night in the Life of a Country Boy	1986	—	—	3.00
B-5647	From Where I Stand/So Far So Good	1986	—	—	3.00
5853	River Deep, Mountain High/Tennessee Waltz	1967	3.75	7.50	15.00
B-44087	Take It Real Easy/You Must Have Been Reading My Heart	1987	—	—	3.00
B-44126	Love Letters/Steady As She Goes	1988	—	—	3.00
CAPRICORN					
0249	If Love Must Go/Lover's Sweat	1975	—	2.00	4.00
0259	Find 'Em, Fool 'Em and Forget 'Em/Mellow Man	1976	—	2.00	4.00
0267	Let Go/Mellow Man	1976	—	2.00	4.00
CHARGER					
105	The "In" Crowd/To Be a Man	1964	3.00	6.00	12.00
107	See You at the "Go-Go"/Walk with Love	1965	2.50	5.00	10.00
109	In Hollywood/Mr. Engineer	1965	2.50	5.00	10.00
113	Monkey Jerk/My Baby	1965	2.50	5.00	10.00
115	No Room to Cry/Out on the Floor	1966	2.50	5.00	10.00
CORDAK					
1602	Look at Me/Walkin' and Whistlin'	1962	3.75	7.50	15.00
DECCA					
33057	Drift Away/City Stars	1973	—	2.50	5.00
INFINITY					
50003	You Can Do It/Sharing the Night Together	1978	—	2.00	4.00
50010	Who's Lovin' You/Thank You for Tonight	1979	—	2.00	4.00
50020	Spending Time, Making Love, and Going Crazy/Let This Man Take Hold of Your Life	1979	—	2.00	4.00
50043	The In Crowd/Let This Man Take Hold of Your Life	1979	—	2.00	4.00
MCA					
40100	Loving Arms/Now That I'm Without You	1973	—	2.00	4.00
40153	Good Old Song/Reachin' for the Feelin'	1973	—	2.00	4.00
40188	Rose/Lovin' the Easy Way	1974	—	2.00	4.00
40201	There's a Honky Tonk Angel (Who'll Take Me Back In)/Lovin' the Easy Way	1974	—	2.00	4.00
40268	Watch Out for Lucy/Turning On You	1974	—	2.00	4.00
40315	The Music's Real/Roll On Sweet Mississippi	1974	—	2.00	4.00
ROBOX					
RRS-117	Decorate the Night (same on both sides)	1979	—	2.50	5.00
WHITE WHALE					
300	Rose Garden/Where's the Girl Gone	1969	2.50	5.00	10.00
330	What a Way to Go/Do You Really Have a Heart	1969	50.00	100.00	200.00
342	Honey, You Can't Take It Back	1970	15.00	30.00	60.00

Albums

Number	Title (A Side/B Side)	Yr	VG	VG+	NM
CAPITOL					
ST-12489	From Where I Stand	1986	2.50	5.00	10.00
CAPRICORN					
CP 0163	New Ray of Sunshine	1976	2.50	5.00	10.00
CHARGER					
CHR-M-2002 [M]	Dobie Gray Sings for "In" Crowders That Go "Go Go"	1965	10.00	20.00	40.00
CHR-S-2002 [S]	Dobie Gray Sings for "In" Crowders That Go "Go Go"	1965	30.00	60.00	120.00
DECCA					
DL 75397	Drift Away	1973	3.00	6.00	12.00
INFINITY					
INF-9001	Midnight Diamond	1979	2.50	5.00	10.00
MCA					
371	Loving Arms	1973	2.50	5.00	10.00
449	Hey Dixie	1974	2.50	5.00	10.00
515	Drift Away	1974	2.50	5.00	10.00
—Reissue of Decca 75397					
ROBOX					
RBX 8102	Welcome Home	1981	2.50	5.00	10.00
STRIPE					
LPM 2001 [M]	Look — Dobie Gray	1963	25.00	50.00	100.00

GRAY, GENE, AND THE STINGRAYS

45s

Number	Title (A Side/B Side)	Yr	VG	VG+	NM
DOT					
16478	Surf Bunny/Surfer's Mood	1963	5.00	10.00	20.00
LINDA					
110	Surf Bunny/Surfer's Mood	1963	10.00	20.00	40.00

GRAY, GLEN

7-Inch Extended Plays

CAPITOL

Number	Title (A Side/B Side)	Yr	VG	VG+	NM
EAP 1-747	No Name Jive//Black Jazz/Smoke Rings	1956	2.50	5.00	10.00
—Sides 1 and 8 of "Album 747"					
EAP 1-747 [PS]	Casa Loma in Hi-Fi! Part 1	1956	2.50	5.00	10.00
EAP 2-747	Memories of You/White Jazz//Dance of the Lame Duck/For You	1956	2.50	5.00	10.00
—Sides 2 and 7 of "Album 747"					
EAP 2-747 [PS]	Casa Loma in Hi-Fi! Part 2	1956	2.50	5.00	10.00
EAP 3-747	(contents unknown)	1956	2.50	5.00	10.00
—Sides 3 and 6 of "Album 747"					
EAP 3-747 [PS]	Casa Loma in Hi-Fi! Part 3	1956	2.50	5.00	10.00
EAP 4-747	Sunrise Serenade/Maniac's Ball//Casa Loma Stomp/Just an Old Manuscript	1956	2.50	5.00	10.00
—Sides 4 and 5 of "Album 747"					
EAP 4-747 [PS]	Casa Loma in Hi-Fi! Part 4	1956	2.50	5.00	10.00
EAP 1-1022	(contents unknown)	195?	2.50	5.00	10.00
EAP 1-1022 [PS]	Sounds of the Great Bands, Part 1	195?	2.50	5.00	10.00
EAP 2-1022	One O'Clock Jump/Contrasts//Boogie Woogie on St. Louis Blues/String of Pearls	195?	2.50	5.00	10.00
EAP 2-1022 [PS]	Sounds of the Great Bands, Part 2	195?	2.50	5.00	10.00

Albums

CAPITOL

Number	Title (A Side/B Side)	Yr	VG	VG+	NM
W 747 [M]	Casa Loma in Hi-Fi!	1956	6.25	12.50	25.00
SM-1022	Sounds of the Great Bands!	197?	2.50	5.00	10.00
—Reissue					
SW 1022 [S]	Sounds of the Great Bands!	1959	3.75	7.50	15.00
W 1022 [M]	Sounds of the Great Bands!	1959	3.00	6.00	12.00

Number	Title (A Side/B Side)	Yr	VG	VG+	NM
SM-1067	Sounds of the Great Bands Volume 2	197?	2.50	5.00	10.00
—Reissue					
ST 1067 [S]	Sounds of the Great Bands Volume 2	1959	3.75	7.50	15.00
T 1067 [M]	Sounds of the Great Bands Volume 2	1959	3.00	6.00	12.00
ST 1234 [S]	Solo Spotlight	1960	3.75	7.50	15.00
T 1234 [M]	Solo Spotlight	1960	3.00	6.00	12.00
ST 1289 [S]	Swingin' Decade	1960	3.75	7.50	15.00
T 1289 [M]	Swingin' Decade	1960	3.00	6.00	12.00
ST 1400 [S]	Swingin' Southern Style	1961	3.75	7.50	15.00
T 1400 [M]	Swingin' Southern Style	1961	3.00	6.00	12.00
ST 1506 [S]	Please Mr. Gray...More Sounds of the Great Bands	1961	3.75	7.50	15.00
T 1506 [M]	Please Mr. Gray...More Sounds of the Great Bands	1961	3.00	6.00	12.00
DT 1588 [R]	Sounds of the Great Casa Loma Band	1961	3.00	6.00	12.00
SM-1588	Sounds of the Great Casa Loma Band	197?	2.50	5.00	10.00
—Reissue					
T 1588 [M]	Sounds of the Great Casa Loma Band	1961	3.75	7.50	15.00
ST 1615 [S]	Shall We Swing?	1961	3.75	7.50	15.00
T 1615 [M]	Shall We Swing?	1961	3.00	6.00	12.00
ST 1739 [S]	Sounds of the Great Bands Volume 5: They All Swung the Blues	1962	3.75	7.50	15.00
T 1739 [M]	Sounds of the Great Bands Volume 5: They All Swung the Blues	1962	3.00	6.00	12.00
SM-1812	Themes of the Great Bands	197?	2.50	5.00	10.00
—Reissue					
ST 1812 [S]	Themes of the Great Bands	1963	3.75	7.50	15.00
T 1812 [M]	Themes of the Great Bands	1963	3.00	6.00	12.00
ST 1938 [S]	Sounds of the Great Bands Volume 7: Today's Best	1963	3.00	6.00	12.00
T 1938 [M]	Sounds of the Great Bands Volume 7: Today's Best	1963	2.50	5.00	10.00
ST 2014 [S]	Sounds of the Great Bands Volume 8: More of Today's Best	1964	3.00	6.00	12.00
T 2014 [M]	Sounds of the Great Bands Volume 8: More of Today's Best	1964	2.50	5.00	10.00
ST 2131 [S]	Sounds of the Great Bands in Latin	1964	3.00	6.00	12.00
T 2131 [M]	Sounds of the Great Bands in Latin	1964	2.50	5.00	10.00
CIRCLE					
16	Glen Gray and the Casa Loma Orchestra	198?	2.50	5.00	10.00
CORAL					
CRL 56006 [10]	Hoagy Carmichael Songs	1950	12.50	25.00	50.00
CRL 56009 [10]	Glen Gray Souvenirs	1950	12.50	25.00	50.00
CREATIVE WORLD					
ST-1055	Shall We Swing?	197?	2.50	5.00	10.00
DECCA					
DL 5089 [10]	Musical Smoke Rings	1950	12.50	25.00	50.00
DL 5397 [10]	No-Name Jive	1953	12.50	25.00	50.00
DL 8570 [M]	Smoke Rings	1957	5.00	10.00	20.00
DL 75016 [R]	Greatest Hits	1968	3.00	6.00	12.00
HARMONY					
HL 7045 [M]	The Great Recordings of Glen Gray	1957	5.00	10.00	20.00
HINDSIGHT					
HSR-104	Glen Gray and the Casa Loma Orchestra, 1939-1940	198?	2.50	5.00	10.00
HSR-120	Glen Gray and the Casa Loma Orchestra, 1943-1946	198?	2.50	5.00	10.00
INSIGHT					
214	Glen Gray and the Casa Loma Orchestra, 1939-1946	198?	2.50	5.00	10.00
MCA					
122	Greatest Hits	1973	2.50	5.00	10.00
—Reissue of Decca 75016					
4076 [(2)]	The Best of Glen Gray	197?	3.00	6.00	12.00
20199	Smoke Rings	198?	2.00	4.00	8.00

GRAY, MAUREEN

45s

Number	Title (A Side/B Side)	Yr	VG	VG+	NM
CHANCELLOR					
1082	Crazy Over You/Today's the Day	1961	6.25	12.50	25.00
1091	Come On and Dance/I Don't Want to Cry	1961	6.25	12.50	25.00
1100	I'm So Young/There's a Boy	1962	6.25	12.50	25.00
LANDA					
689	Dancin' the Strand/Oh My	1962	3.75	7.50	15.00
692	People Are Talking/Oh My	1962	3.75	7.50	15.00
MERCURY					
72131	Story of My Love/Summertime Is Near	1963	3.00	6.00	12.00
72227	I'm a Happy Girl (Tra La La)/Goodbye Baby	1964	3.00	6.00	12.00

GRAY, RUDY

See RUDY GRAYZELL.

GRAYZELL, RUDY

45s

Number	Title (A Side/B Side)	Yr	VG	VG+	NM
ABBOTT					
147	Bonita Chiquita/I'm Gone Again	1953	20.00	40.00	80.00
157	Ocean Paradise/It Ain't My Baby	1954	20.00	40.00	80.00
CAPITOL					
F2946	Hearts Made of Stone/There's Gonna Be a Ball	1954	10.00	20.00	40.00
F3044	You Better Believe It/Ca-Razy	1955	10.00	20.00	40.00
F3149	Please Big Mama/My Heart Is Willing	1955	10.00	20.00	40.00
—Capitol titles as "Rudy Gray"					
MERCURY					
71138	Let's Get Wild/I Love You So	1957	20.00	40.00	80.00
STARDAY					
229	The Moon Is Up/Day by Day	1956	20.00	40.00	80.00
241	Duck Dail/You're Gone	1956	20.00	40.00	80.00
270	You Hurt Me So/Jig-Ga-Lee-Ga	1956	20.00	40.00	80.00
321	Let's Get Wild/I Love You So	1957	25.00	50.00	100.00
SUN					
290	Judy/I Think of You	1958	12.50	25.00	50.00

GREAN, CHARLES RANDOLPH

45s

Number	Title (A Side/B Side)	Yr	VG	VG+	NM
RANWOOD					
840	Quentin's Theme/#1 at the Blue Whale	1969	—	3.50	7.00
858	Josette's Music Box/Back at the Blue Whale	1969	—	2.50	5.00
864	Peter and the Wolf/Georgy	1970	—	2.50	5.00
872	Marcus Welby, M.D. Theme/Come Touch the Sun	1970	—	3.00	6.00
880	The Odd Couple/Theme from "Borsalino"	1970	—	3.00	6.00
891	Bullfrog/Singalong Junk	1970	—	2.50	5.00
901	Any Time of the Year/Although You Make Me Cry	1971	—	2.50	5.00
907	Johnny, Harvey, Charlie, Herbie, Etc. (Part 1 & 2)	1971	—	2.50	5.00
918	Concerto for Knives, Forks, Spoons and Soup Ladle/Gymnopedie	1971	—	2.50	5.00
938	Theme from Star Trek/Rayo de Sol	1972	—	2.50	5.00
952	The Old Piano Roll Blues/Rag-a-Muffin	1972	—	2.50	5.00
973	Karamoja Krackerjack/Two Men of Karamoja	1973	—	2.50	5.00
1010	Very, Very Blue Danube/Now	1974	—	2.00	4.00
1044	Star Trek/Love Theme from "Hustle"	1975	—	2.00	4.00
1064	The $128,000 Question/Sentimentale	1976	—	2.00	4.00
1088	The Masterpiece/Solitary Joe	197?	—	2.00	4.00

Albums

Number	Title (A Side/B Side)	Yr	VG	VG+	NM
HARMONY					
KH 31389	Volume 2	1972	2.50	5.00	10.00
RANWOOD					
8055	Quentin's Theme	1969	3.00	6.00	12.00
8075	The Charles Randolph Grean Sounde	1970	3.00	6.00	12.00
8105	Masterpiece	1972	3.00	6.00	12.00

GREASE BAND

45s

Number	Title (A Side/B Side)	Yr	VG	VG+	NM
SHELTER					
7304	Let It Be Gone/Laughed at the Judge	1971	—	3.00	6.00
7310	All I Wanna Do/Jesse James	1971	—	3.00	6.00

Albums

Number	Title (A Side/B Side)	Yr	VG	VG+	NM
SHELTER					
SW-8904	Grease Band	1971	3.00	6.00	12.00

GREAT LOVE TRIP, THE

45s

Number	Title (A Side/B Side)	Yr	VG	VG+	NM
UNI					
55163	Why Can't We Be/Noah	1969	25.00	5.00	10.00

GREAT SCOTTS, THE

45s

Number	Title (A Side/B Side)	Yr	VG	VG+	NM
EPIC					
9805	Don't Want Your Love/Give Me Lovin'	1965	5.00	10.00	20.00
9866	That's My Girl (Rotten to the Core)/Lost in Conversation	1965	10.00	20.00	40.00
TRIUMPH					
66	Ball and Chain/Run, Run for Your Life	1966	7.50	15.00	30.00
67	Light Hurts My Eyes/You Know What You Can Do	1966	7.50	15.00	30.00

GREAT SOCIETY, THE

Also see GRACE SLICK.

45s

Number	Title (A Side/B Side)	Yr	VG	VG+	NM
COLUMBIA					
44583	Sally Go 'Round the Roses/Didn't Think So	1968	5.00	10.00	20.00
NORTH BEACH					
1001	Someone to Love/Free Advice	1966	62.50	125.00	250.00
—As "The Great!! Society!!"					

Albums

Number	Title (A Side/B Side)	Yr	VG	VG+	NM
COLUMBIA					
CS 9627 [M]	Conspicuous Only In Its Absence	1968	12.50	25.00	50.00
—White label promo only; "Special Mono Radio Station Copy" sticker on front; same number as stereo version					
CS 9627 [S]	Conspicuous Only In Its Absence	1968	6.25	12.50	25.00
—Red label, "360 Sound Stereo"					
CS 9702	How It Was	1968	6.25	12.50	25.00
—Red label, "360 Sound Stereo"					
G 30459 [(2)]	The Great Society Collectors Item	1971	3.75	7.50	15.00
HARMONY					
KH 30391	Somebody to Love	1970	3.00	6.00	12.00

GREAT SPECKLED BIRD

45s

Number	Title (A Side/B Side)	Yr	VG	VG+	NM
AMPEX					
11003	We Sail/Disappearing Woman	1970	2.00	4.00	8.00
11006	Trucker's Café/Smiling Wine	1970	2.00	4.00	8.00

Albums

Number	Title (A Side/B Side)	Yr	VG	VG+	NM
AMPEX					
A-10103	Great Speckled Bird	1970	5.00	10.00	20.00

GREATS, THE

45s

Number	Title (A Side/B Side)	Yr	VG	VG+	NM
EBB					
145	Marching Elvis/Fiddler's Rock	1958	12.50	25.00	50.00

GREAVES, R.B.

45s

Number	Title (A Side/B Side)	Yr	VG	VG+	NM
20TH CENTURY					
2147	Rock and Roll/I'm Married, You're Married	1974	—	2.00	4.00
2203	Let's Try It Again/My Place or Yours	1975	—	2.00	4.00
ATCO					
6714	Take a Letter Maria/Big Bad City	1969	2.00	4.00	8.00
6726	Always Something There to Remind Me/Oh, When I Was a Boy	1969	—	3.00	6.00
6745	Fire and Rain/The Ballad of Leroy	1970	—	3.00	6.00
6778	Oh When I Was a Boy/Georgia Took Her Back	1970	—	3.00	6.00
6789	Whiter Shade of Pale/Show Me the Way to Go	1970	—	3.00	6.00

Number	Title (A Side/B Side)	Yr	VG	VG+	NM
6839	Paperback Writer/Over You Now	1971	—	2.50	5.00
BAREBACK					
523	Margie, Who's Watching the Baby/(B-side unknown)	1977	—	3.00	6.00
MGM					
14483	Margie, Who's Watching the Baby/Area Code 213	1973	—	2.50	5.00
14567	All I Want to Do/Long Live the King	1973	—	2.50	5.00
MIDSONG INT'L.					
72006	Let Me Be the One Tonight/Please Mister Mailman	1980	—	2.00	4.00
SUNFLOWER					
128	Margie, Who's Watching the Baby/Area Code 213	1972	—	3.00	6.00
Albums					
ATCO					
SD 33-311	R.B. Greaves	1969	5.00	10.00	20.00
INTERMEDIA					
QS-5032	Rock and Roll	198?	2.50	5.00	10.00

GRECH, RICH

Number	Title (A Side/B Side)	Yr	VG	VG+	NM
Albums					
RSO					
SO 876	The Last Five Years	1973	3.00	6.00	12.00

—Compiles his work with such groups as Family, Traffic, Blind Faith, Ginger Baker's Air Force and KGB

GRECO, JOHNNY

Number	Title (A Side/B Side)	Yr	VG	VG+	NM
45s					
PAGEANT					
602	Rocket Ride/(B-side unknown)	1963	37.50	75.00	150.00

GREELEY, GEORGE

Number	Title (A Side/B Side)	Yr	VG	VG+	NM
45s					
REPRISE					
0490	Who's Afraid/Jungle Fantasy	1966	—	3.00	6.00
WARNER BROS.					
5100	Malaguena/My Love	1959	2.50	5.00	10.00
5175	Love Music from Tristan & Isolde/My Love	1960	2.00	4.00	8.00
5188	Come Back to Sorrento/Guinevere	1960	2.00	4.00	8.00
5207	Main Theme from "Gone with the Wind"/Tara's Theme	1961	2.00	4.00	8.00
5210	Unchained Melody/Anniversary Song	1961	2.00	4.00	8.00
5218	Lucy's Theme from Parrish/Allison's Theme from Parrish	1961	2.00	4.00	8.00
5239	Tonight/Tender Is the Night	1961	2.00	4.00	8.00
5264	What Now My Love/11th Hour Melody	1962	2.00	4.00	8.00
5293	Ride the High Country/Being in Love	1962	2.00	4.00	8.00
5311	Theme from Mutiny on the Bounty/Love Song from Mutiny on the Bounty	1962	2.00	4.00	8.00
Albums					
CAPITOL					
H 438 [10]	Piano Demitasse	1954	7.50	15.00	30.00
REPRISE					
R 6092 [M]	Piano Rhapsodies of Love	1964	2.50	5.00	10.00
RS 6092 [S]	Piano Rhapsodies of Love	1964	3.00	6.00	12.00
WARNER BROS.					
W 1249 [M]	The World's Greatest Popular Piano Concertos	1958	3.75	7.50	15.00
WS 1249 [S]	The World's Greatest Popular Piano Concertos	1959	5.00	10.00	20.00
W 1291 [M]	World Renowned Popular Piano Concertos	1959	3.75	7.50	15.00
WS 1291 [S]	World Renowned Popular Piano Concertos	1959	5.00	10.00	20.00
W 1319 [M]	The Greatest Motion Picture Piano Concertos	1959	3.75	7.50	15.00
WS 1319 [S]	The Greatest Motion Picture Piano Concertos	1959	5.00	10.00	20.00
WS 1338 [S]	22 Best Loved Christmas Piano Concertos	1959	5.00	10.00	20.00
W 1366 [M]	The Most Beautiful Music of Hawaii	1960	3.00	6.00	12.00
WS 1366 [S]	The Most Beautiful Music of Hawaii	1960	3.75	7.50	15.00
W 1387 [M]	The World's Greatest Love Themes	1960	3.00	6.00	12.00
WS 1387 [S]	The World's Greatest Love Themes	1960	3.75	7.50	15.00
W 1402 [M]	Piano Italiano	1961	3.00	6.00	12.00
WS 1402 [S]	Piano Italiano	1961	3.75	7.50	15.00
W 1410 [M]	The Best of the Popular Piano Concertos	1961	3.00	6.00	12.00
WS 1410 [S]	The Best of the Popular Piano Concertos	1961	3.75	7.50	15.00
W 1415 [M]	Great Broadway Musicals	1961	3.00	6.00	12.00
WS 1415 [S]	Great Broadway Musicals	1961	3.75	7.50	15.00
W 1427 [M]	Famous Film Themes	1961	3.00	6.00	12.00
WS 1427 [S]	Famous Film Themes	1961	3.75	7.50	15.00
W 1451 [M]	George Greeley Plays George Gershwin	1962	3.00	6.00	12.00
WS 1451 [S]	George Greeley Plays George Gershwin	1962	3.75	7.50	15.00
W 1476 [M]	Themes from Mutiny on the Bounty and Other Great Films	1962	3.00	6.00	12.00
WS 1476 [S]	Themes from Mutiny on the Bounty and Other Great Films	1962	3.75	7.50	15.00
W 1503 [M]	A Classic Affair	1963	3.00	6.00	12.00
WS 1503 [S]	A Classic Affair	1963	3.75	7.50	15.00
W 1560 [M]	Best Loved Christmas Piano Concertos	1965	3.00	6.00	12.00
WS 1560 [S]	Best Loved Christmas Piano Concertos	1965	3.75	7.50	15.00

GREEN

Number	Title (A Side/B Side)	Yr	VG	VG+	NM
45s					
ATCO					
6833	Big Dipper/All My Bells	1971	—	2.50	5.00
Albums					
ATCO					
SD 33-282	Green	1969	3.75	7.50	15.00
SD 33-366	To Help Somebody	1971	3.00	6.00	12.00

GREEN, AL

Number	Title (A Side/B Side)	Yr	VG	VG+	NM
12-Inch Singles					
A&M					
12311	As Long As We're Together (4 versions)	1989	—	3.00	6.00
12323	The Message Is Love (6 versions)	1989	—	3.00	6.00
HI					
78510	I Feel Good (7:30)/I Feel Good (3:17)	1978	3.75	7.50	15.00
45s					
A&M					
1427	As Long As We're Together/Blessed	1989	—	—	3.00
2786	Going Away/Building Up	1985	—	2.00	4.00
2807	True Love/He Is the Light	1986	—	2.00	4.00
2919	Everything's Gonna Be Alright/So Real to Me	1987	—	—	3.00
2952	You Know and I Know/True Love	1987	—	—	3.00
2962	Soul Survivor/Jesus Will Fix It	1987	—	—	3.00
BELL					
45258	Guilty/Let Me Help You	1972	—	2.50	5.00
45305	Hot Wire/Don't Leave Me	1973	—	2.50	5.00
CAPITOL					
S7-18869	Tired of Being Alone/Walk On By	1995	—	—	3.00
—B-side by Isaac Hayes					
HI					
2159	I Want to Hold Your Hand/What Am I Gonna Do with Myself	1969	2.00	4.00	8.00
2164	One Woman/Tomorrow's Dream	1969	2.00	4.00	8.00
2172	You Say It/Gotta Find a New World	1969	—	3.00	6.00
2177	Right Now, Right Now/All Because I'm a Foolish One	1970	—	3.00	6.00
2182	I Can't Get Next to You/Ride Sally Ride	1970	—	3.00	6.00
2188	Driving Wheel/True Love	1971	—	3.00	6.00
2194	Tired of Being Alone/Get Back Baby	1971	—	2.50	5.00
2202	Let's Stay Together/Tomorrow's Dream	1971	—	2.50	5.00
2211	Look What You Done for Me/La La for You	1972	—	2.50	5.00
2216	I'm Still in Love with You/Old Time Lovin'	1972	—	2.50	5.00
2227	You Ought to Be with Me/What Is This Feeling	1972	—	2.50	5.00
2235	Call Me (Come Back Home)/What a Wonderful Thing Love Is	1973	—	2.50	5.00
2247	Here I Am (Come and Take Me)/I'm Glad You're Mine	1973	—	2.50	5.00
2257	Livin' for You/It Ain't No Fun to Me	1973	—	2.50	5.00
2262	Let's Get Married/So Good to Be Here	1974	—	2.50	5.00
2274	Sha-La-La (Make Me Happy)/School Days	1974	—	2.50	5.00
2282	L-O-V-E (Love)/I Wish You Were Here	1975	—	2.50	5.00
2288	Oh Me, Oh My (Dreams in My Arms)/Strong As Death (Sweet As Love)	1975	—	2.50	5.00
2300	Full of Fire/Could I Be the One	1975	—	2.50	5.00
2306	Let It Shine/There's No Way	1976	—	2.50	5.00
2319	Keep Me Cryin'/There Is Love	1976	—	2.50	5.00
2322	I Tried to Tell Myself/Something	1977	—	2.50	5.00
2324	Love and Happiness/Glory Glory	1977	—	2.50	5.00
77505	Belle/Chariots of Fire	1977	—	2.00	4.00
77505 [PS]	Belle/Chariots of Fire	1977	—	3.00	6.00
78511	I Feel Good/Feels Like Summer	1978	—	2.00	4.00
78522	Wait Here/To Sir with Love	1978	—	2.00	4.00
78522 [PS]	Wait Here/To Sir with Love	1978	—	3.00	6.00
HOT LINE JOURNAL					
15000	Back Up Train/Don't Leave Me	1967	6.25	12.50	25.00
15001	Don't Hurt Me No More/Get Yourself Together	1967	7.50	15.00	30.00
15002	I'll Be Good to You/Lover's Hideaway	1967	7.50	15.00	30.00
THE RIGHT STUFF					
S7-17524	Let's Stay Together/I'm Still in Love with You	1993	—	—	3.00
S7-18217	I'll Be Home for Christmas/It Feels Like Christmas	1994	—	2.50	5.00
Albums					
A&M					
SP-5150	Soul Survivor	1987	2.50	5.00	10.00
SP-5228	I Get Joy	1989	2.50	5.00	10.00
BELL					
6076	Al Green	1972	5.00	10.00	20.00
—Reissue of Hot Line LP					
HI					
6004	The Belle Album	1977	3.00	6.00	12.00
6009	Truth 'N' Time	1978	3.00	6.00	12.00
8000	Tired of Being Alone	1977	3.00	6.00	12.00
8001	Al Green Gets Next to You	1977	3.00	6.00	12.00
8007	Let's Stay Together	1977	3.00	6.00	12.00
SHL-32055	Green Is Blues	1969	3.75	7.50	15.00
SHL-32062	Al Green Gets Next to You	1971	3.75	7.50	15.00
SHL-32070	Let's Stay Together	1972	3.75	7.50	15.00
SHL-32074	I'm Still in Love with You	1972	3.75	7.50	15.00
SHL-32077	Call Me	1973	3.75	7.50	15.00
SHL-32082	Livin' for You	1973	3.75	7.50	15.00
SHL-32087	Al Green Explores Your Mind	1974	3.75	7.50	15.00
SHL-32089	Al Green/Greatest Hits	1975	3.75	7.50	15.00
SHL-32092	Al Green Is Love	1975	3.75	7.50	15.00
SHL-32097	Full of Fire	1976	3.75	7.50	15.00
SHL-32103	Have a Good Time	1976	3.75	7.50	15.00
SHL-32105	Al Green's Greatest Hits, Volume II	1977	3.75	7.50	15.00
HOT LINE					
1500 [M]	Back Up Train	1967	12.50	25.00	50.00
—As "Al Greene"					
S-1500 [S]	Back Up Train	1967	20.00	40.00	80.00
—As "Al Greene"					
KORY					
1005	Al Green	1977	2.50	5.00	10.00
—Reissue of Bell LP					
MCA					
42308	Love Ritual	1988	2.50	5.00	10.00
MOTOWN					
5283 ML	Al Green/Greatest Hits	198?	2.50	5.00	10.00
—Reissue of Hi 32089					
5284 ML	I'm Still in Love with You	198?	2.50	5.00	10.00
—Reissue of Hi 32074					
5290 ML	Let's Stay Together	198?	2.50	5.00	10.00
—Reissue of Hi 32070					
5291 ML	Al Green's Greatest Hits, Volume II	198?	2.50	5.00	10.00
—Reissue of Hi 32105					
5317 ML	Truth N' Time	198?	2.50	5.00	10.00
MYRRH					
MSB-6661	The Lord Will Make a Way	1980	2.50	5.00	10.00
MSB-6671	Higher Plane	1981	2.50	5.00	10.00
MSB-6702	Precious Lord	1981	2.50	5.00	10.00

Number	Title (A Side/B Side)	Yr	VG	VG+	NM
MSB-6747	I'll Rise Again	1982	2.50	5.00	10.00
MSB-6774	Al Green and the Full Gospel Tabernacle Choir	1984	2.50	5.00	10.00
WR-8113	The Lord Will Make a Way	1985	2.00	4.00	8.00
—Reissue with new number and A&M logo					
WR-8114	Higher Plane	1985	2.00	4.00	8.00
—Reissue with new number and A&M logo					
WR-8115	Precious Lord	1985	2.00	4.00	8.00
—Reissue with new number and A&M logo					
WR-8116	I'll Rise Again	1985	2.00	4.00	8.00
—Reissue with new number and A&M logo					
WR-8117	White Christmas	1985	2.50	5.00	10.00
—Reissue with new number and A&M logo					
WR-8118	Trust in God	1985	2.00	4.00	8.00
—Reissue with new number and A&M logo					
WR-8209	Al Green and the Full Gospel Tabernacle Choir	1986	2.00	4.00	8.00
—Reissue with new number and A&M logo					
7-01-678006-6	White Christmas	1984	3.00	6.00	12.00
MSB-(# unknown)	Trust in God	1984	2.50	5.00	10.00
THE RIGHT STUFF					
T1-27121	Let's Stay Together	1995	3.75	7.50	15.00
—Green vinyl reissue					
T1-27627	I'm Still in Love with You	1995	3.75	7.50	15.00
—Green vinyl reissue					
WORD					
E 77000	One in a Million	1991	3.00	6.00	12.00

GREEN, BARBARA

See BARBARA GREENE.

GREEN, BERNIE, WITH THE STEREO MAD-MEN

Albums

Number	Title (A Side/B Side)	Yr	VG	VG+	NM
RCA VICTOR					
LPM-1929 [M]	Musically Mad	1959	15.00	30.00	60.00
LSP-1929 [S]	Musically Mad	1959	30.00	60.00	120.00

GREEN, FRED

45s

Number	Title (A Side/B Side)	Yr	VG	VG+	NM
BOBBIN					
111	Wham Slam Baby/It's Funny	1959	25.00	50.00	100.00
123	Don't Make a Fool Out of Me/If You Ever Try to Leave Me	1960	25.00	50.00	100.00

GREEN, FRED, AND THE MELLARDS

45s

Number	Title (A Side/B Side)	Yr	VG	VG+	NM
BALLAD					
1012	My Sweetheart/You Can't Keep Love in a Broken Heart	1955	75.00	150.00	300.00
1016	Love Me Crazy/That's Life	1955	50.00	100.00	200.00

GREEN, GARLAND

45s

Number	Title (A Side/B Side)	Yr	VG	VG+	NM
CASINO					
056	I.O.U./It's a Backdoor World	1976	—	2.50	5.00
COTILLION					
44098	Plain and Simple Girl/Hey Cloud	1971	—	3.00	6.00
OCEAN-FRONT					
2000	Tryin' to Hold On/(B-side unknown)	1983	—	2.00	4.00
RCA					
PB-10889	Don't Let Love Walk Out on Us/Ask Me for What You Want	1977	—	3.00	6.00
PB-11023	Shake Your Shaker/Lovin' You Baby	1977	—	2.50	5.00
PB-11126	Let's Celebrate/Let Me Be Your Pacifier	1977	—	2.50	5.00
REVUE					
11001	Girl I Love You/It Rained Forty Days and Nights	1967	3.75	7.50	15.00
11020	Mr. Misery/You Played on a Prayer	196?	3.00	6.00	12.00
11030	Love Now, Pay Later/Ain't That Good Enough	196?	3.00	6.00	12.00
SPRING					
142	He Didn't Know (He Kept On Talkin')/Please Come Home	1973	—	2.50	5.00
146	Sweet Loving Woman/Sending My Best Friend	1974	—	2.50	5.00
151	Let the Good Times Roll/You and I Go Good Together	1974	—	2.50	5.00
158	Bumpin' and Stompin'/Nothing Can Take You from Me	1975	—	2.50	5.00
160	Just Loving You/Nothing Can Take You from Me	1975	—	2.50	5.00
UNI					
55143	Jealous Kind of Fella/I Can't Believe You Quit Me	1969	2.00	4.00	8.00
55188	Don't Think That I Am a Violent Guy/All She Said (Was Goodbye to Me)	1969	2.00	4.00	8.00
55213	Angel Baby/You Played On a Player	1970	2.00	4.00	8.00

Albums

Number	Title (A Side/B Side)	Yr	VG	VG+	NM
RCA VICTOR					
APL1-2351	Love Is What We Came Here For	1977	3.00	6.00	12.00
UNI					
73073	Jealous Kind of Fellow	1969	5.00	10.00	20.00

GREEN, GRANT

45s

Number	Title (A Side/B Side)	Yr	VG	VG+	NM
BLUE NOTE					
1960	Ain't It Funky Now (Part 1)/Ain't It Funky Now (Part 2)	1970	—	2.50	5.00
1965	Sookie, Sookie/Time to Remember	1971	—	2.50	5.00
1969	Does Anybody Really Know What Time It Is?/Never Can Say Goodbye	1971	—	2.50	5.00
1972	The Battle (Part 1)/The Battle (Part 2)	1972	—	2.50	5.00
1983	Afro Party/Father's Lament	1972	—	2.50	5.00
VERVE					
10361	Cantaloupe Woman/Daddy Grapes	1965	2.00	4.00	8.00

Albums

Number	Title (A Side/B Side)	Yr	VG	VG+	NM
BLUE NOTE					
BN-LA037-G [(2)]	Live at the Lighthouse	1973	5.00	10.00	20.00
LT-990	Solid	1980	3.00	6.00	12.00
LT-1032	Nigeria	1980	3.00	6.00	12.00
BLP-4064 [M]	Grant's First Stand	1961	20.00	40.00	80.00
—With W. 63rd St. addresss on label					
BLP-4064 [M]	Grant's First Stand	1963	6.25	12.50	25.00
—With New York, USA address on label					
BLP-4071 [M]	Green Street	1961	15.00	30.00	60.00
—With W. 63rd St. addresss on label					
BLP-4071 [M]	Green Street	1963	6.25	12.50	25.00
—With New York, USA address on label					
BLP-4086 [M]	Grant Stand	1962	15.00	30.00	60.00
—With 61st St. address on label					
BLP-4086 [M]	Grant Stand	1963	6.25	12.50	25.00
—With New York, USA address on label					
BLP-4099 [M]	Sunday Mornin'	1962	15.00	30.00	60.00
—With 61st St. address on label					
BLP-4099 [M]	Sunday Mornin'	1963	6.25	12.50	25.00
—With New York, USA address on label					
BLP-4111 [M]	The Latin Bit	1962	10.00	20.00	40.00
BLP-4132 [M]	Feelin' the Spirit	1963	10.00	20.00	40.00
BLP-4139 [M]	Am I Blue	1963	10.00	20.00	40.00
BLP-4154 [M]	Idle Moments	1964	10.00	20.00	40.00
BLP-4183 [M]	Talkin' About!	1964	10.00	20.00	40.00
BLP-4202 [M]	I Want to Hold Your Hand	1964	10.00	20.00	40.00
BLP-4253 [M]	Street of Dreams	1967	12.50	25.00	50.00
BLP-84064 [S]	Grant's First Stand	1961	15.00	30.00	60.00
—With W. 63rd St. addresss on label					
BLP-84064 [S]	Grant's First Stand	1963	5.00	10.00	20.00
—With New York, USA address on label					
BLP-84064 [S]	Grant's First Stand	1968	3.00	6.00	12.00
—With "A Division of Liberty Records" on label					
BLP-84071 [S]	Green Street	1961	12.50	25.00	50.00
—With W. 63rd St. addresss on label					
BLP-84071 [S]	Green Street	1963	5.00	10.00	20.00
—With New York, USA address on label					
BLP-84071 [S]	Green Street	1968	3.00	6.00	12.00
—With "A Division of Liberty Records" on label					
BLP-84086 [S]	Grant Stand	1962	12.50	25.00	50.00
—With 61st St. address on label					
BLP-84086 [S]	Grant Stand	1963	5.00	10.00	20.00
—With New York, USA address on label					
BLP-84086 [S]	Grant Stand	1968	3.00	6.00	12.00
—With "A Division of Liberty Records" on label					
BLP-84099 [S]	Sunday Mornin'	1962	12.50	25.00	50.00
—With 61st St. address on label					
BLP-84099 [S]	Sunday Mornin'	1963	5.00	10.00	20.00
—With New York, USA address on label					
BLP-84099 [S]	Sunday Mornin'	1968	3.00	6.00	12.00
—With "A Division of Liberty Records" on label					
BLP-84111 [S]	The Latin Bit	1962	10.00	20.00	40.00
—With New York, USA address on label					
BLP-84111 [S]	The Latin Bit	1968	3.00	6.00	12.00
—With "A Division of Liberty Records" on label					
BLP-84132 [S]	Feelin' the Spirit	1963	10.00	20.00	40.00
—With New York, USA address on label					
BLP-84132 [S]	Feelin' the Spirit	1968	3.00	6.00	12.00
—With "A Division of Liberty Records" on label					
BLP-84139 [S]	Am I Blue	1963	10.00	20.00	40.00
—With New York, USA address on label					
BLP-84139 [S]	Am I Blue	1968	3.00	6.00	12.00
—With "A Division of Liberty Records" on label					
BLP-84154 [S]	Idle Moments	1964	10.00	20.00	40.00
—With New York, USA address on label					
BLP-84154 [S]	Idle Moments	1968	3.00	6.00	12.00
—With "A Division of Liberty Records" on label					
BLP-84183 [S]	Talkin' About!	1964	10.00	20.00	40.00
—With New York, USA address on label					
BLP-84183 [S]	Talkin' About!	1968	3.00	6.00	12.00
—With "A Division of Liberty Records" on label					
BLP-84202 [S]	I Want to Hold Your Hand	1964	10.00	20.00	40.00
—With New York, USA address on label					
BLP-84202 [S]	I Want to Hold Your Hand	1968	3.00	6.00	12.00
—With "A Division of Liberty Records" on label					
BLP-84253 [S]	Street of Dreams	1967	10.00	20.00	40.00
BLP-84310	Goin' West	1969	10.00	20.00	40.00
BLP-84327	Carryin' On	1969	10.00	20.00	40.00
BLP-84340	Green Is Beautiful	1970	6.25	12.50	25.00
BLP-84360	Alive!	1970	6.25	12.50	25.00
BLP-84373	Visions	1971	5.00	10.00	20.00
BLP-84413	Shades of Green	1972	5.00	10.00	20.00
BLP-84432	Born to Be Blue	1985	3.00	6.00	12.00
COBBLESTONE					
9001	Iron City	1972	3.75	7.50	15.00
DELMARK					
DL-404 [M]	All the Gin Is Gone	1966	6.25	12.50	25.00
DS-404 [S]	All the Gin Is Gone	1966	6.25	12.50	25.00
DL-427 [M]	Black Forrest	1966	6.25	12.50	25.00
DS-427 [S]	Black Forrest	1966	6.25	12.50	25.00
MOSAIC					
M5-133 [(5)]	The Complete Blue Note Recordings of Grant Green with Sonny Clark	199?	15.00	30.00	60.00
MUSE					
MR-5014	Green Blues	1973	3.75	7.50	15.00
MR-5120	Iron City	197?	3.00	6.00	12.00
VERVE					
V-8627 [M]	His Majesty, King Funk	1965	7.50	15.00	30.00
V6-8627 [S]	His Majesty, King Funk	1965	7.50	15.00	30.00

GREEN, JANICE (THE "OH JULIE" GIRL)

45s

Number	Title (A Side/B Side)	Yr	VG	VG+	NM
NASCO					
6013	With All My Heart/Jackie	1958	5.00	10.00	20.00

GREEN, KEITH

45s

DECCA

Number	Title (A Side/B Side)	Yr	VG	VG+	NM
31799	A Go-Go Letter/The Way I Used to Be	1965	5.00	10.00	20.00
31859	Girl Don't Tell Me/How to Be Your Guy	1965	6.25	12.50	25.00
31973	Home Town Girls/Hear What's Happening, Baby	1966	5.00	10.00	20.00

ERA

Number	Title (A Side/B Side)	Yr	VG	VG+	NM
108	Sgt. Pepper's Epitaph/Country Store	1970	2.50	5.00	10.00
3210	Fantastic/L.A. City Smog Blues	1969	2.50	5.00	10.00

Albums

PRETTY GOOD

Number	Title (A Side/B Side)	Yr	VG	VG+	NM
PGR-1	So You Wanna Go Back to Egypt	1980	3.00	6.00	12.00

SPARROW

Number	Title (A Side/B Side)	Yr	VG	VG+	NM
SPR-1015	For Him Who Has Ears to Hear	1977	3.00	6.00	12.00
SPR-1024	No Compromise	1978	3.00	6.00	12.00
SP-9901	For Him Who Has Ears to Hear	198?	2.00	4.00	8.00
—Reissue of 1015					
SP-9904	No Compromise	198?	2.00	4.00	8.00
—Reissue of 1024					
SP-9927	The Collection	198?	2.50	5.00	10.00

GREEN, LIL

45s

ATLANTIC

Number	Title (A Side/B Side)	Yr	VG	VG+	NM
951	Every Time/I've Got That Feeling	1952	25.00	50.00	100.00

GREEN, PETER

Also see FLEETWOOD MAC.

Albums

REPRISE

Number	Title (A Side/B Side)	Yr	VG	VG+	NM
RS 6436	The End of the Game	1970	5.00	10.00	20.00

SAIL

Number	Title (A Side/B Side)	Yr	VG	VG+	NM
0110	In the Skies	1979	2.50	5.00	10.00
0112	Little Dreamer	1980	2.50	5.00	10.00

GREEN, RUDY

See RUDY GREENE.

GREEN, VERNON, AND THE MEDALLIONS

See THE MEDALLIONS.

GREEN BULLFROG

Albums

DECCA

Number	Title (A Side/B Side)	Yr	VG	VG+	NM
DL 75269	Green Bullfrog	1971	6.25	12.50	25.00

GREENBAUM, NORMAN

Also see DR. WEST'S MEDICINE SHOW AND JUG BAND.

45s

GREGAR

Number	Title (A Side/B Side)	Yr	VG	VG+	NM
71-0107	Nancy Whiskey/Twentieth Century Fox	1969	2.50	5.00	10.00

REPRISE

Number	Title (A Side/B Side)	Yr	VG	VG+	NM
0739	Spirit in the Sky/Canned Ham	1971	—	2.00	4.00
—"Back to Back Hits" series					
0752	Children of Paradise/School for Sweet Talk	1968	2.50	5.00	10.00
0818	Marcy/Children of Paradise	1969	2.50	5.00	10.00
0846	Jubilee/Skyline	1969	2.50	5.00	10.00
0885	Spirit in the Sky/Milk Cow	1969	2.00	4.00	8.00
0919	Canned Ham/Junior Cadillac	1970	—	3.00	6.00
0956	Rhode Island Red/I.J. Foxx	1970	—	3.00	6.00
0956 [PS]	Rhode Island Red/I.J. Foxx	1970	7.50	15.00	30.00
1008	California Earthquake/Rhode Island Red	1971	—	3.00	6.00
1134	Dairy Queen/Petaluma	1972	—	3.00	6.00

Albums

REPRISE

Number	Title (A Side/B Side)	Yr	VG	VG+	NM
MS 2048	Petaluma	1972	3.75	7.50	15.00
RS 6365	Spirit in the Sky	1969	5.00	10.00	20.00
RS 6422	Back Home Again	1970	3.75	7.50	15.00

GREENBEATS, THE

45s

JERDEN

Number	Title (A Side/B Side)	Yr	VG	VG+	NM
757	You Must Be the One/If This Wine Was Mine	1965	3.00	6.00	12.00
763	So Sad/I'm on Fire	1965	3.00	6.00	12.00

GREENE, BARBARA

45s

ATCO

Number	Title (A Side/B Side)	Yr	VG	VG+	NM
6250	Long Tall Sally/Slippin' and Slidin'	1963	10.00	20.00	40.00

RENEE

Number	Title (A Side/B Side)	Yr	VG	VG+	NM
5001	Young Boy/I Should Have Treated You Right	1968	2.50	5.00	10.00

VIVID

Number	Title (A Side/B Side)	Yr	VG	VG+	NM
105	Young Boy/I Should Have Treated You Right	1968	3.00	6.00	12.00

GREENE, JACK

45s

DECCA

Number	Title (A Side/B Side)	Yr	VG	VG+	NM
31768	Don't You Ever Get Tired/The Hurt's On Me	1965	2.50	5.00	10.00
31856	Ever Since My Baby Went Away/Room for One More Heartache	1965	2.00	4.00	8.00
32023	There Goes My Everything/The Hardest Easy Thing	1966	2.00	4.00	8.00
32123	All the Time/Wanting You But Never Having You	1967	2.00	4.00	8.00
32190	What Locks the Door/Left Over Feelings	1967	2.00	4.00	8.00
32261	You Are My Treasure/If God Can Forgive You, So Can I	1968	2.00	4.00	8.00
32352	Love Takes Care of Me/Your Favorite Fool	1968	2.00	4.00	8.00
32423	Until My Dreams Come True/We'll Try a Little Bit Harder	1968	2.00	4.00	8.00
32490	Statue of a Fool/There's More to Love	1969	2.00	4.00	8.00
32558	Back in the Arms of Love/The Key That Fits Her Door	1969	2.00	4.00	8.00
32631	Lord Is That Me/Just a Little While Ago	1970	—	3.50	7.00
32699	The Whole World Comes to Me/If This Is Love	1970	—	3.50	7.00
32755	Something Unseen/What's the Use	1970	—	3.50	7.00
32823	There's a Whole Lot About a Woman (A Man Don't Know)/Makin' Up His Mind	1971	—	3.50	7.00
32863	Hanging Over Me/The Birth of Our Love	1971	—	3.50	7.00
32939	If You Ever Need My Love/Ask Me to Stay	1972	—	3.50	7.00
33008	Satisfaction/From Here On Out	1972	—	3.50	7.00

EMH

Number	Title (A Side/B Side)	Yr	VG	VG+	NM
0015	I'd Be Home On Christmas Day/(B-side unknown)	1982	—	2.50	5.00
0016	The Jukebox Never Plays Home Sweet Home/I Don't Want to Be Alone Tonight	1983	—	2.00	4.00
0019	From Cotton to Satin/I'd Be Home on Christmas Day	1983	—	2.00	4.00
0025	Midnight Tennessee Woman/Goin' Through Hell for an Angel	1983	—	2.00	4.00
0028	I'd Do As Much for You/Singing My Heart Out for You	1984	—	2.00	4.00
0031	Dying to Believe/There Goes My Everything	1984	—	2.00	4.00
0035	If It's Love (Then Bet It All)/Statue of a Fool	1984	—	2.00	4.00

FIRSTLINE

Number	Title (A Side/B Side)	Yr	VG	VG+	NM
709	Devil's Den/(B-side unknown)	1980	—	2.00	4.00

FRONTLINE

Number	Title (A Side/B Side)	Yr	VG	VG+	NM
704	Yours for the Taking/(B-side unknown)	1979	—	2.00	4.00
706	The Rock I'm Leaning On/(B-side unknown)	1980	—	2.00	4.00

MCA

Number	Title (A Side/B Side)	Yr	VG	VG+	NM
40035	The Fool I've Been Today/You Left Me	1973	—	2.50	5.00
40108	I Need Somebody Bad/Joyride	1973	—	2.50	5.00
40179	It's Time to Cross That Bridge/Half That Much	1974	—	2.50	5.00
40263	Sing for the Good Times/Something Seems to Fall Apart Inside	1974	—	2.50	5.00
40354	This Time The Hurtin's On Me/Sawmill Depot	1974	—	2.50	5.00
40415	Cheatin' River/On the Way Home	1975	—	2.50	5.00
40481	He Little Thing'd Her Out of His Arms/Let Me Love You Back Together Again	1975	—	2.50	5.00
40526	Birmingham/My Long Gone Reason	1976	—	2.50	5.00

Albums

DECCA

Number	Title (A Side/B Side)	Yr	VG	VG+	NM
DL 4845 [M]	There Goes My Everything	1967	5.00	10.00	20.00
DL 4904 [M]	All the Time	1967	5.00	10.00	20.00
DL 4939 [M]	What Locks the Door	1968	6.25	12.50	25.00
DL 4979 [M]	You Are My Treasure	1968	7.50	15.00	30.00
DL 74845 [S]	There Goes My Everything	1967	3.75	7.50	15.00
DL 74904 [S]	All the Time	1967	3.75	7.50	15.00
DL 74939 [S]	What Locks the Door	1968	3.75	7.50	15.00
DL 74979 [S]	You Are My Treasure	1968	3.75	7.50	15.00
DL 75080	I Am Not Alone	1969	3.75	7.50	15.00
DL 75124	Statue of a Fool	1969	3.75	7.50	15.00
DL 75188	Lord Is That Me	1970	3.75	7.50	15.00
DL 75208	Greatest Hits	1970	3.75	7.50	15.00
DL 75283	There's a Whole Lot About a Woman	1971	3.75	7.50	15.00
DL 75308	Greene Country	1972	3.75	7.50	15.00

MCA

Number	Title (A Side/B Side)	Yr	VG	VG+	NM
291	Greatest Hits	1973	3.00	6.00	12.00
—Reissue of Decca 75208					
295	Greene Country	1973	3.00	6.00	12.00
—Reissue of Decca 75308					

PICKWICK

Number	Title (A Side/B Side)	Yr	VG	VG+	NM
SPC-6173	I Never Had It So Good	197?	2.50	5.00	10.00

GREENE, JACK, AND JEANNIE SEELY

45s

DECCA

Number	Title (A Side/B Side)	Yr	VG	VG+	NM
32580	Wish I Didn't Have to Miss You/My Tears Don't Show	1969	—	3.50	7.00
32898	Much Oblige/First Day	1971	—	3.50	7.00
32991	What in the World Has Gone Wrong with Our Love/Willingly	1972	—	3.00	6.00

Albums

DECCA

Number	Title (A Side/B Side)	Yr	VG	VG+	NM
DL 75171	Jack Greene and Jeannie Seely	1970	3.75	7.50	15.00
DL 75392	Two for the Show	1972	3.75	7.50	15.00

MCA

Number	Title (A Side/B Side)	Yr	VG	VG+	NM
77	Two for the Show	1973	3.00	6.00	12.00
—Reissue of Decca 75392					

GREENE, LORNE

45s

COLUMBIA

Number	Title (A Side/B Side)	Yr	VG	VG+	NM
44971	The Perfect Woman/It's All in the Game	1969	—	3.00	6.00

GRT

Number	Title (A Side/B Side)	Yr	VG	VG+	NM
32	Daddy (I'm Proud to Be Your Son)/I Love a Rainbow	1969	—	3.00	6.00
37	The First Word/I Love a Rainbow	1970	—	3.00	6.00

RCA VICTOR

Number	Title (A Side/B Side)	Yr	VG	VG+	NM
47-8113	My Sons, My Sons/The Place Where I Worship	1962	2.50	5.00	10.00
47-8229	I'm the Same Old Me/Love Finds a Way	1963	2.50	5.00	10.00
47-8444	Ringo/Bonanza	1964	2.00	4.00	8.00
47-8490	The Man/Pop Goes the Hammer	1964	2.00	4.00	8.00
47-8554	An Ol' Tin Cup/Sand	1965	2.00	4.00	8.00
47-8757	Five Card Stud/Shadow of the Cactus	1965	2.00	4.00	8.00
47-8819	Daddy's Little Girl/I Love a Rainbow	1966	2.00	4.00	8.00
47-8901	Waco/All But the Remembering	1966	2.00	4.00	8.00
47-9037	Must Be Santa/One Solitary Life	1966	2.50	5.00	10.00

Albums

RCA CAMDEN

Number	Title (A Side/B Side)	Yr	VG	VG+	NM
CAS-2391	Five Card Stud	1970	6.25	12.50	25.00

RCA VICTOR

Number	Title (A Side/B Side)	Yr	VG	VG+	NM
SP-33-327 [DJ]	Palaver with The Man	1965	12.50	25.00	50.00
—Promo-only interview record with script					
LPM-2661 [M]	Young at Heart	1963	6.25	12.50	25.00

Number	Title (A Side/B Side)	Yr	VG	VG+	NM
LSP-2661 [S]	Young at Heart	1963	7.50	15.00	30.00
LPM-2843 [M]	Welcome to the Ponderosa	1964	6.25	12.50	25.00
LSP-2843 [S]	Welcome to the Ponderosa	1964	7.50	15.00	30.00
LPM-3302 [M]	The Man	1965	6.25	12.50	25.00
LSP-3302 [S]	The Man	1965	7.50	15.00	30.00
LPM-3409 [M]	Lorne Greene's American West	1965	6.25	12.50	25.00
LSP-3409 [S]	Lorne Greene's American West	1965	7.50	15.00	30.00
LPM-3410 [M]	Have a Happy Holiday	1965	6.25	12.50	25.00
LSP-3410 [S]	Have a Happy Holiday	1965	7.50	15.00	30.00
LPM-3678 [M]	Portrait of the West	1966	6.25	12.50	25.00
LSP-3678 [S]	Portrait of the West	1966	7.50	15.00	30.00
RCA VICTOR RED SEAL					
LM-2783 [M]	Peter and the Wolf	1964	6.25	12.50	25.00
LSC-2783 [S]	Peter and the Wolf	1964	7.50	15.00	30.00
—Above with the London Symphony Orchestra					

GREENE, LORNE; MICHAEL LANDON; DAN BLOCKER

Albums

Number	Title (A Side/B Side)	Yr	VG	VG+	NM
RCA VICTOR					
LPM-2583 [M]	Bonanza — Ponderosa Party Time!	1962	7.50	15.00	30.00
LSP-2583 [S]	Bonanza — Ponderosa Party Time!	1962	10.00	20.00	40.00
LPM-2757 [M]	Christmas on the Ponderosa	1963	6.25	12.50	25.00
LSP-2757 [S]	Christmas on the Ponderosa	1963	7.50	15.00	30.00

GREENE, RUDY

45s

Number	Title (A Side/B Side)	Yr	VG	VG+	NM
CHANCE					
1139	Love Is a Pain/No Need of Your Crying	1953	37.50	75.00	150.00
1146	The Letter/It's You I Love	1953	37.50	75.00	150.00
1151	I Had a Feeling/Meet Me Baby	1954	37.50	75.00	150.00
—Black vinyl					
1151	I Had a Feeling/Meet Me Baby	1954	100.00	200.00	400.00
—Red vinyl					
CLUB 51					
103	Highway No. 1/You Mean Everything to Me	1956	50.00	100.00	200.00
—With the Four Buddies					
EMBER					
1012	Juicy Fruit/You're the One for Me	1957	10.00	20.00	40.00
1020	Lonesome/Wild Life	1957	10.00	20.00	40.00
EXCELLO					
2074	Cool Lovin' Mama/My Mumblin' Baby	1955	12.50	25.00	50.00
2090	Teeny Weeny Baby/Queer Feeling	1956	12.50	25.00	50.00

GREENSLADE

Albums

Number	Title (A Side/B Side)	Yr	VG	VG+	NM
MERCURY					
SRM-1-1015	Spy Guest	1974	3.00	6.00	12.00
SRM-1-1025	Time and Tide	1975	3.00	6.00	12.00
WARNER BROS.					
BS 2698	Greenslade	1973	3.00	6.00	12.00

GREENWICH, ELLIE

Also see THE RAINDROPS.

45s

Number	Title (A Side/B Side)	Yr	VG	VG+	NM
BELL					
855	Ain't That Peculiar/I Don't Want to Be Left Outside	1970	2.50	5.00	10.00
933	That Certain Someone/It's Like a Sad Old Kind of Movie	1970	2.50	5.00	10.00
MADISON					
160	Red Corvette/I Go, You Go	1961	7.50	15.00	30.00
—As "Ellie Gee"					
RED BIRD					
10-034	You Don't Know/Baby	1965	10.00	20.00	40.00
UNITED ARTISTS					
50151	I Want You to Be My Baby/Goodnight, Goodnight	1967	3.75	7.50	15.00
50278	A Long Time Comin'/Niki-Hoeky	1968	3.75	7.50	15.00
VERVE					
10719	Today I Met the Boy I'm Gonna Marry/Maybe I Know	1973	2.50	5.00	10.00
10724	Chapel of Love/River Deep, Mountain High	1973	2.50	5.00	10.00

Albums

Number	Title (A Side/B Side)	Yr	VG	VG+	NM
UNITED ARTISTS					
UAS-6648	Ellie Greenwich Composes, Produces and Sings	1968	12.50	25.00	50.00
VERVE					
V6-5091	Let It Be Written, Let It Be Sung	1973	6.25	12.50	25.00

GREER, BIG JOHN

45s

Number	Title (A Side/B Side)	Yr	VG	VG+	NM
GROOVE					
0002	Bottle It Up and Go/You'll Never Be Mine	1954	10.00	20.00	40.00
0016	When the Roses Bloom in Lover's Lane/Too Long	1954	10.00	20.00	40.00
0038	We Wanna See Santa Do the Mambo/Wait Till After Christmas	1954	10.00	20.00	40.00
0108	Soon, Soon, Soon/I'm Glad for Your Sake	1955	10.00	20.00	40.00
0119	Come Back Maybellene/Night Crawlin'	1955	12.50	25.00	50.00
0131	A Man and a Woman/Blam	1955	15.00	30.00	60.00
—With the Four Students					
KING					
4878	Record Hop/Keep On Loving Me	1956	5.00	10.00	20.00
4941	Let Me Come Home/Come Back, Uncle John	1956	5.00	10.00	20.00
5006	Midnight Ramble/Sweet Slumber	1957	5.00	10.00	20.00
5057	Duck Walk/I Still Love You So	1957	5.00	10.00	20.00
RCA VICTOR					
47-4293	Have Another Drink/I'm Savin' All My Lovin'	1951	10.00	20.00	40.00
47-4348	Got You on My Mind/Woman Is a Five-Letter Word	1951	10.00	20.00	40.00
47-4484	Strong Red Whiskey/If You Let Me	1952	10.00	20.00	40.00
47-5037	I'm the Fat Man/Since You Went Away from Me	1952	10.00	20.00	40.00
47-5170	I'll Never Let You Go/You Played on My Piano	1953	10.00	20.00	40.00
47-5259	Ride Pretty Baby/Don't Worry 'Bout Me	1953	10.00	20.00	40.00
47-5531	Drinkin' Fool/Gettin' Mighty Lonesome for You	1953	10.00	20.00	40.00
50-0007	Drinkin' Wine Spo-Dee-O-Dee/Long Tall Gal	1949	17.50	35.00	70.00
—Orange vinyl					
50-0029	If I Told You Once/I Found a Dream	1949	17.50	35.00	70.00
—Orange vinyl					
50-0051	Rockin' Jenny Jones/I've Just Found Love	1950	17.50	35.00	70.00
—Orange vinyl					
50-0076	I'll Never Do That Again/A Fool Hasn't Got a Chance	1950	15.00	30.00	60.00
—Orange vinyl					
50-0096	Cheatin'/It's Better to Have Been Taken for Granted	1950	15.00	30.00	60.00
—Orange vinyl					
50-0104	Red Juice/Big John's a-Blowin'	1950	15.00	30.00	60.00
—Orange vinyl					
50-0108	Once There Lived a Fool/I Want Ya, I Need Ya	1951	12.50	25.00	50.00
50-0113	Why Did You Go/Our Wedding Time	1951	12.50	25.00	50.00
50-0125	Clambake Boogie/When You Love	1951	12.50	25.00	50.00
50-0137	Big Rock/How Can You Forget?	1951	12.50	25.00	50.00

GREGORY, DICK

45s

Number	Title (A Side/B Side)	Yr	VG	VG+	NM
VEE JAY					
469	They Won't Hire Me/Benefit	1962	3.00	6.00	12.00

Albums

Number	Title (A Side/B Side)	Yr	VG	VG+	NM
COLPIX					
CP 417 [M]	In Living Black and White	1961	6.25	12.50	25.00
CP 420 [M]	East and West	1961	6.25	12.50	25.00
CP 480 [M]	We All Have Problems	1964	6.25	12.50	25.00
GATEWAY					
GLP 9007 [M]	My Brother's Keeper	1963	10.00	20.00	40.00
POPPY					
PP-LA176-G2 [(2)]	Caught in the Act	1973	3.75	7.50	15.00
PYS 40008	Dick Gregory On...	1970	3.75	7.50	15.00
PYS 40011	Dick Gregory at the Village Gate	1972	3.75	7.50	15.00
PYS 60001 [(2)]	The Light Side: The Dark Side	1969	5.00	10.00	20.00
PYS 60004 [(2)]	Frankenstein	1970	3.75	7.50	15.00
PYS 60005 [(2)]	Dick Gregory at Kent State	1971	3.75	7.50	15.00
TOMATO					
9001 [(3)]	The Best of Dick Gregory	1978	5.00	10.00	20.00
VEE JAY					
LP 1093 [M]	Running for President	1964	6.25	12.50	25.00
LP 4001 [M]	Dick Gregory Talks Turkey	1962	6.25	12.50	25.00
LP 4005 [M]	Two Sides of Dick Gregory	1963	6.25	12.50	25.00

GREGORY, IVAN, AND THE BLUE NOTES

45s

Number	Title (A Side/B Side)	Yr	VG	VG+	NM
G&G					
110	Elvis Presley Blues/Kathy	1956	62.50	125.00	250.00

GRENFELL, JOYCE

Albums

Number	Title (A Side/B Side)	Yr	VG	VG+	NM
ELEKTRA					
EKL-184 [M]	Presenting Joyce Grenfell	1960	7.50	15.00	30.00

GRIER, FRANKIE, QUARTET

45s

Number	Title (A Side/B Side)	Yr	VG	VG+	NM
SWAN					
4019	Oh, Gloria/Lonesome for You	1958	100.00	200.00	400.00

GRIER, ROOSEVELT

Most of his 1970s records, and scattered earlier ones, were as "Rosey Grier."

45s

Number	Title (A Side/B Side)	Yr	VG	VG+	NM
20TH CENTURY					
2212	Take the Time to Love Somebody/Your Love Is Right Up My Alley	1975	2.00	4.00	8.00
A					
105	Sincerely/Why Don't You Do Me Right	1959	6.25	12.50	25.00
110	Moonlight in Vermont/Smoky Morning	1960	6.25	12.50	25.00
ABC					
11275	Rat Race/I Don't Want Nobody (To Lead Me On)	1970	—	3.00	6.00
AGP					
109	Bad News/Ring Around the World	1969	2.00	4.00	8.00
AMY					
11004	Who's Got the Ball (Y'All)/Halftime	1967	3.00	6.00	12.00
11015	High Society Woman/C'mon Cupid	1968	3.00	6.00	12.00
11029	Hard to Forget/People Make the World	1968	3.00	6.00	12.00
A&M					
1457	Beautiful People/I'll Be Back Tomorrow	1973	—	2.50	5.00
1500	If You Hit a Good Lick, Lay On It/You're the Violin	1974	—	2.50	5.00
BATTLE					
45911	Why/Lover Set Me Free	1963	6.25	12.50	25.00
BELL					
45459	It's All Right to Cry/(B-side unknown)	1974	2.00	4.00	8.00
D-TOWN					
1058	Pizza Pie Man/Welcome to the Club	1965	10.00	20.00	40.00
LIBERTY					
55413	Struttin' 'n Twistin'/Let the Cool Wind Blow	1962	3.75	7.50	15.00
55453	The Mail Must Go Thru/Your Has Been	1962	3.75	7.50	15.00
MGM					
13698	Slow Drag/Yesterday	1967	3.00	6.00	12.00
13840	Spanish Harlem/I'm Living Good	1967	3.00	6.00	12.00
RIC					
102	Fool, Fool, Fool/Since You've Been Gone	1964	5.00	10.00	20.00
112	Down So Long/In My Tenement	1964	5.00	10.00	20.00
SPINDLE TOP					
102	I'm Going Home/Jinny	1961	5.00	10.00	20.00
UNITED ARTISTS					
50893	Bring Back the Time/Oh How I Miss You Baby	1972	—	3.00	6.00
YOUNGSTOWN					
609	Deputy Dog/(B-side unknown)	1966	7.50	15.00	30.00

Number	Title (A Side/B Side)	Yr	VG	VG+	NM
Albums					
RIC					
M-1008 [M]	Soul City	1964	5.00	10.00	20.00
S-1008 [S]	Soul City	1964	6.25	12.50	25.00
WORD					
WR-8342	Committed	1986	3.00	6.00	12.00

GRIEVES, GRANT

Number	Title (A Side/B Side)	Yr	VG	VG+	NM
45s					
BIG K					
1002	Four in the Floor/Married Woman	196?	15.00	30.00	60.00

GRIFFIN, BUCK

Number	Title (A Side/B Side)	Yr	VG	VG+	NM
45s					
HOLIDAY INN					
109	Pretty Lou/The Girl in Room 1209	1963	10.00	20.00	40.00
LIN					
1005	Meadowlark Boogie/It Don't Make No Never Mind	1954	15.00	30.00	60.00
1007	Rollin' Tears/One Day After Pay Day	1955	15.00	30.00	60.00
1008	Going Home, All Alone/Lookin' for the Green	1955	15.00	30.00	60.00
1014	Next to Mine/Lord, Give Me Strength	1955	15.00	30.00	60.00
1015	Bawlin' and Squallin'/Let's Elope, Baby	1955	18.75	37.50	75.00
1016	Go-Stop-O/Cochise	1955	25.00	50.00	100.00
1018	Little Dan/Neither Do I	1956	15.00	30.00	60.00
METRO					
20007	The Party/Every Night	1958	7.50	15.00	30.00
MGM					
12284	Stutterin' Papa/Watchin' the 7:10 Roll By	1956	25.00	50.00	100.00
12439	Bow My Back/Old Bee Tree	1957	20.00	40.00	80.00
12597	Jessie Lee/You'll Never Come Back	1957	20.00	40.00	80.00

GRIFFIN, JIMMY

Some of these were credited to "James Griffin." Also see BREAD.

Number	Title (A Side/B Side)	Yr	VG	VG+	NM
45s					
IMPERIAL					
66108	These Are the Times/Walking to New Orleans	1965	3.00	6.00	12.00
66152	He Will Break Your Heart/Hard Row to Hoe	1965	3.00	6.00	12.00
POLYDOR					
14213	Breakin' Up Is Easy/Melody Maker	1973	—	2.50	5.00
14236	She Knows/Beachwood Band	1974	—	2.50	5.00
14282	Treat Her Right/How Do You Say Goodbye	1975	—	2.50	5.00
REPRISE					
0268	All My Loving/My Baby Made Me Cry	1964	3.75	7.50	15.00
0280	Gotta Lotta Love/Running to You	1964	3.75	7.50	15.00
0304	You're Nobody Till Somebody Loves You/Try	1964	3.75	7.50	15.00
20114	Girls Grow Up Faster Than Boys/It's a Free Country	1962	5.00	10.00	20.00
20161	What Kind of Girl Are You/A Little Like Lovin' You	1963	5.00	10.00	20.00
20178	Love Letters in the Sand/Summer Holiday	1963	5.00	10.00	20.00
20221	Little Miss Cool/Marie Is Moving	1963	5.00	10.00	20.00
VIVA					
611	Miracle Worker/Looking So Much Better	1967	2.50	5.00	10.00
627	Thank You Love/Light of Your Mind	1968	2.50	5.00	10.00
642	Miracle Worker/Thank You Love	1970	2.50	5.00	10.00
Albums					
POLYDOR					
PD 6018	James Griffin and Co.	1973	3.75	7.50	15.00
REPRISE					
R-6091 [M]	Summer Holiday	1963	12.50	25.00	50.00
R9-6091 [S]	Summer Holiday	1963	15.00	30.00	60.00

GRIFFINS, THE

Number	Title (A Side/B Side)	Yr	VG	VG+	NM
45s					
MERCURY					
70558	I Swear By All the Stars Above/Sing to Me	1955	30.00	60.00	120.00
70650	Bad Little Girl/Scheming	1955	30.00	60.00	120.00
70913	My Baby's Gone/Why Must You Go	1956	10.00	20.00	40.00
WING					
90067	Forever More/Leave It to Me	1956	50.00	100.00	200.00

GRIFFITH, PEGGI

Number	Title (A Side/B Side)	Yr	VG	VG+	NM
45s					
DOLTON					
35	Lovely Girl/You're In My Dreams to Stay	1961	5.00	10.00	20.00

GRIN

Also see NILS LOFGREN.

Number	Title (A Side/B Side)	Yr	VG	VG+	NM
45s					
A&M					
1502	Beggar's Day/You're the Weight	1974	—	2.00	4.00
SPINDIZZY					
4001	If I Were a Song/See What a Love Can Do	1971	—	2.50	5.00
4002	Everybody's Missing the Sun/Eighteen-Faced Lover	1971	—	2.50	5.00
4005	White Lies/Just to Have You	1972	—	2.50	5.00
4006	End Unkind/Slippery Fingers	1972	—	2.50	5.00
THUNDER					
4000	We All Sung Together/See What a Love Can Do	1970	2.00	4.00	8.00
Albums					
A&M					
SP-4405	Gone Crazy	1973	2.50	5.00	10.00
COLUMBIA					
LE 10265	All Out	197?	2.50	5.00	10.00
—Remixed version on Columbia's brown-label "Limited Edition" series					
EPIC					
PE 34247	The Best of Grin	1976	2.50	5.00	10.00
—Without bar code on back					
PE 34247	The Best of Grin	198?	2.00	4.00	8.00
—With bar code on back					
SPINDIZZY					
Z 30321	Grin	1971	3.00	6.00	12.00
Z 31038	1 + 1	1972	3.00	6.00	12.00
KZ 31701	All Out	1973	3.00	6.00	12.00

GRINER, LINDA

Number	Title (A Side/B Side)	Yr	VG	VG+	NM
45s					
MOTOWN					
1037	Good-By Cruel World/Envious	1963	87.50	175.00	350.00
—With incorrect A-side title					
1037	Good-By Cruel Love/Envious	1963	50.00	100.00	200.00
—With corrected A-side title					

GROCE, LARRY

Number	Title (A Side/B Side)	Yr	VG	VG+	NM
45s					
DISNEYLAND					
564	Winnie the Pooh for President (Campaign Song)/(B-side unknown)	1976	5.00	10.00	20.00
MGM					
14621	Muddy Boggy Banjo Man/Sweet Sweet Love	1973	—	2.50	5.00
WARNER BROS.					
8165	Junk Food Junkie/Muddy Boggy Banjo Man	1975	—	2.50	5.00
8221	We've Been Malled/Old Fashioned Girl	1976	—	2.00	4.00
8327	The Ballad of Billy Don Rice/Big White House in Indiana	1977	—	2.00	4.00
8442	Turn On Your TV/Hog and Dog Factory	1977	—	2.00	4.00
Albums					
DAYBREAK					
2000	The Wheat Lies Low	1971	3.00	6.00	12.00
2010	Crescentville	1972	3.00	6.00	12.00
WARNER BROS.					
BS 2933	Junkfood Junkie	1976	2.50	5.00	10.00

GRODECK WHIPPERJENNY

Number	Title (A Side/B Side)	Yr	VG	VG+	NM
Albums					
PEOPLE					
3000	Grodeck Whipperjenny	1969	50.00	100.00	200.00

GROGAN, TOBY

Number	Title (A Side/B Side)	Yr	VG	VG+	NM
45s					
VEE JAY					
560	Angel/Just a Friend	1963	7.50	15.00	30.00
—The Four Seasons sing on this record.					

GROOTNA

Number	Title (A Side/B Side)	Yr	VG	VG+	NM
45s					
COLUMBIA					
45461	Full Time Woman/Is It All Over	1971	—	3.00	6.00
45538	Waitin' for My Ship/That's What You Get	1972	—	3.00	6.00
Albums					
COLUMBIA					
C 31033	Grootna	1971	3.75	7.50	15.00

GROOV-U

Number	Title (A Side/B Side)	Yr	VG	VG+	NM
Albums					
GATEWAY					
GLP-3010	Groov-U On Campus	196?	10.00	20.00	40.00

GROOVIE GOOLIES, THE

Number	Title (A Side/B Side)	Yr	VG	VG+	NM
45s					
RCA VICTOR					
74-0383	The First Annual Semi-Formal Combination Celebration Meet-the-Monster Population Party/Save Your Good Lovin' for Me	1970	2.50	5.00	10.00
Albums					
RCA VICTOR					
LSP-4420	The Groovie Goolies	1970	6.25	12.50	25.00

GROSS, HENRY

Number	Title (A Side/B Side)	Yr	VG	VG+	NM
45s					
ABC					
11322	New York City/My Sunshine	1972	—	3.00	6.00
11334	Close My Eyes/Prayer for All	1972	—	3.00	6.00
A&M					
1494	Fly Away/Simone	1974	—	2.00	4.00
1534	Come On Say It/Ever Lovin' Days	1974	—	2.00	4.00
1613	Meet Me on the Corner/With the Sleep in My Eyes	1974	—	2.00	4.00
1682	One More Tomorrow/Evergreen	1975	—	2.00	4.00
1701	Travelin' Time/All My Love	1975	—	2.00	4.00
CAPITOL					
4946	Better Now We're Friends/You're My Ride Home	1980	—	2.00	4.00
4980	How Long Is Forever/I Love You Now	1981	—	2.00	4.00
LIFESONG					
1761	Only the Beautiful/Creepin' Jenny	1978	—	2.00	4.00
1769	Love Is the Stuff/Shake Down Your Love	1978	—	2.00	4.00
45002	Shannon/Pokey	1976	—	2.50	5.00
45008	Springtime Mama/Overton Square	1976	—	2.00	4.00
45014	Someday (I Didn't Want to Have to Be the One)/Lincoln Road	1976	—	2.00	4.00
45023	String of Hearts/Painting My Love Song	1977	—	2.00	4.00
45024	What a Sound/Painting My Love Song	1977	—	2.00	4.00
Albums					
ABC					
X-747	Henry Gross	1971	3.75	7.50	15.00
A&M					
SP-4416	Henry Gross	1973	3.00	6.00	12.00
SP-4502	Plug Me Into Something	1974	3.00	6.00	12.00
CAPITOL					
ST 12113	What's in a Name	1980	2.50	5.00	10.00

Number	Title (A Side/B Side)	Yr	VG	VG+	NM
LIFESONG					
LS 6002	Release	1976	2.50	5.00	10.00
LS 6010	Show Me to the Stage	1977	2.50	5.00	10.00
PZ 34995	Release	1978	2.00	4.00	8.00
—Reissue of 6002					
PZ 35002	Show Me to the Stage	1978	2.00	4.00	8.00
—Reissue of 6010					
JZ 35280	Love Is the Stuff	1978	2.50	5.00	10.00

GROSS SISTERS, THE

Number	Title (A Side/B Side)	Yr	VG	VG+	NM
45s					
CHECKER					
932	Oom Baby!/My Baby Ain't Nothin' But Bad	1959	10.00	20.00	40.00

GROUNDHOGS, THE

Number	Title (A Side/B Side)	Yr	VG	VG+	NM
45s					
INTERPHON					
7715	Rock Me/Shake It	1965	3.00	6.00	12.00
LIBERTY					
56205	Ship on the Ocean/Sailor	1970	2.00	4.00	8.00
Albums					
CLEVE					
CH-82871	The Groundhogs with John Lee Hooker and John Mayall	196?	25.00	50.00	100.00
IMPERIAL					
LP-12452	Blues Obituary	1969	10.00	20.00	40.00
LIBERTY					
LST-7644	Thank Christ for the Bomb	1970	7.50	15.00	30.00
UNITED ARTISTS					
UA-LA008-F	Hogwash	1973	5.00	10.00	20.00
UA-LA603-G	Crosscut Saw	1976	5.00	10.00	20.00
UA-LA680-G	Black Diamond	1976	5.00	10.00	20.00
UAS-5513	The Groundhogs Split	1971	5.00	10.00	20.00
UAS-5570	Who Will Save the World	1972	5.00	10.00	20.00
WORLD PACIFIC					
WPS-21892	Scratching the Surface	1968	10.00	20.00	40.00

GROUNDSPEED

Number	Title (A Side/B Side)	Yr	VG	VG+	NM
45s					
DECCA					
32344	In a Dream/L-12 East	1968	6.25	12.50	25.00

GROUP, THE

Probably more than one group.

Number	Title (A Side/B Side)	Yr	VG	VG+	NM
45s					
WARNER BROS.					
5840	Baby, Baby It's You/Can't Get Enough of Your Love	1966	3.00	6.00	12.00
Albums					
BELL					
6038	The Group	1970	5.00	10.00	20.00
RCA VICTOR					
LPM-2663 [M]	The Group	1963	5.00	10.00	20.00
LSP-2663 [S]	The Group	1963	6.25	12.50	25.00

GROUP "B"

Number	Title (A Side/B Side)	Yr	VG	VG+	NM
45s					
SCORPIO					
402	Stop Calling Me/She's Gone	1967	6.25	12.50	25.00
406	I Know Your Name Girl/I Never Really Knew	1967	6.25	12.50	25.00

GROUP IMAGE, THE

Number	Title (A Side/B Side)	Yr	VG	VG+	NM
Albums					
COMMUNITY					
A-101	A Mouth in the Clouds	1968	7.50	15.00	30.00

GROUP ONE

Number	Title (A Side/B Side)	Yr	VG	VG+	NM
Albums					
RCA VICTOR					
LPM-3524 [M]	Brothers Go to Mothers and Others	1966	3.75	7.50	15.00
LSP-3524 [S]	Brothers Go to Mothers and Others	1966	5.00	10.00	20.00

GROUP THERAPY

Number	Title (A Side/B Side)	Yr	VG	VG+	NM
45s					
CANTERBURY					
517	Magic in the Air/Bad News	1967	3.00	6.00	12.00
MERCURY					
72702	Thoughts/Come On	1967	3.00	6.00	12.00
PHILIPS					
40598	Can't Stop Lovin' You Baby/I Must Go	1969	2.00	4.00	8.00
RCA VICTOR					
47-9527	People Get Ready/Who'll Be Next	1968	2.00	4.00	8.00
Albums					
PHILIPS					
PHS 600303	37 Minutes of Group Therapy	1969	3.75	7.50	15.00
RCA VICTOR					
LPM-3976 [M]	People Get Ready for Group Therapy	1968	10.00	20.00	40.00
LSP-3976 [S]	People Get Ready for Group Therapy	1968	5.00	10.00	20.00

GROUPIES, THE

Number	Title (A Side/B Side)	Yr	VG	VG+	NM
45s					
ATCO					
6393	I'm a Hog for You/Primitive	1966	7.50	15.00	30.00

GROWING CONCERN, THE

Number	Title (A Side/B Side)	Yr	VG	VG+	NM
45s					
MAINSTREAM					
685	Tomorrow Has Been Canceled/A Boy I Once Knew Well	1968	7.50	15.00	30.00
Albums					
MAINSTREAM					
S-6108 [S]	The Growing Concern	1968	30.00	60.00	120.00
56108 [M]	The Growing Concern	1968	20.00	40.00	80.00

GROWL

Number	Title (A Side/B Side)	Yr	VG	VG+	NM
Albums					
DISCREET					
DS 2209	Growl	1974	5.00	10.00	20.00

GRUNION HUNTERS, THE

Number	Title (A Side/B Side)	Yr	VG	VG+	NM
45s					
HIGHLAND					
1035	The Four-Eyed, Tongue-Tied, Swimmin' Surfer Biter/Sing Along to the Swimmin' Surfer Biter	1963	10.00	20.00	40.00

GRUNIONS, THE

Number	Title (A Side/B Side)	Yr	VG	VG+	NM
45s					
JOCKO					
505	Surfin' Psycho/Big Noise from Winnetka	1963	12.50	25.00	50.00

GRYPHON

Number	Title (A Side/B Side)	Yr	VG	VG+	NM
Albums					
BELL					
1316	Red Queen to Gryphon Three	1974	3.75	7.50	15.00
(NO LABEL)					
12497	Gryphon	197?	20.00	40.00	80.00

GUARALDI, VINCE

Number	Title (A Side/B Side)	Yr	VG	VG+	NM
45s					
FANTASY					
563	Cast Your Fate to the Wind/Samba de Orpheus	1962	2.50	5.00	10.00
567	Zalas/Jitterbug Waltz	1963	2.50	5.00	10.00
571	Mr. Lucky/Treat Street	1963	2.50	5.00	10.00
580	Days of Wine and Roses/(B-side unknown)	1963	2.50	5.00	10.00
593	Linus & Lucy/Oh, Good Grief	1964	5.00	10.00	20.00
606	Humbly I Adore Thee/Theme to Grace	1965	2.50	5.00	10.00
608	Christmas Time Is Here/What Child Is This	1966	5.00	10.00	20.00
613	I'm a Loser/Favela	1966	2.50	5.00	10.00
Albums					
FANTASY					
OJC-149	Vince Guaraldi Trio	198?	2.50	5.00	10.00
—Reissue of 3225					
OJC-235	A Flower Is a Lovesome Thing	198?	2.50	5.00	10.00
—Reissue of 3257					
OJC-272	Modern Music from San Francisco	1987	2.50	5.00	10.00
—Reissue of 3213					
OJC-287	Jazz Impressions	1987	2.50	5.00	10.00
—Reissue of 8359					
OJC-289	Live at the El Matador	1987	2.50	5.00	10.00
—Reissue of 8371					
OJC-437	Jazz Impressions of Black Orpheus (Cast Your Fate to the Wind)	198?	2.50	5.00	10.00
—Reissue of 8089					
3213 [M]	Modern Music from San Francisco	1956	12.50	25.00	50.00
—Red vinyl					
3213 [M]	Modern Music from San Francisco	195?	6.25	12.50	25.00
—Black vinyl, red label, non-flexible vinyl					
3225 [M]	Vince Guaraldi Trio	1956	12.50	25.00	50.00
—Red vinyl					
3225 [M]	Vince Guaraldi Trio	195?	6.25	12.50	25.00
—Black vinyl, red label, non-flexible vinyl					
3225 [M]	Vince Guaraldi Trio	196?	3.75	7.50	15.00
—Black vinyl, red label, flexible vinyl					
3257 [M]	A Flower Is a Lovesome Thing	1958	10.00	20.00	40.00
—Red vinyl					
3257 [M]	A Flower Is a Lovesome Thing	195?	6.25	12.50	25.00
—Black vinyl, red label, non-flexible vinyl					
3257 [M]	A Flower Is a Lovesome Thing	196?	3.75	7.50	15.00
—Black vinyl, red label, flexible vinyl					
3337 [M]	Jazz Impressions of Black Orpheus (Cast Your Fate to the Wind)	1962	10.00	20.00	40.00
—Red vinyl					
3337 [M]	Jazz Impressions of Black Orpheus (Cast Your Fate to the Wind)	1962	6.25	12.50	25.00
—Black vinyl, red label, non-flexible vinyl					
3337 [M]	Jazz Impressions of Black Orpheus (Cast Your Fate to the Wind)	1962	3.75	7.50	15.00
—Black vinyl, red label, flexible vinyl					
3352 [M]	Vince Guaraldi in Person	1963	6.25	12.50	25.00
3356 [M]	Vince Guaraldi and Bola Sete and Friends	1964	6.25	12.50	25.00
3358 [M]	Tour de Force	1964	6.25	12.50	25.00
3359 [M]	Jazz Impressions	1965	6.25	12.50	25.00
3360 [M]	The Latin Side of Vince Guaraldi	1965	6.25	12.50	25.00
3362 [M]	From All Sides	1966	5.00	10.00	20.00
3367 [M]	Vince Guaraldi at Grace Cathedral	1967	5.00	10.00	20.00
3371 [M]	Live at the El Matador	1967	5.00	10.00	20.00
MPF-4505	Vince Guaraldi's Greatest Hits	1981	3.00	6.00	12.00
5019 [M]	A Charlie Brown Christmas	1964	7.50	15.00	30.00
8089 [S]	Jazz Impressions of Black Orpheus (Cast Your Fate to the Wind)	1962	10.00	20.00	40.00
—Blue vinyl					
8089 [S]	Jazz Impressions of Black Orpheus (Cast Your Fate to the Wind)	1962	6.25	12.50	25.00
—Black vinyl, blue label, non-flexible vinyl					
8089 [S]	Jazz Impressions of Black Orpheus (Cast Your Fate to the Wind)	1962	3.75	7.50	15.00
—Black vinyl, blue label, flexible vinyl					
8352 [S]	Vince Guaraldi in Person	1963	6.25	12.50	25.00
8356 [S]	Vince Guaraldi and Bola Sete and Friends	1964	6.25	12.50	25.00
8358 [S]	Tour de Force	1964	6.25	12.50	25.00
8359 [S]	Jazz Impressions	1965	6.25	12.50	25.00
8360 [S]	The Latin Side of Vince Guaraldi	1965	6.25	12.50	25.00

Number	Title (A Side/B Side)	Yr	VG	VG+	NM
8362 [S]	From All Sides	1966	5.00	10.00	20.00
8367 [S]	Vince Guaraldi at Grace Cathedral	1967	5.00	10.00	20.00
8371 [S]	Live at the El Matador	1967	5.00	10.00	20.00
8377	Live-Live-Live	1968	5.00	10.00	20.00
8430	A Boy Named Charlie Brown — Jazz Impressions	1971	5.00	10.00	20.00
—Reissue of 85017					
8431	A Charlie Brown Christmas	1971	6.25	12.50	25.00
—Reissue of 85019; dark blue label					
8431	A Charlie Brown Christmas	1988	3.75	7.50	15.00
—Remastered version with "1988" on back cover. Lighter blue label. Also has a bonus track!					
85017	A Boy Named Charlie Brown — Jazz Impressions	196?	6.25	12.50	25.00
85019 [S]	A Charlie Brown Christmas	1964	10.00	20.00	40.00
MOBILE FIDELITY					
1-112	Jazz Impressions of Black Orpheus (Cast Your Fate to the Wind)	1983	12.50	25.00	50.00
—Audiophile vinyl					
WARNER BROS.					
WS 1747	Oh Good Grief!	1968	5.00	10.00	20.00
WS 1775	Eclectic	1969	3.75	7.50	15.00
WS 1828	Alma-Ville	1970	3.75	7.50	15.00

GUARALDI, VINCE/CONTE CANDOLI

Albums

Number	Title (A Side/B Side)	Yr	VG	VG+	NM
CROWN					
CST-417 [R]	Vince Guaraldi and the Conte Candoli All Stars	1963	2.50	5.00	10.00
CLP-5417 [M]	Vince Guaraldi and the Conte Candoli All Stars	1963	3.00	6.00	12.00
PREMIER					
PM-2009 [M]	Vince Guaraldi-Conte Candoli Quartet	1963	3.00	6.00	12.00
PS-2009 [R]	Vince Guaraldi-Conte Candoli Quartet	1963	2.50	5.00	10.00

GUARALDI, VINCE/FRANK ROSOLINO

Albums

Number	Title (A Side/B Side)	Yr	VG	VG+	NM
PREMIER					
PM-2014 [M]	Vince Guaraldi-Frank Rosolino Quintet	1963	3.00	6.00	12.00
PS-2014 [R]	Vince Guaraldi-Frank Rosolino Quintet	1963	2.50	5.00	10.00

GUARD, DAVE, AND THE WHISKEYHILL SINGERS

Dave Guard had split from THE KINGSTON TRIO.

45s

Number	Title (A Side/B Side)	Yr	VG	VG+	NM
CAPITOL					
4787	Plane Wreck at Los Gatos/Ride On, Railroad Bill	1962	2.50	5.00	10.00

Albums

Number	Title (A Side/B Side)	Yr	VG	VG+	NM
CAPITOL					
ST 1728 [S]	Dave Guard and the Whiskeyhill Singers	1962	6.25	12.50	25.00
T 1728 [M]	Dave Guard and the Whiskeyhill Singers	1962	5.00	10.00	20.00

GUESS WHO, THE

45s

Number	Title (A Side/B Side)	Yr	VG	VG+	NM
AMY					
967	And She's Mine/All Right	1966	5.00	10.00	20.00
—The existence of stock copies of this record has been questioned					
976	His Girl/It's My Pride	1967	7.50	15.00	30.00
—Price is for stock copy; promos go for less					
FONTANA					
1597	This Time Long Ago/There's No Getting Away from It	1967	7.50	15.00	30.00
HILLTAK					
7803	C'mon Little Mama/Moon Wave Maker	1979	—	3.00	6.00
7807	Sweet Young Thing/It's Getting Pretty Bad	1979	—	3.00	6.00
RCA VICTOR					
APBO-0217	Star Baby/Musicione	1974	—	2.50	5.00
SPS-45-223 [DJ]	Friends of Mine (Part 1)/Friends of Mine (Part 2)	1969	3.00	6.00	12.00
APBO-0324	Clap for the Wolfman/Road Food	1974	—	2.50	5.00
PB-10075	Dancin' Fool/Seems Like I Can't Live With You, But I Can't Live Without You	1974	—	2.50	5.00
GB-10161	Clap for the Wolfman/Star Baby	1975	—	2.00	4.00
—Gold Standard Series					
PB-10216	Loves Me Like a Brother/Hoe Down Time	1975	—	2.50	5.00
PB-10360	Dreams/Rosanne	1975	—	2.50	5.00
PB-10410	When the Band Was Singin' (Shakin' All Over)/Women	1975	—	3.00	6.00
PB-10716	Silver Bird/Runnin' Down the Street	1976	3.00	6.00	12.00
74-0102	These Eyes/Lightfoot	1969	—	3.00	6.00
74-0195	Laughing/Undun	1969	—	3.00	6.00
74-0300	No Time/Proper Stranger	1969	—	3.00	6.00
74-0325	American Woman/No Sugar Tonight	1970	—	2.50	5.00
74-0367	Hand Me Down World/Runnin' Down the Street	1970	—	2.50	5.00
74-0388	Share the Land/Bus Rider	1970	—	2.50	5.00
74-0388 [PS]	Share the Land/Bus Rider	1970	2.50	5.00	10.00
74-0414	Hang On to Your Life/Do You Miss Me, Darlin'?	1970	—	2.50	5.00
74-0414 [PS]	Hang On to Your Life/Do You Miss Me, Darlin'?	1970	6.25	12.50	25.00
74-0458	Albert Flasher/Broker	1971	—	2.50	5.00
74-0522	Rain Dance/One Divided	1971	—	2.50	5.00
74-0578	Sour Suite/Life in the Bloodstream	1971	—	2.50	5.00
74-0659	Heartbroken Bopper/Arrividerci Girl	1972	—	2.50	5.00
74-0708	Guns, Guns, Guns/Heaven Only Moved Just Once Yesterday	1972	—	2.50	5.00
74-0803	Runnin' Back to Saskatoon/New Mother Nature	1972	—	2.50	5.00
74-0880	Follow Your Daughter Home/Bye Bye Babe	1973	—	2.50	5.00
74-0926	The Watcher/Orly	1973	—	2.50	5.00
74-0977	Lie Down/Glamour Boy	1973	—	2.50	5.00
SCEPTER					
1295	Shakin' All Over/Till We Kissed	1965	3.75	7.50	15.00
1295	Shakin' All Over/Monkey in a Cage	1965	7.50	15.00	30.00
—B-side by the Discotays					
12108	Hey Ho What You Do to Me/Goodnight Goodnight	1965	3.75	7.50	15.00
12118	Hurting Each Other/Baby's Birthday	1965	5.00	10.00	20.00
12131	Believe Me/Baby Feelin'	1966	5.00	10.00	20.00
12144	One Day/Clock on the Wall	1966	5.00	10.00	20.00

Albums

Number	Title (A Side/B Side)	Yr	VG	VG+	NM
COMPLEAT					
672012-1 [(2)]	The Best of the Gues Who, Live	1986	5.00	10.00	20.00
HILLTAK					
SD 19227	All This for a Song	1979	3.00	6.00	12.00
MGM					
SE-4645	The Guess Who	1969	3.75	7.50	15.00
—Compilation of pre-RCA Victor recordings					
PICKWICK					
SPC-3246	The Guess Who	1970	2.50	5.00	10.00
PRIDE					
PRD 0012	The History of the Guess Who	197?	3.00	6.00	12.00
P.I.P.					
6806	The Guess Who Play Pure Guess Who	197?	3.00	6.00	12.00
RCA					
7622-1-R	The Greatest of the Guess Who	1987	2.50	5.00	10.00
—Late reissue					
RCA VICTOR					
APD1-0130 [Q]	#10	1974	6.25	12.50	25.00
APL1-0130	#10	1973	3.75	7.50	15.00
AFL1-0269	The Best of the Guess Who, Volume II	1977	2.50	5.00	10.00
—Reissue with new prefix					
APD1-0269 [Q]	The Best of the Guess Who, Volume II	1974	6.25	12.50	25.00
APL1-0269	The Best of the Guess Who, Volume II	1973	3.75	7.50	15.00
APD1-0405 [Q]	Road Food	1974	6.25	12.50	25.00
APL1-0405	Road Food	1974	3.75	7.50	15.00
CPD1-0636 [Q]	Flavours	1975	6.25	12.50	25.00
CPL1-0636	Flavours	1975	3.75	7.50	15.00
ANL1-0983	Canned Wheat Packed By the Guess Who	1975	2.50	5.00	10.00
—Reissue of LSP-4157					
APL1-0995	Power in the Music	1975	3.75	7.50	15.00
LSPX-1004	The Best of the Guess Who	1971	3.75	7.50	15.00
ANL1-1117	Wheatfield Soul	1975	2.50	5.00	10.00
—Reissue of LSP-4141					
APL1-1778	The Way They Were	1976	3.75	7.50	15.00
APL1-2253	The Greatest of the Guess Who	1977	3.75	7.50	15.00
AFL1-2594	The Best of the Guess Who	1978	2.50	5.00	10.00
—Reissue of LSPX-1004					
AYL1-3662	The Best of the Guess Who	1979	2.00	4.00	8.00
—"Best Buy Series" reissue					
AYL1-3673	American Woman	1979	2.00	4.00	8.00
—"Best Buy Series" reissue					
AYL1-3746	The Greatest of the Guess Who	1980	2.00	4.00	8.00
—"Best Buy Series" reissue					
LSP-4141	Wheatfield Soul	1969	5.00	10.00	20.00
—Orange label, non-flexible vinyl					
LSP-4141	Wheatfield Soul	1971	3.00	6.00	12.00
—Orange label, flexible vinyl					
LSP-4157	Canned Wheat Packed By the Guess Who	1969	5.00	10.00	20.00
—Orange label, non-flexible vinyl					
LSP-4157	Canned Wheat Packed By the Guess Who	1971	3.00	6.00	12.00
—Orange label, flexible vinyl					
AFL1-4266	American Woman	1977	2.50	5.00	10.00
—Reissue with new prefix					
LSP-4266	American Woman	1970	5.00	10.00	20.00
—Orange label, non-flexible vinyl					
LSP-4266	American Woman	1971	3.00	6.00	12.00
—Orange label, flexible vinyl					
LSP-4359	Share the Land	1970	5.00	10.00	20.00
—Orange label, non-flexible vinyl					
LSP-4359	Share the Land	1971	3.00	6.00	12.00
—Orange label, flexible vinyl					
LSP-4574	So Long, Bannatyne	1971	3.75	7.50	15.00
LSP-4602	Rockin'	1972	3.75	7.50	15.00
LSP-4779	Live at the Paramount (Seattle)	1972	6.25	12.50	25.00
LSP-4830	Artificial Paradise	1973	3.75	7.50	15.00
—Add 1/3 if paper bag is with package					
SCEPTER					
SP-533 [M]	Shakin' All Over	1966	10.00	20.00	40.00
SPS-533 [P]	Shakin' All Over	1966	6.25	12.50	25.00
—The above lists the artist as "The Guess Who's Chad Allan & The Expressions" on the cover					
SPRINGBOARD					
SPB-4022	Shakin' All Over	1972	2.50	5.00	10.00
WAND					
WDS-691	Born in Canada	1969	3.75	7.50	15.00
—Reissue of Scepter LP					

GUIDES, THE

45s

Number	Title (A Side/B Side)	Yr	VG	VG+	NM
GUYDEN					
2023	How Long Must a Fool Go On/You Must Try	1959	7.50	15.00	30.00
—Originally released under the name "The Swallows"					

GUILLOTEENS, THE

45s

Number	Title (A Side/B Side)	Yr	VG	VG+	NM
COLUMBIA					
43852	Wild Child/You Think You're Happy	1966	3.75	7.50	15.00
43852 [PS]	Wild Child/You Think You're Happy	1966	10.00	20.00	40.00
—Sleeve is promo only					
44089	I Love That Girl/Dear Mrs. Applebee	1967	3.00	6.00	12.00
HANNA-BARBERA					
446	I Don't Believe/Hey You	1965	3.75	7.50	15.00
451	Don't Let the Rain Get You Down/For My Own	1965	3.75	7.50	15.00
451 [PS]	Don't Let the Rain Get You Down/For My Own	1965	7.50	15.00	30.00
486	I Sit and Cry/Crying All Over My Time	1966	5.00	10.00	20.00

GUITAR, BILLY

45s

Number	Title (A Side/B Side)	Yr	VG	VG+	NM
DECCA					
30634	Here Comes the Night/You Should Have Loved Her More	1958	17.50	35.00	70.00

GUITAR, BONNIE

45s

Number	Title (A Side/B Side)	Yr	VG	VG+	NM
4 STAR					
1006	I Wanna Spend My Life with You/Maggie	1975	—	2.00	4.00

Number	Title (A Side/B Side)	Yr	VG	VG+	NM
1041	Honey on the Moon/Lonely Eyes	1980	—	2.00	4.00
—Number also listed as 1003. Which is correct? Or are both?					
COLUMBIA					
45643	Just As Soon As I Get Over Loving You/Happy Everything	1972	—	2.50	5.00
DOLTON					
10	Candy Apple Red/Come to Me, I Love You	1959	3.00	6.00	12.00
19	Candy Apple Red/Come to Me, I Love You	1960	2.50	5.00	10.00
DOT					
15550	Dark Moon/Big Mile	1957	3.75	7.50	15.00
15587	Half Your Heart/If You See My Love Dancing	1957	3.00	6.00	12.00
15612	There's a New Moon Over My Shoulder/Mister Fire Eyes	1957	3.00	6.00	12.00
15678	Making Believe/I Saw Your Face in the Moon	1957	3.00	6.00	12.00
15708	A Very Precious Love/Johnny Vagabond	1958	3.00	6.00	12.00
15776	I Found You Out/If You'll Be the Teacher	1958	3.00	6.00	12.00
15862	Rocky Mountain Moon/Whispering Hope	1958	3.00	6.00	12.00
15894	Baby Moon/Solitude	1959	3.00	6.00	12.00
16811	I'm Living in Two Worlds/Goodtime Charlie	1965	—	3.00	6.00
16872	Would You Believe/Get Your Life the Way You Want It	1966	—	3.00	6.00
16919	Are You Sincere/The Tallest Tree	1966	—	3.00	6.00
16968	I'll Be Missing You (Under the Mistletoe)/Blue Christmas	1966	5.00	10.00	20.00
16987	The Kickin' Tree/Only I	1967	—	3.00	6.00
17007	You Can Steal Me/Ramblin' Man	1967	—	3.00	6.00
17029	I Want My Baby/Woman in Love	1967	—	3.00	6.00
17057	Wings of a Dove/Stop the Sun	1967	—	3.00	6.00
17097	Faded Love/I Believe in Love	1968	—	2.50	5.00
17150	Almost Like Being with You/Leaves Are the Tears of Autumn	1968	—	2.50	5.00
17249	Perfect Strangers/I'll Meet You in Denver	1969	—	2.50	5.00
17276	I'll Pick Up My Heart/That See Me Later Look	1969	—	2.50	5.00
FABOR					
138	Ra Ta Ta Ta/Leave Weeping to the Willow Tree	1964	2.00	4.00	8.00
4013	If You See My Love Dancing/Hello, Hello, Please Answer	1956	5.00	10.00	20.00
4017	Clinging Vine/Dream Dreamers	1956	5.00	10.00	20.00
4018	Dark Moon/Big Mile	1957	10.00	20.00	40.00
JERDEN					
707	There'll Be No Teardrops Tonight/The Fool	1963	2.50	5.00	10.00
MCA					
40192	The Bed I Love In/Wishing Star	1974	—	2.00	4.00
40306	From This Moment On/Shine	1974	—	2.00	4.00
PARAMOUNT					
0004	A Truer Love You'll Never Find (Than Mine)/ That's When	1969	—	2.50	5.00
—As "Bonnie and Buddy" (Buddy is Buddy Killen)					
0045	Allegheny/Red Checkered Blazer	1970	—	2.50	5.00
PLAYBACK					
75714	Still the Same/(B-side unknown)	1989	—	2.00	4.00
RADIO					
101	Please, My Love/Love Is Over, Love Is Done	1958	3.00	6.00	12.00
110	Shanty Boat/Only the Moon Man Knows	1958	3.00	6.00	12.00
RCA VICTOR					
47-7951	I'll Step Down/Tell Her Bye	1961	2.50	5.00	10.00
47-8063	Broken Hearted Girl/Who Is She	1962	2.50	5.00	10.00
Albums					
DOT					
DLP-3069 [M]	Moonlight and Shadows	1957	12.50	25.00	50.00
DLP-3151 [M]	Whispering Hope	1958	10.00	20.00	40.00
DLP-3335 [M]	Dark Moon	1961	6.25	12.50	25.00
DLP-3696 [M]	Two Worlds	1966	5.00	10.00	20.00
DLP-3737 [M]	Miss Bonnie Guitar	1966	5.00	10.00	20.00
DLP-3746 [M]	Merry Christmas from Bonnie Guitar	1966	5.00	10.00	20.00
DLP-3793 [M]	Award Winner	1967	5.00	10.00	20.00
DLP-25069 [R]	Moonlight and Shadows	196?	3.75	7.50	15.00
DLP-25151 [S]	Whispering Hope	1958	12.50	25.00	50.00
DLP-25335 [R]	Dark Moon	196?	3.75	7.50	15.00
DLP-25696 [S]	Two Worlds	1966	6.25	12.50	25.00
DLP-25737 [S]	Miss Bonnie Guitar	1966	6.25	12.50	25.00
DLP-25746 [S]	Merry Christmas from Bonnie Guitar	1966	6.25	12.50	25.00
DLP-25793 [S]	Award Winner	1967	5.00	10.00	20.00
DLP-25840	Bonnie Guitar	1968	5.00	10.00	20.00
DLP-25947	Bonnie Guitar Affair!	1969	5.00	10.00	20.00
PARAMOUNT					
PAS-5018	Allegheny	1970	3.75	7.50	15.00
PICKWICK					
SPC-3086	Favorite Lady of Song	196?	3.00	6.00	12.00
RCA CAMDEN					
CAS-2339	Night Train to Memphis	1969	3.75	7.50	15.00

GUITAR SLIM

Number	Title (A Side/B Side)	Yr	VG	VG+	NM
45s					
ATCO					
6072	Oh Yeah/Down Through the Years	1956	10.00	20.00	40.00
6097	It Hurts to Love Someone/If I Should Lose You	1957	7.50	15.00	30.00
6108	I Won't Mind at All/Hello, How Ya' Been, Goodbye	1958	7.50	15.00	30.00
6120	If I Had My Life to Live Over/When There's No Way Out	1958	7.50	15.00	30.00
IMPERIAL					
5278	Woman Troubles/Cryin' in the Mornin'	1954	15.00	30.00	60.00
5310	New Arrival/Standing at the Station	1954	15.00	30.00	60.00
SPECIALTY					
482	The Things That I Used to Do/Well, I Done Get Over It	1954	12.50	25.00	50.00
490	Story of My Life/A Letter to My Girl Friend	1954	10.00	20.00	40.00
527	Later for You Baby/Troubles Don't Last	1954	6.25	12.50	25.00
536	Sufferin' Mind/Twenty-Five Lies	1955	6.25	12.50	25.00
542	Stand By Me/Our Only Child	1955	6.25	12.50	25.00
551	You're Gonna Miss Me/I Got Sumpin' for You	1955	6.25	12.50	25.00
557	Think It Over/Quicksand	1955	6.25	12.50	25.00
569	Sumthin' to Remember Me By/You Give Me Nothin' But the Blues	1956	6.25	12.50	25.00
Albums					
ATLANTIC					
81760	The Atco Sessions	1987	2.50	5.00	10.00
SPECIALTY					
SP-2130	Things That I Used to Do	1969	5.00	10.00	20.00

GUITARS, INC.

Pseudonym for THE FIREBALLS.

Number	Title (A Side/B Side)	Yr	VG	VG+	NM
45s					
HAMILTON					
50035	Little Toy/Holiday Love	1960	6.25	12.50	25.00

GULLIVER

With Daryl Hall. John Oates joined later, but is not on these records.

Number	Title (A Side/B Side)	Yr	VG	VG+	NM
45s					
ELEKTRA					
45689	Angelina/Every Day's a Lovely Day	1970	2.00	4.00	8.00
45698	A Truly Good Song/Every Day's a Lovely Day	1970	2.00	4.00	8.00
Albums					
ELEKTRA					
EKS-74070	Gulliver	1970	5.00	10.00	20.00

GUM DROPS, THE

Number	Title (A Side/B Side)	Yr	VG	VG+	NM
45s					
CORAL					
62003	My Own True Love/On the Wings of the Wind	1958	3.75	7.50	15.00
62102	I Spoke Too Soon/Sie Tu (It's You, It's You)	1959	3.75	7.50	15.00
62138	It Happens Every Day/They Wake Me	1959	3.75	7.50	15.00
DECCA					
30584	You're the One/Gum Drop Shoes and Bells in Her Hair	1958	5.00	10.00	20.00
KING					
1496	Gum Drop/Don't Take It So Hard	1955	5.00	10.00	20.00
1499	I'll Wait for One More Train/Don't Take It So Hard	1955	5.00	10.00	20.00
4913	I Wonder and Wonder/I'll Follow You	1956	6.25	12.50	25.00
4963	Natural Born Lover/Chapel of Hearts	1956	6.25	12.50	25.00
5051	Ba-Bee Da Boat Is Leaving/Pigeon	1957	5.00	10.00	20.00

GUN

Number	Title (A Side/B Side)	Yr	VG	VG+	NM
45s					
EPIC					
10413	Race with the Devil/Sunshine	1968	2.50	5.00	10.00
10537	Don't Look Back/Hobo	1969	2.50	5.00	10.00
10593	Drown Yourself in the River/Long Hair Wildman	1970	2.50	5.00	10.00
Albums					
EPIC					
BN 26468	Gun	1969	5.00	10.00	20.00
BN 26551	Gunsight	1970	6.25	12.50	25.00

GUNHILL ROAD

Number	Title (A Side/B Side)	Yr	VG	VG+	NM
45s					
KAMA SUTRA					
562	Ford, De Soto, Cadillac/(B-side unknown)	1972	—	2.50	5.00
569	Back When My Hair Was Short/We Can't Ride the Roller Coaster Anymore	1973	—	3.00	6.00
582	Ford, De Soto, Cadillac/Sailing	1973	—	2.50	5.00
591	She Made a Man Out of Me/(B-side unknown)	1974	—	2.50	5.00
MERCURY					
73232	42nd Street/(B-side unknown)	1971	—	3.00	6.00
Albums					
KAMA SUTRA					
KLS-2061	Gunhill Road	1972	3.00	6.00	12.00
MERCURY					
SR-61341	Gun Hill Road	1971	3.00	6.00	12.00

GUNTER, ARTHUR

Number	Title (A Side/B Side)	Yr	VG	VG+	NM
45s					
EXCELLO					
2047	Baby Let's Play House/Blues After Hours	1954	30.00	60.00	120.00
2053	She's Mine, All Mine/You Are Doin' Me Wrong	1955	15.00	30.00	60.00
2058	Honey Babe/No Happy Home	1955	15.00	30.00	60.00
2073	Baby You Better Listen/Trouble with My Baby	1955	7.50	15.00	30.00
2084	Hear My Plea Baby/Love Has Got Me	1956	7.50	15.00	30.00
2125	Baby Can't You See/You're Always on My Mind	1958	6.25	12.50	25.00
2137	Ludella/We're Gonna Shake	1959	6.25	12.50	25.00
2147	Crazy Me/Don't Leave Me Now	1959	6.25	12.50	25.00
2164	No Naggin' No Draggin'/I Want Her Back	1959	6.25	12.50	25.00
2191	Little Blue Jeans/Mind Your Own Business Babe	1960	5.00	10.00	20.00
2201	My Heart's Always Lonesome/I'm Fallin', Love's Got Me	1961	5.00	10.00	20.00
Albums					
EXCELLO					
LPS-8017	Black and Blues	1971	6.25	12.50	25.00

GUNTER, CORNEL

Number	Title (A Side/B Side)	Yr	VG	VG+	NM
45s					
ABC-PARAMOUNT					
9698	She Loves to Rock/In Self Defense	1956	10.00	20.00	40.00
—As "Cornel Gunter and the Flairs"					
CHALLENGE					
59281	If I Had the Key to Your Heart/Wishful	1965	2.50	5.00	10.00
DOT					
15654	You Send Me/Call Me a Fool	1957	5.00	10.00	20.00
EAGLE					
301	Baby Come Home/I Want You Madly	1957	7.50	15.00	30.00
LIBERTY					
55096	If We Should Meet Again/Neighborhood Dance	1957	5.00	10.00	20.00

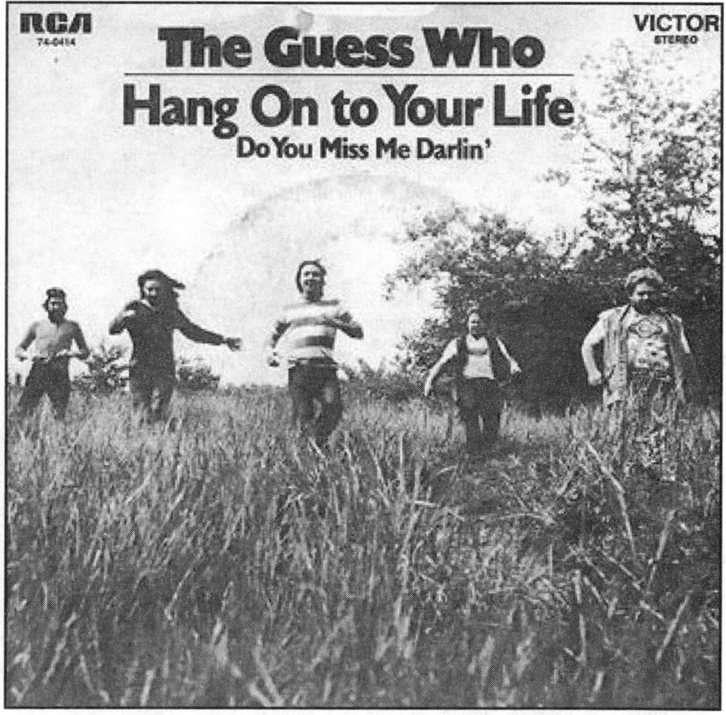

(Top left) The first album by the British band Genesis to be issued in the United States was their second LP, *Trespass*. For unknown reasons, the original issue was on ABC's jazz label, Impulse! It was quickly reissued on the main ABC label. (Top right) In America, Golden Earring is best known for two hits, "Radar Love" and "Twilight Zone." But before either one of them, the group was already recording. This album, named after a remake of the Byrds' hit song, was issued in 1970. (Bottom left) The only hit single the Grateful Dead ever had, "Touch of Grey," came packaged in an attractive poster sleeve with a gray-vinyl 45. This is the outer cover of the sleeve. (Bottom right) There weren't many Guess Who picture sleeves. Even harder to find than the one for "Share the Land" is this one, for "Hang On to Your Life"; it wasn't even listed in the last edition of this book.

Number	Title (A Side/B Side)	Yr	VG	VG+	NM
LOMA					
701	True Love/Peek, Peek-a-Boo	1955	25.00	50.00	100.00
703	You Broke My Heart/(Pretty Baby) I'm Used to You Now	1956	37.50	75.00	150.00
704	Keep Me Alive/Muchacha, Muchacha	1956	20.00	40.00	80.00
705	I'm Sad/One Thing	1956	25.00	50.00	100.00
—The Loma singles credit "The Ermines," and may or may not mention Gunter.					
WARNER BROS.					
5266	Lieft Me Up Angel/Hope of Sand	1962	3.00	6.00	12.00
5292	It Ain't No Use/In a Dream of Love	1962	3.00	6.00	12.00

GUNTER, HARDROCK

45s

Number	Title (A Side/B Side)	Yr	VG	VG+	NM
DECCA					
9-46300	Boogie Woogie on a Saturday Night/Honky Tonk	1951	10.00	20.00	40.00
9-46350	I've Done Gone Hog Wild/I Believe That Mountain Music	1951	6.25	12.50	25.00
9-46363	Sixty Minute Man/Tennessee Blues	1951	6.25	12.50	25.00
9-46367	Dixieland Boogie/If I Could Only Live My Dreams	1951	6.25	12.50	25.00
9-46383	Hesitation Boogie/Don't You Agree	1951	6.25	12.50	25.00
9-46401	Silver and Gold/Senator from Tennessee	1952	6.25	12.50	25.00
KING					
4858	Turn the Other Cheek/Before My Time	1955	5.00	10.00	20.00
MGM					
K-11520	Like the Lovers Do/Naptown, Indiana	1953	6.25	12.50	25.00
K-11596	Sunday Angel/Where Have You Been	1953	6.25	12.50	25.00
SUN					
201	Fallen Angel/Gonna Dance All Night	1954	500.00	1000.	2000.

GUNTER, SHIRLEY

45s

Number	Title (A Side/B Side)	Yr	VG	VG+	NM
FLAIR					
1020	Send Him Back/Since I Fell for You	1953	10.00	20.00	40.00
1027	Found Some Good Lovin'/Strange Romance	1954	7.50	15.00	30.00
1050	Oop Shoop/It's You	1955	7.50	15.00	30.00
1060	You're Mine/Why	1955	7.50	15.00	30.00
1065	What Difference Does It Make/Baby I Love You So	1955	7.50	15.00	30.00
1070	That's the Way I Like It/Gimme, Gimme, Gimme	1955	7.50	15.00	30.00
1076	How Can I Tell You/Ipsy Gypsy Ooh	1955	15.00	30.00	60.00
—With the Flairs					
MODERN					
979	Please Tell Me/Come On	1956	6.25	12.50	25.00
1001	Fortune in Love/Just Got Rid of a Heartache	1956	6.25	12.50	25.00
—With the Flairs					
1011	I'm So Sorry/I've Been Searching	1956	6.25	12.50	25.00
TANGERINE					
949	Stuck Up/You Let My Love Grow Cold	1965	2.50	5.00	10.00
TENDER					
503	Believe Me/Crazy Little Baby	1958	10.00	20.00	40.00

GURUS, THE

45s

Number	Title (A Side/B Side)	Yr	VG	VG+	NM
UNITED ARTISTS					
50089	Come Girl/Blue Snow Night	1966	3.00	6.00	12.00
50089 [PS]	Come Girl/Blue Snow Night	1966	6.25	12.50	25.00
50140	It Just Won't Be That Way/Everybody's Got to Be Alone Sometime	1967	3.00	6.00	12.00

GUTHRIE, ARLO

45s

Number	Title (A Side/B Side)	Yr	VG	VG+	NM
REPRISE					
PRO 304 [DJ]	Motorcycle Song/The Pause of Mr. Claus	1970	5.00	10.00	20.00
0644	Motorcycle Song/Now and Then	1967	3.00	6.00	12.00
0793	Motorcycle Song (Part 1)/Motorcycle Song (Part 2)	1968	3.00	6.00	12.00
0877	Alice's Rock & Roll Restaurant/Coming Into Los Angeles	1969	3.00	6.00	12.00
0951	Gabriel's Mother's Hiway/Ballad #16 Blues	1970	2.00	4.00	8.00
0994	The Ballad of Tricky Fred/Shackles and Chains	1971	—	3.00	6.00
1103	The City of New Orleans/Days Are Short	1972	—	3.00	6.00
1137	Ukulele Lady/Cooper's Lament	1972	—	2.50	5.00
1158	A Week on the Rag/Gypsy Dave	1973	—	2.50	5.00
1211	Nostalgia Rag/Presidential Rag	1974	—	2.00	4.00
1363	Patriot's Dream/Ocean Crossing	1976	—	2.00	4.00
1376	Grocery Blues/Guabi, Guabi	1976	—	2.00	4.00
1388	Massachusetts/My Love	1977	—	2.00	4.00
WARNER BROS.					
49037	Wedding Song/Prologue	1979	—	2.00	4.00
49796	Slow Boat/If I Could Only Touch Your Life	1981	—	2.00	4.00
49889	Oklahoma Nights/Power of Love	1981	—	2.00	4.00

Albums

Number	Title (A Side/B Side)	Yr	VG	VG+	NM
REPRISE					
MS 2060	Hobo's Lullabye	1972	3.00	6.00	12.00
MS 2142	Last of the Brooklyn Cowboys	1973	3.00	6.00	12.00
MS4 2142 [Q]	Last of the Brooklyn Cowboys	1973	5.00	10.00	20.00
MS 2183	Arlo Guthrie	1974	3.00	6.00	12.00
MS 2239	Amigo	1976	3.00	6.00	12.00
R 6267 [M]	Alice's Restaurant	1967	5.00	10.00	20.00
RS 6267 [S]	Alice's Restaurant	1967	3.75	7.50	15.00
—Pink, green and gold label					
RS 6267 [S]	Alice's Restaurant	1968	3.00	6.00	12.00
—With "W7" and "r:" logos on two-tone orange label					
RS 6267 [S]	Alice's Restaurant	1970	2.50	5.00	10.00
—With only "r:" logo on all-orange (tan) label					
RS 6299	Arlo	1968	3.75	7.50	15.00
—With "W7" and "r:" logos on two-tone orange label					
RS 6299	Arlo	1970	2.50	5.00	10.00
—With only "r:" logo on all-orange (tan) label					
RS 6346	Running Down the Road	1969	3.75	7.50	15.00
—With "W7" and "r:" logos on two-tone orange label					
RS 6346	Running Down the Road	1970	2.50	5.00	10.00
—With only "r:" logo on all-orange (tan) label					
RS 6411	Washington County	1970	3.00	6.00	12.00
WARNER BROS.					
BSK 3117	The Best of Arlo Guthrie	1977	2.50	5.00	10.00
—"Burbank" palm trees label					
BSK 3117	The Best of Arlo Guthrie	1979	2.00	4.00	8.00
—White or tan label					
BSK 3232	One Night	1978	2.50	5.00	10.00
BSK 3336	Outlasting the Blues	1979	2.50	5.00	10.00
BSK 3558	Power of Love	1981	2.50	5.00	10.00

GUTHRIE, WOODY

Albums

Number	Title (A Side/B Side)	Yr	VG	VG+	NM
ARCHIVE OF FOLK AND JAZZ					
204	Woody Guthrie	1966	3.00	6.00	12.00
COLLECTABLES					
COL-5095	Golden Classics Vol. 1: Worried Man Blues	198?	3.00	6.00	12.00
COL-5098	Golden Classics Vol. 2: Immortal	198?	3.00	6.00	12.00
ELEKTRA					
EKL-271/2 [(3) M]	The Library of Congress Recordings	1964	10.00	20.00	40.00
—Original pressing has "guitar player" labels					
FOLKWAYS					
FP-11 [10]	Dust Bowl Ballads	1950	150.00	300.00	600.00
FP-715 [10]	Songs to Grow On For Mother and Child	195?	150.00	30.00	600.00
FA-2011 [10]	Dust Bowl Ballads	195?	125.00	250.00	500.00
—Reissue of FP-11					
FA-2481 [M]	Bound for Glory: Songs and Stories of Woody Guthrie	1956	37.50	75.00	150.00
FA-2483 [M]	Woody Guthrie Sings Folk Songs	1964	12.50	25.00	50.00
FA-2484 [M]	Woody Guthrie Sings Folk Songs, Vol. 2	1964	12.50	25.00	50.00
FA-2485 [M]	Struggle	1964	12.50	25.00	50.00
FH-5212 [M]	Dust Bowl Ballads	1964	7.50	15.00	30.00
FH-5485 [M]	Ballds of Sacco and Vanzetti	196?	7.50	15.00	30.00
FC-7005 [10]	Songs to Grow On	1950	125.00	250.00	500.00
FC-7015 [10]	Songs to Grow On For Mother and Child	1953	125.00	250.00	500.00
—Reissue of FP-715					
FC-7027 [10]	Songs to Grow On Vol. 3	1951	125.00	250.00	500.00
31001 [R]	This Land Is Your Land	196?	3.00	6.00	12.00
RCA VICTOR					
LPV-502 [M]	Dust Bowl Ballads	1964	6.25	12.50	25.00
ROUNDER					
1036	Columbia River Collection	1987	2.50	5.00	10.00
1040	Dust Bowl Ballads	1988	2.50	5.00	10.00
1041/2/3 [(3)]	The Library of Congress Recordings	1988	5.00	10.00	20.00
SMITHSONIAN FOLKWAYS					
SF-40007	Woody Guthrie Sings Folk Songs	1989	3.00	6.00	12.00
SF-40025	Struggle	1989	3.00	6.00	12.00
VERVE FOLKWAYS					
FV-9007 [M]	Bed on the Floor	1965	7.50	15.00	30.00
FVS-9007 [R]	Bed on the Floor	1965	5.00	10.00	20.00
FV-9036 [M]	Bonneville Dam & Other Columbia River Songs	1965	7.50	15.00	30.00
FVS-9036 [R]	Bonneville Dam & Other Columbia River Songs	1965	5.00	10.00	20.00

GUTHRIE, WOODY, AND CISCO HOUSTON

Albums

Number	Title (A Side/B Side)	Yr	VG	VG+	NM
STINSON					
SLP-32 [10]	Cowboy Songs	195?	50.00	100.00	200.00
SLP-44 [10]	Folk Songs, Vol. 1	195?	50.00	100.00	200.00
SLP-53 [10]	More Songs	195?	50.00	100.00	200.00

GUTHRIE, WOODY; SONNY TERRY; ALEX STEWART

Albums

Number	Title (A Side/B Side)	Yr	VG	VG+	NM
STINSON					
SLP-7 [10]	Chain Gang, Vol. 1	195?	50.00	100.00	200.00
SLP-8 [10]	Chain Gang, Vol. 2	195?	50.00	100.00	200.00

GUY, ART

45s

Number	Title (A Side/B Side)	Yr	VG	VG+	NM
VALIANT					
762	Where You Gonna Go/Teenage Millionaire	1967	7.50	15.00	30.00

GUY, BOB

Pseudonym for FRANK ZAPPA.

45s

Number	Title (A Side/B Side)	Yr	VG	VG+	NM
DONNA					
1380	Letter from Jeepers/Dear Jeepers	1963	25.00	50.00	100.00

GUY, BOBBY

45s

Number	Title (A Side/B Side)	Yr	VG	VG+	NM
APT					
25052	A Vow/Good Enough	1960	7.50	15.00	30.00

GUY, BROWLEY, AND THE SKYSCRAPERS

45s

Number	Title (A Side/B Side)	Yr	VG	VG+	NM
CHECKER					
779	Watermelon Man/You Look Good to Me	1954	75.00	150.00	300.00
—Black vinyl					
779	Watermelon Man/You Look Good to Me	1954	187.50	375.00	750.00
—Red vinyl					

GUYTON, HOWARD

45s

Number	Title (A Side/B Side)	Yr	VG	VG+	NM
VERVE					
10386	I Watched You Slowly Slip Away/I Got My Own Thing Going	1966	25.00	50.00	100.00

GUYTONES, THE

45s

Number	Title (A Side/B Side)	Yr	VG	VG+	NM
DELUXE					
6144	You Won't Let Me Go/Ooh Bop Sha Boo (Give All Your Love to Me)	1957	20.00	40.00	80.00
6152	She's Mine/Not Wanted	1957	20.00	40.00	80.00

Number	Title (A Side/B Side)	Yr	VG	VG+	NM
6159	Hunky Dory/This Is Love	1958	20.00	40.00	80.00
6163	Baby, I Don't Care/Young Dreamer	1958	15.00	30.00	60.00
6169	Tell Me (How Was I to Know)/Your Heart's Bigger Than Mine	1958	15.00	30.00	60.00

GYPSIES, THE

45s

ATLAS

Number	Title (A Side/B Side)	Yr	VG	VG+	NM
1073	Why/Young Girl to Calypso	1957	20.00	40.00	80.00

GROOVE

Number	Title (A Side/B Side)	Yr	VG	VG+	NM
0117	One, Two, Three, Go/I'm Good to You Baby	1955	5.00	10.00	20.00
0129	Rock Around the Christmas Tree/You've Been Away Too Long	1955	5.00	10.00	20.00

OLD TOWN

Number	Title (A Side/B Side)	Yr	VG	VG+	NM
1168	Blue Bird/Hey There Hey There	1964	5.00	10.00	20.00
1180	Jerk It/Diamonds, Rubies, Gold and Fame	1965	5.00	10.00	20.00
1184	It's a Woman's World/They're Having a Party	1965	20.00	40.00	80.00
1193	Oh I Wonder Why/Diamonds, Rubies, Gold and Fame	1966	6.25	12.50	25.00

GYPSY

45s

METROMEDIA

Number	Title (A Side/B Side)	Yr	VG	VG+	NM
202	Gypsy Queen/Dead and Gone	1970	—	3.00	6.00

RCA VICTOR

Number	Title (A Side/B Side)	Yr	VG	VG+	NM
APBO-0036	Need You Baby/Precious One	1973	—	2.50	5.00
74-0862	Lean On Me/Day After Day	1973	—	2.50	5.00
74-0933	Make Peace with Jesus/Don't Bother Me	1973	—	2.50	5.00

Albums

METROMEDIA

Number	Title (A Side/B Side)	Yr	VG	VG+	NM
MD-1031 [(2)]	Gypsy	1970	5.00	10.00	20.00
MD 1044	In the Garden	1971	3.75	7.50	15.00

RCA VICTOR

Number	Title (A Side/B Side)	Yr	VG	VG+	NM
APL1-0093	Unlock the Gates	1973	3.75	7.50	15.00
LSP-4775	Antithesis	1972	3.75	7.50	15.00

GYPSY TRIPS, THE

45s

WORLD PACIFIC

Number	Title (A Side/B Side)	Yr	VG	VG+	NM
77809	Rock 'n Roll Gypsies/Ain't It Hard	1966	7.50	15.00	30.00

H

H.P. LOVECRAFT

45s

MERCURY

Number	Title (A Side/B Side)	Yr	VG	VG+	NM
73698	Flight/I Feel Better	1975	—	3.00	6.00
—As "Lovecraft"					
73707	We Love You (Whoever You Are)/Ain't Gettin' Home	1975	—	3.00	6.00
—As "Lovecraft"					

PHILIPS

Number	Title (A Side/B Side)	Yr	VG	VG+	NM
40464	Anyway That You Want Me/It's All Over for You	1967	3.00	6.00	12.00
40491	Wayfaring Stranger/The Time Machine	1967	3.00	6.00	12.00
40491 [PS]	Wayfaring Stranger/The Time Machine	1967	6.25	12.50	25.00
40506	The White Ship (Part 1)/The White Ship (Part 2)	1967	3.00	6.00	12.00
40578	Blue Jack of Diamonds/Keeper of the Keys	1968	3.00	6.00	12.00

REPRISE

Number	Title (A Side/B Side)	Yr	VG	VG+	NM
0996	We Can All Have It Together/Will I Know When My Time Comes	1971	2.00	4.00	8.00
—As "Lovecraft"					

Albums

MERCURY

Number	Title (A Side/B Side)	Yr	VG	VG+	NM
SRM-1-1041	We Love You	1975	3.75	7.50	15.00

PHILIPS

Number	Title (A Side/B Side)	Yr	VG	VG+	NM
PHM 200252 [M]	H.P. Lovecraft	1967	5.00	10.00	20.00
PHS 600252 [S]	H.P. Lovecraft	1967	6.25	12.50	25.00
PHS 600279	Lovecraft II	1968	6.25	12.50	25.00

REPRISE

Number	Title (A Side/B Side)	Yr	VG	VG+	NM
RS 6419	Valley of the Moon	1970	5.00	10.00	20.00

H.Y. SLEDGE

Albums

SSS INTERNATIONAL

Number	Title (A Side/B Side)	Yr	VG	VG+	NM
22	Bootleg Music	1971	5.00	10.00	20.00

HA'PENNYS, THE

Albums

FERSCH

Number	Title (A Side/B Side)	Yr	VG	VG+	NM
FL-1110	Love Is Not the Same	1968	50.00	100.00	200.00

HACKAMORE BRICK

45s

KAMA SUTRA

Number	Title (A Side/B Side)	Yr	VG	VG+	NM
521	Searchin'/Radio	1971	—	3.00	6.00

Albums

KAMA SUTRA

Number	Title (A Side/B Side)	Yr	VG	VG+	NM
KSBS-2025	One Kiss Leads to Another	1971	3.00	6.00	12.00

HACKERT, VALINE

45s

BRUNSWICK

Number	Title (A Side/B Side)	Yr	VG	VG+	NM
55151	Billy Boy/Show Me How	1959	50.00	100.00	200.00

HADLEY, RED

45s

METEOR

Number	Title (A Side/B Side)	Yr	VG	VG+	NM
5017	Ring Out Those Bells/Brother, That's All	1955	27.50	75.00	150.00

HAGAN, SAMMY, AND THE VISCOUNTS

45s

CAPITOL

Number	Title (A Side/B Side)	Yr	VG	VG+	NM
F-3772	Out of Your Heart/Shoochie Poochie	1957	10.00	20.00	40.00
F-3818	Wild Bird/Don't Cry	1957	10.00	20.00	40.00
F-3885	Tail Light/Snuggle Bunny	1958	7.50	15.00	30.00

HAGGARD, MERLE

Also see PAYCHECK AND HAGGARD.

45s

CAPITOL

Number	Title (A Side/B Side)	Yr	VG	VG+	NM
2017	Sing Me Back Home/Good Times	1967	2.00	4.00	8.00
2017 [PS]	Sing Me Back Home/Good Times	1967	2.00	4.00	8.00
2123	The Legend of Bonnie and Clyde/Today I Started Loving You Again	1968	2.00	4.00	8.00
2219	Mama Tried/You'll Never Love Me Now	1968	2.00	4.00	8.00
2219 [PS]	Mama Tried/You'll Never Love Me Now	1968	2.00	4.00	8.00
2289	I Take a Lot of Pride in What I Am/Keep Me from Cryin' Today	1968	2.00	4.00	8.00
2289 [PS]	I Take a Lot of Pride in What I Am/Keep Me from Cryin' Today	1968	2.00	4.00	8.00
2383	Hungry Eyes/California Blues	1969	2.00	4.00	8.00
2383 [PS]	Hungry Eyes/California Blues	1969	2.00	4.00	8.00
2503	Workin' Man Blues/Silver Wings	1969	2.00	4.00	8.00
2503 [PS]	Workin' Man Blues/Silver Wings	1969	2.00	4.00	8.00
2626	Okie from Muskogee/If I Had Left It Up to You	1969	2.00	4.00	8.00
2626 [PS]	Okie from Muskogee/If I Had Left It Up to You	1969	2.00	4.00	8.00
2719	The Fightin' Side of Me/Every Fool Has a Rainbow	1970	2.00	4.00	8.00
2719 [PS]	The Fightin' Side of Me/Every Fool Has a Rainbow	1970	2.00	4.00	8.00
2778	Street Singer/Mexicali Rose	1970	2.00	4.00	8.00
2838	Jesus, Take a Hold/No Reason to Quit	1970	2.00	4.00	8.00
2891	I Can't Be Myself/Sidewalks of Chicago	1970	2.00	4.00	8.00
2891 [PS]	I Can't Be Myself/Sidewalks of Chicago	1970	2.00	4.00	8.00
3024	Soldier's Last Letter/The Farmer's Daughter	1971	—	3.00	6.00
3024 [PS]	Soldier's Last Letter/The Farmer's Daughter	1971	2.00	4.00	8.00
3112	Someday We'll Look Back/It's Great to Be Alive	1971	—	3.00	6.00
3144	Song from Sleepwalk/Slow 'n Easy	1971	2.00	4.00	8.00
—By "Merle Haggard's Strangers"					
3198	Daddy Frank (The Guitar Man)/My Heart Would Know	1971	—	3.00	6.00
3294	Grandma Harp/Turnin' Off a Memory	1972	—	3.00	6.00
3419	It's Not Love (But It's Not Bad)/My Woman Keeps Lovin' Her Man	1972	—	3.00	6.00
3488	I Wonder If They Ever Think of Me/I Forget You Every Day	1972	—	3.00	6.00
3552	The Emptiest Arms in the World/Radiator Man from Waco	1973	—	2.50	5.00
3641	Everybody's Had the Blues/Nobody Knows I'm Hurtin'	1973	—	2.50	5.00
3746	If We Make It Through December/Bobby Wants a Puppy Dog for Christmas	1973	—	2.50	5.00
3830	Things Aren't Funny Anymore/Honky Tonk Night Time Man	1974	—	2.50	5.00
3900	Old Man from the Mountain/Holding Things Together	1974	—	2.50	5.00
3974	Kentucky Gambler/I've Got a Darlin' (For a Wife)	1974	—	2.50	5.00
3989	Santa Claus and Popcorn/If We Make It Through December	1974	—	2.50	5.00
4027	Always Wanting You/I've Got a Yearning	1975	—	2.50	5.00
4085	Movin' On/Here in Frisco	1975	—	2.50	5.00
4141	It's All in the Movies/Living with the Shades Pulled Down	1975	—	2.50	5.00
4204	The Roots of My Raising/The Way It Was in '51	1975	—	2.50	5.00
4267	Here Comes the Freedom Train/I Won't Give Up My Train	1976	—	2.50	5.00
4326	Cherokee Maiden/What Have You Got Planned Tonight Diana	1976	—	2.50	5.00
4477	A Workin' Man Can't Get Nowhere Today/Blues Stay Away from Me	1977	—	2.50	5.00
4525	Running Kind/Making Believe	1978	—	2.50	5.00
4636	The Way It Was in '51/Moanin' the Blues	1978	—	2.50	5.00
5460	I'm Gonna Break Every Heart I Can/Falling for You	1965	2.50	5.00	10.00
5523	This Town's Not Big Enough/Shade Tree	1965	2.50	5.00	10.00
5600	Swinging Doors/The Girl Turned Ripe	1966	2.50	5.00	10.00
5704	The Bottle Let Me Down/The Longer You Wait	1966	2.50	5.00	10.00
5803	The Fugitive/Someone Told My Story	1966	3.00	6.00	12.00
5803	I'm a Lonesome Fugitive/Someone Told My Story	1967	2.00	4.00	8.00
—Retitled A-side					
5844	I Threw Away the Rose/Loneliness Is Eating Me Alive	1967	2.00	4.00	8.00
5844 [PS]	I Threw Away the Rose/Loneliness Is Eating Me Alive	1967	2.00	4.00	8.00
5931	Branded Man/You Don't Have Very Far to Go	1967	2.00	4.00	8.00
5931 [PS]	Branded Man/You Don't Have Very Far to Go	1967	2.00	4.00	8.00

CAPITOL NASHVILLE

Number	Title (A Side/B Side)	Yr	VG	VG+	NM
S7-19346	White Christmas/Silver Bells	1996	—	2.00	4.00

CURB

Number	Title (A Side/B Side)	Yr	VG	VG+	NM
76832	When It Rains It Pours/Me and Crippled Soldiers	1990	—	2.00	4.00
76846	Blue Jungle/Me and Crippled Soldiers	1990	—	2.00	4.00
76854	A Bar in Bakersfield/Lucky Old Colorado	1991	—	2.00	4.00

ELEKTRA

Number	Title (A Side/B Side)	Yr	VG	VG+	NM
46634	Bar Room Buddies/The Not So Great Train Robbery	1980	—	2.00	4.00
—With Clint Eastwood					
46634 [PS]	Bar Room Buddies/The Not So Great Train Robbery	1980	—	2.50	5.00

EPIC

Number	Title (A Side/B Side)	Yr	VG	VG+	NM
AE7 1777 [DJ]	Santa Claus and Popcorn/Grandma's Homemade Christmas Card	1982	—	2.50	5.00
02504	My Favorite Memory/Texas Fiddle Song	1981	—	—	3.00
02686	Big City/I Think I'm Gonna Live Forever	1981	—	—	3.00
02894	Are the Good Times Really Over (I Wish a Buck Was Still Silver)/I Always Get Lucky with You	1982	—	—	3.00
03315	Going Where the Lonely Go/Someday You're Gonna Need Your Friends Again	1982	—	—	3.00
03365	Going Where the Lonely Go	1982	2.00	4.00	8.00
—One-sided budget release					
03406	Goin' Home for Christmas/If We Make It Through December	1982	—	2.00	4.00
03723	You Take Me for Granted/I Won't Give Up My Train	1983	—	—	3.00
04006	What Am I Gonna Do (With the Rest of My Life)/I Think I'll Stay	1983	—	—	3.00
04226	That's the Way Love Goes/Don't Seem Like We've Been Together All Our Lives	1983	—	—	3.00
04402	Someday When Things Are Good/If You Hated Me	1984	—	—	3.00
04512	Let's Chase Each Other Around the Room/All I Want to Do Is Sing My Song	1984	—	—	3.00
04830	Natural High/I Never Go Home Anymore	1985	—	—	3.00
05426	Kern River/The Old Water Mill	1985	—	—	3.00
05659	Amber Waves of Grain/I Wish Things Were Simple Again	1985	—	—	3.00
05734	American Waltz/The Farmer's Daughter	1985	—	—	3.00
05782	I Had a Beautiful Time/This Time I Really Do	1986	—	—	3.00
06097	A Friend in California/Mama's Prayers	1986	—	—	3.00
06344	Out Among the Stars/Suzie	1986	—	—	3.00
07036	Almost Persuaded/Love Don't Hurt Everytime	1987	—	—	3.00
07631	Twinkle, Twinkle, Lucky Star/I Don't Have Any Love Around	1987	—	—	3.00
07754	Chill Factor/Thanking the Good Lord	1988	—	—	3.00
07944	We Never Touch at All/Man from Another Time	1988	—	—	3.00
08111	You Babe/Thirty Again	1988	—	—	3.00
68598	5:01 Blues/Man from Another Time	1989	—	—	3.00
68979	A Better Love Next Time/Me and Crippled Soldiers	1989	—	—	3.00
73076	If You Want to Be My Woman/Someday We'll Know	1989	—	—	3.00
73303	Broken Friend/Wouldn't That Be Something	1990	—	2.00	4.00

MCA

Number	Title (A Side/B Side)	Yr	VG	VG+	NM
40700	If We're Not Back in Love By Monday/I Think It's Gone Forever	1977	—	2.00	4.00

Number	Title (A Side/B Side)	Yr	VG	VG+	NM
40743	Ramblin' Fever/When My Blue Moon Turns to Gold Again	1977	—	2.00	4.00
40804	From Graceland to the Promised Land/Are You Lonesome Tonight	1977	—	3.00	6.00
40869	I'm Always on a Mountain When I Fall/The Life of a Rodeo Cowboy	1978	—	2.00	4.00
40936	It's Been a Great Afternoon/Love Me When You Can	1978	—	2.00	4.00
41007	Red Bandana/I Must Have Done Something Bad	1979	—	2.00	4.00
41112	My Own Kind of Hat/Heaven Was a Drink of Wine	1979	—	2.00	4.00
41168	If We Make It Through December/The Fightin' Side of Me	1979	—	2.50	5.00
41200	The Way I Am/Wake Up	1980	—	2.00	4.00
41255	Misery and Gin/No One to Sing For	1980	—	2.00	4.00
41255 [PS]	Misery and Gin/No One to Sing For	1980	—	2.50	5.00
51014	I Think I'll Just Stay Here and Drink/Back to the Barrooms	1980	—	2.00	4.00
51048	Leonard/Our Paths May Never Cross	1981	—	2.00	4.00
51120	Rainbow Stew/Blue Yodel No. 9	1981	—	2.00	4.00
52020	Dealing with the Devil/Fiddle Breakdown	1982	—	2.00	4.00
52276	It's All in the Game/New Cocaine Blues	1983	—	—	3.00
52595	Make-Up and Faded Blue Jeans/Love Me When You Can	1985	—	—	3.00

TALLY

Number	Title (A Side/B Side)	Yr	VG	VG+	NM
152	Singin' My Heart Out/Skid Row	1963	5.00	10.00	20.00
155	Sing a Sad Song/You Don't Even Try	1963	3.75	7.50	15.00
178	Sam Hill/You Don't Have Far to Go	1964	3.75	7.50	15.00
179	(My Friends Are Gonna Be) Strangers/Please Mr. D.J.	1964	3.75	7.50	15.00

Albums

CAPITOL

Number	Title (A Side/B Side)	Yr	VG	VG+	NM
SKAO-168	Pride In What I Am	1969	6.25	12.50	25.00
SM-168	Pride in What I Am	197?	2.50	5.00	10.00
—Reissue with new prefix					
SWBB-223 [(2)]	Same Train, A Different Time	1969	7.50	15.00	30.00
SWBB-259 [(2)]	Close-Up	1969	7.50	15.00	30.00
—Reissue in one package of "Strangers" and "Swinging Doors"					
ST-319	A Portrait of Merle Haggard	1969	5.00	10.00	20.00
ST-384	Okie from Muskogee	1970	5.00	10.00	20.00
ST-451	The Fightin' Side of Me	1970	5.00	10.00	20.00
ST-638	A Tribute to the Best Damn Fiddle Player in the World (Or, My Salute to Bob Wills)	1970	6.25	12.50	25.00
STBB-707 [(2)]	Sing a Sad Song/High on a Hilltop	1971	7.50	15.00	30.00
ST-735	Hag	1971	3.75	7.50	15.00
SWBO-803 [(2)]	The Land of Many Churches	1971	15.00	30.00	60.00
ST-823	Truly the Best of Merle Haggard	1971	10.00	20.00	40.00
ST-835	Someday We'll Look Back	1971	5.00	10.00	20.00
ST-882	Let Me Tell You About a Song	1972	5.00	10.00	20.00
ST 2373 [S]	Strangers	1965	7.50	15.00	30.00
T 2373 [M]	Strangers	1965	6.25	12.50	25.00
SM-2585	Swinging Doors	197?	2.50	5.00	10.00
—Reissue with new prefix					
ST 2585 [S]	Swinging Doors	1966	7.50	15.00	30.00
T 2585 [M]	Swinging Doors	1966	6.25	12.50	25.00
SM-2702	I'm a Lonesome Fugitive	197?	2.50	5.00	10.00
—Reissue with new prefix					
ST 2702 [S]	I'm a Lonesome Fugitive	1967	7.50	15.00	30.00
T 2702 [M]	I'm a Lonesome Fugitive	1967	6.25	12.50	25.00
ST 2789 [S]	Branded Man	1967	7.50	15.00	30.00
T 2789 [M]	Branded Man	1967	6.25	12.50	25.00
ST 2848 [S]	Sing Me Back Home	1968	6.25	12.50	25.00
T 2848 [M]	Sing Me Back Home	1968	7.50	15.00	30.00
ST 2912	The Legend of Bonnie and Clyde	1968	6.25	12.50	25.00
SKAO 2951	The Best of Merle Haggard	1968	6.25	12.50	25.00
ST 2972	Mama Tried	1968	6.25	12.50	25.00
ST-11082	The Best of the Best of Merle Haggard	1972	3.75	7.50	15.00
ST-11127	It's Not Love	1972	3.00	6.00	12.00
ST-11141	Totally Instrumental with One Exception	1973	3.75	7.50	15.00
ST-11200	I Love Dixie Blues...So I Recorded "Live" in New Orleans	1973	3.00	6.00	12.00
ST-11230	Merle Haggard's Christmas Present (Something Old, Something New)	1973	3.00	6.00	12.00
ST-11276	If We Make It Through December	1974	3.00	6.00	12.00
ST-11331	Merle Haggard Presents His 30th Album	1974	3.00	6.00	12.00
ST-11365	Keep Movin' On	1975	3.00	6.00	12.00
ST-11483	It's All in the Movies	1975	3.00	6.00	12.00
SABB-11531 [(2)]	Songs I'll Always Sing	1976	3.75	7.50	15.00
ST-11544	My Love Affair with Trains	1976	3.00	6.00	12.00
ST-11586	The Roots of My Raising	1976	3.00	6.00	12.00
ST-11693	A Working Man Can't Get Nowhere Today	1977	3.00	6.00	12.00
ST-11745	Eleven Winners	1977	3.00	6.00	12.00
SM-11823	My Love Affair with Trains	1978	2.50	5.00	10.00
—Reissue					
SW-11839	The Way It Was	1978	3.00	6.00	12.00
SM-12036	It's All in the Movies	1979	2.50	5.00	10.00
—Reissue					
SN-16052	Sing a Sad Song	1979	2.00	4.00	8.00
—Budget-line reissue					
SN-16053	High on a Hilltop	1979	2.00	4.00	8.00
—Budget-line reissue					
SN-16054	The Best of Merle Haggard	1979	2.00	4.00	8.00
—Budget-line reissue					
SN-16277	Okie from Muskogee	1982	2.00	4.00	8.00
—Budget-line reissue					
SN-16278	The Fightin' Side of Me	1982	2.00	4.00	8.00
—Budget-line reissue					
SN-16279	A Tribute to the Best Damn Fiddle Player in the World (Or, My Salute to Bob Wills)	1982	2.00	4.00	8.00
—Budget-line reissue					
SN-16303	Eleven Winners	1984	2.00	4.00	8.00
—Budget-line reissue					

CAPITOL SPECIAL MARKETS

Number	Title (A Side/B Side)	Yr	VG	VG+	NM
SL-8086 [(2)]	Songs I'll Always Sing	1977	5.00	10.00	20.00

EPIC

Number	Title (A Side/B Side)	Yr	VG	VG+	NM
FE 37593	Big City	1981	2.50	5.00	10.00
PE 37593	Big City	1985	2.00	4.00	8.00
—Budget-line reissue					
FE 38092	Going Where the Lonely Go	1982	2.50	5.00	10.00
PE 38092	Going Where the Lonely Go	1985	2.00	4.00	8.00
—Budget-line reissue					
PE 38307	Goin' Home for Christmas	1982	2.50	5.00	10.00
FE 38815	That's the Way Love Goes	1983	2.50	5.00	10.00
FE 39159	The Epic Collection	1983	2.50	5.00	10.00
PE 39159	The Epic Collection	1985	2.00	4.00	8.00
—Budget-line reissue					
FE 39364	It's All in the Game	1984	2.50	5.00	10.00
FE 39545	His Epic Hits: The First 11	1985	2.50	5.00	10.00
FE 39602	Kern River	1985	2.50	5.00	10.00
FE 40107	Out Among the Stars	1986	2.50	5.00	10.00
PE 40107	Out Among the Stars	1986	2.00	4.00	8.00
—Budget-line reissue					
FE 40224	Amber Waves of Grain	1985	2.50	5.00	10.00
FE 40286	A Friend in California	1986	2.50	5.00	10.00
FE 40986	Chill Factor	1988	2.50	5.00	10.00
FE 44283	5:01 Blues	1989	2.50	5.00	10.00

MCA

Number	Title (A Side/B Side)	Yr	VG	VG+	NM
2267	Ramblin' Fever	1977	3.00	6.00	12.00
2314	My Farewell to Elvis	1977	3.75	7.50	15.00
2375	I'm Always on a Mountain	1978	3.00	6.00	12.00
3089	Serving 190 Proof	1979	3.00	6.00	12.00
3229	The Way I Am	1980	3.00	6.00	12.00
5139	Back to the Barrooms	1980	3.00	6.00	12.00
5250	Songs for the Mamma	1981	3.00	6.00	12.00
5386	Greatest Hits	1982	3.00	6.00	12.00
5573	His Best	1985	2.50	5.00	10.00
37138	Ramblin' Fever	1980	2.00	4.00	8.00
—Budget-line reissue					
37139	My Farewell to Elvis	1980	2.00	4.00	8.00
—Budget-line reissue					
37140	I'm Always on a Mountain	1980	2.00	4.00	8.00
—Budget-line reissue					
37141	Serving 190 Proof	1980	2.00	4.00	8.00
—Budget-line reissue					
37207	The Way I Am	1982	2.00	4.00	8.00
—Budget-line reissue					

HAGGARD, MERLE, AND JANIE FRICKE

45s

EPIC

Number	Title (A Side/B Side)	Yr	VG	VG+	NM
04663	A Place to Fall Apart/All I Want to Do Is Sing My Song	1984	—	—	3.00

HAGGARD, MERLE, AND JEWEL

45s

BNA

Number	Title (A Side/B Side)	Yr	VG	VG+	NM
65895	That's the Way Love Goes/Silver Wings	1999	—	—	3.00

HAGGARD, MERLE, AND GEORGE JONES

Also see each artist's individual listings.

45s

EPIC

Number	Title (A Side/B Side)	Yr	VG	VG+	NM
03072	Yesterday's Wine/I Haven't Found Her Yet	1982	—	—	3.00
03405	C.C. Waterback/After I Sing All My Songs	1982	—	—	3.00

Albums

EPIC

Number	Title (A Side/B Side)	Yr	VG	VG+	NM
FE 38203	A Taste of Yesterday's Wine	1982	2.50	5.00	10.00

HAGGARD, MERLE, AND WILLIE NELSON

Also see each artist's individual listings.

45s

EPIC

Number	Title (A Side/B Side)	Yr	VG	VG+	NM
03494	Reasons to Quit/Half a Man	1983	—	2.00	4.00
ENR-03495	Reasons to Quit	1983	2.00	4.00	8.00
—One-sided budget release					
03842	Pancho and Lefty/Opportunity to Cry	1983	—	2.00	4.00
34-07400	If I Could Only Fly/Without You on My Side	1987	—	—	3.00

Albums

EPIC

Number	Title (A Side/B Side)	Yr	VG	VG+	NM
FE 37958	Poncho and Lefty	1983	3.75	7.50	15.00
—Note misspelled LP title					
FE 37958	Pancho and Lefty	1983	2.50	5.00	10.00
—Reissue corrects spelling of LP title					
FE 40293	Seashores of Old Mexico	1987	2.50	5.00	10.00

HAGGARD, MERLE, AND BONNIE OWENS

45s

TALLY

Number	Title (A Side/B Side)	Yr	VG	VG+	NM
181	Just Between the Two of Us/Slowly But Sure	1964	5.00	10.00	20.00

Albums

CAPITOL

Number	Title (A Side/B Side)	Yr	VG	VG+	NM
ST 2453 [S]	Just Between the Two of Us	1966	7.50	15.00	30.00
T 2453 [M]	Just Between the Two of Us	1966	6.25	12.50	25.00

HAGGARD, MERLE, AND LEONA WILLIAMS

45s

MCA

Number	Title (A Side/B Side)	Yr	VG	VG+	NM
40962	The Bull and the Beaver/I'm Gettin' High	1978	—	2.00	4.00

MERCURY

Number	Title (A Side/B Side)	Yr	VG	VG+	NM
812214-7	We're Strangers Again/Sally Let Your Bangs Hang Down	1983	—	—	3.00
880139-7	Don't Ever Let Your Lover Sleep Alone/It's Cold in California	1984	—	2.00	4.00

Albums

MERCURY

Number	Title (A Side/B Side)	Yr	VG	VG+	NM
812183-1	Heart to Heart	1983	2.50	5.00	10.00

HAGGETT, JIMMY

Number	Title (A Side/B Side)	Yr	VG	VG+	NM
45s					
CAPROCK					
107	All I Have Is You/Without You	1958	10.00	20.00	40.00
METEOR					
5043	Gonna Shut You Off Baby/Tell Her True	1957	50.00	100.00	200.00
SUN					
236	No More/They Call Our Love a Sin	1956	150.00	300.00	600.00

HAIG, RONNIE

Number	Title (A Side/B Side)	Yr	VG	VG+	NM
45s					
ABC-PARAMOUNT					
9912	Don't You Hear Me Calling, Baby/Traveler of Love	1958	7.50	15.00	30.00
10209	Don't You Hear Me Calling, Baby/Traveler of Love	1961	20.00	40.00	80.00
NOTE					
10010	Don't You Hear Me Calling, Baby/Traveler of Love	1958	7.50	15.00	30.00
10014	Rockin' with Rhythm and Blues/Money Is a Thing of the Past	1958	25.00	50.00	100.00

HAINES, CONNIE

Number	Title (A Side/B Side)	Yr	VG	VG+	NM
45s					
MOTOWN					
1092	What's Easy for Two Is Hard for One/Walk in Silence	1966	7.50	15.00	30.00

HAIRCUTS, THE

Number	Title (A Side/B Side)	Yr	VG	VG+	NM
45s					
PARKWAY					
899	She Loves You/Love Me Do	1964	5.00	10.00	20.00
899 [PS]	She Loves You/Love Me Do	1964	10.00	20.00	40.00

HAIRSTON, BROTHER WILL

Number	Title (A Side/B Side)	Yr	VG	VG+	NM
45s					
JVB					
44	The Alabama Bus (Part 1)/The Alabama Bus (Part 2)	1956	75.00	150.00	300.00

HAIRSTON, JACKIE

Number	Title (A Side/B Side)	Yr	VG	VG+	NM
45s					
ATCO					
6464	Monkey on My Back/Hijack	1967	5.00	10.00	20.00

HALE AND THE HUSHABYES

All-star group including BRIAN WILSON, JACKIE DeSHANNON, and SONNY AND CHER.

Number	Title (A Side/B Side)	Yr	VG	VG+	NM
45s					
APOGEE					
104	Yes Sir, That's My Baby/900 Quetzals	1964	75.00	150.00	300.00
REPRISE					
0299	Yes Sir, That's My Baby/Jack's Theme	1964	50.00	100.00	200.00
—Reissued in 1967 by "A Date With Soul"					
YORK					
408	Yes Sir, That's My Baby/Bee Side Soul	1967	12.50	25.00	50.00
—As "A Date with Soul"					

HALEE'S COMET

Roy Halee, later producer for SIMON AND GARFUNKEL.

Number	Title (A Side/B Side)	Yr	VG	VG+	NM
45s					
EPIC					
10207	All I Want Is What's Real/From a Parachute	1967	3.00	6.00	12.00

HALEY, BILL, AND HIS COMETS

Number	Title (A Side/B Side)	Yr	VG	VG+	NM
45s					
APT					
25081	Stop, Look, and Listen/Burn That Candle	1965	5.00	10.00	20.00
25087	Haley A-Go-Go/Tongue Tied Tony	1965	6.25	12.50	25.00
ARZEE					
4677	Yodel Your Blues Away/Within This Broken Heart of Mine	1978	6.25	12.50	25.00
4677 [PS]	Yodel Your Blues Away/Within This Broken Heart of Mine	1978	6.25	12.50	25.00
BUDDAH					
169	Rock Around the Clock/Framed	1970	3.75	7.50	15.00
DECCA					
29124	(We're Gonna) Rock Around the Clock/Thirteen Women (And Only One Man in Town)	1954	15.00	30.00	60.00
—With lines on either side of "Decca"					
29124	(We're Gonna) Rock Around the Clock/Thirteen Women (And Only One Man in Town)	1955	5.00	10.00	20.00
—With star under "Decca"					
29204	Shake, Rattle and Roll/A.B.C. Boogie	1954	10.00	20.00	40.00
—With lines on either side of "Decca"					
29204	Shake, Rattle and Roll/A.B.C. Boogie	1954	5.00	10.00	20.00
—With star under "Decca"					
29317	Dim, Dim the Lights (I Want Some Atmosphere)/Happy Baby	1954	10.00	20.00	40.00
—With lines on either side of "Decca"					
29317	Dim, Dim the Lights (I Want Some Atmosphere)/Happy Baby	1954	5.00	10.00	20.00
—With star under "Decca"					
29418	Mambo Rock/Birth of the Boogie	1955	6.25	12.50	25.00
29552	Razzle-Dazzle/Two Hound Dogs	1955	6.25	12.50	25.00
29713	Burn That Candle/Rock-a-Beatin' Boogie	1955	6.25	12.50	25.00
29791	See You Later, Alligator/The Paper Boy (On Main Street, U.S.A.)	1956	6.25	12.50	25.00
29870	R-O-C-K/The Saints Rock 'N' Roll	1956	6.25	12.50	25.00
29948	Hot Dog Buddy Buddy/Rockin' Through the Rye	1956	6.25	12.50	25.00
30028	Rip It Up/Teenager's Mother (Are You Right?)	1956	6.25	12.50	25.00
30085	Rudy's Rock/Blue Comet Blues	1956	6.25	12.50	25.00
30148	Don't Knock the Rock/Choo Choo Ch'Boogie	1956	6.25	12.50	25.00
30214	Forty Cups of Coffeee/Hook, Line and Sinker	1957	6.25	12.50	25.00
30314	(You Hit the Wrong Note) Billy Goat/Rockin' Rollin' Rover	1957	6.25	12.50	25.00
30314 [PS]	(You Hit the Wrong Note) Billy Goat/Rockin' Rollin' Rover	1957	30.00	60.00	120.00
30394	The Dipsy Doodle/Miss You	1957	6.25	12.50	25.00
30461	Rock the Joint/How Many	1957	6.25	12.50	25.00
30530	It's a Sin/Mary, Mary Lou	1957	6.25	12.50	25.00
30530 [PS]	It's a Sin/Mary, Mary Lou	1957	20.00	40.00	80.00
30592	Skinny Minnie/Sway with Me	1958	7.50	15.00	30.00
30681	Lean Jean/Don't Nobody Move	1958	6.25	12.50	25.00
30741	Chiquita Linda/Whoa Mabel	1958	6.25	12.50	25.00
30781	Corrine, Corrina/B.B. Betty	1958	6.25	12.50	25.00
30844	Charmaine/I Got a Woman	1959	6.25	12.50	25.00
30873	(Now and Then, There's) A Fool Such As I/Where Did You Go Last Night	1959	6.25	12.50	25.00
30926	Caldonia/Shakey	1959	6.25	12.50	25.00
30956	Joey's Song/Ooh, Look-a-There, Ain't She Pretty	1959	6.25	12.50	25.00
31030	Skokiaan (South African Song)/Puerto Rican Peddler	1959	6.25	12.50	25.00
31080	Music, Music, Music/Strictly Instrumental	1960	6.25	12.50	25.00
31649	The Green Door/Yeah, She's Evil	1964	3.00	6.00	12.00
ESSEX					
102	Rock Around the Clock/Crazy Man, Crazy	1955	12.50	25.00	50.00
—Actually a bootleg, but highly sought-after nonetheless					
303	Rock the Joint/Icy Heart	1952	25.00	50.00	100.00
—Black vinyl, block logo ("ESSEX" in all caps)					
303	Rock the Joint/Icy Heart	1952	15.00	30.00	60.00
—Black vinyl, script logo ("Essex" not in all caps)					
303	Rock the Joint/Icy Heart	1952	900.00	1350.	1800.
—Red vinyl					
305	Rocking Chair on the Moon/Dance with a Dolly (With a Hole in Her Stocking)	1952	25.00	50.00	100.00
—Essex 303 and 305 credit "Bill Haley and the Saddlemen"					
310	Real Rock Drive/Stop Beatin' Round the Mulberry Bush	1952	37.50	75.00	150.00
—Blue label					
310	Real Rock Drive/Stop Beatin' Round the Mulberry Bush	1952	20.00	40.00	80.00
—Orange label					
321	Crazy Man, Crazy/Whatcha Gonna Do	1953	15.00	30.00	60.00
327	Pat-a-Cake/Fractured	1953	10.00	20.00	40.00
332	Live It Up/Farewell, So Long, Goodbye	1953	10.00	20.00	40.00
340	Ten Little Indians/I'll Be True	1953	10.00	20.00	40.00
348	Chattanooga Choo Choo/Straight Jacket	1954	10.00	20.00	40.00
374	Sundown Boogie/Jukebox Cannonball	1954	18.75	37.50	75.00
381	Rocket 88/Green Tree Boogie	1955	31.25	62.50	125.00
399	Rock the Joint/Farewell, So Long, Goodbye	1955	18.75	37.50	75.00
GNP CRESCENDO					
475	I'm Walkin'/Crazy Man, Crazy	1974	3.00	6.00	12.00
GONE					
5111	Spanish Twist/My Kind of Woman	1961	6.25	12.50	25.00
5116	Riviera/War Paint	1961	6.25	12.50	25.00
HOLIDAY					
113	Sundown Boogie/Jukebox Cannonball	1951	125.00	250.00	500.00
—The only Holiday single known to exist on a 45. Earlier Holiday singles only exist on 78s.					
JANUS					
162	Travelin' Band/A Little Piece at a Time	1971	3.00	6.00	12.00
KAMA SUTRA					
508	Rock Around the Clock/Framed	1970	5.00	10.00	20.00
KASEY					
7006	A.B.C. Boogie/Rock Around the Clock	1961	5.00	10.00	20.00
—B-side by Phil Flowers					
MCA					
60025	(We're Gonna) Rock Around the Clock/Thirteen Women (And Only One Man in Town)	1973	—	2.50	5.00
—Reissue on black label with rainbow; made the Top 40 in 1974					
NEWTOWN					
5013	Tenor Man/Up Goes My Love	1962	5.00	10.00	20.00
5024	Dance Around the Clock/What Can I Say After I Say I'm Sorry	1963	5.00	10.00	20.00
NICETOWN					
5025	You Call Everybody Darling/Tandy	1963	5.00	10.00	20.00
TRANS WORLD					
718	Real Rock Drive/Yes, Indeed	1954	50.00	100.00	200.00
UNITED ARTISTS					
50483	Ain't Love Funny, Ha Ha Ha/That's How I Got to Memphis	1969	3.00	6.00	12.00
WARNER BROS.					
5145	Candy Kisses/Tamiami	1960	6.25	12.50	25.00
5145 [DJ]	Candy Kisses/Tamiami	1960	12.50	25.00	50.00
—Promo only on yellow vinyl					
5154	Hawk/Chick Safari	1960	6.25	12.50	25.00
5171	Let the Good Times Roll, Creole/So Right Tonight	1960	6.25	12.50	25.00
5228	Flip, Flop and Fly/Honky Tonk	1961	6.25	12.50	25.00
7124	Rock Around the Clock/Shake, Rattle and Roll	1969	3.75	7.50	15.00
7-Inch Extended Plays					
CLAIRE					
4779	*All I Need Is Some More Lovin'/Trouble in Mind/ Life of the Party/I Should Write a Song About You	1978	3.75	7.50	15.00
4779 [PS]	Bill Haley and the Comets	1978	3.75	7.50	15.00
DECCA					
ED 2168	Shake, Rattle and Roll/A.B.C. Boogie//(We're Gonna) Rock Around the Clock/Thirteen Women (And Only One Man in Town)	1954	15.00	30.00	60.00
ED 2168 [PS]	Shake, Rattle and Roll	1954	15.00	30.00	60.00
ED 2209	Dim, Dim the Lights/Happy Baby//Birth of the Boogie/Mambo Rock	1955	15.00	30.00	60.00
ED 2209 [PS]	Dim, Dim the Lights	1955	15.00	30.00	60.00
ED 2322	Razzle-Dazzle/Two Hound Dogs//Burn That Candle/Rock-a-Beatin' Boogie	1956	15.00	30.00	60.00
ED 2322 [PS]	Rock and Roll	1956	15.00	30.00	60.00
ED 2398	See You Later Alligator/R-O-C-K//The Saints Rock 'n Roll/Burn That Candle	1956	12.50	25.00	50.00
ED 2398 [PS]	He Digs Rock 'n' Roll, Part 1	1956	12.50	25.00	50.00

Number	Title (A Side/B Side)	Yr	VG	VG+	NM
ED 2399	(contents unknown)	1956	12.50	25.00	50.00
ED 2399 [PS]	He Digs Rock 'n' Roll, Part 2	1956	12.50	25.00	50.00
ED 2400	(contents unknown)	1956	12.50	25.00	50.00
ED 2400 [PS]	He Digs Rock 'n' Roll, Part 3	1956	12.50	25.00	50.00
ED 2416	(contents unknown)	1956	12.50	25.00	50.00
ED 2416 [PS]	Rock 'n' Roll Stage Show, Part 1	1956	12.50	25.00	50.00
ED 2417	A Rockin' Little Tune/Hide and Seek//Choo Choo Ch' Boogie/Blue Comet Blues	1956-05-01	12.50	25.00	50.00
ED 2417 [PS]	Rock 'n' Roll Stage Show, Part 2	1956	12.50	25.00	50.00
ED 2418	Hey Then, There Now/Goofin' Around//Hot Dog Buddy Buddy/Tonight's the Night	1956	12.50	25.00	50.00
ED 2418 [PS]	Rock 'n' Roll Stage Show, Part 3	1956	12.50	25.00	50.00
ED 2532	(contents unknown)	1957	12.50	25.00	50.00
ED 2532 [PS]	Rockin' the Oldies	1957	12.50	25.00	50.00
ED 2533	(contents unknown)	1957	12.50	25.00	50.00
ED 2533 [PS]	Rock 'n' Roll Party	1957	12.50	25.00	50.00
ED 2534	(contents unknown)	1957	12.50	25.00	50.00
ED 2534 [PS]	Rockin' & Rollin'	1957	12.50	25.00	50.00
ED 2564	(contents unknown)	1957	12.50	25.00	50.00
ED 2564 [PS]	Rockin' Around the World	1957	12.50	25.00	50.00
ED 2576	(contents unknown)	1957	12.50	25.00	50.00
ED 2576 [PS]	Rockin' Around Europe	1957	12.50	25.00	50.00
ED 2577	(contents unknown)	1957	12.50	25.00	50.00
ED 2577 [PS]	Rockin' Around the Americas	1957	12.50	25.00	50.00
ED 2615	Rock Lomond/It's a Sin//Move It On Over/New Rock the Joint	1958-05-01	10.00	20.00	40.00
ED 2615 [PS]	Rockin' the Joint, Part 1	1958	10.00	20.00	40.00
ED 2616	(contents unknown)	1958	10.00	20.00	40.00
ED 2616 [PS]	Rockin' the Joint, Part 2	1958	10.00	20.00	40.00
ED 2638 [M]	(contents unknown)	1958	10.00	20.00	40.00
ED 2638 [PS]	Bill Haley's Chicks	1958	10.00	20.00	40.00
ED 7-2638 [PS]	Bill Haley's Chicks	1959	20.00	40.00	80.00
ED 7-2638 [S]	(contents unknown)	1959	20.00	40.00	80.00
ED 2670 [M]	Joe's Song/Ooh Look-a There Ain't She Pretty//Shakey/Caledonia	1959	10.00	20.00	40.00
ED 2670 [PS]	Bill Haley and His Comets	1959	10.00	20.00	40.00
ED 7-2670 [PS]	Bill Haley and His Comets	1959	20.00	40.00	80.00
ED 7-2670 [S]	Joe's Song/Ooh Look-a There Ain't She Pretty//Shakey/Caledonia	1959	20.00	40.00	80.00
ED 2671 [M]	Strictly Instrumental/South Africa Song//Mack the Knife/In a Little Spanish Town	1959	10.00	20.00	40.00
ED 2671 [PS]	Strictly Instrumental	1959	10.00	20.00	40.00
ED 7-2671 [PS]	Strictly Instrumental	1959	20.00	40.00	80.00
ED 7-2671 [S]	Strictly Instrumental/South Africa Song//Mack the Knife/In a Little Spanish Town	1959	20.00	40.00	80.00
ESSEX					
TWEP-102	Rock the Joint/Rockin' Chair on the Moon//Crazy Man, Crazy/Pat-a-Cake	1954	25.00	50.00	100.00
TWEP-102 [PS]	For Your Dance Party	1954	30.00	60.00	120.00
EP-117	*Live It Up/Farewell, So Long, Goodbye/Real Rock Drive/Fractured	1954	25.00	50.00	100.00
EP-117 [PS]	Rock with Bill Haley and His Comets, Volume 1	1954	30.00	60.00	120.00
EP-118	*Stop Beatin' Round the Mulberry Bush/Watcha Gonna Do/I'll Be True/Juke Box Cannon Ball	1954	25.00	50.00	100.00
EP-118 [PS]	Rock with Bill Haley and His Comets, Volume 2	1954	30.00	60.00	120.00
EP-119	(contents unknown)	1954	25.00	50.00	100.00
EP-119 [PS]	Rock with Bill Haley and His Comets, Volume 3	1954	30.00	60.00	120.00
SOMERSET					
460	(contents unknown)	1955	20.00	40.00	80.00
460 [PS]	Rock with Bill Haley and His Comets	1955	20.00	40.00	80.00
TRANS WORLD					
TWEP-117	(contents unknown)	1955	20.00	40.00	80.00
TWEP-117 [PS]	Rock with Bill Haley and His Comets, Volume 1	1955	20.00	40.00	80.00
TWEP-118	(contents unknown)	1955	20.00	40.00	80.00
TWEP-118 [PS]	Rock with Bill Haley and His Comets, Volume 2	1955	20.00	40.00	80.00
TWEP-119	(contents unknown)	1955	20.00	40.00	80.00
TWEP-119 [PS]	Rock with Bill Haley and His Comets, Volume 3	1955	20.00	40.00	80.00
Albums					
ACCORD					
SN-7125	Rockin' and Rollin'	1981	2.50	5.00	10.00
DECCA					
DL 5560 [10]	Shake, Rattle and Roll	1955	200.00	400.00	800.00
DXSE-7211 [(2)]	Bill Haley's Golden Hits	1972	3.75	7.50	15.00
DL 8225 [M]	Rock Around the Clock	1955	37.50	75.00	150.00
—All-black label with silver print					
DL 8225 [M]	Rock Around the Clock	1960	12.50	25.00	50.00
—Black label with colorband, no mention of MCA on label					
DL 8225 [M]	Rock Around the Clock	1967	7.50	15.00	30.00
—Black label with colorband, "A Division of MCA" on label					
DL 8315 [M]	Music for the Boyfriend	1956	37.50	75.00	150.00
DL 8345 [M]	Rock 'n Roll Stage Show	1956	37.50	75.00	150.00
DL 8569 [M]	Rockin' the Oldies	1957	37.50	75.00	150.00
DL 8692 [M]	Rockin' Around the World	1958	37.50	75.00	150.00
DL 8775 [M]	Rockin' the Joint	1958	37.50	75.00	150.00
DL 8821 [M]	Bill Haley's Chicks	1959	25.00	50.00	100.00
DL 8964 [M]	Strictly Instrumental	1960	25.00	50.00	100.00
DL 75027	Bill Haley's Greatest Hits	1968	3.75	7.50	15.00
DL 78225 [R]	Rock Around the Clock	1959	18.75	37.50	75.00
—All-black label with silver print					
DL 78225 [R]	Rock Around the Clock	1960	6.25	12.50	25.00
—Black label with colorband, no mention of MCA on label					
DL 78225 [R]	Rock Around the Clock	1967	3.75	7.50	15.00
—Black label with colorband, "A Division of MCA" on label					
DL 78821 [S]	Bill Haley's Chicks	1959	37.50	75.00	150.00
DL 78964 [S]	Strictly Instrumental	1960	37.50	75.00	150.00
ESSEX					
LP 202 [M]	Rock with Bill Haley and the Comets	1955	125.00	250.00	500.00
GNP CRESCENDO					
GNPS-2077	Rock 'N' Roll	1973	3.00	6.00	12.00
GNPS-2097	Rock Around the Country	1976	3.00	6.00	12.00
GREAT NORTHWEST					
GNW 4015	Interviewed by Red Robinson	1981	3.00	6.00	12.00
JANUS					
3035	Travelin' Band	1972	6.25	12.50	25.00
7003 [(2)]	Razzle-Dazzle	1972	3.75	7.50	15.00
KAMA SUTRA					
KLPS-2014	Scrapbook	1970	7.50	15.00	30.00
MCA					
161	Bill Haley's Greatest Hits	1973	2.50	5.00	10.00
—Reissue of Decca 75027					
4010 [(2)]	Bill Haley's Golden Hits	1973	3.00	6.00	12.00
—Reissue of Decca 7211					
5539 [(2)]	From the Original Master Tapes	1987	3.00	6.00	12.00
PAIR					
MSM2-35069 [(2)]	Rock and Roll Giant	1986	3.00	6.00	12.00
PICCADILLY					
PIC-3408	Greatest Hits	1980	2.50	5.00	10.00
PICKWICK					
PTP-2077 [(2)]	Rock 'N' Roll	197?	3.00	6.00	12.00
SPC-3256	Bill Haley and the Comets	1970	2.50	5.00	10.00
SPC-3280	Rock 'N' Roll Revival	197?	2.50	5.00	10.00
ROULETTE					
R 25174 [M]	Twistin' Knights at the Roundtable	1962	20.00	40.00	80.00
SR 25174 [S]	Twistin' Knights at the Roundtable	1962	25.00	50.00	100.00
SOMERSET					
P-4600 [M]	Rock with Bill Haley and the Comets	1958	37.50	75.00	150.00
TRANS WORLD					
LP 202 [M]	Rock with Bill Haley and the Comets	1956	75.00	150.00	300.00
VOCALION					
VL 3696 [M]	Bill Haley and the Comets	1963	6.25	12.50	25.00
WARNER BROS.					
W 1378 [M]	Bill Haley and His Comets	1959	12.50	25.00	50.00
WS 1378 [S]	Bill Haley and His Comets	1959	17.50	35.00	70.00
W 1391 [M]	Bill Haley's Jukebox	1960	12.50	25.00	50.00
WS 1391 [S]	Bill Haley's Jukebox	1960	17.50	35.00	70.00
WS 1831	Rock 'N' Roll Revival	1970	3.75	7.50	15.00
ST-93103	Rock 'N' Roll Revival	1070	6.25	12.50	25.00
—Capitol Record Club edition					

HALFNELSON

See SPARKS.

HALL, DARYL

Also see GULLIVER; DARYL HALL AND JOHN OATES.

Number	Title (A Side/B Side)	Yr	VG	VG+	NM
12-Inch Singles					
RCA					
5714-1-RD	Dreamtime (Extended)/(Dub)	1986	—	3.00	6.00
5745-1-RD	Foolish Pride/Let It Out	1986	—	3.00	6.00
5748-1-RD	Foolish Pride (Edit Remix) (Dub)/What's Gonna Happen to Us	1986	—	3.00	6.00
PD-14386 [DJ]	Dreamtime (same on both sides)	1986	—	3.00	6.00
45s					
AMY					
11049	The Princess and the Soldier (Part 1)/The Princess and the Soldier (Part 2)	1969	—	3.00	6.00
EPIC					
77139	I'm in a Philly Mood/Money Changes Everything	1993	—	—	3.00
77258	Stop Lovin' Me, Stop Lovin' You/Stop Lovin' Me, Stop Lovin' You (Churban Remix)	1993	—	—	3.00
PARALLAX					
404	A Lonely Girl/(B-side unknown)	196?	7.50	15.00	30.00
RCA					
5038-7-R	Foolish Pride/What's Gonna Happen to Us	1986	—	—	3.00
5038-7-R [PS]	Foolish Pride/What's Gonna Happen to Us	1986	—	—	3.00
5105-7-R	Someone Like You (The Guitar Solo)/Someone Like You (The Sax Solo)	1987	—	—	3.00
5105-7-R [PS]	Someone Like You (The Guitar Solo)/Someone Like You (The Sax Solo)	1987	—	—	3.00
PB-12001	Something in 4/4 Time/Sacred Songs	1980	—	2.00	4.00
PB-12001 [PS]	Something in 4/4 Time/Sacred Songs	1980	—	2.50	5.00
PB-14387	Dreamtime/Let It Out	1986	—	—	3.00
PB-14387 [PS]	Dreamtime/Let It Out	1986	—	—	3.00

HALL, DARYL, AND JOHN OATES

Number	Title (A Side/B Side)	Yr	VG	VG+	NM
12-Inch Singles					
ARISTA					
9685	Everything Your Heart Desires (54th Street Extended Remix)/If You Want the World (2 mixes)/No Words Can (Dub)/Real Love	1988	—	3.00	6.00
9728	Missed Opportunity (3 mixes)/Soul Love	1988	—	3.00	6.00
9768	Downtown Life (5 mixes)	1989	—	3.00	6.00
RCA					
JD-11302 [DJ]	Do What You Want, Be What You Are/same (Short Version)	1976	3.75	7.50	15.00
JD-11431 [DJ]	August Day/I Don't Wanna Lose You	1977	3.00	6.00	12.00
PD-12297	Private Eyes/Tell Me What You Want	1981	2.00	4.00	8.00
PD-12358	I Can't Go for That (No Can Do)/Unguarded Minute	1981	2.00	4.00	8.00
PD-13080	Did It in a Minute/Head Above Water	1982	2.00	4.00	8.00
PD-13253	Your Imagination/Sara Smile	1982	2.00	4.00	8.00
JD-13403 [DJ]	Maneater (Special Extended Club Mix)/I Can't Go for That (Club Mix)	1982	3.00	6.00	12.00
PD-13428	One on One (Club Mix)/I Can't Go for That (Long)	1983	2.00	4.00	8.00
PD-13508	Family Man/Maneater	1983	2.00	4.00	8.00
JD-13659 [DJ]	Say It Isn't So/Wait for Me (Live)	1983	3.00	6.00	12.00
PD-13679	Say It Isn't So (Special Extended Dance Mix)//Say It Isn't So (Dub)/Kiss on My List	1983	—	3.00	6.00
JM-13705 [DJ]	Jingle Bell Rock from Daryl/Jingle Bell Rock from John	1983	6.25	12.50	25.00
—Promo-only picture disc in plastic sleeve					
PD-13715	Adult Edudation (Special Club Mix)//Adult Education (Special Album Rock Mix)/Maneater	1984	—	3.00	6.00
JD-13736 [DJ]	Adult Education (Special Extended Mix Long)/Adult Education (Special Extended Mix Short)	1984	2.50	5.00	10.00
PD-13917	Out of Touch//Out of Touch (Dub)/Cold, Dark and Yesterday	1984	—	3.00	6.00

Number	Title (A Side/B Side)	Yr	VG	VG+	NM
PD-13971	Method of Modern Love//Method of Modern Love (Dub)/Bank On Your Love	1984	—	3.00	6.00
JD-13972 [DJ]	Method of Modern Love/Bank On Your Love	1984	2.50	5.00	10.00
JD-13983 [DJ]	Jingle Bell Rock (same on both sides)	1984	3.00	6.00	12.00
PD-14036	Some Things Are Better Left Unsaid (Special New Mix)//All American Girl/Some Things Are Better Left Unsaid (Instrumental)	1985	—	3.00	6.00
JD-14038 [DJ]	Some Things Are Better Left Unsaid (Special New Mix) (same on both sides)	1985	2.00	4.00	8.00
PD-14099	Possession Obsession//Dance on Your Knees/ Everytime You Go Away	1985	—	3.00	6.00
JR-14100 [DJ]	Possession Obsession (Special New Mix) (same on both sides)	1985	2.00	4.00	8.00
PD-14179	A Nite at the Apollo Live! The Way You Do the Things You Do-My Girl//Everytime You Go Away/Adult Education	1985	—	3.00	6.00
JR-14180 [DJ]	A Nite at the Apollo Live! The Way You Do the Things You Do-My Girl (same on both sides)	1985	2.00	4.00	8.00
PD-14250	Jingle Bell Rock from Daryl/Jingle Bell Rock from John//Everytime You Go Away/When Something Is Wrong with My Baby	1985	—	—	—
—Canceled					

45s

ARISTA

Number	Title (A Side/B Side)	Yr	VG	VG+	NM
2085	So Close/So Close (Unplugged)	1990	—	—	3.00
2157	Don't Hold Back Your Love/Change of Season	1990	—	—	3.00
9684	Everything Your Heart Desires/Real Love	1988	—	—	3.00
9684 [PS]	Everything Your Heart Desires/Real Love	1988	—	—	3.00
9727	Missed Opportunity/Soul Love	1988	—	—	3.00
9727 [PS]	Missed Opportunity/Soul Love	1988	—	—	3.00
9753	Downtown Life (LP Version)/Downtown Life (Urban Mix)	1988	—	—	3.00
9753 [PS]	Downtown Life (LP Version)/Downtown Life (Urban Mix)	1988	—	—	3.00

ATLANTIC

Number	Title (A Side/B Side)	Yr	VG	VG+	NM
2922	Goodnight & Good Morning/All Our Love	1972	2.50	5.00	10.00
—As "Whole Oats"					
2939	Lilly (Are You Happy)/I'm Sorry	1973	2.00	4.00	8.00
2993	She's Gone/I'm Just a Kid (Don't Make Me Feel Like a Man)	1973	2.00	4.00	8.00
3026	Lady Rain/When the Morning Comes	1974	—	2.50	5.00
3239	Can't Stop the Music/70's Scenario	1975	—	2.50	5.00
3332	She's Gone/I'm Just a Kid (Don't Make Me Feel Like a Man)	1976	—	2.00	4.00
3332 [DJ]	She's Gone (Long Version)/She's Gone	1976	—	3.00	6.00
3397	It's Uncanny/Lilly (Are You Happy)	1977	—	2.00	4.00

CHELSEA

Number	Title (A Side/B Side)	Yr	VG	VG+	NM
3063	If That's What Makes You Happy/The Reason Why	1977	—	2.50	5.00
—B-side by "Daryl Hall and Gulliver"					
3065	Red River Blues/(B-side unknown)	1977	—	2.50	5.00
3069	Perkiomen/The Provider	1977	—	2.50	5.00

RCA

Number	Title (A Side/B Side)	Yr	VG	VG+	NM
PB-10808	Do What You Want, Be What You Are/You'll Never Learn	1976	—	2.00	4.00
PB-10860	Rich Girl/London Luck, & Love	1976	—	2.00	4.00
PB-10860 [PS]	Rich Girl/London Luck, & Love	1976	2.00	4.00	8.00
GB-10942	Sara Smile/Do What You Want, Be What You Are	1977	—	—	3.00
—Gold Standard Series					
PB-10970	Back Together Again/Room to Breathe	1977	—	2.00	4.00
PB-11132	Why Do Lovers (Break Each Other's Heart?)/A Girl Who Used to Be	1977	—	2.00	4.00
PB-11181	Don't Change/The Emptiness	1977	—	2.00	4.00
GB-11324	Rich Girl/Back Together Again	1978	—	—	3.00
—Gold Standard Series					
PB-11371	It's a Laugh/Serious Music	1978	—	2.00	4.00
PB-11424	I Don't Wanna Lose You/August Day	1978	—	2.00	4.00
PB-11747	Wait for Me/No Brain No Pain	1979	—	2.00	4.00
PB-11920	All You Want Is Heaven/Who Said the World Was Fair	1980	—	2.00	4.00
GB-11970	It's a Laugh/I Don't Wanna Lose You	1980	—	—	3.00
—Gold Standard Series					
PB-12048	How Does It Feel to Be Back/United State	1980	—	2.00	4.00
PB-12103	You've Lost That Lovin' Feeling/Diddy Doo Wap (I Hear the Voices)	1980	—	2.00	4.00
PB-12142	Kiss on My List/Africa	1981	—	2.00	4.00
PB-12217	You Make My Dreams/Gotta Lotta Love	1981	—	2.00	4.00
PB-12296	Private Eyes/Tell Me What You Want	1981	—	2.00	4.00
GB-12318	Kiss on My List/You've Lost That Lovin' Feeling	1981	—	—	3.00
—Gold Standard Series					
PB-12357	I Can't Go for That (No Can Do)/Unguarded Minute	1981	—	2.00	4.00
JB-12361 [DJ]	I Can't Go for That (No Can Do)/I Can't Go for That (No Can Do) (Club Mix)	1981	2.50	5.00	10.00
—Promo only					
PB-13065	Did It in a Minute/Head Above Water	1982	—	2.00	4.00
PB-13252	Your Imagination/Sara Smile	1982	—	2.00	4.00
PB-13354	Maneater/Delayed Reaction	1982	—	—	3.00
PB-13354 [PS]	Maneater/Delayed Reaction	1982	—	2.00	4.00
PB-13421	One on One/Art of Heartbreak	1983	—	—	3.00
PB-13421 [PS]	One on One/Art of Heartbreak	1983	—	2.00	4.00
GB-13480	Private Eyes/I Can't Go for That (No Can Do)	1983	—	—	3.00
—Gold Standard Series					
GB-13481	You Make My Dreams/Did It in a Minute	1983	—	—	3.00
—Gold Standard Series					
PB-13507	Family Man/Open All Night	1983	—	—	3.00
PB-13654	Say It Isn't So/Kiss on My List	1983	—	—	3.00
PB-13654 [PS]	Say It Isn't So/Kiss on My List	1983	—	2.00	4.00
PB-13714	Adult Education/Maneater	1984	—	—	3.00
PB-13714 [PS]	Adult Education/Maneater	1984	—	2.00	4.00
GB-13796	Maneater/One on One	1984	—	—	3.00
—Gold Standard Series					
GB-13797	Family Man/Say It Isn't So	1984	—	—	3.00
—Gold Standard Series					
PB-13916	Out of Touch/Cold, Dark, and Yesterday	1984	—	—	3.00
PB-13916 [PS]	Out of Touch/Cold, Dark, and Yesterday	1984	—	—	3.00
PB-13970	Method of Modern Love (Remix Edit)/Method of Modern Love	1984	—	—	3.00
PB-13970 [PS]	Method of Modern Love (Remix Edit)/Method of Modern Love	1984	—	—	3.00
PB-14035	Some Things Are Better Left Unsaid/All American Girl	1985	—	—	3.00
PB-14035 [PS]	Some Things Are Better Left Unsaid/All American Girl	1985	—	—	3.00
GB-14064	Out of Touch/Adult Education	1985	—	—	3.00
—Gold Standard Series					
PB-14098	Possession Obsession/Dance on Your Knees	1985	—	—	3.00
PB-14098 [PS]	Possession Obsession/Dance on Your Knees	1985	—	—	3.00
PB-14178	A Nite at the Apollo Live! The Way You Do the Things You Do-My Girl/Everytime You Go Away	1985	—	—	3.00
—A-side: With David Ruffin and Eddie Kendrick (sic)					
PB-14178 [PS]	A Nite at the Apollo Live! The Way You Do the Things You Do-My Girl/Everytime You Go Away	1985	—	—	3.00
—A-side: With David Ruffin and Eddie Kendrick (sic)					
JR-14259 [DJ]	Jingle Bell Rock from Daryl/Jingle Bell Rock from John	1985	2.50	5.00	10.00
—Promo only on red vinyl					
JR-14259 [DJ]	Jingle Bell Rock from Daryl/Jingle Bell Rock from John	1985	2.50	5.00	10.00
—Promo only on green vinyl					
JR-14259 [PS]	Jingle Bell Rock from Daryl/Jingle Bell Rock from John	1985	2.50	5.00	10.00
GB-14340	Method of Modern Love/Possession Obsession	1986	—	—	3.00
—Gold Standard Series					
GB-14341	Some Things Are Better Left Unsaid/A Nite at the Apollo Live! The Way You Do the Things You Do-My Girl	1986	—	—	3.00
—Gold Standard Series					

RCA VICTOR

Number	Title (A Side/B Side)	Yr	VG	VG+	NM
PB-10373	Camellia/Ennui on the Mountain	1975	—	2.50	5.00
PB-10436	Nothing at All/Alone Too Long	1975	—	2.50	5.00
PB-10530	Sara Smile/Soldering	1975	—	2.50	5.00

SIRE

Number	Title (A Side/B Side)	Yr	VG	VG+	NM
22967	Love Train/"Earth Girls Are Easy" Theme	1989	—	—	3.00
22967 [PS]	Love Train/"Earth Girls Are Easy" Theme	1989	—	—	3.00

Albums

ALLEGIANCE

Number	Title	Yr	VG	VG+	NM
AV-5014	Nucleus	198?	2.00	4.00	8.00

ARISTA

Number	Title	Yr	VG	VG+	NM
AL-8539	Ooh Yeah!	1988	2.50	5.00	10.00
AL-8614	Change of Season	1989	3.00	6.00	12.00

ATLANTIC

Number	Title	Yr	VG	VG+	NM
SD 7242	Whole Oats	1972	3.00	6.00	12.00
SD 7269	Abandoned Luncheonette	1973	3.00	6.00	12.00
SD 18109	War Babies	1974	3.00	6.00	12.00
SD 18213	No Goodbyes	1977	2.50	5.00	10.00
SD 19139	Abandoned Luncheonette	1977	2.00	4.00	8.00

CHELSEA

Number	Title	Yr	VG	VG+	NM
CHL 547	Past Times Behind	1977	3.00	6.00	12.00

INTERMEDIA

Number	Title	Yr	VG	VG+	NM
QS-5040	The Early Years	198?	2.00	4.00	8.00

JEM

Number	Title	Yr	VG	VG+	NM
55002	Early Years	198?	2.00	4.00	8.00

MOBILE FIDELITY

Number	Title	Yr	VG	VG+	NM
1-069	Abandoned Luncheonette	1982	5.00	10.00	20.00
—Audiophile vinyl					

RCA VICTOR

Number	Title	Yr	VG	VG+	NM
APL1-1144	Daryl Hall & John Oates	1976	2.50	5.00	10.00
APL1-1467	Bigger Than Both of Us	1976	2.50	5.00	10.00
AFL1-2300	Beauty on a Back Street	1977	2.50	5.00	10.00
AFL1-2802	Livetime!	1978	2.50	5.00	10.00
AFL1-2804	Along the Red Ledge	1978	2.50	5.00	10.00
AFL1-2804	Along the Red Ledge	1978	3.75	7.50	15.00
—Red vinyl					
ANL1-3463	Daryl Hall & John Oates	1979	2.00	4.00	8.00
AFL1-3494	X-Static	1979	2.50	5.00	10.00
DJL1-3512 [DJ]	Post Static	1979	5.00	10.00	20.00
—Promo-only one-sided 4-song sampler					
AQL1-3646	Voices	1980	3.00	6.00	12.00
—No "RE" of any type on back cover: Embossed lettering and sound waves, Hall's head almost touches the word "Voices" on front					
AQL1-3646	Voices	1980	3.00	6.00	12.00
—"RE" on back cover: Variation unknown					
AQL1-3646	Voices	1980	2.50	5.00	10.00
—"RE 2" on back cover: Cover not embossed; Hall's head 3 inches-plus below "Voices" on front cover					
AQL1-3646	Voices	1980	3.00	6.00	12.00
—"RE 3" on back cover: Cover lettering in black					
AQL1-3646	Voices	1980	2.00	4.00	8.00
—"RE 4" on back cover: Color photo of Hall and Oates on each side					
AQL1-3646	Voices	1981	2.00	4.00	8.00
—"RE 5" on back cover: Variation unknown					
AQL1-3646	Voices	1981	2.00	4.00	8.00
—"RE 6" on back cover: Bar code on upper left back cover					
DJL1-3832	RCA Radio Special Interview Series	1980	3.75	7.50	15.00
AYL1-3836	Daryl Hall & John Oates	1980	2.00	4.00	8.00
AYL1-3866	Bigger Than Both of Us	1980	2.00	4.00	8.00
AFL1-4028	Private Eyes	1981	2.50	5.00	10.00
DJL1-4179	Special Radio Series	1981	3.75	7.50	15.00
AYL1-4230	Beauty on a Back Street	1981	2.00	4.00	8.00
AYL1-4231	Along the Red Ledge	1981	2.00	4.00	8.00
AYL1-4303	X-Static	1982	2.00	4.00	8.00
AFL1-4383	H2O	1982	2.50	5.00	10.00
AYL1-4722	Livetime!	1983	2.00	4.00	8.00
CPL1-4858	Rock 'n Soul Part 1	1983	3.00	6.00	12.00
—Original cover: back cover says "Plus Two New Songs (Recorded September 1983)" WITHOUT mentioning what the songs are					
CPL1-4858	Rock 'n Soul Part 1	1983	2.50	5.00	10.00
—"RE" on lower left back: back cover says "Plus Two New Songs (Recorded September 1983)," then mentions "Say It Isn't So" and "Adult Education"					

Number	Title (A Side/B Side)	Yr	VG	VG+	NM
CPL1-4858	Rock 'n Soul Part 1	1983	2.00	4.00	8.00
—"RE 2" on lower left back: Variation unknown					
AFL1-5309	Big Bam Boom	1984	3.00	6.00	12.00
AJL1-5336	Big Bam Boom	1984	2.50	5.00	10.00
AFL1-7035	Live at the Apollo	1985	2.50	5.00	10.00

HALL, DICKSON

45s

EPIC

Number	Title (A Side/B Side)	Yr	VG	VG+	NM
9262	Cowboy/It's a Long Walk Home	1958	3.75	7.50	15.00
9262 [PS]	Cowboy/It's a Long Walk Home	1958	6.25	12.50	25.00

Albums

EPIC

Number	Title (A Side/B Side)	Yr	VG	VG+	NM
LN 3427 [M]	25 All-Time Country and Western Hits	1958	6.25	12.50	25.00

KAPP

Number	Title (A Side/B Side)	Yr	VG	VG+	NM
KL-1067 [M]	Fabulous Country Hits Way Out West	1957	7.50	15.00	30.00
KL-1464 [M]	24 Fabulous Country Hits	1966	5.00	10.00	20.00
KS-3464 [S]	24 Fabulous Country Hits	1966	6.25	12.50	25.00

MGM

Number	Title (A Side/B Side)	Yr	VG	VG+	NM
E-329 [10]	Outlaws of the Old West	1954	15.00	30.00	60.00
E-3263 [M]	Outlaws of the Old West	1956	10.00	20.00	40.00

PERFECT

Number	Title (A Side/B Side)	Yr	VG	VG+	NM
P-14016 [M]	Country & Western Million Sellers	1960	5.00	10.00	20.00
PS-14016 [S]	Country & Western Million Sellers	1960	6.25	12.50	25.00

HALL, LARRY

45s

HOT

Number	Title (A Side/B Side)	Yr	VG	VG+	NM
1	Sandy/Lovin' Tree	1959	12.50	25.00	50.00

STRAND

Number	Title (A Side/B Side)	Yr	VG	VG+	NM
25007	Sandy/Lovin' Tree	1959	6.25	12.50	25.00
25013	A Girl Like You/Rosemary	1960	5.00	10.00	20.00
25016	For Every Boy/I'll Stay Single	1960	5.00	10.00	20.00
25025	The Girl I Left Behind/Kool Love	1961	5.00	10.00	20.00
25029	Lips of Wine/Rebel Heart	1961	5.00	10.00	20.00
25048	Ladder of Love/The One You Left Behind	1961	5.00	10.00	20.00

Albums

STRAND

Number	Title (A Side/B Side)	Yr	VG	VG+	NM
SL-1005 [M]	Sandy	1960	37.50	75.00	150.00
SLS-1005 [S]	Sandy	1960	50.00	100.00	200.00

HALL, ROY

45s

DECCA

Number	Title (A Side/B Side)	Yr	VG	VG+	NM
29697	Whole Lotta Shakin' Goin' On/All By Myself	1955	20.00	40.00	80.00
29786	See You Later, Alligator/Don't Stop Now	1956	12.50	25.00	50.00
29880	Blue Suede Shoes/Luscious	1956	12.50	25.00	50.00
30060	Three Alley Cats/Diggin' the Boogie	1956	12.50	25.00	50.00

FORTUNE

Number	Title (A Side/B Side)	Yr	VG	VG+	NM
170	Going Down the Road/Jealous Love	1952	10.00	20.00	40.00
—B-side by the Davis Sisters					
521	Corrine, Corrina/Don't Ask Me No Questions	1956	12.50	25.00	50.00

HI-Q

Number	Title (A Side/B Side)	Yr	VG	VG+	NM
5045	Three Alley Cats/Bedspring Motel	196?	15.00	30.00	60.00
5050	Go Go Little Queenie/Everybody Dig That Boogie	196?	15.00	30.00	60.00

HALL, TOM T.

Also see PATTI PAGE.

45s

MERCURY

Number	Title (A Side/B Side)	Yr	VG	VG+	NM
55001	It's All in the Game/The Little Green Flowers	1977	—	2.00	4.00
72700	I Wish My Face in the Morning Dew/Picture of Your Mother	1967	2.00	4.00	8.00
72749	Beauty Is a Fading Flower/Your Love Is Mine Again	1967	2.00	4.00	8.00
72786	The World the Way I Want It/Shame on the Rain	1968	2.00	4.00	8.00
72835	Ain't Got the Time/Hope	1968	2.00	4.00	8.00
72863	Ballad of Forty Dollars/Highways	1968	—	3.00	6.00
72913	Strawberry Farms/3	1969	—	3.00	6.00
72951	Homecoming/Myra	1969	—	3.00	6.00
72998	A Week in a Country Jail/Flat-Footin' It	1969	—	3.00	6.00
73039	Shoeshine Man/Kentucky in the Morning	1970	—	3.00	6.00
73078	Salute to a Switchblade/That'll Be Alright with Me	1970	—	3.00	6.00
73139	Day Drinkin'/Get On with the Show	1970	—	3.00	6.00
—With Dave Dudley					
73140	One Hundred Children/I Took a Memory to Lunch	1970	—	3.00	6.00
73189	Ode to a Half Pound of Ground Round/Pinto the Wonder Horse Is Dead	1971	—	3.00	6.00
73221	The Year That Clayton Delaney Died/Second Handed Flowers	1971	—	2.50	5.00
73278	Me and Jesus/Coot Marseilles Blues	1972	—	2.50	5.00
73297	The Monkey That Became President/She Gave Her Heart to Jethro	1972	—	2.50	5.00
73327	More About John Henry/Windy City Anne	1972	—	2.50	5.00
73346	(Old Dogs-Children and) Watermelon Wine/Grandma Whistled	1972	—	2.50	5.00
73377	Ravishing Ruby/I Flew Over Our House Last Night	1973	—	2.50	5.00
73394	Watergate Blues/Spokane Motel Blues	1973	—	2.50	5.00
73436	I Love/Back When We Were Young	1973	—	2.00	4.00
73488	That Song Is Driving Me Crazy/Forget It	1974	—	2.00	4.00
73617	Country Is/God Came Through Bellville, Ga.	1974	—	2.00	4.00
73641	I Care/Sneaky Snake	1974	—	2.00	4.00
73686	Deal/It Rained in Every Town Except Paducah	1975	—	2.00	4.00
73704	I Like Beer/From a Mansion to a Honky Tonk	1975	—	2.00	4.00
73755	Faster Horses (The Cowboy and the Poet)/No New Friends Please	1975	—	2.00	4.00
73795	Negatory Romance/It's Got to Be Kentucky for Me	1976	—	2.00	4.00
73850	Fox on the Run/Bluegrass Festival in the Sky	1976	—	2.00	4.00
73899	Your Man Loves You Honey/One of the Mysteries of Life	1977	—	2.00	4.00
812835-7	Everything from Jesus to Jack Daniels/(Old Dogs-Children and) Watermelon Wine	1983	—	—	3.00
814560-7	How'd You Get Home So Soon/The Year That Clayton Delaney Died	1983	—	—	3.00
870669-7	Let's Play Remember/Fox Hollow's Animal Train	1988	—	—	3.00
872180-7	Let's Spend Christmas at My House/Let's Go Shopping Today	1988	—	—	3.00
880030-7	Famous in Missouri/I Only Think About You When I'm Drunk	1984	—	—	3.00
880216-7	P.S. I Love You/My Heroes Have Always Been Cowboys	1984	—	—	3.00
880690-7	A Bar with No Beer/Red Sails in the Sunset	1985	—	—	3.00
884017-7	Down in the Florida Keys/Song in a Seashell	1985	—	—	3.00
884850-7	Susie's Beauty Shop/Love Letters in the Sand	1986	—	—	3.00
888155-7	Dowm at the Mall/We're All Through Dancing	1986	—	—	3.00

RCA

Number	Title (A Side/B Side)	Yr	VG	VG+	NM
PB-11158	May the Force Be With You Always/No One Feels My Heart	1977	—	2.50	5.00
PB-11253	I Wish I Loved Somebody Else/Whiskey	1978	—	2.00	4.00
PB-11376	What Have You Got to Lose/The Three Sofa Story	1978	—	2.00	4.00
PB-11453	Son of Clayton Delaney/The Great East Breadway Onion Championship of 1978	1978	—	2.00	4.00
PB-11568	There Is a Miracle in You/Saturday Morning Show	1979	—	2.00	4.00
PB-11713	You Show Me Your Heart (And I'll Show You Mine)/Old Habits Die Hard	1979	—	2.00	4.00
PB-11765	Christmas Is/Thanksgiving Is	1979	—	2.00	4.00
PB-11888	The Old Side of Town/Jesus on the Radio (Daddy on the Phone)	1979	—	2.00	4.00
PB-12005	Soldier of Fortune/The World According to Raymond	1980	—	—	3.00
PB-12066	Back When Gas Was Thirty Cents a Gallon/Texas Never Fell in Love with Me	1980	—	—	3.00
PB-12219	The All New Me/Pour Me (Pour Me Another Drink)	1981	—	—	3.00

Albums

MERCURY

Number	Title (A Side/B Side)	Yr	VG	VG+	NM
SRM-1-500	Songs of Fox Hollow	1975	3.00	6.00	12.00
SRM-1-668	The Rhymer and Other Five and Dimers	1973	3.00	6.00	12.00
SRM-1-687	For the People in the Last Hard Town	1974	3.00	6.00	12.00
SRM-1-1009	Country Is	1974	3.00	6.00	12.00
SRM-1-1033	I Wrote	1975	3.00	6.00	12.00
SRM-1-1044	Greatest Hits, Volume 2	1975	3.00	6.00	12.00
SRM-1-1076	Faster Horses	1976	3.00	6.00	12.00
SRM-1-1111	Magnificent Music	1977	3.00	6.00	12.00
SRM-1-1139	About Love	1977	3.00	6.00	12.00
SRM-1-5008	Greatest Hits, Volume 3	1978	3.00	6.00	12.00
SR-61211	Ballad of Forty Dollars	1969	5.00	10.00	20.00
SR-61247	Homecoming	1969	5.00	10.00	20.00
SR-61277	Witness Life	1970	5.00	10.00	20.00
SR-61307	100 Children	1970	5.00	10.00	20.00
SR-61350	In Search of a Song	1971	3.75	7.50	15.00
SR-61362	We All Got Together And...	1972	3.75	7.50	15.00
SR-61369	Greatest Hits	1972	3.75	7.50	15.00
814025-1	Jesus to Jack Daniels	1983	2.00	4.00	8.00
822425-1	Natural Dreams	1984	2.00	4.00	8.00
822500-1	In Search of a Song	1987	2.00	4.00	8.00
824143-1	Greatest Hits	1985	2.00	4.00	8.00
—Reissue					
824144-1	Greatest Hits, Volume 2	1985	2.00	4.00	8.00
—Reissue					
824145-1	Greatest Hits, Volume 3	1985	2.00	4.00	8.00
—Reissue					
824508-1	Song in a Seashell	1985	2.00	4.00	8.00
832350-1	Songs of Fox Hollow	1987	2.00	4.00	8.00
—Reissue					
834779-1	Country Songs for Children	1988	2.00	4.00	8.00
—Reissue					

PICCADILLY

Number	Title (A Side/B Side)	Yr	VG	VG+	NM
3558	I Like Beer	198?	2.00	4.00	8.00

RCA VICTOR

Number	Title (A Side/B Side)	Yr	VG	VG+	NM
AHL1-2622	New Train	1978	2.50	5.00	10.00
AHL1-3018	Places I've Been	1979	2.50	5.00	10.00
AHL1-3495	T's in Town	1979	2.50	5.00	10.00
AHL1-3685	Soldier of Fortune	1980	2.50	5.00	10.00
AHL1-4749	In Concert: Recorded Live at the Grand Ole Opry	1983	2.50	5.00	10.00
AYL1-5432	In Concert: Recorded Live at the Grand Ole Opry	1985	2.00	4.00	8.00
—"Best Buy Series" reissue					

HALLMARKS, THE

45s

DOT

Number	Title (A Side/B Side)	Yr	VG	VG+	NM
16418	My Little Sailor Boy/Congratulations	1963	5.00	10.00	20.00

EPIC

Number	Title (A Side/B Side)	Yr	VG	VG+	NM
9681	Let There Be You/Royal King	1964	3.00	6.00	12.00

SMASH

Number	Title (A Side/B Side)	Yr	VG	VG+	NM
2115	Soul Shakin' Psychedelic Sally/Girl of My Dreams	1967	7.50	15.00	30.00

HALLOWAY, LARRY

45s

PARKWAY

Number	Title (A Side/B Side)	Yr	VG	VG+	NM
903	Beatle Teen Beat/Going Up	1964	5.00	10.00	20.00

HALLYDAY, JOHNNY

45s

PHILIPS

Number	Title (A Side/B Side)	Yr	VG	VG+	NM
40024	I Got a Woman/Be-Bop-a-Lula	1962	6.25	12.50	25.00
40043	Hey Little Girl/Caravan of Lonely Men	1962	6.25	12.50	25.00

Albums

PHILIPS

Number	Title (A Side/B Side)	Yr	VG	VG+	NM
PHM 200019 [M]	America's Rockin' Hits	1962	20.00	40.00	80.00
PHS 600019 [S]	America's Rockin' Hits	1962	25.00	50.00	100.00

HALOS, THE

45s

7 ARTS

Number	Title (A Side/B Side)	Yr	VG	VG+	NM
709	Nag/Copy Cat	1961	5.00	10.00	20.00

Number	Title (A Side/B Side)	Yr	VG	VG+	NM
720	Come On/What'd I Say	1962	5.00	10.00	20.00
CONGRESS					
244	Do I/Just Keep On Loving Me	1965	3.00	6.00	12.00
249	Since I Fell for You/You're Never Gonna Find	1965	3.00	6.00	12.00
253	Baby What You Want Me to Do/Hey, Hey, Love Me	1965	3.00	6.00	12.00
262 [DJ]	Come Softly to Me/?	1966	3.00	6.00	12.00
—May be promo-only					
Albums					
WARWICK					
W-2046 [M]	The Halos	1962	100.00	200.00	400.00

HAMILTON, CHICO

Number	Title (A Side/B Side)	Yr	VG	VG+	NM
45s					
COLUMBIA					
42045	Afternoon of a Breeze (Part 1)/Afternoon of a Breeze (Part 2)	1961	3.00	6.00	12.00
ENTERPRISE					
9102	Conquistadores '74/Fancy	1974	—	2.50	5.00
IMPULSE!					
238	Forest Flower (Part 1)/Forest Flower (Part 2)	1965	2.50	5.00	10.00
241	Conquistadores (Part 1)/Conquistadores (Part 2)	1966	2.50	5.00	10.00
249	Monday, Monday/Evil Eye	1967	2.00	4.00	8.00
258	For Mods Only/The Dealer	1968	2.00	4.00	8.00
PACIFIC JAZZ					
628	Blue Sands/The Morning After	1955	5.00	10.00	20.00
631	The Squimp/Mr. Jo Jones	1955	5.00	10.00	20.00
WORLD PACIFIC					
88134	Siete Quatro/Satin Doll	1966	2.00	4.00	8.00
Albums					
ABC IMPULSE!					
AS-29 [S]	Passin' Thru	1968	3.75	7.50	15.00
AS-59 [S]	Man from Two Worlds	1968	3.75	7.50	15.00
AS-82 [S]	Chi Chi Chico	1968	3.75	7.50	15.00
AS-9102 [S]	El Chico	1968	3.75	7.50	15.00
AS-9114 [S]	The Further Adventures of El Chico	1968	3.75	7.50	15.00
AS-9130 [S]	The Dealer	1968	3.75	7.50	15.00
AS-9174	The Best of Chico Hamilton	1969	3.75	7.50	15.00
AS-9213 [(2)]	His Great Hits	1971	5.00	10.00	20.00
BLUE NOTE					
BN-LA520-G	Peregrinations	1975	3.00	6.00	12.00
BN-LA622-G	Chico Hamilton & Players	1976	3.00	6.00	12.00
COLUMBIA					
CL 1590 [M]	Selections from "Bye Bye Birdie"	1961	5.00	10.00	20.00
CL 1619 [M]	Chico Hamilton Special	1961	5.00	10.00	20.00
CL 1807 [M]	Drumfusion	1962	5.00	10.00	20.00
CS 8390 [S]	Selections from "Bye Bye Birdie"	1961	6.25	12.50	25.00
CS 8419 [S]	Chico Hamilton Special	1961	6.25	12.50	25.00
CS 8607 [S]	Drumfusion	1962	6.25	12.50	25.00
DECCA					
DL 8614 [M]	Jazz from the Sweet Smell of Success	1957	12.50	25.00	50.00
DISCOVERY					
831	Gongs East	1981	2.50	5.00	10.00
—Reissue of Warner Bros. 1271					
ELEKTRA					
6E-257	Nomad	1980	2.50	5.00	10.00
ENTERPRISE					
SD 7501	The Master	1974	3.00	6.00	12.00
FLYING DUTCHMAN					
10135	Exigente	1971	3.75	7.50	15.00
IMPULSE!					
A-29 [M]	Passin' Thru	1963	6.25	12.50	25.00
AS-29 [S]	Passin' Thru	1963	7.50	15.00	30.00
A-59 [M]	Man from Two Worlds	1964	6.25	12.50	25.00
AS-59 [S]	Man from Two Worlds	1964	7.50	15.00	30.00
A-82 [M]	Chi Chi Chico	1965	5.00	10.00	20.00
AS-82 [S]	Chi Chi Chico	1965	6.25	12.50	25.00
A-9102 [M]	El Chico	1965	5.00	10.00	20.00
AS-9102 [S]	El Chico	1965	6.25	12.50	25.00
A-9114 [M]	The Further Adventures of El Chico	1966	5.00	10.00	20.00
AS-9114 [S]	The Further Adventures of El Chico	1966	6.25	12.50	25.00
A-9130 [M]	The Dealer	1966	5.00	10.00	20.00
AS-9130 [S]	The Dealer	1966	6.25	12.50	25.00
JAZZTONE					
J-1264 [M]	Delightfully Modern	1957	10.00	20.00	40.00
MCA					
637	Man from Two Worlds	198?	2.00	4.00	8.00
—Reissue of Impulse! 59					
638	El Chico	198?	2.00	4.00	8.00
—Reissue of Impulse! 9102					
29037	Passin' Thru	198?	2.50	5.00	10.00
—Reissue of Impulse! 29					
29038	The Best of Chico Hamilton	198?	2.50	5.00	10.00
—Reissue of Impulse! 9174					
MERCURY					
SRM-1-1163	Catwalk	1977	3.00	6.00	12.00
NAUTILUS					
NR-13	Reaching for the Top	1981	7.50	15.00	30.00
—Audiophile vinyl					
PACIFIC JAZZ					
PJLP-17 [10]	Chico Hamilton Trio	1955	25.00	50.00	100.00
PJ-39 [M]	Spectacular	1962	6.25	12.50	25.00
—Reissue of 1209					
PJ-1209 [M]	Chico Hamilton Quintet	1955	18.75	37.50	75.00
PJ-1216 [M]	Chico Hamilton Quintet In Hi-Fi	1956	18.75	37.50	75.00
PJ-1220 [M]	Chico Hamilton Trio	1956	18.75	37.50	75.00
PJ-1225 [M]	Chico Hamilton Quintet	1957	18.75	37.50	75.00
PJ-1231 [M]	Chico Hamilton Plays the Music of Fred Katz	1957	18.75	37.50	75.00
REPRISE					
R-6078 [M]	A Different Journey	1963	7.50	15.00	30.00
R9-6078 [S]	A Different Journey	1963	10.00	20.00	40.00
SOLID STATE					
18043	The Gamut	1969	3.75	7.50	15.00
18050	Headhunters	1969	3.75	7.50	15.00
SOUL NOTE					
121191	Reunion	1989	3.00	6.00	12.00
SUNSET					
SUS-5215	Easy Livin'	196?	3.00	6.00	12.00
WARNER BROS.					
W 1245 [M]	Chico Hamilton Quintet with Strings Attached	1958	12.50	25.00	50.00
WS 1245 [S]	Chico Hamilton Quintet with Strings Attached	1958	15.00	30.00	60.00
W 1271 [M]	Gongs East	1958	12.50	25.00	50.00
WS 1271 [S]	Gongs East	1958	15.00	30.00	60.00
W 1344 [M]	The Three Faces of Chico	1959	12.50	25.00	50.00
WS 1344 [S]	The Three Faces of Chico	1959	15.00	30.00	60.00
WORLD PACIFIC					
ST-1003 [S]	South Pacific in Hi-Fi	1958	10.00	20.00	40.00
ST-1005 [S]	Chico Hamilton Quintet	1958	10.00	20.00	40.00
ST-1008 [S]	The Chico Hamilton Trio Featuring Freddie Gambrell	1958	10.00	20.00	40.00
ST-1016 [S]	Ellington Suite	1959	10.00	20.00	40.00
WP-1216 [M]	Chico Hamilton Quintet In Hi-Fi	1958	12.50	25.00	50.00
WP-1225 [M]	Chico Hamilton Quintet	1958	12.50	25.00	50.00
WP-1231 [M]	Chico Hamilton Plays the Music of Fred Katz	1958	12.50	25.00	50.00
PJ-1238 [M]	South Pacific in Hi-Fi	1957	12.50	25.00	50.00
WP-1238 [M]	South Pacific in Hi-Fi	1958	10.00	20.00	40.00
PJ-1242 [M]	The Chico Hamilton Trio Featuring Freddie Gambrell	1957	12.50	25.00	50.00
WP-1242 [M]	The Chico Hamilton Trio Featuring Freddie Gambrell	1958	10.00	20.00	40.00
WP-1258 [M]	Ellington Suite	1959	12.50	25.00	50.00
WP-1287 [M]	The Original Hamilton Quintet	1960	12.50	25.00	50.00

HAMILTON, GEORGE

Number	Title (A Side/B Side)	Yr	VG	VG+	NM
45s					
ABC-PARAMOUNT					
10734	Loneliness/So Small	1965	2.50	5.00	10.00
10734 [PS]	Loneliness/So Small	1965	5.00	10.00	20.00
MGM					
13178	Don't Envy Me/Little Bitty Falling Star	1963	3.00	6.00	12.00
13215	Does Goodnight Mean Goodbye/Errand of Mercy	1964	3.00	6.00	12.00
UNI					
55303	Evel Knievel/Boy from the Country	1971	2.50	5.00	10.00
Albums					
ABC-PARAMOUNT					
535 [M]	By George	1966	5.00	10.00	20.00
S-535 [S]	By George	1966	6.25	12.50	25.00

HAMILTON, GEORGE, IV

Number	Title (A Side/B Side)	Yr	VG	VG+	NM
45s					
ABC					
12342 [DJ]	Only the Best (mono/stereo)	1978	—	2.50	5.00
—May be promo only					
12376	One Day at a Time/Take This Heart	1978	—	2.00	4.00
ABC-PARAMOUNT					
9765	A Rose and a Baby Ruth/If You Don't Know	1956	7.50	15.00	30.00
9782	Only One Love/If I Possessed a Printing Press	1957	7.50	15.00	30.00
9838	High School Romance/Everybody's Baby	1957	7.50	15.00	30.00
9862	Why Don't They Understand/Even Tho'	1957	7.50	15.00	30.00
9898	Now and For Always/One Heart	1958	6.25	12.50	25.00
9924	I Know Where I'm Goin'/Who's Taking You to the Prom	1958	6.25	12.50	25.00
9946	When Will I Know/Your Cheatin' Heart	1958	6.25	12.50	25.00
9966	Lucy, Lucy/The Two of Us	1958	6.25	12.50	25.00
10009	The Steady Game/Can You Blame Us	1959	5.00	10.00	20.00
10028	Gee/I Know Your Sweetheart	1959	5.00	10.00	20.00
10059	One Little Acre/Little Tom	1959	5.00	10.00	20.00
10090	Why I'm Walkin'/Tremble	1960	5.00	10.00	20.00
10125	Before This Day Ends/Loneliness All Around Me	1960	5.00	10.00	20.00
10167	A Walk on the Wild Side of Life/It's Just the Idea	1960	5.00	10.00	20.00
ABC/DOT					
17687	I Wonder Who's Kissing Her Now/In the Palm of Her Hand	1977	—	2.00	4.00
17708	Cornbread, Beans and Sweet Potato Pie/May the Wind Be Always at Your Back	1977	—	2.00	4.00
17723	Everlasting (Everlasting Love)/In the Palm of Your Hand	1977	—	2.00	4.00
COLONIAL					
420	A Rose and a Baby Ruth/If You Don't Know	1956	20.00	40.00	80.00
451	I've Got a Secret/Sam	1956	10.00	20.00	40.00
GRT					
063	Blue Jeans, Ice Cream and Saturday Shoes/Bad Romancer	1976	—	2.50	5.00
MCA					
41149	Forever Young/'Rangement Blues	1979	—	2.00	4.00
41215	I'll Be Here in the Morning/Spin Spin	1980	—	2.00	4.00
41282	Catfish Bates/Mose Rankin	1980	—	2.00	4.00
RCA					
2722-7-R	Abilene/Oh So Many Tears	1990	—	2.00	4.00
RCA VICTOR					
APBO-0084	Second Cup of Coffee/Farmer's Song	1973	—	2.00	4.00
APBO-0203	Claim on Me/Early Mornin' Rain	1973	—	2.00	4.00
APBO-0314	The Ways of a Country Girl/Pictou County Jail	1974	—	2.00	4.00
47-7881	Three Steps to the Picnic/The Ballad of Widder Jones	1961	3.75	7.50	15.00
47-7934	To You and Yours (From Me and Mine)/I Want a Girl	1961	3.75	7.50	15.00
47-8001	China Doll/Commerce Street and Sixth Avenue North	1962	3.75	7.50	15.00
47-8062	If You Don't Know, I Ain't Gonna Tell You/Where Nobody Knows Me	1962	3.75	7.50	15.00
47-8118	In This Very Same Room/If You Want Me To	1962	3.75	7.50	15.00
47-8181	Abilene/Oh So Many Years	1963	3.00	6.00	12.00

Number	Title (A Side/B Side)	Yr	VG	VG+	NM
47-8250	There's More Pretty Girls Than One/If You Don't, Somebody Else Will	1963	3.00	6.00	12.00
47-8304	Linda with the Lonely Eyes/Fair and Tender Ladies	1963	3.00	6.00	12.00
47-8392	Fort Worth, Dallas or Houston/Life's Railway to Heaven	1964	3.00	6.00	12.00
47-8462	Truck Driving Man/The Little Grave	1964	3.00	6.00	12.00
47-8537	The Last Mister Jones/Anymore	1965	2.50	5.00	10.00
47-8608	Walking the Floor Over You/Driftwood on the River	1965	2.50	5.00	10.00
47-8690	Write Me a Picture/Twist of the Wrist	1965	2.50	5.00	10.00
47-8797	Steel Rail Blues/Tobacco	1966	2.50	5.00	10.00
47-8924	Early Morning Rain/Slightly Used	1966	2.50	5.00	10.00
47-9059	Urge for Going/Changes	1966	2.50	5.00	10.00
47-9239	Break My Mind/Something Special to Me	1967	2.00	4.00	8.00
47-9385	Little World Girl/Song for a Winter's Night	1967	2.00	4.00	8.00
47-9519	It's My Time/Canadian Railroad Trilogy	1968	2.00	4.00	8.00
47-9637	Take My Hand for Awhile/Wonderful World of My Dreams	1968	2.00	4.00	8.00
47-9775	Natividad (The Nativity)/The Little Grave	1969	2.00	4.00	8.00
47-9829	She's a Little Bit Country/My Nova Scotia Home	1970	—	3.00	6.00
47-9886	Back Where It's At/Then I Miss You	1970	—	3.00	6.00
47-9893	Let's Get Together/Everything Is Beautiful	1970	—	3.00	6.00
—With Skeeter Davis					
47-9937	Natividad (The Nativity)/The Little Grave	1970	—	3.00	6.00
47-9945	Anyway/The Best That I Can Do	1971	—	3.00	6.00
74-0100	Back to Denver/Suzanne	1969	2.00	4.00	8.00
74-0171	Canadian Pacific/Sisters of Mercy	1969	2.00	4.00	8.00
74-0256	Carolina in My Mind/I'm Gonna Be a Country Boy Again	1969	2.00	4.00	8.00
74-0469	Countryfied/My North Country Home	1971	—	3.00	6.00
74-0531	West Texas Highway/There's No Room in This Rat Race	1971	—	3.00	6.00
74-0622	10 Degrees and Getting Colder/Tumbleweed	1971	—	3.00	6.00
74-0697	Country Music in My Soul/Child's Song	1972	—	2.50	5.00
74-0776	Travelin' Light/Alberta Bound	1972	—	2.50	5.00
74-0854	Blue Train (Of the Heartbreak Line)/Maritime Farewell	1972	—	2.50	5.00
74-0948	Dirty Old Man/Abilene	1973	—	2.50	5.00

7-Inch Extended Plays

ABC-PARAMOUNT

Number	Title (A Side/B Side)	Yr	VG	VG+	NM
A-220	Clementine/When I Grow Too Old to Dream//Tell Me Why/Let Me Call You Sweetheart	1958	5.00	10.00	20.00
A-220 [PS]	On Campus	1958	5.00	10.00	20.00

Albums

ABC

Number	Title (A Side/B Side)	Yr	VG	VG+	NM
X-750	16 Greatest Hits	1972	2.50	5.00	10.00
AC-30032	The ABC Collection	1975	3.00	6.00	12.00

ABC-PARAMOUNT

Number	Title (A Side/B Side)	Yr	VG	VG+	NM
220 [M]	On Campus	1958	10.00	20.00	40.00
S-220 [S]	On Campus	1958	12.50	25.00	50.00
251 [M]	Sing Me a Sad Song (A Tribute to Hank Williams)	1958	10.00	20.00	40.00
S-251 [S]	Sing Me a Sad Song (A Tribute to Hank Williams)	1958	12.50	25.00	50.00
461 [M]	George Hamilton IV's Big 15	1963	7.50	15.00	30.00
S-461 [P]	George Hamilton IV's Big 15	1963	10.00	20.00	40.00

ABC/DOT

Number	Title (A Side/B Side)	Yr	VG	VG+	NM
DO-2081	Fine Lace	1977	2.50	5.00	10.00

DOT

Number	Title (A Side/B Side)	Yr	VG	VG+	NM
39033	George Hamilton IV	1985	2.50	5.00	10.00

HARMONY

Number	Title (A Side/B Side)	Yr	VG	VG+	NM
HS 11379	Your Cheatin' Heart	1970	2.50	5.00	10.00

LAMB AND LION

Number	Title (A Side/B Side)	Yr	VG	VG+	NM
1015	Bluegrass Gospel	1974	3.00	6.00	12.00

MCA

Number	Title (A Side/B Side)	Yr	VG	VG+	NM
705	Forever Young	198?	2.00	4.00	8.00
—Reissue of 3206					
3206	Forever Young	1980	2.50	5.00	10.00

RCA CAMDEN

Number	Title (A Side/B Side)	Yr	VG	VG+	NM
ACL1-0242	Singin' on the Mountains	1973	2.50	5.00	10.00
CAL-2200 [M]	A Rose and a Baby Ruth	1967	3.75	7.50	15.00
CAS-2200 [S]	A Rose and a Baby Ruth	1967	2.50	5.00	10.00
CAS-2468	Early Morning Rain	1971	2.50	5.00	10.00

RCA VICTOR

Number	Title (A Side/B Side)	Yr	VG	VG+	NM
APL1-0455	Greatest Hits	1974	3.00	6.00	12.00
LPM-2373 [M]	To You and Yours from Me and Mine	1961	6.25	12.50	25.00
LSP-2373 [S]	To You and Yours from Me and Mine	1961	7.50	15.00	30.00
LPM-2778 [M]	Abilene	1963	6.25	12.50	25.00
LSP-2778 [S]	Abilene	1963	7.50	15.00	30.00
LPM-2972 [M]	Fort Worth, Dallas or Houston	1964	6.25	12.50	25.00
LSP-2972 [S]	Fort Worth, Dallas or Houston	1964	7.50	15.00	30.00
LPM-3371 [M]	Mister Sincerity... A Tribute to Ernest Tubb	1965	6.25	12.50	25.00
LSP-3371 [S]	Mister Sincerity... A Tribute to Ernest Tubb	1965	7.50	15.00	30.00
LPM-3510 [M]	Coast Country	1966	6.25	12.50	25.00
LSP-3510 [S]	Coast Country	1966	7.50	15.00	30.00
LPM-3601 [M]	Steel Rail Blues	1966	5.00	10.00	20.00
LSP-3601 [S]	Steel Rail Blues	1966	5.00	10.00	20.00
LPM-3752 [M]	Folk Country Classics	1967	6.25	12.50	25.00
LSP-3752 [S]	Folk Country Classics	1967	5.00	10.00	20.00
LPM-3854 [M]	Folksy	1967	6.25	12.50	25.00
LSP-3854 [S]	Folksy	1967	5.00	10.00	20.00
LPM-3962 [M]	The Gentle Country Sound of George Hamilton IV	1968	10.00	20.00	40.00
LSP-3962 [S]	The Gentle Country Sound of George Hamilton IV	1968	5.00	10.00	20.00
LSP-4066	In the 4th Dimension	1968	5.00	10.00	20.00
LSP-4164	Canadian Pacific	1969	3.75	7.50	15.00
LSP-4265	The Best of George Hamilton IV	1970	3.75	7.50	15.00
LSP-4342	Back Where It's At	1970	3.75	7.50	15.00
LSP-4435	Down Home in the Country	1971	3.75	7.50	15.00
LSP-4517	North Country	1971	3.75	7.50	15.00
LSP-4609	West Texas Highway	1971	3.75	7.50	15.00
LSP-4700	Country Music in My Soul	1972	3.00	6.00	12.00
LSP-4772	Travelin' Light	1972	3.00	6.00	12.00
LSP-4826	International Ambassador	1973	3.00	6.00	12.00

HAMILTON, JUDD

45s

AMERICAN INT'L.

Number	Title (A Side/B Side)	Yr	VG	VG+	NM
151	Rules/Someday Morning	1970	2.00	4.00	8.00
163	Baltimore/Sunshine Man	1970	2.00	4.00	8.00

DOLTON

Number	Title (A Side/B Side)	Yr	VG	VG+	NM
80	Dream/Your Only Boy	1963	7.50	15.00	30.00

HAMILTON, ROY

45s

AGP

Number	Title (A Side/B Side)	Yr	VG	VG+	NM
113	The Dark End of the Street/100 Years	1969	2.00	4.00	8.00
116	Angelica/Hang Ups	1969	2.00	4.00	8.00
125	It's Only Make Believe/100 Years	1969	2.00	4.00	8.00

CAPITOL

Number	Title (A Side/B Side)	Yr	VG	VG+	NM
2057	Let This World Be Free/Wait Until Dark	1967	2.00	4.00	8.00

EPIC

Number	Title (A Side/B Side)	Yr	VG	VG+	NM
9015	You'll Never Walk Alone/I'm Gonna Sit Right Down and Cry	1954	6.25	12.50	25.00
9047	So Let There Be Love/If You Loved Me	1954	6.25	12.50	25.00
9068	Ebb Tide/Beware	1954	6.25	12.50	25.00
9086	Hurt/Star of Love	1954	6.25	12.50	25.00
9092	I Believe/If You Are But a Dream	1955	5.00	10.00	20.00
9102	Unchained Melody/From Here to Eternity	1955	6.25	12.50	25.00
9111	Forgive This Fool/You Wanted to Change Me	1955	5.00	10.00	20.00
9118	A Little Voice/All This Is Mine	1955	5.00	10.00	20.00
9125	Without a Song/Cuban Love Song	1955	5.00	10.00	20.00
9132	Everybody's Got a Home/Take Me with You	1955	5.00	10.00	20.00
9147	There Goes My Heart/Walk Along with Kings	1956	5.00	10.00	20.00
9160	Somebody, Somewhere/Since I Fell for You	1956	5.00	10.00	20.00
9180	I Took My Grief to Him/Chained	1956	5.00	10.00	20.00
9203	The Simple Prayer/A Mother's Love	1957	5.00	10.00	20.00
9212	My Faith, My Hope, My Love/So Long	1957	5.00	10.00	20.00
9224	The Aisle/That Old Feeling	1957	5.00	10.00	20.00
9232	(All of a Sudden) My Heart Sings/I'm Gonna Lock You in My Heart	1957	5.00	10.00	20.00
9257	Don't Let Go/The Night to Love	1957	5.00	10.00	20.00
9268	Crazy Feelin'/In a Dream	1958	3.75	7.50	15.00
9274	Lips/Jungle Fever	1958	3.75	7.50	15.00
9282	Wait for Me/Everything	1958	3.75	7.50	15.00
9294	Pledging My Love/My One and Only Love	1958	3.75	7.50	15.00
9301	It's Never Too Late/Somewhere Along the Way	1959	3.75	7.50	15.00
9307	I Need Your Lovin'/Blue Prelude	1959	3.75	7.50	15.00
9323	Time Marches On/Take It Easy, Joe	1959	3.75	7.50	15.00
9342	Great Romance/On My Way Back Home	1959	3.75	7.50	15.00
9354	The Ten Commandments/Nobody Knows the Trouble I've Seen	1959	5.00	10.00	20.00
9354	The Ten Commandments/Dowm by the Riverside	1959	3.75	7.50	15.00
9372	Down by the Riverside/Nobody Knows the Trouble I've Seen	1960	3.75	7.50	15.00
9373	I Let a Song Go Out of My Heart/I Get the Blues When It Rains	1960	3.75	7.50	15.00
9374	My Story/Please Send Me Someone to Love	1960	3.75	7.50	15.00
9375	Something's Gotta Give/Cheek to Cheek	1960	—	—	—
—Unreleased?					
9376	Sing You Sinners/Blow, Gabriel, Blow	1960	3.75	7.50	15.00
9386	Having Myself a Ball/Slowly	1960	3.75	7.50	15.00
—B-side by Bobby Sykes					
9388	Never Let Me Go/I Get the Blues When It Rains	1960	—	—	—
—Unreleased?					
9390	The Clock/I Get the Blues When It Rains	1960	3.75	7.50	15.00
9398	A Lover's Prayer/Never Let Me Go	1960	3.75	7.50	15.00
9407	Lonely Hands/Your Love	1960	3.75	7.50	15.00
9434	You Can Have Her/Abide With Me	1961	3.75	7.50	15.00
9434 [PS]	You Can Have Her/Abide With Me	1961	7.50	15.00	30.00
9443	You're Gonna Need Magic/To the One I Love	1961	3.75	7.50	15.00
9443 [PS]	You're Gonna Need Magic/To the One I Love	1961	7.50	15.00	30.00
9449	No Substitute for Love/Please Louise	1961	3.75	7.50	15.00
9449 [PS]	No Substitute for Love/Please Louise	1961	7.50	15.00	30.00
9460	Excerpts from "You Can Have Her"	1961	3.75	7.50	15.00
9461	Excerpts from "You Can Have Her"	1961	3.75	7.50	15.00
9462	Excerpts from "You Can Have Her"	1961	3.75	7.50	15.00
9463	Excerpts from "You Can Have Her"	1961	3.75	7.50	15.00
9464	Excerpts from "You Can Have Her"	1961	3.75	7.50	15.00
9466	There We Were/If	1961	3.00	6.00	12.00
9492	Don't Come Cryin' to Me/If Only I Had Known	1962	3.00	6.00	12.00
9520	Climb Ev'ry Mountain/I'll Come Running Back to You	1962	3.00	6.00	12.00
9538	I Am/Earthquake	1962	3.00	6.00	12.00
10559	You'll Never Walk Alone/The Golden Boy	1969	2.00	4.00	8.00

MGM

Number	Title (A Side/B Side)	Yr	VG	VG+	NM
13138	Let Go/You Still Love Him	1963	2.50	5.00	10.00
13157	Midnight Town-Daybreak City/Intermezzo	1963	2.50	5.00	10.00
13175	Theme from "The V.I.P.'s" (The Willow)/The Sinner	1963	2.50	5.00	10.00
13217	The Panic Is On/There She Is	1964	6.25	12.50	25.00
13247	Answer Me, My Love/Unchained Melody	1964	2.50	5.00	10.00
13291	You Can Count on Me/She Makes Me Wanna Dance	1964	6.25	12.50	25.00
13315	Sweet Violets/A Thousand Years Ago	1965	2.50	5.00	10.00

RCA VICTOR

Number	Title (A Side/B Side)	Yr	VG	VG+	NM
47-8641	Heartache/Ain't It the Truth	1965	2.50	5.00	10.00
47-8705	And I Love Her/Tore Up Over You	1965	2.50	5.00	10.00
47-8813	The Impossible Dream/She's Got a Heart	1966	2.50	5.00	10.00
47-8960	Walk Hand in Hand/Crackin' Up Over You	1966	6.25	12.50	25.00
47-9061	I Taught Her Everything She Knows/Lament	1967	2.50	5.00	10.00
47-9171	So High My Love/You Shook Me Up	1967	12.50	25.00	50.00
48-1034	Walk Hand in Hand/Crackin' Up Over You	1972	2.50	5.00	10.00

7-Inch Extended Plays

EPIC

Number	Title (A Side/B Side)	Yr	VG	VG+	NM
EG-7065	(contents unknown)	195?	5.00	10.00	20.00
EG-7065	(contents unknown)	195?	5.00	10.00	20.00
EG-7065 [PS]	Here's Roy Hamilton	195?	5.00	10.00	20.00
EG-7065 [PS]	You'll Never Walk Alone	195?	5.00	10.00	20.00

Number	Title (A Side/B Side)	Yr	VG	VG+	NM
EG-7079	Ebb Tide/Beware//If You Are But a Dream/From Here to Eternity	195?	5.00	10.00	20.00
EG-7079 [PS]	Ebb Tide	195?	5.00	10.00	20.00
EG-7080	(contents unknown)	195?	5.00	10.00	20.00
EG-7080 [PS]	Faith, Hope and Hamilton	195?	5.00	10.00	20.00
EG-7133	(contents unknown)	195?	5.00	10.00	20.00
EG-7133 [PS]	Roy Hamilton	195?	5.00	10.00	20.00
EG-7158	(contents unknown)	195?	3.75	7.50	15.00
EG-7158 [PS]	Roy Hamilton	195?	3.75	7.50	15.00
EG-7159	(contents unknown)	195?	3.75	7.50	15.00
EG-7159 [PS]	Roy Hamilton	195?	3.75	7.50	15.00
EG-7200	(contents unknown)	1958	3.75	7.50	15.00
EG-7200 [PS]	Don't Let Go	1958	3.75	7.50	15.00
EG-7205	(contents unknown)	1958	3.75	7.50	15.00
EG-7205 [PS]	Lips	1958	3.75	7.50	15.00
EG-7210	(contents unknown)	195?	3.75	7.50	15.00
EG-7210 [PS]	With All My Love	195?	3.75	7.50	15.00
EG-7214	(contents unknown)	195?	3.75	7.50	15.00
EG-7214 [PS]	You Belong to My Heart	195?	3.75	7.50	15.00
Albums					
EPIC					
BN 518 [S]	With All My Love	1958	10.00	20.00	40.00
BN 525 [S]	Why Fight The Feeling?	1959	7.50	15.00	30.00
BN 530 [S]	Come Out Swingin'	1959	7.50	15.00	30.00
BN 535 [S]	Have Blues, Must Travel	1959	7.50	15.00	30.00
BN 551 [S]	Spirituals	1960	7.50	15.00	30.00
BN 578 [S]	Soft 'n Warm	1960	7.50	15.00	30.00
BN 595 [S]	You Can Have Her	1961	10.00	20.00	40.00
BN 610 [S]	Only You	1961	7.50	15.00	30.00
BN 632 [R]	You'll Never Walk Alone	1962	5.00	10.00	20.00
LN 1023 [10]	You'll Never Walk Alone	1954	50.00	100.00	200.00
LN 1103 [10]	The Voice of Roy Hamilton	1954	50.00	100.00	200.00
LN 3176 [M]	Roy Hamilton	1955	15.00	30.00	60.00
LN 3294 [M]	You'll Never Walk Alone	1956	17.50	35.00	70.00
LN 3364 [M]	Golden Boy	1957	12.50	25.00	50.00
LN 3519 [M]	With All My Love	1958	7.50	15.00	30.00
LN 3545 [M]	Why Fight The Feeling?	1959	6.25	12.50	25.00
LN 3561 [M]	Come Out Swingin'	1959	6.25	12.50	25.00
LN 3580 [M]	Have Blues, Must Travel	1959	6.25	12.50	25.00
LN 3628 [M]	Roy Hamilton At His Best	1960	10.00	20.00	40.00
LN 3654 [M]	Spirituals	1960	6.25	12.50	25.00
LN 3717 [M]	Soft 'n Warm	1960	6.25	12.50	25.00
LN 3775 [M]	You Can Have Her	1961	7.50	15.00	30.00
LN 3807 [M]	Only You	1961	6.25	12.50	25.00
LN 24000 [M]	Mr. Rock and Soul	1962	6.25	12.50	25.00
LN 24009 [M]	Roy Hamilton's Greatest Hits	1962	5.00	10.00	20.00
LN 24316 [M]	Roy Hamilton's Greatest Hits, Vol. 2	1967	5.00	10.00	20.00
BN 26000 [S]	Mr. Rock and Soul	1962	7.50	15.00	30.00
BN 26009 [S]	Roy Hamilton's Greatest Hits	1962	6.25	12.50	25.00
BN 26316 [S]	Roy Hamilton's Greatest Hits, Vol. 2	1967	6.25	12.50	25.00
MGM					
E-4139 [M]	Warm and Soul	1963	3.75	7.50	15.00
SE-4139 [S]	Warm and Soul	1963	5.00	10.00	20.00
E-4233 [M]	Sentimental, Lonely & Blue	1964	3.75	7.50	15.00
SE-4233 [S]	Sentimental, Lonely & Blue	1964	5.00	10.00	20.00
RCA VICTOR					
LPM-3552 [M]	The Impossible Dream	1966	3.75	7.50	15.00
LSP-3552 [S]	The Impossible Dream	1966	5.00	10.00	20.00

HAMILTON, RUSS

Number	Title (A Side/B Side)	Yr	VG	VG+	NM
45s					
KAPP					
184	Rainbow/We Will Make Love	1957	3.75	7.50	15.00
194	Wedding Ring/I Still Belong to You	1957	3.00	6.00	12.00
204	My Mother's Eyes/I Had a Dream	1957	3.00	6.00	12.00
219	Drifting and Dreaming/Tip Toe Through the Tulips	1958	3.00	6.00	12.00
250	All Alone/The Things I Didn't Say	1958	3.00	6.00	12.00
281	I Found Out/My Unbreakable Heart	1959	3.00	6.00	12.00
612	Valley of Love/The Loneliest Boy in Town	1964	2.50	5.00	10.00
MGM					
12947	Gonna Find Me a Bluebird/Choir Girl	1960	3.00	6.00	12.00
Albums					
KAPP					
KL-1076 [M]	Rainbow	1957	20.00	40.00	80.00

HAMILTON, JOE FRANK & DENNISON

See HAMILTON, JOE FRANK & REYNOLDS.

HAMILTON, JOE FRANK & REYNOLDS

Also includes "Hamilton, Joe Frank & Dennison." Also see THE T-BONES.

Number	Title (A Side/B Side)	Yr	VG	VG+	NM
45s					
ABC DUNHILL					
4276	Don't Pull Your Love/Funk-In-Wagnall	1971	—	3.00	6.00
4287	Annabelle/Goin' Down	1971	—	2.50	5.00
4296	Daisy Mae/It Takes the Best	1971	—	2.50	5.00
4305	Don't Refuse My Love/One Good Woman	1972	—	2.50	5.00
PLAYBOY					
5801	Now That I've Got You/Get On the Bus	1977	—	2.00	4.00
—As "Hamilton, Joe Frank & Dennison"					
6024	Fallin' in Love/So Good at Lovin' You	1975	—	2.50	5.00
6054	Winners and Losers/Barroom Blues	1975	—	2.00	4.00
6068	Everyday Without You/Badman	1976	—	2.00	4.00
6077	Light Up the World with Sunshine/Houdini	1976	—	2.00	4.00
—As "Hamilton, Joe Frank & Dennison"					
6077 [PS]	Light Up the World with Sunshine/Houdini	1976	—	2.50	5.00
—As "Hamilton, Joe Frank & Dennison"					
6088	Don't Fight the Hands (That Need You)/Get On the Bus	1976	—	2.00	4.00
—As "Hamilton, Joe Frank & Dennison"					
6088 [PS]	Don't Fight the Hands (That Need You)/Get On the Bus	1976	—	2.50	5.00
—As "Hamilton, Joe Frank & Dennison"					
Albums					
ABC DUNHILL					
DS-50103	Hamilton, Joe Frank & Reynolds	1971	2.50	5.00	10.00
DSX-50113	Hallway Symphony	1972	2.50	5.00	10.00
PLAYBOY					
PB-407	Fallin' in Love	1975	2.50	5.00	10.00
PZ 34741	Fallin' in Love	1977	2.00	4.00	8.00
—Reissue of 107					

HAMILTON STREETCAR

Number	Title (A Side/B Side)	Yr	VG	VG+	NM
45s					
DOT					
17253	Silver Wings/I See I Am	1969	3.00	6.00	12.00
17279	Brother Speed/Wasn't It You	1969	3.00	6.00	12.00
17306	Honey and Wine/Now I Taste the Tears	1969	3.00	6.00	12.00
LHI					
1206	Confusion/Your Own Come Down	1968	3.75	7.50	15.00
17016	Invisible People/Flash	1967	3.75	7.50	15.00
Albums					
DOT					
DLP-25939	Hamilton Streetcar	1969	6.25	12.50	25.00

HAMLISCH, MARVIN

Number	Title (A Side/B Side)	Yr	VG	VG+	NM
45s					
ARISTA					
0392	Theme from "Ice Castles"/Touch	1979	—	2.00	4.00
A&M					
1775	All I Needed Was the Laughter/If You Hadn't Left Me Crying	1975	—	2.00	4.00
MCA					
40174	The Entertainer/Solace	1974	—	2.50	5.00
40307	Maple Leaf Rag/Mexican Dreams	1974	—	2.00	4.00
52175	The Entertainer/Heliotrope Bouquet	1983	—	2.00	4.00
—B-side by Lalo Schifrin					
PLANET					
45922 [DJ]	Theme from "Ordinary People" (same on both sides)	1980	—	2.00	4.00
UNITED ARTISTS					
XW1082	Bond '77 — James Bond Theme (Part 1)/Bond '77 — James Bond Theme (Part 2)	1977	—	2.00	4.00
50798	Bananas/'Cause I Believe in Loving	1971	—	2.50	5.00
Albums					
MCA					
390	The Sting	1973	2.50	5.00	10.00
2115	The Entertainer	1974	2.50	5.00	10.00
37091	The Sting	198?	2.00	4.00	8.00
—Budget-line reissue					

HAMMER

Number	Title (A Side/B Side)	Yr	VG	VG+	NM
Albums					
SAN FRANCISCO					
SD 203	Hammer	1970	5.00	10.00	20.00

HAMMILL, PETER

Also see VAN DER GRAAF GENERATOR.

Number	Title (A Side/B Side)	Yr	VG	VG+	NM
Albums					
CHARISMA					
CAS-1037	Fool's Mate	1972	3.75	7.50	15.00
CH-1-2202	The Future Now	1978	3.00	6.00	12.00
CH-1-2205	PH 7	1979	3.00	6.00	12.00
ENIGMA					
ST-73206	Skin	1986	2.50	5.00	10.00
ST-73246	And Close As This	1987	2.50	5.00	10.00
PVC					
8902	Sitting Targets	1981	3.00	6.00	12.00

HAMMOND, ALBERT

Number	Title (A Side/B Side)	Yr	VG	VG+	NM
45s					
COLUMBIA					
02470	Memories/I Want You Back with Me	1981	—	2.00	4.00
03412	Before You Change the World/Somewhere in America	1982	—	2.00	4.00
60510	When I'm Gone/World of Love	1981	—	2.00	4.00
EPIC					
50277	Moonlight Lady/Cry Baby	1976	—	2.00	4.00
MUMS					
6009	Down by the River/The Last One to Know	1972	—	2.00	4.00
6011	It Never Rains in Southern California/Anyone Here in the Audience	1972	—	2.50	5.00
—Bizarrely, the stock copy is in rechanneled stereo					
6015	If You Gotta Break Another Heart/That Old American Dream	1973	—	2.00	4.00
6018	The Free Electric Band/You Taught Me to Sing the Blues	1973	—	2.00	4.00
6021	The Peacemaker/Who's for Lunch Today	1973	—	2.00	4.00
6024	Half a Million Miles from Home/I Think I'll Go That Way	1973	—	2.00	4.00
6026	I'm a Train/Brand New Day	1974	—	2.00	4.00
6030	Air Disaster/Candlelight, Sweet Candlelight	1974	—	2.00	4.00
6032	Fountain Avenue/Names, Tags, Numbers, Labels	1974	—	2.00	4.00
6037	99 Miles from L.A./Rivers Are for Boats	1975	—	2.00	4.00
Albums					
COLUMBIA					
JC 36964	Your World and My World	1981	2.50	5.00	10.00
FC 38181	Somewhere in America	1982	2.50	5.00	10.00
EPIC					
JE 35049	When I Need You	1977	2.50	5.00	10.00
MUMS					
KZ 31905	It Never Rains in Southern California	1972	2.50	5.00	10.00
KZ 32267	The Free Electric Band	1973	2.50	5.00	10.00

Number	Title (A Side/B Side)	Yr	VG	VG+	NM
KZ 32834	Albert Hammond	1974	2.50	5.00	10.00

HAMMOND, JOHN

Number	Title (A Side/B Side)	Yr	VG	VG+	NM
45s					
ATLANTIC					
2696	I'm Tore Down/Shake for Me	1969	2.00	4.00	8.00
COLUMBIA					
45372	As the Years Go Passing By/Mellow Down Easy	1971	—	3.00	6.00
RED BIRD					
10-047	I Wish You Would/I Can Tell	1966	5.00	10.00	20.00
Albums					
ATLANTIC					
8152 [M]	I Can Tell	1967	7.50	15.00	30.00
SD 8152 [S]	I Can Tell	1967	7.50	15.00	30.00
SD 8206	Sooner or Later	1968	3.75	7.50	15.00
SD 8251	Southern Fried	1969	3.75	7.50	15.00
CAPRICORN					
CP 0153	Can't Beat the Kid	1975	3.00	6.00	12.00
COLUMBIA					
C 30458	Source Point	1971	3.00	6.00	12.00
KC 31318	I'm Satisfied	1972	3.00	6.00	12.00
FLYING FISH					
FF-502	Nobody But You	1988	2.50	5.00	10.00
ROUNDER					
3042	Mileage	1980	2.50	5.00	10.00
3060	Frogs for Snakes	1982	2.50	5.00	10.00
3074	John Hammond Live	1984	2.50	5.00	10.00
VANGUARD					
VSD 11/12 [(2)]	The Best of John Hammond	1970	3.75	7.50	15.00
VSD-2148 [S]	John Hammond	1964	10.00	20.00	40.00
VRS-9132 [M]	John Hammond	1964	7.50	15.00	30.00
VRS-9153 [M]	Big City Blues	1964	7.50	15.00	30.00
VRS-9178 [M]	So Many Roads	1965	7.50	15.00	30.00
VRS-9198 [M]	Country Blues	1966	7.50	15.00	30.00
VRS-9245 [M]	Mirrors	1967	7.50	15.00	30.00
VSD-79153 [S]	Big City Blues	1964	10.00	20.00	40.00
VSD-79178 [S]	So Many Roads	1965	10.00	20.00	40.00
VSD-79198 [S]	Country Blues	1966	10.00	20.00	40.00
VSD-79245 [S]	Mirrors	1967	7.50	15.00	30.00
VSD-79380	Solo	1976	2.50	5.00	10.00
VSD-79400	Footwork	1978	2.50	5.00	10.00
VSD-79424	Hot Tracks	1979	2.50	5.00	10.00

HAMMOND, JOHNNY

Originally recorded as Johnny "Hammond" Smith; those records are included below.

Number	Title (A Side/B Side)	Yr	VG	VG+	NM
45s					
KUDU					
900	It's Too Late/Workin' on a Groovy Thing	1971	—	3.00	6.00
—Originally recorded as Johnny "Hammond" Smith.					
907	Rock Steady (Part 1)/Rock Steady (Part 2)	1972	—	3.00	6.00
914	Thunder and Lightning (Part 1)/Thunder and Lightning (Part 2)	1973	—	3.00	6.00
MILESTONE					
302	Los Conquistadores Chocolates/Shifting Gears	1975	—	2.50	5.00
NEW JAZZ					
45-501	Sweet Cookies/Secret Love	196?	2.50	5.00	10.00
45-502	All Soul/The Masquerade Is Over	196?	2.50	5.00	10.00
45-509	I'll Remember April/That Good Feeling	196?	2.50	5.00	10.00
PRESTIGE					
193	End of a Love Affair/Sticks An' Stones	196?	2.50	5.00	10.00
209	Swanee River (Part 1)/Swanee River (Part 2)	196?	2.50	5.00	10.00
386	Brother John/Cleopatra and the African Knight	196?	2.00	4.00	8.00
407	Sad Eyes/Opus de Funk	196?	2.00	4.00	8.00
422	Golden Thrush/Stormy Monday Blues	196?	2.00	4.00	8.00
449	Ebb Tide/Stand By Me	196?	2.00	4.00	8.00
455	N.Y.P.D./Dirty Apple	196?	2.00	4.00	8.00
725	Soul Talk (Part 1)/Soul Talk (Part 2)	1970	—	3.00	6.00
748	I'll Be Yours/Smokin' Kool	197?	—	3.00	6.00
Albums					
KUDU					
01	Breakout	1971	3.00	6.00	12.00
04	Wild Horses/Rock Steady	1972	3.00	6.00	12.00
10	The Prophet	1973	3.00	6.00	12.00
16	Higher Ground	1974	3.00	6.00	12.00
MILESTONE					
9062	Gears	1975	3.75	7.50	15.00
9068	Forever Taurus	1976	3.75	7.50	15.00
9076	Storm Warning	1977	3.75	7.50	15.00
9083	Don't Let the System Get You	1978	3.75	7.50	15.00
NEW JAZZ					
NJLP-8221 [M]	All Soul	1959	12.50	25.00	50.00
—Purple label					
NJLP-8221 [M]	All Soul	1965	6.25	12.50	25.00
—Blue label with trident logo					
NJLP-8229 [M]	That Good Feelin'	1959	12.50	25.00	50.00
—Purple label					
NJLP-8229 [M]	That Good Feelin'	1965	6.25	12.50	25.00
—Blue label with trident logo					
NJLP-8241 [M]	Talk That Talk	1960	12.50	25.00	50.00
—Purple label					
NJLP-8241 [M]	Talk That Talk	1965	6.25	12.50	25.00
—Blue label with trident logo					
NJLP-8288 [M]	Look Out!	1962	12.50	25.00	50.00
—Purple label					
NJLP-8288 [M]	Look Out!	1965	6.25	12.50	25.00
—Blue label with trident logo					
PRESTIGE					
PRLP-7203 [M]	Stimulation	1961	10.00	20.00	40.00
—Yellow label					
PRLP-7203 [M]	Stimulation	1965	6.25	12.50	25.00
—Blue label with trident logo					
PRLP-7217 [M]	Gettin' the Message	1961	10.00	20.00	40.00
—Yellow label					
PRLP-7217 [M]	Gettin' the Message	1965	6.25	12.50	25.00
—Blue label with trident logo					
PRLP-7408 [M]	The Stinger	1965	5.00	10.00	20.00
PRST-7408 [S]	The Stinger	1965	6.25	12.50	25.00
PRLP-7420 [M]	Opus de Funk	1966	5.00	10.00	20.00
PRST-7420 [S]	Opus de Funk	1966	6.25	12.50	25.00
PRLP-7464 [M]	The Stinger Meets the Golden Thrush	1966	5.00	10.00	20.00
PRST-7464 [S]	The Stinger Meets the Golden Thrush	1966	6.25	12.50	25.00
PRLP-7482 [M]	Love Potion #9	1967	6.25	12.50	25.00
PRST-7482 [S]	Love Potion #9	1967	5.00	10.00	20.00
PRLP-7494 [M]	Ebb Tide	1967	6.25	12.50	25.00
PRST-7494 [S]	Ebb Tide	1967	5.00	10.00	20.00
PRST-7549	Soul Flowers	1968	5.00	10.00	20.00
PRST-7564	Dirty Grape	1968	5.00	10.00	20.00
PRST-7588	Nasty	1968	5.00	10.00	20.00
PRST-7681	Soul Talk	1969	5.00	10.00	20.00
PRST-7705	The Best of Johnny "Hammond" Smith	1969	3.75	7.50	15.00
PRST-7736	Black Feeling	1969	3.75	7.50	15.00
PRST-7777	Best for Lovers	1970	3.75	7.50	15.00
PRST-7786	Stimulation	1970	3.75	7.50	15.00
PRST-7846	Good 'Nuff	1970	3.75	7.50	15.00
10002	Here It 'Tis	1971	3.75	7.50	15.00
10015	What's Going On	1971	3.75	7.50	15.00
RIVERSIDE					
RLP-442 [M]	Black Coffee	1963	6.25	12.50	25.00
RLP-466 [M]	Mr. Wonderful	1963	6.25	12.50	25.00
RLP-482 [M]	Open House!	1965	5.00	10.00	20.00
RLP-496 [M]	A Little Taste	1965	5.00	10.00	20.00
RS-9442 [S]	Black Coffee	1963	7.50	15.00	30.00
RS-9466 [S]	Mr. Wonderful	1963	7.50	15.00	30.00
RS-9482 [S]	Open House!	1965	6.25	12.50	25.00
RS-9496 [S]	A Little Taste	1965	6.25	12.50	25.00
SALVATION					
702	A Gambler's Life	1974	3.00	6.00	12.00

HAMMOND-HAZLEWOOD

Also see ALBERT HAMMOND.

Number	Title (A Side/B Side)	Yr	VG	VG+	NM
45s					
CAPITOL					
2616	Wendy, Wendy/Broken Hearts Brigade	1969	2.50	5.00	10.00

HAMPTON, JOHN

Number	Title (A Side/B Side)	Yr	VG	VG+	NM
45s					
UNITED					
210	Honey Hush/Shadow Blues	1958	30.00	60.00	120.00

HANCOCK, HERBIE

Also see HEADHUNTERS.

Number	Title (A Side/B Side)	Yr	VG	VG+	NM
12-Inch Singles					
COLUMBIA					
AS 751 [DJ]	Go For It (6:58)/Go For It (7:32)	1980	2.00	4.00	8.00
AS 814 [DJ]	Saturday Night/Making Love	1980	2.00	4.00	8.00
AS 1251 [DJ]	Everybody's Broke (3:53)/Everybody's Broke (7:05)	1981	2.00	4.00	8.00
AS 1262 [DJ]	Magic Number/Everybody's Broke	1981	2.00	4.00	8.00
AS 1333 [DJ]	Magic Number (Remix)/Magic Number (Edit)	1981	2.00	4.00	8.00
AS 1413 [DJ]	Lite Me Up (long)/Lite Me Up (short)	1982	2.00	4.00	8.00
AS 1504 [DJ]	Gettin' to the Good Part/The Fun Tracks	1982	2.00	4.00	8.00
03978	Rockit (2 versions)	1983	2.50	5.00	10.00
04200	Autodrive/Chameleon	1983	—	3.00	6.00
04637	Metal Beat (extended)/Metal Beat (edit)	1984	—	3.00	6.00
04960	Mega-Mix (same on both sides)	1984	2.00	4.00	8.00
05027	Hardrock (long)/Hardrock (short)	1984	—	3.00	6.00
07804	Vibe Alive (extended) (edit) (bonus beats)	1988	—	3.00	6.00
07896	Beat Wise (4 versions)	1988	—	3.00	6.00
10906	Ready or Not (6:43)/You Bet Your Love (8:12)	1979	2.00	4.00	8.00
11019	Tell Everybody (7:48)/Honey from the Jar (5:36)	1979	2.00	4.00	8.00
11310	Stars in Your Eyes/Go For It	1980	2.00	4.00	8.00
45s					
BLUE NOTE					
1862	Watermelon Man/Three Bags Full	1962	2.00	4.00	8.00
1863	Driftin'/Alone Am I	1962	2.00	4.00	8.00
1887	Blind Man (Part 1)/Blind Man (Part 2)	196?	2.00	4.00	8.00
COLUMBIA					
02404	Everybody's Broke/Help Yourself	1981	—	2.00	4.00
02615	Magic Number/Help Yourself	1981	—	2.00	4.00
02824	Lite Me Up/Satisfied with Love	1982	—	2.00	4.00
03004	Gettin' to the Good Part/The Fun Tracks	1982	—	2.00	4.00
03318	Paradise/The Fun Tracks	1982	—	2.00	4.00
04054	Rockit (2 versions)	1983	—	2.50	5.00
04054	Rockit (2 versions)	1984	—	2.00	4.00
—Gold-label "Instant Classic" early reissue					
04268	Autodrive/Chameleon	1983	—	2.00	4.00
04473	Mega-Mix/TFS	1984	—	2.00	4.00
04565	Hardrock (2 versions)	1984	—	2.00	4.00
04565 [PS]	Hardrock (2 versions)	1984	—	2.00	4.00
04633	Metal Beat/Karabali	1984	—	2.00	4.00
07718	Vibe Alive/P. Bop	1988	—	—	3.00
07718 [PS]	Vibe Alive/P. Bop	1988	—	—	3.00
07987	Beat Wise/Chemical Residue	1988	—	—	3.00
10050	Palm Grease/Butterfly	1974	—	2.50	5.00
10094	Spank-a-Lee/Actual Proof	1975	—	2.50	5.00
10239	Suntouch/Hang Up Your Hang-Ups	1975	—	2.50	5.00
10408	Doin' It/People Music	1976	—	2.50	5.00
10563	Maiden Voyage/Spider	1977	—	2.50	5.00
10781	I Thought It Was You/No Means Yes	1978	—	2.50	5.00
10835	Sunlight/Come Running to Me	1978	—	2.50	5.00
10894	Knee Deep/You Get Your Love`	1979	—	2.50	5.00
10936	Ready Or Not/Trust Me	1979	—	2.50	5.00
11021	Tell Everybody/Honey from the Jar	1979	—	2.50	5.00
11122	Doin' It/Honey from the Jar	1979	—	2.00	4.00

Number	Title (A Side/B Side)	Yr	VG	VG+	NM
11227	Go For It/Trust Me	1980	—	—	—
—Canceled?					
11236	Stars in Your Eyes/Go For It	1980	—	2.00	4.00
11323	Making Love/It All Comes Around	1980	—	2.00	4.00
46002	Chameleon/Vein Melter	1974	—	2.50	5.00
46073	Watermelon Man/Sly	1974	—	2.50	5.00
WARNER BROS.					
7358	Fat Mama/Wiggle-Waggle	1969	—	3.00	6.00
7598	Water Torture/Crossings	1972	—	3.00	6.00
Albums					
BLUE NOTE					
BN-LA152-F	Succotash	1974	3.00	6.00	12.00
BN-LA399-H2 [(2)]	Herbie Hancock	1975	3.75	7.50	15.00
BLP-4109 [M]	Takin' Off	1962	12.50	25.00	50.00
BLP-4126 [M]	My Point of View	1963	8.75	17.50	35.00
BLP-4147 [M]	Inventions and Dimensions	1963	8.75	17.50	35.00
BLP-4175 [M]	Empyrean Isles	1964	8.75	17.50	35.00
BLP-4195 [M]	Maiden Voyage	1965	8.75	17.50	35.00
B1-46339	Maiden Voyage	1997	5.00	10.00	20.00
—Audiophile reissue					
B1-91142	The Best of Herbie Hancock	1988	2.50	5.00	10.00
BST-	Speak Like a Child	1968	3.75	7.50	15.00
BST-	The Prisoner	1969	3.75	7.50	15.00
BST-	The Best of Herbie Hancock	1971	3.75	7.50	15.00
BST-	Empyrean Isles	1985	2.50	5.00	10.00
—"The Finest in Jazz Since 1939" reissue					
BST-	Speak Like a Child	1986	2.50	5.00	10.00
—"The Finest in Jazz Since 1939" reissue					
BST-	Inventions and Dimensions	1987	2.50	5.00	10.00
—"The Finest in Jazz Since 1939" reissue					
BST-	My Point of View	1987	2.50	5.00	10.00
—"The Finest in Jazz Since 1939" reissue					
BST-	The Prisoner	1987	2.50	5.00	10.00
—"The Finest in Jazz Since 1939" reissue					
BST-	Takin' Off	1987	2.50	5.00	10.00
—"The Finest in Jazz Since 1939" reissue					
BST- [S]	Takin' Off	1962	10.00	20.00	40.00
—With New York, USA address on label					
BST- [S]	My Point of View	1963	8.75	17.50	35.00
—With New York, USA address on label					
BST- [S]	Inventions and Dimensions	1963	8.75	17.50	35.00
—With New York, USA address on label					
BST- [S]	Empyrean Isles	1964	8.75	17.50	35.00
—With New York, USA address on label					
BST- [S]	Maiden Voyage	1965	8.75	17.50	35.00
—With New York, USA address on label					
BST- [S]	Takin' Off	1967	3.75	7.50	15.00
—With "A Division of Liberty Records" on label					
BST- [S]	My Point of View	1967	3.75	7.50	15.00
—With "A Division of Liberty Records" on label					
BST- [S]	Inventions and Dimensions	1967	3.75	7.50	15.00
—With "A Division of Liberty Records" on label					
BST- [S]	Empyrean Isles	1967	3.75	7.50	15.00
—With "A Division of Liberty Records" on label					
BST- [S]	Maiden Voyage	1967	3.75	7.50	15.00
—With "A Division of Liberty Records" on label					
BST- [S]	Maiden Voyage	1985	2.50	5.00	10.00
—"The Finest in Jazz Since 1939" reissue					
COLUMBIA					
KC 32212	Sextant	1973	3.00	6.00	12.00
PC 32212	Sextant	198?	2.00	4.00	8.00
—Budget-line reissue					
CQ 32371 [Q]	Head Hunters	1973	6.25	12.50	25.00
KC 32371	Head Hunters	1973	3.00	6.00	12.00
PC 32371	Head Hunters	197?	2.00	4.00	8.00
—Reissue (with or without bar code)					
PC 32965	Thrust	1974	3.00	6.00	12.00
—No bar code on cover					
PC 32965	Thrust	198?	2.00	4.00	8.00
—Budget-line reissue with bar code					
PCQ 32965 [Q]	Thrust	1974	6.25	12.50	25.00
PC 33812	Man-Child	1975	3.00	6.00	12.00
—No bar code on cover					
PC 33812	Man-Child	198?	2.00	4.00	8.00
—Budget-line reissue with bar code					
PC 34280	Secrets	1976	3.00	6.00	12.00
—No bar code on cover					
PC 34280	Secrets	198?	2.00	4.00	8.00
—Budget-line reissue with bar code					
PCQ 34280 [Q]	Secrets	1976	6.25	12.50	25.00
PG 34688 [(2)]	V.S.O.P.	1977	3.75	7.50	15.00
JC 34907	Sunlight	1978	3.00	6.00	12.00
C2 34976 [(2)]	V.S.O.P. Quintet	1978	3.75	7.50	15.00
JC 35764	Feets Don't Fail Me Now	1979	3.00	6.00	12.00
PC 35764	Feets Don't Fail Me Now	198?	2.00	4.00	8.00
—Budget-line reissue					
JC 36309	The Best of Herbie Hancock	1979	3.00	6.00	12.00
JC 36415	Monster	1980	2.50	5.00	10.00
PC 36415	Monster	198?	2.00	4.00	8.00
—Budget-line reissue					
JC 36578	Mr. Hands	1980	2.50	5.00	10.00
PC 36578	Mr. Hands	198?	2.00	4.00	8.00
—Budget-line reissue					
FC 37387	Magic Windows	1981	2.50	5.00	10.00
PC 37387	Magic Windows	198?	2.00	4.00	8.00
—Budget-line reissue					
FC 37928	Lite Me Up	1982	2.50	5.00	10.00
PC 37928	Lite Me Up	198?	2.00	4.00	8.00
—Budget-line reissue					
FC 38814	Future Shock	1983	2.50	5.00	10.00
FC 39478	Sound-System	1984	2.50	5.00	10.00
PC 39478	Sound-System	1985	2.00	4.00	8.00
—Budget-line reissue					
FC 39870	Village Life	1985	2.50	5.00	10.00
8C8 39913 [EP]	Hardrock	1984	3.00	6.00	12.00
—Picture disc					
FC 40025	Perfect Machine	1988	2.50	5.00	10.00
SC 40464	'Round Midnight	1986	2.50	5.00	10.00
MGM					
E-4447 [M]	Blow-Up	1967	8.75	17.50	35.00
SE-4447 [S]	Blow-Up	1967	10.00	20.00	40.00
—Also includes one track by the Yardbirds					
PAUSA					
9002	Succotash	198?	2.50	5.00	10.00
TRIP					
UPF-194	Traces	197?	3.00	6.00	12.00
WARNER BROS.					
WS 1834	Fat Albert Rotunda	1970	3.75	7.50	15.00
WS 1898	Mwandishi	1971	3.75	7.50	15.00
BS 2617	Crossings	1972	3.75	7.50	15.00
2WS 2807 [(2)]	Treasure Chest	1974	3.75	7.50	15.00

HANCOCK, HERBIE, AND CHICK COREA

Also see each artist's individual listings.

Number	Title (A Side/B Side)	Yr	VG	VG+	NM
Albums					
COLUMBIA					
PC2 35663 [(2)]	An Evening with Herbie Hancock and Chick Corea	1979	3.00	6.00	12.00
POLYDOR					
PD-2-6238 [(2)]	An Evening with Chick Corea and Herbie Hancock	1979	3.00	6.00	12.00

HANDS OF TIME, THE

Number	Title (A Side/B Side)	Yr	VG	VG+	NM
45s					
SIDEWALK					
903	Got to Get You Into My Life/Midnight Rider	1966	7.50	15.00	30.00

HANDY, JOHN

Number	Title (A Side/B Side)	Yr	VG	VG+	NM
45s					
ABC IMPULSE!					
31005	Hard Work/Young Enough to Dream	1976	—	2.00	4.00
31012	Make Her Mine/Watch Your Money Go	1977	—	2.00	4.00
COLUMBIA					
43706	If Only We Knew/Spanish Lady	1966	2.00	4.00	8.00
Albums					
ABC IMPULSE!					
AS-9314	Hard Work	1976	2.50	5.00	10.00
AS-9324	Carnival	1977	2.50	5.00	10.00
COLUMBIA					
CL 2462 [M]	Recorded Live at the Monterey Jazz Festival	1966	3.75	7.50	15.00
CL 2567 [M]	The Second John Handy Album	1966	3.75	7.50	15.00
CL 2697 [M]	New View	1967	3.75	7.50	15.00
CS 9262 [S]	Recorded Live at the Monterey Jazz Festival	1966	3.75	7.50	15.00
CS 9367 [S]	The Second John Handy Album	1966	3.75	7.50	15.00
CS 9497 [S]	New View	1967	3.00	6.00	12.00
CS 9689	Projections	1968	3.00	6.00	12.00
MILESTONE					
M-9173	Centerpiece, With Class	1989	3.00	6.00	12.00
ROULETTE					
R 52042 [M]	In the Ver-nac'-u-lar	1960	5.00	10.00	20.00
SR 52042 [S]	In the Ver-nac'-u-lar	1960	6.25	12.50	25.00
R 52088 [M]	No Coast Jazz	1962	5.00	10.00	20.00
SR 52088 [S]	No Coast Jazz	1962	6.25	12.50	25.00
R 52121 [M]	John Handy Jazz	1964	3.75	7.50	15.00
SR 52121 [S]	John Handy Jazz	1964	5.00	10.00	20.00
R 52124 [M]	Quote, Unquote	1964	3.75	7.50	15.00
SR 52124 [S]	Quote, Unquote	1964	5.00	10.00	20.00
WARNER BROS.					
BSK 3170	Where Go the Boats	1978	2.50	5.00	10.00
BSK 3242	Handy Dandy Man	1978	2.50	5.00	10.00

HANEY, JACK, AND NIKITER ARMSTRONG

Number	Title (A Side/B Side)	Yr	VG	VG+	NM
45s					
MEL-O-DY					
107	The Interview/Peaceful	1963	5.00	10.00	20.00

HANGMEN, THE

Number	Title (A Side/B Side)	Yr	VG	VG+	NM
45s					
MONUMENT					
910	What a Girl Can't Do/The Girl Who Faded Away	1965	5.00	10.00	20.00
951	Faces/Bad Goodbye	1966	5.00	10.00	20.00
Albums					
MONUMENT					
MLP-8077 [M]	Bitter Sweet	1967	7.50	15.00	30.00
SLP-18077 [S]	Bitter Sweet	1967	10.00	20.00	40.00

HANK AND CAROLEE

Number	Title (A Side/B Side)	Yr	VG	VG+	NM
45s					
MALA					
424	Go On and Go/I've Never Known	1960	10.00	20.00	40.00

HANNAN, JIMMY

Number	Title (A Side/B Side)	Yr	VG	VG+	NM
45s					
ATLANTIC					
2247	Beach Ball/You Gotta Have Love	1964	37.50	75.00	150.00
—Backing Hannan on this record are THE BEE GEES, three years before their first American release!					

HANS CHRISTIAN

With Jon Anderson, pre-YES.

Number	Title (A Side/B Side)	Yr	VG	VG+	NM
45s					
TOWER					
409	Never My Love/All of the Time	1968	25.00	50.00	100.00

HANSON

45s

MANTICORE

Number	Title (A Side/B Side)	Yr	VG	VG+	NM
2001	Love Knows Everything/(B-side unknown)	1973	—	3.00	6.00
2004	Boy Meets Girl/Modern Day Religion	1973	—	3.00	6.00

Albums

MANTICORE

Number	Title (A Side/B Side)	Yr	VG	VG+	NM
MC 66670	Now Hear This	1973	3.00	6.00	12.00
MC 66672	Magic Dragon	1974	2.50	5.00	10.00

HANSSON, BO

Albums

CHARISMA

Number	Title (A Side/B Side)	Yr	VG	VG+	NM
CAS-1059	Lord of the Rings	1973	3.00	6.00	12.00
FC 6062	Magician's Hat	1974	3.00	6.00	12.00

SIRE

Number	Title (A Side/B Side)	Yr	VG	VG+	NM
SR 6044	Music Inspired by Watership Down	1977	2.50	5.00	10.00
SASD-7525	Attic Thoughts	1976	2.50	5.00	10.00

HAPPENINGS, THE

Also see BOB MIRANDA; THE TOKENS.

45s

BIG TREE

Number	Title (A Side/B Side)	Yr	VG	VG+	NM
146	Strawberry Morning/Workin' My Way Back to You	1972	—	2.00	4.00
153	Me Without You/God Bless Joanna	1972	—	2.00	4.00

B.T. PUPPY

Number	Title (A Side/B Side)	Yr	VG	VG+	NM
181 [DJ]	Have Yourself a Merry Little Christmas (same on both sides)	1966	7.50	15.00	30.00

—Stock copies do not exist

Number	Title (A Side/B Side)	Yr	VG	VG+	NM
517	Girls on the Go/Go-Go	1966	2.50	5.00	10.00
520	See You in September/He Thinks He's a Hero	1966	2.50	5.00	10.00
522	Go Away Little Girl/Tea Time	1966	2.00	4.00	8.00
523	Goodnight My Love/Lillies By Money	1966	2.00	4.00	8.00
527	I Got Rhythm/You're in a Bad Way	1967	2.00	4.00	8.00
530	My Mammy/I Believe in Nothing	1967	2.00	4.00	8.00
530 [PS]	My Mammy/I Believe in Nothing	1967	3.75	7.50	15.00
532	Why Do Fools Fall in Love/When the Summer Is Through	1967	2.00	4.00	8.00
532 [PS]	Why Do Fools Fall in Love/When the Summer Is Through	1967	3.75	7.50	15.00
538	Music, Music, Music/When I Lock My Door	1968	2.00	4.00	8.00
538 [PS]	Music, Music, Music/When I Lock My Door	1968	3.75	7.50	15.00
540	Randy/Love Song of Mommy and Daddy	1968	2.00	4.00	8.00
542	Sealed with a Kiss/Anyway	1968	2.00	4.00	8.00
543	Breaking Up Is Hard to Do/Anyway	1968	2.00	4.00	8.00
545	Crazy Rhythm/Love Song of Mommy and Daddy	1968	2.00	4.00	8.00
549	That's All I Want from You/He Thinks He's a Hero	1968	2.00	4.00	8.00

JUBILEE

Number	Title (A Side/B Side)	Yr	VG	VG+	NM
5666	Where Do I Go and Be In/New Day Comin'	1969	—	3.00	6.00
5677	El Paso County Jail/Won't Anybody Listen	1969	—	3.00	6.00
5686	Answer Me, My Love/I Need a Woman	1970	—	3.00	6.00
5698	Tomorrow, Today Will Be Yesterday/Chain of Hands	1970	—	3.00	6.00
5702	Crazy Love/Chain of Hands	1970	—	3.00	6.00
5703	Condition Red/Sweet September	1970	2.50	5.00	10.00

—As "The Honor Society"

Number	Title (A Side/B Side)	Yr	VG	VG+	NM
5712	Lullaby in the Rain/I Wish You Could Know Me (Naomi)	1971	—	3.00	6.00
5721 [DJ]	Make Your Own Kind of Music (mono/stereo)	1971	—	3.00	6.00

—Stock copies may not exist

MIDLAND INT'L.

Number	Title (A Side/B Side)	Yr	VG	VG+	NM
MB-10897	That's Why I Love You/Beyond the Hurt	1977	—	2.00	4.00
MB-11127	Let Me Stay/Someone Special	1977	—	2.00	4.00

PHILCO-FORD

Number	Title (A Side/B Side)	Yr	VG	VG+	NM
HP-7	Go Away Little Girl/See You in September	1967	5.00	10.00	20.00

—4-inch plastic "Hip Pocket Record" with color sleeve

Albums

B.T. PUPPY

Number	Title (A Side/B Side)	Yr	VG	VG+	NM
BT-1001 [M]	The Happenings (Bye-Bye, So Long, Farewell...See You in September)	1966	6.25	12.50	25.00
BTS-1001 [S]	The Happenings (Bye-Bye, So Long, Farewell...See You in September)	1966	7.50	15.00	30.00
BT-1003 [M]	Psycle	1967	6.25	12.50	25.00
BTS-1003 [S]	Psycle	1967	7.50	15.00	30.00
BTS-1004	The Happenings Golden Hits!	1968	10.00	20.00	40.00

JUBILEE

Number	Title (A Side/B Side)	Yr	VG	VG+	NM
JGS-8028	Piece of Mind	1969	6.25	12.50	25.00
JGS-8030	The Happenings' Greatest Hits	1969	6.25	12.50	25.00

HAPPY OTTO

See CRAZY OTTO.

HAPSHASH AND THE COLOURED COAT

Albums

IMPERIAL

Number	Title (A Side/B Side)	Yr	VG	VG+	NM
LP-9377 [M]	Hapshash and the Coloured Coat	1968	12.50	25.00	50.00
LP-12377 [S]	Hapshash and the Coloured Coat	1968	10.00	20.00	40.00
LP-12430	Western Flyer	1969	10.00	20.00	40.00

HARBOR LIGHTS, THE

Early JAY AND THE AMERICANS.

45s

JARO

Number	Title (A Side/B Side)	Yr	VG	VG+	NM
77020	Is That Too Much to Ask/What Would I Do Without You	1960	10.00	20.00	40.00

MALA

Number	Title (A Side/B Side)	Yr	VG	VG+	NM
422	Angel of Love/Tick-a-Tick-a-Tock	1960	12.50	25.00	50.00

HARBOUR LITES, THE

45s

FONTANA

Number	Title (A Side/B Side)	Yr	VG	VG+	NM
1544	Run for Your Life/Lonely Journey	1966	2.50	5.00	10.00

HARD, RANDY

45s

NRC

Number	Title (A Side/B Side)	Yr	VG	VG+	NM
013	Honey Doll/May It Be My Fortune	1959	15.00	30.00	60.00
044	Let Her Go/Make Me a Dreamer	1959	12.50	25.00	50.00

HARD MEAT

Albums

WARNER BROS.

Number	Title (A Side/B Side)	Yr	VG	VG+	NM
WS 1852	Hard Meat	1969	3.75	7.50	15.00
WS 1879	Through a Window	1970	3.75	7.50	15.00

HARD TIMES, THE

45s

WORLD PACIFIC

Number	Title (A Side/B Side)	Yr	VG	VG+	NM
77816	There'll Be a Time/You're Bound to Cry	1966	2.50	5.00	10.00
77826	Come To Your Window/That's All I'll Do	1966	2.50	5.00	10.00
77851	Fortune Teller/Good-By	1966	2.50	5.00	10.00
77873	Blew Mind/Colours	1967	2.50	5.00	10.00

Albums

WORLD PACIFIC

Number	Title (A Side/B Side)	Yr	VG	VG+	NM
WP-1867 [M]	Blew Mind	1968	6.25	12.50	25.00
WPS-21867 [S]	Blew Mind	1968	7.50	15.00	30.00

HARDEN TRIO, THE

45s

COLUMBIA

Number	Title (A Side/B Side)	Yr	VG	VG+	NM
43229	Poor Boy/Let It Be Me	1965	2.00	4.00	8.00
43463	Tippy Toeing/Don't Remind Me	1965	2.00	4.00	8.00
43710	Little Boy Walk Like a Man/Dear Brother	1966	—	3.00	6.00
43844	Seven Days of Crying (Makes One Weak)/Husbands and Wives	1966	—	3.00	6.00
44059	Sneaking 'Cross the Border/Childhood Place	1967	—	3.00	6.00
44249	Forbidden/Manana (Is Soon Enough for Me)	1967	—	3.00	6.00
44420	He Looks a Lot Like You/My Friend Mr. Echo	1968	—	2.50	5.00
44552	Everybody Wants to Be Somebody Else/Diddle Diddle Dumplin'	1968	—	2.50	5.00

Albums

COLUMBIA

Number	Title (A Side/B Side)	Yr	VG	VG+	NM
CL 2506 [M]	Tippy Toeing	1966	5.00	10.00	20.00
CS 9306 [S]	Tippy Toeing	1966	6.25	12.50	25.00

HARDIN, TIM

45s

COLUMBIA

Number	Title (A Side/B Side)	Yr	VG	VG+	NM
44879	Once-Touched by Flame/A Question of Birth	1969	—	3.00	6.00
44920	Simple Song of Freedom/A Question of Birth	1969	—	3.00	6.00
45426	Bird on the Wire/Soft Summer Breeze	1971	—	2.50	5.00
45695	Do the Do/Sweet Lady	1972	—	2.50	5.00

VERVE FOLKWAYS

Number	Title (A Side/B Side)	Yr	VG	VG+	NM
5008	Hang On to a Dream/It'll Never Happen Again	1966	2.50	5.00	10.00
5017	Misty Roses/Don't Make Promises	1966	2.50	5.00	10.00
5031	If I Were a Carpenter/Hang On to a Dream	1966	2.50	5.00	10.00
5042	Green Rocky Road/Never Too Far	1967	2.00	4.00	8.00
5048	Black Sheep Boy/Misty Roses	1967	2.00	4.00	8.00

VERVE FORECAST

Number	Title (A Side/B Side)	Yr	VG	VG+	NM
5059	Tribute to Hank Williams/You Upset the Grace of Living When You Die	1967	—	3.00	6.00
5097	Reason to Believe/Smugglin' Man	1968	—	3.00	6.00
5116	Reason to Believe/Smugglin' Man	1971	—	2.50	5.00

Albums

ANTILLES

Number	Title (A Side/B Side)	Yr	VG	VG+	NM
7023	Nine	1974	3.75	7.50	15.00

ATCO

Number	Title (A Side/B Side)	Yr	VG	VG+	NM
33-210 [M]	This Is Tim Hardin	1967	6.25	12.50	25.00
SD 33-210 [S]	This Is Tim Hardin	1967	5.00	10.00	20.00

COLUMBIA

Number	Title (A Side/B Side)	Yr	VG	VG+	NM
CS 9787	Suite for Susan Moore and Damion — We Are — One, One, All in One	1969	6.25	12.50	25.00

—"360 Sound" label

Number	Title (A Side/B Side)	Yr	VG	VG+	NM
C 30551	Bird on a Wire	1971	5.00	10.00	20.00
KC 31764	Painted Head	1972	5.00	10.00	20.00
PC 37164	The Shock of Grace	1981	3.00	6.00	12.00

MGM

Number	Title (A Side/B Side)	Yr	VG	VG+	NM
GAS-104	Tim Hardin (Golden Archive Series)	1970	5.00	10.00	20.00
M3G-4952	Archetypes	1974	3.75	7.50	15.00

POLYDOR

Number	Title (A Side/B Side)	Yr	VG	VG+	NM
PD-1-6333	Memorial Album	1981	3.00	6.00	12.00

VERVE FOLKWAYS

Number	Title (A Side/B Side)	Yr	VG	VG+	NM
FT-3004 [M]	Tim Hardin/1	1966	6.25	12.50	25.00
FTS-3004 [S]	Tim Hardin/1	1966	7.50	15.00	30.00

VERVE FORECAST

Number	Title (A Side/B Side)	Yr	VG	VG+	NM
FT-3004 [M]	Tim Hardin/1	1967	3.75	7.50	15.00
FTS-3004 [S]	Tim Hardin/1	1967	5.00	10.00	20.00
FTS-3022	Tim Hardin/2	1967	6.25	12.50	25.00
FTS-3049	Tim Hardin/3 — Live in Concert	1968	6.25	12.50	25.00
FTS-3064	Tim Hardin/4	1969	6.25	12.50	25.00
FTS-3078	The Best of Tim Hardin	1970	5.00	10.00	20.00

HARDLY WORTHIT PLAYERS, THE
See SENATOR BOBBY.

HARDWATER
45s
CAPITOL

Number	Title (A Side/B Side)	Yr	VG	VG+	NM
2230	Not So Hard/City Sidewalks	1968	3.00	6.00	12.00

Albums
CAPITOL

Number	Title (A Side/B Side)	Yr	VG	VG+	NM
ST-2954	Hardwater	1968	10.00	20.00	40.00

HARDY, FRANCOISE
45s
4 CORNERS OF THE WORLD

Number	Title (A Side/B Side)	Yr	VG	VG+	NM
103	Catch a Falling Star/Find Me a Boy	196?	2.50	5.00	10.00
123	How Ever Much/Only You Can Do It	196?	2.50	5.00	10.00
125	All Over the World/Another Place	196?	2.50	5.00	10.00
132	The Love of a Boy/Just Call and I'll Be There	196?	2.50	5.00	10.00

REPRISE

Number	Title (A Side/B Side)	Yr	VG	VG+	NM
0808	Loving You/Hang On to a Dream	1969	2.00	4.00	8.00

Albums
4 CORNERS OF THE WORLD

Number	Title (A Side/B Side)	Yr	VG	VG+	NM
FCL-4208 [M]	The "Yeh Yeh" Girl from Paris!	196?	5.00	10.00	20.00
FCS-4208 [S]	The "Yeh Yeh" Girl from Paris!	196?	6.25	12.50	25.00
FCL-4219 [M]	Maid in Paris	196?	5.00	10.00	20.00
FCS-4219 [S]	Maid in Paris	196?	6.25	12.50	25.00
FCL-4231 [M]	Francoise...	196?	5.00	10.00	20.00
FCS-4231 [S]	Francoise...	196?	6.25	12.50	25.00
FCL-4238 [M]	Je Vous Aime	196?	5.00	10.00	20.00
FCS-4238 [S]	Je Vous Aime	196?	6.25	12.50	25.00

REPRISE

Number	Title (A Side/B Side)	Yr	VG	VG+	NM
RS 6290	Francoise Hardy	1968	6.25	12.50	25.00
RS 6318	Loving	1969	5.00	10.00	20.00
RS 6345	Mon Amour, Adieu	1969	5.00	10.00	20.00

HARDY, HAGOOD
45s
CAPITOL

Number	Title (A Side/B Side)	Yr	VG	VG+	NM
4156	The Homecoming/The Queen	1975	—	2.00	4.00
4292	The Missouri Breaks/Afternoon in Venice	1976	—	2.00	4.00

HERITAGE

Number	Title (A Side/B Side)	Yr	VG	VG+	NM
833	I'll Take Love/Just a Little Lovin'	1971	—	2.50	5.00

Albums
CAPITOL

Number	Title (A Side/B Side)	Yr	VG	VG+	NM
ST-11488	The Homecoming	1975	2.50	5.00	10.00
ST-11552	Maybe Tomorrow	1976	2.50	5.00	10.00
SN-16300	The Homecoming	198?	2.00	4.00	8.00
—Budget-line reissue					

HARDY BOYS, THE
45s
RCA VICTOR

Number	Title (A Side/B Side)	Yr	VG	VG+	NM
47-9795	Wheels/Sha-La-La	1969	2.00	4.00	8.00
47-9831	Good, Good Lovin'/Love Train	1970	2.00	4.00	8.00
74-0228	Love and Let Love/Sink or Swim	1969	2.00	4.00	8.00

Albums
RCA VICTOR

Number	Title (A Side/B Side)	Yr	VG	VG+	NM
LSP-4217	Here Come the Hardy Boys	1969	5.00	10.00	20.00
LSP-4315	Wheels	1970	5.00	10.00	20.00

HARGETT, JOHNNIE
45s
CHERRY

Number	Title (A Side/B Side)	Yr	VG	VG+	NM
1016	Rock This Town Tonight/God's Gift to Men	1960	25.00	50.00	100.00

HARGRAVE, RON
45s
CUB

Number	Title (A Side/B Side)	Yr	VG	VG+	NM
9025	Drive-In Movie/Buttercup	1959	3.00	6.00	12.00

MGM

Number	Title (A Side/B Side)	Yr	VG	VG+	NM
12344	A Fool Am I/Too Late	1956	5.00	10.00	20.00
12422	Latch On/Only a Daydream	1957	10.00	20.00	40.00
12475	Hold Me/Song of the Moonlight	1957	5.00	10.00	20.00
12571	If You Should Go/Heartbreaker	1957	5.00	10.00	20.00
12644	Young Romance/Should Have Been Home in Bed	1958	5.00	10.00	20.00

HARLAN, BILLY
45s
BRUNSWICK

Number	Title (A Side/B Side)	Yr	VG	VG+	NM
55066	I Wanna Bop/School House Rock	1958	50.00	100.00	200.00

HARMONAIRES, THE
45s
HOLIDAY

Number	Title (A Side/B Side)	Yr	VG	VG+	NM
2602	Come Back/Lorraine	1957	75.00	150.00	300.00
—Black label					
2602	Come Back/Lorraine	1960	15.00	30.00	60.00
—Red label, double horizontal lines					
2602	Come Back/Lorraine	196?	6.25	12.50	25.00
—Red label, single horizontal line					

HARMONICA FRANK
45s
SUN

Number	Title (A Side/B Side)	Yr	VG	VG+	NM
205	Rockin' Chair Daddy/The Great Musical Menagerist	1954	1500.	3000.	4500.

HARMONY GRITS, THE
Members of the original DRIFTERS formed this group after their firing.
45s
END

Number	Title (A Side/B Side)	Yr	VG	VG+	NM
1051	Am I to Be the One/I Could Have Told You	1959	6.25	12.50	25.00
1063	Gee/I Could Have Told You	1959	6.25	12.50	25.00
1063	Gee/Santa Claus Is Coming to Town	1959	10.00	20.00	40.00

HARNELL, JOE
45s
COLUMBIA

Number	Title (A Side/B Side)	Yr	VG	VG+	NM
43549	Autumn Leaves/Near You	1966	—	2.50	5.00
43756	Our Concerto/Meeskeit	1966	—	2.50	5.00
43756 [DJ]	Our Concerto (same on both sides)	1966	3.75	7.50	15.00
—Promo only on red vinyl					
43902	Nature Boy/Bermuda Concerto	1966	—	2.50	5.00
44148	Un Poco Rio/Sunrise Serenade	1967	—	2.50	5.00
44244	Guantanamera/Seranata	1967	—	2.50	5.00
44365	Blame It on the Bossa Nova/So Soon	1967	—	2.50	5.00
44407	Theme to Candice/Spanish Eyes	1967	—	2.50	5.00
44571	The Mighty Quinn/Simon Says	1968	—	2.50	5.00
44670	Sky Hawk/Work Sunny Work	1968	—	2.50	5.00

EPIC

Number	Title (A Side/B Side)	Yr	VG	VG+	NM
9304	The Way of Love/You Are the Song	1959	2.50	5.00	10.00
9328	What Is This Thing Called Love/My Little Grass Shack in Kealakekua, Hawaii	1959	2.50	5.00	10.00
9406	Time on My Hands/Without a Song	1960	2.00	4.00	8.00

KAPP

Number	Title (A Side/B Side)	Yr	VG	VG+	NM
497	Fly Me to the Moon Bossa Nova/Harlem Nocturne	1962	2.00	4.00	8.00
521	Diane/Walking Song	1963	—	3.00	6.00
528	Our Day Will Come/My One and Only Love	1963	—	3.00	6.00
541	Hud/Come Away with Me	1963	—	3.00	6.00
562	Dawn of Love/Who Am I Kiddin'	1963	—	3.00	6.00
579	You're Nobody Till Somebody Loves You/When the World Was Young	1964	—	3.00	6.00
604	Sonata Portuguese/I'll Set My Love to Music	1964	—	3.00	6.00
633	St. Thomas/Ill Wind	1964	—	3.00	6.00

MCA

Number	Title (A Side/B Side)	Yr	VG	VG+	NM
40953	Theme from "The Incredible Hulk"/Love Theme from "The Incredible Hulk"	1978	—	2.50	5.00

MOTOWN

Number	Title (A Side/B Side)	Yr	VG	VG+	NM
1154	Midnight Cowboy/Green Grow the Lilacs	1969	—	3.00	6.00
1161	My Cherie Amour/Green Grow the Lilacs	1970	—	3.00	6.00

Albums
CAPITOL

Number	Title (A Side/B Side)	Yr	VG	VG+	NM
ST-11657	Harnell	1977	3.00	6.00	12.00

COLUMBIA

Number	Title (A Side/B Side)	Yr	VG	VG+	NM
CL 2466 [M]	Golden Piano Hits	1966	3.00	6.00	12.00
CL 2699 [M]	Bossa Now	1967	3.75	7.50	15.00
CS 9266 [S]	Golden Piano Hits	1966	3.75	7.50	15.00
CS 9499 [S]	Bossa Now	1967	3.00	6.00	12.00

EPIC

Number	Title (A Side/B Side)	Yr	VG	VG+	NM
BN 573 [S]	I Want to Be Happy	1960	5.00	10.00	20.00
LN (# unknown) [M]	I Want to Be Happy	1960	3.75	7.50	15.00

JUBILEE

Number	Title (A Side/B Side)	Yr	VG	VG+	NM
JLP-1015 [M]	Piano Inventions of Jo Harnell	1956	12.50	25.00	50.00
JGM-5020 [M]	Joe Harnell and His Trio	1963	3.75	7.50	15.00
—Reissue of 1015					

KAPP

Number	Title (A Side/B Side)	Yr	VG	VG+	NM
KL 1318 [M]	Fly Me to the Moon and the Bossa Nova Pops	1962	3.75	7.50	15.00
KL 1325 [M]	More Joe Harnell, More Bossa Nova Pops	1963	3.75	7.50	15.00
KL 1339 [M]	Joe Harnell	1963	3.75	7.50	15.00
KL 1416 [M]	The Rhythm and the Fire	1965	3.00	6.00	12.00
KL 1480 [M]	The Best of Joe Harnell	1966	3.00	6.00	12.00
KS 3318 [S]	Fly Me to the Moon and the Bossa Nova Pops	1962	5.00	10.00	20.00
KS 3325 [S]	More Joe Harnell, More Bossa Nova Pops	1963	5.00	10.00	20.00
KS 3339 [S]	Joe Harnell	1963	5.00	10.00	20.00
KS 3416 [S]	The Rhythm and the Fire	1965	3.75	7.50	15.00
KS 3480 [S]	The Best of Joe Harnell	1966	3.75	7.50	15.00

MOTOWN

Number	Title (A Side/B Side)	Yr	VG	VG+	NM
MS-698	Moving On!!	1969	10.00	20.00	40.00

HAROLD AND THE CASUALS
45s
SCOTTY

Number	Title (A Side/B Side)	Yr	VG	VG+	NM
628	Darling Do You Love Me/You Can Shake a Tail Feather	1959	75.00	150.00	300.00

HARPER, CHUCK
As "Chuck Fassert," he recorded with THE REGENTS.
45s
FELSTED

Number	Title (A Side/B Side)	Yr	VG	VG+	NM
8658	Summer Is Thru/Call on Me	1962	7.50	15.00	30.00

HARPER, ROY
45s
EPIC

Number	Title (A Side/B Side)	Yr	VG	VG+	NM
10268	Midspring Dithering/Zengfm	1967	3.75	7.50	15.00

Albums
CHRYSALIS

Number	Title (A Side/B Side)	Yr	VG	VG+	NM
PRO-620 [DJ]	Introduction to Roy Harper	1976	7.50	15.00	30.00
CHR 1105	When An Old Cricketer Leaves the Crease	1976	3.75	7.50	15.00
CHR 1139	One of Those Days in England	1977	3.75	7.50	15.00
CHR 1160	Flat Baroque and Berserk	1978	3.00	6.00	12.00
—Reissue of Harvest LP					
CHR 1161	Stormcock	1978	3.00	6.00	12.00
—Released in the UK in 1971					
CHR 1162	Lifemask	1978	3.00	6.00	12.00
—Released in the UK in 1973					
CHR 1163	Valentine	1978	3.00	6.00	12.00
—Released in the UK in 1974					

Number	Title (A Side/B Side)	Yr	VG	VG+	NM
CH2 1164 [(2)]	Flashes from the Archives of Oblivion	1978	3.75	7.50	15.00
—Released in the UK in 1974					
HARVEST					
SKAO-418	Flat Baroque and Berserk	1970	5.00	10.00	20.00
PVC					
8937	Whatever Happened to Jugula	198?	3.00	6.00	12.00
WORLD PACIFIC					
WPS-21888	Folkjokeopus	1969	6.25	12.50	25.00

HARPERS BIZARRE

45s

Number	Title (A Side/B Side)	Yr	VG	VG+	NM
WARNER BROS.					
5890	The 59th Street Bridge Song (Feelin' Groovy)/ Lost My Love Today	1967	2.50	5.00	10.00
7028	Come to the Sunshine/Debutante's Ball	1967	2.00	4.00	8.00
7063	Anything Goes/Malibu U.	1967	2.00	4.00	8.00
7090	Chattanooga Choo Choo/Hey, You in the Crowd	1967	2.00	4.00	8.00
7106	The 59th Street Bridge Song (Feelin' Groovy)/ Come to the Sunshine	1968	—	3.00	6.00
—"Back to Back Hits" series -- originals have green labels with "W7" logo					
7123	Anything Goes/Chattanooga Choo Choo	1969	—	3.00	6.00
—"Back to Back Hits" series -- originals have green labels with "W7" logo					
7172	Virginia City/Cotton Candy Sandman	1968	—	3.00	6.00
7200	Both Sides Now/Small Talk	1968	—	3.00	6.00
7223	Battle of New Orleans/Green Apple Tree	1968	—	3.00	6.00
7238	I Love You, Alice B. Toklas/Look to the Rainbow	1968	—	3.00	6.00
7296	Knock on Wood/Witchi-Tai-Yo	1969	—	2.50	5.00
7377	Poly High/Soft Soundin' Music	1970	—	2.50	5.00
7388	Anything Goes/Virginia City	1970	—	2.50	5.00
7399	If We Ever Needed the Lord Before/Mad	1970	—	2.50	5.00
7647	Knock on Wood/Poly High	1972	—	2.00	4.00

Albums

Number	Title (A Side/B Side)	Yr	VG	VG+	NM
FOREST BAY					
7545	As Time Goes By	1976	3.75	7.50	15.00
WARNER BROS.					
W 1693 [M]	Feelin' Groovy	1967	6.25	12.50	25.00
WS 1693 [S]	Feelin' Groovy	1967	5.00	10.00	20.00
—Gold label					
WS 1693 [S]	Feelin' Groovy	1968	3.75	7.50	15.00
—Green "W7" label					
WS 1716	Anything Goes	1967	5.00	10.00	20.00
WS 1739	The Secret Life of Harpers Bizarre	1968	5.00	10.00	20.00
WS 1784	Harpers Bizarre Four	1969	5.00	10.00	20.00
ST-91351	Anything Goes	1968	6.25	12.50	25.00
—Capitol Record Club edition					

HARPO, SLIM

45s

Number	Title (A Side/B Side)	Yr	VG	VG+	NM
EXCELLO					
2113	I'm a King Bee/I Got Love If You Want It	1957	15.00	30.00	60.00
2138	Wonderin' and Worryin'/Strange Love	1958	7.50	15.00	30.00
2162	One More Day/You'll Be Sorry One Day	1959	7.50	15.00	30.00
2171	Buzz Me Babe/Late Last Night	1960	7.50	15.00	30.00
2184	Blues Hangover/What a Dream	1960	7.50	15.00	30.00
2194	Rainin' in My Heart/Don't Start Cryin' Now	1961	5.00	10.00	20.00
2239	Buzzin'/I Love the Life I'm Livin'	1963	3.75	7.50	15.00
2246	Little Queen Bee (Got a Brand New King)/I Need Money (Keep Your Alibis)	1964	3.00	6.00	12.00
2253	Still Rainin' in My Heart/We're Two of a Kind	1964	3.00	6.00	12.00
2261	Sittin' Here Wondering/What's Goin' On Baby	1964	3.00	6.00	12.00
2265	Please Don't Turn Me Down/Harpo's Blues	1965	3.00	6.00	12.00
2273	Baby Scratch My Back/I'm Gonna Miss You (LIke the Devil)	1965	3.00	6.00	12.00
2276	Goin' Away Blues/Just a Lonely Stranger	1966	2.50	5.00	10.00
2278	Midnight Blues/Shake Your Hips	1966	2.50	5.00	10.00
2282	I'm Your Bread-Maker, Baby/Loving You (The Way I Do)	1966	2.50	5.00	10.00
2285	Tip On In (Part 1)/Tip On In (Part 2)	1967	2.50	5.00	10.00
2289	I'm Gonna Keep What I've Got/I've Got to Be with You Tonight	1967	2.50	5.00	10.00
2294	Te-Ni-Lee-Ni-Nu/Mailbox Bues	1968	2.50	5.00	10.00
2301	Mohair Sam/I Just Can't Leave You	1969	2.00	4.00	8.00
2305	Just for You/That's Why I Love You	1969	2.00	4.00	8.00
2306	Folsom Prison Blues/Mututal Friend	1969	2.00	4.00	8.00
2309	I've Got My Finger on Your Trigger/The Price Is Too High	1969	2.00	4.00	8.00
2316	Rainin' in My Heart/Jody Man	1970	2.00	4.00	8.00

Albums

Number	Title (A Side/B Side)	Yr	VG	VG+	NM
EXCELLO					
LP-8003 [M]	Raining in My Heart	1961	62.50	125.00	250.00
—Orange and blue label					
LPS-8003 [M]	Raining in My Heart	196?	25.00	50.00	100.00
—All-blue label					
LP-8005 [M]	Baby Scratch My Back	1966	50.00	100.00	200.00
—Orange and blue label					
LPS-8005 [M]	Baby Scratch My Back	196?	25.00	50.00	100.00
—All-blue label					
LPS-8008 [M]	Tip On In	1968	12.50	25.00	50.00
LPS-8010 [M]	The Best of Slim Harpo	1969	12.50	25.00	50.00
LPS-8013 [M]	Slim Harpo Knew the Blues	1970	12.50	25.00	50.00
RHINO					
RNLP-106	The Best of Slim Harpo	198?	3.75	7.50	15.00
R1-70169	Scratch My Back: The Best of Slim Harpo	1989	3.00	6.00	12.00

HARPS, THE

See THE CAMELOTS.

HARPTONES, THE

45s

Number	Title (A Side/B Side)	Yr	VG	VG+	NM
AMBIENT SOUND					
02807	Love Needs a Heart/It's You	1982	—	3.00	6.00
ANDREA					
100	What Is Your Decision/Gimme Some	1956	10.00	20.00	40.00
BRUCE					
101	A Sunday Kind of Love/I'll Never Tell	1953	1000.	2000.	3000.
—"Bruce" in script lettering					
101	A Sunday Kind of Love/I'll Never Tell	1953	20.00	40.00	80.00
—"Bruce" in block lettering					
102	My Memories of You/It Was Just for Laughs	1954	50.00	100.00	200.00
102	My Memories of You/The Laughs on You	1954	30.00	60.00	120.00
—Same B-side with different title (and missing the apostrophe)					
104	I Depended on You/Mambo Boogie	1954	20.00	40.00	80.00
109	Forever Mine/Why Should I Love You	1954	20.00	40.00	80.00
113	Since I Fell for You/Oobidee-Oobidee-Oo	1954	20.00	40.00	80.00
123	High Flying Baby/Loving a Girl Like You	1955	15.00	30.00	60.00
128	I Almost Lost My Mind/Oh Wee Baby	1955	15.00	30.00	60.00
COED					
540	Answer Me My Love/Rain Down Kisses	1960	5.00	10.00	20.00
COMPANION					
102	All in Your Mind/The Last Dance	1961	7.50	15.00	30.00
103	What Will I Tell My Heart/Foolish Me	1961	20.00	40.00	80.00
CUB					
9097	Devil in Velvet/Your Love Is a Good Love	1961	5.00	10.00	20.00
GEE					
1045	Cry Like I Cried/So Good, So Fine, You're Mine	1957	15.00	30.00	60.00
—Red label					
KT					
201	Sunset/I Gotta Have Your Love	1963	12.50	25.00	50.00
PARADISE					
101	Life Is But a Dream/You Know You're Doing Me Wrong	1954	37.50	75.00	150.00
—Maroon label					
101	Life Is But a Dream/You Know You're Doing Me Wrong	1954	15.00	30.00	60.00
—Purple label					
103	My Success/I've Got a Notion	1955	75.00	150.00	300.00
105	It All Depends on You/Guitar Shuffle	1955	37.50	75.00	150.00
—Maroon label					
105	It All Depends on You/Guitar Shuffle	1955	15.00	30.00	60.00
—Purple label					
RAMA					
203	Three Wishes/That's the Way It Goes	1956	20.00	40.00	80.00
214	The Masquerade Is Over/On Sunday Afternoon	1956	20.00	40.00	80.00
221	The Shrine of St. Cecelia/Oo Wee Baby	1957	20.00	40.00	80.00
RAVEN					
8001	A Sunday Kind of Love/Mambo Boogie	1962	3.75	7.50	15.00
TIP TOP					
401	My Memories of You/High Flyin' Baby	1956	10.00	20.00	40.00
WARWICK					
500	I Remember/Laughing on the Outside	1959	6.25	12.50	25.00
512	Love Me Completely/Hep Teenager	1959	6.25	12.50	25.00
551	No Greater Miracle/What Kind of a Fool	1960	6.25	12.50	25.00

7-Inch Extended Plays

Number	Title (A Side/B Side)	Yr	VG	VG+	NM
BRUCE					
BEP 201	A Sunday Kind of Love/Ou Wee Baby//Forever Mine/I Almost Lost My Mind	1954	2500.	3750.	5000.
BEP 201 [PS]	The Sensational Harptones	1954	2500.	3750.	5000.

Albums

Number	Title (A Side/B Side)	Yr	VG	VG+	NM
AMBIENT SOUND					
FZ 37718	Love Needs	1982	3.00	6.00	12.00
HARLEM HIT PARADE					
5006	The Harptones	197?	3.75	7.50	15.00
RELIC					
LP-5001	The Greatest Hits of the Harptones, Vol. 1	197?	3.00	6.00	12.00
LP-5003	The Greatest Hits of the Harptones, Vol. 2	197?	3.00	6.00	12.00

HARRIS, ANITA

45s

Number	Title (A Side/B Side)	Yr	VG	VG+	NM
BRUT					
1345	I Just Need a Lover/Music	197?	—	3.00	6.00
COLUMBIA					
44236	Just Loving You/Butterfly with Coloured Wings	1967	2.00	4.00	8.00
44438	Anniversary Waltz/Comes the Night	1968	2.00	4.00	8.00
LONDON					
9720	Lies/Don't Think About Love	1964	3.00	6.00	12.00
WARNER BROS.					
5638	Trains and Boats and Planes/Upside Down	1965	2.50	5.00	10.00

HARRIS, EDDIE

45s

Number	Title (A Side/B Side)	Yr	VG	VG+	NM
ATLANTIC					
2404	When a Man Loves a Woman/The Tender Storm	1967	2.00	4.00	8.00
2447	Sham Time (Part 1)/Sham Time (Part 2)	1967	2.00	4.00	8.00
2487	Listen Here/A Theme in Search of a Movie	1968	—	3.00	6.00
2561	Live Right Now/It's Crazy	1968	—	3.00	6.00
2607	1974 Blues/Free at Last	1969	—	3.00	6.00
2667	Movin' On Out/Funky Doo	1969	—	3.00	6.00
3216	Is It In/Funkaroma	1974	—	2.00	4.00
3245	I Don't Want Nobody/I Need Some Money	1975	—	2.00	4.00
3256	Get On Down/Time to Do Your Thing	1975	—	2.00	4.00
3288	Get Up and Dance/Why Must We Part	1975	—	2.00	4.00
3347	That Is Why You're Overweight/It's All Right Now	1976	—	2.00	4.00
5052	Love Theme from "The Sandpiper"/Cryin' Blues	1966	2.00	4.00	8.00
5072	Listen Here/Mean Greens	1968	—	3.00	6.00
5101	Foolish/Why Don't You Quit	1971	—	3.00	6.00
5105	Really/Live Right Now	1971	—	3.00	6.00
5106	Boogie Woogie Bossa Nova/Wait Please	1971	—	3.00	6.00
5112	Carry On Brother/Children's Song	1972	—	3.00	6.00
5115	Instant Death/Was	1972	—	3.00	6.00
5116	Two Minutes to Four/Please Let Me Go	1973	—	3.00	6.00
5117	Baby/I've Tried Everything	1973	—	3.00	6.00
5118	Drunk Man/Here Goes Funky	1973	—	3.00	6.00
5120	Is It In/Funkaroma	1974	—	3.00	6.00
COLUMBIA					
43075	Chicago Serenade/More Soul Than Soulful	1964	2.00	4.00	8.00

Number	Title (A Side/B Side)	Yr	VG	VG+	NM
43188	People/Groovy Movies	1964	2.00	4.00	8.00
VEE JAY					
378	Exodus/Alicia	1961	2.50	5.00	10.00
407	God Bless the Child/My Buddy	1961	2.00	4.00	8.00
410	Spartacus/Willow Weep for Me	1961	2.00	4.00	8.00
420	Moon River/Mr. Yunioshi	1962	2.00	4.00	8.00
447	Just Friends/Olifant Gesang	1962	2.00	4.00	8.00
464	Tonight/Be My Love	1962	2.00	4.00	8.00
496	Mima/Lolita Marie	1963	2.00	4.00	8.00
518	Theme from Lawrence of Arabia/Yea! Yea! Yea!	1963	2.00	4.00	8.00
543	Half and Half/K.C. Blues	1963	2.00	4.00	8.00
WARNER BROS.					
49890	Sharkey's Theme/Theme from "Sharkey's Machine"	1980	—	2.00	4.00
—B-side by Sarah Vaughan					
Albums					
ANGELACO					
AN 3002	Sounds Incredible	1980	3.00	6.00	12.00
ATLANTIC					
SD 2-311 [(2)]	Excursions	1973	3.75	7.50	15.00
1448 [M]	The In Sound	1966	3.00	6.00	12.00
SD 1448 [S]	The In Sound	1966	3.75	7.50	15.00
1453 [M]	Mean Greens	1966	3.00	6.00	12.00
SD 1453 [S]	Mean Greens	1966	3.75	7.50	15.00
1478 [M]	The Tender Storm	1967	3.75	7.50	15.00
SD 1478 [S]	The Tender Storm	1967	3.75	7.50	15.00
SD 1495	The Electrifying Eddie Harris	1968	3.75	7.50	15.00
SD 1506	Plug Me In	1968	3.75	7.50	15.00
SD 1517	Silver Cycles	1969	3.75	7.50	15.00
SD 1529	High Voltage	1969	3.75	7.50	15.00
1545 [M-DJ]	The Best of Eddie Harris	1970	6.25	12.50	25.00
—Promo-only white label mono pressing					
SD 1545	The Best of Eddie Harris	1970	3.75	7.50	15.00
SD 1554	Come On Down!	1970	3.75	7.50	15.00
SD 1573	Free Speech	1971	3.75	7.50	15.00
SD 1595	Eddie Harris Live at Newport	1971	3.00	6.00	12.00
SD 1611	Instant Death	1972	3.00	6.00	12.00
SD 1625	Eddie Harris Sings the Blues	1973	3.00	6.00	12.00
SD 1647	E.H. in the U.K.	1974	3.00	6.00	12.00
SD 1659	Is It In	1974	3.00	6.00	12.00
SD 1669	I Need Some Money	1975	3.00	6.00	12.00
SD 1675	Bad Luck Is All I Have	1975	3.00	6.00	12.00
SD 1683	Why You're Overweight	1976	3.00	6.00	12.00
SD 1698	How Can You Live Like That	1977	3.00	6.00	12.00
SD 8807	The Versatile Eddie Harris	1982	2.50	5.00	10.00
SW-94771	Instant Death	1972	3.75	7.50	15.00
—Capitol Record Club edition					
BUDDAH					
BDS 4004	Sculpture	1969	3.00	6.00	12.00
COLUMBIA					
CL 2168 [M]	Cool Sax, Warm Heart	1964	3.75	7.50	15.00
CL 2295 [M]	Cool Sax from Hollywood to Broadway	1965	3.75	7.50	15.00
CS 8968 [S]	Cool Sax, Warm Heart	1964	5.00	10.00	20.00
CS 9095 [S]	Cool Sax from Hollywood to Broadway	1965	5.00	10.00	20.00
CS 9681 [M]	Here Comes the Judge	1968	6.25	12.50	25.00
—Mono copies are promo only					
CS 9681 [S]	Here Comes the Judge	1968	3.75	7.50	15.00
EXODUS					
EX-6002 [M]	For Bird and Bags	1966	3.75	7.50	15.00
GNP CRESCENDO					
GNPS-2073 [(2)]	Black Sax	1973	3.75	7.50	15.00
JANUS					
3020	Smokin'	1970	3.00	6.00	12.00
MUTT & JEFF					
5018	The Real Electrifying Eddie Harris	1982	3.00	6.00	12.00
RCA VICTOR					
APL1-2942	I'm Tired	1978	2.50	5.00	10.00
AFL1-3402	Playin' With Myself	1980	2.50	5.00	10.00
STEEPLECHASE					
1151	Eddie Harris Steps Up	1981	2.50	5.00	10.00
SUNSET					
SUS-5234	The Explosive Eddie Harris	1969	3.00	6.00	12.00
TRADITION					
2067	Genius	1969	3.00	6.00	12.00
TRIP					
5005 [(2)]	Shades of Eddie Harris	1974	3.00	6.00	12.00
VEE JAY					
VJLP 1081 [M]	The Theme from Exodus and Other Film Spectaculars	1964	3.75	7.50	15.00
VJLPS 1081 [S]	The Theme from Exodus and Other Film Spectaculars	1964	5.00	10.00	20.00
LP 3016 [M]	Exodus to Jazz	1961	7.50	15.00	30.00
SR 3016 [S]	Exodus to Jazz	1961	10.00	20.00	40.00
VJS-3016	Exodus to Jazz	198?	2.50	5.00	10.00
—Reissue with thinner vinyl					
LP 3025 [M]	Mighty Like a Rose	1961	7.50	15.00	30.00
SR 3025 [S]	Mighty Like a Rose	1961	10.00	20.00	40.00
LP 3027 [M]	Jazz for "Breakfast at Tiffany's"	1961	7.50	15.00	30.00
SR 3027 [S]	Jazz for "Breakfast at Tiffany's"	1961	10.00	20.00	40.00
LP 3028 [M]	A Study in Jazz	1962	5.00	10.00	20.00
SR 3028 [S]	A Study in Jazz	1962	7.50	15.00	30.00
LP 3031 [M]	Eddie Harris Goes to the Movies	1962	5.00	10.00	20.00
SR 3031 [S]	Eddie Harris Goes to the Movies	1962	7.50	15.00	30.00
LP 3034 [M]	Bossa Nova	1963	5.00	10.00	20.00
SR 3034 [S]	Bossa Nova	1963	7.50	15.00	30.00
LP 3037 [M]	Half and Half	1963	6.25	12.50	25.00
SR 3037 [S]	Half and Half	1963	7.50	15.00	30.00
VJS-3058	For Bird and Bags	198?	2.50	5.00	10.00

HARRIS, EMMYLOU

45s

Number	Title (A Side/B Side)	Yr	VG	VG+	NM
ASYLUM					
64570	Thanks to You/Lovin' You Again	1993	—	—	3.00
64610	High Powered Love/Ballad of a Runaway Horse	1992	—	—	3.00
A&M					
2290	Wish We Were Back in Missouri/Riding with Jesse James	1980	—	2.00	4.00
—B-side by Charlie Daniels					
HUGHES					
53236	I Still Dream of You/Back in Baby's Arms	1988	—	—	3.00
JUBILEE					
5679	I'll Be Your Baby Tonight/I'll Never Fall in Love Again	1969	5.00	10.00	20.00
5697	Paddy/Fugue for the Ox	1970	5.00	10.00	20.00
LITTLE DARLIN'					
7922	Love Doesn't Care Whose House It Lives In/Who's Gonna Love Me Now	1979	—	2.00	4.00
—With Charlie Louvin					
RCA					
PB-13562	Wild Montana Skies/I Remember Romance	1983	—	2.00	4.00
—With John Denver					
REPRISE					
1326	Too Far Gone/Boulder to Birmingham	1975	—	2.50	5.00
1332	If I Could Only Win Your Love/Boulder to Birmingham	1975	—	2.50	5.00
1341	Light of the Stable/Bluebird Wine	1975	2.50	5.00	10.00
—A-side is a longer version than later releases					
1341 [PS]	Light of the Stable/Bluebird Wine	1975	3.00	6.00	12.00
1346	Together Again/Here, There and Everywhere	1976	—	2.50	5.00
1353	Till I Gain Control Again/One of These Days	1976	—	2.50	5.00
1371	Sweet Dreams/Amarillo	1976	—	2.50	5.00
1379	Light of the Stable/Boulder to Birmingham	1976	—	2.50	5.00
19281	Rollin' and Ramblin'/Sweet Dreams Of You	1991	—	—	3.00
19510	Wheels of Love/Better Off Without You	1991	—	—	3.00
19707	Never Be Anyone Else But You/Red, Red Rose	1990	—	—	3.00
19870	Gulf Coast Highway/Evangeline	1990	—	—	3.00
—A-side: With Willie Nelson					
22850	I Still Miss Someone/No Regrets	1989	—	—	3.00
22999	Heaven Only Knows/A River for Him	1989	—	—	3.00
27635	Heartbreak Hill/Icy Blue Heart	1989	—	—	3.00
WARNER BROS.					
PRO-S-2872 [DJ]	Light of the Stable/It Came Upon a Midnight Clear	1987	2.50	5.00	10.00
—B-side by Highway 101					
8388	Making Believe/I'll Be Your San Antone Rose	1977	—	2.50	5.00
8553	Two More Bottles of Wine/I Ain't Living Long Like This	1978	—	2.50	5.00
8623	Easy from Now On/You're Supposed to Be Feeling Good	1978	—	2.50	5.00
8732	Too Far Gone/Tulsa Queen	1979	—	2.00	4.00
8815	Save the Last Dance for Me/Even Cowgirls Get the Blues	1979	—	2.50	5.00
8830	Play Together Again Again/He Don't Deserve You Anymore	1979	—	2.00	4.00
—A-side: With Buck Owens; B-side by Buck Owens solo					
28302	Someday My Ship Will Sail/When He Calls	1987	—	—	3.00
28714	Today I Started Loving You Again/When I Was Young	1986	—	—	3.00
28770	I Had My Heart Set on You/Your Long Journey	1986	—	—	3.00
28852	Timberline/Sweet Chariot	1985	—	2.00	4.00
28952	Rhythm Guitar/Diamond in My Crown	1985	—	—	3.00
29041	White Line/Long Tall Sally Rose	1985	—	2.00	4.00
29138	Someone Like You/Light of the Stable	1984	—	2.00	4.00
29218	Pledging My Love/Baby, Better Start Turnin' 'Em Down	1984	—	2.00	4.00
29329	In My Dreams/Like an Old Fashioned World	1984	—	2.00	4.00
29443	Drivin' Wheel/Good News	1983	—	2.00	4.00
29583	So Sad (To Watch Good Love Go Bad)/Amarillo	1983	—	2.00	4.00
29729	I'm Movin' On/Maybe Tonight	1983	—	2.00	4.00
29898	(Lost His Love) On Our Last Date/Another Pot O' Tea	1982	—	2.00	4.00
29993	Born to Run/Colors of My Heart	1982	—	2.00	4.00
49056	Blue Kentucky Girl/Leaving Louisiana in the Broad Daylight	1979	—	2.00	4.00
49164	Beneath Still Waters/'Til I Gain Control Again	1980	—	2.00	4.00
49239	Wayfaring Stranger/Green Pastures	1980	—	2.00	4.00
49262	That Lovin' You Feeling Again/Lola	1980	—	2.50	5.00
—A-side: With Roy Orbison; B-side by Craig Hundley					
49551	The Boxer/Precious Love	1980	—	2.00	4.00
49633	Beautiful Star of Bethlehem/The Little Drummer Boy	1980	—	2.00	4.00
49645	Light of the Stable/The Little Drummer Boy	1980	—	2.00	4.00
49684	Mister Sandman/Fools' Thin Air	1981	—	2.00	4.00
49739	I Don't Have to Crawl/Colors of Your Heart	1981	—	2.00	4.00
49809	If I Needed You/Ashes By Now	1981	—	2.00	4.00
—With Don Williams					
49892	Tennessee Rose/Mama Help	1982	—	2.00	4.00
Albums					
JUBILEE					
JGS-8031	Gliding Bird	1969	30.00	60.00	120.00
—Originals have color covers; counterfeit covers are black and white					
MOBILE FIDELITY					
1-015	Quarter Moon in a Ten Cent Town	1979	10.00	20.00	40.00
—Audiophile vinyl					
REPRISE					
MS 2213	Pieces of the Sky	1975	2.50	5.00	10.00
MS 2236	Elite Hotel	1976	2.50	5.00	10.00
MSK 2284	Pieces of the Sky	1977	2.00	4.00	8.00
—Reissue of 2213					
MSK 2286	Elite Hotel	1977	2.00	4.00	8.00
—Reissue of 2236					
25776	Bluebird	1989	2.50	5.00	10.00
WARNER BROS.					
BSK 3115	Luxury Liner	1977	2.50	5.00	10.00
BSK 3141	Quarter Moon in a Ten Cent Town	1978	2.50	5.00	10.00
BSK 3258	Profile/Best of Emmylou Harris	1978	2.50	5.00	10.00
BSK 3318	Blue Kentucky Girl	1979	2.50	5.00	10.00
BSK 3422	Roses in the Snow	1980	2.50	5.00	10.00

Number	Title (A Side/B Side)	Yr	VG	VG+	NM
BSK 3484	Light of the Stable: The Christmas Album	1980	2.50	5.00	10.00
BSK 3508	Evangeline	1981	2.50	5.00	10.00
BSK 3603	Cimarron	1981	2.50	5.00	10.00
23740	Last Date	1982	2.50	5.00	10.00
23961	White Shoes	1983	2.50	5.00	10.00
25161	Profile II — The Best of Emmylou Harris	1984	2.50	5.00	10.00
25205	The Ballad of Sally Rose	1985	2.50	5.00	10.00
25352	Thirteen	1986	2.50	5.00	10.00
25585	Angel Band	1987	2.50	5.00	10.00

HARRIS, GENEE

45s

ABC-PARAMOUNT

Number	Title (A Side/B Side)	Yr	VG	VG+	NM
9900	Bye Bye Elvis/You're Like a Jumping Jack	1958	12.50	25.00	50.00

HARRIS, GEORGIA, AND THE LYRICS

45s

HY-TONE

Number	Title (A Side/B Side)	Yr	VG	VG+	NM
111	Let's Exchange Hearts for Christmas/It's Time to Rock	1958	125.00	250.00	500.00
117	Let's Exchange Hearts for Christmas/Kiss, Kiss, Kiss	1958	125.00	250.00	500.00

HARRIS, JET, AND TONY MEECHAN

Also see THE SHADOWS.

45s

LONDON

Number	Title (A Side/B Side)	Yr	VG	VG+	NM
9589	Diamonds/Footstep	1963	3.75	7.50	15.00
9608	Scarlet O'Hara/(Doin' the) Hully Gully	1963	3.75	7.50	15.00
9622	Applejack/Tall Texan	1963	3.75	7.50	15.00

HARRIS, KURT

45s

Number	Title (A Side/B Side)	Yr	VG	VG+	NM
DIAMOND					
158	Go On/Emperor of My Baby's Heart	1964	20.00	40.00	80.00
JOSIE					
898	Let Her Dance/I Can't Love Nobody Else	1962	5.00	10.00	20.00
902	Uh-Uh/You Better Shut Your Mouth	1962	5.00	10.00	20.00

HARRIS, MAJOR

12-Inch Singles

POP ART

Number	Title (A Side/B Side)	Yr	VG	VG+	NM
1401	All My Life/(B-side unknown)	1983	—	3.00	6.00

45s

Number	Title (A Side/B Side)	Yr	VG	VG+	NM
ATLANTIC					
3217	Each Morning I Wake Up/Just a Thing I Do	1974	—	2.50	5.00
3248	Love Won't Let Me Wait/After Loving You	1975	—	2.00	4.00
3299 [DJ]	Loving You Is Mellow (mono/stereo)	1975	—	2.50	5.00
—May be promo-only					
3303	I Got Over Love/Loving You Is Mellow	1975	—	2.00	4.00
3321	Jealousy/Tynisa (What's Your Hurry)	1976	—	2.00	4.00
3336	It's Got to Be Magic/Just a Thing That I Do	1976	—	2.00	4.00
OKEH					
7314	Just Love Me/Loving You More	1968	7.50	15.00	30.00
7327	Like a Rolling Stone/Call Me Tomorrow	1969	15.00	30.00	60.00
WMOT					
02091	Here We Are/Living's Easy Now	1981	—	2.00	4.00
4002	Laid Back Love/This Is What You Mean to Me	1976	—	2.00	4.00

Albums

Number	Title (A Side/B Side)	Yr	VG	VG+	NM
ATLANTIC					
SD 18119	My Way	1974	3.75	7.50	15.00
SD 18160	Jealousy	1976	3.75	7.50	15.00
RCA VICTOR					
APL1-2803	How Do You Take Your Love	1978	3.00	6.00	12.00
WMOT					
627	Mellow Major	1977	3.00	6.00	12.00
PW 37067	The Best of Major Harris, Now and Then	1981	2.50	5.00	10.00

HARRIS, PEPPERMINT

45s

Number	Title (A Side/B Side)	Yr	VG	VG+	NM
ALADDIN					
3097	I Got Loaded/It's You, Yes It's You	1951	25.00	50.00	100.00
—Black vinyl					
3097	I Got Loaded/It's You, Yes It's You	1951	62.50	125.00	250.00
—Green vinyl					
3107	Have Another Drink and Talk to Me/Middle of Winter	1951	20.00	40.00	80.00
3108	Let the Back Door Hit You/P.H. Blues	1951	20.00	40.00	80.00
3130	Right Back On It/Maggie's Boogie	1952	20.00	40.00	80.00
3141	I Cry for My Baby/There's a Dead Cat on the Line	1952	20.00	40.00	80.00
3154	I Sure Do Miss My Baby/Hey Little Schoolgirl	1952	20.00	40.00	80.00
3177	Wasted Love/Goodbye Blues	1953	20.00	40.00	80.00
3183	Don't Leave Me Alone/Wet Rat	1953	20.00	40.00	80.00
3206	I Never Get Enough of You/Three Sheets in the Wind	1953	20.00	40.00	80.00
CASH					
1003	Cadillac Funeral/Treat Me Like I Treat You	1954	37.50	75.00	150.00
COMBO					
114	Love at First Sight/I Don't Care	1956	15.00	30.00	60.00
DART					
103	You Get Me Wondering/Messing Around with the Blues	1959	6.25	12.50	25.00
DUKE					
319	Ain't No Business/Angel Child	1960	6.25	12.50	25.00
JEWEL					
742	Marking Time/Bad, Mad Woman	1965	2.50	5.00	10.00
747	Ma Ma/Anything You Can Do	1965	2.50	5.00	10.00
762	Raining in My Heart/My Time After Awhile	1966	2.50	5.00	10.00
772	Anytime Is the Right Time/Wait Until It Happens to You	1966	2.50	5.00	10.00
789	Bad Bad Whiskey/Lonesome As Can Be	1967	2.50	5.00	10.00
795	24 Hours/Little Girl	1968	2.50	5.00	10.00
MODERN					
936	Bye Bye, Fare Thee Well/Black Cat Bone	1951	25.00	50.00	100.00
SITTIN' IN WITH					
543	Raining in My Heart/My Blues Have Rolled Away	1950	37.50	75.00	150.00
—Other Peppermint Harris 45s on this label may exist.					
"X"					
0142	Need Your Lovin'/Just Me and You	1955	25.00	50.00	100.00

Albums

TIME

Number	Title (A Side/B Side)	Yr	VG	VG+	NM
5 [M]	Peppermint Harris	1962	50.00	100.00	200.00

HARRIS, RAY

45s

SUN

Number	Title (A Side/B Side)	Yr	VG	VG+	NM
254	Come On Little Mama/Where'd You Stay Last Night	1956	37.50	75.00	150.00
272	Greenback Dollar Watch and Chain/Foolish Hearts	1957	25.00	50.00	100.00

HARRIS, RICHARD

45s

Number	Title (A Side/B Side)	Yr	VG	VG+	NM
ABC DUNHILL					
4134	MacArthur Park/Didn't We	1968	—	3.00	6.00
—With both ABC and Dunhill logos at top of label					
4134 [PS]	MacArthur Park/Didn't We	1968	2.00	4.00	8.00
—Regular stock sleeve					
4170	The Yard Went On Forever/Lucky Me	1968	—	2.50	5.00
4185	Watermark/One of the Nicer Things	1969	—	2.50	5.00
4194	Didn't We/Paper Chase	1969	—	2.50	5.00
4218	Fill the World with Love/What a Lot of Flowers	1969	—	2.50	5.00
4218 [PS]	Fill the World with Love/What a Lot of Flowers	1969	—	3.00	6.00
4241	Ballad of a Man Called Horse/Morning of the Mourning for Another	1970	—	2.50	5.00
4293	My Boy/Why Did You Leave Me	1971	—	2.50	5.00
4310	Half of Every Dream/Turning Back the Pages	1972	—	2.50	5.00
4322	There Are Too Many Saviours on My Cross/All the Broken Children	1972	—	2.50	5.00
4322 [PS]	There Are Too Many Saviours on My Cross/All the Broken Children	1972	—	3.00	6.00
4336	How I Spent My Summer/I Don't Have to Tell You	1973	—	2.50	5.00
ATLANTIC					
3238	On Crime and Punishment/Theme from "The Prophet"	1975	—	2.00	4.00
3238 [PS]	On Crime and Punishment/Theme from "The Prophet"	1975	—	2.50	5.00
DUNHILL					
4134	MacArthur Park/Didn't We	1968	2.00	4.00	8.00
—First pressings have Dunhill standing alone at top of label					
4134 [PS]	MacArthur Park/Didn't We	1968	3.75	7.50	15.00
—Special promotional issue, so marked on sleeve					

Albums

Number	Title (A Side/B Side)	Yr	VG	VG+	NM
ABC DUNHILL					
DS-50032	A Tramp Shining	1968	3.75	7.50	15.00
DS-50042	The Yard Went On Forever	1968	3.75	7.50	15.00
DS-50074	The Love Album	1970	3.75	7.50	15.00
DSX-50116	My Boy	1971	3.00	6.00	12.00
DSX-50133	Slides	1972	3.00	6.00	12.00
DSX-50139	The Great Performances	1973	3.00	6.00	12.00
DSX-50159	I, In the Membership	1974	3.00	6.00	12.00
DSX-50160	Jonathan Livingston Seagull	1973	3.00	6.00	12.00
—Spoken-word recording					
ATLANTIC					
QD 18120 [Q]	The Prophet by Kahlil Gibran	1974	5.00	10.00	20.00
—Spoken-word recording					
SD 18120	The Prophet by Kahlil Gibran	1974	3.00	6.00	12.00
—Spoken-word recording					
MCA					
27016	A Tramp Shining	198?	2.00	4.00	8.00
—Budget-line reissue					

HARRIS, ROLF

45s

Number	Title (A Side/B Side)	Yr	VG	VG+	NM
20TH FOX					
207	Tie Me Kangaroo Down, Sport/Nick Teen & Al K. Hall	1960	5.00	10.00	20.00
—Different versions than the Epic recordings					
230	Lost Little Boy/The Big Black Hat	1960	3.75	7.50	15.00
295	Six White Boomers/Tame Eagle	1962	3.75	7.50	15.00
414	Lost Little Boy/The Big Black Hat	1963	3.00	6.00	12.00
EPIC					
9567	Sun Arise/Someone's Pinched My Winkles	1963	3.00	6.00	12.00
9596	Tie Me Kangaroo Down, Sport/The Big Black Hat	1963	3.75	7.50	15.00
9596 [PS]	Tie Me Kangaroo Down, Sport/The Big Black Hat	1963	5.00	10.00	20.00
9615	Nick Teen & Al K. Hall/I Know a Man	1963	3.00	6.00	12.00
9615 [PS]	Nick Teen & Al K. Hall/I Know a Man	1963	5.00	10.00	20.00
9641	Lost Little Boy/Six White Boomers	1963	2.50	5.00	10.00
9641 [PS]	Lost Little Boy/Six White Boomers	1963	5.00	10.00	20.00
9682	The Court of King Caractacus/Two Buffalos	1964	2.50	5.00	10.00
9721	Ringo for President/Click Go the Shears	1964	3.75	7.50	15.00
9756	The Thing/Wild Colonial Boy	1965	2.50	5.00	10.00
9780	Tie My Hunting Dog Down, Jed/Five Young Apprentices	1965	2.50	5.00	10.00
10037	Jake the Peg/Big Dog	1966	2.50	5.00	10.00
MGM					
14103	Two Little Boys/I Love My Love	1970	2.50	5.00	10.00

Albums

EPIC

Number	Title (A Side/B Side)	Yr	VG	VG+	NM
LN 24053 [M]	Tie Me Kangaroo Down, Sport & Sun Arise	1963	5.00	10.00	20.00
LN 24110 [M]	Join Rolf Harris Singing The Count of King Caractacus (And Other Fun Songs)	1964	5.00	10.00	20.00
BN 26053 [S]	Tie Me Kangaroo Down, Sport & Sun Arise	1963	6.25	12.50	25.00

Number	Title (A Side/B Side)	Yr	VG	VG+	NM
BN 26110 [S]	Join Rolf Harris Singing The Count of King Caractacus (And Other Fun Songs)	1964	6.25	12.50	25.00

HARRIS, TED

45s

Number	Title (A Side/B Side)	Yr	VG	VG+	NM
RCA VICTOR					
47-7422	Just Thought I'd Set You Straight/Please Don't Say Take Me Home	1958	7.50	15.00	30.00

HARRIS, THURSTON

45s

Number	Title (A Side/B Side)	Yr	VG	VG+	NM
ALADDIN					
3398	Little Bitty Pretty One/I Hope You Won't Hold It Against Me	1957	10.00	20.00	40.00
3399	Do What You Did/I'm Asking Forgiveness	1957	7.50	15.00	30.00
3415	Be Baby Leba/I'm Out to Getcha	1958	7.50	15.00	30.00
3428	Only One Love Is Blessed/Smokey Joe's	1958	7.50	15.00	30.00
3430	Over and Over/You're Gonna Miss Me	1958	5.00	10.00	20.00
3435	Over Someone Else's Shoulder/Tears from My Heart	1958	5.00	10.00	20.00
3440	Purple Stew/I Heard a Rhapsody	1958	5.00	10.00	20.00
3447	From the Bottom of My Heart/You Don't Know How Much I Love You	1959	5.00	10.00	20.00
3448	Don't You Know/From the Bottom of My Heart	1959	5.00	10.00	20.00
3450	Hey Little Girl/My Love Will Last	1959	5.00	10.00	20.00
3452	Runk Bunk/Bless Your Heart	1959	5.00	10.00	20.00
3456	Slip SLop/Paradise Hill	1959	5.00	10.00	20.00
3462	Moonlight Cocktail/Recess in Heaven	1960	5.00	10.00	20.00
3468	One Scotch, One Bourbon, One Beer/Send Me Some Loving	1960	5.00	10.00	20.00
CUB					
9108	I'd Like to Start Over Again/Mr. Satan	1962	3.00	6.00	12.00
DOT					
16415	Quiet As It's Kept/Goddess of Angels	1963	2.50	5.00	10.00
16427	Poop-A-Loop/She's the One	1963	2.50	5.00	10.00
IMPERIAL					
5928	Got You on My Mind/Tears from My Heart	1963	2.50	5.00	10.00
5971	You're Gonna Need Me/I'm Asking Forgiveness	1963	2.50	5.00	10.00
REPRISE					
0255	Dance On Little Girl/Dancing Silhouettes	1964	2.50	5.00	10.00
UNITED ARTISTS					
0152	Little Bitty Pretty One/Over and Over	1973	—	2.00	4.00
—"Silver Spotlight Series" reissue					

HARRIS, TONY

45s

Number	Title (A Side/B Side)	Yr	VG	VG+	NM
DEE GEE					
3014	Super Man/How Much Do I Love You	1966	4.00	8.00	16.00
EBB					
104	Chicken Baby Chicken/I'll Forever Love You	1957	12.50	25.00	50.00
120	Try This Little Ol' Heart/When I Get You Back	1957	7.50	15.00	30.00
128	You Fascinate Me/Swing, Swing, Swing	1957	7.50	15.00	30.00
TRIUMPH					
60	Go, Go, Little Scrambler/Poor Boy	1964	7.50	15.00	30.00

HARRIS, WEE WILLIE

45s

Number	Title (A Side/B Side)	Yr	VG	VG+	NM
CHARLIE PARKER					
217	I Go Ape/Trouble in Mind	1963	2.50	5.00	10.00

HARRIS, WYNONIE

45s

Number	Title (A Side/B Side)	Yr	VG	VG+	NM
ATCO					
6081	Destination Love/Tell a Whale of a Tale	1956	7.50	15.00	30.00
KING					
4210	Good Rockin' Tonight/Good Morning Mister Blues	1952	37.50	75.00	150.00
—78 originally released in 1948; the only known Wynonie Harris 45 on King before 4461					
4461	Bloodshot Eyes/Confessin' the Blues	1951	30.00	60.00	120.00
4468	I'll Never Give Up/Man Have I Got Troubles	1951	30.00	60.00	120.00
4485	Lovin' Machine/Luscious Woman	1951	30.00	60.00	120.00
—Black vinyl					
4485	Lovin' Machine/Luscious Woman	1951	100.00	200.00	400.00
—Blue vinyl					
4507	My Playful Baby's Gone/Here Comes the Night	1952	25.00	50.00	100.00
4526	Keep On Churnin'/Married Women Stay Married	1952	25.00	50.00	100.00
4555	Do it Again Please/Night Train	1952	25.00	50.00	100.00
4565	Drinking Blues/Adam Come and Get Your Rib	1952	25.00	50.00	100.00
4592	Greyhound/Rot Gut	1953	25.00	50.00	100.00
4593	Bad News Baby (There'll Be Rockin' Tonight)/Bring It Back	1953	25.00	50.00	100.00
4620	Mama Your Daughter Done Lied on Me/Wasn't That Good	1953	25.00	50.00	100.00
4635	Song of the Bayou/The Deacon Doesn't Like It	1953	25.00	50.00	100.00
4662	Tremblin'/Rot Gut	1953	20.00	40.00	80.00
4668	Please Louise/Nearer My Love to Thee	1953	20.00	40.00	80.00
4685	Down Boy Down/Quiet Whiskey	1953	20.00	40.00	80.00
4716	Shake That Thing/Keep A-Talking	1954	20.00	40.00	80.00
4724	I Get a Thrill/Don't Take My Whiskey Away from Me	1954	20.00	40.00	80.00
4763	All She Wants to Do Is Mambo/Christina	1955	15.00	30.00	60.00
4774	Good Mambo Tonight/Git to Gittin' Baby	1955	15.00	30.00	60.00
4789	Fishtail Blues/Mr. Dollar	1955	15.00	30.00	60.00
4814	Drinkin' Sherry Wine/Get With the Guts	1955	12.50	25.00	50.00
4826	Wine, Wine, Sweet Wine/Man's Best Friend	1955	12.50	25.00	50.00
4839	Shot Gun Wedding/I Don't Know Where to Go	1955	12.50	25.00	50.00
4852	Good Morning Judge/Bloodshot Eyes	1955	12.50	25.00	50.00
5050	Big Ole Country Fool/That's Me Right Now	1957	7.50	15.00	30.00
5073	There's No Substitute for Love/A Tale of Woe	1957	7.50	15.00	30.00
5416	Good Rockin' Tonight/Bloodshot Eyes	1960	3.75	7.50	15.00
6011	Big Old Country Fool/Bloodshot Eyes	1965	2.50	5.00	10.00
6304	Good Rockin' Tonight/Good Morning Judge	1970	—	3.00	6.00
ROULETTE					
4291	Bloodshot Eyes/Sweet Lucy Brown	1960	3.00	6.00	12.00

7-Inch Extended Plays

Number	Title (A Side/B Side)	Yr	VG	VG+	NM
KING					
260	(contents unknown)	1954	125.00	250.00	500.00
260 [PS]	Wynonie Harris	1954	125.00	250.00	500.00

Albums

Number	Title (A Side/B Side)	Yr	VG	VG+	NM
KING					
KS-1086	Good Rockin' Blues	1970	6.25	12.50	25.00

HARRISON, GEORGE

Also see THE BEATLES.

12-Inch Singles

Number	Title (A Side/B Side)	Yr	VG	VG+	NM
COLUMBIA					
CAS 2085 [DJ]	I Don't Want to Do It (same on both sides)	1985	5.00	10.00	20.00
DARK HORSE					
PRO-A-949 [DJ]	All Those Years Ago (same on both sides)	1981	6.25	12.50	25.00
PRO-A-1075 [DJ]	Wake Up My Love (same on both sides)	1982	6.25	12.50	25.00
PRO-A-2845 [DJ]	Got My Mind Set on You (same on both sides)	1987	6.25	12.50	25.00
PRO-A-2885 [DJ]	When We Was Fab (same on both sides)	1987	6.25	12.50	25.00
PRO-A-2889 [DJ]	Devil's Radio (Gossip) (same on both sides)	1987	7.50	15.00	30.00

45s

Number	Title (A Side/B Side)	Yr	VG	VG+	NM
APPLE					
1828	What Is Life/Apple Scruffs	1971	3.75	7.50	15.00
—With star on A-side label					
1828	What Is Life/Apple Scruffs	1971	2.00	4.00	8.00
—Without star on A-side label					
1828 [PS]	What Is Life/Apple Scruffs	1971	10.00	20.00	40.00
1836	Bangla-Desh/Deep Blue	1971	6.25	12.50	25.00
—Without star on A-side label					
1836	Bangla-Desh/Deep Blue	1971	2.00	4.00	8.00
—With star on A-side label					
1836 [PS]	Bangla-Desh/Deep Blue	1971	5.00	10.00	20.00
1862	Give Me Love (Give Me Peace on Earth)/Miss O'Dell (2:30)	1973	2.00	4.00	8.00
—With incorrect time for B-side listed					
1862	Give Me Love (Give Me Peace on Earth)/Miss O'Dell (2:20)	1973	2.00	4.00	8.00
—B-side playing time corrected					
P-1862 [DJ]	Give Me Love (Give Me Peace on Earth) (mono/stereo)	1973	12.50	25.00	50.00
1877	Dark Horse/I Don't Care Anymore	1974	2.00	4.00	8.00
—Light blue and white custom photo label					
1877	Dark Horse/I Don't Care Anymore	1974	2.50	5.00	10.00
—White label; NOT a promo					
1877 [PS]	Dark Horse/I Don't Care Anymore	1974	20.00	40.00	80.00
P-1877 [DJ]	Dark Horse (full length mono/stereo)	1974	10.00	20.00	40.00
P-1877 [DJ]	Dark Horse (edited mono/stereo)	1974	15.00	30.00	60.00
1879	Ding Dong, Ding Dong/Hari's on Tour (Express)	1974	5.00	10.00	20.00
—Black and white custom photo label					
1879	Ding Dong, Ding Dong/Hari's on Tour (Express)	1974	62.50	125.00	250.00
—Blue and white custon photo label					
1879 [PS]	Ding Dong, Ding Dong/Hari's on Tour (Express)	1974	5.00	10.00	20.00
P-1879 [DJ]	Ding Dong, Ding Dong (remixed mono/edited stereo)	1974	10.00	20.00	40.00
1884	You/World of Stone	1975	—	3.00	6.00
1884 [PS]	You/World of Stone	1975	3.75	7.50	15.00
P-1884 [DJ]	You (mono/stereo)	1975	10.00	20.00	40.00
1885	This Guitar (Can't Keep from Crying)/Maya Love	1975	6.25	12.50	25.00
—The last Apple 45 until 1995					
P-1885 [DJ]	This Guitar (Can't Keep from Crying) (mono/stereo)	1975	12.50	25.00	50.00
2995	My Sweet Lord/Isn't It a Pity	1970	10.00	20.00	40.00
—With black star on label					
2995	My Sweet Lord/Isn't It a Pity	1970	2.00	4.00	8.00
—With "Mfd. by Apple" on label					
2995	My Sweet Lord/Isn't It a Pity	1975	6.25	12.50	25.00
—With "All Rights Reserved" disclaimer					
2995 [PS]	My Sweet Lord/Isn't It a Pity	1970	10.00	20.00	40.00
CAPITOL					
1828	What Is Life/Apple Scruffs	1976	7.50	15.00	30.00
—Orange label					
1828	What Is Life/Apple Scruffs	1978	—	3.00	6.00
—Purple late-1970s label					
1836	Bangla-Desh/Deep Blue	1976	7.50	15.00	30.00
—Orange label					
1836	Bangla-Desh/Deep Blue	1978	—	3.00	6.00
—Purple late-1970s label					
1836	Bangla-Desh/Deep Blue	1983	3.75	7.50	15.00
—Black colorband label					
1862	Give Me Love (Give Me Peace on Earth)/Miss O'Dell	1978	2.00	4.00	8.00
—Purple late-1970s label					
1862	Give Me Love (Give Me Peace on Earth)/Miss O'Dell	1978	3.75	7.50	15.00
—Black colorband label					
1879	Ding Dong, Ding Dong/Hari's on Tour (Express)	1978	2.00	4.00	8.00
—Purple late-1970s label					
2995	My Sweet Lord/Isn't It a Pity	1976	5.00	10.00	20.00
—Orange label with "Capitol" at bottom					
2995	My Sweet Lord/Isn't It a Pity	1978	—	3.00	6.00
—Purple label; label has reeded edge					
2995	My Sweet Lord/Isn't It a Pity	1983	—	3.00	6.00
—Black label with colorband					
2995	My Sweet Lord/Isn't It a Pity	1988	—	2.50	5.00
—Purple label; label has smooth edge					
COLUMBIA					
04887	I Don't Want to Do It/Queen of the Hop	1985	6.25	12.50	25.00
—B-side by Dave Edmunds					
DARK HORSE					
8294	This Song/Learning How to Love You	1976	2.50	5.00	10.00
—Tan label					
8294	This Song/Learning How to Love You	1976	2.00	4.00	8.00
—White label, NOT a promo					

Number	Title (A Side/B Side)	Yr	VG	VG+	NM
8294 [DJ]	This Song (mono/stereo)	1976	6.25	12.50	25.00
8294 [PS]	This Song/Learning How to Love You	1976	7.50	15.00	30.00
8294 [PS]	This Song (mono/stereo)	1976	10.00	20.00	40.00
—Promotional only sleeve, different from stock sleeve					
8294 [PS]	This Song (mono/stereo)	1976	10.00	20.00	40.00
—Flyer with "The Story Behind This Song"					
8313	Crackerbox Palace/Learning How to Love You	1977	—	2.50	5.00
8763	Blow Away/Soft-Hearted Hana	1979	—	2.50	5.00
—With "RE-1" on label					
8763	Blow Away/Soft-Hearted Hana	1979	5.00	10.00	20.00
—Without "RE-1" on label (no "Loka Productions S.A." on label)					
8763 [PS]	Blow Away/Soft-Hearted Hana	1979	—	2.50	5.00
8844	Love Comes to Everyone/Soft Touch	1979	2.50	5.00	10.00
8844 [PS]	Love Comes to Everyone/Soft Touch	1979	250.00	500.00	750.00
27913	This Is Love/Breath Away from Heaven	1988	—	2.50	5.00
27913 [PS]	This Is Love/Breath Away from Heaven	1988	—	2.50	5.00
28131	When We Was Fab/Zig Zag	1988	—	2.50	5.00
28131 [PS]	When We Was Fab/Zig Zag	1988	—	2.50	5.00
28178	Got My Mind Set on You/Lay His Head	1987	—	2.00	4.00
28178 [PS]	Got My Mind Set on You/Lay His Head	1987	—	2.00	4.00
29744	I Really Love You/Circles	1983	6.25	12.50	25.00
29864	Wake Up My Love/Greece	1982	2.50	5.00	10.00
49725	All Those Years Ago/Writing's on the Wall	1981	—	2.50	5.00
49725 [PS]	All Those Years Ago/Writing's on the Wall	1981	—	2.50	5.00
49785	Teardrops/Save the World	1981	2.50	5.00	10.00
WARNER BROS.					
22807	Cheer Down/That's What It Takes	1989	3.75	7.50	15.00
22807 [DJ]	Cheer Down (same on both sides)	1989	50.00	100.00	200.00
22807 [PS]	Cheer Down/That's What It Takes	1989	3.75	7.50	15.00
Albums					
APPLE					
STCH-639 [(3)]	All Things Must Pass	1970	10.00	20.00	40.00
—Apple labels on first two records and "Apple Jam" labels on third; includes poster and lyric innersleeves					
ST-3350	Wonderwall Music	1968	6.25	12.50	25.00
—With "Mfd. by Apple" on label					
ST-3350	Wonderwall Music	1968	37.50	75.00	150.00
—With Capitol logo on Side 2 bottom					
ST-3350	Wonderwall Music Bonus Photo	1968	—	2.50	5.00
SMAS-3410	Living in the Material World	1973	3.75	7.50	15.00
SMAS-3418	Dark Horse	1974	3.75	7.50	15.00
SW-3420	Extra Texture (Read All About It)	1975	3.75	7.50	15.00
CAPITOL					
STCH-639 [(3)]	All Things Must Pass	1976	7.50	15.00	30.00
—Orange labels with poster and lyric innersleeves					
STCH-639 [(3)]	All Things Must Pass	1978	6.25	12.50	25.00
—Purple labels with poster and lyric innersleeves					
STCH-639 [(3)]	All Things Must Pass	1983	25.00	50.00	100.00
—Black labels, print in colorband, with poster and lyric innersleeves					
ST-11578	The Best of George Harrison	1976	3.75	7.50	15.00
—Custom label, no bar code on back					
ST-11578	The Best of George Harrison	1976	45.00	90.00	180.00
—Orange label					
ST-11578	The Best of George Harrison	1978	2.50	5.00	10.00
—Purple label, large Capitol logo					
ST-11578	The Best of George Harrison	1983	6.25	12.50	25.00
—Black label, print in colorband					
ST-11578	The Best of George Harrison	1988	6.25	12.50	25.00
—Odd reissue with custom label; large stand-alone "S" in trail-off area; bar code on cover					
ST-11578	The Best of George Harrison	1989	20.00	40.00	80.00
—Purple label, small Capitol logo					
SN-16055	Dark Horse	1980	3.75	7.50	15.00
—Budget-line reissue; reverses front and back covers					
SN-16216	Living in the Material World	1980	5.00	10.00	20.00
—Budget-line reissue					
SN-16217	Extra Texture (Read All About It)	1980	6.25	12.50	25.00
—Budget-line reissue					
CAPITOL/APPLE					
STCH-639 [(3)]	All Things Must Pass	1988	20.00	40.00	80.00
—Odd pressing with Apple labels and Capitol cover (look for stand-alone "S" in trail-off wax); with large sticker on back cover					
DARK HORSE					
(no #) [DJ]	Dark Horse Radio Special	1974	100.00	200.00	400.00
—Promo-only; George Harrison introduces his new record label and artists					
PRO 649 [DJ]	A Personal Music Dialogue at Thirty Three and 1/3	1976	12.50	25.00	50.00
DH 3005	Thirty Three and 1/3	1976	2.50	5.00	10.00
—Deduct 30% for cut-outs					
DHK 3255	George Harrison	1979	2.50	5.00	10.00
—Deduct 30% for cut-outs					
DHK 3255	George Harrison	1979	10.00	20.00	40.00
—Columbia House edition (back cover says "Manufactured by Columbia House Under License"					
DHK 3492	Somewhere in England	1981	2.50	5.00	10.00
—Deduct 30% for cut-outs					
23724	Gone Troppo	1982	2.50	5.00	10.00
—Deduct 30% for cut-outs					
23724 [DJ]	Gone Troppo	1982	6.25	12.50	25.00
—Promo on Quiex II vinyl					
25643	Cloud Nine	1987	2.50	5.00	10.00
W1-25643	Cloud Nine	1987	3.00	6.00	12.00
—Columbia House edition					
25726	Best of Dark Horse 1976-1989	1989	6.25	12.50	25.00
W1-25726	Best of Dark Horse 1976-1989	1989	3.75	7.50	15.00
—Columbia House edition					
R 174328	Cloud Nine	1987	3.75	7.50	15.00
—BMG Direct Marketing edition					
R 180307	Best of Dark Horse 1976-1989	1989	3.75	7.50	15.00
—BMG Direct Marketing edition					
ZAPPLE					
ST-3358	Electronic Sound	1969	10.00	20.00	40.00

HARRISON, GEORGE, AND FRIENDS

The "Friends" include BADFINGER; ERIC CLAPTON; BOB DYLAN; BILLY PRESTON; LEON RUSSELL; RAVI SHANKAR; RINGO STARR.

Number	Title (A Side/B Side)	Yr	VG	VG+	NM
Albums					
APPLE					
STCX-3385 [(3)]	The Concert for Bangla Desh	1971	10.00	20.00	40.00
—With 64-page booklet and custom innersleeves					
STCX-3385 [(3)]	The Concert for Bangla Desh	1975	12.50	25.00	50.00
—As above, but with "All Rights Reserved" on labels					
CAPITOL					
SABB-12248 [(2)]	The Concert for Bangla Desh	1982	75.00	150.00	300.00
—Scheduled reissue that was never officially released, though a few copies got out by mistake					

HARRISON, GEORGE/JEFF BECK/DAVE EDMUNDS

Number	Title (A Side/B Side)	Yr	VG	VG+	NM
12-Inch Singles					
COLUMBIA					
CAS 2034 [DJ]	I Don't Want to Do It/Sleepwalk/Queen of the Hop	1985	5.00	10.00	20.00
—Promo sampler from movie "Porky's Revenge"					

HARRISON, NOEL

Number	Title (A Side/B Side)	Yr	VG	VG+	NM
45s					
LONDON					
9755	One Too Many Mornings/Barbara Allen	1965	2.00	4.00	8.00
9795	A Young Girl/The Future Mrs. 'Awkins	1965	2.50	5.00	10.00
9815	It's All Over Now, Baby Blue/Much As I Love You	1966	2.00	4.00	8.00
20011	The Man Behind the Red Balloon/Marlene	1966	2.00	4.00	8.00
20017	Cheryl's Going Home/In a Dusty Old Room	1966	2.00	4.00	8.00
20017 [PS]	Cheryl's Going Home/In a Dusty Old Room	1966	3.00	6.00	12.00
20021	Out for the Day/Fly Sing Song	1967	2.00	4.00	8.00
REPRISE					
0599	Sign of the Queen/Mrs. Williams' Rose	1967	—	3.00	6.00
0615	Life Is a Dream/Suzanne	1967	—	3.00	6.00
0682	Santa Monica Pier/In Your Chidren	1968	—	3.00	6.00
0758	The Windmills of Your Mind/Leitch on the Beach	1968	2.00	4.00	8.00
0795	I'll Be Your Baby Tonight/The Greatest Experiment Is Over	1968	—	3.00	6.00
0914	Another Virgin Spring/Tin Wedding	1970	—	3.00	6.00
Albums					
LONDON					
PS 459 [S]	Noel Harrison	1966	6.25	12.50	25.00
LL 3459 [M]	Noel Harrison	1966	5.00	10.00	20.00
REPRISE					
R-6263 [M]	Collage	1967	3.75	7.50	15.00
RS-6263 [S]	Collage	1967	5.00	10.00	20.00
RS-6295	Santa Monica Pier	1968	3.75	7.50	15.00
RS-6321	The Great Electric Experiment Is Over	1969	3.75	7.50	15.00

HARRISON, WES

Number	Title (A Side/B Side)	Yr	VG	VG+	NM
45s					
LIN					
5002	There Y'Are/Uncle Winnie's Sound Stories	1956	7.50	15.00	30.00
Albums					
PHILIPS					
PHM 200103 [M]	You Won't Believe Your Ears	1963	5.00	10.00	20.00
PHS 600103 [S]	You Won't Believe Your Ears	1963	6.25	12.50	25.00

HARRISON, WILBERT

Number	Title (A Side/B Side)	Yr	VG	VG+	NM
45s					
BELL					
869	C.C. Rider/Since I Fell for You	1970	—	3.00	6.00
BRUNSWICK					
55511	Lovin' Operator/Love You	1974	—	3.00	6.00
55519	I'm Going to the River/I Need Some (Honey Honey)	1975	—	3.00	6.00
CHART					
626	Cool Water/Calypso Man	1956	6.25	12.50	25.00
CONSTELLATION					
122	New York World's Fair/Mama, Mama, Mama	1964	2.50	5.00	10.00
DELUXE					
6002	This Woman of Mine/The Letter	1953	15.00	30.00	60.00
6031	Nobody Knows My Trouble/Gin and Coconut Milk	1954	15.00	30.00	60.00
FURY					
1023	Kansas City/Listen, My Darling	1959	7.50	15.00	30.00
1027	Cheating Baby/Don't Wreck My Life	1959	3.75	7.50	15.00
1028	Goodbye Kansas City/1960	1960	3.75	7.50	15.00
1031	C.C. Rider/Why Did You Leave	1960	3.75	7.50	15.00
1037	Since I Fell for You/Little School Girl	1960	3.75	7.50	15.00
1041	The Horse/Da-De-Ya-Da (I'd Do Anything for You)	1961	3.75	7.50	15.00
1047	Happy in Love/Calypso Dance	1961	3.75	7.50	15.00
1055	Drafted/My Heart Is Yours	1961	3.75	7.50	15.00
1059	Let's Stick Together/Kansas City Twist	1962	3.75	7.50	15.00
1063	Let's Stick Together/My Heart Is Yours	1962	3.00	6.00	12.00
GLADES					
603	Gonna Tell You a Story/Letter Edged in Black	1959	3.00	6.00	12.00
PORT					
3003	Baby Move On/You're Still My Baby	1965	2.00	4.00	8.00
3009	Don't Take It So Hard/Sugar Lump	1965	2.00	4.00	8.00
ROCKIN'					
526	This Woman of Mine/The Letter	1952	25.00	50.00	100.00
ROULETTE					
4752	No One's Love But Yours/Mini-Parade	1967	2.00	4.00	8.00
SAVOY					
1138	Don't Drop It/The Ways of a Woman	1954	10.00	20.00	40.00
1149	Women and Whiskey/Da-De-Ya-Da (I'd Do Anything for You)	1955	7.50	15.00	30.00
1164	Florida Special/Darling, Listen to This Song	1955	7.50	15.00	30.00
1198	Confessin' My Dream/The Way I Feel	1956	7.50	15.00	30.00
1517	My Love Is True/I Know My Baby Loves Me	1957	6.25	12.50	25.00
1531	Baby Don't You Know/My Love for You Lingers On	1958	5.00	10.00	20.00

Number	Title (A Side/B Side)	Yr	VG	VG+	NM
1571	Don't Drop It/Baby Don't You Know	1959	3.75	7.50	15.00
SEA HORN					
502	Say It Again/Near to You	1963	2.00	4.00	8.00
SSS INTERNATIONAL					
830	My Heart Is Yours/Pretty Little Woman	1971	—	3.00	6.00
830 [DJ]	My Heart Is Yours (mono/stereo)	1971	2.50	5.00	10.00
—Promo only on blue vinyl					
SUE					
11	Let's Work Together (Part 1)/Let's Work Together (Part 2)	1969	—	3.00	6.00
WET SOUL					
4	My Heart Is Yours/Pretty Little Woman	1970	2.00	4.00	8.00
Albums					
BUDDAH					
BDS-5002	Wilbert Harrison	1971	7.50	15.00	30.00
CHELSEA					
CH 523	Wilbert Harrison	1977	5.00	10.00	20.00
JUGGERNAUT					
ST-8803	Shoot You Full of Love	1971	12.50	25.00	50.00
SAVOY JAZZ					
SJL-1182	Listen to My Song	1987	3.00	6.00	12.00
SPHERE SOUND					
SSR-7000 [M]	Kansas City	1965	62.50	125.00	250.00
SSSR-7000 [R]	Kansas City	1965	50.00	100.00	200.00
SUE					
SSLP-8801	Let's Work Together	1970	12.50	25.00	50.00
WET SOUL					
1001	Anything You Want	197?	12.50	25.00	50.00

HARSHMAN, ROBERT LUKE

See BOBBY HART.

HART, BILLY AND DON

Number	Title (A Side/B Side)	Yr	VG	VG+	NM
45s					
ROULETTE					
4133	Rock-a-Bop-a-Lena/More and More	1959	15.00	30.00	60.00
4172	Check-Mated and Bingoed/Blabbermouth	1959	7.50	15.00	30.00

HART, BOBBY

Number	Title (A Side/B Side)	Yr	VG	VG+	NM
45s					
ARIOLA AMERICA					
809	Lovers for the Night/You Get Smoke in Your Eyes	1980	—	2.50	5.00
BAMBOO					
507	The Girl I Used to Know/The Spider and the Fly	1961	7.50	15.00	30.00
CHELSEA					
BCBO-0026	Easy Evil/California	1973	—	2.50	5.00
DCP					
1113	That'll Be the Day/Turn On Your Lovelight	1964	5.00	10.00	20.00
1142	Baby Let Your Hair Down/Jealous Feeling	1965	6.25	12.50	25.00
1152	Around the Corner/Cry My Eyes Out	1966	5.00	10.00	20.00
ERA					
3039	Girl in the Window/Journey of Love	1961	5.00	10.00	20.00
GUYDEN					
2022	Is You Is Or Is You Ain't My Baby/Girl of My Dreams	1959	7.50	15.00	30.00
—As "Robert Luke Harshman"					
INFINITY					
017	Too Many Teardrops/The People Next Door	1963	5.00	10.00	20.00
022	Lovesick Blues/I Think It's Called a Heartache	1963	5.00	10.00	20.00
RADIO					
122	Stop Talkin', Start Lovin'/Love Whatcha Doin' to Me	1959	10.00	20.00	40.00
—As "Robert Luke Harshman"					
REEL					
100	Girl in the Window/Journey of Love	1961	10.00	20.00	40.00
WARNER BROS.					
8058	Hard Core Man/To Keep from Crying	1974	—	2.50	5.00
8058 [PS]	Hard Core Man/To Keep from Crying	1974	2.00	4.00	8.00
49079	The Loneliest Night/Sometimes Love	1979	—	2.50	5.00

HART, FREDDIE

Number	Title (A Side/B Side)	Yr	VG	VG+	NM
45s					
CAPITOL					
F2524	Butterfly Love/My Heart Is a Playground	1953	3.75	7.50	15.00
F2588	Secret Kisses/Whole Hog or None	1953	3.75	7.50	15.00
2692	The Whole World Holding Hands/Without You	1969	—	2.50	5.00
F2726	Loose Talk/The Curtain Never Falls	1954	3.75	7.50	15.00
2768	One More Mountain to Climb/Just Another Girl	1970	—	2.50	5.00
2839	Fingerprints/I Can't Keep My Hands Off of You	1970	—	2.50	5.00
F2873	Caught at Last/It Just Don't Seem Like Home	1954	3.75	7.50	15.00
2933	California Grapevine/What's Wrong with Your Head, Fred	1970	—	2.50	5.00
F2991	I'm Going Out on the Front Porch and Cry/Please Don't Tell Her	1954	3.00	6.00	12.00
F3090	Miss Lonely Heart/Oh Heart Let Her Go	1955	3.00	6.00	12.00
3115	Easy Loving/Brother Bluebird	1971	—	2.50	5.00
F3203	Canada to Tennessee/No Thanks to You	1955	3.00	6.00	12.00
3261	My Hang-Up Is You/Big Bad Wolf	1972	—	2.00	4.00
3353	Bless Your Heart/Conscience Makes Cowards	1972	—	2.00	4.00
3453	Got the All Overs for You (All Over Me)/Just Another Girl	1972	—	2.00	4.00
3524	Super Kind of Woman/Mother Nature Made a Believer Out of Me	1973	—	2.00	4.00
3612	Trip to Heaven/Look-a Here	1973	—	2.00	4.00
3730	If You Can't Feel It (It Ain't There)/Skid Row Street	1973	—	2.00	4.00
3789	Blue Christmas/I Believe in Santa Claus	1973	—	2.00	4.00
3827	Hang In There Girl/You Belong to Me	1974	—	2.00	4.00
3898	The Want-To's/Phenix City, Alabama	1974	—	2.00	4.00
3970	My Woman's Man/Let's Clean Up the Country	1974	—	2.00	4.00
4031	I'd Like to Sleep Til I Get Over You/Nothing's Better Than That	1975	—	2.00	4.00
4099	The First Time/Sexy	1975	—	2.00	4.00
4152	Warm Side of You/I Love You, I Just Don't Like You	1975	—	2.00	4.00
4210	You Are the Song (Inside of Me)/I Can Almost See Houston from Here	1976	—	2.00	4.00
4251	She'll Throw Stones at You/Love Makes It Alright	1976	—	2.00	4.00
4313	That Look in Her Eyes/Try My Love for Size	1976	—	2.00	4.00
4363	Why Lovers Turn to Strangers/Paper Sack Full of Memories	1976	—	2.00	4.00
4409	Thank God She's Mine/Falling All Over Me	1977	—	2.00	4.00
4448	The Pleasure's Been All Mine/It's Heaven Loving You	1977	—	2.00	4.00
4498	The Search/Honky Tonk Toys	1977	—	2.00	4.00
4530	So Good, So Rare, So Fine/There's an Angel Living There	1978	—	2.00	4.00
4561	Only You/I Love You, I Just Don't Like You	1978	—	2.00	4.00
4609	Toe to Toe/And Then Some	1978	—	2.00	4.00
4684	My Lady/Guilty	1979	—	2.00	4.00
4720	Wasn't It Easy Baby/My Lady Loves	1979	—	2.00	4.00
COLUMBIA					
21512	Dig Boy Dig/Two of a Kind	1956	12.50	25.00	50.00
21550	Snatch It and Grab It/Human Thing to Do	1956	3.00	6.00	12.00
21558	Drink Up and Go Home/Blue	1956	3.00	6.00	12.00
40821	On the Prowl/Extra	1957	3.00	6.00	12.00
40896	Fraulein/Baby Don't Leave	1957	3.00	6.00	12.00
41005	Say No More/The Outside World	1957	3.00	6.00	12.00
41081	You Are My World/Heaven Only Knows	1957	3.00	6.00	12.00
41144	I Won't Be Home Tonight/Love, Come to Me	1958	3.00	6.00	12.00
41269	I'm No Angel/Midnight Date	1958	3.00	6.00	12.00
41345	The Wall/Davy Jones	1959	2.50	5.00	10.00
41456	Chain Gang/Rock Bottom	1959	2.50	5.00	10.00
41597	The Key's in the Mailbox/Starvation Days	1960	2.50	5.00	10.00
41805	Lying Again/Do My Heart a Favor	1960	2.50	5.00	10.00
42146	What a Laugh!/Heart Attack	1961	2.50	5.00	10.00
42285	Some Do, Some Don't, Some Will, Some Won't/I Like You Are	1962	2.50	5.00	10.00
42491	Stand Up/Ugly Duckling	1962	2.50	5.00	10.00
42679	I'll Hit It with a Stick/Stranger Drive Away	1963	2.00	4.00	8.00
42769	Angels Like You/Mary Ann	1963	2.00	4.00	8.00
EL DORADO					
101	I Don't Want to Lose You/(B-side unknown)	1985	—	2.00	4.00
FIFTH ST.					
1091	Best Love I Never Had/(B-side unknown)	1987	—	2.00	4.00
KAPP					
632	Love Can Make or Break a Heart/Hurts Feel So Good	1964	2.00	4.00	8.00
661	Moon Gal/You've Got It Coming To Ya	1965	2.00	4.00	8.00
694	Hank Williams' Guitar/I Created a Monster	1965	2.00	4.00	8.00
743	Why Should I Cry Over You/Keys in the Mailbox	1966	2.00	4.00	8.00
765	Together Again/Waiting for a Train	1966	2.00	4.00	8.00
794	Misty Blue/Elm Street Pawn Shop	1966	2.00	4.00	8.00
820	I'll Hold You in My Heart/Too Much of You (Left of Me)	1967	—	3.00	6.00
841	Anna Maria/Leon and the Rain	1967	—	3.00	6.00
879	Togetherness/Portrait of a Lonely Man	1967	—	3.00	6.00
910	Born a Fool/Hands of a Man	1968	—	3.00	6.00
944	Don't Cry Baby/Here Lies a Heart	1968	—	3.00	6.00
976	Why Leave Something I Can't Use/Hang On to Her	1969	—	3.00	6.00
993	I Lost All My Tomorrows/That's How High a Man Can Go	1969	—	3.00	6.00
2183	Don't Cry Baby/Loving You Again	1972	—	2.50	5.00
MCA					
40011	Born a Fool/My Anna Maria	1973	—	2.50	5.00
MONUMENT					
826	For a Second There/The Almighty Dollar	1963	2.00	4.00	8.00
838	First You Go Through Me/Valentino	1964	2.00	4.00	8.00
SUNBIRD					
110	Sure Thing/Makin' Love to Memories	1980	—	2.50	5.00
7550	Sure Thing/Makin' Love to Memories	1980	—	2.00	4.00
7553	Roses Are Red/Battle of the Sexes	1980	—	2.00	4.00
7560	You're Crazy Man/Playboy's Centerfolk	1981	—	2.00	4.00
7565	You Were There/The Weaker Sex	1981	—	2.00	4.00
Albums					
CAPITOL					
ST-469	New Sounds	1970	3.00	6.00	12.00
ST-593	California Grapevine	1970	3.00	6.00	12.00
ST-838	Easy Loving	1971	3.00	6.00	12.00
ST-11014	My Hang-Up Is You	1972	3.00	6.00	12.00
ST-11073	Bless Your Heart	1972	3.00	6.00	12.00
ST-11107	Got the All-Overs	1972	3.00	6.00	12.00
ST-11156	Super Kind of Woman	1973	3.00	6.00	12.00
ST-11197	Trip to Heaven	1973	3.00	6.00	12.00
ST-11252	If You Can't Feel It	1974	3.00	6.00	12.00
ST-11296	Hang In There Girl	1974	3.00	6.00	12.00
ST-11353	Country Heart 'N' Soul	1975	3.00	6.00	12.00
ST-11374	Greatest Hits	1975	3.00	6.00	12.00
ST-11449	The First Time	1975	2.50	5.00	10.00
ST-11504	People Put to Music	1976	2.50	5.00	10.00
ST-11568	That Look in Her Eyes	1976	2.50	5.00	10.00
ST-11626	The Pleasure's Been All Mine	1977	2.50	5.00	10.00
ST-11724	Only You	1978	2.50	5.00	10.00
COLUMBIA					
CL 1792 [M]	The Spirited Freddie Hart	1962	10.00	20.00	40.00
G 31550 [(2)]	The World of Freddie Hart	1972	3.75	7.50	15.00
HARMONY					
HL 7412 [M]	The Best of Freddie Hart	1967	3.00	6.00	12.00
HS 11212 [S]	The Best of Freddie Hart	1967	3.00	6.00	12.00
KH 31165	Lonesome Love	1972	2.50	5.00	10.00
KH 32467	You Are My World	1973	2.50	5.00	10.00
HILLTOP					
6117	From Canada to Tennessee	1972	2.50	5.00	10.00
KAPP					
KL-1456 [M]	The Hart of Country Music	1966	3.75	7.50	15.00
KL-1492 [M]	Straight from the Heart	1966	3.75	7.50	15.00

Number	Title (A Side/B Side)	Yr	VG	VG+	NM
KL-1513 [M]	Hurtin' Man	1967	5.00	10.00	20.00
KL-1539 [M]	The Neon and the Rain	1967	5.00	10.00	20.00
KS-3456 [S]	The Hart of Country Music	1966	5.00	10.00	20.00
KS-3492 [S]	Straight from the Heart	1966	5.00	10.00	20.00
KS-3513 [S]	Hurtin' Man	1967	5.00	10.00	20.00
KS-3539 [S]	The Neon and the Rain	1967	5.00	10.00	20.00
KS-3546	Togetherness	1968	5.00	10.00	20.00
KS-3568	Born a Fool	1968	5.00	10.00	20.00
KS-3592	Greatest Hits	1969	3.75	7.50	15.00
MCA					
4088 [(2)]	The Best of Freddie Hart	1975	3.75	7.50	15.00
SUNBIRD					
ST-50100	Sure Thing	1980	3.00	6.00	12.00

HART, MICKEY

Also see THE GRATEFUL DEAD.

45s

Number	Title (A Side/B Side)	Yr	VG	VG+	NM
WARNER BROS.					
7644	Blind John/Pump Man	1972	2.50	5.00	10.00

Albums

Number	Title (A Side/B Side)	Yr	VG	VG+	NM
RELIX					
2026	Rolling Thunder	1987	3.00	6.00	12.00
WARNER BROS.					
BS 2635	Rolling Thunder	1972	7.50	15.00	30.00

HART, MICKEY, AIRTO, FLORA PURIM, BATUCAJE

Albums

Number	Title (A Side/B Side)	Yr	VG	VG+	NM
REFERENCE RECORDINGS					
RR-12	Dafos	1985	3.75	7.50	15.00

HART, ROCKY

45s

Number	Title (A Side/B Side)	Yr	VG	VG+	NM
BIG TOP					
3069	Crying/Baby You've Got It Made	1961	7.50	15.00	30.00
CUB					
9052	Every Day/Come with Me	1959	7.50	15.00	30.00
GLO					
216	I Play the Part of a Fool/Someone Stole My Baby While Doing the Twist	1961	50.00	100.00	200.00

HARTFORD, JOHN

45s

Number	Title (A Side/B Side)	Yr	VG	VG+	NM
AMPEX					
11019	One Too Many Mornings/(B-side unknown)	1971	—	2.50	5.00
FLYING FISH					
4013	Piece of My Heart/(B-side unknown)	1984	—	2.00	4.00
MCA DOT					
53104	Ohio River Rag/Love Wrote This Song	1987	—	2.00	4.00
RCA VICTOR					
47-8987	Tall Tall Grass/Jack's in the Sack	1966	2.00	4.00	8.00
47-9175	Gentle on My Mind/Electric Washing Machine	1967	2.00	4.00	8.00
47-9345	A Simple Thing As Love/Landscape Grown Cold	1967	2.00	4.00	8.00
47-9451	Big Blue Balloon/Six O'Clock Train and a Girl with Green Eyes	1968	2.00	4.00	8.00
47-9507	Shiny Rails of Steel/Natural to Be Gone	1968	2.00	4.00	8.00
47-9668	California Earthquake/Mouth to Mouth Resuscitation	1968	—	3.00	6.00
47-9753	I Didn't Know the World Would Last This Long/Orphan of World War II	1969	—	3.00	6.00
47-9772	Like Unto a Mockingbird/Natural to Be Gone	1969	—	3.00	6.00

Albums

Number	Title (A Side/B Side)	Yr	VG	VG+	NM
FLYING FISH					
FF-020	Mark Twang	1976	2.50	5.00	10.00
FF-028	Nobody Knows What You Do	1977	2.50	5.00	10.00
FF-044	All in the Name of Love	1983	2.50	5.00	10.00
FF-063	Headin' Down Into the Mystery Below	1978	2.50	5.00	10.00
FF-095	Slumberin' on the Cumberland	1979	2.50	5.00	10.00
—With Pat Burton and Benny Martin					
FF-228	You and Me at Home	1980	2.50	5.00	10.00
FF-259	Catalogue	1982	2.50	5.00	10.00
FF-289	Gum Tree Canoe	1984	2.50	5.00	10.00
FF-440	Me Oh My, How Time Flies	1987	2.50	5.00	10.00
MCA					
5861	Annual Waltz	1987	2.00	4.00	8.00
RCA VICTOR					
LPM-3687 [M]	John Hartford Looks at Life	1966	5.00	10.00	20.00
LSP-3687 [S]	John Hartford Looks at Life	1966	3.75	7.50	15.00
LPM-3796 [M]	Earthwords and Music	1967	6.25	12.50	25.00
LSP-3796 [S]	Earthwords and Music	1967	3.75	7.50	15.00
LPM-3884 [M]	The Love Album	1967	6.25	12.50	25.00
LSP-3884 [S]	The Love Album	1967	3.75	7.50	15.00
LSP-3998	Housing Project	1968	3.75	7.50	15.00
LSP-4068	Gentle on My Mind and Other Originals	1968	3.75	7.50	15.00
LSP-4156	John Hartford	1969	3.75	7.50	15.00
LSP-4337	Iron Mountain Depot	1970	3.75	7.50	15.00
WARNER BROS.					
WS 1916	Aereo-Plain	1971	3.00	6.00	12.00
BS 2651	Morning Bugle	1972	3.00	6.00	12.00

HARTFORD, KEN

45s

Number	Title (A Side/B Side)	Yr	VG	VG+	NM
SOUTHERN SOUND					
119	Jay Walker/Little Joe, Go Lightly	1963	6.25	12.50	25.00
—With Frankie Valli					

HARTLEY, KEEF

45s

Number	Title (A Side/B Side)	Yr	VG	VG+	NM
DERAM					
85060	Don't Be Afraid/Don't Give Up	1970	—	3.00	6.00
85069	Roundabout (Part 1)/Roundabout (Part 2)	1971	—	3.00	6.00

Albums

Number	Title (A Side/B Side)	Yr	VG	VG+	NM
DERAM					
DES 18024	Halfbreed	1969	3.75	7.50	15.00
DES 18035	The Battle of North West Six	1970	3.75	7.50	15.00
DES 18047	The Time Is Near	1970	3.75	7.50	15.00
DES 18057	Overdog	1971	3.75	7.50	15.00
XDES 18065	The 72nd Brave	1972	3.75	7.50	15.00
XDES 18070	Lancashire Hustler	1973	3.75	7.50	15.00

HARUMI

45s

Number	Title (A Side/B Side)	Yr	VG	VG+	NM
VERVE FORECAST					
5086	First Impressions/Talk About It	1968	3.00	6.00	12.00

Albums

Number	Title (A Side/B Side)	Yr	VG	VG+	NM
VERVE FORECAST					
FTS-3030	Harumi	1968	6.25	12.50	25.00

HARVEY

Also see ETTA AND HARVEY; THE MOONGLOWS.

45s

Number	Title (A Side/B Side)	Yr	VG	VG+	NM
CHESS					
1713	I Want Somebody/Da Da Goo Goo	1959	10.00	20.00	40.00
1725	Twelve Months of the Year/Don't Be Afraid of Love	1959	10.00	20.00	40.00
—Also see "Moonglows, The"					
1749	Blue Skies/Ooh, Ouch, Stop!	1960	6.25	12.50	25.00
1760	If I Can't Have You/My Heart Cries	1960	6.25	12.50	25.00
—As "Etta and Harvey" (Etta is Etta James)					
1771	Spoonful/It's a Crying Shame	1960	6.25	12.50	25.00
—As "Etta and Harvey" (Etta is Etta James)					
1781	The First Time/Mama	1961	6.25	12.50	25.00
—As "Harvey Fuqua"					
HARVEY					
121	What Can You Do Now/Will I Do	1962	10.00	20.00	40.00
—As "Harvey and Ann"					
TRI-PHI					
1017	She Loves Me So/Any Way You Wanta	1962	10.00	20.00	40.00
1024	Memories of You/Come On and Answer Me	1963	15.00	30.00	60.00

HARVEY, ALEX (1)

British; fronted the Sensational Alex Harvey Band.

45s

Number	Title (A Side/B Side)	Yr	VG	VG+	NM
ATLANTIC					
3293	Delilah/Soul in Chains	1975	—	2.50	5.00
DECCA					
31649	New Orleans/I Just Wanna Make Love to You	1964	5.00	10.00	20.00
VERTIGO					
113	Swamp Snake/Gang Bang	1974	—	2.50	5.00
200	Tomahawk Kid/Sergeant Fury	1974	—	2.50	5.00

Albums

Number	Title (A Side/B Side)	Yr	VG	VG+	NM
ATLANTIC					
SD 18248	Live	1975	3.00	6.00	12.00
VERTIGO					
VEL-1017	Next	1973	3.00	6.00	12.00
VEL-2000	The Impossible Dream	1974	3.00	6.00	12.00
VEL-2004	Tomorrow Belongs to Me	1975	3.00	6.00	12.00

HARVEY, ALEX (2)

American country singer.

45s

Number	Title (A Side/B Side)	Yr	VG	VG+	NM
CAPITOL					
3172	To Make My Life Beautiful/Lady	1971	—	2.00	4.00
3336	Delta Dawn/Momma's Waiting	1972	—	2.00	4.00
3469	Angeline/Devil on My Shoulder	1972	—	2.00	4.00
3493	Good Time Christmas/Someone Who Cares	1972	—	2.00	4.00
—With Son Lex					
3649	Right On/Summer Days	1973	—	2.00	4.00
3703	You Don't Need a Reason/Goodbye Miss Carolina	1973	—	2.00	4.00
3847	Tangerine/Jody's Face	1974	—	2.00	4.00
UNITED ARTISTS					
50494	It Takes a Lot of Tenderness/I'll Be Your Tomorrow	1969	2.00	4.00	8.00

Albums

Number	Title (A Side/B Side)	Yr	VG	VG+	NM
CAPITOL					
ST-789	Alex Harvey	1972	3.00	6.00	12.00
ST-11128	Souvenirs	1973	3.00	6.00	12.00

HARVEY, PHIL

Actually PHIL SPECTOR.

45s

Number	Title (A Side/B Side)	Yr	VG	VG+	NM
IMPERIAL					
5583	Willy Boy/Bumbershoot	1959	37.50	75.00	150.00

HARVEY AND DOC WITH THE DWELLERS

45s

Number	Title (A Side/B Side)	Yr	VG	VG+	NM
ANNETTE					
1002	Oh, Baby/Uncle Kev	1964	62.50	125.00	250.00
—Phil Spector appeared on and produced this					

HARVEY AND THE MOONGLOWS

See THE MOONGLOWS.

HASSAN, ALI

Also see B. BUMBLE AND THE STINGERS.

45s

Number	Title (A Side/B Side)	Yr	VG	VG+	NM
PHILLES					
103	Malaguena/Chop Sticks	1962	7.50	15.00	30.00

HASSLES, THE

BILLY JOEL was in this group.

Number	Title (A Side/B Side)	Yr	VG	VG+	NM
45s					
UNITED ARTISTS					
50215	You've Got Me Hummin'/I'm Thinkin'	1967	3.00	6.00	12.00
—Billy Joel was in this group					
50215 [PS]	You've Got Me Hummin'/I'm Thinkin'	1967	5.00	10.00	20.00
50258	I Hear Voices/Every Step I Take	1968	3.00	6.00	12.00
50450	4 O'Clock in the Morning/Let Me Bring You to the Sunshine	1968	3.00	6.00	12.00
50513	Night After Day/Country Boy	1969	3.00	6.00	12.00
50586	Traveling Band/Great Balls of Fire	1969	3.00	6.00	12.00
Albums					
LIBERTY					
LN-10138	The Hassles	1981	3.00	6.00	12.00
LN-10139	Hour of the Wolf	1981	3.00	6.00	12.00
UNITED ARTISTS					
UAS-6631	The Hassles	1968	6.25	12.50	25.00
UAS-6699	Hour of the Wolf	1969	6.25	12.50	25.00

HATCH, TONY

Number	Title (A Side/B Side)	Yr	VG	VG+	NM
45s					
LONDON					
10505	Ghost Squad/What's All That About	1962	3.00	6.00	12.00
10523	Cyril's Tune/Out of This World	1963	3.00	6.00	12.00
10524	Theme from Dick Powell Theatre/Sharon	1963	3.00	6.00	12.00
REPRISE					
0356	Crossroads/The Marie Celeste	1965	2.50	5.00	10.00
WARNER BROS.					
5887	I Didn't Know What Time It Was/Working in the Coal Mine	1967	2.00	4.00	8.00
7023	Beautiful Rain/While the City Sleeps	1967	2.00	4.00	8.00

HATCHER, WILLIE

Number	Title (A Side/B Side)	Yr	VG	VG+	NM
45s					
COLUMBIA					
44259	Good Things Come to Those Who Wait/Searching	1968	12.50	25.00	50.00
KING					
6360	Head Over Heels/Who's Gotta Woman Like Mine	1971	7.50	15.00	30.00

HATFIELD, BOBBY

Also see THE RIGHTEOUS BROTHERS.

Number	Title (A Side/B Side)	Yr	VG	VG+	NM
45s					
MOONGLOW					
220	I Need a Girl/Hot Tamale	1963	6.25	12.50	25.00
VERVE					
10598	Hang-Ups/Soul Cafe	1968	2.00	4.00	8.00
10621	Brothers/What's the Matter Baby	1968	2.00	4.00	8.00
10634	Only You/The Wonder of You	1969	2.00	4.00	8.00
10639	My Prayer/I Wish I Didn't Love You So	1969	2.00	4.00	8.00
10641	Answer Me My Love/I Only Have Eyes for You	1969	2.00	4.00	8.00
WARNER BROS.					
7566	Rock 'N Roll Woman/Oo Wee Baby, I Love You	1972	—	2.50	5.00
7649	Stay with Me/Rock 'N Roll Woman	1972	—	2.50	5.00
Albums					
MGM					
SE-4727	Messin' in Muscle Shoals	1971	3.00	6.00	12.00

HATHAWAY, DONNY

Also see ROBERTA FLACK.

Number	Title (A Side/B Side)	Yr	VG	VG+	NM
45s					
ATCO					
6719	The Ghetto (Part 1)/The Ghetto (Part 2)	1969	—	3.00	6.00
6759	Thank You Master/Je Vous Aime	1970	—	2.50	5.00
6768	Tryin' Times/Voices Inside	1970	—	2.50	5.00
6799	This Christmas/Be There	1970	2.00	4.00	8.00
6817	Take a Love Song/Magnificent Sanctuary Band	1971	—	2.50	5.00
6828	A Song for You/Put Your Hand in the Hand	1971	—	2.50	5.00
6880	Little Ghetto Boy/We're Still Friends	1972	—	2.50	5.00
6884	Giving Up/Jealous Love	1972	—	2.50	5.00
6899	Bossa Nova/Come Back Charleston Blue	1972	—	2.50	5.00
—With Margie Joseph					
6903	I Love You More Than You'll Ever Know/Lord Help Me	1972	—	2.50	5.00
6928	Love, Love, Love/Someday We'll All Be Free	1973	—	2.50	5.00
6951	Come Little Children/The Slums	1973	—	2.50	5.00
7066	This Christmas/Be There	1975	—	2.50	5.00
7092	You Were Meant for Me/Valdez in the Country	1978	—	2.00	4.00
7320	This Christmas/Be There	1980	—	2.00	4.00
99956	This Christmas/Be There	1982	—	2.00	4.00
CURTOM					
1935	I Thank You Baby/What's This I See	1969	2.00	4.00	8.00
—By "June and Donnie"					
1971	I Thank You/Just Another Reason	1972	—	2.50	5.00
—By "June Conquest and Donnie Hathaway"; same A-side as 1935 but with revised title					
Albums					
ATCO					
SD 38-107	The Best of Donny Hathaway	1978	2.50	5.00	10.00
SD 33-332	Everything Is Everything	1970	3.00	6.00	12.00
SD 33-360	Donny Hathaway	1971	3.00	6.00	12.00
SD 33-386	Donny Hathaway Live	1972	3.00	6.00	12.00
QD 7029 [Q]	Extension of a Man	1974	4.50	9.00	18.00
SD 7029	Extension of a Man	1973	2.50	5.00	10.00
ATLANTIC					
SD 19278	In Performance	1980	2.50	5.00	10.00

HAVEN, SHIRLEY

Number	Title (A Side/B Side)	Yr	VG	VG+	NM
45s					
FEDERAL					
12092	Troubles of My Own/Stop Foolin' Around	1952	75.00	150.00	300.00
—With the Four Jacks					

HAVENS, RICHIE

Number	Title (A Side/B Side)	Yr	VG	VG+	NM
45s					
A&M					
1869	We Can't Hide It Anymore/Dreaming as One	1976	—	2.00	4.00
1882	I'm Not in Love/Dreaming as One	1976	—	2.00	4.00
1901	You Can Close Your Eyes/We Can't Hide It Anymore	1976	—	2.00	4.00
1984	We All Wanna Boogie/Nobody Left to Crown	1977	—	2.00	4.00
ELEKTRA					
46619	Every Night/Here's a Song	1980	—	2.00	4.00
46657	The Girl, the Gold Watch and Everything/Two Hearts in Perfect Time	1980	—	2.00	4.00
MGM					
14141	Sandy/Handsome Johnny	1970	—	2.50	5.00
ODE					
66032	Eyesight to the Blind/Underture	1973	2.00	4.00	8.00
STORMY FOREST					
650	Rocky Raccoon/Stop Pulling and Pushing Me	1970	—	3.00	6.00
651	Minstrel from Gault/There's a Hole in My Future	1970	—	2.50	5.00
653	Give All My Love Away/Nobody Knows	1970	—	2.50	5.00
656	Here Comes the Sun/Younger Men Get Older	1971	2.00	4.00	8.00
—First pressing has an edited version of A-side					
656	Here Comes the Sun/Younger Men Get Older	1971	—	3.00	6.00
—Second (hit) pressing has full-length version of A-side and "REV" on label					
658	Missing Train/I've Got to Get to Know Myself	1971	—	2.50	5.00
660	Fire and Rain/Think About the Children	1971	—	2.50	5.00
664	Where You Gonna Run To/I've Got to Get to Know Myself	1972	—	2.50	5.00
666	Freedom/Handsome Johnny	1972	—	2.50	5.00
671	It Was a Very Good Year/I Know I Won't Be There	1973	—	2.50	5.00
672	Tight Rope/Woman	1973	—	2.50	5.00
VERVE FOLKWAYS					
5022	I Can't Make It Anymore/Morning Morning	1966	2.00	4.00	8.00
5039	I've Gotta Go/Morning Morning	1967	2.00	4.00	8.00
VERVE FORECAST					
5068	Three Day Eternity/No Opportunity Necessary, No Experience Needed	1968	—	3.00	6.00
5092	Indian Rope Man/Just Above My Hobby Horse's Head	1968	—	3.00	6.00
Albums					
A&M					
SP-4598	The End of the Beginning	1976	2.50	5.00	10.00
SP-4641	Mirage	1977	2.50	5.00	10.00
DOUGLAS					
D-779 [M]	Richie Havens' Record	1966	3.75	7.50	15.00
SD-779 [S]	Richie Havens' Record	1966	5.00	10.00	20.00
D-780 [M]	Electric Havens	1966	6.25	12.50	25.00
SD-780 [S]	Electric Havens	1966	5.00	10.00	20.00
ELEKTRA					
6E-242	Connections	1980	2.50	5.00	10.00
MGM					
SE-4698	Mixed Bag	1970	3.75	7.50	15.00
—Reissue of Verve Forecast 3006					
SE-4699	Something Else Again	1970	3.75	7.50	15.00
—Reissue of Verve Forecast 3034					
SE-4700 [(2)]	Richard P. Havens, 1963	1970	5.00	10.00	20.00
—Reissue of Verve Forecast 3047					
RBI					
400	Simple Things	1987	2.50	5.00	10.00
STORMY FOREST					
SFS-6001	Stonehenge	1969	3.75	7.50	15.00
SFS-6005	Alarm Clock	1970	3.00	6.00	12.00
SFS-6010	The Great Blind Degree	1971	3.00	6.00	12.00
SFS-6012 [(2)]	Richie Havens On Stage	1972	3.75	7.50	15.00
SFS-6013	Portfolio	1973	3.00	6.00	12.00
SFS-6201	Mixed Bag II	1974	3.00	6.00	12.00
VERVE FOLKWAYS					
FT-3006 [M]	Mixed Bag	1967	6.25	12.50	25.00
FTS-3006 [S]	Mixed Bag	1967	5.00	10.00	20.00
VERVE FORECAST					
FTS-3006	Mixed Bag	1968	3.75	7.50	15.00
FTS-3034	Something Else Again	1968	5.00	10.00	20.00
FTS-3047 [(2)]	Richard P. Havens, 1983	1968	6.25	12.50	25.00
FTS-3061	Richie Havens	1969	—	—	—
—Canceled					

HAWK, THE

See JERRY LEE LEWIS.

HAWKETTS, THE

Number	Title (A Side/B Side)	Yr	VG	VG+	NM
45s					
CHESS					
1591	Mardi Gras Mambo/Your Time Is Up	1955	25.00	50.00	100.00

HAWKINS, DALE

Number	Title (A Side/B Side)	Yr	VG	VG+	NM
45s					
ABC-PARAMOUNT					
10668	I'll Fly High/La La Song	1965	2.50	5.00	10.00
ABNAK					
110	The Flag/And I Believed You	1965	3.00	6.00	12.00
ATLANTIC					
2126	Stay at Home, Lulu/I Can't Erase You	1961	5.00	10.00	20.00
2150	What a Feeling/Women, That's What's Happening	1962	5.00	10.00	20.00

Number	Title (A Side/B Side)	Yr	VG	VG+	NM
BELL					
807	Back Street/Little Rain Cloud	1969	2.00	4.00	8.00
827	Heavy on My Mind/Joe	1969	2.00	4.00	8.00
CHECKER					
843	See You Soon, Baboon/Four Letter Word	1956	7.50	15.00	30.00
863	Susie-Q/Don't Treat Me This Way	1957	12.50	25.00	50.00
876	Baby, Baby/Mrs. Merguitory's Daughter	1957	7.50	15.00	30.00
892	Little Pig/Tornado	1958	6.25	12.50	25.00
900	La-Do-Dada/Cross Ties	1958	6.25	12.50	25.00
906	My Babe/A House, a Car, and a Wedding Ring	1958	6.25	12.50	25.00
913	Someday, One Day/Take My Heart	1959	6.25	12.50	25.00
916	Class Cutter (Yeah Yeah)/Lonely Nights	1959	6.25	12.50	25.00
923	Ain't That Lovin' You Baby/My Dream	1959	6.25	12.50	25.00
929	Our Turn/Lifeguard Man	1959	6.25	12.50	25.00
934	Liza Jane/Back to School Blues	1959	6.25	12.50	25.00
940	Hot Dog/Don't Break Your Promise to Me	1960	5.00	10.00	20.00
944	Poor Little Rhode Island/Every Little Girl	1960	5.00	10.00	20.00
944 [PS]	Poor Little Rhode Island/Every Little Girl	1960	75.00	150.00	300.00
962	Linda/Who	1960	5.00	10.00	20.00
970	Grandma's House/I Want to Love You	1961	5.00	10.00	20.00
LINCOLN					
002	Johnny B. Goode/Baby We Had It	196?	2.00	4.00	8.00
PAULA					
424	First Cut Is the Deepest/Nothing Left to Do But Say Goodbye	1977	—	2.50	5.00
TILT					
781	Money Honey/The Same Old Way	1962	5.00	10.00	20.00
783	Forbidden Love/Wish I Hadn't Called Home	1962	5.00	10.00	20.00
785	Hawk Blows, Band Plays (Part 1)/Hawk Blows, Band Plays (Part 2)	1962	5.00	10.00	20.00
ZONK					
1002	Gotta Dance/Peaches	1973	—	2.50	5.00
Albums					
BELL					
6036	L.A., Memphis and Tyler, Texas	1969	10.00	20.00	40.00
CHESS					
ACRR-706	Dale Hawkins	1976	3.75	7.50	15.00
LP-1429 [M]	Oh! Susie-Q	1958	500.00	1000.	1500.
ROULETTE					
R 25175 [M]	Let's All Twist at the Miami Beach Peppermint Lounge	1962	50.00	100.00	200.00
SR 25175 [S]	Let's All Twist at the Miami Beach Peppermint Lounge	1962	75.00	150.00	300.00

HAWKINS, EDWIN

Number	Title (A Side/B Side)	Yr	VG	VG+	NM
45s					
BUDDAH					
145	Blowin' in the Wind/Pray for Peace	1970	—	2.50	5.00
155	I Believe/He's a Friend of Mine	1970	—	2.50	5.00
200	Try the Real Thing/Praise Him	1971	—	2.50	5.00
251	Children Get Together/There's a Place for Me	1971	—	2.50	5.00
271	Give Me a Star/Jesus	1971	—	2.50	5.00
324	Jesu, Joy of Man's Desiring/(B-side unknown)	1972	—	2.50	5.00
360	Jubilation/Do My Thing	1973	—	2.50	5.00
PAVILION					
20001	Oh Happy Day/Jesus, Lover of My Soul	1969	—	3.00	6.00
20002	Ain't It Like Him/Lord Don't Move That Mountain	1969	—	3.00	6.00
Albums					
ACCORD					
SN-7120	The Genius of Edwin Hawkins	1981	2.50	5.00	10.00
BIRTHRIGHT					
4020	The Comforter	197?	3.00	6.00	12.00
LS 5904	The Edwin Hawkins Christmas Album	1985	3.75	7.50	15.00
WR-8119	Edwin Hawkins Live	198?	2.50	5.00	10.00
ST-70200	The Edwin Hawkins Christmas Album	1987	2.00	4.00	8.00
—Reissue					
ST-70201	Have Mercy	1987	2.00	4.00	8.00
ST-70202	Angels Will Be Singing	1987	2.00	4.00	8.00
D1-70208	Live with the Oakland Symphony, Vol. 1	1988	2.00	4.00	8.00
—Reissue of Myrrh 6691					
D1-70210	Live with the Oakland Symphony, Vol. 2	1988	2.00	4.00	8.00
—Reissue of Myrrh 6700					
ST-70300	Give Us Peace	1987	2.00	4.00	8.00
D1-70315	The Name	1988	2.50	5.00	10.00
BUDDAH					
BDS-5054	Peace Is Blowin' in the Wind	1969	3.75	7.50	15.00
BDS-5064	More Happy Days	1970	3.75	7.50	15.00
BDS-5070	Oh Happy Day	1970	3.00	6.00	12.00
—Reissue of Pavilion LP					
BDS-5086	Children (Get Together)	1971	3.75	7.50	15.00
BDS-5101	I'd Like to Teach the World to Sing	1972	3.75	7.50	15.00
LECTION					
501	Imagine Heaven	1982	2.50	5.00	10.00
810639-1	The Edwin Hawkins Mass Choir	198?	2.50	5.00	10.00
MYRRH					
6691	Live with the Oakland Symphony, Vol. 1	198?	2.50	5.00	10.00
6700	Live with the Oakland Symphony, Vol. 2	198?	2.50	5.00	10.00
PAVILION					
10001	Let Us Go Into the House of the Lord	1969	3.75	7.50	15.00
SAVOY					
7077 [(2)]	The Best of the Edwin Hawkins Singers	198?	3.00	6.00	12.00

HAWKINS, JALACY

See SCREAMIN' JAY HAWKINS.

HAWKINS, RONNIE

His backing band, The Hawks, evolved into THE BAND.

Number	Title (A Side/B Side)	Yr	VG	VG+	NM
45s					
COTILLION					
44060	Matchbox/Down in the Alley	1970	—	3.00	6.00
44067	Forty Days/Bitter Green	1970	—	3.00	6.00
44076	Little Bird/One More Night	1970	—	3.00	6.00
MONUMENT					
8548	Lawdy Miss Clawdy/Cora Mae	1972	—	2.50	5.00
8561	Lonesome Town/Kinky	1973	—	2.50	5.00
8573	Diddley Daddy/Cora Mae	1973	—	2.50	5.00
8583	Bo Diddley/Lonely Hours	1973	—	2.50	5.00
ROULETTE					
4154 [M]	Forty Days/One of These Days	1959	6.25	12.50	25.00
SSR-4154 [S]	Forty Days/One of These Days	1959	12.50	25.00	50.00
4177 [M]	Mary Lou/Need Your Lovin'	1959	7.50	15.00	30.00
SSR-4177 [S]	Mary Lou/Need Your Lovin'	1959	12.50	25.00	50.00
4209	Southern Love/Love Me Like You Can	1959	5.00	10.00	20.00
4228	Lonely Hours/Clara	1960	5.00	10.00	20.00
4231	The Ballad of Caryl Chessman/The Tale of Floyd Collins	1960	5.00	10.00	20.00
4249	Ruby Baby/Hayride	1960	5.00	10.00	20.00
4267	Sumemrtime/Mister and Mississippi	1960	5.00	10.00	20.00
4311	Cold, Cold Heart/Nobody's Lonesome for Me	1960	5.00	10.00	20.00
4400	Come Love/I Feel Good	1961	5.00	10.00	20.00
4483	Bo Diddley/Who Do You Love	1963	5.00	10.00	20.00
4502	High Blood Pressure/There's a Screw Loose	1963	5.00	10.00	20.00
Albums					
ACCORD					
SN-7213	Premonition	1983	2.50	5.00	10.00
COTILLION					
SD 9019	Ronnie Hawkins	1970	3.75	7.50	15.00
SD 9039	The Hawk	1971	3.75	7.50	15.00
MONUMENT					
KZ 31330	Rock and Roll Resurrection	1972	3.00	6.00	12.00
KZ 32940	The Ghost of Rock and Roll	1973	3.00	6.00	12.00
ZG 33855 [(2)]	Rock and Roll Resurrection/The Ghost of Rock and Roll	1976	3.75	7.50	15.00
ROULETTE					
R 25078 [M]	Ronnie Hawkins	1959	37.50	75.00	150.00
—White label with spokes					
R 25078 [M]	Ronnie Hawkins	1964	12.50	25.00	50.00
—Orange/yellow label					
SR 25078 [S]	Ronnie Hawkins	1959	50.00	100.00	200.00
—White label with spokes; black vinyl					
SR 25078 [S]	Ronnie Hawkins	1959	150.00	300.00	600.00
—White label with spokes; red vinyl					
SR 25078 [S]	Ronnie Hawkins	1964	15.00	30.00	60.00
—Orange/yellow label					
R 25102 [M]	Mr. Dynamo	1960	37.50	75.00	150.00
SR 25102 [S]	Mr. Dynamo	1960	50.00	100.00	200.00
—Black vinyl					
SR 25102 [S]	Mr. Dynamo	1960	150.00	300.00	600.00
—Red vinyl					
R 25120 [M]	The Folk Ballads of Ronnie Hawkins	1960	25.00	50.00	100.00
SR 25120 [S]	The Folk Ballads of Ronnie Hawkins	1960	37.50	75.00	150.00
R 25137 [M]	The Songs of Hank Williams	1960	25.00	50.00	100.00
SR 25137 [S]	The Songs of Hank Williams	1960	37.50	75.00	150.00
SR 42045	The Best of Ronnie Hawkins and His Band	1970	6.25	12.50	25.00
UNITED ARTISTS					
UA-LA968-H	The Hawk	1979	2.50	5.00	10.00

HAWKINS, SCREAMIN' JAY

Number	Title (A Side/B Side)	Yr	VG	VG+	NM
45s					
APOLLO					
506	Please Try to Understand/Not Anymore	1957	6.25	12.50	25.00
528	Baptize Me in Wine/Not Anymore	1958	6.25	12.50	25.00
CHANCELLOR					
1117	Ashes/Nitty Gritty	1962	3.75	7.50	15.00
DECCA					
32019	All Night/I'm Not Made of Clay	1966	3.75	7.50	15.00
32100	I Put a Spell on You/You're an Exception to the Rule	1967	10.00	20.00	40.00
ENRICA					
1010	I Hear Voices/I Just Don't Care	1962	6.25	12.50	25.00
GRAND					
135	Take Me Back/I Is	1957	6.25	12.50	25.00
MERCURY					
70549	This Is All/She Put the Whammee on Me	1955	20.00	40.00	80.00
OKEH					
7072	I Put a Spell on You/Little Demon	1956	12.50	25.00	50.00
7084	You Made Me Love You/Darling, Please Forgive Me	1957	7.50	15.00	30.00
7087	Person to Person/Frenzy	1957	7.50	15.00	30.00
7101	Alligator Wine/There's Something Wrong with You	1958	7.50	15.00	30.00
PHILIPS					
40606	Stone Crazy/I'm Lonely	1969	—	3.00	6.00
40636	Too Many Teardrops/Makaka Ways	1969	—	3.00	6.00
40645	Constipation Blues/Do You Really Love Me	1969	—	3.00	6.00
40668	Moanin'/Do You Really Love Me	1970	—	3.00	6.00
40674	Our Love Is Not for Three/Take Me Back	1970	—	3.00	6.00
PROVIDENCE					
411	My Kind of Love/Po' Folks	1965	3.00	6.00	12.00
QUEEN BEE					
1314	Monkberry Moon Delight/Sweet Ginny	1973	—	3.00	6.00
RCA VICTOR					
PB-10127	You Put the Spell on Me/Voodoo	1974	—	2.50	5.00
ROULETTE					
4579	The Whammy/Strange	1964	3.00	6.00	12.00
TIMELY					
1004	Baptize Me in Wine/Not Anymore	1954	20.00	40.00	80.00
1005	I Found My Way to Wine/Please Try to Understand	1954	20.00	40.00	80.00
WING					
90005	Well, I Tried/You're All of Life to Me	1955	10.00	20.00	40.00
90055	Even Though/Talk About Me	1956	7.50	15.00	30.00

Number	Title (A Side/B Side)	Yr	VG	VG+	NM
Albums					
EPIC					
LN 3448 [M]	At Home with Screamin' Jay Hawkins	1958	300.00	600.00	1200.
LN 3457 [M]	I Put a Spell on You	1958	125.00	250.00	500.00
BN 26457 [R]	I Put a Spell on You	1969	15.00	30.00	60.00
PHILIPS					
PHS 600319	What That Is	1969	10.00	20.00	40.00
PHS 600336	Screamin' Jay Hawkins	1970	10.00	20.00	40.00
SOUNDS OF HAWAII					
5015	A Night at Forbidden City	196?	12.50	25.00	50.00

HAWKS, THE (1)

Number	Title (A Side/B Side)	Yr	VG	VG+	NM
45s					
IMPERIAL					
5266	Joe the Grinder/Candy Girl	1954	62.50	125.00	250.00
5281	She's All Right/Good News	1954	50.00	100.00	200.00
5292	It Ain't That Way/I-Yi	1954	25.00	50.00	100.00
5306	Nobody But You/Give It Up	1954	25.00	50.00	100.00
5317	All Women Are the Same/That's What You Are	1954	25.00	50.00	100.00
5332	It's Too Late Now/I Can't See for Lookin'	1955	25.00	50.00	100.00
MODERN					
990	It's All Over/Ever Since You Been Gone	1956	62.50	125.00	250.00
POST					
2004	These Blues/Why Oh Why	1955	75.00	150.00	300.00

HAWKS, THE (U)

None of these are group (1), but we don't know how many groups are represented below.

Number	Title (A Side/B Side)	Yr	VG	VG+	NM
45s					
ABC-PARAMOUNT					
10116	Grasshopper/The Grissle	1960	6.25	12.50	25.00
DEL-FI					
4108	A Little More Wine, My Dear?/Fussy	1958	10.00	20.00	40.00
MALA					
401	Cupcake/Lupp!!	1959	5.00	10.00	20.00

HAWKWIND

Number	Title (A Side/B Side)	Yr	VG	VG+	NM
45s					
ATCO					
7017	Kings of Speed/Motor Head	1975	—	2.50	5.00
UNITED ARTISTS					
XW314	Urban Guerrilla/Brainbox Position	1973	—	2.50	5.00
50949	Seven by Seven/Silver Necklace	1972	—	2.50	5.00
Albums					
ATCO					
SD 36-115	Warrior on the Edge of Time	1975	3.75	7.50	15.00
GWR					
1237 [(2)]	Live Chronicles	1986	3.00	6.00	12.00
LIBERTY					
LWB-120 [(2)]	Space Ritual/Alive in Liverpool and London	1981	3.00	6.00	12.00
—Reissue of United Artists 120					
LW-5567	In Search of Space	1981	2.00	4.00	8.00
—Reissue of United Artists 5567					
SIRE					
SRK 6047	Quark Strangeness and Charm	1978	3.00	6.00	12.00
UNITED ARTISTS					
UA-LA001-F	Doremi Fasol Latido	1973	3.75	7.50	15.00
UA-LA120-H [(2)]	Space Ritual/Alive in Liverpool and London	1973	5.00	10.00	20.00
UA-LA328-G	Hall of the Mountain Grill	1974	3.75	7.50	15.00
UAS-5519	Hawkwind	1971	3.75	7.50	15.00
UAS-5567	In Search of Space	1972	3.75	7.50	15.00

HAWLEY, DEANE

Number	Title (A Side/B Side)	Yr	VG	VG+	NM
45s					
DORE					
524	New Fad/Pretty Little Mary	1959	3.75	7.50	15.00
536	Good Morning, Mr. Sun/Bossman	1959	3.75	7.50	15.00
543	Where Is My Angel/I'll Never Be a Fool Again	1960	3.75	7.50	15.00
554	Look for a Star/Bossman	1960	3.75	7.50	15.00
569	Like a Fool/Stay at Home Blues	1960	3.75	7.50	15.00
577	Hey There/Rainbow	1960	3.75	7.50	15.00
LIBERTY					
55359	Pocketful of Rainbows/That Dream Could Never Be	1961	5.00	10.00	20.00
55446	Queen of the Angels/You Conquered Me	1962	6.25	12.50	25.00
SUNDOWN					
111	I Hate to See Me Go/Love of the Common People	196?	2.50	5.00	10.00
113	That's the Name of the Game/Canterbury Station	196?	2.50	5.00	10.00
VALOR					
2003	Mummy's Bracelet/Don't Keep Me Guessin'	1961	7.50	15.00	30.00
WARNER BROS.					
5484	I Know She'll Be There/You'll Never Have to Cry Again	1964	3.00	6.00	12.00

HAWN, GOLDIE

Number	Title (A Side/B Side)	Yr	VG	VG+	NM
45s					
REPRISE					
1089	Butterfly/Uncle Pen	1972	2.00	4.00	8.00
1126	Pitta Patta/(Instrumental)	1972	2.00	4.00	8.00
1126 [PS]	Pitta Patta/(Instrumental)	1972	2.50	5.00	10.00
Albums					
REPRISE					
MS 2061	Goldie	1972	6.25	12.50	25.00

HAYES, BILL

Number	Title (A Side/B Side)	Yr	VG	VG+	NM
45s					
ABC-PARAMOUNT					
9785	Wringle, Wrangle/Westward Ho the Wagons	1957	3.00	6.00	12.00
9785 [PS]	Wringle, Wrangle/Westward Ho the Wagons	1957	5.00	10.00	20.00
9809	Ramshackle Daddy/On the Outside	1957	3.00	6.00	12.00
9895	Bop Boy/Uh Huh Oh Yeah	1958	15.00	30.00	60.00
CADENCE					
1245	I Knew an Old Lady/(B-side unknown)	1954	3.00	6.00	12.00
1256	The Ballad of Davy Crockett/Farewell	1955	3.75	7.50	15.00
1261	The Berry Tree/Blue Back Hair	1955	3.00	6.00	12.00
1274	That Do Make It Nice/Kwela Kwela	1955	3.00	6.00	12.00
1275	The Legend of Wyatt Earp/White Buffalo	1955	3.75	7.50	15.00
1294	I Knew an Old Lady/Das Ist Music	1956	3.00	6.00	12.00
1301	A Message from James Dean/The Trail's End	1956	3.75	7.50	15.00
KAPP					
258	Wimoweh/Goin' Down the Road Feelin' Bad	1959	2.50	5.00	10.00
298	Choppin' Mountains/Tall Teller of Tall Tales	1959	2.50	5.00	10.00
MERCURY					
5599	Too Young/Shenandoah Waltz	1951	5.00	10.00	20.00
MGM					
11006	Waltz of the Wind/Mine	1951	3.75	7.50	15.00
11042	The Love of a Gypsy/I've Got an Idea for a Song	1951	3.75	7.50	15.00
11064	I Love You/Never	1951	3.75	7.50	15.00
11112	Charmaine/For All We Know	1951	3.75	7.50	15.00
11142	We Won't Live in A.../Tulips and Heather	1952	3.75	7.50	15.00
11205	April Sings/Golden Haired Boy	1952	3.75	7.50	15.00
11210	When I Dream/Don't Send Me Home	1952	3.75	7.50	15.00
—With Judy Johnson					
11266	High Noon/Padam Padam	1952	3.75	7.50	15.00
11296	Say You'll Wait for Me/My Search for You	1952	3.75	7.50	15.00
11384	My Ever Lovin'/As Long As You Care	1952	3.75	7.50	15.00
11394	How Do You Speak to An Angel/The Donkey Song	1953	3.75	7.50	15.00
11492	I'm So Lonesome/There's Music in You	1953	3.75	7.50	15.00
11556	A Little Kiss Each Morning/Love You	1953	3.75	7.50	15.00
—With Judy Johnson					
12004	Wanderin'/You're Nearer	1955	3.00	6.00	12.00
Albums					
ABC-PARAMOUNT					
194 [M]	Bill Hayes Sings the Best of Disney	1957	10.00	20.00	40.00
DAYBREAK					
DR-2020	The Look of Love	1972	6.25	12.50	25.00
KAPP					
KL-1106 [M]	Jimmy Crack Corn	1958	6.25	12.50	25.00

HAYES, ISAAC

Number	Title (A Side/B Side)	Yr	VG	VG+	NM
45s					
ABC/HBS					
12118	Chocolate Chip/(Instrumental)	1975	—	2.00	4.00
12138	Come Live with Me/Body Language	1975	—	2.00	4.00
12171	Disco Connection/St. Thomas Square	1976	—	2.00	4.00
—By the "Isaac Hayes Movement"					
12176	Rock Me Easy Baby (Pt. 1)/Rock Me Easy Baby (Pt. 2)	1976	—	2.00	4.00
12206	Juicy Fruit (Disco Freak) (Pt. 1)/Juicy Fruit (Disco Freak) (Pt. 2)	1976	—	2.00	4.00
BRUNSWICK					
55258	Sweet Temptation/Laura	1964	2.50	5.00	10.00
CAPITOL					
S7-18869	Walk On By/Tired of Being Alone	1995	—	—	3.00
—B-side by Al Green					
COLUMBIA					
06363	Ike's Rap/Hey Girl (Edited)	1986	—	—	3.00
06363 [PS]	Ike's Rap/Hey Girl (Edited)	1986	—	2.00	4.00
06655	Thing for You/Thank God for Love	1987	—	—	3.00
07104	If You Want My Lovin' (Do Me Right)/(Instrumental)	1987	—	—	3.00
07978	Showdown/(Instrumental)	1988	—	—	3.00
08116	Let Me Be Your Everything/Curious	1988	—	—	3.00
ENTERPRISE					
002	Precious Precious/Going to Chicago Blues	1969	2.00	4.00	8.00
9003	By the Time I Get to Phoenix/Walk On By	1969	—	3.00	6.00
9006	The Mistletoe and Me/Winter Snow	1969	—	3.00	6.00
9017	I Stand Accused/I Just Don't Know What to Do with Myself	1970	—	2.50	5.00
9028	The Look of Love/Ike's Mood	1970	—	2.50	5.00
9031	Never Can Say Goodbye/I Can't Help It If I'm Still in Love with You	1971	—	2.50	5.00
9038	Theme from Shaft/Cafe Regio's	1971	—	2.50	5.00
9042	Do Your Thing/Ellie's Love Theme	1972	—	2.50	5.00
9045	Let's Stay Together/Soulville	1972	—	2.50	5.00
9049	Ain't That Loving You (For More Reasons Than One)/Baby I'm-a Want You	1972	—	2.50	5.00
—With David Porter					
9058	Theme from The Men/Type Thang	1972	—	2.50	5.00
9065	(If Loving You Is Wrong) I Don't Want to Be Right/Rolling Down a Mountainside	1973	—	2.50	5.00
9085	Joy (Part 1)/Joy (Part 2)	1973	—	2.50	5.00
9095	Wonderful/Someone Made You for Me	1974	—	2.50	5.00
9104	Title Theme/Hung Up on My Baby	1974	—	2.50	5.00
POLYDOR					
2011	Don't Let Go/You Can't Hold Your Woman	1979	—	2.00	4.00
2068	A Few More Kisses to Go/What Does It Take	1980	—	2.00	4.00
2090	I Ain't Never/Love Has Been Good to Us	1980	—	2.00	4.00
2102	It's All in the Game/Wherever You Are	1980	—	2.00	4.00
2182	I'm So Proud/I'm Gonna Make Me Love You	1981	—	2.00	4.00
2192	Fugitive/Lifetime Thing	1981	—	2.00	4.00
14446	Out of the Ghetto/It's Heaven to Me	1977	—	2.00	4.00
14464	Moonlight Lovin' (Menage a Trois)/It's Heaven to Me	1978	—	2.00	4.00
14521	Zeke the Freak/If We Ever Needed Peace	1978	—	2.00	4.00
14534	Just the Way You Are (Part 1)/Just the Way You Are (Part 2)	1979	—	2.00	4.00
STAX					
3209	Feel Like Makin' Love (Part 1)/Feel Like Makin' Love (Part 2)	1978	—	2.50	5.00
Albums					
ABC/HBS					
D-874	Chocolate Chip	1975	3.75	7.50	15.00

Number	Title (A Side/B Side)	Yr	VG	VG+	NM
D-923	Disco Connection	1975	3.00	6.00	12.00
D-925	Groove-a-Thon	1976	3.00	6.00	12.00
D-953	Juicy Fruit (Disco Freak)	1976	3.00	6.00	12.00
ATLANTIC					
SD 1599	In the Beginning	1972	3.75	7.50	15.00
—Reissue of Enterprise 100					
COLUMBIA					
FC 40316	U-Turn	1986	2.50	5.00	10.00
FC 40941	Love Attack	1988	2.50	5.00	10.00
ENTERPRISE					
E-100 [M]	Presenting Isaac Hayes	1968	10.00	20.00	40.00
ES-100 [S]	Presenting Isaac Hayes	1968	7.50	15.00	30.00
ENS-1001	Hot Buttered Soul	1969	5.00	10.00	20.00
ENS-1010	The Isaac Hayes Movement	1970	5.00	10.00	20.00
ENS-1014	To Be Continued	1970	5.00	10.00	20.00
ENS-5002 [(2)]	Shaft	1971	5.00	10.00	20.00
ENS-5003 [(2)]	Black Moses	1971	5.00	10.00	20.00
ENS-5005 [(2)]	Live at the Sahara Tahoe	1973	3.75	7.50	15.00
ENS-5007	Joy	1973	3.00	6.00	12.00
ENS-7504	Tough Guys	1974	3.00	6.00	12.00
ENS-7507 [(2)]	Truck Turner	1974	3.75	7.50	15.00
ENS-7510	The Best of Isaac Hayes	1975	3.00	6.00	12.00
POINTBLANK					
SPRO-12787 [DJ]	Funky Junky	1995	3.75	7.50	15.00
—Vinyl is promo only					
POLYDOR					
PD-1-6120	New Horizon	1977	2.50	5.00	10.00
PD-1-6164	For the Sake of Love	1978	2.50	5.00	10.00
PD-1-6224	Don't Let Go	1979	2.50	5.00	10.00
PD-1-6269	And Once Again	1980	2.50	5.00	10.00
STAX					
STX-4102	Hotbed	197?	2.50	5.00	10.00
STX-4114	Hot Buttered Soul	1978	2.50	5.00	10.00
—Reissue of Enterprise 1001					
STX-4129	The Isaac Hayes Movement	197?	2.50	5.00	10.00
—Reissue of Enterprise 1010					
STX-4133	To Be Continued	197?	2.50	5.00	10.00
—Reissue of Enterprise 1014					
MPS-8509	Excerpts from Black Moses	1981	2.50	5.00	10.00
MPS-8515	His Greatest Hit Singles	1982	2.50	5.00	10.00
MPS-8530	Joy	1984	2.50	5.00	10.00
—Reissue of Enterprise 5007					
STX-88002 [(2)]	Shaft	1979	3.00	6.00	12.00
—Reissue of Enterprise 5002					
STX-88003 [(2)]	Enterprise: His Greatest Hits	1980	3.00	6.00	12.00
STX-88004 [(2)]	Live at the Sahara Tahoe	198?	3.00	6.00	12.00
—Reissue of Enterprise 5005					

HAYES, ISAAC, AND DIONNE WARWICK

Number	Title (A Side/B Side)	Yr	VG	VG+	NM
45s					
ABC/HBS					
12253	By the Time I Get to Phoenix—I Say a Little Prayer/That's the Way I Like It—Cry Down	1977	—	2.00	4.00
Albums					
ABC/HBS					
D-996 [(2)]	A Man and a Woman	1977	3.75	7.50	15.00
MCA					
10012 [(2)]	A Man and a Woman	198?	3.00	6.00	12.00
—Reissue of ABC/HBS 996					

HAYES, JIMMY, AND THE SOUL SURFERS

Number	Title (A Side/B Side)	Yr	VG	VG+	NM
45s					
IMPERIAL					
5986	Summer Surfin'/Down on the Beach	1963	6.25	12.50	25.00

HAYES, LINDA

Number	Title (A Side/B Side)	Yr	VG	VG+	NM
45s					
ANTLER					
4000	I Had a Dream/You Ain't Movin' Me	1956	7.50	15.00	30.00
DECCA					
29644	Our Love's Forever Blessed/You're the Only One for Me	1955	7.50	15.00	30.00
HOLLYWOOD					
1003	Take Me Back/Yours for the Asking	1953	12.50	25.00	50.00
1009	No Next Time/Don't Do Nothin' Baby	1954	10.00	20.00	40.00
1016	Play It Right/Your Back's Out	1954	10.00	20.00	40.00
1019	Non-Cooperation/Grrr! Mambo	1954	10.00	20.00	40.00
1027	Change of Heart/Darling Angel	1954	10.00	20.00	40.00
1031	Johnny Ace's Last Letter/Why Johnny Why	1955	12.50	25.00	50.00
—With Johnny Moore					
1032	Our Love's Forever Blessed/You're the Only One for Me	1955	15.00	30.00	60.00
KING					
4752	My Name Ain't Annie/Let's Babalu	1954	18.75	37.50	75.00
4773	Please Have Mercy/Oochi Poochi	1955	12.50	25.00	50.00
RECORDED IN HOLLYWOOD					
244	Yes! I Know (What You're Putting Down)/Sister Ann	1953	12.50	25.00	50.00
246	Big City (Part 1)/Big City (Part 2)	1953	12.50	25.00	50.00

HAYES, TOMMY

Number	Title (A Side/B Side)	Yr	VG	VG+	NM
45s					
PHILIPS					
40259	Trance/Glistening Lights	1965	7.50	15.00	30.00
—The Four Seasons sing backup					

HAYMARKET SQUARE

Number	Title (A Side/B Side)	Yr	VG	VG+	NM
Albums					
CHAPARRAL					
201	Magic Lantern	1968	375.00	750.00	1500.

HAYWARD, JUSTIN

Also see THE MOODY BLUES.

Number	Title (A Side/B Side)	Yr	VG	VG+	NM
45s					
COLUMBIA					
10799	Forever Autumn/The Fighting Machine	1978	2.00	4.00	8.00
DERAM					
401	Night Flight/Suitcase	1980	—	2.00	4.00
402	A Face in the Crowd/It's Not On	1980	—	2.00	4.00
7541	Lay It On Me/Songwriter Part 2	1977	—	2.00	4.00
7542	Country Girl/Songwriter Part 2	1977	—	2.00	4.00
RED BIRD					
10-049	London Is Behind Me/Day Must Come	1966	5.00	10.00	20.00
Albums					
DERAM					
DRL 4801	Night Flight	1980	3.00	5.00	12.00
DES 18073	Songwriter	1977	3.75	7.50	15.00

HAYWARD, JUSTIN, AND JOHN LODGE

Also see JUSTIN HAYWARD; THE MOODY BLUES.

Number	Title (A Side/B Side)	Yr	VG	VG+	NM
45s					
THRESHOLD					
67019	I Dreamed Last Night/Remember Me, My Friend	1975	—	2.00	4.00
67021	Blue Guitar/When You Wake Up	1975	—	2.00	4.00
67021 [PS]	Blue Guitar/When You Wake Up	1975	—	2.50	5.00
Albums					
THRESHOLD					
THS 14	Blue Jays	1975	3.75	7.50	15.00
THSX 101 [DJ]	Blue Jays	1975	12.50	25.00	50.00
—Open-end interview with script; used to promote the LP of the same name					

HAYWOOD, LEON

Number	Title (A Side/B Side)	Yr	VG	VG+	NM
12-Inch Singles					
CASABLANCA					
812164-1	I'm Out to Catch (LP version)/(Dub Version)	1983	—	3.00	6.00
MCA					
13911	Disco Fever/Party	1978	3.00	6.00	12.00
45s					
20TH CENTURY					
2003	One Way Ticket to Loveland/There Ain't Enough Love Around	1972	—	3.00	6.00
2022	La La Song/Sweet Loving Fair	1973	—	3.00	6.00
2065	Keep It in the Family/Long As There's You (I Got Love)	1974	—	2.50	5.00
2103	Sugar Lump/That Sweet Woman of Mine	1974	—	2.50	5.00
2146	Believe Half of What You See (And None of What You Hear)/The Day I Laid Eyes on You	1974	—	2.50	5.00
2191	Come an' Get Yourself Some/B.M.F. Beautiful	1975	—	3.00	6.00
2191	Come an' Get Yourself Some/Who You Been Givin' It Up To	1975	—	2.50	5.00
2228	I Want'a Do Something Freaky to You/I Know What Love Is	1975	—	2.50	5.00
2264	Just Your Fool/Consider the Source	1975	—	2.50	5.00
2285	Strokin' (Part 1)/Strokin' (Part 2)	1976	—	2.50	5.00
2443	Don't Push It Don't Force It/Who You Been Givin' It Up To	1980	—	2.00	4.00
2454	If You're Lookin' for a Night of Fun (Look Past Me, I'm Not the One)/That's What Time It Is	1980	—	2.00	4.00
2469	Daydream/Love Is What We Came Here For	1980	—	2.00	4.00
ATLANTIC					
2799	You and Your Moody Ways/You Know What	1971	—	3.00	6.00
2858	Clean Up Your Own Back Yard/String Bean	1972	—	3.00	6.00
CAPITOL					
2584	Just Your Fool/Consider the Source	1969	3.75	7.50	15.00
2752	I Wanna Thank You/I Was Sent to Love You	1970	3.75	7.50	15.00
CASABLANCA					
812164-7	I'm Out to Catch/Keep It in the Family	1983	—	—	3.00
—With Karen Roberts					
814217-7	T.V. Mama/Steppin' Out	1983	—	—	3.00
COLUMBIA					
10413	The Streets Will Love You to Death - Part 1/The Streets Will Love You to Death - Part 2	1976	—	2.00	4.00
10477	Dream Dream/Let Me Make It Good	1977	—	2.00	4.00
DECCA					
32164	It's Got to Be Mellow/Cornbread & Buttermilk	1967	2.00	4.00	8.00
32230	Mellow Moonlight/Tennessee Waltz	1967	2.00	4.00	8.00
32310	Mercy, Mercy, Mercy/It's the Last Time	1968	2.00	4.00	8.00
32348	I Want to Talk About My Baby/You Don't Have to See Me Cry	1968	2.00	4.00	8.00
32414	Blues Get Off My Shoulder/Everyday Will Be Like a Holiday	1968	2.00	4.00	8.00
FANTASY					
581	The Truth About Money/Would I	1964	6.25	12.50	25.00
FAT FISH					
8005	Soul Cargo/(B-side unknown)	1966	7.50	15.00	30.00
IMPERIAL					
66123	She's With Her Other Love/Pain in My Heart	1965	3.75	7.50	15.00
—As "Leon Hayward"					
66149	Soul-On/1-2-3	1965	3.00	6.00	12.00
MCA					
40793	Super Sexy/Life Goes On	1977	—	2.00	4.00
40849	Double My Pleasure/It's Gonna Be Alright	1978	—	2.00	4.00
40889	Fine and Healthy Thing/She's Built, She's Stacked	1978	—	2.00	4.00
40941	Party/Life Goes On	1978	—	2.00	4.00
40989	Disco Fever/Self Respect	1979	—	2.00	4.00
41035	Energy/You Bring Out the Freak in Me	1979	—	2.00	4.00
MODERN					
99708	Tenderoni/(Instrumental)	1984	—	—	3.00
Albums					
20TH CENTURY					
T-411	Back to Stay	1973	3.00	6.00	12.00

Number	Title (A Side/B Side)	Yr	VG	VG+	NM
T-440	Keep It in the Family	1974	3.00	6.00	12.00
T-476	Come and Get Yourself Some	1975	2.50	5.00	10.00
T-613	Naturally	1980	2.50	5.00	10.00
COLUMBIA					
PC 34363	Intimate	1976	2.50	5.00	10.00
DECCA					
DL 74949	It's Got to Be Mellow	1969	5.00	10.00	20.00
GALAXY					
8206	Mellow, Mellow	196?	5.00	10.00	20.00
MCA					
2322	Double My Pleasure	1978	2.50	5.00	10.00
3090	Energy	1979	2.50	5.00	10.00

HEAD

Albums

Number	Title (A Side/B Side)	Yr	VG	VG+	NM
BUDDAH					
BDS-5062	Head	1970	7.50	15.00	30.00
—With coloring book (deduct 1/3 if missing)					

HEAD, JIM, AND HIS DEL RAYS

Albums

Number	Title (A Side/B Side)	Yr	VG	VG+	NM
HP					
22893 [M]	Jim Head and His Del Rays	1963	75.00	150.00	300.00

HEAD, MURRAY

45s

Number	Title (A Side/B Side)	Yr	VG	VG+	NM
A&M					
1796	Say It Ain't So, Joe/She's Such a Drag	1976	—	2.00	4.00
1836	Somebody's Rockin' My Dreamboat/She's Such a Drag	1976	—	2.00	4.00
DECCA					
32603	Superstar/John Nineteen Forty-One	1969	—	3.00	6.00
—First pressings use this reference on the A-side: "Superstar (From JESUS CHRIST)"					
32603	Superstar/John Nineteen Forty-One	1970	—	2.50	5.00
—Reissues have the word "Superstar" without a subtitle, and small print mentions the LP "Jesus Christ Superstar"					
32603 [PS]	Superstar/John Nineteen Forty-One	1970	2.00	4.00	8.00
—Picture sleeve accompanies second pressings					
32709	Heaven on Their Minds/Strange Thing (Mystifying)	1970	—	2.50	5.00
32709 [PS]	Heaven on Their Minds/Strange Thing (Mystifying)	1970	2.00	4.00	8.00
RCA					
PB-13988	One Night in Bangkok/Merano	1985	—	2.00	4.00
PB-13988 [PS]	One Night in Bangkok/Merano	1985	—	2.00	4.00
PB-14152	Pity the Child/The Deal (No Deal)	1985	—	2.00	4.00
GB-14339	One Night in Bangkok/Pity the Child	1986	—	—	3.00
—Gold Standard Series					

Albums

Number	Title (A Side/B Side)	Yr	VG	VG+	NM
A&M					
SP-4558	Say It Ain't So	1976	3.00	6.00	12.00

HEAD, ROY

45s

Number	Title (A Side/B Side)	Yr	VG	VG+	NM
ABC					
12346	How You See 'Em, Now You Don't/Smooth Whiskey	1978	—	2.00	4.00
12383	Tonight's the Night/A Lady in My Room	1978	—	2.00	4.00
12418	Dixie/Love Survived	1978	—	2.00	4.00
12462 [DJ]	Kiss You and Make It Better (mono/stereo)	1979	—	2.00	4.00
—May be promo only					
ABC DOT					
17608	Lady Luck and Mother Nature/The Door I Used to Close	1976	—	2.00	4.00
17629	Ain't It Funny (How Times Haven't Changed)/A Bridge for Crawling Back	1976	—	2.00	4.00
17650	One Night/Deep Elem Blues	1976	—	2.00	4.00
17669	Just Because/Angel with a Broken Wing	1976	—	2.00	4.00
17706	Julianne/Velvet Strings	1977	—	2.00	4.00
17722	Come to Me/Georgia on My Mind	1977	—	2.00	4.00
ABC DUNHILL					
4240	I'm Not a Fool Anymore/Mama Mama	1970	—	3.00	6.00
ATLANTIC AMERICA					
99529	There's Something on Your Mind/Everything A Man Can Do (And I Love You)	1986	—	—	3.00
AVION					
105	Where Did He Go Right/(B-side unknown)	1983	—	2.00	4.00
BACK BEAT					
543	Teenage Letter/Pain	1965	3.00	6.00	12.00
546	Treat Her Right/So Long, My Love	1965	4.00	8.00	16.00
555	Apple of My Eye/I Pass the Day	1965	3.00	6.00	12.00
560	My Babe/Pain	1966	3.00	6.00	12.00
563	Driving Wheel/Wigglin' and Gigglin'	1966	3.00	6.00	12.00
571	Don't Cry No More/To Make a Big Man Cry	1966	3.00	6.00	12.00
576	You're (Almost) Tough/Tush Hog	1966	3.00	6.00	12.00
582	Nobody But Me/A Good Man Is Hard to Find	1967	2.50	5.00	10.00
CHURCHILL					
7778	After Texas/California Day	1981	—	2.00	4.00
ELEKTRA					
46549	In Our Room/Things I Never Could Have Left Behind	1979	—	2.00	4.00
46582	The Fire of Two Old Flames/Under Suspicion	1980	—	2.00	4.00
46653	Long Drop/Gonna Save It for My Baby	1980	—	2.00	4.00
47029	Drinking Them Long Necks/Baby's Found Another Way to Love Me	1980	—	2.00	4.00
47081	I've Never Gone to Bed With an Ugly Woman/All Night Long Is Gone	1981	—	2.00	4.00
MEGA					
1219	Baby's Not Home/Do What You Can Do	1974	—	2.50	5.00
MERCURY					
72750	Got Down on Saturday (Sunday in the Rain)/The Grass Was Green	1967	2.00	4.00	8.00
72799	Broadway Walk/Turn Out the Lights	1968	2.00	4.00	8.00
72848	Ain't Goin' Down Right/Lovin' Man on Your Hands	1968	2.00	4.00	8.00
NSD					
129	Play Another Gettin' Drunk and Take Somebody Home Song/Your Next One and Only	1982	—	2.00	4.00
146	The Trouble with Hearts/Naughty Smile	1982	—	2.00	4.00
156	Your Mama Don't Dance/Party Time	1982	—	2.00	4.00
SCEPTER					
12116	Just a Little Bit/Treat Me Right	1965	2.50	5.00	10.00
12117	Won't Be Blue/One More Time	1965	2.50	5.00	10.00
12124	Get Back — Part 1/Get Back — Part 2	1965	2.50	5.00	10.00
12138	Convicted/One More Time	1966	2.50	5.00	10.00
SHANNON					
829	The Most Wanted Woman in Town/Gingerbread Man	1975	—	2.50	5.00
833	Help Yourself to Me/To Make a Big Man Cry	1975	—	2.50	5.00
838	I'll Take It/The One That Got Away	1975	—	2.50	5.00
TEXAS CRUDE					
614	Break Out the Good Stuff/(B-side unknown)	1985	—	2.00	4.00
TMI					
75-0103	Rock and Roll Mood/You Got the Power	1972	—	2.50	5.00
75-0106	Why Don't We Go Somewhere and Love/Smell-A-Woman	1972	—	2.50	5.00
BTBO-0111	Small Town Girl/Chug All Night	1973	—	2.50	5.00
75-0113	Carol/Clyde O'Riley	1973	—	2.50	5.00
9000	Puff of Smoke/Lord Take a Bow	1971	—	3.00	6.00
9010	Bit By Bit/Wait Till I Arrive	1972	—	3.00	6.00
TNT					
194	Don't Be Blue/One More Time	1965	3.75	7.50	15.00

Albums

Number	Title (A Side/B Side)	Yr	VG	VG+	NM
ABC					
AB-1054	Tonight's the Night	1978	2.50	5.00	10.00
ABC DOT					
DO-2051	Head First	1976	3.00	6.00	12.00
DO-2066	A Head of His Time	1977	3.00	6.00	12.00
ABC DUNHILL					
DS-50080	Same People	1970	5.00	10.00	20.00
ELEKTRA					
6E-234	In Our Room	1979	2.50	5.00	10.00
6E-298	The Many Sides of Roy Head	1980	2.50	5.00	10.00
MCA					
796	Tonight's the Night	1980	2.00	4.00	8.00
—Reissue of ABC album					
SCEPTER					
S-532 [M]	Treat Me Right	1965	7.50	15.00	30.00
SS-532 [S]	Treat Me Right	1965	10.00	20.00	40.00
TMI					
1000	Dismal Prisoner	1972	3.75	7.50	15.00
TNT					
101 [M]	Roy Head and the Traits	1965	37.50	75.00	150.00
—Counterfeit alert: Authentics do NOT contain the hit "Treat Her Right."					

HEAD EAST

45s

Number	Title (A Side/B Side)	Yr	VG	VG+	NM
A&M					
1718	Never Been Any Reason/One Against the Other	1975	—	2.00	4.00
1784	Love Me Tonight/Brother Jacob	1976	—	2.00	4.00
1930	Gettin' Lucky/Sands of Time	1977	—	2.00	4.00
2026	Since You Been Gone/Pictures	1978	—	2.00	4.00
2026 [PS]	Since You Been Gone/Pictures	1978	2.00	4.00	8.00
2122	Never Been Any Reason/I'm Feelin' Fine	1979	—	2.00	4.00
2208	Got to Be Real/Morning	1979	—	2.00	4.00
2222	Specialty/Morning	1980	—	2.00	4.00
2278	I Surrender/Out of the Blue	1980	—	2.00	4.00

Albums

Number	Title (A Side/B Side)	Yr	VG	VG+	NM
ALLEGIANCE					
AV-432	Onward and Upward	1986	2.00	4.00	8.00
A&M					
SP-3162	Get Yourself Up	198?	2.00	4.00	8.00
—Budget-line reissue					
SP-3196	Flat as a Pancake	198?	2.00	4.00	8.00
—Budget-line reissue					
SP-4537	Flat as a Pancake	1975	2.50	5.00	10.00
SP-4579	Get Yourself Up	1976	2.50	5.00	10.00
SP-4624	Gettin' Lucky	1977	2.50	5.00	10.00
SP-4680	Head East	1978	2.50	5.00	10.00
SP-4795	A Different Kind of Crazy	1979	2.50	5.00	10.00
SP-4826	U.S. 1	1980	2.50	5.00	10.00
SP-6007 [(2)]	Head East Live!	1979	3.00	6.00	12.00

HEAD OVER HEELS

Albums

Number	Title (A Side/B Side)	Yr	VG	VG+	NM
CAPITOL					
ST-797	Head Over Heels	1971	7.50	15.00	30.00

HEAD SHOP, THE

Albums

Number	Title (A Side/B Side)	Yr	VG	VG+	NM
EPIC					
BN 26476	The Head Shop	1969	15.00	30.00	60.00

HEADHUNTERS

Also see HERBIE HANCOCK.

45s

Number	Title (A Side/B Side)	Yr	VG	VG+	NM
ARISTA					
0115	God Made Me Funky/Daffy's Dance	1975	—	2.00	4.00
0137	If You've Got It, You'll Get It/(B-side unknown)	1975	—	2.00	4.00

Albums

Number	Title (A Side/B Side)	Yr	VG	VG+	NM
ARISTA					
AL 4038	Survival of the Fittest	1975	2.50	5.00	10.00
AB 4146	Straight	1978	2.50	5.00	10.00

HEADS, THE

Number	Title (A Side/B Side)	Yr	VG	VG+	NM
45s					
LIBERTY					
56025	Are You Lonely for Me, Baby/You	1968	2.50	5.00	10.00
Albums					
LIBERTY					
LST-7581	Heads Up	1968	6.25	12.50	25.00

HEADS, HANDS AND FEET

Number	Title (A Side/B Side)	Yr	VG	VG+	NM
45s					
ATCO					
6923	One Woman/Dirty, Heavy Weather Road	1973	—	3.00	6.00
Albums					
ATCO					
SD 7025	Old Soldiers Never Die	1973	5.00	10.00	20.00
CAPITOL					
SVBB-680 [(2)]	Heads, Hands and Feet	1971	6.25	12.50	25.00
ST-11051	Tracks	1972	5.00	10.00	20.00

HEADSTONE

Number	Title (A Side/B Side)	Yr	VG	VG+	NM
Albums					
STARR					
(# unknown)	Still Looking	1974	37.50	75.00	150.00

HEART (2)

Number	Title (A Side/B Side)	Yr	VG	VG+	NM
45s					
EMI					
4008	Beautiful Woman/Lovemaker	1974	—	2.00	4.00

HEART (3)

Number	Title (A Side/B Side)	Yr	VG	VG+	NM
45s					
LOOK					
5023	Give Me a Happy Heart/Now	1969	—	3.00	6.00
5029	I Love You/Love	1970	—	3.00	6.00
Albums					
LOOK					
LLP-11000	Heart	1969	3.00	6.00	12.00

HEART (U)

Some of these could be group (3), but others probably are not. None of these, by the way, are the Seattle-based group featuring Ann and Nancy Wilson. That group's first record did not come out in the U.S. until 1976, thus it is not in this book.

Number	Title (A Side/B Side)	Yr	VG	VG+	NM
45s					
REPRISE					
0772	Heartbeat/The Train	1968	—	3.00	6.00
Albums					
KING					
KS-1119	Have a Heart	1970	3.00	6.00	12.00
NATURAL RESOURCES					
NR-102	Heart	1972	3.00	6.00	12.00

HEARTBEATS, THE

Also see SHEP AND THE LIMELITES.

Number	Title (A Side/B Side)	Yr	VG	VG+	NM
45s					
GEE					
1043	When I Found You/Hands Off My Baby	1957	12.50	25.00	50.00
1047	500 Miles to Go/After New Year's Eve	1958	10.00	20.00	40.00
—Red label					
1047	500 Miles to Go/After New Year's Eve	1958	5.00	10.00	20.00
—Gray label					
1061	People Are Talking/Your Way	1960	5.00	10.00	20.00
1062	Darling How Long/Hurry Home Baby	1960	5.00	10.00	20.00
GUYDEN					
2011	One Million Years/Let's Get Married	1959	10.00	20.00	40.00
—Yellow label					
2011	One Million Years/Let's Get Married	1959	7.50	15.00	30.00
—Purple label					
HULL					
711	Crazy for You/Rockin-N-Rollin-N-Rhythm-N-Blues-N	1955	75.00	150.00	300.00
—Pink label, "Sheppard-Miller" as A-side composers					
711	Crazy for You/Rockin-N-Rollin-N-Rhythm-N-Blues-N	1955	50.00	100.00	200.00
—Pink label, "Miller" as A-side composer					
711	Crazy for You/Rockin-N-Rollin-N-Rhythm-N-Blues-N	1955	25.00	50.00	100.00
—Black label					
711 [DJ]	Crazy for You/Rockin-N-Rollin-N-Rhythm-N-Blues-N	1955	150.00	300.00	600.00
—White label					
713	Darling How Long/Hurry Home Baby	1956	50.00	100.00	200.00
716	People Are Talking/Your Way	1956	50.00	100.00	200.00
720	A Thousand Miles Away/Oh Baby Don't	1957	62.50	125.00	250.00
—Black label					
720	A Thousand Miles Away/Oh Baby Don't	1957	20.00	450.00	80.00
—Red label					
JUBILEE					
5202	Finally/Boil and Bubble	1955	7.50	15.00	30.00
NETWORK					
71200	Tormented/After Everybody's Gone	1955	75.00	150.00	300.00
—Cream label, black vinyl					
71200	Tormented/After Everybody's Gone	195?	30.00	60.00	120.00
—Yellow label, black vinyl					
71200	Tormented/After Everybody's Gone	195?	6.25	12.50	25.00
—Red vinyl The Network release as "The Heart Beats Quintet"					
RAMA					
216	A Thousand Miles Away/Oh Baby Don't	1956	20.00	40.00	80.00
222	Wedding Bells/I Won't Be the Fool Anymore	1957	25.00	50.00	100.00
231	I Want to Know/Everybody's Somebody's Fool	1957	25.00	50.00	100.00
ROULETTE					
4054	I Found a Job/Down on My Knees	1958	7.50	15.00	30.00
4091	One Day Next Year/Sometimes I Wonder	1958	7.50	15.00	30.00
4194	Crazy for You/Down on My Knees	1959	7.50	15.00	30.00
Albums					
EMUS					
ES-12033	A Thousand Miles Away	1979	6.25	12.50	25.00
ROULETTE					
R 25107 [M]	A Thousand Miles Away	1960	100.00	200.00	400.00

HEARTBEATS, THE /SHEP AND THE LIMELITES

Also see each artist's individual listings.

Number	Title (A Side/B Side)	Yr	VG	VG+	NM
Albums					
ROULETTE					
RE-115 [(2)]	Echoes of a Rock Era: The Groups	1972	3.75	7.50	15.00

HEARTBREAKERS, THE

Several different groups.

Number	Title (A Side/B Side)	Yr	VG	VG+	NM
45s					
ATCO					
6258	The Willow Wept/You Had Time	1963	5.00	10.00	20.00
BRENT					
7037	I'm Leaving It All Up to You/Corrido Mash	1962	7.50	15.00	30.00
DONNA					
1381	Everytime I See You/Cradle Rock	1963	30.00	60.00	120.00
—Frank Zappa plays guitar on this record					
LINDA					
114	Please Answer/She Is My Baby	1964	3.75	7.50	15.00
MARKAY					
106	Since You've Been Gone/John Law	1962	20.00	40.00	80.00
MGM					
13129	It's Hard Being a Girl/Special Occasions	1963	3.75	7.50	15.00
RCA VICTOR					
47-4327	Heartbreaker/Wanda	1951	150.00	300.00	600.00
47-4508	You're So Necessary to Me/I'm Only Following My Heart	1952	150.00	300.00	600.00
47-4662	Why Don't I/Rockin' Daddy-O	1952	125.00	250.00	500.00
47-4849	There Is Time/It's OK With Me	1952	125.00	250.00	500.00
SWAN					
4242	Baby Baby/I Told You So	1966	3.75	7.50	15.00
VIK					
0261	Without a Cause/One, Two, I Love You	1957	37.50	75.00	150.00
0299	My Love/Love You Till the Day I Die	1957	62.50	125.00	250.00

HEARTS, THE

Number	Title (A Side/B Side)	Yr	VG	VG+	NM
45s					
BATON					
208	Lonely Nights/Oo-Wee	1955	12.50	25.00	50.00
211	All My Love Belongs to You/Talk About Him Girlie	1955	12.50	25.00	50.00
215	Gone, Gone, Gone/Until the Real Thing Comes Along	1955	12.50	25.00	50.00
222	Disappointed Bride/Going Home to Stay	1956	7.50	15.00	30.00
228	He Drives Me Crazy/I Had a Guy	1956	6.25	12.50	25.00
J&S					
425/6	My Love Has Gone/You or Me Have Got to Go	1959	12.50	25.00	50.00
995	A Thousand Years from Today/I Feel So Good	1960	10.00	20.00	40.00
1180/1	You Weren't Home/I Couldn't Let You See Me Crying	1961	12.50	25.00	50.00
1626/7	I Want Your Love Tonight/Like Later Baby	1958	12.50	25.00	50.00
1657	Dancing in a Dream World/You Needn't Tell, I Know	1957	15.00	30.00	60.00
1660	So Long, Baby/You Say You Love Me	1957	15.00	30.00	60.00
4571/2	Goodbye Baby/There Is No Love at All	1959	10.00	20.00	40.00
10002/3	If I Had Known/There Are So Many Ways	1958	12.50	25.00	50.00
TUFF					
370	Dear Abby/(Instrumental)	1963	3.75	7.50	15.00

HEARTS AND FLOWERS

Number	Title (A Side/B Side)	Yr	VG	VG+	NM
45s					
CAPITOL					
2167	She Sang Hymns Out of Tune/Tin Angel (Will You Ever Come Down)	1968	2.50	5.00	10.00
5897	View from Ward 3/Please	1967	2.50	5.00	10.00
Albums					
CAPITOL					
ST 2762 [S]	Now Is the Time for Hearts and Flowers	1967	10.00	20.00	40.00
T 2762 [M]	Now Is the Time for Hearts and Flowers	1967	10.00	20.00	40.00
ST 2868	Of Horses, Kids and Forgotten Women	1968	12.50	25.00	50.00

HEARTS OF STONE

Number	Title (A Side/B Side)	Yr	VG	VG+	NM
45s					
V.I.P.					
25058	It's a Lonesome Road/Yesterday's Love Is Over	1970	2.50	5.00	10.00
25064	If I Could Give You the World/You Gotta Sacrifice	1970	2.50	5.00	10.00
Albums					
V.I.P.					
VIPS-404	Stop the World... We Wanna Get On	1970	10.00	20.00	40.00

HEARTSFIELD

Number	Title (A Side/B Side)	Yr	VG	VG+	NM
45s					
MERCURY					
73449	Music Eyes/Gypsy Rider	1974	—	2.50	5.00
73600	Shine On/Eight Hours at a Time	1974	—	2.50	5.00
73628	Racin' the Sun/Pass Me By	1974	—	2.50	5.00
73706	Nashville/As I Look Into the Fire	1975	—	2.50	5.00
73742	Magic Mood/Rocking Chair	1975	—	2.50	5.00
Albums					
COLUMBIA					
PC 34456	Collector's Item	1976	2.50	5.00	10.00

Number	Title (A Side/B Side)	Yr	VG	VG+	NM
MERCURY					
SRM-1-688	Heartsfield	1973	2.50	5.00	10.00
SRM-1-1003	The Wonder of It All	1974	2.50	5.00	10.00
SRM-1-1034	Foolish Pleasures	1975	2.50	5.00	10.00

HEAT BROTHERS '84

See CANNED HEAT.

HEATH, TED

Number	Title (A Side/B Side)	Yr	VG	VG+	NM
45s					
LONDON					
1006	Sixty Seconds/The Girl in the Little Green Hat	1951	3.00	6.00	12.00
1014	Saxophone Mambo/Take a Letter Miss Smith	1951	3.00	6.00	12.00
1015	This Is the Time/In a Little Spanish Town	1951	3.00	6.00	12.00
1026	London Fog/Romanian Roundabout	1951	3.00	6.00	12.00
1056	The Nearness of You/Lyonia	1951	3.00	6.00	12.00
1057	Button Up Your Overcoat/You're Nearer	1951	3.00	6.00	12.00
1181	Turkey in the Straw/Entry of the Gladiators	1952	3.00	6.00	12.00
1182	L'Heure Bleu/A Kiss in the Dark	1952	3.00	6.00	12.00
1183	Live House Blues/The Black Bottom	1952	3.00	6.00	12.00
1184	Casey Jones/I Want to Be Happy	1952	3.00	6.00	12.00
1198	Obsession/Hawaiian Mambo	1952	3.00	6.00	12.00
1256	Vanessa/Early Autumn	1952	3.00	6.00	12.00
1259	Jungle Fantasy/The Piper's Patrol	1952	3.00	6.00	12.00
1290	Alpine Boogie/Floreintine	1952	3.00	6.00	12.00
1305	Beyond the Sea/On the Bridge	1953	3.00	6.00	12.00
1324	Phantom Regiment/Strike Up the Band	1953	3.00	6.00	12.00
1344	Alouette/Yours Is My Heart	1953	3.00	6.00	12.00
1379	Dragnet/Sloppy Joe	1953	3.00	6.00	12.00
1390	Lullaby of Birdland/Seven-Eleven	1953	3.00	6.00	12.00
1404	Slim Jim/The Original Creep	1954	3.00	6.00	12.00
1418	Jitterbug Waltz/Alligator Crawl	1954	3.00	6.00	12.00
1421	The Champ/Pick Yourself Up	1954	3.00	6.00	12.00
1495	Stomp and Whistle/Bernie's Tune	1954	3.00	6.00	12.00
1500	Skokiaan/Skokiaan	1954	3.00	6.00	12.00
—B-side by the Johnston Brothers					
1531	Asia Minor/Dig Deep	1955	2.50	5.00	10.00
1534	Peg o' My Heart Mambo/In the Mood	1955	2.50	5.00	10.00
1621	Malaguena/Barber Shop Jump	1955	2.50	5.00	10.00
1644	Main Title — The Man with the Golden Arm/ Siboney	1956	2.50	5.00	10.00
1647	Cloudburst/The Trouble with Harry	1956	2.50	5.00	10.00
1675	The Faithful Hussar/Have You Met Miss Jones	1956	2.50	5.00	10.00
1690	Autumn Concerto/Lost	1956	2.50	5.00	10.00
—B-side by Bobbie Britton					
1692	Canadian Sunset/Oriental Holiday	1956	2.50	5.00	10.00
1712	Madagascar/Jungle Drums	1957	2.50	5.00	10.00
1762	Witch Doctor/Headin' North	1957	2.50	5.00	10.00
1800	Little Serenade/I've Got the World on a String	1958	2.50	5.00	10.00
1809	Cha Cha Baby/Tom Hark	1958	2.50	5.00	10.00
1836	Bullfighters Patrol/Strolling Along with the Blues	1958	2.50	5.00	10.00
1867	Frogmarch/9:20 Special	1959	2.00	4.00	8.00
1887	Honky Tonk Train Blues/Bluest Kind of Blue	1959	2.00	4.00	8.00
1893	Swinging Ghosts/Indian Love Call	1959	2.00	4.00	8.00
1920	Slaughter on Tenth Avenue/Sleepy Lagoon	1960	2.00	4.00	8.00
1975	Man from Madrid/Theme from "Dangerman"	1961	2.00	4.00	8.00
2014	Peanut Vendor/Daddy	1961	2.00	4.00	8.00
9503	Charmaine Cha Cha/Sucu Sucu	1962	—	3.00	6.00
9602	Theme from Cleopatra/Mirage	1963	—	3.00	6.00
9629	Theme from "Lord of the Flies"/Paris Mist	1963	—	3.00	6.00
9680	Theme from "The Carpetbaggers"/Wigwam	1964	—	3.00	6.00
Albums					
ARCHIVE OF FOLK AND JAZZ					
215	Ted Heath's Big Band	1970	2.50	5.00	10.00
LONDON					
PS 116 [S]	Hits I Missed	1958	6.25	12.50	25.00
PS 117 [S]	All Time Top Twelve	1958	6.25	12.50	25.00
PS 138 [S]	Swing Session	1958	6.25	12.50	25.00
—New stereo recordings of the same material as appears on LL 802					
PS 140 [S]	Ted Heath Swings in High Stereo	1958	6.25	12.50	25.00
PS 148 [S]	Shall We Dance	1959	6.25	12.50	25.00
PS 159 [S]	Great Film Hits	1959	6.25	12.50	25.00
PS 171 [S]	Pop Hits from the Classics	1959	6.25	12.50	25.00
PS 172 [S]	Big Band Blues	1959	6.25	12.50	25.00
PS 174 [S]	My Very Good Friends The Bandleaders	1959	6.25	12.50	25.00
PS 175 [S]	The Hits of the Twenties	1960	5.00	10.00	20.00
PS 184 [S]	The Big Band Dixie Sound	1960	5.00	10.00	20.00
PS 187 [S]	Ted Heath in Concert	1960	5.00	10.00	20.00
PS 190 [S]	Songs for the Young at Heart	1960	5.00	10.00	20.00
PS 216 [S]	The Hits of the Thirties	1961	5.00	10.00	20.00
PS 219 [S]	Latin Swingers	1961	5.00	10.00	20.00
LPB-340 [10]	Tempo for Dancing	195?	10.00	20.00	40.00
LPB-374 [10]	Ted Heath and His Orchestra	195?	10.00	20.00	40.00
LB-511 [10]	Listen to My Music	195?	10.00	20.00	40.00
PS 535	21st Anniversary Album	1968	3.00	6.00	12.00
LB-732 [10]	Black and White Magic	195?	10.00	20.00	40.00
LL 750 [M]	Ted Heath Strikes Up the Band	1953	5.00	10.00	20.00
LL 802 [M]	Ted Heath at the London Palladium	1953	5.00	10.00	20.00
LL 978 [M]	Ted Heath Plays the Music of Fats Waller	1954	5.00	10.00	20.00
LL 1000 [M]	The 100th London Palladium Concert	1955	5.00	10.00	20.00
LL 1211 [M]	Jazz Concert at the London Palladium, Vol. 3	1955	5.00	10.00	20.00
LL 1217 [M]	Gershwin for Moderns	1956	5.00	10.00	20.00
LL 1279 [M]	Kern for Moderns	1956	5.00	10.00	20.00
LL 1379 [M]	Jazz Concert at the London Palladium, Vol. 4	1956	5.00	10.00	20.00
LL 1475 [M]	Ted Heath Swings in Hi-Fi	1956	5.00	10.00	20.00
LL 1500 [M]	Rodgers for Moderns	1956	5.00	10.00	20.00
LL 1564 [M]	Ted Heath's First American Tour	1956	5.00	10.00	20.00
LL 1566 [M]	Ted Heath at Carnegie Hall	1956	5.00	10.00	20.00
LL 1676 [M]	A Yank in Europe	1956	5.00	10.00	20.00
LL 1716 [M]	All Time Top Twelve	1957	5.00	10.00	20.00
LL 1721 [M]	Spotlight on Sidemen	1957	5.00	10.00	20.00
LL 1737 [M]	Showcase	1957	5.00	10.00	20.00
LL 1743 [M]	Tribute to the Fabulous Dorseys	1957	5.00	10.00	20.00
LL 1749 [M]	Rhapsody in Blue	1957	5.00	10.00	20.00
LL 3047 [M]	Things to Come	1958	5.00	10.00	20.00
LL 3057 [M]	Hits I Missed	1958	5.00	10.00	20.00
LL 3058 [M]	Old English	1958	5.00	10.00	20.00
LL 3062 [M]	Shall We Dance	1959	5.00	10.00	20.00
LL 3106 [M]	Great Film Hits	1959	5.00	10.00	20.00
LL 3124 [M]	Pop Hits from the Classics	1959	5.00	10.00	20.00
LL 3125 [M]	Big Band Blues	1959	5.00	10.00	20.00
LL 3127 [M]	My Very Good Friends The Bandleaders	1959	5.00	10.00	20.00
LL 3128 [M]	The Hits of the Twenties	1960	3.75	7.50	15.00
LL 3138 [M]	The Big Band Dixie Sound	1960	3.75	7.50	15.00
LL 3143 [M]	Ted Heath in Concert	1960	3.75	7.50	15.00
LL 3146 [M]	Songs for the Young at Heart	1960	3.75	7.50	15.00
LL 3192 [M]	The Hits of the Thirties	1961	3.75	7.50	15.00
LL 3195 [M]	Latin Swingers	1961	3.75	7.50	15.00
LL 3325 [M]	Big Band Spirituals	1963	3.00	6.00	12.00
LL 3367 [M]	New Palladium Performances	1964	3.00	6.00	12.00
LONDON PHASE 4					
SP 44002 [S]	Big Band Percussion	1961	3.75	7.50	15.00
SP 44017	Big Band Bash	1962	3.75	7.50	15.00
SP 44023	Satin Strings and Bouncing Brass	1963	3.75	7.50	15.00
SP 44036 [S]	Big Band Spirituals	1963	3.75	7.50	15.00
SP 44038	Swing vs. Latin	1964	3.75	7.50	15.00
SP 44046 [S]	New Palladium Performances	1964	3.00	6.00	12.00
SP 44063	The Sound of Music	1965	3.00	6.00	12.00
SP 44074	Chartbusters	1966	3.00	6.00	12.00
SP 44079	Pow!	1966	3.00	6.00	12.00
P 54002 [M]	Big Band Percussion	1961	3.00	6.00	12.00
RICHMOND					
B 20034 [M]	Big Band Beat	196?	3.00	6.00	12.00
B 20037 [M]	Ted Heath Plays Gershwin	196?	3.00	6.00	12.00
B 20082 [M]	Ted Heath Plays the Music of Fats Waller	196?	3.00	6.00	12.00
B 20096 [M]	Big Band Gershwin	196?	3.00	6.00	12.00
B 20097 [M]	Big Band Kern	196?	3.00	6.00	12.00
B 20098 [M]	Big Band Rodgers	196?	3.00	6.00	12.00

HEATHER BLACK

Number	Title (A Side/B Side)	Yr	VG	VG+	NM
Albums					
AMERICAN PLAYBOY					
1001	Heather Black Live	197?	15.00	30.00	60.00
1001 [(2)]	Heather Black Live	197?	37.50	75.00	150.00
—Evidently, some copies of this were 2-record sets					
DOUBLE BAYOU					
2000	Heather Black	197?	7.50	15.00	30.00

HEATHERTON, JOEY

Number	Title (A Side/B Side)	Yr	VG	VG+	NM
45s					
CORAL					
62422	That's How It Goes/I'll Be Seeing You	1964	7.50	15.00	30.00
62422 [PS]	That's How It Goes/I'll Be Seeing You	1964	10.00	20.00	40.00
62451	Hullaballoo/My Blood Runs Cold	1965	6.25	12.50	25.00
62459	Tomorrow Is Another Day/But He's Not Mine	1965	6.25	12.50	25.00
DECCA					
31962	Live and Learn/When You Call Me Baby	1966	15.00	30.00	60.00
31962 [PS]	Live and Learn/When You Call Me Baby	1966	20.00	40.00	80.00
MGM					
14387	Gone/The Road I Took to You	1972	—	2.50	5.00
14387 [PS]	Gone/The Road I Took to You	1972	2.50	5.00	10.00
14434	I'm Sorry/Crazy	1972	—	3.00	6.00
14434	I'm Sorry/Someone to Watch Over Me	1972	—	2.50	5.00
14499	Crazy/God Only Knows	1973	—	2.50	5.00
Albums					
MGM					
SE-4858	The Joey Heatherton Album	1972	3.75	7.50	15.00

HEAVY BALLOON, THE

Number	Title (A Side/B Side)	Yr	VG	VG+	NM
Albums					
ELEPHANT					
EVS-104	32,000 Lbs.	1969	17.50	35.00	70.00

HEBB, BOBBY

Number	Title (A Side/B Side)	Yr	VG	VG+	NM
45s					
BOOM					
60017	Betty Jo from Ohio/Sam Hall Jr.	1966	2.00	4.00	8.00
CADET					
5690	I Was a Boy When You Needed a Man/Woman in the Window	1972	—	2.50	5.00
LAURIE					
3632	True, I Love You/Proud Soul Heritage	1975	—	2.50	5.00
3638	Sunny '76/Sunny Disco	1976	—	2.50	5.00
PHILIPS					
40365	Sunny/Bread	1966	2.50	5.00	10.00
40400	A Satisfied Mind/Love, Love, Love	1966	2.00	4.00	8.00
40400 [PS]	A Satisfied Mind/Love, Love, Love	1966	3.00	6.00	12.00
40421	Love Me/Crazy Baby	1966	2.00	4.00	8.00
40431	My Pretty Sunshine/Ooh La La	1967	2.00	4.00	8.00
40448	I Love Everything About You/Some Kind of Magic	1967	2.00	4.00	8.00
40482	Everything Is Coming Up Roses/Bound by Love	1967	2.00	4.00	8.00
40551	Dreamy/You Want to Change Me	1968	2.00	4.00	8.00
RICH					
1006	Cherry/Feel So Good	1960	3.75	7.50	15.00
1740	Just a Little Bit More/Walk Me On Alone	1962	3.75	7.50	15.00
SCEPTER					
12166	I Love Mary (Part 1)/I Love Mary (Part 2)	1966	2.00	4.00	8.00
Albums					
EPIC					
BN 26523	Love Games	1970	3.00	6.00	12.00
PHILIPS					
PHM 200212 [M]	Sunny	1966	6.25	12.50	25.00
—With "200-212" in trail-off; this record is mono					
PHM 200212 [S]	Sunny	1966	6.25	12.50	25.00
—With "2/600-212" in trail-off; this record plays stereo, though labeled mono					
PHS 600212 [S]	Sunny	1966	7.50	15.00	30.00

HEDGEHOPPERS ANONYMOUS

Number	Title (A Side/B Side)	Yr	VG	VG+	NM
45s					
PARROT					
3002	Remember/Baby (You're My Everything)	1966	2.50	5.00	10.00
9800	It's Good News Week/Afraid of Love	1965	3.00	6.00	12.00
9817	Don't Push Me/Please Don't Hurt Your Heart for Me	1966	2.50	5.00	10.00

HEINTJE

Number	Title (A Side/B Side)	Yr	VG	VG+	NM
45s					
MGM					
14183	Mama/Mother's Tears	1970	—	2.00	4.00
14272	When the Summer Comes/You Are the Best of All	1971	—	2.00	4.00
Albums					
MGM					
SE-4739	Mama	1970	3.00	6.00	12.00
SE-4772	Best of All	1971	3.00	6.00	12.00

HEINZ

Also see FREDDIE AND THE DREAMERS.

Number	Title (A Side/B Side)	Yr	VG	VG+	NM
45s					
LONDON					
9619	Just Like Eddie/Don't You Knock on My Door	1963	3.75	7.50	15.00
TOWER					
110	Questions I Can't Answer/The Beating of My Heart	1964	5.00	10.00	20.00
172	Digging My Potatoes/Don't Think Twice, It's All Right	1965	5.00	10.00	20.00
195	Don't Worry Baby/Heart Full of Sorrow	1966	7.50	15.00	30.00
253	I'm Not a Bad Boy/Movin' In	1966	5.00	10.00	20.00

HELLERS, THE

Number	Title (A Side/B Side)	Yr	VG	VG+	NM
Albums					
COMMAND					
RS 934 SD	Singers, Talkers, Players, Swingers and Doers	1968	10.00	20.00	40.00

HELLO PEOPLE, THE

Number	Title (A Side/B Side)	Yr	VG	VG+	NM
45s					
ABC					
12160	Book of Love/How High Is the Moon	1976	—	2.50	5.00
ABC DUNHILL					
15023	Future Shock/Destiny	1974	—	2.50	5.00
15031	Just One Victory/Take the Love in Your Body	1975	—	2.50	5.00
MEDIARTS					
109	Pass Me By/Maybe We Should Have Had Rain	1971	2.50	5.00	10.00
PHILIPS					
40481	Let's Go Hide in the Forest/Disparity Waterfront Blues	1967	2.00	4.00	8.00
40522	A Stranger at Her Door/Paisley Teddy Bear	1968	2.00	4.00	8.00
40531	(As I Went Down to) Jerusalem/It's a Monday Kind of Tuesday	1968	2.00	4.00	8.00
40572	If I Should Sing Too Softly/Pray for Rain	1968	2.00	4.00	8.00
40585	Anthem/Jelly Jam	1969	2.00	4.00	8.00
UNITED ARTISTS					
50797	Pass Me By/Maybe We Should Have Had Rain	1971	—	3.00	6.00
Albums					
ABC					
D-882	Bricks	1975	2.50	5.00	10.00
ABC DUNHILL					
DS-50184	The Handsome Devils	1974	2.50	5.00	10.00
MEDIARTS					
41-8	Have You Seen the Light	1970	3.00	6.00	12.00
PHILIPS					
PHS 600265	The Hello People	1968	3.75	7.50	15.00
PHS 600276	Fusion	1969	3.75	7.50	15.00
UNITED ARTISTS					
UAS 5524	Have You Seen the Light	1971	2.50	5.00	10.00
—Reissue of Mediarts LP					

HELMS, BOBBY

Number	Title (A Side/B Side)	Yr	VG	VG+	NM
45s					
CAPITOL					
3003	The Only Thing That Matters/Just Hold My Hand and Sing	1970	2.00	4.00	8.00
CERTRON					
10002	Mary Goes 'Round/Cold Winds Blow on Me	1970	2.00	4.00	8.00
10021	Jingle Bell Rock/The Old Year Is Gone	1970	2.00	4.00	8.00
10023	I Wouldn't Take the World for You/Look What You've Done	1970	2.00	4.00	8.00
COLUMBIA					
4-43031	It's a Girl/Put Your Arms Around Him	1964	2.50	5.00	10.00
DECCA					
9-29947	Tennessee Rock 'N' Roll/I Don't Owe You Nothing	1956	12.50	25.00	50.00
9-30194	Fraulein/(Got a) Heartsick Feeling	1957	5.00	10.00	20.00
9-30194 [PS]	Fraulein/(Got a) Heartsick Feeling	1957	12.50	25.00	50.00
9-30423	My Special Angel/Standing at the End of My World	1957	6.25	12.50	25.00
9-30513	Jingle Bell Rock/Captain Santa Claus	1957	6.25	12.50	25.00
—Black label with star					
9-30513	Jingle Bell Rock/Captain Santa Claus	1960	3.00	6.00	12.00
—Black label with color bars					
9-30513 [PS]	Jingle Bell Rock/Captain Santa Claus	1957	12.50	25.00	50.00
9-30557	Just a Little Lonesome/Love My Baby	1958	5.00	10.00	20.00
9-30619	Jacqueline/Living in the Shadow of the Past	1958	5.00	10.00	20.00
9-30682	Schoolboy Crush/Borrowed Dreams	1958	5.00	10.00	20.00
9-30749	A Hundred Hearts/The Fool and the Angel	1958	5.00	10.00	20.00
9-30831	New River Train/Miss Memory	1959	3.75	7.50	15.00
9-30886	Soon It Can Be Told/I Guess I'll Miss the Prom	1959	3.75	7.50	15.00
9-30928	No Other Baby/You're No Longer Mine	1959	3.75	7.50	15.00
9-30976	My Lucky Day/Hurry Baby	1959	3.75	7.50	15.00
9-31041	To My Sorrow/Someone Was Already There	1960	3.75	7.50	15.00
31103	Let Me Be the One/I Wanna Be with You	1960	3.75	7.50	15.00
31148	Lonely River Rhine/Guess We Thought the World Would End	1960	3.75	7.50	15.00
31230	Sad-Eyed Baby/You're the One	1961	3.00	6.00	12.00
31287	How Can You Divide a Little Child/My Greatest Weakness	1961	3.00	6.00	12.00
31356	One Deep Love/Once in a Lifetime	1962	3.00	6.00	12.00
31403	Then Came You/Yesterday's Champagne	1962	3.00	6.00	12.00
GUSTO					
116	That Heart Belongs to Me/With Jenny on My Mind	1974	—	3.00	6.00
119	Work Things Out with Annie/With Jenny on My Mind	1974	—	3.00	6.00
KAPP					
708	I'm the Man/Have This Love on Me	1965	2.50	5.00	10.00
719	Jingle Bell Rock/The Bell That Couldn't Jingle	1965	3.00	6.00	12.00
732	Those Snowy Glowy Blowy Days of Winter/Sailor	1965	2.50	5.00	10.00
777	The Things I Remember Most/Sorry, My Name Isn't Fred	1966	2.50	5.00	10.00
876	I Miss My Fraulein/Where Does a Shadow Go	1967	2.00	4.00	8.00
LITTLE DARLIN'					
0030	He Thought He'd Die Laughing/You'd Better Make Up Your Mind	1967	2.50	5.00	10.00
0034	The Day You Stop Loving Me/You Can Tell the World	1967	2.50	5.00	10.00
0038	Jingle Bell Rock/I Wanta Go to Santa Claus Land	1967	3.00	6.00	12.00
0041	I Feel You, I Love You/The Day You Stop Loving Me	1968	2.50	5.00	10.00
0049	Or Is It Love/Touch My Heart	1968	2.50	5.00	10.00
0054	My Special Angel/Expressing My Love	1968	2.50	5.00	10.00
0062	So Long/Just Do the Best You Can	1969	2.50	5.00	10.00
0073	Echoes and Shadows/Step Into My Soul	1969	2.50	5.00	10.00
7801	I'm Gonna Love the Devil Out of You/I Can't Promise You	1978	—	3.00	6.00
7807	The Things I Remember Most/I'm Not Sorry	1978	—	3.00	6.00
7809	Jingle Bell Rock/I Wanta Go to Santa Claus Land	1978	—	3.00	6.00
7916	One More Dollar for the Band/Touch My Heart	1979	—	3.00	6.00
MCA					
65026	Jingle Bell Rock/Captain Santa Claus	1973	—	2.50	5.00
—Black label with rainbow					
65026	Jingle Bell Rock/Captain Santa Claus	1980	—	—	3.00
—Blue label with rainbow					
65029	Jingle Bell Rock/The Bell That Couldn't Jingle	1973	—	2.50	5.00
—Black label with rainbow; this contains the 1965 Kapp re-recording of the A-side					
65029	Jingle Bell Rock/The Bell That Couldn't Jingle	1980	—	—	3.00
—Blue label with rainbow					
MILLION					
5	It's the Little Things/Love's Sweet Mystery	1972	—	3.50	7.00
22	It's Starting to Rain Again/Wouldn't Give Up on You	1972	—	3.50	7.00
MISTLETOE					
802	Jingle Bell Rock/Jingle Bells	197?	—	2.50	5.00
802 [PS]	Jingle Bell Rock/Jingle Bells	197?	2.00	4.00	8.00
SPEED					
45-114	Yesterday's Lovin'/Hanging Around	1957	7.50	15.00	30.00
7-Inch Extended Plays					
DECCA					
ED 2555	If Only I Knew/Far Away Heart//My Shoes Keep Walking Back to You/Sugar Moon	1957	5.00	10.00	20.00
ED 2555 [PS]	(title unknown)	1957	5.00	10.00	20.00
ED 2586	Plaything/Magic Song//Tonight's the Night/Just a Little Lonesome	1957	5.00	10.00	20.00
ED 2586 [PS]	Tonight's the Night	1957	5.00	10.00	20.00
ED 2629	Jacqueline/My Special Angel//Borrowed Dreams/Schoolboy Crush	1957	5.00	10.00	20.00
ED 2629 [PS]	Bobby Helms	1957	5.00	10.00	20.00
Albums					
COLUMBIA					
CL 2060 [M]	The Best of Bobby Helms	1963	6.25	12.50	25.00
CS 8860 [S]	The Best of Bobby Helms	1963	7.50	15.00	30.00
DECCA					
DL 8638 [M]	Bobby Helms Sings to My Special Angel	1957	30.00	60.00	120.00
HARMONY					
HL 7409 [M]	Fraulein	1967	3.00	6.00	12.00
HS 11209 [S]	Fraulein	1967	3.00	6.00	12.00
KAPP					
KL 1463 [M]	I'm the Man	1966	3.75	7.50	15.00
KL 1505 [M]	Sorry My Name Isn't Fred	1966	3.75	7.50	15.00
KS 3463 [S]	I'm the Man	1966	5.00	10.00	20.00
KS 3505 [S]	Sorry My Name Isn't Fred	1966	5.00	10.00	20.00
LITTLE DARLIN'					
8088	All New Just for You	1968	6.25	12.50	25.00
MISTLETOE					
MLP-1206	Jingle Bell Rock	197?	3.00	6.00	12.00
POWER PAK					
283	Greatest Hits	197?	2.50	5.00	10.00
VOCALION					
VL 3743 [M]	Someone Already There	1965	3.75	7.50	15.00
VL 73743 [R]	Someone Already There	1965	3.00	6.00	12.00
VL 73874	My Special Angel	1969	3.00	6.00	12.00

HELMS, DON

Number	Title (A Side/B Side)	Yr	VG	VG+	NM
45s					
SMASH					
1781	Fire Ball Mail/I Can't Help It (If I'm Still in Love with You)	1962	5.00	10.00	20.00
Albums					
SMASH					
MGS-27001 [M]	The Steel Guitar Sounds of Hank Williams	1962	5.00	10.00	20.00
MGS-27019 [M]	Don Helms' Steel Guitar	1962	5.00	10.00	20.00
SRS-67001 [S]	The Steel Guitar Sounds of Hank Williams	1962	6.25	12.50	25.00
SRS-67019 [S]	Don Helms' Steel Guitar	1962	6.25	12.50	25.00

HELP

45s

Number	Title (A Side/B Side)	Yr	VG	VG+	NM
DECCA					
32879	Good Time Music/Hold On Child	1971	3.00	6.00	12.00

Albums

Number	Title (A Side/B Side)	Yr	VG	VG+	NM
DECCA					
DL 75257	Help	1970	7.50	15.00	30.00
DL 75304	Second Coming	1971	7.50	15.00	30.00

HEMLOCKS, THE

45s

Number	Title (A Side/B Side)	Yr	VG	VG+	NM
FURY					
1004	Cora Lee/Joys of Love	1957	25.00	50.00	100.00

HENDERSON, JOE

45s

Number	Title (A Side/B Side)	Yr	VG	VG+	NM
FONTANA					
1638	Help Yourself/A Man Without Love	1969	—	3.00	6.00
1658	Don't Forget to Catch Me/Please Don't Go	1969	—	3.00	6.00
KAPP					
590	If We Could Start All Over/You Take One Step, I'll Take Two	1964	2.50	5.00	10.00
RIC					
141	I Ain't Never/The River or the Railroad Track	1964	2.00	4.00	8.00
149	Honey on My Lips/Like a Child	1965	2.00	4.00	8.00
181	Sweet Lovin' Baby/Too Much to Lose	1966	2.00	4.00	8.00
TODD					
1066	Baby Don't Leave Me/Right Now	1961	3.75	7.50	15.00
1072	Snap Your Fingers/If You See Me Cry	1962	3.75	7.50	15.00
1077	Big Love/After Loving You	1962	3.00	6.00	12.00
1079	Three Steps/The Searching Is Over	1962	3.00	6.00	12.00
1082	Cause We're in Love/Sad Teardrops at Dawn	1963	3.00	6.00	12.00
1083	You Can't Lose/All Day Every Day	1963	3.00	6.00	12.00
1085	Love Me Sweet/My Hands Are Tied	1963	3.00	6.00	12.00
1091	Lovin' Part Time/Blues for a Four-String Guitar	1963	3.00	6.00	12.00
1096	If We Could Start All Over/You Take One Step, I'll Take Two	1964	3.00	6.00	12.00

Albums

Number	Title (A Side/B Side)	Yr	VG	VG+	NM
FONTANA					
SRF-67590	Hits, Hits, Hits!	1969	7.50	15.00	30.00
TODD					
MT-2701 [M]	Snap Your Fingers	1962	12.50	25.00	50.00
ST-2701 [S]	Snap Your Fingers	1962	17.50	35.00	70.00

HENDRICKS, BOBBY

45s

Number	Title (A Side/B Side)	Yr	VG	VG+	NM
MERCURY					
71788	Happy Hearts/Pleasing You	1961	3.00	6.00	12.00
71810	Good Lovin'/Honey Crisp	1961	3.00	6.00	12.00
71881	I'm Comin' Home/Every Other Night	1961	3.00	6.00	12.00
MGM					
13179	Let's Get It Over/Love in My Heart	1963	5.00	10.00	20.00
SUE					
706	Itchy Twitchy Feeling/A Thousand Dreams	1958	7.50	15.00	30.00
708	Dreamy Eyes/Molly Be Good	1958	5.00	10.00	20.00
710	Cast Your Vote/It's Misery	1959	5.00	10.00	20.00
712	I'm a Big Boy Now/Good Things Will Come	1959	5.00	10.00	20.00
717	Little John Green/Sincerely, Your Lover	1959	5.00	10.00	20.00
727	City of Angels/If I Just Had Your Love	1960	5.00	10.00	20.00
732	Psycho/Too Good to Be True	1960	5.00	10.00	20.00
UNITED ARTISTS					
0142	Itchy Twitchy Feeling/Psycho	1973	—	2.00	4.00
—"Silver Spotlight Series" reissue					

HENDRIX, AL

45s

Number	Title (A Side/B Side)	Yr	VG	VG+	NM
ABC-PARAMOUNT					
9901	Rhonda Lee/Go, Daddy. Rock	1958	6.25	12.50	25.00
LEGREE					
701	Young and Wild/I Need You	1960	30.00	60.00	120.00
TALLY					
119	Rhonda Lee/Go, Daddy Rock	1957	20.00	40.00	80.00

HENDRIX, JIMI

The albums list includes many posthumous "cash-in" records of early material.

45s

Number	Title (A Side/B Side)	Yr	VG	VG+	NM
AUDIO FIDELITY					
167	No Such Animal (Part 1)/No Such Animal (Part 2)	1970	3.75	7.50	15.00
167 [PS]	No Such Animal (Part 1)/No Such Animal (Part 2)	1970	10.00	20.00	40.00
EXPERIENCE HENDRIX/CLASSIC					
RTH-1007	The Jimi Hendrix Classic Singles Collection	1998	15.00	30.00	60.00
—Boxed set of 10 45s, each with picture sleeves and white sleeve, with booklet					
5651-7	Little Drummer Boy-Auld Lang Syne/Three Little Pigs	1999	3.00	6.00	12.00
—Red vinyl, small hole					
5651-7 [PS]	Little Drummer Boy-Auld Lang Syne/Three Little Pigs	1999	3.00	6.00	12.00
MCA					
55454 [DJ]	Can You Please Crawl Out Your Window?/ Burning of the Midnight Lamp	1998	—	2.00	5.00
—Promo only on orange vinyl					
55454 [PS]	Can You Please Crawl Out Your Window?/ Burning of the Midnight Lamp	1998	—	2.00	5.00
—Cardboard sleeve					
REPRISE					
0572	Hey Joe/51st Anniversary	1967	25.00	50.00	100.00
0572 [PS]	Hey Joe/51st Anniversary	1967	250.00	500.00	1000.
PRO 595 [DJ]	Medley: The Little Drummer Boy-Silent Night/ Auld Lang Syne	1974	37.50	75.00	150.00
PRO 595 [PS]	...And a Happy New Year	1974	20.00	40.00	80.00
0597	Purple Haze/The Wind Cries Mary	1967	6.25	12.50	25.00
0641	Foxey Lady/Hey Joe	1967	6.25	12.50	25.00
0665	Up from the Skies/One Rainy Wish	1968	7.50	15.00	30.00
0728	Purple Haze/Foxey Lady	1968	3.75	7.50	15.00
—"Back to Back Hits" series -- originals have both "r:" and "W7" logos					
0742	All Along the Watchtower/Crosstown Traffic	1971	—	3.00	6.00
—"Back to Back Hits" series					
0767	All Along the Watchtower/Burning of the Midnight Lamp	1968	7.50	15.00	30.00
0792	Crosstown Traffic/Gypsy Eyes	1968	7.50	15.00	30.00
0853	If 6 Was 9/Stone Free	1969	10.00	20.00	40.00
0905	Stepping Stone/Izabella	1970	25.00	50.00	100.00
1000	Freedom/Angel	1971	3.75	7.50	15.00
1044	Star Spangled Banner/Dolly Dagger	1971	3.75	7.50	15.00
1082	Johnny B. Goode/Lover Man	1972	3.75	7.50	15.00
1118	The Wind Cries Mary/Little Wing	1972	3.75	7.50	15.00
EP 2239	Gloria (B-side blank)	1979	—	2.50	5.00
EP 2239 [PS]	Gloria (B-side blank)	1979	—	2.50	5.00
—Above was a bonus record in "The Essential Jimi Hendrix, Volume 2"					
29845	Fire/Little Wing	1982	—	3.00	6.00
TRIP					
3002	Hot Trigger/Suspicious	1972	—	2.50	5.00

Albums

Number	Title (A Side/B Side)	Yr	VG	VG+	NM
ACCORD					
SN-7101	Kaleidoscope	1981	2.50	5.00	10.00
SN-7112	Before London	1981	2.50	5.00	10.00
SN-7139	Cosmic Feeling	1981	2.50	5.00	10.00
CAPITOL					
STAO-472	Band of Gypsys	1970	5.00	10.00	20.00
SWBB-659 [(2)]	Get That Feeling/Flashing	1971	6.25	12.50	25.00
ST 2856 [S]	Get That Feeling	1967	10.00	20.00	40.00
T 2856 [M]	Get That Feeling	1967	20.00	40.00	80.00
ST 2894 [S]	Flashing	1968	10.00	20.00	40.00
T 2894 [M]	Flashing	1968	25.00	50.00	100.00
SJ-12416	Band of Gypsys 2	1986	2.50	5.00	10.00
—Side 2 lists, and plays, three songs					
SJ-12416	Band of Gypsys 2	1986	37.50	75.00	150.00
—Side 2 lists three songs, but plays four completely different songs. Four bands are visible on the record.					
MLP-15022 [EP]	Johnny B. Goode	1986	2.00	4.00	8.00
SN-16319	Band of Gypsys	1985	2.50	5.00	10.00
—Budget-line reissue					
C1-96414	Band of Gypsys	1995	3.75	7.50	15.00
—Numbered reissue					
EXPERIENCE HENDRIX/CAPITOL					
ST-472	Band of Gypsys	1997	6.25	12.50	25.00
—Limited edition on "heavy vinyl" with booklet; distributed by Classic Records					
EXPERIENCE HENDRIX/MCA					
11599 [(2)]	First Rays of the New Rising Sun	1997	12.50	25.00	50.00
—Limited edition on "heavy vinyl" with booklet					
11600 [(2)]	Electric Ladyland	1997	10.00	20.00	40.00
—Limited edition on "heavy vinyl" with booklet					
11601	Axis: Bold As Love	1997	12.50	25.00	50.00
—Limited edition on "heavy vinyl" with booklet					
11602 [(2)]	Are You Experienced?	1997	12.50	25.00	50.00
—Limited edition on "heavy vinyl" with booklet					
11607	Band of Gypsys	1997	6.25	12.50	25.00
—Limited edition on "heavy vinyl" with booklet; pressed in U.S. for export to Europe					
11608	Are You Experienced?	1997	10.00	20.00	40.00
—Limited edition on "heavy vinyl" with booklet; pressed in U.S. for export to Europe; has different cover than US version					
11671 [(2)]	Experience Hendrix: The Best of Jimi Hendrix	1998	6.25	12.50	25.00
—Despite lower number, was released after South Saturn Delta					
11684 [(2)]	South Saturn Delta	1997	6.25	12.50	25.00
—Numbered, limited edition on "heavy vinyl"					
11742 [(3)]	BBC Sessions	1998	7.50	15.00	30.00
11931 [(3)]	Live at the Fillmore East	1999	7.50	15.00	30.00
11987 [(3)]	Live at Woodstock	1999	7.50	15.00	30.00
NUTMEG					
1001	High, Live 'N' Dirty	1978	6.25	12.50	25.00
—Red vinyl					
1001	High, Live 'N' Dirty	1978	6.25	12.50	25.00
—Black vinyl					
1002	Cosmic Turnaround	1981	3.00	6.00	12.00
PICKWICK					
SPC-3528	Jimi	197?	2.50	5.00	10.00
REPRISE					
MS 2025	Smash Hits	1969	10.00	20.00	40.00
—With "W7" and "r:" logos on two-tone orange label					
MS 2025	Smash Hits Bonus Poster	1969	10.00	20.00	40.00
MS 2025	Smash Hits	1970	3.00	6.00	12.00
—With only "r:" logo on all-orange (tan) label					
MS 2025	Smash Hits	198?	2.00	4.00	8.00
—Red and black label or gold and light blue label					
MS 2029	Historic Performances As Recorded at the Monterey International Pop Festival	1970	5.00	10.00	20.00
—Side 1: Jimi Hendrix; Side 2: Otis Redding					
MS 2034	The Cry of Love	1971	125.00	250.00	500.00
—With "W7" and "r:" logos on two-tone orange label					
MS 2034	The Cry of Love	1971	3.75	7.50	15.00
MS 2040	Rainbow Bridge	1971	5.00	10.00	20.00
MS 2049	Hendrix in the West	1972	5.00	10.00	20.00
MS 2103	War Heroes	1972	5.00	10.00	20.00
MS 2204	Crash Landing	1975	3.75	7.50	15.00
MS 2229	Midnight Lightning	1975	3.75	7.50	15.00
2RS 2245 [(2)]	The Essential Jimi Hendrix	1978	5.00	10.00	20.00
MSK 2276	Smash Hits	1977	2.50	5.00	10.00
—Reissue					
HS 2293	The Essential Jimi Hendrix Volume Two	1979	3.75	7.50	15.00
—Add 100% if bonus single of "Gloria" with picture sleeve is enclosed					
HS 2299	Nine to the Universe	1980	2.50	5.00	10.00
R 6261 [M]	Are You Experienced?	1967	50.00	100.00	200.00
RS 6261 [S]	Are You Experienced?	1967	12.50	25.00	50.00
—Pink, gold and green label					
RS 6261 [S]	Are You Experienced?	1968	6.25	12.50	25.00
—With "W7" and "r:" logos on two-tone orange label					

Number	Title (A Side/B Side)	Yr	VG	VG+	NM
RS 6261 [S]	Are You Experienced?	1970	3.00	6.00	12.00
—With only "r:" logo on all-orange (tan) label					
RS 6261 [S]	Are You Experienced?	198?	2.00	4.00	8.00
—Red and black label or gold and light blue label					
R 6281 [M]	Axis: Bold As Love	1968	625.00	1250.	2500.
RS 6281 [S]	Axis: Bold As Love	1968	20.00	40.00	80.00
—Pink, gold and green label					
RS 6281 [S]	Axis: Bold As Love	1968	6.25	12.50	25.00
—With "W7" and "r:" logos on two-tone orange label					
RS 6281 [S]	Axis: Bold As Love	1970	3.00	6.00	12.00
—With only "r:" logo on all-orange (tan) label					
RS 6281 [S]	Axis: Bold As Love	198?	2.00	4.00	8.00
—Red and black label or gold and light blue label					
2R 6307 [(2) M]	Electric Ladyland	1968	2000.	3000.	4000.
—Mono is promo only					
2RS 6307 [(2) S]	Electric Ladyland	1968	25.00	50.00	100.00
—With "W7" and "r:" logos on two-tone orange label					
2RS 6307 [(2) S]	Electric Ladyland	1970	3.75	7.50	15.00
—With only "r:" logo on all-orange (tan) label					
2RS 6307 [(2) S]	Electric Ladyland	198?	3.00	6.00	12.00
—Red and black label or gold and light blue label					
2RS 6481 [(2)]	Soundtrack Recordings from the Film Jimi Hendrix	1973	6.25	12.50	25.00
22306 [(2)]	The Jimi Hendrix Concerts	1982	3.00	6.00	12.00
25119	Kiss the Sky	1984	2.50	5.00	10.00
25358	Jimi Plays Monterey	1986	2.50	5.00	10.00
SMAS-93972	Rainbow Bridge	1971	12.50	25.00	50.00
—Capitol Record Club edition					
RHINO					
RNDF-254 [PD]	The Jimi Hendrix Interview	1982	6.25	12.50	25.00
RYKO ANALOGUE					
RALP-0038 [(2)]	Live at Winterland	1988	3.75	7.50	15.00
RALP-0078 [(2)]	Radio One	1988	3.75	7.50	15.00
—Clear vinyl					
TRACK					
612003 [M]	Axis: Bold As Love	2000	6.25	12.50	25.00
—Classic Records issue of the original U.K. mono mix, on a reproduction of the original British label					
TRIP					
3509 [(2)]	Superpak	197?	3.75	7.50	15.00
TLP-9500	Rare Hendrix	1972	3.75	7.50	15.00
TLP-9501	Roots of Hendrix	1972	3.00	6.00	12.00
TLP-9512	Moods	1973	3.00	6.00	12.00
TLP-9523	The Genius of Jimi Hendrix	1973	3.00	6.00	12.00
UNITED ARTISTS					
UA-LA505-E	The Very Best of Jimi Hendrix	1975	3.00	6.00	12.00
WARNER BROS.					
HS 2299	Nine to the Universe	1980	3.00	6.00	12.00
—Reprise cover, Warner Bros. tan "pinstripe" label; possibly Columbia House edition?					

HENDRIX, JIMI, AND LITTLE RICHARD

Also see each artist's individual listings.

Number	Title (A Side/B Side)	Yr	VG	VG+	NM
45s					
ALA					
1175	Goodnight Irene/Why Don't You Love Me	1972	2.00	4.00	8.00
Albums					
ARCHIVE OF FOLK AND JAZZ					
296	Roots of Rock	1974	3.00	6.00	12.00
PICKWICK					
SPC-3347	Jimi Hendrix and Little Richard Together	1973	3.00	6.00	12.00

HENDRIX, JIMI, AND LONNIE YOUNGBLOOD

Number	Title (A Side/B Side)	Yr	VG	VG+	NM
Albums					
MAPLE					
6004	Two Great Experiences Together	1971	12.50	25.00	50.00

HENHOUSE FIVE PLUS TOO

See RAY STEVENS.

HENRY, CLARENCE

Number	Title (A Side/B Side)	Yr	VG	VG+	NM
45s					
ARGO					
5259	Ain't Got No Home/Troubles, Troubles	1956	5.00	10.00	20.00
5266	I'm a Country Boy/Lonely Tramp	1957	4.00	8.00	16.00
5273	Found a Home/It Won't Be Long	1957	4.00	8.00	16.00
5305	I'm in Love/Baby Baby Please	1958	4.00	8.00	16.00
5378	I Don't Know Why/Just Baby and Me	1960	5.00	10.00	20.00
5378	But I Do/Just Baby and Me	1960	4.00	8.00	16.00
—A-side: Same song, new title					
5388	You Always Hurt the One You Love/Hello, Hello	1961	4.00	8.00	16.00
5395	Lonely Street/Why Can't You	1961	3.75	7.50	15.00
5401	On Bended Knees/Standing in the Need of Love	1961	3.75	7.50	15.00
5408	A Little Too Much/I Wish I Could Stay the Same	1962	3.00	6.00	12.00
5414	Dream Myself a Sweetheart/Lost Without You	1962	3.00	6.00	12.00
5426	Jealous Kind/Come On and Dance	1962	3.00	6.00	12.00
5448	If I Didn't Care/It Takes Two to Tango	1963	3.00	6.00	12.00
5480	Looking Back/Long Lost and Worried	1964	2.50	5.00	10.00
CADET					
5259	Ain't Got No Home/Troubles, Troubles	1966	2.00	4.00	8.00
DIAL					
4057	This Time/Hummin' a Heartache	1967	—	3.00	6.00
4072	Shake Your Money Maker/That's When I Guessed	1968	—	3.00	6.00
PARROT					
45004	Have You Ever Been Lonely/Little Green Frog	1964	2.50	5.00	10.00
45009	I Told My Pillow/Can't Hide My Tear	1964	2.50	5.00	10.00
45015	I Might As Well/Tore Up Over You	1965	2.50	5.00	10.00
Albums					
ARGO					
LP-4009 [M]	You Always Hurt the One You Love	1961	75.00	125.00	250.00
CADET					
LP-4009 [M]	You Always Hurt the One You Love	1966	12.50	25.00	50.00
—Includes copies of Cadet LP in Argo sleeves					

Number	Title (A Side/B Side)	Yr	VG	VG+	NM
ROULETTE					
SR 42039	Alive and Well and Living in New Orleans	1969	6.25	12.50	25.00

HENRY, EARL

Number	Title (A Side/B Side)	Yr	VG	VG+	NM
45s					
DOT					
15756	Whatcha Gonna Do?/I Am the Man	1958	12.50	25.00	50.00
15875	My Suzanne/Believe a Traveler	1958	7.50	15.00	30.00

HENRY TREE

Number	Title (A Side/B Side)	Yr	VG	VG+	NM
45s					
MAINSTREAM					
729	Penfield Town/(B-side unknown)	1970	3.00	6.00	12.00
Albums					
MAINSTREAM					
S-6129	Electric Holy Man	1968	7.50	15.00	30.00

HENSLEE, GENE

Number	Title (A Side/B Side)	Yr	VG	VG+	NM
45s					
IMPERIAL					
8227	Diggin' and Datin'/A Girl Named Haertbreak	1954	17.50	35.00	70.00
8260	Naughty and Nice/Try As I May	1954	15.00	30.00	60.00
8277	Rockin' Baby/What Will I Do	1954	15.00	30.00	60.00
MEL-O-DY					
110	Beautiful Women/Shambles	1963	5.00	10.00	20.00
UNITED ARTISTS					
946	I Don't Wanna Go Home/Shambles	1964	3.75	7.50	15.00

HENSLEY, KEN

Number	Title (A Side/B Side)	Yr	VG	VG+	NM
45s					
MERCURY					
73410	When Evening Comes/Fortune	1973	—	2.50	5.00
Albums					
MERCURY					
SRM-1-661	Proud Words on a Dusty Shelf	1973	3.00	6.00	12.00
WARNER BROS.					
BS 2863	Eager to Please	1975	2.50	5.00	10.00

HEP STARS, THE

With Benny Andersson, later of BJORN & BENNY and ABBA.

Number	Title (A Side/B Side)	Yr	VG	VG+	NM
45s					
CHARTMAKER					
414	It's Now Winter's Day/Musty Dusty	1969	5.00	10.00	20.00
DUNHILL					
4040	Sunny Girl/No Response	1966	6.25	12.50	25.00

HEPSTERS, THE

Number	Title (A Side/B Side)	Yr	VG	VG+	NM
45s					
RONEL					
107	Rockin' N' Rollin' with Santa Claus/I Had To Let You Go	1955	100.00	200.00	400.00
110	I Gotta Sing the Blues/This-a-Way	1956	75.00	150.00	300.00
XMAS					
3711	Rockin' & Rollin' With Santa Claus/Sleigh Bell Rock	19??	2.00	4.00	8.00
—B-side by Three Aces and a Joker; reissue of rare R&B sides					

HERALDS, THE

Number	Title (A Side/B Side)	Yr	VG	VG+	NM
45s					
HERALD					
435	Eternal Love/Gonna Love You	1954	62.50	125.00	250.00

HERD, THE

PETER FRAMPTON was in this group.

Number	Title (A Side/B Side)	Yr	VG	VG+	NM
45s					
FONTANA					
1588	I Can Fly/Understand Me	1967	2.50	5.00	10.00
1602	Sweet William/From the Underworld	1967	2.50	5.00	10.00
1610	Paradise Lost/Come On, Believe Me	1968	2.50	5.00	10.00
1618	Our Fairy Tale/I Don't Want Our Loving to Die	1968	2.50	5.00	10.00
1646	The Game/Beauty Queen	1969	2.50	5.00	10.00
Albums					
FONTANA					
SRF-67579	Lookin' Thru You	1968	6.25	12.50	25.00

HERMAN, WOODY

Number	Title (A Side/B Side)	Yr	VG	VG+	NM
45s					
CADET					
5635	Light My Fire/Hush	1969	—	2.50	5.00
5643	Pontico/Keep On Keeping On	1969	—	2.50	5.00
5659	I Can't Get Next to You/It's Your Thing	1969	—	2.50	5.00
5669	My Cherie Amour/The Hut	1970	—	2.50	5.00
CAPITOL					
F2942	Muskrat Ramble/Woodchopper Mambo	1954	3.00	6.00	12.00
F2960	Mexican Hat Trick/Sleepy Serenade	1954	3.00	6.00	12.00
F3042	Have It Your Way/My Sin Is You	1955	3.00	6.00	12.00
F3173	You're Here My Love/The Girl Upstairs	1955	3.00	6.00	12.00
F3202	Love Is a Many-Splendored Thing/House of Bamboo	1955	3.00	6.00	12.00
F3269	Skinned/Skinned Again	1955	3.00	6.00	12.00
F3488	I Don't Want Nobody (To Have My Love But You)/To Love Again	1956	3.00	6.00	12.00
CHURCHILL					
7735	My Blue Heaven/It Must Be True	1979	—	2.00	4.00
COLUMBIA					
39409	Caldonia/(B-side unknown)	1951	3.00	6.00	12.00
39410	Happiness Is a Thing Called Joe/Bijou	1951	3.00	6.00	12.00
39411	Apple Honey/Wild Root	1951	3.00	6.00	12.00
39412	Northwest Passage/(B-side unknown)	1951	3.00	6.00	12.00
—The above four comprise a box set					

Number	Title (A Side/B Side)	Yr	VG	VG+	NM
43262	My Favorite Things/Do Anything You Wanna	1965	—	3.00	6.00
43449	Mardi Gras/Sting Ray	1965	—	3.00	6.00
43750	Sidewinder/Greasy Sack Blues	1966	—	3.00	6.00
44124	The Duck/Hallelujah, Baby!	1967	—	3.00	6.00
FANTASY					
672	After Hours/(B-side unknown)	1972	—	2.00	4.00
695	Fat Mama/The Raven Speaks	1973	—	2.00	4.00
699	The First Thing I Do/Freedom Jazz Dance	1973	—	2.00	4.00
723	Corazon/America Drinks and Goes Home	1974	—	2.00	4.00
MGM					
11661	Prelude to a Kiss/Cuban Holiday	1954	3.75	7.50	15.00
PHILIPS					
40003	Swing Low, Sweet Chariot/Rose Room	1962	2.00	4.00	8.00
40064	Ramblin' Rose/What Kind of Fool Am I	1962	2.00	4.00	8.00
40125	Days of Wine and Roses/Jazz Me Blues	1963	2.00	4.00	8.00
40187	Taste of Honey/Hallelujah Time	1964	2.00	4.00	8.00
40213	C'mon and Ska/Theme from Golden Boy	1964	2.00	4.00	8.00
VERVE					
10053	I Wonder/Like a House Built on a Strong Foundation	1957	2.50	5.00	10.00
10069	Makin' Whoopee/Comes Love	1957	2.50	5.00	10.00
7-Inch Extended Plays					
COLUMBIA					
B-2521	Caledonia/Bijou//Woodchopper's Ball/Northwest Passage	195?	3.00	6.00	12.00
B-2521 [PS]	Woody Herman (Hall of Fame Series)	195?	3.00	6.00	12.00
Albums					
ACCORD					
SN-7185	All Star Session	1981	2.50	5.00	10.00
AMERICAN RECORDING SOCIETY					
G-410 [M]	The Progressive Big Band Sound	1956	10.00	20.00	40.00
ARCHIVE OF FOLK AND JAZZ					
316	Woody Herman, Vol. 2	197?	2.50	5.00	10.00
338	Woody Herman, Vol. 2	197?	2.50	5.00	10.00
ATLANTIC					
1328 [M]	Woody Herman at the Monterey Jazz Festival	1960	10.00	20.00	40.00
SD 1328 [S]	Woody Herman at the Monterey Jazz Festival	1960	7.50	15.00	30.00
90044	Woody Herman at the Monterey Jazz Festival	1982	2.50	5.00	10.00
—Reissue of 1328					
BRUNSWICK					
BL 54024 [M]	The Swinging Herman Herd	1957	10.00	20.00	40.00
BULLDOG					
2005	20 Golden Pieces of Woody Herman	198?	2.50	5.00	10.00
CADET					
LPS-819	Light My Fire	1969	3.00	6.00	12.00
LPS-835	Heavy Exposure	1969	3.00	6.00	12.00
LPS-845	Woody	1970	3.00	6.00	12.00
CAPITOL					
H 324 [10]	Classics in Jazz	1952	17.50	35.00	70.00
T 324 [M]	Classics in Jazz	1955	10.00	20.00	40.00
T 560 [M]	The Woody Herman Band	1955	10.00	20.00	40.00
T 658 [M]	Road Band	1955	10.00	20.00	40.00
T 748 [M]	Jackpot!	1956	10.00	20.00	40.00
T 784 [M]	Blues Groove	1956	10.00	20.00	40.00
DT 1554 [R]	The Hits of Woody Herman	1961	3.00	6.00	12.00
SM-1554	The Hits of Woody Herman	197?	2.00	4.00	8.00
T 1554 [M]	The Hits of Woody Herman	1961	5.00	10.00	20.00
M-11034	Early Autumn	1972	2.50	5.00	10.00
CENTURY					
CRDD-1080	Road Father	1979	6.25	12.50	25.00
—Direct-to-disc recording					
CR-1110	Chick, Donald, Walter and Woodrow	1978	3.00	6.00	12.00
CHESS					
402 [(2)]	Double Exposure	197?	3.75	7.50	15.00
CLEF					
MGC-745 [M]	Jazz, the Utmost!	1956	20.00	40.00	80.00
COLUMBIA					
C3L 25 [(3) M]	The Thundering Herds	1963	12.50	25.00	50.00
CL 592 [M]	The Three Herds	1955	12.50	25.00	50.00
—Maroon label with gold print					
CL 592 [M]	The Three Herds	1956	7.50	15.00	30.00
—Red and black label with six "eye" logos					
CL 651 [M]	Music for Tired Lovers	1955	10.00	20.00	40.00
CL 2357 [M]	My Kind of Broadway	1965	3.00	6.00	12.00
CL 2436 [M]	Woody's Winners	1965	3.00	6.00	12.00
CL 2491 [M]	Woody Herman's Greatest Hits	1966	3.00	6.00	12.00
CL 2509 [10]	Ridin' Herd	1955	15.00	30.00	60.00
CL 2552 [M]	The Jazz S(w)inger	1966	3.00	6.00	12.00
CL 2563 [10]	Woody!	1955	15.00	30.00	60.00
CL 2693 [M]	Woody Live — East & West	1967	3.75	7.50	15.00
CL 6026 [10]	Sequence in Jazz	1949	17.50	35.00	70.00
CL 6049 [10]	Dance Parade	1949	17.50	35.00	70.00
CL 6092 [10]	Woody Herman and His Woodchoppers	1950	17.50	35.00	70.00
CS 9157 [S]	My Kind of Broadway	1965	3.75	7.50	15.00
CS 9236 [S]	Woody's Winners	1965	3.75	7.50	15.00
CS 9291 [S]	Woody Herman's Greatest Hits	1966	3.75	7.50	15.00
PC 9291	Woody Herman's Greatest Hits	198?	2.00	4.00	8.00
—Reissue with new prefix					
CS 9352 [S]	The Jazz S(w)inger	1966	3.75	7.50	15.00
CS 9493 [S]	Woody Live — East & West	1967	3.00	6.00	12.00
C 32530	Jazz Hoot	1974	3.00	6.00	12.00
CONCORD JAZZ					
CJ-170	Woody Herman and Friends at the Monterey Jazz Festival 1979	198?	3.00	6.00	12.00
CJ-191	Live at the Concord Jazz Festival	1982	3.00	6.00	12.00
CJ-240	World Class	1983	3.00	6.00	12.00
CJ-302	50th Anniversary Tour	1986	3.00	6.00	12.00
CJ-330	Woody's Gold Star	1987	3.00	6.00	12.00
CORAL					
CRL 56005 [10]	Blue Prelude	1950	17.50	35.00	70.00
CRL 56010 [10]	Woody Herman Souvenirs	1950	17.50	35.00	70.00
CRL 56090 [10]	Woody's Best	1953	17.50	35.00	70.00
CROWN					
CLP 5180 [M]	The New Swingin' Herman Band	1960	5.00	10.00	20.00
DECCA					
DL 4484 [M]	Woody Herman's Golden Hits	1964	3.75	7.50	15.00
DL 8133 [M]	Woodchopper's Ball	1955	10.00	20.00	40.00
DL 9229 [M]	The Turning Point — 1943-44	1967	3.75	7.50	15.00
DL 74484 [R]	Woody Herman's Golden Hits	1964	2.50	5.00	10.00
DL 79229 [R]	The Turning Point — 1943-44	1967	2.50	5.00	10.00
DIAL					
LP-210 [10]	Swinging with the Woodchoppers	1950	37.50	75.00	150.00
DISCOVERY					
815	The Third Herd	198?	2.50	5.00	10.00
845	The Third Herd, Volume 2	198?	2.50	5.00	10.00
EVEREST					
SDBR-1003 [S]	The Herd Rides Again…In Stereo	1958	10.00	20.00	40.00
LPBR-1032 [M]	Moody Woody	1958	7.50	15.00	30.00
EV-1222 [M]	The Best of Woody Herman	1963	3.75	7.50	15.00
LPBR-5003 [M]	The Herd Rides Again	1958	7.50	15.00	30.00
SDBR-5032 [S]	Moody Woody	1958	10.00	20.00	40.00
EV-5222 [S]	The Best of Woody Herman	1963	5.00	10.00	20.00
FANTASY					
OJC-344	Giant Steps	198?	2.50	5.00	10.00
—Reissue of 9432					
FPM-4003 [Q]	Children of Lima	1975	5.00	10.00	20.00
8414	Brand New	1971	3.00	6.00	12.00
9416	The Raven Speaks	1972	3.00	6.00	12.00
F-9432	Giant Steps	1973	3.00	6.00	12.00
F-9452	The Thundering Herd	1973	3.00	6.00	12.00
F-9470	The Herd at Montreux	1974	3.00	6.00	12.00
F-9477	Children of Lima	1975	3.00	6.00	12.00
F-9499	King Cobra	1976	3.00	6.00	12.00
F-9609	Feelin' So Blue	1982	2.50	5.00	10.00
FORUM					
F-9016 [M]	Woody Herman Sextet at the Round Table	196?	5.00	10.00	20.00
FS-9016 [S]	Woody Herman Sextet at the Round Table	196?	6.25	12.50	25.00
HARMONY					
HL 7013 [M]	Bijou	1957	5.00	10.00	20.00
HL 7093 [M]	Summer Sequence	1957	5.00	10.00	20.00
HINDSIGHT					
HSR-116	Woody Herman and His Orchestra 1937	198?	2.50	5.00	10.00
HSR-134	Woody Herman and His Orchestra 1944	198?	2.50	5.00	10.00
INSIGHT					
208	Woody Herman and His Orchestra 1937-44	198?	2.50	5.00	10.00
JAZZLAND					
JLP-17 [M]	The Fourth Herd	1960	6.25	12.50	25.00
JLP-917 [S]	The Fourth Herd	1960	6.25	12.50	25.00
LION					
L-70059 [M]	The Herman Herd at Carnegie Hall	1958	6.25	12.50	25.00
MARS					
MRX-1 [10]	Dance Date on Mars	1952	37.50	75.00	150.00
MRX-2 [10]	Woody Herman Goes Native	1953	37.50	75.00	150.00
MCA					
219	Golden Favorites	1973	2.50	5.00	10.00
4077 [(2)]	The Best of Woody Herman	197?	3.75	7.50	15.00
METRO					
M-514 [M]	Woody Herman	1966	3.75	7.50	15.00
MS-514 [R]	Woody Herman	1966	2.50	5.00	10.00
MGM					
E-158 [10]	Woody Herman at Carnegie Hall, 1946, Vol. 1	1952	17.50	35.00	70.00
E-159 [10]	Woody Herman at Carnegie Hall, 1946, Vol. 2	1952	17.50	35.00	70.00
E-192 [10]	The Third Herd	1953	17.50	35.00	70.00
E-284 [10]	Blue Flame	1955	17.50	35.00	70.00
E-3043 [M]	Carnegie Hall 1946	1953	12.50	25.00	50.00
—Compiles 158 and 159 on one 12-inch LP					
E-3385 [M]	Hi-Fi-ing Herd	1956	10.00	20.00	40.00
MOBILE FIDELITY					
1-219	The Fourth Herd	1994	7.50	15.00	30.00
—Audiophile vinyl					
PHILIPS					
PHM 200004 [M]	Swing Low, Sweet Chariot	1962	3.75	7.50	15.00
PHM 200065 [M]	Woody Herman 1963	1963	3.75	7.50	15.00
PHM 200092 [M]	Encore: Woody Herman 1963	1963	3.75	7.50	15.00
PHM 200118 [M]	Woody Herman: 1964	1964	3.75	7.50	15.00
PHM 200131 [M]	The Swinging Herman Herd Recorded Live	1964	3.75	7.50	15.00
PHM 200171 [M]	Woody's Big Band Goodies	1965	3.75	7.50	15.00
PHS 600004 [S]	Swing Low, Sweet Chariot	1962	5.00	10.00	20.00
PHS 600065 [S]	Woody Herman 1963	1963	5.00	10.00	20.00
PHS 600092 [S]	Encore: Woody Herman 1963	1963	5.00	10.00	20.00
PHS 600118 [S]	Woody Herman: 1964	1964	5.00	10.00	20.00
PHS 600131 [S]	The Swinging Herman Herd Recorded Live	1964	5.00	10.00	20.00
PHS 600171 [S]	Woody's Big Band Goodies	1965	5.00	10.00	20.00
PICCADILLY					
3333	It's Coolin' Time	198?	2.50	5.00	10.00
PICKWICK					
SPC-3591	Blowin' Up a Storm	1978	2.50	5.00	10.00
RCA VICTOR					
BGL2-2203 [(2)]	40th Anniversary Carnegie Hall Concert	1977	3.75	7.50	15.00
ROULETTE					
R 25067 [M]	Woody Herman Sextet at the Round Table	1959	7.50	15.00	30.00
SR 25067 [S]	Woody Herman Sextet at the Round Table	1959	10.00	20.00	40.00
SUNBEAM					
206	Woody Herman and His Orchestra 1936	198?	2.50	5.00	10.00
SUNSET					
SUM-1139 [M]	Blowin' Up a Storm	1966	2.50	5.00	10.00
SUS-5139 [S]	Blowin' Up a Storm	1966	3.00	6.00	12.00
TRIP					
5547	Woody 1963	1974	2.50	5.00	10.00
VERVE					
VSP-1 [M]	The First Herd at Carnegie Hall	1966	3.75	7.50	15.00
VSPS-1 [R]	The First Herd at Carnegie Hall	1966	2.50	5.00	10.00
VSP-26 [M]	Woody Herman's Woodchoppers & The First Herd Live at Carnegie Hall	1966	3.75	7.50	15.00

Number	Title (A Side/B Side)	Yr	VG	VG+	NM
VSPS-26 [R]	Woody Herman's Woodchoppers & The First Herd Live at Carnegie Hall	1966	2.50	5.00	10.00
MGV-2030 [M]	Early Autumn	1957	10.00	20.00	40.00
V-2030 [M]	Early Autumn	1963	3.75	7.50	15.00
MGV-2069 [M]	Songs for Hip Lovers	1957	10.00	20.00	40.00
V-2069 [M]	Songs for Hip Lovers	1963	3.75	7.50	15.00
MGV-2096 [M]	Love Is the Sweetest Thing — Sometimes	1958	10.00	20.00	40.00
V-2096 [M]	Love Is the Sweetest Thing — Sometimes	1963	3.75	7.50	15.00
MGV-8014 [M]	Jazz, the Utmost!	1957	10.00	20.00	40.00
—Reissue of Clef LP					
V-8014 [M]	Jazz, the Utmost!	1963	3.75	7.50	15.00
MGV-8216 [M]	Men from Mars	1958	10.00	20.00	40.00
MGV-8255 [M]	Woody Herman '58	1958	10.00	20.00	40.00
V-8255 [M]	Woody Herman '58	1963	3.75	7.50	15.00
V-8558 [M]	Hey! Heard the Herd?	1963	5.00	10.00	20.00
—Reissue of Verve 8216					
V6-8558 [S]	Hey! Heard the Herd?	1963	3.75	7.50	15.00
V6-8764	Concerto for Herd	1968	5.00	10.00	20.00
WHO'S WHO IN JAZZ					
21013	Lionel Hampton Presents Woody Herman	1979	3.00	6.00	12.00
WING					
MGW-12329 [M]	Woody's Big Band Goodies	1966	2.50	5.00	10.00
SRW-16329 [S]	Woody's Big Band Goodies	1966	3.00	6.00	12.00

HERMAN, WOODY/TITO PUENTE

Albums

Number	Title (A Side/B Side)	Yr	VG	VG+	NM
EVEREST					
SDBR-1010 [S]	Herman's Beat of Puente	1958	10.00	20.00	40.00
LPBR-5010 [M]	Herman's Beat of Puente	1958	10.00	20.00	40.00

HERMAN'S HERMITS

Also see PETER NOONE.

45s

Number	Title (A Side/B Side)	Yr	VG	VG+	NM
ABKCO					
4021	Mrs. Brown You've Got a Lovely Daughter/I'm Henry VIII, I Am	1972	—	2.50	5.00
4022	I'm Into Something Good/Can't You Hear My Heartbeat	1972	—	2.50	5.00
4023	There's a Kind of Hush (All Over the World)/Wonderful World	1972	—	2.50	5.00
4024	Listen People/Dandy	1972	—	2.50	5.00
4042	Silhouettes/Just a Little Bit Better	1973	—	2.50	5.00
4043	A Must to Avoid/Leaning on the Lamp Post	1973	—	2.50	5.00
BUDDAH					
516	Lonely Situation (Love Is All I Need)/Blond Haired Blue Eyed Boy	1976	2.00	4.00	8.00
MGM					
(no #) [PS]	Hold On	1966	62.50	125.00	250.00
—Promo-only sleeve similar to the LP cover of the same name; it's not known which single this came with					
13280	I'm Into Something Good/Your Hand in Mine	1964	2.50	5.00	10.00
13310	Can't You Hear My Heartbeat/I Know Why	1964	2.50	5.00	10.00
13310 [PS]	Can't You Hear My Heartbeat/I Know Why	1964	3.75	7.50	15.00
13332	Silhouettes/Walkin' With My Angel	1965	2.50	5.00	10.00
13341	Mrs. Brown You've Got a Lovely Daughter/I Gotta Dream On	1965	2.50	5.00	10.00
13341 [PS]	Mrs. Brown You've Got a Lovely Daughter/I Gotta Dream On	1965	3.75	7.50	15.00
13354	Wonderful World/Traveling Light	1965	2.50	5.00	10.00
13354 [PS]	Wonderful World/Traveling Light	1965	3.75	7.50	15.00
13367	I'm Henry VIII, I Am/The End of the World	1965	2.50	5.00	10.00
13367 [PS]	I'm Henry VIII, I Am/The End of the World	1965	5.00	10.00	20.00
13398	Just a Little Bit Better/Sea Cruise	1965	2.50	5.00	10.00
13398 [PS]	Just a Little Bit Better/Sea Cruise	1965	3.75	7.50	15.00
13437	A Must to Avoid/The Man with the Cigar	1966	2.00	4.00	8.00
13462	Listen People/Got a Feeling	1966	2.00	4.00	8.00
13500	Leaning on the Lamp Post/Hold On	1966	2.00	4.00	8.00
13548	This Door Swings Both Ways/For Love	1966	2.00	4.00	8.00
13603	Dandy/My Reservation's Been Confirmed	1966	2.00	4.00	8.00
13603 [PS]	Dandy/My Reservation's Been Confirmed	1966	3.75	7.50	15.00
13639	East West/What Is Wrong What Is Right	1966	2.00	4.00	8.00
13681	There's a Kind of Hush/No Milk Today	1967	2.00	4.00	8.00
13681	There's a Kind of Hush (All Over the World)/No Milk Today	1967	2.50	5.00	10.00
13681 [PS]	There's a Kind of Hush/No Milk Today	1967	3.75	7.50	15.00
13761	Don't Go Out Into the Rain (You're Going to Melt)/Moonshine Man	1967	2.00	4.00	8.00
13761 [PS]	Don't Go Out Into the Rain (You're Going to Melt)/Moonshine Man	1967	3.75	7.50	15.00
13787	Museum/Last Bus Home	1967	2.00	4.00	8.00
13787 [PS]	Museum/Last Bus Home	1967	3.75	7.50	15.00
13885	I Can Take or Leave Your Loving/Marcel's	1967	2.00	4.00	8.00
13934	Sleepy Joe/Just One Girl	1968	2.50	5.00	10.00
—Black label					
13934	Sleepy Joe/Just One Girl	1968	2.00	4.00	8.00
—Blue and gold label					
13973	Sunshine Girl/Nobody Needs to Know	1968	2.50	5.00	10.00
13994	Ooh, She's Done It Again/The Most Beautiful Thing in My Life	1968	2.50	5.00	10.00
14035	Something's Happening/Little Miss Sorrow, Child of Tomorrow	1969	2.50	5.00	10.00
14060	My Lady/My Sentimental Friend	1969	2.50	5.00	10.00
14100	It's Alright Now/(Here Comes) The Star	1969	2.50	5.00	10.00
PRIVATE STOCK					
45019	Ginny Go Softly/Blond Haired, Blue Eyed Boy	1975	2.00	4.00	8.00
ROULETTE					
7213	Truck Stop Mama/Heart Get Ready for Love	1977	3.75	7.50	15.00

Albums

Number	Title (A Side/B Side)	Yr	VG	VG+	NM
ABKCO					
4227-1	Their Greatest Hits	1988	2.00	4.00	8.00
—Abridged version of AB 4227					
AB-4227 [(2)]	XX (Greatest Hits)	1973	3.00	6.00	12.00
MGM					
E-4282 [M]	Introducing Herman's Hermits	1965	6.25	12.50	25.00
—Version 1: With "Including Their Hit Single 'I'm Into Something Good' " on front cover					
E-4282 [M]	Introducing Herman's Hermits	1965	5.00	10.00	20.00
—Version 2: Same as above, but with a sticker that says "Featuring "Mrs. Brown You Have a Lovely Daughter'."					
E-4282 [M]	Introducing Herman's Hermits	1965	3.75	7.50	15.00
—Version 3: With "Including 'Mrs. Brown You've Got a Lovely Daughter' " on front cover					
SE-4282 [R]	Introducing Herman's Hermits	1965	5.00	10.00	20.00
—Version 1: With "Including Their Hit Single 'I'm Into Something Good' " on front cover					
SE-4282 [R]	Introducing Herman's Hermits	1965	3.75	7.50	15.00
—Version 2: Same as above, but with a sticker that says "Featuring "Mrs. Brown You Have a Lovely Daughter'."					
SE-4282 [R]	Introducing Herman's Hermits	1965	2.50	5.00	10.00
—Version 3: With "Including 'Mrs. Brown You've Got a Lovely Daughter' " on front cover					
E-4295 [M]	Herman's Hermits On Tour	1965	3.00	6.00	12.00
SE-4295 [R]	Herman's Hermits On Tour	1965	2.50	5.00	10.00
E-4315 [M]	The Best of Herman's Hermits	1965	3.00	6.00	12.00
SE-4315 [R]	The Best of Herman's Hermits	1965	2.50	5.00	10.00
E-4342 [M]	Hold On!	1966	2.50	5.00	10.00
SE-4342 [P]	Hold On!	1966	3.00	6.00	12.00
E-4386 [M]	Both Sides of Herman's Hermits	1966	2.50	5.00	10.00
SE-4386 [R]	Both Sides of Herman's Hermits	1966	2.00	4.00	8.00
E-4416 [M]	The Best of Herman's Hermits, Volume 2	1966	3.00	6.00	12.00
—Add 50% if bonus photo of Herman is included					
SE-4416 [P]	The Best of Herman's Hermits, Volume 2	1966	2.50	5.00	10.00
—Add 50% if bonus photo of Herman is included. "Hold On" and "Leaning on the Lamp Post" are in true stereo.					
E-4438 [M]	There's a Kind of Hush All Over the World	1967	2.50	5.00	10.00
SE-4438 [R]	There's a Kind of Hush All Over the World	1967	2.00	4.00	8.00
E-4478 [M]	Blaze	1967	2.50	5.00	10.00
SE-4478 [S]	Blaze	1967	2.50	5.00	10.00
E-4505 [M]	The Best of Herman's Hermits, Volume 3	1967	2.50	5.00	10.00
SE-4505 [P]	The Best of Herman's Hermits, Volume 3	1967	2.50	5.00	10.00
—"Don't Go Out Into the Rain," "Museum," "Last Bus Home" and "Mum and Dad" are in true stereo.					
SE-4548 [P]	Mrs. Brown You've Got a Lovely Daughter	1968	2.50	5.00	10.00
—"Mrs. Brown You've Got a Lovely Daughter" and "There's a Kind of Hush" are rechanneled					
ST-90416 [R]	Introducing Herman's Hermits	1965	5.00	10.00	20.00
—Capitol Record Club edition					
T-90416 [M]	Introducing Herman's Hermits	1965	6.25	12.50	25.00
—Capitol Record Club edition					
ST-90421 [R]	Herman's Hermits On Tour	1965	5.00	10.00	20.00
—Capitol Record Club edition					
T-90421 [M]	Herman's Hermits On Tour	1965	6.25	12.50	25.00
—Capitol Record Club edition					
ST-90646 [R]	Hold On!	1966	5.00	10.00	20.00
—Capitol Record Club edition					
T-90646 [M]	Hold On!	1966	6.25	12.50	25.00
—Capitol Record Club edition					
ST-91286 [S]	Blaze	1967	5.00	10.00	20.00
—Capitol Record Club edition					
T-91286 [M]	Blaze	1967	7.50	15.00	30.00
—Capitol Record Club edition					

HERON, MIKE

45s

Number	Title (A Side/B Side)	Yr	VG	VG+	NM
ELEKTRA					
45739	Call Me Diamond/Brindaban	1971	2.00	4.00	8.00

Albums

Number	Title (A Side/B Side)	Yr	VG	VG+	NM
ELEKTRA					
EKS-74093	Smiling Men with Bad Reputations	1971	5.00	10.00	20.00

HERROLD, DENNIS

45s

Number	Title (A Side/B Side)	Yr	VG	VG+	NM
IMPERIAL					
5482	Hip Hip Baby/Make with the Lovin'	1957	20.00	40.00	80.00

HESITATIONS, THE

45s

Number	Title (A Side/B Side)	Yr	VG	VG+	NM
GWP					
504	Is This the Way to Treat a Girl/Yes I'm Ready	1969	2.00	4.00	8.00
KAPP					
790	Soul Superman/I'm Not Built That Way	1966	2.50	5.00	10.00
810	Soul Kind of Love/Wait a Minute	1967	2.50	5.00	10.00
822	I'll Be Right There/She Won't Come Back	1967	2.50	5.00	10.00
848	You Can't Bypass Love/You'll Never Know	1967	2.50	5.00	10.00
878	Born Free/Love Is Everywhere	1967	2.50	5.00	10.00
899	The Impossible Dream/Nobody Knows You When You're Down and Out	1968	2.50	5.00	10.00
911	Climb Every Mountain/My World	1968	2.50	5.00	10.00
926	Who Will Answer/If You Ever Need a Hand	1968	2.50	5.00	10.00
948	A Whiter Shade of Pale/With Pen in Hand	1968	2.50	5.00	10.00

Albums

Number	Title (A Side/B Side)	Yr	VG	VG+	NM
KAPP					
KL-1525 [M]	Soul Superman	1967	7.50	15.00	30.00
KS-3525 [S]	Soul Superman	1967	6.25	12.50	25.00
KS-3548	The New Born Free	1968	6.25	12.50	25.00
KS-3561	Where We're At	1968	6.25	12.50	25.00
KS-3574	Solid Gold	1969	6.25	12.50	25.00

HESTER, CAROLYN

45s

Number	Title (A Side/B Side)	Yr	VG	VG+	NM
DOT					
16660	Stay Not Late/That's My Song	1964	2.50	5.00	10.00
METROMEDIA					
120	Magic, Man/Big City Streets	1969	2.00	4.00	8.00
RCA VICTOR					
APBO-0008	You Made My Life a Song/Comin' On Back to You	1973	—	3.00	6.00

Albums

Number	Title (A Side/B Side)	Yr	VG	VG+	NM
COLUMBIA					
CL 1796 [M]	Carolyn Hester	1962	15.00	30.00	60.00
—With Bob Dylan on harmonica on three tracks; black and red label with six "eye" logos					

Number	Title (A Side/B Side)	Yr	VG	VG+	NM
CL 1796 [M]	Carolyn Hester	1963	5.00	10.00	20.00
—Red label with "Guaranteed High Fidelity"					
CL 2032 [M]	This Life I'm Living	1963	5.00	10.00	20.00
CS 8596 [S]	Carolyn Hester	1962	20.00	40.00	80.00
—With Bob Dylan on harmonica on three tracks; black and red label with six "eye" logos					
CS 8596 [S]	Carolyn Hester	1963	6.25	12.50	25.00
—Red label, "360 Sound Stereo" in black					
CS 8832 [S]	This Life I'm Living	1963	6.25	12.50	25.00
CORAL					
CRL 57143 [M]	Scarlet Ribbons	1957	12.50	25.00	50.00
DOT					
DLP-3604 [M]	That's My Song	1964	3.75	7.50	15.00
DLP-3638 [M]	Carolyn Hester at Town Hall One	1965	3.75	7.50	15.00
DLP-3649 [M]	Carolyn Hester at Town Hall Two	1965	3.75	7.50	15.00
DLP-25604 [S]	That's My Song	1964	5.00	10.00	20.00
DLP-25638 [S]	Carolyn Hester at Town Hall One	1965	5.00	10.00	20.00
DLP-25649 [S]	Carolyn Hester at Town Hall Two	1965	5.00	10.00	20.00
FOLK ODYSSEY					
32160264	Simply Carolyn Hester	196?	5.00	10.00	20.00
METROMEDIA					
MD-1001	The Carolyn Hester Coalition	1969	5.00	10.00	20.00
MD-1022	Magazine	1970	15.00	30.00	60.00
RCA VICTOR					
APD1-0086 [Q]	Carolyn Hester	1973	5.00	10.00	20.00
—Only released in quadraphonic					
TRADITION					
TLP-1043 [M]	Carolyn Hester	1961	10.00	20.00	40.00

HEWITT, BEN

45s

Number	Title (A Side/B Side)	Yr	VG	VG+	NM
MERCURY					
71413	You Break Me Up/I Ain't Givin' Up Nothin'	1959	25.00	50.00	100.00
71472	Patricia June/For Quite a While	1959	12.50	25.00	50.00
71577	My Search/I Want a New Girl Now	1960	10.00	20.00	40.00
71612	The Queen in the Kingdom/Whirlwind Blues	1960	10.00	20.00	40.00

HEYWOOD, EDDIE

Pianist on the Hugo Winterhalter hit single "Canadian Sunset."

45s

Number	Title (A Side/B Side)	Yr	VG	VG+	NM
20TH CENTURY FOX					
453	Theme from "The Prize"/Li'l Darlin'	1963	2.00	4.00	8.00
COLUMBIA					
39316	Without a Song/A Pretty Girl Is Like a Melody	1951	2.50	5.00	10.00
39317	All the Things You Are/St. Louis Blues	1951	2.50	5.00	10.00
39318	Mighty Like a Rose/When Your Lover Has Gone	1951	2.50	5.00	10.00
39319	Try a Little Tenderness/The Birth of the Blues	1951	2.50	5.00	10.00
—The above four comprise a box set					
DECCA					
28549	Begin the Beguine/On the Sunny Side of the Street	1953	3.00	6.00	12.00
28893	The Moon Was Yellow/You Too, You Too	1953	3.00	6.00	12.00
30007	Jasmine/The Continental	1956	2.50	5.00	10.00
LIBERTY					
55396	The Good Earth/Dream of Olwen	1961	2.00	4.00	8.00
55539	Harlem Blues/The Sidewalks of New York	1963	2.00	4.00	8.00
55575	Canadian Sunset Bossa Nova/The Good Life	1963	2.00	4.00	8.00
MERCURY					
70645	Land of Dreams/Summer Holiday	1955	2.50	5.00	10.00
70677	Love for Love/Sunny Sunday	1955	2.50	5.00	10.00
70863	Soft Summer Breeze/Heywood's Bounce	1956	2.50	5.00	10.00
70950	Secret Love/Let's Fall in Love	1956	2.50	5.00	10.00
71014	Lover/If It's Sunny Sunday	1956	2.50	5.00	10.00
71462	Soft Summer Breeze/Castillian Rhapsody	1959	2.00	4.00	8.00
71504	High on a Windy Hill/Wings in Autumn	1959	2.00	4.00	8.00
71603	Out of Bounds/There You Are	1960	2.00	4.00	8.00
71650	(Love Theme) Rat Race/Everything in Manhattan	1960	2.00	4.00	8.00
71685	Jalousie/Cheek to Cheek	1960	2.00	4.00	8.00
71781	Velvet Rock/Mountains on the Moon	1961	2.00	4.00	8.00
RCA VICTOR					
47-6674	Lost Love/Mozambique	1956	3.00	6.00	12.00
47-6816	Begin the Beguine/No Miracle Needed	1957	2.50	5.00	10.00
47-6956	Love Is All/Virgin Isle Vamp	1957	2.50	5.00	10.00
47-7058	Lies/All About You	1957	2.50	5.00	10.00
47-7262	Haiti Lady/It's Really Nothing	1957	2.50	5.00	10.00
47-7385	St. Louis Blues/Rendezvous	1958	2.50	5.00	10.00

7-Inch Extended Plays

Number	Title (A Side/B Side)	Yr	VG	VG+	NM
DECCA					
ED 2032	Begin the Beguine/Laura//I Don't Know Why/Please Don't Talk About Me When I'm Gone	195?	3.00	6.00	12.00
ED 2032 [PS]	Eddie Heywood, Vol. 1	195?	3.00	6.00	12.00

Albums

Number	Title (A Side/B Side)	Yr	VG	VG+	NM
BRUNSWICK					
BL 58036 [10]	Eddie Heywood '45	1953	12.50	25.00	50.00
CAPITOL					
ST-163	Soft Summer Breeze	1969	3.00	6.00	12.00
ST 2833	With Love and Strings	1968	3.00	6.00	12.00
COLUMBIA					
CL 6157 [10]	Piano Moods	1951	12.50	25.00	50.00
COMMODORE					
XFL-15876	The Biggest Little Band of the Forties	198?	3.00	6.00	12.00
FL-20007 [10]	Eight Selections	1950	18.75	37.50	75.00
CORAL					
CRL 57095 [M]	Featuring Eddie Heywood	1957	10.00	20.00	40.00
DECCA					
DL 8202 [M]	Lightly and Politely	1956	7.50	15.00	30.00
DL 8270 [M]	Swing Low Sweet Heywood	1956	7.50	15.00	30.00
EMARCY					
MG-36042 [M]	Eddie Heywood	1955	10.00	20.00	40.00
EPIC					
LN 3327 [M]	Eddie Heywood at Twilight	1956	7.50	15.00	30.00
LIBERTY					
LRP-3250 [M]	Eddie Heywood's Golden Encores	1962	3.00	6.00	12.00
LRP-3313 [M]	Canadian Sunset Bossa Nova	1963	3.00	6.00	12.00
LST-7250 [S]	Eddie Heywood's Golden Encores	1962	3.75	7.50	15.00
LST-7313 [S]	Canadian Sunset Bossa Nova	1963	3.75	7.50	15.00
MAINSTREAM					
S-6001 [S]	Begin the Beguine	1964	3.75	7.50	15.00
96001 [M]	Begin the Beguine	1964	3.00	6.00	12.00
MERCURY					
MG-20445 [M]	Breezin' Along with the Breeze	1959	5.00	10.00	20.00
MG-20590 [M]	Eddie Heywood at the Piano	1960	5.00	10.00	20.00
MG-20632 [M]	One for My Baby	1960	5.00	10.00	20.00
SR-60115 [S]	Breezin' Along with the Breeze	1959	6.25	12.50	25.00
SR-60248 [S]	Eddie Heywood at the Piano	1960	6.25	12.50	25.00
SR-60632 [S]	One for My Baby	1960	6.25	12.50	25.00
MGM					
E-135 [10]	It's Easy to Remember	1952	12.50	25.00	50.00
E-3093 [M]	Pianorama	1955	10.00	20.00	40.00
E-3260 [M]	Eddie Heywood	1956	10.00	20.00	40.00
RCA VICTOR					
LPM-1466 [M]	The Touch of Eddie Heywood	1957	7.50	15.00	30.00
LPM-1529 [M]	Canadian Sunset	1957	7.50	15.00	30.00
LSP-1529 [S]	Canadian Sunset	1958	10.00	20.00	40.00
LPM-1900 [M]	The Keys and I	1958	7.50	15.00	30.00
SUNSET					
SUM-1121 [M]	An Affair to Remember	196?	3.00	6.00	12.00
SUS-5121 [S]	An Affair to Remember	196?	3.00	6.00	12.00
VOCALION					
VL 3748 [M]	The Piano Stylings of Eddie Heywood	1966	3.75	7.50	15.00
VL 73748 [R]	The Piano Stylings of Eddie Heywood	1966	3.00	6.00	12.00
WING					
MGW-12137 [M]	Eddie Heywood	196?	3.75	7.50	15.00
MGW-12287 [M]	Breezin' Along	196?	3.75	7.50	15.00
SRW-16137 [S]	Eddie Heywood	196?	3.00	6.00	12.00
SRW-16287 [S]	Breezin' Along	196?	3.00	6.00	12.00

HI-FI'S, THE

45s

Number	Title (A Side/B Side)	Yr	VG	VG+	NM
CAMEO					
349	I Keep Forgettin'/Why Can't I Stop Loving You	1965	3.00	6.00	12.00
INTERPHON					
7701	Will Yer or Won't Yer/She's the One	1964	3.00	6.00	12.00
UNITED ARTISTS					
50160	I'm a Box/No Two Ways	1967	2.00	4.00	8.00

HI-FI-DELS, THE

45s

Number	Title (A Side/B Side)	Yr	VG	VG+	NM
ATLANTIC					
2121	Did I Cry/Tricky Tricky	1961	3.75	7.50	15.00

HI-FIVES, THE (1)

45s

Number	Title (A Side/B Side)	Yr	VG	VG+	NM
BELL					
634	Julie/Son of Raunchy	1965	10.00	20.00	40.00
JERDEN					
730	Goin' Away/Tort	1964	3.75	7.50	15.00

HI-FIVES, THE (2)

45s

Number	Title (A Side/B Side)	Yr	VG	VG+	NM
BINGO					
1006	Felicia/Windy City Special	1960	7.50	15.00	30.00
DECCA					
30576	My Friend/How Can I Win?	1958	10.00	20.00	40.00
30657	Dorothy/Just a Shoulder to Cry On	1958	12.50	25.00	50.00
30744	Lonely/What's New	1958	10.00	20.00	40.00

HI-LITERS, THE (1)

With King Bassie and His Three Aces...Ben Vereen was a member.

45s

Number	Title (A Side/B Side)	Yr	VG	VG+	NM
HICO					
2432	Let Me Be True to You/In the Night	1958	25.00	50.00	100.00
2433	Over the Rainbow/(B-side unknown)	1958	37.50	75.00	150.00

HI-LITERS, THE (U)

Probably not group (1), but we don't know if these are the same group or two different groups.

45s

Number	Title (A Side/B Side)	Yr	VG	VG+	NM
VEE JAY					
184	Bobby Sox Baby/Hello Dear	1956	250.00	500.00	1000.
WEN-DEE					
1927	Baby Don't Treat Me This Way/Route 66	1955	15.00	30.00	60.00

HI-LITES, THE (1)

For records on Daran, see THE CHI-LITES.

HI-LITES, THE (2)

45s

Number	Title (A Side/B Side)	Yr	VG	VG+	NM
JULIA					
1105	Gloria/For Your Precious Love	1962	30.00	60.00	120.00
MONOGRAM					
119	Everybody's Somebody's Fool/Moonlight	1976	2.00	4.00	8.00
120	Zoom Zoom Zoom/To the Aisle	1976	2.00	4.00	8.00
121	Pretty Face/Maybe You'll Be There	1976	2.00	4.00	8.00
RECORD FAIR					
500	I'm Falling in Love/Walking My Baby Back Home	1961	12.50	25.00	50.00
501	For Sentimental Reasons/For Your Precious Love	1962	12.50	25.00	50.00

Albums

Number	Title (A Side/B Side)	Yr	VG	VG+	NM
DANDEE					
DLP-206 [M]	For Your Precious Love	1958	500.00	1000.	2000.

HI-LITES, THE (U)

None of these are group (1). Some could be group (2). The rest could be several more groups.

45s

Number	Title (A Side/B Side)	Yr	VG	VG+	NM
BRUNSWICK					
55102	Friday Night Go Go/Chicka-Rocka-Chee-Chi-Cho (Cha Cha)	1958	5.00	10.00	20.00
JET					
501	The Pony (Part 1)/The Pony (Part 2)	1961	5.00	10.00	20.00
502	4000 Miles Away/Woke Up This Morning	1961	7.50	15.00	30.00
KING					
5730	Death of an Angel/Our Winter Love	1963	5.00	10.00	20.00
MERCURY					
70987	The Next Four Years/The Girls with the Bells	1956	6.25	12.50	25.00
OKEH					
7046	I Found a Love/Zanzee	1954	125.00	250.00	500.00
RENO					
1030	Please Believe Me I Love You/Sweet and Lovely	1958	62.50	125.00	250.00
TWIST TIME					
12	Twistin' Time/Twistin' Pony	1962	3.75	7.50	15.00
WASSEL					
701	Groovy/Hey Baby	1965	2.50	5.00	10.00

HI-LO'S, THE

45s

Number	Title (A Side/B Side)	Yr	VG	VG+	NM
COLUMBIA					
40915	A Face in the Crowd/Autumn Rain	1957	2.50	5.00	10.00
41050	A Very Special Love/My Sugar Is So Refined	1957	2.50	5.00	10.00
41197	Whistlin' Down the Lane/When I Remember	1958	2.50	5.00	10.00
41465	Goody Goody/Indiana	1959	2.50	5.00	10.00
41647	Cindy's Prayer/A Lot of Livin' to Do	1960	2.50	5.00	10.00
41867	The Trolley Song/Five Foot Two, Eyes of Blue	1960	2.50	5.00	10.00

7-Inch Extended Plays

Number	Title (A Side/B Side)	Yr	VG	VG+	NM
COLUMBIA					
B-10231	Sunnyside Up/Laura//A Shine on Your Shoes/The Heather on the Hill	195?	3.00	6.00	12.00
B-10231 [PS]	Sunnyside Up	195?	3.00	6.00	12.00

Albums

Number	Title (A Side/B Side)	Yr	VG	VG+	NM
COLUMBIA					
CL 952 [M]	Suddenly It's the Hi-Lo's	1957	7.50	15.00	30.00
CL 1023 [M]	Now Hear This	1957	7.50	15.00	30.00
CL 1259 [M]	The Hi-Lo's and All That Jazz	1958	7.50	15.00	30.00
CL 1416 [M]	Broadway Playbill	1959	7.50	15.00	30.00
CL 1509 [M]	All Over the Place	1960	6.25	12.50	25.00
CL 1723 [M]	This Time It's Love	1962	6.25	12.50	25.00
CS 8057 [S]	Love Nest	1958	10.00	20.00	40.00
CS 8077 [S]	The Hi-Lo's and All That Jazz	1958	10.00	20.00	40.00
CS 8213 [S]	Broadway Playbill	1959	10.00	20.00	40.00
CS 8300 [S]	All Over the Place	1960	7.50	15.00	30.00
CS 8523 [S]	This Time It's Love	1962	7.50	15.00	30.00
COLUMBIA SPECIAL PRODUCTS					
P 14387	Harmony in Jazz	1978	3.00	6.00	12.00
DRG					
SL 5184	Clap Yo' Hands	198?	3.00	6.00	12.00
KAPP					
KL 1027 [M]	The Hi-Lo's and the Jerry Fielding Band	1956	7.50	15.00	30.00
KL 1184 [M]	Under Glass	1959	6.25	12.50	25.00
—Reissue of Starlite 7005					
KL 1194 [M]	On Hand	1960	6.25	12.50	25.00
—Reissue of Starlite 7008					
MCA					
4171 [(2)]	The Hi-Lo's Collection	197?	3.75	7.50	15.00
OMEGA					
OSL-11 [S]	The Hi-Lo's in Stereo	195?	7.50	15.00	30.00
PAUSA					
7040	Back Again	198?	3.00	6.00	12.00
7093	Now	198?	3.00	6.00	12.00
REPRISE					
R-6066 [M]	The Hi-Lo's Happen to Bossa Nova	1963	5.00	10.00	20.00
R9-6066 [S]	The Hi-Lo's Happen to Bossa Nova	1963	6.25	12.50	25.00
STARLITE					
6004 [10]	Listen!	1955	15.00	30.00	60.00
6005 [10]	The Hi-Lo's, I Presume	1955	15.00	30.00	60.00
7005 [M]	Under Glass	1956	10.00	20.00	40.00
7006 [M]	Listen!	1956	10.00	20.00	40.00
—Reissue of 6004					
7007 [M]	The Hi-Lo's. I Presume	1956	10.00	20.00	40.00
—Reissue of 6005					
7008 [M]	On Hand	1956	10.00	20.00	40.00

HIATT, JOHN

45s

Number	Title (A Side/B Side)	Yr	VG	VG+	NM
ATLANTIC					
89461	Snakecharmer/This Is Your Day	1985	—	2.00	4.00
A&M					
1245	Slow Turning/Your Dad Did (Live)	1988	—	—	3.00
2950	Lipstick Sunset/Thank You Girl	1987	—	—	3.00
2970	Have a Little Faith in Me/Thank You Girl	1987	—	—	3.00
CAPITOL					
S7-19626	Little Head/Runaway	1997	—	—	3.00
EPIC					
10990	The Boulevard Ain't So Bad/We Make Spirit	1973	—	3.00	6.00
11095	Sure As I'm Sittin' Here/Ocean	1974	—	2.50	5.00
50022	Hangin' Around the Observatory/Full Moon	1974	—	2.50	5.00
50115	Down Home (Keep On Fallin')/Motorboat to Heaven	1975	—	2.50	5.00
GEFFEN					
29045	Living a Little, Laughing a Little/I'm a Real Man	1985	—	2.00	4.00
29945	I Look for Love/Take Time to Know Her	1982	—	2.00	4.00
MCA					
41019	Radio Girl/Sharon's Got a Drugstore	1979	—	2.00	4.00
41132	Madonna Road/Slug Line	1979	—	2.00	4.00
41300	I Spy (For the FBI)/It Hasn't Happened Yet	1980	—	2.00	4.00
THE RIGHT STUFF					
S7-19856	Johnny 99/I Wish I Were Blind	1998	—	—	3.00
—B-side by the Yell Leaders					

Albums

Number	Title (A Side/B Side)	Yr	VG	VG+	NM
A&M					
SP-5158	Bring the Family	1987	2.50	5.00	10.00
SP-5206	Slow Turning	1988	2.50	5.00	10.00
75021 5310 1	Stolen Moments	1990	3.00	6.00	12.00
EPIC					
KE 32688	Hangin' Around the Observatory	1974	3.75	7.50	15.00
KE 33190	Overcoats	1975	3.75	7.50	15.00
PE 33190	Overcoats	198?	2.00	4.00	8.00
—Budget-line reissue					
GEFFEN					
GHS 2009	All of a Sudden	1982	3.00	6.00	12.00
GHS 4017	Riding with the King	1983	3.00	6.00	12.00
GHS 24055	Warming Up to the Ice Age	1984	3.00	6.00	12.00
MCA					
741	Two-Bit Monster	198?	2.00	4.00	8.00
—Reissue					
747	Slug Line	198?	2.00	4.00	8.00
—Reissue					
3088	Slug Line	1979	3.00	6.00	12.00
5123	Two-Bit Monster	1980	3.00	6.00	12.00
MOBILE FIDEILTY					
1-210	Bring the Family	1994	12.50	25.00	50.00
—Audiophile vinyl					

HIBBLER, AL

45s

Number	Title (A Side/B Side)	Yr	VG	VG+	NM
ALADDIN					
3328	Don't Take Your Love from Me/I Got It So Bad and That Ain't Good	1956	3.75	7.50	15.00
ATLANTIC					
911	Danny Boy/Song of the Wanderer	1950	—	—	—
—Unconfined on 45 rpm					
925	The Blues Come Falling Down/Old Folks	1951	12.50	25.00	50.00
932	Travelin' Light/If I Knew You Were There	1951	12.50	25.00	50.00
945	Now I Lay Me Down to Dream/This Is Always	1951	12.50	25.00	50.00
1071	Danny Boy/Now I Lay Me Down	1955	7.50	15.00	30.00
BRUNSWICK					
55027	Star Dust/Stormy Weather	1957	3.75	7.50	15.00
CLEF					
89095	I'm Getting Sentimental Over You/As Time Goes By	1954	3.75	7.50	15.00
DECCA					
29441	Unchained Melody/Daybreak	1955	5.00	10.00	20.00
29543	I Can't Put My Arms Around a Memory/They Say You're Laughing at Me	1955	3.75	7.50	15.00
29660	He/Breeze (Blow My Baby Back to Me)	1955	5.00	10.00	20.00
29789	11th Hour Melody/Let's Try Again	1956	3.75	7.50	15.00
29950	Away All Boats/Never Turn Back	1956	3.75	7.50	15.00
29982	After the Lights Go Down Low/I Was Telling Her About You	1956	3.75	7.50	15.00
30100	Nightfall/I'm Free	1956	3.75	7.50	15.00
30127	White Christmas/Silent Night	1956	3.75	7.50	15.00
30176	Trees/The Town Crier	1957	3.00	6.00	12.00
30268	Sweet Slumber/Because of You	1957	3.00	6.00	12.00
30337	Around the Corner from the Blues/I Complain	1957	3.00	6.00	12.00
30397	When Will I Forget You/Be Fair	1957	3.00	6.00	12.00
30483	The Crying Wind/A Wish	1957	3.00	6.00	12.00
30547	My Heart Tells Me/I'm Glad I'm Not Young Anymore	1958	3.00	6.00	12.00
30622	Honeysuckle Rose/Ain't Nothin' Wrong with That Baby	1958	3.00	6.00	12.00
30684	Softly, My Love/Your Hands	1958	3.00	6.00	12.00
30752	Love Land/Love Me Long, Hold Me Close	1958	3.00	6.00	12.00
30817	Warm Heart-Cold Feet/Mine All Mine	1959	3.00	6.00	12.00
30870	He Is Always There/What 'Tis, What 'Tis, 'Tis Spring	1959	3.00	6.00	12.00
30946	It Won't Be Easy/Lonesome and Cold	1959	3.00	6.00	12.00
MERCURY					
89011	Please/Believe It Love	1952	3.75	7.50	15.00
REPRISE					
20035	Look Away/Tall the Sky	1961	2.50	5.00	10.00
20077	Walk Away/I've Convinced Everyone But You	1962	2.50	5.00	10.00
TOP RANK					
2089	Strawberry Hill/Stranger	1960	2.50	5.00	10.00

7-Inch Extended Plays

Number	Title (A Side/B Side)	Yr	VG	VG+	NM
DECCA					
ED 2410	*After the Lights Go Down Low/September in the Rain/You'll Never Know/Where Are You?	195?	5.00	10.00	20.00
ED 2410 [PS]	Starring Al Hibbler, Part 1	195?	5.00	10.00	20.00

Albums

Number	Title (A Side/B Side)	Yr	VG	VG+	NM
ARGO					
LP-601 [M]	Melodies by Al Hibbler	1956	10.00	20.00	40.00
—Reissue of Marterry LP					
ATLANTIC					
1251 [M]	After the Lights Go Down Low	1957	12.50	25.00	50.00
—Black label					
1251 [M]	After the Lights Go Down Low	1961	6.25	12.50	25.00
—Mostly red label, white fan logo					
1251 [M]	After the Lights Go Down Low	1963	5.00	10.00	20.00
—Mostly red label, black fan logo					
BRUNSWICK					
BL 54036 [M]	Al Hibbler with the Ellingtonians	1957	12.50	25.00	50.00
DECCA					
DL 8328 [M]	Starring Al Hibbler	1956	7.50	15.00	30.00
DL 8420 [M]	Here's Hibbler	1957	7.50	15.00	30.00
DL 8697 [M]	Torchy and Blue	1958	7.50	15.00	30.00
DL 8757 [M]	Hits by Hibbler	1958	7.50	15.00	30.00

Number	Title (A Side/B Side)	Yr	VG	VG+	NM
DL 8862 [M]	Al Hibbler Remembers the Big Songs of the Big Bands	1959	7.50	15.00	30.00
DL 78862 [S]	Al Hibbler Remembers the Big Songs of the Big Bands	1959	10.00	20.00	40.00
DISCOVERY					
842	It's Monday Every Day	198?	3.00	6.00	12.00
—Reissue of Reprise LP					
LMI					
10001 [M]	Early One Morning	1964	7.50	15.00	30.00
MARTERRY					
LP-601 [M]	Melodies by Al Hibbler	1956	20.00	40.00	80.00
MCA					
4098 [(2)]	The Best of Al Hibbler	197?	3.75	7.50	15.00
NORGRAN					
MGN-4 [10]	Al Hibbler Favorites	1954	37.50	75.00	150.00
MGN-15 [10]	Al Hibbler Sings Duke Ellington	1954	37.50	75.00	150.00
OPEN SKY					
OSR-3126	For Sentimental Reasons	1986	3.00	6.00	12.00
REPRISE					
R-2005 [M]	It's Monday Every Day	1961	7.50	15.00	30.00
R9-2005 [S]	It's Monday Every Day	1961	10.00	20.00	40.00
SCORE					
SLP-4013 [M]	I Surrender, Dear	1957	25.00	50.00	100.00
VERVE					
MGV-4000 [M]	Al Hibbler Sings Love Songs	1956	15.00	30.00	60.00
V-4000 [M]	Al Hibbler Sings Love Songs	1961	5.00	10.00	20.00

HICKEY, ERSEL

Number	Title (A Side/B Side)	Yr	VG	VG+	NM
45s					
APOLLO					
761	Upside Down Love/The Millionaire	1949	12.50	25.00	50.00
EPIC					
9263	Bluebirds Over the Mountain/Hangin' Around	1958	7.50	15.00	30.00
9278	Goin' Down That Road/Lovers' Land	1958	6.25	12.50	25.00
9298	You Never Can Tell/Wedding Day	1958	6.25	12.50	25.00
9309	Don't Be Afraid of Love/You Threw a Dart	1959	6.25	12.50	25.00
9320	I Can't Love Another/People Gotta Talk	1959	6.25	12.50	25.00
9357	Love in Bloom/What Do You Want	1960	6.25	12.50	25.00
9395	Another Wasted Day/Money Brought Me You	1960	6.25	12.50	25.00
JANUS					
151	Bluebirds Over the Mountain/Self Made Man	1971	—	2.50	5.00
KAPP					
372	Teardrops at Dawn/I Guess You Can Call It Love	1961	5.00	10.00	20.00
LAURIE					
3165	Some Enchanted Evening/Put Your Mind at Ease	1963	5.00	10.00	20.00
RAMESES II					
2003	Waitin' for Baby/In Spite of the Fool That I Am	1976	—	3.00	6.00
TOOT					
602	Tryin' to Get to You/Blue Skies	196?	2.50	5.00	10.00
7-Inch Extended Plays					
EPIC					
EG-7206	(contents unknown)	1958	25.00	50.00	100.00
EG-7206 [PS]	Ersel Hickey in Lover's Land	1958	25.00	50.00	100.00
Albums					
BACK-TRAC					
P 18750	The Rockin' Bluebird	1985	15.00	30.00	60.00
—Allegedly, only 200 copies of this were pressed					

HICKMAN, DWAYNE

Starred as Dobie Gillis on TV.

Number	Title (A Side/B Side)	Yr	VG	VG+	NM
45s					
ABC-PARAMOUNT					
9908	School Dance/Pretty Baby	1958	6.25	12.50	25.00
9908 [PS]	School Dance/Pretty Baby	1958	10.00	20.00	40.00
CAPITOL					
4445	I'm a Lover, Not a Fighter/I Pass Your House	1960	5.00	10.00	20.00
Albums					
CAPITOL					
ST 1441 [S]	Dobie!	1960	12.50	25.00	50.00
T 1441 [M]	Dobie!	1960	10.00	20.00	40.00

HICKS, DAN, AND HIS HOT LICKS

Number	Title (A Side/B Side)	Yr	VG	VG+	NM
45s					
BLUE THUMB					
211	Moody Richard/Walkin' One and Only	1972	—	2.50	5.00
213	I'm an Old Cowhand/Woe the Luck	1972	—	2.50	5.00
235	My Old Timey Baby/Cheaters Don't Win	1973	—	2.50	5.00
EPIC					
10511	How Can I Miss You When You Won't Go/Canned Music	1969	—	3.00	6.00
Albums					
BLUE THUMB					
BTS-29	Where's the Money?	1971	3.00	6.00	12.00
BTS-36	Striking It Rich!	1972	3.00	6.00	12.00
BTS-51	Last Train to Hicksville...The Home of Happy Feet	1973	3.00	6.00	12.00
EPIC					
BN 26464	Original Recordings	1969	3.75	7.50	15.00
—Yellow label					
BN 26464	Original Recordings	1973	2.50	5.00	10.00
—Orange label					
PE 26464	Original Recordings	198?	2.00	4.00	8.00
—Reissue with new prefix					
MCA					
670	Striking It Rich!	198?	2.00	4.00	8.00
—Reissue					
671	Last Train to Hicksville...The Home of Happy Feet	198?	2.00	4.00	8.00
—Reissue					

Number	Title (A Side/B Side)	Yr	VG	VG+	NM
WARNER BROS.					
BSK 3158	It Happened One Bite	1978	2.50	5.00	10.00

HIDE-A-WAYS, THE

Number	Title (A Side/B Side)	Yr	VG	VG+	NM
45s					
LOST-NITE					
119	Can't Help Loving That Girl of Mine/I'm Coming Home	196?	—	2.50	5.00
—Reissue label					
MGM					
55004	Cherie/Me Make Em Powwow	1955	125.00	250.00	500.00
RONNI					
1000	Can't Help Lovin' That Girl of Mine/I'm Coming Home	1954	2000.	4000.	6000.

HIGH NUMBERS, THE

See THE WHO.

HIGH TIDE

Number	Title (A Side/B Side)	Yr	VG	VG+	NM
Albums					
LIBERTY					
LST-7638	Sea Shanties	1969	6.25	12.50	25.00

HIGH TREASON

Number	Title (A Side/B Side)	Yr	VG	VG+	NM
Albums					
ABBOTT					
ABS-1209	High Treason	1968	15.00	30.00	60.00

HIGHLIGHTS, THE

Number	Title (A Side/B Side)	Yr	VG	VG+	NM
45s					
BALLY					
1016	City of Angels/Listen, My Love	1956	7.50	15.00	30.00
1027	To Be with You/Will I Ever Know	1957	7.50	15.00	30.00
1044	Indian Style/Turn Around Shoes	1957	6.25	12.50	25.00

HIGHWAYMEN, THE

Number	Title (A Side/B Side)	Yr	VG	VG+	NM
45s					
ABC					
10801	She's Not There/Little Bird, Little Bird	1966	2.00	4.00	8.00
10824	Fling/My Foolish Pride	1966	2.00	4.00	8.00
ABC-PARAMOUNT					
10688	Should I Go, Should I Stay/Permit to Be a Hermit	1965	2.00	4.00	8.00
10716	I'll Show You the Way/Never a Thought for Tomorrow	1965	2.00	4.00	8.00
UNITED ARTISTS					
258	Michael/Santiano	1960	3.75	7.50	15.00
370	Cotton Fields/Gypsy Rover	1961	3.00	6.00	12.00
439	Whiskey in the Jar/I'm On My Way	1962	3.00	6.00	12.00
475	Cindy, Oh Cindy/The Birdman	1962	3.00	6.00	12.00
540	I Know Where I'm Going/Well, Well, Well	1963	3.00	6.00	12.00
568	I Never Will Marry/Pretoria	1963	3.00	6.00	12.00
602	All My Trials/Midnight Train	1963	3.00	6.00	12.00
647	Universal Soldier/I'll Fly Away	1963	3.00	6.00	12.00
679	Roll On Columbia, Roll On/The Tale of Michael Flynn	1963	3.00	6.00	12.00
695	The Sinking of the Reuben James/Bon Soir	1964	2.50	5.00	10.00
752	Nellie/Sweet Mama Tree Top Tall	1964	2.50	5.00	10.00
788	Puttin' On the Style/Michael	1964	2.50	5.00	10.00
801	Michael '65/Puttin' On the Style	1964	2.50	5.00	10.00
Albums					
ABC-PARAMOUNT					
522 [M]	On a New Road	1965	3.00	6.00	12.00
S-522 [S]	On a New Road	1965	3.75	7.50	15.00
UNITED ARTISTS					
UAL 3125 [M]	The Highwaymen	1961	3.75	7.50	15.00
UAL 3168 [M]	Standing Room Only!	1962	3.75	7.50	15.00
UAL 3225 [M]	Encore!	1962	3.75	7.50	15.00
UAL 3245 [M]	March On, Brothers	1963	3.75	7.50	15.00
UAL 3294 [M]	Hootenanny with the Highwaymen	1963	3.75	7.50	15.00
UAL 3323 [M]	One More Time	1964	3.75	7.50	15.00
UAL 3348 [M]	Homecoming	1964	3.75	7.50	15.00
UAS 6125 [S]	The Highwaymen	1961	5.00	10.00	20.00
UAS 6168 [S]	Standing Room Only!	1962	5.00	10.00	20.00
UAS 6225 [S]	Encore!	1962	5.00	10.00	20.00
UAS 6245 [S]	March On, Brothers	1963	5.00	10.00	20.00
UAS 6294 [S]	Hootenanny with the Highwaymen	1963	5.00	10.00	20.00
UAS 6323 [S]	One More Time	1964	5.00	10.00	20.00
UAS 6348 [S]	Homecoming	1964	5.00	10.00	20.00

HIGHWAYMEN, THE (COUNTRY GROUP)

See JOHNNY CASH; WAYLON JENNINGS; KRIS KRISTOFFERSON; WILLIE NELSON.

HILDEBRAND, RAY

See PAUL AND PAULA.

Number	Title (A Side/B Side)	Yr	VG	VG+	NM
45s					
PHILIPS					
40174	It's All Over, Paula/Snow Girl	1964	2.50	5.00	10.00
—As "Paul"					
40318	Hey Little Julie/The Way of the DJ	1965	2.00	4.00	8.00
40339	Hello Viet Nam (Goodbye My Love)/You, Wonderful You	1965	2.00	4.00	8.00
TOWER					
304	Paper Clown/Patsy	1966	2.00	4.00	8.00
—As "Paul (Paul and Paula)"					
Albums					
WORD					
WST-8411	He's Everything to Me	196?	3.00	6.00	12.00
WST-8465	I Need You Every Hour	1971	3.00	6.00	12.00

HILL, BUNKER

45s

MALA

Number	Title (A Side/B Side)	Yr	VG	VG+	NM
451	Hide and Go Seek (Part 1)/Hide and Go Seek (Part 2)	1962	5.00	10.00	20.00
457	Red Ridin' Hood and the Wolf/Nobody Knows	1962	5.00	10.00	20.00
464	The Girl Can't Dance/You Can't Make Me Doubt My Baby	1963	6.25	12.50	25.00

HILL, JESSIE

45s

Number	Title (A Side/B Side)	Yr	VG	VG+	NM
BLUE THUMB					
204	Naturally/Livin' a Lie	1971	—	3.00	6.00
DOWNEY					
115	Chip Chop/Woodshed	1964	2.50	5.00	10.00
117	Understanding/Down the Street	1964	2.50	5.00	10.00
124	Never Thought/TV Guide	1964	2.50	5.00	10.00
MINIT					
607	Ooh Poo Pah Doo — Part 1/Ooh Poo Pah Doo — Part 2	1960	3.75	7.50	15.00
611	Whip It On Me/I Need Your Love	1960	3.00	6.00	12.00
616	Scoop Scoobie Doobie/Highland Blues	1960	3.00	6.00	12.00
622	Oh My Oh My/I Got Mine	1961	3.00	6.00	12.00
628	Oogsey Moo/My Love	1961	3.00	6.00	12.00
638	Sweet Jelly Roll/It's My Fault	1961	3.00	6.00	12.00
646	Can't Get Enough of That Ooh Pah Doo/Pot's on a Strike	1962	3.00	6.00	12.00
UNITED ARTISTS					
0081	Ooh Poo Pah Doo — Part 1/Ooh Poo Pah Doo — Part 2	1973	—	2.00	4.00
—"Silver Spotlight Series" reissue					

HILL, RAYMOND

45s

SUN

Number	Title (A Side/B Side)	Yr	VG	VG+	NM
204	Bourbon Street Jump/The Snuggle	1954	250.00	500.00	750.00

HILL, VERNELL

45s

TUFF

Number	Title (A Side/B Side)	Yr	VG	VG+	NM
381	Long Haired Daddy/Sometimes Love	1964	2.00	4.00	8.00

HILL, VINCE

45s

Number	Title (A Side/B Side)	Yr	VG	VG+	NM
LONDON INT'L.					
10514	The River's Run Dry/Not Any More	1962	3.00	6.00	12.00
PARAMOUNT					
0132	(Love Story) Look Around/In Every Corner of the World	1971	—	2.50	5.00
TOWER					
173	Yesterday's Hero/Unexpectedly	1965	2.00	4.00	8.00
207	Push Push/Take Me to Your Heart Again	1966	2.00	4.00	8.00
223	Looking at Me/Love Me True	1966	2.00	4.00	8.00
254	Heartaches/Merci Cherie	1966	2.00	4.00	8.00
323	Edelweiss/A Woman Needs Love	1967	2.00	4.00	8.00
358	When You Go/When the World Is Ready	1967	2.00	4.00	8.00
389	Why or When or Where/Why Can't I Remember	1968	—	3.00	6.00

HILL, Z.Z.

45s

Number	Title (A Side/B Side)	Yr	VG	VG+	NM
ATLANTIC					
2659	It's a Hang-Up Baby/(Home Just Ain't Home at) Suppertime	1969	2.00	4.00	8.00
COLUMBIA					
10552	Love Is So Good When You're Stealing It/Need You By My Side	1977	—	2.50	5.00
10680	This Time They Told the Truth/Near But Yet So Far	1978	—	2.50	5.00
10748	Universal Love/That's All That's Left	1978	—	2.50	5.00
HILL					
222	Don't Make Me Pay for His Mistakes/(B-side unknown)	1971	—	3.00	6.00
KENT					
404	I Could Do It All Over/You Don't Love Me	1964	2.50	5.00	10.00
416	I Need Someone (To Love Me)/Have Mercy Someone	1965	2.50	5.00	10.00
427	Hey Little Girl/Oh Darlin'	1965	2.50	5.00	10.00
432	That's It/What's More	1965	2.50	5.00	10.00
439	Everybody Has to Cry/Happiness Is All I Need	1965	2.50	5.00	10.00
444	No More Doggin'/The Kind of Love I Want	1966	2.50	5.00	10.00
449	I Found Love/Set Your Sights Higher	1966	2.50	5.00	10.00
453	You Can't Hide a Heartache/Gimme Gimme	1966	2.50	5.00	10.00
460	Oh Darling/Greatest Love	1967	2.50	5.00	10.00
464	Baby I'm Sorry/Where She At	1967	2.50	5.00	10.00
469	You Just Cheat and Lie/Everybody Needs Somebody	1967	2.50	5.00	10.00
478	What Am I Living For/You're Gonna Need My Lovin'	1967	2.50	5.00	10.00
481	Steal Away/Nothing Can Change the Love I Have for You	1967	2.50	5.00	10.00
494	You Got What I Need/Have Mercy Someone	1968	2.50	5.00	10.00
502	Don't Make Promises (You Can't Keep)/Set Your Sights Higher	1968	2.50	5.00	10.00
4547	I Need Someone (To Love Me)/Oh Darling	1971	2.00	4.00	8.00
4550	You Don't Love Me/Have Mercy Someone	1971	2.00	4.00	8.00
4560	If I Could Do It All Over/You Won't Hurt No More	1971	2.00	4.00	8.00
4577	Nothing Can Change This Love/Eveyrbody Has to Cry	1972	2.00	4.00	8.00
MALACO					
2069	Please Don't Make Me (Do Something Bad to You)/Blue Monday	1981	—	2.00	4.00
2074	Separate Ways/Chained to Your Love	1981	—	2.00	4.00
2076	Bump and Grind/Somethin' Goin' On	1981	—	2.00	4.00
2079	Cheating in the Next Room/Right Arm for Your Love	1982	—	2.00	4.00
2082	When It Rains It Pours/When Can We Do This Again	1982	—	2.00	4.00
2085	What Am I Gonna Tell Her/Get You Some Business	1982	—	2.00	4.00
2090	Open House at My House/Who You Been Givin' It To	1983	—	2.00	4.00
2094	Get a Little, Give a Little/Blind Side	1983	—	2.00	4.00
2097	Steal Away/Three Into Two Won't Go	1984	—	2.00	4.00
2103	Someone Else Is Steppin' In/Shade Tree Mechanic	1984	—	2.00	4.00
2109	I'm Gonna Stop You from Givin' Me the Blues/Personally	1984	—	2.00	4.00
2141	Down Home Blues/Please Don't Let Our Good Thing End	1988	—	2.00	4.00
MANKIND					
12003	Faithful and True/I Think I'd Do It	1971	2.00	4.00	8.00
12007	The Chokin' Kind/Hold Back	1971	2.00	4.00	8.00
12012	Second Chance/It Ain't No Use	1972	—	3.50	7.00
12015	It Ain't No Use/Ha Ha	1972	—	3.50	7.00
12017	The Chokin' Kind/A Man Needs a Woman	197?	—	3.50	7.00
M.H.					
200	You Were Wrong/(B-side unknown)	1964	2.50	5.00	10.00
UNITED ARTISTS					
XW225	Ain't Nothing You Can Do/Love in the Street	1973	—	3.00	6.00
XW307	I Don't Need Half a Love/Friendship Only Goes So Far	1973	—	3.00	6.00
XW365	Let Them Talk/Red Rooster	1973	—	3.00	6.00
XW412	Am I Groovin' You/Bad Mouth and Gossip	1974	—	3.00	6.00
XW536	I Keep On Lovin' You/Whatever's Thrilling You Is Killing Me	1974	—	3.00	6.00
XW631	I Created a Monster/Steppin' in the Shoes of a Fool	1975	—	3.00	6.00

Albums

Number	Title (A Side/B Side)	Yr	VG	VG+	NM
COLUMBIA					
JC 35030	Let's Make a Deal	1978	3.00	6.00	12.00
JC 36125	The Mark of Z.Z.	1979	3.00	6.00	12.00
KENT					
KST-528	A Whole Lot of Soul	1969	3.75	7.50	15.00
KST-560	Dues Paid in Full	1971	3.75	7.50	15.00
MALACO					
7411	The Rhyhtm & The Blues	1983	2.50	5.00	10.00
7415	I'm a Blues Man	1984	2.50	5.00	10.00
MANKIND					
201	The Brand New Z.Z. Hill	1971	3.75	7.50	15.00
UNITED ARTISTS					
UA-LA417-G	Keep On Lovin' You	1975	3.00	6.00	12.00
UAS 5589	The Best Thing That's Ever Happened to Me	1972	3.00	6.00	12.00

HILL SISTERS, THE

45s

ANNA

Number	Title (A Side/B Side)	Yr	VG	VG+	NM
103	Hit and Run Away Love/Advertising for Love	1959	125.00	250.00	500.00
1103	Hit and Run Away Love/Advertising for Love	1959	12.50	25.00	50.00

HILLMEN, THE

Albums

TOGETHER

Number	Title (A Side/B Side)	Yr	VG	VG+	NM
STT-1012	The Hillmen	1970	20.00	40.00	80.00

HILLOW HAMMET

Albums

HOUSE OF FOX

Number	Title (A Side/B Side)	Yr	VG	VG+	NM
2	Hammer	1968	37.50	75.00	150.00

HILLSIDE SINGERS, THE

45s

METROMEDIA

Number	Title (A Side/B Side)	Yr	VG	VG+	NM
231	I'd Like to Teach the World to Sing (In Perfect Harmony)/I Believe It All	1971	—	2.50	5.00
241	We're Together/Day by Day	1972	—	2.50	5.00
246	Kum Ba Yah/Tomorrow Belongs to Me	1972	—	2.50	5.00
255	The Last Happy Song/Ah Man, See What You've Done	1972	—	2.50	5.00

Albums

METROMEDIA

Number	Title (A Side/B Side)	Yr	VG	VG+	NM
MD 1051	I'd Like to Teach the World to Sing	1971	3.00	6.00	12.00

HILLSIDERS, THE

45s

MEL-O-DY

Number	Title (A Side/B Side)	Yr	VG	VG+	NM
120	You Only Pass This Way One Time/Rain Is a Lonesome Thing	1964	7.50	15.00	30.00

HILLTOPPERS, THE

45s

DOT

Number	Title (A Side/B Side)	Yr	VG	VG+	NM
15018	Trying/You Made Up My Mind	1952	5.00	10.00	20.00
—As "The Hill Toppers"					
15034	Must I Cry Again/I Keep Telling Myself	1952	4.00	8.00	16.00
15055	If I Were King/I Can't Lie to Myself	1953	4.00	8.00	16.00
15085	P.S. I Love You/I'd Rather Die Young	1953	4.00	8.00	16.00
15105	Love Walked In/To Be Alone	1953	4.00	8.00	16.00
15127	From the Vine Came the Grape/Time Will Tell	1954	4.00	8.00	16.00
15156	Wrapped in a Dream/Poor Butterfly	1954	4.00	8.00	16.00
15201	Sweetheart/Old Cabaret	1954	4.00	8.00	16.00
15220	If I Didn't Care/Bertha	1954	4.00	8.00	16.00
15249	You Try Somebody Else/Time Waits for No One	1954	4.00	8.00	16.00
15318	D-A-R-L-I-N/Frivolette	1955	3.75	7.50	15.00
15351	The Door Is Still Open/Tears from My Eyes	1955	3.75	7.50	15.00

Number	Title (A Side/B Side)	Yr	VG	VG+	NM
15375	The Kentuckian Song/I Must Be Dreaming	1955	3.75	7.50	15.00
15415	Searching/All I Need Is You	1955	3.75	7.50	15.00
15423	Only You (And You Alone)/Until the Real Thing Comes Along	1955	3.75	7.50	15.00
15437	My Treasure/The Last Word in Love	1955	3.75	7.50	15.00
15451	Do the Bop/When You're Alone	1956	3.75	7.50	15.00
15459	So Tired/Faded Rose	1956	3.75	7.50	15.00
15468	I'm Walking Thru Heaven/Eyes of Fire, Lips of Wine	1956	3.75	7.50	15.00
15489	Ka-Ding-Dong/Into Each Life Some Rain Must Fall	1956	3.75	7.50	15.00
—Originals have maroon labels					
15489	Ka-Ding-Dong/Into Each Life Some Rain Must Fall	1956	3.00	6.00	12.00
—Second pressings have black labels					
15511	Until You're Mine/No Regrets	1956	3.00	6.00	12.00
15537	Marianne/You're Wasting Your Time	1957	3.00	6.00	12.00
15560	I Love My Girl/I'm Serious	1957	3.00	6.00	12.00
15594	A Fallen Star/Footsteps	1957	3.00	6.00	12.00
15626	My Cabin of Dreams/Dedicated to You	1957	3.00	6.00	12.00
15662	The Joker (That's What They Call Me)/Chicken Chicken	1957	3.00	6.00	12.00
15712	Starry Eyes/You Sure Look Good to Me	1958	3.00	6.00	12.00
15814	Signorina/Peggy's Sister	1958	3.00	6.00	12.00
15857	You're Nobody Till Somebody Loves You/Trying	1958	3.00	6.00	12.00
15889	I'd Rather Die Young/Welcome to My Heart	1959	2.50	5.00	10.00
15958	Lots of Luck/Lizzie Darlin'	1959	2.50	5.00	10.00
16010	The Prisoner's Song/Phone	1959	2.50	5.00	10.00
16022	Trying/P.S. I Love You	1960	2.50	5.00	10.00
16024	From the Vine Came the Grape/Love Walked In	1960	2.50	5.00	10.00
16025	Only You (And You Alone)/Till Then	1960	2.50	5.00	10.00
16039	Marianne/To Be Alone	1960	2.50	5.00	10.00
16054	To Be Alone/P.S. I Love You	1960	2.50	5.00	10.00
16556	Only You/No Longer Lonely	1963	2.00	4.00	8.00
MGM					
14515	Jamaica Farewell/Sunshine and Love	1973	—	2.50	5.00
—As "Jimmy Sacca and the Hilltoppers"					
14603	Little Things You Do/Sunshine and Love	1973	—	2.50	5.00
—As "Jimmy Sacca and the Hilltoppers"					

7-Inch Extended Plays

DOT

Number	Title	Yr	VG	VG+	NM
DEP-1006	(contents unknown)	195?	3.75	7.50	15.00
DEP-1006 [PS]	The Hilltoppers Sing	195?	3.75	7.50	15.00
DEP-1007	(contents unknown)	195?	3.75	7.50	15.00
DEP-1007 [PS]	The Hilltoppers Sing	195?	3.75	7.50	15.00
DEP-1008	(contents unknown)	195?	3.75	7.50	15.00
DEP-1008 [PS]	The Hilltoppers Sing	195?	3.75	7.50	15.00
DEP-1009	(contents unknown)	195?	3.75	7.50	15.00
DEP-1009 [PS]	The Hilltoppers Sing	195?	3.75	7.50	15.00
DEP-1011	(contents unknown)	195?	3.75	7.50	15.00
DEP-1011 [PS]	The Hilltoppers Sing	195?	3.75	7.50	15.00
DEP-1012	(contents unknown)	195?	3.75	7.50	15.00
DEP-1012 [PS]	The Hilltoppers Sing	195?	3.75	7.50	15.00

Albums

DOT

Number	Title	Yr	VG	VG+	NM
DLP-105 [10]	The Hilltoppers	1954	15.00	30.00	60.00
DLP-106 [10]	The Hilltoppers	1954	15.00	30.00	60.00
DLP-3003 [M]	The Hilltoppers Present Tops in Pops	1955	12.50	25.00	50.00
—Cartoon of female fan on cover					
DLP-3003 [M]	The Hilltoppers Present Tops in Pops	1956	7.50	15.00	30.00
—Four caps with "W" on them on cover					
DLP-3029 [M]	The Towering Hilltoppers	1957	7.50	15.00	30.00
DLP-3073 [M]	Love in Bloom	1958	7.50	15.00	30.00

HIM

See DOUG SAHM.

HINSON, DON, AND THE RIGAMORTICIANS

45s

CAPITOL

Number	Title	Yr	VG	VG+	NM
5314	Riboflavin Flavored, Non-Carbonated, Polyunsaturated Blood/Monster Jerk	1964	3.00	6.00	12.00

Albums

CAPITOL

Number	Title	Yr	VG	VG+	NM
ST 2219 [S]	Monster Dance Party	1964	10.00	20.00	40.00
T 2219 [M]	Monster Dance Party	1964	7.50	15.00	30.00

HINTON, JOE

45s

ARVEE

Number	Title	Yr	VG	VG+	NM
5028	My Love Is Real/I Won't Be Your Fool	1961	3.00	6.00	12.00
—Arvee titles as "Little Joe Hinton"					
5029	Your Kind of Love/Let's Start a Romance	1961	3.00	6.00	12.00
BACK BEAT					
519	I Know/Ladder of Prayer	1958	3.75	7.50	15.00
526	Pretty Little Mama/Will You	1959	3.75	7.50	15.00
526 [PS]	Pretty Little Mama/Will You	1959	7.50	15.00	30.00
532	If You Love Me/A Thousand Cups of Happiness	1960	3.75	7.50	15.00
535	The Girls in My Life/Come On Baby	1961	3.75	7.50	15.00
537	You Know It Ain't Right/Lovre Sick Blues	1963	3.00	6.00	12.00
539	Better to Give Than Receive/There Is No In Between	1963	3.00	6.00	12.00
540	There Oughta Be a Law/You're My Girl	1964	3.00	6.00	12.00
541	Funny/You Gotta Have Love	1964	3.75	7.50	15.00
545	I Want a Little Girl/True Love	1965	3.00	6.00	12.00
547	Darling Come and Talk to Me/Everything	1965	3.00	6.00	12.00
550	Pledging My Love/Just a Kid Named Joe	1965	3.00	6.00	12.00
565	I'm Waiting/How Long Can I Last	1966	2.50	5.00	10.00
574	If I Had Only Known/Lots of Love	1966	2.50	5.00	10.00
581	Close to MyHeart/You've Been Good to Me	1967	2.50	5.00	10.00
589	I'm Satisfied/Be Ever Wonderful	1968	2.50	5.00	10.00
594	Got You on My Mind/Please	1968	2.50	5.00	10.00
SOUL					
35080	Let's Save the Children/You Are Blue	1971	6.25	12.50	25.00

Albums

BACK BEAT

Number	Title	Yr	VG	VG+	NM
B-60 [M]	Funny (How Time Slips Away)	1965	12.50	25.00	50.00
BS-60 [S]	Funny (How Time Slips Away)	1965	17.50	35.00	70.00
DUKE					
DLPS-91	Duke-Peacock Remembers Joe Hinton	1969	5.00	10.00	20.00

HIPPIES, THE

45s

PARKWAY

Number	Title	Yr	VG	VG+	NM
863	Memory Lane/A Lonely Piano	1963	5.00	10.00	20.00
—Originally released as "The Tams"; B-side by Reggie Harrison					

HIPPY DIPPYS, THE

45s

UNI

Number	Title	Yr	VG	VG+	NM
55004	Thoroughly Modern Millie/Jimmy	1967	3.00	6.00	12.00

HIRT, AL

Also see PETE FOUNTAIN.

45s

GWP

Number	Title	Yr	VG	VG+	NM
516	I Still See Elisa/The Gospel of No-Name City	1969	—	3.00	6.00
519	Louisiana Man/Break My Mind	1969	—	3.00	6.00
522	Orange Blossom Special/I Really Don't Want to Know	1970	—	3.00	6.00
529	Glory of Love/I Can Dream, Can't I	1970	—	3.00	6.00
MONUMENT					
8619	Melody for Michele/Sweet Sauce	1974	—	2.00	4.00
8652	Feudin' Pipers (Dueling Banjos)/Southern Scramble	1975	—	2.00	4.00
8671	The Sound of Jazz and the Scent of Jasmine/Monkey Farm	1975	—	2.00	4.00
RCA VICTOR					
47-7854	Janine/Elegie	1961	2.50	5.00	10.00
47-7854 [PS]	Janine/Elegie	1961	3.00	6.00	12.00
47-7903	Perky/I'm On My Way	1961	2.50	5.00	10.00
47-8016	Al Di La/Talkin' About That River	1962	2.50	5.00	10.00
47-8104	Theme from "The Eleventh Hour"/Song from "Two for the See-Saw"	1962	2.50	5.00	10.00
47-8128	Pickin' Cotton/Roman Nocturne	1963	2.50	5.00	10.00
47-8128 [PS]	Pickin' Cotton/Roman Nocturne	1963	3.00	6.00	12.00
47-8280	Java/I Can't Get Started	1963	2.00	4.00	8.00
47-8346	Cotton Candy/Walkin'	1964	2.00	4.00	8.00
47-8391	Sugar Lips/Poupee Brisee	1964	2.00	4.00	8.00
47-8439	Up Above My Head (I Hear Music in the Air)/September Song	1964	2.00	4.00	8.00
47-8478	Hooray for Santa Claus/White Christmas	1964	3.00	6.00	12.00
47-8478 [PS]	Hooray for Santa Claus/White Christmas	1964	3.75	7.50	15.00
47-8487	Fancy Pants/Star Dust	1964	2.00	4.00	8.00
47-8542	Al's Place/Mister Sandman	1965	2.00	4.00	8.00
47-8653	The Silence (Il Silenzio)/Love Theme from "The Sandpiper"	1965	2.00	4.00	8.00
47-8684	Feelin' Fruggy/Louisiana Lullaby	1965	2.00	4.00	8.00
47-8706	Nutty Jingle Bells/Santa Claus Is Comin' to Town	1965	2.50	5.00	10.00
47-8706 [PS]	Nutty Jingle Bells/Santa Claus Is Comin' to Town	1965	3.00	6.00	12.00
47-8736	Yesterday/The Arena	1966	2.00	4.00	8.00
47-8774	Mame/Seven Days to Tahiti	1966	2.00	4.00	8.00
47-8774 [PS]	Mame/Seven Days to Tahiti	1966	2.50	5.00	10.00
47-8854	Skillet Lickin'/Trumpet Pickin'	1966	2.00	4.00	8.00
47-8925	Green Hornet Theme/Strawberry Jam	1966	3.00	6.00	12.00
47-9023	Theme from The Monkees/The Evil One	1966	2.50	5.00	10.00
47-9060	Music to Watch Girls By/His Girl	1967	2.00	4.00	8.00
47-9106	Boywatchers Theme/Yo Yo (Puppet Song)	1967	2.00	4.00	8.00
47-9198	Big Honey/Puppet on a String	1967	2.00	4.00	8.00
47-9285	Calypsoul/Honey Pot	1967	2.00	4.00	8.00
47-9381	Ludwig/Long Gone	1967	2.00	4.00	8.00
47-9417	Keep the Ball Rollin'/Manhattan Safari	1968	2.00	4.00	8.00
47-9500	We Can Fly-Up, Up and Away/The Glory of Love	1968	2.00	4.00	8.00
47-9539	The Odd Couple/Do You Know the Way to San Jose	1968	2.50	5.00	10.00
47-9664	Those Were the Days/The Garbage	1968	2.00	4.00	8.00
47-9717	Penny Arcade/If	1969	2.00	4.00	8.00

Albums

ACCORD

Number	Title	Yr	VG	VG+	NM
SN-7187	Java	1981	2.00	4.00	8.00
ALLEGIANCE					
AV-5018	Showtime	1985	2.00	4.00	8.00
AV-5032	Blues Line	1986	2.00	4.00	8.00
AUDIO FIDELITY					
AFLP-1877 [M]	Swingin' Dixie (At Dan's Pier 600 in New Orleans)	1959	3.75	7.50	15.00
AFLP-1878 [M]	Swingin' Dixie	1959	3.75	7.50	15.00
AFLP-1926 [M]	Swingin' Dixie (Vol. 3)	1961	3.75	7.50	15.00
AFLP-1927 [M]	Swingin' Dixie (Vol. 4)	1961	3.75	7.50	15.00
AFSD-5877 [S]	Swingin' Dixie (At Dan's Pier 600 in New Orleans)	1959	5.00	10.00	20.00
AFSD-5878 [S]	Swingin' Dixie	1959	5.00	10.00	20.00
AFSD-5926 [S]	Swingin' Dixie (Vol. 3)	1961	5.00	10.00	20.00
AFSD-5927 [S]	Swingin' Dixie (Vol. 4)	1961	5.00	10.00	20.00
AF-6282	Hirt...So Good!	1978	2.50	5.00	10.00
CORAL					
CRL 57402 [M]	Al Hirt in New Orleans	1962	3.00	6.00	12.00
CRL 757402 [S]	Al Hirt in New Orleans	1962	3.75	7.50	15.00
CROWN					
CST-457 [S]	The Dawn Busters	196?	3.00	6.00	12.00
CLP-5457 [M]	The Dawn Busters	196?	3.00	6.00	12.00
GHB					
107	Mardi Gras Parade Music	197?	2.50	5.00	10.00
GWP					
2002	Paint Your Wagon	1970	2.50	5.00	10.00
2004	Al Hirt Gold	1971	2.50	5.00	10.00

Number	Title (A Side/B Side)	Yr	VG	VG+	NM
2005	Al Hirt Country	1971	2.50	5.00	10.00
LONGINES SYMPHONETTE					
LWCP 1	The Best of Dixieland Jazz	196?	3.00	6.00	12.00
METRO					
M-517 [M]	Al Hirt	1965	2.50	5.00	10.00
MS-517 [S]	Al Hirt	1965	3.00	6.00	12.00
MONUMENT					
6642	Raw Sugar/Sweet Sauce/Banana Puddin'	1976	2.00	4.00	8.00
—Reissue of 32913					
7603	Jumbo's Gumbo	1977	2.00	4.00	8.00
—Reissue of 33885					
KZ 32913	Raw Sugar/Sweet Sauce/Banana Puddin'	1974	2.50	5.00	10.00
PZ 33885	Jumbo's Gumbo	1975	2.50	5.00	10.00
PAIR					
PDL2-1048 [(2)]	New Orleans By Night	1986	3.00	6.00	12.00
RCA CAMDEN					
CAL-2138 [M]	Struttin' Down Royal Street	1967	3.00	6.00	12.00
CAS-2138 [S]	Struttin' Down Royal Street	1967	2.50	5.00	10.00
CAS-2316	Al's Place	1970	2.50	5.00	10.00
CAS-2573	Have a Merry Little	1971	2.50	5.00	10.00
CXS-9015 [(2)]	Al Hirt Blows His Own Horn	1972	3.00	6.00	12.00
RCA VICTOR					
ANL1-1034	The Best of Al Hirt	1975	2.50	5.00	10.00
LPM-2354 [M]	Al (He's the King) Hirt and His Band	1961	3.00	6.00	12.00
LSP-2354 [S]	Al (He's the King) Hirt and His Band	1961	3.75	7.50	15.00
LPM-2366 [M]	The Greatest Horn in the World	1961	3.00	6.00	12.00
LSP-2366 [S]	The Greatest Horn in the World	1961	3.75	7.50	15.00
LPM-2446 [M]	Horn A-Plenty	1962	3.00	6.00	12.00
LSP-2446 [S]	Horn A-Plenty	1962	3.75	7.50	15.00
LPM-2497 [M]	Al Hirt at the Mardi Gras	1962	3.00	6.00	12.00
LSP-2497 [S]	Al Hirt at the Mardi Gras	1962	3.75	7.50	15.00
LPM-2584 [M]	Trumpet and Strings	1962	3.00	6.00	12.00
LSP-2584 [S]	Trumpet and Strings	1962	3.75	7.50	15.00
LPM-2607 [M]	Our Man in New Orleans	1963	3.00	6.00	12.00
LSP-2607 [S]	Our Man in New Orleans	1963	3.75	7.50	15.00
LM-2729 [M]	"Pops" Goes the Trumpet	1964	3.75	7.50	15.00
LSC-2729 [S]	"Pops" Goes the Trumpet	1964	5.00	10.00	20.00
—With the Boston Pops Orchestra conducted by Arthur Fiedler					
LPM-2733 [M]	Honey in the Horn	1963	3.00	6.00	12.00
LSP-2733 [S]	Honey in the Horn	1963	3.75	7.50	15.00
LPM-2917 [M]	Cotton Candy	1964	3.00	6.00	12.00
LSP-2917 [S]	Cotton Candy	1964	3.75	7.50	15.00
LPM-2965 [M]	Sugar Lips	1964	3.00	6.00	12.00
LSP-2965 [S]	Sugar Lips	1964	3.75	7.50	15.00
LPM-3309 [M]	The Best of Al Hirt	1965	3.00	6.00	12.00
LSP-3309 [S]	The Best of Al Hirt	1965	3.75	7.50	15.00
LPM-3337 [M]	That Honey Horn Sound	1965	3.00	6.00	12.00
LSP-3337 [S]	That Honey Horn Sound	1965	3.75	7.50	15.00
LPM-3416 [M]	Live at Carnegie Hall	1965	3.00	6.00	12.00
LSP-3416 [S]	Live at Carnegie Hall	1965	3.75	7.50	15.00
LPM-3417 [M]	The Sound of Christmas	1965	2.50	5.00	10.00
LSP-3417 [S]	The Sound of Christmas	1965	3.00	6.00	12.00
—Same as above, but in stereo					
LPM-3492 [M]	They're Playing Our Song	1966	3.00	6.00	12.00
LSP-3492 [S]	They're Playing Our Song	1966	3.75	7.50	15.00
LPM-3556 [M]	The Best of Al Hirt, Volume 2	1966	3.00	6.00	12.00
LSP-3566 [S]	The Best of Al Hirt, Volume 2	1966	3.75	7.50	15.00
LPM-3579 [M]	The Happy Trumpet	1966	3.00	6.00	12.00
LSP-3579 [S]	The Happy Trumpet	1966	3.75	7.50	15.00
LPM-3653 [M]	Latin in the Horn	1966	3.00	6.00	12.00
LSP-3653 [S]	Latin in the Horn	1966	3.75	7.50	15.00
LPM-3716 [M]	The Horn Meets the Hornet	1967	3.00	6.00	12.00
LSP-3716 [S]	The Horn Meets the Hornet	1967	3.75	7.50	15.00
LPM-3773 [M]	Music to Watch Girls By	1967	3.75	7.50	15.00
LSP-3773 [S]	Music to Watch Girls By	1967	3.75	7.50	15.00
LPM-3878 [M]	Soul in the Horn	1967	3.75	7.50	15.00
LSP-3878 [S]	Soul in the Horn	1967	3.75	7.50	15.00
LPM-3917 [M]	Al Hirt Plays Bert Kaempfert	1968	5.00	10.00	20.00
LSP-3917 [S]	Al Hirt Plays Bert Kaempfert	1968	3.75	7.50	15.00
LPM-3979 [M]	Unforgettable	1968	6.25	12.50	25.00
LSP-3979 [S]	Unforgettable	1968	3.00	6.00	12.00
LSP-4020	In Love with You	1968	3.00	6.00	12.00
LSP-4101	Al Hirt Now	1969	3.00	6.00	12.00
LSP-4161	Here in My Heart	1969	3.00	6.00	12.00
LSP-4247	Al Hirt	1970	3.00	6.00	12.00
VPS-6025 [(2)]	This Is Al Hirt	1970	3.75	7.50	15.00
VPS-6057 [(2)]	This Is Al Hirt, Volume 2	1972	3.75	7.50	15.00
VERVE					
MGV-1012 [M]	Swinging Dixie from Dan's Pier 600	1957	12.50	25.00	50.00
MGV-1027 [M]	Blockbustin' Dixie!	195?	10.00	20.00	40.00
V-1027 [M]	Blockbustin' Dixie!	1961	5.00	10.00	20.00
VOCALION					
VL 73907	Floatin' Down to Cotton Town	1970	2.50	5.00	10.00
WYNCOTE					
9089	The Dawn Busters	196?	2.50	5.00	10.00

HIRT, AL, AND ANN-MARGRET

Also see each artist's individual listings.

Number	Title (A Side/B Side)	Yr	VG	VG+	NM
Albums					
RCA VICTOR					
LPM-2690 [M]	Beauty and the Beard	1964	6.25	12.50	25.00
LSP-2690 [S]	Beauty and the Beard	1964	7.50	15.00	30.00

HIT PACK, THE

Number	Title (A Side/B Side)	Yr	VG	VG+	NM
45s					
SOUL					
35010	Never Say No to Your Baby/Let's Dance	1965	12.50	25.00	50.00

HO, DON

Number	Title (A Side/B Side)	Yr	VG	VG+	NM
45s					
HEL					
149	Christmas Is for Everyone/Christmas Is You and Me	1977	—	2.00	4.00
149 [PS]	Christmas Is for Everyone/Christmas Is You and Me	1977	—	2.00	4.00
MEGA					
1215	Watch Out Woman/A New Love Song	1974	—	2.00	4.00
1225	Today I Started Loving You Again/Take a Walk in the Country	1975	—	2.00	4.00
REPRISE					
0388	I'll Remember You/E Lei Ka Lei Lei	1965	2.00	4.00	8.00
0441	Suck 'Em Up/La Haina Luna	1965	2.00	4.00	8.00
0451	Sweet Someone/La Haina Luna	1966	2.00	4.00	8.00
0507	Tiny Bubbles/Born Free	1966	2.00	4.00	8.00
0573	I Love You/All That's Left Is the Lemon Tree	1967	2.00	4.00	8.00
0590	Tiny Bubbles/Macao	1967	2.50	5.00	10.00
0591	What Now My Love/One Paddle, Two Paddle	1967	2.00	4.00	8.00
0600	Tomorrow/This Sacred Hour	1967	2.00	4.00	8.00
0609	Forbidden Fruit/Sleepy Summer Days	1967	2.00	4.00	8.00
0643	The Windward Side (Of the Island)/Tu Tu Kane	1967	2.00	4.00	8.00
0669	Instant Happy/White Silver Sands	1968	—	3.00	6.00
0705	Tiny Bubbles/Do I Love You	1968	—	2.00	4.00
—"Back to Back Hits" series					
0754	Remembering/Sunny Days, Starry Nights	1968	—	3.00	6.00
0800	Galveston/Has Anybody Lost a Love	1968	—	3.00	6.00
0871	Honey Come Back/Sands of Waikiki	1969	—	3.00	6.00
0896	It Must Have Been the Wine/Questions	1970	—	2.50	5.00
0936	Melody Fair/Only Foolish People	1970	—	2.50	5.00
0950	Gotta Move Along/Home	1970	—	2.50	5.00
0960	This Is America/United We Stand	1970	—	2.50	5.00
1016	My God and I/What Do I Need to Be Free	1971	—	2.00	4.00
1059	Waikiki/Chotto Matte Kidasi	1971	—	2.00	4.00
Albums					
REPRISE					
R-6161 [M]	The Don Ho Show	1965	3.00	6.00	12.00
RS-6161 [S]	The Don Ho Show	1965	3.75	7.50	15.00
R 6186 [M]	Don Ho...Again!	1966	2.50	5.00	10.00
RS-6186 [S]	Don Ho...Again!	1966	3.00	6.00	12.00
R-6219 [M]	You're Gonna Hear From Me	1966	2.50	5.00	10.00
RS-6219 [S]	You're Gonna Hear From Me	1966	3.00	6.00	12.00
R-6232 [M]	Tiny Bubbles	1966	2.50	5.00	10.00
RS-6232 [S]	Tiny Bubbles	1966	3.00	6.00	12.00
R-6244 [M]	East Coast/West Coast	1967	3.00	6.00	12.00
RS-6244 [S]	East Coast/West Coast	1967	3.00	6.00	12.00
RS-6283	Instant Happy	1968	3.00	6.00	12.00
RS-6303	Hawaii-Ho!	1968	3.00	6.00	12.00
RS-6331	Suck 'Em Up	1969	3.00	6.00	12.00
RS-6357	Don Ho — Greatest Hits!	1969	3.00	6.00	12.00
RS-6367	The Don Ho TV Show	1969	3.00	6.00	12.00
RS-6418	Hawaii's Greatest Hits	1970	2.50	5.00	10.00
RS-6461	Don Ho at the Polynesian Palace	1970	2.50	5.00	10.00

HO-DADS, THE

Number	Title (A Side/B Side)	Yr	VG	VG+	NM
45s					
IMPERIAL					
66001	Legends/Honey	1963	7.50	15.00	30.00
66023	After Dark/Space Race	1964	7.50	15.00	30.00

HOBBITS, THE

Number	Title (A Side/B Side)	Yr	VG	VG+	NM
45s					
DECCA					
32226	Sunny Day Girl/Daffodil Days	1967	3.00	6.00	12.00
32270	Pretty Young Thing/Strawberry Children	1968	3.00	6.00	12.00
ZAR					
25	Frodo Lives/Jolly Good Fellow	1967	5.00	10.00	20.00
Albums					
DECCA					
DL 4920 [M]	Down to Middle-Earth	1967	10.00	20.00	40.00
DL 74920 [S]	Down to Middle-Earth	1967	12.50	25.00	50.00
DL 75009	Men and Doors	1968	7.50	15.00	30.00

HODGE, CHRIS

Number	Title (A Side/B Side)	Yr	VG	VG+	NM
45s					
APPLE					
1850	We're On Our Way/Supersoul	1972	2.00	4.00	8.00
1850 [PS]	We're On Our Way/Supersoul	1972	2.50	5.00	10.00
1858	Goodnight Sweet Lorraine/Contact Love	1973	2.00	4.00	8.00
RCA VICTOR					
APBO-0289	Beautiful Love/Sweet Lady from the Sky	1974	—	2.50	5.00

HODGES, EDDIE

Number	Title (A Side/B Side)	Yr	VG	VG+	NM
45s					
AURORA					
150	Across the Street (Is a Million Miles Away)/She Doesn't Love Me	1965	2.50	5.00	10.00
153	New Orleans/Hard Times for Young Lovers	1965	2.50	5.00	10.00
156	Love Minus Zero (No Limit)/The Water Is Over My Head	1965	2.50	5.00	10.00
161	Hitch Hike/Old Man Rag	1966	2.50	5.00	10.00
CADENCE					
1397	I'm Gonna Knock on Your Door/Ain't Gonna Wash for a Week	1961	3.75	7.50	15.00
1397 [PS]	I'm Gonna Knock on Your Door/Ain't Gonna Wash for a Week	1961	6.25	12.50	25.00
1410	Bandit of My Dreams/Mugmates	1962	5.00	10.00	20.00
1421	(Girls, Girls, Girls) Made to Love/I Make Believe It's You	1962	3.75	7.50	15.00
COLUMBIA					
42649	Seein' Is Believin'/Secret	1962	3.00	6.00	12.00
42649 [PS]	Seein' Is Believin'/Secret	1962	4.00	8.00	16.00
42697	Would You Come Back?/Too Soon to Know	1962	3.00	6.00	12.00
42811	Rainin' in My Heart/Halfway	1963	3.00	6.00	12.00
DECCA					
30675	That Funny Little Dog/What Would It Be Like in Heaven	1958	3.75	7.50	15.00

Number	Title (A Side/B Side)	Yr	VG	VG+	NM
30903	High Hopes/Don't Dance on Momma's Rug	1959	3.75	7.50	15.00
MGM					
13219	Avalanche/Just a Kid in Love	1964	2.50	5.00	10.00

HOFFMAN, ABBIE

Albums

Number	Title (A Side/B Side)	Yr	VG	VG+	NM
BIG TOE					
1	Wake Up, America!	196?	7.50	15.00	30.00

HOG HEAVEN

The Shondells after Tommy James went solo.

45s

Number	Title (A Side/B Side)	Yr	VG	VG+	NM
ROULETTE					
7091	Theme from a Thought/(B-side unknown)	1970	2.00	4.00	8.00
7101	Happy/Prayer	1971	2.00	4.00	8.00
7106	If It Feels Good/(B-side unknown)	1971	2.00	4.00	8.00

Albums

Number	Title (A Side/B Side)	Yr	VG	VG+	NM
ROULETTE					
SR 42057	Hog Heaven	1971	5.00	10.00	20.00

HOGG, SMOKEY

45s

Number	Title (A Side/B Side)	Yr	VG	VG+	NM
COMBO					
11	Where Have You Been/Believe I'll Change My Towns	1952	50.00	100.00	200.00
—Also had releases on Combo 4 and 9, but these are unknown on 45					
EBB					
127	Good Morning Baby/Sure 'Nuff	1958	6.25	12.50	25.00
FEDERAL					
12109	Keep a-Walkin'/Do It No More	1953	25.00	50.00	100.00
12117	Your Little Wagon/Penny Pinching Mama	1953	25.00	50.00	100.00
12127	Gone, Gone, Gone/I Ain't Got Over It Yet	1953	25.00	50.00	100.00
IMPERIAL					
5269	When I've Been Drinkin'/Tear Me Down	1954	25.00	50.00	100.00
5290	My Baby's Gone/Train Whistle	1954	25.00	50.00	100.00
METEOR					
5021	I Declare/Dark Clouds	1955	25.00	50.00	100.00
SPECIALTY					
753	I Want My Baby for Christmas/I Want My Baby for Christmas	197?	2.50	5.00	10.00
—B-side by Jimmy Liggins					

Albums

Number	Title (A Side/B Side)	Yr	VG	VG+	NM
CROWN					
CLP-5226 [M]	Smokey Hogg Sings the Blues	1962	12.50	25.00	50.00
TIME					
6 [M]	Smokey Hogg	1962	20.00	40.00	80.00
UNITED					
US-7745	Smokey Hogg	1970	3.00	6.00	12.00

HOGS, THE

Early version of THE CHOCOLATE WATCH BAND.

45s

Number	Title (A Side/B Side)	Yr	VG	VG+	NM
HANNA-BARBERA					
511	Loose Lip Sync Ships/Blues Theme	1967	37.50	75.00	150.00
—A-side produced by Frank Zappa					

HOLDEN, RANDY

Albums

Number	Title (A Side/B Side)	Yr	VG	VG+	NM
HOBBIT					
5002	Population II	1968	50.00	100.00	200.00

HOLDEN, RON

45s

Number	Title (A Side/B Side)	Yr	VG	VG+	NM
CHALLENGE					
59360	I Tried/I'll Forgive and Forget	1967	10.00	20.00	40.00
DONNA					
1315	Love You So/My Babe	1959	7.50	15.00	30.00
1324	Gee, But I'm Lonesome/Susie Jane	1960	6.25	12.50	25.00
1328	True Love Can Be/Everything's Gonna Be Alright	1960	6.25	12.50	25.00
1331	Who Says There Ain't No Santa Claus/Your Line Is Busy	1960	6.25	12.50	25.00
1335	The Big Shoe/Rock and Roll Call	1961	5.00	10.00	20.00
ELDO					
117	I'll Be Happy/I'll Always Have You	1961	5.00	10.00	20.00
NITE OWL					
10	Love You So/My Babe	1959	200.00	400.00	800.00
NOW					
6	Can You Talk?/I Need Ya	1974	—	3.00	6.00
RAMPART					
645	Girl I Love You/Nothing I Wouldn't Do	1965	3.00	6.00	12.00

Albums

Number	Title (A Side/B Side)	Yr	VG	VG+	NM
DONNA					
DLP-2111 [M]	I Love You So	1960	62.50	125.00	250.00
DLPS-2111 [M]	I Love You So	1960	75.00	150.00	300.00
—Stereo records not known to exist; this is for a mono record in a stereo cover					

HOLIDAY, BILLIE

45s

Number	Title (A Side/B Side)	Yr	VG	VG+	NM
ATLANTIC					
2923	Strange Fruit/I Love My Man	1973	—	3.00	6.00
CLEF					
89089	My Man/He's Funny That Way	1954	3.75	7.50	15.00
89096	Remember/I Can't Face the Music	1954	3.75	7.50	15.00
89108	If the Moon Turns Green/Autumn in New York	1954	3.75	7.50	15.00
89132	How Deep Is the Ocean/What a Little Moonlight Can Do	1955	3.75	7.50	15.00
89150	Love Me or Leave Me/I Thought About You	1955	3.75	7.50	15.00
DECCA					
27145	Them There Eyes/Keeps On Rainin'	1950	6.25	12.50	25.00
48259	Do Your Duty/The Blues Are Brewin'	1951	6.25	12.50	25.00
MAINSTREAM					
614	Strange Fruit/Fine and Mellow	1964	2.00	4.00	8.00
MERCURY					
89002	These Foolish Things/I Only Have Eyes for You	1952	5.00	10.00	20.00
89003	You Turned the Tables on Me/Easy to Love	1952	5.00	10.00	20.00
89004	You Go to My Head/Blue Moon	1952	5.00	10.00	20.00
89005	East o' the Sun/Solitude	1952	5.00	10.00	20.00
89037	Lover Come Back to Me/Yesterdays	1953	5.00	10.00	20.00
89064	Stormy Weather/Tenderly	1953	5.00	10.00	20.00
MGM					
12813	Don't Worry 'Bout Me/Just One More Chance	1959	3.00	6.00	12.00
UNITED ARTISTS					
50999	My Man/Them There Eyes	1973	—	3.00	6.00
VERVE					
10181	Strange Fruit/The Foolish Things	1959	3.00	6.00	12.00

7-Inch Extended Plays

Number	Title (A Side/B Side)	Yr	VG	VG+	NM
DECCA					
ED 2031	Easy Living/What Is This Thing Called Love//Them There Eyes/God Bless the Child	195?	5.00	10.00	20.00
ED 2031 [PS]	Billie Holiday, Vol. 1	195?	5.00	10.00	20.00

Albums

Number	Title (A Side/B Side)	Yr	VG	VG+	NM
AMERICAN RECORDING SOCIETY					
G-409 [M]	Billie Holiday Sings	1956	15.00	30.00	60.00
—Reissue of Clef 713					
G-431 [M]	Lady Sings the Blues	1957	15.00	30.00	60.00
—Reissue of Clef 721					
ARCHIVE OF FOLK AND JAZZ					
265	Billie Holiday	197?	3.00	6.00	12.00
310	Billie Holiday, Vol. 2	197?	3.00	6.00	12.00
ATLANTIC					
1614	Strange Fruit	1972	3.75	7.50	15.00
BLACKHAWK					
BKH-50701	Billie Holiday at Monterey	1986	2.50	5.00	10.00
BULLDOG					
1007	Billie's Blues	198?	2.50	5.00	10.00
CLEF					
MGC-118 [10]	Billie Holiday Sings	1953	45.00	90.00	180.00
MGC-144 [10]	An Evening with Billie Holiday	1954	45.00	90.00	180.00
MGC-161 [10]	Billie Holiday Favorites	1954	45.00	90.00	180.00
MGC-169 [10]	Billie Holiday at Jazz at the Philharmonic	1955	45.00	90.00	180.00
MGC-669 [M]	Music for Torching	1955	25.00	50.00	100.00
MGC-686 [M]	A Recital by Billie Holiday	1956	30.00	60.00	120.00
—Reissue of 144 and 161 as one 12-inch LP					
MGC-690 [M]	Solitude — Songs by Billie Holiday	1956	30.00	60.00	120.00
—Reissue of 118					
MGC-713 [M]	Velvet Moods	1956	30.00	60.00	120.00
MGC-721 [M]	Lady Sings the Blues	1956	30.00	60.00	120.00
COLLECTABLES					
COL-5142	Fine and Mellow	198?	3.00	6.00	12.00
COLUMBIA					
C3L 21 [(3) M]	The Golden Years	1962	12.50	25.00	50.00
—Red and black label with six "eye" logos					
C3L 21 [(3) M]	The Golden Years	1963	6.25	12.50	25.00
—Red "Guaranteed High Fidelity" or "360 Sound" label					
C3L 40 [(3) M]	The Golden Years, Volume 2	1966	7.50	15.00	30.00
CL 637 [M]	Lady Day	1954	17.50	35.00	70.00
—Maroon label, gold print					
CL 637 [M]	Lady Day	1956	10.00	20.00	40.00
—Red and black label with six "eye" logos					
CL 637 [M]	Lady Day	1962	3.75	7.50	15.00
—Red "Guaranteed High Fidelity" or "360 Sound" label					
CL 1157 [M]	Lady in Satin	1958	10.00	20.00	40.00
—Red and black label with six "eye" logos					
CL 1157 [M]	Lady in Satin	1962	3.75	7.50	15.00
—Red "Guaranteed High Fidelity" or "360 Sound" label					
CL 2666 [M]	Billie Holiday's Greatest Hits	1967	3.75	7.50	15.00
CL 6129 [10]	Billie Holiday Sings	1950	50.00	100.00	200.00
CL 6163 [10]	Billie Holiday Favorites	1951	50.00	100.00	200.00
CS 8048 [S]	Lady in Satin	1958	10.00	20.00	40.00
—Red and black label with six "eye" logos					
CS 8048 [S]	Lady in Satin	1962	3.75	7.50	15.00
—Red "Guaranteed High Fidelity" or "360 Sound" label					
CS 8048 [S]	Lady in Satin	1999	6.25	12.50	25.00
—Classic Records reissue on audiophile vinyl					
G 30782 [(2)]	God Bless the Child	1972	5.00	10.00	20.00
C 32060	The Original Recordings	1973	3.75	7.50	15.00
PC 32080	Billie's Blues	198?	2.00	4.00	8.00
—Reissue of Harmony LP					
CG 32121 [(2)]	The Billie Holiday Story, Volume 1	1973	3.75	7.50	15.00
CG 32124 [(2)]	The Billie Holiday Story, Volume 2	1973	3.75	7.50	15.00
CG 32127 [(2)]	The Billie Holiday Story, Volume 3	1973	3.75	7.50	15.00
COLUMBIA JAZZ MASTERPIECES					
CJ 40247	Lady in Satin	1987	2.50	5.00	10.00
CJ 40646	The Quintessential Billie Holiday, Vol. 1	1987	2.50	5.00	10.00
CJ 40790	The Quintessential Billie Holiday, Vol. 2	1987	2.50	5.00	10.00
CJ 44048	The Quintessential Billie Holiday, Vol. 3	1988	2.50	5.00	10.00
CJ 44252	The Quintessential Billie Holiday, Vol. 4	1988	2.50	5.00	10.00
CJ 44423	The Quintessential Billie Holiday, Vol. 5	1989	2.50	5.00	10.00
C 45449	The Quintessential Billie Holiday, Vol. 6	1990	2.50	5.00	10.00
C 46180	The Quintessential Billie Holiday, Vol. 7	1990	2.50	5.00	10.00
COLUMBIA MUSICAL TREASURY					
P3M 5869 [(3)]	The Golden Years	197?	5.00	10.00	20.00
COLUMBIA SPECIAL PRODUCTS					
P 14338	Swing, Brother, Swing	198?	2.50	5.00	10.00
COMMODORE					
FL-20005 [10]	Billie Holiday, Volume 1	1950	62.50	125.00	250.00
FL-20006 [10]	Billie Holiday, Volume 2	1950	62.50	125.00	250.00
DL-30008 [M]	Billie Holiday	1959	12.50	25.00	50.00
—Reissue of 20006					
DL-30011 [M]	Billie Holiday with Eddie Heywood and His Orchestra	1959	12.50	25.00	50.00
—Reissue of 20005					

Number	Title (A Side/B Side)	Yr	VG	VG+	NM
CROWN					
CST-380 [R]	Billie Holiday & Vivian Fears	196?	3.00	6.00	12.00
CLP-5380 [M]	Billie Holiday & Vivian Fears	196?	5.00	10.00	20.00
DECCA					
DXB-161 [(2) M]	The Billie Holiday Story	1959	5.00	10.00	20.00
DL 5345 [10]	Lover Man	1951	50.00	100.00	200.00
DXSB-7161 [(2) R]	The Billie Holiday Story	1959	3.75	7.50	15.00
DL 8215 [M]	The Lady Sings	1956	15.00	30.00	60.00
DL 8701 [M]	The Blues Are Brewin'	1958	15.00	30.00	60.00
DL 8702 [M]	Lover Man	1958	15.00	30.00	60.00
DL 75040	Billie Holiday's Greatest Hits	1968	3.00	6.00	12.00
ESP-DISK'					
3002	The Lady Lives, Vol. 1	1973	3.00	6.00	12.00
3003	The Lady Lives, Vol. 2	1973	3.00	6.00	12.00
HALL					
622	I've Gotta Right to Sing	197?	3.00	6.00	12.00
HARMONY					
KH 32080	Billie's Blues	1973	2.50	5.00	10.00
INTERMEDIA					
QS-5076	Billie Holiday Talks and Sings	198?	2.50	5.00	10.00
JAZZ MAN					
5005	Billie Holiday at Storyville	198?	2.50	5.00	10.00
JAZZTONE					
J-1209 [M]	Billie Holiday Sings	1955	12.50	25.00	50.00
—Reissue of Commodore 20005					
JOLLY ROGER					
5020 [10]	Billie Holiday, Volume 1	1954	25.00	50.00	100.00
5021 [10]	Billie Holiday, Volume 2	1954	25.00	50.00	100.00
5022 [10]	Billie Holiday, Volume 3	1954	25.00	50.00	100.00
MAINSTREAM					
S-6000 [R]	The Commodore Recordings	1965	3.00	6.00	12.00
S-6022 [R]	Once Upon a Time	1965	3.00	6.00	12.00
56000 [M]	The Commodore Recordings	1965	6.25	12.50	25.00
56022 [M]	Once Upon a Time	1965	6.25	12.50	25.00
MCA					
275	Billie Holiday's Greatest Hits	1973	2.50	5.00	10.00
—Reissue of Decca 75040					
4006 [(2)]	The Billie Holiday Story	1973	3.00	6.00	12.00
—Reissue of Decca 7161					
METRO					
M-515 [M]	Billie Holiday	1965	3.75	7.50	15.00
MS-515 [R]	Billie Holiday	1965	3.00	6.00	12.00
MGM					
GAS-122	Billie Holiday (Golden Archive Series)	1970	3.00	6.00	12.00
E-3764 [M]	Billie Holiday	1959	10.00	20.00	40.00
SE-3764 [S]	Billie Holiday	1959	12.50	25.00	50.00
M3G-4948	Archetypes	1974	3.00	6.00	12.00
MOBILE FIDELITY					
1-247	Body and Soul	1996	30.00	60.00	120.00
—Audiophile vinyl					
MONMOUTH/EVERGREEN					
7046	Gallant Lady	1973	3.00	6.00	12.00
PARAMOUNT					
PA-6059	Songs and Conversations	1973	3.00	6.00	12.00
PICKWICK					
PC-3335	Billie Holiday Sings the Blues	197?	2.50	5.00	10.00
RIC					
R-2001 [M]	Rare Live Recordings	1964	6.25	12.50	25.00
SCORE					
SLP-4014 [M]	Billie Holiday Sings the Blues	1957	30.00	60.00	120.00
SOLID STATE					
18040	Lady Love	1969	3.00	6.00	12.00
SUNSET					
SUM-1147 [M]	Shades of Blue	1967	3.00	6.00	12.00
SUS-5147 [R]	Shades of Blue	1967	2.50	5.00	10.00
TOTEM					
1037	Billie Holiday On the Air	198?	2.50	5.00	10.00
TRIP					
5024	Billie Holiday Live	1974	2.50	5.00	10.00
UNITED ARTISTS					
UAS-5625	Lady Love	1972	2.50	5.00	10.00
—Reissue of 15014					
UAJ-14014 [M]	Lady Love	1962	10.00	20.00	40.00
UASJ-15014 [S]	Lady Love	1962	12.50	25.00	50.00
VERVE					
VSP-5 [M]	Lady	1966	3.75	7.50	15.00
VSPS-5 [R]	Lady	1966	3.00	6.00	12.00
VE-2-2503 [(2)]	The First Verve Sessions	1976	3.75	7.50	15.00
VE-2-2515 [(2)]	Stormy Blues	1976	3.75	7.50	15.00
VE-2-2529 [(2)]	All or Nothing at All	198?	3.75	7.50	15.00
MGVS-6021-45 [(2) S]	Songs for Distingue Lovers	1999	5.00	10.00	20.00
—Classic Records reissue on two 12-inch 45-rpm records					
MGVS-6021 [S]	Songs for Distingue Lovers	1960	15.00	30.00	60.00
MGVS-6021 [S]	Songs for Distingue Lovers	199?	6.25	12.50	25.00
—Classic Records reissue on audiophile vinyl					
MGV-8026 [M]	Music for Torching	1957	10.00	20.00	40.00
—Reissue of Clef 669					
V-8026 [M]	Music for Torching	1961	5.00	10.00	20.00
MGV-8027 [M]	A Recital by Billie Holiday	1957	10.00	20.00	40.00
—Reissue of Clef 686					
V-8027 [M]	A Recital by Billie Holiday	1961	5.00	10.00	20.00
MGV-8074 [M]	Solitude — Songs by Billie Holiday	1957	10.00	20.00	40.00
—Reissue of Clef 690					
V-8074 [M]	Solitude — Songs by Billie Holiday	1961	5.00	10.00	20.00
V6-8074 [R]	Solitude — Songs by Billie Holiday	196?	3.00	6.00	12.00
MGV-8096 [M]	Velvet Moods	1957	10.00	20.00	40.00
—Reissue of Clef 713					
V-8096 [M]	Velvet Moods	1961	5.00	10.00	20.00
MGV-8099 [M]	Lady Sings the Blues	1957	10.00	20.00	40.00
—Reissue of Clef 721					
V-8099 [M]	Lady Sings the Blues	1957	5.00	10.00	20.00
MGV-8197 [M]	Body and Soul	1957	15.00	30.00	60.00
V-8197 [M]	Body and Soul	1961	5.00	10.00	20.00
MGV-8257 [M]	Songs for Distingue Lovers	1958	15.00	30.00	60.00
V-8257 [M]	Songs for Distingue Lovers	1961	5.00	10.00	20.00
V6-8257 [S]	Songs for Distingue Lovers	1961	6.25	12.50	25.00
MGV-8302 [M]	Stay with Me	1959	12.50	25.00	50.00
V-8302 [M]	Stay with Me	1961	5.00	10.00	20.00
MGV-8329 [M]	All or Nothing at All	1959	12.50	25.00	50.00
V-8329 [M]	All or Nothing at All	1959	5.00	10.00	20.00
V6-8329 [R]	All or Nothing at All	196?	3.00	6.00	12.00
MGV-8338-2 [(2) M]	The Unforgettable Lady Day	1959	20.00	40.00	80.00
V-8338-2 [(2) M]	The Unforgettable Lady Day	1961	6.25	12.50	25.00
V-8410 [M]	The Essential Billie Holiday	1961	5.00	10.00	20.00
V6-8410 [R]	The Essential Billie Holiday	1961	3.00	6.00	12.00
V-8505 [M]	The Essential Jazz Vocals	1963	5.00	10.00	20.00
V6-8505 [R]	The Essential Jazz Vocals	1963	3.00	6.00	12.00
V6-8808 [R]	The Best of Billie Holiday	1973	2.50	5.00	10.00
2V6S-8816 [(2)]	History of the Real Billie Holiday	1973	3.75	7.50	15.00
817359-1 [(2)]	Embraceable You	198?	3.00	6.00	12.00
823230-1 [(2)]	Stormy Blues	198?	3.00	6.00	12.00
823233-1 [(2)]	History of the Real Billie Holiday	198?	3.00	6.00	12.00
823246-1	The Billie Holiday Songbook	198?	2.50	5.00	10.00
827160-1	All or Nothing at All	1987	2.50	5.00	10.00

HOLIDAY, BILLIE, AND STAN GETZ

Albums

Number	Title (A Side/B Side)	Yr	VG	VG+	NM
DALE					
25 [10]	Billie and Stan	1951	100.00	200.00	400.00

HOLIDAY, BILLIE/AL HIBBLER

Albums

Number	Title (A Side/B Side)	Yr	VG	VG+	NM
IMPERIAL					
LP-9185 [M]	Billie Holiday, Al Hibbler and the Blues	1962	12.50	25.00	50.00
LP-12185 [R]	Billie Holiday, Al Hibbler and the Blues	196?	7.50	15.00	30.00

HOLIDAY, GEORGIE

45s

Number	Title (A Side/B Side)	Yr	VG	VG+	NM
DATE					
1541	Have a Gluey Christmas/Clarence the Cross-Eyed Bear	1966	3.00	6.00	12.00
—As "'Little' Georgie Holiday"					
MAP CITY					
302	Have a Gluey Christmas/A Little Boy's Christmas Prayer	1969	2.50	5.00	10.00

HOLIDAY, JOHN E.

45s

Number	Title (A Side/B Side)	Yr	VG	VG+	NM
ATLANTIC					
2091	Yes I Will Love You Tomorrow/Till the End of Time	1961	5.00	10.00	20.00

HOLIDAY TRIO, THE

45s

Number	Title (A Side/B Side)	Yr	VG	VG+	NM
SANTO					
500	Desperate/Dark Valley	196?	3.75	7.50	15.00

HOLIDAYS, THE (1)

Detroit-based R&B group.

45s

Number	Title (A Side/B Side)	Yr	VG	VG+	NM
GOLDEN WORLD					
36	Makin' Up Time/I'll Love You Forever	1966	6.25	12.50	25.00
47	No Greater Love/Watch Out Girl	1966	6.25	12.50	25.00
GROOVE CITY					
206	Easy Living/I've Lost You	196?	25.00	50.00	100.00
—As "The New Holidays"					
REVILOT					
205	Love's Creeping Up on Me/Never Alone	1967	7.50	15.00	30.00
210	I Know She Cares/I Keep Holding On	1967	7.50	15.00	30.00
226	I'll Keep Coming Back/All That Is Required of You	1968	6.25	12.50	25.00

HOLIDAYS, THE (U)

None of these are group (1), but exactly how many groups are represented here is not known.

45s

Number	Title (A Side/B Side)	Yr	VG	VG+	NM
ANDIE					
5019	The Stars Will Remember/Who Knows, Who Cares	1960	15.00	30.00	60.00
BRENT					
7018	Come Back to Me/No Other Love	1961	5.00	10.00	20.00
BRUNSWICK					
55084	Sands of Gold/French Riviera	1958	3.75	7.50	15.00
CORAL					
62430	Love and Learn/I Want You to Love Me	1964	5.00	10.00	20.00
DIXIE					
1156	Little Miss Hurt/I Got News for You	196?	7.50	15.00	30.00
GALAXY					
714	Send Back My Love/Deacon Brown	1962	5.00	10.00	20.00
714 [DJ]	Send Back My Love/Deacon Brown	1962	7.50	15.00	30.00
—Promo on colored vinyl					
KING					
1217	I'm a-Like a-You (Pizza Pie)/Rolling River	1953	7.50	15.00	30.00
1246	Just Out of Reach/Let the Dice Decide	1953	7.50	15.00	30.00
MELBA					
112	The Robin/Desperately	1957	75.00	150.00	300.00
MONUMENT					
431	Merry Christmas Song/A Very Merry Christmas	1960	3.75	7.50	15.00
NIX					
537	One Little Kiss/My Girl	1961	7.50	15.00	30.00
PAM					
111	Refreshing/Crazy Discharge	1959	50.00	100.00	200.00
ROBBEE					
103	Them There Eyes/The Kiss Cha Cha	1960	15.00	30.00	60.00
107	Lonely Summer/Then I'll Be Tired of You	1960	12.50	25.00	50.00

SPECIALTY

Number	Title (A Side/B Side)	Yr	VG	VG+	NM
533	Irene/Aw-Aw Baby	1954	10.00	20.00	40.00

TRACK

Number	Title (A Side/B Side)	Yr	VG	VG+	NM
101	Patty Ann/Big Brown Eyes	1962	3.75	7.50	15.00

HOLLAND, BRIAN

45s

INVICTUS

Number	Title (A Side/B Side)	Yr	VG	VG+	NM
1265	I'm So Glad (Part 1)/I'm So Glad (Part 2)	1974	—	2.50	5.00
1272	Super Woman/Let's Get Together	1974	—	2.50	5.00

KUDO

Number	Title (A Side/B Side)	Yr	VG	VG+	NM
667	(Where's the Joy?) In Nature Boy/Shock	1958	150.00	300.00	600.00

—First name as "Briant"

HOLLAND, EDDIE

Also see HOLLAND-DOZIER.

45s

MERCURY

Number	Title (A Side/B Side)	Yr	VG	VG+	NM
71290	You/Little Miss Ruby	1958	25.00	50.00	100.00

MOTOWN

Number	Title (A Side/B Side)	Yr	VG	VG+	NM
1021	Jamie/Take a Chance on Me	1961	6.25	12.50	25.00
1026	You Deserve What You Got/Last Night I Had a Vision	1962	6.25	12.50	25.00
1030	If Cleopatra Took a Chance/What About Me	1962	6.25	12.50	25.00
1030 [PS]	If Cleopatra Took a Chance/What About Me	1962	25.00	50.00	100.00
1031	If It's Love (It's All Right)/It's Not Too Late	1962	6.25	12.50	25.00
1036	Darling I Hum Our Song/Just a Few Memories	1963	6.25	12.50	25.00
1043	Brenda/Baby Shake	1963	6.25	12.50	25.00
1049	I'm On the Outside Looking In/I Couldn't Cry If I Wanted To	1963	37.50	75.00	150.00
1052	Leaving Here/Brenda	1964	3.75	7.50	15.00
1058	Just Ain't Enough Love/Last Night I Had a Vision	1964	3.75	7.50	15.00
1063	Candy to Me/If You Don't Want My Love	1964	3.75	7.50	15.00

TAMLA

Number	Title (A Side/B Side)	Yr	VG	VG+	NM
102	Merry-Go-Round/It Moves Me	1959	62.50	125.00	250.00

UNITED ARTISTS

Number	Title (A Side/B Side)	Yr	VG	VG+	NM
172	Merry-Go-Round/It Moves Me	1959	7.50	15.00	30.00
191	Because I Love Her/Everybody's Going	1959	7.50	15.00	30.00
207	Magic Mirror/Will You Love Me	1960	7.50	15.00	30.00
280	The Last Laugh/Why Do You Want to Let Me Go	1960	7.50	15.00	30.00

Albums

MOTOWN

Number	Title (A Side/B Side)	Yr	VG	VG+	NM
604 [M]	Eddie Holland	1963	100.00	200.00	400.00

HOLLAND-DOZIER

Also see LAMONT DOZIER; EDDIE HOLLAND.

45s

INVICTUS

Number	Title (A Side/B Side)	Yr	VG	VG+	NM
1253	Slipping Away/Can't Get Enough	1973	—	2.50	5.00
1254	If You Don't Wanta Be in My Life/New Breed Kinda Woman	1973	—	2.50	5.00
1258	You Took Me from a World Outside/I'm Gonna Hijack Ya, Kidnap Ya, Take What I Want	1973	—	2.50	5.00
9110	Don't Leave Me (Part 1)/Don't Leave Me (Part 2)	1972	—	2.50	5.00
9125	Why Can't We Be Lovers/Don't Leave Me	1972	—	2.50	5.00
9133	Don't Leave Me Starvin' for Your Love (Part 1)/Don't Leave Me Starvin' for Your Love (Part 2)	1972	—	2.50	5.00

MOTOWN

Number	Title (A Side/B Side)	Yr	VG	VG+	NM
1045	What Goes Up Must Come Down/Come On Home	1963	6.25	12.50	25.00

HOLLIDAY, MICHAEL

45s

CAPITOL

Number	Title (A Side/B Side)	Yr	VG	VG+	NM
F3720	Good Luck, Good Health, God Bless You/John and Julie	1957	3.00	6.00	12.00
F4018	Rooney/Keep Your Heart	1958	3.00	6.00	12.00

HOLLIES, THE

Also see ALLAN CLARKE; GRAHAM NASH; TERRY SYLVESTER.

12-Inch Singles

ATLANTIC

Number	Title (A Side/B Side)	Yr	VG	VG+	NM
PR 502 [DJ]	Stop in the Name of Love (same on both sides)	1983	—	3.00	6.00

45s

ATLANTIC

Number	Title (A Side/B Side)	Yr	VG	VG+	NM
89768 [DJ]	Casualty (same on both sides)	1983	—	2.50	5.00
—May be promo only					
89784	Someone Else's Eyes/If the Lights Go Out	1983	—	—	3.00
89819	Stop in the Name of Love/Musical Pictures	1983	—	—	3.00
89819 [PS]	Stop in the Name of Love/Musical Pictures	1983	—	2.50	5.00

EPIC

Number	Title (A Side/B Side)	Yr	VG	VG+	NM
10180	Carrie-Anne/Signs That Will Never Change	1967	2.00	4.00	8.00
10180 [PS]	Carrie-Anne/Signs That Will Never Change	1967	3.75	7.50	15.00
10234	King Midas in Reverse/Water on the Brain	1967	2.00	4.00	8.00
10234 [PS]	King Midas in Reverse/Water on the Brain	1967	3.75	7.50	15.00
10251	Dear Eloise/When Your Light's Turned On	1967	2.00	4.00	8.00
10251 [PS]	Dear Eloise/When Your Light's Turned On	1967	3.75	7.50	15.00
10298	Jennifer Eccles/Try It	1968	2.00	4.00	8.00
10361	Do the Best You Can/Elevated Observations	1968	2.00	4.00	8.00
10400	Listen to Me/Everything Is Sunshine	1968	2.00	4.00	8.00
10454	Sorry Suzanne/Not That Way at All	1969	2.00	4.00	8.00
10532	He Ain't Heavy, He's My Brother/Cos You Like to Love Me	1969	—	3.00	6.00
—A-side: Elton John on piano					
10613	I Can't Tell the Bottom from the Top/Mad Professor Blythe	1970	—	3.00	6.00
10677	Gasoline Alley Bred/Dandelion Wine	1970	2.50	5.00	10.00
10716	Survival of the Fittest/Man Without a Heart	1971	3.00	6.00	12.00
10754	Hey Willy/Row the Boat Together	1971	2.50	5.00	10.00
10842	The Baby/Oh Granny	1972	2.50	5.00	10.00
10842 [PS]	The Baby/Oh Granny	1972	12.50	25.00	50.00
10871	Long Cool Woman (In a Black Dress)/Look What We've Got	1972	—	2.50	5.00
10920	Long Dark Road/Indian Girl	1972	—	2.50	5.00
10951	Magic Woman Touch/Blue in the Morning	1973	—	2.50	5.00
10989	Jesus Was a Crossmaker/I Had a Dream	1973	—	2.50	5.00
11025	Won't We Feel Good/Slow Down	1973	—	2.50	5.00
11051	The Day That Curley Billy Shot Down Crazy Sam McGee/Born a Man	1973	—	2.50	5.00
11100	The Air That I Breathe/No More Riders	1974	—	2.50	5.00
50029	Don't Let Me Down/Layin' to the Music	1974	—	2.50	5.00
50086	Sandy/Second Hand Hangups	1975	—	2.50	5.00
50110	Another Night/Time Machine Jive	1975	—	2.00	4.00
50144	Look Out Johnny/I'm Down	1975	—	2.00	4.00
50204	Crocodile Woman (She Bites)/Write On	1976	—	2.00	4.00
50359	Sandy/Second Hand Hangups	1977	—	2.00	4.00
50422	Draggin' My Heels/I Won't Move Over	1977	—	2.00	4.00
50522	Burn Out/Writing on the Wall	1978	—	2.00	4.00

IMPERIAL

Number	Title (A Side/B Side)	Yr	VG	VG+	NM
54050	Look Through My Window/I'm Alive	196?	3.75	7.50	15.00
—"The Golden Series" gold label reissue with incorrect A-side title					
66026	Just One Look/Keep Off That Friend of Mine	1964	5.00	10.00	20.00
66044	Here I Go Again/Lucille	1964	3.75	7.50	15.00
66070	Come On Back/We're Through	1964	3.75	7.50	15.00
66099	Yes I Will/Nobody	1965	10.00	20.00	40.00
66119	I'm Alive/You Know He Did	1965	3.75	7.50	15.00
66134	Look Through Any Window/So Lonely	1965	3.00	6.00	12.00
66158	I Can't Let Go/I've Got a Way of My Own	1966	3.75	7.50	15.00
66186	Bus Stop/Don't Run and Hide	1966	3.00	6.00	12.00
66214	Stop Stop Stop/It's You	1966	3.00	6.00	12.00
66231	On a Carousel/All the World Is Love	1967	3.00	6.00	12.00
66231 [PS]	On a Carousel/All the World Is Love	1967	7.50	15.00	30.00
66240	Pay You Back With Interest/Whatcha Gonna Do 'Bout It	1967	3.00	6.00	12.00
66258	Just One Look/Running Through the Night	1967	3.00	6.00	12.00
66271	If I Needed Someone/I'll Be True to You (Yes I Will)	1968	10.00	20.00	40.00

LIBERTY

Number	Title (A Side/B Side)	Yr	VG	VG+	NM
55674	Stay/Now's the Time	1964	15.00	30.00	60.00

UNITED ARTISTS

Number	Title (A Side/B Side)	Yr	VG	VG+	NM
50079	After the Fox/The Fox Trot	1966	5.00	10.00	20.00

—With Peter Sellers

Albums

ATLANTIC

Number	Title (A Side/B Side)	Yr	VG	VG+	NM
80076	What Goes Around	1983	2.50	5.00	10.00

CAPITOL

Number	Title (A Side/B Side)	Yr	VG	VG+	NM
N-16056	Hollies' Greatest	1980	2.00	4.00	8.00

COLUMBIA

Number	Title (A Side/B Side)	Yr	VG	VG+	NM
LE 10178	He Ain't Heavy, He's My Brother	1976	3.00	6.00	12.00

EMI AMERICA

Number	Title (A Side/B Side)	Yr	VG	VG+	NM
SN-16397	More Great Hits (1963-1968)	1986	2.00	4.00	8.00

EPIC

Number	Title (A Side/B Side)	Yr	VG	VG+	NM
AS 138 [DJ]	Everything You Always Wanted to Hear by the Hollies But Were Afraid to Ask For	1976	5.00	10.00	20.00
—Promo-only sampler album					
LN 24315 [M]	Evolution	1967	7.50	15.00	30.00
LN 24344 [M]	Dear Eloise/King Midas in Reverse	1967	7.50	15.00	30.00
BN 26315 [S]	Evolution	1967	6.25	12.50	25.00
BN 26344 [S]	Dear Eloise/King Midas in Reverse	1967	6.25	12.50	25.00
BN 26447	Words and Music by Bob Dylan	1969	3.75	7.50	15.00
—Yellow label					
BN 26447	Words and Music by Bob Dylan	1973	2.50	5.00	10.00
—Orange label					
BN 26538	He Ain't Heavy, He's My Brother	1970	5.00	10.00	20.00
E 30255	Moving Finger	1970	5.00	10.00	20.00
KE 30958	Distant Light	1971	3.75	7.50	15.00
—Yellow label					
KE 30958	Distant Light	1974	2.50	5.00	10.00
—Orange label					
PE 30958	Distant Light	1986	2.00	4.00	8.00
—Blue label					
KE 31992	Romany	1972	3.00	6.00	12.00
—Yellow label					
KE 31992	Romany	1974	2.50	5.00	10.00
—Orange label					
KE 32061	The Hollies' Greatest Hits	1973	3.00	6.00	12.00
—Yellow label					
KE 32061	The Hollies' Greatest Hits	1974	2.50	5.00	10.00
—Orange label					
PE 32061	The Hollies' Greatest Hits	1979	2.00	4.00	8.00
—Blue label					
KE 32574	Hollies	1974	2.50	5.00	10.00
PE 33387	Another Night	1975	2.50	5.00	10.00
PE 34714	Clarke, Hicks, Sylvester, Calvert & Elliot	1977	2.50	5.00	10.00
JE 35334	A Crazy Steal	1978	2.50	5.00	10.00

IMPERIAL

Number	Title (A Side/B Side)	Yr	VG	VG+	NM
LP-9265 [M]	Here I Go Again	1964	37.50	75.00	150.00
—Black label with stars					
LP-9265 [M]	Here I Go Again	1964	12.50	25.00	50.00
—Black and pink label					
LP-9299 [M]	Hear! Here!	1965	12.50	25.00	50.00
LP-9312 [M]	The Hollies — Beat Group	1966	7.50	15.00	30.00
LP-9330 [M]	Bus Stop	1966	7.50	15.00	30.00
—Black and pink label					
LP-9330 [M]	Bus Stop	1966	6.25	12.50	25.00
—Black and green label					
LP-9339 [M]	Stop! Stop! Stop!	1966	6.25	12.50	25.00
LP-9350 [M]	The Hollies' Greatest Hits	1967	5.00	10.00	20.00
LP-12265 [R]	Here I Go Again	1964	25.00	50.00	100.00
—Black label with silver print					
LP-12265 [R]	Here I Go Again	1964	7.50	15.00	30.00
—Black and pink label					
LP-12299 [R]	Hear! Here!	1965	7.50	15.00	30.00
LP-12312 [S]	The Hollies — Beat Group	1966	10.00	20.00	40.00

Number	Title (A Side/B Side)	Yr	VG	VG+	NM
LP-12330 [R]	Bus Stop	1966	6.25	12.50	25.00
—Black and pink label					
LP-12330 [R]	Bus Stop	1966	5.00	10.00	20.00
—Black and green label					
LP-12339 [S]	Stop! Stop! Stop!	1966	7.50	15.00	30.00
LP-12350 [P]	The Hollies' Greatest Hits	1967	6.25	12.50	25.00
LIBERTY					
LN-10216	Pay You Back with Interest	1982	2.00	4.00	8.00
PAIR					
PDL2-1041 [(2)]	Hottest Hits	1986	3.75	7.50	15.00
REALM					
2V-8026 [(2)]	The Hollies, Volume 1	1976	3.75	7.50	15.00
—Two-record TV package					
1V-8027	The Hollies, Volume 2	1976	3.00	6.00	12.00
—TV package sold with Realm 8026					
UNITED ARTISTS					
UA-LA329-E	The Very Best of the Hollies	1975	2.50	5.00	10.00

HOLLOWAY, BRENDA

Number	Title (A Side/B Side)	Yr	VG	VG+	NM
45s					
DONNA					
1358	Echo/Hey Fool	1962	10.00	20.00	40.00
1366	Game of Love/Echo-Echo-Echo	1962	12.50	25.00	50.00
1370	I'll Give My Life/More Echo	1962	12.50	25.00	50.00
TAMLA					
54094	Every Little Bit Hurts/Land of 1,000 Boys	1964	3.00	6.00	12.00
54099	I'll Always Love You/Sad Song	1964	3.75	7.50	15.00
54111	When I'm Gone/I've Been Good to You	1965	3.75	7.50	15.00
54111 [PS]	When I'm Gone/I've Been Good to You	1965	25.00	50.00	100.00
54115	Operator/I'll Be Available	1965	3.75	7.50	15.00
54121	You Can Cry on My Shoulder/How Many Times Did You Mean It	1965	5.00	10.00	20.00
54125	Sad Song/Together 'Til the End of Time	1965	5.00	10.00	20.00
54137	Hurt a Little Every Day/Where Were You	1966	7.50	15.00	30.00
54144	'Til Johnny Comes/Where Were You	1967	50.00	100.00	200.00
54148	Just Look What You've Done/Starting the Hurt All Over Again	1967	6.25	12.50	25.00
54155	You've Made Me So Very Happy/I've Got to Find It	1967	5.00	10.00	20.00
206312 [DJ]	Play It Cool, Stay in School	1966	150.00	300.00	600.00
—Promo for Women's Ad Club of Detroit					
Albums					
MOTOWN					
5242 ML	Every Little Bit Hurts	1982	3.00	6.00	12.00
TAMLA					
T 257 [M]	Every Little Bit Hurts	1964	50.00	100.00	200.00
TS 257 [R]	Every Little Bit Hurts	1964	37.50	75.00	150.00

HOLLOWAY, LOLEATTA

Number	Title (A Side/B Side)	Yr	VG	VG+	NM
12-Inch Singles					
GOLD MIND					
402	Catch Me on the Rebound (10:51)/(7:22)	1978	3.75	7.50	15.00
4006	Hit and Run/It's Getting Stronger	1977	5.00	10.00	20.00
SELECT					
5585	Strong Enough (5 versions)	1991	2.00	4.00	8.00
STREETWISE					
2230	Crash Goes Love/Sweet Thing	1984	2.50	5.00	10.00
45s					
AWARE					
033	Our Love/Mother of Shame	1973	—	3.00	6.00
039	H-E-L-P Me My Love/(B-side unknown)	1974	—	3.00	6.00
047	Cry to Me/So Can I	1974	—	3.00	6.00
050	The Show Must Go On/I Know Where You're Coming From	1975	—	3.00	6.00
054	Casanova/Only a Fool	1975	—	3.00	6.00
GALAXY					
780	Rainbow '71/Bring It On Up	1971	2.00	4.00	8.00
GOLD MIND					
4000	Dreamin'/Worn Out Broken Heart	1976	—	3.00	6.00
4001	Hit and Run/Is It Just a Man's Way	1977	—	3.00	6.00
4007	It's Getting Stronger/How Heartaches Are Made	1977	—	3.00	6.00
4012	Only You/Good Good Feeling	1978	—	3.00	6.00
—A-side with Bunny Sigler					
4016	Catch Me on the Rebound/Mama Don't, Papa Won't	1978	—	3.00	6.00
4021	That's What You Said/There'll Come a Time	1979	—	3.00	6.00
4024	Love Sensation/Short End of the Stick	1980	2.50	5.00	10.00
4025	I've Been Loving You Too Long/Two Became a Crowd	1980	—	3.00	6.00
SALSOUL					
2045	Run Away/Run Away (Part 2)	1977	—	3.00	6.00
—With the Salsoul Orchestra					
7034	Seconds/Columbia: The Space Shuttle	1981	—	3.00	6.00
—With the Salsoul Orchestra					
STREETWISE					
1130	Crash Goes Love/Sweet Thing	1984	—	3.00	6.00
Albums					
GOLD MIND					
7500	Loleatta	1977	5.00	10.00	20.00
A-9501	Queen of the Night	1978	5.00	10.00	20.00
GA-9506	Love Sensation	1979	5.00	10.00	20.00

HOLLOWAY, PATRICE

Also see JOSIE AND THE PUSSYCATS.

Number	Title (A Side/B Side)	Yr	VG	VG+	NM
45s					
CAPITOL					
5680	Stolen Hours/Lucky My Boy	1966	20.00	40.00	80.00
5778	Love and Desire/Ecstasy	1967	15.00	30.00	60.00
5985	Stay with Your Own Kind/That's All You Got to Do	1967	12.50	25.00	50.00
TASTE					
125	Do the Del Viking (Pt. 1)/Do the Del Viking (Pt. 2)	1963	7.50	15.00	30.00

HOLLY, BUDDY

Also see THE CRICKETS (1).

Number	Title (A Side/B Side)	Yr	VG	VG+	NM
45s					
CORAL					
61852	Words of Love/Mailman, Bring Me No More Blues	1957	150.00	250.00	400.00
—Promos for any Coral title valued at $50 or under Near Mint are worth 2-4 times the stock copy value.					
61885	Peggy Sue/Everyday	1957	12.50	25.00	50.00
—Orange label					
61885	Peggy Sue/Everyday	196?	6.25	12.50	25.00
—Black color bars label					
61947	I'm Gonna Love You Too/Listen to Me	1958	12.50	25.00	50.00
61985	Rave On/Take Your Time	1958	12.50	25.00	50.00
62006	Early in the Morning/Now We're One	1958	12.50	25.00	50.00
62051	Heartbeat/Well...All Right	1958	12.50	25.00	50.00
62074	It Doesn't Matter Anymore/Raining in My Heart	1959	10.00	20.00	40.00
62134	Peggy Sue Got Married/Crying, Waiting, Hoping	1959	15.00	30.00	60.00
62210	True Love Ways/That Makes It Tough	1960	12.50	25.00	50.00
62283	You're So Square (Baby I Don't Care)/Valley of Tears	1961	40.00	80.00	160.00
—Evidently only released in Canada					
62329	Reminiscing/Wait Till the Sun Shines, Nellie	1962	7.50	15.00	30.00
62352	True Love Ways/Bo Diddley	1963	15.00	30.00	60.00
62369	Brown Eyed Handsome Man/Wishing	1963	10.00	20.00	40.00
62390	Rock Around with Ollie Vee/I'm Gonna Love You Too	1963	10.00	20.00	40.00
62448	Slippin' and Slidin'/What to Do	1965	25.00	50.00	100.00
62554	Rave On/Early in the Morning	1968	7.50	15.00	30.00
62558	Love Is Strange/You're the One	1969	5.00	10.00	20.00
62558 [PS]	Love Is Strange/You're the One	1969	7.50	15.00	30.00
DECCA					
29854	Blue Days, Black Nights/Love Me	1956	150.00	300.00	600.00
—With lines on either side of "Decca"					
29854	Blue Days, Black Nights/Love Me	1956	75.00	150.00	300.00
—With star under "Decca"					
29854 [DJ]	Blue Days, Black Nights/Love Me	1956	100.00	200.00	400.00
—Promos have pink labels					
30166	Modern Don Juan/You Are My One Desire	1956	125.00	250.00	500.00
—With lines on either side of "Decca"					
30166	Modern Don Juan/You Are My One Desire	1956	62.50	125.00	250.00
—With star under "Decca"					
30166 [DJ]	Modern Don Juan/You Are My One Desire	1956	75.00	150.00	300.00
—Promos have pink labels					
30434	That'll Be the Day/Rock Around with Ollie Vee	1957	62.50	125.00	250.00
—With star under "Decca"					
30434	That'll Be the Day/Rock Around with Ollie Vee	1957	100.00	200.00	400.00
—With lines on either side of "Decca"					
30434 [DJ]	That'll Be the Day/Rock Around with Ollie Vee	1957	62.50	125.00	250.00
—Promos have pink labels					
30543	Love Me/You Are My One Desire	1958	75.00	150.00	300.00
30543 [DJ]	Love Me/You Are My One Desire	1958	75.00	150.00	300.00
—Green label promos					
30543 [DJ]	Love Me/You Are My One Desire	1958	50.00	100.00	200.00
—Pink label promos					
30650	Ting-a-Ling/Girl on My Mind	1958	75.00	150.00	300.00
30650 [DJ]	Ting-a-Ling/Girl on My Mind	1958	50.00	100.00	200.00
—Promos have pink labels					
MCA					
40905	It Doesn't Matter Anymore/Peggy Sue	1978	—	2.50	5.00
40905 [PS]	It Doesn't Matter Anymore/Peggy Sue	1978	—	2.50	5.00
7-Inch Extended Plays					
CORAL					
EC 81169	Listen to Me/Peggy Sue//I'm Gonna Love You Too/Everyday	1958	75.00	150.00	300.00
EC 81169 [PS]	Listen to Me	1958	75.00	150.00	300.00
EC 81182	It Doesn't Matter Anymore/Heartbeat//Raining in My Heart/Early in the Morning	1959	75.00	150.00	300.00
EC 81182 [PS]	The Buddy Holly Story	1959	75.00	150.00	300.00
EC 81191	Peggy Sue Got Married/Crying, Waiting, Hoping//Learning the Game/That Makes It Tough	1961	62.50	125.00	250.00
EC 81191 [PS]	Buddy Holly	1961	62.50	125.00	250.00
EC 81193	Brown Eyed Handsome Man/Wishing//Bo Diddley/True Love Ways	1961	62.50	125.00	250.00
EC 81193 [PS]	Brown Eyed Handsome Man	1961	62.50	125.00	250.00
DECCA					
ED 2575	*That'll Be the Day/Blue Days — Black Nights/Ting-a-Ling/You Are My One Desire	1958	150.00	300.00	600.00
ED 2575 [PS]	That'll Be the Day	1958	500.00	1000.	2000.
—Sleeve has liner notes on back					
ED 2575 [PS]	That'll Be the Day	1958	150.00	300.00	600.00
—Sleeve has other EP ads on back					
Albums					
CORAL					
CXB 8 [(2) M]	The Best of Buddy Holly	1966	20.00	40.00	80.00
CXSB 8 [(2) R]	The Best of Buddy Holly	1966	12.50	25.00	50.00
CRL 57210 [M]	Buddy Holly	1958	100.00	200.00	400.00
—Maroon label					
CRL 57210 [M]	Buddy Holly	1964	25.00	50.00	100.00
—Black label with color bars					
CRL 57279 [M]	The Buddy Holly Story	1959	75.00	150.00	300.00
—Maroon label; back color print in black and red					
CRL 57279 [M]	The Buddy Holly Story	1959	37.50	75.00	150.00
—Maroon label; back color print in all black					
CRL 57279 [M]	The Buddy Holly Story	1963	20.00	40.00	80.00
—Black label with color bars					
CRL 57326 [M]	The Buddy Holly Story, Vol. 2	1959	50.00	100.00	200.00
—Maroon label					
CRL 57326 [M]	The Buddy Holly Story, Vol. 2	1963	20.00	40.00	80.00
—Black label with color bars					
CRL 57405 [M]	Buddy Holly and the Crickets	1962	37.50	75.00	150.00
—Reissue of the Crickets LP on Brunswick 54038					
CRL 57426 [M]	Reminiscing	1963	50.00	100.00	200.00
—Maroon label					

Number	Title (A Side/B Side)	Yr	VG	VG+	NM
CRL 57426 [M]	Reminiscing	1964	20.00	40.00	80.00
—Black label with color bars					
CRL 57450 [M]	Buddy Holly Showcase	1964	25.00	50.00	100.00
CRL 57463 [M]	Holly in the Hills	1965	30.00	60.00	120.00
CRL 57492 [M]	Buddy Holly's Greatest Hits	1967	20.00	40.00	80.00
CRL 757279 [R]	The Buddy Holly Story	1963	10.00	20.00	40.00
CRL 757326 [R]	The Buddy Holly Story, Vol. 2	1963	10.00	20.00	40.00
CRL 757405 [R]	Buddy Holly and the Crickets	1963	10.00	20.00	40.00
CRL 757426 [R]	Reminiscing	1964	10.00	20.00	40.00
CRL 757450 [R]	Buddy Holly Showcase	1964	20.00	40.00	80.00
CRL 757463 [R]	Holly in the Hills	1965	25.00	50.00	100.00
CRL 757492 [P]	Buddy Holly's Greatest Hits	1967	12.50	25.00	50.00
CRL 757504 [S]	Giant	1969	12.50	25.00	50.00
CRICKET					
C001000	Buddy Holly Live — Volume 1	197?	5.00	10.00	20.00
C001001	Buddy Holly Live — Volume 1	197?	5.00	10.00	20.00
DECCA					
DXSE 7207 [(2)]	A Rock 'n' Roll Collection	1972	10.00	20.00	40.00
DL 8707 [M]	That'll Be the Day	1958	375.00	750.00	1500.
—Black label with silver print					
DL 8707 [M]	That'll Be the Day	1961	75.00	150.00	300.00
—Black label with color bars					
GREAT NORTHWEST					
GNW-4014	Visions of Buddy	197?	2.50	5.00	10.00
—Interview album					
MCA					
737	The Great Buddy Holly	197?	2.50	5.00	10.00
—Reissue of MCA Coral LP					
1484	Buddy Holly/The Crickets 20 Golden Greats	198?	2.00	4.00	8.00
—Reissue of 3040					
3040	Buddy Holly/The Crickets 20 Golden Greats	1978	3.75	7.50	15.00
4009 [(2)]	A Rock 'n' Roll Collection	1973	5.00	10.00	20.00
—Black labels with rainbow					
4009 [(2)]	A Rock 'n' Roll Collection	1978	3.00	6.00	12.00
—Later pressings on tan or blue/rainbow labels					
4184 [(2)]	Legend	1985	5.00	10.00	20.00
5540 [(2)]	From the Original Master Tapes	1986	6.25	12.50	25.00
11161	Buddy Holly	1995	10.00	20.00	40.00
—Audiophile "Heavy Vinyl" reissue with gatefold cover					
25239	Buddy Holly	1989	3.00	6.00	12.00
—Reissue of Coral 57210					
27059	For the First Time Anywhere	1983	2.50	5.00	10.00
80000 [(6)]	The Complete Buddy Holly	1981	12.50	25.00	50.00
—Box set with booklet and custom innersleeves					
MCA CORAL					
CD-20101	The Great Buddy Holly	1973	3.00	6.00	12.00
VOCALION					
VL 3811 [M]	The Great Buddy Holly	1967	20.00	40.00	80.00
VL 73811 [R]	The Great Buddy Holly	1967	12.50	25.00	50.00
VL 73923	Good Rockin'	1971	30.00	60.00	120.00

HOLLY TWINS, THE

45s

Number	Title (A Side/B Side)	Yr	VG	VG+	NM
LIBERTY					
55015	Take Me Back/It's Easy	1956	6.25	12.50	25.00
55048	I Want Elvis for Christmas/The Tender Age	1956	12.50	25.00	50.00
RENDEZVOUS					
180	Okee-Feenokee/Potato Chips	1962	3.00	6.00	12.00

HOLLYHAWKS, THE

With Niki Sullivan, ex-CRICKETS (1).

45s

Number	Title (A Side/B Side)	Yr	VG	VG+	NM
JUBILEE					
5441	I Cry All the Time/When Came the Fall	1962	20.00	40.00	80.00

HOLLYRIDGE STRINGS, THE

45s

Number	Title (A Side/B Side)	Yr	VG	VG+	NM
CAPITOL					
4557	Lucy's Theme/Hippodrome	1961	2.50	5.00	10.00
4600	The Thunder of Drums/The Guns of Navarone	1961	2.50	5.00	10.00
4631	Moon River/Something Big	1961	2.50	5.00	10.00
4664	The Comancheros/Theme from "The Devil at 4 O'Clock"	1961	2.50	5.00	10.00
4687	My Melancholy Baby/Light in the Piazza	1962	2.00	4.00	8.00
4720	It Happened in Athens/Song of Greece	1962	2.00	4.00	8.00
5165	The Seven Faces of Dr. Lao/The Fall of Love	1964	2.00	4.00	8.00
5207	Love Me Do/All My Loving	1964	3.00	6.00	12.00
5432	L-O-V-E/Those Lazy-Hazy-Crazy Days of Summer	1965	2.00	4.00	8.00
5533	Santa's Got a Brand New Bag/Have Yourself a Merry Little Christmas	1965	2.50	5.00	10.00
5551	Skyscraper/Gaiety	1965	2.00	4.00	8.00

Albums

Number	Title (A Side/B Side)	Yr	VG	VG+	NM
CAPITOL					
ST-883	Hits of the 70's	1971	3.00	6.00	12.00
SM-2116	The Beatles Song Book	197?	2.50	5.00	10.00
ST 2116 [S]	The Beatles Song Book	1964	5.00	10.00	20.00
T 2116 [M]	The Beatles Song Book	1964	3.75	7.50	15.00
SM-2156	The Beach Boys Song Book	197?	2.50	5.00	10.00
ST 2156 [S]	The Beach Boys Song Book	1964	5.00	10.00	20.00
T 2156 [M]	The Beach Boys Song Book	1964	3.75	7.50	15.00
ST 2199 [S]	Hits Made Famous by the Four Seasons	1965	5.00	10.00	20.00
T 2199 [M]	Hits Made Famous by the Four Seasons	1965	3.75	7.50	15.00
ST 2202 [S]	The Beatles Song Book, Vol. 2	1965	5.00	10.00	20.00
T 2202 [M]	The Beatles Song Book, Vol. 2	1965	3.75	7.50	15.00
ST 2221 [S]	Hits Made Famous by Elvis Presley	1965	5.00	10.00	20.00
T 2221 [M]	Hits Made Famous by Elvis Presley	1965	3.75	7.50	15.00
ST 2310 [S]	The Nat King Cole Song Book	1965	5.00	10.00	20.00
T 2310 [M]	The Nat King Cole Song Book	1965	3.75	7.50	15.00
ST 2404 [S]	Christmas Favorites by the Hollyridge Strings	1965	3.75	7.50	15.00
T 2404 [M]	Christmas Favorites by the Hollyridge Strings	1965	3.00	6.00	12.00
SM-2429	The New Beatles Song Book	197?	2.50	5.00	10.00
ST 2429 [S]	The New Beatles Song Book	1966	5.00	10.00	20.00
T 2429 [M]	The New Beatles Song Book	1966	3.75	7.50	15.00
ST 2564 [S]	Oldies But Goldies	1966	5.00	10.00	20.00
T 2564 [M]	Oldies But Goldies	1966	3.75	7.50	15.00
ST 2611 [S]	Skyscraper	1966	5.00	10.00	20.00
T 2611 [M]	Skyscraper	1966	3.75	7.50	15.00
ST 2656 [S]	The Beatles Song Book, Vol. 4	1967	3.75	7.50	15.00
T 2656 [M]	The Beatles Song Book, Vol. 4	1967	5.00	10.00	20.00
ST 2749 [S]	The Beach Boys Song Book, Vol. 2	1967	3.75	7.50	15.00
T 2749 [M]	The Beach Boys Song Book, Vol. 2	1967	5.00	10.00	20.00
ST 2998	Hits Made Famous by Simon and Garfunkel	1968	3.75	7.50	15.00
SM-11830	Christmas Favorites by the Hollyridge Strings	1978	2.50	5.00	10.00
—Abridged reissue of ST 2404					

HOLLYWOOD ARGYLES, THE

Also see FLESH GORDON AND THE NUDE HOLLYWOOD ARGYLES; GARY PAXTON.

45s

Number	Title (A Side/B Side)	Yr	VG	VG+	NM
BRENT					
7004	Vacation Days Are Over/It Takes Time	1959	7.50	15.00	30.00
—As "The Argyles"					
CHATTAHOOCHIE					
691	Long Hair, Unsquare Dude Called Jack/Ole	1965	3.75	7.50	15.00
FELSTED					
8674	Bossy Nover/Find Another Way	1963	5.00	10.00	20.00
FINER ARTS					
1002	The Morning After/See You in the Morning	1961	5.00	10.00	20.00
KAMMY					
105	Alley-Oop '65/Do the Funky Foot	1965	5.00	10.00	20.00
—As "The New Hollywood Argyles"					
LUTE					
5905	Alley Oop/Sho' Know a Lot About Love	1960	6.25	12.50	25.00
5908	Gun Totin' Critter Called Jack/Bug Eyed Man	1960	5.00	10.00	20.00
6002	Hully Gully/So Fine	1960	5.00	10.00	20.00
PAXLEY					
200	Unemployment (same on both sides)	196?	2.50	5.00	10.00
752	You've Been Torturing Me/The Grubble	1960	5.00	10.00	20.00
TRILL					
6311	The Watermelon Song/Short Fat Outlaw	196?	6.25	12.50	25.00

Albums

Number	Title (A Side/B Side)	Yr	VG	VG+	NM
LUTE					
L-9001 [M]	The Hollywood Argyles (Alley Oop)	1960	175.00	350.00	700.00

HOLLYWOOD FLAMES, THE

Also see BOBBY DAY.

45s

Number	Title (A Side/B Side)	Yr	VG	VG+	NM
ATCO					
6155	Every Day, Every Way/If I Thought I Needed You	1959	3.75	7.50	15.00
6164	Ball and Chain/I Found a Boy	1960	3.75	7.50	15.00
6171	Devil or Angel/Do You Ever Think of Me	1960	3.75	7.50	15.00
6180	Money Honey/My Heart's On Fire	1960	3.75	7.50	15.00
CHESS					
1787	Gee/Yes They Do	1961	3.00	6.00	12.00
DECCA					
29285	Peggy/Ooh La La	1954	18.75	37.50	75.00
48331	Let's Talk It Over/I Know	1955	18.75	37.50	75.00
EBB					
119	Buzz-Buzz-Buzz/Crazy	1957	7.50	15.00	30.00
131	Give Me Back My Heart/A Little Bird	1958	6.25	12.50	25.00
144	Frankenstein's Den/Strollin' on the Beach	1958	6.25	12.50	25.00
146	Chains of Love/Let's Talk It Over	1958	6.25	12.50	25.00
149	A Star Fell/I'll Get By	1958	6.25	12.50	25.00
153	I'll Be Seeing You/Just for You	1959	7.50	15.00	30.00
158	So Good/There Is Something on Your Mind	1959	6.25	12.50	25.00
162	Now That You're Gone/Hawaiian Dream	1959	6.25	12.50	25.00
163	Much Too Much/In the Dark	1959	6.25	12.50	25.00
LUCKY					
001	One Night with a Fool/Ride, Helen, Ride	1954	150.00	300.00	600.00
006	Peggy/Ooh-La-La	1954	150.00	300.00	600.00
009	Let's Talk It Over/I Know	1954	100.00	200.00	400.00
MONA-LEE					
135	Buzz-Buzz-Buzz/Crazy	1958	6.25	12.50	25.00
MONEY					
202	Fare Thee Well/I'm Leaving	1954	100.00	200.00	400.00
SWING TIME					
345	Let's Talk It Over/I Know	1953	125.00	250.00	500.00
346	Go and Get Some More/Another Soldier Gone	1953	125.00	250.00	500.00
—B-side by the Question Marks					
SYMBOL					
211	Dance Senorita/Annie Don't Love Me Anymore	1965	3.00	6.00	12.00
215	I'm Coming Home/I'm Gonna Stand By You	1966	3.00	6.00	12.00
VEE JAY					
515	Drop Me a Line/Letter to My Love	1963	3.75	7.50	15.00

HOLLYWOOD PERSUADERS, THE

45s

Number	Title (A Side/B Side)	Yr	VG	VG+	NM
ORIGINAL SOUND					
39	Tijuana/Grunion Run	1964	12.50	25.00	50.00
39	Tijuana Surf/Grunion Run	1964	12.50	25.00	50.00
44	Persuasion/Juarez	1964	6.25	12.50	25.00
50	Drums-A-Go-Go/Agua Caliente	1965	6.25	12.50	25.00
58	Hollywood A-Go-Go/Eve of Destruction	1965	6.25	12.50	25.00

Albums

Number	Title (A Side/B Side)	Yr	VG	VG+	NM
ORIGINAL SOUND					
LPM-5013 [M]	Drums a-Go-Go	1965	12.50	25.00	50.00
LPS-8874 [S]	Drums a-Go-Go	1965	15.00	30.00	60.00

HOLLYWOOD PLAYBOYS, THE

With Nick Massi, later of THE FOUR SEASONS.

45s

Number	Title (A Side/B Side)	Yr	VG	VG+	NM
SURE					
105	Ding Dong School Is Out/Talk to Audrey	1960	7.50	15.00	30.00

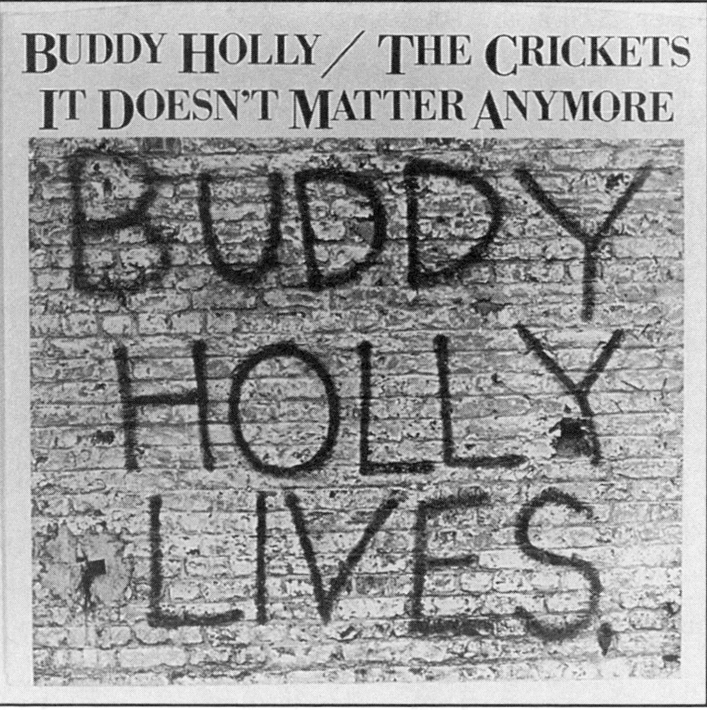

(Top left) Here's one of the obscure early Essex 45s by Bill Haley, "Real Rock Drive." Even before "Crazy Man Crazy" became a moderate hit in 1953, he was releasing material that was prototypical rock 'n' roll. It was also his first record to credit the Comets; before this, his group was known as the Saddlemen. (Top right) The first album by bluesman Slim Harpo, *Raining in My Heart*, is his most collectible. Of course, Harpo is best known for his 1966 hit "Baby Scratch My Back." (Bottom left) The most valuable extended-play single is this one, *The Sensational Harptones*, released by the Bruce label in the mid-1950s. The sleeve alone gets sums in the middle four figures. (Bottom right) The most common Buddy Holly picture sleev comes from this 1978 reissue of "It Doesn't Matter Anymore." It was re-released when the movie *The Buddy Holly Story* brought increased attention to the original recordings.

HOLLYWOOD PRODUCERS, THE

45s

Number	Title (A Side/B Side)	Yr	VG	VG+	NM
PARKWAY					
993	Whits Silk Glove/You're Not Welcome	1966	7.50	15.00	30.00

HOLMAN, EDDIE

45s

Number	Title (A Side/B Side)	Yr	VG	VG+	NM
ABC					
11149	I Love You/I Surrender	1968	2.50	5.00	10.00
11240	Hey There Lonely Girl/It's All in the Game	1969	—	3.00	6.00
11261	Don't Stop Now/Since I Don't Have You	1970	—	3.00	6.00
11265	I'll Be There/Cause You're Mine Little Girl	1970	—	3.00	6.00
11276	Cathy Called/I Need Somebody	1970	—	3.00	6.00
11292	Love Story/Four Walls	1971	—	3.00	6.00
ASCOT					
2142	Go Get Your Own/Laughing at Me	1963	3.75	7.50	15.00
BELL					
712	I'm Not Gonna Give Up/I'll Cry 1,000 Tears	1968	5.00	10.00	20.00
GSF					
6873	My Mind Keeps Telling Me (That I Really Love You, Girl)/Stranded in a Dream	1972	—	3.00	6.00
6885	Young Girl/I'll Call You Joy	1972	—	3.00	6.00
PARKWAY					
106	Am I a Loser/You Know That I Will	1966	5.00	10.00	20.00
133	Somewhere Waits a Lonely Girl/Stay Mine for Heaven's Sake	1967	5.00	10.00	20.00
157	Why Do Fools Fall in Love/Never Let Me Go	1967	5.00	10.00	20.00
960	This Can't Be True/A Free Country	1965	5.00	10.00	20.00
981	Don't Stop Now/Eddie's My Name	1966	5.00	10.00	20.00
994	Return to Me/Stay Mine for Heaven's Sake	1966	5.00	10.00	20.00
SALSOUL					
2026	This Will Be a Night to Remember/Time Will Tell	1977	—	2.50	5.00
2043	You Make My Life Complete/Somehow You Make Me Feel	1977	—	2.50	5.00
SILVER BLUE					
807	You're My Lady (Right Or Wrong)/(Instrumental)	1974	—	2.50	5.00
815	Just Say I Love Her/Darling Take Me Back	1974	—	2.50	5.00
UNITED ARTISTS					
609	Go Get Your Own/Laughing at Me	1963	—	—	—
—Unreleased					

Albums

Number	Title (A Side/B Side)	Yr	VG	VG+	NM
ABC					
S-701	I Love You	1970	7.50	15.00	30.00
SALSOUL					
5511	A Night to Remember	1977	2.50	5.00	10.00

HOLMES, CECIL'S, SOULFUL SOUNDS

45s

Number	Title (A Side/B Side)	Yr	VG	VG+	NM
BUDDAH					
354	Superfly/Soulful Sounds	1973	—	2.50	5.00
391	Kung Fu/Soulful Love	1973	—	2.50	5.00

Albums

Number	Title (A Side/B Side)	Yr	VG	VG+	NM
BUDDAH					
BDS-5129	The Black Motion Picture Experience	1973	3.00	6.00	12.00
BDS-5139	Music for Soulful Lovers	1973	3.00	6.00	12.00

HOLMES, CLINT

45s

Number	Title (A Side/B Side)	Yr	VG	VG+	NM
ATCO					
6958	Playground in My Mind/Goodbye Maria	1974	—	2.50	5.00
7000	Let Me Hear It Out There/When You're No. 1	1974	—	2.50	5.00
7005	Bad Can Be Good/Hang In There Josie	1974	—	2.50	5.00
EPIC					
10891	Playground in My Mind/There's No Future in My Future	1972	—	2.50	5.00
—Originals have yellow labels					
10891	Playground in My Mind/There's No Future in My Future	1973	—	2.00	4.00
—Reissue have orange labels					
11033	Shiddle-Ee-Dee/Like the Fellow Once Said	1973	—	2.00	4.00
PRIVATE STOCK					
45126	I Can Count on You	1976	—	2.00	4.00
45186	It Wouldn't Have Made Any Difference/Got to Give In to Love	1978	—	2.00	4.00
45201	No Walls, No Ceilings, No Floors	1979	—	2.00	4.00

Albums

Number	Title (A Side/B Side)	Yr	VG	VG+	NM
EPIC					
KE 32269	Playground in My Mind	1973	2.50	5.00	10.00

HOLMES, JAKE

45s

Number	Title (A Side/B Side)	Yr	VG	VG+	NM
COLUMBIA					
45517	Trust Me/Just as Lost as Me	1971	—	2.50	5.00
45570	How Much Time/Silence	1972	—	2.50	5.00
POLYDOR					
14006	How Are You/(B-side unknown)	1969	—	2.50	5.00
14011	The Very First Time/Suitcase Room	1969	—	2.50	5.00
14023	A Little Later/Beautiful Girl Goodbye	1970	—	2.50	5.00
14041	So Close/Django and Friend	1970	—	2.50	5.00
TOWER					
392	Genuine Imitation Life/Hard to Keep My Mind on You	1968	—	3.00	6.00
393	Dazed and Confused/Penny's	1968	—	3.00	6.00
451	Saturday Night/Late Sleeping Day	1968	—	3.00	6.00
458	Sleeping Woman/Leaves Never Break	1969	—	3.00	6.00
459	High School Hero/The Diner Song	1969	—	3.00	6.00

Albums

Number	Title (A Side/B Side)	Yr	VG	VG+	NM
COLUMBIA					
C 30996	Jake Holmes	1972	3.00	6.00	12.00
POLYDOR					
24-4007	Jake Holmes	1969	3.00	6.00	12.00
24-4034	So Close, So Very Far to Go	1970	3.00	6.00	12.00
TOWER					
DT 5079 [R]	Above Ground	1967	3.75	7.50	15.00
T 5079 [M]	Above Ground	1967	5.00	10.00	20.00
ST 5127	Letter to Katherine December	1968	3.75	7.50	15.00

HOLMES, MARVIN

45s

Number	Title (A Side/B Side)	Yr	VG	VG+	NM
UNI					
55111	Ooh, Ooh, The Dragon (Part 1)/Ooh, Ooh, The Dragon (Part 2)	1969	6.25	12.50	25.00
55233	Sweet Talk/Thang	1970	6.25	12.50	25.00

Albums

Number	Title (A Side/B Side)	Yr	VG	VG+	NM
BROWN DOOR					
MH-6573	Summer of '73	1973	6.25	12.50	25.00
MH-6581	Honor Thy Father	1975	6.25	12.50	25.00
UNI					
73046	Ooh, Ooh, The Dragon And Other Monsters	1969	7.50	15.00	30.00

HOLMES, RICHARD "GROOVE"

45s

Number	Title (A Side/B Side)	Yr	VG	VG+	NM
BLUE NOTE					
1967	Theme from "Love Story"/Don't Mess with Me	1971	—	2.50	5.00
FLYING DUTCHMAN					
DB-10671	Morning Children/This Is the Me Me (Not the You You)	1976	—	2.00	4.00
—With Brenda Jones					
DB-10735	Caravan/I've Got Love for You	1976	—	2.00	4.00
GROOVE MERCHANT					
1012	Night Glider/Flapjack	1972	—	2.50	5.00
1020	Finger Lickin' Good/The Squirrel	1973	—	2.50	5.00
PACIFIC JAZZ					
321	Harmonica Boogie Shuffle/Them That's Got	1961	2.50	5.00	10.00
330	Groovin' with Jug/Morris the Minor	1961	2.50	5.00	10.00
347	Comin' Through the Apple/Something Special	1962	2.50	5.00	10.00
88130	Secret Love/Hallelujah I Love Her So	1966	2.00	4.00	8.00
88137	It Might As Well Be Spring/This Here	1967	2.00	4.00	8.00
88147	The Odd Couple/Madison Time	1968	2.00	4.00	8.00
88149	I Can't Stop Dancing/Listen Here	1969	—	3.00	6.00
PRESTIGE					
380	Soul Message/Song for My Father	1965	2.50	5.00	10.00
401	Misty/Groove's Groove	1966	2.00	4.00	8.00
427	What Now My Love/Living Soul	1966	2.00	4.00	8.00
428	The More I See You/On the Street Where You Live	1967	2.00	4.00	8.00
431	Never on Sunday/Boo-D-Doo	1967	2.00	4.00	8.00
442	1-2-3/If I Had a Hammer	1967	2.00	4.00	8.00
451	Ain't That Peculiar/Super Soul	1967	2.00	4.00	8.00
460	Gimme Little Sign/Soul Power	1968	2.00	4.00	8.00
718	See See Rider (Part 1)/See See Rider (Part 2)	1968	—	3.00	6.00
723	Misty/What Now My Love	1969	—	3.00	6.00

Albums

Number	Title (A Side/B Side)	Yr	VG	VG+	NM
BLUE NOTE					
BST-84372	Comin' On Home	1971	3.00	6.00	12.00
FANTASY					
OJC-329	Soul Message	1988	2.50	5.00	10.00
—Reissue of Prestige 7435					
FLYING DUTCHMAN					
BDL1-1537	I'm in the Mood for Love	1976	3.00	6.00	12.00
GROOVE MERCHANT					
505	American Pie	1972	3.00	6.00	12.00
512	Night Glider	1972	3.00	6.00	12.00
527	New Groove	1973	3.00	6.00	12.00
4402 [(2)]	Hunk-A-Funk	1975	3.75	7.50	15.00
MUSE					
5134	Shippin' Out	1978	2.50	5.00	10.00
5167	Good Vibrations	1979	2.50	5.00	10.00
5239	Broadway	1981	2.50	5.00	10.00
5358	Blues All Day Long	1989	2.50	5.00	10.00
PACIFIC JAZZ					
PJ-23 [M]	Richard "Groove" Holmes	1961	6.25	12.50	25.00
ST-23 [S]	Richard "Groove" Holmes	1961	7.50	15.00	30.00
PJ-32 [M]	Groovin' with Jug	1961	7.50	15.00	30.00
ST-32 [S]	Groovin' with Jug	1961	10.00	20.00	40.00
PJ-51 [M]	Somethin' Special	1962	5.00	10.00	20.00
ST-51 [S]	Somethin' Special	1962	6.25	12.50	25.00
PJ-59 [M]	After Hours	1962	5.00	10.00	20.00
ST-59 [S]	After Hours	1962	6.25	12.50	25.00
PJ-10105 [M]	Tell It Like It Tis	1966	3.75	7.50	15.00
LN-10130	Groovin' with Jug	198?	2.00	4.00	8.00
—Busget-line reissue					
ST-20105 [S]	Tell It Like It Tis	1966	5.00	10.00	20.00
ST-20153	Workin' on a Groovy Thing	1969	3.75	7.50	15.00
ST-20163	X-77	1969	3.75	7.50	15.00
ST-20171	Come Together	1970	3.75	7.50	15.00
PRESTIGE					
PRLP-7435 [M]	Soul Message	1966	3.75	7.50	15.00
PRST-7435 [S]	Soul Message	1966	5.00	10.00	20.00
PRLP-7468 [M]	Living Soul	1966	3.75	7.50	15.00
PRST-7468 [S]	Living Soul	1966	5.00	10.00	20.00
PRLP-7485 [M]	Misty	1966	3.75	7.50	15.00
PRST-7485 [S]	Misty	1966	5.00	10.00	20.00
PRLP-7493 [M]	Spicy	1967	5.00	10.00	20.00
PRST-7493 [S]	Spicy	1967	3.75	7.50	15.00
PRLP-7497 [M]	Super Cool	1967	5.00	10.00	20.00
PRST-7497 [S]	Super Cool	1967	3.75	7.50	15.00
PRLP-7514 [M]	Get Up and Get It	1967	5.00	10.00	20.00
PRST-7514 [S]	Get Up and Get It	1967	3.75	7.50	15.00
PRST-7543	Soul Power	1968	3.75	7.50	15.00
PRST-7570	The Groover	1968	3.75	7.50	15.00
PRST-7601	That Healin' Feelin'	1969	3.75	7.50	15.00

Number	Title (A Side/B Side)	Yr	VG	VG+	NM
PRST-7700	The Best of Richard "Groove" Holmes	1969	3.75	7.50	15.00
PRST-7741	Soul Mist	1970	3.75	7.50	15.00
PRST-7768	The Best for Beautiful People	1971	3.75	7.50	15.00
PRST-7778	The Best of Soul Organ Giants	1972	3.00	6.00	12.00
VERSATILE					
MSG 6003	Dancing in the Sun	1977	3.75	7.50	15.00
WARNER BROS.					
W 1553 [M]	Book of the Blues	1964	5.00	10.00	20.00
WS 1553 [S]	Book of the Blues	1964	6.25	12.50	25.00
WORLD PACIFIC					
ST-20147	Welcome Home	1968	5.00	10.00	20.00

HOLMES, RUPERT

45s

Number	Title (A Side/B Side)	Yr	VG	VG+	NM
EPIC					
11014	Philly/Talk	1973	—	3.00	6.00
11117	Our National Pastime/Phantom of the Opera	1974	—	3.00	6.00
50013	Terminal/Bagdad	1974	—	3.00	6.00
50096	I Don't Wanna Hold Your Hand/The Man Behind the Woman	1975	—	3.00	6.00
50161	Deco Lady/Terminal	1975	—	3.00	6.00
50223	Weekend Lover/Weekend Lover	1976	—	2.50	5.00
50295	You Make Me Real/Who, What, When, Where, How	1976	—	2.50	5.00
INFINITY					
50035	Escape (The Pina Colada Song)/Drop It	1979	—	2.50	5.00
50051	Him/Get Outta Yourself	1980	—	—	—
—Canceled					
MCA					
41173	Him/Get Outta Yourself	1980	—	2.00	4.00
41235	Answering Machine/Lunch Hour	1980	—	2.00	4.00
50035	Escape (The Pina Colada Song)/Drop It	1980	—	2.00	4.00
51019	Morning Man/The Mask	1980	—	2.00	4.00
51045	Blackjack/Crowd Pleaser	1981	—	2.00	4.00
51092	I Don't Need You/Cold	1981	—	2.00	4.00
PRIVATE STOCK					
45183	Bedside Companions/So Beautiful It Hurts	1978	—	2.50	5.00
45199	Let's Get Crazy Tonight/Long Way Home	1978	—	2.50	5.00

Albums

Number	Title (A Side/B Side)	Yr	VG	VG+	NM
ELEKTRA					
5E-560	Full Circle	1982	2.50	5.00	10.00
EPIC					
KE 32864	Widescreen	1974	3.00	6.00	12.00
KE 33443	Rupert Holmes	1975	3.00	6.00	12.00
PE 34288	Singles	1976	3.00	6.00	12.00
EXCELSIOR					
XMP-6000	Rupert Holmes	1980	2.50	5.00	10.00
XMP-6022	She Lets Her Hair Down	1981	2.50	5.00	10.00
INFINITY					
9020	Partners in Crime	1979	2.50	5.00	10.00
MCA					
5129	Adventure	1980	2.50	5.00	10.00
9020	Partners in Crime	1980	2.00	4.00	8.00
—Reissue of Infinity LP					
37166	Pursuit of Happiness	198?	2.00	4.00	8.00
—Reissue of Private Stock LP					
PRIVATE STOCK					
7006	Pursuit of Happiness	1978	3.00	6.00	12.00

HOLY MACKEREL, THE

Albums

Number	Title (A Side/B Side)	Yr	VG	VG+	NM
REPRISE					
RS-6311	The Holy Mackerel	1968	6.25	12.50	25.00

HOLY MODAL ROUNDERS, THE

45s

Number	Title (A Side/B Side)	Yr	VG	VG+	NM
ELEKTRA					
45644	Bird Song/Dame Fortune	1968	3.75	7.50	15.00
METROMEDIA					
223	Boobs a Lot/Love Is the Closest Thing	1971	2.50	5.00	10.00

Albums

Number	Title (A Side/B Side)	Yr	VG	VG+	NM
ADELPHIA					
1030	Last Round	198?	2.50	5.00	10.00
ELEKTRA					
EKS-74026	The Moray Eels Eat the Holy Modal Rounders	1968	7.50	15.00	30.00
ESP-DISK'					
1068-S [S]	Indian War Whoop	1967	10.00	20.00	40.00
1068 [M]	Indian War Whoop	1967	10.00	20.00	40.00
FANTASY					
F-24711	Stampfel and Weber	1972	5.00	10.00	20.00
FOLKLORE					
FRLP-14031 [M]	The Holy Modal Rounders	1964	20.00	40.00	80.00
METROMEDIA					
MD-1039	Good Taste Is Timeless	1970	7.50	15.00	30.00
PRESTIGE					
PRLP-7410 [M]	The Holy Modal Rounders 2	1965	10.00	20.00	40.00
PRLP-7451 [M]	The Holy Modal Rounders	1966	10.00	20.00	40.00
—Reissue of Folklore LP					
PR-7720	The Holy Modal Rounders	1969	6.25	12.50	25.00
ROUNDER					
3004	Alleged in Their Own Time	198?	2.50	5.00	10.00

HOMBRES, THE

45s

Number	Title (A Side/B Side)	Yr	VG	VG+	NM
SUN					
1104	If This Ain't Loving You Baby/You Made Me What I Am	1969	2.50	5.00	10.00
VERVE FORECAST					
5058	Let It All Hang Out/Go Girl, Go	1967	3.75	7.50	15.00
5058	Let It Out (Let It All Hang Out)/Go Girl, Go	1967	3.00	6.00	12.00
5076	It's a Gas/Am I High	1967	2.50	5.00	10.00
5083	The Prodigal/Mau, Mau, Mau	1968	2.50	5.00	10.00
5093	Pumpkin Man/Take My Overwhelming Love	1968	2.50	5.00	10.00

Albums

Number	Title (A Side/B Side)	Yr	VG	VG+	NM
VERVE FORECAST					
FT-3036 [M]	Let It Out (Let It All Hang Out)	1967	7.50	15.00	30.00
FTS-3036 [S]	Let It Out (Let It All Hang Out)	1967	6.25	12.50	25.00
FTS-3068	The Hombres	1968	—	—	—
—Canceled					

HOMEMADE THEATER

45s

Number	Title (A Side/B Side)	Yr	VG	VG+	NM
A&M					
1776	Santa Jaws (Part 1)/Santa Jaws (Part 2)	1975	3.75	7.50	15.00
1887	C.B. Santa/Soup of the Day	1976	3.75	7.50	15.00

HOMER

45s

Number	Title (A Side/B Side)	Yr	VG	VG+	NM
UNITED					
123-6	I Never Cared for You/(B-side unknown)	1969	6.25	12.50	25.00
123-8	Texas Lights/(B-side unknown)	1970	5.00	10.00	20.00
123-10	Dandelion Wine/(B-side unknown)	1970	5.00	10.00	20.00

Albums

Number	Title (A Side/B Side)	Yr	VG	VG+	NM
UNITED					
HS-101	Grown in U.S.A.	1970	62.50	125.00	250.00

HONDELLS, THE

45s

Number	Title (A Side/B Side)	Yr	VG	VG+	NM
AMOS					
131	Follow the Bouncing Ball/The Legend of Frankie and Johnny	1969	3.00	6.00	12.00
150	Shine On Ruby Mountain/The Legend of Frankie and Johnny	1970	3.00	6.00	12.00
COLUMBIA					
44361	Just One More Chance/Yes to You	1967	5.00	10.00	20.00
44557	Another Woman/Atlanta Georgia Stray	1968	5.00	10.00	20.00
MERCURY					
72324	Little Honda/Hot Rod High	1964	5.00	10.00	20.00
72366	My Buddy Seat/You're Gonna Ride with Me	1964	5.00	10.00	20.00
72366 [PS]	My Buddy Seat/You're Gonna Ride with Me	1964	6.25	12.50	25.00
72405	Little Sidewalk Surfer Girl/Come On Baby (Pack It In)	1965	5.00	10.00	20.00
72443	Sea of Love/Do As I Say	1965	5.00	10.00	20.00
72479	You Meet the Nicest People on a Honda/Sea Cruise	1965	5.00	10.00	20.00
72479 [PS]	You Meet the Nicest People on a Honda/Sea Cruise	1965	7.50	15.00	30.00
72523	Endless Sleep/Follow Your Heart	1966	3.75	7.50	15.00
72563	Younger Girl/All American Girl	1966	3.75	7.50	15.00
72605	Country Love/Kissin' My Life Away	1966	3.75	7.50	15.00
72626	Cheryl's Goin' Home/Show Me	1966	3.75	7.50	15.00

Albums

Number	Title (A Side/B Side)	Yr	VG	VG+	NM
MERCURY					
MG-20940 [M]	Go Little Honda	1964	10.00	20.00	40.00
MG-20982 [M]	The Hondells	1965	12.50	25.00	50.00
SR-60940 [S]	Go Little Honda	1964	15.00	30.00	60.00
SR-60982 [S]	The Hondells	1965	20.00	40.00	80.00

HONEY BEES, THE (1)

45s

Number	Title (A Side/B Side)	Yr	VG	VG+	NM
FONTANA					
1505	You Turn Me On Boy/Some of Your Lovin'	1965	5.00	10.00	20.00
1939	One Wonderful Night/She Don't Deserve You	1964	5.00	10.00	20.00
GARRISON					
3005	Never in a Million Years/Let's Get Back Together	1966	62.50	125.00	250.00
VEE JAY					
611	One Girl, One Boy/No Guy	1964	6.25	12.50	25.00
WAND					
1141	Never in a Million Years/Let's Get Back Together	1966	3.00	6.00	12.00

HONEY BEES, THE (2)

45s

Number	Title (A Side/B Side)	Yr	VG	VG+	NM
IMPERIAL					
5400	Endless/Let's See What's Happening	1956	10.00	20.00	40.00
5436	Just to Live Again/What's to Become of Me	1957	10.00	20.00	40.00

HONEY CONE, THE

45s

Number	Title (A Side/B Side)	Yr	VG	VG+	NM
HOT WAX					
6901	While You're Out Looking for Sugar?/The Feeling's Gone	1969	—	3.00	6.00
6903	Girls It Ain't Easy/The Feeling's Gone	1969	—	3.00	6.00
7001	Take Me With You/Take My Love	1970	—	3.00	6.00
7005	When Will It End/Take Me With You	1970	—	3.00	6.00
7011	Want Ads/We Belong Together	1970	—	3.00	6.00
—Mostly white label					
7011	Want Ads/We Belong Together	1970	—	2.50	5.00
—Mostly orange label					
7106	Stick-Up/V.I.P.	1971	—	3.00	6.00
7110	One Monkey Don't Stop No Show Part I/One Monkey Don't Stop No Show Part II	1971	—	3.00	6.00
7113	The Day I Found Myself/When Will It End	1971	—	3.00	6.00
7205	Sittin' on a Time Bomb (Waitin' for the Hurt to Come)/It's Better to Have Loved and Lost	1972	—	3.00	6.00
7208	Innocent Till Proven Guilty/Don't Send Me an Invitation	1972	—	3.00	6.00
7212	Ace in the Hole/Ooo Baby Baby	1972	—	3.00	6.00
7301	If I Can't Fly/Woman Can't Live by Bread Alone	1973	—	3.00	6.00
9255	The Truth Will Come Out/Somebody Is Always Messing Up a Good Thing	1974	—	3.00	6.00

Number	Title (A Side/B Side)	Yr	VG	VG+	NM
Albums					
HOT WAX					
HA-701	Take Me With You	1970	3.00	6.00	12.00
HA-706	Sweet Replies	1971	3.00	6.00	12.00
HA-707	Soulful Tapestry	1971	3.00	6.00	12.00
HA-713	Love, Peace & Soul	1972	3.00	6.00	12.00

HONEYCOMBS, THE

Number	Title (A Side/B Side)	Yr	VG	VG+	NM
45s					
INTERPHON					
7707	Have I the Right?/Please Don't Pretend Again	1964	3.00	6.00	12.00
7713	I Can't Stop/I'll Cry Tomorrow	1964	2.50	5.00	10.00
7713 [PS]	I Can't Stop/I'll Cry Tomorrow	1964	6.25	12.50	25.00
7716	Color Slide/That's the Way	1965	2.50	5.00	10.00
7716 [PS]	Color Slide/That's the Way	1965	6.25	12.50	25.00
WARNER BROS.					
5634	I'll See You Tomorrow/Something Better Beginning	1965	2.50	5.00	10.00
5655	I Can't Get Through to You/That's the Way	1965	2.50	5.00	10.00
5803	How Will I Know/Who Is Sylvia	1966	2.50	5.00	10.00
Albums					
INTERPHON					
IN-88001 [M]	Here Are the Honeycombs	1964	10.00	20.00	40.00
IN-88001 [R]	Here Are the Honeycombs	1964	7.50	15.00	30.00
VEE JAY					
IN-88001 [M]	Here Are the Honeycombs	1964	12.50	25.00	50.00
IN-88001 [R]	Here Are the Honeycombs	1964	10.00	20.00	40.00

HONEYCONES, THE

Number	Title (A Side/B Side)	Yr	VG	VG+	NM
45s					
EMBER					
1033	Betty Moretti/Cool It Baby	1958	5.00	10.00	20.00
1036	Op/Vision of You	1958	6.25	12.50	25.00
1042	Gee Whiz/Rockin' in the Knees	1958	5.00	10.00	20.00
1049	Tell Me Baby/Your Face	1959	5.00	10.00	20.00

HONEYCUTT, GLENN

Number	Title (A Side/B Side)	Yr	VG	VG+	NM
45s					
FERNWOOD					
142	Campus Love/Tombigbee Queen	1964	25.00	50.00	100.00
SUN					
264	I'll Be Around/I'll Wait Forever	1957	7.50	15.00	30.00

HONEYS, THE

Number	Title (A Side/B Side)	Yr	VG	VG+	NM
45s					
CAPITOL					
2454	Goodnight My Love/Tonight You Belong to Me	1969	20.00	40.00	80.00
4952	Surfin' Down the Swanee River/Shoot the Curl	1963	37.50	75.00	150.00
4952 [PS]	Surfin' Down the Swanee River/Shoot the Curl	1963	200.00	400.00	800.00
5034	Hide Go Seek/Pray for Surf	1963	50.00	100.00	200.00
5093	The One You Can't Have/From Jimmy With Tears	1963	50.00	100.00	200.00
WARNER BROS.					
5430	He's a Doll/The Love of a Boy and Girl	1964	150.00	300.00	600.00
—Stock copy; red label					
5430 [DJ]	He's a Doll/The Love of a Boy and Girl	1964	50.00	100.00	200.00
—Promotional copy; white label					

HONEYTONES, THE

Number	Title (A Side/B Side)	Yr	VG	VG+	NM
45s					
BIG TOP					
3002	Don't Look Now, But/I Know, I Know	1958	5.00	10.00	20.00
MERCURY					
70557	Too Bad/Somewhere, Sometime, Someday	1955	6.25	12.50	25.00
WING					
90013	False Alarm/Honeybun Cha Cha	1955	7.50	15.00	30.00

HONOR SOCIETY, THE

See THE HAPPENINGS.

HOOK, THE

Number	Title (A Side/B Side)	Yr	VG	VG+	NM
45s					
UNI					
55057	Son of Fantasy/Plug Your Head In	1968	2.50	5.00	10.00
55077	Love Theme in E Major/Homes	1968	2.50	5.00	10.00
55149	In the Beginning/Show You the Way	1969	2.50	5.00	10.00
Albums					
UNI					
73023	The Hook Will Grab You	1968	6.25	12.50	25.00
73038	Hooked	1969	6.25	12.50	25.00

HOOKER, JOHN LEE

Number	Title (A Side/B Side)	Yr	VG	VG+	NM
45s					
ABC					
11298	Doin' the Shout/Kick Hit 4 Hit Kix U	1971	—	3.00	6.00
11320	Never Get Out of These Blues Alive/Boogie with the Hook	1972	—	3.00	6.00
BATTLE					
45901	No More Doggin'/I Need Some Money	1962	2.50	5.00	10.00
BLUESWAY					
61010	Motor City Is Burning/Want Ad Blues	1967	2.00	4.00	8.00
61014	Mr. Lucky/Cry Before I Go	1968	—	3.00	6.00
61017	Back Biters and Syndicators/Think Twice Before You Go	1968	—	3.00	6.00
61023	I Don't Wanna Go to Vietnam/Simply the Truth	1969	—	3.00	6.00
CHANCE					
1108	Miss Lorraine/Talkin' Boogie	1951	750.00	1500.	3000.
—As "John Lee Booker"					
1110	Graveyard Blues/I Love to Boogie	1952	750.00	1500.	3000.
—As "John Lee Booker"					
1122	609 Boogie/Road Trouble	1952	500.00	1000.	2000.
—As "John L. Booker"					
CHART					
609	Going South/Wobbling Baby	1955	12.50	25.00	50.00
CHESS					
1505	High Priced Woman/Union Station Blues	1952	300.00	600.00	1200.
1513	Sugar Mama/Walkin' the Boogie	1952	250.00	500.00	1000.
1562	It's My Own Fault/Women and Money	1954	62.50	125.00	250.00
1965	Let's Go Out Tonight/In the Mood	1966	2.50	5.00	10.00
DELUXE					
6004	Blue Monday/Lovin' Guitar Man	1953	125.00	250.00	500.00
—As "John Lee Booker"					
6009	I Came to See You Baby/I'm a Boogie Man	1953	200.00	400.00	800.00
—As "Johnny Lee"					
6032	Stuttering Blues/Pouring Down Rain	1954	100.00	200.00	400.00
—As "John Lee Booker"					
6046	My Baby Don't Love Me/Real, Real Gone	1954	100.00	200.00	400.00
—As "John Lee Booker"					
ELMOR					
303	Blues for Christmas/Big Fine Woman	1959	5.00	10.00	20.00
FEDERAL					
12377	Late Last Night/Don't You Remember Me	1960	3.75	7.50	15.00
FORTUNE					
853	Cry Baby/Love You Baby	1960	5.00	10.00	20.00
855	Crazy About That Walk/We're All God's Chillun	1960	5.00	10.00	20.00
GALAXY					
716	I Lost My Job/You Gotta Shake It Up and Go	1963	2.50	5.00	10.00
HI-Q					
5018	Blues for Christmas/Big Fine Woman	1960	5.00	10.00	20.00
IMPULSE					
242	Honey/Bottle Up and Go	1966	2.50	5.00	10.00
JEWEL					
824	I Feel Good (Part 1)/I Feel Good (Part 2)	1971	—	2.50	5.00
852	Stand By (Part 1)/Stand By (Part 2)	1977	—	2.00	4.00
JVB					
30	Boogie Rambler/No More Doggin'	1953	375.00	750.00	1500.
KING					
4504	Moaning Blues/Stomp Boogie	1952	250.00	500.00	1000.
—As "John Lee Cooker"					
6298	Don't Go Baby/Moanin' and Stompin' Blues	1970	—	3.00	6.00
LAUREN					
361	Ballad to Abraham Lincoln (He Got Assassinated)/Mojo Hand (Louisiana Voodoo)	1961	5.00	10.00	20.00
362	I Lost My Job/You Gotta Shake It Up and Go	1961	5.00	10.00	20.00
MODERN					
835	How Can You Do It/I'm in the Mood	1951	100.00	200.00	400.00
847	Anybody Seen My Baby? (Johnny Says Come Back)/Turn Over a New Leaf	1951	75.00	150.00	300.00
852	Ground Hog Blues/Louise	1951	30.00	60.00	120.00
862	Cold Chills All Over Me/Rock Me, Mama	1952	20.00	40.00	80.00
876	It Hurts Me So/I Got Eyes for You	1952	20.00	40.00	80.00
—With Little Eddie Kirkland					
886	Key to the Highway/Bluebird Blues	1952	20.00	40.00	80.00
893	New Boogie Chillen/I Tried	1952	20.00	40.00	80.00
897	It's Been a Long Time Baby/Rock House Boogie	1952	20.00	40.00	80.00
901	Ride Till I Die/It's Stormin' and Rainin'	1953	15.00	30.00	60.00
908	Please Take Me Back/Love Money Can't Buy	1953	15.00	30.00	60.00
916	Too Much Boogie/Need Somebody	1953	15.00	30.00	60.00
923	Gotta Boogie/Down Child	1953	15.00	30.00	60.00
931	Jump Me/I Wonder Little Darling	1954	15.00	30.00	60.00
935	I Tried Hard/Let's Talk It Over	1954	12.50	25.00	50.00
942	Cool Little Car/Bad Boy	1954	12.50	25.00	50.00
948	Half a Stranger/Shake, Holler and Run	1954	12.50	25.00	50.00
958	Taxi Driver/You Receive Me	1955	12.50	25.00	50.00
966	Hug and Squeeze/The Syndicator	1955	12.50	25.00	50.00
978	Looking for a Woman/I'm Ready	1955	15.00	30.00	60.00
POINTBLANK					
S7-19518	Dimples/Don't Look Back	1997	—	2.00	4.00
38664	Burnin' Hell/Boogie at Russian Hill	1999	—	—	3.00
RIVERSIDE					
438	I Need Some Money/No More Diggin'	1960	6.25	12.50	25.00
ROCKIN'					
524	Blue Monday/Lovin' Guitar Man	1953	250.00	500.00	1000.
—As "John Lee Booker"					
525	Stuttering Blues/Pouring Down Rain	1953	250.00	500.00	1000.
—As "John Lee Booker"					
SPECIALTY					
528	Everybody's Blues/I'm Mad	1954	10.00	20.00	40.00
STAX					
0053	Slow and Easy/Grinder Man	1969	—	3.00	6.00
VEE JAY					
164	Mambo Chillen/Time Is Marching	1955	7.50	15.00	30.00
188	Every Night/Trouble Blues	1956	7.50	15.00	30.00
205	Dimples/Baby Lee	1956	7.50	15.00	30.00
233	The Road Is So Rough/I'm So Worried Baby	1957	6.25	12.50	25.00
245	I'm So Excited/I See You When You're Weak	1957	6.25	12.50	25.00
255	Little Wheel/Rosie Mae	1957	6.25	12.50	25.00
265	You Can Lead Me, Baby/Unfriendly Baby	1958	6.25	12.50	25.00
293	I Love You Honey/You've Taken My Woman	1958	6.25	12.50	25.00
308	Maudie/I'm In the Mood	1959	6.25	12.50	25.00
319	Tennessee Blues/Boogie Chillun	1959	6.25	12.50	25.00
331	Hobo Blues/Crawlin' King Snake	1959	6.25	12.50	25.00
349	No Shoes/Solid Sender	1960	6.25	12.50	25.00
366	Dusty Road/Tupelo	1960	6.25	12.50	25.00
379	I'm Mad Again/I'm Going Upstairs	1961	6.25	12.50	25.00
397	Want Ad Blues/Take Me As I Am	1961	6.25	12.50	25.00
438	Boom Boom/Drug Store Woman	1962	6.25	12.50	25.00
453	She's Mine/A New Leaf	1962	6.25	12.50	25.00
493	Take a Look at Yourself/I Love Her	1963	12.50	25.00	50.00
493	Take a Look at Yourself/Frisco Blues	1963	5.00	10.00	20.00
538	I'm Leaving/Birmingham Blues	1963	3.75	7.50	15.00
575	Send Me Your Pillow/Don't Look Back	1964	3.75	7.50	15.00
670	Big Legs, Tight Skirt/Your Baby Ain't Sweet Like Mine	1965	3.00	6.00	12.00
708	It Serves Me Right/Flowers on the Hour	1966	2.50	5.00	10.00

Number	Title (A Side/B Side)	Yr	VG	VG+	NM
Albums					
ABC					
S-720 [(2)]	Endless Boogie	1971	5.00	10.00	20.00
X-736	Never Get Out of These Blues Alive	1972	5.00	10.00	20.00
XQ-736 [Q]	Never Get Out of These Blues Alive	1974	6.25	12.50	25.00
X-761	Live at Soledad Prison	1972	5.00	10.00	20.00
XQ-761 [Q]	Live at Soledad Prison	1974	6.25	12.50	25.00
X-768	Born in Mississippi, Raised Up in Tennessee	1973	5.00	10.00	20.00
XQ-768 [Q]	Born in Mississippi, Raised Up in Tennessee	1974	6.25	12.50	25.00
X-838	Free Beer and Chicken	1974	3.75	7.50	15.00
XQ-838 [Q]	Free Beer and Chicken	1974	6.25	12.50	25.00
ARCHIVE OF FOLK AND JAZZ					
222	John Lee Hooker	1968	3.00	6.00	12.00
347	Hooked On Blues	1980	3.00	6.00	12.00
ATCO					
33-151 [M]	Don't Turn Me From Your Door	1963	25.00	50.00	100.00
SD 33-151 [R]	Don't Turn Me From Your Door	1967	12.50	25.00	50.00
ATLANTIC					
SD 7228	Detroit Special	1972	5.00	10.00	20.00
BATTLE					
BLP-6113 [M]	John Lee Hooker	196?	37.50	75.00	150.00
BLP-6114 [M]	How Long Blues	196?	37.50	75.00	150.00
BLUESWAY					
BL-6002 [M]	Live at Café A-Go-Go	1967	6.25	12.50	25.00
BLS-6002 [S]	Live at Café A-Go-Go	1967	5.00	10.00	20.00
BL-6012 [M]	Urban Blues	1967	6.25	12.50	25.00
BLS-6012 [S]	Urban Blues	1967	5.00	10.00	20.00
BLS-6023	Simply the Truth	1968	5.00	10.00	20.00
BLS-6038	If You Miss 'Em	1969	5.00	10.00	20.00
BLQ-6052 [Q]	Live at Kabuki-Wuki	1974	6.25	12.50	25.00
BLS-6052	Live at Kabuki-Wuki	1973	3.75	7.50	15.00
BUDDAH					
BDS-4002	The Very Best of John Lee Hooker	1970	3.75	7.50	15.00
BDS-7506	Big Band Blues	1970	3.75	7.50	15.00
CHAMELEON					
D1-74794	The Hook	1989	2.50	5.00	10.00
D1-74808	The Healer	1989	2.50	5.00	10.00
CHESS					
LP-1438 [M]	House of the Blues	1960	75.00	150.00	300.00
—Black label					
LP-1438 [M]	House of the Blues	1966	12.50	25.00	50.00
—Blue and white label					
LP-1454 [M]	John Lee Hooker Plays and Sings the Blues	1961	75.00	150.00	300.00
—Black label					
LP-1454 [M]	John Lee Hooker Plays and Sings the Blues	1966	12.50	25.00	50.00
—Blue and white label					
LP-1508 [M]	Real Folk Blues	1966	12.50	25.00	50.00
LPS-1508 [R]	Real Folk Blues	1966	7.50	15.00	30.00
CH-9199	John Lee Hooker Plays and Sings the Blues	1986	2.00	4.00	8.00
—Reissue					
CH-9258	House of the Blues	1987	2.00	4.00	8.00
CH-9271	The Real Folk Blues	1988	2.00	4.00	8.00
60011 [(2)]	Mad Man Blues	1973	5.00	10.00	20.00
CH2-92507 [(2)]	Mad Man Blues	198?	3.00	6.00	12.00
COLLECTABLES					
COL-5151	Golden Classics	198?	3.00	6.00	12.00
CROWN					
CLP-5157 [M]	The Blues	1960	25.00	50.00	100.00
—Black label with silver "Crown"					
CLP-5157 [M]	The Blues	1962	7.50	15.00	30.00
—Gray label					
CLP-5157 [M]	The Blues	196?	3.00	6.00	12.00
—Black label with multi-color "Crown"					
CLP-5232 [M]	John Lee Hooker Sings the Blues	1962	25.00	50.00	100.00
—Black label with silver "Crown"					
CLP-5232 [M]	John Lee Hooker Sings the Blues	1962	7.50	15.00	30.00
—Gray label					
CLP-5232 [M]	John Lee Hooker Sings the Blues	196?	3.00	6.00	12.00
—Black label with multi-color "Crown"					
CLP-5295 [M]	Folk Blues	1962	7.50	15.00	30.00
—Gray label					
CLP-5295 [M]	Folk Blues	1962	3.00	6.00	12.00
—Black label with multi-color "Crown"					
CLP-5353 [M]	The Great John Lee Hooker	1963	7.50	15.00	30.00
—Gray label					
CLP-5353 [M]	The Great John Lee Hooker	1963	3.00	6.00	12.00
—Black label with multi-color "Crown"					
EXODUS					
325 [M]	Is He the World's Greatest Blues Singer?	1966	6.25	12.50	25.00
FANTASY					
24706 [(2)]	Boogie Chillun	1972	3.75	7.50	15.00
24722 [(2)]	Black Snake	197?	3.75	7.50	15.00
GALAXY					
8201 [M]	I'm John Lee Hooker	1962	62.50	125.00	250.00
8205 [M]	Live at Sugar Hill	196?	62.50	125.00	250.00
GNP CRESCENDO					
GNPS-10007 [(2)]	The Best of John Lee Hooker	1974	3.75	7.50	15.00
GREENE BOTTLE					
3130 [(2)]	Johnny Lee	1972	3.75	7.50	15.00
IMPULSE!					
A-9103 [M]	It Serves You Right to Suffer	1966	7.50	15.00	30.00
AS-9103 [S]	It Serves You Right to Suffer	1966	10.00	20.00	40.00
JEWEL					
5005	I Feel Good	1971	3.75	7.50	15.00
KING					
727 [M]	John Lee Hooker Sings the Blues	1960	125.00	250.00	500.00
KLP-727	John Lee Hooker Sings the Blues	1988	2.00	4.00	8.00
—Reissue of earlier 727					
KS-1085	Moanin' and Stompin' Blues	1970	6.25	12.50	25.00
LABOR					
4	Alone	1982	2.50	5.00	10.00
MUSE					
5205	Sittin' Here Thinkin'	1980	3.00	6.00	12.00
PAUSA					
PR-7197	Jealous	1986	2.50	5.00	10.00
RIVERSIDE					
RLP 12-321 [M]	That's My Story	1960	25.00	50.00	100.00
RLP 12-838 [M]	The Country Blues of John Lee Hooker	1959	25.00	50.00	100.00
SPECIALTY					
SPS-2125	Alone	1970	7.50	15.00	30.00
SPS-2127	Going Down Highway 51	1970	7.50	15.00	30.00
STAX					
STS-2013	That's Where It's At	1970	3.75	7.50	15.00
STX-4134	That's Where It's At	1979	2.50	5.00	10.00
—Reissue of 2013					
TOMATO					
7009 [(2)]	The Cream	1978	3.75	7.50	15.00
TRADITION					
2089	Real Blues	1970	3.75	7.50	15.00
UNITED ARTISTS					
UA-LA127-J [(3)]	John Lee Hooker's Detroit	1974	6.25	12.50	25.00
UAS-5512	Coast to Coast Blues Band	1971	3.75	7.50	15.00
VEE JAY					
LP-1007 [M]	I'm John Lee Hooker	1959	75.00	150.00	300.00
—Maroon label					
LP-1007 [M]	I'm John Lee Hooker	1960	20.00	40.00	80.00
—Black label with colorband					
VJLP-1007	I'm John Lee Hooker	1986	2.00	4.00	8.00
—Reissue of original on flimsier vinyl					
LP-1023 [M]	Travelin'	1960	20.00	40.00	80.00
LP-1033 [M]	The Folk Lore of John Lee Hooker	1961	12.50	25.00	50.00
SR-1033 [S]	The Folk Lore of John Lee Hooker	1961	20.00	40.00	80.00
LP-1043 [M]	Burnin'	1962	12.50	25.00	50.00
SR-1043 [S]	Burnin'	1962	37.50	75.00	150.00
LP-1049 [M]	The Best of John Lee Hooker	1962	12.50	25.00	50.00
SR-1049 [P]	The Best of John Lee Hooker	1962	20.00	40.00	80.00
VJLP-1049	The Best of John Lee Hooker	1986	2.00	4.00	8.00
—Reissue of original on flimsier vinyl					
LP-1058 [M]	The Big Soul of John Lee Hooker	1963	12.50	25.00	50.00
SR-1058 [S]	The Big Soul of John Lee Hooker	1963	37.50	75.00	150.00
VJLP-1058	The Big Soul of John Lee Hooker	1986	2.00	4.00	8.00
—Reissue of original on flimsier vinyl					
LP-1066 [M]	John Lee Hooker On Campus	1963	12.50	25.00	50.00
SR-1066 [S]	John Lee Hooker On Campus	1963	37.50	75.00	150.00
LP-1078 [M]	John Lee Hooker at Newport	1964	12.50	25.00	50.00
SR-1078 [S]	John Lee Hooker at Newport	1964	37.50	751.00	150.00
VJLP-1078	John Lee Hooker at Newport	1986	2.00	4.00	8.00
—Reissue of original on flimsier vinyl					
DY-7301	John Lee Hooker In Person	198?	2.00	4.00	8.00
LP-8502 [M]	Is He the World's Greatest Folk/Blues Singer	1965	10.00	20.00	40.00
VJLP-8502	Is He the World's Greatest Folk/Blues Singer	1986	2.00	4.00	8.00
—Reissue of original on flimsier vinyl					
VERVE FOLKWAYS					
FT-3003 [M]	John Lee Hooker and Seven Nights	1965	6.25	12.50	25.00
FTS-3003 [S]	John Lee Hooker and Seven Nights	1965	10.00	20.00	40.00
WAND					
WDS-689	On the Waterfront	1972	3.75	7.50	15.00

HOOKER, JOHN LEE, AND CANNED HEAT

Also see each artist's individual listings.

Number	Title (A Side/B Side)	Yr	VG	VG+	NM
45s					
UNITED ARTISTS					
50779	Whiskey and Wimmen/Let's Make It	1971	—	2.50	5.00
Albums					
LIBERTY					
35002	Hooker 'n' Heat	1971	5.00	10.00	20.00
RHINO					
RNLP-801	Recorded Live at the Fox Venice Theatre	1985	3.00	6.00	12.00
RNDA-71105	Infinite Boogie	1987	3.00	6.00	12.00

HOOTCH

Number	Title (A Side/B Side)	Yr	VG	VG+	NM
Albums					
PROGRESS					
PRS-4844	Hootch	1974	150.00	300.00	600.00

HOPE, EDDIE

Number	Title (A Side/B Side)	Yr	VG	VG+	NM
45s					
MARLIN					
804	A Fool No More/Lost Child	1956	50.00	100.00	200.00

HOPE, LYNN

Number	Title (A Side/B Side)	Yr	VG	VG+	NM
45s					
ALADDIN					
3095	Blue Moon/Blow, Lynn, Blow	1951	10.00	20.00	40.00
3103	Too Young/Free and Easy	1951	10.00	20.00	40.00
3109	She's Funny That Way/Eleven Till Two	1951	10.00	20.00	40.00
3134	Driftin'/Sentimental Journey	1952	7.50	15.00	30.00
3155	Move It/Don't Worry 'Bout Me	1952	7.50	15.00	30.00
3165	September Song/Blues for Anna Bocoa	1953	6.25	12.50	25.00
3178	Broken Heart/Morocco	1953	6.25	12.50	25.00
3185	Jet/Tenderly	1953	6.25	12.50	25.00
3208	Swing Train/Rose Room	1953	6.25	12.50	25.00
3229	Brazil/C. Jam Blues	1954	6.25	12.50	25.00
3297	All of Me/Summertime	1955	6.25	12.50	25.00
3322	Cherry/Blues in F	1956	6.25	12.50	25.00
KING					
5336	Tenderly/Full Moon	1960	3.00	6.00	12.00
5352	Body and Soul/Sands of Sahara	1960	3.00	6.00	12.00
5378	A Ghost of a Chance/Little Landslide	1960	3.00	6.00	12.00
5431	Shockin'/Blue and Sentimental	1960	3.00	6.00	12.00

HOPEFUL, THE

45s

Number	Title (A Side/B Side)	Yr	VG	VG+	NM
MERCURY					
72637	7 O'Clock News (Silent Night)/6 O'Clock News (America The Beautiful)	1966	3.00	6.00	12.00

HOPKIN, MARY

45s

Number	Title (A Side/B Side)	Yr	VG	VG+	NM
APPLE					
1801	Those Were the Days/Turn, Turn, Turn	1968	2.50	5.00	10.00
1806	Goodbye/Sparrow	1969	2.00	4.00	8.00
1806 [PS]	Goodbye/Sparrow	1969	3.00	6.00	12.00
1816	Temma Harbour/Lantano Dagli Occhi	1970	2.00	4.00	8.00
1816 [PS]	Temma Harbour/Lantano Dagli Occhi	1970	3.00	6.00	12.00
1823	Que Sera, Sera (Whatever Will Be, Will Be)/Fields of St. Etienne	1970	2.00	4.00	8.00
1825	Think About Your Children/Heritage	1970	2.00	4.00	8.00
1825	Think About Your Children/Heritage	1970	3.00	6.00	12.00
—With star on A-side label					
1825 [PS]	Think About Your Children/Heritage	1970	3.00	6.00	12.00
1843	Water, Paper and Clay/Streets of London	1972	2.00	4.00	8.00
1843	Water, Paper and Clay/Streets of London	1972	3.00	6.00	12.00
—With star on A-side label					
1855	Knock Knock Who's There/International	1972	2.00	4.00	8.00
APPLE/AMERICOM					
1801P/M-238	Those Were the Days/Turn, Turn, Turn	1969	150.00	300.00	600.00
—Four-inch flexi-disc sold from vending machines					
RCA VICTOR					
PB-10694	Tell Me Now/If You Love Me	1976	—	2.00	4.00

Albums

Number	Title	Yr	VG	VG+	NM
APPLE					
SW-3351	Post Card	1969	6.25	12.50	25.00
SW-5-3351	Post Card	1969	7.50	15.00	30.00
—Capitol Record Club edition					
SMAS-3381	Earth Song/Ocean Song	1970	6.25	12.50	25.00
SW-3395	Those Were the Days	1972	10.00	20.00	40.00

HOPKINS, LIGHTNIN'

45s

Number	Title (A Side/B Side)	Yr	VG	VG+	NM
ACE					
516	Bad Boogie/Wonder What Is Wrong with Me	1956	10.00	20.00	40.00
ALADDIN					
3063	Shotgun Blues/Rolling Blues	1950	175.00	350.00	700.00
3077	Moonrise Blues/Honey, Honey Blues	1951	50.00	100.00	200.00
3096	Miss Me Blues/Abilene	1951	50.00	100.00	200.00
3117	You Are Not Going to Worry About My Life Anymore/Daddy Will Be Home Someday	1951	50.00	100.00	200.00
3262	So Long/My California	1954	25.00	50.00	100.00
ARHOOLIE					
508	My Woman/Lousiana Blues	1965	3.00	6.00	12.00
513	Come On Baby/Money Taker	1965	3.00	6.00	12.00
BLUESVILLE					
813	So Sorry to Leave You/Got to Move Your Baby	1960	5.00	10.00	20.00
814	Death Bells/Sail On	1961	5.00	10.00	20.00
817	Back to New Orleans/Hard to Love a Woman	1961	5.00	10.00	20.00
820	Happy Blues for John Glenn (Part 1)/Happy Blues for John Glenn (Part 2)	1962	5.00	10.00	20.00
821	Last Night Blues/Walkin' Blues	1962	5.00	10.00	20.00
822	Sinner's Prayer/Angel Child	1962	5.00	10.00	20.00
823	The Business You're Doing/Wake Up Old Lady	1963	5.00	10.00	20.00
824	Going Away/Better Stop Her	1963	5.00	10.00	20.00
825	Katie Mae/My Babe	1963	5.00	10.00	20.00
CHART					
636	Walkin' the Streets/Mussy Haired Woman	1957	7.50	15.00	30.00
DART					
123	Grievance Blues/Unsuccessful Blues	1959	5.00	10.00	20.00
152	Mary Lou/Wait to Go Home	1960	5.00	10.00	20.00
DECCA					
28841	The War Is Over/Policy Game	1953	20.00	40.00	80.00
48306	Merry Christmas/Happy New Year	1953	20.00	40.00	80.00
48312	Highway Blues/Cemetery Blues	1954	20.00	40.00	80.00
48321	I'm Wild About You Baby/Bad Things on My Mind	1954	25.00	50.00	100.00
FIRE					
1034	Mojo Hand/Glory Be	1961	5.00	10.00	20.00
HARLEM					
2321	Contrary Mary/I'm Begging You	1954	50.00	100.00	200.00
2324	Mad Man's Boogie/Nobody Cares for Me	1954	50.00	100.00	200.00
2331	Fast Life/The Jackstropper	1955	50.00	100.00	200.00
2336	Good Old Woman/Untrue	1955	50.00	100.00	200.00
HERALD					
425	Lightnin's Boogie/Don't Think 'Cause You're Pretty	1954	7.50	15.00	30.00
428	Lightnin's Special/Life Is Used to Live	1954	7.50	15.00	30.00
436	Movin' On Out Boogie/Sick Feelin' Blues	1954	7.50	15.00	30.00
443	Nothin' But the Blues/Early Morning Boogie	1954	7.50	15.00	30.00
449	Evil Hearted Woman/They Wonder Who I Am	1955	7.50	15.00	30.00
456	My Baby's Gone/Don't Need No Job	1955	6.25	12.50	25.00
465	I Had a Gal Named Sal/Blues for My Cookie	1955	6.25	12.50	25.00
471	Hopkins Sky Hop/Lonesome in Your Home	1956	6.25	12.50	25.00
476	Grandma's Boogie/I Love You Baby	1956	6.25	12.50	25.00
483	Finally Met My Baby/That's Alright Baby	1956	6.25	12.50	25.00
490	Shine On Moon/Sitting and Thinking	1956	6.25	12.50	25.00
497	Remember Me/Please Don't Go Baby	1957	6.25	12.50	25.00
504	Boogie Woogie Dance/The Blues Is a Mighty Bad Feeling	1957	5.00	10.00	20.00
520	Little Kewpie Doll/Lightnin' Don't Feel Well	1958	5.00	10.00	20.00
531	Hear Me Talkin'/Lightnin's Stomp	1958	5.00	10.00	20.00
542	Let's Move/I'm Achin'	1959	5.00	10.00	20.00
547	Flash Lightnin'/Gonna Change My Ways	1960	5.00	10.00	20.00
IMPERIAL					
5834	Feel So Bad/Shotgun	1962	3.75	7.50	15.00
5852	Picture on the Wall/Lightnin's Boogie	1962	3.75	7.50	15.00
IVORY					
91272	Got Me a Lousiana Woman/War Is Starting Again	196?	3.75	7.50	15.00
JAX					
315	No Good Woman/Been a Bad Man	1953	75.00	150.00	300.00
318	Automobile/Organ Blues	1953	75.00	150.00	300.00
321	Contrary Mary/I'm Begging You	1953	75.00	150.00	300.00
635	Coffee Blues/New Short Haired Woman	1954	62.50	125.00	250.00
642	You Caused My Heart to Weep/Tap Dance Boogie	1954	62.50	125.00	250.00
JEWEL					
788	Back Door Friends/Fishing Clothes	1968	—	3.00	6.00
796	Wig Wearin' Woman/Move On Out, Part 2	1968	—	3.00	6.00
803	Lovin' Arms/Ride in Your New Auto	1969	—	3.00	6.00
807	Play with Your Poodle/Breakfast Time	1970	—	3.00	6.00
809	I'm Comin' Home/You're Too Fast	1970	—	3.00	6.00
816	My Charlie (Part 1)/My Charlie (Part 2)	1970	—	3.00	6.00
819	Rock Me Mama/Love Me This Morning	1971	—	3.00	6.00
825	Uncle Sam the Hip Hit Record Man/Found My Baby Crying	1971	—	3.00	6.00
LIGHTNING					
104	Unsuccessful Blues/(B-side unknown)	1955	125.00	250.00	500.00
MERCURY					
8274	Sad News from Korea/Let Me Fly Your Kite	1952	25.00	50.00	100.00
8293	Gone with the Wind/She's Almost Dead	1952	25.00	50.00	100.00
70081	Ain't It a Shame/Crazy About My Baby	1953	25.00	50.00	100.00
70191	My Mama Told Me/What's the Matter Now	1953	25.00	50.00	100.00
PRESTIGE					
326	I Like to Boogie/Let's Go Sit on the Lawn	1964	2.50	5.00	10.00
343	Mojo Hand/Automobile Blues	1964	2.50	5.00	10.00
374	T Model Blues/You Cook Alright	1965	2.50	5.00	10.00
391	Sinner's Prayer/Got to Move Your Baby	1965	2.50	5.00	10.00
405	I'm Gonna Build Me a Heaven (Part 1)/I'm Gonna Build Me a Heaven (Part 2)	1966	2.50	5.00	10.00
452	Mama Blues/Pneumonia Blues	1968	2.00	4.00	8.00
RPM					
337	Beggin' You to Stay/Bad Luck and Trouble	1951	150.00	300.00	600.00
346	Lonesome Dog Blues/Jake Head	1952	200.00	400.00	800.00
351	Don't Keep My Baby Long/Last Affair	1952	100.00	200.00	400.00
359	Needed Time/One Kind Favor	1952	100.00	200.00	400.00
378	Another Fool in Town/Candy Kitchen	1953	75.00	150.00	300.00
388	Black Cat/Mistreated Blues	1953	75.00	150.00	300.00
398	Santa Fe Blues/Some Day Baby	1954	50.00	100.00	200.00
SHAD					
5011	Hello Central/Mad As I Can Be	1959	3.75	7.50	15.00
SITTIN' IN WITH					
621	Give Me Central 209/New York Boogie	1951	125.00	250.00	500.00
621	Hello Central/New York Boogie	1952	100.00	200.00	400.00
635	Coffee Blues/New Short Haired Woman	1952	125.00	250.00	500.00
642	You Caused My Heart to Weep/Tap Dance Boogie	1952	125.00	250.00	500.00
644	Jail House Blues/"T" Model Blues	1952	125.00	250.00	500.00
647	Bald Headed Woman/Dirty House	1952	125.00	250.00	500.00
649	New Worried Life Blues/One Kind of Favor	1952	—	—	—
—Unreleased on 45 rpm?					
652	Papa Bones Boogie/Everything Happens to Me	1953	125.00	250.00	500.00
658	Freight Train Blues (When I Started Hoboing)/Broken Hearted Blues	1953	125.00	250.00	500.00
660	Mad Blues/Why	1953	125.00	250.00	500.00
661	Gone Again/Down to the River	1953	125.00	250.00	500.00
SPHERE SOUND					
710	Santa/Black Mare Trot	196?	2.50	5.00	10.00
TNT					
8002	Lightnin' Jump/Late in the Evening	1954	175.00	350.00	700.00
8003	Moanin' Blues/Leavin' Blues	1954	175.00	350.00	700.00
VAULT					
965	Easy on Your Heels/No Education	1970	—	3.00	6.00

Albums

Number	Title	Yr	VG	VG+	NM
ANALOGUE PRODUCTIONS					
AAPB-014	Goin' Away	199?	10.00	20.00	40.00
—Audiophile reissue					
ARCHIVE OF FOLK AND JAZZ					
241	Lightnin' Hopkins	1969	3.75	7.50	15.00
313	Lightnin' Hopkins, Vol. 2	197?	3.75	7.50	15.00
342	Autobiography in Blues	1979	3.00	6.00	12.00
ARHOOLIE					
1011	Lightnin' Hopkins and His Guitar	196?	5.00	10.00	20.00
1022	Lightnin' Hopkins, His Brother and Barbara Dane	196?	5.00	10.00	20.00
1030	Blues Festival	196?	3.75	7.50	15.00
1034	Texas Blues Man	1968	3.75	7.50	15.00
1063	Lightnin' Hopkins in Berkeley	1969	3.75	7.50	15.00
1087	Poor Lightnin'	1970	3.75	7.50	15.00
2007	Early Recordings	197?	3.75	7.50	15.00
2010	Early Recordings Volume 2	197?	3.75	7.50	15.00
BARNABY					
Z 30247	Lightnin' Hopkins in New York	1970	3.75	7.50	15.00
BLUES CLASSICS					
30	Historic Recordings 1952-1953	1986	3.00	6.00	12.00
BLUESVILLE					
BVLP-1019 [M]	Lightnin'	1961	25.00	50.00	100.00
—Blue label, silver print					
BVLP-1019 [M]	Lightnin'	1964	7.50	15.00	30.00
—Blue label, trident logo on right					
BVLP-1029 [M]	Last Night Blues	1961	25.00	50.00	100.00
—Blue label, silver print					
BVLP-1045 [M]	Blues in My Bottle	1962	25.00	50.00	100.00
—Blue label, silver print					
BVLP-1045 [M]	Blues in My Bottle	1964	7.50	15.00	30.00
—Blue label, trident logo on right					
BVLP-1057 [M]	Walkin' This Street	1962	25.00	50.00	100.00
—Blue label, silver print					
BVLP-1057 [M]	Walkin' This Street	1964	7.50	15.00	30.00
—Blue label, trident logo on right					

Number	Title (A Side/B Side)	Yr	VG	VG+	NM
BVLP-1061 [M]	Lightnin' & Co.	1963	25.00	50.00	100.00
—Blue label, silver print					
BVLP-1061 [M]	Lightnin' & Co.	1964	7.50	15.00	30.00
—Blue label, trident logo on right					
BVLP-1070 [M]	Smokes Like Lightnin'	1963	25.00	50.00	100.00
—Blue label, silver print					
BVLP-1070 [M]	Smokes Like Lightnin'	1964	7.50	15.00	30.00
—Blue label, trident logo on right					
BVLP-1073 [M]	Goin' Away	1963	25.00	50.00	100.00
—Blue label, silver print					
BVLP-1073 [M]	Goin' Away	1964	7.50	15.00	30.00
—Blue label, trident logo on right					
BVLP-1081 [M]	Gotta Move Your Baby	1964	7.50	15.00	30.00
—Blue label, trident logo on right					
BVLP-1084 [M]	Lightnin' Hopkins' Greatest Hits	1964	10.00	20.00	40.00
BVLP-1086 [M]	Down Home Blues	1964	6.25	12.50	25.00
BLUESWAY					
S-6039	If You Miss 'Im	1969	5.00	10.00	20.00
BULLDOG					
1010	The Texas Bluesman	1965	3.75	7.50	15.00
CANDID					
CM-8010 [M]	Lightnin' in New York	1961	30.00	60.00	120.00
CS-9010 [S]	Lightnin' in New York	1961	37.50	75.00	150.00
COLLECTABLES					
COL-5111	Golden Classics — Mojo Hand	198?	2.50	5.00	10.00
COL-5121	The Herald Recordings/1954	198?	2.50	5.00	10.00
COL-5143	Golden Classics, Part 1: Drinkin' the Blues	198?	2.50	5.00	10.00
COL-5144	Golden Classics, Part 2: Prison Blues	198?	2.50	5.00	10.00
COL-5145	Golden Classics, Part 3: Mama and Papa Hopkins	198?	2.50	5.00	10.00
COL-5146	Golden Classics, Part 4: Nothin' But the Blues	198?	2.50	5.00	10.00
COL-5203	The Lost Texas Tapes, Vol. 1	198?	2.50	5.00	10.00
COL-5204	The Lost Texas Tapes, Vol. 2	198?	2.50	5.00	10.00
COL-5205	The Lost Texas Tapes, Vol. 3	198?	2.50	5.00	10.00
COL-5206	The Lost Texas Tapes, Vol. 4	198?	2.50	5.00	10.00
COL-5207	The Lost Texas Tapes, Vol. 5	198?	2.50	5.00	10.00
CROWN					
CLP-5224 [M]	Lightnin' Hopkins Sings the Blues	1962	25.00	50.00	100.00
—Black label, silver "Crown"					
CLP-5224 [M]	Lightnin' Hopkins Sings the Blues	1962	12.50	25.00	50.00
—Gray label					
CLP-5224 [M]	Lightnin' Hopkins Sings the Blues	196?	6.25	12.50	25.00
—Black label, multi-color logo					
DART					
D-8000 [M]	Lightning Strikes Again	1960	100.00	200.00	400.00
D-8000 [M]	Blues Underground	196?	50.00	100.00	200.00
—Retitled version of above					
FANTASY					
OBC-506	Blues in My Bottle	198?	3.00	6.00	12.00
OBC-522	Goin' Away	1988	3.00	6.00	12.00
OBC-532	Lightnin'	1990	3.00	6.00	12.00
24702 [(2)]	Double Blues	1972	5.00	10.00	20.00
24725 [(2)]	How Many More Years	1981	3.75	7.50	15.00
FIRE					
FLP 104 [M]	Mojo Hand	1960	375.00	750.00	1500.
FOLKLORE					
FRLP-14021 [M]	Hootin' the Blues	1964	15.00	30.00	60.00
FRST-14021 [S]	Hootin' the Blues	1964	17.50	35.00	70.00
FOLKWAYS					
FS-3822 [M]	Lightnin' Hopkins	1962	10.00	20.00	40.00
31011	Roots	196?	3.75	7.50	15.00
GNP CRESCENDO					
10022	Legacy of the Blues, Volume 12	1978	3.00	6.00	12.00
GUEST STAR					
G-1458 [M]	"Live" at the Bird Lounge, Houston, Texas	1964	7.50	15.00	30.00
GS-1458 [R]	"Live" at the Bird Lounge, Houston, Texas	1964	5.00	10.00	20.00
HERALD					
LP 1012 [M]	Lightnin' and the Blues	1959	750.00	1125.	1500.
—Black label					
LP 1012 [M]	Lightnin' and the Blues	1959	200.00	400.00	800.00
—Yellow label					
LP 1012 [M]	Lightnin' and the Blues	196?	125.00	250.00	500.00
—Multi-color label					
IMPERIAL					
LP-9180 [M]	Lightnin' Hopkins On Stage	1962	75.00	150.00	300.00
LP-9186 [M]	Lightnin' Hopkins Sings the Blues	1962	75.00	150.00	300.00
LP-9211 [M]	Lightnin' Hopkins and the Blues	1963	50.00	100.00	200.00
LP-12211 [R]	Lightnin' Hopkins and the Blues	1963	25.00	50.00	100.00
INTERNATIONAL ARTISTS					
IA-6	Free Form Patterns	1968	50.00	100.00	200.00
—With photo on cover					
IA-6	Free Form Patterns	1968	12.50	25.00	50.00
—With psychedelic art on cover					
JAZZ MAN					
BLZ-5502	Lightnin' in New York	1982	2.50	5.00	10.00
JEWEL					
5000	Blue Lightnin'	1967	3.75	7.50	15.00
5001	Talkin' Some Sense	1968	3.75	7.50	15.00
5015	Great Electric Show and Dance	1970	3.75	7.50	15.00
KING					
KS-1085	Moanin' Blues	1969	3.75	7.50	15.00
MAINSTREAM					
311	The Blues	1971	3.75	7.50	15.00
326	Dirty Blues	197?	3.75	7.50	15.00
405	Low Down Dirty Blues	1974	3.75	7.50	15.00
S-6040 [S]	Blues	196?	7.50	15.00	30.00
56040 [M]	Blues	196?	6.25	12.50	25.00
MOUNT VERNON					
104 [M]	Nothin' But the Blues	196?	6.25	12.50	25.00
OLYMPIC GOLD MEDAL					
7110	Blues Giant	1974	3.00	6.00	12.00
POPPY					
60002 [(2)]	Lightnin'!	1969	6.25	12.50	25.00
PRESTIGE					
PRLPT-7370 [(2) M]	My Life with the Blues	1965	15.00	30.00	60.00
PRST-7370 [(S) S]	My Life with the Blues	1965	17.50	35.00	70.00
PRLP-7377 [M]	Soul Blues	1966	12.50	25.00	50.00
PRST-7377 [S]	Soul Blues	1966	15.00	30.00	60.00
PRST-7592	Lightnin' Hopkins' Greatest Hits	1969	3.75	7.50	15.00
PRST-7714	The Best of Lightnin' Hopkins & His Texas Blues Band	1969	3.75	7.50	15.00
PRST-7806	Hootin' the Blues	1969	3.75	7.50	15.00
PRST-7811	The Blues of Lightnin' Hopkins	1969	3.75	7.50	15.00
PRST-7831	Gotta Move Your Baby	1970	3.75	7.50	15.00
RHINO					
RNLP 103	Los Angeles Blues	1982	2.50	5.00	10.00
SCORE					
SLP-4022 [M]	Lightnin' Hopkins Strums the Blues	1958	300.00	600.00	1200.
SMITHSONIAN FOLKWAYS					
SF-40019	Lightnin' Hopkins	1990	3.00	6.00	12.00
SPHERE SOUND					
SSR-7001 [M]	Lightnin' Hopkins	1964	100.00	200.00	400.00
SSSR-7001 [R]	Lightnin' Hopkins	1964	75.00	150.00	300.00
TIME					
1 [M]	Blues/Folk	1960	30.00	60.00	120.00
2 [M]	Blues/Folk Volume 2	1960	30.00	60.00	120.00
ST-70004 [S]	Last of the Great Blues Singers	1962	30.00	60.00	120.00
T-70004 [M]	Last of the Great Blues Singers	1962	30.00	60.00	120.00
TOMATO					
7004 [(2)]	Lightnin'!	1977	3.75	7.50	15.00
TRADITION					
TLP-1035 [M]	Country Blues	1960	7.50	15.00	30.00
TLP-1040 [M]	Autobiography in Blues	1961	7.50	15.00	30.00
TLP-2056 [M]	The Best of Lightnin' Hopkins	1967	5.00	10.00	20.00
TLP-2103 [M]	Lightnin' Strikes	1972	3.75	7.50	15.00
TRIP					
TLP-8015	Lightnin' Hopkins	1971	3.00	6.00	12.00
UNITED					
US-7713	Lightnin' Hopkins Sings the Blues	196?	3.75	7.50	15.00
US-7744	Original Folk Blues	196?	3.75	7.50	15.00
US-7785	A Legend in His Time	196?	3.75	7.50	15.00
UNITED ARTISTS					
UAS-5512	Coast to Coast Blues Band	197?	3.75	7.50	15.00
UP FRONT					
158	Lightnin' Blues	1973	3.00	6.00	12.00
VAULT					
129	California Mudslide	1969	6.25	12.50	25.00
VEE JAY					
LP 1044 [M]	Lightnin' Strikes	1962	12.50	25.00	50.00
VERVE					
V-8453 [M]	Fast Life Woman	1962	10.00	20.00	40.00
VERVE FOLKWAYS					
FV-9000 [M]	The Roots of Lightnin' Hopkins	1965	6.25	12.50	25.00
FVS-9000 [S]	The Roots of Lightnin' Hopkins	1965	7.50	15.00	30.00
FV-9022 [M]	Lightnin' Strikes	1965	6.25	12.50	25.00
FVS-9022 [S]	Lightnin' Strikes	1965	7.50	15.00	30.00
VERVE FORECAST					
FT-3013 [M]	Something Blue	1967	5.00	10.00	20.00
FTS-3013 [S]	Something Blue	1967	6.25	12.50	25.00
FTS-3031	Lightnin' Strikes	1968	5.00	10.00	20.00
WORLD PACIFIC					
ST-1817 [S]	First Meetin'	1963	20.00	40.00	80.00
—Red vinyl					
ST-1817 [S]	First Meetin'	1963	10.00	20.00	40.00
—Black vinyl					
WP-1817 [M]	First Meetin'	1963	7.50	15.00	30.00

HOPKINS, LINDA

Albums

Number	Title (A Side/B Side)	Yr	VG	VG+	NM
PALO ALTO					
PA-8034	How Blue Can You Get	1982	2.50	5.00	10.00

HOPKINS, NICKY

Prominent session keyboardist who played on BEATLES and ROLLING STONES sessions, among dozens of others.

45s

Number	Title (A Side/B Side)	Yr	VG	VG+	NM
COLUMBIA					
45869	Speed On/Sundown in Mexico	1973	—	2.50	5.00
DECCA					
32139	Mister Pleasant/Nothing As Yet	1967	3.00	6.00	12.00

Albums

Number	Title (A Side/B Side)	Yr	VG	VG+	NM
COLUMBIA					
KC 32074	The Tin Man Was a Dreamer	1973	5.00	10.00	20.00

HORNE, LENA

45s

Number	Title (A Side/B Side)	Yr	VG	VG+	NM
20TH CENTURY FOX					
449	Now!/Silent Spring	1963	2.50	5.00	10.00
460	Blowin' in the Wind/The Eagle and Me	1964	2.50	5.00	10.00
BUDDAH					
215	Watch What Happens/Rocky Raccoon	1971	—	3.00	6.00
233	Feels So Good/Nature's Baby	1971	—	3.00	6.00
CAPITOL					
S7-57888	Let It Snow! Let It Snow! Let It Snow!/Jingle Bells	1992	—	2.00	4.00
—B-side by Count Basie					
MCA					
40979	Believe in Yourself/Main Title Overture (Part 1)	1978	—	2.50	5.00
RCA VICTOR					
47-6073	Love Me or Leave Me/I Love to Love	1955	3.00	6.00	12.00
47-6175	It's All Right with Me/It's Love	1955	3.00	6.00	12.00
47-6431	If You Can Dream/What's Right for You	1956	3.00	6.00	12.00
47-7037	Push De Button/Coconut Street	1957	3.00	6.00	12.00
47-7332	When Johnny Comes Marching Home/You'd Better	1957	3.00	6.00	12.00

Number	Title (A Side/B Side)	Yr	VG	VG+	NM
47-8092	Where Is Love/Come On Strong	1962	2.50	5.00	10.00
SKYE					
4523	Watch What Happens/Rocky Raccoon	1970	2.00	4.00	8.00
UNITED ARTISTS					
851	Pleasures and Palaces/Feeling Good	1965	2.00	4.00	8.00
911	The Sand and the Sea/Softly, As I Leave You	1965	2.00	4.00	8.00
1661	Let It Snow! Let It Snow! Let It Snow!/What Are You Doing New Year's Eve	1966	2.50	5.00	10.00
—Silver Spotlight Series					
1661 [DJ]	Let It Snow! Let It Snow! Let It Snow! (same on both sides)	1966	2.00	4.00	8.00
—Silver Spotlight Series promo					
50051	Love Bug/Wonder What I'm Gonna Do	1966	2.00	4.00	8.00
7-Inch Extended Plays					
RCA CAMDEN					
CAE 380	St. Louis Blues/Beale Street Blues//Aunt Hagar's Blues/Careless Love Blues	1956	3.00	6.00	12.00
CAE 380 [PS]	Lena Horne Sings the Blues	1956	3.00	6.00	12.00
RCA VICTOR					
EPA-4038	Ain't It De Truth?/Take It Slow, Joe//Cocoanut Sweet/Push De Button	1957	3.75	7.50	15.00
EPA-4038 [PS]	Jamaica	1957	3.75	7.50	15.00
Albums					
20TH CENTURY FOX					
TF-4115 [M]	Here's Lena Now	1964	3.75	7.50	15.00
TFS-4115 [S]	Here's Lena Now	1964	5.00	10.00	20.00
ACCORD					
SN-7190	Standing Room Only	198?	2.50	5.00	10.00
BLUEBIRD					
9985-1-RB	Stormy Weather: The Legendary Lena	1990	3.00	6.00	12.00
BUDDAH					
BDS-5084	Nature's Baby	1971	3.00	6.00	12.00
BDS-5669 [(2)]	The Essential Lena Horne	197?	3.00	6.00	12.00
BULLDOG					
BDL-2000	20 Golden Pieces of Lena Horne	198?	2.50	5.00	10.00
CHARTER					
CLP-101 [M]	Lena Sings Your Requests	1963	3.75	7.50	15.00
CLS-101 [S]	Lena Sings Your Requests	1963	5.00	10.00	20.00
CLP-106 [M]	Like Latin	1964	3.75	7.50	15.00
CLS-106 [S]	Like Latin	1964	5.00	10.00	20.00
DRG					
MRS-501	Lena Horne With Lennie Hayton & the Marty Paich Orchestra	1985	2.50	5.00	10.00
MRS-510	Lena Goes Latin	1986	2.50	5.00	10.00
JAZZTONE					
J-1262 [M]	Lena and Ivie	1957	12.50	25.00	50.00
LIBERTY					
LN-10194	Lena in Hollywood	198?	2.00	4.00	8.00
LION					
L-70050 [M]	I Feel So Smoochie	1959	5.00	10.00	20.00
MGM					
E-545 [10]	Lena Horne Sings	1952	12.50	25.00	50.00
M3G-5409	The One and Only	197?	2.50	5.00	10.00
MOBILE FIDELITY					
2-094 [(2)]	Lena Horne: The Lady and Her Music	1982	10.00	20.00	40.00
—Audiophile vinyl					
MOVIETONE					
MTM 71005 [M]	Once in a Lifetime	196?	3.75	7.50	15.00
MTS 72005 [S]	Once in a Lifetime	196?	5.00	10.00	20.00
PAIR					
PDL2-1055 [(2)]	Lena	1986	3.00	6.00	12.00
QWEST					
2QW 3597 [(2)]	Lena Horne: The Lady and Her Music	1981	3.00	6.00	12.00
RCA VICTOR					
BGL1-1026	Lena and Michel	1975	3.00	6.00	12.00
—With Michel Legrand					
LOC-1028 [M]	Lena Horne at the Waldorf Astoria	1957	7.50	15.00	30.00
LSO-1028 [S]	Lena Horne at the Waldorf Astoria	1957	10.00	20.00	40.00
LPM-1148 [M]	It's Love	1955	12.50	25.00	50.00
LPM-1375 [M]	Stormy Weather	1956	12.50	25.00	50.00
BGL1-1799	Lena	1976	3.00	6.00	12.00
LPM-1879 [M]	Give the Lady What She Wants	1958	7.50	15.00	30.00
LSP-1879 [S]	Give the Lady What She Wants	1958	10.00	20.00	40.00
LPM-1895 [M]	Songs of Burke and Van Heusen	1959	7.50	15.00	30.00
LSP-1895 [S]	Songs of Burke and Van Heusen	1959	10.00	20.00	40.00
LPM-2364 [M]	Lena Horne at the Sands	1961	6.25	12.50	25.00
LSP-2364 [S]	Lena Horne at the Sands	1961	7.50	15.00	30.00
LPM-2465 [M]	Lena on the Blue Side	1962	6.25	12.50	25.00
LSP-2465 [S]	Lena on the Blue Side	1962	7.50	15.00	30.00
LPM-2587 [M]	Lena...Lovely and Alive	1963	6.25	12.50	25.00
LSP-2587 [S]	Lena...Lovely and Alive	1963	7.50	15.00	30.00
LPT-3061 [10]	This Is Lena Horne	1952	12.50	25.00	50.00
AYL1-4389	Lena, A New Album	1983	2.00	4.00	8.00
—"Best Buy Series" reissue					
SKYE					
15	Lena & Gabor	1970	3.75	7.50	15.00
—With Gabor Szabo					
STANYAN					
POW-3006	Stormy Weather	198?	2.50	5.00	10.00
—Reissue of 10126					
10126	Stormy Weather	197?	3.00	6.00	12.00
SUNBEAM					
212	A Date with Lena Horne	198?	2.50	5.00	10.00
—With Fletcher Henderson and His Orchestra					
THREE CHERRIES					
TC-44411	The Men in My Life	1989	2.50	5.00	10.00
TOPS					
L-910 [10]	Moanin' Low	195?	10.00	20.00	40.00
L-931 [10]	Lena Horne Sings	195?	10.00	20.00	40.00
L-1502 [M]	Lena Horne	1958	5.00	10.00	20.00
UNITED ARTISTS					
UAL 3433 [M]	Feelin' Good	1965	3.75	7.50	15.00
UAL 3470 [M]	Lena in Hollywood	1966	3.75	7.50	15.00
UAL 3496 [M]	Soul	1966	3.75	7.50	15.00
UAS 6433 [S]	Feelin' Good	1965	5.00	10.00	20.00
UAS 6470 [S]	Lena in Hollywood	1966	5.00	10.00	20.00
UAS 6496 [S]	Soul	1966	5.00	10.00	20.00

HORNE, LENA, AND HARRY BELAFONTE

Also see each artist's individual listings.

Number	Title (A Side/B Side)	Yr	VG	VG+	NM
Albums					
RCA VICTOR					
LOC-1507 [M]	Porgy and Bess	1959	6.25	12.50	25.00
LSO-1507 [S]	Porgy and Bess	1959	10.00	20.00	40.00

HORNETS, THE

More than one group.

Number	Title (A Side/B Side)	Yr	VG	VG+	NM
45s					
COLUMBIA					
42999	Fruit Cake/Seven Days to Tahiti	1964	15.00	30.00	60.00
EMERALD					
501	Runt/Breakfast in Bed	196?	7.50	15.00	30.00
FLASH					
125	Crying Over You/Tango Moon	1957	62.50	125.00	250.00
LIBERTY					
55688	Motorcycle U.S.A./On the Track	1964	7.50	15.00	30.00
REV					
3515	Slow Dance/Strollin'	1958	6.25	12.50	25.00
STATES					
127	I Can't Believe/Lonesome Baby	1953	4000.	6000.	8000.
—Black vinyl					
127	I Can't Believe/Lonesome Baby	1953	7500.	10000.	15000.
—Red vinyl					
V.I.P.					
25004	She's My Baby/Give Me a Kiss	1964	15.00	30.00	60.00
Albums					
LIBERTY					
LRP-3348 [M]	Motorcycles U.S.A.	1963	10.00	20.00	40.00
LRP-3364 [M]	Big Drag Boats U.S.A.	1964	12.50	25.00	50.00
LST-7348 [S]	Motorcycles U.S.A.	1963	12.50	25.00	50.00
LST-7364 [S]	Big Drag Boats U.S.A.	1964	15.00	30.00	60.00

HORSES

Don Johnson of "Miami Vice" and "Nash Bridges" fame was in this band.
Don Johnson of "Miami Vice" and "Nash Bridges" fame was in this band.

Number	Title (A Side/B Side)	Yr	VG	VG+	NM
45s					
WHITE WHALE					
301	Class of '69/Country Boy	1969	2.00	4.00	8.00
320	Freight Train/(B-side unknown)	1969	2.50	5.00	10.00
Albums					
WHITE WHALE					
WWS-7121	Horses	1970	10.00	20.00	40.00

HORSLIPS

Number	Title (A Side/B Side)	Yr	VG	VG+	NM
45s					
ATCO					
6935	High Reel/Furniture	1973	2.00	4.00	8.00
DJM					
1026	Warm Sweet Breath of Love/(B-side unknown)	1977	—	2.50	5.00
1032	Trouble (With a Capital T)/(B-side unknown)	1978	—	2.50	5.00
1036	Sure the Boy Was Green/Exiles	1978	2.50	5.00	10.00
—Green vinyl					
1105	Loneliness/Homesick	1979	—	2.50	5.00
MERCURY					
76030	Rescue Me/Soap Opera	1979	—	2.50	5.00
76072 [DJ]	Shakin' All Over (mono/stereo)	1979	—	3.00	6.00
—May be promo only					
RCA VICTOR					
PB-10123	Nighttown Boys/We Bring the Summer With Me	1974	—	3.00	6.00
Albums					
ATCO					
SD 7030	Happy to Meet, Sorry to Part	1973	3.00	6.00	12.00
SD 7039	The Tain	1974	3.00	6.00	12.00
DJM					
10	Book of Invasions	1977	2.50	5.00	10.00
16	Aliens	1978	2.50	5.00	10.00
20	The Man Who Built America	1979	2.50	5.00	10.00
MERCURY					
SRM-1-3809	Short Stories/Tall Tales	1979	2.50	5.00	10.00
SRM-1-3842	Belfast Gigs	1980	2.50	5.00	10.00
RCA VICTOR					
CPL1-0709	Dancehall Sweethearts	1974	3.00	6.00	12.00

HORTON, JAY

Number	Title (A Side/B Side)	Yr	VG	VG+	NM
45s					
MUSTANG					
3010	I Trip on You Girl/(B-side unknown)	1965	7.50	15.00	30.00
3021	It's Love/Come What May	1966	7.50	15.00	30.00

HORTON, JOHNNY

Number	Title (A Side/B Side)	Yr	VG	VG+	NM
45s					
ABBOTT					
100	Candy Jones/Devilish Lovelight	1951	10.00	20.00	40.00
101	Happy Millionaire/Mean Mean Son of a Gun	1951	10.00	20.00	40.00
102	Plaid and Calico/Done Roving	1951	10.00	20.00	40.00
—B-side by Bill Thompson's Westerners					
103	Birds and Butteflies/Coal Smoke, Valve Oil and Steam	1951	10.00	20.00	40.00
104	Go and Wash (Those Dirty Feet)/In My Home in Shelby County	1951	10.00	20.00	40.00
105	Shadows on the Old Bayou/Talk Gobbler Talk	1951	10.00	20.00	40.00
106	Smokey Joe's Barbeque/Words	1951	10.00	20.00	40.00

Number	Title (A Side/B Side)	Yr	VG	VG+	NM
107	Long Rocky Road/On the Banks of the Beautiful Nile	1952	10.00	20.00	40.00
108	Somebody Rocking in My Broken Chair/Betty Lorraine	1952	10.00	20.00	40.00
—With Hillbilly Barton					
109	Rhythm in My Baby's Walk/Bowlin' Baby	1952	10.00	20.00	40.00
135	Plaid and Calico/Shadows on the Old Bayou	1953	7.50	15.00	30.00
COLUMBIA					
21504	Honky Tonk Man/I'm Ready If You're Willing	1956	7.50	15.00	30.00
21538	I'm a One Woman Man/I Don't Like I Did	1956	6.25	12.50	25.00
30568 [S]	Sink the Bismarck/The Same Old Tale the Crow Told Me	1960	6.25	12.50	25.00
—"Stereo Single 33"; small hole, plays at 33 1/3 rpm					
31104 [S]	North to Alaska/Whispering Pines	1961	5.00	10.00	20.00
31105 [S]	Johnny Reb/The Mansion You Stole	1961	5.00	10.00	20.00
31106 [S]	When It's Springtime in Alaska/The Battle of New Orleans	1961	5.00	10.00	20.00
31107 [S]	All for the Love of a Girl/Sink the Bismarck	1961	5.00	10.00	20.00
31108 [S]	The Brave Comanche/Jim Bridger	1961	5.00	10.00	20.00
—The above five all are Columbia "Stereo 7" singles with small center holes					
40813	I'm Coming Home/I Got a Hole in My Picture	1957	7.50	15.00	30.00
40919	She Knows Why/The Woman I Need	1957	5.00	10.00	20.00
40986	I'll Do It Every Time/Let's Take the Long Way Home	1957	5.00	10.00	20.00
41043	You're My Baby/Lover's Rock	1957	7.50	15.00	30.00
41110	Honky Tonk Hardwood Floor/The Wild One	1958	15.00	30.00	60.00
41210	All Grown Up/Counterfeit Love	1958	5.00	10.00	20.00
41308	When It's Springtime in Alaska (It's Forty Below)/Whispering Pines	1958	3.75	7.50	15.00
41308 [PS]	When It's Springtime in Alaska (It's Forty Below)/Whispering Pines	1958	7.50	15.00	30.00
—Promo-only black and white sleeve					
41339	The Battle of New Orleans/All for the Love of a Girl	1959	3.75	7.50	15.00
41339 [PS]	The Battle of New Orleans/All for the Love of a Girl	1959	5.00	10.00	20.00
41437	Johnny Reb/Sal's Got a Sugar Lip	1959	3.75	7.50	15.00
41502	I'm Ready If You're Willing/Take Me Like I Am	1959	3.75	7.50	15.00
41522	They Shined Up Rudolph's Nose/The Electrified Donkey	1959	3.75	7.50	15.00
41568	Sink the Bismarck/The Same Old Tale the Crow Told Me	1960	3.00	6.00	12.00
41568 [PS]	Sink the Bismarck/The Same Old Tale the Crow Told Me	1960	5.00	10.00	20.00
41685	Johnny Freedom/Comanche	1960	3.00	6.00	12.00
41685 [PS]	Johnny Freedom/Comanche	1960	5.00	10.00	20.00
41782	North to Alaska/The Mansion You Stole	1960	3.00	6.00	12.00
41782 [PS]	North to Alaska/The Mansion You Stole	1960	5.00	10.00	20.00
41963	Sleepy Eyed John/They'll Never Take Her Love from Me	1961	3.00	6.00	12.00
41963 [PS]	Sleepy Eyed John/They'll Never Take Her Love from Me	1961	5.00	10.00	20.00
42063	Ole Slewfoot/Miss Marcy	1961	3.00	6.00	12.00
42063 [PS]	Ole Slewfoot/Miss Marcy	1961	5.00	10.00	20.00
42302	Honky Tonk Man/Words	1962	3.75	7.50	15.00
42302 [PS]	Honky Tonk Man/Words	1962	5.00	10.00	20.00
42653	All Grown Up/I'm a One Woman Man	1962	3.00	6.00	12.00
42653 [PS]	All Grown Up/I'm a One Woman Man	1962	5.00	10.00	20.00
42774	Sugar Coated Baby/When It's Springtime in Alaska (It's Forty Below)	1963	2.50	5.00	10.00
42993	Hooray for That Little Difference/Tell My Baby I Love Her	1964	2.50	5.00	10.00
42993 [PS]	Hooray for That Little Difference/Tell My Baby I Love Her	1964	5.00	10.00	20.00
43143	Lost Highway/The Same Old Tale the Crow Told Me	1964	2.50	5.00	10.00
43228	Rock Island Line/I Just Don't Like This Kind of Lovin'	1965	2.50	5.00	10.00
43719	Sam Magee/All for the Love of a Girl	1966	2.00	4.00	8.00
44156	The Battle of New Orleans/All for the Love of a Girl	1967	—	3.00	6.00
CORMAC					
1193	Plaid and Calico/Done Roving	1951	30.00	60.00	120.00
1197	Birds and Butteflies/Coal Smoke, Valve Oil and Steam	1951	30.00	60.00	120.00
DOT					
15966	Plaid and Calico/Shadows on the Old Bayou	1959	3.00	6.00	12.00
MERCURY					
6412	The Devil Sent Me You/First Train Headin' South	1952	7.50	15.00	30.00
6418	The Rest of Your Life/This Won't Be the First Time	1952	7.50	15.00	30.00
70014	I Won't Forget/The Child's Side of Life	1952	7.50	15.00	30.00
70100	Tennessee Jive/The Mansion You Stole	1953	7.50	15.00	30.00
70156	S.S. Loveline/I Won't Get Dreamy-Eyed	1953	7.50	15.00	30.00
70198	You, You, You/Red Lips and Warm Red Wine	1953	7.50	15.00	30.00
70227	All for the Love of a Girl/Broken Hearted	1953	7.50	15.00	30.00
70325	Move On Down the Line/Train with the Rhumba Beat	1954	7.50	15.00	30.00
70399	The Door of Your Mansion/Ha Ha and Moonface	1954	7.50	15.00	30.00
70462	No True Love/There'll Never Be Another Mary	1954	7.50	15.00	30.00
70636	Journey with No End/Ridin' the Sunshine Special	1955	7.50	15.00	30.00
70707	Big Wheels Rollin'/Hey Sweet, Sweet Thing	1955	7.50	15.00	30.00
7-Inch Extended Plays					
COLUMBIA					
B-13621	The Battle of New Orleans/Whispering Pines//The First Train Heading South/Lost Highway	1960	3.00	6.00	12.00
B-13621 [PS]	The Spectacular Johnny Horton, Vol. 1	1960	4.00	8.00	16.00
B-13622	Joe's Been a-Gettin' There/Sam Magee//When It's Springtime in Alaska/Cherokee Boogie	1960	3.00	6.00	12.00
B-13622 [PS]	The Spectacular Johnny Horton, Vol. 2	1960	4.00	8.00	16.00
B-13623	All for the Love of a Girl/The Golden Rocket//Mr. Moonlight/Got the Bull by the Horns	1960	3.00	6.00	12.00
B-13623 [PS]	The Spectacular Johnny Horton, Vol. 3	1960	4.00	8.00	16.00
Albums					
BRIAR					
104 [M]	Done Rovin'	196?	37.50	75.00	150.00
COLUMBIA					
CL 1362 [M]	The Spectacular Johnny Horton	1959	7.50	15.00	30.00
CL 1478 [M]	Johnny Horton Makes History	1960	7.50	15.00	30.00
1596/8396	Johnny Horton's Greatest Hits Bonus Photo	1961	2.50	5.00	10.00
CL 1596 [M]	Johnny Horton's Greatest Hits	1961	6.25	12.50	25.00
CL 1721 [M]	Honky-Tonk Man	1962	7.50	15.00	30.00
CL 2299 [M]	I Can't Forget You	1965	6.25	12.50	25.00
CL 2566 [M]	Johnny Horton on Stage at the Louisiana Hayride	1966	5.00	10.00	20.00
CS 8167 [S]	The Spectacular Johnny Horton	1959	10.00	20.00	40.00
CS 8269 [S]	Johnny Horton Makes History	1960	10.00	20.00	40.00
CS 8396 [S]	Johnny Horton's Greatest Hits	1961	7.50	15.00	30.00
PC 8396	Johnny Horton's Greatest Hits	198?	2.00	4.00	8.00
—Budget-line reissue					
CS 8779 [R]	Honky-Tonk Man	1962	3.75	7.50	15.00
CS 9099 [R]	I Can't Forget You	1965	3.75	7.50	15.00
CS 9366 [S]	Johnny Horton on Stage at the Louisiana Hayride	1966	6.25	12.50	25.00
CS 9940	Johnny Horton On the Road	1969	3.75	7.50	15.00
G 30884 [(2)]	The World of Johnny Horton	1971	3.75	7.50	15.00
DOT					
DLP 3221 [M]	Johnny Horton	1962	7.50	15.00	30.00
DLP 25221 [R]	Johnny Horton	1962	3.75	7.50	15.00
HARMONY					
HS 11291	The Unforgettable Johnny Horton	196?	3.00	6.00	12.00
HS 11384	The Legendary Johnny Horton	1970	3.00	6.00	12.00
KH 30394	The Battle of New Orleans	1971	3.00	6.00	12.00
HILLTOP					
6012	The Voice of Johnny Horton	196?	3.00	6.00	12.00
6060	All for the Love of a Girl	196?	3.00	6.00	12.00
MERCURY					
MG-20478 [M]	The Fantastic Johnny Horton	1959	12.50	25.00	50.00
SESAC					
1201 [M]	Free and Easy Songs	1959	37.50	75.00	150.00

HOSEA, DON

Number	Title (A Side/B Side)	Yr	VG	VG+	NM
45s					
SUN					
368	Since I Met You/Uh Huh Huh	1961	5.00	10.00	20.00

HOT BUTTER

Number	Title (A Side/B Side)	Yr	VG	VG+	NM
45s					
MUSICOR					
1458	Popcorn/At the Movies	1972	—	3.00	6.00
1466	Apache/Hot Butter	1972	—	2.50	5.00
1468	Tequila/Hot Butter	1972	—	2.50	5.00
1473	Percolator/Tristana	1973	—	2.50	5.00
1481	Slay Solution/Kappi Maki	1973	—	2.50	5.00
1491	Pipeline/Apache	1974	—	2.50	5.00
Albums					
MUSICOR					
MS-3242	Popcorn	1972	5.00	10.00	20.00
—Die-cut cover					
MS-3242	Popcorn	1972	3.00	6.00	12.00
—Regular cover					

HOT CHOCOLATE

Number	Title (A Side/B Side)	Yr	VG	VG+	NM
45s					
APPLE					
1812	Give Peace a Chance/Living Without Tomorrow	1969	2.50	5.00	10.00
—As "Hot Chocolate Band"					
BELL					
45390	Rumors/(B-side unknown)	1973	—	2.50	5.00
45466	Emma/(B-side unknown)	1974	—	3.50	7.00
BIG TREE					
16031	Emma/A Love Like Yours	1975	—	2.50	5.00
16038	Disco Queen/Makin' Music	1975	—	2.50	5.00
16047	You Sexy Thing/Amazing Skin Song	1975	—	2.50	5.00
16060	Don't Stop It Now/Beautiful Lady	1976	—	2.50	5.00
16078	Heaven Is in the Back Seat of My Cadillac/(B-side unknown)	1976	—	2.50	5.00
16096	So You Win Again/Part of Being with You	1977	—	2.50	5.00
16101	Man to Man/(B-side unknown)	1977	—	2.50	5.00
EMI-CAPITOL					
S7-19894	You Sexy Thing/So You Win Again	1998	—	—	3.00
EMI AMERICA					
8143	Are You Getting Enough Happiness/One Night's Not Enough	1982	—	2.00	4.00
8157	Bed Games/It Started with a Kiss	1983	—	2.00	4.00
INFINITY					
50002	Every 1's a Winner/Power of Love	1978	—	2.00	4.00
50016	Going Through the Motions/Don't Turn It Off	1979	—	2.00	4.00
50033	I Just Love What You're Doing/Congas Man	1979	—	2.00	4.00
50048	Mindless Boogie/Dance (Get Down To It)	1979	—	2.00	4.00
RAK					
4503	You Could Have Been a Lady/Everybody's Laughing	1972	—	3.00	6.00
4506	I Believe in Love/Caveman Billy	1972	—	3.00	6.00
4508	Mary Anne/Ruth	1972	—	3.00	6.00
4513	Brother Louie/I Want to Be Free	1973	—	3.00	6.00
Albums					
BIG TREE					
BT 76002	10 Greatest Hits	1977	2.50	5.00	10.00
BT 89503	Cicero Park	1975	2.50	5.00	10.00
BT 89512	Hot Chocolate	1975	2.50	5.00	10.00
BT 89519	Man to Man	1976	2.50	5.00	10.00
EMI AMERICA					
ST-17077	Mystery	1982	2.50	5.00	10.00
INFINITY					
INF-9002	Every 1's a Winner	1978	2.50	5.00	10.00
INF-9010	Going Through the Motions	1979	2.50	5.00	10.00

HOT DOGGERS, THE
BRUCE JOHNSTON was in this group.

Albums
EPIC

Number	Title (A Side/B Side)	Yr	VG	VG+	NM
LN 24054 [M]	Surfin' U.S.A.	1963	37.50	75.00	150.00
BN 26054 [S]	Surfin' U.S.A.	1963	50.00	100.00	200.00

HOT POOP
Albums
HOT POOP

Number	Title (A Side/B Side)	Yr	VG	VG+	NM
3072	Hot Poop Does Their Own Thing	1971	75.00	150.00	300.00

HOT RODDERS, THE
Albums
CROWN

Number	Title (A Side/B Side)	Yr	VG	VG+	NM
CST-378 [S]	Big Hot Rod	1963	6.25	12.50	25.00
CLP-5378 [M]	Big Hot Rod	1963	5.00	10.00	20.00

HOT-TODDYS, THE
See ROCKIN' REBELS.

HOT TUNA
Offshoot of JEFFERSON AIRPLANE.

45s
GRUNT

Number	Title (A Side/B Side)	Yr	VG	VG+	NM
65-0502	Water Song/Keep On Truckin'	1972	—	3.00	6.00
65-0502 [PS]	Water Song/Keep On Truckin'	1972	3.00	6.00	12.00
PB-10443	Hot Jellyroll Blues/Surphase Tension	1975	—	2.50	5.00
PB-10776	It's So Easy/I Can't Be Satisfied	1976	—	2.50	5.00

RCA VICTOR

Number	Title (A Side/B Side)	Yr	VG	VG+	NM
74-0528	Candy Man/Been So Long	1971	—	3.00	6.00

Albums
GRUNT

Number	Title (A Side/B Side)	Yr	VG	VG+	NM
BFL1-0348	The Phosphorescent Rat	1974	3.75	7.50	15.00
BFD1-0820 [Q]	America's Choice	1975	6.25	12.50	25.00
BFL1-0820	America's Choice	1975	3.75	7.50	15.00
FTR-1004	Burgers	1972	3.75	7.50	15.00
BFD1-1238 [Q]	Yellow Fever	1975	6.25	12.50	25.00
BFL1-1238	Yellow Fever	1975	3.75	7.50	15.00
BFL1-1920	Hoppkorv	1976	3.75	7.50	15.00
CYL2-2545 [(2)]	Double Dose	1978	5.00	10.00	20.00
BXL1-2591	Burgers	1978	3.00	6.00	12.00
—Reissue of 1004					
BXL1-3357	Final Vinyl	1979	3.00	6.00	12.00

RCA VICTOR

Number	Title (A Side/B Side)	Yr	VG	VG+	NM
AYL1-3864	Hot Tuna	1981	2.00	4.00	8.00
—"Best Buy Series" reissue					
AYL1-3865	First Pull Up Then Pull Down	1981	2.00	4.00	8.00
—"Best Buy Series" reissue					
AYL1-3951	Burgers	1981	2.00	4.00	8.00
—"Best Buy Series" reissue					
LSP-4353	Hot Tuna	1970	3.75	7.50	15.00
LSP-4550	First Pull Up Then Pull Down	1971	3.75	7.50	15.00

HOTLEGS
Early incarnation of 10CC. Also see GRAHAM GOULDMAN.

45s
CAPITOL

Number	Title (A Side/B Side)	Yr	VG	VG+	NM
2886	Neanderthal Man/You Didn't Like It, Because You Didn't Think of It	1970	2.50	5.00	10.00
3043	Run Baby Run/How Many Times	1971	3.75	7.50	15.00

Albums
CAPITOL

Number	Title (A Side/B Side)	Yr	VG	VG+	NM
ST-587	Hotlegs Thinks: School Stinks	1970	6.25	12.50	25.00

HOUK, RALPH
Albums
CARLTON

Number	Title (A Side/B Side)	Yr	VG	VG+	NM
HH-16 [M]	Hear How to Play Better Baseball	1961	10.00	20.00	40.00

HOUND DOG CLOWNS
45s
UNI

Number	Title (A Side/B Side)	Yr	VG	VG+	NM
55047	Superfox/Wicked Witch	1968	5.00	10.00	20.00

HOUR GLASS, THE
Also see DUANE ALLMAN; DUANE AND GREGG ALLMAN; GREGG ALLMAN.

45s
LIBERTY

Number	Title (A Side/B Side)	Yr	VG	VG+	NM
56002	Heartbeat/Nothing But Tears	1967	3.00	6.00	12.00
56029	Power of Love/I Still Want Your Love	1968	3.00	6.00	12.00
56053	D-I-V-O-R-C-E/Changing of the Guard	1968	3.00	6.00	12.00
56065	She Is My Woman/Going Nowhere	1968	3.00	6.00	12.00
56072	Now Is the Time/She Is My Woman	1968	3.00	6.00	12.00
56091	I've Been Trying/Silently	1969	3.00	6.00	12.00

Albums
LIBERTY

Number	Title (A Side/B Side)	Yr	VG	VG+	NM
LRP-3536 [M]	The Hour Glass	1967	6.25	12.50	25.00
LST-7536 [S]	The Hour Glass	1967	7.50	15.00	30.00
LST-7555	The Power of Love	1968	7.50	15.00	30.00

SPRINGBOARD

Number	Title (A Side/B Side)	Yr	VG	VG+	NM
SPB-4016	Duane and Gregg Allman with the Hour Glass	1976	2.50	5.00	10.00

UNITED ARTISTS

Number	Title (A Side/B Side)	Yr	VG	VG+	NM
UA-LA013-G2 [(2)]	The Hour Glass	1973	3.75	7.50	15.00

HOUSTON, CISSY
12-Inch Singles
PRIVATE STOCK

Number	Title (A Side/B Side)	Yr	VG	VG+	NM
PS 5108	Think It Over (6:00)/An Umbrella Song	1978	2.50	5.00	10.00

45s
COLUMBIA

Number	Title (A Side/B Side)	Yr	VG	VG+	NM
11058	Warning-Danger (This Love Affair May Be Hazardous to You)/An Umbrella Song	1979	—	2.00	4.00
11208	Break It To Me Gently/Gonna Take the Easy Way Out	1980	—	2.00	4.00

COMMONWEALTH UNITED

Number	Title (A Side/B Side)	Yr	VG	VG+	NM
3010	I'll Be There/So I Believe	1970	—	3.00	6.00

CONGRESS

Number	Title (A Side/B Side)	Yr	VG	VG+	NM
268	Bring Him Back/World of Broken Hearts	1966	15.00	30.00	60.00
—As "Susie Houston"					

JANUS

Number	Title (A Side/B Side)	Yr	VG	VG+	NM
131	I Just Don't Know What to Do with Myself/Empty Place	1970	—	3.00	6.00
145	Be My Baby/I'll Be There	1971	—	3.00	6.00
159	Hang On to a Dream/Darling Take Me Back	1971	—	3.00	6.00
177	I Love You/Making Love	1971	—	3.00	6.00
190	Didn't We/It's Not Easy	1972	—	3.00	6.00
206	Midnight Train to Georgia/Will You Still Love Me Tomorrow	1972	—	3.00	6.00
230	I'm So Glad I Can Love Again/One Time You Say You Love Me	1973	—	3.00	6.00
255	I Believe/Nothing Can Stop Me	1975	—	3.00	6.00

KAPP

Number	Title (A Side/B Side)	Yr	VG	VG+	NM
814	Don't Come Running to Me/One Broken Heart for Sale	1967	7.50	15.00	30.00
—As "Sissie Houston"					

PRIVATE STOCK

Number	Title (A Side/B Side)	Yr	VG	VG+	NM
45137	Love Is Something That Leads You/If I Ever Lose This Heaven	1977	—	2.50	5.00
45137	Love Is Something That Leads You/It Never Really Ended	1977	—	2.50	5.00
45153	Tomorrow/Love Is Holding On	1977	—	2.50	5.00
45171	Things to Do/It Never Really Ended	1977	—	2.50	5.00
45204	Think It Over/The Umbrella Song	1978	—	2.50	5.00

Albums
COLUMBIA

Number	Title (A Side/B Side)	Yr	VG	VG+	NM
JC 36112	Warning Danger	1979	2.50	5.00	10.00
JC 36193	Step Aside for a Lady	1980	2.50	5.00	10.00

COMMONWEALTH UNITED

Number	Title (A Side/B Side)	Yr	VG	VG+	NM
6008	Cissy Houston	1970	—	—	—
—Canceled?					

JANUS

Number	Title (A Side/B Side)	Yr	VG	VG+	NM
3001	Cissy Houston	1970	3.75	7.50	15.00

PRIVATE STOCK

Number	Title (A Side/B Side)	Yr	VG	VG+	NM
PS 2031	Cissy Houston	1977	3.00	6.00	12.00
PS 7015	Think It Over	1978	3.00	6.00	12.00

HOUSTON, DAVID
45s
COLONIAL

Number	Title (A Side/B Side)	Yr	VG	VG+	NM
101	Waltz of the Angels/(B-side unknown)	1978	2.00	4.00	8.00

COUNTRY INTERNATIONAL

Number	Title (A Side/B Side)	Yr	VG	VG+	NM
145	You're the Perfect Reason/We Couldn't Make It Love	1980	—	3.00	6.00
148	Sad Love Song Lady/Thanks for Being You and Loving Me	1980	—	3.00	6.00
149	The Bottom Line/We Couldn't Make It Love	1980	—	3.00	6.00
155	Bandera Waltz/(B-side unknown)	1981	—	3.00	6.00
220	A Penny for Your Thoughts Tonight Virginia/(B-side unknown)	1989	—	3.00	6.00

DERRICK

Number	Title (A Side/B Side)	Yr	VG	VG+	NM
126	Let Your Love Fall Back on Me/Take Me to Your Heart	1979	—	3.00	6.00
127	Here's to All the Hard Working Husbands (In the World)/Next Sunday I'm Gonna Be Saved	1979	—	3.00	6.00

ELEKTRA

Number	Title (A Side/B Side)	Yr	VG	VG+	NM
45552	Best Friends Make the Worst Enemies/There Won't Be a Wedding	1978	—	2.00	4.00
46028	Faded Love and Winter Roses/Beyond the Blue Horizon	1979	—	2.00	4.00

EPIC

Number	Title (A Side/B Side)	Yr	VG	VG+	NM
9625	Mountain of Love/Angeline	1963	2.00	4.00	8.00
9658	Chickashay/Passing Through	1964	2.00	4.00	8.00
9690	One If For Him, Two If For Me/Your Memories	1964	2.00	4.00	8.00
9720	Love Looks Good on You/My Little Lady	1964	2.00	4.00	8.00
9746	Sweet, Sweet Judy/Too Many Times (Away from You)	1964	2.00	4.00	8.00
9782	Rose Colored Glasses/Ballad of the Fool Killer	1965	2.50	5.00	10.00
9831	Livin' in a House Full of Love/Cowpoke	1965	2.00	4.00	8.00
9884	Sammy/I'll Take You Home Again, Kathleen	1966	2.00	4.00	8.00
9884 [PS]	Sammy/I'll Take You Home Again, Kathleen	1966	2.50	5.00	10.00
10025	Almost Persuaded/We Got Love	1966	2.00	4.00	8.00
10102	A Loser's Cathedral/Where Could I Go? (But to Her)	1966	—	3.00	6.00
10102 [PS]	A Loser's Cathedral/Where Could I Go? (But to Her)	1966	2.50	5.00	10.00
10154	With One Exception/Sweet, Sweet Judy	1967	—	3.00	6.00
10154 [PS]	With One Exception/Sweet, Sweet Judy	1967	2.50	5.00	10.00
10224	You Mean the World to Me/Don't Mention Tomorrow	1967	—	3.00	6.00
10224 [PS]	You Mean the World to Me/Don't Mention Tomorrow	1967	2.50	5.00	10.00
10291	Have a Little Faith/Too Far Gone	1968	—	3.00	6.00
10291 [PS]	Have a Little Faith/Too Far Gone	1968	2.50	5.00	10.00
10338	Already It's Heaven/Lighter Shade of Pale	1968	—	3.00	6.00
10338 [PS]	Already It's Heaven/Lighter Shade of Pale	1968	2.50	5.00	10.00
10394	Where Love Used to Live/I Love a Rainbow	1968	—	3.00	6.00
10430	My Woman's Good to Me/Lullaby to a Little Girl	1968	—	3.00	6.00
10488	I'm Down to My Last "I Love You"/Watching My World Walk Away	1969	—	3.00	6.00
10539	Baby, Baby (I Know You're a Lady)/True Love's a Lasting Thing	1969	—	3.00	6.00

Number	Title (A Side/B Side)	Yr	VG	VG+	NM
10596	I Do My Swinging at Home/Then I'll Know You Care	1970	—	3.00	6.00
10643	Wonders of the Wine/If God Can Forgive Me	1970	—	3.00	6.00
10696	A Woman Always Knows/The Rest of My Life	1970	—	3.00	6.00
10748	Nashville/That's Why I Cry	1971	—	3.00	6.00
10778	Maiden's Prayer/Home Sweet Home	1971	—	3.00	6.00
10830	The Day That Love Walked In/Sweet Lovin'	1972	—	3.00	6.00
10870	Soft, Sweet and Warm/The Rest of My Life	1972	—	3.00	6.00
10911	I Wonder How John Felt (When He Baptized Jesus)/Will the Circle Be Unbroken	1972	2.00	4.00	8.00
10939	Good Things/The Love She Gives	1973	—	3.00	6.00
10995	She's All Woman/Sweet Lovin'	1973	—	2.50	5.00
11048	The Lady of the Night/Thank You Teardrop	1973	—	2.50	5.00
11096	That Same Ol' Look of Love/Clinging Vine	1974	—	2.50	5.00
50009	Can't You Feel It/I Walk and I Walk and I Walk	1974	—	2.50	5.00
50066	A Man Needs Love/Flower of Love	1975	—	2.50	5.00
50113	I'll Be Your Steppin' Stone/Then I'll Know You Care	1975	—	2.50	5.00
50134	Sweet Molly/Old Blind Fiddler	1975	—	2.50	5.00
—With Calvin Crawford					
50156	The Woman on My Mind/I Can't Sit Still	1975	—	2.50	5.00
50186	What a Night/From the Bottom of My Heart	1976	—	2.50	5.00
50241	Lullaby Song/White Circle	1976	—	2.50	5.00
50275	Come On Down (To Our Favorite Forget-About-Her Place)/Me and Susan Wright	1976	—	2.50	5.00
EXCELSIOR					
1012	Texas Ida Red/(B-side unknown)	1981	—	3.00	6.00
1015	After All/(B-side unknown)	1981	—	2.00	4.00
NRC					
047	It's Been So Long/Kalua	1959	5.00	10.00	20.00
PHILLIPS INTERNATIONAL					
3583	Sherry's Lips/Miss Brown	1961	7.50	15.00	30.00
RCA VICTOR					
47-6611	Sugar Sweet/Hasta Luego	1956	7.50	15.00	30.00
47-6606	Blue Prelude/I'll Always Have It on My Mind	1956	7.50	15.00	30.00
47-6837	Someone Else's Arms/Ain't Going There No More	1957	7.50	15.00	30.00
47-6927	One and Only/Hackin' Around	1957	12.50	25.00	50.00
47-7001	The Teenage Frankie and Johnny/I'll Follow	1957	7.50	15.00	30.00
SOUNDWAVES					
4712	E.T. Still Means Ernest Tubb to Me/One Good Cry Away from Happiness	1982	—	2.00	4.00
STARDAY/GUSTO					
156	So Many Ways/Touch My World	1977	—	3.00	6.00
161	Amazing Grace/Return to Me	1977	—	3.00	6.00
—Canceled					
162	Ain't That Lovin' You Baby/Love Is a Mystery	1977	—	3.00	6.00
168	The Twelfth of Never/Barroom Champagne	1977	—	3.00	6.00
172	It Started All Over Again/Touch My World	1977	—	3.00	6.00
184	No Tell Motel/Hate to Tell Baby a Lie	1978	—	3.00	6.00
SUN					
403	Sherry's Lips/Miss Brown	1966	5.00	10.00	20.00
1127	Sherry's Lips/Miss Brown	1972	2.00	4.00	8.00
Albums					
EPIC					
EGP 502 [(2)]	The World of David Houston	1970	5.00	10.00	20.00
LN 24112 [M]	New Voice from Nashville	1964	3.75	7.50	15.00
LN 24156 [M]	12 Great Country Hits	1965	3.75	7.50	15.00
LN 24213 [M]	Almost Persuaded	1966	3.75	7.50	15.00
LN 24303 [M]	A Loser's Cathedral	1967	5.00	10.00	20.00
LN 24320 [M]	Golden Hymns	1967	5.00	10.00	20.00
LN 24338 [M]	You Mean the World to Me	1967	5.00	10.00	20.00
LN 24342 [M]	David Houston's Greatest Hits	1968	7.50	15.00	30.00
BN 26112 [S]	New Voice from Nashville	1964	5.00	10.00	20.00
BN 26156 [S]	12 Great Country Hits	1965	5.00	10.00	20.00
BN 26213 [S]	Almost Persuaded	1966	5.00	10.00	20.00
BN 26303 [S]	A Loser's Cathedral	1967	3.75	7.50	15.00
BN 26320 [S]	Golden Hymns	1967	3.75	7.50	15.00
BN 26338 [S]	You Mean the World to Me	1967	3.75	7.50	15.00
BN 26342 [S]	David Houston's Greatest Hits	1968	3.75	7.50	15.00
BN 26391	Already It's Heaven	1968	3.75	7.50	15.00
BN 26432	Where Love Used to Live	1969	3.75	7.50	15.00
BN 26482	David	1969	3.75	7.50	15.00
BN 26539	Baby, Baby	1970	3.75	7.50	15.00
E 30108	Wonders of the Wine	1970	3.75	7.50	15.00
E 30437	Sweet Lovin'	1971	3.75	7.50	15.00
E 30602	David Houston's Greatest Hits, Volume 2	1971	3.75	7.50	15.00
E 30657	A Woman Always Knows	1971	3.75	7.50	15.00
KE 31385	The Day Love Walked In	1972	3.00	6.00	12.00
KE 32189	Good Things	1973	3.00	6.00	12.00
KE 33948	What a Night	1976	3.00	6.00	12.00
GUSTO					
0012	The Best of David Houston	1978	2.50	5.00	10.00
HARMONY					
HS 11412	David Houston	1970	2.50	5.00	10.00
KH 31778	The Many Sides of David Houston	1972	2.50	5.00	10.00
KH 32287	Old Time Religion	1973	2.50	5.00	10.00
RCA CAMDEN					
CAL-2126 [M]	David Houston Sings	1966	3.75	7.50	15.00
CAS-2126 [R]	David Houston Sings	1966	2.50	5.00	10.00
STARDAY					
990	David Houston	1978	2.50	5.00	10.00

HOUSTON, DAVID, AND BARBARA MANDRELL

Number	Title (A Side/B Side)	Yr	VG	VG+	NM
45s					
EPIC					
10656	After Closing Time/My Song of Love	1970	—	3.00	6.00
10779	We've Got Everything But Love/Try a Little Harder	1971	—	3.00	6.00
10908	A Perfect Match/Almost Persuaded	1972	—	3.00	6.00
11068	I Love You, I Love You/Let's Go Down Together	1973	—	2.50	5.00
11120	Lovin' You Is Worth It/How Can It Be Wrong	1974	—	2.50	5.00
20005	Ten Commandments of Love/Try a Little Harder	1974	—	2.50	5.00
Albums					
EPIC					
KE 31705	A Perfect Match	1972	3.00	6.00	12.00
KE 32915	The Best of David Houston and Barbara Mandrell	1974	3.00	6.00	12.00

HOUSTON, DAVID, AND TAMMY WYNETTE

Number	Title (A Side/B Side)	Yr	VG	VG+	NM
45s					
EPIC					
10194	My Elusive Dreams/Marriage on the Rocks	1967	2.00	4.00	8.00
10274	It's All Over/Together We Stand	1967	2.00	4.00	8.00
Albums					
EPIC					
LN 24325 [M]	My Elusive Dreams	1967	5.00	10.00	20.00
BN 26325 [S]	My Elusive Dreams	1967	3.75	7.50	15.00

HOUSTON, JOHNNY

Number	Title (A Side/B Side)	Yr	VG	VG+	NM
45s					
EVENT					
4277	Slick Chick/Playboy	1959	7.50	15.00	30.00
4280	Torrid Tessie Lee/Our Very First Kiss	1959	7.50	15.00	30.00

HOUSTON, SOLDIER BOY

Number	Title (A Side/B Side)	Yr	VG	VG+	NM
45s					
ATLANTIC					
971	Western Rider Blues/Hug Me Baby	1952	62.50	125.00	250.00

HOUSTON, THELMA

Number	Title (A Side/B Side)	Yr	VG	VG+	NM
12-Inch Singles					
CENTURY 2000					
1001	Hold On (4 versions)/Athens Grooves/Olympus Thunder	1990	—	3.00	6.00
MCA					
L33-1253 [DJ]	I'd Rather Spend the Bad Times with You (3 versions)	1984	2.00	4.00	8.00
L33-1795 [DJ]	Working Girl (3:45)/(5:00)	1983	2.00	4.00	8.00
13963	Working Girl/Running in Circles	1983	—	3.00	6.00
23520	You Used to Hold Me So Tight (12" Version)/(Dub) (LP)	1984	—	3.00	6.00
23552	Fantasy and Heartbreak (Dance Version)/(LP Version)	1985	—	3.00	6.00
MOTOWN					
00053	Ride to the Rainbow/Love Machine	1979	2.00	4.00	8.00
RCA VICTOR					
PD-12293	96 Tears/There's No Runnin' Away from Love	1981	—	3.50	7.00
REPRISE					
PRO-A-4475 [DJ]	High (4 versions)	1990	2.00	4.00	8.00
PRO-A-4487 [DJ]	Out of My Hands (Remix) (same on both sides)	1990	2.00	4.00	8.00
21765	High (5 versions)	1990	—	3.00	6.00
21769	Our of My Hands (5 versions)	1990	—	3.00	6.00
40080	Throw You Down (4 version)/What He Has (2 versions)	1990	—	3.00	6.00
45s					
ABC DUNHILL					
11 [DJ]	Everybody Gets to Go to the Moon (same on both sides)	1969	3.75	7.50	15.00
—Special Apollo 11 promotional item					
11 [PS]	Everybody Gets to Go to the Moon (same on both sides)	1969	5.00	10.00	20.00
—Special Apollo 11 promotional item					
4197	Sunshower/If This Was the Last Song	1969	2.50	5.00	10.00
4212	Jumpin' Jack Flash/This Is Your Life	1969	2.50	5.00	10.00
4222	Save the Country/I Just Can't Stay Away	1970	2.00	4.00	8.00
4260	The Good Earth/Ride, Louie, Ride	1970	2.00	4.00	8.00
CAPITOL					
5767	Baby Mine/Woman Behind Her Man	1966	12.50	25.00	50.00
5882	Don't Cry, My Soldier Boy/Let's Try to Make It	1967	12.50	25.00	50.00
MCA					
52196	Working Girl/Running in Circles	1983	—	—	3.00
52239	Make It Last/Just Like All the Rest	1983	—	—	3.00
52489	(I Guess) It Must Be Love/Running in Circles	1984	—	—	3.00
52491	Love Is a Dangerous Game/You Used to Hold Me So Tight	1984	—	—	3.00
52574	Keep It Light/My Lucille	1985	—	—	3.00
—B-side by B.B. King					
52582	What a Woman Feels Inside/Fantasy and Heartbreak	1985	—	—	3.00
MOTOWN					
1245	I'm Just a Part of Yesterday/Piano Man	1973	—	2.50	5.00
1260	Do You Know Where You're Going/Together	1973	—	2.50	5.00
1316	You've Been Doing Wrong for So Long/Pick Up the Week	1974	—	2.50	5.00
1385	The Bingo Long Song/Razzle Dazzle	1976	—	2.50	5.00
—B-side by William Goldstein					
1385 [PS]	The Bingo Long Song/Razzle Dazzle	1976	—	3.00	6.00
—B-side by William Goldstein					
MOWEST					
5008	I Want to Go Back There Again/Pick Up the Week	1972	—	3.00	6.00
5013	Me and Bobby McGee/No One's Gonna Be a Fool Forever	1972	—	3.00	6.00
5023	Piano Man/Me and Bobby McGee	1972	—	3.00	6.00
5027	What If/There Is a Fool	1972	—	3.00	6.00
5046	If It's the Last Thing I Do/And I Never Did	1973	—	—	—
—Unreleased					
5050	I'm Just a Part of Yesterday/Piano Man	1973	—	3.00	6.00
RCA					
PB-11913	Suspicious Minds/Gone	1980	—	2.50	5.00
PB-12215	If You Feel It/Hollywood	1981	—	2.00	4.00
PB-12285	96 Tears/There's No Runnin' Away from Love	1981	—	2.00	4.00
TAMLA					
54275	One Out of Every Six (Censored)/Pick of the Week	1976	2.50	5.00	10.00

Number	Title (A Side/B Side)	Yr	VG	VG+	NM
54278	Don't Leave Me This Way (Short Version)/Today Will Soon Be Yesterday	1977	—	2.00	4.00
54278 [DJ]	Don't Leave Me This Way (Long Version)/Don't Leave Me This Way (Short Version)	1977	—	3.00	6.00
54283	If It's the Last Thing I Do/If You Won't Let Me Walk on the Water	1977	—	2.00	4.00
54287	I'm Here Again/Sharin' Something Perfect	1977	—	2.00	4.00
54292	I Can't Go On Living Without Your Love/Any Way You Like It	1978	—	2.00	4.00
54295	I'm Not Strong Enough to Love You/Triplin'	1978	—	2.00	4.00
54297	Saturday Night, Sunday Morning/Come to Me	1979	—	2.00	4.00

Albums

Number	Title (A Side/B Side)	Yr	VG	VG+	NM
ABC DUNHILL					
DS-50054	Sun Shower	1969	6.25	12.50	25.00
MCA					
5395	Thelma Houston	1983	2.50	5.00	10.00
5527	Qualifying Heat	1984	2.50	5.00	10.00
MOTOWN					
M5-120V1	Superstar Series, Vol. 20	1981	2.50	5.00	10.00
M5-127V1	Sunshower	1981	2.00	4.00	8.00
M5-226V1	Any Way You Like It	1982	2.50	5.00	10.00
MOWEST					
MW-102	Thelma Houston	1972	5.00	10.00	20.00
RCA VICTOR					
AFL1-3500	Breakwater Cat	1980	2.50	5.00	10.00
AFL1-3842	Never Gonna Be Another One	1981	2.50	5.00	10.00
REPRISE					
26234	Throw You Down	1990	3.75	7.50	15.00
SHEFFIELD LABS					
2	I've Got the Music in Me	1975	10.00	20.00	40.00
SHEFFIELD TREASURY					
ST-200	I've Got the Music in Me	1983	5.00	10.00	20.00
—Reissue of Sheffield Labs 2					
TAMLA					
T6-345R1	Any Way You Like It	1976	3.00	6.00	12.00
T7-358R1	The Devil in Me	1977	2.50	5.00	10.00
T7-361R1	Ready to Roll	1978	2.50	5.00	10.00

HOUSTON, THELMA, AND JERRY BUTLER

Also see each artist's individual listings.

45s

Number	Title (A Side/B Side)	Yr	VG	VG+	NM
MOTOWN					
1422	It's a Lifetime Thing/Kiss Me Now	1977	—	2.50	5.00

Albums

Number	Title (A Side/B Side)	Yr	VG	VG+	NM
MOTOWN					
M6-887	Thelma and Jerry	1977	2.50	5.00	10.00
M7-903	Two to One	1978	2.50	5.00	10.00

HOUSTON FEARLESS

45s

Number	Title (A Side/B Side)	Yr	VG	VG+	NM
IMPERIAL					
66354	Race with the Devil/Someone Else's Blues	1969	—	—	—
—Canceled					

Albums

Number	Title (A Side/B Side)	Yr	VG	VG+	NM
IMPERIAL					
LP-12421	Houston Fearless	1969	5.00	10.00	20.00

HOWARD, EDDY

45s

Number	Title (A Side/B Side)	Yr	VG	VG+	NM
MERCURY					
5433	American Beauty Rose/Seems Like Only Yesterday	1950	3.75	7.50	15.00
—Note: Earlier Eddy Howard releases on Mercury may exist on 45.					
5439	Put Your Arms Around Me Honey/Lassus Trombone	1950	3.75	7.50	15.00
5453	My Heart Isn't In It/I Do Better in the Mountains	1950	3.75	7.50	15.00
5475	Daddy's Little Boy/They Put the Lights Out	1950	3.75	7.50	15.00
5490	I'm Forever Blowing Bubbles/Red We Want	1950	3.75	7.50	15.00
5491	Patricia/So Long, Sally	1950	3.75	7.50	15.00
5516	I'll Be Home for Christmas/Dearest Santa	1950	3.75	7.50	15.00
5517	To Think You've Chosen Me/The One Rose	1950	3.75	7.50	15.00
5567	A Penny a Kiss — A Penny a Hug/I Still Feel the Same About You	1951	3.75	7.50	15.00
5576	When You Return/Little Small Town Girl	1951	3.75	7.50	15.00
5578	Daddy's Little Girl/Daddy's Little Boy	1951	3.75	7.50	15.00
5590	Around the World/That's All That's Left	1951	3.75	7.50	15.00
5623	One Kind Word/How Thoughtful of You	1951	3.75	7.50	15.00
5630	What Will I Tell My Heart/The Strange Little Girl	1951	3.75	7.50	15.00
5663	(A Woman Is a) Deadly Weapon/I'm in Love Again	1951	3.75	7.50	15.00
5678	Hello Young Lovers/We Kiss in a Shadow	1951	3.75	7.50	15.00
5697	I'm Cryin'/Put All Your Kisses in an Envelope	1951	3.75	7.50	15.00
5711	Sin/My Wife and I	1951	3.75	7.50	15.00
—Revised A-side title					
5711	It's No Sin/My Wife and I	1951	5.00	10.00	20.00
5722	Uncle Mistletoe/When Christmas Rolls Around	1951	3.75	7.50	15.00
5748	It's All Over But the Memories/Chances Are	1951	3.75	7.50	15.00
5752	There's a Christmas Tree/Auld Lang Syne	1951	3.75	7.50	15.00
5771	Stolen Love/I'll See You in My Dreams	1952	3.75	7.50	15.00
5791	My Adobe Hacienda/Wishin'	1952	3.75	7.50	15.00
5815	Be Anything (But Be Mine)/She Took	1952	3.75	7.50	15.00
5832	Singing in the Rain/All I Do Is Dream of You	1952	3.75	7.50	15.00
5837	The Family That Prays Together/(B-side unknown)	1952	3.75	7.50	15.00
5871	Auf Wiederseh'n Sweetheart/I Don't Want to Take a Chance	1952	3.75	7.50	15.00
5898	Mademoiselle/I Don't Know Any Better	1952	3.75	7.50	15.00
70015	It's Worth Any Price You Pay/Kentucky Babe	1952	3.00	6.00	12.00
70071	Your Mother and Mine/You've Got Me Crying	1953	3.00	6.00	12.00
70107	Gomen Nasai (Forgive Me)/Someone to Kiss Your Tears Away	1953	3.00	6.00	12.00
70134	Say You're Mine Again/Broken Wings	1953	3.00	6.00	12.00
70135	Am I Loving You/Almost Always	1953	3.00	6.00	12.00
70176	Love Every Moment That You Live/The Right Way	1953	3.00	6.00	12.00
70225	That's the Price I Paid for You/Skirts	1953	3.00	6.00	12.00
70272	Ebenezer Scrooge/Bimbo	1953	3.75	7.50	15.00
70293	Little Miss One/Till We Two Are One	1954	3.00	6.00	12.00
70301	Bimbo/Call Me Darling	1954	3.00	6.00	12.00
70304	Melancholy Me/I Wonder What's Become of Sally	1954	3.00	6.00	12.00
70388	Vieni Su/Don't Worry Baby	1954	3.00	6.00	12.00
70467	Love Me Tonight/You're Always Welcome Home	1954	3.00	6.00	12.00
70475	Happy Birthday/Anniversary Waltz	1954	3.75	7.50	15.00
70513	All of You/I'll Wrap You in My Arms	1954	3.00	6.00	12.00
70533	Old Memories/Finger of Suspicion	1955	3.00	6.00	12.00
70566	Words of Love/Forevermore	1955	3.00	6.00	12.00
70639	The Man from Laramie/The Three of Us	1955	3.00	6.00	12.00
70700	The Teen-Agers' Waltz/Choo Choo Cha Cha	1955	3.00	6.00	12.00
70763	Round, Round the Christmas Tree/Silver Bells	1955	3.00	6.00	12.00
70800	Why Is Your Dog Following Me/Rustic Old Cathedral	1956	2.50	5.00	10.00
70881	Whatever Will Be, Will Be/You Can't Keep Running	1956	2.50	5.00	10.00
70946	Never, Never, Never/Thank You Lord	1956	2.50	5.00	10.00
70989	Confidential/Tiger Lily	1956	2.50	5.00	10.00
71002	Uncle Mistletoe/Silver Bells	1956	3.00	6.00	12.00
71008	Driftwood/The Hour of Love	1956	2.50	5.00	10.00
71072	Delia's Gone/Love Me a Little Bit	1957	2.50	5.00	10.00
71300	Just Foolin'/My Last Goodbye	1958	2.50	5.00	10.00
71773	I Want You to Want Me to Want You/Just a Year Ago Tonight	1961	2.50	5.00	10.00

7-Inch Extended Plays

Number	Title (A Side/B Side)	Yr	VG	VG+	NM
MERCURY					
EP 1-3213	I Wonder What's Become of Sally/Little Miss One //Call Me Darling/Yellow Roses	195?	3.75	7.50	15.00
EP 1-3213 [PS]	Yellow Roses	195?	3.75	7.50	15.00

Albums

Number	Title (A Side/B Side)	Yr	VG	VG+	NM
CIRCLE					
29	Eddy Howard 1949-1952	198?	2.50	5.00	10.00
79	Eddy Howard 1949-1953	1985	2.50	5.00	10.00
COLUMBIA					
CL 6067 [10]	Eddy Howard	1949	15.00	30.00	60.00
HINDSIGHT					
HSR-119	Eddy Howard 1946-1951	198?	2.50	5.00	10.00
HSR-156	Eddy Howard 1945-1948	198?	2.50	5.00	10.00
HSR-405 [(2)]	Eddy Howard and His Orchestra Play 22 Original Big Band Favorites	198?	3.00	6.00	12.00
INSIGHT					
205	Eddy Howard and His Orchestra 1945-1951	198?	2.50	5.00	10.00
MERCURY					
MG-20112 [M]	Singing in the Rain	195?	6.25	12.50	25.00
MG-20312 [M]	Paradise Isle	195?	6.25	12.50	25.00
MG-20432 [M]	Great for Dancing	1958	5.00	10.00	20.00
MG-20562 [M]	Eddy Howard's Golden Hits	1961	3.75	7.50	15.00
MG-20593 [M]	More Eddy Howard's Golden Hits	1962	3.75	7.50	15.00
MG-20665 [M]	Eddy Howard Sings and Plays the Great Old Waltzes	1962	3.75	7.50	15.00
MG-20817 [M]	Eddy Howard Sings and Plays the Great Band Hits	196?	3.75	7.50	15.00
MG-20910 [M]	Intimately Yours	1965	3.75	7.50	15.00
MG-21014 [M]	Softly and Sincerely	196?	3.75	7.50	15.00
SR-60104 [S]	Great for Dancing	1959	6.25	12.50	25.00
SR-60562 [S]	Eddy Howard's Golden Hits	1961	5.00	10.00	20.00
SR-60593 [S]	More Eddy Howard's Golden Hits	1962	5.00	10.00	20.00
SR-60665 [S]	Eddy Howard Sings and Plays the Great Old Waltzes	1962	5.00	10.00	20.00
SR-60817 [S]	Eddy Howard Sings and Plays the Great Band Hits	196?	5.00	10.00	20.00
SR-60910 [S]	Intimately Yours	1965	5.00	10.00	20.00
SR-61014 [S]	Softly and Sincerely	196?	5.00	10.00	20.00
WING					
MGW-12104 [M]	Saturday Night Dance Date	196?	3.00	6.00	12.00
MGW-12171 [M]	Eddy Howard Sings Words of Love	196?	3.00	6.00	12.00
MGW-12171 [M]	Words of Love	196?	3.00	6.00	12.00
MGW-12194 [M]	Sleepy Serenade	196?	3.00	6.00	12.00
MGW-12249 [M]	The Velvet Voice	196?	3.00	6.00	12.00
SRW-16104 [S]	Saturday Night Dance Date	196?	3.00	6.00	12.00
SRW-16171 [S]	Eddy Howard Sings Words of Love	196?	3.00	6.00	12.00
SRW-16171 [S]	Words of Love	196?	3.00	6.00	12.00
SRW-16194 [S]	Sleepy Serenade	196?	3.00	6.00	12.00
SRW-16249 [S]	The Velvet Voice	196?	3.00	6.00	12.00

HOWARD, RONNIE

45s

Number	Title (A Side/B Side)	Yr	VG	VG+	NM
BIG TOP					
3093	If Santa Fell/Give My Toy to the Boy Next Door	1961	3.75	7.50	15.00

HOWE, STEVE

Also see YES.

Albums

Number	Title (A Side/B Side)	Yr	VG	VG+	NM
ATLANTIC					
SD 18154	Beginnings	1975	2.50	5.00	10.00
SD 19243	The Steve Howe Album	1980	2.50	5.00	10.00

HOWELL, BILL

45s

Number	Title (A Side/B Side)	Yr	VG	VG+	NM
PALLADIUM					
513	Rocket Rollin' Blues/Bayou City Blues	195?	12.50	25.00	50.00

HOWL THE GOOD

45s

Number	Title (A Side/B Side)	Yr	VG	VG+	NM
RARE EARTH					
5045	Long Way from Home/Why Do You Cry	1972	2.00	4.00	8.00

Number	Title (A Side/B Side)	Yr	VG	VG+	NM
Albums					
RARE EARTH					
RS-537	Howl the Good	1972	5.00	10.00	20.00

HOWLIN' WOLF

Number	Title (A Side/B Side)	Yr	VG	VG+	NM
45s					
CADET CONCEPT					
7013	Evil/Tail Dragger	1969	2.00	4.00	8.00
CHESS					
1528	Oh! Red/My Last Affair	1952	175.00	350.00	700.00
—Note: Howlin' Wolf releases on Chess before 1528 are unknown on 45 rpm					
1557	All Night Boogie/I Love My Baby	1953	75.00	150.00	300.00
1566	No Place to Go/Rockin' Daddy	1954	25.00	50.00	100.00
1575	How Long/Evil Is Going On	1954	25.00	50.00	100.00
1584	I'll Be Around/Forty Four	1955	12.50	25.00	50.00
1593	Who Will Be Next/I Have a Little Girl	1955	10.00	20.00	40.00
1607	Come to Me Baby/Don't Mess with My Baby	1955	10.00	20.00	40.00
1618	Smoke Stack Lightning/You Can't Be Beat	1956	10.00	20.00	40.00
1632	I Asked for Water/So Glad	1956	10.00	20.00	40.00
1648	Goin' Back Home/My Life	1957	10.00	20.00	40.00
1668	Somebody in My Home/Nature	1957	10.00	20.00	40.00
1679	Sittin' On Top of the World/Poor Boy	1958	10.00	20.00	40.00
1695	Moaning for My Baby/I Didn't Know	1958	10.00	20.00	40.00
1712	I'm Leaving You/Change My Way	1959	10.00	20.00	40.00
1726	Howlin' Blues/I Better Go Now	1959	10.00	20.00	40.00
1735	Mr. Airplane Man/I've Been Abused	1959	10.00	20.00	40.00
1744	The Natchez Burning/You Gonna Wreck My Life	1959	10.00	20.00	40.00
1762	Spoonful/Howlin' for My Baby	1960	7.50	15.00	30.00
1777	Wang Dang Doodle/Back Door Man	1961	7.50	15.00	30.00
1793	Little Baby/Down in the Bottom	1961	7.50	15.00	30.00
1804	The Red Rooster/Shake for Me	1961	6.25	12.50	25.00
1813	You'll Be Mine/Goin' Down Slow	1962	6.25	12.50	25.00
1823	Just Like I Treat You/I Ain't Superstitious	1962	6.25	12.50	25.00
1844	Do the Do/Mama's Baby	1962	6.25	12.50	25.00
1870	300 Pounds of Joy/Built for Comfort	1963	5.00	10.00	20.00
1890	Tail Dragger/Hidden Charms	1964	5.00	10.00	20.00
1911	Love Me Darlin'/My Country Sugar Mama	1964	5.00	10.00	20.00
1923	Killin' Floor/Louise	1965	5.00	10.00	20.00
1928	Tell Me What I've Done/Ooh Baby	1965	3.75	7.50	15.00
1945	I Walked from Dallas/Don't Laugh at Me	1965	3.75	7.50	15.00
1968	New Crawlin' King Snake/Wild Ramblin'	1966	3.75	7.50	15.00
2009	I Had a Dream/Pop It to Me	1967	3.75	7.50	15.00
2081	Mary Sue/Hard Luck	1970	2.00	4.00	8.00
2108	I Smell a Rat/Just As Long	1971	2.00	4.00	8.00
2118	Do the Do/Red Rooster	1971	2.00	4.00	8.00
2145	Back Door Wolf/Coon on the Moon	1973	2.00	4.00	8.00
RPM					
340	Passing By Blues/Crying at Daybreak	1952	1000.	2000.	3000.
—Note: Howlin' Wolf releases on RPM before 340 are unknown on 45 rpm					
347	My Baby Stole Off/I Want Your Picture	1952	800.00	1600.	2400.
Albums					
CADET					
LPS-319	This Is Howlin' Wolf's New Album	1969	6.25	12.50	25.00
CHESS					
201 [(2)]	Howlin' Wolf	1976	3.75	7.50	15.00
LP-1434 [M]	Moanin' in the Moonlight	1958	150.00	300.00	600.00
LP-1469 [M]	Howlin' Wolf	1962	150.00	300.00	600.00
LP-1502 [M]	The Real Folk Blues	1966	12.50	25.00	50.00
LP-1512 [M]	More Real Folk Blues	1966	12.50	25.00	50.00
LP-1540	Evil	1969	6.25	12.50	25.00
CH-9107	His Greatest Sides, Vol. 1	1985	2.50	5.00	10.00
CH-9182	Chicago — 26 Golden Years	1985	2.50	5.00	10.00
CH-9195	Moanin' in the Moonlight	1986	2.00	4.00	8.00
—Reissue of 1434					
CH-9273	The Real Folk Blues	1988	2.50	5.00	10.00
—Reissue of 1502					
CH-9279	More Real Folk Blues	1988	2.50	5.00	10.00
—Reissue of 1512					
CH-9297	The London Howlin' Wolf Sessions	1989	2.50	5.00	10.00
—Reissue of 60008					
CH5-9332 [(5)]	The Chess Box	1991	10.00	20.00	40.00
CH-50002	Message to the Young	1971	5.00	10.00	20.00
CH-50015	Live and Cookin'	1972	5.00	10.00	20.00
CH-50045	Back Door Wolf	1974	5.00	10.00	20.00
CH-60008	The London Howlin' Wolf Sessions	1971	5.00	10.00	20.00
CH-60016 [(2)]	Howlin' Wolk, AKA Chester Burnett	1972	6.25	12.50	25.00
CH-93001	Change My Way	198?	2.50	5.00	10.00
CROWN					
CLP-5240 [M]	Howlin' Wolf Sings the Blues	1962	6.25	12.50	25.00
CUSTOM					
CM-2055 [M]	Big City Blues	196?	10.00	20.00	40.00
CS-2055 [R]	Big City Blues	196?	5.00	10.00	20.00
KENT					
KLP-526 [M]	Original Folk Blues	1967	3.75	7.50	15.00
KST-526 [R]	Original Folk Blues	1967	3.00	6.00	12.00
KST-527	Howlin' Wolf's 20 Greatest R&B Hits	1968	3.00	6.00	12.00
KST-535	Underground Blues	1968	3.00	6.00	12.00
ROUNDER					
SS-28	Cadillac Daddy: Memphis Recordings, 1952	1989	3.00	6.00	12.00

HUBBARD, FREDDIE

Number	Title (A Side/B Side)	Yr	VG	VG+	NM
12-Inch Singles					
FANTASY					
F 204	Splash (5:05)/You're Gonna Lose Me (5:28)	1981	2.00	4.00	8.00
45s					
ATLANTIC					
2677	Wichita Lineman/Lonely Soul	1969	2.00	4.00	8.00
BLUE NOTE					
1779	One Mint Julep/Gypsy Blues	196?	2.50	5.00	10.00
1809	Changing Scene/I Wish I Knew	196?	2.50	5.00	10.00
1810	Cry Me Not/Osie Mae	196?	2.50	5.00	10.00
1908	Blue Frenzy/Mirrors	196?	2.50	5.00	10.00
COLUMBIA					
10060	Baraka Sasa/Crisis	1974	—	2.50	5.00
10434	Neo Terra (New Land)/Rock Me Arms	1976	—	2.50	5.00
CTI					
6	Red Clay (Part 1)/Red Clay (Part 2)	1970	—	3.00	6.00
514	Here's That Rainy Day (Part 1)/Here's That Rainy Day (Part 2)	197?	—	3.00	6.00
519	Red Clay (Part 1)/Red Clay (Part 2)	197?	—	3.00	6.00
Albums					
ABC IMPULSE!					
AS-27 [S]	The Artistry of Freddie Hubbard	1968	3.00	6.00	12.00
AS-38 [S]	The Body and Soul of Freddie Hubbard	1968	3.00	6.00	12.00
AS-9237 [(2)]	Re-Evaluation: The Impulse Years	1973	3.75	7.50	15.00
ATLANTIC					
SD 2-314 [(2)]	The Art of Freddie Hubbard	1974	3.75	7.50	15.00
1477 [M]	Backlash	1967	6.25	12.50	25.00
SD 1477 [S]	Backlash	1967	3.75	7.50	15.00
SD 1501	High Pressure Blues	1969	3.75	7.50	15.00
SD 1526	Soul Experiment	1970	3.00	6.00	12.00
SD 1549	Black Angel	1971	3.00	6.00	12.00
80108	Sweet Return	1983	2.50	5.00	10.00
90466	Backlash	1986	2.00	4.00	8.00
—Reissue of SD 1477					
BASF					
10726	The Hub of Hubbard	1972	3.00	6.00	12.00
BLUE NOTE					
BN-LA356-H [(2)]	Freddie Hubbard	1975	3.75	7.50	15.00
BLP-4040 [M]	Open Sesame	1960	30.00	60.00	120.00
—"Deep groove" version (deep indentation under label on both sides)					
BLP-4040 [M]	Open Sesame	1960	20.00	40.00	80.00
—Regular version with W. 63rd St. address on label					
BLP-4040 [M]	Open Sesame	1963	5.00	10.00	20.00
—With New York, USA address on label					
BLP 4056 [M]	Goin' Up	1960	20.00	40.00	80.00
—With W. 63rd St. address on label					
BLP-4056 [M]	Goin' Up	1963	5.00	10.00	20.00
—With New York, USA address on label					
BLP-4073 [M]	Hub Cap	1961	20.00	40.00	80.00
—With W. 63rd St. address on label					
BLP-4073 [M]	Hub Cap	1963	5.00	10.00	20.00
—With New York, USA address on label					
BLP-4085 [M]	Ready for Freddie	1961	20.00	40.00	80.00
—With 61st St. address on label					
BLP-4085 [M]	Ready for Freddie	1963	5.00	10.00	20.00
—With New York, USA address on label					
BLP-4115 [M]	Hub Tones	1962	6.25	12.50	25.00
4135/84135	Here to Stay	1963	—	—	—
—Scheduled, but unreleased until 1985					
BLP-4172 [M]	Breaking Point	1964	6.25	12.50	25.00
BLP-4196 [M]	Blue Spirits	1965	6.25	12.50	25.00
BLP-4207 [M]	The Night of the Cookers — Live at Club Le Marchal, Vol. 1	1965	6.25	12.50	25.00
BLP-4208 [M]	The Night of the Cookers — Live at Club Le Marchal, Vol. 2	1965	6.25	12.50	25.00
B1-32094	Ready for Freddie	1995	3.00	6.00	12.00
—"The Finest in Jazz Since 1939" reissue					
BJT-48017	The Eternal Triangle	1988	3.00	6.00	12.00
BST-84040	Open Sesame	1989	2.50	5.00	10.00
—"The Finest in Jazz Since 1939" reissue					
BST-84040 [S]	Open Sesame	1960	15.00	30.00	60.00
—With W. 63rd St. addresss on label					
BST-84040 [S]	Open Sesame	1963	6.25	12.50	25.00
—With New York, USA address on label					
BST-84040 [S]	Open Sesame	1967	3.75	7.50	15.00
—With "A Division of Liberty Records" on label					
BST-84040 [S]	Open Sesame	199?	6.25	12.50	25.00
—Classic Records reissue on audiophile vinyl					
BST-84056 [S]	Goin' Up	1960	15.00	30.00	60.00
—With W. 63rd St. addresss on label					
BST-84056 [S]	Goin' Up	1963	6.25	12.50	25.00
—With New York, USA address on label					
BST-84056 [S]	Goin' Up	1967	3.75	7.50	15.00
—With "A Division of Liberty Records" on label					
BST-84073	Hub Cap	198?	2.50	5.00	10.00
—"The Finest in Jazz Since 1939" reissue					
BST-84073 [S]	Hub Cap	1961	15.00	30.00	60.00
—With W. 63rd St. addresss on label					
BST-84073 [S]	Hub Cap	1963	6.25	12.50	25.00
—With New York, USA address on label					
BST-84073 [S]	Hub Cap	1967	3.75	7.50	15.00
—With "A Division of Liberty Records" on label					
BST-84085 [S]	Ready for Freddie	1961	15.00	30.00	60.00
—With 61st St. addresss on label					
BST-84085 [S]	Ready for Freddie	1963	6.25	12.50	25.00
—With New York, USA address on label					
BST-84085 [S]	Ready for Freddie	1967	3.75	7.50	15.00
—With "A Division of Liberty Records" on label					
BST-84115	Hub-Tones	1985	2.50	5.00	10.00
—"The Finest in Jazz Since 1939" reissue					
BST-84115 [S]	Hub-Tones	1962	7.50	15.00	30.00
—With New York, USA address on label					
BST-84115 [S]	Hub-Tones	1967	3.75	7.50	15.00
—With "A Division of Liberty Records" on label					
BST-84135	Here to Stay	1985	3.00	6.00	12.00
BST-84172 [S]	Breaking Point	1964	7.50	15.00	30.00
—With New York, USA address on label					
BST-84172 [S]	Breaking Point	1967	3.75	7.50	15.00
—With "A Division of Liberty Records" on label					
BST-84196	Blue Spirits	1987	2.50	5.00	10.00
—"The Finest in Jazz Since 1939" reissue					
BST-84196 [S]	Blue Spirits	1965	7.50	15.00	30.00
—With New York, USA address on label					
BST-84196 [S]	Blue Spirits	1967	3.75	7.50	15.00
—With "A Division of Liberty Records" on label					

Number	Title (A Side/B Side)	Yr	VG	VG+	NM
BST-84207 [S]	The Night of the Cookers — Live at Club Le Marchal, Vol. 1	1965	7.50	15.00	30.00
—With New York, USA address on label					
BST-84207 [S]	The Night of the Cookers — Live at Club Le Marchal, Vol. 1	1967	3.75	7.50	15.00
—With "A Division of Liberty Records" on label					
BST-84208 [S]	The Night of the Cookers — Live at Club Le Marchal, Vol. 2	1965	7.50	15.00	30.00
—With New York, USA address on label					
BST-84208 [S]	The Night of the Cookers — Live at Club Le Marchal, Vol. 2	1967	3.75	7.50	15.00
—With "A Division of Liberty Records" on label					
B1-85121	Doubletake	1987	2.50	5.00	10.00
B1-85139	Life-Flight	1987	2.50	5.00	10.00
B1-90905	Times 'R Changin'	1989	3.00	6.00	12.00
B1-93202	The Best of Freddie Hubbard	1989	3.00	6.00	12.00
COLUMBIA					
KC 33048	High Energy	1974	2.50	5.00	10.00
PC 33556	Liquid Love	1975	2.50	5.00	10.00
PC 34166	Windjammer	1976	2.50	5.00	10.00
PC 34902	Bundle of Joy	1977	2.50	5.00	10.00
JC 35386	Super Blue	1978	2.50	5.00	10.00
JC 36015	Love Connection	1979	2.50	5.00	10.00
JC 36358	The Best of Freddie Hubbard	1979	2.50	5.00	10.00
FC 36418	Skagly	1980	2.50	5.00	10.00
CTI					
CTS-6001	Red Clay	1970	3.00	6.00	12.00
CTS-6007	The Straight Life	1971	3.00	6.00	12.00
CTS-6013	First Light	1972	3.00	6.00	12.00
CTS-6018	Sky Dive	1973	2.50	5.00	10.00
CTS-6036	Keep Your Soul Together	1974	2.50	5.00	10.00
CTS-6044	Freddie Hubbard In Concert	1974	2.50	5.00	10.00
CTS-6047	The Baddest Hubbard	1974	2.50	5.00	10.00
CTS-6056	Polar AC	1975	2.50	5.00	10.00
8016	Red Clay	198?	2.00	4.00	8.00
—Reissue of 6001					
8017	First Light	198?	2.00	4.00	8.00
—Reissue of 6013					
8022	The Straight Life	198?	2.00	4.00	8.00
—Reissue of 6007					
CTI/CBS ASSOCIATED					
FZ 40687	First Light	1987	2.50	5.00	10.00
ELEKTRA MUSICIAN					
60029	Ride Like the Wind	1982	2.50	5.00	10.00
ENJA					
3095	Outpost	1981	2.50	5.00	10.00
FANTASY					
9610	Splash	1981	2.50	5.00	10.00
9615	Keystone Bop	1982	2.50	5.00	10.00
9626	A Little Night Music	1983	2.50	5.00	10.00
9635	Classics	1984	2.50	5.00	10.00
IMPULSE!					
A-27 [M]	The Artistry of Freddie Hubbard	1962	6.25	12.50	25.00
AS-27 [S]	The Artistry of Freddie Hubbard	1962	7.50	15.00	30.00
A-38 [M]	The Body and Soul of Freddie Hubbard	1963	6.25	12.50	25.00
AS-38 [S]	The Body and Soul of Freddie Hubbard	1963	7.50	15.00	30.00
LIBERTY					
LT-1110	Mistral	1981	2.50	5.00	10.00
PABLO					
2310884	The Best of Freddie Hubbard	1983	2.50	5.00	10.00
2312134	Born to Be Blue	1982	2.50	5.00	10.00
PABLO LIVE					
2620113 [(2)]	Live at the Northsea Jazz Festival, The Hague, 1980	1983	3.00	6.00	12.00
PABLO TODAY					
2312134	Born to Be Blue	198?	2.50	5.00	10.00
PAUSA					
7122	Rollin'	1982	2.50	5.00	10.00
PHOENIX 10					
PHX 318	Extended	1981	2.00	4.00	8.00
PICCADILLY					
3467	Intrepid Fox	198?	2.50	5.00	10.00
QUINTESSENCE					
25161	Skylark	1978	2.50	5.00	10.00
REAL TIME					
305	Back to Birdland	198?	2.50	5.00	10.00

HUBBARD, FREDDIE, AND OSCAR PETERSON

Also see each artist's individual listings.

Albums

Number	Title (A Side/B Side)	Yr	VG	VG+	NM
PABLO					
2310876	Face to Face	198?	2.50	5.00	10.00

HUBBARD, FREDDIE, AND STANLEY TURRENTINE

Also see each artist's individual listings.

Albums

Number	Title (A Side/B Side)	Yr	VG	VG+	NM
CTI					
CTS-6044	In Concert, Volume 1	1974	2.50	5.00	10.00
CTS-6049	In Concert, Volume 2	1975	2.50	5.00	10.00

HUBCAPS, THE

ERNIE MARESCA is in this group.

45s

Number	Title (A Side/B Side)	Yr	VG	VG+	NM
LAURIE					
3219	Hot Rod City (Vocal)/Hot Rod City (Instrumental)	1964	3.75	7.50	15.00

HUDDLE, JACK

45s

Number	Title (A Side/B Side)	Yr	VG	VG+	NM
KAPP					
207	Starlight/Believe Me	1959	50.00	100.00	200.00
—Buddy Holly plays guitar on these tracks					
PETSY					
1002	Starlight/Believe Me	1958	125.00	250.00	500.00

HUDSON, POOKIE

Lead singer with THE SPANIELS.
Lead singer with THE SPANIELS.

45s

Number	Title (A Side/B Side)	Yr	VG	VG+	NM
DOUBLE L					
711	Jealous Heart/I Know, I Know	1963	5.00	10.00	20.00
720	I Love You For Sentimental Reasons/Miracles	1963	5.00	10.00	20.00
JAMIE					
1319	This Gets To Me/All the Places I've Been	1966	15.00	30.00	60.00
PARKWAY					
839	John Brown/Turn Out the Lights	1962	5.00	10.00	20.00

HUDSON, ROCK

45s

Number	Title (A Side/B Side)	Yr	VG	VG+	NM
DECCA					
30966	Pillow Talk/Roly Poly	1959	3.75	7.50	15.00
30966 [PS]	Pillow Talk/Roly Poly	1959	6.25	12.50	25.00

Albums

Number	Title (A Side/B Side)	Yr	VG	VG+	NM
STANYAN					
SR-10014	Rock Gently	1971	6.25	12.50	25.00

HUDSON AND LANDRY

45s

Number	Title (A Side/B Side)	Yr	VG	VG+	NM
DORE					
852	The Hippie and the Redneck/Top 40 DJ's	1971	2.50	5.00	10.00
855	Ajax Liquor Store/The Hippie and the Redneck	1971	2.50	5.00	10.00
868	Ajax Airlines/Bruiser La Rue	1972	2.50	5.00	10.00
874	Obscene Phone Bust/The Prospectors	1972	2.50	5.00	10.00
879	Soul Bowl/Friar Shuck	1972	2.50	5.00	10.00
880	Frontier Christmas (Harlowe and The Mrs.)/The Soul Bowl	1972	2.50	5.00	10.00
881	Ajax Mortuary/Ajax Pet Store	1973	2.50	5.00	10.00
891	The Chocolate Freak/The Fate of the Mightiest Nation	1973	2.50	5.00	10.00
895	The Gas Man/Sir Basil	1974	2.50	5.00	10.00
898	The Weird Kingdom/Montague for President	1974	2.50	5.00	10.00

Albums

Number	Title (A Side/B Side)	Yr	VG	VG+	NM
DORE					
324	Hanging In There	1971	5.00	10.00	20.00
326	Losing Their Heads	1971	5.00	10.00	20.00
329	Right-Off!	1972	5.00	10.00	20.00
331	Weird Kingdom	1973	5.00	10.00	20.00
333	The Best of Hudson and Landry	1974	3.75	7.50	15.00
334	The Best of Hudson and Landry 2	1975	3.75	7.50	15.00

HUDSON BROTHERS, THE

45s

Number	Title (A Side/B Side)	Yr	VG	VG+	NM
ARISTA					
0208	Help Wanted/Last Time I Looked	1976	—	2.50	5.00
0286	I Don't Wanna Be Lonely/Pauline	1977	—	2.50	5.00
0371	The Runaway/You Can't Make Me Cry	1978	—	2.50	5.00
CASABLANCA					
0108	So You Are a Star/Ma Ma Ma Baby	1974	—	3.00	6.00
—With long version of A-side					
801	So You Are a Star/Ma Ma Ma Baby	1974	—	2.50	5.00
—With short version of A-side					
816	Me and My Guitar/Coochie Coochie Coo	1975	—	2.50	5.00
COLUMBIA					
03976	Don't Try to Fight It/You Keep Me Up	1983	—	2.00	4.00
—As "The Hudsons"					
DECCA					
32634	Love Is a Word/Laugh, Funny, Funny	1970	—	3.00	6.00
—As "Everyday Hudson"					
ELEKTRA					
46648	Annie/Joni	1980	—	2.00	4.00
—As "Hudson"					
47049	Afraid to Love/Sidewalk	1980	—	2.00	4.00
—As "Hudson"					
LIONEL					
3211	Love Nobody/The World Would Be a Little Bit Better	1971	—	3.00	6.00
—As "Hudson"					
PLAYBOY					
50001	Someday/Leavin' It's Over	1972	—	3.00	6.00
ROCKET					
40141	America — Fight Back/If You Really Need Me	1973	—	3.00	6.00
—As "Hudson"					
40317	Sunday Driver/Be a Man	1974	—	3.00	6.00
40417	Rendezvous/Medley	1975	—	2.50	5.00
40464	Lonely School Year/If You Really Need Me	1975	—	2.50	5.00
40464 [PS]	Lonely School Year/If You Really Need Me	1975	2.00	4.00	8.00
40508	Spinning the Wheel (With the Girl You Love)/ Bernie Was a Friend of Ours	1976	—	2.50	5.00

Albums

Number	Title (A Side/B Side)	Yr	VG	VG+	NM
ARISTA					
AB 4199	The Truth About Us	1978	2.50	5.00	10.00
CASABLANCA					
NBLP-7004	Hollywood Situation	1974	2.50	5.00	10.00
ELEKTRA					
6E-299	Damn Those Kids	1980	2.50	5.00	10.00
—As "Hudson"					
FIRST AMERICAN					
7708	The Hudson Brothers	1980	2.50	5.00	10.00
PLAYBOY					
102	Hudson	1972	3.75	7.50	15.00
ROCKET					
PIG-460	Totally Out of Control	1974	2.50	5.00	10.00
PIG-2169	Ba-Fa	1975	2.50	5.00	10.00

HUES CORPORATION, THE

45s

LIBERTY

Number	Title (A Side/B Side)	Yr	VG	VG+	NM
56204	Goodfootin'/We're Keepin' Our Business Together	1970	—	3.00	6.00
—As "The Hughes Corporation"					

RCA VICTOR

Number	Title (A Side/B Side)	Yr	VG	VG+	NM
APBO-0139	Go to the Poet/Miracle Maker	1973	—	2.50	5.00
APBO-0232	Rock the Boat/All Goin' Down Together	1974	—	2.50	5.00
PB-10066	Rockin' Soul/Go to the Poet	1974	—	2.50	5.00
PB-10200	Love Corporation/He's My Home	1975	—	2.50	5.00
PB-10311	One Good Night Together/When You Look Down the Road	1975	—	2.50	5.00
PB-10390	You Showed Me What Love Is/When You Look Down the Road	1975	—	2.50	5.00
GB-10480	Rockin' Soul/Go to the Poet	1975	—	—	3.00
—Gold Standard Series					
GB-10481	Rock the Boat/All Goin' Down Together	1975	—	—	3.00
—Gold Standard Series					
74-0813	There He Is Again/Main Chance	1972	—	2.50	5.00
74-0900	Freedom for the Stallion/Off My Cloud	1973	—	2.50	5.00

WARNER BROS.

Number	Title (A Side/B Side)	Yr	VG	VG+	NM
8400	I Caught Your Act/Natural Find	1977	—	2.00	4.00
8559	Give Me Everything/Needed	1978	—	2.00	4.00
8638	Love Dance/With All My Love and Affection	1978	—	2.00	4.00

Albums

RCA VICTOR

Number	Title (A Side/B Side)	Yr	VG	VG+	NM
APL1-0323	Freedom for the Stallion	1973	2.50	5.00	10.00
APL1-0755	Rockin' Soul	1974	2.50	5.00	10.00
APL1-0938	Love Corporation	1975	2.50	5.00	10.00
ANL1-2147	Rock the Boat	1976	2.00	4.00	8.00
APL1-2408	The Best of the Hues Corporation	1977	2.50	5.00	10.00

WARNER BROS.

Number	Title (A Side/B Side)	Yr	VG	VG+	NM
BS 3043	I Caught Your Act	1977	2.50	5.00	10.00
BSK 3196	Your Place or Mine	1978	2.50	5.00	10.00

HUGHES, JIMMY

45s

ATLANTIC

Number	Title (A Side/B Side)	Yr	VG	VG+	NM
2454	Uncle Sam/It Ain't What You've Got	1967	2.00	4.00	8.00

FAME

Number	Title (A Side/B Side)	Yr	VG	VG+	NM
1000	Midnight Affair/When It Comes to Dancing	1965	2.50	5.00	10.00
1003	Neighbor, Neighbor/It's a Good Thing	1966	2.00	4.00	8.00
1006	I Worship the Ground You Walk On/A Shot of Rhythm and Blues	1966	2.00	4.00	8.00
1011	Why Not Tonight/I'm a Man of Action	1967	2.00	4.00	8.00
1014	Don't Lose Your Good Thing/You Can't Believe Everything That You Hear	1967	2.00	4.00	8.00
1015	Hi-Heel Sneakers/Time Will Bring You Back	1967	2.00	4.00	8.00
6401	Steal Away/Lollipops, Lace and Lipstick	1964	5.00	10.00	20.00
—Black label					
6401	Steal Away/Lollipops, Lace and Lipstick	1964	3.00	6.00	12.00
—Red label					
6403	Try Me/Lovely Ladies	1964	2.50	5.00	10.00
6404	I Want Justice/I'm Getting Better	1964	2.50	5.00	10.00
6407	Goodbye My Lover, Goodbye/It Was Nice	1965	2.50	5.00	10.00
6410	You Really Know How to Hurt a Guy/The Loving Physician	1965	2.50	5.00	10.00

GUYDEN

Number	Title (A Side/B Side)	Yr	VG	VG+	NM
2075	I'm Qualified/My Loving Time	1962	5.00	10.00	20.00

JAMIE

Number	Title (A Side/B Side)	Yr	VG	VG+	NM
1280	I'm Qualified/My Loving Time	1964	3.75	7.50	15.00

VOLT

Number	Title (A Side/B Side)	Yr	VG	VG+	NM
4002	I Like Everything About You/What Side of the Door	1968	2.00	4.00	8.00
4008	Let 'Em Down Baby/The Sweet Things You Do	1969	2.00	4.00	8.00
4017	Chains of Love/I'm Not Ashamed to Beg or Plead	1969	2.00	4.00	8.00
4024	I'm So Glad/Lay It on the Line	1969	2.00	4.00	8.00

Albums

ATCO

Number	Title (A Side/B Side)	Yr	VG	VG+	NM
33-209 [M]	Why Not Tonight	1967	5.00	10.00	20.00
SD 33-209 [S]	Why Not Tonight	1967	5.00	10.00	20.00

VEE JAY

Number	Title (A Side/B Side)	Yr	VG	VG+	NM
VJ-1102 [M]	Steal Away	1965	6.25	12.50	25.00
VJS-1102 [R]	Steal Away	1965	6.25	12.50	25.00

VOLT

Number	Title (A Side/B Side)	Yr	VG	VG+	NM
VOS-6003	Something Special	1969	5.00	10.00	20.00

HUGO AND LUIGI

45s

MERCURY

Number	Title (A Side/B Side)	Yr	VG	VG+	NM
70563	Medley: Nobody's Sweetheart-Somebody Stole My Gal/The Crazy Otto Rag	1955	3.00	6.00	12.00
70676	A Satisfied Mind/The Goodbye Song	1955	3.00	6.00	12.00
70721	Young Abe Lincoln/Two-Thirds of the Tennessee River	1955	3.00	6.00	12.00
70803	Our Melody/Anywhere Is Home with You	1956	3.00	6.00	12.00

RCA VICTOR

Number	Title (A Side/B Side)	Yr	VG	VG+	NM
SP-45-101 [DJ]	RCA Victor Special DJ Spots	1959	2.50	5.00	10.00
47-7518	La Plume de Ma Tante/Honolulu Lu	1959	2.00	4.00	8.00
47-7569	Watusi Wedding/Yalaloo	1959	2.00	4.00	8.00
47-7639	Just Come Home/Lonesome Stranger	1959	2.00	4.00	8.00
47-7808	Smile/Tweedle Dee	1960	2.00	4.00	8.00
47-7868	La Pachange/Bimbombey	1961	2.00	4.00	8.00
47-7955	Brotherhood of Man/Love from a Heart of Gold	1961	2.00	4.00	8.00

ROULETTE

Number	Title (A Side/B Side)	Yr	VG	VG+	NM
4012	Rockabilly Party/Shenandoah Rose	1957	3.75	7.50	15.00
4050	76 Trombones/Twilight in Tennessee	1958	3.00	6.00	12.00
4074	Cha-Hua-Hua/Something's Always Happening on the River	1958	3.00	6.00	12.00

Albums

RCA VICTOR

Number	Title (A Side/B Side)	Yr	VG	VG+	NM
LPM-2254 [M]	The Sound of Children at Christmas	1960	3.75	7.50	15.00
LSP-2254 [S]	The Sound of Children at Christmas	1960	5.00	10.00	20.00
LPM-2641 [M]	The Cascading Voices of the Hugo & Luigi Chorus	1963	2.50	5.00	10.00
LSP-2641 [S]	The Cascading Voices of the Hugo & Luigi Chorus	1963	3.00	6.00	12.00
LPM-2717 [M]	Let's Fall in Love	1963	2.50	5.00	10.00
LSP-2717 [S]	Let's Fall in Love	1963	3.00	6.00	12.00
LPM-2789 [M]	The Cascading Voices of the Hugo & Luigi Chorus — With Brass	1964	2.50	5.00	10.00
LSP-2789 [S]	The Cascading Voices of the Hugo & Luigi Chorus — With Brass	1964	3.00	6.00	12.00
LPM-2863 [M]	The Cascading Voices of the Hugo & Luigi Chorus — With Strings	1964	2.50	5.00	10.00
LSP-2863 [S]	The Cascading Voices of the Hugo & Luigi Chorus — With Strings	1964	3.00	6.00	12.00
LSP-4083	Maggie Flynn	1968	2.50	5.00	10.00

ROULETTE

Number	Title (A Side/B Side)	Yr	VG	VG+	NM
R-25044 [M]	When Good Fellows Get Together	1959	5.00	10.00	20.00
R-25283 [M]	Cascading Voices	1965	3.00	6.00	12.00
SR-25283 [S]	Cascading Voices	1965	3.75	7.50	15.00

WING

Number	Title (A Side/B Side)	Yr	VG	VG+	NM
MGW 12207 [M]	Sing Along by the Fireside	195?	3.00	6.00	12.00

HULLABALLOOS, THE

45s

ROULETTE

Number	Title (A Side/B Side)	Yr	VG	VG+	NM
4587	I'm Gonna Love You Too/Party Doll	1964	5.00	10.00	20.00
4587 [PS]	I'm Gonna Love You Too/Party Doll	1964	10.00	20.00	40.00
4593	Beware/Did You Ever	1965	5.00	10.00	20.00
4593 [PS]	Beware/Did You Ever	1965	10.00	20.00	40.00
4612	Learning the Game/Don't Stop	1965	5.00	10.00	20.00
4612 [PS]	Learning the Game/Don't Stop	1965	10.00	20.00	40.00
4622	I Won't Turn Around Now/My Heart Keeps Telling Me	1965	5.00	10.00	20.00
4622 [PS]	I Won't Turn Around Now/My Heart Keeps Telling Me	1965	10.00	20.00	40.00

Albums

ROULETTE

Number	Title (A Side/B Side)	Yr	VG	VG+	NM
R-25297 [M]	England's Newest Singing Sensations	1965	12.50	25.00	50.00
SR-25297 [P]	England's Newest Singing Sensations	1965	18.75	37.50	75.00
R-25310 [M]	The Hullabaloos on Hullabaloo	1965	12.50	25.00	50.00
SR-25310 [P]	The Hullabaloos on Hullabaloo	1965	18.75	37.50	75.00

HULLABALOO SINGERS AND ORCHESTRA, THE

Albums

COLUMBIA

Number	Title (A Side/B Side)	Yr	VG	VG+	NM
CL 2410 [M]	The Hullabaloo Show	1965	5.00	10.00	20.00
CS 9210 [S]	The Hullabaloo Show	1965	6.25	12.50	25.00

HUMAN BEINZ, THE

45s

CAPITOL

Number	Title (A Side/B Side)	Yr	VG	VG+	NM
2119	Turn On Your Love Light/It's Fun to Be Clean	1968	2.50	5.00	10.00
2119 [PS]	Turn On Your Love Light/It's Fun to Be Clean	1968	5.00	10.00	20.00
2198	Every Time Woman/The Face	1968	2.50	5.00	10.00
2431	I've Got to Keep On Pushin'/This Little Girl of Mine	1969	2.50	5.00	10.00
5990	Nobody But Me/Sueno	1967	3.75	7.50	15.00

GATEWAY

Number	Title (A Side/B Side)	Yr	VG	VG+	NM
828	Gloria/The Times They Are a-Changin'	1967	3.75	7.50	15.00
838	You Can't Make Me Cry/The Pied Piper	1967	3.75	7.50	15.00

Albums

CAPITOL

Number	Title (A Side/B Side)	Yr	VG	VG+	NM
ST 2906	Nobody But Me	1968	7.50	15.00	30.00
ST 2926	Evolutions	1968	10.00	20.00	40.00

GATEWAY

Number	Title (A Side/B Side)	Yr	VG	VG+	NM
GLP-3012	Nobody But Me	1968	10.00	20.00	40.00
—With added tracks by The Mammals					

HUMAN EXPRESSION, THE

45s

ACCENT

Number	Title (A Side/B Side)	Yr	VG	VG+	NM
1214	Every Night/Love at Psychedelic Velocity	1967	50.00	100.00	200.00
1226	Calm Me Down/Optical Sound	1967	25.00	50.00	100.00
1252	I Don't Need Nobody/Sweet Child of Nothingness	1967	25.00	50.00	100.00

HUMBLE PIE

45s

ATCO

Number	Title (A Side/B Side)	Yr	VG	VG+	NM
7216	Fool for a Pretty Face/You Soppy Pratt	1980	—	2.50	5.00

A&M

Number	Title (A Side/B Side)	Yr	VG	VG+	NM
1282	I Don't Need No Doctor/Song for Jenny	1971	—	2.00	4.00
1282 [PS]	I Don't Need No Doctor/Song for Jenny	1971	—	3.00	6.00
1349	Hot and Nasty/You're So Good for Me	1972	—	2.00	4.00
1349 [PS]	Hot and Nasty/You're So Good for Me	1972	—	3.00	6.00
1366	Sweet Peace and Time/30 Days in the Hole	1972	—	2.00	4.00
1406	Say No More/Black Coffee	1973	—	2.00	4.00
1440	Honky Tonk Woman/Get Down to It	1973	—	2.00	4.00
1484	Oh La De Da/The Out Crowd	1974	—	2.00	4.00
1530	Rally with Ali/Ninety-Nine Pounds	1974	—	2.00	4.00
1711	Road Hog/Rock and Roll Music	1975	—	2.00	4.00

IMMEDIATE

Number	Title (A Side/B Side)	Yr	VG	VG+	NM
001	Natural Born Woman/I'll Go Alone	1969	2.00	4.00	8.00

Albums

ACCORD

Number	Title (A Side/B Side)	Yr	VG	VG+	NM
SN-7192	Recaptured	1981	2.50	5.00	10.00

ATCO

Number	Title (A Side/B Side)	Yr	VG	VG+	NM
SD 38-122	On to Victory	1980	2.50	5.00	10.00
SD 38-131	Go for the Throat	1981	2.50	5.00	10.00

Number	Title (A Side/B Side)	Yr	VG	VG+	NM
A&M					
SP-3127	Humble Pie	1981	2.00	4.00	8.00
—Budget-line reissue					
SP-3132	Smokin'	1981	2.00	4.00	8.00
—Budget-line reissue					
SP-3208	The Best of Humble Pie	1982	2.50	5.00	10.00
SP-3506 [(2)]	Performance — Rockin' the Fillmore	1971	3.75	7.50	15.00
SP-3513 [(2)]	Lost and Found	1972	3.75	7.50	15.00
SP-3611	Thunderbox	1974	3.00	6.00	12.00
SP-3701 [(2)]	Eat It	1973	3.75	7.50	15.00
SP-4270	Humble Pie	1970	3.00	6.00	12.00
SP-4301	Rock On	1971	3.00	6.00	12.00
SP-4342	Smokin'	1972	3.00	6.00	12.00
SP-4514	Street Rats	1975	3.00	6.00	12.00
SP-6008 [(2)]	Performance — Rockin' the Fillmore	1981	2.50	5.00	10.00
—Budget-line reissue					
SP-6009 [(2)]	Lost and Found	1981	2.50	5.00	10.00
—Budget-line reissue					
SP-6503 [(2)]	Eat It	1981	2.50	5.00	10.00
—Budget-line reissue					
COMPLEAT					
672009-1 [(2)]	A Slice of Humble Pie	1985	3.00	6.00	12.00

HUMBLEBUMS, THE

GERRY RAFFERTY was in this group.

Number	Title (A Side/B Side)	Yr	VG	VG+	NM
45s					
UNITED ARTISTS					
50771	All the Best People Do It/Cruisin'	1971	2.50	5.00	10.00
Albums					
LIBERTY					
LST-7636	The Humblebums	1969	7.50	15.00	30.00
LST-7656	Open Up the Door	1970	7.50	15.00	30.00

HUMES, ANITA

Number	Title (A Side/B Side)	Yr	VG	VG+	NM
45s					
ROULETTE					
4564	Don't Fight It Baby/When Somethin's Hard to Get	1964	3.75	7.50	15.00
4575	I'm Making It Over/Just for the Boy	1964	3.75	7.50	15.00
4750	Are You Going My Way/Everybody's Got You	1967	2.50	5.00	10.00

HUMPERDINCK, ENGELBERT

Number	Title (A Side/B Side)	Yr	VG	VG+	NM
45s					
EPIC					
AE7 1170 [DJ]	Christmas Song/Silent Night	1978	—	2.00	4.00
AE7 1170 [PS]	Christmas Song/Silent Night	1978	—	2.00	4.00
02060	Don't You Love Me Anymore/Till I Get It Right	1981	—	—	3.00
02245	Maybe This Time/When the Night Ends	1981	—	—	3.00
03817	Till You and Your Lover Are Lovers Again/What Will I Write	1983	—	—	3.00
50270	After the Lovin'/Let's Remember the Good Times	1976	—	2.50	5.00
50365	I Believe in Miracles/Goodbye My Friend	1977	—	2.00	4.00
50447	A Lover's Holiday/Look at Me	1977	—	2.00	4.00
50488	A Night to Remember/Silent Night	1977	—	2.00	4.00
50526	The Last of the Romantics/I Have Paid the Toll	1978	—	2.00	4.00
50566	Love Me Tender/This Time One Year Ago	1978	—	2.00	4.00
50579	Love's In Need of Love Today/Sweet Marjorene	1978	—	2.00	4.00
50632	This Moment in Time/And the Day Begins	1978	—	2.00	4.00
50692	Can't Help Falling in Love/You Know Me	1979	—	2.00	4.00
50732	Lovin' Too Well/Much, Much Greater Love	1979	—	2.00	4.00
50844	Love's Only Love/Burning Ember	1980	—	—	3.00
50899	A Chance to Be a Hero/Any Kind of Love at All	1980	—	—	3.00
50933	Don't Cry Out Loud/Don't Touch That Dial	1980	—	—	3.00
50958	It's Not Easy to Live Together/Royal Affair	1980	—	—	3.00
HICKORY					
1337	Baby Turn Around/If I Could Do the Things I Want to Do	1965	4.00	8.00	16.00
—As "Gerry Dorsey"					
PARROT					
40011 [M]	Release Me (And Let Me Love Again)/Ten Guitars	1967	2.00	4.00	8.00
40011 [S]	Release Me (And Let Me Love Again)/Ten Guitars	1967	5.00	10.00	20.00
—Both sides in true stereo. Letters "XDR" are stamped in run-off area before the matrix number					
40015	There Goes My Everything/You Love	1967	2.00	4.00	8.00
40019	The Last Waltz/That Promise	1967	2.00	4.00	8.00
40019 [PS]	The Last Waltz/That Promise	1967	3.00	6.00	12.00
40023	Am I That Easy to Forget/Pretty Ribbons	1967	2.00	4.00	8.00
40023 [PS]	Am I That Easy to Forget/Pretty Ribbons	1967	3.00	6.00	12.00
40027	A Man Without Love/Call on Me	1968	2.00	4.00	8.00
40032	Les Bicyclettes De Belsize/Three Little Words	1968	2.00	4.00	8.00
40032 [PS]	Les Bicyclettes De Belsize/Three Little Words	1968	3.00	6.00	12.00
40036	The Way It Used to Be/A Good Thing Going	1969	—	3.00	6.00
40036 [PS]	The Way It Used to Be/A Good Thing Going	1969	2.50	5.00	10.00
40040	I'm a Better Man/Cafe	1969	—	3.00	6.00
40044	Winter World of Love/Take My Heart	1969	—	3.00	6.00
40044 [PS]	Winter World of Love/Take My Heart	1969	2.50	5.00	10.00
40049	My Marie/Our Song (La Paloma)	1970	—	3.00	6.00
40049 [PS]	My Marie/Our Song (La Paloma)	1970	2.00	4.00	8.00
40054	Sweetheart/Born to Be Wanted	1970	—	3.00	6.00
40054 [PS]	Sweetheart/Born to Be Wanted	1970	2.00	4.00	8.00
40059	When There's No You/Stranger, Step In My World	1971	—	3.00	6.00
40059 [PS]	When There's No You/Stranger, Step In My World	1971	2.00	4.00	8.00
40065	Another Time, Another Place/You're the Window of My World	1971	—	3.00	6.00
40069	Too Beautiful to Last/A Hundred Times a Day	1972	—	2.50	5.00
40071	In Time/How Does It Feel	1972	—	2.50	5.00
40072	I Never Said Goodbye/Time After Time	1972	—	2.50	5.00
40073	I'm Leavin' You/My Summer Song	1973	—	2.00	4.00
40076	Love Is All/Lady of the Night	1973	—	2.00	4.00
40077	Free as the Wind/My Friend the Wind	1974	—	2.00	4.00
40079	Catch Me I'm Falling/Love, Oh Precious Love	1974	—	2.00	4.00
40082	Forever and Ever/Precious Love	1974	—	2.00	4.00
40085	This Is What You Mean to Me/A World Without Music	1975	—	2.00	4.00
Albums					
EPIC					
(no #) [PD]	Last of the Romantics	1978	6.25	12.50	25.00
PE 34381	After the Lovin'	1976	2.50	5.00	10.00
—Orange label					
PE 34381	After the Lovin'	198?	2.00	4.00	8.00
—Reissue with bar code; dark blue label					
E 34436	The Ultimate	1977	2.50	5.00	10.00
—Orange label					
PE 34436	The Ultimate	198?	2.00	4.00	8.00
—Reissue with bar code; dark blue label					
E 34719	Golden Love Songs	1977	2.50	5.00	10.00
—Orange label					
PE 34719	Golden Love Songs	198?	2.00	4.00	8.00
—Reissue with bar code; dark blue label					
PE 34730	Miracles	1977	2.50	5.00	10.00
—Orange label					
PE 34730	Miracles	198?	2.00	4.00	8.00
—Reissue with bar code; dark blue label					
JE 35020	Last of the Romantics	1978	2.50	5.00	10.00
—Orange label					
PE 35020	Last of the Romantics	198?	2.00	4.00	8.00
—Reissue with bar code; dark blue label					
PE 35031	Christmas Tyme	1977	3.00	6.00	12.00
JE 35791	This Moment in Time	1979	2.50	5.00	10.00
PE 35791	This Moment in Time	198?	2.00	4.00	8.00
—Budget-line reissue					
JE 36431	Love's Only Love	1980	2.50	5.00	10.00
PE 36765	A Merry Christmas with Engelbert Humperdinck	1980	2.50	5.00	10.00
—Some copies of the record have a "JE" prefix					
E2X 36782 [(2)]	All of Me/Live in Concert	1980	3.00	6.00	12.00
FE 37128	Don't You Love Me Anymore	1981	2.50	5.00	10.00
PE 37128	Don't You Love Me Anymore	1983	2.00	4.00	8.00
—Budget-line reissue					
FE 38087	You and Your Lover	1983	2.50	5.00	10.00
PE 39469	White Christmas	1984	2.50	5.00	10.00
LONDON					
BP 688/9 [(2)]	Engelbert Humperdinck Sings for You	1977	3.75	7.50	15.00
PS 709	Love Letters	1978	2.50	5.00	10.00
PARROT					
PA 61012 [M]	Release Me	1967	5.00	10.00	20.00
PA 61015 [M]	The Last Waltz	1967	5.00	10.00	20.00
PAS 71012 [S]	Release Me	1967	3.75	7.50	15.00
PAS 71015 [S]	The Last Waltz	1967	3.75	7.50	15.00
PAS 71022	A Man Without Love	1968	3.75	7.50	15.00
PAS 71026	Engelbert	1969	3.75	7.50	15.00
XPAS 71030	Engelbert Humperdinck	1969	3.75	7.50	15.00
XPAS 71038	We Made It Happen	1970	3.75	7.50	15.00
XPAS 71043	Sweetheart	1971	3.75	7.50	15.00
XPAS 71048	Another Time, Another Place	1971	3.75	7.50	15.00
XPAS 71051	Live at the Riviera, Las Vegas	1971	3.75	7.50	15.00
XPAS 71056	In Time	1972	3.75	7.50	15.00
XPAS 71061	King of Hearts	1973	3.75	7.50	15.00
APAS 71065	My Love	1974	3.75	7.50	15.00
PAS 71067	His Greatest Hits	1974	3.75	7.50	15.00

HUMPHREY, BOBBI

Number	Title (A Side/B Side)	Yr	VG	VG+	NM
12-Inch Singles					
EPIC					
50537	Home-Made Jam/Sunset Burgundy	1978	2.50	5.00	10.00
50746	Love When I'm In Your Arms/Sweet and Low	1979	2.50	5.00	10.00
WARNER BROS.					
21716	Let's Get Started (2 versions)/Rainbows	1990	—	3.00	6.00
45s					
BLUE NOTE					
XW395	Chicago, Damn/Just a Love Child	1974	—	2.50	5.00
XW455	Harlem River Drive/Black and Blues	1974	—	2.50	5.00
XW592	Fun House/San Francisco Lights	1975	—	2.50	5.00
XW785	Uno Esta/Sweeter Than Sugar	1976	—	2.50	5.00
1971	Spanish Harlem/Sad Bag	1971	2.00	4.00	8.00
1974	Ain't No Sunchine/Sad Bag	1972	2.00	4.00	8.00
1980	Is This All/Lonely Town, Lonely Street	1972	2.00	4.00	8.00
EPIC					
50448	Dancin' to Keep From Cryin'/Theme I	1977	—	2.50	5.00
50529	Home-Made Jam/Sunset Burgundy	1978	—	2.50	5.00
50745	Love When I'm In Your Arms/Sweet and Low	1979	—	2.50	5.00
Albums					
BLUE NOTE					
BN-LA142-G	Blacks and Blues	1974	2.50	5.00	10.00
BN-LA344-G	Satin Doll	1974	2.50	5.00	10.00
BN-LA550-G	Fancy Dancer	1975	2.50	5.00	10.00
BN-LA699-G	The Best of Bobbi Humphrey	1976	2.50	5.00	10.00
BST-84379	Flute-In	1971	3.00	6.00	12.00
BST-84421	Dig This	1972	3.00	6.00	12.00
EPIC					
PE 34704	Tailor Made	1977	2.50	5.00	10.00
JE 35338	Freestyle	1978	2.50	5.00	10.00
JE 35607	The Good Life	1979	2.50	5.00	10.00
JE 36368	The Best of Bobbi Humphrey	1980	2.50	5.00	10.00

HUMPHREY, PAUL

Number	Title (A Side/B Side)	Yr	VG	VG+	NM
45s					
LIZARD					
1009	Funky L.A./Baby Rice	1971	—	3.00	6.00
21006	Cool Aid/Detroit	1971	—	3.00	6.00
Albums					
BLUE THUMB					
BTS 47	Supermellow	1973	3.00	6.00	12.00
BTS 66	America, Wake Up!	1974	3.00	6.00	12.00
DISCOVERY					
DS-850	Paul Humphrey Sextet	1981	2.50	5.00	10.00
LIZARD					
20106	Paul Humphrey & the Cool Aid Chemists	1971	3.75	7.50	15.00

HUNGER

45s

PUBLIC

Number	Title (A Side/B Side)	Yr	VG	VG+	NM
101	Mind Machine/(B-side unknown)	1968	6.25	12.50	25.00
103	No Shame/(B-side unknown)	1968	6.25	12.50	25.00
1001	Colors/(B-side unknown)	1969	7.50	15.00	30.00

Albums

PUBLIC

Number	Title (A Side/B Side)	Yr	VG	VG+	NM
1006	Strictly from Hunger	1969	150.00	300.00	600.00

HUNT, DANNY

45s

DYNAMITE

Number	Title (A Side/B Side)	Yr	VG	VG+	NM
8663	What's Happening to Our Love Affair/(B-side unknown)	1974	5.00	10.00	20.00

HUNT, GERALDINE

45s

Number	Title (A Side/B Side)	Yr	VG	VG+	NM
ABC					
10859	Winner Take All/For Lovers Only	1966	7.50	15.00	30.00
BOMBAY					
4501	He's for Real/(B-side unknown)	1964	25.00	50.00	100.00
CHECKER					
1028	I Let Myself Go/I Wished I Had Listened	1962	7.50	15.00	30.00
PRISM					
315	Can't Fake the Feeling/(B-side unknown)	1980	—	2.00	4.00
323	Heart Heart/(B-side unknown)	1981	—	2.00	4.00
ROULETTE					
7068	Never, Never Leave Me/Push, Sweet	1970	—	3.00	6.00
7109	Now That There's You/Shades of Blue	1971	—	3.00	6.00
7129	Baby, I Need Your Loving/(B-side unknown)	1972	—	3.00	6.00
7132	Cold Blood/Just Believe in Me	1972	—	3.00	6.00
7149	You Brought Joy/Shades of Blue	1973	—	3.00	6.00
U.S.A.					
732	Sneak Around/It Never Happened Before	1962	7.50	15.00	30.00
737	Sneak Around/It Never Happened Before	1963	6.25	12.50	25.00

HUNTER, CHRISTINE

45s

ROULETTE

Number	Title (A Side/B Side)	Yr	VG	VG+	NM
4589	Santa Bring Me Ringo/Where Were You Daddy	1964	3.75	7.50	15.00

HUNTER, IAN

Also see MOTT THE HOOPLE.

45s

Number	Title (A Side/B Side)	Yr	VG	VG+	NM
CHRYSALIS					
2324	When the Daylight Comes/Life After Death	1979	—	2.50	5.00
2352	Cleveland Rocks/Just Another Night	1979	—	2.50	5.00
2405	We Gotta Get Out of Here/Sons and Daughters	1980	—	2.00	4.00
2542	I Need Your Love/(B-side unknown)	1981	—	2.00	4.00
2569	Central Park 'N' West/(B-side unknown)	1981	—	2.00	4.00
COLUMBIA					
03929	All of the Good Ones Are Taken/Death 'N' Glory Boys	1983	—	2.00	4.00
04166	Seeing Double/That Girl Is Rock 'N' Roll	1983	—	2.00	4.00
10161	Once Bitten Twice Shy/3000 Miles from Here	1975	—	3.00	6.00

Albums

Number	Title (A Side/B Side)	Yr	VG	VG+	NM
CHRYSALIS					
CHS 1214	You're Never Alone with a Schizophrenic	1979	2.50	5.00	10.00
2CHS 1269 [(2)]	Ian Hunter Live/Welcome to the Club	1980	3.00	6.00	12.00
CHS 1326	Short Back N' Sides	1981	2.50	5.00	10.00
PV 41214	You're Never Alone with a Schizophrenic	1982	2.00	4.00	8.00
—Budget-line reissue					
PV 41326	Short Back N' Sides	1982	2.00	4.00	8.00
—Budget-line reissue					
COLUMBIA					
PC 33480	Ian Hunter	1975	2.50	5.00	10.00
—No bar code on cover					
PC 33480	Ian Hunter	198?	2.00	4.00	8.00
—Budget-line reissue with bar code					
PC 34142	All American Alien Boy	1976	2.50	5.00	10.00
—No bar code on cover					
PC 34142	All American Alien Boy	198?	2.00	4.00	8.00
—Budget-line reissue with bar code					
PC 34721	Overnight Angels	1977	2.50	5.00	10.00
—No bar code on cover					
C2 36251 [(2)]	Shades of Ian Hunter	1980	3.00	6.00	12.00
FC 38628	All of the Good Ones Are Taken	1983	2.50	5.00	10.00

HUNTER, IVORY JOE

45s

Number	Title (A Side/B Side)	Yr	VG	VG+	NM
ATLANTIC					
1049	It May Sound Silly/I Got to Learn to Do the Mambo	1954	6.25	12.50	25.00
1066	I Want Somebody/Heven Came Down to Earth	1955	6.25	12.50	25.00
1086	A Tear Fell/I Need You By My Side	1956	6.25	12.50	25.00
1095	You Mean Everything to Me/That's Why I Dream	1956	6.25	12.50	25.00
1111	Since I Met You Baby/You Can't Stop This Rocking and Rolling	1956	7.50	15.00	30.00
1128	Empty Arms/Love's a Hurting Game	1957	5.00	10.00	20.00
1151	She's Gone/Everytime I Hear That Song	1957	5.00	10.00	20.00
1164	All About the Blues/If Only You Were Here with Me	1957	5.00	10.00	20.00
1173	You're On My Mind/Baby, Baby, Count on Me	1958	5.00	10.00	20.00
1183	I'm So Glad I Found You/Shooty Booty	1958	5.00	10.00	20.00
1191	You Flip Me Baby/Yes, I Want You	1958	5.00	10.00	20.00
2020	I Just Want to Love You/Now I Don't Worry No More	1959	3.75	7.50	15.00
CAPITOL					
4587	I'm Hooked/Because I Love You	1961	3.00	6.00	12.00
4648	May the Best Man Win/You Better Believe It Baby	1961	3.00	6.00	12.00
4688	The Life I Live/A Great Big Heart Full of Love	1962	3.00	6.00	12.00
DOT					
15880	City Lights/Stolen Moments	1958	3.75	7.50	15.00
15930	Old Fashioned Love/Cottage for Sale	1959	3.75	7.50	15.00
15957	I Love You So Much It Hurts/Welcome Home Baby	1959	3.75	7.50	15.00
15986	My Search Was Ended/Did You Mean It	1959	3.75	7.50	15.00
EPIC					
10725	Heartbreak and Misery/We All Like That Groovy Feeling	1971	—	3.00	6.00
10725	Heartbreak and Misery/I'm Coming Down with the Blues	1971	—	3.00	6.00
GOLDISC					
3010	It's Love, It's Love, It's Love/You Satisfy Me Baby	1960	3.75	7.50	15.00
GOLDWAX					
307	Every Little Bit Helped Me/I Can Make You Happy	1966	5.00	10.00	20.00
KING					
4424	False Friend Blues/Send Me Pretty Mama	1951	10.00	20.00	40.00
—Ivory Joe Hunter records on King before 4422 are unconfirmed on 45 rpm					
4443	She's Gone Blues/Stop Rockin' That Train	1951	10.00	20.00	40.00
4455	Old Gal and New Gal Blues/Woo Wee Blues	1951	10.00	20.00	40.00
5166	Jealous Heart/I Like It	1958	3.75	7.50	15.00
5271	Guess Who/Don't Fall in Love with Me	1959	—	—	—
—Unreleased					
5280	Guess Who/Don't Fall in Love with Me	1959	3.75	7.50	15.00
MGM					
8011	I Almost Lost My Mind/If I Give You My Love	1949	12.50	25.00	50.00
—Original 45 issue of this record					
10578	I Almost Lost My Mind/If I Give You My Love	1949	10.00	20.00	40.00
10618	S.P. Blues/Why Fool Yourself	1950	7.50	15.00	30.00
10663	I Need You So/Leave Her Alone	1950	7.50	15.00	30.00
10733	Let Me Dream/Gimme a Pound of Round Ground	1950	7.50	15.00	30.00
10761	Old Man's Boogie/Living a Lie	1950	7.50	15.00	30.00
10818	It's A Sin/Don't You Believe Me	1950	7.50	15.00	30.00
10899	I Found My Baby/I Ain't Got No Gal	1951	7.50	15.00	30.00
10951	I Can't Get You Off My Mind/I Can't Resist You	1951	7.50	15.00	30.00
10995	You Lied/When I Lost You	1951	7.50	15.00	30.00
11052	I'm Yours/Wrong Woman Blues	1951	7.50	15.00	30.00
11132	Blue Moon/U Name It	1952	7.50	15.00	30.00
11165	Laugh/Where Shall I Go	1952	7.50	15.00	30.00
11195	I'm Sorry for You My Friend/I Will Be	1952	7.50	15.00	30.00
11263	I Get That Lonesome Feeling/I Thought I Had Loved	1952	7.50	15.00	30.00
11325	Big Bounce/Tell Her for Me	1952	7.50	15.00	30.00
11378	Rockin' Chair Boogie/Music Before Dawn	1952	7.50	15.00	30.00
11459	I Had a Girl/If You See My Baby	1953	7.50	15.00	30.00
11549	I'm Afraid/Don't Make Me Cry	1953	7.50	15.00	30.00
11599	I Must Be Talking to Myself/My Best Wishes	1953	7.50	15.00	30.00
11702	I Have a Secret/I Feel So Good	1954	6.25	12.50	25.00
11818	Do You Miss Me/Whose Arms Are You Missing	1954	6.25	12.50	25.00
PARAMOUNT					
0253	He'll Never Love You/San Antonio Rose	1973	—	3.00	6.00
SMASH					
1825	My Arms Are Waiting/Congratulations	1963	3.00	6.00	12.00
1860	There's No Forgetting You/My Lover's Prayer	1963	3.00	6.00	12.00
SOUND STAGE 7					
2623	Ivory Tower/I'll Give You All Night to Stop	1968	2.00	4.00	8.00
2635	Until the Day I Die/I Built a Wall Around Me	1969	2.00	4.00	8.00
2643	Straighten Up Baby/Baby Me Baby	1969	2.00	4.00	8.00
STAX					
155	This Kind of Woman/Can't Explain Why It Happened	1964	3.00	6.00	12.00
TEARDROP					
3058	I've Asked You for the Last Time/Heart	196?	2.50	5.00	10.00
VEE JAY					
452	Somebody's Stealing My Love/You Only Want Me When You Need Me	1962	3.00	6.00	12.00
VEEP					
1258	What's the Matter Baby/Don't You Believe Me	1967	2.00	4.00	8.00
1270	Did She Ask About Me/From the First Time We Met	1967	2.00	4.00	8.00

7-Inch Extended Plays

Number	Title (A Side/B Side)	Yr	VG	VG+	NM
ATLANTIC					
589	*Since I Met You Baby/I Got to Learn to Do the Mambo/It May Sound Silly/A Tear Fell	1958	12.50	25.00	50.00
589 [PS]	Ivory Joe Hunter (Since I Met You Baby)	1958	12.50	25.00	50.00
608	(contents unknown)	1958	15.00	30.00	60.00
608 [PS]	Rock with Ivory Joe Hunter	1958	15.00	30.00	60.00
KING					
265	(contents unknown)	1954	20.00	40.00	80.00
265 [PS]	Ivory Joe Hunter	1954	20.00	40.00	80.00
MGM					
X-1376	(contents unknown)	1957	12.50	25.00	50.00
X-1376 [PS]	I Get That Lonesome Feeling, Volume 1	1957	12.50	25.00	50.00
X-1377	(contents unknown)	1957	12.50	25.00	50.00
X-1377 [PS]	I Get That Lonesome Feeling, Volume 2	1957	12.50	25.00	50.00
X-1378	(contents unknown)	1957	12.50	25.00	50.00
X-1378 [PS]	I Get That Lonesome Feeling, Volume 3	1957	12.50	25.00	50.00

Albums

Number	Title (A Side/B Side)	Yr	VG	VG+	NM
ARCHIVE OF FOLK AND JAZZ					
289	Ivory Joe Hunter	1974	3.00	6.00	12.00
ATLANTIC					
8008 [M]	Ivory Joe Hunter	1957	50.00	100.00	200.00
—Black label					
8008 [M]	Ivory Joe Hunter	1960	25.00	50.00	100.00
—Purple and red label					
8015 [M]	The Old and the New	1958	50.00	100.00	200.00
—Black label					
8015 [M]	The Old and the New	1960	25.00	50.00	100.00
—Purple and red label					
DOT					
DLP-3569 [M]	This Is Ivory Joe Hunter	1964	10.00	20.00	40.00
DLP-25569 [S]	This Is Ivory Joe Hunter	1964	12.50	25.00	50.00

Number	Title (A Side/B Side)	Yr	VG	VG+	NM
EPIC					
E 30348	The Return of Ivory Joe Hunter	1971	5.00	10.00	20.00
GOLDISC					
403 [M]	The Fabulous Ivory Joe Hunter	1961	15.00	30.00	60.00
HOME COOKING					
112	I'm Coming Down with the Blues	1989	3.00	6.00	12.00
KING					
605 [M]	16 of His Greatest Hits	1958	100.00	200.00	400.00
LION					
L-70068 [M]	I Need You So	1959	15.00	30.00	60.00
MGM					
E-3488 [M]	I Get That Lonesome Feeling	1957	75.00	150.00	300.00
PARAMOUNT					
PAS-6080	I've Always Been Country	1974	3.00	6.00	12.00
POLYDOR					
830897-1	Since I Met You Baby	1987	3.00	6.00	12.00
SMASH					
MGS-27037 [M]	Ivory Joe Hunter's Golden Hits	1963	10.00	20.00	40.00
SRS-67037 [S]	Ivory Joe Hunter's Golden Hits	1963	12.50	25.00	50.00
SOUND					
M-603 [M]	Ivory Joe Hunter	1959	37.50	75.00	150.00
STRAND					
SL-1123 [M]	The Artistry of Ivory Joe Hunter	196?	10.00	20.00	40.00
SLS-1123 [S]	The Artistry of Ivory Joe Hunter	196?	12.50	25.00	50.00

HUNTER, ROBERT

Albums

Number	Title (A Side/B Side)	Yr	VG	VG+	NM
RELIX					
2002 [PD]	Promontory Rider	1982	5.00	10.00	20.00
—Limited edition of 1,000 picture discs					
ROUND					
RX-101	Tales of the Great Rum Runners	1974	10.00	20.00	40.00
RX-105	Tiger Rose	1975	10.00	20.00	40.00

HUNTER, TAB

45s

Number	Title (A Side/B Side)	Yr	VG	VG+	NM
DOT					
15533	Young Love/Red Sails in the Sunset	1957	6.25	12.50	25.00
15548	Ninety-Nine Ways/Don't Get Around Much Anymore	1957	6.25	12.50	25.00
15657	Don't Let It Get Around/I'm Alone Because I Love You	1957	5.00	10.00	20.00
15767	I'm a Runaway/It's All Over Town	1958	5.00	10.00	20.00
16036	Young Love/Ninety-Nine Ways	1960	5.00	10.00	20.00
16187	My Devotion/You Cheated	1961	3.75	7.50	15.00
16205	Wild Side of Life/My Devotion	1961	3.75	7.50	15.00
16264	The Way You Look Tonight/You Cheated	1961	3.75	7.50	15.00
16355	I Can't Stop Loving You/Born to Lose	1962	3.75	7.50	15.00
WARNER BROS.					
5008	Jealous Heart/Lonesome Road	1958	5.00	10.00	20.00
5032 [M]	I'll Be With You in Apple Blossom Time/My Only Love	1959	5.00	10.00	20.00
S-5032 [S]	I'll Be With You in Apple Blossom Time/My Only Love	1959	6.25	12.50	25.00
5051 [M]	There's No Fool Like a Young Fool/I'll Never Smile Again	1959	5.00	10.00	20.00
S-5051 [S]	There's No Fool Like a Young Fool/I'll Never Smile Again	1959	6.25	12.50	25.00
5093	Our Love/Waitin' for Fall	1959	5.00	10.00	20.00
5093 [PS]	Our Love/Waitin' for Fall	1959	6.25	12.50	25.00
5160	Again/Love Is Just Around the Corner	1960	5.00	10.00	20.00
5160 [PS]	Again/Love Is Just Around the Corner	1960	6.25	12.50	25.00

7-Inch Extended Plays

Number	Title (A Side/B Side)	Yr	VG	VG+	NM
WARNER BROS.					
EA 1221 [M]	(contents unknown)	1958	5.00	10.00	20.00
EA 1221 [PS]	Tab Hunter	1958	5.00	10.00	20.00
ESB 1221 [PS]	Tab Hunter	1959	6.25	12.50	25.00
ESB 1221 [S]	(contents unknown)	1959	6.25	12.50	25.00

Albums

Number	Title (A Side/B Side)	Yr	VG	VG+	NM
DOT					
DLP-3370 [M]	Young Love	1961	7.50	15.00	30.00
DLP-25370 [S]	Young Love	1961	7.50	15.00	30.00
WARNER BROS.					
W 1221 [M]	Tab Hunter	1958	7.50	15.00	30.00
WS 1221 [S]	Tab Hunter	1958	10.00	20.00	40.00
W 1292 [M]	When I Fall in Love	1959	7.50	15.00	30.00
WS 1292 [S]	When I Fall in Love	1959	10.00	20.00	40.00
W 1367 [M]	R.F.D. Tab Hunter	1960	7.50	15.00	30.00
WS 1367 [S]	R.F.D. Tab Hunter	1960	10.00	20.00	40.00

HUNTER MUSKETT

Albums

Number	Title (A Side/B Side)	Yr	VG	VG+	NM
BRADLEY					
1003	Hunter Muskett	1973	20.00	40.00	80.00

HURRICANES, THE

45s

Number	Title (A Side/B Side)	Yr	VG	VG+	NM
KING					
4817	Poor Little Dancin' Girl/Pistol Packin' Mama	1955	50.00	100.00	200.00
4867	Maybe It's All for the Best/Yours	1956	50.00	100.00	200.00
4898	Raining in My Heart/Tell Me Baby	1956	50.00	100.00	200.00
4926	Little Girl of Mine/Your Promise to Me	1956	37.50	75.00	150.00
4947	Dear Mother/You May Not Know	1956	30.00	60.00	120.00
5018	Fallen Angel/I'll Always Be in Love with You	1957	25.00	50.00	100.00
5042	Priceless/Now That I Need You	1957	25.00	50.00	100.00

HURT, MISSISSIPPI JOHN

Albums

Number	Title (A Side/B Side)	Yr	VG	VG+	NM
BIOGRAPH					
C-4 [M]	1928: His First Recordings	1972	6.25	12.50	25.00
PIEDMONT					
PLP-13157 [M]	Folk Songs and Blues	1963	20.00	40.00	80.00
PLP-13181 [M]	Worried Blues	1964	20.00	40.00	80.00
VANGUARD					
VSD-19/20 [(2)]	The Best of Missisippi John Hurt	197?	6.25	12.50	25.00
VRS-9145 [M]	Blues at Newport	1965	6.25	12.50	25.00
VRS-9220 [M]	Mississippi John Hurt/Today	1966	6.25	12.50	25.00
VRS-9248 [M]	The Immortal Mississippi John Hurt	1967	6.25	12.50	25.00
VSD-79145 [S]	Blues at Newport	1965	7.50	15.00	30.00
VSD-79220 [S]	Mississippi John Hurt/Today	1966	7.50	15.00	30.00
VSD-79248 [S]	The Immortal Mississippi John Hurt	1967	7.50	15.00	30.00
VSD-79327	The Last Session	1972	5.00	10.00	20.00

HURVITZ, SANDY

Albums

Number	Title (A Side/B Side)	Yr	VG	VG+	NM
VERVE					
V6-5064	Sandy's Album Is Here at Last	1968	7.50	15.00	30.00
—Produced by FRANK ZAPPA					

HUSKY, FERLIN

Also includes records as "Terry Preston" and "Simon Crum."

45s

Number	Title (A Side/B Side)	Yr	VG	VG+	NM
4 STAR					
1516	Guilty Feeling/Road to Heaven	1950	7.50	15.00	30.00
—All 4 Star records as "Terry Preston"; it's possible that not all these exist on 45s					
1518	Let's Keep the Communists Out/The Sabbath	1950	7.50	15.00	30.00
1542	Irma/Put Me in Your Pocket	1950	7.50	15.00	30.00
1566	Wise Guy/Cross Eyed Gal from the Ozarks	1951	7.50	15.00	30.00
1571	Jezebel/Tennessee Hillbilly Ghost	1951	7.50	15.00	30.00
1572	Crying Heart Blues/If You Don't Believe I'm Leaving (Just Count the Days I'm Gone)	1951	7.50	15.00	30.00
1573	Rotation Blues/Deadly Weapon	1951	7.50	15.00	30.00
ABC					
11345	True True Lovin'/A Legend in My Time	1973	—	3.00	6.00
11360	Between Me and Blue/(B-side unknown)	1973	—	3.00	6.00
11381	Baby's Blue/One	1973	—	3.00	6.00
11395	Rosie Cries a Lot/Shoes	1973	—	3.00	6.00
11432	Freckles and Polliwog Days/Everything Is Nothing Without You	1974	—	3.00	6.00
12020	Drinkin' Man/Cuzz Yore So Sweet	1974	—	3.00	6.00
—As "Simon Crum"					
12021	A Room for a Boy...Never Used/A Ring of String	1974	—	2.50	5.00
12048	Champagne Ladies and Blue Ribbon Babies/I Feel Better All Over	1974	—	2.50	5.00
12085	Burning/A Touch of Yesterday	1975	—	2.50	5.00
ABC DOT					
17574	An Old Memory (Got in My Eye)/She's Not Yours Anymore	1975	—	2.50	5.00
CAPITOL					
F1861	China Doll/Tennessee Central #9	1951	6.25	12.50	25.00
F1947	I Want You So/Time	1952	5.00	10.00	20.00
—As "Terry Preston"					
2023	Christmas Dream/Christmas Is Holy	1967	2.00	4.00	8.00
F2024	Words/I'm Missin' Lots of Lovin'	1952	5.00	10.00	20.00
—As "Terry Preston"					
2048	Just for You/Don't Hurt Me Anymore	1967	2.00	4.00	8.00
F2105	Counting My Heartaches/I Love You	1952	5.00	10.00	20.00
—As "Terry Preston"					
2154	I Promised You the World/You Should Live My Life	1968	2.00	4.00	8.00
F2211	I'm Only Wishing/Are You Afraid	1952	5.00	10.00	20.00
—As "Terry Preston"					
2288	White Fences and Evergreen Trees/Love's Been Good to Me	1968	2.00	4.00	8.00
F2298	Gone/Out of Reach	1952	7.50	15.00	30.00
—As "Terry Preston"					
F2391	My Foolish Heart/Undesired	1953	5.00	10.00	20.00
—As "Terry Preston"					
2411	Flat River, Mo./One Life to Live	1969	2.00	4.00	8.00
F2467	I've Got a Woman's Love/Watch the Company You Keep	1953	5.00	10.00	20.00
—As "Terry Preston"					
F2495	Mini Ha Cha/I Lost My Love Today	1953	5.00	10.00	20.00
F2502	A Dear John Letter/I'd Rather Die Young	1953	5.00	10.00	20.00
—With Jean Shepard					
2512	That's Why I Love You So Much/Forever Yours	1969	2.00	4.00	8.00
F2558	How Much Are You Mine/You'll Die a Thousand Deaths	1953	5.00	10.00	20.00
F2586	Forgive Me, John/My Wedding Ring	1953	5.00	10.00	20.00
—With Jean Shepard					
F2627	Walkin' and Hummin'/I Wouldn't Treat a Dog Like You're Treating Me	1953	5.00	10.00	20.00
2666	Every Step of the Way/That's What I'd Do	1969	2.00	4.00	8.00
F2706	The Glass That Stands Beside You/Let's Kiss and Try Again	1954	5.00	10.00	20.00
—With Jean Shepard					
F2746	Eli the Camel/Somebody Lied	1954	5.00	10.00	20.00
2793	Heavenly Sunshine/All My Little Loving Ways	1970	—	3.00	6.00
F2814	Each Time You Leave/Deceived	1954	5.00	10.00	20.00
—As "Terry Preston"					
F2835	The Drunken Driver/Homesick	1954	5.00	10.00	20.00
2882	Your Sweet Love Lifted Me/You're the Happy Song I Sing	1970	—	3.00	6.00
F2914	King of a Lonely Castle/Very Seldom Frequently Ever	1954	5.00	10.00	20.00
2999	Sweet Misery/Because You're Mine	1970	—	3.00	6.00
F3001	I Feel Better All Over (More Than Anywhere's Else)/Little Tom	1954	3.75	7.50	15.00
F3063	Cuzz Yore So Sweet/My Gallina	1955	5.00	10.00	20.00
—As "Simon Crum"					
3069	One More Time/Don't Let the Good Life Pass You By	1971	—	3.00	6.00
F3097	I'll Baby Sit with You/She's Always There	1955	3.75	7.50	15.00

Number	Title (A Side/B Side)	Yr	VG	VG+	NM
3165	Open Up the Book (And Take a Look)/Even If It's True	1971	—	3.00	6.00
F3183	Don't Blame the Children/Saith the Lord	1955	3.75	7.50	15.00
F3233	Dear Mr. Brown/I'll Be Here for a Lifetime	1955	3.75	7.50	15.00
F3270	A Hillbilly Deck of Cards/Ooh I Want You	1955	5.00	10.00	20.00
—As "Simon Crum"					
3308	Just Plain Lonely/Always in All Ways	1972	—	3.00	6.00
F3316	A Sinful Secret/Slow Down Brother	1956	3.75	7.50	15.00
3415	How Could You Be Anything But Love/I'd Walk a Mile for a Smile	1972	—	3.00	6.00
F3428	Aladdin's Lamp/That Big Old Moon	1956	3.75	7.50	15.00
F3460	Bop Cat Bop/Muki Ruki	1956	5.00	10.00	20.00
—As "Simon Crum"					
F3522	Nothing Looks As Good As You/Waiting	1956	3.75	7.50	15.00
F3628	Gone/Missing Persons	1957	3.75	7.50	15.00
F3742	A Fallen Star/Prize Possession	1957	3.00	6.00	12.00
F3790	Make Me Live Again/This Moment of Love	1957	3.00	6.00	12.00
F3862	What'cha Doin' After School/Wang Dang Doo	1957	3.00	6.00	12.00
F3943	Kingdom of Love/Terrific Together	1958	3.00	6.00	12.00
F4000	I Saw God/I Feel That Old Heartache Again	1958	3.00	6.00	12.00
F4046	I Will/All of the Time	1958	3.00	6.00	12.00
F4073	Country Music Is Here to Stay/Stand Up, Sit Down, Shut Your Mouth	1958	5.00	10.00	20.00
—As "Simon Crum"					
F4123	My Reason for Living/Wrong	1959	3.00	6.00	12.00
F4186	Draggin' the River/Sea Sand	1959	3.00	6.00	12.00
F4252	Morgan Poisoned the Water Hole/I Fell Out of Love with You	1959	3.75	7.50	15.00
—As "Simon Crum"					
F4278	Black Sheep/I'll Always Return	1959	3.00	6.00	12.00
4343	My Love for You/Asi Es La Vida	1960	3.00	6.00	12.00
4406	Wings of a Dove/Next to Jimmy	1960	3.00	6.00	12.00
4464	Country Music Fiddler/I Feel Better All Over	1960	3.75	7.50	15.00
—As "Simon Crum"					
4499	Enormity in Motion/Cuzz Yore So Sweet	1961	3.75	7.50	15.00
—As "Simon Crum"					
4548	Before I Lose My Mind/What Good Will I Ever Be	1961	3.00	6.00	12.00
4594	Willow Tree/Take a Look	1961	3.00	6.00	12.00
4650	The Waltz You Saved for Me/Out of a Clear Blue Sky	1961	3.00	6.00	12.00
4721	Somebody Save Me/Just Another Lonely Night	1962	2.50	5.00	10.00
4779	Stand Up/It Scares Me	1962	2.50	5.00	10.00
4853	It Was You/Near You	1962	2.50	5.00	10.00
4908	You Hurt Me/My Reason for Living	1963	2.50	5.00	10.00
4966	Don't Be Mad/Little Red Webb	1963	3.00	6.00	12.00
—As "Simon Crum"					
4977	Who's Next/As Close As We'll Ever Be	1963	2.50	5.00	10.00
5067	Face of a Clown/Love Looks Good on You	1963	2.50	5.00	10.00
5111	Timber I'm Falling/Don't Count the Diamonds	1964	2.50	5.00	10.00
5206	Up on the Mountain Top/Weaker Moments	1964	2.50	5.00	10.00
5355	True, True Lovin'/Love Built the House	1965	2.50	5.00	10.00
5438	Willie Was a Gamblin' Man/Picking Up the Pieces	1965	2.50	5.00	10.00
5522	Money Greases the Wheels/Lasting Love	1965	2.50	5.00	10.00
5615	I Could Sing All Night/What Does Your Conscience Say to You	1966	2.50	5.00	10.00
5679	I Hear Little Rock Calling/Stand Beside Me	1966	2.50	5.00	10.00
5775	Once/Why Do I Put Up with You	1966	2.50	5.00	10.00
5852	What Am I Gonna Do Now/General G	1967	2.00	4.00	8.00
5938	You Pushed Me Too Far/A Bridge I Have Never Crossed	1967	2.00	4.00	8.00

KING

Number	Title (A Side/B Side)	Yr	VG	VG+	NM
5434	Irma/Cotton Pickin' Heart	1960	3.00	6.00	12.00
5476	Electrified Donkey/Guilty Feeling	1961	3.00	6.00	12.00

7-Inch Extended Plays

CAPITOL

Number	Title (A Side/B Side)	Yr	VG	VG+	NM
EAP 1-609	(contents unknown)	1955	5.00	10.00	20.00
EAP 1-609 [PS]	Ferlin Husky	1955	5.00	10.00	20.00
EAP 1-718	Hang Your Head in Shame/That Silver Haired Daddy of Mine//Honky-Tonkin' Party Girl/Useless	1956	3.75	7.50	15.00
EAP 1-718 [PS]	Songs of the Home and Heart, Part 1	1956	3.75	7.50	15.00
EAP 2-718	I Can't Go On This Way/That Little Girl of Mine//You Make Me Feel Funny, Honey/Rockin' Alone in an Old Rockin' Chair	1956	3.75	7.50	15.00
EAP 2-718 [PS]	Songs of the Home and Heart, Part 2	1956	3.75	7.50	15.00
EAP 3-718	Farther and Farther Apart/Never Have, Never Will//I Dreamed of an Old Love Affair/Daddy's Little Girl	1956	3.75	7.50	15.00
EAP 3-718 [PS]	Songs of the Home and Heart, Part 3	1956	3.75	7.50	15.00
EAP 1-880	(contents unknown)	1957	3.75	7.50	15.00
EAP 1-880 [PS]	Boulevard of Broken Dreams, Part 1	1957	3.75	7.50	15.00
EAP 2-880	(contents unknown)	1957	3.75	7.50	15.00
EAP 2-880 [PS]	Boulevard of Broken Dreams, Part 2	1957	3.75	7.50	15.00
EAP 3-880	(contents unknown)	1957	3.75	7.50	15.00
EAP 3-880 [PS]	Boulevard of Broken Dreams, Part 3	1957	3.75	7.50	15.00
EAP 1-921	Don't Walk Away/Somewhere There's Sunshine//My Home Town/This Whole Wide World	1958	3.00	6.00	12.00
EAP 1-921 [PS]	Country Music Holiday	1958	3.00	6.00	12.00
EAP 1-1280	(contents unknown)	1960	3.00	6.00	12.00
EAP 1-1280 [PS]	Ferlin Favorites, Part 1	1960	3.00	6.00	12.00
EAP 2-1280	(contents unknown)	1960	3.00	6.00	12.00
EAP 2-1280 [PS]	Ferlin Favorites, Part 2	1960	3.00	6.00	12.00
EAP 3-1280	(contents unknown)	1960	3.00	6.00	12.00
EAP 3-1280 [PS]	Ferlin Favorites, Part 3	1960	3.00	6.00	12.00
EAP 1-1516	(contents unknown)	1961	3.00	6.00	12.00
EAP 1-1516 [PS]	Wings of a Dove	1961	3.00	6.00	12.00

Albums

ABC

Number	Title (A Side/B Side)	Yr	VG	VG+	NM
X-776	True True Lovin'	1973	3.00	6.00	12.00
X-818	Freckles and Polliwog Days	1974	3.00	6.00	12.00
X-849	Champagne Ladies and Blue Ribbon Babies	1974	3.00	6.00	12.00
X-884	The Foster-Rice Songbook	1975	3.00	6.00	12.00

CAPITOL

Number	Title (A Side/B Side)	Yr	VG	VG+	NM
ST-115	White Fences and Evergreen Trees	1968	3.75	7.50	15.00
SKAO-143	The Best of Ferlin Husky	1969	3.75	7.50	15.00
SM-143	The Best of Ferlin Husky	197?	2.50	5.00	10.00
—Reissue with new prefix					
ST-239	That's Why I Love You So Much	1969	3.75	7.50	15.00
ST-433	Your Love Is Heavenly Sunshine	1970	3.75	7.50	15.00
ST-591	Your Sweet Love Has Lifted Me	1970	3.75	7.50	15.00
T 718 [M]	Songs of the Home and Heart	1956	15.00	30.00	60.00
—Turquoise label					
T 718 [M]	Songs of the Home and Heart	1959	10.00	20.00	40.00
—Black colorband label, Capitol logo at left					
T 718 [M]	Songs of the Home and Heart	1962	6.25	12.50	25.00
—Black colorband label, Capitol logo at top					
ST-768	One More Time	1971	3.75	7.50	15.00
T 880 [M]	Boulevard of Broken Dreams	1957	15.00	30.00	60.00
—Turquoise label					
T 976 [M]	Sittin' On a Rainbow	1958	15.00	30.00	60.00
—Turquoise label					
T 1204 [M]	Born to Lose	1959	10.00	20.00	40.00
—Black colorband label, Capitol logo at left					
T 1204 [M]	Born to Lose	1962	6.25	12.50	25.00
—Black colorband label, Capitol logo at top					
T 1280 [M]	Ferlin's Favorites	1960	10.00	20.00	40.00
—Black colorband label, Capitol logo at left					
T 1280 [M]	Ferlin's Favorites	1962	6.25	12.50	25.00
—Black colorband label, Capitol logo at top					
DT 1383 [R]	Gone	196?	3.00	6.00	12.00
T 1383 [M]	Gone	1960	10.00	20.00	40.00
—Black colorband label, Capitol logo at left					
T 1383 [M]	Gone	1962	6.25	12.50	25.00
—Black colorband label, Capitol logo at top					
ST 1546 [S]	Walkin' and Hummin'	1961	7.50	15.00	30.00
—Black colorband label, Capitol logo at left					
ST 1546 [S]	Walkin' and Hummin'	1962	5.00	10.00	20.00
—Black colorband label, Capitol logo at top					
T 1546 [M]	Walkin' and Hummin'	1961	6.25	12.50	25.00
—Black colorband label, Capitol logo at left					
T 1546 [M]	Walkin' and Hummin'	1962	3.75	7.50	15.00
—Black colorband label, Capitol logo at top					
ST 1633 [S]	Memories of Home	1961	7.50	15.00	30.00
—Black colorband label, Capitol logo at left					
ST 1633 [S]	Memories of Home	1962	5.00	10.00	20.00
—Black colorband label, Capitol logo at top					
T 1633 [M]	Memories of Home	1961	6.25	12.50	25.00
—Black colorband label, Capitol logo at left					
T 1633 [M]	Memories of Home	1962	3.75	7.50	15.00
—Black colorband label, Capitol logo at top					
ST 1720 [S]	Some of My Favorites	1962	5.00	10.00	20.00
T 1720 [M]	Some of My Favorites	1962	3.75	7.50	15.00
ST 1885 [S]	The Heart and Soul of Ferlin Husky	1963	5.00	10.00	20.00
T 1885 [M]	The Heart and Soul of Ferlin Husky	1963	3.75	7.50	15.00
DT 1991 [R]	The Hits of Ferlin Husky	1963	3.00	6.00	12.00
T 1991 [M]	The Hits of Ferlin Husky	1963	3.75	7.50	15.00
ST 2101 [S]	By Request	1964	5.00	10.00	20.00
T 2101 [M]	By Request	1964	3.75	7.50	15.00
ST 2305 [S]	True, True Lovin'	1965	5.00	10.00	20.00
T 2305 [M]	True, True Lovin'	1965	3.75	7.50	15.00
ST 2439 [S]	Ferlin Husky Sings the Songs of Music City, U.S.A.	1966	5.00	10.00	20.00
T 2439 [M]	Ferlin Husky Sings the Songs of Music City, U.S.A.	1966	3.75	7.50	15.00
ST 2548 [S]	I Could Sing All Night	1966	5.00	10.00	20.00
T 2548 [M]	I Could Sing All Night	1966	3.75	7.50	15.00
ST 2705 [S]	What Am I Gonna Do Now?	1967	3.75	7.50	15.00
T 2705 [M]	What Am I Gonna Do Now?	1967	5.00	10.00	20.00
ST 2793 [S]	Christmas All Year Long	1967	3.75	7.50	15.00
T 2793 [M]	Christmas All Year Long	1967	3.75	7.50	15.00
ST 2870	Just for You	1968	3.75	7.50	15.00
ST 2913	Where No One Stands Alone	1968	3.75	7.50	15.00
ST-11069	Just Plain Lonely	1972	3.75	7.50	15.00

HILLTOP

Number	Title (A Side/B Side)	Yr	VG	VG+	NM
6005	Ole Opry Favorites	196?	3.00	6.00	12.00
6086	Green, Green Grass of Home	1970	3.00	6.00	12.00
6099	Wings of a Dove	197?	3.00	6.00	12.00

KING

Number	Title (A Side/B Side)	Yr	VG	VG+	NM
647 [M]	Country Tunes Sung from the Heart	1959	17.50	35.00	70.00
728 [M]	Easy Livin'	1960	17.50	35.00	70.00

STARDAY

Number	Title (A Side/B Side)	Yr	VG	VG+	NM
3018	Greatest Hits	197?	3.00	6.00	12.00

HUTCH, WILLIE

45s

DUNHILL

Number	Title (A Side/B Side)	Yr	VG	VG+	NM
4012	The Duck/Love Runs Out	1965	15.00	30.00	60.00

MAVERICK

Number	Title (A Side/B Side)	Yr	VG	VG+	NM
1003	Use What You Got (Part 1)/Use What You Got (Part 2)	1968	3.75	7.50	15.00

MODERN

Number	Title (A Side/B Side)	Yr	VG	VG+	NM
1021	I Can't Get Enough/Your Love Has Made Me a Man	1966	10.00	20.00	40.00

MOTOWN

Number	Title (A Side/B Side)	Yr	VG	VG+	NM
1222	Brother's Gonna Work It Out/I Choose You	1973	—	2.50	5.00
1252	Slick/Mother's Theme	1973	—	2.50	5.00
1252 [PS]	Slick/Mother's Theme	1973	—	3.00	6.00
1282	Sunshine Lady/I Just Wanted to Make Her Happy	1973	—	2.50	5.00
1287	If You Ain't Got No Money (You Can't Get No Honey) Pt. 1/Pt. 2	1974	—	2.50	5.00
1292	Theme of Foxy Brown/Give Me Some of That Good Old Love	1974	—	2.50	5.00
1331	I'm Gonna Stay/Woman You Touched Me	1975	—	2.50	5.00
1339	Get Ready for the Get Down/Don't Let Nobody Tell You How to Do Your Thing	1975	—	2.50	5.00
1360	Love Power/Talk to Me	1975	—	2.00	4.00
1371	Party Down/Just Another Day	1976	—	2.00	4.00
1406	Let Me Be the One, Baby/She's Just Doing Her Thing	1976	—	2.00	4.00
1411	Shake It, Shake It/I Feel Like We Can Make It	1976	—	2.00	4.00

Number	Title (A Side/B Side)	Yr	VG	VG+	NM
1416	We Gonna Have a House Party/Never Had It So Good	1977	—	2.00	4.00
1424	We Gonna Party Tonight/Precious Pearl	1977	—	2.00	4.00
1433	What You Gonna Do After the Party/I Feel Like We Can Make It	1977	—	2.00	4.00
1637	In and Out/Girl	1982	—	2.00	4.00
RCA VICTOR					
74-0189	Ain't Gonna Stop/Do What You Wanna Do	1969	2.50	5.00	10.00
74-0294	When a Boy Falls in Love (Part 1)/When a Boy Falls in Love (Part 2)	1969	2.50	5.00	10.00
74-0327	Magic of Love/Walking on My Love	1970	2.50	5.00	10.00
WHITFIELD					
8615	All American Funkathon/And All Hell Broke Loose	1978	—	2.00	4.00
8689	Paradise/Hip Shakin' Sexy Lady	1978	—	2.00	4.00
49015	Deep in Your Love/Everybody Needs Money	1979	—	2.00	4.00
49102	Down Here on Disco Street/Kelly Green	1979	—	2.00	4.00

Albums

Number	Title	Yr	VG	VG+	NM
MOTOWN					
M 766	The Mack	1973	3.00	6.00	12.00
M 784	Fully Exposed	1973	3.00	6.00	12.00
M6-811	Foxy Brown	1974	3.00	6.00	12.00
M6-815	Mark of the Beast	1974	3.00	6.00	12.00
M6-838	Ode to My Lady	1975	3.00	6.00	12.00
M6-854	Concert in Blues	1976	3.00	6.00	12.00
M6-871	Color Her...	1977	3.00	6.00	12.00
M6-874	Havin' a House Party	1977	3.00	6.00	12.00
5281 ML	The Mack	1983	2.00	4.00	8.00
—Reissue of 766					
RCA VICTOR					
LSP-4213	Soul Portrait: Willie Hutch	1969	3.75	7.50	15.00
WHITFIELD					
BSK 3226	In Tune	1978	2.50	5.00	10.00
BSK 3352	Midnight Dancer	1979	2.50	5.00	10.00

HUTTO, J.B.

45s

Number	Title (A Side/B Side)	Yr	VG	VG+	NM
CHANCE					
1155	Now She's Gone/Combination Boogie	1954	250.00	500.00	1000.
1160	Lovin' You/Pet Cream Man	1954	1000.	2000.	4000.
—The above two may be listed on the label as "J.B. and the Hawks"					
1165	Dim Lights/Things Are So Slow	1955	750.00	1500.	3000.

HUTTON, DANNY

Also see THREE DOG NIGHT.

45s

Number	Title (A Side/B Side)	Yr	VG	VG+	NM
ALMO					
213	Why Don't You Love Me Anymore/Home in Pasadena	1964	5.00	10.00	20.00
—As "Daring Dan Hutton"					
HANNA-BARBERA					
447	Roses and Rainbows/Monster Shindig	1965	3.75	7.50	15.00
447 [PS]	Roses and Rainbows/Monster Shindig	1965	7.50	15.00	30.00
453	Big Bright Eyes/Monester Shindig (Part 2)	1965	3.75	7.50	15.00
MGM					
13502	Funny How Love Can Be/Dreamin' Isn't Good for You	1966	2.50	5.00	10.00
13502 [PS]	Funny How Love Can Be/Dreamin' Isn't Good for You	1966	5.00	10.00	20.00
13613	Hang On to a Dream/Hit the Wall	1966	2.50	5.00	10.00

Albums

Number	Title	Yr	VG	VG+	NM
MGM					
SE-4664	Pre-Dog Night	1970	7.50	15.00	30.00

HYLAND, BRIAN

45s

Number	Title (A Side/B Side)	Yr	VG	VG+	NM
ABC-PARAMOUNT					
10236	Let Me Belong to You/Let It Die	1961	2.50	5.00	10.00
10262	I'll Never Stop Wanting You/The Night I Cried	1961	2.50	5.00	10.00
10262 [PS]	I'll Never Stop Wanting You/The Night I Cried	1961	5.00	10.00	20.00
10294	Ginny Come Lately/I Should Be Gettin' Better	1962	2.50	5.00	10.00
10294 [PS]	Ginny Come Lately/I Should Be Gettin' Better	1962	5.00	10.00	20.00
10336	Sealed with a Kiss/Summer Job	1962	3.00	6.00	12.00
10336 [PS]	Sealed with a Kiss/Summer Job	1962	5.00	10.00	20.00
10359	Warmed Over Kisses (Left Over Love)/Walk a Lonely Mile	1962	2.50	5.00	10.00
10359 [PS]	Warmed Over Kisses (Left Over Love)/Walk a Lonely Mile	1962	5.00	10.00	20.00
10374	I May Not Live to See Tomorrow/It Ain't That Way at All	1962	2.50	5.00	10.00
10374 [PS]	I May Not Live to See Tomorrow/It Ain't That Way at All	1962	5.00	10.00	20.00
10400	If Mary's There/Remember Me	1963	2.50	5.00	10.00
10400 [PS]	If Mary's There/Remember Me	1963	5.00	10.00	20.00
10427	Somewhere in the Night/I Wish Today Was Yesterday	1963	2.50	5.00	10.00
10452	I'm Afraid to Go Home/Save Your Heart for Me	1963	2.50	5.00	10.00
10494	Nothing Matters But You/Let Us Make Our Own Mistakes	1963	2.50	5.00	10.00
10549	Act Naturally/Out of Sight, Out of Mind	1964	2.50	5.00	10.00
DOT					
17050	Apologize/Words on Paper	1967	—	3.00	6.00
17061	It's Christmas Time Once Again/Words on Paper	1967	3.00	6.00	12.00
17078	Come with Me/Delilah	1968	—	3.00	6.00
17109	The Lover/Springfield, Illinois	1968	—	3.00	6.00
17176	Tragedy/You'd Better Stop and Think It Over	1968	—	3.00	6.00
17222	A Million to One/It Could All Begin Again	1969	—	3.00	6.00
17258	Early April Morning/Stay and Love Me All Summer	1969	—	3.00	6.00
17291	Dreamy Eyes/Gonna Make a Woman Out of You	1970	—	3.00	6.00
KAPP					
342	Itsy Bitsy Teeny Weeny Yellow Polka Dot Bikini/Don't Dilly Dally, Sally	1960	3.75	7.50	15.00
342 [PS]	Itsy Bitsy Teeny Weeny Yellow Polka Dot Bikini/Don't Dilly Dally, Sally	1960	7.50	15.00	30.00
352	Four Little Heels (The Clickety Clack Song)/That's How Much	1960	3.00	6.00	12.00
352 [PS]	Four Little Heels (The Clickety Clack Song)/That's How Much	1960	6.25	12.50	25.00
363	I Gotta Go/Lopsided, Over Loaded	1960	3.00	6.00	12.00
363 [PS]	I Gotta Go/Lopsided, Over Loaded	1960	6.25	12.50	25.00
401	Lipstick on Your Lips/When Will I Know	1961	3.00	6.00	12.00
LEADER					
801	Library Love Affair/Rosemary	1960	5.00	10.00	20.00
805	Itsy Bitsy Teeny Weeny Yellow Polka Dot Bikini/Don't Dilly Dally, Sally	1960	7.50	15.00	30.00
PHILIPS					
40179	Here's to Our Love/Two Kinds of Girls	1964	2.00	4.00	8.00
40179 [PS]	Here's to Our Love/Two Kinds of Girls	1964	3.00	6.00	12.00
40203	Devoted to You/Pledging My Love	1964	2.00	4.00	8.00
40203 [PS]	Devoted to You/Pledging My Love	1964	3.00	6.00	12.00
40221	Now I Belong to You/One Step Forward, Two Steps Back	1964	2.00	4.00	8.00
40263	He Don't Understand You/Love Will Find a Way	1965	2.00	4.00	8.00
40263 [PS]	He Don't Understand You/Love Will Find a Way	1965	3.00	6.00	12.00
40306	Stay Away from Her/I Can't Keep a Secret	1965	2.00	4.00	8.00
40354	3000 Miles/Sometimes They Do, Sometimes They Don't	1966	2.00	4.00	8.00
40377	The Joker Went Wild/I Can Hear the Rain	1966	2.50	5.00	10.00
40405	Why Did You Do It/Run, Run, Look and See	1966	2.00	4.00	8.00
40424	Hung Up in Your Eyes/Why Mine	1967	2.00	4.00	8.00
40424 [PS]	Hung Up in Your Eyes/Why Mine	1967	3.00	6.00	12.00
40444	Holiday for Clowns/Yesterday I Had a Girl	1967	2.00	4.00	8.00
40472	Get the Message/Kinda Groovy	1967	—	3.00	6.00
UNI					
55193	You and Me/Could You Dig It	1970	—	3.00	6.00
55240	Gypsy Woman/You and Me (#2)	1970	—	3.00	6.00
55272	Lonely Teardrops/Lorraine	1971	—	2.50	5.00
55287	So Long, Marianne/No Place to Run	1971	—	2.50	5.00
55306	Out of the Blue/If You Came Back	1971	—	2.50	5.00
55323	I Love Every Little Thing About You/With My Eyes Wide Open	1972	—	2.50	5.00
55334	Only Wanna Make You Happy/When You're Lovin' Me	1972	—	2.50	5.00

Albums

Number	Title	Yr	VG	VG+	NM
ABC-PARAMOUNT					
400 [M]	Let Me Belong to You	1961	7.50	15.00	30.00
S-400 [S]	Let Me Belong to You	1961	10.00	20.00	40.00
431 [M]	Sealed with a Kiss	1962	7.50	15.00	30.00
S-431 [S]	Sealed with a Kiss	1962	10.00	20.00	40.00
463 [M]	Country Meets Folk	1964	7.50	15.00	30.00
S-463 [S]	Country Meets Folk	1964	10.00	20.00	40.00
DOT					
DLP 25926	Tragedy/A Million to One	1969	3.75	7.50	15.00
DLP 25954	Stay and Love Me All Summer	1969	3.75	7.50	15.00
KAPP					
KL 1202 [M]	The Bashful Blonde	1960	12.50	25.00	50.00
KS 3202 [S]	The Bashful Blonde	1960	20.00	40.00	80.00
PHILIPS					
PHM 200136 [M]	Here's to Our Love	1964	5.00	10.00	20.00
PHM 200158 [M]	Rockin' Folk	1965	5.00	10.00	20.00
PHM 200217 [M]	Run, Run, Look and See/The Joker Went Wild	1966	5.00	10.00	20.00
—With "200-217" in trail-off; this record plays mono					
PHM 200217 [S]	Run, Run, Look and See/The Joker Went Wild	1966	5.00	10.00	20.00
—With "2/600-217" in trail-off; this record plays stereo, though labeled mono					
PHS 600136 [S]	Here's to Our Love	1964	6.25	12.50	25.00
PHS 600158 [S]	Rockin' Folk	1965	6.25	12.50	25.00
PHS 600217 [S]	Run, Run, Look and See/The Joker Went Wild	1966	6.25	12.50	25.00
PICKWICK					
SPC-3261	Young Years	197?	2.50	5.00	10.00
PRIVATE STOCK					
PS-7003	In a State of Bayou	1977	3.00	6.00	12.00
RHINO					
RNLP-70226	Greatest Hots	1987	2.50	5.00	10.00
UNI					
73097	Brian Hyland	1970	3.75	7.50	15.00
WING					
MGW-12341 [M]	Here's To Our Love	1967	3.00	6.00	12.00
SRW-16341 [S]	Here's To Our Love	1967	3.00	6.00	12.00

I

I.V. LEAGUERS, THE

45s

Number	Title (A Side/B Side)	Yr	VG	VG+	NM
DOT					
15677	Ring Chimes/The Story	1957	5.00	10.00	20.00
NAU-VOO					
803	Told by the Stars/Jim Jam	1959	100.00	200.00	400.00
PORTER					
1004	Ring Chimes/The Story	1957	12.50	25.00	50.00

IAN, JANIS

45s

Number	Title (A Side/B Side)	Yr	VG	VG+	NM
CAPITOL					
3107	He's a Rainbow/Here in Spain	1971	2.00	4.00	8.00
CASABLANCA					
2245	Night Rains/Fly Too High	1980	—	2.50	5.00
COLUMBIA					
02176	Sugar Mountain/Under the Covers	1981	—	2.00	4.00
02546	Restless Eyes/I Remember Yesterday	1981	—	2.00	4.00
10119	When the Party's Over/Bright Lights and Promises	1975	—	2.50	5.00
10154	At Seventeen/Stars	1975	—	2.50	5.00
10154 [PS]	At Seventeen/Stars	1975	2.00	4.00	8.00
10228	In the Winter/Thankyouse	1975	—	2.50	5.00
10297	Aftertones/Boy, I Really Tied One On	1976	—	2.50	5.00
10331	I Would Like to Dance/Goodbye to Morning	1976	—	2.50	5.00
10391	Roses/Love Is Blind	1976	—	2.50	5.00
10484	Miracle Row/Take It to the Sky	1977	—	2.50	5.00
10526	Candlelight/I Want to Make You Love Me	1977	—	2.50	5.00
10813	That Grand Illusion/Hopper Paining	1978	—	2.50	5.00
10864	The Bridge/Do You Wanna Dance	1978	—	2.50	5.00
10979	Here Comes the Night/Tonight Will Last Forever	1979	—	2.00	4.00
11111	Night Rains/Fly Too High	1979	—	2.00	4.00
11327	The Other Side of the Sun/Memories	1980	—	2.00	4.00
46034	Jesse/The Man You Are in Me	1974	—	2.50	5.00
POLYDOR					
14299	Society's Child (Baby I've Been Thinking)/I'll Give You a Stone If You Throw It	1975	—	3.00	6.00
VERVE					
5027	Society's Child (Baby I've Been Thinking)/Letter to Jon	1967	2.50	5.00	10.00
VERVE FOLKWAYS					
5027	Society's Child (Baby I've Been Thinking)/Letter to Jon	1966	3.00	6.00	12.00
VERVE FORECAST					
5027	Society's Child (Baby I've Been Thinking)/Letter to Jon	1967	2.00	4.00	8.00
5041	I'll Give You a Stone If You'll Throw It/Younger Generation Blues	1967	2.00	4.00	8.00
5072	Insanity Comes Quietly to the Structured Mind/Snowflakes Fall, Snowrays Call	1967	2.00	4.00	8.00
5079	Somg for All the Seasons of Your Mind/Lonely One	1968	2.00	4.00	8.00
5090	Lady of the Night/Friends Again	1968	2.00	4.00	8.00
5099	Everybody Knows/Janey's Blues	1968	2.00	4.00	8.00
5113	Month of May/Calling Your Name	1969	2.00	4.00	8.00

Albums

Number	Title (A Side/B Side)	Yr	VG	VG+	NM
ANALOGUE PRODUCTIONS					
AAP 027	Breaking Silence	1995	6.25	12.50	25.00
—Audiophile vinyl					
CAPITOL					
SKAO-683	Present Company	1971	3.75	7.50	15.00
SN-683	Present Company	1975	2.50	5.00	10.00
COLUMBIA					
KC 32857	Stars	1974	2.50	5.00	10.00
PC 32857	Stars	197?	2.00	4.00	8.00
PC 33394	Between the Lines	1975	2.50	5.00	10.00
—No bar code on cover					
PC 33394	Between the Lines	1979	2.00	4.00	8.00
—With bar code on cover					
PCQ 33394 [Q]	Between the Lines	1975	3.75	7.50	15.00
PC 33919	Aftertones	1976	2.50	5.00	10.00
—No bar code on cover					
PC 33919	Aftertones	1979	2.00	4.00	8.00
—With bar code on cover					
PCQ 33919 [Q]	Aftertones	1976	3.75	7.50	15.00
JC 34440	Miracle Row	1977	2.50	5.00	10.00
JC 35325	Janis Ian	1978	2.50	5.00	10.00
JC 36139	Night Rains	1979	2.50	5.00	10.00
PC 36139	Night Rains	198?	2.00	4.00	8.00
FC 37360	Restless Eyes	1981	2.50	5.00	10.00
MGM					
GAS-121	Janis Ian (Golden Archive Series)	1970	6.25	12.50	25.00
POLYDOR					
PD-6058	Janis Ian	1976	2.50	5.00	10.00
VERVE					
V/VS-5027	Janis Ian	1967	—	—	—
—Scheduled, possibly not released; same LP is Verve Forecast 3017					
VERVE FORECAST					
FT-3017 [M]	Janis Ian	1967	5.00	10.00	20.00
FTS-3017 [S]	Janis Ian	1967	3.75	7.50	15.00
FT-3024 [M]	For All the Seasons of Your Mind	1967	5.00	10.00	20.00
FTS-3024 [S]	For All the Seasons of Your Mind	1967	3.75	7.50	15.00
FTS-3048	The Secret Life of J. Eddy Fink	1968	3.75	7.50	15.00
FTS-3063	Who Really Cares?	1969	3.75	7.50	15.00

IAN AND SYLVIA

45s

Number	Title (A Side/B Side)	Yr	VG	VG+	NM
COLUMBIA					
45430	Creatures of Rain/Summer Wages	1971	—	3.00	6.00
45475	More Often Than Not/Some Kind of Fool	1971	—	3.00	6.00
45680	You Were On My Mind/Salmon in the Sea	1972	—	3.00	6.00
MGM					
13686	Lovin' Sound/Pilgrimage to Paradise	1967	2.00	4.00	8.00
14082	Give It to the World/Shinbone Alley	1969	2.00	4.00	8.00
VANGUARD					
35021	Four Strong Winds/C.C. Rider	1963	2.50	5.00	10.00
35025	You Were On My Mind/Someday Soon	1964	2.50	5.00	10.00
35035	Play One More/The French Girl	1964	2.50	5.00	10.00
35062	House of Cards/90" By 90"	1968	2.00	4.00	8.00

Albums

Number	Title (A Side/B Side)	Yr	VG	VG+	NM
AMPEX					
A-10103	Great Speckled Bird	1970	5.00	10.00	20.00
COLUMBIA					
C 30736	Ian and Sylvia	1971	3.00	6.00	12.00
KC 31337	You Were On My Mind	1972	3.00	6.00	12.00
G 32516 [(2)]	The Best of Ian and Sylvia	1973	3.75	7.50	15.00
MGM					
GAS-115	Ian and Sylvia (Golden Archive Series)	1970	3.75	7.50	15.00
E-4388 [M]	Lovin' Sound	1967	5.00	10.00	20.00
SE-4388 [S]	Lovin' Sound	1967	3.75	7.50	15.00
SE-4550	Full Circle	1968	5.00	10.00	20.00
VANGUARD					
VSD-5/6 [(2)]	Ian and Sylvia's Greatest Hits	1969	3.75	7.50	15.00
VSD-23/24 [(2)]	Ian and Sylvia's Greatest Hits, Vol. 2	1970	3.75	7.50	15.00
VSD-2113 [S]	Ian and Sylvia	1963	7.50	15.00	30.00
VSD-2149 [S]	Four Strong Winds	1963	6.25	12.50	25.00
VRS-9109 [M]	Ian and Sylvia	1963	6.25	12.50	25.00
VRS-9133 [M]	Four Strong Winds	1963	5.00	10.00	20.00
VRS-9154 [M]	Northern Journey	1964	5.00	10.00	20.00
VRS-9175 [M]	Early Morning Rain	1965	5.00	10.00	20.00
VRS-9215 [M]	Play One More	1966	5.00	10.00	20.00
VRS-9241 [M]	So Much for Dreaming	1967	5.00	10.00	20.00
VSD-73114	Greatest Hits	1985	2.50	5.00	10.00
VSD-79154 [S]	Northern Journey	1964	6.25	12.50	25.00
VSD-79175 [S]	Early Morning Rain	1965	6.25	12.50	25.00
VSD-79215 [S]	Play One More	1966	6.25	12.50	25.00
VSD-79241 [S]	So Much for Dreaming	1967	6.25	12.50	25.00
VSD-79269	The Best of Ian & Sylvia	1968	3.75	7.50	15.00
VSD-79284	Nashville	1968	3.75	7.50	15.00

IAN AND THE ZODIACS

45s

Number	Title (A Side/B Side)	Yr	VG	VG+	NM
PHILIPS					
40244	The Cryin' Game/Livin' Lovin' Wreck	1964	2.50	5.00	10.00
40277	Good Morning Little Schoolgirl/Message to Martha	1965	2.50	5.00	10.00
40291	So Much in Love with You/This Empty Place	1965	2.50	5.00	10.00
40291 [PS]	So Much in Love with You/This Empty Place	1965	6.25	12.50	25.00
40343	Why Can't It Be Me/Leave It to Me	1965	2.50	5.00	10.00
40369	No Money, No Honey/Where Were You	1966	2.50	5.00	10.00

Albums

Number	Title (A Side/B Side)	Yr	VG	VG+	NM
PHILIPS					
PHM 200176 [M]	Ian and the Zodiacs	1965	10.00	20.00	40.00
PHS 600176 [S]	Ian and the Zodiacs	1965	12.50	25.00	50.00

ID, THE

45s

Number	Title (A Side/B Side)	Yr	VG	VG+	NM
RCA VICTOR					
47-9136	Short Circuit/Boil the Kettle, Mother	1967	3.00	6.00	12.00
47-9195	Wild Times/The Take	1967	3.00	6.00	12.00

Albums

Number	Title (A Side/B Side)	Yr	VG	VG+	NM
AURA					
1000	Where Are We Going?	1976	12.50	25.00	50.00
RCA VICTOR					
LPM-3805 [M]	The Inner Sound of the Id	1967	10.00	20.00	40.00
LSP-3805 [S]	The Inner Sound of the Id	1967	10.00	20.00	40.00

IDEALS, THE (1)

Chicago-based group that, at one time, featured MAJOR LANCE. He is not on the Satellite singles, however.

45s

Number	Title (A Side/B Side)	Yr	VG	VG+	NM
PASO					
6401	Together/What's the Matter with You Sam	1961	12.50	25.00	50.00
6402	Magic/Teens	1961	12.50	25.00	50.00
SATELLITE					
2007	You Lost and I Won/You Hurt Me	1965	6.25	12.50	25.00
2009	Kissing/I Had a Dream	1966	6.25	12.50	25.00
2011	Go Go Gorilla/Kissing Won't Go Out of Style	1966	6.25	12.50	25.00

IDEALS, THE (2)

45s

Number	Title (A Side/B Side)	Yr	VG	VG+	NM
CHECKER					
920	Knee Socks/Mary's Lamb	1959	6.25	12.50	25.00
979	Knee Socks/Mary's Lamb	1961	3.75	7.50	15.00
—As "Johnny Brantley and the Ideals"					

IDEALS, THE (U)

Some of these could be groups (1) or (2), but others are likely other groups.

45s

Number	Title (A Side/B Side)	Yr	VG	VG+	NM
COOL					
108	Do I Have the Right/You Won't Like It	1958	75.00	150.00	300.00
CORTLAND					
110	Don Juan/Gorilla	1963	5.00	10.00	20.00
113	Mo Joe Hanna/Simple Simon	1964	3.75	7.50	15.00
115	Feeling of a Kiss/You Came a Long Way from St. Louis	1964	3.75	7.50	15.00

Number	Title (A Side/B Side)	Yr	VG	VG+	NM
117	Local Boy/L.A.	1964	3.75	7.50	15.00
DECCA					
30720	Annie Has a Stroller/My Girl	1959	10.00	20.00	40.00
30800	Ivy League Lover/Don't Be a Baby, Baby	1959	6.25	12.50	25.00
FARGO					
1024	The Duchess/Trans Zizstor	1962	5.00	10.00	20.00
STARS OF HOLLYWOOD					
1001	Please, Jan/Always Yours	1959	10.00	20.00	40.00
ST. LAWRENCE					
1001	Cathy's Clown/Go Get a Wig	1965	3.00	6.00	12.00
1020	I Got Lucky (When I Found You)/Tell Her I Apologize	1966	3.75	7.50	15.00

IDES OF MARCH, THE

45s

Number	Title (A Side/B Side)	Yr	VG	VG+	NM
KAPP					
992	Nobody Loves Me/Strawberry Sunday	1969	2.50	5.00	10.00
PARROT					
304	I'll Keep Searching/You Wouldn't Listen	1966	2.50	5.00	10.00
310	Roller Coaster/Things Aren't Always What They Seem	1966	2.50	5.00	10.00
312	You Need Love/Sha-La-La-La-Lee	1966	2.50	5.00	10.00
321	My Foolish Pride/Give Your Mind Wings	1967	2.50	5.00	10.00
326	Hole in My Soul/Girls Don't Grow on Trees	1967	2.50	5.00	10.00
RCA VICTOR					
APBO-0052	Hot Water/Heavy on the Country	1973	—	2.50	5.00
74-0850	Mother America/Ladyland	1972	—	2.50	5.00
SUNDAZED					
142	I'm Gonna Say My Prayers/The Sun Ain't Gonna Shine Anymore	1999	—	—	2.00
142 [PS]	I'm Gonna Say My Prayers/The Sun Ain't Gonna Shine Anymore	1999	—	—	2.00
WARNER BROS.					
7140	Vehicle/L.A. Goodbye	1972	—	2.00	4.00
—"Back to Back Hits" series -- originals have green labels					
7334	High on a Hillside/One Woman Man	1969	—	3.00	6.00
7378	Vehicle/Lead Me Down, Gently	1970	2.00	4.00	8.00
7403	Superman/Home	1970	—	3.00	6.00
7426	Melody/The Sky Is Falling	1970	—	3.00	6.00
7466	L.A. Goodbye/Mrs. Grayson's Farm	1971	—	3.00	6.00
7507	Tie-Dye Princess/Friends of Feeling	1971	—	3.00	6.00
7526	Giddy-Up, Ride Me/Freedom Sweet	1971	—	3.00	6.00

Albums

Number	Title	Yr	VG	VG+	NM
RCA VICTOR					
APL1-0143	Midnight Oil	1973	3.75	7.50	15.00
LSP-4812	World Woven	1972	3.75	7.50	15.00
WARNER BROS.					
WS 1863	Vehicle	1970	5.00	10.00	20.00
—Green "W7" label					
WS 1863	Vehicle	1970	3.75	7.50	15.00
—Green "WB" label					
WS 1896	Common Bond	1971	3.75	7.50	15.00

IDLE RACE, THE

Jeff Lynne, later of THE MOVE and ELECTRIC LIGHT ORCHESTRA, was in this group.

45s

Number	Title (A Side/B Side)	Yr	VG	VG+	NM
LIBERTY					
55997	Here We Go 'Round the Lemon Tree/My Father's Son	1967	5.00	10.00	20.00
56064	The End of the Road/The Morning Sunshine	1968	6.25	12.50	25.00

Albums

Number	Title	Yr	VG	VG+	NM
LIBERTY					
LST-7603	Birthday Party	1969	12.50	25.00	50.00

IDOLS, THE

Probably more than one group.

45s

Number	Title (A Side/B Side)	Yr	VG	VG+	NM
DOT					
16210	Just a Little Bit More/Why Must I Cry	1961	3.75	7.50	15.00
—B-side by the Swans					
E-Z					
1	Jeannine/Can't Tag Along	1961	10.00	20.00	40.00
RCA VICTOR					
47-7339	30 Days/The Prowler	1958	5.00	10.00	20.00
47-7417	Here in My Heart/The Counterfeiter	1958	5.00	10.00	20.00
REVEILLE					
1002	Just a Little Bit More/Why Must I Cry	1961	7.50	15.00	30.00
—B-side by the Swans					

IF

45s

Number	Title (A Side/B Side)	Yr	VG	VG+	NM
CAPITOL					
2909	The Promised Land/I'm Reaching Out on All Sides	1970	2.00	4.00	8.00
2990	Raise the Level of Your Conscious Mind/What Did I Say About the Box, Jack	1970	2.00	4.00	8.00
3068	Your City Is Falling/Woman Can't You See	1971	2.00	4.00	8.00
3932	I Believe in Rock and Roll/Still Alive	1974	—	3.00	6.00
METROMEDIA					
258	Waterfall/(B-side unknown)	1972	—	3.00	6.00

Albums

Number	Title	Yr	VG	VG+	NM
CAPITOL					
ST-539	If	1970	5.00	10.00	20.00
SW-676	If2	1971	5.00	10.00	20.00
SMAS-820	If3	1971	5.00	10.00	20.00
ST-11299	Not Just Another Bunch of Pretty Faces	1974	3.00	6.00	12.00
ST-11344	Tea Break Over — Back On Your 'Eads!	1974	3.00	6.00	12.00
METROMEDIA					
BML1-0174	Double Diamond	1973	3.00	6.00	12.00
KMD-1057	Waterfall	1972	3.00	6.00	12.00

IFIELD, FRANK

Also see THE BEATLES.

45s

Number	Title (A Side/B Side)	Yr	VG	VG+	NM
CAPITOL					
5032	I'm Confessin' (That I Love You)/Waltzing Matilda	1963	2.50	5.00	10.00
5089	Please/Mule Train	1963	2.50	5.00	10.00
5134	Don't Blame Me/Say It Isn't So	1964	2.50	5.00	10.00
5170	Sweet Lorraine/You Came a Long Way from St. Louis	1964	2.50	5.00	10.00
5275	True Love Ways/I Should Care	1964	2.50	5.00	10.00
5349	Without You/Don't Make Me Laugh	1965	2.50	5.00	10.00
HICKORY					
1397	No One Will Ever Know/I'm Saving All My Love (For You)	1966	2.00	4.00	8.00
1411	Call Her Your Sweetheart/Give Myself a Party	1966	2.00	4.00	8.00
1435	I Remember You/Stranger to You	1967	2.00	4.00	8.00
1454	Kaw-Liga/Out of Nowhere	1967	2.00	4.00	8.00
1473	Just Let Me Make Believe/Fireball Mail	1967	2.00	4.00	8.00
1486	Oh, Such a Stranger/Then You Can Tell Me Goodbye	1967	2.00	4.00	8.00
1499	Adios Matador/Movin' Lover	1968	2.00	4.00	8.00
1507	Don't Forget to Cry/Morning in Your Eyes	1968	2.00	4.00	8.00
1514	Good Morning Dear/Innocent Years	1968	2.00	4.00	8.00
1525	Maurie/I'm Learning Child	1968	2.00	4.00	8.00
1540	Let Me Into Your Life/Mary in the Morning	1969	—	3.00	6.00
1550	I Love You Because/It's My Time	1969	—	3.00	6.00
1556	Lights of Home/Love Hurts	1969	—	3.00	6.00
1574	Sweet Memories/You've Still Got a Place in My Heart	1970	—	3.00	6.00
1595	Someone/One More Mile, One More Town (One More Time)	1971	—	3.00	6.00
MAM					
3612	Lonesome Jubilee/Teach Me Little Children	1971	—	2.50	5.00
VEE JAY					
457	I Remember You/I Listen to My Heart	1962	3.75	7.50	15.00
—With Frank Ifield's name spelled correctly on label					
457	I Remember You/I Listen to My Heart	1962	5.00	10.00	20.00
—With both labels misspelled "Farnk Ifield"					
477	Lovesick Blues/Anytime	1962	3.00	6.00	12.00
499	The Wayward Wind/I'm Smiling Now	1963	3.00	6.00	12.00
525	Unchained Melody/Nobody's Darlin' But Mine	1963	3.00	6.00	12.00
553	I'm Confessin' (That I Love You)/Heart and Soul	1963	3.00	6.00	12.00
WARNER BROS.					
8730	Why Don't We Leave Together/Crawling Back	1979	—	2.00	4.00
8853	Crystal/Touch the Morning	1979	—	2.00	4.00
49095	Play Born to Lose Again/Yesterday Just Passed My Way Again	1979	—	2.00	4.00

Albums

Number	Title	Yr	VG	VG+	NM
CAPITOL					
ST 10356 [S]	I'm Confessin'	1963	6.25	12.50	25.00
T 10356 [M]	I'm Confessin'	1963	5.00	10.00	20.00
HICKORY					
LPM-132 [M]	The Best of Frank Ifield	1966	5.00	10.00	20.00
LPS-132 [P]	The Best of Frank Ifield	1966	5.00	10.00	20.00
LPM-136 [M]	Tale of Two Cities	1967	3.75	7.50	15.00
LPS-136 [S]	Tale of Two Cities	1967	5.00	10.00	20.00
ST-90753 [S]	The Best of Frank Ifield	1966	6.25	12.50	25.00
—Capitol Record Club edition					
T-90753 [M]	The Best of Frank Ifield	1966	6.25	12.50	25.00
—Capitol Record Club edition					
VEE JAY					
LP 1054 [M]	I Remember You	1962	7.50	15.00	30.00
SR 1054 [S]	I Remember You	1962	12.50	25.00	50.00

IGGY AND THE STOOGES

12-Inch Singles

Number	Title (A Side/B Side)	Yr	VG	VG+	NM
BOMP!					
12139	I Got a Right/Gimme Some Skin	1991	—	2.50	5.00

45s

Number	Title (A Side/B Side)	Yr	VG	VG+	NM
BOMP!					
139	I Got a Right/Gimme Some Skin	1991	—	—	2.00
139 [PS]	I Got a Right/Gimme Some Skin	1991	—	—	2.00
COLUMBIA					
45877	Search and Destroy/Penetration	1973	2.50	5.00	10.00
ELEKTRA					
45664	I Wanna Be Your Dog (Part 1)/I Wanna Be Your Dog (Part 2)	1970	7.50	15.00	30.00
—As "The Stooges"					
45695	Down on the Street/I Feel Alright	1970	7.50	15.00	30.00
—As "The Stooges"					
SIAMESE					
001	I Got a Right/Gimme Some Skin	1977	6.25	12.50	25.00
001	I Got a Right/Gimme Some Skin	1977	2.50	5.00	10.00
—Second pressing: "Siamese" in fake Asian lettering with iguana logo					
001 [PS]	I Got a Right/Gimme Some Skin	1977	—	3.00	6.00
—Only issued with Bomp!-distributed copies; has "Iggy & & The Stooges" on cover					

7-Inch Extended Plays

Number	Title	Yr	VG	VG+	NM
BOMP!					
114	Jesus Loves the Stooges	1977	—	3.75	7.50
114 [PS]	Jesus Loves the Stooges	1977	—	3.75	7.50

Albums

Number	Title	Yr	VG	VG+	NM
BOMP!					
1018	Kill City	1978	2.00	4.00	8.00
—By "Iggy Pop and James Williamson"					
COLUMBIA					
KC 32111	Raw Power	1973	12.50	25.00	50.00
ELEKTRA					
EKS 74051	The Stooges	1969	12.50	25.00	50.00
—By "The Stooges"; red label with large stylized "E" (butterfly label, deduct 60%)					
EKS 74101	Fun House	1970	12.50	25.00	50.00
—By "The Stooges"; red label with large stylized "E" (butterfly label, deduct 60%)					

Number	Title (A Side/B Side)	Yr	VG	VG+	NM
IMPORT/BOMP!					
1015	Metallic K.O.	1977	4.50	9.00	18.00
1018	Kill City	1978	3.00	6.00	12.00
—By "Iggy Pop and James Williamson"; original issue on green vinyl					

IKETTES, THE
Also see THE MIRETTES.

Number	Title (A Side/B Side)	Yr	VG	VG+	NM
45s					
ATCO					
6212	I'm Blue (The Gong-Gong Song)/Find My Baby	1961	5.00	10.00	20.00
6223	Troubles on My Mind/Come On and Truck	1962	3.75	7.50	15.00
6232	Zizzy Zee Zum Zum/Heavenly Love	1962	3.75	7.50	15.00
6243	I Do Love You/I Had a Dream the Other Night	1962	3.75	7.50	15.00
MODERN					
1005	Peaches 'N' Cream/The Biggest Players	1965	2.50	5.00	10.00
1008	(He's Gonna Be) Fine, Fine, Fine/How Come	1965	2.50	5.00	10.00
1011	I'm So Thankful/Don't Feel Sorry for Me	1965	2.00	4.00	8.00
1015	Sally Go Round the Roses/Lonely for You	1965	2.00	4.00	8.00
1024	Da Doo Ron Ron/Not That I Recall	1966	2.00	4.00	8.00
PHI-DAN					
5009	Down Down/What'cha Gonna Do	1966	2.50	5.00	10.00
POMPEII					
66683	Beauty Is Just Skin Deep/Make Them Wait	1968	—	3.00	6.00
UNITED ARTISTS					
50866	If You Take a Close Look/Got What It Takes	1971	—	2.50	5.00
51103	I'm Just Not Ready for Love/Two Timin' Double Dealin'	1973	—	2.50	5.00
Albums					
MODERN					
M-102 [M]	Soul Hits	1965	7.50	15.00	30.00
MST-102 [S]	Soul Hits	1965	10.00	20.00	40.00
UNITED ARTISTS					
UA-LA190-F	(G)Old and New	1973	3.00	6.00	12.00

ILL WIND, THE

Number	Title (A Side/B Side)	Yr	VG	VG+	NM
45s					
ABC					
11107	In My Dark World/Walkin' and Singin'	1968	6.25	12.50	25.00
Albums					
ABC					
S-641	Flashes	1968	25.00	50.00	100.00

ILL WINDS, THE
Later incarnation of CHANTAY'S.

Number	Title (A Side/B Side)	Yr	VG	VG+	NM
45s					
REPRISE					
0423	So Be On Your Way (I Won't Cry)/Fear of the Rain	1965	3.75	7.50	15.00
0492	I Idolize You/A Letter	1966	3.75	7.50	15.00

ILLINOIS SPEED PRESS, THE

Number	Title (A Side/B Side)	Yr	VG	VG+	NM
45s					
COLUMBIA					
44564	Get In the Wind (Part 1)/Get In the Wind (Part 2)	1968	2.50	5.00	10.00
45166	Country Dumplin'/Sadly Out of Place	1970	2.50	5.00	10.00
Albums					
COLUMBIA					
CS 9792	The Illinois Speed Press	1969	3.75	7.50	15.00
CS 9976	Duet	1970	3.75	7.50	15.00

ILLUSION, THE

Number	Title (A Side/B Side)	Yr	VG	VG+	NM
45s					
DYNO VOICE					
914	It's Groovy Time/My Party	1968	2.50	5.00	10.00
STEED					
712	Did You See Her Eyes/Falling in Love	1969	2.50	5.00	10.00
717	Run Run Run/I Love You Yes I Do	1969	2.00	4.00	8.00
718	Did You See Her Eyes/Falling in Love	1969	—	3.00	6.00
721	How Does It Feel/Once in a Lifetime	1969	—	3.00	6.00
722	Together/Don't Push It	1969	—	3.00	6.00
726	Let's Make Each Other Happy/Beside You	1970	—	3.00	6.00
732	Collection/Wait a Minute	1970	—	3.00	6.00
Albums					
STEED					
ST-37003	The Illusion	1969	5.00	10.00	20.00
ST-37005	Together (As a Way of Life)	1969	3.75	7.50	15.00
ST-37006	If It's So	1970	3.75	7.50	15.00

ILLUSIONS, THE
More than one group.

Number	Title (A Side/B Side)	Yr	VG	VG+	NM
45s					
COLUMBIA					
43700	I Know/Take My Heart	1966	2.50	5.00	10.00
CORAL					
62173	The Letter/Henry and Henrietta	1960	10.00	20.00	40.00
DIAL					
4004	I Don't Believe It/The World Outside	1965	2.50	5.00	10.00
DOT					
16752	Secrets of Love/Don't Put Me Down	1965	5.00	10.00	20.00
EMBER					
1071	How High Is the Mountain/Can't We Fall in Love	1961	7.50	15.00	30.00
KAPE					
1001	The Closer You Are/For Sentimental Reasons	196?	2.50	5.00	10.00
LAURIE					
3245	Maybe/In the Beginning	1964	5.00	10.00	20.00
LITTLE DEBBIE					
105	Story of My Life/Walking Boy	1964	37.50	75.00	150.00
MALI					
104	Hey Boy/Lonely Soldier	1962	12.50	25.00	50.00
NORTHEAST					
801	Hey Boy/Lonely Soldier	1962	3.75	7.50	15.00
RELIC					
512	Hey Boy/Lonely Soldier	1964	2.50	5.00	10.00
ROUND					
1018	Jezebel/Nightmare	1963	20.00	40.00	80.00
SHERATON					
104	Hey Boy/Lonely Soldier	1962	6.25	12.50	25.00

ILLUSTRATION

Number	Title (A Side/B Side)	Yr	VG	VG+	NM
Albums					
JANUS					
JLP-3010	Illustration	1969	6.25	12.50	25.00

ILMO SMOKEHOUSE

Number	Title (A Side/B Side)	Yr	VG	VG+	NM
Albums					
BEAUTIFUL SOUND					
3002	Ilmo Smokehouse	1971	10.00	20.00	40.00
ROULETTE					
RS-3002	Ilmo Smokehouse	1971	5.00	10.00	20.00

IMAGINATIONS, THE (1)

Number	Title (A Side/B Side)	Yr	VG	VG+	NM
45s					
BALLAD					
500	Wait a Little Longer Son/Mama's Little Baby	1962	5.00	10.00	20.00
BO MARC					
301	Guardian Angel/Hey You	1961	10.00	20.00	40.00
DUEL					
507	Guardian Angel/Hey You	1961	5.00	10.00	20.00
MUSIC MAKERS					
103	Goodnight Baby/The Search Is Over	1961	12.50	25.00	50.00
108	Guardian Angel/Hey You	1961	12.50	25.00	50.00
Albums					
RELIC					
LP-5058	The Imaginations (1961-1962)	198?	2.50	5.00	10.00

IMAGINATIONS, THE (2)
Another concoction of STEVE BARRI and P.F. SLOAN.

Number	Title (A Side/B Side)	Yr	VG	VG+	NM
45s					
DUNHILL					
4092	I Love You When You're Mad/Summer in New York	1967	5.00	10.00	20.00

IMAGINATIONS, THE (3)

Number	Title (A Side/B Side)	Yr	VG	VG+	NM
45s					
FRATERNITY					
1001	I Just Can't Get Over Losing You/Strange Neighborhood	1967	7.50	15.00	30.00
1006	No One Ever Lost More/Strange Voice	1968	6.25	12.50	25.00

IMPACS, THE

Number	Title (A Side/B Side)	Yr	VG	VG+	NM
45s					
KING					
5851	Jo-Ann/Two Strangers	1964	2.50	5.00	10.00
5863	Shimmy, Shimmy/Zot	1964	2.50	5.00	10.00
5891	She Didn't Even Say Hello/Kool It	1964	2.50	5.00	10.00
5910	Ain't That the Way Life Is/Don't Cry Baby	1964	2.50	5.00	10.00
5965	Your Mama Put the Hurt on Me/Cape Kennedy, Florida	1964	2.50	5.00	10.00
PARKWAY					
865	I'm Gonna Make You Cry/Tears in My Heart	1963	3.00	6.00	12.00
Albums					
KING					
886 [M]	Impact!	1964	50.00	100.00	200.00
KS-886 [S]	Impact!	1964	75.00	150.00	300.00
916 [M]	A Weekend with the Impacs	1964	50.00	100.00	200.00
KS-916 [S]	A Weekend with the Impacs	1964	75.00	150.00	300.00

IMPACTS, THE
Several different groups.

Number	Title (A Side/B Side)	Yr	VG	VG+	NM
45s					
ANDERSON					
104	Summer/Linda	1964	12.50	25.00	50.00
CARLTON					
548	Darling, No You're Mine/Help Me Somebody	1961	12.50	25.00	50.00
—With incorrect A-side title					
548	Darling, Now You're Mine/Help Me Somebody	1961	7.50	15.00	30.00
DCP					
1147	Wishing Well/Heartaches	1965	12.50	25.00	50.00
—As "Kenny and the Impacts"					
1150	Just Because/Pigtails	1965	10.00	20.00	40.00
KIP					
1890	Burnt Valves/Chrome Reverse	1963	12.50	25.00	50.00
RCA VICTOR					
47-7583	Bobby Sox Squaw/Croc-O-Doll	1959	5.00	10.00	20.00
47-7609	Canadian Sunset/They Say	1959	12.50	25.00	50.00
WATTS					
5599	Now Is the Time/Soup	1959	20.00	40.00	80.00
Albums					
DEL-FI					
DFLP-1234 [M]	Wipe Out	1963	15.00	30.00	60.00
DFS-1234 [S]	Wipe Out	1963	20.00	40.00	80.00
DLF-1234	Wipe Out	199?	3.00	6.00	12.00
—Reissue with bar code					

IMPALA SYNDROME, THE

Number	Title (A Side/B Side)	Yr	VG	VG+	NM
Albums					
PARALLAX					
4002	The Impala Syndrome	1970	25.00	50.00	100.00

IMPALAS, THE

45s

Number	Title (A Side/B Side)	Yr	VG	VG+	NM
20TH FOX					
428	Last Night I Saw a Girl/There Is Nothin' Like a Dame	1963	3.00	6.00	12.00
BUNKY					
7760	Whay Should He Do/I Still Love You	1969	2.00	4.00	8.00
7762	Whip it On Me/I Still Love You	1969	2.00	4.00	8.00
CAPITOL					
2709	Speed Up/Soul	1969	2.00	4.00	8.00
CHECKER					
999	For the Love of Mike/I Need You So Much	1961	3.00	6.00	12.00
CUB					
9022	I Ran All the Way Home/Fool, Fool, Fool	1959	15.00	30.00	60.00
—Original A-side title					
9022	Sorry (I Ran All the Way Home)/Fool, Fool, Fool	1959	5.00	10.00	20.00
9033	Oh What a Fool/Sandy Went Away	1959	5.00	10.00	20.00
9053	Peggy Darling/Bye Everybody	1959	5.00	10.00	20.00
9066	All Alone/When My Heart Does All the Talking	1960	5.00	10.00	20.00
—As "Speedo and the Impalas"					
HAMILTON					
50026	I Was a Fool/First Date	1960	5.00	10.00	20.00
RED BOY					
113	When You Dance/I Can't See Me Without You	1966	6.25	12.50	25.00
RITE-ON					
101	I Can't See Me Without You/Old Man Mose	196?	5.00	10.00	20.00
STEADY					
044	When You Dance/I Can't See Me Without You	1967	5.00	10.00	20.00
SUNDOWN					
115	The Lonely One/Lost Boogie	1959	3.75	7.50	15.00

7-Inch Extended Plays

Number	Title (A Side/B Side)	Yr	VG	VG+	NM
CUB					
5000	(contents unknown)	1959	100.00	200.00	400.00
5000 [PS]	Sorry (I Ran All the Way Home)	1959	100.00	200.00	400.00

Albums

Number	Title (A Side/B Side)	Yr	VG	VG+	NM
CUB					
8003 [M]	Sorry (I Ran All the Way Home)	1959	100.00	200.00	400.00
S-8003 [S]	Sorry (I Ran All the Way Home)	1959	150.00	300.00	600.00

IMPERIALITES, THE

45s

Number	Title (A Side/B Side)	Yr	VG	VG+	NM
IMPERIAL					
66015	Have Love, Will Travel/Let's Get One	1964	5.00	10.00	20.00

IMPERIALS, THE (1)

See LITTLE ANTHONY AND THE IMPERIALS.

IMPERIALS, THE (2)

45s

Number	Title (A Side/B Side)	Yr	VG	VG+	NM
BUZZY					
1	My Darling/You Should Have Told Me	1962	5.00	10.00	20.00
—Red vinyl					
SAVOY					
1104	My Darling/You Should Have Told Me	1954	50.00	100.00	200.00

IMPERIALS, THE (3)

45s

Number	Title (A Side/B Side)	Yr	VG	VG+	NM
NEWTIME					
503	A Short Prayer/Where Will You Be	1962	3.75	7.50	15.00
505	The Letter/Go and Get Your Heart Broken	1962	3.75	7.50	15.00

IMPERIALS, THE (4)

45s

Number	Title (A Side/B Side)	Yr	VG	VG+	NM
OMNI					
5501	Who's Gonna Love Me/Better Take Time to Love	1978	—	2.50	5.00

IMPERIALS, THE (U)

We're not sure which group these are.

45s

Number	Title (A Side/B Side)	Yr	VG	VG+	NM
CAPITOL					
4921	I'm Still Dancing/Bermuda Wonderful	1963	3.75	7.50	15.00
CARLTON					
566	Faithfully Yours/Vut Vut	1961	5.00	10.00	20.00

IMPERIALS MINUS TWO, THE

45s

Number	Title (A Side/B Side)	Yr	VG	VG+	NM
IMPERIAL					
5787	A Swingin' Dream/In Any Language	1961	5.00	10.00	20.00

IMPOSSIBLES, THE

More than one group.

45s

Number	Title (A Side/B Side)	Yr	VG	VG+	NM
BLANCHE					
029	Chapel Bells/Little by Little	1960	100.00	200.00	400.00
REPRISE					
0305	Lonely Bluebird/Paint Me a Pretty Picture	1964	6.25	12.50	25.00
RMP					
501	Everywhere I Go/Well, It's Alright	1966	6.25	12.50	25.00
1030	Mr. Maestro/Well, It's Alright	1964	6.25	12.50	25.00
ROULETTE					
4745	I Wanna Know/It's All Right	1967	5.00	10.00	20.00

IMPRESSIONS, THE

Also see JERRY BUTLER; CURTIS MAYFIELD.

45s

Number	Title (A Side/B Side)	Yr	VG	VG+	NM
20TH FOX					
172	All Through the Night/Meanwhile, Back in My Heart	1959	10.00	20.00	40.00
ABC					
10831	Can't Satisfy/This Must End	1966	2.00	4.00	8.00
10869	Love's a-Comin'/Wade in the Water	1966	2.00	4.00	8.00
10900	You Always Hurt Me/Little Girl	1967	2.00	4.00	8.00
10932	It's Hard to Believe/You've Got Me Runnin'	1967	2.00	4.00	8.00
10964	I Can't Stay Away from You/You Ought to Be in Heaven	1967	2.00	4.00	8.00
11022	We're a Winner/It's All Over	1967	2.00	4.00	8.00
11071	We're Rolling On (Part 1)/We're Rolling On (Part 2)	1968	2.00	4.00	8.00
11103	I Loved and I Lost/Up, Up and Away	1968	2.00	4.00	8.00
11135	Don't Cry My Love/Sometimes I Wonder	1968	2.00	4.00	8.00
11188	East of Java/Just Before Sunrise	1969	2.00	4.00	8.00
ABC-PARAMOUNT					
10241	Gypsy Woman/As Long As You Love Me	1961	3.75	7.50	15.00
10289	Grow Closer Together/Can't You See	1962	3.75	7.50	15.00
10328	Little Young Lover/Never Let Me Go	1962	3.75	7.50	15.00
10357	You've Come Home/Minstrel and Queen	1962	3.75	7.50	15.00
10386	I'm the One Who Loves You/I Need Your Love	1962	3.75	7.50	15.00
10431	Sad, Sad Girl and Boy/Twist and Limbo	1963	3.75	7.50	15.00
10487	It's All Right/You'll Want Me Back	1963	3.75	7.50	15.00
10511	Talking About My Baby/Never Too Much Love	1963	3.75	7.50	15.00
10537	Girl You Don't Know Me/A Woman Who Loves Me	1964	3.75	7.50	15.00
10544	I'm So Proud/I Made a Mistake	1964	3.75	7.50	15.00
10554	Keep On Pushing/I Love You (Yeah)	1964	3.75	7.50	15.00
10581	You Must Believe Me/See the Real Me	1964	3.75	7.50	15.00
10602	Amen/Long, Long Winter	1964	3.75	7.50	15.00
10622	People Get Ready/I've Been Trying	1965	3.75	7.50	15.00
10647	Woman's Got Soul/Get Up and Move	1965	3.00	6.00	12.00
10670	Meeting Over Yonder/I've Found That I've Lost	1965	3.00	6.00	12.00
10710	I Need You/Never Could You Be	1965	3.00	6.00	12.00
10725	Just One Kiss from You/Twilight Time	1965	3.00	6.00	12.00
10750	You've Been Cheatin'/Man, Oh Man	1965	3.00	6.00	12.00
10761	Since I Lost the One I Love/Falling in Love with You	1966	2.50	5.00	10.00
10789	Too Slow/No One Else	1966	2.50	5.00	10.00
ABNER					
1013	For Your Precious Love/Sweet Was the Wine	1958	10.00	20.00	40.00
—As "Jerry Butler and the Impressions"					
1017	Come Back My Love/Love Me	1958	7.50	15.00	30.00
1023	The Gift of Love/At the County Fair	1959	7.50	15.00	30.00
1025	Lonely One/Senorita I Love You	1959	7.50	15.00	30.00
1034	Say That You Love Me/A New Love	1960	7.50	15.00	30.00
BANDERA					
2504	Listen/Shorty's Got to Go	1959	12.50	25.00	50.00
CHI-SOUND					
2418	Sorry/All I Wanna Do Is Make Love to You	1979	—	2.50	5.00
2438	Maybe I'm Mistaken/All I Wanna Do Is Make Love to You	1980	—	2.50	5.00
2491	For Your Precious Love/You're Mine	1981	—	2.50	5.00
2499	Love, Love, Love/Fan the Fire	1981	—	2.50	5.00
COTILLION					
44210	This Time/I'm a Fool for Love	1976	—	2.50	5.00
44211	Silent Night/I Saw Mommy Kissing Santa Claus	1976	—	3.00	6.00
44214	You'll Never Find/Stardust	1977	—	2.50	5.00
44222	Can't Get Along/You're So Right for Me	1977	—	2.50	5.00
CURTOM					
SP-3 [DJ]	Merry Christmas Happy New Year	197?	3.00	6.00	12.00
0103	Sooner or Later/Miracle Woman	1975	—	2.50	5.00
0106	Same Thing It Took/I'm So Glad	1975	—	2.50	5.00
0110	Loving Power/First Impressions	1975	—	2.50	5.00
0116	Sunshine/I Wish I'd Stayed in Bed	1976	—	2.50	5.00
1932	Fool for You/I'm Loving Nothing	1968	—	3.00	6.00
1932 [PS]	Fool for You/I'm Loving Nothing	1968	3.75	7.50	15.00
1934	This Is My Country/My Woman's Love	1968	—	3.00	6.00
1937	My Deceiving Heart/You Want Somebody Else	1969	—	3.00	6.00
1940	Seven Years/The Girl I Find	1969	—	3.00	6.00
1943	Choice of Colors/Mighty Mighty Spade and Whitey	1969	—	3.00	6.00
1946	Say You Love Me/You'll Be Always Mine	1969	—	3.00	6.00
1948	Wherever She Leadeth Me/Amen (1970)	1970	—	3.00	6.00
1951	Check Out Your Mind/Can't You See	1970	—	3.00	6.00
1954	(Baby) Turn On to Me/Soulful Love	1970	—	3.00	6.00
1957	Ain't Got Time/I'm So Proud	1971	—	3.00	6.00
1959	Love Me/Do You Wanna Win	1971	—	3.00	6.00
1966	Inner City Blues/We Must Be in Love	1971	—	3.00	6.00
1970	This Loves for Real/Times Have Changed	1972	—	3.00	6.00
1973	I Need to Belong to Someone/Love Me	1972	—	3.00	6.00
1982	Preacher Man/Times Have Changed	1973	—	3.00	6.00
1985	Thin Line/I'm Loving You	1973	—	3.00	6.00
1994	If It's In You to Do Wrong/Times Have Changed	1973	—	3.00	6.00
1997	Finally Got Myself Together (I'm a Changed Man)/I'll Always Be Here	1974	—	3.00	6.00
2003	Something's Mighty, Mighty Wrong/Three the Hard Way	1974	—	3.00	6.00
FALCON					
1013	For Your Precious Love/Sweet Was the Wine	1958	15.00	30.00	60.00
—As "Jerry Butler and the Impressions"					
MCA					
52995	Can't Wait 'Til Tomorrow/Love Workin' On Me	1987	—	—	3.00
PORT					
70031	Listen/Shorty's Got to Go	1962	3.75	7.50	15.00
SWIRL					
107	I Need Your Love/Don't Leave Me	1962	5.00	10.00	20.00
VEE JAY					
280	For Your Precious Love/Sweet Was the Wine	1958	4000.	6000.	8000.
—As "Jerry Butler and the Impressions"					
424	Say That You Love Me/Senorita I Love You	1962	5.00	10.00	20.00
574	The Gift of Love/At the County Fair	1963	3.75	7.50	15.00
621	Say That You Love Me/Senorita I Love You	1964	3.75	7.50	15.00

Albums

Number	Title (A Side/B Side)	Yr	VG	VG+	NM
ABC					
606 [M]	The Fabulous Impressions	1967	6.25	12.50	25.00
S-606 [S]	The Fabulous Impressions	1967	5.00	10.00	20.00

Number	Title (A Side/B Side)	Yr	VG	VG+	NM
S-635	We're a Winner	1968	3.75	7.50	15.00
S-654	The Best of the Impressions	1968	3.75	7.50	15.00
S-668	The Versatile Impressions	1969	3.75	7.50	15.00
S-727	16 Greatest Hits	1971	3.00	6.00	12.00
D-780 [(2)]	Curtis Mayfield/His Early Years with the Impressions	1973	5.00	10.00	20.00
ABC-PARAMOUNT					
450 [M]	The Impressions	1963	7.50	15.00	30.00
S-450 [S]	The Impressions	1963	10.00	20.00	40.00
468 [M]	The Never Ending Impressions	1964	7.50	15.00	30.00
S-468 [S]	The Never Ending Impressions	1964	10.00	20.00	40.00
493 [M]	Keep On Pushing	1964	7.50	15.00	30.00
S-493 [S]	Keep On Pushing	1964	10.00	20.00	40.00
505 [M]	People Get Ready	1965	7.50	15.00	30.00
S-505 [S]	People Get Ready	1965	10.00	20.00	40.00
515 [M]	The Impressions' Greatest Hits	1965	5.00	10.00	20.00
S-515 [S]	The Impressions' Greatest Hits	1965	6.25	12.50	25.00
523 [M]	One By One	1965	5.00	10.00	20.00
S-523 [S]	One By One	1965	6.25	12.50	25.00
545 [M]	Ridin' High	1966	5.00	10.00	20.00
S-545 [S]	Ridin' High	1966	6.25	12.50	25.00
ST-90520 [S]	One By One	1965	7.50	15.00	30.00
—Capitol Record Club edition					
T-90520 [M]	One By One	1965	6.25	12.50	25.00
—Capitol Record Club edition					
CHI-SOUND					
T-596	Come to My Party	1979	2.50	5.00	10.00
T-624	Fan the Fire	1981	2.50	5.00	10.00
COTILLION					
SD 9912	It's About Time	1976	3.00	6.00	12.00
CURTOM					
CUR-2006	Lasting Impressions	198?	2.50	5.00	10.00
CU 5003	First Impressions	1975	3.00	6.00	12.00
CU 5009	Loving Power	1976	3.00	6.00	12.00
CRS-8001	This Is My Country	1968	3.75	7.50	15.00
CRS-8003	The Young Mods' Forgotten Story	1969	3.75	7.50	15.00
CRS-8004	Best Impressions — Curtis, Sam, Dave	1969	3.75	7.50	15.00
CRS-8006	Check Out Your Mind	1970	3.75	7.50	15.00
CRS-8012	Times Have Changed	1972	3.75	7.50	15.00
CRS-8016	Preacher Man	1973	3.75	7.50	15.00
CRS-8019	Finally Got Myself Together	1974	3.75	7.50	15.00
LOST-NITE					
LLP-22 [10]	Jerry Butler and the Impressions	1981	3.75	7.50	15.00
—Red vinyl					
MCA					
1500	The Impressions Greatest Hits	1982	2.00	4.00	8.00
5373	In the Heat of the Night	1982	2.50	5.00	10.00
PICKWICK					
SPC-3602	The Impressions	1978	2.00	4.00	8.00
SCEPTER CITATION					
CTN-18018	The Best of Curtis Mayfield and the Impressions	1972	2.50	5.00	10.00
SIRE					
SASH-3717 [(2)]	The Vintage Years	1977	3.75	7.50	15.00
—Includes solo hits by Jerry Butler and Curtis Mayfield					

IMUS, DON

Number	Title (A Side/B Side)	Yr	VG	VG+	NM
45s					
HAPPY TIGER					
576	From Adam's Rib to Women's Lib/The Ballad of Rick Nelson	1971	2.00	4.00	8.00
—As "Imus in the Morning"					
RCA VICTOR					
PB-10170	Everybody Needs Milk/Play That Country Juke Box	1975	2.00	4.00	8.00
48-1031	Rev. Billy Sol Hargus/1200 Hamburgers to Go	1972	2.00	4.00	8.00
—As "Imus in the Morning"					
74-0789	Holy Land Record Package/Rent-A-Car Phone Call	1972	2.00	4.00	8.00
—As "Imus in the Morning"					
74-0982	Son of Checkers (The Watergate Case)/Oh, Billy Sol, Please Heal Us All	1973	2.00	4.00	8.00
Albums					
BANG					
407	This Honky's Nuts	1974	6.25	12.50	25.00
RCA VICTOR					
LSP-4699	1200 Hamburgers to Go	1972	6.25	12.50	25.00
LSP-4819	One Sacred Chicken to Go	1973	6.25	12.50	25.00

IN-BETWEENS, THE

Early incarnation of SLADE.

Number	Title (A Side/B Side)	Yr	VG	VG+	NM
45s					
HIGHLAND					
1173	Girl Child, I Am An Evil Witchman/Security	1966	75.00	150.00	300.00

IN CROWD, THE (1)

Also see JON AND ROBIN & THE IN CROWD.

Number	Title (A Side/B Side)	Yr	VG	VG+	NM
45s					
ABNAK					
121	Inside Out/Big Cities	1967	2.00	4.00	8.00
121 [DJ]	Inside Out/Big Cities	1967	3.00	6.00	12.00
—Promo only on yellow vinyl					
129	Let's Take a Walk/Hangin' From Your Lovin' Tree	1968	2.00	4.00	8.00
129 [DJ]	Let's Take a Walk/Hangin' From Your Lovin' Tree	1968	3.00	6.00	12.00
—Promo only on yellow vinyl					

IN CROWD, THE (2)

Includes two members of THE ELIGIBLES.

Number	Title (A Side/B Side)	Yr	VG	VG+	NM
45s					
VIVA					
604	Questions and Answers/Happiness in My Heart	1966	2.00	4.00	8.00
610	If I Knew a Magic Word/Never Ending Symphony	1967	2.00	4.00	8.00

IN CROWD, THE (3)

British group.

Number	Title (A Side/B Side)	Yr	VG	VG+	NM
45s					
TOWER					
147	That's How Strong My Love Is/Things She Says	1965	6.25	12.50	25.00
196	Why Must They Criticize/I Don't Mind	1966	6.25	12.50	25.00

IN CROWD, THE (U)

It's doubtful that any of these are group (1) or (3). Some may be group (2), though.

Number	Title (A Side/B Side)	Yr	VG	VG+	NM
45s					
BRENT					
7046	Grapevine/Cat Dance	1965	3.75	7.50	15.00
HICKORY					
1378	Speed Queen/Cry, Boy, Cry	1966	3.75	7.50	15.00
1413	In the Midnight Hour/Just Give Me Time	1966	3.00	6.00	12.00
MUSICOR					
1111	Do the Surfer Jerk/Girl in the Black Bikini	1965	5.00	10.00	20.00
RONN					
1	In the Midnight Hour/Nothing You Do	1967	2.50	5.00	10.00
SWAN					
4204	Let's Shindig/Klink	1965	3.75	7.50	15.00

IN GROUP, THE

Number	Title (A Side/B Side)	Yr	VG	VG+	NM
Albums					
IN					
I-1002 [M]	Swinging 12 String	1964	5.00	10.00	20.00
IS-1002 [S]	Swinging 12 String	1964	6.25	12.50	25.00

IN-SECT, THE

Number	Title (A Side/B Side)	Yr	VG	VG+	NM
Albums					
RCA CAMDEN					
CAL-909 [M]	Introducing the In-Sect Direct from England	1964	10.00	20.00	40.00
CAS-909 [S]	Introducing the In-Sect Direct from England	1964	12.50	25.00	50.00

INCREDIBLE BONGO BAND, THE

Number	Title (A Side/B Side)	Yr	VG	VG+	NM
45s					
MGM					
14588	Bongo Rock/Bongolia	1973	—	2.50	5.00
14635	Let There Be Drums/Dueling Bongos	1973	—	2.50	5.00
PRIDE					
1015	Bongo Rock/Bongolia	1972	2.00	4.00	8.00
7601	Kirburi/When the Bed Breaks Down, I'll Mee You in the Spring	1974	—	2.50	5.00
Albums					
PRIDE					
0028	Bongo Rock	1973	2.50	5.00	10.00
6010	The Return of the Incredible Bongo Band	1974	2.50	5.00	10.00

INCREDIBLE STRING BAND, THE

Number	Title (A Side/B Side)	Yr	VG	VG+	NM
45s					
ELEKTRA					
45696	This Moment/Big Ted	1970	2.00	4.00	8.00
Albums					
CARTHAGE					
CGLP-4421	The Hangman's Beautiful Daughter	198?	3.00	6.00	12.00
ELEKTRA					
EKM-322 [M]	The Incredible String Band	1967	7.50	15.00	30.00
7E-2002 [(2)]	'U'	1971	6.25	12.50	25.00
—Butterfly label					
7E-2004 [(2)]	Relics of the Incredible String Band	1971	5.00	10.00	20.00
—Butterfly label					
EKM-4010 [M]	The 5,000 Spirits	1967	7.50	15.00	30.00
EKS-7322 [S]	The Incredible String Band	1967	5.00	10.00	20.00
—Brown label					
EKS-7322	The Incredible String Band	1969	3.75	7.50	15.00
—Red label, large stylized "E"					
EKS-7322	The Incredible String Band	1971	3.00	6.00	12.00
—Butterfly label					
EKS-74010 [S]	The 5,000 Spirits	1967	5.00	10.00	20.00
—Brown label					
EKS-74010	The 5,000 Spirits	1969	3.75	7.50	15.00
—Red label, large stylized "E"					
EKS-74010	The 5,000 Spirits	1971	3.00	6.00	12.00
—Butterfly label					
EKS-74021	The Hangman's Beautiful Daughter	1968	5.00	10.00	20.00
—Brown label					
EKS-74021	The Hangman's Beautiful Daughter	1969	3.75	7.50	15.00
—Red label, large stylized "E"					
EKS-74021	The Hangman's Beautiful Daughter	1971	3.00	6.00	12.00
—Butterfly label					
EKS-74036	Wee Tam	1969	5.00	10.00	20.00
—Brown label					
EKS-74036	Wee Tam	1969	3.75	7.50	15.00
—Red label, large stylized "E"					
EKS-74036	Wee Tam	1971	3.00	6.00	12.00
—Butterfly label					
EKS-74037	The Big Huge	1969	5.00	10.00	20.00
—Brown label					
EKS-74037	The Big Huge	1969	3.75	7.50	15.00
—Red label, large stylized "E"					
EKS-74037	The Big Huge	1971	3.00	6.00	12.00
—Butterfly label					
EKS-74057	Changing Horses	1969	3.75	7.50	15.00
—Red label, large stylized "E"					
EKS-74057	Changing Horses	1971	3.00	6.00	12.00
—Butterfly label					
EKS-74061	I Looked Up	1970	3.75	7.50	15.00
—Red label, large stylized "E"					
EKS-74061	I Looked Up	1971	3.00	6.00	12.00
—Butterfly label					

Number	Title (A Side/B Side)	Yr	VG	VG+	NM
EKS-74112	Liquid Acrobat As Regards the Air	1972	3.75	7.50	15.00
—Butterfly label					
REPRISE					
MS 2122	Earthspan	1973	3.00	6.00	12.00
MS 2139	No Ruinous Feud	1973	3.00	6.00	12.00
MS 2198	Hard Rope and Silver Twine	1974	3.00	6.00	12.00

INCREDIBLES, THE

45s

Number	Title (A Side/B Side)	Yr	VG	VG+	NM
AUDIO ARTS					
60001	I'll Make It Easy (If You Come On Home)/Crying Heart	1966	3.00	6.00	12.00
60006	There's Nothing Else to Say/Another Dirty Deal	1967	2.50	5.00	10.00
60007	Heart and Soul/I Found Another Love	1967	2.50	5.00	10.00
60009	Without a Word/Standing Here Crying	1967	2.50	5.00	10.00
60014	Fool, Fool, Fool/Lost Without You	1968	2.50	5.00	10.00
60016	Miss Treatment/All of a Sudden	1968	2.50	5.00	10.00
60017	Standing Here Crying/All of a Sudden	1968	2.50	5.00	10.00
60018	Stop the Raindrops/Fool, Fool, Fool	1968	2.50	5.00	10.00
TETRAGRAMMATON					
1515	All of a Sudden/Standing Here Crying	1969	2.00	4.00	8.00

Albums

Number	Title (A Side/B Side)	Yr	VG	VG+	NM
AUDIO ARTS					
AAS-7000	Heart and Soul	1970	5.00	10.00	20.00

INDEPENDENTS, THE

45s

Number	Title (A Side/B Side)	Yr	VG	VG+	NM
WAND					
11245	Just As Long As You Need Me, Part 1/Part 2	1972	—	3.00	6.00
11249	I Just Want to Be There/Can't Understand It	1972	—	3.00	6.00
11252	Leaving Me/I Love You Yes I Do	1973	—	3.00	6.00
11258	Baby I've Been Missing You/Couldn't Hear Nobody Say	1973	—	3.00	6.00
11263	It's All Over/Sara Lee	1973	—	3.00	6.00
11267	The First Time We Met/Show Me How	1973	—	3.00	6.00
11273	Arise and Shine (Let's Get It On)/I Found Love	1974	—	3.00	6.00
11279	Let This Be a Lesson to You/No Wind, No Rain	1974	—	3.00	6.00

Albums

Number	Title (A Side/B Side)	Yr	VG	VG+	NM
WAND					
WDS-694	The First Time We Met	1973	6.25	12.50	25.00
WDS-696	The Independents	1973	6.25	12.50	25.00
WDS-699	Discs of Gold	1974	6.25	12.50	25.00

INDEX

Albums

Number	Title (A Side/B Side)	Yr	VG	VG+	NM
DC					
71	The Index	1968	1500.	2250.	3000.
—Black label; issued with black and white jacket; number is from deal wax					
4736	The Index	1968	1000.	1500.	2000.
—Red label; issued with generic white jacket, though sometimes found in first LP's jacket; number in dead wax					

INDIAN SUMMER

Albums

Number	Title (A Side/B Side)	Yr	VG	VG+	NM
RCA/NEON					
NE-3	Indian Summer	1971	5.00	10.00	20.00

INFLUENCE

Albums

Number	Title (A Side/B Side)	Yr	VG	VG+	NM
ABC					
ABCS-630	Influence	1968	7.50	15.00	30.00

INGMANN, JORGEN

45s

Number	Title (A Side/B Side)	Yr	VG	VG+	NM
ATCO					
6184	Apache/Echo Boogie	1960	3.75	7.50	15.00
6195	Anna/Cherokee	1961	3.00	6.00	12.00
6205	Milord/Oceans of Love	1961	2.50	5.00	10.00
6216	Violetta/Pinetop's Boogie Woogie	1962	2.50	5.00	10.00
6235	Africa/Johnny's Tune	1962	2.50	5.00	10.00
6277	Fourth Man Theme/Drina	1963	2.00	4.00	8.00
6305	Tovarisch/Desert March	1964	2.00	4.00	8.00
6370	Theme from "Zorba the Greek"/Gorilla	1965	2.00	4.00	8.00
6403	Corfu/Seven Roses	1966	2.00	4.00	8.00
PARROT					
45006	Sunrise Serenade/Tokyo Melody	1964	2.50	5.00	10.00

Albums

Number	Title (A Side/B Side)	Yr	VG	VG+	NM
ATCO					
33-130 [M]	Apache	1961	10.00	20.00	40.00
33-139 [M]	The Many Guitars of Jorgen Ingmann	1962	10.00	20.00	40.00
MERCURY					
MG-20200 [M]	Swinging Guitar	1956	15.00	30.00	60.00
MG-20292 [M]	Swing Softly	1956	15.00	30.00	60.00

INGRAM, LUTHER

45s

Number	Title (A Side/B Side)	Yr	VG	VG+	NM
DECCA					
31794	Ain't That Nice/You Never Miss Your Water	1965	3.00	6.00	12.00
HIB					
698	If It's All the Same To You Babe/Exus Trek	1967	20.00	40.00	80.00
KOKO					
101	I Can't Stop/You Got to Give Love to Get Love	1968	2.50	5.00	10.00
103	Missing You/Since You Don't Want Me	1968	2.50	5.00	10.00
721	Ain't Good for Nothing/These Are the Things	1976	—	3.00	6.00
724	Let's Steal Away to the Hideaway/I've Got Your Love in My Life	1977	—	3.00	6.00
725	I Like the Feeling/Gonna Be the Next Time	1977	—	3.00	6.00
728	Do You Love Somebody/How I Miss My Baby	1977	—	3.00	6.00
731	Get to Me/Trying to Find My Love	1978	—	3.00	6.00
2101	You Can Depend on Me/Looking for a New Love	1969	2.00	4.00	8.00
2102	Pity for the Lonely/Looking for a New Love	1969	2.00	4.00	8.00
2103	Puttin' Game Down/Since You Don't Want Me	1969	2.00	4.00	8.00
2104	My Honey and Me/I Can't Stop	1969	2.00	4.00	8.00
2105	Ain't That Loving You (For More Reasons Than One)/Home Don't Seem Like Home	1970	2.00	4.00	8.00
2106	To the Other Man/I'll Just Call You Honey	1970	2.00	4.00	8.00
2107	Be Good to Me Baby/Since You Don't Want Me	1971	2.00	4.00	8.00
2108	I'll Love You Until the End/Ghetto Train	1971	2.00	4.00	8.00
2110	You Were Made for Me/Missing You	1972	2.00	4.00	8.00
2111	(If Loving You Is Wrong) I Don't Want to Be Right/Puttin' Game Down	1972	2.00	4.00	8.00
2113	I'll Be Your Shelter (In Time of Storm)/I Can't Stop	1972	2.00	4.00	8.00
2115	Always/Help Me Love	1973	2.00	4.00	8.00
2116	Love Ain't Gonna Run Me Away/To the Other Man	1973	2.00	4.00	8.00
PROFILE					
5125	Baby Don't Go Too Far/How Sweet It Would Be	1986	—	—	3.00
5132	Don't Turn Around/(B-side unknown)	1987	—	—	3.00
5143	Gotta Serve Somebody/All in the Name of Love	1987	—	—	3.00
SMASH					
2019	(I Spy) For the F.B.I./Foxey Devil	1966	5.00	10.00	20.00

Albums

Number	Title (A Side/B Side)	Yr	VG	VG+	NM
KOKO					
KOS-2201	I've Been Here All the Time	1971	3.75	7.50	15.00
KOS-2202	If Loving You Is Wrong I Don't Want to Be Right	1972	3.75	7.50	15.00

INITIALS, THE (1)

45s

Number	Title (A Side/B Side)	Yr	VG	VG+	NM
CONGRESS					
207	School Day/The Song Is Number One	1964	3.00	6.00	12.00
219	Dancing on the Sand/Seventeen Guys on a Blanket at the Beach	1964	3.00	6.00	12.00
229	Someday She'll Love Me/I Should Have Listened	1964	3.00	6.00	12.00
—As "Angelo and the Initials"					

INITIALS, THE (2)

45s

Number	Title (A Side/B Side)	Yr	VG	VG+	NM
DEE					
1001	You/Bells of Joy	1959	50.00	100.00	200.00
SHERRY					
667	You/Bells of Joy	1959	12.50	25.00	50.00

INK SPOTS

45s

Number	Title (A Side/B Side)	Yr	VG	VG+	NM
DECCA					
9-5 [PS]	Ink Spots, Volume 2	1950	3.75	7.50	15.00
—Box for 25238, 25239 and 25240					
23632	If I Didn't Care/Whispering Grass (Don't Tell the Trees)	1950	6.25	12.50	25.00
—Black label, lines on either side of "Decca"					
23632	If I Didn't Care/Whispering Grass (Don't Tell the Trees)	1955	3.00	6.00	12.00
—Black label, star under "Decca"					
23632	If I Didn't Care/Whispering Grass (Don't Tell the Trees)	1961	2.50	5.00	10.00
—Black label, color bars at right					
25238	I'll Get By (As Long As I Have You)/Just for a Thrill	1950	5.00	10.00	20.00
—Side 1 and 6 of "Album No. 9-5"					
25239	I'd Climb the Highest Mountain/I'm Gettin' Sentimental Over You	1950	5.00	10.00	20.00
—From "Album No. 9-5"					
25240	Coquette/When the Swallows Come Back to Capistrano	1950	5.00	10.00	20.00
—From "Album No. 9-5"					
25505	It's a Sin to Tell a Lie/That's When Your Heartaches Begin	1961	2.50	5.00	10.00
25533	All My Life/You Were Only Fooling	1961	3.00	6.00	12.00
27102	Sometime/I Was Dancing with Someone	1950	6.25	12.50	25.00
27214	The Way It Used to Be/Right About Now	1950	6.25	12.50	25.00
27256	Our Lady of Fatima/Stranger in the City	1950	6.25	12.50	25.00
27259	Dream Awhile/Time Out for Tears	1950	6.25	12.50	25.00
27391	If/A Friend of Johnny's	1951	5.00	10.00	20.00
27464	Tell Me You Love Me/Castles in the Sand	1951	5.00	10.00	20.00
27493	Do Something for Me/A Fool Grows Wise	1951	5.00	10.00	20.00
27632	More of the Same Sweet You/What Can You Do	1951	5.00	10.00	20.00
27742	I Don't Stand a Ghost of a Chance/I'm Lucky I Have You	1951	5.00	10.00	20.00
27996	Honest and Truly/All My Life	1952	5.00	10.00	20.00
29750	Memories of You/It's Funny to Everyone But Me	1955	5.00	10.00	20.00
29991	My Prayer/Bewildered	1956	5.00	10.00	20.00
30058	The Best Things in Life Are Free/I Don't Stand a Ghost of a Chance	1956	3.75	7.50	15.00
GRAND AWARD					
1001	Rock and Roll Rag/Do I Worry	1956	5.00	10.00	20.00
KING					
1297	Ebb Tide/If You Should Say Goodbye	1953	15.00	30.00	60.00
1304	Changing Partners/Stranger in Paradise	1954	17.50	35.00	70.00
1336	Melody of Love/Am I Too Late	1954	17.50	35.00	70.00
1378	Yesterdays/Planting Rice	1954	15.00	30.00	60.00
1425	When You Come to the End of the Day/Someone's Rocking My Dreamboat	1955	12.50	25.00	50.00
1429	Melody of Love/There Is Something Missing	1955	10.00	20.00	40.00
1512	Don't Laugh at Me/Keep It Movin'	1955	10.00	20.00	40.00
4670	Here in My Lonely Room/A Fool in Love	1953	37.50	75.00	150.00
4857	Command Me/I'll Walk a Country Mile	1955	10.00	20.00	40.00
SWIFT					
1001	If I Didn't Care//Into Each Life Some Rain Must Fall/We Three	195?	3.75	7.50	15.00
VERVE					
10198	Secret Love/A Little Bird Told Me	1960	3.00	6.00	12.00

7-Inch Extended Plays

Number	Title (A Side/B Side)	Yr	VG	VG+	NM
DECCA					
ED 2047	*It's Funny to Everyone But Me/It's a Sin to Tell a Lie/Don't Get Around Much Anymore/My Prayer	195?	6.25	12.50	25.00

Number	Title (A Side/B Side)	Yr	VG	VG+	NM
ED 2047 [PS]	The Ink Spots, Volume 2	195?	6.25	12.50	25.00
Albums					
ARCHIVE OF FOLK AND JAZZ					
350	The Ink Spots in London	197?	2.50	5.00	10.00
COLORTONE					
4901 [M]	The Ink Spots	1958	15.00	30.00	60.00
4947 [M]	The Ink Spots, Vol. 2	1959	15.00	30.00	60.00
CROWN					
CST-144 [S] *—Black vinyl*	The Ink Spots' Greatest Hits	1959	6.25	12.50	25.00
CST-144 [S] *—Red vinyl*	The Ink Spots' Greatest Hits	1959	12.50	25.00	50.00
CST-175 [S] *—Black vinyl*	The Ink Spots	1961	6.25	12.50	25.00
CST-175 [S] *—Red vinyl*	The Ink Spots	1961	12.50	25.00	50.00
CST-217 [S]	The Sensational Ink Spots	1962	6.25	12.50	25.00
CLP-5112 [M]	The Ink Spots' Greatest Hits	1959	5.00	10.00	20.00
CLP-5142 [M]	The Ink Spots	1961	5.00	10.00	20.00
CLP-5187 [M]	The Sensational Ink Spots	1962	5.00	10.00	20.00
DECCA					
DXB 182 [(2) M]	The Best of the Ink Spots	1965	7.50	15.00	30.00
DL 4297 [M]	Our Golden Favorites	1962	6.25	12.50	25.00
DL 5056 [10]	The Ink Spots	1950	12.50	25.00	50.00
DL 5071 [10]	The Ink Spots, Vol. 2	1950	12.50	25.00	50.00
DL 5333 [10]	Precious Memories	1951	12.50	25.00	50.00
DL 5541 [10]	Street of Dreams	1954	12.50	25.00	50.00
DXSB 7182 [(2) P]	The Best of the Ink Spots	1965	5.00	10.00	20.00
DL 8154 [M] *—Black label, silver print*	The Best of the Ink Spots	1955	10.00	20.00	40.00
DL 8232 [M] *—Black label, silver print*	Time Our for Tears	1956	10.00	20.00	40.00
DL 8768 [M] *—Black label, silver print*	Torch Time	1958	10.00	20.00	40.00
DL 74297 [S]	Our Golden Favorites	1962	5.00	10.00	20.00
GRAND AWARD					
GA 232 SD [S]	The Ink Spots' Greatest, Volume 3	1959	10.00	20.00	40.00
GA 33-328 [M]	The Ink Spots' Greatest, Volume 1	1958	6.25	12.50	25.00
GA 33-354 [M]	The Ink Spots' Greatest, Volume 2	1958	6.25	12.50	25.00
GA 33-396 [M]	The Ink Spots' Greatest, Volume 3	1959	6.25	12.50	25.00
KING					
535 [M]	Something Old, Something New	1956	100.00	200.00	400.00
642 [M] *—Reissue of 535*	Songs That Will Live Forever	1959	75.00	150.00	300.00
5001	18 Hits by the Ink Spots	197?	2.50	5.00	10.00
MCA					
4005 [(2)]	The Best of the Ink Spots	197?	3.00	6.00	12.00
OPEN SKY					
3125	Just Like Old Times	198?	2.50	5.00	10.00
PAULA					
2212	The Ink Spots Sing Country	1972	2.50	5.00	10.00
TOPS					
L-1561 [M]	The Ink Spots	1957	10.00	20.00	40.00
L-1668 [M]	The Ink Spots, Vol. 2	1959	10.00	20.00	40.00
VERVE					
MGV-2124 [M]	The Ink Spots' Favorites	1959	6.25	12.50	25.00
MGVS-6096 [S]	The Ink Spots' Favorites	1959	10.00	20.00	40.00
VOCALION					
VL 3606 [M]	Sincerely Yours	196?	3.00	6.00	12.00
VL 3725 [M]	Lost in a Dream	1965	3.00	6.00	12.00
VL 73606 [R]	Sincerely Yours	196?	2.50	5.00	10.00
VL 73725 [R]	Lost in a Dream	1965	2.50	5.00	10.00
WALDORF MUSIC HALL					
MH 33-144 [10]	Songs of the South Seas	195?	20.00	40.00	80.00
MH 33-152 [10]	The Ink Spots Quartet	195?	20.00	40.00	80.00

INMAN, AUTRY

Number	Title (A Side/B Side)	Yr	VG	VG+	NM
45s					
DECCA					
28592	I'll Miss My Heart/Stop Stallin'	1953	5.00	10.00	20.00
28629	That's All Right/Uh Huh Honey	1953	6.25	12.50	25.00
28778	Pucker Up/That's When I Need You the Most	1953	5.00	10.00	20.00
28798	A Dear John Letter/Brown Eyed Baby	1953	5.00	10.00	20.00
28960	It Hurts Too Much to Cry/Happy Go Lucky	1953	5.00	10.00	20.00
29060	Just Reminiscing/Under the Moon	1954	5.00	10.00	20.00
29170	Little One/Once More	1954	5.00	10.00	20.00
29362	Finally I'm Free/Don't Put It Off	1954	5.00	10.00	20.00
29447	You Said Goodbye/It's a Shame	1955	5.00	10.00	20.00
29635	Tell Me Now/A Friend	1955	5.00	10.00	20.00
29690	Blue Monday/Look Over Your Shoulder	1955	6.25	12.50	25.00
29936	Be-Bop Baby/It Would Be a Doggone Lie	1956	25.00	50.00	100.00
46407	Let's Take the Long Way Home Tonight/I Hope Tomorrow Never Comes	1952	5.00	10.00	20.00
EPIC					
10232	Don't Call Me (I'll Call You)/Love Has to Die (All By Itself)	1967	2.00	4.00	8.00
10276	There Stands the Glass/This Heart Was Made for Lovin'	1968	2.00	4.00	8.00
10327	I Can See an Angel/Wish in One Hand (Cry in the Other)	1968	2.00	4.00	8.00
10389	Ballad of Two Brothers/Don't Call Me (I'll Call You)	1968	2.00	4.00	8.00
10452	Home Is Heavy on My Mind/You're the Only One in My Heart	1969	2.00	4.00	8.00
10494	I'll Be Waiting/Traveling Salesman	1969	2.00	4.00	8.00
GLAD					
1002	I'm Still in Love with Mary/Please Cut Me Down	1960	3.75	7.50	15.00
JUBILEE					
9001	The Drinks Are On Me/You Don't Live There Anymore	196?	2.00	4.00	8.00
MERCURY					
71983	Living with One and Loving Two/I Guess I'm Crazy	1962	3.00	6.00	12.00
MILLION					
4	Please Let Me Love You/Maybe This Is the Day	1972	—	3.00	6.00
24	If You Were Mine/Please Let Me Love You	1972	—	3.00	6.00
RCA VICTOR					
47-7173	Dream Boat/Remember the Night	1958	7.50	15.00	30.00
47-7260	Mary Nell/The Hard Way	1958	7.50	15.00	30.00
SIMS					
131	The Volunteer/Unlucky Am I	1963	2.50	5.00	10.00
140	Big Sam/My Word	1963	2.50	5.00	10.00
170	The Ballad of John F. Kennedy/The World's Worst Lover	1964	2.50	5.00	10.00
188	My Past/You're Welcome Dear	1964	2.50	5.00	10.00
219	Give Me 40 Acres (To Turn This Rig Around)/Six Rounds of Love and Hate	1964	2.50	5.00	10.00
UNITED ARTISTS					
278	That's All Right/Farther to Go Than I've Been	1960	3.75	7.50	15.00
303	Let's Take the Long Way Home/Too Blue to Cry	1961	3.75	7.50	15.00
Albums					
EPIC					
BN 26428	Ballad of Two Brothers	1968	5.00	10.00	20.00
JUBILEE					
JGM-2055 [M]	Riscotheque Saturday Night	1964	5.00	10.00	20.00
JGS-2055 [S]	Riscotheque Saturday Night	1964	6.25	12.50	25.00
JGM-2056 [M]	New Year's Eve with Autry Inman	1964	5.00	10.00	20.00
JGS-2056 [S]	New Year's Eve with Autry Inman	1964	6.25	12.50	25.00
MOUNTAIN DEW					
7022 [M]	Autry Inman	1963	5.00	10.00	20.00
S-7022 [S]	Autry Inman	1963	6.25	12.50	25.00
SIMS					
107 [M]	Autry Inman at the Frontier Club	1964	5.00	10.00	20.00
S-107 [S]	Autry Inman at the Frontier Club	1964	6.25	12.50	25.00

INNER CIRCLE, THE

Another STEVE BARRI and P.F. SLOAN creation.

Number	Title (A Side/B Side)	Yr	VG	VG+	NM
45s					
DUNHILL					
4128	So Long Mary Ann/Goes to Show	1968	5.00	10.00	20.00
IMPACT					
1019	Sally Go Round the Roses/Sugar	1967	5.00	10.00	20.00

INNOCENCE, THE

Number	Title (A Side/B Side)	Yr	VG	VG+	NM
45s					
KAMA SUTRA					
214	There's Got to Be a Word!/It's Not Gonna Take Too Long	1966	2.00	4.00	8.00
222	Mairzy Doats/Lifetime Lovin' You	1967	2.50	5.00	10.00
228	All I Do Is Think About You/Whence, I Make Thee Mine	1967	2.00	4.00	8.00
232	Someone Got Caught in My Eye/Your Show Is Over	1967	2.00	4.00	8.00
237	Day Turns Me On (The Bufferin Song)/It's Not Gonna Take Too Long	1967	2.00	4.00	8.00
Albums					
KAMA SUTRA					
KLP-8059 [M]	The Innocence	1967	5.00	10.00	20.00
KLPS-8059 [S]	The Innocence	1967	7.50	15.00	30.00

INNOCENTS, THE

Also see KATHY YOUNG AND THE INNOCENTS.

Number	Title (A Side/B Side)	Yr	VG	VG+	NM
45s					
DECCA					
31519	Don't Cry/Come On Lover	1963	5.00	10.00	20.00
INDIGO					
105	Honest I Do/My Baby Hully Gullys	1960	5.00	10.00	20.00
111	Gee Whiz/Please Mr. Sun	1960	5.00	10.00	20.00
116	Kathy/In the Beginning	1961	5.00	10.00	20.00
124	Beware/Because I Love You	1961	5.00	10.00	20.00
128	Donna/You Got Me Goin'	1961	5.00	10.00	20.00
132	Pains in My Heart/When I Become a Man	1961	5.00	10.00	20.00
PORT					
3026	Gee Whiz/Please Mr. Sun	196?	2.00	4.00	8.00
REPRISE					
20112	Be Mine/Oh How I Miss My Baby	1962	6.25	12.50	25.00
20122 *—Unreleased*	Be Mine/Oh How I Miss My Baby	1962	—	—	—
20125	You're Never Satisfied/Oh How I Miss My Baby	1962	5.00	10.00	20.00
TRANS WORLD					
7001	Tick Tock/The Rut	196?	5.00	10.00	20.00
WARNER BROS.					
5450	My Heart Stood Still/Don't Call Me Lonely Anymore	1964	7.50	15.00	30.00
Albums					
INDIGO					
503 [M]	Inocently Yours	1961	20.00	40.00	80.00
503 [M-DJ] *—Plain white cover*	Inocently Yours	1961	125.00	250.00	500.00

INSECT TRUST, THE

Number	Title (A Side/B Side)	Yr	VG	VG+	NM
45s					
ATCO					
6764	Reciprocity/Reincarnations	1970	2.50	5.00	10.00
CAPITOL					
2386	Miss Fun City/Special Rider Blues	1969	3.75	7.50	15.00
Albums					
ATCO					
SD 33-313	Hoboken Saturday Night	1970	10.00	20.00	40.00
CAPITOL					
SKAO-109	The Insect Trust	1968	10.00	20.00	40.00

INSECTS, THE

45s

Number	Title (A Side/B Side)	Yr	VG	VG+	NM
APPLAUSE					
1002	Let's Bug the Beatles/Dear Beatles	1964	6.25	12.50	25.00

—B-side by the Little Lady Beatles

INSIDE OUT

Albums

Number	Title (A Side/B Side)	Yr	VG	VG+	NM
FREDLO					
6834	Bringing It All Back	1968	50.00	100.00	200.00

INSIDERS, THE

45s

Number	Title (A Side/B Side)	Yr	VG	VG+	NM
RCA VICTOR					
47-9225	I'm Just a Man/I'm Better Off Without You	1967	6.25	12.50	25.00
47-9325	If You Had a Heart/Movin' On	1967	3.75	7.50	15.00
RED BIRD					
10-055	Chapel Bells Are Calling/I'm Stuck on You	1966	3.75	7.50	15.00

INSIGHT, THE

45s

Number	Title (A Side/B Side)	Yr	VG	VG+	NM
CASCADE					
364	Please Come Home For Christmas/Out Of Sight	1964	7.50	15.00	30.00

INSPIRATIONS, THE

More than one group.

45s

Number	Title (A Side/B Side)	Yr	VG	VG+	NM
AL-BRITE					
1651	Angel in Disguise/Stool Pigeon	1960	20.00	40.00	80.00
BELTONE					
2037	The Girl By My Side/Neckin'	1963	15.00	30.00	60.00
GONE					
5097	Angel in Disguise/Stool Pigeon	1961	6.25	12.50	25.00
JAMIE					
1034	Dry Your Eyes/Good-Bye	1956	18.75	37.50	75.00
1212	Dry Your Eyes/Good-Bye	1962	5.00	10.00	20.00
RONDAK					
9787	Ring Those Bells/The Cumberland and the Merrimac	1961	200.00	400.00	800.00
SPARKLE					
102	Angel in Disguise/Stool Pigeon	1960	37.50	75.00	150.00
SULTAN					
1	The Genie/The Feeling of Her Kiss	1959	7.50	15.00	30.00
1 [PS]	The Genie/The Feeling of Her Kiss	1959	12.50	25.00	50.00

INTENTIONS, THE

Probably more than one group.

45s

Number	Title (A Side/B Side)	Yr	VG	VG+	NM
JAMIE					
1253	Summertime Angel/Mr. Misery	1963	375.00	750.00	1500.
MELRON					
5014	I'm in Love with a Go-Go Girl/Wonderful Girl	1965	50.00	100.00	200.00
PHILIPS					
40428	Don't Forget That I Love You/Night Rider	1967	6.25	12.50	25.00

INTERLUDES, THE

Probably more than one group.

45s

Number	Title (A Side/B Side)	Yr	VG	VG+	NM
ABC-PARAMOUNT					
10213	Number 1 in the Nation/Beautiful, Wonderful, Heavenly You	1961	3.75	7.50	15.00
KING					
5633	Darling I'll Be True/Wilted Rose Bud	1962	7.50	15.00	30.00
RCA VICTOR					
47-7281	I Shed a Million Tears/Oo-Wee	1958	6.25	12.50	25.00
STAR-HI					
103	I Want You to Know/Split a Kiss	1959	3.75	7.50	15.00
VALLEY					
105	Heartbreaker/Scandalous	1959	3.75	7.50	15.00
106	No One for Me/Fort Lauderdale	1960	3.75	7.50	15.00
107	White Sailor Hat/Evil	1960	3.75	7.50	15.00

INTERNATIONAL SUBMARINE BAND, THE

Also see GRAM PARSONS.

45s

Number	Title (A Side/B Side)	Yr	VG	VG+	NM
ASCOT					
2218	The Russians Are Coming/Truck Driving Man	1966	3.75	7.50	15.00
2218 [PS]	The Russians Are Coming/Truck Driving Man	1966	12.50	25.00	50.00

—Counterfeit identification: Fake copies are missing the Ascot logo and catalog number.

Number	Title (A Side/B Side)	Yr	VG	VG+	NM
COLUMBIA					
43935	Sum Up Broke/One Day Week	1966	7.50	15.00	30.00
LHI					
1205	Luxury Liner/Blue Eyes	1968	3.75	7.50	15.00
1217	Miller's Cave/I Must Be Somebody Else	1968	3.75	7.50	15.00

Albums

Number	Title (A Side/B Side)	Yr	VG	VG+	NM
LHI					
12001	Safe at Home	1968	25.00	50.00	100.00

—Counterfeits have white labels, legitimate copies have multi-color labels

INTERNS, THE

45s

Number	Title (A Side/B Side)	Yr	VG	VG+	NM
CAPITOL					
5747	Is It Really What You Want/Just Like Me	1966	3.00	6.00	12.00
UPTOWN					
730	Hard to Get/And I'm Glad	1966	3.00	6.00	12.00

INTIMATES, THE

45s

Number	Title (A Side/B Side)	Yr	VG	VG+	NM
EPIC					
9743	I've Got a Tiger in My Tank/Smart, Too Late	1964	3.75	7.50	15.00

INTRIGUES, THE

45s

Number	Title (A Side/B Side)	Yr	VG	VG+	NM
TOOT					
609	Soul Brother (Part 1)/Soul Brother (Part 2)	1968	2.50	5.00	10.00
YEW					
1001	In a Moment/Scotchman Rock	1969	3.00	6.00	12.00
1002	I'm Gonna Love You/I Gotta Find Out for Myself	1969	2.50	5.00	10.00
1007	Just a Little Bit More/Let's Dance	1970	2.50	5.00	10.00
1010	Tuck a Little Love Away/I Know There's Love	1970	2.50	5.00	10.00
1012	The Language of Love/I Got Love	1971	2.50	5.00	10.00
1013	Mojo Hannah/To Make a World	1971	2.50	5.00	10.00

Albums

Number	Title (A Side/B Side)	Yr	VG	VG+	NM
YEW					
YS-777	In a Moment	1970	7.50	15.00	30.00

INTRUDERS, THE (1)

Early Philly Soul group.

45s

Number	Title (A Side/B Side)	Yr	VG	VG+	NM
GAMBLE					
201	(We'll Be) United/Up and Down the Ladder	1966	2.50	5.00	10.00
203	Devil with an Angel's Smile/A Book for the Broken Hearted	1966	2.50	5.00	10.00
203 [PS]	Devil with an Angel's Smile/A Book for the Broken Hearted	1966	3.75	7.50	15.00
204	It Must Be Love/Check Yourself	1966	2.50	5.00	10.00
205	Together/Up and Down the Ladder	1967	2.50	5.00	10.00
209	Baby I'm Lonely/A Love That's Real	1967	2.50	5.00	10.00
214	Cowboys to Girls/Turn the Hands of Time	1968	2.50	5.00	10.00
217	(Love Is Like a) Baseball Game/Friends No More	1968	2.50	5.00	10.00
221	Slow Drag/So Glad I'm Yours	1968	2.50	5.00	10.00
223	Give Her a Transplant/Girls, Girls, Girls	1969	2.50	5.00	10.00
225	Me Tarzan You Jane/Favorite Candidate	1969	2.50	5.00	10.00
231	Lollipop (I Like You)/Don't Give It Away	1969	2.50	5.00	10.00
235	Sad Girl/Let's Go Downtown	1969	2.50	5.00	10.00
240	Old Love/Every Day Is a Holiday	1969	2.50	5.00	10.00
2501	(Win, Place or Show) She's a Winner/Memories Are Here to Stay	1972	2.00	4.00	8.00
2506	I'll Always Love My Mama (Part 1)/I'll Always Love My Mama (Part 2)	1973	2.00	4.00	8.00
2508	I Wanna Know Your Name/Hang On In There	1973	2.00	4.00	8.00
4001	Tender (Was the Love We Knew)/By the Time I Get to Phoenix	1970	2.00	4.00	8.00
4004	When We Get Married/Doctor Doctor	1970	2.00	4.00	8.00
4007	This Is My Love Song/Let Me in Your Mind	1970	2.00	4.00	8.00
4009	I'm Girl Scoutin'/Wonder What Kind of Bag She's In	1971	2.00	4.00	8.00
4014	Pray for Me/Best Days of My Life	1971	2.00	4.00	8.00
4016	I Bet He Don't Love You (Like I Love You)/Do You Remember Yesterday	1971	2.00	4.00	8.00
4019	(Win, Place or Show) She's a Winner/Memories Are Here to Stay	1972	2.50	5.00	10.00
GOWEN					
1401	I'm Sold on You/Come Home Soon	1961	10.00	20.00	40.00
PHILADELPHIA INT'L.					
3624	I'll Always Love My Mama (Part 1)/I'll Always Love My Mama (Part 2)	1977	—	2.50	5.00
3689	I'll Always Love My Mama/Save the Children	1979	—	2.50	5.00
TSOP					
4758	A Nice Girl Like You/To Be Happy Is the Real Thing	1974	—	3.00	6.00
4766	Rainy Days and Mondays/Be on Time	1975	—	3.00	6.00
4771	Plain Old Fashioned Girl/Energy of Love	1975	—	3.00	6.00

Albums

Number	Title (A Side/B Side)	Yr	VG	VG+	NM
GAMBLE					
G-5001 [M]	The Intruders Are Together	1967	10.00	20.00	40.00
GS-5001 [S]	The Intruders Are Together	1967	12.50	25.00	50.00
GS-5004	Cowboys to Girls	1968	12.50	25.00	50.00
GS-5005	The Intruders Greatest Hits	1969	10.00	20.00	40.00
GS-5008	When We Get Married	1970	12.50	25.00	50.00
KZ 31991	Save the Children	1973	5.00	10.00	20.00
KZ 32131	Super Hits	1973	5.00	10.00	20.00
PHILADELPHIA INT'L.					
PZ 32131	Super Hits	198?	2.00	4.00	8.00

—Reissue of Gamble 32131

Number	Title (A Side/B Side)	Yr	VG	VG+	NM
TSOP					
KZ 33149	Energy of Love	1974	3.75	7.50	15.00

INTRUDERS, THE (2)

Instrumental group from New Jersey.

45s

Number	Title (A Side/B Side)	Yr	VG	VG+	NM
BELTONE					
1009	Camptown Rock/Morse Code	1961	3.75	7.50	15.00
FAME					
101	Fried Eggs/Jeffrie's Rock	1959	6.25	12.50	25.00
313	Creepin'/Frankfurters and Sauerkraut	1959	6.25	12.50	25.00
616	Rock-A-Ma-Roll/Era-Rock-A	1959	6.25	12.50	25.00

INVITATIONS, THE

45s

Number	Title (A Side/B Side)	Yr	VG	VG+	NM
DIAMOND					
253	Got to Have It Now/Swingin' on the Love Vine	1968	3.00	6.00	12.00
DYNO VOICE					
206	Written on the Wall/Hallelujah	1965	7.50	15.00	30.00
210	What's Wrong with Me Baby/Why Did My Baby Turn Bad	1965	7.50	15.00	30.00
215	Skiing in the Snow/Why Did My Baby Turn Bad	1966	15.00	30.00	60.00

Number	Title (A Side/B Side)	Yr	VG	VG+	NM
MGM					
13574	The Skate/Girl I'm Leavin' You	1966	3.75	7.50	15.00
13666	Watch Out Little Girl/You're Like a Mystery	1967	3.75	7.50	15.00
SILVER BLUE					
801	They Say the Girl's Crazy/For Your Precious Love	1973	2.00	4.00	8.00
804	Let's Love/Love Has to Grow	1973	2.00	4.00	8.00
809	Living Together Is Keeping Us Apart/I Didn't Know	1974	2.00	4.00	8.00
818	Look on the Good Side/Look on the Good Side (Part 2)	1974	2.00	4.00	8.00

IRIDESCENTS, THE

Number	Title (A Side/B Side)	Yr	VG	VG+	NM
45s					
HUDSON					
8102	Three Coins in the Fountain/Strong Love	1963	25.00	50.00	100.00
—Blue vinyl					
8102	Three Coins in the Fountain/Strong Love	1963	6.25	12.50	25.00
ULTRASONIC					
109	I Know/The Angels Sang	1960	100.00	200.00	400.00

IRISH ROVERS, THE

Number	Title (A Side/B Side)	Yr	VG	VG+	NM
45s					
DECCA					
32254	The Unicorn/Black Velvet Band	1968	2.50	5.00	10.00
32333	(The Puppet Song) Whiskey on a Sunday/The Orange and the Green	1968	2.00	4.00	8.00
32371	Liverpool Lou/The Bi-Plane, Ever More	1968	2.00	4.00	8.00
32444	Lily the Pink/Mrs. Crandall's Boardinghouse	1969	2.00	4.00	8.00
32529	Peter Knight/Did She Mention My Name	1969	2.00	4.00	8.00
32575	Fifi O'Toole/Winkin', Blinkin', and Nod	1969	2.00	4.00	8.00
32616	Rhymes and Reasons/Penny Whistler Peddler	1970	—	3.00	6.00
32616 [PS]	Rhymes and Reasons/Penny Whistler Peddler	1970	2.50	5.00	10.00
32723	Two Little Boys/Years May Come, Years May Go	1970	—	3.00	6.00
32775	The Marvelous Toy/Marika's Lullaby	1970	—	3.00	6.00
Albums					
DECCA					
DL 4835 [M]	First	1967	5.00	10.00	20.00
DL 4951 [M]	The Unicorn	1968	6.25	12.50	25.00
DL 74835 [S]	First	1967	3.75	7.50	15.00
DL 74951 [S]	The Unicorn	1968	3.75	7.50	15.00
DL 75037	All Hung Up	1968	3.75	7.50	15.00
DL 75081	Tales to Warm Your Mind	1969	3.75	7.50	15.00
DL 75157	Life of the Rover	1969	3.75	7.50	15.00
DL 75302	On the Shores of Americay	1971	3.75	7.50	15.00
MCA					
15	The Unicorn	1973	2.50	5.00	10.00
—Reissue of Decca 74951					
175	On the Shores of Americay	1973	2.50	5.00	10.00
—Reissue of Decca 75302					
249	First	1973	2.50	5.00	10.00
—Reissue of Decca 74835					
284	Life of the Rover	1973	2.50	5.00	10.00
—Reissue of Decca 75157					
4066 [(2)]	Greatest Hits	1976	3.75	7.50	15.00

IRON BUTTERFLY

Number	Title (A Side/B Side)	Yr	VG	VG+	NM
45s					
ATCO					
6573	Possession/Unconscious Power	1968	2.00	4.00	8.00
6606	In-A-Gadda-Da-Vida/Iron Butterfly Theme	1968	2.50	5.00	10.00
6647	Soul Experience/In the Crowds	1969	2.00	4.00	8.00
6676	In the Times of Our Lives/It Must Be Love	1969	2.00	4.00	8.00
6712	Little Girl/I Can't Help But Deceive You	1969	2.00	4.00	8.00
6782	Easy Rider (Let the Wind Pay the Way)/Soldier in Town	1970	2.00	4.00	8.00
6818	Silly Sally/Stone Believer	1971	—	3.00	6.00
MCA					
40379	Pearly Gates/Searchin' Circles	1975	—	2.00	4.00
40493	Beyond the Milky Way/Get It Out	1975	—	2.00	4.00
Albums					
ATCO					
33-227 [M]	Heavy	1967	7.50	15.00	30.00
SD 33-227 [S]	Heavy	1967	6.25	12.50	25.00
—Brown and purple label					
SD 33-227 [S]	Heavy	1969	3.75	7.50	15.00
—Yellow label					
33-250 [M]	In-A-Gadda-Da-Vida	1968	12.50	25.00	50.00
SD 33-250 [S]	In-A-Gadda-Da-Vida	1968	6.25	12.50	25.00
—Brown and purple label					
SD 33-250 [S]	In-A-Gadda-Da-Vida	1969	3.75	7.50	15.00
—Yellow label					
SD 33-250 [S]	In-A-Gadda-Da-Vida	197?	2.50	5.00	10.00
—Any later Atco label; LP was in print into the late 1980s					
SD 33-280	Ball	1969	3.75	7.50	15.00
SD 33-318	Iron Butterfly Live	1970	3.75	7.50	15.00
—Yellow label					
SD 33-318	Iron Butterfly Live	197?	2.50	5.00	10.00
—Any later Atco label; LP was in print into the late 1980s					
SD 33-339	Metamorphosis	1970	3.75	7.50	15.00
SD 33-369	The Best of Iron Butterfly/Evolution	1971	3.75	7.50	15.00
MCA					
465	Scorching Beauty	1975	3.00	6.00	12.00
2164	Sun and Steel	1976	3.00	6.00	12.00
PAIR					
PDL2-1065 [(2)]	Rare Flight	1986	3.75	7.50	15.00

IRRIDESCENTS, THE

Number	Title (A Side/B Side)	Yr	VG	VG+	NM
45s					
HAWK					
4001	Bali Ha'i/Swamp Surfer	1963	12.50	25.00	50.00
INFINITY					
037	Bali Ha'i/Swamp Surfer	1963	6.25	12.50	25.00
OLDIES 45					
183	Bali Ha'i/Swamp Surfer	1964	3.00	6.00	12.00

IRWIN, BIG DEE

Number	Title (A Side/B Side)	Yr	VG	VG+	NM
45s					
CUB					
9155	I Only Get This Feeling/Wrong Direction	1968	2.00	4.00	8.00
—As "Dee Erwin"					
DIMENSION					
1021	The Christmas Song/I Wish You a Merry Christmas	1963	3.75	7.50	15.00
—With Little Eva					
IMPERIAL					
66295	Wrong Direction/I Only Get This Feeling	1968	2.50	5.00	10.00
—As "Dee Irwin"					
66320	I Can't Stand the Pain/My Hope to Die Girl	1968	2.50	5.00	10.00
66334	All I Want for Christmas Is Your Love//By the Time I Get to Phoenix/I Say a Little Prayer	1968	3.00	6.00	12.00
—With Mamie Galore					
66359	Day Tripper/I Didn't Wanna Do It, But I Did	1969	2.00	4.00	8.00
—With Mamie Galore					
66420	Ain't No Way/Cherish	1969	2.00	4.00	8.00
PHIL-LA OF SOUL					
303	Better to Have Loved and Lost/Linda	1967	3.75	7.50	15.00
—As "Dee Erwin"					
ROULETTE					
4596	Discotheque/The Sun's Gonna Shine Tomorrow	1965	2.50	5.00	10.00
—As "Big Dee Erwin"					

ISLE, JIMMY

Number	Title (A Side/B Side)	Yr	VG	VG+	NM
45s					
BALLY					
1034	Baby-O/Hssle	1957	6.25	12.50	25.00
EVEREST					
19320	Oh Judy/Billy Boy	1959	6.25	12.50	25.00
MALA					
459	Our Town/Everybody Gotta Little Girl But Me	1963	5.00	10.00	20.00
ROULETTE					
4065	Goin' Wild/You and Johnny Smith	1958	7.50	15.00	30.00
SUN					
306	Diamond Ring/I've Been Waiting	1958	6.25	12.50	25.00
318	Time Will Tell/Without a Love	1959	6.25	12.50	25.00
332	What a Life/Together	1959	6.25	12.50	25.00

ISLEY BROTHERS, THE

Number	Title (A Side/B Side)	Yr	VG	VG+	NM
12-Inch Singles					
T-NECK					
AS 947 [DJ]	Hurry Up and Wait (3:54) (4:09)	1981	2.00	4.00	8.00
2267	Livin' in the Life/Go for Your Guns	1977	3.75	7.50	15.00
2276	Tell Me When You Need It Again/Take Me to the Next Phase	1977	3.75	7.50	15.00
2283	I Wanna Be with You (6:20)/Rockin' with Fire (5:57)	1978	3.00	6.00	12.00
2289	It's a Disco Night (Rock Don't Stop)/Ain't Givin' Up on Love	1979	3.00	6.00	12.00
03282	It's Alright with Me (Vocal) (Instrumental)	1982	2.50	5.00	10.00
04148	I Need Your Body/(Instrumental)	1983	2.00	4.00	8.00
WARNER BROS.					
PRO-A-2378 [DJ]	Colder Are My Night (Edit Version) (LP Version)	1985	2.00	4.00	8.00
PRO-A-4511 [DJ]	Spend the Night (Edit)/Colder Are My Nights (Edit)/Smooth Sailin' Tonight (Edit)	1989	2.00	4.00	8.00
PRO-A-5417 [DJ]	Sensitive Lover (4 versions)	1992	2.00	4.00	8.00
20827	I Wish (Vocal) (Instrumental)	1987	2.00	4.00	8.00
21415	You'll Never Walk Alone (4 versions)/One of a Kind	1989	2.00	4.00	8.00
45s					
ATLANTIC					
2092	Jeepers Creepers/Teach Me How to Shimmy	1961	3.75	7.50	15.00
2100	Shine On Harvest Moon/Standing on the Dance Floor	1961	3.75	7.50	15.00
2110	Your Old Lady/Write to Me	1961	3.75	7.50	15.00
2122	A Fool for You/Just One More Time	1961	3.75	7.50	15.00
2263	Looking for a Love/The Last Girl	1964	2.50	5.00	10.00
2277	Simon Says/Wild As a Tiger	1965	2.50	5.00	10.00
2303	Move Over and Let Me Dance/Have You Ever Been Disappointed	1965	3.75	7.50	15.00
CINDY					
3009	Don't Be Jealous/This Is the End	1958	37.50	75.00	150.00
—"Cindy" in shadow print					
3009	Don't Be Jealous/This Is the End	1958	18.75	37.50	75.00
—"Cindy" in regular print					
GONE					
5022	I Wanna Know/Everybody's Gonna Rock and Roll	1958	20.00	40.00	80.00
5048	My Love/The Drag	1958	20.00	40.00	80.00
MARK-X					
7003	The Drag/Rockin' MacDonald	1957	25.00	50.00	100.00
8000	The Drag/Rockin' MacDonald	1959	7.50	15.00	30.00
PHILCO-FORD					
HP-41	Twist and Shout/Rubberleg Twist	1969	6.25	12.50	25.00
—4-inch plastic "Hip Pocket Record" with color sleeve					
RCA					
447-0589	Shout (Part 1)/Shout (Part 2)	1976	—	2.00	4.00
—Gold Standard Series; black label, dog near top					
RCA VICTOR					
47-7537	I'm Gonna Knock on Your Door/Turn to Me	1959	6.25	12.50	25.00
47-7588	Shout (Part 1)/Shout (Part 2)	1959	7.50	15.00	30.00
47-7657	Respectable/Without a Song	1959	6.25	12.50	25.00
47-7718	He's Got the Whole World in His Hands/How Deep Is the Ocean	1960	6.25	12.50	25.00
47-7746	Gypsy Love Song/Open Up Your Heart	1960	6.25	12.50	25.00
47-7787	Say You Love Me Too/Tell Me Who	1960	6.25	12.50	25.00

Number	Title (A Side/B Side)	Yr	VG	VG+	NM
61-7588 [S]	Shout (Part 1)/Shout (Part 2)	1959	15.00	30.00	60.00
—"Living Stereo" (large hole, plays at 45 rpm)					
447-0589	Shout (Part 1)/Shout (Part 2)	1962	3.00	6.00	12.00
—Gold Standard Series; black label, dog on top (this charted with this number in 1962)					
447-0589	Shout (Part 1)/Shout (Part 2)	1965	2.00	4.00	8.00
—Gold Standard Series; black label, dog on side					
447-0589	Shout (Part 1)/Shout (Part 2)	1969	—	2.50	5.00
—Gold Standard Series; red label					
T-NECK					
501	Testify (Part 1)/Testify (Part 2)	1964	3.75	7.50	15.00
901	It's Your Thing/Don't Give It Away	1969	—	3.00	6.00
902	I Turned You On/I Know Who You Been Socking It To	1969	—	3.00	6.00
906	Black Berries — Pt. 1/Black Berries — Pt. 2	1969	—	3.00	6.00
908	Was It Good to You/I Got to Get Myself Together	1969	—	3.00	6.00
912	Bless Your Heart/Give the Women What They Want	1969	—	3.00	6.00
914	Keep On Doin'/Save Me	1970	—	3.00	6.00
919	If He Can, You Can/Holdin' On	1970	—	3.00	6.00
921	Girls Will Be Girls, Boys Will Be Boys/Get Down Off of the Train	1970	—	3.00	6.00
924	Get Into Something/Get Into Something (Part 2)	1970	—	3.00	6.00
927	Freedom/I Need You So	1970	—	3.00	6.00
929	Warpath/I Got to Find Me One	1971	—	3.00	6.00
930	Love the One You're With/He's Got Your Love	1971	—	3.00	6.00
932	Spill the Wine/Take Inventory	1971	—	3.00	6.00
933	Lay Lady Lay/Vacuum Cleaner	1971	—	3.00	6.00
934	Lay-Away/Feel Like the World	1972	—	3.00	6.00
935	Pop That Thang/I Got to Find Me One	1972	—	3.00	6.00
936	Work to Do/Beautiful	1972	—	3.00	6.00
937	It's Too Late/Nothing to Do But Today	1973	—	3.00	6.00
02033	Hurry Up and Wait/(Instrumental)	1981	—	2.50	5.00
02151	Don't Say Goodnight (It's Time for Love) (Parts 1 & 2)	1981	—	2.00	4.00
—Reissue					
02179	I Once Had Your Love (And I Can't Let Go)/(Instrumental)	1981	—	2.50	5.00
2251	That Lady (Part 1)/That Lady (Part 2)	1973	—	2.50	5.00
2252	What It Comes Down To/Highways of My Life	1973	—	2.50	5.00
2253	Summer Breeze (Part 1)/Summer Breeze (Part 2)	1974	—	2.50	5.00
2254	Live It Up (Part 1)/Live It Up (Part 2)	1974	—	2.50	5.00
2255	Midnight Sky (Part 1)/Midnight Sky (Part 2)	1974	—	2.50	5.00
2256	Fight the Power Part 1/Fight the Power Part 2	1975	—	2.50	5.00
2259	For the Love of You (Part 1&2)/You Walk Your Way	1975	—	2.50	5.00
2260	Who Loves You Better-Part 1/Who Loves You Better-Part 2	1976	—	2.50	5.00
2261	Harvest for the World/Harvest for the World (Part 2)	1976	—	2.50	5.00
2262	The Pride (Part 1)/The Pride (Part 2)	1977	—	2.50	5.00
2264	Livin' in the Life/Go for Your Guns	1977	—	2.50	5.00
2270	Voyage to Atlantis/Do You Wanna Stay Down	1977	—	2.50	5.00
02270	Voyage to Atlantis/Do You Wanna Stay Down	1981	—	2.00	4.00
—Reissue					
2272	Take Me to the Next Phase (Part 1)/Take Me to the Next Phase (Part 2)	1978	—	2.50	5.00
2277	Groove with You/Footsteps in the Dark	1978	—	2.50	5.00
2278	Showdown (Part 1)/Showdown (Part 2)	1978	—	2.50	5.00
2279	I Wanna Be with You (Part 1)/I Wanna Be with You (Part 2)	1979	—	2.50	5.00
2284	Winner Takes All/Fun and Games	1979	—	2.50	5.00
2287	It's a Disco Night (Rock Don't Stop)/Ain't Givin' Up on Love	1979	—	2.50	5.00
2290	Don't Say Goodnight (It's Time for Love) (Part 1)/Don't Say Goodnight (It's Time for Love) (Part 2)	1980	—	2.50	5.00
2291	Here We Go Again (Part 1)/Here We Go Again (Part 2)	1980	—	2.50	5.00
2292	Say You Will (Part 1)/Say You Will (Part 2)	1980	—	2.50	5.00
2293	Who Said?/(Can't You See) What You've Done to Me	1980	—	2.50	5.00
02293	Who Said?/(Can't You See) What You Do to Me	1981	—	2.00	4.00
—Reissue					
02531	Inside You (Part 1)/Inside You (Part 2)	1981	—	2.50	5.00
02705	Party Night/Welcome Into My Night	1982	—	2.50	5.00
02985	The Real Deal/(Instrumental)	1982	—	2.50	5.00
03281	It's Alright with Me/(Instrumental)	1982	—	2.50	5.00
03797	Between the Sheets/(Instrumental)	1983	—	2.50	5.00
03994	Choosey Lover/(Instrumental)	1983	—	2.50	5.00
04320	Let's Make Love Tonight/(Instrumental)	1984	—	2.50	5.00
TAMLA					
54128	This Old Heart of Mine (Is Weak for You)/There's No Love Left	1966	3.75	7.50	15.00
54133	Take Some Time Out for Love/Who Could Ever Doubt My Love	1966	3.00	6.00	12.00
54135	I Guess I'll Always Love You/I Hear a Symphony	1966	3.00	6.00	12.00
54146	Got to Have You Back/Just Ain't Enough Love	1967	3.00	6.00	12.00
54154	One Too Many Heartaches/That's the Way Love Is	1967	3.00	6.00	12.00
54164	Take Me in Your Arms (Rock Me a Little While)/Why When Love Is Gone	1968	3.00	6.00	12.00
54175	Behind a Painted Smile/All Because I Love You	1968	3.00	6.00	12.00
54182	Take Some Time Out for Love/Just Ain't Enough Love	1969	3.00	6.00	12.00
TEENAGE					
1004	Angels Cried/The Cow Jumped Over the Moon	1957	200.00	400.00	800.00
UNITED ARTISTS					
605	She's Gone/Tango	1963	5.00	10.00	20.00
638	Surf and Shout/Whatcha Gonna Do	1963	5.00	10.00	20.00
659	Please, Please, Please/You'll Never Leave Him	1963	5.00	10.00	20.00
714	Who's That Lady/My Little Girl	1964	5.00	10.00	20.00
798	Love Is a Wonderful Thing/Open Up Her Eyes	1964	—	—	—
—Unreleased					
923	Love Is a Wonderful Thing/Open Up Her Eyes	1965	—	—	—
—Unreleased					

Number	Title (A Side/B Side)	Yr	VG	VG+	NM
VEEP					
1230	Love Is a Wonderful Thing/Open Up Her Eyes	1966	2.50	5.00	10.00
V.I.P.					
25020	I Hear a Symphony/Who Could Ever Doubt My Love	1965	200.00	400.00	800.00
WAND					
118	Right Now/The Snake	1962	3.75	7.50	15.00
124	Twist and Shout/Spanish Twist	1962	5.00	10.00	20.00
127	Twistin' with Linda/You Better Come Home	1962	3.00	6.00	12.00
131	Nobody But Me/I'm Laughing to Keep from Crying	1963	3.00	6.00	12.00
137	I Say Love/Hold On Baby	1963	3.00	6.00	12.00
WARNER BROS.					
22748	One of a Kind/You'll Never Walk Alone	1989	—	—	3.00
22900	Spend the Night (Ce Soir)/(Instrumental)	1989	—	—	3.00
22900 [PS]	Spend the Night (Ce Soir)/(Instrumental)	1989	—	—	3.00
27954	It Takes a Good Woman/(Instrumental)	1988	—	2.00	4.00
28129	I Wish/(Instrumental)	1988	—	2.00	4.00
28129 [PS]	I Wish/(Instrumental)	1988	—	2.00	4.00
28241	Come My Way/(Instrumental)	1987	—	2.00	4.00
28385	Smooth Sailin' Tonight/(Instrumental)	1987	—	2.00	4.00
28385 [PS]	Smooth Sailin' Tonight/(Instrumental)	1987	—	2.00	4.00
28764	May I?/(Instrumental)	1986	—	2.00	4.00
28860	Colder Are My Nights/(Instrumental)	1985	—	2.00	4.00

Albums

Number	Title	Yr	VG	VG+	NM
BUDDAH					
BDS-5652 [(2)]	The Best of the Isley Brothers	1976	3.75	7.50	15.00
COLLECTABLES					
COL-5103	Shout!	198?	2.50	5.00	10.00
ISLAND					
7243 [(2) DJ]	Mission to Please	1996	5.00	10.00	20.00
—Promo-only vinyl in generic cover					
MOTOWN					
M5-106V1	Motown Superstar Series, Volume 6	1981	2.00	4.00	8.00
M5-128V1	This Old Heart of Mine	1981	2.00	4.00	8.00
—Reissue of Tamla 269					
M5-143V1	Doin' Their Thing (Best of the Isley Brothers)	1981	2.00	4.00	8.00
—Reissue of Tamla 287					
PICKWICK					
SPC-3331	Soul Shout!	197?	2.50	5.00	10.00
RCA CAMDEN					
ACL1-0126	Rock On Brother	1973	3.00	6.00	12.00
ACL1-0861	Rock Around the Clock	1975	3.00	6.00	12.00
RCA VICTOR					
LPM-2156 [M]	Shout!	1959	30.00	60.00	120.00
—"Long Play" label					
LSP-2156 [S]	Shout!	1959	50.00	100.00	200.00
—"Living Stereo" label					
SCEPTER					
SC-552 [M]	Take Some Time Out for the Isley Brothers	1966	7.50	15.00	30.00
SCS-552 [S]	Take Some Time Out for the Isley Brothers	1966	10.00	20.00	40.00
SUNSET					
SUS-5257	The Isley Brothers Do Their Thing	1969	3.75	7.50	15.00
T-NECK					
ASZ 137 [DJ]	Everything You Always Wanted to Hear by the Isley Brothers But Were Afraid to Ask For	1976	5.00	10.00	20.00
—Promo-only compilation					
TNS-3001	It's Our Thing	1969	5.00	10.00	20.00
TNS-3002	The Brothers: Isley	1969	5.00	10.00	20.00
TNS-3006	Get Into Something	1970	3.75	7.50	15.00
TNS-3007	In the Beginning (With Jimi Hendrix)	1970	5.00	10.00	20.00
TNS-3008	Givin' It Back	1971	3.75	7.50	15.00
TNS-3009	Brother, Brother, Brother	1972	3.75	7.50	15.00
TNS-3010 [(2)]	The Isleys Live	1973	5.00	10.00	20.00
TNS-3011	Isleys' Greatest Hits	1973	3.75	7.50	15.00
KZ 32453	3 + 3	1973	3.00	6.00	12.00
PZ 32453	3 + 3	197?	2.00	4.00	8.00
—Reissue with new prefix					
ZQ 32453 [Q]	3 + 3	1974	5.00	10.00	20.00
PZ 33070	Live It Up	1974	3.00	6.00	12.00
—No bar code on cover					
PZQ 33070 [Q]	Live It Up	1974	5.00	10.00	20.00
PZ 33536	The Heat Is On	1975	3.00	6.00	12.00
—No bar code on cover					
PZ 33536	The Heat Is On	198?	2.00	4.00	8.00
—Budget-line reissue with bar code					
PZ 33809	Harvest for the World	1976	3.00	6.00	12.00
—No bar code on cover					
PZQ 33809 [Q]	Harvest for the World	1976	5.00	10.00	20.00
PZ 34432	Go for Your Guns	1977	3.00	6.00	12.00
—No bar code on cover					
PZ 34432	Go for Your Guns	198?	2.00	4.00	8.00
—Budget-line reissue with bar code					
PZQ 34432 [Q]	Go for Your Guns	1977	5.00	10.00	20.00
PZ 34452	Forever Gold	1977	2.50	5.00	10.00
JZ 34930	Showdown	1978	2.50	5.00	10.00
PZ 34930	Showdown	198?	2.00	4.00	8.00
—Budget-line reissue					
KZ2 35650 [(2)]	Timeless	1978	3.00	6.00	12.00
PZ2 36077 [(2)]	Winner Takes All	1979	3.00	6.00	12.00
FZ 36305	Go All the Way	1980	2.50	5.00	10.00
PZ 36305	Go All the Way	198?	2.00	4.00	8.00
—Budget-line reissue					
FZ 37080	Grand Slam	1981	2.50	5.00	10.00
PZ 37080	Grand Slam	198?	2.00	4.00	8.00
—Budget-line reissue					
FZ 37533	Inside You	1981	2.50	5.00	10.00
FZ 38047	The Real Deal	1982	2.50	5.00	10.00
FZ 38674	Between the Sheets	1983	2.50	5.00	10.00
PZ 38674	Between the Sheets	1985	2.00	4.00	8.00
—Budget-line reissue					
FZ 39240	Greatest Hits, Vol. 1	1984	2.50	5.00	10.00
PZ 39240	Greatest Hits, Vol. 1	1985	2.00	4.00	8.00
—Budget-line reissue					

Number	Title (A Side/B Side)	Yr	VG	VG+	NM
TAMLA					
T-269 [M]	This Old Heart of Mine	1966	6.25	12.50	25.00
TS-269 [S]	This Old Heart of Mine	1966	7.50	15.00	30.00
T-275 [M]	Soul on the Rocks	1967	6.25	12.50	25.00
TS-275 [S]	Soul on the Rocks	1967	7.50	15.00	30.00
TS-287	Doin' Their Thing (Best of the Isley Brothers)	1969	5.00	10.00	20.00
UNITED ARTISTS					
UA-LA500-E	The Very Best of the Isley Brothers	1975	2.50	5.00	10.00
UAL-3313 [M]	The Famous Isley Brothers	1963	12.50	25.00	50.00
UAS-6313 [S]	The Famous Isley Brothers	1963	15.00	30.00	60.00
WAND					
WD-653 [M]	Twist & Shout	1962	20.00	40.00	80.00
WDS-653 [S]	Twist & Shout	1962	25.00	50.00	100.00
WARNER BROS.					
25347	Masterpiece	1985	2.50	5.00	10.00
25586	Smooth Sailin'	1987	2.50	5.00	10.00
25940	Spend the Night	1989	2.50	5.00	10.00

IT'S A BEAUTIFUL DAY

45s

Number	Title (A Side/B Side)	Yr	VG	VG+	NM
COLUMBIA					
44928	White Bird/Wasted Union Blues	1969	2.00	4.00	8.00
45152	Good Lovin'/Soapstone Mountain	1970	—	3.00	6.00
45309	Do You Remember the Sun/Dolphin	1971	—	2.50	5.00
45536	Anytime/Apples and Oranges	1972	—	2.50	5.00
45788	White Bird/Wasted Union Blues	1973	—	2.50	5.00
45853	Ain't That Lovin' You Baby/Time	1973	—	3.00	6.00
SAN FRANCISCO SOUND					
11680	Aquarian Dream/Bulgaria	198?	2.50	5.00	10.00

Albums

Number	Title (A Side/B Side)	Yr	VG	VG+	NM
COLUMBIA					
CS 1058	Marrying Maiden	1970	7.50	15.00	30.00
—Red "360 Sound" label					
CS 1058	Marrying Maiden	1970	3.75	7.50	15.00
—Orange label					
CS 9768	It's A Beautiful Day	1969	7.50	15.00	30.00
—Red "360 Sound" label					
CS 9768	It's A Beautiful Day	1970	5.00	10.00	20.00
—Orange label					
C 30734	Choice Quality Stuff/Anytime	1971	3.75	7.50	15.00
KC 31338	It's a Beautiful Day at Carnegie Hall	1972	3.75	7.50	15.00
KC 32181	It's a Beautiful Day...Today	1973	3.75	7.50	15.00
KC 32660 [DJ]	A Thousand and One Nights	1973	12.50	25.00	50.00
—Canceled before commercial release?					
SAN FRANCISCO SOUND					
11790	It's a Beautiful Day	1985	6.25	12.50	25.00
—Limited reissue					

ITALIAN ASPHALT AND PAVEMENT COMPANY, THE

See THE DUPREES.

IVAN

45s

Number	Title (A Side/B Side)	Yr	VG	VG+	NM
CORAL					
62017	Real Wild Child/Oh You Beautiful Doll	1958	50.00	100.00	200.00
—With Buddy Holly on guitar					
62081	That'll Be Alright/Frankie Frankenstein	1959	100.00	200.00	400.00
65607	Real Wild Child/That'll Be Alright	1967	12.50	25.00	50.00

IVERS, PETER

Albums

Number	Title (A Side/B Side)	Yr	VG	VG+	NM
EPIC					
BN 26500	Knight of the Blue Communion	1970	10.00	20.00	40.00
WARNER BROS.					
BS 2804	Terminal Love	1974	3.00	6.00	12.00

IVES, BURL

45s

Number	Title (A Side/B Side)	Yr	VG	VG+	NM
BELL					
930	Real Roses/Roll Up Some Inspiration	1970	—	2.50	5.00
943	Time/(B-side unknown)	1970	—	2.50	5.00
BIG TREE					
130	Gingerbread House/Tumbleweed Snowman	1971	—	2.50	5.00
BUENA VISTA					
419	On the Front Porch/Ugly Bug Ball	1963	2.00	4.00	8.00
419 [PS]	On the Front Porch/Ugly Bug Ball	1963	3.00	6.00	12.00
COLUMBIA					
4-124	Grandfather Kringle/The 12 Days Of Christmas	1951	3.00	6.00	12.00
—Yellow-label "Chidren's Series" record; alternate number is 90138					
4-124 [PS]	Grandfather Kringle/The 12 Days Of Christmas	1951	3.75	7.50	15.00
1-173	Riders in the Sky (Cowboy Legend)/Wayfaring Stranger-Woolie Boogie Bee	1949	10.00	20.00	40.00
—Microgroove 33 1/3 rpm 7-inch single					
1-418	Mule Train/Greer County Bachelor	1950	7.50	15.00	30.00
—Microgroove 33 1/3 rpm 7-inch single					
1-550 (?)	John Henry/Mah Lindy Lou	1950	7.50	15.00	30.00
—Microgroove 33 1/3 rpm 7-inch single					
1-580 (?)	The Doughnut Song/I Got a Fever in My Bones	1950	7.50	15.00	30.00
—Microgroove 33 1/3 rpm 7-inch single					
1-630 (?)	Got the World by the Tail/My Momma Told Me	1950	7.50	15.00	30.00
—Microgroove 33 1/3 rpm 7-inch single					
1-780 (?)	Pig Pig/Last Night the Nightingale Woke Me	1950	7.50	15.00	30.00
—Microgroove 33 1/3 rpm 7-inch single					
6-780 (?)	Pig Pig/Last Night the Nightingale Woke Me	1950	6.25	12.50	25.00
1-910 (?)	There's a Little White House/Little White Duck	1950	7.50	15.00	30.00
—Microgroove 33 1/3 rpm 7-inch single					
6-910 (?)	There's a Little White House/Little White Duck	1950	6.25	12.50	25.00
39328	On Top of Old Smoky/The Syncopated Clock	1951	3.75	7.50	15.00
—With Percy Faith co-credited					
44606	Little Green Apples/One Too Many Mornings	1968	—	3.00	6.00
44711	Santa Mouse/Oh What a Lucky Boy Am I	1968	—	3.00	6.00
44711 [PS]	Santa Mouse/Oh What a Lucky Boy Am I	1968	2.50	5.00	10.00
44974	Montego Bay/Tessie's Bar Mystery	1969	—	3.00	6.00
CYCLONE					
75014	One More Time Billy Brown/Tied Down Here at Home	1970	—	2.50	5.00
DECCA					
25524	Mockin' Bird Hill/Royal Telephone (Telephone to Glory)	196?	2.00	4.00	8.00
25585	Twelve Days of Christmas/The Indian Christmas Carol	1962	2.50	5.00	10.00
25691	You Know You Belong to Someone Else/Jealous	196?	2.00	4.00	8.00
25754	I Talk to the Trees/They Call the Wind Maria	1970	—	3.00	6.00
27079	This Time Tomorrow/One Hour Ahead of the Posse	1950	5.00	10.00	20.00
28055	Wild Side of Life/It's So Long and Goodbye to You	1952	3.75	7.50	15.00
28079	This Time Tomorrow/One Hour Ahead of the Posse	1952	3.75	7.50	15.00
28299	There's a Mule Up in Tombstone, Arizona/ Lonesome, So Lonesome	1952	3.75	7.50	15.00
28347	The Friendly Beasts/There Were Three Ships	1952	3.00	6.00	12.00
28348	Jesous Anatonia/What Child Is This	1952	3.00	6.00	12.00
28349	The Seven Joys of Mary (Part 1)/The Seven Joys of Mary (Part 2)	1952	3.00	6.00	12.00
28350	King Herod and the Clock/Down in Yon Forest	1952	3.00	6.00	12.00
—The above four comprise a box set					
28708	Close the Door Richard/Left My Gal in the Mountains	1953	3.75	7.50	15.00
28849	Great White Bird/Brighten the Corner Where You Are	1953	3.75	7.50	15.00
28935	The Crawdad Song/Hound Dog	1953	3.75	7.50	15.00
29039	There's Plenty of Fish in the Ocean/The Old Red Barn	1954	3.75	7.50	15.00
29088	True Love Goes On and On/Brave Man	1954	3.75	7.50	15.00
29129	Wait for Me Darling/Casey Jones	1954	3.00	6.00	12.00
29282	The Mission San Miquel/Tangled Web	1954	3.75	7.50	15.00
29423	The Ballad of Davy Crockett/Goober Peas	1955	3.75	7.50	15.00
29533	I Wonder What's Become of Sally/Wabash Cannonball	1955	3.00	6.00	12.00
29549	Be Sure You're Right (Then Go Ahead)/Ol' Betsy	1955	3.75	7.50	15.00
29910	Jack Was Every Inch a Sailor/Harlem Man	1956	3.00	6.00	12.00
30046	The Bus Stop Song/That's My Heart Strings	1956	3.00	6.00	12.00
30217	Marianne/Pretty Girl	1957	3.00	6.00	12.00
30855	We Love Ye, Jimmy/I Never See Maggie Alone	1959	3.00	6.00	12.00
31248	Long Black Veil/Forty Hour Week	1961	2.50	5.00	10.00
31330	A Little Bitty Tear/Shanghaid	1961	2.50	5.00	10.00
31371	Funny Way of Laughin'/Mother Wouldn't Do That	1962	2.50	5.00	10.00
31405	Call Me Mr. In-Between/What You Gonna Do, Leroy	1962	2.50	5.00	10.00
31433	Mary Ann Regrets/How Do You Fall Out of Love	1962	2.50	5.00	10.00
31453	The Same Old Hurt/Curry Road	1963	2.50	5.00	10.00
31479	Roses and Orchids/Baby Come Home to Me	1963	2.50	5.00	10.00
31504	I'm the Boss/The Moon Is High	1963	2.50	5.00	10.00
31518	This Is All I Ask/There Goes Another Pal of Mine	1963	2.50	5.00	10.00
31543	It Comes and Goes/I Found My Best Friend in the Dog Pound	1963	2.50	5.00	10.00
31571	True Love Goes On and On/I Wonder What's Become of Sally	1963	2.50	5.00	10.00
31610	Four Initials on a Tree/This Is Your Day	1964	2.00	4.00	8.00
31659	Pearly Shells/What Little Tears Are Made Of	1964	2.00	4.00	8.00
31695	A Holly Jolly Christmas/Snow for Johnny	1964	2.50	5.00	10.00
31772	On the Beach at Waikiki/Some Hangin' Round You All the Time	1965	2.00	4.00	8.00
31811	Salt Water Guitar/The Story of Bobby Lee Trent	1965	2.00	4.00	8.00
31857	Frangipani/A Girl Sittin' Up in a Tree	1965	2.00	4.00	8.00
31918	The Sixties/Don't Forget Your Paddle	1966	2.00	4.00	8.00
31981	Here She Comes (There She Goes)/Atlantic Coastal Line	1966	2.00	4.00	8.00
31997	Evil Off My Mind/Taste of Heaven	1966	2.00	4.00	8.00
32078	Lonesome 7-7203/Hollow Words	1967	2.00	4.00	8.00
32165	Funny Little Show/Holding Hands for Joe	1967	2.00	4.00	8.00
32282	Bury the Bottle/That's Where My Baby Used to Be	1968	2.00	4.00	8.00
32990	Stayin' Song/The Best Is Yet to Come	1972	—	3.00	6.00
33049	Miss Johnson's Happiness Emporium/Anytime You Say	1972	—	3.00	6.00
DISNEYLAND					
F-130	Chim Chim Chiree/Lavender Blue	1964	2.00	4.00	8.00
F-130 [PS]	Chim Chim Chiree/Lavender Blue	1964	3.00	6.00	12.00
MCA					
31695	A Holly Jolly Christmas/Snow For Johnny	1989	—	2.50	5.00
—Double the NM value if insert is enclosed					
40082	Payin' My Dues Again/All Around	1973	—	2.50	5.00
40175	Tale of the Comet Kohoutek/A Very Fine Lady	1974	—	2.50	5.00
MONKEY JOE					
MJ-1 [DJ]	The Christmas Legend of Monkey Joe/It's Gonna Be A Mixed Up Xmas	1978	2.50	5.00	10.00
UNITED ARTISTS					
293	Alexander's Ragtime Band/Say It Isn't So	1961	2.00	4.00	8.00
1568	Go 'Way from My House/Two Maidens Went Milking	196?	2.00	4.00	8.00
1569	Willie Boy/Irish Rover	196?	2.00	4.00	8.00
1570	Alexander's Ragtime Band/What'll I Do	196?	2.00	4.00	8.00
1571	All Alone/Always	196?	2.00	4.00	8.00
—The above four all are "Silver Spotlight Series" releases					

7-Inch Extended Plays

Number	Title (A Side/B Side)	Yr	VG	VG+	NM
DECCA					
ED 2235	*The Locktender's Lament/Ox Driver's Song/The Bold Soldier/The Young Married Man (Cod Liver Oil)/Sad Man's Song (Fare Thee Well, O Honey)/ The Harlem Man	195?	3.00	6.00	12.00
ED 2235 [PS]	Songs For and About Men, Part 1	195?	3.00	6.00	12.00
ED 2236	The Western Settler/Waltzing Matilda (The Jolly Swagman's Song)//The Wild Rover/Frankie and Johnny/The Deceiver	195?	3.00	6.00	12.00
ED 2236 [PS]	Songs For and About Men, Part 2	195?	3.00	6.00	12.00
ED 2714	(contents unknown)	1961	2.50	5.00	10.00
ED 2714 [PS]	Burl Ives	1961	2.50	5.00	10.00

Number	Title (A Side/B Side)	Yr	VG	VG+	NM
ED 2720	Funny Way of Laughin'/Mother Wouldn't Do That//What You Gonna Do Leroy/I Ain't Comin' Home Tonight	1962	2.50	5.00	10.00
ED 2720 [PS]	It's Just My Funny Way of Laughin'	1962	2.50	5.00	10.00
ED 2726	Call Me Mr. In-Between/Poor Little Jimmie//In Foggy Old London/Thumbin' Johnny Brown	1962	2.50	5.00	10.00
ED 2726 [PS]	Call Me Mr. In-Between	1962	2.50	5.00	10.00
ED 2741	(contents unknown)	1962	2.50	5.00	10.00
ED 2741 [PS]	Mary Ann Regrets	1962	2.50	5.00	10.00
ED 2771	True Love Goes On and On/This Is All I Ask//It Comes and Goes/I'm the Boss	1963	2.50	5.00	10.00
ED 2771 [PS]	True Love Goes On and On	1963	2.50	5.00	10.00
Albums					
ARCHIVE OF FOLK AND JAZZ					
340	Burl Ives Live	1978	2.50	5.00	10.00
BELL					
6055	Time	1971	2.50	5.00	10.00
COLUMBIA					
CL 628 [M]	The Wayfaring Stranger	1955	7.50	15.00	30.00
CL 980 [M]	Burl Ives Sings Songs for All Ages	1956	7.50	15.00	30.00
CL 1459 [M]	Return of the Wayfaring Stranger	1960	7.50	15.00	30.00
CL 2570 [10]	Children's Favorites	1955	10.00	20.00	40.00
—"House Party Series" issue					
CL 6058 [10]	The Return of the Wayfaring Stranger	1949	12.50	25.00	50.00
CL 6109 [10]	The Wayfaring Stranger	1950	12.50	25.00	50.00
CL 6144 [10]	More Folk Songs	1950	12.50	25.00	50.00
CS 9041 [R]	The Wayfaring Stranger	1964	3.00	6.00	12.00
CS 9675	The Times They Are a-Changin'	1969	3.00	6.00	12.00
CS 9728	Burl Ives Christmas Album	1968	3.00	6.00	12.00
CS 9925	Softly and Tenderly	1969	3.00	6.00	12.00
DECCA					
DXB 167 [(2) M]	The Best of Burl Ives	1961	6.25	12.50	25.00
DL 4152 [M]	The Versatile Burl Ives	1961	3.75	7.50	15.00
DL 4179 [M]	Songs of the West	1961	3.75	7.50	15.00
DL 4279 [M]	It's Just My Funny Way of Laughin'	1962	3.75	7.50	15.00
DL 4304 [M]	Sing Out, Sweet Land	1962	3.75	7.50	15.00
DL 4320 [M]	Sunshine in My Soul	1962	3.75	7.50	15.00
DL 4361 [M]	Burl	1963	3.75	7.50	15.00
DL 4390 [M]	The Best of Burl's for Boys and Girls	1963	3.75	7.50	15.00
DL 4433 [M]	Singin' Easy	1964	3.75	7.50	15.00
DL 4533 [M]	True Love	1964	3.75	7.50	15.00
DL 4578 [M]	Pearly Shells	1964	3.75	7.50	15.00
DL 4606 [M]	My Gal Sal	1965	3.00	6.00	12.00
DL 4668 [M]	On the Beach at Waikiki	1965	3.00	6.00	12.00
DL 4689 [M]	Have a Holly Jolly Christmas	1965	3.00	6.00	12.00
DL 4734 [M]	Burl's Choice	1966	3.00	6.00	12.00
DL 4789 [M]	Something Special	1966	3.00	6.00	12.00
DL 4850 [M]	Burl Ives' Greatest Hits	1967	3.75	7.50	15.00
DL 4876 [M]	Broadway	1967	3.75	7.50	15.00
DL 4972 [M]	Big Country Hits	1968	3.75	7.50	15.00
DL 5013 [10]	Ballads and Folk Songs	1949	12.50	25.00	50.00
DL 5080 [10]	Ballads and Folk Songs, Volume 2	1949	12.50	25.00	50.00
DL 5093 [10]	Ballads, Folk and Country Songs	1949	12.50	25.00	50.00
DL 5428 [10]	Christmas Day in the Morning	1952	12.50	25.00	50.00
DL 5467 [10]	Folk Songs Dramatic and Dangerous	1953	12.50	25.00	50.00
DL 5490 [10]	Women: Folk Songs About the Fair Sex	1954	12.50	25.00	50.00
DXSB 7167 [(2) S]	The Best of Burl Ives	1961	7.50	15.00	30.00
DL 8080 [M]	Coronation Concert	1953	10.00	20.00	40.00
DL 8107 [M]	The Wild Side of Life	1955	6.25	12.50	25.00
DL 8125 [M]	Men	1956	6.25	12.50	25.00
DL 8245 [M]	Down to the Sea in Ships	1956	6.25	12.50	25.00
DL 8246 [M]	Women	1956	6.25	12.50	25.00
DL 8247 [M]	In the Quiet of Night	1956	6.25	12.50	25.00
DL 8248 [M]	Burl Ives Sings for Fun	1956	6.25	12.50	25.00
DL 8391 [M]	Christmas Eve	1957	6.25	12.50	25.00
DL 8444 [M]	Songs of Ireland	1958	6.25	12.50	25.00
DL 8587 [M]	Captain Burl Ives' Ark	1958	6.25	12.50	25.00
DL 8637 [M]	Old Time Varieties	1958	6.25	12.50	25.00
DL 8749 [M]	Australian Folk Songs	1959	6.25	12.50	25.00
DL 8886 [M]	Cheers	1959	6.25	12.50	25.00
DL 74152 [S]	The Versatile Burl Ives	1961	5.00	10.00	20.00
DL 74179 [S]	Songs of the West	1961	5.00	10.00	20.00
DL 74279 [S]	It's Just My Funny Way of Laughin'	1962	5.00	10.00	20.00
DL 74304 [S]	Sing Out, Sweet Land	1962	5.00	10.00	20.00
DL 74320 [S]	Sunshine in My Soul	1962	5.00	10.00	20.00
DL 74361 [S]	Burl	1963	5.00	10.00	20.00
DL 74390 [S]	The Best of Burl's for Boys and Girls	1963	5.00	10.00	20.00
DL 74433 [S]	Singin' Easy	1964	5.00	10.00	20.00
DL 74533 [S]	True Love	1964	5.00	10.00	20.00
DL 74578 [S]	Pearly Shells	1964	5.00	10.00	20.00
DL 74606 [S]	My Gal Sal	1965	3.75	7.50	15.00
DL 74668 [S]	On the Beach at Waikiki	1965	3.75	7.50	15.00
DL 74689 [S]	Have a Holly Jolly Christmas	1965	3.75	7.50	15.00
DL 74734 [S]	Burl's Choice	1966	3.75	7.50	15.00
DL 74789 [S]	Something Special	1966	3.75	7.50	15.00
DL 74850 [S]	Burl Ives' Greatest Hits	1967	3.00	6.00	12.00
DL 74876 [S]	Broadway	1967	3.00	6.00	12.00
DL 74972 [S]	Big Country Hits	1968	3.00	6.00	12.00
DL 78391 [R]	Christmas Eve	196?	2.50	5.00	10.00
DL 78886 [S]	Cheers	1959	7.50	15.00	30.00
DISNEYLAND					
ST-3927 [M]	Chim Chim Chiree and Other Children's Choices	1964	3.75	7.50	15.00
STER-3927 [S]	Chim Chim Chiree and Other Children's Choices	1964	5.00	10.00	20.00
HARMONY					
HL 9507 [M]	The Little White Duck	196?	3.75	7.50	15.00
HL 9551 [M]	The Lollipop Tree	196?	3.75	7.50	15.00
HS 11275	Got the World by the Tail	196?	2.50	5.00	10.00
MCA					
114	Burl Ives' Greatest Hits	1973	2.50	5.00	10.00
—Reissue of Decca 74850					
318	Paying My Dues Again	1973	2.50	5.00	10.00
4034 [(2)]	The Best of Burl Ives	197?	3.00	6.00	12.00
4089 [(2)]	The Best of Burl Ives Volume 2	197?	3.00	6.00	12.00
15002	Have a Holly Jolly Christmas	1973	3.00	6.00	12.00
—Reissue of Decca 74689; black label with rainbow					
15002	Have a Holly Jolly Christmas	1980	2.00	4.00	8.00
—Blue label with rainbow					
15030	Santa Claus Is Coming to Town	198?	2.50	5.00	10.00
NATIONAL GEOGRAPHIC					
7806	We Americans	1978	3.00	6.00	12.00
PICKWICK					
SPC-1018	Twelve Days of Christmas	197?	2.50	5.00	10.00
STINSON					
SLP-1 [10]	The Wayfaring Stranger	1949	15.00	30.00	60.00
SUNSET					
SUS-5280	Favorites	1970	2.50	5.00	10.00
UNITED ARTISTS					
UAL 3060 [M]	Ballads	1959	3.75	7.50	15.00
UAS 6060 [S]	Ballads	1959	5.00	10.00	20.00
WORD					
3259 [M]	Faith and Joy	196?	3.75	7.50	15.00
3339 [M]	Shall We Gather at the River	1966	3.00	6.00	12.00
3391 [M]	I Do Believe	1967	3.00	6.00	12.00
8140 [S]	Faith and Joy	196?	5.00	10.00	20.00
8339 [S]	Shall We Gather at the River	1966	3.75	7.50	15.00
8391 [S]	I Do Believe	1967	3.75	7.50	15.00
8537	How Great Thou Art	1971	3.00	6.00	12.00

IVEYS, THE

See BADFINGER.

IVOLEERS, THE

Number	Title (A Side/B Side)	Yr	VG	VG+	NM
45s					
BUZZ					
101	Lover's Quarrel/Come with Me	1959	100.00	200.00	400.00

IVORY

Number	Title (A Side/B Side)	Yr	VG	VG+	NM
Albums					
PLAYBOY					
115	Ivory	1973	3.00	6.00	12.00
TETRAGRAMMATON					
T-104	Ivory	1968	5.00	10.00	20.00

IVORY, JACKIE

Number	Title (A Side/B Side)	Yr	VG	VG+	NM
45s					
ATCO					
6398	Hi-Heel Sneakers/Three Tickets to Georgia	1966	2.50	5.00	10.00
Albums					
ATCO					
33-178 [M]	Soul Discovery	1965	5.00	10.00	20.00
SD 33-178 [S]	Soul Discovery	1965	6.25	12.50	25.00

IVORYS, THE

Number	Title (A Side/B Side)	Yr	VG	VG+	NM
45s					
DARLA					
1000	Wishing Well/Deep Freeze	1962	100.00	200.00	400.00
SPARTA					
001	Why Don't You Write Me/Deep Freeze	1962	20.00	40.00	80.00

IVY LEAGUE, THE

Number	Title (A Side/B Side)	Yr	VG	VG+	NM
45s					
CAMEO					
343	Wait a Minute/What More Do You Want	1965	3.75	7.50	15.00
356	Lonely Room/Funny How Love Can Be	1965	3.75	7.50	15.00
365	A Girl Like You/That's Why I'm Crying	1965	3.75	7.50	15.00
377	Tossing & Turning/Graduation Day	1965	3.75	7.50	15.00
388	Our Love Is Slipping Away/I Could Make You Fall in Love	1966	3.75	7.50	15.00
388 [PS]	Our Love Is Slipping Away/I Could Make You Fall in Love	1966	6.25	12.50	25.00
402	Rain Rain Go Away/Running Around in Circles	1966	3.75	7.50	15.00
449	When You're Young/My World Fell Down	1966	3.75	7.50	15.00
Albums					
CAMEO					
C 2000 [M]	Tossing and Turning	1965	7.50	15.00	30.00
CS 2000 [R]	Tossing and Turning	1965	7.50	15.00	30.00

IVY THREE, THE

Number	Title (A Side/B Side)	Yr	VG	VG+	NM
45s					
SHELL					
302	Nine Out of Ten/I've Cried Enough for Two	1961	7.50	15.00	30.00
—Gold label					
302	Nine Out of Ten/I've Cried Enough for Two	1961	5.00	10.00	20.00
—Multicolored label					
306	Bagoo/Suicide	1961	3.75	7.50	15.00
720	Yogi/Was Judy There	1960	5.00	10.00	20.00
—Originals have blue labels					
720	Yogi/Was Judy There	1961	3.75	7.50	15.00
—Reissues have multicolored labels					
723	Alone in the Chapel/Hush Little Baby	1960	6.25	12.50	25.00

IVY-TONES, THE

Number	Title (A Side/B Side)	Yr	VG	VG+	NM
45s					
RED TOP					
105	Oo-Wee Baby/Each Time	1958	5.00	10.00	20.00
—Blue label					
105	Oo-Wee Baby/Each Time	1958	3.75	7.50	15.00
—Red label					

J

J.B.'S, THE

See FRED WESLEY.

J.B. AND THE HAWKS

See J.B. HUTTO.

J.K. AND COMPANY

Albums

WHITE WHALE

Number	Title (A Side/B Side)	Yr	VG	VG+	NM
WWS-7117	Suddenly One Summer	1969	6.25	12.50	25.00

JACKIE AND JILL

45s

U.S.A.

Number	Title (A Side/B Side)	Yr	VG	VG+	NM
791	I Want a Beatle for Christmas/Jingle Bells	1964	5.00	10.00	20.00

JACKIE AND THE RAINDROPS

45s

COLPIX

Number	Title (A Side/B Side)	Yr	VG	VG+	NM
738	Down Our Street/My Heart Is Your Heart	1964	2.50	5.00	10.00

JACKS, TERRY

Also see THE POPPY FAMILY.

45s

Number	Title (A Side/B Side)	Yr	VG	VG+	NM
BELL					
45432	Seasons in the Sun/Put the Bone In	1974	—	2.50	5.00
45467	If You Go Away/Me and You	1974	—	2.00	4.00
45606	Love Game/Rock and Roll	1974	—	2.00	4.00
LONDON					
181	Concrete Sea/She Even Took the Cat	1972	—	2.50	5.00
188	I'm Gonna Love You, Too/Something Good Was Over Before It Ever Got to Start	1972	—	2.50	5.00
PARROT					
347	A Good Thing Lost/I'm Gonna Capture You	1970	—	3.00	6.00
PRIVATE STOCK					
45023	Christina/The Feeling That We've Lost	1975	—	2.00	4.00
45094	In My Father's Footsteps/Until You're Down	1976	—	2.00	4.00

Albums

Number	Title (A Side/B Side)	Yr	VG	VG+	NM
BELL					
1307	Seasons in the Sun	1974	2.50	5.00	10.00

JACKS, THE

Also see THE CADETS.

45s

Number	Title (A Side/B Side)	Yr	VG	VG+	NM
KENT					
344	Why Don't You Write Me/This Empty Heart	1960	3.75	7.50	15.00
RPM					
428	Why Don't You Write Me/Smack Dab in the Middle	1955	50.00	100.00	200.00
428	Why Don't You Write Me/My Darling	1955	15.00	30.00	60.00
433	I'm Confessin'/Since My Baby's Been Gone	1955	15.00	30.00	60.00
444	This Empty Heart/My Clumsy Heart	1955	12.50	25.00	50.00
454	So Wrong/How Soon	1956	12.50	25.00	50.00
458	Sugar Baby/Why Did I Fall in Love	1956	15.00	30.00	60.00
467	Let's Make Up/Dream a Little Longer	1956	15.00	30.00	60.00

Albums

Number	Title (A Side/B Side)	Yr	VG	VG+	NM
CROWN					
CST-372 [R]	Jumpin' with the Jacks	1962	12.50	25.00	50.00
CLP-5021 [M]	Jumpin' with the Jacks	1960	50.00	100.00	200.00
CLP-5372 [M]	Jumpin' with the Jacks	1962	25.00	50.00	100.00
RELIC					
5023	The Jacks' Greatest Hits	198?	2.50	5.00	10.00
RPM					
LRP-3006 [M]	Jumpin' with the Jacks	1956	1000.	1500.	2000.
UNITED					
US-7797	Rock 'n' Roll Hits of the 50's	197?	3.75	7.50	15.00

JACKSON, BULL MOOSE

45s

Number	Title (A Side/B Side)	Yr	VG	VG+	NM
KING					
4181	I Love You Yes I Do/Sneaky Pete	1951	15.00	30.00	60.00
—78 originally released in 1947					
4189	I Want a Bowlegged Woman/All My Love Belongs to You	1951	20.00	40.00	80.00
—78 originally released in 1948 -- 5191 and 5198 are the only legitimate 45s known before 4451					
4451	Trust in Me/Wonder When My Baby's Coming Home	1951	15.00	30.00	60.00
4462	Unless/End This Misery	1951	15.00	30.00	60.00
4472	Cherokee Boogie/I'm Lucky I Have You	1951	15.00	30.00	60.00
4493	I'll Be Home for Christmas/I Never Loved Anyone But You	1951	15.00	30.00	60.00
4524	Nosey Joe/Sad	1952	20.00	40.00	80.00
4535	(Let Me Love You) All Night Long/Bootsie	1952	15.00	30.00	60.00
4551	Bearcat Blues/There Is No Greater Love	1952	15.00	30.00	60.00
4580	Big Ten Inch Record/I Needed You	1952	50.00	100.00	200.00
4634	Meet Me with Your Black Dress On/Try to Forget Him	1953	10.00	20.00	40.00
4655	If You'll Let Me/Hodge Podge	1953	10.00	20.00	40.00
4775	If You Ain't Lovin'/I Wanna Hug Ya, Kiss Ya	1955	6.25	12.50	25.00
4802	I'm Glad for Your Sake/Must You Keep On Pretending	1955	6.25	12.50	25.00
SEVEN ARTS					
705	I Love YouYes I Do/Aw Shucks Baby	1961	5.00	10.00	20.00
WARWICK					
575	I Found My Love/More of the Same	1960	5.00	10.00	20.00

Albums

Number	Title (A Side/B Side)	Yr	VG	VG+	NM
AUDIO LAB					
AL-1524 [M]	Bull Moose Jackson	1959	150.00	300.00	600.00

JACKSON, CHUCK

45s

Number	Title (A Side/B Side)	Yr	VG	VG+	NM
ABC					
11368	I Only Get This Feeling/Slowly But Surely	1973	—	3.00	6.00
11398	I Can't Break Away/Just a Little Tear	1973	—	3.00	6.00
11423	If Only You Believe/Maybe This Will Be the Morning	1974	—	3.00	6.00
12024	Take Off Your Make-Up/Talk a Little Less	1974	—	3.00	6.00
ALL PLATINUM					
2357	Love Lights/(Instrumental)	1975	—	2.50	5.00
2360	I'm Needing You, Wanting You/We Can't Hide It Anymore	1975	—	2.50	5.00
2363	If You Were My Woman (Part 1)/If You Were My Woman (Part 2)	1976	—	2.50	5.00
2370	One of Those Yesterdays/Love Lights	1976	—	2.50	5.00
2373	I Fell Asleep/One of Those Yesterdays	1976	—	2.50	5.00
AMY					
849	Come On and Love Me/Ooh Baby	1962	3.75	7.50	15.00
868	I'm Yours/Hula Lula	1962	3.75	7.50	15.00
ATCO					
6197	Never Let Me Go/Baby I Want to Marry You	1961	3.00	6.00	12.00
BELTONE					
1005	Mr. Price/Hula Lula	1961	5.00	10.00	20.00
CLOCK					
1015	Come On and Love Me/Ooh Baby	1959	6.25	12.50	25.00
—Clock sides as "Charles Jackson"					
1022	Hula Hula/I'm Yours	1960	6.25	12.50	25.00
1027	This Is It/Mr. Pride	1960	6.25	12.50	25.00
DAKAR					
4512	I Forgot to Tell You/The Man and the Woman	1972	—	3.00	6.00
DOT					
15673	Woke Up This Morning/Wilette	1957	7.50	15.00	30.00
—With Kripp Johnson					
EMI AMERICA					
8042	I Wanna Give You Some Love/Waiting in Vain	1980	—	2.00	4.00
8056	After You/Let's Get Together	1980	—	2.00	4.00
MOTOWN					
1118	(Don't Let the Boy Overpower) The Man in You/Girls, Girls, Girls	1968	2.50	5.00	10.00
1144	Are You Lonely for Me Baby/Your Wonderful Love	1969	2.50	5.00	10.00
1152	Honey Come Back/What Am I Gonna Do Without You	1969	2.50	5.00	10.00
1160	The Day My World Stood Still/Baby, I'll Get It	1970	125.00	250.00	500.00
SUGARHILL					
764	Sometimes When We Touch/(B-side unknown)	1981	—	2.00	4.00
VIBRATION					
569	We Can't Hide It Anymore/I'm Needing You, Wanting You	1977	—	2.50	5.00
—With Sylvia					
V.I.P.					
25052	The Day My World Stood Still/Baby, I'll Get It	1970	2.50	5.00	10.00
25056	Let Somebody Love Me/Two Feet from Happiness	1970	2.50	5.00	10.00
25059	Is There Anything Love Can't Do/Pet Names	1971	2.50	5.00	10.00
25067	Who You Gonna Run To/Forgive My Jealousy	1971	100.00	200.00	400.00
WAND					
106	I Don't Want to Cry/Just Once	1961	3.00	6.00	12.00
108	(It Never Happens) In Real Life/The Same Old Story	1961	3.00	6.00	12.00
110	I Wake Up Crying/Everybody Needs Love	1961	3.00	6.00	12.00
115	The Breaking Point/My Willow Tree	1961	3.00	6.00	12.00
119	What'cha Gonna Say Tomorrow/Angel of Angels	1962	3.00	6.00	12.00
122	Any Day Now (My Wild Beautiful Bird)/The Prophet	1962	3.75	7.50	15.00
126	I Keep Forgetting/Who's Gonna Pick Up the Pieces	1962	2.50	5.00	10.00
128	Gettin' Ready for the Heartbreak/In Between Tears	1962	2.50	5.00	10.00
132	Tell Him I'm Not Home/Lonely Am I	1963	2.50	5.00	10.00
132 [PS]	Tell Him I'm Not Home/Lonely Am I	1963	6.25	12.50	25.00
138	I Will Never Turn My Back on You/Tears of Joy	1963	2.50	5.00	10.00
141	Any Other Way/Big New York	1963	2.50	5.00	10.00
149	Hand It Over/Look Over Your Shoulder	1964	2.00	4.00	8.00
154	Beg Me/This Broken Heart	1964	2.00	4.00	8.00
161	Somebody New/Stand By Me	1964	2.00	4.00	8.00
169	Since I Don't Have Yopu/Hand It Over	1964	2.00	4.00	8.00
179	I Need You/Soul Brother Twist	1965	2.00	4.00	8.00
188	If I Didn't Love You/Just a Little Bit of Your Soul	1965	2.00	4.00	8.00
1105	Good Things Come to Those Who Wait/Yah	1965	2.00	4.00	8.00
1119	All in My Mind/And That's Saying a Lot	1966	2.00	4.00	8.00
1129	These Chains of Love/Theme to the Blues	1966	2.00	4.00	8.00
1142	I've Got to Be Strong/Where Did She Stay	1967	2.00	4.00	8.00
1151	Every Man Needs a Down Home Girl/Need You There	1967	2.00	4.00	8.00
1159	Hound Dog/Love Me Tender	1967	2.00	4.00	8.00
1166	Shame on Me/Candy	1967	2.00	4.00	8.00
1178	My Child's Child/Theme to the Blues	1968	2.00	4.00	8.00

Albums

Number	Title (A Side/B Side)	Yr	VG	VG+	NM
ABC					
X-798	Through All Times	1973	3.75	7.50	15.00
ALL PLATINUM					
3014	Needing You, Wanting You	1976	3.75	7.50	15.00
COLLECTABLES					
COL-5115	Golden Classics	198?	2.50	5.00	10.00
EMI AMERICA					
SW-17031	I Wanna Give You Some Love	1980	2.50	5.00	10.00
GUEST STAR					
GS-1912 [M]	Chuck Jackson	196?	5.00	10.00	20.00

Number	Title (A Side/B Side)	Yr	VG	VG+	NM
GSS-1912 [R]	Chuck Jackson	196?	3.00	6.00	12.00
MOTOWN					
M-667 [M]	Chuck Jackson Arrives!	1967	10.00	20.00	40.00
MS-667 [S]	Chuck Jackson Arrives!	1967	6.25	12.50	25.00
MS-687	Goin' Back to Chuck Jackson	1969	6.25	12.50	25.00
SCEPTER					
5100	A Tribute to Burt Bacharach	1972	3.75	7.50	15.00
SPIN-O-RAMA					
123 [M]	Starring Chuck Jackson	196?	5.00	10.00	20.00
S-123 [R]	Starring Chuck Jackson	196?	3.00	6.00	12.00
STRAND					
SL-1125 [M]	The Great Chuck Jackson	196?	6.25	12.50	25.00
SLS-1125 [S]	The Great Chuck Jackson	196?	7.50	15.00	30.00
UNITED ARTISTS					
UA-LA499-E	The Very Best of Chuck Jackson	1974	2.50	5.00	10.00
V.I.P.					
403	Teardrops Keep Fallin' on My Heart	1970	10.00	20.00	40.00
WAND					
WD-650 [M]	I Don't Want to Cry	1961	10.00	20.00	40.00
WD-654 [M]	Any Day Now	1962	10.00	20.00	40.00
WD-655 [M]	Encore	1963	10.00	20.00	40.00
WD-658 [M]	Chuck Jackson On Tour	1964	10.00	20.00	40.00
WD-667 [M]	Mr. Everything	1965	7.50	15.00	30.00
WDS-667 [S]	Mr. Everything	1965	10.00	20.00	40.00
WD-673 [M]	A Tribute to Rhythm and Blues	1966	7.50	15.00	30.00
WDS-673 [S]	A Tribute to Rhythm and Blues	1966	10.00	20.00	40.00
WD-676 [M]	A Tribute to Rhythm and Blues, Volume 2	1966	7.50	15.00	30.00
WDS-676 [S]	A Tribute to Rhythm and Blues, Volume 2	1966	10.00	20.00	40.00
WD-680 [M]	Dedicated to the King!!	1966	10.00	20.00	40.00
WDS-680 [S]	Dedicated to the King!!	1966	12.50	25.00	50.00
WD-683 [M]	Chuck Jackson's Greatest Hits	1967	5.00	10.00	20.00
WDS-683 [S]	Chuck Jackson's Greatest Hits	1967	6.25	12.50	25.00

JACKSON, CHUCK, AND MAXINE BROWN

Also see each artist's individual listings.

Number	Title (A Side/B Side)	Yr	VG	VG+	NM
45s					
WAND					
181	Something You Got/Baby Take Me	1965	2.00	4.00	8.00
191	Don't Go/Can't Let You Out of My Sight	1965	2.00	4.00	8.00
198	I Need You So/Cause We're in Love	1965	2.00	4.00	8.00
1109	Plerase Don't Hurt Me/I'm Satisfied	1966	2.00	4.00	8.00
1148	Hold On I'm Comin'/Never Had It So Good	1967	2.00	4.00	8.00
1155	Daddy's Home/Don't Go	1967	2.00	4.00	8.00
1162	See See Rider/Tennessee Waltz	1967	2.00	4.00	8.00
Albums					
WAND					
WD-669 [M]	Say Something	1965	7.50	15.00	30.00
WDS-669 [S]	Say Something	1965	10.00	20.00	40.00
WD-678 [M]	Hold On, We're Coming	1966	7.50	15.00	30.00
WDS-678 [S]	Hold On, We're Coming	1966	10.00	20.00	40.00

JACKSON, CHUCK, AND TAMMI TERRELL

Also see each artist's individual listings.

Number	Title (A Side/B Side)	Yr	VG	VG+	NM
Albums					
WAND					
WD-682 [M]	The Early Show	1967	7.50	15.00	30.00
WDS-682 [S]	The Early Show	1967	7.50	15.00	30.00

JACKSON, DEON

Number	Title (A Side/B Side)	Yr	VG	VG+	NM
45s					
ATLANTIC					
2213	Hush Little Baby/You Said You Loved Me	1963	2.50	5.00	10.00
2252	Come Back Home/Nursery Rhymes	1964	2.50	5.00	10.00
CARLA					
1900	I Can't Go On/I Need a Love Like Yours	1968	2.00	4.00	8.00
1903	You'll Wake Up Wiser Baby/You Gotta Love	1968	2.00	4.00	8.00
2526	Love Makes the World Go Round/You Said You Loved Me	1966	2.50	5.00	10.00
2527	Love Takes a Long Time Growing/Hush Little Baby	1966	2.00	4.00	8.00
2530	I Can't Do Without You/That's What You Do to Me	1966	2.00	4.00	8.00
2533	When Your Love Has Gone/Hard to Get Thing Called Love	1967	2.00	4.00	8.00
2537	Ooh Baby/All on a Sunny Day	1967	2.00	4.00	8.00
SHOUT					
254	I'll Always Love You/Life Can Be That Way	1969	6.25	12.50	25.00
Albums					
ATCO					
33-188 [M]	Love Makes the World Go Round	1966	7.50	15.00	30.00
SD 33-188 [S]	Love Makes the World Go Round	1966	10.00	20.00	40.00
COLLECTABLES					
COL-5106	Golden Classics	198?	2.50	5.00	10.00

JACKSON, EARL

Number	Title (A Side/B Side)	Yr	VG	VG+	NM
45s					
ABC					
11142	Self Soul Satisfaction/Looking Through the Eyes of Love	1968	7.50	15.00	30.00

JACKSON, GEORGE

Number	Title (A Side/B Side)	Yr	VG	VG+	NM
45s					
ATLANTIC					
1024	Uh Huh/I'm Sorry	1954	12.50	25.00	50.00
CAMEO					
460	When I Stop Lovin' You/That Lonely Night	1967	3.00	6.00	12.00
CHESS					
2167	Things Are Gettin' Better/Mackin' on You	1975	—	3.00	6.00
DOT					
16724	Blinkety Blink/There Goes My Pride	1965	3.00	6.00	12.00
FAME					
1457	Find 'Em, Fool 'Em, and Forget 'Em/My Desires Are Getting the Best of Me	1969	2.00	4.00	8.00
1468	That's How Much You Mean to Me/I'm Gonna Hold On	1970	2.00	4.00	8.00
HI					
2130	I'm Gonna Wait/So Good to Me	1967	3.00	6.00	12.00
2212	Aretha, Sing One for Me/I'm Gonna Wait	1972	2.00	4.00	8.00
2236	Let Them Know You Care/Patricia	1973	2.00	4.00	8.00
MERCURY					
72736	Kiss Me/Tossin' and Turnin'	1967	2.50	5.00	10.00
72782	I Don't Have the Time to Love You/Don't Use Me	1968	2.50	5.00	10.00
MGM					
14680	We've Only Just Begun/You Can't Run Away from Love	1973	—	3.00	6.00
14732	Willie Lump Lump/How Can I Get Next to You	1974	—	3.00	6.00
14767	Soul Train/Smoking and Drinking	1974	—	3.00	6.00
RPM					
441	Hold Me Up/Heaven on Earth	1955	6.25	12.50	25.00
VERVE					
10658	Love Highjacker/I Found What I Wanted	1970	6.25	12.50	25.00

JACKSON, GEORGE, AND DAN GREER

See GEORGE AND GREER.

JACKSON, J.J.

Number	Title (A Side/B Side)	Yr	VG	VG+	NM
45s					
CALLA					
119	But It's Alright/Boogaloo Baby	1966	3.00	6.00	12.00
125	I Dig Girls/That Ain't Right	1966	2.50	5.00	10.00
130	Til Love Goes Out of Style/Seems Like I've Been Here Before	1967	2.50	5.00	10.00
133	Four Walls (Three Windows and Two Doors)/ Here We Go Again	1967	2.50	5.00	10.00
CONGRESS					
6008	Fat, Black and Together/That Woman Loving	1969	2.00	4.00	8.00
EVEREST					
2012	False Face/Ring Telephone	1963	3.00	6.00	12.00
LOMA					
2082	Try Me/Sho Nuff (Gotta Good Thing Goin')	1967	2.00	4.00	8.00
2090	Down But Not Out/Why Does It Take So Long	1968	2.00	4.00	8.00
2096	Come See Me (I'm Your Man)/I Don't Want to Live My Life Alone	1968	2.00	4.00	8.00
2102	Too Late/You Do It Cause You Wanna	1968	2.00	4.00	8.00
2104	That Ain't Right/Courage Ain't Strength	1968	2.00	4.00	8.00
PERCEPTION					
7	Nobody's Gonna Help You/Help Me Get to My Grits	1970	2.00	4.00	8.00
WARNER BROS.					
7130	But It's Alright/Four Walls (Three Windows and Two Doors)	1970	—	3.00	6.00
—"Back to Back Hits" series					
7278	But It's Alright/Ain't Too Proud to Beg	1969	2.00	4.00	8.00
7321	Four Walls (Three Windows and Two Doors)/That Ain't Right	1969	2.00	4.00	8.00
Albums					
CALLA					
C-1101 [M]	But It's Alright/I Dig Girls	1967	5.00	10.00	20.00
CS-1101 [S]	But It's Alright/I Dig Girls	1967	6.25	12.50	25.00
CONGRESS					
CS-7000	The Greatest Little Soul Band in the World	1968	6.25	12.50	25.00
PERCEPTION					
3	J.J. Jackson's Dilemma	1970	3.75	7.50	15.00
WARNER BROS.					
WS 1797	The Great J.J. Jackson	1969	5.00	10.00	20.00

JACKSON, JACKIE

Number	Title (A Side/B Side)	Yr	VG	VG+	NM
12-Inch Singles					
POLYDOR					
871549	Stay (4 versions)/Who's Loving You Now	1989	2.00	4.00	8.00
889035	Cruzin' (5 versions)	1989	2.00	4.00	8.00
45s					
POLYDOR					
871548-7	Stay/Who's Loving You Now	1989	—	—	3.00
871548-7 [PS]	Stay/Who's Loving You Now	1989	—	—	3.00
889034-7	Cruzin/(B-side unknown)	1989	—	—	3.00
889034-7 [PS]	Cruzin/(B-side unknown)	1989	—	—	3.00
Albums					
MOTOWN					
M 785L	Jackie Jackson	1973	3.00	6.00	12.00
POLYDOR					
837766-1	Be the One	1989	2.50	5.00	10.00

JACKSON, JERMAINE

Number	Title (A Side/B Side)	Yr	VG	VG+	NM
12-Inch Singles					
ARISTA					
ADP 9189 [DJ]	Tell Me I'm Not Dreamin' (Too Good to Be True)/ Do What You Do/Escape from the Planet	1984	2.50	5.00	10.00
AD1 9222 [DJ]	Dynamite/(Instrumental)/Tell Me I'm Not Dreaming (Instrumental)	1984	—	3.00	6.00
9317	When the Rain Begins to Fall/Come to Me	1985	2.00	4.00	8.00
—A-side with Pia Zadora					
AD1 9357	(Closest Thing to) Perfect/(Instrumental)	1985	—	3.00	6.00
AD1 9445	I Think It's Love (4 versions)	1986	—	3.00	6.00
AD1 9501	Do You Remember Me (6 versions)	1986	—	3.00	6.00
ADP 9876 [DJ]	Don't Take It Personal (same on both sides)	1989	2.00	4.00	8.00
AD1 9878	Don't Take It Personal (3 versions)	1989	—	3.00	6.00
AD1 9934	Two Ships in the Night (4 versions)	1990	—	3.00	6.00
LAFACE					
24004	You Said, You Said (5 versions)	1991	—	3.00	6.00
24012	Word to the Badd!! (5 versions)	1991	2.50	5.00	10.00

Number	Title (A Side/B Side)	Yr	VG	VG+	NM
24017	I Dream, I Dream (5 versions)	1992	—	3.00	6.00

MOTOWN

Number	Title (A Side/B Side)	Yr	VG	VG+	NM
PR 108 [DJ]	Very Special Part/(Instrumental)	1982	2.50	5.00	10.00

45s

ARISTA

Number	Title (A Side/B Side)	Yr	VG	VG+	NM
2029	I'd Like to Get to Know You/Spare the Rod, Love the Child	1990	—	—	3.00
9190	Dynamite/Tell Me I'm Not Dreaming (Too Good to Be True) (Instrumental)	1984	—	—	3.00
9190 [PS]	Dynamite/Tell Me I'm Not Dreaming (Too Good to Be True) (Instrumental)	1984	—	—	3.00
9275	Take Good Care of My Heart/Tell Me I'm Not Dreaming (Too Good to Be True) (Instrumental)	1984	—	—	3.00
—A-side with Whitney Houston					
9279	Do What You Do/Tell Me I'm Not Dreaming (Too Good to Be True)	1984	—	—	3.00
9356	(Closest Thing to) Perfect/(Instrumental)	1985	—	—	3.00
9356 [PS]	(Closest Thing to) Perfect/(Instrumental)	1985	—	—	3.00
9444	I Think It's Love/Voices in the Dark	1985	—	—	3.00
9444 [PS]	I Think It's Love/Voices in the Dark	1985	—	—	3.00
9495	Words Into Action/Our Love Story	1986	—	—	3.00
9495 [PS]	Words Into Action/Our Love Story	1986	—	—	3.00
9502	Do You Remember Me/Whatcha' Doin'	1986	—	—	3.00
9502 [PS]	Do You Remember Me/Whatcha' Doin'	1986	—	—	3.00
9690	If You Say My Eyes Are Beautiful/Just the Lonely Talking Again	1988	—	—	3.00
—A-side with Whitney Houston; B-side: Whitney Houston solo					
9788	Clean Up Your Act/I'm Gonna Git Ya Sucka	1988	—	—	3.00
—B-side by the Gap Band					
9788 [PS]	Clean Up Your Act/I'm Gonna Git Ya Sucka	1988	—	—	3.00
9875	Don't Take It Personal/Clean Up Your Act	1989	—	—	3.00
9875 [PS]	Don't Take It Personal/Clean Up Your Act	1989	—	—	3.00
9933	Two Ships (In the Night)/Next to You	1990	—	—	3.00
9933 [PS]	Two Ships (In the Night)/Next to You	1990	—	—	3.00

LAFACE

Number	Title (A Side/B Side)	Yr	VG	VG+	NM
24003	You Said, You Said/(Instrumental)	1991	—	—	3.00

MCA CURB

Number	Title (A Side/B Side)	Yr	VG	VG+	NM
52521	When the Rain Begins to Fall/Substitute	1984	—	—	3.00
—With Pia Zadora					
52521 [PS]	When the Rain Begins to Fall/Substitute	1984	—	—	3.00

MOTOWN

Number	Title (A Side/B Side)	Yr	VG	VG+	NM
1201	That's How Love Goes/I Lost My Love in the Big City	1972	—	2.50	5.00
1216	Daddy's Home/Take Me in Your Arms (Rock Me a Little While)	1972	—	2.50	5.00
1244	You're in Good Hands/Does Your Mama Know About Me	1973	—	2.50	5.00
1386	She's the Ideal Girl/I'm So Glad You Chose Me	1976	—	—	—
—Unreleased					
1401	Let's Be Young Tonight/Boss Odyssey	1976	—	2.50	5.00
1409	You Need to Be Loved/My Touch of Madness	1977	—	2.50	5.00
1441	Castles of Sand/I Love Every Little Thing About You	1978	—	2.50	5.00
1469	Let's Get Serious/Je Vous Aime Beaucoups	1980	—	2.00	4.00
1490	You're Supposed to Keep Your Love for Me/Let It Ride	1980	—	2.00	4.00
1499	Little Girl Don't You Worry/We Can Put It Back Together	1980	—	2.00	4.00
1503	You Like Me Don't You/(Instrumental)	1981	—	2.00	4.00
1525	I'm Just Too Shy/All Because of You	1981	—	2.00	4.00
1600	Paradise in Your Eyes/I'm My Brother's Keeper	1982	—	2.00	4.00
1628	Let Me Tickle Your Fancy/Maybe Next Time	1982	—	2.00	4.00
—Devo is the backing group					
1649	Very Special Part/You're Givin' Me the Runaround	1982	—	2.00	4.00

Albums

ARISTA

Number	Title (A Side/B Side)	Yr	VG	VG+	NM
AL-8203	Jermaine Jackson	1984	2.50	5.00	10.00
AL-8277	Precious Moments	1986	2.50	5.00	10.00
AL-8421	Jermaine Jackson	1986	2.00	4.00	8.00
—Budget-line reissue					
AL-8493	Don't Take It Personal	1989	2.50	5.00	10.00

MOTOWN

Number	Title (A Side/B Side)	Yr	VG	VG+	NM
M5-117V1	Motown Superstar Series, Vol. 17	1981	2.50	5.00	10.00
M-752	Jermaine	1972	2.50	5.00	10.00
M-775	Come Into My Life	1973	2.50	5.00	10.00
M6-842	My Name Is Jermaine	1976	2.50	5.00	10.00
M6-888	Feel the Fire	1977	2.50	5.00	10.00
M7-898	Frontiers	1978	2.50	5.00	10.00
M7-928	Let's Get Serious	1980	2.50	5.00	10.00
M8-948	Jermaine	1980	2.50	5.00	10.00
M8-952	I Like Your Style	1981	2.50	5.00	10.00
6017 ML	Let Me Tickle Your Fancy	1982	2.50	5.00	10.00

JACKSON, JERRY

45s

CAPITOL

Number	Title (A Side/B Side)	Yr	VG	VG+	NM
2112	Miss You/Take Over Now	1968	2.50	5.00	10.00

COLUMBIA

Number	Title (A Side/B Side)	Yr	VG	VG+	NM
43056	Shrimp Boats/Always	1964	3.00	6.00	12.00
43158	Tell Her Johnny Said Goodbye/Are You Glad When We're Apart	1964	3.00	6.00	12.00
43231	You're Mine (And I Love You)/Hey, Sugarfoot	1965	3.00	6.00	12.00

KAPP

Number	Title (A Side/B Side)	Yr	VG	VG+	NM
387	Time/Se Habla Espanol	1961	5.00	10.00	20.00
420	I Don't Play Games/You Might Be There With Him	1961	5.00	10.00	20.00
438	If I Had Only Know How to Keep Her (She Would Never Have Gone to You)/Till the End of Time	1961	5.00	10.00	20.00
448	La-Dee-Dah (Ha-Ha-Ha)/You Don't Wanna Hurt Me	1962	3.75	7.50	15.00
464	They Really Don't Know You/Blues in the Night	1962	3.75	7.50	15.00
496	She Lied/Wide Awake in a Dream	1962	3.75	7.50	15.00
511	Gypsy Eyes/Turn Back	1963	3.75	7.50	15.00
543	Blowin' in the Wind (Part 1)/Blowin' in the Wind (Part 2)	1963	3.75	7.50	15.00

PARKWAY

Number	Title (A Side/B Side)	Yr	VG	VG+	NM
100	It's Rough Out There/I'm Gonna Paint a Picture	1966	5.00	10.00	20.00

TOP RANK

Number	Title (A Side/B Side)	Yr	VG	VG+	NM
2042	A Chance to Prove My Love/For Every One There's Someone	1960	5.00	10.00	20.00
2072	Every Time You Kiss Me/Meaning of My Love	1960	5.00	10.00	20.00

JACKSON, JILL

Also see PAUL AND PAULA.

45s

REPRISE

Number	Title (A Side/B Side)	Yr	VG	VG+	NM
0297	Hey Handsome Boy/All Over Again	1964	3.75	7.50	15.00
0323	Pixie Girl/I Just Don't Know What to Do With Myself	1964	3.75	7.50	15.00
0362	Born Too Late/Here Comes the Night	1965	3.75	7.50	15.00
0411	Treasure of Love/I'll Love You for a While	1965	3.75	7.50	15.00

JACKSON, JUNE

45s

BELL

Number	Title (A Side/B Side)	Yr	VG	VG+	NM
45173	Little Dog Heaven/Tenderly with Feeling	1972	5.00	10.00	20.00

IMPERIAL

Number	Title (A Side/B Side)	Yr	VG	VG+	NM
66185	It's What's Up Front That Counts/Fifty Per Cent Won't Do	1966	7.50	15.00	30.00

JACKSON, LIL' SON

45s

IMPERIAL

Number	Title (A Side/B Side)	Yr	VG	VG+	NM
5204	Journey Back Home/Rockin' and Rollin' #2	1952	25.00	50.00	100.00
—Note: Lil' Son Jackson records on Imperial before 5204 are unconfirmed on 45 rpm					
5218	Black and Brown/Sad Letter Blues	1953	25.00	50.00	100.00
5229	Lonely Blues/Freight Train Blues	1953	25.00	50.00	100.00
5237	Spending Money Blues/All Alone	1953	25.00	50.00	100.00
5248	Movin' to the Country/Confession	1953	25.00	50.00	100.00
5259	Dirty Work/Little Girl	1953	25.00	50.00	100.00
5267	Thrill Me, Baby/Doctor, Doctor	1954	20.00	40.00	80.00
5276	Big Rat/Piggly Wiggly	1954	20.00	40.00	80.00
5286	Trouble Don't Last Always/Blues by the Hour	1954	20.00	40.00	80.00
5300	Get High Everybody/Let Me Down Easy	1954	20.00	40.00	80.00
5312	How Long/Good Ole Wagon	1954	20.00	40.00	80.00
5319	My Younger Days/I Wish to Go Home	1954	20.00	40.00	80.00
5339	Sugar Mama/Messin' Up	1955	20.00	40.00	80.00
5703	Rockin' and Rollin'/Peace Breaking People	1960	3.75	7.50	15.00
5851	Everybody's Blues/Travelin' Woman	1962	3.75	7.50	15.00
5963	Prison Bound/Rolling Mill	1963	3.00	6.00	12.00

POST

Number	Title (A Side/B Side)	Yr	VG	VG+	NM
2014	No Money/Lonely Blues	1955	10.00	20.00	40.00

Albums

ARHOOLIE

Number	Title (A Side/B Side)	Yr	VG	VG+	NM
1004 [M]	Lil' Son Jackson	1960	6.25	12.50	25.00

IMPERIAL

Number	Title (A Side/B Side)	Yr	VG	VG+	NM
LP-9142 [M]	Rockin' and Rollin'	1961	100.00	200.00	400.00

JACKSON, MAHALIA

45s

APOLLO

Number	Title (A Side/B Side)	Yr	VG	VG+	NM
235	Silent Night, Holy Night/Go Tell It On The Mountain	1951	5.00	10.00	20.00
—Note: Earlier Mahalia Jackson 45s on Apollo may exist					
240	Get Away Jordan/I Gave Up Everything	1951	5.00	10.00	20.00
245	Bless This House/The Lord's Prayer	1951	5.00	10.00	20.00
246	His Eyes Are On the Sparrow/It Is No Secret (What God Can Do)	1951	5.00	10.00	20.00
248	How I Got Over/Just As I Am	1951	5.00	10.00	20.00
258	He's the One/I'm Getting Nearer My Home	1952	5.00	10.00	20.00
262	In the Upper Room (Part 1)/In the Upper Room (Part 2)	1952	5.00	10.00	20.00
269	He Said He Would/God Spoke to Me	1953	5.00	10.00	20.00
273	I'm Going Down the River/Do You Know Him	1953	5.00	10.00	20.00
278	I Wonder If I Will Ever Rest/Coming to Jesus	1953	5.00	10.00	20.00
282	Hands of God/It's Real	1954	5.00	10.00	20.00
286	I'm On My Way/My Story	1954	5.00	10.00	20.00
289	Walking to Jerusalem/What Then	1954	5.00	10.00	20.00
291	I Walked Into the Garden/I'm Going to Tell God	1955	5.00	10.00	20.00
298	Nobody Knows/Run All the Way	1955	5.00	10.00	20.00
304	He's My Light/If You Just Keep Still	1956	4.50	9.00	18.00
311	His Eyes Are On the Sparrow/I Can Put My Trust in Jesus	1956	4.50	9.00	18.00
313	Didn't It Rain/Nobody Knows	1956	4.50	9.00	18.00
314	I'm On My Way/My Story	1956	4.50	9.00	18.00
539	Silent Night/The Lord's Prayer	1959	3.75	7.50	15.00
750	Silent Night/The Lord's Prayer	1962	3.00	6.00	12.00
750 [PS]	Silent Night/The Lord's Prayer	1962	5.00	10.00	20.00

COLUMBIA

Number	Title (A Side/B Side)	Yr	VG	VG+	NM
40411	A Rusty Old Halo/The Treasure of Love	1955	3.75	7.50	15.00
40412	Walk Over God's Heaven/Jesus Met the Woman	1955	3.75	7.50	15.00
40473	You'll Never Walk Alone/One God	1955	3.75	7.50	15.00
40529	His Hands/I See God	1955	3.75	7.50	15.00
40554	The Bible Tells Me So/Satisfied Mind	1955	3.75	7.50	15.00
40610	The Lord Is a Busy Man/You're Not Living in Vain	1955	3.75	7.50	15.00
40712	Round the Rainbow/An Evening Star	1956	3.75	7.50	15.00
40721	I Ask the Lord/I'm Going to Live	1956	3.75	7.50	15.00
40753	The Lord's Prayer/Precious Lord	1956	3.75	7.50	15.00
40777	Silent Night, Holy Night/Mary's Little Boy Chile	1956	3.75	7.50	15.00
40854	God Is So Good/I Complained	1957	3.75	7.50	15.00
41000	Trouble/He's a Light Unto My Pathway	1957	3.75	7.50	15.00
41055	Sweet Little Jesus Boy/A Star Stood Still	1957	3.00	6.00	12.00
41150	He's Got the Whole World In His Hands/Didn't It Rain	1958	3.00	6.00	12.00
41258	For My Good Fortune/Have You Any Rivers	1958	3.00	6.00	12.00
41322	Elijah Rock/Hold Me	1959	3.00	6.00	12.00

Number	Title (A Side/B Side)	Yr	VG	VG+	NM
41382	Tell the World About This/Trouble of the World	1959	3.00	6.00	12.00
41779	My Country 'Tis of Thee (America)/Onward, Christian Soldiers	1960	3.00	6.00	12.00
42633	Joy To The World!/Go Tell It On The Mountain	1962	2.50	5.00	10.00
42910	We Shall Overcome/Let's Pray Together	1963	2.50	5.00	10.00
42946	In the Summer of His Years/Song for My Brother	1964	2.50	5.00	10.00
43474	Sunrise, Sunset/Like the Breeze Blows	1965	2.50	5.00	10.00
44529	Take My Hand, Precious Lord/We Shall Overcome	1968	2.00	4.00	8.00
45068	Abraham, Martin and John/Day Is Done	1970	—	3.00	6.00
JZSP 137705/6 [DJ]	Happy Birthday To You, Our Lord/Silver Bells	1968	—	2.50	5.00
GRAND AWARD					
1025	Dig a Little Deeper/I'm On My Way	1959	3.75	7.50	15.00
KENWOOD					
300	In the Upper Room (Part 1)/In the Upper Room (Part 2)	1964	2.00	4.00	8.00
301	His Eyes Are On the Sparrow/Walking to Jerusalem	196?	2.00	4.00	8.00
302	How I Got Over/Didn't It Rain	196?	2.00	4.00	8.00
303	Go Tell It On the Mountain/Bless This House	196?	2.00	4.00	8.00
304	Move On Up a Little Higher (Part 1)/Move On Up a Little Higher (Part 2)	196?	2.00	4.00	8.00
305	These Are They/Get Away Jordan	196?	2.00	4.00	8.00
750	Silent Night/The Lord's Prayer	1964	2.50	5.00	10.00
NASHBORO					
750 [DJ]	Silent Night/The Lord's Prayer	197?	—	2.00	4.00
—Reissue of Kenwood 750					
U.S.A.					
109	The Holy Bible (Part 1)/The Holy Bible (Part 2)	196?	2.50	5.00	10.00

Albums

Number	Title	Yr	VG	VG+	NM
APOLLO					
201/202 [M]	Spirituals	1954	7.50	15.00	30.00
482 [M]	No Matter How You Pray	1959	6.25	12.50	25.00
499 [M]	Mahalia Jackson	1962	6.25	12.50	25.00
1001/2 [M]	Command Performance	1961	6.25	12.50	25.00
COLUMBIA					
CL 644 [M]	Mahalia Jackson	1955	10.00	20.00	40.00
CL 702 [M]	Sweet Little Jesus Boy	1955	10.00	20.00	40.00
CL 899 [M]	Bless This House	1956	7.50	15.00	30.00
CL 1244 [M]	Newport 1958	1959	5.00	10.00	20.00
CL 1343 [M]	That Great Gettin' Up Morning	1959	5.00	10.00	20.00
CL 1428 [M]	Come On Children, Let's Sing	1960	5.00	10.00	20.00
CL 1473 [M]	The Power and the Glory	1960	5.00	10.00	20.00
CL 1549 [M]	I Believe	1960	3.75	7.50	15.00
CL 1643 [M]	Every Time I Feel the Spirit	1961	3.75	7.50	15.00
CL 1726 [M]	Recorded in Europe During Her Latest Concert Tour	1962	3.75	7.50	15.00
CL 1824 [M]	Great Songs of Love and Faith	1962	3.75	7.50	15.00
CL 1903 [M]	Silent Night	1962	3.75	7.50	15.00
CL 1936 [M]	Make a Joyful Noise Unto the Lord	1962	3.75	7.50	15.00
CL 2004 [M]	Mahalia Jackson's Greatest Hits	1963	3.00	6.00	12.00
CL 2130 [M]	Let's Pray Together	1964	3.00	6.00	12.00
CL 2452 [M]	Mahalia Sings	1966	3.00	6.00	12.00
CL 2546 [M]	Garden of Prayer	1967	3.75	7.50	15.00
CL 2605 [M]	My Faith	1967	3.75	7.50	15.00
CL 2690 [M]	Mahalia Jackson In Concert, Easter Sunday 1967	1967	3.75	7.50	15.00
CS 8071 [S]	Newport 1958	1959	7.50	15.00	30.00
CS 8153 [S]	That Great Gettin' Up Morning	1959	6.25	12.50	25.00
CS 8225 [S]	Come On Children, Let's Sing	1960	6.25	12.50	25.00
CS 8264 [S]	The Power and the Glory	1960	6.25	12.50	25.00
CS 8349 [S]	I Believe	1960	5.00	10.00	20.00
CS 8443 [S]	Every Time I Feel the Spirit	1961	5.00	10.00	20.00
CS 8526 [S]	Recorded in Europe During Her Latest Concert Tour	1962	5.00	10.00	20.00
CS 8624 [S]	Great Songs of Love and Faith	1962	5.00	10.00	20.00
CS 8703 [S]	Silent Night	1962	5.00	10.00	20.00
CS 8736 [S]	Make a Joyful Noise Unto the Lord	1962	5.00	10.00	20.00
CS 8759 [R]	Mahalia Jackson	1963	3.00	6.00	12.00
CS 8761 [R]	Bless This House	1963	3.00	6.00	12.00
PC 8761	Bless This House	198?	2.00	4.00	8.00
—Budget-line reissue					
CS 8804 [S]	Mahalia Jackson's Greatest Hits	1963	3.75	7.50	15.00
CS 8930 [S]	Let's Pray Together	1964	3.75	7.50	15.00
CS 9252 [S]	Mahalia Sings	1966	3.75	7.50	15.00
CS 9346 [S]	Garden of Prayer	1967	3.00	6.00	12.00
CS 9405 [S]	My Faith	1967	3.00	6.00	12.00
CS 9490 [S]	Mahalia Jackson In Concert, Easter Sunday 1967	1967	3.00	6.00	12.00
CS 9659	A Mighty Fortress	1968	3.00	6.00	12.00
CS 9686	The Best-Loved Hymns of Dr. Martin Luther King Jr.	1968	3.75	7.50	15.00
PC 9686	The Best-Loved Hymns of Dr. Martin Luther King Jr.	198?	2.00	4.00	8.00
—Budget-line reissue					
CS 9727	Christmas with Mahalia	1968	3.00	6.00	12.00
CS 9813	Right Out of the Church	1969	3.00	6.00	12.00
CS 9950	What the World Needs Now	1970	3.00	6.00	12.00
CG 30744 [(2)]	America's Favorite Hymns	1971	3.75	7.50	15.00
KG 31379 [(2)]	The Great Mahalia Jackson	1972	3.75	7.50	15.00
KC 34073	How I Got Over	1976	2.50	5.00	10.00
PC 37710	Mahalia Jackson's Greatest Hits	198?	2.00	4.00	8.00
3C 38304	Silent Night	1982	2.00	4.00	8.00
—Reissue					
FOLKWAYS					
31101	I Sing Because I'm Happy, Volume 1	198?	2.50	5.00	10.00
31102	I Sing Because I'm Happy, Volume 2	198?	2.50	5.00	10.00
GRAND AWARD					
GA 265 SD	I Believe	1966	3.75	7.50	15.00
—Reissue of 326					
GA 33-326 [M]	Mahalia Jackson	1955	7.50	15.00	30.00
GA 33-390 [M]	Mahalia Jackson	195?	7.50	15.00	30.00
HARMONY					
HS 11279	You'll Never Walk Alone	196?	2.50	5.00	10.00
HS 11372	Abide With Me	1970	2.50	5.00	10.00
H 30019	Sunrise, Sunset	1970	2.50	5.00	10.00
KH 31111	Lord Don't Let Me Fall	1972	2.50	5.00	10.00
KENWOOD					
474	In the Upper Room	196?	3.75	7.50	15.00
479	Just As I Am	196?	3.75	7.50	15.00
482	No Matter How You Pray	196?	3.75	7.50	15.00
486	Mahalia	196?	3.75	7.50	15.00
489	Mahalia Jackson With the Greatest Spiritual Singers	196?	3.75	7.50	15.00
500	The Best of Mahalia Jackson	196?	3.75	7.50	15.00
501	I Lift My Voice	196?	3.75	7.50	15.00
502	Sing Out	196?	3.75	7.50	15.00
1001/2 [(2)]	Command Performance	196?	5.00	10.00	20.00
PICKWICK					
SPC-3510	I Believe	197?	2.50	5.00	10.00
PRIORITY					
PU 37710	Mahalia Jackson's Greatest Hits	1981	2.50	5.00	10.00

JACKSON, MICHAEL

12-Inch Singles

Number	Title (A Side/B Side)	Yr	VG	VG+	NM
EPIC					
03915	Wanna Be Startin' Somethin' (6:30)/(Instrumental)	1983	3.00	6.00	12.00
ES 4533 [(2) DJ]	In the Closet (11 versions)	1991	7.50	15.00	30.00
ES 4580 [(2) DJ]	Jam (13 versions)	1991	7.50	15.00	30.00
04961	Thriller/(Instrumental)	1983	2.50	5.00	10.00
07462	Bad (5 versions)	1987	2.50	5.00	10.00
07487	The Way You Make Me Feel (4 versions)	1987	2.00	4.00	8.00
07583	Dirty Diana/(Instrumental)	1988	—	3.00	6.00
50658	You Can't Win (7:14)/(2:58)	1978	6.25	12.50	25.00
74099	Black or White (7 versions)	1991	2.00	4.00	8.00
74201	Remember the Time (4 versions)/Black or White (The Underground Club Mix)`	1991	2.00	4.00	8.00
74267	In the Closet (4 versions)	1992	2.00	4.00	8.00
74334	Jam (4 versions)	1992	2.00	4.00	8.00
74420	Who Is It (4 versions)/Beat It (Moby's Sub Mix)	1993	2.00	4.00	8.00
78001	Scream (5 versions)/Childhood	1995	2.00	4.00	8.00
78003	You Are Not Alone (2 versions)/MJ Megamix/Scream Louder	1995	2.50	5.00	10.00
78212 [(2)]	They Don't Care About Us (7 versions)/Earth Song/Rock with You (Club Mix)/This Time Around	1996	3.00	6.00	12.00

45s

Number	Title (A Side/B Side)	Yr	VG	VG+	NM
EPIC					
02156	Rock with You/Off the Wall	1981	—	—	3.00
—Reissue					
02157	She's Out of My Life/Lovely One	1981	—	—	3.00
—Reissue; B-side by The Jacksons					
03509	Billie Jean/Can't Get Outta the Rain	1983	—	2.00	4.00
03575	Billie Jean	1983	3.00	6.00	12.00
—One-sided budget release					
03759	Beat It/Get On the Floor	1983	—	2.00	4.00
03914	Wanna Be Startin' Somethin'/(Instrumental)	1983	—	2.00	4.00
03914 [PS]	Wanna Be Startin' Somethin'/(Instrumental)	1983	—	2.50	5.00
04026	Human Nature/Baby Be Mine	1983	—	2.00	4.00
04026 [PS]	Human Nature/Baby Be Mine	1983	—	2.50	5.00
04165	P.Y.T. (Pretty Young Thing)/Working Day and Night	1983	—	2.00	4.00
04165 [PS]	P.Y.T. (Pretty Young Thing)/Working Day and Night	1983	—	2.50	5.00
04364	Thriller/Can't Get Outta the Rain	1984	—	2.00	4.00
07253	I Just Can't Stop Loving You/Baby Be Mine	1987	—	—	3.00
07253 [PS]	I Just Can't Stop Loving You/Baby Be Mine	1987	—	—	3.00
07418	Bad/I Can't Help It	1987	—	—	3.00
07418 [PS]	Bad/I Can't Help It	1987	—	—	3.00
07645	The Way You Make Me Feel/(Instrumental)	1987	—	—	3.00
07645 [PS]	The Way You Make Me Feel/(Instrumental)	1987	—	—	3.00
07668	Man in the Mirror/(Instrumental)	1988	—	—	3.00
07668 [PS]	Man in the Mirror/(Instrumental)	1988	—	—	3.00
07739	Dirty Diana/(Instrumental)	1988	—	—	3.00
07739 [PS]	Dirty Diana/(Instrumental)	1988	—	—	3.00
07962	Another Part of Me/(Instrumental)	1988	—	—	3.00
07962 [PS]	Another Part of Me/(Instrumental)	1988	—	—	3.00
08044	Smooth Criminal/(Instrumental)	1988	—	—	3.00
08044 [PS]	Smooth Criminal/(Instrumental)	1988	—	—	3.00
50654	You Can't Win (Part 1)/You Can't Win (Part 2)	1979	—	3.00	6.00
50742	Don't Stop 'Til You Get Enough/I Can't Help It	1979	—	2.00	4.00
50797	Rock with You/Working Day and Night	1979	—	2.00	4.00
50838	Off the Wall/Get On the Floor	1980	—	2.00	4.00
50871	She's Out of My Life/Get On the Floor	1980	—	2.00	4.00
74100	Black or White/(Instrumental)	1991	—	—	3.00
74200	Remember the Time/Black or White (The Underground Club Mix)	1992	—	—	3.00
74266	In the Closet (7" Edit)/In the Closet (The Mission Radio Edit)	1992	—	—	3.00
74333	Jam/Rock with You (Masters At Work Remix)	1992	—	—	3.00
74406	Who Is It/Wanna Be Startin' Somethin'	1992	—	—	3.00
74708	Heal the World/She Drives Me Wild	1992	—	—	3.00
77060	Will You Be There/(Instrumental)	1993	—	—	3.00
77312	Gone Too Soon/(Instrumental)	1993	—	—	3.00
78000	Scream/Childhood	1995	—	—	3.00
—A-side: With Janet Jackson					
78002	You Are Not Alone/Scream Louder	1995	—	—	3.00
78007	Blood on the Dance Floor/Dangerous (Roger's Dangerous Edit)	1997	—	—	3.00
78012	Stranger in Moscow (Radio Edit)/(Tee's Radio Mix)	1997	—	—	3.00
78264	They Don't Care About Us/Rock with You (Frankie Knuckles Mix)	1996	—	—	3.00
MCA					
S45-1786 [DJ]	Someone in the Dark (same on both sides)	1982	12.50	25.00	50.00
S45-1786 [PS]	Someone in the Dark (same on both sides)	1982	12.50	25.00	50.00
40947	Ease On Down the Road/Poppy Girls	1978	—	2.50	5.00
40947 [PS]	Ease On Down the Road/Poppy Girls	1978	—	2.50	5.00
—With Diana Ross					
MOTOWN					
1191	Got to Be There/Maria (You Were the Only One)	1971	—	2.50	5.00

Number	Title (A Side/B Side)	Yr	VG	VG+	NM
1197	Rockin' Robin/Love Is Here and Now You're Gone	1972	—	2.50	5.00
1202	I Wanna Be Where You Are/We Got a Good Thing Going	1972	—	2.50	5.00
1202 [PS]	I Wanna Be Where You Are/We Got a Good Thing Going	1972	2.50	5.00	10.00
1207	Ben/You Can Cry on My Shoulder	1972	—	2.50	5.00
1218	With a Child's Heart/Morning Glow	1973	—	2.50	5.00
1270	Doggin' Around/Up Again	1974	—	—	—
—Unreleased					
1341	We're Almost There/Take Me Back	1975	—	2.50	5.00
1349	Just a Little Bit of You/Dear Michael	1975	—	2.50	5.00
1512	One Day in Your Life/Take Me Back	1981	—	2.00	4.00
1739	Farewell My Summer Love/Call On Me	1984	—	2.00	4.00
1739 [PS]	Farewell My Summer Love/Call On Me	1984	—	2.50	5.00
1757	Girl You're So Together/Touch the One You Love	1984	—	2.00	4.00
1914	Twenty-Five Miles/Up on the House Top	1987	2.00	4.00	8.00
1914 [PS]	Twenty-Five Miles/Up on the House Top	1987	2.00	4.00	8.00

Albums

EPIC

Number	Title (A Side/B Side)	Yr	VG	VG+	NM
FE 35745	Off the Wall	1979	2.00	4.00	8.00
QE 38112	Thriller	1982	2.00	4.00	8.00
8E8 38867 [PD]	Thriller	1983	3.75	7.50	15.00
OE 40600	Bad	1987	2.00	4.00	8.00
9E9 44043 [PD]	Bad	1987	3.00	6.00	12.00
E2 45400 [(2)]	Dangerous	1991	3.75	7.50	15.00
HE 47545	Off the Wall	1982	10.00	20.00	40.00
—Half-speed mastered edition					
HE 48112	Thriller	1982	10.00	20.00	40.00
—Half-speed mastered edition					
E3 59000 [(3)]	HIStory: Past, Present and Future — Book I	1995	5.00	10.00	20.00
—Box set with 12x12 booklet					
E2 68000 [(2)]	Blood on the Dance Floor: HIStory in the Mix	1997	3.75	7.50	15.00

MOTOWN

Number	Title (A Side/B Side)	Yr	VG	VG+	NM
M5-107V1	Motown Superstar Series, Vol. 7	1981	2.00	4.00	8.00
M5-130V1	Got to Be There	1981	2.50	5.00	10.00
—Reissue of Motown 747					
M5-153V1	Ben	1981	2.50	5.00	10.00
—Reissue of Motown 755					
M5-194V1	The Best of Michael Jackson	1981	2.50	5.00	10.00
—Reissue of Motown 851					
M 747	Got to Be There	1972	3.75	7.50	15.00
M 755	Ben	1972	3.75	7.50	15.00
—With only Michael Jackson on front cover					
M 755	Ben	1972	15.00	30.00	60.00
—With Michael Jackson on top half of cover, rats on the bottom half					
M 767	Music and Me	1973	3.75	7.50	15.00
M6-825S	Forever, Michael	1975	3.00	6.00	12.00
M6-851S	The Best of Michael Jackson	1975	3.00	6.00	12.00
M8-956	One Day in Your Life	1981	2.50	5.00	10.00
6099 ML	Michael Jackson and The Jackson 5 — 14 Greatest Hits	1984	2.50	5.00	10.00
—Picture disc packaged with one glove					
6101 ML	Farewell My Summer Love 1984	1984	2.50	5.00	10.00

JACKSON, MICHAEL, AND PAUL MCCARTNEY

Also see each artist's individual listings.

12-Inch Singles

COLUMBIA

Number	Title (A Side/B Side)	Yr	VG	VG+	NM
04169	Say Say Say//(Instrumental)/Ode to a Koala Bear	1983	2.50	5.00	10.00

45s

COLUMBIA

Number	Title (A Side/B Side)	Yr	VG	VG+	NM
04168	Say, Say, Say/Ode to a Koala Bear	1983	—	2.00	4.00
—B-side by Paul McCartney					
04168 [PS]	Say, Say, Say/Ode to a Koala Bear	1983	—	2.00	4.00

EPIC

Number	Title (A Side/B Side)	Yr	VG	VG+	NM
03288	The Girl Is Mine/Can't Get Outta the Rain	1982	—	2.50	5.00
—B-side by Michael Jackson					
03288 [PS]	The Girl Is Mine/Can't Get Outta the Rain	1982	—	2.50	5.00
03372	The Girl Is Mine	1982	2.50	5.00	10.00
—Michael Jackson/Paul McCartney; one-sided budget release					

JACKSON, MILLIE

12-Inch Singles

JIVE

Number	Title (A Side/B Side)	Yr	VG	VG+	NM
1015	Hot! Wild! Unrestricted! Crazy Love (4 versions)	1986	—	3.00	6.00
1022	Love Is a Dangerous Game/(Instrumental)	1986	—	3.00	6.00
1057	It's a Thang (4 versions)	1987	—	3.00	6.00
1109	Something You Can Feel (3 versions)	1988	—	3.00	6.00
1194	You Knocked the Love (Right Out of My Heart) (3 versions)/Let Me Show You	1989	—	3.00	6.00
1247	Will You Love Me Tomorrow (same on both sides)	1989	—	3.00	6.00

SPRING

Number	Title (A Side/B Side)	Yr	VG	VG+	NM
028 [DJ]	All the Way Lover/You Created a Monster	1977	2.50	5.00	10.00
099	We Got to Hit It Off (same on both sides)	1979	2.50	5.00	10.00
195	Mess on Your Hands-Finger Rap (censored & uncensored)	1982	3.00	6.00	12.00

45s

JIVE

Number	Title (A Side/B Side)	Yr	VG	VG+	NM
1007-7-J	Hot! Wild! Unrestricted! Crazy Love (long & short version)	1986	—	—	3.00
1007-7-J [PS]	Hot! Wild! Unrestricted! Crazy Love (long & short version)	1986	—	—	3.00
1009-7-J	Love Is a Dangerous Game/(Instrumental)	1986	—	—	3.00
1009-7-J [PS]	Love Is a Dangerous Game/(Instrumental)	1986	—	—	3.00
1040-7-J	An Imitation of Love/Mind Over Matter	1987	—	—	3.00
1040-7-J [PS]	An Imitation of Love/Mind Over Matter	1987	—	—	3.00
1056-7-J	It's a Thang/(Instrumental)	1987	—	—	3.00
1108-7-J	The Tide Is Turning/Cover Me (Wall to Wall)	1988	—	—	3.00
1111-7-J	Something You Can Feel/(Instrumental)	1988	—	—	3.00
1111-7-J [PS]	Something You Can Feel/(Instrumental)	1988	—	—	3.00
1246-7-J	Will You Love Me Tomorrow/Muffle That Fart	1989	—	2.00	4.00

MGM

Number	Title (A Side/B Side)	Yr	VG	VG+	NM
14050	Little Bit of Something/My Heart Took a Licking	1969	2.00	4.00	8.00

SPRING

Number	Title (A Side/B Side)	Yr	VG	VG+	NM
119	A Child of God (It's Hard to Believe)/You're the Joy of My Life	1971	—	2.50	5.00
123	Ask Me What You Want/I Just Can't Stand It	1972	—	2.50	5.00
127	My Man, a Sweet Man/I Gotta Get Away	1972	—	2.50	5.00
131	I Miss You Baby/I Ain't Giving Up	1972	—	2.50	5.00
134	Breakaway/Strange Things	1973	—	2.50	5.00
139	Hurts So Good/Love Doctor	1973	—	2.50	5.00
144	I Got to Try It One Time/Get Your Love Right	1974	—	2.50	5.00
147	How Do You Feel the Morning After/In the Wash	1974	—	2.50	5.00
155	The Rap/If Loving You Is Wrong I Don't Want to Be Right	1974	—	2.50	5.00
157	I'm Through Trying to Prove My Love to You/All I Want Is a Fighting Chance	1975	—	2.50	5.00
161	Leftovers/Loving Arms	1975	—	2.50	5.00
164	Bad Risk/There You Are	1976	—	2.50	5.00
167	Feel Like Making Love/I'm in Love Again	1976	—	2.50	5.00
170	I Can't Say Goodbye/Help Me Finish My Song	1977	—	2.50	5.00
173	A Love of Your Own/Live My Love for You	1977	—	2.50	5.00
175	If You're Not Back in Love by Monday/A Taste of Outside Love	1977	—	2.50	5.00
179	All the Way Lover/Cheatin' Is	1978	—	2.50	5.00
185	Sweet Music Man/Go Out and Get Some	1978	—	2.50	5.00
189	Keep the Home Fire Burnin'/Logs and Thangs	1978	—	2.50	5.00
192	Never Change Lovers in the Middle of the Night/Seeing You Again	1979	—	2.50	5.00
197	A Moment's Pleasure/Once You've Had It	1979	—	2.50	5.00
3002	We Got to Hit It Off/What Went Wrong Last Night	1979	—	2.00	4.00
3007	Didn't I Blow Your Mind/Be a Sweetheart	1980	—	2.00	4.00
3011	Despair/Wish That I Could Have Hurt That Way Again	1980	—	2.00	4.00
3013	This Is It (Part 1)/This Is It (Part 2)	1980	—	2.00	4.00
3017	I Had to Say It/It's Going to Take Some Time This Time	1981	—	2.00	4.00
3019	I Can't Stop Loving You/Loving You	1981	—	2.00	4.00
3021	Anybody That Don't Like Millie Jackson/Rose Colored Glasses	1981	—	2.50	5.00
3024	Passion/Lovers and Girlfriends	1982	—	2.00	4.00
3028	Special Occasion/Blues Don't Get Tired of Me	1982	—	2.00	4.00
3034	I Feel Like Walking in the Rain/(B-side unknown)	1983	—	2.00	4.00
3036	E.S.P./(B-side unknown)	1984	—	2.00	4.00
3040	Sister in the System/(B-side unknown)	1984	—	2.00	4.00

Albums

JIVE

Number	Title (A Side/B Side)	Yr	VG	VG+	NM
1016-1-J	An Imitation of Love	1986	2.00	4.00	8.00
1103-1-J	The Tide Is Turning	1988	2.00	4.00	8.00
1186-1-J	Back to the Shit	1989	2.50	5.00	10.00
1447-1-J	Young Man, Older Woman	1991	3.00	6.00	12.00

SPRING

Number	Title (A Side/B Side)	Yr	VG	VG+	NM
SPR-5703	Millie Jackson	1972	3.00	6.00	12.00
SPR-5706	It Hurts So Good	1973	3.00	6.00	12.00
SPR-6701	Millie	1974	2.50	5.00	10.00
SPR-6703	Caught Up	1974	2.50	5.00	10.00
SPR-6708	Still Caught Up	1975	2.50	5.00	10.00
SP-6712	Lovingly Yours	1976	2.50	5.00	10.00
SP-6715	Feelin' Bitchy	1977	2.50	5.00	10.00
SP-1-6719	Get It Out'cha System	1978	2.50	5.00	10.00
SP-1-6722	A Moment's Pleasure	1979	2.50	5.00	10.00
SP-2-6725 [(2)]	Live & Uncensored	1979	3.00	6.00	12.00
SP-1-6727	For Men Only	1980	2.50	5.00	10.00
SP-1-6730	I Had to Say It	1981	2.50	5.00	10.00
SP-1-6735	Live and Outrageous (Rated XXX)	1982	2.50	5.00	10.00
SP-1-6737	Hard Times	1983	2.50	5.00	10.00

JACKSON, MILLIE, AND ISAAC HAYES

45s

POLYDOR

Number	Title (A Side/B Side)	Yr	VG	VG+	NM
2036	Do You Wanna Make Love/I Changed My Mind	1979	—	2.00	4.00
2063	You Never Cross My Mind/Feels Like the First Time	1980	—	2.00	4.00

Albums

POLYDOR

Number	Title (A Side/B Side)	Yr	VG	VG+	NM
PD-1-6229	Royal Rappin's	1979	2.50	5.00	10.00

JACKSON, RUDY

45s

IMPERIAL

Number	Title (A Side/B Side)	Yr	VG	VG+	NM
5425	Teasing Me/Give Me Your Hand	1957	10.00	20.00	40.00
5945	Go On Lover, Go On/Who Do You Think You Are	1963	3.00	6.00	12.00

R & B

Number	Title (A Side/B Side)	Yr	VG	VG+	NM
1310	I'm Crying/Enfold Me	1955	20.00	40.00	80.00

JACKSON, SHIRLEY

45s

METRO

Number	Title (A Side/B Side)	Yr	VG	VG+	NM
20031	The Wedding/Wait for Me	1960	3.00	6.00	12.00

JACKSON, TONY, AND THE VIBRATIONS

45s

KAPP

Number	Title (A Side/B Side)	Yr	VG	VG+	NM
639	This Little Girl of Mine/You Beat Me to the Punch	1965	3.75	7.50	15.00

RED BIRD

Number	Title (A Side/B Side)	Yr	VG	VG+	NM
10-038	That's What I Want/Stage Door	1965	3.75	7.50	15.00

JACKSON, WALTER

45s

BRUNSWICK

Number	Title (A Side/B Side)	Yr	VG	VG+	NM
55502	It Doesn't Take Much/Let Me Come Back	1973	—	3.00	6.00

CHI-SOUND

Number	Title (A Side/B Side)	Yr	VG	VG+	NM
XW908	Feelings/Words (Are Impossible)	1976	—	2.50	5.00
XW964	Baby, I Love Your Way/What Would You Do	1977	—	2.50	5.00
XW1044	It's All Over/Gonna Find Me an Angel	1977	—	2.50	5.00

Number	Title (A Side/B Side)	Yr	VG	VG+	NM
XW1140	If I Had My Way/We Could Fly	1978	—	2.50	5.00
XW1216	Manhattan Skyline/I Won't Remember Ever Loving You	1978	—	2.50	5.00
2426	Magic Man/Golden Rays	1979	—	2.00	4.00
COLUMBIA					
02037	Tell Me Where It Hurts/When I See You	1981	—	2.00	4.00
02294	What If I Walked Out on You/Come to Me	1981	—	2.00	4.00
42528	This World of Mine/I Don't Want to Suffer	1962	6.25	12.50	25.00
42659	Starting Tomorrow/Then, Only Then	1963	5.00	10.00	20.00
42823	Opportunity/It Will Be the Last Time	1963	5.00	10.00	20.00
COTILLION					
44053	Anyway That You Want Me/Life Has Its Ups and Downs	1969	2.00	4.00	8.00
EPIC					
10408	Ad Lib/No Butterflies	1968	2.00	4.00	8.00
KELLI-ARTS					
1006	If I Had a Chance/(B-side unknown)	1982	—	2.50	5.00
OKEH					
7189	That's What Mama Say/What Would You Do	1964	3.00	6.00	12.00
7204	It's All Over/Lee Cross	1964	2.50	5.00	10.00
7215	Suddenly I'm All Alone/Special Love	1965	2.50	5.00	10.00
7219	Welcome Home/Blowin' in the Wind	1965	2.50	5.00	10.00
7229	I'll Keep On Trying/Where Have All the Flowers Gone	1965	2.50	5.00	10.00
7236	Funny (Not Much)/One Heart Lonely	1965	2.50	5.00	10.00
7247	It's an Uphill Climb to the Bottom/Tear for Tear	1966	2.00	4.00	8.00
7247 [PS]	It's an Uphill Climb to the Bottom/Tear for Tear	1966	5.00	10.00	20.00
7256	After You There Can Be Nothing/My Funny Valentine	1966	2.00	4.00	8.00
7260	A Corner in the Sun/Not You	1966	2.00	4.00	8.00
7272	Speak Her Name/They Don't Give Medals (To Yesterday's Heroes)	1967	2.00	4.00	8.00
7272 [PS]	Speak Her Name/They Don't Give Medals (To Yesterday's Heroes)	1967	5.00	10.00	20.00
7285	Deep in the Heart of Harlem/My One Chance to Make It	1967	2.00	4.00	8.00
7285 [PS]	Deep in the Heart of Harlem/My One Chance to Make It	1967	5.00	10.00	20.00
7295	Cold, Cold Winter/My Ship Is Comin' In	1967	2.00	4.00	8.00
7305	Everything/Road to Ruin	1968	2.00	4.00	8.00
U.S.A.					
104	Fool for You/Walls That Separate	196?	3.00	6.00	12.00

Albums

Number	Title	Yr	VG	VG+	NM
CHI-SOUND					
CS-LA656-G	Feeling Good	1976	3.00	6.00	12.00
CS-LA733-G	I Want to Come Back As A Song	1977	3.00	6.00	12.00
CS-LA844-G	Good to See You	1978	3.00	6.00	12.00
COLUMBIA					
FC 37132	Tell Me Where It Hurts	1981	2.50	5.00	10.00
EPIC					
E 34657	Greatest Hits	1977	2.50	5.00	10.00
PE 40434	Greatest Hits	1987	2.00	4.00	8.00
OKEH					
OKM 12107 [M]	It's All Over	1965	6.25	12.50	25.00
OKM 12108 [M]	Welcome Home	1966	6.25	12.50	25.00
OKM 12120 [M]	Speak Her Name	1967	6.25	12.50	25.00
OKS 14107 [S]	It's All Over	1965	7.50	15.00	30.00
OKS 14108 [S]	Welcome Home	1966	7.50	15.00	30.00
OKS 14120 [S]	Speak Her Name	1967	7.50	15.00	30.00
OKS 14128	Walter Jackson's Greatest Hits	1969	3.75	7.50	15.00

JACKSON, WANDA

45s

Number	Title (A Side/B Side)	Yr	VG	VG+	NM
ABC					
12116	Take a Look/I Can't Stand to Hear You Say Goodbye	1975	—	2.50	5.00
CAPITOL					
2021	A Girl Don't Have to Drink to Have Fun/My Days Are Darker Than Your Nights	1967	2.50	5.00	10.00
2085	By the Time You Get to Phoenix/Wishing Well	1968	2.00	4.00	8.00
2151	My Baby Walked Right Out on Me/No Place to Go But Home	1968	2.00	4.00	8.00
2245	Little Boy Soldier/I Talk a Pretty Story	1968	2.00	4.00	8.00
2315	I Wish I Was Your Friend/Poor Old Me	1968	2.00	4.00	8.00
2379	If I Had a Hammer/The Pain of It All	1969	2.00	4.00	8.00
2472	Your Tender Love/As the Day Wears On	1969	2.00	4.00	8.00
2524	Everything's Leaving/You Cheated Me	1969	2.00	4.00	8.00
2614	My Big Iron Skillet/The Hunter	1969	2.00	4.00	8.00
2693	Two Separate Bar Stools/Two Wrongs Don't Make a Right	1969	2.00	4.00	8.00
2761	A Woman Lives for Love/What Have We Done	1970	—	3.00	6.00
2872	Who Shot John/Stop the World	1970	—	3.00	6.00
2986	Fancy Satin Pillows/Why Don't We Love Like That Anymore	1970	—	3.00	6.00
3070	People Gotta Be Loving/Glory Hallelujah	1971	—	3.00	6.00
3143	Back Then/I'm Gonna Walk Out of Your Life	1971	—	3.00	6.00
3218	I Already Know (What I'm Gettin' for My Birthday)/The Man You Could Have Been	1971	—	3.00	6.00
3293	I'll Be Whatever You Say/The More You See Me Less	1972	—	3.00	6.00
3385	I Wouldn't Want You Any Other Way/Song of the Wind	1972	—	3.00	6.00
F3485	I Gotta Know/Half As Good a Girl	1956	10.00	20.00	40.00
3498	Roll with the Tide/Tennessee Women's Prison	1972	—	3.00	6.00
F3575	The Hot Dog That Made Him Mad/Silver Threads and Golden Needles	1956	10.00	20.00	40.00
3599	I Don't Know How to Tell Him/Your Memory Comes and Gets Me	1973	—	3.00	6.00
F3637	Cryin' Through the Night/Baby Loves Him	1957	12.50	25.00	50.00
F3683	Don'a Wana/Let Me Explain	1957	7.50	15.00	30.00
F3764	Cool Love/Did You Miss Me	1957	7.50	15.00	30.00
F3843	Fujiyama Mama/No Wedding Bells for Joe	1957	7.50	15.00	30.00
F3941	Just a Queen for a Day/Honey Bop	1958	7.50	15.00	30.00
F4026	(Every Time They Play) Our Song/Mean, Mean Man	1958	7.50	15.00	30.00
F4081	Sinful Heart/Rock Your Baby	1958	7.50	15.00	30.00
F4142	Savin' My Love/I Wanna Waltz	1959	6.25	12.50	25.00
F4207	A Date with Jerry/You're the One for Me	1959	6.25	12.50	25.00
F4286	Reaching/I'd Rather Have You	1959	6.25	12.50	25.00
4354	My Destiny/Please Call Today	1960	6.25	12.50	25.00
4397	Let's Have a Party/Cool Love	1960	10.00	20.00	40.00
4469	Mean, Mean Man/Happy, Happy Birthday	1960	6.25	12.50	25.00
4520	Riot in Cell Black #9/Little Charm Bracelet	1961	6.25	12.50	25.00
4553	Right or Wrong/Funnel of Love	1961	6.25	12.50	25.00
4635	In the Middle of a Heartache/I'd Be Ashamed	1961	6.25	12.50	25.00
4681	A Little Bitty Tear/I Don't Wanta Go	1962	5.00	10.00	20.00
4723	If I Cried Every Time You Hurt Me/Let My Love Walk In	1962	5.00	10.00	20.00
4723 [PS]	If I Cried Every Time You Hurt Me/Let My Love Walk In	1962	7.50	15.00	30.00
4785	I Misunderstood/Between the Window and the Phone	1962	3.75	7.50	15.00
4833	The Greatest Actor/You Bug Me Bad	1962	3.75	7.50	15.00
4884	Whirlpool/One Teardrop at a Time	1962	3.75	7.50	15.00
4917	But I Was Lying/Sympathy	1963	3.75	7.50	15.00
4973	This Should Go On Forever/We Haven't a Moment to Lose	1963	3.75	7.50	15.00
5015	Memory Mountain/Let Me Talk to You	1963	3.75	7.50	15.00
5072	Slippin'/Just for You	1963	3.75	7.50	15.00
5142	The Violet and a Rose/To Tell You the Truth	1964	3.00	6.00	12.00
5228	Leave My Baby Alone/I'm Mad at Me	1964	3.00	6.00	12.00
5287	Candy Man/Weary Blues From Waitin'	1964	3.00	6.00	12.00
5364	My Baby's Gone/If I Were You	1965	3.00	6.00	12.00
5433	Have I Grown Used to Missing You/Take Me Home	1965	3.00	6.00	12.00
5491	My First Day Without You/Send Me No Roses	1965	3.00	6.00	12.00
5559	The Box It Came In/Look Out Heart	1965	3.00	6.00	12.00
5645	Because It's You/Long As I Have You	1966	2.50	5.00	10.00
5712	This Gun Don't Care/I Wonder If She Knows	1966	2.50	5.00	10.00
5789	Tears Will Be the Chaser for Your Wine/Reckless Love Affair	1967	2.50	5.00	10.00
5863	Both Sides of the Line/Famous Last Words	1967	2.50	5.00	10.00
5960	My Heart Gets All the Breaks/You'll Always Have My Love	1967	2.50	5.00	10.00
DECCA					
29140	You Can't Have My Love/Lovin' Country Style	1954	15.00	30.00	60.00
—With Billy Gray					
29253	The Right to Love/If You Knew What I Know	1954	15.00	30.00	60.00
29267	If You Don't, Somebody Else Will/You'd Be the First One to Know	1954	12.50	25.00	50.00
—With Billy Gray					
29514	Tears at the Grand Ole Opry/Nobody's Darlin' But Mine	1955	12.50	25.00	50.00
29677	Don't Do the Things He'd Do/It's the Same World	1955	7.50	15.00	30.00
29803	Wasted/I Cried Again	1956	12.50	25.00	50.00
30153	You Won't Forget (About Me)/A Heart You Could Have Had	1956	7.50	15.00	30.00
JIN					
300	Lonely Days, Lonely Nights/My Memories	197?	—	2.50	5.00
MYRRH					
122	When It's Time to Fall in Love Again/Say "I Do"	1973	—	2.50	5.00
126	Come On Home (To This Lonely Heart)/It's a Long, Long Time to Cry	1973	—	2.50	5.00
143	Jesus Put a Yodel in My Soul/(B-side unknown)	1974	—	2.50	5.00
152	Where Do I Put His Memory/Take a Look	1975	—	2.50	5.00

Albums

Number	Title	Yr	VG	VG+	NM
CAPITOL					
ST-129	The Many Moods of Wanda Jackson	1969	3.75	7.50	15.00
ST-238	The Happy Side of Wanda Jackson	1969	3.75	7.50	15.00
ST-345	Wanda Jackson In Person	1970	3.75	7.50	15.00
ST-434	Wanda Jackson Country!	1970	3.75	7.50	15.00
ST-554	A Woman Lives for Love	1970	3.75	7.50	15.00
ST-669	I've Gotta Sing!	1971	3.75	7.50	15.00
T 1041 [M]	Wanda Jackson	1958	75.00	150.00	300.00
—Black colorband label, Capitol logo at left					
T 1041 [M]	Wanda Jackson	1962	25.00	50.00	100.00
—Black colorband label, Capitol logo at top					
T 1384 [M]	Rockin' with Wanda	1960	100.00	200.00	400.00
—Black colorband label, Capitol logo at left					
T 1384 [M]	Rockin' with Wanda	1962	62.50	125.00	250.00
—Gold "Star Line" label					
T 1384 [M]	Rockin' with Wanda	1963	37.50	75.00	150.00
—Black "Star Line" label					
ST 1511 [S]	There's a Party Goin' On	1961	100.00	200.00	400.00
—Black colorband label, Capitol logo at left					
T 1511 [M]	There's a Party Goin' On	1961	62.50	125.00	250.00
—Black colorband label, Capitol logo at left					
ST 1596 [S]	Right or Wrong	1961	12.50	25.00	50.00
—Black colorband label, Capitol logo at left					
ST 1596 [S]	Right or Wrong	1962	6.25	12.50	25.00
—Black colorband label, Capitol logo at top					
T 1596 [M]	Right or Wrong	1961	10.00	20.00	40.00
—Black colorband label, Capitol logo at left					
T 1596 [M]	Right or Wrong	1962	5.00	10.00	20.00
—Black colorband label, Capitol logo at top					
ST 1776 [S]	Wonderful Wanda	1962	7.50	15.00	30.00
T 1776 [M]	Wonderful Wanda	1962	6.25	12.50	25.00
ST 1911 [S]	Love Me Forever	1963	7.50	15.00	30.00
T 1911 [M]	Love Me Forever	1963	6.25	12.50	25.00
ST 2030 [S]	Two Sides of Wanda	1964	7.50	15.00	30.00
T 2030 [M]	Two Sides of Wanda	1964	6.25	12.50	25.00
ST 2306 [S]	Blues in My Heart	1965	7.50	15.00	30.00
T 2306 [M]	Blues in My Heart	1965	6.25	12.50	25.00
ST 2438 [S]	Wanda Jackson Sings Country Songs	1965	7.50	15.00	30.00
T 2438 [M]	Wanda Jackson Sings Country Songs	1965	6.25	12.50	25.00
ST 2606 [S]	Wanda Jackson Salutes the Country Music Hall of Fame	1966	5.00	10.00	20.00

Number	Title (A Side/B Side)	Yr	VG	VG+	NM
T 2606 [M]	Wanda Jackson Salutes the Country Music Hall of Fame	1966	3.75	7.50	15.00
ST 2704 [S]	Reckless Love Affair	1967	3.75	7.50	15.00
T 2704 [M]	Reckless Love Affair	1967	5.00	10.00	20.00
ST 2812 [S]	You'll Always Have My Love	1967	3.75	7.50	15.00
T 2812 [M]	You'll Always Have My Love	1967	5.00	10.00	20.00
ST 2883	The Best of Wanda Jackson	1968	3.75	7.50	15.00
ST 2976	Cream of the Crop	1968	3.75	7.50	15.00
ST-11023	Praise the Lord	1972	3.75	7.50	15.00
ST-11096	I Wouldn't Want You Any Other Way	1972	3.75	7.50	15.00
ST-11161	Country Keepsakes	1973	3.75	7.50	15.00
DECCA					
DL 4224 [M]	Lovin' Country Style	1962	12.50	25.00	50.00
HILLTOP					
6058	Please Help Me I'm Falling	197?	2.50	5.00	10.00
6074	Leave My Baby Alone	197?	3.00	6.00	12.00
6116	We'll Sing in the Sunshine	197?	3.00	6.00	12.00
6123	Phoenix	197?	2.50	5.00	10.00
6182	Tears at the Grand Ole Opry	197?	2.50	5.00	10.00
MYRRH					
6533	Now I Have Everything	197?	3.00	6.00	12.00
6556	Make Me Like a Child Again	197?	3.00	6.00	12.00
PICKWICK					
PTP-2053 [(2)]	Wanda Jackson	197?	3.00	6.00	12.00
VARRICK					
VR-025	Rock 'n' Roll Away Your Blues	1987	3.00	6.00	12.00
WORD					
WST-8614	Country Gospel	197?	3.00	6.00	12.00
WST-8781	Closer to Jesus	197?	3.00	6.00	12.00

JACKSON FIVE, THE

See THE JACKSONS.

JACKSON HEIGHTS

45s

Number	Title (A Side/B Side)	Yr	VG	VG+	NM
VERVE					
10706	Long Time Dying/Maureen	1973	2.00	4.00	8.00

Albums

Number	Title (A Side/B Side)	Yr	VG	VG+	NM
MERCURY					
SR-61331	King Progress	1970	6.25	12.00	25.00
VERVE					
V6-5089	Jackson Heights	1973	5.00	10.00	20.00

JACKSONS, THE

Includes records as "The Jackson Five." Also see JACKIE JACKSON; JERMAINE JACKSON; MICHAEL JACKSON.

12-Inch Singles

Number	Title (A Side/B Side)	Yr	VG	VG+	NM
EPIC					
05022	State of Shock/(Instrumental)	1984	2.00	4.00	8.00
50721	Shake Your Body (Down to the Ground)/That's What You Get (For Being Polite)	1978	5.00	10.00	20.00

45s

Number	Title (A Side/B Side)	Yr	VG	VG+	NM
DYNAMO					
146	You Don't Have to Be Over Twenty-One to Fall in Love/Some Girls Want Me for Their Love	1971	10.00	20.00	40.00
EPIC					
01032	Can You Feel It/Everybody	1981	—	2.00	4.00
02132	Walk Right Now/Your Ways	1981	—	2.00	4.00
02157	Lovely One/She's Out of My Life	1981	—	—	3.00
—Reissue; B-side by Michael Jackson					
02720	The Things I Do for You/Working Day and Night	1982	—	2.00	4.00
04503	State of Shock/Your Ways	1984	—	2.00	4.00
—A-side: With Mick Jagger					
04503 [PS]	State of Shock/Your Ways	1984	—	2.00	4.00
04575	Torture/(Instrumental)	1984	—	2.00	4.00
04575 [PS]	Torture/(Instrumental)	1984	—	2.00	4.00
04673	Body/(Instrumental)	1984	—	2.00	4.00
04673 [PS]	Body/(Instrumental)	1984	—	2.00	4.00
50595	Blame It on the Boogie/Ease On Down the Road	1978	—	2.00	4.00
50656	Shake Your Body (Down to the Ground)/That's What You Get (For Being Polite)	1979	—	2.50	5.00
—Original issue has orange label					
50656	Shake Your Body (Down to the Ground)/That's What You Get (For Being Polite)	1979	—	2.00	4.00
—Second issue has dark blue label					
50938	Lovely One/Bless His Soul	1980	—	2.00	4.00
50959	Heartbreak Hotel/The Things I Do for You	1980	—	2.00	4.00
68688	Nothing (That Compares 2 U)/Alright with Me	1989	—	—	3.00
69022	2300 Jackson Street/When I Look at You	1989	—	—	3.00
EPIC/PHILA. INT'L.					
50289	Enjoy Yourself/Style of Life	1976	—	2.50	5.00
50350	Show You the Way to Go/Blues Away	1977	—	2.50	5.00
50454	Goin' Places/Do What You Wanna	1977	—	2.50	5.00
50496	Find Me a Girl/Different Kind of Lady	1977	—	2.50	5.00
MCA					
53032	Time Out for the Burglar/News at Eleven	1987	—	—	3.00
—B-side by the Distants					
53032 [PS]	Time Out for the Burglar/News at Eleven	1987	—	—	3.00
MOTOWN					
1157	I Want You Back/Who's Lovin' You	1969	2.00	4.00	8.00
1163	ABC/The Young Folks	1970	2.00	4.00	8.00
1166	The Love You Save/I Found That Girl	1970	2.00	4.00	8.00
1166 [DJ]	I Found That Girl (same on both sides)	1970	5.00	10.00	20.00
—Red vinyl					
1166 [DJ]	The Love You Save	1970	7.50	15.00	30.00
—Blank back promo					
1171	I'll Be There/One More Chance	1970	2.00	4.00	8.00
1174	Santa Claus Is Coming to Town/Christmas Won't Be the Same This Year	1970	3.00	6.00	12.00
1177	Mama's Pearl/Darling Dear	1971	—	3.00	6.00
1177 [PS]	Mama's Pearl/Darling Dear	1971	3.75	7.50	15.00
1179	Never Can Say Goodbye/She's Good	1971	—	3.00	6.00
1186	Maybe Tomorrow/I Will Find a Way	1971	—	3.00	6.00
1194	Sugar Daddy/I'm So Happy	1971	—	3.00	6.00
1199	Little Bitty Pretty One/If I Had to Move a Mountain	1972	—	3.00	6.00
1205	Looking Through the Windows/Love Song	1972	—	3.00	6.00
1214	Corner of the Sky/To Know	1972	—	3.00	6.00
1224	Hallelujah Day/You Made Me What I Am	1973	—	3.00	6.00
1230	Boogie Man/Don't Let Your Baby Catch You	1973	—	—	—
—Unreleased					
1277	Get It Together/Touch	1973	—	3.00	6.00
1286	Dancing Machine/It's Too Late to Change the Time	1974	—	3.00	6.00
1308	Whatever You Got, I Want/I Can't Quit Your Love	1974	—	3.00	6.00
1310	I Am Love (Parts 1 & 2)/I Am Love (Part 2)	1975	—	3.00	6.00
1310	I Am Love (Part 1)/I Am Love (Part 2)	1975	2.00	4.00	8.00
1356	Forever Came Today/All I Do Is Think of You	1975	—	3.00	6.00
1365	Body Language/Call of the Wild	1975	—	—	—
—Unreleased					
2193	Who's Lovin' You/In the Still of the Night (I'll Remember)	1992	—	2.00	4.00
—B-side by Boyz II Men					
STEELTOWN					
681	Big Boy/You've Changed	1968	25.00	50.00	100.00
684	You Don't Have to Be Over Twenty-One to Fall in Love/Some Girls Want Me for Their Love	1968	25.00	50.00	100.00
689	Let Me Carry Your School Books/I Never Had a Girl	1969	20.00	40.00	80.00
—By "The Ripples and Waves plus Michael"					

Albums

Number	Title (A Side/B Side)	Yr	VG	VG+	NM
EPIC					
PE 34229	The Jacksons	1976	2.50	5.00	10.00
—Orange label					
PE 34229	The Jacksons	198?	—	3.00	6.00
—Budget-line reissue with bar code and dark blue label					
JE 34835	Goin' Places	1977	2.50	5.00	10.00
—Orange label					
PE 34835	Goin' Places	198?	—	3.00	6.00
—Budget-line reissue					
JE 35552	Destiny	1978	2.50	5.00	10.00
—Orange label					
JE 35552	Destiny	1979	2.00	4.00	8.00
—Dark blue label					
FE 36424	Triumph	1980	2.00	4.00	8.00
KE2 37545 [(2)]	Jacksons Live	1981	3.00	6.00	12.00
QE 38946	Victory	1984	2.00	4.00	8.00
8E8 39576 [PD]	Victory	1984	3.75	7.50	15.00
OE 40911	2300 Jackson Street	1989	2.00	4.00	8.00
HE 46424	Triumph	1982	15.00	30.00	60.00
—Half-speed mastered edition					
MOTOWN					
M5-112V1	Motown Superstar Series, Vol. 12	1981	2.50	5.00	10.00
M5-129V1	Diana Ross Presents the Jackson Five	1981	2.00	4.00	8.00
M5-152V1	ABC	1981	2.00	4.00	8.00
M5-157V1	Third Album	1981	2.00	4.00	8.00
M5-201V1	Jackson 5 Greatest Hits	1981	2.00	4.00	8.00
MS 700	Diana Ross Presents the Jackson 5	1969	6.25	12.50	25.00
MS 709	ABC	1970	6.25	12.50	25.00
MS 713	Christmas Album	1970	6.25	12.50	25.00
MS 718	Third Album	1970	3.75	7.50	15.00
M-735	Maybe Tomorrow	1971	3.75	7.50	15.00
M-741	Jackson 5 Greatest Hits	1971	3.75	7.50	15.00
M-742	Goin' Back to Indiana	1971	3.75	7.50	15.00
M-750	Lookin' Through the Windows	1972	3.75	7.50	15.00
M-761	Skywriter	1973	3.00	6.00	12.00
M6-780	Dancing Machine	1974	3.00	6.00	12.00
M6-783	Get It Together	1973	3.00	6.00	12.00
M6-829	Moving Violation	1975	3.00	6.00	12.00
M6-865	Joyful Jukebox Music	1976	3.00	6.00	12.00
M7-868 [(3)]	Anthology	1976	5.00	10.00	20.00
37463 1294-1 [DJ]	Soulsation!	1995	5.00	10.00	20.00
—Vinyl is promo only; 4-song sampler from box set					
5228 ML	Maybe Tomorrow	1982	2.00	4.00	8.00
5250 ML	Christmas Album	1982	2.00	4.00	8.00
—Reissue of Motown 713					

JACOBI, LOU

Albums

Number	Title (A Side/B Side)	Yr	VG	VG+	NM
CAPITOL					
ST 2596 [S]	Al Tijuana and His Jewish Brass	1966	5.00	10.00	20.00
T 2596 [M]	Al Tijuana and His Jewish Brass	1966	3.75	7.50	15.00

JADE, FAINE

45s

Number	Title (A Side/B Side)	Yr	VG	VG+	NM
RSVP					
1130	Introspection/(B-side unknown)	1968	6.25	12.50	25.00

Albums

Number	Title (A Side/B Side)	Yr	VG	VG+	NM
RSVP					
8002	Introspection: A Faine Jade Recital	1968	100.00	200.00	400.00

JADE WARRIOR

45s

Number	Title (A Side/B Side)	Yr	VG	VG+	NM
VERTIGO					
106	We Have Reason to Believe/Barazinbar	1972	2.00	4.00	8.00
108	A Winter's Tale/The Demon Trucker	1972	2.00	4.00	8.00

Albums

Number	Title (A Side/B Side)	Yr	VG	VG+	NM
ANTILLES					
AN-7045	Floating World	198?	2.00	4.00	8.00
—Reissue of Island 9290					
AN-7048	Waves	198?	2.00	4.00	8.00
—Reissue of Island 9318					
AN-7056	Kites	198?	2.00	4.00	8.00
—Reissue of Island 9393					
AN-7068	Way of the Sun	1978	2.50	5.00	10.00

Number	Title (A Side/B Side)	Yr	VG	VG+	NM
ISLAND					
ILPS 9290	Floating World	1974	2.50	5.00	10.00
ILPS 9318	Waves	1975	2.50	5.00	10.00
ILPS 9393	Kites	1976	2.50	5.00	10.00
VERTIGO					
VEL-1007	Jade Warrior	1971	3.00	6.00	12.00
VEL-1009	Released	1972	3.00	6.00	12.00
VEL-1012	Last Autumn's Dream	1972	3.00	6.00	12.00

JADES, THE

Many different groups.

45s

Number	Title (A Side/B Side)	Yr	VG	VG+	NM
ADONA					
1445	Hey Senorita/(B-side unknown)	1962	7.50	15.00	30.00
CAPITOL					
2281	Ain't It Funny What Love Can Do/Baby I Need Your Love	1968	—	3.00	6.00
CHRISTY					
110	Oh Why/Big Beach Party	1959	125.00	250.00	500.00
111	Tell Me Pretty Baby/Applesauce	1959	62.50	125.00	250.00
113	Don't Be a Fool/Friday Night with My Baby	1959	125.00	250.00	500.00
114	Look for a Lie/Blue Memories	1959	375.00	750.00	1500.
DORE					
687	Hold Back the Dawn/When They Ask About You	1963	5.00	10.00	20.00
DOT					
15822	I'm Pretending/Beverly	1958	20.00	40.00	80.00
GAITY					
2-23-64	Surfin' Crow/Blue Black Hair	1964	45.00	90.00	180.00
IMPERIAL					
66383	Wheel of Fortune/Gotta Find Somebody to Love	1969	—	3.00	6.00
66425	L-O-V-E I Love You/Don't Give What's Mine Away	1969	—	3.00	6.00
LIBERTY					
56192	All's Quiet on West 23rd/Love of a Woman	1970	—	2.50	5.00
MGM					
13399	There's a Kinder Way to Say Goodbye/You're So Right for Me	1965	3.00	6.00	12.00
NAU VOO					
807	Walking All Alone/Hey Little Girl	1959	37.50	75.00	150.00
OXBORO					
2002	Surfin' Crow/Blue Black Hair	1964	30.00	60.00	120.00
2005	Little Marlene/Shake Baby Shake	1965	30.00	60.00	120.00
PORT					
70042	He's My Guy/There Will Come a Day	1964	6.25	12.50	25.00
TIME					
1002	Leave Her For Me/So Blue	1957	50.00	100.00	200.00
—Lou Reed is alleged to have been in this group, but he would have been 15 at the time.					
UNI					
55019	The Glide/Flower Power	1967	2.00	4.00	8.00
55032 [DJ]	Privilege (same on both sides)	1967	2.00	4.00	8.00
VERVE					
10385	For Just Another Day/I'm By Your Side (Baby)	1966	3.00	6.00	12.00

Albums

Number	Title (A Side/B Side)	Yr	VG	VG+	NM
JARRETT					
21517 [M]	Live at the Disco a-Go-Go	1965	30.00	60.00	120.00

JAGGED EDGE, THE

45s

Number	Title (A Side/B Side)	Yr	VG	VG+	NM
RCA VICTOR					
47-8880	Baby You Don't Know/Deep Inside	1966	2.50	5.00	10.00
TWIRL					
2024	How Many Times/Midnight to Six Man	1966	7.50	15.00	30.00

JAGGER, CHRIS

45s

Number	Title (A Side/B Side)	Yr	VG	VG+	NM
ASYLUM					
11028	Riddle Song/Handful of Dust	1973	—	3.00	6.00

Albums

Number	Title (A Side/B Side)	Yr	VG	VG+	NM
ASYLUM					
7E-1009	The Adventures of Valentine Vox the Ventriloquist	1974	3.00	6.00	12.00
SD 5069	Chris Jagger	1973	3.00	6.00	12.00

JAGGERZ, THE

45s

Number	Title (A Side/B Side)	Yr	VG	VG+	NM
GAMBLE					
218	(That's Why) Baby I Love You/Bring It Back	1968	2.00	4.00	8.00
226	Gotta Find My Way Back Home/Forever Together, Together Forever	1968	2.00	4.00	8.00
238	Together/Let Me Be the One	1969	2.00	4.00	8.00
4008	Higher and Higher/Ain't No Sun	1970	2.00	4.00	8.00
4012	Need Your Love/Here's a Heart	1970	2.00	4.00	8.00
KAMA SUTRA					
502	The Rapper/Born Poor	1970	2.00	4.00	8.00
509	I Call My Baby Candy/Will She Believe Me	1970	—	3.00	6.00
513	What a Bummer/Memories of the Traveller	1970	—	3.00	6.00
517	Let's Talk About Love/I'll Never Forget You	1971	—	2.50	5.00
583	Let's Talk About Love/Ain't That Sad	1973	—	2.00	4.00
WOODEN NICKEL					
PB-10194	Don't It Make You Want to Dance/2 Plus 2	1975	—	2.00	4.00

Albums

Number	Title (A Side/B Side)	Yr	VG	VG+	NM
GAMBLE					
GS-5006	Introducing the Jaggerz	1969	5.00	10.00	20.00
KAMA SUTRA					
KSBS-2017	We Went to Different Schools Together	1970	3.75	7.50	15.00
WOODEN NICKEL					
BWL1-0772	Come Again	1975	3.00	6.00	12.00

JAGUARS, THE (1)

45s

Number	Title (A Side/B Side)	Yr	VG	VG+	NM
AARDELL					
0003	Rock It Davy, Rock It/I Wanted You	1955	12.50	25.00	50.00
0006	Be My Sweetie/Why Don't You Believe Me	1956	12.50	25.00	50.00
0011	The Way You Look Tonight/Moonlight and You	1956	62.50	125.00	250.00
—Black vinyl					
0011	The Way You Look Tonight/Moonlight and You	1956	150.00	300.00	600.00
—Red vinyl					
BARONET					
1	The Way You Look Tonight/Baby, Baby, Baby	1962	6.25	12.50	25.00
CLASSIC ARTISTS					
117	Happy Holiday/More Than Enough for Me	1989	—	3.00	6.00
—B-side by Johnny Staton and the Feathers					
136	Merry Christmas, Darling/Lost and Found	1990	—	3.00	6.00
ORIGINAL SOUND					
6	Thinking of You/Look Into My Eyes	1959	20.00	40.00	80.00
20	Thinking of You/Look Into My Eyes	1962	10.00	20.00	40.00
59	The Way You Look Tonight/Baby, Baby, Baby	1966	5.00	10.00	20.00
R-DELL					
11	The Way You Look Tonight/Baby, Baby, Baby	1956	12.50	25.00	50.00
16	I Love You Baby/Baby, Baby, Baby	1957	30.00	60.00	120.00
45	Rock It Davy, Rock It/I Wanted You	1958	10.00	20.00	40.00
107	Rock It Davy, Rock It/The Big Bear	1958	10.00	20.00	40.00
117	Girl of My Dreams/Don't Go Home	1960	15.00	30.00	60.00

JAGUARS, THE (2)

45s

Number	Title (A Side/B Side)	Yr	VG	VG+	NM
DOT					
16723	Dead Sea/Supersonic	1965	2.50	5.00	10.00
16931	The Gorilla/He'll Turn Away	1966	2.50	5.00	10.00

JAGUARS, THE (3)

45s

Number	Title (A Side/B Side)	Yr	VG	VG+	NM
EPIC					
9325	Drive-In/Exit 6	1959	5.00	10.00	20.00

JAGUARS, THE (4)

45s

Number	Title (A Side/B Side)	Yr	VG	VG+	NM
FARO					
618	Where Lovers Go/Discover a Lover	1965	3.00	6.00	12.00

JAGUARS, THE (U)

Some of these could be the above groups.

45s

Number	Title (A Side/B Side)	Yr	VG	VG+	NM
EBB					
129	Hold Me Tight/Piccadilly	1958	25.00	50.00	100.00
RENDEZVOUS					
159	Fine, Fine, Fine/It Finally Happened	1961	5.00	10.00	20.00
216	Fine, Fine, Fine/It Finally Happened	1963	3.00	6.00	12.00
SKOOP					
1067	It's Gonna Be Alright/(B-side unknown)	1966	6.25	12.50	25.00
SPAY					
121	Rendezvous/(B-side unknown)	196?	15.00	30.00	60.00

JAIM

Albums

Number	Title (A Side/B Side)	Yr	VG	VG+	NM
ETHEREAL					
1001	Prophecy Fulfilled	1970	12.50	25.00	50.00

JAMAL, AHMAD

45s

Number	Title (A Side/B Side)	Yr	VG	VG+	NM
20TH CENTURY					
2026	Peace at Last/The World Is a Ghetto	1973	—	2.50	5.00
2053	M*A*S*H Theme/Keep On Trucking	1973	2.00	4.00	8.00
2260	Pablo Sierra/(B-side unknown)	1975	—	2.50	5.00
2448	Don't Ask My Neighbors/Chaser	1980	—	2.50	5.00
ARGO					
5294	But Not for Me/Music, Music, Music	1958	2.50	5.00	10.00
5306	Poinciana/Soft Winds	1958	2.50	5.00	10.00
5317	Secret Love/Taking a Chance on Love	1958	2.50	5.00	10.00
5337	Tangerine/Seleritus	1959	2.50	5.00	10.00
5354	Should I/I Like to Recognize the Tune	1959	2.50	5.00	10.00
5370	Billy Boy/Poor Butterfly	1960	2.50	5.00	10.00
5379	It's a Wonderful World/Valentina	1960	2.50	5.00	10.00
5397	The Breeze and I/We Kiss in a Shadow	1961	2.00	4.00	8.00
5416	All of You/You're Blase	1962	2.00	4.00	8.00
5419	April in Paris/Like Someone in Love	1962	2.00	4.00	8.00
5429	Night Mist Blues/We Live in Two Different Worlds	1962	2.00	4.00	8.00
5434	Haitian Market Place/Montevidas Has Macanudo	1963	2.00	4.00	8.00
5441	Bossa Nova Do Marilia (Part 1)/Bossa Nova Do Marilia (Part 2)	1963	2.00	4.00	8.00
5487	Naked City Theme/Haitian Market Place	1965	2.00	4.00	8.00
5504	Feeling Good/A Wonderful Day Like Today	1965	2.00	4.00	8.00
5508	Who Can I Turn To/Look at the Face	1965	2.00	4.00	8.00
5512	This Terrible Planet/Dance to the Lady	1965	2.00	4.00	8.00
5513	Extensions (Part 1)/Extensions (Part 2)	1965	2.00	4.00	8.00
ATLANTIC					
89476 [DJ]	It's That Time Of Year Again (same on both sides)	1985	—	2.50	5.00
—With Larry Goshorn; may be promo only					
CADET					
5527	Love Theme from "The Sandpiper"/This Could Be the Start of Something Big	1966	—	3.00	6.00
5569	Nature Boy/Little Ditty	1967	—	3.00	6.00
5581	Minor Moods/Beautiful Friendship	1967	—	3.00	6.00
5605	Wild Is the Wind/I Wish I Knew (How It Would Feel to Be Free)	1968	—	3.00	6.00
OKEH					
6855	The Surrey with the Fringe on Top/Rica Pulpa	1952	5.00	10.00	20.00
6889	Billy Boy/Perfidia	1952	5.00	10.00	20.00
6921	A Gal in Calico/Aki And Ukthay	1952	5.00	10.00	20.00

Number	Title (A Side/B Side)	Yr	VG	VG+	NM
6945	Will You Still Be Mine/Ahmad's Blues	1953	5.00	10.00	20.00
PARROT					
810	But Not for Me/Seleritus	1955	6.25	12.50	25.00
818	It Could Happen to You/Excerpts from the Blues	1955	6.25	12.50	25.00
Albums					
20TH CENTURY					
T-417	Ahmad Jamal '73	1973	2.50	5.00	10.00
T-432	Jamaica	1974	2.50	5.00	10.00
T-459	Jamal Plays Jamal	1975	2.50	5.00	10.00
T-515	Steppin' Out with a Dream	1977	2.50	5.00	10.00
T-600	Genetic Walk	1980	2.50	5.00	10.00
T-622	Intervals	1980	2.50	5.00	10.00
T-631	Greatest Hits	1981	2.50	5.00	10.00
ABC					
S-660	Tranquility	1968	3.00	6.00	12.00
ABC IMPULSE!					
AS-9176	At the Top — Poinciana Revisited	1969	3.75	7.50	15.00
AS-9194	Awakening	1970	3.75	7.50	15.00
AS-9217	Freelight	1971	3.00	6.00	12.00
AS-9226	Outertimeinnerspace	1972	3.00	6.00	12.00
AS-9260 [(2)]	Re-Evaluations: The Impulse Years	1975	3.00	6.00	12.00
ARGO					
LP-602 [M]	Chamber Music of New Jazz	1956	7.50	15.00	30.00
—Reissue of Creative 602					
LP-610 [M]	Count 'Em 88	1957	7.50	15.00	30.00
LP-628 [M]	But Not for Me/Ahmad Jamal at the Pershing	1958	7.50	15.00	30.00
LPS-628 [S]	But Not for Me/Ahmad Jamal at the Pershing	1958	10.00	20.00	40.00
LP-636 [M]	Ahmad Jamal, Volume IV	1958	7.50	15.00	30.00
LPS-636 [S]	Ahmad Jamal, Volume IV	1958	10.00	20.00	40.00
LP-638 [(2) M]	Portfolio of Ahmad Jamal	1959	10.00	20.00	40.00
LPS-638 [(2) S]	Portfolio of Ahmad Jamal	1959	12.50	25.00	50.00
LP-646 [M]	Jamal at the Penthouse	1959	7.50	15.00	30.00
LPS-646 [S]	Jamal at the Penthouse	1959	10.00	20.00	40.00
LP-662 [M]	Happy Moods	1960	5.00	10.00	20.00
LPS-662 [S]	Happy Moods	1960	6.25	12.50	25.00
LP-667 [M]	Ahmad Jamal at the Pershing Volume 2	1961	5.00	10.00	20.00
LPS-667 [S]	Ahmad Jamal at the Pershing Volume 2	1961	6.25	12.50	25.00
LP-673 [M]	Listen to Ahmad Jamal	1961	5.00	10.00	20.00
LPS-673 [S]	Listen to Ahmad Jamal	1961	6.25	12.50	25.00
LP-685 [M]	Alhambra	1961	5.00	10.00	20.00
LPS-685 [S]	Alhambra	1961	6.25	12.50	25.00
LP-691 [M]	All of You	1962	5.00	10.00	20.00
LPS-691 [S]	All of You	1962	6.25	12.50	25.00
LP-703 [M]	Ahmad Jamal at the Blackhawk	1962	5.00	10.00	20.00
LPS-703 [S]	Ahmad Jamal at the Blackhawk	1962	6.25	12.50	25.00
LP-712 [M]	Macanudo	1963	5.00	10.00	20.00
LPS-712 [S]	Macanudo	1963	6.25	12.50	25.00
LP-719 [M]	Poin'-ci-an'a	1963	5.00	10.00	20.00
LPS-719 [S]	Poin'-ci-an'a	1963	6.25	12.50	25.00
LP-733 [M]	"Naked City" Theme	1964	5.00	10.00	20.00
LPS-733 [S]	"Naked City" Theme	1964	6.25	12.50	25.00
LP-751 [M]	The Roar of the Greasepaint	1965	5.00	10.00	20.00
LPS-751 [S]	The Roar of the Greasepaint	1965	6.25	12.50	25.00
LP-758 [M]	Extensions	1965	5.00	10.00	20.00
LPS-758 [S]	Extensions	1965	6.25	12.50	25.00
ATLANTIC					
81258 [(2)]	Digital Works	1985	3.00	6.00	12.00
81645	Rossiter Road	1986	2.50	5.00	10.00
81699 [(2)]	Live at the Montreal Jazz Festival 1985	1986	3.00	6.00	12.00
81793	Crystal	1987	2.50	5.00	10.00
CADET					
LP-628 [M]	But Not for Me/Ahmad Jamal at the Pershing	1966	3.00	6.00	12.00
LPS-628 [S]	But Not for Me/Ahmad Jamal at the Pershing	1966	3.75	7.50	15.00
LP-636 [M]	Ahmad Jamal, Volume IV	1966	3.00	6.00	12.00
LPS-636 [S]	Ahmad Jamal, Volume IV	1966	3.75	7.50	15.00
LP-638 [(2) M]	Portfolio of Ahmad Jamal	1966	3.75	7.50	15.00
LPS-638 [(2) S]	Portfolio of Ahmad Jamal	1966	5.00	10.00	20.00
LP-646 [M]	Jamal at the Penthouse	1966	3.00	6.00	12.00
LPS-646 [S]	Jamal at the Penthouse	1966	3.75	7.50	15.00
LP-662 [M]	Happy Moods	1966	3.00	6.00	12.00
LPS-662 [S]	Happy Moods	1966	3.75	7.50	15.00
LP-667 [M]	Ahmad Jamal at the Pershing Volume 2	1966	3.00	6.00	12.00
LPS-667 [S]	Ahmad Jamal at the Pershing Volume 2	1966	3.75	7.50	15.00
LP-673 [M]	Listen to Ahmad Jamal	1966	3.00	6.00	12.00
LPS-673 [S]	Listen to Ahmad Jamal	1966	3.75	7.50	15.00
LP-685 [M]	Alhambra	1966	3.00	6.00	12.00
LPS-685 [S]	Alhambra	1966	3.75	7.50	15.00
LP-691 [M]	All of You	1966	3.00	6.00	12.00
LPS-691 [S]	All of You	1966	3.75	7.50	15.00
LP-703 [M]	Ahmad Jamal at the Blackhawk	1966	3.00	6.00	12.00
LPS-703 [S]	Ahmad Jamal at the Blackhawk	1966	3.75	7.50	15.00
LP-712 [M]	Macanudo	1966	3.00	6.00	12.00
LPS-712 [S]	Macanudo	1966	3.75	7.50	15.00
LP-719 [M]	Poin'-ci-an'a	1966	3.00	6.00	12.00
LPS-719 [S]	Poin'-ci-an'a	1966	3.75	7.50	15.00
LP-733 [M]	"Naked City" Theme	1966	3.00	6.00	12.00
LPS-733 [S]	"Naked City" Theme	1966	3.75	7.50	15.00
LP-751 [M]	The Roar of the Greasepaint	1966	3.00	6.00	12.00
LPS-751 [S]	The Roar of the Greasepaint	1966	3.75	7.50	15.00
LP-758 [M]	Extensions	1966	3.00	6.00	12.00
LPS-758 [S]	Extensions	1965	3.75	7.50	15.00
LP-764 [M]	Rhapsody	1966	3.75	7.50	15.00
LPS-764 [S]	Rhapsody	1966	5.00	10.00	20.00
LP-777 [M]	Heat Wave	1966	3.75	7.50	15.00
LPS-777 [S]	Heat Wave	1966	5.00	10.00	20.00
LP-786 [M]	Standard Eyes	1967	3.75	7.50	15.00
LPS-786 [S]	Standard Eyes	1967	5.00	10.00	20.00
LP-792 [M]	Cry Young	1967	5.00	10.00	20.00
LPS-792 [S]	Cry Young	1967	3.75	7.50	15.00
LPS-807	The Bright, the Blue and the Beautiful	1968	3.75	7.50	15.00
50035 [(2)]	Inspiration	1974	3.75	7.50	15.00
CATALYST					
7606	Live at Oil Can Harry's	1978	3.00	6.00	12.00

Number	Title (A Side/B Side)	Yr	VG	VG+	NM
CHESS					
CH-91553	Poinciana	198?	2.50	5.00	10.00
CREATIVE					
LP-602 [M]	Chamber Music of New Jazz	1956	12.50	25.00	50.00
EPIC					
BN 627 [R]	Ahmad Jamal Trio	196?	5.00	10.00	20.00
BN 634 [S]	The Piano Scene of Ahmad Jamal	1959	5.00	10.00	20.00
LN 3212 [M]	Ahmad Jamal Trio	1956	12.50	25.00	50.00
—Yellow label with lines around rim					
LN 3212 [M]	Ahmad Jamal Trio	1963	6.25	12.50	25.00
—Yellow label, no lines around rim					
LN 3631 [M]	The Piano Scene of Ahmad Jamal	1959	7.50	15.00	30.00
GRP/IMPULSE!					
226	The Awakening	199?	3.75	7.50	15.00
—Reissue on audiophile vinyl					
MCA					
29041	At the Top — Poinciana Revisited	198?	2.00	4.00	8.00
—Reissue of Impulse! 9178					
29042	Awakening	198?	2.00	4.00	8.00
—Reissue of Impulse! 9194					
29043	Freelight	198?	2.00	4.00	8.00
—Reissue of Impulse! 9217					
MCA/IMPULSE!					
5644	Awakening	1986	2.50	5.00	10.00
—Another reissue of Impulse! 9194					
MOTOWN					
M8-945	Night Song	1981	2.50	5.00	10.00

JAMES, BOB

Number	Title (A Side/B Side)	Yr	VG	VG+	NM
45s					
CTI					
22	In the Garden/Soulero	1974	—	2.50	5.00
23	Night on Bald Mountain/In the Garden	1974	—	2.50	5.00
24	Feel Like Makin' Love/Soulero	1974	—	2.50	5.00
26	I Feel a Song (In My Heart)/Golden Apple	1975	—	2.50	5.00
31	Westchester Lady (Part 1)/Westchester Lady (Part 2)	1976	—	2.50	5.00
37	Where the Wind Blows Free/El Verano	1977	—	2.50	5.00
TAPPAN ZEE					
02530	Sign of the Times/Enchanted Forest	1981	—	2.00	4.00
02672	Steamin' Feelin'/Enchanted Forest	1982	—	2.00	4.00
03191	Janus/Spunky	1982	—	2.00	4.00
04532	Courtship (Basketball Theme)/Marco Polo	1984	—	2.00	4.00
10668	We're All Alone/Heads	1978	—	2.00	4.00
10715	You Are So Beautiful/Night Crawler	1978	—	2.00	4.00
10896	Angela (Theme from "Taxi")/Caribbean Nights	1979	—	3.00	6.00
10969	Touchdown/Sun Runner	1979	—	2.00	4.00
11096	Friends/Blue Lick	1979	—	2.00	4.00
11171	Main Theme from "Star Trek (The Motion Picture)"/I Want to Thank You	1980	—	3.00	6.00
Albums					
CBS MASTERWORKS					
IM 39540	Rameau	1985	2.50	5.00	10.00
COLUMBIA					
FC 38678	The Genie (Themes & Variations from the TV Series "Taxi")	1983	2.50	5.00	10.00
CTI					
CTS-6043	One	1974	3.00	6.00	12.00
CTS-6057	Two	1975	3.00	6.00	12.00
CTS-6063	Three	1976	3.00	6.00	12.00
7074	BJ4	1977	3.00	6.00	12.00
ESP-DISK'					
1009 [M]	Explosions	1965	5.00	10.00	20.00
S-1009 [S]	Explosions	1965	6.25	12.50	25.00
MERCURY					
MG-20768 [M]	Bold Conceptions	1963	5.00	10.00	20.00
SR-60768 [S]	Bold Conceptions	1963	6.25	12.50	25.00
TAPPAN ZEE					
JC 34896	Heads	1977	2.50	5.00	10.00
PC 34896	Heads	1985	—	3.00	6.00
—Budget-line reissue					
JC 35594	Touchdown	1978	2.50	5.00	10.00
PC 35594	Touchdown	1985	—	3.00	6.00
—Budget-line reissue					
JC 36056	Lucky Seven	1979	2.50	5.00	10.00
PC 36056	Lucky Seven	1985	—	3.00	6.00
—Budget-line reissue					
JC 36422	"H"	1980	2.50	5.00	10.00
C2X 36786 [(2)]	All Around the Town	1981	3.00	6.00	12.00
FC 36835	One	1981	2.50	5.00	10.00
—Reissue of CTI 6043					
PC 36835	One	1985	—	3.00	6.00
—Budget-line reissue					
FC 36836	Two	1981	2.50	5.00	10.00
—Reissue of CTI 6057					
PC 36836	Two	1985	—	3.00	6.00
—Budget-line reissue					
FC 36837	Three	1981	2.50	5.00	10.00
—Reissue of CTI 6063					
PC 36837	Three	1985	—	3.00	6.00
—Budget-line reissue					
FC 36838	BJ4	1981	2.50	5.00	10.00
—Reissue of CTI 7074					
PC 36838	BJ4	1985	—	3.00	6.00
—Budget-line reissue					
FC 37495	Sign of the Times	1981	2.50	5.00	10.00
FC 38067	Hands Down	1982	2.50	5.00	10.00
FC 38801	Foxie	1983	2.50	5.00	10.00
FC 39580	12	1985	2.50	5.00	10.00
HC 45594	Touchdown	1982	7.50	15.00	30.00
—Half-speed mastered edition					
HC 47495	Sign of the Times	1982	7.50	15.00	30.00
—Half-speed mastered edition					

Number	Title (A Side/B Side)	Yr	VG	VG+	NM
WARNER BROS.					
25495	Obsession	1986	2.50	5.00	10.00
25757	Ivory Coast	1988	2.50	5.00	10.00
26256	Grand Piano Canyon	1990	3.00	6.00	12.00

JAMES, DICK

45s

Number	Title (A Side/B Side)	Yr	VG	VG+	NM
LONDON					
1002	Eleanor/Mary Rose	1950	3.75	7.50	15.00
1013	Theater/My Life's Desire	1950	3.75	7.50	15.00
1027	Unless/Now That You've Left Me	1950	3.75	7.50	15.00
1044	We'll Keep a Welcome/The Minute Waltz	1951	3.75	7.50	15.00
1050	Happy Valley/My Truly Truly Fair	1951	3.75	7.50	15.00
1053	Tell Me Again/With All My Heart and Soul	1951	3.75	7.50	15.00
1139	Unforgettable/My Love for You	1951	3.75	7.50	15.00
1162	Pretending/It Would Break My Heart	1951	3.75	7.50	15.00

JAMES, ELMORE

Some of the below were as "Elmo James."

45s

Number	Title (A Side/B Side)	Yr	VG	VG+	NM
ACE					
508	I Believe My Time Ain't Long/I Wish I Was a Catfish	1955	62.50	125.00	250.00
CHECKER					
777	Country Boogie/She Just Won't Do Right	1953	250.00	500.00	1000.
CHESS					
1756	I Can't Hold Out/The Sun Is Shining	1960	3.75	7.50	15.00
CHIEF					
7001	The Twelve Year Old Boy/Coming Home	1957	20.00	40.00	80.00
7004	It Hurts Me Too/Elmore's Contribution to Jazz	1957	20.00	40.00	80.00
7006	Cry for Me Baby/Take Me Where You Go	1957	15.00	30.00	60.00
7020	Knocking at Your Door/Calling All Blues	1960	10.00	20.00	40.00
ENJOY					
2015	It Hurts Me Too/Bleeding Heart	1965	5.00	10.00	20.00
2015	It Hurts Me Too/Pickin' the Blues	1965	3.75	7.50	15.00
2020	Mean Mistreatin' Mama/Bleeding	1965	3.75	7.50	15.00
2027	Dust My Broom/Everyday I Have the Blues	1965	3.75	7.50	15.00
FIRE					
504	Shake Your Moneymaker/Look on Yonder Wall	1962	10.00	20.00	40.00
1011	Make My Dreams Come True/Bobby's Rock	1960	7.50	15.00	30.00
1016	The Sky Is Crying/Held My Baby Last Night	1960	10.00	20.00	40.00
1024	I'm Worried/Rollin' and Tumblin'	1960	5.00	10.00	20.00
1031	Fine Little Mama/Done Somebody Wrong	1961	5.00	10.00	20.00
1503	Stranger Blues/Anna Lee	1963	3.75	7.50	15.00
2020	It Hurts Me Too/Pickin' the Blues	196?	3.75	7.50	15.00
—Red vinyl					
FLAIR					
1011	Early in the Morning/Hawaiian Boogie	1953	125.00	250.00	500.00
1014	Can't Stop Lovin'/Make a Little Love	1953	50.00	100.00	200.00
1022	Strange Kinda Feeling/Please Find My Baby	1953	50.00	100.00	200.00
1031	Make My Dreams Come True/Hand in Hand	1954	75.00	150.00	300.00
1039	Sho'nuff, I Do/1839 Blues	1954	75.00	150.00	300.00
1048	Dark and Dreary/Rock My Baby Right	1954	75.00	150.00	300.00
1057	Standing at the Cross Roads/Sunny Land	1955	62.50	125.00	250.00
1062	Late Hours at Midnight/The Way You Treat Me	1955	37.50	75.00	150.00
1069	Happy Home/No Love in My Heart	1955	37.50	75.00	150.00
1074	Dust My Blues/I Was a Fool	1955	62.50	125.00	250.00
1079	Blues Before Sunrise/Goodbye Baby	1955	50.00	100.00	200.00
JEWEL					
764	Dust My Broom/Gotta Find My Baby	1966	2.50	5.00	10.00
783	Catfish Blues/Make a Little Love	1967	2.50	5.00	10.00
KENT					
331	Dust My Blues/Happy Home	1960	3.00	6.00	12.00
394	Dust My Blues/Happy Home	1964	2.50	5.00	10.00
465	Sunnyland/Goodbye Baby	1967	2.00	4.00	8.00
508	I Believe/1839 Blues	1969	—	3.00	6.00
M-PAC					
7231	Cry for Me/Take Me Where You Go	1966	2.50	5.00	10.00
MEL					
7011	Cry for Me Baby/(B-side unknown)	197?	—	3.00	6.00
METEOR					
5000	I Believe/I Held My Baby Last Night	1953	200.00	400.00	800.00
5003	Baby What's Wrong/Sinful Woman	1953	125.00	250.00	500.00
5016	Saxony Boogie/Dumb Woman Blues	1954	75.00	150.00	300.00
5024	San Symphonic Boogie/Flaming Blues	1955	62.50	125.00	250.00
MODERN					
983	Wild About You/Long Tall Woman	1956	75.00	150.00	300.00
VEE JAY					
249	Coming Home/The 12-Year-Old Boy	1957	6.25	12.50	25.00
259	It Hurts Me Too/Elmore's Contribution to Jazz	1957	6.25	12.50	25.00
269	Cry for Me Baby/Take Me Where You Go	1958	6.25	12.50	25.00

Albums

Number	Title (A Side/B Side)	Yr	VG	VG+	NM
BELL					
6037	Elmore James	1969	6.25	12.50	25.00
CHESS					
LP-1537	Whose Muddy Shoes	1969	6.25	12.50	25.00
COLLECTABLES					
COL-5112	Golden Classics	198?	3.00	6.00	12.00
COL-5184	The Complete Fire and Enjoy Sessions, Part 1	198?	2.50	5.00	10.00
COL-5185	The Complete Fire and Enjoy Sessions, Part 2	198?	2.50	5.00	10.00
COL-5186	The Complete Fire and Enjoy Sessions, Part 3	198?	2.50	5.00	10.00
COL-5187	The Complete Fire and Enjoy Sessions, Part 4	198?	2.50	5.00	10.00
CROWN					
CLP-5168 [M]	Blues After Hours	1961	62.50	125.00	250.00
—Black label, silver "Crown"					
CLP-5168 [M]	Blues After Hours	1962	12.50	25.00	50.00
—Gray label					
INTERMEDIA					
QS-5034	Red Hot Blues	198?	2.50	5.00	10.00
KENT					
KST-522 [R]	Original Folk Blues	1964	6.25	12.50	25.00
KLP-5022 [M]	Original Folk Blues	1964	10.00	20.00	40.00
KLP-9001	Anthology of the Blues Legend	196?	6.25	12.50	25.00
KLP-9010	The Resurrection of Elmore James	196?	6.25	12.50	25.00
SPHERE SOUND					
SR-7002 [M]	The Sky Is Crying	1965	45.00	90.00	180.00
SSR-7002 [R]	The Sky Is Crying	1965	30.00	60.00	120.00
SR-7008 [M]	I Need You	1966	37.50	75.00	150.00
SSR-7008 [R]	I Need You	1966	30.00	60.00	120.00
UP FRONT					
UP-122	The Great Elmore James	1970	3.00	6.00	12.00

JAMES, ETTA

45s

Number	Title (A Side/B Side)	Yr	VG	VG+	NM
ARGO					
5359	All I Could Do Was Cry/Girl of My Dreams	1960	3.00	6.00	12.00
5368	My Dearest Darling/Tough Mary	1960	3.00	6.00	12.00
5380	At Last/I Just Want to Make Love to You	1961	3.75	7.50	15.00
5385	Trust in Me/Anything to Say You're Mine	1961	2.50	5.00	10.00
5390	Dream/Fool That I Am	1961	2.50	5.00	10.00
5393	Sunday Kind of Love/Don't Cry, Baby	1961	2.50	5.00	10.00
5402	It's Too Soon to Know/Seven Day Fool	1961	2.50	5.00	10.00
5409	Something's Got a Hold on Me/Waiting for Charlie to Come Home	1962	2.50	5.00	10.00
5418	Stop the Wedding/Street of Tears	1962	2.50	5.00	10.00
5424	Next Door to the Blues/Fools Rush In	1962	2.50	5.00	10.00
5430	How Do You Speak to An Angel/Would It Make Any Difference to You	1962	2.50	5.00	10.00
5437	Pushover/I Can't Hold It In Anymore	1963	2.50	5.00	10.00
5445	Be Honest with Me/Pay Back	1963	2.50	5.00	10.00
5452	Two Sides (To Every Story)/Worry 'Bout You	1963	2.50	5.00	10.00
5459	Baby What You Want Me to Do/What I Say	1964	2.50	5.00	10.00
5465	Look Who's Blue/Loving You More Every Day	1964	2.50	5.00	10.00
5477	Breaking Point/That Man Belongs Back Here with Me	1964	2.50	5.00	10.00
5485	Mellow Fellow/Bobby Is His Name	1964	2.50	5.00	10.00
CADET					
5519	Somewhere Down the Line/Do I Make Myself Clear	1966	2.00	4.00	8.00
—With Sugar Pie DeSanto					
5526	Only Time Will Tell/I'm Sorry for You	1966	2.00	4.00	8.00
5539	In the Basement — Part 1/In the Basement — Part 2	1966	2.00	4.00	8.00
—With Sugar Pie DeSanto					
5552	I Prefer You/I'm So Glad	1966	2.00	4.00	8.00
5564	Don't Take Me for Your Fool/It Must Be Your Love	1967	2.00	4.00	8.00
5568	Happiness/842-3089 (Call My Name)	1967	2.00	4.00	8.00
5578	Tell Mama/I'd Rather Go Blind	1967	2.00	4.00	8.00
5594	Security/I'm Gonna Take What He's Got	1968	2.00	4.00	8.00
5606	I Got You Babe/I Worship the Ground You Walk On	1968	2.00	4.00	8.00
5620	Fire/You Got It	1968	2.00	4.00	8.00
5630	Almost Persuaded/Steal Away	1968	2.00	4.00	8.00
5655	Miss Pitiful/Bobby Is His Name	1969	2.00	4.00	8.00
5664	Tighten Up Your Own Thing/What Fools We Mortals Be	1970	2.00	4.00	8.00
5671	The Sound of Love/When I Stop Dreaming	1970	2.00	4.00	8.00
5676	Losers Weepers — Part 1/Losers Weepers — Part 2	1970	2.00	4.00	8.00
CAPITOL					
B-44333	Avenue D/My Head Is a City	1989	—	2.00	4.00
—With David A. Stewart					
CHESS					
2100	The Love of My Man/Nothing from Nothing Leaves Nothing	1971	—	3.00	6.00
2112	I Think It's You/Take Out Some Insurance	1971	—	3.00	6.00
2125	I Found a Love/Nothing from Nothing Leaves Nothing	1972	—	3.00	6.00
2144	All the Way Down/Lay Back Daddy	1973	—	3.00	6.00
2148	Leave Your Hat On/Only a Fool	1974	—	3.00	6.00
2153	Out on the Street Again/Feeling Uneasy	1974	—	3.00	6.00
2171	Lovin' Arms/Take Out Some Insurance	1975	—	3.00	6.00
31001	Jump Into Love/(B-side unknown)	1976	—	2.50	5.00
EPIC					
68593	Baby What You Want Me to Do/Max's Theme (Instrumental)	1989	—	2.00	4.00
KENT					
304	Baby, Baby, Every Night/Sunshine of Love	1958	7.50	15.00	30.00
345	Roll with Me Henry/Good Rockin' Daddy	1960	6.25	12.50	25.00
352	How Big a Fool/Good Rockin' Daddy	1961	6.25	12.50	25.00
370	Do Something Crazy/Good Rockin' Daddy	1962	6.25	12.50	25.00
MODERN					
947	The Wallflower (Roll With Me Henry)/Hold Me, Squeeze Me	1955	10.00	20.00	40.00
947	The Wallflower (Dance With Me Henry)/Hold Me, Squeeze Me	1955	6.25	12.50	25.00
957	Hey Henry (Doin' Fine, Henry)/Be Mine	1955	6.25	12.50	25.00
962	Good Rockin' Daddy/Crazy Feeling	1955	7.50	15.00	30.00
972	That's All/W-O-M-A-N	1955	6.25	12.50	25.00
984	I'm a Fool/Number One (My One and Only)	1956	6.25	12.50	25.00
988	Shortnin' Bread Rock/Tears of Joy	1956	6.25	12.50	25.00
998	Fools We Mortals Be/Tough Lover	1956	7.50	15.00	30.00
1007	Good Lookin'/Then I'll Care	1957	6.25	12.50	25.00
1016	The Pick-Up/Market Place	1957	6.25	12.50	25.00
1022	By the Light of the Silvery Moon/Come What May	1957	6.25	12.50	25.00
PHILCO-FORD					
HP-31	Tell Mama/Security	1968	5.00	10.00	20.00
—4-inch plastic "Hip Pocket Record" with color sleeve					
T-ELECTRIC					
41264	It Takes Love to Keep a Woman/Mean Mother	1980	—	2.50	5.00
WARNER BROS.					
8545	Piece of My Heart/Lovesick Blues	1978	—	2.50	5.00
8611	Sugar on the Floor/Lovesick Blues	1978	—	2.50	5.00

Albums

Number	Title (A Side/B Side)	Yr	VG	VG+	NM
ARGO					
LP-4003 [M]	At Last!	1961	10.00	20.00	40.00

Number	Title (A Side/B Side)	Yr	VG	VG+	NM
LPS-4003 [S]	At Last!	1961	15.00	30.00	60.00
LP-4011 [M]	The Second Time Around	1961	7.50	15.00	30.00
LPS-4011 [S]	The Second Time Around	1961	10.00	20.00	40.00
LP-4013 [M]	Etta James	1962	7.50	15.00	30.00
LPS-4013 [S]	Etta James	1962	10.00	20.00	40.00
LP-4018 [M]	Etta James Sings for Lovers	1962	7.50	15.00	30.00
LPS-4018 [S]	Etta James Sings for Lovers	1962	10.00	20.00	40.00
LP-4025 [M]	Etta James Top Ten	1963	7.50	15.00	30.00
LPS-4025 [S]	Etta James Top Ten	1963	10.00	20.00	40.00
LP-4032 [M]	Etta James Rocks the House	1964	25.00	50.00	100.00
LPS-4032 [S]	Etta James Rocks the House	1964	37.50	75.00	150.00
LP-4040 [M]	The Queen of Soul	1965	7.50	15.00	30.00
LPS-4040 [S]	The Queen of Soul	1965	10.00	20.00	40.00
CADET					
LP-802 [M]	Tell Mama	1968	6.25	12.50	25.00
LPS-802 [S]	Tell Mama	1968	5.00	10.00	20.00
LPS-832	Funk	1969	5.00	10.00	20.00
LPS-847	Losers Weepers	1970	3.75	7.50	15.00
LP-4003 [M]	At Last!	1966	3.00	6.00	12.00
LPS-4003 [S]	At Last!	1966	3.75	7.50	15.00
LP-4011 [M]	The Second Time Around	1966	3.00	6.00	12.00
LPS-4011 [S]	The Second Time Around	1966	3.75	7.50	15.00
LP-4013 [M]	Etta James	1966	3.00	6.00	12.00
LPS-4013 [S]	Etta James	1966	3.75	7.50	15.00
LP-4018 [M]	Etta James Sings for Lovers	1966	3.00	6.00	12.00
LPS-4018 [S]	Etta James Sings for Lovers	1966	3.75	7.50	15.00
LP-4025 [M]	Etta James Top Ten	1966	3.00	6.00	12.00
LPS-4025 [S]	Etta James Top Ten	1966	3.75	7.50	15.00
LP-4040 [M]	The Queen of Soul	1966	3.00	6.00	12.00
LPS-4040 [S]	The Queen of Soul	1966	3.75	7.50	15.00
LP-4055 [M]	Call My Name	1967	3.75	7.50	15.00
LPS-4055 [S]	Call My Name	1967	5.00	10.00	20.00
CHESS					
CH2-6028 [(2)]	The Sweetest Peaches	1989	3.00	6.00	12.00
CH-9110	Her Greatest Sides, Vol. 1	1984	2.50	5.00	10.00
CH-9184	Etta James Rocks the House	1986	2.00	4.00	8.00
—Reissue					
CH-9266	At Last!	1987	2.00	4.00	8.00
—Reissue					
CH-9269	Tell Mama	1987	2.00	4.00	8.00
—Reissue					
CH-9287	The Second Time Around	1989	2.00	4.00	8.00
—Reissue					
CH-50042	Etta James	1973	3.75	7.50	15.00
2CH-60004 [(2)]	Peaches	1971	5.00	10.00	20.00
CH-60029	Come a Little Closer	1974	3.75	7.50	15.00
CH-91509	Come a Little Closer	198?	2.00	4.00	8.00
—Reissue					
CROWN					
CST-360 [R]	Etta James	1963	5.00	10.00	20.00
—With Etta smiling on cover					
CST-360 [R]	Etta James	1963	5.00	10.00	20.00
—With Etta somber on cover					
CLP-5209 [M]	Miss Etta James	1961	25.00	50.00	100.00
—First edition, with framed picture on cover					
CLP-5209 [M]	Miss Etta James	1962	15.00	30.00	60.00
—Second edition, all-white cover with "Miss Etta James"					
CLP-5234 [M]	The Best of Etta James	1962	15.00	30.00	60.00
—Black label					
CLP-5234 [M]	The Best of Etta James	1963	7.50	15.00	30.00
—Gray label					
CLP-5250 [M]	Twist with Etta James	1962	15.00	30.00	60.00
—Black label					
CLP-5250 [M]	Twist with Etta James	1963	7.50	15.00	30.00
—Gray label					
CLP-5360 [M]	Etta James	1963	7.50	15.00	30.00
—With Etta smiling on cover					
CLP-5360 [M]	Etta James	1963	7.50	15.00	30.00
—With Etta somber on cover					
INTERMEDIA					
QS-5014	Etta, Red Hot 'N' Live!	198?	2.50	5.00	10.00
ISLAND					
91018	Seven Year Itch	1988	2.50	5.00	10.00
842926-1	Sticking to My Guns	1990	3.00	6.00	12.00
KENT					
KST-500 [R]	Miss Etta James	1964	20.00	40.00	80.00
—Red vinyl					
KST-500 [R]	Miss Etta James	1964	6.25	12.50	25.00
—Black vinyl					
KLP-5000 [M]	Miss Etta James	1964	7.50	15.00	30.00
UNITED					
US 7712	Etta James Sings	197?	2.50	5.00	10.00
WARNER BROS.					
BSK 3156	Deep in the Night	1978	3.00	6.00	12.00

JAMES, JIMMY, AND THE VAGABONDS

12-Inch Singles

Number	Title (A Side/B Side)	Yr	VG	VG+	NM
PYE					
121	I Am Somebody (same on both sides)	1976	3.75	7.50	15.00
125	Now Is the Time/I Go Where the Music Takes Me	1976	3.75	7.50	15.00

45s

Number	Title (A Side/B Side)	Yr	VG	VG+	NM
ATCO					
6551	Come to Me Softly/Hi-Diddley Dee Dum Dum	1968	2.00	4.00	8.00
6608	Red Red Wine/No Good to Cry	1968	2.00	4.00	8.00
PYE					
71017	You Don't Stand a Chance If You Can't Dance (Part 1 & 2)	1975	—	3.00	6.00
71019	Lay Some Lovin' on Me/You Don't Stand a Chance If You Can't Dance	1975	—	2.50	5.00
71057	I Am Somebody/Chains of Love	1975	—	2.50	5.00
71068	I Go Where the Music Takes Me/Let's Love Together	1976	—	2.50	5.00
71075	Now Is the Time/Never Had This Dream Before	1976	—	2.50	5.00

Albums

Number	Title (A Side/B Side)	Yr	VG	VG+	NM
ATCO					
33-222 [M]	The New Religion	1967	5.00	10.00	20.00
SD 33-222 [S]	The New Religion	1967	5.00	10.00	20.00
PYE					
12111	You Don't Stand a Chance If You Can't Dance	1975	2.50	5.00	10.00

JAMES, JONI

45s

Number	Title (A Side/B Side)	Yr	VG	VG+	NM
MGM					
11223	Let There Be Love/My Baby Just Cares for Me	1952	6.25	12.50	25.00
11295	You Belong to Me/Yes, Yes, Yes	1952	6.25	12.50	25.00
11333	Why Don't You Believe Me/Purple Shades	1952	7.50	15.00	30.00
11390	Have You Heard/Wishing Ring	1953	5.00	10.00	20.00
11426	Your Cheatin' Heart/I'll Be Waiting for You	1953	5.00	10.00	20.00
11470	Is It Any Wonder/Almost Always	1953	5.00	10.00	20.00
11543	My Love, My Love/You're Fooling Someone	1953	5.00	10.00	20.00
11606	I'll Never Stand in Your Way/Why Can't I	1953	5.00	10.00	20.00
11637	Christmas and You/Nina-Non	1953	5.00	10.00	20.00
11696	Am I in Love/Maybe Next Time	1954	5.00	10.00	20.00
11753	In a Garden of Roses/Every Day	1954	5.00	10.00	20.00
11802	Mama, Don't Cry at My Wedding/Pa Pa Pa	1954	5.00	10.00	20.00
11865	Everytime You Tell Me You Love Me/When We Come of Age	1954	5.00	10.00	20.00
11919	How Important Can It Be?/This Is My Confession	1955	5.00	10.00	20.00
11960	When You Wish Upon a Star/Is This the End of the Line	1955	5.00	10.00	20.00
12020	The Moment I Saw You/Where Is That Someone for Me	1955	5.00	10.00	20.00
12066	You Are My Love/I Lay Me Down to Sleep	1955	5.00	10.00	20.00
12091	The Christmas Song/Have Yourself a Merry Little Christmas	1955	6.25	12.50	25.00
12126	My Believing Heart/You Never Fall in Love Again	1955	5.00	10.00	20.00
12175	Don't Tell Me Not to Love You/Somewhere Someone Is Lonely	1956	3.75	7.50	15.00
12213	I Woke Up Crying/The Maverick Queen	1956	3.75	7.50	15.00
12288	Give Us This Day/How Lucky You Are	1956	3.75	7.50	15.00
12353	Love Letters/Don't Take Your Love from Me	1956	3.75	7.50	15.00
12368	White Christmas/I'll Be Home for Christmas	1956	5.00	10.00	20.00
12369	Danny Boy/To You I Give My Heart	1956	3.75	7.50	15.00
12450	I Need You So/Only Trust Your Heart	1957	3.75	7.50	15.00
12480	Summer Love/I'm Sorry for You, My Friend	1957	3.75	7.50	15.00
12531	Crying in the Shadows/Day Dreaming	1957	3.75	7.50	15.00
12565	Never 'Til Now/I Give You My Heart	1957	3.75	7.50	15.00
12565 [PS]	Never 'Til Now/I Give You My Heart	1957	6.25	12.50	25.00
12607	Dansero/Love Works Miracles	1958	3.75	7.50	15.00
12627	Nothing Will Ever Change/Does It Show	1958	3.75	7.50	15.00
12639	Arrividerci Roma/Non Dimenticar	1958	3.75	7.50	15.00
12660	Coming from You/Junior Prom	1958	3.75	7.50	15.00
12706	There Goes My Heart/Funny	1958	3.75	7.50	15.00
12706 [PS]	There Goes My Heart/Funny	1958	12.50	25.00	50.00
SK-12706 [S]	There Goes My Heart/Funny	1958	10.00	20.00	40.00
—Note different prefix. Also, label will say "Stereo."					
12746	There Must Be a Way/Sorry for Myself	1959	3.75	7.50	15.00
12779	I Still Get a Thrill (Thinking of You)/Perhaps	1959	3.75	7.50	15.00
12779 [PS]	I Still Get a Thrill (Thinking of You)/Perhaps	1959	6.25	12.50	25.00
12807	I Still Get Jealous/My Prayer of Love	1959	3.75	7.50	15.00
12828	Are You Sorry/What I Don't Know Won't Hurt Me	1959	3.75	7.50	15.00
12849	Little Things Mean a Lot/I Laughed at Love	1959	3.75	7.50	15.00
12885	I Need You Now/You Belong to Me	1960	3.00	6.00	12.00
12895	They Really Don't Know You/We Know	1960	3.00	6.00	12.00
12933	My Last Date (With You)/I Can't Give You Anything But Love	1960	3.00	6.00	12.00
12933 [PS]	My Last Date (With You)/I Can't Give You Anything But Love	1960	5.00	10.00	20.00
12948	Be My Love/Tall As a Tree	1960	3.00	6.00	12.00
12948 [PS]	Be My Love/Tall As a Tree	1960	5.00	10.00	20.00
12990	Theme from "Carnival"/Can You Imagine That	1961	3.00	6.00	12.00
13016	Go Away (Bother Me No More)/I Gave My Love	1961	3.00	6.00	12.00
13037	Somebody Else Is Taking My Place/You Were Wrong	1961	3.00	6.00	12.00
13037 [PS]	Somebody Else Is Taking My Place/You Were Wrong	1961	5.00	10.00	20.00
13080	It's Magic/Tender and True	1962	3.00	6.00	12.00
13092	You Are My Sunshine/Lend Me Your Handkerchief	1962	3.75	7.50	15.00
13117	Anyone But Her/Forgive a Fool	1962	3.75	7.50	15.00
13159	Hey, Good Lookin'/He Says the Same Things to Me	1963	3.75	7.50	15.00
13180	Red Sails in the Sunset/Every Time I Meet You	1963	3.75	7.50	15.00
13206	Teach Me to Forget You/Un Cafe	1964	5.00	10.00	20.00
13243	Break, My Heart, Break/Don't Let the Neighbors Know	1964	5.00	10.00	20.00
13267	Pearly Shells/Hawaiian War Chant	1964	5.00	10.00	20.00
13288	Sentimental Me/You're Nearer	1964	20.00	40.00	80.00
13304	Dondi/Once I Loved	1964	5.00	10.00	20.00
13365	There Goes My Heart/I Still Get Jealous	1965	5.00	10.00	20.00
SK-50111 [S]	There Must Be a Way/Sorry for Myself	1959	7.50	15.00	30.00
SHARP					
46	Let There Be Love/My Baby Just Cares for Me	1952	75.00	150.00	300.00
50	You Belong to Me/Yes, Yes, Yes	1952	62.50	125.00	250.00

7-Inch Extended Plays

Number	Title (A Side/B Side)	Yr	VG	VG+	NM
MGM					
X-222 [PS]	Let There Be Love	1953	12.50	25.00	50.00
—Cover for X-4047 and X-4048					
X-234 [PS]	Joni James	1954	12.50	25.00	50.00
—Cover with X-4090 and X-4091					
X-1160	I'm in the Mood for Love/Where Can I Go Without You//People Will Say We're in Love/Love Letters	1955	15.00	30.00	60.00
X-1160 [PS]	Joni James	1955	15.00	30.00	60.00
X-1172	(contents unknown)	1955	15.00	30.00	60.00
X-1172 [PS]	Have Yourself a Merry Little Christmas	1955	15.00	30.00	60.00
X-1211	(contents unknown)	1956	10.00	20.00	40.00
X-1211 [PS]	In the Still of the Night, Part 1	1956	10.00	20.00	40.00
X-1212	(contents unknown)	1956	10.00	20.00	40.00

Number	Title (A Side/B Side)	Yr	VG	VG+	NM
X-1212 [PS]	In the Still of the Night, Part 2	1956	10.00	20.00	40.00
X-1213	In the Still of the Night/What's New//Deep Purple/ You'd Be So Nice to Come Home To	1956	10.00	20.00	40.00
X-1213 [PS]	In the Still of the Night, Vol. 3	1956	10.00	20.00	40.00
X-1219	(contents unknown)	1956	10.00	20.00	40.00
X-1219 [PS]	Award Winning Album, Part 1	1956	10.00	20.00	40.00
X-1220	(contents unknown)	1956	10.00	20.00	40.00
X-1220 [PS]	Award Winning Album, Part 2	1956	10.00	20.00	40.00
X-1221	(contents unknown)	1956	10.00	20.00	40.00
X-1221 [PS]	Award Winning Album, Part 3	1956	10.00	20.00	40.00
X-1223	In Love in Vain/Too Late Now//Autumn Leaves/ That Old Feeling	1956	10.00	20.00	40.00
X-1223 [PS]	Little Girl Blue	1956	10.00	20.00	40.00
X-1227	I Need You Now/This Is My Confession//The Moment I Saw You/Am I in Love	1956	10.00	20.00	40.00
X-1227 [PS]	Let There Be Love	1956	10.00	20.00	40.00
X-1343	My Foolish Heart/I Don't Stand a Ghost of a Chance with You//Stella by Starlight/A Hundred Years from Today	1956	10.00	20.00	40.00
X-1343 [PS]	Joni Sings Songs by Victor Young (Vol. 1)	1956	10.00	20.00	40.00
X-1344	Song of Surrender/Everything I Do//If I Were a Bell.My Darling, My Darling	1956	10.00	20.00	40.00
X-1344 [PS]	Joni Sings Songs by Victor Young/Songs by Frank Loesser (Vol. 2)	1956	10.00	20.00	40.00
X-1345	On a Slow Boat to China/I'll Know//Spring Will Be a Little Late This Year/Anywhere I Wander	1956	10.00	20.00	40.00
X-1345 [PS]	Joni Sings Songs by Frank Loesser (Vol. 3)	1956	10.00	20.00	40.00
X-1389	(contents unknown)	1957	10.00	20.00	40.00
X-1389 [PS]	Give Us This Day, Vol. 1	1957	10.00	20.00	40.00
X-1390	Look for the Silver Lining/Panis Angelicus//I Believe/The Rosary	1957	10.00	20.00	40.00
X-1390 [PS]	Give Us This Day, Vol. 2	1957-05-0110.00		20.00	40.00
X-1391	Count Your Blessings/Ave Maria (Gounod)// Abide with Me/May the Good Lord Bles and Keep You	1957	10.00	20.00	40.00
X-1391 [PS]	Give Us This Day, Vol. 3	1957	10.00	20.00	40.00
X-1399	(contents unknown)	1957	15.00	30.00	60.00
X-1399 [PS]	Merry Christmas from Joni, Part 1	1957	15.00	30.00	60.00
X-1400	(contents unknown)	1957	15.00	30.00	60.00
X-1400 [PS]	Merry Christmas from Joni, Part 2	1957	15.00	30.00	60.00
X-1401	(contents unknown)	1957	15.00	30.00	60.00
X-1401 [PS]	Merry Christmas from Joni, Part 3	1957	15.00	30.00	60.00
X-1545	Always/When You Were Sweet Sixteen//Let Me Call You Sweetheart/Alice Blue Gown	1957	10.00	20.00	40.00
X-1545 [PS]	Among My Souvenirs, Vol. I	1957	10.00	20.00	40.00
X-1546	(contents unknown)	1957	10.00	20.00	40.00
X-1546 [PS]	Among My Souvenirs, Vol. II	1957	10.00	20.00	40.00
X-1547	(contents unknown)	1957	10.00	20.00	40.00
X-1547 [PS]	Among My Souvenirs, Vol. III	1957	10.00	20.00	40.00
X-1652	(contents unknown)	1959	10.00	20.00	40.00
X-1652 [PS]	Songs of Hank Williams, Part 1	1959	10.00	20.00	40.00
X-1653	(contents unknown)	1959	10.00	20.00	40.00
X-1653 [PS]	Songs of Hank Williams, Part 2	1959	10.00	20.00	40.00
X-1654	(contents unknown)	1959	10.00	20.00	40.00
X-1654 [PS]	Songs of Hank Williams, Part 3	1959	10.00	20.00	40.00
X-1656	(contents unknown)	1959	10.00	20.00	40.00
X-1656 [PS]	100 Strings and Joni, Part 1	1959	10.00	20.00	40.00
X-1657	(contents unknown)	1959	10.00	20.00	40.00
X-1657 [PS]	100 Strings and Joni, Part 2	1959	10.00	20.00	40.00
X-1658	(contents unknown)	1959	10.00	20.00	40.00
X-1658 [PS]	100 Strings and Joni, Part 3	1959	10.00	20.00	40.00
X-4047	Let There Be Love/My Romance//The Nearness of You/You're Mine You	1953	12.50	25.00	50.00
—One record of "X222"					
X-4048	You're My Everything/You're Nearer//Love Is Here to Stay/I'll Be Seeing You	1953	12.50	25.00	50.00
—One record of "X222"					
X-4090	Have You Heard/Almost Always//Purple Shades/ Your Cheatin' Heart	1954	12.50	25.00	50.00
—One record of "X234"					
X-4091	Why Don't You Believe Me/Is It Any Wonder// Wishing Ring/My Love, My Love	1954	12.50	25.00	50.00
—One record of "X234"					

Albums

MGM

Number	Title (A Side/B Side)	Yr	VG	VG+	NM
E-222 [10]	Let There Be Love	1953	50.00	100.00	200.00
E-234 [10]	Award Winning Album	1954	50.00	100.00	200.00
E-272 [10]	Little Girl Blue	1955	50.00	100.00	200.00
E-3240 [M] *—Yellow label*	When I Fall in Love	1955	20.00	40.00	80.00
E-3240 [M] *—Black label*	When I Fall in Love	1960	10.00	20.00	40.00
E-3328 [M] *—Yellow label*	In the Still of the Night	1956	20.00	40.00	80.00
E-3328 [M] *—Black label*	In the Still of the Night	1960	10.00	20.00	40.00
E-3346 [M] *—Yellow label*	Award Winning Album	1956	20.00	40.00	80.00
E-3346 [M] *—Black label*	Award Winning Album	1960	10.00	20.00	40.00
E-3347 [M] *—Yellow label*	Little Girl Blue	1956	20.00	40.00	80.00
E-3347 [M] *—Black label*	Little Girl Blue	1960	10.00	20.00	40.00
E-3348 [M] *—Yellow label*	Let There Be Love	1956	20.00	40.00	80.00
E-3348 [M] *—Black label*	Let There Be Love	1960	10.00	20.00	40.00
E-3449 [M] *—Yellow label*	Songs by Victor Young and Frank Loesser	1956	20.00	40.00	80.00
E-3449 [M] *—Black label*	Songs by Victor Young and Frank Loesser	1960	10.00	20.00	40.00
E-3468 [M] *—Yellow label original*	Merry Christmas from Joni	1956	30.00	60.00	120.00
E-3468 [M] *—Black label reissue*	Merry Christmas from Joni	1960	15.00	30.00	60.00
E-3528 [M] *—Yellow label*	Give Us This Day	1957	20.00	40.00	80.00
E-3528 [M] *—Black label*	Give Us This Day	1960	10.00	20.00	40.00
E-3533 [M] *—Yellow label*	Songs by Jerome Kern and Harry Warren	1957	20.00	40.00	80.00
E-3533 [M] *—Black label*	Songs by Jerome Kern and Harry Warren	1960	10.00	20.00	40.00
E-3602 [M] *—Yellow label*	Among My Souvenirs	1958	20.00	40.00	80.00
E-3602 [M] *—Black label*	Among My Souvenirs	1960	10.00	20.00	40.00
E-3623 [M] *—Yellow label*	Ti Voglio Bene	1958	20.00	40.00	80.00
E-3623 [M] *—Black label*	Ti Voglio Bene	1960	10.00	20.00	40.00
E-3706 [M] *—Yellow label*	Award Winning Album, Volume 2	1958	20.00	40.00	80.00
E-3706 [M] *—Black label*	Award Winning Album, Volume 2	1960	10.00	20.00	40.00
E-3718 [M] *—Yellow label*	Je T'aime (I Love You)	1958	20.00	40.00	80.00
E-3718 [M] *—Black label*	Je T'aime (I Love You)	1960	10.00	20.00	40.00
SE-3718 [S] *—Yellow label*	Je T'aime (I Love You)	1958	30.00	60.00	120.00
SE-3718 [S] *—Black label*	Je T'aime (I Love You)	1960	12.50	25.00	50.00
E-3739 [M] *—Yellow label*	Songs of Hank Williams	1959	20.00	40.00	80.00
E-3739 [M] *—Black label*	Songs of Hank Williams	1960	10.00	20.00	40.00
SE-3739 [S] *—Yellow label*	Songs of Hank Williams	1959	30.00	60.00	120.00
SE-3739 [S] *—Black label*	Songs of Hank Williams	1960	12.50	25.00	50.00
E-3749 [M] *—Yellow label*	Irish Favorites	1959	20.00	40.00	80.00
E-3749 [M] *—Black label*	Irish Favorites	1960	10.00	20.00	40.00
SE-3749 [S] *—Yellow label*	Irish Favorites	1959	30.00	60.00	120.00
SE-3749 [S] *—Black label*	Irish Favorites	1960	12.50	25.00	50.00
E-3755 [M] *—Yellow label*	100 Strings and Joni	1959	20.00	40.00	80.00
E-3755 [M] *—Black label*	100 Strings and Joni	1960	10.00	20.00	40.00
SE-3755 [S] *—Yellow label*	100 Strings and Joni	1959	30.00	60.00	120.00
SE-3755 [S] *—Black label*	100 Strings and Joni	1960	12.50	25.00	50.00
E-3772 [M]	Joni James Swings Sweet	1959	15.00	30.00	60.00
SE-3772 [S]	Joni James Swings Sweet	1959	20.00	40.00	80.00
E-3800 [M]	Joni James at Carnegie Hall	1959	15.00	30.00	60.00
SE-3800 [S]	Joni James at Carnegie Hall	1959	20.00	40.00	80.00
E-3837 [M]	I'm In the Mood for Love	1960	15.00	30.00	60.00
SE-3837 [S]	I'm In the Mood for Love	1960	20.00	40.00	80.00
E-3839 [M]	100 Strings and Joni On Broadway	1960	15.00	30.00	60.00
SE-3839 [S]	100 Strings and Joni On Broadway	1960	17.50	35.00	70.00
E-3840 [M]	100 Strings and Joni In Hollywood	1960	15.00	30.00	60.00
SE-3840 [S]	100 Strings and Joni In Hollywood	1960	17.50	35.00	70.00
E-3885 [M]	More Joni Hits	1960	12.50	25.00	50.00
SE-3885 [S]	More Joni Hits	1960	15.00	30.00	60.00
E-3892 [M]	100 Voices, 100 Strings	1960	12.50	25.00	50.00
SE-3892 [S]	100 Voices, 100 Strings	1960	15.00	30.00	60.00
E-3958 [M]	Folk Songs by Joni James	1961	12.50	25.00	50.00
SE-3958 [S]	Folk Songs by Joni James	1961	15.00	30.00	60.00
E-3987 [M]	The Mood Is Swinging	1961	12.50	25.00	50.00
SE-3987 [S]	The Mood Is Swinging	1961	15.00	30.00	60.00
E-3990 [M]	The Mood Is Romance	1961	12.50	25.00	50.00
SE-3990 [S]	The Mood Is Romance	1961	15.00	30.00	60.00
E-3991 [M]	The Mood Is Blue	1961	12.50	25.00	50.00
SE-3991 [S]	The Mood Is Blue	1961	15.00	30.00	60.00
E-4008 [M]	After Hours	1962	12.50	25.00	50.00
SE-4008 [S]	After Hours	1962	15.00	30.00	60.00
E-4053 [M]	I Feel a Song Comin' On	1962	12.50	25.00	50.00
SE-4053 [S]	I Feel a Song Comin' On	1962	15.00	30.00	60.00
E-4054 [M]	I'm Your Girl	1962	12.50	25.00	50.00
SE-4054 [S]	I'm Your Girl	1962	15.00	30.00	60.00
E-4101 [M]	Country Girl Style	1962	12.50	25.00	50.00
SE-4101 [S]	Country Girl Style	1962	15.00	30.00	60.00
E-4151 [M]	The Very Best of Joni James	1963	10.00	20.00	40.00
SE-4151 [S]	The Very Best of Joni James	1963	12.50	25.00	50.00
E-4158 [M]	Something for the Boys	1963	10.00	20.00	40.00
SE-4158 [S]	Something for the Boys	1963	12.50	25.00	50.00
E-4182 [M]	Three O'Clock in the Morning	1963	10.00	20.00	40.00
SE-4182 [S]	Three O'Clock in the Morning	1963	12.50	25.00	50.00
E-4200 [M]	My Favorite Things	1963	10.00	20.00	40.00
SE-4200 [S]	My Favorite Things	1963	12.50	25.00	50.00
E-4208 [M]	Italianissime!	1963	10.00	20.00	40.00
SE-4208 [S]	Italianissime!	1963	12.50	25.00	50.00
E-4248 [M]	Put On a Happy Face	1964	10.00	20.00	40.00
SE-4248 [S]	Put On a Happy Face	1964	12.50	25.00	50.00
E-4255 [M]	Joni James Sings the Gershwins	1964	10.00	20.00	40.00
SE-4255 [S]	Joni James Sings the Gershwins	1964	12.50	25.00	50.00
E-4263 [M]	Beyond the Reef	1964	10.00	20.00	40.00
SE-4263 [S]	Beyond the Reef	1964	12.50	25.00	50.00
E-4286 [M]	Bossa Nova Style	1965	10.00	20.00	40.00
SE-4286 [S]	Bossa Nova Style	1965	12.50	25.00	50.00

JAMES, LEONARD

Albums

DECCA

Number	Title (A Side/B Side)	Yr	VG	VG+	NM
DL 8772 [M]	Boppin' and a-Strollin'	1958	12.50	25.00	50.00

JAMES, RICK

12-Inch Singles

MOTOWN

Number	Title (A Side/B Side)	Yr	VG	VG+	NM
00012	High on Your Love Suite (7:20)/You and I (8:04)	1978	3.00	6.00	12.00
PR-60 [DJ]	Love Gun (10:03) (3:45)	1979	3.00	6.00	12.00
PR-81 [DJ]	Give It To Me Baby (3 versions)	1981	3.00	6.00	12.00
144	17 (6:40 vocal) (5:38 instrumental)	1984	—	3.00	6.00
981 [DJ]	You and I (8:04) (same on both sides)	1978	2.50	5.00	10.00
4511	Cold Blooded/(Instrumental)	1983	—	3.00	6.00
4528	Can't Stop/Oh What a Night	1985	—	3.00	6.00
4561	Sweet and Sexy Thing (3 versions)	1986	—	3.00	6.00
4565	Forever and a Day/(Instrumental)	1986	—	3.00	6.00

REPRISE

Number	Title (A Side/B Side)	Yr	VG	VG+	NM
PRO-A-3376 [DJ]	Sexual Love Affair (Club) (Remix Edit) (LP)	1988	2.00	4.00	8.00
20941	Loosey's Rap (5 versions)	1988	—	3.00	6.00
21035	This Magic Moment (3 versions)	1988	—	3.00	6.00
21036	Sexual Luv Affair (4 versions)/In the Girls Room	1988	—	3.00	6.00

45s

A&M

Number	Title (A Side/B Side)	Yr	VG	VG+	NM
1615	Funkin' Around/My Mama	1974	6.25	12.50	25.00

GORDY

Number	Title (A Side/B Side)	Yr	VG	VG+	NM
1619	Dance Wit' Me — Part 1/Dance Wit' Me — Part 2	1982	—	2.00	4.00
1619 [PS]	Dance Wit' Me — Part 1/Dance Wit' Me — Part 2	1982	—	2.50	5.00
1634	Hard to Get/My Love	1982	—	2.00	4.00
1646	She Blew My Mind (69 Times)/(B-side unknown)	1982	—	2.00	4.00
1658	Teardrops/Throwdown	1983	—	2.00	4.00
1687	Cold Blooded/(Instrumental)	1983	—	2.00	4.00
1703	U Bring the Freak Out/He Talks	1983	—	2.00	4.00
1714	Ebony Eyes/1,2,3	1983	—	2.50	5.00
—As "Rick James and Friend"					
1714	Ebony Eyes/1,2,3	1983	—	2.00	4.00
—As "Rick James and Smokey Robinson"					
1730	17/(Instrumental)	1984	—	2.00	4.00
1763	You Turn Me On/Fire and Desire	1981	—	2.00	4.00
1776	Can't Stop/Oh What a Night	1985	—	2.00	4.00
1776 [PS]	Can't Stop/Oh What a Night	1985	—	2.50	5.00
1796	Glow/(Instrumental)	1985	—	2.00	4.00
1806	Spend the Night with Me/(Instrumental)	1985	—	2.00	4.00
7156	You & I/Hollywood	1978	—	2.50	5.00
7162	Mary Jane/Dream Maker	1978	—	2.50	5.00
7164	High on Your Love Suite/Stone City Band High	1979	—	2.50	5.00
7164 [PS]	High on Your Love Suite/Stone City Band High	1979	—	3.00	6.00
7167	Bustin' Out/Sexy Lady	1979	—	2.50	5.00
7171	Fool on the Street/Jefferson Hall	1979	—	2.50	5.00
7176	Love Gun/Stormy Love	1979	—	2.50	5.00
7177	Come Into My Life (Part 1)/Come Into My Life (Part 2)	1980	—	2.50	5.00
7185	Big Time/Island Lady	1980	—	2.50	5.00
7191	Gettin' it On (In the Summertime)/Summer Love	1980	—	2.50	5.00
7197	Give It to Me Baby/Don't Give Up on Love	1981	—	2.00	4.00
7205	Super Freak (Part 1)/Super Freak (Part 2)	1981	—	2.00	4.00
7215	Ghetto Life/Below the Funk (Pass the J)	1981	—	2.00	4.00

MOTOWN

Number	Title (A Side/B Side)	Yr	VG	VG+	NM
1844	Sweet and Sexy Thing/(Instrumental)	1986	—	—	3.00
1862	Forever and a Day/(Instrumental)	1986	—	—	3.00

REPRISE

Number	Title (A Side/B Side)	Yr	VG	VG+	NM
27764	Sexual Love Affair/In the Girls' Room	1988	—	—	3.00
27828	Wonderful/(Instrumental)	1988	—	—	3.00
27828 [PS]	Wonderful/(Instrumental)	1988	—	—	3.00
27885	Loosey's Rap/(Instrumental)	1988	—	—	3.00
—With Roxanne Shante					
27885 [PS]	Loosey's Rap/(Instrumental)	1988	—	—	3.00

WARNER BROS.

Number	Title (A Side/B Side)	Yr	VG	VG+	NM
27763	This Magic Moment-Dance with Me/(Instrumental)	1989	—	—	3.00
27763 [PS]	This Magic Moment-Dance with Me/(Instrumental)	1989	—	—	3.00

Albums

GORDY

Number	Title (A Side/B Side)	Yr	VG	VG+	NM
G7-981	Come Get It!	1978	2.50	5.00	10.00
G7-984	Bustin' Out of L. Seven	1979	2.50	5.00	10.00
G8-990	Fire It Up	1979	2.50	5.00	10.00
G8-995	Garden of Love	1980	2.50	5.00	10.00
G8-1002	Street Songs	1981	2.00	4.00	8.00
6005 GL	Throwin' Down	1982	2.00	4.00	8.00
6043 GL	Cold Blooded	1983	2.00	4.00	8.00
6095 GL	Reflections	1984	2.00	4.00	8.00
6135 GL	Glow	1985	2.00	4.00	8.00

MOTOWN

Number	Title (A Side/B Side)	Yr	VG	VG+	NM
5263 ML	Come Get It!	198?	2.00	4.00	8.00
5382 ML	Greatest Hits	1986	2.00	4.00	8.00
MOT-5405	Street Songs	1987	—	3.00	6.00

REPRISE

Number	Title (A Side/B Side)	Yr	VG	VG+	NM
25659	Wonderful	1988	2.50	5.00	10.00

JAMES, SONNY

45s

CAPITOL

Number	Title (A Side/B Side)	Yr	VG	VG+	NM
2067	A World of Our Own/An Old Sweetheart of Mine	1967	2.00	4.00	8.00
2155	Heaven Says Hello/Fairy Tales	1968	—	3.00	6.00
2155 [PS]	Heaven Says Hello/Fairy Tales	1968	2.00	4.00	8.00
F2164	Short Cut/It's So Nice to Make Up	1952	6.25	12.50	25.00
F2259	That's Me Without You/Cool, Cold and Colder	1952	6.25	12.50	25.00
2271	Born to Be With You/In Waikiki	1968	—	3.00	6.00
2271 [PS]	Born to Be With You/In Waikiki	1968	2.00	4.00	8.00
2370	Only the Lonely/The Journey	1968	—	3.00	6.00
2370 [PS]	Only the Lonely/The Journey	1968	2.00	4.00	8.00
F2399	The One I Can't Forget/Somebody's Heartache	1953	6.25	12.50	25.00
2486	Running Bear/Midnight Mood	1969	—	3.00	6.00
2486 [PS]	Running Bear/Midnight Mood	1969	2.00	4.00	8.00
F2508	I Forgot More Than You'll Ever Know/Poor Boy, Rich Lovin'	1953	6.25	12.50	25.00
2595	Since I Met You, Baby/Clinging to a Hope	1969	—	3.00	6.00
2595 [PS]	Since I Met You, Baby/Clinging to a Hope	1969	2.00	4.00	8.00
F2641	Won't Somebody Tell Me/My Greatest Thrill	1953	6.25	12.50	25.00
2700	It's Just a Matter of Time/This World of Ours	1969	—	3.00	6.00
2700 [PS]	It's Just a Matter of Time/This World of Ours	1969	2.00	4.00	8.00
F2734	I've Always Wanted You/That's How I Need You	1954	5.00	10.00	20.00
2782	My Love/Blue for You	1970	—	2.50	5.00
F2829	Table Next to Mine/Believe Another's Lips	1954	5.00	10.00	20.00
2834	Don't Keep Me Hangin' On/Woodbine Valley	1970	—	2.50	5.00
F2906	She Done Give Her Heart to Me/Oceans of Tears	1954	5.00	10.00	20.00
2914	Endlessly/Happy Memories	1970	—	2.50	5.00
F2958	Christmas in My Home Town/I Forgot to Remember Santa Claus	1954	5.00	10.00	20.00
3015	Empty Arms/Everything Begins and Ends with You	1971	—	2.50	5.00
3015 [PS]	Empty Arms/Everything Begins and Ends with You	1971	2.00	4.00	8.00
F3025	Lovin' Season/This Kiss Must Last Forever	1955	5.00	10.00	20.00
F3112	Deceive Me Once Again/Ain't Gonna Take No Chance	1955	5.00	10.00	20.00
3114	Bright Lights, Big City/True Love Lasts Forever	1971	—	2.50	5.00
3114 [PS]	Bright Lights, Big City/True Love Lasts Forever	1971	2.00	4.00	8.00
F3163	Til the Last Leaf Shall Fall/You Don't Have to Walk Alone	1955	5.00	10.00	20.00
3174	Here Comes Honey Again/The Only Ones We Truly Hurt	1971	—	2.50	5.00
F3198	Too Much/Let's Go Bunny Huggin'	1955	5.00	10.00	20.00
3232	Only Love Can Break a Heart/He Has Walked This Way Before	1971	—	2.50	5.00
F3281	Careless with My Heart/Pigtails and Ribbons	1955	5.00	10.00	20.00
3322	That's Why I Love You Like I Do/Still Water Runs Deep	1972	—	2.50	5.00
F3357	For Rent (One Empty Heart)/My Stolen Love	1956	3.75	7.50	15.00
3398	Traces/I'm in Love with You	1972	—	2.50	5.00
F3441	Twenty Feet of Muddy Water/All Mixed Up	1956	3.75	7.50	15.00
3475	Downfall of Me/I'll Follow You	1972	—	2.50	5.00
F3542	The Cat Came Back/Hello, Old Broken Heart	1956	3.75	7.50	15.00
3564	Reach Out Your Hand and Touch Me/Just Keep Thinking of Me	1973	—	2.50	5.00
F3602	Young Love/You're the Reason I'm in Love	1956	4.00	8.00	16.00
3653	Heaven on Earth/She Believes in Me	1973	—	2.50	5.00
F3674	First Date, First Kiss, First Love/Speak to Me	1957	3.75	7.50	15.00
F3734	Lovesick Blues/Dear Love	1957	3.75	7.50	15.00
3779	Surprise, Surprise/What Am I Living For	1973	—	2.50	5.00
F3792	Love Conquered/Mighty Loveable Man	1957	3.75	7.50	15.00
F3840	Uh Huh-mm/Why Can't They Remember	1957	3.75	7.50	15.00
F3888	Kathleen/Walk to the Dance	1958	3.75	7.50	15.00
3931	All the Way Together/Clinging Vine	1974	—	2.50	5.00
F3962	Are You Mine/Let's Play Love	1958	3.75	7.50	15.00
F4020	You Got That Touch/I Can See It in Your Eyes	1958	3.75	7.50	15.00
F4066	Let Me Be the One to Love You/I Can't Stay Away from You	1958	3.75	7.50	15.00
F4127	Yo-Yo/Dream Big	1959	3.75	7.50	15.00
F4178	Talk of the School/The Table	1959	3.75	7.50	15.00
F4229	Pure Love/This Love of Mine	1959	3.75	7.50	15.00
F4268	Who's Next in Line/Red Mud	1959	3.75	7.50	15.00
F4268 [PS]	Who's Next in Line/Red Mud	1959	7.50	15.00	30.00
4307	Till Tomorrow/I Forgot More Than You'll Ever Know	1959	3.75	7.50	15.00
4969	The Minute You're Gone/Gold and Silver	1963	2.50	5.00	10.00
5057	Going Through the Motions (Of Living)/Bad Times a-Comin'	1963	2.50	5.00	10.00
5129	Baltimore/Least of All You	1964	2.50	5.00	10.00
5197	Ask Marie/Sugar Lump	1964	2.50	5.00	10.00
5280	You're the Only World I Know/Tying Pieces Together	1964	2.50	5.00	10.00
5375	I'll Keep Holding On (Just to Your Love)/I'm Getting Gray from Being Blue	1965	2.00	4.00	8.00
5454	Behind the Tear/Runnin'	1965	2.00	4.00	8.00
5536	True Love's a Blessing/Just Ask Your Heart	1965	2.00	4.00	8.00
5612	Take Good Care of Her/On the Fingers of One Hand	1966	2.00	4.00	8.00
5690	Room in Your Heart/How Many Times Can a Man Be a Fool	1966	2.00	4.00	8.00
5733	My Christmas Dream/Barefoot Santa Claus	1966	2.00	4.00	8.00
5733 [PS]	My Christmas Dream/Barefoot Santa Claus	1966	3.00	6.00	12.00
5833	Need You/On and On	1967	2.00	4.00	8.00
5914	I'll Never Find Another You/Goodbye, Maggie, Goodbye	1967	2.00	4.00	8.00
5914 [PS]	I'll Never Find Another You/Goodbye, Maggie, Goodbye	1967	3.00	6.00	12.00
5987	It's the Little Things/Don't Cut Timber on a Windy Day	1967	2.00	4.00	8.00

COLUMBIA

Number	Title (A Side/B Side)	Yr	VG	VG+	NM
10001	A Mi Esposa Con Amor (To My Wife with Love)/Just Don't Stop Lovin' Me	1974	—	2.50	5.00
10072	A Little Bit South of Saskatoon/Home Style Lovin'	1974	—	2.50	5.00
10121	Little Band of Gold/Pop and Me	1975	—	2.50	5.00
10139	Indian Love Call/Maria Elena	1975	—	2.50	5.00
—As "The Guitars of Sonny James"					
10184	What in the World's Come Over You/Walking the Railroad Trestle	1975	—	2.50	5.00
10249	Eres Tu (Touch the Wind)/Apache	1975	—	2.50	5.00
10276	The Prisoner's Song/Back in the Saddle Again	1975	—	2.50	5.00
10335	When Something Is Wrong with My Baby/Big Silver Bird	1976	—	2.50	5.00
10392	Come On In/Baby's Eyes	1976	—	2.50	5.00
10466	You're Free to Go/Puttin' On the Dog Tonight	1976	—	2.50	5.00
10551	In the Jailhouse Now/Amazing Grace	1977	—	2.50	5.00
10628	Abilene/Pistol Packin' Mama	1977	—	2.50	5.00
10703	This Is the Love/It'll Still Be Worth It All	1978	—	2.50	5.00
10764	Caribbean/Each Time I Look at You	1978	—	2.50	5.00
10852	Building Memories/Little Band of Gold	1978	—	2.50	5.00
45644	When the Snow Is On the Roses/Love is a Rainbow	1972	—	2.50	5.00
45706	White Silver Sands/Why Is It I'm the Last to Know	1972	—	2.50	5.00

Number	Title (A Side/B Side)	Yr	VG	VG+	NM
45770	I Love You More and More Everyday/I'll Think About That Tomorrow	1973	—	2.50	5.00
45871	If She Just Helps Me Get Over You/I Won't Think About It Now	1973	—	2.50	5.00
46003	Is It Wrong (For Loving You)/Suddenly There's a Valley	1974	—	2.50	5.00
DIMENSION					
1026	Innocent Lies/Don't Let the Stars Get in Your Eyes	1981	—	2.00	4.00
1033	A Place in the Sun/Leqan On Me Girl	1982	—	2.00	4.00
1036	I'm Looking Over the Rainbow/Something's Got a Hold on Me	1982	—	2.00	4.00
1040	The Fool in Me/Little Rainbow	1982	—	2.00	4.00
1045	A Free Roamin' Mind/(B-side unknown)	1983	—	2.00	4.00
DOT					
16381	A Mile and a Quarter/Just One More Lie	1962	3.00	6.00	12.00
16419	On the Longest Day/The Only Cure	1963	3.00	6.00	12.00
GROOVE					
1	Young Love/Broken Wings	1961	3.00	6.00	12.00
MONUMENT					
45280	Hold What You've Got/Hanging On to Yesterday	1979	—	2.00	4.00
45288	Lorelei/If I Ever Wanted You	1979	—	2.00	4.00
NRC					
050	Jenny Lou/Passin' Through	1960	3.75	7.50	15.00
050 [PS]	Jenny Lou/Passin' Through	1960	6.25	12.50	25.00
056	Cold in the Morning/Wondering	1960	3.00	6.00	12.00
061	Bimbo/I Wish This Night Would Never End	1960	3.00	6.00	12.00
RCA VICTOR					
47-7858	Apache/Magnetism	1961	3.00	6.00	12.00
47-7919	Innocent Angel/Hey Little Ducky	1961	3.00	6.00	12.00
47-7998	The Day's Not Over Yet/The Legend of Brown Mountain Light	1962	3.00	6.00	12.00
7-Inch Extended Plays					
CAPITOL					
EAP 1-779	Can't Get Over Missin' You/Cold, Cold Heart//Only One Heart to Give/I Got the Feeling	1957	5.00	10.00	20.00
EAP 1-779 [PS]	Southern Gentleman, Part 1	1957	5.00	10.00	20.00
EAP 2-779	I Wish I Knew/Forgive Me//I'll Always Wonder (But I'll Never Know)/Lonesome	1957	5.00	10.00	20.00
EAP 2-779 [PS]	Southern Gentleman, Part 2	1957	5.00	10.00	20.00
EAP 3-779	'Til the Last Leaf Shall Fall/Only a Shadow Between//May God Be With You/My God and I	1957	5.00	10.00	20.00
EAP 3-779 [PS]	Southern Gentleman, Part 3	1957	5.00	10.00	20.00
EAP 1-827	Young Love/Twenty Feet of Muddy Water//For Rent/Hello Old Broken Heart	1957	6.25	12.50	25.00
EAP 1-827 [PS]	Young Love	1957	6.25	12.50	25.00
Albums					
ABC					
AC-30027	The ABC Collection	1976	3.00	6.00	12.00
CAPITOL					
ST-111	Born to Be with You	1968	3.75	7.50	15.00
SKAO-144	The Best of Sonny James Vol. 2	1969	3.75	7.50	15.00
ST-193	Only the Lonely	1969	3.75	7.50	15.00
SWBB-258 [(2)]	Close-Up	1969	5.00	10.00	20.00
—Combines ST 2500 and ST 2788 in one package					
ST-320	The Astrodome Presents In Person Sonny James	1969	3.75	7.50	15.00
ST-432	It's Just a Matter of Time	1970	3.75	7.50	15.00
ST-478	My Love/Don't Keep Me Hangin' On	1970	3.75	7.50	15.00
STBB-535 [(2)]	You're the Only World I Know/I'll Never Find Another You	1970	5.00	10.00	20.00
—Combines the two listed albums in one package					
ST-629	#1	1970	3.75	7.50	15.00
ST-734	Empty Arms	1971	3.75	7.50	15.00
T 779 [M]	The Southern Gentleman	1957	12.50	25.00	50.00
—Turquoise label					
T 779 [M]	The Southern Gentleman	1964	5.00	10.00	20.00
—Black label with colorband, logo on top					
ST-804	The Sensational Sonny James	1971	3.75	7.50	15.00
ST-849	Here Comes Honey Again	1971	3.75	7.50	15.00
T 887 [M]	Sonny	1957	12.50	25.00	50.00
—Turquoise label					
T 887 [M]	Sonny	1964	5.00	10.00	20.00
—Black label with colorband, logo on top					
T 988 [M]	Honey	1958	12.50	25.00	50.00
—Turquoise label					
T 988 [M]	Honey	1964	5.00	10.00	20.00
—Black label with colorband, logo on top					
T 1178 [M]	This Is Sonny James	1959	10.00	20.00	40.00
—Black label with colorband, logo at left					
T 1178 [M]	This Is Sonny James	1964	5.00	10.00	20.00
—Black label with colorband, logo on top					
ST 2017 [S]	The Minute You're Gone	1964	6.25	12.50	25.00
T 2017 [M]	The Minute You're Gone	1964	5.00	10.00	20.00
ST 2209 [S]	You're the Only World I Know	1965	6.25	12.50	25.00
T 2209 [M]	You're the Only World I Know	1965	5.00	10.00	20.00
ST 2317 [S]	I'll Keep Holding On	1965	6.25	12.50	25.00
T 2317 [M]	I'll Keep Holding On	1965	5.00	10.00	20.00
ST 2415 [S]	Behind the Tear	1965	6.25	12.50	25.00
T 2415 [M]	Behind the Tear	1965	5.00	10.00	20.00
ST 2500 [S]	True Love's a Blessing	1966	6.25	12.50	25.00
T 2500 [M]	True Love's a Blessing	1966	5.00	10.00	20.00
ST 2561 [S]	Till the Last Leaf Shall Fall	1966	6.25	12.50	25.00
T 2561 [M]	Till the Last Leaf Shall Fall	1966	5.00	10.00	20.00
ST 2589 [S]	My Christmas Dream	1966	6.25	12.50	25.00
T 2589 [M]	My Christmas Dream	1966	5.00	10.00	20.00
SM-2615	The Best of Sonny James	197?	2.50	5.00	10.00
ST 2615 [S]	The Best of Sonny James	1966	5.00	10.00	20.00
—Black Starline label					
T 2615 [M]	The Best of Sonny James	1966	3.75	7.50	15.00
ST 2703 [S]	Need You	1967	3.75	7.50	15.00
T 2703 [M]	Need You	1967	5.00	10.00	20.00
ST 2788 [S]	I'll Never Find Another You	1967	3.75	7.50	15.00
T 2788 [M]	I'll Never Find Another You	1967	5.00	10.00	20.00
ST 2884 [S]	A World of Our Own	1968	3.75	7.50	15.00
T 2884 [M]	A World of Our Own	1968	6.25	12.50	25.00
ST 2937	Heaven Says Hello	1968	3.75	7.50	15.00
SM-11013	The Biggest Hits of Sonny James	197?	2.50	5.00	10.00
ST-11013	The Biggest Hits of Sonny James	1972	3.75	7.50	15.00
ST-11067	That's Why I Love You Like I Do	1972	3.75	7.50	15.00
ST-11108	Traces	1972	3.00	6.00	12.00
ST-11144	The Gentleman from the South	1973	3.00	6.00	12.00
ST-11196	Young Love	1973	3.00	6.00	12.00
COLUMBIA					
KC 31646	When the Snow Is On the Roses	1972	3.00	6.00	12.00
KC 32028	Sonny James Sings the Greatest Country Hits of '72	1973	3.00	6.00	12.00
KC 32291	If She Just Helps Me Get Over You	1973	3.00	6.00	12.00
KC 32805	Is It Wrong	1974	3.00	6.00	12.00
KC 33056	A Mi Esposa Con Amor (To My Wife with Love)	1974	3.00	6.00	12.00
KC 33428	A Little Bit South of Saskatoon/Little Band of Gold	1975	3.00	6.00	12.00
PC 33477	The Guitars of Sonny James	1975	3.00	6.00	12.00
CG 33627 [(2)]	When the Snow Is On the Roses/If She Just Helps Me Get Over You	1975	3.75	7.50	15.00
PC 33846	Country Male Artist of the Decade	1975	3.00	6.00	12.00
PC 34035	200 Years of Country Music	1976	3.00	6.00	12.00
PC 34309	When Something Is Wrong with My Baby	1976	3.00	6.00	12.00
PC 34472	You're Free to Go	1977	3.00	6.00	12.00
PC 34706	Sonny James In Prison, In Person	1977	3.00	6.00	12.00
KC 35379	This Is the Love	1978	3.00	6.00	12.00
KC 35626	Sonny James' Greatest Hits	1978	3.00	6.00	12.00
DOT					
DLP 3462 [M]	Young Love	1962	10.00	20.00	40.00
DLP 25462 [S]	Young Love	1962	12.50	25.00	50.00
DOT/MCA					
39087	Sonny James	198?	2.50	5.00	10.00
HILLTOP					
6067	Invisible Tears	1969	2.50	5.00	10.00
6079	Timberline	1969	2.50	5.00	10.00
PICKWICK					
SPC-3594	Young Love	1977	2.00	4.00	8.00
RCA CAMDEN					
CAL-2140 [M]	Young Love	1967	3.75	7.50	15.00
CAS-2140 [S]	Young Love	1967	3.00	6.00	12.00

JAMES, TOMMY

Number	Title (A Side/B Side)	Yr	VG	VG+	NM
45s					
21 RECORDS					
105	Two-Time Lover/Say Please	1983	—	—	3.00
105 [PS]	Two-Time Lover/Say Please	1983	—	2.00	4.00
FANTASY					
761	I Love You Love Me Love/Devil Gate Drive	1976	—	2.00	4.00
761 [PS]	I Love You Love Me Love/Devil Gate Drive	1976	—	2.50	5.00
776	Tighter, Tighter/Comin' Down	1976	—	2.50	5.00
811	Love Is Gonna Find a Way/I Don't Love You Anymore	1977	—	2.50	5.00
886	Tighter, Tighter/Comin' Down	1980	—	2.00	4.00
MCA					
40289	Glory, Glory/Comin' Down	1974	—	2.50	5.00
MILLENNIUM					
YB-11785	Three Times in Love/I Just Wanna Play the Music	1980	—	2.00	4.00
YB-11787	No Hay Dos Sin Tres (Three Times in Love)/I Just Wanna Play the Music	1980	—	2.50	5.00
YB-11787 [PS]	No Hay Dos Sin Tres (Three Times in Love)/I Just Wanna Play the Music	1980	2.50	5.00	10.00
YB-11788	It's Alright (For Now)/You Got Me	1980	—	2.00	4.00
YB-11802	You're So Easy to Love/Halfway to Heaven	1981	—	2.00	4.00
YB-11814	The Lady in White/Payin' for My Lover's Mistake	1981	—	2.00	4.00
ROULETTE					
7084	Ball and Chain/Candy Maker	1970	—	3.00	6.00
7093	Church Street Soul Revival/Draggin' the Line	1970	2.00	4.00	8.00
7100	Adrienne/Light of Day	1971	—	3.00	6.00
7103	Draggin' the Line/Bits & Pieces	1971	—	3.00	6.00
7110	I'm Coming Home/Sing, Sing, Sing	1971	—	2.50	5.00
7114	Nothing to Hide/Walk a Country Mile	1971	—	2.50	5.00
7119	Tell 'Em Willie Boy's A-Comin'/Forty Days and Dorty Nights	1972	—	2.50	5.00
7126	Cat's Eye in the Window/Dark Is the Night	1972	—	2.50	5.00
7130	Love Song/Kingston Highway	1972	—	2.50	5.00
7135	Celebration/The Last One to Know	1972	—	2.50	5.00
7140	Boo, Boo, Don't Cha Be Blue/Rings and Things	1973	—	2.50	5.00
7147	Calico/Hey, My Lady	1973	—	2.50	5.00
Albums					
FANTASY					
9509	In Touch	1976	3.00	6.00	12.00
9532	Midnight Rider	1977	3.00	6.00	12.00
MILLENNIUM					
BXL1-7748	Three Times in Love	1980	2.50	5.00	10.00
BXL1-7758	Easy to Love	1981	2.50	5.00	10.00
ROULETTE					
3001	Christian of the World	1971	3.75	7.50	15.00
3007	My Head, My Bed, My Red Guitar	1972	3.75	7.50	15.00
SR-42061	Tommy James	1970	3.75	7.50	15.00

JAMES, TOMMY, AND THE SHONDELLS

Also see HOG HEAVEN; TOMMY JAMES.

Number	Title (A Side/B Side)	Yr	VG	VG+	NM
45s					
PHILCO-FORD					
HP-1	Mirage/I Think We're Alone Now	1967	3.75	7.50	15.00
—4-inch plastic "Hip Pocket Record" with color sleeve					
HP-2	Hanky Panky/Gettin' Together	1967	3.75	7.50	15.00
—4-inch plastic "Hip Pocket Record" with color sleeve					
RED FOX					
110	Hanky Panky/Thunderbolt	1966	10.00	20.00	40.00
—As "The Shondells"					
ROULETTE					
4686	Hanky Panky/Thunderbolt	1966	2.50	5.00	10.00
4695	Say I Am (What I Am)/Lots of Pretty Girls	1966	2.00	4.00	8.00
4695 [PS]	Say I Am (What I Am)/Lots of Pretty Girls	1966	3.75	7.50	15.00

Number	Title (A Side/B Side)	Yr	VG	VG+	NM
4710	It's Only Love/Don't Let My Love Pass You By	1966	2.00	4.00	8.00
4710	It's Only Love/Ya Ya	1966	3.00	6.00	12.00
4720	I Think We're Alone Now/Gone, Gone, Gone	1967	2.50	5.00	10.00
4720 [PS]	I Think We're Alone Now/Gone, Gone, Gone	1967	3.75	7.50	15.00
4736	Mirage/Run, Run, Baby, Run	1967	2.00	4.00	8.00
4736 [PS]	Mirage/Run, Run, Baby, Run	1967	3.75	7.50	15.00
4756	I Like the Way/(Baby) Baby I Can't Take It No More	1967	2.00	4.00	8.00
4762	Gettin' Together/Real Girl	1967	2.00	4.00	8.00
4762 [PS]	Gettin' Together/Real Girl	1967	3.75	7.50	15.00
4775	Out of the Blue/Love's Closin' In on Me	1967	2.00	4.00	8.00
7000	Get Out Now/Wish It Were True	1968	2.00	4.00	8.00
7008	Mony Mony/One Two Three and I Fell	1968	2.50	5.00	10.00
7016	Somebody Cares/Do Unto Me	1968	2.00	4.00	8.00
7024	Do Something to Me/Ginger Bread Man	1968	2.00	4.00	8.00
7028	Crimson and Clover/(I'm) Taken	1968	3.75	7.50	15.00
7028	Crimson and Clover/Some Kind of Love	1968	2.50	5.00	10.00
7039	Sweet Cherry Wine/Breakaway	1969	2.00	4.00	8.00
7050	Crystal Blue Persuasion/I'm Alive	1969	2.50	5.00	10.00
7060	Ball of Fire/Makin' Good Time	1969	2.00	4.00	8.00
7066	She/Loved One	1969	2.00	4.00	8.00
7071	Gotta Get Back to You/Red Rover	1970	2.00	4.00	8.00
7076	Come to Me/Talkin' and Signifyin'	1970	2.00	4.00	8.00
SNAP					
102	Hanky Panky/Thunderbolt	1963	20.00	40.00	80.00
—As "The Shondells"; no mention of Red Fox Records on label					
102	Hanky Panky/Thunderbolt	1966	7.50	15.00	30.00
—As "The Shondells"; with "Dist. by Red Fox Records, Pgh, Pa." on label					
Albums					
RHINO					
R1-70920 [(2)]	Anthology	1989	3.75	7.50	15.00
ROULETTE					
R 25336 [M]	Hanky Panky	1966	5.00	10.00	20.00
SR 25336 [P]	Hanky Panky	1966	6.25	12.50	25.00
—"Hanky Panky" is rechanneled					
R 25344 [M]	It's Only Love	1967	7.50	15.00	30.00
SR 25344 [S]	It's Only Love	1967	6.25	12.50	25.00
R 25353 [M]	I Think We're Alone Now	1967	7.50	15.00	30.00
SR 25353 [P]	I Think We're Alone Now	1967	6.25	12.50	25.00
—Footprints cover; "I Think We're Alone Now" is rechanneled					
SR 25353 [P]	I Think We're Alone Now	1967	3.75	7.50	15.00
—Photo cover					
SR 25355	Something Special! The Best of Tommy James & The Shondells	1968	6.25	12.50	25.00
R 25357 [M]	Gettin' Together	1968	10.00	20.00	40.00
SR 25357 [S]	Gettin' Together	1968	6.25	12.50	25.00
SR 42005	Something Special! The Best of Tommy James & The Shondells	1968	3.75	7.50	15.00
SR 42012	Mony Mony	1968	5.00	10.00	20.00
SR 42023	Crimson and Clover	1969	5.00	10.00	20.00
SR 42030	Cellophane Symphony	1969	5.00	10.00	20.00
SR 42040	The Best of Tommy James & The Shondells	1969	5.00	10.00	20.00
—Original versions are in a Unipak (gatefold must be opened to remove record)					
SR 42040	The Best of Tommy James & The Shondells	197?	3.75	7.50	15.00
—Later versions have gatefold covers, but record can be removed without opening it					
SR 42044	Travelin'	1970	3.75	7.50	15.00

JAMES GANG, THE (1)

Also see TOMMY BOLIN; JOE WALSH.

45s

Number	Title (A Side/B Side)	Yr	VG	VG+	NM
ABC					
11272	Funk #49/Thanks	1970	—	3.00	6.00
11301	Walk Away/Yadig?	1971	—	3.00	6.00
11312	White Man—Black Man/Midnight	1971	—	3.00	6.00
11325	Looking for My Lady/Hairy Hypochondriac	1972	—	3.00	6.00
11336	Had Enough/Kick Back Man	1972	—	3.00	6.00
ATCO					
6953	Must Be Love/Got No Time for Trouble	1974	—	2.50	5.00
6966	Standing in the Rain/From Another Time	1974	—	2.50	5.00
7006	Cruisin' Down the Highway/Miami Two-Step	1974	—	2.50	5.00
7021	Merry Go Round/Red Satin Lover	1975	—	2.50	5.00
7067	I Need Love/Feelin' Alright	1975	—	2.50	5.00
BLUESWAY					
61027	I Don't Have the Time/Fred	1969	2.00	4.00	8.00
61030	Funk #48/Collage	1969	2.50	5.00	10.00
61033	Take a Look Around/Stop	1970	2.00	4.00	8.00
Albums					
ABC					
S-688	Yer' Album	1970	3.00	6.00	12.00
S-711	James Gang Rides Again	1970	6.25	12.50	25.00
—First pressing with a short version of Ravel's "Bolero" as part of the song "The Bomber"; exists on both promos and early stock copies; no "RE-1" in trail-off wax					
S-711	James Gang Rides Again	1970	3.00	6.00	12.00
—Standard pressing without "Bolero" as part of "The Bomber"; "RE-1" in trail-off wax					
X-721	Thirds	1971	3.00	6.00	12.00
X-733	James Gang Live in Concert	1971	3.00	6.00	12.00
X-741	Straight Shooter	1972	3.00	6.00	12.00
X-760	Passin' Thru	1972	3.00	6.00	12.00
ABCX-774	The Best of the James Gang Featuring Joe Walsh	1973	3.00	6.00	12.00
—Most copies of this LP contain the edited version of "The Bomber." The full title of the LP is on the spine, and the record's trail-off wax has the number "ABCX-774-A-RE-1".					
ABCX-774	The Best of the James Gang Featuring Joe Walsh	1973	5.00	10.00	20.00
—A few copies of this LP contain the full version of "The Bomber" with the "Bolero" excerpt. The words "The Best Of" do NOT appear on the spine, and the record's trail-off wax has the number "ABCX-774-A".					
X-801 [(2)]	16 Greatest Hits	1973	3.75	7.50	15.00
ATCO					
SD 36-102	Miami	1974	2.50	5.00	10.00
SD 36-112	Newborn	1975	2.50	5.00	10.00
SD 36-141	Jesse Come Home	1976	2.50	5.00	10.00
SD 7037	Bang	1973	2.50	5.00	10.00
BLUESWAY					
BLS-6034	Yer' Album	1969	3.75	7.50	15.00
MCA					
6012 [(2)]	16 Greatest Hits	1980	2.50	5.00	10.00
—Reissue					
37111	James Gang Rides Again	1980	2.00	4.00	8.00
—Reissue					
37112	The Best of the James Gang Featuring Joe Walsh	1980	2.00	4.00	8.00
—Reissue					

JAMES GANG, THE (2)

45s

Number	Title (A Side/B Side)	Yr	VG	VG+	NM
ASCOT					
2168	Everybody Knows/Ladies' Man	1965	3.00	6.00	12.00
2196	Georgia Pines/Baby Take Me Back	1965	3.00	6.00	12.00
2205	Right String But the Wrong Yo-Yo/Satin and Lace	1966	3.00	6.00	12.00

JAMESON, BOBBY

45s

Number	Title (A Side/B Side)	Yr	VG	VG+	NM
CURRENT					
103	All Alone/Your Sweet Lovin'	1964	3.00	6.00	12.00
LONDON					
9730	All I Want Is My Baby/Each and Everyday	1965	10.00	20.00	40.00

JAMIE AND JANE

"Jamie" is GENE PITNEY.

45s

Number	Title (A Side/B Side)	Yr	VG	VG+	NM
DECCA					
30862	Snuggle Up Baby/Strollin' Thru the Park	1959	7.50	15.00	30.00
30934	Faithful Our Love/Classical Rock and Roll	1959	7.50	15.00	30.00

JAMIES, THE

45s

Number	Title (A Side/B Side)	Yr	VG	VG+	NM
EPIC					
9281	Summertime, Summertime/Searching for You	1958	3.00	6.00	12.00
—Reissued in 1962 with the same catalog number and label design					
9281 [PS]	Summertime, Summertime/Searching for You	1958	5.00	10.00	20.00
9299	When the Sun Goes Down/Snow Train	1958	5.00	10.00	20.00
9565	When the Sun Goes Down/Snow Train	1963	3.00	6.00	12.00
11129	Summertime, Summertime/Searching for You	1974	—	2.50	5.00
UNITED ARTISTS					
193	The Evening Star/Don't Darken My Door	1959	5.00	10.00	20.00

JAMME

45s

Number	Title (A Side/B Side)	Yr	VG	VG+	NM
ABC DUNHILL					
4231	Poor Widow/She Sits There	1970	2.00	4.00	8.00
Albums					
ABC DUNHILL					
DS-50072	Jamme	1970	5.00	10.00	20.00

JAN AND ARNIE

Also see JAN AND DEAN.

45s

Number	Title (A Side/B Side)	Yr	VG	VG+	NM
ARWIN					
108	Jennie Lee/Gotta Getta Date	1958	10.00	20.00	40.00
111	Gas Money/Bonnie Lou	1958	10.00	20.00	40.00
113	I Love Linda/The Beat That Can't Be Beat	1958	15.00	30.00	60.00
DORE					
522	Baby Talk/Jeannette Get Your Hair Done	1959	150.00	300.00	600.00
—Actually by Jan and Dean, but incorrectly credited					
DOT					
16116	Gas Money/Gotta Getta Date	1960	12.50	25.00	50.00
7-Inch Extended Plays					
DOT					
DEP-1097	(contents unknown)	1960	125.00	250.00	500.00
DEP-1097 [PS]	Jan and Arnie	1960	125.00	250.00	500.00

JAN AND DEAN

Also see JAN BERRY; THE LEGENDARY MASKED SURFERS; THE RALLY PACKS.

45s

Number	Title (A Side/B Side)	Yr	VG	VG+	NM
CHALLENGE					
9111	Heart and Soul/Those Words	1961	10.00	20.00	40.00
9111	Heart and Soul/A Midsummer Night's Dream	1961	5.00	10.00	20.00
9120	Wanted: One Girl/Something a Little Bit Different	1961	7.50	15.00	30.00
COLUMBIA					
44036	Yellow Balloon/Taste of Rain	1967	7.50	15.00	30.00
DORE					
522	Baby Talk/Jeannette Get Your Hair Done	1959	7.50	15.00	30.00
531	There's a Girl/My Heart Sings	1959	6.25	12.50	25.00
539	Clementine/You're On My Mind	1960	6.25	12.50	25.00
548	Cindy/Whiter Tennis Sneakers	1960	6.25	12.50	25.00
555	We Go Together/Rosilane	1960	6.25	12.50	25.00
555	We Go Together/Rosie Lane	1960	6.25	12.50	25.00
—B-side title was altered after the record no longer was issued with picture sleeve					
555 [PS]	We Go Together/Rosilane	1960	30.00	60.00	120.00
576	Gee/Such a Good Night to Be Together	1960	6.25	12.50	25.00
576 [PS]	Gee/Such a Good Night to Be Together	1960	75.00	150.00	300.00
583	Baggy Pants/Judy's an Angel	1961	7.50	15.00	30.00
610	Julie/Don't Fly Away	1961	7.50	15.00	30.00
EVATONE					
7801X	Surf Bunkey	1980	2.00	4.00	8.00
—6-inch red flexi-disc; Dutch version of "Surf City"					
JAN & DEAN					
10	Hawaii/Tijuana	1966	18.75	37.50	75.00
11	Fan Tan/Love and Hate	1966	30.00	60.00	120.00
J&D					
001	California Lullabye/Summertime	1966	7.50	15.00	30.00
402	Like a Summer Rain/Louisiana Man	1966	7.50	15.00	30.00
1271 [DJ]	Ocean Park Angel/Wipe Out	1981	—	—	—
—B-side by the Surfaris					

Number	Title (A Side/B Side)	Yr	VG	VG+	NM
LIBERTY					
S7-19770	Frosty (The Snow Man)/Rudolph the Red-Nosed Reindeer	1997	—	—	3.00
—B-side by the Ventures on Dolton					
55397	A Sunday Kind of Love/Poor Little Puppet	1961	6.25	12.50	25.00
55454	Tennessee/Your Heart Has Changed Its Mind	1962	6.25	12.50	25.00
55496	Who Put the Bomp/My Favorite Dream	1962	12.50	25.00	50.00
55522	Frosty (The Snow Man)/(She's Still Talking) Baby Talk	1962	37.50	75.00	150.00
—Promos worth about half this value					
55531	Linda/When I Learn How to Cry	1963	6.25	12.50	25.00
55580	Surf City/She's My Summer Girl	1963	3.75	7.50	15.00
55580 [PS]	Surf City/She's My Summer Girl	1963	10.00	20.00	40.00
55613	Honolulu Lulu/Someday	1963	3.75	7.50	15.00
55613 [PS]	Honolulu Lulu/Someday	1963	10.00	20.00	40.00
55641	Drag City/Schlock Rod (Part 1)	1963	3.75	7.50	15.00
55641 [PS]	Drag City/Schlock Rod (Part 1)	1963	10.00	20.00	40.00
55672	Dead Man's Curve/The New Girl in School	1964	3.75	7.50	15.00
55672 [PS]	Dead Man's Curve/The New Girl in School	1964	10.00	20.00	40.00
55704	The Little Old Lady (From Pasadena)/My Mighty G.T.O.	1964	3.75	7.50	15.00
55704 [PS]	The Little Old Lady (From Pasadena)/My Mighty G.T.O.	1964	10.00	20.00	40.00
55724	Ride the Wild Surf/The Anaheim, Azusa and Cucamonga Sewing Circle, Book Review and Timing Association	1964	3.75	7.50	15.00
55724 [PS]	Ride the Wild Surf/The Anaheim, Azusa and Cucamonga Sewing Circle, Book Review and Timing Association	1964	10.00	20.00	40.00
55727	Sidewalk Surfin'/When It's Over	1964	3.75	7.50	15.00
55727 [PS]	Sidewalk Surfin'/When It's Over	1964	10.00	20.00	40.00
55766	(Here They Come) From All Over the World/ Freeway Flyer	1965	3.00	6.00	12.00
55766 [PS]	(Here They Come) From All Over the World/ Freeway Flyer	1965	50.00	100.00	200.00
55792	You Really Know How to Hurt a Guy/It's As Easy As 1-2-3	1965	3.00	6.00	12.00
55792 [PS]	You Really Know How to Hurt a Guy/It's As Easy As 1-2-3	1965	7.50	15.00	30.00
55816	It's a Shame to Say Goodbye/The Submarine Races	1965	—	—	—
—Unreleased					
55833	I Found a Girl/It's a Shame to Say Goodbye	1965	3.00	6.00	12.00
55849	Folk City/A Beginning from an End	1965	3.00	6.00	12.00
55849 [PS]	Folk City/A Beginning from an End	1965	7.50	15.00	30.00
55856	Norwegian Wood/I Can't Wait to Love You	1966	—	—	—
—Unreleased					
55860	Batman/Bucket "T"	1966	6.25	12.50	25.00
55886	Popsicle/Norwegian Wood	1966	3.00	6.00	12.00
55905	Fiddle Around/Surfer's Dream	1966	3.00	6.00	12.00
55923	The New Girl in School/School Days	1966	3.00	6.00	12.00
MAGIC LAMP					
401	California Lullabye/Summertime	1966	7.50	15.00	30.00
ODE					
66111	Fun City/Totally Wild	1975	6.25	12.50	25.00
UNITED ARTISTS					
0089	Jennie Lee/Baby Talk	1973	3.75	7.50	15.00
—0089 through 0094 are "Silver Spotlight Series" reissues					
0090	Linda/The New Girl in School	1973	3.75	7.50	15.00
0091	Surf City/Ride the Wild Surf	1973	3.75	7.50	15.00
0092	Dead Man's Curve/Drag City	1973	3.75	7.50	15.00
0093	Honolulu Lulu/Sidewalk Surfin'	1973	3.75	7.50	15.00
0094	The Little Old Lady (From Pasadena)/Popsicle	1973	3.75	7.50	15.00
XW670	Sidewalk Surfin'/Gonna Hustle You	1975	3.75	7.50	15.00
50859	Jennie Lee/Vegetables	1971	3.75	7.50	15.00
50859 [PS]	Jennie Lee/Vegetables	1971	6.25	12.50	25.00
WARNER BROS.					
7151	Only a Boy/Love and Hate	1967	10.00	20.00	40.00
7219	Laurel and Hardy/I Know My Mind	1968	12.50	25.00	50.00
7240 [DJ]	In the Still of the Night/Girl, You're Blowing My Mind	1968	20.00	40.00	80.00
—Stock copy may not exist					

7-Inch Extended Plays

Number	Title (A Side/B Side)	Yr	VG	VG+	NM
SUNDAZED					
SEP 125	Yellow Balloon/Raindrops//California Lullaby/ Here Comes the Rain	1996	—	—	2.50
—Light blue marbled vinyl; instrumental versions of songs on the reissue of the "Save for a Rainy Day" LP					
SEP 125 [PS]	Sounds for a Rainy Day	1996	—	—	2.50

Albums

Number	Title (A Side/B Side)	Yr	VG	VG+	NM
COLUMBIA					
CL 2661 [M]	Save for a Rainy Day	1967	—	—	—
—Canceled					
CS 9461 [S]	Save for a Rainy Day	1967	2000.	3000.	4000.
—LP not known to exist, but an acetate does, and possibly an import on this label and number					
DEADMAN'S CURVE					
(no #)	Live at the Keystone Berkeley	1981	12.50	25.00	50.00
—Plain jacket with front and back cover inserts					
(no #)	Live at the Keystone Berkeley	1981	6.25	12.50	25.00
—With front and back covers pasted on					
DORE					
LP-101	Jan and Dean Bonus Photo	1960	30.00	60.00	120.00
LP-101	Jan and Dean	197?	3.75	7.50	15.00
—Reissue with black label					
LP-101 [M]	Jan and Dean	1960	100.00	200.00	400.00
—Original with blue label					
J&D					
101 [M]	Save for a Rainy Day	1967	75.00	150.00	300.00
—Private pressing by Dean Torrence of unreleased Columbia album					
LIBERTY					
LRP-3248 [M]	Jan and Dean's Golden Hits	1962	7.50	15.00	30.00
LRP-3294 [M]	Jan and Dean Take Linda Surfin'	1963	12.50	25.00	50.00
LRP-3314 [M]	Surf City and Other Swingin' Cities	1963	10.00	20.00	40.00
LRP-3339 [M]	Drag City	1963	10.00	20.00	40.00
LRP-3361 [M]	Dead Man's Curve/The New Girl in School	1964	10.00	20.00	40.00
—Black and white cover with pink tint					
LRP-3361 [M]	Dead Man's Curve/The New Girl in School	1964	7.50	15.00	30.00
—Full-color cover					
LRP-3361 [M]	The New Girl in School/Dead Man's Curve	1964	5.00	10.00	20.00
—Reissue with reversed title					
LRP-3368 [M]	Ride the Wild Surf	1964	7.50	15.00	30.00
LRP-3377 [M]	The Little Old Lady from Pasadena	1964	7.50	15.00	30.00
LRP-3403 [M]	Command Performance/Live in Person	1965	7.50	15.00	30.00
LRP-3417 [M]	Jan and Dean's Golden Hits, Volume 2	1965	6.25	12.50	25.00
LRP-3431 [M]	Folk 'N' Roll	1965	7.50	15.00	30.00
LRP-3441 [M]	Filet of Soul	1966	7.50	15.00	30.00
LRP-3444 [M]	Jan and Dean Meet Batman	1966	12.50	25.00	50.00
LRP-3458 [M]	Popsicle	1966	7.50	15.00	30.00
LRP-3460 [M]	Jan and Dean's Golden Hits, Volume 3	1966	6.25	12.50	25.00
LST-7248 [S]	Jan and Dean's Golden Hits	1962	10.00	20.00	40.00
LST-7294 [S]	Jan and Dean Take Linda Surfin'	1963	20.00	40.00	80.00
LST-7314 [S]	Surf City and Other Swingin' Cities	1963	12.50	25.00	50.00
LST-7339 [S]	Drag City	1963	12.50	25.00	50.00
LST-7361 [S]	Dead Man's Curve/The New Girl in School	1964	12.50	25.00	50.00
—Black and white cover with pink tint					
LST-7361 [S]	Dead Man's Curve/The New Girl in School	1964	10.00	2.00	40.00
—Full-color cover					
LST-7361 [S]	The New Girl in School/Dead Man's Curve	1964	7.50	15.00	30.00
—Reissue with reversed title					
LST-7368 [S]	Ride the Wild Surf	1964	10.00	20.00	40.00
LST-7377 [S]	The Little Old Lady from Pasadena	1964	10.00	20.00	40.00
LST-7403 [S]	Command Performance/Live in Person	1965	10.00	20.00	40.00
LST-7417 [S]	Jan and Dean's Golden Hits, Volume 2	1965	7.50	15.00	30.00
LST-7431 [S]	Folk 'N' Roll	1965	10.00	20.00	40.00
LST-7441 [S]	Filet of Soul	1966	10.00	20.00	40.00
LST-7444 [S]	Jan and Dean Meet Batman	1966	17.50	35.00	70.00
LST-7458 [S]	Popsicle	1966	10.00	20.00	40.00
LST-7460 [S]	Jan and Dean's Golden Hits, Volume 3	1966	7.50	15.00	30.00
LN-10011	Dead Man's Curve	1980	2.00	4.00	8.00
—Budget-line reissue					
LN-10115	The Best of Jan and Dean	1981	2.00	4.00	8.00
LN-10151	The Little Old Lady from Pasadena	1982	2.00	4.00	8.00
—Budget-line reissue					
PAIR					
PDL2-1071 [(2)]	California Gold	1986	3.00	6.00	12.00
RHINO					
RNDA 1498 [(2)]	One Summer Night — Live	1982	5.00	10.00	20.00
SUNDAZED					
LP 5022 [(2)]	Save for a Rainy Day	1996	3.75	7.50	15.00
—First release to the general public; colored vinyl					
LP 5040	Jan and Dean (The Dore Album)	1996	2.50	5.00	10.00
—Reissue of Dore LP on colored vinyl with extra tracks and poster					
SUNSET					
SUM-1156 [M]	Jan and Dean	1967	3.75	7.50	15.00
SUS-5156 [S]	Jan and Dean	1967	3.75	7.50	15.00
UNITED ARTISTS					
UA-LA341-H2 [(2)]	Gotta Take That One Last Ride	1974	3.75	7.50	15.00
UA-LA443-E	The Very Best of Jan and Dean	1975	2.50	5.00	10.00
UA-LA515-E	The Very Best of Jan and Dean, Volume 2	1975	2.50	5.00	10.00
UAS-9961 [(2)]	Anthology (Legendary Masters Series, Vol. 3)	1971	6.25	12.50	25.00

JAN AND LORRAINE

Albums

Number	Title (A Side/B Side)	Yr	VG	VG+	NM
ABC					
S-691	Gypsy People	1969	6.25	12.50	25.00

JANKOWSKI, HORST

45s

Number	Title (A Side/B Side)	Yr	VG	VG+	NM
MERCURY					
72425	A Walk in the Black Forest/Nola	1965	2.00	4.00	8.00
72465	Simple Gimple/Charming Vienna	1965	—	3.00	6.00
72465 [PS]	Simple Gimple/Charming Vienna	1965	2.00	4.00	8.00
72492	Heide/Happy Frankfurt	1965	—	3.00	6.00
72520	Cruisin' Down the River/Play a Simple Melody	1966	—	3.00	6.00
72567	Black Forest Holiday/Elmer's Tune	1966	—	3.00	6.00
72615	A Place in the Sun/So What's New	1966	—	3.00	6.00
72647	Spy with a Cold Nose/Big, Big River	1966	—	3.00	6.00
72740	A Man and a Woman/A Lover's Concerto	1967	—	3.00	6.00
72766	Glory of Love/Lazy	1968	—	2.50	5.00
72809	And We Got Love/Zabadak	1968	—	2.50	5.00
72851	Chitty Chitty Bang Bang/This Guy's in Love with You	1968	—	2.50	5.00
72948	Dream Flight/Pink Balloon	1969	—	2.50	5.00

Albums

Number	Title (A Side/B Side)	Yr	VG	VG+	NM
MERCURY					
MG-20993 [M]	The Genius of Jankowski	1965	3.00	6.00	12.00
MG-21054 [M]	More Genius of Jankowski	1965	3.00	6.00	12.00
MG-21076 [M]	Still More Genius of Jankowski	1966	3.00	6.00	12.00
MG-21093 [M]	So What's New?	1966	3.00	6.00	12.00
MG-21106 [M]	Baby But Grand	1967	3.00	6.00	12.00
MG-21125 [M]	With Love	1967	3.00	6.00	12.00
SR-60993 [S]	The Genius of Jankowski	1965	3.75	7.50	15.00
SR-61054 [S]	More Genius of Jankowski	1965	3.75	7.50	15.00
SR-61076 [S]	Still More Genius of Jankowski	1966	3.75	7.50	15.00
SR-61093 [S]	So What's New?	1966	3.75	7.50	15.00
SR-61106 [S]	Baby But Grand	1967	3.75	7.50	15.00
SR-61125 [S]	With Love	1967	3.75	7.50	15.00
SR-61160	And We Got Love	1968	3.00	6.00	12.00
SR-61195	Piano Affairs	1968	3.00	6.00	12.00
SR-61219	Jankowski Plays Jankowski	1969	3.00	6.00	12.00
SR-61232	A Walk in the Evergreens	1970	3.00	6.00	12.00

JANSSEN, DAVID

Albums

Number	Title (A Side/B Side)	Yr	VG	VG+	NM
EPIC					
LN 24150 [M]	Hidden Island	1965	5.00	10.00	20.00
BN 26150 [S]	Hidden Island	1965	6.25	12.50	25.00

JAPANESE BEATLES, THE

45s

Number	Title (A Side/B Side)	Yr	VG	VG+	NM
GOLDEN CREST					
584	The Beatle Song (Japanese Style) (Part 1)/The Beatle Song (Japanese Style) (Part 2)	1964	5.00	10.00	20.00

JARMELS, THE

45s

Number	Title (A Side/B Side)	Yr	VG	VG+	NM
LAURIE					
3085	Little Lonely One/She Loves to Dance	1961	3.75	7.50	15.00
3098	A Little Bit of Soap/The Way You Look Tonight	1961	5.00	10.00	20.00
3116	I'll Follow You/Gee Oh Gosh	1962	3.75	7.50	15.00
3124	Red Sails in the Sunset/Loneliness	1962	3.75	7.50	15.00
3142	Little Bug/One By One	1962	3.75	7.50	15.00
3174	Come On Girl/Keep Your Mind on Me	1963	3.75	7.50	15.00

Albums

Number	Title (A Side/B Side)	Yr	VG	VG+	NM
COLLECTABLES					
COL-5044	Golden Classics	198?	2.50	5.00	10.00

JARRETT, KEITH

12-Inch Singles

Number	Title (A Side/B Side)	Yr	VG	VG+	NM
ECM					
PRO-A-768 [DJ]	Country/My Song	1978	2.50	5.00	10.00
PRO-A-1088 [DJ]	Mon Coeur Est Rouge (2 versions)/Heartland	1982	2.00	4.00	8.00
PRO-A-2072 [DJ]	God Bless the Child (Edit)/The Masquerade Is Over	1983	—	3.00	6.00
PRO-A-2186 [DJ]	Flying Part 1 and 2/Prism	1984	—	3.00	6.00

45s

Number	Title (A Side/B Side)	Yr	VG	VG+	NM
ABC IMPULSE!					
31001	Treasure Island/Sister Fortune	1975	—	2.50	5.00
ATLANTIC					
5110	All I Want/Standing Outside	1971	—	3.00	6.00
ECM					
29483	God Bless the Child/Meaning of the Blues	1983	—	2.00	4.00

Albums

Number	Title (A Side/B Side)	Yr	VG	VG+	NM
ABC IMPULSE!					
AS-9240	Fort Yawuh	1973	3.00	6.00	12.00
AS-9274	Treasure Island	1974	3.00	6.00	12.00
AS-9301	Death and the Flower	1974	3.00	6.00	12.00
AS-9305	Backhand	1975	2.50	5.00	10.00
AS-9315	Mysteries	1976	2.50	5.00	10.00
AS-9322	Shades	1976	2.50	5.00	10.00
AS-9331	Byablue	1977	2.50	5.00	10.00
IA-9334	Bop-Be	1977	2.50	5.00	10.00
IA-9348	The Best of Keith Jarrett	1978	2.50	5.00	10.00
ATLANTIC					
SD 1596	Mourning of a Star	1971	3.00	6.00	12.00
SD 1612	Birth	1972	3.00	6.00	12.00
SD 1673	El Juicio (The Judgment)	1975	2.50	5.00	10.00
SD 8808	Somewhere Before	198?	2.00	4.00	8.00
—Reissue of Vortex 2012					
COLUMBIA					
KG 31580 [(2)]	Expectations	1972	3.75	7.50	15.00
ECM					
1017	Facing You	1973	2.50	5.00	10.00
1033/4 [(2)]	In the Light	1976	3.00	6.00	12.00
1035/6/7 [(3)]	Solo Concerts	1974	5.00	10.00	20.00
1049	Luminessence	1974	2.50	5.00	10.00
1050	Belonging	1974	2.50	5.00	10.00
1064/5 [(2)]	The Koln Concert	1976	3.00	6.00	12.00
1070	Arbour Zena	1976	2.50	5.00	10.00
1085	Survivors' Suite	1977	2.50	5.00	10.00
1086/7 [(2)]	Hymns/Spheres	1977	3.00	6.00	12.00
1090	Staircase/Hourglass/Sundial/Sand	1977	3.00	6.00	12.00
1100 [(10)]	The Sun Bear Concerts	1977	20.00	40.00	80.00
1115	My Song	1978	2.50	5.00	10.00
1150	Eyes of the Heart	1979	2.50	5.00	10.00
1171 [(2)]	Nude Ants	1979	3.00	6.00	12.00
1174	Sacred Hymns	1981	2.50	5.00	10.00
1201 [(2)]	Invocations/The Moth and the Flame	1981	3.00	6.00	12.00
1227 [(3)]	Concerts	1982	5.00	10.00	20.00
1228	Concerts	1982	2.50	5.00	10.00
—Abridged version of 1227					
23793	Standards, Volume 1	1983	2.50	5.00	10.00
25007	Changes	1984	2.50	5.00	10.00
25023	Standards, Volume 2	1985	2.50	5.00	10.00
25041	Standards Live	1986	2.50	5.00	10.00
MCA					
29044	Fort Yawuh	1980	2.00	4.00	8.00
—Reissue of Impulse 9240					
29045	Treasure Island	1980	2.00	4.00	8.00
—Reissue of Impulse 9274					
29046	Death and the Flower	1980	2.00	4.00	8.00
—Reissue of Impulse 9301					
29047	Byablue	1980	2.00	4.00	8.00
—Reissue of Impulse 9331					
29048	Bop-Be	1980	2.00	4.00	8.00
—Reissue of Impulse 9334					
39106	Treasure Island	198?	2.50	5.00	10.00
—Another reissue of Impulse 9274					
VORTEX					
2006	Life Between the Exit Signs	1969	5.00	10.00	20.00
2008	Restoration Ruin	1969	5.00	10.00	20.00
2012	Somewhere Before	1970	5.00	10.00	20.00

JARRETT, KEITH, AND JACK DEJOHNETTE

Albums

Number	Title (A Side/B Side)	Yr	VG	VG+	NM
ECM					
1021	Ruta & Daitya	1973	2.50	5.00	10.00

JARVIS, FELTON

45s

Number	Title (A Side/B Side)	Yr	VG	VG+	NM
ABC-PARAMOUNT					
10570	Be-I-Bye/Ski King	1964	3.75	7.50	15.00
10610	Honky Tonk Song/Everybody's Going to the Party	1964	3.75	7.50	15.00
10641	Too Many Tigers/Knuckie, Knuckie	1965	3.75	7.50	15.00
MGM					
12982	Indian Love Call/Goin' Downtown	1961	5.00	10.00	20.00
THUNDER INT'L.					
1023	Swingin' Cat/Honest John the Workin' Man's Friend	1960	25.00	50.00	100.00
VIVA					
1001	Don't Knock Elvis/Honest John	1959	10.00	20.00	40.00

JASPER WRATH

45s

Number	Title (A Side/B Side)	Yr	VG	VG+	NM
SUNFLOWER					
107	It's Up to You/Did You Know That	1971	2.50	5.00	10.00

Albums

Number	Title (A Side/B Side)	Yr	VG	VG+	NM
SUNFLOWER					
SNF-5003	Jasper Wrath	1971	10.00	20.00	40.00

JAXON, BOB

45s

Number	Title (A Side/B Side)	Yr	VG	VG+	NM
20TH CENTURY FOX					
441	Weep, Mary, Weep/Do the People	1963	2.50	5.00	10.00
ABC-PARAMOUNT					
10364	It's a Cruel, Cruel Thing/One Way to Love Me	1962	3.00	6.00	12.00
CADENCE					
1264	Ali Baba/Why Does a Woman Cry	1955	3.75	7.50	15.00
RCA VICTOR					
47-6945	Beach Party/I'm Hangin' Around	1957	3.75	7.50	15.00
47-7006	(Gotta Have Something in the) Bank Frank/Come On Down	1957	5.00	10.00	20.00
47-7106	Declaration of Love/I'm Hurtin' Inside	1957	3.75	7.50	15.00
47-7168	Me! Please! Me!/All About Me	1958	3.75	7.50	15.00
47-7232	For the Love of You/(Well It's) No Lie	1958	3.75	7.50	15.00

JAY, IRA

45s

Number	Title (A Side/B Side)	Yr	VG	VG+	NM
SUN					
351	You Don't Love Me/More Than Anything	1960	5.00	10.00	20.00

JAY, JERRY

California DJ, better known as Jerry Osborne.

45s

Number	Title (A Side/B Side)	Yr	VG	VG+	NM
QUALITY					
201	The King's Country/Merry Christmas To You	1966	50.00	100.00	200.00

JAY, PETER, AND THE JAYWALKERS

45s

Number	Title (A Side/B Side)	Yr	VG	VG+	NM
WAND					
180	What's Easy/Parchment Farm	1965	2.50	5.00	10.00

JAY AND THE AMERICANS

Also see JAY BLACK; JAY TRAYNOR.

45s

Number	Title (A Side/B Side)	Yr	VG	VG+	NM
EEOC					
1140	Things Are Changing/Things Are Changing	1965	37.50	75.00	150.00
1140 [PS]	Things Are Changing/Things Are Changing	1965	37.50	75.00	150.00
—Promotional item for the Equal Employment Opportunity Commission					
UNITED ARTISTS					
0026	She Cried/Come a Little Bit Closer	1973	—	2.50	5.00
0027	Cara Mia/Let's Lock the Door (And Throw Away the Key)	1973	—	2.50	5.00
0028	This Magic Moment/Walking in the Rain	1973	—	2.50	5.00
—0026, 0027, 0028 are "Silver Spotlight Series" reissues					
353	Tonight/The Other Girls	1961	3.00	6.00	12.00
415	She Cried/Dawning	1962	3.75	7.50	15.00
479	It's My Turn to Cry/This Is It	1962	3.00	6.00	12.00
504	Tomorrow/Yes	1962	3.00	6.00	12.00
566	What's the Use/Strangers Tomorrow	1963	2.50	5.00	10.00
626	Only in America/My Clair De Lune	1963	2.50	5.00	10.00
669	Come Dance with Me/Look in My Eyes Maria	1963	2.50	5.00	10.00
693	To Wait for Love/Friday	1964	2.50	5.00	10.00
759	Come a Little Bit Closer/Goodbye Boys, Goodbye	1964	2.50	5.00	10.00
805	Let's Lock the Door (And Throw Away the Key)/I'll Remember You	1965	2.50	5.00	10.00
845	Think of the Good Times/If You Were Mine, Girl	1965	2.50	5.00	10.00
881	Cara Mia/When It's All Over	1965	2.50	5.00	10.00
919	Some Enchanted Evening/Girl	1965	2.50	5.00	10.00
919 [PS]	Some Enchanted Evening/Girl	1965	3.75	7.50	15.00
948	Sunday and Me/Through This Doorway	1965	2.50	5.00	10.00
948 [PS]	Sunday and Me/Through This Doorway	1965	12.50	25.00	50.00
992	Why Can't You Bring Me Home/Baby Stop Your Cryin'	1966	2.00	4.00	8.00
50016	Crying/I Don't Need a Friend	1966	2.00	4.00	8.00
50016 [PS]	Crying/I Don't Need a Friend	1966	3.00	6.00	12.00
50046	Livin' Above Your Head/Look at Me, What Do You See	1966	2.00	4.00	8.00
50046 [PS]	Livin' Above Your Head/Look at Me, What Do You See	1966	3.00	6.00	12.00
50086	Baby Come Home/Stop the Clock	1966	2.00	4.00	8.00
50094	(He's) Raining in My Sunshine/The Reason for Living (For You My Darling)	1966	2.00	4.00	8.00
50139	Nature Boy/You Ain't As Hip As All That, Baby	1967	2.00	4.00	8.00
50196	(We'll Meet in the) Yellow Forest/Got Hung Up Along the Way	1967	2.00	4.00	8.00
50222	Shanghai Noodle Factory/French Provincial	1967	2.00	4.00	8.00
50282	No Other Love/No, I Don't Know Her	1968	2.00	4.00	8.00
50448	You Ain't Gonna Wake Up Cryin'/Gemini	1968	2.00	4.00	8.00

Number	Title (A Side/B Side)	Yr	VG	VG+	NM
50475	This Magic Moment/Since I Don't Have You	1969	3.00	6.00	12.00
50510	When You Dance/No, I Don't Know Her	1969	—	3.00	6.00
50535	Hushabye/Gypsy Woman	1969	—	3.00	6.00
50567	(I'd Kill) For the Love of a Lady/Learnin' How to Fly	1969	—	3.00	6.00
50605	Walkin' in the Rain/(I'd Kill) For the Love of a Lady	1969	2.00	4.00	8.00
50654	Do You Ever Think of Me/Capture the Moment	1970	—	3.00	6.00
50683	Do I Love You?/Tricia (Tell Your Daddy)	1970	—	3.00	6.00
50858	There Goes My Baby/Solitary Man	1971	—	3.00	6.00
Albums					
LIBERTY					
LM-1010	Jay and the Americans Greatest Hits	1981	2.00	4.00	8.00
—Another reissue					
RHINO					
RNLP 70224	All-Time Greatest Hits	1986	3.00	6.00	12.00
SUNSET					
SUS-5252	Jay and the Americans!!	1968	3.00	6.00	12.00
SUS-5278	Early American Hits	1969	3.75	7.50	15.00
UNART					
M-20018 [M]	Jay and the Americans!!	196?	3.00	6.00	12.00
MS-21018 [S]	Jay and the Americans!!	196?	3.00	6.00	12.00
UNITED ARTISTS					
UA-LA357-E	The Very Best of Jay and the Americans	1975	3.00	6.00	12.00
LM-1010	Jay and the Americans Greatest Hits	1980	2.50	5.00	10.00
—Reissue					
UAL-3222 [M]	She Cried	1962	12.50	25.00	50.00
UAL-3300 [M]	At the Café Wha?	1963	12.50	25.00	50.00
UAL-3407 [M]	Come a Little Bit Closer	1964	6.25	12.50	25.00
UAL-3417 [M]	Blockbusters	1965	6.25	12.50	25.00
UAL-3453 [M]	Jay and the Americans Greatest Hits	1965	5.00	10.00	20.00
UAL-3474 [M]	Sunday and Me	1966	5.00	10.00	20.00
UAL-3534 [M]	Livin' Above Your Head	1966	5.00	10.00	20.00
UAL-3555 [M]	Jay and the Americans Greatest Hits, Volume 2	1966	5.00	10.00	20.00
UAL-3562 [M]	Try Some of This	1967	5.00	10.00	20.00
UAS-6222 [S]	She Cried	1962	25.00	50.00	100.00
UAS-6300 [S]	At the Café Wha?	1963	25.00	50.00	100.00
UAS-6407 [S]	Come a Little Bit Closer	1964	7.50	15.00	30.00
UAS-6417 [S]	Blockbusters	1965	7.50	15.00	30.00
UAS-6453 [S]	Jay and the Americans Greatest Hits	1965	6.25	12.50	25.00
UAS-6474 [S]	Sunday and Me	1966	6.25	12.50	25.00
UAS-6534 [S]	Livin' Above Your Head	1966	6.25	12.50	25.00
UAS-6555 [S]	Jay and the Americans Greatest Hits, Volume 2	1966	5.00	10.00	20.00
UAS-6582 [S]	Try Some of This	1967	5.00	10.00	20.00
UAS-6671	Sands of Time	1969	5.00	10.00	20.00
UAS-6719	Wax Museum	1970	5.00	10.00	20.00
UAS-6751	Wax Museum, Volume 2	1970	5.00	10.00	20.00
UAS-6762	Capture the Moment	1970	5.00	10.00	20.00
ST-90814 [S]	Jay and the Americans Greatest Hits	1966	7.50	15.00	30.00
—Capitol Record Club edition					
ST-90815 [S]	Jay and the Americans Greatest Hits, Volume 2	1966	7.50	15.00	30.00
—Capitol Record Club edition					

JAY AND THE DELTAS

Number	Title (A Side/B Side)	Yr	VG	VG+	NM
45s					
WARNER BROS.					
5404	Bells Are Ringing/Super Hawk	1964	12.50	25.00	50.00

JAY AND THE TECHNIQUES

Number	Title (A Side/B Side)	Yr	VG	VG+	NM
45s					
EVENT					
222	I Feel Love Coming On/World of Mine	1975	—	2.50	5.00
228	Number Onederful/Don't Forget to Ask	1975	—	2.50	5.00
GORDY					
7123	I'll Be Here/Robot Man	1973	—	3.00	6.00
PHILCO-FORD					
HP-22	Apples Peaches Pumpkin Pie/Loving for Money	1968	3.75	7.50	15.00
—4-inch plastic "Hip Pocket Record" with color sleeve					
SMASH					
2086	Apples, Peaches, Pumpkin Pie/Stronger Than Dirt	1967	2.00	4.00	8.00
2124	Keep the Ball Rollin'/Here We Go Again	1967	2.00	4.00	8.00
2124 [PS]	Keep the Ball Rollin'/Here We Go Again	1967	3.00	6.00	12.00
2142	Strawberry Shortcake/Still (In Love with You)	1967	2.00	4.00	8.00
2142 [PS]	Strawberry Shortcake/Still (In Love with You)	1967	3.00	6.00	12.00
2154	Baby Make Your Own Sweet Music/Help Yourself to All My Lovin'	1968	2.00	4.00	8.00
2154 [PS]	Baby Make Your Own Sweet Music/Help Yourself to All My Lovin'	1968	3.00	6.00	12.00
2171	The Singles Game/Baby How Easy Your Heart Forgets Me	1968	2.00	4.00	8.00
2171 [PS]	The Singles Game/Baby How Easy Your Heart Forgets Me	1968	3.00	6.00	12.00
2185	Hey Diddle Diddle/If I Should Lose You	1968	2.00	4.00	8.00
2217	Change Your Mind/Are You Ready for This	1969	2.00	4.00	8.00
2237	Dancin' Mood/If I Should Lose You	1969	2.00	4.00	8.00
Albums					
SMASH					
MGS-27095 [M]	Apples, Peaches, Pumpkin Pie	1967	7.50	15.00	30.00
SRS-67095 [S]	Apples, Peaches, Pumpkin Pie	1967	7.50	15.00	30.00
—First cover with "live" photo of the band					
SRS-67095 [S]	Apples, Peaches, Pumpkin Pie	1968	5.00	10.00	20.00
—Second cover with "posed" photo of the band					
SRS-67102	Love Lost and Found	1968	7.50	15.00	30.00

JAYBEES, THE

Number	Title (A Side/B Side)	Yr	VG	VG+	NM
45s					
RCA VICTOR					
47-8904	Do You Think I'm in Love/I'm a Lover	1966	5.00	10.00	20.00

JAYE, JERRY

Number	Title (A Side/B Side)	Yr	VG	VG+	NM
45s					
COLUMBIA					
10170	It's All in the Game/Love Me 'Til the Morning Comes	1975	—	2.00	4.00
10269	Maybellene/Because It's Love	1975	—	2.00	4.00
HI					
2120	My Girl Josephine/Five Miles from Home	1967	2.00	4.00	8.00
2128	Let the Four Winds Blow/Singin' the Blues	1967	2.00	4.00	8.00
2139	Brown-Eyed Handsome Man/In the Middle of Nowhere	1968	—	3.00	6.00
2150	Long Black Veil/(Today) I Started Loving You Again	1968	—	3.00	6.00
2171	Never Going Back/You've Got to Go	1969	—	3.00	6.00
2310	Honky Tonk Women Love Redneck Men/What's Left	1976	—	2.00	4.00
2318	Hot and Still Heatin'/Crazy	1976	—	2.00	4.00
2323	When Morning Comes to Memphis/(B-side unknown)	1977	—	2.00	4.00
MEGA					
0033	I Didn't Hear a Thing/Love Is a Job	1971	—	2.50	5.00
0045	Don't Bring the Rain Back Again/Tiny Praying Hands	1971	—	2.50	5.00
—As "K.C. and the Sunshine Junkanoo Band"					
0066	Share Your Love with Me/When My Ship Comes In	1972	—	2.50	5.00
0116	Honky Tonk Livin'/I'm Gonna Spend My Whole Life Lovin' You	1973	—	2.50	5.00
209	Walkin' My Baby Back Home/I Slipped But I Didn't Fall	1974	—	2.00	4.00
1218	Poor Side of Town/Lay Down	1974	—	2.00	4.00
STEPHENY					
1820	Sugar Dumplin'/How Could You Lose Your Trust in Me	1958	10.00	20.00	40.00
Albums					
HI					
HL-12038 [M]	My Girl Josephine	1967	5.00	10.00	20.00
SHL-32038 [S]	My Girl Josephine	1967	5.00	10.00	20.00
SHL-32102	Honky Tonk Women Love Redneck Men	1976	3.00	6.00	12.00

JAYHAWKS, THE

Also see THE MARATHONS; THE VIBRATIONS.

Number	Title (A Side/B Side)	Yr	VG	VG+	NM
45s					
ALADDIN					
3393	Everyone Should Know/The Creature	1957	20.00	40.00	80.00
ARGYLE					
1005	Lonely Highway/La Macerena	1961	6.25	12.50	25.00
EASTMAN					
792	Start the Fire/I Wish the World Owed Me a Living	1958	37.50	75.00	150.00
798	New Love/Betty Brown	1958	37.50	75.00	150.00
FLASH					
105	Counting Teardrops/The Devil's Cousin	1955	50.00	100.00	200.00
109	Starnded in the Jungle/My Only Darling	1956	12.50	25.00	50.00
111	Love Train/Don't Mind Dyin'	1956	7.50	15.00	30.00

JAYNELLS, THE

Number	Title (A Side/B Side)	Yr	VG	VG+	NM
45s					
CAMEO					
286	I'll Stay Home New Year's Eve/Down Home	1963	5.00	10.00	20.00
DIAMOND					
153	I'll Stay Home (New Year's Eve)/Down Home	1963	10.00	20.00	40.00

JAYNETTS, THE

Number	Title (A Side/B Side)	Yr	VG	VG+	NM
45s					
J&S					
1177	Out Behind the Daisies/Is It My Imagination	196?	2.00	4.00	8.00
1468/9	Chicken, Chicken, Crance or Crow/Winky Dinky	196?	2.00	4.00	8.00
1473	Peepin' In and Out the Window/Extra, Extra, Read All About It	196?	2.00	4.00	8.00
1477	Who Stole the Cookie/That's My Boy	196?	2.50	5.00	10.00
1686	Looking for Wonderland, My Lover/Make It an Extra	1965	2.00	4.00	8.00
1765/6	I Wanted to Be Free/Where Are You Tonight	196?	2.50	5.00	10.00
4418/9	Vangie Don't You Cry/My Guy Is As Sweet As Can Be	196?	2.00	4.00	8.00
TUFF					
369	Sally, Go 'Round the Roses/(Instrumental)	1963	3.75	7.50	15.00
371	Keep an Eye on Her/(Instrumental)	1963	2.50	5.00	10.00
374	Snowman, Snowman, Sweet Potato Nose/(Instrumental)	1963	3.75	7.50	15.00
377	No Love at All/Tonight You Belong to Me	1964	3.00	6.00	12.00
Albums					
TUFF					
LP 13 [M]	Sally Go 'Round the Roses	1963	75.00	150.00	300.00

JAYTONES, THE

Number	Title (A Side/B Side)	Yr	VG	VG+	NM
45s					
BRUNSWICK					
55087	The Clock/Gasoline	1958	30.00	60.00	120.00
CUB					
9057	My Only Love/Absolutely Right	1960	15.00	30.00	60.00
TIMELY					
1003/4	My Darling/The Bells	1958	375.00	750.00	1500.

JAZZ CRUSADERS, THE

See THE CRUSADERS.

JEFFERSON

Also see ROCKIN' BERRIES.

Number	Title (A Side/B Side)	Yr	VG	VG+	NM
45s					
DECCA					
32501	The Colour of My Love/Look No Further	1969	2.00	4.00	8.00
JANUS					
106	Baby Take Me in Your Arms/I Fell Flat on My Face	1969	2.00	4.00	8.00
117	You Know How It Is with a Woman/Are You Growing Tired of My Love	1970	2.00	4.00	8.00

Number	Title (A Side/B Side)	Yr	VG	VG+	NM
Albums					
JANUS					
JLS-3006	Baby, Take Me in Your Arms	1969	6.25	12.50	25.00

JEFFERSON, BLIND LEMON

Number	Title (A Side/B Side)	Yr	VG	VG+	NM
Albums					
MILESTONE					
MLP-2004 [M]	The Immortal Blind Lemon Jefferson	1968	6.25	12.50	25.00
MLP-2007 [M]	The Immortal Blind Lemon Jefferson, Vol. 2	1969	6.25	12.50	25.00
MLP-2013 [M]	Black Snake Moan	1970	6.25	12.50	25.00
RIVERSIDE					
RLP 12-125 [M]	Blind Lemon Jefferson — Classic Folk Blues	1957	30.00	60.00	120.00
RLP 12-136 [M]	Blind Lemon Jefferson, Volume 2	1958	30.00	60.00	120.00
1014 [10]	The Folk Blues of Blind Lemon Jefferson	1953	62.50	125.00	250.00
1053 [10]	Penitentiary Blues	1955	62.50	125.00	250.00

JEFFERSON AIRPLANE

Also see MARTY BALIN; PAPA JOHN CREACH; HOT TUNA; JEFFERSON STARSHIP; PAUL KANTNER; JORMA KAUKONEN; GRACE SLICK.

Number	Title (A Side/B Side)	Yr	VG	VG+	NM
45s					
EPIC					
73044	Summer of Love/Panda	1989	—	2.50	5.00
GRUNT					
65-0500	Pretty As You Feel/Wild Turkey	1971	—	2.50	5.00
65-0500 [PS]	Pretty As You Feel/Wild Turkey	1971	2.50	5.00	10.00
65-0506	Long John Silver/Milk Train	1972	—	2.50	5.00
65-0506 [PS]	Long John Silver/Milk Train	1972	3.75	7.50	15.00
65-0511	Trial by Fire/Twilight Double Leader	1972	—	2.50	5.00
JB-10988 [DJ]	White Rabbit (mono/stereo)	1978	7.50	15.00	30.00
—White vinyl					
RCA					
5156-7-R	White Rabbit/Plastic Fantastic Lover	1987	—	2.50	5.00
—White vinyl					
5156-7-R [PS]	White Rabbit/Plastic Fantastic Lover	1987	—	2.50	5.00
RCA VICTOR					
47-8769	It's No Secret/Runnin' 'Round This World	1966	3.75	7.50	15.00
47-8848	Come Up the Years/Blues from an Airplane	1966	3.75	7.50	15.00
47-8967	Bringing Me Down/Let Me In	1966	3.75	7.50	15.00
47-9063	My Best Friend/How Do You Feel	1967	3.75	7.50	15.00
47-9140	Somebody to Love/She Has Funny Cars	1967	3.75	7.50	15.00
47-9248	White Rabbit/Plastic Fantastic Lover	1967	3.75	7.50	15.00
47-9297	Ballad of You & Me & Pooneil/Two Heads	1967	2.50	5.00	10.00
47-9389	Watch Her Ride/Martha	1967	2.50	5.00	10.00
47-9496	Greasy Heart/Share a Little Joke (With the World)	1968	2.00	4.00	8.00
47-9644	Crown of Creation/Lather	1968	2.00	4.00	8.00
47-9644 [PS]	Crown of Creation/Lather	1968	5.00	10.00	20.00
74-0150	Plastic Fantastic Lover/Other Side of This Life	1969	—	3.00	6.00
74-0150 [PS]	Plastic Fantastic Lover/Other Side of This Life	1969	5.00	10.00	20.00
74-0245	Volunteers/We Can Be Together	1969	—	3.00	6.00
74-0245 [PS]	Volunteers/We Can Be Together	1969	3.75	7.50	15.00
74-0343	Have You Seen the Saucers/Mexico	1970	—	3.00	6.00
74-0343 [PS]	Have You Seen the Saucers/Mexico	1970	3.75	7.50	15.00
Albums					
DCC COMPACT CLASSICS					
LPZ-2033	Surrealistic Pillow	1997	6.25	12.50	25.00
—Audiophile vinyl					
EPIC					
OE 45271	Jefferson Airplane	1989	3.75	7.50	15.00
GRUNT					
BFL1-0147	Thirty Seconds Over Winterland	1973	3.00	6.00	12.00
APL1-0437	Early Flight	1974	3.00	6.00	12.00
FTR-1001	Bark	1971	3.75	7.50	15.00
—With brown paper bag					
FTR-1001	Bark	1971	2.50	5.00	10.00
—Without brown paper bag					
FTR-1007	Long John Silver	1972	3.00	6.00	12.00
CYL2-1255 [(2)]	Flight Log 1966-1976	1977	3.00	6.00	12.00
AYL1-4386	Bark	1981	2.00	4.00	8.00
AYL1-4391	Thirty Seconds Over Winterland	1981	2.00	4.00	8.00
MOBILE FIDELITY					
1-148	Crown of Creation	1984	5.00	10.00	20.00
—Audiophile vinyl					
PAIR					
PDL2-1090 [(2)]	Time Machine	1986	3.00	6.00	12.00
RCA					
5724-1-R [(2)]	2400 Fulton Street: An Anthology	1987	3.75	7.50	15.00
RCA VICTOR					
APD1-0320 [Q]	Volunteers	1973	20.00	40.00	80.00
—Yellow/orange label					
APD1-0320 [Q]	Volunteers	1975	12.50	25.00	50.00
—Tan label					
LOP-1511 [M]	After Bathing at Baxter's	1967	12.50	25.00	50.00
LSO-1511 [S]	After Bathing at Baxter's	1967	5.00	10.00	20.00
—Black label, dog on top					
LSO-1511 [S]	After Bathing at Baxter's	1969	3.00	6.00	12.00
—Orange label					
LSO-1511 [S]	After Bathing at Baxter's	1975	2.50	5.00	10.00
—Tan label					
LPM-3584 [M]	Jefferson Airplane Takes Off!	1966	1500.	2250.	3000.
—Version 1: With "Runnin' 'Round This World" as last song on side 1. Count the number of bands on Side 1 of the record; don't rely on the cover listing, as some jackets list the title when it's not on the record					
LPM-3584 [M]	Jefferson Airplane Takes Off!	1966	250.00	500.00	1000.
—Version 2: No "Runnin' 'Round This World", but "questionable" lyrics remain in "Let Me In" ("Don't tell me you want money") and "Run Around" ("That sway as you lay under me"). Until the exact matrix numbers are known, it must be heard to confirm.					
LPM-3584 [M]	Jefferson Airplane Takes Off!	1966	6.25	12.50	25.00
—Version 3: No "Runnin' 'Round This World", altered lyrics to "Let Me In" ("Don't tell me it's so funny") and "Run Around ("That sway as you stay here by me"). All later versions confirm to Version 3.					
LSP-3584 [S]	Jefferson Airplane Takes Off!	1966	2000.	3500.	5000.
—Version 1: See Version 1 note under mono version					
LSP-3584 [S]	Jefferson Airplane Takes Off!	1966	450.00	900.00	1800.
—Version 2: See Version 2 note under mono version					
LSP-3584 [S]	Jefferson Airplane Takes Off!	1966	6.25	12.50	25.00
—Version 3: See Version 3 note under mono version					
LSP-3584 [S]	Jefferson Airplane Takes Off!	1969	3.00	6.00	12.00
—Orange label					
LSP-3584 [S]	Jefferson Airplane Takes Off!	1975	2.50	5.00	10.00
—Tan label					
AYL1-3661	The Worst of Jefferson Airplane	1980	2.00	4.00	8.00
AYL1-3738	Surrealistic Pillow	1980	2.00	4.00	8.00
AYL1-3739	Jefferson Airplane Takes Off!	1980	2.00	4.00	8.00
LPM-3766 [M]	Surrealistic Pillow	1967	15.00	30.00	60.00
LSP-3766 [S]	Surrealistic Pillow	1967	7.50	15.00	30.00
—Black label, dog on top					
LSP-3766 [S]	Surrealistic Pillow	1969	3.00	6.00	12.00
—Orange label					
LSP-3766 [S]	Surrealistic Pillow	1975	2.50	5.00	10.00
—Tan label					
AYL1-3797	Crown of Creation	1980	2.00	4.00	8.00
AYL1-3798	Bless Its Pointed Little Head	1980	2.00	4.00	8.00
AYL1-3867	Volunteers	1980	2.00	4.00	8.00
LSP-4048	Crown of Creation	1968	7.50	15.00	30.00
—Black label, dog on top					
LSP-4048	Crown of Creation	1969	3.00	6.00	12.00
—Orange label					
LSP-4048	Crown of Creation	1975	2.50	5.00	10.00
—Tan label					
LSP-4133	Bless Its Pointed Little Head	1969	3.00	6.00	12.00
—Orange label					
LSP-4133	Bless Its Pointed Little Head	1975	2.50	5.00	10.00
—Tan label					
LSP-4238	Volunteers	1969	3.00	6.00	12.00
—Orange label					
LSP-4238	Volunteers	1975	2.50	5.00	10.00
—Tan label					
LSP-4459	The Worst of Jefferson Airplane	1970	3.00	6.00	12.00
AFL1-4545	After Bathing at Baxter's	1981	2.00	4.00	8.00
AYL1-4718	After Bathing at Baxter's	1983	2.00	4.00	8.00

JEFFERSON STARSHIP

See cross-references under JEFFERSON AIRPLANE.

Number	Title (A Side/B Side)	Yr	VG	VG+	NM
45s					
GRUNT					
FB-10080	Ride the Tiger/Devil's Den	1974	—	2.00	4.00
FB-10206	Caroline/Be Young You	1975	—	2.00	4.00
FB-10367	Miracles/Al Garimaso (There Is Love)	1975	—	2.50	5.00
FB-10456	Play on Love/I Want to See Another World	1975	—	2.00	4.00
FB-10746	With Your Love/Switchblade	1976	—	2.50	5.00
FB-10791	St. Charles/Love Lovely Day	1976	—	2.00	4.00
GB-10941	Miracles/With Your Love	1977	—	—	3.00
—Gold Standard Series					
FB-11196	Count on Me/Show Yourself	1978	—	2.00	4.00
FB-11196 [PS]	Count on Me/Show Yourself	1978	—	2.50	5.00
FB-11274	Runaway/Hot Water	1978	—	2.00	4.00
FB-11274 [PS]	Runaway/Hot Water	1978	—	2.50	5.00
JB-11274 [DJ]	Runaway (Long)/Runaway (Short)	1978	—	2.50	5.00
JB-11274 [PS]	Runaway (Long)/Runaway (Short)	1978	—	3.00	6.00
—Promo-only sleeve (one song listed on jacket)					
FB-11374	Crazy Feelin'/Love Too Good	1978	—	2.00	4.00
FB-11374 [PS]	Crazy Feelin'/Love Too Good	1978	—	2.50	5.00
FB-11426	Light the Sky On Fire/Hyperdrive	1978	—	2.00	4.00
FB-11426 [PS]	Light the Sky On Fire/Hyperdrive	1978	—	2.50	5.00
GB-11506	Count on Me/Runaway	1979	—	—	3.00
—Gold Standard Series					
FB-11750	Jane/Freedom at Point Zero	1979	—	2.00	4.00
FB-11750 [PS]	Jane/Freedom at Point Zero	1979	—	2.50	5.00
FB-11921	Girl with the Hungry Eyes/Just the Same	1980	—	2.00	4.00
FB-11921 [PS]	Girl with the Hungry Eyes/Just the Same	1980	—	2.50	5.00
FB-11961	Rock Music/Lightning Rose	1980	—	2.00	4.00
FB-12211	Find Your Way Back/Modern Times	1981	—	2.00	4.00
FB-12212	Mary/Modern Times	1981	—	—	—
—Unreleased					
FB-12275	Stranger/Free	1981	—	2.00	4.00
FB-12332	Save Your Love/Wild Eyes	1981	—	2.00	4.00
FB-13350	Be My Lady/Out of Control	1982	—	2.00	4.00
FB-13439	Winds of Change/Black Widow	1983	—	2.00	4.00
FB-13531	Can't Find Love/I Will Stay	1983	—	2.00	4.00
FB-13811	No Way Out/Rose Goes to Yale	1984	—	2.00	4.00
FB-13872	Layin' It on the Line/Showdown	1984	—	2.00	4.00
FB-13872 [PS]	Layin' It on the Line/Showdown	1984	—	2.00	4.00
Albums					
DCC COMPACT CLASSICS					
LPZ-2036	Red Octopus	1997	6.25	12.50	25.00
—Audiophile vinyl					
GRUNT					
BFD1-0717 [Q]	Dragon Fly	1974	3.75	7.50	15.00
BFL1-0717	Dragon Fly	1974	2.50	5.00	10.00
BFD1-0999 [Q]	Red Octopus	1975	3.75	7.50	15.00
BFL1-0999	Red Octopus	1975	2.50	5.00	10.00
BFD1-1557 [Q]	Spitfire	1976	3.75	7.50	15.00
BFL1-1557	Spitfire	1976	2.50	5.00	10.00
BXL1-2515	Earth	1978	2.50	5.00	10.00
BZL1-3247	Gold	1978	2.50	5.00	10.00
DJL1-3363 [PD]	Gold	1978	3.75	7.50	15.00
—Promo-only picture disc					
BZL1-3452	Freedom at Point Zero	1979	2.50	5.00	10.00
AYL1-3660	Red Octopus	1980	2.00	4.00	8.00
AYL1-3796	Dragon Fly	1980	2.00	4.00	8.00
BZL1-3848	Modern Times	1981	2.50	5.00	10.00
AYL1-3953	Spitfire	1981	2.00	4.00	8.00
AYL1-4172	Earth	1981	2.00	4.00	8.00
BXL1-4372	Winds of Change	1982	2.50	5.00	10.00
BXL1-4921	Nuclear Furniture	1984	2.50	5.00	10.00
AYL1-5161	Freedom at Point Zero	1984	2.00	4.00	8.00

JEFFREY, JOE, GROUP

Number	Title (A Side/B Side)	Yr	VG	VG+	NM
45s					
WAND					
11200	My Pledge of Love/Margie	1969	2.00	4.00	8.00
11207	The Train/Dreamin' Till Then	1969	—	3.00	6.00
11213	Chance of Loving You/Hey Hey Woman	1969	—	3.00	6.00
11219	My Baby Loves Lovin'/Chance of Loving You	1970	—	3.00	6.00
11235	A Hundred Pounds of Clay/Power of Love	1971	—	3.00	6.00
Albums					
WAND					
WDS-686	My Pledge of Love	1969	7.50	15.00	30.00

JEFFREYS, GARLAND

Number	Title (A Side/B Side)	Yr	VG	VG+	NM
12-Inch Singles					
EPIC					
AS 962 [DJ]	Modern Lovers/R.O.C.K./Ghost of a Chance	1981	2.50	5.00	10.00
RCA					
62175	Hail Hail Rock 'N' Roll (5 versions)	1992	2.00	4.00	8.00
62295	The Answer (6 versions)	1992	2.50	5.00	10.00
45s					
ARISTA					
0119	The Disco Kid Part 1/The Disco Kid Part 2	1975	—	2.50	5.00
ATLANTIC					
2948	She Didn't Lie/Lon Chaney	1973	—	2.50	5.00
2981	Wild in the Streets/Lon Chaney	1973	—	2.50	5.00
A&M					
1934	Wild in the Streets/Ghost Writer	1977	—	2.00	4.00
1952	New York Skyline/Cool Down Boy	1977	—	2.00	4.00
2030	One-Eyed Jack/Reelin'	1978	—	2.00	4.00
2074	She Didn't Lie/Scream in the Night	1979	—	2.00	4.00
2178	American Boy and Girl/Livin' for Me	1979	—	2.00	4.00
2244	American Boy and Girl/Matador	1980	—	2.00	4.00
EPIC					
AE7 1225 [DJ]	Interview with Garland Jeffreys	1981	2.00	4.00	8.00
AE7 1225 [PS]	Interview with Garland Jeffreys	1981	2.00	4.00	8.00
02073	Modern Lovers/Spanish Manners	1981	—	—	3.00
02173	R.O.C.K./Miami Beach	1981	—	—	3.00
03189	Surrender/Rebel Love	1982	—	—	3.00
03687	Rebel Love/What Does It Take (To Win Your Love)	1983	—	—	3.00
51008	96 Tears/Escape Goat Dab	1981	—	—	3.00
7-Inch Extended Plays					
EPIC					
AE7 1223 [DJ]	(contents unknown)	1981	2.00	4.00	8.00
AE7 1223 [PS]	Escapades	1981	2.00	4.00	8.00
Albums					
ATLANTIC					
SD 7253	Garland Jeffreys	1973	3.75	7.50	15.00
A&M					
SP-4629	Ghost Writer	1977	3.00	6.00	12.00
SP-4681	One-Eyed Jack	1978	2.50	5.00	10.00
SP-4778	American Boy and Girl	1979	2.50	5.00	10.00
EPIC					
PE 36983	Escape Artist	1981	2.50	5.00	10.00
FE 37436	Rock 'N' Roll Adult	1981	2.50	5.00	10.00
ARE 38190	Guts for Love	1983	2.50	5.00	10.00

JELLY BEAN BANDITS, THE

Number	Title (A Side/B Side)	Yr	VG	VG+	NM
45s					
MAINSTREAM					
674	Country Woman/Generation	1967	7.50	15.00	30.00
Albums					
MAINSTREAM					
S-6103 [S]	The Jelly Bean Bandits	1967	37.50	75.00	150.00
56103 [M]	The Jelly Bean Bandits	1967	25.00	50.00	100.00

JELLY BEANS, THE

Number	Title (A Side/B Side)	Yr	VG	VG+	NM
45s					
ESKEE					
001	I'm Hip to You/You Don't Mean No Good to Me	1965	3.75	7.50	15.00
RED BIRD					
10-003	I Wanna Love Him So Bad/So Long	1964	5.00	10.00	20.00
10-011	The Kind of Boy You Can't Forget/Baby Be Mine	1964	5.00	10.00	20.00

JELLYBREAD

Number	Title (A Side/B Side)	Yr	VG	VG+	NM
Albums					
BLUE HORIZON					
BH-4801	First Slice	1970	7.50	15.00	30.00

JENKINS, FLORENCE FOSTER

One of the worst singers ever to be recorded — and unlike MRS. MILLER, Jenkins sang arias!

Number	Title (A Side/B Side)	Yr	VG	VG+	NM
Albums					
RCA VICTOR					
LM-2597 [M]	The Glory (????) of the Human Voice	1961	5.00	10.00	20.00
LRT-7001 [10]	A Florence! Foster!! Jenkins!!! Recital!!!!	195?	12.50	25.00	50.00

JENNIFER

Later recorded as Jennifer Warnes.

Number	Title (A Side/B Side)	Yr	VG	VG+	NM
45s					
PARROT					
324	Here, There and Everywhere/Sunny Day Blue	1968	3.00	6.00	12.00
328	Chelsea Morning/The Park	1969	2.50	5.00	10.00
333	I Am Waiting/The Leaves	1969	2.50	5.00	10.00
336	Easy to Be Hard/Let the Sunshine In	1969	2.50	5.00	10.00
343	We're Not Gonna Take It/The Weather's Better	1970	2.00	4.00	8.00
346	Old Folks/Cajun Train	1970	2.00	4.00	8.00
REPRISE					
1070	Last Song/These Days	1972	—	3.00	6.00
Albums					
PARROT					
PAS-71020	I Can Remember Anything	1968	5.00	10.00	20.00
PAS-71034	See Me	1970	5.00	10.00	20.00

JENNINGS, WAYLON

Also see WAYLON AND JESSI; WAYLON AND WILLIE.

Number	Title (A Side/B Side)	Yr	VG	VG+	NM
12-Inch Singles					
RCA					
WJ-01 [DJ]	Don't You Think This Outlaw Bit's Done Got Out of Hand/Medley of Buddy Holly Hits	1979	3.75	7.50	15.00
WJ-0283 [DJ]	Medley of Hits (7:14) (same on both sides)	1983	3.75	7.50	15.00
45s					
ARK 21					
S7-58711	I Know About Me, Don't Know About You/Closing In on the Fire	1998	—	—	3.00
A&M					
722	Rave On/Love, Denise	1963	5.00	10.00	20.00
739	Four Strong Winds/Just to Satisfy You	1964	3.75	7.50	15.00
753	The Race Is On/Sing the Girls a Song	1964	3.75	7.50	15.00
BAT					
121636	White Lightning/(B-side unknown)	1962	12.50	25.00	50.00
121639	Dream Baby/Crying	1962	10.00	20.00	40.00
BRUNSWICK					
55130	Jole Blon/When Sin Stops	1959	75.00	150.00	300.00
COLUMBIA					
04881	Highwayman/The Human Condition	1985	—	—	3.00
—A-side: Willie Nelson/Waylon Jennings/Johnny Cash/Kris Kristofferson; B-side: Nelson, Cash					
04881 [PS]	Highwayman/The Human Condition	1985	—	2.00	4.00
—A-side: Willie Nelson/Waylon Jennings/Johnny Cash/Kris Kristofferson; B-side: Nelson, Cash					
05594	Desperadoes Waiting for a Train/The Twentieth Century Is Almost Over	1985	—	—	3.00
—A-side: Willie Nelson/Waylon Jennings/Johnny Cash/Kris Kristofferson; B-side: Nelson, Cash					
08406	Highwayman/Desperadoes Waiting for a Train	1988	—	—	3.00
—Waylon Jennings/Willie Nelson/Johnny Cash/Kris Kristofferson; reissue					
73233	Silver Stallion/America Remains	1990	—	—	3.00
—Waylon Jennings/Willie Nelson/Johnny Cash/Kris Kristofferson					
73381	Born and Raised in Black and White/Texas	1990	—	—	3.00
—The Highwaymen (Waylon Jennings/Willie Nelson/Johnny Cash/Kris Kristofferson)					
73572	American Remains/Texas	1990	—	—	3.00
—The Highwaymen (Waylon Jennings/Willie Nelson/Johnny Cash/Kris Kristofferson)					
EPIC					
73352	Wrong/Waking Up with You	1990	—	—	3.00
73519	Where Corn Don't Grow/Waking Up with You	1990	—	—	3.00
73647	What Bothers Me Most/Wrong	1990	—	—	3.00
73718	The Eagle/What Bothers Me Most	1991	—	—	3.00
74403	Just Talkin'/I've Got My Faults	1992	—	—	3.00
74705	Too Dumb for New York City, Too Smart for L.A./I've Got My Faults	1992	—	—	3.00
LIBERTY					
S7-18486	It Is What It Is/The Devil's Right Hand	1995	—	—	3.00
—By The Highwaymen					
MCA					
52776	Working Without a Net/They Ain't Got 'Em All	1986	—	—	3.00
52830	Will the Wolf Survive/I've Got Me a Woman	1986	—	—	3.00
52915	What You'll Do When I'm Gone/That Dog Won't Hunt	1986	—	—	3.00
53009	Rose in Paradise/Crying Don't Even Come Close	1987	—	—	3.00
53088	Fallin' Out/Deep in the West	1987	—	—	3.00
53158	My Rough and Rowdy Days/Love Song (I Can't Sing Anymore)	1987	—	—	3.00
53243	If Ole Hank Could Only See Us Now (Chapter Five...Nashville)/You Went Out with Rock 'n' Roll	1988	—	—	3.00
53314	How Much Is It Worth to Live in L.A./G.I. Joe	1988	—	—	3.00
53476	Which Way Do I Go (Now That I'm Gone)/Hey Willie	1988	—	—	3.00
53634	Trouble Man/Yoyos, Bozos, Bimbos and Heroes	1989	—	—	3.00
53710	You Put the Soul in the Song/Woman I Hate It	1989	—	—	3.00
RAMCO					
1997	My World/Another Blue Day	1968	3.00	6.00	12.00
RCA					
5034-7-R	The Broken Promise Land/I Don't Have Any More Love Songs	1986	—	2.00	4.00
PB-10842	Are You Ready for the Country/So Good Woman	1976	—	2.50	5.00
PB-10924	Luckenbach, Texas (Back to the Basics of Love)/Belle of the Ball	1977	—	2.50	5.00
GB-10927	Dreaming My Dreams with You/Can't You See	1977	—	—	3.00
—Gold Standard Series					
PB-11118	The Wurlitzer Prize (I Don't Want to Get Over You)/Lookin' for a Feeling	1977	—	2.50	5.00
PB-11344	I've Always Been Crazy/I Never Said It Would Be Easy	1978	—	2.00	4.00
PB-11390	Don't You Think This Outlaw Bit's Done Got Out of Hand/Girl I Can Tell (You're Trying to Work It Out)	1978	—	2.00	4.00
GB-11500	Are You Ready for the Country/The Wurlitzer Prize (I Don't Want to Get Over You)	1978	—	—	3.00
—Gold Standard Series					
PB-11596	Amanda/Lonesome, On'ry and Mean	1979	—	2.00	4.00
PB-11596 [PS]	Amanda/Lonesome, On'ry and Mean	1979	—	2.50	5.00
PB-11723	Come with Me/Mes'kin	1979	—	2.00	4.00
GB-11757	Luckenbach, Texas (Back to the Basics of Love)/Belle of the Ball	1979	—	—	3.00
—Gold Standard Series					
PB-11898	I Ain't Living Long Like This/The World's Crazy	1979	—	2.00	4.00
GB-11991	I've Always Been Crazy/Don't You Think This Outlaw Bit's Done Got Out of Hand	1980	—	—	3.00
—Gold Standard Series					
PB-12007	Clyde/I Came Here to Party	1980	—	2.00	4.00
PB-12067	Theme from "The Dukes of Hazzard" (Good Ol' Boys)/It's Alright	1980	—	2.00	4.00
PB-12067 [PS]	Theme from "The Dukes of Hazzard" (Good Ol' Boys)/It's Alright	1980	—	2.50	5.00

Number	Title (A Side/B Side)	Yr	VG	VG+	NM
GB-12187	Theme from "The Dukes of Hazzard" (Good Ol' Boys)/Come with Me	1981	—	—	3.00
—Gold Standard Series					
GB-12313	Amanda/I Ain't Living Long Like This	1981	—	—	3.00
—"Gold Standard Series" reissue					
PB-12367	Shine/White Water	1981	—	2.00	4.00
PB-13257	Women Do Know How to Carry On/Honky Tonk Blues	1982	—	2.00	4.00
PB-13465	Lucille (You Won't Do Your Daddy's Will)/Medley of Hits	1983	—	2.00	4.00
PB-13543	Breakin' Down/Livin' Legends (A Dyin' Breed)	1983	—	2.00	4.00
PB-13631	The Conversation/Fancy Free	1983	—	2.00	4.00
—A-side with Hank Williams, Jr.					
PB-13729	I May Be Used (But Baby I Ain't Used Up)/So You Want to Be a Cowboy Singer	1984	—	2.00	4.00
PB-13827	Never Could Toe the Mark/Talk Good Boogie	1984	—	2.00	4.00
PB-13903	Silent Night, Holy Night/Precious Memories	1984	—	2.00	4.00
—A-side with Jessi Colter					
PB-13908	America/People Up in Texas	1984	—	2.00	4.00
PB-13984	Waltz Me to Heaven/Dream On	1984	—	2.00	4.00
PB-14094	Drinkin' and Dreamin'/Prophets Show Up in Strange Places	1985	—	2.00	4.00
PB-14215	The Devil's on the Loose/Good Morning John	1985	—	2.00	4.00
PB-14291	Sweet Mother Texas/Hanging On	1985	—	2.00	4.00

RCA VICTOR

Number	Title (A Side/B Side)	Yr	VG	VG+	NM
APBO-0086	You Asked Me To/Willy, the Wandering Gypsy and Me	1973	2.00	4.00	8.00
AMAO-0122	MacArthur Park/The Taker	1973	—	2.50	5.00
APBO-0251	This Time/Mona	1974	—	3.00	6.00
PB-10020	I'm a Ramblin' Man/Got a Lot Going for Me	1974	—	3.00	6.00
PB-10142	Rainy Day Woman/Let's All Help the Cowboys (Sing the Blues)	1974	—	3.00	6.00
GB-10169	This Time/You Asked Me To	1975	—	2.00	4.00
—Gold Standard Series					
PB-10270	Dreaming My Dreams with You/Waymore's Blues	1975	—	3.00	6.00
PB-10379	Are You Sure Hank Done It This Way/Bob Wills Is Still the King	1975	—	3.00	6.00
GB-10498	I'm a Ramblin' Man/Got a Lot Going for Me	1975	—	2.00	4.00
—Gold Standard Series					
GB-10499	Rainy Day Woman/Let's All Help the Cowboys (Sing the Blues)	1975	—	2.00	4.00
—Gold Standard Series					
GB-10673	Are You Sure Hank Done It This Way/Bob Wills Is Still the King	1976	—	2.00	4.00
—Gold Standard Series					
PB-10721	Can't You See/I'll Go Back to Her	1976	—	2.50	5.00
47-8572	That's the Chance I'll Have to Take/I Wonder Just Where I Went Wrong	1965	2.50	5.00	10.00
47-8652	Stop the World (And Let Me Off)/The Dark Side of Fame	1965	2.50	5.00	10.00
47-8729	Anita, You're Dreaming/Look Into My Teardrops	1965	2.50	5.00	10.00
47-8822	Time to Bum Again/Norwegian Wood	1966	2.50	5.00	10.00
47-8917	(That's What You Get) For Lovin' Me/Time Will Tell the Story	1966	2.50	5.00	10.00
47-9025	Green River/Silver Ribbons	1966	2.50	5.00	10.00
47-9146	Mental Revenge/Born to Love You	1967	2.50	5.00	10.00
47-9259	The Chokin' Kind/Love of the Common People	1967	2.50	5.00	10.00
47-9414	Walk On Out of My Mind/Julie	1967	2.50	5.00	10.00
47-9480	I Got You/No One's Gonna Miss Me	1968	2.50	5.00	10.00
—A-side with Anita Carter					
47-9561	Only Daddy That'll Walk the Line/Right Before My Eyes	1968	2.50	5.00	10.00
47-9642	Yours Love/Six Strings Away	1968	2.50	5.00	10.00
47-9819	Singer of Sad Songs/Lila	1970	2.00	4.00	8.00
47-9885	The Taker/Shadows of the Gallows	1970	2.00	4.00	8.00
47-9925	(Don't Let the Sun Set on You) Tulsa/You'll Look for Me	1970	2.00	4.00	8.00
47-9967	Mississippi Woman/Life Goes On	1971	2.00	4.00	8.00
48-1003	Cedartown, Georgia/I Think It's Time She Learned	1971	2.00	4.00	8.00
74-0105	Something's Wrong in California/Farewell Party	1969	2.00	4.00	8.00
74-0157	The Days of Sand and Shovels/Delia's Gone	1969	2.00	4.00	8.00
74-0210	MacArthur Park/But You Know I Love You	1969	2.00	4.00	8.00
74-0281	Brown Eyed Handsome Man/Sorrow (Breaks a Good Man Down)	1969	2.00	4.00	8.00
74-0615	Good Hearted Woman/It's All Over Now	1971	2.00	4.00	8.00
74-0716	Sweet Dream Woman/Sure Didn't Take Him Long	1972	2.00	4.00	8.00
74-0808	Pretend I Never Happened/Nothin' Worth Takin' or Leavin'	1972	2.00	4.00	8.00
74-0886	You Can Have Her/Gone to Denver	1973	2.00	4.00	8.00
74-0961	We Had It All/Do No Good Woman	1973	2.00	4.00	8.00

TREND

Number	Title (A Side/B Side)	Yr	VG	VG+	NM
102	Another Blue Day/Never Again	1962	7.50	15.00	30.00
106	The Stage/My Baby Walks All Over Me	1963	25.00	50.00	100.00

Albums

A&M

Number	Title	Yr	VG	VG+	NM
SP-4238	Don't Think Twice	1969	10.00	20.00	40.00

BAT

Number	Title	Yr	VG	VG+	NM
1001 [M]	Waylon Jennings at JD's	1964	175.00	350.00	700.00
—Approximately 500 copies pressed					

MCA

Number	Title	Yr	VG	VG+	NM
731	Waylon Jennings	198?	3.00	6.00	12.00
—Reissue of Vocalion LP					
5688	Will the Wolf Survive	1986	2.50	5.00	10.00
5911	Hangin' Tough	1987	2.50	5.00	10.00
42038	A Man Called Hoss	1987	2.50	5.00	10.00
42222	Full Circle	1988	2.50	5.00	10.00
42287	New Classic Waylon	1989	2.50	5.00	10.00

PAIR

Number	Title	Yr	VG	VG+	NM
PDL1-1005 [(2)]	Waylon!	1986	3.00	6.00	12.00
PDL1-1033 [(2)]	A Couple More Years	1986	3.00	6.00	12.00
PDL1-1110 [(2)]	Honly Tonk Hero	1986	3.00	6.00	12.00

RCA

Number	Title	Yr	VG	VG+	NM
5620-1-RB	The Best of Waylon	1987	2.50	5.00	10.00
9561-1-R	The Early Years (1965-1969)	1989	2.50	5.00	10.00

RCA CAMDEN

Number	Title	Yr	VG	VG+	NM
ACL1-0306	Only Daddy That'll Walk the Line	1973	2.50	5.00	10.00
CAL-2183 [M]	The One and Only Waylon Jennings	1967	3.75	7.50	15.00
CAS-2183 [S]	The One and Only Waylon Jennings	1967	3.00	6.00	12.00
CAS-2556	Heartaches by the Number	1972	3.00	6.00	12.00
CAS-2608	Ruby, Don't Take Your Love to Town	1972	3.00	6.00	12.00

RCA VICTOR

Number	Title	Yr	VG	VG+	NM
APL1-0240	Honky Tonk Heroes	1973	3.75	7.50	15.00
APL1-0539	This Time	1974	3.00	6.00	12.00
APL1-0734	The Ramblin' Man	1974	3.00	6.00	12.00
APL1-1062	Dreaming My Dreams	1975	2.50	5.00	10.00
APL1-1108	Waylon Live	1976	2.50	5.00	10.00
APL1-1816	Are You Ready for the Country	1976	2.50	5.00	10.00
AAL1-2317	Ol' Waylon	198?	2.00	4.00	8.00
—Reissue					
APL1-2317	Ol' Waylon	1977	2.50	5.00	10.00
AFL1-2979	I've Always Been Crazy	1978	2.50	5.00	10.00
AHL1-3378	Greatest Hits	1979	2.50	5.00	10.00
AHL1-3493	What Goes Around Comes Around	1979	2.50	5.00	10.00
LPM-3523 [M]	Folk-Country	1966	7.50	15.00	30.00
LSP-3523 [S]	Folk-Country	1966	10.00	20.00	40.00
AHL1-3602	Music Man	1980	2.50	5.00	10.00
LPM-3620 [M]	Leavin' Town	1966	7.50	15.00	30.00
LSP-3620 [S]	Leavin' Town	1966	10.00	20.00	40.00
LPM-3660 [M]	Waylon Sings Ol' Harlan	1967	7.50	15.00	30.00
LSP-3660 [S]	Waylon Sings Ol' Harlan	1967	10.00	20.00	40.00
AYL1-3663	Are You Ready for the Country	1980	2.00	4.00	8.00
—Budget-line reissue					
LPM-3736 [M]	Nashville Rebel	1967	10.00	20.00	40.00
LSP-3736 [S]	Nashville Rebel	1967	12.50	25.00	50.00
LPM-3825 [M]	Love of the Common People	1967	7.50	15.00	30.00
LSP-3825 [S]	Love of the Common People	1967	6.25	12.50	25.00
AYL1-3897	Honky Tonk Heroes	1980	2.00	4.00	8.00
—Budget-line reissue					
LPM-3918 [M]	Hangin' On	1968	25.00	50.00	100.00
LSP-3918 [S]	Hangin' On	1968	6.25	12.50	25.00
LPM-4023 [M]	Only the Greatest	1968	—	—	—
—Canceled?					
LSP-4023 [S]	Only the Greatest	1968	6.25	12.50	25.00
AYL1-4072	Dreaming My Dreams	1981	2.00	4.00	8.00
—Budget-line reissue					
AYL1-4073	The Ramblin' Man	1981	2.00	4.00	8.00
—Budget-line reissue					
LSP-4085	Jewels	1968	6.25	12.50	25.00
LSP-4137	Just to Satisfy You	1969	6.25	12.50	25.00
AYL1-4163	Waylon Live	1981	2.00	4.00	8.00
—Budget-line reissue					
AYL1-4164	I've Always Been Crazy	1981	2.00	4.00	8.00
—Budget-line reissue					
LSP-4180	Country-Folk	1969	6.25	12.50	25.00
AHL1-4247	Black On Black	1982	2.50	5.00	10.00
AYL1-4250	Music Man	1982	2.00	4.00	8.00
—Budget-line reissue					
LSP-4260	Waylon	1970	5.00	10.00	20.00
LSP-4341	The Best of Waylon Jennings	1970	5.00	10.00	20.00
LSP-4418	Singer of Sad Songs	1970	5.00	10.00	20.00
LSP-4487	The Taker/Tulsa	1971	5.00	10.00	20.00
LSP-4567	Cedartown, Georgia	1971	5.00	10.00	20.00
LSP-4647	Good Hearted Woman	1972	5.00	10.00	20.00
AFL1-4673	It's Only Rock & Roll	1983	2.50	5.00	10.00
LSP-4751	Ladies Love Outlaws	1972	5.00	10.00	20.00
AHL1-4826	Waylon and Company	1983	2.50	5.00	10.00
AYL1-4828	The Best of Waylon Jennings	1983	2.00	4.00	8.00
—Budget-line reissue					
LSP-4854	Lonesome, On'ry and Mean	1973	3.75	7.50	15.00
AHL1-5017	Never Could Toe the Mark	1984	2.50	5.00	10.00
AYL1-5126	Ol' Waylon	1984	2.00	4.00	8.00
—Budget-line reissue					
AHL1-5325	Waylon's Greatest Hits, Vol. 2	1984	2.50	5.00	10.00
AHL1-5428	Turn the Page	1985	2.50	5.00	10.00
AYL1-5433	Waylon and Company	1985	2.00	4.00	8.00
—Budget-line reissue					
AHL1-5473	Collector's Series	1985	2.50	5.00	10.00
AYL1-7046	Never Could Toe the Mark	1985	2.00	4.00	8.00
—Budget-line reissue					
AHL1-7184	Sweet Mother Texas	1986	2.50	5.00	10.00

SOUNDS

Number	Title	Yr	VG	VG+	NM
1001 [M]	Waylon Jennings at JD's	1964	125.00	250.00	500.00
—Approximately 500 copies pressed; reissue of Bat 1001					

VOCALION

Number	Title	Yr	VG	VG+	NM
DL 73873	Waylon Jennings	1969	6.25	12.50	25.00

JENNINGS, WAYLON; WILLIE NELSON; JESSI COLTER; TOMPALL GLASER

Also see JESSI COLTER; WAYLON JENNINGS; WILLIE NELSON; WAYLON AND JESSI; WAYLON AND WILLIE.

Albums

RCA VICTOR

Number	Title	Yr	VG	VG+	NM
AAL1-1321	Wanted! The Outlaws	198?	2.00	4.00	8.00
—Reissue					
APL1-1321	Wanted! The Outlaws	1976	3.00	6.00	12.00
—Tan label					
APL1-1321	Wanted! The Outlaws	1976	2.50	5.00	10.00
—Black label, dog near top					

JENNINGS, WAYLON, AND JERRY REED

45s

RCA

Number	Title (A Side/B Side)	Yr	VG	VG+	NM
PB-13580	Hold On, I'm Comin'/Waiting On Down the Line	1983	—	2.00	4.00
GB-13789	Hold On, I'm Comin'/The Conversation	1984	—	—	3.00
—Gold Standard Series; B-side by Waylon and Hank Williams, Jr.					

JENSEN, KRIS

45s

Number	Title (A Side/B Side)	Yr	VG	VG+	NM
A&M					
1204	Dead End Street/Me and Bobby McGee	1970	—	2.50	5.00
COLPIX					
118	Bonnie Baby/Staying Up Late	1959	3.00	6.00	12.00
HICKORY					
1173	Torture/Let's Sit Down	1962	3.00	6.00	12.00
1195	Claudette/Don't Take Her from Me	1962	2.00	4.00	8.00
1203	Poor Unlucky Me/Cut Me Down (From Your Whipping Post)	1963	2.00	4.00	8.00
1224	Big As I Can Dream/Donna, Donna	1963	2.00	4.00	8.00
1243	In Time/Lookin' for Love	1964	2.00	4.00	8.00
1256	Come Back to Me (My Love)/You've Only Got Me to Lose	1964	2.00	4.00	8.00
1285	Little Wind-Up Doll/Somebody's Smilin'	1964	2.00	4.00	8.00
1311	That's a Whole Lotta Love/What Should I Do	1965	2.00	4.00	8.00
KAPP					
393	The Jackie Look/Tender Hearted Baby	1961	2.50	5.00	10.00
410	Danny'd Dream/3 Vanilla, 2 Chocolate, 1 Pistachio Ice Cream Cones	1961	2.50	5.00	10.00
433	Busy Signal/Mary, Mary	1961	2.50	5.00	10.00
493	Busy Signal/Mary, Mary	1962	2.00	4.00	8.00
LEADER					
808	Perfect Love/School Bus	1960	3.00	6.00	12.00
813	Please Let Me Love You Tonight/Your Daddy Don't Like Me	1961	3.00	6.00	12.00
WHITE WHALE					
229	I Got You/I Can't Get Nowhere with You	1966	—	3.00	6.00
240	I Love to Call You Sweetheart/Good Pop Music	1966	—	3.00	6.00

Albums

Number	Title (A Side/B Side)	Yr	VG	VG+	NM
HICKORY					
LP 110 [M]	Torture	1963	20.00	40.00	80.00

JEREMY'S FRIENDS

Alan Arkin was a member of this group.

Albums

Number	Title (A Side/B Side)	Yr	VG	VG+	NM
WARWICK					
W-2019 [M]	Jeremy's Friends	1960	12.50	25.00	50.00

JEREMY AND THE SATYRS

45s

Number	Title (A Side/B Side)	Yr	VG	VG+	NM
REPRISE					
0664	Let's Go to the Movie Show/Lonely Child of Tears	1968	2.50	5.00	10.00

Albums

Number	Title (A Side/B Side)	Yr	VG	VG+	NM
REPRISE					
RS-6282	Jeremy and the Satyrs	1968	5.00	10.00	20.00

JERICHO

45s

Number	Title (A Side/B Side)	Yr	VG	VG+	NM
BEARSVILLE					
31003	Cheater Man/Make It Better	1971	2.00	4.00	8.00

Albums

Number	Title (A Side/B Side)	Yr	VG	VG+	NM
AMPEX					
A-10112	Jericho	1971	6.25	12.50	25.00

JERRY AND WAYNE

45s

Number	Title (A Side/B Side)	Yr	VG	VG+	NM
ABC-PARAMOUNT					
9806	Baby Baby Baby/I'm Sad, Blue and Lonesome	1957	5.00	10.00	20.00
9808	Baby Baby Baby, Be Mine/I'm Sad, Blue and Lonesome	1957	6.25	12.50	25.00

JESSE AND MARVIN

"Jesse" is JESSE BELVIN. "Marvin" later was with MARVIN AND JOHNNY.

45s

Number	Title (A Side/B Side)	Yr	VG	VG+	NM
SPECIALTY					
447	Dream Girl/Daddy Loves Baby	1952	50.00	100.00	200.00
—Red vinyl					
447	Dream Girl/Daddy Loves Baby	1952	18.75	37.50	75.00
—Black vinyl					

JESTERS, THE

Also see THE PARAGONS/THE JESTERS.

45s

Number	Title (A Side/B Side)	Yr	VG	VG+	NM
AMY					
859	Alexander Graham Bell/Buffalo	1962	2.00	4.00	8.00
CYCLONE					
5011	I Laughed/Now That You're Gone	1958	12.50	25.00	50.00
FEATURE					
101	Panther Pounce/Tiger Tail	1964	12.50	25.00	50.00
SIDEWALK					
910	Leave Me Alone/Don't Try to Crawl Back	1967	2.50	5.00	10.00
916	Hands of Time/If You Love Her, Tell Her So	1967	2.50	5.00	10.00
SUN					
400	Cadillac Man/My Babe	1966	7.50	15.00	30.00
ULTIMA					
705	Drag Like Boogie/A-Rab	1964	7.50	15.00	30.00
WINLEY					
218	So Strange/Love No One But You	1957	12.50	25.00	50.00
221	I'm Falling in Love/Please Let Me Love You	1957	12.50	25.00	50.00
225	The Plea/Oh Baby	1958	10.00	20.00	40.00
242	The Wind/Sally Green	1959	10.00	20.00	40.00
248	That's How It Goes/Tutti Frutti	1961	12.50	25.00	50.00
—Red vinyl					
248	That's How It Goes/Tutti Frutti	1961	7.50	15.00	30.00
—Black vinyl					
252	Come Let Me Show You/Uncle Henry's Basement	1961	7.50	15.00	30.00

Albums

Number	Title (A Side/B Side)	Yr	VG	VG+	NM
COLLECTABLES					
COL-5036	The Best of the Jesters	198?	2.50	5.00	10.00

JET SET, THE

45s

Number	Title (A Side/B Side)	Yr	VG	VG+	NM
CAPITOL					
5358	True to You/You Got Me Hooked	1965	6.25	12.50	25.00
5421	How Can I Know/Dancing Yet	1965	6.25	12.50	25.00
—As "Liza and the Jet Set"					

JETHRO TULL

12-Inch Singles

Number	Title (A Side/B Side)	Yr	VG	VG+	NM
CHRYSALIS					
CHS 3 PDJ [DJ]	Ring Out, Solstice Bells/March, The Mad Scientist//Christmas Song/Pan Dance	1976	6.25	12.50	25.00

45s

Number	Title (A Side/B Side)	Yr	VG	VG+	NM
CHRYSALIS					
2006	Living in the Past/Christmas Song	1972	—	3.00	6.00
2012	A Passion Play (Edit #9)/A Passion Play (Edit #8)	1973	—	3.00	6.00
2017	A Passion Play (Edit #6)/A Passion Play (Edit #10)	1973	—	2.50	5.00
2101	Bungle in the Jungle/Back Door Angels	1974	—	2.50	5.00
2101 [PS]	Bungle in the Jungle/Back Door Angels	1974	2.50	5.00	10.00
2103	Skating Away (On the Thin Ice of a New Day)/ Sealion	1975	—	2.50	5.00
2106	Minstrel in the Gallery/Sumer Day Sand	1975	—	2.50	5.00
2110	Locomotive Breath/Fat Man	1975	—	2.50	5.00
2114	Too Old to Rock and Roll, Too Young to Die/Bad Eyed and Loveless	1976	—	2.50	5.00
2135	The Whistler/Strip Cartoon	1977	—	2.50	5.00
2387	Home/Warm Sporran	1979	—	2.50	5.00
2613	Fallen on Hard Times/Pussy Willow	1982	—	2.00	4.00
S7-18211	Christmas Song/Skating Away on the Thin Ice of a New Day	1994	—	2.50	5.00
—Green vinyl					
43172	Steel Monkey/Down at the End of Your Road	1987	—	2.00	4.00
REPRISE					
0815 [DJ]	Love Story/Song for Jeffrey	1969	3.75	7.50	15.00
—May be promo-only					
0845 [DJ]	Living in the Past/Driving Song	1969	5.00	10.00	20.00
—May be promo-only					
0886	Reasons for Waiting/Sweet Dream	1970	3.75	7.50	15.00
0899	Teacher/Witch's Promise	1970	3.75	7.50	15.00
0927	Inside/Time for Everything	1970	—	2.50	5.00
1024	Hymn 43/Mother Goose	1971	—	2.50	5.00
1054	Locomotive Breath/Wind-Up	1971	—	2.50	5.00
1153	Thick as a Brick (Edit)/Hymn 43	1972	—	2.50	5.00
—"Back to Back Hits" series					

Albums

Number	Title (A Side/B Side)	Yr	VG	VG+	NM
CHRYSALIS					
PRO 623 [DJ]	The Jethro Tull Radio Show	1975	12.50	25.00	50.00
CHR 1003	Thick as a Brick	1973	3.00	6.00	12.00
—Green label, "3300 Warner Blvd." address					
CHR 1003	Thick as a Brick	1977	2.50	5.00	10.00
—Blue label, New York address					
2CH 1035 [(2)]	Living in the Past	1972	5.00	10.00	20.00
—Two-record set with booklet; green labels					
CHR 1035 [(2)]	Living in the Past	1977	3.75	7.50	15.00
—Blue label, New York address					
CHR 1040	A Passion Play	1973	3.00	6.00	12.00
—Green label, "3300 Warner Blvd." address					
CHR 1040	A Passion Play	1977	2.50	5.00	10.00
—Blue label, New York address					
CHR 1041	This Was	1973	3.00	6.00	12.00
—Green label, "3300 Warner Blvd." address					
CHR 1041	This Was	1977	2.50	5.00	10.00
—Blue label, New York address					
CHR 1042	Stand Up	1973	3.00	6.00	12.00
—Green label, "3300 Warner Blvd." address					
CHR 1042	Stand Up	1977	2.50	5.00	10.00
—Blue label, New York address					
CHR 1043	Benefit	1973	3.00	6.00	12.00
—Green label, "3300 Warner Blvd." address					
CHR 1043	Benefit	1977	2.50	5.00	10.00
—Blue label, New York address					
CH4 1044 [Q]	Aqualung	1974	10.00	20.00	40.00
CHR 1044	Aqualung	1973	3.00	6.00	12.00
—Green label, "3300 Warner Blvd." address					
CHR 1044	Aqualung	1977	2.50	5.00	10.00
—Blue label, New York address					
CH4 1067 [Q]	War Child	1974	10.00	20.00	40.00
CHR 1067	War Child	1974	3.00	6.00	12.00
—Green label, "3300 Warner Blvd." address					
CHR 1067	War Child	1974	2.50	5.00	10.00
—Blue label, New York address					
CHR 1078	M.U. — The Best of Jethro Tull	1975	3.00	6.00	12.00
—Green label, "3300 Warner Blvd." address					
CHR 1078	M.U. — The Best of Jethro Tull	1977	2.50	5.00	10.00
—Blue label, New York address					
CHR 1082	Minstrel in the Gallery	1975	3.00	6.00	12.00
—Green label, "3300 Warner Blvd." address					
CHR 1082	Minstrel in the Gallery	1977	2.50	5.00	10.00
—Blue label, New York address					
CHR 1111	Too Old to Rock 'N' Roll; Too Young to Die!	1976	3.00	6.00	12.00
—Green label, "3300 Warner Blvd." address					
CHR 1111	Too Old to Rock 'N' Roll; Too Young to Die!	1977	2.50	5.00	10.00
—Blue label, New York address					
CHR 1132	Songs from the Wood	1977	2.50	5.00	10.00
CHR 1135	Repeat — The Best of Jethro Tull, Vol. II	1977	2.50	5.00	10.00
CHR 1175	Heavy Horses	1978	2.50	5.00	10.00
CHR2 1201 [(2)]	Jethro Tull Live — Bursting Out	1978	3.00	6.00	12.00
CHR 1238	Stormwatch	1979	2.50	5.00	10.00
CHR 1301	"A"	1980	2.50	5.00	10.00

Number	Title (A Side/B Side)	Yr	VG	VG+	NM
CHR 1380	The Broadsword and the Beast	1982	2.50	5.00	10.00
F1-21708	Rock Island	1989	2.50	5.00	10.00
FV 41003	Thick as a Brick	1983	2.00	4.00	8.00
PV 41003	Thick as a Brick	1986	2.00	4.00	8.00
KV2 41035 [(2)]	Living in the Past	1983	3.00	6.00	12.00
PV 41040	A Passion Play	1983	2.00	4.00	8.00
PV 41041	This Was	1983	2.00	4.00	8.00
PV 41042	Stand Up	1983	2.00	4.00	8.00
PV 41043	Benefit	1983	2.00	4.00	8.00
FV 41044	Aqualung	1983	2.00	4.00	8.00
PV 41067	War Child	1983	2.00	4.00	8.00
FV 41078	M.U. — The Best of Jethro Tull	1983	2.00	4.00	8.00
PV 41082	Minstrel in the Gallery	1983	2.00	4.00	8.00
PV 41111	Too Old to Rock 'N' Roll; Too Young to Die!	1983	2.00	4.00	8.00
PV 41132	Songs from the Wood	1983	2.00	4.00	8.00
FV 41135	Repeat — The Best of Jethro Tull, Vol. II	1983	2.00	4.00	8.00
PV 41135	Repeat — The Best of Jethro Tull, Vol. II	1986	2.00	4.00	8.00
PV 41175	Heavy Horses	1983	2.00	4.00	8.00
V2X 41201 [(2)]	Jethro Tull Live — Bursting Out	1983	3.00	6.00	12.00
PV 41238	Stormwatch	1983	2.00	4.00	8.00
PV 41301	"A"	1983	2.00	4.00	8.00
FV 41380	The Broadsword and the Beast	1983	2.00	4.00	8.00
PV 41380	The Broadsword and the Beast	1986	2.00	4.00	8.00
FV 41461	Under Wraps	1984	2.50	5.00	10.00
PV 41461	Under Wraps	1986	2.00	4.00	8.00
FV 41515	Original Masters	1985	2.50	5.00	10.00
FV 41590	Crest of a Knave	1987	2.50	5.00	10.00
V5X 41653 [(5)]	20 Years of Jethro Tull	1988	20.00	40.00	80.00
VX2 41655 [(2)]	20 Years of Jethro Tull	1989	6.25	12.50	25.00
—Abridged version of Chrysalis 41653					
DCC COMPACT CLASSICS					
LPZ 2033	Aqualung	1997	6.25	12.50	25.00
—Audiophile vinyl					
LPZ-2059	Original Masters	1998	6.25	12.50	25.00
—Audiophile vinyl					
MOBILE FIDELITY					
1-061	Aqualung	1980	17.50	35.00	70.00
—Audiophile vinyl					
1-092	The Broadsword and the Beast	1982	10.00	20.00	40.00
—Audiophile vinyl					
1-187	Thick as a Brick	1985	7.50	15.00	30.00
—Audiophile vinyl					
REPRISE					
MS 2035	Aqualung	1971	3.75	7.50	15.00
MS 2072	Thick as a Brick	1972	3.75	7.50	15.00
2MS 2106 [(2)]	Living in the Past	1972	6.25	12.50	25.00
—Two-record set with booklet; original edition, rather than using cardboard outer sleeve for the records, has record sleeves attached to enclosed booklet, and thus is difficult to find intact					
RS 6336	This Was	1969	5.00	10.00	20.00
—Two-tone orange label with "r:" and "W7" logos on label					
RS 6336	This Was	1970	3.75	7.50	15.00
—All-one-color (orange/brown) label with no "W7" on label					
RS 6360	Stand Up	1969	5.00	10.00	20.00
—Two-tone orange label with "r:" and "W7" logos on label; band "stands up" when gatefold is opened					
RS 6360	Stand Up	1970	3.75	7.50	15.00
—All-one-color (orange/brown) label with no "W7" on label					
RS 6400	Benefit	1970	5.00	10.00	20.00
—Two-tone orange label with "r:" and "W7" logos on label					
RS 6400	Benefit	1970	3.75	7.50	15.00
—All-one-color (orange/brown) label with no "W7" on label					

JEWEL AND EDDIE

JEWEL AKENS and Eddie Daniels; EDDIE COCHRAN plays guitar.

Number	Title (A Side/B Side)	Yr	VG	VG+	NM
45s					
SILVER					
1004	Opportunity/Doin' the Hully Gully	1960	10.00	20.00	40.00
1004	Opportunity/Strollin' Guitar	1960	7.50	15.00	30.00
1008	My Eyes Are Cryin' for You/Sixteen Tons	1960	7.50	15.00	30.00

JEWELL AND THE RUBIES

Number	Title (A Side/B Side)	Yr	VG	VG+	NM
45s					
ABC-PARAMOUNT					
10485	The Kidnapper/A Thrill	1963	3.00	6.00	12.00
LA LOUISIANNE					
8041	The Kidnapper/A Thrill	1963	7.50	15.00	30.00

JEWELS, THE (1)

Female vocal group.

Number	Title (A Side/B Side)	Yr	VG	VG+	NM
45s					
DIMENSION					
1034	Opportunity/Gotta Find a Way	1964	5.00	10.00	20.00
1048	Smokey Joe/But I Do	1965	3.75	7.50	15.00

JEWELS, THE (2)

Male vocal group, did the original version of the hit "Hearts of Stone."

Number	Title (A Side/B Side)	Yr	VG	VG+	NM
45s					
ANTLER					
1102	The Wind/Pearlie Mae	1959	10.00	20.00	40.00
IMPERIAL					
5351	Angel in My Life/Hearts Can Be Broken	1955	25.00	50.00	100.00
5362	Natural, Natural Ditty/Please Return	1955	25.00	50.00	100.00
5377	How/Rickety Rock	1956	25.00	50.00	100.00
5387	My Baby/Goin', Goin', Goin'	1956	25.00	50.00	100.00
ORIGINAL SOUND					
38	Hearts of Stone/Oh Yes I Know	1964	5.00	10.00	20.00
RPM					
474	She's a Flirt/Be-Bomp Baby	1956	17.50	35.00	70.00
R&B					
1301	Hearts of Stone/Runnin'	1954	50.00	100.00	200.00
1303	Oh Yes I Know/A Fool in Paradise	1954	75.00	150.00	300.00

JEWELS, THE (3)

Number	Title (A Side/B Side)	Yr	VG	VG+	NM
45s					
DYNAMITE					
2000	Papa Left Mama Holdin' the Bag/This Is My Story	1966	3.75	7.50	15.00
FEDERAL					
12541	My Song/This Is My Story	1966	5.00	10.00	20.00
KING					
6068	Smokie Joe's/Lookie Lookie	1967	3.00	6.00	12.00

JEWELS, THE (4)

Probably an instrumental group.

Number	Title (A Side/B Side)	Yr	VG	VG+	NM
45s					
FERN					
806	Jewel Rock/Space Guitar	1961	5.00	10.00	20.00

JEWELS, THE (5)

For recordings on Rama, see THE CROWS.

JEWELS, THE (U)

We can't definitely put these with any of the above groups. This could be as many as three more groups!

Number	Title (A Side/B Side)	Yr	VG	VG+	NM
45s					
MGM					
13577	We Got Togetherness/I'm Forever Blowing Bubbles	1966	5.00	10.00	20.00
OLIMPIC					
244	Jimmy Lee/The Hash	1964	7.50	15.00	30.00
SHASTA					
115	I Worry 'Bout You/Are You Coming to the Party	1959	5.00	10.00	20.00

JIANTS, THE

Number	Title (A Side/B Side)	Yr	VG	VG+	NM
45s					
CLAUDRA					
112	Tornado/She's My Woman	1959	50.00	100.00	200.00

JILL AND RAY

See PAUL AND PAULA.

JIMENEZ, JOSE

Also includes records under his real name, Bill Dana.

Number	Title (A Side/B Side)	Yr	VG	VG+	NM
45s					
A&M					
773	Jose's Dream/Cry	1965	2.00	4.00	8.00
—As "Bill Dana"					
779	All I Need Is You/Make Nice	1965	2.00	4.00	8.00
—As "Bill Dana"					
811	Jose Jimenezchevitz/Childhood Scenes	1966	2.00	4.00	8.00
—As "Bill Dana"					
KAPP					
409	The Astronaut (Part 1)/The Astronaut (Part 2)	1961	2.00	4.00	8.00
409 [PS]	The Astronaut (Part 1)/The Astronaut (Part 2)	1961	3.00	6.00	12.00
434	Christmas Sing Along with Jose: Jingle Bells/Sing Along with Jose: Shine On Harvest Moon	1961	3.75	7.50	15.00
443	Jose Jimenez in Orbit/Press Conference with Jose Jimenez in Orbit	1962	2.50	5.00	10.00
540	Jose and Cleopatra (Part 1)/Jose and Cleopatra (Part 2)	1963	2.50	5.00	10.00
552	King of the Surf (Part 1)/King of the Surf (Part 2)	1963	3.75	7.50	15.00
SIGNATURE					
12041	My Name — Jose Jimenez/In the Wee Small Hours	1960	3.00	6.00	12.00
12046	Bob Sled Racer/U.S. Senator	1960	3.00	6.00	12.00
—As "Bill Dana"					
Albums					
A&M					
SP-4144	Mashuganishi Yogi	1968	3.75	7.50	15.00
CAPITOL					
ST-464	Hoo Ha! Direct from Noshville	1970	3.75	7.50	15.00
KAPP					
KL 1215 [M]	Jose Jimenez the Submarine Officer	1961	6.25	12.50	25.00
—Original title					
KL 1215 [M]	More Jose Jimenez	1961	5.00	10.00	20.00
KL 1238 [M]	Jose Jimenez — The Astronaut (The First Man in Space)	1961	5.00	10.00	20.00
KL 1238 [M]	Jose Jimenez at the Hungry I	196?	3.75	7.50	15.00
—Reissue with new title					
KL-1257 [M]	Jose Jimenez in Orbit — Bill Dana on Earth	1961	5.00	10.00	20.00
KL 1304 [M]	Jose Jimenez Talks to Teenagers of All Ages	1962	5.00	10.00	20.00
KL-1320 [M]	Jose Jimenez — Our Secret Weapon	1963	5.00	10.00	20.00
KL-1332 [M]	Jose Jimenez in Jollywood	1963	5.00	10.00	20.00
KL-1402 [M]	Bill Dana in Las Vegas	1964	5.00	10.00	20.00
KS 3238 [S]	Jose Jimenez at the Hungry I	196?	3.75	7.50	15.00
KS-3332 [S]	Jose Jimenez in Jollywood	1963	6.25	12.50	25.00
ROULETTE					
R 25161 [M]	My Name...Jose Jimenez	1961	5.00	10.00	20.00
—Reissue of Signature LP					
SIGNATURE					
SM 1013 [M]	My Name...Jose Jimenez	1960	6.25	12.50	25.00

JIMMIE DALE AND THE FLATLANDERS

Number	Title (A Side/B Side)	Yr	VG	VG+	NM
45s					
PLANTATION					
92	Dallas/Tonight I'm Gonna Go Downtown	1972	12.50	25.00	50.00
106	Jole Blon/You've Never Seen Me Cry	1972	12.50	25.00	50.00
Albums					
PLANTATION					
22	One Road More	1972	—	—	—
—May exist only as an 8-track tape. Should an LP exist, its value would be in the hundreds.					
ROUNDER					
SS-34	More a Legend Than a Band	1990	3.00	6.00	12.00
—As "The Flatlanders"; reissue of Plantation material					

JIMMY AND DUANE
"Duane" is DUANE EDDY.

45s
EB X. PRESTON

Number	Title (A Side/B Side)	Yr	VG	VG+	NM
213	Soda Fountain Girl/(B-side unknown)	1955	62.50	125.00	250.00

JIMMY AND WALTER
45s
SUN

Number	Title (A Side/B Side)	Yr	VG	VG+	NM
180	Before Long/Easy	1953	500.00	1000.	2000.
—The earliest known 45 on Sun					

JIVE BOMBERS, THE
45s
SAVOY

Number	Title (A Side/B Side)	Yr	VG	VG+	NM
1508	Bad Boy/When Your Hair Has Turned to Silver	1957	6.25	12.50	25.00
1513	If I Had a Talking Picture of You/The Blues Don't Mean a Thing	1957	5.00	10.00	20.00
1515	You Took My Love/Cherry	1957	5.00	10.00	20.00
1535	Just Around the Corner/Is This the End	1958	5.00	10.00	20.00
1560	Star Dust/You Give Your Love to Me	1959	5.00	10.00	20.00

Albums
SAVOY JAZZ

Number	Title (A Side/B Side)	Yr	VG	VG+	NM
SJL-1150	Bad Boy	1986	2.50	5.00	10.00

JIVE FIVE, THE
45s
AMBIENT SOUND

Number	Title (A Side/B Side)	Yr	VG	VG+	NM
02742	Magic Maker, Music Maker/Oh Baby	1982	—	2.50	5.00
03053	Hey Sam/Don't Believe Him Donna	1982	—	2.50	5.00

AVCO

Number	Title (A Side/B Side)	Yr	VG	VG+	NM
4568	Come Down in Time/Love Is Pain	1971	—	3.00	6.00
4589	Follow the Lamb/Let the Feeling Belong	1972	—	3.00	6.00
4589	Follow the Lamb/Lay Lady Lay	1972	—	3.00	6.00

BELTONE

Number	Title (A Side/B Side)	Yr	VG	VG+	NM
1006	My True Story/When I Was Single	1961	7.50	15.00	30.00
1014	Never, Never/People from Another World	1961	5.00	10.00	20.00
2019	Hully Gully Calling Time/No, Not Again	1962	5.00	10.00	20.00
2024	What Time Is It?/Beggin' You Please	1962	5.00	10.00	20.00
2029	These Golden Rings/Do You Hear Wedding Bells	1962	5.00	10.00	20.00
2030	Lily Marlene/Johnny Never Knew	1963	5.00	10.00	20.00
2034	She's My Girl/Rain	1963	5.00	10.00	20.00

BRUT

Number	Title (A Side/B Side)	Yr	VG	VG+	NM
814	All I Ever Do Is Dream About You/Super Woman (Part 2)	1973	—	3.00	6.00

DECCA

Number	Title (A Side/B Side)	Yr	VG	VG+	NM
32671	(If You Let Me Make Love to You) Why Can't I Touch You/You Showed Me the Light of Love	1970	2.00	4.00	8.00
32736	I Want You to Be My Baby/Give Me Just a Chance	1970	2.00	4.00	8.00

LANA

Number	Title (A Side/B Side)	Yr	VG	VG+	NM
105	My True Story/When I Was Single	196?	2.00	4.00	8.00
—Early reissue					

MUSICOR

Number	Title (A Side/B Side)	Yr	VG	VG+	NM
1250	Crying Like a Baby/You'll Fall in Love	1967	3.00	6.00	12.00
1270	No More Tears/You'll Fall in Love	1967	3.00	6.00	12.00
1305	Sugar (Don't Take Away My Candy)/Blues in the Ghetto	1968	3.00	6.00	12.00

SKETCH

Number	Title (A Side/B Side)	Yr	VG	VG+	NM
219	United/Prove Every Word You Say	1964	3.75	7.50	15.00

UNITED ARTISTS

Number	Title (A Side/B Side)	Yr	VG	VG+	NM
0100	I'm a Happy Man/It Will Stand	1973	—	2.50	5.00
—"Silver Spotlight Series" reissue; B-side by The Showmen					
807	United/Prove Every Word You Say	1965	5.00	10.00	20.00
853	I'm a Happy Man/Kiss Kiss Kiss	1965	5.00	10.00	20.00
936	Please Baby Please/A Bench in the Park	1965	5.00	10.00	20.00
50004	Goin' Wild/Main Street	1966	3.75	7.50	15.00
50033	In My Neighborhood/Then Came Heartbreak	1966	3.75	7.50	15.00
50069	You're a Puzzle/Ha Ha	1966	3.75	7.50	15.00
50107	You/You Promised Me Great Things	1966	3.75	7.50	15.00

Albums
AMBIENT SOUND

Number	Title (A Side/B Side)	Yr	VG	VG+	NM
FZ 37717	Here We Are	1982	3.75	7.50	15.00

AMBIENT SOUND/ROUNDER

Number	Title (A Side/B Side)	Yr	VG	VG+	NM
ASR-801	Way Back	1985	3.00	6.00	12.00

COLLECTABLES

Number	Title (A Side/B Side)	Yr	VG	VG+	NM
COL-5022	Greatest Hits	198?	2.50	5.00	10.00

RELIC

Number	Title (A Side/B Side)	Yr	VG	VG+	NM
5020	The Jive Five's Greatest Hits (1961-1963)	198?	2.50	5.00	10.00

UNITED ARTISTS

Number	Title (A Side/B Side)	Yr	VG	VG+	NM
UAL-3455 [M]	The Jive Five	1965	12.50	25.00	50.00
UAS-6455 [S]	The Jive Five	1965	18.75	37.50	75.00

JIVERS, THE
45s
ALADDIN

Number	Title (A Side/B Side)	Yr	VG	VG+	NM
3329	Cherie/Little Mama	1956	40.00	80.00	160.00
3347	Ray Pearl/Dear Little One	1956	30.00	60.00	120.00

JO JO GUNNE
45s
ASYLUM

Number	Title (A Side/B Side)	Yr	VG	VG+	NM
11003	Run Run Run/Take It Easy	1972	—	2.50	5.00
11007	Shake That Fat/I Make Love	1972	—	2.50	5.00
11018	Ready Freddie/Wait a Lifetime	1973	—	2.50	5.00
11020	Take Me Down Easy/Rock Around the Symbol	1973	—	2.50	5.00
11031	I Wanna Love You/New City	1974	—	2.50	5.00
45225	Where Is the Show/Into My Life	1975	—	2.50	5.00

Albums
ASYLUM

Number	Title (A Side/B Side)	Yr	VG	VG+	NM
7E-1022	So...Where's the Show?	1974	2.50	5.00	10.00
SD 5053	Jo Jo Gunne	1972	3.75	7.50	15.00
SD 5065	Bite Down Hard	1973	3.75	7.50	15.00
SD 5071	Jumpin' the Gunne	1973	3.75	7.50	15.00
—Gatefold cover					
SD 5071	Jumpin' the Gunne	1974	2.50	5.00	10.00
—Regular cover					

JODIMARS, THE
Contains ex-members of BILL HALEY AND HIS COMETS.

45s
CAPITOL

Number	Title (A Side/B Side)	Yr	VG	VG+	NM
F3285	Well Now — Dig This/Let's All Rock Together	1955	6.25	12.50	25.00
F3360	Dancin' the Bop/Boom Boom My Bayou Baby	1956	6.25	12.50	25.00
F3436	Lotsa Love/Rattle My Bones	1956	6.25	12.50	25.00
F3512	Rattle Shakin' Daddy/Eat Your Heart Out, Annie	1956	6.25	12.50	25.00
F3588	Clarabella/Midnight	1956	6.25	12.50	25.00
F3633	Cloud 99/Later	1957	6.25	12.50	25.00

PRESIDENT

Number	Title (A Side/B Side)	Yr	VG	VG+	NM
1017	Shoo-Sue/Story-Telling Baby	1957	5.00	10.00	20.00

JOE & EDDIE
45s
CAPITOL

Number	Title (A Side/B Side)	Yr	VG	VG+	NM
F4149	The Fox/Lonesome Road	1959	2.50	5.00	10.00
F4209	Green Grass/And I Believe	1959	2.50	5.00	10.00
F4288	Take My Hand/Remember Me	1959	2.50	5.00	10.00

GNP CRESCENDO

Number	Title (A Side/B Side)	Yr	VG	VG+	NM
185	I Got Shoes/Water Boy	1962	2.00	4.00	8.00
195	Lonesome Traveler/There's a Meetin' Here Tonight	1963	2.00	4.00	8.00
305	Children Go/I Laid Around	1963	2.00	4.00	8.00
306	What's That I Hear/Farewell My Cindy Jane	1963	2.00	4.00	8.00
316	Wild Is the Wind/Swing Down Chariot	1964	—	3.00	6.00
321	Frankie and Johnny Blues/Gonna Build a Mountain	1964	—	3.00	6.00
324	Goodnight Irene/Pearly Shells	1964	—	3.00	6.00
333	Lonesome Road/Tear Down the Walls	1964	—	3.00	6.00
338	He's Got the Whole World in His Hands/Gabrielle	1965	—	3.00	6.00
344	Depend On Yourself/With You in Mind	1965	—	3.00	6.00
353	It Ain't Me Babe/Walkin' Down the Line	1965	—	3.00	6.00
355	I Got You (I've Got Everything)/Petticoat White (Summer Blue Sky)	1965	—	3.00	6.00
366	Michael, Row the Boat Ashore/That Was the Last Thing on My Mind	1965	—	3.00	6.00

Albums
GNP CRESCENDO

Number	Title (A Side/B Side)	Yr	VG	VG+	NM
GNP-75 [M]	Joe & Eddie	1963	5.00	10.00	20.00
GNP-86 [M]	There's a Meetin' Here Tonite	1963	5.00	10.00	20.00
GNP-96 [M]	Coast to Coast	1964	5.00	10.00	20.00
GNPS-96 [S]	Coast to Coast	1964	6.25	12.50	25.00
GNP-99 [M]	Joe & Eddie, Volume 4	1964	5.00	10.00	20.00
GNPS-99 [S]	Joe & Eddie, Volume 4	1964	6.25	12.50	25.00
GNP-2005 [M]	Tear Down the Walls	1965	3.75	7.50	15.00
GNPS-2005 [S]	Tear Down the Walls	1965	5.00	10.00	20.00
GNP-2007 [M]	Joe & Eddie Live in Hollywood	1965	3.75	7.50	15.00
GNPS-2007 [S]	Joe & Eddie Live in Hollywood	1965	5.00	10.00	20.00
GNP-2014 [M]	Walkin' Down the Line	1965	3.75	7.50	15.00
GNPS-2014 [S]	Walkin' Down the Line	1965	5.00	10.00	20.00
GNP-2021 [M]	The Magic of Their Singing	1966	3.75	7.50	15.00
GNPS-2021 [S]	The Magic of Their Singing	1966	5.00	10.00	20.00

JOEL, BILLY
45s
COLUMBIA

Number	Title (A Side/B Side)	Yr	VG	VG+	NM
02518	Say Goodbye to Hollywood/Summer, Highland Falls	1981	—	2.00	4.00
02518 [PS]	Say Goodbye to Hollywood/Summer, Highland Falls	1981	—	2.00	4.00
02628	She's Got a Way/The Ballad of Billy the Kid	1981	—	2.00	4.00
02628 [PS]	She's Got a Way/The Ballad of Billy the Kid	1981	—	2.00	4.00
03238	It's Still Rock and Roll to Me/Don't Ask Me Why	1982	—	—	3.00
—Reissue					
03239	You May Be Right/She's Got a Way	1982	—	—	3.00
—Reissue					
03241	Honesty/Sometimes a Fantasy	1982	—	—	3.00
—Reissue					
03244	Pressure/Laura	1982	—	2.00	4.00
03244 [PS]	Pressure/Laura	1982	—	2.00	4.00
CNR-03321	Pressure	1982	—	3.00	6.00
—One-sided budget release (Large hole)					
03413	Allentown/Elvis Presley Blvd.	1982	—	2.00	4.00
03413 [PS]	Allentown/Elvis Presley Blvd.	1982	—	2.00	4.00
CNR-03426	Allentown	1982	—	3.00	6.00
—One-sided budget release					
03780	Goodnight Saigon/A Room of Our Own	1983	—	2.00	4.00
03780 [PS]	Goodnight Saigon/A Room of Our Own	1983	—	2.00	4.00
04012	Tell Her About It/Easy Money	1983	—	—	3.00
04012 [PS]	Tell Her About It/Easy Money	1983	—	2.00	4.00
04149	Uptown Girl/Careless Talk	1983	—	—	3.00
04149 [PS]	Uptown Girl/Careless Talk	1983	—	2.00	4.00
04259	An Innocent Man/I'll Cry Instead	1983	—	—	3.00
04259 [PS]	An Innocent Man/I'll Cry Instead	1983	—	2.00	4.00
04400	The Longest Time/Christie Lee	1984	—	—	3.00
04400 [PS]	The Longest Time/Christie Lee	1984	—	2.00	4.00
04514	Leave a Tender Moment Alone/This Night	1984	—	—	3.00
04514 [PS]	Leave a Tender Moment Alone/This Night	1984	—	2.00	4.00
04681	Keeping the Faith (Special Mix)/She's Right On Time	1984	—	—	3.00
04681 [PS]	Keeping the Faith (Special Mix)/She's Right On Time	1984	—	2.00	4.00
05417	You're Only Human (Second Wind)/Surprises	1985	—	—	3.00
05417 [PS]	You're Only Human (Second Wind)/Surprises	1985	—	—	3.00
05657	The Night Is Still Young/Summer, Highland Falls	1985	—	—	3.00
05657 [PS]	The Night Is Still Young/Summer, Highland Falls	1985	—	2.00	4.00

Number	Title (A Side/B Side)	Yr	VG	VG+	NM
05657 [PS]	The Night Is Still Young/Summer, Highland Falls	1985	2.50	5.00	10.00
—Promotional sleeve, different that stock sleeve					
06108	A Matter of Trust/Getting Closer	1986	—	—	3.00
06526	This Is the Time/Code of Silence	1986	—	—	3.00
06526 [PS]	This Is the Time/Code of Silence	1986	—	—	3.00
06994	Baby Grand/Big Man on Mulberry Street	1987	—	—	3.00
—A-side: With Ray Charles					
06994 [PS]	Baby Grand/Big Man on Mulberry Street	1987	—	—	3.00
07626	Back in the U.S.S.R./Big Shot	1987	—	—	3.00
07626 [PS]	Back in the U.S.S.R./Big Shot	1987	—	2.00	4.00
07664	The Times They Are a-Changin'/Back in the U.S.S.R.	1987	—	2.00	4.00
08415	Tell Her About It/Easy Money	1988	—	—	3.00
—Reissue					
08416	An Innocent Man/I'll Cry Instead	1988	—	—	3.00
—Reissue					
08417	The Longest Time/Christie Lee	1988	—	—	3.00
—Reissue					
08418	Leave a Tender Moment Alone/This Night	1988	—	—	3.00
—Reissue					
08419	Keeping the Faith/She's Right on Time	1988	—	—	3.00
—Reissue					
08420	You're Only Human (Second Wind)/Surprises	1988	—	—	3.00
—Reissue					
10015	Travelin' Prayer/Ain't No Crime	1974	—	3.00	6.00
10064	The Entertainer/The Mexican Connection	1974	—	3.00	6.00
10412	James/Summer, Highland Falls	1976	—	3.00	6.00
10562	Say Goodbye to Hollywood/I've Loved These Days	1977	—	3.00	6.00
10624	Movin' Out (Anthony's Song)/She's Always a Woman	1977	2.50	5.00	10.00
10646	Just the Way You Are/Get It Right the First Time	1977	—	2.50	5.00
10708	Movin' Out (Anthony's Song)/Everybody Has a Dream	1978	—	2.50	5.00
10750	Only the Good Die Young/Get It Right the First Time	1978	—	2.50	5.00
10788	She's Always a Woman/Vienna	1978	—	2.50	5.00
10853	My Life/52nd Street	1978	—	2.50	5.00
10913	Big Shot/Root Beer Rag	1979	—	2.50	5.00
10959	Honesty/The Mexican Connection	1979	—	2.50	5.00
11229	All for Leyna/Souvenir	1980	—	—	—
—Canceled					
11231	You May Be Right/Close to the Borderline	1980	—	2.00	4.00
11231 [PS]	You May Be Right/Close to the Borderline	1980	—	3.00	6.00
11276	It's Still Rock and Roll to Me/Through the Long Night	1980	—	2.00	4.00
11276 [PS]	It's Still Rock and Roll to Me/Through the Long Night	1980	—	3.00	6.00
11331	Don't Ask Me Why/C'etait Toi (You Were the One)	1980	—	2.00	4.00
11331 [PS]	Don't Ask Me Why/C'etait Toi (You Were the One)	1980	—	3.00	6.00
11379	Sometimes a Fantasy/All for Leyna	1980	—	2.50	5.00
11379 [PS]	Sometimes a Fantasy/All for Leyna	1980	2.00	4.00	8.00
45963	Piano Man/You're My Home	1973	—	3.00	6.00
46055	Worse Comes to Worst/Somewhere Along the Line	1974	—	3.00	6.00
73021	We Didn't Start the Fire/House of Blue Light	1989	—	—	3.00
73091	I Go to Extremes/When in Rome	1989	—	—	3.00
73442	That's Not Her Style/And So It Goes	1990	—	—	3.00
77086	The River of Dreams/No Man's Land	1993	—	—	3.00
77254	All About Soul/Picked a Real Bad Time	1993	—	—	3.00
77363	Lullabye (Goodnight, My Angel)/Two Thousand Years	1994	—	—	3.00
78641	To Make You Feel My Love//Intro/Summer, Highland Falls/Summer, Highland Falls	1997	—	—	3.00

EPIC

Number	Title (A Side/B Side)	Yr	VG	VG+	NM
06118	Modern Woman/Sleeping with the Television On	1986	—	—	3.00
06118 [PS]	Modern Woman/Sleeping with the Television On	1986	—	2.00	4.00
74422	All Shook Up/Wear My Ring Around Your Neck	1992	—	—	3.00
—B-side is instrumental track of Ricky Van Shelton's recording					

FAMILY PRODUCTIONS

Number	Title (A Side/B Side)	Yr	VG	VG+	NM
0900	She's Got a Way/Everybody Loves You Now	1971	6.25	12.50	25.00
0906	Tomorrow Is Today/Everybody Loves You Now	1971	6.25	12.50	25.00

Albums

COLUMBIA

Number	Title	Yr	VG	VG+	NM
AS 326 [DJ]	Souvenir	1976	7.50	15.00	30.00
—Promo-only LP with one side live, one side a compilation of studio tracks					
AS 1343 [DJ]	Billy Joel Interview	1982	6.25	12.50	25.00
CQ 32544 [Q]	Piano Man	1974	5.00	10.00	20.00
KC 32544	Piano Man	1973	3.00	6.00	12.00
—Some copies have the first song spelled "Travelin' Prayer," others have it "Travellin' Prayer." No difference in value.					
PC 32544	Piano Man	1976	2.50	5.00	10.00
—No bar code on back cover					
PC 32544	Piano Man	1979	2.00	4.00	8.00
—With bar code on back cover					
PC 33146	Streetlife Serenade	1975	2.50	5.00	10.00
—No bar code on back cover					
PC 33146	Streetlife Serenade	1979	2.00	4.00	8.00
—With bar code on back cover					
PCQ 33146 [Q]	Streetlife Serenade	1975	5.00	10.00	20.00
PC 33848	Turnstiles	1976	2.50	5.00	10.00
—No bar code on back cover					
PC 33848	Turnstiles	1976	2.00	4.00	8.00
—With bar code on back cover					
PCQ 33848 [Q]	Turnstiles	1976	5.00	10.00	20.00
HC 34987	The Stranger	1981	7.50	15.00	30.00
—Half-speed mastered edition (original)					
JC 34987	The Stranger	1977	2.50	5.00	10.00
PC 34987	The Stranger	1979	2.00	4.00	8.00
FC 35609	52nd Street	1978	2.50	5.00	10.00
PC 35609	52nd Street	1985	2.00	4.00	8.00
FC 36384	Glass Houses	1980	2.50	5.00	10.00
PC 36384	Glass Houses	1986	2.00	4.00	8.00
PC 37461	Songs in the Attic	1984	2.00	4.00	8.00
TC 37461	Songs in the Attic	1981	2.50	5.00	10.00
QC 38200	The Nylon Curtain	1982	2.50	5.00	10.00
QC 38837	An Innocent Man	1983	2.50	5.00	10.00
PC 38984	Cold Spring Harbor	1983	2.00	4.00	8.00
—Remixed, remastered version of Family Productions album					
C2 40121 [(2)]	Greatest Hits, Volumes 1 and 2	1985	3.00	6.00	12.00
OC 40402	The Bridge	1986	2.50	5.00	10.00
C2 40996 [(2)]	KOHUEPT	1987	3.75	7.50	15.00
OC 44366	Storm Front	1989	3.00	6.00	12.00
HC 44987	The Stranger	1982	6.25	12.50	25.00
—Half-speed mastered edition (reissue)					
HC 45609	52nd Street	1982	6.25	12.50	25.00
—Half-speed mastered edition					
HC 47461	Songs in the Attic	1982	17.50	35.00	70.00
—Half-speed mastered edition					
HC 48837	An Innocent Man	1983	7.50	15.00	30.00
—Half-speed mastered edition					

FAMILY PRODUCTIONS

Number	Title	Yr	VG	VG+	NM
FPS-2700	Cold Spring Harbor	1971	10.00	20.00	40.00
—Authentic copies have mostly dark blue labels; when reissued on Columbia, the entire LP was remixed and remastered, and "You Can Make Me Free" was shortened by three minutes					

JOEY AND DANNY

45s

SWAN

Number	Title (A Side/B Side)	Yr	VG	VG+	NM
4276	Santa's Got a Brand New Bag/Rats in My Room	1967	5.00	10.00	20.00

JOEY AND THE CONTINENTALS

45s

CLARIDGE

Number	Title (A Side/B Side)	Yr	VG	VG+	NM
304	She Rides with Me/Rudy Vahoo	1966	6.25	12.50	25.00
—Reissued on Claridge 312 as "The G.T.O.'s"					

KOMET

Number	Title (A Side/B Side)	Yr	VG	VG+	NM
1001	Linda/Will Love Ever Come My Way	196?	3.75	7.50	15.00

LAURIE

Number	Title (A Side/B Side)	Yr	VG	VG+	NM
3294	Sad Girl/Baby	1965	6.25	12.50	25.00

JOEY AND THE LEXINGTONS

45s

COMET

Number	Title (A Side/B Side)	Yr	VG	VG+	NM
2154	Heaven/The Girl I Love	1962	37.50	75.00	150.00

DUNES

Number	Title (A Side/B Side)	Yr	VG	VG+	NM
2029	Bobbie/Tears from My Eyes	1963	25.00	50.00	100.00

JOEY AND THE TEENAGERS

45s

COLUMBIA

Number	Title (A Side/B Side)	Yr	VG	VG+	NM
42054	What's On Your Mind/The Draw	1961	20.00	40.00	80.00

JOHN, ELTON

12-Inch Singles

GEFFEN

Number	Title (A Side/B Side)	Yr	VG	VG+	NM
PRO-A-948 [DJ]	Nobody Wins/Nobody Wins (French Version)	1981	3.00	6.00	12.00
PRO-A-1463 [DJ]	Empty Garden (Hey Hey Johnny) (Long)/(Short)	1981	2.50	5.00	10.00
PRO-A-2025 [DJ]	I'm Still Standing (same on both sides)	1983	2.00	4.00	8.00
PRO-A-2066 [DJ]	Kiss the Bride (LP Version) (Edit)	1983	—	3.00	6.00
—B-side by Liz Lands; "Gordy" on top of label					
PRO-A-2160 [DJ]	Sad Songs (Say So Much) (same on both sides)	1984	—	3.00	6.00
PRO-A-2176 [DJ]	Sasson Presents Elton John	1983	5.00	10.00	20.00
—One-sided promo with two versions of "Sad Songs (Say So Much)" and an etched facsimile autograph on B-side					
PRO-A-2188 [DJ]	Who Wears These Shoes? (same on both sides)	1984	—	3.00	6.00
PRO-A-2374 [DJ]	Wrap Her Up (same on both sides)	1985	—	3.00	6.00
PRO-A-2569 [DJ]	Heartache All Over the World (2 edit versions)	1986	—	3.00	6.00
20563	Heartache All Over the World (2 versions)/Highlander	1986	—	3.00	6.00

MCA

Number	Title (A Side/B Side)	Yr	VG	VG+	NM
L33-1172 [DJ]	Bite Your Lip (Get Up and Dance) (same on both sides)	1977	2.50	5.00	10.00
L33-1850 [DJ]	Victim of Love (same on both sides)	1979	—	3.00	6.00
L33-1854 [DJ]	Johnny B. Goode (same on both sides)	1979	2.00	4.00	8.00
L33-17458 [DJ]	Candle in the Wind (Live) (same on both sides)	1987	—	3.00	6.00
L33-17475 [DJ]	Take Me to the Pilot (Live) (same on both sides)	1987	—	3.00	6.00
23870	I Don't Wanna Go On with You Like That (3 versions)	1988	2.00	4.00	8.00
23917	Mona Lisas and Mad Hatters (3 versions)/A Word in Spanish	1986	2.00	4.00	8.00

45s

CONGRESS

Number	Title (A Side/B Side)	Yr	VG	VG+	NM
6017	Lady Samantha/It's Me That You Need	1970	12.50	25.00	50.00
6017 [DJ]	Lady Samantha/It's Me That You Need	1970	7.50	15.00	30.00
6022	Border Song/Bad Side of the Moon	1970	12.50	25.00	50.00
6022 [DJ]	Border Song/Bad Side of the Moon	1970	7.50	15.00	30.00

DJM

Number	Title (A Side/B Side)	Yr	VG	VG+	NM
70008	Lady Samantha/All Across the Havens	1969	75.00	150.00	300.00
70008 [DJ]	Lady Samantha/All Across the Havens	1969	25.00	50.00	100.00

GEFFEN

Number	Title (A Side/B Side)	Yr	VG	VG+	NM
28578	Heartache All Over the World/Highlander	1986	—	—	3.00
28578 [PS]	Heartache All Over the World/Highlander	1986	—	—	3.00
28800	Nikita/Restless	1985	—	—	3.00
28800 [PS]	Nikita/Restless	1985	—	—	3.00
28873	Wrap Her Up/The Man Who Never Died	1985	—	—	3.00
28873 [PS]	Wrap Her Up/The Man Who Never Died	1985	—	—	3.00
29111	In Neon/Tactics	1984	—	—	3.00
29189	Who Wears These Shoes?/Lonely Boy	1984	—	—	3.00
29189 [PS]	Who Wears These Shoes?/Lonely Boy	1984	—	—	3.00
29292	Sad Songs (Say So Much)/A Simple Man	1984	—	—	3.00
29292 [DJ]	Sad Songs (Say So Much) (2 mixes)	1984	2.50	5.00	10.00
—One side features a 4:05 mix unavailable elsewhere					
29402	Cold As Christmas (In the Middle of the Year)/(B-side unassigned)	1983	—	—	—
—Unreleased					
29460	I Guess That's Why They Call It the Blues/The Retreat	1983	—	—	3.00

Number	Title (A Side/B Side)	Yr	VG	VG+	NM
29460 [PS]	I Guess That's Why They Call It the Blues/The Retreat	1983	—	—	3.00
29568	Kiss the Bride/Choc Ice Goes Mental	1983	—	—	3.00
29568 [PS]	Kiss the Bride/Choc Ice Goes Mental	1983	—	—	3.00
29639	I'm Still Standing/Love So Cold	1983	—	—	3.00
29639 [PS]	I'm Still Standing/Love So Cold	1983	—	—	3.00
29846	Ball & Chain/Where Have All the Good Times Gone?	1982	—	2.00	4.00
29954	Blue Eyes/Hey Papa Legba	1982	—	2.00	4.00
29954 [PS]	Blue Eyes/Hey Papa Legba	1982	—	2.50	5.00
49722	Nobody Wins/Fools in Fashion	1981	—	2.00	4.00
49722 [PS]	Nobody Wins/Fools in Fashion	1981	—	2.50	5.00
49788	Chloe/Tortured	1981	—	2.00	4.00
49788 [DJ]	Chloe//Fanfare/Chloe	1981	2.00	4.00	8.00
—B-side of this promo-only single is full-length version					
50049	Empty Garden (Hey Hey Johnny)/Take Me Down to the Ocean	1982	—	2.00	4.00
50049 [DJ]	Empty Garden (LP version)/Empty Garden (Edit)	1982	2.00	4.00	8.00
50049 [PS]	Empty Garden (Hey Hey Johnny)/Take Me Down to the Ocean	1982	—	2.50	5.00
MCA					
S45-1938	Love Song (Long)/Love Song (Short)	1976	5.00	10.00	20.00
—Promo-only release from the Here And There live album					
40000	Crocodile Rock/Elderberry Wine	1972	—	3.00	6.00
—Original pressings have a solid black label					
40046	Daniel/Skyline Pigeon	1973	—	2.50	5.00
40105	Saturday Night's Alright for Fighting//Jack Rabbit/Whenever You're Ready	1973	—	2.50	5.00
40148	Goodbye Yellow Brick Road/Young Man's Blues	1973	—	2.50	5.00
40198	Bennie and the Jets/Harmony	1974	—	2.50	5.00
40259	Don't Let the Sun Go Down on Me/Sick City	1974	—	2.50	5.00
40297	The Bitch Is Back/Cold Highway	1974	—	2.50	5.00
40344	Lucy in the Sky with Diamonds/One Day at a Time	1974	—	2.50	5.00
—Both sides feature "Dr. Winston O'Boogie" (John Lennon)					
40344 [PS]	Lucy in the Sky with Diamonds/One Day at a Time	1974	2.50	5.00	10.00
40364	Philadelphia Freedom/I Saw Her Standing There	1975	—	2.50	5.00
—B-side features John Lennon					
40364 [PS]	Philadelphia Freedom/I Saw Her Standing There	1975	—	3.00	6.00
40364 [PS]	Philadelphia Freedom/I Saw Her Standing There	1975	10.00	20.00	40.00
—Promo-only sleeve from WFIL radio in Philadelphia					
40421	Someone Saved My Life Tonight/House of Cards	1975	—	2.50	5.00
—Original copies have "Captain Fantastic" label					
40421	Someone Saved My Life Tonight/House of Cards	1975	—	2.00	4.00
—With MCA black/rainbow label					
40461	Island Girl/Sugar on the Floor	1975	—	2.00	4.00
40505	Grow Some Funk of Your Own/I Feel Like a Bullet (in the Gun of Robert Ford)	1976	—	2.00	4.00
40892	Ego/Flinstone Boy	1978	—	2.00	4.00
40892 [PS]	Ego/Flinstone Boy	1978	2.50	5.00	10.00
40973	Part-Time Love/I Cry at Night	1978	—	2.00	4.00
40973 [PS]	Part-Time Love/I Cry at Night	1978	—	2.00	4.00
40993	Song for Guy/Lovesick	1979	2.50	5.00	10.00
—The stock copy is much scarcer than the promo, the only Elton John MCA single where this is the case.					
40993 [DJ]	Song for Guy/Lovesick	1979	—	2.50	5.00
40993 [PS]	Song for Guy/Lovesick	1979	—	2.50	5.00
41042	Mama Can't Buy You Love/Three Way Love Affair	1979	—	2.00	4.00
41042 [PS]	Mama Can't Buy You Love/Three Way Love Affair	1979	—	2.00	4.00
41126	Victim of Love/Strangers	1979	2.00	4.00	8.00
—Label incorrectly says "From the MCA LP...'Thunder in the Night'"					
41126	Victim of Love/Strangers	1979	—	2.00	4.00
—Label correctly says "From the MCA LP...'Victim of Love'"					
41159	Johnny B. Goode/Georgia	1980	—	2.50	5.00
41236	Little Jeannie/Conquer the Sun	1980	—	2.00	4.00
—Originals have a colorful custom label					
41236 [PS]	Little Jeannie/Conquer the Sun	1980	—	2.50	5.00
41293	(Sartorial Eloquence) Don't Ya Wanna Play This Game No More?//Cartier/White Man Danger	1980	—	2.00	4.00
53196	Candle in the Wind/Sorry Seems to Be the Hardest Word	1987	—	—	3.00
53196 [PS]	Candle in the Wind/Sorry Seems to Be the Hardest Word	1987	—	2.00	4.00
—White sleeve					
53196 [PS]	Candle in the Wind/Sorry Seems to Be the Hardest Word	1987	—	—	3.00
—Yellow sleeve with album jackets pictured on back					
53260	Take Me to the Pilot/Tonight	1988	—	2.00	4.00
53260 [PS]	Take Me to the Pilot/Tonight	1988	—	2.00	4.00
53345	I Don't Wanna Go On with You Like That/Rope Around a Fool	1988	—	—	3.00
53345 [PS]	I Don't Wanna Go On with You Like That/Rope Around a Fool	1988	—	—	3.00
53408	A Word in Spanish/Heavy Traffic	1988	—	—	3.00
53408 [PS]	A Word in Spanish/Heavy Traffic	1988	—	—	3.00
53692	Healing Hands/Dancing in the End Zone	1989	—	—	3.00
53750	Sacrifice/Love Is a Cannibal	1989	—	—	3.00
54423	The One/Suit of Wolves	1992	—	—	3.00
54452	Runaway Train/Understanding Women	1992	—	—	3.00
—A-side: Elton John and Eric Clapton					
54581	Simple Life/The North	1993	—	—	3.00
65018	Step Into Christmas/Ho! Ho! Ho! (Who'd Be a Turkey at Christmas)	1973	—	2.50	5.00
—Originals have black labels with rainbow					
65018	Step Into Christmas/Ho! Ho! Ho! (Who'd Be a Turkey at Christmas)	1978	—	2.00	4.00
—Second edition: Tan label					
65018	Step Into Christmas/Ho! Ho! Ho! (Who'd Be a Turkey at Christmas)	1980	—	—	3.00
—Third edition: Blue label with rainbow					
79026	Club at the End of the Street/Sacrifice	1990	—	—	3.00
POLYDOR					
PRO-002	Pinball Wizard/Acid Queen	1975	10.00	20.00	40.00
—Promo-only release; B-side by Tina Turner					
ROCKET					
31456 8108 7	Something About the Way You Look Tonight/Candle in the Wind 1997	1997	—	2.50	5.00
40645	Sorry Seems to Be the Hardest Word/Shoulder Holster	1976	—	2.00	4.00
40677	Bite Your Lip (Get up and dance!)/Chameleon	1977	—	2.00	4.00
852172-7	Made in England/Lucy in the Sky with Diamonds	1995	—	2.00	4.00
—B-side recorded live at Madison Square Garden in 1974 with John Lennon					
852394-7	Blessed/Latitude	1995	—	2.00	4.00
856014-7	Believe/The One (Live)	1995	—	—	3.00
856014-7 [PS]	Believe/The One (Live)	1995	—	—	3.00
UNI					
55246	Border Song/Bad Side of the Moon	1970	—	3.00	6.00
55265	Your Song/Take Me to the Pilot	1970	—	3.00	6.00
55277	Friends/Honey Roll	1971	—	3.00	6.00
55314	Levon/Goodbye	1971	—	3.00	6.00
55318	Tiny Dancer/Razor Face	1971	—	3.00	6.00
—Stock copies have full-length version of A-side					
55318 [DJ]	Tiny Dancer/Razor Face	1971	2.50	5.00	10.00
—With a severely truncated version of the A-side					
55328	Rocket Man/Suzie (Dramas)	1972	—	3.00	6.00
55343	Honky Cat/Slave	1972	—	3.00	6.00
VIKING					
1010	From Denver to L.A./Warm Summer Rain	1970	15.00	30.00	60.00
—B-side by The Barbara Moore Singers					
1010 [DJ]	From Denver to L.A. (same on both sides)	1970	6.25	12.50	25.00
—The promo version of this has been counterfeited; some say all are counterfeits.					

7-Inch Extended Plays

Number	Title (A Side/B Side)	Yr	VG	VG+	NM
UNI					
1903 [DJ]	Come Down in Time/Country Comfort//Amoreena/Love Song	1971	3.75	7.50	15.00
—Jukebox issue, small hole, plays at 33 1/3 rpm					
1903 [PS]	Tumbleweed Connection	1971	3.75	7.50	15.00
—Part of Little LP series (LLP 143)					

Albums

Number	Title (A Side/B Side)	Yr	VG	VG+	NM
COLUMBIA SPECIAL PRODUCTS					
P 16196	The Best of Elton John, Volume One	1981	3.00	6.00	12.00
P 16197	The Best of Elton John, Volume Two	1981	3.00	6.00	12.00
—Both of the above "Distributed Exclusively by Scott Distributing Corp."					
DCC COMPACT CLASSICS					
LPZ-2004	Madman Across the Water	1994	5.00	10.00	20.00
—Audiophile vinyl					
LPZ-2013	Elton John's Greatest Hits	1995	5.00	10.00	20.00
—Audiophile vinyl					
LPZ-2020	Elton John's Greatest Hits, Volume 2	1996	—	—	—
—Canceled					
DIRECT DISC					
SD-16614 [(2)]	Goodbye Yellow Brick Road	1980	12.50	25.00	50.00
—Audiophile vinyl					
GEFFEN					
GHS 2002	The Fox	1981	2.50	5.00	10.00
GHS 2013	Jump Up!	1982	2.50	5.00	10.00
GHS 4006	Too Low for Zero	1983	2.50	5.00	10.00
GHS 24031	Breaking Hearts	1984	2.50	5.00	10.00
GHS 24031 [DJ]	Breaking Hearts	1984	5.00	10.00	20.00
—Promo pressing on Quiex II vinyl					
GHS 24077	Ice on Fire	1985	2.50	5.00	10.00
GHS 24114	Leather Jackets	1986	2.50	5.00	10.00
GHS 24153	Elton John's Greatest Hits, Vol. 3, 1979-1987	1987	2.50	5.00	10.00
MCA					
619	11-17-70	1979	2.00	4.00	8.00
620	Empty Sky	1979	2.00	4.00	8.00
621	Rock of the Westies	1979	2.00	4.00	8.00
622	Here and There	1979	2.00	4.00	8.00
771	Victim of Love	1981	2.00	4.00	8.00
772	21 at 33	1981	2.00	4.00	8.00
1689	Elton John's Greatest Hits	198?	2.00	4.00	8.00
L33-1995 [PD]	A Single Man	1978	10.00	20.00	40.00
—Promo picture disc					
2012	Elton John	1973	2.50	5.00	10.00
2014	Tumbleweed Connection	1973	2.50	5.00	10.00
—With booklet					
2015	11-17-70	1973	2.50	5.00	10.00
2016	Madman Across the Water	1973	2.50	5.00	10.00
—With booklet					
2017	Honky Chateau	1973	2.50	5.00	10.00
2100	Don't Shoot Me, I'm Only the Piano Player	1973	5.00	10.00	20.00
—With all-black label (no rainbow) and booklet					
2100	Don't Shoot Me, I'm Only the Piano Player	1973	2.50	5.00	10.00
—With black rainbow label and booklet					
2116	Caribou	1974	2.50	5.00	10.00
2128	Elton John's Greatest Hits	1974	2.50	5.00	10.00
2130	Empty Sky	1975	2.50	5.00	10.00
—First American issue of his 1969 debut					
2142	Captain Fantastic and the Brown Dirt Cowboy	1975	3.00	6.00	12.00
—With custom label, two booklets and poster					
2142 [DJ]	Captain Fantastic and the Brown Dirt Cowboy	1975	75.00	150.00	300.00
—Brown vinyl promo, autographed by Elton John and Bernie Taupin					
2163	Rock of the Westies	1975	2.50	5.00	10.00
2197	Here and There	1976	2.50	5.00	10.00
3001	Tumbleweed Connection	1977	2.00	4.00	8.00
3003	Madman Across the Water	1977	2.00	4.00	8.00
3027	Elton John's Greatest Hits, Volume 2	1977	2.50	5.00	10.00
3065	A Single Man	1978	2.50	5.00	10.00
5104	Victim of Love	1979	2.50	5.00	10.00
5121	21 at 33	1980	2.50	5.00	10.00
—Originals have custom labels					
5224	Elton John's Greatest Hits	1981	2.00	4.00	8.00
5225	Elton John's Greatest Hits, Volume 2	1981	2.00	4.00	8.00
6011 [(2)]	Blue Moves	1979	2.50	5.00	10.00
6240	Reg Strikes Back	1988	2.50	5.00	10.00
6321	Sleeping with the Past	1989	2.50	5.00	10.00
6894 [(2)]	Goodbye Yellow Brick Road	1980	2.50	5.00	10.00
8022 [(2)]	Live in Australia with the Melbourne Symphony Orchestra	1987	3.75	7.50	15.00
10003 [(2)]	Goodbye Yellow Brick Road	1973	3.75	7.50	15.00
13921 [EP]	The Thom Bell Sessions	1979	2.00	4.00	8.00

Number	Title (A Side/B Side)	Yr	VG	VG+	NM
14951 [PD]	A Single Man	1978	5.00	10.00	20.00
—Stock picture disc					
37064	Honky Chateau	1979	2.00	4.00	8.00
37065	Caribou	1979	2.00	4.00	8.00
37066	Captain Fantastic and the Brown Dirt Cowboy	1979	2.00	4.00	8.00
37067	Elton John	1979	2.00	4.00	8.00
37068	A Single Man	1979	2.00	4.00	8.00
37113	Don't Shoot Me, I'm Only the Piano Player	1979	2.00	4.00	8.00
37199	Tumbleweed Connection	1982	2.00	4.00	8.00
37200	Madman Across the Water	1982	2.00	4.00	8.00
37215	Elton John's Greatest Hits	1983	2.00	4.00	8.00
37216	Elton John's Greatest Hits	1983	2.00	4.00	8.00
37266	Your Songs	1986	2.50	5.00	10.00
39115	The Complete Thom Bell Sessions	1989	3.75	7.50	15.00

MCA/ROCKET

Number	Title (A Side/B Side)	Yr	VG	VG+	NM
2-11004 [(2)]	Blue Moves	1976	3.75	7.50	15.00
—Originals have light blue labels with a train at the top of the label					

MOBILE FIDELITY

Number	Title (A Side/B Side)	Yr	VG	VG+	NM
2-160 [(2)]	Goodbye Yellow Brick Road	1984	10.00	20.00	40.00
—Audiophile vinyl					

NAUTILUS

Number	Title (A Side/B Side)	Yr	VG	VG+	NM
NR-42	Elton John's Greatest Hits	198?	25.00	50.00	100.00
—Audiophile vinyl					

ROCKET

Number	Title (A Side/B Side)	Yr	VG	VG+	NM
526915-1	Made in England	1995	5.00	10.00	20.00
—U.S. version is on 180-gram vinyl, distributed by Classic Records					

UNI

Number	Title (A Side/B Side)	Yr	VG	VG+	NM
73090	Elton John	1970	3.75	7.50	15.00
73096	Tumbleweed Connection	1971	3.75	7.50	15.00
—With booklet					
93090	Elton John	1971	3.00	6.00	12.00
93096	Tumbleweed Connection	1971	3.00	6.00	12.00
—With booklet					
93105	11-17-70	1971	3.75	7.50	15.00
93120	Madman Across the Water	1971	3.75	7.50	15.00
—With booklet					
93135	Honky Chateau	1972	3.75	7.50	15.00

JOHN, ELTON, AND KIKI DEE

Also see each artist's individual listings.

45s

MCA

Number	Title (A Side/B Side)	Yr	VG	VG+	NM
54762	True Love/Runaway Train	1993	—	—	3.00
—B-side by Elton John and Eric Clapton					

ROCKET

Number	Title (A Side/B Side)	Yr	VG	VG+	NM
40585	Don't Go Breakin' My Heart/Snow Queen	1976	—	2.00	4.00
—By "Elton John and Kiki Dee"					
40585 [PS]	Don't Go Breakin' My Heart/Snow Queen	1976	—	2.50	5.00
—By "Elton John and Kiki Dee"					

JOHN, ELTON, AND MILLIE JACKSON

Also see each artist's individual listings.

12-Inch Singles

GEFFEN

Number	Title (A Side/B Side)	Yr	VG	VG+	NM
PRO-A-2324 [DJ]	Act of War (Edit)/(Instrumental)	1985	—	3.00	6.00
20347	Act of War (8:32)/Act of War (5:04)	1985	—	3.00	6.00

45s

GEFFEN

Number	Title (A Side/B Side)	Yr	VG	VG+	NM
28956	Act of War, Part 1/Act of War, Part 2	1985	—	2.00	4.00
28956 [PS]	Act of War, Part 1/Act of War, Part 2	1985	—	2.00	4.00

JOHN, LITTLE WILLIE

45s

ATLANTIC

Number	Title (A Side/B Side)	Yr	VG	VG+	NM
89189	Fever/Ruby Baby	1987	—	—	3.00
—B-side by the Drifters					
89189 [PS]	Fever/Ruby Baby	1987	—	—	3.00
—From the movie "Big Town"					

KING

Number	Title (A Side/B Side)	Yr	VG	VG+	NM
4818	All Around the World/Don't Leave Me Dear	1955	6.25	12.50	25.00
4841	Need Your Love So Bad/Home at Last	1955	6.25	12.50	25.00
4893	Are You Ever Coming Back/I'm Stickin' with You Baby	1956	6.25	12.50	25.00
4935	Fever/Letter from My Darling	1956	7.50	15.00	30.00
4960	Do Something for Me/My Nerves	1956	6.25	12.50	25.00
4989	I've Been Around/Suffering with the Blues	1956	6.25	12.50	25.00
5003	Will the Sun Shine Tomorrow/A Little Bit of Loving	1956	6.25	12.50	25.00
5023	Love, Life and Money/You Got to Get Up Early in the Morning	1957	6.25	12.50	25.00
5045	I've Got to Go Cry/Look What You've Done to Me	1957	6.25	12.50	25.00
5066	Young Girl/If I Thought You Needed Me	1957	6.25	12.50	25.00
5083	Uh Uh Baby/Summer Date	1957	6.25	12.50	25.00
5091	Person to Person/Until You Do	1957	6.25	12.50	25.00
5108	Talk to Me, Talk to Me/Spasms	1958	6.25	12.50	25.00
5142	Let's Rock While the Rockin's Good/You're a Sweetheart	1958	6.25	12.50	25.00
5147	Tell It Like It Is/Don't Be Ashamed to Call My Name	1958	6.25	12.50	25.00
5154	All My Love Belongs to You/Why Don't You Haul Off and Love Me	1958	6.25	12.50	25.00
5170	No Regrets/I'll Carry Your Love Wherever I Go	1959	5.00	10.00	20.00
5179	Made for Me/Do More in Life	1959	5.00	10.00	20.00
5219	Leave My Kitten Alone/Let Nobody Love You	1959	5.00	10.00	20.00
5274	Let Them Talk/Right There	1959	5.00	10.00	20.00
5318	Loving Care/My Love Is	1960	5.00	10.00	20.00
5342	I'm Shakin'/Cottage for Sale	1960	5.00	10.00	20.00
5356	Heartbreak (It's Hurtin' Me)/Do You Love Me	1960	5.00	10.00	20.00
5394	Sleep/There's a Difference	1960	5.00	10.00	20.00
5428	Walk Slow/You Hurt Me	1960	3.75	7.50	15.00
5452	Leave My Kitten Alone/I'll Never Go Back on My Word	1961	3.75	7.50	15.00
5458	I'm Sorry/The Very Thought of You	1961	3.75	7.50	15.00
5503	(I've Got) Spring Fever/Flamingo	1961	3.75	7.50	15.00
5516	Take My Love (I Want to Give It All to You)/Now You Know	1961	3.75	7.50	15.00
5539	Need Your Love So Bad/Drive Me Home	1961	3.75	7.50	15.00
5577	There Is Someone in This World for Me/Autumn Leaves	1961	3.75	7.50	15.00
5591	Fever/Bo-Da-Ley Dino-Ley	1962	3.75	7.50	15.00
5602	The Masquerade Is Over/Katanga	1962	3.75	7.50	15.00
5628	Until Again My Love/Mister Glenn	1962	3.75	7.50	15.00
5641	Every Beat of My Heart/I Wish I Could Cry	1962	3.75	7.50	15.00
5667	She Thinks I Still Care/Come Back to Me	1962	3.75	7.50	15.00
5681	Doll Face/Big Blue Diamonds	1962	3.75	7.50	15.00
5694	Without a Friend/Half a Love	1962	3.75	7.50	15.00
5717	Don't Play with Love/Heaven All Around Me	1963	3.00	6.00	12.00
5744	My Baby's in Love with Another Guy/Come On Sugar	1963	3.00	6.00	12.00
5799	Let Them Talk/Talk to Me	1963	3.00	6.00	12.00
5818	So Lovely/Inside Information	1963	3.00	6.00	12.00
5823	Person to Person/I'm Shakin'	1963	3.00	6.00	12.00
5850	Bill Bailey/My Love Will Never Change	1964	3.00	6.00	12.00
5870	Rock Love/It Only Hurts for a Little While	1964	3.00	6.00	12.00
5886	All Around the World/All My Love Belongs to You	1964	3.00	6.00	12.00
5949	Do Something for Me/Don't You Know I'm in Love	1964	3.00	6.00	12.00
6003	Talk to Me/Take My Love	1965	2.50	5.00	10.00
6170	Fever/Let Them Talk	1968	2.50	5.00	10.00
6302	All Around the World/Need Your Love So Bad	1970	2.00	4.00	8.00

7-Inch Extended Plays

KING

Number	Title (A Side/B Side)	Yr	VG	VG+	NM
423	(contents unknown)	1958	62.50	125.00	250.00
423 [PS]	Talk to Me	1958	62.50	125.00	250.00

Albums

BLUESWAY

Number	Title (A Side/B Side)	Yr	VG	VG+	NM
BLS-6069	Free at Last	1973	6.25	12.50	25.00

KING

Number	Title (A Side/B Side)	Yr	VG	VG+	NM
564 [M]	Fever	1957	150.00	300.00	600.00
—White cover with "Fever" in large colorful letters					
395-564 [M]	Fever	1956	250.00	500.00	1000.
—"Nurse with thermometer" cover					
596 [M]	Talk to Me	1958	75.00	150.00	300.00
603 [M]	Mister Little Willie John	1958	62.50	125.00	250.00
691 [M]	Little Willie John In Action	1960	62.50	125.00	250.00
739 [M]	Sure Things	1961	37.50	75.00	150.00
767 [M]	The Sweet, the Hot, the Teenage Beat	1961	37.50	75.00	150.00
802 [M]	Come On and Join Little Willie John	1962	30.00	60.00	120.00
895 [M]	These Are My Favorite Songs	1964	25.00	50.00	100.00
949 [M]	Little Willie Sings All Originals	1966	25.00	50.00	100.00
KS-949 [S]	Little Willie Sings All Originals	1966	37.50	75.00	150.00
KS-1081	Free at Last	1970	10.00	20.00	40.00

JOHN, MABLE

45s

MOTOWN

Number	Title (A Side/B Side)	Yr	VG	VG+	NM
54031	Who Wouldn't Love a Man Like That/You Made a Fool Out of Me	1960	125.00	250.00	500.00
—Mispress with wrong label; may have been promo only					

STAX

Number	Title (A Side/B Side)	Yr	VG	VG+	NM
0016	Running Out/Shouldn't I Love Him	1968	5.00	10.00	20.00
192	Your Good Thing (Is About to End)/It's Catching	1966	5.00	10.00	20.00
205	If You Give Up What You Got/You're Taking Up Another Man's Place	1967	5.00	10.00	20.00
215	Same Time, Same Place/Bigger and Better	1967	5.00	10.00	20.00
225	I'm a Big Girl Now/Wait You Dog	1967	5.00	10.00	20.00
234	Don't Hit Me No More/Left Over Love	1967	5.00	10.00	20.00
249	Don't Get Caught/Able Mable	1968	5.00	10.00	20.00

TAMLA

Number	Title (A Side/B Side)	Yr	VG	VG+	NM
54031	Who Wouldn't Love a Man Like That/You Made a Fool Out of Me	1960	37.50	75.00	150.00
54040	No Love/Looking for a Love	1961	30.00	60.00	120.00
—Version with long intro					
54040	No Love/Looking for a Love	1961	25.00	50.00	100.00
—Version with no intro					
54050	Take Me/Action Speaks Louder Than Words	1962	20.00	40.00	80.00
54081	Who Wouldn't Love a Man Like That/Say You'll Never Let Me Go	1963	30.00	60.00	120.00

JOHN, ROBERT

45s

ARIOLA AMERICA

Number	Title (A Side/B Side)	Yr	VG	VG+	NM
7693	Poor Side of Town/Give a Little More	1978	—	2.00	4.00

ATLANTIC

Number	Title (A Side/B Side)	Yr	VG	VG+	NM
2846	The Lion Sleeps Tonight (Wimoweh) (Mbube)/Janet	1971	—	3.00	6.00
2884	Hushabye/To Touch, To Feel	1972	—	2.50	5.00
2906	The Way You Do the Things You Do/To Touch, To Feel	1972	—	2.50	5.00
2930	You and Me/You Don't Need a Gypsy	1973	—	2.50	5.00

A&M

Number	Title (A Side/B Side)	Yr	VG	VG+	NM
1210	When the Party Is Over/Raindrops, Love and Sunshine	1970	—	2.50	5.00
1250	You Can't Hold On/You're What's Been Missing from My Life	1971	—	2.50	5.00
1341	I'm Gonna Be Strong/I Don't Want to Make You Love Me	1972	—	2.50	5.00

BIG TOP

Number	Title (A Side/B Side)	Yr	VG	VG+	NM
3004	White Bucks and Saddle Shoes/Stranded	1958	12.50	25.00	50.00
—As "Bobby Pedrick, Jr."					
3008	Betty Blue Eyes/Pajama Party	1958	10.00	20.00	40.00
—As "Bobby Pedrick, Jr."					
3024	My Private Joy/Summer Nights	1959	10.00	20.00	40.00
—As "Bobby Pedrick, Jr."					

COLUMBIA

Number	Title (A Side/B Side)	Yr	VG	VG+	NM
44435	If You Don't Want My Love/Don't Go	1968	2.00	4.00	8.00
44639	Don't Leave Me/Children	1968	2.00	4.00	8.00
44697	Can't Stop Loving You/Thirteen Times	1968	3.00	6.00	12.00

Number	Title (A Side/B Side)	Yr	VG	VG+	NM
44706	Ooh Baby Baby/Children	1968	2.00	4.00	8.00
44950	Who Could Ever Believe It/Children in the Making	1969	2.00	4.00	8.00
DUEL					
504	That Girl Is You/I'm Scared	1962	5.00	10.00	20.00
—As "Bobby Pedrick, Jr."					
516	Dining and Dancing/Two Ton Tessie	1962	5.00	10.00	20.00
—As "Bobby Pedrick, Jr."					
525	If I Had My Life to Live Over/If Mary Only Knew	1963	5.00	10.00	20.00
—As "Bobby Pedrick, Jr."					
EMI AMERICA					
8013	Only Time/That's What Keeps Us Together	1979	—	2.00	4.00
8015	Sad Eyes/Am I Ever Gonna Hold You	1979	—	2.00	4.00
8023	Stay a Little Longer/Only Time	1979	—	2.00	4.00
8030	Lonely Eyes/Dance the Night Away	1979	—	2.00	4.00
8049	Hey There Lonely Girl/You Could Have Told Me	1980	—	2.00	4.00
8061	Sherry/On My Own	1980	—	2.00	4.00
MGM					
13384	Don't Try to Change My Ways/(I Have to) Teach Myself How to Cry	1965	3.75	7.50	15.00
—As "Bobby Pedrick"					
MOSAIC					
04445	Greased Lightning/(Instrumental)	1984	—	—	3.00
MOTOWN					
1664	Bread and Butter/If You Don't Want My Love	1983	—	—	3.00
SHELL					
722	School Crush/Come Out, Come Out	1960	5.00	10.00	20.00
—As "Bobby Pedrick"					
VERVE					
10402	Maybe/Karine	1966	12.50	25.00	50.00
—As "Bobby Pedrick"					
Albums					
COLUMBIA					
CS 9687	If You Don't Want My Love	1968	5.00	10.00	20.00
EMI AMERICA					
SW-17007	Robert John	1979	2.50	5.00	10.00
SW-17027	Back on the Street	1980	2.50	5.00	10.00
HARMONY					
KH 31353	On the Way Up	1972	3.00	6.00	12.00

JOHN'S CHILDREN

Number	Title (A Side/B Side)	Yr	VG	VG+	NM
45s					
WHITE WHALE					
239	Strange Affair/Smashed, Blocked	1966	5.00	10.00	20.00
Albums					
WHITE WHALE					
WWS 7128	Orgasm	1970	50.00	100.00	200.00

JOHN AND ERNEST

Also see DICKIE GOODMAN.

Number	Title (A Side/B Side)	Yr	VG	VG+	NM
45s					
RAINY WEDNESDAY					
201	Super Fly Meets Shaft/Problems	1973	—	2.50	5.00
201	Super Fly Meets Shaft/Part Two	1973	—	2.50	5.00
203	Soul President Number One/Crossover	1973	—	2.50	5.00

JOHNNIE AND JOE

Number	Title (A Side/B Side)	Yr	VG	VG+	NM
45s					
ABC-PARAMOUNT					
10079	I Adore You/I Want You Here Beside Me	1960	3.75	7.50	15.00
10117	Your Love/Why Do You Hurt Me So	1960	3.75	7.50	15.00
AMBIENT SOUND					
03410	Kingdom of Love/Tossin' Turnin' (Yearnin' Burnin' For Your Love)	1982	—	2.50	5.00
CHESS					
1641	I'll Be Spinning/Feel Alright	1956	5.00	10.00	20.00
1654	Over the Mountain; Across the Sea/My Baby's Gone, On, On	1957	6.25	12.50	25.00
—Originals with blue and silver "chess pieces" label					
1654	Over the Mountain; Across the Sea/My Baby's Gone, On, On	1958	3.00	6.00	12.00
—Reissues on blue labels					
1654	Over the Mountain; Across the Sea/My Baby's Gone, On, On	1963	2.50	5.00	10.00
—Reissues on other labels (multicolor, black)					
1677	I Was So Lonely/If You Tell Me You're Mine	1957	5.00	10.00	20.00
1693	Why Oh Why/Why Did She Go	1958	5.00	10.00	20.00
1706	My Baby's Gone/Darling	1958	5.00	10.00	20.00
1769	Across the Sea/You Said It, And Don't Forget It	1960	3.75	7.50	15.00
GONE					
5024	Who Do You Love/Trust in Me	1958	7.50	15.00	30.00
J&S					
1008	Over the Mountain (Part 2)/Won't You Come Back to Me	1959	6.25	12.50	25.00
1603	I Was So Lonely/If You Tell Me You're Mine	1957	6.25	12.50	25.00
1605/6	Who Do You Love/Trust in Me	1958	6.25	12.50	25.00
1630/1	Warm, Soft and Lovely/False Love Has Got to Go	1958	6.25	12.50	25.00
1654	Over the Mountain; Across the Sea/My Baby's Gone, On, On	1957	37.50	75.00	150.00
—With horizontal lines on label					
1654	Over the Mountain; Across the Sea/My Baby's Gone, On, On	1962	5.00	10.00	20.00
—Without horizontal lines on label					
1659	It Was There/There Goes My Heart	1957	6.25	12.50	25.00
1701	Where Did She Go/Red Sails in the Sunset	1959	6.25	12.50	25.00
4420	The Devil Said No, Gone With You Bad Self/You Can Always Count on Me	196?	3.75	7.50	15.00
8719	Tell Me/Sincere Love	196?	3.75	7.50	15.00
42832	You're the Loveliest Song/Let Your Mind Do the Walking	196?	3.75	7.50	15.00
87187	False Love Has Got to Go/Jamaica — Our Thing	196?	3.75	7.50	15.00
TUFF					
379	Here We Go Baby/That's the Way You Go	1964	3.00	6.00	12.00
Albums					
AMBIENT SOUND					
FZ 38345	Kingdom of Love	1982	3.00	6.00	12.00

JOHNNY AND JON

Number	Title (A Side/B Side)	Yr	VG	VG+	NM
45s					
JEWEL					
776	Christmas in Viet Nam/Why Did You Leave Me Crawl	1966	7.50	15.00	30.00

JOHNNY AND THE BLUE BEATS

Number	Title (A Side/B Side)	Yr	VG	VG+	NM
Albums					
WINSOR					
1001	Smile	196?	10.00	20.00	40.00

JOHNNY AND THE DREAMS

Number	Title (A Side/B Side)	Yr	VG	VG+	NM
45s					
RICHIE					
457	You're Too Young/Are You for Me	1961	125.00	250.00	500.00
—Red vinyl					
457	You're Too Young/Are You for Me	1961	62.50	125.00	250.00
—Black vinyl					

JOHNNY AND THE HURRICANES

Number	Title (A Side/B Side)	Yr	VG	VG+	NM
45s					
ATILA					
211	Saga of the Beatles/Rene	1967	2.50	5.00	10.00
214	Judy's Moody/I Love You	1967	2.50	5.00	10.00
215	Because I Love You/Wisdom's 5th Take	1967	2.50	5.00	10.00
216	Red River Rock '67/The Psychedlic Woman	1967	2.50	5.00	10.00
BIG TOP					
3036	Down Yonder/Sheba	1960	5.00	10.00	20.00
3036 [PS]	Down Yonder/Sheba	1960	10.00	20.00	40.00
3051	Revival/Rocking Goose	1960	5.00	10.00	20.00
3051 [PS]	Revival/Rocking Goose	1960	10.00	20.00	40.00
3056	You Are My Sunshine/Molly-O	1960	5.00	10.00	20.00
3056 [PS]	You Are My Sunshine/Molly-O	1960	10.00	20.00	40.00
3063	Ja-Da/Mr. Lonely	1961	5.00	10.00	20.00
3063 [PS]	Ja-Da/Mr. Lonely	1961	10.00	20.00	40.00
3076	Old Smokey/High Voltage	1961	5.00	10.00	20.00
3076 [PS]	Old Smokey/High Voltage	1961	10.00	20.00	40.00
3090	Traffic Jam/Farewell, Farewell	1961	5.00	10.00	20.00
3103	Misirlou/Salvation	1962	5.00	10.00	20.00
3113	San Antonio Rose/Come On Train	1962	5.00	10.00	20.00
3125	Shiek of Araby/Minnesota Fats	1962	5.00	10.00	20.00
3132	Whatever Happened to Baby Jane/Greens and Beans	1963	5.00	10.00	20.00
3146	James Bond Theme/Hungry Eye	1963	5.00	10.00	20.00
3159	Rough road/Kaw-Liga	1963	5.00	10.00	20.00
JEFF					
211	Saga of the Beatles/Rene	1964	3.75	7.50	15.00
MALA					
470	It's a Mad, Mad, Mad, Mad World/Shadows	1963	2.50	5.00	10.00
483	That's All/Honey, Honey	1964	2.50	5.00	10.00
TWIRL					
1001	Crossfire/Lazy	1958	12.50	25.00	50.00
WARWICK					
502	Crossfire/Lazy	1959	6.25	12.50	25.00
509 ST [S]	Red River Rock/Buckeye	1959	12.50	25.00	50.00
509 [M]	Red River Rock/Buckeye	1959	6.25	12.50	25.00
513 ST [S]	Reveille Rock/Time Bomb	1959	12.50	25.00	50.00
513 [M]	Reveille Rock/Time Bomb	1959	6.25	12.50	25.00
520	Beatnik Fly/Sand Storm	1960	5.00	10.00	20.00
520 [PS]	Beatnik Fly/Sand Storm	1960	15.00	30.00	60.00
7-Inch Extended Plays					
WARWICK					
EX-700	Red River Rock/Storm Warning//Joy Ride/Bam Boo	1959	20.00	40.00	80.00
EX-700 [PS]	Johnny and the Hurricanes	1959	30.00	60.00	120.00
—Came with paper sleeve rather than cardboard sleeve					
Albums					
ATILA					
1030 [M]	Live at the Star-Club	1964	75.00	150.00	300.00
BIG TOP					
13-1302 [M]	The Big Sound of Johnny and the Hurricanes	1960	62.50	125.00	250.00
ST 13-1302 [S]	The Big Sound of Johnny and the Hurricanes	1960	75.00	150.00	300.00
WARWICK					
W-2007ST [S]	Johnny and the Hurricanes	1959	75.00	150.00	300.00
W-2007 [M]	Johnny and the Hurricanes	1959	37.50	75.00	150.00
W-2010ST [S]	Stormsville	1960	62.50	125.00	250.00
W-2010 [M]	Stormsville	1960	37.50	75.00	150.00

JOHNNY AND THE JAMMERS

"Johnny" is JOHNNY WINTER. His debut single.

Number	Title (A Side/B Side)	Yr	VG	VG+	NM
45s					
DART					
131	School Day Blues/You Know I Love You	1959	75.00	150.00	300.00

JOHNNY AND THE TOKENS

Also see THE TOKENS.

Number	Title (A Side/B Side)	Yr	VG	VG+	NM
45s					
WARWICK					
658	The Taste of a Tear/Never Till Now	1961	5.00	10.00	20.00

JOHNS, SAMMY

Number	Title (A Side/B Side)	Yr	VG	VG+	NM
45s					
ELEKTRA					
47189	Common Man/Easy to Be with You	1981	—	2.00	4.00
47248	Love Me Off the Road/This Time	1981	—	2.00	4.00
GRC					
1001	Shake a Hand/(B-side unknown)	1973	—	2.00	4.00

(Top left) A nice, rare EP comes from the Impalas. It features their only hit, "Sorry (I Ran All the Way Home)," plus three other tracks. (Top right) Most likely, this EP on Dot of Jan and Arnie was issued to capitalize on the early success of Jan and Dean. In near-mint condition, the sleeve and record combined can fetch in the $1,000 neighborhood. (Bottom left) If you have a copy of *Jefferson Airplane Takes Off!* that you purchased in 1966, check it carefully. Some very early pressings have 12 tracks instead of the standard 11 (the deleted track is the single B-side "Runnin' 'Round This World"). Second pressings have uncensored versions of two songs. Check the listing for this LP for more information. (Bottom right) Johnny and the Hurricanes are best known for their rockin' instrumental versions of "Red River Valley" (as "Red River Rock") and "Blue Tail Fly" (as "Beatnik Fly"). The group continued to record for some years after those hits on Warwick. This is one of the four Big Top singles that had picture sleeves.

Number	Title (A Side/B Side)	Yr	VG	VG+	NM
1007	America/(B-side unknown)	1973	—	2.00	4.00
2021	Early Morning Love/Holy Mother, Aging Father	1974	—	2.00	4.00
2046	Chevy Van/Hang My Head and Moan	1975	—	2.50	5.00
2062	Rag Doll/Friends of Mine	1975	—	2.00	4.00
MCA					
53398	Chevy Van/Love Me Off the Road	1988	—	—	3.00
REAL WORLD					
7307	Falling Over You/Six Feet Tall and Handsome	1980	—	2.00	4.00
WARNER BROS.					
8224	Peas in a Pod/Friends of Mine	1976	—	2.00	4.00
8270	America/Bless Our Soul	1976	—	2.00	4.00
8335	Hey Mr. Dreamer/Female Chauvinist Sow	1977	—	2.00	4.00
8441	Chevy Van/Music of the Band	1977	—	2.00	4.00
Albums					
GRC					
5003	Sammy Johns	1975	2.50	5.00	10.00

JOHNSON, BETTY

Number	Title (A Side/B Side)	Yr	VG	VG+	NM
45s					
ATLANTIC					
1169	The Little Blue Man/Winter in Miami	1958	3.75	7.50	15.00
1186	Dream/How Much	1958	3.00	6.00	12.00
2002	Hoopa Hoola/One More Time	1958	3.00	6.00	12.00
2009	You Can't Get to Heaven on Roller Skates/I Want a Good Home for My Cat	1958	3.00	6.00	12.00
2019	Does Your Heart Beat for Me?/You and Only You	1959	3.00	6.00	12.00
2039	The Lonely Willow Tree/Waltz Me Around	1959	3.00	6.00	12.00
2056	Fantastic/Don't You Care a Rowboat	1960	3.00	6.00	12.00
BALLY					
1000	I'll Wait/Please Tell Me Why	1956	3.00	6.00	12.00
1005	Honky Tonk Rock/Say It Ain't So, Joe	1956	3.75	7.50	15.00
1013	Clay Idol/Why Do You Cry?	1956	3.00	6.00	12.00
1020	I Dreamed/If It's Wrong to Love You	1956	3.00	6.00	12.00
1033	Little White Lies/1492	1957	3.00	6.00	12.00
1041	The Song You Heard When You Fell in Love/I'm Beginning to Wonder	1957	3.00	6.00	12.00
COED					
532	There's a Star Spangled Banner Waving Somewhere/Take a Little Look (In the Good Book)	1960	2.50	5.00	10.00
DOT					
16127	Slipping Around/One Has My Name, The Other Has My Heart	1960	2.50	5.00	10.00
NEW-DISC					
10013	I Want Eddie Fisher For Christmas/Show Me	1954	6.25	12.50	25.00
RCA VICTOR					
47-6034	Seven Pretty Dreams/Be a Lover	1955	3.00	6.00	12.00
47-6158	That's Happiness/Give Me Something I Can Dream About	1955	3.00	6.00	12.00
47-6268	I'm a Sinner/Beginner's Luck	1955	3.00	6.00	12.00
47-8143	Betty's Bossa Nova/Ginny's Got a Phone	1963	2.00	4.00	8.00
REPUBLIC					
2011	Depend on Me/I Don't Want to Go to Sleep Tonight	1961	2.50	5.00	10.00
2017	Let Me Be the One/Only When I Dream	1961	2.50	5.00	10.00
2021	My Kind of Guy/A Gal's Best Friend Is Her Makeup	1961	2.50	5.00	10.00
2025	How Do You Tell Your Heart/Why, Why	1961	2.50	5.00	10.00
2026	I Dreamed/Luna Caprese	1962	2.50	5.00	10.00
WORLD ARTISTS					
1014	Wednesday's Child/What's the Matter	1963	2.00	4.00	8.00
Albums					
ATLANTIC					
8017 [M]	Betty Johnson	1958	12.50	25.00	50.00
8027 [M]	The Song You Heard When You Fell in Love	1959	12.50	25.00	50.00
—Black label					
8027 [M]	The Song You Heard When You Fell in Love	1960	5.00	10.00	20.00
—White "fan" logo on right					
SD 8027 [S]	The Song You Heard When You Fell in Love	1959	20.00	40.00	80.00
—Green label					
SD 8027 [S]	The Song You Heard When You Fell in Love	1960	6.25	12.50	25.00
—White "fan" logo on right					

JOHNSON, BILL

Number	Title (A Side/B Side)	Yr	VG	VG+	NM
45s					
SUN					
340	Bobaloo/Bad Times Ahead	1960	5.00	10.00	20.00

JOHNSON, BLIND WILLIE

Number	Title (A Side/B Side)	Yr	VG	VG+	NM
Albums					
FOLKWAYS					
FG-3585 [M]	Blind Willie Johnson: His Story	1957	25.00	50.00	100.00
RBF					
10 [M]	Blind Willie Johnson 1927-1930	1965	17.50	35.00	70.00

JOHNSON, BUBBER

Number	Title (A Side/B Side)	Yr	VG	VG+	NM
45s					
KING					
4793	Drop Me a Line/Ding Dang Doo	1955	5.00	10.00	20.00
4822	Come Home/There'll Be No One	1955	5.00	10.00	20.00
4855	It's Christmas Time/Let's Make Everyday a Christmas Day	1955	5.00	10.00	20.00
4872	Wonderful Things Happen/Keep a Light in the Window	1956	5.00	10.00	20.00
4924	My One Desire/I Lost Track of Everything	1956	5.00	10.00	20.00
4939	My Lonely Heart/Have a Little Faith in Me	1956	5.00	10.00	20.00
4988	Confidential/Let's Take a Walk	1956	5.00	10.00	20.00
5014	Butterfly/Too Many Hearts	1957	5.00	10.00	20.00
5034	Little Girls Don't Cry/The Search	1957	5.00	10.00	20.00
5068	Crazy Afternoon/So Much Tonight	1957	5.00	10.00	20.00
5089	Muddy Water/The Whisperers	1957	5.00	10.00	20.00
5117	Dedicated to the One I Love/Prince of Players	1958	3.75	7.50	15.00
5132	Finger Tips/I'm Confessin'	1958	3.75	7.50	15.00
5143	I Surrender Dear/Everybody's With You When You're Winning	1958	3.75	7.50	15.00
5148	I Can't See Why/As Long As I Live	1958	3.75	7.50	15.00
5174	One Good Reason/Time Was	1959	3.75	7.50	15.00
5193	House of Love/Until Sunrise	1959	3.75	7.50	15.00
5232	I Do (Love You)/Come On	1959	3.75	7.50	15.00
5267	Tell Me Who/I Know My Way	1959	3.75	7.50	15.00
5298	Those Who Dream/Atlanta	1959	3.75	7.50	15.00
MERCURY					
8285	I've Got an Invitation/Forget It If You Can	1952	15.00	30.00	60.00
Albums					
KING					
569 [M]	Come Home	1957	50.00	100.00	200.00
624 [M]	Bubber Johnson Sings Sweet Love Songs	1959	37.50	75.00	150.00

JOHNSON, BUDDY

Number	Title (A Side/B Side)	Yr	VG	VG+	NM
45s					
ATLANTIC					
1013	Don't Take Your Love from Me/Off Shore	1953	6.25	12.50	25.00
DECCA					
28907	Talkin' About Another Man's Wife/Jeannette	1953	6.25	12.50	25.00
29058	A Handful of Stars/Two Cigarettes in the Dark	1954	6.25	12.50	25.00
MERCURY					
70173	Jit Jit/That's What I Feel About You	1953	5.00	10.00	20.00
70488	I Never Had It So Good/There's No One Like You	1954	3.75	7.50	15.00
70656	Send Out for a Bottle of Beer/Bitter Sweet	1955	3.75	7.50	15.00
70695	It's Obdacious/Save Your Love for Me	1955	3.75	7.50	15.00
71017	Why Don't Cha Stop It/Kool Kitty	1956	3.00	6.00	12.00
71159	I've Surrendered/Slide's Mambo	1957	3.00	6.00	12.00
71262	Minglin'/I Wonder Where Our Love Has Gone	1958	3.00	6.00	12.00
71799	The Last Laugh's on You (Ha, Ha, Baby)/Good Time Man	1961	2.50	5.00	10.00
WING					
90064	Doot Doot Dow/I Don't Want Nobody	1956	3.75	7.50	15.00
90074	Buddy's Boogie/I'll Dearly Love You	1956	3.75	7.50	15.00
90084	Goodbye Baby/I Still Love You	1956	3.75	7.50	15.00
Albums					
MCA					
1356	Fine Brown Frame	198?	2.50	5.00	10.00
MERCURY					
MG-20209 [M]	Rock 'n' Roll	195?	20.00	40.00	80.00
MG-20322 [M]	Walkin'	195?	20.00	40.00	80.00
MG-20330 [M]	Buddy Johnson Wails	195?	20.00	40.00	80.00
MG-20347 [M]	Swing Me	195?	20.00	40.00	80.00
SR-60072 [S]	Buddy Johnson Wails	195?	25.00	50.00	100.00
WING					
MGW-12005 [M]	Rock 'n' Roll	1956	37.50	75.00	150.00
MGW-12111 [M]	Rock 'n' Roll Stage Show	1963	10.00	20.00	40.00

JOHNSON, BUDDY & ELLA

Also see BUDDY JOHNSON.

Number	Title (A Side/B Side)	Yr	VG	VG+	NM
45s					
MERCURY					
70251	I'm Just Your Fool/A-12	1953	5.00	10.00	20.00
70321	One More Time/Mush Mouth	1954	5.00	10.00	20.00
70377	Ain't Cha Got Me/Let's Start All Over Again	1954	5.00	10.00	20.00
70421	Any Day Now/A Pretty Girl, a Cadillac and Money	1954	5.00	10.00	20.00
70459	We'll Do It/It Used to Hurt Me	1954	5.00	10.00	20.00
70523	Crazy 'Bout a Saxophone/Gotta Go Upside Your Head	1955	3.75	7.50	15.00
70775	Doot Doot Dow/I Don't Want Nobody	1956	3.00	6.00	12.00
70912	Bring It Home to Me/You Got It Made	1956	3.00	6.00	12.00
71723	I Don't Want Nobody (To Have My Love But You)/I'm Just Your Fool	1960	2.50	5.00	10.00
ROULETTE					
4134	Tune No. 1/Don't Fail Me Baby	1959	3.00	6.00	12.00
4188	Keep My Love for You/A Woman, a Lover, a Friend	1959	3.00	6.00	12.00
Albums					
MERCURY					
MG-20347 [M]	Swing Me	195?	20.00	40.00	80.00
ROULETTE					
R 25085 [M]	Go Ahead and Rock and Roll	1959	20.00	40.00	80.00
SR 25085 [S]	Go Ahead and Rock and Roll	1959	30.00	60.00	120.00

JOHNSON, CLIFF

Number	Title (A Side/B Side)	Yr	VG	VG+	NM
45s					
COLUMBIA					
40865	Go 'Way Hound Dog/Twenty Four Hours a Day	1957	20.00	40.00	80.00

JOHNSON, HOYT

Number	Title (A Side/B Side)	Yr	VG	VG+	NM
45s					
ERWIN					
555	Eeny Meany Minie Mo/(B-side unknown)	1957	50.00	100.00	200.00
RCA VICTOR					
47-7522	Sylvia/Bella Renee	1959	10.00	20.00	40.00
47-7607	Little Boy Blue/My Special Girl	1959	37.50	75.00	150.00
47-7731	Too Shy/Eca-La	1960	10.00	20.00	40.00
SATELLITE					
110	Cindy/I Just Can't Learn	1961	6.25	12.50	25.00

JOHNSON, JIMMY

Number	Title (A Side/B Side)	Yr	VG	VG+	NM
45s					
ALLIGATOR					
792	Serves Me Right to Suffer/Your Turn to Cry	1979	—	2.00	4.00
CLASS					
237	Cool, Cool School/Lone Ranger Gonna Get Married	1958	15.00	30.00	60.00
MID WEST					
1002	Mean Woman Blues/(B-side unknown)	195?	62.50	125.00	250.00

Number	Title (A Side/B Side)	Yr	VG	VG+	NM
RENDEZVOUS					
145	Cool, Cool School/Lone Ranger Gonna Get Married	1961	6.25	12.50	25.00
VIV					
3001	How About Me? Pretty Baby/Cat Daddy	1956	50.00	100.00	200.00

JOHNSON, JOHNNY, AND THE BANDWAGON
See THE BANDWAGON.

JOHNSON, LONNIE

45s

Number	Title (A Side/B Side)	Yr	VG	VG+	NM
BLUESVILLE					
806	Don't Ever Love/You Don't Move Me	196?	3.00	6.00	12.00
812	I'll Get Along Somehow/Memories of You	196?	3.00	6.00	12.00
FEDERAL					
12376	Friendless Blues/What a Real Woman	1960	3.75	7.50	15.00
KING					
4201	Tomorrow Night/What a Woman	1951	15.00	30.00	60.00
—78 released in 1948					
4459	Take Me I'm Yours/Why Should I Cry	1951	10.00	20.00	40.00
4473	It Was All in Vain/You Only Want Me When You're Lonely	1951	10.00	20.00	40.00
4492	Happy New Year, Darling/Christmas Blues	1951	12.50	25.00	50.00
—B-side by Gatemouth Moore					
4503	Seven Long Days/Darlin'	1951	10.00	20.00	40.00
4510	My Mother's Eyes/My Crazy Self	1951	10.00	20.00	40.00
4553	I'm Guilty/Can't Sleep Anymore	1952	10.00	20.00	40.00
4572	You Can't Buy Love/Just Another Day	1952	10.00	20.00	40.00
4758	Tomorrow Night/Pleasing You	1954	10.00	20.00	40.00
5293	Tomorrow Night/Pleasing You	1959	3.75	7.50	15.00
5907	Love Me Tonight/Brenda	1964	2.50	5.00	10.00
6303	Tomorrow Night/Blues Stay Away from Me	1970	—	3.00	6.00
PRESTIGE					
310	Mr. Jelly Roll Baker/I'll Get Along Somehow	1964	2.50	5.00	10.00
RAMA					
9	My Woman Is Gone/Don't Make Me Cry Baby	1953	15.00	30.00	60.00
—Black vinyl					
9	My Woman Is Gone/Don't Make Me Cry Baby	1953	37.50	75.00	150.00
—Red vinyl					
14	Stick With It Baby/Will You Remember	1953	15.00	30.00	60.00
19	It's Been So Long/Vaya Con Dios	1953	15.00	30.00	60.00
20	This Love of Mine/I Love a Dream	1953	15.00	30.00	60.00

Albums

Number	Title (A Side/B Side)	Yr	VG	VG+	NM
BLUESVILLE					
BVLP-1007 [M]	Blues by Lonnie	1960	50.00	100.00	200.00
—Blue label, silver print					
BVLP-1007 [M]	Blues by Lonnie	1964	15.00	30.00	60.00
—Blue label with trident logo at right					
BVLP-1011 [M]	Blues and Ballads	1960	50.00	100.00	200.00
—Blue label, silver print					
BVLP-1011 [M]	Blues and Ballads	1964	15.00	30.00	60.00
—Blue label with trident logo at right					
BVLP-1024 [M]	Losing Game	1961	50.00	100.00	200.00
—Blue label, silver print					
BVLP-1024 [M]	Losing Game	1964	15.00	30.00	60.00
—Blue label with trident logo at right					
BVLP-1062 [M]	Another Night to Cry	1963	50.00	100.00	200.00
—Blue label, silver print					
BVLP-1062 [M]	Another Night to Cry	1964	15.00	30.00	60.00
—Blue label with trident logo at right					
COLUMBIA					
C 46221	Steppin' On the Blues	1990	5.00	10.00	20.00
FANTASY					
OBC-502	Blues by Lonnie	198?	3.00	6.00	12.00
OBC-531	Blues and Ballads	1990	3.00	6.00	12.00
KING					
395-520 [M]	Lonesome Road	1958	750.00	1375.	2000.
958 [M]	Lonnie Johnson 24 Twelve-Bar Blues	1966	15.00	30.00	60.00
KS-958 [R]	Lonnie Johnson 24 Twelve-Bar Blues	1966	15.00	30.00	60.00
KS-1083	Tomorrow Night	1970	6.25	12.50	25.00
PRESTIGE					
PRST-7724	The Blues of Lonnie Johnson	1970	5.00	10.00	20.00

JOHNSON, LONNIE, AND VICTORIA SPIVEY

Albums

Number	Title (A Side/B Side)	Yr	VG	VG+	NM
BLUESVILLE					
BVLP-1044 [M]	Idle Hours	1962	37.50	75.00	150.00
—Blue label, silver print					
BVLP-1044 [M]	Idle Hours	1964	12.50	25.00	50.00
—Blue label with trident logo at right					
BVLP-1054 [M]	Woman Blues	1962	37.50	75.00	150.00
—Blue label, silver print					
BVLP-1054 [M]	Woman Blues	1964	12.50	25.00	50.00
—Blue label with trident logo at right					
FANTASY					
OBC-518	Idle Hours	198?	3.00	6.00	12.00

JOHNSON, MARV

45s

Number	Title (A Side/B Side)	Yr	VG	VG+	NM
GORDY					
7042	Why Do You Want to Let Me Go/I'm Not a Plaything	1965	3.75	7.50	15.00
7051	Just the Way You Are/Miss You Baby	1966	3.75	7.50	15.00
7077	I'll Pick a Rose for My Rose/You Got the Love I Love	1968	3.75	7.50	15.00
KUDO					
663	My Baby-O/Once Upon a Time	1958	150.00	300.00	600.00
TAMLA					
101	Come to Me/Whisper	1959	75.00	150.00	300.00
—No address on label					
101	Come to Me/Whisper	1959	62.50	125.00	250.00
—With Gladstone St., Detroit, address on label					
UNITED ARTISTS					
0030	You've Got What It Takes/I Love the Way You Love	1973	—	2.50	5.00
—"Silver Spotlight Series" reissue					
0031	Move Two Mountains/Come to Me	1973	—	2.50	5.00
—"Silver Spotlight Series" reissue					
160	Come to Me/Whisper	1959	6.25	12.50	25.00
175	River of Tears/I'm Coming Home	1959	5.00	10.00	20.00
185	You Got What It Takes/Don't Leave Me	1959	5.00	10.00	20.00
208	I Love the Way You Love/Let Me Love You	1960	5.00	10.00	20.00
226	Ain't Gonna Be That Way/All the Love I've Got	1960	5.00	10.00	20.00
241	(You've Got to) Move Two Mountains/I Need You	1960	3.75	7.50	15.00
273	Happy Days/Baby, Baby	1960	3.75	7.50	15.00
294	Merry-Go-Round/Tell Me That You Love Me	1961	3.75	7.50	15.00
322	How Can We Tell Him/I've Got a Notion	1961	5.00	10.00	20.00
359	Show Me/Oh Mary	1961	5.00	10.00	20.00
386	Easier Said Than Done/Johnny One Stop	1961	5.00	10.00	20.00
423	Magic Mirror/With All That's In Me	1962	5.00	10.00	20.00
454	He Gave Me You/That's How Bad	1962	5.00	10.00	20.00
483	Let Yourself Go/That's Where I Lost My Baby	1962	5.00	10.00	20.00
556	Keep Tellin' Yourself/Everyone Who's Been in Love with You	1963	5.00	10.00	20.00
590	He's Got the Whole World In His Hands/Another Tear Falls	1963	5.00	10.00	20.00
617	Come On and Stop/Not Available	1963	5.00	10.00	20.00
643	Congratulations, You've Hurt Me Again/Crying on My Pillow	1963	5.00	10.00	20.00
691	Unbreakable Love/A Man Who Don't Believe in Love	1964	6.25	12.50	25.00

7-Inch Extended Plays

Number	Title (A Side/B Side)	Yr	VG	VG+	NM
UNITED ARTISTS					
10,007	I Love the Way You Love/Let Me Love You//You Got What It Takes/Don't Leave Me	1960	25.00	50.00	100.00
10,007 [PS]	Marv Johnson	1960	25.00	50.00	100.00
10,009	(contents unknown)	1960	25.00	50.00	100.00
10,009 [PS]	Marv Johnson	1960	25.00	50.00	100.00

Albums

Number	Title (A Side/B Side)	Yr	VG	VG+	NM
UNITED ARTISTS					
UAL 3081 [M]	Marvelous Marv Johnson	1960	37.50	75.00	150.00
UAL 3118 [M]	More Marv Johnson	1961	37.50	75.00	150.00
UAL 3187 [M]	I Believe	1962	37.50	75.00	150.00
UAS 6081 [S]	Marvelous Marv Johnson	1960	50.00	100.00	200.00
UAS 6118 [S]	More Marv Johnson	1961	50.00	100.00	200.00
UAS 6187 [S]	I Believe	1962	50.00	100.00	200.00

JOHNSON, MIRRIAM
See JESSI COLTER.

JOHNSON, ROBERT

Albums

Number	Title (A Side/B Side)	Yr	VG	VG+	NM
COLUMBIA					
CL 1654 [M]	King of the Delta Blues Singers	1961	125.00	250.00	500.00
—Red and black label with six "eye" logos					
CL 1654 [M]	King of the Delta Blues Singers	1963	12.50	25.00	50.00
—"Guaranteed High Fidelity" label					
CL 1654 [M]	King of the Delta Blues Singers	1965	6.25	12.50	25.00
—"360 Sound Mono" label					
CL 1654 [M]	King of the Delta Blues Singers	1970	3.00	6.00	12.00
—Orange label with "Columbia" circling the edge					
CL 1654 [M]	King of the Delta Blues Singers	1998	2.50	5.00	10.00
—Red label, "Columbia" in white at top, "Sony Music" under side numbers					
C 30034 [M]	King of the Delta Blues Singers, Volume 2	1970	5.00	10.00	20.00
PC 30034 [M]	King of the Delta Blues Singers, Volume 2	1979	2.50	5.00	10.00
C3 46222 [(3)]	Robert Johnson — The Complete Recordings	1990	12.50	25.00	50.00

JOHNSON, TERRY

45s

Number	Title (A Side/B Side)	Yr	VG	VG+	NM
GORDY					
7091	My Springtime/Suzie	1969	30.00	60.00	120.00
7095	Whatcha Gonna Do/Suzie	1970	6.25	12.50	25.00

JOHNSON BROTHERS, THE

45s

Number	Title (A Side/B Side)	Yr	VG	VG+	NM
IMPERIAL					
5550	Love Ain't Got a Thing/Find Another Heart	1958	5.00	10.00	20.00
VALOR					
2006	Zombie Lou/Castin' My Spell	1958	25.00	50.00	100.00

JOHNSTON, BRUCE
Also see THE BEACH BOYS; BRUCE AND TERRY; THE GAMBLERS; THE KUSTOM KINGS; PAPA DOO RUN RUN; THE REVERES (3); THE VETTES.

45s

Number	Title (A Side/B Side)	Yr	VG	VG+	NM
COLUMBIA					
10568	Pipeline/Disney Girls	1977	2.50	5.00	10.00
—Promos (with "Pipeline" on both sides) worth 50% less					
DEL-FI					
4202	The Original Surfer Stomp/Pajama Party	1963	15.00	30.00	60.00
—Originals credit "The Surf Stompers"					
4202	The Original Surfer Stomp/Pajama Party	1963	7.50	15.00	30.00
DONNA					
1354	Do the Surfer Stomp (Part 1)/Do the Surfer Stomp (Part 2)	1962	12.50	25.00	50.00
—Originals credit "The Surf Stompers"					
1354	Do the Surfer Stomp (Part 1)/Do the Surfer Stomp (Part 2)	1962	7.50	15.00	30.00
1354 [PS]	Do the Surfer Stomp (Part 1)/Do the Surfer Stomp (Part 2)	1962	25.00	50.00	100.00
1364	Soupy Shuffle Stomp (SSS)/Moon Shot	1962	7.50	15.00	30.00
1374	The Original Surfer Stomp (Part 1)/The Original Surfer Stomp (Part 2)	1962	7.50	15.00	30.00
RONDA					
1003	Do the Surfer Stomp (Part 1)/Do the Surfer Stomp (Part 2)	1962	10.00	20.00	40.00

Albums

COLUMBIA

Number	Title (A Side/B Side)	Yr	VG	VG+	NM
CL 2057 [M]	Surfin' 'Round the World	1963	37.50	75.00	150.00
CS 8857 [S]	Surfin' 'Round the World	1963	75.00	150.00	300.00
PC 34459	Going Public	1976	3.75	7.50	15.00

DEL-FI

Number	Title (A Side/B Side)	Yr	VG	VG+	NM
DFLP-1228 [M]	Surfers' Pajama Party	1963	25.00	50.00	100.00
DFST-1228 [S]	Surfers' Pajama Party	1963	50.00	100.00	200.00

JOHNSTON, COLONEL JUBILATION B., AND THE MYSTIC KNIGHTS BAND AND STREET SINGERS

Albums

COLUMBIA

Number	Title (A Side/B Side)	Yr	VG	VG+	NM
CL 2532 [M]	Moldy Goldies	1966	6.25	12.50	25.00
CS 9332 [S]	Moldy Goldies	1966	7.50	15.00	30.00

JOINER, ARKANSAS, JUNIOR HIGH SCHOOL BAND

45s

LIBERTY

Number	Title (A Side/B Side)	Yr	VG	VG+	NM
55244	National City/Big Ben	1959	2.50	5.00	10.00
55276	Arkansas Traveler/Hot Time in the Old Town	1960	2.50	5.00	10.00
55341	Highland Rock/Hop-Scotch	1960	2.50	5.00	10.00

—This one by the "Joiner, Arkansas, State College Band"

JOLLY, PETE

45s

AVA

Number	Title (A Side/B Side)	Yr	VG	VG+	NM
116	Falling in Love with Love/Little Bird	1963	2.00	4.00	8.00
149	Sweet September/Kiss Me Baby	1963	2.00	4.00	8.00
167	A Hard Day's Night/Three, Four, Five	1964	2.00	4.00	8.00
169	Moment of Truth/Sweet September	1964	2.00	4.00	8.00

A&M

Number	Title (A Side/B Side)	Yr	VG	VG+	NM
934	Dancing in the Streets/A Love So Fine	1968	—	3.00	6.00
963	Like a Lover/Serenta	1968	—	3.00	6.00
1032	Give a Damn/A Love So Fine	1969	—	3.00	6.00
1089	Little Green Apples/What the World Needs Now Is Love	1969	—	3.00	6.00

MAINSTREAM

Number	Title (A Side/B Side)	Yr	VG	VG+	NM
699	Sweet September/Little Bird	1969	—	3.00	6.00

Albums

AVA

Number	Title (A Side/B Side)	Yr	VG	VG+	NM
A-22 [M]	Little Bird	1963	5.00	10.00	20.00
AS-22 [S]	Little Bird	1963	6.25	12.50	25.00
A-39 [M]	Sweet September	1963	5.00	10.00	20.00
AS-39 [S]	Sweet September	1963	6.25	12.50	25.00
A-51 [M]	Hello Jolly	1964	5.00	10.00	20.00
AS-51 [S]	Hello Jolly	1964	6.25	12.50	25.00

A&M

Number	Title (A Side/B Side)	Yr	VG	VG+	NM
SP-3033	Seasons	1969	3.00	6.00	12.00
SP-4145	Herb Alpert Presents Pete Jolly	1968	3.00	6.00	12.00
SP-4184	Give a Damn	1970	3.00	6.00	12.00

CHARLIE PARKER

Number	Title (A Side/B Side)	Yr	VG	VG+	NM
PLP-825S [S]	Pete Jolly Gasses Everybody	1962	6.25	12.50	25.00
PLP-825 [M]	Pete Jolly Gasses Everybody	1962	5.00	10.00	20.00

COLUMBIA

Number	Title (A Side/B Side)	Yr	VG	VG+	NM
CL 2397 [M]	Too Much, Baby	1965	5.00	10.00	20.00
CS 9197 [S]	Too Much, Baby	1965	6.25	12.50	25.00

MAINSTREAM

Number	Title (A Side/B Side)	Yr	VG	VG+	NM
S-6114	The Best of Pete Jolly	196?	3.75	7.50	15.00

METROJAZZ

Number	Title (A Side/B Side)	Yr	VG	VG+	NM
E-1014 [M]	Impossible	1958	8.75	17.50	35.00
SE-1014 [S]	Impossible	1958	8.75	17.50	35.00

MGM

Number	Title (A Side/B Side)	Yr	VG	VG+	NM
E-4127 [M]	5 O'Clock Shadows	1963	5.00	10.00	20.00
SE-4127 [S]	5 O'Clock Shadows	1963	6.25	12.50	25.00

RCA VICTOR

Number	Title (A Side/B Side)	Yr	VG	VG+	NM
LPM-1105 [M]	Jolly Jumps In	1955	12.50	25.00	50.00
LPM-1125 [M]	Duo, Trio, Quartet	1955	12.50	25.00	50.00
LPM-1367 [M]	When Lights Are Low	1957	12.50	25.00	50.00

STEREO FIDELITY

Number	Title (A Side/B Side)	Yr	VG	VG+	NM
SFS-11000 [S]	Continental Jazz	1960	6.25	12.50	25.00

TRIP

Number	Title (A Side/B Side)	Yr	VG	VG+	NM
TLP-5817	A Touch of Jazz	197?	2.50	5.00	10.00

JOLSON, AL

Almost his entire recording career predates the 45 and the LP. It's likely that Decca 78s from the 23000 and 24000 series were reissued onto 45s, but we don't have confirmation as to which ones.

45s

DECCA

Number	Title (A Side/B Side)	Yr	VG	VG+	NM
9-27024	The Old Piano Roll Blues/Way Down Yonder in New Orleans	1950	5.00	10.00	20.00
9-27043	Are You Lonesome Tonight/No Sad Songs for Me	1950	5.00	10.00	20.00
9-27181	De Camptown Races/Oh Susannah	1950	5.00	10.00	20.00
9-27362	Beautiful Dreamer/Old Folks at Home	1951	3.75	7.50	15.00
9-27364	I Dream of Jeannie with the Light Brown Hair/Old Black Joe	1951	3.75	7.50	15.00
9-27365	Massa's in De Cold, Cold Ground/My Old Kentucky Home	1951	3.75	7.50	15.00
—The above four comprise a box set					
9-27410	In Our House/I'm Crying Just for You	1951	3.75	7.50	15.00

MCA

Number	Title (A Side/B Side)	Yr	VG	VG+	NM
60037	Swanee/April Showers	1973	—	2.50	5.00
—Black label with rainbow					
60038	Avalon/Anniversary Song	1973	—	2.50	5.00
—Black label with rainbow					
60048	You Made Me Love You/Ma Blushin' Rosie	1973	—	2.50	5.00
—Black label with rainbow					
60096	My Mammy/Sonny Boy	197?	—	2.50	5.00
—Black label with rainbow					
60136	California Here I Come/Rock-a-Bye Your Baby with a Dixie Melody	197?	—	2.50	5.00
—Black label with rainbow					

Albums

DECCA

Number	Title (A Side/B Side)	Yr	VG	VG+	NM
DXA 169 [(2) M]	The Best of Jolson	196?	6.25	12.50	25.00
DLP 5006 [10]	Jolson Sings Again	1949	7.50	15.00	30.00
DLP 5026 [10]	Al Jolson In Songs He Made Famous	1949	7.50	15.00	30.00
DLP 5029 [10]	Souvenir Album, Vol. II	1949	7.50	15.00	30.00
DLP 5030 [10]	Al Jolson, Vol. III	1949	7.50	15.00	30.00
DLP 5031 [10]	Souvenir Album, Vol. IV	1949	7.50	15.00	30.00
DL 5308 [10]	Stephen Foster Songs	1950	25.00	50.00	100.00
DL 5314 [10]	Souvenir Album, Vol. V	1951	7.50	15.00	30.00
DL 5315 [10]	Souvenir Album, Vol. VI	1951	7.50	15.00	30.00
DXSA 7169 [(2) R]	The Best of Jolson	196?	3.75	7.50	15.00
DL 9034 [M]	You Made Me Love You	1957	6.25	12.50	25.00
—Black label, silver print					
DL 9034 [M]	You Made Me Love You	196?	3.75	7.50	15.00
—Black label with color bars					
DL 9035 [M]	Rock-a-Bye Your Baby	1957	6.25	12.50	25.00
—Black label, silver print					
DL 9035 [M]	Rock-a-Bye Your Baby	196?	3.75	7.50	15.00
—Black label with color bars					
DL 9036 [M]	Rainbow 'Round My Shoulder	1957	6.25	12.50	25.00
—Black label, silver print					
DL 9036 [M]	Rainbow 'Round My Shoulder	196?	3.75	7.50	15.00
—Black label with color bars					
DL 9037 [M]	You Ain't Heard Nothin' Yet!	1957	6.25	12.50	25.00
—Black label, silver print					
DL 9037 [M]	You Ain't Heard Nothin' Yet!	1957	3.75	7.50	15.00
—Black label with color bars					
DL 9038 [M]	Memories	1957	6.25	12.50	25.00
—Black label, silver print					
DL 9038 [M]	Memories	1957	3.75	7.50	15.00
—Black label with color bars					
DL 9050 [M]	Among My Souvenirs	1957	6.25	12.50	25.00
—Black label, silver print					
DL 9050 [M]	Among My Souvenirs	196?	3.75	7.50	15.00
—Black label with color bars					
DL 9063 [M]	The Immortal Al Jolson	1958	6.25	12.50	25.00
—Black label, silver print					
DL 9063 [M]	The Immortal Al Jolson	196?	3.75	7.50	15.00
—Black label with color bars					
DL 9070 [M]	Overseas	1959	7.50	15.00	30.00
—Black label, silver print					
DL 9070 [M]	Overseas	196?	3.75	7.50	15.00
—Black label with color bars					
DL 9074 [M]	The World's Greatest Entertainer	1959	6.25	12.50	25.00
—Black label, silver print					
DL 9074 [M]	The World's Greatest Entertainer	196?	3.75	7.50	15.00
—Black label with color bars					
DL 9095 [M]	Al Jolson with Oscar Levant at the Piano	1961	7.50	15.00	30.00
DL 9095 [M]	Al Jolson with Oscar Levant at the Piano	1961	7.50	15.00	30.00
DL 9099 [M]	Jolie	196?	6.25	12.50	25.00
—Black label, silver print					
DL 79034 [R]	You Made Me Love You	196?	3.00	6.00	12.00
DL 79035 [R]	Rock-a-Bye Your Baby	196?	3.00	6.00	12.00
DL 79036 [R]	Rainbow 'Round My Shoulder	196?	3.00	6.00	12.00
DL 79037 [R]	You Ain't Heard Nothin' Yet!	196?	3.00	6.00	12.00
DL 79038 [R]	Memories	196?	3.00	6.00	12.00
DL 79050 [R]	Among My Souvenirs	196?	3.00	6.00	12.00
DL 79070 [R]	Overseas	196?	3.00	6.00	12.00
DL 79074 [R]	The World's Greatest Entertainer	196?	3.00	6.00	12.00

MCA

Number	Title (A Side/B Side)	Yr	VG	VG+	NM
2057	You Made Me Love You	197?	2.50	5.00	10.00
2058	Rock-a-Bye Your Baby	197?	2.50	5.00	10.00
2059	Rainbow 'Round My Shoulder	197?	2.50	5.00	10.00
2060	You Ain't Heard Nothin' Yet!	197?	2.50	5.00	10.00
2061	Memories	197?	2.50	5.00	10.00
2064	Among My Souvenirs	197?	2.50	5.00	10.00
2066	The Immortal Al Jolson	197?	2.50	5.00	10.00
2067	The World's Greatest Entertainer	197?	2.50	5.00	10.00
10002 [(2)]	The Best of Jolson	1973	3.00	6.00	12.00
27051	You Made Me Love You	198?	2.00	4.00	8.00
27052	Rock-a-Bye Your Baby	198?	2.00	4.00	8.00
27053	Rainbow 'Round My Shoulder	198?	2.00	4.00	8.00
27054	You Ain't Heard Nothin' Yet!	198?	2.00	4.00	8.00
27055	Memories	198?	2.00	4.00	8.00
27057	The Immortal Al Jolson	198?	2.00	4.00	8.00
27058	The World's Greatest Entertainer	198?	2.00	4.00	8.00

SUNBEAM

Number	Title (A Side/B Side)	Yr	VG	VG+	NM
503	Steppin' Out	197?	2.50	5.00	10.00
505	California, Here I Come	197?	2.50	5.00	10.00

TOTEM

Number	Title (A Side/B Side)	Yr	VG	VG+	NM
1006	Al Jolson On the Air, Volume 1	197?	2.50	5.00	10.00
1012	Al Jolson On the Air, Volume 2	197?	2.50	5.00	10.00
1019	Al Jolson On the Air, Volume 3	197?	2.50	5.00	10.00
1030	Al Jolson On the Air, Volume 4	197?	2.50	5.00	10.00
1040	Al Jolson On the Air, Volume 5	197?	2.50	5.00	10.00

JON AND ROBIN AND THE IN CROWD

Also see THE IN CROWD (1).

45s

ABNAK

Number	Title (A Side/B Side)	Yr	VG	VG+	NM
111	Lonely One/How Come	1965	2.50	5.00	10.00
111 [DJ]	Lonely One/How Come	1965	3.75	7.50	15.00
—Promo only on yellow vinyl					
113	Can't Make It With You/If I Need Someone	1966	2.50	5.00	10.00
113 [DJ]	Can't Make It With You/If I Need Someone	1966	3.75	7.50	15.00
—Promo only on yellow vinyl					
115	Hey Girl/If I Need Someone	1966	2.50	5.00	10.00
115 [DJ]	Hey Girl/If I Need Someone	1966	3.75	7.50	15.00
—Promo only on yellow vinyl					
119	Do It Again A Little Bit Slower/If I Need Someone	1967	3.00	6.00	12.00

Number	Title (A Side/B Side)	Yr	VG	VG+	NM
119 [DJ]	Do It Again A Little Bit Slower/If I Need Someone	1967	4.00	8.00	16.00
—Promo only on yellow vinyl					
122	Drums/You Don't Care	1967	2.50	5.00	10.00
122 [DJ]	Drums/You Don't Care	1967	3.75	7.50	15.00
—Promo only on yellow vinyl					
124	I Want Some More/Love Me Baby	1967	2.50	5.00	10.00
124 [DJ]	I Want Some More/Love Me Baby	1967	3.75	7.50	15.00
—Promo only on yellow vinyl					
127	Dr. Jon (The Medicine Man)/Love Me Baby	1968	2.00	4.00	8.00
127 [DJ]	Dr. Jon (The Medicine Man)/Love Me Baby	1968	3.00	6.00	12.00
—Promo only on yellow vinyl					
130	You Got Style/Thursday Morning	1968	2.00	4.00	8.00
130 [DJ]	You Got Style/Thursday Morning	1968	3.00	6.00	12.00
—Promo only on yellow vinyl					
133	Save Me, Save Me/Thursday Morning	1968	2.00	4.00	8.00
—As "Jon and the In Crowd"					
133 [DJ]	Save Me, Save Me/Thursday Morning	1968	3.00	6.00	12.00
—Promo only on yellow vinyl					
135	Gift of Love/Gift of Love (Country Style)	1969	2.00	4.00	8.00
135 [DJ]	Gift of Love/Gift of Love (Country Style)	1969	3.00	6.00	12.00
—Promo only on yellow vinyl					
138	Give Me Your Love/Lonely One	1969	2.00	4.00	8.00
138 [DJ]	Give Me Your Love/Lonely One	1969	3.00	6.00	12.00
—Promo only on yellow vinyl					
140	There's An American Flag on the Moon (Part 1)/ There's An American Flag on the Moon (Part 2)	1969	2.00	4.00	8.00
140 [DJ]	There's An American Flag on the Moon (Part 1)/ There's An American Flag on the Moon (Part 2)	1969	3.00	6.00	12.00
—Promo only on yellow vinyl					
141	If You Got It, Flaunt It/I'll Come Running to You	1969	2.00	4.00	8.00
141 [DJ]	If You Got It, Flaunt It/I'll Come Running to You	1969	3.00	6.00	12.00
—Promo only on yellow vinyl					
Albums					
ABNAK					
ABM-2068 [M]	Soul of a Boy and Girl	1967	5.00	10.00	20.00
ABST-2068 [S]	Soul of a Boy and Girl	1967	5.00	10.00	20.00
ABST-2070	Elastic Event	1968	5.00	10.00	20.00

JONES, BRIAN

Also see THE ROLLING STONES.

Number	Title (A Side/B Side)	Yr	VG	VG+	NM
Albums					
ROLLING STONES					
COC 49100	Brian Jones Presents the Pipes of Pan at Joujouka	1971	15.00	30.00	60.00

JONES, CORKY

See BUCK OWENS.

JONES, DAVY

Also see DOLENZ, JONES & TORK; DOLENZ, JONES, BOYCE & HART; THE MONKEES.

Number	Title (A Side/B Side)	Yr	VG	VG+	NM
45s					
BELL					
45111	Rainy Jane/Welcome to My Love	1971	2.50	5.00	10.00
45136	I Really Love You/Sitting in the Apple Tree	1971	2.50	5.00	10.00
45159	Girl/Take My Love	1971	12.50	25.00	50.00
45178	I'll Believe in You/The Road to Love	1972	5.00	10.00	20.00
COLPIX					
764	Dream Girl/Take Me to Paradise	1965	5.00	10.00	20.00
—Colpix sides as "David Jones"					
764 [PS]	Dream Girl/Take Me to Paradise	1965	7.50	15.00	30.00
784	What Are We Going to Do/This Bouquet	1965	5.00	10.00	20.00
784 [PS]	What Are We Going to Do/This Bouquet	1965	7.50	15.00	30.00
789	The Girl from Chelsea/Theme for a New Love	1965	5.00	10.00	20.00
789 [PS]	The Girl from Chelsea/Theme for a New Love	1965	10.00	20.00	40.00
MGM					
14458	You're a Lady/Who Was It	1972	7.50	15.00	30.00
14524	Rubberene/Who Was It	1973	7.50	15.00	30.00
Albums					
BELL					
6067	Davy Jones	1971	5.00	10.00	20.00
COLPIX					
CP 493 [M]	David Jones	1965	6.25	12.50	25.00
CPS 493 [S]	David Jones	1965	10.00	20.00	40.00
—This album charted in 1967 thanks to the singer's membership in The Monkees					

JONES, DOROTHY

Number	Title (A Side/B Side)	Yr	VG	VG+	NM
45s					
COLUMBIA					
4-42062	Take That Long Walk Home/It's Unbelievable	1961	2.50	5.00	10.00

JONES, GEORGE

Also see GENE PITNEY.

Number	Title (A Side/B Side)	Yr	VG	VG+	NM
45s					
D					
1226	New Baby for Christmas/Maybe Next Christmas	1961	3.00	6.00	12.00
EPIC					
02526	Still Doin' Time/Good Ones and Bad Ones	1981	—	—	3.00
02696	Same Ol' Me/Together Alone	1982	—	—	3.00
03489	Shine On (Shine All Your Sweet Love on Me)/ Memories of Mama	1982	—	—	3.00
03883	I Always Get Lucky with You/I'd Rather Have What We Had	1983	—	—	3.00
04082	Tennessee Whiskey/Almost Persuaded	1983	—	—	3.00
04413	You've Still Got a Place in My Heart/I'm Ragged But Right	1984	—	—	3.00
04609	She's My Rock/(What Love Can Do) The Second Time Around	1984	—	—	3.00
04876	Size Seven Round (Made of Gold)/All I Want to Do in Life	1985	—	—	3.00
—A-side with Lacy J. Dalton; B-side with Janie Frickie					
05439	Who's Gonna Fill Their Shoes/A Whole Lot of Trouble for You	1985	—	—	3.00
05698	The One I Loved Back Then (The Corvette Song)/ If Only You'd Love Me Again	1985	—	—	3.00
05862	Somebody Wants Me Out of the Way/Call the Wrecker for My Heart	1986	—	—	3.00
06296	Wine Colored Roses/These Old Eyes Have Seen It All	1986	—	—	3.00
06593	The Right Left Hand/The Very Best on Me	1986	—	—	3.00
07107	I Turn to You/Don't Leave Without Taking Your Silver	1987	—	—	3.00
07655	The Bird/I'm Goin' Home Like I Never Did Before	1987	—	—	3.00
07748	I'm a Survivor/The Real McCoy	1988	—	—	3.00
07913	The Old Man No One Loves/One Hell of a Song	1988	—	—	3.00
08011	If I Could Bottle This Up/I Always Get It Right with You	1988	—	—	3.00
—With Shelby Lynne					
08509	I'm a One Woman Man/Pretty Little Lady from Beaumont, Texas	1988	—	—	3.00
10831	We Can Make It/One of These Days	1972	—	2.50	5.00
10858	Loving You Could Never Be Better/Try It, You'll Like It	1972	—	2.50	5.00
10917	A Picture of Me (Without You)/The Man Worth Loving You	1972	—	2.50	5.00
10959	What My Woman Can't Do/My Loving Wife	1973	—	2.50	5.00
11006	Nothing Ever Hurt Me (Half As Bad As Losing You)/Wine	1973	—	2.50	5.00
11053	Once You've Had the Best/Mary Don't Go Round	1973	—	2.50	5.00
11122	The Grand Tour/Our Private Life	1974	—	2.50	5.00
50038	The Door/Wean Me	1974	—	2.50	5.00
50088	These Days (I Barely Get By)/Baby, There's Nothing Like You	1975	—	2.50	5.00
50127	Memories of Us/I Just Don't Give a Damn	1975	—	2.50	5.00
50187	The Battle/I'll Come Back	1976	—	2.50	5.00
50227	You Always Look Your Best (Here in My Arms)/ Have You Seen My Chicken	1976	—	2.50	5.00
50271	Her Name Is.../Diary of My Mind	1976	—	2.50	5.00
50385	Old King Kong/It's a 10-33 (Let's Get Jesus on the Line)	1977	—	2.00	4.00
50423	If I Could Put Them All Together (I'd Have You)/ You've Got the Best of Me Again	1977	—	2.00	4.00
50495	Bartender's Blues/Rest in Peace	1977	—	2.00	4.00
50564	I'll Just Take It Out in Love/Leaving Love All Over the Place	1978	—	2.00	4.00
50684	Someday My Day Will Come/We Oughta Be Ashamed	1979	—	2.00	4.00
50867	He Stopped Loving Her Today/A Hard Act to Follow	1980	—	3.00	6.00
50922	I'm Not Ready Yet/Garage Sale Today	1980	—	2.00	4.00
50968	If Drinkin' Don't Kill Me (Her Memory Will)/Brother to the Blues	1980	—	2.00	4.00
68743	Ya Ba Da Ba Do (So Are You)/Don't You Ever Get Tired (Of Hurting Me)	1989	—	2.50	5.00
68743	The King Is Gone (So Are You)/Don't You Ever Get Tired (Of Hurting Me)	1989	—	—	3.00
—Same song, different title (changed for legal reasons)					
68743 [PS]	Ya Ba Da Ba Do (So Are You)/Don't You Ever Get Tired (Of Hurting Me)	1989	—	2.50	5.00
68991	Writing on the Wall/Burning Bridges	1989	—	—	3.00
73070	Radio Lover/Burning Bridges	1989	—	—	3.00
73424	Six Foot Deep, Six Foot Down/He Never Got the Picture at All	1990	—	2.00	4.00
MCA					
54187	You Couldn't Get the Picture/Heckle and Jeckle	1991	—	2.00	4.00
54272	She Loved a Lot in Her Time/Come Home to Me	1991	—	2.00	4.00
54370	Honky Tonk Myself to Death/Where the Tall Grass Grows	1992	—	2.00	4.00
54470	I Don't Need Your Rockin' Chair/Finally Friday	1992	—	2.50	5.00
54604	Wrong's What I Do Best/The Bottle Let Me Down	1993	—	2.00	4.00
54687	Walls Can Fall/You Must Have Walked Across My Mind Again	1993	—	—	3.00
54749	High-Tech Redneck/Forever's Here to Stay	1993	—	2.00	4.00
54969	A Good Year for the Roses/I've Still Got Some Hurtin' Left to Do	1994	—	2.00	4.00
—A-side with Alan Jackson					
55228	Honky Tonk Song/The Lone Ranger	1996	—	2.00	4.00
55287	Billy B. Bad/Back Down to Hung Up on You	1996	—	2.00	4.00
72038	Wild Irish Rose/No Future for Me in Our Past	1998	—	—	3.00
MERCURY					
7045 [S]	White Lightning/Treasure of Love	196?	10.00	20.00	40.00
7046 [S]	Why Baby Why/Hearts in My Dream	196?	10.00	20.00	40.00
7047 [S]	The Window Up Above/Color of the Blues	196?	10.00	20.00	40.00
7048 [S]	Tall, Tall Trees/Don't Stop the Music	196?	10.00	20.00	40.00
7049 [S]	Who Shot Sam/Accidentally on Purpose	196?	10.00	20.00	40.00
71029	Don't Stop the Music/Uh, Uh, No	1957	6.25	12.50	25.00
71049	Just One More/Gonna Come Get You	1957	6.25	12.50	25.00
71096	Too Much Water/All I Want to Do	1957	6.25	12.50	25.00
71139	Nothing Can Stop Me/I'm With the Wrong One	1957	6.25	12.50	25.00
71176	Tall, Tall Trees/Hearts in My Dream	1957	5.00	10.00	20.00
71224	Take the Devil Out of Me/A Cup of Loneliness	1957	5.00	10.00	20.00
71225	New Baby for Christmas/Maybe Next Christmas	1957	5.00	10.00	20.00
71257	Color of the Blues/Eskimo Pie	1958	5.00	10.00	20.00
71340	Wandering Soul/Jesus Wants Me	1958	5.00	10.00	20.00
71373	Treasure of Love/If I Don't Love You (Grits Ain't Groceries)	1958	5.00	10.00	20.00
71406	White Lightning/Long Time to Forget	1959	3.75	7.50	15.00
71464	Who Shot Sam/Into My Arms Again	1959	3.75	7.50	15.00
71506	My Lord Has Called Me/If You Want to Wear a Crown	1959	5.00	10.00	20.00
71514	Money to Burn/Big Harlan Taylor	1959	3.75	7.50	15.00
71583	Accidently on Purpose/Sparkling Blue Eyes	1960	3.75	7.50	15.00
71615	Have Mercy on Me/If You Believe	1960	5.00	10.00	20.00
71636	Family Bible/Your Old Standby	1960	5.00	10.00	20.00
71641	Out of Control/Just Little Boy Blue	1960	3.75	7.50	15.00
71700	The Window Up Above/Candy Hearts	1960	3.75	7.50	15.00
71721	Family Bible/Taggin' Along	1961	3.75	7.50	15.00
71804	Tender Years/Battle of Love	1961	3.00	6.00	12.00
71804 [PS]	Tender Years/Battle of Love	1961	3.75	7.50	15.00

Number	Title (A Side/B Side)	Yr	VG	VG+	NM
71910	Aching, Breaking Heart/When My Heart Hurts No More	1962	3.00	6.00	12.00
71910 [PS]	Aching, Breaking Heart/When My Heart Hurts No More	1962	3.75	7.50	15.00
72010	You're Still on My Mind/Cold, Cold Heart	1962	3.00	6.00	12.00
72010 [PS]	You're Still on My Mind/Cold, Cold Heart	1962	3.75	7.50	15.00
72087	I Love You Because/Revenoor Man	1963	3.00	6.00	12.00
72087 [PS]	I Love You Because/Revenoor Man	1963	3.75	7.50	15.00
72159	Are You Mine/I Didn't Hear You	1963	3.00	6.00	12.00
72200	Mr. Fool/One Is a Lonely Number	1963	3.00	6.00	12.00
72233	The Last Town I Painted/Tarnished Angel	1964	3.00	6.00	12.00
72233 [PS]	The Last Town I Painted/Tarnished Angel	1964	3.75	7.50	15.00
72293	Oh Lonesome Me/Life to Go	1964	3.00	6.00	12.00
72293 [PS]	Oh Lonesome Me/Life to Go	1964	3.75	7.50	15.00
72362	I Wouldn't Know About That/You Better Treat Your Man Right	1964	3.00	6.00	12.00

MUSICOR

Number	Title (A Side/B Side)	Yr	VG	VG+	NM
1067	Things Have Gone to Pieces/Wearing My Heart Away	1965	2.00	4.00	8.00
1067 [PS]	Things Have Gone to Pieces/Wearing My Heart Away	1965	3.75	7.50	15.00
1098	Love Bug/I Can't Get Used to Being Lonely	1965	2.00	4.00	8.00
1117	Take Me/Ship of Love	1965	2.00	4.00	8.00
1143	I'm a People/I Woke Up from Dreaming	1966	2.00	4.00	8.00
1174	Old Brush Arbors/Flowers for Mama	1966	2.00	4.00	8.00
1181	Four-O-Thirty Three/Don't Think I Don't	1966	2.00	4.00	8.00
1226	Walk Through This World with Me/Developing My Pictures	1967	2.00	4.00	8.00
1243	I Can't Get There from Here/A Poor Man's Riches	1967	2.00	4.00	8.00
1244	A Cup of Loneliness/That the World But Give Me Jesus	1967	3.00	6.00	12.00
1267	If My Heart Had Windows/Honky Tonk Downstairs	1967	2.00	4.00	8.00
1289	Say It's Not You/Poor Chinee	1968	2.00	4.00	8.00
1297	Small Time Laboring Man/Well It's Alright	1968	2.00	4.00	8.00
1298	As Long As I Live/Your Angel Steps Out of Heaven	1968	2.00	4.00	8.00
1333	When the Grass Grows Over Me/Heartaches and Hangovers	1968	2.00	4.00	8.00
1339	Lonely Christmas Call/My Mom and Santa Claus	1968	2.00	4.00	8.00
1351	I'll Share My World with You/I'll See You a While Ago	1969	2.00	4.00	8.00
1366	If Not for You/When the Wife Runs Off	1969	2.00	4.00	8.00
1381	She's Mine/No Blues Is Good News	1969	2.00	4.00	8.00
1392	Where Grass Won't Grow/Shoulder to Shoulder	1970	—	3.00	6.00
1404	Going Life's Way/Uncloudy Day	1970	—	3.00	6.00
1408	Tell Me My Lying Eyes Are Wrong/You've Become My Everything	1970	—	3.00	6.00
1425	A Good Year for the Roses/Let a Little Loving Come In	1970	2.00	4.00	8.00
1432	Sometimes You Just Can't Win/Brothers of a Bottle	1971	—	3.00	6.00
1440	Right Won't Touch a Hand/Someone Sweet to Love	1971	—	3.00	6.00
1446	I'll Follow You (Up to Our Cloud)/Getting Over the Storm	1971	—	3.00	6.00

RCA VICTOR

Number	Title (A Side/B Side)	Yr	VG	VG+	NM
AMBO-0123	Tender Years/White Lightnin'	1973	—	2.50	5.00
APBO-0218	My Favorite Lies/You Gotta Be My Baby	1974	—	2.50	5.00
PB-10052	I Can Love You Enough/Talk to Me Lonesome Heart	1974	—	2.50	5.00
74-0625	A Day in the Life of a Fool/Old, Old House	1971	—	3.00	6.00
74-0700	I Made Leaving (Easy for You)/How Proud I Would Have Been	1972	—	3.00	6.00
74-0792	Wrapped Around Her Finger/With Half a Heart	1972	—	3.00	6.00
74-0878	I Can Still See Him in Your Eyes/She's Mine	1973	—	3.00	6.00

STARDAY

Number	Title (A Side/B Side)	Yr	VG	VG+	NM
130	No Money in This Deal/You're in My Heart	1954	25.00	50.00	100.00
146	Play It Cool, Man/Wrong About You	1954	15.00	30.00	60.00
—B-side with Sonny Burns					
160	Let Him Know/Let Me Catch My Breath	1954	15.00	30.00	60.00
162	You All Goodnight/Let Him Know	1954	15.00	30.00	60.00
165	Tell Her/Heartbroken Me	1954	15.00	30.00	60.00
—B-side with Sonny Burns					
188	Hold Everything/What's Wrong with You	1955	12.50	25.00	50.00
202	Why Baby Why/Season of My Heart	1955	12.50	25.00	50.00
216	What Am I Worth/Still Hurtin'	1955	10.00	20.00	40.00
234	I'm Ragged But I'm Right/Your Heart	1956	10.00	20.00	40.00
240	Rock It/How Come It	1956	50.00	100.00	200.00
—As "Thumper Jones"					
247	You Gotta Be My Baby/It's OK	1956	10.00	20.00	40.00
256	Boat of Life/Taggin' Along	1956	10.00	20.00	40.00
264	Just One More/Gonna Come Get You	1956	10.00	20.00	40.00
7003	Seasons of My Heart/I'm Ragged But I'm Right	197?	—	2.50	5.00
7020	Wasted Words/Any Old Time	197?	—	2.50	5.00
7036	Why Baby Why/You Gotta Be My Baby	197?	—	2.50	5.00
8012	Why Baby Why/Seasons of My Heart	197?	—	2.50	5.00

UNITED ARTISTS

Number	Title (A Side/B Side)	Yr	VG	VG+	NM
424	She Thinks I Still Care/Sometimes You Just Can't Win	1962	2.50	5.00	10.00
424 [PS]	She Thinks I Still Care/Sometimes You Just Can't Win	1962	3.75	7.50	15.00
442	Beacon in the Night/He Made Me Free	1962	3.00	6.00	12.00
462	Open Pit Mine/Geronimo	1962	2.50	5.00	10.00
463	He Is So Good to Me/Magic Valley	1962	3.00	6.00	12.00
500	A Girl I Used to Know/Big Fool of the Year	1962	2.50	5.00	10.00
528	Not What I Had in Mind/I Saw Me	1962	2.50	5.00	10.00
530	Lonely Christmas Call/My Mom and Santa Claus	1962	3.75	7.50	15.00
578	You Comb Her Hair/Ain't It Funny What a Fool Will Do	1963	2.50	5.00	10.00
578 [PS]	You Comb Her Hair/Ain't It Funny What a Fool Will Do	1963	3.75	7.50	15.00
683	Your Heart Turned Left (And I Was On the Right)/ My Tears Are Overdue	1964	2.50	5.00	10.00
724	Where Does a Little Tear Come From/Something I Dreamed	1964	2.50	5.00	10.00
751	The Race Is On/She's Lonesome Again	1964	2.50	5.00	10.00
804	Least of All/Brown to Blue	1965	2.50	5.00	10.00
858	Wrong Number/Old Old House	1965	2.50	5.00	10.00
901	What's Money/I Get Lonely in a Hurry	1965	2.50	5.00	10.00
965	World's Worse Loser/I Can't Change Overnight	1965	2.50	5.00	10.00
50014	Best Guitar Picker/A Good Old Fashioned Cry	1966	2.50	5.00	10.00

Albums

ACCORD

Number	Title	Yr	VG	VG+	NM
SN-7201	Tender Years	1982	2.50	5.00	10.00

ALLEGIANCE

Number	Title	Yr	VG	VG+	NM
AV-5015	Cold Cold Heart	198?	2.50	5.00	10.00

ARCHIVE OF FOLK AND JAZZ

Number	Title	Yr	VG	VG+	NM
353	George Jones Sings Country Hits	198?	2.50	5.00	10.00

BULLDOG

Number	Title	Yr	VG	VG+	NM
BDL-2009	20 Golden Pieces of George Jones	198?	2.50	5.00	10.00

EPIC

Number	Title	Yr	VG	VG+	NM
KE 31321	George Jones	1972	3.75	7.50	15.00
—Yellow label					
KE 31321	George Jones	1973	3.00	6.00	12.00
—Orange label					
KE 31718	A Picture of Me (Without You)	1972	3.75	7.50	15.00
—Yellow label					
KE 31718	A Picture of Me (Without You)	1973	3.00	6.00	12.00
—Orange label					
KE 32414	Nothing Ever Hurt Me (Half As Bad As Losing You)	1973	3.75	7.50	15.00
KE 32563	In a Gospel Way	1974	3.75	7.50	15.00
KE 33083	The Grand Tour	1974	3.75	7.50	15.00
KE 33352	The Best of George Jones	1975	3.75	7.50	15.00
PE 33352	The Best of George Jones	198?	2.00	4.00	8.00
—Budget-line reissue					
KE 33547	Memories of Us	1975	3.75	7.50	15.00
BG 33749 [(2)]	George Jones/A Picture of Me (Without You)	1976	3.75	7.50	15.00
KE 34034	The Battle	1976	3.00	6.00	12.00
KE 34290	Alone Again	1976	3.00	6.00	12.00
PE 34692	All-Time Greatest Hits Volume 1	1977	3.00	6.00	12.00
—Orange label					
PE 34692	All-Time Greatest Hits Volume 1	198?	2.00	4.00	8.00
—Dark blue label					
PE 34717	I Wanta Sing	1977	3.00	6.00	12.00
—Orange label					
PE 34717	I Wanta Sing	198?	2.00	4.00	8.00
—Dark blue label					
KE 35414	Bartender's Blues	1978	3.00	6.00	12.00
PE 35414	Bartender's Blues	198?	2.00	4.00	8.00
—Budget-line reissue					
JE 35544	My Very Special Guests	1979	3.00	6.00	12.00
PE 35544	My Very Special Guests	198?	2.00	4.00	8.00
—Budget-line reissue					
JE 36586	I Am What I Am	1980	3.00	6.00	12.00
FE 37106	Still the Same Old Me	1981	2.50	5.00	10.00
PE 37106	Still the Same Ole Me	198?	2.00	4.00	8.00
—Budget-line reissue					
FE 37346	Encore	1981	2.50	5.00	10.00
KE2 38323 [(2)]	Anniversary — 10 Years of Hits	1982	3.00	6.00	12.00
FE 38406	Shine On	1983	2.50	5.00	10.00
PE 38406	Shine On	198?	2.00	4.00	8.00
—Budget-line reissue					
FE 38978	Jones Country	1983	2.50	5.00	10.00
PE 38978	Jones Country	1985	2.00	4.00	8.00
—Budget-line reissue					
FE 39002	You've Still Got a Place in My Heart	1984	2.50	5.00	10.00
FE 39272	Ladies' Choice	1984	2.50	5.00	10.00
FE 39546	By Request	1984	2.50	5.00	10.00
FE 39598	Who's Gonna Fill Their Shoes	1985	2.50	5.00	10.00
FE 39899	First Time Live!	1985	2.50	5.00	10.00
FE 40413	Wine Colored Roses	1986	2.50	5.00	10.00
FE 40776	Super Hits	1987	2.50	5.00	10.00
FE 40781	Too Wild Too Long	1988	2.50	5.00	10.00
FE 44078	One Woman Man	1989	2.50	5.00	10.00

HILLTOP

Number	Title	Yr	VG	VG+	NM
6048	You're In My Heart	1968	3.75	7.50	15.00
6092	Heartaches by the Number	1969	3.75	7.50	15.00
6133	Oh Lonesome Me	1970	3.75	7.50	15.00

INTERMEDIA

Number	Title	Yr	VG	VG+	NM
QS-5044	I Can't Change Overnight	198?	2.50	5.00	10.00
QS-5061	How I Love These Old Songs	198?	2.50	5.00	10.00

LIBERTY

Number	Title	Yr	VG	VG+	NM
LN-10167	Trouble in Mind	1981	2.00	4.00	8.00
LN-10168	I Get Lonely in a Hurry	1981	2.00	4.00	8.00

MCA

Number	Title	Yr	VG	VG+	NM
10398	And Along Came Jones	1991	5.00	10.00	20.00
—Vinyl issued only through Columbia House					

MERCURY

Number	Title	Yr	VG	VG+	NM
ML-8014	Greatest Hits	1980	3.00	6.00	12.00
MG-20282 [M]	Hillbilly Hit Parade, Volume 1	1957	37.50	75.00	150.00
—Five tracks by George Jones, one by George Jones with Benny Barnes, and four by other artists					
MG-20306 [M]	14 Country Favorites	1957	37.50	75.00	150.00
MG-20462 [M]	Country Church Time	1959	50.00	100.00	200.00
MG-20477 [M]	George Jones Sings White Lightning and Other Favorites	1959	37.50	75.00	150.00
MG-20596 [M]	George Jones Salutes Hank Williams	1960	20.00	40.00	80.00
MG-20621 [M]	George Jones' Greatest Hits	1961	10.00	20.00	40.00
MG-20624 [M]	Country and Western Hits	1961	10.00	20.00	40.00
MG-20694 [M]	George Jones Sings From the Heart	1962	10.00	20.00	40.00
MG-20793 [M]	The Novelty Side of George Jones	1963	20.00	40.00	80.00
MG-20836 [M]	The Ballad Side of George Jones	1963	10.00	20.00	40.00
MG-20906 [M]	Blue and Lonesome	1964	6.25	12.50	25.00
MG-20937 [M]	Country and Western No. 1 Male Singer	1964	6.25	12.50	25.00
MG-20990 [M]	Heartaches and Tears	1965	6.25	12.50	25.00
MG-21029 [M]	Singing the Blues	1965	6.25	12.50	25.00
MG-21048 [M]	George Jones' Greatest Hits Volume 2	1965	6.25	12.50	25.00

Number	Title (A Side/B Side)	Yr	VG	VG+	NM
SR-60257 [S]	George Jones Salutes Hank Williams	1960	25.00	50.00	100.00
SR-60621 [P]	George Jones' Greatest Hits	1961	12.50	25.00	50.00
SR-60624 [P]	Country and Western Hits	1961	12.50	25.00	50.00
SR-60694 [S]	George Jones Sings From the Heart	1962	12.50	25.00	50.00
SR-60793 [S]	The Novelty Side of George Jones	1963	25.00	50.00	100.00
SR-60836 [S]	The Ballad Side of George Jones	1963	12.50	25.00	50.00
SR-60906 [S]	Blue and Lonesome	1964	7.50	15.00	30.00
SR-60937 [S]	Country and Western No. 1 Male Singer	1964	7.50	15.00	30.00
SR-60990 [S]	Heartaches and Tears	1965	7.50	15.00	30.00
SR-61029 [S]	Singing the Blues	1965	7.50	15.00	30.00
SR-61048 [S]	George Jones' Greatest Hits Volume 2	1965	7.50	15.00	30.00
822646-1	George Jones Salutes Hank Williams	1985	2.50	5.00	10.00
826095-1	Rockin' the Country	1985	2.50	5.00	10.00
826248-1	Greatest Hits	1986	2.50	5.00	10.00
MUSICOR					
MM-2046 [M]	Mr. Country and Western Music	1965	7.50	15.00	30.00
MM-2060 [M]	New Country Hits	1965	7.50	15.00	30.00
MM-2061 [M]	Old Brush Arbors	1966	7.50	15.00	30.00
MM-2088 [M]	Love Bug	1966	7.50	15.00	30.00
MM-2099 [M]	I'm a People	1966	6.25	12.50	25.00
MM-2106 [M]	We Found Heaven Right Here on Earth	1966	6.25	12.50	25.00
MM-2116 [M]	George Jones' Greatest Hits	1967	6.25	12.50	25.00
MM-2119 [M]	Walk Through This World with Me	1967	7.50	15.00	30.00
MM-2124 [M]	Cup of Loneliness	1967	7.50	15.00	30.00
MM-2128 [M]	Hits by George	1967	7.50	15.00	30.00
MS-3046 [S]	Mr. Country and Western Music	1965	10.00	20.00	40.00
MS-3060 [S]	New Country Hits	1965	10.00	20.00	40.00
MS-3061 [S]	Old Brush Arbors	1966	10.00	20.00	40.00
MS-3088 [S]	Love Bug	1966	10.00	20.00	40.00
MS-3099 [S]	I'm a People	1966	7.50	15.00	30.00
MS-3106 [S]	We Found Heaven Right Here on Earth	1966	7.50	15.00	30.00
MS-3116 [S]	George Jones' Greatest Hits	1967	6.25	12.50	25.00
MS-3119 [S]	Walk Through This World with Me	1967	5.00	10.00	20.00
MS-3124 [S]	Cup of Loneliness	1967	5.00	10.00	20.00
MS-3128 [S]	Hits by George	1967	5.00	10.00	20.00
MS-3149	The Songs of Dallas Frazier	1968	5.00	10.00	20.00
MS-3158	If My Heart Had Windows	1968	5.00	10.00	20.00
M2S-3159 [(2)]	The George Jones Story: The Musical Loves, Life and Sorrows of America's Great Country Star	1968	7.50	15.00	30.00
M2S-3169 [(2)]	My Country	1969	7.50	15.00	30.00
MS-3177	I'll Share My World with You	1969	5.00	10.00	20.00
MS-3181	Where Grass Won't Grow	1969	5.00	10.00	20.00
MS-3188	Will You Visit Me on Sunday?	1970	5.00	10.00	20.00
MS-3191	The Best of George Jones	1970	5.00	10.00	20.00
MS-3194	George Jones With Love	1971	5.00	10.00	20.00
MS-3203	The Best of Sacred Music	1971	5.00	10.00	20.00
MS-3204	The Great Songs of Leon Payne	1971	5.00	10.00	20.00
NASHVILLE					
2076	Seasons of My Heart	1970	3.75	7.50	15.00
PAIR					
PDL2-1074 [(2)]	The Best of George Jones	1986	3.00	6.00	12.00
PDL2-1080 [(2)]	Country, By George!	1986	3.00	6.00	12.00
POWER PAK					
271	The Crown Prince of Country Music	197?	2.50	5.00	10.00
QUICKSILVER					
QS-1011	Frozen in Time	198?	2.50	5.00	10.00
QS-1012	If My Heart Had Windows	198?	2.50	5.00	10.00
RCA CAMDEN					
ACL1-0377	The Race Is On	1973	3.00	6.00	12.00
CAS-2591	Flowers for Mama	1973	3.00	6.00	12.00
RCA VICTOR					
APL1-0316	Best of George Jones Vol. II	1973	3.75	7.50	15.00
APL1-0486	You Gotta Be My Baby	1974	3.75	7.50	15.00
APL1-0612	His Songs	1974	3.75	7.50	15.00
APL1-0815	I Can Love You Enough	1974	3.75	7.50	15.00
APL1-1113	The Best of the Best	1975	3.75	7.50	15.00
LSP-4672	First in the Hearts of Country Music Lovers	1972	3.75	7.50	15.00
LSP-4716	Best of George Jones Vol. I	1972	3.75	7.50	15.00
LSP-4725	Poor Man's Riches	1972	3.75	7.50	15.00
LSP-4726	I Made Leaving (Easy for You)	1972	3.75	7.50	15.00
LSP-4727	Country Singer	1972	3.75	7.50	15.00
LSP-4733	George Jones And Friends	1972	3.75	7.50	15.00
LSP-4785	Four-O Thirty-Three	1972	3.75	7.50	15.00
LSP-4786	Tender Years	1972	3.75	7.50	15.00
LSP-4787	Take Me	1972	3.75	7.50	15.00
LSP-4801	Wrapped Around Her Finger	1973	3.75	7.50	15.00
LSP-4847	I Can Still See Him	1973	3.75	7.50	15.00
ROUNDER					
SS-15	Burn the Honky Tonk Down	198?	2.50	5.00	10.00
SS-17	Heartaches & Hangovers	198?	2.50	5.00	10.00
SEARS					
SPS-125	Maybe, Little Baby	196?	5.00	10.00	20.00
STARDAY					
SLP 101 [M]	The Grand Ole Opry's New Star	1958	300.00	600.00	1200.
SLP 125 [M]	The Crown Prince of Country Music	1960	40.00	80.00	160.00
SLP 150 [M]	George Jones Sings His Greatest Hits	1962	12.50	25.00	50.00
SLP 151 [M]	The Fabulous Country Music Sound of George Jones	1962	12.50	25.00	50.00
SLP 335 [M]	George Jones	1965	10.00	20.00	40.00
SLP 344 [M]	Long Live King George	1965	10.00	20.00	40.00
SLP 366	The George Jones Story Bonus Photo	1966	5.00	10.00	20.00
SLP 366 [(2) M]	The George Jones Story	1966	7.50	15.00	30.00
SLP 401	The George Jones Song Book & Picture Album	1967	12.50	25.00	50.00
—With book					
SLP 401 [M]	The George Jones Song Book & Picture Album	1967	7.50	15.00	30.00
—Without book					
SLP 440 [M]	The Golden Country Hits of George Jones	1969	7.50	15.00	30.00
3021	16 Greatest Hits	197?	2.50	5.00	10.00
DT-90080 [R]	George Jones Sings His Greatest Hits	1964	20.00	40.00	80.00
—Capitol Record Club edition					
UNITED ARTISTS					
UXS-85 [(2)]	George Jones Superpak	1972	5.00	10.00	20.00
UAL-3193 [M]	The New Favorites of George Jones	1962	7.50	15.00	30.00
UAL-3218 [M]	George Jones Sings the Hits of His Country Cousins	1962	7.50	15.00	30.00
UAL-3219 [M]	Homecoming in Heaven	1962	7.50	15.00	30.00
UAL-3220 [M]	My Favorites of Hank Williams	1962	7.50	15.00	30.00
UAL-3221 [M]	George Jones Sings Bob Wills	1962	10.00	20.00	40.00
UAL-3270 [M]	I Wish the Night Would Never End	1963	6.25	12.50	25.00
UAL-3291 [M]	The Best of George Jones	1963	6.25	12.50	25.00
UAL-3338 [M]	More New Favorites	1964	6.25	12.50	25.00
UAL-3364 [M]	George Jones Sings Like the Dickens	1964	10.00	20.00	40.00
UAL-3388 [M]	I Get Lonely in a Hurry	1964	7.50	15.00	30.00
UAL-3408 [M]	Trouble in Mind	1965	7.50	15.00	30.00
UAL-3422 [M]	The Race Is On	1965	7.50	15.00	30.00
—With photo of George Jones on front					
UAL-3422 [M]	The Race Is On	1965	5.00	10.00	20.00
—With cartoon on front					
UAL-3442 [M]	King of Broken Hearts	1965	7.50	15.00	30.00
UAL-3457 [M]	The Great George Jones	1966	7.50	15.00	30.00
UAL-3532 [M]	George Jones' Golden Hits, Volume 1	1966	5.00	10.00	20.00
UAL-3558 [M]	The Young George Jones	1967	7.50	15.00	30.00
UAL-3566 [M]	George Jones' Golden Hits, Volume 2	1967	7.50	15.00	30.00
UAS-6193 [S]	The New Favorites of George Jones	1962	10.00	20.00	40.00
UAS-6218 [S]	George Jones Sings the Hits of His Country Cousins	1962	10.00	20.00	40.00
UAS-6219 [S]	Homecoming in Heaven	1962	10.00	20.00	40.00
UAS-6220 [S]	My Favorites of Hank Williams	1962	10.00	20.00	40.00
UAS-6221 [S]	George Jones Sings Bob Wills	1962	12.50	25.00	50.00
UAS-6270 [S]	I Wish the Night Would Never End	1963	7.50	15.00	30.00
UAS-6291 [S]	The Best of George Jones	1963	7.50	15.00	30.00
UAS-6328 [S]	More New Favorites	1964	7.50	15.00	30.00
UAS-6364 [S]	George Jones Sings Like the Dickens	1964	12.50	25.00	50.00
UAS-6388 [S]	I Get Lonely in a Hurry	1964	10.00	20.00	40.00
UAS-6408 [S]	Trouble in Mind	1965	10.00	20.00	40.00
UAS-6422 [S]	The Race Is On	1965	10.00	20.00	40.00
—With photo of George Jones on front					
UAS-6422 [S]	The Race Is On	1965	6.25	12.50	25.00
—With cartoon on front					
UAS-6442 [S]	King of Broken Hearts	1965	10.00	20.00	40.00
UAS-6457 [S]	The Great George Jones	1966	10.00	20.00	40.00
UAS-6532 [S]	George Jones' Golden Hits, Volume 1	1966	6.25	12.50	25.00
UAS-6558 [S]	The Young George Jones	1967	5.00	10.00	20.00
UAS-6566 [S]	George Jones' Golden Hits, Volume 2	1967	5.00	10.00	20.00
WING					
MGW-12266 [M]	The Great George Jones	196?	3.75	7.50	15.00
SRW-16266 [S]	The Great George Jones	196?	3.75	7.50	15.00

JONES, GEORGE, AND BRENDA CARTER

45s

Number	Title (A Side/B Side)	Yr	VG	VG+	NM
MUSICOR					
1325	Milwaukee, Here I Come/Great Big Spirit of Love	1968	2.00	4.00	8.00

JONES, GEORGE, AND JEANETTE HICKS

45s

Number	Title (A Side/B Side)	Yr	VG	VG+	NM
MERCURY					
71061	Yearning/Cry, Cry	1957	6.25	12.50	25.00
STARDAY					
279	Yearning/So Near Yet So Far Away	1956	7.50	15.00	30.00

JONES, GEORGE, AND BRENDA LEE

Also see each artist's individual listings.

45s

Number	Title (A Side/B Side)	Yr	VG	VG+	NM
EPIC					
04723	Hallelujah I Love Her So/(What Love Can Do) The Second Time Around	1984	—	2.00	4.00

JONES, GEORGE, AND MELBA MONTGOMERY

45s

Number	Title (A Side/B Side)	Yr	VG	VG+	NM
MUSICOR					
1204	Close Together (As You and Me)/Long As We're Dreaming	1966	2.00	4.00	8.00
1238	Party Pickin'/Simply Divine	1967	2.00	4.00	8.00
UNITED ARTISTS					
575	We Must Have Been Out of Our Minds/Until Then	1963	2.50	5.00	10.00
635	Let's Invite Them Over/What's In Our Hearts	1963	2.50	5.00	10.00
704	There's a Friend in the Way/Suppose Tonight Would Be Our Last	1964	2.50	5.00	10.00
732	Please Be My Love/Will There Ever Be Another	1964	2.50	5.00	10.00
784	Multiply the Heartaches/Once More	1964	2.50	5.00	10.00
828	House of Gold/I Dreamed My Baby Came Home	1965	2.50	5.00	10.00
899	Don't Go/I Let You Go	1965	2.50	5.00	10.00
941	Blue Moon of Kentucky/I Can't Get Over You	1965	2.50	5.00	10.00
50015	Afraid/Now Tell Me	1966	2.50	5.00	10.00

Albums

Number	Title (A Side/B Side)	Yr	VG	VG+	NM
LIBERTY					
LN-10169	Singing What's In Our Hearts	1981	2.00	4.00	8.00
MUSICOR					
MM-2109 [M]	Close Together (As You and Me)	1966	5.00	10.00	20.00
MM-2127 [M]	Let's Get Together	1967	7.50	15.00	30.00
MM-2127 [M]	Boy Meets Girl	1967	7.50	15.00	30.00
—Alternate title					
MS-2127 [S]	Let's Get Together	1967	5.00	10.00	20.00
MS-2127 [S]	Boy Meets Girl	1967	5.00	10.00	20.00
—Alternate title					
MS-3109 [S]	Close Together (As You and Me)	1966	6.25	12.50	25.00
UNITED ARTISTS					
UAL-3301 [M]	Singing What's In Our Heart	1963	6.25	12.50	25.00
UAL-3352 [M]	Bluegrass Hootenanny	1964	6.25	12.50	25.00
UAL-3472 [M]	Blue Moon of Kentucky	1966	5.00	10.00	20.00
UAS-6301 [S]	Singing What's In Our Heart	1963	7.50	15.00	30.00
UAS-6352 [S]	Bluegrass Hootenanny	1964	7.50	15.00	30.00
UAS-6472 [S]	Blue Moon of Kentucky	1966	6.25	12.50	25.00

JONES, GEORGE, AND JOHNNY PAYCHECK

Also see each artist's individual listings.

45s

EPIC

Number	Title (A Side/B Side)	Yr	VG	VG+	NM
50647	Mabellene/Don't Want No Stranger Sleepin' in My Bed	1978	—	2.00	4.00
50708	You Can Have Her/Along Came Jones	1979	—	2.00	4.00
50891	When You're Ugly Like Us (You Just Naturally Got to Be Cool)/Kansas City	1980	—	2.00	4.00
50949	You Better Move On/Smack Dab in the Middle	1980	—	2.00	4.00

Albums

EPIC

Number	Title (A Side/B Side)	Yr	VG	VG+	NM
JE 35783	Double Trouble	1980	2.50	5.00	10.00

JONES, GEORGE, AND MARGIE SINGLETON

45s

MERCURY

Number	Title (A Side/B Side)	Yr	VG	VG+	NM
71856	Did I Ever Tell You/Not Even Friends	1961	3.00	6.00	12.00
71955	Waltz of the Angels/Talk About Lovin'	1962	3.00	6.00	12.00

Albums

MERCURY

Number	Title (A Side/B Side)	Yr	VG	VG+	NM
MG-20747 [M]	Duets Country Style	1962	7.50	15.00	30.00
SR-60747 [S]	Duets Country Style	1962	10.00	20.00	40.00

JONES, GEORGE, AND TAMMY WYNETTE

Also see each artist's individual listings; TINA WITH DADDY AND MOMMY.

45s

EPIC

Number	Title (A Side/B Side)	Yr	VG	VG+	NM
10815	Take Me/We Go Together	1971	—	2.50	5.00
10881	The Ceremony/The Great Divide	1972	—	2.50	5.00
10923	Old Fashioned Singing/We Love to Sing About Jesus	1972	—	2.50	5.00
10963	Let's Build a World Together/Touching Shoulders	1973	—	2.50	5.00
11031	We're Gonna Hold On/My Elusive Dreams	1973	—	2.50	5.00
11077	Mr. and Mrs. Santa Claus/The Greatest Christmas Gift	1973	—	2.50	5.00
11083	(We're Not) The Jet Set/The Crawdad Song	1974	—	2.50	5.00
11151	We Loved It Away/Ain't It Been Good	1974	—	2.50	5.00
50099	God's Gonna Getcha (For That)/Those Were the Good Times	1975	—	2.50	5.00
50235	Golden Ring/We're Putting It Back Together	1976	—	2.50	5.00
50314	Near You/Tattletale Eyes	1976	—	2.50	5.00
50418	Southern California/Keep the Change	1977	—	2.00	4.00
50849	Two Story House/It Sure Was Good	1980	—	2.00	4.00
50930	A Pair of Old Sneakers/We'll Talk About It Later	1980	—	2.00	4.00

MCA

Number	Title (A Side/B Side)	Yr	VG	VG+	NM
55048	One/Golden Ring	1995	—	2.00	4.00

JONES, JACK

45s

CAPITOL

Number	Title (A Side/B Side)	Yr	VG	VG+	NM
F3808	Good Luck Good Buddy/Baby Come Home	1957	3.00	6.00	12.00
F3844	For Crying Out Loud/Born to Be Lucky	1957	3.00	6.00	12.00
F3929	A Very Precious Love/What's the Use	1958	2.50	5.00	10.00
F3991	Come On Baby Let's Go/You Laugh	1958	2.50	5.00	10.00
F4089	Laffin' at Me/Deeply Devoted	1958	2.50	5.00	10.00
F4161	Make Room for the Joy/When I Love I'll Love Forever	1959	2.50	5.00	10.00
F4161 [PS]	Make Room for the Joy/When I Love I'll Love Forever	1959	3.75	7.50	15.00

KAPP

Number	Title (A Side/B Side)	Yr	VG	VG+	NM
341	It's a Lonesome Town/A Lot of Livin' to Do	1960	2.50	5.00	10.00
380	Big Time/She's My Darling, She's My Heart	1961	2.50	5.00	10.00
435	Lollipops and Roses/This Was My Love	1961	2.00	4.00	8.00
461	Gift of Love/Pick Up the Pieces	1962	2.00	4.00	8.00
477	Poetry/Dreamin' All the Time	1962	2.00	4.00	8.00
495	I've Got My Pride/That's Her Little Way	1962	2.00	4.00	8.00
507	La Paloma/The Lonely Bull	1963	2.00	4.00	8.00
516	Call Me Irresponsible/Mutiny on the Bounty	1963	2.00	4.00	8.00
534	Love Is a Ticklish Affair/That's the Way I Come to You	1963	2.00	4.00	8.00
551	Wives and Lovers/Toys in the Attic	1963	—	3.00	6.00
551 [PS]	Wives and Lovers/Toys in the Attic	1963	2.00	4.00	8.00
571	Love with the Proper Stranger/The Mood I'm In	1964	—	3.00	6.00
571 [PS]	Love with the Proper Stranger/The Mood I'm In	1964	2.00	4.00	8.00
589	The First Night of the Full Moon/Far Away	1964	—	3.00	6.00
589 [PS]	The First Night of the Full Moon/Far Away	1964	2.00	4.00	8.00
608	Where Love Has Gone/The Lorelei	1964	—	3.00	6.00
608 [PS]	Where Love Has Gone/The Lorelei	1964	2.00	4.00	8.00
629	Lullaby for Christmas Eve/The Village of St. Bernadette	1964	2.00	4.00	8.00
635	Dear Heart/Emily	1964	—	3.00	6.00
635 [PS]	Dear Heart/Emily	1964	2.00	4.00	8.00
651	The Race Is On/I Can't Believe I'm Losing You	1965	—	3.00	6.00
651 [PS]	The Race Is On/I Can't Believe I'm Losing You	1965	2.00	4.00	8.00
672	Seein' the Right Love Go Wrong/Travelin' On	1965	—	3.00	6.00
699	The True Picture/Just Yesterday	1965	—	3.00	6.00
722	Love Bug/And I Love Her	1965	—	3.00	6.00
722 [PS]	Love Bug/And I Love Her	1965	2.00	4.00	8.00
736	The Weekend/Wildflower	1966	—	3.00	6.00
755	The Impossible Dream (The Quest)/Strangers in the Night	1966	—	3.00	6.00
781	A Day in the Life of a Fool/Shining Sea	1966	—	3.00	6.00
781 [PS]	A Day in the Life of a Fool/Shining Sea	1966	—	—	—
—Rumored to exist, but without conclusive evidence, we will delete this from future editions					
800	Lady/Afraid to Love	1966	—	3.00	6.00
818	I'm Indestructible/Afterthoughts	1967	—	3.00	6.00
833	Now I Know/More and More	1967	—	3.00	6.00
847	Our Song/Michelle	1967	—	3.00	6.00
860	Open for Business As Usual/The Mood I'm In	1967	—	3.00	6.00
880	Don't Give Your Love Away/Oh How Much I Love You	1967	—	3.00	6.00
900	Brother, Where Are You/Gypsies, Jugglers and Clowns	1968	—	3.00	6.00
937	People/Don't Rain on My Parade	1968	—	3.00	6.00
964	Far Away/Meditation	1968	—	3.00	6.00
2022	Mathilda/Far Away	1969	—	2.50	5.00
2063	It Only Takes a Moment/Once Upon a Time	1969	—	2.50	5.00
2138	Mirrored Door/Feather Bed	1971	—	2.50	5.00
2143	Breathe Deep/Trippin' on a Country Road	1971	—	2.50	5.00
2154	I'll See You Through/No Concern	1971	—	2.50	5.00

MGM

Number	Title (A Side/B Side)	Yr	VG	VG+	NM
14851	The Love Boat Theme/Ready to Take a Chance Again	197?	2.00	4.00	8.00
14852	Love Theme from "A Star Is Born" (Evergreen)/I Could Have Been a Sailor	197?	—	2.00	4.00

POLYDOR

Number	Title (A Side/B Side)	Yr	VG	VG+	NM
815096-7	The Love Boat Theme/The Rockford Files	1983	—	2.00	4.00
—Reissue; B-side by Mike Post					

RCA VICTOR

Number	Title (A Side/B Side)	Yr	VG	VG+	NM
APBO-0220	Do Me Wrong, But Do Me/Fools in Love	1974	—	2.00	4.00
PB-10025	She Doesn't Live Here Anymore/Write Me a Love Song Charlie	1974	—	2.00	4.00
PB-10317	What I Did for Love/Don't Mention Love	1975	—	2.00	4.00
PB-10845	Send In the Clowns/You Need a Man	1976	—	2.00	4.00
PB-10955	Try It Again/With One More Look at You	1977	—	2.00	4.00
PB-11076	Dixie Chicken/Perfect Strangers	1977	—	2.00	4.00
47-9365	Live for Life/That Tiny World	1967	—	2.50	5.00
47-9441	If You Ever Leave Me/Pretty	1968	—	2.50	5.00
47-9510	Without Her/Follow Me	1968	—	2.50	5.00
47-9564	I Really Want You to Know/This World Is Yours	1968	—	2.50	5.00
47-9639	The Way That I Live/Dirty Word	1968	—	2.50	5.00
47-9687	Love Story/L.A. Breakdown (And Take Me In)	1968	—	2.50	5.00
74-0185	Sweet Child/The Last Seven Days	1969	—	2.50	5.00
74-0278	Little Altar Boy/What's Out There for Me	1969	—	2.50	5.00
74-0350	Sweet Changes/I Wish We'd All Been Ready	1970	—	2.50	5.00
74-0425	Pieces of Dreams/Years of My Youth	1971	—	2.50	5.00
74-0475	Let Me Be the One/Talk It Over in the Morning	1971	—	2.50	5.00
74-0573	The Kind of Girl She Is/What Have They Done to the Moon	1971	—	2.50	5.00
74-0683	The Mountain/How Can We Run Away	1972	—	2.50	5.00
74-0734	Coming Apart/A Game of Magic	1972	—	2.50	5.00

Albums

CAPITOL

Number	Title (A Side/B Side)	Yr	VG	VG+	NM
ST 1274 [S]	This Love of Mine	1959	7.50	15.00	30.00
T 1274 [M]	This Love of Mine	1959	6.25	12.50	25.00
ST 2100 [S]	In Love	1964	5.00	10.00	20.00
—Reissue of 1274					
T 2100 [M]	In Love	1964	3.75	7.50	15.00

KAPP

Number	Title (A Side/B Side)	Yr	VG	VG+	NM
KL-1228 [M]	Shall We Dance	1961	3.00	6.00	12.00
KL-1259 [M]	This Was My Love	1962	3.00	6.00	12.00
KL-1265 [M]	I've Got a Lot of Livin' to Do	1962	3.00	6.00	12.00
KL-1328 [M]	Call Me Irresponsible	1963	3.00	6.00	12.00
KL-1337 [M]	She Loves Me	1963	3.00	6.00	12.00
KL-1352 [M]	Wives and Lovers	1963	3.00	6.00	12.00
KL-1365 [M]	Bewitched	1964	3.00	6.00	12.00
KL-1396 [M]	Where Love Has Gone	1964	3.00	6.00	12.00
KL 1399 [M]	Jack Jones' Christmas Album	1964	3.00	6.00	12.00
KL-1415 [M]	Dear Heart	1964	3.00	6.00	12.00
KL-1433 [M]	My Kind of Town	1965	3.00	6.00	12.00
KL-1435 [M]	There's Love & There's Love & There's Love	1965	3.00	6.00	12.00
KL-1465 [M]	For the "In" Crowd	1966	3.00	6.00	12.00
KL-1486 [M]	The Impossible Dream	1966	3.00	6.00	12.00
KL-1500 [M]	Jack Jones Sings	1966	3.00	6.00	12.00
KL-1511 [M]	Lady	1967	3.75	7.50	15.00
KL-1531 [M]	Our Song	1967	3.75	7.50	15.00
KL-1559 [M]	Greatest Hits	1968	5.00	10.00	20.00
—May exist only as a white label promo					
KS-3228 [S]	Shall We Dance	1961	3.75	7.50	15.00
KS-3259 [S]	This Was My Love	1962	3.75	7.50	15.00
KS-3265 [S]	I've Got a Lot of Livin' to Do	1962	3.75	7.50	15.00
KS-3328 [S]	Call Me Irresponsible	1963	3.75	7.50	15.00
KS-3337 [S]	She Loves Me	1963	3.75	7.50	15.00
KS-3352 [S]	Wives and Lovers	1963	3.75	7.50	15.00
KS-3365 [S]	Bewitched	1964	3.75	7.50	15.00
KS-3396 [S]	Where Love Has Gone	1964	3.75	7.50	15.00
KS 3399 [S]	Jack Jones' Christmas Album	1964	3.75	7.50	15.00
KS-3415 [S]	Dear Heart	1964	3.75	7.50	15.00
KS-3433 [S]	My Kind of Town	1965	3.75	7.50	15.00
KS-3435 [S]	There's Love & There's Love & There's Love	1965	3.75	7.50	15.00
KS-3465 [S]	For the "In" Crowd	1966	3.75	7.50	15.00
KS-3486 [S]	The Impossible Dream	1966	3.75	7.50	15.00
KS-3500 [S]	Jack Jones Sings	1966	3.75	7.50	15.00
KS-3511 [S]	Lady	1967	3.00	6.00	12.00
KS-3531 [S]	Our Song	1967	3.00	6.00	12.00
KS-3551	What the World Needs Now Is Love!	1968	3.00	6.00	12.00
KS-3559	Greatest Hits	1968	3.00	6.00	12.00
KS-3566	Curtain Time	1968	3.00	6.00	12.00
KS-3602	Greatest Hits Vol. 2	1970	3.00	6.00	12.00

MCA

Number	Title (A Side/B Side)	Yr	VG	VG+	NM
4115 [(2)]	The Best of Jack Jones	197?	3.00	6.00	12.00
15014	Jack Jones' Christmas Album	197?	2.50	5.00	10.00
—Reissue					
15036	White Christmas	198?	2.00	4.00	8.00

MGM

Number	Title (A Side/B Side)	Yr	VG	VG+	NM
MG-1-5023	Nobody Does It Better	1979	2.50	5.00	10.00
MG-1-5024	Don't Stop Now	1980	2.50	5.00	10.00

PICKWICK

Number	Title (A Side/B Side)	Yr	VG	VG+	NM
PC-3001 [M]	This Love of Mine	196?	3.00	6.00	12.00
SPC-3001 [S]	This Love of Mine	196?	3.00	6.00	12.00
SPC-3041	A Very Precious Love	196?	2.50	5.00	10.00

RCA VICTOR

Number	Title (A Side/B Side)	Yr	VG	VG+	NM
APL1-0139	Together	1973	2.50	5.00	10.00
APL1-0408	Harbour	1974	2.50	5.00	10.00
APL1-0773	Write Me a Letter	1975	2.50	5.00	10.00

Number	Title (A Side/B Side)	Yr	VG	VG+	NM
ANL1-1081 *—Reissue*	Jack Jones Sings Michel Legrand	1975	2.00	4.00	8.00
APL1-1111	What I Did for Love	1975	2.50	5.00	10.00
APL1-2067	A Full Life	1976	2.50	5.00	10.00
APL1-2361	With One More	1977	2.50	5.00	10.00
LPM-3911 [M]	Without Her	1967	5.00	10.00	20.00
LSP-3911 [S]	Without Her	1967	3.00	6.00	12.00
LPM-3969 [M]	If You Ever Leave Me	1968	5.00	10.00	20.00
LSP-3969 [S]	If You Ever Leave Me	1968	3.00	6.00	12.00
LSP-4048	Where Is Love	1968	3.00	6.00	12.00
LSP-4108	L.A. Break Down	1969	3.00	6.00	12.00
LSP-4209	A Time for Us	1969	3.00	6.00	12.00
LSP-4234	Christmas	1969	3.00	6.00	12.00
LSP-4413	In Person at the Sands, Las Vegas	1970	3.00	6.00	12.00
LSP-4480	Jack Jones Sings Michel Legrand	1970	3.00	6.00	12.00
LSP-4613	A Song for You	1971	3.00	6.00	12.00
LSP-4692	Bread Winners	1972	2.50	5.00	10.00
VOCALION					
VL 73913	Jack Jones Showcase	1970	2.50	5.00	10.00

JONES, JIMMY

45s

Number	Title (A Side/B Side)	Yr	VG	VG+	NM
ABC-PARAMOUNT					
10094 *—As "Jimmy Jones and the Pretenders"*	Blue and Lonely/Daddy Needs Baby	1960	37.50	75.00	150.00
ARROW					
717 *—As "Jimmy Jones and the Jones Boys"*	Heaven in Your Eyes/The Whistlin' Man	1957	45.00	90.00	180.00
BELL					
682	Personal Property/39-21-40	1967	2.00	4.00	8.00
689	True Love Ways/Snap My Fingers	1967	2.00	4.00	8.00
CAPITOL					
3849	If I Knew Then (What I Know Now)/Everything's Gonna Be All Right	1974	—	2.50	5.00
CONCHILLO					
1	Ain't Nothing Wrong Makin' Love the First Night/ Time and Changes	1976	—	3.00	6.00
CUB					
9049	Handy Man/The Search Is Over	1959	6.25	12.50	25.00
9067	Good Timin'/My Precious Angel	1960	6.25	12.50	25.00
9072	That's When I Cried/I Just Go for You	1960	5.00	10.00	20.00
9072 [PS]	That's When I Cried/I Just Go for You	1960	12.50	25.00	50.00
9076	Itchin'/Ee-I-Ee-I-Oh	1960	5.00	10.00	20.00
9082	Ready for Love/For You	1960	5.00	10.00	20.00
9085	I Told You So/You Got It	1961	3.75	7.50	15.00
9093	Dear One/I Say Love	1961	3.75	7.50	15.00
9102	Mr. Music Man/Holler Hey	1961	3.75	7.50	15.00
9110	You're Much Too Young/Nights of Mexico	1962	3.75	7.50	15.00
EPIC					
9339	Whenever You Need Me/You for Me to Love	1959	30.00	60.00	120.00
PARKWAY					
988	Don't You Just Know It/Dynamite	1966	2.50	5.00	10.00
RAMA					
210 *—As "Jimmy Jones and the Pretenders"*	Lover/Plain Old Love	1956	30.00	60.00	120.00
ROULETTE					
4232 *—As "Jimmy 'Handyman' Jones"*	Lover/Plain Old Love	1960	7.50	15.00	30.00
VEE JAY					
505	No Insurance (For a Broken Heart)/Mr. Fix-It	1963	3.75	7.50	15.00

Albums

Number	Title (A Side/B Side)	Yr	VG	VG+	NM
JEN JILLUS					
1001	The Handy Man's Back in Town	1977	3.00	6.00	12.00
MGM					
E-3847 [M]	Good Timin'	1960	30.00	60.00	120.00
SE-3847 [S]	Good Timin'	1960	40.00	80.00	160.00

JONES, JOE

45s

Number	Title (A Side/B Side)	Yr	VG	VG+	NM
CAPITOL					
F2951	Adam Bit the Apple/Will Call	1954	10.00	20.00	40.00
HERALD					
488	You Done Me Wrong/When Your Hair Has Turned to Silver	1956	10.00	20.00	40.00
RIC					
972	You Talk Too Much/I Love You Still	1960	6.25	12.50	25.00
ROULETTE					
4304	You Talk Too Much/I Love You Still	1960	3.75	7.50	15.00
4316	One Big Mouth/Here's What You Gotta Do	1960	3.00	6.00	12.00
4344	California Sun/Please Don't Talk About Me When I'm Gone	1961	3.00	6.00	12.00
4377	The Big Mule/I've Got a Uh Uh Wife	1961	3.00	6.00	12.00

Albums

Number	Title (A Side/B Side)	Yr	VG	VG+	NM
ROULETTE					
R 25143 [M]	You Talk Too Much	1961	37.50	75.00	150.00
SR 25143 [R]	You Talk Too Much	1961	25.00	50.00	100.00

JONES, JOHN PAUL

Also see LED ZEPPELIN.

45s

Number	Title (A Side/B Side)	Yr	VG	VG+	NM
COTILLION					
44102	Got to Get Together Now/Man from Nazareth	1971	6.25	12.50	25.00
JERDEN					
761 *—B-side by Rosemary and Howard*	Sound City/Broken Promises	1965	7.50	15.00	30.00
PARKWAY					
915	Baja/A Foggy Day in Vietnam	1964	10.00	20.00	40.00

Albums

Number	Title (A Side/B Side)	Yr	VG	VG+	NM
COLUMBIA					
KC 32047	John Paul Jones	1973	5.00	10.00	20.00

JONES, JONAH

45s

Number	Title (A Side/B Side)	Yr	VG	VG+	NM
BETHLEHEM					
11014	You're the Cream in My Coffee/The Sheik of Araby	1959	3.00	6.00	12.00
CAPITOL					
F3747	On the Street Where You Live/Rose Room	1957	2.50	5.00	10.00
F3893	76 Trombones/Baubles, Bangles and Beads	1958	2.50	5.00	10.00
F3999	Ballin' the Jack/Slowly But Surely	1958	2.50	5.00	10.00
F4057	Night Train/Lots of Luck, Charlie	1958	2.50	5.00	10.00
F4199	Cherry/I Dig Chicks	1959	2.50	5.00	10.00
F4238	High Hopes/Hit Me Again	1959	2.50	5.00	10.00
F4297	Where Did We Go? Out/Gentleman Jimmy	1959	2.50	5.00	10.00
4375	Blueberry Hill/Shanghai	1960	2.50	5.00	10.00
4497	I Ain't Down Yet/Blue Champagne	1961	2.00	4.00	8.00
4878	The Bells of St. Mary's/Brotherhood of Man	1962	2.00	4.00	8.00
4944	The Work Song/Jonah's Sermon	1963	2.00	4.00	8.00
4993	Doodles/Pink Shutters	1963	2.00	4.00	8.00
DECCA					
25672	People/Who Can I Turn To	196?	—	3.00	6.00
31765	Think Beautiful/Don't Forget 127th Street (127th Street March)	1965	—	3.00	6.00
GROOVE					
0140	Come Sit By Me/God Loves You Child	1956	3.75	7.50	15.00
MOTOWN					
1145	For Better or Worse/Don't Mess with Bill	1969	30.00	60.00	120.00

7-Inch Extended Plays

Number	Title (A Side/B Side)	Yr	VG	VG+	NM
CAPITOL					
EAP 1-839	*Rose Room/Mack the Knife/My Blue Heaven/ Royal Garden Blues	1958	3.00	6.00	12.00
EAP 1-839 [PS]	Muted Jazz, Part 1	1958	3.00	6.00	12.00
EAP 1-963	*Baubles, Bangles and Beads/The Party's Over/ Till There Was You/Seventy Six Trombones	1958	3.00	6.00	12.00
EAP 1-963 [PS]	Swingin' on Broadway, Part 1	1958	3.00	6.00	12.00
EAP 2-963	You're So Right for Me/Just My Luck//I Could Have Danced All Night/Whatever Lola Wants	195?	3.00	6.00	12.00
EAP 2-963 [PS]	Swingin' on Broadway, Part 2	195?	3.00	6.00	12.00
EAP 3-963	(contents unknown)	1958	3.00	6.00	12.00
EAP 3-963 [PS]	Swingin' on Broadway, Part 3	1958	3.00	6.00	12.00

Albums

Number	Title (A Side/B Side)	Yr	VG	VG+	NM
ANGEL					
ANG.60005 [10]	Jonah Wails — 1st Blast	1954	18.75	37.50	75.00
ANG.60006 [10]	Jonah Wails — 2nd Blast	1954	18.75	37.50	75.00
BETHLEHEM					
BCP-1014 [10]	Jonah Jones Sextet	1954	20.00	40.00	80.00
CAPITOL					
T 839 [M]	Muted Jazz	1957	10.00	20.00	40.00
T 963 [M]	Swingin' On Broadway	1958	10.00	20.00	40.00
ST 1039 [S]	Jumpin' with Jonah	1958	7.50	15.00	30.00
T 1039 [M]	Jumpin' with Jonah	1958	6.25	12.50	25.00
ST 1083 [S]	Swingin' at the Cinema	1958	7.50	15.00	30.00
T 1083 [M]	Swingin' at the Cinema	1958	6.25	12.50	25.00
ST 1115 [S]	Jonah Jumps Again	1959	7.50	15.00	30.00
T 1115 [M]	Jonah Jumps Again	1959	6.25	12.50	25.00
ST 1193 [S]	I Dig Chicks	1959	6.25	12.50	25.00
T 1193 [M]	I Dig Chicks	1959	5.00	10.00	20.00
ST 1237 [S]	Swingin' 'Round the World	1959	6.25	12.50	25.00
T 1237 [M]	Swingin' 'Round the World	1959	5.00	10.00	20.00
ST 1375 [S]	Hit Me Again!	1960	6.25	12.50	25.00
T 1375 [M]	Hit Me Again!	1960	5.00	10.00	20.00
ST 1405 [S]	A Touch of Blue	1960	6.25	12.50	25.00
T 1405 [M]	A Touch of Blue	1960	5.00	10.00	20.00
ST 1532 [S]	The Unsinkable Molly Brown	1961	6.25	12.50	25.00
T 1532 [M]	The Unsinkable Molly Brown	1961	5.00	10.00	20.00
ST 1557 [S]	Great Instrumental Hits Styled by Jonah Jones	1961	6.25	12.50	25.00
T 1557 [M]	Great Instrumental Hits Styled by Jonah Jones	1961	5.00	10.00	20.00
ST 1641 [S]	Broadway Swings Again	1961	6.25	12.50	25.00
T 1641 [M]	Broadway Swings Again	1961	5.00	10.00	20.00
SM-1660	Jonah Jones/Glenn Gray	197?	2.50	5.00	10.00
ST 1660 [S]	Jonah Jones/Glenn Gray	1961	6.25	12.50	25.00
T 1660 [M]	Jonah Jones/Glenn Gray	1961	5.00	10.00	20.00
ST 1773 [S]	Jazz Bonus	1962	5.00	10.00	20.00
T 1773 [M]	Jazz Bonus	1962	3.75	7.50	15.00
ST 1948 [S]	And Now, In Person — Jonah Jones	1963	5.00	10.00	20.00
T 1948 [M]	And Now, In Person — Jonah Jones	1963	3.75	7.50	15.00
ST 2087 [S]	Blowin' Up a Storm	1964	5.00	10.00	20.00
T 2087 [M]	Blowin' Up a Storm	1964	3.75	7.50	15.00
ST 2594 [S]	The Best of Jonah Jones	1966	3.00	6.00	12.00
T 2594 [M]	The Best of Jonah Jones	1966	3.75	7.50	15.00
CIRCLE					
CLP-83	1944: Butterflies in the Rain	198?	2.50	5.00	10.00
DECCA					
DL 4638 [M]	Hello Broadway	1965	3.00	6.00	12.00
DL 4688 [M]	On the Sunny Side of the Street	1966	3.00	6.00	12.00
DL 4765 [M]	Tijuana Taxi	1966	3.00	6.00	12.00
DL 4800 [M]	Sweet with a Beat	1967	3.75	7.50	15.00
DL 74638 [S]	Hello Broadway	1965	3.75	7.50	15.00
DL 74688 [S]	On the Sunny Side of the Street	1966	3.75	7.50	15.00
DL 74765 [S]	Tijuana Taxi	1966	3.75	7.50	15.00
DL 74800 [S]	Sweet with a Beat	1967	3.00	6.00	12.00
GROOVE					
LG-1001 [M]	Jonah Jones at the Embers	1956	12.50	25.00	50.00
HALL OF FAME					
613	After Hours Jazz	198?	2.50	5.00	10.00
JAZZ MAN					
5009	Confessin'	1981	2.50	5.00	10.00
MOTOWN					
M-683	Along Came Jonah	1969	10.00	20.00	40.00
M-690	Little Dis, Little Dat	1970	10.00	20.00	40.00
PICKWICK					
SPC-3008	Swing Along	196?	3.00	6.00	12.00

Number	Title (A Side/B Side)	Yr	VG	VG+	NM
RCA CAMDEN					
CAS-2328	Jonah Jones Quartet	1969	3.00	6.00	12.00
RCA VICTOR					
LPM-2004 [M]	Jonah Jones at the Embers	1959	10.00	20.00	40.00
—Reissue of Groove and Vik LP					
SWING					
8408	Paris 1954	198?	2.50	5.00	10.00
VIK					
LXA-1135 [M]	Jonah Jones at the Embers	1958	10.00	20.00	40.00
—Reissue of Groove LP					

JONES, LITTLE ANTHONY
Not the same Little Anthony who was with the Imperials.

Number	Title (A Side/B Side)	Yr	VG	VG+	NM
45s					
EMBER					
1090	Dear Gesu Bambino (Part 1)/Dear Gesu Bambino (Part 2)	1962	3.75	7.50	15.00

JONES, LITTLE JOHNNY

Number	Title (A Side/B Side)	Yr	VG	VG+	NM
45s					
ATLANTIC					
1045	Hoy, Hoy/Doin' the Best I Can	1954	20.00	40.00	80.00
FLAIR					
1010	Sweet Little Woman/I May Be Wrong	1953	200.00	400.00	800.00

JONES, LITTLE SONNY

Number	Title (A Side/B Side)	Yr	VG	VG+	NM
45s					
IMPERIAL					
5275	I Got Booted/Tend to Your Business Blues	1954	25.00	50.00	100.00
5287	Winehead Baby/Going to the Country	1954	25.00	50.00	100.00
SPECIALTY					
443	Is Everything All Right/Do You Really Love Me	1952	20.00	40.00	80.00

JONES, PAUL
Original lead singer for MANFRED MANN.

Number	Title (A Side/B Side)	Yr	VG	VG+	NM
45s					
BELL					
805	It's Getting Better/Not Before Time	1969	2.00	4.00	8.00
CAPITOL					
5745	I Can't Hold On Much Longer/Baby Tomorrow	1966	2.00	4.00	8.00
5800	High Time/It Is Coming Closer	1966	2.00	4.00	8.00
5857	Sonny Boy Williamson/I've Been a Bad, Bad Boy	1967	2.00	4.00	8.00
5970	Privilege/Free Me	1967	2.00	4.00	8.00
LONDON					
168	Mighty Ship/Who Are the Masters	1972	—	2.50	5.00
178	The Pod That Came Back/Construction Worker's Song	1972	—	2.50	5.00
PRIVATE STOCK					
45004	Love Enough	1974	—	2.50	5.00
Albums					
CAPITOL					
ST 2795 [S]	Paul Jones Sings Songs from the Film "Privilege" and Others	1967	7.50	15.00	30.00
T 2795 [M]	Paul Jones Sings Songs from the Film "Privilege" and Others	1967	7.50	15.00	30.00
LONDON					
XPS 605	Crucifix in a Horseshoe	1971	3.00	6.00	12.00

JONES, QUINCY

Number	Title (A Side/B Side)	Yr	VG	VG+	NM
45s					
ABC					
11086	For Love of Ivy/The Pussyfoot	1968	2.00	4.00	8.00
A&M					
1115	Oh Happy Day/Love and Peace	1969	—	3.00	6.00
1139	Oh Happy Day/Love and Peace	1969	—	2.50	5.00
1163	Killer Joe/Maybe Tomorrow	1970	—	2.50	5.00
1184	Bridge Over Troubled Water (Part 1)/Bridge Over Troubled Water (Part 2)	1970	—	2.50	5.00
1316	What's Going On (Part 1)/What's Going On (Part 2)	1971	—	2.50	5.00
1323	Ironside/Cast Your Fate to the Wind	1972	—	2.50	5.00
1404	Love Theme from "The Getaway" (Part 1)/Love Theme from "The Getaway" (Part 2)	1973	—	2.00	4.00
1455	Sanford & Son Theme/Summer in the City	1973	—	2.00	4.00
1606	If I Ever Lose This Heaven/Along Came Betty	1974	—	2.00	4.00
1606 [PS]	If I Ever Lose This Heaven/Along Came Betty	1974	—	3.00	6.00
1638	Soul Saga/Boogie Joe, The Grinder	1974	—	2.00	4.00
1663	Body Heat/One Track Mind	1975	—	2.00	4.00
1743	Is It Love That We're Missing/Cry Baby	1975	—	2.00	4.00
1743 [PS]	Is It Love That We're Missing/Cry Baby	1975	—	3.00	6.00
1791	Mellow Madness/Paranoid	1976	—	2.00	4.00
1878	Midnight Soul Patrol/Brown Soft Shoe	1976	—	2.00	4.00
1909	"Roots" Medley/Many Rains Ago (Oluwu)	1977	—	2.00	4.00
1909 [PS]	"Roots" Medley/Many Rains Ago (Oluwu)	1977	—	3.00	6.00
1923	What Shall I Do (Hush, Hush, Somebody's Calling My Name)/Oh, Lord, Come By Here	1977	—	2.00	4.00
2043	Stuff Like That/There's a Train Leavin'	1978	—	2.00	4.00
2043 [PS]	Stuff Like That/There's a Train Leavin'	1978	—	3.00	6.00
2080	Love, I Never Had It So Good/I Heard That	1978	—	2.00	4.00
2309	Ai No Corrida/Lenta Letina	1981	—	2.00	4.00
2334	Razzamatazz/Velas	1981	—	2.00	4.00
—Featuring Patti Austin					
2357	Just Once/The Dude	1981	—	2.00	4.00
—Featuring James Ingram					
2387	One Hundred Ways/Velas	1981	—	2.00	4.00
—Featuring James Ingram					
2417	There's a Train Leavin'/Something Special	1981	—	2.00	4.00
—Featuring Patti Austin					
BELL					
832	I'm a Believer/The Time for Love Is Anytime	1969	—	3.00	6.00
833	Cactus Flower Theme/The Time for Love Is Anytime	1969	—	3.00	6.00
838	Bob & Carol & Ted & Alice/Giggle Grass	1969	—	3.00	6.00
COLGEMS					
66-1016	Hangin' Paper/Lonely Bottles	1968	2.00	4.00	8.00
IMPULSE					
206	Quintessence/For Lena and Lennie	1962	3.00	6.00	12.00
MERCURY					
71425	The Syncopated Clock/Tuxedo Junction	1959	3.00	6.00	12.00
71460	Choo Choo Ch-Boogie/Marchin' the Blues	1959	3.00	6.00	12.00
71489	Moanin'/The Preacher	1959	3.00	6.00	12.00
71546	Birth of a Band/Change of Pace	1959	3.00	6.00	12.00
71665	Love Is Here to Stay/Moonglow	1960	3.00	6.00	12.00
71737	G-Man Train/Pleasingly Plump	1960	3.00	6.00	12.00
71825	Mack the Knife/Hot Saki	1961	3.00	6.00	12.00
71940	St. Louis Blues/Twistin' Chicken	1962	3.00	6.00	12.00
72012	A Taste of Honey/Shagnasty	1962	3.00	6.00	12.00
72105	Boogie Bossa Nova/Morning of the Carnival	1963	2.50	5.00	10.00
72160	Jive Samba/Comin' Home Baby	1963	2.50	5.00	10.00
72289	Baby Elephant Walk/Mr. Lucky	1964	2.50	5.00	10.00
72306	Theme from "Golden Boy"/Sea Weed	1964	2.50	5.00	10.00
72348	A Hard Day's Night/Soul Serenade	1964	2.50	5.00	10.00
72423	Non-Stop to Brazil/Gentle Rain	1965	2.50	5.00	10.00
72436	The Pawnbroker/Harlem Drive	1965	2.50	5.00	10.00
72460	Mirage/Pack It Up	1965	2.50	5.00	10.00
72496	(I Can't Get No) Satisfaction/What's New Pussycat	1965	2.50	5.00	10.00
72533	Baby Cakes/Mohair Sam	1966	2.50	5.00	10.00
QWEST					
17528	Stomp (Frankie Knuckles Mix)/Stomp (Mousse T.'s Radio Mix)	1996	—	—	3.00
17673	Slow Jams (New Edit)/Slow Jams (Remix)	1996	—	—	3.00
—Featuring Babyface and Tamia with Portrait and Barry White					
19881	Tomorrow (A Better You, A Better Me)/(Instrumental)	1990	—	—	3.00
—Featuring Tevin Campbell					
19992	The Secret Garden (Sweet Seduction Suite)/(Instrumental)	1990	—	—	3.00
—With Al B. Sure!, James Ingram, El DeBarge and Barry White					
19992 [PS]	The Secret Garden (Sweet Seduction Suite)/(Instrumental)	1990	—	—	3.00
22697	I'll Be Good to You/(Instrumental)	1990	—	—	3.00
—With Ray Charles and Chaka Khan					
22697 [PS]	I'll Be Good to You/(Instrumental)	1990	—	—	3.00
RCA VICTOR					
74-0221	Ole Turkey Buzzard/Soul Full of Gold	1969	—	3.00	6.00
REPRISE					
1072	Passin' the Buck/Money Runner	1972	—	2.50	5.00
UNI					
55142	The Lost Man/Main Squeeze	1969	—	3.00	6.00
UNITED ARTISTS					
50706	Call Me Mister Tibbs/Soul Flower	1970	—	2.50	5.00
Albums					
ABC					
D-782 [(2)]	Mode	1973	3.00	6.00	12.00
ABC-PARAMOUNT					
149 [M]	This Is How I Feel About Jazz	1956	25.00	50.00	100.00
186 [M]	Go West, Man!	1957	25.00	50.00	100.00
ABC IMPULSE!					
AS-11 [S]	The Quintessence	1968	3.75	7.50	15.00
IA-9342 [(2)]	Quintessential Charts	1978	3.00	6.00	12.00
A&M					
SP-3023	Walking in Space	1969	3.00	6.00	12.00
SP-3030	Gula Matari	1970	3.00	6.00	12.00
SP-3037	Smackwater Jack	1971	3.00	6.00	12.00
SP-3041	You've Got It Bad Girl	1973	3.00	6.00	12.00
SP-3191	Body Heat	1982	2.00	4.00	8.00
—Budget-line reissue					
SP-3200	The Best	1982	2.00	4.00	8.00
SP-3248	The Dude	198?	2.00	4.00	8.00
—Budget-line reissue					
SP-3249	Sounds...And Stuff Like That!	198?	2.00	4.00	8.00
—Budget-line reissue					
SP-3278	The Best, Vol. 2	1985	2.00	4.00	8.00
SP-3617	Body Heat	1974	2.50	5.00	10.00
SP-3705 [(2)]	I Heard That!!	1976	3.00	6.00	12.00
SP-3721	The Dude	1981	2.50	5.00	10.00
SP-4526	Mellow Madness	1975	2.50	5.00	10.00
SP-4626	Roots	1977	2.50	5.00	10.00
SP-4685	Sounds...And Stuff Like That!	1978	2.50	5.00	10.00
SP-6507 [(2)]	I Heard That!!	198?	2.50	5.00	10.00
—Budget-line reissue					
QU-53041 [Q]	You've Got It Bad Girl	1974	5.00	10.00	20.00
QU-53617 [Q]	Body Heat	1974	5.00	10.00	20.00
QU-54526 [Q]	Mellow Madness	1975	5.00	10.00	20.00
CHESS					
CH-91562	The Music of Quincy Jones	198?	2.50	5.00	10.00
COLGEMS					
COM-107 [M]	In Cold Blood	1967	5.00	10.00	20.00
COS-107 [S]	In Cold Blood	1967	6.25	12.50	25.00
EMARCY					
MG-36083 [M]	Jazz Abroad	1956	25.00	50.00	100.00
818177-1 [(2)]	The Birth of a Band	1984	3.00	6.00	12.00
GRP/IMPULSE!					
222	The Quintessence	199?	3.75	7.50	15.00
—Reissue on audiophile vinyl					
IMPULSE!					
A-11 [M]	The Quintessence	1962	7.50	15.00	30.00
AS-11 [S]	The Quintessence	1962	10.00	20.00	40.00
LIBERTY					
LOM-16004 [M]	Enter Laughing	1967	6.25	12.50	25.00
LOS-17004 [S]	Enter Laughing	1967	7.50	15.00	30.00
MCA					
4145 [(2)]	Quintessential Charts	198?	2.50	5.00	10.00
—Reissue of ABC Impulse 9342					

Number	Title (A Side/B Side)	Yr	VG	VG+	NM
5578	The Slugger's Wife	1985	3.00	6.00	12.00
MCA/IMPULSE!					
5728	The Quintessence	1986	2.00	4.00	8.00
MERCURY					
SRM-2-623 [(2)]	Ndeda	1972	3.75	7.50	15.00
PPS-2014 [M]	Around the World	1961	7.50	15.00	30.00
PPS-6014 [S]	Around the World	1961	10.00	20.00	40.00
MG-20444 [M]	Birth of a Band	1959	12.50	25.00	50.00
MG-20561 [M]	The Great, Wide World of Quincy Jones	1960	12.50	25.00	50.00
MG-20612 [M]	I Dig Dancers	1960	10.00	20.00	40.00
MG-20653 [M]	Quincy Jones at Newport '61	1961	7.50	15.00	30.00
MG-20751 [M]	Big Band Bossa Nova	1962	7.50	15.00	30.00
MG-20799 [M]	Quincy Jones Plays Hip Hits	1963	7.50	15.00	30.00
MG-20863 [M]	Quincy Jones Explores the Music of Henry Mancini	1964	5.00	10.00	20.00
MG-20938 [M]	Golden Boy	1964	5.00	10.00	20.00
MG-21011 [M]	The Pawnbroker	1964	5.00	10.00	20.00
MG-21025 [M]	Mirage	1965	5.00	10.00	20.00
MG-21050 [M]	Quincy Jones Plays for Pussycats	1965	5.00	10.00	20.00
MG-21063 [M]	Quincy's Got a Brand New Bag	1965	5.00	10.00	20.00
MG-21070 [M]	Slender Thread	1966	5.00	10.00	20.00
SR-60129 [S]	Birth of a Band	1959	15.00	30.00	60.00
SR-60221 [S]	The Great, Wide World of Quincy Jones	1960	15.00	30.00	60.00
SR-60612 [S]	I Dig Dancers	1960	12.50	25.00	50.00
SR-60653 [S]	Quincy Jones at Newport '61	1961	10.00	20.00	40.00
SR-60751 [S]	Big Band Bossa Nova	1962	10.00	20.00	40.00
SR-60799 [S]	Quincy Jones Plays Hip Hits	1963	10.00	20.00	40.00
SR-60863 [S]	Quincy Jones Explores the Music of Henry Mancini	1964	6.25	12.50	25.00
SR-60938 [S]	Golden Boy	1964	6.25	12.50	25.00
SR-61011 [S]	The Pawnbroker	1964	6.25	12.50	25.00
SR-61025 [S]	Mirage	1965	6.25	12.50	25.00
SR-61050 [S]	Quincy Jones Plays for Pussycats	1965	6.25	12.50	25.00
SR-61063 [S]	Quincy's Got a Brand New Bag	1965	6.25	12.50	25.00
SR-61070 [S]	Slender Thread	1966	6.25	12.50	25.00
MOBILE FIDELITY					
1-078	You've Got It Bad Girl	1981	6.25	12.50	25.00
—Audiophile vinyl					
NAUTILUS					
NR-52	The Dude	198?	10.00	20.00	40.00
—Audiophile vinyl					
PRESTIGE					
PRLP-172 [10]	Quincy Jones with the Swedish-American All Stars	1953	50.00	100.00	200.00
QWEST					
25356 [(2)]	The Color Purple	1985	5.00	10.00	20.00
—Boxed set on purple vinyl					
25389 [(2)]	The Color Purple	1985	3.75	7.50	15.00
—Gatefold package on purple vinyl					
26020	Back on the Block	1989	3.00	6.00	12.00
TRIP					
5514	The Great Wide World of Quincy Jones	1974	2.00	4.00	8.00
5554	Live at Newport '61	197?	2.00	4.00	8.00
UNITED ARTISTS					
UAS-5214	They Call Me Mister Tibbs	1970	6.25	12.50	25.00
WING					
SRW-16398	Around the World	1969	3.00	6.00	12.00

JONES, RONNIE, AND THE CLASSMATES

45s

Number	Title (A Side/B Side)	Yr	VG	VG+	NM
END					
1002	Teenage Rock/Little Girl Next Door	1957	30.00	60.00	120.00
1014	Lonely Boy/Baby Cries	1958	30.00	60.00	120.00
1125	Teenage Rock/Little Girl Next Door	1963	6.25	12.50	25.00

JONES, SPIKE, AND THE CITY SLICKERS

45s

Number	Title (A Side/B Side)	Yr	VG	VG+	NM
KAPP					
314	I Want the South to Win the War for Christmas/Let's All Sing a Song for Christmas	1959	10.00	20.00	40.00
—B-side by the Happy Harts					
314 [PS]	I Want the South to Win the War for Christmas/Let's All Sing a Song for Christmas	1959	15.00	30.00	60.00
LIBERTY					
55191	The Late Late Late Movies (Part 1)/The Late Late Late Movies (Part 2)	1959	3.00	6.00	12.00
55253	Ah-1, Ah-2, Ah-Sunset Strip (Part 1)/Ah-1, Ah-2, Ah-Sunset Strip (Part 2)	1960	3.00	6.00	12.00
55317	Keystone Kapers/Silence Please	1961	3.00	6.00	12.00
55649	The Ballad of Jed Clampett/Green, Green	1963	2.50	5.00	10.00
55684	Dominique/Sweet and Lovely	1964	2.50	5.00	10.00
55718	I'm in the Mood for Love/Paradise	1964	2.50	5.00	10.00
55788	Let's Kiss, Kiss, Kiss/Star Jenka	1965	2.50	5.00	10.00
RCA VICTOR					
WP 143 [(3)]	The Nutcracker Suite	1949	20.00	40.00	80.00
—Includes aqua label records 47-2795, 47-2796 and 47-2797 plus box					
WP 143 [(3)]	The Nutcracker Suite	1951	15.00	30.00	60.00
—Includes black label records 47-2795, 47-2796 and 47-2797 plus box					
WY-461	Barnyard Christmas/Socko the Smallest Snowball	1952	5.00	10.00	20.00
—With the Bell Sisters; "Little Nipper" children's series					
27-0030	Cocktails for Two/Chloe	195?	5.00	10.00	20.00
47-2795	Nutcracker Suite — 1 (The Little Girl's Dream)/Nutcracker Suite — 6 (End of the Little Girl's Dream)	1949	5.00	10.00	20.00
—Originals with aqua labels and gold print					
47-2795	Nutcracker Suite — 1 (The Little Girl's Dream)/Nutcracker Suite — 6 (End of the Little Girl's Dream)	1951	3.75	7.50	15.00
—Reissue on black label with white print, outline of dog on right					
47-2796	Nutcracker Suite — 2 (Land of the Sugar Plum Fairy)/Nutcracker Suite — 5 (Back to the Fairy Ball)	1949	5.00	10.00	20.00
—Originals with aqua labels and gold print					
47-2796	Nutcracker Suite — 2 (Land of the Sugar Plum Fairy)/Nutcracker Suite — 5 (Back to the Fairy Ball)	1951	3.75	7.50	15.00
—Reissue on black label with white print, outline of dog on right					
47-2797	Nutcracker Suite — 3 (The Fairy Ball)/Nutcracker Suite — 4 (The Mysterious Room)	1949	5.00	10.00	20.00
—Originals with aqua labels and gold print					
47-2797	Nutcracker Suite — 3 (The Fairy Ball)/Nutcracker Suite — 4 (The Mysterious Room)	1951	3.75	7.50	15.00
—Reissue on black label with white print, outline of dog on right					
47-2894	Ya Wanna Buy a Bunny/Knock Knock	1949	5.00	10.00	20.00
47-2963	(All I Want for Christmas Is) My Two Front Teeth/Happy New Year	1949	7.50	15.00	30.00
47-2992	Dance of the Hours/None But the Lonely Heart	1949	5.00	10.00	20.00
47-3126	Wild Bill Hiccup/Morpheus	1949	5.00	10.00	20.00
47-3198	The Charleston/Charlestone-Mio	1949	5.00	10.00	20.00
47-3199	Black Bottom/Doin' the New Raccoon	1949	5.00	10.00	20.00
47-3200	I Wonder Where My Baby Is Tonight/The Varsity Drag	1949	5.00	10.00	20.00
—The above three comprise a box set					
47-3287	That Old Black Magic/Liebestraum	1949	5.00	10.00	20.00
47-3288	Love in Bloom/My Old Flame	1949	5.00	10.00	20.00
47-3289	William Tell Overture/I Kiss Your Hand Madame	1949	5.00	10.00	20.00
—The above three comprise a box set					
47-3741	Chinese Mule Train/Riders in the Sky	1950	5.00	10.00	20.00
47-3827	I Know a Secret/Charlestone-Mio	1950	5.00	10.00	20.00
47-3912	Yaaha Hula Hickey Dula/Yes! We Have No Bananas	1950	5.00	10.00	20.00
47-3934	Rudolph the Red-Nosed Reindeer/Mommy, Won't You Buy a Baby Brother	1950	5.00	10.00	20.00
47-4012	Tennessee Waltz/I Haven't Been Home	1950	5.00	10.00	20.00
47-4055	Peter Cottontail/Rhapsody from Hungary	1951	5.00	10.00	20.00
47-4125	My Daddy Is a General to Me/Ill Barkio	1951	5.00	10.00	20.00
47-4209	Too Young/So 'Elp Me	1951	5.00	10.00	20.00
47-4315	Rudolph the Red-Nosed Reindeer/(All I Want for Christmas Is) My Two Front Teeth	1951	5.00	10.00	20.00
47-4546	Deep Purple/It Never Rains in Sunny California	1952	5.00	10.00	20.00
47-4568	Down South/I've Turned a Gadabout	1952	5.00	10.00	20.00
47-4669	There's a Blue Sky Way Out Yonder/Stop Your Gamblin'	1952	5.00	10.00	20.00
47-4731	A Din Skal, A Min Skal (Swedish Polka)	1952	—	—	—
—Canceled?					
47-4831	(All of a Sudden) My Heart Sings/I'll Never Work There Anymore	1952	5.00	10.00	20.00
47-4875	Hotter Than a Pistol/Hot Lips	1952	5.00	10.00	20.00
47-5015	Barnyard Christmas/Socko the Smallest Snowball	1952	5.00	10.00	20.00
—With the Bell Sisters					
47-5067	I Saw Mommy Kissing Santa Claus/Winter	1952	5.00	10.00	20.00
47-5067 [PS]	I Saw Mommy Kissing Santa Claus/Winter	1952	10.00	20.00	40.00
47-5107	I Went to Your Wedding/I'll Never Work There Anymore	1952	5.00	10.00	20.00
47-5320	Three Little Fishes/A Din Skal, A Min Skal (Swedish Polka)	1953	5.00	10.00	20.00
47-5392	Captain of the Spaceship/Are My Ears On Straight	1953	—	—	—
—Canceled					
47-5472	Pal-Yat-Chee/Dragnet	1953	5.00	10.00	20.00
47-5497	Where Did My Snowman Go/Santa Brought Me Choo Choo Trains	1953	5.00	10.00	20.00
47-5602	Ricketshaw/My Heart Went Boom Boom	1954	—	—	—
—Canceled					
47-5742	Secret Love/I'm in the Mood for Love	1954	5.00	10.00	20.00
47-5917	Japanese Skokiaan/My Heart Went Boom Boom	1954	5.00	10.00	20.00
47-5920	I Want Eddie Fisher for Christmas/Japanese Skokiaan	1954	5.00	10.00	20.00
47-6064	This Song Is For the Birds/Hi Mister	1955	5.00	10.00	20.00
447-0172	(All I Want for Christmas Is) My Two Front Teeth/Rudolph the Red-Nosed Reindeer	195?	3.75	7.50	15.00
—Reissue (Gold Standard Series); black label, dog on top					
VERVE					
2026	My Birthday Comes on Christmas/Wouldn't It Be Fun	1956	3.75	7.50	15.00
10037	I'm Popeye the Sailor Man/My Heart Went Boom Boom	1957	3.75	7.50	15.00
WARNER BROS.					
5116	Monster Movie Babe/Teenage Brain Surgeon	1959	3.75	7.50	15.00

7-Inch Extended Plays

Number	Title (A Side/B Side)	Yr	VG	VG+	NM
VERVE					
2003	Love and Marriage/Memories Are Made of This//16 Tacos/The Trouble with Pascual	1956	3.75	7.50	15.00

Albums

Number	Title (A Side/B Side)	Yr	VG	VG+	NM
CORNOGRAPHIC					
1001	King of Corn	197?	2.50	5.00	10.00
HINDSIGHT					
HSR-185	The Uncollected Spike Jones 1946	198?	2.50	5.00	10.00
LIBERTY					
LRP-3140 [M]	Omnibust	1959	12.50	25.00	50.00
LRP-3154 [M]	60 Years of Music America Hates Best	1960	12.50	25.00	50.00
LRP-3338 [M]	Washington Square	1963	5.00	10.00	20.00
LRP-3349 [M]	Spike Jones' New Band	1964	7.50	15.00	30.00
LRP-3370 [M]	My Man	1964	5.00	10.00	20.00
LRP-3401 [M]	Spike Jones Plays Hank Williams Hits	1965	5.00	10.00	20.00
LST-7140 [S]	Omnibust	1959	18.75	37.50	75.00
—Black vinyl					
LST-7140 [S]	Omnibust	1959	37.50	75.00	150.00
—Red vinyl					
LST-7154 [S]	60 Years of Music America Hates Best	1960	18.75	37.50	75.00
LST-7338 [S]	Washington Square	1963	6.25	12.50	25.00
LST-7349 [S]	Spike Jones' New Band	1964	10.00	20.00	40.00
LST-7370 [S]	My Man	1964	6.25	12.50	25.00
LST-7401 [S]	Spike Jones Plays Hank Williams Hits	1965	6.25	12.50	25.00
RCA GOLD SEAL					
AGL1-4142	Spike Jones Is Murdering the Classics!	1982	2.00	4.00	8.00
—Reissue					

Number	Title (A Side/B Side)	Yr	VG	VG+	NM
RCA RED SEAL					
LSC-3235 [R]	Spike Jones Is Murdering the Classics!	1971	5.00	10.00	20.00
RCA VICTOR					
LPT-18 [10]	Spike Jones Plays the Charleston	1952	50.00	100.00	200.00
ANL1-1035	The Best of Spike Jones	1975	2.50	5.00	10.00
—Reissue					
LPM-2224 [M]	Thank You Music Lovers	1960	12.50	25.00	50.00
ANL1-2312	The Best of Spike Jones, Volume 2	1977	2.50	5.00	10.00
—Reissue					
LPM-3054 [10]	Bottoms Up	1952	50.00	100.00	200.00
LPM-3128 [10]	Spike Jones Murders Carmen and Kids the Classics	1953	50.00	100.00	200.00
AYL1-3748	The Best of Spike Jones, Volume 1	1980	2.00	4.00	8.00
—"Best Buy Series" reissue					
LPM-3849 [M]	The Best of Spike Jones	1967	6.25	12.50	25.00
LSP-3849 [R]	The Best of Spike Jones	1967	5.00	10.00	20.00
AYL1-3870	The Best of Spike Jones, Volume 2	1981	2.00	4.00	8.00
—"Best Buy Series" reissue					
RHINO					
R1 70196	It's a Spike Jones Christmas	1988	3.00	6.00	12.00
R1 70261	Dinner Music...For People Who Aren't Very Hungry	1988	3.00	6.00	12.00
UNITED ARTISTS					
UA-LA439-E	The Very Best of Spike Jones	1975	3.00	6.00	12.00
VERVE					
MGV-2021 [M]	Let's Sing a Song for Christmas	1956	12.50	25.00	50.00
V-2021 [M]	Let's Sing a Song for Christmas	1961	7.50	15.00	30.00
MGV-4005 [M]	Dinner Music...For People Who Aren't Very Hungry	1957	12.50	25.00	50.00
V-4005 [M]	Dinner Music...For People Who Aren't Very Hungry	1961	6.25	12.50	25.00
WARNER BROS.					
W 1332 [M]	Spike Jones in Hi-Fi	1959	10.00	20.00	40.00
WS 1332 [S]	Spike Jones in Stereo	1959	12.50	25.00	50.00

JONES, THUMPER

See GEORGE JONES.

JONES, TOM

12-Inch Singles

Number	Title (A Side/B Side)	Yr	VG	VG+	NM
INTERSCOPE					
2172 [DJ]	If I Only Knew (4 versions)	1994	2.50	5.00	10.00
2194 [DJ]	Situation (5 versions)	1994	2.50	5.00	10.00
MCA					
55144	She's a Lady (3 versions)	1995	2.50	5.00	10.00

45s

Number	Title (A Side/B Side)	Yr	VG	VG+	NM
CHINA					
871038-7	Kiss/E.F.L.	1989	—	—	3.00
—A-side: The Art of Noise with Tom Jones; B-side by Art of Noise					
871038-7 [PS]	Kiss/E.F.L.	1989	—	—	3.00
EPIC					
50308	Say You'll Stay Until Tomorrow/Lady Lay	1976	—	2.00	4.00
50382	Take Me Tonight/I Hope You'll Understand	1977	—	2.00	4.00
50468	What a Night/That's Where I Belong	1977	—	2.00	4.00
50506	There's Nothing Stronger Than Our Love/No One Gave Me Love	1978	—	2.00	4.00
50636	Hey Love/Baby, As You Turn Away	1978	—	2.00	4.00
MCA					
41127	Dancing Endlessly/Never Had a Lady Before	1979	—	2.00	4.00
MERCURY					
76100	Darlin'/I Don't Want to Know You That Way	1981	—	2.00	4.00
76115	What in the World's Come Over You/The Things That Matter Most to Me	1981	—	2.00	4.00
76125	Lady Lay Down/A Daughter's Question	1981	—	2.00	4.00
76172	A Woman's Touch/I'll Never Get Over You	1982	—	2.00	4.00
810445-7	Touch Me (I'll Be Your Fool Once More)/We're Wasting Our Time	1983	—	—	3.00
812631-7	It'll Be Me/If I Ever Had to Say Goodbye to You	1983	—	—	3.00
814820-7	I've Been Rained On Too/That Old Piano	1983	—	—	3.00
818801-7	This Time/Memphis, Tennessee	1984	—	—	3.00
870233-7	Things That Matter Most to Me/Green, Green Grass of Home	1988	—	—	3.00
880173-7	All the Love Is On the Radio/(B-side unknown)	1984	—	—	3.00
880402-7	I'm an Old Rock and Roller (Dancin' to a Different Beat)/My Kind of Girl	1984	—	—	3.00
880569-7	Give Her All the Roses (Don't Wait Until Tomorrow)/A Picture of You	1985	—	—	3.00
884039-7	Not Another Heart Song/Only My Heart Knows	1985	—	—	3.00
884252-7	It's Four in the Morning/I'll Never Get Over You	1985	—	—	3.00
888911-7	Lover to Lover/A Daughter's Question	1987	—	—	3.00
PARROT					
9737	It's Not Unusual/To Wait for Love (Is to Waste Your Life Away)	1965	2.50	5.00	10.00
9765	What's New Pussycat/Once Upon a Time	1965	2.50	5.00	10.00
9765 [PS]	What's New Pussycat/Once Upon a Time	1965	3.75	7.50	15.00
9787	With These Hands/Some Other Guy	1965	2.00	4.00	8.00
9787 [PS]	With These Hands/Some Other Guy	1965	3.00	6.00	12.00
9801	Thunderball/Key to My Heart	1965	2.00	4.00	8.00
9801 [PS]	Thunderball/Key to My Heart	1965	5.00	10.00	20.00
—Version 1: with a dead female and a spear gun					
9801 [PS]	Thunderball/Key to My Heart	1965	3.00	6.00	12.00
—Version 2: without the above elements on sleeve					
9800	Promise Her Anything/Little You	1966	2.00	4.00	8.00
40006	Not Responsible/Once There Was a Time	1966	2.00	4.00	8.00
40008	City Girl/What a Party	1966	2.00	4.00	8.00
40009	Green, Green Grass of Home/If I Had You	1966	2.00	4.00	8.00
40012	Detroit City/Ten Guitars	1967	2.00	4.00	8.00
40014	Funny Familiar Forgotten Feelings/I'll Never Let You Go	1967	2.00	4.00	8.00
40016	Sixteen Tons/Things I Wanna Do	1967	2.00	4.00	8.00
40018	I'll Never Fall in Love Again/Once Upon a Time	1967	3.00	6.00	12.00
—First pressings contain the full-length version of the A-side; time is listed at over four minutes					
40018	I'll Never Fall in Love Again/Once Upon a Time	1967	2.00	4.00	8.00
—Later pressings delete a verse from the A-side; time is listed at 2:55					
40020	Land of a Thousand Dances/I Can't Stop Loving You	1967	5.00	10.00	20.00
—May be promo only					
40024	I'm Coming Home/Lonely One	1967	2.00	4.00	8.00
40025	Delilah/Smile Away Your Blues	1968	2.00	4.00	8.00
40029	Help Yourself/Day by Day	1968	2.00	4.00	8.00
40035	A Minute of Your Time/Looking Out My Window	1968	2.00	4.00	8.00
40038	Love Me Tonight/Hide and Seek	1969	—	3.00	6.00
40038 [PS]	Love Me Tonight/Hide and Seek	1969	2.00	4.00	8.00
40045	Without Love (There Is Nothing)/The Man Who Knows Too Much	1969	—	3.00	6.00
40045 [PS]	Without Love (There Is Nothing)/The Man Who Knows Too Much	1969	2.00	4.00	8.00
40048	Daughter of Darkness/Tupelo Mississippi Flash	1970	—	3.00	6.00
40048 [PS]	Daughter of Darkness/Tupelo Mississippi Flash	1970	2.00	4.00	8.00
40051	I (Who Have Nothing)/Stop Breaking My Heart	1970	—	3.00	6.00
40051 [PS]	I (Who Have Nothing)/Stop Breaking My Heart	1970	2.00	4.00	8.00
40056	Can't Stop Loving You/Never Give Away Love	1970	—	3.00	6.00
40056 [PS]	Can't Stop Loving You/Never Give Away Love	1970	2.00	4.00	8.00
40058	She's a Lady/My Way	1971	—	3.00	6.00
40058 [PS]	She's a Lady/My Way	1971	2.00	4.00	8.00
40062	Puppet Man/Every Mile	1971	—	3.00	6.00
40064	Puppet Man/Resurrection Shuffle	1971	—	2.50	5.00
40067	Till/One Day Soon	1971	—	2.50	5.00
40070	The Young New Mexican Puppeteer/All That I Need Is Time	1972	—	2.50	5.00
40074	Letter to Lucille/Thank the Lord	1973	—	2.50	5.00
40078	La, La, La (Just Having You Here)/Love, Love, Love	1973	—	2.50	5.00
40080	Somethin' 'Bout You Baby I Like/Keep a-Talkin' 'Bout Love	1973	—	2.50	5.00
40081	Pledging My Love/I'm Too Far Gone	1974	—	2.50	5.00
40083	Ain't No Love/When the Band Goes Home	1974	—	2.50	5.00
40084	I Got Your Number/The Pain of Love	1974	—	2.50	5.00
40086	Memories Don't Leave Like People Do/Helping Hand	1975	—	2.50	5.00
SYMBOL					
205	Nothing But Fine/Trying to Get to My Grits	1965	3.00	6.00	12.00
TOWER					
126	Little Lonely One/That's What We'll All Do	1965	3.00	6.00	12.00
126 [PS]	Little Lonely One/That's What We'll All Do	1965	5.00	10.00	20.00
176	Lonely One/I Was a Fool	1965	3.00	6.00	12.00
176 [PS]	Lonely One/I Was a Fool	1965	5.00	10.00	20.00
190	Baby I'm in Love/Chills and Fever	1966	2.50	5.00	10.00

Albums

Number	Title (A Side/B Side)	Yr	VG	VG+	NM
EPIC					
PE 34383	Classic Tom Jones	1976	3.00	6.00	12.00
PE 34468	Say You'll Stay Until Tomorrow	1977	3.00	6.00	12.00
PE 34720	Tom Is Love	1977	2.50	5.00	10.00
JE 35023	What a Night	1978	2.50	5.00	10.00
JIVE					
1214-1-J	Move Closer	1989	3.00	6.00	12.00
LONDON					
PS 717	The Country Side of Tom Jones	1978	2.50	5.00	10.00
LC-50002	Tom Jones' Greatest Hits	1977	3.00	6.00	12.00
820234-1	This Is Tom Jones	1985	2.00	4.00	8.00
820319-1	Tom Jones' Greatest Hits	1985	2.50	5.00	10.00
MCA					
3182	Tom Jones	1979	2.50	5.00	10.00
37114	Rescue Me	1980	2.00	4.00	8.00
MERCURY					
SRM-1-4010	Darlin'	1981	2.50	5.00	10.00
SRM-1-4062	Tom Jones Country	1982	2.50	5.00	10.00
814448-1	Don't Let Our Dreams Die Young	1983	2.50	5.00	10.00
822701-1	Love Is on the Radio	1984	2.50	5.00	10.00
826140-1	Tender Loving Care	1985	2.50	5.00	10.00
830409-1	Things That Matter Most to Me	1987	2.50	5.00	10.00
PARROT					
XPAS-1 [DJ]	Special Tom Jones Interview	1970	25.00	50.00	100.00
—Promo-only open-end interview with gatefold cover and script					
PA 61004 [M]	It's Not Unusual	1965	3.75	7.50	15.00
PA 61006 [M]	What's New Pussycat?	1965	3.75	7.50	15.00
PA 61007 [M]	A-Tom-Ic Jones	1966	3.75	7.50	15.00
PA 61009 [M]	Green, Green Grass of Home	1967	3.75	7.50	15.00
PA 61011 [M]	Funny Familiar Forgotten Feelings	1967	3.75	7.50	15.00
PA 61014 [M]	Tom Jones Live	1967	3.75	7.50	15.00
PAS 71004 [S]	It's Not Unusual	1965	3.75	7.50	15.00
PAS 71006 [S]	What's New Pussycat?	1965	3.75	7.50	15.00
PAS 71007 [S]	A-Tom-Ic Jones	1966	3.75	7.50	15.00
PAS 71009 [S]	Green, Green Grass of Home	1967	3.75	7.50	15.00
PAS 71011 [S]	Funny Familiar Forgotten Feelings	1967	3.75	7.50	15.00
PAS 71014 [S]	Tom Jones Live	1967	3.75	7.50	15.00
PAS 71019	The Tom Jones Fever Zone	1968	3.00	6.00	12.00
PAS 71025	Help Yourself	1969	3.00	6.00	12.00
PAS 71028	This Is Tom Jones	1969	3.00	6.00	12.00
PAS 71031	Live in Las Vegas	1969	3.00	6.00	12.00
PAS 71037	Tom	1970	3.00	6.00	12.00
PAS 71039	I (Who Have Nothing)	1970	3.00	6.00	12.00
PAS 71046	She's a Lady	1971	3.00	6.00	12.00
PAS 71049	Live at Caesar's Palace	1971	3.00	6.00	12.00
XPAS 71055	Close Up	1972	3.00	6.00	12.00
XPAS 71060	The Body and Soul of Tom Jones	197?	3.00	6.00	12.00
XPAS 71062	Tom Jones' Greatest Hits	1973	3.00	6.00	12.00
PAS 71066	Somethin' 'Bout You Baby I Like	1974	3.00	6.00	12.00
PAS 71068	Memories Don't Leave Like People Do	197?	3.00	6.00	12.00

JONES, TONI

45s

Number	Title (A Side/B Side)	Yr	VG	VG+	NM
SMASH					
1814	Love Is Strange/Dear (Here Comes My Baby)	1963	2.50	5.00	10.00

JONES BROTHERS, THE

45s

SUN

Number	Title (A Side/B Side)	Yr	VG	VG+	NM
213	Every Night/Look to Jesus	1954	200.00	400.00	800.00

JOPLIN, JANIS

Also see BIG BROTHER AND THE HOLDING COMPANY.

45s

COLUMBIA

Number	Title (A Side/B Side)	Yr	VG	VG+	NM
45023	Kozmik Blues/Little Girl Blue	1969	—	3.00	6.00
45080	One Good Man/Try (Just a Little Bit Harder)	1970	—	3.00	6.00
45128	Wake Me, Lord/Maybe	1970	—	3.00	6.00
45314	Me and Bobby McGee/Half Moon	1971	—	2.50	5.00
45379	Mercedez Benz/Cry Baby	1971	—	2.50	5.00
45433	Get It While You Can/Move Over	1971	—	2.50	5.00
45630	Bye Bye Baby/Down on Me	1972	—	2.50	5.00

Albums

COLUMBIA

Number	Title (A Side/B Side)	Yr	VG	VG+	NM
AS 1377 [DJ]	A Collection	1982	5.00	10.00	20.00
KCS 9913	I Got Dem Ol' Kozmik Blues Again Mama!	1969	5.00	10.00	20.00
—"360 Sound Stereo" on label					
KCS 9913	I Got Dem Ol' Kozmik Blues Again Mama!	1970	3.00	6.00	12.00
—Orange label					
PC 9913	I Got Dem Ol' Kozmik Blues Again Mama!	198?	2.00	4.00	8.00
—Budget-line reissue					
CQ 30322 [Q]	Pearl	1974	5.00	10.00	20.00
KC 30322	Pearl	1971	3.75	7.50	15.00
PC 30322	Pearl	1975	3.00	6.00	12.00
—Reissue without bar code					
PC 30322	Pearl	198?	2.00	4.00	8.00
—Reissue with bar code					
C2X 31160 [(2)]	Joplin in Concert	1972	5.00	10.00	20.00
CG 31160	Joplin in Concert	198?	3.00	6.00	12.00
KC 32168	Janis Joplin's Greatest Hits	1973	3.75	7.50	15.00
PC 32168	Janis Joplin's Greatest Hits	197?	2.00	4.00	8.00
CG 33345 [(2)]	Janis	198?	3.00	6.00	12.00
PG 33345 [(2)]	Janis	1975	3.75	7.50	15.00
PC 37569	Farewell Song	1982	2.50	5.00	10.00

COLUMBIA SPECIAL PRODUCTS

Number	Title (A Side/B Side)	Yr	VG	VG+	NM
2P 13792 [(2)]	The Greatest Hits of Janis Joplin	1977	5.00	10.00	20.00

JORDAN, JERRY

45s

MCA

Number	Title (A Side/B Side)	Yr	VG	VG+	NM
40639	What It Was, Was Football/Phone Call from God	1976	—	2.00	4.00

Albums

MCA

Number	Title (A Side/B Side)	Yr	VG	VG+	NM
473	Phone Call from God	1975	2.50	5.00	10.00
2174	Don't Call Me... I'll Call You	1976	2.50	5.00	10.00

JORGENSON, CHRISTINE

Albums

J RECORDS

Number	Title (A Side/B Side)	Yr	VG	VG+	NM
J-1 [M]	Christine Jorgenson Reveals	1958	12.50	25.00	50.00

JOSEFUS

45s

MAINSTREAM

Number	Title (A Side/B Side)	Yr	VG	VG+	NM
725	Jimmy Jimmy/Sephus Blues	1970	3.75	7.50	15.00

Albums

HOOKAH

Number	Title (A Side/B Side)	Yr	VG	VG+	NM
330	Dead Man	1969	75.00	150.00	300.00

MAINSTREAM

Number	Title (A Side/B Side)	Yr	VG	VG+	NM
S-6127	Josefus	1970	25.00	50.00	100.00

JOSEPH

Albums

SCEPTER

Number	Title (A Side/B Side)	Yr	VG	VG+	NM
SRS-674	Stoned Age Man	1970	20.00	40.00	80.00

JOSEPH, MARGIE

12-Inch Singles

H.C.R.C.

Number	Title (A Side/B Side)	Yr	VG	VG+	NM
03338	Knockout (Part 1)/Knockout (Part 2)	1982	2.00	4.00	8.00

45s

ATLANTIC

Number	Title (A Side/B Side)	Yr	VG	VG+	NM
2907	Born to Wander/Let's Go Somewhere and Love	1972	—	2.50	5.00
2933	Touch Your Woman/I'm So Glad I'm Your Woman	1973	—	2.50	5.00
2954	Let's Stay Together/I'd Rather Go Blind	1973	—	2.50	5.00
2988	Come Lay Some Lovin' on Me/Ridin' High	1973	—	2.50	5.00
3032	My Love/Sweet Surrender	1974	—	2.50	5.00
3220	Words (Are Impossible)/I Still Love You	1974	—	2.50	5.00
3269	I Can't Move No Mountains/Just As Soon As the Feeling's Over	1975	—	2.50	5.00
3290	Stay Still/Just As Soon As the Feeling's Over	1975	—	2.50	5.00
3445	Come On Back to Me Lover/He Came Into My Life	1978	—	2.00	4.00
3509	I Feel His Love Getting Stronger/How Will I Know	1978	—	2.00	4.00
3525	I Don't Want to Get Over You/Love Takes Tears	1978	—	2.00	4.00

COTILLION

Number	Title (A Side/B Side)	Yr	VG	VG+	NM
44201	Hear the Words, Feel the Feeling/I Get Carried Away	1976	—	2.00	4.00
44207	Don't Turn the Lights Off/All Cried Out	1976	—	2.00	4.00
99737	Big Strong Man/(B-side unknown)	1984	—	2.00	4.00
99771	Ready for the Night/(B-side unknown)	1984	—	2.00	4.00

H.C.R.C.

Number	Title (A Side/B Side)	Yr	VG	VG+	NM
03337	Knockout (Part 1)/Knockout (Part 2)	1982	—	2.00	4.00

VOLT

Number	Title (A Side/B Side)	Yr	VG	VG+	NM
4012	One More Chance/Never Can You Be	1969	2.00	4.00	8.00
4023	What You Gonna Do/Nobody	1969	2.00	4.00	8.00
4037	Your Sweet Lovin'/What's Wrong Baby	1970	—	3.00	6.00
4046	Punish Me/A Sweeter Tomorrow	1970	—	3.00	6.00
4056	Stop! In the Name of Love/Make Me Believe You'll Stay	1971	—	3.00	6.00
4061	The Other Woman Got My Man and Gone/I'll Always Love You	1971	—	3.00	6.00

Albums

ATLANTIC

Number	Title (A Side/B Side)	Yr	VG	VG+	NM
SD 7248	Margie Joseph	1973	3.00	6.00	12.00
SD 7277	Sweet Surrender	1974	3.00	6.00	12.00
SD 18126	Margie	1975	3.00	6.00	12.00
SD 19182	Feeling My Way	1978	2.50	5.00	10.00

COTILLION

Number	Title (A Side/B Side)	Yr	VG	VG+	NM
SD 9906	Hear the Words, Feel the Feeling	1976	3.00	6.00	12.00

H.C.R.C.

Number	Title (A Side/B Side)	Yr	VG	VG+	NM
20009	Knockout	1983	2.50	5.00	10.00

VOLT

Number	Title (A Side/B Side)	Yr	VG	VG+	NM
VOS-6012	Margie Joseph Makes a New Impression	1971	7.50	15.00	30.00
VOS-6016	Phase II	1971	7.50	15.00	30.00

JOSEPH, MARGIE, AND BLUE MAGIC

Also see each artist's individual listings.

45s

ATCO/WMOT

Number	Title (A Side/B Side)	Yr	VG	VG+	NM
7030	What's Come Over Me/You and Me (Got a Good Thing Goin')	1975	—	2.50	5.00

JOSHUA FOX

45s

TETRAGRAMMATON

Number	Title (A Side/B Side)	Yr	VG	VG+	NM
1527	Goin' Down for Big Numbers/Moontime Bore	1969	3.00	6.00	12.00
1532	Don't Tell Me a Story/It's Just Meant to Be	1969	3.00	6.00	12.00

Albums

TETRAGRAMMATON

Number	Title (A Side/B Side)	Yr	VG	VG+	NM
T-125	Joshua Fox	1969	7.50	15.00	30.00

JOSIE AND THE PUSSYCATS

Also see PATRICE HOLLOWAY; CHERYL LADD.

45s

CAPITOL

Number	Title (A Side/B Side)	Yr	VG	VG+	NM
CP 58-1	Letter to Mama/Inside, Outside, Upside Down	1970	5.00	10.00	20.00
CP 58-1 [PS]	Letter to Mama/Inside, Outside, Upside Down	1970	7.50	15.00	30.00
CP 59-2	With Every Beat of My Heart/Josie	1970	5.00	10.00	20.00
CP 59-2 [PS]	With Every Beat of My Heart/Josie	1970	7.50	15.00	30.00
CP 60-3	Voodoo/If That Isn't Love	1970	5.00	10.00	20.00
CP 60-3 [PS]	Voodoo/If That Isn't Love	1970	7.50	15.00	30.00
CP 61-4	I Wanna Make You Happy/It's Gotta Be Him	1970	5.00	10.00	20.00
CP 61-4 [PS]	I Wanna Make You Happy/It's Gotta Be Him	1970	7.50	15.00	30.00
2967	Every Beat of My Heart/It's All Right with Me	1970	5.00	10.00	20.00
—Same song as CP 59, but a slightly different title and a mono mix					
3045	Stop, Look and Listen/You've Come a Long Way, Baby	1971	5.00	10.00	20.00

Albums

CAPITOL

Number	Title (A Side/B Side)	Yr	VG	VG+	NM
ST-665	Josie and the Pussycats	1970	50.00	100.00	200.00

JOURNEY

Original lead singer Gregg Rolie was also the original lead singer of SANTANA.

12-Inch Singles

COLUMBIA

Number	Title (A Side/B Side)	Yr	VG	VG+	NM
AS 568 [DJ]	Just the Same Way (stereo/mono)	1979	2.50	5.00	10.00

GEFFEN

Number	Title (A Side/B Side)	Yr	VG	VG+	NM
PRO-A-2240 [DJ]	Only the Young (same on both sides)	1985	—	3.00	6.00

45s

COLUMBIA

Number	Title (A Side/B Side)	Yr	VG	VG+	NM
02241	Who's Crying Now/Mother, Father	1981	—	—	3.00
02241 [PS]	Who's Crying Now/Mother, Father	1981	—	2.00	4.00
02567	Don't Stop Believin'/Natural Thing	1981	—	—	3.00
02567 [PS]	Don't Stop Believin'/Natural Thing	1981	—	2.00	4.00
02687	Open Arms/Little Girl	1982	—	—	3.00
02687 [PS]	Open Arms/Little Girl	1982	—	2.00	4.00
02883	Still They Ride/La Raza Del Sol	1982	—	—	3.00
02883 [PS]	Still They Ride/La Raza Del Sol	1982	—	2.00	4.00
03133	Open Arms/The Party's Over	1982	—	—	3.00
—Reissue					
03134	Who's Crying Now/Don't Stop Believin'	1982	—	—	3.00
—Reissue					
03513	Separate Ways (Worlds Apart)/Frontiers	1983	—	—	3.00
03513 [PS]	Separate Ways (Worlds Apart)/Frontiers	1983	—	2.00	4.00
CNR-03568	Separate Ways (Worlds Apart)	1983	—	2.50	5.00
—One-sided budget release					
03840	Faithfully/Frontiers	1983	—	—	3.00
04004	After the Fall/Only Solutions	1983	—	—	3.00
04151	Send Her My Love/Chain Reaction	1983	—	—	3.00
05869	Be Good to Yourself/Only the Young	1986	—	—	3.00
05869 [PS]	Be Good to Yourself/Only the Young	1986	—	—	3.00
06134	Suzanne/Ask the Lonely	1986	—	—	3.00
06134 [PS]	Suzanne/Ask the Lonely	1986	—	—	3.00
06301	I'll Be Alright Without You/The Eyes of a Woman	1986	—	—	3.00
06301 [PS]	I'll Be Alright Without You/The Eyes of a Woman	1986	—	—	3.00
06302	Girl Can't Help It/It Could Have Been You	1986	—	—	3.00
06302 [PS]	Girl Can't Help It/It Could Have Been You	1986	—	—	3.00
07043	Why Can't This Night Go On Forever/Positive Touch	1987	—	—	3.00
07043 [PS]	Why Can't This Night Go On Forever/Positive Touch	1987	—	—	3.00
10137	To Play Some Music/Topaz	1975	—	3.00	6.00
10324	On a Saturday Night/To Play Some Music	1976	—	3.00	6.00
10370	It's All Too Much/She Makes Me (Feel Alright)	1976	—	3.00	6.00
10522	Spaceman/Nickel and Dime	1977	—	3.00	6.00
10700	Wheel in the Sky/Can Do	1978	—	2.50	5.00
10757	Anytime/Can Do	1978	—	2.50	5.00
10800	Lights/Somethin' to Hide	1978	—	2.50	5.00

Number	Title (A Side/B Side)	Yr	VG	VG+	NM
10928	Just the Same Way/Somethin' to Hide	1979	—	2.00	4.00
11036	Lovin', Touchin', Squeezin'/Daydream	1979	—	2.00	4.00
11143	Too Late/Do You Recall	1979	—	2.00	4.00
11213	Any Way You Want It/When You're Alone (It Ain't Easy)	1980	—	2.00	4.00
11275	Walks Like a Lady/People and Places	1980	—	2.00	4.00
11339	Good Morning Girl/Stay Awhile	1980	—	2.00	4.00
60505	The Party's Over (Hopelessly in Love)/Just the Same Way	1981	—	2.00	4.00
78428	When You Love a Woman/Message of Love	1996	—	—	3.00
GEFFEN					
29090	Only the Young/I'll Only Fall in Love Again	1985	—	2.00	4.00
—B-side by Sammy Hagar					
29090 [PS]	Only the Young/I'll Only Fall in Love Again	1985	—	2.00	4.00
Albums					
COLUMBIA					
AS 914 [DJ]	Journey	1975	3.75	7.50	15.00
—Promo-only sampler					
AS 1606 [DJ]	A Candid Conversation with Journey	197?	3.75	7.50	15.00
—Promo-only interview and songs LP					
PC 33388	Journey	1975	2.50	5.00	10.00
—No bar code on cover					
PC 33388	Journey	198?	—	3.00	6.00
—With bar code on cover					
PC 33904	Look Into the Future	1976	2.50	5.00	10.00
—No bar code on cover					
PC 33904	Look Into the Future	198?	—	3.00	6.00
—With bar code on cover					
PCQ 33904 [Q]	Look Into the Future	1976	3.75	7.50	15.00
PC 34311	Next	1977	2.50	5.00	10.00
—No bar code on cover					
PC 34311	Next	198?	—	3.00	6.00
—With bar code on cover					
JC 34912	Infinity	1978	2.50	5.00	10.00
—No bar code on cover					
JC 34912	Infinity	1979	—	3.00	6.00
—With bar code on cover					
FC 35797	Evolution	1979	2.00	4.00	8.00
PC 35797	Evolution	1985	—	3.00	6.00
—Budget-line reissue					
C2 36324 [(2)]	In the Beginning	1979	2.50	5.00	10.00
FC 36339	Departure	1980	2.00	4.00	8.00
KC2 37016 [(2)]	Captured	1981	2.50	5.00	10.00
TC 37408	Escape	1981	2.00	4.00	8.00
FC 37998	Dream After Dream	1982	3.00	6.00	12.00
PC 37998	Dream After Dream	1986	2.00	4.00	8.00
—Budget-line reissue					
QC 38504	Frontiers	1983	2.00	4.00	8.00
OC 39936	Raised on Radio	1986	2.00	4.00	8.00
OC 44493	Greatest Hits	1988	2.50	5.00	10.00
HC 44912	Infinity	1982	7.50	15.00	30.00
—Half-speed mastered edition					
HC 46339	Departure	1980	5.00	10.00	20.00
—Half-speed mastered edition					
HC 47408	Escape	1982	5.00	10.00	20.00
—Half-speed mastered edition					
HC 47998	Dream After Dream	1982	7.50	15.00	30.00
—Half-speed mastered edition					
HC 48504	Frontiers	1983	7.50	15.00	30.00
—Half-speed mastered edition					
MOBILE FIDELITY					
1-144	Escape	1984	50.00	100.00	200.00
—Audiophile vinyl					

JOURNEYMEN, THE (1)

Also see SCOTT McKENZIE; JOHN PHILLIPS.

Number	Title (A Side/B Side)	Yr	VG	VG+	NM
45s					
AMY					
821	Cup-E-Co/Hush Storm	1961	3.00	6.00	12.00
CAPITOL					
4625	500 Miles/The River She Comes Down	1961	2.50	5.00	10.00
4678	Soft Blow the Summer Winds/Kumbaya	1962	2.50	5.00	10.00
4737	Don't Turn Around/Hush Now Sally	1962	2.50	5.00	10.00
4829	What'll I Do/Loadin' Coal	1962	2.50	5.00	10.00
4943	Rag Mama/I Never Will Marry	1963	2.50	5.00	10.00
4943 [PS]	Rag Mama/I Never Will Marry	1963	10.00	20.00	40.00
5031	Kumbaya/Ja Da	1963	2.50	5.00	10.00
Albums					
CAPITOL					
ST 1629 [S]	The Journeymen	1961	7.50	15.00	30.00
T 1629 [M]	The Journeymen	1961	6.25	12.50	25.00
ST 1770 [S]	Coming Attraction — Live!	1962	7.50	51.00	30.00
T 1770 [M]	Coming Attraction — Live!	1962	6.25	12.50	25.00
ST 1951 [S]	New Directions in Folk Music	1963	7.50	15.00	30.00
T 1951 [M]	New Directions in Folk Music	1963	6.25	12.50	25.00

JOURNEYMEN, THE (2)

Number	Title (A Side/B Side)	Yr	VG	VG+	NM
45s					
IONA					
1111	Work Out/Bag's Groove	1961	12.50	25.00	50.00
1115	Surfer's Blues/Surfer's Rule	1963	12.50	25.00	50.00
1115	Surfer's Blues/Surfer's Rule	1963	10.00	20.00	40.00
—Rerelease as "The Baylanders"					

JOY, BENNY

Number	Title (A Side/B Side)	Yr	VG	VG+	NM
45s					
ANTLER					
4011	Crash the Party/Little Red Book	1959	125.00	250.00	500.00
DECCA					
31199	New York, Hey Hey/Sincerely, Your Friend	1961	3.75	7.50	15.00
31280	Birds of a Feather Fly Together/You Go Your Way (And I'll Go Mine)	1961	3.75	7.50	15.00
DIXIE					
2001	Steady with Betty/Spin the Bottle	1958	125.00	250.00	500.00
DOT					
16445	I'm of No More Use to You Old Earth/Harry's Harem	1963	3.75	7.50	15.00
RAM					
1107	Ittie Bittie Everything/(B-side unknown)	1959	125.00	250.00	500.00
TRI-DEC					
8667	Steady with Betty/Spin the Bottle	1958	150.00	300.00	600.00

JOY, RODDIE

Number	Title (A Side/B Side)	Yr	VG	VG+	NM
45s					
PARKWAY					
101	Something Strange Is Going On/Stop	1966	3.00	6.00	12.00
134	Every Breath I Take/Walkin' Back	1967	3.00	6.00	12.00
151	I Want You Back/Let's Start All Over	1967	3.00	6.00	12.00
991	A Boy Is Just a Toy/Stop	1966	3.75	7.50	15.00
RED BIRD					
10-021	Love Hit Me with a Wallop/Come Back Baby	1965	5.00	10.00	20.00
10-031	The La La Song/He's So Easy to Love	1965	6.25	12.50	25.00
10-037	If There's Anything Else You Want (Let Me Know)/Stop	1965	10.00	20.00	40.00

JOY OF COOKING

Number	Title (A Side/B Side)	Yr	VG	VG+	NM
45s					
CAPITOL					
3075	Brownsville/Only Time Will Tell Me	1971	—	3.00	6.00
3224	Closer to the Ground/Pilot	1971	—	2.50	5.00
3330	Let Love Carry You Along/Home Town Man	1972	—	2.50	5.00
3396	Don't the Moon Look Fat and Round/All Around the Sun and the Moon	1972	—	2.50	5.00
Albums					
CAPITOL					
ST-661	Joy of Cooking	1971	3.75	7.50	15.00
SMAS-828	Closer to the Ground	1971	3.75	7.50	15.00
ST-11050	Castles	1972	3.00	6.00	12.00

JOY TONES, THE

Number	Title (A Side/B Side)	Yr	VG	VG+	NM
45s					
COED					
600	This Love (That I'm Giving You)/I Wanna Party Some More	1965	3.00	6.00	12.00

JOYE, COL, AND THE JOY BOYS

Number	Title (A Side/B Side)	Yr	VG	VG+	NM
45s					
DECCA					
30933	(Rockin' Rollin') Clementine/Bye Bye Baby Goodbye	1959	7.50	15.00	30.00

JOYETTES, THE

Number	Title (A Side/B Side)	Yr	VG	VG+	NM
45s					
ONYX					
502	Story of Love/The Boy Next Door	1956	25.00	50.00	100.00

JOYOUS NOISE

Number	Title (A Side/B Side)	Yr	VG	VG+	NM
Albums					
CAPITOL					
SMAS-844	Joyous Noise	1971	5.00	10.00	20.00

JOYTONES, THE

Number	Title (A Side/B Side)	Yr	VG	VG+	NM
45s					
RAMA					
191	All My Love Belongs to You/You Just Won't Treat Me Right	1956	37.50	75.00	150.00
202	Gee What a Boy/Is This Really the End	1956	75.00	150.00	300.00
215	My Foolish Heart/Jimbo Jango	1956	125.00	250.00	500.00

JULIAN, DON, AND THE MEADOWLARKS

Also see THE LARKS.

Number	Title (A Side/B Side)	Yr	VG	VG+	NM
45s					
CLASSIC ARTISTS					
101	Quickie Wedding/Our Love	1988	—	2.00	4.00
105	White Christmas/Marry Christmas, Baby	1988	—	3.00	6.00
DOOTO					
424	Blue Moon/Big Mama Wants to Rock	1957	12.50	25.00	50.00
DOOTONE					
359	Heaven and Paradise/Embarrassing Moments	1955	75.00	150.00	300.00
367	Always and Always/I Got Tore Up	1955	18.75	37.50	75.00
—Red label					
367	Always and Always/I Got Tore Up	1955	12.50	25.00	50.00
—Maroon label					
372	This Must Be Paradise/Mine All Mine	1955	15.00	30.00	60.00
394	Please Love a Fool/Oop Boopy Oop	1956	12.50	25.00	50.00
405	I Am a Believer/Boogie Woogie Teenager	1956	20.00	40.00	80.00
DYNAMITE					
1112	Heaven Only Knows/Popeye	1962	7.50	15.00	30.00
ORIGINAL SOUND					
3	Please Say You Want Me/Doin' the Cha Cha Cha	1959	10.00	20.00	40.00
12	There's a Girl/Blue Moon	1960	7.50	15.00	30.00
RPM					
399	Love Only You/Heal Pretty Mama	1954	75.00	150.00	300.00
—As "The Meadow Larks"					
406	LSMFT Blues (Lord Find My Sweet Theresa)/Pass the Gin	1954	750.00	1500.	3000.
—As "The Meadow Larks"					
7-Inch Extended Plays					
DOOTO					
203	(contents unknown)	1958	50.00	100.00	200.00
203 [PS]	Don Julian and the Meadowlarks	1958	50.00	100.00	200.00
—Reissue of Dootone 203					

Number	Title (A Side/B Side)	Yr	VG	VG+	NM
DOOTONE					
203	(contents unknown)	1956	100.00	200.00	400.00
203 [PS]	Don Julian and the Meadowlarks	1956	100.00	200.00	400.00

JULIAN'S TREATMENT

Albums

Number	Title (A Side/B Side)	Yr	VG	VG+	NM
DECCA					
DL 75224	A Time Before This	1970	5.00	10.00	20.00

JULIANA

45s

Number	Title (A Side/B Side)	Yr	VG	VG+	NM
RCA VICTOR					
47-7906	You Can Have Any Boy/You're Saying Goodnight	1961	15.00	30.00	60.00

JULY

Albums

Number	Title (A Side/B Side)	Yr	VG	VG+	NM
EPIC					
BN 26416	July	1969	50.00	100.00	200.00

JUMPIN' JACKS, THE

45s

Number	Title (A Side/B Side)	Yr	VG	VG+	NM
DECCA					
29973	You'll Wonder Where the Yellow Went/A Frantic Antic	1956	7.50	15.00	30.00
29973 [PS]	You'll Wonder Where the Yellow Went/A Frantic Antic	1956	10.00	20.00	40.00

JUNIOR'S EYES

Albums

Number	Title (A Side/B Side)	Yr	VG	VG+	NM
A&M					
SP-4189	Junior's Eyes	1970	5.00	10.00	20.00

JUNIOR AND HIS FRIENDS

45s

Number	Title (A Side/B Side)	Yr	VG	VG+	NM
ABC-PARAMOUNT					
10089	Who's Our Pet, Annette!/A.B.C. Love	1960	7.50	15.00	30.00

JUSTICE, JIMMY

45s

Number	Title (A Side/B Side)	Yr	VG	VG+	NM
BLUE CAT					
101	Don't Let the Stars Get In Your Eyes/Guitar Player (Her and Him)	1964	2.50	5.00	10.00
KAPP					
469	Ain't That Funny/One	1962	3.00	6.00	12.00
482	When My Little Girl Is Smiling/If I Lost Your Love	1962	3.00	6.00	12.00
514	I Wake Up Crying/World of Lonely People	1963	3.00	6.00	12.00

Albums

Number	Title (A Side/B Side)	Yr	VG	VG+	NM
KAPP					
KL-1308 [M]	Justice for All	1963	6.25	12.50	25.00
KS-3308 [S]	Justice for All	1963	10.00	20.00	40.00

JUSTIS, BILL

45s

Number	Title (A Side/B Side)	Yr	VG	VG+	NM
BELL					
921	Electric Dreams/Dark Continent Contribution	1970	—	2.50	5.00
MCA					
40810	Foxy Lady/Orange Blossom Special	1977	—	2.00	4.00
MONUMENT					
956	Yellow Summer/So Until I See You	1966	2.50	5.00	10.00
8699	Sea Dream/Touching, Feeling, Dreaming	1976	—	2.50	5.00
NRC					
1119	Blowing Rock/Boogie Woogie Rock	1959	5.00	10.00	20.00
PHILLIPS INTERNATIONAL					
3519	Raunchy/Midnight Man	1957	5.00	10.00	20.00
3522	College Man/The Stranger	1958	5.00	10.00	20.00
3525	Wild Ride/Scroungie	1958	5.00	10.00	20.00
3529	Cattywampus/Summer Holiday	1958	5.00	10.00	20.00
3535	Bop Train/String of Pearls	1958	5.00	10.00	20.00
3544	Flea Circus/Cloud Nine	1959	5.00	10.00	20.00
SMASH					
1812	I'm Gonna Learn to Dance/Tamoure	1963	2.50	5.00	10.00
1812 [PS]	I'm Gonna Learn to Dance/Tamoure	1963	4.00	8.00	16.00
1851	Sunday in Madrid/Satin and Velvet	1963	2.50	5.00	10.00
1902	Lavender Sax/Fia, Fia	1964	2.50	5.00	10.00
1955	How Soon/Ska-Ha	1964	2.50	5.00	10.00
1977	Late Game/Last Farewell	1965	2.50	5.00	10.00

Albums

Number	Title (A Side/B Side)	Yr	VG	VG+	NM
HARMONY					
KH 31189	Enchanted Sea	1972	3.00	6.00	12.00
MONUMENT					
MLP 8078 [M]	The Eternal Sea	1967	3.75	7.50	15.00
SLP 18078 [S]	The Eternal Sea	1967	3.75	7.50	15.00
PHILLIPS INTERNATIONAL					
PLP-1950 [M]	Cloud Nine	1959	100.00	200.00	400.00
SMASH					
MGS-27021 [M]	Bill Justis Plays 12 Big Instrumental Hits (Alley Cat/Green Onions)	1962	3.75	7.50	15.00
MGS-27030 [M]	Bill Justis Plays 12 More Big Instrumental Hits (Telstar/The Lonely Bull)	1963	3.75	7.50	15.00
MGS-27031 [M]	Bill Justis Plays 12 Smash Instrumental Hits	1963	3.75	7.50	15.00
MGS-27036 [M]	Bill Justis Plays 12 Top Tunes	1963	3.75	7.50	15.00
MGS-27043 [M]	Bill Justis Plays 12 Other Instrumental Hits	1964	3.75	7.50	15.00
MGS-27047 [M]	Dixieland Folk Style	1964	3.75	7.50	15.00
MGS-27065 [M]	More Instrumental Hits	1965	3.75	7.50	15.00
MGS-27077 [M]	Taste of Honey/The "In" Crowd	1966	3.75	7.50	15.00
SRS-67021 [S]	Bill Justis Plays 12 Big Instrumental Hits (Alley Cat/Green Onions)	1962	5.00	10.00	20.00
SRS-67030 [S]	Bill Justis Plays 12 More Big Instrumental Hits (Telstar/The Lonely Bull)	1963	5.00	10.00	20.00
SRS-67031 [S]	Bill Justis Plays 12 Smash Instrumental Hits	1963	5.00	10.00	20.00
SRS-67036 [S]	Bill Justis Plays 12 Top Tunes	1963	5.00	10.00	20.00
SRS-67043 [S]	Bill Justis Plays 12 Other Instrumental Hits	1964	5.00	10.00	20.00
SRS-67047 [S]	Dixieland Folk Style	1964	5.00	10.00	20.00
SRS-67065 [S]	More Instrumental Hits	1965	5.00	10.00	20.00
SRS-67077 [S]	Taste of Honey/The "In" Crowd	1966	5.00	10.00	20.00
830898-1	Raunchy	1987	2.50	5.00	10.00
SUN					
LP-109	Raunchy	1969	3.00	6.00	12.00

K

K.C. AND THE SUNSHINE BAND

Includes K.C. as a solo performer.

12-Inch Singles

Number	Title (A Side/B Side)	Yr	VG	VG+	NM
EPIC					
03187	(You Said) You'd Gimme Some More (7:33)/(Instrumental)	1982	2.00	4.00	8.00
SUNSHINE SOUND					
207	Do You Wanna Go Party (7:27) (10:00)	1979	2.00	4.00	8.00

45s

Number	Title (A Side/B Side)	Yr	VG	VG+	NM
CASABLANCA					
2227	Yes I'm Ready/With Your Love	1979	—	2.00	4.00
—As "Teri DeSario with K.C."					
2278	Dancin' in the Streets/Moonlight Madness	1980	—	2.00	4.00
—As "Teri DeSario with K.C."					
812991-7	Yes I'm Ready/Dancin' in the Streets	1983	—	2.00	4.00
—As "Teri DeSario with K.C."; reissue					
EPIC					
03286	When You Dance to the Music/(You Said) You'd Gimme Some More	1982	—	2.00	4.00
03356	On the Line/Don't Run	1983	—	2.00	4.00
—B-side features Teri DeSario					
MECA					
1001	Give It Up/(Instrumental)	1983	—	2.00	4.00
—K.C. solo					
SUNSHINE SOUND					
02545	Love Me/Don't Say No	1981	—	2.00	4.00
02652	It Happens Every Night/Stand Up	1981	—	2.00	4.00
T.K.					
1001	Blow Your Whistle/I'm Going to Do Something Good	1973	—	2.50	5.00
—As "K.C. and the Sunshine Junkanoo Band"					
1003	Sound Your Funky Horn/Why Don't We Get Together	1974	—	2.50	5.00
1005	Queen of Clubs/Do It Good	1974	—	2.50	5.00
1008	I'm a Pushover/You Don't Know	1974	—	2.50	5.00
1009	Get Down Tonight/You Don't Know	1975	—	2.00	4.00
1010	Shotgun Shuffle/Hey J	1975	—	2.00	4.00
—As "The Sunshine Band"					
1015	That's the Way (I Like It)/What Makes You Happy	1975	—	2.00	4.00
1018	Rock Your Baby/S.O.S.	1976	—	2.00	4.00
—As "The Sunshine Band"					
1019	(Shake, Shake, Shake) Shake Your Booty/Boogie Shoes	1976	—	2.00	4.00
1020	I Like to Do It/Come On In	1976	—	2.00	4.00
1022	I'm Your Boogie Man/Wrap Your Arms Around Me	1977	—	2.00	4.00
1023	Keep It Comin' Love/Baby I Love You	1977	—	2.00	4.00
1023 [PS]	Keep It Comin' Love/Baby I Love You	1977	—	2.50	5.00
1025	Boogie Shoes/I Get Lifted	1978	—	2.00	4.00
1025 [PS]	Boogie Shoes/I Get Lifted	1978	—	3.00	6.00
1026	Black Water Gold (Part 1)/Black Water Gold (Part 2)	1978	—	2.00	4.00
—As "The Sunshine Band"					
1028	It's the Same Old Song/Let's Go Party	1978	—	2.00	4.00
1028 [PS]	It's the Same Old Song/Let's Go Party	1978	—	2.00	4.00
1030	Do You Feel All Right/I Will Love You Tomorrow	1978	—	2.00	4.00
1030 [PS]	Do You Feel All Right/I Will Love You Tomorrow	1978	—	2.00	4.00
1031	Who Do Ya Love/Sho-Nuff	1978	—	2.00	4.00
1031 [PS]	Who Do Ya Love/Sho-Nuff	1978	—	2.00	4.00
1033	Do You Wanna Go Party/Come to My Island	1979	—	2.00	4.00
1035	Please Don't Go/I Betcha Didn't Know That	1979	—	2.00	4.00
1036	Let's Go Rock and Roll/I've Got the Feeling	1980	—	2.00	4.00
1037	Que Pasa?/Por Favor No Te Vayas	1980	—	2.00	4.00
1038	Make Me a Star/Do Me	1980	—	2.00	4.00
—K.C. solo					
1044	Space Cadet/Do Me	1981	—	2.00	4.00
—K.C. solo					
1048	Redlight/I Don't Wanna Make Love	1982	—	2.00	4.00
—K.C. solo					

Albums

Number	Title (A Side/B Side)	Yr	VG	VG+	NM
EPIC					
FE 37490	The Painter	1981	2.50	5.00	10.00
PE 37490	The Painter	1982	2.00	4.00	8.00
—Budget-line reissue					
FE 38073	All in a Night's Work	1982	2.50	5.00	10.00
PE 38073	All in a Night's Work	1984	2.00	4.00	8.00
—Budget-line reissue					
MECA					
8301	KC Ten	1984	2.50	5.00	10.00
SUNSHINE SOUND					
614	Space Cadet/Solo Flight	1981	2.50	5.00	10.00
T.K.					
500	Do It Good	1974	3.00	6.00	12.00
603	K.C. and the Sunshine Band	1975	2.50	5.00	10.00
604	The Sound of Sunshine	1975	2.50	5.00	10.00
—By "The Sunshine Band" (all instrumental)					
605	Part 3	1976	2.50	5.00	10.00
607	Who Do Ya (Love)	1978	2.50	5.00	10.00
611	Do You Wanna Go Party	1979	2.50	5.00	10.00
612	Greatest Hits	1980	2.50	5.00	10.00

K.C. AND THE SUNSHINE BAND AND KOOL & THE GANG FEATURING JT TAYLOR

45s

Number	Title (A Side/B Side)	Yr	VG	VG+	NM
EMI-CAPITOL					
S7-19725	Casper, the Friendly Ghost/Delicious	1997	—	—	3.00
—B-side by Shampoo					

K-DOE, ERNIE

45s

Number	Title (A Side/B Side)	Yr	VG	VG+	NM
DUKE					
378	My Mother-in-Law (Is In My Hair Again)/Looking Into the Future	1964	2.00	4.00	8.00
387	Little Bit of Everything/Someone	1965	2.00	4.00	8.00
400	Please Don't Stop/Boomerang	1966	2.00	4.00	8.00
404	Little Marie/Somebody Told Me	1966	2.00	4.00	8.00
411	Later for Tomorrow/Dancin' Man	1966	2.00	4.00	8.00
420	Love Me Like I Wanna/Don't Kill My Groove	1967	2.00	4.00	8.00
423	(It Will Have to Do) Until the Real Thing Comes Along/Little Marie	1967	2.00	4.00	8.00
437	Gotta Pack My Bag/How Sweet You Are	1968	2.00	4.00	8.00
450	I'm Sorry/Trying to Make You Love Me	1969	2.00	4.00	8.00
456	I'll Make Everything Be Alright/Wishing in Vain	1969	2.00	4.00	8.00
EMBER					
1050	My Love for You/Tuff-Enuff	1959	6.25	12.50	25.00
1075	My Love for You/Shirley's Tuff	1961	3.75	7.50	15.00
INSTANT					
3260	Baby, Since I Met You/Sufferin' So	1963	2.50	5.00	10.00
3264	Reaping What I Sow/Talking Out of My Head	1964	2.50	5.00	10.00
ISLAND					
031	Let Me Love You/So Good	1975	—	3.00	6.00
JANUS					
167	Here Come the Girls/Long Way Home	1971	—	3.00	6.00
MINIT					
604	Make You Love Me/There's a Will, There's a Way	1959	7.50	15.00	30.00
614	'Tain't It the Truth/Hello My Lover	1960	5.00	10.00	20.00
623	Mother-in-Law/Wanted, $10,000 Reward	1961	6.25	12.50	25.00
—Side 1 is at the correct speed. Trail-off number is "SO-738-2"					
623	Mother-in-Law/Wanted, $10,000 Reward	1961	50.00	100.00	200.00
—Side 1 was accidentally mis-mastered at 33 1/3 rpm. Trail-off number is "45-SO-738"					
627	Te-Ta-Te-Ta-Ta/Real Man	1961	3.75	7.50	15.00
634	A Certain Girl/I Cried My Last Tear	1961	3.75	7.50	15.00
641	Popeye Joe/Come On Home	1962	3.75	7.50	15.00
645	Hey Hey Hey/Love You the Best	1962	3.75	7.50	15.00
651	Beating Like a Tom-Tom/I Got to Find Somebody	1962	3.75	7.50	15.00
656	Loving You/Get Out of My House	1962	3.75	7.50	15.00
661	Easier Said Than Done/Be Sweet	1963	3.75	7.50	15.00
665	I'm the Boss/Pennies Worth o' Happiness	1963	3.75	7.50	15.00
SANSU					
1006	Stoop Down/(B-side unknown)	197?	5.00	10.00	20.00
1016	Hotcha Mama/She Gave It All to Me	197?	5.00	10.00	20.00
SPECIALTY					
563	Eternity/Do Baby Do	1955	10.00	20.00	40.00
—As "Ernest Kador"					
UNITED ARTISTS					
0110	Mother-in-Law/A Wonderful Dream	1973	—	2.50	5.00
—"Silver Spotlight Series" reissue; B-side by the Majors					

Albums

Number	Title (A Side/B Side)	Yr	VG	VG+	NM
JANUS					
JLS-3030	Ernie K-Doe	1971	6.25	12.50	25.00
MINIT					
LP-0002 [M]	Mother-in-Law	1961	50.00	100.00	200.00
—Orange label					
LP-24002 [R]	Mother-in-Law	196?	37.50	75.00	150.00
—Black label, not issued until after Imperial bought Minit					

KACT-TIES, THE

45s

Number	Title (A Side/B Side)	Yr	VG	VG+	NM
ATCO					
6299	Oh What a Night/Let Me In Your Life	1964	3.75	7.50	15.00
—As "The Kac-Ties"					
KAPE					
501	Happy Birthday/Girl in My Heart	1965	3.75	7.50	15.00
—As "The Kac-Ties"					
502	Walkin' in the Rain/Smile	1965	3.75	7.50	15.00
—As "The Kac-Ties"					
503	Let Your Love Light Shine/Were-Wolf	1965	3.75	7.50	15.00
—As "The Kac-Ties"					
SHELLEY					
163	Let Your Love Light Shine/Were-Wolf	1963	6.25	12.50	25.00
165	Oh What a Night/Let Me In Your Life	1963	6.25	12.50	25.00
TRANS ATLAS					
695	Walkin' in the Rain/Smile	1962	75.00	150.00	300.00
—With thunderstorm sound effects					
695	Walkin' in the Rain/Smile	1962	37.50	75.00	150.00
—Without thunderstorm sound effects					

KAEMPFERT, BERT

45s

Number	Title (A Side/B Side)	Yr	VG	VG+	NM
DECCA					
30616	Midnight Blues/Ducky	1958	2.50	5.00	10.00
30866	Cerveza/Catalina	1959	2.00	4.00	8.00
31141	Wonderland by Night/Dreaming the Blues	1960	2.00	4.00	8.00
31236	Tenderly/Without Your Love	1961	2.00	4.00	8.00
31279	Now and Forever/Only Those in Love	1961	2.00	4.00	8.00
31350	Afrikaan Beat/Echo in the Night	1961	2.00	4.00	8.00
31388	That Happy Feeling/Take Me	1962	2.00	4.00	8.00
31420	Goden Wings in the Sun/Cinderella After Midnight	1962	2.00	4.00	8.00
31439	Happy Trumpeter/Tootsie Flutie	1962	2.00	4.00	8.00
31463	Gentleman Jim/Tipsy Gypsy	1963	—	3.00	6.00
31498	Danke Schoen/Give and Take	1963	—	3.00	6.00
31532	The Bass Walks/Don't Talk to Me	1963	—	3.00	6.00
31560	Little Drummer Boy/Jingo Jango	1963	2.50	5.00	10.00
31611	Dancing in a Dream/Big Build Up	1964	—	3.00	6.00
31638	L-O-V-E/Blue Midnight	1964	—	3.00	6.00
31666	Almost There/Treat for Trumpet	1964	—	3.00	6.00
31722	Red Roses for a Blue Lady/Lonely Nightingale	1965	—	3.00	6.00
31778	Three O'Clock in the Morning/Nothing's New	1965	—	3.00	6.00
31812	Moon Over Naples/The Moon Is Making Eyes	1965	—	3.00	6.00
31873	Holiday for Bells/Jumpin' Jiminy Christmas	1965	2.00	4.00	8.00

Number	Title (A Side/B Side)	Yr	VG	VG+	NM
31882	Bye Bye Blues/Remember When	1965	—	3.00	6.00
31882 [PS]	Bye Bye Blues/Remember When	1965	—	—	—

—Rumored to exist, but without conclusive evidence, we will delete this from future editions

Number	Title (A Side/B Side)	Yr	VG	VG+	NM
31945	Strangers in the Night/But Not Today	1966	—	3.00	6.00
32008	I Can't Give You Anything But Love/Milica	1966	—	3.00	6.00
32051	So What's New/Hold Back the Dawn	1966	—	3.00	6.00
32094	Pussy Footin'/Hold Me	1967	—	3.00	6.00
32159	Talk/Night Dreams	1967	—	3.00	6.00
32204	Love for Love/You Are My Sunshine	1967	—	3.00	6.00
32241	Caravan/Milina	1967	—	3.00	6.00
32283	The First Waltz/Somebody Loves You	1968	—	2.50	5.00
32329	Mister Sandman/Lonely Is the Name	1968	—	2.50	5.00
32379	My Way of Life/Malaysian Melody	1968	—	2.50	5.00
32471	One Lonely Night/The Maltese Melody	1969	—	2.50	5.00
32518	Games People Play/Here's My Life (Here's My Love)	1969	—	2.50	5.00
32647	Someday We'll Be Together/We Can Make It Girl	1970	—	2.50	5.00
32715	Theme from "You Can't Win Them All"/Flight to Mecca	1970	—	2.50	5.00
32772	Something/Sweet Caroline	1971	—	2.50	5.00
32809	(I'll Be With You) In Apple Blossom Time/My Life	1971	—	2.50	5.00
32875	Proud Mary/In Our Time	1971	—	2.50	5.00
32935	Lonely Is the Name/Only a Fool	1972	—	2.50	5.00

MCA

Number	Title (A Side/B Side)	Yr	VG	VG+	NM
40221	The Most Beautiful Girl/Moon Over Baja	1974	—	2.00	4.00

7-Inch Extended Plays

DECCA

Number	Title (A Side/B Side)	Yr	VG	VG+	NM
ED 2697	Wonderland by Night/Dreaming the Blues//As I Love You/Tammy	1961	2.50	5.00	10.00
ED 2697 [PS]	Wonderland by Night	1961	2.50	5.00	10.00
ED 2721	That Happy Feeling/Take Me//Happy Trumpeter/Sunday in Madrid	196?	2.50	5.00	10.00
ED 2721 [PS]	That Happy Feeling	196?	2.50	5.00	10.00
ED 2766	Danke Schoen/Bass Walks//Gentleman Jim/Tipsy Wipsy	196?	2.50	5.00	10.00
ED 2766 [PS]	Danke Schoen	196?	2.50	5.00	10.00
ED 2796	(contents unknown)	196?	2.50	5.00	10.00
ED 2796 [PS]	Red Roses for a Blue Lady	196?	2.50	5.00	10.00

Albums

DECCA

Number	Title (A Side/B Side)	Yr	VG	VG+	NM
DL 4101 [M]	Wonderland by Night	1960	3.75	7.50	15.00
DL 4117 [M]	The Wonderland of Bert Kaempfert	1961	3.75	7.50	15.00
DL 4161 [M]	Dancing in Wonderland	1961	3.75	7.50	15.00
DL 4228 [M]	With a "Sound" in My Heart	1962	3.00	6.00	12.00
DL 4265 [M]	Lights Out, Sweet Dreams	1963	3.00	6.00	12.00
DL 4273 [M]	Afrikaan Beat and Other Favorites	1962	3.00	6.00	12.00
DL 4305 [M]	That Happy Feeling	1962	3.00	6.00	12.00
DL 4374 [M]	Living It Up!	1963	3.00	6.00	12.00
DL 4441 [M]	Christmas Wonderland	1963	3.75	7.50	15.00
DL 4490 [M]	That Latin Feeling	1964	3.00	6.00	12.00
DL 4569 [M]	Blue Midnight	1965	3.00	6.00	12.00
DL 4616 [M]	The Magic Music of Far Away Places	1965	3.00	6.00	12.00
DL 4670 [M]	Three O'Clock in the Morning	1965	3.00	6.00	12.00
DL 4693 [M]	Bye Bye Blues	1966	3.00	6.00	12.00
DL 4795 [M]	Strangers in the Night	1966	3.00	6.00	12.00
DL 4810 [M]	Bert Kaempfert's Greatest Hits	1966	3.00	6.00	12.00
DL 4860 [M]	Hold Me	1967	3.00	6.00	12.00
DL 4925 [M]	The World We Knew	1967	5.00	10.00	20.00
DL 4986 [M]	Love That	1968	5.00	10.00	20.00
DXS 7200 [(2)]	The Best of Bert Kaempfert	197?	5.00	10.00	20.00
DL 8881 [M]	April in Portugal	1959	3.75	7.50	15.00
DL 34485	The Best of Bert Kaempfert	197?	5.00	10.00	20.00

—Special Decca Custom Division edition

Number	Title (A Side/B Side)	Yr	VG	VG+	NM
DL 74101 [S]	Wonderland by Night	1960	5.00	10.00	20.00
DL 74117 [S]	The Wonderland of Bert Kaempfert	1961	5.00	10.00	20.00
DL 74161 [S]	Dancing in Wonderland	1961	5.00	10.00	20.00
DL 74228 [S]	With a "Sound" in My Heart	1962	3.75	7.50	15.00
DL 74265 [S]	Lights Out, Sweet Dreams	1963	3.75	7.50	15.00
DL 74273 [S]	Afrikaan Beat and Other Favorites	1962	3.75	7.50	15.00
DL 74305 [S]	That Happy Feeling	1962	3.75	7.50	15.00
DL 74374 [S]	Living It Up!	1963	3.75	7.50	15.00
DL 74441 [S]	Christmas Wonderland	1963	4.00	8.00	16.00

—Same as above, but in stereo

Number	Title (A Side/B Side)	Yr	VG	VG+	NM
DL 74490 [S]	That Latin Feeling	1964	3.75	7.50	15.00
DL 74569 [S]	Blue Midnight	1965	3.75	7.50	15.00
DL 74616 [S]	The Magic Music of Far Away Places	1965	3.75	7.50	15.00
DL 74670 [S]	Three O'Clock in the Morning	1965	3.75	7.50	15.00
DL 74693 [S]	Bye Bye Blues	1966	3.75	7.50	15.00
DL 74795 [S]	Strangers in the Night	1966	3.75	7.50	15.00
DL 74810 [S]	Bert Kaempfert's Greatest Hits	1966	3.75	7.50	15.00
DL 74860 [S]	Hold Me	1967	3.75	7.50	15.00
DL 74925 [S]	The World We Knew	1967	3.75	7.50	15.00
DL 74986 [S]	Love That	1968	3.75	7.50	15.00
DL 75059	My Way of Life	1968	3.75	7.50	15.00
DL 75089	Warm and Wonderful	1969	3.75	7.50	15.00
DL 75140	Traces of Love	1969	3.75	7.50	15.00
DL 75175	The Kaempfert Touch	1970	3.75	7.50	15.00
DL 75234	Free and Easy	1970	3.75	7.50	15.00
DL 75256	Orange Colored Sky	1971	3.75	7.50	15.00
DL 75305	Bert Kaempfert Now!	1971	3.75	7.50	15.00
DL 75322	Six Plus Six	1972	3.75	7.50	15.00
DL 78881 [S]	April in Portugal	1959	5.00	10.00	20.00

MCA

Number	Title (A Side/B Side)	Yr	VG	VG+	NM
11	Bert Kaempfert's Greatest Hits	1973	2.50	5.00	10.00

—Reissue of Decca 74810

Number	Title (A Side/B Side)	Yr	VG	VG+	NM
314	The Fabulous Fifties	1973	3.00	6.00	12.00
447	Gallery	1974	3.00	6.00	12.00

KAK

Gary Yoder of BLUE CHEER was in this group.

45s

EPIC

Number	Title (A Side/B Side)	Yr	VG	VG+	NM
10383 [DJ]	Everything's Changing (Long Version)/Everything's Changing (Edited Version)	1968	5.00	10.00	20.00

—May be promo only

Number	Title (A Side/B Side)	Yr	VG	VG+	NM
10446	I've Got Time/Disbelievin'	1969	5.00	10.00	20.00

Albums

EPIC

Number	Title (A Side/B Side)	Yr	VG	VG+	NM
BN 26429	Kak	1969	62.50	125.00	250.00

KALABASH CORP., THE

Albums

UNCLE BILL

Number	Title (A Side/B Side)	Yr	VG	VG+	NM
KB-3114	The Kalabash Corp.	1970	20.00	40.00	80.00

KALEIDOSCOPE, THE

45s

EPIC

Number	Title (A Side/B Side)	Yr	VG	VG+	NM
10117	Elevator Man/Please	1967	7.50	15.00	30.00
10219	Little Orphan Annie/Why Try	1967	7.50	15.00	30.00
10239	I Found Out/Rampe Rampe	1967	7.50	15.00	30.00
10332	Just a Taste/Hello Trouble	1968	7.50	15.00	30.00
10481	Lie to Me/Let the Good Love Flow	1969	7.50	15.00	30.00
10500	Killing Floor/Lie to Me	1969	7.50	15.00	30.00

FONTANA

Number	Title (A Side/B Side)	Yr	VG	VG+	NM
1633	Jimmy Artichoke/Just How Much You Are	1968	—	—	—

—Unreleased

Albums

EPIC

Number	Title (A Side/B Side)	Yr	VG	VG+	NM
LN 24304 [M]	Side Trips	1967	7.50	15.00	30.00
LN 24333 [M]	Beacon from Mars	1967	15.00	30.00	60.00
BN 26304 [S]	Side Trips	1967	10.00	20.00	40.00
BN 26333 [S]	Beacon from Mars	1967	25.00	50.00	100.00
BN 26467	Incredible Kaleidoscope	1969	7.50	15.00	30.00
BN 26508	Bernice	1970	7.50	15.00	30.00

PACIFIC ARTS

Number	Title (A Side/B Side)	Yr	VG	VG+	NM
102	When Scopes Collide	1978	3.00	6.00	12.00

KALIN TWINS, THE

45s

AMY

Number	Title (A Side/B Side)	Yr	VG	VG+	NM
969	Thinkin' About You Baby/Sometimes It Comes	1966	2.00	4.00	8.00

DECCA

Number	Title (A Side/B Side)	Yr	VG	VG+	NM
30552	Jumpin' Jack/Walkin' to School	1958	5.00	10.00	20.00
30642	When/Three O'Clock Thrill	1958	6.25	12.50	25.00
30745	Forget Me Not/Dream of Me	1958	6.25	12.50	25.00
30807	It's Only the Beginning/Oh My Goodness	1959	5.00	10.00	20.00
30868	Cool/When I Look in the Mirror	1959	5.00	10.00	20.00
30911	Sweet Sugar Lips/Moody	1959	5.00	10.00	20.00
30977	Why Don't You Believe Me/The Meaning of the Blues	1959	5.00	10.00	20.00
30977 [PS]	Why Don't You Believe Me/The Meaning of the Blues	1959	7.50	15.00	30.00
31064	Loneliness/Chicken Thief	1960	3.75	7.50	15.00
31111	True to You/Blue, Blue Town	1960	3.75	7.50	15.00
31169	Zing! Went the Strings of My Heart/No Money Can Buy	1960	3.75	7.50	15.00
31220	Momma-Poppa/You Mean the World to Me	1961	3.75	7.50	15.00
31286	Bubbles (I'm Forever Blowing Bubbles)/One More Time	1961	3.75	7.50	15.00
31410	Trouble/A Picture of You	1962	3.75	7.50	15.00

7-Inch Extended Plays

DECCA

Number	Title (A Side/B Side)	Yr	VG	VG+	NM
ED 2623	(contents unknown)	1958	15.00	30.00	60.00
ED 2623 [PS]	When	1958	20.00	40.00	80.00
ED 2641	(contents unknown)	1958	12.50	25.00	50.00
ED 2641 [PS]	Forget Me Not	1958	15.00	30.00	60.00

Albums

DECCA

Number	Title (A Side/B Side)	Yr	VG	VG+	NM
DL 8812 [M]	The Kalin Twins	1959	25.00	50.00	100.00

VOCALION

Number	Title (A Side/B Side)	Yr	VG	VG+	NM
VL 3771 [M]	When	1966	3.75	7.50	15.00
VL 73771 [R]	When	1966	3.00	6.00	12.00

KALLEN, KITTY

45s

20TH CENTURY FOX

Number	Title (A Side/B Side)	Yr	VG	VG+	NM
471	Make Somebody Love You/Lies and More Lies	1964	2.00	4.00	8.00

BELL

Number	Title (A Side/B Side)	Yr	VG	VG+	NM
673	Summer, Summer Wind/Oba, Oba	1967	2.00	4.00	8.00

COLUMBIA

Number	Title (A Side/B Side)	Yr	VG	VG+	NM
40298	The High and the Mighty/Still You'd Break My Heart	1954	3.75	7.50	15.00

—With Harry James

Number	Title (A Side/B Side)	Yr	VG	VG+	NM
41236	When Will I Know/Love Is a Sacred Thing	1958	3.00	6.00	12.00
41473	If I Give My Heart to You/The Door That Won't Open	1959	3.00	6.00	12.00
41546	That Old Feeling/Need Me	1959	3.00	6.00	12.00
41622	Always in My Heart/Got a Date with an Angel	1960	3.00	6.00	12.00
41671	Make Love to Me/Heaven Help Me	1960	3.00	6.00	12.00
41769	Come Live with Me/Be True to Me	1960	3.00	6.00	12.00
41857	I Believe in You/The Things You Left in My Heart	1960	3.00	6.00	12.00
41934	Hey Good Lookin'/Raining in My Heart	1961	3.00	6.00	12.00
42038	Summertime Lies/Yassu	1961	3.00	6.00	12.00
42247	It Wasn't God Who Made Honky Tonk Angels/You Are My Sunshine	1961	3.00	6.00	12.00

DECCA

Number	Title (A Side/B Side)	Yr	VG	VG+	NM
28813	Lonely/Heartless Heart	1953	3.75	7.50	15.00
28904	A Little Lie/Are You Looking for a Sweetheart	1953	3.75	7.50	15.00

Number	Title (A Side/B Side)	Yr	VG	VG+	NM
29037	Little Things Mean a Lot/I Don't Think You Love Me Anymore	1954	3.75	7.50	15.00
29130	In the Chapel in the Moonlight/Take Everything But You	1954	3.75	7.50	15.00
29268	I Want You All to Myself (Just You)/Don't Let the Kitty Geddin	1954	3.75	7.50	15.00
29315	The Spirit of Christmas/Baby Brother (Santa Claus, Dear Santa Claus)	1954	3.00	6.00	12.00
29417	I'd Never Forgive Myself/Honestly	1955	3.00	6.00	12.00
29473	By Bayou Bay/Kitty Who?	1955	3.00	6.00	12.00
29548	If It's a Dream/Forgive Me	1955	3.00	6.00	12.00
29593	Let's Make the Most of Tonight/Just Between Friends	1955	3.00	6.00	12.00
29663	Only Forever/Come Spring	1955	3.00	6.00	12.00
29708	Sweet Kentucky Rose/How Lonely Can I Get?	1955	3.00	6.00	12.00
29959	True Love/Will I Always Be Your Sweetheart	1956	3.00	6.00	12.00
30049	How About Me/The Lonely One	1956	3.00	6.00	12.00
30144	Saturday Blues/Ah, Ah, Ah (The Song That Haunts)	1956	3.00	6.00	12.00
30267	Star Bright/Gently, Johnny	1957	3.00	6.00	12.00
30346	Teen-Age Heart/Hideaway Heart	1957	3.00	6.00	12.00
30516	Crying Roses/I Never Was the One	1957	3.00	6.00	12.00
88181	The Spirit of Christmas/Baby Brother (Santa Claus, Dear Santa Claus)	1954	3.00	6.00	12.00
—Children's Series issue					
88181 [PS]	The Spirit of Christmas/Baby Brother (Santa Claus, Dear Santa Claus)	1954	5.00	10.00	20.00
—Children's Series issue					
MERCURY					
5417	Juke Box Annie/Choo'n Gum	1950	5.00	10.00	20.00
5587	If You Want Some Lovin'/Last Night	1951	3.75	7.50	15.00
5700	I Wish I Had a Daddy in the White House/The Old Soft Shoe	1951	3.75	7.50	15.00
5727	Another Human Being of the Opposite Sex/More, More, More	1951	3.75	7.50	15.00
PHILIPS					
40375	One Grain of Sand/From Your Lips to the Arms of an Angel	1966	2.00	4.00	8.00
RCA VICTOR					
47-8124	My Coloring Book/Here's to Us	1962	2.50	5.00	10.00
47-8202	I'll Teach You How to Cry/We'll Cross That Bridge	1963	2.50	5.00	10.00
7-Inch Extended Plays					
DECCA					
ED 2164	(contents unknown)	1954	10.00	20.00	40.00
ED 2164 [PS]	Kitty Kallen Sings	1954	10.00	20.00	40.00
ED 2467	(contents unknown)	1956	6.25	12.50	25.00
ED 2467 [PS]	It's a Lonesome Old Town, Part 1	1956	6.25	12.50	25.00
ED 2468	(contents unknown)	1956	6.25	12.50	25.00
ED 2468 [PS]	It's a Lonesome Old Town, Part 2	1956	6.25	12.50	25.00
ED 2469	(contents unknown)	1956	6.25	12.50	25.00
ED 2469 [PS]	It's a Lonesome Old Town, Part 3	1956	6.25	12.50	25.00
MERCURY					
EP 1-3293	(contents unknown)	1955	10.00	20.00	40.00
EP 1-3293 [PS]	Pretty Kitty Kallen Sings, Vol. 1	1955	10.00	20.00	40.00
EP 1-3294	(contents unknown)	1955	10.00	20.00	40.00
EP 1-3294 [PS]	Pretty Kitty Kallen Sings, Vol. 2	1955	10.00	20.00	40.00
Albums					
COLUMBIA					
CL 1404 [M]	If I Give My Heart to You	1960	5.00	10.00	20.00
CL 1662 [M]	Honky Tonk Angel	1961	5.00	10.00	20.00
CS 8204 [S]	If I Give My Heart to You	1960	6.25	12.50	25.00
CS 8462 [S]	Honky Tonk Angel	1961	6.25	12.50	25.00
DECCA					
DL 8397 [M]	It's a Lonesome Old Town	1958	10.00	20.00	40.00
MERCURY					
MG 25206 [10]	Pretty Kitty Kallen Sings	1955	12.50	25.00	50.00
MOVIETONE					
71026 [M]	Delightfully	1967	3.75	7.50	15.00
S-72026 [S]	Delightfully	1967	3.75	7.50	15.00
RCA VICTOR					
LPM-2640 [M]	My Coloring Book	1963	5.00	10.00	20.00
LSP-2640 [S]	My Coloring Book	1963	6.25	12.50	25.00
VOCALION					
VL 3679 [M]	Little Things Mean a Lot	1959	6.25	12.50	25.00
WING					
MGW-12241 [M]	Kitty Kallen Sings	196?	3.75	7.50	15.00
SRW-16241 [R]	Kitty Kallen Sings	196?	3.00	6.00	12.00

KALLEN, KITTY (WITH RICHARD HAYES)

Number	Title (A Side/B Side)	Yr	VG	VG+	NM
45s					
MERCURY					
5466	Our Lady of Fatima/Honestly I Love You	1950	3.75	7.50	15.00
5499	Halls of Ivy/Dream	1950	3.75	7.50	15.00
5501	Silver Bells/A Bushel and a Peck	1950	3.75	7.50	15.00
5532	Silver Bells/Jing-a-Ling	1950	3.75	7.50	15.00
5564	It Is No Secret (What God Can Do)/Get Out the Old Records	1950	3.75	7.50	15.00
5586	The Aba Daba Honeymoon/I Don't Want to Love	1951	3.75	7.50	15.00
5661	Everyone Is Welcome (In the House of the Lord)/Good Luck	1951	3.75	7.50	15.00

KALLEN, KITTY, AND GEORGIE SHAW

Number	Title (A Side/B Side)	Yr	VG	VG+	NM
45s					
DECCA					
29776	Go On with the Wedding/The Second Greatest Sex	1955	3.00	6.00	12.00

KALLMANN, GUNTER, CHORUS

Number	Title (A Side/B Side)	Yr	VG	VG+	NM
45s					
4 CORNERS OF THE WORLD					
119	Music for Falling in Love/Serenade	1965	—	3.00	6.00
138	Wish Me a Rainbow/The Day the Rains Came	1966	—	3.00	6.00
139	Morning, Noon and Night/Chanson d'Amour	1967	—	3.00	6.00
144	Paint Yourself a Rainbow/This Is My Song	1967	—	3.00	6.00
146	Tammy/You Know What to Do	1967	—	3.00	6.00
148	Counting the Days/Our Day Will Come	1968	—	3.00	6.00
150	Talk to the Animals/In the Heat of the Night	1968	—	3.00	6.00
POLYDOR					
15008	Where's the Playground Susie/Once in Each Life	1969	—	2.50	5.00
Albums					
4 CORNERS OF THE WORLD					
FCL-4209 [M]	Serenade for Elisabeth	1965	3.00	6.00	12.00
FCS-4209 [S]	Serenade for Elisabeth	1965	3.75	7.50	15.00
FCL-4218 [M]	Serenade for a Lady in Love	1965	3.00	6.00	12.00
FCS-4218 [S]	Serenade for a Lady in Love	1965	3.75	7.50	15.00
FCL-4226 [M]	Songs for My Love	1966	3.00	6.00	12.00
FCS-4226 [S]	Songs for My Love	1966	3.75	7.50	15.00
FCL-4235 [M]	Wish Me a Rainbow	1966	3.00	6.00	12.00
FCS-4235 [S]	Wish Me a Rainbow	1966	3.75	7.50	15.00
FCL-4237 [M]	With All My Heart	1967	3.00	6.00	12.00
FCS-4237 [S]	With All My Heart	1967	3.75	7.50	15.00
FCS-4248	Live for Love	1968	3.00	6.00	12.00
FCS-4256	Love Is Blue	1968	3.00	6.00	12.00
POLYDOR					
24-	Once in Each Life	1969	2.50	5.00	10.00
24-	Early in the Morning	1970	2.50	5.00	10.00

KANE, EDEN

Number	Title (A Side/B Side)	Yr	VG	VG+	NM
45s					
FONTANA					
1891	Boys Cry/Don't Come Crying to Me	1964	3.00	6.00	12.00
1961	Hangin' Around/Do Something About You	1964	3.00	6.00	12.00
LONDON					
1993	Well, I Ask You/Before I Lose My Mind	1961	3.75	7.50	15.00
9508	Get Lost/I'm Telling You	1961	3.75	7.50	15.00
9516	Forget Me Not/New Kind of Lovin'	1962	3.75	7.50	15.00
9532	I Don't Know Why/Music for Strings	1962	3.75	7.50	15.00
T-A					
193	Reason to Believe/(B-side unknown)	1970	—	3.00	6.00

KANE, PAUL

See PAUL SIMON.

KANE'S COUSINS

Number	Title (A Side/B Side)	Yr	VG	VG+	NM
Albums					
SHOVE LOVE					
9827	Undergum Bubbleground	1969	10.00	20.00	40.00

KANGAROO

Number	Title (A Side/B Side)	Yr	VG	VG+	NM
45s					
MGM					
13960	I Never Tell Me Twice/Such a Long Long Time	1968	3.00	6.00	12.00
13961	Daydream Stallion/The Only Thing I Had	1968	3.00	6.00	12.00
—As "Barbara Keith and Kangaroo"					
13962	Frogg Giggin'/Maybe Tomorrow	1968	3.00	6.00	12.00
—As "N.D. Smart and Kangaroo"					
Albums					
MGM					
SE-4586	Kangaroo	1968	6.25	12.50	25.00

KANNIBAL KOMIX

Number	Title (A Side/B Side)	Yr	VG	VG+	NM
45s					
COLOSSUS					
118	Little Little/Neurotic Reaction	1970	2.00	4.00	8.00
Albums					
COLOSSUS					
1004	Kannibal Komix	1970	5.00	10.00	20.00

KANSAS

Number	Title (A Side/B Side)	Yr	VG	VG+	NM
12-Inch Singles					
CBS ASSOCIATED					
1747 [DJ]	Mainstream/Everybody's My Friend	1983	—	3.00	6.00
KIRSHNER					
1451 [DJ]	Play the Game Tonight/Confessions Pre-Release Montage	1982	2.00	4.00	8.00
1534 [DJ]	Right Away/Diamonds and Pearls	1982	2.00	4.00	8.00
MCA					
L33-17306 [DJ]	Can't Cry Anymore (same on both sides)	1987	—	3.00	6.00
45s					
CBS ASSOCIATED					
04057	Fight Fire with Fire/Incident on a Bridge	1983	—	—	3.00
04057 [PS]	Fight Fire with Fire/Incident on a Bridge	1983	—	2.00	4.00
04213	Everybody's My Friend/End of the Age	1983	—	—	3.00
04213 [PS]	Everybody's My Friend/End of the Age	1983	—	2.00	4.00
KIRSHNER					
02903	Play the Game Tonight/Play On	1982	—	2.00	4.00
03084	Right Away/Windows	1982	—	2.00	4.00
03084 [PS]	Right Away/Windows	1982	—	2.50	5.00
4253	Can I Tell You/The Pilgrimage	1974	—	3.00	6.00
4256	Bringing It Back/Lonely Wind	1974	—	3.00	6.00
4258	Song for America (Part 1)/Song for America (Part 2)	1975	—	3.00	6.00
4259	It's You/It Takes a Woman's Love to Make a Man	1975	—	3.00	6.00
4267	Carry On Wayward Son/Questions of My Childhood	1976	—	2.50	5.00
4270	What's On My Mind/Lonely Street	1977	—	2.00	4.00
4273	Point of Know Return/Closet Chronicles	1977	—	2.00	4.00
4274	Dust in the Wind/Paradox	1978	—	2.50	5.00
4276	Portrait (He Knew)/Lightning's Hand	1978	—	2.00	4.00
4280	Lonely Wind/Song for America	1979	—	2.00	4.00
4284	People of the South Wind/Stay Out of Trouble	1979	—	2.00	4.00
4285	Reason to Be/How My Soul Cries Out for You	1979	—	2.00	4.00
4291	Hold On/Don't Open Your Eyes	1980	—	2.00	4.00

Number	Title (A Side/B Side)	Yr	VG	VG+	NM
4292	Got to Rock On/No Room for a Stranger	1980	—	2.00	4.00
MCA					
52958	All I Wanted/We're Not Alone Anymore	1986	—	—	3.00
52958 [PS]	All I Wanted/We're Not Alone Anymore	1986	—	—	3.00
53027	Power/To 19	1987	—	—	3.00
53027 [PS]	Power/To 19	1987	—	—	3.00
53070	Can't Cry Anymore/Three Pretenders	1987	—	—	3.00
53070 [PS]	Can't Cry Anymore/Three Pretenders	1987	—	—	3.00
53425	Stand Beside Me/House on Fire	1988	—	—	3.00
Albums					
CBS ASSOCIATED					
QZ 38733	Drastic Measures	1983	2.00	4.00	8.00
QZ 39283	The Best of Kansas	1984	2.00	4.00	8.00
KIRSHNER					
AS 555 [DJ]	Two for the Show (Sampler)	1978	5.00	10.00	20.00
—Promo-only single disc of selections from 35660					
KZ 32817	Kansas	1974	3.00	6.00	12.00
PZ 32817	Kansas	197?	2.00	4.00	8.00
—Reissue					
PZ 33385	Song for America	1975	3.00	6.00	12.00
—Without bar code on cover					
PZ 33385	Song for America	198?	2.00	4.00	8.00
—With bar code on cover					
PZ 33806	Masque	1975	3.00	6.00	12.00
—Without bar code on cover					
PZ 33806	Masque	198?	2.00	4.00	8.00
—With bar code on cover					
JZ 34224	Leftoverture	1976	2.50	5.00	10.00
PZ 34224	Leftoverture	198?	2.00	4.00	8.00
—Budget-line reissue					
JZ 34929	Point of Know Return	1977	2.50	5.00	10.00
PZ2 35660 [(2)]	Two for the Show	1978	3.75	7.50	15.00
FZ 36008	Monolith	1979	2.50	5.00	10.00
PZ 36008	Monolith	198?	2.00	4.00	8.00
—Budget-line reissue					
FZ 36588	Audio-Visions	1980	2.50	5.00	10.00
PZ 36588	Audio-Visions	198?	2.00	4.00	8.00
—Budget-line reissue					
FZ 38002	Vinyl Confessions	1982	2.50	5.00	10.00
PZ 38002	Vinyl Confessions	198?	2.00	4.00	8.00
—Budget-line reissue					
HZ 44224	Leftoverture	1982	10.00	20.00	40.00
—Half-speed mastered edition					
HZ 44929	Point of Know Return	1982	10.00	20.00	40.00
—Half-speed mastered edition					
HZ 46008	Monolith	1982	12.50	25.00	50.00
—Half-speed mastered edition					
HZ 48002	Vinyl Confessions	1982	25.00	50.00	100.00
—Half-speed mastered edition					
MCA					
5838	Power	1986	2.00	4.00	8.00
6254	In the Spirit of Things	1988	2.00	4.00	8.00

KANTNER, PAUL/JEFFERSON STARSHIP

Also see JEFFERSON STARSHIP.

Number	Title (A Side/B Side)	Yr	VG	VG+	NM
45s					
RCA VICTOR					
74-0426	Let's Go Together/A Child Is Coming	1971	—	2.50	5.00
74-0426 [PS]	Let's Go Together/A Child Is Coming	1971	2.00	4.00	8.00
—As "Paul Kantner/Jefferson Starship"					
Albums					
RCA VICTOR					
AYL1-3868	Blows Against the Empire	1981	2.00	4.00	8.00
—Budget-line reissue					
LSP-4448	Blows Against the Empire	1970	3.75	7.50	15.00
LSP-4448 [DJ]	Blows Against the Empire	1970	37.50	75.00	150.00
—Clear vinyl promo					

KANTNER, PAUL, AND GRACE SLICK

Number	Title (A Side/B Side)	Yr	VG	VG+	NM
45s					
GRUNT					
BFBO-0094	Sketches of China/Ballad of Chrome Men	1973	—	2.50	5.00
—With David Freiberg					
65-0503	Sunfighter/China	1971	—	2.50	5.00
65-0503 [PS]	Sunfighter/China	1971	—	3.00	6.00
Albums					
GRUNT					
BXL1-0148	Baron Von Tollbooth and the Chrome Nun	1973	3.00	6.00	12.00
FTR-1002	Sunfighter	1971	3.75	7.50	15.00
—With booklet (deduct 33% if missing)					
AYL1-3799	Baron Von Tollbooth and the Chrome Nun	1980	2.00	4.00	8.00
—Budget-line reissue					

KAPLAN, GABRIEL

Number	Title (A Side/B Side)	Yr	VG	VG+	NM
45s					
ABC					
12027	De Amerikans/Ed Sullivan, Ed Sullivan	1974	2.00	4.00	8.00
ELEKTRA					
45369	Up Your Nose/Bye Centennial Minutes	1976	—	3.00	6.00
45369 [PS]	Up Your Nose/Bye Centennial Minutes	1976	2.00	4.00	8.00
Albums					
ABC					
D-815	Holes and Mellow Rolls	1974	3.75	7.50	15.00
—Original release with painting of ice-cream bars on cover					
D-905	Holes and Mellow Rolls	1976	3.00	6.00	12.00
—Reissue with photo of the "Welcome Back, Kotter" cast on cover					

KARTUNES, THE

Number	Title (A Side/B Side)	Yr	VG	VG+	NM
45s					
MGM					
12598	Raindrops/Will You Marry Me	1957	7.50	15.00	30.00
12680	Dedicated to Love/Willie the Weeper	1958	6.25	12.50	25.00

KASANDRA

Number	Title (A Side/B Side)	Yr	VG	VG+	NM
45s					
CAPITOL					
2342	Don't Pat Me On the Back and Call Me Brother/ Just Look in My Face	1968	2.00	4.00	8.00
Albums					
CAPITOL					
ST-2957	John W. Anderson Presents KaSandra	1968	3.75	7.50	15.00

KASENETZ-KATZ SINGING ORCHESTRAL CIRCUS

Number	Title (A Side/B Side)	Yr	VG	VG+	NM
45s					
BELL					
966	When He Come/Ah-La	1970	2.50	5.00	10.00
—As "Kasenetz-Katz Fighter Squadron"					
BUDDAH					
52	Down in Tennessee/Mrs. Green	1968	2.00	4.00	8.00
64	Quick Joey Small (Run Joey Run)/Mr. Jensen	1968	2.00	4.00	8.00
82	I'm in Love with You/To You, With Love	1969	2.00	4.00	8.00
90	Embrasez-Moi/Mrs. Green	1969	2.00	4.00	8.00
EPIC					
50443	Heart Get Ready for Love/Jungle Junk	1977	—	2.50	5.00
—As "K&K Super Cirkus"					
SUPER K					
109	Bubblegum March/Dong-Dong-Diki-Di-Ki-Dong	1970	2.00	4.00	8.00
Albums					
BUDDAH					
BDS-5020	Kasenetz-Katz Singing Orchestral Circus	1968	3.75	7.50	15.00
BDS-5028	Kasenetz-Katz Super Circus	1969	3.75	7.50	15.00

KATMANDU

Number	Title (A Side/B Side)	Yr	VG	VG+	NM
Albums					
MAINSTREAM					
S-6131	Katmandu	1971	10.00	20.00	40.00

KAUKONEN, JORMA

Also see HOT TUNA; JEFFERSON AIRPLANE.

Number	Title (A Side/B Side)	Yr	VG	VG+	NM
Albums					
GRUNT					
BFL1-0209	Quah	1973	3.00	6.00	12.00
BXL1-0209	Quah	197?	2.50	5.00	10.00
—Reissue with new prefix					
AYL1-3747	Quah	1981	2.00	4.00	8.00
—"Best Buy Series" reissue					
RCA VICTOR					
AFL1-3446	Jorma	1979	2.50	5.00	10.00
AFL1-3725	Barbecue King	1981	2.50	5.00	10.00

KAY, JOHN

Also see SPARROW; STEPPENWOLF.

Number	Title (A Side/B Side)	Yr	VG	VG+	NM
45s					
ABC DUNHILL					
4309	I'm Movin' On/Walk Beside Me	1972	—	2.00	4.00
4319	You Win Again/Somebody	1972	—	2.00	4.00
4351	Moonshine/Nobody Lives Here Anymore	1973	—	2.00	4.00
4360	Dance to My Song/Easy Evil	1973	—	2.00	4.00
COLUMBIA					
44769	Twistin'/Square-Headed People	1969	2.00	4.00	8.00
MERCURY					
74004	Say You Will/Give Me Some News I Can Use	1978	—	2.00	4.00
Albums					
ABC DUNHILL					
DSX-50120	Forgotten Songs & Unsung Heroes	1972	2.50	5.00	10.00
DSX-50147	My Sportin' Life	1973	2.50	5.00	10.00
MERCURY					
SRM-1-3715	All in Good Time	1978	2.50	5.00	10.00

KAY, JOHN, AND SPARROW

See SPARROW.

KAY, JOHN, AND STEPPENWOLF

See STEPPENWOLF.

KAY-GEES, THE

Number	Title (A Side/B Side)	Yr	VG	VG+	NM
45s					
DELITE					
903	Kilowatt/Kilowatt Invasion	1978	—	2.00	4.00
906	Cheek to Cheek/Tango Hustle	1978	—	2.00	4.00
913	Heavenly Love/Burn Me Up	1979	—	2.00	4.00
GANG					
321	You've Got to Keep On Bumpin' (Pt 1)/You've Got to Keep On Bumpin' (Pt 2)	1974	—	2.50	5.00
1322	Master Plan/(B-side unknown)	1974	—	2.50	5.00
1323	Get Down/My Favorite Song	1975	—	2.50	5.00
1325	Hustle Wit Every Muscle (Theme from "Party" TV Show)/(Instrumental)	1975	—	2.50	5.00
1326	Waiting at the Bus Stop (Part 1)/Waiting at the Bus Stop (Part 2)	1976	—	2.50	5.00
Albums					
DE-LITE					
9505	Kilowatt	1978	2.50	5.00	10.00
9510	Burn Me Up	1979	2.50	5.00	10.00
GANG					
101	Keep On Bumpin' & Masterplan	1975	2.50	5.00	10.00
102	Find a Friend	1975	2.50	5.00	10.00

KAYAK

Number	Title (A Side/B Side)	Yr	VG	VG+	NM
45s					
JANUS					
274	I Want You to Be Mine/Irene	1978	—	2.50	5.00
278	Keep the Change/Ivory Dance	1979	—	2.50	5.00

Number	Title (A Side/B Side)	Yr	VG	VG+	NM
MERCURY					
76059	Periscope Life/Stop That Song	1980	—	2.00	4.00
Albums					
HARVEST					
ST-11305	See See the Sun	1973	3.75	7.50	15.00
JANUS					
(no #) [PD]	Phantom of the Night	1979	6.25	12.50	25.00
—Numbered limited edition of 3,000					
NXS-7023	Royal Bed Bouncer	1975	2.50	5.00	10.00
NXS-7034	Starlight Dancer	1978	2.50	5.00	10.00
NXS-7039	Phantom of the Night	1979	2.50	5.00	10.00
MERCURY					
SRM-1-3824	Periscope Life	1980	2.50	5.00	10.00

KAYE, SAMMY

Number	Title (A Side/B Side)	Yr	VG	VG+	NM
45s					
COLUMBIA					
1-740 (?)	Guilty/Checky-Checky Hoopla	1950	7.50	15.00	30.00
—Microgroove 33 1/3 rpm 7-inch single					
6-740 (?)	Guilty/Checky-Checky Hoopla	1950	5.00	10.00	20.00
38963	Harbor Lights/Sugar Sweet	1950	3.75	7.50	15.00
39030	Patricia/Petite Waltz	1950	3.75	7.50	15.00
39036	To Think You've Chosen Me/You Oughta Be in Pictures	1950	3.75	7.50	15.00
39113	Tennessee Waltz/Get Out Those Old Records	1950	3.75	7.50	15.00
39140	Tell Me You Love Me/Dear Little Girl of Theta Chi	1950	3.75	7.50	15.00
39156	You and Beautiful You/Tonda Wonda Hoy	1951	3.75	7.50	15.00
39186	Peter Cottontail/Easter Parade	1951	3.75	7.50	15.00
39270	I Love You Because/Pretty Little Bells	1951	3.75	7.50	15.00
3-39270	I Love You Because/Pretty Little Bells	1951	5.00	10.00	20.00
—Microgroove 33 1/3 rpm 7-inch single (note prefix)					
39325	I'm Yours to Command/Shenandoah Waltz	1951	3.75	7.50	15.00
39360	My Prayer/Down the Trail of Aching Hearts	1951	3.75	7.50	15.00
39376	Come Back to Angeuleme/Please Don't Talk About Me	1951	3.75	7.50	15.00
39421	Del Rio/Would Mind	1951	3.75	7.50	15.00
39492	Dixie/Tennessee Tears	1951	3.75	7.50	15.00
39499	Longing for You/Mary Rose	1951	3.75	7.50	15.00
39531	It's All in the Game/Be Mine Tonight	1951	3.75	7.50	15.00
39567	(It's No) Sin/Jealous Eyes	1951	3.75	7.50	15.00
39572	Silent Night-O Little Town Of Bethlehem/Joy To The World-Hark the Herald Angels Sing-O Come All Ye Faithful	1951	3.00	6.00	12.00
39573	White Christmas/Jingle Bells	1951	3.00	6.00	12.00
39574	Winter Wonderland/Rudolph the Red-Nosed Reindeer	1951	3.00	6.00	12.00
39575	Frosty the Snow Man/Santa Claus Is Coming to Town	1951	3.00	6.00	12.00
—The above four comprise a box set					
39583	Daddy/Bouquet of Roses	1951	3.75	7.50	15.00
39602	The Three Bells/I Only Have One Life	1951	3.75	7.50	15.00
39633	You Know You Belong to Someone Else/My Lei-Ee-Yana	1952	3.75	7.50	15.00
39667	Wheel of Fortune/Goodbye Sweetheart	1952	3.75	7.50	15.00
39688	Winnipesaukee/I Ain't Lazy	1952	3.75	7.50	15.00
39724	You/Oh How I Miss You	1952	3.75	7.50	15.00
39731	You/Pittsburgh, Pennsylvania	1952	3.00	6.00	12.00
—B-side by Guy Mitchell; part of a 4-record box set					
39769	Walkin' to Missouri/One for the Wonder	1952	3.75	7.50	15.00
39771	Girl of My Dreams/My Extraordinary Girl	1952	3.00	6.00	12.00
39772	All the Things You Are/Who	1952	3.00	6.00	12.00
39773	Josephine/Would You Like to Take a Walk	1952	3.00	6.00	12.00
39774	Little Girl/We'll Meet Again	1952	3.00	6.00	12.00
—The above four comprise a box set					
39816	I Don't Know Any Better/God's Little Candles	1952	3.75	7.50	15.00
39856	It Wasn't God Who Made Honky Tonk Angels/I Went to Your Wedding	1952	3.75	7.50	15.00
39883	Forget Me Not/Sailin' Along the Ohio	1952	3.75	7.50	15.00
39894	All Around the Christmas Tree/Santa, Santa, Santa Claus	1952	3.75	7.50	15.00
39917	Hurry, Hurry, Hurry/Dance of Mexico	1953	3.00	6.00	12.00
39936	Lighthouse in the Harbor/Angel Made of Ice	1953	3.00	6.00	12.00
39957	Gomen-Sasai (Forgive Me)/Until Tomorrow	1953	3.00	6.00	12.00
39977	Sweet Sue-Just You/I Couldn't Keep from Crying	1953	3.00	6.00	12.00
39999	Orange Blossom Serenade/The Tattle-Tale Duck	1953	3.00	6.00	12.00
40025	The Midnight Ride/The One in Your Heart	1953	3.00	6.00	12.00
40061	In the Mission of St. Augustine/No Stone Unturned	1953	3.00	6.00	12.00
40151	Bella Bella Donna Mis/Y (That's Why)	1954	3.00	6.00	12.00
40205	Godspeed to You/Till You Kiss Me at the Altar	1954	3.00	6.00	12.00
40248	Dream for Sale/Sittin' 'n' Waitin'	1954	3.00	6.00	12.00
40269	Friends and Neighbors/Through	1954	3.00	6.00	12.00
40299	Sentimental/If We Should Ever Meet Again	1954	3.00	6.00	12.00
40417	Melody of Love/You Are the One	1955	3.00	6.00	12.00
40431	Hindustan/She Went That-a-Way	1955	3.00	6.00	12.00
40485	Impossible/Jim, Johnny and Jonas	1955	3.00	6.00	12.00
40517	The Banjo's Back in Town/Joe, Joe, Joe	1955	3.00	6.00	12.00
40518	Sweet and Lovely/Yearning	1955	3.00	6.00	12.00
40556	Queen of My Lonesome Heart/I'll Never Learn Cha-Cha-Cha	1955	3.00	6.00	12.00
40574	The Lucky Little Bell/Don't Cry Baby	1955	3.00	6.00	12.00
40621	Hey Pretty Girl/In the Valley of the Moon	1955	3.00	6.00	12.00
40645	We All Need Love/Try Another Cherry Tree	1956	3.00	6.00	12.00
40698	Once Again/Every Sunday Morning	1956	3.00	6.00	12.00
40707	I Could Have Danced All Night/I've Grown Accustomed to Your Face	1956	3.00	6.00	12.00
40752	The Rich People of Brooklyn/Dreamy River	1956	3.00	6.00	12.00
40795	Faded Roses/I'm Through with Love	1956	3.00	6.00	12.00
40839	I Met a Girl/Mountain of Kisses	1957	2.50	5.00	10.00
40869	Money/The Ship That Never Sailed	1957	2.50	5.00	10.00
40909	What a Saturday Night/A Young Lover's Dream	1957	2.50	5.00	10.00
40936	Past My Prime/Charm Bracelet	1957	2.50	5.00	10.00
40966	Charleston/Posin'	1957	2.50	5.00	10.00
40988	Mary Lou/Moonlight Swim	1957	2.50	5.00	10.00
41028	Ha, Ha, Ha/You'd Be Surprised	1957	2.50	5.00	10.00
41084	Garden of Allah/Well, Anyway	1957	2.50	5.00	10.00
41140	That Girl Next Door/Our First Formal Dance	1958	2.50	5.00	10.00
41178	That Daffodil Feelin'/Spain	1958	2.50	5.00	10.00
41206	Why Can't This Night Go On Forever/Yearning	1958	2.50	5.00	10.00
41255	Roses Remind Me of You/At the High School Prom	1958	2.50	5.00	10.00
41293	Sweet Leilani/How Good Can a Good Girl Be	1958	2.50	5.00	10.00
41348	Leave the Door Wide Open/Dah Dee (Daddy)	1959	2.50	5.00	10.00
41398	Until Tomorrow/Sammy Kaye's Theme Song	1959	2.50	5.00	10.00
41508	Deep Purple/Till Tomorrow	1959	2.50	5.00	10.00
41552	My Happiness/Melody of Love	1960	2.50	5.00	10.00
41656	Chopsticks Boogie/Harvey's Melody	1960	2.50	5.00	10.00
DECCA					
25511	Oh Johnny, Oh Johnny, Oh!/Got a Date with an Angel	1962	2.00	4.00	8.00
25555	After You've Gone/Who's Sorry Now	1962	2.00	4.00	8.00
25604	Roses Are Red/Ramblin' Rose	1963	2.00	4.00	8.00
25722	The Whiffenpoof Song/There Is a Tavern in the Town	1967	—	3.00	6.00
25752	Charley, My Boy/Hot Lips	1969	—	2.50	5.00
31174	Merry Merry Christmas (To You)/Silver Bells	1960	2.50	5.00	10.00
31175	Christmas Child (Loo, Loo, Loo)/Let It Snow, Let It Snow, Let It Snow	1960	2.50	5.00	10.00
31204	Welcome Home/What's New at the Zoo	1961	2.00	4.00	8.00
31264	I'm a Big Girl Now/Strange Interlude	1961	2.00	4.00	8.00
31294	Lydia, the Tattooed Lady/I'm Married to a Strip Tease Dancer	1961	2.00	4.00	8.00
31336	Swing and Sway Twist/Mama and Papa Twist	1961	3.00	6.00	12.00
31448	Big Deal/Shoot the Piano Player	1962	2.00	4.00	8.00
31589	Charade/Maria Elena	1964	—	3.00	6.00
31642	Night Train/Bedtime Story	1964	—	3.00	6.00
31700	House of the Rising Sun/Theme from Golden Boy	1964	—	3.00	6.00
31738	Night Walker/Sophia	1965	—	3.00	6.00
31773	Goldfinger/Blue Prelude	1965	—	3.00	6.00
31854	Hush...Hush, Sweet Charlotte/The Hucklebuck	1965	—	3.00	6.00
31935	Lara's Theme (from Dr. Zhivago)/Swedish Rhapsody (Madame X Love Theme)	1966	—	3.00	6.00
32034	Smile/In the Arms of Love	1966	—	3.00	6.00
32071	Oh, How I Miss You Tonight/Gambit	1966	—	3.00	6.00
32258	Talk to the Animals/Glory of Love	1968	—	2.50	5.00
32442	I Love to Cry at Weddings/I'm a Brass Band	1969	—	2.50	5.00
32624	Something/Juanita (Love Theme from "Topaz")	1970	—	2.50	5.00
PROJECT 3					
1421	For the Good Times/If You've Got the Time	1972	—	2.00	4.00
RCA VICTOR					
47-2810	Cuddle Up a Little Closer, Lovey Mine/I Want a Girl (Just Like the Girl That Married Dear Old Dad)	1949	3.75	7.50	15.00
47-2811	Down Among the Sheltering Palms/The World Is Waiting for the Sunrise	1949	3.75	7.50	15.00
47-2812	There But For You Go I/My Son	1949	3.75	7.50	15.00
47-2813	I Still Love You/We Just Couldn't Say Goodbye	1949	3.75	7.50	15.00
47-2862	April Showers/June Is Bustin' Out All Over	1949	3.75	7.50	15.00
47-2863	Indian Summer/September Song	1949	3.75	7.50	15.00
47-2864	White Christmas/Winter Wonderland	1949	3.75	7.50	15.00
47-2901	Careless Hands/Powder Your Face with Sunshine	1949	3.75	7.50	15.00
47-2908	Room Full of Roses/It's Springtime Again	1949	3.75	7.50	15.00
47-2923	The Four Winds and the Seven Seas/Out of Love	1949	3.75	7.50	15.00
47-2936	Belmont Boogie/Hollywood Square Dance	1949	3.75	7.50	15.00
47-2942	Fiddle Dee Dee/It's a Great Feeling	1949	3.75	7.50	15.00
47-3010	Dime a Dozen/Everything They Said Came True	1949	3.75	7.50	15.00
47-3038	The Last Mile Home/Hawaiian Sunset	1949	3.75	7.50	15.00
47-3048	Let's Harmonize/Makin' Love Ukulele Style	1949	3.75	7.50	15.00
47-3067	Funny Face/Toot Toot Tootsie	1949	3.75	7.50	15.00
47-3071	Here Comes Santa Claus/I Want to Wish You a Merry Christmas	1949	3.75	7.50	15.00
47-3075	My Little Grass Shack in Kaelakekua, Hawaii/My Tan	1949	3.75	7.50	15.00
47-3076	My Isle of Golden Dreams/Sweet Leilani	1949	3.75	7.50	15.00
47-3077	Hawaiian War Chant/Hawaiian Sunset	1949	3.75	7.50	15.00
47-3101	Careless Kisses/Echoes	1949	3.75	7.50	15.00
47-3115	It Isn't Fair/My Lily and My Rose	1950	3.75	7.50	15.00
47-3168	Always/Blue Skies	1950	3.75	7.50	15.00
47-3169	How Deep Is the Ocean/Say It Isn't So	1950	3.75	7.50	15.00
47-3170	Alexander's Ragtime Band/A Pretty Girl Is Like a Melody	1950	3.75	7.50	15.00
47-3203	Wanderin'/The Bicycle Song	1950	3.75	7.50	15.00
47-3754	Roses/Tiddley Winkle Woe	1950	3.75	7.50	15.00
47-3828	The Object of My Affection/I Thought She Was a Local	1950	3.75	7.50	15.00
47-3891	Miss You/There's No Use	1950	3.75	7.50	15.00
7-Inch Extended Plays					
COLUMBIA					
B-2546	Daddy/Harbor Lights//Walkin' to Missouri/In the Mission of St. Augustine	195?	3.75	7.50	15.00
B-2546 [PS]	Sammy Kaye (Hall of Fame Series)	195?	3.75	7.50	15.00
RCA CAMDEN					
CAE-264	You Always Hurt the One You Love/Taking a Chance on Love//Amapola/Taboo	195?	2.50	5.00	10.00
CAE-264 [PS]	Sammy Kaye and His Orchestra Play	195?	2.50	5.00	10.00
CAE-271	Easter Parade/Baby Face//Begin the Beguine/Pretty Baby	195?	2.50	5.00	10.00
CAE-271	Sammy Kaye and His Orchestra	195?	2.50	5.00	10.00
Albums					
COLUMBIA					
CL 561 [M]	Swing and Sway with Sammy Kaye	195?	7.50	15.00	30.00
CL 668 [M]	Music, Maestro, Please!	195?	7.50	15.00	30.00
CL 885 [M]	My Fair Lady (For Dancing)	1956	5.00	10.00	20.00
CL 891 [M]	What Makes Sammy Swing and Sway	1956	5.00	10.00	20.00
CL 964 [M]	Sunday Serenade	1957	5.00	10.00	20.00
CL 1018 [M]	Popular American Waltzes	1957	5.00	10.00	20.00
CL 1236 [M]	Strauss Waltzes for Dancing	1959	3.75	7.50	15.00
CL 2541 [10]	Christmas Serenade	1955	10.00	20.00	40.00
—"House Party Series" issue					

Number	Title (A Side/B Side)	Yr	VG	VG+	NM
CL 6155 [10]	Sunday Serenade	1953	10.00	20.00	40.00
DECCA					
DL 4070 [M]	Christmas Day with Sammy Kaye	1960	3.00	6.00	12.00
DL 4071 [M]	Sing and Sway with Sammy Kaye	1960	3.00	6.00	12.00
DL 4121 [M]	Dance to My Golden Favorites	1961	3.00	6.00	12.00
DL 4154 [M]	Songs I Wish I Had Played...The First Time Around	1961	3.00	6.00	12.00
DL 4215 [M]	Sexy Strings and Subtle Saxes	1962	3.00	6.00	12.00
DL 4247 [M]	New Twists on Old Favorites	1962	3.00	6.00	12.00
DL 4306 [M]	For Your Dancing Pleasure	1962	3.00	6.00	12.00
DL 4357 [M]	Come Dance with Me	1963	3.00	6.00	12.00
DL 4424 [M]	Dreamy Serenades	1963	3.00	6.00	12.00
DL 4502 [M]	Come Dance to the Hits	1964	3.00	6.00	12.00
DL 4590 [M]	Come Dance with Me (Vol. 2)	1965	3.00	6.00	12.00
DL 4655 [M]	Dancetime	1965	3.00	6.00	12.00
DL 4687 [M]	Swing and Sway Au-Go-Go	1965	3.00	6.00	12.00
DL 4754 [M]	Shall We Dance	1966	3.00	6.00	12.00
DL 4823 [M]	Let's Face the Music	1967	3.00	6.00	12.00
DL 4862 [M]	Swing & Sway in Hawaii	1967	3.75	7.50	15.00
DL 4924 [M]	Dance and Be Happy	1967	3.75	7.50	15.00
DL 4970 [M]	Glory of Love	1967	3.75	7.50	15.00
DL 74070 [S]	Christmas Day with Sammy Kaye	1960	3.75	7.50	15.00
DL 74071 [S]	Sing and Sway with Sammy Kaye	1960	3.75	7.50	15.00
DL 74121 [S]	Dance to My Golden Favorites	1961	3.75	7.50	15.00
DL 74154 [S]	Songs I Wish I Had Played...The First Time Around	1961	3.75	7.50	15.00
DL 74215 [S]	Sexy Strings and Subtle Saxes	1962	3.75	7.50	15.00
DL 74247 [S]	New Twists on Old Favorites	1962	3.75	7.50	15.00
DL 74306 [S]	For Your Dancing Pleasure	1962	3.75	7.50	15.00
DL 74357 [S]	Come Dance with Me	1963	3.75	7.50	15.00
DL 74424 [S]	Dreamy Serenades	1963	3.75	7.50	15.00
DL 74502 [S]	Come Dance to the Hits	1964	3.75	7.50	15.00
DL 74590 [S]	Come Dance with Me (Vol. 2)	1965	3.75	7.50	15.00
DL 74655 [S]	Dancetime	1965	3.75	7.50	15.00
DL 74687 [S]	Swing and Sway Au-Go-Go	1965	3.75	7.50	15.00
DL 74754 [S]	Shall We Dance	1966	3.75	7.50	15.00
DL 74823 [S]	Let's Face the Music	1967	3.75	7.50	15.00
DL 74862 [S]	Swing & Sway in Hawaii	1967	3.00	6.00	12.00
DL 74924 [S]	Dance and Be Happy	1967	3.00	6.00	12.00
DL 74970 [S]	Glory of Love	1967	3.00	6.00	12.00
DL 75106	The 30's Are Here to Stay	1968	3.00	6.00	12.00
HARMONY					
HL 7187 [M]	Dancing with Sammy Kaye in Hi-Fi	196?	3.75	7.50	15.00
HL 7230 [M]	In a Dancing Mood	196?	3.75	7.50	15.00
HL 7321 [M]	My Fair Lady	1964	3.75	7.50	15.00
HL 7357 [M]	Beautiful Waltzes for Dancing	196?	3.75	7.50	15.00
HS 11087 [R]	Dancing with Sammy Kaye in Hi-Fi	196?	3.00	6.00	12.00
HS 11121 [R]	My Fair Lady	1964	3.00	6.00	12.00
HS 11157 [R]	Beautiful Waltzes for Dancing	196?	3.00	6.00	12.00
HS 11261	All-Time Waltz Favorites	1968	3.00	6.00	12.00
HS 11377	Harbor Lights	1970	2.50	5.00	10.00
KH 32013	Best of the Big Bands	1971	2.50	5.00	10.00
HINDSIGHT					
HSR-158	1940-41	198?	2.50	5.00	10.00
HSR-163	1942-43	198?	2.50	5.00	10.00
HSR-207	1944-46	198?	2.50	5.00	10.00
HSR-402 [(2)]	22 Original Big Band Recordings	198?	3.00	6.00	12.00
MCA					
191	Dance to My Golden Favorites	1973	2.50	5.00	10.00
—Reissue of Decca 74121					
205	Plays Swing & Sway	1973	2.50	5.00	10.00
—Reissue of Decca 74306					
278	The 30's Are Here to Stay	197?	2.50	5.00	10.00
—Reissue of Decca material					
4027 [(2)]	The Best of Sammy Kaye	197?	3.00	6.00	12.00
PROJECT 3					
5065	Brand New Recordings	1972	3.00	6.00	12.00
RCA CAMDEN					
CAL-355 [M]	Swing and Sway with Sammy Kaye	1957	5.00	10.00	20.00
RCA VICTOR					
LPM-3966 [M]	The Best of Sammy Kaye	1967	5.00	10.00	20.00
LSP-3966 [R]	The Best of Sammy Kaye	1967	3.00	6.00	12.00
VPM-6070 [(2)]	This Is Sammy Kaye	1972	3.00	6.00	12.00
VOCALION					
VL 73919	Theme from "Love Story"	1971	2.50	5.00	10.00

KAYLI, BOB

45s

Number	Title (A Side/B Side)	Yr	VG	VG+	NM
ANNA					
1104	Never More/Peppermint (You Know What to Do)	1959	10.00	20.00	40.00
CARLTON					
482	Everyone Was There/I Took a Dare	1958	7.50	15.00	30.00
GORDY					
7004	Toodle Loo/Everyone Was There	1962	20.00	40.00	80.00
7008	Toodle Loo/Hold On Pearl	1962	7.50	15.00	30.00
TAMLA					
54051	Small Sad Sam/Tie Me Tight	1962	7.50	15.00	30.00

KAZAN, LAINIE

45s

Number	Title (A Side/B Side)	Yr	VG	VG+	NM
COLPIX					
768	Color of Love/Ouzo	1965	2.50	5.00	10.00
MGM					
13479	I'm Shooting High/No More Songs for Me	1966	2.00	4.00	8.00
13526	Can I Trust You/I Can't Remember (Ever Loving You)	1966	2.00	4.00	8.00
13657	Kiss Tomorrow Goodbye/Sweet Talk	1967	2.00	4.00	8.00
13777	Road to Ruin/What Did I Lose by Loving You	1967	2.00	4.00	8.00
13877	Sunny/When I Look in Your Eyes	1967	2.00	4.00	8.00
13943	Night Song/They Don't Give Medals	1968	2.00	4.00	8.00
POMPEII					
7001	Window on My Mind/It's You	1971	—	3.00	6.00

Albums

Number	Title (A Side/B Side)	Yr	VG	VG+	NM
MGM					
E-4340 [M]	Right Now	1966	5.00	10.00	20.00
SE-4340 [S]	Right Now	1966	6.25	12.50	25.00
E-4385 [M]	Lainie Kazan	1966	5.00	10.00	20.00
SE-4385 [S]	Lainie Kazan	1966	6.25	12.50	25.00
E-4451 [M]	The Love Album	1967	6.25	12.50	25.00
SE-4451 [S]	The Love Album	1967	5.00	10.00	20.00
SE-4496	Love Is	1968	5.00	10.00	20.00
SE-4631	The Best of Lainie Kazan	1969	5.00	10.00	20.00

KEGGS, THE

45s

Number	Title (A Side/B Side)	Yr	VG	VG+	NM
ORBIT					
20959	To Find Out/(B-side unknown)	1967	1000.	2000.	4000.

—Counterfeit identification: The producer's first name, "Yolanda," is misspelled "Yalanda" on fakes.

KEITH

45s

Number	Title (A Side/B Side)	Yr	VG	VG+	NM
COLUMBIA					
43268	Dream/Caravan of Lonely Men	1965	3.75	7.50	15.00
—As "Keith and the Admirations"					
DISCREET					
1193	What Did You Do in the Revolution, Dad/In and Out of Love	1974	—	2.50	5.00
MERCURY					
72596	Ain't Gonna Lie/Our Love Started All Over Again	1966	2.00	4.00	8.00
72639	98.6/The Teenie Bopper Song	1966	2.50	5.00	10.00
72639 [PS]	98.6/The Teenie Bopper Song	1966	3.75	7.50	15.00
72652	Tell Me To My Face/Pretty Little Shy One	1967	2.00	4.00	8.00
72652 [PS]	Tell Me To My Face/Pretty Little Shy One	1967	3.75	7.50	15.00
72695	Daylight Savin' Time/Happy Walking Around	1967	2.00	4.00	8.00
72695 [PS]	Daylight Savin' Time/Happy Walking Around	1967	3.00	6.00	12.00
72715	Easy-As-Pie/Sugar Man	1967	2.00	4.00	8.00
72715 [PS]	Easy-As-Pie/Sugar Man	1967	3.00	6.00	12.00
72746	I'm So Proud/Candy Candy	1967	2.00	4.00	8.00
72794	Hurry/Pleasure of Your Company	1968	2.00	4.00	8.00
72824	Always Tomorrow/I Can't Go Wrong	1968	2.00	4.00	8.00
PHILCO-FORD					
HP-20	98.6/Ain't Gonna Lie	1968	3.75	7.50	15.00
—4-inch plastic "Hip Pocket Record" with color sleeve					
RCA VICTOR					
74-0140	Marstrand/The Problem	1969	—	3.00	6.00
74-0222	Trixin's Election/A Fairy Tale or Two	1969	—	3.00	6.00

Albums

Number	Title (A Side/B Side)	Yr	VG	VG+	NM
MERCURY					
MG-21102 [M]	98.6/Ain't Gonna Lie	1967	3.75	7.50	15.00
MG-21129 [M]	Out of Crank	1967	3.75	7.50	15.00
SR-61102 [S]	98.6/Ain't Gonna Lie	1967	5.00	10.00	20.00
SR-61129 [S]	Out of Crank	1967	5.00	10.00	20.00
RCA VICTOR					
LSP-4143	The Adventures of Keith	1969	5.00	10.00	20.00

KEITH AND DONNA

Also see THE GRATEFUL DEAD.

Albums

Number	Title (A Side/B Side)	Yr	VG	VG+	NM
ROUND					
RX-104	Keith and Donna	1975	7.50	15.00	30.00

KELLEM, MANNY

45s

Number	Title (A Side/B Side)	Yr	VG	VG+	NM
EPIC					
10282	Love Is Blue/Claudine	1968	—	3.00	6.00
10308	Trains and Boats and Planes/Free Again	1968	—	3.00	6.00
METROMEDIA					
104	Red White and Maddox/Jubilee Joe	1969	—	3.00	6.00

Albums

Number	Title (A Side/B Side)	Yr	VG	VG+	NM
EPIC					
BN 26367	Love Is Blue	1968	2.50	5.00	10.00

KELLER, JERRY

45s

Number	Title (A Side/B Side)	Yr	VG	VG+	NM
CAPITOL					
4630	Never Wake Up/Be Careful How You Drive, Young Joey	1961	3.00	6.00	12.00
4668	I'll Get By/My Year of Love	1961	3.00	6.00	12.00
CORAL					
62348	It's Too Late/What Will I Tell My Darling	1963	2.50	5.00	10.00
62361	Sume Summer/Goodnight Pretty Girl	1963	2.50	5.00	10.00
62378	Sea Shell Sherry/What Happens When He Comes Home	1963	2.50	5.00	10.00
62409	Small Wonder/The Tears Keep Falling Down	1964	2.50	5.00	10.00
KAPP					
277 [M]	Here Comes Summer/Time Has a Way	1959	3.75	7.50	15.00
277 [PS]	Here Comes Summer/Time Has a Way	1959	6.25	12.50	25.00
KS-277 [S]	Here Comes Summer/Time Has a Way	1959	7.50	15.00	30.00
295	If I Had a Girl/Lovable	1959	3.00	6.00	12.00
295 [PS]	If I Had a Girl/Lovable	1959	6.25	12.50	25.00
310	Now, Now, Now/There Are Such Things	1959	3.00	6.00	12.00
322	American Beauty Rose/Lonesome Lullaby	1960	3.00	6.00	12.00
337	My Name Ain't Joe/White for You and Bless for Me	1960	3.00	6.00	12.00
353	What More Can I Say/Whole-Heartedly	1960	3.00	6.00	12.00
RCA VICTOR					
47-9221	You're Leanin' On My Mind/My Heart Loves the Samba (Best of All)	1967	2.00	4.00	8.00
REPRISE					
0351	Fickle Finger of Fate/Glory of Love	1965	2.00	4.00	8.00
0397	Ma (She's Such a Quiet Girl)/The Mack	1965	2.00	4.00	8.00

Albums

KAPP

Number	Title (A Side/B Side)	Yr	VG	VG+	NM
KL-1178 [M]	Here Comes Jerry Keller	1959	10.00	20.00	40.00
KS-3178 [S]	Here Comes Jerry Keller	1959	12.50	25.00	50.00

KELLERMAN, SALLY

45s

DECCA

Number	Title (A Side/B Side)	Yr	VG	VG+	NM
33024	Roll with the Feelin'/Child of Mine	1972	—	3.00	6.00

Albums

DECCA

Number	Title (A Side/B Side)	Yr	VG	VG+	NM
DL 75359	Roll with the Feelin'	1972	5.00	10.00	20.00

KELLIN, MIKE

Albums

VERVE FORECAST

Number	Title (A Side/B Side)	Yr	VG	VG+	NM
FT-3028 [M]	Mike Kellin	1967	6.25	12.50	25.00
FTS-3028 [S]	Mike Kellin	1967	6.25	12.50	25.00

KELLUM, MURRY

45s

CINNAMON

Number	Title (A Side/B Side)	Yr	VG	VG+	NM
765	Walking Tall/Huckleberry's Ferry Boat Building Blues	1973	—	2.50	5.00
777	Lovely Lady/Alive and Doing Well	1973	—	2.50	5.00
794	Girl of My Life/Since You've Been Gone	1974	—	2.50	5.00

EPIC

Number	Title (A Side/B Side)	Yr	VG	VG+	NM
10741	Joy to the World/In a Phone Booth on My Knees	1971	—	2.50	5.00
10784	Train Train (Carry Me Away)/What's Made Milwaukee Famous	1971	—	2.50	5.00
10832	Love You to Sleep Tonight/You Do the Callin' (I'll Do the Crawlin')	1972	—	2.50	5.00

M.O.C.

Number	Title (A Side/B Side)	Yr	VG	VG+	NM
653	Long, Tall Texan/I Gotta Leave This Town	1963	3.00	6.00	12.00

—B-side by Glenn Sutton

Number	Title (A Side/B Side)	Yr	VG	VG+	NM
657	Red Ryder/Texas Lil	1964	3.00	6.00	12.00
658	I Dreamed I Was a Beatle/Oh How Sweet It Could Be	1964	5.00	10.00	20.00

PLANTATION

Number	Title (A Side/B Side)	Yr	VG	VG+	NM
176 [DJ]	Memphis Sun (mono/stereo)	1978	—	2.50	5.00

—Released only as a promo

RANWOOD

Number	Title (A Side/B Side)	Yr	VG	VG+	NM
1047	Shoot Low Sheriff/How Long Has It Been (Since They Played Something You Could Dance To)	1976	—	2.50	5.00

KELLY, EMMETT

Albums

ROULETTE

Number	Title (A Side/B Side)	Yr	VG	VG+	NM
R-25130 [M]	Sing Along with Emmett Kelly	1962	6.25	12.50	25.00
SR-25130 [S]	Sing Along with Emmett Kelly	1962	7.50	15.00	30.00

KELLY, PAT

45s

CHIC

Number	Title (A Side/B Side)	Yr	VG	VG+	NM
1009	She's a Devil/The Stranger Dressed in Black	1957	7.50	15.00	30.00

JUBILEE

Number	Title (A Side/B Side)	Yr	VG	VG+	NM
5315	Hey Doll Baby/Cloud 13	1958	15.00	30.00	60.00
5333	Patsy/That Is Where My Money Goes	1958	6.25	12.50	25.00

KELLY, PAUL

45s

DIAL

Number	Title (A Side/B Side)	Yr	VG	VG+	NM
4021	Chills and Fever/Only Your Love	1965	2.50	5.00	10.00
4025	Since I Found You/Can't Help It	1966	2.50	5.00	10.00
4088	Call Another Doctor/We're Gonna Make It	1968	2.50	5.00	10.00

HAPPY TIGER

Number	Title (A Side/B Side)	Yr	VG	VG+	NM
541	Stealing in the Name of the Lord/Day After Forever	1970	—	3.00	6.00
555	Sailing/509	1970	—	3.00	6.00
568	Poor But Proud/Hot Runnin' Soul	1971	—	3.00	6.00
573	Hangin' On In There/Soul Flow	1971	—	3.00	6.00

PHILIPS

Number	Title (A Side/B Side)	Yr	VG	VG+	NM
40409	I Need Your Love So Bad/Nine Times Out of Ten	1966	3.75	7.50	15.00
40457	Cryin' for My Baby/Sweet Sweet Lovin'	1967	3.75	7.50	15.00
40480	If This Old House Could Talk/You Don't Know, You Just Don't Know	1967	3.75	7.50	15.00
40513	Glad to Be Sad/My Love Is Growing Stronger	1968	3.75	7.50	15.00

WARNER BROS.

Number	Title (A Side/B Side)	Yr	VG	VG+	NM
7614	Travelin' Man/Here Comes Old Jezebel	1972	—	2.50	5.00
7657	Don't Burn Me/Love Me Now	1972	—	2.50	5.00
7707	Come Lay Some Lovin' on Me/Come By Here	1973	—	2.50	5.00
7765	I'm Into Something I Can't Shake Loose/Joy	1974	—	2.50	5.00
7823	Hooked, Hogtied & Collared/I Wanna Be Close to You	1974	—	2.50	5.00
8040	Let Your Love Come Down (Let It Fall on Me)/I Wanna Be Close to You	1974	—	2.50	5.00
8067	Take It Away from Him (Put It On Me)/Try My Love	1975	—	2.50	5.00
8120	Get Sexy/I Believe I Can	1975	—	2.50	5.00
8187	Play Me a Love Song/Stealin' Love on the Side	1976	—	2.50	5.00

Albums

HAPPY TIGER

Number	Title (A Side/B Side)	Yr	VG	VG+	NM
1015	Stealing in the Name of the Lord	1970	3.75	7.50	15.00

WARNER BROS.

Number	Title (A Side/B Side)	Yr	VG	VG+	NM
BS 2605	Dirt	1972	3.00	6.00	12.00
BS 2689	Don't Burn Me	1973	3.00	6.00	12.00
BS 2812	Hooked, Hogtied & Collared	1974	3.00	6.00	12.00
BS 3026	Stand on the Positive Side	1976	3.00	6.00	12.00

KELLY FOUR, THE

45s

CANDIX

Number	Title (A Side/B Side)	Yr	VG	VG+	NM
325	Annie Had a Party/Sweet Angelina	1961	6.25	12.50	25.00

—A-side is an alternate take of Silver 1006

Number	Title (A Side/B Side)	Yr	VG	VG+	NM
325	Annie Had a Party/Sweet Angelina	1961	6.25	12.50	25.00

—As "Big Daddy Greenfield"; same recordings as above

SILVER

Number	Title (A Side/B Side)	Yr	VG	VG+	NM
1001	Strollin' Guitar/Guybo	1959	10.00	20.00	40.00

—A-side was reissued on Silver 1004 by "Jewel and Eddie"

Number	Title (A Side/B Side)	Yr	VG	VG+	NM
1006	Annie Had a Party/So Fine, Be Mine	1960	10.00	20.00	40.00

—A-side was reissued on Crest 1088 by "The Gee Cees"

KEMPER, JIMMY, AND THE TIERS

45s

LE MANS

Number	Title (A Side/B Side)	Yr	VG	VG+	NM
002	Lonely for Kathy/I'm Free to Choose	1964	37.50	75.00	150.00

KENDALL SISTERS, THE

45s

ARGO

Number	Title (A Side/B Side)	Yr	VG	VG+	NM
5278	I'm Available/Don't Bother Me	1957	3.75	7.50	15.00
5291	Yea, Yea/Won't You Be My Baby	1958	3.75	7.50	15.00
5310	Billy, Billy, Billy/Let's Wait	1958	3.75	7.50	15.00

CHECKER

Number	Title (A Side/B Side)	Yr	VG	VG+	NM
884	Make It Soon/Three Wishes	1958	3.75	7.50	15.00
889	Yea, Yea/Won't You Be My Baby	1958	6.25	12.50	25.00

KENDRICK, NAT, AND THE SWANS

James Brown's backing band, later known as the J.B.'s. Also see FRED WESLEY.

45s

DADE

Number	Title (A Side/B Side)	Yr	VG	VG+	NM
1804	(Do the) Mashed Potatoes (Part 1)/(Do the) Mashed Potatoes (Part 2)	1959	3.75	7.50	15.00
1808	Dish Rag (Part 1)/Dish Rag (Part 2)	1960	3.75	7.50	15.00
1812	Hot Chili/Slow Down	1960	3.75	7.50	15.00
5003	Wobble Wobble (Part 1)/Wobble Wobble (Part 2)	1961	3.75	7.50	15.00
5004	(Do the) Mashed Potatoes (Part 1)/(Do the) Mashed Potatoes (Part 2)	1961	3.00	6.00	12.00

KENDRICKS, EDDIE

Also see DARYL HALL AND JOHN OATES; THE TEMPTATIONS.

12-Inch Singles

ARISTA

Number	Title (A Side/B Side)	Yr	VG	VG+	NM
SP-15 [DJ]	Ain't No Smoke Without Fire (5:58)/Whip (5:05)	1978	3.00	6.00	12.00

CORNER STONE

Number	Title (A Side/B Side)	Yr	VG	VG+	NM
3001	Surprise Attack (3 versions)	1984	2.00	4.00	8.00

45s

ARISTA

Number	Title (A Side/B Side)	Yr	VG	VG+	NM
0325	Ain't No Smoke Without Fire/Love, Love, Love	1978	—	2.00	4.00
0346	The Best of Strangers Now/Don't Underestimate the Power of Love	1978	—	2.00	4.00
0466	I Just Want to Be the One in Your Life/I Can't Let You Walk Away	1979	—	2.00	4.00
0500	Your Love Has Been So Good/I Never Used to Dance	1980	—	2.00	4.00

ATLANTIC

Number	Title (A Side/B Side)	Yr	VG	VG+	NM
3796	Looking for Love/Need Your Lovin'	1981	—	2.00	4.00
3874 [DJ]	I Don't Need Nobody Else (same on both sides)	1981	—	2.50	5.00

—May be promo only

CORNER STONE

Number	Title (A Side/B Side)	Yr	VG	VG+	NM
1001	Surprise Attack/(B-side unknown)	1984	—	2.00	4.00

TAMLA

Number	Title (A Side/B Side)	Yr	VG	VG+	NM
54203	It's So Hard for Me to Say Good-Bye/This Used to Be the Home of Johnnie Mae	1971	—	2.50	5.00
54210	Can I/I Did It All for You	1971	—	2.50	5.00
54218	Eddie's Love/Let Me Run Into Your Lonely Heart	1972	—	2.50	5.00
54222	If You Let Me/Just Memories	1972	—	2.50	5.00
54230	Girl You Need a Change of Mind (Part 1)/Girl You Need a Change of Mind (Part 2)	1973	—	2.50	5.00
54236	Darling Come Back Home/Loving You the Second Time Around	1973	—	2.50	5.00
54238	Keep On Truckin' (Part 1)/Keep On Truckin' (Part 2)	1973	—	2.50	5.00
54243	Boogie Down/Can't Help What I Am	1974	—	2.50	5.00
54247	Son of Sagittarius/Trust Your Heart	1974	—	2.50	5.00
54249	Tell Her Love Has Felt the Need/Loving You the Second Time Around	1974	—	2.50	5.00
54255	One Tear/The Thin Man	1974	—	2.50	5.00
54257	Shoeshine Boy/Hooked on Your Love	1975	—	2.50	5.00
54260	Get the Cream Off the Top/Honey Brown	1975	—	2.50	5.00
54263	Happy/Deep and Quiet Love	1975	—	2.50	5.00
54266	He's a Friend/All of My Life	1976	—	2.50	5.00
54270	Get It While It's Hot/Never Gonna Leave You	1976	—	2.50	5.00
54277	Goin' Up in Smoke/Thanks for the Memories	1976	—	2.50	5.00
54285	Date with the Rain/Born Again	1977	—	2.50	5.00
54289	Baby/I Want to Live (My Life with You)	1977	—	—	—

—Unreleased

Number	Title (A Side/B Side)	Yr	VG	VG+	NM
54290	Baby/Intimate Friends	1977	—	2.50	5.00

Albums

ARISTA

Number	Title (A Side/B Side)	Yr	VG	VG+	NM
AB 4170	Vintage '78	1978	2.50	5.00	10.00
AB 4250	Something More	1979	2.50	5.00	10.00

ATLANTIC

Number	Title (A Side/B Side)	Yr	VG	VG+	NM
SD 19294	Love Keys	1981	2.50	5.00	10.00

MOTOWN

Number	Title (A Side/B Side)	Yr	VG	VG+	NM
M5-151V1	Eddie Kendricks	1981	2.00	4.00	8.00

—Reissue of Tamla 327

Number	Title (A Side/B Side)	Yr	VG	VG+	NM
M5-196V1	He's a Friend	1981	2.00	4.00	8.00

—Reissue of Tamla 343

TAMLA

Number	Title (A Side/B Side)	Yr	VG	VG+	NM
T-309	All By Myself	1971	2.50	5.00	10.00

Number	Title (A Side/B Side)	Yr	VG	VG+	NM
T6-315	People...Hold On	1972	2.50	5.00	10.00
T6-327	Eddie Kendricks	1973	2.50	5.00	10.00
T6-330	Boogie Down!	1974	2.50	5.00	10.00
T6-335	For You	1974	2.50	5.00	10.00
T6-338	The Hit Man	1975	2.50	5.00	10.00
T6-343	He's a Friend	1976	2.50	5.00	10.00
T6-346	Goin' Up in Smoke	1976	2.50	5.00	10.00
T7-354	Eddie Kendricks at His Best	1977	2.50	5.00	10.00
T8-356	Slick	1978	2.50	5.00	10.00

KENNEDY, JOHN FITZGERALD

Various tribute records, most of which were released in the immediate aftermath of his assassination in 1963.

Albums

Number	Title (A Side/B Side)	Yr	VG	VG+	NM
20TH CENTURY					
TCF 3127 [M]	The Presidential Years 1960-1963	1963	5.00	10.00	20.00
—Narrated by David Teig					
CAEDMON					
TC-2021 [(2)]	Self-Portrait	196?	5.00	10.00	20.00
CAPITOL					
ST 2486 [S]	Years of Lightning, Day of Drums	1966	7.50	15.00	30.00
T 2486 [M]	Years of Lightning, Day of Drums	1966	5.00	10.00	20.00
—Narrated by Gregory Peck; U.S. Information Agency movie soundtrack					
COLPIX					
CP 2500 [M]	Four Days That Shocked the World	1964	12.50	25.00	50.00
—Narrated by Reid Collins; covers Nov. 22-25, 1963					
DECCA					
DL 9116 [M]	That Was The Week That Was	1963	5.00	10.00	20.00
—BBC show's tribute to JFK, broadcast Nov. 23, 1963					
DIPLOMAT					
10000 [M]	John F. Kennedy — A Memorial Album	1963	3.75	7.50	15.00
DOCUMENTARIES UNLIMITED					
(no #) [M]	JFK The Man, The President	1963	5.00	10.00	20.00
—Narrated by Barry Gray					
HARMONICA					
HLP-3005 [M]	Kennedy Speaks	1963	5.00	10.00	20.00
LEGACY					
L2L 1017 [(2) M]	John Fitzgerald Kennedy...As We Remember Him	1965	6.25	12.50	25.00
—Narrated by Charles Kuralt; with 240-page book					
PICKWICK					
169 [M]	The Presidential Years (1960-1963)	1963	3.75	7.50	15.00
PREMIER					
2099 [M]	A Memorial Album	1963	5.00	10.00	20.00
—From WMCA Radio, New York, Nov. 22, 1963					
RCA VICTOR					
VDM-101 [M]	The Kennedy Wit	1964	3.75	7.50	15.00
—Narrated by David Brinkley with introduction by Adlai E. Stevenson					
SOMERSET					
16100 [M]	Actual Speeches of Franklin D. Roosevelt and John F. Kennedy	1963	3.75	7.50	15.00
—One side has FDR speeches, the other, JFK speeches					

KENNEDY, ROBERT FRANCIS

Tribute album released shortly after his death.

Albums

Number	Title (A Side/B Side)	Yr	VG	VG+	NM
COLUMBIA					
C2S 792 [(2)]	A Memorial	1968	5.00	10.00	20.00

KENNER, CHRIS

45s

Number	Title (A Side/B Side)	Yr	VG	VG+	NM
BATON					
220	Grandma's House/Don't Let Her Pin That Charge	1956	10.00	20.00	40.00
IMPERIAL					
5448	Sick and Tired/Nothing Will Keep Me from You	1957	6.25	12.50	25.00
5488	Will You Be Mine/I Have News for You	1958	6.25	12.50	25.00
5767	Sick and Tired/Nothing Will Keep Me from You	1961	3.00	6.00	12.00
INSTANT					
3229	I Like It Like That, Part 1/I Like It Like That, Part 2	1961	3.75	7.50	15.00
3234	A Very True Story/Packin' Up	1961	3.00	6.00	12.00
3237	Something You Got/Come See About Me	1961	3.00	6.00	12.00
3244	How Far/Time	1962	3.00	6.00	12.00
3247	Let Me Show You How (To Twist)/Johnny Little	1962	3.00	6.00	12.00
3252	Land of 1000 Dances/That's My Girl	1962	3.00	6.00	12.00
3257	Come Back and See/Go Thru Life	1963	3.00	6.00	12.00
3263	What's Wrong with Life/Never Reach Perfection	1963	3.00	6.00	12.00
3265	She Can Dance/Anybody Here See My Baby	1964	3.00	6.00	12.00
3277	I'm Lonely, Take Me/Cinderella	1966	2.50	5.00	10.00
3280	All Night Rambler, Part 1/All Night Rambler, Part 2	1966	2.50	5.00	10.00
3283	Shoo Rah/Stretch My Hands to You	1967	2.50	5.00	10.00
3286	Fumigate Funky Broadway/Wind the Clock	1967	2.50	5.00	10.00
3290	Memories of a King (Let Freedom Ring), Part 1/ Memories of a King (Let Freedom Ring), Part 2	1968	3.00	6.00	12.00
3293	Mini-Skirts and Soul/Sad Mistake	1968	2.50	5.00	10.00
RON					
335	Rocket to the Moon/Life's Just a Struggle	1961	3.00	6.00	12.00
UPTOWN					
708	Life of My Baby/They Took My Money	1965	2.50	5.00	10.00
716	I'm the Greatest/Get On This Train	1965	2.50	5.00	10.00
VALIANT					
3229	I Like It Like That, Part 1/I Like It Like That, Part 2	1960	10.00	20.00	40.00

Albums

Number	Title (A Side/B Side)	Yr	VG	VG+	NM
ATLANTIC					
8117 [M]	Land of 1,000 Dances	1965	20.00	40.00	80.00
COLLECTABLES					
COL-5116	Golden Classics: I Like It Like That	198?	3.00	6.00	12.00

KENNY AND CORKY

45s

Number	Title (A Side/B Side)	Yr	VG	VG+	NM
BIG TOP					
3031	Nuttin' for Christmas/Suzy Snowflake	1959	5.00	10.00	20.00
3031 [PS]	Nuttin' for Christmas/Suzy Snowflake	1959	10.00	20.00	40.00

KENNY AND THE CADETS

Also see THE BEACH BOYS.

45s

Number	Title (A Side/B Side)	Yr	VG	VG+	NM
RANDY					
422	Barbie/What Is a Young Man Made Of	1962	100.00	200.00	400.00
—Pink label original (white labels are counterfeits)					
422	Barbie/What Is a Young Man Made Of	1962	250.00	500.00	1000.
—Red and gold vinyl					

KENNY AND THE FIENDS

45s

Number	Title (A Side/B Side)	Yr	VG	VG+	NM
DOT					
16568	House on Haunted Hill (Part 1)/House on Haunted Hill (Part 2)	1963	5.00	10.00	20.00
16596	Moon Shot/One-Two-Three-Four	1964	5.00	10.00	20.00
POSEA					
80	The Raven (Part 1)/The Raven (Part 2)	1963	7.50	15.00	30.00
87	House on Haunted Hill/Green Door	1963	10.00	20.00	40.00
—As "Kenny and the Beach Fiends"					
PRINCESS					
51	House on Haunted Hill (Part 1)/House on Haunted Hill (Part 2)	1963	7.50	15.00	30.00

KENNY AND THE KASUALS

45s

Number	Title (A Side/B Side)	Yr	VG	VG+	NM
MARK IV					
911	Nothin' Better to Do/Floatin'	1965	7.50	15.00	30.00
1002	Don't Let Your Baby Go/(B-side unknown)	1966	7.50	15.00	30.00
1003	It's All Right/You Make Me Feel So Good	1966	7.50	15.00	30.00
1004	Strings of Time/(B-side unknown)	1966	7.50	15.00	30.00
1006	I'm Gonna Make It/Journey to Tyme	1966	10.00	20.00	40.00
1008	See-Saw Ride/As I Knew	1967	7.50	15.00	30.00
UNITED ARTISTS					
50085	I'm Gonna Make It/Journey to Tyme	1966	5.00	10.00	20.00

Albums

Number	Title (A Side/B Side)	Yr	VG	VG+	NM
MARK					
5000 [M]	The Impact Sound of Kenny and the Kasuals Live at the Studio Club	1966	250.00	500.00	1000.
5000 [M]	The Impact Sound of Kenny and the Kasuals Live at the Studio Club	1977	6.25	12.50	25.00
—"Reissue, 1977" appears on cover					
6000 [M]	Teen Dreams	1978	62.50	125.00	250.00
—Red vinyl; numbered, signed limited edition					
7000 [S]	Garage Kings	1979	6.25	12.50	25.00

KENNY AND THE SOCIALITES

45s

Number	Title (A Side/B Side)	Yr	VG	VG+	NM
CROSSTOWN					
001	I'll Have to Decide/King Tut Rock	1958	37.50	75.00	150.00

KENSINGTON MARKET

45s

Number	Title (A Side/B Side)	Yr	VG	VG+	NM
WARNER BROS.					
7221	I Would Be the One/Speaking of Dreams	1968	2.00	4.00	8.00

Albums

Number	Title (A Side/B Side)	Yr	VG	VG+	NM
WARNER BROS.					
WS 1754	Avenue Road	1968	5.00	10.00	20.00
WS 1780	Aardvark	1969	5.00	10.00	20.00

KENT, AL

45s

Number	Title (A Side/B Side)	Yr	VG	VG+	NM
BARITONE					
942	Hold Me/Tell Me Why	1960	37.50	75.00	150.00
CHECKER					
881	Dat's Why (I Love You So)/Am I the Man	1958	15.00	30.00	60.00
RIC-TIC					
123	The Way You Been Acting Lately/(Instrumental)	1967	5.00	10.00	20.00
127	You've Got to Pay the Price/Where Do I Go from Here	1967	5.00	10.00	20.00
133	Finders Keepers/Ooh! Pretty Lady	1967	5.00	10.00	20.00
140	Bless You (My Love)/(Instrumental)	1968	3.75	7.50	15.00
WINGATE					
004	You Know I Love You/Country Boy	1965	6.25	12.50	25.00
WIZARD					
100	Hold Me/You Know Me	1959	25.00	50.00	100.00

KENT, BILLY, AND THE ANDANTES

45s

Number	Title (A Side/B Side)	Yr	VG	VG+	NM
MAH'S					
000.2	Your Love/Take All of Me	1960	30.00	60.00	120.00
—First pressing, with Detroit address on label					
000.2	Your Love/Take All of Me	1960	15.00	30.00	60.00
—Second pressing, without address and with Roulette distribution mentioned on label					

KENTON, STAN

45s

Number	Title (A Side/B Side)	Yr	VG	VG+	NM
CAPITOL					
F1043	Evening in Pakistan/Jolly Rogers	1950	5.00	10.00	20.00
—Note: Earlier Stan Kenton 45s on Capitol may exist					
F1191	Easy Go/But Then You Kissed Me	1950	5.00	10.00	20.00
F1236	Love for Sale/Be Easy, Be Tender	1950	5.00	10.00	20.00
F1279	Viva Prado/I'm So in the Mood	1950	5.00	10.00	20.00
F1480	September Song/Artistry in Tango1	1951	3.75	7.50	15.00
F1535	Tortillas and Beans/Dynaflow	1951	3.75	7.50	15.00
F1616	The Spider and the Fly/Are You Livin' Old Man	1951	3.00	6.00	12.00
—Reissue of 78 rpm material					
F1636	Artistry in Rhythm/Artistry Jumps	1951	3.00	6.00	12.00
—Reissue of 78 rpm material					
F1661	Across the Alley from the Alamo/After You	1951	3.00	6.00	12.00
—Reissue of 78 rpm material					

Number	Title (A Side/B Side)	Yr	VG	VG+	NM
F1680	September Song/Laura	195?	3.00	6.00	12.00
—Reissue					
F1704	Laura/Jump for Joe	1951	3.75	7.50	15.00
F1774	Francesca/Night Watch	1951	3.75	7.50	15.00
F1823	Daddy/Street of Dreams	1951	3.75	7.50	15.00
—A-side with June Christy, vocals					
F1874	Blues in Burlesque (Part 1)/Blues in Burlesque (Part 2)	1951	3.75	7.50	15.00
F2040	Delicado/Bag and Baggage	1952	3.75	7.50	15.00
F2064	Cool Eyes/She's a Comely Wench	1952	3.75	7.50	15.00
F2214	Stardust/Beehive	1952	3.75	7.50	15.00
F2250	Taboo/Lonesome Train	1952	3.75	7.50	15.00
2278	The Odd Couple/MacArthur Park	1968	2.50	5.00	10.00
F2373	Hushabye/Harlem Nocturne	1953	3.75	7.50	15.00
F2388	Jeepers Creepers/And the Bull Walked Around Olay	1953	3.75	7.50	15.00
F2409	Do Nothing Till You Hear from Me/How Many Hearts Have You Broken	1953	3.00	6.00	12.00
F2410	Sweet Dreams Sweetheart/Gotta Be Gettin'	1953	3.00	6.00	12.00
F2411	Don't Let Me Dream/It's Been a Long, Long Time	1953	3.00	6.00	12.00
F2412	Every Time We Say Goodbye/Four Months, Three Weeks, Two Days	1953	3.00	6.00	12.00
F2413	Shoo Fly Pie and Apple Pie Down/I Been Down in Texas	1953	3.00	6.00	12.00
F2414	It's a Pity to Say Goodnight/There Is No Greater Love	1953	3.00	6.00	12.00
F2415	Curiosity/Theme to the West	1953	3.00	6.00	12.00
F2416	Unison Riff/I Told Ya I Love Ya Now Get Out	1953	3.00	6.00	12.00
F2418	Harlem Holiday/Don't Want That Man Around	1953	3.00	6.00	12.00
F2419	How Am I to Know/He Was a Good Man	1953	3.00	6.00	12.00
F2446	Sophisticated Lady/Begin the Beguine	1953	3.00	6.00	12.00
F2447	There's a Small Hotel/Shadow Waltz	1953	3.00	6.00	12.00
F2449	Fascinating Rhythm/Over the Rainbow	1953	3.00	6.00	12.00
F2511	Baja/All About Ronnie	1953	3.00	6.00	12.00
F2685	Tenderly/The Creep	1953	3.00	6.00	12.00
F2789	Alone Too Long/Don't Take Your Love from Me	1954	3.00	6.00	12.00
F2822	The Lady in Red/Under a Blanket of Blue	1954	3.00	6.00	12.00
F2879	Sambo Mambo/Mambo Riff	1954	3.00	6.00	12.00
F3046	A-Ting-a-Ling/Malaguena	1955	3.00	6.00	12.00
F3110	Casanova/Dark Eyes	1955	3.00	6.00	12.00
F3134	23 Degrees N — 82 Degrees W/Falling	1955	3.00	6.00	12.00
F3151	Freddy/Handwriting on the Wall	1955	3.00	6.00	12.00
F3243	Sunset Tower/Opus in Chartreuse	1955	3.00	6.00	12.00
F3345	Baa Too Kee/Winter in Madrid	1956	3.00	6.00	12.00
F3836	Lemon Twist/Baby You're Through	1957	2.50	5.00	10.00
F3928	Tequila/Cuban Mumble	1958	2.50	5.00	10.00
F4196	Whistle Walk/Tamer Lane	1959	2.50	5.00	10.00
4370	Opus in Chartreuse Cha Cha Cha/Chocolate Caliente	1960	2.50	5.00	10.00
4500	Carnival/Malibu Moonlight	1961	2.00	4.00	8.00
4629	Theme from "Splendor in the Grass"/Officer Krupke	1961	2.00	4.00	8.00
4707	Magic Moment/Waltz of the Prophet	1962	2.00	4.00	8.00
4764	Come On Back/Warm Blue Stream	1962	2.00	4.00	8.00
4847	Mama Sang a Song/Whispering Hope	1962	2.00	4.00	8.00
5085	O Tannenbaum/What Is a Santa Claus	1963	2.50	5.00	10.00
5480	Peyton Place Theme/007	1965	2.00	4.00	8.00
5572	Patch of Blue/Make Me Love You	1966	2.00	4.00	8.00
5828	Dragnet/Spanish Eyes	1967	2.50	5.00	10.00
F15530	Artistry in Bolero/Come Back to Sorrento	1950	3.75	7.50	15.00
F15531	Willow Weep for Me/Fantasy	1950	3.75	7.50	15.00
F15532	Safranski (Artistry in Bass)/Opus in Pastels	1950	3.75	7.50	15.00
F15533	Artistry in Percussion/Ain't No Misery in Me	1950	3.75	7.50	15.00
—The above four comprise a box set					

CREATIVE WORLD

Number	Title (A Side/B Side)	Yr	VG	VG+	NM
1001 [DJ]	The Twelve Days of Christmas//O Tannenbaum/We Three Kings Of Orient Are	197?	—	2.00	4.00

Albums

CAPITOL

Number	Title (A Side/B Side)	Yr	VG	VG+	NM
H 155 [10]	Encores	1950	15.00	30.00	60.00
T 155 [M]	Encores	195?	10.00	20.00	40.00
—Turquoise label					
DT 167 [R]	Artistry in Rhythm	1969	2.50	5.00	10.00
H 167 [10]	Artistry in Rhythm	1950	15.00	30.00	60.00
SM-167 [R]	Artistry in Rhythm	1975	2.00	4.00	8.00
—Reissue with new prefix					
T 167 [M]	Artistry in Rhythm	1959	3.75	7.50	15.00
—Black label with colorband, Capitol logo at left					
T 167 [M]	Artistry in Rhythm	195?	10.00	20.00	40.00
—Turquoise label					
T 167 [M]	Artistry in Rhythm	1962	3.00	6.00	12.00
—Black label with colorband, Capitol logo at top					
H 172 [10]	A Presentation of Progressive Jazz	1950	15.00	30.00	60.00
T 172 [M]	A Presentation of Progressive Jazz	195?	10.00	20.00	40.00
P 189 [10]	Innovations in Modern Music	1950	15.00	30.00	60.00
H 190 [10]	Milestones	1950	15.00	30.00	60.00
T 190 [M]	Milestones	195?	10.00	20.00	40.00
—Turquoise label					
PRO-206/7 [DJ]	The Kenton Era (Excerpts)	1955	10.00	20.00	40.00
L 248 [10]	Stan Kenton Presents	1951	15.00	30.00	60.00
T 248 [M]	Stan Kenton Presents	195?	10.00	20.00	40.00
—Turquoise label					
ST-305	Music from "Hair"	1969	3.75	7.50	15.00
H 353 [10]	City of Glass	1952	15.00	30.00	60.00
H 358 [10]	Classics	1952	15.00	30.00	60.00
T 358 [M]	Classics	195?	10.00	20.00	40.00
—Turquoise label					
H 383 [10]	New Concepts of Artistry in Rhythm	1953	15.00	30.00	60.00
T 383 [M]	New Concepts of Artistry in Rhythm	195?	10.00	20.00	40.00
—Turquoise label					
H 386 [10]	Prologue: This Is an Orchestra	1953	15.00	30.00	60.00
H 421 [10]	Popular Favorites	1953	15.00	30.00	60.00
T 421 [M]	Popular Favorites	195?	10.00	20.00	40.00
—Turquoise label					
H 426 [10]	Sketches on Standards	1953	15.00	30.00	60.00
T 426 [M]	Sketches on Standards	195?	10.00	20.00	40.00
—Turquoise label					
H 460 [10]	This Modern World	1953	15.00	30.00	60.00
H 462 [10]	Portraits on Standards	1953	15.00	30.00	60.00
T 462 [M]	Portraits on Standards	195?	10.00	20.00	40.00
—Turquoise label					
W 524 [M]	Kenton Showcase	1954	10.00	20.00	40.00
H 525 [10]	Kenton Showcase — The Music of Bill Russo	1954	15.00	30.00	60.00
H 526 [10]	Kenton Showcase — The Music of Bill Holman	1954	15.00	30.00	60.00
TDB 569 [(4) M]	The Kenton Era	1955	25.00	50.00	100.00
—Box set with 44-page book					
STCL-575 [(3)]	Stan Kenton	1970	5.00	10.00	20.00
T 656 [M]	Duet	1955	10.00	20.00	40.00
—With June Christy; turquoise label					
T 666 [M]	Contemporary Concepts	1955	10.00	20.00	40.00
—Turquoise label					
W 724 [M]	Kenton in Hi-Fi	1956	10.00	20.00	40.00
—Turquoise label					
T 731 [M]	Cuban Fire!	1956	10.00	20.00	40.00
—Turquoise label					
T 731 [M]	Cuban Fire!	1959	5.00	10.00	20.00
—Black label with colorband, Capitol logo at left					
T 731 [M]	Cuban Fire!	1962	3.75	7.50	15.00
—Black label with colorband, Capitol logo at top					
T 736 [M]	City of Glass/This Modern World	1956	10.00	20.00	40.00
—Combination of 353 and 460 onto one 12-inch LP, turquoise label					
T 810 [M]	Kenton with Voices	1957	10.00	20.00	40.00
—Turquoise label					
T 932 [M]	Rendezvous with Kenton	1957	10.00	20.00	40.00
—Turquoise label					
T 995 [M]	Back to Balboa	1958	10.00	20.00	40.00
—Turquoise label					
ST 1068 [S]	The Ballad Style of Stan Kenton	1959	5.00	10.00	20.00
—Black label with colorband, Capitol logo at left					
ST 1068 [S]	The Ballad Style of Stan Kenton	1962	3.00	6.00	12.00
—Black label with colorband, Capitol logo at top					
T 1068 [M]	The Ballad Style of Stan Kenton	1959	6.25	12.50	25.00
—Black label with colorband, Capitol logo at left					
T 1068 [M]	The Ballad Style of Stan Kenton	1962	3.75	7.50	15.00
—Black label with colorband, Capitol logo at top					
ST 1130 [S]	Lush Interlude	1959	5.00	10.00	20.00
—Black label with colorband, Capitol logo at left					
T 1130 [M]	Lush Interlude	1959	6.25	12.50	25.00
—Black label with colorband, Capitol logo at left					
ST 1166 [S]	The Stage Door Swings	1959	5.00	10.00	20.00
—Black label with colorband, Capitol logo at left					
T 1166 [M]	The Stage Door Swings	1959	6.25	12.50	25.00
—Black label with colorband, Capitol logo at left					
ST 1276 [S]	The Kenton Touch	1960	5.00	10.00	20.00
—Black label with colorband, Capitol logo at left					
T 1276 [M]	The Kenton Touch	1960	6.25	12.50	25.00
—Black label with colorband, Capitol logo at left					
SW 1305 [S]	Viva Kenton!	1960	5.00	10.00	20.00
—Black label with colorband, Capitol logo at left					
W 1305 [M]	Viva Kenton!	1960	6.25	12.50	25.00
—Black label with colorband, Capitol logo at left					
STBO 1327 [(2) S]	Road Show	1960	7.50	15.00	30.00
—Black label with colorband, Capitol logo at left					
STBO 1327 [(2) S]	Road Show	1962	3.75	7.50	15.00
—Black label with colorband, Capitol logo at top					
TBO 1327 [(2) M]	Road Show	1960	10.00	20.00	40.00
—Black label with colorband, Capitol logo at left					
TBO 1327 [(2) M]	Road Show	1962	5.00	10.00	20.00
—Black label with colorband, Capitol logo at top					
ST 1394 [S]	Standards in Silhouette	1960	5.00	10.00	20.00
—Black label with colorband, Capitol logo at left					
ST 1394 [S]	Standards in Silhouette	1962	3.00	6.00	12.00
—Black label with colorband, Capitol logo at top					
T 1394 [M]	Standards in Silhouette	1960	6.25	12.50	25.00
—Black label with colorband, Capitol logo at left					
T 1394 [M]	Standards in Silhouette	1962	3.75	7.50	15.00
—Black label with colorband, Capitol logo at top					
ST 1460 [S]	Kenton at the Las Vegas Tropicana	1961	5.00	10.00	20.00
—Black label with colorband, Capitol logo at left					
T 1460 [M]	Kenton at the Las Vegas Tropicana	1961	6.25	12.50	25.00
—Black label with colorband, Capitol logo at left					
ST 1533 [S]	The Romantic Approach	1961	5.00	10.00	20.00
—Black label with colorband, Capitol logo at left					
ST 1533 [S]	The Romantic Approach	1961	3.00	6.00	12.00
—Black label with colorband, Capitol logo at top					
T 1533 [M]	The Romantic Approach	1961	6.25	12.50	25.00
—Black label with colorband, Capitol logo at left					
T 1533 [M]	The Romantic Approach	1961	3.75	7.50	15.00
—Black label with colorband, Capitol logo at top					
ST 1609 [S]	Kenton's West Side Story	1961	5.00	10.00	20.00
—Black label with colorband, Capitol logo at left					
ST 1609 [S]	Kenton's West Side Story	1961	3.00	6.00	12.00
—Black label with colorband, Capitol logo at top					
T 1609 [M]	Kenton's West Side Story	1961	6.25	12.50	25.00
—Black label with colorband, Capitol logo at left					
T 1609 [M]	Kenton's West Side Story	1961	3.75	7.50	15.00
—Black label with colorband, Capitol logo at top					
ST 1621 [S]	A Merry Christmas	1961	5.00	10.00	20.00
T 1621 [M]	A Merry Christmas	1961	3.75	7.50	15.00
ST 1674 [S]	The Sophisticated Approach	1962	3.75	7.50	15.00
—Black label with colorband, Capitol logo at top					
T 1674 [M]	The Sophisticated Approach	1962	3.00	6.00	12.00
—Black label with colorband, Capitol logo at top					
ST 1796 [S]	Adventures in Jazz	1962	3.75	7.50	15.00
—Black label with colorband, Capitol logo at top					
T 1796 [M]	Adventures in Jazz	1962	3.00	6.00	12.00
—Black label with colorband, Capitol logo at top					
ST 1844 [S]	Adventures in Time	1963	3.75	7.50	15.00
—Black label with colorband, Capitol logo at top					
T 1844 [M]	Adventures in Time	1963	3.00	6.00	12.00
—Black label with colorband, Capitol logo at top					

Number	Title (A Side/B Side)	Yr	VG	VG+	NM
ST 1931 [S]	Artistry in Bossa Nova	1963	3.75	7.50	15.00
T 1931 [M]	Artistry in Bossa Nova	1963	3.00	6.00	12.00
ST 1985 [S]	Adventures in Blues	1963	3.75	7.50	15.00
—Black label with colorband, Capitol logo at top					
T 1985 [M]	Adventures in Blues	1963	3.00	6.00	12.00
—Black label with colorband, Capitol logo at top					
ST 2132 [S]	Artistry in Voices and Brass	1964	3.75	7.50	15.00
—Black label with colorband, Capitol logo at top					
T 2132 [M]	Artistry in Voices and Brass	1964	3.00	6.00	12.00
—Black label with colorband, Capitol logo at top					
STAO 2217 [S]	Kenton Plays Wagner	1964	3.75	7.50	15.00
—Black label with colorband, Capitol logo at top					
TAO 2217 [M]	Kenton Plays Wagner	1964	3.00	6.00	12.00
—Black label with colorband, Capitol logo at top					
DT 2327 [R]	Stan Kenton's Greatest Hits	1965	2.50	5.00	10.00
—Black label with colorband, Capitol logo at top					
SM-2327	Stan Kenton's Greatest Hits	197?	2.00	4.00	8.00
—Reissue with new prefix					
T 2327 [M]	Stan Kenton's Greatest Hits	1965	3.00	6.00	12.00
—Black label with colorband, Capitol logo at top					
MAS 2424 [M]	Stan Kenton Conducts the Los Angeles Neophonic Orchestra	1966	3.00	6.00	12.00
—Black label with colorband, Capitol logo at top					
SMAS 2424 [S]	Stan Kenton Conducts the Los Angeles Neophonic Orchestra	1966	3.75	7.50	15.00
—Black label with colorband, Capitol logo at top					
ST 2655 [S]	Kenton Plays for Today	1966	3.75	7.50	15.00
—Black label with colorband, Capitol logo at top					
T 2655 [M]	Kenton Plays for Today	1966	3.00	6.00	12.00
—Black label with colorband, Capitol logo at top					
ST 2810	The World We Know	1968	3.00	6.00	12.00
ST 2932	Jazz Compositions of Dee Barton	1968	3.00	6.00	12.00
ST 2974	Finian's Rainbow	1968	3.00	6.00	12.00
STCL 2989 [(3)]	The Stan Kenton Deluxe Set	1968	5.00	10.00	20.00
M-11027	Artistry in Jazz	1972	2.50	5.00	10.00
SM-11794 [M]	Cuban Fire!	1978	2.50	5.00	10.00
—Reissue of Capitol T 731					
STBB-12016 [(2)]	The Comprehensive Kenton	1979	3.75	7.50	15.00
SM-12037	Kenton's West Side Story	1979	2.50	5.00	10.00
—Reissue of Capitol ST 1609					
N-16182	Stan Kenton's Greatest Hits	1984	2.00	4.00	8.00
—Budget-line reissue					

CREATIVE WORLD

Number	Title (A Side/B Side)	Yr	VG	VG+	NM
ST 1001	Kenton's Christmas	1970	3.00	6.00	12.00
ST 1002 [R]	New Concepts of Artistry in Rhythm	197?	2.50	5.00	10.00
—Reissue of Capitol T 383					
ST 1003 [R]	Contemporary Concepts	197?	2.00	4.00	8.00
—Reissue of Capitol T 666					
ST 1004 [R]	Kenton in Stereo	197?	2.50	5.00	10.00
—Reissue of Capitol W 724					
ST 1005	Lush Interlude	197?	2.50	5.00	10.00
—Reissue of Capitol ST 1130					
ST 1006 [R]	City of Glass/This Modern World	197?	2.00	4.00	8.00
—Reissue of Capitol T 736					
ST 1007	Kenton's West Side Story	197?	2.50	5.00	10.00
—Reissue of Capitol ST 1609					
ST 1008 [R]	Cuban Fire!	197?	2.00	4.00	8.00
—Reissue of Capitol T 731					
ST 1009 [R]	Innovations in Modern Music	197?	2.00	4.00	8.00
—Reissue of Capitol P 189					
ST 1010	Adventures in Jazz	197?	2.50	5.00	10.00
—Reissue of Capitol ST 1796					
ST 1011	Adventures in Time	197?	2.50	5.00	10.00
—Reissue of Capitol ST 1844					
ST 1012	Adventures in Blues	197?	2.50	5.00	10.00
—Reissue of Capitol ST 1985					
ST 1013	Stan Kenton Conducts the Los Angeles Neophonic Orchestra	197?	2.50	5.00	10.00
—Reissue of Capitol SMAS 2424					
ST 1015 [(2)]	Live at Redlands University	1971	2.50	5.00	10.00
ST 1017	The Romantic Approach	197?	2.00	4.00	8.00
—Reissue of Capitol ST 1533					
ST 1018	The Sophisticated Approach	197?	2.50	5.00	10.00
—Reissue of Capitol ST 1674					
ST 1019	Road Show, Volume 1	197?	2.50	5.00	10.00
—Partial reissue of Capitol STBO 1327					
ST 1020	Road Show, Volume 2	197?	2.50	5.00	10.00
—Partial reissue of Capitol STBO 1327					
ST 1022	Jazz Compositions of Dee Barton	197?	2.50	5.00	10.00
—Reissue of Capitol ST 2932					
ST 1023 [R]	Stan Kenton Presents	197?	2.00	4.00	8.00
—Reissue of Capitol T 248					
ST 1024	Kenton Plays Wagner	197?	2.50	5.00	10.00
—Reissue of Capitol STAO 2217					
ST 1025	Adventures in Standards	197?	2.50	5.00	10.00
ST 1026 [R]	Kenton Showcase	197?	2.00	4.00	8.00
—Reissue of Capitol W 524					
ST 1027 [R]	Collector's Choice	197?	2.00	4.00	8.00
ST 1028 [R]	The Fabulous Alumni of Stan Kenton	197?	2.00	4.00	8.00
ST 1029 [R]	Some Women I've Known	197?	2.00	4.00	8.00
ST 1030 [(4) R]	The Kenton Era	197?	5.00	10.00	20.00
—Reissue of Capitol TDB 569					
ST 1031	Back to Balboa	197?	2.50	5.00	10.00
—Reissue of Capitol T 995					
ST 1032	Kenton at the Las Vegas Tropicana	197?	2.50	5.00	10.00
—Reissue of Capitol ST 1460					
ST 1033	The Kenton Touch	197?	2.50	5.00	10.00
—Reissue of Capitol ST 1276					
ST 1034 [R]	Encores	197?	2.00	4.00	8.00
—Reissue of Capitol T 155					
ST 1035 [R]	The Christy Years	197?	2.00	4.00	8.00
ST 1036 [R]	Kenton By Request, Vol. I	197?	2.00	4.00	8.00
ST 1037 [R]	A Concert in Progessive Jazz	197?	2.00	4.00	8.00
—Reissue of Capitol T 172					
ST 1038	Artistry in Voices and Brass	197?	2.50	5.00	10.00
—Reissue of Capitol ST 2132					
ST 1039 [Q]	Live at Brigham Young	1971	3.75	7.50	15.00
ST 1040 [R]	Kenton By Request, Vol. II	197?	2.00	4.00	8.00
ST 1041 [R]	Sketches on Standards	197?	2.00	4.00	8.00
—Reissue of Capitol T 426					
ST 1042 [R]	Portraits on Standards	197?	2.00	4.00	8.00
—Reissue of Capitol T 462					
ST 1043 [R]	Artistry in Rhythm	197?	2.00	4.00	8.00
—Reissue of Capitol DT 167					
ST 1044	The Stage Door Swings	197?	2.50	5.00	10.00
—Reissue of Capitol ST 1166					
ST 1045	Artistry in Bossa Nova	197?	2.50	5.00	10.00
ST 1046	Stan Kenton with Jean Turner	197?	2.50	5.00	10.00
ST 1047 [R]	Milestones	197?	2.00	4.00	8.00
—Reissue of Capitol T 190					
ST 1048 [R]	Duet	197?	2.00	4.00	8.00
—Reissue of Capitol T 656					
ST 1049	Standards in Silhouette	197?	2.50	5.00	10.00
—Reissue of Capitol ST 1394					
ST 1050 [R]	The Lighter Side of Stan Kenton	197?	2.00	4.00	8.00
ST 1057	Rendezvous with Kenton	197?	2.50	5.00	10.00
—Reissue of Capitol T 932					
ST 1058 [(2) Q]	Live at Butler University	1972	5.00	10.00	20.00
ST 1059 [(2) Q]	Stan Kenton with the Four Freshmen at Butler University	1972	5.00	10.00	20.00
ST 1060 [(2) Q]	National Anthems of the World	1972	5.00	10.00	20.00
ST 1061 [R]	Stan Kenton — Formative Years	197?	2.00	4.00	8.00
—Reissue of Decca DL 8259					
ST 1062 [R]	Kenton By Request, Vol. III	197?	2.00	4.00	8.00
ST 1063	Viva Kenton!	197?	2.50	5.00	10.00
—Reissue of Capitol SW 1305					
ST 1064 [R]	Kenton By Request, Vol. IV	197?	2.00	4.00	8.00
ST 1065	Birthday in Britain	1973	2.50	5.00	10.00
ST 1066 [R]	Kenton By Request, Vol. V	197?	2.00	4.00	8.00
ST 1067	Too Much	197?	2.50	5.00	10.00
ST 1068	The Ballad Style of Stan Kenton	197?	2.00	4.00	8.00
—Reissue of Capitol ST 1068					
ST 1069	Kenton By Request, Vol. VI	197?	2.50	5.00	10.00
ST 1070	7.5 on the Richter Scale	197?	2.50	5.00	10.00
ST 1071	Solo	1973	2.50	5.00	10.00
ST 1072	Kenton Plays Chicago	1974	2.50	5.00	10.00
ST 1073	Fire, Fury and Fun	1974	2.50	5.00	10.00
ST 1074	Hits in Concert	197?	2.50	5.00	10.00
ST 1076	Kenton '76	1976	2.50	5.00	10.00
ST 1077	Journey Into Capricorn	1977	2.50	5.00	10.00
ST 1078 [R]	The Jazz Compositions of Stan Kenton	197?	2.00	4.00	8.00
ST 1079	Street of Dreams	197?	2.50	5.00	10.00
ST 1080	The Exciting Stan Kenton	197?	2.50	5.00	10.00
CW-3005	Stan Kenton Presents Gabe Baltazar	1979	2.50	5.00	10.00

DECCA

Number	Title (A Side/B Side)	Yr	VG	VG+	NM
DL 8259 [M]	Stan Kenton — Formative Years	195?	6.25	12.50	25.00
—All-black label with silver print					
DL 8259 [M]	Stan Kenton — Formative Years	1960	3.75	7.50	15.00
—Black label with color bars					

HINDSIGHT

Number	Title (A Side/B Side)	Yr	VG	VG+	NM
HSR-118	Stan Kenton 1941	1984	2.00	4.00	8.00
HSR-124	Stan Kenton 1941, Volume 2	1984	2.00	4.00	8.00
HSR-136	Stan Kenton 1943-44	1984	2.00	4.00	8.00
HSR-147	Stan Kenton 1944-45	1984	2.00	4.00	8.00
HSR-157	Stan Kenton 1945-47	1984	2.00	4.00	8.00
HSR-195	Stan Kenton 1962	1984	2.00	4.00	8.00

INSIGHT

Number	Title (A Side/B Side)	Yr	VG	VG+	NM
206	Stan Kenton and His Orchestra, Volume 1	197?	2.50	5.00	10.00
217	Stan Kenton and His Orchestra, Volume 2	197?	2.50	5.00	10.00

LONDON PHASE 4

Number	Title (A Side/B Side)	Yr	VG	VG+	NM
BP 44179/80 [(2)]	Stan Kenton Today	1972	10.00	20.00	40.00
ST-44276	Live in Europe	1976	2.50	5.00	10.00

MOBILE FIDELITY

Number	Title (A Side/B Side)	Yr	VG	VG+	NM
1-091	Kenton Plays Wagner	1982	6.25	12.50	25.00
—Audiophile vinyl					

MOSAIC

Number	Title (A Side/B Side)	Yr	VG	VG+	NM
M6-136 [(6)]	The Complete Capitol Recordings of the Holmanand Russo Charts	199?	30.00	60.00	120.00
MQ10-163 [(10)]	The Complete Capitol Studio Recordings of Stan Kenton 1943-47	199?	50.00	100.00	200.00

SUNBEAM

Number	Title (A Side/B Side)	Yr	VG	VG+	NM
213	Artistry in Rhythm, 1944-45	197?	2.50	5.00	10.00

KENTON, STAN, AND TEX RITTER

Albums

CAPITOL

Number	Title (A Side/B Side)	Yr	VG	VG+	NM
ST 1757 [S]	Stan Kenton/Tex Ritter	1962	20.00	40.00	80.00
T 1757 [M]	Stan Kenton/Tex Ritter	1962	15.00	30.00	60.00

KENTS, THE

45s

ARGO

Number	Title (A Side/B Side)	Yr	VG	VG+	NM
5299	I Found My Girl/With All My Heart and Soul	1958	7.50	15.00	30.00

DOME

Number	Title (A Side/B Side)	Yr	VG	VG+	NM
501	I Love You So/Happy Beat	1958	125.00	250.00	500.00

KEROUAC, JACK

Albums

DOT

Number	Title (A Side/B Side)	Yr	VG	VG+	NM
DLP-3154 [M]	Poetry for the Beat Generation	1959	250.00	500.00	1000.
—Acknowledged to be extremely rare; the same performance is on Hanover 5000					

HANOVER

Number	Title (A Side/B Side)	Yr	VG	VG+	NM
HML-5000 [M]	Poetry for the Beat Generation	1959	62.50	125.00	250.00
HML-5006 [M]	Blues and Haikus	1959	62.50	125.00	250.00
—STEVE ALLEN plays piano behind Kerouac on this album					

RHINO

Number	Title (A Side/B Side)	Yr	VG	VG+	NM
R1-70939 [(4)]	The Jack Kerouac Collection	1990	15.00	30.00	60.00
—Box set compiling the Hanover and Verve LPs plus an LP of unreleased material					

Number	Title (A Side/B Side)	Yr	VG	VG+	NM
VERVE					
MGV-15005 [M]	Readings on the Beat Generation	1960	62.50	125.00	250.00

KERR, ANITA, SINGERS

Also see THE LITTLE DIPPERS.

45s

Number	Title (A Side/B Side)	Yr	VG	VG+	NM
AMPEX					
11042	Eli's Comin'/Something in the Way She Moves	1971	—	2.50	5.00
11050	Shine, Shine//Medley: O Come All Ye Faithful-Noel	1970	—	3.00	6.00
11051	Oh Holy Night/Medley: Angels We Have Heard on High-What Child Is This?-Joy to the World	1970	—	3.00	6.00
DECCA					
27767	Borrowed Angel/My Evening	1951	3.00	6.00	12.00
27872	Have Faith/Pray	1951	3.00	6.00	12.00
28053	The Road Up Ahead/God Has Been Good to Me	1952	2.50	5.00	10.00
28260	A Promise and a Prayer/Mt Grandmother's Place	1952	2.50	5.00	10.00
28962	A Vision of the Blessed Mother/God Is Everywhere	1953	2.50	5.00	10.00
28996	After You/Not Mine	1954	2.50	5.00	10.00
30756	Give In, Give In/Keep Your Belt Buttoned Up, Baby	1958	2.00	4.00	8.00
33032	Mary Kaye's Theme/Where Do I Go from Here	1972	—	3.00	6.00
DOT					
17210	Alfie/A House Is Not a Home	1969	—	2.50	5.00
17270	Lalena/Suppose	1969	—	2.50	5.00
17315	Ob-La-Di, Ob-La-Da/You and I	1969	—	2.50	5.00
17334	Coco/Money Rings Out Like Freedom	1969	—	2.50	5.00
RCA VICTOR					
PB-10388	The Masterpiece/At Seventeen	1975	—	2.00	4.00
47-8246	Guitar Country/Waitin' for the Evening Train	1963	3.00	6.00	12.00
—With Chet Atkins					
47-8332	Copper Kettle/Summer Green and Winter White	1964	—	3.00	6.00
WARNER BROS.					
5866	A Man and a Woman/Just Say Goodbye	1966	—	3.00	6.00
7010	One in a Row/The Ever Constant Sea	1967	—	3.00	6.00
7065	For Bert/I Can't Help Remembering You	1967	—	3.00	6.00
7085	In the Morning/The Smile You Save for Strangers	1967	—	3.00	6.00
7161	All This (She Does to Me)/No Salt on Her Tail	1967	—	3.00	6.00
7185	One Day/One Up on Me	1968	—	2.50	5.00
7211	Happiness/Wine in the Wind	1968	—	2.50	5.00

7-Inch Extended Plays

Number	Title (A Side/B Side)	Yr	VG	VG+	NM
SESAC					
AD-49 [DJ]	On This Holy Night/Bring a Torch, Jeanette, Isabella//Sleep, Sweet Jesus, Sleep/The 12 Days Of Christmas	197?	—	3.00	6.00
AD-56 [DJ]	Deck the Halls/All Through The Night//Rise Up Shepherd and Foller/Christmas Is the Day	197?	—	3.00	6.00
AD-56 [PS]	Deck the Halls/All Through The Night//Rise Up Shepherd and Foller/Christmas Is the Day	197?	—	3.00	6.00

Albums

Number	Title (A Side/B Side)	Yr	VG	VG+	NM
AMPEX					
A-10136	Grow to Know Me	1971	2.50	5.00	10.00
A-10142	A Christmas Story	1971	3.00	6.00	12.00
—With the Royal Philharmonic Orchestra					
BAINBRIDGE					
6224	Slightly Baroque	1981	2.50	5.00	10.00
6226	I Sang with Jim Reeves	1981	2.50	5.00	10.00
6227	The Simon and Garfunkel Songbook	1981	2.50	5.00	10.00
6228	'Round Midnight	1981	2.50	5.00	10.00
CENTURY					
1160	Anita Kerr Performs Wonder's	1979	2.50	5.00	10.00
DECCA					
DL 4061 [M]	For You, For Me, Forevermore	1960	3.75	7.50	15.00
DL 8647 [M]	Quartet Voices in Hi-Fi	1958	3.75	7.50	15.00
DL 74061 [S]	For You, For Me, Forevermore	1960	5.00	10.00	20.00
DL 75159	Till the End of Time	1970	2.50	5.00	10.00
DOT					
DLP 25906	The Anita Kerr Singers Reflect on the Hits of Burt Bacharach & Hal David	1969	2.50	5.00	10.00
DLP 25944	Precious Teresa	1969	2.50	5.00	10.00
DLP 25961	Velvet Voices and Bold Brass	1969	2.50	5.00	10.00
DLP 25970	Touchlove	1970	2.50	5.00	10.00
RCA CAMDEN					
CAS-2209	Gentle on My Mind	1968	2.50	5.00	10.00
RCA VICTOR					
APL1-1166	The Anita Kerr Singers	1975	2.50	5.00	10.00
APL1-2298	Anite Kerr and the French Connection	1977	2.50	5.00	10.00
LPM-2480 [M]	From Nashville...The Hit Sound	1962	3.00	6.00	12.00
LSP-2480 [S]	From Nashville...The Hit Sound	1962	3.75	7.50	15.00
LPM-2581 [M]	"The Genius" In Harmony	1962	3.00	6.00	12.00
LSP-2581 [S]	"The Genius" In Harmony	1962	3.75	7.50	15.00
LPM-2679 [M]	Tender Words	1963	3.00	6.00	12.00
LSP-2679 [S]	Tender Words	1963	3.75	7.50	15.00
LPM-3322 [M]	Mellow Moods of Love	1965	3.00	6.00	12.00
LSP-3322 [S]	Mellow Moods of Love	1965	3.75	7.50	15.00
LPM-3428 [M]	We Dig Mancini	1965	3.00	6.00	12.00
LSP-3428 [S]	We Dig Mancini	1965	3.75	7.50	15.00
LPM-3485 [M]	Sunday Serenade	1966	3.00	6.00	12.00
LSP-3485 [S]	Sunday Serenade	1966	3.75	7.50	15.00
VOCALION					
VL 73899	For You	1969	2.50	5.00	10.00
WARNER BROS.					
W 1665 [M]	Slightly Baroque	1966	3.00	6.00	12.00
WS 1665 [S]	Slightly Baroque	1966	3.75	7.50	15.00
W 1724 [M]	All You Need Is Love	1967	3.75	7.50	15.00
WS 1724 [S]	All You Need Is Love	1967	3.00	6.00	12.00
WORD					
8647	Hallelujah Brass	197?	2.50	5.00	10.00
8692	Hymns	197?	2.50	5.00	10.00
—With Kurt Kaiser					
8696	Walk a Little Slower	197?	2.50	5.00	10.00
8706	Precious Memories	197?	2.50	5.00	10.00
8707	Hallelujah Guitars	197?	2.50	5.00	10.00
8741	Hallelujah Woodwinds	197?	2.50	5.00	10.00
8808	Hallelujah Voices	197?	2.50	5.00	10.00

KERSHAW, RUSTY AND DOUG

45s

Number	Title (A Side/B Side)	Yr	VG	VG+	NM
HICKORY					
1027	So Lovely, Baby/Why Cry for You	1955	7.50	15.00	30.00
1036	Can I Be Dreaming/Look Around	1955	7.50	15.00	30.00
1042	Honey Honey/Let's Stay Together	1956	7.50	15.00	30.00
1048	Hey You There/Your Crazy, Crazy Heart	1956	7.50	15.00	30.00
1055	I'll Understand/Mister Love	1956	7.50	15.00	30.00
1061	If I Win, I Win/Money	1957	7.50	15.00	30.00
—B-side by Al Terry					
1063	Going Down the Road/You'll See	1957	10.00	20.00	40.00
1068	Love Me to Pieces/I Never Had the Blues	1957	10.00	20.00	40.00
1072	Dream Queen/Take My Love	1957	7.50	15.00	30.00
1077	Hey Mae/Why Don't You Love Me	1958	7.50	15.00	30.00
1083	Hey Sheriff/Sweet Thing	1958	7.50	15.00	30.00
1091	It's Too Late/We'll Do It Anyway	1958	7.50	15.00	30.00
1095	Kaw-Liga/Never Love Again	1959	15.00	30.00	60.00
1101	Dancing Shoes/I Love You Like This	1959	15.00	30.00	60.00
1110	The Love I Want/Oh Love	1959	7.50	15.00	30.00
1137	Louisiana Man/Make Me Realize	1960	12.50	25.00	50.00
1151	Diggy Liggy Lo/Hey Mae	1961	15.00	30.00	60.00
1163	Cheated Too/So Lovely Baby	1961	7.50	15.00	30.00
1177	Cajun Joe (Bully of the Bayou)/Sweet Sweet to Me	1962	7.50	15.00	30.00

Albums

Number	Title (A Side/B Side)	Yr	VG	VG+	NM
HICKORY					
LPM-103 [M]	Rusty and Doug Sing Louisiana Man	1960	30.00	60.00	120.00
HICKORY/MGM					
H3G-4506	Louisiana Man	1974	5.00	10.00	20.00

KESEY, KEN

Albums

Number	Title (A Side/B Side)	Yr	VG	VG+	NM
SOUND CITY					
27690 [M]	The Acid Test	1967	75.00	150.00	300.00
—THE GRATEFUL DEAD appear on this LP					

KESNER, DICK

Albums

Number	Title (A Side/B Side)	Yr	VG	VG+	NM
BRUNSWICK					
BL 54044 [M]	Lawrence Welk Presents Dick Kesner	1958	5.00	10.00	20.00
BL 54051 [M]	Dick Kesner and His Magic Stradivarius	1959	3.75	7.50	15.00
BL 54054 [M]	Intermezzo	1960	3.75	7.50	15.00
BL 754044 [S]	Lawrence Welk Presents Dick Kesner	1959	6.25	12.50	25.00
BL 754051 [S]	Dick Kesner and His Magic Stradivarius	1959	5.00	10.00	20.00
BL 754054 [S]	Intermezzo	1960	5.00	10.00	20.00
CORAL					
CRL 57352 [M]	Music of Hawaii	1960	3.00	6.00	12.00
CRL 57360 [M]	A "New" Old Refrain	1961	3.00	6.00	12.00
CRL 57376 [M]	The Sound of Gypsy Music	1961	3.00	6.00	12.00
CRL 57393 [M]	Amor Latino	1962	3.00	6.00	12.00
CRL 57435 [M]	Golden Favorites	1964	3.00	6.00	12.00
CRL 757352 [S]	Music of Hawaii	1960	3.75	7.50	15.00
CRL 757360 [S]	A "New" Old Refrain	1961	3.75	7.50	15.00
CRL 757376 [S]	The Sound of Gypsy Music	1961	3.75	7.50	15.00
CRL 757393 [S]	Amor Latino	1962	3.75	7.50	15.00
CRL 757435 [S]	Golden Favorites	1964	3.75	7.50	15.00
VOCALION					
VL 3777 [M]	Latin Favorites	196?	3.00	6.00	12.00
VL 73777 [S]	Latin Favorites	196?	3.75	7.50	15.00

KESTRELS, THE

45s

Number	Title (A Side/B Side)	Yr	VG	VG+	NM
LAURIE					
3053	There Comes a Time/In the Chapel in the Moonlight	1960	6.25	12.50	25.00

KEYES, TROY

45s

Number	Title (A Side/B Side)	Yr	VG	VG+	NM
ABC					
11027	Love Explosion/I'm Crying (Inside)	1967	2.50	5.00	10.00
11060	No Sad Songs/You Told Your Story (Now Let Me Tell Mine)	1968	3.75	7.50	15.00
11116	A Good Love Gone Bad/I Can Wait My Turn	1968	5.00	10.00	20.00
—With Norma Jenkins					

KEYMEN, THE

45s

Number	Title (A Side/B Side)	Yr	VG	VG+	NM
ABC-PARAMOUNT					
9976	Sentimental Journey/Like Help, Man	1958	3.75	7.50	15.00
9977 [M]	Miss You/Isle of Capri	1958	3.75	7.50	15.00
S-9977 [S]	Miss You/Isle of Capri	1958	6.25	12.50	25.00
9991 [M]	Gazachstahagen/Miss You	1959	3.75	7.50	15.00
S-9991 [S]	Gazachstahagen/Miss You	1959	6.25	12.50	25.00
10016	Dream/Nancy Lee	1959	3.00	6.00	12.00
10039	Camilia/Cha Cha Marcha Congo	1959	3.00	6.00	12.00

Albums

Number	Title (A Side/B Side)	Yr	VG	VG+	NM
ABC-PARAMOUNT					
258 [M]	Dance with Dick Clark	1958	7.50	15.00	30.00
S-258 [S]	Dance with Dick Clark	1958	12.50	25.00	50.00
288 [M]	Dance with Dick Clark, Volume 2	1959	7.50	15.00	30.00
S-288 [S]	Dance with Dick Clark, Volume 2	1959	12.50	25.00	50.00
CORAL					
CRL 57112 [M]	Vocal Sounds of the Keymen	1957	7.50	15.00	30.00
GOLDUST					
LPS-153 [M]	The Keymen Live	196?	12.50	25.00	50.00

KEYNOTES, THE

Possibly all the same group.

45s

Number	Title (A Side/B Side)	Yr	VG	VG+	NM
APOLLO					
478	Suddenly/Zenda	1955	37.50	75.00	150.00
484	I Don't Know/A Star	1955	20.00	40.00	80.00
493	Really Wish You Were Here/Bye Bye Baby	1956	30.00	60.00	120.00
498	Now I Know/Zup Zup	1956	25.00	50.00	100.00
503	In the Evening/O Yeah Hm-m-m	1956	20.00	40.00	80.00
513	One Little Kiss/Now I Know	1957	20.00	40.00	80.00
DOT					
15225	Who/They Say	1954	7.50	15.00	30.00
POP					
111	Carelessly/Congratulations Baby	1957	20.00	40.00	80.00
TOP RANK					
2005	With These Rings/We're Not Getting Along	1959	3.75	7.50	15.00

KEYSTONERS, THE

45s

Number	Title (A Side/B Side)	Yr	VG	VG+	NM
EPIC					
9187	The Magic Kiss/After I Propose	1956	15.00	30.00	60.00
G&M					
102	The Magic Kiss/I'd Write About the Blues	1956	75.00	150.00	300.00
OKEH					
7210	The Magic Kiss/After I Propose	1964	5.00	10.00	20.00
RIFF					
202	Sleep and Dream/T.V. Gal	1961	50.00	100.00	200.00

KEYTONES, THE

45s

Number	Title (A Side/B Side)	Yr	VG	VG+	NM
OLD TOWN					
1041	Wonders of the World/A Fool in Love	1957	75.00	150.00	300.00
1041	Seven Wonders of the World/A Fool in Love	1957	25.00	50.00	100.00

KHAZAD DOOM

Albums

Number	Title (A Side/B Side)	Yr	VG	VG+	NM
LPL					
892	Level 6 1/2	1970	250.00	500.00	1000.

KICKSTANDS, THE

Albums

Number	Title (A Side/B Side)	Yr	VG	VG+	NM
CAPITOL					
ST 2078 [S]	Black Boots and Bikes	1964	37.50	75.00	150.00
T 2078 [M]	Black Boots and Bikes	1964	30.00	60.00	120.00
T/ST 2078	Black Boots and Bikes Bonus Fold-Out	1964	12.50	25.00	50.00

KID, THE

45s

Number	Title (A Side/B Side)	Yr	VG	VG+	NM
RUMBLE					
1347	Sleep Tight/True Love	1959	45.00	90.00	180.00

KIDD, JOHNNY, AND THE PIRATES

45s

Number	Title (A Side/B Side)	Yr	VG	VG+	NM
APT					
25040	Shakin' All Over/Yes Sir, That's My Baby	1960	6.25	12.50	25.00
CAPITOL					
5065	I'll Never Get Over You/Then I Got Everything	1963	3.75	7.50	15.00

KIDDS, THE

45s

Number	Title (A Side/B Side)	Yr	VG	VG+	NM
IMPERIAL					
5335	Are You Forgetting Me/Drunk, Drunk, Drunk	1955	125.00	250.00	500.00
POST					
2003	You Broke My Heart/I Won't Be Back	1955	75.00	150.00	300.00

KILLING FLOOR

Albums

Number	Title (A Side/B Side)	Yr	VG	VG+	NM
SIRE					
SES-97019	Killing Floor	1970	12.50	25.00	50.00

KIM, ANDY

45s

Number	Title (A Side/B Side)	Yr	VG	VG+	NM
20TH CENTURY FOX					
6709	Give Me Your Love/That Girl	1968	2.00	4.00	8.00
CAPITOL					
3895	Rock Me Gently/Rock Me Gently (Part 2)	1974	—	2.50	5.00
3962	Fire, Baby, I'm on Fire/Here Comes the Mornin'	1974	—	2.00	4.00
3962 [PS]	Fire, Baby, I'm on Fire/Here Comes the Mornin'	1974	—	3.00	6.00
4032	Hang Up Those Rock 'N' Roll Shoes/Essence of Joan	1975	—	2.00	4.00
4086	Mary Ann/You Are My Everything	1975	—	2.00	4.00
4130	(She Got Me) Dancin'/Baby, You're All I Got	1975	—	2.00	4.00
4234	Oh, Pretty Woman/Baby You're All I Got	1976	—	2.00	4.00
RED BIRD					
10-040	I Hear You Say (I Love You Baby)/Falling in Love	1965	3.75	7.50	15.00
STEED					
707	How'd We Ever Get This Way/Are You Ever Coming Home	1968	2.00	4.00	8.00
710	Shoot 'Em Up Baby/Ordinary Kind of Girl	1968	2.00	4.00	8.00
711	Rainbow Ride/Resurrection	1968	2.00	4.00	8.00
715	Foundation of My Soul/Tricia Tell Your Daddy	1969	2.00	4.00	8.00
716	Baby I Love You/Gee Girl	1969	2.00	4.00	8.00
720	So Good Together/I Got to Know	1969	—	3.00	6.00
720 [PS]	So Good Together/I Got to Know	1969	3.00	6.00	12.00
723	A Friend in the City/You	1970	—	3.00	6.00
723 [PS]	A Friend in the City/You	1970	3.00	6.00	12.00
727	It's Your Life/To Be Continued	1970	—	3.00	6.00
729	Be My Baby/Love That Little Woman	1970	—	3.00	6.00
731	I Wish I Were/Walking My La De La	1971	—	3.00	6.00
734	I Been Moved/If I Had You Here	1971	—	3.00	6.00
734 [PS]	I Been Moved/If I Had You Here	1971	3.00	6.00	12.00
TCF					
5	Give Me Your Love/Li'l Liz (I Love You)	1964	3.75	7.50	15.00
UNI					
55332	Who Has the Answers?/Shady Hollow Dreamers	1972	—	2.50	5.00
55353	Love Song/Love the Poor Boy	1972	—	2.50	5.00
55356	Oh What a Day/Sunshine	1972	—	2.50	5.00
UNITED ARTISTS					
591	Love Me, Love Me/I Loved You Once	1963	3.75	7.50	15.00

Albums

Number	Title (A Side/B Side)	Yr	VG	VG+	NM
ABC DUNHILL					
DSDP-50193	Andy Kim's Greatest Hits	1974	3.00	6.00	12.00
—Reissue of Steed 37008					
CAPITOL					
ST-11318	Andy Kim	1974	3.00	6.00	12.00
ST-11368	The Pilot	1975	3.00	6.00	12.00
STEED					
STS-37001	How'd We Ever Get This Way	1968	3.75	7.50	15.00
STS-37002	Rainbow Ride	1969	3.75	7.50	15.00
STS-37004	Baby I Love You	1969	3.75	7.50	15.00
STS-37008	Andy Kim's Greatest Hits	1970	3.75	7.50	15.00
UNI					
73137	Andy Kim	1972	3.00	6.00	12.00

KIMBERLY, ADRIAN

Actually DON EVERLY.

45s

Number	Title (A Side/B Side)	Yr	VG	VG+	NM
CALLIOPE					
6501	The Graduation Song...Pomp and Circumstance/Black Mountain Stomp	1961	10.00	20.00	40.00
6503	Greensleeves/God Bless America	1961	10.00	20.00	40.00
6504	When You Wish Upon a Star/Draggin' Dragon	1961	10.00	20.00	40.00

KIME, WARREN, AND HIS BRASS IMPACT ORCHESTRA

45s

Number	Title (A Side/B Side)	Yr	VG	VG+	NM
COMMAND					
4093	The Breeze and I/Mas Que Nada	1967	—	2.50	5.00
4106	Feeling Good/No Moon at All	1967	—	2.50	5.00
4118	Let's Get Away From It All/On My Mind	1968	—	2.50	5.00

Albums

Number	Title (A Side/B Side)	Yr	VG	VG+	NM
COMMAND					
33-910 [M]	Brass Impact	1967	2.50	5.00	10.00
SD-910 [S]	Brass Impact	1967	3.00	6.00	12.00
33-919 [M]	Explosive Brass Impact	1967	2.50	5.00	10.00
SD-919 [S]	Explosive Brass Impact	1967	3.00	6.00	12.00

KING, ALBERT

45s

Number	Title (A Side/B Side)	Yr	VG	VG+	NM
ATLANTIC					
2604	The Hunter/As the Years Go Passing By	1969	2.00	4.00	8.00
BOBBIN					
114	Why Are You So Mean to Me/Ooh-Ee Baby	1959	6.25	12.50	25.00
119	Need You By My Side/The Time Has Come	1960	6.25	12.50	25.00
126	Blues at Sunrise/Let's Have a Natural Ball	1960	6.25	12.50	25.00
129	I Walked All Night Long/I've Made Nights By Myself	1961	6.25	12.50	25.00
130	Travelin' to California/Dyna-Flow	1961	6.25	12.50	25.00
131	Don't Thow Your Love on Me So Strong/This Morning	1961	6.25	12.50	25.00
135	I Get Evil/What Can I Do to Change Your Mind	1962	6.25	12.50	25.00
141	I'll Do Anything for You/Got to Be Some Changes Made	1963	6.25	12.50	25.00
143	Old Blue Ribbon/I've Made Nights By Myself	1963	6.25	12.50	25.00
KING					
5575	Don't Throw Your Love on Me So Strong/This Morning	1961	3.00	6.00	12.00
5588	Travelin' to California/Dyna-Flow	1961	3.00	6.00	12.00
5751	This Funny Feeling/Had You Told It Like It Was	1963	3.00	6.00	12.00
6265	Travelin' to California/Don't Throw Your Love on Me So Strong	1969	2.00	4.00	8.00
PARROT					
798	Bad Luck Blues/Be On Your Merry Way	1954	400.00	800.00	1200.
STAX					
0020	Night Stomp/Blues Power	1968	2.00	4.00	8.00
0034	Drowning on Dry Land (Vocal)/(Instrumental)	1969	2.00	4.00	8.00
0058	Wrapped Up in Love Again/Cockroach	1969	2.00	4.00	8.00
0069	Can't You See What You're Doing to Me/Cold Sweat	1970	2.00	4.00	8.00
0101	Everybody Wants to Go to Heaven/Lovejoy, Ill.	1971	—	3.50	7.00
0121	Angel of Mercy/Funky London	1972	—	3.50	7.00
0135	I'll Play the Blues for You (Part 1)/I'll Play the Blues for You (Part 2)	1972	—	3.50	7.00
0147	Breaking Up Somebody's Home/Little Brother	1972	—	3.50	7.00
0166	The High Cost of Loving/Playing on Me	1973	—	3.50	7.00
0189	That's What the Blues Is All About/I Wanna Get Funky	1973	—	3.50	7.00
190	Laundromat Blues/Overall Junction	1966	2.50	5.00	10.00
197	Funk-Shun/Pretty Woman (Can't Make You Love Me)	1966	2.50	5.00	10.00
201	Crosscut Saw/Down Don't Bother Me	1966	2.50	5.00	10.00
217	Born Under a Bad Sign/Personal Manager	1967	2.50	5.00	10.00
0217	I Can Hear Nothing But the Blues/Flat Tire	1974	—	3.50	7.00
0228	Crosscut Saw/Don't Burn Down the Bridge	1974	—	3.50	7.00
0234	Santa Claus Wants Some Lovin'/Don't Burn Down the Bridges	1974	—	3.50	7.00
241	Cold Feet/Drive a Hard Bargain	1967	2.50	5.00	10.00
252	(I Love) Lucy/You're Gonna Need Me	1968	2.50	5.00	10.00
1056	What Do The Lonely Do At Christmas?/Santa Claus Wants Some Lovin'	197?	—	3.00	6.00
—B-side by Emotions; reissue					

Number	Title (A Side/B Side)	Yr	VG	VG+	NM
1073	Christmas Comes Once A Year/I'll Be Your Santa Claus	197?	—	2.50	5.00

—B-side by Rufus Thomas; reissue

Number	Title (A Side/B Side)	Yr	VG	VG+	NM
3203	The Pinch Paid Off (Part 1)/The Pinch Paid Off (Part 2)	1978	—	2.50	5.00
3225	Santa Claus Wants Some Lovin'/Don't Burn Down the Bridges	1979	—	3.00	6.00

TOMATO

Number	Title (A Side/B Side)	Yr	VG	VG+	NM
10001	Call My Job/Love Shack	1978	—	2.50	5.00
10002	Chump Change/Good Time Charlie	1978	—	2.50	5.00
10009	The Very Thought of You/I Get Evil	1979	—	2.50	5.00
10012	Born Under a Bad Sign/I've Got the Blues	1979	—	2.50	5.00

UTOPIA

Number	Title (A Side/B Side)	Yr	VG	VG+	NM
PB-10544	Cadillac Assembly Line/Nobody Wants a Loser	1976	—	2.50	5.00
PB-10682	Sensation, Communication Together/Gonna Make It Somehow	1976	—	2.50	5.00
PB-10770	Guitar Man/Rub My Back	1976	—	2.50	5.00
PB-10879	Ain't Nothing You Can Do/I Don't Care What My Baby Do	1977	—	2.50	5.00

Albums

ATLANTIC

Number	Title	Yr	VG	VG+	NM
SD 8213	King of the Blues Guitar	1969	6.25	12.50	25.00

FANTASY

Number	Title	Yr	VG	VG+	NM
9627	San Francisco '83	1983	2.50	5.00	10.00
9633	I'm in a Phone Booth, Baby	1984	2.50	5.00	10.00

KING

Number	Title	Yr	VG	VG+	NM
852 [M]	Big Blues	1963	125.00	250.00	500.00
KS-1060	Travelin' to California	1969	6.25	12.50	25.00

MODERN BLUES

Number	Title	Yr	VG	VG+	NM
MBLP-723	Let's Have a Natural Ball	198?	2.50	5.00	10.00

STAX

Number	Title	Yr	VG	VG+	NM
ST-723 [M]	Born Under a Bad Sign	1967	20.00	40.00	80.00
STS-723 [S]	Born Under a Bad Sign	1967	30.00	60.00	120.00
STS-2003	Live Wire/Blues Power	1968	12.50	25.00	50.00
STS-2010	Years Gone By	1969	6.25	12.50	25.00
STS-2015	King Does the King's Thing	1969	6.25	12.50	25.00
STS-2040	Lovejoy	1971	5.00	10.00	20.00
STS-3009	I'll Play the Blues for You	1972	5.00	10.00	20.00
STX-4101	The Pinch	1977	3.00	6.00	12.00
STX-4128	Live Wire/Blues Power	1979	2.50	5.00	10.00
—Reissue of 2003					
STX-4132	Montreux Festival	1980	2.50	5.00	10.00
—Retitled reissue of 5520					
STS-5505	I Wanna Get Funky	1974	3.75	7.50	15.00
STS-5520	Montreux Festival	1975	3.75	7.50	15.00
MPS-8504	Blues for Elvis	1981	2.50	5.00	10.00
—Retitled reissue of 2015					
MPS-8513	I'll Play the Blues for You	1981	2.50	5.00	10.00
—Reissue of 3309					
MPS-8517	Lovejoy	1981	2.50	5.00	10.00
—Reissue of 2040					
MPS-8522	Years Gone By	1982	2.50	5.00	10.00
—Reissue of 2010					
MPS-8534	The Lost Session	1986	2.50	5.00	10.00
MPS-8536	I Wanna Get Funky	1987	2.50	5.00	10.00
—Reissue of 5505					
MPS-8546	Blues at Sunrise	1988	2.50	5.00	10.00
MPS-8556	Wednesday Night in San Francisco	1990	2.50	5.00	10.00
MPS-8557	Tuesday Night in San Francisco	1990	2.50	5.00	10.00

SUNDAZED

Number	Title	Yr	VG	VG+	NM
LP 5031	Born Under a Bad Sign	1999	3.75	7.50	15.00

—Reissue on 180-gram vinyl

TOMATO

Number	Title	Yr	VG	VG+	NM
TOM-6002	King Albert	1978	3.00	6.00	12.00
TOM-7022	New Orleans Heat	1979	3.00	6.00	12.00

UTOPIA

Number	Title	Yr	VG	VG+	NM
BUL1-1387	Truckload of Lovin'	1976	3.00	6.00	12.00
BUL1-1731	Albert	1976	3.00	6.00	12.00
CUL2-2205 [(2)]	Albert Live	1977	3.75	7.50	15.00

KING, ALBERT/STEVE CROPPER/POP STAPLES

45s

STAX

Number	Title (A Side/B Side)	Yr	VG	VG+	NM
0047	Tupelo (Part 1)/Tupelo (Part 2)	1969	2.00	4.00	8.00
0048	Water/Opus de Soul	1969	2.00	4.00	8.00

Albums

STAX

Number	Title	Yr	VG	VG+	NM
STS-2020	Jammed Together	1969	6.25	12.50	25.00
MPS-8544	Jammed Together	1988	2.50	5.00	10.00

—Reissue

KING, ALBERT/LITTLE MILTON

Albums

STAX

Number	Title	Yr	VG	VG+	NM
STX-4123	Chronicle	1979	3.00	6.00	12.00

—One side devoted to each artist

KING, ALBERT/OTIS RUSH

Albums

CHESS

Number	Title	Yr	VG	VG+	NM
LPS 1538	Door to Door	1969	6.25	12.50	25.00
CH-9322	Door to Door	1990	2.50	5.00	10.00

—Reissue

KING, B.B.

Also see BOBBY BLAND AND B.B. KING.

12-Inch Singles

MCA

Number	Title (A Side/B Side)	Yr	VG	VG+	NM
L33-1284 [DJ]	My Lucille (Extended)/Into the Night	1985	2.00	4.00	8.00
2118 [DJ]	The Blues Come Over Me (6 versions)	1991	—	3.00	6.00
L33-17810 [DJ]	Lay Another Log on the Fire/Go On	1989	—	3.00	6.00
23831	Habit to Me (LP Version) (TV Mix)	1988	—	3.00	6.00

45s

ABC

Number	Title (A Side/B Side)	Yr	VG	VG+	NM
10856	Don't Answer the Door (Part 1)/Don't Answer the Door (Part 2)	1966	3.75	7.50	15.00
10889	Waitin' on You/Night Life	1966	3.75	7.50	15.00
11268	Hummingbird/Ask Me No Questions	1970	2.00	4.00	8.00
11280	Chains and Things/King's Special	1970	2.00	4.00	8.00
11290	Ask Me No Questions/Nobody Loves Me But My Mother	1971	2.00	4.00	8.00
11302	Help the Poor/Lucille's Granny	1971	2.00	4.00	8.00
11310	Ghetto Woman/Seven Minutes	1971	2.00	4.00	8.00
11316	Ain't Nobody Home/Alexi's Boogie	1971	2.00	4.00	8.00
11319	Sweet Sixteen/I've Been Blue Too Long	1972	—	3.00	6.00
11321	I Got Some Help I Don't Need/Lucille's Granny	1972	—	3.00	6.00
11330	Guess Who/Better Lovin' Man	1972	—	3.00	6.00
11339	Summer in the City/Five Long Years	1972	—	3.00	6.00
11373	To Know You Is to Love You/I Can't Leave	1973	—	3.00	6.00
11406	I Like to Live the Love/Love	1973	—	3.00	6.00
11433	Who Are You/On to Me	1974	—	3.00	6.00
12029	Philadelphia/Up at 5 A.M.	1974	—	3.00	6.00
12053	Friends/My Song	1974	—	3.00	6.00
12158	When I'm Wrong/Have Faith	1976	—	3.00	6.00
12247	Slow and Easy/I Wonder Why	1977	—	3.00	6.00
12380	Never Make a Move Too Soon/Let Me Make You Cry a Little Longer	1978	—	3.00	6.00
12412	I Just Can't Leave Your Love Alone/Midnight Believer	1978	—	3.00	6.00

ABC-PARAMOUNT

Number	Title (A Side/B Side)	Yr	VG	VG+	NM
10316	I'm Gonna Sit In Till You Give In/You Ask Me	1962	3.75	7.50	15.00
10334	Blues at Midnight/My Baby's Coming Home	1962	3.75	7.50	15.00
10361	Chains of Love/Sneakin' Around	1962	3.75	7.50	15.00
10367	Tomorrow Night/Mother's Love	1962	3.75	7.50	15.00
10390	Guess Who/By Myself	1962	3.75	7.50	15.00
10455	On My Word of Honor/Young Dreamers	1963	3.75	7.50	15.00
10486	How Do I Love You/Slowly Losing My Mind	1963	3.75	7.50	15.00
10527	How Blue Can You Get/Please Accept My Love	1964	3.75	7.50	15.00
10552	Help the Poor/I Wouldn't Have It Any Other Way	1964	3.75	7.50	15.00
10576	Whole Lotta Lovin'/The Hurt	1964	3.75	7.50	15.00
10597	Never Trust a Woman/Worryin' Blues	1964	3.75	7.50	15.00
10616	Please Send Me Someone to Love/The Worst Thing in My Life	1965	3.75	7.50	15.00
10634	Everyday I Have the Blues/It's My Own Fault	1965	3.75	7.50	15.00
10675	Tired of Your Jive/Night Owl	1965	3.75	7.50	15.00
10724	All Over Again/The Things You Put Me Through	1965	3.75	7.50	15.00
10754	Goin' to Chicago Blues/I'd Rather Drink Muddy Water	1965	3.75	7.50	15.00
10766	Tormented/You're Still a Square	1966	3.75	7.50	15.00

BLUESWAY

Number	Title (A Side/B Side)	Yr	VG	VG+	NM
61004	Think It Over/I Don't Want You Cutting Off Your Hair	1967	2.50	5.00	10.00
61007	Worried Dream/That's Wrong, Little Mama	1967	2.50	5.00	10.00
61011	Raining in My Heart/Heartbreaker	1967	2.50	5.00	10.00
61012	Sweet Sixteen (Part 1)/Sweet Sixteen (Part 2)	1968	2.50	5.00	10.00
61015	Paying the Cost to Be the Boss/Having My Say	1968	2.50	5.00	10.00
61018	I'm Gonna Do What They Do to Me/Losing Faith in You	1968	2.50	5.00	10.00
61019	You Put It On Me/B.B. Jones	1968	2.50	5.00	10.00
61021	Dance with Me/Please Send Me Someone to Love	1968	2.50	5.00	10.00
61022	Don't Waste My Time/Get Myself Somebody	1969	2.50	5.00	10.00
61024	Why I Sing the Blues/Friends	1969	2.50	5.00	10.00
61026	Get Off My Back Woman/I Want You So Bad	1969	2.50	5.00	10.00
61029	Just a Little Love/My Mood	1969	2.50	5.00	10.00
61032	The Thrill Is Gone/You're Mean	1969	3.00	6.00	12.00
61032 [PS]	The Thrill Is Gone/You're Mean	1969	5.00	10.00	20.00
61035	So Excited/Confessin' the Blues	1970	2.00	4.00	8.00

KENT

Number	Title (A Side/B Side)	Yr	VG	VG+	NM
301	You Know I Go for You/Why Do Everything Happen to Me	1958	5.00	10.00	20.00
307	Days of Old/Don't Look Now, But You Got the Blues	1958	5.00	10.00	20.00
315	Please Accept My Love/You've Been an Angel	1958	6.25	12.50	25.00
—With the Vocal Chords					
317	Worry Worry/I Am	1959	5.00	10.00	20.00
319	The Fool/Come By Here	1959	5.00	10.00	20.00
325	A Lonely Lover's Plea/Woman in Love	1959	5.00	10.00	20.00
327	Everyday I Have the Blues/Time to Say Goodbye	1959	5.00	10.00	20.00
329	Sugar Mama/Mean Old Friend	1959	5.00	10.00	20.00
330	Sweet Sixteen, Pt. 1/Sweet Sixteen, Pt. 2	1960	5.00	10.00	20.00
333	Got a Right to Love My Baby/My Own Fault	1960	3.75	7.50	15.00
336	Please Love Me/Crying Won't Help You	1960	3.75	7.50	15.00
337	Blind Love/You Upset Me Baby	1960	3.75	7.50	15.00
338	Ten Long Years/Everyday I Have the Blues	1960	3.75	7.50	15.00
339	Did You Ever Love a Woman/Three O'Clock Blues	1960	3.75	7.50	15.00
340	Sweet Little Angel/You Done Lost Your Good Thing Now	1960	3.75	7.50	15.00
346	Partin' Time/Good Man Gone Bad	1960	3.75	7.50	15.00
350	Waking Dr. Bill/You Done Lost Your Good Thing Now	1960	3.75	7.50	15.00
351	Things Are Not the Same/Fishin' After Me	1961	3.75	7.50	15.00
353	Bad Luck Soul/Get Out of Here	1961	3.75	7.50	15.00
358	Hold That Train/Understand	1961	3.75	7.50	15.00
360	Peace of Mind/Someday	1961	3.75	7.50	15.00
362	You're Breaking My Heart/Bad Case of Love	1961	3.75	7.50	15.00
365	My Sometime Baby/Lonely	1962	3.00	6.00	12.00
372	Gonna Miss You Around Here/Hully Gully Twist	1962	3.00	6.00	12.00
373	3 O'Clock Stomp/Mashed Potato Twist	1962	3.00	6.00	12.00
381	Tell Me Baby/Mashing the Popeye	1962	3.00	6.00	12.00
383	Going Down Slow/When My Heart Beats Like a Hammer	1962	3.00	6.00	12.00
386	Your Letter/Blues for Me	1962	3.00	6.00	12.00
387	Christmas Celebration/Easy Listening	1962	3.00	6.00	12.00
388	Whole Lot of Loving/Down Now	1963	3.00	5.00	10.00
389	Trouble in Mind/Long Nights	1963	3.00	5.00	10.00

Number	Title (A Side/B Side)	Yr	VG	VG+	NM
390	My Reward/The Road I Travel	1963	3.00	5.00	10.00
391	The Letter/You Never Know	1963	3.00	5.00	10.00
392	Army of the Lord/Precious Lord	1964	3.00	7.50	15.00
393	Rock Me Baby/I Can't Lose	1964	3.00	5.00	10.00
396	Let Me Love You/You're Gonna Miss Me	1964	3.00	5.00	10.00
403	Beautician Blues/I Can Hear My Name	1964	3.00	5.00	10.00
412	Christmas Celebration/Easy Listening	1964	3.00	6.00	12.00
415	Got 'Em Bad/The Worst Thing in My Life	1965	3.00	6.00	12.00
421	Please Love Me/Baby Look at You	1965	3.00	6.00	12.00
426	Blue Shadows/And Like That	1965	3.00	6.00	12.00
429	Just a Dream/Why Do Everything Happen to Me	1965	3.00	6.00	12.00
435	Mercy, Mercy, Mercy/Broken Promise	1965	3.00	6.00	12.00
441	Eyesight to the Blind/Just Like a Woman	1966	3.00	6.00	12.00
445	Five Long Years/Love, Honor and Obey	1966	3.00	6.00	12.00
447	Ain't Nobody's Business/I Wonder Why	1966	3.00	6.00	12.00
450	I Stay in the Mood/Early Every Morning	1966	3.00	6.00	12.00
458	It's a Mean World/Blues Stay Away	1966	2.00	4.00	8.00
462	The Jungle/Long Gone Baby	1967	2.00	4.00	8.00
467	Treat Me Right/Who Can Your Good Man Be	1967	2.00	4.00	8.00
470	Bad Breaks/Growing Old	1967	2.00	4.00	8.00
475	Sweet Thing/Soul Beat	1967	2.00	4.00	8.00
484	Worry, Worry, Worry/Why Do Everything Happen to Me	1968	—	3.00	6.00
492	The Woman I Love/Blues for Me	1968	—	3.00	6.00
499	Slow Burn/3 O'Clock Blues	1968	—	3.00	6.00
510	Your Fool/Shoutin' the Blues	1969	—	3.00	6.00
4513	I'm Cracking Up Over You/Powerhouse	1969	2.50	5.00	10.00
4515	Dreams/House Rocker	1970	2.50	5.00	10.00
4526	Worried Life/Walkin' Dr. Bill	1970	2.50	5.00	10.00
4542	That Evil Child/Tell Me Baby	1971	2.00	4.00	8.00
4549	I'll Survive/Long Nights	1971	2.00	4.00	8.00
4562	Precious Lord/Swing Low, Sweet Chariot	1972	2.00	4.00	8.00
4566	Don't Get Around Much Anymore/Poontanging	1972	2.00	4.00	8.00
4572	Recession Blues/Walkin' Dr. Bill	1972	2.00	4.00	8.00

MCA

Number	Title (A Side/B Side)	Yr	VG	VG+	NM
41062	Happy Birtday Blues/Better Not Look Down	1979	—	2.00	4.00
51101	There Must Be a Better World Somewhere/You're Going with Me	1981	—	2.00	4.00
52057	Since I Met You Baby/One of Those Nights	1982	—	—	3.00
52098	Street Life/Overture	1982	—	—	3.00
—With the Crusaders and the London Symphony Orchestra					
52125	Love Me Tender/The World I Never Made	1982	—	—	3.00
52218	Sell My Monkey/Inflation Blues	1983	—	—	3.00
52530	Into the Night/Century City Chase of J.B. in Teheran	1985	—	—	3.00
52530 [PS]	Into the Night/Century City Chase of J.B. in Teheran	1985	—	—	3.00
52574	My Lucille/Keep It Light	1985	—	—	3.00
—B-side by Thelma Houston					
52675	Big Boss Man/My Guitar Sings the Blues	1985	—	—	3.00
52751	Memory Lane/Six Silver Strings	1985	—	—	3.00
53269	(You've Become a) Habit to Me/(You've Become a) Habit to Me (Long)	1988	—	—	3.00
53644	Lay Another Log on the Fire/Go On	1989	—	—	3.00
54339	The Blues Come Over Me (Wild & Bluesy Club Mix Edit)/The Blues Come Over Me (Integrity Mix)	1992	—	2.00	4.00

POINTBLANK

Number	Title (A Side/B Side)	Yr	VG	VG+	NM
58820	Christmas Celebration/White Christmas	1999	—	—	3.00
—B-side by Hadda Brooks					

RPM

Number	Title (A Side/B Side)	Yr	VG	VG+	NM
339	3 O'Clock Blues/That Ain't the Way to Do It	1951	225.00	450.00	900.00
—B.B. King singles on RPM before 339 are unconfirmed on 45 rpm					
348	Fine Lookin' Woman/She Don't Move Me No More	1952	75.00	150.00	300.00
355	Shake It Up and Go/My Own Fault, Darling	1952	37.50	75.00	150.00
360	Gotta Find My Baby/Someday Somewhere	1952	25.00	50.00	100.00
363	You Know I Love You/You Didn't Want Me	1952	20.00	40.00	80.00
374	Story from My Heart and Soul/Boogie Woogie Woman	1952	37.50	75.00	150.00
380	Woke Up This Morning (My Baby She Was Gone)/Don't Have to Cry	1953	25.00	50.00	100.00
386	Please Love Me/Highway Bound	1953	37.50	75.00	150.00
391	Please Hurry Home/Neighborhood Affair	1953	20.00	40.00	80.00
395	Why Did You Leave Me/Blind Love	1953	20.00	40.00	80.00
403	Praying to the Lord/Please Help Me	1954	7.50	15.00	30.00
408	Love Me Baby/The Woman I Love	1954	7.50	15.00	30.00
411	Everything I Do Is Wrong/Don't You Want a Man Like Me	1954	7.50	15.00	30.00
412	When My Heart Beats Like a Hammer/Bye Bye Baby	1954	7.50	15.00	30.00
416	You Upset Me Baby/Whole Lotta' Love	1954	7.50	15.00	30.00
421	Every Day I Have the Blues/Sneakin' Around	1955	7.50	15.00	30.00
425	Lonely and Blue/Jump with You Baby	1955	7.50	15.00	30.00
430	I'm in Love/Shut Your Mouth	1955	7.50	15.00	30.00
435	Talkin' the Blues/Boogie Rock	1955	7.50	15.00	30.00
437	Ten Long Years/What Can I Do	1955	7.50	15.00	30.00
450	I'm Cracking Up Over You/Ruby Lee	1956	6.25	12.50	25.00
451	Crying Won't Help You/Sixteen Tons	1956	6.25	12.50	25.00
451	Crying Won't Help You/Can't We Talk It Over	1956	6.25	12.50	25.00
457	Did You Ever Love a Woman/Let's Do the Boogie	1956	6.25	12.50	25.00
459	Dark Is the Night (Part 1)/Dark Is the Night (Part 2)	1956	6.25	12.50	25.00
468	Bad Luck/Sweet Little Angel	1956	6.25	12.50	25.00
479	On My Word of Honor/Bim Bam	1956	6.25	12.50	25.00
486	You Don't Know/Early in the Morning	1957	6.25	12.50	25.00
490	How Do I Love You/You Can't Fool My Heart	1957	6.25	12.50	25.00
492	Troubles, Troubles, Troubles/I Want to Get Married	1957	6.25	12.50	25.00
494	Quit My Baby/Be Careful with a Fool	1957	6.25	12.50	25.00
498	I Wonder/I Need You So Bad	1957	6.25	12.50	25.00
501	The Key to My Kingdom/My Heart Belongs to Only You	1957	6.25	12.50	25.00

Albums

ABC

Number	Title (A Side/B Side)	Yr	VG	VG+	NM
D-704	Blues Is King	1970	3.00	6.00	12.00
—Reissue of BluesWay 6001					
D-709	Blues on Top of Blues	1970	3.00	6.00	12.00
—Reissue of BluesWay 6011					
D-712	Lucille	1970	3.00	6.00	12.00
—Reissue of BluesWay 6016					
D-713	Indianola Mississippi Seeds	1970	3.00	6.00	12.00
D-723	Live in Cook County Jail	1971	3.00	6.00	12.00
D-724	Live at the Regal	1971	3.00	6.00	12.00
—Reissue of ABC-Paramount 509					
D-730	B.B. King in London	1971	3.00	6.00	12.00
D-743	L.A. Midnight	1972	3.00	6.00	12.00
X-759	Guess Who	1972	3.00	6.00	12.00
X-767	The Best of B.B. King	1973	3.00	6.00	12.00
X-794	To Know You Is to Love You	1973	3.00	6.00	12.00
D-813	His Best/The Electric B.B. King	1974	3.00	6.00	12.00
—Reissue of BluesWay 6022					
D-819	Live and Well	1974	3.00	6.00	12.00
—Reissue of BluesWay 6031					
D-825	Friends	1974	3.00	6.00	12.00
D-868	Completely Well	1975	3.00	6.00	12.00
—Reissue of BluesWay 6037					
D-878	Back in the Alley	1975	3.00	6.00	12.00
—Reissue of BluesWay 6050					
D-898	Lucille Talks Back	1975	3.00	6.00	12.00
AB-977	King Size	1977	3.00	6.00	12.00
AA-1061	Midnight Believer	1978	3.00	6.00	12.00

ABC-PARAMOUNT

Number	Title (A Side/B Side)	Yr	VG	VG+	NM
456 [M]	Mr. Blues	1963	7.50	15.00	30.00
S-456 [S]	Mr. Blues	1963	10.00	20.00	40.00
509 [M]	Live at the Regal	1965	10.00	20.00	40.00
S-509 [S]	Live at the Regal	1965	12.50	25.00	50.00
528 [M]	Confessin' the Blues	1965	7.50	15.00	30.00
S-528 [S]	Confessin' the Blues	1965	10.00	20.00	40.00

BLUESWAY

Number	Title (A Side/B Side)	Yr	VG	VG+	NM
BL-6001 [M]	Blues Is King	1967	10.00	20.00	40.00
BLS-6001 [S]	Blues Is King	1967	6.25	12.50	25.00
BLS-6011	Blues on Top of Blues	1968	6.25	12.50	25.00
BLS-6016	Lucille	1968	6.25	12.50	25.00
BLS-6022	His Best/The Electric B.B. King	1969	5.00	10.00	20.00
BLS-6031	Live and Well	1969	5.00	10.00	20.00
BLS-6037	Completely Well	1969	5.00	10.00	20.00
BLS-6050	Back in the Alley	1970	5.00	10.00	20.00

CROWN

Number	Title (A Side/B Side)	Yr	VG	VG+	NM
CST-147 [R]	B.B. King Wails	1960	3.00	6.00	12.00
—Black vinyl					
CST-147 [R]	B.B. King Wails	1960	25.00	50.00	100.00
—Red vinyl					
CST-152 [R]	B.B. King Sings Spirituals	1960	3.00	6.00	12.00
—Black vinyl					
CST-152 [R]	B.B. King Sings Spirituals	1960	25.00	50.00	100.00
—Red vinyl					
CST-195 [S]	King of the Blues	1961	5.00	10.00	20.00
—Black vinyl; this album is in true stereo, contrary to prior reports					
CST-195 [S]	King of the Blues	1961	30.00	60.00	120.00
—Red vinyl; this album is in true stereo, contrary to prior reports					
CST-309 [R]	Blues in My Heart	1963	3.00	6.00	12.00
CST-359 [P]	B.B. King	1963	3.00	6.00	12.00
—Half of the album is in stereo, half is rechanneled					
CLP-5020 [M]	Singin' the Blues	1957	25.00	50.00	100.00
—Black label, silver "Crown"					
CLP-5020 [M]	Singin' the Blues	1963	5.00	10.00	20.00
—Gray label, black "Crown"					
CLP-5020 [M]	Singin' the Blues	196?	3.00	6.00	12.00
—Black label, multi-color "Crown"					
CLP-5063 [M]	The Blues	1958	20.00	40.00	80.00
—Black label, silver "Crown"					
CLP-5063 [M]	The Blues	1963	5.00	10.00	20.00
—Gray label, black "Crown"					
CLP-5063 [M]	The Blues	196?	3.00	6.00	12.00
—Black label, multi-color "Crown"					
CLP-5115 [M]	B.B. King Wails	1959	20.00	40.00	80.00
—Black label, silver "Crown"					
CLP-5115 [M]	B.B. King Wails	1963	5.00	10.00	20.00
—Gray label, black "Crown"					
CLP-5115 [M]	B.B. King Wails	196?	3.00	6.00	12.00
—Black label, multi-color "Crown"					
CLP-5119 [M]	B.B. King Sings Spirituals	1960	15.00	30.00	60.00
—Gray label, black "Crown"					
CLP-5119 [M]	B.B. King Sings Spirituals	196?	3.00	6.00	12.00
—Black label, multi-color "Crown"					
CLP-5143 [M]	The Great B.B. King	1961	15.00	30.00	60.00
—Gray label, black "Crown"					
CLP-5143 [M]	The Great B.B. King	196?	3.00	6.00	12.00
—Black label, multi-color "Crown"					
CLP-5167 [M]	King of the Blues	1961	15.00	30.00	60.00
—Gray label, black "Crown"					
CLP-5167 [M]	King of the Blues	196?	3.00	6.00	12.00
—Black label, multi-color "Crown"					
CLP-5188 [M]	My Kind of Blues	1961	15.00	30.00	60.00
—Gray label, black "Crown"					
CLP-5188 [M]	My Kind of Blues	196?	3.00	6.00	12.00
—Black label, multi-color "Crown"					
CLP-5230 [M]	More B.B. King	1962	15.00	30.00	60.00
—Gray label, black "Crown"					
CLP-5230 [M]	More B.B. King	196?	3.00	6.00	12.00
—Black label, multi-color "Crown"					
CLP-5248 [M]	Twist with B.B. King	1962	15.00	30.00	60.00
—Gray label, black "Crown"					
CLP-5248 [M]	Twist with B.B. King	196?	3.00	6.00	12.00
—Black label, multi-color "Crown"					
CLP-5286 [M]	Easy Listening Blues	1962	15.00	30.00	60.00
—Gray label, black "Crown"					

Number	Title (A Side/B Side)	Yr	VG	VG+	NM
CLP-5286 [M]	Easy Listening Blues	196?	3.00	6.00	12.00
—Black label, multi-color "Crown"					
CLP-5309 [M]	Blues in My Heart	1963	10.00	20.00	40.00
—Gray label, black "Crown"					
CLP-5309 [M]	Blues in My Heart	196?	3.00	6.00	12.00
—Black label, multi-color "Crown"					
CLP-5359 [M]	B.B. King	1963	10.00	20.00	40.00
—Gray label, black "Crown"					
CLP-5359 [M]	B.B. King	196?	3.00	6.00	12.00
—Black label, multi-color "Crown"					
CRUSADERS					
16013	Live in London	1982	6.25	12.50	25.00
—Part of MCA's "Audiophile Series"					
CUSTOM					
CM-2046 [M]	Blues for Me	196?	3.00	6.00	12.00
CM-2049 [M]	I Love You So	196?	3.00	6.00	12.00
CM-2052 [M]	The Soul of B.B. King	196?	3.00	6.00	12.00
DIRECT DISK					
SD-16616	Midnight Believer	1980	12.50	25.00	50.00
—Audiophile vinyl					
GALAXY					
202 [M]	16 Greatest Hits	1963	15.00	30.00	60.00
8202 [S]	16 Greatest Hits	1963	20.00	40.00	80.00
GRP					
GR-9637	Live at the Apollo	1991	3.75	7.50	15.00
KENT					
KST-512 [R]	Rock Me Baby	1964	3.75	7.50	15.00
KST-513 [R]	Let Me Love You	1965	3.75	7.50	15.00
KST-515 [R]	B.B. King Live on Stage	1965	3.75	7.50	15.00
KST-516 [R]	The Soul of B.B. King	1966	3.75	7.50	15.00
KST-517 [R]	Pure Soul	1966	3.75	7.50	15.00
KST-521 [R]	The Jungle	1967	3.75	7.50	15.00
KST-529 [R]	Boss of the Blues	1968	3.75	7.50	15.00
KST-533 [(2)]	From the Beginning	1969	5.00	10.00	20.00
KST-535	Underground Blues	1969	3.75	7.50	15.00
KST-539	The Incredible Soul of B.B. King	1970	3.75	7.50	15.00
KST-548	Turn On with B.B. King	1970	3.75	7.50	15.00
KST-552	Greatest Hits, Volume 1	1971	3.75	7.50	15.00
KST-561	Better Than Ever	1971	3.75	7.50	15.00
KST-563	Doing My Thing, Lord	1971	3.75	7.50	15.00
KST-565	B.B. King Live	1972	3.75	7.50	15.00
KST-568	The Original Sweet Sixteen	1972	3.75	7.50	15.00
KLP-5012 [M]	Rock Me Baby	1964	5.00	10.00	20.00
KLP-5013 [M]	Let Me Love You	1965	5.00	10.00	20.00
KLP-5015 [M]	B.B. King Live on Stage	1965	5.00	10.00	20.00
KLP-5016 [M]	The Soul of B.B. King	1966	5.00	10.00	20.00
KLP-5017 [M]	Pure Soul	1966	5.00	10.00	20.00
KLP-5021 [M]	The Jungle	1967	5.00	10.00	20.00
KLP-5029 [M]	Boss of the Blues	1968	5.00	10.00	20.00
MCA					
3151	Take It Home	1979	2.50	5.00	10.00
5162	There Must Be a Better World Somewhere	1981	2.50	5.00	10.00
5307	Love Me Tender	1982	2.50	5.00	10.00
5413	Blues 'N' Jazz	1983	2.50	5.00	10.00
5616	Six Silver Strings	1985	2.50	5.00	10.00
6455	Live at San Quentin	1990	3.00	6.00	12.00
2-8016 [(2)]	"Now Appearing" at Ole Miss	1980	3.00	6.00	12.00
27005	Live in Cook County Jail	1980	2.00	4.00	8.00
—Reissue of ABC 723					
27006	Live at the Regal	1980	2.00	4.00	8.00
—Reissue of ABC 724					
27007	His Best/The Electric B.B. King	1980	2.00	4.00	8.00
—Reissue of ABC 813					
27008	Live and Well	1980	2.00	4.00	8.00
—Reissue of ABC 819					
27009	Completely Well	1980	2.00	4.00	8.00
—Reissue of ABC 868					
27010	Back in the Alley	1980	2.00	4.00	8.00
—Reissue of ABC 878					
27011	Midnight Believer	1980	2.00	4.00	8.00
—Reissue of ABC 1061					
27028	Take It Home	1981	2.00	4.00	8.00
—Reissue of MCA 3151					
27034	There Must Be a Better World Somewhere	1983	2.00	4.00	8.00
—Reissue of MCA 5162					
27074	The Best of B.B. King	1984	2.00	4.00	8.00
—Reissue of ABC 767					
42183	The King of the Blues: 1989	1989	2.50	5.00	10.00
MOBILE FIDELITY					
1-235	Lucille	1995	6.25	12.50	25.00
—Audiophile vinyl					
PICKWICK					
SPC-3593	Live at the Regal	197?	2.00	4.00	8.00
SPC-3654	Live in Cook County Jail	197?	2.00	4.00	8.00
STAX					
ORS-4508	16 Original Big Hits	198?	2.00	4.00	8.00
UNITED					
US-7703	Heart Full of Blues	197?	2.00	4.00	8.00
US-7705	Easy Listening Blues	197?	2.00	4.00	8.00
—Reissue of Crown 5286					
US-7708	Blues for Me	197?	2.00	4.00	8.00
—Reissue of Custom 2046					
US-7711	I Love You So	197?	2.00	4.00	8.00
—Reissue of Custom 2049					
US-7714	The Soul of B.B. King	197?	2.00	4.00	8.00
—Reissue of Custom 2052					
US-7721	Swing Low	197?	2.00	4.00	8.00
US-7724	My Kind of Blues	197?	2.00	4.00	8.00
—Reissue of Crown 5188					
US-7726	Singin' the Blues	197?	2.00	4.00	8.00
—Reissue of Crown 5020					
US-7728	The Great B.B. King	197?	2.00	4.00	8.00
—Reissue of Crown 5143					
US-7732	The Blues	197?	2.00	4.00	8.00
—Reissue of Crown 5063					
US-7733	Rock Me, Baby	197?	2.00	4.00	8.00
—Reissue of Kent 5012					
US-7734	Let Me Love You	197?	2.00	4.00	8.00
—Reissue of Kent 513					
US-7736	B.B. King Live on Stage	197?	2.00	4.00	8.00
—Reissue of Kent 515					
US-7742	The Jungle	197?	2.00	4.00	8.00
—Reissue of Kent 521					
US-7750	Boss of the Blues	197?	2.00	4.00	8.00
—Reissue of Kent 529					
US-7756	The Incredible Soul of B.B. King	197?	2.00	4.00	8.00
—Reissue of Kent 539					
US-7763	Turn On with B.B. King	197?	2.00	4.00	8.00
—Reissue of Kent 548					
US-7766	Greatest Hits, Volume 1	197?	2.00	4.00	8.00
—Reissue of Kent 552					
US-7773	The Original Sweet Sixteen	197?	2.00	4.00	8.00
—Reissue of Kent 568					
US-7788	9 x 9	197?	2.00	4.00	8.00

KING, B.B./ERIC CLAPTON

Also see each artist's individual listings.

45s

Number	Title (A Side/B Side)	Yr	VG	VG+	NM
REPRISE					
7-16831	Riding with the King/Key to the Highway	2000	—	—	3.00
7-16832	Worried Life Blues/Days of Old	2000	—	—	3.00
7-16833	Marry You/Three O'Clock Blues (Edit)	2000	—	—	3.00
7-16834	When My Heart Beats Like a Hammer (Edit)/I Wanna Be	2000	—	—	3.00
7-16835	Help the Poor/Hold On I'm Coming	2000	—	—	3.00
7-16836	Come Rain or Come Shine/Ten Long Years	2000	—	—	3.00

KING, BEN E.

Also see AVERAGE WHITE BAND; THE DRIFTERS.

45s

Number	Title (A Side/B Side)	Yr	VG	VG+	NM
ATCO					
6166	Show Me the Way/Brace Yourself	1960	4.00	8.00	16.00
6185	Spanish Harlem/First Taste of Love	1960	5.00	10.00	20.00
6194	Stand By Me/On the Horizon	1961	5.00	10.00	20.00
6203	Amor/Souvenir of Mexico	1961	4.00	8.00	16.00
6207	Young Boy Blues/Here Comes the Night	1961	4.00	8.00	16.00
6215	Ecstasy/Yes	1962	4.00	8.00	16.00
6222	Don't Play That Song (You Lied)/Hermit of Misty Mountain	1962	4.00	8.00	16.00
6231	Too Bad/My Heart Cries for You	1962	3.00	6.00	12.00
6237	I'm Standing By/Walking in the Footsteps of a Fool	1962	3.00	6.00	12.00
6246	Tell Daddy/Auf Weidersehn, My Dear	1962	3.00	6.00	12.00
6256	How Can I Forget/Gloria Gloria	1963	3.00	6.00	12.00
6267	I (Who Have Nothing)/The Beginning of Time	1963	3.00	6.00	12.00
6275	I Could Have Danced All Night/Gypsy	1963	3.00	6.00	12.00
6284	What Now My Love/Groovin'	1964	2.50	5.00	10.00
6288	That's When It Hurts/Around the Corner	1964	2.50	5.00	10.00
6303	What Can a Man Do/Si, Senor	1964	2.50	5.00	10.00
6315	It's All Over/Let the Water Run Down	1964	2.50	5.00	10.00
6328	Seven Letters/River of Tears	1964	2.50	5.00	10.00
6343	The Record (Baby I Love You)/The Way You Shake It	1965	2.50	5.00	10.00
6357	She's Gone Again/Not Now (I'll Tell You When)	1965	2.50	5.00	10.00
6371	Cry No More/There's No Place to Hide	1965	2.50	5.00	10.00
6390	Goodnight My Love/I Can't Break the News to Myself	1965	2.50	5.00	10.00
6413	So Much Love/Don't Drive Me Away	1966	2.00	4.00	8.00
6431	Get in a Hurry/I Swear by Stars Above	1966	2.00	4.00	8.00
6454	They Don't Give Medals to Yesterday's Heroes/What Is Soul	1966	2.00	4.00	8.00
6472	A Man Without a Dream/Tears, Tears, Tears	1967	2.00	4.00	8.00
6493	Katherine/Teeny Weeny Little Bit	1967	2.00	4.00	8.00
6527	Don't Take Your Sweet Love Away/She Knows What to Do for Me	1967	2.50	5.00	10.00
6557	We Got a Thing Goin' On/What 'Cha Gonna Do About It	1968	2.00	4.00	8.00
—With Dee Dee Sharp					
6571	Don't Take Your Love from Me/Forgive This Soul	1968	2.00	4.00	8.00
6596	Where's the Girl/It's Amazing	1968	2.00	4.00	8.00
6637	It Ain't Fair/Till I Can't Take It Anymore	1968	2.00	4.00	8.00
6666	Hey Little One/When You Love Someone	1969	2.50	5.00	10.00
ATLANTIC					
3241	Supernatural Thing — Part 1/Supernatural Thing — Part 2	1975	—	2.50	5.00
3274	Do It in the Name of Love/Imagination	1975	—	2.50	5.00
3308	We Got Love/I Had a Love	1975	—	2.50	5.00
3337	I Betch'a You Didn't Know/Smooth Sailing	1976	—	2.50	5.00
3359	One More Time/Somebody's Knocking	1976	—	2.50	5.00
3402	Get It Up/Keepin' It To Myself	1977	—	2.50	5.00
—With the Average White Band					
3427	A Star in the Ghetto/What Is Soul?	1977	—	2.50	5.00
—With the Average White Band					
3444	Fool for You Anyway/The Message	1977	—	2.50	5.00
—With the Average White Band					
3494	I See the Light/Tippin'	1978	—	2.50	5.00
3535	Fly Away to My Wonderland/Spoiled	1978	—	2.50	5.00
3635	Music Trance/And This Is Love	1979	—	2.00	4.00
3808	Street Tough/Why Is the Question	1981	—	2.00	4.00
3839	You Made the Difference in My Life/Souvenirs of Love	1981	—	2.00	4.00
89234	Spanish Harlem/First Taste of Love	1987	—	—	3.00
89361	Stand By Me/Yakety Yak	1986	—	—	3.00
—B-side by the Coasters					
89361 [DJ]	Stand By Me Medley (same on both sides)	1986	2.00	4.00	8.00
—Contains excerpts from all 10 songs on the "Stand By Me" soundtrack album. It is listed here because it uses the same number as the stock release of "Stand By Me."					
89361 [PS]	Stand By Me/Yakety Yak	1986	—	—	3.00

Number	Title (A Side/B Side)	Yr	VG	VG+	NM
89361 [PS]	Stand By Me Medley	1986	2.00	4.00	8.00
—Promo-only sleeve accompanying above medley. Stock and promo sleeves are identical in front but different on back.					
ICHIBAN					
254	You've Got All of Me/It's All Right	1992	—	—	3.00
257	You Still Move Me/I'm Gonna Be Somebody	1992	—	—	3.00
MANDALA					
2512	Take Me to the Pilot/I Guess It's Goodbye	1972	—	2.50	5.00
2513	Into the Mystic/White Moon	1972	—	2.50	5.00
2518	Spread Myself Around/Travellin' Woman	1973	—	2.50	5.00
MANHATTAN					
50078	Save the Last Dance for Me/Wheel of Love	1987	—	—	3.00
50078 [PS]	Save the Last Dance for Me/Wheel of Love	1987	—	—	3.00
MAXWELL					
800	I Can't Take It Like a Man/(B-side unknown)	1969	2.00	4.00	8.00
THE RIGHT STUFF					
S7-19728	4th of July, Asbury Park (Sandy)/Janey, Don't You Lose Heart	1997	—	—	3.00
—B-side by Mrs. Fun/Tina & The B-Side Movement					

Albums

Number	Title (A Side/B Side)	Yr	VG	VG+	NM
ATCO					
33-133 [M]	Spanish Harlem	1961	25.00	50.00	100.00
—Yellow label with harp					
33-133 [M]	Spanish Harlem	1962	10.00	20.00	40.00
—Gold and gray label					
SD 33-133 [S]	Spanish Harlem	1961	37.50	75.00	150.00
—Yellow label with harp					
SD 33-133 [S]	Spanish Harlem	1962	12.50	25.00	50.00
—Purple and brown label					
33-137 [M]	Ben E. King Sings for Soulful Lovers	1962	10.00	20.00	40.00
SD 33-137 [S]	Ben E. King Sings for Soulful Lovers	1962	15.00	30.00	60.00
33-142 [M]	Don't Play That Song	1962	10.00	20.00	40.00
SD 33-142 [S]	Don't Play That Song	1962	15.00	30.00	60.00
33-165 [M]	Ben E. King's Greatest Hits	1964	7.50	15.00	30.00
SD 33-165 [S]	Ben E. King's Greatest Hits	1964	10.00	20.00	40.00
—Purple and brown label					
SD 33-165 [S]	Ben E. King's Greatest Hits	1969	3.00	6.00	12.00
—Yellow label					
SD 33-165 [S]	Ben E. King's Greatest Hits	197?	2.00	4.00	8.00
—Any other color label					
33-174 [M]	Seven Letters	1965	10.00	20.00	40.00
SD 33-174 [S]	Seven Letters	1965	12.50	25.00	50.00
ATLANTIC					
SD 18132	Supernatural	1975	3.00	6.00	12.00
SD 18169	I Have a Love	1976	3.00	6.00	12.00
SD 18191	Rhapsody	1976	3.00	6.00	12.00
SD 19200	Let Me Live in Your Life	1978	3.00	6.00	12.00
SD 19269	Music Trance	1980	2.50	5.00	10.00
SD 19300	Street Tough	1981	2.50	5.00	10.00
81716	Stand By Me: The Best of Ben E. King	1987	2.00	4.00	8.00
—Includes seven Ben E. King tracks and three by the Drifters					
CLARION					
606 [M]	Young Boy Blues	1966	6.25	12.50	25.00
SD 606 [S]	Young Boy Blues	1966	7.50	15.00	30.00
MANDALA					
MLP-3008 [DJ]	Audio Biography	1972	7.50	15.00	30.00
—Promo-only interview by Richard Robinson					
MAXWELL					
88001	Rough Edges	1969	5.00	10.00	20.00

KING, CAROLE

Also see THE CITY; BERTELL DACHE.

12-Inch Singles

Number	Title (A Side/B Side)	Yr	VG	VG+	NM
ATLANTIC					
PR 427 [DJ]	One to One (same on both sides)	1982	2.00	4.00	8.00
CAPITOL					
SPRO-8863/4 [DJ]	Main Street Saturday Night/Disco Tech	1978	3.00	6.00	12.00

45s

Number	Title (A Side/B Side)	Yr	VG	VG+	NM
ABC-PARAMOUNT					
9921	Goin' Wild/The Right Girl	1958	37.50	75.00	150.00
9986	Baby Sittin'/Under the Stars	1958	37.50	75.00	150.00
ALPINE					
57	Oh, Neil/A Very Special Boy	1959	175.00	350.00	700.00
ATLANTIC					
4026	One to One/Goat Annie	1982	—	2.00	4.00
4026 [PS]	One to One/Goat Annie	1982	—	2.50	5.00
4062	Read Between the Lines/Life Without Love	1982	—	2.00	4.00
89694 [DJ]	Speeding Time (same on both sides)	1984	—	2.00	4.00
—May be promo only					
89756	Crying in the Rain/Sacred Heart of Stone	1983	—	2.00	4.00
CAPITOL					
4455	Hard Rock Cafe/To Know That I Love You	1977	—	2.00	4.00
4455 [PS]	Hard Rock Cafe/To Know That I Love You	1977	—	2.50	5.00
4497	Simple Things/Hold On	1977	—	2.00	4.00
4593	Main Street Saturday Night/Changes	1978	—	2.00	4.00
4649	Sunbird/Morning Sun	1978	—	2.00	4.00
4718	Move Lightly/Whiskey	1979	—	2.00	4.00
4718 [PS]	Move Lightly/Whiskey	1979	—	2.50	5.00
4766	Time Gone By/Dreamlike I Wander	1979	—	2.00	4.00
4864	One Fine Day/Rulers of This World	1980	—	2.00	4.00
4864 [PS]	One Fine Day/Recipients of History	1980	2.00	4.00	8.00
—First pressing sleeves list the wrong title for the B-side (no records are known to exist with this title)					
4864 [PS]	One Fine Day/Rulers of This World	1980	—	2.00	4.00
—Second pressing sleeves don't list a B-side at all					
4911	The Locomotion/Oh No Not My Baby	1980	—	2.00	4.00
4941	Chains/Bad Girl	1980	—	2.00	4.00
B-44336	City Streets/Time Heals All Wounds	1989	—	—	3.00
B-44336 [PS]	City Streets/Time Heals All Wounds	1989	—	—	3.00
7PRO-79520 [DJ]	City Streets (same on both sides)	1989	—	2.00	4.00
7PRO-79520 [PS]	City Streets (same on both sides)	1989	—	2.00	4.00
7PRO-79873 [DJ]	Lovelight (same on both sides)	1989	—	2.50	5.00
—Vinyl is promo only					
COMPANION					
2000	It Might As Well Rain Until September/Nobody's Perfect	1962	75.00	150.00	300.00
DIMENSION					
1004	School Bells Are Ringing/I Didn't Have Any Summer Romance	1962	5.00	10.00	20.00
1009	He's a Bad Boy/We Grew Up Together	1963	5.00	10.00	20.00
2000	It Might As Well Rain Until September/Nobody's Perfect	1962	3.00	6.00	12.00
ODE					
66006	Eventually/Up On the Roof	1970	2.00	4.00	8.00
66015	It's Too Late/I Feel the Earth Move	1971	—	2.00	4.00
66015 [PS]	It's Too Late/I Feel the Earth Move	1971	—	2.50	5.00
66019	So Far Away/Smackwater Jack	1971	—	2.00	4.00
66019 [PS]	So Far Away/Smackwater Jack	1971	—	2.50	5.00
66022	Sweet Seasons/Pocket Money	1971	—	2.00	4.00
66022 [PS]	Sweet Seasons/Pocket Money	1971	—	2.50	5.00
66026	It's Going to Take Some Time/Brother Brother	1972	—	3.00	6.00
66031	Been to Canaan/Bitter with the Sweet	1972	—	2.00	4.00
66031 [PS]	Been to Canaan/Bitter with the Sweet	1972	—	2.50	5.00
66035	Believe in Humanity/You Light Up My Life	1973	—	2.00	4.00
66035 [PS]	Believe in Humanity/You Light Up My Life	1973	—	2.50	5.00
66039	Corazon/That's How Things Go Down	1973	—	2.00	4.00
66047	Jazzman/You Go Your Way, I'll Go Mine	1974	—	2.50	5.00
66047 [PS]	Jazzman/You Go Your Way, I'll Go Mine	1974	—	3.00	6.00
66101	Jazzman/You Go Your Way, I'll Go Mine	1974	—	2.00	4.00
66101 [PS]	Jazzman/You Go Your Way, I'll Go Mine	1974	—	2.50	5.00
66106	Nightingale/You're Something New	1975	—	2.00	4.00
66112 SP	Chicken Soup with Rice/Pierre	1975	2.00	[illegible]	8.00
—33 1/3 rpm 7-inch record					
66112 SP [PS]	Chicken Soup with Rice/Pierre	1975	2.50	5.00	10.00
66119	Only Love Is Real/Still Here Thinking of You	1976	—	2.00	4.00
66123	High Out of Time/I'd Like to Know You Better	1976	—	2.00	4.00
RCA VICTOR					
47-7560	Short Mort/Queen of the Beach	1959	25.00	50.00	100.00
TOMORROW					
7502	A Road to Nowhere/Some of Your Lovin'	1966	10.00	20.00	40.00

Albums

Number	Title (A Side/B Side)	Yr	VG	VG+	NM
ATLANTIC					
SD 19344	One to One	1982	2.50	5.00	10.00
80118	Speeding Time	1983	2.50	5.00	10.00
CAPITOL					
SPRO-9103/4 [EP]	Touch the Sky Sampler	1979	3.75	7.50	15.00
—Promo-only four-song excerpt from "Touch the Sky"					
SMAS-11667	Simple Things	1977	2.50	5.00	10.00
SW-11785	Welcome Home	1978	2.50	5.00	10.00
SW-11785	Welcome Home	1978	2.50	5.00	10.00
ST-11953	Touch the Sky	1979	2.50	5.00	10.00
SWAK-11963	Touch the Sky	1979	2.50	5.00	10.00
SOO-12073	Pearls — Songs of Goffin and King	1980	2.50	5.00	10.00
SN-16057	Simple Things	1980	2.00	4.00	8.00
—Budget-line reissue					
SN-16058	Welcome Home	1980	2.00	4.00	8.00
—Budget-line reissue					
SN-16059	Touch the Sky	1980	2.00	4.00	8.00
—Budget-line reissue					
C1-90885	City Streets	1989	3.00	6.00	12.00
ODE					
PE 34944	Carole King: Writer	1977	2.50	5.00	10.00
—Reissue of 77006					
FE 34946	Tapestry	1979	2.50	5.00	10.00
—Reissue with new prefix					
PE 34946	Tapestry	1977	2.50	5.00	10.00
—Reissue of 77009					
PE 34949	Music	1977	2.50	5.00	10.00
—Reissue of 77013					
PE 34950	Rhymes and Reasons	1977	2.50	5.00	10.00
—Reissue of 77016					
PE 34953	Wrap Around Joy	1977	2.50	5.00	10.00
—Reissue of 77024					
PE 34955	Really Rosie	1977	2.50	5.00	10.00
—Reissue of 77027					
PE 34962	Fantasy	1977	2.50	5.00	10.00
—Reissue of 77018					
PE 34963	Thoroughbred	1977	2.50	5.00	10.00
—Reissue of 77034					
JE 34967	Her Greatest Hits	1978	2.50	5.00	10.00
HE 44946	Tapestry	1980	12.50	25.00	50.00
—Half-speed mastered edition					
SP-77006	Writer: Carole King	1970	3.00	6.00	12.00
SP-77009	Tapestry	1971	3.00	6.00	12.00
SP-77013	Music	1971	3.00	6.00	12.00
SP-77016	Rhymes and Reasons	1972	3.00	6.00	12.00
SP-77018	Fantasy	1973	3.00	6.00	12.00
SP-77024	Wrap Around Joy	1974	3.00	6.00	12.00
SP-77027	Really Rosie	1975	3.00	6.00	12.00
SP-77034	Thoroughbred	1976	3.00	6.00	12.00
SQ-88013 [Q]	Music	1974	5.00	10.00	20.00

KING, CLAUDE

45s

Number	Title (A Side/B Side)	Yr	VG	VG+	NM
CINNAMON					
808	Don't Do Me Mad/It's Such a Perfect Day for Making Love	1974	—	2.50	5.00
COLUMBIA					
42043	Big River, Big Man/Sweet Lovin'	1961	2.50	5.00	10.00
42196	The Comancheros/I Can't Get Over the Way You Got Over Me	1961	2.50	5.00	10.00
42196 [PS]	The Comancheros/I Can't Get Over the Way You Got Over Me	1961	3.75	7.50	15.00
42352	Wolverton Mountain/Little Bitty Heart	1962	3.00	6.00	12.00
42352 [PS]	Wolverton Mountain/Little Bitty Heart	1962	3.75	7.50	15.00
42581	The Burning of Atlanta/Don't That Moon Look Lonesome	1962	2.50	5.00	10.00

Number	Title (A Side/B Side)	Yr	VG	VG+	NM
42581 [PS]	The Burning of Atlanta/Don't That Moon Look Lonesome	1962	3.75	7.50	15.00
42630	I've Got the World by the Tail/Shopping Center	1962	2.50	5.00	10.00
42630 [PS]	I've Got the World by the Tail/Shopping Center	1962	3.75	7.50	15.00
42688	Sheepskin Valley/I Backed Out	1963	2.50	5.00	10.00
42688 [PS]	Sheepskin Valley/I Backed Out	1963	3.75	7.50	15.00
42782	Building a Bridge/What Will I Do	1963	2.50	5.00	10.00
42782 [PS]	Building a Bridge/What Will I Do	1963	3.75	7.50	15.00
42833	Hey Lucille!/Scarlett O'Hara	1963	2.50	5.00	10.00
42833 [PS]	Hey Lucille!/Scarlett O'Hara	1963	3.75	7.50	15.00
42959	That's What Makes the World Go Around/A Lace Mantilla and a Rose of Red	1964	2.00	4.00	8.00
43083	Sam Hill/Big Ole Shoulder	1964	2.00	4.00	8.00
43157	Whirlpool (Of Your Love)/This Land of Yours and Mine	1964	2.00	4.00	8.00
43298	Tiger Woman/When You Gotta Go	1965	2.00	4.00	8.00
43416	Little Buddy/Come On Home	1965	2.00	4.00	8.00
43510	Catch a Little Raindrop/Hold That Tiger	1966	2.00	4.00	8.00
43714	The Juggler/I Won't Be Long in Your Town	1966	2.50	5.00	10.00
43867	Little Things That Every Girl Should Know/The Right Place	1966	2.00	4.00	8.00
44035	The Watchman/That's the Way the Wind Blows	1967	2.00	4.00	8.00
44237	Laura (What's He Got That I Ain't Got)/Good-By My Love	1967	2.00	4.00	8.00
44340	Yellow Haired Woman/Ninety-Nine Years	1967	2.00	4.00	8.00
44504	Parchman Farm Blues/Birmingham Bus Station	1968	2.00	4.00	8.00
44642	The Power of Your Sweet Love/Beertops and Teardrops	1968	2.00	4.00	8.00
44749	Sweet Love on My Mind/Four Roses	1969	2.00	4.00	8.00
44833	All for the Love of a Girl/I Remember Johnny	1969	2.00	4.00	8.00
44833 [PS]	All for the Love of a Girl/I Remember Johnny	1969	3.00	6.00	12.00
45015	Friend, Lover, Woman, Wife/The House of the Rising Sun	1969	2.00	4.00	8.00
45142	I'll Be Your Baby Tonight/It's Good to Have My Baby Home	1970	—	3.00	6.00
45248	Mary's Vineyard/Johnny Valentine	1970	—	3.00	6.00
45340	Chip 'n' Dale's Place/Highway Lonely	1971	—	3.00	6.00
45441	When You're Twenty-One/Heart	1971	—	3.00	6.00
45515	Darlin' Raise the Shade (Let the Sun Shine In)/ Sweet Mary Ann	1971	—	3.00	6.00
45614	The Lady of Our Town/Just As Soon As I Get Over Loving You	1972	—	3.00	6.00
45704	He Ain't Country/This Time I'm Through	1972	—	3.00	6.00
TRUE					
103	Cotton Dan/(B-side unknown)	1977	—	2.50	5.00
Albums					
COLUMBIA					
CS 1024	Friend, Lover, Woman, Wife	1970	3.75	7.50	15.00
CL 1810 [M]	Meet Claude King	1962	6.25	12.50	25.00
—Six "eye" logos on label					
CL 1810 [M]	Meet Claude King	1963	3.75	7.50	15.00
—"Guaranteed High Fidelity" or "Mono" on red label					
CL 2415 [M]	Tiger Woman	1965	5.00	10.00	20.00
CS 8610 [S]	Meet Claude King	1962	10.00	20.00	40.00
—Six "eye" logos on label					
CS 8610 [S]	Meet Claude King	1963	5.00	10.00	20.00
—"360 Sound Stereo" on red label					
CS 9215 [S]	Tiger Woman	1965	6.25	12.50	25.00
—"360 Sound Stereo" on red label					
CS 9789	I Remember Johnny Horton	1968	3.75	7.50	15.00
—"360 Sound Stereo" on red label					
C 30804	Chip 'n' Dale's Place	1971	3.75	7.50	15.00
HARMONY					
HS 11300	The Best of Claude King	1969	3.00	6.00	12.00

KING, CLYDIE

Number	Title (A Side/B Side)	Yr	VG	VG+	NM
45s					
IMPERIAL					
66109	The Thrill Is Gone/If You Were a Man	1965	5.00	10.00	20.00
66139	My Love Grows Deeper/Missin' My Baby	1965	5.00	10.00	20.00
66172	He Always Comes Back to Me/Soft and Gentle Ways	1966	5.00	10.00	20.00
LIZARD					
21007	'Bout Love/(B-side unknown)	1971	—	3.00	6.00
MINIT					
32025	Good for Cryin' Over You Days/Mistakes of Yesterday	1967	3.00	6.00	12.00
32054	Love Now, Pay Later/One Part, Two Part	1969	2.00	4.00	8.00
PHILIPS					
40001	Boys in My Life/Promises	1962	5.00	10.00	20.00
40051	Turn Around/Don't Hang Up the Phone	1962	5.00	10.00	20.00
40107	Only the Guilty Cry/By Noro	1963	5.00	10.00	20.00
SPECIALTY					
605	Our Romance/Written on the Wall	1957	7.50	15.00	30.00
Albums					
LIZARD					
A-20104	Direct Me	1971	3.00	6.00	12.00

KING, CURTIS

No, not King Curtis.

Number	Title (A Side/B Side)	Yr	VG	VG+	NM
45s					
COLUMBIA					
44096	Bad Habits/So Nice While It Lasted	1967	5.00	10.00	20.00

KING, EARL

Number	Title (A Side/B Side)	Yr	VG	VG+	NM
45s					
ACE					
509	Those Lonely, Lonely Nights/Baby You Can Get Your Gun	1955	15.00	30.00	60.00
514	My Love Is Strong/Little Girl	1956	12.50	25.00	50.00
517	It Must Have Been Love/I'll Take You Back Home	1956	12.50	25.00	50.00
520	Is Everything Alright/Mother Told Me Not to Go	1956	12.50	25.00	50.00
529	Those Lonely, Lonely Feelings/You Can Fly High	1957	12.50	25.00	50.00
543	I'll Never Get Tired/Well'o, Well'o, Well'o Baby	1958	12.50	25.00	50.00
564	Weary Silent Night/Everybody's Carried Away	1959	10.00	20.00	40.00
598	Don't You Know You're Wrong/Buddy It's Time to Go	1960	10.00	20.00	40.00
IMPERIAL					
5713	Come On — Part 1/Come On — Part 2	1960	6.25	12.50	25.00
5730	Love Me Now/The Things That I Used to Do	1961	6.25	12.50	25.00
5750	Come Along with Me/You're More to Me Than Gold	1961	6.25	12.50	25.00
5774	You Better Know/Mama and Papa	1961	6.25	12.50	25.00
5811	Trick Bag/Always a First Time	1962	6.25	12.50	25.00
5858	We Are Just Friends/You're More to Me That Gold	1962	6.25	12.50	25.00
5891	Come Along with Me/Case of Love	1962	6.25	12.50	25.00
REX					
1015	I Can't Help Myself/Darling Honey, Angel Child	1961	5.00	10.00	20.00
SPECIALTY					
495	A Mother's Love/I'm Your Best Bet Baby	1954	15.00	30.00	60.00
531	No One But Me/Eating and Sleeping	1954	15.00	30.00	60.00
558	Funny Face/Sittin' and Wonderin'	1955	15.00	30.00	60.00

KING, FREDDIE

Number	Title (A Side/B Side)	Yr	VG	VG+	NM
45s					
COTILLION					
44015	Funky/Play It Cool	1968	2.00	4.00	8.00
44058	I Wonder Why/Yonder Wall	1970	2.00	4.00	8.00
EL-BEE					
157	Country Boy/That's What You Think	1956	100.00	200.00	400.00
FEDERAL					
12384	Have You Ever Loved a Woman/You've Got to Love Her with a Feeling	1960	10.00	20.00	40.00
12401	Hideaway/I Love the Woman	1961	7.50	15.00	30.00
12415	Lonesome Whistle Blues/It's Too Bad Things Are Going So Tough	1961	7.50	15.00	30.00
12428	San-Ho-Zay/See See Baby	1961	7.50	15.00	30.00
12432	I'm Tore Down/Sen-Say-Shun	1961	7.50	15.00	30.00
12439	Christmas Tears/I Hear Jingle Bells	1961	7.50	15.00	30.00
12443	If You Believe in What You Do/Heads Up	1961	5.00	10.00	20.00
12450	Takin' Care of Business/The Stumble	1962	5.00	10.00	20.00
12456	Side Tracked/Sittin' on the Boat Dock	1962	5.00	10.00	20.00
12462	What About Love/Texas Oil	1962	5.00	10.00	20.00
12470	Come On/Just Pickin'	1962	5.00	10.00	20.00
12475	In the Open/I'm On My Way to Atlanta	1962	5.00	10.00	20.00
12482	The Bossa Nova Watusi Twist/Look Ma, I'm Crying	1963	3.75	7.50	15.00
12491	(I'd Love To) Make Love to You/One Hundred Years	1963	3.75	7.50	15.00
12499	(The Welfare) Turns Its Back on You/You're Barkin' Up the Wrong Tree	1963	3.75	7.50	15.00
12509	Surf Monkey/Monkey Donkey	1963	5.00	10.00	20.00
12515	Meet Me at the Station/Ting-a-Ling	1964	3.75	7.50	15.00
12518	Driving Sideways/Someday After Awhile (You'll Be Gone)	1964	3.00	6.00	12.00
12521	She Put the Whammy on Me/High Rise	1964	3.00	6.00	12.00
12529	Now I've Got a Woman/Onion Rings	1964	3.00	6.00	12.00
12532	Some Other Day, Some Other Time/Manhole	1965	3.00	6.00	12.00
12535	If You Have It/I Love You More Every Day	1965	3.00	6.00	12.00
12537	Full Time Love/She's the One	1965	3.00	6.00	12.00
KING					
6057	Use What You've Got/Double Eyed Whammy	1966	3.00	6.00	12.00
6080	You've Got Me Licked/The Girl from Kookamunga	1967	3.00	6.00	12.00
6264	Have You Ever Loved a Woman/Hideaway	1969	2.00	4.00	8.00
RSO					
505	My Credit Didn't Go Through/Texas Flyer	1975	—	2.50	5.00
516	Boogie Bump/It's Your Love	1975	—	2.50	5.00
SHELTER					
7303	Going Down/Toke Down	1971	—	3.00	6.00
7320	Me and My Guitar/Downtown in Lodi	1972	—	3.00	6.00
7333	Woman Across the River/Help Me Through the Day	1973	—	3.00	6.00
40410	Going Down/Me and My Guitar	1975	—	2.50	5.00
Albums					
COTILLION					
SD 9004	Freddie King Is a Blues Master	1969	6.25	12.50	25.00
SD 9016	My Feeling for the Blues	1970	6.25	12.50	25.00
KING					
762 [M]	Freddie King Sings the Blues	1961	62.50	125.00	250.00
773 [M]	Let's Hide Away and Dance Away	1961	62.50	125.00	250.00
821 [M]	Bossa Nova and Blues	1962	37.50	75.00	150.00
856 [M]	Freddie King Goes Surfin'	1963	20.00	40.00	80.00
KS-856 [S]	Freddie King Goes Surfin'	1963	30.00	60.00	120.00
928 [M]	A Bonanza of Instrumentals	1965	12.50	25.00	50.00
KS-928 [S]	A Bonanza of Instrumentals	1965	15.00	30.00	60.00
964 [M]	24 Vocals and Instrumentals	1966	6.25	12.50	25.00
KS-1059	Hide Away	1969	3.75	7.50	15.00
MCA					
690	The Best of Freddie King	1979	2.00	4.00	8.00
—Reissue of Shelter 52021					
MODERN BLUES					
MB2LP-721 [(2)]	Just Pickin'	198?	3.75	7.50	15.00
MBLP-722	Freddie King Sings	198?	2.50	5.00	10.00
RSO					
RS-1-3025	Freddie King 1934-1976	1977	3.00	6.00	12.00
SD 4803	Burglar	1974	3.00	6.00	12.00
SD 4811	Larger Than Life	1975	3.00	6.00	12.00
SHELTER					
2140	The Best of Freddie King	1975	3.75	7.50	15.00
—Original with MCA distribution					
SW-8905	Getting Ready	1971	3.75	7.50	15.00
SW-8913	Texas Cannonball	1972	3.75	7.50	15.00
SW-8919	Woman Across the River	1973	3.75	7.50	15.00
SRL 52021	The Best of Freddie King	1977	3.00	6.00	12.00
—Second edition with ABC distribution					

Number	Title (A Side/B Side)	Yr	VG	VG+	NM
STARDAY/GUSTO					
5012	17 Original Hits	1977	2.50	5.00	10.00
5033	Hide Away	1978	2.50	5.00	10.00

KING, FREDDIE/LULA REED/BOBBY THOMPSON

Albums

Number	Title (A Side/B Side)	Yr	VG	VG+	NM
KING					
777 [M]	Boy-Girl-Boy	1962	62.50	125.00	250.00

KING, JEAN

45s

Number	Title (A Side/B Side)	Yr	VG	VG+	NM
HANNA-BARBERA					
497	Don't Say Goodbye/It's Good Enough for Me	1966	2.50	5.00	10.00

Albums

Number	Title (A Side/B Side)	Yr	VG	VG+	NM
HANNA-BARBERA					
HLP-8505 [M]	Jean King Sings for the In Crowd	1966	5.00	10.00	20.00

KING, JONATHAN

Also see HEDGEHOPPERS ANONYMOUS.

45s

Number	Title (A Side/B Side)	Yr	VG	VG+	NM
PARROT					
3005	Just Like a Woman/Land of the Golden Tree	1966	2.00	4.00	8.00
3008	Icicles (Fell from the Heart of a Bluebird)/In a Hundred Years from Now	1966	2.00	4.00	8.00
3011	Round, Round/Time and Motion	1967	2.00	4.00	8.00
3021	1968 (Message to the Presidential Candidates)/Colloquial Sex	1968	2.00	4.00	8.00
3027	Lazy Bones/Just Want to Say Thank You	1968	2.00	4.00	8.00
3029	Hooked on a Feeling/I Don't Want to Be Gay	1969	—	3.00	6.00
3030	Flirt/Hey Jim	1969	—	3.00	6.00
9774	Everyone's Gone to the Moon/Summer's Coming	1965	2.50	5.00	10.00
9804	Green Is the Grass/Where the Sun Has Never Shown	1965	2.00	4.00	8.00
40047	Let It All Hang Out/Colloquial Sex	1970	—	3.00	6.00
40055	Cherry Cherry/Gay Girl	1970	—	3.00	6.00
UK					
49002	It's a Tall Order for a Short Guy/Learned Tax Counsel	1972	—	2.50	5.00
49014	Mary, My Love/A Little Bit Left of Right	1973	—	2.50	5.00
49018	The Kung Fu Anthem/A Little Bit Left of Right	1973	—	2.50	5.00
49034	The Way You Look Tonight/The True Story of Molly Malone	1974	—	2.50	5.00

Albums

Number	Title (A Side/B Side)	Yr	VG	VG+	NM
PARROT					
PA 61013 [M]	Jonathan King Or Then Again....	1967	10.00	20.00	40.00
PAS 71013 [P]	Jonathan King Or Then Again....	1967	12.50	25.00	50.00
—Only "Where the Sun Has Never Shown" is rechanneled.					
U.K.					
53101	Bubble Rock Is Here to Stay	1972	6.25	12.50	25.00
53104	Pandora's Box	1973	6.25	12.50	25.00

KING, MORGANA

45s

Number	Title (A Side/B Side)	Yr	VG	VG+	NM
20TH FOX					
142	Give Me Love/Lost, Lonely and Looking for Love	1959	3.00	6.00	12.00
MAINSTREAM					
600	A Taste of Honey/Corcavado	1964	2.50	5.00	10.00
623	Try to Remember/Cuore di Mama	1964	2.50	5.00	10.00
MERCURY					
70927	Homesick in Paris/For You and Me	1956	3.75	7.50	15.00
70967	Four Walls, Two Windows, One Broken Heart/Mine for the Taking	1956	3.75	7.50	15.00
PARAMOUNT					
0245	A Song for You/You Are the Sunshine of My Life	1973	—	2.50	5.00
0275	Jennifer Had/Like a Seed	1974	—	2.50	5.00
REPRISE					
0481	If You Should Leave Me (E Se Domani)/Mountain High, Valley Low	1966	2.00	4.00	8.00
0604	The Look of Love/I Have Loved Me a Man	1967	2.00	4.00	8.00
VERVE					
10615	I Know How It Feels to Be Lonely/I Only Know I Loved You	1968	—	3.00	6.00
10630	Didn't We/Eleanor Rigby	1968	—	3.00	6.00
WING					
90073	In the Wee Small Hours of the Morning/It's De-Lovely	1956	3.75	7.50	15.00

Albums

Number	Title (A Side/B Side)	Yr	VG	VG+	NM
ASCOT					
AM 13014 [M]	The Winter of My Discontent	1964	6.25	12.50	25.00
AM 13019 [M]	The End of a Love Affair	1965	6.25	12.50	25.00
—Reissue of United Artists 30020					
AM 13020 [M]	Everybody Loves Saturday Night	1965	6.25	12.50	25.00
AM 13025 [M]	More Morgana	1965	6.25	12.50	25.00
AS 16014 [S]	The Winter of My Discontent	1964	7.50	15.00	30.00
AS 16019 [S]	The End of a Love Affair	1965	7.50	15.00	30.00
—Reissue of United Artists 40020					
AS 16020 [S]	Everybody Loves Saturday Night	1965	7.50	15.00	30.00
AS 16025 [S]	More Morgana	1965	7.50	15.00	30.00
EMARCY					
MG-36079 [M]	For You, For Me, Forever More	1956	20.00	40.00	80.00
MAINSTREAM					
MRL-321	Taste of Honey	1972	3.75	7.50	15.00
MRL-355	Cuore di Mama	1974	3.75	7.50	15.00
S-6015 [S]	With a Taste of Honey	1964	6.25	12.50	25.00
S-6052 [S]	Miss Morgana King	1965	6.25	12.50	25.00
56015 [M]	With a Taste of Honey	1964	5.00	10.00	20.00
56052 [M]	Miss Morgana King	1965	5.00	10.00	20.00
MERCURY					
MG-20231 [M]	Morgana King Sings the Blues	1958	20.00	40.00	80.00
MUSE					
MR-5166	Stretchin' Out	1977	2.50	5.00	10.00
MR-5190	Everything Must Change	1978	2.50	5.00	10.00
MR-5224	Higher Ground	1979	2.50	5.00	10.00
MR-5257	Looking Through the Eyes of Love	1981	2.50	5.00	10.00
MR-5301	Portraits	1983	2.50	5.00	10.00
MR-5326	Simply Eloquent	1986	2.50	5.00	10.00
MR-5339	Another Time, Another Space	1988	2.50	5.00	10.00
PARAMOUNT					
PAS-6067	New Beginnings	1973	3.00	6.00	12.00
RCA CAMDEN					
CAL-543 [M]	The Greatest Songs Ever Swung	1959	5.00	10.00	20.00
CAS-543 [S]	The Greatest Songs Ever Swung	1959	7.50	15.00	30.00
REPRISE					
R 6192 [M]	It's a Quiet Thing	1966	5.00	10.00	20.00
RS 6192 [S]	It's a Quiet Thing	1966	6.25	12.50	25.00
R 6205 [M]	Wild Is Love	1966	5.00	10.00	20.00
RS 6205 [S]	Wild Is Love	1966	6.25	12.50	25.00
R 6257 [M]	Gemini Changes	1967	5.00	10.00	20.00
RS 6257 [S]	Gemini Changes	1967	6.25	12.50	25.00
TRIP					
5533	Morgana King Sings	197?	2.50	5.00	10.00
UNITED ARTISTS					
UAL 3028 [M]	Folk Songs A La King	1960	10.00	20.00	40.00
UAS 6028 [S]	Folk Songs A La King	1960	12.50	25.00	50.00
UAL 30020 [M]	Let Me Love You	1960	12.50	25.00	50.00
UAS 40020 [S]	Let Me Love You	1960	15.00	30.00	60.00
VERVE					
V-5061 [M]	I Know How It Feels	1968	6.25	12.50	25.00
V6-5061 [S]	I Know How It Feels	1968	6.25	12.50	25.00
WING					
MGW-12307 [M]	More Morgana King	1965	3.75	7.50	15.00
SRW-16307 [S]	More Morgana King	1965	5.00	10.00	20.00

KING, REV. MARTIN LUTHER

The 1968 releases are posthumous tributes.

45s

Number	Title (A Side/B Side)	Yr	VG	VG+	NM
GORDY					
7023	I Have a Dream/We Shall Overcome	1963	7.50	15.00	30.00
7023	I Have a Dream/We Shall Overcome	1968	2.00	4.00	8.00
—B-side by Liz Lands; "Gordy" on side of label					
MERCURY					
72814	I Have a Dream/I've Been to the Mountain Top-Eulogy	1968	2.00	4.00	8.00

Albums

Number	Title (A Side/B Side)	Yr	VG	VG+	NM
20TH CENTURY					
TCF-3110 [M]	Freedom March on Washington	1963	7.50	15.00	30.00
S-3201	The Rev. Dr. Martin Luther King, Jr.	1968	5.00	10.00	20.00
BUDDAH					
BDS-2002	Man of Love	1968	5.00	10.00	20.00
CREED					
3201 [M]	I Have a Dream	1968	5.00	10.00	20.00
DOOTO					
DTL-831 [M]	Martin Luther King at Zion Hill	1962	7.50	15.00	30.00
DTL-841	The American Dream	1968	5.00	10.00	20.00
GORDY					
G-906 [M]	The Great March to Freedom	1963	10.00	20.00	40.00
—"Gordy" in script at top of label					
G-906 [M]	The Great March to Freedom	1968	3.75	7.50	15.00
—Later pressings					
G-908 [M]	The Great March on Washington	1963	10.00	20.00	40.00
—"Gordy" in script at top of label					
G-908 [M]	The Great March on Washington	1968	3.75	7.50	15.00
—Later pressings					
G-929	...Free at Last	1968	7.50	15.00	30.00
—Original with gatefold cover					
MERCURY					
SR-61170	In Search of Freedom	1968	5.00	10.00	20.00
MR. MAESTRO					
1000 [M]	The March on Washington	1963	7.50	15.00	30.00
SUNSET					
21033	The Struggle for Freedom	1968	3.75	7.50	15.00
UNART					
S 21033	In the Struggle for Freedom and Human Dignity	1968	5.00	10.00	20.00

KING BEES, THE

More than one group.

45s

Number	Title (A Side/B Side)	Yr	VG	VG+	NM
CHECKER					
909	Buzzin'/Good Rockin' Tonight	1958	20.00	40.00	80.00
FLIP					
323	Puppy Love/Give Me Your Number	1957	10.00	20.00	40.00
KRC					
302	Lovely Love/Can't You Understand?	1957	10.00	20.00	40.00
NOBLE					
715	Tender Love/What Could Have Been Can't Be	1959	62.50	125.00	250.00
RCA VICTOR					
47-8688	What She Does to Me/That Ain't Love	1965	3.00	6.00	12.00
47-8787	On Your Way Down the Drain/Rhythm and Blues	1966	3.00	6.00	12.00
47-8979	Lost in the Shuffle/Hardly (Part 3)	1966	3.00	6.00	12.00

KING BISCUIT BOY

45s

Number	Title (A Side/B Side)	Yr	VG	VG+	NM
EPIC					
50129	New Orleans/I'm Writing You a Letter	1975	—	2.50	5.00
PARAMOUNT					
0052	Corrina, Corrina/Cookin' Little Baby	1970	—	2.50	5.00
0076	King Biscuit's Boogie/Badly Bent	1971	—	2.50	5.00

Albums

Number	Title (A Side/B Side)	Yr	VG	VG+	NM
EPIC					
KE 32891	King Biscuit Boy	1974	3.00	6.00	12.00
PARAMOUNT					
PAS-5023	Gooduns	1969	3.75	7.50	15.00

Number	Title (A Side/B Side)	Yr	VG	VG+	NM
PAS-5030	Official Music	1970	3.75	7.50	15.00
—As "King Biscuit Boy with Crowbar"					

KING CRIMSON

12-Inch Singles

Number	Title (A Side/B Side)	Yr	VG	VG+	NM
WARNER BROS.					
PRO-A-2131 [DJ]	Sleepless (Long Version)/Sleepless (Short Version)	1984	2.00	4.00	8.00
PRO-A-2148 [DJ]	3 of a Perfect Pair/Man with an Open Heart	1984	2.00	4.00	8.00
20193	Sleepless (Dance Mix)/(Instrumental)	1984	—	3.00	6.00

45s

Number	Title (A Side/B Side)	Yr	VG	VG+	NM
ATLANTIC					
2702	In the Court of the Crimson King (Part 1)/In the Court of the Crimson King (Part 2)	1970	3.00	6.00	12.00
3016	Night Watch/The Great Deceiver	1974	—	3.00	6.00
WARNER BROS.					
29309	Sleepless/Nuages (That Which Passes, Passes Like Clouds)	1984	—	2.50	5.00
29964	Heartbeat/Requiem	1982	—	2.50	5.00

Albums

Number	Title (A Side/B Side)	Yr	VG	VG+	NM
ATLANTIC					
SD 7212	Islands	1972	5.00	10.00	20.00
SD 7263	Larks' Tongues in Aspic	1973	5.00	10.00	20.00
SD 7298	Starless and Bible Black	1974	5.00	10.00	20.00
SD 8245	In the Court of the Crimson King — An Observation by King Crimson	1969	5.00	10.00	20.00
SD 8266	In the Wake of Poseidon	1970	5.00	10.00	20.00
SD 8278	Lizard	1971	5.00	10.00	20.00
SD 18110	Red	1974	3.75	7.50	15.00
SD 18136	USA	1975	3.75	7.50	15.00
SD 19155	In the Court of the Crimson King — An Observation by King Crimson	1978	3.00	6.00	12.00
—Reissue of Atlantic 8245					
EDITIONS EG					
EGKC-1	In the Court of the Crimson King — An Observation by King Crimson	1985	2.50	5.00	10.00
—Reissue of Atlantic 19155					
EGKC-2	In the Wake of Poseidon	1985	2.50	5.00	10.00
—Reissue of Atlantic 8266					
EGKC-3	Lizard	1985	2.50	5.00	10.00
—Reissue of Atlantic 8278					
EGKC-4	Islands	1985	2.50	5.00	10.00
—Reissue of Atlantic 7212					
EGKC-6	Lark's Tongue in Aspic	1985	2.50	5.00	10.00
—Reissue of Atlantic 7263					
EGKC-7	Starless and Bible Black	1985	2.50	5.00	10.00
—Reissue of Atlantic 7298					
EGKC-8	Red	1985	2.50	5.00	10.00
—Reissue of Atlantic 18110					
EGKC-9	USA	1985	2.50	5.00	10.00
—Reissue of Atlantic 18135					
EGKC-10 [(2)]	The Young Person's Guide to King Crimson	1985	3.75	7.50	15.00
MOBILE FIDELITY					
1-075	In the Court of the Crimson King	1981	20.00	40.00	80.00
—Audiophile vinyl					
WARNER BROS.					
WBMS-119 [DJ]	The Return of King Crimson	1981	15.00	30.00	60.00
—Promo-only interview and music show					
BSK 3629	Discipline	1981	2.50	5.00	10.00
23692	Beat	1982	2.50	5.00	10.00
25071	Three of a Perfect Pair	1984	2.50	5.00	10.00

KING CROONERS, THE

45s

Number	Title (A Side/B Side)	Yr	VG	VG+	NM
EXCELLO					
2168	Won't You Let Me Know/Now That She's Gone	1959	10.00	20.00	40.00
2187	Memoirs/School Daze	1960	15.00	30.00	60.00
HART					
1002	She's Mine All Mine/Lonely Nights	1959	100.00	200.00	400.00

KING CURTIS

45s

Number	Title (A Side/B Side)	Yr	VG	VG+	NM
ABC-PARAMOUNT					
10133	Beatnick Hoedown/King Neptune's Guitar	1960	3.75	7.50	15.00
ALCOR					
1016	Jay Walk/The Lone Prairie	1961	5.00	10.00	20.00
APOLLO					
507	King's Rock/Dynamite at Midnight	1957	7.50	15.00	30.00
ATCO					
6114	The Birth of the Blues/Just Smoochin'	1958	5.00	10.00	20.00
6124	You Made Me Love You/Ific	1958	5.00	10.00	20.00
6135	Castle Rock/Chili	1959	5.00	10.00	20.00
6143	Honey Dripper (Part 1)/Honey Dripper (Part 2)	1959	5.00	10.00	20.00
6152	Heavenly Blues/Restless Guitar	1959	5.00	10.00	20.00
6387	Spanish Harlem/The Boss	1965	2.50	5.00	10.00
6406	On Broadway/Quicksand	1966	2.00	4.00	8.00
6419	Make the World Go Away/You've Lost That Lovin' Feeling	1966	2.00	4.00	8.00
6429	Dancing in the Streets/He'll Have to Go	1966	2.00	4.00	8.00
6447	Pots and Pans (Part 1)/Pots and Pans (Part 2)	1966	2.00	4.00	8.00
6457	Something on Your Mind/Soul Theme	1966	2.00	4.00	8.00
6476	Jump Back/When Something Is Wrong with My Baby	1967	2.00	4.00	8.00
6496	You Don't Miss Your Water/Green Onions	1967	2.00	4.00	8.00
6511	Memphis Soul Stew/Blue Nocturne	1967	2.00	4.00	8.00
6516	Ode to Billie Joe/In the Pocket	1967	2.00	4.00	8.00
—As "The Kingpins"					
6534	For What It's Worth/Cook Out	1968	2.00	4.00	8.00
6547	I Never Loved a Man (The Way I Love You)/I Was Made to Love Her	1968	2.00	4.00	8.00
6562	(Sittin' On) The Dock of the Bay/This Is Soul	1968	2.00	4.00	8.00
6582	(Theme from) Valley of the Dolls/Eighth Wonder	1968	2.00	4.00	8.00
6598	I Heard It Through the Grapevine/Whiter Shade of Pale	1968	2.00	4.00	8.00
6613	Harper Valley P.T.A./Makin' Hey	1968	2.00	4.00	8.00
6630	The Christmas Song/What Are You Doing New Year's Eve?	1968	3.00	6.00	12.00
6664	Games People Play/Foot Pattin' (Part 2)	1969	2.00	4.00	8.00
6680	Instant Groove/Sweet Inspiration	1969	2.00	4.00	8.00
6695	Little Green Apples/La Jeanne	1969	2.00	4.00	8.00
6711	C.C. Rider/Rocky Roll	1969	2.00	4.00	8.00
6720	Pop Corn Willie/Patty Cake	1969	2.00	4.00	8.00
6738	Soulin'/Teasin'	1970	—	3.00	6.00
6762	Get Ready/Bridge Over Troubled Water	1970	—	3.00	6.00
6779	Whole Lotta Love/Floatin'	1970	—	3.00	6.00
6785	Changes (Part 1)/Changes (Part 2)	1970	—	3.00	6.00
6834	Changes (Part 1)/Changes (Part 2)	1971	—	3.00	6.00
6908	Ridin' Thumb (Part 1)/Ridin' Thumb (Part 2)	1972	—	3.00	6.00
CAPITOL					
4788	Beach Party/Turn 'Em On	1962	2.50	5.00	10.00
4841	Beautiful Brown Eyes/Your Cheatin' Heart	1962	2.50	5.00	10.00
4891	Strollin' Home/Mess Around	1962	2.50	5.00	10.00
4998	Do the Monkey/Feel All Right	1963	2.50	5.00	10.00
5061	Theme from "Lilies of the Field" (Part 1)/Theme from "Lilies of the Field" (Part 2)	1963	2.50	5.00	10.00
5109	Soul Serenade/More Soul	1964	2.50	5.00	10.00
5212	Summer Dream/Melancholy Serenade	1964	2.50	5.00	10.00
5270	Stranger on the Shore/Hide Away	1964	2.50	5.00	10.00
5324	Sister Sadie/Tanya	1964	2.50	5.00	10.00
5377	Bill Bailey/Soul Twine	1965	2.50	5.00	10.00
5490	The Prance/Slow Drag	1965	2.50	5.00	10.00
DELUXE					
6142	The Stranger/Steel Guitar Rag	1957	6.25	12.50	25.00
6157	Wicky Wacky (Part 1)/Wicky Wacky (Part 2)	1958	6.25	12.50	25.00
ENJOY					
1000	Soul Twist/Twisting Time	1962	3.75	7.50	15.00
1001	Twisting with the King/Wobble Twist	1962	3.75	7.50	15.00
EVEREST					
19406	Jay Walk/The Lone Prairie	1961	3.75	7.50	15.00
EVERLAST					
5030	Soul Twist/Twisting Time	1965	2.50	5.00	10.00
GEM					
208	Tenor in the Sky/No More Crying on My Pillow	1954	10.00	20.00	40.00
GROOVE					
1060	Movin' On/Rockabye Baby	1956	6.25	12.50	25.00
KING					
5647	King Curtis Stomp/Steel Guitar Rag	1962	3.00	6.00	12.00
MONARCH					
702	Wine Head/I've Got News for You Baby	1953	15.00	30.00	60.00
NEW JAZZ					
45-510	Soul Meeting/All the Way	1961	3.75	7.50	15.00
SEG-WAY					
1006	Hot Rod/Bonaparte's Retreat	1962	3.75	7.50	15.00
SKY ROCKET					
106	Madisonville (Part 1)/Madisonville (Part 2)	1960	5.00	10.00	20.00
TRU SOUND					
401	Trouble in Mind/But That's Alright	1961	3.75	7.50	15.00
406	Twistin' and Jivin'/I Have to Worry	1961	3.75	7.50	15.00
412	So Rare/Hucklebuck Twist	1961	3.75	7.50	15.00
415	Free for All/When the Saints Go Marching In	1962	3.75	7.50	15.00
422	Low Down/I'll Wait for You	1962	3.75	7.50	15.00

Albums

Number	Title (A Side/B Side)	Yr	VG	VG+	NM
ATCO					
33-113 [M]	Have Tenor Sax, Will Blow	1959	10.00	20.00	40.00
SD 33-113 [S]	Have Tenor Sax, Will Blow	1959	15.00	30.00	60.00
33-189 [M]	That Lovin' Feeling	1966	5.00	10.00	20.00
SD 33-189 [S]	That Lovin' Feeling	1966	6.25	12.50	25.00
33-198 [M]	Live at Small's Paradise	1966	5.00	10.00	20.00
SD 33-198 [S]	Live at Small's Paradise	1966	6.25	12.50	25.00
33-211 [M]	The Great Memphis Hits	1967	5.00	10.00	20.00
SD 33-211 [S]	The Great Memphis Hits	1967	6.25	12.50	25.00
33-231 [M]	King Size Soul	1967	6.25	12.50	25.00
SD 33-231 [S]	King Size Soul	1967	5.00	10.00	20.00
33-247 [M]	Sweet Soul	1968	7.50	15.00	30.00
SD 33-247 [S]	Sweet Soul	1968	5.00	10.00	20.00
SD 33-266	The Best of King Curtis	1968	5.00	10.00	20.00
SD 33-293	Instant Groove	1969	5.00	10.00	20.00
SD 33-338	Get Ready	1970	5.00	10.00	20.00
SD 33-359	Live at Fillmore West	1971	5.00	10.00	20.00
SD 33-385	Everybody's Talkin'	1972	5.00	10.00	20.00
ATLANTIC					
SD 1637	Blues Montreux	1973	3.00	6.00	12.00
CAPITOL					
ST 1756 [S]	Country Soul	1963	10.00	20.00	40.00
T 1756 [M]	Country Soul	1963	7.50	15.00	30.00
ST 2095 [S]	Soul Serenade	1964	7.50	15.00	30.00
T 2095 [M]	Soul Serenade	1964	6.25	12.50	25.00
ST 2341 [S]	King Curtis Plays the Hits Made Famous by Sam Cooke	1965	7.50	15.00	30.00
T 2341 [M]	King Curtis Plays the Hits Made Famous by Sam Cooke	1965	6.25	12.50	25.00
ST 2858	The Best of King Curtis	1968	6.25	12.50	25.00
SM-11798	Soul Serenade	1978	2.50	5.00	10.00
—Reissue					
SM-11963	The Best of King Curtis	1979	2.50	5.00	10.00
—Reissue					
CLARION					
615 [M]	The Great "K" Curtis	1966	5.00	10.00	20.00
SD 615 [S]	The Great "K" Curtis	1966	6.25	12.50	25.00
COLLECTABLES					
COL-5119	Soul Twist	198?	2.50	5.00	10.00
COL-5156	Golden Classics: Enjoy…The Best of King Curtis	198?	2.50	5.00	10.00
ENJOY					
ENLP-2001 [M]	Soul Twist	1962	12.50	25.00	50.00

Number	Title (A Side/B Side)	Yr	VG	VG+	NM
EVEREST					
SDBR-1121 [S]	Azure	1961	18.75	37.50	75.00
LPBR-5121 [M]	Azure	1961	12.50	25.00	50.00
FANTASY					
OJC-198	The New Scene of King Curtis	1985	2.50	5.00	10.00
—Reissue of New Jazz 8237					
OBC-512	Trouble in Mind	1988	2.50	5.00	10.00
—Reissue of Tru-Sound 15001					
NEW JAZZ					
NJLP-8237 [M]	The New Scene of King Curtis	1960	15.00	30.00	60.00
—Purple label					
NJLP-8237 [M]	The New Scene of King Curtis	1965	7.50	15.00	30.00
—Blue label with trident logo on right					
PRESTIGE					
PRLP-7222 [M]	Soul Meeting	1962	12.50	25.00	50.00
PRST-7222 [S]	Soul Meeting	1962	18.75	37.50	75.00
PRST-7709	The Best of King Curtis	1969	3.75	7.50	15.00
PRST-7775	The Best of King Curtis — One More Time	1970	3.75	7.50	15.00
PRST-7789	King Soul	1970	3.75	7.50	15.00
PRST-7833	Soul Meeting	1971	3.75	7.50	15.00
—Reissue of 7222					
24033 [(2)]	Jazz Groove	198?	3.75	7.50	15.00
RCA CAMDEN					
CAS-2242	Sax in Motion	1968	3.75	7.50	15.00
RCA VICTOR					
LPM-2492 [M]	Arthur Murray's Music for Dancing: The Twist!	1962	6.25	12.50	25.00
LSP-2492 [S]	Arthur Murray's Music for Dancing: The Twist!	1962	7.50	15.00	30.00
TRU-SOUND					
TS-15001 [M]	Trouble in Mind	1961	12.50	25.00	50.00
TS-15008 [M]	It's Party Time	1962	12.50	25.00	50.00
TS-15009 [M]	Doin' the Dixie Twist	1962	12.50	25.00	50.00

KING FAMILY, THE

Number	Title (A Side/B Side)	Yr	VG	VG+	NM
45s					
WARNER BROS.					
PRO 216 [DJ]	Go Tell It on the Mountain/Here the Sledges with the Bells	1965	2.50	5.00	10.00
5647	The Sweetheart Tree/Amen	1965	—	3.00	6.00
5678	Just One Smile/Today I'm in Love	1965	—	3.00	6.00
5869	The Men in My Little Girl's Life/Bill Bailey (Won't You Please Come Home)	1966	—	3.00	6.00
Albums					
CAPITOL					
DT 2352 [R]	Love at Home	1965	3.00	6.00	12.00
T 2352 [M]	Love at Home	1965	3.75	7.50	15.00
FANNY FARMER/FLEETWOOD					
FCLP 3039	Fanny Farmer Presents The King Family Christmas Album	196?	3.00	6.00	12.00
HARMONY					
HS 11293	The Wonderful King Family	196?	2.50	5.00	10.00
WARNER BROS.					
W 1601 [M]	The King Family Show!	1965	3.00	6.00	12.00
WS 1601 [S]	The King Family Show!	1965	3.75	7.50	15.00
W 1613 [M]	The King Family Album	1965	3.00	6.00	12.00
WS 1613 [S]	The King Family Album	1965	3.75	7.50	15.00
W 1627 [M]	Christmas with the King Family	1965	3.00	6.00	12.00
WS 1627 [S]	Christmas with the King Family	1965	3.75	7.50	15.00
W 1633 [M]	Sunday with the King Family	1966	3.00	6.00	12.00
WS 1633 [S]	Sunday with the King Family	1966	3.75	7.50	15.00

KING FLOYD

Number	Title (A Side/B Side)	Yr	VG	VG+	NM
45s					
CHIMNEYVILLE					
435	Groove Me/What Our Love Needs	1970	—	3.00	6.00
437	Baby Let Me Kiss You/Please Don't Leave Me Lonely	1971	—	2.50	5.00
437 [PS]	Baby Let Me Kiss You/Please Don't Leave Me Lonely	1971	2.00	4.00	8.00
439	Got to Have Your Lovin'/Let Us Be	1971	—	2.50	5.00
442	It's Wonderful/Let Me See You Do That Thing	1971	—	2.50	5.00
443	Woman Don't Go Astray/Everybody Needs Somebody	1972	—	2.50	5.00
446	Think About It/Here It Is	1973	—	2.50	5.00
1779	So Much Confusion/So Much Confusion (Part 2)	1973	—	2.50	5.00
10202	I Feel Like Dynamite/Handle with Care	1974	—	2.50	5.00
10205	Don't Cry No More/I'm Missing You	1974	—	2.50	5.00
10206	Can't Give It Up/I'm Gonna Fall in Love with You	1975	—	2.50	5.00
10207	We Can Love/Making Love	1975	—	2.50	5.00
—With Dorothy Moore					
10209	Hey Baby/I Really Love You	1976	—	2.50	5.00
10212	Body English/I Really Love You	1976	—	2.50	5.00
10218	Stop, Look and Listen/Trouble	1977	—	2.50	5.00
10222	So True/Doing That No More	197?	—	2.50	5.00
10224	I Wanna Slow Dance Wit 'Cha/Stop, Look and Listen	197?	—	2.50	5.00
DIAL					
1027	Can You Dig It/Learning to Forget You	1974	—	3.00	6.00
ORIGINAL SOUND					
52	Why Did She Leave Me/Walkin' and Thinkin'	1964	3.75	7.50	15.00
PULSAR					
2401	Times Have Changed/Groov-a-Ling	1969	2.50	5.00	10.00
—With the Three Queens					
2406	Together We Can Do It/You Got the Love I Need	1969	2.50	5.00	10.00
UPTOWN					
719	Love Makes the World Go Round/Walkin' and Thinkin'	1965	3.00	6.00	12.00
733	Come On Home (Where You Belong)/I Don't Care (No More)	1966	3.00	6.00	12.00
V.I.P.					
25061	Heartaches/Together We Can Do Anything	1970	5.00	10.00	20.00
Albums					
CHIMNEYVILLE					
SD 9047	King Floyd	1971	3.75	7.50	15.00
PULSAR					
10602	A Man in Love	1969	5.00	10.00	20.00
V.I.P.					
407	The Heart of the Matter	1970	10.00	20.00	40.00

KING HARVEST

Number	Title (A Side/B Side)	Yr	VG	VG+	NM
45s					
A&M					
1726	Little Bit Like Magic/Vaea	1975	—	2.00	4.00
1761	Lovestruck/Hickory	1975	—	2.00	4.00
PERCEPTION					
515	Dancing in the Moonlight/Marty and the Captain	1972	—	2.50	5.00
527	A Little Bit Like Magic/Elmore Bacon	1973	—	2.00	4.00
534	Take It Slow/Idaho	1973	—	2.00	4.00
556	Celestial Navigator/Angels of Mercy	1974	—	2.00	4.00
Albums					
A&M					
SP-4540	King Harvest	1975	2.50	5.00	10.00
PERCEPTION					
36	Dancing in the Moonlight	1973	3.00	6.00	12.00

KING PINS, THE (1)

Number	Title (A Side/B Side)	Yr	VG	VG+	NM
45s					
FEDERAL					
12480	Believe in Me/Don't Wait Pretty Baby	1963	5.00	10.00	20.00
12484	It Won't Be This Way (Always)/How Long Will It Last	1963	5.00	10.00	20.00
12505	The Monkey One More Time/With the Other Guy	1963	3.75	7.50	15.00
12512	Hop Scotch/Wonderful One	1964	3.75	7.50	15.00
12517	Two Hearts/I Won't Have It	1964	3.75	7.50	15.00
12519	I Got the Monkey Off My Back/You're Using Me	1964	3.75	7.50	15.00
Albums					
KING					
865 [M]	It Won't Be This Way Always	1963	75.00	150.00	300.00

KING PINS, THE (2)

Number	Title (A Side/B Side)	Yr	VG	VG+	NM
45s					
LARSE					
101	94 Second Turf/Rod Hot Rod	1966	10.00	20.00	40.00
MGM					
13535	Rod Hot Rod/Door Banger	1966	7.50	15.00	30.00

KING RICHARD'S FLUEGEL KNIGHTS

Number	Title (A Side/B Side)	Yr	VG	VG+	NM
45s					
MTA					
101	Milord/Happiness Is	1966	—	3.00	6.00
107	A Sign of the Times/England Swings	1966	—	3.00	6.00
110	The Crusades/Castle Holiday	1966	—	3.00	6.00
115	Cabaret/Sing, Sing, Sing	1966	—	3.00	6.00
120	Two Different Worlds/Everybody Loves My Baby	1967	—	3.00	6.00
131	Miniskirt Waltz/Horn Duey	1967	—	3.00	6.00
138	Camelot/Bye Bye Blues	1967	—	3.00	6.00
151	Feelin' Good/To Life	1968	—	2.50	5.00
154	Mrs. Robinson/Dessert	1968	—	2.50	5.00
161	Gentle on My Mind/Something Classic	1968	—	2.50	5.00
166	Memories Are Made of This/One of Those Songs	1969	—	2.50	5.00
187	Everybody Loves My Baby/Horn Duey	1970	—	2.50	5.00
Albums					
MTA					
5001	A Sign of the Times	1966	3.00	6.00	12.00
5005	Something Super	1967	3.00	6.00	12.00
5005	Something Super!	1968	3.00	6.00	12.00
5014	One of Those Songs	1969	3.00	6.00	12.00

KINGDOM

Number	Title (A Side/B Side)	Yr	VG	VG+	NM
45s					
SPECIALTY					
722	Seven Fathoms Deep/If I Never Was to See Her Again	1970	3.00	6.00	12.00
Albums					
SPECIALTY					
SPS-2135	Kingdom	1970	15.00	30.00	60.00

KINGS, THE

Several different groups.

Number	Title (A Side/B Side)	Yr	VG	VG+	NM
45s					
BATON					
245	Long Lonely Nights/Let Me Know	1957	10.00	20.00	40.00
EPIC					
9370	I Want to Know/Bomp-I-Ty Bump	1960	7.50	15.00	30.00
GONE					
5013	Don't Go/Love Is Something from Within	1957	25.00	50.00	100.00
GOTHAM					
316	God Made You Mine/The Good Book	1956	25.00	50.00	100.00
HARLEM					
2322	Fire in My Heart/You Never Know	1954	37.50	75.00	150.00
JALO					
203	Angel/Come On Little Baby	1958	10.00	20.00	40.00
JAY-WING					
5805	Surrender/Hold Me	1959	37.50	75.00	150.00
JOX					
052	I've Got a License/Just a Little Bit of You	1965	10.00	20.00	40.00
LOOKIE					
18	I Want to Know/Bomp-I-Ty Bump	1960	10.00	20.00	40.00
RCA VICTOR					
47-7419	Till You/Elephant Walk	1958	6.25	12.50	25.00

Number	Title (A Side/B Side)	Yr	VG	VG+	NM
47-7544	Troubles Don't Last/Your Sweet Love	1959	6.25	12.50	25.00
SPECIALTY					
497	What Can I Do/Till I Say Well Done	1954	30.00	60.00	120.00

KINGSMEN, THE (1)

Northwest garage band. Also see JACK EELY.

45s

Number	Title (A Side/B Side)	Yr	VG	VG+	NM
JERDEN					
712	Louie Louie/Haunted Castle	1963	15.00	30.00	60.00
WAND					
143	Louie, Louie/Haunted Castle	1963	5.00	10.00	20.00
143	Louie Louie 64-65-66.../Haunted Castle	1966	3.75	7.50	15.00
143	Louie Louie/Little Green Thing	196?	3.75	7.50	15.00
150	Money/Bent Scepter	1964	3.00	6.00	12.00
157	Little Latin Lupe Lu/David's Mood	1964	2.50	5.00	10.00
164	Death of an Angel/Searchin' for Love	1964	2.50	5.00	10.00
172	The Jolly Green Giant/Long Green	1965	3.00	6.00	12.00
183	The Climb/I'm Waiting	1965	2.50	5.00	10.00
189	Annie Fanny/Give Her Lovin'	1965	2.50	5.00	10.00
1107	(You Got) Gamma Goochie/It's Only the Dog	1965	3.75	7.50	15.00
1115	Killer Joe/Little Green Thing	1966	3.75	7.50	15.00
1118	The Krunch/The Climb	1966	3.75	7.50	15.00
1118 [PS]	The Krunch/The Climb	1966	6.25	12.50	25.00
1127	My Wife Can't Dance/Little Sally Tease	1966	2.50	5.00	10.00
1137	If I Need Someone/The Grass Is Green	1966	2.50	5.00	10.00
1147	Trouble/Daytime Shadows	1967	2.00	4.00	8.00
1154	The Wolf of Manhattan/Children's Caretaker	1967	2.00	4.00	8.00
1157	(I Have Found) Another Girl/Don't Say No	1967	2.00	4.00	8.00
1164	Bo Diddley Bach/Just Before the Break of Day	1968	2.00	4.00	8.00
1174	Get Out of My Life Woman/Since You've Been Gone	1968	2.00	4.00	8.00
1180	I Guess I Was Dreamin'/Oh Love	1968	2.00	4.00	8.00

Albums

Number	Title (A Side/B Side)	Yr	VG	VG+	NM
RHINO					
RNLP-126	The Best of the Kingsmen	1985	2.50	5.00	10.00
SCEPTER					
CTN-18002	The Best of the Kingsmen	1972	2.50	5.00	10.00
WAND					
WD-657 [M]	The Kingsmen In Person	1964	7.50	15.00	30.00
WDS-657 [P]	The Kingsmen In Person	1964	10.00	20.00	40.00
WD-659 [M]	The Kingsmen, Volume II	1964	7.50	15.00	30.00
—With "Death of an Angel"					
WD-659 [M]	The Kingsmen, Volume II	1964	10.00	20.00	40.00
—Without "Death of an Angel" (replaced by untitled instrumental)					
WDS-659 [S]	The Kingsmen, Volume II	1964	10.00	20.00	40.00
—With "Death of an Angel"					
WDS-659 [S]	The Kingsmen, Volume II	1964	12.50	25.00	50.00
—Without "Death of an Angel" (replaced by untitled instrumental)					
WD-662 [M]	The Kingsmen, Volume 3	1965	6.25	12.50	25.00
WDS-662 [S]	The Kingsmen, Volume 3	1965	7.50	15.00	30.00
WD-670 [M]	The Kingsmen On Campus	1965	6.25	12.50	25.00
WDS-670 [S]	The Kingsmen On Campus	1965	7.50	15.00	30.00
WD-674 [M]	15 Great Hits	1966	5.00	10.00	20.00
WDS-674 [P]	15 Great Hits	1966	6.25	12.50	25.00
WD-675 [M]	Up and Away	1966	5.00	10.00	20.00
WDS-675 [S]	Up and Away	1966	6.25	12.50	25.00
WD-681 [M]	The Kingsmen's Greatest Hits	1967	3.75	7.50	15.00
WDS-681 [S]	The Kingsmen's Greatest Hits	1967	5.00	10.00	20.00
ST-91011 [S]	Up and Away	1966	7.50	15.00	30.00
—Capitol Record Club edition					

KINGSMEN, THE (2)

Instrumental group composed of former members of BILL HALEY AND HIS COMETS.

45s

Number	Title (A Side/B Side)	Yr	VG	VG+	NM
EASTWEST					
115	Week End/Better Believe It	1958	10.00	20.00	40.00
120	Conga Rock/The Cat Walk	1958	10.00	20.00	40.00

KINGSMEN, THE (3)

45s

Number	Title (A Side/B Side)	Yr	VG	VG+	NM
ALL STAR					
500	Guardian Angel/I'm Your Lover Man	1957	20.00	40.00	80.00

KINGSMEN, THE (U)

Some of these could have been by groups (1), (2) or (3).

45s

Number	Title (A Side/B Side)	Yr	VG	VG+	NM
ARNOLD					
2106	Goodnight Sweetheart/Humpty Dumpty	196?	30.00	60.00	120.00
CAPITOL					
3576	You Better Do Right/Today	1973	—	2.50	5.00
JALYNNE					
108	Ladies Choice/Dig This	1960	5.00	10.00	20.00
NEIL					
102	One Foolish Mistake/Stranded Love	1956	15.00	30.00	60.00

KINGSTON TRIO, THE

Also see DAVE GUARD AND THE WHISKEYHILL SINGERS; BOB SHANE; JOHN STEWART.

45s

Number	Title (A Side/B Side)	Yr	VG	VG+	NM
CAPITOL					
PRO 856 [DJ]	The Merry Minuet/Tick, Tick, Tick	1959	10.00	20.00	40.00
X1-1407 [S]	When I Was Young/Leave My Woman Alone	1960	5.00	10.00	20.00
—33 1/3 rpm, small hole jukebox pressing					
X2-1407 [S]	This Mornin', This Evenin', So Soon/Everglades	1960	5.00	10.00	20.00
—33 1/3 rpm, small hole jukebox pressing					
X3-1407 [S]	Buddy Better Get On Down the Line/South Wind	1960	5.00	10.00	20.00
—33 1/3 rpm, small hole jukebox pressing					
X4-1407 [S]	Who's Gonna Hold Her Hand/To Morrow	1960	5.00	10.00	20.00
—33 1/3 rpm, small hole jukebox pressing					
X5-1407 [S]	Colorado Trail/The Tattooed Lady	1960	5.00	10.00	20.00
—33 1/3 rpm, small hole jukebox pressing					
XE1-1446 [S]	We Wish You a Merry Christmas/The Last Month of the Year	1960	3.75	7.50	15.00
—33 1/3 rpm, small hole jukebox pressing					
XE2-1446 [S]	Sing We Noel/Go Where I Send Thee	1960	3.75	7.50	15.00
—33 1/3 rpm, small hole jukebox pressing					
XE3-1446 [S]	The White Snows of Winter/All Through the Night	1960	3.75	7.50	15.00
—33 1/3 rpm, small hole jukebox pressing					
XE4-1446 [S]	Follow Now, Oh Shepherd/Somerset Gloucestershire Wassail	1960	3.75	7.50	15.00
—33 1/3 rpm, small hole jukebox pressing					
XE5-1446 [S]	Bye Bye Thou Little Tiny Child/Mary Mild	1960	3.75	7.50	15.00
—33 1/3 rpm, small hole jukebox pressing					
SM-1705 [S]	Billy Goat Hill/Take Her Out of Pity	1962	3.75	7.50	15.00
—Small hole, plays at 33 1/3 rpm					
SXE1-1809 [S]	Some Fool Made a Soldier Out of Me/To Be Redeemed	1963	3.75	7.50	15.00
—33 1/3 rpm, small hole jukebox pressing					
SXE2-1809 [S]	Honey, Are You Mad at Your Man/Adios Farewell	1963	3.75	7.50	15.00
—33 1/3 rpm, small hole jukebox pressing					
SXE3-1809 [S]	Poor Ellie Smith/My Lord What a Mornin'	1963	3.75	7.50	15.00
—33 1/3 rpm, small hole jukebox pressing					
SXE4-1809 [S]	Long Black Veil/Genny Glen	1963	3.75	7.50	15.00
—33 1/3 rpm, small hole jukebox pressing					
SXE5-1809 [S]	The First Time/Dogie's Lament	1963	3.75	7.50	15.00
—33 1/3 rpm, small hole jukebox pressing					
2006/7 [DJ]	Farewell Adelita/Corey, Corey	1960	3.75	7.50	15.00
2006/7 [PS]	Farewell Adelita/Corey, Corey	1960	6.25	12.50	25.00
—Promo item for Welgrume Sportswear					
2782/3 [DJ]	Molly Dee/Haul Away	1959	3.75	7.50	15.00
2782/3 [PS]	Molly Dee/Haul Away	1959	6.25	12.50	25.00
—Promo item for "The New March of Dimes"					
3149	Tell the Riverboat Captain/Windy Wakefield	1971	2.50	5.00	10.00
—As "The New Kingston Trio"					
F3970	Scarlet Ribbons (For Her Hair)/Three Jolly Coachmen	1958	5.00	10.00	20.00
F4049	Tom Dooley/Ruby Red	1958	6.25	12.50	25.00
F4114	Raspberries, Strawberries/Sally	1959	5.00	10.00	20.00
F4167 [M]	The Tijuana Jail/Oh Cindy	1959	5.00	10.00	20.00
SF4167 [S]	The Tijuana Jail/Oh Cindy	1959	12.50	25.00	50.00
F4221	M.T.A./All My Sorrows	1959	5.00	10.00	20.00
F4271	A Worried Man/San Miguel	1959	5.00	10.00	20.00
4303	Coo Coo-U/Green Grasses	1959	3.75	7.50	15.00
4338	El Matador/Home from the Hill	1960	3.75	7.50	15.00
4338 [PS]	El Matador/Home from the Hill	1960	10.00	20.00	40.00
—This sleeve's existence has been confirmed					
4379	Bad Man Blunder/Escape of Old John Webb	1960	3.75	7.50	15.00
4441	Everglades/This Mornin', This Evenin', So Soon	1960	3.75	7.50	15.00
4475	Somerset Gloucestershire Wassail/Goodnight My Baby	1960	3.75	7.50	15.00
4475 [PS]	Somerset Gloucestershire Wassail/Goodnight My Baby	1960	15.00	30.00	60.00
4536	You're Gonna Miss Me/En El Aqua	1961	3.75	7.50	15.00
4642	Coming from the Mountains/Nothing More to Look Forward To	1961	3.75	7.50	15.00
4671	Where Have All the Flowers Gone/O Ken Karanga	1961	3.75	7.50	15.00
4740	Scotch and Soda/Jane, Jane, Jane	1962	2.50	5.00	10.00
4740 [PS]	Scotch and Soda/Jane, Jane, Jane	1962	7.50	15.00	30.00
4808	Old Joe Clark/C'mon Betty Home	1962	2.50	5.00	10.00
4842	One More Town/She Was Too Good to Me	1962	2.50	5.00	10.00
4842 [PS]	One More Town/She Was Too Good to Me	1962	7.50	15.00	30.00
4898	Greenback Dollar/New Frontier	1963	2.50	5.00	10.00
4898 [PS]	Greenback Dollar/New Frontier	1963	10.00	20.00	40.00
4951	Reverend Mr. Black/One More Round	1963	2.50	5.00	10.00
5005	Desert Pete/Ballad of the Thresher	1963	2.50	5.00	10.00
5078	Ally Ally Oxen Free/Marcelle Vanine	1963	2.50	5.00	10.00
5132	Last Night I Had the Strangest Dream/Patriot Game	1964	2.50	5.00	10.00
5166	Seasons in the Sun/If You Don't Look Around	1964	2.50	5.00	10.00
6002	Tom Dooley/M.T.A.	1962	2.00	4.00	8.00
—Originals have two-tone green swirl labels					
6046	A Worried Man/Scotch and Soda	1964	2.00	4.00	8.00
—Originals have two-tone green swirl labels					
6071	Greenback Dollar/Reverend Mr. Black	1965	2.00	4.00	8.00
—Originals have two-tone green swirl labels; "Greenback Dollar" does NOT have the word "damn" obliterated by a guitar chord, as the original 45 does					
S7-19762	Somerset Gloucestershire Wassail/Goodnight My Baby	1997	—	2.00	4.00
CAPITOL CUSTOM					
KB-2670/1	Tom Dooley/A Worried Man//The Hunter/With You My Johnny	1960	7.50	15.00	30.00
KB-2670/1 [PS]	Cool Cargo	1960	7.50	15.00	30.00
—Promotional item for 7-Up					
DECCA					
31702	My Ramblin' Boy/Hope You Understand	1964	3.75	7.50	15.00
31702 [PS]	My Ramblin' Boy/Hope You Understand	1964	6.25	12.50	25.00
31730	Little Play Soldiers/I'm Going Home	1965	2.50	5.00	10.00
31790	Stay Awhile/Yes I Can Feel It	1965	2.50	5.00	10.00
31790 [PS]	Stay Awhile/Yes I Can Feel It	1965	6.25	12.50	25.00
31860	The Runaway Song/Parchment Farm (Blues)	1965	2.50	5.00	10.00
31860 [PS]	The Runaway Song/Parchment Farm (Blues)	1965	6.25	12.50	25.00
31922	Norwegian Wood/Put Your Money Away	1966	2.50	5.00	10.00
31961	The Spinnin' of the World/A Little Soul Is Born	1966	2.50	5.00	10.00
32010	Lock All the Windows/Hit and Run	1966	2.50	5.00	10.00
32040	Babe, You've Been On My Mind/Texas Across the River	1966	2.50	5.00	10.00
MOUNTAIN CREEK					
301/2	Big Ship Glory/Johnson Party of Four	1977	6.25	12.50	25.00
NAUTILUS					
NR2-45	Aspen Gold/Longest Beer of the Night	1979	—	2.50	5.00
TETRAGRAMMATON					
1526	One Too Many Mornings/Scotch and Soda	1969	2.50	5.00	10.00
XERES					
10004	Looking for the Sunshine/Reverend Mr. Black	1982	—	2.00	4.00
10004 [PS]	Looking for the Sunshine/Reverend Mr. Black	1982	—	2.00	4.00

7-Inch Extended Plays

CAPITOL

Number	Title (A Side/B Side)	Yr	VG	VG+	NM
EAP 1-996	Three Jolly Coachmen/Wreck of the "John B"//Bay of Mexico/Saro Jane	1958	7.50	15.00	30.00
EAP 1-996 [PS]	The Kingston Trio	1958	7.50	15.00	30.00
EAP 1-1119	M.T.A./Como Se Viene//All My Sorrows/Sail Away Ladies	1959	7.50	15.00	30.00
EAP 1-1119 [PS]	M.T.A.	1959	7.50	15.00	30.00
EAP 1-1129	The Tijuana Jail/Oh Cindy//Coplas/Tom Dooley	1959	7.50	15.00	30.00
EAP 1-1129 [PS]	Tijuana Jail	1959	7.50	15.00	30.00
EAP 1-1136	Tom Dooley/Coplas//Banua/Santy Ano	1959	7.50	15.00	30.00
EAP 1-1136 [PS]	Tom Dooley	1959	7.50	15.00	30.00
EAP 1-1182	Raspberries, Strawberries/Ruby Red//Sally/Scarlet Ribbons	1959	7.50	15.00	30.00
EAP 1-1182 [PS]	Raspberries, Strawberries	1959	7.50	15.00	30.00
EAP 1-1199	M.T.A./All My Sorrows//Scarlet Ribbons/Remember the Alamo	1959	6.25	12.50	25.00
EAP 1-1199 [PS]	The Kingston Trio at Large, Part 1	1959	6.25	12.50	25.00
EAP 2-1199	Blow Ye Winds/Corey Corey//The Long Black Rifle/Early in the Mornin'	1959	6.25	12.50	25.00
EAP 2-1199 [PS]	The Kingston Trio at Large, Part 2	1959	6.25	12.50	25.00
EAP 3-1199	The Seine/I Bawled//Good News/Getaway John	1959	6.25	12.50	25.00
EAP 3-1199 [PS]	The Kingston Trio at Large, Part 3	1959	6.25	12.50	25.00
EAP 1-1258	Molly Dee/Across the Wide Missouri//Goober Peas/A Worried Man	1959	6.25	12.50	25.00
EAP 1-1258 [PS]	Here We Go Again! Part 1	1959	6.25	12.50	25.00
EAP 2-1258	Haul Away/The Wanderer//E Inu Tatou E/A Rollin' Stone	1959	6.25	12.50	25.00
EAP 2-1258 [PS]	Here We Go Again! Part 2	1959	6.25	12.50	25.00
EAP 3-1258	Round About a Mountain/Oleanna//The Unfortunate Miss Bailey/San Miguel	1959	6.25	12.50	25.00
EAP 3-1258 [PS]	Here We Go Again! Part 3	1959	6.25	12.50	25.00
EAP 1-1322	A Worried Man/Molly Dee//San Miguel/Oleanna	1959	6.25	12.50	25.00
EAP 1-1322 [PS]	A Worried Man	1959	6.25	12.50	25.00
EAP 1-1352	El Matador/The Mountains o' Mourne//The Hunter/Farewell Adelita	1960	6.25	12.50	25.00
EAP 1-1352 [PS]	Sold Out, Part 1	1960	6.25	12.50	25.00
EAP 2-1352	Don't Cry Katie/Medley: Tanga Tiki-Toerau//Mangwani Mpulele/With You My Johnny	1960	6.25	12.50	25.00
EAP 2-1352 [PS]	Sold Out, Part 2	1960	6.25	12.50	25.00
EAP 3-1352	With Her Head Tucked Underneath Her Arm/Carrier Pigeon//Bimini/Raspberries, Strawberries	1960	6.25	12.50	25.00
EAP 3-1352 [PS]	Sold Out, Part 3	1960	6.25	12.50	25.00
EAP 1-1407	Bad Man Blunder/The Escape of Old John Webb//Colorado Trail/The Tattooed Lady	1960	6.25	12.50	25.00
EAP 1-1407 [PS]	String Along, Part 1	1960	6.25	12.50	25.00
EAP 2-1407	When I Was Young/Leave My Woman Alone//Who's Gonna Hold Her Hand/To Morrow	1960	6.25	12.50	25.00
EAP 2-1407 [PS]	String Along, Part 2	1960	6.25	12.50	25.00
EAP 3-1407	This Mornin', This Evenin', So Soon/Everglades//Buddy Better Get On Down the Line/South Wind	1960	6.25	12.50	25.00
EAP 3-1407 [PS]	String Along, Part 3	1960	6.25	12.50	25.00
EAP 1-1446	Bye Bye Thou Little Tiny Child/The Snows of Winter//Sing We Noel/The Last Month of the Year	1960	6.25	12.50	25.00
EAP 1-1446 [PS]	The Last Month of the Year, Part 1	1960	6.25	12.50	25.00
EAP 2-1446	We Wish You a Merry Christmas/All Through the Night//Mary Mild/A Round About Christmas	1960	6.25	12.50	25.00
EAP 2-1446 [PS]	The Last Month of the Year, Part 2	1960	6.25	12.50	25.00
EAP 3-1446	Goodnight My Baby Goodnight/Go Where I Send Thee//Follow Now, Oh Shepherds/Somerset Gloucestershire Wassail	1960	6.25	12.50	25.00
EAP 3-1446 [PS]	The Last Month of the Year, Part 3	1960	6.25	12.50	25.00
EAP 1-1474	En El Agua/Come All You Fair and Tender Ladies//Blow the Candle Out/Blue Eyed Gal	1961	6.25	12.50	25.00
EAP 1-1474 [PS]	Make Way, Part 1	1961	6.25	12.50	25.00
EAP 2-1474	The Jug of Punch/Bonny Heilan' Laddie//The River Is Wide/Oh Yes, Oh	1961	6.25	12.50	25.00
EAP 2-1474 [PS]	Make Way, Part 2	1961	6.25	12.50	25.00
EAP 3-1474	Utawena/Hear Travelin'//Hangman/Speckled Roan	1961	6.25	12.50	25.00
EAP 3-1474 [PS]	Make Way, Part 3	1961	6.25	12.50	25.00
EAP 1-1642	Coming from the Mountains/Oh Sail Away//Weeping Willow/Reuben James	1961	6.25	12.50	25.00
EAP 1-1642 [PS]	Close Up, Part 1	1961	6.25	12.50	25.00
EAP 2-1642	Take Her Out of Pity/Don't You Weep, Mary//When My Love Was Here/Karu	1961	6.25	12.50	25.00
EAP 2-1642 [PS]	Close Up, Part 2	1961	6.25	12.50	25.00
EAP 3-1642	The Whistling Gypsy/O Ken Karanga//Jessie James/Glorious Kingdom	1961	6.25	12.50	25.00
EAP 3-1642 [PS]	Close Up, Part 3	1961	6.25	12.50	25.00

Albums

CAPITOL

Number	Title (A Side/B Side)	Yr	VG	VG+	NM
STBB-513 [(2)]	Tom Dooley/Scarlet Ribbons	1970	5.00	10.00	20.00
DT 996 [R]	The Kingston Trio	196?	3.00	6.00	12.00
T 996 [M]	The Kingston Trio	1958	12.50	25.00	50.00
—Turquoise label					
T 996 [M]	The Kingston Trio	1958	10.00	20.00	40.00
—Black label with colorband, Capitol logo at left					
T 996 [M]	The Kingston Trio	1962	5.00	10.00	20.00
—Black label with colorband, Capitol logo at top					
T 1107 [M]	From the Hungry I	1959	10.00	20.00	40.00
—Black label with colorband, Capitol logo at left					
T 1107 [M]	From the Hungry I	1962	5.00	10.00	20.00
—Black label with colorband, Capitol logo at top					
ST 1183 [S]	Stereo Concert	1959	12.50	25.00	50.00
—Black label with colorband, Capitol logo at left					
ST 1183 [S]	Stereo Concert	1962	6.25	12.50	25.00
—Black label with colorband, Capitol logo at top					
ST 1199 [S]	The Kingston Trio at Large	1959	10.00	20.00	40.00
—Black label with colorband, Capitol logo at left					
ST 1199 [S]	The Kingston Trio at Large	1962	5.00	10.00	20.00
—Black label with colorband, Capitol logo at top					
T 1199 [M]	The Kingston Trio at Large	1959	7.50	15.00	30.00
—Black label with colorband, Capitol logo at left					
T 1199 [M]	The Kingston Trio at Large	1962	3.75	7.50	15.00
—Black label with colorband, Capitol logo at top					
ST 1258 [S]	Here We Go Again!	1959	10.00	20.00	40.00
—Black label with colorband, Capitol logo at left					
ST 1258 [S]	Here We Go Again!	1962	5.00	10.00	20.00
—Black label with colorband, Capitol logo at top					
T 1258 [M]	Here We Go Again!	1959	7.50	15.00	30.00
—Black label with colorband, Capitol logo at left					
T 1258 [M]	Here We Go Again!	1962	3.75	7.50	15.00
—Black label with colorband, Capitol logo at top					
ST 1352 [S]	Sold Out	1960	10.00	20.00	40.00
—Black label with colorband, Capitol logo at left					
ST 1352 [S]	Sold Out	1962	5.00	10.00	20.00
—Black label with colorband, Capitol logo at top					
T 1352 [M]	Sold Out	1960	7.50	15.00	30.00
—Black label with colorband, Capitol logo at left					
T 1352 [M]	Sold Out	1962	3.75	7.50	15.00
—Black label with colorband, Capitol logo at top					
ST 1407 [S]	String Along	1960	10.00	20.00	40.00
—Black label with colorband, Capitol logo at left					
ST 1407 [S]	String Along	1962	5.00	10.00	20.00
—Black label with colorband, Capitol logo at top					
T 1407 [M]	String Along	1960	7.50	15.00	30.00
—Black label with colorband, Capitol logo at left					
T 1407 [M]	String Along	1962	3.75	7.50	15.00
—Black label with colorband, Capitol logo at top					
ST 1446 [S]	The Last Month of the Year	1960	10.00	20.00	40.00
—Same as above, but in stereo					
T 1446 [M]	The Last Month of the Year	1960	7.50	15.00	30.00
ST 1474 [S]	Make Way!	1961	10.00	20.00	40.00
—Black label with colorband, Capitol logo at left					
ST 1474 [S]	Make Way!	1962	5.00	10.00	20.00
—Black label with colorband, Capitol logo at top					
T 1474 [M]	Make Way!	1961	7.50	15.00	30.00
—Black label with colorband, Capitol logo at left					
T 1474 [M]	Make Way!	1962	3.75	7.50	15.00
—Black label with colorband, Capitol logo at top					
ST 1564 [S]	Goin' Places	1961	10.00	20.00	40.00
—Black label with colorband, Capitol logo at left					
ST 1564 [S]	Goin' Places	1962	5.00	10.00	20.00
—Black label with colorband, Capitol logo at top					
T 1564 [M]	Goin' Places	1961	7.50	15.00	30.00
—Black label with colorband, Capitol logo at left					
T 1564 [M]	Goin' Places	1962	3.75	7.50	15.00
—Black label with colorband, Capitol logo at top					
DT 1612 [R]	Encores	1961	5.00	10.00	20.00
—Black label with colorband, Capitol logo at left					
DT 1612 [R]	Encores	1962	2.50	5.00	10.00
—Black label with colorband, Capitol logo at top					
T 1612 [M]	Encores	1961	7.50	15.00	30.00
—Black label with colorband, Capitol logo at left					
T 1612 [M]	Encores	1962	3.75	7.50	15.00
—Black label with colorband, Capitol logo at top					
ST 1642 [S]	Close-Up	1961	10.00	20.00	40.00
—Black label with colorband, Capitol logo at left					
ST 1642 [S]	Close-Up	1962	5.00	10.00	20.00
—Black label with colorband, Capitol logo at top					
T 1642 [M]	Close-Up	1961	7.50	15.00	30.00
—Black label with colorband, Capitol logo at left					
T 1642 [M]	Close-Up	1962	3.75	7.50	15.00
—Black label with colorband, Capitol logo at top					
ST 1658 [S]	College Concert	1962	6.25	12.50	25.00
T 1658 [M]	College Concert	1962	5.00	10.00	20.00
SM-1705	The Best of the Kingston Trio	197?	2.50	5.00	10.00
ST 1705 [P]	The Best of the Kingston Trio	1962	5.00	10.00	20.00
T 1705 [M]	The Best of the Kingston Trio	1962	5.00	10.00	20.00
ST 1747 [S]	Something Special	1962	6.25	12.50	25.00
T 1747 [M]	Something Special	1962	5.00	10.00	20.00
ST 1809 [S]	New Frontier	1962	6.25	12.50	25.00
T 1809 [M]	New Frontier	1962	5.00	10.00	20.00
ST 1871 [S]	The Kingston Trio #16	1963	6.25	12.50	25.00
T 1871 [M]	The Kingston Trio #16	1963	5.00	10.00	20.00
ST 1935 [S]	Sunny Side!	1963	6.25	12.50	25.00
T 1935 [M]	Sunny Side!	1963	5.00	10.00	20.00
KAO 2005 [M]	Sing a Song with the Kingston Trio	1963	6.25	12.50	25.00
SKAO 2005 [S]	Sing a Song with the Kingston Trio	1963	7.50	15.00	30.00
ST 2011 [S]	Time to Think	1964	5.00	10.00	20.00
T 2011 [M]	Time to Think	1964	3.75	7.50	15.00
ST 2081 [S]	Back in Town	1964	5.00	10.00	20.00
T 2081 [M]	Back in Town	1964	3.75	7.50	15.00
STCL 2180 [(3) S]	The Folk Era	1964	12.50	25.00	50.00
—Box set with booklet					
TCL 2180 [(3) M]	The Folk Era	1964	10.00	20.00	40.00
—Box set with booklet					
SM-2280	The Best of the Kingston Trio, Volume 2	197?	2.50	5.00	10.00
ST 2280 [S]	The Best of the Kingston Trio, Volume 2	1965	5.00	10.00	20.00
T 2280 [M]	The Best of the Kingston Trio, Volume 2	1965	3.75	7.50	15.00
SM-2614	The Best of the Kingston Trio, Volume 3	197?	2.50	5.00	10.00
ST 2614 [S]	The Best of the Kingston Trio, Volume 3	1966	5.00	10.00	20.00
T 2614 [M]	The Best of the Kingston Trio, Volume 3	1966	3.75	7.50	15.00
M-11577	The Kingston Trio	1976	2.50	5.00	10.00
M-11968	From the Hungry I	1979	2.50	5.00	10.00
SN-16183	The Best of the Kingston Trio	1981	2.00	4.00	8.00
—Budget-line reissue					
SN-16184	The Best of the Kingston Trio, Volume 2	1981	2.00	4.00	8.00
—Budget-line reissue					
N-16185	Tom Dooley	1981	2.00	4.00	8.00
SN-16186	Scarlet Ribbons	1981	2.00	4.00	8.00

DECCA

Number	Title (A Side/B Side)	Yr	VG	VG+	NM
DL 4613 [M]	The Kingston Trio (Nick-Bob-John)	1965	6.25	12.50	25.00
DL 4656 [M]	Stay Awhile	1965	6.25	12.50	25.00
DL 4694 [M]	Somethin' Else	1965	6.25	12.50	25.00
DL 4758 [M]	Children of the Morning	1966	6.25	12.50	25.00
DL 74613 [S]	The Kingston Trio (Nick-Bob-John)	1965	7.50	15.00	30.00

Number	Title (A Side/B Side)	Yr	VG	VG+	NM
DL 74656 [S]	Stay Awhile	1965	7.50	15.00	30.00
DL 74694 [S]	Somethin' Else	1965	7.50	15.00	30.00
DL 74758 [S]	Children of the Morning	1966	7.50	15.00	30.00
FOLK ERA					
FE-2001	Rediscover the Kingston Trio	198?	2.50	5.00	10.00
FE-2036	Hidden Treasures	198?	2.50	5.00	10.00
NAUTILUS					
NR-2	Aspen Gold	1979	10.00	20.00	40.00
—Audiophile vinyl					
PAIR					
PDL2-1067 [(2)]	Early American Heroes	1986	3.00	6.00	12.00
PICKWICK					
SPC-3260	Tom Dooley	196?	3.00	6.00	12.00
TETRAGRAMMATON					
T-5101 [(2)]	Once Upon a Time	1969	6.25	12.50	25.00

KINKS, THE

Also see DAVE DAVIES.

Number	Title (A Side/B Side)	Yr	VG	VG+	NM
12-Inch Singles					
ARISTA					
SP-34 [DJ]	Father Christmas/A Rock 'n' Roll Fantasy	1978	6.25	12.50	25.00
SP-45 [DJ]	(Wish I Could Fly Like) Superman (3:45) (5:58)	1979	3.75	7.50	15.00
SP-152 [DJ]	Come Dancing (same on both sides)	1983	3.75	7.50	15.00
CP 700	(Wish I Could Fly Like) Superman/Low Budget	1979	2.00	4.00	8.00
ADP 9095 [DJ]	Don't Forget to Dance (same on both sides)	1983	—	3.00	6.00
ADP 9297 [DJ]	Do It Again (same on both sides)	1984	—	3.00	6.00
ADP 9337 [DJ]	Summer's Gone (same on both sides)	1983	—	3.00	6.00
MCA					
L33-17207 [DJ]	Rock 'n' Roll Cities (same on both sides)	1987	—	3.00	6.00
L33-17260 [DJ]	Lost and Found (same on both sides)	1987	—	3.00	6.00
L33-17345 [DJ]	How Are You (same on both sides)	1987	—	3.00	6.00
L33-17460 [DJ]	The Road (same on both sides)	1988	2.00	4.00	8.00
L33-17498 [DJ]	The Road (Edit) (same on both sides)	1988	—	3.00	6.00
L33-17531 [DJ]	Art Lover (Live)/Destroyer (Live)	1988	—	3.00	6.00
45s					
ARISTA					
SP-5 [DJ]	Sleepwalker/All the Kids on the Street	1977	2.50	5.00	10.00
—Gold vinyl; B-side by the Hollywood Stars					
SP-5 [PS]	Sleepwalker/All the Kids on the Street	1977	2.50	5.00	10.00
0240	Sleepwalker/Full Moon	1977	—	2.00	4.00
0247	Life Goes On/Juke Box Music	1977	—	2.00	4.00
0296	Father Christmas/Prince of the Punks	1977	—	2.50	5.00
0296 [PS]	Father Christmas/Prince of the Punks	1977	—	2.50	5.00
0342	A Rock and Roll Fantasy/Live Life	1978	—	2.00	4.00
0372	Black Messiah/Live Life	1978	—	2.00	4.00
0409	Superman/Low Budget	1979	—	2.50	5.00
0409	(Wish I Could Fly Like) Superman/Party Line	1979	—	2.00	4.00
0448	Low Budget/A Gallon of Gas	1979	—	2.00	4.00
0458	Catch Me Now I'm Falling/Low Budget	1979	—	2.00	4.00
0541	Lola/Celluloid Heroes	1980	—	2.00	4.00
0541 [PS]	Lola/Celluloid Heroes	1980	—	2.50	5.00
0577	You Really Got Me/Attitude	1980	—	2.00	4.00
0619	Destroyer/Back to Back	1981	—	2.00	4.00
0649	Better Things/Yo-Yo	1981	—	2.00	4.00
1054	Come Dancing/Noise	1983	—	2.00	4.00
1054 [PS]	Come Dancing/Noise	1983	—	2.00	4.00
9016	Come Dancing/Noise	1983	—	—	3.00
9016 [PS]	Come Dancing/Noise	1983	—	—	3.00
9075	Don't Forget to Dance/Young Conservatives	1983	—	—	3.00
9309	Do It Again/Guilty	1984	—	—	3.00
9309 [PS]	Do It Again/Guilty	1984	—	—	3.00
9334	Summer's Gone/Going Solo	1985	—	—	3.00
CAMEO					
308	Long Tall Sally/I Took My Baby Home	1964	150.00	300.00	600.00
345	Long Tall Sally/I Took My Baby Home	1965	75.00	150.00	300.00
348	You Still Want Me/You Do Something to Me	1965	—	—	—
—Canceled. NOTE: An EP on Cameo, which contains the four songs assigned to Cameo in the U.S., is a bootleg with little collector value.					
MCA					
52960	Rock 'N' Roll Cities/Sleazy Town	1986	—	—	3.00
52960 [PS]	Rock 'N' Roll Cities/Sleazy Town	1986	—	—	3.00
53015	Lost and Found/Killing Time	1987	—	—	3.00
53015 [PS]	Lost and Found/Killing Time	1987	—	—	3.00
53093	Working at the Factory/How Are You	1987	2.50	5.00	10.00
53699	How Do I Get Close/War Is Over	1989	2.50	5.00	10.00
RCA VICTOR					
APBO-0275	Money Talks/Here Comes Flash	1974	2.50	5.00	10.00
DJBO-0275 [DJ]	Money Talks (short/long versions)	1974	2.00	4.00	8.00
LPBO-5001	Sitting in the Midday Sun/Sweet Lady Genevieve	1973	2.50	5.00	10.00
PB-10019	Mirror of Love/It's Evil	1974	—	3.00	6.00
PB-10121	Preservation/Salvation Road	1974	—	3.00	6.00
PB-10251	Everybody's a Star (Starmaker)/Ordinary People	1975	—	3.00	6.00
PB-10551	I'm in Disgrace/The Hard Way	1976	—	3.00	6.00
74-0620	20th Century Man/Skin and Bones	1971	2.00	4.00	8.00
74-0807	Supersonic Rocket Ship/You Don't Know My Name	1972	2.00	4.00	8.00
74-0852	Celluloid Heroes/Hot Potatoes	1972	2.00	4.00	8.00
74-0940	One of the Survivors/Scrap Heap City	1973	50.00	100.00	200.00
—Released with acoustic versions of the two songs rather than the LP versions and quickly deleted					
REPRISE					
0306	You Really Got Me/It's All Right	1964	6.25	12.50	25.00
—Originals have peach labels					
0306	You Really Got Me/It's All Right	1964	3.75	7.50	15.00
—Second pressings have orange and brown labels					
0334	All Day and All of the Night/I Gotta Move	1964	5.00	10.00	20.00
0347	Tired of Waiting for You/Come On Now	1965	5.00	10.00	20.00
0366	Who'll Be the Next in Line/Everybody's Gonna Be Happy	1965	5.00	10.00	20.00
0379	Set Me Free/I Need You	1965	5.00	10.00	20.00
0409	See My Friends/Never Met a Girl Like You Before	1965	3.75	7.50	15.00
0420	A Well Repected Man/Such a Shame	1965	3.75	7.50	15.00
0454	Till the End of the Day/Where Have All the Good Times Gone	1966	3.75	7.50	15.00
0471	Dedicated Follower of Fashion/Sittin' on My Sofa	1966	3.75	7.50	15.00
0497	Sunny Afternoon/I'm Not Like Everybody Else	1966	3.75	7.50	15.00
0540	Dead End Street/Big Black Smoke	1966	10.00	20.00	40.00
0587	Mr. Pleasant/Harry Rag	1967	10.00	20.00	40.00
0612	Waterloo Sunset/Two Sisters	1967	10.00	20.00	40.00
0647	Autumn Almanac/David Watts	1967	10.00	20.00	40.00
0691	Wonderboy/Polly	1968	10.00	20.00	40.00
0708	Sunny Afternoon/Dead End Street	1968	2.50	5.00	10.00
0712	Dedicated Follower of Fashion/Who'll Be the Next in Line	1968	2.50	5.00	10.00
0715	A Well Respected Man/Set Me Free	1968	2.50	5.00	10.00
0719	Tired of Waiting for You/All Day and All of the Night	1968	2.50	5.00	10.00
0722	You Really Got Me/It's All Right	1968	2.50	5.00	10.00
—0708 through 0722 are "Back to Back Hits" series -- originals have both "r:" and "W7" on label					
0743	Lola/Apeman	1972	—	2.50	5.00
—"Back to Back Hits" series					
0762	Days/She's Got Everything	1968	10.00	20.00	40.00
0806	Starstruck/Picture Book	1969	10.00	20.00	40.00
0847	The Village Green Preservation Society/Do You Remember Walter	1969	10.00	20.00	40.00
0863	Victoria/Brainwashed	1969	3.75	7.50	15.00
0930	Lola/Mindless Child of Motherhood	1970	2.50	5.00	10.00
0979	Apeman/Rats	1970	2.50	5.00	10.00
1017	God's Children/The Way Love Used to Be	1971	5.00	10.00	20.00
1094	King Kong/Waterloo Sunset	1972	3.75	7.50	15.00
7-Inch Extended Plays					
CAMEO					
315	Long Tall Sally/I Took My Baby Home//You Still Want Me/You Do Something To Me	196?	—	—	—
—Bootleg; also comes with bootleg title sleeve					
Albums					
ARISTA					
SP-69 [DJ]	Low Budget Radio Interview	1979	10.00	20.00	40.00
—Promo-only radio show featuring Ray Davies					
SP-85 [EP]	A Fistful of Kinks	1980	6.25	12.50	25.00
—Promo-only four-song sampler from "One for the Road"					
AL 4106	Sleepwalker	1977	2.50	5.00	10.00
AL 4106 [DJ]	Sleepwalker	1977	7.50	15.00	30.00
—White label promo					
AL 4167	Misfits	1978	2.50	5.00	10.00
AL 4167 [DJ]	Misfits	1978	7.50	15.00	30.00
—White label promo					
AL 4240	Low Budget	1979	2.50	5.00	10.00
AL 8018	State of Confusion	1983	2.50	5.00	10.00
AL13 8041 [(2)]	One for the Road	1983	2.50	5.00	10.00
—Reissue of 8609					
AL 8264	Word of Mouth	1984	2.50	5.00	10.00
ALB6 8300	Low Budget	1985	2.00	4.00	8.00
—Budget-line reissue					
ALB6 8328	Give the People What They Want	1985	2.00	4.00	8.00
—Budget-line reissue					
ALB6 8375	Sleepwalker	1985	2.00	4.00	8.00
—Budget-line reissue					
ALB6 8377	Misfits	1985	2.00	4.00	8.00
—Budget-line reissue					
AL11 8428 [(2)]	Come Dancing with the Kinks	1986	3.00	6.00	12.00
A2L 8609 [(2)]	One for the Road	1980	3.75	7.50	15.00
AL 9567	Give the People What They Want	1981	2.50	5.00	10.00
COMPLEAT					
CPL2-2001 [(2)]	A Compleat Collection	1984	3.00	6.00	12.00
CPL2-2003 [(2)]	20th Anniversary Edition	1984	3.00	6.00	12.00
MCA					
5822	Think Visual	1987	2.50	5.00	10.00
6337	UK Jive	1989	3.00	6.00	12.00
L33-17281 [DJ]	A Look at "Think Visual"	1987	12.50	25.00	50.00
—Promo only in white jacket					
42107	Live: The Road	1988	2.50	5.00	10.00
MOBILE FIDELITY					
1-070	Misfits	1981	5.00	10.00	20.00
—Audiophile vinyl					
PYE					
505	The Kinks	1975	3.00	6.00	12.00
509	The Kinks, Vol. 2	1976	3.00	6.00	12.00
RCA VICTOR					
APL1-1743	Celluloid Heroes (The Kinks' Greatest)	1976	2.50	5.00	10.00
APL1-3520	Second Time Around	1980	2.50	5.00	10.00
AYL1-3749	Schoolboys in Disgrace	1980	2.00	4.00	8.00
—Budget-line reissue					
AYL1-3750	Soap Opera	1980	2.00	4.00	8.00
—Budget-line reissue					
AYL1-3869	Celluloid Heroes (The Kinks' Greatest)	1981	2.00	4.00	8.00
—Budget-line reissue					
AYL1-4558	Muswell Hillbillies	1982	2.00	4.00	8.00
—Budget-line reissue					
LSP-4644	Muswell Hillbillies	1971	7.50	15.00	30.00
AYL1-4719	Second Time Around	1983	2.00	4.00	8.00
—Budget-line reissue					
LPL1-5002	Preservation Act 1	1973	3.75	7.50	15.00
CPL2-5040 [(2)]	Preservation Act 2	1974	5.00	10.00	20.00
APL1-5081	Soap Opera	1975	3.75	7.50	15.00
—Orange label					
APL1-5081	Soap Opera	1975	2.50	5.00	10.00
—Brown label					
LPL1-5102	Schoolboys in Disgrace	1975	2.50	5.00	10.00
VPS-6065 [(2)]	Everybody's in Showbiz	1972	5.00	10.00	20.00
—Orange label					
VPS-6065 [(2)]	Everybody's in Showbiz	1975	3.00	6.00	12.00
—Brown label					
REPRISE					
PRO 328 [P-DJ]	God Save the Kinks	1969	125.00	250.00	500.00
—Mail-order box with decal, postcard, bag of grass, two pins, letter, Kinks consumer guide and "Then Now and In Between" LP. Price is for complete package.					
PRO 328 [P-DJ]	Then Now and In Between	1969	12.50	25.00	50.00
—Album that came with above box is sometimes found by itself without all the other goodies.					
MS-2127	The Great Lost Kinks Album	1973	12.50	25.00	50.00

Number	Title (A Side/B Side)	Yr	VG	VG+	NM
R-6143 [M]	You Really Got Me	1965	15.00	30.00	60.00
R-6143 [M-DJ]	You Really Got Me	1965	100.00	200.00	400.00
—White label promo					
RS-6143 [P]	You Really Got Me	1965	20.00	40.00	80.00
—Pink, gold and green label					
RS-6143 [P]	You Really Got Me	1971	2.50	5.00	10.00
—Orange label with "r:" and steamboat at top					
R-6158 [M]	Kinks-Size	1965	12.50	25.00	50.00
R-6158 [M-DJ]	Kinks-Size	1965	50.00	100.00	200.00
—White label promo					
RS-6158 [R]	Kinks-Size	1965	7.50	15.00	30.00
R-6173 [M]	Kinda Kinks	1965	12.50	25.00	50.00
R-6173 [M-DJ]	Kinda Kinks	1965	50.00	100.00	200.00
—White label promo					
RS-6173 [R]	Kinda Kinks	1965	7.50	15.00	30.00
R-6184 [M]	Kinks Kinkdom	1965	12.50	25.00	50.00
R-6184 [M-DJ]	Kinks Kinkdom	1965	50.00	100.00	200.00
—White label promo					
RS-6184 [R]	Kinks Kinkdom	1965	7.50	15.00	30.00
R-6197 [M]	The Kink Kontroversy	1966	12.50	25.00	50.00
R-6197 [M-DJ]	The Kink Kontroversy	1966	50.00	100.00	200.00
—White label promo					
RS-6197 [R]	The Kink Kontroversy	1966	7.50	15.00	30.00
R-6217 [M]	The Kinks Greatest Hits!	1966	10.00	20.00	40.00
RS-6217 [R]	The Kinks Greatest Hits!	1966	6.25	12.50	25.00
—Pink, gold and green label					
RS-6217 [R]	The Kinks Greatest Hits!	1971	2.50	5.00	10.00
—Orange label with "r:" and steamboat at top					
R-6228 [M]	Face to Face	1967	10.00	20.00	40.00
RS-6228 [P]	Face to Face	1967	7.50	15.00	30.00
—Pink, gold and green label					
RS-6228 [P]	Face to Face	1971	2.50	5.00	10.00
—Orange label with "r:" and steamboat at top					
R-6260 [M]	The Live Kinks	1967	8.75	17.50	35.00
RS-6260 [S]	The Live Kinks	1967	6.25	12.50	25.00
—Pink, gold and green label					
RS-6260 [S]	The Live Kinks	1971	2.50	5.00	10.00
—Orange label with "r:" and steamboat at top					
R-6272 [M-DJ]	Something Else by the Kinks	1968	75.00	150.00	300.00
—White label promo; no stock copies were issued in mono					
RS-6272 [S]	Something Else by the Kinks	1968	7.50	15.00	30.00
—Pink, gold and green label					
RS-6272 [S]	Something Else by the Kinks	1968	5.00	10.00	20.00
—Two-tone orange label with "r: and "W7" logos with steamboat					
RS-6272 [S]	Something Else by the Kinks	1971	2.50	5.00	10.00
—Orange label with "r:" and steamboat at top					
RS-6327	The Kinks Are the Village Green Preservation Society	1969	7.50	15.00	30.00
—Two-tone orange label with "r: and "W7" logos with steamboat					
RS-6327	The Kinks Are the Village Green Preservation Society	1971	2.50	5.00	10.00
—Orange label with "r:" and steamboat at top					
RS-6366	Arthur (Or The Decline and Fall of the British Empire)	1969	6.25	12.50	25.00
—Two-tone orange label with "r: and "W7" logos with steamboat					
RS-6366	Arthur (Or The Decline and Fall of the British Empire)	1971	2.50	5.00	10.00
—Orange label with "r:" and steamboat at top					
RS-6423	Lola Versus Powerman and the Moneygoround, Part One	1970	3.75	7.50	15.00
—Original pressings have blue printing on a white cover					
RS-6423	Lola Versus Powerman and the Moneygoround, Part One	1971	2.50	5.00	10.00
—Later pressings have black printing on a white cover					
RS-6454 [(2)]	The Kink Kronicles	1972	3.75	7.50	15.00
SMAS-93034	Arthur (Or The Decline and Fall of the British Empire)	1970	10.00	20.00	40.00
—Capitol Record Club edition					
RHINO					
R1 70086	The Kinks Greatest Hits! Vol. 1	1989	3.00	6.00	12.00
R1 70315	You Really Got Me	1988	3.00	6.00	12.00
R1 70316	Kinda Kinks	1988	3.00	6.00	12.00
R1 70317	Kinks-Size	1988	3.00	6.00	12.00
R1 70318	Kinks Kinkdom	1988	3.00	6.00	12.00

KIPPINGTON LODGE

With Nick Lowe.

45s

Number	Title (A Side/B Side)	Yr	VG	VG+	NM
CAPITOL					
2236	And She Cried/Rumors	1968	7.50	15.00	30.00

KIRBY, KATHY

45s

Number	Title (A Side/B Side)	Yr	VG	VG+	NM
ASCOT					
2232	In All the World/Time	1967	2.00	4.00	8.00
LONDON					
9572	(He's a) Big Man/Slowly	1963	3.75	7.50	15.00
9621	Dance On/Playboy	1963	3.75	7.50	15.00
9628	Secret Love/Too Bad for Johnny	1964	3.75	7.50	15.00
9645	Let Me Go Lover/Sweetest Sounds	1964	3.75	7.50	15.00
9677	Love Me Baby/You're the One	1964	3.75	7.50	15.00
9750	I Belong/I'll Try Not to Cry	1965	3.75	7.50	15.00
PARROT					
9767	Secret Love/Soon I'll Wed My Love	1965	3.00	6.00	12.00
9775	The Way of Love/Oh Darling How I Miss You	1965	3.00	6.00	12.00
9805	Where in the World/Wonderful Feeling of Love	1965	3.00	6.00	12.00
9827	Till the End of Time/Spanish Flea	1966	2.50	5.00	10.00

KIRK, DAVE

45s

Number	Title (A Side/B Side)	Yr	VG	VG+	NM
HI-Q					
5024	Oh! Baby/Those Lonely Blue Nights	1962	12.50	25.00	50.00

KISS

12-Inch Singles

Number	Title (A Side/B Side)	Yr	VG	VG+	NM
CASABLANCA					
20169	I Was Made for Lovin' You/Charisma	1979	6.25	12.50	25.00
MERCURY					
229-1 [DJ]	Lick It Up (same on both sides)	1983	3.75	7.50	15.00
244-1 [DJ]	All Hell's Breaking Loose (same on both sides)	1983	3.75	7.50	15.00
311-1 [DJ]	Heaven's on Fire (same on both sides)	1984	3.75	7.50	15.00
326-1 [DJ]	Thrills in the Night (same on both sides)	1984	3.75	7.50	15.00
377-1 [DJ]	Tears Are Falling (same on both sides)	1985	3.75	7.50	15.00
531-1 [DJ]	Crazy Nights (same on both sides)	1987	3.00	6.00	12.00
559-1 [DJ]	Reason to Live (same on both sides)	1987	3.00	6.00	12.00
572-1 [DJ]	Turn On the Night (same on both sides)	1987	3.00	6.00	12.00

45s

Number	Title (A Side/B Side)	Yr	VG	VG+	NM
CASABLANCA					
0004	Love Theme from Kiss/Nothin' to Lose	1974	3.00	6.00	12.00
0011	Kissin' Time/Nothin' to Lose	1974	3.00	6.00	12.00
0015	Strutter/100,000 Years	1974	3.00	6.00	12.00
823	Let Me Go, Rock and Roll/Hotter Than Hell	1975	3.00	6.00	12.00
829	Rock and Roll All Nite/Getaway	1975	3.00	6.00	12.00
841	C'mon and Love Me/Getaway	1975	3.00	6.00	12.00
850	Rock and Roll All Nite (Live)/Rock and Roll All Night (Studio)	1975	2.50	5.00	10.00
854	Shout It Out Loud/Sweet Pain	1976	2.50	5.00	10.00
858	Flaming Youth/God of Thunder	1976	2.50	5.00	10.00
858 [PS]	Flaming Youth/God of Thunder	1976	15.00	30.00	60.00
863	Detroit Rock City/Beth	1976	2.50	5.00	10.00
—With "Detroit Rock City" listed as "Side A"					
863	Beth/Detroit Rock City	1976	—	2.50	5.00
—With "Beth" listed as "Side A"					
873	Hard Luck Woman/Mr. Speed	1976	—	3.00	6.00
880	Calling Dr. Love/Take Me	1977	—	3.00	6.00
889	Christine Sixteen/Shock Me	1977	—	3.00	6.00
895	Love Gun/Hooligan	1977	—	3.00	6.00
906	Shout It Out Loud (Live)/Nothin' to Lose	1977	—	3.00	6.00
915	Rocket Ride/Tomorrow and Tonight	1978	—	3.00	6.00
928	Strutter '78/Shock Me	1978	—	3.00	6.00
983	I Was Made for Lovin' You/Hard Times	1979	—	2.50	5.00
2205	Sure Know Something/Dirty Livin'	1979	—	2.50	5.00
2282	Shandi/She's So European	1980	—	2.50	5.00
2299	Tomorrow/Naked City	1980	—	2.50	5.00
2343	A World Without Heroes/Dark Light	1981	—	2.50	5.00
2365	I Love It Loud/Danger	1982	—	2.50	5.00
2365 [PS]	I Love It Loud/Danger	1982	5.00	10.00	20.00
MERCURY					
814671-7	Lick It Up/Dance All Over Your Face	1983	—	2.00	4.00
818216-7	Young and Wasted/All Hell Is Breaking Loose	1984	—	2.00	4.00
858894-7	Detroit Rock City/Detroit Rock City	1994	—	2.00	4.00
—B-side by Mighty Mighty Bosstones; small center hole; green vinyl					
858894-7 [PS]	Detroit Rock City/Detroit Rock City	1994	—	2.00	4.00
870022-7	Reason to Live/Thief in the Night	1987	—	2.00	4.00
870022-7 [PS]	Reason to Live/Thief in the Night	1987	—	2.50	5.00
870215-7	Turn On the Night/Hell or High Water	1988	—	2.00	4.00
870215-7 [PS]	Turn On the Night/Hell or High Water	1988	—	2.50	5.00
872244-7	Let's Put the X in Sex/Calling Dr. Love	1989	—	2.50	5.00
872244-7 [PS]	Let's Put the X in Sex/Calling Dr. Love	1989	—	3.00	6.00
876146-7	Hide Your Heart/Betrayed	1989	—	2.50	5.00
876716-7	Forever/The Street Giveth and the Street Taketh Away	1990	—	2.50	5.00
880205-7	Heaven's on Fire/Lonely Is the Hunter	1984	—	2.00	4.00
880535-7	Thrills in the Night/Burn Bitch Burn	1985	—	2.00	4.00
884141-7	Tears Are Falling/Any Way You Slice It	1985	—	2.00	4.00
884141-7 [PS]	Tears Are Falling/Any Way You Slice It	1985	—	2.50	5.00
888796-7	Crazy Crazy Nights/No, No, No	1987	—	2.00	4.00
888796-7 [PS]	Crazy Crazy Nights/No, No, No	1987	—	2.50	5.00

Albums

Number	Title (A Side/B Side)	Yr	VG	VG+	NM
CASABLANCA					
NBLP 7001	Kiss	1974	7.50	15.00	30.00
—All renumbered versions have "Kissin' Time"; dark blue label					
NBLP 7001	Kiss	1976	3.75	7.50	15.00
—Tan label with desert scene, "Casablanca" label					
NBLP 7001	Kiss	1977	3.00	6.00	12.00
—Tan label with desert scene, "Casablanca Record and FilmWorks" label					
NBLP 7006	Hotter Than Hell	1974	7.50	15.00	30.00
—Dark blue label					
NBLP 7006	Hotter Than Hell	1976	3.75	7.50	15.00
—Tan label with desert scene, "Casablanca" label					
NBLP 7006	Hotter Than Hell	1977	3.00	6.00	12.00
—Tan label with desert scene, "Casablanca Record and FilmWorks" label					
NBLP 7016	Dressed to Kill	1975	7.50	15.00	30.00
—Dark blue label					
NBLP 7016	Dressed to Kill	1976	3.75	7.50	15.00
—Tan label with desert scene, "Casablanca" label					
NBLP 7016	Dressed to Kill	1977	3.00	6.00	12.00
—Tan label with desert scene, "Casablanca Record and FilmWorks" label					
NBLP 7020 [(2)]	Alive!	1975	10.00	20.00	40.00
—Dark blue labels; with booklet					
NBLP 7020 [(2)]	Alive!	1976	5.00	10.00	20.00
—Tan labels with desert scene, "Casablanca" label					
NBLP 7020 [(2)]	Alive!	1977	3.75	7.50	15.00
—Tan labels with desert scene, "Casablanca Record and FilmWorks" label					
NBLP 7025	Destroyer	1976	7.50	15.00	30.00
—Dark blue label					
NBLP 7025	Destroyer	1976	3.75	7.50	15.00
—Tan label with desert scene, "Casablanca" label					
NBLP 7025	Destroyer	1977	3.00	6.00	12.00
—Tan label with desert scene, "Casablanca Record and FilmWorks" label					
NBLP 7032 [(3)]	The Originals	1976	37.50	75.00	150.00
—Tan label with desert scene, "Casablanca" label; with booklet, four Kiss cards, a Kiss Army sticker					
NBLP 7032 [(3)]	The Originals	1976	25.00	50.00	100.00
—Tan label with desert scene, "Casablanca" label; without extras					
NBLP 7032 [(3)]	The Originals	1977	18.75	37.50	75.00
—Tan label with desert scene, "Casablanca Record and FilmWorks" label; with extras listed above					

Number	Title (A Side/B Side)	Yr	VG	VG+	NM
NBLP 7032 [(3)]	The Originals	1977	6.25	12.50	25.00
—Tan label with desert scene, "Casablanca Record and FilmWorks" label; without extras					
NBLP 7037	Rock and Roll Over	1976	5.00	10.00	20.00
—Tan label with desert scene, "Casablanca" label; comes with order form and sheet of stickers					
NBLP 7037	Rock and Roll Over	1977	3.00	6.00	12.00
—Tan label with desert scene, "Casablanca Record and FilmWorks" label					
NBLP 7057	Love Gun	1977	10.00	20.00	40.00
—With insert (cardboard gun)					
NBLP 7057	Love Gun	1977	3.00	6.00	12.00
—Without insert					
NBLP 7076 [(2)]	Alive II	1977	100.00	200.00	400.00
—With three tracks, "Take Me," "Hooligan" and "Do You Love Me," that are not on later editions. Perhaps as few as 50 copies were made.					
NBLP 7076 [(2)]	Alive II	1977	25.00	50.00	100.00
—With 8-page insert of tattoos. LP cover lists three tracks, "Take Me," "Hooligan" and "Do You Love Me," that are not on the record.					
NBLP 7076 [(2)]	Alive II	1977	18.75	37.50	75.00
—Without 8-page insert of tattoos. LP cover lists three tracks, "Take Me," "Hooligan" and "Do You Love Me," that are not on the record.					
NBLP 7076 [(2)]	Alive II	1977	10.00	20.00	40.00
—With 8-page insert of tattoos. Without "Take Me," "Hooligan" and "Do You Love Me" listed on cover					
NBLP 7076 [(2)]	Alive II	1977	3.75	7.50	15.00
—Without 8-page insert of tattoos. Without "Take Me," "Hooligan" and "Do You Love Me" listed on cover					
NBLP 7100 [(2)]	Double Platinum	1978	10.00	20.00	40.00
—Contains cardboard platinum award, or an order form for it					
NBLP 7100 [(2)]	Double Platinum	1978	3.75	7.50	15.00
—With neither platinum award nor the order form					
NBLP 7152	Dynasty	1979	3.75	7.50	15.00
—With poster or order form for it					
NBLP 7152	Dynasty	1979	2.50	5.00	10.00
—With neither poster nor order form					
NBLP 7225	Kiss Unmasked	1980	3.75	7.50	15.00
—With poster or order form for it					
NBLP 7225	Kiss Unmasked	1980	2.50	5.00	10.00
—With neither poster nor order form					
NBLP 7261	Music from The Elder	1981	7.50	15.00	30.00
NBLP 7270	Creatures of the Night	1982	10.00	20.00	40.00
—Original version has band with makeup					
NB 9001	Kiss	1974	20.00	40.00	80.00
—First Warner Bros.-distributed version does NOT have "Kissin' Time"					
NB 9001	Kiss	1974	12.50	25.00	50.00
—Second Warner Bros.-distributed version DOES have "Kissin' Time" on Side 2 (RE-1 on label)					
NB 20128 [DJ]	A Taste of Platinum	1978	12.50	25.00	50.00
—Promo-only sampler from Double Platinum					
NB 20137 [DJ]	Criss, Frehley, Simmons, Stanley	1978	10.00	20.00	40.00
—Promo-only sampler from the band's solo albums					
812770-1	Dynasty	1983	2.00	4.00	8.00
—Reissue					
822780-1 [(2)]	Alive!	1984	2.50	5.00	10.00
—Reissue					
822781-1 [(2)]	Alive II	1984	2.50	5.00	10.00
—Reissue					
824146-1	Kiss	1984	2.00	4.00	8.00
—Reissue					
824147-1	Hotter Than Hell	1984	2.00	4.00	8.00
—Reissue					
824148-1	Dressed to Kill	1984	2.00	4.00	8.00
—Reissue					
824149-1	Destroyer	1984	2.00	4.00	8.00
—Reissue					
824150-1	Rock and Roll Over	1984	2.00	4.00	8.00
—Reissue					
824151-1	Love Gun	1984	2.00	4.00	8.00
—Reissue					
824153-1	Music from The Elder	1984	2.00	4.00	8.00
—Reissue					
824154-1	Creatures of the Night	1984	2.00	4.00	8.00
—Reissue; features band without its makeup on cover					
824155-1 [(2)]	Double Platinum	1984	2.50	5.00	10.00
—Reissue					
826242-1	Unmasked	1985	2.00	4.00	8.00
—Reissue					
MERCURY					
792-1 [DJ]	First Kiss, Last Licks	1990	25.00	50.00	100.00
—Promo-only sampler					
522647-1 [(2)]	Alive III	1994	6.25	12.50	25.00
—Limited edition black vinyl					
522647-1 [(2)]	Alive III	1994	6.25	12.50	25.00
—Limited edition white vinyl					
522647-1 [(2)]	Alive III	1994	6.25	12.50	25.00
—Limited edition blue vinyl					
522647-1 [(2)]	Alive III	1994	6.25	12.50	25.00
—Limited edition red vinyl					
528950-1 [(2)]	MTV Unplugged	1996	5.00	10.00	20.00
532741-1 [(2)]	You Wanted the Best, You Got the Best!!	1996	5.00	10.00	20.00
814297-1	Lick It Up	1983	3.00	6.00	12.00
822495-1	Animalize	1984	3.00	6.00	12.00
826099-1	Asylum	1985	2.50	5.00	10.00
832632-1	Crazy Nights	1987	2.50	5.00	10.00
832903-1 [PD]	Crazy Nights	1987	6.25	12.50	25.00
836427-1	Smashes, Thrashes and Hits	1988	2.50	5.00	10.00
836887-1 [PD]	Smashes, Thrashes and Hits	1988	6.25	12.50	25.00
838913-1	Hot in the Shade	1989	2.50	5.00	10.00

KISSOON, MAC AND KATIE

45s

Number	Title (A Side/B Side)	Yr	VG	VG+	NM
ABC					
11306	Chirpy Chirpy Cheep Cheep/Walking Around	1971	—	3.00	6.00
BELL					
45198	I Found My Freedom/Love Game Today	1972	—	2.50	5.00
45436	Love Will Keep Us Together/I'm Up in Heaven	1974	—	2.50	5.00
MCA					
40409	Black Rose/Sugar Candy Kisses	1975	—	2.00	4.00
40482	Like a Butterfly/Beautiful Day	1975	—	2.00	4.00
40550	Two of Us/Dream of Me	1976	—	2.00	4.00
40609	Fly Away/Where Would Our Love Be	1976	—	2.00	4.00

Albums

Number	Title (A Side/B Side)	Yr	VG	VG+	NM
STATE/MCA					
2192	The Two of Us	1976	3.00	6.00	12.00

KIT AND THE OUTLAWS

45s

Number	Title (A Side/B Side)	Yr	VG	VG+	NM
PHILIPS					
40420	Midnight Hour/Don't Tread on Me	1966	3.00	6.00	12.00

KIT KATS, THE

45s

Number	Title (A Side/B Side)	Yr	VG	VG+	NM
JAMIE					
1321	That's the Way/Won't Find Better Than Me	1966	3.00	6.00	12.00
1326	Let's Get Lost on a Country Road/Find Someone (Who'll Make You Happy)	1966	3.00	6.00	12.00
1331	You've Got to Know/Cold Walls	1967	3.00	6.00	12.00
1337	Breezy/Won't Find Better Than Me	1967	3.00	6.00	12.00
1343	Sea of Love/Cold Walls	1967	3.00	6.00	12.00
1345	Distance/Find Someone	1968	2.50	5.00	10.00
1346	I Got the Feeling/That's the Way	1968	2.50	5.00	10.00
1353	I Want to Be/Need You	1968	2.50	5.00	10.00
1354	You're So Good to Me/Need You	1968	2.50	5.00	10.00
1362	Hey Saturday Noon/That's the Way	1968	2.50	5.00	10.00
1381	Won't Find Better (Than Me)/(They Call It) Love	1969	2.00	4.00	8.00
—As "New Hope"					
1385	Rain/Let's Get Lost on a Country Road	1970	2.00	4.00	8.00
—As "New Hope"					
1388	Look Away/The Money Game	1970	2.00	4.00	8.00
—As "New Hope"					
1422	Find Someone/Breezy	1974	—	3.00	6.00
—As "New Hope"					
LAURIE					
3186	Good Luck Charlie/Aba Daba Honeymoon	1963	5.00	10.00	20.00
LAWN					
249	You're No Angel/Cold Walls	1964	3.75	7.50	15.00
PARAMOUNT					
0110	That You Love/Taking My Time	1971	2.00	4.00	8.00

Albums

Number	Title (A Side/B Side)	Yr	VG	VG+	NM
JAMIE					
LPM-3029 [M]	It's Just a Matter of Time	1966	6.25	12.50	25.00
LPS-3029 [S]	It's Just a Matter of Time	1966	7.50	15.00	30.00
LPM-3032 [M]	The Kit Kats Do Their Thing — Live!	1967	7.50	15.00	30.00
LPS-3032 [S]	The Kit Kats Do Their Thing — Live!	1967	10.00	20.00	40.00
JLPS-3034	To Understand Is to Love	1970	7.50	15.00	30.00
—As "New Hope"					

KITCHEN CINQ, THE

45s

Number	Title (A Side/B Side)	Yr	VG	VG+	NM
DECCA					
32262	Good Lovin'/For Never We Met	1968	2.50	5.00	10.00
32374	She's So Fine/The Minstrel	1968	2.50	5.00	10.00
LHI					
17000	You'll Be Sorry Someday/Determination	1966	3.00	6.00	12.00
17005	If You Think/Ride the Wind	1967	3.00	6.00	12.00
17010	Still in Love with You Baby/Ride the Wind	1967	3.00	6.00	12.00
17015	Street Song/When the Rain Disappears	1967	3.00	6.00	12.00

Albums

Number	Title (A Side/B Side)	Yr	VG	VG+	NM
LHI					
E-12000 [M]	Everything But the Kitchen Cinq	1967	7.50	15.00	30.00
E7-12000 [S]	Everything But the Kitchen Cinq	1967	10.00	20.00	40.00

KITTENS, THE

Probably more than one group.

45s

Number	Title (A Side/B Side)	Yr	VG	VG+	NM
ABC					
10835	The Masquerade Is Over/It's Gotta Be Love	1966	2.50	5.00	10.00
ABC-PARAMOUNT					
10619	Shindig/I Got to Know Him	1965	3.00	6.00	12.00
10730	Lookie Lookie/We Find Him Guilty	1965	3.00	6.00	12.00
10783	Is It Our Baby/Undecided You	1966	3.00	6.00	12.00
ALPINE					
64	Dark, Dark Sunglasses/Itsy Bitsy Teeny Weeny Yellow Polka Dot Bikini	1960	7.50	15.00	30.00
67	A Letter on His Sweater/Broken Dreams	1960	7.50	15.00	30.00
CHESS					
2027	Hey Operator/Ain't No More Room	1967	2.00	4.00	8.00
2055	How Long Can I Go On/I've Got to Get Over You	1968	2.00	4.00	8.00
CHESTNUT					
203	Count Every Star/I'm Worried	1963	12.50	25.00	50.00
DON-EL					
122	Walter/Lite Bulb	1963	3.75	7.50	15.00
205	I Need Your Love Tonight/Johnny's Place	1963	3.75	7.50	15.00
MURBO					
1015	Joey Has a New Love/Lonely Summer	1967	2.50	5.00	10.00
UNART					
2010	It's All Over Now/Letter to Donna	1959	12.50	25.00	50.00

KLAATU

45s

Number	Title (A Side/B Side)	Yr	VG	VG+	NM
CAPITOL					
4377	Calling Occupants/Doctor Marvello	1976	2.00	4.00	8.00
4412	Calling Occupants/Sub-Rosa Subway	1977	—	2.50	5.00
4516	Around the Universe in 80 Days/We're Off You Know	1977	—	2.50	5.00
4627	Dear Christine/Older	1978	—	2.50	5.00
4866	Knee Deep in Love/Dog Star	1980	—	2.50	5.00
ISLAND					
011	California Jam/Doctor Marvello	1975	2.50	5.00	10.00

Albums

CAPITOL

Number	Title (A Side/B Side)	Yr	VG	VG+	NM
ST-11542	Klaatu	1976	3.75	7.50	15.00
ST-11633	Hope	1977	3.00	6.00	12.00
SW-11836	Sir Army Suit	1978	3.00	6.00	12.00
ST-12080	Endangered Species	1980	3.00	6.00	12.00
SN-16060	Klaatu	1980	2.00	4.00	8.00
—Budget-line reissue					
SN-16061	Hope	1980	2.00	4.00	8.00
—Budget-line reissue					
SN-16062	Sir Army Suit	1980	2.00	4.00	8.00
—Budget-line reissue					

KLEIN, GEORGE

45s

SUN

Number	Title (A Side/B Side)	Yr	VG	VG+	NM
358	U.T. Party (Part 1)/U.T. Party (Part 2)	1961	5.00	10.00	20.00

KLEIN, ROBERT

45s

BRUT

Number	Title (A Side/B Side)	Yr	VG	VG+	NM
802	The Fabulous Fifties/(B-side unknown)	1973	—	3.00	6.00

CASABLANCA

Number	Title (A Side/B Side)	Yr	VG	VG+	NM
972	Fallin'/Fill In the Words	1979	—	2.00	4.00

Albums

BRUT

Number	Title (A Side/B Side)	Yr	VG	VG+	NM
6001	Child of the 50's	1973	3.00	6.00	12.00
6600	Mind Over Matter	1974	3.00	6.00	12.00

CAEDMON

Number	Title (A Side/B Side)	Yr	VG	VG+	NM
TC 9100	The Unauthorized Biography of Howard Who	1969	3.00	6.00	12.00

EPIC

Number	Title (A Side/B Side)	Yr	VG	VG+	NM
PE 33535	New Teeth	1975	2.50	5.00	10.00

KLEMMER, JOHN

45s

ABC

Number	Title (A Side/B Side)	Yr	VG	VG+	NM
12172	Touch/Glass Dolphins	1976	—	2.50	5.00
12228	Forest Child/At Seventeen	1976	—	2.50	5.00
12301	Caress/Quiet Afternoon	1977	—	2.00	4.00

CADET

Number	Title (A Side/B Side)	Yr	VG	VG+	NM
5603	And We Were Lovers/Look to the Sky	1968	2.00	4.00	8.00

CADET CONCEPT

Number	Title (A Side/B Side)	Yr	VG	VG+	NM
7023	Here Comes the Child/Soliloquy for Tenor and Voice	197?	—	3.00	6.00

ELEKTRA

Number	Title (A Side/B Side)	Yr	VG	VG+	NM
47050	Magnificent Madness/Heart	1980	—	2.00	4.00
47170	Let's Make Love/Hush	1981	—	2.00	4.00

Albums

ABC

Number	Title (A Side/B Side)	Yr	VG	VG+	NM
D-836	Fresh Feathers	1974	3.75	7.50	15.00
D-922	Touch	1975	3.75	7.50	15.00
D-950	Barefoot Ballet	1976	3.00	6.00	12.00
AB-1007	LifeStyle (Living & Loving)	1977	3.00	6.00	12.00
AA-1068	Arabesque	1978	3.00	6.00	12.00
AA-1106	Cry	1978	3.00	6.00	12.00
AA-1116	Brazilia	1979	3.00	6.00	12.00

ABC IMPULSE!

Number	Title (A Side/B Side)	Yr	VG	VG+	NM
AS-9214	Constant Throb	1973	3.75	7.50	15.00
AS-9220	Waterfalls	1973	3.75	7.50	15.00
AS-9244	Intensity	1974	3.75	7.50	15.00
AS-9269	Magic and Movement	1974	3.75	7.50	15.00

ARISTA/NOVUS

Number	Title (A Side/B Side)	Yr	VG	VG+	NM
3500	Nexus	1979	3.00	6.00	12.00

BLUEBIRD

Number	Title (A Side/B Side)	Yr	VG	VG+	NM
6577-1-RB	Nexus One	1987	2.50	5.00	10.00

CADET

Number	Title (A Side/B Side)	Yr	VG	VG+	NM
LP 797 [M]	Involvement	1967	7.50	15.00	30.00
LPS 797 [S]	Involvement	1967	5.00	10.00	20.00
LPS 808	And We Were Lovers	1968	5.00	10.00	20.00

CADET CONCEPT

Number	Title (A Side/B Side)	Yr	VG	VG+	NM
LPS 321	Blowin' Gold	1969	5.00	10.00	20.00
LPS 326	All the Children Cried	1970	5.00	10.00	20.00
LPS 330	Eruptions	1971	5.00	10.00	20.00

CHESS

Number	Title (A Side/B Side)	Yr	VG	VG+	NM
2ACMJ-401 [(2)]	Magic Moments	1976	3.75	7.50	15.00
CH2-92501 [(2)]	Blowin' Gold	198?	3.00	6.00	12.00

ELEKTRA

Number	Title (A Side/B Side)	Yr	VG	VG+	NM
6E-284	Magnificent Madness	1980	2.50	5.00	10.00
5E-527	Hush	1981	2.50	5.00	10.00
5E-566	Solo Saxophone II: Life	1982	2.50	5.00	10.00

ELEKTRA/MUSICIAN

Number	Title (A Side/B Side)	Yr	VG	VG+	NM
60197	Finesse	1983	2.50	5.00	10.00

MCA

Number	Title (A Side/B Side)	Yr	VG	VG+	NM
AA-1116	Brazilia	1979	2.50	5.00	10.00
—Reissue of ABC 1116					
6007 [(2)]	The Best of John Klemmer, Volume One/Mosaic	198?	2.50	5.00	10.00
—Reissue of MCA 8014					
6017 [(2)]	The Best of John Klemmer, Volume Two/The Impulse Years	1982	3.00	6.00	12.00
6246	Music	1989	2.50	5.00	10.00
8014 [(2)]	The Best of John Klemmer, Volume One/Mosaic	1979	3.75	7.50	15.00
37012	Fresh Feathers	1980	2.00	4.00	8.00
—Reissue of ABC 836					
37013	Barefoot Ballet	1980	2.00	4.00	8.00
—Reissue of ABC 950					
37014	LifeStyle (Living & Loving)	1980	2.00	4.00	8.00
—Reissue of ABC 1007					
37015	Arabesque	1980	2.00	4.00	8.00
—Reissue of ABC 1068					
37016	Cry	1980	2.00	4.00	8.00
—Reissue of ABC 1106					
37017	Constant Throb	1980	2.00	4.00	8.00
—Reissue					
37018	Waterfalls	1980	2.00	4.00	8.00
—Reissue					
37019	Intensity	1980	2.00	4.00	8.00
—Reissue					
37020	Magic and Movement	1980	2.00	4.00	8.00
—Reissue					
37115	Brazilia	1980	2.00	4.00	8.00
—Reissue of MCA 1116					
37152	Touch	198?	2.00	4.00	8.00
—Reissue of ABC 922					

MOBILE FIDELITY

Number	Title (A Side/B Side)	Yr	VG	VG+	NM
1-006	Touch	1979	7.50	15.00	30.00
—Audiophile vinyl					

NAUTILUS

Number	Title (A Side/B Side)	Yr	VG	VG+	NM
NR-4	Straight from the Heart	1980	20.00	40.00	80.00
—Audiophile vinyl					
NR-22	Finesse	1981	20.00	40.00	80.00
—Audiophile vinyl					

KLEMMER, JOHN, AND EDDIE HARRIS

Also see each artist's individual listings.

Albums

CRUSADERS

Number	Title (A Side/B Side)	Yr	VG	VG+	NM
16015	Two Tone	1982	6.25	12.50	25.00
—Part of MCA's "Audiophile Series"					

KLOWNS, THE

45s

RCA VICTOR

Number	Title (A Side/B Side)	Yr	VG	VG+	NM
74-0393	Lady Love/If You Can't Be a Clown	1970	—	2.50	5.00
74-0393 [PS]	Lady Love/If You Can't Be a Clown	1970	2.00	4.00	8.00
74-0485	Flower in My Garden/I Don't Believe in Magic	1971	—	2.50	5.00

Albums

RCA VICTOR

Number	Title (A Side/B Side)	Yr	VG	VG+	NM
LSP-4438	The Klowns	1970	2.50	5.00	10.00

KNACK, THE

No relation to the late-1970s pop group.

45s

CAPITOL

Number	Title (A Side/B Side)	Yr	VG	VG+	NM
2075	Freedom Now/Lady in the Window	1968	2.50	5.00	10.00
5774	Time Waits for No One/I'm Aware	1966	2.50	5.00	10.00
5889	The Spell/Softly, Softly	1967	2.50	5.00	10.00
5940	Banana Man/Pretty Daisy	1967	2.50	5.00	10.00

KNICKERBOCKERS, THE

45s

CHALLENGE

Number	Title (A Side/B Side)	Yr	VG	VG+	NM
59268	All I Need Is You/Bite, Bite Barracuda	1965	10.00	20.00	40.00
59293	Jerktown/Room for One More	1965	3.75	7.50	15.00
59321	Lies/The Coming Generation	1965	4.00	8.00	16.00
59326	One Track Mind/I Must Be Doing Something Right	1966	3.75	7.50	15.00
59332	High on Love/Stick with Me	1966	3.75	7.50	15.00
59335	Just One Girl/Chapel in the Fields	1966	3.75	7.50	15.00
59341	Love Is a Bird/Rumors, Gossip, Words Untrue	1966	3.75	7.50	15.00
59348	Can You Help Me/Please Don't Love Him	1966	3.75	7.50	15.00
59359	What Does That Make You/Sweet Green Fields	1967	3.75	7.50	15.00
59366	Come and Get It/Wishful Thinking	1967	3.75	7.50	15.00
59380	You'll Never Walk Alone/I Can Do It Better	1967	3.75	7.50	15.00
59384	As a Matter of Fact/They Ran for Their Lives	1968	3.75	7.50	15.00

Albums

CHALLENGE

Number	Title (A Side/B Side)	Yr	VG	VG+	NM
CH-621 [M]	Jerk and Twine Time	1965	100.00	200.00	400.00
CH-622 [M]	Lies	1966	25.00	50.00	100.00
CHS-622 [S]	Lies	1966	50.00	100.00	200.00
LP-12664 [M]	Llyod Thaxton Presents the Knickerbockers	1965	50.00	100.00	200.00

SUNDAZED

Number	Title (A Side/B Side)	Yr	VG	VG+	NM
LP-5000	The Great Lost Knickerbockers Album	1990	3.00	6.00	12.00
—Blue vinyl					

KNIGHT, CHRIS

"Peter Brady" of THE BRADY BUNCH.

45s

PARAMOUNT

Number	Title (A Side/B Side)	Yr	VG	VG+	NM
0177	Good for Each Other/Over and Over	1972	3.75	7.50	15.00
0177 [PS]	Good for Each Other/Over and Over	1972	3.75	7.50	15.00

KNIGHT, CHRIS, AND MAUREEN MCCORMICK

Also see each artist's individual listings; THE BRADY BUNCH.

45s

PARAMOUNT

Number	Title (A Side/B Side)	Yr	VG	VG+	NM
0246	Little Bird/Just a-Singin' Along	1973	3.75	7.50	15.00

Albums

PARAMOUNT

Number	Title (A Side/B Side)	Yr	VG	VG+	NM
PAS-6062	Chris Knight and Maureen McCormick	1973	30.00	60.00	120.00

KNIGHT, FREDERICK

45s

1-2-3

Number	Title (A Side/B Side)	Yr	VG	VG+	NM
1724	Have a Little Mercy/Sauerkraut	1970	3.75	7.50	15.00

JUANA

Number	Title (A Side/B Side)	Yr	VG	VG+	NM
1948	Let Me Ring Your Bell Again/When It Ain't Right	1980	—	2.50	5.00
3402	I'm Falling in Love Again/Done Got Over Lover	1976	—	2.50	5.00
3404	Sugar/I'm Falling in Love	1976	—	2.50	5.00
3408	High Society/(Instrumental)	1976	—	2.50	5.00
3411	Staying Power/Wrapped in Your Love	1977	—	2.50	5.00
3415	Sit Down on Your Love/Staying Power	1977	—	2.50	5.00
3418	You and Me/When It Ain't Right with My Baby	1978	—	2.50	5.00

Number	Title (A Side/B Side)	Yr	VG	VG+	NM
3420	My Music Makes Me Feel Good/When It Ain't Right with My Baby	1978	—	2.50	5.00
3423	You Can't Deny Me/If You Love Your Baby	1979	—	2.50	5.00
3700	The Old Songs/Bundle of Love	1981	—	2.50	5.00
3702	You're the Best Thing in My Life/(B-side unknown)	1981	—	2.50	5.00
STAX					
0117	I've Been Lonely for So Long/Lean on Me	1972	2.00	4.00	8.00
0139	Trouble/A Friend	1972	—	3.50	7.00
0167	Take Me On Home Witcha/This Is My Song of Love to You	1973	—	3.50	7.00
0201	I Let My Chance Go By/Suzy	1974	—	3.50	7.00
TRUTH					
3202	Passing Through/Sometimes Storm	1974	—	3.00	6.00
3216	I Betcha Didn't Know That/Let's Make a Deal	1974	—	3.00	6.00
3228	I Wanna Play with You/I Miss You	1975	—	3.00	6.00
Albums					
STAX					
STS-3011	I've Been Lonely So Long	1973	5.00	10.00	20.00

KNIGHT, GLADYS, AND THE PIPS

Includes Gladys Knight solo.

12-Inch Singles

Number	Title (A Side/B Side)	Yr	VG	VG+	NM
BUDDAH					
DSC 115	Love Is Always On Your Mind/(Instrumental)	1977	3.00	6.00	12.00
DSC 126	It's a Better Than Good Time/(Instrumental)	1978	3.00	6.00	12.00
COLUMBIA					
AS 803 [DJ]	Taste of Bitter Love/Bourgie, Bourgie	1980	2.50	5.00	10.00
AS 1307 [DJ]	I Will Fight/God Is	1981	2.00	4.00	8.00
03969	Save the Overtime (For Me)/(Instrumental)	1983	2.00	4.00	8.00
04965	When You're Far Away/(Instrumental)	1983	—	3.00	6.00
05161	My Time (2 versions)	1984	—	3.00	6.00
10996	You Bring Out the Best in Me/You Loved Away the Pain	1979	2.00	4.00	8.00
MCA					
1456 [DJ]	Men (5 versions)	1990	2.00	4.00	8.00
1621 [DJ]	Where Would I Be (3 versions)	1991	2.00	4.00	8.00
1694 [DJ]	Superwoman (4 versions)	1991	2.00	4.00	8.00
2080 [DJ]	Meet Me in the Middle (6 versions)	1991	2.00	4.00	8.00
3311 [DJ]	This Time (4 versions)	1994	2.00	4.00	8.00
L33-17429 [DJ]	Lovin' On Next to Nothin' (4 versions)	1987	2.00	4.00	8.00
L33-17431 [DJ]	Love Overboard (4 versions)	1987	2.00	4.00	8.00
L33-17444 [DJ]	Love Overboard (6:10) (5:44)	1987	2.00	4.00	8.00
L33-17561 [DJ]	It's Gonna Take All Our Love (same on both sides)	1988	2.00	4.00	8.00
23713	Send It To Me/When You Love Somebody	1986	2.00	4.00	8.00
23803	Love Overboard (6:00)/(Instrumental)	1987	—	3.00	6.00
23804	Lovin' On Next to Nothin'/(Instrumental)	1987	—	3.00	6.00
23871	It's Gonna Take All Our Love/(Instrumental)	1988	—	3.00	6.00
54130	Men/(Instrumental)	1990	—	3.00	6.00

45s

Number	Title (A Side/B Side)	Yr	VG	VG+	NM
BRUNSWICK					
55048	Whistle My Love/Ching Ching	1958	30.00	60.00	120.00
BUDDAH					
363	Where Peaceful Waters Flow/Perfect Love	1973	—	2.50	5.00
363 [PS]	Where Peaceful Waters Flow/Perfect Love	1973	2.00	4.00	8.00
383	Midnight Train to Georgia/(Instrumental)	1973	—	3.00	6.00
383	Midnight Train to Georgia/Window Raising Granny	1973	—	2.50	5.00
393	I've Got to Use My Imagination/I Can See Clearly Now	1973	—	2.50	5.00
403	Best Thing That Ever Happened to Me/Once in a Lifetime	1974	—	2.50	5.00
423	On and On/The Makings of You	1974	—	2.50	5.00
423 [PS]	On and On/The Makings of You	1974	2.00	4.00	8.00
433	I Feel a Song (In My Heart)/Don't Burn Down the Bridge	1974	—	2.50	5.00
453	Love FInds It's Own Way/Better You Go Your Way	1975	—	2.50	5.00
463	The Way We Were-Try to Remember/The Need to Be	1975	—	2.50	5.00
487	Money/Street Brothers	1975	—	2.50	5.00
513	Part Time Love/Where Did I Put His Memory	1975	—	2.50	5.00
523	Make Yours a Happy Home/The Going Up and the Coming Down	1976	—	2.50	5.00
544	So Sad the Song/(Instrumental)	1976	—	2.50	5.00
569	Baby Don't Change Your Mind/I Love to Feel That Feelin'	1977	—	2.50	5.00
584	Sorry Doesn't Always Make It Right/You Put a New Life in My Body	1977	—	2.50	5.00
592	The One and Only/Pipe Dreams	1978	—	2.50	5.00
598	It's a Better Than Good Time/Everybody's Got to Find a Way	1978	—	2.50	5.00
601	I'm Coming Home Again/Love Gives You the Power	1978	—	2.50	5.00
605	Sail Away/I'm Still Caught Up with You	1979	—	2.50	5.00
1974 [DJ]	Do You Hear What I Hear/Silent Night	1974	—	3.00	6.00
1974 [PS]	Do You Hear What I Hear/Silent Night	1974	—	3.00	6.00
CASABLANCA					
912	If I Could Bring Back Yesterday/Since I Found Love	1978	—	2.00	4.00
—As "The Pips"					
949	Baby I'm Your Fool/Lights of the City	1978	—	2.00	4.00
—As "The Pips"					
COLUMBIA					
02113	Forever Yesterday (For the Children)/(Instrumental)	1981	—	2.00	4.00
02113 [PS]	Forever Yesterday (For the Children)/(Instrumental)	1981	—	2.50	5.00
02413	If That'll Make You Happy/Love Was Made for Two	1981	—	2.00	4.00
02549	I Will Fight/God Is	1981	—	2.00	4.00
02706	Friend of Mine/Reach High	1982	—	2.00	4.00
03418	That Special Time of Year/Santa Claus Is Comin' to Town	1982	—	2.00	4.00
03761	Save the Overtime (For Me)/Ain't No Greater Love	1983	—	2.00	4.00
04033	You're Number 1 in My Book/Oh La De Dah	1983	—	2.00	4.00
04219	Hero (The Wind Beneath My Wings)/Seconds	1983	—	2.50	5.00
04333	Here's That Sunny Day/Oh La De Da	1984	—	2.00	4.00
04369	When You're Far Away/Seconds	1984	—	2.00	4.00
04761	My Time/(Instrumental)	1985	—	2.00	4.00
04761 [PS]	My Time/(Instrumental)	1985	—	2.50	5.00
04873	Keep Givin' Me Love/Do You Wanna Have Some Fun	1985	—	2.00	4.00
05679	Till I See You Again/Strivin'	1985	—	2.00	4.00
10922	Am I Too Late/It's the Same Old Song	1979	—	2.00	4.00
10997	You Bring Out the Best in Me/You Loved Away the Pain	1979	—	2.00	4.00
11088	The Best Thing We Can Do Is Say Goodbye/You Don't Have to Say I Love You	1979	—	2.00	4.00
11239	Landlord/We Need Hearts	1980	—	2.00	4.00
11330	Taste of Bitter Love/Add It Up	1980	—	2.00	4.00
11375	Bourgie', Bourgie'/Get the Love	1980	—	2.00	4.00
11409	When a Child Is Born/The Lord's Prayer	1980	—	2.00	4.00
—With Johnny Mathis					
ENJOY					
2012	What Shall I Do/Love Call	1964	3.75	7.50	15.00
EVERLAST					
5025	Happiness/I Had a Dream Last Night	1963	6.25	12.50	25.00
—As "The Pips"					
FURY					
1050	Every Beat of My Heart/Room in Your Heart	1961	6.25	12.50	25.00
—Re-recordings of the same songs on Huntom and Vee Jay					
1052	Guess Who/Stop Running Around	1961	3.75	7.50	15.00
1054	Letter Full of Tears/You Broke Your Promise	1961	3.75	7.50	15.00
1064	Operator/I'll Trust in You	1962	3.75	7.50	15.00
1067	Darling/Linda	1962	5.00	10.00	20.00
—As "The Pips"					
1073	Come See About Me/I Want That Kind of Love	1963	7.50	15.00	30.00
HUNTOM					
2510	Every Beat of My Heart/Room in Your Heart	1961	125.00	250.00	500.00
—As "The Pips"					
MAXX					
326	Giving Up/Maybe, Maybe Baby	1964	3.75	7.50	15.00
329	Lovers Always Forget/Another Love	1964	3.75	7.50	15.00
331	Either Way I Lose/Go Away, Stay Away	1964	3.75	7.50	15.00
334	Who Knows/Stop and Get a Hold of Myself	1965	3.75	7.50	15.00
335	Tell Her You're Mine/If I Should Ever Be in Love	1965	3.75	7.50	15.00
MCA					
53002	Send It to Me/When You Love Somebody (It's Christmas Every Day)	1987	—	—	3.00
53002 [PS]	Send It to Me/When You Love Somebody (It's Christmas Every Day)	1987	—	—	3.00
53210	Love Overboard/(Instrumental)	1987	—	—	3.00
53210 [PS]	Love Overboard/(Instrumental)	1987	—	—	3.00
53211	Lovin' on Next to Nothin'/(Instrumental)	1988	—	—	3.00
53211 [PS]	Lovin' on Next to Nothin'/(Instrumental)	1988	—	—	3.00
53351	It's Gonna Take All Our Love/(Instrumental)	1988	—	—	3.00
53657	Licence to Kill/You	1989	—	—	3.00
53676	Licence to Kill/Pam	1989	—	—	3.00
—B-side by National Philharmonic Orchestra					
54117	Men/(Instrumental)	1991	—	—	3.00
SCOTTI BROS.					
06267	Loving on Borrowed Time (Love Theme from Cobra)/Angel of the City	1986	—	—	3.00
—A-side: Gladys Knight and Bill Medley; B-side: Robert Tepper					
SOUL					
35023	Just Walk in My Shoes/Stepping Closer to Your Heart	1966	2.00	4.00	8.00
35033	Take Me in Your Arms and Love Me/Do You Love Me Just a Little More?	1967	2.00	4.00	8.00
35034	Everybody Needs Love/Since I've Lost You	1967	2.00	4.00	8.00
35039	I Heard It Through the Grapevine/It's Time to Go Now	1967	2.50	5.00	10.00
35042	The End of Our Road/Don't Let Her Take Your Love from Me	1968	2.00	4.00	8.00
35045	It Should Have Been Me/You Don't Love MeNo More	1968	2.00	4.00	8.00
35047	I Wish It Would Rain/It's Summer	1968	2.00	4.00	8.00
35057	Didn't You Know (You'd Have to Cry Sometime)/Keep an Eye	1969	2.00	4.00	8.00
35063	The Nitty Gritty/Got Myself a Good Man	1969	2.00	4.00	8.00
35068	Friendship Train/Cloud Nine	1969	2.00	4.00	8.00
35071	You Need Love Like I Do (Don't You)/You're My Everything	1970	2.00	4.00	8.00
35078	If I Were Your Woman/The Tracks of My Tears	1970	—	3.50	7.00
35083	I Don't Want to Do Wrong/Is There a Place In His Heart for Me	1971	—	3.00	6.00
35091	Make Me the Woman You Come Home To/If You're Gonna Leave (Just Leave)	1972	—	3.00	6.00
35094	Help Me Make It Through the Night/If You're Gonna Leave (Just Leave)	1972	—	3.00	6.00
35098	Neither One of Us (Wants to Be the First to Say Goodbye)/Can't Give It Up No More	1972	—	3.00	6.00
35105	Daddy Could Swear I Declare/For Once in My Life	1973	—	3.00	6.00
35107	All I Need Is Time/The Only Time You Love Me (Is When You're Losing Me)	1973	—	3.00	6.00
35111	Betwen Her Goodbye and My Hello/This Child Needs Its Father	1974	—	3.00	6.00
TRIP					
3004	It Hurt Me So Bad/What Will Become of Me	1973	—	3.00	6.00
3004 [PS]	It Hurt Me So Bad/What Will Become of Me	1973	3.00	6.00	12.00
VEE JAY					
386	Every Beat of My Heart/Room in Your Heart	1961	5.00	10.00	20.00
—By "The Pips"					
386	Every Beat of My Heart/Ain'tcha Got Some Room (In Your Heart for Me)	1961	5.00	10.00	20.00
—By "The Pips"; same B-side, different title					
545	A Love Like Mine/Queen of Tears	1963	5.00	10.00	20.00

Number	Title (A Side/B Side)	Yr	VG	VG+	NM
Albums					
ACCORD					
SN-7103	Every Beat of My Heart	1981	2.50	5.00	10.00
SN-7105	Letter Full of Tears	1981	2.50	5.00	10.00
SN-7131	I Feel a Song	1981	2.50	5.00	10.00
SN-7188	It's Showtime	1982	2.50	5.00	10.00
ALLEGIANCE					
AV-5002	Glad to Be...	198?	2.50	5.00	10.00
BELL					
1323	In the Beginning	1975	3.00	6.00	12.00
6013	Tastiest Hits	1968	5.00	10.00	20.00
BUDDAH					
BDS-5141	Imagination	1973	3.00	6.00	12.00
BDS-5602	Claudine	1974	7.50	15.00	30.00
BDS-5612	I Feel a Song	1974	3.00	6.00	12.00
BDS-5639	2nd Anniversary	1975	3.00	6.00	12.00
BDS-5653	The Best of Gladys Knight & The Pips	1976	3.00	6.00	12.00
BDS-5676	Pipe Dreams	1976	3.00	6.00	12.00
BDS-5689	Still Together	1977	3.00	6.00	12.00
BDS-5701	The One and Only	1978	3.00	6.00	12.00
BDS-5714	Miss Gladys Knight	1978	3.00	6.00	12.00
CASABLANCA					
NBLP 7081	At Last...The Pips	1977	2.50	5.00	10.00
—As "The Pips"					
NBLP 7113	Callin'	1978	2.50	5.00	10.00
—As "The Pips"					
COLLECTABLES					
COL-5154	Golden Classics: Letter Full of Tears	198?	2.50	5.00	10.00
COLUMBIA					
JC 35704	Gladys Knight	1979	2.50	5.00	10.00
PC 35704	Gladys Knight	198?	2.00	4.00	8.00
—Budget-line reissue					
JC 36387	About Love	1980	2.50	5.00	10.00
PC 36387	About Love	198?	2.00	4.00	8.00
—Budget-line reissue					
FC 37086	Touch	1981	2.50	5.00	10.00
PC 37086	Touch	198?	2.00	4.00	8.00
—Budget-line reissue					
FC 38114	That Special Time of Year	1982	2.50	5.00	10.00
PC 38114	That Special Time of Year	1983	2.00	4.00	8.00
—Same as above with new prefix					
FC 38205	Visions	1983	2.50	5.00	10.00
PC 38205	Visions	198?	2.00	4.00	8.00
—Budget-line reissue					
FC 39423	Life	1985	2.50	5.00	10.00
PC 39423	Life	198?	2.00	4.00	8.00
—Budget-line reissue					
FC 40376	Greatest Hits	1986	2.50	5.00	10.00
FC 40878	The Best of Gladys Knight and the Pips/The Columbia Years	1988	2.50	5.00	10.00
FURY					
1003 [M]	Letter Full of Tears	1962	125.00	250.00	500.00
LOST-NITE					
LLP-17 [10]	Gladys Knight and the Pips	1981	3.00	6.00	12.00
—Red vinyl; generic cover					
MAXX					
3000 [M]	Gladys Knight and the Pips	1964	37.50	75.00	150.00
MCA					
10329	Good Woman	1991	3.75	7.50	15.00
42004	All Our Love	1987	2.50	5.00	10.00
MOTOWN					
M5-113V	Motown Superstar Series, Vol. 13	1981	2.50	5.00	10.00
M5-126V1	Everybody Needs Love	1981	3.00	6.00	12.00
—Reissue of Soul 706					
M5-148V1	Nitty Gritty	1981	3.00	6.00	12.00
—Reissue of Soul 713					
M5-193V1	Neither One of Us	1981	3.00	6.00	12.00
—Reissue of Soul 737					
M 792S [(2)]	Anthology	1974	3.75	7.50	15.00
MOT 5303	All the Great Hits of Gladys Knight and the Pips	198?	2.00	4.00	8.00
NATURAL RESOURCES					
NR 4004T1	Silk N' Soul	1978	2.50	5.00	10.00
—Reissue of Soul 711					
PAIR					
PDL2-1198	The Best of Gladys Knight and the Pips	1987	3.00	6.00	12.00
PICKWICK					
SPC-3349	Every Beat of My Heart	197?	2.50	5.00	10.00
SOUL					
S 706 [M]	Everybody Needs Love	1967	5.00	10.00	20.00
SS 706 [S]	Everybody Needs Love	1967	6.25	12.50	25.00
S 707 [M]	Feelin' Bluesy	1968	10.00	20.00	40.00
—Mono copies are promo only					
SS 707 [S]	Feelin' Bluesy	1968	6.25	12.50	25.00
SS 711	Silk N' Soul	1968	6.25	12.50	25.00
SS 713	Nitty Gritty	1969	6.25	12.50	25.00
SS 723	Gladys Knight and the Pips Greatest Hits	1970	3.75	7.50	15.00
SS 730	All in a Knight's Work	1970	3.75	7.50	15.00
SS 731	If I Were Your Woman	1971	3.75	7.50	15.00
S 736L	Standing Ovation	1971	3.75	7.50	15.00
S 737L	Neither One of Us	1973	3.75	7.50	15.00
S 739L	All I Need Is Time	1973	3.75	7.50	15.00
S 741	Knight Time	1974	3.00	6.00	12.00
S 744	A Little Knight Music	1975	3.00	6.00	12.00
SPHERE SOUND					
SR-7006 [M]	Gladys Knight and the Pips	196?	50.00	100.00	200.00
SSR-7006 [R]	Gladys Knight and the Pips	196?	30.00	60.00	120.00
SPRINGBOARD					
SPB-4035	Early Hits	1972	2.50	5.00	10.00
SPB-4050	How Do You Say Goodbye	1973	2.50	5.00	10.00
UNITED ARTISTS					
UA-LA503-E	The Very Best of Gladys Knight and the Pips	1975	3.00	6.00	12.00
UPFRONT					
UPF 130	Gladys Knight and the Pips	197?	2.50	5.00	10.00
UPF 185	Gladys Knight and the Pips	197?	2.50	5.00	10.00
VEE JAY					
D1-74796	Every Beat of My Heart: The Greatest Hits of the Early Years	1989	3.75	7.50	15.00

KNIGHT, JEAN

Number	Title (A Side/B Side)	Yr	VG	VG+	NM
45s					
CHELSEA					
3020	Don't Ask for 24 Hours/Hold Back the Night	1975	—	2.50	5.00
3035	Jesse James Is an Outlaw/Hold Back the Night	1975	—	2.50	5.00
COTILLION					
46020	You Got the Papers (But I Got the Man)/Anything You Can Do (I Can Do As Well)	1981	—	2.00	4.00
46027	Keep It Comin'/One on One	1981	—	2.00	4.00
47002	You Show Me Yours, I'll Show You Mine/(B-side unknown)	1982	—	2.00	4.00
—All of the above with Premium					
DIAL					
1026	Dirt/Jesse Joe	1974	—	2.50	5.00
ICHIBAN					
97-422	Bill/Bus Stop	1997	—	—	3.00
JETSTREAM					
706	Doggin' Around/The Man That Left Me	1965	2.50	5.00	10.00
MIRAGE					
99606	Let the Good Times Roll/Magic	1985	—	—	3.00
99643	My Toot Toot/My Heart Is Willing (And My Body Is Too)	1985	—	—	3.00
99643 [PS]	My Toot Toot/My Heart Is Willing (And My Body Is Too)	1985	—	—	3.00
STAX					
0088	Mr. Big Stuff/Why I Keep Living These Memories	1971	—	3.00	6.00
0105	You Think You're Hot Stuff/Don't Talk About Jody	1971	—	2.50	5.00
0116	Carry On/Call Me Your Fool	1972	—	2.50	5.00
0136	Helping Man/Pick Up the Pieces	1972	—	2.50	5.00
0150	Do Me/Save the Last Kiss for Me	1972	—	2.50	5.00
TRIBE					
8304	Lonesome Tonight/Love	1964	3.00	6.00	12.00
8306	T'Ain't It the Truth/I'm So Glad for Your Sake	1965	3.00	6.00	12.00
8313	Anyone Can Love Him/A Tear	1966	3.00	6.00	12.00
Albums					
COTILLION					
SD 5230	Jean Knight and Premium	1981	3.75	7.50	15.00
MIRAGE					
90282	My Toot Toot	1985	2.50	5.00	10.00
STAX					
STS-2045	Mr. Big Stuff	1971	10.00	20.00	40.00
MPS-8554	Mr. Big Stuff	198?	2.50	5.00	10.00

KNIGHT, ROBERT

Also see THE PARAMOUNTS (3).

Number	Title (A Side/B Side)	Yr	VG	VG+	NM
45s					
DOT					
16256	Because/Dance Only with Me	1961	3.00	6.00	12.00
16303	Free Me/The Other Half of Man	1962	3.00	6.00	12.00
ELF					
90019	Isn't It Lonely Together/We'd Better Stop	1968	—	3.00	6.00
90030	Smokey/If I Had My Way	1969	—	3.00	6.00
90037	I Only Have Eyes for You/I'm Sticking with You	1969	—	3.00	6.00
MONUMENT					
8612	Better Get Ready for Love/Somebody's Baby	1974	—	2.50	5.00
8629	Dynamite/The Outsider	1974	—	2.50	5.00
PRIVATE STOCK					
45038	I'm Coming Home to You/(B-side unknown)	1975	—	2.50	5.00
45069	Second Chance/Glitter Lady	1976	—	2.50	5.00
45118	I've Got News for You/(B-side unknown)	1976	—	2.50	5.00
RISING SONS					
705	Everlasting Love/Somebody's Baby	1967	2.00	4.00	8.00
707	Blessed Are the Lonely/It's Been Worth It All	1967	—	3.00	6.00
708	Power of Love/Love on a Mountain Top	1968	—	3.00	6.00
Albums					
RISING SONS					
RSM-7000 [M]	Everlasting Love	1967	7.50	15.00	30.00
RSS-17000 [S]	Everlasting Love	1967	10.00	20.00	40.00

KNIGHT, SONNY

Number	Title (A Side/B Side)	Yr	VG	VG+	NM
45s					
ALADDIN					
3357	But Officer/Dear Wonderful God	1957	7.50	15.00	30.00
AURA					
403	If You Want This Love/I Just Called to Say Hello	1964	2.00	4.00	8.00
4505	Love Me As Though There Were No Tomorrow/Fool Like Me	1964	2.00	4.00	8.00
4505 [PS]	Love Me As Though There Were No Tomorrow/Fool Like Me	1964	5.00	10.00	20.00
4508	Rose Mary/(B-side unknown)	1965	2.00	4.00	8.00
A&M					
718	Evil Minded Woman/Georgia Town	1963	2.50	5.00	10.00
728	Be True to Your Dog/State Street	1964	2.50	5.00	10.00
DOT					
15507	Confidential/Jailbird	1956	5.00	10.00	20.00
—Originals have maroon labels					
15507	Confidential/Jailbird	1956	3.75	7.50	15.00
—Second pressings have black labels					
15542	End of a Dream/Worthless and Lowdown	1957	3.75	7.50	15.00
15597	Lovesick Blues/Insha Allot	1957	3.75	7.50	15.00
15635	Dedicated to You/Short Walk	1957	3.75	7.50	15.00
FIFO					
102	Cold, Cold Night/Saving My Love	1961	3.75	7.50	15.00
105	A Swingin' Door/(B-side unknown)	1961	3.75	7.50	15.00
MERCURY					
72033	Just One More Chance/Lost Child	1962	2.50	5.00	10.00

Number	Title (A Side/B Side)	Yr	VG	VG+	NM
ORIGINAL SOUND					
2	Once in Awhile/School's Out	1959	5.00	10.00	20.00
18	Those Oldies But Goodies Are Dedicated to You/ She Had Me Reelin'	1961	3.75	7.50	15.00
SPECIALTY					
594	Keep a-Walkin'/My Baby Don't Want Me	1957	3.75	7.50	15.00
STARLA					
1	Dedicated to You/Short Walk	1957	7.50	15.00	30.00
10	Once in a While/School's Out	1958	3.75	7.50	15.00
VITA					
137	Confidential/Jailbird	1956	10.00	20.00	40.00
WORLD PACIFIC					
403	If You Want This Love/I Just Called to Say Hello	1964	3.00	6.00	12.00
77811	If I May/Need Your Love So Bad	1966	2.00	4.00	8.00
77832	Angel Love/If I Ruled the World	1966	2.00	4.00	8.00
77858	The Quiet Man/I Can't Let You Go	1966	—	—	—
—Unreleased					
Albums					
AURA					
AR-3001 [M]	If You Want This Love	1964	6.25	12.50	25.00
AS-3001 [S]	If You Want This Love	1964	7.50	15.00	30.00

KNIGHT, TERRY, AND THE PACK

Group evloved into GRAND FUNK RAILROAD.

Number	Title (A Side/B Side)	Yr	VG	VG+	NM
45s					
A&M					
769	Kids Will Be the Same/You Lie	1965	3.75	7.50	15.00
CAMEO					
482	Forever and a Day/Lizbeth Peach	1967	2.50	5.00	10.00
495	Come Home Baby/Dirty Lady	1967	2.50	5.00	10.00
CAPITOL					
2174	Without a Woman/Let Me Stand Next to Your Fire	1968	3.00	6.00	12.00
—As "The Pack"					
2409	Such a Lonely Life/Lullaby	1969	2.50	5.00	10.00
2506	St. Paul/(Legend of) William and Mary	1969	2.50	5.00	10.00
2737	I'll Keep Waiting Patiently/Lullaby	1970	2.50	5.00	10.00
LUCKY ELEVEN					
003	Harlem Shuffle/I've Got News for You	1965	4.00	8.00	16.00
—As "The Pack"					
007	Does It Matter to You Girl/Wide Trackin'	1965	4.00	8.00	16.00
—As "The Fabulous Pack"					
007 [PS]	Does It Matter to You Girl/Wide Trackin'	1965	6.25	12.50	25.00
—As "The Fabulous Pack"					
225	How Much More/I've Been Told	1966	3.75	7.50	15.00
226	I Got Love/Better Man Than I	1966	3.75	7.50	15.00
228	Lady Jane/Lovin' Kind	1966	3.75	7.50	15.00
229	What's On Your Mind/A Change on the Way	1966	3.75	7.50	15.00
230	I (Who Have Nothing)/Numbers	1966	3.75	7.50	15.00
235	This Precious Time/Love, Love, Love, Love, Love	1967	3.75	7.50	15.00
236	One Monkey Don't Stop No Show/The Train	1967	3.75	7.50	15.00
WINGATE					
007	The Tears Come Rollin'/The Colour of My Love	1965	6.25	12.50	25.00
—As "The Pack"					
Albums					
ABKCO					
AB-4217 [(2)]	Mark, Don and Terry 1966-67	1972	5.00	10.00	20.00
CAMEO					
C 2007 [M]	Reflections	1967	5.00	10.00	20.00
—Reissue of Lucky Eleven LE-8001					
CS 2007 [S]	Reflections	1967	6.25	12.50	25.00
—Reissue of Lucky Eleven LES-8001					
LUCKY ELEVEN					
LE-8000 [M]	Terry Knight and the Pack	1966	10.00	20.00	40.00
LES-8000 [R]	Terry Knight and the Pack	1966	6.25	12.50	25.00
LE-8001 [M]	Reflections	1967	6.25	12.50	25.00
LES-8001 [S]	Reflections	1967	10.00	20.00	40.00

KNIGHT RIDERS, THE

Featuring BILLY VERA.

Number	Title (A Side/B Side)	Yr	VG	VG+	NM
45s					
UNITED ARTISTS					
366	Annie's Place/Unchained Melody	1961	6.25	12.50	25.00

KNIGHTS, THE

At least three, and perhaps four, different groups.

Number	Title (A Side/B Side)	Yr	VG	VG+	NM
45s					
CAPITOL					
5302	Hot Rod High/Theme for Teen Love	1964	12.50	25.00	50.00
FELSTED					
8640	White Fang/Night Train	1962	3.00	6.00	12.00
Albums					
ACE					
4763	Cold Days, Hot Knights	196?	100.00	200.00	400.00
200854	Across the Board	1966	100.00	200.00	400.00
201302	The Knights 1967	1967	100.00	200.00	400.00
CAPITOL					
DT 2189 [R]	Hot Rod High	1964	100.00	200.00	400.00
T 2189 [M]	Hot Rod High	1964	100.00	200.00	400.00
JUSTICE					
JLP-156	On the Move	196?	75.00	150.00	300.00

KNOCKOUTS, THE (1)

Number	Title (A Side/B Side)	Yr	VG	VG+	NM
45s					
SHAD					
5013	Darling Lorraine/Riot in Room 3C	1959	12.50	25.00	50.00
—With long ending on A-side					
5013	Darling Lorraine/Riot in Room 3C	1959	6.25	12.50	25.00
—With short ending on A-side					
5018	Please Be Mine/Rich Boy, Poor Boy	1960	6.25	12.50	25.00

KNOCKOUTS, THE (U)

The records on Scepter and Tribute are by the same group, but we're not sure if they are by group (1) or a different group. The MGM group may be different or the same, too; again, we're not sure.

Number	Title (A Side/B Side)	Yr	VG	VG+	NM
45s					
MGM					
13010	Fever/You Can Take My Girl	1961	5.00	10.00	20.00
SCEPTER					
1269	Got My Mojo Workin'/Every Day of the Week	1964	3.00	6.00	12.00
TRIBUTE					
199	Got My Mojo Working (Part 1)/Got My Mojo Working (Part 2)	1964	3.75	7.50	15.00
201	Tweet-Tweet/What's On Your Mind	1964	4.00	8.00	16.00
Albums					
TRIBUTE					
1202 [M]	Go Ape with the Knockouts	1964	50.00	100.00	200.00

KNOTT SISTERS, THE

Number	Title (A Side/B Side)	Yr	VG	VG+	NM
45s					
BIG TOP					
3003	Undivided Attention/Sun Glasses	1958	25.00	50.00	100.00

KNOX, BUDDY

Number	Title (A Side/B Side)	Yr	VG	VG+	NM
45s					
LIBERTY					
55290	Lovey Dovey/I Got You	1960	3.00	6.00	12.00
55305	Ling, Ting, Tong/The Kisses	1961	3.00	6.00	12.00
55305 [PS]	Ling, Ting, Tong/The Kisses	1961	7.50	15.00	30.00
55366	All By Myself/Three Eyed Man	1961	3.00	6.00	12.00
55411	Cha-Hua-Hua/Open	1962	3.00	6.00	12.00
55473	She's Gone/There's Only Me	1962	3.00	6.00	12.00
55503	Dear Abby/Three Way Love Affair	1962	3.00	6.00	12.00
55592	Shadaroom/Tomorrow Is a-Comin'	1963	2.50	5.00	10.00
55650	Thanks a Lot/Hitchhike Back to Georgia	1963	2.50	5.00	10.00
55694	Good Lovin'/All Time Loser	1964	2.50	5.00	10.00
REPRISE					
0395	Livin' in a House Full of Love/Good Time Girl	1965	2.50	5.00	10.00
0431	A Lover's Question/You Said Goodbye	1965	2.50	5.00	10.00
0463	A White Sport Coat/That Don't Do Me No Good	1966	2.50	5.00	10.00
0501	Love Has Many Ways/Sixteen Feet of Patio	1966	2.50	5.00	10.00
ROULETTE					
4002	Party Doll/My Baby's Gone	1957	12.50	25.00	50.00
—Maroon label, silver print, with roulette wheel around outside					
4002	Party Doll/My Baby's Gone	1957	7.50	15.00	30.00
—Red label, roulette wheel on top half of label					
4002	Party Doll/My Baby's Gone	1957	6.25	12.50	25.00
—Red label, no roulette wheel					
4002	Party Doll/My Baby's Gone	1957	10.00	20.00	40.00
—Red label, black print, with roulette wheel around outside					
4002	Party Doll/My Baby's Gone	1958	3.75	7.50	15.00
—White label with color spokes					
4009	Rock Your Little Baby to Sleep/Don't Make Me Cry	1957	10.00	20.00	40.00
—Red label with roulette wheel around outside					
4009	Rock Your Little Baby to Sleep/Don't Make Me Cry	1957	6.25	12.50	25.00
—Red label, roulette wheel on top half of label					
4009	Rock Your Little Baby to Sleep/Don't Make Me Cry	1957	5.00	10.00	20.00
—Red label, no roulette wheel					
4018	Hula Love/Devil Woman	1957	6.25	12.50	25.00
4042	Swingin' Daddy/Whenever I'm Lonely	1958	6.25	12.50	25.00
4082	Somebody Touched Me/C'mon Baby	1958	6.25	12.50	25.00
4120	That's Why I Cry/Teaseable, Pleaseable You	1958	6.25	12.50	25.00
4140	I Think I'm Gonna Kill Myself/To Be with You	1959	6.25	12.50	25.00
4179	Taste of the Blues/I Ain't Sharin' Sharon	1959	6.25	12.50	25.00
4262	Long Lonely Nights/Storm Clouds	1960	6.25	12.50	25.00
RUFF					
1001	Jo-Ann/Don't Make a Ripple	1965	2.50	5.00	10.00
TRIPLE D					
798	Party Doll/I'm Stickin' With You	1956	250.00	500.00	1000.
—B-side by Jimmy Bowen					
UNITED ARTISTS					
50301	This Time Tomorrow/Gypsy Man	1968	2.00	4.00	8.00
50463	Today My Sleepless Nights Came Back to Town/ A Million Years or So	1968	2.00	4.00	8.00
50526	God Knows I Love You/Night Runners	1969	2.00	4.00	8.00
50596	Salt Lake City/I'm Only Rockin'	1969	2.00	4.00	8.00
50644	Yesterday Is Gone/Back to New Orleans	1970	—	3.00	6.00
50722	White Dove/Glory Train	1970	—	3.00	6.00
50789	Come Softly to Me/Travelin' Light	1971	—	3.00	6.00
Albums					
ACCORD					
SN-7218	Party Doll and Other Hits	1981	2.50	5.00	10.00
LIBERTY					
LRP-3251 [M]	Buddy Knox's Golden Hits	1962	7.50	15.00	30.00
LST-7251 [S]	Buddy Knox's Golden Hits	1962	10.00	20.00	40.00
ROULETTE					
R 25003 [M]	Buddy Knox	1957	50.00	100.00	200.00
—Black label, all silver print (original)					
R 25003 [M]	Buddy Knox	1957	37.50	75.00	150.00
—Black label, red and silver print					
R 25003 [M]	Buddy Knox	1959	25.00	50.00	100.00
—White label with colored spokes					
R 25048 [M]	Buddy Knox and Jimmy Bowen	1959	50.00	100.00	200.00
—Black label, red and silver print					
R 25048 [M]	Buddy Knox and Jimmy Bowen	1959	25.00	50.00	100.00
—White label with colored spokes					
UNITED ARTISTS					
UAS 6689	Gypsy Man	1969	6.25	12.50	25.00

(Top left) Not everyone dug what Stan Kenton was doing with his so-called "progessive jazz," but he was quite popular at doing it. Here's one of the scarce Capitol 10-inch LPs, *A Presentation of Progressive Jazz*. (Top right) Capitol Compact 33 singles were 7-inch stereo records for jukeboxes. Here's one by the Kingston Trio of a title that was not issued on regular 45. (Bottom left) Kiss is the most collectible 1970s rock group. One of their most sought-after items is *First Kiss, Last Licks*, a promo-only compilation of both "masked" and "unmasked" hits. Unusally, it also contains photos of both versions of the band. (Bottom right) Before Buddy Knox had the first hit single ever on Roulette Records, that hit, "Party Doll," was issued on the obscure Triple D label. On the B-side was Jimmy Bowen's biggest hit, "I'm Stickin' With You."

KOALA, THE

45s

CAPITOL

Number	Title (A Side/B Side)	Yr	VG	VG+	NM
2365	Don't You Know What I Mean/Scattered Children's Toys	1968	3.75	7.50	15.00

Albums

CAPITOL

Number	Title (A Side/B Side)	Yr	VG	VG+	NM
SKAO-176	The Koala	1969	15.00	30.00	60.00

KOKOMO (1)

Pseudonym for producer Jimmy "Wiz" Wisner.

45s

FELSTED

Number	Title (A Side/B Side)	Yr	VG	VG+	NM
8612	Asia Minor/Roy's Tune	1961	2.50	5.00	10.00
8612 [PS]	Asia Minor/Roy's Tune	1961	3.75	7.50	15.00
8622	Humorous/Theme from a Silent Movie	1961	2.00	4.00	8.00
8628	Piano Rhapsody/Sweet Memories	1961	2.00	4.00	8.00
8635	Journey Home/Like Teen	1961	2.00	4.00	8.00
8641	Poinciana/The Good Earth	1962	2.00	4.00	8.00

Albums

FELSTED

Number	Title (A Side/B Side)	Yr	VG	VG+	NM
7513 [M]	Asia Minor	1961	10.00	20.00	40.00
17513 [S]	Asia Minor	1961	12.50	25.00	50.00

KOKOMO (2)

45s

COLUMBIA

Number	Title (A Side/B Side)	Yr	VG	VG+	NM
3-10207	Kitty Sittin' Pretty/It Ain't Cool (To Be Cool No More)	1975	—	2.50	5.00
3-10213	Kitty Sittin' Pretty/Anytime	1975	—	2.50	5.00
3-10283	Rise and Shine/Do It Right	1976	—	2.50	5.00
3-10380	Use Your Imagination/That's Enough	1976	—	2.50	5.00

Albums

COLUMBIA

Number	Title (A Side/B Side)	Yr	VG	VG+	NM
PC 33442	Kokomo	1975	2.50	5.00	10.00
PC 34031	Rise and Shine!	1976	2.50	5.00	10.00

KOKOMOS, THE

45s

Number	Title (A Side/B Side)	Yr	VG	VG+	NM
GONE					
5134	Mama's Boy/Yours Truly	1962	3.75	7.50	15.00
JOSIE					
906	Open House Party/No Lies	1963	3.00	6.00	12.00

KOLE, JERRY, AND THE STRINGERS

Albums

CROWN

Number	Title (A Side/B Side)	Yr	VG	VG+	NM
CST-385 [S]	Hot Rod Alley	1963	10.00	20.00	40.00
CLP-5385 [M]	Hot Rod Alley	1963	7.50	15.00	30.00

KONGOS, JOHN

45s

Number	Title (A Side/B Side)	Yr	VG	VG+	NM
ELEKTRA					
45729	He's Gonna Step on You Again/Sometimes It's Not Enough	1971	—	3.00	6.00
45760	Tokoloshe Man/Can Someone Please Direct Me Back to Earth	1972	—	2.50	5.00
45779	Jubilee Cloud/I Would Have Had a Good Time	1972	—	2.50	5.00
45809	He's Gonna Step on You Again/Tokoloshe Man	1972	—	2.50	5.00
GROOVE					
58-0009	Johnny and the Mermaid/Raunchy Twist	1963	3.00	6.00	12.00
KAPP					
799	I Love Mary/Good Time Party Companion	1966	2.50	5.00	10.00
RCA VICTOR					
47-8226	The Enchanted Sea/Tulips for 'Toinette	1963	3.00	6.00	12.00

Albums

Number	Title (A Side/B Side)	Yr	VG	VG+	NM
ELEKTRA					
EKS-75019	Kongos	1971	3.00	6.00	12.00
JANUS					
JLS 3032	Confusions About a Goldfish	1970	3.75	7.50	15.00

KONRADS, THE

45s

DECCA

Number	Title (A Side/B Side)	Yr	VG	VG+	NM
32060	I Didn't Know How Much/I Thought of You Last Night	1966	2.00	4.00	8.00

KOOBAS, THE

45s

Number	Title (A Side/B Side)	Yr	VG	VG+	NM
CAPITOL					
2416	First Cut Is the Deepest/Walking Out	1969	2.00	4.00	8.00
KAPP					
737	Take Me for a Little While/Give a Little Bit	1965	3.75	7.50	15.00
737 [PS]	Take Me for a Little While/Give a Little Bit	1965	5.00	10.00	20.00

KOOL AND THE GANG

Also see K.C. AND THE SUNSHINE BAND.

12-Inch Singles

Number	Title (A Side/B Side)	Yr	VG	VG+	NM
DE-LITE					
179-1 [DJ]	Take My Heart (same on both sides)	1983	—	3.00	6.00
261-1 [DJ]	Tonight (same on both sides)	1983	—	3.00	6.00
278-1 [DJ]	Straight Ahead (same on both sides)	1983	—	3.00	6.00
884199-1	Emergency (3 versions)	1984	—	3.00	6.00
MERCURY					
478-1 [DJ]	Stone Love (2 versions)/Dance Champion	1986	—	3.00	6.00
739-1 [DJ]	Raindrops (3 versions)	1989	—	2.50	5.00
874403-1	Raindrops (3 versions)/Amor, Amore	1989	—	3.00	6.00
888074-1	Victory (2 versions)/Bad Woman	1986	—	3.00	6.00
888292-1	Stone Love (Club Version)	1986	—	3.00	6.00
888712-1	Holiday (4 versions)	1988	—	3.00	6.00

45s

Number	Title (A Side/B Side)	Yr	VG	VG+	NM
DE-LITE					
519	Kool and the Gang/Raw Hamburger	1969	—	3.00	6.00
523	The Gangs Back Again/Kools Back Again	1969	—	3.00	6.00
525	Kool It (Here Comes the Fuzz)/Can't Stop	1970	—	3.00	6.00
529	Let the Music Take Your Mind/Chocolate Buttermilk	1970	—	3.00	6.00
534	Funky Man/1,2,3,4,5,6,7,8	1970	—	3.00	6.00
538	Who's Gonna Take the Weight (Part One)/Who's Gonna Take the Weight (Part Two)	1970	—	3.00	6.00
540	I Want to Take You Higher/Pneumonia	1971	—	3.00	6.00
543	The Penguin/Lucky for Me	1971	—	3.00	6.00
544	N.T. (Part One)/N.T. (Part Two)	1971	—	3.00	6.00
546	Love the Life You Live, Part I/Love the Life You Live, Part II	1972	—	3.00	6.00
547	You've Lost That Lovin' Feeling/Ike's Mood	1972	—	3.00	6.00
550	Music Is the Messenger, Part I/Music Is the Messenger, Part II	1972	—	3.00	6.00
552	Good Times/The Frog	1972	—	3.00	6.00
553	Funky Granny/Blowing with the Wind	1973	—	3.00	6.00
555	Country Junkie/I Remember John W. Coltrane	1973	—	3.00	6.00
557	Funky Stuff/More Funky Stuff	1973	—	3.00	6.00
559	Jungle Boogie/North, East, South, West	1973	—	2.50	5.00
561	Hollywood Swinging/Dujii	1974	—	2.50	5.00
801	Ladies Night/If You Feel Like Dancin'	1979	—	2.00	4.00
802	Too Hot/Tonight's the Night	1979	—	2.00	4.00
804	Hangin' Out/Got You Into My Life	1980	—	2.00	4.00
807	Celebration/Morning Star	1980	—	2.00	4.00
810	Take It to the Top/Love Affair	1981	—	2.00	4.00
813	Jones Vs. Jones/Night People	1981	—	2.00	4.00
815	Take My Heart/Just Friends	1981	—	2.50	5.00
—First pressings have no subtitle					
815	Take My Heart (You Can Have It If You Want It)/Just Friends	1981	—	2.00	4.00
816	Steppin' Out/Love Festival	1982	—	2.00	4.00
818	Get Down On It/Steppin' Out	1982	—	2.00	4.00
822	Big Fun/No Show	1982	—	2.00	4.00
824	Let's Go Dancin' (Ooh, La, La, La)/Be My Lady	1982	—	2.00	4.00
825	Street Kids/As One	1983	—	2.00	4.00
829	Joanna/A Place for Us	1983	—	—	3.00
830	Tonight/September Love	1984	—	—	3.00
831	Straight Ahead/September Love	1984	—	—	3.00
901	Slick Superchick/Life's a Song	1978	—	2.50	5.00
905	A Place in Space/The Force	1978	—	2.50	5.00
909	I Like Music/It's All You Need	1978	—	2.50	5.00
910	Everybody's Dancin'/Stay Awhile	1978	—	2.50	5.00
1562	Higher Plane/Wild Is Love	1974	—	2.50	5.00
1563	Rhyme Tyme People/Father, Father	1974	—	2.50	5.00
1567	Spirit of the Boogie/Summer Madness	1975	—	2.50	5.00
1573	Caribbean Festival/Caribbean Festival (Disco Version)	1975	—	2.50	5.00
1577	Winter Sadness/Father, Father	1975	—	2.50	5.00
1579	Love and Understanding (Come Together)/Sunshine and Love	1976	—	2.50	5.00
1583	Universal Sound/Ancestral Ceremony	1976	—	2.50	5.00
1586	Open Sesame — Part 1/Open Sesame — Part 2	1976	—	2.50	5.00
1590	Super Band/Sunshine	1977	—	2.50	5.00
880431-7	Misled/Rollin'	1984	—	—	3.00
880623-7	Fresh/In the Heart	1985	—	—	3.00
880623-7 [PS]	Fresh/In the Heart	1985	—	2.00	4.00
880869-7	Cherish/(Instrumental)	1985	—	—	3.00
880869-7 [PS]	Cherish/(Instrumental)	1985	—	2.00	4.00
884199-7	Emergency/You Are the One	1985	—	—	3.00
MERCURY					
870513-7	Rags to Riches/Rags to Riches (Remix)	1988	—	—	3.00
870513-7 [PS]	Rags to Riches/Rags to Riches (Remix)	1988	—	—	3.00
872038-7	Strong/Funky Stuff	1988	—	—	3.00
874402-7	Raindrops/(B-side unknown)	1989	—	—	3.00
876072-7	Never Give Up/(B-side unknown)	1989	—	—	3.00
888074-7	Victory/Bad Woman	1986	—	—	3.00
888074-7 [PS]	Victory/Bad Woman	1986	—	—	3.00
888292-7	Stone Love/Dance Champion	1987	—	—	3.00
888292-7 [PS]	Stone Love/Dance Champion	1987	—	—	3.00
888712-7	Holiday/Holiday (Jam Mix)	1987	—	—	3.00
888712-7 [PS]	Holiday/Holiday (Jam Mix)	1987	—	—	3.00
888867-7	In a Special Way/God's Country	1987	—	—	3.00
888867-7 [PS]	In a Special Way/God's Country	1987	—	—	3.00

Albums

Number	Title (A Side/B Side)	Yr	VG	VG+	NM
DE-LITE					
MK-48 [DJ]	History of Kool and the Gang	1979	3.75	7.50	15.00
2003	Kool and the Gang	1969	6.25	12.50	25.00
2008	Live at the Sex Machine	1971	3.00	6.00	12.00
2009	The Best of Kool and the Gang	1971	3.00	6.00	12.00
2010	Live at PJ's	1971	3.00	6.00	12.00
2011	Music Is the Message	1972	3.00	6.00	12.00
2012	Good Times	1973	3.00	6.00	12.00
2013	Wild and Peaceful	1973	2.50	5.00	10.00
2014	Light of Worlds	1974	2.50	5.00	10.00
2015	Kool & The Gang Greatest Hits!	1975	2.50	5.00	10.00
2016	Spirit of the Boogie	1975	2.50	5.00	10.00
2018	Love and Understanding	1976	2.50	5.00	10.00
2023	Open Sesame	1976	2.50	5.00	10.00
4001	Kool Jazz	1973	2.50	5.00	10.00
8502	Something Special	1981	2.50	5.00	10.00
8505	As One	1982	2.50	5.00	10.00
8508	In the Heart	1983	2.50	5.00	10.00
9501	The Force	1978	2.50	5.00	10.00
9507	Kool & The Gang Spin Their Top Ten Hits	1978	2.50	5.00	10.00
9509	Everybody's Dancin'	1979	2.50	5.00	10.00
9513	Ladies Night	1979	2.50	5.00	10.00
9518	Celebrate!	1980	2.50	5.00	10.00
814351-1	In the Heart	1984	2.00	4.00	8.00
—Reissue					

Number	Title (A Side/B Side)	Yr	VG	VG+	NM
822534-1	Something Special	1984	2.00	4.00	8.00
—Reissue					
822535-1	As One	1984	2.00	4.00	8.00
—Reissue					
822536-1	Kool & The Gang Spin Their Top Ten Hits	1984	2.00	4.00	8.00
—Reissue					
822537-1	Ladies Night	1984	2.00	4.00	8.00
—Reissue					
822538-1	Celebrate!	1984	2.00	4.00	8.00
—Reissue					
822943-1	Emergency	1984	2.00	4.00	8.00
MERCURY					
830398-1	Forever	1986	2.00	4.00	8.00
834780-1	Everything's Kool & the Gang: Greatest Hits & More	1988	2.00	4.00	8.00
838233-1	Sweat	1989	2.00	4.00	8.00

KOOL GENTS

DEE CLARK was a member of this group.

45s

Number	Title (A Side/B Side)	Yr	VG	VG+	NM
VEE JAY					
173	This Is the Night/Do Ya Do	1956	50.00	100.00	200.00
207	You Know/I Can't Help Myself	1956	50.00	100.00	200.00

KOOPER, AL

Also see BLOOD, SWEAT AND TEARS; MIKE BLOOMFIELD; THE BLUES PROJECT.

45s

Number	Title (A Side/B Side)	Yr	VG	VG+	NM
AURORA					
164	New York's My Town/My Voice, My Piano	1967	3.00	6.00	12.00
COLUMBIA					
03312	Two Sides (To Every Situation)/Snowblind	1982	—	2.00	4.00
44748	You Never Know Who Your Friends Are/Soft Landing on the Moon	1969	—	2.50	5.00
44811	I Stand Alone/Hey, Western Union Man	1969	—	2.50	5.00
45093	One Room Country Shack/Bury My Body	1970	—	2.50	5.00
45148	She Gets Me Where I Live/God Sheds His Grace on Thee	1970	—	2.50	5.00
45179	Love Theme from "The Landlord"/Brand New Day	1970	—	2.50	5.00
45243	I Got a Woman/Easy Does It	1970	—	2.50	5.00
45412	John the Baptist/Back on My Feet	1971	—	2.50	5.00
45566	The Monkey Time/Bended Knees (Please Don't Let Me Down)	1972	—	2.50	5.00
45691	Sam Stone/Be Real	1972	—	2.50	5.00
45735	Jolie/Be Real	1972	—	2.50	5.00
UNITED ARTISTS					
XW879	This Diamond Ring/Hollywood Vampire	1976	—	2.00	4.00
VERVE FOLKWAYS					
5026	Changes/Pack Up Your Sorrows	1966	3.00	6.00	12.00

Albums

Number	Title (A Side/B Side)	Yr	VG	VG+	NM
COLUMBIA					
CS 9718	I Stand Alone	1969	3.75	7.50	15.00
—"360 Sound" label					
CS 9718	I Stand Alone	1970	2.50	5.00	10.00
—Orange label					
CS 9855	You Never Know Who Your Friends Are	1969	3.75	7.50	15.00
—"360 Sound" label					
CS 9855	You Never Know Who Your Friends Are	1970	2.50	5.00	10.00
—Orange label					
CS 9951	Kooper Session	1970	3.75	7.50	15.00
—With Shuggie Otis; "360 Sound" label					
CS 9951	Kooper Session	1970	2.50	5.00	10.00
—With Shuggie Otis; orange label					
C2 30031 [(2)]	Easy Does It	1970	5.00	10.00	20.00
KC 30506	New York City (You're a Woman)	1971	3.75	7.50	15.00
KC 31159	A Possible Projection of the Future/Childhood's End	1972	3.75	7.50	15.00
KC 31723	Naked Songs	1973	3.75	7.50	15.00
PG 33169 [(2)]	Unclaimed Freight (Al's Big Deal)	1975	3.75	7.50	15.00
FC 38137	Championship Wrestling	1982	2.50	5.00	10.00
UNITED ARTISTS					
UA-LA702-G	Act Like Nothing's Wrong	1976	3.00	6.00	12.00

KORNER, ALEXIS

45s

Number	Title (A Side/B Side)	Yr	VG	VG+	NM
COLUMBIA					
10166	Get Off My Cloud/Strange N' Deranged	1975	2.00	4.00	8.00

Albums

Number	Title (A Side/B Side)	Yr	VG	VG+	NM
COLUMBIA					
PC 33427	Get Off of My Cloud	1975	3.75	7.50	15.00
JUST SUNSHINE					
13	All Star Blues Incorporated	1974	3.00	6.00	12.00
MOBILE FIDELITY					
1-265	Blues at the Marquee	1996	5.00	10.00	20.00
—Audiophile vinyl					
WARNER BROS.					
2XS 1966 [(2)]	Bootleg Him	1972	6.25	12.50	25.00
BS 2647	Accidentally Borne in New Orleans	1972	3.75	7.50	15.00

KOSSOFF, PAUL

Also see FREE.

Albums

Number	Title (A Side/B Side)	Yr	VG	VG+	NM
DJM					
2300 [(2)]	Koss	1977	3.75	7.50	15.00
ISLAND					
ILPS 9264	Back Street Crawler	1975	2.50	5.00	10.00

KOSTELANETZ, ANDRE

45s

Number	Title (A Side/B Side)	Yr	VG	VG+	NM
COLUMBIA					
40044	Playing Around/Time on My Hands	1953	2.50	5.00	10.00
40350	Sweet Surrender/April in Paradise	1954	2.50	5.00	10.00
41534	Sabre Dance/Gypsy Fiddler	1959	2.00	4.00	8.00
42604	Washington Twist/Secret Service	1962	2.00	4.00	8.00
43034	Bluesette/Fall in Love	1964	—	3.00	6.00
44147	The Impossible Dream/Born Free	1967	—	3.00	6.00
44255	You Are There/One of These Songs	1967	—	3.00	6.00
45061	Come Saturday Morning/Leaving on a Jet Plane	1970	—	2.50	5.00
45244	Things of Life/Valse de Rothschild	1970	—	2.50	5.00
45357	Theme from "Love Story"/Mr. Bojangles	1971	—	2.00	4.00
JZSP 76389/90 [DJ]	Medley: Santa Claus Is Coming To Town & Have Yourself A Merry Little Christmas/Christmas Chopsticks	1963	2.50	5.00	10.00
JZSP 111905/6 [DJ]	O Come All Ye Faithful/Oh Tannenbaum	1965	3.00	6.00	12.00
—Green vinyl					
JZSP 111905/6 [DJ]	O Come All Ye Faithful/Oh Tannenbaum	1965	2.00	4.00	8.00
—Black vinyl					
JZSP 116040/1 [DJ]	Galop from "Moscow, Cheremushki"/Galop from "Ballet Suite No. 2"	1966	2.00	4.00	8.00
—White label promo only					
JZSP 116040/1 [PS]	Galop from "Moscow, Cheremushki"/Galop from "Ballet Suite No. 2"	1966	3.00	6.00	12.00
—Title on sleeve: "Kosty Plays Shosty"					
COLUMBIA MASTERWORKS					
A-753 [(4)]	Carnival Tropicana	195?	2.50	5.00	10.00
—Box for 4-record set					
A-925 [(5)]	Swan Lake	195?	2.50	5.00	10.00
—Box for five-record set					
4-7603-M	Malaguena/No Taboleiro De Bahiana	195?	2.00	4.00	8.00
4-7604-M	La Cumparasita/Adios	195?	2.00	4.00	8.00
4-7605-M	Mexicana/Caminito	195?	2.00	4.00	8.00
4-7606-M	Yours/Siboney	195?	2.00	4.00	8.00
—The above four comprise box set A-753					
4-7648-M	Swan Lake (Part 1)/Swan Lake (Part 10)	195?	2.00	4.00	8.00
4-7649-M	Swan Lake (Part 2)/Swan Lake (Part 9)	195?	2.00	4.00	8.00
4-7650-M	Swan Lake (Part 3)/Swan Lake (Part 8)	195?	2.00	4.00	8.00
4-7651-M	Swan Lake (Part 4)/Swan Lake (Part 7)	195?	2.00	4.00	8.00
4-7652-M	Swan Lake (Part 5)/Swan Lake (Part 6)	195?	2.00	4.00	8.00
—The above five comprise box set A-925					

Albums

Number	Title (A Side/B Side)	Yr	VG	VG+	NM
COLUMBIA					
AK 1 [M]	Musical Tour of the World	195?	5.00	10.00	20.00
KZ 1 [M]	Meet Andre Kostelanetz	1955	5.00	10.00	20.00
—Red and black label with six "eye" logos					
GP 10 [(2)]	Sounds of Love	1969	3.00	6.00	12.00
C2L 11 [M]	The Romantic Music of Tchaikovsky	195?	6.25	12.50	25.00
—Red and black label with six "eye" logos					
CL 720 [M]	Peter and the Wolf; Carnival of the Animals	1956	5.00	10.00	20.00
—Red and black label with six "eye" logos					
CL 734 [M]	The Music of Victor Youmans	1956	5.00	10.00	20.00
—Red and black label with six "eye" logos					
CL 765 [M]	The Music of Victor Herbert	1956	5.00	10.00	20.00
—Red and black label with six "eye" logos					
CL 768 [M]	Music of Irving Berlin	1956	5.00	10.00	20.00
—Red and black label with six "eye" logos					
CL 780 [M]	Lure of the Tropics	1956	5.00	10.00	20.00
—Red and black label with six "eye" logos					
CL 781 [M]	Stardust	1956	5.00	10.00	20.00
—Red and black label with six "eye" logos					
CL 797 [M]	La Boheme for Orchestra	1956	5.00	10.00	20.00
—Red and black label with six "eye" logos					
CL 806 [M]	Show Boat/South Pacific/Slaughter on 10th Avenue	1956	5.00	10.00	20.00
—Red and black label with six "eye" logos					
CL 811 [M]	Calendar Girl	1956	5.00	10.00	20.00
—Red and black label with six "eye" logos					
CL 843 [M]	The Very Thought of You	1956	5.00	10.00	20.00
—Red and black label with six "eye" logos					
CL 863 [M]	Café Continental	1956	5.00	10.00	20.00
—Red and black label with six "eye" logos					
CL 864 [M]	Beautiful Dreamer	1956	5.00	10.00	20.00
—Red and black label with six "eye" logos					
CL 1220 [M]	Romantic Music of...	1958	3.75	7.50	15.00
CL 1335 [M]	The Lure of Paradise	1959	3.00	6.00	12.00
CL 1354 [M]	Strauss Waltzes	1959	3.00	6.00	12.00
CL 1431 [M]	Gypsy Passion	1960	3.00	6.00	12.00
CL 1495 [M]	Gershwin: Rhapsody in Blue; Previn: Concerto in F	1960	3.00	6.00	12.00
CL 1528 [M]	Joy to the World: Music for Christmas	1959	3.75	7.50	15.00
CL 1657 [M]	Wonderland of Sound	1961	3.00	6.00	12.00
CL 1718 [M]	Star-Spangled Marches	1962	3.00	6.00	12.00
CL 1827 [M]	Wonderland of Sound (Broadway's Greatest Hits)	1962	3.00	6.00	12.00
CL 1898 [M]	Wonderland of Sound (Fire and Jealousy)	1962	3.00	6.00	12.00
CL 1938 [M]	Wonderland of Sound (The World's Greatest Waltzes)	1963	2.50	5.00	10.00
CL 1995 [M]	Wonderland of Opera	1963	2.50	5.00	10.00
CL 2039 [M]	Wonderland of Golden Hits	1963	2.50	5.00	10.00
CL 2068 [M]	Wonderland of Christmas	1963	3.00	6.00	12.00
CL 2078 [M]	Kostelanetz in Wonderland	1964	2.50	5.00	10.00
CL 2133 [M]	Gershwin Wonderland	1964	2.50	5.00	10.00
CL 2138 [M]	New York Wonderland	1964	2.50	5.00	10.00
CL 2185 [M]	I Wish You Love	1964	2.50	5.00	10.00
CL 2250 [M]	New Orleans Wonderland	1965	2.50	5.00	10.00
CL 2359 [M]	Thunder (The Spectacular Sound of John Philip Sousa)	1965	2.50	5.00	10.00
CL 2467 [M]	The Shadow of Your Smile and Other Great Movie Themes	1966	2.50	5.00	10.00
CL 2534 [M]	Today's Golden Hits	1966	2.50	5.00	10.00
CL 2581 [M]	Exotic Nights	1966	2.50	5.00	10.00
CL 2609 [M]	The Kostelanetz Sound of Today	1967	2.50	5.00	10.00
CL 2688 [M]	Concert in the Park	1967	2.50	5.00	10.00
CL 2756 [M]	Today's Greatest Movie Hits	1967	3.00	6.00	12.00
CS 8144 [S]	The Lure of Paradise	1959	3.75	7.50	15.00
CS 8162 [S]	Strauss Waltzes	1959	3.75	7.50	15.00
CS 8228 [S]	Gypsy Passion	1960	3.75	7.50	15.00
CS 8286 [S]	Gershwin: Rhapsody in Blue; Previn: Concerto in F	1960	3.75	7.50	15.00
CS 8328 [S]	Joy to the World: Music for Christmas	1959	5.00	10.00	20.00
—Red and black label with six "eye" logos					

Number	Title (A Side/B Side)	Yr	VG	VG+	NM
CS 8457 [S]	Wonderland of Sound	1961	3.75	7.50	15.00
CS 8518 [S]	Star-Spangled Marches	1962	3.75	7.50	15.00
CS 8627 [S]	Wonderland of Sound (Broadway's Greatest Hits)	1962	3.75	7.50	15.00
CS 8698 [S]	Wonderland of Sound (Fire and Jealousy)	1962	3.75	7.50	15.00
CS 8738 [S]	Wonderland of Sound (The World's Greatest Waltzes)	1963	3.00	6.00	12.00
CS 8795 [S]	Wonderland of Opera	1963	3.00	6.00	12.00
CS 8839 [S]	Wonderland of Golden Hits	1963	3.00	6.00	12.00
CS 8868 [S]	Wonderland of Christmas	1963	3.75	7.50	15.00
CS 8878 [S]	Kostelanetz in Wonderland	1964	3.00	6.00	12.00
CS 8933 [S]	Gershwin Wonderland	1964	3.00	6.00	12.00
CS 8938 [S]	New York Wonderland	1964	3.00	6.00	12.00
CS 8985 [S]	I Wish You Love	1964	3.00	6.00	12.00
CS 9050 [S]	New Orleans Wonderland	1965	3.00	6.00	12.00
CS 9159 [S]	Thunder (The Spectacular Sound of John Philip Sousa)	1965	3.00	6.00	12.00
CS 9267 [S]	The Shadow of Your Smile and Other Great Movie Themes	1966	2.50	5.00	10.00
CS 9334 [S]	Today's Golden Hits	1966	3.00	6.00	12.00
CS 9381 [S]	Exotic Nights	1966	2.50	5.00	10.00
CS 9409 [S]	The Kostelanetz Sound of Today	1967	2.50	5.00	10.00
CS 9488 [S]	Concert in the Park	1967	2.50	5.00	10.00
CS 9556 [S]	Today's Greatest Movie Hits	1967	2.50	5.00	10.00
CS 9623	Scarborough Fair	1968	2.50	5.00	10.00
CS 9691	For the Young at Heart	1968	2.50	5.00	10.00
CS 9724	Hits from Funny Girl, Finian's Rainbow, and Star!	1968	2.50	5.00	10.00
CS 9740	Andre Kostelanetz' Greatest Hits	1969	2.50	5.00	10.00
CS 9823	Traces	1969	2.50	5.00	10.00
CS 9973	Greatest Hits of the 60's	1970	2.50	5.00	10.00
CS 9998	I'll Never Fall in Love Again	1970	2.50	5.00	10.00
LE 10083	Joy to the World: Music for Christmas	197?	2.50	5.00	10.00
—Reissue of CS 8328					
LE 10086	Wonderland of Christmas	197?	2.50	5.00	10.00
—Reissue of CS 8868					
C 30037	Everything Is Beautiful	1970	2.50	5.00	10.00
C 30501	Love Story	1971	2.50	5.00	10.00
C 30672	For All We Know	1971	2.50	5.00	10.00
C 31002	Kostelanetz Plays Chicago	1971	2.50	5.00	10.00
KG 31491 [(2)]	Andre Kostelanetz Plays Cole Porter	1972	3.75	7.50	15.00
KG 32002 [(2)]	The World's Greatest Love Songs	1973	3.00	6.00	12.00
KC 32187	Last Tango in Paris	1973	2.50	5.00	10.00
KC 32451	Kostelanetz Plays Great Hits of Today	1973	2.50	5.00	10.00
KC 32580	Andre Kostelanetz Plays Legrand's Greatest Hits	1974	2.50	5.00	10.00
KG 32825 [(2)]	Andre Kostelanetz Plays Gershwin	1974	3.00	6.00	12.00
CQ 32856 [Q]	Quadraphonic Pop Concert	1973	3.75	7.50	15.00
KC 33061	Musical Reflections of Broadway and Hollywood	1974	2.50	5.00	10.00
KG 33065 [(2)]	Strike Up the Band	1974	3.00	6.00	12.00
KC 33437	Orient Express	1975	2.50	5.00	10.00
C 33550	Never Can Say Goodbye	1975	2.00	4.00	8.00
KC 33550	Never Can Say Goodbye	1975	2.50	5.00	10.00
KC 33954	Music from A Chorus Line and Treemonisha	1975	2.50	5.00	10.00
KC 34157	I'm Easy and Other Themes	1976	2.50	5.00	10.00
PC 34352	Dance with Me	1977	2.50	5.00	10.00
PC 34660	Music of Charlie Chaplin and Duke Ellington	1977	2.50	5.00	10.00
JC 35328	You Light Up My Life	1978	2.50	5.00	10.00
JC 35788	Superman	1979	2.00	4.00	8.00
JC 36382	Various Themes	1980	2.00	4.00	8.00
COLUMBIA MASTERWORKS					
ML 2007 [10]	Music of Stephen Foster	195?	6.25	12.50	25.00
ML 2011 [10]	Waltzes of Johann Strauss	195?	6.25	12.50	25.00
ML 2014 [10]	Songs of Cole Porter	195?	7.50	15.00	30.00
ML 2022 [10]	Motion Picture Favorites	195?	6.25	12.50	25.00
ML 2056 [10]	Chopin-Kostelanetz	195?	6.25	12.50	25.00
ML 4065 [M]	Favorites	195?	5.00	10.00	20.00
ML 4066 [M]	Clair de Lune	195?	5.00	10.00	20.00
ML 4082 [M]	Carnival Tropicana	195?	5.00	10.00	20.00
ML 4253 [M]	Music of Fritz Kreisler and Sigmund Romberg	195?	5.00	10.00	20.00
ML 4308 [M]	Swan Lake (Highlights)	195?	5.00	10.00	20.00
ML 4409 [M]	Bizet: L'arlesienne Suites 1 & 2	195?	5.00	10.00	20.00
ML 4455 [M]	An American in Paris	195?	5.00	10.00	20.00
ML 4822 [M]	Lure of the Tropics	1956	5.00	10.00	20.00
MS 6106 [S]	Offenbach: Gaite Parisienne; Bizet: Carmen (Highlights)	195?	5.00	10.00	20.00
ML 6111 [M]	Romantic Strings	1960	3.00	6.00	12.00
ML 6129 [M]	Showstoppers	1960	3.00	6.00	12.00
ML 6179 [M]	Wishing You a Merry Christmas	1960	3.00	6.00	12.00
ML 6206 [M]	Promenade Favorites	1966	3.00	6.00	12.00
ML 6224 [M]	Romantic Waltzes of Tchaikovsky	1961	3.00	6.00	12.00
ML 6226 [M]	Favorite Romantic Concertos	1961	3.00	6.00	12.00
MS 6711 [S]	Romantic Strings	1960	3.75	7.50	15.00
MS 6729 [S]	Showstoppers	1960	3.75	7.50	15.00
MS 6779 [S]	Wishing You a Merry Christmas	1960	3.75	7.50	15.00
MS 6806 [S]	Promenade Favorites	1966	3.75	7.50	15.00
MS 6824 [S]	Romantic Waltzes of Tchaikovsky	1961	3.75	7.50	15.00
MS 6826 [S]	Favorite Romantic Concertos	1961	3.75	7.50	15.00
MS 7087	Vienna, City of Dreams	1968	3.00	6.00	12.00
MS 7108 [S]	Andre Kostelanetz Conducts Great Romantic Ballads	196?	2.50	5.00	10.00
MS 7319	Musical Evenings	1969	2.50	5.00	10.00
MS 7427	Extravaganza	1970	2.50	5.00	10.00
M 30075	Music for Strings	1970	2.50	5.00	10.00
M 35114	Festive Overtures	1978	2.00	4.00	8.00
COLUMBIA SPECIAL PRODUCTS					
C 10975	Wishing You a Merry Christmas	1972	2.50	5.00	10.00
—Reissue of Columbia Masterworks MS 6779					
P 13286	Scarborough Fair	197?	2.00	4.00	8.00
HARMONY					
HL 7368 [M]	You and the Night and the Music	196?	2.50	5.00	10.00
HL 7371 [M]	Broadway Theatre Party	196?	2.50	5.00	10.00
HL 7395 [M]	Grand Canyon Suite	196?	2.50	5.00	10.00
HL 7432 [M]	Joy to the World: Music for Christmas	1967	3.00	6.00	12.00
—Reissue of Columbia 1528					
HS 11168 [S]	You and the Night and the Music	196?	2.50	5.00	10.00
HS 11171 [S]	Broadway Theatre Party	196?	2.50	5.00	10.00
HS 11195 [S]	Grand Canyon Suite	196?	2.50	5.00	10.00
HS 11232 [S]	Joy to the World: Music for Christmas	1967	3.00	6.00	12.00
—Reissue of Columbia 8328					
HS 11281	The Magic of Music	1968	2.50	5.00	10.00
H 30014	Be My Love	1970	2.50	5.00	10.00
KH 31414	Greatest Hits of Broadway and Hollywood	1972	2.50	5.00	10.00
KH 31500	Love Theme from "The Godfather"	1972	2.50	5.00	10.00
KH 31571	Andre Kostelanetz Plays Richard Rogers	1973	2.50	5.00	10.00
KH 32170	Strike Up the Band	1973	2.50	5.00	10.00
READER'S DIGEST					
RD-120-A [(8)]	The Best of Andre Kostelanetz	197?	7.50	15.00	30.00

KOTTKE, LEO

45s

CAPITOL

Number	Title (A Side/B Side)	Yr	VG	VG+	NM
3854	Pamela Brown/A Child Should Be a Fish	1974	—	3.00	6.00
4177	Can't Quite Put It Into Words/Power Failure	1975	—	2.50	5.00

Albums

Number	Title (A Side/B Side)	Yr	VG	VG+	NM
CAPITOL					
ST-682	Mudlark	1971	3.00	6.00	12.00
ST-11000	Greenhouse	1972	2.50	5.00	10.00
ST-11164	My Feet Are Smiling	1973	2.50	5.00	10.00
ST-11262	Ice Water	1974	2.50	5.00	10.00
ST-11335	Dreams and All That Stuff	1974	2.50	5.00	10.00
ST-11446	Chewing Pine	1975	2.50	5.00	10.00
ST-11576	Leo Kottke 1971-1976 — Did You Hear Me?	1976	2.50	5.00	10.00
SWBC-11867 [(2)]	The Best of Leo Kottke	1979	3.00	6.00	12.00
SN-16063	Mudlark	1979	2.00	4.00	8.00
—Budget-line reissue					
SN-16064	Ice Water	1979	2.00	4.00	8.00
—Budget-line reissue					
SN-16065	Greenhouse	1979	2.00	4.00	8.00
—Budget-line reissue					
SN-16187	Dreams and All That Stuff	1980	2.00	4.00	8.00
—Budget-line reissue					
SN-16188	Chewing Pine	1980	2.00	4.00	8.00
—Budget-line reissue					
SN-16189	Leo Kottke 1971-1976 — Did You Hear Me?	1980	2.00	4.00	8.00
—Budget-line reissue					
CHRYSALIS					
CHR 1106	Leo Kottke	1977	2.50	5.00	10.00
CHR 1191	Burnt Lips	1978	2.50	5.00	10.00
CHR 1234	Balance	1979	2.50	5.00	10.00
CHR 1328	Guitar Music	1981	2.50	5.00	10.00
PV 41106	Leo Kottke	1985	2.00	4.00	8.00
—Budget-line reissue					
PV 41191	Burnt Lips	1985	2.00	4.00	8.00
—Budget-line reissue					
PV 41234	Balance	1985	2.00	4.00	8.00
—Budget-line reissue					
PV 41328	Guitar Music	1983	2.00	4.00	8.00
—Budget-line reissue					
FV 41411	Time Step	1983	2.50	5.00	10.00
PV 41411	Time Step	1986	2.00	4.00	8.00
—Budget-line reissue					
OBLIVION					
S-1	12-String Blues/Live at the Scholar Coffee House	1969	6.25	12.50	25.00
PRIVATE MUSIC					
2007-1-P	A Shout Toward Noon	1986	2.50	5.00	10.00
2025-1-P	Regards from Chuck Pink	1988	2.50	5.00	10.00
2050-1-P	My Father's Face	1989	2.50	5.00	10.00
SYMPOSIUM					
2001	Circle Round the Sun	1970	3.00	6.00	12.00
TAKOMA					
1024	6 and 12 String Guitar	1969	3.00	6.00	12.00

KOTTKE, LEO/PETER LANG/JOHN FAHEY

Also see JOHN FAHEY; LEO KOTTKE.

Albums

TAKOMA

Number	Title (A Side/B Side)	Yr	VG	VG+	NM
1040	Leo Kottke/Peter Lang/John Fahey	1974	3.00	6.00	12.00

KRAFTWERK

12-Inch Singles

Number	Title (A Side/B Side)	Yr	VG	VG+	NM
CAPITOL					
8502	Showroom Dummies (6:00)/Les Mannequins (6:02)	1977	5.00	10.00	20.00
8526	Neon Lights (9:03)/The Model	1978	6.25	12.50	25.00
ELEKTRA					
ED 5551 [DJ]	Robotnik/The Robots/Robotronik	1991	3.00	6.00	12.00
WARNER BROS.					
PRO-A-951 [DJ]	Pocket Calculator/Dentaku	1981	3.00	6.00	12.00
20549	Musique Nonstop (LP Version)/Musique Nonstop (7" Version)	1986	2.00	4.00	8.00

45s

Number	Title (A Side/B Side)	Yr	VG	VG+	NM
CAPITOL					
4211	Radioactivity/Antenna	1976	—	2.50	5.00
4211 [PS]	Radioactivity/Antenna	1976	2.00	4.00	8.00
4460	Trans-Europe Express/Franz Schubert	1977	—	2.50	5.00
4620	Neon Lights/The Robots	1978	—	2.50	5.00
VERTIGO					
203	Autobahn/Morgan Spaziergance	1975	2.00	4.00	8.00
204	Mitternacht (Midnight)/Kometen Melodie (Comet Melody 2)	1975	2.00	4.00	8.00
WARNER BROS.					
28441	The Telephone Call/Der Telefon Anruf	1987	—	—	3.00
28441 [PS]	The Telephone Call/Der Telefon Anruf	1987	—	—	3.00
28532	Musique Non-Stop (Long)/Musique Non-Stop (Short)	1986	—	—	2.00
28532 [PS]	Musique Non-Stop (Long)/Musique Non-Stop (Short)	1986	—	—	2.00
29342	Tour de France (Remix)/Tour de France (French)	1984	—	—	3.00
49723	Pocket Calculator/Dentaku	1981	—	—	3.00

Number	Title (A Side/B Side)	Yr	VG	VG+	NM
49723	Pocket Calculator/Dentaku	1981	—	2.50	5.00
—Yellow vinyl					
49723 [PS]	Pocket Calculator/Dentaku	1981	—	2.50	5.00
—Plastic sleeve that goes with yellow vinyl pressing					
49795	Numbers/Computer Love	1981	—	—	3.00
Albums					
CAPITOL					
ST-11457	Radio-Activity	1975	4.00	8.00	16.00
SW 11603	Trans-Europe Express	1977	4.00	8.00	16.00
SW-11728	The Man-Machine	1978	4.00	8.00	16.00
SN-16301	Trans-Europe Express	198?	2.50	5.00	10.00
—Reissue					
SN-16302	The Man-Machine	198?	2.50	5.00	10.00
—Reissue					
SN-16380	Radio-Activity	1986	2.50	5.00	10.00
—Reissue					
ELEKTRA					
60789	Computer World	1988	2.00	4.00	8.00
—Reissue					
60797	Autobahn	1988	2.00	4.00	8.00
—Still another reissue of this album					
60798	Electric Cafe	1988	2.00	4.00	8.00
—Reissue					
60869 [(2)]	The Mix	1991	3.00	6.00	12.00
MERCURY					
SRM-1-3704	Autobahn	1977	3.75	7.50	15.00
—Reissue of Vertigo VEL-2003					
VERTIGO					
VEL-2003	Autobahn	1974	5.00	10.00	20.00
VEL-2006	Ralf & Florian	1976	4.00	8.00	16.00
—Recorded in 1973					
WARNER BROS.					
HS 3549	Computer World	1981	2.50	5.00	10.00
25326	Autobahn	1985	3.00	6.00	12.00
—Another reissue of Vertigo VEL-2003					
25525	Electric Cafe	1986	3.00	6.00	12.00

KRAMER, BILLY J., AND THE DAKOTAS

Number	Title (A Side/B Side)	Yr	VG	VG+	NM
45s					
EPIC					
10331	1941/His Love Is Just a Lie	1968	2.50	5.00	10.00
IMPERIAL					
66027	Little Children/Bad to Me	1964	3.00	6.00	12.00
66048	I'll Keep You Satisfied/I Know	1964	3.00	6.00	12.00
66051	From a Window/I'll Be On My Way	1964	3.00	6.00	12.00
66051 [PS]	From a Window/I'll Be On My Way	1964	6.25	12.50	25.00
66085	It's Gotta Last Forever/They Remind Me of You	1965	3.00	6.00	12.00
66115	Trains and Boats and Planes/I'll Be On My Way	1965	3.00	6.00	12.00
66115	Trains and Boats and Planes/That's the Way I Feel	1965	2.50	5.00	10.00
66135	Irresistible You/Twilight Time	1965	2.50	5.00	10.00
66143	I'll Be Doggone/Neon City	1965	2.50	5.00	10.00
66210	You Make Me Feel Like Someone/Take My Hand	1966	2.50	5.00	10.00
LIBERTY					
55586	Do You Want to Know a Secret/I'll Be On My Way	1963	7.50	15.00	30.00
55618	The Cruel Surf/The Millionaire	1963	10.00	20.00	40.00
55626	Bad to Me/I Call Your Name	1963	7.50	15.00	30.00
55643	I'll Keep You Satisfied/I Know	1963	7.50	15.00	30.00
55667	Bad to Me/Do You Want to Know a Secret	1964	6.25	12.50	25.00
55687	Little Children/They Remind Me of You	1964	—	—	—
—Unreleased					
Albums					
CAPITOL					
SM-11897 [P]	The Best of Billy J. Kramer and the Dakotas	1979	2.50	5.00	10.00
IMPERIAL					
LP 9267 [M]	Little Children	1964	12.50	25.00	50.00
—Black label with stars					
LP 9267 [M]	Little Children	1964	7.50	15.00	30.00
—Black and pink label					
LP 9273 [M]	I'll Keep You Satisfied/From a Window	1964	7.50	15.00	30.00
LP 9291 [M]	Trains and Boats and Planes	1965	7.50	15.00	30.00
LP 12267 [P]	Little Children	1964	20.00	40.00	80.00
—Black label with silver print					
LP 12267 [P]	Little Children	1964	10.00	20.00	40.00
—Black and pink label					
LP 12273 [P]	I'll Keep You Satisfied/From a Window	1964	10.00	20.00	40.00
LP 12921 [R]	Trains and Boats and Planes	1965	6.25	12.50	25.00

KREED

Number	Title (A Side/B Side)	Yr	VG	VG+	NM
Albums					
VISION OF SOUND					
71-56	Kreed	1971	300.00	600.00	1200.

KRISTOFFERSON, KRIS

Also see WILLIE NELSON.

Number	Title (A Side/B Side)	Yr	VG	VG+	NM
45s					
COLUMBIA					
04881	Highwayman/The Human Condition	1985	—	—	3.00
—A-side: Willie Nelson/Waylon Jennings/Johnny Cash/Kris Kristofferson; B-side: Nelson, Cash					
04881 [PS]	Highwayman/The Human Condition	1985	—	2.00	4.00
—A-side: Willie Nelson/Waylon Jennings/Johnny Cash/Kris Kristofferson; B-side: Nelson, Cash					
05594	Desperadoes Waiting for a Train/The Twentieth Century Is Almost Over	1985	—	—	3.00
—A-side: Willie Nelson/Waylon Jennings/Johnny Cash/Kris Kristofferson; B-side: Nelson, Cash					
08406	Highwayman/Desperadoes Waiting for a Train	1988	—	—	3.00
—Waylon Jennings/Willie Nelson/Johnny Cash/Kris Kristofferson; reissue					
08406	Highwayman/Desperadoes Waiting for a Train	1988	—	—	3.00
—Waylon Jennings/Willie Nelson/Johnny Cash/Kris Kristofferson; reissue					
10525	Watch Closely Now/Crippled Crow	1977	—	2.00	4.00
10731	The Fighter/Forever in Your Love	1978	—	2.00	4.00
11160	Prove It to You One More Time Again/Fallen Angel	1979	—	2.00	4.00
11383	I'll Take Any Chance I Can with You/Maybe You Heard	1980	—	2.00	4.00
60507	Nobody Loves Anybody Anymore/Maybe You Heard	1981	—	2.00	4.00
73381	Born and Raised in Black and White/Texas	1990	—	—	3.00
—The Highwaymen (Waylon Jennings/Willie Nelson/Johnny Cash/Kris Kristofferson)					
73572	American Remains/Texas	1990	—	—	3.00
—The Highwaymen (Waylon Jennings/Willie Nelson/Johnny Cash/Kris Kristofferson)					
EPIC					
10225	Golden Idol/Killing Time	1967	3.75	7.50	15.00
LIBERTY					
S7-18486	It Is What It Is/The Devil's Right Hand	1995	—	—	3.00
—By The Highwaymen					
MERCURY					
888345-7	They Killed Him/Anthem '84	1987	—	—	3.00
888554-7	Love Is the Way/This Old Road	1987	—	—	3.00
888723-7	El Coyote/They Killed Him	1987	—	—	3.00
MONUMENT					
1210	Sunday Morning Comin' Down/To Beat the Devil	1970	2.00	4.00	8.00
8525	Loving Her Was Easier (Than Anything I'll Ever Do Again)/Epitaph	1971	—	3.00	6.00
8531	The Taker/Pilgrim: Chapter 33	1971	—	3.00	6.00
8536	Josie/Border Lord	1972	—	3.00	6.00
8558	Jesus Was a Capricorn/Enough for You	1972	—	3.00	6.00
8564	Jesse Younger/Give It Time to Be Tender	1973	—	3.00	6.00
8571	Why Me/Help Me	1973	—	2.50	5.00
8618	I May Smoke Too Much/Lights of Magdala	1974	—	2.50	5.00
8658	Easy, Come On/Rocket to Star	1975	—	2.00	4.00
8679	If It's All the Same to You/The Year 2000 Minus 25	1975	—	2.00	4.00
8707	The Prisoner/It's Never Gonna Be the Same Again	1976	—	2.00	4.00
21000	Here Comes That Rainbow Again/(B-side unknown)	1981	—	2.00	4.00
Albums					
COLUMBIA					
PZ 30679	The Silver Tongued Devil and I	1976	2.00	4.00	8.00
—Reissue					
PZ 30817	Me and Bobby McGee	1976	2.00	4.00	8.00
—Reissue					
PZ 31302	Border Lord	1976	2.00	4.00	8.00
—Reissue					
PZ 31909	Jesus Was a Capricorn	1976	2.00	4.00	8.00
—Reissue					
PZ 32914	Spooky Lady's Sideshow	1976	2.00	4.00	8.00
—Reissue					
PZ 33379	Who's to Bless...And Who's to Blame	1976	2.00	4.00	8.00
—Reissue					
PZ 34254	Surreal Thing	1976	3.00	6.00	12.00
PZ 34687	Songs of Kristofferson	1977	3.00	6.00	12.00
JZ 35310	Easter Island	1978	3.00	6.00	12.00
JZ 36135	Shake Hands with the Devil	1979	3.00	6.00	12.00
JZ 36885	To the Bone	1980	3.00	6.00	12.00
MERCURY					
830406-1	Repossessed	1987	2.50	5.00	10.00
MONUMENT					
SLP-18139	Kristofferson	1970	6.25	12.50	25.00
—Original label is light green with a yellow ring					
Z 30679	The Silver Tongued Devil and I	1971	3.00	6.00	12.00
ZQ 30679 [Q]	The Silver Tongued Devil and I	1972	5.00	10.00	20.00
Z 30817	Me and Bobby McGee	1971	3.00	6.00	12.00
—Reissue of 18139 with new title					
KZ 31302	Border Lord	1972	3.00	6.00	12.00
KZ 31909	Jesus Was a Capricorn	1972	3.00	6.00	12.00
ZQ 31909 [Q]	Jesus Was a Capricorn	1973	5.00	10.00	20.00
PZ 32914	Spooky Lady's Sideshow	1974	3.00	6.00	12.00
PZQ 32914 [Q]	Spooky Lady's Sideshow	1974	5.00	10.00	20.00
PZ 33379	Who's to Bless...And Who's to Blame	1975	3.00	6.00	12.00
PW 38392	Songs of Kristofferson	1982	2.00	4.00	8.00
—Reissue of 34687					
PAIR					
PDL2-1078 [(2)]	My Songs	1986	3.00	6.00	12.00

KRISTOFFERSON, KRIS, AND RITA COOLIDGE

Also see each artist's individual listings.

Number	Title (A Side/B Side)	Yr	VG	VG+	NM
45s					
A&M					
1475	A Song I'd Like to Sing/From the Bottle to the Bottom	1973	—	2.00	4.00
1475 [PS]	A Song I'd Like to Sing/From the Bottle to the Bottom	1973	—	3.00	6.00
1498	Loving Arms/I'm Down	1974	—	2.00	4.00
2121	Not Everyone Knows/Blue As I Do	1979	—	2.00	4.00
MONUMENT					
8630	Rain/What'cha Gonna Do	1974	—	2.00	4.00
8636	Lover Please/Slow Down	1975	—	2.00	4.00
8646	We Must Have Been Out of Our Minds/Sweet Susannah	1975	—	2.00	4.00
Albums					
A&M					
SP-4403	Full Moon	1973	3.00	6.00	12.00
SP-4690	Natural Act	1979	2.50	5.00	10.00
MONUMENT					
PZ 33278	Breakaway	1974	3.00	6.00	12.00

KRISTYL

Number	Title (A Side/B Side)	Yr	VG	VG+	NM
Albums					
(NO LABEL)					
(no #)	Kristyl	1975	50.00	100.00	200.00

KUBAN, BOB, AND THE IN-MEN

45s

MUSICLAND U.S.A.

Number	Title (A Side/B Side)	Yr	VG	VG+	NM
20001	The Cheater/Try Me Baby	1966	5.00	10.00	20.00
—With "Vocal by Walter Scott" on both sides' labels					
20001	The Cheater/Try Me Baby	1966	3.00	6.00	12.00
—With "Vocal by Walter Scott" on only B-side label					
20001	The Cheater/Try Me Baby	1966	2.50	5.00	10.00
—With no mention of "Vocal by Walter Scott"					
20006	The Teaser/All I Want	1966	2.50	5.00	10.00
20007	Drive My Car/The Pretzel	1966	2.50	5.00	10.00
20013	Harlem Shuffle/Theme from "Virginia Wolff"	1967	2.00	4.00	8.00
20017	Batman Theme/You Better Run, You Better Hide	1967	2.00	4.00	8.00

NORMAN

Number	Title (A Side/B Side)	Yr	VG	VG+	NM
558	Jerkin' Time/Turn On Your Lovelight	1965	3.00	6.00	12.00
567	Little Girl/I Don't Want to Know	1965	3.00	6.00	12.00

REPRISE

Number	Title (A Side/B Side)	Yr	VG	VG+	NM
0937	Soul Man/Hard to Handle	1970	2.00	4.00	8.00

Albums

MUSICLAND U.S.A.

Number	Title (A Side/B Side)	Yr	VG	VG+	NM
LP-3500 [M]	Look Out for the Cheater	1966	7.50	15.00	30.00
SLP-3500 [S]	Look Out for the Cheater	1966	10.00	20.00	40.00

KUF-LINX, THE

45s

CHALLENGE

Number	Title (A Side/B Side)	Yr	VG	VG+	NM
1013	So Tough/What'cha Gonna Do	1957	10.00	20.00	40.00
1013	So Tough/What'cha Gonna Do	1958	6.25	12.50	25.00
59004	Eyeballin'/Service with a Smile	1958	3.75	7.50	15.00
59015	Climb Love Mountain/All That's Good	1958	3.75	7.50	15.00
59102	So Tough/What'cha Gonna Do	1961	3.00	6.00	12.00

KUSTOM KINGS, THE

BRUCE JOHNSTON appears on the below.

45s

SMASH

Number	Title (A Side/B Side)	Yr	VG	VG+	NM
1883	In My '40 Ford/Clutch Rider	1964	12.50	25.00	50.00

Albums

SMASH

Number	Title (A Side/B Side)	Yr	VG	VG+	NM
MGS-27051 [M]	Kustom City, U.S.A.	1964	30.00	60.00	120.00
SRS-67051 [S]	Kustom City, U.S.A.	1964	50.00	100.00	200.00

KWESKIN, JIM

45s

REPRISE

Number	Title (A Side/B Side)	Yr	VG	VG+	NM
0624	The Sheik of Araby/Minglewood	1967	2.00	4.00	8.00

VANGUARD

Number	Title (A Side/B Side)	Yr	VG	VG+	NM
35027	Rag Momma/Don't You Leave Me Here	1964	2.50	5.00	10.00

Albums

MOUNTAIN RAILROAD

Number	Title (A Side/B Side)	Yr	VG	VG+	NM
MR-52672	Jug Band Blues	198?	2.50	5.00	10.00
MR-52782	Jim Kweskin Lives Again	198?	2.50	5.00	10.00
MR-52790	Side by Side	198?	2.50	5.00	10.00
MR-52793	Swing on a Star	198?	2.50	5.00	10.00

REPRISE

Number	Title (A Side/B Side)	Yr	VG	VG+	NM
R 6266 [M]	Garden of Joy	1967	5.00	10.00	20.00
RS 6266 [S]	Garden of Joy	1967	3.75	7.50	15.00
RS 6464	America	1971	3.75	7.50	15.00

VANGUARD

Number	Title (A Side/B Side)	Yr	VG	VG+	NM
VSD 13/14 [(2)]	Greatest Hits	1970	3.75	7.50	15.00
VSD-2158 [S]	Jim Kweskin and the Jug Band	1963	6.25	12.50	25.00
VRS-9139 [M]	Jim Kweskin and the Jug Band	1963	5.00	10.00	20.00
VRS-9163 [M]	Jug Band Music	1965	5.00	10.00	20.00
VRS-9188 [M]	Relax Your Mind	1966	5.00	10.00	20.00
VRS-9234 [M]	See Reverse Side for Title	1967	5.00	10.00	20.00
VRS-9243 [M]	Jump for Joy	1967	5.00	10.00	20.00
VSD-79163 [S]	Jug Band Music	1965	6.25	12.50	25.00
VSD-79188 [S]	Relax Your Mind	1966	6.25	12.50	25.00
VSD-79234 [S]	See Reverse Side for Title	1967	6.25	12.50	25.00
VSD-79243 [S]	Jump for Joy	1967	5.00	10.00	20.00
VSD-79270	The Best of Jim Kweskin and the Jug Band	1968	3.75	7.50	15.00

L

L.T.D.

45s

A&M

Number	Title (A Side/B Side)	Yr	VG	VG+	NM
1514	Elegant Love/Success	1974	—	2.50	5.00
1537	What Goes Around/To the Bone	1974	—	2.50	5.00
1665	Don't Lose Your Cool/Thank You Mother	1975	—	2.50	5.00
1681	Trying to Find a Way/I Told You I'd Be Back	1975	—	2.50	5.00
1731	Rated X/Ain't No Way	1975	—	2.50	5.00
1847	Love Ballad/Let the Music Keep Playing	1976	—	2.50	5.00
1847 [PS]	Love Ballad/Let the Music Keep Playing	1976	—	3.00	6.00
1897	Love to the World/Get Your It Together	1976	—	2.50	5.00
1974	(Every Time I Turn Around) Back in Love Again/ Material Things	1977	—	2.50	5.00
1974 [PS]	(Every Time I Turn Around) Back in Love Again/ Material Things	1977	2.00	4.00	8.00
2005	Never Get Enough of Your Love/Make Someone Smile Today	1978	—	2.50	5.00
2005 [PS]	Never Get Enough of Your Love/Make Someone Smile Today	1978	—	3.00	6.00
2057	Holding On (When Love Is Gone)/Together Forever	1978	—	2.50	5.00
2095	We Both Deserve Each Other's Love/It's Time to Be Real	1978	—	2.50	5.00
2142	Dance "N" Sing "N"/Give It All	1979	—	2.50	5.00
2142 [PS]	Dance "N" Sing "N"/Give It All	1979	—	3.00	6.00
2176	Share My Love/Sometimes	1979	—	2.50	5.00
2192	Stranger/Sometimes	1979	—	2.50	5.00
2250	Where Did We Go Wrong/Stand Up L.T.D.	1980	—	2.50	5.00
2283	Shine On/Love Is What You Need	1980	—	2.50	5.00
2346	Shine On (Spanish Version)/Where Did We Go Wrong	1981	—	2.50	5.00
2382	Kickin' Back/Now	1981	—	2.50	5.00
2395	April Love/Stay on the One	1982	—	2.50	5.00
2414	Cuttin' It Up/Love Magic	1982	—	2.00	4.00

MONTAGE

Number	Title (A Side/B Side)	Yr	VG	VG+	NM
908	For You/(B-side unknown)	1983	—	2.00	4.00

Albums

A&M

Number	Title (A Side/B Side)	Yr	VG	VG+	NM
SP-3119	L.T.D.	198?	2.00	4.00	8.00
—Budget-line reissue					
SP-3146	Love to the World	198?	2.00	4.00	8.00
—Budget-line reissue					
SP-3148	Something to Love	198?	2.00	4.00	8.00
—Budget-line reissue					
SP-3602	L.T.D.	1974	3.00	6.00	12.00
SP-3660	Gittin' Down	1975	3.00	6.00	12.00
SP-4589	Love to the World	1976	2.50	5.00	10.00
SP-4646	Something to Love	1977	2.50	5.00	10.00
SP-4705	Togetherness	1978	2.50	5.00	10.00
SP-4771	Devotion	1979	2.50	5.00	10.00
SP-4819	Shine On	1980	2.50	5.00	10.00
SP-4881	Love Magic	1981	2.50	5.00	10.00

LA LUPE

45s

ROULETTE

Number	Title (A Side/B Side)	Yr	VG	VG+	NM
7043	Down on Me/Touch Me	1969	2.00	4.00	8.00
7054	Don't Ever Leave Me/(B-side unknown)	1969	2.00	4.00	8.00
7141	Unchained Melody/Carlos Dominguez	1973	—	3.00	6.00

Albums

ROULETTE

Number	Title (A Side/B Side)	Yr	VG	VG+	NM
SR-42024	The Queen Does Her Thing	1969	7.50	15.00	30.00

LABEEF, SLEEPY

45s

COLUMBIA

Number	Title (A Side/B Side)	Yr	VG	VG+	NM
43452	Everybody's Got to Have Somebody (To Love)/ You Can't Catch Me	1965	3.00	6.00	12.00
43875	I Feel a Lot More Like I Do Now/I'm Too Broke	1966	3.00	6.00	12.00
44068	Sure Beats the Heck Out of Settlin' Down/ Schneider	1967	2.50	5.00	10.00
44261	Completely Destroyed/Go Ahead On Baby	1967	2.50	5.00	10.00
44455	Every Day/If I'm Right I'm Wrong	1968	2.50	5.00	10.00

CRESCENT

Number	Title (A Side/B Side)	Yr	VG	VG+	NM
102	Turn Me Loose/(B-side unknown)	195?	50.00	100.00	200.00

MERCURY

Number	Title (A Side/B Side)	Yr	VG	VG+	NM
71112	I'm Through/All Alone	1957	25.00	50.00	100.00
71179	All the Time/Lonely	1957	25.00	50.00	100.00

PICTURE

Number	Title (A Side/B Side)	Yr	VG	VG+	NM
1937	Ride On Josephine/(B-side unknown)	1959	37.50	75.00	150.00

PLANTATION

Number	Title (A Side/B Side)	Yr	VG	VG+	NM
55	Too Much Monkey Business/Got You on My Mind	1970	6.25	12.50	25.00
66	Asphalt Cowboy/Got You on My Mind	1971	2.50	5.00	10.00
74	Blackland Farmer/Got You on My Mind	1971	2.50	5.00	10.00
74 [DJ]	Blackland Farmer (mono/stereo)	1971	3.00	6.00	12.00
—Promo only on green vinyl					

STARDAY

Number	Title (A Side/B Side)	Yr	VG	VG+	NM
292	I'm Through/All Alone	1957	37.50	75.00	150.00

SUN

Number	Title (A Side/B Side)	Yr	VG	VG+	NM
1132	Thunder Road/A Hundred Pounds of Lovin'	1974	—	2.00	4.00
1133 [DJ]	Ghost Riders in the Sky (same on both sides)	1975	—	2.00	4.00
—Promo only					
1134	There Ain't Much After Taxes/A Hundred Pounds of Lovin'	1976	—	2.00	4.00
1137	Good Rockin' Boogie (Part 1)/Good rockin' Boogie (Part 2)	1978	—	2.00	4.00
1145	Flying Saucers Rock and Roll/Boogie Woogie Country Girl	1979	—	2.00	4.00

WAYSIDE

Number	Title (A Side/B Side)	Yr	VG	VG+	NM
1651	Ride On Josephine/(B-side unknown)	1959	50.00	100.00	200.00
—Wayside titles as "Tommy LaBeef"					
1652	Walkin' Slowly/(B-side unknown)	1959	62.50	125.00	250.00
1654	Tore Up/Lonely	1959	75.00	150.00	300.00

Albums

ROUNDER

Number	Title (A Side/B Side)	Yr	VG	VG+	NM
3052	It Ain't What You Eat...	198?	2.50	5.00	10.00
3070	Electricity	198?	2.50	5.00	10.00
3072	Nothin' But the Truth	198?	2.50	5.00	10.00

SUN

Number	Title (A Side/B Side)	Yr	VG	VG+	NM
130	Bull's Night Out	1974	3.00	6.00	12.00
138	Western Gold	197?	3.00	6.00	12.00
1004	Rockabilly 1977	1977	3.00	6.00	12.00
1018	Downtown Rockabilly	1978	3.00	6.00	12.00

LABELLE

Also see PATTI LaBELLE; PATTI LaBELLE AND THE BLUE BELLES.

45s

EPIC

Number	Title (A Side/B Side)	Yr	VG	VG+	NM
50048	Lady Marmalade/Space Children	1974	—	3.00	6.00
50097	Night Bird/What Can I Do for You	1975	—	3.00	6.00
50140	Messin' My Mind/Take the Night Off	1975	—	3.00	6.00
50168	Slow Burn/Far As We Felt Like Going	1975	—	3.00	6.00
50262	Get You Somebody New/Who's Watching the Watcher	1976	—	3.00	6.00
50315	Isn't It a Shame/Gypsy Moths	1976	—	3.00	6.00

RCA VICTOR

Number	Title (A Side/B Side)	Yr	VG	VG+	NM
APBO-0157	Mr. Sunshine Man/Sunshine	1973	2.00	4.00	8.00
74-0965	Open Up Your Heart/Going Up a Holiday	1973	2.00	4.00	8.00

WARNER BROS.

Number	Title (A Side/B Side)	Yr	VG	VG+	NM
7512	Morning Much Better/Shades of Difference	1971	2.00	4.00	8.00
7579	Moonshadow/If I Can't Have You	1972	2.00	4.00	8.00
7624	Touch Me All Over/Ain't It Sad It's All Over	1972	2.00	4.00	8.00

Albums

EPIC

Number	Title (A Side/B Side)	Yr	VG	VG+	NM
KE 33075	Nightbirds	1974	3.00	6.00	12.00
PE 33075	Nightbirds	197?	2.00	4.00	8.00
—Reissue with new prefix					
PE 33579	Phoenix	1975	2.50	5.00	10.00
PEQ 33579 [Q]	Phoenix	1975	3.75	7.50	15.00
PE 34189	Chameleon	1976	2.50	5.00	10.00
—Original with no bar code and orange label					
PE 34189	Chameleon	198?	2.00	4.00	8.00
—Reissue with bar code and dark blue label					

RCA VICTOR

Number	Title (A Side/B Side)	Yr	VG	VG+	NM
APL1-0205	Pressure Cookin'	1973	3.00	6.00	12.00
AYL1-4176	Pressure Cookin'	1982	2.00	4.00	8.00
—"Best Buy Series" reissue					

WARNER BROS.

Number	Title (A Side/B Side)	Yr	VG	VG+	NM
WS 1943	LaBelle	1971	3.75	7.50	15.00
BS 2618	Moonshadow	1972	3.75	7.50	15.00

LABELLE, PATTI

Also see LaBELLE; PATTI LaBELLE AND THE BLUE BELLES.

12-Inch Singles

EPIC

Number	Title (A Side/B Side)	Yr	VG	VG+	NM
50664	Music Is My Way of Life (2 versions)	1979	3.00	6.00	12.00

MCA

Number	Title (A Side/B Side)	Yr	VG	VG+	NM
1131 [DJ]	'Twas Love/Reason for the Season	1990	2.00	4.00	8.00
2074 [DJ]	Somebody Loves You Baby (4 versions)	1991	2.00	4.00	8.00
2433 [DJ]	All Right Now (6 versions)	1992	2.00	4.00	8.00
3140 [DJ]	All This Love (3 versions)	1994	2.00	4.00	8.00
3160 [DJ]	All This Love (4 versions)	1994	2.00	4.00	8.00
L33-17339 [DJ]	Just the Facts (same on both sides)	1987	2.00	4.00	8.00
L33-18014 [DJ]	Yo Mister (same on both sides)	1989	2.00	4.00	8.00
L33-18108 [DJ]	I Can't Complain/(Instrumental)	1989	2.00	4.00	8.00
23534	New Attitude (Extended Mix)/Axel F (Extended Mix)	1985	2.50	5.00	10.00
—B-side by Harold Faltermeyer					
23567	Stir It Up (3 versions)	1985	2.50	5.00	10.00
23607	On My Own/Stir It Up	1986	—	3.00	6.00
—A-side with Michael McDonald					
23649	Something Special (5 versions)	1986	2.00	4.00	8.00
23651	Oh, People (Extended)/(Instrumental)	1986	2.00	4.00	8.00
23773	Just the Facts (4 versions)	1987	2.50	5.00	10.00
23984	Yo Mister (3 versions)	1989	2.00	4.00	8.00
54541	All Right Now (Extended) (Remix) (Dub)	1992	2.00	4.00	8.00
54851	The Right Kinda Lover (Fusion Extended Remix) (Def Jam Remix) (Club Remix)	1994	2.50	5.00	10.00
54933	All This Love (Hip Hop Mix) (Patti's Buttah Mix)/ Our World	1994	2.00	4.00	8.00
55113	Turn It Out (4 mixes)	1995	2.00	4.00	8.00

PHILADELPHIA INT'L.

Number	Title (A Side/B Side)	Yr	VG	VG+	NM
04176	If Only You Knew/I'll Never, Never Give Up	1983	2.50	5.00	10.00
05296	Shy (Remix)/Shy (Dub Mix)	1985	2.00	4.00	8.00

45s

ARISTA

Number	Title (A Side/B Side)	Yr	VG	VG+	NM
12929	My Love, Sweet Love/Sittin' Up in My Room	1996	—	—	3.00
—B-side by Brandy					

BEVERLY GLEN

Number	Title (A Side/B Side)	Yr	VG	VG+	NM
2012	Love Has Finally Come at Last/American Dream	1984	—	2.00	4.00
—With Bobby Womack					
2018	It Takes a Lot of Strength to Say Goodbye/Who's Foolin' Who	1984	—	2.00	4.00
—With Bobby Womack					

ELEKTRA

Number	Title (A Side/B Side)	Yr	VG	VG+	NM
69887	The Best Is Yet to Come/Bye Bye Love	1982	—	2.00	4.00
—With Grover Washington Jr.					

EPIC

Number	Title (A Side/B Side)	Yr	VG	VG+	NM
50445	Joy to Have Your Love/Do I Stand a Chance	1977	—	3.00	6.00
50487	You Are My Friend/I Think About You	1977	—	3.00	6.00
50510	Since I Don't Have You/Dan Swit Me	1978	—	3.00	6.00

Number	Title (A Side/B Side)	Yr	VG	VG+	NM
50550	Teach Me Tonight/Quiet Time	1978	—	3.00	6.00
50583	Little Girls/You Make It So Hard	1978	—	3.00	6.00
50659	It's Alright with Me/Music Is My Way of Life	1979	—	2.50	5.00
50718	Music Is My Way of Life/My Best Was Good Enough	1979	—	2.50	5.00
50763	Love Is Just a Touch Away/Love and Learn	1979	—	2.50	5.00
50852	Come and Dance with Me/Release	1980	—	2.50	5.00
50872	I Don't Go Shopping/Come and Dance with Me	1980	—	2.50	5.00
50910	Ain't That Enough/Don't Make Your Angel Cry	1980	—	2.50	5.00
MCA					
52517	New Attitude/Shoot Out	1984	—	2.00	4.00
—B-side by Harold Faltermeyer					
52517 [PS]	New Attitude/Shoot Out	1984	—	2.00	4.00
52610	Stir It Up/The Discovery	1985	—	2.00	4.00
—B-side by Harold Faltermeyer					
52610 [PS]	Stir It Up/The Discovery	1985	—	2.00	4.00
52770	On My Own/Stir It Up	1986	—	—	3.00
—A-side: With Michael McDonald					
52770 [PS]	On My Own/Stir It Up	1986	—	2.00	4.00
52876	Something Special (Is Gonna Happen Tonight)/(Instrumental)	1986	—	—	3.00
52877	Oh, People/Love Attack	1986	—	—	3.00
52877 [PS]	Oh, People/Love Attack	1986	—	2.00	4.00
52945	Kiss Away the Pain/(Instrumental)	1986	—	—	3.00
53064	The Last Unbroken Heart/Miami Vice: New York Theme	1987	—	—	3.00
—A-side: With Bill Champlin; B-side by Harold Faltermeyer					
53064 [PS]	The Last Unbroken Heart/Miami Vice: New York Theme	1987	—	—	3.00
53100	Just the Facts/(Instrumental)	1987	—	—	3.00
53358	If You Asked Me To/(Instrumental)	1988	—	—	3.00
53728	Yo Mister/I Can Fly	1989	—	—	3.00
53774	I Can't Complain/I Can Fly	1989	—	—	3.00
54481	When You Love Somebody (I'm Saving My Love for You)/Temptation	1992	—	—	3.00
54513	All Right Now/All Right Now (Remix Dub)	1992	—	—	3.00
54673	The Right Kinda Lover/(Instrumental)	1993	—	—	3.00
PHILADELPHIA INT'L.					
02309	Rocking Pneumonia and the Boogie Woogie Flu/Over the Rainbow	1981	—	2.00	4.00
02655	The Spirit's In It/The Family	1981	—	2.00	4.00
04248	If Only You Knew/I'll Never, Never Give Up	1983	—	2.00	4.00
04399	I'm in Love Again/Love, Need and Want It	1984	—	2.00	4.00
05436	I Can't Forget You/Living Doubt	1985	—	2.00	4.00
05755	If You Don't Know Me By Now/(Instrumental)	1986	—	2.00	4.00
05877	Look to the Rainbow/What Can I Do for You	1986	—	2.00	4.00
Albums					
EPIC					
PE 34847	Patti LaBelle	1977	2.50	5.00	10.00
—Original with no bar code and orange label					
PE 34847	Patti LaBelle	1986	2.00	4.00	8.00
—Reissue with bar code and dark blue label					
JE 35335	Tasty	1978	2.50	5.00	10.00
JE 35772	It's Alright with Me	1979	2.50	5.00	10.00
JE 36381	Released	1980	2.50	5.00	10.00
FE 36997	Best of Patti LaBelle	1981	2.50	5.00	10.00
PE 36997	Best of Patti LaBelle	198?	2.00	4.00	8.00
—Budget-line reissue					
MCA					
5737	Winner in You	1986	2.50	5.00	10.00
6292	Be Yourself	1989	2.50	5.00	10.00
10439	Burnin'	1991	3.00	6.00	12.00
PHILADELPHIA INT'L.					
FZ 37380	The Spirit's In It	1981	2.50	5.00	10.00
PZ 37380	The Spirit's In It	198?	2.00	4.00	8.00
—Budget-line reissue					
FZ 38539	I'm in Love Again	1983	2.50	5.00	10.00
FZ 40020	Patti	1985	2.50	5.00	10.00

LABELLE, PATTI, AND THE BLUE BELLES

Also see THE BLUE BELLES; LaBELLE; PATTI LaBELLE AND THE BLUE BELLES.

Number	Title (A Side/B Side)	Yr	VG	VG+	NM
45s					
ATLANTIC					
2311	All or Nothing/You Forgot How to Love	1965	3.00	6.00	12.00
2318	A Groovy Kind of Love/Over the Rainbow	1966	2.50	5.00	10.00
2333	Ebb Tide/Patti's Prayer	1966	2.50	5.00	10.00
2347	I'm Still Waiting/Family Man	1966	2.50	5.00	10.00
2373	Take Me for a Little While/I Don't Want to Go On Without You	1967	2.50	5.00	10.00
2390	(There's) Always Something There to Remind Me/Tender Words	1967	2.50	5.00	10.00
2408	Unchained Melody/Dreamer	1967	2.50	5.00	10.00
2446	Oh My Love/I Need Your Love	1967	2.50	5.00	10.00
2548	He's My Man/Wonderful	1968	2.50	5.00	10.00
2610	Dance to the Rhythm of Love/He's Gone	1969	2.50	5.00	10.00
2629	Loving Blues/Pride's No Match for Love	1969	2.50	5.00	10.00
2712	Suffer/Trustin' in You	1970	2.50	5.00	10.00
KING					
5777	Down the Aisle (Wedding Song)/C'est La Vie	1963	3.75	7.50	15.00
NEWTIME					
510	Love Me Just a Little/The Joke's On You	1962	5.00	10.00	20.00
NEWTOWN					
5000	I Sold My Heart to the Junkman/Itty Bitty Twist	1962	5.00	10.00	20.00
—Credited to "The Blue-Belles" but actually recorded by The Starlets					
5006	I Found a New Love/Pitter Patter	1962	5.00	10.00	20.00
—Most of the Newtown sides credit "The Blue-Belles"					
5007	Tear After Tear/Go On, This Is Goodbye	1962	5.00	10.00	20.00
5009	Cool Water/When Johnny Comes Marching Home	1962	5.00	10.00	20.00
5019	Academy Award/Decatur Street	1963	5.00	10.00	20.00
5777	Down the Aisle (Wedding Song)/C'est La Vie	1963	3.75	7.50	15.00
NICETOWN					
5020	You'll Never Walk Alone/Where Are You	1963	3.75	7.50	15.00
PARKWAY					
896	You'll Never Walk Alone/Decatur Street	1964	3.00	6.00	12.00
896 [PS]	You'll Never Walk Alone/Decatur Street	1964	20.00	40.00	80.00
913	One Phone Call/You Will Fill My Eyes No More	1964	3.00	6.00	12.00
935	Danny Boy/I Believe	1964	3.00	6.00	12.00
PEAK					
7042	I've Got to Let Him Know/I Sold My Heart to the Junkman	1962	6.25	12.50	25.00
—Credited to "The Blue-Belles" but actually recorded by The Starlets					
Albums					
ATLANTIC					
8119 [M]	Over the Rainbow	1966	7.50	15.00	30.00
SD 8119 [S]	Over the Rainbow	1966	10.00	20.00	40.00
8147 [M]	Dreamer	1967	7.50	15.00	30.00
SD 8147 [S]	Dreamer	1967	10.00	20.00	40.00
MISTLETOE					
MLP-1204	Merry Christmas from LaBelle	1976	5.00	10.00	20.00
NEWTOWN					
631 [M]	Sweethearts of the Apollo	1963	100.00	200.00	400.00
632 [M]	Sleigh Bells, Jingle Bells and Blue Bells	1963	75.00	150.00	300.00
PARKWAY					
P-7043 [M]	The Bluebelles On Stage	1965	37.50	75.00	150.00
—With bonus single					
P-7043 [M]	The Bluebelles On Stage	1965	30.00	60.00	120.00
—Without bonus single					
TRIP					
3508	Patti LaBelle and the Bluebelles	197?	2.50	5.00	10.00
8000	Patti LaBelle and the Bluebelles' Greatest Hits	1971	2.50	5.00	10.00
9525	Early Hits	197?	2.50	5.00	10.00
UNITED ARTISTS					
UA-LA504-E	The Very Best of Patti LaBelle and the Bluebelles	1975	2.50	5.00	10.00

LACEWING

Number	Title (A Side/B Side)	Yr	VG	VG+	NM
45s					
MAINSTREAM					
731	Paradox/(B-side unknown)	1971	3.00	6.00	12.00
Albums					
MAINSTREAM					
S-6132	Lacewing	1971	12.50	25.00	50.00

LADD, CHERYL

Also see JOSIE AND THE PUSSYCATS.

Number	Title (A Side/B Side)	Yr	VG	VG+	NM
45s					
CAPITOL					
4215	Country Love/He's Lookin' More Everyday Like the Man Who Broke My Heart	1976	—	2.50	5.00
4599	Think It Over/Here Is a Song	1978	—	2.00	4.00
4599 [PS]	Think It Over/Here Is a Song	1978	—	3.00	6.00
4650	Good Good Lovin'/Skinnydippin'	1978	—	2.00	4.00
4650 [PS]	Good Good Lovin'/Skinnydippin'	1978	—	3.00	6.00
4698	Missing You/Thunder in the Distance	1979	—	2.00	4.00
B-5115	Can't Say No to You/You Make It Beautiful	1982	—	2.00	4.00
—With Frankie Valli					
B-5115 [PS]	Can't Say No to You/You Make It Beautiful	1982	—	2.00	4.00
WARNER BROS.					
7821	Mama Don't Be Blue/The Family	1974	—	3.00	6.00
7821 [PS]	Mama Don't Be Blue/The Family	1974	2.50	5.00	10.00
Albums					
CAPITOL					
SW-11808	Cheryl Ladd	1978	3.00	6.00	12.00
ST-11927	Dance Forever	1979	3.00	6.00	12.00

LADDERS, THE

Number	Title (A Side/B Side)	Yr	VG	VG+	NM
45s					
HOLIDAY					
2611	Counting the Stars/I Want to Know	1957	75.00	150.00	300.00
—Red label, double lines					
2611	Counting the Stars/I Want to Know	196?	20.00	40.00	80.00
—Red label, single line					
VEST					
826	My Love Is Gone/Hey, Pretty Baby	1959	37.50	75.00	150.00
—No stars around "Vest" logo					
826	My Love Is Gone/Hey, Pretty Baby	1960	12.50	25.00	50.00
—With stars around "Vest" logo					

LADY BUGS, THE

May be three different groups, two different groups, or all the same group.

Number	Title (A Side/B Side)	Yr	VG	VG+	NM
45s					
CHATTAHOOCHIE					
637	How Do You Do It/Liverpool	1964	3.75	7.50	15.00
DEL-FI					
4233	Sooner or Later/It's the Last Time	1964	5.00	10.00	20.00
LEGRAND					
1033	Who Sends the Love Note/Fraternity U.S.A.	1964	5.00	10.00	20.00

LADYBIRDS, THE

Number	Title (A Side/B Side)	Yr	VG	VG+	NM
45s					
ATCO					
6329	Memories/Lady Bird	1964	3.00	6.00	12.00
LAWN					
231	Handsome Boy/Yes I Know	1964	2.50	5.00	10.00

LAINE, DENNY

Also see THE MOODY BLUES; WINGS.

Number	Title (A Side/B Side)	Yr	VG	VG+	NM
45s					
ARISTA					
0511	Japanese Tears/Guess I'm Only Fooling	1980	—	2.00	4.00
CAPITOL					
4340	It's So Easy-Listen to Me/I'm Lookin' for Someone to Love	1976	—	3.00	6.00

Number	Title (A Side/B Side)	Yr	VG	VG+	NM
4425	Heartbeat/Moondreams	1977	—	3.00	6.00
DERAM					
7509	Ask the People/Say You Don't Mind	1967	3.75	7.50	15.00
Albums					
CAPITOL					
ST-11588	Holly Days	1977	3.75	7.50	15.00
REPRISE					
MS 2190	Ah, Laine!	1972	3.00	6.00	12.00
TAKOMA					
7034	Japanese Tears	1983	2.50	5.00	10.00

LAINE, FRANKIE

Number	Title (A Side/B Side)	Yr	VG	VG+	NM
45s					
ABC					
10891	I'll Take Care of Your Cares/Every Street's a Boulevard	1966	—	3.00	6.00
10924	Making Memories/Moment of Truth	1967	—	3.00	6.00
10946	You Wanted Someone to Play With (I Wanted Someone to Love)/The Real Meaning of Love	1967	—	3.00	6.00
10967	Laura, What's He Got That I Ain't Got/Sometimes (I Just Can't Stand You)	1967	—	3.00	6.00
10983	You, No One But You/Somewhere There's Someone	1967	—	3.00	6.00
11032	To Each His Own/I'm Happy to Hear You're Sorry	1967	—	3.00	6.00
11057	I Don't Want to Set the World On Fire/I Found You	1968	—	3.00	6.00
11097	Forsaking All Others/Take Me Back	1968	—	3.00	6.00
11129	Please Forgive Me/Pretty Little Princess	1968	—	3.00	6.00
11174	You Gave Me a Mountain/The Secret of Happiness	1969	—	3.00	6.00
11224	Dammit Isn't God's Last Name/Fresh Out of Tears	1969	—	3.00	6.00
11231	If I Didn't Believe in You/Allegra	1969	—	3.00	6.00
AMOS					
138	I Believe/On the Sunny Side of the Street	1970	—	2.50	5.00
153	Put Your Hand in the Hand/Going to Newport	1971	—	2.50	5.00
161	Don't Blame the Child/My God and I	1971	—	2.50	5.00
CAPITOL					
5299	Go On With Your Dancing/Halfway	1964	2.00	4.00	8.00
5472	House of Laughter/A Girl	1965	2.00	4.00	8.00
5525	Seven Days of Love/Heartaches Can Be Fun	1965	2.00	4.00	8.00
5569	The Meaning of It All/Pray and He Will Answer You	1966	2.00	4.00	8.00
5658	Johnny Willow/What Do You Know	1966	2.00	4.00	8.00
COLUMBIA					
39367	Jezebel/Rose, Rose, I Love You	1951	3.75	7.50	15.00
39489	Wonderful, Wasn't It?/The Girl in the Wood	1951	3.75	7.50	15.00
39585	Jealousy (Jalousie)/Flamenco	1951	3.75	7.50	15.00
39597	One for My Baby/Tomorrow Mountain	1951	3.00	6.00	12.00
39598	Song of the Islands/Necessary Evil	1951	3.00	6.00	12.00
39599	She Reminds Me of You/Love Is Such a Cheat	1951	3.00	6.00	12.00
39600	Sleepy Time Down South/To Be Worthy	1951	3.00	6.00	12.00
—The above four comprise a box set					
39662	Jealousy (Jalousie)/Charmaine	1952	3.00	6.00	12.00
—B-side by Paul Weston; part of a box set					
39665	The Gandy Dancers' Ball/When You're in Love	1952	3.75	7.50	15.00
39716	That's How It Goes/Snow in Lover's Lane	1952	3.75	7.50	15.00
39770	High Noon (Do Not Forsake Me)/Rock of Gibraltar	1952	3.75	7.50	15.00
39798	There's a Rainbow 'Round My Shoulder/She's Funny That Way	1952	3.00	6.00	12.00
39799	Wonderful, Wasn't It?/The Girl in the Wood	1952	3.00	6.00	12.00
39862	The Mermaid/The Ruby and the Pearl	1952	3.75	7.50	15.00
39903	I'm Just a Poor Bachelor/Tonight You Belong to Me	1952	3.75	7.50	15.00
39938	I Believe/Your Cheatin' Heart	1953	3.75	7.50	15.00
39979	Ramblin' Man/I Let Her Go	1953	3.75	7.50	15.00
40022	When the Wind Blows/Te Amo	1953	3.75	7.50	15.00
40036	Hey Joe!/Sittin' in the Sun	1953	3.75	7.50	15.00
40079	Another Me/Blowing Wild	1953	3.75	7.50	15.00
40136	Granada/I'd Give My Life	1953	3.75	7.50	15.00
40178	The Kid's Last Fight/Long Distance Love	1954	3.75	7.50	15.00
40235	Some Day/There Must Be a Reason	1954	3.75	7.50	15.00
40295	Rain, Rain, Rain/Your Heart, My Heart	1954	3.75	7.50	15.00
—With the Four Lads					
40378	In the Beginning/Old Shoes	1954	3.75	7.50	15.00
40433	The Tarrier Song/Bubbles	1955	3.00	6.00	12.00
40457	Cool Water/Strange Lady in Town	1955	3.00	6.00	12.00
40526	Humming Bird/My Little One	1955	3.00	6.00	12.00
40558	Hawk-Eye/Your Love	1955	3.00	6.00	12.00
40583	A Woman in Love/Walking the Night Away	1955	3.00	6.00	12.00
40600	I Heard the Angels Singing/Ain't It a Pity and a Shame	1955	3.00	6.00	12.00
—With the Four Lads					
40663	Hell Hath No Fury/The Most Happy Fella	1956	3.00	6.00	12.00
40669	Moby Dick/A Capitol Ship	1956	3.00	6.00	12.00
40693	Don't Cry/Ticky Ticky Tick (I'm Gonna Tell on You)	1956	3.00	6.00	12.00
—With Paul Weston					
40720	Make Me a Child Again/The Thief	1956	3.00	6.00	12.00
40741	On the Road to Mandalay/Only If We Love	1956	3.00	6.00	12.00
40780	Moonlight Gambler/Lotus Land	1956	3.00	6.00	12.00
40780 [PS]	Moonlight Gambler/Lotus Land	1956	6.25	12.50	25.00
40856	Love Is a Golden Ring/There's Not a Moment to Spare	1957	3.00	6.00	12.00
40916	Gunfight at the O.K. Corral/Without Him	1957	3.00	6.00	12.00
40962	The 3:10 to Yuma/You Know How It Is	1957	3.00	6.00	12.00
41036	East Is East/The Greater Sin	1957	3.00	6.00	12.00
41106	Annabelle Lee/All of These…And More	1958	3.00	6.00	12.00
41139	My Gal and a Prayer/Lonesome Road	1958	3.00	6.00	12.00
41163	Lovin' Up a Storm/A Kiss Can Change the World	1958	3.00	6.00	12.00
41187	I Have to Cry/Choombala Bay	1958	3.00	6.00	12.00
41230	Rawhide/Magnificent Obsession	1958	6.25	12.50	25.00
41283	A Cottage for Sale/When I Speak Your Name	1958	3.00	6.00	12.00
41299	When I Speak Your Name/Midnight on a Rainy Monday	1958	3.00	6.00	12.00
41331	That's My Desire/In My Wildest Dreams	1959	2.50	5.00	10.00
41376	My Little Love/Journey's End	1959	2.50	5.00	10.00
41430	El Diablo/The Valley of a Hundred Hills	1959	2.50	5.00	10.00
41486	Rockin' Mother/Rocks and Gravel	1959	2.50	5.00	10.00
41613	St. James Infirmary/Et Voila	1960	2.50	5.00	10.00
41700	Seven Women/And Doesn't She Roll	1960	2.50	5.00	10.00
41787	Kisses That Shake the World/Here She Comes Now	1960	2.50	5.00	10.00
41974	Gunslinger/Wanted Man	1961	2.50	5.00	10.00
42233	Miss Satan/Ride Through the Night	1961	2.50	5.00	10.00
42383	A Wedded Man/We'll Be Together Again	1962	2.50	5.00	10.00
42767	The Moment of Truth/Don't Make Me Baby Blue	1963	2.50	5.00	10.00
42843	I'm Gonna Be Strong/And Doesn't She Roll	1963	2.50	5.00	10.00
42884	Take Her/I'm Gonna Be Strong	1963	2.50	5.00	10.00
42966	Lonely Days of Winter/Up Among the Stars	1964	2.50	5.00	10.00
50006	Jezebel/(B-side unknown)	1954	2.50	5.00	10.00
—Early "Hall of Fame Series" issue					
MAINSTREAM					
5579	Tell Me 'Bout the Hard Times/(B-side unknown)	1975	—	2.00	4.00
MERCURY					
526	Exactly Like You/You're Wonderful	195?	5.00	10.00	20.00
1026	Black and Blue/Wrap Your Troubles in Dreams	195?	6.25	12.50	25.00
1275	The Cry of the Wild Goose/Don't Cry Little Children	195?	5.00	10.00	20.00
—Part of box set A-113					
1277	Mule Train/God Bless the Child	195?	5.00	10.00	20.00
—Part of box set A-113					
5028	Stay As Sweet As You Are/I May Be Wrong	1950	6.25	12.50	25.00
—Reissue of 78 rpm					
5177	You're All I Want for Christmas/Tara Talara Tara	1950	7.50	15.00	30.00
—Reissue of 78 rpm					
5316	That Lucky Old Sun/I Get Sentimental Over Nothing	1950	6.25	12.50	25.00
—Reissue of 78 rpm					
5358	Satan Wears a Satin Gown/Baby Just for Me	1950	6.25	12.50	25.00
5363	The Cry of the Wild Goose/Black Lace	1950	6.25	12.50	25.00
—Maroon label					
5363	The Cry of the Wild Goose/Black Lace	1950	7.50	15.00	30.00
—Turquoise label					
5390	Swamp Girl/A Kiss for Tomorrow	1950	6.25	12.50	25.00
5421	Stars and Stripes Forever/Thanks for the Kisses	1950	6.25	12.50	25.00
5458	Music, Maestro, Please/Dream a Little Dream of Me	1950	5.00	10.00	20.00
5495	Nevertheless/I Was Dancing with Someone	1950	5.00	10.00	20.00
5500	If I Were a Bell/Sleepy Ol' River	1950	5.00	10.00	20.00
5544	I'm Gonna Live 'Til I Die/A Man Gets Awfully Lonesome	1950	5.00	10.00	20.00
5553	Merry Christmas Everywhere/What Am I Gonna Do This Christmas	1950	5.00	10.00	20.00
5580	Dear, Dear, Dear/May the Good Lord Bless and Keep You	1951	5.00	10.00	20.00
5581	Metro Polka/The Jalopy Song	1951	5.00	10.00	20.00
5656	The Gang That Sang Heart of My Heart/Out in the Rain	1951	5.00	10.00	20.00
5685	Isle of Capri/The Day Isn't Long Enough	1951	5.00	10.00	20.00
5733	Get Happy/I Would Do Most Anything for You	1951	5.00	10.00	20.00
5768	Baby I Need You/Yes My Darling Daughter	1951	5.00	10.00	20.00
5892	All of Me/South of the Border	1952	5.00	10.00	20.00
70099	Ain't Misbehavin'/How Rhythm Was Born	1953	3.75	7.50	15.00
70262	(The Gang That Sang) Heart of My Heart/South of the Border	1953	3.75	7.50	15.00
70275	West End Blues/I Can't Believe That You're in Love with Me	1953	3.75	7.50	15.00
SUNFLOWER					
125	My Own True Love/Time to Ride	1972	—	2.50	5.00
WARNER BROS.					
7774	Blazing Saddles/I'm Tired	1974	—	3.00	6.00
—B-side by Madeline Kahn					
7-Inch Extended Plays					
COLUMBIA					
5-1169	There's a Rainbow 'Round My Shoulder/She's Funny That Way//Wonderful Wasn't It?/The Girl in the Wood	195?	5.00	10.00	20.00
—Alternate number is B-1512					
5-1325	Jezebel/Jealousy (Jalousie)//The Gandy Dancers' Ball/When You're in Love	195?	5.00	10.00	20.00
—Alternate number is B-1582					
B-1512 [PS]	Rainbow 'Round My Shoulder	195?	5.00	10.00	20.00
5-1569	Your Cheatin' Heart/I Believe//Love Is Such a Cheat/High Noon (Do Not Forsake Me)	195?	5.00	10.00	20.00
—Alternate number is B-1685					
B-1582 [PS]	Frankie Laine Spotlite	195?	5.00	10.00	20.00
B-1685 [PS]	Frankie Laine Favorites	195?	5.00	10.00	20.00
B-1897	(contents unknown)	195?	5.00	10.00	20.00
B-1897 [PS]	Popular Favorites	195?	5.00	10.00	20.00
B-2086	(contents unknown)	1956	5.00	10.00	20.00
B-2086 [PS]	Bring Your Smile Along	1956	5.00	10.00	20.00
B-2121	(contents unknown)	1957	5.00	10.00	20.00
B-2121 [PS]	Moonlight Gambler	1957	5.00	10.00	20.00
B-2132	(contents unknown)	1957	5.00	10.00	20.00
B-2132 [PS]	Love Is a Golden Ring and Other Hits	1957	5.00	10.00	20.00
B-2590	*Shine/That's My Desire/That Lucky Old Sun/Moonlight Gambler	1960	3.75	7.50	15.00
B-2590 [PS]	Frankie Laine (Hall of Fame Series)	1960	3.75	7.50	15.00
B-11161	(contents unknown)	195?	5.00	10.00	20.00
B-11161 [PS]	Foreign Affair	195?	5.00	10.00	20.00
B-11162	(contents unknown)	195?	5.00	10.00	20.00
B-11162 [PS]	Foreign Affair	195?	5.00	10.00	20.00
MERCURY					
EP 1-3001	(contents unknown)	195?	6.25	12.50	25.00
EP 1-3001 [PS]	Music, Maestro, Please	195?	6.25	12.50	25.00
EP 1-3010	Two Loves Have I/I May Be Wrong//All of Me/Old Fashioned Love	195?	6.25	12.50	25.00
EP 1-3010 [PS]	Frankie Laine	195?	6.25	12.50	25.00
EP 1-3021	But Beautiful/That's My Desire//We Will Be Together Again/Shine	195?	6.25	12.50	25.00

Number	Title (A Side/B Side)	Yr	VG	VG+	NM
EP 1-3021 [PS]	Frankie Laine Favorites	195?	6.25	12.50	25.00
EP 1-3028	(contents unknown)	195?	6.25	12.50	25.00
EP 1-3028 [PS]	Christmas Favorites	195?	6.25	12.50	25.00
EP-1-3057	I May Be Wrong/On the Sunny Side of the Street //Too Marvelous for Words/I Get a Kick Out of You	195?	5.00	10.00	20.00
—B-side by Billy Daniels					
EP-1-3057	(title unknown)	195?	5.00	10.00	20.00
EP 1-3071	(contents unknown)	195?	6.25	12.50	25.00
EP 1-3071 [PS]	Georgia on My Mind	195?	6.25	12.50	25.00
EP 1-3165	(contents unknown)	195?	6.25	12.50	25.00
EP 1-3165 [PS]	Get Happy	195?	6.25	12.50	25.00
EP 1-3175	(contents unknown)	195?	6.25	12.50	25.00
EP 1-3175 [PS]	With All My Heart	195?	6.25	12.50	25.00

Albums

Number	Title (A Side/B Side)	Yr	VG	VG+	NM
ABC					
604 [M]	I'll Take Care of Your Cares	1967	3.00	6.00	12.00
S-604 [S]	I'll Take Care of Your Cares	1967	3.75	7.50	15.00
608 [M]	I Wanted Someone to Love	1967	3.00	6.00	12.00
S-608 [S]	I Wanted Someone to Love	1967	3.75	7.50	15.00
628 [M]	To Each His Own	1968	5.00	10.00	20.00
S-628 [S]	To Each His Own	1968	3.75	7.50	15.00
S-657	Take Me Back to Laine Country	1968	3.75	7.50	15.00
S-682	You Gave Me a Mountain	1969	3.75	7.50	15.00
AMOS					
7009	Frankie Laine's Greatest Hits	1970	3.00	6.00	12.00
7013	Brand New Day	1971	3.00	6.00	12.00
BULLDOG					
BDL-1035	All of Me	198?	2.50	5.00	10.00
CAPITOL					
ST 2277 [S]	I Believe	1965	3.75	7.50	15.00
T 2277 [M]	I Believe	1965	3.00	6.00	12.00
COLUMBIA					
CL 625 [M]	Command Performance	1954	10.00	20.00	40.00
CL 808 [M]	Jazz Spectacular	1956	7.50	15.00	30.00
CL 975 [M]	Rockin'	1957	7.50	15.00	30.00
CL 1116 [M]	Foreign Affair	1958	7.50	15.00	30.00
CL 1176 [M]	Torchin'	1959	5.00	10.00	20.00
CL 1231 [M]	Frankie Laine's Greatest Hits	1958	6.25	12.50	25.00
—Red and black label with six "eye" logos					
CL 1231 [M]	Frankie Laine's Greatest Hits	1962	3.75	7.50	15.00
—"Guaranteed High Fidelity" or "360 Sound Mono" label					
CL 1317 [M]	You Are My Love	1960	5.00	10.00	20.00
CL 1393 [M]	Frankie Laine, Balladeer	1960	5.00	10.00	20.00
CL 1615 [M]	Hell Bent for Leather!	1961	5.00	10.00	20.00
—Red and black label with six "eye" logos					
CL 1615 [M]	Hell Bent for Leather!	1962	3.75	7.50	15.00
—"Guaranteed High Fidelity" or "360 Sound Mono" label					
CL 1696 [M]	Deuces Wild	1962	5.00	10.00	20.00
—Red and black label with six "eye" logos					
CL 1696 [M]	Deuces Wild	1962	3.75	7.50	15.00
—"Guaranteed High Fidelity" or "360 Sound Mono" label					
CL 1829 [M]	Call of the Wild	1962	3.75	7.50	15.00
CL 1962 [M]	Wanderlust	1963	3.75	7.50	15.00
CL 2504 [10]	Lover's Laine	1955	10.00	20.00	40.00
CL 2548 [10]	One for My Baby	1955	10.00	20.00	40.00
CL 6200 [10]	One for My Baby	1952	12.50	25.00	50.00
CL 6278 [10]	Mr. Rhythm	1954	12.50	25.00	50.00
CS 8024 [S]	Torchin'	1959	7.50	15.00	30.00
CS 8087 [S]	Reunion in Rhythm	1959	7.50	15.00	30.00
CS 8119 [S]	You Are My Love	1960	6.25	12.50	25.00
CS 8188 [S]	Frankie Laine, Balladeer	1960	6.25	12.50	25.00
CS 8415 [S]	Hell Bent for Leather!	1961	7.50	15.00	30.00
—Red and black label with six "eye" logos					
CS 8415 [S]	Hell Bent for Leather!	1962	5.00	10.00	20.00
—"360 Sound Stereo" label					
CS 8496 [S]	Deuces Wild	1962	6.25	12.50	25.00
—Red and black label with six "eye" logos					
CS 8496 [S]	Deuces Wild	1962	5.00	10.00	20.00
—"360 Sound Stereo" label					
CS 8629 [S]	Call of the Wild	1962	5.00	10.00	20.00
CS 8636 [R]	Frankie Laine's Greatest Hits	1963	3.00	6.00	12.00
PC 8636	Frankie Laine's Greatest Hits	198?	2.00	4.00	8.00
—Reissue with new prefix					
CS 8762 [S]	Wanderlust	1963	5.00	10.00	20.00
CL (# unknown) [M]	Reunion in Rhythm	1959	5.00	10.00	20.00
GALAXY SERIES					
4821 [M]	Frankie Laine Sings	195?	3.00	6.00	12.00
HARMONY					
HL 7329 [M]	Roving Gambler	196?	3.00	6.00	12.00
HL 7382 [M]	That's My Desire	196?	3.00	6.00	12.00
HL 7425 [M]	Memories	196?	3.00	6.00	12.00
HS 11129 [S]	Roving Gambler	196?	3.00	6.00	12.00
HS 11182 [S]	That's My Desire	196?	3.00	6.00	12.00
HS 11225 [S]	Memories	196?	3.00	6.00	12.00
HS 11345	I'm Gonna Live 'Til I Die	1969	3.00	6.00	12.00
H 30406	High Noon	1971	3.00	6.00	12.00
HINDSIGHT					
HSR-216	Frankie Laine with Carl Fischer and His Orchestra, 1947	1985	2.50	5.00	10.00
MERCURY					
PKW-2-111 [(2)]	The Great Years	1969	3.75	7.50	15.00
MG-20069 [M]	Songs by Frankie Laine	1956	10.00	20.00	40.00
MG-20080 [M]	That's My Desire	1957	10.00	20.00	40.00
MG-20083 [M]	Frankie Laine Sings For Us	1957	10.00	20.00	40.00
MG-20085 [M]	Concert Date	1957	10.00	20.00	40.00
MG-20105 [M]	With All My Heart	1957	10.00	20.00	40.00
MG-20587 [M]	Frankie Laine's Golden Hits	1960	6.25	12.50	25.00
MG-25007 [10]	Favorites	1949	12.50	25.00	50.00
MG-25024 [10]	Songs from the Heart	1950	12.50	25.00	50.00
MG-25025 [10]	Frankie Laine	1950	12.50	25.00	50.00
MG-25026 [10]	Frankie Laine	1950	12.50	25.00	50.00
MG-25027 [10]	Frankie Laine	1950	12.50	25.00	50.00
MG-25082 [10]	Christmas Favorites	1951	12.50	25.00	50.00
MG-25097 [10]	Mr. Rhythm Sings	1951	12.50	25.00	50.00
MG-25124 [10]	Listen to Laine	1952	12.50	25.00	50.00
SR-60587 [R]	Frankie Laine's Golden Hits	196?	3.00	6.00	12.00
PICKWICK					
SPC-3526	That Lucky Old Sun	197?	2.50	5.00	10.00
SPC-3601	You Gave Me a Mountain	197?	2.50	5.00	10.00
TOWER					
ST 5092 [S]	Memory Laine	1967	3.75	7.50	15.00
T 5092 [M]	Memory Laine	1967	3.00	6.00	12.00
WING					
MGW 12110 [M]	All-Time Favorites	196?	3.75	7.50	15.00
MGW 12158 [M]	Singing the Blues	196?	3.75	7.50	15.00
MGW 12202 [M]	That's My Desire	196?	3.75	7.50	15.00
SRW 16110 [R]	All-Time Favorites	196?	3.00	6.00	12.00
SRW 16158 [R]	Singing the Blues	196?	3.00	6.00	12.00
SRW 16202 [R]	That's My Desire	196?	3.00	6.00	12.00

LAINE, FRANKIE, AND JIMMY BOYD

Also see each artist's individual listings.

45s

Number	Title (A Side/B Side)	Yr	VG	VG+	NM
COLUMBIA					
39945	Tell Me a Story/The Little Boy and the Old Man	1953	3.75	7.50	15.00
40069	Let's Go Fishin'/Poor Little Piggy Bank	1953	3.75	7.50	15.00
40650	Little Child/Let's Go Fishin'	1956	3.00	6.00	12.00

LAINE, FRANKIE, AND PATTI PAGE

Also see each artist's individual listings.

45s

Number	Title (A Side/B Side)	Yr	VG	VG+	NM
MERCURY					
5442	I Love You for That/If I Were You Baby, I'd Love Me	1950	5.00	10.00	20.00

LAINE, FRANKIE, AND JO STAFFORD

Also see each artist's individual listings.

45s

Number	Title (A Side/B Side)	Yr	VG	VG+	NM
COLUMBIA					
39388	Pretty Eyed Baby/That's One for Me	1951	3.75	7.50	15.00
39466	In the Cool of the Evening/That's Good, That's Bad	1951	3.75	7.50	15.00
39570	Hey, Good Lookin'/Gambella (The Gamblin' Lady)	1951	3.75	7.50	15.00
39672	Hambone/Let's Have a Party	1952	3.75	7.50	15.00
39867	Settin' the Woods on Fire/Piece a-Puddin'	1952	3.75	7.50	15.00
39893	Christmas Roses/Chow Willy	1952	3.75	7.50	15.00
40116	Way Down Yonder in New Orleans/Floatin' Down to Cotton Town	1953	3.75	7.50	15.00
40198	Rollin' Down the Line/Goin' Like Wildfire	1954	3.75	7.50	15.00
40401	High Society/Back Where I Belong	1954	3.75	7.50	15.00

LAINE, LINDA, AND THE SINNERS

Also see FREDDIE AND THE DREAMERS.

45s

Number	Title (A Side/B Side)	Yr	VG	VG+	NM
TOWER					
108	Low Grades and High Fever/After Today	1964	3.00	6.00	12.00
—Also see "Freddie and the Dreamers"					

LAKE, GREG

45s

Number	Title (A Side/B Side)	Yr	VG	VG+	NM
ATLANTIC					
3305	I Believe in Father Christmas/Humbug	1975	—	3.00	6.00
3305 [PS]	I Believe in Father Christmas/Humbug	1975	2.50	5.00	10.00
3405	C'est La Vie/Jeremy Bender	1977	—	2.50	5.00
CHRYSALIS					
2517	Let Me Love You Once/(B-side unknown)	1981	—	2.00	4.00
2571	Retribution Drive/Let Me Love You Once	1981	—	2.00	4.00

Albums

Number	Title (A Side/B Side)	Yr	VG	VG+	NM
CHRYSALIS					
CHR 1357	Greg Lake	1981	2.50	5.00	10.00

LAKE, KAREN

45s

Number	Title (A Side/B Side)	Yr	VG	VG+	NM
ABC-PARAMOUNT					
10050	Nine O'Clock/Will I Know	1959	5.00	10.00	20.00
10087	Kiss Me Quick and Go/When I'm Not Teen Age Anymore	1960	5.00	10.00	20.00
BIG TOP					
3077	Air Mail Special Delivery/I'd Like to Miss My Graduation	1961	7.50	15.00	30.00
—Produced by Phil Spector					

LALA AND THE LALARETTES

45s

Number	Title (A Side/B Side)	Yr	VG	VG+	NM
ELPECO					
2922	This Day of Ours/Getting Ready for Freddy	1963	15.00	30.00	60.00

LAMARR, GENE

45s

Number	Title (A Side/B Side)	Yr	VG	VG+	NM
SPRY					
113	Crazy Little House on the Hill/You Don't Love Me Anymore	1959	37.50	75.00	150.00
114	You Can Count on Me/Just a Little Bit Longer	1959	37.50	75.00	150.00
115	Close to Me/Moon Eyes	1959	25.00	50.00	100.00

LAMAS, FERNANDO

Albums

Number	Title (A Side/B Side)	Yr	VG	VG+	NM
ROULETTE					
R-25041 [M]	With Love, Fernando Lamas	1958	10.00	20.00	40.00

LAMB

Number	Title (A Side/B Side)	Yr	VG	VG+	NM
Albums					
FILLMORE					
F 30003	Sign of Change	1970	5.00	10.00	20.00
WARNER BROS.					
WS 1920	Cross Between	1971	5.00	10.00	20.00
WS 1952	Bring Out the Sun	1972	5.00	10.00	20.00

LAMB, BECKY

Number	Title (A Side/B Side)	Yr	VG	VG+	NM
45s					
WARNER BROS.					
7154	Little Becky's Christmas Wish/Go to Sleep, Little Lambs	1967	3.00	6.00	12.00
—B-side by Bill Lamb					

LAMBERT, RUDY

See THE MONDELLOS.

LAMM, ROBERT

Of CHICAGO.

Number	Title (A Side/B Side)	Yr	VG	VG+	NM
45s					
COLUMBIA					
10068	Skinny Boy/Temporary Jones	1974	—	2.50	5.00
Albums					
COLUMBIA					
PC 33095	Skinny Boy	1974	3.00	6.00	12.00

LAMONT, BILLY

Number	Title (A Side/B Side)	Yr	VG	VG+	NM
45s					
KING					
5403	Come On Right Now/Hear Me Now	1960	3.00	6.00	12.00
OKEH					
7125	Country Boy/Can't Make It By Myself	1959	6.25	12.50	25.00
7131	I'm Gonna Try/Now Darling	1960	6.25	12.50	25.00
SAVOY					
1522	I'm So Lonely/I Got a Rock 'n' Roll Gal	1957	3.75	7.50	15.00
THREE-D					
850	Country Boy/Can't Make It By Myself	1959	37.50	75.00	150.00

LAMP, BUDDY

Number	Title (A Side/B Side)	Yr	VG	VG+	NM
45s					
ABC-PARAMOUNT					
10398	I'm Comin' Home/Promised Land	1963	3.75	7.50	15.00
D-TOWN					
1064	Next Best Thing/Just a Little Bit of Lovin'	1966	7.50	15.00	30.00
DOUBLE L					
716	Thank You Love/My Tears	1963	7.50	15.00	30.00
DUKE					
438	I'm Coming Home/Where Have You Been	1968	2.50	5.00	10.00
461	Devil's Gonna Get You/Wall Around Your Heart	1970	2.00	4.00	8.00
468	Hen Pecked/If You See Kate	1971	2.00	4.00	8.00
GONE					
5104	Good News/What Here Can I Do	1961	3.75	7.50	15.00
WHEELSVILLE					
113	You've Got the Lovin' Touch/I Wanna Go Home	196?	10.00	20.00	40.00
120	Confusion/I Wanna Go Home	196?	10.00	20.00	40.00
122	Save Your Love/I Wanna Go Home	196?	17.50	35.00	70.00

LAMP OF CHILDHOOD, THE

Number	Title (A Side/B Side)	Yr	VG	VG+	NM
45s					
DUNHILL					
4051	Season of the Witch/You Can't Blame Me	1966	2.00	4.00	8.00
4063	First Time Last Time/2 O'Clock Morning	1967	2.00	4.00	8.00
4063 [PS]	First Time Last Time/2 O'Clock Morning	1967	3.00	6.00	12.00
4089	No More Running Around/2 O'Clock Morning	1967	2.00	4.00	8.00

LAMPLIGHTERS, THE

Number	Title (A Side/B Side)	Yr	VG	VG+	NM
45s					
FEDERAL					
12149	Part of Me/Turn Me Loose	1953	75.00	150.00	300.00
12152	Give Me/Be-Bop Wino	1953	37.50	75.00	150.00
12166	Smootchie/I Can't Stand It	1954	37.50	75.00	150.00
12176	Tell Me You Came/I Used to Cry Mercy, Mercy	1954	37.50	75.00	150.00
12182	Salty Dog/Ride, Jockey, Ride	1954	37.50	75.00	150.00
12192	Five Minutes Longer/You Hear	1954	37.50	75.00	150.00
12197	Yum! Yum!/Goody Good Times	1954	37.50	75.00	150.00
12206	I Wanna Know/Believe in Me	1955	37.50	75.00	150.00
12212	Roll On/Love, Rock and Thrill	1955	37.50	75.00	150.00
12242	Don't Make It So Good/Hug a Little, Kiss a Little	1955	37.50	75.00	150.00
12255	You Were Sent Down from Heaven/Bo-Peep	1956	25.00	50.00	100.00
12261	It Ain't Right/Everything's All Right	1956	25.00	50.00	100.00
KING					
5890	Be-Bop Wino/Thunderbird	1964	3.75	7.50	15.00
—B-side by Dossie Terry					

LANCASTRIANS, THE

Number	Title (A Side/B Side)	Yr	VG	VG+	NM
45s					
CAPITOL					
5501	Never Gonna Come On Home/There'll Be No More Goodbyes	1965	2.50	5.00	10.00
JERDEN					
798	The World Keeps Going Round/Not the Same Anymore	1966	2.50	5.00	10.00

LANCE, HERB

Number	Title (A Side/B Side)	Yr	VG	VG+	NM
45s					
DELUXE					
6150	You Can't Be Sure of Anything/By the Candleglow	1957	12.50	25.00	50.00
MALA					
404	Like a Baby/My Good Mind	1959	5.00	10.00	20.00
405	Some Love/Until the Real Thing	1959	5.00	10.00	20.00
426	Deep in My Heart/Prayer in My Heart	1961	5.00	10.00	20.00
Albums					
CHESS					
LP-1506 [M]	The Comeback	1966	6.25	12.50	25.00
LPS-1506 [S]	The Comeback	1966	7.50	15.00	30.00

LANCE, MAJOR

Number	Title (A Side/B Side)	Yr	VG	VG+	NM
45s					
COLUMBIA					
10488	Come On, Have Yourself a Good Time/Come What May	1977	—	2.50	5.00
CURTOM					
1953	Stay Away from Me (I Love You Too Much)/Gypsy Woman	1970	—	3.00	6.00
1956	Must Be Love Coming Down/Little Young Lover	1970	—	3.00	6.00
DAKAR					
608	Follow the Leader/Since You've Been Gone	1969	2.00	4.00	8.00
612	Shadows of a Memory/Sweeter As the Days Go By	1969	2.00	4.00	8.00
KAT FAMILY					
03024	I Wanna Go Home/(Instrumental)	1982	—	2.00	4.00
04185	Are You Leaving Me/I Wanna Go Home	1983	—	2.00	4.00
MERCURY					
71582	I've Got a Girl/Phyllis	1960	7.50	15.00	30.00
OKEH					
7175	The Monkey Time/Mama Didn't Know	1963	3.75	7.50	15.00
7181	Hey Little Girl/Crying in the Rain	1963	3.00	6.00	12.00
7187	Um, Um, Um, Um, Um, Um/Sweet Music	1964	3.75	7.50	15.00
7187 [PS]	Um, Um, Um, Um, Um, Um/Sweet Music	1964	7.50	15.00	30.00
7191	The Matador/Gonna Get Married	1964	2.50	5.00	10.00
7197	It Ain't No Use/Girls	1964	2.50	5.00	10.00
7200	Think Nothing About It/It's Alright	1964	12.50	25.00	50.00
7203	Rhythm/Please Don't Say No More	1964	2.50	5.00	10.00
7203 [PS]	Rhythm/Please Don't Say No More	1964	3.75	7.50	15.00
7209	Sometimes I Wonder/I'm So Lost	1965	2.50	5.00	10.00
7216	Come See/You Belong to Me My Love	1965	2.50	5.00	10.00
7216 [PS]	Come See/You Belong to Me My Love	1965	3.75	7.50	15.00
7223	Ain't It a Shame/Gotta Get Away	1965	2.50	5.00	10.00
7226	Too Hot to Hold/Dark and Lovely	1965	2.50	5.00	10.00
7233	Everybody Loves a Good Time/I Just Can't Help It	1965	3.75	7.50	15.00
7250	Little Young Lover/Investigate	1966	3.75	7.50	15.00
7250 [PS]	Little Young Lover/Investigate	1966	5.00	10.00	20.00
7255	It's the Beat/You'll Want Me Back	1966	2.50	5.00	10.00
7266	Ain't No Soul (In These Shoes)/I	1966	3.75	7.50	15.00
7284	You Don't Want Me No More/Wait Till I Get You in Your Arms	1967	12.50	25.00	50.00
7298	Without a Doubt/Forever	1967	2.50	5.00	10.00
OSIRIS					
001	You're Everything I Need/(Instrumental)	1975	—	2.50	5.00
PLAYBOY					
6017	Um, Um, Um, Um, Um, Um/Last of the Red Hot Lovers	1974	—	2.50	5.00
6020	Sweeter/Wild and Free	1975	—	2.50	5.00
SOUL					
35123	I Never Thought I'd Be Losing You/Chicago Disco	1977	—	2.50	5.00
VOLT					
4079	I Wanna Make Up/That's the Story of My Life	1972	—	3.00	6.00
4085	Ain't No Sweat/Since I Lost My Baby's Love	1972	—	3.00	6.00
Albums					
KAT FAMILY					
FZ 38898	The Major's Back	1983	3.00	6.00	12.00
OKEH					
OKM-12105 [M]	The Monkey Time	1963	10.00	20.00	40.00
OKM-12106 [M]	Um, Um, Um, Um, Um, Um	1964	10.00	20.00	40.00
OKM-12110 [M]	Major's Greatest Hits	1965	7.50	15.00	30.00
OKS-14105 [S]	The Monkey Time	1963	12.50	25.00	50.00
OKS-14106 [S]	Um, Um, Um, Um, Um, Um	1964	12.50	25.00	50.00
OKS-14110 [S]	Major's Greatest Hits	1965	10.00	20.00	40.00
SOUL					
S7-751	Now Arriving	1978	3.00	6.00	12.00

LANCELOT LINK AND THE EVOLUTION REVOLUTION

Number	Title (A Side/B Side)	Yr	VG	VG+	NM
45s					
ABC					
11278	Sha La Love You/Blind Date	1970	2.50	5.00	10.00
11285	Daydreams/Magic Feelings	1970	2.50	5.00	10.00
Albums					
ABC					
S-715	Lancelot Link and the Evolution Revolution	1970	10.00	20.00	40.00

LANCERS, THE

Number	Title (A Side/B Side)	Yr	VG	VG+	NM
45s					
CLOUD					
500	Baja/When Johnny Comes Draggin' Home	1965	6.25	12.50	25.00
CORAL					
61288	Mr. Sandman/Little White Light	1954	3.00	6.00	12.00
61314	'Twas the Night Before Christmas/I Wanna Do More Than Whistle (Under the Mistletoe)	1954	3.00	6.00	12.00
61332	Tweedlee Dee/Open Up Your Heart (And Let the Sun Shine In)	1955	3.00	6.00	12.00
61343	Timberjack/Crazy Music	1955	3.00	6.00	12.00
—With Lawrence Welk and His Orchestra					
61374	Somebody Else Is Taking My Place/Cherry	1955	3.00	6.00	12.00
61382	Two Hearts, Two Kisses/Afraid	1955	3.00	6.00	12.00
61416	Leave the Door Partly Open/The Lucky Black Cat	1955	3.00	6.00	12.00
61468	It Shouldn't Hurt to Love You/It Takes a Heap of Livin'	1955	3.00	6.00	12.00
61527	Alphabet Rock/How Lonely Can I Get	1955	3.00	6.00	12.00
61550	Rock Around the Island/The Walking Doll	1956	3.00	6.00	12.00
61611	Sorry/A Man Is As Good As His Word	1956	3.00	6.00	12.00
61614	Joey, Joey, Joey/When You're in Love	1956	3.00	6.00	12.00

Number	Title (A Side/B Side)	Yr	VG	VG+	NM
61616	Little Fool/A Man Is As Good As His Word	1956	3.00	6.00	12.00
61665	The First Traveling Saleslady/Free	1956	3.00	6.00	12.00
61686	The Bonnie Banks of Loch Lomon'/Maybe Now	1956	3.00	6.00	12.00
61712	I Came Back to Say I'm Sorry/Never Leave Me	1956	3.00	6.00	12.00
61769	Freckle Face Sara Jane/It Happened in Monterey	1957	3.00	6.00	12.00
61831	Charm Bracelets/And I Don't Feel Bad	1957	3.00	6.00	12.00
61866	Lover's Rendezvous/Follow the River	1957	3.00	6.00	12.00
61887	I'm Awfully Strong for You/I'd Move Heaven and Earth	1957	3.00	6.00	12.00
61899	Don't Go Near the Water/A Hundred Heartbeats	1957	3.00	6.00	12.00
61930	The Stroll/Jo-Ann	1958	3.00	6.00	12.00
61966	Sorry/The Sound	1958	3.00	6.00	12.00
61998	It Was Great While It Lasted/The Lord Is a Generous Man	1958	3.00	6.00	12.00
OLD TIMER					
604	Baja/When Johnny Comes Draggin' Home	1965	10.00	20.00	40.00
—Black vinyl					
604	Baja/When Johnny Comes Draggin' Home	1965	2.50	5.00	10.00
—Red vinyl (reissue)					
VEE JAY					
654	The Warmth of the Sun/Hush-A-Bye	1965	2.50	5.00	10.00
Albums					
CORAL					
CRL 57100 [M]	Dixieland Ball	1957	6.25	12.50	25.00
IMPERIAL					
LP-9075 [M]	Concert in Contrasts	1959	7.50	15.00	30.00
LP-12023 [S]	Concert in Contrasts	1959	10.00	20.00	40.00
TREND					
TL-1009 [10]	The Lancers	1954	10.00	20.00	40.00

LANDIS, JERRY

See PAUL SIMON.

LANDS, HOAGY

Number	Title (A Side/B Side)	Yr	VG	VG+	NM
45s					
ABC-PARAMOUNT					
10171	(I'm Gonna) Cry Some Tears/Lighted Windows	1960	6.25	12.50	25.00
10392	Tender Years/I'm Yours	1963	3.75	7.50	15.00
ATLANTIC					
2217	Baby Come On Home/Baby Let Me Hold Your Hand	1964	3.75	7.50	15.00
JUDI					
054	(I'm Gonna) Cry Some Tears/Lighted Windows	1960	20.00	40.00	80.00
LAURIE					
3349	Theme from The Other Side/Friends and Lovers Don't Go Together	1966	5.00	10.00	20.00
3372	Yesterday/Forever	1967	5.00	10.00	20.00
3381	The Next in Line/Please Don't Talk About Me When I'm Gone	1967	6.25	12.50	25.00
—Backing group: THE CHIFFONS.					
MGM					
K-13041	My Tears Are Dry/It's Gonna Be Morning	1961	5.00	10.00	20.00
K-13062	Goodnight Irene/It Ain't As Easy As That	1962	5.00	10.00	20.00

LANDS, LIZ

Number	Title (A Side/B Side)	Yr	VG	VG+	NM
45s					
GORDY					
7023	We Shall Overcome/I Have a Dream	1963	6.25	12.50	25.00
—B-side by Rev. Martin Luther King					
7026	May What He Lived For Live/He's Got the Whole World in His Hands	1963	7.50	15.00	30.00
7030	Midnight Journey/Keep Me	1964	12.50	25.00	50.00
—The Temptations sing backup					
ONE-DERFUL					
4847	One Man's Poison/Don't Shut Me Out	1967	3.75	7.50	15.00
T&L					
201	Silent Night (Part 1)/Silent Night (Part 2)	19??	2.00	4.00	8.00

LANDSLIDE

Number	Title (A Side/B Side)	Yr	VG	VG+	NM
Albums					
CAPITOL					
ST-11006	Two-Sided Fantasy	1972	10.00	20.00	40.00

LANE, BILLY

Number	Title (A Side/B Side)	Yr	VG	VG+	NM
45s					
TABA					
201	Beginner in Love/Space Ship Blues	196?	40.00	80.00	160.00

LANE, MICKEY

Number	Title (A Side/B Side)	Yr	VG	VG+	NM
45s					
BRUNSWICK					
55098	Daddy's Little Baby/Toasted Love	1958	5.00	10.00	20.00
LAURIE					
3071	Dum Dee Dee Dum/Night Cap	1960	6.25	12.50	25.00

LANE, MICKEY LEE

Number	Title (A Side/B Side)	Yr	VG	VG+	NM
45s					
MALA					
12032	Tutti Frutti/With Your Love	1968	2.00	4.00	8.00
SWAN					
4183	Shaggy Dog/Oo-Oo	1964	3.00	6.00	12.00
4199	The Zoo/(They're All in the) Senior Class	1965	2.50	5.00	10.00
4210	Little Girl (I Was Wrong)/When You're in Love	1965	2.50	5.00	10.00
4222	Hey Sah-Lo-Ney/Of Yesterday	1965	2.50	5.00	10.00
4252	The Only Thing to Do/She Don't Want To	1966	2.50	5.00	10.00

LANE, ROCKI, AND THE GROSS GROUP

Number	Title (A Side/B Side)	Yr	VG	VG+	NM
45s					
EPIC					
10556	Happy Hairy Hippy Harry Claus/Santa Soul	1969	6.25	12.50	25.00

LANI & BONI

See DELANEY AND BONNIE.

LANIN, LESTER

Number	Title (A Side/B Side)	Yr	VG	VG+	NM
45s					
AUDIO FIDELITY					
134	All You Need Is Love/The Windows of the World	1968	—	2.50	5.00
135	Mame/Cabaret	1968	—	2.50	5.00
148	Up-Up and Away/The Windows of the World	1968	—	2.50	5.00
EPIC					
9279	Lester Lanin Cha-Cha-Cha (And Medley)/Toreador Song	1958	2.50	5.00	10.00
9296	Over the Rainbow Cha-Cha-Cha/I Want My Mama	1958	2.50	5.00	10.00
9349	Winter Wonderland/Dance of the Sugar-Plum Fairies	1959	3.00	6.00	12.00
9350	Sleigh Ride/Christmas Carol Medley	1959	3.00	6.00	12.00
9396	Glow-Worm Cha Cha/Yellow Rose of Texas Meringue	1960	2.00	4.00	8.00
9426	Blue Tango Rock/This Could Be the Start of Something Big	1960	2.00	4.00	8.00
9444	The Bells/Bow and Arrow	1961	2.00	4.00	8.00
9482	Organ Twist/Sweet Georgia Brown	1961	2.00	4.00	8.00
9501	Russian Roulette/Twelfth Street Rag	1962	2.00	4.00	8.00
9514	Give Me a Song/You Can't Be True, Dear	1962	2.00	4.00	8.00
9571	Ballad of the Red River Valley/Tumbling Tumbleweeds	1963	2.00	4.00	8.00
9618	Theme from "The Seven Capital Sins"/Hora (Happiness)	1963	2.00	4.00	8.00
9624	Tamoure Shake/Theme from "The Seven Capital Sins"	1963	2.00	4.00	8.00
JZSP 123255/6 [DJ]	Winter Wonderland/Sleigh Ride	1967	2.00	4.00	8.00
JZSP 123257/8 [DJ]	Dance of the Sugar-Plum Fairies/Ring In the New	1967	2.00	4.00	8.00
JZSP 123259/60 [DJ]	Christmas Medley/Jingle Bells	1967	2.00	4.00	8.00
METROMEDIA					
118	Love Theme from Romeo and Juliet/Aquarius	1969	—	2.00	4.00
135	Ob-La-Di, Ob-La-Da/Dizzy	1969	—	2.00	4.00
PHILIPS					
40217	Down by the Riverside/West Indies Ska	1964	—	3.00	6.00
40344	Theme from "The Yearling"/Dancing Tambourines	1965	—	3.00	6.00
7-Inch Extended Plays					
EPIC					
EG 7184	*September Song/Marianne/Ballin' the Jack/Waltz from "Eugen Onegin"/Anything Goes/Love for Sale/Sunny/Greensleeves/At the Darktown Strutters' Ball	195?	2.50	5.00	10.00
EG 7184 [PS]	Dance to the Music of Lester Lanin, Volume 1	195?	2.50	5.00	10.00
EG 7203	*Laura/Deep Purple/Tin Roof Blues/After You've Gone/Do I Love You Because You're Beautiful/Hawaiian War Chant/It's Delovely/You're Sensational/Everything I've Got/Love Walked In/Charleston/Alexander's Ragtime Band	195?	2.50	5.00	10.00
EG 7203 [PS]	Lester Lanin Goes to College	195?	2.50	5.00	10.00
Albums					
AUDIO FIDELITY					
AFLP-2180 [M]	Thoroughly Modern	1968	3.75	7.50	15.00
AFSD-6180 [S]	Thoroughly Modern	1968	3.00	6.00	12.00
EPIC					
BSN 146 [(2) S]	The Dance Album	1964	5.00	10.00	20.00
BN 505 [S]	Lester Lanin at the Tiffany Ball	1959	5.00	10.00	20.00
BN 516 [S]	Cocktail Dancing	1959	5.00	10.00	20.00
BN 517 [S]	Have Band, Will Travel	1959	5.00	10.00	20.00
BN 556 [S]	Dance to the Lester Lanin Beat	1960	5.00	10.00	20.00
BN 570 [S]	High Society	1961	3.75	7.50	15.00
BN 620 [S]	Twistin' in High Society!	1961	3.75	7.50	15.00
BN 628 [R]	Lester Lanin and His Orchestra	1962	3.00	6.00	12.00
BN 633 [R]	Dance to the Music of Lester Lanin	1962	3.00	6.00	12.00
LN 3242 [M]	Lester Lanin and His Orchestra	1956	3.75	7.50	15.00
LN 3340 [M]	Dance to the Music of Lester Lanin	1957	3.75	7.50	15.00
LN 3410 [M]	Lester Lanin at the Tiffany Ball	1957	3.75	7.50	15.00
LN 3474 [M]	Lester Lanin Goes to College	1958	3.75	7.50	15.00
LN 3525 [M]	Have Band, Will Travel	1958	3.75	7.50	15.00
LN 3531 [M]	Cocktail Dancing	1959	3.75	7.50	15.00
LN 3617 [M]	Christmas Dance Party (Volume 9)	1959	3.75	7.50	15.00
LN 3656 [M]	Dance to the Lester Lanin Beat	1960	3.75	7.50	15.00
LN 3699 [M]	High Society	1961	3.00	6.00	12.00
LN 3825 [M]	Twistin' in High Society!	1961	3.00	6.00	12.00
SN 6046 [(2) M]	The Dance Album	1964	3.75	7.50	15.00
LN 24016 [M]	Dancing Theatre Party	1962	3.00	6.00	12.00
LN 24105 [M]	Richard Rogers Hits	1964	3.00	6.00	12.00
LN 24317 [M]	Cole Porter's Greatest Hits	1967	3.00	6.00	12.00
BN 26016 [S]	Dancing Theatre Party	1962	3.75	7.50	15.00
BN 26105 [S]	Richard Rogers Hits	1964	3.75	7.50	15.00
BN 26317 [S]	Cole Porter's Greatest Hits	1967	3.00	6.00	12.00
BN (# unknown) [S]	Christmas Dance Party (Volume 9)	1959	5.00	10.00	20.00
BN (# unknown) [S]	Lester Lanin Goes to College	1959	5.00	10.00	20.00
HARMONY					
HS 11262	Everybody Dance	1968	2.50	5.00	10.00
HINDSIGHT					
HSR-210	Dance Instrumentals: 1960-1962	198?	2.00	4.00	8.00
METROMEDIA					
MD-1006	Narrowing the Generation Gap	1969	3.00	6.00	12.00
PHILIPS					
PHM 200132 [M]	Lester Lanin Plays for Dancing	1964	2.50	5.00	10.00
PHM 200145 [M]	Dancing at the Discotheque	1964	2.50	5.00	10.00
PHM 200165 [M]	I Had a Ball	1965	2.50	5.00	10.00
PHM 200181 [M]	Hits for Dancing	1965	2.50	5.00	10.00
PHM 200192 [M]	Lester Lanin at the Country Club	1966	2.50	5.00	10.00
PHM 200211 [M]	Forty Beatles Hits	1966	3.00	6.00	12.00
PHS 600132 [S]	Lester Lanin Plays for Dancing	1964	3.00	6.00	12.00
PHS 600145 [S]	Dancing at the Discotheque	1964	3.00	6.00	12.00

Number	Title (A Side/B Side)	Yr	VG	VG+	NM
PHS 600165 [S]	I Had a Ball	1965	3.00	6.00	12.00
PHS 600181 [S]	Hits for Dancing	1965	3.00	6.00	12.00
PHS 600192 [S]	Lester Lanin at the Country Club	1966	3.00	6.00	12.00
PHS 600211 [S]	Forty Beatles Hits	1966	3.75	7.50	15.00

LANZA, MARIO

45s

RCA VICTOR

Number	Title (A Side/B Side)	Yr	VG	VG+	NM
WDM-1649 [(4)]	Sings Christmas Songs	195?	12.50	25.00	50.00
—4 records, all red vinyl, plus box					
WDM-1649 [(4)]	Sings Christmas Songs	195?	10.00	20.00	40.00
—4 records, all black vinyl, plus box					
47-6334	Ave Maria/I'll Walk with God	1955	3.75	7.50	15.00
47-6644	Earthbound/This Land	1956	3.00	6.00	12.00
47-6915	A Night to Remember/Behold	1957	3.00	6.00	12.00
47-7119	Come Dance with Me/Never Till Now	1957	3.00	6.00	12.00
47-7164	Arrivederci Roma/Younger Than Springtime	1958	3.00	6.00	12.00
47-7439	For the First Time/O Sole Mio	1959	3.00	6.00	12.00
47-7622	I'll Walk with God/Guardian Angels	1959	3.00	6.00	12.00
49-1353	Be My Love/I'll Never Love You	1950	6.25	12.50	25.00
—Red vinyl					
49-1353	Be My Love/I'll Never Love You	1951	5.00	10.00	20.00
—Black vinyl					
49-3207	Because/For You Alone	1951	5.00	10.00	20.00
—Red vinyl					
49-3228	Vesti La Giubba (On with the Play)/Ave Maria (Bach-Gounod)	1951	5.00	10.00	20.00
—Red vinyl					
49-3300	The Loveliest Night of the Year/La Donna E Mobile	1951	5.00	10.00	20.00
—Red vinyl					
49-3639	The Lord's Prayer/Guardian Angels	195?	3.00	6.00	12.00
—Side 1 and Side 8 of WDM-1649; red vinyl					
49-3639	The Lord's Prayer/Guardian Angels	195?	2.00	4.00	8.00
—Side 1 and Side 8 of WDM-1649; black vinyl					
49-3640	The First Noel/Silent Night	195?	2.00	4.00	8.00
—Side 2 and Side 7 of WDM-1649; black vinyl					
49-3640	The First Noel/Silent Night	195?	3.00	6.00	12.00
—Side 2 and Side 7 of WDM-1649; red vinyl					
49-3641	O Come, All Ye Faithful/Oh Little Town of Bethlehem	195?	3.00	6.00	12.00
—Side 3 and Side 6 of WDM-1649; red vinyl					
49-3641	O Come, All Ye Faithful/Oh Little Town of Bethlehem	195?	2.00	4.00	8.00
—Side 3 and Side 6 of WDM-1649; black vinyl					
49-3642	Away in a Manger/We Three Kings of Orient Are	195?	2.00	4.00	8.00
—Side 4 and Side 5 of WDM-1649; black vinyl					
49-3642	Away in a Manger/We Three Kings of Orient Are	195?	3.00	6.00	12.00
—Side 4 and Side 5 of WDM-1649; red vinyl					
49-3914	Because You're Mine/The Song Angels Sing	1952	3.75	7.50	15.00
—Red vinyl					
49-4209	Song of India/(B-side unknown)	1953	3.75	7.50	15.00
49-4218	Deep in My Heart, Dear/Serenade	1954	3.75	7.50	15.00
49-4220	Drink, Drink, Drink/(B-side unknown)	1954	3.75	7.50	15.00
447-0774	Ave Maria/The Lord's Prayer	196?	2.00	4.00	8.00
—Reissue; black label, dog on top					
447-0777	Oh, Holy Night/I'll Walk With God	196?	2.00	4.00	8.00
—Reissue; black label, dog on top					

7-Inch Extended Plays

RCA VICTOR

Number	Title (A Side/B Side)	Yr	VG	VG+	NM
ERA 51	Addio Alla Madre (Turiddu's Farewell)/Granada//Mama Mia Che Vo Sape?/The Lord's Prayer	195?	3.00	6.00	12.00
ERA 51 [PS]	(title unknown)	195?	3.00	6.00	12.00
ERA 110	Un Diall-Azzurro Spazio/Questa O Quella//Come Un Bel Di Di Maggio/La Donna E Mobile	195?	3.00	6.00	12.00
ERA 110 [PS]	Rigoletto	195?	3.00	6.00	12.00
ERA 115	O Come All Ye Faithful/Silent Night//We Three Kings Of Orient Are/The First Noel	195?	3.00	6.00	12.00
ERA 115 [PS]	Four Favorite Christmas Carols	195?	3.00	6.00	12.00
—Ornament-shaped sleeve					
LPC-117	Deep in My Heart, Dear/Gaudeamus Igitur//Serenade/Drink, Drink, Drink	1961	3.75	7.50	15.00
—33 1/3 rpm, small hole					
LPC-117 [PS]	The Student Prince	1961	3.75	7.50	15.00
ERA 130	I Know, I Know, I Know/Be My Love//The Loveliest Night of the Year/Because You're Mine	195?	3.00	6.00	12.00
ERA 130 [PS]	Mario Lanza In Movie Hits	195?	3.00	6.00	12.00
ERA 222	Because/Vesta La Giubba//Core 'Ingrato/Toselli's Serenade	1954	3.00	6.00	12.00
ERA 222 [PS]	Mario Lanza Sings Because	1954	3.00	6.00	12.00
ERB 1860 [PS]	A Kiss and Other Love Songs	1955	3.00	6.00	12.00
EPA-4222	*Seven Hills of Rome/Arrivederci Roman/Come Dance with Me/Lolita	1958	3.00	6.00	12.00
EPA-4222 [PS]	Seven Hills of Rome	1958	3.00	6.00	12.00
EPA-4344	*Come Prima/Pineapple Pickers/O, Mon Amour/O Sole Mio/Hofbrauhaus Song	1959	3.00	6.00	12.00
EPA-4344 [PS]	For the First Time	1959	3.00	6.00	12.00
549-5127	A Kiss/Begin the Beguine//My Romance/Night and Day	195?	3.00	6.00	12.00
—Record 1 of 2-EP set ERB 1860					
549-5128	Long Ago/The Night Is Young and You're So Beautiful//My Heart Stood Still/The Moon Was Yellow	195?	3.00	6.00	12.00
—Record 1 of 2-EP set ERB 1860					

Albums

Number	Title (A Side/B Side)	Yr	VG	VG+	NM
PAIR					
PDL2-1059 [(2)]	The Voice of the Century	1986	3.00	6.00	12.00
PICKWICK					
CAS-777(e) [R]	Christmas Hymns and Carols	1977	2.00	4.00	8.00
—Same contents as RCA Camden CAS-777(e)					
RCA CAMDEN					
CAL-450 [M]	You Do Something to Me	195?	3.75	7.50	15.00
CAS-450(e) [R]	You Do Something to Me	195?	3.00	6.00	12.00
CAL-777 [M]	Christmas Hymns and Carols	196?	3.75	7.50	15.00
CAS-777(e) [R]	Christmas Hymns and Carols	196?	3.00	6.00	12.00
RCA RED SEAL					
ARL1-0134	Lanza Sings Caruso	1973	2.50	5.00	10.00
CRL1-1750	A Legendary Performer	1976	2.50	5.00	10.00
ANL1-2874	Pure Gold	1978	2.50	5.00	10.00
CRM5-4158 [(5)]	The Mario Lanza Collection	1981	15.00	30.00	60.00
ARL1-4405	The Great Caruso	198?	2.00	4.00	8.00
VCS-6192 [(3)]	Mario Lanza's Greatest Hits	1970	6.25	12.50	25.00
VCS-7073 [(2)]	Opera's Greatest Hits	1971	4.50	9.00	18.00
RCA VICTOR RED SEAL					
LM-1127 [M]	The Great Caruso	195?	10.00	20.00	40.00
LSC-1127(e) [R]	The Great Caruso	196?	3.00	6.00	12.00
LM-1188 [M]	Love Songs and a Neapolitan Serenade	195?	10.00	20.00	40.00
LSC-1188(e) [R]	Love Songs and a Neapolitan Serenade	196?	3.00	6.00	12.00
LM-1860 [M]	"A Kiss" and Other Love Songs	1955	10.00	20.00	40.00
LSC-1860(e) [R]	"A Kiss" and Other Love Songs	196?	3.00	6.00	12.00
LM-1927 [M]	The Touch of Your Hand	1955	10.00	20.00	40.00
LSC-1927(e) [R]	The Touch of Your Hand	196?	3.00	6.00	12.00
LM-1943 [M]	Magic Mario	1955	10.00	20.00	40.00
LM-1996 [M]	Serenade	1956	10.00	20.00	40.00
LM-2070 [M]	Lanza on Broadway	1956	7.50	15.00	30.00
LSC-2070(e) [R]	Lanza on Broadway	196?	3.00	6.00	12.00
LM-2090 [M]	Cavalcade of Show Tunes	1957	7.50	15.00	30.00
LSC-2090(e) [R]	Cavalcade of Show Tunes	196?	3.00	6.00	12.00
LM-2211 [M]	Seven Hills of Rome	1958	7.50	15.00	30.00
LM-2331 [M]	Mario	1959	5.00	10.00	20.00
LSC-2331 [S]	Mario!	1959	7.50	15.00	30.00
LM-2333 [M]	Lanza Sings Christmas Carols	1959	3.75	7.50	15.00
LSC-2333 [S]	Lanza Sings Christmas Carols	1959	5.00	10.00	20.00
—Original copies have "shaded dog" on labels					
LM-2338 [M]	For the First Time	1959	3.75	7.50	15.00
LSC-2338 [S]	For the First Time	1959	5.00	10.00	20.00
LM-2339 [M]	The Student Prince	1959	3.75	7.50	15.00
LSC-2339 [S]	The Student Prince	1959	5.00	10.00	20.00
LM-2393 [M]	Mario Lanza Sings Caruso Favorites	1960	3.75	7.50	15.00
LSC-2393 [S]	Mario Lanza Sings Caruso Favorites	1960	5.00	10.00	20.00
LM-2422 [M]	Double Feature — Mario Lanza	1960	5.00	10.00	20.00
LM-2454 [M]	A Mario Lanza Program	1960	3.75	7.50	15.00
LSC-2454 [S]	A Mario Lanza Program	1960	5.00	10.00	20.00
LM-2509 [M]	The Vagabond King	1961	3.75	7.50	15.00
LSC-2509 [S]	The Vagabond King	1961	5.00	10.00	20.00
LM-2607 [M]	I'll Walk with God	1962	5.00	10.00	20.00
LSC-2607(e) [R]	I'll Walk with God	1962	3.00	6.00	12.00
LM-2720 [M]	I'll See You in My Dreams	1964	3.00	6.00	12.00
LSC-2720 [S]	I'll See You in My Dreams	1964	3.75	7.50	15.00
LM-2748 [M]	The Best of Mario Lanza	1964	3.00	6.00	12.00
LSC-2748 [S]	The Best of Mario Lanza	1964	3.75	7.50	15.00
LM-2790 [M]	If You Are But a Dream	196?	3.00	6.00	12.00
LSC-2790 [S]	If You Are But a Dream	196?	3.75	7.50	15.00
LM-2932 [M]	His Favorite Arias	196?	3.00	6.00	12.00
LSC-2932 [S]	His Favorite Arias	196?	3.75	7.50	15.00
LM-2998 [M]	The Best of Mario Lanza, Volume 2	1968	5.00	10.00	20.00
LSC-2998 [S]	The Best of Mario Lanza, Volume 2	1968	3.75	7.50	15.00
LSC-3049	Younger Than Springtime	1968	3.00	6.00	12.00
LSC-3101	Mario Lanza in Opera	1969	3.75	7.50	15.00
LSC-3102	Mario Lanza Memories	1969	3.75	7.50	15.00
LSC-3103	Mario Lanza…Speak to Me of Love	1969	3.75	7.50	15.00
LSC-3216	The Student Prince	1971	3.00	6.00	12.00
LSC-3289	Be My Love	1972	3.00	6.00	12.00

LAPELS, THE

45s

Number	Title (A Side/B Side)	Yr	VG	VG+	NM
DOT					
16129	Sneakin' Around/Sneakin' Blues	1960	3.00	6.00	12.00
MELKER					
103	Sneakin' Around/Sneakin' Blues	1960	10.00	20.00	40.00

LARADOS, THE

Members of this group were later in THE REFLECTIONS.

45s

Number	Title (A Side/B Side)	Yr	VG	VG+	NM
FOX					
962/3	Now the Parting Begins/Bad Guitar Man	1958	50.00	100.00	200.00
MADOG					
801	Will You Love Me Tomorrow/You Didn't Care	1980	3.75	7.50	15.00

LARKIN, BILLY

Includes The Delegates; Billy Larkin and the Delegates.

45s

Number	Title (A Side/B Side)	Yr	VG	VG+	NM
AURA					
4504	Pigmy (Part 1)/Pigmy (Part 2)	1965	3.75	7.50	15.00
—As "The Delegates"					
4508	The Peeper/Hainty	1965	3.75	7.50	15.00
—As "The Delegates"					
CASINO					
097	Here's to the Next Time/Lonely Woman	1975	—	2.00	4.00
SUNBIRD					
107	I Can't Stop Now/(B-side unknown)	1980	—	2.00	4.00
7557	20-20 Hindsight/Lonely Woman	1981	—	2.00	4.00
7562	Longing for the High/Is There Nothing Left to Say	1981	—	2.00	4.00
WORLD PACIFIC					
4504	Pigmy (Part 1)/Pigmy (Part 2)	1965	3.00	6.00	12.00
—As "The Delegates"					
77844	Hold On! I'm a-Comin'/Dirty Water	1966	2.00	4.00	8.00
88120	Pigmy (Part 1)/The Peeper	1966	2.50	5.00	10.00
—As "The Delegates"					

Albums

Number	Title (A Side/B Side)	Yr	VG	VG+	NM
AURA					
23002 [S]	Pigmy	1964	6.25	12.50	25.00
—As "The Delegates"					
ARS 23003 [S]	Blue Lights	196?	6.25	12.50	25.00
83002 [M]	Pigmy	1964	5.00	10.00	20.00
—As "The Delegates"					
AR 83003 [M]	Blue Lights	196?	5.00	10.00	20.00

Number	Title (A Side/B Side)	Yr	VG	VG+	NM
WORLD PACIFIC					
WP-1837 [M]	Hole in the Wall	1966	5.00	10.00	20.00
—Also see THE DELEGATES.					
WP-1843 [M]	Ain't That a Groove	1966	5.00	10.00	20.00
WP-1850 [M]	Hold On	1967	5.00	10.00	20.00
WPS-21837 [S]	Hole in the Wall	1966	6.25	12.50	25.00
WPS-21843 [S]	Ain't That a Groove	1966	6.25	12.50	25.00
WPS-21850 [S]	Hold On	1967	6.25	12.50	25.00

LARKS, THE (1)

Also see DON JULIAN AND THE MEADOWLARKS.

Number	Title (A Side/B Side)	Yr	VG	VG+	NM
45s					
MONEY					
106	The Jerk/Forget Me	1964	5.00	10.00	20.00
109	Mickey's East Coast Jerk/Soul Jerk	1965	3.00	6.00	12.00
110	The Slauson Shuffle/Soul Jerk	1965	3.00	6.00	12.00
112	The Roman/Heavenly Father	1965	3.00	6.00	12.00
115	Can You Do the Duck/Sad Sad Boy	1965	3.00	6.00	12.00
119	Lost My Love Yesterday/The Answer Came Too Late	1966	3.00	6.00	12.00
122	Philly Dog/Heaven Only Knows	1966	3.00	6.00	12.00
127	The Skate/Come Back Baby	1967	3.00	6.00	12.00
601	I Love You/I Want You Back	1973	—	3.00	6.00
604	My Favorite Beer Joint/(Instrumental)	1973	—	3.00	6.00
607	Shorty the Pimp (Part 1)/Shorty the Pimp (Part 2)	1974	—	3.00	6.00
—Money 604 and 607 as "Don Julian and the Larks"					
Albums					
COLLECTABLES					
COL-5176	Golden Classics: The Jerk	198?	2.50	5.00	10.00
MONEY					
LP-1102 [M]	The Jerk	1965	10.00	20.00	40.00
ST-1102 [S]	The Jerk	1965	12.50	25.00	50.00
LP-1107 [M]	Soul Kaleidoscope	1966	10.00	20.00	40.00
ST-1107 [S]	Soul Kaleidoscope	1966	12.50	25.00	50.00
LP-1110 [M]	Superslick	1967	10.00	20.00	40.00
ST-1110 [S]	Superslick	1967	12.50	25.00	50.00

LARKS, THE (2)

Number	Title (A Side/B Side)	Yr	VG	VG+	NM
45s					
SHERYL					
334	It's Unbelievable/I Can't Believe It	1961	7.50	15.00	30.00
338	There Is a Girl/Let's Drink a Toast	1961	6.25	12.50	25.00

LARKS, THE (3)

Number	Title (A Side/B Side)	Yr	VG	VG+	NM
45s					
APOLLO					
429	Little Side Car/Hey Little Girl	1951	1000.	2000.	4000.
430	Ooh, It Feels So Good/I Don't Believe in Tomorrow	1951	1000.	2000.	4000.
435	My Lost Love/How Long Must I Wait for You	1952	250.00	500.00	1000.
437	Darlin'/Lucy Brown	1952	250.00	500.00	1000.
475	No Mama No/Honey from the Bee	1955	100.00	200.00	400.00
1180	Hopefully Yours/When I Leave These Prison Walls	1951	1000.	2000.	4000.
1184	My Reverie/Let's Say a Prayer	1951	500.00	1000.	2000.
—Black vinyl					
1184	My Reverie/Let's Say a Prayer	1951	4000.	6000.	8000.
—Red vinyl					
1189	Shadrack/Honey in the Rock	1952	500.00	1000.	2000.
1190	Stolen Love/In My Lonely Room	1952	625.00	1250.	2500.
—Black vinyl					
1190	Stolen Love/In My Lonely Room	1952	2500.	3750.	5000.
—Red vinyl					
1194	I Live True to You/Hold Me	1952	250.00	500.00	1000.
LLOYDS					
108	Margie/Rockin' in the Rockin' Room	1954	200.00	400.00	800.00
110	Tippin' In/If It's a Crime	1954	200.00	400.00	800.00
112	No Other Girl/The World Is Waiting for the Sunrise	1954	200.00	400.00	800.00
114	Forget It/I Live True to You	1954	150.00	300.00	600.00

LARKS, THE (U)

It's doubtful that any of these are groups (1) or (3). Some could be by group (2).

Number	Title (A Side/B Side)	Yr	VG	VG+	NM
45s					
CROSS FIRE					
74-49/50	Fabulous Cars and Diamond Rings/Life Is Sweeter Now	1961	5.00	10.00	20.00
GUYDEN					
2098	I Want Her to Love Me/(Instrumental)	1963	3.00	6.00	12.00
2103	Fabulous Cars and Diamond Rings/Life Is Sweeter Now	1964	3.00	6.00	12.00
JETT					
3001	Love You So/Love Me True	1965	15.00	30.00	60.00
NASCO					
028	I Love You/I Want You Back	1972	2.00	4.00	8.00
STACY					
969	Food Sticks/Scavenger	1963	3.00	6.00	12.00
VIOLET					
1051	I Want Her to Love Me/(Instrumental)	1962	5.00	10.00	20.00

LARKTONES, THE

Number	Title (A Side/B Side)	Yr	VG	VG+	NM
45s					
ABC-PARAMOUNT					
9909	The Letter/Rockin' Swingin' Man	1958	7.50	15.00	30.00
RIKI					
140	Why Are You Tearing Us Apart/Nosy Neighbor	1960	15.00	30.00	60.00

LAROSA, JULIUS

Number	Title (A Side/B Side)	Yr	VG	VG+	NM
45s					
ABC					
10959	For Once in My Life/Summer Love	1967	—	3.00	6.00
CADENCE					
1230	Anywhere I Wander/This Is Heaven	1953	3.75	7.50	15.00
1231	My Lady Loves to Dance/Let's Make Up Before We Say Goodnight	1953	3.75	7.50	15.00
1232	Eh, Cumpari/Till They're All Gone Home	1953	3.75	7.50	15.00
1235	The Big Bell and the Little Bell/I Couldn't Believe My Eyes	1954	3.00	6.00	12.00
1236	My Funny Valentine/Roseanne	1954	3.00	6.00	12.00
1237	When You're in Love/Have a Heart	1954	3.00	6.00	12.00
1240	Three Coins in the Fountain/Me Gotta Have You	1954	3.00	6.00	12.00
1244	My Heart's on a Fast Express/In My Own Quiet Way	1954	3.00	6.00	12.00
1251	Mobile/I Hate to Say Hello	1954	3.00	6.00	12.00
1252	Campanelle (Jingle Bells)/I Hope You'll Be Very Happy	1954	3.00	6.00	12.00
1253	Jingle Dingle/Campanelle (Jingle Bells)	1954	3.00	6.00	12.00
1258	Let's Stay Home Tonight/Pass It On	1955	3.00	6.00	12.00
1265	Domani (Tomorrow)/Mama Rosa	1955	3.00	6.00	12.00
1270	Suddenly There's a Valley/Everytime That I Kiss Carrie	1955	3.00	6.00	12.00
1440	David and Lisa's Love Song/Suddenly There's a Valley	1963	2.00	4.00	8.00
1444	Gonna Build a Mountain/JE	1964	2.00	4.00	8.00
GP					
592	A Christmas Gift/To Find Our Children	1981	—	3.00	6.00
KAPP					
323	Green Fields/Your Hand in Mine	1960	2.00	4.00	8.00
348	Bewitched/It's Alright with Me	1960	2.00	4.00	8.00
371	Let Your Lips Tell Me/Seventeen	1961	2.00	4.00	8.00
417	There's No Other Love/Caress Me	1961	2.00	4.00	8.00
444	You Can't Keep Me from Loving You/If I Had My Way	1962	2.00	4.00	8.00
METROMEDIA					
186	Brooklyn Roads/Being Alive	1970	—	2.50	5.00
MGM					
CS5-5	Celebrity Scene: Julius LaRosa	1967	12.50	25.00	50.00
—Box set of five singles (13671-13675). Price includes box, all 5 singles, jukebox title strips, bio. Records are sometimes found by themselves, so they are also listed separately.					
13454	Small, Small World/Unless	1966	—	3.00	6.00
13497	Lonely As I Leave You/You're Gonna Hear from Me	1966	—	3.00	6.00
13575	I Think It's Going to Rain Today/You Only See Her	1966	—	3.00	6.00
13651	We Need A Little Christmas/Our Venetian Affair	1966	2.00	4.00	8.00
13671	(titles unknown)	1967	2.00	4.00	8.00
13672	Somethin' Special/You're Gonna Hear from Me	1967	2.00	4.00	8.00
13673	(titles unknown)	1967	2.00	4.00	8.00
13674	What Did I Have That I Don't Have/Spring	1967	2.00	4.00	8.00
13675	Who Am I/What'll I Do	1967	2.00	4.00	8.00
RCA VICTOR					
47-6416	Lipstick and Candy and Rubber Sole Shoes/Winter in New England	1956	2.50	5.00	10.00
47-6499	I've Got Love/Augustine	1956	2.50	5.00	10.00
47-6567	Get Me to the Church On Time/I've Grown Accustomed to Her Face	1956	2.50	5.00	10.00
47-6648	The Opposite Sex/Namely You	1956	2.50	5.00	10.00
47-6700	All I Want/Priscilla	1956	2.50	5.00	10.00
47-6802	Jeanette/Stashu Pandowski	1957	2.50	5.00	10.00
47-6878	Mama Guitar/Man to Man	1957	2.50	5.00	10.00
47-6923	Crying My Heart Out for You/When You're With the One You Love	1957	2.50	5.00	10.00
47-6998	Worlds Apart/Famous Last Words	1957	2.50	5.00	10.00
47-7059	Just Forever/Since When (Is It a Sin)	1957	2.50	5.00	10.00
47-7186	Lover, Lover/A Heart for a Heart	1958	2.50	5.00	10.00
47-7227	Torero/Milano	1958	2.50	5.00	10.00
74-0938	The Good Life/Sing Me a Song	1973	—	2.50	5.00
ROULETTE					
4135	Where's the Girl/Protect Me	1959	2.50	5.00	10.00
4162	Honey Bunch/Port of Love	1959	2.50	5.00	10.00
7-Inch Extended Plays					
CADENCE					
EP 1233	No Other Love/I Believe//My Funny Valentine/Roseanne	1953	3.75	7.50	15.00
EP 1233 [PS]	(title unknown)	1953	3.75	7.50	15.00
EP 1234	Ave Maria/Adeste Fideles//Silent Night/Oh Holy Night	1953	3.75	7.50	15.00
EP 1234 [PS]	Julius LaRosa Sings…	1953	3.75	7.50	15.00
RCA VICTOR					
EPA 841	(contents unknown)	1956	3.75	7.50	15.00
EPA 841 [PS]	Julius LaRosa	1956	3.75	7.50	15.00
Albums					
AUDIOPHILE					
AP-190	It's a Wrap!	1985	3.00	6.00	12.00
CADENCE					
CLP 1007 [M]	Julius LaRosa (Julie's Best)	1955	10.00	20.00	40.00
FORUM					
F-16012 [M]	Just Say I Love Her	1960	3.75	7.50	15.00
FS-16012 [S]	Just Say I Love Her	1960	5.00	10.00	20.00
KAPP					
KL-1245 [M]	The New Julie LaRosa	1961	3.75	7.50	15.00
KS-3245 [S]	The New Julie LaRosa	1961	5.00	10.00	20.00
METROMEDIA					
MD-1036	Words	1971	3.00	6.00	12.00
MGM					
E-4398 [M]	You're Gonna Hear from Me	1966	3.00	6.00	12.00
SE-4398 [S]	You're Gonna Hear from Me	1966	3.75	7.50	15.00
E-4437 [M]	Hey Look Me Over	1967	3.00	6.00	12.00
SE-4437 [S]	Hey Look Me Over	1967	3.75	7.50	15.00
RCA VICTOR					
LPM-1299 [M]	Julius LaRosa	1956	10.00	20.00	40.00
ROULETTE					
R 25054 [M]	Love Songs A LaRosa	1959	5.00	10.00	20.00
SR 25054 [S]	Love Songs A LaRosa	1959	6.25	12.50	25.00
R 25083 [M]	On the Sunny Side	1960	5.00	10.00	20.00
SR 25083 [S]	On the Sunny Side	1960	6.25	12.50	25.00

LARRY AND THE CROSSFIRES

Number	Title (A Side/B Side)	Yr	VG	VG+	NM
45s					
SEARCY					
711	Torquay '65/Wee Wee Hours	1965	12.50	25.00	50.00

LARRY AND THE LEGENDS

Number	Title (A Side/B Side)	Yr	VG	VG+	NM
45s					
ATLANTIC					
2220	Don't Pick On My Baby/The Creep	1964	6.25	12.50	25.00
—With the Four Seasons					

LASALLE, DENISE

Number	Title (A Side/B Side)	Yr	VG	VG+	NM
45s					
ABC					
12225	Hellfire Loving/I Get What I Want	1976	—	2.50	5.00
12238	Freedom to Express Yourself/Second Breath	1977	—	2.00	4.00
12312	Love Me Right/Fool Me Good	1977	—	2.00	4.00
12353	One Life to Live/Before You Take It to the Streets	1978	—	2.00	4.00
12419	Workin' Overtime/No Matter What They Say	1978	—	2.00	4.00
12443	P.A.R.T.Y. (Where It Is)/Under the Influence	1979	—	2.00	4.00
CHESS					
2005	A Love Reputation/One Little Thing	1967	2.50	5.00	10.00
2044	Private Property/I've Been Waiting	1968	2.50	5.00	10.00
2058	Count Down (And Fly Me to the Moon)/A Promise Is a Promise	1968	2.50	5.00	10.00
MALACO					
2089	Lady in the Street/I Was Not the Best Woman	198?	—	2.00	4.00
2092	Lay Me Down/I Was Telling Him About You	198?	—	2.00	4.00
2095	Down Home Blues/Down Home Blues (X-Rated)	198?	—	2.00	4.00
2098	Right Place, Right Time/He's Not Available	1984	—	2.00	4.00
—With Latimore					
2105	Treat Your Man Like a Baby/Come to Bed	1985	—	2.00	4.00
2112	My Tu-Tu/Give Me Yo' Strongest Whiskey	1985	—	2.00	4.00
2124	Santa Claus Got the Blues/Love Is a Five Letter Word	1985	—	2.50	5.00
2131	What's Going On in My House/He's That Way Sometime	1986	—	2.00	4.00
2138	Hold What You Got/Footsteps of a Fool	1986	—	2.00	4.00
2152	Bring It On Home to Me/Write This One Off (As Actors)	1987	—	2.00	4.00
2156	Caught in Your Mess/I Forgot to Remember	1987	—	2.00	4.00
2167	Drop That Zero/Chain Letter	1988	—	2.00	4.00
MCA					
41222	I'm So Hot/Miracle, You and Me	1980	—	2.00	4.00
51046	I'm Trippin' on You/I'll Get You Some Help	1981	—	2.00	4.00
51098	Sharing Your Love/I'll Get You Some Help	1981	—	2.00	4.00
TARPEN					
6603	A Love Reputation/One Little Thing	1967	6.25	12.50	25.00
WESTBOUND					
162	Heartbreaker of the Year/Hung Up, Strung Out	1971	2.00	4.00	8.00
182	Trapped by a Thing Called Love/Keep It Coming	1971	—	3.00	6.00
201	Now Run and Tell That/The Deeper I Go	1972	—	3.00	6.00
206	Man Sized Job/I'm Over You	1972	—	3.00	6.00
215	What It Takes to Get a Good Woman (That's What It's Gonna Take to Keep Her)/Making a Good Thing Better	1973	—	3.00	6.00
219	Your Man and Your Best Friend/What Am I Doing Wrong	1973	—	3.00	6.00
221	Don't Nobody Live Here (By the Name of Fool)/Goody Goody Getter	1973	—	3.00	6.00
223	Get Up Off My Mind/The Best Thing I Ever Had	1974	—	3.00	6.00
229	Trying to Forget/We've Got Love	1974	—	3.00	6.00
5004	My Brand on You/Anytime Is the Right Time	1975	—	2.50	5.00
5008	Here I Am Again/Hung Up, Strung Out	1975	—	2.50	5.00
5019	Married, But Not to Each Other/Who's the Fool	1976	—	2.50	5.00
Albums					
ABC					
D-966	Second Breath	1976	3.00	6.00	12.00
D-1027	The Bitch Is Bad	1977	3.00	6.00	12.00
AA-1087	Under the Influence	1978	3.00	6.00	12.00
MALACO					
7412	A Lady in the Street	198?	2.50	5.00	10.00
7417	Right Place, Right Time	1984	2.50	5.00	10.00
7422	Love Talkin'	198?	2.50	5.00	10.00
7434	Rain and Fire	198?	2.50	5.00	10.00
7441	It's Lying Time Again	198?	2.50	5.00	10.00
7447	Hittin' Where It Hurts	198?	2.50	5.00	10.00
7454	Still Trapped	198?	2.50	5.00	10.00
7464	Love Me Right	198?	2.50	5.00	10.00
MCA					
759	Unwrapped	198?	2.00	4.00	8.00
—Reissue of 3089					
760	I'm So Hot	198?	2.00	4.00	8.00
—Reissue of 3239					
3089	Unwrapped	1979	2.50	5.00	10.00
3239	I'm So Hot	1980	2.50	5.00	10.00
WESTBOUND					
209	Here I Am Again	1975	3.00	6.00	12.00
2012	Trapped by a Thing Called Love	1972	3.75	7.50	15.00
2016	On the Loose	1973	3.75	7.50	15.00

LAST, JAMES

Number	Title (A Side/B Side)	Yr	VG	VG+	NM
45s					
MGM					
13599	Lara's Theme/Games That Lovers Play	1966	2.50	5.00	10.00
POLYDOR					
2071	The Seduction (Love Theme)/Night Drive	1980	—	—	3.00
2108	Fantasy/Last Glow	1980	—	—	3.00
2119	So Excited/Last Glow	1980	—	—	3.00
15004	Happy Heart/A Man and a Woman	1969	—	2.00	4.00
15017	Proud Mary/Washington Square	1970	—	2.00	4.00
15024	Girl of the North Country/The Party Is Over	1971	—	2.00	4.00
15028	Music from Across the Way/Endless Journey	1971	—	2.00	4.00
15045	Wedding Song (There Is Love)/Love Must Be the Reason	1972	—	2.00	4.00
15050	Heart of Gold/It's Going to Take Some Time	1972	—	2.00	4.00
15082	Jenny Jenny/But I Can Sleep in a Park	1973	—	2.00	4.00
15108	Summertime/Love for Sale	1975	—	2.00	4.00
15115	Theme from Prisoner of Second Avenue/Jubilation	197?	—	2.00	4.00
Albums					
POLYDOR					
24-4512	Good Times	1971	3.00	6.00	12.00
PD-5505	Music from Across the Way	1972	2.50	5.00	10.00
PD-5506	The Love Album	197?	2.50	5.00	10.00
PD-5512	Love Must Be the Reason	1972	2.50	5.00	10.00
PD-5534	Non Stop Dancing	1973	2.50	5.00	10.00
PD-5538	M.O.R.	1973	2.50	5.00	10.00
24-6004	Hair	1969	3.00	6.00	12.00
PD-6040	Well Kept Secret	1975	2.50	5.00	10.00
PD-1-6283	Seduction	1980	2.50	5.00	10.00
24-	Classics Up to Date	1970	3.00	6.00	12.00
24-	Soft Rock	1970	3.00	6.00	12.00
24-	El Condor Pasa	1971	3.00	6.00	12.00

LAST CALL OF SHILOH, THE

Number	Title (A Side/B Side)	Yr	VG	VG+	NM
Albums					
LAST CALL					
5136	The Last Call	196?	50.00	100.00	200.00

LAST POETS, THE

Number	Title (A Side/B Side)	Yr	VG	VG+	NM
45s					
BLUE THUMB					
216	Tribute to Orabi/Bird's Word	1972	3.00	6.00	12.00
DOUGLAS					
ADS 8	O.D./Black Thighs	1971	3.75	7.50	15.00
ADS 8 [PS]	O.D./Black Thighs	1971	7.50	15.00	30.00
Albums					
BLUE THUMB					
BT-39	Chastisement	1972	7.50	15.00	30.00
BT-52	At Last	1973	7.50	15.00	30.00
CASABLANCA					
NBLP 7051	Delights of the Garden	1977	6.25	12.50	25.00
CELLULOID					
6101	The Last Poets	198?	2.50	5.00	10.00
6105	This Is Madness	198?	2.50	5.00	10.00
6108	Oh My People	198?	2.50	5.00	10.00
6136	Delights of the Garden	198?	2.50	5.00	10.00
COLLECTABLES					
COL-6500	Right On!	198?	2.50	5.00	10.00
DOUGLAS					
3	The Last Poets	1970	12.50	25.00	50.00
Z 30583	This Is Madness	1971	12.50	25.00	50.00
Z 30811	The Last Poets	1971	10.00	20.00	40.00
JUGGERNAUT					
8802	Right On!	1971	12.50	25.00	50.00
—As "The Original Last Poets"					

LATEEF, YUSEF

Number	Title (A Side/B Side)	Yr	VG	VG+	NM
45s					
ARGO					
5292	Cookin'/Marching Piper Blues	1958	3.00	6.00	12.00
ATLANTIC					
2562	Othelia/Stay with Me	1968	—	3.00	6.00
2641	Raymond Winchester/Bishop's School	1969	—	3.00	6.00
2997	Superfine/Down in Atlanta	1973	—	2.50	5.00
5104	Buddy and Lou/Russell and Elliott	1971	—	2.50	5.00
5114	Nubian Lady/Below Yellow Bell	1972	—	2.50	5.00
IMPULSE!					
223	Theme from "The Prize"/Megeve	1963	2.00	4.00	8.00
225	Trouble in Mind/Yusef's French Brother	196?	2.00	4.00	8.00
233	Sister Mamie (Part 1)/Sister Mamie (Part 2)	196?	2.00	4.00	8.00
NEW JAZZ					
45-506	Yesterdays/Dopolous	196?	2.00	4.00	8.00
PRESTIGE					
127	Love and Humor/Meditation	1957	3.00	6.00	12.00
254	Love Theme from "Spartacus"/Snafu	1960	2.50	5.00	10.00
332	Blues for the Orient/I'll Remember April	1964	2.00	4.00	8.00
419	Love Theme from "Spartacus"/Sea Breeze	196?	2.00	4.00	8.00
RIVERSIDE					
445	Goin' Home/Salt Water Blues	1960	2.50	5.00	10.00
4504	Jungle Fantasy/Titoro	1961	2.50	5.00	10.00
Albums					
ABC IMPULSE!					
AS-56 [S]	Jazz Around the World	1968	3.00	6.00	12.00
AS-69 [S]	Live at Pep's	1968	3.00	6.00	12.00
AS-84 [S]	1984	1968	3.00	6.00	12.00
AS-92 [S]	Psychicemotus	1968	3.00	6.00	12.00
AS-9117 [S]	A Flat, G Flat and C	1968	3.00	6.00	12.00
AS-9125 [S]	The Golden Flute	1968	3.00	6.00	12.00
AS-9259 [(2)]	Re-evaluations: The Impulse Years	1974	3.75	7.50	15.00
AS-9310	Club Date	197?	3.00	6.00	12.00
IA-9353 [(2)]	Yusef Lateef Live!	1978	3.75	7.50	15.00
ARCHIVE OF FOLK AND JAZZ					
285	Yusef Lateef	197?	2.50	5.00	10.00
ARGO					
LP-634 [M]	Live at Cranbrook	1959	7.50	15.00	30.00
ATLANTIC					
SD 2-1000 [(2)]	10 Years	1977	3.75	7.50	15.00
SD 1499	The Complete Lateef	1968	3.75	7.50	15.00
SD 1508	The Blue Lateef	1969	3.75	7.50	15.00
SD 1525	Yusef Lateef's Detroit	1969	3.75	7.50	15.00
SD 1548	The Diverse Lateef	1971	3.75	7.50	15.00

Number	Title (A Side/B Side)	Yr	VG	VG+	NM
SD 1563	Suite 16	1970	3.75	7.50	15.00
SD 1591	The Best of Yusef Lateef	1971	3.75	7.50	15.00
SD 1602	Gentle Giant	1972	3.00	6.00	12.00
SD 1635	Hush 'n' Thunder	1973	3.00	6.00	12.00
SD 1650	Part of the Search	1974	3.00	6.00	12.00
SD 1685	The Doctor Is In... And Out	1976	3.00	6.00	12.00
81663	Concerto for Yusef Lateef	1988	2.50	5.00	10.00
CADET					
LP-634 [M]	Live at Cranbrook	1966	3.75	7.50	15.00
LPS-816	Live at Cranbrook	1969	3.00	6.00	12.00
CHARLIE PARKER					
PLP-814S [S]	Lost in Sound	1962	7.50	15.00	30.00
PLP-814 [M]	Lost in Sound	1962	6.25	12.50	25.00
CTI					
7082	Autophysiopsychic	1978	3.00	6.00	12.00
7088	In a Temple Garden	1979	3.00	6.00	12.00
DELMARK					
DL-407 [M]	Yusef!	1965	5.00	10.00	20.00
DS-407 [S]	Yusef!	1965	6.25	12.50	25.00
FANTASY					
OJC-399	Other Sounds	1989	2.50	5.00	10.00
OJC-482	Cry! Tender	1991	3.00	6.00	12.00
OJC-612	Eastern Sounds	1991	3.00	6.00	12.00
IMPULSE!					
A-56 [M]	Jazz Around the World	1963	6.25	12.50	25.00
AS-56 [S]	Jazz Around the World	1963	7.50	15.00	30.00
A-69 [M]	Live at Pep's	1964	6.25	12.50	25.00
AS-69 [S]	Live at Pep's	1964	7.50	15.00	30.00
A-84 [M]	1984	1965	6.25	12.50	25.00
AS-84 [S]	1984	1965	7.50	15.00	30.00
A-92 [M]	Psychicemotus	1966	6.25	12.50	25.00
AS-92 [S]	Psychicemotus	1966	7.50	15.00	30.00
A-9117 [M]	A Flat, G Flat and C	1966	6.25	12.50	25.00
AS-9117 [S]	A Flat, G Flat and C	1966	7.50	15.00	30.00
A-9125 [M]	The Golden Flute	1966	6.25	12.50	25.00
AS-9125 [S]	The Golden Flute	1966	7.50	15.00	30.00
LANDMARK					
LLP-502	Yusef Lateef in Nigeria	1985	2.50	5.00	10.00
MCA					
4146 [(2)]	Live Session	198?	3.00	6.00	12.00
MILESTONE					
47009 [(2)]	The Many Faces of Yusef Lateef	1973	3.75	7.50	15.00
MOODSVILLE					
MVLP-22 [M]	Eastern Sounds	1961	10.00	20.00	40.00
—Green label, silver print					
MVST-22 [S]	Eastern Sounds	1961	12.50	25.00	50.00
—Green label, silver print					
NEW JAZZ					
NJLP-8218 [M]	Other Sounds	1959	12.50	25.00	50.00
—Purple label					
NJLP-8218 [M]	Other Sounds	1965	6.25	12.50	25.00
—Blue label, trident logo at right					
NJLP-8234 [M]	Cry! Tender	1960	12.50	25.00	50.00
—Purple label					
NJLP-8234 [M]	Cry! Tender	1965	6.25	12.50	25.00
—Blue label, trident logo at right					
NJLP-8261 [M]	The Sounds of Yusef	1961	12.50	25.00	50.00
—Reissue of Prestige 7122; purple label					
NJLP-8261 [M]	The Sounds of Yusef	1965	6.25	12.50	25.00
—Blue label, trident logo at right					
NJLP-8272 [M]	Into Something	1962	12.50	25.00	50.00
—Purple label					
NJLP-8272 [M]	Into Something	1965	6.25	12.50	25.00
—Blue label, trident logo at right					
PRESTIGE					
PRLP-7122 [M]	The Sounds of Yusef	1957	25.00	50.00	100.00
—Yellow label					
PRLP-7319 [M]	Eastern Sounds	1964	6.25	12.50	25.00
PRST-7319 [S]	Eastern Sounds	1964	6.25	12.50	25.00
—Reissue of Moodsville 22					
PRLP-7398 [M]	The Sounds of Yusef Lateef	1966	5.00	10.00	20.00
PRST-7398 [S]	The Sounds of Yusef Lateef	1966	6.25	12.50	25.00
PRLP-7447 [M]	Yusef Lateef Plays for Lovers	1967	6.25	12.50	25.00
PRST-7447 [S]	Yusef Lateef Plays for Lovers	1967	5.00	10.00	20.00
PRST-7637	Into Something	1966	3.75	7.50	15.00
PRST-7653	Expressions	1969	3.75	7.50	15.00
PRST-7748	Cry! Tender	1970	3.75	7.50	15.00
PRST-7832	Imagination	1971	3.75	7.50	15.00
24007 [(2)]	Yusef Lateef	1972	3.75	7.50	15.00
24035 [(2)]	Blues for the Orient	1974	3.75	7.50	15.00
24105 [(2)]	Yusef's Bag	197?	3.75	7.50	15.00
RIVERSIDE					
RLP 12-325 [M]	Three Faces of Yusef Lateef	1960	10.00	20.00	40.00
RLP-337 [M]	The Centaur and the Phoenix	1960	10.00	20.00	40.00
RLP-1176 [S]	Three Faces of Yusef Lateef	1960	10.00	20.00	40.00
RS-3011	This Is Yusef Lateef	1968	3.75	7.50	15.00
RLP-9337 [S]	The Centaur and the Phoenix	1960	10.00	20.00	40.00
SAVOY					
MG-12103 [M]	Jazz Mood	1957	12.50	25.00	50.00
MG-12109 [M]	Jazz for the Thinker	1957	12.50	25.00	50.00
MG-12117 [M]	Prayer to the East	1957	12.50	25.00	50.00
MG-12120 [M]	Jazz and the Sounds of Nature	1958	12.50	25.00	50.00
MG-12139 [M]	The Dreamer	1958	12.50	25.00	50.00
MG-12140 [M]	The Fabric of Jazz	1958	12.50	25.00	50.00
SR-13007 [S]	The Dreamer	1959	12.50	25.00	50.00
SR-13008 [S]	The Fabric of Jazz	1959	12.50	25.00	50.00
SAVOY JAZZ					
SJL-2205	Morning	1976	3.00	6.00	12.00
SJL-2226	Gong!	197?	3.00	6.00	12.00
SJL-2238 [(2)]	Angel Eyes	1979	3.75	7.50	15.00
TRIP					
5018	Outside Blues	1973	2.50	5.00	10.00
VERVE					
MGV-8217 [M]	Before Dawn	1958	25.00	50.00	100.00
V-8217 [M]	Before Dawn	1961	6.25	12.50	25.00

LATIMORE

12-Inch Singles

Number	Title (A Side/B Side)	Yr	VG	VG+	NM
T.K. DISCO					
400	Goodbye Heartache/We Got to Hit It Off	1979	3.75	7.50	15.00

45s

Number	Title (A Side/B Side)	Yr	VG	VG+	NM
ATLANTIC					
2639	I Pity the Fool/I'm Just an Ordinary Man	1969	2.00	4.00	8.00
DADE					
2013	Girl, I Got News for You/Ain't Gonna Cry No More	1967	2.50	5.00	10.00
2014	There She Is/It Was So Nice While It Lasted	1967	2.50	5.00	10.00
2015	It's Just a Matter of Time/Let's Move and Groove Together	1967	2.50	5.00	10.00
2017	The Power and the Glory/Love Don't Love Me	1968	2.50	5.00	10.00
2020	Have a Little Faith/I'm a Believer	1968	2.50	5.00	10.00
2022	I Pity the Fool/I'm Just an Ordinary Man	1968	2.50	5.00	10.00
2026	I'll Be Good to You/Life's Little Ups and Downs	1969	2.50	5.00	10.00
GLADES					
1714	Jolie/There's No End	1973	2.00	4.00	8.00
1716	Stormy Monday/There's No End	1973	—	3.00	6.00
1720	If You Were My Woman/Put Pride Aside	1974	—	3.00	6.00
1722	Let's Straighten It Out/Ain't Nobody Gonna Make Me Change My Mind	1974	—	3.00	6.00
1726	Keep the Home Fires Burnin'/That's How It Is	1975	—	3.00	6.00
1729	There's a Red-Neck in the Soul Band/Just One Step	1975	—	3.00	6.00
1733	Qualified Man/She Don't Lose Her Groove	1976	—	3.00	6.00
1739	Somethin' 'Bout 'Cha/Sweet Vibrations	1976	—	3.00	6.00
1742	I Get Lifted/All the Way Lover	1977	—	3.00	6.00
1744	Let Me Live the Life I Love/It Ain't Where You Been	1977	—	3.00	6.00
1750	Dig a Little Deeper/Let Me Go	1978	—	3.00	6.00
1752	Long Distance Love/Out to Get 'Cha	1979	—	3.00	6.00
1755	Goodbye Heartache/We Got to Hit It Off	1979	—	3.00	6.00
1756	Discoed to Death/Just One Step	1979	—	3.00	6.00
1761	Take Me to the Mountaintop/Joy	1980	—	3.00	6.00
MALACO					
2083	Let the Doorknob Hit'cha/Do That To Me One More Time	1982	—	2.00	4.00
2084	Ain't Nothing You Can Do/Bad Risk	198?	—	2.00	4.00
2093	I'll Do Anything for You/Hell Fire Lovin'	198?	—	2.00	4.00
2098	Right Place, Right Time/He's Not Available	1984	—	2.00	4.00
—With Denise LaSalle					
2099	One Shirt, Soulless Shoes/You	1984	—	2.00	4.00
2119	Good Time Man/You Crowed in My Bed	198?	—	2.00	4.00
2130	Sunshine Lady/There's No Limit to My Love	1986	—	2.00	4.00

Albums

Number	Title (A Side/B Side)	Yr	VG	VG+	NM
GLADES					
6502	Latimore	1973	3.00	6.00	12.00
6503	More, More, More	1974	3.00	6.00	12.00
7505	Latimore 3	1975	3.00	6.00	12.00
7509	It Ain't Where You Been	1976	2.50	5.00	10.00
7515	Dig a Little Deeper	1978	2.50	5.00	10.00
MALACO					
7409	Singing in the Key of Love	198?	2.50	5.00	10.00
7414	I'll Do Anything for You	198?	2.50	5.00	10.00
7423	Good Time Man	198?	2.50	5.00	10.00
7436	Every Way But Wrong	198?	2.50	5.00	10.00
7443	Slow Down	198?	2.50	5.00	10.00
7456	The Only Way Is Up	198?	2.50	5.00	10.00
7468	Catchin' Up	1993	3.00	6.00	12.00

LATIN SOULS, THE

45s

Number	Title (A Side/B Side)	Yr	VG	VG+	NM
KAPP					
844	La Bamba/The Party Is Over	1967	2.00	4.00	8.00
898	I've Got You/Look But Don't Touch	1968	2.00	4.00	8.00

Albums

Number	Title (A Side/B Side)	Yr	VG	VG+	NM
KAPP					
KL-1524 [M]	Boo-Ga-Loo and Shing-a-Ling	1967	6.25	12.50	25.00
KS-3524 [S]	Boo-Ga-Loo and Shing-a-Ling	1967	5.00	10.00	20.00
KS-3553	Tigar Boo-Ga-Loo	1968	5.00	10.00	20.00

LAUGHING GRAVY

45s

Number	Title (A Side/B Side)	Yr	VG	VG+	NM
WHITE WHALE					
261	Vegetables/Snow Flakes on Laughing Gravy's Whiskers	1968	50.00	100.00	200.00

LAURELS, THE (1)

45s

Number	Title (A Side/B Side)	Yr	VG	VG+	NM
ABC-PARAMOUNT					
10048	Hand in Hand/Picture of Love	1959	12.50	25.00	50.00

LAURELS, THE (2)

45s

Number	Title (A Side/B Side)	Yr	VG	VG+	NM
"X"					
0143	Truly, Truly/'Tis Night	1955	62.50	125.00	250.00

LAURELS, THE (U)

May also be by group (2), but we're not sure.

45s

Number	Title (A Side/B Side)	Yr	VG	VG+	NM
SPRING					
1112	Baby Talk/You Left Me	1959	15.00	30.00	60.00

LAUREN, ROD

45s

Number	Title (A Side/B Side)	Yr	VG	VG+	NM
CHANCELLOR					
1126	I Ain't Got You/Mexicali Rose	1962	3.00	6.00	12.00
1132	Oh How I Miss You Tonight/Blame Your Friends	1963	3.00	6.00	12.00

Number	Title (A Side/B Side)	Yr	VG	VG+	NM
1136	Yesterday's Lovers/I Know	1963	3.00	6.00	12.00
1141	I Wanna Know/Searcher for Love	1963	3.00	6.00	12.00
1146	Let Me Tell You 'Bout My Baby/I can't Get You Out of My Heart	1963	3.00	6.00	12.00
RCA VICTOR					
47-7645	If I Had a Girl/No Wonder	1959	3.75	7.50	15.00
47-7645 [PS]	If I Had a Girl/No Wonder	1959	5.00	10.00	20.00
47-7720	Listen My Love/This I Know	1960	3.75	7.50	15.00
47-7786	A Wild Imagination/The One Finger Symphony	1960	3.75	7.50	15.00
47-8020	I Dreamed/A Wondrous Place	1962	3.00	6.00	12.00
Albums					
RCA VICTOR					
LPM-2176 [M]	I'm Rod Lauren	1961	10.00	20.00	40.00
LSP-2176 [S]	I'm Rod Lauren	1961	12.50	25.00	50.00

LAURIE, ANNIE

Number	Title (A Side/B Side)	Yr	VG	VG+	NM
45s					
DELUXE					
6107	It Hurts to Be in Love/Hand in Hand	1957	5.00	10.00	20.00
6135	It Must Be You/Please Honey Don't Go	1957	3.75	7.50	15.00
6140	You're the Only One for Me/Out of My Mind	1957	3.75	7.50	15.00
6151	Love Is a Funny Thing/Nobody's Gonna Hurt You Baby	1957	3.75	7.50	15.00
6173	Someday Someway/Hold On to What You Got	1958	3.75	7.50	15.00
6182	Since I Fell for You/Lost Love	1959	3.75	7.50	15.00
6189	If You're Lonely/It's Gonna Come Out in the Wash Someday	1960	3.75	7.50	15.00
OKEH					
6915	You Belong to Me/I Feel So Right Tonight	1952	6.25	12.50	25.00
6933	Stop Talkin' and Start Walkin'/Give Me Half a Chance	1953	6.25	12.50	25.00
6973	It's Been a Long, Long Time/I Ain't Got It Bad No More	1953	6.25	12.50	25.00
7025	I'm in the Mood for You/Feeling the Need	1954	5.00	10.00	20.00
SAVOY					
1197	You Promised Love/Rockin' and Rollin' Again	1956	5.00	10.00	20.00
Albums					
AUDIO LAB					
AL-1510 [M]	It Hurts to Be in Love	1959	75.00	150.00	300.00

LAURIE, LINDA

Number	Title (A Side/B Side)	Yr	VG	VG+	NM
45s					
ANDIE					
5015	All Winter Long/Stay with Me	1960	3.00	6.00	12.00
GLORY					
290	Ambrose (Part Five)/Ooh! What a Lover	1958	3.75	7.50	15.00
294	Forever Ambrose/Wherever He Goes, I Go	1959	3.00	6.00	12.00
KEETCH					
6001	Jose He Say/Chico	197?	—	2.50	5.00
MCA					
40119	Leave Me Alone (Ruby Red Dress)/Sweet Deceiver	1973	—	3.00	6.00
RUST					
5022	Prince Charming/Soupin' Up Your Motor	1960	2.50	5.00	10.00
5042	Stay at Home Sue/Lazy Love	1961	2.50	5.00	10.00
5061	The Return of Ambrose/Chicken Little	1963	2.50	5.00	10.00

LAVETTE, BETTY

Number	Title (A Side/B Side)	Yr	VG	VG+	NM
45s					
ATCO					
6891	Heart of Gold/You'll Wake Up Wisely	1972	—	3.00	6.00
6913	Your Turn to Cry/Soul Tambourine	1973	—	3.00	6.00
ATLANTIC					
2160	My Man — He's a Lovin' Man/Shut Your Mouth	1962	3.00	6.00	12.00
—As "Betty LaVett"					
2198	You'll Never Change/Here I Am	1963	3.00	6.00	12.00
—As "Betty LaVett"					
CALLA					
102	Let Me Down Easy/What I Don't Know (Won't Hurt Me)	1965	2.50	5.00	10.00
104	I Feel Good (All Over)/Only Your Love Can Save Me	1965	2.50	5.00	10.00
106	Stand Up Like a Man/I'm Just a Fool for You	1965	2.50	5.00	10.00
KAREN					
1540	Love Makes the World Go Round/Almost	1968	2.00	4.00	8.00
1544	Get Away/What Condition My Condition Was In	1968	2.00	4.00	8.00
1545	With a Little Help from My Friends/Hey Love	1969	2.00	4.00	8.00
1548	Ticket to the Moon/Let Me Down Easy	1969	2.00	4.00	8.00
LUPINE					
123	Witch Craft in the Air/You Killed the Love	1964	10.00	20.00	40.00
—As "Betty LaVett"					
1021	Witch Craft in the Air/You Killed the Love	1964	6.25	12.50	25.00
—As "Betty LaVett"					
MOTOWN					
1532	Right in the Middle (Of Falling in Love)/You Seen One, You Seen 'Em All	1981	—	2.50	5.00
—As "Bettye LaVette"					
1614	Either Way, We Lose/I Can't Stop	1982	—	2.50	5.00
—As "Bettye LaVette"					
SILVER FOX					
17	He Made a Woman Out of Me/Nearer to You	1969	—	3.00	6.00
21	Do Your Duty/Love's Made a Fool Out of Me	1970	—	3.00	6.00
24	Games People Play/My Train's Comin' In	1970	—	3.00	6.00
SSS INTERNATIONAL					
839	Take Another Piece of My Heart/At the Mercy of a Man	1971	—	3.00	6.00
WEST END					
1213	Doin' the Best That I Can/(Instrumental)	1983	—	2.50	5.00
—As "Bettye LaVette"					
Albums					
MOTOWN					
6000 ML	Tell Me a Lie	1982	3.00	6.00	12.00
—As "Bettye LaVette"					

LAVOIE, KENT

See LOBO.

LAWRENCE, BILL

Number	Title (A Side/B Side)	Yr	VG	VG+	NM
45s					
BERTRAM INT'L.					
207	Hey Baby!/Caribbean	1959	25.00	50.00	100.00
227	Please Don't Leave Me/Billy Boy	1960	15.00	30.00	60.00
FREEDOM					
44004	Hey Baby!/Caribbean	1958	37.50	75.00	150.00
MOOD					
1013	Little Girl/(B-side unknown)	195?	17.50	35.00	70.00
Albums					
TOPS					
L-1576 [M]	Bill Lawrence Sings I'm in the Mood for Love	1957	5.00	10.00	20.00

LAWRENCE, EDDIE

Number	Title (A Side/B Side)	Yr	VG	VG+	NM
45s					
CORAL					
61168	Old, Old Vienna (Part 1)/Old, Old Vienna (Part 2)	1954	3.00	6.00	12.00
61671	The Old Philosopher/King Arthur's Mine	1956	3.75	7.50	15.00
61713	The New Philosopher/Loco Baseball	1956	3.00	6.00	12.00
61799	German Baseball/Golden Baskos	1957	3.00	6.00	12.00
61821	Abner the Baseball (Part 1)/Abner the Baseball (Part 2)	1957	3.00	6.00	12.00
61863	The Old Philosopher on the Range/Memories of Louise	1957	3.00	6.00	12.00
61915	The Merry Old Philosopher/That Holiday Spirit	1957	5.00	10.00	20.00
61940	The Visitor/Fix Your Watch	1958	3.00	6.00	12.00
61978	The Philosopher Strikes Back/Frankensteiner Polka	1958	3.00	6.00	12.00
62005	The Good Old Days/Hi-Fi Blues	1958	3.00	6.00	12.00
62049	The Space Philosopher/Outta This World	1958	3.00	6.00	12.00
62070	The Mother Philosopher/The Salesman's Philosopher	1959	2.50	5.00	10.00
62267	The Suburban Philosopher/We Sure Had Fun	1961	2.50	5.00	10.00
62298	The Philosopher Twist/The D.J. Philosopher Returns	1961	2.50	5.00	10.00
62367	The Mets' Philosopher/We Love the Mets	1963	3.75	7.50	15.00
EPIC					
9804	The World's Fair Philosopher/The Old Philosopher and the Single Girl	1965	3.00	6.00	12.00
SHASTA					
139	Stardust/Harlem Nocturne	196?	2.00	4.00	8.00
144	Cattle Call/Cielito Lindo	196?	2.00	4.00	8.00
SIGNATURE					
12010	The Doctor's Philosopher/Blackouts of 1984	1960	2.50	5.00	10.00
12031	Anyone for President/Unequal	1960	2.50	5.00	10.00
Albums					
CORAL					
CRL 57103 [M]	The Old Philosopher	1956	7.50	15.00	30.00
CRL 57155 [M]	Eddie "The Old Philosopher" Lawrence	1957	7.50	15.00	30.00
CRL 57203 [M]	The Kingdom of Eddie Lawrence	1958	7.50	15.00	30.00
CRL 57371 [M]	The Side Splitting Personality of Eddie Lawrence	1961	7.50	15.00	30.00
CRL 57411 [M]	Seven Characters In Search of Eddie Lawrence	1962	7.50	15.00	30.00
CRL 757411 [S]	Seven Characters In Search of Eddie Lawrence	1962	10.00	20.00	40.00
EPIC					
LN 24149 [M]	Is That What's Bothering You Bunkie?	1965	7.50	15.00	30.00
BN 26149 [S]	Is That What's Bothering You Bunkie?	1965	10.00	20.00	40.00
SIGNATURE					
SM-1003 [M]	The Garden of Eddie Lawrence	1960	10.00	20.00	40.00

LAWRENCE, MARK

Number	Title (A Side/B Side)	Yr	VG	VG+	NM
45s					
GNP CRESCENDO					
419	Is There A Santa Claus?/The Heavenly Forest	1968	—	3.00	6.00
JERDEN					
110	Is There A Santa Claus/Santa Claus Square Dance	196?	2.00	4.00	8.00

LAWRENCE, STEVE

Number	Title (A Side/B Side)	Yr	VG	VG+	NM
45s					
20TH CENTURY					
2246	N[illegible]at We're in Love/I Just Needed Your L[illegible]vin'	1975	—	2.00	4.00
ABC-PARAMOUNT					
10005	(I Don't Care) Only Love Me/Loving Is a Way of Living	1959	2.50	5.00	10.00
10031	There'll Be Some Changes Made/You're Everything Wonderful	1959	2.50	5.00	10.00
10058	Pretty Blue Eyes/You're Nearer	1959	2.50	5.00	10.00
10085	Footsteps/You Don't Know	1960	2.50	5.00	10.00
10113	You're Everything Wonderful/Why Why Why	1960	2.50	5.00	10.00
10146	Come Back Silly Girl/Going Steady	1960	2.50	5.00	10.00
CALENDAR					
63-1001	I've Gotta Be Me/Love's a Game	1968	—	3.00	6.00
63-1005	Runaround/I'm Falling Down	1968	—	3.00	6.00
COLUMBIA					
31545 [S]	(titles unknown)	1962	3.00	6.00	12.00
31546 [S]	(titles unknown)	1962	3.00	6.00	12.00
31547 [S]	(titles unknown)	1962	3.00	6.00	12.00
31548 [S]	(titles unknown)	1962	3.00	6.00	12.00
31549 [S]	(titles unknown)	1962	3.00	6.00	12.00
—Anyone who can fill in these gaps -- the above five all are Columbia "Stereo 7" singles -- please let us know.					
42396	The Lady Wants to Twist/Tell Her I Said Hello	1962	2.50	5.00	10.00
42455	A House Without Windows/The Endless Night	1962	2.50	5.00	10.00

Number	Title (A Side/B Side)	Yr	VG	VG+	NM
42601	Go Away Little Girl/If You Love Her Tell Her So	1962	2.00	4.00	8.00
42601 [PS]	Go Away Little Girl/If You Love Her Tell Her So	1962	3.00	6.00	12.00
42699	Don't Be Afraid, Little Darlin'/Don't Come Runnin' Back	1963	2.00	4.00	8.00
42699 [PS]	Don't Be Afraid, Little Darlin'/Don't Come Runnin' Back	1963	3.00	6.00	12.00
42795	Poor Little Rich Girl/More (Theme from Mondo Cane)	1963	2.00	4.00	8.00
42837	One Love Too Late/Walking Proud	1963	—	—	—
—Canceled?					
42865	Walking Proud/All the Way Home	1963	2.00	4.00	8.00
42865 [PS]	Walking Proud/All the Way Home	1963	3.00	6.00	12.00
42952	My Home Town/A Room Without Windows	1964	2.00	4.00	8.00
43047	Everybody Knows/One Love Too Late	1964	2.00	4.00	8.00
43095	Yet…I Know/Put Away Your Teardrops	1964	2.00	4.00	8.00
43192	I Will Wait for You/Bewitched	1964	2.00	4.00	8.00
43303	Where Can I Go/Last Night I Made a Girl Cry	1965	—	3.50	7.00
43362	The Sounds of Summer/Millions of Roses	1965	—	3.50	7.00
43487	Only the Young/The Week-End	1965	—	3.50	7.00
43610	Today Will Be Yesterday Tomorrow/I'm Making the Same Mistakes	1966	—	3.50	7.00
43681	The Warm Hours/Good Times	1966	—	3.50	7.00
43758	I'm a Fool to Want You/The Ballad of the Sad Young Men	1966	—	3.50	7.00
44022	Did I Ever Really Live/Girl in the White Glove	1967	—	3.00	6.00
44084	The Impossible Dream/Sweet Maria	1967	—	3.00	6.00
44384	Remember When/You've Got to Learn	1967	—	3.00	6.00
44514	I Want to Be with You/Dulcinea	1968	—	3.00	6.00
CORAL					
61279	Tell Me What to Do (To Make You Mine)/Willow	1954	3.00	6.00	12.00
61327	Kiss Me Now/How Do I Break Away	1954	3.00	6.00	12.00
61486	Open Up the Gates of Mercy/My Impression of Jamie	1955	3.00	6.00	12.00
61537	Adelaide/The Lord Is a Busy Man	1955	3.00	6.00	12.00
61563	Speedoo/The Chicken and the Hawk	1956	3.00	6.00	12.00
61667	Ethel Baby/Never My Love	1956	3.00	6.00	12.00
61708	Never Mind/If You Would Say You're Mine	1956	3.00	6.00	12.00
61761	The Banana Boat Song/Long Before I Knew You	1956	3.00	6.00	12.00
61792	Party Doll/(The Bad Donkey) Pum-Pa-Lum	1957	3.75	7.50	15.00
61834	Can't Wait for Summer/Fabulous	1957	3.00	6.00	12.00
61876	Fraulein/Blue Rememberin' You	1957	3.00	6.00	12.00
61904	A Long Last Look/At a Time Like This	1957	3.00	6.00	12.00
61925	Geisha Girl/I Don't Know	1958	3.00	6.00	12.00
61950	Uh-Huh, Oh Yeah/Lover in the House	1958	2.50	5.00	10.00
61992	Stranger in Mexico/Those Nights at the Round Table	1958	2.50	5.00	10.00
62025	Many a Time/All About Love	1958	2.50	5.00	10.00
62052	I Only Have Eyes for You/These Things Are Free	1958	2.50	5.00	10.00
62080	Blah, Blah, Blah/Lover in the House	1959	2.50	5.00	10.00
KING					
1223	To the Birds/With Every Breath I Take	1953	5.00	10.00	20.00
1252	King for a Day/You Can't Hold a Memory in Your Arms	1953	5.00	10.00	20.00
1315	Remember Me/Too Little Time	1954	5.00	10.00	20.00
5360	Poinciana/Mine and Mine Alone	1960	2.50	5.00	10.00
5913	King for a Day/Liebscher	1964	2.00	4.00	8.00
15185	Never Leave Me/(B-side unknown)	1952	6.25	12.50	25.00
15190	Poinciana/All My Love Belongs to You	1952	5.00	10.00	20.00
15199	Sudden Fear/Always Love Me	1952	5.00	10.00	20.00
15208	How Many Stars Have to Shine/Tango	1952	5.00	10.00	20.00
15218	Tomorrow/If Not for You	1953	5.00	10.00	20.00
MGM					
14257	Lookin' Good/Frosty Morning	1971	—	2.00	4.00
14288	The Last Run/Frosty Morning	1971	—	2.00	4.00
14368	Ain't No Sunshine-You Are My Sunshine/In My Own Lifetime	1972	—	2.00	4.00
14531	The Best Thing That Ever Happened (To Me)/Hello, Los Angeles	1973	—	2.00	4.00
14631	The End/You Light Up My Life	1973	—	2.00	4.00
RCA VICTOR					
74-0169	Pickin' Up the Pieces/I've Got My Eyes on You	1969	—	2.50	5.00
74-0237	The Drifter/To Say Goodbye	1969	—	2.50	5.00
74-0303	Cry for Us All/Mama, a Rainbow	1969	—	2.50	5.00
74-0357	Groovin'/Being Alone	1970	—	2.50	5.00
UNITED ARTISTS					
240	Tears from Heaven/Hold Back the Dike	1960	2.50	5.00	10.00
291	Portrait of My Love/Oh How You Lied	1961	2.00	4.00	8.00
335	My Clair de Lune/In Time	1961	2.00	4.00	8.00
364	Somewhere Along the Way/While There's Still Time	1961	2.00	4.00	8.00
403	Our Concerto/Send Someone to Love Me	1962	2.00	4.00	8.00
XW927	You Take My Heart Away/(Everybody Has To) Begin Again	1976	—	2.00	4.00
XW1050	Everytime I Sing a Love Song/I Wasn't Man Enough	1977	—	2.00	4.00
WARNER BROS.					
8584	Take My Hand/Don't Wish Too Hard	1978	—	2.00	4.00
Albums					
ABC-PARAMOUNT					
290 [M]	Swing Softly with Me	1959	6.25	12.50	25.00
S-290 [S]	Swing Softly with Me	1959	7.50	15.00	30.00
392 [M]	The Best of Steve Lawrence	1960	5.00	10.00	20.00
S-392 [S]	The Best of Steve Lawrence	1960	6.25	12.50	25.00
APPLAUSE					
1001	Take It On Home	1981	2.50	5.00	10.00
COLUMBIA					
CL 1953 [M]	Winners!	1963	3.00	6.00	12.00
CL 2121 [M]	Academy Award Losers	1964	3.00	6.00	12.00
CL 2227 [M]	Everybody Knows	1964	3.00	6.00	12.00
CL 2419 [M]	The Steve Lawrence Show	1965	3.00	6.00	12.00
CL 2540 [M]	Of Love and… Sad Young Men	1966	3.00	6.00	12.00
CS 8753 [S]	Winners!	1963	3.75	7.50	15.00
CS 8921 [S]	Academy Award Losers	1964	3.75	7.50	15.00
CS 9027 [S]	Everybody Knows	1964	3.75	7.50	15.00

Number	Title (A Side/B Side)	Yr	VG	VG+	NM
CS 9219 [S]	The Steve Lawrence Show	1965	3.75	7.50	15.00
CS 9340 [S]	Of Love and… Sad Young Men	1966	3.75	7.50	15.00
CS 9565	Greatest Hits	1968	3.00	6.00	12.00
PC 9565	Greatest Hits	198?	2.00	4.00	8.00
—Reissue with new prefix					
CORAL					
CRL 57050 [M]	About That Girl	1956	10.00	20.00	40.00
CRL 57182 [M]	Songs by Steve Lawrence	1957	10.00	20.00	40.00
CRL 57204 [M]	Here's Steve Lawrence	1958	10.00	20.00	40.00
CRL 57268 [M]	All About Love	1959	7.50	15.00	30.00
CRL 57434 [M]	Songs Everybody Knows	1963	6.25	12.50	25.00
CRL 757268 [S]	All About Love	1959	10.00	20.00	40.00
CRL 757434 [S]	Songs Everybody Knows	1963	7.50	15.00	30.00
HARMONY					
HS 11257	Moon River	196?	2.50	5.00	10.00
HS 11327	Ramblin' Rose	1969	2.50	5.00	10.00
HS 11397	Love Me	1970	2.50	5.00	10.00
KING					
593 [M]	Steve Lawrence	1959	20.00	40.00	80.00
MGM					
SE-4824	Portrait	1973	2.50	5.00	10.00
RCA VICTOR					
LSP-4167	I've Gotta Be Me	1969	3.00	6.00	12.00
LSP-4347	On a Clear Day	1970	3.00	6.00	12.00
UNITED ARTISTS					
UAL-3098 [M]	The Steve Lawrence Sound	1960	5.00	10.00	20.00
UAL-3114 [M]	Steve Lawrence Goes Latin	1960	5.00	10.00	20.00
UAL-3150 [M]	Portrait of My Love	1961	5.00	10.00	20.00
UAL-3190 [M]	The Very Best of Steve Lawrence	1962	5.00	10.00	20.00
UAL-3265 [M]	People Will Say We're in Love	1963	5.00	10.00	20.00
UAL-3368 [M]	Steve Lawrence Conquers Broadway	1964	3.75	7.50	15.00
UAS-6098 [S]	The Steve Lawrence Sound	1960	6.25	12.50	25.00
UAS-6114 [S]	Steve Lawrence Goes Latin	1960	6.25	12.50	25.00
UAS-6150 [S]	Portrait of My Love	1961	6.25	12.50	25.00
UAS-6190 [S]	The Very Best of Steve Lawrence	1962	6.25	12.50	25.00
UAS-6265 [S]	People Will Say We're in Love	1963	6.25	12.50	25.00
UAS-6368 [S]	Steve Lawrence Conquers Broadway	1964	5.00	10.00	20.00
VOCALION					
VL 3775 [M]	Here's Steve Lawrence	196?	3.00	6.00	12.00
VL 73775 [R]	Here's Steve Lawrence	196?	2.50	5.00	10.00
VL 73886	The More I See You	1970	2.50	5.00	10.00

LAWRENCE, STEVE, AND EYDIE GORME

Also see each artist's individual listings.

Number	Title (A Side/B Side)	Yr	VG	VG+	NM
45s					
ABC-PARAMOUNT					
10104	This Could Be the Start of Something Big/Darn It, Baby, That's Love	1960	2.50	5.00	10.00
CALENDAR					
63-1003	Two of Us/Mr. Spoons	1968	—	3.00	6.00
COLUMBIA					
42815	I Want to Stay Here/Ain't Love	1963	2.00	4.00	8.00
42932	I Can't Stop Talking About You/To the Movies We Go	1963	2.00	4.00	8.00
43179	Happy Holiday/That Holiday Feeling	1964	2.50	5.00	10.00
43930	The Honeymoon Is Over/Together Forever	1966	—	3.50	7.00
44123	Cabaret/Mame	1967	—	3.00	6.00
44228	Summer Wind/Be Still	1967	—	3.00	6.00
CORAL					
61313	Make Yourself Comfortable/I've Gotta Crow	1954	3.00	6.00	12.00
61411	Besame Mucho/Close Your Eyes, Take a Deep Breath	1955	3.00	6.00	12.00
61440	Knickerbocker Mambo/Give a Fool a Chance	1955	3.00	6.00	12.00
MGM					
14340	Lead Me On/Tea for Two	1971	—	2.00	4.00
14383	We Can Make It Together/E Fini	1972	—	2.00	4.00
—With the Osmonds					
14493	Feelin'/Lead Me On	1973	—	2.00	4.00
RCA VICTOR					
47-9656	Dear World/A Break at Love	1968	—	2.50	5.00
47-9694	Hurry Home for Christmas/Dedicated to Love	1968	2.00	4.00	8.00
74-0123	Chapter One/Real True Lovin'	1969	—	2.50	5.00
74-0334	(You're My) Soul and Inspiration/Now I Love the World Again	1970	—	2.50	5.00
74-0386	For All We Know/Did You Give the World My Love Today, Babe	1970	—	2.50	5.00
74-0420	Love Is Blue-Autumn Leaves/Hi Sweetie	1971	—	2.50	5.00
UNITED ARTISTS					
282	The Facts of Life/I'm a Girl, You're a Boy	1960	2.50	5.00	10.00
XW1163	You Take My Heart Away/What I Did for Love	1978	—	2.00	4.00
—Steve Lawrence is on A-side, Eydie Gorme on B-side					
Albums					
ABC					
X-764 [(2)]	20 Golden Performances	1974	3.00	6.00	12.00
ABC-PARAMOUNT					
300 [M]	We Got Us	1960	5.00	10.00	20.00
S-300 [S]	We Got Us	1960	6.25	12.50	25.00
311 [M]	Steve and Eydie Sing the Golden Hits	1960	5.00	10.00	20.00
S-311 [S]	Steve and Eydie Sing the Golden Hits	1960	6.25	12.50	25.00
469 [M]	Our Best to You	1964	3.75	7.50	15.00
S-469 [S]	Our Best to You	1964	5.00	10.00	20.00
CALENDAR					
KOM-1001 [M]	Golden Rainbow	1968	7.50	15.00	30.00
KOS-1001 [S]	Golden Rainbow	1968	10.00	20.00	40.00
COLUMBIA					
CL 2021 [M]	Steve and Eydie at the Movies	1964	3.00	6.00	12.00
CL 2262 [M]	That Holiday Feeling	1964	3.00	6.00	12.00
CL 2636 [M]	Steve and Eydie Together On Broadway	1967	3.00	6.00	12.00
CL 2730 [M]	Bonfa and Brazil	1968	3.75	7.50	15.00
CS 8821 [S]	Steve and Eydie at the Movies	1964	3.75	7.50	15.00
CS 9062 [S]	That Holiday Feeling	1964	3.75	7.50	15.00
CS 9436 [S]	Steve and Eydie Together On Broadway	1967	3.75	7.50	15.00
CS 9530 [S]	Bonfa and Brazil	1968	3.00	6.00	12.00

Number	Title (A Side/B Side)	Yr	VG	VG+	NM
CORAL					
CRL 57336 [M]	Steve and Eydie	1962	5.00	10.00	20.00
HARMONY					
H 30292	Something's Gotta Give	1971	2.50	5.00	10.00
MATI-MOR					
8003	It's Us Again	196?	5.00	10.00	20.00
—Promotional item for Silvirkin shampoo					
MGM					
SE-4803	The World of Steve Lawrence and Eydie Gorme	1972	2.50	5.00	10.00
SE-4881	Feelin'	1973	2.50	5.00	10.00
RCA VICTOR					
LSP-4107	Real True Lovin'	1969	3.00	6.00	12.00
LSP-4115	What It Was, Was Love	1969	3.00	6.00	12.00
LSP-4393	A Man and a Woman	1971	3.00	6.00	12.00
VPS-6035 [(2)]	This Is Steve Lawrence and Eydie Gorme	1971	3.75	7.50	15.00
VPS-6050 [(2)]	This Is Steve Lawrence and Eydie Gorme, Vol. 2	1972	3.75	7.50	15.00
STAGE 2					
712	Hallelujah	198?	2.50	5.00	10.00
UNITED ARTISTS					
UAL-3191 [M]	The Very Best of Eydie and Steve	1962	5.00	10.00	20.00
UAL-3268 [M]	Two on the Aisle	1963	5.00	10.00	20.00
WWL-4509 [M]	Cozy	1961	5.00	10.00	20.00
UAS-6191 [S]	The Very Best of Eydie and Steve	1962	6.25	12.50	25.00
UAS-6268 [S]	Two on the Aisle	1963	6.25	12.50	25.00
WWS-8509 [S]	Cozy	1961	6.25	12.50	25.00
VOCALION					
VL 3825 [M]	Presenting Steve and Eydie	1968	3.00	6.00	12.00
VL 73825 [R]	Presenting Steve and Eydie	1968	2.50	5.00	10.00

LAWRENCE, SYD

45s

Number	Title (A Side/B Side)	Yr	VG	VG+	NM
COSMIC					
1001	The Answer to the Flying Saucer/Haunted Guitar	1956	10.00	20.00	40.00
—B-side by Billy Mure					

LAWRENCE, VICKI

45s

Number	Title (A Side/B Side)	Yr	VG	VG+	NM
BELL					
45303	The Night the Lights Went Out in Georgia/Dime a Dance	1973	—	2.50	5.00
45362	He Did with Me/Mr. Allison	1973	—	2.00	4.00
45409	Sensual Man/Ships in the Night	1973	—	2.00	4.00
45437	Mama's Gonna Make It Better/Cameo	1974	—	2.00	4.00
ELF					
90035	And I'll Go/The Whole State of Alabama	1970	—	3.00	6.00
PRIVATE STOCK					
45036	The Other Woman/Cameo	1975	—	2.00	4.00
45067	There's a Gun Still Smokin' in Nashville	1976	—	2.00	4.00
45121	Love in the Hot Afternoon/(B-side unknown)	1976	—	2.00	4.00
SOMA					
5248	The Night the Lights Went Out in Georgia/He Did with Me	197?	—	2.50	5.00
—Original, reissue or bootleg? Please advise.					
UNITED ARTISTS					
50748	No, No/Lincoln Street Chapel	1971	—	3.00	6.00

Albums

Number	Title (A Side/B Side)	Yr	VG	VG+	NM
BELL					
1120	The Night the Lights Went Out in Georgia	1973	3.00	6.00	12.00

LAWRENCE, WALT

45s

Number	Title (A Side/B Side)	Yr	VG	VG+	NM
HOLLYWOOD INT'L.					
2	Cascade/Twilight Adrift	195?	10.00	20.00	40.00

LAWS, HUBERT

45s

Number	Title (A Side/B Side)	Yr	VG	VG+	NM
ATLANTIC					
5046	Miss Thing/Blue Eyed Peas and Rice	1965	2.00	4.00	8.00
COLUMBIA					
02694	Goodbye for Now (Theme from "Reds")/(Instrumental)	1982	—	2.00	4.00
10736	False Faces/The Baron	1978	—	2.00	4.00
10811	It Happens Every Day/Love Gets Better	1978	—	2.00	4.00
11022	Land of Passion/Heartbeats	1979	—	2.00	4.00
11368	Wildfire/Family	1980	—	2.00	4.00
CTI					
3	Fire and Rain/Theme from Love Story	1971	—	2.50	5.00
13	Amazing Grace (Part 1)/Amazing Grace (Part 2)	1973	—	2.50	5.00
21	Mean Lene/Come All Ye Disconsolate	1974	—	2.50	5.00
27	The Chicago Theme (Love Loop)/I Had a Dream	1975	—	2.50	5.00
501	La Jean/Let It Be	197?	—	2.00	4.00
505	Feelin' Alright/Let It Be	197?	—	2.00	4.00

Albums

Number	Title (A Side/B Side)	Yr	VG	VG+	NM
ATLANTIC					
1432 [M]	The Laws of Jazz	1965	3.00	6.00	12.00
SD 1432 [S]	The Laws of Jazz	1965	3.75	7.50	15.00
1452 [M]	Flute By-Laws	1966	3.00	6.00	12.00
SD 1452 [S]	Flute By-Laws	1966	3.75	7.50	15.00
SD 1509	Laws Cause	1970	3.00	6.00	12.00
SD 1624	Wild Flower	1973	2.50	5.00	10.00
SD 8813	The Laws of Jazz	198?	2.00	4.00	8.00
—Reissue of 1432					
CBS					
M 39858	Blanchard: New Earth Symphony; Telemann: Suite in A; Amazing Grace	1985	3.00	6.00	12.00
COLUMBIA					
PC 34330	Romeo and Juliet	1976	3.00	6.00	12.00
JC 35022	Say It with Silence	1978	2.50	5.00	10.00
JC 35708	Land of Passion	1979	2.50	5.00	10.00
FC 36365	The Best of Hubert Laws	198?	2.50	5.00	10.00
JC 36396	Family	1980	2.50	5.00	10.00
FC 38850	Make It Last	1983	2.50	5.00	10.00
CTI					
CTX-3 + 3 [(2)]	In the Beginning	1974	3.75	7.50	15.00
1002	Crying Song	1970	5.00	10.00	20.00
6000	Crying Song	1970	3.00	6.00	12.00
—Reissue of 1002					
6006	Afro-Classic	1971	3.00	6.00	12.00
6012	Rite of Spring	1972	3.00	6.00	12.00
6022	Morning Star	1972	3.00	6.00	12.00
6025	Carnegie Hall	1973	3.00	6.00	12.00
6058	The Chicago Theme	1975	3.00	6.00	12.00
6065	Then There Was Light, Vol. 1	1976	3.00	6.00	12.00
6066	Then There Was Light, Vol. 2	1976	3.00	6.00	12.00
7075	San Francisco	1976	3.00	6.00	12.00
8015	The Chicago Theme	198?	2.00	4.00	8.00
—Reissue of 6058					
8019	Afro-Classic	198?	2.00	4.00	8.00
—Reissue of 6006					
8020	Rite of Spring	198?	2.00	4.00	8.00
—Reissue of 6012					

LAWS, RONNIE

45s

Number	Title (A Side/B Side)	Yr	VG	VG+	NM
BLUE NOTE					
XW738	Always There/Tidal Wave	1975	—	2.50	5.00
XW848	Carmen/All the Time	1976	—	2.50	5.00
XW1007	Just Love/Nuthin' But Nuthin'	1977	—	2.50	5.00
XW1036	Friends and Strangers/Goodtime Ride	1977	—	2.50	5.00
CAPITOL					
B-5241	In the Groove/Summer Fool	1983	—	—	3.00
B-5241 [PS]	In the Groove/Summer Fool	1983	—	2.00	4.00
B-5274	Mr. Nice Guy/Off and On Again	1983	—	—	3.00
B-5421	City Girl/Rolling	1984	—	—	3.00
B-5405	(You Are) Paradise/Stay Awake	1985	—	—	3.00
COLUMBIA					
06240	Come to Me/Take a Chance	1986	—	—	3.00
06574	Mirror Town/Midnight Side	1986	—	—	3.00
07629	Rhythm of Romance/Nite Life	1987	—	—	3.00
07787	Smoke House/All Day Rhythm	1988	—	—	3.00
LIBERTY					
1424	Stay Awake/Summer Fool	1981	—	2.00	4.00
1442	There's a Way/Just As You Are	1981	—	2.00	4.00
1459	Heavy On Easy/Just As You Are	1982	—	2.00	4.00
UNITED ARTISTS					
1264	Love Is Here/Grace	1978	—	2.00	4.00
1278	All for You/These Days	1979	—	2.00	4.00
1334	Every Generation/Every Generation (Part 2)	1980	—	2.00	4.00
1334 [PS]	Every Generation/Every Generation (Part 2)	1980	—	2.50	5.00
1354	Love's Victory/It's One	1980	—	2.00	4.00
1376	Young Child/(B-side unknown)	1980	—	2.00	4.00

Albums

Number	Title (A Side/B Side)	Yr	VG	VG+	NM
BLUE NOTE					
BN-LA452-G	Pressure Sensitive	1975	3.00	6.00	12.00
BN-LA628-G	Fever	1976	3.00	6.00	12.00
BN-LA730-H	Friends and Strangers	1977	2.50	5.00	10.00
CAPITOL					
ST-12261	Mr. Nice Guy	1983	2.50	5.00	10.00
ST-12375	Classic Masters	1984	2.50	5.00	10.00
COLUMBIA					
BFC 40089	Mirror Town	1986	2.50	5.00	10.00
FC 40902	All Day Rhythm	1987	2.50	5.00	10.00
LIBERTY					
LO-628	Fever	198?	2.00	4.00	8.00
—Reissue of Blue Note 628					
LW-730	Friends and Strangers	198?	2.00	4.00	8.00
—Reissue of Blue Note 730					
LO-881	Flame	198?	2.00	4.00	8.00
—Reissue of United Artists 881					
LT-1001	Every Generation	1981	2.00	4.00	8.00
—Reissue of United Artists 1001					
LN-10164	Pressure Sensitive	198?	2.00	4.00	8.00
—Reissue of Blue Note 452					
LN-10232	Flame	198?	2.00	4.00	8.00
—Budget-line reissue					
LN-10255	Fever	198?	2.00	4.00	8.00
—Budget-line reissue					
LN-10307	Solid Ground	1986	2.00	4.00	8.00
—Budget-line reissue					
LO-51087	Solid Ground	1981	2.50	5.00	10.00
UNITED ARTISTS					
UA-LA881-H	Flame	1978	2.50	5.00	10.00
LT-1001	Every Generation	1980	2.50	5.00	10.00

LAWSON, LINDA

Albums

Number	Title (A Side/B Side)	Yr	VG	VG+	NM
CHANCELLOR					
CHL-5010 [M]	Introducing Linda Lawson	1960	5.00	10.00	20.00

LAY, SAM

Albums

Number	Title (A Side/B Side)	Yr	VG	VG+	NM
BLUE THUMB					
BTS 14	Sam Lay in Bluesland	1970	6.25	12.50	25.00

LEADBELLY

Albums

Number	Title (A Side/B Side)	Yr	VG	VG+	NM
ALLEGRO					
L-4027 [10]	Sinful Songs	195?	62.50	125.00	250.00
CAPITOL					
H 369 [10]	Classics in Jazz	1953	62.50	125.00	250.00
T 1821 [M]	Leadbelly: Huddie Ledbetter's Best	1962	10.00	20.00	40.00
ELEKTRA					
EKL-301/2 [(2)]	The Library of Congress Recordings	1966	6.25	12.50	25.00

Number	Title (A Side/B Side)	Yr	VG	VG+	NM
FOLKWAYS					
FP-4 [10]	Lead Belly's Legacy, Vol. 1: Take This Hammer	1950	30.00	60.00	120.00
FP-14 [10]	Lead Belly's Legacy, Vol. 2: Rock Island Line	1951	30.00	60.00	120.00
FP-24 [10]	Lead Belly's Legacy, Vol. 3: Early Recordings	1951	30.00	60.00	120.00
FP-34 [10]	Lead Belly's Legacy, Vol. 4: Easy Rider	1951	30.00	60.00	120.00
FP-241 [(2) M]	Leadbelly's Last Sessions, Vol. 1	196?	10.00	20.00	40.00
FP-242 [(2) M]	Leadbelly's Last Sessions, Vol. 2	196?	10.00	20.00	40.00
FA-2004 [10]	Lead Belly's Legacy, Vol. 1: Take This Hammer	195?	12.50	25.00	50.00
—Reissue of FP-4					
FA-2014 [10]	Lead Belly's Legacy, Vol. 2: Rock Island Line	195?	12.50	25.00	50.00
—Reissue of FP-14					
FA-2024 [10]	Lead Belly's Legacy, Vol. 3: Early Recordings	195?	12.50	25.00	50.00
—Reissue of FP-24					
FA-2034 [10]	Lead Belly's Legacy, Vol. 4: Easy Rider	195?	12.50	25.00	50.00
—Reissue of FP-34					
FA-2941 [M]	Leadbelly's Last Sessions, Vol. 3	196?	6.25	12.50	25.00
FA-2942 [M]	Leadbelly's Last Sessions, Vol. 4	196?	6.25	12.50	25.00
FA-3106 [M]	Leadbelly Sings Folk Songs	196?	6.25	12.50	25.00
RCA VICTOR					
LPV-505 [M]	Midnight Special	1964	10.00	20.00	40.00
ROYALE					
18131 [10]	Blues Songs	1954	30.00	60.00	120.00
—As "The Lonesome Blues Singer"					
VERVE FOLKWAYS					
FT-3019 [M]	From the Last Sessions	1967	6.25	12.50	25.00
FTS-3019 [R]	From the Last Sessions	1967	3.75	7.50	15.00
FV-9001 [M]	Take This Hammer	1965	6.25	12.50	25.00
FVS-9001 [R]	Take This Hammer	1965	3.75	7.50	15.00
FV-9021 [M]	Keep Your Hands Off Her	1965	6.25	12.50	25.00
FVS-9021 [R]	Keep Your Hands Off Her	1965	3.75	7.50	15.00

LEAPER, BOB

Number	Title (A Side/B Side)	Yr	VG	VG+	NM
45s					
REPRISE					
0276	Sunday Morning/Come and Join Us	1964	2.50	5.00	10.00
Albums					
LONDON					
LL 3391 [M]	Big Band Beatle Songs	1964	3.75	7.50	15.00
SP 4056 [S]	Big Band Beatle Songs	1964	5.00	10.00	20.00

LEAPING FERNS, THE

Also recorded as CHANTAY'S.

Number	Title (A Side/B Side)	Yr	VG	VG+	NM
45s					
X-PANDED SOUND					
103	It Never Works Out for Me/Maybe Baby	1964	7.50	15.00	30.00

LEAPY LEE

Number	Title (A Side/B Side)	Yr	VG	VG+	NM
45s					
CADET					
5635	It's All Happening/It's Great	1969	—	3.50	7.00
DECCA					
32380	Little Arrows/Time Will Tell	1968	2.00	4.00	8.00
32436	Here Comes the Rain/I'm Gonna Spend My Love	1969	—	3.50	7.00
32492	Little Yellow Aeroplane/Boom Boom (That's How My Heart Beats)	1969	—	3.50	7.00
32584	Someone's in Love/Best to Forget	1969	—	3.50	7.00
32625	Good Morning/Teresa	1970	—	3.50	7.00
32692	Tupelo Mississippi Flash/Green Green Trees	1970	—	3.00	6.00
32808	Best to Forget/I'll Be Your Baby Tonight	1971	—	3.00	6.00
MAM					
3618	Just Another Night/My Advice to You	1972	—	3.00	6.00
3622	Summer Rain/No Full Moon	1972	—	3.00	6.00
MCA					
40470	Every Road Leads Back to You/Honey Go Drift Away	1975	—	2.50	5.00
Albums					
DECCA					
DL 75076	Little Arrows	1968	5.00	10.00	20.00
DL 75237	Leapy Lee	1970	3.75	7.50	15.00

LEARY, DR. TIMOTHY

Number	Title (A Side/B Side)	Yr	VG	VG+	NM
45s					
MERCURY					
72713	Turn On, Tune In, Drop Out (Part 1)/Turn On, Tune In, Drop Out (Part 2)	1967	7.50	15.00	30.00
Albums					
DOUGLAS					
1	You Can Be Anyone This Time Around	1969	25.00	50.00	100.00
ESP-DISK'					
1027 [M]	Turn On, Tune In, Drop Out	1966	37.50	75.00	150.00
MERCURY					
MG-21131 [M]	Turn On, Tune In, Drop Out	1967	10.00	20.00	40.00
SR-61131 [S]	Turn On, Tune In, Drop Out	1967	12.50	25.00	50.00
PIXIE					
CA-1069 [M]	L.S.D.	1966	20.00	40.00	80.00

LEATHER BOY

Number	Title (A Side/B Side)	Yr	VG	VG+	NM
45s					
FLOWER					
100	My Prayer/You Gotta Have Soul	1968	7.50	15.00	30.00
MGM					
13724	I'm a Leather Boy/Shadows	1967	7.50	15.00	30.00
13724 [PS]	I'm a Leather Boy/Shadows	1967	15.00	30.00	60.00
13790	On the Go/Soulin'	1967	7.50	15.00	30.00
PARKWAY					
125	Jersey Thursday/Black Friday	1966	7.50	15.00	30.00

LEATHERCOATED MINDS, THE

Number	Title (A Side/B Side)	Yr	VG	VG+	NM
Albums					
VIVA					
V-6003 [M]	Trip Down Sunset Strip	1967	15.00	30.00	60.00
V-36003 [S]	Trip Down Sunset Strip	1967	20.00	40.00	80.00

LEAVES, THE

Number	Title (A Side/B Side)	Yr	VG	VG+	NM
45s					
CAPITOL					
5799	Lemon Princess/Twilight Sanctuary	1966	3.00	6.00	12.00
MIRA					
202	Love Minus Zero-No Limit/Too Many People	1965	12.50	25.00	50.00
207	Hey Joe, Where You Gonna Go/Be with You	1965	25.00	50.00	100.00
213	You Better Move On/A Different Story	1966	12.50	25.00	50.00
220	Be with You/Funny Little World	1966	12.50	25.00	50.00
222	Hey Joe/Funny Little World	1966	12.50	25.00	50.00
222	Hey Joe/Girl from the East	1966	10.00	20.00	40.00
227	Too Many People/Girl from the East	1966	10.00	20.00	40.00
231	Get Out of My Life Woman/Girl from the East	1966	10.00	20.00	40.00
234	Be with You/You Better Move On	1966	10.00	20.00	40.00
Albums					
CAPITOL					
ST 2638 [S]	All the Good That's Happening	1967	7.50	15.00	30.00
T 2638 [M]	All the Good That's Happening	1967	6.25	12.50	25.00
MIRA					
LP-3005 [M]	Hey Joe	1966	10.00	20.00	40.00
LPS-3005 [S]	Hey Joe	1966	12.50	25.00	50.00
SURREY					
LPS-3005	Hey Joe	196?	37.50	75.00	150.00
—Issued in Mira jackets					

LED ZEPPELIN

Number	Title (A Side/B Side)	Yr	VG	VG+	NM
45s					
ATLANTIC					
PR 157 [DJ]	Gallows Pole (mono/stereo)	1971	50.00	100.00	200.00
PR 175 [DJ]	Stairway to Heaven (mono/stereo)	1972	25.00	50.00	100.00
PR 175 [PS]	Stairway to Heaven (mono/stereo)	1972	62.50	125.00	250.00
PR 269 [DJ]	Stairway to Heaven (stereo/stereo)	1973	12.50	25.00	50.00
2613	Communication Breakdown/Good Times Bad Times	1969	6.25	12.50	25.00
2690	Whole Lotta Love/Living Loving Maid (She's Just a Woman)	1969	3.75	7.50	15.00
—With A-side time of 3:12					
2690	Whole Lotta Love/Living Loving Maid (She's Just a Woman)	1969	5.00	10.00	20.00
—With A-side time of 5:33					
2777	Immigrant Song/Hey, Hey, What Can I Do	1970	6.25	12.50	25.00
—First pressings with "Do What Thou Wilt Shalt Be the Whole of the Law" in trail-off					
2777	Immigrant Song/Hey, Hey, What Can I Do	1970	3.75	7.50	15.00
—Second pressings without "Do What Thou Wilt Shalt Be the Whole of the Law" in trail-off					
2777	Immigrant Song/Hey, Hey, What Can I Do	1970	—	2.50	5.00
—Third pressings with smaller, bolder type; in print well into the late 1980s					
2777 [DJ]	Immigrant Song	1970	30.00	60.00	120.00
—One-sided promo					
2849	Black Dog/Misty Mountain Hop	1971	2.50	5.00	10.00
2865	Rock and Roll/Four Sticks	1972	2.50	5.00	10.00
2970	Over the Hills & Far Away/Dancing Days	1973	2.50	5.00	10.00
2986	D'yer Mak'er/The Crunge	1973	—	3.00	6.00
—Defective pressing -- the left channel starts to fade out midway through the A-side, making it sound like rechanneled stereo. The number "3" follows the matrix number in the trail-off wax of those copies we've encountered.					
2986	D'yer Mak'er/The Crunge	1973	2.50	5.00	10.00
—Normal pressing in true stereo throughout.					
SWAN SONG					
70102	Trampled Under Foot/Black Country Woman	1975	—	3.00	6.00
70110	Candy Store Rock/Royal Orleans	1976	—	3.00	6.00
71003	Fool in the Rain/Hot Dog	1979	—	3.00	6.00
Albums					
ATLANTIC					
7201 [M]	Led Zeppelin III	1970	50.00	100.00	200.00
—White label promo only					
SD 7201	Led Zeppelin III	2000	6.25	12.50	25.00
—Classic Records reissue on audioiphile vinyl					
SD 7201 [DJ]	Led Zeppelin III	1970	50.00	100.00	200.00
—Stereo white label promo					
SD 7201 [S]	Led Zeppelin III	1970	3.75	7.50	15.00
—Die-cut cover with movable wheel; "1841 Broadway" address on label					
SD 7201 [S]	Led Zeppelin III	1974	2.50	5.00	10.00
—"75 Rockefeller Plaza" address on label					
7208 [M]	Led Zeppelin (IV) (Runes)	1971	75.00	150.00	300.00
—White label promo only					
SD 7208	Led Zeppelin (IV) (Runes)	2000	6.25	12.50	25.00
—Classic Records reissue on audioiphile vinyl					
SD 7208 [DJ]	Led Zeppelin (IV) (Runes)	1971	37.50	75.00	150.00
—Stereo white label promo					
SD 7208 [S]	Led Zeppelin (IV) (Runes)	1971	3.00	6.00	12.00
—"1841 Broadway" address on label					
SD 7208 [S]	Led Zeppelin (IV) (Runes)	1974	2.50	5.00	10.00
—"75 Rockefeller Plaza" address on label					
7255 [M]	Houses of the Holy	1973	250.00	500.00	1000.
—White label promo only					
SD 7255 [S]	Houses of the Holy	1973	3.00	6.00	12.00
—"1841 Broadway" address on label					
SD 7255 [S]	Houses of the Holy	1974	2.50	5.00	10.00
—"75 Rockefeller Plaza" address on label					
8216 [M]	Led Zeppelin	1969	100.00	200.00	400.00
—White label promo only					
SD 8216	Led Zeppelin	1969	62.50	125.00	250.00
—Possible mispress with purple and brown labels					
SD 8216	Led Zeppelin	2000	6.25	12.50	25.00
—Classic Records reissue on audioiphile vinyl					
SD 8216 [DJ]	Led Zeppelin	1969	50.00	100.00	200.00
—Stereo white label promo					
SD 8216 [S]	Led Zeppelin	1969	5.00	10.00	20.00
—"1841 Broadway" address on label					
SD 8216 [S]	Led Zeppelin	1974	2.50	5.00	10.00
—"75 Rockefeller Plaza" address on label					

Number	Title (A Side/B Side)	Yr	VG	VG+	NM
8236 [M]	Led Zeppelin II	1969	50.00	100.00	200.00
—White label promo only					
SD 8236	Led Zeppelin II	2000	6.25	12.50	25.00
—Classic Records reissue on audioiphile vinyl					
SD 8236 [DJ]	Led Zeppelin II	1969	75.00	150.00	300.00
—Stereo white label promo					
SD 8236 [S]	Led Zeppelin II	1969	5.00	10.00	20.00
—"1841 Broadway" address on label					
SD 8236 [S]	Led Zeppelin II	1974	2.50	5.00	10.00
—"75 Rockefeller Plaza" address on label					
SD 19126	Led Zeppelin	1977	2.00	4.00	8.00
SD 19127	Led Zeppelin II	1977	2.00	4.00	8.00
SD 19128	Led Zeppelin III	1977	2.00	4.00	8.00
SD 19129	Led Zeppelin (IV) (Runes)	1977	2.00	4.00	8.00
SD 19130	Houses of the Holy	1977	2.00	4.00	8.00
82144 [(6)]	Led Zeppelin (Box Set)	1990	25.00	50.00	100.00
83061 [(4)]	BBC Sessions	2000	15.00	30.00	60.00
—Classic Records limited edition; each LP is in its own cardboard sleeve inside a box with a sheet of liner notes					
83268 [(2)]	Early Days: The Best of Led Zeppelin Vol. 1	1999	3.75	7.50	15.00
83278 [(2)]	Latter Days: The Best of Led Zeppelin Vol. 2	2000	3.75	7.50	15.00
SMAS-94019	Led Zeppelin (IV) (Runes)	1972	10.00	20.00	40.00
—Capitol Record Club edition					
MOBILE FIDELITY					
1-065	Led Zeppelin II	1981	20.00	40.00	80.00
—Audiophile vinyl					
SWAN SONG					
SS 2-200 [(2)]	Physical Graffiti	1975	3.75	7.50	15.00
SS 2-201 [(2)]	The Song Remains the Same	1976	3.75	7.50	15.00
SS 8416	Presence	1976	2.50	5.00	10.00
SS 16002	In Through the Out Door	1979	2.50	5.00	10.00
—Released with six different covers, numbered "A" through "F" on the spine. Add 50% if brown paper bag is still with jacket.					
90051	Coda	1982	2.50	5.00	10.00

LEE

See LEE MARENO.

LEE, ALVIN

Also see TEN YEARS AFTER.

12-Inch Singles

Number	Title (A Side/B Side)	Yr	VG	VG+	NM
21 RECORDS					
PR 918 [DJ]	Detroit Diesel (same on both sides)	1986	—	3.00	6.00
PR 956 [DJ]	Shot in the Dark (same on both sides)	1986	—	3.00	6.00

45s

Number	Title (A Side/B Side)	Yr	VG	VG+	NM
21 RECORDS					
99501	Heart of Stone/She's So Cute	1986	—	—	3.00
99527	Detroit Diesel/Let's Go	1986	—	—	3.00
ATLANTIC					
3792 [DJ]	Ridin' Truckin' (same on both sides)	1981	—	2.00	4.00
—May be promo only					
4004 [DJ]	Can't Stop (same on both sides)	1982	—	2.00	4.00
—May be promo only					
COLUMBIA					
45987	So Sad/Riffin'	1974	—	2.00	4.00
—With Mylon LeFevre					
RSO					
936	Ride On Cowboy/Can't Sleep at Night	1979	—	2.00	4.00
—With "Ten Years Later"					

Albums

Number	Title (A Side/B Side)	Yr	VG	VG+	NM
21 RECORDS					
90517	Detroit Diesel	1986	2.50	5.00	10.00
ATLANTIC					
SD 19287	Free Fall	1980	2.50	5.00	10.00
SD 19306	RX5	1981	2.50	5.00	10.00
COLUMBIA					
KC 32729	On the Road to Freedom	1973	3.00	6.00	12.00
—With Mylon LeFevre					
PC 32729	On the Road to Freedom	197?	2.00	4.00	8.00
—With Mylon LeFevre; reissue with new prefix					
PG 33187 [(2)]	In Flight	1974	3.75	7.50	15.00
PC 33796	Pump Iron!	1975	3.00	6.00	12.00
RSO					
RS-1-3033	Rocket Fuel	1978	3.00	6.00	12.00
—With "Ten Years Later"					
RS-1-3049	Ride On	1979	3.00	6.00	12.00
—With "Ten Years Later"					

LEE, ARTHUR

Also see LOVE.

45s

Number	Title (A Side/B Side)	Yr	VG	VG+	NM
A&M					
1361	Everybody's Gotta Live/Love Jumped Through My Window	1972	—	2.00	4.00
1381	Sad Song/You Want Change for Your Re-Run	1972	—	2.00	4.00
CAPITOL					
4980	Ninth Wave/Rumble Still Skins	1963	7.50	15.00	30.00

Albums

Number	Title (A Side/B Side)	Yr	VG	VG+	NM
A&M					
SP-4356	Vindicator	1972	7.50	15.00	30.00
RHINO					
RNLP 020	Arthur Lee	1981	2.50	5.00	10.00

LEE, BILLY, AND THE RIVIERAS

Early version of MITCH RYDER AND THE DETROIT WHEELS.

45s

Number	Title (A Side/B Side)	Yr	VG	VG+	NM
HYLAND					
3016	Won't You Dance with Me/You Know	1964	6.25	12.50	25.00

LEE, BRENDA

45s

Number	Title (A Side/B Side)	Yr	VG	VG+	NM
DECCA					
30050	Jambalaya (On the Bayou)/Bigelow 6-2000	1956	7.50	15.00	30.00
30107	Christy Christmas/I'm Gonna Lasso Santa Claus	1956	6.25	12.50	25.00
30198	One Step at a Time/Fairyland	1957	6.25	12.50	25.00
30333	Dynamite/Love You 'Til I Die	1957	6.25	12.50	25.00
30411	Ain't That Love/One Teenager to Another	1957	6.25	12.50	25.00
30535	Rock-a-Bye Baby Blues/Rock the Bop	1958	6.25	12.50	25.00
30673	Ring-a My Phone/Little Jonah	1958	7.50	15.00	30.00
30776	Rockin' Around the Christmas Tree/Papa Noel	1958	6.25	12.50	25.00
—Originals have black labels with star under "Decca"					
30776	Rockin' Around the Christmas Tree/Papa Noel	1960	3.75	7.50	15.00
—Reissues have black labels with color bars					
30776 [PS]	Rockin' Around the Christmas Tree/Papa Noel	1960	12.50	25.00	50.00
30806	Bill Bailey Won't You Please Come Home/Hummin' the Blues	1959	6.25	12.50	25.00
30885	Let's Jump the Broomstick/One of These Days	1959	7.50	15.00	30.00
30967	Sweet Nothin's/Weep No More My Baby	1959	5.00	10.00	20.00
30967 [PS]	Sweet Nothin's/Weep No More My Baby	1959	30.00	60.00	120.00
31093	I'm Sorry/That's All You Gotta Do	1960	5.00	10.00	20.00
31093 [PS]	I'm Sorry/That's All You Gotta Do	1960	12.50	25.00	50.00
31149	I Want to Be Wanted/Just a Little	1960	3.75	7.50	15.00
31149 [PS]	I Want to Be Wanted/Just a Little	1960	10.00	20.00	40.00
31195	Emotions/I'm Learning About Love	1961	3.75	7.50	15.00
31195 [PS]	Emotions/I'm Learning About Love	1961	7.50	15.00	30.00
31231	You Can Depend on Me/It's Never Too Late	1961	3.75	7.50	15.00
31231 [PS]	You Can Depend on Me/It's Never Too Late	1961	7.50	15.00	30.00
31272	Dum Dum/Eventually	1961	3.75	7.50	15.00
31272 [PS]	Dum Dum/Eventually	1961	—	—	—
—Rumored to exist, but without conclusive evidence, we will delete this from future editions					
31309	Fool #1/Anybody But Me	1961	3.75	7.50	15.00
31309 [PS]	Fool #1/Anybody But Me	1961	7.50	15.00	30.00
31348	Break It To Me Gently/So Deep	1962	3.75	7.50	15.00
31348 [PS]	Break It To Me Gently/So Deep	1962	6.25	12.50	25.00
31379	Everybody Loves Me But You/Here Comes That Feelin'	1962	3.75	7.50	15.00
31407	Heart in Hand/It Started All Over Again	1962	3.75	7.50	15.00
31424	All Alone Am I/Save All Your Lovin' for Me	1962	3.75	7.50	15.00
31424 [PS]	All Alone Am I/Save All Your Lovin' for Me	1962	6.25	12.50	25.00
31454	Your Used to Be/She'll Never Know	1963	3.75	7.50	15.00
31454 [PS]	Your Used to Be/She'll Never Know	1963	6.25	12.50	25.00
31478	Losing You/He's So Heavenly	1963	3.75	7.50	15.00
31478 [PS]	Losing You/He's So Heavenly	1963	6.25	12.50	25.00
31510	My Whole World Is Falling Down/I Wonder	1963	3.75	7.50	15.00
31510 [PS]	My Whole World Is Falling Down/I Wonder	1963	6.25	12.50	25.00
31539	The Grass Is Greener/Sweet Impossible You	1963	3.75	7.50	15.00
31539 [PS]	The Grass Is Greener/Sweet Impossible You	1963	6.25	12.50	25.00
31570	As Usual/Lonely Lonely Lonely Me	1963	3.75	7.50	15.00
31599	Think/The Waiting Game	1964	2.50	5.00	10.00
31599 [PS]	Think/The Waiting Game	1964	3.75	7.50	15.00
31628	Alone with You/My Dreams	1964	2.50	5.00	10.00
31628 [PS]	Alone with You/My Dreams	1964	3.75	7.50	15.00
31654	When You Loved Me/He's Sure to Remember Me	1964	2.50	5.00	10.00
31654 [PS]	When You Loved Me/He's Sure to Remember Me	1964	3.75	7.50	15.00
31687	Jingle Bell Rock/Winter Wonderland	1964	3.00	6.00	12.00
31687 [PS]	Jingle Bell Rock/Winter Wonderland	1964	4.00	8.00	16.00
31688	This Time of the Year/Christmas Will Be Just Another Lonely Day	1964	3.00	6.00	12.00
31688 [PS]	This Time of the Year/Christmas Will Be Just Another Lonely Day	1964	4.00	8.00	16.00
31690	Is It True/Just Behind the Rainbow	1964	2.50	5.00	10.00
31690 [PS]	Is It True/Just Behind the Rainbow	1964	3.75	7.50	15.00
31728	Thanks a Lot/The Crying Game	1965	2.50	5.00	10.00
31762	Truly, Truly, True/I Still Miss Someone	1965	2.50	5.00	10.00
31762 [PS]	Truly, Truly, True/I Still Miss Someone	1965	3.75	7.50	15.00
31792	Too Many Rivers/No One	1965	2.50	5.00	10.00
31849	Rusty Bells/If You Don't (Not Like You)	1965	2.50	5.00	10.00
31917	Too Little Time/Time and Time Again	1966	2.00	4.00	8.00
31970	Ain't Gonna Cry No More/It Takes One to Know One	1966	2.00	4.00	8.00
32018	Coming On Strong/You Keep Coming Back to Me	1966	2.00	4.00	8.00
32079	Ride, Ride, Ride/Lonely People Do Foolish Things	1967	2.00	4.00	8.00
32119	Born to Be By Your Side/Take Me	1967	2.00	4.00	8.00
32161	My Heart Keeps Hangin' On/Where Love Is	1967	2.00	4.00	8.00
32213	Where's the Melody/Save Me for a Rainy Day	1967	2.00	4.00	8.00
32248	That's All Right/Fantasy	1967	2.00	4.00	8.00
32299	Cabaret/Mood Indigo	1968	2.00	4.00	8.00
—With Pete Fountain					
32330	Kansas City/Each Day Is a Rainbow	1968	2.00	4.00	8.00
32428	Johnny One Time/I Must Have Been Out of My Mind	1968	2.00	4.00	8.00
32428 [PS]	Johnny One Time/I Must Have Been Out of My Mind	1968	3.75	7.50	15.00
32491	You Don't Need Me for Anything Anymore/Bring Me Sunshine	1969	—	3.00	6.00
32560	Let It Be Me/You Better Move On	1969	—	3.00	6.00
32675	I Think I Love You Again/Hello Love	1970	—	3.00	6.00
32734	Do Right Woman, Do Right Man/Sisters in Sorrow	1970	—	3.00	6.00
32848	If This Is Our Last Time/Everybody's Reaching Out for Someone	1971	—	3.00	6.00
32918	I'm a Memory/Misty Memories	1972	—	3.00	6.00
32975	Always on My Mind/That Ain't Right	1972	—	3.00	6.00
34494 [DJ]	Where's the Melody? (same on both sides)	1967	3.75	7.50	15.00
—Promo-only number, pink label					
38236 [DJ]	Voice Tracks by Brenda Lee: For Brenda Lee Day, March 29, 1961/Introduction and Station Breaks for General Use	1961	10.00	20.00	40.00
—Pink label promo					
88215	Christy Christmas/I'm Gonna Lasso Santa Claus	1956	12.50	25.00	50.00
—As "Little Brenda Lee" on Decca's Children's Series					
88215 [PS]	Christy Christmas/I'm Gonna Lasso Santa Claus	1956	20.00	40.00	80.00
ELEKTRA					
45492	Left-Over Love/Could It Be I Found Love Tonight	1978	—	2.50	5.00

Number	Title (A Side/B Side)	Yr	VG	VG+	NM
MCA					
40003	Nobody Wins/We Had a Good Thing Goin'	1973	—	2.50	5.00
40107	Sunday Sunrise/Must I Believe	1973	—	2.50	5.00
40171	Wrong Ideas/Something For A Rainy Day	1973	—	2.50	5.00
40262	Big Four Poster Bed/Castles In The Sand	1974	—	2.50	5.00
40318	Rock On Baby/More Than A Memory	1974	—	2.50	5.00
40385	He's My Rock/Feel Free	1975	—	2.50	5.00
40442	Bringing It Back/Papa's Knee	1975	—	2.50	5.00
40511	Find Yourself Another Puppet/What I Had With You	1976	—	2.50	5.00
40584	Brother Shelton/Now He's Coming Home	1976	—	2.50	5.00
40640	Takin' What I Can Get/Your Favorite Wornout Nightmare's Coming Home	1976	—	2.50	5.00
40683	Ruby's Lounge/Oklahoma Superstar	1977	—	2.50	5.00
41130	Tell Me What It's Like/Let Your Love Fall Back On Me	1979	—	2.50	5.00
41187	The Cowgirl And The Dandy/Do You Wanna Spend The Night	1980	—	2.50	5.00
41262	Keeping Me Warm For You/At The Moonlight	1980	—	2.50	5.00
41270	Don't Promise Me Anything (Do It)/You Only Broke My Heart	1980	—	2.50	5.00
41322	Broken Trust/Right Behind The Rain	1980	—	2.50	5.00
—With the Oak Ridge Boys					
51047	Every Now And Then/He'll Play The Music	1981	—	2.00	4.00
51113	Fool, Fool/Right Behind The Rain	1981	—	2.00	4.00
51154	Enough For You/What Am I Gonna Do	1981	—	2.00	4.00
51195	Only When I Laugh/Too Many Nights Alone	1981	—	2.00	4.00
51230	From Levis To Calvin Klein Jeans/I Know A Lot About Love	1982	—	2.00	4.00
52060	Keeping Me Warm For You/There's More To Me Than You Can See	1982	—	2.00	4.00
52124	Just For The Moment/Love Letters	1982	—	2.00	4.00
—With the Oak Ridge Boys					
52268	Didn't We Do It Good/We're So Close	1983	—	2.00	4.00
52394	A Sweeter Love (I'll Never Know)/A Woman's Mind	1984	—	2.00	4.00
52654	I'm Takin' My Time/That's The Way It Was Then	1985	—	2.00	4.00
52720	Why You Been Gone So Long/He Can't Make Your Kind of Love	1985	—	2.00	4.00
52720 [PS]	Why You Been Gone So Long/He Can't Make Your Kind of Love	1985	—	2.00	4.00
52804	Two Hearts/Loving Arms	1986	—	2.00	4.00
52804 [DJ]	Two Hearts (same on both sides)	1986	2.50	5.00	10.00
—Promo only on red vinyl					
60069	Sweet Nothin's/I Want to Be Wanted	197?	—	2.00	4.00
—Reissue; originals have black rainbow label					
60070	I'm Sorry/All Alone Am I	197?	—	2.00	4.00
—Reissue; originals have black rainbow label					
65027	Rockin' Around the Christmas Tree/Papa Noel	1973	—	2.00	4.00
—Black label with rainbow					
65027	Rockin' Around the Christmas Tree/Papa Noel	1980	—	—	3.00
—Blue label with rainbow					
65028	Jingle Bell Rock/Winter Wonderland	1973	—	2.00	4.00
—Black label with rainbow					
65028	Jingle Bell Rock/Winter Wonderland	1980	—	—	3.00
—Blue label with rainbow					
MONUMENT					
03781	You're Gonna Love Yourself (In the Morning)/What Do You Think About Lovin'	1983	—	2.00	4.00
—A-side: With Willie Nelson; B-side: With Dolly Parton					
WARNER BROS.					
19303	A Little Unfair/Some of These Days	1991	—	—	3.00
19397	Your One and Only/You Better Do Better	1991	—	—	3.00
7-Inch Extended Plays					
DECCA					
ED 2678	(contents unknown)	1960	5.00	10.00	20.00
ED 2678 [PS]	Sweet Nothin's	1960	5.00	10.00	20.00
ED 2682	Be My Love Again/Just Let Me Dream//Jambalaya/Wee Wee Willie	1960	5.00	10.00	20.00
ED 2682 [PS]	(title unknown)	1960	5.00	10.00	20.00
ED 2683	Dynamite/Heading Home//I'm Sorry/That's All You Gotta Do	1960	5.00	10.00	20.00
ED 2683 [PS]	I'm Sorry	1960	5.00	10.00	20.00
ED 2695	I Want to Be Wanted/Just a Little//Teach Me Tonite/Walkin' to New Orleans	1961	5.00	10.00	20.00
ED 2695 [PS]	(title unknown)	1961	5.00	10.00	20.00
ED 2702	Dum Dum/Eventually//When I Fall in Love/Build a Big Fence	1961	5.00	10.00	20.00
ED 2702 [PS]	(title unknown)	1961	5.00	10.00	20.00
ED 2704	(contents unknown)	1961	5.00	10.00	20.00
ED 2704 [PS]	Lover Come Back to Me	1961	5.00	10.00	20.00
ED 2712	Fool #1/Anybody But Me//You Can Depend on Me/It's Never Too Late	1961	5.00	10.00	20.00
ED 2712 [PS]	(title unknown)	1961	5.00	10.00	20.00
ED 2716	Break It to Me Gently/Will You Love Me Tomorrow//Tragedy/So Deep	1962	5.00	10.00	20.00
ED 2716 [PS]	Break It to Me Gently	1962	5.00	10.00	20.00
ED 2725	Here Comes That Feeling/Everybody Loves Me But You//You've Got Me Crying Again/Lazy River	1962	5.00	10.00	20.00
ED 2725 [PS]	Everybody Loves Me But You	1962	5.00	10.00	20.00
ED 2730	It Started All Over Again/Heart in Hand//You Always Hurt the One You Love/Cry	1962	5.00	10.00	20.00
ED 2730 [PS]	(title unknown)	1962	5.00	10.00	20.00
ED 2738	All Alone Am I/Why Me//It's a Lonely Old Town/Save All Your Loving for Me	1962	5.00	10.00	20.00
ED 2738 [PS]	All Alone Am I	1962	5.00	10.00	20.00
ED 2745	My Coloring Book/I Left My Heart in San Francisco//What Kind of Fool Am I/Fly Me to the Moon	1962	5.00	10.00	20.00
ED 2745 [PS]	Fly Me to the Moon	1962	5.00	10.00	20.00
ED 2764	The Grass Is Greener/I Wonder//My Whole World Is Falling Down/Losing You	1963	5.00	10.00	20.00
ED 2764 [PS]	The Grass Is Greener	1963	5.00	10.00	20.00
ED 2775	As Usual/The End of the World//There Goes My Heart/Out in the Cold Again	1963	5.00	10.00	20.00
ED 2775 [PS]	As Usual	1963	5.00	10.00	20.00
ED 2801	Thanks a Lot/Think//Is It True/When You Love Me	1965	5.00	10.00	20.00
ED 2801 [PS]	(title unknown)	1965	5.00	10.00	20.00
7-4216 [DJ]	You Always Hurt the One You Love/Lazy River/You've Got Me Crying//I Miss You So/Fools Rush In/I'll Be Seeing You	1962	5.00	10.00	20.00
—Jukebox EP, stereo, small hole, plays at 33 1/3 rpm					
7-4216 [PS]	Sincerely	1962	5.00	10.00	20.00
7-4439 [DJ]	I Wanna Be Around/Our Day Will Come/You're the Reason I'm in Love//End of the World/Losing You/Break It to Me Gently	1963	5.00	10.00	20.00
—Jukebox EP, stereo, small hole, plays at 33 1/3 rpm					
7-4439 [PS]	Let Me Sing	1963	5.00	10.00	20.00
7-4825 [DJ]	What Now My Love/You Don't Have to Say You Love Me/You've Got Your Troubles//Up Tight/Strangers in the Night/Call Me	1966	5.00	10.00	20.00
—Jukebox EP, stereo, small hole, plays at 33 1/3 rpm					
7-4825 [PS]	Coming On Strong	1966	5.00	10.00	20.00
7-34254	This Time of the Year/Blue Christmas/Jingle Bell Rock//Rockin' Around the Christmas Tree/Marshmallow World/Winter Wonderland	1964	6.25	12.50	25.00
—Jukebox EP, stereo, small hole, plays at 33 1/3 rpm					
7-34254 [PS]	Merry Christmas	1964	6.25	12.50	25.00
—Sleeve says this is "DL 74583"; price includes title strips					
7-34363 [DJ]	Bye Bye Blues/September in the Rain/What a Difference a Day Makes//The Good Life/Shadow of Your Smile/Softly As I Leave You	1966	5.00	10.00	20.00
—Jukebox EP, stereo, small hole, plays at 33 1/3 rpm					
7-34363 [PS]	Bye Bye Blues	1966	5.00	10.00	20.00
Albums					
DECCA					
DL 4039 [M]	Brenda Lee	1960	6.25	12.50	25.00
DL 4082 [M]	This Is...Brenda	1960	6.25	12.50	25.00
DL 4104 [M]	Emotions	1961	6.25	12.50	25.00
DL 4176 [M]	All the Way	1961	6.25	12.50	25.00
DL 4216 [M]	Sincerely	1962	6.25	12.50	25.00
DL 4326 [M]	Brenda, That's All	1962	6.25	12.50	25.00
DL 4370 [M]	All Alone Am I	1963	6.25	12.50	25.00
DL 4439 [M]	Let Me Sing	1963	6.25	12.50	25.00
DL 4509 [M]	By Request	1964	5.00	10.00	20.00
DL 4583 [M]	Merry Christmas from Brenda Lee	1964	5.00	10.00	20.00
DL 4626 [M]	Top Teen Hits	1965	5.00	10.00	20.00
DL 4661 [M]	The Versatile Brenda Lee	1965	5.00	10.00	20.00
DL 4684 [M]	Too Many Rivers	1965	5.00	10.00	20.00
DL 4755 [M]	Bye Bye Blues	1966	5.00	10.00	20.00
DL 4757 [M]	10 Golden Years	1966	6.25	12.50	25.00
—With gatefold cover					
DL 4757 [M]	10 Golden Years	196?	3.75	7.50	15.00
—With regular cover					
DL 4825 [M]	Coming On Strong	1966	3.75	7.50	15.00
DL 4941 [M]	Reflections in Blue	1967	5.00	10.00	20.00
DL 8873 [M]	Grandma, What Great Songs You Sang	1960	10.00	20.00	40.00
DL 74039 [S]	Brenda Lee	1960	7.50	15.00	30.00
DL 74082 [S]	This Is...Brenda	1960	7.50	15.00	30.00
DL 74104 [S]	Emotions	1961	7.50	15.00	30.00
DL 74176 [S]	All the Way	1961	7.50	15.00	30.00
DL 74216 [S]	Sincerely	1962	7.50	15.00	30.00
DL 74326 [S]	Brenda, That's All	1962	7.50	15.00	30.00
DL 74370 [S]	All Alone Am I	1963	7.50	15.00	30.00
DL 74439 [S]	Let Me Sing	1963	7.50	15.00	30.00
DL 74509 [S]	By Request	1964	6.25	12.50	25.00
DL 74583 [S]	Merry Christmas from Brenda Lee	1964	6.25	12.50	25.00
DL 74626 [S]	Top Teen Hits	1965	6.25	12.50	25.00
DL 74661 [S]	The Versatile Brenda Lee	1965	6.25	12.50	25.00
DL 74684 [S]	Too Many Rivers	1965	6.25	12.50	25.00
DL 74755 [S]	Bye Bye Blues	1966	6.25	12.50	25.00
DL 74757 [S]	10 Golden Years	1966	7.50	15.00	30.00
—With gatefold cover					
DL 74757 [S]	10 Golden Years	196?	5.00	10.00	20.00
—With regular cover					
DL 74825 [S]	Coming On Strong	1966	5.00	10.00	20.00
DL 74941 [S]	Reflections in Blue	1967	3.75	7.50	15.00
DL 74955	For the First Time	1968	3.75	7.50	15.00
—With Pete Fountain					
DL 75111	Johnny One Time	1969	3.75	7.50	15.00
DL 75232	Memphis Portrait	1970	3.75	7.50	15.00
DL 78873 [S]	Grandma, What Great Songs You Sang	1960	12.50	25.00	50.00
ST-92062	Johnny One Time	1969	5.00	10.00	20.00
—Capitol Record Club edition					
R 103619 [S]	Merry Christmas from Brenda Lee	1971	5.00	10.00	20.00
—RCA Music Service edition					
MCA					
232 [S]	Merry Christmas from Brenda Lee	1973	3.00	6.00	12.00
305	Brenda	1973	3.75	7.50	15.00
375	New Sunrise	1973	3.00	6.00	12.00
433	Brenda Lee Now	1974	3.00	6.00	12.00
477	Sincerely, Brenda Lee	1975	2.50	5.00	10.00
758	Even Better	198?	2.00	4.00	8.00
—Reissue of 3211					
824	Only When I Laugh	1982	2.00	4.00	8.00
—Reissue of 5278					
2233	L.A. Sessions	1976	2.50	5.00	10.00
3211	Even Better	1979	2.50	5.00	10.00
4012 [(2)]	The Brenda Lee Story — Her Greatest Hits	1973	5.00	10.00	20.00
5143	Take Me Back	1980	2.50	5.00	10.00
5278	Only When I Laugh	1981	2.50	5.00	10.00
5342	Greatest Country Hits	1982	2.50	5.00	10.00
5626	Feels So Right	1985	2.50	5.00	10.00
15021 [S]	Merry Christmas from Brenda Lee	197?	2.50	5.00	10.00
15038	Rockin' Around the Christmas Tree	198?	2.50	5.00	10.00
MCA CORAL					
CB-20044	Let It Be Me	197?	2.50	5.00	10.00

Number	Title (A Side/B Side)	Yr	VG	VG+	NM
VOCALION					
VL 3795 [M]	Here's Brenda Lee	1967	3.00	6.00	12.00
VL 73795 [S]	Here's Brenda Lee	1967	3.00	6.00	12.00
VL 73890	Let It Be Me	1970	3.00	6.00	12.00

LEE, BRENDA (2)

Not the same Brenda Lee as the others; this one's real name is Brenda Lee Jones.

45s

Number	Title (A Side/B Side)	Yr	VG	VG+	NM
APOLLO					
490	I Ain't Gonna Give Nobody None/I'll Never Get Rich Again	1956	7.50	15.00	30.00

LEE, CURTIS

Also see C.L. AND THE PICTURES.

45s

Number	Title (A Side/B Side)	Yr	VG	VG+	NM
DUNES					
801	California GH-903/Then I'll Know	1960	5.00	10.00	20.00
2001	Special Love/"D" in Love	1960	5.00	10.00	20.00
2003	Pledge of Love/Then I'll Know	1961	5.00	10.00	20.00
2003 [PS]	Pledge of Love/Then I'll Know	1961	6.25	12.50	25.00
2007	Pretty Little Angel Eyes/Gee, How I Wish	1961	6.25	12.50	25.00
2008	Under the Moon of Love/Beverly Jean	1961	6.25	12.50	25.00
—2007 and 2208 were Phil Spector productions					
2012	Just Another Fool/A Night at Daddy G's	1962	5.00	10.00	20.00
2015	Does He Mean That Much to You/The Wobble	1962	5.00	10.00	20.00
2020	Lonely Weekends/Better Him Than Me	1963	5.00	10.00	20.00
2021	Pickin' Up the Pieces of My Heart/Mr. Mistaker	1963	5.00	10.00	20.00
HOT					
7	I Never Knew What Love Could Do/Gotta Have You	1960	18.75	37.50	75.00
MIRA					
240	Sweet Baby/Is She In Your Town	1967	5.00	10.00	20.00
ROJAC					
114	Get In My Bag/Everybody's Going Wild	1967	3.00	6.00	12.00
SABRA					
517	Let's Take a Ride/I'm Asking Forgiveness	1960	6.25	12.50	25.00
WARRIOR					
1555	With All My Heart/Pure Love	1959	7.50	15.00	30.00

LEE, DICKEY

45s

Number	Title (A Side/B Side)	Yr	VG	VG+	NM
ATCO					
6546	Run Right Back/Red, Green, Yellow, Blue	1968	2.00	4.00	8.00
6580	All My Life/Hang-Ups	1968	2.00	4.00	8.00
6609	You're Young and You'll Forget/Waitin' for Love to Come My Way	1968	2.00	4.00	8.00
DIAMOND					
266	Ruby Baby/I Remember Barbara	1969	2.00	4.00	8.00
DOT					
16087	Life in a Teenage World/Why Don't You Write On	1960	3.75	7.50	15.00
HALLWAY					
1924	Big Brother/She's Walking Away	1964	2.50	5.00	10.00
MERCURY					
55068	I'm Just a Heartache Away/Midnight Flyer	1979	—	2.00	4.00
57005	He's an Old Rock 'N' Roller/It Hurts to Be in Love	1979	—	2.00	4.00
57017	Don't Look Back/I'm Trustin' a Feelin'	1980	—	2.00	4.00
57027	Workin' My Way to Your Heart/If You Want Me	1980	—	2.00	4.00
57036	Lost in Love/Again	1980	—	2.00	4.00
—A-side with Kathy Burdick					
57052	Honky Tonk Hearts/Best I Hit the Road	1981	—	2.00	4.00
57056	I Wonder If I Care As Much/Further Than a Country Mile	1981	—	2.00	4.00
76129	Everybody Loves a Winner/You Won't Be Here Tonight	1982	—	2.00	4.00
RCA					
PB-10764	9,999,999 Tears/I Never Will Get Over You	1976	—	2.00	4.00
PB-10914	If You Gotta Make a Fool of Somebody/My Love Shows Thru	1977	—	2.00	4.00
GB-10929	Rocky/9,999,999 Tears	1977	—	—	3.00
—Gold Standard Series					
PB-11009	Virginia, How Far Will You Go/My Love Shows Thru	1977	—	2.00	4.00
PB-11125	Peanut Butter/Breezy Was Her Name	1977	—	2.00	4.00
PB-11191	Love Is a Word/I'll Be Leaving Alone	1978	—	2.00	4.00
PB-11294	My Heart Won't Cry Anymore/Danna	1978	—	2.00	4.00
PB-11389	It's Not Easy/I've Been Honky-Tonkin' Too Long	1978	—	2.00	4.00
RCA VICTOR					
APBO-0082	Sparklin' Brown Eyes/Country Song	1973	—	2.50	5.00
APBO-0227	I Use the Soap/Strawberry Women	1974	—	2.50	5.00
PB-10014	Give Me One Good Reason/Sweet Fever	1974	—	2.50	5.00
PB-10091	The Busiest Memory in Town/Way to Go On	1974	—	2.50	5.00
PB-10289	You Make It Look So Easy/The Door's Always Open	1975	—	2.00	4.00
PB-10361	Rocky/The Closest Thing to You	1975	—	2.00	4.00
PB-10543	Angels, Roses and Rain/Danna	1976	—	2.00	4.00
PB-10684	Makin' Love Don't Always Make Love Grow/I Never Will Get Over You	1976	—	2.00	4.00
47-9862	All Too Soon/Charlie	1970	—	3.00	6.00
47-9941	Home To/Special	1971	—	3.00	6.00
47-9988	The Mahogany Pulpit/Everybody's Reaching Out for Someone	1971	—	3.00	6.00
48-1013	Never Ending Song of Love/On the Southbound	1971	—	3.00	6.00
74-0623	I Saw My Lady/What We Used to Hang On To	1971	—	3.00	6.00
74-0710	Ashes of Love/The Kingdom I Call Home	1972	—	2.50	5.00
74-0798	Baby, Bye Bye/She Thinks I Still Care	1972	—	2.50	5.00
74-0892	Crying Over You/My World Around You	1973	—	2.50	5.00
74-0980	Put Me Down Softly/If She Turns Up in Atlanta	1973	—	2.50	5.00
RENDEZVOUS					
188	Dream Boy/Stay True Baby	1962	6.25	12.50	25.00
SMASH					
1758	Patches/More or Less	1962	3.75	7.50	15.00
1791	I Saw Linda Yesterday/The Girl I Can't Forget	1962	3.00	6.00	12.00
1808	Don't Wanna Talk About Paula/Just a Friend	1963	3.00	6.00	12.00
1822	I Go Lonely/Ten Million Faces	1963	3.00	6.00	12.00
1844	She Wants to Be Bobby's Girl/The Day the Sawmill Closed Down	1963	3.00	6.00	12.00
1871	To the Aisle/Mother Nature	1964	3.00	6.00	12.00
1913	Me and My Teardrops/Only Trust in Me	1964	3.00	6.00	12.00
SUN					
280	Good Lovin'/Memories Never Grow Old	1957	7.50	15.00	30.00
297	Dreamy Nights/Fool, Fool, Fool	1958	20.00	40.00	80.00
TAMPA					
131	Dream Boy/Stay True Baby	1957	7.50	15.00	30.00
TCF HALL					
102	Laurie (Strange Things Happen)/Party Doll	1965	2.50	5.00	10.00
111	The Girl from Peyton Place/The Girl I Used to Know	1965	2.50	5.00	10.00
118	Good Girl Goin' Bad/Pretty White Dress	1965	2.50	5.00	10.00
128	Good Guy/Annie	1966	2.50	5.00	10.00

Albums

Number	Title (A Side/B Side)	Yr	VG	VG+	NM
MERCURY					
SRM-1-5020	Dickey Lee	1979	2.50	5.00	10.00
SRM-1-5026	Dickey Lee Again	1980	2.50	5.00	10.00
RCA VICTOR					
APL1-0311	Sparklin' Brown Eyes	1974	3.00	6.00	12.00
APL1-1243	Rocky	1975	3.00	6.00	12.00
APL1-1725	Angels, Roses and Rain	1976	3.00	6.00	12.00
LSP-4637	Never Ending Song of Love	1971	3.00	6.00	12.00
LSP-4715	Ashes of Love	1972	3.00	6.00	12.00
LSP-4791	Baby, Bye Bye	1972	3.00	6.00	12.00
LSP-4857	Crying Over You	1973	3.00	6.00	12.00
SMASH					
MGS-27020 [M]	The Tale of Patches	1962	7.50	15.00	30.00
SRS-67020 [S]	The Tale of Patches	1962	10.00	20.00	40.00
TCF HALL					
ST-9001 [S]	"Laurie" and "The Girl from Peyton Place"	1965	6.25	12.50	25.00
T-9001 [M]	"Laurie" and "The Girl from Peyton Place"	1965	5.00	10.00	20.00

LEE, JACKIE (1)

Male R&B singer whose biggest hit was "The Duck."

45s

Number	Title (A Side/B Side)	Yr	VG	VG+	NM
ABC					
11146	One for the Road/Darkest Days	1968	5.00	10.00	20.00
CAPITOL					
3145	25 Miles to Louisiana/Pershing Square	1971	—	3.00	6.00
KEYMEN					
109	Glory of Love/Bring It Home	1968	2.50	5.00	10.00
114	African Boo-Ga-Loo/(B-side unknown)	1968	2.50	5.00	10.00
MIRWOOD					
5502	The Duck/Let Your Conscience Be Your Guide	1965	3.00	6.00	12.00
5509	Your P-E-R-S-O-N-A-L-I-T-Y/Try My Method	1966	2.50	5.00	10.00
5510	The Shotgun and the Duck/Do the Temptation Walk	1966	2.50	5.00	10.00
5519	You're Everything/Would You Believe	1966	2.50	5.00	10.00
5527	Don't Be Ashamed/Oh, My Darlin'	1966	2.50	5.00	10.00
5528	Baby I'm Satisfied/Whether It's Right or Wrong	1966	2.50	5.00	10.00
—With Dolores Hall					
UNI					
55206	The Chicken/I Love You	1970	2.00	4.00	8.00
55259	Your Sweetness Is My Weakness/You Were Searching for a Love	1970	2.00	4.00	8.00

Albums

Number	Title (A Side/B Side)	Yr	VG	VG+	NM
MIRWOOD					
MW-7000 [M]	The Duck	1966	5.00	10.00	20.00
SW-7000 [S]	The Duck	1966	6.25	12.50	25.00

LEE, JACKIE (2)

Philadelphia-based keyboard player.

45s

Number	Title (A Side/B Side)	Yr	VG	VG+	NM
ABC-PARAMOUNT					
9892	The Storm/Bye Bye Blues	1958	2.50	5.00	10.00
CORAL					
61214	The Donkey Serenade/Mr. Hot Piano	1954	3.00	6.00	12.00
61259	Bei Mir Bist Du Schoen/Missouri Waltz	1954	3.00	6.00	12.00
61304	I Can't Give You Anything But Love/Blue Boogie	1954	3.00	6.00	12.00
61400	Chop Sticks/Luigi's Wedding	1955	3.00	6.00	12.00
61461	Cannibal King/The Spoon Song	1955	3.00	6.00	12.00
61534	Aloha Oe/More, More, More	1955	3.00	6.00	12.00
61579	A String of Pearls/Always Love Me	1956	2.50	5.00	10.00
61638	Crazy Polka/Elmer's Tune	1956	2.50	5.00	10.00
61734	Chatterbox/Dardanella	1956	2.50	5.00	10.00
61827	Baby Buggy Boogie/Sippin' Soda	1957	2.50	5.00	10.00
SURE					
1738	Do the New Hully Gully/Patricia	1962	2.50	5.00	10.00
1767	Hungarian Rhapsody Boogie/Bumpy	1962	2.50	5.00	10.00
SWAN					
4034	Happy Vacation/The Hucklebuck	1959	3.00	6.00	12.00
4039	Like Sunset/Rancho	1959	3.00	6.00	12.00

LEE, JACKIE (3)

Female singer.

45s

Number	Title (A Side/B Side)	Yr	VG	VG+	NM
EPIC					
9807	I Cry Alone/'Cause I Love Him	1965	2.50	5.00	10.00
10183	Love Is Gone/The Lonely Clown	1967	2.00	4.00	8.00

LEE, JACKIE, AND THE RAINDROPS

45s

Number	Title (A Side/B Side)	Yr	VG	VG+	NM
LONDON INT'L.					
10602	The Last One to Know/There's No One in the Whole Wide World	1962	3.00	6.00	12.00

LEE, JENNY, AND THE STARLETS

Number	Title (A Side/B Side)	Yr	VG	VG+	NM
45s					
CONGRESS					
107	What I Gotta Do/Show Me a Man	1962	3.75	7.50	15.00

LEE, JOHNNY

For records on DeLuxe, see JOHN LEE HOOKER.

LEE, LAURA

Number	Title (A Side/B Side)	Yr	VG	VG+	NM
12-Inch Singles					
FANTASY					
D-133	Sat-Is-Fac-Tion (6:20)/Your Song	1979	3.00	6.00	12.00
45s					
ARIOLA AMERICA					
7652	Love's Got Me Tired (But I Ain't Tired of Love)/ You're Barking Up the Wrong Tree	1976	—	2.50	5.00
CHESS					
1989	Stop Giving Your Man Away/You Need Me	1967	3.00	6.00	12.00
2013	Dirty Man/It's Mighty Hard	1967	2.50	5.00	10.00
2030	Wanted: Lover, No Experience Necessary/Up Tight, Good Man	1967	2.50	5.00	10.00
2041	As Long As I Got You/A Man with Some Backbone	1968	2.50	5.00	10.00
2052	Need to Belong/He Will Break Your Heart	1968	2.50	5.00	10.00
2062	Hang It Up/It's How You Make It Good	1968	2.50	5.00	10.00
2068	Mama's Got a Good Thing/Love More Than Pride	1969	2.50	5.00	10.00
COTILLION					
44054	What a Man/Separation Line	1970	2.00	4.00	8.00
44073	Together/But You Know I Love You	1970	2.00	4.00	8.00
FANTASY					
865	Sat-Is-Fac-Tion/Your Song	1979	—	2.50	5.00
HOT WAX					
7007	Wedlock Is a Padlock/Her Picture Matches Mine	1970	2.00	4.00	8.00
7105	Women's Love Rights/Her Picture Matches Mine	1971	2.00	4.00	8.00
7111	Love and Liberty/I Don't Want Nothing Old But Money	1971	2.00	4.00	8.00
7201	Since I Fell for You/I Don't Want Nothing Old But Money	1972	—	3.50	7.00
7204	Rip Off/Two Lovely Pillows	1972	—	3.50	7.00
7207	If You Can Beat Me Rockin' (You Can Have My Chair)/If I'm Good Enough to Love	1972	—	3.50	7.00
7210	Crumbs Off the Table/You've Got to Save Me	1972	—	3.50	7.00
7302	(If You Want to Try Love Again) Remember Me/ If I'm Good Enough to Love	1973	—	3.50	7.00
7305	I'll Catch You When You Fall/I Can't Hold On Much Longer	1973	—	3.50	7.00
INVICTUS					
1264	I Need It Just As Bad As You/If I'm Good Enough to Love	1974	—	3.00	6.00
1273	Don't Leave Me Starving for Your Love/ Remember Me	1974	—	3.00	6.00
RIC-TIC					
111	To Win Your Heart/So Will I	1966	3.75	7.50	15.00
Albums					
CHESS					
CH-50031	Love More Than Pride	1972	5.00	10.00	20.00
HOT WAX					
HA-708	Women's Love Rights	1971	3.75	7.50	15.00
HA-714	Laura Lee	1972	3.75	7.50	15.00
HA-715	The Best of Laura Lee	1973	3.75	7.50	15.00
INVICTUS					
KZ 33133	Laura Lee	1974	2.50	5.00	10.00

LEE, MICHELE

Number	Title (A Side/B Side)	Yr	VG	VG+	NM
45s					
ABC-PARAMOUNT					
10365	I'm Sorry Missus Murray (But I Cannot Baby-Sit for You Tonight)/Havin' a Party for One	1962	3.75	7.50	15.00
10365 [PS]	I'm Sorry Missus Murray (But I Cannot Baby-Sit for You Tonight)/Havin' a Party for One	1962	7.50	15.00	30.00
10411	He's Not Good Enough for You/I See It All Now	1963	3.75	7.50	15.00
COLUMBIA					
4-43288	Pretty Lies, Pretty Make Believe/Somewhere in the World	1965	2.00	4.00	8.00
4-43376	Call Me/You Were There	1965	2.00	4.00	8.00
4-43476	Feeling Good/Steady, Steady	1965	2.00	4.00	8.00
4-43575	Laugh, Clown, Laugh/I'll Never Go There Anymore	1966	2.00	4.00	8.00
4-43923	If You Go Away/Wednesday's Child	1966	2.00	4.00	8.00
4-44165	Being Good Isn't Good Enough/I Believe in You	1967	2.00	4.00	8.00
4-44413	L. David Sloane/Everybody Loves My Baby (But My Baby Don't Love Nobody But Me)	1967	2.00	4.00	8.00
4-44554	I Can't Believe I'm Losing You/I Didn't Come to New York to Meet a Guy from My Home Town	1968	2.00	4.00	8.00
4-44698	Knowing When to Leave/The Look of Love	1968	2.00	4.00	8.00
4-44835	It's a Long Way to Fall/You'll Remember Me	1969	—	3.00	6.00
Albums					
COLUMBIA					
CL 2486 [M]	A Taste of the Fantastic	1966	3.75	7.50	15.00
CS 9286 [S]	A Taste of the Fantastic	1966	5.00	10.00	20.00
CS 9682	L. David Sloane and Other Hits of Today	1968	5.00	10.00	20.00

LEE, PEGGY

Number	Title (A Side/B Side)	Yr	VG	VG+	NM
45s					
ATLANTIC					
3215	Let's Love/Always	1974	—	2.00	4.00
A&M					
1771	I Remember/Some Cats Know	1975	—	2.00	4.00
CAPITOL					
F791	The Old Master Painter/Bless You	1949	6.25	12.50	25.00
—With Mel Torme					
F801	My Small Senor/When You Speak with Your Eyes	1950	5.00	10.00	20.00
F810	Save Your Sorrow for Tomorrow/Sugar	1950	5.00	10.00	20.00
F849	Sunshine Cake/Goodbye John	1950	5.00	10.00	20.00
F898	Crazy He Calls Me/Them There Eyes	1950	5.00	10.00	20.00
F961	Cry, Cry, Cry/Once Around the Moon	1950	5.00	10.00	20.00
F1105	Show Me the Way to Get Out of This World ('Cause That's Where Everything Is)/Happy Music	1950	5.00	10.00	20.00
F1161	Lover Come Back to Me/Helpless	1950	5.00	10.00	20.00
F1244	Once in a Lifetime/Love Is So Peculiar	1950	5.00	10.00	20.00
F1298	Where Are You/Ay-Ay-Chug-a-Lug	1950	5.00	10.00	20.00
F1366	Climb Up the Mountain/The Mill on the Floss	1951	3.75	7.50	15.00
F1428	Yeah, Yeah, Yeah/Rock Me to Sleep	1951	3.75	7.50	15.00
F1450	That Ol' Devil/Cannonball Express	1951	3.75	7.50	15.00
F1513	He's Only Wonderful/It Never Happens to Me	1951	3.75	7.50	15.00
F1544	Boulevard Café/If You Turn Me Down	1951	3.75	7.50	15.00
F1573	(When I Dance with You) I Get Ideas/Tonight You Belong to Me	1951	3.75	7.50	15.00
F1586	My Magic Heart/So Far So Good	1951	3.75	7.50	15.00
F1601	It's a Good Day/Them There Eyes	1951	3.75	7.50	15.00
—Reissue of 78 rpm recordings from the 1940s					
F1602	Manana (Is Soon Enough for Me)/Why Don't You Do It Right	1951	3.75	7.50	15.00
—Reissue of 78 rpm recordings from the 1940s					
F1609	That Old Feeling/Solitude	1951	3.75	7.50	15.00
—B-side by the Capitol Jazzmen; reissue of 1940s material					
F1667	I Can't Give You Anything But Love/I Don't Know Enough About You	1951	3.75	7.50	15.00
—Reissue of 78 rpm recordings from the 1940s					
F1683	While We're Young/Golden Earrings	195?	3.00	6.00	12.00
—Reissue					
F1749	I Love You But I Don't Like You/Wandering Swallow	1951	3.75	7.50	15.00
F1776	While We're Young/Birmingham Jail	1951	3.75	7.50	15.00
SM-1857 [S]	Mack the Knife/(B-side unknown)	1963	3.75	7.50	15.00
—Small hole, plays at 33 1/3 rpm					
F1926	Shame on You/Would You Dance	1952	3.75	7.50	15.00
F2025	Everytime/Goin' On a Hayride	1952	3.75	7.50	15.00
2171	Reason to Believe/Didn't Want to Have to Do It	1968	—	3.00	6.00
2308	Misty Roses/It'll Never Happen Again	1968	—	3.00	6.00
2477	Spinning Wheel/Lean On Me	1969	—	3.00	6.00
2602	Is That All There Is/Me and My Shadow	1969	—	3.00	6.00
2696	Something/Whistle for Happiness	1969	—	3.00	6.00
2721	My Old Flame/Love Story	1970	—	2.50	5.00
2817	Have You Seen My Baby/You'll Remember Me	1970	—	2.50	5.00
2910	One More Ride on the Merry-Go-Round/Pieces of Dreams	1970	—	2.50	5.00
3113	Where Did They Go/All I Want	1971	—	2.50	5.00
3439	Someone Who Cares/Love Song	1972	—	2.50	5.00
F3722	Every Night/Baby, Baby, Wait for Me	1957	3.00	6.00	12.00
F3811	Listen to the Rockin' Bird/Uninvited Dream	1957	3.00	6.00	12.00
F3998	Fever/You Don't Know	1958	3.00	6.00	12.00
F4071	Light of Love/Sweetheart	1958	3.00	6.00	12.00
F4115	Alright, OK, You Win/My Man	1959	3.00	6.00	12.00
F4189	Hallelujah I Love Him So/I'm Looking Out the Window	1959	3.00	6.00	12.00
F4243	You Came a Long Way from St. Louis/I Lost My Sugar in Salt Lake City	1959	3.00	6.00	12.00
4298	You Deserve/Where Do I Go from Here	1959	3.00	6.00	12.00
4311	The Tree/The Christmas List	1959	3.75	7.50	15.00
4311 [PS]	The Tree/The Christmas List	1959	5.00	10.00	20.00
4349	Heart/C'est Magnifique	1960	2.50	5.00	10.00
4449	I'm Gonna Go Fishin'/My Gentle Young Johnny	1960	2.50	5.00	10.00
4474	I Like a Sleighride (Jingle Bells)/Christmas Carousel	1960	3.00	6.00	12.00
4474 [PS]	I Like A Sleighride (Jingle Bells)/Christmas Carousel	1960	10.00	20.00	40.00
4498	Bucket of Tears/I Love Being Here with You	1961	2.50	5.00	10.00
4576	Boston Beans/Yes Indeed	1961	2.50	5.00	10.00
4610	Hey, Look Me Over/When He Makes Music	1961	2.50	5.00	10.00
4750	The Sweetest Sounds/Loads of Love	1962	2.50	5.00	10.00
4812	Tell All the World About You/Amazing	1962	2.50	5.00	10.00
4888	I'm a Woman/Big Bad Bill	1962	2.50	5.00	10.00
4942	Alley Cat Song/O Barquinho (Little Boat)	1963	2.50	5.00	10.00
5001	The Doodlin' Song/Got That Magic	1963	2.50	5.00	10.00
5121	I Can't Stop Loving You/A Lot of Livin' to Do	1964	2.50	5.00	10.00
5241	In the Name of Love/My Sin	1964	2.50	5.00	10.00
5289	Talk to Me Baby/After You've Gone	1964	2.50	5.00	10.00
5346	That's What It Takes/Pass Me By	1965	2.00	4.00	8.00
5404	Bewitched/Sneakin' Up on You	1965	2.00	4.00	8.00
5469	The Sandpiper Love Theme (The Shadow of Your Smile)/Maybe This Summer	1965	2.00	4.00	8.00
5488	I Go to Sleep/Stop Living in the Past	1965	2.00	4.00	8.00
5521	Everybody Has the Right to Be Wrong/Free Spirits	1965	2.00	4.00	8.00
5557	Big Spender/Trapped	1965	2.00	4.00	8.00
5605	That Man/You Don't Know	1966	2.00	4.00	8.00
5653	Come Back to Me/You've Got Possibilities	1966	2.00	4.00	8.00
5678	Stay with Me/Happy Feet	1966	2.00	4.00	8.00
5758	So What's New/Walking Happy	1966	2.00	4.00	8.00
5988	I Feel It/Lonesome Road	1967	—	3.00	6.00
S7-19343	Happy Holiday/Auld Lang Syne	1996	—	—	3.00
—B-side by Guy Lombardo					
DECCA					
27238	Watermelon Weather/The Moon Came Up	1950	3.75	7.50	15.00
—With Bing Crosby					
27813	Just One of Those Things/I'm Glad There Is You	1951	3.75	7.50	15.00
28142	Be Anything/Forgive Me	1952	3.75	7.50	15.00
28215	Lover/You Go to My Head	1952	3.75	7.50	15.00
28313	Just One of Those Things/I'm Glad There Is You	1952	3.75	7.50	15.00
28395	San Souci/River, River	1952	3.75	7.50	15.00
28565	This Is a Very Special Day/I Hear the Music Now	1953	3.75	7.50	15.00
28631	Who's Gonna Pay the Check/Sorry, Baby, You Let My Love Get Cold	1953	3.75	7.50	15.00
28737	I've Got You Under My Skin/My Heart Belongs to Daddy	1953	3.75	7.50	15.00

Number	Title (A Side/B Side)	Yr	VG	VG+	NM
28889	Apples, Peaches and Cherries/Night Holds No Fear	1953	3.75	7.50	15.00
28890	Baubles, Bangles and Beads/Love You So	1953	3.75	7.50	15.00
28939	Ring Those Christmas Bells/It's Christmas Time Again	1953	3.75	7.50	15.00
29003	Go You Where You Go/Where Can I Go Without You	1954	3.75	7.50	15.00
29076	Juhnny Guitar/Autumn in Rome	1954	3.75	7.50	15.00
29164	Summer Vacation/That's What a Woman Is For	1954	3.75	7.50	15.00
29250	Love, You Didn't Do Right by Me/Sisters	1954	3.75	7.50	15.00
29342	God Rest Ye Merry Gentlemen/White Christmas	1954	3.75	7.50	15.00
—A-side with Trudi Stevens; B-side by Bing Crosby and Danny Kaye					
29359	It Must Be So/Straight Ahead	1954	3.00	6.00	12.00
—With the Mills Brothers					
29373	Let Me Go Lover/Bouquet of Roses	1954	3.00	6.00	12.00
29427	He's a Tramp/The Siamese Cat Song	1955	3.00	6.00	12.00
29429	I Belong to You/How Bitter, My Sweet	1955	3.00	6.00	12.00
29460	Bella Notte/La La Lu	1955	3.00	6.00	12.00
29534	Ooh, That Kiss/Oh! No!	1955	3.00	6.00	12.00
29605	Sing a Rainbow/He Needs Me	1955	3.00	6.00	12.00
29608	What Can I Say After I Say I'm Sorry/Sugar	1955	3.00	6.00	12.00
29681	Me/Pablo Pasablo	1955	3.00	6.00	12.00
29834	Mr. Wonderful/Crazy in the Heart	1956	3.00	6.00	12.00
29837	The Comeback/You've Got to See Mamma Every Night	1956	3.00	6.00	12.00
29877	Joey, Joey, Joey/They Can't Take That Away from Me	1956	3.00	6.00	12.00
29994	That's Alright Honey/We Laughed at Love	1956	3.00	6.00	12.00
30059	You Oughta Be Mine/I Don't Know Enough About You	1956	3.00	6.00	12.00
30117	Where Flamingos Fly/Gypsy with Fire in Her Shoes	1956	3.00	6.00	12.00
30494	Never Mind/Wrong, Wrong, Wrong	1957	2.50	5.00	10.00
30879	It Ain't Necessarily So/Swing Low Sweet Chariot	1959	2.50	5.00	10.00

Albums

ARCHIVE OF FOLK AND JAZZ

Number	Title (A Side/B Side)	Yr	VG	VG+	NM
294	Peggy Lee	197?	2.50	5.00	10.00

ATLANTIC

Number	Title (A Side/B Side)	Yr	VG	VG+	NM
SD 18108	Let's Love	1974	3.00	6.00	12.00

A&M

Number	Title (A Side/B Side)	Yr	VG	VG+	NM
SP-4547	Mirrors	1975	3.00	6.00	12.00

CAPITOL

Number	Title (A Side/B Side)	Yr	VG	VG+	NM
ST-105	Two Shows Nightly	1969	50.00	100.00	200.00
—Withdrawn immediately after release					
H 151 [10]	Rendezvous with Peggy Lee	1952	25.00	50.00	100.00
T 151 [M]	Rendezvous with Peggy Lee	1954	12.50	25.00	50.00
—Turquoise or gray label					
T 151 [M]	Rendezvous with Peggy Lee	1959	6.25	12.50	25.00
—Black label with colorband, Capitol logo at left					
H 204 [10]	My Best to You	1952	25.00	50.00	100.00
T 204 [M]	My Best to You	1954	12.50	25.00	50.00
—Turquoise or gray label					
T 204 [M]	My Best to You	1959	6.25	12.50	25.00
—Black label with colorband, Capitol logo at left					
DKAO-377	Peggy Lee's Greatest	1969	3.00	6.00	12.00
ST-382	Is That All There Is?	1969	3.00	6.00	12.00
SM-386	Is That All There Is?	197?	2.50	5.00	10.00
—Reissue with new prefix					
ST-463	Bridge Over Troubled Water	1970	3.00	6.00	12.00
STBB-517 [(2)]	Folks Who Live on the Hill/Broadway Ala Lee	1970	3.75	7.50	15.00
STCL-576 [(3)]	Peggy Lee	1970	6.25	12.50	25.00
ST-622	Make It with You	1970	3.00	6.00	12.00
ST-810	Where Did They Go	1971	3.00	6.00	12.00
ST 864 [S]	The Man I Love	1959	7.50	15.00	30.00
T 864 [M]	The Man I Love	1957	12.50	25.00	50.00
—Turquoise label					
T 864 [M]	The Man I Love	1959	6.25	12.50	25.00
—Black label with colorband, Capitol logo at left					
ST 975 [S]	Jump for Joy	1959	7.50	15.00	30.00
T 975 [M]	Jump for Joy	1958	10.00	20.00	40.00
—Turquoise or gray label					
T 975 [M]	Jump for Joy	1959	6.25	12.50	25.00
—Black label with colorband, Capitol logo at left					
ST 1049 [S]	Things Are Swingin'	1959	7.50	15.00	30.00
T 1049 [M]	Things Are Swingin'	1958	6.25	12.50	25.00
ST 1131 [S]	I Like Men	1959	7.50	15.00	30.00
T 1131 [M]	I Like Men	1959	6.25	12.50	25.00
ST 1213 [S]	Alright, Okay, You Win	1959	7.50	15.00	30.00
T 1213 [M]	Alright, Okay, You Win	1959	6.25	12.50	25.00
ST 1219 [S]	Beauty and the Beast	1959	7.50	15.00	30.00
—With George Shearing; black label with colorband, Capitol logo at left					
ST 1219 [S]	Beauty and the Beast	1962	5.00	10.00	20.00
—With George Shearing; black label with colorband, Capitol logo at top					
T 1219 [M]	Beauty and the Beast	1959	6.25	12.50	25.00
—With George Shearing; black label with colorband, Capitol logo at left					
T 1219 [M]	Beauty and the Beast	1962	3.75	7.50	15.00
—With George Shearing; black label with colorband, Capitol logo at top					
SM-1290	Latin Ala Lee!	1977	2.50	5.00	10.00
—Reissue with new prefix					
ST 1290 [S]	Latin Ala Lee!	1960	6.25	12.50	25.00
—Black label with colorband, Capitol logo at left					
ST 1290 [S]	Latin Ala Lee!	1962	3.75	7.50	15.00
—Black label with colorband, Capitol logo at top					
T 1290 [M]	Latin Ala Lee!	1960	5.00	10.00	20.00
—Black label with colorband, Capitol logo at left					
T 1290 [M]	Latin Ala Lee!	1962	3.00	6.00	12.00
—Black label with colorband, Capitol logo at top					
ST 1366 [S]	All Aglow Again	1960	6.25	12.50	25.00
—Black label with colorband, Capitol logo at left					
ST 1366 [S]	All Aglow Again	1962	3.75	7.50	15.00
—Black label with colorband, Capitol logo at top					
T 1366 [M]	All Aglow Again	1960	5.00	10.00	20.00
—Black label with colorband, Capitol logo at left					
T 1366 [M]	All Aglow Again	1962	3.00	6.00	12.00
—Black label with colorband, Capitol logo at top					
ST 1401 [S]	Pretty Eyes	1960	6.25	12.50	25.00
—Black label with colorband, Capitol logo at left					
ST 1401 [S]	Pretty Eyes	1962	3.75	7.50	15.00
—Black label with colorband, Capitol logo at top					
T 1401 [M]	Pretty Eyes	1960	5.00	10.00	20.00
—Black label with colorband, Capitol logo at left					
T 1401 [M]	Pretty Eyes	1962	3.00	6.00	12.00
—Black label with colorband, Capitol logo at top					
ST 1423 [S]	Christmas Carousel	1960	6.25	12.50	25.00
T 1423 [M]	Christmas Carousel	1960	5.00	10.00	20.00
ST 1475 [S]	Ole Ala Lee!	1961	6.25	12.50	25.00
T 1475 [M]	Ole Ala Lee!	1961	5.00	10.00	20.00
SM-1520	Basin Street East	1977	2.50	5.00	10.00
—Reissue with new prefix					
ST 1520 [S]	Basin Street East	1961	6.25	12.50	25.00
—Black label with colorband, Capitol logo at left					
ST 1520 [S]	Basin Street East	1962	3.75	7.50	15.00
—Black label with colorband, Capitol logo at top					
T 1520 [M]	Basin Street East	1961	5.00	10.00	20.00
—Black label with colorband, Capitol logo at left					
T 1520 [M]	Basin Street East	1962	3.00	6.00	12.00
—Black label with colorband, Capitol logo at top					
ST 1630 [S]	If You Go	1962	6.25	12.50	25.00
T 1630 [M]	If You Go	1962	5.00	10.00	20.00
ST 1671 [S]	Blue Cross Country	1962	6.25	12.50	25.00
T 1671 [M]	Blue Cross Country	1962	5.00	10.00	20.00
DT 1743 [R]	Bewitching-Lee!	1962	3.75	7.50	15.00
T 1743 [M]	Bewitching-Lee!	1962	6.25	12.50	25.00
—Black "The Star Line" label					
ST 1772 [S]	Sugar 'n' Spice	1962	6.25	12.50	25.00
T 1772 [M]	Sugar 'n' Spice	1962	5.00	10.00	20.00
ST 1850 [S]	Mink Jazz	1963	6.25	12.50	25.00
T 1850 [M]	Mink Jazz	1963	5.00	10.00	20.00
SM-1857	I'm a Woman	1977	2.50	5.00	10.00
—Heissue with new prefix					
ST 1857 [S]	I'm a Woman	1963	6.25	12.50	25.00
T 1857 [M]	I'm a Woman	1963	5.00	10.00	20.00
ST 1969 [S]	In Love Again	1963	6.25	12.50	25.00
T 1969 [M]	In Love Again	1963	5.00	10.00	20.00
ST 2096 [S]	In the Name of Love	1964	5.00	10.00	20.00
T 2096 [M]	In the Name of Love	1964	3.75	7.50	15.00
ST 2320 [S]	Pass Me By	1965	5.00	10.00	20.00
T 2320 [M]	Pass Me By	1965	3.75	7.50	15.00
ST 2388 [S]	That Was Then, Now Is Now	1965	5.00	10.00	20.00
T 2388 [M]	That Was Then, Now Is Now	1965	3.75	7.50	15.00
ST 2390 [S]	Happy Holiday	1965	3.75	7.50	15.00
T 2390 [M]	Happy Holiday	1965	3.00	6.00	12.00
ST 2469 [S]	Guitars Ala Lee	1966	5.00	10.00	20.00
T 2469 [M]	Guitars Ala Lee	1966	3.75	7.50	15.00
ST 2475 [S]	Big $pender	1966	5.00	10.00	20.00
T 2475 [M]	Big $pender	1966	3.75	7.50	15.00
ST 2732 [S]	Extra Special	1967	3.75	7.50	15.00
T 2732 [M]	Extra Special	1967	5.00	10.00	20.00
ST 2781	Somethin' Groovy	1968	3.75	7.50	15.00
ST 2887	The Hits of Peggy Lee	1968	3.75	7.50	15.00
ST-11077	Norma Deloris Egstrom from Jamestown, North Dakota	1972	3.00	6.00	12.00
SN-16140	Peggy Lee Sings Songs of Cy Coleman	198?	2.00	4.00	8.00

COLUMBIA

Number	Title (A Side/B Side)	Yr	VG	VG+	NM
CL 6033 [10]	Benny Goodman and Peggy Lee	1949	15.00	30.00	60.00

DECCA

Number	Title (A Side/B Side)	Yr	VG	VG+	NM
DXB 164 [(2) M]	The Best of Peggy Lee	1964	7.50	15.00	30.00
DL 4458 [M]	Lover	1964	6.25	12.50	25.00
DL 4461 [M]	The Fabulous Peggy Lee	1964	6.25	12.50	25.00
DL 5482 [10]	Black Coffee	1953	25.00	50.00	100.00
DL 5539 [10]	Songs in an Intimate Style	1953	20.00	40.00	80.00
DXSB 7164 [(2) R]	The Best of Peggy Lee	1964	5.00	10.00	20.00
DL 8358 [M]	Black Coffee	1956	15.00	30.00	60.00
DL 8411 [M]	Dream Street	1957	15.00	30.00	60.00
DL 8591 [M]	Sea Shells	1958	15.00	30.00	60.00
DL 8816 [M]	Miss Wonderful	1959	15.00	30.00	60.00
DL 74458 [R]	Lover	1964	3.75	7.50	15.00
DL 74461 [R]	The Fabulous Peggy Lee	1964	3.75	7.50	15.00

DRG

Number	Title (A Side/B Side)	Yr	VG	VG+	NM
SL-5190	Close Enough for Love	1979	3.00	6.00	12.00

GLENDALE

Number	Title (A Side/B Side)	Yr	VG	VG+	NM
6023	You Can Depend on Me	1982	2.50	5.00	10.00

HARMONY

Number	Title (A Side/B Side)	Yr	VG	VG+	NM
HL 7005 [M]	Peggy Lee Sings with Benny Goodman	195?	6.25	12.50	25.00
H 30024	Miss Peggy Lee	1970	2.50	5.00	10.00

HINDSIGHT

Number	Title (A Side/B Side)	Yr	VG	VG+	NM
HSR-220	Peggy Lee with the David Barbour and Billy May Bands, 1948	1985	2.50	5.00	10.00

MCA

Number	Title (A Side/B Side)	Yr	VG	VG+	NM
4049 [(2)]	The Best of Peggy Lee	197?	3.00	6.00	12.00

MERCURY

Number	Title (A Side/B Side)	Yr	VG	VG+	NM
SRM-1-1172	Live in London	1977	3.00	6.00	12.00

MUSICMASTERS

Number	Title (A Side/B Side)	Yr	VG	VG+	NM
5005	Peggy Sings the Blues	1988	3.00	6.00	12.00

PAUSA

Number	Title (A Side/B Side)	Yr	VG	VG+	NM
PR-9043	Sugar 'n' Spice	1985	2.50	5.00	10.00

PICKWICK

Number	Title (A Side/B Side)	Yr	VG	VG+	NM
SPC-3090	Once More with Feeling	196?	2.50	5.00	10.00
SPC-3192	I've Got the World	1971	2.50	5.00	10.00

VOCALION

Number	Title (A Side/B Side)	Yr	VG	VG+	NM
VL 3776 [M]	So Blue	1966	3.75	7.50	15.00
VL 73776 [R]	So Blue	1966	2.50	5.00	10.00
VL 73903	Crazy in the Heart	1969	2.50	5.00	10.00

LEE AND THE LEOPARDS

45s

FORTUNE

Number	Title (A Side/B Side)	Yr	VG	VG+	NM
867	What About Me/Don't Press Your Luck	1964	12.50	25.00	50.00

Number	Title (A Side/B Side)	Yr	VG	VG+	NM
GORDY					
7002	Come Into My Palace/Trying to Make It	1962	15.00	30.00	60.00
LAURIE					
3197	Come Into My Palace/Trying to Make It	1963	6.25	12.50	25.00

LEFEVRE, RAYMOND

45s

Number	Title (A Side/B Side)	Yr	VG	VG+	NM
4 CORNERS OF THE WORLD					
142	When a Man Loves a Woman/Black Is Black	1967	—	2.50	5.00
145	Groovin'/A Whiter Shade of Pale	1967	—	2.50	5.00
147	Ame Caline (Soul Coaxing)/If I Were a Carpenter	1968	—	2.50	5.00
149	La, La, La (He Gives Me Love)/C'est La Rose	1968	—	2.50	5.00
151	Delilah/If I Only Had Time	1968	—	2.50	5.00
ATLANTIC					
2093	Come Softly to Me/Havah Nagilah	1961	2.50	5.00	10.00
BUDDAH					
269	Mammy Blue/What Have They Done to My Song, Ma	1971	—	2.50	5.00
JAMIE					
1161	Never on Sunday/Sleepy Time	1960	2.50	5.00	10.00
1171	Rendezvous/The Right Girl on the Left Bank	1960	2.50	5.00	10.00
KAPP					
231	The Day the Rains Came/Butterfingers	1958	2.50	5.00	10.00
279	You Are My Destiny/Le Belle Helene	1959	2.50	5.00	10.00
766	You Don't Have to Say You Love Me/La Boheme	1966	—	3.00	6.00
809	Spanish Eyes/Stars of the Way	1967	—	3.00	6.00
AS-949 [DJ]	Silver Bells (mono/stereo)	196?	2.00	4.00	8.00
MERCURY					
71599	What Good Does It Do Me/(Instrumental)	1960	2.50	5.00	10.00
VERVE					
10263	Come Une Symphonie/Un Voms Vivo	1962	2.00	4.00	8.00

Albums

Number	Title (A Side/B Side)	Yr	VG	VG+	NM
4 CORNERS OF THE WORLD					
FCL-4239 [M]	Love Me, Please Love Me	1967	3.00	6.00	12.00
FCS-4239 [S]	Love Me, Please Love Me	1967	3.00	6.00	12.00
FCS-4244	Soal Coaxing (Ame Caline)	1968	3.00	6.00	12.00
FCS-4250	La La La (He Gives Me Love)	1968	3.00	6.00	12.00
FCS-4257	Merry Christmas	1968	3.00	6.00	12.00
ATLANTIC					
8044 [M]	Romantica	1961	5.00	10.00	20.00
SD 8044 [S]	Romantica	1961	6.25	12.50	25.00
BUDDAH					
BDS-5095	Raymond Lefevre	1971	2.50	5.00	10.00
BDS-5109	Oh Happy Day	1972	2.50	5.00	10.00
KAPP					
KL-1510 [M]	You Don't Have to Stay	1967	3.75	7.50	15.00
KS-3510 [S]	You Don't Have to Stay	1967	3.00	6.00	12.00
MONUMENT					
MLP-8067 [M]	Paris Cancan	1967	3.75	7.50	15.00
SLP-18067 [S]	Paris Cancan	1967	3.00	6.00	12.00

LEFT BANKE, THE

45s

Number	Title (A Side/B Side)	Yr	VG	VG+	NM
CAMERICA					
005	Queen of Paradise/And One Day	1978	—	2.50	5.00
SMASH					
2041	Walk Away Renee/I Haven't Got the Nerve	1966	3.75	7.50	15.00
2074	Pretty Ballerina/Lazy Day	1966	3.75	7.50	15.00
2089	Ivy, Ivy/And Suddenly	1967	3.00	6.00	12.00
2097	She May Call You Up Tonight/Barterers and Their Wives	1967	3.00	6.00	12.00
2119	Desiree/I've Got Something on My Mind	1967	3.00	6.00	12.00
2119 [PS]	Desiree/I've Got Something on My Mind	1967	6.25	12.50	25.00
2165	Dark Is the Bark/My Friend Today	1968	3.00	6.00	12.00
2198	Goodbye Holly/Sing, Little Bird, Sing	1968	3.00	6.00	12.00
2209	Bryant Hotel/Give the Man a Hand	1969	3.00	6.00	12.00
2243	Myrah/Pedestal	1969	10.00	20.00	40.00
—Picture sleeves are bootlegs					

Albums

Number	Title (A Side/B Side)	Yr	VG	VG+	NM
RHINO					
RNLP-123	History of the Left Banke	1985	2.50	5.00	10.00
SMASH					
MGS-27088 [M]	Walk Away Renee/Pretty Ballerina	1967	10.00	20.00	40.00
SRS-67088	Walk Away Renee/Pretty Ballerina	198?	2.50	5.00	10.00
—Reissue with thinner vinyl					
SRS-67088 [S]	Walk Away Renee/Pretty Ballerina	1967	10.00	20.00	40.00
SRS-67113	The Left Banke, Too	1968	12.50	25.00	50.00

LEGENDARY MASKED SURFERS, THE

45s

Number	Title (A Side/B Side)	Yr	VG	VG+	NM
UNITED ARTISTS					
XW270	Summer Means Fun/Gonna Hustle You	1973	5.00	10.00	20.00
—Original pressings have a Jan & Dean recording on them by mistake					
XW270	Summer Means Fun/Gonna Hustle You	1973	30.00	60.00	120.00
—With the intended recording, a newly-recorded vocal track					
XW270 [PS]	Summer Means Fun/Gonna Hustle You	1973	7.50	15.00	30.00
50958	Summertime, Summertime/Gonna Hustle You	1972	7.50	15.00	30.00

LEGENDARY STARDUST COWBOY, THE

45s

Number	Title (A Side/B Side)	Yr	VG	VG+	NM
MERCURY					
72862	Paralyzed/Who's Knocking on My Door	1968	5.00	10.00	20.00
72891	Down in the Wrecking Yard/I Took a Trip on a Gemini Spaceship	1969	5.00	10.00	20.00
72912	Everything's Getting Bigger But Our Love/Kiss and Run	1969	5.00	10.00	20.00
NORTON					
012	I Hate CD's/Linda	199?	—	—	2.00
012 [PS]	I Hate CD's/Linda	199?	—	—	2.00
PSYCHO-SUAVE					
1033	Paralyzed/Who's Knocking on My Door	1968	7.50	15.00	30.00

LEGENDS, THE

Several different groups.

45s

Number	Title (A Side/B Side)	Yr	VG	VG+	NM
BRIDGE SOCIETY					
2204	Keep On Running/Cheating	1968	10.00	20.00	40.00
CALDWELL					
410	Go Away with Me/Jungle Lullaby	1962	6.25	12.50	25.00
CAPITOL					
5014	Summertime Blues/Run to the Movies	1963	5.00	10.00	20.00
COLUMBIA					
41949	Theme from "Exodus"/Later	1961	3.00	6.00	12.00
DOC HOLLIDAY					
107	Surf's Up/Dance with the Drummer Man	1963	10.00	20.00	40.00
107 [PS]	Surf's Up/Dance with the Drummer Man	1963	12.50	25.00	50.00
EPIC					
10937	Rock and Roll Woman/Problems	1973	2.00	4.00	8.00
ERMINE					
39	My Love for You/Say Mama	1962	12.50	25.00	50.00
41	Lariat/Late Train	1962	10.00	20.00	40.00
43	Bop-A-Lena/I Wish I Knew	1962	12.50	25.00	50.00
45	Temptation/Marionette	1962	10.00	20.00	40.00
HART-VAN					
18003	Traction/As Long As I Live	1962	7.50	15.00	30.00
HEART					
7672	Rock and Roll Woman/Problems	1972	5.00	10.00	20.00
HULL					
727	The Legend of Love/Now I'm Telling You	1958	25.00	50.00	100.00
—Red label					
727	The Legend of Love/Now I'm Telling You	1962	7.50	15.00	30.00
—Multicolor label					
JAMIE					
1228	Tell the Truth/You'll Never See the Forest	1962	5.00	10.00	20.00
KEY					
1002	Lariat/Gail	1961	10.00	20.00	40.00
1002	Lariat/Late Train	1961	10.00	20.00	40.00
MELBA					
109	I'll Never Fall in Love Again/Eyes of an Angel	1957	37.50	75.00	150.00
—Label with double horizontal lines					
109	I'll Never Fall in Love Again/Eyes of an Angel	1961	10.00	20.00	40.00
—Label with no horizontal lines					
PARROT					
45010	Just in Case/If I Only Had Her Back	1965	3.00	6.00	12.00
45011	Alright/How Can I Find Her	1965	3.00	6.00	12.00
RAILROAD HOUSE					
12003	High Towers/Fever Games	1969	5.00	10.00	20.00
12003 [PS]	High Towers/Fever Games	1969	7.50	15.00	30.00
THAMES					
104	Raining in My Heart/(B-side unknown)	1964	7.50	15.00	30.00
UP					
2202	Baby, Get Your Head Screwed On/Why	1968	12.50	25.00	50.00
WARNER BROS.					
5457	Here Comes the Rain/Don't Be Ashamed	1964	3.75	7.50	15.00

Albums

Number	Title (A Side/B Side)	Yr	VG	VG+	NM
CAPITOL					
ST 1925 [S]	The Legends Let Loose	1963	20.00	40.00	80.00
T 1925 [M]	The Legends Let Loose	1963	15.00	30.00	60.00
COLUMBIA					
CL 1707 [M]	Hit Sounds of Today's Smash Hit Combos	1961	7.50	15.00	30.00
CS 8507 [S]	Hit Sounds of Today's Smash Hit Combos	1961	10.00	20.00	40.00
ERMINE					
LP-101 [M]	The Legends Let Loose	1963	50.00	100.00	200.00

LEGRAND, MICHEL

45s

Number	Title (A Side/B Side)	Yr	VG	VG+	NM
20TH CENTURY					
2346	The Other Side of Midnight (Noelle's Theme)/Drive to Demeris	1977	—	2.00	4.00
BELL					
45118	The Summer Knows/I Will Say Goodbye	1971	—	2.50	5.00
45171	Brian's Song/Theme from "The Go-Between"	1972	—	2.50	5.00
45215	Jesus Christ Superstar-Day by Day/Amy's Theme	1972	—	2.50	5.00
COLUMBIA					
40661	Under Paris Skies/Merry-Go-Round	1956	3.00	6.00	12.00
40692	Smile/Bon Jour, Paris	1956	3.00	6.00	12.00
40732	Love Theme from "La Strada"/Paris Canaille	1956	3.00	6.00	12.00
40751	Friendly Persuasion/Lovers and Lollipops	1956	3.00	6.00	12.00
41312	Cheek to Cheek/Only You	1958	2.50	5.00	10.00
DECCA					
32287	Pretty Polly/The Race Is to the Swift	1968	—	3.00	6.00
MCA					
40160	Walking on the Beach/Breezy's Song	1973	—	2.00	4.00
40523	Gable and Lombard Love Theme/I Can't Give You Anything But Love, Baby	1976	—	2.00	4.00
MGM					
13816	Tara's Theme (Part 1)/Tara's Theme (Part 2)	1967	—	3.00	6.00
13816	Tara's Theme (Part 1)/Theme from Orfell Negro	1967	—	3.00	6.00
13894	Love Theme from "Elvira Madigan"/Melange	1968	—	3.00	6.00
PHILIPS					
40098	Love Is a Ball/Millie's Theme	1963	2.00	4.00	8.00
40188	Monkey Business/Come Ray or Come Charles	1964	2.00	4.00	8.00
40257	Love Theme from Parapailies de Cherbourg/Garage Scene	1965	2.00	4.00	8.00
40357	I Will Wait for You/Melody from the Stars	1966	2.00	4.00	8.00
RCA VICTOR					
PB-10234	Blue, Green, Gray and Gone/Brian's Song	1975	—	2.00	4.00
UNITED ARTISTS					
50618	What Are You Doing the Rest of Your Life/Floating Time	1969	—	3.50	7.00

Number	Title (A Side/B Side)	Yr	VG	VG+	NM
50662	What Are You Doing the Rest of Your Life (English)/What Are You Doing the Rest of Your Life (French)	1970	—	3.00	6.00
WARNER BROS.					
7486	Theme from "Summer of '42"/Summer Song	1971	—	2.50	5.00
Albums					
BELL					
4200 [(2)]	Twenty Songs of the Century	1974	3.00	6.00	12.00
6071	Brian's Song Themes & Variations	1972	2.50	5.00	10.00
COLUMBIA					
CL 555 [M]	I Love Paris	1954	10.00	20.00	40.00
CL 647 [M]	Holiday in Rome	1955	6.25	12.50	25.00
CL 706 [M]	Vienna Holiday	1955	6.25	12.50	25.00
CL 888 [M]	Castles in Spain	1956	6.25	12.50	25.00
CL 1115 [M]	Michel Legrand Plays Cole Porter	1957	6.25	12.50	25.00
CL 1139 [M]	Legrand in Rio	1957	6.25	12.50	25.00
CL 1250 [M]	Legrand Jazz	1958	10.00	20.00	40.00
—Miles Davis appears on this record					
CL 1437 [M]	I Love Paris	1960	6.25	12.50	25.00
CS 8079 [S]	Legrand Jazz	1959	10.00	20.00	40.00
—Miles Davis appears on this record					
CS 8237 [S]	I Love Paris	1960	5.00	10.00	20.00
PC 9237	I Love Paris	1987	2.00	4.00	8.00
—Reissue with new prefix					
GRYPHON					
786	Jazz Grand	1978	2.50	5.00	10.00
HARMONY					
HL 7331 [M]	I Love Paris	196?	3.00	6.00	12.00
HS 11131 [S]	I Love Paris	196?	3.00	6.00	12.00
KH 31540	Cole Porter, Volume II	1972	2.50	5.00	10.00
KH 31549	Cole Porter, Volume I	1972	2.50	5.00	10.00
MGM					
SE-4491	Cinema La Grand	1967	3.75	7.50	15.00
MOBILE FIDELITY					
1-504	Jazz Grand	198?	12.50	25.00	50.00
—Audiophile vinyl					
PABLO TODAY					
2312139	After the Rain	198?	2.50	5.00	10.00
PHILIPS					
PHM 200074 [M]	The Michel Legrand Big Band Plays Richard Rogers	1963	5.00	10.00	20.00
PHM 200143 [M]	Michel Legrand Sings	1964	6.25	12.50	25.00
PHS 600074 [S]	The Michel Legrand Big Band Plays Richard Rogers	1963	6.25	12.50	25.00
PHS 600143 [S]	Michel Legrand Sings	1964	7.50	15.00	30.00
RCA VICTOR					
BGL1-0850	Jimmy's	1975	2.50	5.00	10.00
BXL1-0850	Jimmy's	1978	2.00	4.00	8.00
—Reissue with new prefix					
BGL1-1028	Concert	1976	2.50	5.00	10.00
BXL1-1028	Concert	1978	2.00	4.00	8.00
—Reissue with new prefix					
BGL1-1392	Michel Legrand and Friends	1976	2.50	5.00	10.00
BXL1-1392	Michel Legrand and Friends	1978	2.00	4.00	8.00
—Reissue with new prefix					
VERVE					
V6-8760	Michel Legrand at Shelly's Mann-Hole	1969	3.00	6.00	12.00

LEHRER, TOM

Number	Title (A Side/B Side)	Yr	VG	VG+	NM
45s					
REPRISE					
0862	Pollution/Who's Next	1969	2.00	4.00	8.00
Albums					
LEHRER					
TLP-1 [10]	Songs by Tom Lehrer	1953	25.00	50.00	100.00
TL-101 [M]	Songs by Tom Lehrer	1959	10.00	20.00	40.00
TL-102S [S]	More of Tom Lehrer	1959	10.00	20.00	40.00
TL-102 [M]	More of Tom Lehrer	1958	10.00	20.00	40.00
TL-201 [M]	Tom Lehrer Revisited	1959	6.25	12.50	25.00
TL-202S [S]	An Evening Wasted with Tom Lehrer	1959	10.00	20.00	40.00
TL-202 [M]	An Evening Wasted with Tom Lehrer	1959	6.25	12.50	25.00
REPRISE					
R-6179 [M]	That Was the Year That Was	1965	5.00	10.00	20.00
RS-6179 [S]	That Was the Year That Was	1965	6.25	12.50	25.00
—Pink, yellow and green label					
RS-6179 [S]	That Was the Year That Was	1968	3.75	7.50	15.00
—Two-tone orange label with "W7" and "r:" logos					
RS-6179 [S]	That Was the Year That Was	1970	2.50	5.00	10.00
—Orange/tan label with "r:" logo					
R 6199 [M]	An Evening Wasted with Tom Lehrer	1966	5.00	10.00	20.00
—Reissue of Lehrer 202					
RS 6199 [S]	An Evening Wasted with Tom Lehrer	1966	6.25	12.50	25.00
—Reissue of Lehrer 202					
R-6216 [M]	Songs of Tom Lehrer	1966	5.00	10.00	20.00
RS-6216 [S]	Songs of Tom Lehrer	1966	6.25	12.50	25.00

LEIBER, JERRY

Number	Title (A Side/B Side)	Yr	VG	VG+	NM
Albums					
KAPP					
KL-1127 [M]	Scooby-Doo	1959	12.50	25.00	50.00

LEIBER AND STOLLER BIG BAND, THE

Number	Title (A Side/B Side)	Yr	VG	VG+	NM
45s					
UNITED ARTISTS					
441	Blue Baion/Café Expresso	1962	3.00	6.00	12.00
Albums					
ATLANTIC					
8047 [M]	Yakety Yak	1960	10.00	20.00	40.00
—White "fan" logo on right side of label					
8047 [M]	Yakety Yak	1962	5.00	10.00	20.00
—Black "fan" logo on right side of label					
SD 8047 [S]	Yakety Yak	1960	12.50	25.00	50.00
—White "fan" logo on right side of label					
SD 8047 [S]	Yakety Yak	1962	6.25	12.50	25.00
—Black "fan" logo on right side of label					

LEIGH, LINDA

Number	Title (A Side/B Side)	Yr	VG	VG+	NM
45s					
AMERICAN INT'L.					
540	I Promise You/My Guy	1959	6.25	12.50	25.00
543	Beri-Beri/The Plan	1959	12.50	25.00	50.00
546	Foolish Dreams/The Scent	1960	5.00	10.00	20.00
KASH					
1028	Heart/Here I Go Out of Your Life	1965	3.00	6.00	12.00
RENDEZVOUS					
103	Move Out/It's Real	1958	5.00	10.00	20.00
106	Please Please (Let Me Go Steady)/Teardrops	1959	5.00	10.00	20.00
REPRISE					
20060	Someone Special/Please	1962	3.00	6.00	12.00
20078	Lover's Beach/A Thousand Violins	1962	3.00	6.00	12.00

LEMMON, JACK

Number	Title (A Side/B Side)	Yr	VG	VG+	NM
45s					
EPIC					
9318	Daphne/Sleepy Lagoon	1959	2.50	5.00	10.00
9364	I Cover the Waterfront/I'm Forever Blowing Bubbles	1960	2.50	5.00	10.00
9399	Theme from The Apartment/Lemmon Flavored Blues	1960	2.50	5.00	10.00
9399 [PS]	Theme from The Apartment/Lemmon Flavored Blues	1960	5.00	10.00	20.00
Albums					
CAPITOL					
ST 1943 [S]	Jack Lemmon Plays Piano Selections from Irma La Douce	1963	15.00	30.00	60.00
T 1943 [M]	Jack Lemmon Plays Piano Selections from Irma La Douce	1963	12.50	25.00	50.00
EPIC					
BN 523 [S]	A Twist of Lemmon	1959	12.50	25.00	50.00
BN 528 [S]	Jack Lemmon Sings and Plays Music from Some Like It Hot	1959	12.50	25.00	50.00
LN 3491 [M]	A Twist of Lemmon	1959	10.00	20.00	40.00
LN 3559 [M]	Jack Lemmon Sings and Plays Music from Some Like It Hot	1959	10.00	20.00	40.00

LEMON PIPERS, THE

Number	Title (A Side/B Side)	Yr	VG	VG+	NM
45s					
BUDDAH					
11	Turn Around and Take a Look/Danger	1967	2.50	5.00	10.00
23	Green Tambourine/No Help from Me	1967	3.00	6.00	12.00
31	Rice Is Nice/Blueberry Blue	1968	2.50	5.00	10.00
31 [PS]	Rice Is Nice/Blueberry Blue	1968	3.75	7.50	15.00
41	Jelly Jungle (Of Orange Marmalade)/Shoe Shine Boy	1968	2.50	5.00	10.00
63	Wine and Violet/Lonely Atmosphere	1968	2.50	5.00	10.00
136	I Was Not Born to Follow/Rainbow Tree	1969	2.00	4.00	8.00
CAROL					
107	Quiet Please/Monaural 78	1966	3.75	7.50	15.00
Albums					
BUDDAH					
BD-5009 [M]	Green Tambourine	1968	6.25	12.50	25.00
BDS-5009 [S]	Green Tambourine	1968	6.25	12.50	25.00
BDS-5016	Jungle Marmalade	1968	6.25	12.50	25.00

LENNON, FREDDIE

Number	Title (A Side/B Side)	Yr	VG	VG+	NM
45s					
JERDEN					
792	That's My Life (My Love and My Home)/Next Time You Feel Important	1966	20.00	40.00	80.00

LENNON, JOHN

Includes records as "Plastic Ono Band," "John Ono Lennon," "John Lennon/Plastic Ono Band" and other records he made with Yoko Ono. Also see THE BEATLES.

Number	Title (A Side/B Side)	Yr	VG	VG+	NM
12-Inch Singles					
CAPITOL					
SPRO-9585/6 [DJ]	Imagine/Come Together	1986	10.00	20.00	40.00
SPRO-9894 [DJ]	Happy Xmas (War Is Over) (same on both sides)	1986	50.00	100.00	200.00
—Limited edition for the Central Virginia Food Bank					
SPRO-9917 [DJ]	Rock and Roll People (same on both sides)	1986	15.00	30.00	60.00
SPRO-9929 [DJ]	Happy Xmas (War Is Over)/Listen, the Snow Is Falling	1986	12.50	25.00	50.00
—Custom silver label, plastic sleeve with sticker					
SPRO-79463 [DJ]	Stand By Me (same on both sides)	1988	10.00	20.00	40.00
GEFFEN					
PRO-A-919 [DJ]	(Just Like) Starting Over/Kiss Kiss Kiss	1980	20.00	40.00	80.00
—A-side is slightly longer (4:17) than any other release of this song					
PRO-A-1079 [DJ]	Happy Xmas (War Is Over)/Beautiful Boy (Darling Boy)	1982	7.50	15.00	30.00
POLYDOR					
PRO 250-1 [DJ]	Nobody Told Me/O' Sanity	1983	7.50	15.00	30.00
45s					
APPLE					
1809	Give Peace a Chance/Remember Love	1969	—	2.50	5.00
—As "Plastic Ono Band"					
1809 [PS]	Give Peace a Chance/Remember Love	1969	3.75	7.50	15.00
—As "Plastic Ono Band"					
1813	Cold Turkey/Don't Worry Kyoko (Mummy's Only Looking for a Hand in the Snow)	1969	—	2.50	5.00
—As "Plastic Ono Band"; most copies skip on A-side on the third chorus because of a pressing defect					
1813	Cold Turkey/Don't Worry Kyoko (Mummy's Only Looking for a Hand in the Snow)	1969	2.50	5.00	10.00
—As "Plastic Ono Band"; some copies don't skip on A-side. They tend to have wider, bolder print than those that do.					

Number	Title (A Side/B Side)	Yr	VG	VG+	NM
1813 [PS]	Cold Turkey/Don't Worry Kyoko (Mummy's Only Looking for a Hand in the Snow)	1969	10.00	20.00	40.00
—As "Plastic Ono Band"					
1818	Instant Karma! (We All Shine On)/Who Has Seen the Wind?	1970	—	2.00	4.00
—As "John Ono Lennon"; B-side by "Yoko Ono Lennon"					
1818 [DJ]	Instant Karma! (We All Shine On)	1970	50.00	100.00	200.00
—As "John Ono Lennon"; one-sided promo					
1818 [PS]	Instant Karma! (We All Shine On)/Who Has Seen the Wind?	1970	3.75	7.50	15.00
—As "John Ono Lennon"; B-side by "Yoko Ono Lennon"					
1827	Mother/Why	1970	2.00	4.00	8.00
—As "John Lennon/Plastic Ono Band"; B-side by "Yoko Ono/Plastic Ono Band"					
1827	Mother/Why	1970	3.00	6.00	12.00
—As "John Lennon/Plastic Ono Band"; star on A-side label					
1827	Mother/Why	1970	10.00	20.00	40.00
—As "John Lennon/Plastic Ono Band"; "MONO" on A-side label					
1827 [PS]	Mother/Why	1970	30.00	60.00	120.00
—As "John Lennon/Plastic Ono Band"; B-side by "Yoko Ono/Plastic Ono Band"					
1830	Power to the People/Touch Me	1971	2.00	4.00	8.00
—As "John Lennon/Plastic Ono Band"; B-side by "Yoko Ono/Plastic Ono Band"					
1830	Power to the People/Touch Me	1971	2.00	4.00	8.00
—As "John Lennon/Plastic Ono Band"; with star on A-side label					
1830 [PS]	Power to the People/Touch Me	1971	7.50	15.00	30.00
—As "John Lennon/Plastic Ono Band"; B-side by "Yoko Ono/Plastic Ono Band"					
1840	Imagine/It's So Hard	1971	2.00	4.00	8.00
—As "John Lennon Plastic Ono Band"; tan label					
1840	Imagine/It's So Hard	1975	3.00	6.00	12.00
—As "John Lennon Plastic Ono Band"; green label with "All Rights Reserved"					
1842	Happy Xmas (War Is Over)/Listen, the Snow Is Falling	1971	3.75	7.50	15.00
—As "John & Yoko/Plastic Ono Band with the Harlem Community Choir"; green vinyl, faces label					
1842	Happy Xmas (War Is Over)/Listen, the Snow Is Falling	1971	2.50	5.00	10.00
—As "John & Yoko/Plastic Ono Band with the Harlem Community Choir"; green vinyl, Apple label					
1842 [PS]	Happy Xmas (War Is Over)/Listen, the Snow Is Falling	1971	5.00	10.00	20.00
—As "John & Yoko/Plastic Ono Band with the Harlem Community Choir"					
1848	Woman Is the Nigger of the World/Sisters O Sisters	1972	2.00	4.00	8.00
—As "John Lennon/Plastic Ono Band..."; B-side by "Yoko Ono/Plastic Ono Band..."					
1848 [PS]	Woman Is the Nigger of the World/Sisters O Sisters	1972	6.25	12.50	25.00
—As "John Lennon/Plastic Ono Band..."; B-side by "Yoko Ono/Plastic Ono Band..."					
1868	Mind Games/Meat City	1973	—	3.00	6.00
1868 [PS]	Mind Games/Meat City	1973	3.75	7.50	15.00
P-1868 [DJ]	Mind Games (mono/stereo)	1973	12.50	25.00	50.00
1874	Whatever Gets You Thru the Night/Beef Jerky	1974	—	3.00	6.00
—As "John Lennon and the Plastic Ono Nuclear Band"					
P-1874 [DJ]	Whatever Gets You Thru the Night (mono/stereo)	1974	12.50	25.00	50.00
—As "John Lennon and the Plastic Ono Nuclear Band"					
1878	#9 Dream/What You Got	1974	2.00	4.00	8.00
P-1878 [DJ]	#9 Dream (edited mono/stereo)	1974	12.50	25.00	50.00
P-1878 [DJ]	What You Got (mono/stereo)	1974	25.00	50.00	100.00
1881	Stand By Me/Move Over Ms. L.	1975	2.00	4.00	8.00
P-1881 [DJ]	Stand By Me (mono/stereo)	1975	12.50	25.00	50.00
P-1883 [DJ]	Ain't That a Shame (mono/stereo)	1975	50.00	100.00	200.00
—No stock copies issued					
P-1883 [DJ]	Slippin' and Slidin' (mono/stereo)	1975	50.00	100.00	200.00
—No stock copies issued					
S45X-47663/4 [DJ]	Happy Xmas (War Is Over)/Listen, the Snow Is Falling	1971	187.50	375.00	750.00
—As "John & Yoko/Plastic Ono Band with the Harlem Community Choir"; white label on styrene					
APPLE/AMERICOM					
1809P/M-435	Give Peace a Chance/Remember Love	1969	187.50	375.00	750.00
—As "Plastic Ono Band"; four-inch flexi-disc sold in vending machines					
ATLANTIC					
PR-104/5 [DJ]	John Lennon on Ronnie Hawkins: The Short Rap/The Long Rap	1970	25.00	50.00	100.00
CAPITOL					
1840	Imagine/It's So Hard	1978	—	3.00	6.00
—As "John Lennon Plastic Ono Band"; purple late 1970s label					
1840	Imagine/It's So Hard	1983	—	3.00	6.00
—As "John Lennon Plastic Ono Band"; black colorband label					
1840	Imagine/It's So Hard	1988	—	2.50	5.00
—As "John Lennon Plastic Ono Band"; purple late-1980s label (wider)					
1842	Happy Xmas (War Is Over)/Listen, the Snow Is Falling	1976	12.50	25.00	50.00
—As "John & Yoko/Plastic Ono Band with the Harlem Community Choir"; orange label					
1842	Happy Xmas (War Is Over)/Listen, the Snow Is Falling	1978	—	3.00	6.00
—As "John & Yoko/Plastic Ono Band with the Harlem Community Choir"; purple late-1970s label					
1842	Happy Xmas (War Is Over)/Listen, the Snow Is Falling	1983	—	3.00	6.00
—As "John & Yoko/Plastic Ono Band with the Harlem Community Choir"; black colorband label					
1842	Happy Xmas (War Is Over)/Listen, the Snow Is Falling	1988	5.00	10.00	20.00
—As "John & Yoko/Plastic Ono Band with the Harlem Community Choir"; purple late-1980s label (wider)					
1868	Mind Games/Meat City	1978	—	3.00	6.00
—Purple late-1970s label					
1868	Mind Games/Meat City	1983	3.00	6.00	12.00
—Black colorband label					
1874	Whatever Gets You Thru the Night/Beef Jerky	1978	—	3.00	6.00
—Purple late-1970s label					
1874	Whatever Gets You Thru the Night/Beef Jerky	1983	—	3.00	6.00
—Black colorband label					
1874	Whatever Gets You Thru the Night/Beef Jerky	1988	—	3.00	6.00
—Purple late-1980s label					
1878	#9 Dream/What You Got	1976	10.00	20.00	40.00
—Orange label					
1878	#9 Dream/What You Got	1978	—	3.00	6.00
—Purple late-1970s label					
1878	#9 Dream/What You Got	1983	2.50	5.00	10.00
—Black colorband label					

Number	Title (A Side/B Side)	Yr	VG	VG+	NM
S7-17644	Happy Xmas (War Is Over)/Listen, the Snow Is Falling	1993	—	2.00	4.00
—John & Yoko/The Plastic Ono Band; green vinyl					
S7-17783	Give Peace a Chance/Remember Love	1994	25.00	50.00	100.00
—CEMA Special Markets issue; meant for gold-plating in a special plaque. About 100 were not.					
B-44230	Jealous Guy/Give Peace a Chance	1988	—	2.50	5.00
B-44230 [PS]	Jealous Guy/Give Peace a Chance	1988	—	2.50	5.00
S7-57849	Imagine/It's So Hard	1992	12.50	25.00	50.00
—CEMA Special Markets issue; meant for gold-plating in a special plaque. About 1,000 were not.					
COTILLION					
PR-104/5 [DJ]	John Lennon on Ronnie Hawkins: The Short Rap/The Long Rap	1970	20.00	40.00	80.00
—White label with promo markings					
PR-104/5 [DJ]	John Lennon on Ronnie Hawkins: The Short Rap/The Long Rap	1970	22.50	45.00	90.00
—No promo markings on white label					
GEFFEN					
29855	Happy Xmas (War Is Over)/Beautiful Boy (Darling Boy)	1982	—	2.50	5.00
29855 [PS]	Happy Xmas (War Is Over)/Beautiful Boy (Darling Boy)	1982	—	2.50	5.00
49604	(Just Like) Starting Over/Kiss Kiss Kiss	1980	—	2.00	4.00
—B-side by Yoko Ono					
49604 [PS]	(Just Like) Starting Over/Kiss Kiss Kiss	1980	—	2.00	4.00
—B-side by Yoko Ono					
49644	Woman/Beautiful Boys	1980	—	2.00	4.00
—B-side by Yoko Ono					
49644 [PS]	Woman/Beautiful Boys	1980	—	2.00	4.00
—B-side by Yoko Ono					
49695	Watching the Wheels/Yes, I'm Your Angel	1981	—	2.00	4.00
—B-side by Yoko Ono					
49695 [PS]	Watching the Wheels/Yes, I'm Your Angel	1981	—	2.00	4.00
—B-side by Yoko Ono					
KYA					
1260 [DJ]	The KYA 1969 Peace Talk	1969	50.00	100.00	200.00
NOISEVILLE					
43	John Lennon Talks About David Peel	199?	10.00	20.00	40.00
—Red vinyl, signed by David Peel					
43	John Lennon Talks About David Peel	199?	2.50	5.00	10.00
—Black vinyl					
43 [PS]	John Lennon Talks About David Peel	199?	2.50	5.00	10.00
POLYDOR					
817254-7	Nobody Told Me/O' Sanity	1983	2.50	5.00	10.00
—With "Manufactured by Polydor Incorporated..." on label; B-side by Yoko Ono					
817254-7	Nobody Told Me/O' Sanity	1983	—	2.50	5.00
—With "Manufactured and Marketed by Polygram..." on label; B-side by Yoko Ono					
817254-7 [PS]	Nobody Told Me/O' Sanity	1983	—	2.50	5.00
821107-7	I'm Stepping Out/Sleepless Night	1984	—	2.00	4.00
—B-side by Yoko Ono					
821107-7 [PS]	I'm Stepping Out/Sleepless Night	1984	—	2.00	4.00
821204-7	Borrowed Time/Your Hands	1984	—	2.50	5.00
—B-side by Yoko Ono					
821204-7 [PS]	Borrowed Time/Your Hands	1984	—	2.50	5.00
881378-7	Every Man Has a Woman Who Loves Him/It's Alright	1984	2.00	4.00	8.00
—B-side by Sean Ono Lennon					
881378-7 [PS]	Every Man Has a Woman Who Loves Him/It's Alright	1984	2.00	4.00	8.00
QUAKER GRANOLA DIPPS					
(no #)	A Tribute to John Lennon	1986	3.75	7.50	15.00
—Cardboard record included in specially marked boxes of Quaker Granola Dipps					
QUAYE/TRIDENT					
SK 3419 [DJ]	Rock 'N' Roll	1975	125.00	250.00	500.00
—Radio spot to promote the album Rock 'N' Roll					

Albums

Number	Title	Yr	VG	VG+	NM
ADAM VIII					
A-8018	John Lennon Sings the Great Rock & Roll Hits (Roots)	1975	250.00	500.00	1000.
—Counterfeits abound. On authentic copies, cover is posterboard (not slicks); labels are normal size (not overly large); printing on cover is sharp, not blurry; the word "Greatest" does NOT appear on the spine. Authentic copies usually have ad sleeve also.					
APPLE					
SMAX-3361	Wedding Album	1969	37.50	75.00	150.00
—With photo strip, postcard, poster of wedding photos, poster of lithographs, "Bagism" bag, booklet, photo of slice of wedding cake. Missing inserts reduce the value.					
SW-3362	Live Peace in Toronto 1969	1970	3.75	7.50	15.00
—By "The Plastic Ono Band" -- without calendar					
SW-3362	Live Peace in Toronto 1969	1970	5.00	10.00	20.00
—By "The Plastic Ono Band"; with calendar					
SW-3372	John Lennon Plastic Ono Band	1970	5.00	10.00	20.00
SW-3379	Imagine	1971	5.00	10.00	20.00
—With either of two postcard inserts, lyric sleeve, poster					
SW-3379	Imagine	1975	5.00	10.00	20.00
—"All Rights Reserved" label					
SVBB-3392 [(2)]	Some Time in New York City	1972	7.50	15.00	30.00
—By John and Yoko; with photo card and petition					
SVBB-3392 [(2) DJ]	Some Time in New York City	1972	250.00	500.00	1000.
—White label promo					
SW-3414	Mind Games	1973	5.00	10.00	20.00
SW-3416	Walls and Bridges	1974	5.00	10.00	20.00
—With fold-open segmented front cover					
SK-3419	Rock 'n' Roll	1975	5.00	10.00	20.00
SW-3421	Shaved Fish	1975	5.00	10.00	20.00
T-5001	Two Virgins — Unfinished Music No. 1	1968	12.50	25.00	50.00
—With Yoko Ono; without brown bag					
T-5001	Two Virgins — Unfinished Music No. 1	1968	37.50	75.00	150.00
—With Yoko Ono; price with brown bag					
T-5001	Two Virgins — Unfinished Music No. 1	1968	37.50	75.00	150.00
—With Yoko Ono; with die-cut bag					
T-5001	Two Virgins — Unfinished Music No. 1	1985	3.75	7.50	15.00
—With Yoko Ono; reissue, flat label					
CAPITOL					
SW-3372	John Lennon Plastic Ono Band	1978	3.00	6.00	12.00
—Purple label, large Capitol logo					

Number	Title (A Side/B Side)	Yr	VG	VG+	NM
SW-3372	John Lennon Plastic Ono Band	1982	5.00	10.00	20.00
—Black label, print in colorband					
SW-3372	John Lennon Plastic Ono Band	1988	7.50	15.00	30.00
—Purple label, small Capitol logo					
SW-3379	Imagine	1978	2.50	5.00	10.00
—Purple label, large Capitol logo					
SW-3379	Imagine	1986	7.50	15.00	30.00
—Black label, print in colorband					
SW-3379	Imagine	1987	6.25	12.50	25.00
—Black label, print in colorband; "Digitally Re-Mastered" at top of front cover					
SW-3379	Imagine	1988	7.50	15.00	30.00
—Purple label, small Capitol logo					
SVBB-3392 [(2)]	Some Time in New York City	197?	6.25	12.50	25.00
—By John and Yoko; purple label, large Capitol logo					
SVBB-3392 [(2)]	Some Time in New York City	197?	25.00	50.00	100.00
—Both discs in single-pocket gatefold (the other pocket is glued shut)					
SW-3414	Mind Games	1978	10.00	20.00	40.00
—Purple label, large Capitol logo					
SW-3416	Walls and Bridges	1978	3.75	7.50	15.00
—Purple label, large Capitol logo; standard front cover					
SW-3416	Walls and Bridges	1982	7.50	15.00	30.00
—Black label, print in colorband					
SW-3416	Walls and Bridges	1989	7.50	15.00	30.00
—Purple label, small Capitol logo					
SK-3419	Rock 'n' Roll	1978	10.00	20.00	40.00
—Purple label, large Capitol logo					
SW-3421	Shaved Fish	1978	3.00	6.00	12.00
—Purple Capitol label with Apple logo on cover					
SW-3421	Shaved Fish	1978	10.00	20.00	40.00
—Purple Capitol label with Capitol logo on cover					
SW-3421	Shaved Fish	1983	5.00	10.00	20.00
—Black Capitol label with Apple logo on cover					
SW-3421	Shaved Fish	1983	10.00	20.00	40.00
—Black Capitol label with Capitol logo on cover					
SW-3421	Shaved Fish	1989	10.00	20.00	40.00
—Purple Capitol label (small logo) with Capitol logo on cover					
ST-12239	Live Peace in Toronto 1969	1982	2.50	5.00	10.00
—By "The Plastic Ono Band"; reissue, purple Capitol label					
ST-12239	Live Peace in Toronto 1969	1983	12.50	25.00	50.00
—By "The Plastic Ono Band"; reissue, black Capitol label					
SV-12451	Live in New York City	1986	3.00	6.00	12.00
SJ-12533	Menlove Ave.	1986	3.75	7.50	15.00
SN-16068	Mind Games	1980	3.00	6.00	12.00
—Budget-line reissue					
SN-16069	Rock 'n' Roll	1980	3.00	6.00	12.00
—Budget-line reissue					
C1-90803 [(2)]	Imagine: Music from the Motion Picture	1988	5.00	10.00	20.00
C1-91425	Double Fantasy	1989	5.00	10.00	20.00
—Very briefly available reissue					
R 144136	Menlove Ave.	1986	12.50	25.00	50.00
—RCA Music Service edition					
R 144136	Menlove Ave.	198?	12.50	25.00	50.00
—BMG Direct Marketing edition					
R 144497	Live in New York City	1986	3.75	7.50	15.00
—RCA Music Service edition					
SV-512451	Live in New York City	1986	3.75	7.50	15.00
—Columbia House edition					
C1-591425	Double Fantasy	1989	15.00	30.00	60.00
—Columbia House edition of reissue					

GEFFEN

Number	Title (A Side/B Side)	Yr	VG	VG+	NM
GHS 2001	Double Fantasy	1980	2.50	5.00	10.00
—Seven tracks by John, seven by Yoko; off-white label; titles on back cover out of order					
GHS 2001	Double Fantasy	1981	18.75	37.50	75.00
—Columbia House edition (all have corrected back cover) with "CH" on label					
GHS 2001	Double Fantasy	1981	3.00	6.00	12.00
—Off-white label, titles in order on the back cover					
GHS 2001	Double Fantasy	1981	3.00	6.00	12.00
—Columbia House edition (all have corrected back cover) without "CH" on label					
GHS 2001	Double Fantasy	1986	12.50	25.00	50.00
—Same as above, but with black Geffen label					
GHSP 2023	The John Lennon Collection	1982	5.00	10.00	20.00
GHSP 2023 [DJ]	The John Lennon Collection	1982	12.50	25.00	50.00
—Promo only on Quiex II audiophile vinyl					
R 104689	Double Fantasy	1981	10.00	20.00	40.00
—RCA Music Service edition					

MOBILE FIDELITY

Number	Title (A Side/B Side)	Yr	VG	VG+	NM
1-153	Imagine	1984	12.50	25.00	50.00
—Audiophile vinyl					

NAUTILUS

Number	Title (A Side/B Side)	Yr	VG	VG+	NM
NR-47	Double Fantasy	1982	20.00	40.00	80.00
—Half-speed master					
NR-47	Double Fantasy	1982	500.00	1000.	2000.
—Half-speed master; alternate experimental cover with yellow and red added to black and white front					

PARLOPHONE

Number	Title (A Side/B Side)	Yr	VG	VG+	NM
21954 [(2)]	Lennon Legend	1998	5.00	10.00	20.00
—"Made in U.S.A." on back cover					

POLYDOR

Number	Title (A Side/B Side)	Yr	VG	VG+	NM
817160-1	Milk and Honey	1983	2.50	5.00	10.00
—Six tracks by John, six by Yoko					
817160-1	Milk and Honey	1984	37.50	75.00	150.00
—Yellow or green vinyl; unauthorized "inside jobs"					
817238-1	Heart Play (Unfinished Dialogue)	1983	3.00	6.00	12.00
—Interviews with John Lennon and Yoko Ono					

SILHOUETTE

Number	Title (A Side/B Side)	Yr	VG	VG+	NM
SM-10012 [(2)]	Reflections and Poetry	1984	6.25	12.50	25.00

ZAPPLE

Number	Title (A Side/B Side)	Yr	VG	VG+	NM
ST-3357	Life with the Lions — Unfinished Music No. 2	1969	5.00	10.00	20.00
—With Yoko Ono					

LENNON SISTERS, THE

Also see LAWRENCE WELK.

45s

BRUNSWICK

Number	Title (A Side/B Side)	Yr	VG	VG+	NM
55000	Young and In Love/Teenage Waltz	1957	2.50	5.00	10.00
55013	White Silver Sands/One Day a Little Girl	1957	2.50	5.00	10.00
55028	Shake Me I Rattle/Pocahontas	1957	2.50	5.00	10.00
55044	Let's Light the Christmas Tree/Merry, Merry Christmas	1957	3.00	6.00	12.00
55051	To Know You Is to Love You/Hide Your Troubles Behind a Smile	1958	2.50	5.00	10.00
55058	Dear One/Mr. Clarinet Man	1958	2.50	5.00	10.00
55063	How Will I Know My Love/Graduation Dance	1958	2.50	5.00	10.00
55075	Bubble Gum/Have You Ever Been Lonely	1958	2.50	5.00	10.00
—With Larry Dean					
55082	Walk with Me/Goodnight God	1958	2.50	5.00	10.00
55113	The Children's Marching Song/Slumber Party	1959	2.50	5.00	10.00

DOT

Number	Title (A Side/B Side)	Yr	VG	VG+	NM
15965	A Hundred and One in the Sun/Vacation Waltz	1959	2.00	4.00	8.00
16131	Freckles/I Wakled with the Wind	1960	2.00	4.00	8.00
16184	Did'Ja Know/What a Sky	1961	2.00	4.00	8.00
16215	Darlin' Meggie/On the Double	1961	2.00	4.00	8.00
16255	Sad Movies (Make Me Cry)/I Don't Know Why	1961	2.00	4.00	8.00
16277	Kaw-Liga/We Live in Two Different Worlds	1961	2.00	4.00	8.00
16423	Bei Mir Bist Du Schoen/Lida Rose	1963	2.00	4.00	8.00
16489	The Heartstrings/Speak, Sugar, Speak	1963	2.00	4.00	8.00
16681	Little Stranger/Little Lady Make Believe	1964	—	3.00	6.00
16748	Chim Chim Cheree/A Step in Time	1965	—	3.00	6.00
17010	He's Got a Lotta Lovin'/I'm Coming Back to You	1967	—	3.00	6.00
17046	I Love/Gypsy, What Can I Do	1967	—	3.00	6.00

MERCURY

Number	Title (A Side/B Side)	Yr	VG	VG+	NM
72830	As Long As There's an Apple Tree/I'm So Glad That You've Found Me	1968	—	3.00	6.00
72883	The Christmas Waltz/Lullaby for Christmas	1968	—	3.00	6.00

Albums

BRUNSWICK

Number	Title (A Side/B Side)	Yr	VG	VG+	NM
BL 54031 [M]	Let's Get Acquainted	1957	6.25	12.50	25.00
BL 54039 [M]	Lawrence Welk Presents the Lennon Sisters	1958	6.25	12.50	25.00

DOT

Number	Title (A Side/B Side)	Yr	VG	VG+	NM
DLP-3250 [M]	Best-Loved Catholic Hymns	1959	3.75	7.50	15.00
DLP-3292 [M]	The Lennon Sisters Sing 12 Great Hits	1960	3.75	7.50	15.00
DLP 3343 [M]	Christmas with the Lennon Sisters	1961	3.75	7.50	15.00
DLP-3398 [M]	Sad Movies (Make Me Cry)	1961	3.75	7.50	15.00
DLP-3417 [M]	Can't Help Falling in Love	1962	3.00	6.00	12.00
DLP-3481 [M]	The Lennon Sisters' Favorites	1963	3.00	6.00	12.00
DLP-3557 [M]	Dominique and Other Great Folk Songs	1964	3.00	6.00	12.00
DLP-3589 [M]	No. 1 Hits of the 1960s	1964	3.00	6.00	12.00
DLP-3622 [M]	Twelve Great Hits, Volume 2	1965	3.00	6.00	12.00
DLP-3659 [M]	Solos	1965	3.00	6.00	12.00
DLP-3797 [M]	Somethin' Stupid	1967	3.75	7.50	15.00
DLP-25250 [S]	Best-Loved Catholic Hymns	1959	5.00	10.00	20.00
DLP-25292 [S]	The Lennon Sisters Sing 12 Great Hits	1960	5.00	10.00	20.00
DLP 25343 [S]	Christmas with the Lennon Sisters	1961	5.00	10.00	20.00
DLP-25398 [S]	Sad Movies (Make Me Cry)	1961	5.00	10.00	20.00
DLP-25417 [S]	Can't Help Falling in Love	1962	3.75	7.50	15.00
DLP-25481 [S]	The Lennon Sisters' Favorites	1963	3.75	7.50	15.00
DLP-25557 [S]	Dominique and Other Great Folk Songs	1964	3.75	7.50	15.00
DLP-25589 [S]	No. 1 Hits of the 1960s	1964	3.75	7.50	15.00
DLP-25622 [S]	Twelve Great Hits, Volume 2	1965	3.75	7.50	15.00
DLP-25659 [S]	Solos	1965	3.75	7.50	15.00
DLP-25797 [S]	Somethin' Stupid	1967	3.00	6.00	12.00

HAMILTON

Number	Title (A Side/B Side)	Yr	VG	VG+	NM
HLP-119 [M]	Melody of Love	196?	3.00	6.00	12.00
HLP-12119 [S]	Melody of Love	196?	3.00	6.00	12.00

MERCURY

Number	Title (A Side/B Side)	Yr	VG	VG+	NM
SR-61164	The Lennon Sisters Today!!	1968	3.00	6.00	12.00
SR-61201	Pop Country	1969	3.00	6.00	12.00

PICKWICK

Number	Title (A Side/B Side)	Yr	VG	VG+	NM
PTP-2014 [(2)]	America's Sweethearts	1973	3.00	6.00	12.00
SPC-3084	Our Favorite Songs	196?	2.50	5.00	10.00
SPC-3110	Goodnight Sweetheart	197?	2.50	5.00	10.00

RANWOOD

Number	Title (A Side/B Side)	Yr	VG	VG+	NM
7027 [(2)]	22 Songs of Faith and Inspiration	198?	2.50	5.00	10.00
8205	Best of the Lennon Sisters	198?	2.00	4.00	8.00
8212	How Great Thou Art	198?	2.00	4.00	8.00

VOCALION

Number	Title (A Side/B Side)	Yr	VG	VG+	NM
VL 73864	Too Marvelous for Words	1969	2.50	5.00	10.00
VL 73887	The Lennon Sisters with Lawrence Welk	1970	2.50	5.00	10.00

LENNY AND THE CHIMES

45s

VEE JAY

Number	Title (A Side/B Side)	Yr	VG	VG+	NM
605	Only Forever/Two Times Two	1964	3.00	6.00	12.00

LENNY AND THE THUNDERTONES

45s

DOT

Number	Title (A Side/B Side)	Yr	VG	VG+	NM
16177	The Street Beat/Happy Little Jug	1961	6.25	12.50	25.00

LENOIR, J.B.

45s

CHECKER

Number	Title (A Side/B Side)	Yr	VG	VG+	NM
844	Let Me Die with the One I Love/If I Give My Love to You	1956	10.00	20.00	40.00
856	Don't Touch My Head/I've Been Down So Long	1957	10.00	20.00	40.00
874	What About Your Daughter/Five Years	1957	7.50	15.00	30.00
901	Daddy Talk to Your Son/She Don't Know	1958	7.50	15.00	30.00

J.O.B.

Number	Title (A Side/B Side)	Yr	VG	VG+	NM
1012	The Mojo/How Can I Leave	1952	50.00	100.00	200.00
1102	Play a Little While/Louise	1952	30.00	60.00	120.00

PARROT

Number	Title (A Side/B Side)	Yr	VG	VG+	NM
802	Eisenhower Blues/I'm in Korea	1954	100.00	200.00	400.00
802	Tax Paying Blues/I'm in Korea	1954	250.00	500.00	1000.
—A-side is similar, though not identical, to "Eisenhower Blues"					
802	Tax Paying Blues/I'm in Korea	1954	500.00	1000.	2000.
—Red vinyl					
809	Mama Talk to Your Daughter/Man, Watch Your Woman	1955	20.00	40.00	80.00

Number	Title (A Side/B Side)	Yr	VG	VG+	NM
814	Mama Your Daughter Is Going to Miss Me/What Have I Done	1955	25.00	50.00	100.00
821	Fine Girls/I Lost My Baby	1955	37.50	75.00	150.00
SHAD					
5012	Back Door/Louella	1959	5.00	10.00	20.00
U.S.A.					
744	I Feel So Good/Sing Um the Way I Feel	1963	5.00	10.00	20.00
VEE JAY					
352	Do What I Say/Oh Baby	1960	3.00	6.00	12.00
—As "J.B. Lenore"					
Albums					
CHESS					
LP-410	Natural Man	1970	10.00	20.00	40.00
CH-9323	Natural Man	1990	3.00	6.00	12.00
POLYDOR					
24-4011	J.B. Lenoir	1970	3.75	7.50	15.00

LEONARD, JACK E.

Number	Title (A Side/B Side)	Yr	VG	VG+	NM
Albums					
VIK					
LX-1080 [M]	Rock 'n Roll for People Over Sixteen	1957	10.00	20.00	40.00

LESTER, BOBBY, AND THE MOONLIGHTERS

The Moonlighters are THE MOONGLOWS.

Number	Title (A Side/B Side)	Yr	VG	VG+	NM
45s					
CHECKER					
806	So All Alone/Shoo Doo-Be Do (My Loving Baby)	1954	25.00	50.00	100.00
—Maroon label with checkerboard top					
806	So All Alone/Shoo Doo-Be Do (My Loving Baby)	1958	10.00	20.00	40.00
—Maroon label, vertical logo					
813	New Gal/The Hug and a Kiss	1955	20.00	40.00	80.00

LESTER, KETTY

Number	Title (A Side/B Side)	Yr	VG	VG+	NM
45s					
ERA					
3068	Love Letters/I'm a Fool to Want You	1962	3.00	6.00	12.00
3080	But Not for Me/Once Upon a Time	1962	2.50	5.00	10.00
3088	You Can't Lie to a Liar/River of Salt	1962	2.50	5.00	10.00
3094	This Land Is Your Land/Love Is for Everyone	1962	2.50	5.00	10.00
3103	Fallen Angel/Lullaby for Lovers	1963	2.50	5.00	10.00
EVEREST					
20007	Queen for a Day/I Said Goodbye to My Love	1962	2.50	5.00	10.00
PETE					
706	I Wil Lead You/Now That I Need Him	1968	—	3.00	6.00
710	Measure of a Man/Cracker Box Living	1968	—	3.00	6.00
714	Show Me/Since I Fell for You	1969	—	3.00	6.00
RCA VICTOR					
47-8331	The House Is Haunted/Some Things Are Better Left Unsaid	1964	2.00	4.00	8.00
47-8371	Please Don't Cry Anymore/Roses Grow With Thorns	1964	2.00	4.00	8.00
47-8424	I Trust You Baby/Theme from The Luck of Ginger Coffey	1964	2.00	4.00	8.00
47-8471	You Go Your Way/Variations on a Theme by Byrd	1964	2.00	4.00	8.00
47-8573	(Looking for a) Better World/Pretty Lies, Pretty Make Believes	1965	2.00	4.00	8.00
TOWER					
166	I'll Be Looking Back/West Coast	1965	2.00	4.00	8.00
208	Secret Love/Love Me Just a Little Bit	1966	2.00	4.00	8.00
236	When a Woman Loves a Man/We'll Be Together Again	1966	2.00	4.00	8.00
Albums					
AVI					
6116	A Collection of Her Best	1982	3.75	7.50	15.00
ERA					
EL-108 [M]	Love Letters	1962	10.00	20.00	40.00
ES-108 [S]	Love Letters	1962	15.00	30.00	60.00
PETE					
1109	Ketty Lester	1969	3.75	7.50	15.00
RCA VICTOR					
LPM-2945 [M]	The Soul of Me	1964	6.25	12.50	25.00
LSP-2945 [S]	The Soul of Me	1964	7.50	15.00	30.00
LPM-3326 [M]	Where Is Love	1965	6.25	12.50	25.00
LSP-3326 [S]	Where Is Love	1965	7.50	15.00	30.00
SHEFFIELD					
15	Ketty Lester In Concert	1977	3.75	7.50	15.00
TOWER					
ST 5029 [S]	When a Woman Loves a Man	1966	6.25	12.50	25.00
T 5029 [M]	When a Woman Loves a Man	1966	6.25	12.50	25.00

LETTERMEN, THE

Number	Title (A Side/B Side)	Yr	VG	VG+	NM
45s					
ALPHA OMEGA					
078501	It Feels Like Christmas/I Believe	1985	—	2.00	4.00
078501 [PS]	It Feels Like Christmas/I Believe	1985	—	2.00	4.00
APPLAUSE					
104	What I Did for Love/Cherish-Precious and Few	1983	—	2.00	4.00
CAPITOL					
2054	Goin' Out of My Head-Can't Take My Eyes Off You/I Believe	1967	2.00	4.00	8.00
2132	Sherry Don't Go/Never My Love	1968	—	3.00	6.00
2196	Anyone Who Had a Heart/All the Gray-Haired Men	1968	—	3.00	6.00
2218	Love Is Blue-Greensleeves/Where Were You When the Lights Went Out	1968	—	3.00	6.00
2254	Playing the Piano/Sally Le Roy	1968	—	3.00	6.00
2324	Put Your Head on My Shoulder/Mary's Rainbow	1968	—	3.00	6.00
2414	I Have Dreamed/The Pendulum Swings Both Ways	1969	—	3.00	6.00
2482	Hurt So Bad/Catch the Wind	1969	—	3.00	6.00
2643	Shangri-La/When Summer Ends	1969	—	3.00	6.00
2697	Traces-Memories Medley/For Once in a Lifetime	1969	—	3.00	6.00
2774	Hang On Sloopy/For Love	1970	—	2.50	5.00
2820	She Cried/For Love	1970	—	2.50	5.00
2938	Hey Girl/Worlds	1970	—	2.50	5.00
3020	Everything Is Good About You/It's Over	1971	—	2.50	5.00
3098	Love Is a Hurtin' Thing/Feelings	1971	—	2.50	5.00
3192	Love/Maybe Tomorrow	1971	—	2.50	5.00
3285	Oh My Love/An Old Fashioned Love Song	1972	—	2.00	4.00
3449	Maybe We Should/Spin Away	1972	—	2.00	4.00
3512	Sandman/Love Song	1973	—	2.00	4.00
3619	A Summer Song/Mac Arthur Park	1973	—	2.00	4.00
3810	Goodbye/The You Part of Me	1973	—	2.00	4.00
3912	The Way We Were-Isn't It a Shame/Touch Me in the Morning	1974	—	2.00	4.00
4005	Song from Some Came Running (To Love and Be Loved)/Eastward	1974	—	2.00	4.00
4096	You Are My Sunshine Girl/Make a Time for Lovin'	1975	—	2.00	4.00
4161	If You Feel the Way I Do/Love Me Like a Stranger	1975	—	2.00	4.00
4226	Storms of Troubled Times/The Way You Look Tonight	1976	—	2.00	4.00
4586	The Way You Look Tonight/That's My Desire	1961	3.00	6.00	12.00
4586 [PS]	The Way You Look Tonight/That's My Desire	1961	5.00	10.00	20.00
4658	When I Fall in Love/Smile	1961	3.00	6.00	12.00
4658 [PS]	When I Fall in Love/Smile	1961	5.00	10.00	20.00
4699	Come Back Silly Girl/A Song for Young Love	1962	3.00	6.00	12.00
4699 [PS]	Come Back Silly Girl/A Song for Young Love	1962	5.00	10.00	20.00
4746	How Is Julie?/Turn Around, Look at Me	1962	3.00	6.00	12.00
4746 [PS]	How Is Julie?/Turn Around, Look at Me	1962	5.00	10.00	20.00
4810	Silly Boy (She Doesn't Love You)/I Told the Stars	1962	3.00	6.00	12.00
4810 [PS]	Silly Boy (She Doesn't Love You)/I Told the Stars	1962	5.00	10.00	20.00
4851	Again/Tree in the Meadow	1962	3.00	6.00	12.00
4914	No Other Love/Heartache on Heartache	1963	2.50	5.00	10.00
4976	Two Brothers/The Allentown Jail	1963	2.50	5.00	10.00
5091	Where or When/Be My Girl	1963	2.50	5.00	10.00
5218	Put Away Your Teardrops/Seventh Dawn Theme	1964	2.50	5.00	10.00
5273	When Summer Ends/You Don't Know Just How Lucky You Are	1964	2.50	5.00	10.00
5370	The Girl with a Little Tin Heart/It's Over	1965	2.00	4.00	8.00
5437	Theme from "A Summer Place"/Sealed with a Kiss	1965	2.00	4.00	8.00
5499	Secretly/The Things We Did Last Summer	1965	2.00	4.00	8.00
5499 [PS]	Secretly/The Things We Did Last Summer	1965	3.00	6.00	12.00
5544	I Believe/Sweet September	1965	2.00	4.00	8.00
5583	You'll Be Needin' Me/Run to My Loving Arms	1966	2.00	4.00	8.00
5649	I Only Have Eyes for You/Love Letters	1966	2.00	4.00	8.00
5649 [PS]	I Only Have Eyes for You/Love Letters	1966	3.00	6.00	12.00
5749	Chanson D'Amour/She Don't Want Me Now	1966	2.00	4.00	8.00
5813	Our Winter Love/Warm	1966	2.00	4.00	8.00
5913	Volare/Mr. Sun	1967	2.00	4.00	8.00
WARNER BROS.					
5152	Their Hearts Were Full of Spring/When	1960	3.75	7.50	15.00
5178	Two Hearts/Magic Sound	1960	3.75	7.50	15.00
Albums					
APPLAUSE					
1006	Love Is...	198?	2.50	5.00	10.00
CAPITOL					
SKAO-138	The Best of the Lettermen, Vol. 2	1969	3.00	6.00	12.00
SM-147	Put Your Head on My Shoulder	1977	2.00	4.00	8.00
—Reissue with new prefix					
ST-147	Put Your Head on My Shoulder	1968	3.75	7.50	15.00
ST-202	I Have Dreamed	1969	3.00	6.00	12.00
SWBB-251 [(2)]	Close-Up	1969	3.75	7.50	15.00
—Reissue of ST 2013 and ST 2083 in one package					
ST-269	Hurt So Bad	1969	3.00	6.00	12.00
ST-390	Traces/Memories	1970	3.00	6.00	12.00
ST-496	Reflections	1970	3.00	6.00	12.00
STCL-577 [(3)]	The Lettermen	1970	6.25	12.50	25.00
ST-634	Everything's Good About You	1971	3.00	6.00	12.00
STBB-710 [(2)]	Let It Be Me/And I Love Her	1971	3.75	7.50	15.00
SW-781	Feelings	1971	3.00	6.00	12.00
ST-836	Love Book	1971	3.00	6.00	12.00
ST 1669 [S]	A Song for Young Love	1962	5.00	10.00	20.00
T 1669 [M]	A Song for Young Love	1962	3.75	7.50	15.00
ST 1711 [S]	Once Upon a Time	1962	5.00	10.00	20.00
T 1711 [M]	Once Upon a Time	1962	3.75	7.50	15.00
ST 1761 [S]	Jim, Tony and Bob	1962	5.00	10.00	20.00
T 1761 [M]	Jim, Tony and Bob	1962	3.75	7.50	15.00
ST 1829 [S]	College Standards	1963	5.00	10.00	20.00
T 1829 [M]	College Standards	1963	3.75	7.50	15.00
ST 1936 [S]	The Lettermen In Concert	1963	5.00	10.00	20.00
T 1936 [M]	The Lettermen In Concert	1963	3.75	7.50	15.00
ST 2013 [S]	A Lettermen Kind of Love	1964	3.75	7.50	15.00
T 2013 [M]	A Lettermen Kind of Love	1964	3.00	6.00	12.00
ST 2083 [S]	The Lettermen Look at Love	1964	3.75	7.50	15.00
T 2083 [M]	The Lettermen Look at Love	1964	3.00	6.00	12.00
ST 2142 [S]	She Cried	1964	3.75	7.50	15.00
T 2142 [M]	She Cried	1964	3.00	6.00	12.00
ST 2213 [S]	You'll Never Walk Alone	1965	3.75	7.50	15.00
T 2213 [M]	You'll Never Walk Alone	1965	3.00	6.00	12.00
ST 2270 [S]	Portrait of My Love	1965	3.75	7.50	15.00
T 2270 [M]	Portrait of My Love	1965	3.00	6.00	12.00
ST 2359 [S]	The Hit Sounds of the Lettermen	1965	3.75	7.50	15.00
T 2359 [M]	The Hit Sounds of the Lettermen	1965	3.00	6.00	12.00
ST 2428 [S]	More Hit Sounds of the Lettermen!	1966	3.75	7.50	15.00
T 2428 [M]	More Hit Sounds of the Lettermen!	1966	3.00	6.00	12.00
ST 2496 [S]	A New Song for Young Love	1966	3.75	7.50	15.00
T 2496 [M]	A New Song for Young Love	1966	3.00	6.00	12.00
ST 2554 [S]	The Best of the Lettermen	1966	3.75	7.50	15.00
T 2554 [M]	The Best of the Lettermen	1966	3.00	6.00	12.00
ST-8-2587 [S]	For Christmas This Year	1966	5.00	10.00	20.00
—Capitol Record Club edition					
ST 2587 [S]	For Christmas This Year	1966	3.75	7.50	15.00
T 2587 [M]	For Christmas This Year	1966	3.00	6.00	12.00
ST 2633 [S]	Warm	1967	3.75	7.50	15.00
T 2633 [M]	Warm	1967	3.75	7.50	15.00

Number	Title (A Side/B Side)	Yr	VG	VG+	NM
SM-2711	Spring!	1977	2.00	4.00	8.00
—Reissue with new prefix					
ST 2711 [S]	Spring!	1967	3.75	7.50	15.00
T 2711 [M]	Spring!	1967	3.75	7.50	15.00
ST 2758 [S]	The Lettermen!!!... And "Live!"	1967	3.75	7.50	15.00
T 2758 [M]	The Lettermen!!!... And "Live!"	1967	5.00	10.00	20.00
ST 2865	Goin' Out of My Head	1968	3.75	7.50	15.00
ST 2934	Special Request	1968	3.75	7.50	15.00
SW-11010	Lettermen 1	1972	2.50	5.00	10.00
SW-11124	Spin Away	1972	2.50	5.00	10.00
SW-11183	"Alive" Again ... Naturally	1973	2.50	5.00	10.00
SW-11249	All-Time Greatest Hits	1973	2.50	5.00	10.00
SW-11319	Now and Forever	1974	2.50	5.00	10.00
SW-11364	There Is No Greater Love	1974	2.50	5.00	10.00
SW-11424	Make Time	1975	2.50	5.00	10.00
SW-11470	The Time Is Right	1975	2.50	5.00	10.00
SW-11508	Kind of Country	1976	2.50	5.00	10.00
SM-11678	Hurt So Bad	1977	2.00	4.00	8.00
—Reissue of 269					
SM-11814	The Lettermen!!! ... And "Live!"	1978	2.00	4.00	8.00
—Reissue of 2758					
SM-11970	Goin' Out of My Head	1979	2.00	4.00	8.00
—Reissue of 2865					
SN-16071	The Best of the Lettermen	1980	2.00	4.00	8.00
—Budget-line reissue					
SN-16190	Let It Be Me	1981	2.00	4.00	8.00
—Budget-line reissue					
SN-16191	And I Love Her	1981	2.00	4.00	8.00
—Budget-line reissue					
SN-16222	The Best of the Lettermen, Vol. 2	198?	2.00	4.00	8.00
—Budget-line reissue					
SN-16312	All-Time Greatest Hits	198?	2.00	4.00	8.00
—Budget-line reissue					
LONGINES SYMPHONETTE					
220 [(5)]	A Time for Us	1972	7.50	15.00	30.00
PICKWICK					
SPC-3294	Soft Hits	1972	2.50	5.00	10.00
SPC-3565	With Love	1978	2.00	4.00	8.00

LETTERMEN, THE (2)

Different group from above.

45s

Number	Title (A Side/B Side)	Yr	VG	VG+	NM
LIBERTY					
55141	Hey, Big Brain/Guiro	1958	2.50	5.00	10.00

LEVIATHAN

Albums

Number	Title (A Side/B Side)	Yr	VG	VG+	NM
MACH					
XMA-12501	Leviathan	1974	10.00	20.00	40.00

LEVON AND THE HAWKS

45s

Number	Title (A Side/B Side)	Yr	VG	VG+	NM
ATCO					
6383	He Don't Love You (And He'll Break Your Heart)/ Stones I Throw	1965	7.50	15.00	30.00
6625	He Don't Love You (And He'll Break Your Heart)/ Go Go Lisa Jane	1968	7.50	15.00	30.00

LEWIS, BARBARA

45s

Number	Title (A Side/B Side)	Yr	VG	VG+	NM
ATLANTIC					
2141	My Heart Went Do Dat Da/The Longest Night of the Year	1962	3.00	6.00	12.00
2159	My Mama Told Me/Gonna Love You Till the Day I Die	1962	3.00	6.00	12.00
2184	Hello Stranger/Think a Little Sugar	1963	5.00	10.00	20.00
2200	Straighten Up Your Heart/If You Love Her	1963	3.00	6.00	12.00
2214	Puppy Love/Snap Your Fingers	1963	3.00	6.00	12.00
2227	Someday We're Gonna Love Again/Spend a Little Time	1964	2.50	5.00	10.00
2255	Come Home/Pushin' a Good Thing Too Far	1964	2.50	5.00	10.00
2283	Baby, I'm Yours/I Say Love	1965	3.75	7.50	15.00
2300	Make Me Your Baby/Love to Be Loved	1965	3.75	7.50	15.00
2316	Don't Forget About Me/It's Magic	1965	2.50	5.00	10.00
2346	Make Me Belong to You/Girls Need Loving Care	1966	2.00	4.00	8.00
2361	I Remember the Feeling/Baby What You Want Me to Do	1966	2.00	4.00	8.00
2400	Love Makes the World Go Round/I'll Make Him Love Me	1967	2.00	4.00	8.00
2413	Fool, Fool, Fool/Only All the Time	1967	2.00	4.00	8.00
2482	Thankful for What I Got/Sho Nuff	1968	2.00	4.00	8.00
2514	On Bended Knees/I'll Keep Believing	1968	2.00	4.00	8.00
2550	I'm All You've Got/You're a Dream Maker	1968	2.00	4.00	8.00
ENTERPRISE					
9012	You Made Me a Woman/Just the Way You Are Today	1970	—	3.00	6.00
9027	Ask the Lonely/Why Did It Take You So Long	1970	—	3.00	6.00
9029	Anyway/That's the Way I Like It	1970	—	3.00	6.00
KAREN					
313	My Heart Went Do Dat Da/The Longest Night of the Year	1961	7.50	15.00	30.00
REPRISE					
1146	Rock and Roll Lullaby/I'm So Thankful	1972	—	2.50	5.00

7-Inch Extended Plays

Number	Title (A Side/B Side)	Yr	VG	VG+	NM
ATLANTIC					
LSD 8110 [DJ]	Baby I'm Yours/Hy Heart Went Do Da Dat/Puppy Love//Hello Stranger/Someday We're Gonna Love Again/Snap Your Fingers	196?	3.75	7.50	15.00
—Jukebox mini-LP, small hole, plays at 33 1/3 rpm					
LSD 8110 [PS]	Baby I'm Yours	196?	3.75	7.50	15.00

Albums

Number	Title (A Side/B Side)	Yr	VG	VG+	NM
ATLANTIC					
8086 [M]	Hello Stranger	1963	10.00	20.00	40.00
SD 8086 [S]	Hello Stranger	1963	12.50	25.00	50.00
8090 [M]	Snap Your Fingers	1964	10.00	20.00	40.00
SD 8090 [S]	Snap Your Fingers	1964	12.50	25.00	50.00
8110 [M]	Baby, I'm Yours	1965	10.00	20.00	40.00
SD 8110 [S]	Baby, I'm Yours	1965	12.50	25.00	50.00
8118 [M]	It's Magic	1966	7.50	15.00	30.00
SD 8118 [S]	It's Magic	1966	10.00	20.00	40.00
SD 8173	Workin' on a Groovy Thing	1968	6.25	12.50	25.00
SD 8286	The Best of Barbara Lewis	1971	5.00	10.00	20.00
COLLECTABLES					
COL-5104	Golden Classics	198?	2.50	5.00	10.00
ENTERPRISE					
ENS-1006	The Many Grooves of Barbara Lewis	1970	6.25	12.50	25.00

LEWIS, BOBBY (1)

R&B singer.

45s

Number	Title (A Side/B Side)	Yr	VG	VG+	NM
ABC-PARAMOUNT					
10565	That's Right/Fannie Lewis	1964	3.00	6.00	12.00
10592	Jealous Love/Stark Raving Wild	1964	3.00	6.00	12.00
BELTONE					
1002	Tossin' and Turnin'/Oh Yes I Love You	1961	6.25	12.50	25.00
1012	One Track Mind/Are You Ready	1961	6.25	12.50	25.00
1015	What a Walk/Cry No More	1961	3.75	7.50	15.00
1016	Yes, Oh Yes, It Did/Mamie in the Afternoon	1962	3.75	7.50	15.00
2018	A Man's Gotta Be a Man/Day by Day I Need Your Love	1962	3.75	7.50	15.00
2023	I'm Tossin' and Turnin' Again/Nothin' But the Blues	1962	3.75	7.50	15.00
2026	Lonely Teardrops/Boom-a-Chick-Chick	1962	3.75	7.50	15.00
2035	Nothin' But the Blues/Intermission	1963	3.75	7.50	15.00
MERCURY					
71245	Mumbles Blues/Oh Baby	1957	6.25	12.50	25.00
PHILIPS					
40519	Soul Seekin'/Give Me Your Yesterdays	1968	5.00	10.00	20.00
ROULETTE					
4182	You Better Stop/Fire of Love	1959	3.75	7.50	15.00
4382	Solid as a Rock/Oh Mr. Somebody	1961	3.75	7.50	15.00
SPOTLIGHT					
394	Mumbles Blues/Oh Baby	1957	7.50	15.00	30.00
397	Solid as a Rock/You Even Forgot My Name	1957	7.50	15.00	30.00

Albums

Number	Title (A Side/B Side)	Yr	VG	VG+	NM
BELTONE					
4000 [M]	Tossin' and Turnin'	1961	50.00	100.00	200.00

LEWIS, BOBBY (2)

Country singer.

45s

Number	Title (A Side/B Side)	Yr	VG	VG+	NM
ACE OF HEARTS					
0463	Already Gone to My Heart/Mr. President	1973	—	3.00	6.00
0466	Here with You/Where Happiness Is	1973	—	3.00	6.00
0472	Too Many Memories/With Meaning	1973	—	3.00	6.00
0480	I Never Get Through Missing You/Lady Lover	1974	—	3.00	6.00
0502	Let Me Take Care of You/Where Happiness Is	1975	—	3.00	6.00
7503	It's So Nice to Be with You/(B-side unknown)	1975	—	3.00	6.00
CAPRICORN					
0318	She's Been Keeping Me Up Nights/I Keep Falling in Love with You	1979	—	2.50	5.00
0331	Love Won't Be Love Without You/This Is a Man and Woman Kind of Night	1979	—	2.50	5.00
GRT					
007	Lady Lover/I Never Get Through Missing You	1974	—	3.00	6.00
008	I See Love/Your Love	1974	—	3.00	6.00
HME					
04853	Love Is An Overload/Treat Her Like a Stranger	1985	—	2.00	4.00
RPA					
7603	For Your Love/(B-side unknown)	1976	—	3.00	6.00
7613	I'm Getting High Remembering/With Meaning	1976	—	3.00	6.00
7622	What a Diff'rence a Day Made/I Can Feel It	1977	—	3.00	6.00
UNITED ARTISTS					
842	Everybody's Baby/Perfect Example of a Fool	1965	2.50	5.00	10.00
920	Why Me/Six Days a Week, Twice on Sunday	1965	2.50	5.00	10.00
50009	You Remind Me Of Myself/I Hope You Find in Him What You Were Looking For in Me	1966	2.00	4.00	8.00
50067	How Long Has It Been/Easy to Say, Hard to Do	1966	2.00	4.00	8.00
50133	Two of the Usual/Your B.A.B.Y. Baby Don't Love You	1967	2.00	4.00	8.00
50161	Love Me and Make It All Better/My Tears Don't Care (They Fall Anywhere)	1967	2.00	4.00	8.00
50208	I Doubt It/Laughing Girl, She's Not Happy	1967	2.00	4.00	8.00
50263	Ordinary Miracle/These Are Things I Miss	1968	2.00	4.00	8.00
50327	From Heaven to Heartache/Only for Me	1968	2.00	4.00	8.00
50476	Each and Every Part of Me/My (Is Such a Lonely Word)	1969	2.00	4.00	8.00
50528	Til Something Better Comes Along/I'm Only a Man	1969	2.00	4.00	8.00
50573	Things for You and I/Somebody Lied to Me	1969	2.00	4.00	8.00
50620	I'm Going Home/I May Never Be Free	1969	2.00	4.00	8.00
50668	Hello Mary Lou/Love, Wonderful Love	1970	—	3.50	7.00
50719	Simple Days and Simple Ways/Love's Garden	1970	—	3.50	7.00
50754	Come Sundown/He Gives Us All His Love	1971	—	3.50	7.00
50791	If I Had You/Doggone This Heartache	1971	—	3.50	7.00
50850	Today's Teardrops/Love's Satisfaction	1971	—	3.50	7.00
50885	Only Love Can Break a Heart/We Ran Out of Time	1972	—	3.50	7.00

Albums

Number	Title (A Side/B Side)	Yr	VG	VG+	NM
ACE OF HEARTS					
1002	Too Many Memories	1974	3.75	7.50	15.00
RPA					
1002	Portrait in Love	1976	2.50	5.00	10.00
1013	Soul Full of Music	1977	2.50	5.00	10.00
UNITED ARTISTS					
UAL-3582 [M]	How Long Has It Been	1967	6.25	12.50	25.00

Number	Title (A Side/B Side)	Yr	VG	VG+	NM
UAS-6582 [S]	How Long Has It Been	1967	6.25	12.50	25.00
UAS-6616	A World of Love from Bobby Lewis	1967	5.00	10.00	20.00
UAS-6629	An Ordinary Miracle	1968	5.00	10.00	20.00
UAS-6673	From Heaven to Heartache	1968	5.00	10.00	20.00
UAS-6717	Thanks for You and I	1969	5.00	10.00	20.00
UAS-6760	The Best of Bobby Lewis, Vol. 1	1970	3.75	7.50	15.00

LEWIS, CLARENCE

45s

Number	Title (A Side/B Side)	Yr	VG	VG+	NM
FURY					
1032	Cupid's Little Helper/Half a Heart	1960	3.75	7.50	15.00
RED ROBIN					
136	Lost Everything/Your Heart Must Be Made of Stone	1955	20.00	40.00	80.00

LEWIS, EARL, AND THE CHANNELS

See THE CHANNELS.

LEWIS, GARY, AND THE PLAYBOYS

45s

Number	Title (A Side/B Side)	Yr	VG	VG+	NM
EPIC					
50068	One Good Woman/Ooh Baby	1975	2.00	4.00	8.00
—Gary Lewis solo					
LIBERTY					
(no #) [DJ]	Way Way Out (same on both sides)	1967	125.00	250.00	500.00
65-227 [DJ]	Doin' the Flake//This Diamond Ring/Little Miss Go-Go	1965	6.25	12.50	25.00
65-227 [PS]	Doin' the Flake//This Diamond Ring/Little Miss Go-Go	1965	12.50	25.00	50.00
—Kellogg's Corn Flakes giveaway					
55756	This Diamond Ring/Hard to Find	1964	3.00	6.00	12.00
55756	This Diamond Ring/Tijuana Wedding	1964	2.50	5.00	10.00
55778	Count Me In/Little Miss Go-Go	1965	2.50	5.00	10.00
55809	Save Your Heart for Me/Without a Word of Warning	1965	2.50	5.00	10.00
55818	Everybody Loves a Clown/Time Stands Still	1965	2.50	5.00	10.00
55818 [PS]	Everybody Loves a Clown/Time Stands Still	1965	3.75	7.50	15.00
55846	She's Just My Style/I Won't Make That Mistake Again	1965	2.50	5.00	10.00
55846 [PS]	She's Just My Style/I Won't Make That Mistake Again	1965	3.75	7.50	15.00
55865	Sure Gonna Miss Her/I Don't Wanna Say Goodnight	1966	2.50	5.00	10.00
55865 [PS]	Sure Gonna Miss Her/I Don't Wanna Say Goodnight	1966	3.75	7.50	15.00
55880	Green Grass/I Can Read Between the Lines	1966	2.50	5.00	10.00
55880 [PS]	Green Grass/I Can Read Between the Lines	1966	3.75	7.50	15.00
55898	My Heart's Symphony/Tina	1966	2.50	5.00	10.00
55898 [PS]	My Heart's Symphony/Tina	1966	3.75	7.50	15.00
55914	(You Don't Have to) Paint Me a Picture/Looking for the Stars	1966	2.50	5.00	10.00
55914 [PS]	(You Don't Have to) Paint Me a Picture/Looking for the Stars	1966	3.75	7.50	15.00
55932	Down on the Sloop John B/Ice Melts in the Sun	1966	—	—	—
—Unreleased					
55933	Where Will the Words Come From/May the Best Man Win	1966	2.50	5.00	10.00
55949	The Loser (With a Broken Heart)/Ice Melts in the Sun	1967	2.50	5.00	10.00
55949 [PS]	The Loser (With a Broken Heart)/Ice Melts in the Sun	1967	3.75	7.50	15.00
55971	Girls in Love/Let's Be More Than Friends	1967	2.00	4.00	8.00
55985	Jill/New in Town	1967	2.00	4.00	8.00
56011	Has She Got the Nicest Eyes/Happiness	1967	2.00	4.00	8.00
56037	Sealed with a Kiss/Sara Jane	1968	2.00	4.00	8.00
56075	C.C. Rider/Main Street	1968	—	3.00	6.00
56093	Rhythm of the Rain/Mister Memory	1969	—	3.00	6.00
56093	Every Day I Have to Cry Some/Mister Memory	1969	—	3.00	6.00
56121	Hayride/Gary's Groove	1969	—	3.00	6.00
56144	I Saw Elvis Presley Last Night/Something Is Wrong	1969	3.00	6.00	12.00
56158	Great Balls of Fire/I'm On the Road Right Now	1970	—	3.00	6.00
SCEPTER					
12359	Peace of Mind/Then Again Maybe	1972	2.00	4.00	8.00
—Gary Lewis solo					
UNITED ARTISTS					
0064	This Diamond Ring/My Heart's Symphony	1973	—	2.00	4.00
0065	Count Me In/Save Your Heart for Me	1973	—	2.00	4.00
0066	Everybody Loves a Clown/Sure Gonna Miss Her	1973	—	2.00	4.00
0067	She's Just My Style/Green Grass	1973	—	2.00	4.00
—0064 through 0067 are "Silver Spotlight Series" reissues					

Albums

Number	Title (A Side/B Side)	Yr	VG	VG+	NM
LIBERTY					
LM-1003	This Diamond Ring	1981	2.00	4.00	8.00
—Reissue of United Artists 1008					
LRP-3408 [M]	This Diamond Ring	1965	5.00	10.00	20.00
LRP-3419 [M]	A Session with Gary Lewis and the Playboys	1965	5.00	10.00	20.00
LRP-3428 [M]	Everybody Loves a Clown	1965	5.00	10.00	20.00
LRP-3435 [M]	She's Just My Style	1966	3.75	7.50	15.00
LRP-3452 [M]	Hits Again!	1966	3.75	7.50	15.00
LRP-3468 [M]	Golden Greats	1966	3.75	7.50	15.00
LRP-3487 [M]	(You Don't Have to) Paint Me a Picture	1967	3.75	7.50	15.00
—Side 1 plays as listed					
LRP-3487 [M]	(You Don't Have to) Paint Me a Picture	1967	5.00	10.00	20.00
—Side 1, Song 4 claims to be "Tina" but plays "Ice Melts in the Sun"					
LRP-3519 [M]	New Directions	1967	3.75	7.50	15.00
LRP-3524 [M]	Listen	1967	3.75	7.50	15.00
LST-7408 [S]	This Diamond Ring	1965	6.25	12.50	25.00
LST-7419 [S]	A Session with Gary Lewis and the Playboys	1965	6.25	12.50	25.00
LST-7428 [S]	Everybody Loves a Clown	1965	6.25	12.50	25.00
LST-7435 [S]	She's Just My Style	1966	5.00	10.00	20.00
LST-7452 [S]	Hits Again!	1966	5.00	10.00	20.00
LST-7468 [S]	Golden Greats	1966	5.00	10.00	20.00
—Side 2 plays as listed					
LST-7468 [S]	Golden Greats	1966	7.50	15.00	30.00
—Side 2, Song 2 claims to be "I Won't Make That Mistake Again" but it plays "You've Got to Hide Your Love Away"					
LST-7487 [S]	(You Don't Have to) Paint Me a Picture	1967	5.00	10.00	20.00
—Side 1 plays as listed					
LST-7487 [S]	(You Don't Have to) Paint Me a Picture	1967	6.25	12.50	25.00
—Side 1, Song 4 claims to be "Tina" but plays "Ice Melts in the Sun"					
LST-7519 [S]	New Directions	1967	3.75	7.50	15.00
LST-7524 [S]	Listen	1967	3.75	7.50	15.00
LST-7568	Gary Lewis Now!	1968	3.75	7.50	15.00
LST-7589	More Golden Greats	1968	3.75	7.50	15.00
LST-7606	Close Cover Before Playing	1969	3.75	7.50	15.00
LST-7623	Rhythm of the Rain	1969	3.75	7.50	15.00
LST-7633	I'm On the Right Road Now	1970	3.75	7.50	15.00
LN-10241	Golden Greats	198?	2.00	4.00	8.00
—Budget-line reissue					
RHINO					
RNLP-163	Greatest Hits (1965-1968)	1985	2.50	5.00	10.00
SUNSET					
SUM-1168 [M]	Gary Lewis and the Playboys	1967	3.00	6.00	12.00
SUS-5168 [S]	Gary Lewis and the Playboys	1967	3.00	6.00	12.00
SUS-5262	Rhythm!	1969	3.00	6.00	12.00
UNITED ARTISTS					
UA-LA430-E	The Very Best of Gary Lewis and the Playboys	1975	2.50	5.00	10.00
LM-1003	This Diamond Ring	1980	2.50	5.00	10.00
—Edited reissue of Liberty 7408					

LEWIS, JERRY

Also see DEAN MARTIN.

45s

Number	Title (A Side/B Side)	Yr	VG	VG+	NM
CAPITOL					
F1045	I'm a Little Busybody/Sunday Driving	1950	5.00	10.00	20.00
F1385	The Navy Gets the Gravy/Pa-Pa-Pa Polka	1951	3.75	7.50	15.00
F1482	A-Hunting We Will Go/Never Been Kissed	1951	3.75	7.50	15.00
F1740	I Like It, I Like It/I'll Tell a Policeman on You	1951	3.75	7.50	15.00
F1868	I Love Girls/Lay Something on the Bar	1951	3.75	7.50	15.00
F1969	The Book Was So Much Better Than the Picture/North Dakota, South Dakota	1952	3.75	7.50	15.00
F2141	Crazy Words/I Can't Carry a Tune	1952	3.75	7.50	15.00
F2202	They Go Wild, Simply Wild Over Me/I Keep Her Picture Hanging	1952	3.75	7.50	15.00
F2317	I've Had a Very Merry Christmas/Strictly for the Birds	1952	5.00	10.00	20.00
F2481	If You Love Me Truly/Little Man You've Had a Busy Day	1953	3.75	7.50	15.00
—With Patti Lewis					
F2576	Give Me a Little Kiss, Will Ya Huh/Yyyup	1953	3.75	7.50	15.00
DECCA					
30124	Rock-a-Bye Your Baby with a Dixie Melody/Come Rain or Come Shine	1956	3.00	6.00	12.00
30263	Let Me Sing and I'm Happy/It All Depends on You	1957	2.50	5.00	10.00
30345	My Mammy/With These Arms	1957	2.50	5.00	10.00
30370	By Myself/No One	1957	2.50	5.00	10.00
30503	Sad Sack/The Lord Loves a Laughing Man	1957	2.50	5.00	10.00
30607	Long Black Nylons/Back to Kenya	1958	2.50	5.00	10.00
30664	Dormi-Dormi-Dormi/Love Is a Lonely Thing	1958	2.50	5.00	10.00
30808	Song from "The Geisha Boy"/The More I See	1959	2.50	5.00	10.00
31019	Makin' Whoopee/Have a Girl, Have a Boy	1959	2.50	5.00	10.00
31115	Smile/Everything's Coming Up Roses	1960	2.00	4.00	8.00
31400	My Mammy/Let Me Sing and I'm Happy	1962	2.00	4.00	8.00
DOT					
16164	Somebody/Turn It On	1960	2.00	4.00	8.00
16772	Green, Green/I'll See Your Light	1965	—	3.00	6.00
—As "The Jerry Lewis Singers"					
LIBERTY					
55633	Kids/Witchcraft	1963	2.00	4.00	8.00

7-Inch Extended Plays

Number	Title (A Side/B Side)	Yr	VG	VG+	NM
DECCA					
ED 2455	(contents unknown)	1957	3.75	7.50	15.00
ED 2455 [PS]	Jerry Lewis Just Sings, Vol. 1	1957	3.75	7.50	15.00
ED 2456	(contents unknown)	1957	3.75	7.50	15.00
ED 2456 [PS]	Jerry Lewis Just Sings, Vol. 2	1957	3.75	7.50	15.00
ED 2457	Birth of the Blues/Bye Bye Baby//Back in Your Own Backyard/Sometimes I'm Happy	1957	3.75	7.50	15.00
ED 2457 [PS]	Jerry Lewis Just Sings, Vol. 3	1957	3.75	7.50	15.00

Albums

Number	Title (A Side/B Side)	Yr	VG	VG+	NM
DECCA					
DL 8410 [M]	Jerry Lewis Just Sings	1956	15.00	30.00	60.00
DL 8595 [M]	More Jerry Lewis	1957	15.00	30.00	60.00
DL 8936 [M]	Big Songs for Little People	1959	12.50	25.00	50.00
DL 78936 [S]	Big Songs for Little People	1959	15.00	30.00	60.00
DOT					
DLP 3664 [M]	The Jerry Lewis Singers	1964	3.75	7.50	15.00
DLP 25664 [S]	The Jerry Lewis Singers	1964	5.00	10.00	20.00

LEWIS, JERRY LEE

45s

Number	Title (A Side/B Side)	Yr	VG	VG+	NM
CURB					
10521	Never Too Old to Rock and Roll/Rock and Roll Kiss	1988	—	2.50	5.00
—A-side with Ronnie McDowell; B-side is Ronnie McDowell solo					
ELEKTRA					
46030	Rockin' My Life Away/I Wish I Was Eighteen Again	1979	—	2.00	4.00
46067	Who Will the Next Fool Be/Rita May	1979	—	2.00	4.00
46591	When Two Worlds Collide/Good News Travels Fast	1980	—	2.00	4.00
46642	Honky Tonk Stuff/Rockin' Jerry Lee	1980	—	2.00	4.00
47026	Over the Rainbow/Folsom Prison Blues	1980	—	2.00	4.00
47095	Thirty-Nine and Holding/Change Places with Me	1980	—	2.00	4.00
69962	I'd Do It All Again/Who Will Buy the Wine	1982	—	2.00	4.00
MCA					
52151	My Fingers Do the Talkin'/Forever Forgiving	1983	—	—	3.00

Number	Title (A Side/B Side)	Yr	VG	VG+	NM
52188	Come As You Were/Circumstantial Evidence	1983	—	—	3.00
52233	She Sings Amazing Grace/Why You Been Gone So Long	1983	—	—	3.00
52369	I Am What I Am/That Was the Way It Was Then	1984	—	—	3.00

MERCURY

Number	Title (A Side/B Side)	Yr	VG	VG+	NM
55011	Middle Age Crazy/Georgia on My Mind	1977	—	2.00	4.00
55021	Come On In/Who's Sorry Now	1977	—	2.00	4.00
55028	I'll Find It Where I Can/Don't Let the Stars Get In Your Eyes	1977	—	2.00	4.00
73099	There Must Be More to Love Than This/Home Away from Home	1970	—	3.00	6.00
73155	I Can't Have a Merry Christmas, Mary (Without You)/In Loving Memories	1970	—	3.00	6.00
73192	Touching Home/Woman, Woman	1971	—	3.00	6.00
73227	When He Walks on You (Like You Have Walked on Me)/Foolish Kind of Man	1971	—	3.00	6.00
73248	Would You Take Another Chance on Me/Me and Bobby McGee	1971	—	3.00	6.00
73273	Chantilly Lace/Think About It Darlin'	1972	—	2.50	5.00
73296	Lonely Weekends/Turn On Your Love Light	1972	—	2.50	5.00
73303	Writing on the Wall/Me and Jesus	1972	—	2.50	5.00

—With Linda Gail Lewis

Number	Title (A Side/B Side)	Yr	VG	VG+	NM
73328	Who's Gonna PlayThis Old Piano/No Honky Tonks in Heaven	1972	—	2.50	5.00
73361	No More Hanging On/Mercy of a Letter	1973	—	2.50	5.00
73374	Drinking Wine Spo-Dee O'Dee/Rock and Roll Medley	1973	—	2.50	5.00
73402	No Headstone on My Grave/Jack Daniels	1973	—	2.50	5.00
73423	Sometimes a Memory Ain't Enough/I Think I Need to Pray	1973	—	2.50	5.00
73452	I'm Left, You're Right, She's Gone/I've Fallen to the Bottom	1974	—	2.50	5.00
73491	Tell Tale Signs/Cold, Cold Morning Light	1974	—	2.50	5.00
73618	He Can't Fill My Shoes/Tomorrow's Taking Baby Away	1974	—	2.50	5.00
73661	I Can Still Hear the Music in the Restroom/Remember Me	1975	—	2.00	4.00
73685	Boogie Woogie Country Man/I'm Still Jealous of You	1975	—	2.00	4.00
73729	A Damn Good Country Song/When I Take My Vacation in Heaven	1975	—	2.00	4.00
73763	Don't Boogie Woogie/That Kind of Fool	1976	—	2.00	4.00
73822	Let's Put It Back Together Again/Jerry Lee's Rock and Roll Revival Show	1976	—	2.00	4.00
73872	The Closest Thing to You/You Belong to Me	1976	—	2.00	4.00
76148	I'm So Lonesome I Could Cry/Pick Me Up on Your Way Down	1982	—	2.00	4.00

PHILLIPS INT'L.

Number	Title (A Side/B Side)	Yr	VG	VG+	NM
3559	In the Mood/I Get the Blues When It Rains	1960	12.50	25.00	50.00

—As "The Hawk"

POLYDOR

Number	Title (A Side/B Side)	Yr	VG	VG+	NM
889312-7	Breathless/Great Balls of Fire	1989	—	2.00	4.00
889312-7 [PS]	Breathless/Great Balls of Fire	1989	—	2.00	4.00
889798-7	Crazy Arms/Great Balls of Fire	1989	—	2.00	4.00

SCR

Number	Title (A Side/B Side)	Yr	VG	VG+	NM
386	Get Out Your Big Roll, Daddy/Honky Tonkin' Rock 'N' Roll Piano Man	1985	—	2.50	5.00

SIRE

Number	Title (A Side/B Side)	Yr	VG	VG+	NM
19809	It Was the Whiskey Talkin' (Not Me)/same (Rock and Roll Version)	1990	—	—	3.00
64423	Goose Bumps/Crown Victoria 51	1995	—	2.50	5.00

SMASH

Number	Title (A Side/B Side)	Yr	VG	VG+	NM
1857	Pen and Paper/Hit the Road Jack	1963	3.75	7.50	15.00
1886	I'm on Fire/Bread and Butter Man	1964	10.00	20.00	40.00
1906	She Was My Baby (He Was My Friend)/The Hole He Said He'd Dig for Me	1964	3.75	7.50	15.00
1930	High Heel Sneakers/You Went Back on Your Word	1964	3.75	7.50	15.00
1969	Baby Hold Me Close/I Believe in You	1965	3.75	7.50	15.00
1992	This Must Be the Place/Rocking Pneumonia and the Boogie Woogie Flu	1965	3.75	7.50	15.00
2006	Green, Green Grass of Home/You've Got What It Takes	1965	3.75	7.50	15.00
2027	Sticks and Stones/What a Heck of a Mess	1966	3.00	6.00	12.00
2053	If I Had It All to Do Over/Memphis Beat	1966	3.00	6.00	12.00
2103	Holding On/It's a Hang-Up, Baby	1967	3.00	6.00	12.00
2122	Turn On Your Love Light/Shotgun Man	1967	3.00	6.00	12.00
2146	Another Place, Another Time/Walking the Floor Over You	1968	2.50	5.00	10.00
2164	What's Made Milwaukee Famous (Has Made a Loser Out of Me)/All the Good Is Gone	1968	2.50	5.00	10.00
2186	She Still Comes Around (To Love What's Left of Me)/Slipping Around	1968	2.50	5.00	10.00
2202	To Make Love Sweeter for You/Let's Talk About Us	1968	2.50	5.00	10.00
2220	Don't Let Me Cross Over/We Live in Two Different Worlds	1969	2.00	4.00	8.00

—With Linda Gail Lewis

Number	Title (A Side/B Side)	Yr	VG	VG+	NM
2224	One Has My Name (The Other Has My Heart)/I Can't Stop Loving You	1969	2.00	4.00	8.00
2244	She Even Woke Me Up to Say Goodbye/Echoes	1969	2.00	4.00	8.00
2254	Roll Over Beethoven/Secret Places	1969	2.00	4.00	8.00

—With Linda Gail Lewis

Number	Title (A Side/B Side)	Yr	VG	VG+	NM
2257	Once More with Feeling/You Went Out of Your Way (To Walk on Me)	1970	2.00	4.00	8.00
884934-7	Sixteen Candles/Rock and Roll (Fais-Do-Do)	1986	—	2.00	4.00

—B-side with Roy Orbison, Carl Perkins and Johnny Cash

Number	Title (A Side/B Side)	Yr	VG	VG+	NM
888142-7	We Remember the King/Class of '55	1987	—	2.00	4.00

—With Johnny Cash, Roy Orbison and Carl Perkins; B-side by Carl Perkins solo

SUN

Number	Title (A Side/B Side)	Yr	VG	VG+	NM
259	Crazy Arms/End of the Road	1957	25.00	50.00	100.00

—As "Jerry Lee Lewis"

Number	Title (A Side/B Side)	Yr	VG	VG+	NM
259	Crazy Arms/End of the Road	1957	12.50	25.00	50.00

—As "Jerry Lee Lewis and His Pumping Piano"

Number	Title (A Side/B Side)	Yr	VG	VG+	NM
267	Whole Lot of Shakin' Going On/It'll Be Me	1957	10.00	20.00	40.00
281	Great Balls of Fire/You Win Again	1957	10.00	20.00	40.00
281 [PS]	Great Balls of Fire/You Win Again	1957	20.00	40.00	80.00
288	Breathless/Down the Line	1958	10.00	20.00	40.00
296	High School Confidential/Fools Like Me	1958	7.50	15.00	30.00
296 [PS]	High School Confidential/Fools Like Me	1958	20.00	40.00	80.00
301	Lewis Boogie/The Return of Jerry Lee	1958	7.50	15.00	30.00

—B-side by George and Louis

Number	Title (A Side/B Side)	Yr	VG	VG+	NM
303	I'll Make It All Up to You/Break-Up	1958	6.25	12.50	30.00
312	I'll Sail My Ship Alone/It Hurt Me So	1958	6.25	12.50	25.00
317	Lovin' Up a Storm/Big Blon' Baby	1959	6.25	12.50	25.00
324	Let's Talk About Us/Ballad of Billy Joe	1959	6.25	12.50	25.00
330	Little Queenie/I Could Never Be Ashamed of You	1959	6.25	12.50	25.00
337	Old Black Joe/Baby Baby, Bye Bye	1960	5.00	10.00	20.00
344	Hang Up My Rock and Roll Shoes/John Henry	1960	5.00	10.00	20.00
352	Love Made a Fool of Me/When I Get Paid	1960	5.00	10.00	20.00
356	What'd I Say/Livin' Lovin' Wreck	1961	5.00	10.00	20.00
364	Cold, Cold Heart/It Won't Happen with Me	1961	5.00	10.00	20.00
367	Save the Last Dance for Me/As Long As I Live	1961	5.00	10.00	20.00
371	Money/Bonnie B	1961	5.00	10.00	20.00
374	I've Been Twistin'/Ramblin' Rose	1962	5.00	10.00	20.00
379	Sweet Little Sixteen/How's My Ex Treating You	1962	5.00	10.00	20.00
382	Good Golly Miss Molly/I Can't Trust Me	1962	5.00	10.00	20.00
384	Teenage Letter/Seasons of My Heart	1963	5.00	10.00	20.00
396	Carry Me Back to Old Virginny/I Know What It Means	1965	5.00	10.00	20.00
1101	Invitation to Your Party/I Could Never Be Ashamed of You	1969	—	3.00	6.00
1107	One Minute Past Eternity/Frankie and Johnny	1969	—	3.00	6.00
1115	I Can't Seem to Say Goodbye/Goodnight Irene	1970	—	2.50	5.00
1119	Waiting for the Train (All Around the Watertank)/Big Legged Woman	1970	—	2.50	5.00
1125	Love on Broadway/Matchbox	1971	—	2.50	5.00
1128	Your Loving Ways/I Can't Trust Me in Your Arms Anymore	1972	—	2.50	5.00
1130	Good Rockin' Tonight/I Can't Trust Me in Your Arms Anymore	1973	—	2.50	5.00
1138	Matchbox/Am I to Be the One	1978	—	2.00	4.00
1139	Save the Last Dance for Me/Am I to Be the One	1978	—	2.00	4.00

—With uncredited "duet" partner, actually Orion (Jimmy Ellis); a shameless attempt to concoct a "lost Elvis Presley duet"

Number	Title (A Side/B Side)	Yr	VG	VG+	NM
1141	Cold, Cold Heart/Hello Josephine	1979	—	2.00	4.00
1151	Be-Bop-a-Lula/The Breakup	1980	—	2.00	4.00

—B-side by Charlie Rich; both sides are duets with Orion

7-Inch Extended Plays

SUN

Number	Title (A Side/B Side)	Yr	VG	VG+	NM
EPA-107	Mean Woman Blues/I'm Feelin' Sorry//Whole Lot of Shakin' Goin' On/Turn Around	1958	20.00	30.00	80.00
EPA-107 [PS]	The Great Ball of Fire	1958	20.00	30.00	80.00
EPA-108	Don't Be Cruel/Goodnight Irene//Put Me Down/It All Depends	1958	12.50	25.00	50.00
EPA-108 [PS]	Jerry Lee Lewis	1958	12.50	25.00	50.00
EPA-109	(contents unknown)	1958	12.50	25.00	50.00
EPA-109 [PS]	Jerry Lee Lewis	1958	12.50	25.00	50.00
EPA-110	(contents unknown)	1958	12.50	25.00	50.00
EPA-110 [PS]	Jerry Lee Lewis	1958	12.50	25.00	50.00

Albums

ACCORD

Number	Title (A Side/B Side)	Yr	VG	VG+	NM
SN-7133	I Walk the Line	1981	2.50	5.00	10.00

DESIGN

Number	Title (A Side/B Side)	Yr	VG	VG+	NM
DLP-165 [M]	Rockin' with Jerry Lee Lewis	1963	6.25	12.50	25.00
DST-165 [R]	Rockin' with Jerry Lee Lewis	1963	5.00	10.00	20.00

ELEKTRA

Number	Title (A Side/B Side)	Yr	VG	VG+	NM
6E-184	Jerry Lee Lewis	1979	3.00	6.00	12.00
6E-254	When Two Worlds Collide	1980	3.00	6.00	12.00
6E-291	Killer Country	1980	3.00	6.00	12.00
60191	The Best of Jerry Lee Lewis Featuring 39 and Holding	1982	2.50	5.00	10.00

HILLTOP

Number	Title (A Side/B Side)	Yr	VG	VG+	NM
6102	Sunday After Church	1971	2.50	5.00	10.00
6110	Roll Over Beethoven	1972	2.50	5.00	10.00
6120	Rural Route #1	1972	2.50	5.00	10.00

MCA

Number	Title (A Side/B Side)	Yr	VG	VG+	NM
5387	My Fingers Do the Talkin'	1983	2.50	5.00	10.00
5478	I Am What I Am	1984	2.50	5.00	10.00

MERCURY

Number	Title (A Side/B Side)	Yr	VG	VG+	NM
SRM-1-637	The "Killer" Rocks On	1972	3.75	7.50	15.00
SRM-1-677	Sometimes a Memory Ain't Enough	1973	3.75	7.50	15.00
690 [DJ]	A Jerry Lee Lewis Radio Special	1973	12.50	25.00	50.00
SRM-1-690	Southern Roots — Back Home to Memphis	1973	3.75	7.50	15.00
SRM-1-710	I-40 Country	1974	3.75	7.50	15.00
SRM-2-803 [(2)]	The Session	1973	5.00	10.00	20.00
SRM-1-1030	Boogie Woogie Country Man	1975	3.75	7.50	15.00
SRM-1-1064	Odd Man In	1975	3.75	7.50	15.00
SRM-1-1109	Country Class	1976	3.75	7.50	15.00
SRM-1-5004	Country Memories	1977	3.75	7.50	15.00
SRM-1-5006	The Best of Jerry Lee Lewis Volume II	1978	3.75	7.50	15.00
SRM-1-5010	Jerry Lee Lewis Keeps Rockin'	1978	3.75	7.50	15.00
SR-61278	Live at the International, Las Vegas	1970	3.75	7.50	15.00
SR-61318	In Loving Memories	1970	7.50	15.00	30.00
SR-61323	There Must Be More to Love Than This	1971	3.75	7.50	15.00
SR-61343	Touching Home	1971	3.75	7.50	15.00

—With photo of Jerry Lee in front of a brick wall

Number	Title (A Side/B Side)	Yr	VG	VG+	NM
SR-61343	Touching Home	1971	5.00	10.00	20.00

—With drawing on cover and small photo of Jerry Lee

Number	Title (A Side/B Side)	Yr	VG	VG+	NM
SR-61346	Would You Take Another Chance on Me?	1971	3.75	7.50	15.00
SR-61366	Who's Gonna PlayThis Old Piano... (Think About It Darlin')	1972	3.75	7.50	15.00
822789-1	The Best of Jerry Lee Lewis Volume II	198?	2.50	5.00	10.00
826251-1	Greatest Hits	198?	2.50	5.00	10.00
830399-1	Would You Take Another Chance on Me	1987	2.50	5.00	10.00

—Reissue of 61346

Number	Title (A Side/B Side)	Yr	VG	VG+	NM
836935-1	Killer: The Mercury Years Volume One, 1963-1968	1989	3.00	6.00	12.00
836938-1	Killer: The Mercury Years Volume Two, 1969-1972	1989	3.00	6.00	12.00

Number	Title (A Side/B Side)	Yr	VG	VG+	NM
836941-1	Killer: The Mercury Years Volume Three, 1973-1977	1989	3.00	6.00	12.00
PAIR					
PDL2-1132 [(2)]	Solid Gold	1986	3.00	6.00	12.00
PICKWICK					
PTP-2055 [(2)]	Jerry Lee Lewis	1973	3.00	6.00	12.00
SPC-3224	High Heel Sneakers	1970	2.50	5.00	10.00
SPC-3344	Drinking Wine Spo-Dee-O-Dee	1973	2.50	5.00	10.00
POLYDOR					
826139-1	I'm on Fire	1985	2.50	5.00	10.00
839516-1	Great Balls of Fire!	1989	3.00	6.00	12.00
POWER PAK					
247	From the Vaults of Sun	1974	2.50	5.00	10.00
RHINO					
RNDF-255 [PD]	Original Sun Greatest Hits	1983	3.75	7.50	15.00
RNDA-1499 [(2)]	Milestones	1985	3.75	7.50	15.00
R1-70255	Original Sun Greatest Hits	1989	2.50	5.00	10.00
—Reissue of 255 on black vinyl					
R1-70656	Jerry Lee Lewis	1989	3.00	6.00	12.00
—Reissue of Sun 1230					
R1-70657	Jerry Lee's Greatest	1989	3.00	6.00	12.00
—Reissue of Sun 1265					
R1-70899	Wild One: Rare Tracks from Jerry Lee Lewis	1989	3.00	6.00	12.00
R1-71499 [(2)]	Milestones	1989	3.00	6.00	12.00
—Reissue of 1499					
SEARS					
SPS-610	Hound Dog	1970	6.25	12.50	25.00
SMASH					
SL-7001	Golden Hits	1980	3.00	6.00	12.00
MGS-27040 [M]	The Golden Hits of Jerry Lee Lewis	1964	6.25	12.50	25.00
MGS-27056 [M]	The Greatest Live Show on Earth	1964	25.00	50.00	100.00
MGS-27063 [M]	The Return of Rock	1965	7.50	15.00	30.00
MGS-27071 [M]	Country Songs for City Folks	1965	6.25	12.50	25.00
MGS-27079 [M]	Memphis Beat	1966	6.25	12.50	25.00
MGS-27086 [M]	By Request — More of the Greatest Live Show on Earth	1966	7.50	15.00	30.00
MGS-27097 [M]	Soul My Way	1967	7.50	15.00	30.00
SRS-67040 [S]	The Golden Hits of Jerry Lee Lewis	1964	7.50	15.00	30.00
SRS-67040 [S]	The Golden Rock Hits of Jerry Lee Lewis	1969	3.75	7.50	15.00
—Retitled reissue					
SRS-67056 [S]	The Greatest Live Show on Earth	1964	37.50	75.00	150.00
SRS-67063 [S]	The Return of Rock	1965	10.00	20.00	40.00
SRS-67071	All Country	1969	3.75	7.50	15.00
—Retitled reissue					
SRS-67071 [S]	Country Songs for City Folks	1965	7.50	15.00	30.00
SRS-67079 [S]	Memphis Beat	1966	7.50	15.00	30.00
SRS-67086 [S]	By Request — More of the Greatest Live Show on Earth	1966	10.00	20.00	40.00
SRS-67097 [S]	Soul My Way	1967	10.00	20.00	40.00
SRS-67104	Another Place Another Time	1968	5.00	10.00	20.00
SRS-67112	She Still Comes Around (To Love What's Left of Me)	1969	5.00	10.00	20.00
SRS-67117	Jerry Lee Lewis Sings the Country Music Hall of Fame Hits, Vol. 1	1969	5.00	10.00	20.00
SRS-67118	Jerry Lee Lewis Sings the Country Music Hall of Fame Hits, Vol. 2	1969	5.00	10.00	20.00
SRS-67126	Together	1969	5.00	10.00	20.00
—With Linda Gail Lewis					
SRS-67128	She Even Woke Me Up to Say Goodbye	1970	5.00	10.00	20.00
SRS-67131	The Best of Jerry Lee Lewis	1970	5.00	10.00	20.00
SUN					
LP-102	Original Golden Hits — Volume 1	1969	3.75	7.50	15.00
LP-103	Original Golden Hits — Volume 2	1969	3.75	7.50	15.00
LP-107	Rockin' Rhythm and Blues	1969	3.75	7.50	15.00
LP-108	The Golden Cream of the Country	1969	3.75	7.50	15.00
LP-114	A Taste of Country	1970	3.75	7.50	15.00
LP-124	Monsters	1971	3.75	7.50	15.00
LP-128	Original Golden Hits — Volume 3	1972	3.75	7.50	15.00
1005	The Original	1978	3.00	6.00	12.00
1011	Duets	1978	3.00	6.00	12.00
—With Orion (uncredited)					
1018	Trio +	1979	3.00	6.00	12.00
—With Carl Perkins, Charlie Rich and (uncredited) Orion					
SLP-1230 [M]	Jerry Lee Lewis	1958	50.00	100.00	200.00
SLP-1265 [M]	Jerry Lee's Greatest	1961	62.50	125.00	250.00
SLP-1265 [M-DJ]	Jerry Lee's Greatest	1961	200.00	400.00	800.00
—White label promo					
SUNNYVALE					
905	The Sun Story, Vol. 5	1977	2.50	5.00	10.00
WING					
PKW2-125 [(2)]	The Legend of Jerry Lee Lewis	1969	6.25	12.50	25.00
MGW-12340 [M]	The Return of Rock	1967	3.00	6.00	12.00
SRW-16340	In Demand	1968	2.50	5.00	10.00
SRW-16340 [S]	The Return of Rock	1967	3.00	6.00	12.00
SRW-16406	Unlimited	1968	3.00	6.00	12.00

LEWIS, RAMSEY

12-Inch Singles

Number	Title (A Side/B Side)	Yr	VG	VG+	NM
COLUMBIA					
05311	This Ain't No Fantasy (Extended with Male)/(Extended with Female)	1985	—	3.00	6.00
06850	7-11 (Club Mix) (Booster Mix)	1987	—	3.00	6.00
10937	Aquarius-Let the Sunshine In/Just Can't Give You Up	1979	3.00	6.00	12.00

45s

Number	Title (A Side/B Side)	Yr	VG	VG+	NM
ARGO					
108-S [S]	Scarlet Ribbons/Here 'Tis	1960	5.00	10.00	20.00
110-S [S]	Solo Para Ti/These Foolish Things	1960	5.00	10.00	20.00
5303	Black Eyed Peas/Carmen	1958	3.00	6.00	12.00
5322	Tracy Blues/Delilah	1958	3.00	6.00	12.00
5344	C.C. Rider/Consider the Source	1959	3.00	6.00	12.00
5351	Ol' Devil Moon/Please Send Me Someone to Love	1959	3.00	6.00	12.00
5352	The Chant/Here 'Tis	1959	3.00	6.00	12.00
5362	Little Liza Jane/Put Your Little Foot Right Out	1960	3.00	6.00	12.00
5377	Santa Claus Is Coming to Town/Winter Wonderland	1960	3.00	6.00	12.00
5387	Blues for the Night Owl/Hello, Cello	1961	2.50	5.00	10.00
5398	Never on Sunday/The Ripper	1961	2.50	5.00	10.00
5407	Sound of Christmas/Merry Christmas Baby	1961	3.00	6.00	12.00
5411	I Got Plenty of Nothin'/Thanks for the Memory	1962	2.50	5.00	10.00
5413	Blue Spring/Spring Fever	1962	2.50	5.00	10.00
5423	Blueberry Hill/Memphis in June	1962	2.50	5.00	10.00
5431	Maha de Carnaval/Tangleweed 'Round My Heart	1963	2.00	4.00	8.00
5438	Look-a Here/Andaluza	1963	2.00	4.00	8.00
5454	Lonely Avenue/Come On Baby	1963	2.00	4.00	8.00
5467	Dance Mystique/For the Love of a Princess	1964	2.00	4.00	8.00
5474	Why Don't You Do It Right/Travel On	1964	2.00	4.00	8.00
5481	Something You Got/My Babe	1964	2.00	4.00	8.00
5488	Jingle Bells/Egg Nog	1964	2.50	5.00	10.00
5496	Let It Be Me/It Had Better Be Tonight	1965	2.00	4.00	8.00
5506	The "In" Crowd/Since I Fell for You	1965	2.50	5.00	10.00
CADET					
5377	Santa Claus Is Coming To Town/Winter Wonderland	1966	2.00	4.00	8.00
—Reissue of Argo 5377					
5423	Blueberry Hill/Memphis in June	1966	—	3.00	6.00
5431	Maha de Carnaval/Tangleweed 'Round My Heart	1966	—	3.00	6.00
5481	Something You Got/My Babe	1966	—	3.00	6.00
5496	Let It Be Me/It Had Better Be Tonight	1966	—	3.00	6.00
5506	The "In" Crowd/Since I Fell for You	1966	—	3.00	6.00
5522	Hang On Sloopy/Movin' Easy	1965	2.00	4.00	8.00
5525	A Hard Day's Night/All My Love Belongs to You	1966	2.00	4.00	8.00
5531	Hi Heel Sneakers — Pt. 1/Hi Heel Sneakers — Pt. 2	1966	2.00	4.00	8.00
5541	Wade in the Water/Ain't That Peculiar	1966	2.00	4.00	8.00
5547	Up Tight/Money in the Pocket	1966	2.00	4.00	8.00
5553	Rudolph the Red-Nosed Reindeer/Day Tripper	1966	2.00	4.00	8.00
5556	One, Two, Three/Down by the Riverside	1967	2.00	4.00	8.00
5562	Function at the Junction/Hey, Mrs. Jones	1967	2.00	4.00	8.00
5565	Saturday Night After the Movies/China Gate	1967	2.00	4.00	8.00
5573	Dancing in the Street/Girls Talk	1967	2.00	4.00	8.00
5583	Soul Man/Struttin' Lightly	1967	2.00	4.00	8.00
5593	The Look of Love/Bear Mash	1968	—	3.00	6.00
5596	Jade Easy/Party Time	1968	—	3.00	6.00
5609	Since You've Been Gone/Les Fleurs	1968	—	3.00	6.00
5629	Mary's Boy Child/Have Yourself a Merry Little Christmas	1968	—	3.00	6.00
5640	Julia/Do What You Wanna	1969	—	3.00	6.00
5645	If You've Got It, Flaunt It/Wanderin' Rose	1969	—	3.00	6.00
5662	Mary's Boy Child/My Cherie Amour	1969	—	3.00	6.00
5668	Everybody's Talkin'/Love I Feel for You	1970	—	3.00	6.00
5674	Them Changes/Unsilent Minority	1970	—	3.00	6.00
5678	Do Whatever Sets You Free/Close Your Eyes and Remember	1970	—	3.00	6.00
5681	Candida/Love Me Now	1971	—	3.00	6.00
5684	He Ain't Heavy, He's My Brother/Up in Yonder	1971	—	3.00	6.00
5695	Summertime/Look-a There	1973	—	3.00	6.00
COLUMBIA					
02043	So Much More/Romance Me	1981	—	2.00	4.00
02572	Lakeshore Cowboy/Michelle	1981	—	2.00	4.00
02704	You Never Know/Lynn	1982	—	2.00	4.00
03274	Up Where We Belong/Chance Encounter	1982	—	2.00	4.00
04524	The Two of Us/Song Without Words (Remembering)	1984	—	2.00	4.00
04655	Quiet Storm/Ram	1984	—	2.00	4.00
05640	This Ain't No Fantasy/The Quest	1985	—	—	3.00
05819	Ram Jam/Slow Dancin'	1986	—	—	3.00
07220	7-11/My Love Will Lead You Home	1987	—	—	3.00
10056	Hot Dawgit/R.L. Tambura	1974	—	2.50	5.00
—A-side with Earth, Wind and Fire					
10103	Sun Goddess/Jungle Strut	1975	—	2.50	5.00
—A-side with Earth, Wind and Fire					
10235	What's the Name of This Funk (Spider Man)/Juacklyn	1975	—	2.50	5.00
10293	Don't It Feel Good/Fish Bite	1976	—	2.50	5.00
10382	Brazilica/Salongo	1976	—	2.50	5.00
10571	Spring High/The Messenger	1977	—	2.50	5.00
10643	Skippin'/Camino El Bueno	1977	—	2.50	5.00
10698	Tequila Mockingbird/My Angel's Smile	1978	—	2.50	5.00
10827	All the Way Live/Toccata	1978	—	2.50	5.00
10932	Aquarius-Let the Sunshine In/Just Can't Give You Up	1979	—	2.50	5.00
11042	Wearin' It Out/Spanoletta	1979	—	2.50	5.00
45634	Slipping Into Darkness/Collage	1972	—	2.50	5.00
45707	Upendo Mi Pamoja/Eternal Peace	1972	—	2.50	5.00
45766	Kufanya Mapenzi (Making Love)/What It Is	1973	—	2.50	5.00
45847	Dreams/Hang On Sloopy	1973	—	2.50	5.00
45973	Hi-Heel Sneakers/Wade in the Water	1973	—	2.50	5.00
46037	Summer Breeze/Everywhere Calypso	1974	—	2.50	5.00

7-Inch Extended Plays

Number	Title (A Side/B Side)	Yr	VG	VG+	NM
ARGO					
EP-1084	Sleigh Ride/Christmas Blues//Sound of Christmas/The Christmas Song	1961	2.50	5.00	10.00
EP-1084 [PS]	Sound of Christmas	1961	3.00	6.00	12.00

Albums

Number	Title (A Side/B Side)	Yr	VG	VG+	NM
ARGO					
611S [S]	Gentleman of Swing	1959	15.00	30.00	60.00
611 [M]	Gentleman of Swing	1958	12.50	25.00	50.00
627S [S]	Gentleman of Jazz	1959	15.00	30.00	60.00
627 [M]	Gentleman of Jazz	1958	12.50	25.00	50.00
642S [S]	The Ramsey Lewis Trio with Lee Winchester	1959	12.50	25.00	50.00
642 [M]	The Ramsey Lewis Trio with Lee Winchester	1959	10.00	20.00	40.00
645S [S]	An Hour with the Ramsey Lewis Trio	1959	12.50	25.00	50.00
645 [M]	An Hour with the Ramsey Lewis Trio	1959	10.00	20.00	40.00
665S [S]	Stretching Out	1960	12.50	25.00	50.00
665 [M]	Stretching Out	1960	10.00	20.00	40.00
671S [S]	The Ramsey Lewis Trio in Chicago	1961	12.50	25.00	50.00
671 [M]	The Ramsey Lewis Trio in Chicago	1961	10.00	20.00	40.00

Number	Title (A Side/B Side)	Yr	VG	VG+	NM
680S [S]	More Music from the Soil	1961	12.50	25.00	50.00
680 [M]	More Music from the Soil	1961	10.00	20.00	40.00
687-S [S]	Sound of Christmas	1961	12.50	25.00	50.00
687 [M]	Sound of Christmas	1961	10.00	20.00	40.00
693S [S]	The Sound of Spring	1962	7.50	15.00	30.00
693 [M]	The Sound of Spring	1962	6.25	12.50	25.00
701S [S]	Country Meets the Blues	1962	7.50	15.00	30.00
701 [M]	Country Meets the Blues	1962	6.25	12.50	25.00
705S [S]	Bossa Nova	1962	7.50	15.00	30.00
705 [M]	Bossa Nova	1962	6.25	12.50	25.00
715S [S]	Pot Luck	1963	7.50	15.00	30.00
715 [M]	Pot Luck	1963	6.25	12.50	25.00
723S [S]	Barefoot Sunday Blues	1963	7.50	15.00	30.00
723 [M]	Barefoot Sunday Blues	1963	6.25	12.50	25.00
732S [S]	Bach to the Blues	1964	7.50	15.00	30.00
732 [M]	Bach to the Blues	1964	6.25	12.50	25.00
741S [S]	The Ramsey Lewis Trio at the Bohemian Caverns	1964	7.50	15.00	30.00
741 [M]	The Ramsey Lewis Trio at the Bohemian Caverns	1964	6.25	12.50	25.00
745-S [S]	More Sounds of Christmas	1964	7.50	15.00	30.00
745 [M]	More Sounds of Christmas	1964	6.25	12.50	25.00
LP-755 [M]	Choice! The Best of the Ramsey Lewis Trio	1965	7.50	15.00	30.00
LPS-755 [S]	Choice! The Best of the Ramsey Lewis Trio	1965	10.00	20.00	40.00
757S [S]	The In Crowd	1965	7.50	15.00	30.00
757 [M]	The In Crowd	1965	6.25	12.50	25.00

CADET

Number	Title (A Side/B Side)	Yr	VG	VG+	NM
611S [S]	Gentleman of Swing	1966	3.75	7.50	15.00
611 [M]	Gentleman of Swing	1966	3.00	6.00	12.00
627S [S]	Gentleman of Jazz	1966	3.75	7.50	15.00
627 [M]	Gentleman of Jazz	1966	3.00	6.00	12.00
645S [S]	An Hour with the Ramsey Lewis Trio	1966	3.75	7.50	15.00
645 [M]	An Hour with the Ramsey Lewis Trio	1966	3.00	6.00	12.00
665S [S]	Stretching Out	1966	3.75	7.50	15.00
665 [M]	Stretching Out	1966	3.00	6.00	12.00
671S [S]	The Ramsey Lewis Trio in Chicago	1966	3.75	7.50	15.00
671 [M]	The Ramsey Lewis Trio in Chicago	1966	3.00	6.00	12.00
680S [S]	More Music from the Soil	1966	3.75	7.50	15.00
680 [M]	More Music from the Soil	1966	3.00	6.00	12.00
687X [M]	Sound of Christmas	1966	5.00	10.00	20.00
—Reissue of Argo 687					
687X-S [S]	Sound of Christmas	1966	5.00	10.00	20.00
—Reissue of Argo 687-S					
693S [S]	The Sound of Spring	1966	3.75	7.50	15.00
693 [M]	The Sound of Spring	1966	3.00	6.00	12.00
701S [S]	Country Meets the Blues	1966	3.75	7.50	15.00
701 [M]	Country Meets the Blues	1966	3.00	6.00	12.00
705S [S]	Bossa Nova	1966	3.75	7.50	15.00
705 [M]	Bossa Nova	1966	3.00	6.00	12.00
LP-715 [M]	Pot Luck	1966	3.00	6.00	12.00
LPS-715 [S]	Pot Luck	1966	3.75	7.50	15.00
723S [S]	Barefoot Sunday Blues	1966	3.75	7.50	15.00
723 [M]	Barefoot Sunday Blues	1966	3.00	6.00	12.00
732S [S]	Bach to the Blues	1966	3.75	7.50	15.00
732 [M]	Bach to the Blues	1966	3.00	6.00	12.00
741S [S]	The Ramsey Lewis Trio at the Bohemian Caverns	1964	3.75	7.50	15.00
741 [M]	The Ramsey Lewis Trio at the Bohemian Caverns	1964	3.00	6.00	12.00
745-S [S]	More Sounds of Christmas	1964	5.00	10.00	20.00
745 [M]	More Sounds of Christmas	1964	3.75	7.50	15.00
750S [S]	You Better Believe It	1966	3.75	7.50	15.00
750 [M]	You Better Believe It	1966	3.00	6.00	12.00
LP-755 [M]	Choice! The Best of the Ramsey Lewis Trio	1965	3.75	7.50	15.00
LPS-755 [S]	Choice! The Best of the Ramsey Lewis Trio	1965	5.00	10.00	20.00
757S [S]	The In Crowd	1965	3.75	7.50	15.00
757 [M]	The In Crowd	1965	3.00	6.00	12.00
LP-761 [M]	Hang On Ramsey!	1966	3.75	7.50	15.00
LPS-761 [S]	Hang On Ramsey!	1966	5.00	10.00	20.00
LP-771 [M]	Swingin'	1966	3.75	7.50	15.00
LPS-771 [S]	Swingin'	1966	5.00	10.00	20.00
LP-774 [M]	Wade in the Water	1966	3.75	7.50	15.00
LPS-774 [S]	Wade in the Water	1966	5.00	10.00	20.00
LP-782 [M]	The Movie Album	1967	5.00	10.00	20.00
LPS-782 [S]	The Movie Album	1967	3.75	7.50	15.00
LP-790 [M]	Goin' Latin	1967	5.00	10.00	20.00
LPS-790 [S]	Goin' Latin	1967	3.75	7.50	15.00
LP-794 [M]	Dancing in the Street	1967	5.00	10.00	20.00
LPS-794 [S]	Dancing in the Street	1967	3.75	7.50	15.00
LPS-799	Up Pops Ramsey Lewis	1968	3.75	7.50	15.00
LPS-811	Maiden Voyage	1968	3.75	7.50	15.00
LPS-821	Mother Nature's Son	1969	3.75	7.50	15.00
LPS-827	Another Voyage	1969	3.75	7.50	15.00
LPS-836	Ramsey Lewis, The Piano Player	1970	3.75	7.50	15.00
LPS-839	The Best of Ramsey Lewis	1970	3.75	7.50	15.00
LPS-844	Them Changes	1970	3.75	7.50	15.00
50020	Groover	1973	3.00	6.00	12.00
50058 [(2)]	Solid Ivory	1974	3.75	7.50	15.00
60001	Back to the Roots	1971	3.00	6.00	12.00
60018 [(2)]	Inside Ramsey Lewis	1972	3.75	7.50	15.00

CBS

Number	Title (A Side/B Side)	Yr	VG	VG+	NM
FM 42661	A Classic Encounter	1988	2.50	5.00	10.00

CHESS

Number	Title (A Side/B Side)	Yr	VG	VG+	NM
9001 [(2)]	Solid Ivory	197?	3.00	6.00	12.00
—Reissue of Cadet 50058					
CH 9716	Sound of Christmas	1984	2.50	5.00	10.00
—Reissue of Argo 687-S					

COLUMBIA

Number	Title (A Side/B Side)	Yr	VG	VG+	NM
CQ 31096 [Q]	Upendo Ni Pamoja	1972	4.50	9.00	18.00
KC 31096	Upendo Ni Pamoja	1972	3.00	6.00	12.00
KC 32030	Funky Serenity	1973	3.00	6.00	12.00
KC 32490	Ramsey Lewis' Newly Recorded All-Time, Non-Stop Golden Hits	1973	3.00	6.00	12.00
PC 32490	Ramsey Lewis' Newly Recorded All-Time, Non-Stop Golden Hits	197?	2.00	4.00	8.00
—Reissue with new prefix					
KC 32897	Solar Wind	1974	3.00	6.00	12.00
KC 33194	Sun Goddess	1974	2.50	5.00	10.00
PC 33194	Sun Goddess	197?	2.00	4.00	8.00
—Reissue with new prefix					
CG 33663 [(2)]	Upendo Ni Pamoja/Funky Serenity	1975	3.00	6.00	12.00
PC 33800	Don't It Feel Good	1975	2.50	5.00	10.00
—Originals have no bar code					
PC 33800	Don't It Feel Good	198?	2.00	4.00	8.00
—Budget-line reissue with bar code					
PC 34173	Salongo	1976	2.50	5.00	10.00
—Originals have no bar code					
PC 34173	Salongo	198?	2.00	4.00	8.00
—Budget-line reissue with bar code					
PC 34696	Love Notes	1977	2.50	5.00	10.00
JC 35018	Tequila Mockingbird	1977	2.50	5.00	10.00
JC 35483	Legacy	1978	2.50	5.00	10.00
PC 35483	Legacy	198?	2.00	4.00	8.00
—Budget-line reissue					
JC 35815	Ramsey	1979	2.50	5.00	10.00
FC 36364	The Best of Ramsey Lewis	1980	2.50	5.00	10.00
JC 36423	Routes	1980	2.50	5.00	10.00
PC 36423	Routes	198?	2.00	4.00	8.00
—Budget-line reissue					
FC 37153	Three Piece Suite	1981	2.50	5.00	10.00
FC 37687	Live at the Savoy	1982	2.50	5.00	10.00
PC 37687	Live at the Savoy	198?	2.00	4.00	8.00
—Budget-line reissue					
FC 38294	Chance Encounter	1983	2.50	5.00	10.00
FC 38787	Les Fleurs	1983	2.50	5.00	10.00
FC 39158	Reunion	1983	2.50	5.00	10.00
FC 40108	Fantasy	1985	2.50	5.00	10.00
FC 40677	Keys to the City	1987	2.50	5.00	10.00
HC 43194	Sun Goddess	1982	12.50	25.00	50.00
—Half-speed mastered edition					
FC 44190	Urban Renewal	1989	3.75	7.50	15.00
HC 47687	Live at the Savoy	1982	20.00	40.00	80.00
—Half-speed mastered edition					

COLUMBIA JAZZ ODYSSEY

Number	Title (A Side/B Side)	Yr	VG	VG+	NM
PC 37019	Blues for the Night Owl	1981	2.50	5.00	10.00

EMARCY

Number	Title (A Side/B Side)	Yr	VG	VG+	NM
MG-36150 [M]	Down to Earth	1958	10.00	20.00	40.00
SR-80029 [S]	Down to Earth	1958	12.50	25.00	50.00

MERCURY

Number	Title (A Side/B Side)	Yr	VG	VG+	NM
MG-20536 [M]	Down to Earth	1965	5.00	10.00	20.00
SR-60536 [S]	Down to Earth	1965	6.25	12.50	25.00

LEWIS, RAMSEY, AND JEAN DUSHON

Albums

ARGO

Number	Title (A Side/B Side)	Yr	VG	VG+	NM
750S [S]	You Better Believe It	1965	7.50	15.00	30.00
750 [M]	You Better Believe It	1965	6.25	12.50	25.00

LEWIS, RAMSEY, AND NANCY WILSON

Also see each artist's individual listings.

Albums

COLUMBIA

Number	Title (A Side/B Side)	Yr	VG	VG+	NM
FC 39326	The Two of Us	1984	2.50	5.00	10.00

LEWIS, RUDY

Also see THE DRIFTERS.

45s

ATLANTIC

Number	Title (A Side/B Side)	Yr	VG	VG+	NM
2193	I've Loved You So Long/Baby I Dig Love	1963	3.00	6.00	12.00

RCA VICTOR

Number	Title (A Side/B Side)	Yr	VG	VG+	NM
47-7792	Moonbeam/Beer, Beer and More Beer	1960	5.00	10.00	20.00
—With the Sputnicks					

LEWIS, SABBY

45s

ABC-PARAMOUNT

Number	Title (A Side/B Side)	Yr	VG	VG+	NM
9685	Ding-a-Ling/Kenny's Blues	1956	10.00	20.00	40.00
9687	Forgive Me, My Love/Regretting	1956	10.00	20.00	40.00

GONE

Number	Title (A Side/B Side)	Yr	VG	VG+	NM
5074	Swana/Sabby	1959	6.25	12.50	25.00
—With the Uniques					

LEWIS, SAMMIE

45s

SUN

Number	Title (A Side/B Side)	Yr	VG	VG+	NM
218	So Long Baby Goodbye/I Feel So Worried	1955	20.00	40.00	80.00

LEWIS, SMILEY

45s

DOT

Number	Title (A Side/B Side)	Yr	VG	VG+	NM
16674	I Wonder/Lookin' for My Woman	1964	2.50	5.00	10.00

IMPERIAL

Number	Title (A Side/B Side)	Yr	VG	VG+	NM
5194	The Bells Are Ringing/Lillie Mae	1952	30.00	60.00	120.00
—Note: Smiley Lewis records on Imperial before 5194 are unconfirmed on 45 rpm					
5208	Gumbo Blues/It's So Peaceful	1952	25.00	50.00	100.00
5224	Gypsy Blues/You're Not the One	1953	25.00	50.00	100.00
5234	Play Girl/Big Mamou	1953	20.00	40.00	80.00
5234	Play Girl/Big Mamou	1953	62.50	125.00	250.00
—Red vinyl					
5241	Caldonia's Party/Oh Baby	1953	20.00	40.00	80.00
5252	Little Fernandez/It's Music	1953	20.00	40.00	80.00
5268	Down the Road/Blue Monday	1954	20.00	40.00	80.00
5279	I Love You for Sentimental Reasons/The Rocks	1954	20.00	40.00	80.00
5296	Can't Stop Loving You/That Certain Door	1954	20.00	40.00	80.00
5316	Too Many Drivers/Ooh La La	1954	20.00	40.00	80.00
5325	Jailbird/Farewell	1955	20.00	40.00	80.00
5349	Real Gone Lover/Nobody Knows	1955	20.00	40.00	80.00
5356	I Hear You Knocking/Bumpity Bump	1955	20.00	40.00	80.00
5372	Queen of Hearts/Come On	1956	20.00	40.00	80.00
5380	One Night/Ain't Gonna Do It	1956	20.00	40.00	80.00

Number	Title (A Side/B Side)	Yr	VG	VG+	NM
5389	She's Got Me (Hook, Line and Sinker)/Please Listen to Me	1956	20.00	40.00	80.00
5404	Down Yonder We Go Ballin'/Someday You'll Want Me	1956	20.00	40.00	80.00
5418	Shame, Shame, Shame/No No	1957	15.00	30.00	60.00
5431	You Are My Sunshine/Sweeter Words Have Never Been Spoken	1957	10.00	20.00	40.00
5450	Go On Fool/Goin' to Jump and Shout	1957	7.50	15.00	30.00
5470	Rootin' and Tootin'/I Can't Believe	1957	7.50	15.00	30.00
5478	Bad Luck Blues/School Days Are Back Again	1957	7.50	15.00	30.00
5531	Lil' Liza Jane/My Love Is Gone	1958	6.25	12.50	25.00
5662	Oh Red!/I Want to Be with Her	1960	3.75	7.50	15.00
5676	Last Night/Ain't Goin' There No More	1960	3.75	7.50	15.00
5719	Stormy Monday Blues/Tell Me Who	1961	3.75	7.50	15.00
5820	Gumbo Blues/Tee Nah Nah	1962	3.75	7.50	15.00
KNIGHT					
2007	Baby Please/I Shall Not Be Moved	1959	3.75	7.50	15.00
2011	Lost Weekend/By the Water	1959	3.75	7.50	15.00
LOMA					
2024	Bells Are Ringing/Walkin' the Girl	1965	2.50	5.00	10.00
OKEH					
7146	I'm Coming Down with the Blues/Tune-Up	1962	3.00	6.00	12.00
Albums					
IMPERIAL					
LP-9141 [M]	I Hear You Knocking	1961	150.00	300.00	600.00
—Black vinyl					
LP-9141 [M]	I Hear You Knocking	1961	1500.	3000.	6000.
—Green vinyl (one copy known)					

LEWIS AND CLARKE EXPEDITION, THE

45s

Number	Title (A Side/B Side)	Yr	VG	VG+	NM
CHARTMAKER					
402	Expedition West/For Your Freedom Tonight	1966	2.00	4.00	8.00
COLGEMS					
66-1006	I Feel Good (I Feel Bad)/Blue Revelations	1967	2.00	4.00	8.00
66-1006 [PS]	I Feel Good (I Feel Bad)/Blue Revelations	1967	3.75	7.50	15.00
66-1011	Destination Unknown/Freedom Bird	1967	2.00	4.00	8.00
66-1011 [PS]	Destination Unknown/Freedom Bird	1967	3.75	7.50	15.00
66-1022	Chain Around the Flowers/Why Need They Pretend	1968	2.00	4.00	8.00
66-1028	Daddy's Plastic Child/Gypsy Song Man	1968	2.00	4.00	8.00
Albums					
COLGEMS					
COM-105 [M]	The Lewis and Clarke Expedition	1967	6.25	12.50	25.00
COS-105 [S]	The Lewis and Clarke Expedition	1967	7.50	15.00	30.00

LEYTON, JOHN

45s

Number	Title (A Side/B Side)	Yr	VG	VG+	NM
ABC-PARAMOUNT					
10292	Son, This Is She/Six White Horses	1962	3.00	6.00	12.00
ATCO					
6319	Make Love to Me/I'll Cut Your Tail Off	1964	3.00	6.00	12.00
LIVERPOOL SOUND					
901	Beautiful Dreamer/I Guess You Are Always On My Mind	1964	3.00	6.00	12.00

LIBERACE

45s

Number	Title (A Side/B Side)	Yr	VG	VG+	NM
AVI					
101	The Way We Were/The Entertainer	1976	—	2.00	4.00
112	My Melody of Love/El Bimbo	1976	—	2.00	4.00
COLUMBIA					
39709	September Song/I Want My Mama	1952	3.75	7.50	15.00
39777	Star Dust/Malaguena	1952	3.00	6.00	12.00
39778	As Time Goes By/Liebestraum	1952	3.00	6.00	12.00
39779	Carioca/Warsaw Concerto	1952	3.00	6.00	12.00
39780	Polish National Dance/Moonlight Sonata	1952	3.00	6.00	12.00
—The above four comprise a box set					
39895	I Miss You So/I Don't Care	1952	3.75	7.50	15.00
39919	Yakety Yak Polka/Begin the Beguine	1953	3.00	6.00	12.00
39920	Chopsticks/The Old Piano Roll Blues	1953	3.00	6.00	12.00
39921	Cement Mixer/Slaughter on Tenth Avenue	1953	3.00	6.00	12.00
39922	Cumana/Lover	1953	3.00	6.00	12.00
—The above four comprise a box set					
39984	Tchakovsky's Piano Concerto #1/September Song	1953	3.00	6.00	12.00
39985	I Don't Care/Jalousie	1953	3.00	6.00	12.00
39986	Autumn Nocturne/Concerto #2 in A Major for Piano and Orchestra	1953	3.00	6.00	12.00
39987	Tales from the Vienna Woods/I'll Be Seeing You	1953	3.00	6.00	12.00
—The above four comprise a box set					
39995	I'm Loved/I'd Never Forgive Myself	1953	3.75	7.50	15.00
40065	Warsaw Concerto (Beginning)/Cornish Rhapsody (Conclusion)	1953	3.00	6.00	12.00
40066	Warsaw Concerto (Conclusion)/Cornish Rhapsody (Beginning)	1953	3.00	6.00	12.00
40067	Grieg's Piano Concerto (Beginning)/Chopin's Fantasia (Conclusion)	1953	3.00	6.00	12.00
40068	Grieg's Piano Concerto (Conclusion)/Chopin's Fantasia (Beginning)	1953	3.00	6.00	12.00
—The above four comprise a box set					
40099	A Story of Three Loves/Maiden's Wish Samba	1953	3.75	7.50	15.00
40145	Spellbound Concerto (Beginning)/Rachmaninoff Fantasia (Conclusion)	1953	3.00	6.00	12.00
40146	Spellbound Concerto (Conclusion)/Rachmaninoff Fantasia (Beginning)	1953	3.00	6.00	12.00
40147	Dream of Olwen/Laura (Conclusion)	1953	3.00	6.00	12.00
40148	Stella by Starlight/Laura (Beginning)	1953	3.00	6.00	12.00
—The above four comprise a box set					
40217	Twelfth Street Rag/Beer Barrel Polka	1954	3.00	6.00	12.00
40285	Polonaise/Liebestraum (Love's Dream)	1954	3.00	6.00	12.00
40314	Rhapsody by Candlelight/Star of India	1954	3.00	6.00	12.00
40331	Waltz in C-Sharp Minor/Polonaise in A Major	1954	2.50	5.00	10.00
40332	Nocturne No. 5 in E-Flat Major/Etude in A-Flat Major	1954	2.50	5.00	10.00
40333	Fantasie-Impromptu (Beginning)/Nocturne No. 2 in E Flat Major (Conclusion)	1954	2.50	5.00	10.00
40334	Fantasie-Impromptu (Conclusion)/Nocturne No. 2 in E Flat Major (Beginning)	1954	2.50	5.00	10.00
—The above four comprise a box set					
40335	Polonaise in A-Flat Major (Beginning)/Grande Valse	1954	2.50	5.00	10.00
40336	Polonaise in A-Flat Major (Conclusion)/Prelude No. 4 in E Minor	1954	2.50	5.00	10.00
40337	Etude No. 3 in E Major (Beginning)/Etude in F Minor	1954	2.50	5.00	10.00
40338	Etude No. 3 in E Major (Conclusion)/Waltz No. 6 in D-Flat Major	1954	2.50	5.00	10.00
—The above four comprise a box set					
40379	The Spirit of Christmas/O Holy Night	1954	3.00	6.00	12.00
40380	The Christmas Song/The Toy Piano//The Beauty of Holiness/Santa Claus Medley	1954	3.00	6.00	12.00
40381	Gesu Bambino/Sleigh Ride//Star Bright/Ave Maria	1954	3.00	6.00	12.00
40382	Twas the Night Before Christmas/Christmas Medley	1954	3.00	6.00	12.00
40394	Cornish Rhapsody/Rhapsody by Candlelight	1954	2.50	5.00	10.00
40395	Alexander's Ragtime Band/El Cumbanchero	1954	2.50	5.00	10.00
40396	My TV Sponsors/Clair de Lune	1954	2.50	5.00	10.00
40397	Cement Mixer/Beer Barrel Polka	1954	2.50	5.00	10.00
—The above four comprise a box set					
40454	I'll Get By/Finger of Suspicion	1955	3.00	6.00	12.00
40455	Unchained Melody/The Bridges at Toko-Ri	1955	3.00	6.00	12.00
40570	Sincerely Yours/Under Paris Skies	1955	3.00	6.00	12.00
40647	We All Need Love/Dancing Skeletons	1956	3.00	6.00	12.00
40686	Faith Unlocks the Door/Nocturne No. 2	1956	3.00	6.00	12.00
40768	The Magic of Believing/Cuba	1956	3.00	6.00	12.00
48001	Ave Maria/Christmas Medley (White Christmas/Jingle Bells/O Come All Ye Faithful/Silent Night)	1954	3.75	7.50	15.00
48001 [PS]	Ave Maria/Christmas Medley (White Christmas/Jingle Bells/O Come All Ye Faithful/Silent Night)	1954	5.00	10.00	20.00
48008	I Love You Truly/Oh Promise Me	1954	3.00	6.00	12.00
48008 [PS]	I Love You Truly/Oh Promise Me	1954	3.75	7.50	15.00
CORAL					
62112	Gigi/This Earth Is Mine	1959	2.50	5.00	10.00
65539	I Believe/Gigi	1961	2.00	4.00	8.00
65556	I'll Be Seeing You/Laura	1961	2.00	4.00	8.00
DECCA					
28279	Velvet Moon/It's Shadow Time	1952	3.75	7.50	15.00
DOT					
16594	Alley Cat/Theme from "Outer Space"	1964	—	3.00	6.00
17033	Happy Barefoot Boy/Two for the Road	1967	—	3.00	6.00
MGM					
14518	The Morning After/Theme from "Above San Francisco"	1973	—	2.50	5.00
WARNER BROS.					
7465	Ciao/Theme from Love Story	1971	—	2.50	5.00
7-Inch Extended Plays					
COLUMBIA					
5-2050	The Spirit of Christmas/Christmas Medley//Star Bright/The Beauty of Holiness	1954	3.00	6.00	12.00
5-2050 [PS]	(title unknown)	1954	3.75	7.50	15.00
5-2051	O Holy Night/The Toy Piano//Sleigh Ride/The Christmas Song	1954	3.00	6.00	12.00
5-2051 [PS]	(title unknown)	1954	3.75	7.50	15.00
DECCA					
ED 2197	(contents unknown)	195?	5.00	10.00	20.00
ED 2197 [PS]	Piano Solos	195?	5.00	10.00	20.00
Albums					
ABC					
4002	16 Great Performances	1974	3.00	6.00	12.00
AVI					
1023	Candlelight Classics	1973	3.00	6.00	12.00
1029	The World of Liberacte	1974	3.00	6.00	12.00
CBS					
FM 42244	Concert Favorites	1986	2.50	5.00	10.00
COLUMBIA					
CL 575 [M]	Liberace at the Piano	1954	10.00	20.00	40.00
—Maroon label, gold print					
CL 589 [M]	Christmas at Liberace's	1954	12.50	25.00	50.00
—Maroon label, gold print					
CL 600 [M]	Liberace at the Hollywood Bowl	1955	10.00	20.00	40.00
CL 645 [M]	Hollywood Bowl Encore	1955	10.00	20.00	40.00
CL 661 [M]	Liberace by Candlelight	1955	10.00	20.00	40.00
CL 800 [M]	Sincerely Yours	1956	12.50	25.00	50.00
CL 896 [M]	Liberace at Home	1956	12.50	25.00	50.00
CL 2516 [10]	Piano Reverie	1955	15.00	30.00	60.00
CL 2592 [10]	Kiddin' on the Keys	1955	15.00	30.00	60.00
CL 6217 [10]	Liberace at the Piano	1952	20.00	40.00	80.00
CL 6239 [10]	An Evening with Liberace	1953	20.00	40.00	80.00
CL 6251 [10]	Liberace by Candlelight	1953	20.00	40.00	80.00
CL 6269 [10]	Concertos for You	1953	20.00	40.00	80.00
CL 6283 [10]	Concertos for You, Volume 2	1953	20.00	40.00	80.00
CL 6327 [10]	Liberace Plays Chopin	1954	20.00	40.00	80.00
CL 6328 [10]	Liberace Plays Chopin, Volume 2	1954	20.00	40.00	80.00
CS 9845	Liberace's Greatest Hits	1969	3.00	6.00	12.00
—Red "360 Sound" label					
CORAL					
7CXB 9 [(2) S]	The Best of Liberace	1965	5.00	10.00	20.00
CXB 9 [(2) M]	The Best of Liberace	1965	3.75	7.50	15.00
CRL 57292 [M]	Piano Song Book — Movie Themes	1959	3.75	7.50	15.00
CRL 57305 [M]	The Magic Pianos of Liberace	1960	3.00	6.00	12.00
CRL 57305 [M]	The Magic Pianos of Liberace	1960	3.75	7.50	15.00
CRL 57344 [M]	My Inspiration	1961	3.00	6.00	12.00
CRL 57346 [M]	Liberace at the Palladium	1961	3.00	6.00	12.00
CRL 57377 [M]	My Parade of Golden Favorites	1961	3.00	6.00	12.00
CRL 57392 [M]	As Time Goes By	1962	3.00	6.00	12.00

Number	Title (A Side/B Side)	Yr	VG	VG+	NM
CRL 57395 [M]	Rhapsody by Candlelight	1962	3.00	6.00	12.00
CRL 57452 [M]	Golden Themes from Hollywood	1964	3.00	6.00	12.00
CRL 757292 [S]	Piano Song Book — Movie Themes	1959	5.00	10.00	20.00
CRL 757305 [S]	The Magic Pianos of Liberace	1960	3.75	7.50	15.00
CRL 757305 [S]	The Magic Pianos of Liberace	1960	5.00	10.00	20.00
CRL 757344 [S]	My Inspiration	1961	3.75	7.50	15.00
CRL 757346 [S]	Liberace at the Palladium	1961	3.75	7.50	15.00
CRL 757377 [S]	My Parade of Golden Favorites	1961	3.75	7.50	15.00
CRL 757392 [S]	As Time Goes By	1962	3.75	7.50	15.00
CRL 757395 [S]	Rhapsody by Candlelight	1962	3.75	7.50	15.00
CRL 757452 [S]	Golden Themes from Hollywood	1964	3.75	7.50	15.00
DOT					
DLP-3547 [M]	Mr. Showmanship	1964	3.00	6.00	12.00
DLP-3550 [M]	A Liberace Christmas	1964	3.00	6.00	12.00
DLP-3563 [M]	My Most Requested	1965	3.00	6.00	12.00
DLP-3595 [M]	Liberace at the Americana, Volume 1	1965	3.00	6.00	12.00
DLP-3596 [M]	Liberace at the Americana, Volume 2	1965	3.00	6.00	12.00
DLP-3755 [M]	New Sounds	1966	3.00	6.00	12.00
DLP-3816 [M]	Liberace Now!	1967	3.75	7.50	15.00
DLP-9502 [M]	Silver Anniversary	1965	3.00	6.00	12.00
DLP-25547 [S]	Mr. Showmanship	1964	3.75	7.50	15.00
DLP-25550 [S]	A Liberace Christmas	1964	3.75	7.50	15.00
DLP-25563 [S]	My Most Requested	1965	3.75	7.50	15.00
DLP-25595 [S]	Liberace at the Americana, Volume 1	1965	3.75	7.50	15.00
DLP-25596 [S]	Liberace at the Americana, Volume 2	1965	3.75	7.50	15.00
DLP-25755 [S]	New Sounds	1966	3.75	7.50	15.00
DLP-25816 [S]	Liberace Now!	1967	3.75	7.50	15.00
DLP-25858	The Love Album	1968	3.00	6.00	12.00
DLP-25901	Sound of Love	1969	3.00	6.00	12.00
DLP-29502 [S]	Silver Anniversary	1965	3.75	7.50	15.00
HARMONY					
HL 7154 [M]	The Liberace Show	1959	3.75	7.50	15.00
HL 7237 [M]	Rhapsody in Blue	196?	3.00	6.00	12.00
HL 7361 [M]	Concerto by Candlelight	196?	3.00	6.00	12.00
HS 11054 [R]	The Liberace Show	196?	2.50	5.00	10.00
HS 11161 [R]	Concerto by Candlelight	196?	3.00	6.00	12.00
HL 11175 [R]	Rhapsody in Blue	196?	2.50	5.00	10.00
HS 11325	Tenderly	1969	2.50	5.00	10.00
HS 11391	The Very Thought of You	1970	2.50	5.00	10.00
MCA					
740	Here's Liberace	198?	2.00	4.00	8.00
—Reissue of Vocalion 73821					
4060 [(2)]	The Best of Liberace	197?	3.00	6.00	12.00
4167 [(2)]	The Artistry of Liberace	198?	3.00	6.00	12.00
MISTLETOE					
MLP-1208	Twas the Night Before Christmas	1974	2.50	5.00	10.00
PARAMOUNT					
PAS-1009	The Best of Liberace	1973	3.00	6.00	12.00
PAS-1032 [(2)]	Liberace In Concert	1974	3.75	7.50	15.00
PICKWICK					
SPC-3085	You Made Me Love You	196?	2.50	5.00	10.00
SPC-3124	Strangers in the Night	196?	2.50	5.00	10.00
SPC-3159	What Now My Love	1969	2.50	5.00	10.00
SPC-3208	By the Time I Get to Phoenix	197?	2.50	5.00	10.00
VOCALION					
VL 3821 [M]	Here's Liberace	196?	3.00	6.00	12.00
VL 73821 [R]	Here's Liberace	196?	3.00	6.00	12.00
WARNER BROS.					
WS 1847	A Brand New Me	1969	3.00	6.00	12.00
WS 1889	Love and Music Festival "Live"	1970	3.00	6.00	12.00

LIEBERMAN, LORI

Number	Title (A Side/B Side)	Yr	VG	VG+	NM
45s					
CAPITOL					
3370	L.A. Texas Boy/Louisiana Cock Fight	1972	—	2.50	5.00
3379	Killing Me Softly with His Song/Back to Before	1972	—	3.00	6.00
3577	And the Feeling's Good/My Lover Do You Know	1973	—	2.50	5.00
3709	Becoming/House Full of Women	1973	—	2.50	5.00
3889	Make No Mistake/The World Is Turning	1974	—	2.50	5.00
4020	Raise Up Off of Me/Legacy	1974	—	2.50	5.00
MILLENNIUM					
622	Let Me Down Easy/Boston	1978	—	2.00	4.00
Albums					
CAPITOL					
ST-11081	Lori Lieberman	1972	3.00	6.00	12.00
ST-11203	Becoming	1973	3.00	6.00	12.00
ST-11297	A Piece of Time	1974	3.00	6.00	12.00

LIFEGUARDS, THE (1)

Number	Title (A Side/B Side)	Yr	VG	VG+	NM
45s					
ABC-PARAMOUNT					
10021	Everybody Out'a the Pool/Teenage Tango	1959	10.00	20.00	40.00
CASA BLANCA					
5535	Everybody Out'a the Pool/Teenage Tango	1959	12.50	25.00	50.00
DR					
69	Everybody Out'a the Pool/Teenage Tango	1965	3.75	7.50	15.00

LIFEGUARDS, THE (2)

Yet another production of STEVE BARRI and P.F. SLOAN.

Number	Title (A Side/B Side)	Yr	VG	VG+	NM
45s					
CATCH					
104	State Beach/Big Swim	1964	7.50	15.00	30.00
REPRISE					
0277	Swim Party/Swimtime U.S.A.	1964	6.25	12.50	25.00

LIFEGUARDS, THE (U)

May be group (1); may be group (2); may be neither.

Number	Title (A Side/B Side)	Yr	VG	VG+	NM
Albums					
WYNCOTE					
SW-9043 [S]	C'mon and Swim	1964	3.75	7.50	15.00
W-9043 [M]	C'mon and Swim	1964	3.00	6.00	12.00

LIGHT, ENOCH

Includes records made by the same musicians under other names; examples include "Terry Snyder and the All-Stars" and "The Command All-Stars."

Number	Title (A Side/B Side)	Yr	VG	VG+	NM
45s					
COMMAND					
4008	The Private Life of a Private Eye/Gum Shoe Lullaby	1960	2.50	5.00	10.00
4009	Young at Heart Cha Cha/Travel Now, Pay Next Year, Pleasure Cruise	1960	2.50	5.00	10.00
4010	Mack the Knife Cha Cha/(B-side unknown)	1960	2.50	5.00	10.00
4011	Rock-a-Bongo Boogie/Blue Is the Night	1960	2.50	5.00	10.00
—By "Terry Snyder and the All-Stars"					
4013	No Rest for the Drummer Man/American Patrol	196?	2.50	5.00	10.00
4014	Waltzing Matilda/Sunrise Over Sumatra	196?	2.50	5.00	10.00
4019	Satan Never Sleeps/The Four Horsemen of the Apocalypse	1961	2.00	4.00	8.00
4028	Perdido/Rio Junction	1962	2.00	4.00	8.00
4029	Meditation (Meditacao)/Big Ben Bossa	1962	2.00	4.00	8.00
4031	Ching Ching Chow Chow/Istanbul	196?	2.00	4.00	8.00
4033	Nola/Big Ben Bossa	196?	2.00	4.00	8.00
4035	Hud/Speak Not a Word	196?	2.00	4.00	8.00
4050	A Hard Day's Night/Carribe	1964	2.00	4.00	8.00
4062	Begin the Beguine/(B-side unknown)	196?	2.00	4.00	8.00
4067	Downtown/Easy Baby, Go Easy Baby	1965	2.00	4.00	8.00
4068	Forget Domani/Love Me Now	1965	2.00	4.00	8.00
4069	Theme from "Zorba the Greek"/Von Ryan's Express	1965	2.00	4.00	8.00
4072	Love Theme from "The Sandpiper"/Forget Domani	1966	2.00	4.00	8.00
GRAND AWARD					
1020	I Want to Be Happy Cha Cha/Cara Mia Cha Cha	1958	3.00	6.00	12.00
1026	Baby, It's Cold Outside Cha Cha/Chiquita Cha Cha	1958	3.00	6.00	12.00
1032	With My Eyes Wide Open I'm Dreaming/I Cried for You	1959	3.00	6.00	12.00
1035	Scarlet Ribbons/Greensleeves	1959	3.00	6.00	12.00
PROJECT 3					
1305	Is Paris Burning/And We Were Lovers	1967	—	3.00	6.00
1310	Come On, Come On, Come On, Don't Be Timid/I Love, I Live, I Love	1967	—	3.00	6.00
1322	In the Heat of the Night/Live for Life	1967	—	3.00	6.00
1330	Green Tambourine/I Wonder What She's Doing Tonight	1968	—	3.00	6.00
1339	Lullaby from "Rosemary's Baby"/The Windmills of Your Mind	1968	—	3.00	6.00
1341	Hang 'Em High/The Windmills of Your Mind	1968	—	3.00	6.00
1344	A Man Without Love/Whoever You Are, I Love You	1969	—	3.00	6.00
1346	Interlude/Now	1969	—	3.00	6.00
1348	Funny Girl/Ol' Devil Moon	1969	—	3.00	6.00
1354	Blowin' in the Wind/Happy Ever After	1969	—	3.00	6.00
1359	Hair/(B-side unknown)	1969	—	3.00	6.00
1367	Alice's Restaurant/Raindrops Keep Fallin' on My Head	1970	—	2.50	5.00
1368	My Silent Song/Little Fugue for You and Me	1970	—	2.50	5.00
1369	Day of Anger/Song from "The Wild Bunch"	1970	—	2.50	5.00
1379	A Lover's Concerto/Bond Street	197?	—	2.50	5.00
1385	The Out-of-Towners/Patton Theme	197?	—	2.50	5.00
1389	In the Mood/Let's Dance	197?	—	2.50	5.00
1394	One O'Clock Jump/Take the "A" Train	197?	—	2.50	5.00
1395	South Rampart Street Parade/Woodchopper's Ball	197?	—	2.50	5.00
1396	Marie/I'll Never Smile Again	197?	—	2.50	5.00
1397	Jersey Bounce/Tuxedo Junction	197?	—	2.50	5.00
1398	I'm Getting Sentimental Over You/A String of Pearls	197?	—	2.50	5.00
1399	Cherokee/Flying Home	197?	—	2.50	5.00
1401	Moonlight Serenade/Snowfall	197?	—	2.50	5.00
1405	Chicago/Happy Days Are Here Again	197?	—	2.50	5.00
1406	Bye Bye Blackbird/Charleston	197?	—	2.50	5.00
1407	If You Knew Susie/I'm Looking Over a Four-Leaf Clover	197?	—	2.50	5.00
1408	Ain't She Sweet/Yes Sir, That's My Baby	197?	—	2.50	5.00
1409	Tea for Two/Toot, Toot, Tootsie	197?	—	2.50	5.00
1411	The Theme from "Shaft"/The Night They Drove Old Dixie Down	197?	—	2.50	5.00
1412	Diamonds Are Forever/Fiddler on the Roof	197?	—	2.50	5.00
1416	The Godfather Waltz/The French Connection	197?	—	2.50	5.00
1420	Cecelia/Eglantine	197?	—	2.50	5.00
1427	Give Joy to the World/(B-side unknown)	197?	—	2.50	5.00
Albums					
ABC WESTMINSTER/GRAND AWARD					
68008	Sing Along with the Original Roaring 20's	1974	2.50	5.00	10.00
68009	The Flirty 30's	1974	2.50	5.00	10.00
68012	The Torchy Thirties	1974	2.50	5.00	10.00
COMMAND					
800 SD [S]	Persuasive Percussion	1960	3.75	7.50	15.00
—By "Terry Snyder and the All-Stars"					
33-800 [M]	Persuasive Percussion	1960	3.00	6.00	12.00
—By "Terry Snyder and the All-Stars"					
804 SD [S]	The Sound of Strings	1960	3.75	7.50	15.00
33-804 [M]	The Sound of Strings	1960	3.00	6.00	12.00
805 SD [S]	Paperback Ballet	1960	3.75	7.50	15.00
33-805 [M]	Paperback Ballet	1960	3.00	6.00	12.00
806 SD [S]	Provocative Percussion	1960	3.75	7.50	15.00
—By "The Command All-Stars"					
33-806 [M]	Provocative Percussion	1960	3.00	6.00	12.00
—By "The Command All-Stars"					
808 SD [S]	Persuasive Percussion, Volume 2	1960	3.75	7.50	15.00
—By "Terry Snyder and the All-Stars"					
33-808 [M]	Persuasive Percussion, Volume 2	1960	3.00	6.00	12.00
—By "Terry Snyder and the All-Stars"					
810 SD [S]	Provocative Percussion, Volume 2	1960	3.75	7.50	15.00
33-810 [M]	Provocative Percussion, Volume 2	1960	3.00	6.00	12.00

Number	Title (A Side/B Side)	Yr	VG	VG+	NM
814 SD [S]	Pertinent Percussion Cha-Cha's	1960	3.75	7.50	15.00
33-814 [M]	Pertinent Percussion Cha-Cha's	1960	3.00	6.00	12.00
817 SD [S]	Persuasive Percussion, Volume 3	1961	3.75	7.50	15.00
—By "The Command All-Stars"					
33-817 [M]	Persuasive Percussion, Volume 3	1961	3.00	6.00	12.00
—By "The Command All-Stars"					
818 SD [S]	Big Bold and Brassy	1961	3.75	7.50	15.00
33-818 [M]	Big Bold and Brassy	1961	3.00	6.00	12.00
821 SD [S]	Provocative Percussion, Volume 3	1961	3.75	7.50	15.00
33-821 [M]	Provocative Percussion, Volume 3	1961	3.00	6.00	12.00
822 SD [S]	Far Away Places	1961	3.75	7.50	15.00
33-822 [M]	Far Away Places	1961	3.00	6.00	12.00
826 SD [S]	Stereo 35/MM	1961	3.75	7.50	15.00
830 SD [S]	Persuasive Percussion, Volume 4	1962	3.75	7.50	15.00
33-830 [M]	Persuasive Percussion, Volume 4	1962	3.00	6.00	12.00
831 SD [S]	Stereo 35/MM, Volume Two	1962	3.75	7.50	15.00
833 SD [S]	Vibrations	1962	3.75	7.50	15.00
33-833 [M]	Vibrations	1962	3.00	6.00	12.00
834 SD [S]	Provocative Percussion, Volume 4	1962	3.75	7.50	15.00
33-834 [M]	Provocative Percussion, Volume 4	1962	3.00	6.00	12.00
835 SD [S]	Great Themes from Hit Films	1962	3.75	7.50	15.00
33-835 [M]	Great Themes from Hit Films	1962	3.00	6.00	12.00
840 SD [S]	Enoch Light and His Orchestra At Carnegie Hall Play Irving Berlin	1962	3.75	7.50	15.00
33-840 [M]	Enoch Light and His Orchestra At Carnegie Hall Play Irving Berlin	1962	3.00	6.00	12.00
844 SD [S]	Big Band Bossa Nova	1962	3.75	7.50	15.00
33-844 [M]	Big Band Bossa Nova	1962	3.00	6.00	12.00
850 SD [S]	Far Away Places, Volume 2	1963	3.75	7.50	15.00
33-850 [M]	Far Away Places, Volume 2	1963	3.00	6.00	12.00
851 SD [S]	Let's Dance the Bossa Nova	1963	3.75	7.50	15.00
33-851 [M]	Let's Dance the Bossa Nova	1963	3.00	6.00	12.00
854 SD [S]	1963 — The Year's Most Popular Themes	1963	3.75	7.50	15.00
33-854 [M]	1963 — The Year's Most Popular Themes	1963	3.00	6.00	12.00
863 SD [S]	Rome 35/MM	1964	3.75	7.50	15.00
33-863 [M]	Rome 35/MM	1964	3.00	6.00	12.00
867 SD [S]	Dimension "3"	1964	3.75	7.50	15.00
33-867 [M]	Dimension "3"	1964	3.00	6.00	12.00
868 SD [S]	Command Performances	1964	3.75	7.50	15.00
33-868 [M]	Command Performances	1964	3.00	6.00	12.00
871 SD [S]	Great Themes from Hit Films	1964	3.75	7.50	15.00
33-871 [M]	Great Themes from Hit Films	1964	3.00	6.00	12.00
873 SD [S]	Discotheque Dance...Dance...Dance	1964	3.75	7.50	15.00
33-873 [M]	Discotheque Dance...Dance...Dance	1964	3.00	6.00	12.00
879 SD [S]	Great Cole Porter Songs	1965	3.75	7.50	15.00
33-879 [M]	Great Cole Porter Songs	1965	3.00	6.00	12.00
882 SD [S]	Discotheque Dance...Dance...Dance, Volume 2	1965	3.75	7.50	15.00
33-882 [M]	Discotheque Dance...Dance...Dance, Volume 2	1965	3.00	6.00	12.00
887 SD [S]	Magnificent Movie Themes	1965	3.75	7.50	15.00
33-887 [M]	Magnificent Movie Themes	1965	3.00	6.00	12.00
895 SD [S]	Persuasive Percussion 1966	1966	3.75	7.50	15.00
33-895 [M]	Persuasive Percussion 1966	1966	3.00	6.00	12.00
915 SD	Command Performances, Volume 2	1969	3.75	7.50	15.00
QD-40002 [Q]	A New Concept	1972	3.75	7.50	15.00

GRAND AWARD

Number	Title (A Side/B Side)	Yr	VG	VG+	NM
GA-201 SD [S]	The Roaring Twenties	1958	6.25	12.50	25.00
GA-202 SD [S]	The Flirty Thirties	1958	6.25	12.50	25.00
GA-203 SD [S]	Waltzes for Dancing	1958	6.25	12.50	25.00
GA-206 SD [S]	Tommy Dorsey's Song Hits	1958	6.25	12.50	25.00
GA-207 SD [S]	Glenn Miller's Song Hits	1958	6.25	12.50	25.00
GA-211 SD [S]	The Roaring Twenties, Volume 2	1958	6.25	12.50	25.00
GA-214 SD [S]	Around the World in 80 Days	1958	6.25	12.50	25.00
GA-215 SD [S]	Gigi	1958	6.25	12.50	25.00
GA-216 SD [S]	My Fair Lady	1958	6.25	12.50	25.00
GA-217 SD [S]	Oklahoma/South Pacific	1958	6.25	12.50	25.00
GA-220 SD [S]	The Torchy Thirties	1958	6.25	12.50	25.00
GA-222 SD [S]	I Want to Be Happy Cha Cha's	1959	6.25	12.50	25.00
GA-224 SD [S]	New World Symphony	1958	6.25	12.50	25.00
GA-225 SD [S]	The Great Themes of America's Great Bands	1958	6.25	12.50	25.00
GA-227 SD [S]	Happy Cha Cha's, Vol. 2	1959	6.25	12.50	25.00
GA-228 SD [S]	Show Spectacular	1959	6.25	12.50	25.00
GA-229 SD [S]	The Roaring Twenties, Volume 3	1959	6.25	12.50	25.00
GA-236 SD [S]	All the Things You Are	1959	6.25	12.50	25.00
GA-237 SD [S]	Come to Hawaii	1959	6.25	12.50	25.00
GA-238 SD [S]	With My Eyes Wide Open I'm Dreaming	1959	6.25	12.50	25.00
GA-242 SD [S]	Something to Remember You By	1959	6.25	12.50	25.00
GA-246 SD [S]	Just for Kicks	1959	6.25	12.50	25.00
GA-251 SD [S]	Sing Along with the Original Roaring 20's	1959	6.25	12.50	25.00
GA 33-327 [M]	The Roaring Twenties	1958	5.00	10.00	20.00
GA 33-353 [M]	The Roaring Twenties, Volume 3	1959	5.00	10.00	20.00
GA 33-371 [M]	The Flirty Thirties	1958	5.00	10.00	20.00
GA 33-372 [M]	Waltzes for Dancing	1958	5.00	10.00	20.00
GA 33-380 [M]	Paris Spectacular	1958	5.00	10.00	20.00
GA 33-381 [M]	Glenn Miller's Song Hits	1958	5.00	10.00	20.00
GA 33-382 [M]	Tommy Dorsey's Song Hits	1958	5.00	10.00	20.00
GA 33-388 [M]	I Want to Be Happy Cha Cha's	1959	5.00	10.00	20.00
GA 33-391 [M]	Happy Cha Cha's, Vol. 2	1959	5.00	10.00	20.00
GA 33-392 [M]	The Great Themes of America's Great Bands	1958	5.00	10.00	20.00
GA 33-399 [M]	All the Things You Are	1959	5.00	10.00	20.00
GA 33-405 [M]	Come to Hawaii	1959	5.00	10.00	20.00
GA 33-406 [M]	With My Eyes Wide Open I'm Dreaming	1959	5.00	10.00	20.00
GA 33-410 [M]	Something to Remember You By	1959	5.00	10.00	20.00
GA 33-419 [M]	Sing Along with the Original Roaring 20's	1959	5.00	10.00	20.00

PROJECT 3

Number	Title (A Side/B Side)	Yr	VG	VG+	NM
PR-5000 SD	Spanish Strings	1967	3.00	6.00	12.00
PR4C-5000 [Q]	Spanish Strings	1973	3.75	7.50	15.00
PR-5004 SD	It's Happening	1967	3.00	6.00	12.00
PR-5005 SD	Film on Film — Great Movie Themes	1967	3.00	6.00	12.00
PR-5013 SD	Film Fame	1968	3.00	6.00	12.00
PR-5021 SD	Twelve Smash Hits	1968	3.00	6.00	12.00
PR-5027 SD	The Best of Hollywood '68-'69	1968	3.00	6.00	12.00
PR-5030 SD	Whoever You Are, I Love You	1968	3.00	6.00	12.00
PR-5036 SD	Enoch Light and the Brass Menagerie	1969	3.00	6.00	12.00
PR4C-5036 [Q]	Enoch Light and the Brass Menagerie	1973	3.75	7.50	15.00
PR-5038 SD	Glittering Guitars	1969	3.00	6.00	12.00
PR-5042 SD	Enoch Light and the Brass Menagerie, Volume 2	1969	3.00	6.00	12.00
PR4C-5042 [Q]	Enoch Light and the Brass Menagerie, Volume 2	1973	3.75	7.50	15.00
PR-5043 SD	Spaced Out	1970	3.00	6.00	12.00
PR4C-5043 [Q]	Spaced Out	1973	3.75	7.50	15.00
PR-5046 SD	Best of the Movie Themes 1970	1970	3.00	6.00	12.00
PR4C-5046 [Q]	Best of the Movie Themes 1970	1973	3.75	7.50	15.00
PR-5048 SD	Permissive Polyphonics	1970	3.00	6.00	12.00
PR4C-5048 [Q]	Permissive Polyphonics	1973	3.75	7.50	15.00
PR-5049 SD	Big Band Hits of the 30's	1971	3.00	6.00	12.00
PR4C-5049 [Q]	Big Band Hits of the 30's	1973	3.75	7.50	15.00
PR-5051 SD	Hit Movie Themes	1971	3.00	6.00	12.00
PR4C-5051 [Q]	Hit Movie Themes	1973	3.75	7.50	15.00
PR-5056 SD	Big Band Hits of the 30's & 40's!	1971	3.00	6.00	12.00
PR4C-5056 [Q]	Big Band Hits of the 30's & 40's!	1973	3.75	7.50	15.00
PR-5059 SD	Big Hits of the 20's	1971	3.00	6.00	12.00
PR4C-5059 [Q]	Big Hits of the 20's	1973	3.75	7.50	15.00
PR-5060 SD	Enoch Light and the Brass Menagerie 1973	1972	3.00	6.00	12.00
PR4C-5060 [Q]	Enoch Light and the Brass Menagerie 1973	1973	3.75	7.50	15.00
PR-5063 SD	Movie Hits!	1972	3.00	6.00	12.00
PR4C-5063 [Q]	Movie Hits!	1973	3.75	7.50	15.00
PR4C-5068 [Q]	4 Channel Dynamite!	1973	3.75	7.50	15.00
PR4C-5073 [Q]	Charge!	1973	3.75	7.50	15.00
PR4C-5076 [Q]	Big Band Hits of the 40's & 50's	1973	3.75	7.50	15.00
PR4C-5077 [Q]	Future Sound Shock	1973	3.75	7.50	15.00
PR-5084 SD	Beatles Classics	1974	3.00	6.00	12.00
PR4C-5084 [Q]	Beatles Classics	1974	3.75	7.50	15.00
PR-5086 SD	Great Hits from the Gatsby Era	1974	3.00	6.00	12.00
PR4C-5086 [Q]	Great Hits from the Gatsby Era	1974	3.75	7.50	15.00
PR-5089 SD	Big Band Hits of the 30's, Volume 2	1975	3.00	6.00	12.00
PR4C-5089 [Q]	Big Band Hits of the 30's, Volume 2	1975	3.75	7.50	15.00
PR-5092 SD	Disco Disque	197?	3.00	6.00	12.00
PR4C-5092 [Q]	Disco Disque	197?	3.75	7.50	15.00
PR-5100	Let It Be	197?	3.00	6.00	12.00
PR-5109	The Most Beautiful Music in the World	1981	3.00	6.00	12.00
PR-6003/4 [(2)]	Big Hits of the Seventies	1974	3.75	7.50	15.00
PR4C-6003/4 [(2) Q]	Big Hits of the Seventies	1974	5.00	10.00	20.00
PR-6005/6 [(2)]	Big Band Hits of the 30's, 40's & 50's	1974	3.75	7.50	15.00
PR4C-6005/6 [(2) Q]	Big Band Hits of the 30's, 40's & 50's	1974	5.00	10.00	20.00
PR-6011/12 [(2)]	Music Maestro, Please	197?	3.75	7.50	15.00
PR-6013/14 [(2)]	Big Band Hits of the 30's and 40's	197?	3.75	7.50	15.00
PR4C-6013/14 [(2) Q]	Big Band Hits of the 30's and 40's	197?	5.00	10.00	20.00
PR-6034 [(2)]	20 Great Movie Themes	1980	3.75	7.50	15.00

SEAGULL

Number	Title (A Side/B Side)	Yr	VG	VG+	NM
LG-8204	Blowin' in the Wind	198?	2.50	5.00	10.00
LG-8207	Music from the Movies	198?	2.50	5.00	10.00

LIGHTFOOT, GORDON

45s

ABC-PARAMOUNT

Number	Title (A Side/B Side)	Yr	VG	VG+	NM
10352	Daisy-Doo/I'm the One (Remember Me)	1962	6.25	12.50	25.00
—As "Gord Lightfoot"					
10373	It's Too Late, He Wins/Negotiations	1962	6.25	12.50	25.00

CHATEAU

Number	Title (A Side/B Side)	Yr	VG	VG+	NM
142	Daisy-Doo/I'm the One (Remember Me)	1962	12.50	25.00	50.00
148	It's Too Late, He Wins/Negotiations	1962	12.50	25.00	50.00
152	I'll Meet You in Michigan/Is My Baby Blue Tonight	1962	10.00	20.00	40.00

REPRISE

Number	Title (A Side/B Side)	Yr	VG	VG+	NM
0744	If You Could Read My Mind/Me and Bobby McGee	1972	—	2.00	4.00
—"Back to Back Hits" series					
0745	Talking in Your Sleep/Summer Side of Life	1972	—	2.00	4.00
—"Back to Back Hits" series					
0926	Me and Bobby McGee/Pony Man	1970	—	2.50	5.00
0974	If You Could Read My Mind/Poor Little Allison	1970	—	3.00	6.00
1020	Talking in Your Sleep/Nous Vivons Ensemble	1971	—	2.50	5.00
1035	Summer Side of Life/Love and Maple Syrup	1971	—	2.50	5.00
1088	Beautiful/Don Quixote	1972	—	2.50	5.00
1128	You Are What I Am/The Same Old Obsession	1972	—	2.50	5.00
1145	Can't Depend on You/It's Worth Believin'	1972	—	2.50	5.00
1194	Sundown/Too Late for Prayin'	1974	—	2.00	4.00
1309	Carefree Highway/Seven Island Suite	1974	—	2.00	4.00
1328	Rainy Day People/Cherokee Bend	1975	—	2.00	4.00
1369	The Wreck of the Edmund Fitzgerald/The House You Live In	1976	—	2.00	4.00
1380	Race Among the Ruins/Protocol	1976	—	2.00	4.00

UNITED ARTISTS

Number	Title (A Side/B Side)	Yr	VG	VG+	NM
929	Just Like Tom Thumb's Blues/Ribbon of Darkness	1965	2.50	5.00	10.00
50055	For Lovin' Me/Spin, Spin	1966	2.00	4.00	8.00
50114	I'll Be Alright/Go Go Round	1967	2.00	4.00	8.00
50152	The Way I Feel/Peaceful Waters	1967	2.00	4.00	8.00
50281	Pussywillows, Cat-Tails/Black Day in July	1968	2.00	4.00	8.00
50447	Does Your Mother Know/Bitter Green	1968	2.00	4.00	8.00
50765	If I Could/Softly	1971	—	2.50	5.00

WARNER BROS.

Number	Title (A Side/B Side)	Yr	VG	VG+	NM
5621	For Lovin' Me/I'm Not Sayin'	1965	3.75	7.50	15.00
8518	The Circle Is Small/Sweet Guinevere	1978	—	2.50	5.00
—Without A-side subtitle					
8518	The Circle Is Small (I Can See It In Your Eyes)/Sweet Guinevere	1978	—	2.00	4.00
—Subtitle added to later pressings					
8579	Daylight Katy/Hangdog Hotel Room	1978	—	2.00	4.00
8644	Dreamland/Songs the Minstrel Sang	1978	—	2.00	4.00
28222	Ecstasy Made Easy/Morning Glory	1987	—	—	3.00
28422	East of Midnight/I'll Tag Along	1987	—	—	3.00
28553	Stay Loose/Morning Glory	1986	—	—	3.00
28655	Anything for Love/Let It Ride	1986	—	—	3.00
28655 [PS]	Anything for Love/Let It Ride	1986	—	2.00	4.00
29466	Someone to Believe In/Without You	1983	—	2.00	4.00
29511	Knotty Pine/Salute	1983	—	2.00	4.00
29859	Shadows/In My Fashion	1982	—	2.00	4.00
29963	Blackberry Wine/(B-side unknown)	1982	—	2.00	4.00
49230	Dream Street Rose/Make Way for the Lady	1980	—	2.00	4.00
49516	If You Need Me/Mister Rock of Ages	1980	—	2.00	4.00
50012	Baby Step Back/Thank You for the Promises	1982	—	2.00	4.00

Number	Title (A Side/B Side)	Yr	VG	VG+	NM
Albums					
LIBERTY					
LN-10038	The Best of Lightfoot	198?	2.00	4.00	8.00
—Budget-line reissue					
LN-10039	Sunday Concert	198?	2.00	4.00	8.00
—Budget-line reissue					
LN-10040	Back Here on Earth	198?	2.00	4.00	8.00
—Budget-line reissue					
LN-10041	Did She Mention My Name	198?	2.00	4.00	8.00
—Budget-line reissue					
LN-10043	The Way I Feel	198?	2.00	4.00	8.00
—Budget-line reissue					
LN-10044	Lightfoot	198?	2.00	4.00	8.00
—Budget-line reissue					
MOBILE FIDELITY					
1-018	Sundown	1979	10.00	20.00	40.00
—Audiophile vinyl					
PAIR					
PDL2-1081 [(2)]	Songbook	1986	3.00	6.00	12.00
REPRISE					
MS 2037	Summer Side of Life	1971	3.00	6.00	12.00
MS 2056	Don Quixote	1972	3.00	6.00	12.00
MS 2116	Old Dan's Records	1972	3.00	6.00	12.00
MS 2177	Sundown	1974	3.00	6.00	12.00
MS 2206	Cold on the Shoulder	1975	3.00	6.00	12.00
2RS 2237 [(2)]	Gord's Gold	1975	3.75	7.50	15.00
MS 2246	Summertime Dream	1976	3.00	6.00	12.00
RS 6392	Sit Down Young Stranger	1970	3.75	7.50	15.00
RS 6392	If You Could Read My Mind	1971	2.50	5.00	10.00
—Retitled version					
ST-93228	Sit Down Young Stranger	1970	5.00	10.00	20.00
—Capitol Record Club edition					
UNITED ARTISTS					
UA-LA243-G	The Very Best of Gordon Lightfoot	1974	3.00	6.00	12.00
UAL 3487 [M]	Lightfoot	1966	5.00	10.00	20.00
UAL-3587 [M]	The Way I Feel	1967	5.00	10.00	20.00
UAS-5510	Classic Lightfoot (The Best of Lightfoot/Volume 2)	1971	3.75	7.50	15.00
UAS-6487 [S]	Lightfoot	1966	6.25	12.50	25.00
UAS-6587 [S]	The Way I Feel	1967	6.25	12.50	25.00
UAS-6649	Did She Mention My Name	1968	5.00	10.00	20.00
UAS-6672	Back Here on Earth	1969	5.00	10.00	20.00
UAS-6714	Sunday Concert	1969	3.75	7.50	15.00
UAS-6754	The Best of Lightfoot	1970	3.75	7.50	15.00
WARNER BROS.					
BSK 3149	Endless Wire	1978	2.50	5.00	10.00
HS 3426	Dream Street Rose	1980	2.50	5.00	10.00
BSK 3633	Shadows	1982	2.50	5.00	10.00
23901	Salute	1983	2.50	5.00	10.00
25482	East of Midnight	1986	2.50	5.00	10.00
25784	Gord's Gold, Volume II	1989	3.00	6.00	12.00

LIGHTFOOT, PAPA

Number	Title (A Side/B Side)	Yr	VG	VG+	NM
45s					
ALADDIN					
3171	After a While (Blue Lights)/P.L.'s Blues	1953	50.00	100.00	200.00
3304	Blue Lights/Jumpin' with Jarvis	1955	37.50	75.00	150.00
IMPERIAL					
5289	Wine, Women, Whiskey/Mean Old Train	1954	37.50	75.00	150.00
SAVOY					
1161	Mean Old Train/Wild Fire	1955	7.50	15.00	30.00
Albums					
VAULT					
130	Natchez Trace	1969	3.75	7.50	15.00
—As "Papa George Lightfoot"					

LIGHTHOUSE

Number	Title (A Side/B Side)	Yr	VG	VG+	NM
45s					
EVOLUTION					
1041	Hats Off/Sing, Sing, Sing	1971	—	2.50	5.00
1048	One Fine Morning/Little Kind Words	1971	—	3.00	6.00
1052	Take It Slow (Out in the Country)/Sweet Lullaby	1971	—	2.50	5.00
1058	I Just Wanna Be Your Friend/1849	1972	—	2.50	5.00
1061	I'd Be So Happy/Old Man	1972	—	2.50	5.00
1069	Sunny Days/Lonely Places	1972	—	2.50	5.00
1072	You Girl/Merlin	1972	—	2.50	5.00
1076	Broken Guitar Blues/Merlin	1973	—	2.50	5.00
POLYDOR					
14197	Can You Feel It/Bright Side	1973	—	2.00	4.00
14198	Pretty Lady/Bright Side	1973	—	2.00	4.00
14220	Magic's in the Dancing/Disagreeable man	1974	—	2.00	4.00
14246	Good Day/Going Downtown	1974	—	2.00	4.00
RCA VICTOR					
47-9808	The Chant (Nam-Myo-Ho Renge Kyo)/Could You Be Concerned	1969	—	3.00	6.00
74-0224	Eight Miles High/If There Ever Was a Time	1969	—	3.00	6.00
74-0285	Feel So Good/Places on Faces Four Blue Carpet Traces	1969	—	3.00	6.00
Albums					
EVOLUTION					
3007	One Fine Morning	1971	3.75	7.50	15.00
3010	Thoughts of Movin' On	1972	3.75	7.50	15.00
3014 [(2)]	Lighthouse Live!	1972	5.00	10.00	20.00
3016	Sunny Days	1973	3.75	7.50	15.00
JANUS					
JSX-7025	The Best of Lighthouse	1976	3.00	6.00	12.00
POLYDOR					
PD-5056	Can You Feel It	1973	3.00	6.00	12.00
PD-1-6028	Good Day	1974	3.00	6.00	12.00
RCA VICTOR					
LSP-4173	Lighthouse	1969	3.75	7.50	15.00
LSP-4241	Suite Feeling	1969	3.75	7.50	15.00
LSP-4325	Peacing It All Together	1970	3.75	7.50	15.00

LIGHTNIN' SLIM

Number	Title (A Side/B Side)	Yr	VG	VG+	NM
45s					
ACE					
505	Bad Feeling Blues/Lightning Slim Boogie	1955	37.50	75.00	150.00
EXCELLO					
2066	I Can't Be Successful/Lightnin' Blues	1955	10.00	20.00	40.00
2075	Sugar Plum/Just Made Twenty One	1956	7.50	15.00	30.00
2080	Goin' Home/Wonderin' and Goin'	1956	7.50	15.00	30.00
2096	Have Your Way/Bad Luck and Trouble	1956	7.50	15.00	30.00
2106	Mean Old Lonesome Train/I'm Grown	1957	7.50	15.00	30.00
2116	I'm a Rollin' Stone/Love Me Mama	1957	7.50	15.00	30.00
2131	Hoo-Doo Blues/It's Mighty Crazy	1958	7.50	15.00	30.00
2142	My Starter Won't Work/Long Leanie Mama	1958	7.50	15.00	30.00
2150	Feelin' Awful Blues/I'm Leavin' You Baby	1959	7.50	15.00	30.00
2160	Sweet Little Woman/Lightnin's Troubles	1959	7.50	15.00	30.00
2169	Rooster Blues/G.I. Slim	1959	7.50	15.00	30.00
2179	My Little Angel Child/Too Close Blues	1960	6.25	12.50	25.00
2186	Cool Down Baby/Nothin' But the Devil	1960	6.25	12.50	25.00
2195	Somebody Knockin'/I Just Don't Know	1961	6.25	12.50	25.00
2203	Hello Mary Lee/I'm Tired Waitin' Baby	1961	6.25	12.50	25.00
2215	Mind Your Own Business/You're Old Enough to Understand	1962	6.25	12.50	25.00
2224	Winter Time Blues/I'm Warnin' You Baby	1962	6.25	12.50	25.00
2228	If You Ever Need Me/I'm Evil	1963	6.25	12.50	25.00
2234	Loving Around the Clock/You Know You're So Fine	1963	6.25	12.50	25.00
2240	Blues at Night/Don't Mistreat Me Baby	1963	6.25	12.50	25.00
2245	You Give Me the Blues/Strangest Feelin'	1964	6.25	12.50	25.00
2252	Greyhound Blues/She's My Crazy Little Baby	1964	6.25	12.50	25.00
2258	Baby Please Come Back/You Move Me Baby	1964	6.25	12.50	25.00
2262	Have Mercy on Me Baby/I've Been a Fool for You Darlin'	1965	6.25	12.50	25.00
2267	Bad Luck Blues/Can't Live This Life No More	1965	6.25	12.50	25.00
2269	Don't Start Me Talkin'/Darlin' You're the One	1965	5.00	10.00	20.00
2272	I Hate to See You Leave/Love Is Just a Gamble	1965	5.00	10.00	20.00
2320	My Babe/Good Morning Heartaches	1971	2.50	5.00	10.00
FEATURE					
3006	Rock Me, Mama/Bad Luck	1954	75.00	150.00	300.00
3008	I Can't Live Happy/New Orleans Bound	1954	15.00	30.00	60.00
3012	Bugger Bugger Boy/Ethel Mae	1954	15.00	30.00	60.00
Albums					
EXCELLO					
LP 8000 [M]	Rooster Blues	1960	200.00	400.00	800.00
LPS 8000 [M]	Rooster Blues	196?	12.50	25.00	50.00
—Thogh labeled "Electronic Stereo," this record is mono					
LP 8004 [M]	Lightnin' Slim's Bell Ringer	1965	75.00	150.00	300.00
LPS 8004 [M]	Lightnin' Slim's Bell Ringer	196?	12.50	25.00	50.00
—Thogh labeled "Electronic Stereo," this record is mono					
LPS 8018	High and Low Down	1971	3.75	7.50	15.00
LPS 8023	London Gumbo	1972	3.75	7.50	15.00
INTERMEDIA					
QS-5062	That's All Right	198?	2.50	5.00	10.00

LIGHTNING

Number	Title (A Side/B Side)	Yr	VG	VG+	NM
45s					
P.I.P.					
8921	Hideaway/Freedom	1970	5.00	10.00	20.00
Albums					
P.I.P.					
6807	Lightning	1971	7.50	15.00	30.00

LIMELIGHTERS, THE

Number	Title (A Side/B Side)	Yr	VG	VG+	NM
45s					
JOSIE					
795	Cabin Hideaway/My Sweet Norma Lee	1956	37.50	75.00	150.00

LIMELITERS, THE

Also see GLENN YARBROUGH.

Number	Title (A Side/B Side)	Yr	VG	VG+	NM
45s					
RCA VICTOR					
47-7859	A Dollar Down/When Twice the Moon Has Come and Gone	1961	2.00	4.00	8.00
47-7859 [PS]	A Dollar Down/When Twice the Moon Has Come and Gone	1961	3.00	6.00	12.00
47-7913	Paco Peco/A Hundred Years Ago	1961	2.00	4.00	8.00
47-7942	Milk and Honey/Red Roses and White Wine	1961	2.00	4.00	8.00
47-7966	Jonah/Just an Honest Mistake	1961	2.00	4.00	8.00
47-8069	The Riddle Song/I Had a Mule	1962	2.00	4.00	8.00
47-8094	Who Will Buy/Funk	1962	2.00	4.00	8.00
47-8094 [PS]	Who Will Buy/Funk	1962	3.00	6.00	12.00
47-8255	Midnight Special/McClintock's Theme	1963	2.00	4.00	8.00
47-8361	No Man Is an Island/A Casinda Pequenina	1964	2.00	4.00	8.00
WARNER BROS.					
7254	Time to Gather Seed/The Importance of the Rose	1968	—	3.00	6.00
7-Inch Extended Plays					
RCA VICTOR					
VLP 2445 [PS]	(title unknown)	196?	5.00	10.00	20.00
VLP 2445 [S]	A Wayfaring Stranger/Charmin' Betsy/Gotta Travel On//(B-side unknown)	196?	5.00	10.00	20.00
Albums					
ELEKTRA					
EKM-180 [M]	The Limeliters	1960	5.00	10.00	20.00
EKS-7180 [S]	The Limeliters	1960	6.25	12.50	25.00
GNP CRESCENDO					
GNPS-2188	Alive! In Concert, Vol. 1	1986	2.50	5.00	10.00
GNPS-2190	Alive! In Concert, Vol. 2	1987	2.50	5.00	10.00
LEGACY					
113	Their First Historic Album	1970	3.00	6.00	12.00
RCA CAMDEN					
ACL1-602	This Train	1974	2.50	5.00	10.00

Number	Title (A Side/B Side)	Yr	VG	VG+	NM
RCA VICTOR					
LPM-2272 [M]	Tonight: In Person	1961	5.00	10.00	20.00
LSP-2272 [S]	Tonight: In Person	1961	6.25	12.50	25.00
ANL1-2336	Pure Gold	1977	2.00	4.00	8.00
LPM-2393 [M]	The Slightly Fabulous Limeliters	1961	5.00	10.00	20.00
LSP-2393 [S]	The Slightly Fabulous Limeliters	1961	6.25	12.50	25.00
LPM-2445 [M]	Sing Out!	1962	5.00	10.00	20.00
LSP-2445 [S]	Sing Out!	1962	6.25	12.50	25.00
LPM-2512 [M]	Through Children's Eyes	1962	5.00	10.00	20.00
LSP-2512 [S]	Through Children's Eyes	1962	6.25	12.50	25.00
LPM-2547 [M]	Folk Matinee	1962	5.00	10.00	20.00
LSP-2547 [S]	Folk Matinee	1962	6.25	12.50	25.00
LPM-2588 [M]	Makin' a Joyful Noise	1963	5.00	10.00	20.00
LSP-2588 [S]	Makin' a Joyful Noise	1963	6.25	12.50	25.00
LPM-2609 [M]	Our Men in San Francisco	1963	5.00	10.00	20.00
LSP-2609 [S]	Our Men in San Francisco	1963	6.25	12.50	25.00
LPM-2671 [M]	Fourteen 14K Folk Songs	1963	5.00	10.00	20.00
LSP-2671 [S]	Fourteen 14K Folk Songs	1963	6.25	12.50	25.00
LPM-2844 [M]	More of Everything!	1964	3.75	7.50	15.00
LSP-2844 [S]	More of Everything!	1964	5.00	10.00	20.00
LPM-2889 [M]	The Best of the Limeliters	1964	3.75	7.50	15.00
LSP-2889 [S]	The Best of the Limeliters	1964	5.00	10.00	20.00
LPM-2906 [M]	Leave It to the Limeliters	1964	3.75	7.50	15.00
LSP-2906 [S]	Leave It to the Limeliters	1964	5.00	10.00	20.00
LPM-2907 [M]	London Concert	1964	3.75	7.50	15.00
LSP-2907 [S]	London Concert	1964	5.00	10.00	20.00
LPM-3385 [M]	The Limeliters Look at Love... In Depth	1965	3.75	7.50	15.00
LSP-3385 [S]	The Limeliters Look at Love... In Depth	1965	5.00	10.00	20.00
LSP-4100	The Original "Those Were the Days"	1969	3.75	7.50	15.00
WEST KNOLL					
WK-1001	Alive! In Concert, Vol. 1	198?	2.50	5.00	10.00
WK-1002	Alive! In Concert, Vol. 2	198?	2.50	5.00	10.00

LIMEYS, THE

Number	Title (A Side/B Side)	Yr	VG	VG+	NM
45s					
DOT					
16725	Don't Cry/I Can't Find My Way Through	1965	3.75	7.50	15.00
SCEPTER					
12156	Come Back/Scraped: Green and Blue	1966	3.75	7.50	15.00

LIMOUSINE

Number	Title (A Side/B Side)	Yr	VG	VG+	NM
Albums					
GSF					
1002	Limousine	1972	5.00	10.00	20.00

LIND, BOB

Number	Title (A Side/B Side)	Yr	VG	VG+	NM
45s					
CAPITOL					
3169	Theme from the Music Box/She Can Get Along	1971	—	2.50	5.00
UNITED ARTISTS					
0032	Elusive Butterfly/Truly Julie's Blues	1973	—	2.00	4.00
—"Silver Spotlight Series" reissue					
VERVE FOLKWAYS					
5018	Wandering/Hey Nellie Hellie	1966	2.00	4.00	8.00
5029	Black Night/White Snow	1966	2.00	4.00	8.00
WORLD PACIFIC					
77808	Elusive Butterfly/Cheryl's Goin' Home	1965	2.50	5.00	10.00
77822	Remember the Rain/Truly Julie's Blues (I'll Be There)	1966	2.00	4.00	8.00
77830	We've Never Spoken/I Just Let It Take Me	1966	2.00	4.00	8.00
77839	San Francisco Woman/Baby Take Me Home	1966	2.00	4.00	8.00
77865	Good Time Special/Just My Love	1967	2.00	4.00	8.00
77879	Goodbye Neon Lies/We May Have Touched	1967	2.00	4.00	8.00
Albums					
CAPITOL					
ST-780	Since There Were Circles	1971	3.75	7.50	15.00
VERVE FOLKWAYS					
FT-3005 [M]	The Elusive Bob Lind	1966	6.25	12.50	25.00
FTS-3005 [S]	The Elusive Bob Lind	1966	7.50	15.00	30.00
WORLD PACIFIC					
WP-1841 [M]	Don't Be Concerned	1966	5.00	10.00	20.00
WP-1851 [M]	Photographs of Feeling	1966	5.00	10.00	20.00
ST-21841 [S]	Don't Be Concerned	1966	6.25	12.50	25.00
ST-21851 [S]	Photographs of Feeling	1966	6.25	12.50	25.00

LINDEN, KATHY

Number	Title (A Side/B Side)	Yr	VG	VG+	NM
45s					
CAPITOL					
4700	Remember Me (To Jimmy)/Beautiful Brown Eyes	1962	2.00	4.00	8.00
4770	Words/There'll Always Be Sadness	1962	2.00	4.00	8.00
4811	If You Really Love Me/Jimmy	1962	2.00	4.00	8.00
5018	People Say/There'll Always Be Sadness	1963	2.00	4.00	8.00
FELSTED					
8510	Billy/If I Could Hold You in My Arms	1958	3.75	7.50	15.00
8521	You'd Be Surprised/Why Oh Why	1958	3.75	7.50	15.00
8533	Oh Johnny Oh/Georgie	1958	3.75	7.50	15.00
8544	Kissin' Conversation/Just a Sandy Haired Boy Called Sandy	1958	3.75	7.50	15.00
8554	Somebody Loves You/You Walked Into My Life	1959	3.75	7.50	15.00
8571	Goodbye, Jimmy, Goodbye/Heartaches at Sweet Sixteen	1959	3.75	7.50	15.00
8587	You Don't Know Girls/So Close to My Heart	1959	3.00	6.00	12.00
8596	Think Love/Mary Lou Wilson and Johnny Brown	1959	3.00	6.00	12.00
MONUMENT					
420	Allentown Jail/That's What Love Is	1960	2.50	5.00	10.00
423	Midnight/The Willow Weeps	1960	2.50	5.00	10.00
428	Take Me Home (To My Lover)/We Had Words	1960	2.50	5.00	10.00
436	So in Love (With You)/Take Me Home, Jimmy	1961	2.50	5.00	10.00
Albums					
FELSTED					
7501 [M]	That Certain Boy	1959	15.00	30.00	60.00

LINDISFARNE

Number	Title (A Side/B Side)	Yr	VG	VG+	NM
45s					
ATCO					
7093	Run for Home/Stick Together	1978	—	2.00	4.00
7095	Warm Feeling/Woman	1979	—	2.00	4.00
ELEKTRA					
45733	We Can Swing Together/Float Me Down the River	1971	—	—	—
—Canceled					
45799	Lady Eleanor/Down	1972	—	3.00	6.00
45819	Don't Ask Him/All Fall Down	1972	—	2.50	5.00
45835	Court in the Act/Poor Old Ireland	1973	—	2.50	5.00
Albums					
ATCO					
SD 38-108	Back and Forth	1978	3.00	6.00	12.00
ELEKTRA					
7E-1018	Happy Daze	1975	3.00	6.00	12.00
EKS-74099	Nicely Out of Tune	1971	3.75	7.50	15.00
EKS-75021	Fog on the Tyne	1972	3.75	7.50	15.00
EKS-75043	Dingly Dell	1972	3.75	7.50	15.00
EKS-75077	Roll On, Ruby	1974	3.75	7.50	15.00

LINDSAY, MARK

Also see PAUL REVERE AND THE RAIDERS; THE UNKNOWNS.

Number	Title (A Side/B Side)	Yr	VG	VG+	NM
45s					
COLUMBIA					
10081	Mamacita/Song for a Friend	1974	—	2.50	5.00
10114	Photograph/Song for a Friend	1975	—	2.50	5.00
44875	The Old Man at the Fair/First Hymn from Grand Terrace	1969	—	3.00	6.00
45037	Arizona/Man from Houston	1969	—	3.00	6.00
45125	Miss America/Small Town Woman	1970	—	3.00	6.00
45180	Silver Bird/So Hard to Leave You	1970	—	3.00	6.00
45229	And the Grass Won't Pay No Mind/Funny How Little Men Care	1970	—	3.00	6.00
45286	Problem Child/Bookends	1970	—	3.00	6.00
45385	Been Too Long on the Road/All I Really See Is You	1971	—	2.50	5.00
45462	Are You Old Enough/Don't You Know	1971	—	2.50	5.00
45506	Pretty Pretty/Something Big	1971	—	2.50	5.00
45895	California/Someone's Been Hiding	1973	—	2.50	5.00
ELKA					
310	Sing Your Own Song/Sing Your Own Song (Theme)	1976	2.50	5.00	10.00
GREEDY					
106	Sing Your Own Song/Sing Your Own Song (Theme)	1976	—	3.00	6.00
WARNER BROS.					
8359	Sing Me High, Sing Me Low/Flips-Eyed	1977	—	2.00	4.00
8479	Little Ladies of the Night/Flips-Eyed	1977	—	2.00	4.00
Albums					
COLUMBIA					
CS 9986	Arizona	1970	3.75	7.50	15.00
—Red "360 Sound" label					
CS 9986	Arizona	1970	3.00	6.00	12.00
—Orange label					
C 30111	Silver Bird	1970	3.00	6.00	12.00
C 30735	You've Got a Friend	1971	3.00	6.00	12.00

LINK-EDDY COMBO

Number	Title (A Side/B Side)	Yr	VG	VG+	NM
45s					
REPRISE					
20002	Big Mr. C./The Man with the Golden Arm	1961	3.75	7.50	15.00
20008	Katrina/The Cat's Pajamas	1961	3.75	7.50	15.00

LINKLETTER, BOB

Number	Title (A Side/B Side)	Yr	VG	VG+	NM
45s					
CHATTAHOOCHIE					
702	The Out Crowd/Final Season	1965	5.00	10.00	20.00

LINKS, THE

Number	Title (A Side/B Side)	Yr	VG	VG+	NM
45s					
TEENAGE					
1009	Ba-Bee/She's the One	1958	250.00	500.00	1000.

LINN COUNTY

Number	Title (A Side/B Side)	Yr	VG	VG+	NM
45s					
MERCURY					
72852	Cave Song/Think	1968	2.00	4.00	8.00
72882	Fast Days/Lower Lemons	1969	2.00	4.00	8.00
72907	The Girl Can't Help It/Fever Shot	1969	2.00	4.00	8.00
PHILIPS					
40644	Let the Music Begin/Wine Take Me Away	1969	2.00	4.00	8.00
Albums					
MERCURY					
SR-61181	Proud Flesh Soothseer	1968	5.00	10.00	20.00
SR-61218	Fever Shot	1969	5.00	10.00	20.00
PHILIPS					
PHS 600326	Till the Break of Dawn	1970	3.75	7.50	15.00

LINNEAS, THE

Number	Title (A Side/B Side)	Yr	VG	VG+	NM
45s					
DIAMOND					
241	It's a Good Kind of Hurt/Forever Baby	1968	3.00	6.00	12.00
248	My Baby Comes Home Today/Born to Be Your Baby	1968	3.00	6.00	12.00

LIONS, THE

Number	Title (A Side/B Side)	Yr	VG	VG+	NM
45s					
EVEREST					
19388	No One But You/Giggles	1961	3.75	7.50	15.00

Number	Title (A Side/B Side)	Yr	VG	VG+	NM
IMPERIAL					
5678	Hickory Dickory/The Yodel	1960	3.75	7.50	15.00
RENDEZVOUS					
116	The Feast of the Beasts/Two-Timing Lovers	1960	3.75	7.50	15.00

LIPTON, PEGGY

45s

Number	Title (A Side/B Side)	Yr	VG	VG+	NM
ODE					
111	Let Me Pass By/Stoney End	1968	2.00	4.00	8.00
114	San Francisco Glide/Stoney End	1968	2.00	4.00	8.00
114 [PS]	San Francisco Glide/Stoney End	1968	3.00	6.00	12.00
118	Just a Little Lovin' (Early in the Morning)/Red Clay County Line	1969	2.00	4.00	8.00
124	Lu/Let Me Pass By	1969	2.00	4.00	8.00
124 [PS]	Lu/Let Me Pass By	1969	3.00	6.00	12.00
66001	Wear Your Love Like Heaven/Honey Won't Let Me	1970	—	3.00	6.00
66001 [PS]	Wear Your Love Like Heaven/Honey Won't Let Me	1970	3.00	6.00	12.00

Albums

Number	Title	Yr	VG	VG+	NM
ODE					
Z12 44006	Peggy Lipton	1968	6.25	12.50	25.00

LIQUID SMOKE

45s

Number	Title (A Side/B Side)	Yr	VG	VG+	NM
AVCO EMBASSY					
4522	I Who Have Nothing/Warm Touch	1970	2.00	4.00	8.00
4532	The Shelter of Your Arms/Let Me Down Easy	1970	2.00	4.00	8.00
4546	Hard to Handle/(B-side unknown)	1970	2.00	4.00	8.00
ROULETTE					
7166	Dance, Dance, Dance/Where's Our Love	1975	—	3.00	6.00

Albums

Number	Title	Yr	VG	VG+	NM
AVCO EMBASSY					
AVE-33005	Liquid Smoke	1970	6.25	12.50	25.00

LISTEN

With Robert Plant, later of LED ZEPPELIN.

45s

Number	Title (A Side/B Side)	Yr	VG	VG+	NM
COLUMBIA					
43967	You Better Run/Everybody's Gonna Say	1967	75.00	150.00	300.00
—Promotional copies go for about half these values					

LISTENING

45s

Number	Title (A Side/B Side)	Yr	VG	VG+	NM
VANGUARD					
35077	I Can Teach You/Cuando	1968	5.00	10.00	20.00
35094	Life Stories/Hello You	1968	5.00	10.00	20.00

Albums

Number	Title	Yr	VG	VG+	NM
VANGUARD					
VSD-6504	Listening	1968	15.00	30.00	60.00

LITTER

45s

Number	Title (A Side/B Side)	Yr	VG	VG+	NM
PROBE					
461	Silly People/Feeling	1968	6.25	12.50	25.00
467	Blue Ice/On Our Minds	1969	6.25	12.50	25.00
SCOTTY					
6710	Action Woman/A Legal Matter	1967	25.00	50.00	100.00
WARICK					
6711	Somebody Help Me/I'm a Man	1967	50.00	100.00	200.00
6712	Action Woman/Whatcha Gonna Do About It	1967	37.50	75.00	150.00

Albums

Number	Title	Yr	VG	VG+	NM
EVA					
12013	Rare Tracks	1983	3.75	7.50	15.00
HEXAGON					
681	$100 Fine	1968	100.00	200.00	400.00
PROBE					
4504	Emerge	1969	12.50	25.00	50.00
WARICK					
671	Distortions	1967	125.00	250.00	500.00

LITTLE ANTHONY AND THE IMPERIALS

45s

Number	Title (A Side/B Side)	Yr	VG	VG+	NM
APOLLO					
521	The Fires Burn No More/Lift Up Your Hands	1957	15.00	30.00	60.00
—As "The Chesters"					
AVCO					
4635	I'm Falling in Love with You/What Good Am I Without You	1974	—	2.50	5.00
4645	I Don't Have to Worry/Loneliest House on the Block	1974	—	2.50	5.00
4651	Hold On (Just a Little Bit Longer)/I've Got to Let You Go (Part 1)	1975	—	2.50	5.00
4655	I'll Be Loving You Sooner or Later/Young Girl	1975	—	2.50	5.00
DCP					
1104	I'm On the Outside (Looking In)/Please Go	1964	2.50	5.00	10.00
1119	Goin' Out of My Head/Make It Easy on Yourself	1964	2.50	5.00	10.00
1128	Hurt So Bad/Reputation	1965	2.50	5.00	10.00
1128 [PS]	Hurt So Bad/Reputation	1965	10.00	20.00	40.00
1136	Take Me Back/Our Song	1965	2.00	4.00	8.00
1149	I Miss You So/Get Out of My Life	1965	2.00	4.00	8.00
1154	Hurt/Never Again	1966	2.00	4.00	8.00
END					
1027	Tears on My Pillow/Two People in the World	1958	10.00	20.00	40.00
—As "The Imperials"					
1027	Tears on My Pillow/Two People in the World	1958	6.25	12.50	25.00
—As "Little Anthony and the Imperials"					
1036	So Much/Oh Yeah	1958	6.25	12.50	25.00
1038	The Diary/Cha Cha Henry	1959	6.25	12.50	25.00
1039	When You Wish Upon a Star/Wishful Thinking	1959	6.25	12.50	25.00
1047	A Prayer and a Juke Box/River Path	1959	6.25	12.50	25.00
1053	So Near and Yet So Far/I'm Alright	1959	6.25	12.50	25.00
1060	Shimmy, Shimmy, Ko-Ko Bop/I'm Still in Love with You	1959	7.50	15.00	30.00
1067	My Empty Room/Bayou, Bayou, Baby	1960	3.75	7.50	15.00
1074	I'm Taking a Vacation from Love/Only Sympathy	1960	3.75	7.50	15.00
1080	Limbo (Part 1)/Limbo (Part 2)	1960	3.75	7.50	15.00
1083	Formula of Love/Dream	1961	3.75	7.50	15.00
1086	Please Say You Want Me/So Near and Yet So Far	1961	3.75	7.50	15.00
1091	Traveling Stranger/Say Yea	1961	3.75	7.50	15.00
1104	Dream/A Lovely Way to Spend an Evening	1961	3.75	7.50	15.00
JANUS					
160	Father, Father/Each One, Teach One	1971	—	3.00	6.00
166	Madeline/Universe	1971	—	3.00	6.00
178	(Where Do I Begin) Love Story/There's an Island	1972	—	3.00	6.00
LIBERTY					
55119	The Glory of Love/C'mon Tiger (Gimme a Growl)	1958	7.50	15.00	30.00
—As "The Imperials"					
MCA					
41258	Daylight/Your Love	1980	—	2.00	4.00
—Little Anthony solo					
PCM					
202	This Time We're Winning/Your Love	1983	—	2.00	4.00
PURE GOLD					
101	Nothing from Nothing/Running with the Wrong Crowd	1976	—	2.50	5.00
ROULETTE					
4379	That Lil' Ole Lovemaker Me/It Just Ain't Fair	1961	3.00	6.00	12.00
—Little Anthony solo					
4477	Lonesome Romeo/I've Got a Lot to Offer Darling	1963	3.00	6.00	12.00
—Little Anthony solo					
UNITED ARTISTS					
0117	Goin' Out of My Head/I'm On the Outside (Looking In)	1973	—	2.00	4.00
—"Silver Spotlight Series" reissue					
0118	Hurt So Bad/Take Me Back	1973	—	2.00	4.00
—"Silver Spotlight Series" reissue					
50552	Out of Sight, Out of Mind/Summer's Comin'	1969	—	3.00	6.00
50598	The Ten Commandments of Love/Let the Sunshine In	1969	—	3.00	6.00
50625	It'll Never Be the Same Again/Don't Get Close	1970	—	3.00	6.00
50677	World of Darkness/The Change	1970	—	3.00	6.00
50720	Help Me Find a Way (To Say I Love You)/If I Love You	1970	—	3.00	6.00
VEEP					
1228	Better Use Your Head/The Wonder of It All	1966	2.00	4.00	8.00
1228 [PS]	Better Use Your Head/The Wonder of It All	1966	10.00	20.00	40.00
1233	You Better Take It Easy Baby/Gonna Fix You Good (Every Time You're Bad)	1966	2.00	4.00	8.00
1239	Tears on My Pillow/Who's Sorry Now	1966	—	3.00	6.00
1240	I'm On the Outside (Looking In)/Please Go	1966	—	3.00	6.00
1241	Goin' Out of My Head/Shing-a-Ling	1966	—	3.00	6.00
1242	Hurt So Bad/Reputation	1966	—	3.00	6.00
1243	Take Me Back/Our Song	1966	—	3.00	6.00
1244	I Miss You So/Get Out of My Life	1966	—	3.00	6.00
1245	Hurt/Never Again	1966	—	3.00	6.00
1248	It's Not the Same/Down on Love	1966	2.00	4.00	8.00
1255	Don't Tie Me Down/Where There's a Will There's a Way	1967	2.00	4.00	8.00
1262	Hold On to Someone/Lost in Love	1967	2.00	4.00	8.00
1269	You Only Live Twice/Hungry Heart	1967	2.00	4.00	8.00
1275	Beautiful People/If I Remember to Forget	1967	2.00	4.00	8.00
1278	I'm Hypnotized/Hungry Heart	1968	2.00	4.00	8.00
1283	What Greater Love/In the Back of My Heart	1968	2.00	4.00	8.00
1285	Yesterday Has Gone/My Love Is a Rainbow	1968	2.00	4.00	8.00
1293	The Flesh Failures (Let the Sunshine In)/Gentle Rain	1969	2.00	4.00	8.00
1303	Anthem (Revelation)/Goodbye Good Times	1969	2.00	4.00	8.00

7-Inch Extended Plays

Number	Title	Yr	VG	VG+	NM
END					
203	(contents unknown)	1959	50.00	100.00	200.00
203 [PS]	Little Anthony and the Imperials	1959	75.00	150.00	300.00
204	(contents unknown)	1959	50.00	100.00	200.00
204 [PS]	We Are Little Anthony and the Imperials	1959	75.00	150.00	300.00

Albums

Number	Title	Yr	VG	VG+	NM
ACCORD					
SN-7216	Tears on My Pillow	1983	2.50	5.00	10.00
AVCO					
AV-11012	On a New Street	1973	5.00	10.00	20.00
DCP					
DCL-3801 [M]	I'm On the Outside Looking In	1964	6.25	12.50	25.00
DCL-3808 [M]	Goin' Out of My Head	1965	6.25	12.50	25.00
DCL-3809 [M]	The Best of Little Anthony and the Imperials	1965	5.00	10.00	20.00
DCS-6801 [S]	I'm On the Outside Looking In	1964	7.50	15.00	30.00
DCS-6808 [S]	Goin' Out of My Head	1965	7.50	15.00	30.00
DCS-6809 [S]	The Best of Little Anthony and the Imperials	1965	6.25	12.50	25.00
END					
LP 303 [M]	We Are The Imperials Featuring Little Anthony	1959	62.50	125.00	250.00
LP 311 [M]	Shades of the 40's	1960	50.00	100.00	200.00
FORUM					
F-9107 [M]	Little Anthony and the Imperials' Greatest Hits	196?	3.75	7.50	15.00
FS-9107 [R]	Little Anthony and the Imperials' Greatest Hits	196?	3.00	6.00	12.00
LIBERTY					
LM-1017	Out of Sight, Out of Mind	1981	2.00	4.00	8.00
—Reissue of United Artists 1017					
LN-10133	The Best of Little Anthony and the Imperials	1981	2.00	4.00	8.00
—Budget-line reissue					
PICKWICK					
SPC-3029	The Hits of Little Anthony and the Imperials	196?	3.00	6.00	12.00
RHINO					
R1-70919	The Best of Little Anthony and the Imperials	1989	3.00	6.00	12.00
ROULETTE					
R-25294 [M]	Little Anthony and the Imperials' Greatest Hits	1965	6.25	12.50	25.00

Number	Title (A Side/B Side)	Yr	VG	VG+	NM
SR-25294 [R]	Little Anthony and the Imperials' Greatest Hits	1965	5.00	10.00	20.00
SR-42007	Forever Yours	1968	3.75	7.50	15.00
SONGBIRD					
3245	Daylight	1980	2.50	5.00	10.00
SUNSET					
SUS-5287	Little Anthony and the Imperials	1970	3.75	7.50	15.00
UNITED ARTISTS					
UA-LA026-G [(2)]	Legendary Masters Series	1972	6.25	12.50	25.00
UA-LA255-G	The Very Best of Little Anthony and the Imperials	1974	2.50	5.00	10.00
LM-1017	Out of Sight, Out of Mind	1980	2.50	5.00	10.00
—Reissue of United Artists 6720					
UAS 6720	Out of Sight, Out of Mind	1969	5.00	10.00	20.00
VEEP					
VP 13510 [M]	I'm On the Outside Looking In	1966	3.75	7.50	15.00
VP 13511 [M]	Goin' Out of My Head	1966	3.75	7.50	15.00
VP 13512 [M]	The Best of Little Anthony and the Imperials	1966	3.75	7.50	15.00
VP 13513 [M]	Payin' Our Dues	1966	3.75	7.50	15.00
VP 13514 [M]	Reflections	1967	3.75	7.50	15.00
VP 13516 [M]	Movie Grabbers	1967	3.75	7.50	15.00
VPS 16510 [S]	I'm On the Outside Looking In	1966	5.00	10.00	20.00
VPS 16511 [S]	Goin' Out of My Head	1966	5.00	10.00	20.00
VPS 16512 [S]	The Best of Little Anthony and the Imperials	1966	5.00	10.00	20.00
VPS 16513 [S]	Payin' Our Dues	1966	5.00	10.00	20.00
VPS 16514 [S]	Reflections	1967	5.00	10.00	20.00
VPS 16516 [S]	Movie Grabbers	1967	5.00	10.00	20.00
VPS 16519	The Best of Little Anthony, Volume 2	1968	3.75	7.50	15.00

LITTLE BILL AND THE BLUENOTES

Number	Title (A Side/B Side)	Yr	VG	VG+	NM
45s					
DOLTON					
4	I Love an Angel/Bye Bye Baby	1959	7.50	15.00	30.00
Albums					
CAMELOT					
102 [M]	The Fiesta Club Presents Little Bill and the Bluenotes	1960	100.00	200.00	400.00

LITTLE BILLY

Number	Title (A Side/B Side)	Yr	VG	VG+	NM
45s					
ABC-PARAMOUNT					
9896	I Found Me a Girl/Say It Like You Mean It	1958	3.75	7.50	15.00

LITTLE BOOKER

Number	Title (A Side/B Side)	Yr	VG	VG+	NM
45s					
ACE					
547	Open the Door/Teen-Age Rock	1958	6.25	12.50	25.00
IMPERIAL					
5293	Thinkin' 'Bout My Baby/Doing the Ham Bone	1954	25.00	50.00	100.00

LITTLE BOY BLUES

Number	Title (A Side/B Side)	Yr	VG	VG+	NM
45s					
FONTANA					
1623	It's Only You/Is Love?	1968	3.75	7.50	15.00
IRC					
6928	Look at the Sun/Love for a Day	1966	5.00	10.00	20.00
6936	I'm Ready/Little Boy Blues' Blues	1966	7.50	15.00	30.00
6939	I Can Only Give You Everything/You Don't Love Me	1966	7.50	15.00	30.00
Albums					
FONTANA					
SRF-67578	In the Woodland of Weir	1968	75.00	15.00	30.00

LITTLE BUBBER

Number	Title (A Side/B Side)	Yr	VG	VG+	NM
45s					
IMPERIAL					
5225	High Class Woman/Come Back Baby	1953	20.00	40.00	80.00
5238	Runnin' Around/Never Trust a Woman	1953	20.00	40.00	80.00

LITTLE CAESAR

Number	Title (A Side/B Side)	Yr	VG	VG+	NM
45s					
BIG TOWN					
106	Can't Stand It All Alone/Big Eyes	195?	15.00	30.00	60.00
110	What Kind of Fool Is He/Wonder Why I'm Leaving (Rat Song)	195?	15.00	30.00	60.00
RCA VICTOR					
47-7270	Who Slammed the Door/I'm Reachin'	1958	6.25	12.50	25.00
RECORDED IN HOLLYWOOD					
234	Long Time Baby/(Going Down to) The River	1952	15.00	30.00	60.00
235	Goodbye Baby/If I Could See My Baby	1952	15.00	30.00	60.00
236	Move Me/Lying Woman	1953	15.00	30.00	60.00
237	You're Part of Me/Here Is a Letter	1953	15.00	30.00	60.00
238	Do Right/Money Ain't Long Enough	1953	15.00	30.00	60.00
239	Atomic Love/You Can't Bring Me Down	1953	15.00	30.00	60.00
RPM					
393	Chains of Love Have Disappeared/Tried to Reason with You Baby	1953	15.00	30.00	60.00

LITTLE CAESAR AND THE CONSULS

Number	Title (A Side/B Side)	Yr	VG	VG+	NM
45s					
MALA					
512	(My Girl) Sloopy/Poison Ivy	1965	3.75	7.50	15.00
518	You've Really Got a Hold on Me/It's So Easy	1965	3.00	6.00	12.00
523	Hey Girl/You Laugh Too Much	1966	3.00	6.00	12.00

LITTLE CAESAR AND THE EMPIRE

Number	Title (A Side/B Side)	Yr	VG	VG+	NM
45s					
PARKWAY					
152	Everybody Dance Now/(Instrumental)	1967	6.25	12.50	25.00

LITTLE CAESAR AND THE ROMANS

Number	Title (A Side/B Side)	Yr	VG	VG+	NM
45s					
DEL-FI					
4158	Those Oldies But Goodies (Remind Me of You)/She Don't Wanna Dance	1961	7.50	15.00	30.00
4164	Hully Gully Again/Frankie and Johnny	1961	6.25	12.50	25.00
4166	Memories of Those Oldies But Goodies/Fever	1961	15.00	30.00	60.00
4170	Ten Commandments of Love/C.C. Rider	1961	12.50	25.00	50.00
4176	Popeye One More Time/Yoyo Yo Yoyo	1962	6.25	12.50	25.00
SCEPTER					
12237	Baby Love/When Will I Get Over You	1969	2.00	4.00	8.00
—As "Caesar and the Romans"					
12264	Jailhouse Rock/Leavin' My Past Behind	1969	2.00	4.00	8.00
—As "Caesar and the Romans"					
Albums					
DEL-FI					
DFLP-1218 [M]	Memories of Those Oldies But Goodies	1961	75.00	150.00	300.00

LITTLE CHARLES AND THE SIDEWINDERS

Number	Title (A Side/B Side)	Yr	VG	VG+	NM
45s					
DECCA					
31980	I'm Available/It's a Heartache	1966	10.00	20.00	40.00
32095	Talkin' About You, Babe/A Taste of the Good Life	1967	7.50	15.00	30.00
32233	The Loner (Part 1)/The Loner (Part 2)	1967	5.00	10.00	20.00
32321	Sweet Lorene/Twice as Much for My Baby	1968	5.00	10.00	20.00
JEWEL					
752	Give Me a Chance/Guess I'll Have to Take What's Left	1965	5.00	10.00	20.00

LITTLE CHERYL

Number	Title (A Side/B Side)	Yr	VG	VG+	NM
45s					
CAMEO					
270	Heaven Only Knows/Can't We Just Be Friends	1963	10.00	20.00	40.00
276	Mama Let the Phone Bell Ring/Can't We Just Be Friends	1963	3.00	6.00	12.00
292	Come On Home/I Love You Conrad	1964	3.00	6.00	12.00
307	Yeh Yeh We Love 'Em All/Nick and Joe Callin'	1964	4.00	8.00	16.00
REPRISE					
20109	Jim/Pocketful of Money	1962	3.75	7.50	15.00

LITTLE COOLBREEZERS, THE

See THE COOLBREEZERS.

LITTLE DIPPERS, THE

Also see ANITA KERR SINGERS.

Number	Title (A Side/B Side)	Yr	VG	VG+	NM
45s					
DOT					
16602	Sails/For Just a Little While Tonight	1964	2.00	4.00	8.00
UNIVERSITY					
210	Forever/Two by Four	1959	2.50	5.00	10.00
603	Tonight/Be Sincere	1960	2.50	5.00	10.00
608	Lonely/I Wonder, I Wonder, I Wonder	1960	2.50	5.00	10.00

LITTLE DOUG

See DOUG SAHM.

LITTLE ESTHER

See LITTLE ESTHER PHILLIPS.

LITTLE EVA

Number	Title (A Side/B Side)	Yr	VG	VG+	NM
45s					
AMY					
943	Stand By Me/That's My Man	1965	2.00	4.00	8.00
BELL					
45264	The Loco-Motion/Will You Love Me Tomorrow	1972	—	2.50	5.00
DIMENSION					
1000	The Loco-Motion/He Is the Boy	1962	5.00	10.00	20.00
1003	Keep Your Hands Off/Where Do I Go	1962	3.75	7.50	15.00
—Some copies have this shortened title					
1003	Keep Your Hands Off My Baby/Where Do I Go	1962	3.00	6.00	12.00
—Most copies have longer, and correct, title					
1006	Let's Turkey Trot/Down Home	1963	3.00	6.00	12.00
1011	Old Smokey Locomotion/Just a Little Girl	1963	3.00	6.00	12.00
1013	The Trouble with Boys/What I Gotta Do	1963	3.00	6.00	12.00
1019	Let's Start the Party Again/Please Hurt Me	1963	3.00	6.00	12.00
1021	The Christmas Song/I Wish You a Merry Christmas	1963	3.75	7.50	15.00
—With Big Dee Irwin					
1035	Makin' with the Magilla/Run to Her	1964	2.50	5.00	10.00
1035	Makin' with the Magilla/Conga	1964	2.50	5.00	10.00
1035 [PS]	Makin' with the Magilla/Run to Her	1964	10.00	20.00	40.00
1042	Wake Up John/Takin' Back What I Said	1964	2.50	5.00	10.00
SPRING					
101	Mama Said/Something About You Boy	1970	—	3.00	6.00
107	Night After Night/Something About You Boy	1970	—	3.00	6.00
VERVE					
10459	Bend It/Just One Word Isn't Enough	1966	2.00	4.00	8.00
10529	Everything Is Beautiful About You Boy/Take a Step in My Direction	1967	2.00	4.00	8.00
Albums					
DIMENSION					
DLP-6000 [M]	LLLLLoco-Motion	1962	37.50	75.00	150.00
—Without "Keep Your Hands Off My Baby"					
DLP-6000 [M]	LLLLLoco-Motion	1962	50.00	100.00	200.00
—With "Keep Your Hands Off My Baby"					
DLPS-6000 [R]	LLLLLoco-Motion	1962	37.50	75.00	150.00
—Without "Keep Your Hands Off My Baby"					
DLPS-6000 [R]	LLLLLoco-Motion	1962	50.00	100.00	200.00
—With "Keep Your Hands Off My Baby"					

LITTLE FEAT

45s

WARNER BROS.

Number	Title (A Side/B Side)	Yr	VG	VG+	NM
7431	Strawberry Flats/Hamburger Midnight	1970	2.00	4.00	8.00
7553	Easy to Slip/Cat Fever	1972	2.00	4.00	8.00
7689	Dixie Chicken/Lafayette Railroad	1973	—	3.00	6.00
8054	Oh Atlanta/Down the Road	1974	—	2.50	5.00
8174	Long Distance Love/Romance Dance	1975	—	2.50	5.00
8219	All That You Dream/One Love Stand	1976	—	2.50	5.00
8420	Time Loves a Hero/Sailin' Shoes	1977	—	2.50	5.00
8566	Oh Atlanta/Willin'	1978	—	2.50	5.00
27684	One Clear Moment/Changin' Luck	1988	—	—	3.00
27684 [PS]	One Clear Moment/Changin' Luck	1988	—	—	3.00
27728	Hate to Lose Your Lovin'/Cajun Girl	1988	—	—	3.00
27728 [PS]	Hate to Lose Your Lovin'/Cajun Girl	1988	—	—	3.00
49169	Wake Up Dreaming/Front Page News	1980	—	2.50	5.00
49801	Front Page News/Easy to Sleep	1981	—	2.50	5.00
49841	Strawberry Flats/Gringo	1981	—	2.50	5.00

Albums

MOBILE FIDELITY

Number	Title (A Side/B Side)	Yr	VG	VG+	NM
1-013 [(2)]	Waiting for Columbus	1979	20.00	40.00	80.00
—Audiophile vinyl					

NAUTILUS

Number	Title (A Side/B Side)	Yr	VG	VG+	NM
NR-24	Time Loves a Hero	198?	12.50	25.00	50.00
—Audiophile vinyl					

WARNER BROS.

Number	Title (A Side/B Side)	Yr	VG	VG+	NM
PRO-A-984 [DJ]	Hoy-Hoy!	1981	5.00	10.00	20.00
—Single-album sampler of 2-LP set					
WS 1890	Little Feat	1971	5.00	10.00	20.00
—Green "WB" label; with photo on back cover					
WS 1890	Little Feat	1971	3.75	7.50	15.00
—Green "WB" label; without photo on back cover					
WS 1890	Little Feat	1973	2.50	5.00	10.00
—"Burbank" palm trees label					
WS 1890	Little Feat	1979	2.00	4.00	8.00
—Tan or white label					
BS 2600	Sailin' Shoes	1972	3.75	7.50	15.00
—Green "WB" label					
BS 2600	Sailin' Shoes	1973	2.50	5.00	10.00
—"Burbank" palm trees label					
BS 2600	Sailin' Shoes	1979	2.00	4.00	8.00
—Tan or white label					
BS 2686	Dixie Chicken	1973	3.75	7.50	15.00
—"Burbank" palm trees label					
BS 2686	Dixie Chicken	1979	2.00	4.00	8.00
—Tan or white label					
BS 2748	Feats Don't Fail Me Now	1974	3.75	7.50	15.00
—"Burbank" palm trees label					
BS 2748	Feats Don't Fail Me Now	1979	2.00	4.00	8.00
—Tan or white label					
BS 2884	The Last Record Album	1975	3.75	7.50	15.00
—"Burbank" palm trees label					
BS 2884	The Last Record Album	1979	2.00	4.00	8.00
—Tan or white label					
BS 3015	Time Loves a Hero	1977	3.00	6.00	12.00
—"Burbank" palm trees label					
BS 3015	Time Loves a Hero	1979	2.00	4.00	8.00
—Tan or white label					
2WS 3140 [(2)]	Waiting for Columbus	1978	3.75	7.50	15.00
—"Burbank" palm trees label					
2WS 3140 [(2)]	Waiting for Columbus	1979	2.50	5.00	10.00
—Tan or white label					
HS 3345	Down on the Farm	1979	2.50	5.00	10.00
2BSK 3538 [(2)]	Hoy-Hoy!	1981	3.00	6.00	12.00
25750	Let It Roll	1988	2.50	5.00	10.00
26263	Representing the Mambo	1990	3.75	7.50	15.00

ZOO/CLASSIC

Number	Title (A Side/B Side)	Yr	VG	VG+	NM
11097 [(2)]	Ain't Had Enough Fun	1995	5.00	10.00	20.00
—180-gram vinyl					
11097 [(2)]	Ain't Had Enough Fun	1995	4.50	9.00	18.00
—150-gram vinyl					

LITTLE GUY AND THE GIANTS

45s

LAWN

Number	Title (A Side/B Side)	Yr	VG	VG+	NM
103	It's You/So Young	1960	50.00	100.00	200.00

LITTLE IKE

45s

CHAMPION

Number	Title (A Side/B Side)	Yr	VG	VG+	NM
1011	She Can Rock/Am I Losin' You	1959	25.00	50.00	100.00

LITTLE IVA AND HER BAND

45s

MIRACLE

Number	Title (A Side/B Side)	Yr	VG	VG+	NM
2	When I Needed You/Continental Strut	1960	500.00	1000.	1500.

LITTLE JOE

45s

BRUNSWICK

Number	Title (A Side/B Side)	Yr	VG	VG+	NM
55369	Holiday/Fool on the Hill	1968	2.00	4.00	8.00

Albums

BRUNSWICK

Number	Title (A Side/B Side)	Yr	VG	VG+	NM
BL 754135	Little Joe (Sure Can Sing)	1968	5.00	10.00	20.00

LITTLE JOE AND THE THRILLERS

45s

ENJOY

Number	Title (A Side/B Side)	Yr	VG	VG+	NM
2011	Peanuts and Popcorn/Chicken Little Boo Boo	1964	2.50	5.00	10.00

EPIC

Number	Title (A Side/B Side)	Yr	VG	VG+	NM
9293	Mine/It's Too Bad We Had to Say Goodbye	1958	3.75	7.50	15.00
9431	Run Little Girl/Public Opinion	1961	3.00	6.00	12.00

MGM

Number	Title (A Side/B Side)	Yr	VG	VG+	NM
14129	Somehow, Someway/Days 'Til Morning	1970	—	2.50	5.00
14230	People Show/Baby I Could Be So Good at Lovin' You	1971	—	2.50	5.00
14290	Don't Take the Rain Away/The Children	1971	—	2.50	5.00
14361	Shelly Made Me Smile/Words and Music	1972	—	2.50	5.00
14466	Baby I Could Be So Good at Lovin' You/Cherry Pink and Apple Blossom White	1972	—	2.50	5.00
14662	Folks Who Live on the Hill/Baby I Could Be So Good at Lovin' You	1973	—	2.50	5.00

OKEH

Number	Title (A Side/B Side)	Yr	VG	VG+	NM
7075	Let's Do the Slop/This I Know	1956	3.75	7.50	15.00
7088	Peanuts/Lilly Lou	1957	5.00	10.00	20.00
7094	Lonesome/The Echoes Keep Calling Me	1957	3.75	7.50	15.00
7099	Don't Leave Me Alone/What's Happened to Your Halo	1958	3.75	7.50	15.00
7107	Mine/It's Too Bad We Had to Say Goodbye	1958	3.75	7.50	15.00
7116	Cherry (Part 1)/Cherry (Part 2)	1959	3.00	6.00	12.00
7121	I'm Tryin'/Strange Dreams	1959	3.00	6.00	12.00
7127	Give Me All Your Love/I'll Never Let You Go	1959	3.00	6.00	12.00
7134	Ev'ry Now and Then/Goodnight, Little Girl	1960	3.00	6.00	12.00
7136	Stay/Please Don't Go	1960	3.00	6.00	12.00
7140	Run Little Girl/Public Opinion	1961	3.00	6.00	12.00

REPRISE

Number	Title (A Side/B Side)	Yr	VG	VG+	NM
20142	Peanuts/No, No, I Can't Stop	1963	2.50	5.00	10.00

7-Inch Extended Plays

EPIC

Number	Title (A Side/B Side)	Yr	VG	VG+	NM
EG-7198	(contents unknown)	1958	25.00	50.00	100.00
EG-7198 [PS]	Little Joe and the Thrillers	1958	25.00	50.00	100.00

LITTLE JOEY AND THE FLIPS

45s

JOY

Number	Title (A Side/B Side)	Yr	VG	VG+	NM
262	Bongo Stomp/Lost Love	1962	3.75	7.50	15.00
268	Bongo Gully/It Was Like Heaven	1962	3.00	6.00	12.00

LITTLE JUNIOR'S BLUE FLAMES

See JUNIOR PARKER.

LITTLE LADY BEATLES, THE

See THE INSECTS.

LITTLE MILTON

45s

BOBBIN

Number	Title (A Side/B Side)	Yr	VG	VG+	NM
101	I'm a Lonely Man/That Will Never Do	1958	6.25	12.50	25.00
103	Long Distance Operator/I Found Me a New Love	1959	6.25	12.50	25.00
112	Strange Dreams/I'm Tryin'	1959	6.25	12.50	25.00
117	Hold Me Tight/Same Old Blues	1959	6.25	12.50	25.00
120	Dead Love/My Baby Pleases Me	1960	6.25	12.50	25.00
125	Let It Be Known/Hey Girl	1960	6.25	12.50	25.00
128	I'm in Love/Cross My Heart	1961	6.25	12.50	25.00

CHECKER

Number	Title (A Side/B Side)	Yr	VG	VG+	NM
977	Saving My Love for You/Lonely No More	1961	3.75	7.50	15.00
994	So Mean to Me/I Need Somebody	1961	3.75	7.50	15.00
1012	Satisfied/Someone to Love	1962	3.75	7.50	15.00
1020	I Wonder Why/Losing Hand	1962	3.75	7.50	15.00
1048	She Put a Spell on Me/Never Too Old	1963	3.75	7.50	15.00
1063	Meddlin'/One of These Old Days	1963	3.75	7.50	15.00
1078	Sacrifice/What Kind of Love Is This	1964	3.75	7.50	15.00
1096	Blind Man/Blues in the Night	1964	3.75	7.50	15.00
1105	We're Gonna Make It/Can't Hold Back the Tears	1965	3.75	7.50	15.00
1113	Who's Cheating Who?/Ain't No Big Deal on You	1965	3.75	7.50	15.00
1118	Help Me Help You/Without My Sweet Baby	1965	3.75	7.50	15.00
1128	My Baby's Something Else/Your People	1965	3.75	7.50	15.00
1132	Sometimes/We Got the Winning Hand	1965	3.75	7.50	15.00
1138	I'm Mightry Grateful/When Does Heartache End	1966	3.75	7.50	15.00
1149	Man Loves Two/Believe in Me	1966	3.75	7.50	15.00
1162	Feel So Bad/You Colored My Blues Right	1966	5.00	10.00	20.00
1172	I'll Never Turn My Back on You/Don't Leave Her	1967	3.00	6.00	12.00
1178	I'm Shorty/Sitting Home Alone	1967	3.00	6.00	12.00
1186	A Whole Lot of Fun Before the Weekend Is Done/Real True Love	1967	3.00	6.00	12.00
1189	More and More/Cost of Living	1967	3.00	6.00	12.00
1194	I Know What I Want/You Mean Everything to Me	1968	3.00	6.00	12.00
1203	At the Dark End of the Street/I (Who Have Nothing)	1968	3.00	6.00	12.00
1208	Let Me Down Easy/Lonely Drifter	1968	3.00	6.00	12.00
1212	Grits Ain't Groceries (All Around the World)/I Can't Quit You Baby	1969	3.00	6.00	12.00
1217	Just a Little Bit/Spring	1969	3.00	6.00	12.00
1221	Poor Man/So Blue	1969	3.00	6.00	12.00
1225	Let's Get Together/I'll Always Love You	1969	3.00	6.00	12.00
1226	If Walls Could Talk/Loving You	1969	3.00	6.00	12.00
1227	Baby I Love You/Don't Talk Back	1970	3.00	6.00	12.00
1231	Somebody's Changin' My Sweet Baby's Mind/I'm Tired	1970	3.00	6.00	12.00
—As "Little Milton Campbell"					
1236	Many Rivers to Cross/Mother's Love	1970	3.00	6.00	12.00
1239	I Play Dirty/Nothing Beats a Failure	1971	2.00	4.00	8.00

GLADES

Number	Title (A Side/B Side)	Yr	VG	VG+	NM
1734	Friend of Mine/(Instrumental)	1976	—	2.50	5.00
1738	Baby It Ain't No Way/Bring It On Back	1976	—	2.50	5.00
1741	Just One Step/(Instrumental)	1977	—	2.50	5.00
1743	Loving You (Is the Best Thing to Happen to Me)/9:59 A.M.	1977	—	2.50	5.00
1747	Me for You, You for Me/My Thing Is You	1977	—	2.50	5.00

MALACO

Number	Title (A Side/B Side)	Yr	VG	VG+	NM
2104	The Blues Is All Right/Come Back Kind of Loving	1985	—	2.00	4.00
2108	Misty Blue/Catch You on the Way Down	1985	—	2.00	4.00
2123	Lonesome Christmas/Come To Me	1985	—	2.00	4.00
2127	I Will Survive/4:59 A.M.	1986	—	2.00	4.00
2134	Real Good Woman/Annie Mae's Café	198?	—	2.00	4.00
2147	His Old Lady and My Old Lady/(B-side unknown)	198?	—	2.00	4.00

Number	Title (A Side/B Side)	Yr	VG	VG+	NM
2162	Bad Dream/The Woman I Love	198?	—	2.00	4.00
MCA					
52184	Age Ain't Nothin' But a Number/(Instrumental)	1983	—	2.00	4.00
52254	Living on the Dark Side of Love/Why Are You So Hard to Please	1983	—	2.00	4.00
METEOR					
5040	Love at First Sight/Let's Boogie Baby	1957	50.00	100.00	200.00
5045	Let My Baby Be/Oh My Little Baby	1957	200.00	400.00	800.00
STAX					
0100	If That Ain't a Reason (For Your Woman to Leave You)/Mr. Mailman	1971	—	3.00	6.00
0111	That's What Love Will Make You Do/I'm Livin' Off the Love You Give	1972	—	3.00	6.00
0124	Walking the Back Streets and Crying/Before the Honeymoon	1972	—	3.00	6.00
0141	I'm Gonna Cry a River/What It Is	1972	—	3.00	6.00
0148	Lovin' Stick/Rainy Day	1972	—	3.00	6.00
0174	What It Is/Who Can Handle Me Is You	1973	—	3.00	6.00
0191	Tin Pan Alley/Sweet Woman of Mine	1974	—	3.00	6.00
0210	Behind Closed Doors/Bet You I Win	1974	—	3.00	6.00
0229	Let Me Back In/Let Your Loss Be Your Lesson	1974	—	3.00	6.00
0238	If You Talk in Your Sleep/Sweet Woman of Mine	1975	—	3.00	6.00
0252	How Could You Do It to Me/Packed Up and Took My Mind	1975	—	3.00	6.00
SUN					
194	Beggin' My Baby/Somebody Told Me	1954	75.00	150.00	300.00
200	If You Love Me/Alone and Blue	1954	150.00	300.00	600.00
220	Looking for My Baby/Lonesome for My Baby	1955	200.00	400.00	800.00

Albums

Number	Title (A Side/B Side)	Yr	VG	VG+	NM
CHECKER					
LP-2995 [M]	We're Gonna Make It	1965	25.00	50.00	100.00
—Black label					
LP-2995 [M]	We're Gonna Make It	1966	17.50	35.00	70.00
—Blue label with red and black checkers					
LP-2995 [M]	We're Gonna Make It	196?	6.25	12.50	25.00
—Blue, fading to white, label					
LP-3002 [M]	Little Milton Sings Big Blues	1966	12.50	25.00	50.00
LP-3011	Grits Ain't Groceries	1969	6.25	12.50	25.00
LP-3012	If Walls Could Talk	1970	6.25	12.50	25.00
CHESS					
204 [(2)]	Little Milton	1976	3.75	7.50	15.00
CH-9252	We're Gonna Make It	1986	2.50	5.00	10.00
—Reissue of Checker 2995					
CH-9265	Little Milton Sings Big Blues	1987	2.50	5.00	10.00
—Reissue of Checker 3002					
CH-9289	If Walls Could Talk	1989	2.50	5.00	10.00
—Reissue of Checker 3012					
CH-50013	Little Milton's Greatest Hits	1972	3.75	7.50	15.00
GLADES					
7508	Friend of Mine	1976	3.00	6.00	12.00
7511	Me for You, You for Me	1977	3.00	6.00	12.00
MALACO					
7419	Playin' for Keeps	198?	3.00	6.00	12.00
7427	I Will Survive	198?	3.00	6.00	12.00
7435	Annie Mae's Café	198?	3.00	6.00	12.00
7445	Movin' to the Country	198?	3.00	6.00	12.00
7448	Back to Back	198?	3.00	6.00	12.00
7453	Too Much Pain	198?	3.00	6.00	12.00
MCA					
5414	Age Ain't Nothin' But a Number	1983	2.50	5.00	10.00
ROUNDER					
SS-35	The Sun Masters	198?	3.00	6.00	12.00
STAX					
STS-3012	Waiting for Little Milton	1973	5.00	10.00	20.00
4117	Waiting for Little Milton	1978	3.00	6.00	12.00
—Reissue of 3012					
5514	Blues 'n' Soul	1974	5.00	10.00	20.00
MPS-8514	Walking the Back Streets	1981	2.50	5.00	10.00
MPS-8518	Blues 'n' Soul	1981	2.50	5.00	10.00
—Reissue of 5514					
MPS-8529	Grits Ain't Groceries	198?	2.50	5.00	10.00
—Reissue of Checker 3011					
MPS-8550	What It Is	198?	2.50	5.00	10.00

LITTLE MISS CORNSHUCKS

45s

Number	Title (A Side/B Side)	Yr	VG	VG+	NM
CHESS					
1785	No Teasing Around/It Do Me No Good	1961	3.75	7.50	15.00

Albums

Number	Title (A Side/B Side)	Yr	VG	VG+	NM
CHESS					
LP-1453 [M]	The Loneliest Gal in Town	1961	50.00	100.00	200.00

LITTLE OTIS

45s

Number	Title (A Side/B Side)	Yr	VG	VG+	NM
TAMLA					
54058	I Out-Duked the Duke/Baby I Need You	1962	7.50	15.00	30.00

LITTLE RICHARD

Also see THE DEUCES OF RHYTHM AND THE TEMPO TOPPERS; JIMI HENDRIX.

12-Inch Singles

Number	Title (A Side/B Side)	Yr	VG	VG+	NM
MCA					
L33-17101 [DJ]	Great Gosh A' Mighty! (same on both sides)	1986	2.00	4.00	8.00
SPECIALTY					
SPS 4000	Lucille/Heebie-Jeebies Love	198?	2.00	4.00	8.00
WTG					
08169	Twins (5 versions)	1988	—	3.00	6.00
—With Philip Bailey					

45s

Number	Title (A Side/B Side)	Yr	VG	VG+	NM
ATLANTIC					
2181	Crying in the Chapel/Hole in the Wall	1963	3.00	6.00	12.00
2192	It Is No Secret (What God Can Do)/Travelin' Shoes	1963	3.00	6.00	12.00
BELL					
45385	Good Golly Miss Molly/Good Golly Miss Molly (Part 2)	1973	—	2.50	5.00
BRUNSWICK					
55362	She's Together/Try Some of Mine	1968	2.00	4.00	8.00
55377	Stingy Jenny/Baby Don't You Tear My Clothes	1968	2.00	4.00	8.00
55386	Soul Train/Can I Count on You	1968	2.00	4.00	8.00
CORAL					
62366	Milky White Way/Need Him	1963	2.50	5.00	10.00
CRITIQUE					
99392	Happy Endings/California Girls	1987	—	—	3.00
—A-side: With the Beach Boys; B-side: The Beach Boys without Little Richard					
ELEKTRA					
69370	Tutti Frutti/Rave On	1988	—	—	3.00
—B-side by John Cougar Mellencamp					
69384	Tutti Frutti/Powerful Stuff	1988	—	—	3.00
—B-side by the Fabulous Thunderbirds					
69385	Tutti Frutti/Kokomo	1988	—	—	3.00
—B-side by the Beach Boys					
END					
1057	Troubles of the World/Save Me Lord	1959	3.75	7.50	15.00
1058	Milky White Way/I've Just Come From the Fountain	1959	3.75	7.50	15.00
GREEN MOUNTAIN					
413	In the Middle of the Night/Where Will I Find a Place to Sleep This Evening	1973	—	2.50	5.00
KENT					
4567	Mississippi/In the Name	1972	—	—	—
—Unreleased					
4568	Don't You Know I/In the Name	1972	—	2.50	5.00
MAINSTREAM					
5572	Try to Help Your Brother/Funk Proof	1975	—	2.50	5.00
MANTICORE					
7007	Call My Name/Steal Miss Liza (Miss Liza Jane)	1975	—	2.00	4.00
MCA					
52780	Great Gosh A-Mighty! (It's a Matter of Time)/The Ride	1986	—	—	3.00
—B-side by Charlie Midnight					
52780 [PS]	Great Gosh A-Mighty! (It's a Matter of Time)/The Ride	1986	—	—	3.00
MERCURY					
71884	He's Not Just a Soldier/Joy, Joy, Joy	1962	3.75	7.50	15.00
71911	Do You Care/Ride On King Jesus	1962	3.75	7.50	15.00
71965	Why Don't You Change Your Ways/He Got What He Wanted	1962	3.75	7.50	15.00
MODERN					
1018	Holy Mackeral/Baby, Don't You Want a Man Like Me	1966	3.00	6.00	12.00
1018 [PS]	Holy Mackeral/Baby, Don't You Want a Man Like Me	1966	5.00	10.00	20.00
1019	Do You Feel It (Part 1)/Do You Feel It (Part 2)	1966	3.00	6.00	12.00
1022	Directly from My Heart to You/I'm Back	1966	3.00	6.00	12.00
1030	Slippin' and Slidin'/Bring It Back Home to Me	1967	3.00	6.00	12.00
1043	Baby What You Want Me to Do (Part 1)/Baby What You Want Me to Do (Part 2)	1967	3.00	6.00	12.00
OKEH					
7251	Poor Dog (Who Can't Wag His Own Tail)/Well	1966	3.75	7.50	15.00
7251 [PS]	Poor Dog (Who Can't Wag His Own Tail)/Well	1966	6.25	12.50	25.00
7262	I Need Love/Commandments of Love	1966	3.00	6.00	12.00
7271	Hurry Sundown/I Don't Want to Discuss It	1967	3.00	6.00	12.00
7278	Don't Deceive Me (Please Don't Go)/Never Gonna Let You Go	1967	3.00	6.00	12.00
7286	Money/Little Bit of Something	1967	3.00	6.00	12.00
7325	Lucille/Whole Lotta Shakin' Goin' On	1969	2.50	5.00	10.00
PEACOCK					
1658	Little Richard's Boogie/Directly from My Heart to You	1956	37.50	75.00	150.00
1673	Maybe I'm Right/I Love My Baby	1957	20.00	40.00	80.00
RCA VICTOR					
47-4392	Taxi Blues/Every Hour	1951	225.00	450.00	900.00
47-4582	Get Rich Quick/Thinkin' 'Bout My Mother	1952	200.00	400.00	800.00
47-4772	Why Did You Leave Me?/Ain't Nothin' Happenin'	1952	200.00	400.00	800.00
47-5025	Please Have Mercy on Me/I Brought It All on Myself	1952	150.00	300.00	600.00
REPRISE					
0907	Freedom Blues/Dew Drop Inn	1970	2.50	5.00	10.00
0942	Greenwood Mississippi/I Saw Her Standing There	1970	2.50	5.00	10.00
1005	Shake a Hand (If You Can)/Somebody Saw You	1971	2.00	4.00	8.00
1043	Green Power/Dancing in the Street	1971	2.00	4.00	8.00
1062	Money Is/Money Runner	1972	2.00	4.00	8.00
—B-side by Quincy Jones					
1130	Mockingbird Sally/Nuki Suki	1972	2.00	4.00	8.00
SPECIALTY					
561	Tutti-Frutti/I'm Just a Lonely Guy	1955	12.50	25.00	50.00
572	Long Tall Sally/Slippin' and Slidin' (Peepin' and Hidin')	1956	10.00	20.00	40.00
579	Rip It Up/Ready Teddy	1956	10.00	20.00	40.00
584	Heebie-Jeebies/She's Got it	1956	10.00	20.00	40.00
591	The Girl Can't Help It/All Around the World	1956	10.00	20.00	40.00
598	Lucille/Send Me Some Lovin'	1957	10.00	20.00	40.00
606	Jenny, Jenny/Miss Ann	1957	10.00	20.00	40.00
606 [PS]	Jenny, Jenny/Miss Ann	1957	15.00	30.00	60.00
611	Keep a Knockin'/Can't Believe You Wanna Leave	1957	7.50	15.00	30.00
611 [PS]	Keep a Knockin'/Can't Believe You Wanna Leave	1957	15.00	30.00	60.00
624	Good Golly, Miss Molly/Hey-Hey-Hey-Hey!	1958	7.50	15.00	30.00
624 [PS]	Good Golly, Miss Molly/Hey-Hey-Hey-Hey!	1958	12.50	25.00	50.00
633	Ooh! My Soul/True, Fine Mama	1958	6.25	12.50	25.00
633 [PS]	Ooh! My Soul/True, Fine Mama	1958	12.50	25.00	50.00
645	Baby Face/I'll Never Let You Go	1958	6.25	12.50	25.00
652	She Knows How to Rock/Early One Morning	1958	6.25	12.50	25.00
660	By the Light of the Silvery Moon/Wonderin'	1959	6.25	12.50	25.00
664	Kansas City/Lonesome and Blue	1959	6.25	12.50	25.00

Number	Title (A Side/B Side)	Yr	VG	VG+	NM
670	Shake a Hand/All Night Long	1959	6.25	12.50	25.00
680	Whole Lotta Shakin' Goin' On/Maybe I'm Right	1959	6.25	12.50	25.00
681	I Got It/Baby	1960	6.25	12.50	25.00
686	The Most I Can Offer/Directly from My Heart	1964	3.75	7.50	15.00
692	Bama Lama Bama Loo/Annie's Back	1964	3.75	7.50	15.00
697	Keep a Knockin'/Bama Lama Bama Loo	1964	3.75	7.50	15.00
699	Poor Boy Paul/Wonderin'	1964	3.75	7.50	15.00
734	Chicken Little Baby/Oh Why	1974	—	3.00	6.00
VEE JAY					
612	Whole Lotta Shakin' Goin' On/Goodnight Irene	1964	2.50	5.00	10.00
625	Blueberry Hill/Cherry Red	1964	2.50	5.00	10.00
652	It Ain't Whatcha Do/Cross Over	1965	2.50	5.00	10.00
665	Without Love/Dance What You Wanna	1965	2.50	5.00	10.00
698	I Don't Know What You've Got But It's Got Me — Part I/I Don't Know What You've Got But It's Got Me — Part II	1965	2.50	5.00	10.00
WARNER BROS.					
28491	Big House Reunion/Somebody's Comin'	1987	—	2.00	4.00
WTG					
08492	Twins (Long)/Twins (Short)	1988	—	2.00	4.00
—With Philip Bailey					
7-Inch Extended Plays					
RCA CAMDEN					
CAE-416	Ain't Nothin' Happenin'/Why Did You Leave Me//Every Hour/I Brought It All on Myself	1955	37.50	75.00	150.00
CAE-416 [PS]	Little Richard	1955	37.50	75.00	150.00
CAE-446	Taxi Blues/Please Have Mercy on Me//Get Rich Quick/Thinkin' 'Bout My Mother	1956	25.00	50.00	100.00
CAE-446 [PS]	Little Richard Rocks	1956	25.00	50.00	100.00
SPECIALTY					
SEP-400	Long Tall Sally/Miss Ann//She's Got It/Can't Believe You Wanna Leave	1957	25.00	50.00	100.00
SEP-400 [PS]	Here's Little Richard	1957	25.00	50.00	100.00
SEP-401	Slippin' and Slidin'/Oh Why//Ready Teddy/Baby	1957	25.00	50.00	100.00
SEP-401 [PS]	Here's Little Richard	1957	25.00	50.00	100.00
SEP-402	Tutti-Frutti/True, Fine Mama//Rip It Up/Jenny, Jenny	1957	25.00	50.00	100.00
SEP-402 [PS]	Here's Little Richard	1957	25.00	50.00	100.00
SEP-403	(contents unknown)	1958	20.00	40.00	80.00
SEP-403 [PS]	Little Richard	1958	20.00	40.00	80.00
SEP-404	Ooh! My Soul/All Around the World//Good Golly, Miss Molly/Babyface	1958	20.00	40.00	80.00
SEP-404 [PS]	Little Richard	1958	20.00	40.00	80.00
SEP-405	(contents unknown)	1958	20.00	40.00	80.00
SEP-405 [PS]	Little Richard	1958	20.00	40.00	80.00
Albums					
20TH FOX					
FXG-5010 [M]	Little Richard Sings Gospel	1959	25.00	50.00	100.00
SGM-5010 [S]	Little Richard Sings Gospel	1959	37.50	75.00	150.00
ACCORD					
SN-7123	Tutti Frutti	1981	2.50	5.00	10.00
AUDIO ENCORES					
1002	Little Richard	1980	6.25	12.50	25.00
BUDDAH					
BDS-7501	Little Richard	1969	7.50	15.00	30.00
CORAL					
CRL 57446 [M]	Coming Home	1963	10.00	20.00	40.00
CRL 757446 [S]	Coming Home	1963	12.50	25.00	50.00
CROWN					
CLP-5362 [M]	Little Richard Sings Freedom Songs	1963	5.00	10.00	20.00
CUSTOM					
2061 [M]	Little Richard Sings Spirituals	196?	3.00	6.00	12.00
EPIC					
EG 30428 [(2)]	Cast a Long Shadow	1971	5.00	10.00	20.00
PE 40389	Little Richard's Greatest Hits	1986	2.50	5.00	10.00
PE 40390	The Explosive Little Richard	1986	2.50	5.00	10.00
EXACT					
206	The Best of Little Richard	1980	2.50	5.00	10.00
GNP CRESCENDO					
GNP-9033	The Big Hits	1974	3.00	6.00	12.00
GRT					
2103	The Original Little Richard	1977	2.50	5.00	10.00
GUEST STAR					
GS-1429 [M]	Little Richard with Sister Rosetta Tharpe	196?	3.00	6.00	12.00
GSS-1429 [R]	Little Richard with Sister Rosetta Tharpe	196?	3.00	6.00	12.00
KAMA SUTRA					
KSBS-2023	Little Richard	1970	6.25	12.50	25.00
MERCURY					
MG-20656 [M]	It's Real	1961	12.50	25.00	50.00
SR-60656 [S]	It's Real	1961	15.00	30.00	60.00
MODERN					
100 [M]	His Greatest Hits/Recorded Live	1966	5.00	10.00	20.00
103 [M]	The Explosive Little Richard	1966	5.00	10.00	20.00
1000 [S]	His Greatest Hits/Recorded Live	1966	6.25	12.50	25.00
1003 [S]	The Explosive Little Richard	1966	6.25	12.50	25.00
OKEH					
OKM 12117 [M]	The Explosive Little Richard	1967	6.25	12.50	25.00
OKM 12121 [M]	Little Richard's Greatest Hits	1967	6.25	12.50	25.00
OKS 14117 [S]	The Explosive Little Richard	1967	5.00	10.00	20.00
OKS 14121 [S]	Little Richard's Greatest Hits	1967	5.00	10.00	20.00
PICKWICK					
SPC-3258	King of the Gospel Singers	197?	2.50	5.00	10.00
RCA CAMDEN					
CAL-420 [M]	Little Richard	1956	50.00	100.00	200.00
CAS-2430	Every Hour with Little Richard	1970	3.00	6.00	12.00
REPRISE					
MS 2107	The Second Coming	1973	5.00	10.00	20.00
RS 6406	The Rill Thing	1971	5.00	10.00	20.00
RS 6462	King of Rock and Roll	1972	5.00	10.00	20.00
RHINO					
R1-70236	Shut Up! A Collection of Rare Tracks, 1951-1964	1988	3.00	6.00	12.00

Number	Title (A Side/B Side)	Yr	VG	VG+	NM
SCEPTER					
CTN-18020	The Best of Little Richard	1972	3.00	6.00	12.00
SPECIALTY					
100 [M]	Here's Little Richard	1957	175.00	350.00	700.00
SP-2100 [M]	Here's Little Richard	1957	50.00	100.00	200.00
—Thick vinyl					
SP-2103 [M]	Little Richard	1958	37.50	75.00	150.00
—Front cover photo occupies the entire cover					
SP-2103 [M]	Little Richard	196?	25.00	50.00	100.00
—Front cover photo partially obscured by a black triangle at uper right; thick vinyl					
SP-2103 [M]	Little Richard	197?	5.00	10.00	20.00
—Reissue with thinner vinyl					
SP-2104 [M]	The Fabulous Little Richard	1958	37.50	75.00	150.00
—Thick vinyl					
SP-2104 [M]	The Fabulous Little Richard	197?	5.00	10.00	20.00
—Reissue with thinner vinyl					
SP-2111	Little Richard — His Biggest Hits	1963	12.50	25.00	50.00
—Thick vinyl					
SP-2111 [M]	Little Richard — His Biggest Hits	197?	5.00	10.00	20.00
—Reissue with thinner vinyl					
SP-2113	Little Richard's Grooviest 17 Original Hits	1968	6.25	12.50	25.00
—Thick vinyl					
SP-2136	Well Alright!	1970	5.00	10.00	20.00
SP-8508 [(5)]	The Specialty Sessions	1989	10.00	20.00	40.00
SPIN-O-RAMA					
119 [M]	Clap Your Hands	196?	3.00	6.00	12.00
TRIP					
8013 [(2)]	Greatest Hits	1972	3.00	6.00	12.00
UNITED					
US-7775	His Greatest Hits/Recorded Live	197?	2.50	5.00	10.00
US-7777	The Wild and Frantic Little Richard	197?	2.50	5.00	10.00
UNITED ARTISTS					
UA-LA497-E	The Very Best of Little Richard	1975	2.50	5.00	10.00
UPFRONT					
UPF-123	The Best of Little Richard	197?	2.50	5.00	10.00
UPF-197	Little Richard Sings Gospel	197?	2.50	5.00	10.00
VEE JAY					
LP-1107 [M]	Little Richard Is Back!	1964	12.50	25.00	50.00
LPS-1107 [S]	Little Richard Is Back!	1964	17.50	35.00	70.00
VJLP-1107	Little Richard's Back	198?	2.50	5.00	10.00
—Reissue with thin vinyl					
LP-1124 [M]	Little Richard's Greatest Hits	1965	6.25	12.50	25.00
LPS-1124 [S]	Little Richard's Greatest Hits	1965	10.00	20.00	40.00
VJLP-1124	Little Richard's Greatest Hits	198?	2.50	5.00	10.00
—Reissue with thin vinyl					
DY-7304	Talkin' 'Bout Soul	198?	3.00	6.00	12.00
VEE JAY/CHAMELEON					
D1-74797	Rip It Up	1989	3.00	6.00	12.00
WING					
MGW-12288 [M]	King of the Gospel Singers	1964	3.75	7.50	15.00
SRW-16288 [S]	King of the Gospel Singers	1964	5.00	10.00	20.00

LITTLE SAMMY AND THE TONES

Number	Title (A Side/B Side)	Yr	VG	VG+	NM
45s					
JACLYN					
1761	Christine/Over the Rainbow	1962	12.50	25.00	50.00

LITTLE SYLVIA

See SYLVIA (1).

LITTLE TOMMY AND THE ELGINS

Number	Title (A Side/B Side)	Yr	VG	VG+	NM
45s					
ABC-PARAMOUNT					
10358	Never Love Again/I Walk On	1962	6.25	12.50	25.00
ELMAR					
1084	Never Love Again/I Walk On	1962	15.00	30.00	60.00

LITTLE WALTER

Number	Title (A Side/B Side)	Yr	VG	VG+	NM
45s					
CHANCE					
1116	That's All Right/Just Keep Loving Her	1952	1000.	2000.	3000.
—As "Little Walter J."					
CHECKER					
758	Juke/Can't Hold On Much Longer	1952	50.00	100.00	200.00
764	Mean Old World/Sad Hours	1952	30.00	60.00	120.00
767	Don't Have to Hunt No More/Tonight with a Fool	1953	20.00	40.00	80.00
770	Off the Wall/Tell Me Mama	1953	20.00	40.00	80.00
—Black vinyl					
770	Off the Wall/Tell Me Mama	1953	750.00	1500.	3000.
—Red vinyl					
780	Blues with a Feeling/Quarter to Twelve	1953	25.00	50.00	100.00
786	Lights Out/You're So Fine	1953	12.50	25.00	50.00
793	Oh Baby/Rocker	1954	10.00	20.00	40.00
799	You'd Better Watch Yourself/Blue Light	1954	10.00	20.00	40.00
—Black vinyl					
799	You'd Better Watch Yourself/Blue Light	1954	25.00	50.00	100.00
—Red vinyl					
805	Last Night/Mellow Down Easy	1954	15.00	30.00	60.00
811	My Babe/Thunder Bird	1955	10.00	20.00	40.00
817	Roller Coaster/I Got to Go	1955	10.00	20.00	40.00
825	Too Late/I Hate to See You Go	1955	10.00	20.00	40.00
833	Who/It Ain't Right	1956	10.00	20.00	40.00
838	Flying Saucer/One More Chance with You	1956	10.00	20.00	40.00
845	Teenage Beat/What a Feeling	1956	10.00	20.00	40.00
852	It's Too Late Brother/Take Me Back	1957	10.00	20.00	40.00
859	Everybody Needs Somebody/Nobody But You	1957	10.00	20.00	40.00
867	Boom, Boom — Out Goes the Light/Temperature	1957	10.00	20.00	40.00
890	The Toddle/Confessin' the Blues	1958	7.50	15.00	30.00
904	Key to the Highway/Rock Bottom	1958	7.50	15.00	30.00
919	My Baby's Sweeter/Crazy Mixed-Up World	1959	6.25	12.50	25.00
930	Everything's Gonna Be All Right/Back Track	1959	6.25	12.50	25.00
938	Break It Up/Me and Piney Brown	1960	5.00	10.00	20.00
945	Ah'w Baby/I Had My Fun	1960	5.00	10.00	20.00

Number	Title (A Side/B Side)	Yr	VG	VG+	NM
955	My Babe/Blue Midnight	1960	5.00	10.00	20.00
968	I Don't Play/As Long As I Have You	1961	5.00	10.00	20.00
986	Crazy Legs/Crazy for My Baby	1961	5.00	10.00	20.00
1013	Just You Fool/I Got to Find My Baby	1962	3.75	7.50	15.00
1043	Up the Line/Southern Feeling	1963	3.75	7.50	15.00
1071	Diggin' My Potatoes/Snake Dancer	1964	3.75	7.50	15.00
1081	Dead Presidents/I'm a Business Man	1964	3.75	7.50	15.00
1117	Mean Ole Frisco/Blue and Lonesome	1965	3.75	7.50	15.00

Albums

CHECKER

Number	Title (A Side/B Side)	Yr	VG	VG+	NM
LP-1428 [M]	The Best of Little Walter	1957	125.00	250.00	500.00
—Black or maroon label					
LP-3004 [M]	The Best of Little Walter	1967	12.50	25.00	50.00
—Reissue of 1428					

CHESS

Number	Title (A Side/B Side)	Yr	VG	VG+	NM
2ACMB-202 [(2)]	Little Walter	1976	5.00	10.00	20.00
—Reissue of 60014					
CHV-416 [M]	Confessin' the Blues	1974	3.00	6.00	12.00
LP-1535 [M]	Hate to See You Go	1969	6.25	12.50	25.00
2CH-60014 [(2)]	Boss Blues Harmonica	1972	5.00	10.00	20.00

LITTLE WHEELS, THE

With RAY HILDEBRAND and JILL JACKSON, better known as PAUL AND PAULA.

45s

DOT

Number	Title (A Side/B Side)	Yr	VG	VG+	NM
16676	Four Wheeles, Ball Bearing Surfing Board/The Bumper	1964	7.50	15.00	30.00

LITTLEFIELD, LITTLE WILLIE

45s

BULLSEYE

Number	Title (A Side/B Side)	Yr	VG	VG+	NM
1005	Ruby-Ruby/Easy Go	1958	7.50	15.00	30.00

FEDERAL

Number	Title (A Side/B Side)	Yr	VG	VG+	NM
12101	Sticking on You Baby/Blood Is Redder Than Wine	1952	25.00	50.00	100.00
12110	K.C. Loving/Pleading at Midnight	1953	25.00	50.00	100.00
12137	The Midnight Hour Was Shining/My Best Wishes and Regards	1953	25.00	50.00	100.00
12148	Miss K.C.'s Fine/Rock-a-Bye Baby	1953	25.00	50.00	100.00
12163	Please Don't Go-o-o-o-oh/Don't Take My Heart Little Girl	1954	20.00	40.00	80.00
12174	Goofy Dust Blues/Falling Tears	1954	20.00	40.00	80.00
12221	Jim Wilson's Boogie/Sitting on the Curbstone	1955	15.00	30.00	60.00
12351	Kansas City/Midnight Hour Was Shining	1959	7.50	15.00	30.00

RHYTHM

Number	Title (A Side/B Side)	Yr	VG	VG+	NM
107	Baby Shame/Mistreated	1956	37.50	75.00	150.00
108	Ruby-Ruby/Easy Go	1956	37.50	75.00	150.00
115	I Need a Pay Day/I Want a Little Girl	195?	25.00	50.00	100.00
124	Theresa/The Day the Rains Came	195?	20.00	40.00	80.00
130	I Wanna Love You/Goodbye Baby	195?	20.00	40.00	80.00

LITTLES, HATTIE

45s

GORDY

Number	Title (A Side/B Side)	Yr	VG	VG+	NM
7004	Back in My Arms Again/(B-side unknown)	1962	200.00	400.00	800.00
7007	Here You Come/Your Love Is Wonderful	1962	20.00	40.00	80.00

LITTLETON, JOHN, AND THE CAPISTRANOS

45s

DUKE

Number	Title (A Side/B Side)	Yr	VG	VG+	NM
179	Po Mary/Now Darling	1959	20.00	40.00	80.00

LIVELY ONES, THE

45s

DEL-FI

Number	Title (A Side/B Side)	Yr	VG	VG+	NM
4184	Guitarget/Crying Guitar	1962	7.50	15.00	30.00
4189	Misirlou/Blue Tears	1962	7.50	15.00	30.00
4189	Misirlou/Livin'	1962	7.50	15.00	30.00
4196	Surf Rider/Surfer's Lament	1963	7.50	15.00	30.00
4205	Surfer Boogie/Ric-a-Tic	1963	6.25	12.50	25.00
4210	High Tide/Goofy Foot	1963	6.25	12.50	25.00
4217	Surf City/Telstar Surf	1963	6.25	12.50	25.00

MGM

Number	Title (A Side/B Side)	Yr	VG	VG+	NM
13691	Bugalu Movement/Take It While You Can	1967	3.75	7.50	15.00

SMASH

Number	Title (A Side/B Side)	Yr	VG	VG+	NM
1880	Night and Day/Hey Scrounge	1964	6.25	12.50	25.00

Albums

DEL-FI

Number	Title (A Side/B Side)	Yr	VG	VG+	NM
DFLP-1226 [M]	Surf Rider	1963	25.00	50.00	100.00
DFST-1226 [S]	Surf Rider	1963	37.50	75.00	150.00
DFLP-1231 [M]	Surf Drums	1963	12.50	25.00	50.00
DFST-1231 [S]	Surf Drums	1963	17.50	35.00	70.00
DLF 1231	Surf Drums	1997	3.00	6.00	12.00
DFLP-1237 [M]	Surf City	1963	10.00	20.00	40.00
DFST-1237 [S]	Surf City	1963	12.50	25.00	50.00
DLF 1237	Surf City	1997	3.00	6.00	12.00
DFLP-1240 [M]	Surfin' South of the Border	1964	10.00	20.00	40.00
DFST-1240 [S]	Surfin' South of the Border	1964	12.50	25.00	50.00

MGM

Number	Title (A Side/B Side)	Yr	VG	VG+	NM
E-4449 [M]	Bugalu Party	1967	5.00	10.00	20.00
SE-4449 [S]	Bugalu Party	1967	6.25	12.50	25.00

LIVERBIRDS, THE

45s

PHILIPS

Number	Title (A Side/B Side)	Yr	VG	VG+	NM
40276	Shop Around/It's Got to Be You	1965	2.50	5.00	10.00
40288	Why Do You Hang Around Me/Diddley Daddy	1965	2.50	5.00	10.00

LIVERPOOL BEATS, THE

Albums

RONDO

Number	Title (A Side/B Side)	Yr	VG	VG+	NM
2026 [M]	The New Merseyside Sound	1964	7.50	15.00	30.00

LIVERPOOL SPINNERS, THE

British group; because of its existence, the R&B group The Spinners was called the "Motown Spinners" or the "Detroit Spinners" in the U.K. So in the U.S. we added "Liverpool" to this group's name for the same reason.

45s

FONTANA

Number	Title (A Side/B Side)	Yr	VG	VG+	NM
1574	Seth Davey/All For Me Grog	1967	2.50	5.00	10.00

LIVERPOOLS, THE

Albums

WYNCOTE

Number	Title (A Side/B Side)	Yr	VG	VG+	NM
SW-9001 [S]	Beatle Mania! In the U.S.A.	1964	6.25	12.50	25.00
W-9001 [M]	Beatle Mania! In the U.S.A.	1964	5.00	10.00	20.00
SW-9061 [S]	The Hit Sounds from England	1964	5.00	10.00	20.00
W-9061 [M]	The Hit Sounds from England	1964	3.75	7.50	15.00

LIVERS, THE

45s

CONSTELLATION

Number	Title (A Side/B Side)	Yr	VG	VG+	NM
118	Beatle Time/This Is the Night	1964	3.75	7.50	15.00

LIVIN' BLUES

Albums

DWARF

Number	Title (A Side/B Side)	Yr	VG	VG+	NM
2003	Dutch Treat	1971	7.50	15.00	30.00

LLOYD, CHARLES

45s

ATLANTIC

Number	Title (A Side/B Side)	Yr	VG	VG+	NM
2435	Love-In/Sunday Morning	1967	2.00	4.00	8.00
5071	Sombrero Sam (Part 1)/Sombrero Sam (Part 2)	1966	2.00	4.00	8.00
5078	Forest Flower Sunday (Part 1)/Forest Flower Sunday (Part 2)	1967	2.00	4.00	8.00

A&M

Number	Title (A Side/B Side)	Yr	VG	VG+	NM
1415	Seagull/TM	1973	—	2.50	5.00

COLUMBIA

Number	Title (A Side/B Side)	Yr	VG	VG+	NM
43290	She's a Woman/You Know	1965	2.50	5.00	10.00

KAPP

Number	Title (A Side/B Side)	Yr	VG	VG+	NM
2118	Moonman/I Don't Care What You Tell Me	1971	—	3.00	6.00

Albums

ATLANTIC

Number	Title (A Side/B Side)	Yr	VG	VG+	NM
1459 [M]	Dream Weaver	1966	3.75	7.50	15.00
SD 1459 [S]	Dream Weaver	1966	5.00	10.00	20.00
1473 [M]	Forest Flower	1967	3.75	7.50	15.00
SD 1473 [S]	Forest Flower	1967	5.00	10.00	20.00
1481 [M]	Love-In	1967	5.00	10.00	20.00
SD 1481 [S]	Love-In	1967	3.75	7.50	15.00
SD 1493	Journey Within	1968	3.75	7.50	15.00
SD 1500	Charles Lloyd in Europe	1969	3.75	7.50	15.00
SD 1519	Soundtrack	1970	3.75	7.50	15.00
SD 1556	The Best of Charles Lloyd	1970	3.75	7.50	15.00
SD 1571	Charles Lloyd in the Soviet Union	1971	3.75	7.50	15.00
SD 1586	Flowering of the Original	1972	3.00	6.00	12.00

A&M

Number	Title (A Side/B Side)	Yr	VG	VG+	NM
SP-3044	Waves	1973	3.00	6.00	12.00
SP-3046	Geeta	1973	3.00	6.00	12.00

BLUE NOTE

Number	Title (A Side/B Side)	Yr	VG	VG+	NM
BT-85104	A Night in Copenhagen	198?	2.50	5.00	10.00

COLUMBIA

Number	Title (A Side/B Side)	Yr	VG	VG+	NM
CL 2267 [M]	Discovery!	1965	6.25	12.50	25.00
CL 2412 [M]	Of Course, Of Course	1966	6.25	12.50	25.00
CS 9067 [S]	Discovery!	1965	7.50	15.00	30.00
CS 9212 [S]	Of Course, Of Course	1966	7.50	15.00	30.00
CS 9609	Nirvana	1968	6.25	12.50	25.00

ELEKTRA MUSICIAN

Number	Title (A Side/B Side)	Yr	VG	VG+	NM
60220	Montreux '82	1983	2.50	5.00	10.00

KAPP

Number	Title (A Side/B Side)	Yr	VG	VG+	NM
KS-3634	Moon Man	1971	3.00	6.00	12.00
KS-3647	Warm Waters	1971	3.00	6.00	12.00

PACIFIC ARTS

Number	Title (A Side/B Side)	Yr	VG	VG+	NM
7-123	Weavings	1978	3.00	6.00	12.00
7-139	Big Sur Tapestry	1979	3.00	6.00	12.00

LLOYD, DAVID

Albums

EPIC

Number	Title (A Side/B Side)	Yr	VG	VG+	NM
LN 24151 [M]	Confidential (Sounds for a Secret Agent)	1965	5.00	10.00	20.00
BN 26151 [S]	Confidential (Sounds for a Secret Agent)	1965	6.25	12.50	25.00

LLOYD, JIMMY

45s

ROULETTE

Number	Title (A Side/B Side)	Yr	VG	VG+	NM
4062	I Got a Rocket in My Pocket/You're Gone Baby	1958	25.00	50.00	100.00
7001	Where the Rio De Rosa Flows/The Beginning of the End	1957	15.00	30.00	60.00

LOAD OF MISCHIEF

45s

HOLIDAY INN

Number	Title (A Side/B Side)	Yr	VG	VG+	NM
2205	I'm a Lover/Back in My Arms Again	1967	5.00	10.00	20.00

SUN

Number	Title (A Side/B Side)	Yr	VG	VG+	NM
407	I'm a Lover/Back in My Arms Again	1967	20.00	40.00	80.00
—The last of the Sam Phillips Sun 45s					

LOBO

45s

ATLANTIC

Number	Title (A Side/B Side)	Yr	VG	VG+	NM
3851 [DJ]	Caribbean Carnival (same on both sides)	1981	—	2.50	5.00
—May be promo only					

Number	Title (A Side/B Side)	Yr	VG	VG+	NM
BIG TREE					
112	Me and You and a Dog Named Boo/Walk Away from It All	1971	—	3.00	6.00
116	She Didn't Do Magic/I'm the Only One	1971	—	2.50	5.00
119	California Kid and Reemo/A Little Different	1971	—	2.50	5.00
134	The Albatross/We'll Make It, I Know We Will	1972	—	2.50	5.00
141	A Simple Man/Don't Expect Me to Be Your Friend	1972	—	2.50	5.00
147	I'd Love You to Want Me/Am I True to Myself	1972	—	2.50	5.00
158	Don't Expect Me to Be Your Friend/A Simple Man	1973	—	2.00	4.00
15001	Standing at the End of the Line/Stoney	1974	—	2.00	4.00
15008	Rings/I'm Just Dreaming	1974	—	2.00	4.00
16001	It Sure Took a Long, Long Time/Running Deer	1973	—	2.00	4.00
16004	How Can I Tell Her/Hope You're Proud of Me Girl	1973	—	2.00	4.00
16012	There Ain't No Way/Love Me for What I Am	1973	—	2.00	4.00
16033	Don't Tell Me Goodnight/My Mama Had Soul	1975	—	2.00	4.00
16040	Would I Still Have You/Morning Sun	1975	—	2.00	4.00
ELEKTRA					
47099	I Can't Believe You Anymore/Fight Fire with Fire	1980	—	2.00	4.00
EVERGREEN					
1028	Am I Going Crazy (Or Just Out of My Mind) /(B-side unknown)	1985	—	2.00	4.00
—Stock copies have corrected title					
1028 [DJ]	Am I Going Crazy (Or Just Out of Her Mind) (same on both sides)	1985	—	2.50	5.00
—Promo copies have incorrect title					
1033	Paint the Town Blue/(B-side unknown)	1985	—	2.00	4.00
—With Robin Lee					
LAURIE					
3526	Happy Days in New York City/My Friend Is Here	1969	3.75	7.50	15.00
—As "Kent LaVoie"					
LOBO					
I	I Don't Want to Want You/No One Will Ever Know	1981	—	2.00	4.00
IV	Come Looking for Me/(B-side unknown)	1982	—	2.00	4.00
X	Living My Life Without You/(B-side unknown)	1982	—	2.00	4.00
MCA					
41065	Where Were You When I Was Falling in Love/I Don't Wanna Make Love Anymore	1979	—	2.00	4.00
41152	Holdin' On for Dear Love/Gus, the Dancing Dog	1979	—	2.00	4.00
WARNER BROS.					
8493	Afterglow/Our Best Time	1977	—	2.00	4.00
8537	You Are All I'll Ever Need/Our Best Time	1978	—	2.00	4.00

Albums

Number	Title	Yr	VG	VG+	NM
BIG TREE					
2003	Introducing Lobo	1971	3.75	7.50	15.00
2013	Of a Simple Man	1972	3.75	7.50	15.00
2100	Introducing Lobo	1973	3.00	6.00	12.00
—Reissue of 2003 with new cover					
2101	Calumet	1973	3.75	7.50	15.00
BT 89501	Just a Singer	1974	3.00	6.00	12.00
BT 89505	A Cowboy Afraid of Horses	1975	3.00	6.00	12.00
BT 89513	The Best of Lobo	1976	3.00	6.00	12.00
MCA					
3194	Lobo	1979	2.50	5.00	10.00

LOCKETS, THE

45s

Number	Title	Yr	VG	VG+	NM
ARGO					
5455	Little Boy/Don'tcha Know	1963	3.00	6.00	12.00

LOCOMOTIONS, THE

45s

Number	Title	Yr	VG	VG+	NM
GONE					
5142	Little Eva/Adios My Love	1962	5.00	10.00	20.00
SWAN					
4237	Weekend Workout/Make It Saturday Night	1965	2.50	5.00	10.00

LODI

45s

Number	Title	Yr	VG	VG+	NM
MOWEST					
5003	Happiness/I Hope I See It in My Lifetime	1971	2.00	4.00	8.00

Albums

Number	Title	Yr	VG	VG+	NM
MOWEST					
MW 101L	Happiness	1972	6.25	12.50	25.00

LOE AND JOE

45s

Number	Title	Yr	VG	VG+	NM
HARVEY					
112	Little Ole Boy, Little Ole Girl/That's How I Am Without You	1962	7.50	15.00	30.00

LOFGREN, NILS

Also see GRIN. Also was a member of BRUCE SPRINGSTEEN's E Street Band in the 1980s.

12-Inch Singles

Number	Title	Yr	VG	VG+	NM
BACKSTREET					
L33-1127 [DJ]	Across the Tracks/Daddy Dream	1983	2.00	4.00	8.00
COLUMBIA					
CAS 2100 [DJ]	Secrets in the Street (same on both sides)	1985	—	3.00	6.00
CAS 2173 [DJ]	Delivery Night (same on both sides)	1985	—	3.00	6.00

45s

Number	Title	Yr	VG	VG+	NM
A&M					
1692	Back It Up/If I Say It, It's So	1975	—	2.50	5.00
1812	Cry Tough/Share a Little	1976	—	2.50	5.00
1839	It's Not a Crime/Share a Little	1976	—	2.50	5.00
1927	I Came to Dance/Code of the Road	1977	—	2.00	4.00
2173	Kool Skool/No Mercy	1979	—	2.00	4.00
BACKSTREET					
51191	Night Fades Away/Ancient History	1981	—	2.00	4.00
COLUMBIA					
05406	Secrets in the Street/From the Heart	1985	—	—	3.00
05598	Delivery Night/Flip Ya Flip	1985	—	—	3.00

Albums

Number	Title	Yr	VG	VG+	NM
A&M					
SP-3145	Cry Tough	198?	2.00	4.00	8.00
—Reissue of 4573					
SP-3201	The Best	1982	2.50	5.00	10.00
SP-3707 [(2)]	Night After Night	1977	3.00	6.00	12.00
SP-4509	Nils Lofgren	1975	2.50	5.00	10.00
SP-4573	Cry Tough	1976	2.50	5.00	10.00
SP-4628	I Came to Dance	1977	2.50	5.00	10.00
SP-4756	Nils	1979	2.50	5.00	10.00
SP-6509 [(2)]	Night After Night	198?	2.50	5.00	10.00
—Reissue of 3707					
SP-8362 [DJ]	Authorized Bootleg	1976	6.25	12.50	25.00
BACKSTREET					
5251	Night Fades Away	1981	2.50	5.00	10.00
5421	Wonderland	1983	2.50	5.00	10.00
COLUMBIA					
BFC 39982	Flip	1985	2.50	5.00	10.00

LOGGINS, DAVE

45s

Number	Title	Yr	VG	VG+	NM
EPIC					
02152	Please Come to Boston/Someday	1981	—	—	3.00
—Reissue					
11115	Please Come to Boston/Let Me Go Now	1974	—	2.50	5.00
50035	Someday/Girl from Knoxville	1974	—	2.00	4.00
50069	Second Hand Lady/So You Couldn't Get to Me	1975	—	2.00	4.00
50221	Saviour of My Natural Life/You've Got Me to Hold On To	1976	—	2.00	4.00
50246	Movin' to the Country/Wild Millie the Country Girl	1976	—	2.00	4.00
50326	Three Little Words (I Love You)/Don't Treat Me Like a Stranger	1976	—	2.00	4.00
50491	Ship in a Bottle/The Ballad of Cowboy 20	1977	—	2.00	4.00
50500	One-Way Ticket to Paradise/Crowd of Lonely People	1978	—	2.00	4.00
50578	So Much for Dreams/You Found It Now	1978	—	2.00	4.00
50711	Pieces of April/Color of My Mood	1979	—	2.00	4.00
50783	One Way Ticket to Paradise/The Fool in Me	1979	—	2.00	4.00
VANGUARD					
35147	Claudia/Think'n of You	1972	—	2.50	5.00
35167	Pieces of April/Think'n of You	1972	—	2.50	5.00
35177	Building Condemned/Lady in an Orange Silk Blouse	1973	—	2.50	5.00

Albums

Number	Title	Yr	VG	VG+	NM
EPIC					
KE 32833	Apprentice (In a Musical Workshop)	1974	2.50	5.00	10.00
PE 33946	Country Suite	1975	2.50	5.00	10.00
PE 34713	One Way	1977	2.50	5.00	10.00
JE 35792	David Loggins	1979	2.50	5.00	10.00
VANGUARD					
VSD-6580	Personal Belongings	1972	3.75	7.50	15.00

LOGGINS AND MESSINA

Also see JIM MESSINA.

45s

Number	Title	Yr	VG	VG+	NM
COLUMBIA					
JBQ 507	Your Mama Don't Dance/Thinking of You	1973	2.50	5.00	10.00
—Quadraphonic single, "Special Coin Operator Release"					
10077	Changes/Get a Hold	1974	—	2.50	5.00
10118	Growin'/Keep Me in Mind	1975	—	2.50	5.00
10188	I Like It Like That/Angry Eyes	1975	—	2.50	5.00
10222	A Lover's Question/Angry Eyes	1975	—	2.50	5.00
10311	When I Was a Child/Peacemaker	1976	—	2.50	5.00
10376	Native Son/Pretty Princess	1976	—	2.50	5.00
10444	Angry Eyes/Watching the River Run	1976	—	2.50	5.00
45550	Same Old Wine/Vahevelia	1972	—	3.00	6.00
—As "Kenny Loggins and Jim Messina"					
45617	Nobody But You/Danny's Song	1972	—	3.00	6.00
—As "Kenny Loggins and Jim Messina"					
45664	Peace of Mind/House at Pooh Corner	1972	—	3.00	6.00
—As "Kenny Loggins and Jim Messina"					
45719	Your Mama Don't Dance/Golden Ribbons	1972	—	3.00	6.00
—As "Kenny Loggins and Jim Messina"; gray label					
45719	Your Mama Don't Dance/Golden Ribbons	1972	—	2.50	5.00
—As "Kenny Loggins and Jim Messina"; orange label					
45815	Thinking of You/Till the Ends Meet	1973	—	2.50	5.00
—A-side is a different version than on most LPs					
45952	My Music/A Love Song	1973	—	2.50	5.00
46010	Watching the River Run/Travelin' Blues	1974	—	2.50	5.00

Albums

Number	Title	Yr	VG	VG+	NM
COLUMBIA					
C 31044	Kenny Loggins with Jim Messina Sittin' In	1972	2.50	5.00	10.00
PC 31044	Kenny Loggins with Jim Messina Sittin' In	197?	2.00	4.00	8.00
—Reissue with new prefix					
CQ 31748 [Q]	Loggins and Messina	1973	3.75	7.50	15.00
KC 31748	Loggins and Messina	1972	2.50	5.00	10.00
PC 31748	Loggins and Messina	197?	2.00	4.00	8.00
—Reissue with new prefix					
CQ 32540 [Q]	Full Sail	1973	3.75	7.50	15.00
KC 32540	Full Sail	1973	2.50	5.00	10.00
PC 32540	Full Sail	197?	2.00	4.00	8.00
—Reissue with new prefix					
PG 32848 [(2)]	On Stage	1974	3.00	6.00	12.00
—Original with no bar code					
PG 32848 [(2)]	On Stage	198?	2.50	5.00	10.00
—With bar code					
PC 33175	Mother Lode	1974	2.50	5.00	10.00
—Original with no bar code					
PC 33175	Mother Lode	198?	2.00	4.00	8.00
—With bar code					
PC 33578	Native Sons	1976	2.50	5.00	10.00
—Original with no bar code					

Number	Title (A Side/B Side)	Yr	VG	VG+	NM
PC 33578	Native Sons	198?	2.00	4.00	8.00
—With bar code					
PCQ 33578 [Q]	Native Sons	1976	3.75	7.50	15.00
PC 33810	So Fine	1975	2.50	5.00	10.00
—Original with no bar code					
PC 33810	So Fine	198?	2.00	4.00	8.00
—With bar code					
JG 34167 [(2)]	Finale	1977	3.00	6.00	12.00
PC 34388	The Best of Friends	1976	2.50	5.00	10.00
—Original with no bar code					
PC 34388	The Best of Friends	198?	2.00	4.00	8.00
—With bar code					
HC 44388	The Best of Friends	1982	12.50	25.00	50.00
—Half-speed mastered edition					
DIRECT DISC					
SD 16606	Full Sail	198?	7.50	15.00	30.00
—Audiophile vinyl					
EPIC					
PC 34388	The Best of Friends	1976	5.00	10.00	20.00
—Mispressing with wrong label					

LOLITA

45s

Number	Title (A Side/B Side)	Yr	VG	VG+	NM
4 CORNERS OF THE WORLD					
131	Come Back/When Our Father Is Happy	1965	—	3.50	7.00
KAPP					
349	Sailor (Your Home Is the Sea)/La Luna (Quando La Luna)	1960	3.00	6.00	12.00
—Maroon and silver label					
349	Sailor (Your Home Is the Sea)/La Luna (Quando La Luna)	1960	2.00	4.00	8.00
—Black label					
349 [PS]	Sailor (Your Home Is the Sea)/La Luna (Quando La Luna)	1960	5.00	10.00	20.00
370	Cowboy Jimmy Joe (Die Sterne Der Prarie)/Theme from "A Summer Place"	1961	2.00	4.00	8.00
370 [PS]	Cowboy Jimmy Joe (Die Sterne Der Prarie)/Theme from "A Summer Place"	1961	5.00	10.00	20.00
402	For the First Time (I've Fallen in Love)/Souvenir d'Amour	1961	2.00	4.00	8.00

Albums

Number	Title (A Side/B Side)	Yr	VG	VG+	NM
KAPP					
KL-1219 [M]	Sailor	1961	6.25	12.50	25.00
KL-1229 [M]	Songs You Will Never Forget	1961	6.25	12.50	25.00
KS-3219 [S]	Sailor	1961	7.50	15.00	30.00
KS-3229 [S]	Songs You Will Never Forget	1961	7.50	15.00	30.00

LOLLIPOP SHOPPE, THE

45s

Number	Title (A Side/B Side)	Yr	VG	VG+	NM
SHAMLEY					
44005	Someone I Know/Through My Window	1969	3.00	6.00	12.00
UNI					
55050	You Must Be a Witch/Don't Close the Door	1968	3.75	7.50	15.00
55050 [PS]	You Must Be a Witch/Don't Close the Door	1968	6.25	12.50	25.00

Albums

Number	Title (A Side/B Side)	Yr	VG	VG+	NM
UNI					
73019	The Lollipop Shoppe	1968	20.00	40.00	80.00

LOLLIPOPS, THE (1)

45s

Number	Title (A Side/B Side)	Yr	VG	VG+	NM
ATCO					
6787	Nothing's Gonna Stop Our Love/I Believe in Love	1970	—	3.00	6.00
GORDY					
7089	Cheating Is Telling On You/Need Your Love	1969	200.00	400.00	800.00
IMPACT					
1021	Lovin' Good Feelin'/Step Aside Baby	1967	7.50	15.00	30.00
V.I.P.					
25051	Cheating Is Telling On You/Need Your Love	1968	6.25	12.50	25.00

LOLLIPOPS, THE (2)

45s

Number	Title (A Side/B Side)	Yr	VG	VG+	NM
SSS INTERNATIONAL					
777	You Don't Know/Feel So Comfortable	1969	3.75	7.50	15.00

LOLLIPOPS, THE (3)

45s

Number	Title (A Side/B Side)	Yr	VG	VG+	NM
WARNER BROS.					
5122	Mister Santa/Little Donkey (Carry Mary Safely on Her Way)	1959	3.00	6.00	12.00

LOLLIPOPS, THE (U)

Some of these could be group (1).

45s

Number	Title (A Side/B Side)	Yr	VG	VG+	NM
RCA VICTOR					
47-8344	Peggy Got Engaged/I'll Set My Love to Music	1964	5.00	10.00	20.00
47-8390	Don't Monkey With Me/Love Is the Only Answer	1964	5.00	10.00	20.00
47-8430	Billy, Billy Baby/Big Brother	1964	5.00	10.00	20.00
47-8494	Busy Signal/I Want You Back Again	1965	3.75	7.50	15.00
SMASH					
2057	He's the Boy/Gee Whiz Baby	1966	3.00	6.00	12.00

LOMAX, JACKIE

45s

Number	Title (A Side/B Side)	Yr	VG	VG+	NM
APPLE					
1802	Sour Milk Sea/The Eagle Laughs at You	1968	5.00	10.00	20.00
—With B-side author listed as "(George Harrison)"					
1802	Sour Milk Sea/The Eagle Laughs at You	1968	5.00	10.00	20.00
—With B-side author listed as "(Jackie Lomax)"					
1807	New Day/Thumbin' a Ride	1969	18.75	37.50	75.00
—With star on A-side label					
1807	New Day/Thumbin' a Ride	1969	15.00	30.00	60.00
—Without star on A-side label					
1819	How the Web Was Woven/I Fall Inside Your Eyes	1970	2.00	4.00	8.00
1819 [PS]	How the Web Was Woven/I Fall Inside Your Eyes	1970	2.50	5.00	10.00
1834	Sour Milk Sea/(I) Fall Inside Your Eyes	1971	2.00	4.00	8.00
PRO-6240/1 [DJ]	Sour Milk Sea/(I) Fall Inside Your Eyes	1971	7.50	15.00	30.00
CAPITOL					
4384	More (Livin' for Lovin')/I Remember (Memorabilia)	1976	—	2.50	5.00
EPIC					
10270	One Minute Woman/Genuine Imitation of Life	1967	3.00	6.00	12.00
WARNER BROS.					
7503	Helluva Woman/Higher Ground	1971	—	3.00	6.00
7564	Lavender Dream/Lost	1972	—	3.00	6.00
7589	Roll On/Hellfire, Night Crier	1972	—	3.00	6.00

LOMAX. JACKIE

Albums

Number	Title (A Side/B Side)	Yr	VG	VG+	NM
APPLE					
ST-3354	Is This What You Want?	1969	6.25	12.50	25.00
CAPITOL					
ST-11558	Livin' for Lovin'	1976	2.50	5.00	10.00
ST-11668	Did You Ever	1977	2.50	5.00	10.00
WARNER BROS.					
PRO 520 [DJ]	An Interview with Jackie Lomax	1972	10.00	20.00	40.00
WS 1914	Home Is In My Head	1971	3.00	6.00	12.00
BS 2591	Three	1972	3.00	6.00	12.00

LONDON, JULIE

45s

Number	Title (A Side/B Side)	Yr	VG	VG+	NM
BETHLEHEM					
11003	Sometimes I Feel Like a Motherless Child/A Foggy Day	1958	5.00	10.00	20.00
11015	Don't Worry 'Bout Me/You're Blase	1959	3.00	6.00	12.00
LIBERTY					
33007 [S]	When I Fall in Love/The More I See You	1960	5.00	10.00	20.00
33008 [S]	Blue Moon/I Guess I'll Have to Change My Plan	1960	5.00	10.00	20.00
33009 [S]	Bye Bye Blues/Basin Street Blues	1960	5.00	10.00	20.00
33010 [S]	Daddy/Bye Bye Blackbird	1960	5.00	10.00	20.00
—The above four are 33 1/3 rpm jukebox singles					
55006	Cry Me a River/S'Wonderful	1955	3.00	6.00	12.00
55009	Baby, Baby, All the Time/Shadow Woman	1955	2.50	5.00	10.00
55025	September in the Rain/Lonely Girl	1956	2.50	5.00	10.00
55032	Tall Boy/Now, Baby, Now	1956	2.50	5.00	10.00
55052	The Meaning of the Blues/Boy on a Dolphin	1957	2.50	5.00	10.00
55074	It Had to Be You/Dark	1957	2.50	5.00	10.00
55108	I'd Like You for Christmas/Saddle the Wind	1957	3.00	6.00	12.00
55131	Tell Me You're Home/The Freshman	1958	2.50	5.00	10.00
55139	It's Easy/Voice in the Mirror	1958	2.50	5.00	10.00
55157	Blue Moon/Man of the West	1958	2.50	5.00	10.00
55175	Come On-a My House/My Strange Affair	1959	2.50	5.00	10.00
55182	Must Be Catchin'/Something I Dreamed Last Night	1959	2.50	5.00	10.00
55216	Comin' Through the Rye/Makin' Whoopee	1959	2.50	5.00	10.00
55227	Cry Me a River/It's a Blue World	1959	2.50	5.00	10.00
55269	In the Wee Small Hours of the Morning/Time for Lovers	1960	2.50	5.00	10.00
55300	Send for Me/Evenin'	1961	2.00	4.00	8.00
55309	Sanctuary/Every Chance I Get	1961	2.00	4.00	8.00
55337	My Darling, My Darling/My Love, My Love	1961	2.00	4.00	8.00
55512	Desafinado/Where Did the Gentleman Go	1962	2.00	4.00	8.00
55605	I'm Coming Back to You/When Snowflakes Fall in the Summer	1963	2.00	4.00	8.00
55666	Guilty Heart/I Want to Find Out for Myself	1964	—	3.00	6.00
55702	Girl (Boy) from Ipanema/My Lover Is a Stranger	1964	—	3.00	6.00
55759	We Proved Them Wrong/You're Free to Go	1964	—	3.00	6.00
55830	Girl Talk/Won't Somebody Please Belong to Me	1965	—	3.00	6.00
55911	Nice Girls Don't Stay for Breakfast/Bill Bailey (Won't You Please Come Home)	1966	—	3.00	6.00
55966	Mickey Mouse March/Baby Won't You Please	1967	—	3.00	6.00
56074	Yummy, Yummy, Yummy/Come to Me Slowly	1968	—	2.50	5.00
56085	Louie Louie/Hushabye Mountain	1969	—	2.50	5.00
56112	Too Much of a Man/Sittin' Pretty	1969	—	—	—
—Unreleased					
UNITED ARTISTS					
0013	Cry Me a River/Come On-a My House	1973	—	2.00	4.00
—"Silver Spotlight Series" reissue					

7-Inch Extended Plays

Number	Title (A Side/B Side)	Yr	VG	VG+	NM
LIBERTY					
LEP-1-3006	Laura/S' Wonderful//I'm in the Mood for Love/Can't Help Lovin' That Man	1956	3.00	6.00	12.00
LEP-1-3006 [PS]	Julie Is Her Name, Part One	1956	3.00	6.00	12.00
LEP-2-3006	(contents unknown)	1956	3.00	6.00	12.00
LEP-2-3006 [PS]	Julie Is Her Name, Part Two	1956	3.00	6.00	12.00
LEP-3-3006	(contents unknown)	1956	3.00	6.00	12.00
LEP-3-3006 [PS]	Julie Is Her Name, Part Three	1956	3.00	6.00	12.00
LEP-1-3012	*Lonely Girl/Fools Rush In/How Deep Is the Ocean/Mean to Me	195?	3.00	6.00	12.00
LEP-1-3012 [PS]	Lonely Girl, Part One	195?	3.00	6.00	12.00
LEP-2-3012	(contents unknown)	195?	3.00	6.00	12.00
LEP-2-3012 [PS]	Lonely Girl, Part Two	195?	3.00	6.00	12.00
LEP-3-3012	(contents unknown)	195?	3.00	6.00	12.00
LEP-3-3012 [PS]	Lonely Girl, Part Three	195?	3.00	6.00	12.00

Albums

Number	Title (A Side/B Side)	Yr	VG	VG+	NM
LIBERTY					
MCR-1 [M]	By Myself	196?	6.25	12.50	25.00
—Columbia Record Club exclusive					
SCR-1 [S]	By Myself	196?	7.50	15.00	30.00
—Columbia Record Club exclusive					
LRP-3006 [M]	Julie Is Her Name	1956	12.50	25.00	50.00
—Green label					
LRP-3006 [M]	Julie Is Her Name	1960	5.00	10.00	20.00
—Black label, colorband and logo at left					

Number	Title (A Side/B Side)	Yr	VG	VG+	NM
LRP-3012 [M]	Lonely Girl	1956	12.50	25.00	50.00
—Green label					
LRP-3012 [M]	Lonely Girl	1960	5.00	10.00	20.00
—Black label, colorband and logo at left					
LRP-3043 [M]	About the Blues	1957	10.00	20.00	40.00
—Green label					
LRP-3043 [M]	About the Blues	1960	5.00	10.00	20.00
—Black label, colorband and logo at left					
LRP-3060 [M]	Make Love to Me	1957	10.00	20.00	40.00
—Green label					
LRP-3060 [M]	Make Love to Me	1960	5.00	10.00	20.00
—Black label, colorband and logo at left					
LRP-3096 [M]	Julie	1957	10.00	20.00	40.00
—Green label					
LRP-3100 [M]	Julie Is Her Name, Volume 2	1958	10.00	20.00	40.00
—Green label					
LRP-3100 [M]	Julie Is Her Name, Volume 2	1960	5.00	10.00	20.00
—Black label, colorband and logo at left					
LRP-3105 [M]	London By Night	1958	7.50	15.00	30.00
—Green label					
LRP-3119 [M]	Swing Me an Old Song	1959	7.50	15.00	30.00
—Green label					
LRP-3130 [M]	Your Number Please	1959	7.50	15.00	30.00
—Green label					
LRP-3130 [M]	Your Number Please	1960	5.00	10.00	20.00
—Black label, colorband and logo at left					
LRP-3152 [M]	Julie…At Home	1960	7.50	15.00	30.00
LRP-3164 [M]	Around Midnight	1960	7.50	15.00	30.00
LRP-3171 [M]	Send for Me	1961	7.50	15.00	30.00
LRP-3192 [M]	Whatever Julie Wants	1961	7.50	15.00	30.00
LRP-3203 [M]	Sophisticated Lady	1962	6.25	12.50	25.00
LRP-3231 [M]	Love Letters	1962	6.25	12.50	25.00
LRP-3249 [M]	Love on the Rocks	1963	6.25	12.50	25.00
LRP-3278 [M]	Latin in a Satin Mood	1963	6.25	12.50	25.00
LRP-3291 [M]	Julie's Golden Hits	1963	6.25	12.50	25.00
—White cover					
LRP-3291 [M]	Julie's Golden Hits	1963	6.25	12.50	25.00
—Black cover					
LRP-3300 [M]	The End of the World	1963	6.25	12.50	25.00
LRP-3324 [M]	The Wonderful World of Julie London	1963	6.25	12.50	25.00
LRP-3342 [M]	Julie London	1964	6.25	12.50	25.00
LRP-3375 [M]	Julie London In Person at the Americana	1964	6.25	12.50	25.00
LRP-3392 [M]	Our Fair Lady	1965	6.25	12.50	25.00
LRP-3416 [M]	Feeling Good	1965	6.25	12.50	25.00
LRP-3434 [M]	All Through the Night	1965	6.25	12.50	25.00
LRP-3478 [M]	For the Night People	1966	6.25	12.50	25.00
LRP-3493 [M]	Nice Girls Don't Stay for Breakfast	1967	6.25	12.50	25.00
LRP-3514 [M]	With Body and Soul	1967	7.50	15.00	30.00
L-5501 [M]	The Best of Julie London	1962	7.50	15.00	30.00
S-6601 [S]	The Best of Julie London	1962	10.00	20.00	40.00
LST-7004 [S]	Julie	1958	17.50	35.00	70.00
—Black label, silver print					
LST-7012 [S]	About the Blues	1958	17.50	35.00	70.00
—Black label, silver print					
LST-7012 [S]	About the Blues	1960	6.25	12.50	25.00
—Black label, colorband and logo at left					
LST-7027 [S]	Julie Is Her Name	1958	25.00	50.00	100.00
—Blue vinyl					
LST-7027 [S]	Julie Is Her Name	1958	25.00	50.00	100.00
—Red vinyl					
LST-7027 [S]	Julie Is Her Name	1958	10.00	20.00	40.00
—Black label, silver print					
LST-7027 [S]	Julie Is Her Name	1960	6.25	12.50	25.00
—Black label, colorband and logo at left					
LST-7029 [S]	Lonely Girl	1958	10.00	20.00	40.00
—Black label, silver print					
LST-7029 [S]	Lonely Girl	1960	6.25	12.50	25.00
—Black label, colorband and logo at left					
LST-7060 [S]	Make Love to Me	1958	10.00	20.00	40.00
—Black label, silver print					
LST-7060 [S]	Make Love to Me	1960	6.25	12.50	25.00
—Black label, colorband and logo at left					
LST-7100 [S]	Julie Is Her Name, Volume 2	1958	10.00	20.00	40.00
—Black label, silver print					
LST-7100 [S]	Julie Is Her Name, Volume 2	1960	6.25	12.50	25.00
—Black label, colorband and logo at left					
LST-7105 [S]	London By Night	1958	10.00	20.00	40.00
—Black label, silver print					
LST-7119 [S]	Swing Me an Old Song	1959	10.00	20.00	40.00
—Black label, silver print					
LST-7130 [S]	Your Number Please	1959	10.00	20.00	40.00
—Black label, silver print					
LST-7130 [S]	Your Number Please	1960	6.25	12.50	25.00
—Black label, colorband and logo at left					
LST-7152 [S]	Julie…At Home	1960	25.00	50.00	100.00
—Blue vinyl					
LST-7152 [S]	Julie…At Home	1960	10.00	20.00	40.00
—Black vinyl					
LST-7164 [S]	Around Midnight	1960	10.00	20.00	40.00
LST-7171 [S]	Send for Me	1961	10.00	20.00	40.00
LST-7192 [S]	Whatever Julie Wants	1961	10.00	20.00	40.00
LST-7203 [S]	Sophisticated Lady	1962	7.50	15.00	30.00
LST-7231 [S]	Love Letters	1962	7.50	15.00	30.00
LST-7249 [S]	Love on the Rocks	1963	7.50	15.00	30.00
LST-7278 [S]	Latin in a Satin Mood	1963	7.50	15.00	30.00
LST-7291 [S]	Julie's Golden Hits	1963	7.50	15.00	30.00
—White cover					
LST-7291 [S]	Julie's Golden Hits	1963	7.50	15.00	30.00
—Black cover					
LST-7300 [S]	The End of the World	1963	7.50	15.00	30.00
LST-7324 [S]	The Wonderful World of Julie London	1963	7.50	15.00	30.00
LST-7342 [S]	Julie London	1964	7.50	15.00	30.00
LST-7375 [S]	Julie London In Person at the Americana	1964	7.50	15.00	30.00
LST-7392 [S]	Our Fair Lady	1965	7.50	15.00	30.00
LST-7416 [S]	Feeling Good	1965	7.50	15.00	30.00
LST-7434 [S]	All Through the Night	1965	7.50	15.00	30.00
LST-7478 [S]	For the Night People	1966	7.50	15.00	30.00
LST-7493 [S]	Nice Girls Don't Stay for Breakfast	1967	6.25	12.50	25.00
LST-7514 [S]	With Body and Soul	1967	6.25	12.50	25.00
LST-7546	Easy Does It	1968	5.00	10.00	20.00
LST-7609	Yummy, Yummy, Yummy	1969	5.00	10.00	20.00
SL-9002 [M]	Calendar Girl	1956	25.00	50.00	100.00
SUNSET					
SUM-1104 [M]	Julie London	196?	3.00	6.00	12.00
SUM-1161 [M]	Soft and Sweet	196?	3.00	6.00	12.00
SUS-5104 [S]	Julie London	196?	3.75	7.50	15.00
SUS-5161 [S]	Soft and Sweet	196?	3.75	7.50	15.00
SUS-5207	Gone with the Wind	196?	3.00	6.00	12.00
UNITED ARTISTS					
UA-LA437-E	The Very Best of Julie London	1975	3.00	6.00	12.00

LONDON, LAURIE

45s

Number	Title (A Side/B Side)	Yr	VG	VG+	NM
CAPITOL					
F3891	He's Got the Whole World (In His Hands)/Handed Down	1958	3.75	7.50	15.00
F3973	Joshua/I Gotta Robe	1958	3.00	6.00	12.00
F4133	My Mother/Three O'Clock	1959	3.00	6.00	12.00
ROULETTE					
4176	Pretty Eyed Baby/Boom Ladda Boom Boom	1959	2.50	5.00	10.00

Albums

Number	Title (A Side/B Side)	Yr	VG	VG+	NM
CAPITOL					
T 1016 [M]	Laurie London	1958	12.50	25.00	50.00

LONDON SOUND 70 ORCHESTRA AND CHORUS

Albums

Number	Title (A Side/B Side)	Yr	VG	VG+	NM
DECCA					
DEB 7-7 [(3)]	The Sounds of Christmas	1970	6.25	12.50	25.00

LONE TWISTER, THE

45s

Number	Title (A Side/B Side)	Yr	VG	VG+	NM
ATLANTIC					
2130	The Lone Twister/Twistin' Up a Storm	1961	3.75	7.50	15.00

LONESOME BLUES SINGER, THE

See LEADBELLY.

LONESOME DRIFTER, THE

45s

Number	Title (A Side/B Side)	Yr	VG	VG+	NM
K					
5812	Eager Boy/Teardrop Valley	1958	500.00	1000.	2000.

LONESOME RHODES

45s

Number	Title (A Side/B Side)	Yr	VG	VG+	NM
RCA VICTOR					
47-9305	The Delight of My Day/(B-side unknown)	1967	5.00	10.00	20.00

Albums

Number	Title (A Side/B Side)	Yr	VG	VG+	NM
RCA VICTOR					
LPM-3759 [M]	Lonesome Rhodes	1967	7.50	15.00	30.00
LSP-3759 [S]	Lonesome Rhodes	1967	5.00	10.00	20.00

LONG, HUEY

45s

Number	Title (A Side/B Side)	Yr	VG	VG+	NM
FIDELITY					
4054	How to Tell My Heart/Waiting for a Letter	1962	5.00	10.00	20.00
4055	Elvis Stole My Gal/Ballad of John Glenn	1962	12.50	25.00	50.00

LONG, SHORTY (1)

R&B singer.

45s

Number	Title (A Side/B Side)	Yr	VG	VG+	NM
SOUL					
35001	Devil with the Blue Dress/Wind It Up	1964	6.25	12.50	25.00
35005	It's a Crying Shame/Out to Get You	1964	6.25	12.50	25.00
35021	Function at the Junction/Call On Me	1966	3.75	7.50	15.00
35031	Chantilly Lace/Your Love Is Amazing	1966	3.75	7.50	15.00
35040	Night Fo' Last/(Instrumental)	1968	2.50	5.00	10.00
35044	Here Comes the Judge/Sing What You Wanna	1968	2.50	5.00	10.00
35054	I Had a Dream/Ain't No Justice	1969	2.50	5.00	10.00
35064	A Whiter Shade of Pale/When You Are Available	1969	2.50	5.00	10.00
TRI-PHI					
1006	I'll Be There/Bad Willie	1962	12.50	25.00	50.00
1015	Too Smart/I'll Be There	1962	17.50	35.00	70.00
1021	What's the Matter/Going Away	1963	15.00	30.00	60.00

Albums

Number	Title (A Side/B Side)	Yr	VG	VG+	NM
SOUL					
SS-709	Here Comes the Judge	1968	5.00	10.00	20.00
SS-719	The Prime of Shorty Long	1969	3.75	7.50	15.00

LONG, SHORTY (2)

C&W singer.

45s

Number	Title (A Side/B Side)	Yr	VG	VG+	NM
KING					
5605	Take Me to the Happy Land/Mary, Oh Mary	1962	6.25	12.50	25.00
RCA VICTOR					
47-6472	Hey, Doll Baby/Luscious	1956	25.00	50.00	100.00
47-6572	Vacation Rock/Burnt Toast and Black Coffee	1956	25.00	50.00	100.00
47-6804	Another Love Has Ended/Little White Horse	1957	25.00	50.00	100.00
47-6873	You Don't Have to Be a Baby to Cry/I'd Crawl Back	1957	25.00	50.00	100.00
48-0057	The Morning After/Please Daddy Forgive	1949	10.00	20.00	40.00
—Originals on green vinyl; second pressing on black vinyl is unconfirmed					
48-0098	The Warm Red Wine/I Got Mine	1949	10.00	20.00	40.00
—Originals on green vinyl; second pressing on black vinyl is unconfirmed					
48-0347	A Bottle and a Blonde/Waltz of Colorado	1950	10.00	20.00	40.00
—Originals on green vinyl; second pressing on black vinyl is unconfirmed					

Number	Title (A Side/B Side)	Yr	VG	VG+	NM
Albums					
FORD					
FXM-712 [M]	Country Jamboree	1963	5.00	10.00	20.00

LONGBRANCH PENNYWHISTLE

GLENN FREY, J.D. SOUTHER and RY COODER all were members of this group.

Number	Title (A Side/B Side)	Yr	VG	VG+	NM
45s					
AMOS					
121	Don't Talk Now/Jubilee Anne	1969	3.75	7.50	15.00
129	Lucky Love/Rebecca	1969	3.75	7.50	15.00
148	Star Spangled Bus/Bring Back Founky Women	1970	3.75	7.50	15.00
Albums					
AMOS					
AAS-7007	Longbranch Pennywhistle	1969	12.50	25.00	50.00

LONGET, CLAUDINE

Number	Title (A Side/B Side)	Yr	VG	VG+	NM
45s					
A&M					
817	Meditation (Meditacao)/Sunrise, Sunset	1966	—	3.00	6.00
832	A Man and a Woman/Here, There and Everywhere	1967	—	3.00	6.00
846	Hello, Hello/Wonderlove	1967	—	3.00	6.00
864	Good Day Sunshine/The Look of Love	1967	—	3.00	6.00
877	Small Talk/A Man in a Raincoat	1967	—	3.00	6.00
895	Snow/I Don't Intend to Spend My Christmas Without You	1967	2.00	4.00	8.00
897	When I'm Sixty-Four/I Love How You Love Me	1968	—	2.50	5.00
909	Love Is Blue (L'amour Est Bleu)/Think of Rain	1968	—	2.50	5.00
936	Nothing to Lose/White Horses	1968	—	2.50	5.00
954	Lullaby from "Rosemary's Baby" (Sleep Safe and Warm)/It's Hard to Say Goodbye	1968	—	2.50	5.00
967	A Walk in the Park/Who Needs You	1968	—	2.50	5.00
1002	Am I Blue/Flea in Her Ear	1968	—	2.50	5.00
1024	I Think It's Gonna Rain Today/Hurry On Down	1969	—	2.50	5.00
1059	Colours/Love Can Never Die	1969	—	2.50	5.00
1098	Quentin's Theme/Lazy Summer Night	1969	—	2.50	5.00
1181	A Bushel and a Peck/Run Wild, Run Free	1970	—	2.50	5.00
BARNABY					
603	Goodbye Jimmy Goodbye/(B-side unknown)	1974	—	2.00	4.00
2022	Broomstick Cowboy/Long Long Time	1970	—	2.00	4.00
2028	Ain't No Mountain High Enough/Electric Moon	1971	—	2.00	4.00
2033	Anytime of the Year/Guess Who I Saw in Paris	1971	—	2.00	4.00
2060	Let's Spend the Night Together/Wake Up to Me Gentle	1972	—	2.00	4.00
5001	Remember the Good/While You're Sleeping	1972	—	2.00	4.00
5021	Every Beat of My Heart/Sugar Me	1973	—	2.00	4.00
Albums					
A&M					
LP-121 [M]	Claudine	1967	3.75	7.50	15.00
LP-128 [M]	The Look of Love	1967	3.75	7.50	15.00
SP-4121 [S]	Claudine	1967	3.00	6.00	12.00
SP-4128 [S]	The Look of Love	1967	3.00	6.00	12.00
SP-4142	Love Is Blue	1968	3.00	6.00	12.00
SP-4163	Colours	1969	3.00	6.00	12.00
SP-4232	Run Wild, Run Free	1970	3.00	6.00	12.00
BARNABY					
Z 30377	We've Only Just Begun	1971	3.00	6.00	12.00
KZ 31383	Let's Spend the Night Together	1972	3.00	6.00	12.00

LONNIE AND THE CAROLLONS

Number	Title (A Side/B Side)	Yr	VG	VG+	NM
45s					
MOHAWK					
108	Chapel of Tears/My Heart	1958	37.50	75.00	150.00
—Green label					
108	Chapel of Tears/My Heart	1961	7.50	15.00	30.00
—Red label					
108	Chapel of Tears/My Heart	1965	5.00	10.00	20.00
—White label					
111	Hold Me Close/Trudy	1958	12.50	25.00	50.00
112	Back Yard Rock/You Say	1958	12.50	25.00	50.00
113	The Gang All Knows/Ike Hammer	1959	15.00	30.00	60.00
122	Need Your Lovin'/Beeline	1960	6.25	12.50	25.00
—As "Lonnie"					

LONNIE AND THE CRISIS

Number	Title (A Side/B Side)	Yr	VG	VG+	NM
45s					
RELIC					
532	Bells in the Chapel/Santa Town USA	196?	—	3.00	6.00
—Reissue of Universal 103					
TIMES SQUARE					
25	Bells in the Chapel/Santa Town USA	196?	2.00	4.00	8.00
—Reissue of Universal 103					
UNIVERSAL					
103	Bells in the Chapel/Santa Town USA	1961	50.00	100.00	200.00

LOOKING GLASS

Also see ELLIOTT LURIE.

Number	Title (A Side/B Side)	Yr	VG	VG+	NM
45s					
EPIC					
10834	Don't It Make You Feel Good/Catherine Street	1972	—	2.50	5.00
10874	Brandy (You're a Fine Girl)/One by One	1972	—	3.00	6.00
10900	Jenn-Lyne/Golden Rainbow	1972	—	2.50	5.00
10953	Sweet Somethin'/Rainbow Man	1973	—	2.50	5.00
11001	Jimmy Loves Mary-Anne/Wooly Eyes	1973	—	2.50	5.00
11061	City Lady/Who's Gonna Sing My Rock 'N' Roll Song	1973	—	2.50	5.00
11085	Sweet Somethin'/Who's Gonna Sing My Rock 'N' Roll Song	1974	—	2.50	5.00
20001	Rock This Town/Highway to Hollywood	1974	—	2.50	5.00
Albums					
EPIC					
KE 31320	Looking Glass	1972	3.75	7.50	15.00
KE 32167	Subway Serenade	1973	3.75	7.50	15.00

LOOKING GLASS, THE

This group pre-dates the one on Epic, which did not use the word "The" in its name.

Number	Title (A Side/B Side)	Yr	VG	VG+	NM
45s					
UNI					
55034	Virginia Day's Ragtime/Cry//Memories/What Am I Doin'	1967	2.50	5.00	10.00
VALIANT					
750	Silver and Sunshine (How Wonderful My Love)/If I Never Love Again	1966	2.50	5.00	10.00
WARNER BROS.					
7050	Lonely Stranger/Love Is Not Everything	1967	2.50	5.00	10.00

LOOKINLAND, MIKE

"Bobby Brady" of THE BRADY BUNCH.

Number	Title (A Side/B Side)	Yr	VG	VG+	NM
45s					
CAPITOL					
3914	Gum Drop/Love Doesn't Care Who's In It	1974	2.50	5.00	10.00
3914 [PS]	Gum Drop/Love Doesn't Care Who's In It	1974	3.75	7.50	15.00

LOOSE

Number	Title (A Side/B Side)	Yr	VG	VG+	NM
45s					
NOCTURNE					
1909	Freaky Billy the Wheelie King/It's Happenin'	1969	2.50	5.00	10.00
Albums					
NOCTURNE					
906	Freaky Billie, The Wheelie King	1970	7.50	15.00	30.00

LOPEZ, TRINI

Number	Title (A Side/B Side)	Yr	VG	VG+	NM
45s					
CAPITOL					
3195	Some Kind of a Summer/Poor Old Billy	1971	—	2.50	5.00
3312	Ruby Mountain/Y Voluere	1972	—	2.50	5.00
3402	Mammy Blue/Viva	1972	—	2.50	5.00
D.R.A.					
7008	Rosita/Only in My Dreams	1962	3.75	7.50	15.00
GRIFFIN					
504	Butterfly/Don't Burn Your Bridges Behind You	1973	—	2.50	5.00
508	Bring Back the Sunshine/We Gotta Make It Together	1974	—	2.50	5.00
KING					
5173	Rosalia/Nola	1959	5.00	10.00	20.00
5187	Since I Don't Have You/Rock On	1959	6.25	12.50	25.00
5198	Love Me Tonight/Here Comes Sally	1959	5.00	10.00	20.00
5234	Don't Let Your Sweet Love Die/I'm Grateful	1959	5.00	10.00	20.00
5284	Nobody Loves Me/Nobody Listens to Our Teenage Problems	1959	5.00	10.00	20.00
5304	Chain of Love/Sweet Thing	1960	5.00	10.00	20.00
5324	Schemes/Jeannie Marie	1960	5.00	10.00	20.00
5344	It Hurts to Be in Love/The Search Goes On	1960	5.00	10.00	20.00
5418	Don't Treat Me That Way/Then You Know	1960	5.00	10.00	20.00
5487	One Heart, One Life, One Love/You Broke the Only Heart	1961	5.00	10.00	20.00
5801	Jeannie Marie/Love Me Tonight	1963	3.00	6.00	12.00
5820	Don't Go/It Seems	1963	3.00	6.00	12.00
5824	Nobody Loves Me/The Club for Broken Hearts	1963	3.00	6.00	12.00
5849	Yes You Do/Won't You Be	1964	3.00	6.00	12.00
6000	Jeannie Marie/Nobody Listens, Nobody Cares	1965	2.00	4.00	8.00
6021	The Search Goes On/Chain of Love	1966	2.00	4.00	8.00
PRIVATE STOCK					
45024	Somethin' 'Bout You Baby I Like/Sweet Life	1975	—	2.50	5.00
45035	Seco Sulto Y Tonton	1975	—	2.50	5.00
45044	Heavy Makes You Happy (Sha-La-Boom-Boom-Yeah)/Satisfaction	1975	—	2.50	5.00
REPRISE					
0260	Jailer, Bring Me Water/You Can't Say Goodbye	1964	2.00	4.00	8.00
0276	Ya Ya/What Have I Got of My Own	1964	2.00	4.00	8.00
0300	Michael/San Fancisco De Assisi	1964	2.00	4.00	8.00
0328	Sad Tomorrows/I've Lost My Love for You	1964	2.00	4.00	8.00
0328 [PS]	Sad Tomorrows/I've Lost My Love for You	1964	3.75	7.50	15.00
0336	Lemon Tree/Pretty Eyes	1965	2.50	5.00	10.00
0336 [PS]	Lemon Tree/Pretty Eyes	1965	3.75	7.50	15.00
0376	Are You Sincere/You'll Be Sorry	1965	2.00	4.00	8.00
0405	Sinner Man/Double Trouble	1965	2.00	4.00	8.00
0405 [PS]	Sinner Man/Double Trouble	1965	3.75	7.50	15.00
0421	Regressa A Mi/Mi Felicidad	1965	2.00	4.00	8.00
0435	Made in Paris/Pretty Little Girl	1965	2.00	4.00	8.00
0435 [PS]	Made in Paris/Pretty Little Girl	1965	3.75	7.50	15.00
0455	The 32nd of May/I'm Coming Home, Cindy	1966	2.00	4.00	8.00
0480	La Bamba — Part 1/Trini's Tune	1966	2.00	4.00	8.00
0508	Hall of Fame/Pancho Lopez	1966	2.00	4.00	8.00
0536	Your Ever Changin' Mind/Takin' the Back Roads	1966	2.00	4.00	8.00
0547	Gonna Get Along Without Ya' Now/Love Letters	1967	—	3.00	6.00
0574	In the Land of Plenty/Up To Now	1967	—	3.00	6.00
0596	Ballad of the Dirty Dozen/The Bramble Bush	1967	—	3.00	6.00
0618	I Wanna Be Free/Together	1967	—	3.00	6.00
0648	It's a Great Life/Let's Take a Walk	1967	—	3.00	6.00
0659	Sally Was a Good Old Girl/It's a Great Life	1968	—	3.00	6.00
0687	Good Old Mountain Dew/Mental Journey	1968	—	3.00	6.00
0700	If I Had a Hammer/Lemon Tree	1968	—	2.50	5.00
—"Back to Back Hits" series					
0725	La Bamba/Kansas City	1968	—	2.50	5.00
—"Back to Back Hits" series					
0770	Something Tells Me/Malaguena Salerosa	1968	—	3.00	6.00
0801 [DJ]	El Nino Del Tambor/Nocho De Paz (Let There Be Peace)	1968	2.00	4.00	8.00
—Stock copy may not exist					
0814	Come a Little Bit Closer/My Baby Loves Sad Songs	1969	—	3.00	6.00
0825	Don't Let the Sun Catch You Crryin'/My Baby Loves Sad Songs	1969	—	3.00	6.00
0879	Games People Play/Love Story	1969	—	3.00	6.00

Number	Title (A Side/B Side)	Yr	VG	VG+	NM
0912	5 O'Clock World/You Make My Day	1970	—	2.50	5.00
0933	Mexican Medicine Man/Time to Get It Together	1970	—	2.50	5.00
0947	Su-Kal-De-Don/Mexican Medicine Man	1970	—	2.50	5.00
0975	Let's Think About Living/There Was a Crooked Man	1970	—	2.50	5.00
20168	A-M-E-R-I-C-A/Let It Be Known	1963	2.50	5.00	10.00
20190	La Bamba (Part 1)/La Bamba (Part 2)	1963	2.50	5.00	10.00
20198	If I Had a Hammer/Unchain My Heart	1963	3.00	6.00	12.00
20236	Kansas City/Lonesome Traveler	1963	2.00	4.00	8.00
ROULETTE					
7214	Beautiful People/Helplessly	1977	—	2.50	5.00
VOLK					
101	The Right to Rock/Just Once More	1958	7.50	15.00	30.00
7-Inch Extended Plays					
FRESCA					
ZTEP-124178	If I Had a Hammer/A-Me-Ri-Ca//Kansas City/The Blizzard Song	1967	2.50	5.00	10.00
ZTEP-124178 [PS]	Trini Lopez Sings His Greatest Hits	1967	3.75	7.50	15.00
—Available on specially marked packages of Fresca soda					
KING					
EP-483	Jeanie Marie/It Seems//Don't Go/Love Me Tonight	1963	10.00	20.00	40.00
—Possibly promo only; not known if issued with sleeve					
Albums					
CAPITOL					
SK 11009	Viva	1972	2.50	5.00	10.00
GUEST STAR					
GS-1499 [M]	Trini Lopez and Scott Gregory	1964	12.50	25.00	50.00
—"Scott Gregory" is said to be a pseudonym for BILL HALEY.					
HARMONY					
H 30012	Bye Bye Love	1970	2.50	5.00	10.00
KING					
863 [M]	Teenage Love Songs	1963	15.00	30.00	60.00
877 [M]	More of Trini Lopez	1964	15.00	30.00	60.00
962 [M]	24 Songs by the Great Trini Lopez	1966	7.50	15.00	30.00
REPRISE					
R-6083 [M]	Trini Lopez at PJ's	1963	3.00	6.00	12.00
R9-6083 [S]	Trini Lopez at PJ's	1963	3.75	7.50	15.00
R-6103 [M]	More Trini Lopez at PJ's	1963	3.00	6.00	12.00
R9-6103 [S]	More Trini Lopez at PJ's	1963	3.75	7.50	15.00
R-6112 [M]	On the Move	1964	3.00	6.00	12.00
R9-6112 [S]	On the Move	1964	3.75	7.50	15.00
R-6125 [M]	The Latin Album	1964	3.00	6.00	12.00
RS-6125 [S]	The Latin Album	1964	3.75	7.50	15.00
R-6134 [M]	Live at Basin St. East	1964	3.00	6.00	12.00
RS-6134 [S]	Live at Basin St. East	1964	3.75	7.50	15.00
R-6147 [M]	The Folk Album	1965	3.00	6.00	12.00
RS-6147 [S]	The Folk Album	1965	3.75	7.50	15.00
R-6165 [M]	The Love Album	1965	3.00	6.00	12.00
RS-6165 [S]	The Love Album	1965	3.75	7.50	15.00
R-6171 [M]	The Rhythm & Blues Album	1965	3.00	6.00	12.00
RS-6171 [S]	The Rhythm & Blues Album	1965	3.75	7.50	15.00
R-6183 [M]	The Sing-Along World of Trini Lopez	1965	3.00	6.00	12.00
RS-6183 [S]	The Sing-Along World of Trini Lopez	1965	3.75	7.50	15.00
R-6196 [M]	Trini	1966	3.00	6.00	12.00
RS-6196 [S]	Trini	1966	3.75	7.50	15.00
R-6215 [M]	The Second Latin Album	1966	3.00	6.00	12.00
RS-6215 [S]	The Second Latin Album	1966	3.75	7.50	15.00
R-6226 [M]	Greatest Hits!	1966	3.00	6.00	12.00
RS-6226 [S]	Greatest Hits!	1966	3.75	7.50	15.00
R-6238 [M]	Trini Lopez in London	1967	3.75	7.50	15.00
RS-6238 [S]	Trini Lopez in London	1967	3.00	6.00	12.00
R-6255 [M]	Trini Lopez — Now!	1967	3.75	7.50	15.00
RS-6255 [S]	Trini Lopez — Now!	1967	3.00	6.00	12.00
RS-6285	It's a Great Life	1968	3.00	6.00	12.00
RS-6300	Welcome to Trini Country	1968	3.00	6.00	12.00
RS-6337	The Whole Enchilada	1969	3.00	6.00	12.00
RS-6361	The Trini Lopez Show	1970	3.75	7.50	15.00
ROULETTE					
3020	Transformed by Time	1978	2.50	5.00	10.00

LORD, BOBBY

Number	Title (A Side/B Side)	Yr	VG	VG+	NM
45s					
COLUMBIA					
21339	No More No More/Why Were You Only Fooling Me	1955	12.50	25.00	50.00
—With longer A-side title					
21339	No More/Why Were You Only Fooling Me	1955	6.25	12.50	25.00
21367	I'm the Devil Who Made Her That Way/Ain'tcha Ever Gonna	1955	6.25	12.50	25.00
21397	Something's Missing/Sittin' Home Prayin' for Rain	1955	5.00	10.00	20.00
21437	Hawk-Eye/I Can't Make My Dreams Understand	1955	7.50	15.00	30.00
21459	I Can't Do Without You Anymore/Don't Make Me Laugh	1955	5.00	10.00	20.00
21498	So Doggone Lonesome/Pie Peachie Pie Pie	1956	5.00	10.00	20.00
21539	Everybody's Rockin' But Me/Without Your Love	1956	20.00	40.00	80.00
—"Without Your Love" was the hit, but "Everybody's Rockin' But Me" is the collectible side					
40666	Fire of Love/Beautiful Baby	1956	7.50	15.00	30.00
40819	Your Sweet Love/My Baby's Not My Baby Anymore	1957	5.00	10.00	20.00
40927	High Voltage/Just Wonderful	1957	10.00	20.00	40.00
41030	Am I a Fool/I Know It Was You	1957	5.00	10.00	20.00
41155	Sack/Fire of Love	1958	6.25	12.50	25.00
41288	When I've Learned/Walking Alone	1958	5.00	10.00	20.00
41352	Party Pooper/What a Thrill	1959	6.25	12.50	25.00
41505	Too Many Miles/Swamp Fox	1959	6.25	12.50	25.00
41596	Give Me a Woman/Where Did My Woman Go	1960	5.00	10.00	20.00
41824	Before I Lose My Mind/When the Snow Falls	1960	5.00	10.00	20.00
42012	A Rose and a Thorn/Fascination	1961	5.00	10.00	20.00
DECCA					
32115	Look What You're Doing/On and On Goes the Hurt	1967	2.00	4.00	8.00
32174	Shadows on the Wall/One Day Down	1967	2.00	4.00	8.00
32277	Live Your Life Out Loud/Charlotte, North Carolina	1968	—	3.00	6.00
32373	The True and Lasting Kind/It's My Life	1968	—	3.00	6.00
32431	Yesterday's Letters/Don't Forget to Smell the Flowers (Along the Way)	1969	—	3.00	6.00
32578	Rainbow Girl/Do You Ever Think of Me	1969	—	3.00	6.00
32657	You and Me Against the World/Something Real	1970	—	3.00	6.00
32718	Wake Me Up Early in the Morning/Violets Are Red	1970	—	3.00	6.00
32797	Do It to Someone You Love/So in Love with You	1970	2.00	4.00	8.00
32797	Goodbye Jukebox/Do It to Someone You Love	1971	—	3.00	6.00
32841	They've Got Something in the Country/Peace of Mind	1971	—	3.00	6.00
32932	Everybody's Here/Sweet Inspiration	1972	—	3.00	6.00
HICKORY					
1158	I'll Go On Alone/My Heart Tells Me So	1961	3.00	6.00	12.00
1169	Precious Jewel/Trail of Tears	1962	3.00	6.00	12.00
1190	Don't Shed Any Tears for Me/Out Behind the Barn	1962	3.00	6.00	12.00
1210	Cry, Cry Darling/Shopping Center	1963	2.50	5.00	10.00
1232	Life Can Have Meaning/Pickin' White Gold	1963	2.50	5.00	10.00
1259	A Man Needs a Woman/Take a Bucket to the Wall	1964	2.50	5.00	10.00
1310	I'm Going Home Next Summer/That Room in the Corner of the House	1965	2.50	5.00	10.00
1361	Cash on the Barrelhead/That's Love	1965	2.50	5.00	10.00
1389	It Only Hurts When I'm Laughing/Losers Like Me	1966	2.00	4.00	8.00
Albums					
DECCA					
DL 75246	Bobby Lord	1970	3.00	6.00	12.00
HARMONY					
HL 7322 [M]	Bobby Lord's Best	1964	6.25	12.50	25.00
HICKORY					
LP-126 [M]	The Bobby Lord Show	1965	5.00	10.00	20.00

LORD, BRIAN, AND THE MIDNIGHTERS

FRANK ZAPPA was a member of this group.

Number	Title (A Side/B Side)	Yr	VG	VG+	NM
45s					
CAPITOL					
4981	Big Surfer/Not Another One	1963	37.50	75.00	150.00
VIGAH					
001	Big Surfer/Not Another One	1963	75.00	150.00	300.00

LORD ROCKINGHAM'S XI

Number	Title (A Side/B Side)	Yr	VG	VG+	NM
45s					
LONDON					
1810	Fried Onions/The Squelch	1958	3.00	6.00	12.00
1839	Hoots Mon/Blue Train	1958	3.00	6.00	12.00

LORD SITAR

Sometimes rumored to be GEORGE HARRISON, but it's not.

Number	Title (A Side/B Side)	Yr	VG	VG+	NM
45s					
CAPITOL					
5972	Black Is Black/Have You Seen Your Mother, Baby, Standing in the Shadow	1967	5.00	10.00	20.00
Albums					
CAPITOL					
ST 2916	Lord Sitar	1968	7.50	15.00	30.00

LORDAN, JERRY

Number	Title (A Side/B Side)	Yr	VG	VG+	NM
45s					
CAPITOL					
4389	Who Could Be Bluer/Do I Worry	1960	3.75	7.50	15.00

LORDS OF LONDON, THE

Number	Title (A Side/B Side)	Yr	VG	VG+	NM
45s					
DECCA					
32196	Time Waits for No One/Cornflakes and Ice Cream	1967	5.00	10.00	20.00
MGM					
13919	Candy Rainbow/Within Your Mind	1968	5.00	10.00	20.00

LORELEIS, THE

Number	Title (A Side/B Side)	Yr	VG	VG+	NM
45s					
BRUNSWICK					
55271	Strange Way/Why Do I Put Up with You	1964	2.00	4.00	8.00

LORRAINE AND THE SOCIALITES

Number	Title (A Side/B Side)	Yr	VG	VG+	NM
45s					
MERCURY					
72163	Any Old Way/The Conqueror	1963	3.00	6.00	12.00

LORY, DICK

Number	Title (A Side/B Side)	Yr	VG	VG+	NM
45s					
COLUMBIA					
41224	Wild Blooded Woman/No One But You Knows When	1958	12.50	25.00	50.00
41276	Crazy Little Daisy/Don't Be a Fool for Love	1958	10.00	20.00	40.00
DOT					
15496	Cool It Baby/Ball Room Baby	1956	15.00	30.00	60.00
LIBERTY					
55306	The Pain Is Here/You	1961	3.75	7.50	15.00
55319	Hello Walls/City of Love	1961	3.75	7.50	15.00
55529	I Got Over You/Welcome Home Again	1963	3.75	7.50	15.00
55600	Crazy Arms/There's Going to Be a Fight	1963	3.75	7.50	15.00
55707	I Will/I Catch Myself Crying	1964	3.00	6.00	12.00

LOS ADMIRADORES

Number	Title (A Side/B Side)	Yr	VG	VG+	NM
Albums					
COMMAND					
809 SD [S]	Bongos Bongos Bongos	1960	3.75	7.50	15.00
812 SD [S]	Bongos/Flutes/Guitars	1960	3.75	7.50	15.00

LOS BRAVOS

45s

Number	Title (A Side/B Side)	Yr	VG	VG+	NM
PARROT					
3020	Bring a Little Lovin'/Make It Last	1968	3.00	6.00	12.00
3023	Dirty Street/Two People in Me	1968	2.50	5.00	10.00
PRESS					
60002	Black Is Black/I Want a Name	1966	3.75	7.50	15.00
60003	Going Nowhere/Brand New Baby	1966	2.50	5.00	10.00
60004	You'll Never Get the Chance Again/I'm All Ears	1967	2.50	5.00	10.00

Albums

Number	Title (A Side/B Side)	Yr	VG	VG+	NM
PARROT					
PAS 71021	Bring a Little Lovin'	1968	20.00	40.00	80.00
—Among the other tracks, "Black Is Black" in in true stereo.					
PRESS					
PR 73003 [M]	Black Is Black	1966	12.50	25.00	50.00
PRS 83003 [R]	Black Is Black	1966	7.50	15.00	30.00

LOS INDIOS TABAJARAS

45s

Number	Title (A Side/B Side)	Yr	VG	VG+	NM
RCA VICTOR					
47-8216	Maria Elena/Jungle Dream	1963	2.00	4.00	8.00
47-8313	Always in My Heart/Moonlight and Shadows	1964	—	3.00	6.00
47-8401	Marta/St. Louis Blues	1964	—	3.00	6.00
47-8510	Darktown Strutters' Ball/The Third Man Theme	1965	—	3.00	6.00
47-9094	The Petite Waltz/Sentimental Journey	1967	—	2.50	5.00
47-9388	Rio Antigo/Os Quindins De Ya Ya	1967	—	2.50	5.00

Albums

Number	Title (A Side/B Side)	Yr	VG	VG+	NM
RCA CAMDEN					
CXS-9031 [(2)]	Los Indios Tabajaras	1973	3.75	7.50	15.00
RCA INTERNATIONAL					
IL5-7367	Los Grandes Exitos	198?	3.00	6.00	12.00
RCA VICTOR					
AFL1-0210	Favorite Movie Themes	1977	2.50	5.00	10.00
—Reissue with new prefix					
APL1-0210	Favorite Movie Themes	1973	3.00	6.00	12.00
FSP-296	Maria Elena	1971	3.00	6.00	12.00
FSP-300	Siempre En Mi Corazon	1972	3.00	6.00	12.00
FSP-310	Softly	1972	3.00	6.00	12.00
AFL1-0668	Classical Guitars	1977	2.50	5.00	10.00
—Reissue with new prefix					
CPL1-0668	Classical Guitars	1974	3.00	6.00	12.00
AFL1-1033	Secret Love	1977	2.50	5.00	10.00
—Reissue with new prefix					
APL1-1033	Secret Love	1975	3.00	6.00	12.00
ANL1-1179	Maria Elena	1976	2.50	5.00	10.00
—Reissue					
LPM-1788 [M]	Sweet and Savage	1958	10.00	20.00	40.00
LSP-1788 [S]	Sweet and Savage	1958	12.50	25.00	50.00
APL1-2082	Mellow Nostalgia	1977	3.00	6.00	12.00
ANL1-2321	In a Sentimental Mood	1977	2.50	5.00	10.00
AFL1-2526	Masterpieces	1978	3.00	6.00	12.00
LPM-2822 [M]	Maria Elena	1963	5.00	10.00	20.00
—Reissue of LPM-1788					
LSP-2822 [S]	Maria Elena	1963	6.25	12.50	25.00
—Reissue of LSP-1788					
AFL1-2912	Always in My Heart	1977	2.50	5.00	10.00
—Reissue with new prefix					
LPM-2912 [M]	Always in My Heart	1964	3.75	7.50	15.00
LSP-2912 [S]	Always in My Heart	1964	5.00	10.00	20.00
LPM-2959 [M]	Twin Guitar Moods	1964	3.75	7.50	15.00
LSP-2959 [S]	Twin Guitar Moods	1964	5.00	10.00	20.00
AFL1-3241	Two Guitars	1979	2.50	5.00	10.00
LPM-3413 [M]	Many-Splendored Guitars	1965	3.75	7.50	15.00
LSP-3413 [S]	Many-Splendored Guitars	1965	5.00	10.00	20.00
AFL1-3505	Casually Classical	1977	2.50	5.00	10.00
—Reissue with new prefix					
LPM-3505 [M]	Casually Classical	1966	3.75	7.50	15.00
LSP-3505 [S]	Casually Classical	1966	5.00	10.00	20.00
AFL1-3535	Rainbows	1980	2.50	5.00	10.00
LPM-3611 [M]	Twin Guitars — In a Mood for Lovers	1966	3.75	7.50	15.00
LSP-3611 [S]	Twin Guitars — In a Mood for Lovers	1966	5.00	10.00	20.00
LPM-3723 [M]	Their Very Special Touch	1967	3.75	7.50	15.00
LSP-3723 [S]	Their Very Special Touch	1967	5.00	10.00	20.00
LPM-3909 [M]	Fascinating Rhythms of Their Brazil	1968	5.00	10.00	20.00
LSP-3909 [S]	Fascinating Rhythms of Their Brazil	1968	3.75	7.50	15.00
AFL1-3990	Beautiful Sounds	1981	2.50	5.00	10.00
AFL1-4007	The Best of Los Indios Tabajaras	1977	2.50	5.00	10.00
—Reissue with new prefix					
LSP-4007	The Best of Los Indios Tabajaras	1968	3.75	7.50	15.00
LSP-4013	In a Sentimental Mood	1968	3.75	7.50	15.00
LSP-4129	Song of the Islands	1969	3.75	7.50	15.00
AFL1-4273	Music for Romance	1982	2.50	5.00	10.00
LSP-4365	Dreams of Love	1970	3.75	7.50	15.00
LSP-4496	The Very Thought of You	1971	3.75	7.50	15.00
LSP-4615	What the World Needs Now	1971	3.00	6.00	12.00
AFL1-4649	Guitars on the Go	1983	2.50	5.00	10.00

LOS LOCOS DEL RITMO

Albums

Number	Title (A Side/B Side)	Yr	VG	VG+	NM
DIMSA					
8178	Rock!	196?	25.00	50.00	100.00

LOS SEVEN DAYS

Albums

Number	Title (A Side/B Side)	Yr	VG	VG+	NM
ECO					
314	Sha-La-La	196?	12.50	25.00	50.00

LOST, THE

45s

Number	Title (A Side/B Side)	Yr	VG	VG+	NM
CAPITOL					
5519	Back Door Blues/Maybe More Than You Do	1965	3.75	7.50	15.00
5708	Mean Motorcycle/Violet Gown	1966	3.75	7.50	15.00
5725	No Reason Why/Violet Gown	1966	3.75	7.50	15.00
JANUS					
109	I Shall Be Released/Shame	1969	2.50	5.00	10.00

LOST & FOUND

45s

Number	Title (A Side/B Side)	Yr	VG	VG+	NM
INTERNATIONAL ARTISTS					
120	Everybody's Here/Forever Lasting Plastic Words	1968	6.25	12.50	25.00
125	When Will You Come Through/Professor Black	1968	6.25	12.50	25.00

Albums

Number	Title (A Side/B Side)	Yr	VG	VG+	NM
INTERNATIONAL ARTISTS					
IA-3	Everybody's Here	1968	25.00	50.00	100.00
—Original pressing, no "Masterfonics" in dead wax					
IA-3	Everybody's Here	1979	3.75	7.50	15.00
—Reissue with "Masterfonics" in trail-off wax					

LOST NATION, THE

Albums

Number	Title (A Side/B Side)	Yr	VG	VG+	NM
RARE EARTH					
RS-518	Paradise Lost	1970	5.00	10.00	20.00

LOTHAR AND THE HAND PEOPLE

45s

Number	Title (A Side/B Side)	Yr	VG	VG+	NM
CAPITOL					
2008	Have Mercy (Mercy, Mercy, Mercy)/Let the Boy Pretend	1967	2.50	5.00	10.00
2376	Machines/Milkweed Love	1969	2.00	4.00	8.00
2556	Midnight Ranger/Yes, I Love You	1969	2.00	4.00	8.00
5874	L-O-V-E/Rose Colored Glasses	1967	2.50	5.00	10.00
5945	Comic Strip/Every Single Word	1967	2.50	5.00	10.00

Albums

Number	Title (A Side/B Side)	Yr	VG	VG+	NM
CAPITOL					
ST-247	Space Hymn	1969	10.00	20.00	40.00
SM-2997	Presenting Lothar and the Hand People	1977	2.00	4.00	8.00
—Reissue with new prefix					
ST 2997	Presenting Lothar and the Hand People	1968	10.00	20.00	40.00

LOU, HERB B., AND THE LEGAL EAGLES

Break-in record with HERB ALPERT involvement.

45s

Number	Title (A Side/B Side)	Yr	VG	VG+	NM
ARCH					
1607	The Trial/Kiss Me	1958	10.00	20.00	40.00

LOUDERMILK, JOHN D.

45s

Number	Title (A Side/B Side)	Yr	VG	VG+	NM
COLONIAL					
430	Sittin' in the Balcony/A-Plus in Love	1957	7.50	15.00	30.00
—As "Johnny Dee"					
430 [PS]	Sittin' in the Balcony/A-Plus in Love	1957	100.00	200.00	400.00
—As "Johnny Dee"					
435	Teenage Queen/It's Gotta Be You	1957	7.50	15.00	30.00
—As "Johnny Dee"					
COLUMBIA					
4-41165	Yearbook/Susie's House	1958	3.75	7.50	15.00
4-41165 [PS]	Yearbook/Susie's House	1958	6.25	12.50	25.00
4-41209	Lover's Lane/Yo Yo	1958	3.75	7.50	15.00
4-41247	Goin' Away to School/This Cold War with You	1958	3.75	7.50	15.00
4-41507	The Happy Wanderer/Red Headed Stranger	1959	3.75	7.50	15.00
4-41562	Tobacco Road/Midnight Bus	1960	5.00	10.00	20.00
DOT					
15699	Somebody Sweet/They Were Right	1958	7.50	15.00	30.00
—As "Johnny Dee"					
RCA VICTOR					
47-7938	Language of Love/Darling Jane	1961	3.00	6.00	12.00
47-7993	Thou Shalt Not Steal/Mister Jones	1962	3.00	6.00	12.00
47-8054	Callin' Doctor Casey/Oh How Sad	1962	3.00	6.00	12.00
47-8101	Road Hog/Angela Jones	1962	3.00	6.00	12.00
47-8101 [PS]	Road Hog/Angela Jones	1962	5.00	10.00	20.00
47-8154	Bad News/The Guitar Player	1963	3.00	6.00	12.00
47-8308	Blue Train (Of the Heartbreak Line)/Rhythm and Blues	1962	3.00	6.00	12.00
47-8389	Th' Wife/Nothing to Gain	1964	3.00	6.00	12.00
47-8826	Run On Home Baby Brother/Silver Cloud Talking Blues	1966	2.50	5.00	10.00
47-8973	I Hear It Now/You're the Guilty One	1966	2.50	5.00	10.00
47-9189	It's My Time/Bahama Mama	1967	2.50	5.00	10.00
47-9592	Sidewalks/The Odd Folks of Okracoke	1968	2.00	4.00	8.00
74-0121	Brown Girl/The Jones'	1969	2.00	4.00	8.00
WARNER BROS.					
7489	When I Was Nine/Lord Have Mercy	1971	—	3.50	7.00

Albums

Number	Title (A Side/B Side)	Yr	VG	VG+	NM
RCA VICTOR					
LPM-2434 [M]	Language of Love	1961	6.25	12.50	25.00
LSP-2434 [S]	Language of Love	1961	7.50	15.00	30.00
LPM-2539 [M]	Twelve Sides of Loudermilk	1962	5.00	10.00	20.00
LSP-2539 [S]	Twelve Sides of Loudermilk	1962	6.25	12.50	25.00
LPM-3497 [M]	A Bizarre Collection of the Most Unusual Songs	1965	5.00	10.00	20.00
LSP-3497 [S]	A Bizarre Collection of the Most Unusual Songs	1965	6.25	12.50	25.00
LPM-3807 [M]	Suburban Attitudes in Country Music	1967	6.25	12.50	25.00
LSP-3807 [S]	Suburban Attitudes in Country Music	1967	5.00	10.00	20.00
LSP-4040	Country Love Songs	1968	5.00	10.00	20.00
LSP-4097	The Open Mind of John D. Loudermilk	1968	5.00	10.00	20.00
WARNER BROS.					
WS 1922	Volume 1, Elloree	1971	3.75	7.50	15.00

LOUIE AND THE LOVERS

45s

Number	Title (A Side/B Side)	Yr	VG	VG+	NM
EPIC					
5-10616	Driver Go Slow/I Know You Know	1970	2.00	4.00	8.00
5-10678	Rise/I Don't Want to Be Seen with You	1970	2.00	4.00	8.00
5-10825	Little Georgie Baker/Tomorrows Just Might Change	1972	2.00	4.00	8.00

Number	Title (A Side/B Side)	Yr	VG	VG+	NM

Albums

EPIC

Number	Title (A Side/B Side)	Yr	VG	VG+	NM
E 30026	Rise	1970	5.00	10.00	20.00

LOUIS, BOBBY

45s

CAPITOL

Number	Title (A Side/B Side)	Yr	VG	VG+	NM
F4224	Adult Western/Love at First Sight	1959	7.50	15.00	30.00
F4272	I'm a Coward/Cell of Love	1959	7.50	15.00	30.00

LOUISE, TINA

Albums

CONCERT HALL

Number	Title (A Side/B Side)	Yr	VG	VG+	NM
H-1503 [M]	Her Portrait in Hi-Fi	1958	12.50	25.00	50.00
H-1521 [M]	It's Time for Tina	1958	50.00	100.00	200.00

URANIA

Number	Title (A Side/B Side)	Yr	VG	VG+	NM
ULM-2005 [M]	It's Time for Tina	1959	50.00	100.00	200.00
USD-2005 [S]	It's Time for Tina	1959	75.00	150.00	300.00

LOVE

45s

BLUE THUMB

Number	Title (A Side/B Side)	Yr	VG	VG+	NM
106	Stand Out/I'll Pray for You	1970	—	3.00	6.00
7116	Keep On Shining/Everlasting First	1970	—	3.00	6.00

ELEKTRA

Number	Title (A Side/B Side)	Yr	VG	VG+	NM
45603	My Little Red Book/Message to Pretty	1966	2.50	5.00	10.00
45605	7 and 7 Is/No. Fourteen	1966	2.50	5.00	10.00
45608	Stephanie Knows Who/Orange Sky	1966	7.50	15.00	30.00
45608	She Comes in Colors/Orange Sky	1966	2.50	5.00	10.00
45613	Que Vida/Hey Joe	1967	12.50	25.00	50.00
45629	Alone Again Or/A House Is Not a Motel	1968	2.50	5.00	10.00
45633	Laughing Stock/You're Mine and We Belong Together	1968	3.75	7.50	15.00
45700	Alone Again Or/Good Times	1970	2.00	4.00	8.00

RSO

Number	Title (A Side/B Side)	Yr	VG	VG+	NM
502	Time Is Like a River/With a Little Energy	1974	—	2.50	5.00
506	Good Old Fashioned Dream/You Said You Would	1975	—	2.50	5.00

Albums

BLUE THUMB

Number	Title (A Side/B Side)	Yr	VG	VG+	NM
BTS-8822	False Start	1970	5.00	10.00	20.00
BTS-9000 [(2)]	Out Here	1969	6.25	12.50	25.00

ELEKTRA

Number	Title (A Side/B Side)	Yr	VG	VG+	NM
EKL-4001 [M]	Love	1966	25.00	50.00	100.00
EKL-4001 [M-DJ]	Love	1966	75.00	150.00	300.00
—White label promo					
EKL-4005 [M]	Da Capo	1967	25.00	50.00	100.00
EKL-4013 [M]	Forever Changes	1967	12.50	25.00	50.00
EKL-4013 [M-DJ]	Forever Changes	1967	37.50	75.00	150.00
—White label promo					
EKS-74001 [S]	Love	1966	12.50	25.00	50.00
—Brown label					
EKS-74001 [S]	Love	1969	3.75	7.50	15.00
—Red label with large stylized "E"					
EKS-74001 [S]	Love	1971	3.00	6.00	12.00
—Butterfly label					
EKS-74005 [S]	Da Capo	1967	10.00	20.00	40.00
—Brown label					
EKS-74005 [S]	Da Capo	1969	3.75	7.50	15.00
—Red label with large stylized "E"					
EKS-74005 [S]	Da Capo	1971	3.00	6.00	12.00
—Butterfly label					
EKS-74013 [S]	Forever Changes	1967	7.50	15.00	30.00
—Brown label					
EKS-74013 [S]	Forever Changes	1969	3.75	7.50	15.00
—Red label with large stylized "E"					
EKS-74013 [S]	Forever Changes	1971	3.00	6.00	12.00
—Butterfly label					
EKS-74013 [S]	Forever Changes	1980	2.50	5.00	10.00
—Red label, small "E," Warner Communications logo on label					
EKS-74013 [S]	Forever Changes	1984	2.00	4.00	8.00
—Red and black label					
EKS-74049	Four Sail	1969	6.25	12.50	25.00
—Red label with large stylized "E"					
EKS-74049	Four Sail	1971	3.00	6.00	12.00
—Butterfly label					
EKS-74049 [DJ]	Four Sail	1969	20.00	40.00	80.00
—White label promo					
EKS-74058	Revisited	1970	6.25	12.50	25.00
—Red label with large stylized "E"					
EKS-74058	Revisited	1971	3.00	6.00	12.00
—Butterfly label					
EKS-74058	Revisited	1984	2.00	4.00	8.00
—Red and black label					
EKS-74058	Revisited	198?	2.50	5.00	10.00
—Red label, small "E," Warner Communications logo on label					

MCA

Number	Title (A Side/B Side)	Yr	VG	VG+	NM
27025	Studio/Live	1982	2.50	5.00	10.00

RHINO

Number	Title (A Side/B Side)	Yr	VG	VG+	NM
RNDF-251 [PD]	Love Live	1981	3.75	7.50	15.00
RNLP-800	Best of Love	1980	2.50	5.00	10.00
RNLP-70175	The Best of Love (1966-1969) (Golden Archive Series)	1987	2.50	5.00	10.00

RSO

Number	Title (A Side/B Side)	Yr	VG	VG+	NM
SO 4804	Reel to Real	1974	3.75	7.50	15.00

LOVE, DARLENE

Also see THE BLOSSOMS; THE CRYSTALS.

45s

COLUMBIA

Number	Title (A Side/B Side)	Yr	VG	VG+	NM
07984	He's Sure the Man I Love/Everybody Needs	1988	—	2.50	5.00

ELEKTRA

Number	Title (A Side/B Side)	Yr	VG	VG+	NM
69647	River Deep, Mountain High/Leader of the Pack	1985	—	2.00	4.00
—B-side by Leader of the Pack					
69647 [PS]	River Deep, Mountain High/Leader of the Pack	1985	—	2.00	4.00

PASSPORT

Number	Title (A Side/B Side)	Yr	VG	VG+	NM
7926	Christmas (Baby Please Come Home)/Playing for Keeps	1983	3.00	6.00	12.00

PHILLES

Number	Title (A Side/B Side)	Yr	VG	VG+	NM
111	(Today I Met) The Boy I'm Gonna Marry/My Heart Beat a Little Faster	1963	7.50	15.00	30.00
111	(Today I Met) The Boy I'm Gonna Marry/Playing for Keeps	1963	5.00	10.00	20.00
114	Wait 'Til My Bobby Gets Home/Take It From Me	1963	5.00	10.00	20.00
117	A Fine Fine Boy/Nino & Sonny (Big Trouble)	1963	5.00	10.00	20.00
119	Christmas (Baby Please Come Home)/Harry and Milt Meet Hal B.	1963	10.00	20.00	40.00
123	Stumble and Fall/(He's a) Quiet Guy	1964	200.00	400.00	800.00
—Yellow and red label stock copy; has been verified to exist					
123	Stumble and Fall/(He's a) Quiet Guy	1964	75.00	150.00	300.00
—Yellow and red label, "D.J. Copy Not for Sale" on label					
123 [DJ]	Stumble and Fall/(He's a) Quiet Guy	1964	37.50	75.00	150.00
—White label promo					
125X	Christmas (Baby Please Come Home)/Winter Wonderland	1965	6.25	12.50	25.00
125	Christmas (Baby Please Come Home)/X-Mas Blues	1964	100.00	200.00	400.00

REPRISE

Number	Title (A Side/B Side)	Yr	VG	VG+	NM
0534	Too Late to Say You're Sorry/If	1966	2.50	5.00	10.00

WARNER/SPECTOR

Number	Title (A Side/B Side)	Yr	VG	VG+	NM
0401	Christmas (Baby Please Come Home)/Winter Wonderland	1974	2.50	5.00	10.00
0410	Lord, If You're a Woman/Stumble and Fall	1975	2.50	5.00	10.00

Albums

COLUMBIA

Number	Title (A Side/B Side)	Yr	VG	VG+	NM
FC 40605	Paint Another Picture	1988	3.00	6.00	12.00

LOVE, HONEY, AND THE LOVE NOTES

45s

CAMEO

Number	Title (A Side/B Side)	Yr	VG	VG+	NM
380	We Belong Together/Mary Ann	1965	3.00	6.00	12.00
409	Baby Baby You/Beg Me	1966	3.00	6.00	12.00
—As "The Lovenotes"					

LOVE, HOT SHOT

45s

SUN

Number	Title (A Side/B Side)	Yr	VG	VG+	NM
196	Wolf Call Boogie/Harmonica Jam	1954	1000.	2000.	4000.

LOVE, MICHAEL

Not the Beach Boy.

45s

COLUMBIA

Number	Title (A Side/B Side)	Yr	VG	VG+	NM
44253	Mrs. MacAbee/I Love Those Trees	1967	2.00	4.00	8.00

LOVE CHILDS AFRO CUBAN BLUES BAND

12-Inch Singles

MIDSONG INT'L.

Number	Title (A Side/B Side)	Yr	VG	VG+	NM
MD-10983	Oye Como Va (9:56)/Medley: Spanish Harlem-Dancin' to Spandisco	1977	3.00	6.00	12.00

45s

ROULETTE

Number	Title (A Side/B Side)	Yr	VG	VG+	NM
7172	Life and Death in G & A/Bang Bang	1975	—	2.50	5.00
7180	Black Skin Blue Eyed Boys/Ask Me	1975	—	2.50	5.00

Albums

MIDSONG INT'L.

Number	Title (A Side/B Side)	Yr	VG	VG+	NM
BKL1-2292	Spandisco	1977	2.50	5.00	10.00

ROULETTE

Number	Title (A Side/B Side)	Yr	VG	VG+	NM
3016	Out Among 'Em	1975	2.50	5.00	10.00

LOVE EXCHANGE, THE

45s

UPTOWN

Number	Title (A Side/B Side)	Yr	VG	VG+	NM
755	Swallow the Sun/Mellow Memory	1968	6.25	12.50	25.00

Albums

TOWER

Number	Title (A Side/B Side)	Yr	VG	VG+	NM
ST 5115	The Love Exchange	1968	6.25	12.50	25.00

LOVE GENERATION, THE

45s

IMPERIAL

Number	Title (A Side/B Side)	Yr	VG	VG+	NM
66243	Groovy Summertime/Playin' on the Strings of the Wind	1967	2.00	4.00	8.00
66254	Meet Me at the Love-In/She Touched Me	1967	2.00	4.00	8.00
66275	Maman (Mama)/W.C. Fields	1968	2.00	4.00	8.00
66289	Love and Sunshine/Magic Land	1968	2.00	4.00	8.00
66310	Montage from "How Sweet It Is" (I Know That You Know)/Consciousness Expansion	1968	2.00	4.00	8.00
66336	Let the Good Time In/Catching Up on Fun	1968	2.00	4.00	8.00

Albums

IMPERIAL

Number	Title (A Side/B Side)	Yr	VG	VG+	NM
LP-9351 [M]	The Love Generation	1967	5.00	10.00	20.00
LP-12351 [S]	The Love Generation	1967	5.00	10.00	20.00
LP-12364	A Generation of Love	1968	5.00	10.00	20.00
LP-12408	Montage	1968	5.00	10.00	20.00

LOVE NOTES, THE (1)

45s

HOLIDAY

Number	Title (A Side/B Side)	Yr	VG	VG+	NM
2605	United/Tonight	1957	15.00	30.00	60.00
—Glossy label					

Number	Title (A Side/B Side)	Yr	VG	VG+	NM
2605	United/Tonight	1957	5.00	10.00	20.00
—Flat (matte) label					
2607	If I Could Make You Mine/Don't Go	1957	10.00	20.00	40.00

LOVE NOTES, THE (2)

Number	Title (A Side/B Side)	Yr	VG	VG+	NM
45s					
IMPERIAL					
5254	Surrender Your Heart/Get On My Train	1953	300.00	600.00	1200.
RAINBOW					
266	I'm Sorry/Sweet Lulu	1954	75.00	150.00	300.00
RIVIERA					
970	I'm Sorry/Sweet Lulu	1954	200.00	400.00	800.00
975	Since I Fell for You/Don't Be No Fool	1954	250.00	500.00	1000.
—Authentic copies have a lavender (light purple) label, counterfeits have a pink label					

LOVE NOTES, THE (3)

Number	Title (A Side/B Side)	Yr	VG	VG+	NM
45s					
WILSHIRE					
200	Nancy/Our Songs of Love	1963	10.00	20.00	40.00
203	Gloria/The Mathematics of Love	1963	25.00	50.00	100.00

LOVE, PEACE AND HAPPINESS

Also see THE NEW BIRTH; THE NITE-LITERS.

Number	Title (A Side/B Side)	Yr	VG	VG+	NM
45s					
RCA VICTOR					
74-0402	Don't Blame the Young Folks for the Drug Society/You've Got to Be the One for Me	1970	—	3.00	6.00
74-0468	Message to the Establishment/Love Is Far Stronger Than We	1971	—	2.50	5.00
74-0584	Strip Me Naked/Unborn Child	1971	—	2.50	5.00
74-0740	I Don't Want to Do Wrong/Lonely Room	1972	—	2.50	5.00
Albums					
RCA VICTOR					
LSP-4535	Love Is Stronger	1971	3.00	6.00	12.00
LSP-4721	Here 'Tis	1972	3.00	6.00	12.00

LOVE POTION, THE

Number	Title (A Side/B Side)	Yr	VG	VG+	NM
45s					
KAPP					
979	This Love/Moby Binks	1969	2.00	4.00	8.00
TCB					
1601	This Love/Mr. Farouk	1968	3.75	7.50	15.00

LOVE SCULPTURE

DAVE EDMUNDS was in this group.

Number	Title (A Side/B Side)	Yr	VG	VG+	NM
45s					
PARROT					
335	Sabre Dance/Think of Love	1969	3.75	7.50	15.00
362	In the Land of the Few/Farandole	1970	3.75	7.50	15.00
Albums					
EMI AMERICA					
SQ-17208	Blues Helping	1986	3.00	6.00	12.00
—Reissue of Rare Earth LP					
PARROT					
PAS 71035	Forms and Feelings	1970	6.25	12.50	25.00
RARE EARTH					
RS-505	Blues Helping	1969	10.00	20.00	40.00

LOVE SOCIETY, THE

Number	Title (A Side/B Side)	Yr	VG	VG+	NM
45s					
MERCURY					
73130	America/Wanda	1970	3.75	7.50	15.00
RCA VICTOR					
74-0257	Don't Worry Baby/You Know How I Feel (And Why)	1969	2.50	5.00	10.00
SCEPTER					
12223	Without You/Do You Wanna Dance	1968	3.00	6.00	12.00
12236	Tobacco Road/Drops of Rain	1969	3.00	6.00	12.00

LOVE UNLIMITED

Number	Title (A Side/B Side)	Yr	VG	VG+	NM
12-Inch Singles					
UNLIMITED GOLD					
1410	High Steppin', Hip Dressin' Fella (You Got It Together)/(Instrumental)	1979	3.00	6.00	12.00
45s					
20TH CENTURY					
2025	Oh Love, Well We Finally Made It/Yes, We Finally Made It	1973	—	2.50	5.00
2062	It May Be Winter Outside (But In My Heart It's Spring)/It's Winter Again	1973	—	2.50	5.00
2082	Under the Influence of Love/(Instrumental)	1974	—	2.50	5.00
2110	People of Tomorrow Are the Children of Today/So Nice to Hear	1974	—	2.50	5.00
2141	I Belong to You/And Only You	1974	—	2.50	5.00
2183	Share a Little Love in Your Heart/I Love You So, Never Gonna Let You Go	1975	—	2.50	5.00
MCA					
40009	Fragile/I'll Be Yours Forever	1973	—	3.00	6.00
UNI					
55319	Walkin' in the Rain with the One I Love/I Should Have Known	1972	—	3.00	6.00
55342	Is It Really True Boy — Is It Really Me?/Another Chance	1972	—	3.00	6.00
55349	Are You Really Sure/Another Chance	1972	—	3.00	6.00
UNLIMITED GOLD					
1409	High Steppin', Hip Dressin' Fella (You Got It Together)/(Instrumental)	1979	—	2.50	5.00
1412	I'm So Glad That I'm a Woman/Gotta Be Where You Are	1980	—	2.50	5.00
1417	If You Want Me, Say It/When I'm In Your Arms, Everything's Okay	1980	—	2.50	5.00
7001	I Did It for Love/(Instrumental)	1977	—	2.50	5.00
Albums					
20TH CENTURY					
T-414	Under the Influence of...	1973	2.50	5.00	10.00
T-443	In Heat	1974	2.50	5.00	10.00
MCA					
181	Love Unlimited	1973	3.00	6.00	12.00
—Reissue of Uni 73131					
316	Under the Influence of...	1973	—	—	—
—Canceled; issued on 20th Century 414					
UNI					
73131	Love Unlimited	1972	3.75	7.50	15.00
UNLIMITED GOLD					
101	He's All I Got	1977	2.50	5.00	10.00
JZ 36130	Love Is Back	1979	2.50	5.00	10.00

LOVE UNLIMITED ORCHESTRA

Number	Title (A Side/B Side)	Yr	VG	VG+	NM
12-Inch Singles					
20TH CENTURY					
TCD-66	Don't You Know How Much I Love You/Hey Look at Me, I'm in Love	1978	3.75	7.50	15.00
UNLIMITED GOLD					
1406	Jamaican Girl/I'm in the Mood	1979	3.00	6.00	12.00
1414	Young America/Freeway Flyer	1980	3.00	6.00	12.00
02135	Lift Your Voice and Say (United We Can Live in Peace Today)/My Fantasies	1981	2.50	5.00	10.00
02479	Welcome Aboard/Strange	1981	2.50	5.00	10.00
02636	Night Life in the City/Wind	1981	2.50	5.00	10.00
03882	My Laboratory Is Ready for You/Goodbye Concerto	1983	2.50	5.00	10.00
45s					
20TH CENTURY					
2069	Love's Theme/Sweet Moments	1973	—	2.50	5.00
2090	Rhapsody in White/Barry's Theme	1974	—	2.50	5.00
2107	Theme from "Together Brothers"/Find the Man Brothers	1974	—	2.50	5.00
2145	Baby Blues/What a Groove	1974	—	2.50	5.00
2162	Satin Soul/Just Living It Up	1975	—	2.50	5.00
2197	Forever in Love/Only You Can Make Me Blue	1975	—	2.50	5.00
2281	Midnight Groove/It's Only What I Feel	1976	—	2.50	5.00
2301	My Sweet Summer Suite/Just Living It Up	1976	—	2.50	5.00
2325	Theme from King Kong (Pt. 1)/Theme from King Kong (Pt. 2)	1977	—	2.50	5.00
2348	Brazilian Love Song/My Sweet Summer Suite	1977	—	2.50	5.00
2364	Whisper Softly/Hey Look at Me, I'm in Love	1978	—	2.50	5.00
2367	Don't You Know How Much I Love You/Hey Look at Me, I'm in Love	1978	—	2.50	5.00
2399	Theme from "Superman"/Theme from "Shaft"	1978	—	2.50	5.00
UNLIMITED GOLD					
1405	Jamaican Girl/I'm in the Mood	1979	—	2.50	5.00
1413	Young America/Freeway Flyer	1980	—	2.50	5.00
1421	I Wanna Boogie and Woogie with You/I'm in the Mood	1980	—	2.50	5.00
1423	Vieni Qua Bella Mi/Bayou	1980	—	2.50	5.00
02134	Lift Your Voice and Say (United We Can Live in Peace Today)/My Fantasies	1981	—	2.00	4.00
02478	Welcome Aboard/Strange	1981	—	2.00	4.00
02635	Night Life in the City/Wind	1981	—	2.00	4.00
03881	My Laboratory Is Ready for You/Goodbye Concerto	1983	—	2.00	4.00
Albums					
20TH CENTURY					
T-101	Together Brothers	1974	3.00	6.00	12.00
T-433	Rhapsody in White	1974	2.50	5.00	10.00
T-458	White Gold	1974	2.50	5.00	10.00
T-480	Music Maestro Please	1975	2.50	5.00	10.00
T-517	My Sweet Summer Suite	1976	2.50	5.00	10.00
T-554	My Musical Bouquet	1978	2.50	5.00	10.00
T-582	Movie Themes	1978	2.50	5.00	10.00
UNLIMITED GOLD					
FZ 37425	Welcome Aboard	1981	2.50	5.00	10.00
FZ 38366	Rise	1983	2.50	5.00	10.00

LOVECRAFT

See H.P. LOVECRAFT.

LOVEJOYS, THE

Number	Title (A Side/B Side)	Yr	VG	VG+	NM
45s					
RED BIRD					
10-004	Payin'/It's Mighty Nice	1964	7.50	15.00	30.00

LOVELITES, THE

Number	Title (A Side/B Side)	Yr	VG	VG+	NM
45s					
BANDERA					
2515	I Found Me a Lover/You Better Stop It	1967	3.75	7.50	15.00

LOVENOTES, THE

See HONEY LOVE AND THE LOVE NOTES.

LOVERS, THE (1)

Husband-and-wife R&B duo.

Number	Title (A Side/B Side)	Yr	VG	VG+	NM
45s					
ALADDIN					
3419	Tell Me/Love Bug Bit Me	1958	10.00	20.00	40.00
IMPERIAL					
5845	Darling It's Wonderful/I Want to Be Loved	1962	5.00	10.00	20.00
5960	Tell Me/Let's Elope	1963	5.00	10.00	20.00
66055	Darling It's Wonderful/I Want to Be Loved	1964	3.75	7.50	15.00

Number	Title (A Side/B Side)	Yr	VG	VG+	NM
LAMP					
2005	Darling It's Wonderful/Gotta Whole Lot of Livin' to Do	1957	12.50	25.00	50.00
2013	I Wanna Be Loved/Let's Elope	1957	12.50	25.00	50.00
2018	Tell Me/Love Bug Bit Me	1958	12.50	25.00	50.00
POST					
10007	Darling It's Wonderful/Gotta Whole Lot of Livin' to Do	1963	3.75	7.50	15.00

LOVERS, THE (2)

45s

Number	Title (A Side/B Side)	Yr	VG	VG+	NM
AGON					
1011	Caravan of Lonely Men/In My Tenement	1965	6.25	12.50	25.00
GATE					
501	Someone/Do This For Me	1965	25.00	50.00	100.00
PHILIPS					
40353	Someone/Do This for Me	1966	5.00	10.00	20.00

LOVERS, THE (3)

45s

Number	Title (A Side/B Side)	Yr	VG	VG+	NM
CASINO					
103	Let's/Big Axe	1958	5.00	10.00	20.00

LOVERS, THE (4)

45s

Number	Title (A Side/B Side)	Yr	VG	VG+	NM
MARLIN					
3313	Discomania (Part 1)/Discomania (Part 2)	1977	—	2.50	5.00

LOVERS, THE (U)

These could be groups (1) or (2).

45s

Number	Title (A Side/B Side)	Yr	VG	VG+	NM
CHECKER					
1100	It's Too Late/Security	1965	2.50	5.00	10.00
DECCA					
29862	Don't Touch Me/Let Me Be the First to Know	1956	10.00	20.00	40.00
KELLER					
101	Party Line/Strange As It Seems	1961	10.00	20.00	40.00

LOVETONES, THE

45s

Number	Title (A Side/B Side)	Yr	VG	VG+	NM
LOVE-TONE					
101	You Can Tell Me That This Is Christmas/When I Asked My Love	1961	5.00	10.00	20.00
PLUS					
108	Talk to an Angel/Take It Easy, Baby	1956	125.00	250.00	500.00

LOVIN' SPOONFUL, THE

45s

Number	Title (A Side/B Side)	Yr	VG	VG+	NM
KAMA SUTRA					
201	Do You Believe in Magic/On the Road Again	1965	3.75	7.50	15.00
—Originals have a mostly red-orange label					
201	Do You Believe in Magic/On the Road Again	1965	2.50	5.00	10.00
—Second pressings have a mostly yellow label with "Kama Sutra" in red					
201	Do You Believe in Magic/On the Road Again	1965	2.00	4.00	8.00
—Third pressings have a mostly yellow label with "Kama Sutra" in black					
205	You Didn't Have to Be So Nice/My Gal	1965	3.00	6.00	12.00
—Originals have a mostly red-orange label					
205	You Didn't Have to Be So Nice/My Gal	1965	2.50	5.00	10.00
—Second pressings have a mostly yellow label with "Kama Sutra" in red					
205	You Didn't Have to Be So Nice/My Gal	1965	2.00	4.00	8.00
—Third pressings have a mostly yellow label with "Kama Sutra" in black					
205 [PS]	You Didn't Have to Be So Nice/My Gal	1965	3.75	7.50	15.00
208	Daydream/Night Owl Blues	1966	3.00	6.00	12.00
—Originals have a mostly yellow label with "Kama Sutra" in red					
208	Daydream/Night Owl Blues	1966	2.50	5.00	10.00
—Second pressings have a mostly yellow label with "Kama Sutra" in black					
208 [PS]	Daydream/Night Owl Blues	1966	3.75	7.50	15.00
209	Did You Ever Have to Make Up Your Mind/Didn't Want to Have to Do It	1966	2.50	5.00	10.00
209 [PS]	Did You Ever Have to Make Up Your Mind/Didn't Want to Have to Do It	1966	3.75	7.50	15.00
211	Summer in the City/Butchie's Tune	1966	2.50	5.00	10.00
211 [PS]	Summer in the City/Butchie's Tune	1966	3.75	7.50	15.00
216	Rain on the Roof/Pow	1966	2.50	5.00	10.00
216 [PS]	Rain on the Roof/Pow	1966	3.75	7.50	15.00
219	Nashville Cats/Full Measure	1966	2.50	5.00	10.00
219 [PS]	Nashville Cats/Full Measure	1966	3.75	7.50	15.00
220	Darling Be Home Soon/Darlin' Companion	1967	2.50	5.00	10.00
220 [PS]	Darling Be Home Soon/Darlin' Companion	1967	3.75	7.50	15.00
225	Six O'Clock/The Finale	1967	2.50	5.00	10.00
225 [PS]	Six O'Clock/The Finale	1967	3.75	7.50	15.00
231	Lonely (Amy's Theme)/You're a Big Boy Now	1967	3.75	7.50	15.00
239	She Is Still a Mystery/Only Pretty, What a Pity	1967	2.50	5.00	10.00
239 [PS]	She Is Still a Mystery/Only Pretty, What a Pity	1967	3.75	7.50	15.00
241	Money/Close Your Eyes	1967	2.00	4.00	8.00
250	Never Going Back/Forever	1968	2.00	4.00	8.00
251	Revelation Revolution '69/Run with You	1968	2.00	4.00	8.00
255	Me About You/Amazing Air	1968	2.00	4.00	8.00
551	Summer in the City/You and Me and Rain on the Roof	1972	—	3.00	6.00
608 [DJ]	Daydream (mono/stereo)	1976	—	3.00	6.00
—Stock copy not known to exist					

Albums

Number	Title (A Side/B Side)	Yr	VG	VG+	NM
ACCORD					
SN-7196	Distant Echoes	1981	2.50	5.00	10.00
BUDDAH					
BDM-5706	The Best of the Lovin' Spoonful	197?	3.00	6.00	12.00
BLB6-8339	The Best of the Lovin' Spoonful	198?	2.50	5.00	10.00
—Reissue of 5706					
KAMA SUTRA					
KOPS-750 [(2)]	24 Karat Hits	1968	5.00	10.00	20.00
KSBS-2011	The John Sebastian Song Book	1970	3.75	7.50	15.00
KSBS-2013	The Very Best of the Lovin' Spoonful	1970	3.75	7.50	15.00
KSBS-2029	Once Upon a Time	1971	3.75	7.50	15.00
KSBS-2608 [(2)]	The Best...Lovin' Spoonful	1976	5.00	10.00	20.00
KLP-8050 [M]	Do You Believe in Magic	1965	5.00	10.00	20.00
KLPS-8050 [S]	Do You Believe in Magic	1965	7.50	15.00	30.00
KLP-8051 [M]	Daydream	1966	5.00	10.00	20.00
KLPS-8051 [S]	Daydream	1966	7.50	15.00	30.00
KLP-8053 [M]	What's Up, Tiger Lily?	1966	5.00	10.00	20.00
KLPS-8053 [S]	What's Up, Tiger Lily?	1966	7.50	15.00	30.00
KLP-8054 [M]	Hums of the Lovin' Spoonful	1966	5.00	10.00	20.00
KLPS-8054 [S]	Hums of the Lovin' Spoonful	1966	7.50	15.00	30.00
KLP-8056 [M]	The Best of the Lovin' Spoonful	1967	3.75	7.50	15.00
—Came with four bonus photos of the band, which are priced separately					
KLPS-8056 [S]	The Best of the Lovin' Spoonful	1967	3.75	7.50	15.00
—Came with four bonus photos of the band, which are priced separately					
KLP/S-8056	The Best of the Lovin' Spoonful Bonus Photos (4)	1967	2.50	5.00	10.00
KLP-8058 [M]	You're a Big Boy Now	1967	5.00	10.00	20.00
KLPS-8058 [S]	You're a Big Boy Now	1967	5.00	10.00	20.00
KLP-8061 [M]	Everything Playing	1968	7.50	15.00	30.00
KLPS-8061 [S]	Everything Playing	1968	5.00	10.00	20.00
KLPS-8064	The Best of the Lovin' Spoonful, Volume 2	1968	5.00	10.00	20.00
KLPS-8073	Revelation: Revolution '69	1969	6.25	12.50	25.00
ST-90597 [S]	Do You Believe in Magic	1965	10.00	20.00	40.00
—Capitol Record Club edition					
T-90597 [M]	Do You Believe in Magic	1965	7.50	15.00	30.00
—Capitol Record Club edition					
ST-91102 [S]	The Best of the Lovin' Spoonful	1967	5.00	10.00	20.00
—Capitol Record Club edition					
ST-91198 [S]	You're a Big Boy Now	1967	6.25	12.50	25.00
—Capitol Record Club edition					
PAIR					
PDL2-1200 [(2)]	The Best of the Lovin' Spoonful	1986	3.00	6.00	12.00
RHINO					
RNLP-114	The Best of the Lovin' Spoonful, Vol. 2	1985	2.50	5.00	10.00

LOWE, JIM

45s

Number	Title (A Side/B Side)	Yr	VG	VG+	NM
20TH CENTURY FOX					
426	Hootenanny Granny/These Bones Gonna Rise Again	1963	2.00	4.00	8.00
BUDDAH					
44	Michael J. Polalrd for President/The Ol' Racetrack	1968	—	3.00	6.00
DECCA					
31153	Someone Else's Arms/Man of the Cloth	1960	2.50	5.00	10.00
31198	That Do Make It Nice/Two Sides to Every Story	1961	2.50	5.00	10.00
DOT					
15381	Close the Door/Nuevo Laredo	1955	3.00	6.00	12.00
15407	Maybellene/Rene La Rue	1955	3.00	6.00	12.00
15429	John Jacob Jingleheimer Smith/St. James Avenue	1955	3.00	6.00	12.00
15456	The Sixty-Four Thousand Dollar Question/Blue Suede Shoes	1956	3.00	6.00	12.00
15486	The Green Door/(The Story of) The Little Man in Chinatown	1956	3.75	7.50	15.00
—Originals have maroon labels					
15486	The Green Door/(The Story of) The Little Man in Chinatown	1956	3.00	6.00	12.00
—Second pressings have black labels					
15525	By You, By You, By You/I Feel the Beat	1957	2.50	5.00	10.00
15569	Four Walls/Talkin' to the Blues	1957	3.00	6.00	12.00
15611	From a Jack to a King/Slow Train	1957	2.50	5.00	10.00
15665	Rick-a-Chickie/The Bright Light	1957	2.50	5.00	10.00
15693	Kewpie Doll/The Lady from Johannesburg	1958	2.50	5.00	10.00
15753	Take Us To Your President/Later On Tonight	1958	2.50	5.00	10.00
15832	Chapel Bells on Chapel Hill/Ja, Ja, Ja	1958	2.50	5.00	10.00
15869	Play Number Eleven/Come Away from Her Arms	1958	2.50	5.00	10.00
15954	I'm Movin' On/Without You	1959	2.50	5.00	10.00
16046	He'll Have to Go/Dress Rehearsal	1960	2.50	5.00	10.00
16074	The Midnight Ride of Paul Revere/A Tomorrow That Never Comes	1960	2.50	5.00	10.00
16636	Addis Ababa/Have You Ever Been Lonely	1964	—	3.00	6.00
MERCURY					
70163	Gambler's Guitar/The Martins and the Coys	1953	5.00	10.00	20.00
70265	Santa Claus Rides a Strawberry Roan/Love in Both Directions	1953	5.00	10.00	20.00
70319	Goodbye Little Sweetheart/River Boat	1954	5.00	10.00	20.00
71016	Prince of Peace/Santa Claus Rides a Strawberry Roan	1956	3.75	7.50	15.00
UNITED ARTISTS					
874	Mr. Moses/Make Your Back Strong	1965	—	3.00	6.00
50124	Gambler's Guitar/Blotson Bottom	1967	—	3.00	6.00

Albums

Number	Title (A Side/B Side)	Yr	VG	VG+	NM
DOT					
DLP-3051 [M]	The Green Door	1956	37.50	75.00	150.00
DLP-3114 [M]	Wicked Women	1958	25.00	50.00	100.00
DLP-3681 [M]	Songs They Sing Behind the Green Door	1965	6.25	12.50	25.00
DLP-25881 [S]	Songs They Sing Behind the Green Door	1965	7.50	15.00	30.00
MERCURY					
MG-20246 [M]	The Door of Fame	1957	37.50	75.00	150.00

LOWE, VIRGINIA

45s

Number	Title (A Side/B Side)	Yr	VG	VG+	NM
MELBA					
107	I'm in Love with Elvis Presley/Empty Feeling	1956	12.50	25.00	50.00

LRY

Albums

Number	Title (A Side/B Side)	Yr	VG	VG+	NM
CONGRESS OF THE CROW					
8031002	The LRY Record	1968	50.00	100.00	200.00

LUCAS, AL

45s

Number	Title (A Side/B Side)	Yr	VG	VG+	NM
CHALLENGE					
59042	She's My Baby/Got the Ring	1959	15.00	30.00	60.00
59050	Sweet Tooth for My Baby Ruth/Always	1959	10.00	20.00	40.00

LUDDEN, ALLEN

Albums

Number	Title (A Side/B Side)	Yr	VG	VG+	NM
RCA VICTOR					
LPM-2934 [M]	Allen Ludden Sings His Favorite Songs	1964	5.00	10.00	20.00
LSP-2934 [S]	Allen Ludden Sings His Favorite Songs	1964	6.25	12.50	25.00

LUKE, ROBIN

45s

Number	Title (A Side/B Side)	Yr	VG	VG+	NM
BERTRAM INTERNATIONAL					
206	Susie Darlin'/Living's Loving You	1958	15.00	30.00	60.00
206 [PS]	Susie Darlin'/Living's Loving You	1958	25.00	50.00	100.00
208	My Girl/Chicka Chicka Honey	1958	7.50	15.00	30.00
210	Strollin' Blues/You Can't Stop Me from Dreaming	1959	7.50	15.00	30.00
212	Five Minutes More/Who's Gonna Hold Your Hand	1959	7.50	15.00	30.00
DOT					
15781	Susie Darlin'/Living's Loving You	1958	6.25	12.50	25.00
15839	My Girl/Chicka Chicka Honey	1958	5.00	10.00	20.00
15899	Strollin' Blues/You Can't Stop Me from Dreaming	1959	5.00	10.00	20.00
15959	Five Minutes More/Who's Gonna Hold Your Hand	1959	5.00	10.00	20.00
16001	Make Me a Dreamer/Walkin' in the Moonlight	1959	5.00	10.00	20.00
16040	Bad Boy/School Bus Love Affair	1960	5.00	10.00	20.00
16096	Everlovin'/Well Oh Well Oh	1960	5.00	10.00	20.00
16096 [PS]	Everlovin'/Well Oh Well Oh	1960	15.00	30.00	60.00
16170	So Alone/All Because of You	1960	5.00	10.00	20.00
16229	Part of a Fool/Poor Little Rich Boy	1961	3.75	7.50	15.00
16366	Foggin' Up the Windows/Time	1962	3.75	7.50	15.00
—With Roberta Shore					
INTERNATIONAL					
206	Susie Darlin'/Living's Loving You	1958	250.00	500.00	1000.
—Light blue label					

7-Inch Extended Plays

Number	Title (A Side/B Side)	Yr	VG	VG+	NM
DOT					
DEP-1092	(contents unknown)	1958	100.00	200.00	400.00
DEP-1092 [PS]	Susie Darlin'	1958	100.00	200.00	400.00

LUKE THE DRIFTER

See HANK WILLIAMS.

LUKE THE DRIFTER, JR.

See HANK WILLIAMS, JR.

LULU

12-Inch Singles

Number	Title (A Side/B Side)	Yr	VG	VG+	NM
SBK					
19777	Independence (5 versions)	1993	2.00	4.00	8.00

45s

Number	Title (A Side/B Side)	Yr	VG	VG+	NM
ALFA					
7006	I Could Never Miss You (More Than I Do)/Dance to the Feeling	1981	—	2.00	4.00
7006 [PS]	I Could Never Miss You (More Than I Do)/Dance to the Feeling	1981	—	2.50	5.00
—With Lulu wearing a spotted headband					
7006 [PS]	I Could Never Miss You (More Than I Do)/Dance to the Feeling	1981	—	3.00	6.00
—With Lulu not wearing a headband (original)					
7011	If I Were You/You Win, I Lose	1981	—	2.00	4.00
7011 [PS]	If I Were You/You Win, I Lose	1981	—	2.50	5.00
7021	Who's Foolin' Who/You Win, I Lose	1982	—	2.00	4.00
ATCO					
6722	Oh Me Oh My (I'm a Fool for You Baby)/Sweep Around Your Own Back Door	1969	2.00	4.00	8.00
6749	Hum a Song (From Your Heart)/Where's Eddie	1970	—	3.00	6.00
6761	Good Day Sunshine/After the Feeling Is Gone	1970	—	3.00	6.00
6774	Melody Fair/To the Other Woman	1970	—	3.00	6.00
6819	Goodbye My Love, Goodbye/Everybody's Got to Clap	1971	—	3.00	6.00
6885	It Takes a Real Man/You Ain't Wrong, You Just Ain't Right	1972	—	3.00	6.00
CHELSEA					
78-0121	Make Believe World/Help Me Help You	1973	2.00	4.00	8.00
3001	The Man Who Sold the World/Watch That Man	1974	7.50	15.00	30.00
—A David Bowie song on the A-side...and produced by Bowie, too					
3009	The Man with a Golden Gun/Baby I Don't Care	1974	5.00	10.00	20.00
3011	Take Your Mama for a Ride (Long)/Take Your Mama for a Ride (Short)	1975	2.50	5.00	10.00
3019	Boy Meets Girl/(B-side unknown)	1975	2.50	5.00	10.00
3038	Heaven and Earth and the Stars/(B-side unknown)	1976	5.00	10.00	20.00
EPIC					
10187	To Sir with Love/The Boat That I Row	1967	2.50	5.00	10.00
10210	Dreamy Nights and Days/Let's Pretend	1967	2.00	4.00	8.00
10260/65 [DJ]	Best of Both Worlds/Everybody Knows	1968	6.25	12.50	25.00
—B-side by the Dave Clark Five; odd promo					
10260	Best of Both Worlds/Love Loves to Love Love	1967	2.00	4.00	8.00
10260 [PS]	Best of Both Worlds/Love Loves to Love Love	1967	5.00	10.00	20.00
10302	Me, the Peaceful Heart/Look Out	1968	2.00	4.00	8.00
10302 [PS]	Me, the Peaceful Heart/Look Out	1968	5.00	10.00	20.00
10346	Sad Memories/Boy	1968	2.00	4.00	8.00
10367	Morning Dew/You and I	1968	2.00	4.00	8.00
10403	Without Him/This Time	1968	2.00	4.00	8.00
10420	Rattler/I'm a Tiger	1968	2.00	4.00	8.00
PARROT					
9678	Shout/Forget Me Baby	1964	5.00	10.00	20.00
9714	Here Comes the Night/I'll Come Running	1964	5.00	10.00	20.00
9778	Leave a Little Love/He Don't Want Your Love Anymore	1965	5.00	10.00	20.00
9791	Try to Understand/Not in This Whole World	1965	5.00	10.00	20.00
40021	Shout/When He Touches Me	1967	2.50	5.00	10.00
ROCKET					
YB-11355	Don't Take Love for Granted/Love Is the Sweetest Mistake	1978	—	2.50	5.00

7-Inch Extended Plays

Number	Title (A Side/B Side)	Yr	VG	VG+	NM
EPIC					
5-26339 [DJ]	To Sir With Love/Morning Dew/Love Loves to Love Love//Best of Both Worlds/Day Tripper/Take Me in Your Arms (And Love Me)	1967	3.75	7.50	15.00
—Jukebox mini-LP, small hole, plays at 33 1/3 rpm					
5-26339 [PS]	To Sir With Love	1967	3.75	7.50	15.00

Albums

Number	Title (A Side/B Side)	Yr	VG	VG+	NM
ALFA					
10006	Lulu	1981	3.00	6.00	12.00
ATCO					
33-310 [M-DJ]	New Routes	1970	7.50	15.00	30.00
—White label promo; no stock copies were issued in mono					
SD 33-310 [S]	New Routes	1970	3.00	6.00	12.00
33-330 [M-DJ]	Melody Fair	1970	7.50	15.00	30.00
—White label promo; no stock copies were issued in mono					
SD 33-330 [S]	Melody Fair	1970	3.00	6.00	12.00
CHELSEA					
BCL1-0144	Lulu	1973	3.00	6.00	12.00
CHL-518	Heaven and Earth and the Stars	1976	5.00	10.00	20.00
EPIC					
LN 24339 [M]	To Sir with Love	1967	6.25	12.50	25.00
BN 26339 [P]	To Sir with Love	1967	7.50	15.00	30.00
BN 26536	It's Lulu	1970	3.00	6.00	12.00
HARMONY					
H 30249	To Love Somebody	1970	5.00	10.00	20.00
PARROT					
PA 61016 [M]	From Lulu with Love	1967	15.00	30.00	60.00
PAS 71016 [S]	From Lulu with Love	1967	20.00	40.00	80.00
PICKWICK					
SPC-3237	Lulu	1973	2.00	4.00	8.00
ROCKET					
BXL1-3073	Don't Take Love for Granted	1978	3.00	6.00	12.00

LUMAN, BOB

45s

Number	Title (A Side/B Side)	Yr	VG	VG+	NM
CAPITOL					
F3972	Try Me/I Know My Baby Cares	1958	7.50	15.00	30.00
F4059	Precious/Svengali	1958	7.50	15.00	30.00
EPIC					
10312	Ain't Got Time to Be Unhappy/I Can't Remember to Forget	1968	—	3.00	6.00
10381	I Like Trains/A World of Unhappiness	1968	—	3.00	6.00
10416	I'm In This Town for Good/A Woman Without Love	1968	—	3.00	6.00
10439	Come On Home and Sing the Blues to Daddy/Big, Big World	1969	—	3.00	6.00
10480	Every Day I Have to Cry Some/Livin' in a House Full of Love	1969	—	3.00	6.00
10535	The Gun/Cleanin' Up the Streets of Memphis	1969	—	3.00	6.00
10581	Gettin' Back to Norma/Maybelline	1970	—	3.00	6.00
10631	Honky Tonk Man/I Ain't Built That Way	1970	—	3.00	6.00
10667	What About the Hurt/The Time to Remember	1970	—	3.00	6.00
10699	Is It Any Wonder That I Love You?/Give Us One More Chance	1971	—	2.50	5.00
10755	I Got a Woman/One Hundred Songs on the Jukebox	1971	—	2.50	5.00
10786	A Chain Don't Take to Me/Don't Let Love Pass You By	1971	—	2.50	5.00
10823	When You Say Love/Have a Little Faith	1972	—	2.50	5.00
10869	It Takes You/Let's Think About Livin'	1972	—	2.50	5.00
10905	Lonely Women Make Good Lovers/Love Ought to Be a Happy Thing	1972	—	2.50	5.00
10943	Neither One of Us/Anything But Lonesome	1973	—	2.00	4.00
10994	A Good Love Is Like a Good Song/Have I Ever Said "I Love You" to a Lady	1973	—	2.00	4.00
11039	Still Loving You/I'm Gonna Write a Song	1973	—	2.00	4.00
11087	Just Enough to Make Me Stay/Baby Make It Good	1974	—	2.00	4.00
11138	Let Me Make the Bright Lights Shine for You/The Closest Thing to Heaven That I Love	1974	—	2.00	4.00
50065	Proud of You Baby/Tonight Your Baby's Coming Home	1975	—	2.00	4.00
50136	Shame on Me/How Do You Start Over	1975	—	2.00	4.00
50183	A Satisfied Mind/Cleanin' Up the Streets of Memphis	1975	—	2.00	4.00
50216	The Man from Bowling Green/It's Only Make Believe	1976	—	2.00	4.00
50247	How Do You Start Over/Red Cadillac and Black Mustache	1976	—	2.00	4.00
50297	Labor of Love/Blond Haired Woman	1976	—	2.00	4.00
50323	He's Got a Way with Women/Here We Are Making Love Again	1976	—	2.00	4.00
HICKORY					
1201	You're Welcome/Interstate 40	1963	3.00	6.00	12.00
1219	Can't Take the Country from the Boy/I'm Gonna Write a Song of Love	1963	3.00	6.00	12.00
1221	Too Hot to Dance/I Like Your Kind of Love	1963	3.00	6.00	12.00
—With Sue Thompson					
1238	The File/Bigger Men Than I (Have Cried)	1964	3.00	6.00	12.00
1266	Lonely Room (Empty Walls)/Run On Home Baby Brother	1964	3.00	6.00	12.00
1277	Fire Engine Red/Old George Dickel	1964	3.00	6.00	12.00
1289	Bad, Bad Day/Tears from Out of Nowhere	1965	2.50	5.00	10.00
1307	Jealous Heart/Go On Home Boy	1965	2.50	5.00	10.00
1333	I Love You Because/Love Worked a Miracle	1965	2.50	5.00	10.00
1355	Five Miles from Home (Soon I'll See Mary)/(I Get So) Sentimental	1965	2.50	5.00	10.00
1382	Poor Boy Blues/(Can't Get You) Off My Mind	1966	2.50	5.00	10.00
1410	Come On and Sing/It's a Sin	1966	2.50	5.00	10.00

(Top left) Among the most popular female singers of the early 1960s was Brenda Lee. She had a long string of hits that only abated at the start of the psychedelic era; she later comfortably moved into country music. One of her big hits was "Fool #1." (Top right) One of the rarest John Lennon albums is *Roots*, the collection of rock 'n' roll standards that Morris Levy released on his Adam VIII Ltd. record label in early 1975. It was quickly removed from the market. Counterfeits are around but can be easily identified. See the listings for this album for more information. (Bottom left) An interesting picture sleeve, this one adorns the last Lovin' Spoonful Top 20 song, "Six O' Clock." (Bottom right) Robin Luke's hit "Susie Darlin'" was originally issued on International Records with a picture sleeve. The popular issue on Dot was only issued with a generic Dot sleeve.

Number	Title (A Side/B Side)	Yr	VG	VG+	NM
1430	Hardly Anymore/Freedom of Living	1967	2.00	4.00	8.00
1460	If You Don't Love Me (Then Why Don't You Leave Me Alone)/Throwin' Kisses	1967	2.00	4.00	8.00
1481	Running Scared/The Best Years of My Wife	1967	2.00	4.00	8.00
1536	It's All Over (But the Shouting)/Still Loving You	1969	—	3.00	6.00
1564	Still Loving You/Meet Mr. Mud	1970	—	3.00	6.00
IMPERIAL					
5705	A Red Cadillac and a Black Moustache/All Night Long	1960	6.25	12.50	25.00
8311	A Red Cadillac and a Black Moustache/All Night Long	1957	20.00	40.00	80.00
8313	Red Hot/Whenever You're Ready	1957	20.00	40.00	80.00
8315	Make Up Your Mind, Baby/Your Love	1958	15.00	30.00	60.00
—The same coupling was slated for Imperial 8314 but not released.					
POLYDOR					
14408	I'm a Honky-Tonk Woman's Man/Lonely Women Make Good Lovers	1977	—	2.00	4.00
14431	The Pay Phone/He'll Be the One	1977	—	2.00	4.00
14444	A Christmas Tribute/Give Someone You Love (A Little Bit of Love This Year)	1977	—	2.00	4.00
14454	Proud Lady/Let Me Love Him Out of You	1978	—	2.00	4.00
ROLLIN' ROCK					
028	Stranger Than Fiction/You're the Cause of It All	1978	—	2.00	4.00
WARNER BROS.					
5081	My Baby Walks All Over Me/Class of '59	1959	6.25	12.50	25.00
5105	Dreamy Doll/Buttercup	1959	6.25	12.50	25.00
5172	Let's Think About Living/You've Got Everything	1960	5.00	10.00	20.00
5172 [PS]	Let's Think About Living/You've Got Everything	1960	10.00	20.00	40.00
5184	Why, Why, Bye, Bye/Oh Lonesome Me	1960	5.00	10.00	20.00
5184 [PS]	Why, Why, Bye, Bye/Oh Lonesome Me	1960	10.00	20.00	40.00
5204	The Great Snow Man/The Pig Latin Song	1961	5.00	10.00	20.00
5204 [PS]	The Great Snow Man/The Pig Latin Song	1961	10.00	20.00	40.00
5233	Private Eyes/You've Turned Down the Lights	1961	5.00	10.00	20.00
5233 [PS]	Private Eyes/You've Turned Down the Lights	1961	10.00	20.00	40.00
5255	Louisiana Man/Rocks of Reno	1962	5.00	10.00	20.00
5272	Big River Rose/Belonging to You	1962	5.00	10.00	20.00
5299	Hey Joe/The Fool	1962	5.00	10.00	20.00
5321	You're Everything/Envy	1962	5.00	10.00	20.00
5506	Boston Rocker/Old Friends//Bad Bad Day/Let's Think About Living	1960	25.00	50.00	100.00
—Part of Warner Bros. "+2" series, with two new songs and excerpts of two prior hits					
5506 [PS]	Boston Rocker/Old Friends//Bad Bad Day/Let's Think About Living	1960	25.00	50.00	100.00

Albums

Number	Title	Yr	VG	VG+	NM
EPIC					
BN 26393	Ain't Got Time to Be Unhappy	1968	5.00	10.00	20.00
BN 26463	Come On Home and Sing the Blues	1969	5.00	10.00	20.00
BN 26541	Gettin' Back	1970	5.00	10.00	20.00
E 30617	Is It Any Wonder	1971	5.00	10.00	20.00
E 30923	Chain Don't Take to Me	1972	5.00	10.00	20.00
KE 31375	When You Say Love	1972	5.00	10.00	20.00
KE 31746	Lonely Women Make Good Lovers	1972	5.00	10.00	20.00
KE 32191	Neither One of Us	1973	3.75	7.50	15.00
KE 32759	Bob Luman's Greatest Hits	1974	3.75	7.50	15.00
KE 33942	Satisfied Mind	1975	3.00	6.00	12.00
KE 34445	Alive and Well!	1976	3.00	6.00	12.00
HARMONY					
KH 32006	Bob Luman	1973	3.00	6.00	12.00
HICKORY					
LPM-124 [M]	Livin' Lovin' Sounds	1965	6.25	12.50	25.00
LPS-124 [S]	Livin' Lovin' Sounds	1965	7.50	15.00	30.00
HICKORY/MGM					
H3G-4508	Still Loving You	1974	3.75	7.50	15.00
POLYDOR					
PD-1-6135	Bob Luman	1978	3.00	6.00	12.00
WARNER BROS.					
W 1396 [M]	Let's Think About Livin'	1960	12.50	25.00	50.00
WS 1396 [S]	Let's Think About Livin'	1960	17.50	35.00	70.00

LUMPKIN, HENRY

45s

Number	Title	Yr	VG	VG+	NM
MOTOWN					
1005	I've Got a Notion/We Really Love Each Other	1961	20.00	40.00	80.00
1013	What Is a Man/Don't Leave Me	1961	10.00	20.00	40.00
1029	Mo Jo Hanna/Break Down and Sing	1962	10.00	20.00	40.00

LUND, GARRETT

Albums

Number	Title	Yr	VG	VG+	NM
(NO LABEL)					
(no #)	Almost Grown	1975	75.00	150.00	300.00

LUREX, LARRY

See FREDDIE MERCURY.

LURIE, ELLIOTT

Also see LOOKING GLASS.

45s

Number	Title	Yr	VG	VG+	NM
ARISTA					
0219	Rich Girl/Night Ride Part 2	1976	—	2.00	4.00
EPIC					
11153	Your Love Song/(B-side unknown)	1974	—	2.00	4.00
50083	Disco/I Don't Wanna Lose You	1975	—	2.00	4.00
50101	I Think I'm Fallin'/Rainbow Girl	1975	—	2.00	4.00

Albums

Number	Title	Yr	VG	VG+	NM
EPIC					
PE 33337	Elliott Lurie	1975	2.50	5.00	10.00

LY-DELLS, THE

45s

Number	Title	Yr	VG	VG+	NM
MASTER					
111	Genie of the Lamp/Teenage Tears	1961	62.50	125.00	250.00
251	Wizard of Love/Let This Night Last	1961	15.00	30.00	60.00
PAM					
103	There Goes the Boy/Talking to Myself	1959	50.00	100.00	200.00
PARKWAY					
897	There Goes the Boy/Talking to Myself	1964	5.00	10.00	20.00
ROULETTE					
4493	Karen/Doing the Wiggle Wobble	1963	6.25	12.50	25.00
SCA					
18001	Book of Songs/Hear That Train	1962	10.00	20.00	40.00
SOUTHERN SOUND					
122	Three Little Monkeys/Playing Hide and Seek	1965	15.00	30.00	60.00

LYMAN, ARTHUR

45s

Number	Title	Yr	VG	VG+	NM
GNP CRESCENDO					
315	Shangri-La/Pearly Shells	1964	—	3.00	6.00
349	Cast Your Fate to the Wind/Night Train	1965	—	3.00	6.00
497	Skybird/Puka Shells	1975	—	2.00	4.00
HIFI					
533	76 Trombones/House on a Haunted Hill	1959	2.50	5.00	10.00
550	Taboo/Dahil Sayo	1959	2.50	5.00	10.00
564	Bahia/Jungle Jalopy	1959	2.50	5.00	10.00
591	Legend of the Rain/Vera Cruz	1960	2.50	5.00	10.00
599	Jungle Fantasy/Koni Au I Ka Wai	1960	2.50	5.00	10.00
5002	Taboo Tu/Ebb Tide	1960	2.50	5.00	10.00
5024	Yellow Bird/Havah Nagilah	1961	2.50	5.00	10.00
5040	(The Sloop) John B/Honolulu Nites	1961	2.50	5.00	10.00
5047	Never on Sunday/I Talk to the Trees	1961	2.50	5.00	10.00
5049	Moanin'/Aloha No Honolulu	1962	2.50	5.00	10.00
5055	Anna/(B-side unknown)	1962	2.50	5.00	10.00
5057	America (West Side Story)/Planning Rice	1962	2.50	5.00	10.00
5058	We Three Kings/Little Drummer Boy	1962	3.00	6.00	12.00
5065	Mutiny on the Bounty/Pagan Love Song	1963	2.00	4.00	8.00
5066	Love for Sale/Dahil Sayo	1963	2.00	4.00	8.00
5071	Cottonfields/Limbo Rock	1963	2.00	4.00	8.00
5076	Sentimental Journey/Jungle Drums	1963	2.00	4.00	8.00
5078	Blowin' in the Wind/I've Been Workin' on the Railroad	1963	2.00	4.00	8.00
5079	He's Gone Away/Suzy's Waltz	1963	2.00	4.00	8.00
5080	Charade/Arthur's Line	1963	2.00	4.00	8.00
5081	Winter Wonderland/Rudolph, the Red-Nosed Reindeer	1963	3.00	6.00	12.00
5082	Petticoat Junction/Gently, Gently	1963	3.00	6.00	12.00
5083	We Three Kings/Little Drummer Boy	1963	3.00	6.00	12.00
5088	Swingin' Shephard Blues/(B-side unknown)	1964	2.00	4.00	8.00
5089	Wheel of Fortune/La Montana	1964	2.00	4.00	8.00
5091	Hello, Dolly/Get Me to the Church On Time	1964	2.00	4.00	8.00
5092	Taboo/Black Orchid	1965	2.00	4.00	8.00
5096	Afro Blues/Waltzing Matilda	1965	2.00	4.00	8.00
5100	Lemon Tree/The Car	1966	2.00	4.00	8.00
5101	The Shadow of Your Smile/Imua Kamehameha	1966	2.00	4.00	8.00
5105	The Windmills of Your Mind/Lonely Winds	1969	2.00	4.00	8.00

Albums

Number	Title	Yr	VG	VG+	NM
GNP CRESCENDO					
GNP-605 [M]	Exotic Sounds	1963	3.75	7.50	15.00
GNPS-605 [S]	Exotic Sounds	1963	5.00	10.00	20.00
GNP-606 [M]	Paradise	1964	3.75	7.50	15.00
GNPS-606 [S]	Paradise	1964	5.00	10.00	20.00
GNP-607 [M]	Cast Your Fate to the Wind	1965	3.75	7.50	15.00
GNPS-607 [S]	Cast Your Fate to the Wind	1965	5.00	10.00	20.00
GNPS-2091	Puka Shells	1975	2.50	5.00	10.00
HIFI					
R-607 [M]	Leis of Jazz	1958	5.00	10.00	20.00
SR-607 [S]	Leis of Jazz	1958	7.50	15.00	30.00
R-806 [M]	Taboo	1958	5.00	10.00	20.00
SR-806 [S]	Taboo	1958	7.50	15.00	30.00
R-807 [M]	Hawaiian Sunset	1959	5.00	10.00	20.00
SR-807 [S]	Hawaiian Sunset	1959	7.50	15.00	30.00
R-808 [M]	Bwan-A	1959	5.00	10.00	20.00
SR-808 [S]	Bwan-A	1959	7.50	15.00	30.00
R-813 [M]	The Legend of Pele	1959	5.00	10.00	20.00
SR-813 [S]	The Legend of Pele	1959	7.50	15.00	30.00
R-815 [M]	Bahia	1959	5.00	10.00	20.00
SR-815 [S]	Bahia	1959	7.50	15.00	30.00
R-818 [M]	Arthur Lyman On Broadway	1960	5.00	10.00	20.00
SR-818 [S]	Arthur Lyman On Broadway	1960	7.50	15.00	30.00
R-822 [M]	Taboo (Volume 2)	1960	5.00	10.00	20.00
SR-822 [S]	Taboo (Volume 2)	1960	7.50	15.00	30.00
LIFE					
L 1004 [M]	Percussion Spectacular	1961	7.50	15.00	30.00
L 1004 [M]	Yellow Bird	1961	5.00	10.00	20.00
—Reissue with new title reflecting the hit single					
SL 1004 [S]	Percussion Spectacular	1961	10.00	20.00	40.00
SL 1004 [S]	Yellow Bird	1961	6.25	12.50	25.00
—Reissue with new title reflecting the hit single					
L 1005 [M]	The Colorful Percussions of Arthur Lyman	1962	5.00	10.00	20.00
SL 1005 [S]	The Colorful Percussions of Arthur Lyman	1962	6.25	12.50	25.00
L 1007 [M]	The Many Moods of Arthur Lyman	1962	5.00	10.00	20.00
SL 1007 [S]	The Many Moods of Arthur Lyman	1962	6.25	12.50	25.00
L 1009 [M]	I Wish You Love	1963	5.00	10.00	20.00
L 1009 [M]	Love for Sale!	1963	6.25	12.50	25.00
—Alternate title					
SL 1009 [S]	I Wish You Love	1963	6.25	12.50	25.00
SL 1009 [S]	Love for Sale!	1963	7.50	15.00	30.00
—Alternate title					
L 1010 [M]	Cotton Fields	1963	5.00	10.00	20.00
SL 1010 [S]	Cotton Fields	1963	6.25	12.50	25.00
L 1014 [M]	Blowin' in the Wind	1963	5.00	10.00	20.00
SL 1014 [S]	Blowin' in the Wind	1963	6.25	12.50	25.00
L 1018 [M]	Mele Kalikimaka (Merry Christmas)	1963	5.00	10.00	20.00
SL 1018 [S]	Mele Kalikimaka (Merry Christmas)	1963	6.25	12.50	25.00
L 1023 [M]	Isle of Enchantment	1964	5.00	10.00	20.00
SL 1023 [S]	Isle of Enchantment	1964	6.25	12.50	25.00
L 1024 [M]	Call of the Midnight Sun	1964	5.00	10.00	20.00
SL 1024 [S]	Call of the Midnight Sun	1964	6.25	12.50	25.00

Number	Title (A Side/B Side)	Yr	VG	VG+	NM
L 1025 [M]	Hawaiian Sunset, Volume 2	1965	3.75	7.50	15.00
SL 1025 [S]	Hawaiian Sunset, Volume 2	1965	5.00	10.00	20.00
L 1027 [M]	Polynesia	1965	3.75	7.50	15.00
SL 1027 [S]	Polynesia	1965	5.00	10.00	20.00
L 1030 [M]	Greatest Hits	1965	3.00	6.00	12.00
SL 1030 [S]	Greatest Hits	1965	3.75	7.50	15.00
L 1031 [M]	Lyman '66	1965	3.75	7.50	15.00
SL 1031 [S]	Lyman '66	1965	5.00	10.00	20.00
L 1033 [M]	The Shadow of Your Smile	1966	3.75	7.50	15.00
SL 1033 [S]	The Shadow of Your Smile	1966	5.00	10.00	20.00
L 1034 [M]	Aloha, Amigo	1966	3.75	7.50	15.00
SL 1034 [S]	Aloha, Amigo	1966	5.00	10.00	20.00
L 1035 [M]	Ilikai	1967	3.75	7.50	15.00
SL 1035 [S]	Ilikai	1967	5.00	10.00	20.00
L 1036 [M]	Arthur Lyman at the Port of L.A.	1967	3.75	7.50	15.00
SL 1036 [S]	Arthur Lyman at the Port of L.A.	1967	5.00	10.00	20.00
SL 1037	Latitude 20	1968	3.75	7.50	15.00
SL 1038	Aphrodisia	1968	3.75	7.50	15.00
SL 1039	Winner's Circle	1969	3.75	7.50	15.00
SL 1040	Today's Greatest Hits	1970	3.75	7.50	15.00

LYMAN, JONI

45s

Number	Title (A Side/B Side)	Yr	VG	VG+	NM
REPRISE					
0378	Happy Birthday Blue/I Just Don't Know What to Do with Myself	1965	10.00	20.00	40.00

LYMON, FRANKIE

Also see FRANKIE LYMON AND THE TEENAGERS.

45s

Number	Title (A Side/B Side)	Yr	VG	VG+	NM
BIG KAT					
7008	I Want You to Be My Girl/Portable on My Shoulder	1968	2.50	5.00	10.00
7008 [PS]	I Want You to Be My Girl/Portable on My Shoulder	1968	3.00	6.00	12.00
COLUMBIA					
43094	Somewhere/Sweet and Lovely	1964	12.50	25.00	50.00
GEE					
1039	Goody Goody/Creation of Love	1957	6.25	12.50	25.00
1052	I'm Not Too Young to Dream/Goody Good Girl	1959	6.25	12.50	25.00
ROULETTE					
4026	So Goes My Love/My Girl	1957	6.25	12.50	25.00
4035	It's Christmas Once Again/Little Girl	1957	6.25	12.50	25.00
4044	Footsteps/Thumb Thumb	1958	5.00	10.00	20.00
4068	Mama Don't Allow It/Portable on My Shoulder	1958	5.00	10.00	20.00
4093	Melinda/The Only Way to Love	1958	5.00	10.00	20.00
4128	No Matter What You've Done/Up Jumped a Rabbit	1959	5.00	10.00	20.00
4150	Before I Fall Asleep/What a Little Moonlight Can Do	1959	5.00	10.00	20.00
4257	Little Bitty Pretty One/Creation of Love	1960	5.00	10.00	20.00
4283	Buzz, Buzz, Buzz/Waitin' in School	1960	5.00	10.00	20.00
4310	Jailhouse Rock/Silhouettes	1961	5.00	10.00	20.00
4348	Change Partners/So Young	1961	5.00	10.00	20.00
4391	I Put the Bomp/So Young	1962	5.00	10.00	20.00
TCF					
11	Teacher Teacher/To Each His Own	1964	3.75	7.50	15.00

7-Inch Extended Plays

Number	Title (A Side/B Side)	Yr	VG	VG+	NM
ROULETTE					
EPR-1-304	Let's Fall in Love/My Baby Just Cares for Me//Goody Goody/Somebody Loves Me	1958	50.00	100.00	200.00
EPR-1-304 [PS]	Frankie Lymon at the London Palladium	1958	50.00	100.00	200.00

Albums

Number	Title (A Side/B Side)	Yr	VG	VG+	NM
GUEST STAR					
GS-1406 [M]	Teen Time Tunes Starring Frankie Lymon	1959	10.00	20.00	40.00
—Various-artists compilation; color cover					
GS-1406 [M]	Rock & Roll Party Starring Frankie Lymon	196?	6.25	12.50	25.00
—Various-artists compilation; retitled, black and white cover					
ROULETTE					
R-25013 [M]	Frankie Lymon at the London Palladium	1958	75.00	150.00	300.00
R-25036 [M]	Rock 'n' Roll	1958	75.00	150.00	300.00
R-25250 [M]	Frankie Lymon's Greatest	1964	7.50	15.00	30.00
SR-25250 [R]	Frankie Lymon's Greatest	1964	6.25	12.50	25.00

LYMON, FRANKIE, AND THE TEENAGERS

Also see FRANKIE LYMON.

45s

Number	Title (A Side/B Side)	Yr	VG	VG+	NM
GEE					
1002	Why Do Fools Fall in Love/Please Be Mine	1956	20.00	40.00	80.00
—Red and gold label					
1002	Why Do Fools Fall in Love/Please Be Mine	1956	12.50	25.00	50.00
—Red and black label; vocal duet on B-side					
1002	Why Do Fools Fall in Love/Please Be Mine	1956	7.50	15.00	30.00
—Red and black label; vocal solo on B-side. All of the above credit "The Teenagers featuring Frankie Lymon"					
1002	Why Do Fools Fall in Love/My Girl	1958	6.25	12.50	25.00
—White label, "Gee Records" at top; note different B-side					
1012	I Want You to Be My Girl/I'm Not a Know-It-All	1956	12.50	25.00	50.00
—As "The Teenagers featuring Frankie Lymon"					
1012	I Want You to Be My Girl/I'm Not a Know-It-All	1956	7.50	15.00	30.00
—As "Frankie Lymon and the Teenagers"					
1018	I Promise to Remember/Who Can Explain	1956	7.50	15.00	30.00
1022	The ABC's of Love/Share	1956	7.50	15.00	30.00
1026	I'm Not a Juvenile Delinquent/Baby Baby	1957	7.50	15.00	30.00
1032	Teenage Love/Paper Castles	1957	7.50	15.00	30.00
1035	Am I Fooling Myself Again/Love Is a Clown	197?	—	—	—
—Evidently a 1970s bootleg to fill in a gap in the Gee Records discography					
1036	Miracle of Love/Out in the Cold Again	1957	7.50	15.00	30.00
1039	Goody Goody/Creation of Love	1957	10.00	20.00	40.00
—Actually a Frankie Lymon solo recording; the first pressing credited the entire group					

7-Inch Extended Plays

Number	Title (A Side/B Side)	Yr	VG	VG+	NM
GEE					
GEP-601	Teenage Love/Why Do Fools Fall in Love//I Want You to Be My Girl/Love Is a Clown	1956	37.50	75.00	150.00
GEP-601 [PS]	The Teenagers Go Rock'n	1956	50.00	100.00	200.00
GEP-602	(contents unknown)	1957	50.00	100.00	200.00
GEP-602 [PS]	The Teenagers Go Romantic	1957	50.00	100.00	200.00

Albums

Number	Title (A Side/B Side)	Yr	VG	VG+	NM
ACCORD					
SN-7203	Why Do Fools Fall in Love	1982	2.50	5.00	10.00
GEE					
GLP-701 [M]	The Teenagers Featuring Frankie Lymon	1956	125.00	250.00	500.00
—Red label					
GLP-701 [M]	The Teenagers Featuring Frankie Lymon	1961	37.50	75.00	150.00
—Gray label					
GLP-701 [M]	The Teenagers Featuring Frankie Lymon	197?	3.00	6.00	12.00
—White label on thinner vinyl					
MURRAY HILL					
148 [(5)]	Frankie Lymon and the Teenagers	198?	17.50	35.00	70.00
RHINO					
R1-70918	The Best of Frankie Lymon and the Teenagers	1989	3.00	6.00	12.00

LYMON, LEWIS, AND THE TEENCHORDS

45s

Number	Title (A Side/B Side)	Yr	VG	VG+	NM
END					
1003	Too Young/Your Last Chance	1957	25.00	50.00	100.00
1007	I Found Out Why/Tell Me Love	1958	20.00	40.00	80.00
1113	Too Young/Your Last Chance	1962	5.00	10.00	20.00
FURY					
1000	I'm So Happy (Tra-La-La-La-La-La)/Lydia	1957	50.00	100.00	200.00
—Maroon label					
1000	I'm So Happy (Tra-La-La-La-La-La)/Lydia	1958	10.00	20.00	40.00
—Yellow label					
1003	Honey, Honey (You Don't Know)/Please Tell the Angels	1957	20.00	40.00	80.00
1006	I'm Not Too Young to Fall in Love/Falling in Love	1957	20.00	40.00	80.00
JUANITA					
101	Dance Girl/Them There Eyes	1958	12.50	25.00	50.00

Albums

Number	Title (A Side/B Side)	Yr	VG	VG+	NM
COLLECTABLES					
COL-5049	Lewis Lymon and the Teenchords Meet the Kodaks	198?	2.50	5.00	10.00
LOST-NITE					
LLP-13 [10]	Lewis Lymon and the Teenchords	1981	2.50	5.00	10.00
—Red vinyl					

LYNCH, KENNY

45s

Number	Title (A Side/B Side)	Yr	VG	VG+	NM
ARLEN					
750	Make It Easy on Yourself/Monument	1964	3.00	6.00	12.00
BIG TOP					
3140	Poof (Up in Smoke)/Happy That's Me	1963	3.00	6.00	12.00
IMPERIAL					
66088	So Much to Love You For/My Own Two Feet	1964	3.00	6.00	12.00
LIBERTY					
55740	That's What Girls Are Made For/What Am I to You	1964	3.00	6.00	12.00
55811	For Lovin' You Baby/I'll Stay By You	1965	2.50	5.00	10.00
WHITE WHALE					
307	Along Comes Love/Sweet Situation	1969	—	3.00	6.00

LYNN, BARBARA

45s

Number	Title (A Side/B Side)	Yr	VG	VG+	NM
ATLANTIC					
2450	This Is the Thanks I Get/Ring, Telephone, Ring	1967	2.00	4.00	8.00
2513	Why Can't You Love Me/You're Losing Me	1968	2.00	4.00	8.00
2553	Love Ain't Never Hurt Nobody/You're Gonna See a Lot More	1968	2.00	4.00	8.00
2585	People Like Me/He Ain't Gonna Do Right	1968	2.00	4.00	8.00
2812	(Until Then) I'll Suffer/Take Your Love and Run	1971	—	3.00	6.00
2853	Nice and Easy/I'm a One Woman Man	1972	—	3.00	6.00
2880	(Daddy Hotstuff) You're Too Hot to Hold/You Better Quit It	1972	—	3.00	6.00
2931	You Make Me So Hot/It Ain't No Good to Be Too Good	1973	—	3.00	6.00
JAMIE					
1220	You'll Lose a Good Thing/Lonely Heartache	1962	5.00	10.00	20.00
1233	Second Fiddle Girl/Letter to Mommy and Daddy	1962	3.00	6.00	12.00
1240	You're Gonna Need Me/I'm Sorry I Met You	1962	3.00	6.00	12.00
1244	Don't Be Cruel/You Can't Be Satisfied	1963	3.00	6.00	12.00
1251	To Love or Not to Love/Promises	1963	3.00	6.00	12.00
1260	(I Cried at) Laura's Wedding/You Better Stop	1963	3.00	6.00	12.00
1265	Everybody Loves Somebody/Dedicate the Blues to Me	1963	3.00	6.00	12.00
1269	Money/Jealous Love	1964	3.00	6.00	12.00
1277	Oh! Baby (We Got a Good Thing Goin')/Unfair	1964	3.00	6.00	12.00
1286	Don't Spread It Around/Let Her Knock Herself Out	1964	3.00	6.00	12.00
1292	It's Better to Have It/People Gonna Talk	1964	3.00	6.00	12.00
1295	(Don't Pretend) Just Lay It on the Line/Careless Hands	1965	2.00	4.00	8.00
—With Lee Maye					
1297	Keep On Pushing Your Luck/I've Taken All I'm Gonna Take	1965	2.00	4.00	8.00
1301	Can't Buy Me Love/That's What Friends Are For	1965	2.00	4.00	8.00
1304	All I Need Is Your Love/You're Gonna Be Sorry	1965	2.00	4.00	8.00
TRIBE					
8316	Running Back/I'm a Good Woman	1966	2.00	4.00	8.00
8319	You Left the Water Running/Until I'm Free	1966	2.00	4.00	8.00
8322	Watch the One That Brings Bad News/AUB A-Go-Go	1967	2.00	4.00	8.00
8324	I Don't Want a Playboy/New Kind of Love	1967	2.00	4.00	8.00

Albums

Number	Title (A Side/B Side)	Yr	VG	VG+	NM
ATLANTIC					
8171 [M]	Here Is Barbara Lynn	1968	12.50	25.00	50.00
SD 8171 [S]	Here Is Barbara Lynn	1968	10.00	20.00	40.00
JAMIE					
JLP-3023 [M]	You'll Lose a Good Thing	1962	12.50	25.00	50.00
JLPS-3023 [R]	You'll Lose a Good Thing	1962	12.50	25.00	50.00

Number	Title (A Side/B Side)	Yr	VG	VG+	NM
JLP-3026 [M]	Sister of Soul	1964	—	—	—
—Canceled					
JLPS-3026 [S]	Sister of Soul	1964	—	—	—
—Canceled					

LYNN, DONNA

45s

CAPITOL

Number	Title (A Side/B Side)	Yr	VG	VG+	NM
5087	Ronnie/That's Me, I'm the Brother	1963	3.75	7.50	15.00
5127	My Boyfriend Got a Beatle Haircut/That Winter Weekend	1964	5.00	10.00	20.00
5156	Java Jones/Things That I Feel	1964	3.75	7.50	15.00
5213	Silly Girl/There Goes the Boy I Love with Mary	1964	3.75	7.50	15.00
5378	I'd Much Rather Be with the Girls/I'm Sorry More Than You Know	1965	3.00	6.00	12.00
5456	True Blue/When Your Heart Rings, Answer	1965	3.00	6.00	12.00

PALMER

Number	Title (A Side/B Side)	Yr	VG	VG+	NM
5016	Don't You Dare/I Was Raining	1967	6.25	12.50	25.00

Albums

CAPITOL

Number	Title (A Side/B Side)	Yr	VG	VG+	NM
ST 2085 [S]	Java Jones/My Boyfriend Got a Beatle Haircut	1964	7.50	15.00	30.00
T 2085 [M]	Java Jones/My Boyfriend Got a Beatle Haircut	1964	5.00	10.00	20.00

LYNN, LORETTA

Also see ERNEST TUBB AND LORETTA LYNN; CONWAY TWITTY AND LORETTA LYNN.

45s

DECCA

Number	Title (A Side/B Side)	Yr	VG	VG+	NM
31323	The Girl That I Am Now/I Walked Away from the Wreck	1961	3.75	7.50	15.00
31384	Success/Hundred Proof Heartache	1962	3.00	6.00	12.00
31435	World of Forgotten People/Get Set for a Heartache	1962	3.75	7.50	15.00
31471	The Other Woman/Who'll Help Me Get Over You	1963	2.50	5.00	10.00
31541	Before I'm Over You/Where Were You	1963	2.50	5.00	10.00
31608	Wine, Women and Song/This Haunted House	1964	2.50	5.00	10.00
31707	Happy Birthday/When Lonely Hits Your Heart	1964	2.50	5.00	10.00
31769	Blue Kentucky Girl/Two Steps Forward	1965	2.50	5.00	10.00
31836	The Home You're Tearin' Down/The Farther You Go	1965	2.50	5.00	10.00
31879	When I Hear My Children Play/Everybody Wants to Go to Heaven	1965	3.00	6.00	12.00
31893	Dear Uncle Sam/Hurtin' for Certain	1966	2.50	5.00	10.00
31966	You Ain't Woman Enough/God Gave Me a Heart to Forgive	1966	2.50	5.00	10.00
32043	It Won't Seem Like Christmas/To Heck with Santa Claus	1966	2.50	5.00	10.00
32043 [PS]	It Won't Seem Like Christmas/To Heck with Santa Claus	1966	3.75	7.50	15.00
32045	Don't Come Home a-Drinkin' (With Lovin' on Your Mind)/A Saint to a Sinner	1966	2.50	5.00	10.00
32127	If You're Not Gone Too Long/A Man I Hardly Know	1967	2.50	5.00	10.00
32184	What Kind of a Girl (Do You Think I Am?)/Bargain Basement Dress	1967	2.50	5.00	10.00
32264	Fist City/Slowly Killing Me	1968	2.00	4.00	8.00
32332	You've Just Stepped In (From Stepping Out on Me)/Taking the Place of My Man	1968	2.00	4.00	8.00
32392	Your Squaw Is On the Warpath/Let Me Go, You're Hurtin' Me	1968	2.00	4.00	8.00
32439	Woman of the World (Leave My World Alone)/Sneakin' In	1969	2.00	4.00	8.00
32513	To Make a Man (Feel Like a Man)/One Little Reason	1969	2.00	4.00	8.00
32586	Wings Upon Your Horns/Let's Get Back Down to Earth	1969	2.00	4.00	8.00
32637	I Know How/The End of My World	1970	2.00	4.00	8.00
32693	You Wanna Give Me a Lift/What's the Bottle Done Today Baby	1970	2.00	4.00	8.00
32749	Coal Miner's Daughter/Man of the House	1970	2.50	5.00	10.00
32749 [PS]	Coal Miner's Daughter/Man of the House	1970	3.00	6.00	12.00
32763	I Love You/That Ain't a Woman's Way	1970	2.00	4.00	8.00
32796	I Wanna Be Free/If I Never Love Again	1971	—	3.50	7.00
32851	You're Lookin' at Country/When You're Poor	1971	—	3.50	7.00
32900	Here in Topeka/Kinfolks Holler	1971	5.00	10.00	20.00
32900	One's On the Way/Kinfolks Holler	1971	—	3.50	7.00
—Retitled version of A-side					
32974	Here I Am Again/My Kind of Man	1972	—	3.50	7.00
33039	Rated "X"/'Til the Pain Outwears the Shame	1972	—	3.50	7.00

MCA

Number	Title (A Side/B Side)	Yr	VG	VG+	NM
40058	Love Is the Foundation/What Sundown Does to You	1973	—	2.50	5.00
40150	Hey Loretta/Turn Me Any Way But Loose	1973	—	2.50	5.00
40223	They Don't Make 'Em Like My Daddy/Nothin'	1974	—	2.50	5.00
40283	Trouble in Paradise/We've Already Tasted Love	1974	—	2.50	5.00
40358	The Pill/Will You Be There	1975	—	2.50	5.00
40438	Home/You Take Me to Heaven Every Night	1975	—	2.50	5.00
40484	When the Tingle Becomes a Chill/All I Want from You (Is Away)	1975	—	2.50	5.00
40541	Red, White and Blue/Sounds of a New Love (Being Born)	1976	—	2.50	5.00
40607	Somebody Somewhere (Don't Know What He's Missin' Tonight)/Sundown Tavern	1976	—	2.50	5.00
40679	She's Got You/The Lady That Lived Here Before	1977	—	2.50	5.00
40747	Why Can't He Be You/I Keep On Putting On	1977	—	2.50	5.00
40832	Out of My Head and Back in My Bed/Old Rooster	1977	—	2.50	5.00
40910	Spring Fever/God Bless the Children	1978	—	2.00	4.00
40954	We've Come a Long Way, Baby/I Can't Feel You Anymore	1978	—	2.00	4.00
40954 [PS]	We've Come a Long Way, Baby/I Can't Feel You Anymore	1978	—	3.00	6.00
41021	I Can't Feel You Anymore/True Love Needs to Keep in Touch	1979	—	2.00	4.00
41129	I've Got a Picture of Us on My Mind/I Don't Feel Like a Movie Tonight	1979	—	2.00	4.00
41185	Pregnant Again/You're a Cross I Can't Bear	1980	—	2.00	4.00
41250	Naked in the Rain/I Should Be Over You by Now	1980	—	2.00	4.00
51015	Cheatin' On a Cheater/Until I Met You	1980	—	2.00	4.00
51058	Somebody Led Me Away/Everybody's Lookin' for Somebody New	1981	—	2.00	4.00
51226	I Lie/If I Ain't Got It	1982	—	2.50	5.00
52005	I Lie/If I Ain't Got It	1982	—	2.00	4.00
52092	Making Love from Memory/Don't It Feel Good	1982	—	2.00	4.00
52158	Breakin' It/There's All Kinds of Smoke (In the Barroom)	1983	—	2.00	4.00
52219	Lyin', Cheatin', Woman Chasin', Honky Tonkin', Whiskey Drinkin' You/Star Light, Star Bright	1983	—	2.00	4.00
52289	Walking with My Memories/It's Gone	1983	—	2.00	4.00
52621	Heart Don't Do This to Me/Adam's Rib	1985	—	—	3.00
52706	Wouldn't It Be Great/One Man Band	1985	—	—	3.00
52766	Just a Woman/Take Me in Your Arms (And Hold Me)	1986	—	—	3.00
53320	Who Was That Stranger/Elsie Banks	1988	—	—	3.00
53397	Fly Away/Your Used to Be	1988	—	—	3.00
65034	Shadrack, the Black Reindeer/Let's Put Christ Back in Christmas	1974	—	2.00	4.00
—Black label with rainbow					
65034	Shadrack, the Black Reindeer/Let's Put Christ Back in Christmas	1980	—	—	3.00
—Blue label with rainbow					

ZERO

Number	Title (A Side/B Side)	Yr	VG	VG+	NM
107	I'm a Honky Tonk Girl/Whispering Sea	1960	125.00	250.00	500.00
110	New Rainbow/Heartaches Meet Mr. Blues	1960	100.00	200.00	400.00
112	The Darkest Day/Gonna Pack My Troubles	1961	100.00	200.00	400.00

7-Inch Extended Plays

DECCA

Number	Title (A Side/B Side)	Yr	VG	VG+	NM
ED 2762	The Other Woman/Where Were You//Success/Before I'm Over You	1964	5.00	10.00	20.00
ED 2762 [PS]	The Other Woman	1964	5.00	10.00	20.00
ED 2784	(contents unknown)	1965	5.00	10.00	20.00
ED 2784 [PS]	Wine, Women and Song	1965	5.00	10.00	20.00
ED 2793	(contents unknown)	1965	5.00	10.00	20.00
ED 2793 [PS]	The End of the World	1965	5.00	10.00	20.00
ED 2800	(contents unknown)	1965	5.00	10.00	20.00
ED 2800 [PS]	Songs from the Heart	1965	5.00	10.00	20.00

Albums

DECCA

Number	Title (A Side/B Side)	Yr	VG	VG+	NM
DL 4457 [M]	Loretta Lynn Sings	1963	15.00	30.00	60.00
DL 4541 [M]	Before I'm Over You	1964	7.50	15.00	30.00
DL 4620 [M]	Songs from My Heart	1965	7.50	15.00	30.00
DL 4665 [M]	Blue Kentucky Girl	1965	7.50	15.00	30.00
DL 4695 [M]	Hymns	1965	7.50	15.00	30.00
DL 4744 [M]	I Like 'Em Country	1966	6.25	12.50	25.00
DL 4783 [M]	You Ain't Woman Enough	1966	6.25	12.50	25.00
DL 4817 [M]	Country Christmas	1966	6.25	12.50	25.00
DL 4842 [M]	Don't Come Home a-Drinkin' (With Lovin' on Your Mind)	1967	7.50	15.00	30.00
DL 4928 [M]	Who Says God Is Dead!	1967	10.00	20.00	40.00
DL 4930 [M]	Singin' with Feelin'	1967	7.50	15.00	30.00
DL 74457 [S]	Loretta Lynn Sings	1963	20.00	40.00	80.00
DL 74541 [S]	Before I'm Over You	1964	10.00	20.00	40.00
DL 74620 [S]	Songs from My Heart	1965	10.00	20.00	40.00
DL 74665 [S]	Blue Kentucky Girl	1965	10.00	20.00	40.00
DL 74695 [S]	Hymns	1965	10.00	20.00	40.00
DL 74744 [S]	I Like 'Em Country	1966	7.50	15.00	30.00
DL 74783 [S]	You Ain't Woman Enough	1966	7.50	15.00	30.00
DL 74817 [S]	Country Christmas	1966	7.50	15.00	30.00
DL 74842 [S]	Don't Come Home a-Drinkin' (With Lovin' on Your Mind)	1967	6.25	12.50	25.00
DL 74928 [S]	Who Says God Is Dead!	1967	6.25	12.50	25.00
DL 74930 [S]	Singin' with Feelin'	1967	6.25	12.50	25.00
DL 74997	Fist City	1968	6.25	12.50	25.00
DL 75000	Loretta Lynn's Greatest Hits	1968	6.25	12.50	25.00
DL 75084	Your Squaw Is On the Warpath	1969	10.00	20.00	40.00
—First editions had a track called "Barney"					
DL 75084	Your Squaw Is On the Warpath	1969	6.25	12.50	25.00
—Later editions delete the track "Barney"					
DL 75113	Woman of the World/To Make a Man	1969	6.25	12.50	25.00
DL 75163	Wings Upon Your Horns	1970	6.25	12.50	25.00
DL 75198	Loretta Lynn Writes 'Em and Sings 'Em	1970	6.25	12.50	25.00
DL 75253	Coal Miner's Daughter	1971	5.00	10.00	20.00
DL 75282	I Wanna Be Free	1971	5.00	10.00	20.00
DL 75310	You're Lookin' at Country	1971	5.00	10.00	20.00
DL 75334	One's On the Way	1972	5.00	10.00	20.00
DL 75351	God Bless America Again	1972	5.00	10.00	20.00
DL 75381	Here I Am Again	1972	5.00	10.00	20.00

MCA

Number	Title (A Side/B Side)	Yr	VG	VG+	NM
1	Loretta Lynn's Greatest Hits	1973	3.75	7.50	15.00
—Reissue of Decca 75000					
5	Hymns	1973	3.75	7.50	15.00
—Reissue of Decca 74695					
6	You Ain't Woman Enough	1973	3.75	7.50	15.00
—Reissue of Decca 74783					
7	Who Says God Is Dead!	1973	3.75	7.50	15.00
—Reissue of Decca 74928					
58	Here I Am Again	1973	3.75	7.50	15.00
—Reissue of Decca 75381					
113	Don't Come Home a-Drinkin' (With Lovin' on Your Mind)	1973	3.75	7.50	15.00
—Reissue of Decca 74842					
248	Country Christmas	1973	3.75	7.50	15.00
—First reissue of Decca LP					
300	Entertainer of the Year — Loretta	1973	3.75	7.50	15.00
355	Love Is the Foundation	1973	3.75	7.50	15.00
420	Loretta Lynn's Greatest Hits Vol. II	1974	3.75	7.50	15.00
444	They Don't Make 'Em Like My Daddy	1974	3.75	7.50	15.00
471	Back to the Country	1975	3.00	6.00	12.00
628	When the Tingle Becomes a Chill	198?	2.00	4.00	8.00
—Budget-line reissue					
630	Somebody Somewhere	198?	2.00	4.00	8.00
—Budget-line reissue					

Number	Title (A Side/B Side)	Yr	VG	VG+	NM
721	We've Come a Long Way, Baby	198?	2.00	4.00	8.00
—Budget-line reissue					
735	Alone with You	198?	2.50	5.00	10.00
L33-1934 [DJ]	Loretta Lynn	1974	10.00	20.00	40.00
—Promo-only compilation					
2146	Home	1975	3.00	6.00	12.00
2179	When the Tingle Becomes a Chill	1976	3.00	6.00	12.00
2228	Somebody Somewhere	1976	3.00	6.00	12.00
2265	I Remember Patsy	1977	3.00	6.00	12.00
2330	Out of My Head and Back in My Bed	1978	3.00	6.00	12.00
2341	Loretta Lynn's Greatest Hits	1978	3.00	6.00	12.00
—Reissue of MCA 1					
2342	Coal Miner's Daughter	1978	3.00	6.00	12.00
—Reissue					
2353	Loretta Lynn's Greatest Hits Vol. II	1978	3.00	6.00	12.00
—Reissue of MCA 420					
3073	We've Come a Long Way, Baby	1979	3.00	6.00	12.00
3217	Loretta	1980	2.50	5.00	10.00
5148	Lookin' Good	1980	2.50	5.00	10.00
5293	I Lie	1982	2.50	5.00	10.00
5426	Lyin', Cheatin', Woman Chasin', Honky Tonkin', Whiskey Drinkin' You	1983	2.50	5.00	10.00
5613	Just a Woman	1985	2.50	5.00	10.00
15022	Country Christmas	1974	3.00	6.00	12.00
—Second reissue of Decca LP; black rainbow label					
15022	Country Christmas	1980	2.50	5.00	10.00
—Blue rainbow label					
15032	Christmas Without Daddy	198?	3.00	6.00	12.00
35013	Allis-Chalmers Presents Loretta Lynn	1978	10.00	20.00	40.00
—Special products compilation					
35018	Crisco Presents Loretta Lynn's Country Classics	1979	10.00	20.00	40.00
—Special products compilation					
37080	I Remember Patsy Cline	198?	2.00	4.00	8.00
—Budget-line reissue					
37165	Loretta	198?	2.00	4.00	8.00
—Budget-line reissue					
37205	Loretta Lynn's Greatest Hits Vol. II	198?	2.00	4.00	8.00
—Budget-line reissue					
37235	Loretta Lynn's Greatest Hits	198?	2.00	4.00	8.00
—Budget-line reissue					
37236	Coal Miner's Daughter	198?	2.00	4.00	8.00
—Budget-line reissue					
42174	Who Was That Stranger	1988	2.50	5.00	10.00
VOCALION					
VL 73853	Here's Loretta Lynn	1968	3.75	7.50	15.00

LYNN, LORETTA, AND ERNEST TUBB

See ERNEST TUBB AND LORETTA LYNN.

LYNN, LORETTA, AND CONWAY TWITTY

See CONWAY TWITTY AND LORETTA LYNN.

LYNN, SANDRA

45s

Number	Title (A Side/B Side)	Yr	VG	VG+	NM
CONSTELLATION					
140	Where Would I Be/Sometime	1964	3.00	6.00	12.00

LYNNE, GLORIA

45s

Number	Title (A Side/B Side)	Yr	VG	VG+	NM
ABC IMPULSE!					
31003	Out of This World/Thank You Early Bird	1976	—	2.00	4.00
CANYON					
36	Love's Finally Found Me/If You Don't Get It Yourself	1970	—	2.50	5.00
EVEREST					
2023	I'll Buy You a Star/Record Company Blues	1963	2.00	4.00	8.00
2030	Stormy Monday Blues/Humming Blues	1963	2.00	4.00	8.00
2036	I Wish You Love/Through a Long and Sleepless Night	1963	2.00	4.00	8.00
2042	I Should Care/Indian Love Call	1964	2.00	4.00	8.00
2044	Don't Take Your Love from Me/You Don't Know What Love Is	1964	2.00	4.00	8.00
2047	Serenade in Blue/Without a Song	1964	2.00	4.00	8.00
2051	On Christmas Day/Wouldn't It Be Loverly	1964	2.00	4.00	8.00
2055	Fly Me to the Moon/The Night Has a Thousand Eyes	1965	2.00	4.00	8.00
2058	Out of This World/Squeeze Me	1965	2.00	4.00	8.00
2059	Lonely Street/Try a Little Tenderness	1965	2.00	4.00	8.00
2061	Folks Who Live on the Hill/That's a Joy	1965	2.00	4.00	8.00
2062	My Devotion/I'm Glad There Is You	1965	2.00	4.00	8.00
19303	June Night/Perdido	1959	3.00	6.00	12.00
19308	But Not for Me/Just in Time	1959	3.00	6.00	12.00
19326	Be My Love/My Prayer for You	1960	2.50	5.00	10.00
19337	Happiness Is Just a Thing Called Joe/My Reverie	1960	2.50	5.00	10.00
19346	Am I Blue/Little Girl Blue	1960	2.50	5.00	10.00
19347	Without a Song/They Didn't Believe Me	1960	2.50	5.00	10.00
19367	Gypsy Boy/Recommend to Love	1960	2.50	5.00	10.00
19373	Condemned Without Trial/Dreamy	1960	2.50	5.00	10.00
19390	Jazz in You/Love, I've Found You	1961	2.00	4.00	8.00
19409	He Needs Me/The Lamp Is Low	1961	2.00	4.00	8.00
19418	Impossible/This Little Boy of Mine	1961	2.00	4.00	8.00
19428	You Don't Have to Be a Tower of Strength/I Will Follow You	1961	3.00	6.00	12.00
19431	I'm Glad There Is You/And This Is My Beloved	1962	2.00	4.00	8.00
20008	I Know Love/It Just Happened to Me	1962	2.00	4.00	8.00
FONTANA					
1507	The Touch of Your Lips/Intimate Moments	1965	—	3.00	6.00
1511	Watermelon Man/All Alone	1965	—	3.00	6.00
1523	The Whisperers/I Understand	1965	—	3.00	6.00
1538	Speaking of Happiness/Somtimes It Be's That Way	1966	—	3.00	6.00
1554	Strangers in the Night/Hey, Candy Man	1966	—	3.00	6.00
1560	Honey Machine/I Got What You Want	1966	—	3.00	6.00
1567	Love Is/It's Not the Truth	1967	—	3.00	6.00
1594	Foolish Dreamer/I Can't Stand It	1967	—	3.00	6.00
1617	I've Never Ever Loved Before/Down Here on the Ground	1968	—	2.50	5.00
1627	The Guy Who Lived Up There/Hold Back the Dawn	1968	—	2.50	5.00
1639	I've Got to Be Someone/Problem Child	1969	—	2.50	5.00
1660	No Easy Way Down/Darlin'	1969	—	2.50	5.00
1674	Hold It/Untouched by Human Love	1969	—	2.50	5.00
1890	Be Anything (But Be Mine)/Soul Serenade	1964	2.00	4.00	8.00
1890 [PS]	Be Anything (But Be Mine)/Soul Serenade	1964	3.00	6.00	12.00
1966	Soul Serenade/Do Anything	1965	—	3.00	6.00
HIFI					
5103	I Wish You Love/Long Long Story	1966	—	3.00	6.00
MERCURY					
73267	Never My Love/The Summer Knows	1972	—	2.50	5.00
73294	Just Let Me Be Me/Kickin' Life	1972	—	2.50	5.00
SEECO					
6037	Little Boy Blues/Way Beyond the Hills	1959	3.00	6.00	12.00
6077	Is There Someone for Me/I'm Not Afraid Anymore	1961	2.50	5.00	10.00

Albums

Number	Title (A Side/B Side)	Yr	VG	VG+	NM
ABC IMPULSE!					
AS-9311	Don't Know	1976	3.00	6.00	12.00
CANYON					
7709	Happy and In Love	1970	3.75	7.50	15.00
COLLECTABLES					
COL-5138	Golden Classics	198?	2.50	5.00	10.00
DESIGN					
D-177 [M]	My Funny Valentine	196?	2.50	5.00	10.00
DS-177 [S]	My Funny Valentine	196?	3.00	6.00	12.00
EVEREST					
ES-1001 [S]	Gloria Lynne Live! Take 1	1959	10.00	20.00	40.00
SDBR-1022 [S]	Miss Gloria Lynne	1959	7.50	15.00	30.00
SDBR-1063 [S]	Lonely and Sentimental	1960	7.50	15.00	30.00
SDBR-1090 [S]	Try a Little Tenderness	1960	7.50	15.00	30.00
SDBR-1101 [S]	Day In, Day Out	1961	7.50	15.00	30.00
SDBR-1126 [S]	I'm Glad There Is You	1961	7.50	15.00	30.00
SDBR-1128 [S]	He Needs Me	1961	7.50	15.00	30.00
SDBR-1131 [S]	This Little Boy of Mine	1961	7.50	15.00	30.00
SDBR-1132 [S]	Gloria Lynne at Basin Street East	1962	7.50	15.00	30.00
SDBR-1203 [S]	Gloria Blue	1962	7.50	15.00	30.00
SDBR-1208 [S]	Gloria Lynne at the Las Vegas Thunderbird	1963	7.50	15.00	30.00
EV-1220 [S]	Gloria, Marty & Strings	1963	7.50	15.00	30.00
EV-1226 [S]	I Wish You Love	1964	6.25	12.50	25.00
EV-1228 [S]	Glorious Gloria Lynne	1964	6.25	12.50	25.00
EV-1230 [S]	After Hours	1965	6.25	12.50	25.00
EV-1231 [S]	The Best of Gloria Lynne	1965	5.00	10.00	20.00
EV-1237 [S]	Go, Go, Go	1965	5.00	10.00	20.00
EV-1238 [S]	Gloria Lynne '66	1966	5.00	10.00	20.00
E-5001 [M]	Gloria Lynne Live! Take 1	1959	7.50	15.00	30.00
LPBR-5022 [M]	Miss Gloria Lynne	1959	5.00	10.00	20.00
LPBR-5063 [M]	Lonely and Sentimental	1960	5.00	10.00	20.00
LPBR-5090 [M]	Try a Little Tenderness	1960	5.00	10.00	20.00
LPBR-5101 [M]	Day In, Day Out	1961	5.00	10.00	20.00
LPBR-5126 [M]	I'm Glad There Is You	1961	5.00	10.00	20.00
LPBR-5128 [M]	He Needs Me	1961	5.00	10.00	20.00
LPBR-5131 [M]	This Little Boy of Mine	1961	5.00	10.00	20.00
LPBR-5132 [M]	Gloria Lynne at Basin Street East	1962	5.00	10.00	20.00
LPBR-5203 [M]	Gloria Blue	1962	5.00	10.00	20.00
LPBR-5208 [M]	Gloria Lynne at the Las Vegas Thunderbird	1963	5.00	10.00	20.00
EV-5220 [M]	Gloria, Marty & Strings	1963	5.00	10.00	20.00
EV-5226 [M]	I Wish You Love	1964	5.00	10.00	20.00
EV-5228 [M]	Glorious Gloria Lynne	1964	5.00	10.00	20.00
EV-5230 [M]	After Hours	1965	5.00	10.00	20.00
EV-5231 [M]	The Best of Gloria Lynne	1965	3.75	7.50	15.00
EV-5237 [M]	Go, Go, Go	1965	3.75	7.50	15.00
EV-5238 [M]	Gloria Lynne '66	1966	3.75	7.50	15.00
FONTANA					
MGF-27528 [M]	Intimate Moments	1964	3.75	7.50	15.00
MGF-27541 [M]	Soul Serenade	1965	3.75	7.50	15.00
MGF-27546 [M]	Love and a Woman	1965	3.75	7.50	15.00
MGF-27555 [M]	Where It's At	1966	3.75	7.50	15.00
MGF-27561 [M]	Gloria	1966	3.75	7.50	15.00
MGF-27571 [M]	The Other Side of Gloria Lynne	1967	5.00	10.00	20.00
SRF-67528 [S]	Intimate Moments	1964	5.00	10.00	20.00
SRF-67541 [S]	Soul Serenade	1965	5.00	10.00	20.00
SRF-67546 [S]	Love and a Woman	1965	5.00	10.00	20.00
SRF-67555 [S]	Where It's At	1966	5.00	10.00	20.00
SRF-67561 [S]	Gloria	1966	5.00	10.00	20.00
SRF-67571 [S]	The Other Side of Gloria Lynne	1967	3.75	7.50	15.00
SRF-67577	Here, There and Everywhere	1968	3.75	7.50	15.00
HIFI					
R-440 [M]	Gloria Lynne	1966	3.75	7.50	15.00
SR-440 [S]	Gloria Lynne	1966	5.00	10.00	20.00
SR-441	Greatest Hits	1969	3.75	7.50	15.00
INTERMEDIA					
QS-5069	Classics	198?	2.50	5.00	10.00
MERCURY					
SRM-1-633	A Very Gentle Sound	1972	3.75	7.50	15.00
MUSE					
MR-5381	A Time for Love	198?	2.50	5.00	10.00
SUNSET					
SUM-1145 [M]	Gloria Lynne	1966	3.00	6.00	12.00
SUM-1171 [M]	I Wish You Love	1967	3.00	6.00	12.00
SUS-5145 [S]	Gloria Lynne	1966	3.00	6.00	12.00
SUS-5171 [S]	I Wish You Love	1967	3.00	6.00	12.00
SUS-5221	Golden Greats	1968	3.00	6.00	12.00
UPFRONT					
146	Gloria Lynne	197?	3.00	6.00	12.00

LYNYRD SKYNYRD

12-Inch Singles

Number	Title (A Side/B Side)	Yr	VG	VG+	NM
MCA					
L33-17385 [DJ]	Truck Drivin' Man/Simple Man	1987	2.00	4.00	8.00

Number	Title (A Side/B Side)	Yr	VG	VG+	NM
L33-17444 [DJ]	Georgia Peaches (same on both sides)	1987	2.00	4.00	8.00
L33-17488 [DJ]	Swamp Music (same on both sides)	1987	2.00	4.00	8.00
L33-17569 [DJ]	Gimme Back My Bullets/Comin' Home	198?	2.00	4.00	8.00
45s					
ATINA					
129	Need All My Friends/Michelle	1978	3.75	7.50	15.00
COLUMBIA					
78284	White Knuckle Ride/Tearin' It Up	1996	—	—	3.00
—B-side by Joe Diffie					
MCA					
L45-1966 [DJ]	Gimme Back My Bullets (same on both sides)	1976	6.25	12.50	25.00
40258	Sweet Home Alabama/Take Your Time	1974	—	2.50	5.00
40328	Free Bird/Down South Jukin'	1974	—	2.50	5.00
40416	Saturday Night Special/Made in the Shade	1975	—	2.50	5.00
40532	Double Trouble/Roll Gypsy Roll	1975	—	2.50	5.00
40565	Gimme Back My Bullets/All I Can Do Is Write About It	1976	—	2.50	5.00
40647	Gimme Three Steps/Travelin' Man	1976	—	2.50	5.00
40665	Free Bird/Searching	1976	—	2.50	5.00
40819	What's Your Name/I Know a Little	1977	—	2.50	5.00
—"What's Your Name" is a different mix than that on the Street Survivors LP.					
40888	You Got That Right/Ain't No Good Life	1978	—	2.50	5.00
40957	Down South Jukin'/Wino	1978	—	2.50	5.00
53206	When You Got Good Friends/Truck Drivin' Man	1987	—	2.00	4.00
60191	Sweet Home Alabama/Saturday Night Special	1976	—	2.00	4.00
—Reissue					
SHADE TREE					
101	Need All My Friends/Michelle	1971	375.00	750.00	1500.
—As "Lynard Skynard"; approximately 300 copies pressed					
SOUNDS OF THE SOUTH					
40158	Gimme Three Steps/Mr. Banker	1973	2.00	4.00	8.00
40231	Don't Ask Me No Questions/Take Your Time	1974	2.00	4.00	8.00
40258	Sweet Home Alabama/Take Your Time	1974	2.00	4.00	8.00
Albums					
ATLANTIC					
A1-82258	Lynyrd Skynyrd 1991	1991	5.00	10.00	20.00
—The only U.S. vinyl version was released through Columbia House					
MCA					
363	(pronounced leh-nerd skin-nerd)	1975	3.00	6.00	12.00
—Reissue on black rainbow label					
413	Second Helping	1975	3.00	6.00	12.00
—Reissue on black rainbow label					
1448	Best of the Rest	1985	2.00	4.00	8.00
L33-1946 [(2) DJ]	One More From the Road	1976	6.25	12.50	25.00
—Promo only on black vinyl					
L33-1946 [(2) DJ]	One More From the Road	1976	12.50	25.00	50.00
—Promo on blue, gold, purple or red vinyl (each has the same value)					
L33-1988 [DJ]	Skynyrd's First and...Last	1978	6.25	12.50	25.00
—Promo sampler					
2137	Nuthin' Fancy	1975	3.00	6.00	12.00
3019	(pronounced leh-nerd skin-nerd)	1976	2.50	5.00	10.00
—Second reissue with new number on black rainbow label					
3020	Second Helping	1976	2.50	5.00	10.00
—Second reissue with new number on black rainbow label					

Number	Title (A Side/B Side)	Yr	VG	VG+	NM
3021	Nuthin' Fancy	1976	2.50	5.00	10.00
—Reissue with new number on black rainbow label					
3022	Gimme Back My Bullets	1976	3.00	6.00	12.00
3029	Street Survivors	1977	6.25	12.50	25.00
—Originals with the band in flames on the front cover and a smaller band photo on the back cover					
3029	Street Survivors	1977	2.50	5.00	10.00
—After the band's plane crash, the "flames" photo was replaced with the back cover photo; the back cover is black with only the song titles					
3047	Skynyrd's First and...Last	1978	3.00	6.00	12.00
—Originals with tan labels and gatefold cover					
5221	(pronounced leh-nerd skin-nerd)	1980	2.00	4.00	8.00
5222	Second Helping	1980	2.00	4.00	8.00
5223	Street Survivors	1980	2.00	4.00	8.00
5370	Best of the Rest	1982	2.50	5.00	10.00
—Original version					
6001 [(2)]	One More From the Road	1976	3.75	7.50	15.00
—Originals with black rainbow label and gatefold cover					
6897 [(2)]	One More From the Road	1985	2.50	5.00	10.00
—Most, if not all, of these pressings have no gatefold					
6898 [(2)]	Gold & Platinum	1985	2.50	5.00	10.00
—Most, if not all, of these pressings have no gatefold					
8027 [(2)]	Southern by the Grace of God	1988	3.00	6.00	12.00
10014 [(2)]	One More From the Road	1980	2.50	5.00	10.00
11008 [(2)]	Gold & Platinum	1979	3.00	6.00	12.00
—Originals with embossed gatefold cover					
37069	Gimme Back My Bullets	1980	2.00	4.00	8.00
37070	Nuthin' Fancy	1980	2.00	4.00	8.00
37071	Skynyrd's First and...Last	1980	2.00	4.00	8.00
37211	(pronounced leh-nerd skin-nerd)	1985	2.00	4.00	8.00
37212	Second Helping	1985	2.00	4.00	8.00
37213	Street Survivors	1985	2.00	4.00	8.00
42084	Legend	1987	2.50	5.00	10.00
42293	Skynyrd's Innyrds	1989	3.00	6.00	12.00
SOUNDS OF THE SOUTH					
363	(pronounced leh-nerd skin-nerd)	1973	5.00	10.00	20.00
413	Second Helping	1974	5.00	10.00	20.00
—Both of the above are original pressings with yellow labels					
LYONS, MARIE					
45s					
DELUXE					
101	Drown in My Own Tears/Try Me	1968	3.00	6.00	12.00
—As "Queenie Lyons"					
103	Fever/Your Key Don't Fit No More	1969	2.50	5.00	10.00
—As "Marie 'Queenie' Lyons"					
123	Daddy's House/See and Don't See	1970	2.50	5.00	10.00
Albums					
DELUXE					
12001	Soul Fever	1970	6.25	12.50	25.00
LYZER, TONY					
45s					
LAURIE					
3019	Six Little Men/Loco	1958	37.50	75.00	150.00

M

M.H. ROYALS, THE

Number	Title (A Side/B Side)	Yr	VG	VG+	NM
45s					
ABC					
10907	Tomorrow's Dead/She's Gone Forever	1967	6.25	12.50	25.00
10957	Old Town/Now She's Crying	1967	6.25	12.50	25.00

M.P.D. LIMITED

Number	Title (A Side/B Side)	Yr	VG	VG+	NM
45s					
LTD					
400	Little Boy Sad/Wendy Don't Go	1965	10.00	20.00	40.00

M-3'S, THE

Number	Title (A Side/B Side)	Yr	VG	VG+	NM
45s					
ABC-PARAMOUNT					
10772	Funny Cafe/So Give Me Love	1966	6.25	12.50	25.00
UNITED ARTISTS					
737	When the Party's Over/Magic Kiss	1964	3.00	6.00	12.00
889	Three Lonely Nights/I See a Rainbow	1965	3.00	6.00	12.00

MABLEY, MOMS

Number	Title (A Side/B Side)	Yr	VG	VG+	NM
45s					
MERCURY					
72935	Abraham, Martin and John/Sunny	1969	—	3.00	6.00
72958	His Way/Yes Indeed	1969	—	3.00	6.00
72974	It's Your Thing/He's Got the Whole World in His Hands	1969	—	3.00	6.00
73240	I Surrender Dear/That's Pops	1971	—	2.50	5.00
Albums					
CHESS					
LP-1447 [M]	Moms Mabley, Funniest Woman in the World, Onstage	1961	6.25	12.50	25.00
LP-1452 [M]	Moms Mabley at the "UN"	1961	6.25	12.50	25.00
LP-1460 [M]	Moms Mabley at the Playboy Club	1961	6.25	12.50	25.00
LP-1463 [M]	Moms Mabley at Geneva Conference	1962	6.25	12.50	25.00
LP-1472 [M]	Moms Mabley Breaks It Up	1962	6.25	12.50	25.00
LP-1477 [M]	Young Men, Si — Old Men, No	1962	6.25	12.50	25.00
LP-1479 [M]	I Got Somethin' to Tell You!	1963	6.25	12.50	25.00
LP-1482 [M]	The Funny Sides of Moms Mabley	1963	6.25	12.50	25.00
LP-1486 [M]	Moms Wows	1964	6.25	12.50	25.00
LP-1487 [M]	The Best of Moms	1964	6.25	12.50	25.00
LP-1497 [M]	The Man in My Life	1965	5.00	10.00	20.00
LPS-1525	Moms Mabley Breaks Up the Network	1968	5.00	10.00	20.00
LPS-1530	Moms Mabley Sings	1969	5.00	10.00	20.00
MERCURY					
MG-20889 [M]	Out on a Limb	1964	3.75	7.50	15.00
MG-20907 [M]	Moms the Word	1964	3.75	7.50	15.00
MG-21012 [M]	Now Hear This	1965	3.75	7.50	15.00
MG-21090 [M]	Moms Mabley at the White House	1966	3.75	7.50	15.00
MG-21139 [M]	The Best of Moms Mabley	1967	6.25	12.50	25.00
SR-60889 [S]	Out on a Limb	1964	5.00	10.00	20.00
SR-60907 [S]	Moms the Word	1964	5.00	10.00	20.00
SR-61012 [S]	Now Hear This	1965	5.00	10.00	20.00
SR-61090 [S]	Moms Mabley at the White House	1966	5.00	10.00	20.00
SR-61139 [S]	The Best of Moms Mabley	1967	3.75	7.50	15.00
SR-61205	Her Young Thing	1969	3.75	7.50	15.00
SR-61229	The Youngest Teenager	1969	3.75	7.50	15.00
SR-61235	Abraham, Martin and John	1969	3.75	7.50	15.00
SR-61263	Live at Sing Sing	1970	3.75	7.50	15.00

MACH, LEON

Number	Title (A Side/B Side)	Yr	VG	VG+	NM
45s					
LAVENDER					
1554	You Hurt Me So/It's You I Love	1960	25.00	50.00	100.00

MACK, LONNIE

Number	Title (A Side/B Side)	Yr	VG	VG+	NM
45s					
BUCCANEER					
3001	Memphis/Lonnie on the Move	196?	2.00	4.00	8.00
—Reissue of Fraternity material					
CAPITOL					
4441	Running Wild/Funky Country Living	1977	—	2.50	5.00
ELEKTRA					
45638	Memphis/Why	1968	2.50	5.00	10.00
45652	Save Your Money/In the Band	1969	2.50	5.00	10.00
45715	She Even Woke Me Up to Say Goodbye/Lay It Down	1971	2.00	4.00	8.00
45761	Rings/Florida	1972	2.00	4.00	8.00
EPIC					
07973	Too Rock for Country, Too Country for Rock and Roll/Lucille	1988	—	2.00	4.00
08117	Hard Life/50's-60's Man	1988	—	2.00	4.00
FRATERNITY					
906	Memphis/Down in the Dumps	1963	3.75	7.50	15.00
912	Wham!/Susie-Q	1963	3.75	7.50	15.00
918	Baby, What's Wrong/Where There's a Will	1963	3.00	6.00	12.00
920	Say Something Nice to Me/Lonnie on the Move	1964	3.00	6.00	12.00
925	I've Had It/Nashville	1964	3.00	6.00	12.00
932	Chicken Pickin'/Sa-Ba-Hoola	1964	3.00	6.00	12.00
938	Don't Make My Baby Blue/Georgia Boy	1964	3.00	6.00	12.00
942	Crying Over You/Coastin'	1965	3.00	6.00	12.00
946	Tonky Go Go/When I'm Alone	1965	3.00	6.00	12.00
951	Honky Tonk '65/Chicken Pickin'	1965	3.00	6.00	12.00
957	Crying Over You/Are You Guilty	1966	3.00	6.00	12.00
959	The Circus/Bucaroo	1966	3.00	6.00	12.00
967	Tension (Part 1)/Tension (Part 2)	1966	3.00	6.00	12.00
969	Wildwood Flower/Snow on the Mountain	1966	3.00	6.00	12.00
981	I Left My Heart in San Francisco/Omaha	1967	2.50	5.00	10.00
986	Save Your Money/Snow on the Mountain	1967	2.50	5.00	10.00
1004	Soul Express/Down and Out	1968	2.50	5.00	10.00
1278	Soul Express/I Found a Love	197?	—	3.00	6.00
ROULETTE					
7175	All We Need Is Love, You and Me/Highway 56	1975	—	3.00	6.00
Albums					
ALLIGATOR					
AL-3903	The Wham of That Memphis Man	1987	2.50	5.00	10.00
—Reissue of Fraternity LP					
AL-4739	Strike Like Lightning	1985	2.50	5.00	10.00
AL-4750	Second Sight	1987	2.50	5.00	10.00
AL-4786	Live!: Attack of the Killer V	1990	3.00	6.00	12.00
CAPITOL					
ST-11619	Home at Last	1976	3.00	6.00	12.00
ST-11703	Lonnie Mack and Pismo	1977	3.00	6.00	12.00
ELEKTRA					
EKS-74040	Glad I'm In the Band	1969	6.25	12.50	25.00
EKS-74050	Whatever's Right	1969	6.25	12.50	25.00
EKS-74077	For Collectors Only	1970	6.25	12.50	25.00
EKS-74102	The Hills of Indiana	1971	6.25	12.50	25.00
EPIC					
FE 44075	Roadhouses and Dance Halls	1989	3.00	6.00	12.00
FRATERNITY					
SF-1014 [M]	The Wham of That Memphis Man	1963	30.00	60.00	120.00
SSF-1014 [S]	The Wham of That Memphis Man	1963	75.00	150.00	300.00
TRIP					
TLX-9522 [(2)]	The Memphis Sounds of Lonnie Mack	1975	3.00	6.00	12.00

MACKENZIE, GISELE

Number	Title (A Side/B Side)	Yr	VG	VG+	NM
45s					
CAPITOL					
F1722	Jolie Jacqueline/Fairyland	1951	3.75	7.50	15.00
F1768	J'Attendrai/My Greatest Love	1951	3.75	7.50	15.00
F1807	On Rosary Hill/Lovers' Waltz	1951	3.75	7.50	15.00
—With Gordon MacRae					
F1826	Sans Souci/I Never Was Loved by Anyone Else	1951	3.75	7.50	15.00
F1865	Sweetheart/It's All Over But the Memories	1951	3.75	7.50	15.00
F1907	La Fiacre/Thu Pocket Thu Pocket	1951	3.75	7.50	15.00
F1959	My Buick, My Lover and I/Lovers' Waltz	1952	3.00	6.00	12.00
—With Gordon MacRae					
F1983	Wishin'/Goodbye Sweetheart	1952	3.00	6.00	12.00
F1997	Eggbert the Easter Egg/Benny the Bob-Tailed Bunny	1952	3.75	7.50	15.00
F2059	What'll I Do/I'm So Easy to Satisfy	1952	3.00	6.00	12.00
F2110	Johnny/Whistle My Love	1952	3.00	6.00	12.00
F2156	Adios/Darling You Can't Love Two	1952	3.00	6.00	12.00
F2256	Don't Let the Stars Get In Your Eyes/My Favorite Song	1952	3.00	6.00	12.00
F2307	Gone/The New Wears Off Too Fast	1952	3.00	6.00	12.00
F2354	Let Me Know/Friend of the Family	1953	3.00	6.00	12.00
F2404	Lipstick and Powder and Paint/Get It While You're Young	1953	3.00	6.00	12.00
—With Helen O'Connell					
F2501	I'd Rather Die Young/I Didn't Want to Love You	1953	3.00	6.00	12.00
F2521	Give Me a Name/When the Hands of the Clock Pray at Midnight	1953	3.00	6.00	12.00
—With Helen O'Connell					
F2556	Half Hearted/Till They've All Come Home	1953	3.00	6.00	12.00
F2600	Walkin' Tune/Embrasse	1953	3.00	6.00	12.00
F2695	A Letter and a Ring/Le Gros Bill	1954	3.00	6.00	12.00
F2743	Doggone It Baby, I'm in Love/Ridin' to Tennessee	1954	3.00	6.00	12.00
F2827	El Recicario/The One Who Broke My Heart Is Back in Town	1954	3.00	6.00	12.00
EVEREST					
19352	In Milano/You Dream of Me (And I'll Dream of You)	1960	2.00	4.00	8.00
MERCURY					
72113	Loser's Lullaby/By Myself	1963	—	3.50	7.00
RCA VICTOR					
47-7086	Never Go Away/This I Know	1957	2.50	5.00	10.00
47-7183	They're Playing Our Song/Come to Me My True Love	1958	2.00	4.00	8.00
VIK					
0233	The Star You Wished Upon Last Night/It's Delightful to Be Married	1956	2.50	5.00	10.00
0249	He Knows/Hello There	1957	2.50	5.00	10.00
0274	The Waltz That Broke My Heart/Oh Pain, Oh Agony	1957	2.50	5.00	10.00
0300	Too Fat for the Chimney/Jingle Bells	1957	3.00	6.00	12.00
0300 [PS]	Too Fat for the Chimney/Jingle Bells	1957	5.00	10.00	20.00
"X"					
0137	Hard to Get/Boston Fancy	1955	3.00	6.00	12.00
0137 [PS]	Hard to Get/Boston Fancy	1955	5.00	10.00	20.00
0172	Pepper Hot Baby/That's the Chance I've Got to Take	1955	2.50	5.00	10.00
0189	Reserved/The Little Child	1956	2.50	5.00	10.00
—With Billy Quinn					
0202	Mr. Telephone/Dance If You Want to Dance	1956	2.50	5.00	10.00
Albums					
EVEREST					
SDBR-1069 [S]	In Person at the Empire Room	1959	7.50	15.00	30.00
LPBR-5069 [M]	In Person at the Empire Room	1959	6.25	12.50	25.00
GLENDALE					
6017	Gisele MacKenzie Sings	1978	3.00	6.00	12.00
RCA VICTOR					
LPM-1790 [M]	Gisele	1958	7.50	15.00	30.00
LSP-1790 [S]	Gisele	1958	10.00	20.00	40.00
LPM-2006 [M]	Christmas with Gisele	1959	7.50	15.00	30.00
LSP-2006 [S]	Christmas with Gisele	1959	10.00	20.00	40.00
SUNSET					
SUM-1155 [M]	In Person at the Empire Room	196?	3.00	6.00	12.00
SUS-5155 [S]	In Person at the Empire Room	196?	3.75	7.50	15.00

Number	Title (A Side/B Side)	Yr	VG	VG+	NM
VIK					
LX-1055 [M]	Gisele MacKenzie	1956	10.00	20.00	40.00
LX-1075 [M]	Mam'selle MacKenzie	1956	10.00	20.00	40.00
LX-1099 [M]	Christmas with Gisele	1957	10.00	20.00	40.00

MACRAE, GORDON, AND JO STAFFORD
See JO STAFFORD AND GORDON MacRAE.

MACRAE, SHEILA
Albums

Number	Title (A Side/B Side)	Yr	VG	VG+	NM
ABC					
ABCS-611	How Sweet She Is	1968	6.25	12.50	25.00

MAD HATTERS, THE
45s

Number	Title (A Side/B Side)	Yr	VG	VG+	NM
ASCOT					
2197	I Need Love/Blowin' in the Wind	1965	6.25	12.50	25.00
FONTANA					
1582	I'll Come Running/Hello Girl	1967	5.00	10.00	20.00
IGL					
117	Her Love/Route 66	196?	3.75	7.50	15.00

MAD LADS, THE
45s

Number	Title (A Side/B Side)	Yr	VG	VG+	NM
CAPITOL					
5284	Don't Cry at the Party/I'll Survive	1964	3.75	7.50	15.00
STAX					
160	Surf Jerk/Sidewalk Surf	1964	3.75	7.50	15.00
VOLT					
127	Don't Have to Shop Around/Tear-Maker	1965	2.50	5.00	10.00
131	I Want Someone/Nothing Can Break Through	1965	2.50	5.00	10.00
135	Come Closer to Me/Sugar Sugar	1966	2.50	5.00	10.00
137	I Want a Girl/What Will Love Tend to Make You Do	1966	2.50	5.00	10.00
139	Patch My Heart/You Mean So Much to Me	1966	2.50	5.00	10.00
143	These Simple Reasons/I Don't Want to Lose Your Love	1967	2.50	5.00	10.00
150	My Inspiration/Mr. Fix-It	1967	2.50	5.00	10.00
162	Whatever Hurts You/No Time Is Better Than Right Now	1968	2.50	5.00	10.00
4003	So Nice/Make Room	1968	2.00	4.00	8.00
4009	Love Is Here Today and Gone Tomorrow/Make This Young Lady Mine	1969	2.00	4.00	8.00
4016	By the Time I Get to Phoenix/No Strings Attached	1969	2.00	4.00	8.00
4041	Seeing Is Believing/These Old Memories	1970	2.00	4.00	8.00
4068	Gone! The Promises of Yesterday/I'm So Glad I Fell in Love with You	1971	2.00	4.00	8.00
4080	Let Me Repair Your Heart/Did My Baby Call	1972	2.00	4.00	8.00
4098	I Forgot to Be Your Lover/I'm So Glad I Fell in Love with You	1973	2.00	4.00	8.00
WAND					
11221	Let's Have Some Fun (Part 1)/Let's Have Some Fun (Part 2)	1970	2.50	5.00	10.00

Albums

Number	Title (A Side/B Side)	Yr	VG	VG+	NM
STAX					
MPS-8525	The Best of the Mad Lads	198?	2.50	5.00	10.00
VOLT					
414 [M]	The Mad Lads In Action	1966	7.50	15.00	30.00
S-414 [S]	The Mad Lads In Action	1966	10.00	20.00	40.00
VOS-6005	The Mad, Mad, Mad, Mad, Mad Lads	1969	7.50	15.00	30.00
VOS-6020	A New Beginning	1973	5.00	10.00	20.00

MAD MILO
45s

Number	Title (A Side/B Side)	Yr	VG	VG+	NM
COMBO					
131	Elvis on Trial/A Date with Elvis	1957	12.50	25.00	50.00
MILLION					
20018	Elvis for Christmas/New Year	1957	12.50	25.00	50.00
—B-side by Ron Tan and Combo					

MAD RIVER
45s

Number	Title (A Side/B Side)	Yr	VG	VG+	NM
CAPITOL					
2310	A Gazelle/High All the Time	1968	3.00	6.00	12.00
2559	Copper Plates/Harfy Magnum	1969	3.00	6.00	12.00

Albums

Number	Title (A Side/B Side)	Yr	VG	VG+	NM
CAPITOL					
ST-185	Paradise Bar and Grill	1969	10.00	20.00	40.00
ST 2985	Mad River	1968	12.50	25.00	50.00

MADHATTANS, THE
45s

Number	Title (A Side/B Side)	Yr	VG	VG+	NM
ATLANTIC					
1142	Wowie/A Basketful of Blueberries	1957	5.00	10.00	20.00

MADISONS, THE
45s

Number	Title (A Side/B Side)	Yr	VG	VG+	NM
LAWN					
240	Can You Imagine It/The Wind and the Rain	1964	10.00	20.00	40.00
LIMELIGHT					
3018	Bad Baboon/Because I Got You	1964	5.00	10.00	20.00
MGM					
13312	Cheryl Anne/Looking for True Love	1965	10.00	20.00	40.00

MADRIGAL
45s

Number	Title (A Side/B Side)	Yr	VG	VG+	NM
SSS INTERNATIONAL					
824	I Believe in Sunshine/Lady	1971	2.00	4.00	8.00

Albums

Number	Title (A Side/B Side)	Yr	VG	VG+	NM
SSS INTERNATIONAL					
18	Madrigal	1971	7.50	15.00	30.00

MADURA
45s

Number	Title (A Side/B Side)	Yr	VG	VG+	NM
COLUMBIA					
45483	Johnny B. Goode/(B-side unknown)	1971	2.00	4.00	8.00
46022	Save the Miracle/Windy One	1974	2.00	4.00	8.00

Albums

Number	Title (A Side/B Side)	Yr	VG	VG+	NM
COLUMBIA					
G 30794 [(2)]	Madura	1971	5.00	10.00	20.00
KC 32545	Madura II	1973	3.75	7.50	15.00

MAESTRO, JOHNNY
Also see THE BROOKLYN BRIDGE; THE CRESTS.

45s

Number	Title (A Side/B Side)	Yr	VG	VG+	NM
APT					
25075	Phone Booth on the Highway/She's All Mine Alone	1965	12.50	25.00	50.00
BUDDAH					
201	The Rains Came/Never Knew THis Kind of Hurt Before	1971	2.50	5.00	10.00
236	Yours Until Tomorrow/Man in a Band	1971	2.50	5.00	10.00
289 [DJ]	Snow (mono/stereo)	1971	2.50	5.00	10.00
—May be promo only					
CAMEO					
256	Over the Weekend/I'll Be There	1963	7.50	15.00	30.00
305	Lean on Me/(It's Harder to) Make Up My Mind	1964	5.00	10.00	20.00
COED					
527	Say It Isn't So/The Great Physician	1960	6.25	12.50	25.00
—As "Johnny Masters"					
545	Model Girl/We've Got to Tell Them	1961	6.25	12.50	25.00
—As "Johnny Mastro"					
549	What a Surprise/Warning Voice	1961	6.25	12.50	25.00
552	Mr. Happiness/Test of Love	1961	6.25	12.50	25.00
557	I.O.U./The Way You Look Tonight	1961	7.50	15.00	30.00
562	Besame Baby/It Must Be Love	1962	25.00	50.00	100.00
PARKWAY					
118	My Times/Is It You	1966	5.00	10.00	20.00
987	Heartburn/Try Me	1966	3.75	7.50	15.00
987 [DJ]	Heartburn	1966	15.00	30.00	60.00
—One-sided white label promo					
999	I Care About You/Come See Me (I'm Your Man)	1966	3.75	7.50	15.00
UNITED ARTISTS					
474	Before I Loved Her/Fifty Million Heartbeats	1962	10.00	20.00	40.00

Albums

Number	Title (A Side/B Side)	Yr	VG	VG+	NM
BUDDAH					
BDS-5091	The Johnny Maestro Story	1971	10.00	20.00	40.00
—With inserts; deduct 40% if missing					

MAGI, THE
Albums

Number	Title (A Side/B Side)	Yr	VG	VG+	NM
UNCLE DIRTY					
6102-N13	Win or Lose	1975	75.00	150.00	300.00

MAGIC CHRISTIANS, THE
Trevor Burton of THE MOVE was in this studio group.

45s

Number	Title (A Side/B Side)	Yr	VG	VG+	NM
COMMONWEALTH UNITED					
3006	Come and Get It/Nats	1970	3.00	6.00	12.00

MAGIC FERN, THE
45s

Number	Title (A Side/B Side)	Yr	VG	VG+	NM
JERDEN					
813	Maggie/I Wonder Why	1966	5.00	10.00	20.00
PICCADILLY					
240	Nellie/Candy Day	1967	3.75	7.50	15.00

Albums

Number	Title (A Side/B Side)	Yr	VG	VG+	NM
PANORAMA					
108	The Magic Fern	1980	25.00	50.00	100.00
108	The Magic Fern	1980	37.50	75.00	150.00

MAGIC LANTERNS
Contrary to some opinions, Ozzy Osbourne was never in this group. (The bass player was Michael "Oz" Osborne; notice the difference in last name spelling.) But ALBERT HAMMOND was.

45s

Number	Title (A Side/B Side)	Yr	VG	VG+	NM
ATLANTIC					
2560	Shame, Shame/Baby, I Gotta Go Now	1968	2.50	5.00	10.00
2600	Give Me Love/Biding My Time	1969	2.00	4.00	8.00
2626	Melt All Your Troubles Away/Bossa Nova 1940-Hello You Lovers	1969	2.00	4.00	8.00
2715	One Night Stand/Frisco Annie	1970	2.00	4.00	8.00
BIG TREE					
109	One Night Stand/Frisco Annie	1970	—	3.00	6.00
113	Let the Sunshine In/Old Pa Bradley	1971	—	3.00	6.00
CHARISMA					
100	Country Woman/Pa Bradley	1972	—	2.50	5.00
EPIC					
10062	Excuse Me Baby/Greedy Girl	1966	2.00	4.00	8.00
10062 [PS]	Excuse Me Baby/Greedy Girl	1966	5.00	10.00	20.00
10111	Knight in Rusty Armour/Simple Things	1966	2.00	4.00	8.00

Albums

Number	Title (A Side/B Side)	Yr	VG	VG+	NM
ATLANTIC					
SD 8217	Shame, Shame	1969	5.00	10.00	20.00

MAGIC MUSHROOM, THE
45s

Number	Title (A Side/B Side)	Yr	VG	VG+	NM
WARNER BROS.					
5846	I'm Gone/Cry Baby	1966	6.25	12.50	25.00

MAGIC MUSHROOMS, THE

45s

A&M

Number	Title (A Side/B Side)	Yr	VG	VG+	NM
815	It's a-Happening/Never More	1966	3.75	7.50	15.00

PHILIPS

Number	Title (A Side/B Side)	Yr	VG	VG+	NM
40483	Look in My Face/Never Let Go	1968	3.75	7.50	15.00

MAGIC SAND

Albums

UNI

Number	Title (A Side/B Side)	Yr	VG	VG+	NM
73094	Magic Sand	1971	6.25	12.50	25.00

MAGIC TOUCH, THE (1)

Female group.

45s

BLACK FALCON

Number	Title (A Side/B Side)	Yr	VG	VG+	NM
19102	Step Into My World/Step Into My World (Part 2)	1971	2.00	4.00	8.00

MAGIC TOUCH, THE (2)

Male group.

45s

ROULETTE

Number	Title (A Side/B Side)	Yr	VG	VG+	NM
7143	Baby You Belong to Me/Lost and Lonely Boy	1973	3.00	6.00	12.00

MAGISTRATES, THE

45s

MGM

Number	Title (A Side/B Side)	Yr	VG	VG+	NM
13946	Here Comes the Judge/Girl	1968	3.00	6.00	12.00
13980	After the Fox/Tear Down the Walls	1968	3.00	6.00	12.00

MAGNETS, THE (1)

45s

GROOVE

Number	Title (A Side/B Side)	Yr	VG	VG+	NM
58-0058	Surprise/You Just Say the Word	1965	10.00	20.00	40.00

MAGNETS, THE (2)

45s

LONDON INT'L.

Number	Title (A Side/B Side)	Yr	VG	VG+	NM
10036	Drag Race/Joker	1963	6.25	12.50	25.00

MAGNETS, THE (3)

45s

RCA VICTOR

Number	Title (A Side/B Side)	Yr	VG	VG+	NM
47-7391	When the School Bells Ring/Don't Tarry, Little Mary	1958	6.25	12.50	25.00

MAGNIFICENT FOUR, THE

45s

BLAST

Number	Title (A Side/B Side)	Yr	VG	VG+	NM
210	The Closer You Are/Uncle Sam	1963	10.00	20.00	40.00

WHALE

Number	Title (A Side/B Side)	Yr	VG	VG+	NM
506	The Closer You Are/Uncle Sam	1961	20.00	40.00	80.00

MAGNIFICENT MEN, THE

45s

CAPITOL

Number	Title (A Side/B Side)	Yr	VG	VG+	NM
2062	Baby, I'm Crazy About You/Forever Together	1967	2.00	4.00	8.00
2134	By the Time I Get to Phoenix/Tired of Pushing	1968	2.00	4.00	8.00
2202	Almost Persuaded/I Found What I Wanted in You	1968	2.00	4.00	8.00
2319	Save the Country/So Much Love Waiting	1968	2.00	4.00	8.00
5608	Peace of Mind/All Your Lovin's Gone To My Head	1966	2.00	4.00	8.00
5732	I've Got News/Maybe, Baby	1966	2.00	4.00	8.00
5812	Stormy Weather/Much, Much More of Your Love	1966	2.00	4.00	8.00
5905	I Could Be So Happy/You Changed My Life	1967	2.00	4.00	8.00
5976	Swet Soul Medley — Part 1/Sweet Soul Medley — Part 2	1967	2.00	4.00	8.00

MERCURY

Number	Title (A Side/B Side)	Yr	VG	VG+	NM
72988	Holly Go Softly/Open Up and Get Richer	1969	—	3.00	6.00
73028	Lay Lady Lay/Whatever It Takes	1970	—	3.00	6.00

Albums

CAPITOL

Number	Title (A Side/B Side)	Yr	VG	VG+	NM
ST 2678 [S]	The Magnificent Men	1967	3.75	7.50	15.00
T 2678 [M]	The Magnificent Men	1967	5.00	10.00	20.00
ST 2775 [S]	The Magnificent Men "Live!"	1967	3.75	7.50	15.00
T 2775 [M]	The Magnificent Men "Live!"	1967	5.00	10.00	20.00
ST 2846 [S]	World of Soul	1968	3.75	7.50	15.00
T 2846 [M]	World of Soul	1968	5.00	10.00	20.00

MERCURY

Number	Title (A Side/B Side)	Yr	VG	VG+	NM
SR-61252	Better Than a Ten Cent Movie	1970	3.75	7.50	15.00

MAGNIFICENT 7, THE

45s

DIAL

Number	Title (A Side/B Side)	Yr	VG	VG+	NM
4074	Ooh, Baby Baby/Never Will I (Make My Baby Cry)	1968	6.25	12.50	25.00

DIMENSION

Number	Title (A Side/B Side)	Yr	VG	VG+	NM
1050	Show Me/Boogidy	1965	5.00	10.00	20.00
—As "Magnificent VII"					

EASTERN

Number	Title (A Side/B Side)	Yr	VG	VG+	NM
611	She's Called a Woman/Since You've Been Gone So Long	1966	10.00	20.00	40.00

MAGNIFICENTS, THE

45s

CHECKER

Number	Title (A Side/B Side)	Yr	VG	VG+	NM
1016	The Dribble Twist/Do You Mind	1962	3.75	7.50	15.00

KANSOMA

Number	Title (A Side/B Side)	Yr	VG	VG+	NM
03	The Dribble Twist/Do You Mind	1962	7.50	15.00	30.00

VEE JAY

Number	Title (A Side/B Side)	Yr	VG	VG+	NM
183	Up On the Mountain/Why Did She Go	1956	18.75	37.50	75.00
208	Hiccup/Caddy Bo	1956	25.00	50.00	100.00
235	Off the Mountain/Lost Lovers	1957	18.75	37.50	75.00
281	Don't Leave Me/Ozeta	1958	25.00	50.00	100.00
367	Up On the Mountain/Let's Do the Cha Cha	1960	5.00	10.00	20.00

MAHAL, TAJ

45s

COLUMBIA

Number	Title (A Side/B Side)	Yr	VG	VG+	NM
10055	Why Did You Have to Desert Me/Cajun Waltz	1974	—	2.00	4.00
10109	Salve Drive/Cajun Waltz	1975	—	2.00	4.00
10260	Why, And We Repeat Why, And We Repeat.../(B-side unknown)	1975	—	2.00	4.00
10368	Ain't Nobody's Business/Easy to Love	1976	—	2.00	4.00
44051	Let the Good Times Roll/Shimmy Like My Sister Kate	1967	2.00	4.00	8.00
44405	E-Z Rider/Leaving Trunk	1967	2.00	4.00	8.00
44476	Statesboro Blues/Everybody's Got to Change Sometime	1968	2.00	4.00	8.00
44696	You Don't Miss Your Water/Going Down to the Country-Paint My Mailbox Blue	1968	2.00	4.00	8.00
44767	Corinna/A Lot of Love	1969	2.00	4.00	8.00
44991	Six Days on the Road/Light Rain Blues	1969	2.00	4.00	8.00
45419	Fishin' Blues/Diving Duck Blues	1971	—	2.50	5.00
45455	Ain't Gwine to Whistle Dixie Anymore (Part 1/Part 2)	1971	—	2.50	5.00
45539	Chevrolet/Oh Susanna	1972	—	2.50	5.00
45990	Buck Dancer's Choice/Little Red Hen	1974	—	2.50	5.00
46031	Built for Comfort/Teacup's Jazzy Blues Tune	1974	—	2.50	5.00

WARNER BROS.

Number	Title (A Side/B Side)	Yr	VG	VG+	NM
8528	Sing a Happy Song/Southbound with the Hammer Down	1978	—	2.00	4.00

Albums

COLUMBIA

Number	Title (A Side/B Side)	Yr	VG	VG+	NM
CG 18 [(2)]	Giant Step/De Old Folks at Home	198?	2.50	5.00	10.00
—Reissue with new prefix					
GP 18 [(2)]	Giant Step/De Old Folks at Home	1969	5.00	10.00	20.00
—Red "360 Sound" label					
GP 18 [(2)]	Giant Step/De Old Folks at Home	1971	3.75	7.50	15.00
—Orange label					
CL 2779 [M]	Taj Mahal	1967	7.50	15.00	30.00
CS 9579 [S]	Taj Mahal	1967	3.75	7.50	15.00
—Red "360 Sound" label					
CS 9579 [S]	Taj Mahal	1971	3.00	6.00	12.00
—Orange label					
PC 9579 [S]	Taj Mahal	198?	2.00	4.00	8.00
—Reissue with new prefix					
CS 9698	The Natch'l Blues	1968	3.75	7.50	15.00
—Red "360 Sound" label					
CS 9698	The Natch'l Blues	1971	3.00	6.00	12.00
—Orange label					
PC 9698	The Natch'l Blues	198?	2.00	4.00	8.00
—Reissue with new prefix					
CG 30619 [(2)]	The Real Thing	198?	2.50	5.00	10.00
—Reissue with new prefix					
G 30619 [(2)]	The Real Thing	1971	5.00	10.00	20.00
C 30767	Happy to Be Like I Am	1971	3.00	6.00	12.00
PC 30767	Happy to Be Like I Am	198?	2.00	4.00	8.00
—Budget-line reissue					
KC 31605	Recycling the Blues & Other Related Stuff	1972	3.00	6.00	12.00
PC 31605	Recycling the Blues & Other Related Stuff	198?	2.00	4.00	8.00
—Budget-line reissue					
KC 32600	Oooh So Good 'N Blues	1973	3.00	6.00	12.00
PC 32600	Oooh So Good 'N Blues	198?	2.00	4.00	8.00
—Budget-line reissue					
KC 33051	Mo' Roots	1974	3.00	6.00	12.00
PC 33051	Mo' Roots	198?	2.00	4.00	8.00
—Budget-line reissue					
PC 33801	Music Keeps Me Together	1975	3.00	6.00	12.00
PC 34103	Satisfied & Tickled Too	1976	3.00	6.00	12.00
PC 34466	Anthology Volume 1	1977	3.00	6.00	12.00
FC 36528	The Best of Taj Mahal	1981	2.50	5.00	10.00
PC 36528	The Best of Taj Mahal	198?	2.00	4.00	8.00
—Budget-line reissue					

CRYSTAL CLEAR

Number	Title (A Side/B Side)	Yr	VG	VG+	NM
5011	Live and Direct	1980	6.25	12.50	25.00
—Direct-to-disc recording					

WARNER BROS.

Number	Title (A Side/B Side)	Yr	VG	VG+	NM
BS 2994	Music Fuh Ya' (Musica Para Tu)	1977	2.50	5.00	10.00
BS 3024	Brothers	1977	2.50	5.00	10.00
BS 3094	Evolution (Recent)	1978	2.50	5.00	10.00

MAHARIS, GEORGE

45s

EPIC

Number	Title (A Side/B Side)	Yr	VG	VG+	NM
9504	Teach Me Tonight/After the Lights Go Down Low	1962	2.00	4.00	8.00
9504 [PS]	Teach Me Tonight/After the Lights Go Down Low	1962	2.50	5.00	10.00
9522	Love Me as I Love You/They Knew About You	1962	2.00	4.00	8.00
9522 [PS]	Love Me as I Love You/They Knew About You	1962	2.50	5.00	10.00
9555	Baby Has Gone Bye Bye/After One Kiss	1962	2.00	4.00	8.00
9555 [PS]	Baby Has Gone Bye Bye/After One Kiss	1962	2.50	5.00	10.00
9569	Don't Fence Me In/Alright, Okay, You Win	1963	2.00	4.00	8.00
9569 [PS]	Don't Fence Me In/Alright, Okay, You Win	1963	2.50	5.00	10.00
9580	Donna Loves Jerry/Oh, I'm in Love	1963	2.00	4.00	8.00
—By Donna Lynn with George Maharis					
9600	Where Can You Go (For a Broken Heart)/Kiss Me	1963	2.00	4.00	8.00
9600 [PS]	Where Can You Go (For a Broken Heart)/Kiss Me	1963	2.50	5.00	10.00
9613	That's How It Goes/It Isn't There	1963	2.00	4.00	8.00
9613 [PS]	That's How It Goes/It Isn't There	1963	2.50	5.00	10.00
9653	It's a Sin to Tell a Lie/Sara Darling	1964	—	3.00	6.00
9696	The Object of My Affection/Tonight You Belong to Me	1964	—	3.00	6.00
9753	I'm Coming Back for You/Lonely People Do Foolish Things	1965	—	3.00	6.00
9772	More I Cannot Do/Where Does Happiness Go	1965	—	3.00	6.00

Number	Title (A Side/B Side)	Yr	VG	VG+	NM
9844	Quien Sabe (Who Knows, Who Knows)/You Always Hurt the One You Love	1965	—	3.00	6.00
9858	Ivy/A World Without Sunshine	1965	—	3.00	6.00
10039	Never Is a Long, Long Time/Goodbye, Good Luck and God Bless You	1966	—	3.00	6.00
Albums					
EPIC					
LN 24001 [M]	George Maharis Sings!	1962	3.00	6.00	12.00
LN 24021 [M]	Portrait in Music	1962	3.00	6.00	12.00
LN 24037 [M]	Just Turn Me Loose!	1963	3.00	6.00	12.00
LN 24064 [M]	Where Can You Go for a Broken Heart?	1963	3.00	6.00	12.00
LN 24079 [M]	Make Love to Me	1964	3.00	6.00	12.00
LN 24111 [M]	Tonight You Belong to Me	1964	3.00	6.00	12.00
LN 24191 [M]	A New Route: George Maharis	1966	3.00	6.00	12.00
BN 26001 [S]	George Maharis Sings!	1962	3.75	7.50	15.00
BN 26021 [S]	Portrait in Music	1962	3.75	7.50	15.00
BN 26037 [S]	Just Turn Me Loose!	1963	3.75	7.50	15.00
BN 26064 [S]	Where Can You Go for a Broken Heart?	1963	3.75	7.50	15.00
BN 26079 [S]	Make Love to Me	1964	3.75	7.50	15.00
BN 26111 [S]	Tonight You Belong to Me	1964	3.75	7.50	15.00
BN 26191 [S]	A New Route: George Maharis	1966	3.75	7.50	15.00

MAHAVISHNU ORCHESTRA

Also see JOHN McLAUGHLIN.

Number	Title (A Side/B Side)	Yr	VG	VG+	NM
45s					
COLUMBIA					
10134	Can't Stand Your Funk/Eternity's Breath Part 2	1975	—	2.50	5.00
45836	Open Country Joy/Celestial Commuters	1973	—	2.50	5.00
Albums					
COLUMBIA					
KC 31067	The Inner Mounting Flame	1972	3.00	6.00	12.00
—As "Mahavishnu Orchestra with John McLaughlin"					
PC 31067	The Inner Mounting Flame	197?	2.00	4.00	8.00
—Reissue with new prefix					
CQ 31996 [Q]	Birds of Fire	1973	5.00	10.00	20.00
KC 31996	Birds of Fire	1973	2.50	5.00	10.00
PC 31996	Birds of Fire	197?	2.00	4.00	8.00
—Reissue with new prefix					
CQ 32766 [Q]	Between Nothingness and Eternity	1973	5.00	10.00	20.00
KC 32766	Between Nothingness and Eternity	1973	2.50	5.00	10.00
PC 32766	Between Nothingness and Eternity	197?	2.00	4.00	8.00
—Reissue with new prefix					
KC 32957	Apocalypse	1974	2.50	5.00	10.00
PC 32957	Apocalypse	197?	2.00	4.00	8.00
—Reissue with new prefix					
PC 33411	Visions of the Emerald Beyond	1975	2.50	5.00	10.00
—Original with no bar code					
PC 33411	Visions of the Emerald Beyond	198?	2.00	4.00	8.00
—Reissue with bar code					
PC 33908	Inner Worlds	1976	2.50	5.00	10.00
—Original with no bar code					
PC 33908	Inner Worlds	198?	2.00	4.00	8.00
—Reissue with bar code					
JC 36394	The Best of Mahavishnu Orchestra	1980	2.50	5.00	10.00

MAHOGANY RUSH

Number	Title (A Side/B Side)	Yr	VG	VG+	NM
45s					
20TH CENTURY					
2111	New Rock and Roll/Child of the Novelty	1974	—	2.50	5.00
2166	Buddy/Satisfy Your Soul	1975	—	2.50	5.00
Albums					
20TH CENTURY					
T-451	Child of the Novelty	1974	6.25	12.50	25.00
T-463	Maxoom	1975	6.25	12.50	25.00
T-482	Strange Universe	1975	5.00	10.00	20.00
COLUMBIA					
PC 34190	Mahogany Rush IV	1976	3.75	7.50	15.00
—Original with no bar code					
PC 34190	Mahogany Rush IV	198?	2.00	4.00	8.00
—Reissue with bar code					
PC 34677	World Anthem	1977	3.75	7.50	15.00
—Original with no bar code					
PC 34677	World Anthem	198?	2.00	4.00	8.00
—Reissue with bar code					
JC 35257	Frank Marino & Mahogany Rush Live	1978	3.75	7.50	15.00
PC 35257	Frank Marino & Mahogany Rush Live	198?	2.00	4.00	8.00
—Budget-line reissue					
JC 35753	Tales of the Unexpected	1979	3.75	7.50	15.00
PC 35753	Tales of the Unexpected	198?	2.00	4.00	8.00
—Budget-line reissue					
JC 36204	What's Next	1980	3.75	7.50	15.00
PC 36204	What's Next	198?	2.00	4.00	8.00
—Budget-line reissue					

MAIN ATTRACTION, THE

Number	Title (A Side/B Side)	Yr	VG	VG+	NM
45s					
TOWER					
420	I Remember Yesterday/If I'm Wrong	1968	2.50	5.00	10.00
435	Everyday/One Must Cry	1968	2.50	5.00	10.00
464	Friends/Jonathan	1969	2.50	5.00	10.00
Albums					
TOWER					
ST-5177	And Now…The Main Attraction	1968	6.25	12.50	25.00

MAIN INGREDIENT, THE

Number	Title (A Side/B Side)	Yr	VG	VG+	NM
12-Inch Singles					
RCA					
PD-13046	Party People/Save Me	1981	3.00	6.00	12.00
45s					
MERCURY					
73831	Magic Touch/Very White	1976	—	2.50	5.00
—As "Tony Sylvester and the New Ingredient"					
73871	Puzuzu/Soca	1977	—	2.50	5.00
—As "Tony Sylvester and the New Ingredient"					
POLYDOR					
889910-7	I Just Wanna Love You/When We Need It Bad	1989	—	—	3.00
RCA					
PB-12060	Think Positive/Spoiled	1980	—	2.00	4.00
—RCA 1980s titles as "Cuba Gooding and the Main Ingredient"					
PB-12107	What Can a Miracle Do/Makes No Diff'rence to Me	1980	—	2.00	4.00
PB-12320	Evening of Love/(Instrumental)	1981	—	—	—
—Unreleased					
PB-12340	I Only Have Eyes for You/Only	1981	—	2.00	4.00
PB-13045	Party People/Save Me	1982	—	2.00	4.00
RCA VICTOR					
APBO-0046	Girl Blue/Movin' On	1973	—	2.50	5.00
AMBO-0124	Everybody Plays the Fool/I'm So Proud	1973	—	2.00	4.00
—Gold Standard Series					
APBO-0205	Just Don't Want to Be Lonely/Goodbye My Love	1974	—	2.50	5.00
APBO-0305	Happiness Is Just Around the Bend/Why Can't We All Unite	1974	—	2.50	5.00
PB-10095	California My Way/Looks Like Rain	1974	—	2.50	5.00
PB-10224	Rolling Down a Mountainside/Family Man	1975	—	2.50	5.00
PB-10334	The Good Old Days/I Want to Make You Glad	1975	—	2.50	5.00
PB-10431	Shame on the World/Lillian	1975	—	2.50	5.00
GB-10482	Why Can't We All Unite/Happiness Is Just Around the Corner	1975	—	2.00	4.00
—Gold Standard Series					
GB-10483	Just Don't Want to Be Lonely/Goodbye My Love	1975	—	2.00	4.00
—Gold Standard Series					
47-9748	I Was Born to Lose You/Psychedelic Ride	1969	—	3.00	6.00
74-0252	Get Back/Brotherly Love	1969	—	3.00	6.00
74-0313	The Girl I Left Behind/Can't Stand Your Love	1970	—	2.50	5.00
74-0340	You've Been My Inspiration/Life Won't Be the Same (Without You)	1970	—	2.50	5.00
74-0385	Need Your Love/I'm Better Off Without You	1970	—	2.50	5.00
74-0401	I'm So Proud/Brother Love	1970	—	2.50	5.00
74-0456	Spinning Around (I Must Be Falling in Love)/Magic Shoes	1971	—	2.50	5.00
74-0517	Black Seeds Keep On Growing/Baby Change Your Mind	1971	—	2.50	5.00
74-0603	I'm Leaving This Time/Another Day Has Come	1971	—	2.50	5.00
74-0731	Everybody Plays the Fool/Who Can I Turn To	1972	—	3.00	6.00
74-0856	You've Got to Take It (If You Want It)/Travelling	1973	—	2.50	5.00
74-0939	You Can Call Me Rover/I'm Better Off Without You	1973	—	2.50	5.00
ZAKIA					
015	Do Me Right/(B-side unknown)	1986	—	2.00	4.00
Albums					
COLLECTABLES					
COL-5101	Golden Classics	198?	2.50	5.00	10.00
POLYDOR					
841249-1	I Just Wanna Love You	1989	3.00	6.00	12.00
RCA VICTOR					
APL1-0314	Greatest Hits	1974	3.00	6.00	12.00
APL1-0335	Euphrates River	1974	3.00	6.00	12.00
APL1-0644	Rolling Down a Mountainside	1975	3.00	6.00	12.00
APL1-1003	Shame On the World	1975	3.00	6.00	12.00
APL1-1558	Music Maximus	1977	3.00	6.00	12.00
APL1-1858	Super Hits	1977	3.00	6.00	12.00
ANL1-2667	Rolling Down a Mountainside	1978	2.50	5.00	10.00
—Reissue of APL1-0644					
AFL1-3641	Ready for Love	1980	2.50	5.00	10.00
AFL1-3963	I Only Have Eyes for You	1981	2.50	5.00	10.00
LSP-4253	The Main Ingredient L.T.D.	1970	3.00	6.00	12.00
LSP-4412	Tasteful Soul	1971	3.00	6.00	12.00
LSP-4483	Black Seeds	1971	3.00	6.00	12.00
LSP-4677	Bitter Sweet	1972	3.00	6.00	12.00
LSP-4834	Afrodisiac	1973	3.00	6.00	12.00

MAJESTICS, THE (1)

Number	Title (A Side/B Side)	Yr	VG	VG+	NM
45s					
CHESS					
1802	Oasis (Part 1)/Oasis (Part 2)	1961	5.00	10.00	20.00
V.I.P.					
25028 [DJ]	Say You/All for Someone	1965	250.00	500.00	1000.
—Promo only; stock copies credited "The Monitors"					

MAJESTICS, THE (2)

Number	Title (A Side/B Side)	Yr	VG	VG+	NM
45s					
CHEX					
1000	Give Me a Cigarette/Shoppin' and Hoppin'	1962	25.00	50.00	100.00
1000	Give Me a Cigarette/So I Can Forget	1962	10.00	20.00	40.00
1004	Unhappy and Blue/Treat Me Like You Want	1962	12.50	25.00	50.00
1006	Lonely Heart/Gwendolyn	1962	7.50	15.00	30.00
1009	Baby/Teach Me How to Limbo	1963	6.25	12.50	25.00

MAJESTICS, THE (3)

Number	Title (A Side/B Side)	Yr	VG	VG+	NM
45s					
20TH FOX					
171	The Lone Stranger/Sweet One	1959	6.25	12.50	25.00
CONTOUR					
501	Teen Age Gossip/Hard Times	1960	20.00	40.00	80.00
FARO					
592	TV Cowboys/So You Want to Rock	1959	6.25	12.50	25.00
FOXIE					
7004	The Lone Stranger/Sweet One	1960	5.00	10.00	20.00
NRC					
502	Please Don't Say No/Divided Heart	1958	62.50	125.00	250.00
SIOUX					
91459	The Lone Stranger/Sweet One	1959	12.50	25.00	50.00

MAJESTICS, THE (4)

45s

DUNES

Number	Title (A Side/B Side)	Yr	VG	VG+	NM
2014	The Boss Walk (Part 1)/The Boss Walk (Part 2)	1962	10.00	20.00	40.00

SAM

Number	Title (A Side/B Side)	Yr	VG	VG+	NM
112	Jaguar/Blue Feeling	1962	12.50	25.00	50.00
117	Riptide/Big Noise from Makaba	1962	12.50	25.00	50.00
123	XL-3/My Little Baby	1963	12.50	25.00	50.00

MAJESTICS, THE (5)

45s

JORDAN

Number	Title (A Side/B Side)	Yr	VG	VG+	NM
1057 *—Yellow vinyl*	Angel of Love/Searching for a New Love	1961	75.00	150.00	300.00
1057 *—Black vinyl*	Angel of Love/Searching for a New Love	1961	12.50	25.00	50.00

LINDA

Number	Title (A Side/B Side)	Yr	VG	VG+	NM
111	Strange World/Everything Is Gonna Be All Right	1963	15.00	30.00	60.00
121	Girl of My Dreams/It Hurts Me	1963	25.00	50.00	100.00

NU-TONE

Number	Title (A Side/B Side)	Yr	VG	VG+	NM
123	Angel of Love/Searching for a New Love	1961	17.50	35.00	70.00

PIXIE

Number	Title (A Side/B Side)	Yr	VG	VG+	NM
6901	Angel of Love/Searching for a New Love	1961	7.50	15.00	30.00

MAJESTICS, THE (6)

Sam Moore of SAM AND DAVE was in this group.

45s

MARLIN

Number	Title (A Side/B Side)	Yr	VG	VG+	NM
802	Nitey Nite/Cave Man Rock	1956	250.00	500.00	1000.

MAJESTICS, THE (7)

45s

MGM

Number	Title (A Side/B Side)	Yr	VG	VG+	NM
13488	Love Has Forgotten Me/Smile Through My Tears	1966	3.00	6.00	12.00

MAJOR LANCE

See listing under LANCE, MAJOR.

MAJORETTES, THE

45s

TROY

Number	Title (A Side/B Side)	Yr	VG	VG+	NM
1000	White Levi's/Please Come Back	1963	5.00	10.00	20.00
1000 [PS]	White Levi's/Please Come Back	1963	10.00	20.00	40.00

MAJORS, THE (1)

45s

IMPERIAL

Number	Title (A Side/B Side)	Yr	VG	VG+	NM
5855	A Wonderful Dream/Time Will Tell	1962	5.00	10.00	20.00
5879	She's a Troublemaker/A Little Bit Now, A Little Bit Later	1962	3.75	7.50	15.00
5914	What in the World/Anything You Can Do	1963	3.00	6.00	12.00
5936	Tra La La/What Have You Been Doin'	1963	3.00	6.00	12.00
5968	One Happy Ending/Get Up Now	1963	3.00	6.00	12.00
5991	Which Way Did She Go/Your Life Begins (Sweet 16)	1963	3.00	6.00	12.00
66009	I'll Be There/Ooh Wee Baby	1963	3.00	6.00	12.00

UNITED ARTISTS

Number	Title (A Side/B Side)	Yr	VG	VG+	NM
0110	A Wonderful Dream/Mother-in-Law	1973	—	2.50	5.00

—"Silver Spotlight Series" reissue; B-side by Ernie K-Doe

Albums

IMPERIAL

Number	Title (A Side/B Side)	Yr	VG	VG+	NM
LP-9222 [M]	Meet the Majors	1963	37.50	75.00	150.00
LP-12222 [S]	Meet the Majors	1963	75.00	150.00	300.00

MAJORS, THE (2)

45s

DERBY

Number	Title (A Side/B Side)	Yr	VG	VG+	NM
763	At Last/You Ran Away from My Heart	1951	200.00	400.00	800.00
779	Laughing on the Outside/Come On Up to My Room	1951	150.00	300.00	600.00

MAJORS, THE (3)

45s

FELSTED

Number	Title (A Side/B Side)	Yr	VG	VG+	NM
8501	Blue Sunset/Rockin' the Boogie	1958	7.50	15.00	30.00
8576	Come Go with Me/Les Qua	1959	6.25	12.50	25.00
8707	Come Go with Me/Les Qua	1964	3.75	7.50	15.00

MAJORS, THE (4)

45s

ORIGINAL

Number	Title (A Side/B Side)	Yr	VG	VG+	NM
1003	Big Eyes/Go 'Way	1954	100.00	200.00	400.00

MAKEBA, MIRIAM

Also see HARRY BELAFONTE.

45s

KAPP

Number	Title (A Side/B Side)	Yr	VG	VG+	NM
452	Carnival/Can't Cross Over	1962	3.00	6.00	12.00

LONDON

Number	Title (A Side/B Side)	Yr	VG	VG+	NM
1610	Lovely Lies/Kilimanjaro	1956	3.75	7.50	15.00

—With the Manhattan Brothers

MERCURY

Number	Title (A Side/B Side)	Yr	VG	VG+	NM
72642	Ballad of the Sad Young Men/Mommy, Mommy, What Is Heaven Like	1966	2.00	4.00	8.00

RCA VICTOR

Number	Title (A Side/B Side)	Yr	VG	VG+	NM
47-8326	Dubula/Forbidden Games	1964	2.50	5.00	10.00

REPRISE

Number	Title (A Side/B Side)	Yr	VG	VG+	NM
0578	Reza/When I've Passed On	1967	—	3.00	6.00
0606	Pata Pata/Ballad of the Sad Young Men	1967	2.00	4.00	8.00
0654	Malaysha/Ring Bell, Ring Bell	1967	—	3.00	6.00
0671	What Is Love/Ho Po Zamani	1968	—	3.00	6.00
0732	Pata Pata/Malaysha	1969	—	2.00	4.00

—"Back to Back Hits" series

Number	Title (A Side/B Side)	Yr	VG	VG+	NM
0755	Ibabalazie/Emavungivini (Down in the Dumps)	1968	—	3.00	6.00
0804	I Shall Be Released/Iphi Ndilela	1969	—	3.00	6.00
0921	I Shall Sing/In My Life	1970	—	3.00	6.00

Albums

KAPP

Number	Title (A Side/B Side)	Yr	VG	VG+	NM
KL-1274 [M]	The Many Voices of Miriam Makeba	1962	5.00	10.00	20.00
KS-3274 [S]	The Many Voices of Miriam Makeba	1962	6.25	12.50	25.00

MERCURY

Number	Title (A Side/B Side)	Yr	VG	VG+	NM
MG-21082 [M]	The Magnificent Miriam Makeba	1966	3.00	6.00	12.00
MG-21095 [M]	All About Miriam	1967	3.00	6.00	12.00
SR-61082 [S]	The Magnificent Miriam Makeba	1966	3.75	7.50	15.00
SR-61095 [S]	All About Miriam	1967	3.75	7.50	15.00

MERCURY/URBAN AFRICA

Number	Title (A Side/B Side)	Yr	VG	VG+	NM
838208-1	Welela	1989	3.00	6.00	12.00

RCA VICTOR

Number	Title (A Side/B Side)	Yr	VG	VG+	NM
LPM-2267 [M]	Miriam Makeba	1960	5.00	10.00	20.00
LSP-2267 [S]	Miriam Makeba	1960	6.25	12.50	25.00
LPM-2750 [M]	The World of Miriam Makeba	1963	3.75	7.50	15.00
LSP-2750 [S]	The World of Miriam Makeba	1963	5.00	10.00	20.00
LPM-2845 [M]	The Voice of Africa	1964	3.75	7.50	15.00
LSP-2845 [S]	The Voice of Africa	1964	5.00	10.00	20.00
LPM-3321 [M]	Makeba Sings	1965	3.75	7.50	15.00
LSP-3321 [S]	Makeba Sings	1965	5.00	10.00	20.00
LPM-3512 [M]	The Magic of Makeba	1966	3.75	7.50	15.00
LSP-3512 [S]	The Magic of Makeba	1966	5.00	10.00	20.00
LPM-3982 [M]	The Best of Miriam Makeba	1968	6.25	12.50	25.00
LSP-3982 [S]	The Best of Miriam Makeba	1968	3.00	6.00	12.00

REPRISE

Number	Title (A Side/B Side)	Yr	VG	VG+	NM
R-6253 [M]	Miriam Makeba In Concert!	1967	3.75	7.50	15.00
RS-6253 [S]	Miriam Makeba In Concert!	1967	3.00	6.00	12.00
R-6274 [M]	Pata Pata	1967	3.75	7.50	15.00
RS-6274 [S]	Pata Pata	1967	3.00	6.00	12.00
RS-6310	Makeba!	1968	3.00	6.00	12.00
RS-6381	Keep Me in Mind	1970	3.00	6.00	12.00

WARNER BROS.

Number	Title (A Side/B Side)	Yr	VG	VG+	NM
25673	Sangoma	1988	2.50	5.00	10.00

MALACHI

Albums

VERVE

Number	Title (A Side/B Side)	Yr	VG	VG+	NM
V-5024 [M]	Holy Music	1967	7.50	15.00	30.00
V6-5024 [S]	Holy Music	1967	10.00	20.00	40.00

MALCOLM X

Albums

DOUGLAS

Number	Title (A Side/B Side)	Yr	VG	VG+	NM
SD 795 [M]	Malcolm X Talks to Young People	1968	7.50	15.00	30.00
Z 30743 [M]	By Any Means Necessary	1971	7.50	15.00	30.00

MALLETT, SAUNDRA, AND THE VANDELLAS

45s

TAMLA

Number	Title (A Side/B Side)	Yr	VG	VG+	NM
54067	Camel Walk/It's Gonna Be Hard Times	1962	250.00	500.00	1000.

MALO

45s

WARNER BROS.

Number	Title (A Side/B Side)	Yr	VG	VG+	NM
7559	Suavecito/Nena	1972	—	2.50	5.00
7605	Café/Peace	1972	—	2.50	5.00
7651	Suavecito/Café	1973	—	2.00	4.00

—"Back to Back Hits" reissue

Number	Title (A Side/B Side)	Yr	VG	VG+	NM
7668	Oye Mama/I'm For Real	1972	—	2.50	5.00
7677	Latin Bugaloo/Midnight Thoughts	1973	—	2.50	5.00
7692	I Don't Know/Merengue	1973	—	2.50	5.00

Albums

WARNER BROS.

Number	Title (A Side/B Side)	Yr	VG	VG+	NM
BS 2584	Malo	1972	3.00	6.00	12.00
BS 2652	Dos	1972	3.00	6.00	12.00
BS 2702	Evolution	1973	3.00	6.00	12.00
BS 2769	Ascencion	1974	3.00	6.00	12.00

MALTAIS, GENE

45s

DECCA

Number	Title (A Side/B Side)	Yr	VG	VG+	NM
30387	Crazy Baby/Deep River Blues	1957	50.00	100.00	200.00

LILAC

Number	Title (A Side/B Side)	Yr	VG	VG+	NM
3159	The Raging Sea/(B-side unknown)	1957	100.00	200.00	400.00

REGAL

Number	Title (A Side/B Side)	Yr	VG	VG+	NM
7502	Lovemakin'/The Bug	1958	37.50	75.00	150.00

MAMA CASS

See CASS ELLIOT.

MAMA LION

45s

FAMILY PRODUCTIONS

Number	Title (A Side/B Side)	Yr	VG	VG+	NM
0903	Ain't Too Proud to Beg/Cry	1971	2.00	4.00	8.00
0921	Sister Sister/Give It Everything I've Got	1972	2.00	4.00	8.00

Albums

FAMILY PRODUCTIONS

Number	Title (A Side/B Side)	Yr	VG	VG+	NM
FPS-2702	Mama Lion	1972	5.00	10.00	20.00
FPS-2713	Give It Everything I've Got	1973	5.00	10.00	20.00

MAMAS AND THE PAPAS, THE

Also see DENNY DOHERTY; CASS ELLIOT; JILL GIBSON; JOHN PHILLIPS; MICHELLE PHILLIPS.

45s

Number	Title (A Side/B Side)	Yr	VG	VG+	NM
ABC DUNHILL					
4125	Safe in My Garden/Too Late	1968	2.00	4.00	8.00
4150	For the Love of Ivy/Strange Young Girls	1968	2.00	4.00	8.00
4171	Do You Wanna Dance/My Girl	1968	2.00	4.00	8.00
4301	Step Out/Shooting Star	1972	—	3.00	6.00
DUNHILL					
4018 [DJ]	Go Where You Wanna Go/Somebody Groovy	1966	5.00	10.00	20.00
—Withdrawn before stock copies were released					
4020	California Dreamin'/Somebody Groovy	1966	2.50	5.00	10.00
—Most of the 1966 Dunhill singles credited "The Mama's and the Papa's"					
4020 [PS]	California Dreamin'/Somebody Groovy	1966	75.00	150.00	300.00
—Sleeve is promo only					
4026	Monday, Monday/Got a Feeling	1966	2.50	5.00	10.00
4031	I Saw Her Again/Even If I Could	1966	2.50	5.00	10.00
4050	Look Through My Window/Once Was a Time I Thought	1966	2.50	5.00	10.00
4057	Words of Love/Dancing in the Street	1966	2.50	5.00	10.00
4077	Dedicated to the One I Love/Free Advice	1967	2.50	5.00	10.00
4083	Creeque Alley/Did You Ever Want to Cry	1967	2.50	5.00	10.00
4083 [PS]	Creeque Alley/Did You Ever Want to Cry	1967	10.00	20.00	40.00
—Sleeve is promo only					
4099	Twelve Thirty (Young Girls Are Coming to the Canyon)/Straight Shooter	1967	2.50	5.00	10.00
4107	Glad to Be Unhappy/Hey Girl	1967	2.50	5.00	10.00
4113	Dancing Bear/John's Music Box	1967	2.50	5.00	10.00
4113 [PS]	Dancing Bear/John's Music Box	1967	3.00	6.00	12.00
4125	Safe in My Garden/Too Late	1968	6.25	12.50	25.00
—Without the "ABC" logo at top of label					

Albums

Number	Title	Yr	VG	VG+	NM
ABC					
AC-30005	The ABC Collection	1976	3.75	7.50	15.00
ABC DUNHILL					
DS-50006	If You Can Believe Your Eyes and Ears	1968	3.00	6.00	12.00
DS-50010	The Mamas and the Papas	1968	3.00	6.00	12.00
DS-50014	The Mamas and the Papas Deliver	1968	3.00	6.00	12.00
DS-50025	Farewell to the First Golden Era	1968	3.00	6.00	12.00
DS-50031	The Papas and the Mamas	1968	3.75	7.50	15.00
—The five LPs above are reissues of records originally without the ABC logo					
DS-50036	Golden Era, Volume 2	1968	5.00	10.00	20.00
DS-50064	16 of Their Greatest Hits	1969	3.75	7.50	15.00
DS-50073 [(2)]	A Gathering of Flowers	1970	6.25	12.50	25.00
DSX-50100	Monterey International Pop Festival	1970	3.75	7.50	15.00
DSX-50106	People Like Us	1971	3.00	6.00	12.00
DSX-50145 [(2)]	20 Golden Hits	1973	5.00	10.00	20.00
DUNHILL					
D-50006 [M]	If You Can Believe Your Eyes and Ears	1966	20.00	40.00	80.00
—With toilet completely visible in lower right					
D-50006 [M]	If You Can Believe Your Eyes and Ears	1966	5.00	10.00	20.00
—With scroll over toilet					
D-50006 [M]	If You Can Believe Your Eyes and Ears	1966	10.00	20.00	40.00
—Black cover with photo cropped to render toilet invisible					
DS-50006 [S]	If You Can Believe Your Eyes and Ears	1966	25.00	50.00	100.00
—With toilet completely visible in lower right					
DS-50006 [S]	If You Can Believe Your Eyes and Ears	1966	6.25	12.50	25.00
—With scroll over toilet proclaiming "Includes California Dreamin' "					
DS-50006 [S]	If You Can Believe Your Eyes and Ears	1966	12.50	25.00	50.00
—Black cover with photo cropped to render toilet invisible					
DS-50006 [S]	If You Can Believe Your Eyes and Ears	1966	6.25	12.50	25.00
—With scroll over toilet proclaiming "Includes California Dreamin'...Monday Monday...I Call Your Name"					
D-50010 [M]	The Mamas and the Papas	1966	5.00	10.00	20.00
DS-50010 [S]	The Mamas and the Papas	1966	6.25	12.50	25.00
D-50014 [M]	The Mamas and the Papas Deliver	1967	5.00	10.00	20.00
DS-50014 [S]	The Mamas and the Papas Deliver	1967	6.25	12.50	25.00
D-50025 [M]	Farewell to the First Golden Era	1967	5.00	10.00	20.00
DS-50025 [S]	Farewell to the First Golden Era	1967	5.00	10.00	20.00
DS-50031	The Papas and the Mamas	1968	6.25	12.50	25.00
ST-90797 [S]	If You Can Believe Your Eyes and Ears	1966	12.50	25.00	50.00
—Capitol Record Club edition; known copies have scroll proclaiming "Includes California Dreamin'."					
MCA					
709	Farewell to the First Golden Era	1980	2.00	4.00	8.00
710	The Papas and the Mamas	1980	2.00	4.00	8.00
6019 [(2)]	The Best of the Mamas and the Papas	1986	3.00	6.00	12.00
37145	16 of Their Greatest Hits	1980	2.00	4.00	8.00
PICKWICK					
SPC-3352	California Dreaming	1972	3.00	6.00	12.00

MANCHA, STEVE

45s

Number	Title (A Side/B Side)	Yr	VG	VG+	NM
GROOVESVILLE					
1001	You're Still in My Heart/She's So Good	1965	6.25	12.50	25.00
1002	I Don't Want to Lose You/Need to Be Needed	1966	5.00	10.00	20.00
1004	Friday Night/Monday Through Thursday	1966	25.00	50.00	100.00
1005	Don't Make Me a Storyteller/I Won't Love and Leave You	1967	5.00	10.00	20.00
1007	Just Keep On Loving Me/Sweet Baby Don't Ever Be Untrue	1967	6.25	12.50	25.00
WHEELSVILLE					
102	Did My Baby Call/Whirlpool	1965	37.50	75.00	150.00

MANCHESTER, MELISSA

Also see NATIONAL LAMPOON.

12-Inch Singles

Number	Title (A Side/B Side)	Yr	VG	VG+	NM
MCA					
23563	Energy (Vocal)/Energy (Dub)	1985	—	3.00	6.00

45s

Number	Title (A Side/B Side)	Yr	VG	VG+	NM
ANGEL					
S7-19771	Have Yourself a Merry Little Christmas/I've Got My Love to Keep Me Warm	1997	—	—	3.00
ARISTA					
0116	Midnight Blue/I Got Eyes	1975	—	2.00	4.00
0146	Just Too Many People/This Lady's Not Home	1975	—	2.00	4.00
0168	Just You and I/My Sweet Thing	1976	—	2.00	4.00
0183	Better Days/Sing, Sing, Sing	1976	—	2.00	4.00
0196	Happy Endings/Rescue Me	1976	—	2.00	4.00
0218	Monkey See, Monkey Do/So's My Old Man	1976	—	2.00	4.00
0237	Dirty Work/Be Somebody	1977	—	2.00	4.00
0267	I Wanna Be Where You Are/No One's Ever Seen This Side of Me	1977	—	2.00	4.00
0373	Don't Cry Out Loud/We Had This Time	1978	—	2.00	4.00
—Originals have black labels					
0373	Don't Cry Out Loud/We Had This Time	1979	—	—	3.00
—Second pressings have whitish labels					
0405	Theme from "Ice Castles"/Such a Night	1979	—	2.00	4.00
0456	Pretty Girls/It's All in the Sky Above	1979	—	2.00	4.00
0485	Fire in the Morning/Lights of Dawn	1980	—	2.00	4.00
0551	If This Is Love/Talk	1980	—	2.00	4.00
0579	Without You/Boys in the Back Room	1980	—	2.00	4.00
0587	Lovers After All/Happier Than I've Ever Been	1981	—	2.00	4.00
—With Peabo Bryson					
0657	Race to the End/Long Goodbyes	1982	—	2.00	4.00
0676	You Should Hear How She Talks About You/Long Goodbyes	1982	—	2.00	4.00
1028	Come In from the Rain/Hey Ricky (You're a Low Down Heel)	1982	—	2.00	4.00
1045	Nice Girls/Hey Ricky (You're a Low Down Heel)	1983	—	2.00	4.00
1057	My Boyfriend's Back/Looking for the Perfect Aah	1983	—	2.00	4.00
9014	My Boyfriend's Back/Looking for the Perfect Aah	1983	—	—	3.00
9087	No One Can Love You More Than Me/White Rose	1983	—	—	3.00
9162	I Don't Care What the People Say/Emergency	1984	—	—	3.00
BELL					
45399	Never Never Land/Be Happy Now	1973	—	2.50	5.00
45465	Heaven/Inclined	1974	—	2.50	5.00
CASABLANCA					
880308-7	Thief of Hearts/(B-side unknown)	1984	—	—	3.00
MB					
1005	Beautiful People/A Song for You	1967	3.75	7.50	15.00
MCA					
52575	Mathematics/So Full of Yourself	1985	—	—	3.00
52575 [PS]	Mathematics/So Full of Yourself	1985	—	—	3.00
52616	Energy/So Full of Yourself	1985	—	—	3.00
52616 [PS]	Energy/So Full of Yourself	1985	—	—	3.00
52688	Just One Lifetime/So Full of Yourself	1985	—	—	3.00
52784	Music of Goodbye (Love Theme from Out of Africa)/Have You Got a Story for Me	1986	—	—	3.00
—With Al Jarreau					
52784 [PS]	Music of Goodbye (Love Theme from Out of Africa)/Have You Got a Story for Me	1986	—	—	3.00
—With Al Jarreau					
RCA VICTOR					
74-0366	Tellin' the World/(B-side unknown)	1970	3.00	6.00	12.00
—With Grover Kimball					

Albums

Number	Title	Yr	VG	VG+	NM
ARISTA					
AL 4006	Home to Myself	1975	2.50	5.00	10.00
—Reissue of Bell 1123					
AL 4011	Bright Eyes	1975	2.50	5.00	10.00
—Reissue of Bell 1303					
AL 4031	Melissa	1975	2.50	5.00	10.00
AQ 4031 [Q]	Melissa	1975	3.75	7.50	15.00
AL 4067	Better Days & Happy Endings	1976	2.50	5.00	10.00
AQ 4067 [Q]	Better Days & Happy Endings	1976	3.75	7.50	15.00
AL 4095	Help Is On the Way	1976	2.50	5.00	10.00
AL 4136	Singin'	1977	2.50	5.00	10.00
AB 4186	Don't Cry Out Loud	1978	2.50	5.00	10.00
AL 8055	Melissa	1983	2.00	4.00	8.00
—Budget-line reissue of 4031					
AL 8094	Emergency	1983	2.50	5.00	10.00
AL 8293	Greatest Hits	198?	2.00	4.00	8.00
—Budget-line reissue of 9611					
AL 8350	Hey Ricky	198?	2.00	4.00	8.00
—Budget-line reissue of 9574					
AL 8373	Don't Cry Out Loud	198?	2.00	4.00	8.00
—Budget-line reissue of 4186					
AL 9506	Melissa Manchester	1979	2.50	5.00	10.00
AL 9533	For the Working Girl	1980	2.50	5.00	10.00
AL 9574	Hey Ricky	1982	2.50	5.00	10.00
AL 9611	Greatest Hits	1983	2.50	5.00	10.00
BELL					
1123	Home to Myself	1973	3.00	6.00	12.00
1303	Bright Eyes	1974	3.00	6.00	12.00
MCA					
5587	Mathematics	1985	2.50	5.00	10.00
MIKA					
841273-1	Tribute	1989	3.00	6.00	12.00
MOBILE FIDELITY					
1-028	Melissa	1980	5.00	10.00	20.00
—Audiophile vinyl					
NAUTILUS					
NR-33	Don't Cry Out Loud	198?	10.00	20.00	40.00
—Audiophile vinyl					
PAIR					
PDL2-1086 [(2)]	The Many Moods of Melissa Manchester	1986	3.00	6.00	12.00

MANCHESTERS, THE (1)

Albums

Number	Title	Yr	VG	VG+	NM
DIPLOMAT					
D-2307 [M]	Beatlerama	1964	3.75	7.50	15.00
—No artist credited on label or cover					
D-2307 [M]	Beatlerama	1964	3.75	7.50	15.00
—With artist credited					
DS-2307 [S]	Beatlerama	1964	5.00	10.00	20.00
—No artist credited on label or cover					

Number	Title (A Side/B Side)	Yr	VG	VG+	NM
DS-2307 [S]	Beatlerama	1964	5.00	10.00	20.00
—With artist credited					
GUEST STAR					
G-2307 [M]	Beatlerama	1964	3.75	7.50	15.00
GS-2307 [S]	Beatlerama	1964	5.00	10.00	20.00

MANCHESTERS, THE (2)

Featuring DAVID GATES.

45s

Number	Title (A Side/B Side)	Yr	VG	VG+	NM
VEE JAY					
700	I Don't Come from England/Dragonfly	1965	6.25	12.50	25.00

MANCINI, HENRY

45s

Number	Title (A Side/B Side)	Yr	VG	VG+	NM
AVCO EMBASSY					
4531	Love Theme from Sunflower/Giovanna	1970	—	2.50	5.00
CORAL					
61974	The Long Hot Summer/Paris Holiday	1958	3.00	6.00	12.00
61990	Love Theme from "The Brothers Karamazov"/ Tana's Theme	1958	3.00	6.00	12.00
LIBERTY					
1489	Trail of the Pink Panther (Soundtrack)/The Inspector Clouseau Theme (Soundtrack)	1983	—	2.00	4.00
55045	(Main Theme from) Four Girls in Town/Cha Cha Cha for Gia	1956	3.00	6.00	12.00
55060	Hot Rod/Big Band Rock and Roll	1957	3.00	6.00	12.00
55184	Pow/Cha Cha Cha for Gia	1959	2.50	5.00	10.00
RCA					
PB-10888	Theme from "Charlie's Angels"/Bumper's Theme	1977	—	2.50	5.00
PB-11054	What's Happening Theme/Silver Streak	1977	—	2.50	5.00
PB-11142	The Money Changers/Just You and Me Together, Love	1977	—	2.50	5.00
PB-11423	Theme from Battlestar Galactica/NBC Nightly News Theme	1978	—	2.50	5.00
RCA VICTOR					
APBO-0117	Ludmilla's Theme/Pretty Girls	1973	—	2.50	5.00
APBO-0249	Olympic Village/Dolce	1974	—	2.50	5.00
APBO-0323	Hangin' Out/Send a Little Love My Way	1974	—	2.50	5.00
PB-10060	Sex Symbol/Theme from "White Dawn"	1974	—	2.50	5.00
PB-10288	The Greatest Gift/The Pink Penther Theme	1975	—	2.50	5.00
PB-10355	Once Is Not Enough/The Greatest Gift	1975	—	2.50	5.00
PB-10463	Satin Soul/African Symphony	1975	—	2.50	5.00
PB-10731	Slow Hot Wind/Symphonic Soul	1976	—	2.50	5.00
47-7442	Fallout/Dreamsville	1959	3.00	6.00	12.00
47-7460	Peter Gunn/The Brothers Go to Mother's	1959	3.00	6.00	12.00
47-7512	Spook!/Timothy	1959	3.00	6.00	12.00
47-7682	Bijou/Let's Walk	1960	3.00	6.00	12.00
47-7705	Mr. Lucky/Floating Pad	1960	3.00	6.00	12.00
47-7785	Big Noise from Winnetka/The Blues	1960	3.00	6.00	12.00
47-7791	High Time/The Second Time Around	1960	3.00	6.00	12.00
47-7830	Theme from The Great Impostor/Love Music	1961	2.50	5.00	10.00
47-7830 [PS]	Theme from The Great Impostor/Love Music	1961	3.75	7.50	15.00
47-7902	Fanny/My Cousin from Naples	1961	2.50	5.00	10.00
47-7916	Moon River/Breakfast at Tiffany's	1961	2.00	4.00	8.00
47-7916 [PS]	Moon River/Breakfast at Tiffany's	1961	3.75	7.50	15.00
47-8008	Experiment in Terror/Tooty Tooty	1962	2.00	4.00	8.00
47-8037	Theme from "Hatari!"/Your Father's Feathers	1962	2.00	4.00	8.00
47-8037 [PS]	Theme from "Hatari!"/Your Father's Feathers	1962	3.75	7.50	15.00
47-8099	Love Theme from Phaedra/Dreamsville	1962	2.00	4.00	8.00
47-8120	Days of Wine and Roses/76 Trombones	1962	2.00	4.00	8.00
47-8120 [PS]	Days of Wine and Roses/76 Trombones	1962	3.75	7.50	15.00
47-8184	Banzai Pipeline/Rhapsody in Blue	1963	5.00	10.00	20.00
47-8184 [PS]	Banzai Pipeline/Rhapsody in Blue	1963	6.25	12.50	25.00
47-8256	Charade/Orange Tamoure	1963	2.00	4.00	8.00
47-8256 [PS]	Charade/Orange Tamoure	1963	3.75	7.50	15.00
47-8286	The Pink Panther Theme/It Had Better Be Tonight	1963	2.00	4.00	8.00
47-8286 [PS]	The Pink Panther Theme/It Had Better Be Tonight	1963	3.75	7.50	15.00
47-8381	A Shot in the Dark/The Shadows of Paris	1964	2.00	4.00	8.00
47-8381 [PS]	A Shot in the Dark/The Shadows of Paris	1964	3.00	6.00	12.00
47-8458	Dear Heart/How Soon	1964	2.00	4.00	8.00
47-8458 [PS]	Dear Heart/How Soon	1964	3.00	6.00	12.00
47-8574	Senor Peter Gunn/La Raspa	1965	2.00	4.00	8.00
47-8624	Pie in the Face Polka/Sweetheart Tree	1965	2.00	4.00	8.00
47-8691	He Shouldn't-A, Hadn't-A, Oughtn't-A Swang on Me/Push the Button, Man	1965	2.00	4.00	8.00
47-8718	Moment to Moment/Soldier in the Rain	1965	2.00	4.00	8.00
47-8798	House of the Rising Sun/Turtles	1966	—	3.00	6.00
47-8856	Arabesque/We've Loved Before	1966	—	3.00	6.00
47-8857	In the Arms of Love/Swing March	1966	—	3.00	6.00
47-8951	Hawaii/Driftwood and Dreams	1966	—	3.00	6.00
47-9200	Two for the Road/Happy Barefoot Boy	1967	—	3.00	6.00
47-9340	Wait Until Dark/Theme for Three	1967	—	3.00	6.00
47-9483	The Party/Party Poop	1968	—	3.00	6.00
47-9483 [PS]	The Party/Party Poop	1968	2.50	5.00	10.00
47-9521	Nothing to Lose/Norma De La Guadalajara	1968	—	3.00	6.00
47-9585	The Magnificent Seven/Springtime for Hitler	1968	2.00	4.00	8.00
47-9654	A Man, a Horse, and a Gun/Las Cruces	1968	—	3.00	6.00
47-9857	Love Theme from Sunflower/Darling Lili	1970	—	2.50	5.00
47-9927	Theme from Love Story/Phone Call to the Past	1970	—	2.50	5.00
74-0131	Love Theme from Romeo and Juliet/The Windmills of Your Mind	1969	2.50	5.00	10.00
74-0212	Moonlight Sonata/Natalie	1969	—	3.00	6.00
74-0297	Midnight Cowboy/There's Enough to Go Around	1969	—	3.00	6.00
74-0315	Theme from "The Molly Maguires"/Theme from "Z"	1970	—	2.50	5.00
74-0454	Theme from "The Night Visitor"/Whistling Away the Dark	1971	—	2.50	5.00
74-0575	Mystery Movie Theme/Theme from "Cade's Country"	1971	—	2.50	5.00
74-0618	Nicholas and Alexandra's Theme/Two for the Road	1971	—	2.50	5.00
74-0685	Brass on Ivory/Poor Butterfly	1972	—	2.50	5.00
—With Doc Severinson					
74-0756	Theme from The Mancini Generation/Bluish Bag	1972	—	2.50	5.00
74-0890	Theme from "The Thief Who Came to Dinner"/ Charade	1973	—	2.50	5.00
74-0974	Oklahoma Crude/Amazing Grace	1973	—	2.50	5.00
UNITED ARTISTS					
XW1237	Pink Panther Theme '78/Touch of Red	1978	—	2.00	4.00
WARNER BROS.					
5019	The Star Spangled Banner/The Stars and Stripes Forever	1959	2.50	5.00	10.00
29697	The Thorn Birds Theme/Luke and Meggie	1983	—	2.00	4.00
49139	Ravel's Bolero/It's Easy to Say	1979	—	2.00	4.00
—B-side by Julie Andrews and Dudley Moore					
49139 [PS]	Ravel's Bolero/It's Easy to Say	1979	3.00	6.00	12.00
—Fold-out poster sleeve of Bo Derek and scenes from the movie "10"					

7-Inch Extended Plays

Number	Title (A Side/B Side)	Yr	VG	VG+	NM
RCA VICTOR					
EPA-4333 [M]	Peter Gunn/A Profound Gass//Fallout!/Sorta Blue	1959	3.00	6.00	12.00
EPA-4333 [PS]	The Music from Peter Gunn	1959	3.00	6.00	12.00
ESP-4333 [PS]	The Music from Peter Gunn	1959	5.00	10.00	20.00
ESP-4333 [S]	Peter Gunn/A Profound Gass//Fallout!/Sorta Blue	1959	5.00	10.00	20.00
EPA-4339 [M]	*Walkin' Bass/Spook!/The Little Man Theme/ Goofin' at the Coffee House	1959	3.00	6.00	12.00
EPA-4339 [PS]	More Music from Peter Gunn	1959	3.00	6.00	12.00
ESP-4339 [PS]	More Music from Peter Gunn	1959	3.75	7.50	15.00
ESP-4339 [S]	*Walkin' Bass/Spook!/The Little Man Theme/ Goofin' at the Coffee House	1959	3.75	7.50	15.00
EPA-4363	Mr. Lucky/My Friend Andamo//Lightly Latin/Tipsy	1960	3.00	6.00	12.00
EPA-4363 [PS]	Music from Mr. Lucky	1960	3.00	6.00	12.00

Albums

Number	Title (A Side/B Side)	Yr	VG	VG+	NM
AVCO EMBASSY					
AVE 0110	Sunflower	1970	3.75	7.50	15.00
DECCA					
DL 79185	Sometimes a Great Notion	1971	3.75	7.50	15.00
LIBERTY					
LRP-3121 [M]	The Versatile Henry Mancini	1959	5.00	10.00	20.00
LST-7121 [S]	The Versatile Henry Mancini	1959	7.50	15.00	30.00
LT-51135	Trail of the Pink Panther	1982	2.50	5.00	10.00
MCA					
2085	The Great Waldo Pepper	1975	3.00	6.00	12.00
6222	The Glass Menagerie	1987	2.50	5.00	10.00
PAIR					
PDL2-1092 [(2)]	The Mancini Collection (Film Music)	1986	3.00	6.00	12.00
PARAMOUNT					
PAS-6000	The Molly Maguires	1970	5.00	10.00	20.00
RCA CAMDEN					
ACL2-0293 [(2)]	Film Music	1973	3.00	6.00	12.00
CAL-928 [M]	The Second Time Around and Others	1966	3.00	6.00	12.00
CAS-928 [S]	The Second Time Around and Others	1966	3.00	6.00	12.00
CAL-2158 [M]	Mancini Plays Mancini and Other Composers	1968	3.00	6.00	12.00
CAS-2158 [S]	Mancini Plays Mancini and Other Composers	1968	2.50	5.00	10.00
CAS-2510	Dream of You	1971	2.50	5.00	10.00
CXS-9005 [(2)]	Mancini Magic	1971	3.00	6.00	12.00
CXS-9034	Everybody's Favorite	1972	2.50	5.00	10.00
RCA VICTOR					
APD1-0013 [Q]	Mancini Salutes Sousa	1973	4.50	9.00	18.00
APL1-0013	Mancini Salutes Sousa	1972	3.00	6.00	12.00
APD1-0098 [Q]	Brass, Ivory and Strings	1973	4.50	9.00	18.00
APL1-0098	Brass, Ivory and Strings	1973	3.00	6.00	12.00
PRM-175 [M]	Academy Award Songs, Volume Two	1965	3.75	7.50	15.00
—Made for the B.F. Goodrich tire company					
PRS-175 [S]	Academy Award Songs, Volume Two	1965	5.00	10.00	20.00
—Made for the B.F. Goodrich tire company					
ABL1-0231	Visions of Eight	1973	3.00	6.00	12.00
AFL1-0270	Country Gentlemen	1977	2.50	5.00	10.00
—Reissue with new prefix					
APD1-0270 [Q]	Country Gentlemen	1973	4.50	9.00	18.00
APL1-0270	Country Gentlemen	1973	3.00	6.00	12.00
APL1-0271	Oklahoma Crude	1973	3.00	6.00	12.00
AFL1-0672	Hangin' Out	1977	2.50	5.00	10.00
—Reissue with new prefix					
APD1-0672 [Q]	Hangin' Out	1974	4.50	9.00	18.00
CPL1-0672	Hangin' Out	1974	3.00	6.00	12.00
ABD1-0968 [Q]	Return of the Pink Panther	1975	4.50	9.00	18.00
ABL1-0968	Return of the Pink Panther	1975	3.00	6.00	12.00
ANL1-0980	Pure Gold	1975	2.50	5.00	10.00
AFL1-1025	Symphonic Soul	1977	2.00	4.00	8.00
—Reissue with new prefix					
APD1-1025 [Q]	Symphonic Soul	1975	4.50	9.00	18.00
APL1-1025	Symphonic Soul	1975	2.50	5.00	10.00
APL1-1379	Concert of Film Music	1975	2.50	5.00	10.00
CPL1-1843	A Legendary Performer	1976	2.50	5.00	10.00
APL1-1896	Cop Show Themes	1976	2.50	5.00	10.00
ANL1-1928 [S]	A Merry Mancini Christmas	1976	2.00	4.00	8.00
—Reissue with new number and new front cover					
LPM-1956 [M]	The Music from Peter Gunn	1959	10.00	20.00	40.00
—Original cover is a "block" design with "Peter Gunn" at top					
LPM-1956 [M]	The Music from Peter Gunn	1959	5.00	10.00	20.00
—Reissue cover is green/blue with huge "Peter Gunn" in center					
LSP-1956 [S]	The Music from Peter Gunn	1959	12.50	25.00	50.00
—Original cover is a "block" design with "Peter Gunn" at top					
LSP-1956 [S]	The Music from Peter Gunn	1959	6.25	12.50	25.00
—Reissue cover is green/blue with huge "Peter Gunn" in center					
LPM-2040 [M]	More Music from Peter Gunn	1959	5.00	10.00	20.00
LSP-2040 [S]	More Music from Peter Gunn	1959	6.25	12.50	25.00
LPM-2101 [M]	The Mancini Touch	1959	5.00	10.00	20.00
LSP-2101 [S]	The Mancini Touch	1959	6.25	12.50	25.00
LPM-2147 [M]	The Blues and the Beat	1960	6.25	12.50	25.00
LSP-2147 [S]	The Blues and the Beat	1960	7.50	15.00	30.00
LPM-2198 [M]	Music from Mr. Lucky	1960	5.00	10.00	20.00
LSP-2198 [S]	Music from Mr. Lucky	1960	6.25	12.50	25.00
LPM-2258 [M]	Combo!	1960	5.00	10.00	20.00
LSP-2258 [S]	Combo!	1960	6.25	12.50	25.00
APL1-2290	Mancini's Angels	1977	2.50	5.00	10.00

Number	Title (A Side/B Side)	Yr	VG	VG+	NM
LPM-2360 [M]	Mr. Lucky Goes Latin	1961	5.00	10.00	20.00
LSP-2360 [S]	Mr. Lucky Goes Latin	1961	6.25	12.50	25.00
LPM-2362 [M]	Breakfast at Tiffany's	1961	5.00	10.00	20.00
LSP-2362 [S]	Breakfast at Tiffany's	1961	6.25	12.50	25.00
LPM-2442 [M]	Experiment in Terror	1962	6.25	12.50	25.00
—Original cover has Lee Remick under attack					
LPM-2442 [M]	Experiment in Terror	1962	5.00	10.00	20.00
—Reissue cover has two mannequins					
LSP-2442 [S]	Experiment in Terror	1962	10.00	20.00	40.00
—Original cover has Lee Remick under attack					
LSP-2442 [S]	Experiment in Terror	1962	6.25	12.50	25.00
—Reissue cover has two mannequins					
ANL1-2484	Mancini Plays the Theme from Love Story	1977	2.50	5.00	10.00
—Reissue of LSP-4466					
LPM-2559 [M]	Hatari!	1962	5.00	10.00	20.00
LSP-2559 [S]	Hatari!	1962	6.25	12.50	25.00
LPM-2604 [M]	Our Man in Hollywood	1963	3.75	7.50	15.00
LSP-2604 [S]	Our Man in Hollywood	1963	5.00	10.00	20.00
LPM-2692 [M]	Uniquely Mancini	1963	3.75	7.50	15.00
LSP-2692 [S]	Uniquely Mancini	1963	5.00	10.00	20.00
AFL1-2693	The Best of Mancini	1977	2.50	5.00	10.00
—Reissue with new prefix					
LPM-2693 [M]	The Best of Mancini	1964	3.00	6.00	12.00
LSP-2693 [S]	The Best of Mancini	1964	3.75	7.50	15.00
LPM-2755 [M]	Charade	1963	3.75	7.50	15.00
LSP-2755 [S]	Charade	1963	5.00	10.00	20.00
LPM-2795 [M]	The Pink Panther	1964	3.75	7.50	15.00
LSP-2795 [S]	The Pink Panther	1964	5.00	10.00	20.00
LPM-2897 [M]	The Concert Sound of Henry Mancini	1964	3.00	6.00	12.00
LSP-2897 [S]	The Concert Sound of Henry Mancini	1964	3.75	7.50	15.00
LPM-2990 [M]	Dear Heart and Other Songs About Love	1965	3.00	6.00	12.00
LSP-2990 [S]	Dear Heart and Other Songs About Love	1965	3.75	7.50	15.00
AQL1-3052	The Theme Scene	1978	2.50	5.00	10.00
AQL1-3347	The Best of Mancini, Volume 3	1979	2.50	5.00	10.00
LPM-3356 [M]	The Latin Sound of Henry Mancini	1965	3.00	6.00	12.00
LSP-3356 [S]	The Latin Sound of Henry Mancini	1965	3.75	7.50	15.00
LPM-3402 [M]	The Great Race	1965	3.00	6.00	12.00
LSP-3402 [S]	The Great Race	1965	3.75	7.50	15.00
AFL1-3557	The Best of Mancini, Volume 2	1977	2.50	5.00	10.00
—Reissue with new prefix					
LPM-3557 [M]	The Best of Mancini, Volume 2	1966	3.00	6.00	12.00
LSP-3557 [S]	The Best of Mancini, Volume 2	1966	3.75	7.50	15.00
LPM-3612 [M]	A Merry Mancini Christmas	1966	2.50	5.00	10.00
—Original front cover has a photo of Henry Mancini and family					
LSP-3612 [S]	A Merry Mancini Christmas	1966	3.00	6.00	12.00
—Same as above, but in stereo					
LPM-3623 [M]	Arabesque	1966	3.00	6.00	12.00
LSP-3623 [S]	Arabesque	1966	3.75	7.50	15.00
LPM-3648 [M]	What Did You Do in the War, Daddy?	1966	3.00	6.00	12.00
LSP-3648 [S]	What Did You Do in the War, Daddy?	1966	3.75	7.50	15.00
AYL1-3667	Pure Gold	1980	2.00	4.00	8.00
—"Best Buy Series" reissue					
AYL1-3668	Mancini Country	1980	2.00	4.00	8.00
—"Best Buy Series" reissue					
LPM-3694 [M]	Mancini '67	1967	3.75	7.50	15.00
LSP-3694 [S]	Mancini '67	1967	3.75	7.50	15.00
AFL1-3713	Music of Hawaii	1977	2.50	5.00	10.00
—Reissue with new prefix					
LPM-3713 [M]	Music of Hawaii	1966	3.00	6.00	12.00
LSP-3713 [S]	Music of Hawaii	1966	3.75	7.50	15.00
AYL1-3756	Brass On Ivory	1980	2.00	4.00	8.00
—"Best Buy Series" reissue					
AYL1-3757	A Warm Shade of Ivory	1980	2.00	4.00	8.00
—"Best Buy Series" reissue					
LPM-3802 [M]	Two for the Road	1967	5.00	10.00	20.00
LSP-3802 [S]	Two for the Road	1967	3.75	7.50	15.00
AYL1-3822	The Best of Mancini	1981	2.00	4.00	8.00
—"Best Buy Series" reissue					
LPM-3840 [M]	Gunn	1967	5.00	10.00	20.00
LSP-3840 [S]	Gunn	1967	7.50	15.00	30.00
AYL1-3877	Music of Hawaii	1981	2.00	4.00	8.00
—"Best Buy Series" reissue					
LPM-3887 [M]	Encore! More of the Concert Sound of Henry Mancini	1967	5.00	10.00	20.00
LSP-3887 [S]	Encore! More of the Concert Sound of Henry Mancini	1967	3.75	7.50	15.00
AYL1-3954	Country Gentlemen	1981	2.00	4.00	8.00
—"Best Buy Series" reissue					
LPM-3997 [M]	Party	1968	6.25	12.50	25.00
LSP-3997 [S]	Party	1968	3.75	7.50	15.00
LSP-4049	The Big Latin Band of Henry Mancini	1968	3.75	7.50	15.00
AFL1-4140	A Warm Shade of Ivory	1977	2.00	4.00	8.00
—Reissue with new prefix					
LSP-4140	A Warm Shade of Ivory	1969	3.75	7.50	15.00
LSP-4239	Six Hours Past Sunset	1969	3.75	7.50	15.00
AFL1-4307	Mancini Country	1977	2.50	5.00	10.00
—Reissue with new prefix					
LSP-4307	Mancini Country	1970	3.75	7.50	15.00
LSP-4350	Theme from "Z" and Other Film Music	1970	3.75	7.50	15.00
LSP-4466	Mancini Plays the Theme from Love Story	1971	3.75	7.50	15.00
AFL1-4542	Mancini Concert	1977	2.50	5.00	10.00
—Reissue with new prefix					
LSP-4542	Mancini Concert	1971	3.75	7.50	15.00
AFL1-4629	Brass On Ivory	1977	2.00	4.00	8.00
—Reissue with new prefix					
LSP-4629	Brass on Ivory	1972	3.00	6.00	12.00
LSP-4630	Big Screen — Little Screen	1972	3.75	7.50	15.00
LSP-4689	The Mancini Generation	1972	3.00	6.00	12.00
LPM-6013 [(2) M]	The Academy Award Songs	1966	3.75	7.50	15.00
LSP-6013 [(2) S]	The Academy Award Songs	1966	5.00	10.00	20.00
VPS-6029 [(2)]	This Is Henry Mancini	1970	5.00	10.00	20.00
VPS-6053 [(2)]	This Is Henry Mancini, Volume 2	1972	5.00	10.00	20.00
SUNSET					
SUM-1105 [M]	Sounds and Voices	1966	3.00	6.00	12.00
SUS-5105 [S]	Sounds and Voices	1966	3.00	6.00	12.00

Number	Title (A Side/B Side)	Yr	VG	VG+	NM
UNITED ARTISTS					
UA-LA694-G	The Pink Panther Strikes Again	1976	3.75	7.50	15.00
UAS-5210	The Hawaiians	1970	3.00	6.00	12.00
SW-93297	The Hawaiians	1970	5.00	10.00	20.00
—Capitol Record Club edition					
WARNER BROS.					
W 1312 [M]	March Step in Hi-Fi	1959	5.00	10.00	20.00
WS 1312 [S]	March Step in Stereo	1959	7.50	15.00	30.00
W 1465 [M]	Sousa's Greatest Marches	1962	3.75	7.50	15.00
WS 1465 [S]	Sousa's Greatest Marches	1962	5.00	10.00	20.00
W 1491 [M]	Marches	1963	3.75	7.50	15.00
WS 1491 [S]	Marches	1963	5.00	10.00	20.00
BS 2700	The Thief Who Came to Dinner	1973	3.75	7.50	15.00
BSK 3399	10	1979	3.75	7.50	15.00

MANDEL, HARVEY

Number	Title (A Side/B Side)	Yr	VG	VG+	NM
45s					
JANUS					
144	Midnight Sun/Baby Batter	1970	—	3.00	6.00
198	Pegasus/Uni Ino	1972	—	3.00	6.00
PHILIPS					
40566	Cristo Redentor/Bradley's Barn	1968	2.00	4.00	8.00
40579	Wade in the Water (Part 1)/Wade in the Water (Part 2)	1968	2.00	4.00	8.00
40607	Campus Blues/Righteous	1969	2.00	4.00	8.00
40627	Moontan/Summer Sequence	1969	2.00	4.00	8.00
40643	Dry Your Eyes/Ridin' High	1969	2.00	4.00	8.00
Albums					
EDITIONS EG					
CAROL-1535-1	Cristo Redentor	198?	2.50	5.00	10.00
—Reissue of Philips 600-281					
JANUS					
JLS-3017	Baby Batter	1970	3.00	6.00	12.00
JLS-3037	The Snake	1972	3.00	6.00	12.00
JLS-3047	Shangrenade	1973	3.00	6.00	12.00
JSX-3067	Feel the Sound of Harvey Mandel	1974	3.00	6.00	12.00
JXS-7014	The Best of Harvey Mandel	1975	3.00	6.00	12.00
OVATION					
OV-1415	Get Off in Chicago	1971	3.75	7.50	15.00
PHILIPS					
PHS 600281	Cristo Redentor	1969	6.25	12.50	25.00
PHS 600306	Righteous	1969	6.25	12.50	25.00
PHS 600325	Games Guitars Play	1970	6.25	12.50	25.00

MANDEL, MIKE

Number	Title (A Side/B Side)	Yr	VG	VG+	NM
Albums					
VANGUARD					
VSD-79409	Sky Music	1978	3.00	6.00	12.00
VSD-79437	Utopia Parkway	1979	3.00	6.00	12.00

MANDO AND THE CHILI PEPPERS

Number	Title (A Side/B Side)	Yr	VG	VG+	NM
Albums					
GOLDEN CREST					
CR-3023 [M]	On the Road with Rock and Roll	1957	125.00	250.00	500.00

MANDRAKE MEMORIAL

Number	Title (A Side/B Side)	Yr	VG	VG+	NM
45s					
POPPY					
90103	Something in the Air/Musical Man	1969	2.50	5.00	10.00
Albums					
POPPY					
PYS 40002	Mandrake Memorial	1968	10.00	20.00	40.00
PYS 40003	Medium	1969	10.00	20.00	40.00
PYS 40006	Puzzle	1970	10.00	20.00	40.00

MANDRELL, BARBARA

Number	Title (A Side/B Side)	Yr	VG	VG+	NM
45s					
ABC					
12362	Tonight/If I Were a River	1978	—	2.00	4.00
12403	Sleeping Single in a Double Bed/Just One More of Your Goodbyes	1978	—	2.00	4.00
12451	(If Loving You Is Wrong) I Don't Want to Be Right/I Feel the Hurt Coming On	1979	—	2.50	5.00
ABC DOT					
17601	Standing Room Only/Can't Help But Wonder	1975	—	2.00	4.00
17623	Beginning of the End/That's What Friends Are For	1976	—	2.00	4.00
17644	Love Is Thin Ice/Will We Ever Make Love In Love Again	1976	—	2.00	4.00
17668	Midnight Angel/I Count on You	1976	—	2.00	4.00
17688	Married But Not to Each Other/Fools Gold	1977	—	2.00	4.00
17716	Hold Me/This Is Not Another Cheatin' Song	1977	—	2.00	4.00
17736	Woman to Woman/Let the Rain Out	1977	—	2.00	4.00
CAPITOL					
B-44220	I Wish That I Could Fall in Love Today/I'll Be Your Jukebox Tonight	1988	—	—	3.00
B-44276	My Train of Thought/Blanket of Love	1989	—	—	3.00
B-44383	Mirror Mirror/Blanket of Love	1989	—	—	3.00
B-44494	Why Do Bad Things Happen to Good People/You Wouldn't Know Love	1990	—	2.00	4.00
CAPITOL NASHVILLE					
7PRO-79029 [DJ]	You've Become the Dream (same on both sides)	1990	—	2.50	5.00
—Vinyl is promo only					
7PRO-79334 [DJ]	Men and Trains (same on both sides)	1991	—	2.50	5.00
—Vinyl is promo only					
COLUMBIA					
10082	Wonder When My Baby's Comin' Home/Kiss the Hurt Away	1974	—	2.50	5.00
44955	I've Been Loving You Too Long (To Stop Now)/Baby Come Home	1969	—	3.00	6.00
45143	Playin' Around with Love/I Almost Lost My Mind	1970	—	2.50	5.00
45307	Do Right Woman — Do Right Man/The Letter	1971	—	2.50	5.00
45391	Treat Him Right/Break My Mind	1971	—	2.50	5.00

Number	Title (A Side/B Side)	Yr	VG	VG+	NM
45505	Tonight My Baby's Coming Home/He'll Never Take the Place of You	1971	—	2.50	5.00
45580	Show Me/Satisfied	1972	—	2.50	5.00
45702	Holdin' On (To the Love I Got)/Smile, Somebody Loves You	1972	—	2.50	5.00
45819	Give a Little, Take a Little/Ain't It Good	1973	—	2.50	5.00
45904	The Midnight Oil/In the Name of Love	1973	—	2.50	5.00
46054	This Time I Almost Made It/Son-of-a-Gun	1974	—	2.50	5.00
EMI AMERICA					
43032	Child Support/I'm Glad I Married You	1987	—	—	3.00
43042	Angels Love Bad Men/Sunshine Street	1988	—	—	3.00
EMI MANHATTAN					
50102	Sure Feels Good/Sunshine Street	1987	—	—	3.00
MCA					
S45-1241 [DJ]	Santa, Bring My Baby Back Home//It Must Have Been the Mistletoe/From Our House to Yours	1984	2.50	5.00	10.00
12451	(If Loving You Is Wrong) I Don't Want to Be Right/ I Feel the Hurt Coming On	1979	—	2.00	4.00
—Reissue of ABC 12451					
41077	Fooled by a Feeling/Love Takes a Long Time to Die	1979	—	—	3.00
41162	Years/Darlin'	1979	—	—	3.00
41162 [PS]	Years/Darlin'	1979	—	2.00	4.00
41263	Crackers/Using Him to Get to You	1980	—	—	3.00
51001	The Best of Strangers/Sometime, Somewhere, Somehow	1980	—	—	3.00
51062	Love Is Fair/Sometime, Somewhere, Somehow	1981	—	—	3.00
51107	I Was Country When Country Wasn't Cool/ Woman's Got a Right	1981	—	2.00	4.00
51171	Wish You Were Here/She's Out There Dancin' Alone	1981	—	—	3.00
52038	'Till You're Gone/You're Not Supposed to Be Here	1982	—	—	3.00
52111	Operator, Long Distance Please/Black and White	1982	—	—	3.00
52206	In Times Like These/Loveless	1983	—	—	3.00
52258	One of a Kind Pair of Fools/As Well As Can Be Expected	1983	—	—	3.00
52340	Happy Birthday Dear Heartache/A Man's Not a Man ('Til He's Loved by a Woman)	1984	—	—	3.00
52397	Only a Lonely Heart Knows/I Wonder What the Rich Folk Are Doin' Tonight	1984	—	—	3.00
52465	Crossword Puzzle/If It's Not One Thing It's Another	1984	—	—	3.00
52537	There's No Love in Tennessee/Sincerely I'm Yours	1985	—	—	3.00
52537 [PS]	There's No Love in Tennessee/Sincerely I'm Yours	1985	—	—	3.00
52645	Angel in Your Arms/Don't Look in My Eyes	1985	—	—	3.00
52737	Fast Lanes and Country Roads/You Only You	1985	—	—	3.00
52737 [DJ]	Fast Lanes and Country Roads (same on both sides)	1985	2.50	5.00	10.00
—Promo only on yellow vinyl					
52737 [PS]	Fast Lanes and Country Roads/You Only You	1985	—	—	3.00
52802	When You Get to the Heart/Survivors	1986	—	—	3.00
—With the Oak Ridge Boys					
52802 [DJ]	When You Get to the Heart (same on both sides)	1986	2.50	5.00	10.00
—Promo only on red vinyl					
52900	No One Mends a Broken Heart Like You/Love Is Adventure in the Great Unknown	1986	—	—	3.00
MOSRITE					
190	Queen for a Day/Alone in the Crowd	196?	6.25	12.50	25.00
Albums					
ABC					
AB-1088	Moods	1978	3.00	6.00	12.00
AB-1119	The Best of Barbara Mandrell	1979	3.00	6.00	12.00
ABC DOT					
DOSD-2045	This Is Barbara Mandrell	1976	3.00	6.00	12.00
DOSD-2067	Midnight Angel	1976	3.00	6.00	12.00
DO-2076	Lovers, Friends and Strangers	1977	3.00	6.00	12.00
DO-2098	Love's Ups and Downs	1977	3.00	6.00	12.00
CAPITOL					
C1-90416	I'll Be Your Jukebox Tonight	1988	2.50	5.00	10.00
C1-91977	Morning Sun	1990	3.00	6.00	12.00
COLUMBIA					
C 30967	Treat Him Right	1971	5.00	10.00	20.00
KC 32743	The Midnight Oil	1973	3.75	7.50	15.00
PC 32743	The Midnight Oil	198?	2.00	4.00	8.00
—Budget-line reissue					
KC 32959	This Time I Almost Made It	1974	3.75	7.50	15.00
PC 34876	The Best of Barbara Mandrell	1977	3.00	6.00	12.00
—No bar code on cover					
PC 34876	The Best of Barbara Mandrell	198?	2.00	4.00	8.00
—Reissue with bar code on cover					
FC 37437	Looking Back	1982	2.50	5.00	10.00
PC 37437	Looking Back	198?	2.00	4.00	8.00
—Budget-line reissue					
EMI AMERICA					
ET-46956	Sure Feels Good	1987	2.50	5.00	10.00
MCA					
641	Midnight Angel	198?	2.00	4.00	8.00
—Reissue of ABC Dot 2067					
672	This Is Barbara Mandrell	198?	2.00	4.00	8.00
—Reissue of ABC Dot 2045					
673	Lovers, Friends and Strangers	198?	2.00	4.00	8.00
—Reissue of ABC Dot 2076					
674	Love's Ups and Downs	198?	2.00	4.00	8.00
—Reissue of ABC Dot 2098					
3165	Just for the Record	1979	2.50	5.00	10.00
3280	Moods	1980	2.00	4.00	8.00
—Reissue of ABC 1088					
5136	Love Is Fair	1980	2.50	5.00	10.00
5243	Barbara Mandrell Live	1981	2.50	5.00	10.00
5295	...In Black and White	1982	2.50	5.00	10.00
5330	He Set My Life to Music	1982	2.50	5.00	10.00
5377	Spun Gold	1983	2.50	5.00	10.00
5474	Clean Cut	1984	2.50	5.00	10.00
5519	Christmas at Our House	1984	3.00	6.00	12.00
5566	Greatest Hits	1985	2.50	5.00	10.00
5619	Get to the Heart	1985	2.50	5.00	10.00
37173	Just for the Record	198?	2.00	4.00	8.00
—Budget-line reissue					
37202	Moods	198?	—	3.00	6.00
—Budget-line reissue					
37224	Barbara Mandrell Live	198?	2.00	4.00	8.00
—Budget-line reissue					
PAIR					
PDL1-1079 [(2)]	The Best of Barbara Mandrell	1986	3.00	6.00	12.00

MANDRELL, BARBARA, AND LEE GREENWOOD

Number	Title (A Side/B Side)	Yr	VG	VG+	NM
45s					
MCA					
52415	To Me/We Were Meant for Each Other	1984	—	—	3.00
52525	It Should Have Been Love By Now/Can't Get Too Much of a Good Thing	1985	—	2.00	4.00

MANDRILL

Number	Title (A Side/B Side)	Yr	VG	VG+	NM
45s					
ARISTA					
0274	Funky Monkey/Gilley Hines	1977	—	2.00	4.00
0304	Can You Get It/Holiday	1978	—	2.00	4.00
0326	Happy Beat/Holiday	1978	—	2.00	4.00
0375	Too Late/Holiday	1978	—	2.00	4.00
0490	My Kind of Girl/Lo Siento Mucho	1980	—	2.00	4.00
0507	Getting in the Mood/(B-side unknown)	1980	—	2.00	4.00
0529	Dance of Love/When You Shake	1980	—	2.00	4.00
MONTAGE					
1222	Put Your Money Where the Funk Is/(B-side unknown)	1982	—	2.00	4.00
1224	Soar Like an Eagle/Starry-Eyed	1982	—	2.00	4.00
POLYDOR					
14070	Mandrill/Warning Blues	1971	—	2.50	5.00
14085	Rollin' On/Symphonic Revolution	1971	—	2.50	5.00
14127	Kofijahm/I Refuse to Smile	1972	—	2.50	5.00
14142	Cohelo/Git It All	1972	—	2.50	5.00
14156	Children of the Sun/Ace Is High	1972	—	2.50	5.00
14163	Fencewalk/Hagalo	1973	—	2.50	5.00
14187	Hang Loose/Polk Street Carnival	1973	—	2.50	5.00
14200	Mango Meat/Afrikus Retrospectus	1973	—	2.50	5.00
14214	Love Song/Two Sisters of Mystery	1974	—	2.50	5.00
14235	Positive Thing/Positive Thing Plus	1974	—	2.50	5.00
14257	Road to Love/Armadillo	1974	—	2.50	5.00
UNITED ARTISTS					
XW673	Tee Vee/Silk	1975	—	2.00	4.00
XW778	Disco-Lypso/Solid	1976	—	2.00	4.00
Albums					
ARISTA					
AL 4144	We Are One	1977	2.50	5.00	10.00
AL 4195	New Worlds	1978	2.50	5.00	10.00
AL 9527	Getting In the Mood	1980	2.50	5.00	10.00
LIBERTY					
LN-10196	Rebirth	1983	2.00	4.00	8.00
MONTAGE					
ST-72008	Energize	1982	3.00	6.00	12.00
POLYDOR					
24-4060	Mandrill	1971	3.00	6.00	12.00
PD-5025	Mandrill Is	1972	3.00	6.00	12.00
PD-5043	Composite Truth	1973	3.00	6.00	12.00
PD-5059	Just Outside of Town	1973	3.00	6.00	12.00
PD-1-6047	The Best of Mandrill	1975	3.00	6.00	12.00
PD-2-9002 [(2)]	Mandrilland	1976	3.75	7.50	15.00
UNITED ARTISTS					
UA-LA408-G	Solid	1975	3.00	6.00	12.00
UA-LA577-G	Beast from the East	1976	3.00	6.00	12.00

MANGIONE, CHUCK

Number	Title (A Side/B Side)	Yr	VG	VG+	NM
12-Inch Singles					
A&M					
8448 [DJ]	Feels So Good (4:40) (same on both sides)	1978	3.00	6.00	12.00
COLUMBIA					
AS 1903 [DJ]	Love Wears No Disguise/Diana "D"	1984	2.00	4.00	8.00
07827	Long Hair Soulful (Extended) (Edit)	1988	2.00	4.00	8.00
45s					
A&M					
1707	Chase the Clouds Away/Soft	1975	—	2.00	4.00
1773	Bellavia/Listen to the Wind	1975	—	2.00	4.00
1827	Soft/Can't We Do This All Night	1976	—	2.00	4.00
1886	Main Squeeze/Come Take a Ride with Me	1976	—	2.00	4.00
1886 [PS]	Main Squeeze/Come Take a Ride with Me	1976	—	3.00	6.00
1919	Bellavia/Doin' Everything With You	1977	—	2.00	4.00
2001	Feels So Good/Maui-Waui	1977	—	2.00	4.00
2001 [PS]	Feels So Good/Maui-Waui	1977	—	2.50	5.00
2088	Children of Sanchez/Doin' Everything with You	1978	—	2.00	4.00
2088 [PS]	Children of Sanchez/Doin' Everything with You	1978	—	2.50	5.00
2118	Bellavia/(B-side unknown)	1979	—	2.00	4.00
2167	Land of Make Believe/Children of Sanchez	1979	—	2.00	4.00
2211	Give It All You Got/B'Bye	1980	—	2.00	4.00
2211 [PS]	Give It All You Got/B'Bye	1980	—	2.00	4.00
2236	Fun and Games/Children of Sanchez (Finale)	1980	—	2.00	4.00
2236 [PS]	Fun and Games/Children of Sanchez (Finale)	1980	—	2.00	4.00
2341	Give It All You Got, But Slowly/Neapolitan Tarantella	1981	—	—	3.00
2354	Cannonball Run Theme/Can't We Do This All Night	1981	—	—	3.00
COLUMBIA					
03008	Steppin' Out/Memories of Scirocco	1982	—	—	3.00
03329	No Problem/Memories of Scirocco	1982	—	—	3.00
03986	Journey to a Rainbow/Please Stay the Night	1983	—	—	3.00

Number	Title (A Side/B Side)	Yr	VG	VG+	NM
04649	Diana "D"/Josephine	1984	—	—	3.00
05866	Save Tonight for Me/T.J.'s Gingerbread House	1986	—	—	3.00
07917	Long Hair Soulful/Do You Ever Think About Me	1988	—	—	3.00
MERCURY					
73208	Hill Where the Lord Hides/Friends and Lovers	1971	2.00	4.00	8.00
73238	And In the Beginning/Feel a Vision	1972	—	3.00	6.00
73262	Freddie's Walkin'/Look to the Children	1972	—	3.00	6.00
73371	Last Tango in Paris/Legend of the One-Eyed Sailor	1973	—	3.00	6.00
73453	As Long As We're Together/Legend of the One-Eyed Sailor	1974	—	3.00	6.00
73635	Land of Make Believe/As Long As We're Together	1975	—	3.00	6.00
73920	Land of Make Believe/As Long As We're Together	1977	—	2.50	5.00
74016	Hill Where the Lord Hides/Land of Make Believe	1978	—	2.50	5.00
Albums					
A&M					
SP-3115	Chase the Clouds Away	198?	—	3.00	6.00
—Budget-line reissue					
SP-3172	Bellavia	198?	—	3.00	6.00
—Budget-line reissue					
SP-3193	Fun and Games	1983	—	3.00	6.00
—Budget-line reissue					
SP-3219	Feels So Good	198?	—	3.00	6.00
—Budget-line reissue					
SP-3220	Main Squeeze	198?	—	3.00	6.00
—Budget-line reissue					
SP-3237	70 Miles Young	198?	—	3.00	6.00
—Budget-line reissue					
SP-3282	The Best of Chuck Mangione	1985	2.50	5.00	10.00
SP-3715	Fun and Games	1980	2.50	5.00	10.00
SP-4518	Chase the Clouds Away	1975	2.50	5.00	10.00
SP-4557	Bellavia	1975	2.50	5.00	10.00
SP-4612	Main Squeeze	1976	2.50	5.00	10.00
SP-4658	Feels So Good	1977	2.50	5.00	10.00
SP-4911	70 Miles Young	1982	2.50	5.00	10.00
SP-6513 [(2)]	Tarantella	1981	3.00	6.00	12.00
SP-6700 [(2)]	Children of Sanchez	1978	3.00	6.00	12.00
SP-6701 [(2)]	An Evening of Magic — Chuck Mangione Live at the Hollywood Bowl	1979	3.00	6.00	12.00
QU-54518 [Q]	Chase the Clouds Away	1975	4.50	9.00	18.00
QU-54557 [Q]	Bellavia	1975	4.50	9.00	18.00
COLUMBIA					
FC 38101	Love Notes	1982	2.50	5.00	10.00
PC 38101	Love Notes	198?	—	3.00	6.00
—Budget-line reissue					
FC 38686	Journey to a Rainbow	1983	2.50	5.00	10.00
PC 38686	Journey to a Rainbow	1986	—	3.00	6.00
—Budget-line reissue					
FC 39479	Disguise	1984	2.50	5.00	10.00
FC 40254	Save Tonight for Me	1986	2.50	5.00	10.00
FC 40984	Eyes of the Veiled Temptress	1988	2.50	5.00	10.00
FANTASY					
OJC-495	Recuerdo	1991	3.00	6.00	12.00
—Reissue of Jazzland 984					
JAZZLAND					
JLP-84 [M]	Recuerdo	1962	10.00	20.00	40.00
JLP-984 [S]	Recuerdo	1962	12.50	25.00	50.00
MERCURY					
SRM-1-631	The Chuck Mangione Quartet	1972	3.00	6.00	12.00
SRM-1-650	Alive!	1973	3.00	6.00	12.00
SRM-1-681	Friends & Love/Highlights	1973	3.00	6.00	12.00
SRM-1-684	Land of Make Believe	1973	3.00	6.00	12.00
SRM-2-800 [(2)]	Friends & Love — A Chuck Mangione Concert	1971	3.75	7.50	15.00
SRM-1-1050	Encore/The Chuck Mangione Concerts	1975	2.50	5.00	10.00
SRM-2-7501 [(2)]	Together: A New Chuck Mangione Concert	1971	3.75	7.50	15.00
SRM-2-8601 [(2)]	The Best of Chuck Mangione	1978	3.00	6.00	12.00
824301-1	Alive!	198?	2.00	4.00	8.00
—Reissue of 650					
MILESTONE					
47042 [(2)]	Jazz Brother	1977	3.00	6.00	12.00
—Reissue of material issued by "The Jazz Brothers"					
MOBILE FIDELITY					
1-068	Feels So Good	1981	6.25	12.50	25.00
—Audiophile vinyl					

MANHATTAN TRANSFER

12-Inch Singles

Number	Title (A Side/B Side)	Yr	VG	VG+	NM
ATLANTIC					
PR 525 [DJ]	Spice of Life/The Night That Monk Returned to Heaven	1983	—	3.00	6.00
PR 560 [DJ]	American Pop/Why Not	1983	—	3.00	6.00
PR 2272 [DJ]	So You Say (same on both sides)	1987	—	3.00	6.00
45s					
ATLANTIC					
3277	Sweet Talking Guy/Clap Your Hands	1975	2.00	4.00	8.00
3292	Operator/Tuxedo Junction	1975	—	2.50	5.00
3349	Helpless/My Cat Fell in the Well	1976	—	2.50	5.00
3374	Chanson d'Amour/Popsicle Toes	1976	—	2.50	5.00
3472	Where Did Our Love Go/Inside and Out	1978	—	2.50	5.00
3491	Four Brothers/It's Not the Spotlight	1978	—	2.50	5.00
3636	Birdland/Shaker Song	1979	—	2.50	5.00
3649	Twilight Zone-Twilight Tone/Body and Soul	1980	—	2.50	5.00
3756 [DJ]	Nothin' You Can Do About It (same on both sides)	1980	—	2.50	5.00
—May be promo only					
3772	Trickle, Trickle/Foreign Affair	1980	2.50	5.00	10.00
3816	Boy from New York City/(The World of) Confirmation	1981	—	2.00	4.00
3855	Smile Again/Until I Met You	1981	—	2.00	4.00
3877	Spies in the Night/Kafka	1981	—	2.00	4.00
4034	Route 66/On the Boulevard	1982	—	2.00	4.00
89094	So You Say/Notes from the Underground	1988	—	2.00	4.00
89094 [PS]	So You Say/Notes from the Underground	1988	—	2.00	4.00
89156	Soul Food to Go/Hear the Voices	1988	—	2.00	4.00
89156 [PS]	Soul Food to Go/Hear the Voices	1988	—	2.00	4.00
89467	That's Killer Joe/Airegin II	1985	—	2.50	5.00
89533	Ray's Rockhouse/Another Life in Tunisia	1985	—	2.00	4.00
89533 [PS]	Ray's Rockhouse/Another Life in Tunisia	1985	—	2.00	4.00
89594	Baby Come Back to Me (Morse Code of Love)/ That's the Way It Goes	1984	2.50	5.00	10.00
89647	This Independence/Code of Ethics	1984	—	2.50	5.00
89695	Mystery/Goodbye Love	1984	—	2.00	4.00
89720	American Pop/Why	1983	—	2.00	4.00
—Featuring Frankie Valli					
89786	Spice of Life/The Night That Monk Returned to Heaven	1983	—	2.00	4.00
89786 [PS]	Spice of Life/The Night That Monk Returned to Heaven	1983	—	2.50	5.00
CAPITOL					
2968	Care for Me/Rosianna	1970	2.50	5.00	10.00
—With Gene Pistilli					
3036	Maybe Mexico/Winterlude	1971	2.50	5.00	10.00
—With Gene Pistilli					
3108	Java Jive/Chicken Bone Bone	1971	2.50	5.00	10.00
—With Gene Pistilli					
(NO LABEL)					
1984 [DJ]	The Christmas Song (same on both sides)	1984	10.00	20.00	40.00
1984 [PS]	The Christmas Song (same on both sides)	1984	10.00	20.00	40.00
—Above sleeve and record are a private pressing for friends and associates of the group					
Albums					
ATLANTIC					
SD 16036	Mecca for Moderns	1981	2.50	5.00	10.00
SD 18133	The Manhattan Transfer	1975	2.50	5.00	10.00
SD 18183	Coming Out	1976	2.50	5.00	10.00
SD 19163	Pastiche	1978	2.50	5.00	10.00
SD 19258	Extensions	1979	2.50	5.00	10.00
SD 19319	The Best of the Manhattan Transfer	1981	2.50	5.00	10.00
80104	Bodies and Souls	1983	2.50	5.00	10.00
81233	Bop Doo-Wopp	1984	3.00	6.00	12.00
81266	Vocalese	1985	2.50	5.00	10.00
81723	Live	1987	2.50	5.00	10.00
81803	Brasil	1987	2.50	5.00	10.00
CAPITOL					
ST-778	Jukin'	1971	3.75	7.50	15.00
—With Gene Pistilli					
ST-11405	Jukin'	1975	2.50	5.00	10.00
—With Gene Pistilli; reissue of 778					
SN-16223	Jukin'	198?	2.00	4.00	8.00
—With Gene Pistilli; budget-line reissue					
COLUMBIA					
C 47079	The Offbeat of Avenues	1991	3.75	7.50	15.00
MOBILE FIDELITY					
1-022	Manhattan Transfer Live	1979	5.00	10.00	20.00
—Audiophile vinyl					
1-199	Extensions	1994	6.25	12.50	25.00
—Audiophile vinyl					

MANHATTANS, THE (1)

Well-known male R&B vocal group.

12-Inch Singles

Number	Title (A Side/B Side)	Yr	VG	VG+	NM
COLUMBIA					
AS 1316 [DJ]	Let Your Love Come Down (same on both sides)	1981	2.50	5.00	10.00
03940	Crazy (5:00) (Instrumental)	1983	2.00	4.00	8.00
05973	Maybe Tomorrow/Where Did We Go Wrong	1986	2.00	4.00	8.00
45s					
CARNIVAL					
504	I've Got Everything But You/For the Very First Time	1964	5.00	10.00	20.00
506	There Goes a Fool/Call Somebody Please	1964	10.00	20.00	40.00
507	I Wanna Be (Your Everything)/What's It Gonna Be	1965	3.75	7.50	15.00
509	Searchin' for My Baby/I'm the One That Love Forgot	1965	3.75	7.50	15.00
512	Follow Your Heart/The Boston Money	1965	3.75	7.50	15.00
514	Baby I Need You/Teach Me the Philly Dog	1966	3.75	7.50	15.00
517	Can I/That New Girl	1966	3.75	7.50	15.00
522	I Betcha (Couldn't Love Me)/Sweet Little Girl	1966	3.75	7.50	15.00
524	It's That Time of the Year/Alone on New Year's Eve	1966	5.00	10.00	20.00
526	All I Need Is Your Love/Our Love Will Never Die	1967	3.75	7.50	15.00
529	When We're Made As One/Baby I'm Sorry	1967	3.75	7.50	15.00
533	I Call It Love/Manhattan Stomp	1967	3.75	7.50	15.00
542	I Don't Wanna Go/Love Is Breaking Out	1968	3.75	7.50	15.00
545	Til You Come Back to Me/Call Somebody Please	1968	3.75	7.50	15.00
COLUMBIA					
02164	Shining Star/Summertime in the City	1981	—	—	3.00
—Reissue					
02191	Just One Moment Away/When I Leave Tomorrow	1981	—	2.00	4.00
02548	Let Your Love Come Down/I Gotta Thank You	1981	—	2.00	4.00
02666	Money, Money/I Wanta Thank You	1982	—	2.00	4.00
03939	Crazy/Gonna Find You	1983	—	2.00	4.00
04110	Forever By Your Side/Locked Up in Your Love	1983	—	2.00	4.00
04754	You Send Me/You're Gonna Love Being Loved By Me	1985	—	2.00	4.00
04754 [PS]	You Send Me/You're Gonna Love Being Loved By Me	1985	—	2.00	4.00
04930	Don't Say No/Dreamin'	1985	—	2.00	4.00
06376	Where Did We Go Wrong/Maybe Tomorrow	1986	—	2.00	4.00
—With Regina Belle					
07010	Mr. D.J./All I Need	1987	—	2.00	4.00
10045	Don't Take Your Love/The Day the Robins Sang to Me	1974	—	2.50	5.00
10140	Hurt/Nursery Rhymes	1975	—	2.50	5.00
10310	Kiss and Say Goodbye/Wonderful World of Love	1976	—	2.50	5.00
10430	I Kinda Miss You/Gypsy Man	1976	—	2.50	5.00
10495	It Feels So Good to Be Loved By You/On the Street (Where I Live)	1977	—	2.50	5.00
10586	We Never Danced to a Love Song/Let's Start It All Over Again	1977	—	2.50	5.00

Number	Title (A Side/B Side)	Yr	VG	VG+	NM
10674	Am I Losing You/Movin'	1978	—	2.50	5.00
10766	Everybody Has a Dream/Happiness	1978	—	2.50	5.00
10921	Here Comes the Hurt Again/Don't Say Goodbye	1979	—	2.50	5.00
11024	The Way We Were-Memories/New York City	1979	—	2.50	5.00
11222	Shining Star/I'll Never Run Away from Love Again	1980	—	2.00	4.00
11321	Girl of My Dreams/The Closer You Are	1980	—	2.00	4.00
11398	I'll Never Find Another (Another Just Like You)/ Rendezvous	1980	—	2.00	4.00
45838	There's No Me Without You/I'm Not a Run-Around	1973	—	3.00	6.00
45927	You'd Better Believe It/Soul Train	1973	—	3.00	6.00
45971	Wish That You Were Mine/It's So Hard Loving You	1973	—	3.00	6.00
46081	Summertime in the City/The Other Side of Me	1974	—	3.00	6.00
60511	Do You Really Mean Goodbye/Rendezvous	1981	—	2.00	4.00
DELUXE					
109	The Picture Became Quite Clear/Oh Lord, How I Wish I Could Sleep	1969	2.50	5.00	10.00
115	It's Gonna Take a Lot to Bring Me Back/Give Him Up	1970	2.50	5.00	10.00
122	If My Heart Could Speak/Loneliness	1970	2.50	5.00	10.00
129	From Atlanta to Goodbye/Fantastic Journey	1970	2.50	5.00	10.00
132	Let Them Talk/Straight to My Heart	1970	2.50	5.00	10.00
136	Do You Ever/I Can't Stand for You to Leave Me	1971	2.50	5.00	10.00
137	A Million to One/Cry If You Wanna Cry	1971	2.50	5.00	10.00
139	One Life to Live/It's the Only One	1972	2.50	5.00	10.00
144	Back Up/Fever	1972	2.50	5.00	10.00
146	Rainbow Week/Loneliness	1973	2.50	5.00	10.00
152	Do You Ever/If My Heart Could Speak	1973	2.50	5.00	10.00
STARFIRE					
121	Alone on New Year's Eve/It's That Time of the Year	1979	—	2.50	5.00
VALLEY VUE					
75723	Sweet Talk/(B-side unknown)	1989	—	3.00	6.00
75749	Why You Wanna Love Me Like That/(B-side unknown)	1989	—	3.00	6.00
Albums					
CARNIVAL					
CMLP-201 [M]	Dedicated to You	1966	62.50	125.00	250.00
CSLP-201 [S]	Dedicated to You	1966	125.00	250.00	500.00
CMLP-202 [M]	For You and Yours	1967	37.50	75.00	150.00
CSLP-202 [S]	For You and Yours	1967	75.00	150.00	300.00
COLLECTABLES					
COL-5135	Dedicated to You: Golden Carnival Classics, Part One	198?	2.50	5.00	10.00
COL-5136	For You and Yours: Golden Carnival Classics, Part Two	198?	2.50	5.00	10.00
COLUMBIA					
KC 32444	There's No Me Without You	1973	3.75	7.50	15.00
PC 32444	There's No Me Without You	198?	2.00	4.00	8.00
—Budget-line reissue					
KC 33064	That's How Much I Love You	1975	3.75	7.50	15.00
PC 33820	The Manhattans	1976	3.00	6.00	12.00
—No bar code on back cover					
PC 33820	The Manhattans	198?	2.00	4.00	8.00
—With bar code on back cover					
PC 34450	It Feels So Good	1977	3.00	6.00	12.00
—No bar code on back cover					
PC 34450	It Feels So Good	198?	2.00	4.00	8.00
—With bar code on back cover					
PCQ 34450 [Q]	It Feels So Good	1977	5.00	10.00	20.00
JC 35252	There's No Good in Goodbye	1978	3.00	6.00	12.00
JC 35693	Love Talk	1979	3.00	6.00	12.00
PC 35693	After Midnight	198?	2.00	4.00	8.00
—Budget-line reissue					
JC 36411	After Midnight	1980	3.00	6.00	12.00
JC 36861	Manhattans Greatest Hits	1980	3.00	6.00	12.00
FC 37156	Black Tie	1981	2.50	5.00	10.00
PC 37156	Black Tie	198?	2.00	4.00	8.00
—Budget-line reissue					
FC 38600	Forever By Your Side	1983	2.50	5.00	10.00
FC 39277	Too Hot to Stop It	1985	2.50	5.00	10.00
DELUXE					
12000	With These Hands	1971	6.25	12.50	25.00
12004	A Million to One	1972	6.25	12.50	25.00
SOLID SMOKE					
8007	Follow Your Heart	1981	2.50	5.00	10.00
VALLEY VUE					
D1-72946	Sweet Talk	1989	3.00	6.00	12.00

MANHATTANS, THE (2)

Number	Title (A Side/B Side)	Yr	VG	VG+	NM
45s					
COLPIX					
115	Big Wheel Express/Powder Blue	1959	7.50	15.00	30.00

MANHATTANS, THE (U)

Some of these are likely group (1); others could be group (2); others are probably neither.

Number	Title (A Side/B Side)	Yr	VG	VG+	NM
45s					
AVANTI					
1401	What Should I Do/Later for You	1963	6.25	12.50	25.00
BIG MACK					
3911	Why Should I Cry/The Feeling Is Mutual	196?	50.00	100.00	200.00
CAPITOL					
4591	Molly Brown Medley/I Ain't Down Yet	1961	5.00	10.00	20.00
4730	La La La/Sing All the Day	1962	5.00	10.00	20.00
ENJOY					
2008	Come On Back/Long Time No See	1964	5.00	10.00	20.00
—As "Ronnie and the Manhattans"					
GOLDEN WORLD					
14	Just a Little Loving/Beautiful Brown Eyes	1964	7.50	15.00	30.00
KING					
5228	Ebb Tide (Part 1)/Ebb Tide (Part 2)	1959	3.75	7.50	15.00
5259	Sugar Tooth/Like Saying Something	1959	3.75	7.50	15.00

Number	Title (A Side/B Side)	Yr	VG	VG+	NM
PINEY					
107	Live It Up/Go Baby Go	1962	15.00	30.00	60.00
108	Crazy Love/The Hawk and the Crow	1962	12.50	25.00	50.00
WARNER					
1015	How Do I Say I'm Sorry/Love Is Where You Find It	1958	30.00	60.00	120.00

MANILOW, BARRY

Also see FEATHERBED.

Number	Title (A Side/B Side)	Yr	VG	VG+	NM
12-Inch Singles					
ARISTA					
SP-21 [DJ]	En El Copa (same on both sides)	1978	6.25	12.50	25.00
—Spanish version of "Copacabana"					
9295 [DJ]	When October Goes (same on both sides)	1984	2.50	5.00	10.00
9665	Hey Mambo (2 versions)	1988	3.00	6.00	12.00
13379	I'd Really Love to See You Tonight (2 mixes)/ Could It Be Magic (1993 remix)	1997	3.00	6.00	12.00
(# unknown)	En El Copa (Long) (Short)	1978	7.50	15.00	30.00
RCA					
PD-14330	I'm Your Man (Club Mix)/I'm Your Man (Dub)	1986	2.50	5.00	10.00
45s					
ARISTA					
SP-11 [DJ]	It's Just Another New Year's Eve (same on both sides)	1977	2.00	4.00	8.00
SP-11 [PS]	It's Just Another New Year's Eve (same on both sides)	1977	3.00	6.00	12.00
SP-25 [DJ]	Ready to Take a Chance Again (same on both sides)	1978	2.00	4.00	8.00
SP-25 [PS]	Ready to Take a Chance Again (same on both sides)	1978	3.00	6.00	12.00
0108	It's a Miracle/One of These Days	1975	—	2.00	4.00
0126	Could It Be Magic/I Am Your Child	1975	—	2.00	4.00
0157	I Write the Songs/A Nice Boy Like Me	1975	—	2.00	4.00
0172	Tryin' to Get the Feeling Again/Beautiful Music	1976	—	2.00	4.00
0206	This One's for You/Riders to the Stars	1976	—	2.00	4.00
0212	Weekend in New England/Say the Words	1976	—	2.00	4.00
0244	Looks Like We Made It/New York City Rhythm	1977	—	2.00	4.00
0273	Daybreak/Jump Shout Boogie	1977	—	2.00	4.00
0305	Can't Smile Without You/Sunrise	1978	—	2.00	4.00
0330	Even Now/I Was a Fool (To Let You Go)	1978	—	2.00	4.00
0330 [PS]	Even Now/I Was a Fool (To Let You Go)	1978	—	2.00	4.00
0339	Copacabana (Short Version)/Copacabana (Long Version)	1978	—	2.00	4.00
0357	Ready to Take a Chance Again/Sweet Life	1978	—	2.00	4.00
0382	Somewhere in the Night/Leavin' in the Morning	1978	—	2.00	4.00
0464	Ships/They Gave In to the Blues	1979	—	2.00	4.00
0481	When I Wanted You/Bobbie Lee (What's the Difference I Gotta Live)	1979	—	2.00	4.00
0501	I Don't Want to Walk Without You/One Voice	1980	—	2.00	4.00
0566	I Made It Through the Rain/Only in Chicago	1980	—	2.00	4.00
0596	Lonely Together/The Last Duet	1981	—	2.00	4.00
—B-side with Lily Tomlin					
0633	The Old Songs/Don't Fall in Love with Me	1981	—	2.00	4.00
0658	Somewhere Down the Road/Let's Take All Night to Say Goodbye	1982	—	2.00	4.00
0675	Let's Hang On/No Other Love	1982	—	2.00	4.00
0698	Oh Julie/Break Down the Door	1982	—	2.00	4.00
1025	Memory/Heart of Steel	1982	—	2.00	4.00
1046	Some Kind of Friend/Heaven	1983	—	2.00	4.00
2094	Jingle Bells/Because It's Christmas (For All the Children)	1990	—	—	3.00
—A-side with Expose					
9003	Some Kind of Friend/Heaven	1983	—	—	3.00
9101	Read 'Em and Weep/One Voice	1983	—	—	3.00
9185	You're Lookin' Hot Tonight/Put a Quarter in the Jukebox	1984	—	—	3.00
—B-side with Ronnie Milsap					
9666	Hey Mambo/When October Goes	1988	—	—	3.00
—With Kid Creole and the Coconuts					
9666 [PS]	Hey Mambo/When October Goes	1988	—	—	3.00
9811	Please Don't Be Scared/A Little Traveling Music, Please	1989	—	—	3.00
9838	Keep Each Other Warm/A Little Traveling Music, Please	1989	—	2.50	5.00
9838 [PS]	Keep Each Other Warm/A Little Traveling Music, Please	1989	—	2.50	5.00
BELL					
45357	Sweetwater Jones/One of These Days	1973	—	3.00	6.00
45422	Cloudburst/Could It Be Magic	1973	—	3.00	6.00
45443	Let's Take Some Time to Say Goodbye/Seven More Years	1974	—	3.00	6.00
45613	Mandy/Something's Comin' Up	1974	—	2.50	5.00
RCA					
PB-14223	In Search of Love/At the Dance	1985	—	—	3.00
PB-14223 [PS]	In Search of Love/At the Dance	1985	—	2.00	4.00
PB-14302	He Doesn't Care (But I Do)/It's All Behind Us Now	1986	—	—	3.00
PB-14302 [PS]	He Doesn't Care (But I Do)/It's All Behind Us Now	1986	—	2.00	4.00
PB-14397	I'm Your Man/I'm Your Man (Dub)	1986	—	—	3.00
PB-14397 [PS]	I'm Your Man/I'm Your Man (Dub)	1986	—	—	3.00
SBK					
S7-17906	Let Me Be Your Wings/Follow Your Heart	1994	—	2.00	4.00
—A-side with Debra Byrd; B-side by Gino Conforti					
Albums					
ARISTA					
AB 2500 [EP]	Oh, Julie!	1982	5.00	10.00	20.00
AL 4007	Barry Manilow I	1975	2.50	5.00	10.00
—Revised version of Bell 1129 with new cover; "Could It Be Magic" especially is noticeably different between the Bell and Arista versions					
AL 4016	Barry Manilow II	1975	2.50	5.00	10.00
—Reissue of Bell 1314					
AQ 4016 [Q]	Barry Manilow II	1975	3.75	7.50	15.00
AL 4060	Tryin' to Get the Feeling	1975	2.50	5.00	10.00
AQ 4060 [Q]	Tryin' to Get the Feeling	1975	3.75	7.50	15.00
AB 4090	This One's for You	1976	2.50	5.00	10.00
AL 4164	Even Now	1978	2.00	4.00	8.00

Number	Title (A Side/B Side)	Yr	VG	VG+	NM
AL13-8039 [(2)]	Greatest Hits	1983	2.50	5.00	10.00
AL13-8049 [(2)]	Barry Manilow/Live	1983	2.50	5.00	10.00
AL8-8102	Barry Manilow/Greatest Hits, Vol. II	1983	2.00	4.00	8.00
AL8-8254	2:00 A.M. Paradise Café	1984	2.00	4.00	8.00
AL9-8274	The Manilow Collection — 20 Classic Hits	1985	2.00	4.00	8.00
AL8-8291	Barry Manilow/Greatest Hits, Vol. II	1985	—	3.00	6.00
AL8-8322	Even Now	1985	—	3.00	6.00
AL8-8331	This One's for You	1985	—	3.00	6.00
AL8-8336	Tryin' to Get the Feeling	1985	—	3.00	6.00
AL8-8370	Barry Manilow II	1985	—	3.00	6.00
AL8-8372	Barry Manilow I	1985	—	3.00	6.00
AL 8500 [(2)]	Barry Manilow/Live	1977	3.00	6.00	12.00
AL-8527	Swing Street	1987	2.00	4.00	8.00
AL-8570	Barry Manilow	1989	2.00	4.00	8.00
AL-8598	Greatest Hits, Vol. 1	1989	2.50	5.00	10.00
AL-8599	Greatest Hits, Vol. 2	1989	2.50	5.00	10.00
AL-8600	Greatest Hits, Vol. 3	1989	2.50	5.00	10.00
A2L 8601 [(2)]	Greatest Hits	1978	3.00	6.00	12.00
A2L 8601 [(2) PD]	Greatest Hits	1979	10.00	20.00	40.00
—Entire contents on two picture discs (yes, it has the same number as the regular issue)					
AL-8638 [(2)]	Live on Broadway	1990	5.00	10.00	20.00
AL-8644	Because It's Christmas	1990	3.75	7.50	15.00
AL 9505	One Voice	1979	2.00	4.00	8.00
AL 9537	Barry	1980	2.00	4.00	8.00
AL 9573	If I Should Love Again	1981	2.00	4.00	8.00
AL-9610	Here Comes the Night	1982	2.00	4.00	8.00
NU 9740	Manilow Magic	1982	3.00	6.00	12.00
BELL					
1129	Barry Manilow	1973	6.25	12.50	25.00
1314	Barry Manilow II	1974	3.75	7.50	15.00
MOBILE FIDELITY					
1-097	Barry Manilow I	1981	5.00	10.00	20.00
—Audiophile vinyl					
RCA VICTOR					
AFL1-7044	Manilow	1985	2.00	4.00	8.00

MANN, BARRY

45s

Number	Title (A Side/B Side)	Yr	VG	VG+	NM
ABC-PARAMOUNT					
10143	War Paint/Counting Teardrops	1960	5.00	10.00	20.00
10180	Happy Birthday, Broken Heart/Millionaire	1961	5.00	10.00	20.00
10237	Who Put the Bomp (In the Bomp, Bomp, Bomp)/ Love, True Love	1961	6.25	12.50	25.00
10263	Little Miss U.S.A./Find Another Fool	1961	5.00	10.00	20.00
10356	Hey Baby I'm Dancin'/Like I Don't Love You	1962	5.00	10.00	20.00
10380	Teenage Has-Been/Bless You	1962	5.00	10.00	20.00
ARISTA					
0194	The Princess and the Punk/Jennifer	1976	—	2.00	4.00
CAPITOL					
2082	Young Electric Psychedelic Hippy Flippy Folk & Funky Philosophic Turned On Groovy Twelve-String Band/Take Your Love	1968	3.75	7.50	15.00
2217	I Just Can't Help Believin'/Where Do I Go from Here	1968	2.50	5.00	10.00
5695	Looking at Tomorrow/Angelica	1966	2.50	5.00	10.00
5894	Where Do I Go from Here/She Is Today	1967	2.50	5.00	10.00
CASABLANCA					
2287	Brown-Eyed Woman/In My Own Way	1980	—	2.00	4.00
COLPIX					
691	Graduation Time/Johnny Surfboard	1963	5.00	10.00	20.00
JDS					
5002	I Love to Last a Lifetime/All the Things You Are	1959	7.50	15.00	30.00
NEW DESIGN					
1000	Carry Me Home/Sundown	1971	—	2.50	5.00
1005	When You Get Right Down to It/Don't Give Up on Me	1972	—	2.50	5.00
1006	Too Many Mornings/On Broadway	1972	—	2.50	5.00
1006	Too Many Mornings/Lay It All Out	1972	—	2.50	5.00
RCA VICTOR					
PB-10104	Nobody But You/Woman, Woman, Woman	1974	—	2.50	5.00
PB-10230	Nothing Good Comes Easy/Woman, Woman, Woman	1975	—	2.50	5.00
PB-10319	Don't Seem Right/I'm a Survivor	1975	—	2.50	5.00
RED BIRD					
10-015	Talk to Me Baby/Amy	1964	3.75	7.50	15.00
SCEPTER					
12281	Feelings/Let Me Stay with You	1970	—	3.00	6.00
UNITED ARTISTS					
XW1021	Best That I Know How/Lettin' Good Times Get Away	1977	—	2.00	4.00
WARNER BROS.					
8752	For No Reason at All/Almost Gone	1979	—	2.00	4.00
8752 [PS]	For No Reason at All/Almost Gone	1979	—	2.50	5.00

Albums

Number	Title (A Side/B Side)	Yr	VG	VG+	NM
ABC-PARAMOUNT					
399 [M]	Who Put the Bomp	1963	30.00	60.00	120.00
S-399 [S]	Who Put the Bomp	1963	75.00	150.00	300.00
CASABLANCA					
NBLP 7226	Barry Mann	1980	2.50	5.00	10.00
NEW DESIGN					
Z 30876	Lay It All Out	1971	3.00	6.00	12.00
RCA VICTOR					
APL1-0860	Survivor	1975	3.00	6.00	12.00
DJL1-1162 [DJ]	Flo and Eddie Interview Barry Mann	1975	12.50	25.00	50.00

MANN, BOBBY

See BOBBY BLOOM.

MANN, CARL

45s

Number	Title (A Side/B Side)	Yr	VG	VG+	NM
ABC					
12035	Burnin' Holes in the Eyes of Abraham Lincoln/ Ballad of Johnny Clyde	1974	—	2.50	5.00
12071	Neon Lights/Just About Out	1975	—	2.50	5.00
12092	It's Not the Coffee/Cheatin' Time	1975	—	2.50	5.00
ABC/DOT					
17596	Back Loving/Annie Over Time	1975	—	2.50	5.00
17621	Twilight Time/Belly-Rubbin' Country Soul	1976	—	2.50	5.00
JAXON					
502	Gonna Rock and Roll Tonight/Rockin' Love	1957	750.00	1500.	3000.
PHILLIPS INT'L.					
3539	Mona Lisa/Foolish One	1959	6.25	12.50	25.00
3546	Pretend/Rockin' Love	1959	6.25	12.50	25.00
3550	Some Enchanted Evening/I Can't Forget	1960	6.25	12.50	25.00
3555	South of the Border/I'm Comin' Home	1960	6.25	12.50	25.00
3564	The Wayward Wind/Born to Be Bad	1961	6.25	12.50	25.00
3569	I Ain't Got No Home/If I Could Change You	1961	6.25	12.50	25.00
3579	When I Grow Too Old to Dream/Mountain Dew	1962	6.25	12.50	25.00

Albums

Number	Title (A Side/B Side)	Yr	VG	VG+	NM
PHILLIPS INT'L.					
PLP-1960 [M]	Like Mann	1960	150.00	300.00	600.00

MANN, HERBIE

12-Inch Singles

Number	Title (A Side/B Side)	Yr	VG	VG+	NM
ATLANTIC					
DSKO 172 [DJ]	Jisco Dazz/Body Oil	1979	2.50	5.00	10.00
DK 4708	Superman/Etagui	1978	2.50	5.00	10.00

45s

Number	Title (A Side/B Side)	Yr	VG	VG+	NM
ATLANTIC					
2262	Theme from Malamondo/Fiddler on the Roof	1964	2.50	5.00	10.00
2363	Is Paris Burning?/Happy Brass	1966	2.00	4.00	8.00
2379	The Honeydripper/The Puppet	1967	—	3.00	6.00
2392	Day Tripper/A Good Thing (Is Hard to Come By)	1967	2.00	4.00	8.00
—With Tamiko Jones					
2393	Uskudar/Turkish Coffee	1967	—	3.00	6.00
2399	The Beat Goes On/Free for All	1967	—	3.00	6.00
2444	To Sir with Love/Hold Back (Just a Little Longer)	1967	—	3.00	6.00
2451	Cottage for Sale/Live for Life	1967	—	3.00	6.00
—With Carmen McRae					
2498	By the Time I Get to Phoenix/Sports Car	1968	—	3.00	6.00
2621	Memphis Underground/New Orleans	1969	—	3.00	6.00
2661	Battle Hymn of the Republic/Hold On, I'm Comin'	1969	—	3.00	6.00
2671	It's a Funky Thing — Right On (Part 1)/It's a Funky Thing — Right On (Part 2)	1969	—	3.00	6.00
2882	Respect Yourself/Mississippi Gambler	1972	—	2.50	5.00
2960	Do It Again/Turtle Baby	1973	—	2.50	5.00
3009	Now I've Found a Lady/Spin Ball	1974	—	2.50	5.00
3037	Anata/Sound of Wood Wind	1974	—	2.50	5.00
3219	My Girl/Rivers of Babylon	1974	—	2.50	5.00
3246	Hijack/Orient Express	1975	—	2.00	4.00
3282	Waterbed/Body Oil	1975	—	2.00	4.00
3313	Stars and Stripes Forever (Part 1)/Stars and Stripes Forever (Part 2)	1976	—	2.50	5.00
3343	Cajun Moon/So Git It While You Can	1976	—	2.00	4.00
3390	Birdwalk/Aria	1977	—	2.00	4.00
3536	The Closer I Get to You/Watermelon Man	1978	—	2.00	4.00
3547	Superman/Etagui	1978	—	2.00	4.00
3547 [PS]	Superman/Etagui	1978	—	3.00	6.00
3575	Jisco Dazz/Time Is a Thief	1979	—	2.00	4.00
5009	Uhuru/High Life	1960	3.00	6.00	12.00
5010	Walkin'/(B-side unknown)	1961	3.00	6.00	12.00
5015	This Little Girl of Mine/Why Don't You Do Right	1961	3.00	6.00	12.00
5019	Carnival/La La La	1962	3.00	6.00	12.00
5020	Sumemrtime/Comin' Home Baby	1962	3.00	6.00	12.00
5023	Right Now/Boroquino	1962	3.00	6.00	12.00
5026	Blues Walk Bossa Nova/It Must Be Love Bossa Nova	1962	3.00	6.00	12.00
5031	Bag's Groove/New York Is a Jungle Festival	1963	2.50	5.00	10.00
5032	The Girl from Ipanema/Soft Winds	1964	2.50	5.00	10.00
5036	Love in Peace/One Note Samba	1964	2.50	5.00	10.00
5037	Harlem Nocturne/Not Now — Not Later	1964	2.50	5.00	10.00
5038	Down By the Riverside/Insensatez	1964	2.50	5.00	10.00
5044	Soul Guajira/Hushi Mushi	1965	2.00	4.00	8.00
5048	The Joker/Feeling Good	1965	2.00	4.00	8.00
5064	Today/Arrastao	1966	2.00	4.00	8.00
5065	Our Man Flint/Yesterday	1966	2.00	4.00	8.00
5070	Theme from This Is My Beloved/Scratch	1966	2.00	4.00	8.00
5074	Philly Dog/Frere Jacques	1966	2.00	4.00	8.00
89880	Theme from "Tootsie"/(B-side unknown)	1983	—	2.00	4.00
A&M					
896	Unchain My Heart/Glory of Love	1968	2.00	4.00	8.00
BETHLEHEM					
3040	Chicken Little/My Little Suede Shoes	1962	2.50	5.00	10.00
11036	Love Is a Simple Thing/Jasmine	1959	3.00	6.00	12.00
11037	Surrey with the Fringe on Top/Sorimao	1959	3.00	6.00	12.00
11038	Cuban Love Song/Scuffles	1959	3.00	6.00	12.00
PRESTIGE					
113	Let's March (Part 1)/Let's March (Part 2)	1957	5.00	10.00	20.00
318	Cherry Point/Early Morning Blues	1964	2.50	5.00	10.00
416	Tutti Flutee (Part 1)/Tutti Flutee (Part 2)	1966	2.00	4.00	8.00

Albums

Number	Title (A Side/B Side)	Yr	VG	VG+	NM
ATLANTIC					
SD 2-300 [(2)]	The Evolution of Mann	1972	3.75	7.50	15.00
1343 [M]	The Common Ground	1960	3.75	7.50	15.00
SD 1343 [S]	The Common Ground	1960	5.00	10.00	20.00
1371 [M]	The Family of Mann	1961	3.75	7.50	15.00
SD 1371 [S]	The Family of Mann	1961	5.00	10.00	20.00
1380 [M]	Herbie Mann at the Village Gate	1962	3.75	7.50	15.00

Number	Title (A Side/B Side)	Yr	VG	VG+	NM
SD 1380 [S]	Herbie Mann at the Village Gate	1962	5.00	10.00	20.00
1384 [M]	Right Now	1962	3.75	7.50	15.00
SD 1384 [S]	Right Now	1962	5.00	10.00	20.00
1397 [M]	Do the Bossa Nova with Herbie Mann	1962	3.75	7.50	15.00
SD 1397 [S]	Do the Bossa Nova with Herbie Mann	1962	5.00	10.00	20.00
1407 [M]	Herbie Mann Returns to the Village Gate	1963	3.75	7.50	15.00
SD 1407 [S]	Herbie Mann Returns to the Village Gate	1963	5.00	10.00	20.00
1413 [M]	Herbie Mann Live at Newport	1963	3.75	7.50	15.00
SD 1413 [S]	Herbie Mann Live at Newport	1963	5.00	10.00	20.00
1422 [M]	Latin Fever	1964	3.75	7.50	15.00
SD 1422 [S]	Latin Fever	1964	5.00	10.00	20.00
1426 [M]	Nirvana	1964	3.75	7.50	15.00
SD 1426 [S]	Nirvana	1964	5.00	10.00	20.00
1433 [M]	My Kinda Groove	1965	3.75	7.50	15.00
SD 1433 [S]	My Kinda Groove	1965	5.00	10.00	20.00
1437 [M]	The Roar of the Greasepaint, The Smell of the Crowd	1965	3.75	7.50	15.00
SD 1437 [S]	The Roar of the Greasepaint, The Smell of the Crowd	1965	5.00	10.00	20.00
1445 [M]	Standing Ovation at Newport	1965	3.75	7.50	15.00
SD 1445 [S]	Standing Ovation at Newport	1965	5.00	10.00	20.00
1454 [M]	Herbie Mann Today	1966	3.75	7.50	15.00
SD 1454 [S]	Herbie Mann Today	1966	5.00	10.00	20.00
1462 [M]	Monday Night at the Village Gate	1966	3.75	7.50	15.00
SD 1462 [S]	Monday Night at the Village Gate	1966	5.00	10.00	20.00
1464 [M]	Our Mann Flute	1966	3.75	7.50	15.00
SD 1464 [S]	Our Mann Flute	1966	5.00	10.00	20.00
1471 [M]	New Mann at Newport	1967	5.00	10.00	20.00
SD 1471 [S]	New Mann at Newport	1967	3.75	7.50	15.00
1475 [M]	Impressions of the Middle East	1967	5.00	10.00	20.00
SD 1475 [S]	Impressions of the Middle East	1967	3.75	7.50	15.00
1483 [M]	The Beat Goes On	1967	5.00	10.00	20.00
SD 1483 [S]	The Beat Goes On	1967	3.75	7.50	15.00
1490 [M]	The Herbie Mann String Album	1968	6.25	12.50	25.00
SD 1490 [S]	The Herbie Mann String Album	1968	3.75	7.50	15.00
SD 1497	Wailing Dervishes	1968	3.75	7.50	15.00
SD 1507	Windows Open	1969	3.00	6.00	12.00
SD 1513	The Inspiration I Feel	1969	3.75	7.50	15.00
SD 1522	Memphis Underground	1969	3.00	6.00	12.00
SD 1536	Live at the Whisky A-Go-Go	1969	3.00	6.00	12.00
SD 1540	Concerto Grosso in D Blues	1969	3.00	6.00	12.00
SD 1544	The Best of Herbie Mann	1970	3.00	6.00	12.00
SD 1610	Mississippi Gambler	1972	3.00	6.00	12.00
QD 1632 [Q]	Hold On, I'm Comin'	1973	5.00	10.00	20.00
SD 1632	Hold On, I'm Comin'	1973	3.00	6.00	12.00
SD 1642	Turtle Bay	1973	3.00	6.00	12.00
SD 1648	London Underground	1974	3.00	6.00	12.00
SD 1655	Reggae	1974	3.00	6.00	12.00
SD 1658	First Light	1974	3.00	6.00	12.00
SD 1670	Discotheque	1975	3.00	6.00	12.00
SD 1676	Waterbed	1975	3.00	6.00	12.00
SD 1682	Surprises	1976	3.00	6.00	12.00
8141 [M]	Mann and a Woman	1967	5.00	10.00	20.00
SD 8141 [S]	Mann and a Woman	1967	3.75	7.50	15.00
SD 16046	Mellow	1981	2.50	5.00	10.00
SD 18209	Bird in a Silver Cage	1977	2.50	5.00	10.00
SD 19112	Herbie Mann & Fire Island	1977	2.50	5.00	10.00
SD 19169	Brazil — Once Again	1978	2.50	5.00	10.00
SD 19221	Super Mann	1979	2.50	5.00	10.00
SD 19252	Yellow Fever	1980	2.50	5.00	10.00
80077	Astral Island	1983	2.50	5.00	10.00
81285	See Through Spirits	1986	2.50	5.00	10.00
90141	Nirvana	1984	2.50	5.00	10.00
A&M					
2003 [M]	Glory of Love	1967	5.00	10.00	20.00
SP-3003	Glory of Love *—Audiophile reissue (labeled as such)*	198?	3.75	7.50	15.00
SP-3003 [S]	Glory of Love	1967	3.00	6.00	12.00
SP-3008	Trust in Me/Soul Flutes	1969	3.00	6.00	12.00
BETHLEHEM					
BCP-24 [M]	Flamingo, My Goodness — Four Flutes, Vol. 2	1955	12.50	25.00	50.00
BCP-40 [M]	The Herbie Mann-Sam Most Quintet	1956	12.50	25.00	50.00
BCP-58 [M]	Herbie Mann Plays	1956	12.50	25.00	50.00
BCP-63 [M]	Love and the Weather	1956	12.50	25.00	50.00
BCP-1018 [10]	East Coast Jazz 4	1954	25.00	50.00	100.00
BCP-6020 [M]	The Mann with the Most	1960	10.00	20.00	40.00
BCP-6067 [M]	The Epitome of Jazz	1963	7.50	15.00	30.00
COLUMBIA					
CS 1068	Big Boss	1970	3.00	6.00	12.00
CL 2388 [M]	Latin Mann	1965	3.75	7.50	15.00
CS 9188 [S]	Latin Mann	1965	5.00	10.00	20.00
EMBRYO					
520	Stone Flute	1970	3.00	6.00	12.00
526	Muscle Shoals Nitty Gritty	1970	3.00	6.00	12.00
531	Memphis Two-Step	1971	3.00	6.00	12.00
532	Push Push	1971	3.00	6.00	12.00
EPIC					
LN 3395 [M]	Salute to the Flute	1957	15.00	30.00	60.00
LN 3499 [M]	Herbie Mann with the Ilcken Trio	1958	15.00	30.00	60.00
FINNADAR					
9014	Gagaku and Beyond	197?	2.50	5.00	10.00
JAZZLAND					
JLP-5 [M]	Herbie Mann Quintet *—Reissue of Riverside 245*	1960	7.50	15.00	30.00
MILESTONE					
47010	Let Me Tell You	1973	3.00	6.00	12.00
NEW JAZZ					
NJLP-8211 [M]	Just Walkin' *—Purple label*	1958	12.50	25.00	50.00
NJLP-8211 [M]	Just Walkin' *—Blue label with trident logo*	1964	6.25	12.50	25.00
PRESTIGE					
PRLP-7101 [M]	Flute Souffle	1957	20.00	40.00	80.00
PRLP-7124 [M]	Flute Flight	1957	20.00	40.00	80.00
PRLP-7136 [M]	Mann in the Morning	1958	20.00	40.00	80.00
PRLP-7432 [M]	The Best of Herbie Mann	1965	3.75	7.50	15.00
PRST-7432 [R]	The Best of Herbie Mann	1965	3.00	6.00	12.00
PRST-7659	Herbie Mann in Sweden	1969	3.00	6.00	12.00
RIVERSIDE					
RLP 12-234 [M]	Sultry Serenade *—Blue on white label*	1957	15.00	30.00	60.00
RLP 12-234 [M]	Sultry Serenade *—Blue label with reel and microphone logo*	1958	10.00	20.00	40.00
RLP 12-245 [M]	Great Ideas of Western Mann	1957	10.00	20.00	40.00
S-3029	Moody Mann	1969	3.00	6.00	12.00
6084	Great Ideas of Western Mann	197?	2.50	5.00	10.00
SAVOY					
MG-12102 [M]	Flute Suite	1957	12.50	25.00	50.00
MG-12107 [M]	Mann Alone	1957	12.50	25.00	50.00
MG-12108 [M]	Yardbird Suite	1957	12.50	25.00	50.00
SAVOY JAZZ					
SJL-1102	Be Bop Synthesis	197?	2.50	5.00	10.00
SOLID STATE					
SS-18020	Jazz Impressions of Brazil	1968	3.00	6.00	12.00
SS-18023	St. Thomas	1968	3.00	6.00	12.00
SURREY					
S-1015 [M]	Big Band	1965	3.75	7.50	15.00
SS-1015 [S]	Big Band	1965	5.00	10.00	20.00
TRIP					
5031	Super Mann	1974	2.50	5.00	10.00
UNITED ARTISTS					
UAL-4042 [M]	African Suite	1959	7.50	15.00	30.00
UAS-5042 [S]	African Suite	1959	10.00	20.00	40.00
UAS-5638	Brazil Blues	1972	3.00	6.00	12.00
UAJ-14009 [M]	Brasil, Bossa Nova and Blue	1962	7.50	15.00	30.00
UAJ-14022 [M]	St. Thomas	1962	7.50	15.00	30.00
UAJS-15009 [S]	Brasil, Bossa Nova and Blue	1962	10.00	20.00	40.00
UAJS-15022 [S]	St. Thomas	1962	10.00	20.00	40.00
VERVE					
VSP-8 [M]	Bongo, Conga and Flute	1966	3.75	7.50	15.00
VSPS-8 [R]	Bongo, Conga and Flute	1966	3.00	6.00	12.00
VSP-19 [M]	Big Band Mann	1966	3.75	7.50	15.00
VSPS-19 [R]	Big Band Mann	1966	3.00	6.00	12.00
MGVS-6074 [S]	Flautista! — Herbie Mann Plays Afro-Cuban Jazz	1960	7.50	15.00	30.00
MGV-8247 [M]	The Magic Flute of Herbie Mann	1958	10.00	20.00	40.00
V-8247 [M]	The Magic Flute of Herbie Mann	1961	5.00	10.00	20.00
MGV-8336 [M]	Flautista! — Herbie Mann Plays Afro-Cuban Jazz	1959	10.00	20.00	40.00
V-8336 [M]	Flautista! — Herbie Mann Plays Afro-Cuban Jazz	1961	5.00	10.00	20.00
V6-8336 [S]	Flautista! — Herbie Mann Plays Afro-Cuban Jazz	1961	3.75	7.50	15.00
MGV-8392 [M]	Flute, Brass, Vibes and Percussion	1960	7.50	15.00	30.00
V-8392 [M]	Flute, Brass, Vibes and Percussion	1961	5.00	10.00	20.00
V-8527 [M]	The Sound of Mann	1963	5.00	10.00	20.00
V6-8527 [S]	The Sound of Mann	1963	3.75	7.50	15.00
V6-8821 [(2)]	Et Tu Flute	1973	3.75	7.50	15.00

MANN, HERBIE, AND BUDDY COLLETTE

Albums

Number	Title (A Side/B Side)	Yr	VG	VG+	NM
INTERLUDE					
MO-503 [M]	Flute Fraternity *—Reissue of Mode 114*	1959	10.00	20.00	40.00
ST-1103 [S]	Flute Fraternity	1959	7.50	15.00	30.00
MODE					
LP-114 [M]	Flute Fraternity	1957	17.50	35.00	70.00

MANN, HERBIE, AND JOAO GILBERTO

Albums

Number	Title (A Side/B Side)	Yr	VG	VG+	NM
ATLANTIC					
8105 [M]	Herbie Mann and Joao Gilberto with Antonio Carlos Jobim	1965	3.75	7.50	15.00
SD 8105 [S]	Herbie Mann and Joao Gilberto with Antonio Carlos Jobim	1965	5.00	10.00	20.00

MANN, HERBIE, AND MACHITO

Albums

Number	Title (A Side/B Side)	Yr	VG	VG+	NM
ROULETTE					
R-52122 [M]	Afro-Jazziac	1963	3.75	7.50	15.00
SR-52122 [S]	Afro-Jazziac	1963	5.00	10.00	20.00

MANN, JOHNNY, SINGERS

45s

Number	Title (A Side/B Side)	Yr	VG	VG+	NM
EPIC					
10895	Stand Up and Cheer/America, There's So Much to Say	1972	—	2.50	5.00
LIBERTY					
55249	Varsity Drag/Sweet Georgia Brown	1959	2.50	5.00	10.00
55327	East of the Sun/(B-side unknown)	1961	2.00	4.00	8.00
55355	Don't/Love Me	1961	2.00	4.00	8.00
55466	Summersong/Mr. and Mrs. Millionaire	1962	2.00	4.00	8.00
55525	Cotton Fields/Shenandoah	1962	2.00	4.00	8.00
55653	African Noel/Children, Board That Train *—By "The Johnny Mann Children's Choir"*	1963	2.00	4.00	8.00
55799	The Voice of Freedom/Try to Remember	1965	—	3.00	6.00
55871	Cinnamint Shuffle/Rovin' Gambler	1966	—	3.00	6.00
55938	Whither Thou Goest/A Joyful Noise	1966	—	3.00	6.00
55972	Up-Up and Away/Joey Is the Name	1967	—	3.00	6.00
56010	Don't Look Back/Instant Happy	1967	—	3.00	6.00
56083	Snow/If I Only Had Time	1968	2.00	4.00	8.00
56107	Carolina on My Mind/Little Sister	1969	—	3.00	6.00

Albums

Number	Title (A Side/B Side)	Yr	VG	VG+	NM
EPIC					
KE 31954	Stand Up and Cheer!	1973	3.00	6.00	12.00
LIBERTY					
LRP-3134 [M]	Alma Mater	1959	3.75	7.50	15.00
LRP-3149 [M]	Roar Along with the Singing Twenties	1960	3.75	7.50	15.00
LRP-3156 [M]	Swing Along with the Singing Thirties	1960	3.75	7.50	15.00
LRP-3198 [M]	Ballads of the King	1961	3.75	7.50	15.00
LRP-3217 [M]	Ballads of the King, Volume 2	1961	3.75	7.50	15.00

Number	Title (A Side/B Side)	Yr	VG	VG+	NM
LRP-3253 [M]	Golden Folk Song Hits	1963	3.00	6.00	12.00
LRP-3296 [M]	Golden Folk Song Hits, Volume 2	1963	3.00	6.00	12.00
LRP-3355 [M]	Golden Folk Song Hits, Volume 3	1964	3.00	6.00	12.00
LRP-3387 [M]	Invisible Tears	1964	3.00	6.00	12.00
LRP-3391 [M]	The Ballad Sound (Beatle Songs)	1964	3.75	7.50	15.00
LRP-3411 [M]	If I Loved You	1965	3.00	6.00	12.00
LRP-3436 [M]	I'll Remember You	1965	3.00	6.00	12.00
LRP-3447 [M]	Daydream	1966	3.00	6.00	12.00
LRP-3522 [M]	We Wish You a Merry Christmas	1967	3.75	7.50	15.00
LRP-3523 [M]	We Can Fly! Up-Up and Away	1967	3.00	6.00	12.00
LST-7134 [S]	Alma Mater	1959	5.00	10.00	20.00
LST-7149 [S]	Roar Along with the Singing Twenties	1960	5.00	10.00	20.00
LST-7156 [S]	Swing Along with the Singing Thirties	1960	5.00	10.00	20.00
LST-7198 [S]	Ballads of the King	1961	5.00	10.00	20.00
LST-7217 [S]	Ballads of the King, Volume 2	1961	5.00	10.00	20.00
LST-7253 [S]	Golden Folk Song Hits	1963	3.75	7.50	15.00
LST-7296 [S]	Golden Folk Song Hits, Volume 2	1963	3.75	7.50	15.00
LST-7355 [S]	Golden Folk Song Hits, Volume 3	1964	3.75	7.50	15.00
LST-7387 [S]	Invisible Tears	1964	3.75	7.50	15.00
LST-7391 [S]	The Ballad Sound (Beatle Songs)	1964	5.00	10.00	20.00
LST-7411 [S]	If I Loved You	1965	3.75	7.50	15.00
LST-7426 [S]	I'll Remember You	1965	3.75	7.50	15.00
LST-7447 [S]	Daydream	1966	3.75	7.50	15.00
LST-7522 [S]	We Wish You a Merry Christmas	1967	3.75	7.50	15.00
LST-7523 [S]	We Can Fly! Up-Up and Away	1967	3.75	7.50	15.00
LST-7629	Golden	1969	3.00	6.00	12.00
LMM-13017 [M]	The Great Bands with Great Voices Swing the Great Voices of the Great Bands	1962	3.75	7.50	15.00
LSS-14017 [S]	The Great Bands with Great Voices Swing the Great Voices of the Great Bands	1962	5.00	10.00	20.00
SUNSET					
SUM-1115 [M]	The Flowing Voices of the Johnny Mann Singers	196?	2.50	5.00	10.00
SUS-5115 [S]	The Flowing Voices of the Johnny Mann Singers	196?	3.00	6.00	12.00
SUS-5196	Heart Full of Song	1968	3.00	6.00	12.00
SUS-5231	Country Style	1969	3.00	6.00	12.00
SUS-5288	At Our Best	1970	3.00	6.00	12.00
UNITED ARTISTS					
UXS-87 [(2)]	The Johnny Mann Singers Superpak	1972	3.75	7.50	15.00

MANN, MANFRED

Also see MIKE D'ABO; PAUL JONES; MANFRED MANN'S EARTH BAND.

45s

Number	Title (A Side/B Side)	Yr	VG	VG+	NM
ASCOT					
2151	Hubble Bubble (Toil and Trouble)/I'm Your Kingpin	1964	50.00	100.00	200.00
2157	Do Wah Diddy Diddy/What You Gonna Do?	1964	3.75	7.50	15.00
2165	Sha La La/John Hardy	1964	2.50	5.00	10.00
2165 [PS]	Sha La La/John Hardy	1964	6.25	12.50	25.00
2170	Come Tomorrow/What Did I Do Wrong	1965	2.50	5.00	10.00
2170 [PS]	Come Tomorrow/What Did I Do Wrong	1965	6.25	12.50	25.00
2181	Poison Ivy/I Can't Believe What You Say	1965	—	—	—
—Unreleased?					
2184	My Little Red Book/What Am I Doing Wrong	1965	2.50	5.00	10.00
2194	If You Gotta Go, Go Now/The One in the Middle	1965	2.50	5.00	10.00
2210	She Needs Company/Hi Lili, Hi Lo	1966	2.50	5.00	10.00
2241	My Little Red Book/I Can't Believe What You Say	1967	2.50	5.00	10.00
MERCURY					
72607	Just Like a Woman/I Wanna Be Rich	1966	2.50	5.00	10.00
72607 [PS]	Just Like a Woman/I Wanna Be Rich	1966	6.25	12.50	25.00
72629	Semi-Detached Suburban Mr. Jones/Each and Every Day	1966	2.50	5.00	10.00
72675	Ha, Ha, Said the Clown/Feeling So Good	1967	2.50	5.00	10.00
72770	The Mighty Quinn (Quinn the Eskimo)/By Request — Edwin Garvey	1968	2.50	5.00	10.00
—Orange and red swirl label					
72770	The Mighty Quinn (Quinn the Eskimo)/By Request — Edwin Garvey	1968	3.00	6.00	12.00
—Red label with "Mercury" in all capital letters					
72770	The Mighty Quinn (Quinn the Eskimo)/By Request — Edwin Garvey	1968	2.00	4.00	8.00
—Red label with white "Mercury" in a circle					
72770	Quinn the Eskimo/By Request — Edwin Garvey	1968	3.00	6.00	12.00
—Orange and red swirl label					
72770	Quinn the Eskimo/By Request — Edwin Garvey	1968	2.50	5.00	10.00
—Red label with white "Mercury" in a circle					
72822	My Name Is Jack/There Is a Man	1968	2.00	4.00	8.00
72822 [PS]	My Name Is Jack/There Is a Man	1968	3.75	7.50	15.00
72879	Fox on the Run/Too Many People	1968	2.00	4.00	8.00
72921	Ragamuffin Man/A B-Side	1969	2.00	4.00	8.00
POLYDOR					
14026	Sometimes/Snakeskin Garter	1970	—	3.00	6.00
14074	California Coastline/Part Time	1971	—	—	—
—Unreleased					
14097	Please Mrs. Henry/Prayers	1971	—	2.50	5.00
PRESTIGE					
312	5-4-3-2-1/Without You	1964	10.00	20.00	40.00
314	Blue Brave/Brother Jack	1964	25.00	50.00	100.00
UNITED ARTISTS					
0048	Do Wah Diddy Diddy/Sha La La	1973	—	2.50	5.00
—"Silver Spotlight Series" reissue					
0049	Pretty Flamingo/Come Tomorrow	1973	—	2.50	5.00
—"Silver Spotlight Series" reissue					
50040	Pretty Flamingo/You're Standing By	1966	2.50	5.00	10.00
50066	When Will I Be Loved/Do You Have to Do That	1966	2.50	5.00	10.00

Albums

Number	Title (A Side/B Side)	Yr	VG	VG+	NM
ASCOT					
AM-13015 [M]	The Manfred Mann Album	1964	10.00	20.00	40.00
AM-13018 [M]	The Five Faces of Manfred Mann	1965	10.00	20.00	40.00
AM-13021 [M]	My Little Red Book of Winners	1965	10.00	20.00	40.00
AM-13024 [M]	Mann Made	1966	10.00	20.00	40.00
AS-16015 [P]	The Manfred Mann Album	1964	12.50	25.00	50.00
AS-16018 [P]	The Five Faces of Manfred Mann	1965	12.50	25.00	50.00
AS-16021 [S]	My Little Red Book of Winners	1965	12.50	25.00	50.00
AS-16024 [S]	Mann Made	1966	12.50	25.00	50.00
CAPITOL					
SM-11688	The Best of Manfred Mann	1977	2.50	5.00	10.00
SN-16073	The Best of Manfred Mann	1980	2.00	4.00	8.00
JANUS					
JXS-3064	The Best of Manfred Mann	1974	3.00	6.00	12.00
MERCURY					
SR-61168	The Mighty Quinn	1968	6.25	12.50	25.00
POLYDOR					
24-4013	Chapter Three	1970	3.75	7.50	15.00
UNITED ARTISTS					
94 [DJ]	Manfred Mann Interview	1966	50.00	100.00	200.00
—Promotional album in plain white jacket					
UAL 3549 [M]	Pretty Flamingo	1966	7.50	15.00	30.00
UAL 3551 [M]	Manfred Mann's Greatest Hits	1966	7.50	15.00	30.00
UAS 6549 [S]	Pretty Flamingo	1966	10.00	20.00	40.00
UAS 6551 [P]	Manfred Mann's Greatest Hits	1966	10.00	20.00	40.00
—"Do Wah Diddy Diddy," "Sha La La," "I Got You Babe" and "Satisfaction" are rechanneled.					

MANN, MANFRED'S, EARTH BAND

Also see MANFRED MANN.

12-Inch Singles

Number	Title (A Side/B Side)	Yr	VG	VG+	NM
ARISTA					
ADP 9110 [DJ]	Demolition Man (same on both sides)	1983	2.00	4.00	8.00
ADP 9147 [DJ]	Runner (same on both sides)	1983	2.00	4.00	8.00

45s

Number	Title (A Side/B Side)	Yr	VG	VG+	NM
ARISTA					
9143	Runner/Where Do They Send Them	1984	—	2.00	4.00
—First pressing has whitish label					
9143	Runner/Where Do They Send Them	1984	—	—	3.00
—Second pressing has black label					
9203	Rebel/Figures on a Rock	1984	—	—	3.00
POLYDOR					
14113	Living Without You/Tribute	1972	—	2.50	5.00
14130	I'm Up and Leaving/Part Time Man	1972	—	2.50	5.00
14130 [PS]	I'm Up and Leaving/Part Time Man	1972	2.50	5.00	10.00
14160	It's All Over Now, Baby Blue/Ashes	1973	—	2.50	5.00
14173	Mardi Gras Day/Sad Joy	1973	—	2.50	5.00
14191	Get Your Rocks Off/Wind	1973	—	2.50	5.00
14205	Joybringer/Cloudy Eyes	1973	—	2.50	5.00
14225	Father of Night/Solar Fire Two	1974	—	2.50	5.00
WARNER BROS.					
8152	Spirit in the Night/As Above So Below	1975	—	—	—
—Unreleased?					
8176	Spirit in the Night/As Above So Below	1976	—	3.00	6.00
8176 [DJ]	Spirit in the Night (Long)/Spirit in the Night (Short)	1976	—	3.00	6.00
8252	Blinded by the Light/Starbird No. 2	1976	—	2.50	5.00
8252 [PS]	Blinded by the Light/Starbird No. 2	1976	2.00	4.00	8.00
8355	Spirit in the Night/Questions	1977	—	2.50	5.00
—This has newly-recorded vocal tracks by Chris Thompson					
8574	California/Bouillabaise	1978	—	2.50	5.00
8620	Davy's on the Road Again/Bouillabaise	1978	—	2.50	5.00
8850	You Angel You/"Belle" of the Earth	1979	—	2.00	4.00
49678	For You/Fool I Am	1981	—	2.50	5.00
49762	Adolescent Dream/Lies (Through the 80's)	1981	—	2.00	4.00

Albums

Number	Title (A Side/B Side)	Yr	VG	VG+	NM
ARISTA					
AL 8194	Somewhere in Afrika	1983	2.50	5.00	10.00
POLYDOR					
PD-5015	Manfred Mann's Earth Band	1971	3.75	7.50	15.00
PD-5031	Glorified, Magnified	1972	3.75	7.50	15.00
PD-5050	Get Your Rocks Off	1973	3.75	7.50	15.00
PD-1-6019	Solar Fire	1974	3.75	7.50	15.00
WARNER BROS.					
BS 2826	The Good Earth	1974	3.00	6.00	12.00
BS 2877	Nightingales and Bombers	1975	3.00	6.00	12.00
BS 2965	The Roaring Silence	1976	3.00	6.00	12.00
—Orange cover					
BSK 3055	The Roaring Silence	1977	2.50	5.00	10.00
—Blue cover; re-recording of "Spirit in the Night" is added					
BSK 3157	Watch	1978	2.50	5.00	10.00
BSK 3302	Angel Station	1979	2.50	5.00	10.00
BSK 3498	Chance	1980	2.50	5.00	10.00

MANN, REV. COLUMBUS

45s

Number	Title (A Side/B Side)	Yr	VG	VG+	NM
CYE					
1001	Soon Very Soon (He's Coming Back)/(B-side unknown)	196?	10.00	20.00	40.00
TAMLA					
54047	Jesus Loves/They Shall Be Mine	1961	12.50	25.00	50.00

Albums

Number	Title (A Side/B Side)	Yr	VG	VG+	NM
TAMLA					
T-227 [M]	They Shall Be Mine	1962	2000.	3000.	4000.
WINGATE					
701 [M]	He Satisfies Me	196?	300.00	600.00	900.00

MANN, SHADOW

Albums

Number	Title (A Side/B Side)	Yr	VG	VG+	NM
TOMORROW					
TPS-69001	Come Live with Me	1974	15.00	30.00	60.00

MANNA, CHARLIE

45s

Number	Title (A Side/B Side)	Yr	VG	VG+	NM
DECCA					
31320	I Want Me Crayons (Part 1)/I Want Me Crayons (Part 2)	1961	2.50	5.00	10.00
31320 [PS]	I Want Me Crayons (Part 1)/I Want Me Crayons (Part 2)	1961	3.00	6.00	12.00
JUBILEE					
5498	Dear Sally, Mary, Lou/Give Me a Chance to Explain	1965	2.00	4.00	8.00

Albums

DECCA

Number	Title (A Side/B Side)	Yr	VG	VG+	NM
DL 4159 [M]	Manna Overboard!!	1961	6.25	12.50	25.00
DL 4213 [M]	Manna Live!!	1962	6.25	12.50	25.00
DL 74159 [R]	Manna Overboard!!	1961	3.75	7.50	15.00
DL 74213 [R]	Manna Live!!	1962	3.75	7.50	15.00

VERVE

Number	Title (A Side/B Side)	Yr	VG	VG+	NM
V-15051 [M]	The Rise and Fall of the Great Society	1966	3.00	6.00	12.00
V6-15051 [S]	The Rise and Fall of the Great Society	1966	3.75	7.50	15.00

MANNING, TERRY

Albums

ENTERPRISE

Number	Title (A Side/B Side)	Yr	VG	VG+	NM
ENS-1008	Home Sweet Home	1969	10.00	20.00	40.00

MANNO, TOMMY

45s

ATLANTIC

Number	Title (A Side/B Side)	Yr	VG	VG+	NM
2149	Too Good to Be True/That's for Me to Know	1962	3.00	6.00	12.00

MANSON, CHARLES

Albums

AWARENESS

Number	Title (A Side/B Side)	Yr	VG	VG+	NM
08903-1056	Lie: The Love and Terror Cult	1987	5.00	10.00	20.00
LP-2144	Lie: The Love and Terror Cult	197?	10.00	20.00	40.00

ESP-DISK'

Number	Title (A Side/B Side)	Yr	VG	VG+	NM
2003	Lie: The Love and Terror Cult	1970	50.00	100.00	200.00

MANTLE, MICKEY

Also see TERESA BREWER.

Albums

RCA VICTOR

Number	Title (A Side/B Side)	Yr	VG	VG+	NM
LPM 1704 [M]	My Favorite Hits	1958	100.00	200.00	400.00

MANTOVANI

45s

LONDON

Number	Title (A Side/B Side)	Yr	VG	VG+	NM
1000	Tell Me You Love Me/Le Chaland Qui Passe	1951	3.00	6.00	12.00
1017	Wyoming/Under the Roofs of Paris	1951	3.00	6.00	12.00
1018	For You/Kisses in the Dark	1951	3.00	6.00	12.00
1019	Diane/Babette	1951	3.00	6.00	12.00
1020	Charmaine/Just for a Little While	1951	3.00	6.00	12.00
1170	At Dawning/I Love You Truly	1952	3.00	6.00	12.00
1171	Greensleeves/Love Makes the World Go Round	1952	3.00	6.00	12.00
1173	Love Here in My Heart/Poeme	1952	3.00	6.00	12.00
1174	Lovely Lady/Mexicali Rose	1952	3.00	6.00	12.00
1175	Dancing with Tears in My Eyes/Dear Love, My Love	1952	3.00	6.00	12.00
1205	Was It a Dream/It Happened in Monterey	1952	3.00	6.00	12.00
1223	Symphony/Faith	1952	3.00	6.00	12.00
1236	Agnes Waltz/Die Schonbrunner Waltz	1952	3.00	6.00	12.00
1237	Some Enchanted Evening/Gypsy Love Waltz	1952	3.00	6.00	12.00
1245	La Comparsita/Tango Della Luna	1952	3.00	6.00	12.00
1253	Teddy Bear's Christmas/The Whistling Boy	1952	3.00	6.00	12.00
1268	Roses from the South/Blue Danube	1952	3.00	6.00	12.00
1269	Wine, Women and Song Waltz/Village Swallows	1952	3.00	6.00	12.00
1271	Acceleration/Emperor Waltz	1952	3.00	6.00	12.00
1272	Vienna Blood Waltz/You and You	1952	3.00	6.00	12.00
1273	Voices of Spring Waltz/An Artist's Life	1952	3.00	6.00	12.00
1274	Treasure Waltz/1001 Nights	1952	3.00	6.00	12.00
1280	White Christmas/Adeste Fideles	1952	3.00	6.00	12.00
1287	Gypsy Legend/Czardas	1953	2.50	5.00	10.00
1300	Love's Dream After the Ball/Red Petticoats	1953	2.50	5.00	10.00
1307	Ah! Sweet Mystery of Life/Kiss in the Dark	1953	2.50	5.00	10.00
1308	Kiss Me Again/Italian Street Song	1953	2.50	5.00	10.00
1309	Sweethearts/Falling in Love with Someone	1953	2.50	5.00	10.00
1310	Indian Summer/Land of Romance	1953	2.50	5.00	10.00
1328	The Moulin Rouge Theme (Where Is Your Heart)/ Vola Columba	1953	2.50	5.00	10.00
1332	Adios Muchachos/Speakeasy	1953	2.50	5.00	10.00
1333	Ave Maria/Ombra Mai Fa (Largo)	1953	2.50	5.00	10.00
1354	Queen Elizabeth Waltz/Royal Blue Waltz	1953	2.50	5.00	10.00
1355	Suddenly/Beautiful Dreamer	1953	2.50	5.00	10.00
1361	Chiquita Mia/Ramona	1953	2.50	5.00	10.00
1369	Jamaican Rumba/Swedish Rhapsody	1953	2.50	5.00	10.00
1380	The Melba Waltz/We'll Gather Lilacs	1953	2.50	5.00	10.00
1394	The Skaters' Waltz/The Midnight Waltz	1953	2.50	5.00	10.00
1443	I Live for You/Luxembourg Polka	1954	2.50	5.00	10.00
1466	Wanting You/I Bring a Love Song	1954	2.50	5.00	10.00
1467	Desert Song/When I Grow Too Old to Dream	1954	2.50	5.00	10.00
1468	Lover, Come Back to Me/You Will Remember Vienna	1954	2.50	5.00	10.00
1469	Will You Remember/Softly As In Morning Sunrise	1954	2.50	5.00	10.00
1471	Dream, Dream, Dream/Bewitched	1954	2.50	5.00	10.00
1483	June Night/Little Swiss Waltz	1954	2.50	5.00	10.00
1507	Lonely Ballerina/You Stepped Out of a Dream	1954	2.50	5.00	10.00
1510	Lazy Gondolier/Longing	1954	2.50	5.00	10.00
1543	Begin the Beguine/Our Dream Waltz	1955	2.50	5.00	10.00
1547	Me Chere Amie/Amoreuse	1955	2.50	5.00	10.00
1604	Brass Buttons/Edelma	1955	2.50	5.00	10.00
1617	When You Lose the One You Love/Angelus	1956	2.00	4.00	8.00
1646	Candlelight/Spring in Montmartre	1956	2.00	4.00	8.00
1669	Hearts of Paris/Merry-Go-Round Waltz	1956	2.00	4.00	8.00
1698	Song of Sorrento/Valse Campestre	1957	2.00	4.00	8.00
1708	Toyshop Ballet/Habanero	1957	2.00	4.00	8.00
1746	Around the World/The Road to Ballingarry	1957	2.00	4.00	8.00
1746 [PS]	Around the World/The Road to Ballingarry	1957	3.00	6.00	12.00
1761	Let Me Be Loved/Call of the West	1957	3.75	7.50	15.00
1761 [PS]	Let Me Be Loved/Call of the West	1957	15.00	30.00	60.00
—Sought-after sleeve has a photo of James Dean					
1790	To My Love/The Story of Three Loves	1958	2.00	4.00	8.00
1823	Only Yesterday/Tulips from Amsterdam	1958	2.00	4.00	8.00
1840	Come Prima/The Canary	1958	2.00	4.00	8.00
1859	Summertime/This Nearly Was Mine	1959	2.00	4.00	8.00
1919	Tenderly/Jamaica Farewell	1960	2.00	4.00	8.00
1927	In the Spring/Song Without End	1960	2.00	4.00	8.00
1946	Theme from "The Sundowners"/Mine Alone	1960	2.00	4.00	8.00
1947	Irma La Douce/Count of Luxembourg Waltz	1960	2.00	4.00	8.00
1953	Main Theme from Exodus (Ari's Theme)/Karen	1960	2.00	4.00	8.00
1953 [PS]	Main Theme from Exodus (Ari's Theme)/Karen	1960	2.50	5.00	10.00
1983	Theme from "The Valiant Years"/Non Dimenticar	1961	2.00	4.00	8.00
1999	Theme from "Carnival"/Do Re Mi	1961	2.00	4.00	8.00
2000	Theme from "Greengage Summer"/Theme from "Rocco and His Brothers"	1961	2.00	4.00	8.00
2021	Moon River/Sail Away	1961	2.00	4.00	8.00
9520	The Waltz You Saved for Me/Whistle Down the Wind	1962	—	3.00	6.00
9543	Advise and Consent/Let Me Call You Sweetheart	1962	—	3.00	6.00
9552	What Kind of Fool Am I/Someone Nice Like You	1962	—	3.00	6.00
9567	Mutiny on the Bounty Theme/Love Song from Mutiny on the Bounty	1962	—	3.00	6.00
9595	Elizabethan Serenade/A Girl Named Tamiko	1963	—	3.00	6.00
9604	My Moonlight Madonna/Home in the Meadow	1963	—	3.00	6.00
9624	Take the "A" Train/Manhattan Lullaby	1963	—	3.00	6.00
9626	The Bowery/Take the "A" Train	1963	—	3.00	6.00
9653	Two Guitars/Hava Nagila	1964	—	3.00	6.00
9655	Charade/The Fall of Love	1964	—	3.00	6.00
9674	The Churchill March/Love Theme from The Carpetbaggers	1964	—	3.00	6.00
9711	Return to Peyton Place/I Left My Heart in San Francisco	1964	—	3.00	6.00
9734	Fiddler on the Roof/Kanshi I (Sad Am I)	1965	—	3.00	6.00
20013	Ebb Tide/Games That Lovers Play	1966	—	3.00	6.00
20040	The Willow Tree/Villa Rides	1967	—	3.00	6.00
20045	Delilah/Both Sides Now	1968	—	2.50	5.00
20056	Aquarius/Where Did Our Summers Go	1969	—	2.50	5.00
20064	Theme from "Love Story"/Loss of Love	1970	—	2.00	4.00
20070	All of a Sudden/Winter World of Love	1971	—	2.00	4.00

7-Inch Extended Plays

LONDON

Number	Title (A Side/B Side)	Yr	VG	VG+	NM
BEP 6001	*Blue Danube/Roses from the South/Wine, Women and Song/Village Swallows	195?	2.50	5.00	10.00
BEP 6001 [PS]	Strauss Waltzes	195?	2.50	5.00	10.00
BEP 6002	*Tales from the Vienna Woods/Morning Papers/ You and You/Vienna Blood	195?	2.50	5.00	10.00
BEP 6002 [PS]	Strauss Waltzes	195?	2.50	5.00	10.00
BEP 6003	*Emperor Waltz/Accelerations/Voices of Spring/ Artists Life	195?	2.50	5.00	10.00
BEP 6003 [PS]	Strauss Waltzes	195?	2.50	5.00	10.00
BEP 6004	*Greensleeves/Love Makes the World Go Round/ A Dawning/I Love You Truly	195?	2.50	5.00	10.00
BEP 6004 [PS]	Favorite Waltzes	195?	2.50	5.00	10.00
BEP 6005	*Mexicali Rose/Lovely Lady Love/Here Is My Heart/My Moonlight Madonna	195?	2.50	5.00	10.00
BEP 6005 [PS]	Favorite Waltzes	195?	2.50	5.00	10.00
BEP 6006	*Dancing with Tears in My Eyes/Dear Love, My Love/Was It a Dream?/It Happened in Monterey	195?	2.50	5.00	10.00
BEP 6006 [PS]	Favorite Waltzes	195?	2.50	5.00	10.00
BEP 6007	*El Gracio/Tango D'Amore/The Agnes Waltz/Die Schonbrunner Waltz	195?	2.50	5.00	10.00
BEP 6007 [PS]	Dance Time	195?	2.50	5.00	10.00
BEP 6008	*Tell Me You Love Me/Le Chaland Qui Passe/ Symphony/Faith	195?	2.50	5.00	10.00
BEP 6008 [PS]	Dance Time	195?	2.50	5.00	10.00
BEP 6009	*Carriage and Pair/Bees in the Bonnet/Oh Mama Mama/Gypsy Trumpeter	195?	2.50	5.00	10.00
BEP 6009 [PS]	Highlights	195?	2.50	5.00	10.00
BEP 6010	*La Cumpasita/Tango de la Luna/Mexican Starlight/Tango Bolero	195?	2.50	5.00	10.00
BEP 6010 [PS]	Dance Time	195?	2.50	5.00	10.00
BEP 6011	*Some Enchanted Evening/Gypsy Love/Hejra Kati/Love Is a Song	195?	2.50	5.00	10.00
BEP 6011 [PS]	Highlights	195?	2.50	5.00	10.00
BEP 6012	*Under the Roofs of Paris/Wyoming/Kisses in the Dark/For You	195?	2.50	5.00	10.00
BEP 6012 [PS]	Waltzing with Mantovani	195?	2.50	5.00	10.00
BEP 6013	*Diane/Babette/Charmaine/Just for Awhile	195?	2.50	5.00	10.00
BEP 6013 [PS]	Waltzing with Mantovani	195?	2.50	5.00	10.00
BEP 6014	*Beyond the Sea (La Mer)/Night and Day/The Green Cockatoo/El Toreador	195?	2.50	5.00	10.00
BEP 6014 [PS]	Mantovani Concert	195?	2.50	5.00	10.00
BEP 6015	Clair de Lune//Lullaby of the Bells	195?	2.50	5.00	10.00
BEP 6015 [PS]	Music from the Films	195?	2.50	5.00	10.00
BEP 6016	*Prelude to the Stars/The Way to the Stars/Nature Boy/Ritual Fire Dance	195?	2.50	5.00	10.00
BEP 6016 [PS]	Mantovani Concert	195?	2.50	5.00	10.00
BEP 6017	Warsaw Concerto//Cornish Rhapsody	195?	2.50	5.00	10.00
BEP 6017 [PS]	Music from the Films	195?	2.50	5.00	10.00
BEP 6074	*Indian Summer/A Kiss in the Dark/Sweethearts/ Falling in Love with Someone	195?	2.00	4.00	8.00
BEP 6074 [PS]	The Music of Victor Herbert	195?	2.00	4.00	8.00
BEP 6075	*Ah! Sweet Mystery of Life/To the Land of My Own Romance/Kiss Me Again/Indian Street Song	195?	2.00	4.00	8.00
BEP 6075 [PS]	The Music of Victor Herbert	195?	2.00	4.00	8.00
BEP 6320	*September Song/Intermezzo/Over the Rainbow/Laura	195?	2.00	4.00	8.00
BEP 6320 [PS]	Mantovani Film Encores, Vol. 1	195?	2.00	4.00	8.00

Albums

BAINBRIDGE

Number	Title (A Side/B Side)	Yr	VG	VG+	NM
BT-6277	Mantovani's Italia	1988	2.00	4.00	8.00
8001 [(2)]	The Magic of Mantovani: Live at the Royal Festival Hall	1982	3.00	6.00	12.00

FLEETWOOD

Number	Title (A Side/B Side)	Yr	VG	VG+	NM
FMS 1019	90 Minutes with Mantovani	1978	3.00	6.00	12.00
—Side 1: Great Songs of Christmas (reissue of London recordings); Side 2: Great Songs for All Seasons					

HOLIDAY

Number	Title (A Side/B Side)	Yr	VG	VG+	NM
HDY 1928	Holy Night	1981	2.50	5.00	10.00

Number	Title (A Side/B Side)	Yr	VG	VG+	NM
LONDON					
SS 1 [S]	Mantovani Stereo Showcase	1959	5.00	10.00	20.00
PS 106 [S]	Gems Forever	1959	5.00	10.00	20.00
PS 112 [S]	Music from the Films	1959	3.75	7.50	15.00
PS 118 [S]	Strauss Waltzes	1959	5.00	10.00	20.00
PS 119 [S]	Waltz Encores	1959	5.00	10.00	20.00
PS 124 [S]	Film Encores	1959	3.75	7.50	15.00
PS 125 [S]	Song Hits from Theatreland	1959	3.75	7.50	15.00
PS 133 [S]	Concert Encores	1959	5.00	10.00	20.00
PS 142 [S]	Christmas Carols	1959	5.00	10.00	20.00
—Originals have blue back cover, "Stereophonic" on upper left front cover and dark blue "FFSS" labels					
PS 142 [S]	Christmas Carols	196?	3.75	7.50	15.00
—Reissue with white back cover					
PS 147 [S]	Continental Encores	1959	5.00	10.00	20.00
PS 164 [S]	Film Encores, Vol. 2	1959	5.00	10.00	20.00
PS 165 [S]	The Music of Victor Herbert and Sigmund Romberg	1959	5.00	10.00	20.00
PS 165/6 [(2) S]	All-American Showcase	1959	6.25	12.50	25.00
PS 166 [S]	The Music of Irving Berlin and Rudolf Friml	1959	5.00	10.00	20.00
PS 182 [S]	The American Scene	1960	3.75	7.50	15.00
PS 193 [S]	Songs to Remember	1960	3.75	7.50	15.00
PS 202 [S]	Operetta Memories	1960	3.75	7.50	15.00
PS 224 [S]	Mantovani Plays Music from Exodus and Other Great Themes	1960	3.75	7.50	15.00
PS 232 [S]	Italia Mia	1961	3.75	7.50	15.00
PS 242 [S]	Themes from Broadway (Carnival)	1961	3.75	7.50	15.00
PS 245 [S]	Songs of Praise	1961	3.00	6.00	12.00
PS 248 [S]	American Waltzes	1962	3.00	6.00	12.00
PS 249 [S]	Moon River and Other Great Film Themes	1962	3.00	6.00	12.00
PS 269 [S]	Classical Encores	1963	3.00	6.00	12.00
PS 270 [S]	Stop the World—I Want to Get Off/Oliver	1962	3.00	6.00	12.00
PS 280 [S]	The World's Great Love Songs	1963	3.00	6.00	12.00
PS 295 [S]	Latin Rendezvous	1963	3.00	6.00	12.00
PS 328 [S]	Mantovani/Manhattan	1963	3.00	6.00	12.00
PS 338 [S]	Christmas Greetings from Mantovani	1963	3.75	7.50	15.00
PS 360 [S]	Folk Songs Around the World	1964	3.00	6.00	12.00
PS 392 [S]	The Incomparable Mantovani	1964	3.00	6.00	12.00
PS 419 [S]	The Mantovani Sound — Big Hits from Broadway and Hollywood	1965	3.00	6.00	12.00
PS 422 [S]	Mantovani Ole	1965	3.00	6.00	12.00
PS 448 [S]	Mantovani Magic	1966	3.00	6.00	12.00
PS 474 [S]	Mr. Music...Mantovani	1966	3.00	6.00	12.00
PS 483 [S]	Mantovani's Golden Hits	1967	3.00	6.00	12.00
PS 516 [S]	Mantovani/Hollywood	1967	3.00	6.00	12.00
PS 526 [S]	The Mantovani Touch	1968	3.00	6.00	12.00
PS 532 [S]	Mantovani/Tango	1968	3.00	6.00	12.00
PS 542 [S]	Mantovani...Memories	1968	3.00	6.00	12.00
PS 548 [S]	The Mantovani Scene	1969	3.00	6.00	12.00
PS 565 [S]	The World of Mantovani	1969	3.00	6.00	12.00
LL 570 [M]	Greensleeves (A Selection of Favorite Waltzes)	1952	5.00	10.00	20.00
PS 570	Greensleeves	1970	3.00	6.00	12.00
PS 572 [S]	Mantovani Today	1970	3.00	6.00	12.00
PS 578 [S]	Mantovani In Concert	1970	3.00	6.00	12.00
XPS 585/6 [(2) S]	From Monty with Love	1971	3.75	7.50	15.00
XPS 598 [S]	To Lovers Everywhere U.S.A.	1971	3.00	6.00	12.00
XPS 610 [S]	Annunzio Paolo Mantovani (25th Anniversary)	1972	3.00	6.00	12.00
LL 685 [M]	Strauss Waltzes	1953	5.00	10.00	20.00
BP 720/1 [(2)]	Christmas Favorites	19??	3.75	7.50	15.00
LL 766 [M]	An Enchanted Evening with Mantovani	1953	5.00	10.00	20.00
LL 768 [M]	Mantovani Plays Tangos	1953	5.00	10.00	20.00
XPS 900	Gypsy Soul	1972	2.50	5.00	10.00
XPS 902	An Evening with Mantovani	1973	2.50	5.00	10.00
XPS 906	All-Time Greatest Hits, Volume 1	1973	2.50	5.00	10.00
APS 907	Musical Moments	1974	2.50	5.00	10.00
BP 910/1 [(2)]	Romantic Hits	197?	3.00	6.00	12.00
LL 913 [M]	Christmas Carols	1953	3.75	7.50	15.00
—Original recordings in mono					
LL 913 [M]	Christmas Carols	1959	3.00	6.00	12.00
—Mono versions of stereo re-recordings					
XPS 913	The Greatest Gift Is Love	197?	2.50	5.00	10.00
XPS 914	More Golden Hits	197?	2.50	5.00	10.00
XPS 915	American Encores	1976	2.50	5.00	10.00
XPS 917	Strictly Mantovani	1977	2.50	5.00	10.00
PS 921	Favorite Melodies from Opera	1978	2.50	5.00	10.00
LL 979 [M]	Romantic Melodies	1954	5.00	10.00	20.00
LL 1094 [M]	Waltz Time	1954	5.00	10.00	20.00
LL 1150 [M]	The Music of Rudolf Frimi	1955	5.00	10.00	20.00
LL 1219 [M]	Song Hits from Theatreland	1955	5.00	10.00	20.00
LL 1259 [M]	Lonely Ballerina (Musical Modes)	1956	5.00	10.00	20.00
LL 1262 [M]	Gershwin: Concerto	1955	5.00	10.00	20.00
LL 1262 [M]	Gershwin: Rhapsody in Blue	1955	5.00	10.00	20.00
LL 1331 [M]	Operatic Arias	1955	5.00	10.00	20.00
LL 1452 [M]	Waltzes of Irving Berlin	1956	5.00	10.00	20.00
LL 1502 [M]	Candlelight	195?	3.75	7.50	15.00
LL 1513 [M]	Music from the Films	1956	5.00	10.00	20.00
LL 1525 [M]	Music from the Ballet	1956	5.00	10.00	20.00
LL 1700 [M]	Film Encores	1957	5.00	10.00	20.00
LL 1748 [M]	The World's Favorite Love Songs	1957	5.00	10.00	20.00
LL 3004 [M]	Concert Encores	1958	3.75	7.50	15.00
LL 3032 [M]	Gems Forever	1958	3.75	7.50	15.00
LL 3095 [M]	Continental Encores	1959	3.75	7.50	15.00
LL 3117 [M]	Film Encores, Vol. 2	1959	3.75	7.50	15.00
LL 3122 [M]	The Music of Victor Herbert and Sigmund Romberg	1959	3.75	7.50	15.00
LL 3122/3 [(2) M]	All-American Showcase	1959	5.00	10.00	20.00
LL 3123 [M]	The Music of Irving Berlin and Rudolf Friml	1959	3.75	7.50	15.00
LL 3136 [M]	The American Scene	1960	3.00	6.00	12.00
LL 3149 [M]	Songs to Remember	1960	3.00	6.00	12.00
LL 3181 [M]	Operetta Memories	1960	3.00	6.00	12.00
LL 3231 [M]	Mantovani Plays Music from Exodus and Other Great Themes	1960	3.00	6.00	12.00
LL 3239 [M]	Italia Mia	1961	3.00	6.00	12.00
LL 3250 [M]	Themes from Broadway (Carnival)	1961	3.00	6.00	12.00
LL 3251 [M]	Songs of Praise	1961	2.50	5.00	10.00
LL 3260 [M]	American Waltzes	1962	2.50	5.00	10.00
LL 3261 [M]	Moon River and Other Great Film Themes	1962	2.50	5.00	10.00
LL 3269 [M]	Classical Encores	1963	2.50	5.00	10.00
LL 3270 [M]	Stop the World—I Want to Get Off/Oliver	1962	2.50	5.00	10.00
LL 3280 [M]	The World's Great Love Songs	1963	2.50	5.00	10.00
LL 3295 [M]	Latin Rendezvous	1963	2.50	5.00	10.00
LL 3328 [M]	Mantovani/Manhattan	1963	2.50	5.00	10.00
LL 3338 [M]	Christmas Greetings from Mantovani	1963	3.00	6.00	12.00
LL 3360 [M]	Folk Songs Around the World	1964	2.50	5.00	10.00
LL 3392 [M]	The Incomparable Mantovani	1964	2.50	5.00	10.00
LL 3419 [M]	The Mantovani Sound — Big Hits from Broadway and Hollywood	1965	2.50	5.00	10.00
LL 3422 [M]	Mantovani Ole	1965	2.50	5.00	10.00
LL 3448 [M]	Mantovani Magic	1966	2.50	5.00	10.00
LL 3474 [M]	Mr. Music...Mantovani	1966	2.50	5.00	10.00
LL 3483 [M]	Mantovani's Golden Hits	1967	3.00	6.00	12.00
LL 3516 [M]	Mantovani/Hollywood	1967	3.00	6.00	12.00
LL 3526 [M]	The Mantovani Touch	1968	3.75	7.50	15.00
PM 55001 [M]	Kismet	1964	3.00	6.00	12.00
820085-1	Mantovani's Golden Hits	198?	2.00	4.00	8.00
—Reissue of 483					
820333-1	Mantovani/Tango	198?	2.00	4.00	8.00
—Reissue of 532					
820334-1	The Incomparable Mantovani	198?	2.00	4.00	8.00
—Reissue of 392					
LONDON PHASE 4					
SP-44043 [S]	Kismet	1964	3.75	7.50	15.00
BP 44302/3 [(2)]	Million Sellers	1978	3.00	6.00	12.00

MANZAREK, RAY

Also see THE DOORS; RICK AND THE RAVENS.

Number	Title (A Side/B Side)	Yr	VG	VG+	NM
45s					
MERCURY					
73477	Solar Boat/Moorish Idol	1974	—	2.50	5.00
73601	Downbound Train/Choose Up and Choose Off	1974	—	2.50	5.00
73644	The Whole Thing Started with Rock and Roll (And Now It's Out of Control)/Art Deco Fandango	1974	—	2.50	5.00
Albums					
A&M					
SP-4945	Carmina Burana	1984	2.50	5.00	10.00
MERCURY					
SRM-1-703	The Golden Scarab	1974	3.00	6.00	12.00
SRM-1-1014	The Whole Thing Started with Rock & Roll Now It's Out of Control	1975	3.00	6.00	12.00

MAR-KEYS

Number	Title (A Side/B Side)	Yr	VG	VG+	NM
45s					
SATELLITE					
107	Last Night/Night Before	1960	7.50	15.00	30.00
STAX					
112	Morning After/Diana	1961	3.00	6.00	12.00
114	About Noon/Sack-O-Woe	1961	3.00	6.00	12.00
115	Foxy/One Degree North	1961	3.00	6.00	12.00
121	Pop-Eye Stroll/Po-Dunk	1962	3.00	6.00	12.00
124	What's Happening/You Got It	1962	3.00	6.00	12.00
129	Sailor Man Waltz/Sack-O-Woe	1963	3.00	6.00	12.00
133	The Dribble/Bo Time	1963	3.00	6.00	12.00
156	Beach Bash/Bush Bash	1964	2.50	5.00	10.00
166	The Shovel/Banana Juice	1965	2.50	5.00	10.00
181	Grab This Thing (Part 1)/Grab This Thing (Part 2)	1965	2.50	5.00	10.00
185	Philly Dog/Honey Pot	1966	2.50	5.00	10.00
Albums					
ATLANTIC					
8055 [M]	Last Night	1961	25.00	50.00	100.00
—White "fan" logo on right					
8055 [M]	Last Night	1962	12.50	25.00	50.00
—Black "fan" logo on right					
SD 8055 [R]	Last Night	1966	10.00	20.00	40.00
8062 [M]	Do the Pop-Eye with the Mar-Keys	1962	12.50	25.00	50.00
SD 8062 [R]	Do the Pop-Eye with the Mar-Keys	1966	10.00	20.00	40.00
STAX					
ST-707 [M]	The Great Memphis Sound	1966	12.50	25.00	50.00
STS-707 [R]	The Great Memphis Sound	1966	10.00	20.00	40.00
STS-2025	Damifiknew	1969	5.00	10.00	20.00
STS-2036	Memphis Experience	1971	5.00	10.00	20.00

MAR-KEYS/BOOKER T. AND THE MG'S

Also see each artist's individual listings.

Number	Title (A Side/B Side)	Yr	VG	VG+	NM
Albums					
STAX					
ST-720 [M]	Back to Back	1967	5.00	10.00	20.00
STS-720 [S]	Back to Back	1967	6.25	12.50	25.00

MAR-VELS, THE

Number	Title (A Side/B Side)	Yr	VG	VG+	NM
45s					
ANGIE					
1005	Go On and Have Yourself a Ball/How Do I Keep the Girls Away	1963	5.00	10.00	20.00
BUTANE					
778	Go On and Have Yourself a Ball/How Do I Keep the Girls Away	1963	3.75	7.50	15.00
IN					
102	Surfing at Makeha/Endless Nights	1964	12.50	25.00	50.00
LOVE					
5011/2	Cherry Lips/Could Be You	1958	7.50	15.00	30.00
TAMMY					
1016	Somewhere in Life/Voo Doo Hurt	1961	75.00	150.00	300.00
1019	My Guardian Angel/Marble Stomp	1961	75.00	150.00	300.00

MARAINEY, BIG MEMPHIS

Number	Title (A Side/B Side)	Yr	VG	VG+	NM
45s					
SUN					
184	Call Me Anything, But Call Me/Baby No, No	1953	2000.	3000.	4000.

MARATHONS, THE (1)

Two different groups posing as one. After the success of "Peanut Butter" on Arvee, the label hired another group to be The Marathons after losing a legal battle to keep the "real" group, which was really THE VIBRATIONS in disguise. And the Vibrations had formerly been THE JAYHAWKS. Confused yet?

Number	Title (A Side/B Side)	Yr	VG	VG+	NM
45s					
ARGO					
5389	Peanut Butter/Down in New Orleans	1961	3.75	7.50	15.00
—As "Vibrations Named By Others As MARATHONS"					
ARVEE					
5027	Peanut Butter/Talkin' Trash	1961	5.00	10.00	20.00
5038	Tight Sweater/C. Percy Mercy of Scotland	1961	3.00	6.00	12.00
5048	Chicken Spaceman/You Bug Me Baby	1962	3.00	6.00	12.00
CHESS					
1790	Peanut Butter/Down in New Orleans	1961	4.00	8.00	16.00
PLAZA					
507	Mashed Potatoes One More Time/Little Pancho	1962	3.00	6.00	12.00
Albums					
ARVEE					
A-428 [M]	Peanut Butter	1961	45.00	90.00	180.00

MARATHONS, THE (2)

Completely unrelated to groups (1).

Number	Title (A Side/B Side)	Yr	VG	VG+	NM
45s					
SABRINA					
334	Don't Know Why/The Stranger	1959	30.00	60.00	120.00

MARAUDERS, THE

More than one group.

Number	Title (A Side/B Side)	Yr	VG	VG+	NM
45s					
ALMO					
221	Like You/Slippin' and Slidin'	1965	3.75	7.50	15.00
HAWK					
4002	Sand Flea/Stomp Watch	1962	12.50	25.00	50.00
LAURIE					
3356	Out of Sight, Out of Mind/Jug Band Music	1966	5.00	10.00	20.00
LEE					
9449	Nightmare/Lovin'	1965	7.50	15.00	30.00
SKYVIEW					
001	Since I Met You/I Don't Know How	1966	5.00	10.00	20.00
001 [PS]	Since I Met You/I Don't Know How	1966	12.50	25.00	50.00

MARBLE PHROGG, THE

Number	Title (A Side/B Side)	Yr	VG	VG+	NM
45s					
DERRICK					
8568	Fire/(B-side unknown)	1968	20.00	40.00	80.00
Albums					
DERRICK					
8868	The Marble Phrogg	1968	250.00	500.00	1000.

MARCEAU, MARCEL

Number	Title (A Side/B Side)	Yr	VG	VG+	NM
Albums					
GONE					
LP 1F	The Best of Marcel Marceau	196?	12.50	25.00	50.00
MGM					
SE-	The Best of Marcel Marceau	196?	10.00	20.00	40.00
—The above records are identical: 38 minutes of silence and 2 minutes of applause!					

MARCELS, THE

Number	Title (A Side/B Side)	Yr	VG	VG+	NM
45s					
888					
101	How Deep Is the Ocean/Lonely Boy	1964	3.75	7.50	15.00
ALL EARS					
810085	Blue Moon/Clap Your Hands (When I Clap My Hands)	1981	—	3.00	6.00
BARON					
109	Betty Lou/Take Me Back	197?	2.00	4.00	8.00
CHARTBOUND					
009	Letter Full of Tears/Tell Me	197?	2.00	4.00	8.00
COLPIX					
186	Blue Moon/Goodybe to Love	1961	7.50	15.00	30.00
186 [PS]	Blue Moon/Goodybe to Love	1961	15.00	30.00	60.00
196	Summertime/Teeter-Totter Love	1961	6.25	12.50	25.00
606	You Are My Sunshine/Find Another Fool	1961	6.25	12.50	25.00
612	Heartaches/My Love for You	1961	6.25	12.50	25.00
612 [PS]	Heartaches/My Love for You	1961	25.00	50.00	100.00
617	Merry Twist-Mas/Don't Cry for Me This Christmas	1961	6.25	12.50	25.00
617 [PS]	Merry Twist-Mas/Don't Cry for Me This Christmas	1961	30.00	60.00	120.00
624	My Melancholy Baby/Really Need Your Love	1962	5.00	10.00	20.00
629	Footprints in the Sand/Twistin' Fever	1962	12.50	25.00	50.00
640	Flowerpot/Hold On	1962	7.50	15.00	30.00
651	Loved Her the Whole Week Through/Friendly Loans	1962	6.25	12.50	25.00
665	Alright, Okay, You Win/Lollipop Baby	1962	6.25	12.50	25.00
683	That Old Black Magic/Don't Turn Your Back on Me	1963	6.25	12.50	25.00
687	Give Me Back Your Love/I Wanna Be the Leader	1963	7.50	15.00	30.00
694	One Last Kiss/Teeter-Totter Love	1963	25.00	50.00	100.00
694	One Last Kiss/You Got to Be Sincere	1963	50.00	100.00	200.00
KYRA					
100	Comes Love/Your Red Wagon	1964	25.00	50.00	100.00
—Red vinyl					
100	Comes Love/Your Red Wagon	1964	12.50	25.00	50.00
MONOGRAM					
112	I'll Be Forever Loving You/A Fallen Tear	1974	3.00	6.00	12.00
113	Sweet Was the Wine/Over the Rainbow	1974	3.00	6.00	12.00
115	Two People in the World/Most of All	1974	3.00	6.00	12.00
OWL					
324	(You Gave Me) Peace of Mind/Crazy Bells	197?	2.00	4.00	8.00
QUEEN BEE					
47001	In the Still of the Night/High on a Hill	1973	3.75	7.50	15.00
ROCKY					
13711	(You Gave Me) Peace of Mind/That Lucky Old Sun	1975	2.00	4.00	8.00
—As "The Fabulous Marcels"					
ST. CLAIR					
13711	(You Gave Me) Peace of Mind/That Lucky Old Sun	1975	2.50	5.00	10.00
—As "The Fabulous Marcels"					
Albums					
COLPIX					
CP- [M]	Blue Moon	1961	87.50	175.00	350.00
—Gold label					
CP- [M]	Blue Moon	1963	30.00	60.00	120.00
—Blue label					

MARCH, LITTLE PEGGY

Number	Title (A Side/B Side)	Yr	VG	VG+	NM
45s					
OLDE WORLD					
1105	Average People/Isn't This the Way We Are	1975	2.00	4.00	8.00
RCA VICTOR					
47-8107	Little Me/Pagan Love Song	1962	3.75	7.50	15.00
47-8139	I Will Follow Him/Wind-Up Doll	1963	5.00	10.00	20.00
47-8189	I Wish I Were a Princess/My Teenage Castle	1963	3.75	7.50	15.00
47-8189 [PS]	I Wish I Were a Princess/My Teenage Castle	1963	7.50	15.00	30.00
47-8221	Hello Heartache, Goodbye Love/Boy Crazy	1963	3.75	7.50	15.00
47-8221 [PS]	Hello Heartache, Goodbye Love/Boy Crazy	1963	7.50	15.00	30.00
47-8267	The Impossible Happened/Waterfall	1963	3.00	6.00	12.00
47-8291	My Heart Keeps Telling Me/His	1963	—	—	—
—Unreleased					
47-8302	(I'm Watching) Every Little Move You Make/After You	1963	3.00	6.00	12.00
47-8357	Takin' the Long Way Home/Leave Me Alone	1964	2.50	5.00	10.00
—All records from 1964 on are as "Peggy March"					
47-8418	Oh My, What a Guy/Only You Could Do That to My Heart	1964	2.50	5.00	10.00
47-8460	Watch What You Do With My Baby/Can't Stop Thinking About Him	1964	2.50	5.00	10.00
47-8534	Why Can't He Be You/Losin' My Touch	1965	2.50	5.00	10.00
47-8605	Let Her Go/Your Girl	1965	2.50	5.00	10.00
47-8710	He Couldn't Care Less/Heaven for Lovers	1965	2.50	5.00	10.00
47-8840	Ein Boy Wie Du (A Boy Like You)/Sechs Tage Lang (Six Long Days)	1966	5.00	10.00	20.00
47-8877	Play a Simple Melody/Old Fashioned Wedding	1966	2.50	5.00	10.00
—With Gary Marshall					
47-8903	He's Back Again/Running Scared	1966	2.50	5.00	10.00
47-9033	Fool, Fool, Fool (Look in the Mirror)/Try to See It My Way	1966	2.50	5.00	10.00
47-9143	January First/How Can I Tell Him	1967	2.50	5.00	10.00
47-9223	Mama Dear, Papa Dear/Your Good Girl's Gonna Go Bad	1967	2.50	5.00	10.00
47-9283	This Heart Wasn't Made to Kick Around/Foolin' Around	1967	2.50	5.00	10.00
47-9359	Have a Good Time/Let Me Down Hard	1967	2.50	5.00	10.00
47-9494	If You Would Love Me/Thinking Through My Tears	1968	2.50	5.00	10.00
47-9566	Roses on the Sea/Time and Time Again	1968	2.50	5.00	10.00
47-9627	I've Been Here Before/Aren't You Glad	1968	2.50	5.00	10.00
47-9718	Purple Hat/Try to See It My Way	1969	2.50	5.00	10.00
74-0136	Boom Bang-a Bang/Lilac Skies	1969	2.50	5.00	10.00
Albums					
RCA VICTOR					
LPM-3883 [M]	No Foolin'	1968	10.00	20.00	40.00
LPM- [M]	I Will Follow Him	1963	15.00	30.00	60.00
LSP- [S]	I Will Follow Him	1963	20.00	40.00	80.00
LSP- [S]	No Foolin'	1968	6.25	12.50	25.00

MARCH, LITTLE PEGGY/BENNIE THOMAS

Number	Title (A Side/B Side)	Yr	VG	VG+	NM
Albums					
RCA VICTOR					
LPM- [M]	In Our Fashion	1965	10.00	20.00	40.00
LSP- [S]	In Our Fashion	1965	12.50	25.00	50.00

MARCHAN, BOBBY

Number	Title (A Side/B Side)	Yr	VG	VG+	NM
45s					
ACE					
523	Chickee Wah-Wah/Don't Take Your Love from Me	1956	10.00	20.00	40.00
532	I'll Never Let You Go/I Can't Stop Loving You	1957	7.50	15.00	30.00
557	Rockin' Behind the Iron Curtain/You Can't Stop Her	1959	7.50	15.00	30.00
3004	Push the Button/My Day Is Coming	1974	—	2.50	5.00
3008	God Bless Our Love/My Day Is Coming	1975	—	2.50	5.00
3016	Baby Get Your Yo-Yo/What Can I Do	1975	—	2.50	5.00
ALADDIN					
3189	Just a Little Walk/Have Mercy	1953	15.00	30.00	60.00
BOBBY ROBINSON					
(# unknown)	There's Something on Your Mind/(B-side unknown)	1973	—	3.00	6.00
CAMEO					
405	There's Something About My Baby/Everything a Poor Fool Needs	1966	2.50	5.00	10.00
429	Shake Your Tambourine/Just Be Yourself	1966	2.50	5.00	10.00
453	Meet Me in Church/Hooked	1967	2.00	4.00	8.00
469	You Better Hold On/Help Yourself	1967	2.00	4.00	8.00
489	Rockin' Pneumonia/Someone to Take Your Place	1967	2.00	4.00	8.00
DIAL					
1152	Bump Your Bootie/Ain't Nothing Wrong with Whitey	1975	—	2.50	5.00
3022	I Gotta Sit Down and Cry/I Got a Thing Going	1964	2.50	5.00	10.00
4002	Get Down to It/Half a Mind	1964	2.50	5.00	10.00

Number	Title (A Side/B Side)	Yr	VG	VG+	NM
4007	Hello Happiness/Funny Style	1965	2.50	5.00	10.00
4020	I Feel It Coming/Gimme Your Love	1965	2.50	5.00	10.00
4065	I Just Want What Belongs to Me/Sad Sack	1967	2.00	4.00	8.00
FIRE					
510	Yes It's Written All Over Your Face/Look at My Heart	1962	3.75	7.50	15.00
1014	Snoopin' and Accusin'/This Is the Life	1959	3.75	7.50	15.00
1022	There's Something On Your Mind (Part 1)/There's Something On Your Mind (Part 2)	1960	6.25	12.50	25.00
1027	Booty Green/It Hurts Me to My Heart	1960	3.75	7.50	15.00
1028	You're Still My Baby (Part 1)/You're Still My Baby (Part 2)	1960	3.75	7.50	15.00
1035	All in My Mind/I Miss You So	1961	3.75	7.50	15.00
1037	What You Don't Know Don't Hurt You/I Need Someone (I Need You)	1961	3.75	7.50	15.00
GALE					
4M-101	Chickee Wah Wah/Give a Helping Hand	1957	6.25	12.50	25.00
GAMBLE					
216	(Ain't No Reason) For Girls to Be Lonely Part 1/Part 2	1968	2.00	4.00	8.00
MERCURY					
73908	I Wanna Bump with the Big Fat Woman/Disco Rabbit	1977	—	2.50	5.00
VOLT					
108	What Can I Do (Part 1)/What Can I Do (Part 2)	1963	3.00	6.00	12.00
Albums					
COLLECTABLES					
COL-	Golden Classics	198?	2.50	5.00	10.00
SPHERE SOUND					
SR- [M]	There's Something on Your Mind	1964	50.00	100.00	200.00
SSR- [S]	There's Something on Your Mind	1964	75.00	150.00	300.00

MARCHING OTTO
See CRAZY OTTO.

MARENO, LEE

Number	Title (A Side/B Side)	Yr	VG	VG+	NM
45s					
NEW ART					
103	Goddess of Love/He's Gone	1961	30.00	60.00	120.00
SCEPTER					
1222	Goddess of Love/He's Gone	1961	7.50	15.00	30.00
12222	Goddess of Love/Lonely Summer	1968	3.00	6.00	12.00
—As "Lee"					

MARESCA, ERNIE

Number	Title (A Side/B Side)	Yr	VG	VG+	NM
45s					
LAURIE					
3345	The Good Life/A Bum Can't Cry	1966	2.50	5.00	10.00
3371	My Son/My Shadow and Me	1967	2.50	5.00	10.00
3447	What Is a Marine/The Night My Papa Died	1968	2.00	4.00	8.00
3496	Blind Date/People Get Jealous	1969	2.00	4.00	8.00
3519	The Spirit of Woodstock/Web of Love	1969	2.00	4.00	8.00
3671	The Night My Poppa Died/Please Don't Play Me a Seven	1978	—	3.00	6.00
3698	You're the Only Girl for Me/Medley	1980	—	3.00	6.00
—B-side by the Belmonts					
PROVIDENCE					
417	Rockin' Blvd. St./Am I Better Off Than Them	1965	12.50	25.00	50.00
RUST					
5076	The Beetle Dance/Theme from Lilly, Lilly	1964	3.75	7.50	15.00
SEVILLE					
107	Lonesome Blues/I Don't Know Why	1960	3.75	7.50	15.00
117	Shout! Shout! (Knock Yourself Out)/Crying Like a Baby	1962	6.25	12.50	25.00
119	Down on the Beach/Mary Jane	1962	3.75	7.50	15.00
119 [PS]	Down on the Beach/Mary Jane	1962	5.00	10.00	20.00
122	Something to Shout About/How Many Times	1962	3.75	7.50	15.00
125	Love Express/Lorelei	1963	12.50	25.00	50.00
129	The Rovin' Kind/Please Be Fair	1963	3.75	7.50	15.00
138	I Can't Dance/It's Their World	1965	3.75	7.50	15.00
Albums					
SEVILLE					
SV 77001 [M]	Shout! Shout! Knock Yourself Out	1962	30.00	60.00	120.00
SV 87001 [S]	Shout! Shout! Knock Yourself Out	1962	50.00	100.00	200.00

MARGO AND THE MARVETTES

Number	Title (A Side/B Side)	Yr	VG	VG+	NM
45s					
AMERICAN ARTS					
8	Cherry Pie/Say You Will	1965	3.75	7.50	15.00

MARGO, MARGO, MEDRESS AND SIEGEL
See THE TOKENS.

MARGULIS, CHARLIE

Number	Title (A Side/B Side)	Yr	VG	VG+	NM
45s					
CARLTON					
456	Heartache for Sale/Gigi	1958	3.00	6.00	12.00
494	Malaguena/Theme from El Salon Mexico	1959	3.00	6.00	12.00
Albums					
CARLTON					
LP 12-103 [M]	Marvelous Margulis	1958	6.25	12.50	25.00
STLP 12-103 [S]	Marvelous Margulis	1959	7.50	15.00	30.00

MARIACHI BRASS, THE

Number	Title (A Side/B Side)	Yr	VG	VG+	NM
45s					
WORLD PACIFIC					
77815	Tequila/Flowers on the Wall	1966	2.00	4.00	8.00
77823	Bang Bang/Happiness Is	1966	2.00	4.00	8.00
77848	Dancing in the Street/When You're Smiling	1966	2.00	4.00	8.00
77853	La Bamba/Colonel Bogey March	1966	2.00	4.00	8.00
77857	A Man and a Woman/All	1966	2.00	4.00	8.00
77863	The Dating Game/In the Mood	1967	5.00	10.00	20.00
—Contrary to popular belief, the A-side was never done by Herb Alpert and the Tijuana Brass					
Albums					
WORLD PACIFIC					
WP- [M]	A Taste of Tequila	1966	3.00	6.00	12.00
WP- [M]	Hats Off!!!	1966	3.00	6.00	12.00
WP- [M]	Double Shot	1966	3.00	6.00	12.00
WP- [M]	In the Mood	1967	3.00	6.00	12.00
WPS- [S]	A Taste of Tequila	1966	3.75	7.50	15.00
WPS- [S]	Hats Off!!!	1966	3.75	7.50	15.00
WPS- [S]	Double Shot	1966	3.75	7.50	15.00
WPS- [S]	In the Mood	1967	3.75	7.50	15.00

MARIE AND THE DECCORS

Number	Title (A Side/B Side)	Yr	VG	VG+	NM
45s					
CUB					
9115	I'm the One/Queen of Fools	1962	6.25	12.50	25.00

MARINO, FRANK, AND MAHOGANY RUSH
See MAHOGANY RUSH.

MARIONETTES, THE

Number	Title (A Side/B Side)	Yr	VG	VG+	NM
45s					
LONDON					
9738	Whirlpool of Love/Nobody But You	1965	3.00	6.00	12.00

MARK-ALMOND

Number	Title (A Side/B Side)	Yr	VG	VG+	NM
45s					
ABC					
12221	New York State of Mind/Return to the City	1976	—	2.00	4.00
BLUE THUMB					
201	The City/The Ghetto	1971	—	3.00	6.00
206	One Way Sunday/The Bay	1971	—	3.00	6.00
COLUMBIA					
45745	Organ Grinder/What Am I Living For	1972	—	2.50	5.00
45951	Get Yourself Together/Lonely Girl	1973	—	2.50	5.00
HORIZON					
118	You Look Just Like a Girl Again/The City	1978	—	2.00	4.00
Albums					
ABC					
D-945	To the Heart	1976	2.50	5.00	10.00
BLUE THUMB					
BTS 27	Mark-Almond	1971	3.00	6.00	12.00
—Reissue of 8827					
BTS 32	Mark-Almond II	1971	3.00	6.00	12.00
BTS 50	The Best of Mark-Almond	1973	3.00	6.00	12.00
BTS-8827	Mark-Almond	1971	3.75	7.50	15.00
COLUMBIA					
KC 31917	Rising	1972	3.00	6.00	12.00
PC 31917	Rising	198?	2.00	4.00	8.00
—Budget-line reissue					
KC 32486	Mark-Almond 73	1973	3.00	6.00	12.00
CG 33648 [(2)]	Rising/Mark-Almond 73	1976	3.75	7.50	15.00
HORIZON					
SP-730	Other People's Rooms	1978	2.50	5.00	10.00
MCA					
711	Mark-Almond II	198?	2.00	4.00	8.00
—Reissue of Blue Thumb 32					
792	The Best of Mark-Almond	198?	2.00	4.00	8.00
—Reissue of Blue Thumb 50					
793	To the Heart	198?	2.00	4.00	8.00
—Reissue of ABC 945					
PACIFIC ARTS					
7-142	The Best of the Mark-Almond Band...Live	1980	2.50	5.00	10.00

MARKETTS, THE

Number	Title (A Side/B Side)	Yr	VG	VG+	NM
45s					
ARVEE					
5063	Beach Bum/Sweet Potatoes	1962	5.00	10.00	20.00
CALLIOPE					
8003	Mary Hartman, Mary Hartman/(B-side unknown)	1977	—	2.50	5.00
—As "The New Marketts"					
8009	City Nights/Soul Coaxing	1977	—	2.50	5.00
—As "The New Marketts"					
FARR					
007	Song from M.A.S.H./Song from M.A.S.H. (Disco Version)	1976	—	2.50	5.00
—As "The New Marketts"					
019	The Hustle/Song from M.A.S.H.	1977	—	2.50	5.00
—As "The New Marketts"					
021	Looking for Mr. Goodbar (Terry's Theme)/Black	1977	—	2.50	5.00
—As "Danny Welton and the New Marketts"					
LIBERTY					
55401	Surfer's Stomp/Start	1962	5.00	10.00	20.00
—As "The Mar-Kets"					
55443	Balboa Blue/Stompede	1962	5.00	10.00	20.00
—As "The Mar-Kets"					
55506	Stomping Room Only/Canadian Sunset	1962	5.00	10.00	20.00
—As "The Mar-Kets"					
MERCURY					
73433	Mystery Movie Theme/Sister Candy	1973	2.00	4.00	8.00
SEMINOLE					
501	Song from M.A.S.H./Song from M.A.S.H. (Disco Version)	1976	2.00	4.00	8.00
—As "The New Marketts"					
UNI					
55173	The Undefeated/They Call the Wind Maria	1969	2.00	4.00	8.00
UNION					
501	Surfer's Stomp/Start	1961	7.50	15.00	30.00
504	Balboa Blue/Stompede	1962	7.50	15.00	30.00
507	Stomping Room Only/Canadian Sunset	1962	7.50	15.00	30.00

Number	Title (A Side/B Side)	Yr	VG	VG+	NM
UNITED ARTISTS					
0043	Surfer's Stomp/Balboa Blue	1973	—	2.50	5.00
—"Silver Spotlight Series" reissue					
WARNER BROS.					
5365	Woody Wagon/Cobra	1963	3.75	7.50	15.00
5391	Outer Limits/Bella Dalena	1963	7.50	15.00	30.00
—Original title of A-side					
5391	Out of Limits/Bella Dalena	1963	5.00	10.00	20.00
5423	Vanishing Point/Borealis	1964	3.00	6.00	12.00
5468	Come See, Come Ska/Look for a Star	1964	3.00	6.00	12.00
5641	Miami's Blue/Napoleon's Solo	1965	2.50	5.00	10.00
5670	Ready Steady Go/Lady in the Cage	1965	2.50	5.00	10.00
5696	Batman Theme/Richie's Theme	1966	3.00	6.00	12.00
5814	Theme from "The Avengers"/A Touch of Velvet, a Sting of Brass	1966	5.00	10.00	20.00
5847	Tarzan/Stirrin' Up Some Soul	1966	2.50	5.00	10.00
7116	Out of Limits/Batman Theme	1968	—	3.00	6.00
—"Back to Back Hits" series -- originals have green labels with "W7" logo					
WORLD PACIFIC					
77874	Sunshine Girl/Sun Power	1967	2.50	5.00	10.00
77899	California Summer (People Moving West)/Groovin' Time	1968	2.50	5.00	10.00
Albums					
LIBERTY					
LRP-3226 [M]	Surfer's Stomp	1962	10.00	20.00	40.00
—Add 20% if "Surfer's Stomp" instruction sheet is enclosed					
LRP-3226 [M]	The Surfing Scene	196?	7.50	15.00	30.00
—Retitled version of above					
LST-7226 [S]	Surfer's Stomp	1962	12.50	25.00	50.00
—Add 20% if "Surfer's Stomp" instruction sheet is enclosed					
LST-7226 [S]	The Surfing Scene	196?	10.00	20.00	40.00
—Retitled version of above					
MERCURY					
SRM-1-679	AM, FM, Etc.	1973	3.75	7.50	15.00
WARNER BROS.					
W 1509 [M]	The Marketts Take to Wheels	1963	10.00	20.00	40.00
WS 1509 [S]	The Marketts Take to Wheels	1963	12.50	25.00	50.00
W 1537 [M]	Out of Limits!	1964	7.50	15.00	30.00
WS 1537 [S]	Out of Limits!	1964	10.00	20.00	40.00
W 1642 [M]	The Batman Theme	1966	10.00	20.00	40.00
WS 1642 [S]	The Batman Theme	1966	12.50	25.00	50.00
WORLD PACIFIC					
WP-1870 [M]	Sun Power	1967	6.25	12.50	25.00
WPS-21870 [S]	Sun Power	1967	5.00	10.00	20.00

MARKEYS, THE

No relation to THE MAR-KEYS.

Number	Title (A Side/B Side)	Yr	VG	VG+	NM
45s					
20TH CENTURY					
1210	Eternal Love/You've Got Me on a String	1956	12.50	25.00	50.00
GONE					
5028	Special Delivery/Along Came Love	1958	7.50	15.00	30.00
RCA VICTOR					
47-7256	Hot Rod/Yakkaty Yal	1958	6.25	12.50	25.00
47-7412	Time to Love/Make a Record Man	1958	6.25	12.50	25.00

MARKHAM, PIGMEAT

Number	Title (A Side/B Side)	Yr	VG	VG+	NM
45s					
CHESS					
1828	Hold That Ladder (Part 1)/Hold That Ladder (Part 2)	1962	2.50	5.00	10.00
1891	Open the Door, Richard (Part 1)/Open the Door, Richard (Part 2)	1964	2.00	4.00	8.00
2049	Here Comes the Judge/The Trial	1968	—	3.50	7.00
2059	Sock It To 'Em Judge/The Hip Judge	1968	—	3.00	6.00
2087	Pig's Popcorn/Who's Got the Number	1969	—	3.00	6.00
Albums					
CHESS					
LP-1451 [M]	The Trial	1961	6.25	12.50	25.00
LP-1462 [M]	Pigmeat Markham At the Party	1962	6.25	12.50	25.00
LP-1467 [M]	Anything Goes	1962	6.25	12.50	25.00
LP-1475 [M]	The World's Greatest Clown	1963	6.25	12.50	25.00
LP-1484 [M]	Open the Door, Richard	1964	6.25	12.50	25.00
LP-1493 [M]	Mr. Funny Man	1965	6.25	12.50	25.00
LP-1500 [M]	This'll Kill Ya	1965	6.25	12.50	25.00
LP-1505 [M]	If You Can't Be Good, Be Careful	1966	3.75	7.50	15.00
LPS-1505 [S]	If You Can't Be Good, Be Careful	1966	5.00	10.00	20.00
LP-1515 [M]	Mr. Vaudeville	1967	3.75	7.50	15.00
LPS-1515 [S]	Mr. Vaudeville	1967	5.00	10.00	20.00
LP-1517 [M]	Save Your Soul, Baby	1967	5.00	10.00	20.00
LPS-1517 [S]	Save Your Soul, Baby	1967	5.00	10.00	20.00
LP-1521 [M]	Backstage	1968	5.00	10.00	20.00
LPS-1521 [S]	Backstage	1968	5.00	10.00	20.00
LPS-1525	Here Comes the Judge	1968	5.00	10.00	20.00
LPS-1526	Tune Me In	1968	3.75	7.50	15.00
LPS-1529	Hustlers	1969	3.75	7.50	15.00
LPS-1534	Bag	1970	3.75	7.50	15.00
CH-9166	Here Comes the Judge	1985	2.50	5.00	10.00
—Reissue of 1525					
JEWEL					
5007	Crap-Shootin' Rev	1972	3.00	6.00	12.00
5012	Will the Real Pigmeat Markham Please Sit Down	1973	3.00	6.00	12.00

MARKLEY

Number	Title (A Side/B Side)	Yr	VG	VG+	NM
Albums					
FORWARD					
1007	A Group	1969	7.50	15.00	30.00

MARKS, GUY

Number	Title (A Side/B Side)	Yr	VG	VG+	NM
45s					
ABC					
11055	Loving You Has Made Me Bananas/Forgive Me, My Love	1968	2.00	4.00	8.00
11099	Meet Me Tonight by the Postage Machine/This Is Forever	1968	—	3.00	6.00
11148	How the West Was Really Won/This Is Forever	1968	—	3.00	6.00
ARIOLA AMERICA					
7646	The Bridge/Man in the Glass	1976	—	2.00	4.00
Albums					
ABC					
549 [M]	Hollywood Sings	1966	3.75	7.50	15.00
S-549 [S]	Hollywood Sings	1966	3.75	7.50	15.00
S-648	Loving You Has Made Me Bananas	1968	5.00	10.00	20.00

MARKSMEN, THE (1)

With Don Wilson of THE VENTURES.

Number	Title (A Side/B Side)	Yr	VG	VG+	NM
45s					
BLUE HORIZON					
6052	Night Run/Scratch	1960	37.50	75.00	150.00

MARKSMEN, THE (2)

Number	Title (A Side/B Side)	Yr	VG	VG+	NM
45s					
JUBILEE					
5531	Coming In on a Wing and a Prayer/Just One More Mile	1966	3.00	6.00	12.00

MARLEY, BOB, AND THE WAILERS

Number	Title (A Side/B Side)	Yr	VG	VG+	NM
12-Inch Singles					
COTILLION					
PR 201 [DJ]	Reggae on Broadway (6:00) (3:15)	1981	3.00	6.00	12.00
PR 414 [DJ]	Chances Are (same on both sides)	1981	3.75	7.50	15.00
ISLAND					
DMD 628 [DJ]	Buffalo Soldier/Buffalo Dub	1983	2.50	5.00	10.00
DMD 668 [DJ]	Mix Up, Mix Up (LP Version) (Edit Version)	1983	2.50	5.00	10.00
TUFF GONG					
864693-1	Iron Zion Lion (4 versions)/Could You Be Loved	1992	3.00	6.00	12.00
45s					
COTILLION					
46023	Reggae on Broadway/Gonna Get You	1981	—	2.50	5.00
46029	Chances Are/(B-side unknown)	1981	—	2.50	5.00
ISLAND					
004	I Shot the Sheriff/Put It On	1974	—	3.00	6.00
027	Lively Up Yourself/So Jah Seh	1975	—	3.00	6.00
037	No Woman, No Cry/Kinky Reggae	1975	—	3.00	6.00
060	Roots, Rock, Reggae/Cry to Me	1976	—	3.00	6.00
072	Who the Cap Fit/(B-side unknown)	1976	—	3.00	6.00
089	Exodus/(Instrumental)	1977	—	3.00	6.00
092	Waiting in Vain/Roots	1977	—	3.00	6.00
099	Is This Love/Crisis	1978	—	3.00	6.00
1211	Rock It Baby/Stop That Train	1972	2.00	4.00	8.00
1215	Concrete Jungle/No More Trouble	1973	2.00	4.00	8.00
1218	Get Up, Stand Up/Slave Driver	1973	2.00	4.00	8.00
49080	Wake Up and Live/Wake Up and Live (Dub)	1979	—	3.00	6.00
49156	Kaya/One Drop	1980	—	3.00	6.00
49547	Ride Natty Ride/Could You Be Loved	1980	—	3.00	6.00
49636	Redemption Song/Coming In from the Cold	1980	—	3.00	6.00
49755	Jamming/No Woman, No Cry	1981	—	3.00	6.00
99740	Blackman Redemption/Is This Love	1984	—	2.00	4.00
99837	Mix Up, Mix Up/(B-side unknown)	1983	—	2.00	4.00
99882	Buffalo Soldier/Buffalo Dub	1983	—	2.00	4.00
99882 [PS]	Buffalo Soldier/Buffalo Dub	1983	—	3.00	6.00
562356-7	Kinky Reggae (Raga Mix)/Kinky Reggae (Kinky Mix)	1999	—	2.00	4.00
SHELTER					
7309	Doppy Conquer/Justice	1971	3.00	6.00	12.00
—B-side by the Upsetters					
Albums					
ACCORD					
SN-7211	Jamaican Storm	1982	2.50	5.00	10.00
CALLA					
CAS-1240 [(2)]	The Birth of a Legend	1976	3.75	7.50	15.00
ZX 34759	The Birth of a Legend	1977	2.50	5.00	10.00
—Reissue of Record 1 of Calla 1240					
ZX 34760	Early Music	1977	2.50	5.00	10.00
—Reissue of Record 2 of Calla 1240					
COLUMBIA					
PZ 34759	The Birth of a Legend	198?	2.00	4.00	8.00
—Budget-line reissue of Calla 34759					
PZ 34760	Early Music	198?	2.00	4.00	8.00
—Budget-line reissue of Calla 34760					
COTILLION					
SD 5228	Chances Are	1981	2.50	5.00	10.00
ISLAND					
ISLD 11 [(2)]	Babylon by Bus	1978	3.75	7.50	15.00
—Island distribution					
ISLD 11 [(2)]	Babylon by Bus	1979	3.00	6.00	12.00
—Warner Bros. distribution					
ILPS 9241	Catch a Fire	1975	3.75	7.50	15.00
—Reissue with standard cover; Island distribution					
ILPS 9241	Catch a Fire	1978	3.00	6.00	12.00
—Reissue; Warner Bros. distribution					
SW-9241	Catch a Fire	1973	12.50	25.00	50.00
—"Cigarette lighter" cover with flip-open top; Capitol distribution					
ILPS 9256	Burnin'	1974	3.75	7.50	15.00
—Island distribution					
ILPS 9256	Burnin'	1978	3.00	6.00	12.00
—Warner Bros. distribution					
SW-9256	Burnin'	1973	5.00	10.00	20.00
—Capitol distribution					

Number	Title (A Side/B Side)	Yr	VG	VG+	NM
ILPS 9281	Natty Dread	1974	3.75	7.50	15.00
—Island distribution					
ILPS 9281	Natty Dread	1978	3.00	6.00	12.00
—Warner Bros. distribution					
ILPS 9376	Live!	1975	3.00	6.00	12.00
—Island distribution					
ILPS 9376	Live!	1978	2.50	5.00	10.00
—Warner Bros. distribution					
ILPS 9383	Rastaman Vibration	1976	3.00	6.00	12.00
—Island distribution					
ILPS 9383	Rastaman Vibration	1978	2.50	5.00	10.00
—Warner Bros. distribution					
ILPS 9383 [DJ]	Rastaman Vibration	1976	25.00	50.00	100.00
—Promotional package with burlap box and press kit					
ILPS 9498	Exodus	1977	3.00	6.00	12.00
—Island distribution (all have multicolor labels)					
ILPS 9498	Exodus	1978	2.50	5.00	10.00
—Warner Bros. distribution					
ILPS 9517	Kaya	1978	3.00	6.00	12.00
—Island distribution					
ILPS 9517	Kaya	1979	2.50	5.00	10.00
—Warner Bros. distribution					
ILPS 9542	Survival	1979	3.00	6.00	12.00
ILPS 9596	Uprising	1980	3.00	6.00	12.00
90029 [(2)]	Babylon by Bus	1983	3.00	6.00	12.00
90030	Catch a Fire	1983	2.00	4.00	8.00
90031	Burnin'	1983	2.00	4.00	8.00
90032	Live!	1983	2.00	4.00	8.00
90033	Rastaman Vibration	1983	2.00	4.00	8.00
90034	Exodus	1983	2.00	4.00	8.00
90035	Kaya	1983	2.00	4.00	8.00
90036	Uprising	1983	2.00	4.00	8.00
90037	Natty Dread	1983	2.00	4.00	8.00
—90029-90037 are reissues with Atco distribution					
90085	Confrontation	1983	2.50	5.00	10.00
90169	Legend	1984	2.50	5.00	10.00
90520	Rebel Music	1986	2.50	5.00	10.00
524419-1	Dreams of Freedom	1997	3.00	6.00	12.00
546404-1	Chant Down Babylon	1999	3.00	6.00	12.00
MOBILE FIDELITY					
1-221	Exodus	1995	6.25	12.50	25.00
—Audiophile vinyl					
1-236	Catch a Fire	1995	6.25	12.50	25.00
—Audiophile vinyl					
TUFF GONG					
524103-1	Natural Mystic	1995	3.75	7.50	15.00
846197-1 [(2)]	Babylon by Bus	1990	3.75	7.50	15.00
846200-1	Burnin'	1990	3.00	6.00	12.00
846201-1	Catch a Fire	1990	3.00	6.00	12.00
846202-1	Survival	1990	3.00	6.00	12.00
846203-1	Live!	1990	3.00	6.00	12.00
846204-1	Natty Dread	1990	3.00	6.00	12.00
846205-1	Rastaman Vibration	1990	3.00	6.00	12.00
846206-1	Rebel Music	1990	3.00	6.00	12.00
846207-1	Confrontation	1990	3.00	6.00	12.00
846208-1	Exodus	1990	3.00	6.00	12.00
846209-1	Kaya	1990	3.00	6.00	12.00
846210-1	Legend	1990	3.00	6.00	12.00
846211-1	Uprising	1990	3.00	6.00	12.00
848243-1	Talkin' Blues	1991	3.00	6.00	12.00

MARLO, MICKI

45s

Number	Title (A Side/B Side)	Yr	VG	VG+	NM
ABC-PARAMOUNT					
9762	Little By Little/It All Started With Your Kiss	1956	6.25	12.50	25.00
9807	Ain't That Love/The Beginning of Love	1957	3.75	7.50	15.00
9841	What You've Done to Me/That's Right	1957	7.50	15.00	30.00
—With "Vocal assist by Paul Anka"					
9841	What You've Done to Me/That's Right	1957	3.75	7.50	15.00
—New mix, without "Vocal assist by Paul Anka"					
CAPITOL					
F2736	I'm Gonna Rock, Rock, Rock/Love's Like That	1954	5.00	10.00	20.00
F2801	I'm Going to Sit Right Down and Cry Over You/ Forever Is Now	1954	5.00	10.00	20.00
F2874	I'm Flying/Why Should I Cry	1954	3.75	7.50	15.00
F2932	Show Me/Every Road Must Have a Turning	1954	3.75	7.50	15.00
F3016	Don't Go, Don't Go/Can You	1955	3.75	7.50	15.00
F3062	Prize of Gold/Foolish Notion	1955	3.75	7.50	15.00
F3148	I've Got Rhythm in My Nursery Rhymes/Dream Boy	1955	3.75	7.50	15.00
F3266	Pet Me, Poppa/Like I Love Nobody Before	1955	3.75	7.50	15.00
F3346	How Come You Love Me Like You Do/Way Down by the Cherry Tree	1956	3.75	7.50	15.00

Albums

Number	Title (A Side/B Side)	Yr	VG	VG+	NM
ABC-PARAMOUNT					
295 [M]	Married I Can Always Get	1959	5.00	10.00	20.00
S-295 [S]	Married I Can Always Get	1959	6.25	12.50	25.00

MARMALADE, THE

45s

Number	Title (A Side/B Side)	Yr	VG	VG+	NM
ARIOLA AMERICA					
7619	Falling Apart at the Seams/Fly, Fly, Fly	1976	—	2.00	4.00
7631	My Everything/Walking a Tightrope	1976	—	2.00	4.00
EMI					
3676	Engine Driver/Wishing Well	1973	—	2.00	4.00
EPIC					
10162	Can't Stop Now/There Ain't No Use in Hanging On	1967	2.50	5.00	10.00
10236	Otherwise It's Been a Perfect Day/I See the Rain	1967	2.50	5.00	10.00
10284	Cry/Man in a Shop	1968	2.00	4.00	8.00
10340	Hey Joe/Lovin' Things	1968	2.00	4.00	8.00
10404	Wait for Me Mary-Ann/Mess Around	1968	2.00	4.00	8.00
10428	Ob-La-Di, Ob-La-Da/Chains	1969	2.50	5.00	10.00
10493	Time Is On My Side/Baby Make It Soon	1969	2.00	4.00	8.00
LONDON					
20058	Reflections of My Life/Rollin' Thing	1970	—	3.00	6.00
20059	Rainbow/The Ballad of Cherry Flavar	1970	—	2.50	5.00
20066	My Little One/Is Your Life Your Own	1971	—	2.50	5.00
20068	Lonely Man/Cousin Norman	1971	—	2.50	5.00
20072	Just One Woman/Radancer	1971	—	2.50	5.00

Albums

Number	Title (A Side/B Side)	Yr	VG	VG+	NM
EPIC					
BN 26553	The Best of the Marmalade	1970	5.00	10.00	20.00
LONDON					
PS 575	Reflections of My Life	1970	5.00	10.00	20.00

MARQUEES, THE (1)

45s

Number	Title (A Side/B Side)	Yr	VG	VG+	NM
DAY-SEL					
1001	Ecstasy/Close to Me	1959	150.00	300.00	600.00

MARQUEES, THE (2)

45s

Number	Title (A Side/B Side)	Yr	VG	VG+	NM
GRAND					
141	The Bells/The Rain	1956	75.00	150.00	300.00
—With no address on label					
141	The Bells/The Rain	195?	12.50	25.00	50.00
—With address on label					

MARQUEES, THE (3)

45s

Number	Title (A Side/B Side)	Yr	VG	VG+	NM
JO-ANN					
128	Stay with Me/That's the Way I Feel	1960	37.50	75.00	150.00
130	I Need a Helping Hand/Don't You Do Me Like That	1961	25.00	50.00	100.00

MARQUEES, THE (4)

45s

Number	Title (A Side/B Side)	Yr	VG	VG+	NM
LEN					
100	Say Hey/I'm in Misery	1958	25.00	50.00	100.00

MARQUEES, THE (5)

MARVIN GAYE was in this group.

45s

Number	Title (A Side/B Side)	Yr	VG	VG+	NM
OKEH					
7096	Hey Little School Girl/Wyatt Earp	1957	30.00	60.00	120.00

MARQUEES, THE (6)

45s

Number	Title (A Side/B Side)	Yr	VG	VG+	NM
WARNER BROS.					
5072	Who Will Be the First One/Love Machine	1959	10.00	20.00	40.00
5127	Christmas in the Crowd/Sunset to Sunrise	1959	10.00	20.00	40.00
5139	Until the Day I Die/Don't Be Mean, Geraldine	1960	20.00	40.00	80.00

MARS, SYLVIA

Albums

Number	Title (A Side/B Side)	Yr	VG	VG+	NM
LYRIC					
124	Blues Walk Right In	196?	15.00	30.00	60.00

MARSDEN, BERYL

45s

Number	Title (A Side/B Side)	Yr	VG	VG+	NM
CAPITOL					
5552	Who You Gonna Hurt/Gonna Make Him My Baby	1965	2.50	5.00	10.00

MARSDEN, GERRY

Also see GERRY AND THE PACEMAKERS.

45s

Number	Title (A Side/B Side)	Yr	VG	VG+	NM
COLUMBIA					
44309	Gilbert Green/Please Let Them Be	1967	2.50	5.00	10.00

MARSH, RICHIE

Also known as Dick Marsh, he later recorded as "Sky Saxon" in THE SEEDS.

45s

Number	Title (A Side/B Side)	Yr	VG	VG+	NM
ACAMA					
125	Baby, Baby, Baby/Half Angel	1960	7.50	15.00	30.00
AVA					
122	Goodbye/Crying Inside My Heart	1963	5.00	10.00	20.00
ROSCO					
412	There's Only One Girl/What Chance Have I	1960	5.00	10.00	20.00
SHEPHERD					
2203	They Say Darling/I Swear That It's True	1962	6.25	12.50	25.00

MARSHALL, CHUCK

Albums

Number	Title (A Side/B Side)	Yr	VG	VG+	NM
DECCA					
DL 4267 [M]	Twist to Songs Everybody Knows	1962	3.75	7.50	15.00
DL 74267 [S]	Twist to Songs Everybody Knows	1962	5.00	10.00	20.00

MARSHALL, PETER

Albums

Number	Title (A Side/B Side)	Yr	VG	VG+	NM
DOT					
DLP-25930	For the Love of Pete	1969	6.25	12.50	25.00

MARSHALL BROTHERS, THE

45s

Number	Title (A Side/B Side)	Yr	VG	VG+	NM
SAVOY					
825	Mr. Santa's Boogie/Who'll Be the Fool from Now On	1951	125.00	250.00	500.00
833	Why Make a Fool Out of Me/Just a Poor Boy in Love	1952	100.00	200.00	400.00

MARSHALL TUCKER BAND, THE

12-Inch Singles

Number	Title (A Side/B Side)	Yr	VG	VG+	NM
WARNER BROS.					
PRO-A-816 [DJ]	Running Like the Wind (Edit)/Last of the Singing Cowboys	1979	2.50	5.00	10.00
PRO-A-863 [DJ]	It Takes Time (Single Version)//Sing My Blues/ Cattle Drive	1980	3.00	6.00	12.00

45s

Number	Title (A Side/B Side)	Yr	VG	VG+	NM
CAPRICORN					
0021	Can't You See/See You Later, I'm Gone	1973	—	3.00	6.00
0030	Take the Highway/Jesus Told Me So	1973	—	3.00	6.00
0049	Another Cruel Love/Blue Ridge Mountain Sky	1974	—	2.50	5.00
0228	This Ol' Cowboy/Try One More Time	1975	—	2.50	5.00
0244	Fire on the Mountain/Bop Away My Blues	1975	—	2.50	5.00
0251	Searchin' for a Rainbow/Walkin' and Talkin'	1976	—	2.50	5.00
0258	Long Hard Ride/Windy City Blues	1976	—	2.50	5.00
0270	Heard It in a Love Song/Life in a Song	1977	—	2.50	5.00
0278	Can't You See/Fly Like an Eagle	1977	—	2.50	5.00
0300	Dream Lover/A Change Is Gonna Come	1978	—	2.50	5.00
0307	I'll Be Seeing You/Everybody Needs Somebody	1978	—	2.50	5.00
MERCURY					
870050-7	Once You Get the Feel of It/Slow Down	1987	—	—	3.00
870505-7	Dancin' Shoes/I'm Glad It's Gone	1988	—	—	3.00
872096-7	Still Holdin' On/Same Old Moon	1989	—	—	3.00
888774-7	Hangin' Out in Smokey Places/He Don't Know	1987	—	—	3.00
WARNER BROS.					
8841	Last of the Singing Cowboys/Pass It On	1979	—	2.50	5.00
8841 [PS]	Last of the Singing Cowboys/Pass It On	1979	—	3.00	6.00
29355	I May Be Easy But You Make It Hard/Shot Down Where You Stand	1984	—	2.00	4.00
29619	A Place I've Never Been/8:05	1983	—	2.00	4.00
29939	Reachin' for a Little Bit More/Sweet Elaine	1982	—	2.00	4.00
29995	Mr. President/The Sea, Dreams and Fairy Tales	1982	—	2.00	4.00
49068	Running Like the Wind/(B-side unknown)	1979	—	2.50	5.00
49215	It Takes Time/Jimi	1980	—	2.50	5.00
49259	Disillusioned/Without You	1980	—	2.00	4.00
49724	This Time I Believe/Tell the Blues to Take Off the Night	1981	—	2.00	4.00
49764	Time Has Come/Love Some	1981	—	2.00	4.00

Albums

Number	Title (A Side/B Side)	Yr	VG	VG+	NM
CAPRICORN					
CP 0112	The Marshall Tucker Band	1973	3.00	6.00	12.00
CP 0124	A New Life	1974	3.00	6.00	12.00
2CP 0145 [(2)]	Where We All Belong	1974	3.75	7.50	15.00
CP 0161	Searchin' for a Rainbow	1975	3.00	6.00	12.00
CP 0170	Long Hard Ride	1976	3.00	6.00	12.00
CPK 0180	Carolina Dreams	1977	3.00	6.00	12.00
CP 0205	Together Forever	1978	3.00	6.00	12.00
CP 0214	Greatest Hits	1978	3.00	6.00	12.00
MERCURY					
832794-1	Still Holdin' On	1988	2.50	5.00	10.00
WARNER BROS.					
BSK 3317	Running Like the Wind	1979	2.50	5.00	10.00
HS 3410	Tenth	1980	2.50	5.00	10.00
HS 3525	Dedicated	1981	2.50	5.00	10.00
BSK 3606	The Marshall Tucker Band	1982	2.50	5.00	10.00
—Reissue of Capricorn 0112					
2WS 3608 [(2)]	Where We All Belong	1982	3.00	6.00	12.00
—Reissue of Capricorn 0145					
BSK 3609	Searchin' for a Rainbow	1982	2.50	5.00	10.00
—Reissue of Capricorn 0161					
BSK 3610	Carolina Dreams	1982	2.50	5.00	10.00
—Reissue of Capricorn 0180					
BSK 3611	Greatest Hits	1982	2.50	5.00	10.00
—Reissue of Capricorn 0214					
BSK 3662	A New Life	1982	2.50	5.00	10.00
—Reissue of Capricorn 0124					
BSK 3663	Long Hard Ride	1982	2.50	5.00	10.00
—Reissue of Capricorn 0170					
BSK 3664	Together Forever	1982	2.50	5.00	10.00
—Reissue of Capricorn 0205					
BSK 3684	Tuckerized	1982	2.50	5.00	10.00
23803	Just Us	1983	2.50	5.00	10.00

MARSHANS, THE

45s

Number	Title (A Side/B Side)	Yr	VG	VG+	NM
ETIQUETTE					
8	I Remember/It's Almost Tomorrow	1964	5.00	10.00	20.00
JOHNSON					
736	My Letter To Santa/Main Man	1966	5.00	10.00	20.00

MARSHMALLOW WAY

45s

Number	Title (A Side/B Side)	Yr	VG	VG+	NM
UNITED ARTISTS					
50611	Good Day/Music, Music	1969	2.00	4.00	8.00

Albums

Number	Title (A Side/B Side)	Yr	VG	VG+	NM
UNITED ARTISTS					
UAS-6708	Marshmallow Way	1969	5.00	10.00	20.00

MARTELLS, THE

45s

Number	Title (A Side/B Side)	Yr	VG	VG+	NM
BELLA					
20	Rockin' Santa Claus/Carol Lee	1959	10.00	20.00	40.00
—B-side by Eulis Mason					
45	Forgotten Spring/Va Va Voom	1961	12.50	25.00	50.00
CESSNA					
477	Forgotten Spring/Va Va Voom	1961	20.00	40.00	80.00
RELIC					
517	Forgotten Spring/Va Va Voom	1964	2.50	5.00	10.00

MARTHA AND THE VANDELLAS

Also see SAUNDRA MALLETT AND THE VANDELLAS; MARTHA REEVES.

45s

Number	Title (A Side/B Side)	Yr	VG	VG+	NM
A&M					
3022	Nowhere to Run/I Got You (I Feel Good)	1988	—	2.00	4.00
—B-side by James Brown					
3022 [PS]	Nowhere to Run/I Got You (I Feel Good)	1988	—	2.00	4.00
—"Good Morning Vietnam" sleeve					
GORDY					
7011	I'll Have to Let Him Go/My Baby Won't Come Back	1962	6.25	12.50	25.00
7014	Come and Get These Memories/Jealous Love	1963	7.50	15.00	30.00
7022	Heat Wave/A Love Like Yours	1963	5.00	10.00	20.00
7025	Quicksand/Darling, I Hum Our Song	1963	3.75	7.50	15.00
7027	Live Wire/Old Love	1964	3.75	7.50	15.00
7031	In My Lonely Room/A Tear for the Girl	1964	3.75	7.50	15.00
7033	Dancing in the Street/There He Is (At My Door)	1964	3.75	7.50	15.00
7033 [PS]	Dancing in the Street/There He Is (At My Door)	1964	30.00	60.00	120.00
7036	Wild One/Dancing Slow	1964	3.00	6.00	12.00
7039	Nowhere to Run/Motoring	1965	3.00	6.00	12.00
7045	You've Been in Love Too Long/Love (Makes You Do Foolish Things)	1965	3.00	6.00	12.00
7048	My Baby Loves Me/Never Leave Your Baby's Side	1965	3.00	6.00	12.00
7053	What Am I Gonna Do Without Your Love/Go Ahead and Laugh	1966	3.00	6.00	12.00
7056	I'm Ready for Love/He Doesn't Love Her Anymore	1966	3.00	6.00	12.00
7058	Jimmy Mack/Third Finger, Left Hand	1967	2.50	5.00	10.00
7062	Love Bug Leave My Heart Alone/One Way Out	1967	2.50	5.00	10.00
7067	Honey Chile/Show Me the Way	1967	2.50	5.00	10.00
—Starting here, as "Martha Reeves and the Vandellas"					
7070	I Promise to Wait My Love/Forget Me Not	1968	2.50	5.00	10.00
7075	I Can't Dance to That Music You're Playin'/I Tried	1968	2.50	5.00	10.00
7080	Sweet Darlin'/Without You	1968	2.50	5.00	10.00
7085	(We've Got) Honey Love/I'm In Love (And I Know It)	1969	2.00	4.00	8.00
7094	Taking My Love (And Leaving Me)/Heartless	1969	2.00	4.00	8.00
7098	I Should Be Pround/Love, Guess Who	1970	2.00	4.00	8.00
7103	I Gotta Let You Go/You're the Loser Now	1970	2.00	4.00	8.00
7110	Bless You/Hope I Don't Get My Heart Broke	1971	2.00	4.00	8.00
7113	In and Out of My Life/Your Love Makes It All Worthwhile	1972	2.00	4.00	8.00
7118	Tear It On Down/I Want You Back	1972	2.00	4.00	8.00
7127	Baby Don't Leave Me/I Won't Be the Fool I've Been Again	1973	2.00	4.00	8.00
TOPPS/MOTOWN					
7	Dancing in the Street	1967	18.75	37.50	75.00
—Cardboard record					
14	Love Is Like a Heat Wave	1967	18.75	37.50	75.00
—Cardboard record					

Albums

Number	Title (A Side/B Side)	Yr	VG	VG+	NM
GORDY					
G-902 [M]	Come and Get These Memories	1963	100.00	200.00	400.00
GS-902 [S]	Come and Get These Memories	1963	200.00	400.00	800.00
G-907 [M]	Heat Wave	1963	37.50	75.00	150.00
GS-907 [R]	Heat Wave	1963	37.50	75.00	150.00
—"Stereo" banner pre-printed on cover					
GS-907 [S]	Heat Wave	1963	100.00	200.00	400.00
—Mono cover with "Stereo" sticker					
G-915 [M]	Dance Party	1965	10.00	20.00	40.00
GS-915 [S]	Dance Party	1965	15.00	30.00	60.00
G-917 [M]	Greatest Hits	1966	6.25	12.50	25.00
GS-917 [S]	Greatest Hits	1966	7.50	15.00	30.00
G-920 [M]	Watchout!	1966	6.25	12.50	25.00
GS-920 [S]	Watchout!	1966	7.50	15.00	30.00
G-925 [M]	Martha and the Vandellas Live!	1967	7.50	15.00	30.00
GS-925 [S]	Martha and the Vandellas Live!	1967	6.25	12.50	25.00
G-926 [M]	Ridin' High	1968	10.00	20.00	40.00
—Mono is promo only					
GS-926 [S]	Ridin' High	1968	5.00	10.00	20.00
GS-944	Sugar 'N Spice	1969	5.00	10.00	20.00
GS-952	Natural Resources	1970	5.00	10.00	20.00
GS-958	Black Magic	1972	5.00	10.00	20.00
MOTOWN					
M5-111V1	Motown Superstar Series, Vol. 11	1981	2.50	5.00	10.00
M5-145V1	Heat Wave	1981	2.50	5.00	10.00
—Reissue of Gordy 907					
M5-204V1	Greatest Hits	1981	2.50	5.00	10.00
—Reissue of Gordy 917					
M7-778 [(2)]	Anthology	1974	3.75	7.50	15.00

MARTIN, BARRY

45s

Number	Title (A Side/B Side)	Yr	VG	VG+	NM
FREEDOM					
44019	Minnie the Moocher/The Willies	1959	3.00	6.00	12.00
RCA VICTOR					
47-7834	Got a Whole Lot of Lovin' to Do/Why'd I Have to Fa;;	1961	5.00	10.00	20.00

MARTIN, BOBBI

45s

Number	Title (A Side/B Side)	Yr	VG	VG+	NM
BUDDAH					
217	No Love at All/A Place for Me	1971	—	2.00	4.00
227	Devotion/A Place for Me	1971	—	2.00	4.00
253	Tomorrow/Sentimental Journey	1971	—	2.00	4.00
286	Something Tells Me (Something's Gonna Happen Tonight)/Give Me a Star to Live On	1972	—	2.00	4.00
CORAL					
62263	I Need Your Love/Cry, Cry, Cry (I Never Thought I'd Make You Cry)	1961	2.00	4.00	8.00
62285	Wooden Heart/How Should I Cry	1961	2.00	4.00	8.00
62321	Forgive Me/Tired and Blue	1962	2.00	4.00	8.00
62340	Afraid/Brenda, Brenda	1962	2.00	4.00	8.00
62351	I'll Never Stop Loving You/Why, Tell Me Why	1963	2.00	4.00	8.00

Number	Title (A Side/B Side)	Yr	VG	VG+	NM
62384	"A" You're Adorable/A Girl's Prayer	1963	2.00	4.00	8.00
62410	I'm a Fool (To Go On Loving You)/Does Your Heart Hurt a Little	1964	—	3.00	6.00
62426	Don't Forget I Still Love You/On the Outside (Looking In)	1964	—	3.00	6.00
62447	I Can't Stop Thinking of You/A Million Thanks to You	1965	—	3.00	6.00
62452	I Love You So/When Will the Torch Go Out	1965	—	3.00	6.00
62452 [PS]	I Love You So/When Will the Torch Go Out	1965	2.50	5.00	10.00
62457	Holding Back the Tears/I Don't Want to Love	1965	—	3.00	6.00
62466	Auf Wiedersehn Good Bye/There Are No Rules	1965	—	3.00	6.00
62472	Just One Time/Trying to Get You Off My Mind	1965	—	3.00	6.00
62475	Don't Take It Out on Me/Something on My Mind	1965	—	3.00	6.00
62485	I Can Give You Love/Sometimes	1966	—	3.00	6.00
62488	It's a Sin to Tell a Lie/Oh, Lonesome Me	1966	—	3.00	6.00
62503	Just As Much As Ever/You Have No Idea	1966	—	3.00	6.00
62512	Anytime/How Long	1967	—	3.00	6.00

MGM

Number	Title (A Side/B Side)	Yr	VG	VG+	NM
14587	Smile for Me/Now Lonely Is Only a Word	1973	—	2.00	4.00

UNITED ARTISTS

Number	Title (A Side/B Side)	Yr	VG	VG+	NM
0148	For the Love of Him/I Think of You	1973	—	2.00	4.00
—"Silver Spotlight Series" reissue					
50253	Only You (And You Alone)/Would You Believe	1968	—	2.50	5.00
50297	A Man and a Woman/Before You	1968	—	2.50	5.00
50443	Harper Valley P.T.A./He Called Me Baby	1968	—	2.50	5.00
50456	I Love Him/I Think of You	1968	—	2.50	5.00
50523	Your Cheatin' Heart/Tennessee Waltz	1969	—	2.50	5.00
50602	For the Love of Him/I Think of You	1969	—	2.50	5.00
50687	Goin' South/Give a Woman Love	1970	—	2.50	5.00
50728	No Love at All/What Greater Love	1970	—	2.50	5.00

Albums

BUDDAH

Number	Title	Yr	VG	VG+	NM
BDS-5090	Tomorrow	1971	3.00	6.00	12.00

CORAL

Number	Title	Yr	VG	VG+	NM
CRL 57472 [M]	Don't Forget I Still Love You	1965	3.75	7.50	15.00
CRL 57478 [M]	I Love You So	1965	3.75	7.50	15.00
CRL 757472 [S]	Don't Forget I Still Love You	1965	5.00	10.00	20.00
CRL 757478 [S]	I Love You So	1965	5.00	10.00	20.00

SUNSET

Number	Title	Yr	VG	VG+	NM
SUS-5319	Thinking of You	197?	2.50	5.00	10.00

UNITED ARTISTS

Number	Title	Yr	VG	VG+	NM
UAS-6668	Harper Valley P.T.A.	1968	3.00	6.00	12.00
UAS-6700	For the Love of Him	1969	3.00	6.00	12.00
UAS-6755	With Love	1970	3.00	6.00	12.00

VOCALION

Number	Title	Yr	VG	VG+	NM
VL 73906	Have You Ever Been Lonely	196?	2.50	5.00	10.00

MARTIN, DEAN

45s

CAPITOL

Number	Title (A Side/B Side)	Yr	VG	VG+	NM
54-691	Just for Fun/My One, My Only, My All	1949	5.00	10.00	20.00
—Note: Dean Martin singles on Capitol before 691 are unconfirmed on 45 rpm					
54-726	That Lucky Old Sun/Vieni Su	1949	5.00	10.00	20.00
F937	Rain/Zing-a, Zing-a, Boom	1950	3.75	7.50	15.00
F948	Muskrat Ramble/I'm Gonna Paper All My Walls with Love Letters	1950	3.75	7.50	15.00
F981	Choo'n Gum/I Don't Care If the Sun Don't Shine	1950	3.75	7.50	15.00
F1002	I Still Get a Thrill/Be Honest with Me	1950	3.75	7.50	15.00
F1028	I'll Always Love You/Baby Obey Me	1950	3.75	7.50	15.00
F1052	Bye Bye Blackbird/Happy Feet	1950	3.75	7.50	15.00
F1139	Peddler's Serenade/Wham, Bam, Thank You, Ma'am	1950	3.75	7.50	15.00
F1160	Don't Rock the Boat/I'm in Love with You	1950	3.75	7.50	15.00
—With Margaret Whiting					
F1342	If/I Love the Way	1950	3.75	7.50	15.00
F1358	You and Your Beautiful Eyes/Tonda Wanda Hoy	1951	3.75	7.50	15.00
F1458	Beside You/Who's Sorry Now	1951	3.75	7.50	15.00
F1682	Oh Marie/I'll Always Love You	1951	3.00	6.00	12.00
F1703	In the Cool, Cool, Cool of the Evening/Bonne Nuit	1951	3.75	7.50	15.00
F1797	Hanging Around with You/Aw C'mon	1951	3.75	7.50	15.00
F1811	Meanderin'/Bella Bimba	1951	3.75	7.50	15.00
F1817	Solitaire/I Ran All the Way Home	1951	3.75	7.50	15.00
F1885	Night Train to Memphis/Blue Smoke	1951	3.75	7.50	15.00
F1901	Never Before/Sailors Polka	1951	3.75	7.50	15.00
F1921	As You Are/Oh Boy	1952	3.75	7.50	15.00
F1938	Until/My Heart Found Home	1952	3.75	7.50	15.00
F1975	All I Have to Give/When You're Smiling	1952	3.75	7.50	15.00
F2001	Pretty as a Picture/Won't You Surrender	1952	3.75	7.50	15.00
F2071	Bet-i-Cha/I Passed Your House Tonight	1952	3.75	7.50	15.00
F2140	Oh Marie/Come Back to Sorrento	1952	3.75	7.50	15.00
F2165	You Belong to Me/Hominy Grits	1952	3.75	7.50	15.00
F2240	I Know a Dream When I See One/Second Chance	1952	3.75	7.50	15.00
F2319	What Could Be More Beautiful/The Kiss	1953	3.00	6.00	12.00
F2378	Little Did We Know/There's My Lover	1953	3.00	6.00	12.00
F2485	Love Me, Love Me/Till I Find YouLove Me, Love Me/Till I Find You	1953	3.00	6.00	12.00
F2555	If I Could Sing Like Bing/Don't You Remember	1953	3.00	6.00	12.00
F2589	That's Amore/You're the Right One	1953	3.75	7.50	15.00
F2640	The Christmas Blues/If I Should Love Again	1953	3.00	6.00	12.00
F2749	Hey Brother Pass the Wine/I'd Cry Like a Baby	1954	3.00	6.00	12.00
F2818	Money Burns a Hole in My Pocket/Sway	1954	3.00	6.00	12.00
F2870	That's What I Like/Peddler Man	1954	3.00	6.00	12.00
F2911	Try Again/One More Time	1954	3.00	6.00	12.00
F2985	Open Up the Doghouse/Long, Long Ago	1954	3.75	7.50	15.00
—With Nat King Cole					
F3011	Confused/Belle from Barcelona	1955	2.50	5.00	10.00
F3036	Young and Foolish/Under the Bridges of Paris	1955	2.50	5.00	10.00
F3133	Chee Chee Oo-Chee/Ridin' Into Love	1955	2.50	5.00	10.00
F3153	Simpatico/Love Is All That Matters	1955	2.50	5.00	10.00
F3196	Two Sleepy People/Relax Ay Voo	1955	2.50	5.00	10.00
—With Line Renaud					
F3238	I Like Them All/In Napoli	1955	2.50	5.00	10.00
F3295	Memories Are Made of This/Change of Heart	1955	3.00	6.00	12.00
F3352	Innamorata/Lady with a Big Umbrella	1956	2.50	5.00	10.00
F3414	Standing on the Corner/Watching the World Go By	1956	2.50	5.00	10.00
F3468	Street of Love/I'm Gonna Steal You Away	1956	2.50	5.00	10.00
F3521	Mississippi Dreamboat/Test of Time	1956	2.50	5.00	10.00
F3577	The Look/Give Me a Sign	1956	2.50	5.00	10.00
F3604	Just Kiss Me/I Know I Can't Forget	1956	2.50	5.00	10.00
F3648	Captured/The Man Who Plays the Mandolino	1957	2.50	5.00	10.00
F3680	Bamboozled/Only Trust Your Heart	1957	2.50	5.00	10.00
F3718	I Can't Give You Anything But Love/I Never Had a Chance	1957	2.50	5.00	10.00
F3752	Write to Me from Naples/Beau James	1957	2.50	5.00	10.00
F3787	Promise Her Anything/Triche Trache	1957	2.50	5.00	10.00
F3842	Makin' Love Ukulele Style/Good Morning Life	1957	2.50	5.00	10.00
F3894	Return to Me/Forgetting You	1958	2.00	4.00	8.00
F3988	Angel Baby/I'll Gladly Make the Same Mistake Again	1958	2.00	4.00	8.00
F4028	Volare (Nel Blu Dipinto Di Blu)/Outa My Mind	1958	2.00	4.00	8.00
F4028 [PS]	Volare (Nel Blu Dipinto Di Blu)/Outa My Mind	1958	6.25	12.50	25.00
F4065	Once Upon a Time/The Magician	1958	2.00	4.00	8.00
F4124	It Takes So Long/You Were Made for Love	1959	2.00	4.00	8.00
F4174	Rio Bravo/My Rifle, My Pony and Me	1959	2.00	4.00	8.00
F4222	On an Evening in Roma/You Can't Love 'Em All	1959	2.00	4.00	8.00
F4222 [PS]	On an Evening in Roma/You Can't Love 'Em All	1959	6.25	12.50	25.00
F4287	I Ain't Gonna Lead This Life No More/Career	1959	2.00	4.00	8.00
4328	Love Me, My Love/Who Was That Lady	1960	2.00	4.00	8.00
4361	Napoli/Professor, Professor	1960	2.00	4.00	8.00
4391	Just in Time/Buttercup a Golden Hair	1960	2.00	4.00	8.00
4420	Ain't That a Kick in the Head/Humdinger	1960	2.00	4.00	8.00
4472	How Sweet It Is/Sogni D'Oro	1960	2.00	4.00	8.00
4518	Sparklin' Eyes/Tu Sei Bella Signorina	1961	2.00	4.00	8.00
4551	Bella, Bella Bambina/All in a Night's Work	1961	2.00	4.00	8.00
4570	The Story of Life/Giuggiola	1961	2.00	4.00	8.00
B-44153	That's Amore/It Must Be Him	1988	—	2.00	4.00
—B-side by Vikki Carr					
S7-57889	Rudolph, the Red-Nosed Reindeer/White Christmas	1992	—	2.50	5.00
58742	The Christmas Blues/Let It Snow! Let It Snow! Let It Snow!	1998	—	—	3.00

MCA

Number	Title (A Side/B Side)	Yr	VG	VG+	NM
52662	L.A. Is My Home/Drinking Champagne	1985	—	2.00	4.00

REPRISE

Number	Title (A Side/B Side)	Yr	VG	VG+	NM
PRO 248 [DJ]	White Christmas (same on both sides)	1966	2.50	5.00	10.00
0252	La Giostra (Merry-Go-Round)/Grazie, Prego, Scusi	1964	2.00	4.00	8.00
0281	Everybody Loves Somebody/A Little Voice	1964	2.50	5.00	10.00
0307	The Door Is Still Open to My Heart/Every Minute, Every Hour	1964	2.00	4.00	8.00
0333	You're Nobody Till Somebody Loves You/You'll Always Be the One I Love	1964	2.00	4.00	8.00
0344	Send Me the Pillow You Dream On/I'll Be Seeing You	1965	2.00	4.00	8.00
0369	(Remember Me) I'm the One Who Loves You/Born to Lose	1965	2.00	4.00	8.00
0393	Houston/Bumming Around	1965	2.00	4.00	8.00
0415	I Will/You're the Reason I'm in Love	1965	2.00	4.00	8.00
0443	Somewhere There's a Someone/That Old Clock on the Wall	1965	2.00	4.00	8.00
0466	Come Running Back/Bouquet of Roses	1966	—	3.00	6.00
0500	A Million and One/Shades	1966	—	3.00	6.00
0516	Nobody's Baby Again/It Just Happened That Way	1966	—	3.00	6.00
0538	(Open Up the Door) Let the Good Times In/I'm Not the Marrying Kind	1966	—	3.00	6.00
0542	Blue Christmas/A Marshmallow World	1966	—	3.00	6.00
0571	Lay Some Happiness on Me/Think About Me	1967	—	3.00	6.00
0601	In the Chapel in the Moonlight/Welcome to My World	1967	—	3.00	6.00
0608	Little Ole Wine Drinker, Me/I Can't Help Remembering You	1967	—	3.00	6.00
0640	In the Misty Moonlight/Wallpaper Roses	1967	—	3.00	6.00
0640	In the Misty Moonlight/The Glory of Love	1967	—	3.00	6.00
0672	You've Still Got a Place in My Heart/Old Yellow Line	1968	—	2.50	5.00
0703	Lay Some Happiness on Me/(Open Up the Door) Let the Good Times In	1968	—	2.50	5.00
0709	Everybody Loves Somebody/A Million and One	1968	—	2.50	5.00
0711	Somewhere There's a Someone/Come Running Back	1968	—	2.50	5.00
0714	Houston/I Will	1968	—	2.50	5.00
0717	You're Nobody Till Somebody Loves You/(Remember Me) I'm the One Who Loves You	1968	—	2.50	5.00
0718	Send Me the Pillow You Dream On/The Door Is Still Open to My Heart	1968	—	2.50	5.00
0730	In the Chapel in the Moonlight/Little Ole Wine Drinker, Me	1968	—	2.50	5.00
0735	In the Misty Moonlight/Not Enough Indians	1970	—	2.00	4.00
—0703 through 0735 are "Back to Back Hits" reissues					
0761	April Again/That Old Time Feelin'	1968	—	2.50	5.00
0765	Five Card Stud/One Lonely Boy	1968	—	2.50	5.00
0780	Not Enough Indians/Rainbows Are Back in Style	1968	—	2.50	5.00
0812	Gentle on My Mind/That's When I See the Blues	1969	—	2.50	5.00
0841	I Take a Lot of Pride in What I Am/Drowning in My Tears	1969	—	2.50	5.00
0857	Crying TIme/One Cup of Happiness	1969	—	2.50	5.00
0893	Down Home/Come On Down	1970	—	2.50	5.00
0915	For the Love of a Woman/The Tracks of My Tears	1970	—	2.50	5.00
0934	My Woman, My Woman, My Wife/Here We Go Again	1970	—	2.50	5.00
0955	Detroit City/Turn the World Around	1970	—	2.50	5.00
0973	For the Good Times/Georgia Sunshine	1970	—	2.50	5.00
1004	She's a Little Bit Country/Raining in My Heart	1971	—	2.50	5.00
1060	What's Yesterday/The Right Kind of Woman	1971	—	2.50	5.00
1085	I Can Give You What You Want Now/Guess Who	1972	—	2.50	5.00
1141	Amor Mio/You Made Me Love You	1972	—	2.50	5.00
1166	Smile/Get On With Your Livin'	1973	—	2.50	5.00
1178	You're the Best Thing That Ever Happened to Me/Free to Carry On	1973	—	2.50	5.00

Number	Title (A Side/B Side)	Yr	VG	VG+	NM
20058	Just Close Your Eyes/Tik-A-Tee Tik-A-Tay	1962	3.00	6.00	12.00
20082	Baby-O/Dame Su Amor	1962	2.50	5.00	10.00
20116	From the Bottom of My Heart (Dammi, Dammi, Dammi)/Who's Got the Action	1962	2.50	5.00	10.00
20116 [PS]	From the Bottom of My Heart (Dammi, Dammi, Dammi)/Who's Got the Action	1962	5.00	10.00	20.00
20128	Sam's Song/Me and My Shadow	1962	3.75	7.50	15.00
—A-side: With Sammy Davis, Jr.; B-side: Sammy Davis Jr. and Frank Sinatra					
20140	Who's Got the Action/Send a Fine	1963	2.50	5.00	10.00
20150	Ain't Gonna Try Anymore/A Face in the Crowd	1963	2.50	5.00	10.00
20194	Corrine, Corrina/My Sugar's Gone	1963	2.50	5.00	10.00
20215	Via Veneto/Mama Roma	1963	2.50	5.00	10.00
20217	Fugue for Tinhorns/The Oldest Established (Permanent Floating Crap Game in New York)	1963	3.75	7.50	15.00
—By Frank Sinatra/Bing Crosby/Dean Martin					
20217 [PS]	Fugue for Tinhorns/The Oldest Established (Permanent Floating Crap Game in New York)	1963	20.00	40.00	80.00
—By Frank Sinatra/Bing Crosby/Dean Martin					
WARNER BROS.					
29480	Drinking Champagne/Since I Met You Baby	1983	—	2.00	4.00
29584	Hangin' Around/My First Country Song	1983	—	2.00	4.00
7-Inch Extended Plays					
CAPITOL					
EAP 1-401	(contents unknown)	195?	5.00	10.00	20.00
EAP 1-401 [PS]	Dean Martin Sings	195?	5.00	10.00	20.00
EAP 1-481	That's Amore/Oh Marie//Come Back to Sorrento/Luna Mezzo Mare	1954	5.00	10.00	20.00
EAP 1-481 [PS]	Sunny Italy	1954	5.00	10.00	20.00
EAP 1-701	(contents unknown)	1956	3.75	7.50	15.00
EAP 1-701 [PS]	Memories Are Made of This	1956	3.75	7.50	15.00
EAP 1-702	(contents unknown)	1956	3.75	7.50	15.00
EAP 1-702 [PS]	Artists and Models	1956	3.75	7.50	15.00
EAP 1-806	(contents unknown)	1957	3.75	7.50	15.00
EAP 1-806 [PS]	Hollywood or Bust	1957	3.75	7.50	15.00
EAP 1-840	(contents unknown)	1957	3.75	7.50	15.00
EAP 1-840 [PS]	Ten Thousand Bedrooms	1957	3.75	7.50	15.00
EAP 1-849	(contents unknown)	1957	3.00	6.00	12.00
EAP 1-849 [PS]	Pretty Baby, Part 1	1957	3.00	6.00	12.00
EAP 2-849	(contents unknown)	1957	3.00	6.00	12.00
EAP 2-849 [PS]	Pretty Baby, Part 2	1957	3.00	6.00	12.00
EAP 3-849	(contents unknown)	1957	3.00	6.00	12.00
EAP 3-849 [PS]	Pretty Baby, Part 3	1957	3.00	6.00	12.00
EAP 1-939	*Return to Me/Don't You Remember/Forgetting You/Buona Sera	1958	3.75	7.50	15.00
EAP 1-939 [PS]	Return to Me	1958	3.75	7.50	15.00
EAP 1-1285	(contents unknown)	1959	3.00	6.00	12.00
EAP 1-1285 [PS]	A Winter Romance, Part 1	1959	3.00	6.00	12.00
EAP 2-1285	(contents unknown)	1959	3.00	6.00	12.00
EAP 2-1285 [PS]	A Winter Romance, Part 2	1959	3.00	6.00	12.00
EAP 3-1285	(contents unknown)	1959	3.00	6.00	12.00
EAP 3-1285 [PS]	A Winter Romance, Part 3	1959	3.00	6.00	12.00
Albums					
CAPITOL					
SKAO-140	The Best of Dean Martin, Vol. 2	1968	3.75	7.50	15.00
H 401 [10]	Dean Martin Sings	1953	25.00	50.00	100.00
T 401 [M]	Dean Martin Sings	1953	12.50	25.00	50.00
STBB-523 [(2)]	You're Nobody 'Til Somebody Loves You/Return to Me	1970	5.00	10.00	20.00
T 576 [M]	Swingin' Down Yonder	1955	7.50	15.00	30.00
T 849 [M]	Pretty Baby	1957	7.50	15.00	30.00
DT 1047 [R]	This Is Dean Martin	196?	3.00	6.00	12.00
T 1047 [M]	This Is Dean Martin	1958	7.50	15.00	30.00
ST 1150 [S]	Sleep Warm	1959	7.50	15.00	30.00
T 1150 [M]	Sleep Warm	1959	6.25	12.50	25.00
ST 1285 [S]	A Winter Romance	1959	7.50	15.00	30.00
T 1285 [M]	A Winter Romance	1959	5.00	10.00	20.00
ST 1442 [S]	This Time I'm Swingin'	1961	7.50	15.00	30.00
T 1442 [M]	This Time I'm Swingin'	1961	5.00	10.00	20.00
SW 1580 [S]	Dean Martin	1961	7.50	15.00	30.00
W 1580 [M]	Dean Martin	1961	5.00	10.00	20.00
SM-1659	Dino — Italian Love Songs	197?	2.50	5.00	10.00
—Reissue with new prefix					
ST 1659 [S]	Dino — Italian Love Songs	1962	7.50	15.00	30.00
T 1659 [M]	Dino — Italian Love Songs	1962	5.00	10.00	20.00
ST 1702 [S]	Cha Cha De Amor	1962	7.50	15.00	30.00
T 1702 [M]	Cha Cha De Amor	1962	5.00	10.00	20.00
DT 2212 [R]	Hey Brother Pour the Wine	1964	3.00	6.00	12.00
T 2212 [M]	Hey Brother Pour the Wine	1964	5.00	10.00	20.00
ST 2297 [S]	Dean Martin Sings — Sinatra Conducts	1965	5.00	10.00	20.00
T 2297 [M]	Dean Martin Sings — Sinatra Conducts	1965	3.75	7.50	15.00
DT 2333 [R]	Dean Martin — Southern Style	1965	3.00	6.00	12.00
T 2333 [M]	Dean Martin — Southern Style	1965	3.75	7.50	15.00
STT 2343 [S]	Holiday Cheer	1965	5.00	10.00	20.00
—Some copies of this LP have labels that state the title as "Baby, It's Cold Outside."					
TT 2343 [M]	Holiday Cheer	1965	3.75	7.50	15.00
—Reissue of 1285 with one fewer track					
DT 2601 [R]	The Best of Dean Martin	1966	3.00	6.00	12.00
SM-2601	The Best of Dean Martin	197?	2.50	5.00	10.00
—Reissue with new prefix					
T 2601 [M]	The Best of Dean Martin	1966	3.75	7.50	15.00
DTCL 2815 [(3) R]	The Dean Martin Deluxe Set	1967	5.00	10.00	20.00
TCL 2815 [(3) M]	The Dean Martin Deluxe Set	1967	7.50	15.00	30.00
PAIR					
PDL2-1029 [(2)]	Dreams and Memories	1986	3.00	6.00	12.00
PICKWICK					
PTP-2051 [(2)]	Dean Martin	197?	3.00	6.00	12.00
SPC-3057	You Can't Love 'Em All	196?	2.50	5.00	10.00
SPC-3089	I Can't Give You Anything But Love	196?	2.50	5.00	10.00
SPC-3136	Young and Foolish	196?	2.50	5.00	10.00
SPC-3175	You Were Made for Love	197?	2.50	5.00	10.00
SPC-3283	Deluxe	197?	2.50	5.00	10.00
REPRISE					
MS 2053	Dino	1972	3.75	7.50	15.00
MS 2174	You're the Best Thing That Ever Happened to Me	1973	3.75	7.50	15.00
MS 2267	Once in a Lifetime	1978	3.00	6.00	12.00
R-6021 [M]	French Style	1962	3.75	7.50	15.00
R9-6021 [S]	French Style	1962	5.00	10.00	20.00
R-6054 [M]	Dino Latino	1962	3.75	7.50	15.00
R9-6054 [S]	Dino Latino	1962	5.00	10.00	20.00
R-6061 [M]	Country Style	1963	3.75	7.50	15.00
R9-6061 [S]	Country Style	1963	5.00	10.00	20.00
R-6085 [M]	Dean "Tex" Martin Rides Again	1963	3.75	7.50	15.00
R9-6085 [S]	Dean "Tex" Martin Rides Again	1963	5.00	10.00	20.00
R-6123 [M]	Dream with Dean	1964	3.00	6.00	12.00
RS-6123 [S]	Dream with Dean	1964	3.75	7.50	15.00
R-6130 [M]	Everybody Loves Somebody	1964	3.00	6.00	12.00
RS-6130 [S]	Everybody Loves Somebody	1964	3.75	7.50	15.00
R-6140 [M]	The Door Is Still Open to My Heart	1964	3.00	6.00	12.00
RS-6140 [S]	The Door Is Still Open to My Heart	1964	3.75	7.50	15.00
R-6146 [M]	Dean Martin Hits Again	1965	3.00	6.00	12.00
RS-6146 [S]	Dean Martin Hits Again	1965	3.75	7.50	15.00
R-6170 [M]	(Remember Me) I'm the One Who Loves You	1965	3.00	6.00	12.00
RS-6170 [S]	(Remember Me) I'm the One Who Loves You	1965	3.75	7.50	15.00
R-6181 [M]	Houston	1965	3.00	6.00	12.00
RS-6181 [S]	Houston	1965	3.75	7.50	15.00
R-6201 [M]	Somewhere There's a Someone	1966	3.00	6.00	12.00
RS-6201 [S]	Somewhere There's a Someone	1966	3.75	7.50	15.00
R-6211 [M]	The Silencers	1966	5.00	10.00	20.00
RS-6211 [S]	The Silencers	1966	6.25	12.50	25.00
R-6213 [M]	The Hit Sound of Dean Martin	1966	3.00	6.00	12.00
RS-6213 [S]	The Hit Sound of Dean Martin	1966	3.75	7.50	15.00
R 6222 [M]	The Dean Martin Christmas Album	1966	3.75	7.50	15.00
RS 6222 [S]	The Dean Martin Christmas Album	1966	5.00	10.00	20.00
R-6233 [M]	The Dean Martin TV Show	1966	3.00	6.00	12.00
RS-6233 [S]	The Dean Martin TV Show	1966	3.75	7.50	15.00
R-6242 [M]	Happiness Is Dean Martin	1967	3.75	7.50	15.00
RS-6242 [S]	Happiness Is Dean Martin	1967	3.75	7.50	15.00
R-6250 [M]	Welcome to My World	1967	3.75	7.50	15.00
RS-6250 [S]	Welcome to My World	1967	3.75	7.50	15.00
RS-6301	Dean Martin's Greatest Hits! Vol. 1	1968	3.75	7.50	15.00
RS-6320	Dean Martin's Greatest Hits! Vol. 2	1968	3.75	7.50	15.00
RS-6330	Gentle on My Mind	1968	3.75	7.50	15.00
RS-6338	I Take a Lot of Pride in What I Am	1969	3.75	7.50	15.00
RS-6403	My Woman, My Woman, My Wife	1970	3.75	7.50	15.00
RS-6428	For the Good Times	1971	3.75	7.50	15.00
TOWER					
DT 5006 [R]	The Lush Years	1965	3.75	7.50	15.00
T 5006 [M]	The Lush Years	1965	5.00	10.00	20.00
DT 5018 [R]	Relaxin'	1966	3.75	7.50	15.00
T 5018 [M]	Relaxin'	1966	5.00	10.00	20.00
ST 5036 [S]	Happy in Love	1966	5.00	10.00	20.00
T 5036 [M]	Happy in Love	1966	3.75	7.50	15.00
WARNER BROS.					
23870	The Nashville Sessions	1983	3.00	6.00	12.00

MARTIN, DEAN, AND JERRY LEWIS

Number	Title (A Side/B Side)	Yr	VG	VG+	NM
7-Inch Extended Plays					
CAPITOL					
EAP 1-533	(contents unknown)	1954	20.00	40.00	80.00
EAP 1-533 [PS]	Livin' It Up	1954	20.00	40.00	80.00
EAP 1-733	(contents unknown)	1956	15.00	30.00	60.00
EAP 1-733 [PS]	Pardners	1956	15.00	30.00	60.00

MARTIN, DEWEY, AND MEDICINE BALL

Dewey is a former member of BUFFALO SPRINGFIELD.

Number	Title (A Side/B Side)	Yr	VG	VG+	NM
45s					
RCA VICTOR					
74-0489	There Must Be a Reason/Caress Me Pretty Music	1971	2.00	4.00	8.00
UNI					
55178	Jambalaya (On the Bayou)/Ala-Bam	1969	2.00	4.00	8.00
55245	Indian Child/I Do Believe	1970	2.00	4.00	8.00
Albums					
UNI					
73088	Dewey Martin and Medicine Ball	1970	6.25	12.50	25.00

MARTIN, GEORGE

Number	Title (A Side/B Side)	Yr	VG	VG+	NM
45s					
UNITED ARTISTS					
745	Ringo's Theme (This Boy)/And I Love Her	1964	6.25	12.50	25.00
745 [PS]	Ringo's Theme (This Boy)/And I Love Her	1964	75.00	150.00	300.00
750	A Hard Day's Night/I Should Have Known Better	1964	25.00	50.00	100.00
750 [PS]	A Hard Day's Night/I Should Have Known Better	1964	500.00	1000.	2000.
831	All Quiet on the Mersey Front/Cast Your Fate to the Wind	1965	3.75	7.50	15.00
873	I Feel Fine/Downtown	1965	3.75	7.50	15.00
50148	Love in the Open Air/Bahama Sound	1967	7.50	15.00	30.00
Albums					
UNITED ARTISTS					
UAL 3377 [M]	Off the Beatle Track	1964	20.00	40.00	80.00
UAL 3383 [M]	A Hard Day's Night	1964	10.00	20.00	40.00
UAL 3420 [M]	George Martin	1965	10.00	20.00	40.00
UAL 3448 [M]	George Martin Plays "Help"	1965	12.50	25.00	50.00
UAL 3539 [M]	George Martin Salutes the Beatle Girls	1966	12.50	25.00	50.00
UAL 3647 [M]	London by George	1967	7.50	15.00	30.00
UAS 6377 [S]	Off the Beatle Track	1964	25.00	50.00	100.00
UAS 6383 [S]	A Hard Day's Night	1964	12.50	25.00	50.00
UAS 6420 [S]	George Martin	1965	12.50	25.00	50.00
UAS 6448 [S]	George Martin Plays "Help"	1965	20.00	40.00	80.00
UAS 6539 [S]	George Martin Salutes the Beatle Girls	1966	20.00	40.00	80.00
UAS 6647 [S]	London by George	1967	10.00	20.00	40.00

MARTIN, JANIS

Number	Title (A Side/B Side)	Yr	VG	VG+	NM
45s					
PALETTE					
5058	Hard Times Ahead/Here Today and Gone Tomorrow	1960	6.25	12.50	25.00
5071	Teen Street/Cry Guitar	1961	6.25	12.50	25.00

Number	Title (A Side/B Side)	Yr	VG	VG+	NM
RCA VICTOR					
47-6491	Drugstore Rock and Roll/Will You, Willyum	1956	10.00	20.00	40.00
47-6560	Ooby-Dooby/One More Year to Go	1956	10.00	20.00	40.00
47-6652	My Boy Elvis/Little Bit	1956	17.50	35.00	70.00
47-6744	Let's Elope, Baby/Barefoot Baby	1956	7.50	15.00	30.00
47-6832	Love Me to Pieces/Two Long Years	1957	7.50	15.00	30.00
47-6983	Love and Kisses/I'll Never Be Free	1957	7.50	15.00	30.00
47-7104	All Right Baby/Billy Boy, Billy Boy	1957	7.50	15.00	30.00
47-7184	Cracker Jack/Good Love	1958	7.50	15.00	30.00

7-Inch Extended Plays

Number	Title (A Side/B Side)	Yr	VG	VG+	NM
RCA VICTOR					
EPA-4093	Just Squeeze Me (But Don't Tease Me)/My Confession//I Don't Hurt Anymore/Half Loved	1957	37.50	75.00	150.00
EPA-4093 [PS]	Just Squeeze Me	1957	50.00	100.00	200.00

MARTIN, MARTY

45s

Number	Title (A Side/B Side)	Yr	VG	VG+	NM
ANVIL					
1001	All I Got for Christmas Was a Broken Heart/ Hootenanny Santa	1963	2.50	5.00	10.00

MARTIN, VINCE

45s

Number	Title (A Side/B Side)	Yr	VG	VG+	NM
20TH FOX					
214	The Sea Is Green/Is There Somebody Somewhere	1960	3.00	6.00	12.00
ABC-PARAMOUNT					
9992	Goodnight Irene/The Old Grey Goose	1959	3.00	6.00	12.00
10029	Strawberry Fair/Homing Pigeon	1959	3.00	6.00	12.00
CAPITOL					
2565	Summer Wind/I Can't Escape from You	1969	—	3.00	6.00
GLORY					
247	Cindy, Oh Cindy/Only If You Praise the Lord	1956	5.00	10.00	20.00
—With the Tarriers					
252	Katie-O/Anyplace Road	1957	3.75	7.50	15.00
259	Big Dreams/Wait for Me	1957	3.75	7.50	15.00
262	The Midnight Special/Ginny My Joy	1957	3.75	7.50	15.00
266	Goodbye My Love/Oh My Darling, Oh	1957	3.75	7.50	15.00
283	Keep a-Movin'/Sail Me Back	1958	3.75	7.50	15.00

MARTIN, VINCE, AND FRED NEIL

45s

Number	Title (A Side/B Side)	Yr	VG	VG+	NM
ELEKTRA					
45009	Tear Down the Walls/I Know You Rider	1964	2.50	5.00	10.00

Albums

Number	Title (A Side/B Side)	Yr	VG	VG+	NM
ELEKTRA					
EKL-248 [M]	Tear Down the Walls	1964	12.50	25.00	50.00
EKS-7248 [S]	Tear Down the Walls	1964	15.00	30.00	60.00

MARTINEZ, TONY

Albums

Number	Title (A Side/B Side)	Yr	VG	VG+	NM
DEL-FI					
DFLP-1205S [S]	The Many Sides of Pepino	1959	10.00	20.00	40.00
DFLP-1205 [M]	The Many Sides of Pepino	1959	7.50	15.00	30.00

MARTINI, LUIGI, AND THE BAY CITY 5

45s

Number	Title (A Side/B Side)	Yr	VG	VG+	NM
JAGUAR					
3001	Basin Street Blues/Please Don't Talk About Me	1954	75.00	150.00	300.00
3002	Oh Marie/I'm Sorry I Made You Cry	1954	75.00	150.00	300.00

MARTINO, AL

45s

Number	Title (A Side/B Side)	Yr	VG	VG+	NM
20TH CENTURY FOX					
508	My Side of the Story/It's All Over But the Shouting	1964	2.00	4.00	8.00
530	I Can't Get You Out of My Heart/Come Back to Me	1964	2.00	4.00	8.00
575	Mama/My Bella Amore	1965	2.00	4.00	8.00
20TH FOX					
132	I Can't Get You Out of My Heart/Two Hearts Are Better Than One	1959	3.00	6.00	12.00
153	Darling, I Love You/Memory of You	1959	3.00	6.00	12.00
173	I Sold My Heart/Summertime	1960	3.00	6.00	12.00
180	Mama/And I Have You My Love	1960	3.00	6.00	12.00
184	Dearest (Cara)/Hello My Love	1960	3.00	6.00	12.00
200	Journey to Love/Only the Broken Hearted	1960	3.00	6.00	12.00
213	Heart of Hearts/Our Concerto	1960	3.00	6.00	12.00
232	Come Back to Me/It's All Over But the Shouting	1960	3.00	6.00	12.00
237	Little Boy, Little Girl/My Side of the Story	1961	3.00	6.00	12.00
BBS					
101	Here in My Heart/I Cried Myself to Sleep	1952	7.50	15.00	30.00
—With "BBS Records" at top of label					
101	Here in My Heart/I Cried Myself to Sleep	1952	10.00	20.00	40.00
—With "BBS Record Co., Phila. 7, Pa." at top of label					
101	Here in My Heart/I Cried Myself to Sleep	1952	15.00	30.00	60.00
—Red vinyl					
CAPITOL					
2053	A Voice in the Choir/The Glory of Love	1967	—	3.00	6.00
2102	Love Is Blue/I'm Carrying the World on My Shoulders	1968	—	3.00	6.00
F2122	Take My Heart/I Never Cared	1952	5.00	10.00	20.00
2158	Lili Marlene/Georgia	1968	—	3.00	6.00
F2185	Say You'll Wait for Me/I've Never Seen	1952	5.00	10.00	20.00
F2260	Now/In All This World	1952	5.00	10.00	20.00
2285	Wake Up to Me Gentle/If You Must Leave My Life	1968	—	3.00	6.00
F2353	One Lonely Night/Rachel	1953	5.00	10.00	20.00
2355	I Can't Help It (If I'm Still in Love with You)/I Can Only See You	1968	—	3.00	6.00
F2431	Here Are My Arms/There's Music in You	1953	5.00	10.00	20.00
2468	Sausalito/Take My Hand for Awhile	1969	—	3.00	6.00
F2480	This Night I'll Remember/When You're Mine	1953	5.00	10.00	20.00
F2535	All I Want Is a Chance/You Can't Go On Forever Breaking My Heart	1953	5.00	10.00	20.00
F2649	Before/Sweetheart of Mine	1953	5.00	10.00	20.00
2674	I Started Loving You Again/Let Me Stay Awhile (With You)	1969	—	3.00	6.00
F2737	Melancholy Serenade/Way Paesano	1954	5.00	10.00	20.00
2746	Can't Help Falling in Love/You're All the Woman That I Need	1970	—	2.50	5.00
F2826	On and On/Give Me Something to Go with the Wine	1954	5.00	10.00	20.00
2830	Walking in the Sand/One More Mile (And Darlin' I'll Be Home)	1970	—	2.50	5.00
F2899	Don't Go to Strangers/When	1954	5.00	10.00	20.00
2956	True Love Is Greater Than Friendship/The Call	1970	—	2.50	5.00
F2982	Say It Again/The Story of Tina	1954	5.00	10.00	20.00
3056	Come Into My Life/One Pair of Hands	1971	—	2.50	5.00
F3080	Love Is Eternal/Snowy, Snowy Mountains	1955	3.75	7.50	15.00
3120	Too Many Mornings/Losing My Mind	1971	—	2.50	5.00
F3171	To Please My Lady/The Man from Laramie	1955	3.75	7.50	15.00
3256	More Than Ever Now/The Summer Knows	1972	—	2.50	5.00
F3307	Close to Me/The Journey's End	1955	3.75	7.50	15.00
3313	Speak Softly Love/I Have But One Heart	1972	—	2.00	4.00
3444	Take Me Back/Canta Libre	1972	—	2.00	4.00
F3501	The Girl I Left in Rome/Love to Call My Own	1956	3.75	7.50	15.00
3604	If I Give My Heart to You/Hey Mama	1973	—	2.00	4.00
F3605	I'm Sorry/I'm a Funny Guy	1956	3.75	7.50	15.00
3748	Roses in the Sky/Daddy Let's Play	1973	—	2.00	4.00
3763	She/Mary Go Lightly (Como Un Nino)	1973	—	2.00	4.00
3771	Mary Go Lightly (Como Un Nino)/Daddy Let's Play	1973	—	2.00	4.00
3918	Daddy Loves You Honey/More Than Ever Now	1974	—	2.00	4.00
3987	To the Door of the Sun (Alle Porte Del Sol)/Mary Go Lightly	1974	—	2.00	4.00
4071	Charmer/Wake Up	1975	—	2.00	4.00
4134	Volare/You Belong to Me	1975	—	2.00	4.00
4241	The More I See You/My Thrill	1976	—	2.00	4.00
4322	May I Have the Next Dream with You/Sing My Love Song	1976	—	2.00	4.00
4362	Dream of Me/There's Nothing Greater Than Our Love	1976	—	2.00	4.00
4444	Kentucky Mornin'/Sweet Marjorene	1977	—	2.00	4.00
4508	The Next Hundred Years/After the Lovin'	1977	—	2.00	4.00
4551	One Last Time/Here I Go Again	1978	—	2.00	4.00
4593	Here in My Heart/Granada	1961	2.50	5.00	10.00
4643	Pardon/Another Time, Another Place	1961	2.50	5.00	10.00
4681	Torero/Now That I Found You	1979	—	2.00	4.00
4710	Exodus/Love, Where Are You Now	1962	2.50	5.00	10.00
4797	Make Me Believe/Because You're Mine	1962	2.50	5.00	10.00
4798	I Think About You/Only a Dream Away	1979	—	2.00	4.00
—With Kathy Keates					
4897	Almost Gone/Doors	1980	—	2.00	4.00
4930	I Love You Because/Merry-Go-Round	1963	2.00	4.00	8.00
4957	Look Around (You'll Find Me There)/More Than Ever Now	1980	—	2.00	4.00
5000	Painted, Tainted Rose/That's the Way It's Got to Be	1963	2.00	4.00	8.00
5060	Living a Lie/I Love You Truly	1963	2.00	4.00	8.00
A-5094	You and I/Warm Is When You Touch Me	1982	—	—	3.00
5108	I Love You More and More Every Day/I'm Living My Heaven with You	1964	2.00	4.00	8.00
5183	Tears and Roses/A Year Ago Tonight	1964	2.00	4.00	8.00
B-5191	What Your Love Did for Me/Warm Is When You Touch Me	1982	—	—	3.00
5239	Always Together/Thank You for Loving Me	1964	2.00	4.00	8.00
5293	We Could/Sunrise to Sunrise	1964	2.00	4.00	8.00
5311	Silver Bells/You're All I Want for Christmas	1964	2.00	4.00	8.00
5341	My Heart Would Know/Hush, Hush, Sweet Charlotte	1965	2.00	4.00	8.00
5341 [PS]	My Heart Would Know/Hush, Hush, Sweet Charlotte	1965	3.00	6.00	12.00
5384	Somebody Else Is Taking My Place/With All My Heart	1965	2.00	4.00	8.00
5434	My Cherie/Romana	1965	2.00	4.00	8.00
5506	Forgive Me/What Now My Love	1965	2.00	4.00	8.00
5542	Spanish Eyes/Melody of Love	1965	2.00	4.00	8.00
5598	Think I'll Go Somewhere and Cry Myself to Sleep/ Hello Memory	1966	—	3.00	6.00
5652	Wiederseh'n/The Minute You're Gone	1966	—	3.00	6.00
5652 [PS]	Wiederseh'n/The Minute You're Gone	1966	2.50	5.00	10.00
5702	Just Yesterday/By the River of Roses	1966	—	3.00	6.00
5741	The Wheel of Hurt/Somewhere in This World	1966	—	3.00	6.00
5825	Daddy's Little Girl/Devotion	1967	—	3.00	6.00
5904	Mary in the Morning/I Love You and You Love Me	1967	—	3.00	6.00
5989	More Than the Eye Can See/Red Is Red	1967	—	3.00	6.00

Albums

Number	Title (A Side/B Side)	Yr	VG	VG+	NM
20TH CENTURY FOX					
SF-3025 [M]	Al Martino	1959	6.25	12.50	25.00
SFX-3025 [S]	Al Martino	1959	7.50	15.00	30.00
SF-3032 [M]	Sing Along with Al Martino	1959	6.25	12.50	25.00
SFX-3032 [S]	Sing Along with Al Martino	1959	7.50	15.00	30.00
TF-4168 [M]	Al Martino Sings	196?	5.00	10.00	20.00
TFS-4168 [S]	Al Martino Sings	196?	6.25	12.50	25.00
TF-5009 [M]	Love Notes	196?	5.00	10.00	20.00
TFS-5009 [S]	Love Notes	196?	6.25	12.50	25.00
CAPITOL					
ST-180	Sausalito	1969	3.00	6.00	12.00
ST-379	Jean	1969	3.00	6.00	12.00
ST-405	Can't Help Falling in Love	1970	3.00	6.00	12.00
ST-497	My Heart Sings	1970	3.00	6.00	12.00
STBB-526 [(2)]	Here in My Heart/Yesterday	1970	3.75	7.50	15.00
STCL-572 [(3)]	Al Martino	1971	6.25	12.50	25.00
STBB-713 [(2)]	I Wish You Love/Losing You	1971	3.75	7.50	15.00
ST-793	Summer of '42	1971	3.00	6.00	12.00
ST 1774 [S]	The Exciting Voice of Al Martino	1962	5.00	10.00	20.00
T 1774 [M]	The Exciting Voice of Al Martino	1962	3.75	7.50	15.00
ST 1907 [S]	The Italian Voice of Al Martino	1963	5.00	10.00	20.00
T 1907 [M]	The Italian Voice of Al Martino	1963	3.75	7.50	15.00

Number	Title (A Side/B Side)	Yr	VG	VG+	NM
ST 1914 [S]	I Love You Because	1963	3.75	7.50	15.00
T 1914 [M]	I Love You Because	1963	3.00	6.00	12.00
ST 1975 [S]	Painted, Tainted Rose	1963	3.75	7.50	15.00
T 1975 [M]	Painted, Tainted Rose	1963	3.00	6.00	12.00
ST 2040 [S]	Living a Lie	1964	3.75	7.50	15.00
T 2040 [M]	Living a Lie	1964	3.00	6.00	12.00
ST 2107 [S]	I Love You More and More Every Day/Tears and Roses	1964	3.75	7.50	15.00
T 2107 [M]	I Love You More and More Every Day/Tears and Roses	1964	3.00	6.00	12.00
ST 2165 [S]	A Merry Christmas from Al Martino	1964	3.75	7.50	15.00
T 2165 [M]	A Merry Christmas from Al Martino	1964	3.00	6.00	12.00
ST 2200 [S]	We Could	1964	3.75	7.50	15.00
T 2200 [M]	We Could	1964	3.00	6.00	12.00
ST 2312 [S]	Somebody Else Is Taking My Place	1965	3.75	7.50	15.00
T 2312 [M]	Somebody Else Is Taking My Place	1965	3.00	6.00	12.00
ST 2362 [S]	My Cherie	1965	3.75	7.50	15.00
T 2362 [M]	My Cherie	1965	3.00	6.00	12.00
ST 2435 [S]	Spanish Eyes	1966	3.75	7.50	15.00
T 2435 [M]	Spanish Eyes	1966	3.00	6.00	12.00
ST 2528 [S]	Think I'll Go Somewhere and Cry Myself to Sleep	1966	3.75	7.50	15.00
T 2528 [M]	Think I'll Go Somewhere and Cry Myself to Sleep	1966	3.00	6.00	12.00
ST 2592 [S]	This Is Love	1966	3.75	7.50	15.00
T 2592 [M]	This Is Love	1966	3.00	6.00	12.00
ST 2654 [S]	This Love for You	1967	3.75	7.50	15.00
T 2654 [M]	This Love for You	1967	3.75	7.50	15.00
ST 2733 [S]	Daddy's Little Girl	1967	3.75	7.50	15.00
T 2733 [M]	Daddy's Little Girl	1967	3.75	7.50	15.00
ST 2780 [S]	Mary in the Morning	1967	3.75	7.50	15.00
T 2780 [M]	Mary in the Morning	1967	3.75	7.50	15.00
ST 2843	This Is Al Martino	1968	3.75	7.50	15.00
ST 2908	Love Is Blue	1968	3.75	7.50	15.00
SKAO 2946	The Best of Al Martino	1968	3.75	7.50	15.00
SM-2946	The Best of Al Martino	197?	2.50	5.00	10.00
—Reissue with new prefix					
ST 2983	Wake Up to Me Gentle	1968	3.75	7.50	15.00
SM-11071	Love Theme from "The Godfather"	1977	2.00	4.00	8.00
—Reissue with new prefix					
ST-11071	Love Theme from "The Godfather"	1972	2.50	5.00	10.00
ST-11302	I Won't Last a Day Without You	1974	2.50	5.00	10.00
ST-11366	To the Door of the Sun	1975	2.50	5.00	10.00
ST-11572	Sing My Love Songs	1976	2.50	5.00	10.00
SM-11679	To the Door of the Sun	1977	2.00	4.00	8.00
—Reissue of 11366					
ST-11741	The Next Hundred Years	1978	2.50	5.00	10.00
SN-16074	The Best of Al Martino	1981	2.00	4.00	8.00
—Budget-line reissue					

MOVIETONE

Number	Title (A Side/B Side)	Yr	VG	VG+	NM
MTM 2002 [M]	That Old Feeling	196?	3.75	7.50	15.00
MTM 2015 [M]	All of Me	1967	5.00	10.00	20.00
MTS 72002 [S]	That Old Feeling	196?	5.00	10.00	20.00
MTS 72015 [S]	All of Me	1967	3.75	7.50	15.00

PICKWICK

Number	Title (A Side/B Side)	Yr	VG	VG+	NM
SPC-3049	Don't Go to Strangers	196?	3.00	6.00	12.00
SPC-3276	Mary in the Morning	197?	2.50	5.00	10.00

SPRINGBOARD

Number	Title (A Side/B Side)	Yr	VG	VG+	NM
4074	Time After Time	1978	2.00	4.00	8.00

MARTY

45s

NOVELTY

Number	Title (A Side/B Side)	Yr	VG	VG+	NM
101	Marty on Planet Mars (Part 1)/Marty on Planet Mars (Part 2)	1956	10.00	20.00	40.00

MARTY AND THE SYMBOLS

45s

GRAPHIC ARTS

Number	Title (A Side/B Side)	Yr	VG	VG+	NM
1000	You're the One/Rip Van Winkle	1963	20.00	40.00	80.00

MARVELETTES, THE

45s

A&M

Number	Title (A Side/B Side)	Yr	VG	VG+	NM
1201	Danger Heartbreak Dead Ahead/Baby Please Don't Go	1988	—	2.00	4.00
—B-side by Them					
1201 [PS]	Danger Heartbreak Dead Ahead/Baby Please Don't Go	1988	—	2.00	4.00
—"Good Morning Vietnam" sleeve					

GORDY

Number	Title (A Side/B Side)	Yr	VG	VG+	NM
7024	Too Hurt to Cry, Too Much in Love to Say Goodbye/Come On Home	1963	20.00	40.00	80.00
—As "The Darnells"					

TAMLA

Number	Title (A Side/B Side)	Yr	VG	VG+	NM
54046	Please Mr. Postman/So Long Baby	1961	6.25	12.50	25.00
54046 [PS]	Please Mr. Postman/So Long Baby	1961	30.00	60.00	120.00
54054	Twistin' Postman/I Want a Guy	1962	5.00	10.00	20.00
54054 [PS]	Twistin' Postman/I Want a Guy	1962	25.00	50.00	100.00
54060	Playboy/All the Love I've Got	1962	5.00	10.00	20.00
54065	Beechwood 4-5789/Someday, Someway	1962	5.00	10.00	20.00
54072	Strange I Know/Too Strong to Be Strung Along	1962	3.75	7.50	15.00
54077	Forever/Locking Up My Heart	1963	3.75	7.50	15.00
54082	Tie a String Around My Finger/My Daddy Knows Best	1963	5.00	10.00	20.00
54088	As Long As I Know He's Mine/Little Girl Blue	1963	3.00	6.00	12.00
54091	He's a Good Guy (Yes He Is)/Goddess of Love	1964	3.00	6.00	12.00
54091 [DJ]	Yes He Is	1964	18.75	37.50	75.00
—One-sided promo with different title than stock copy					
54097	You're My Remedy/A Little Bit of Sympathy, A Little Bit of Love	1964	2.50	5.00	10.00
54097 [PS]	You're My Remedy/A Little Bit of Sympathy, A Little Bit of Love	1964	15.00	30.00	60.00
54105	Too Many Fish in the Sea/A Need for Love	1964	2.50	5.00	10.00
54116	I'll Keep Holding On/No Time for Tears	1965	2.50	5.00	10.00
54120	Danger, Heartbreak Dead Ahead/Your Cheating Ways	1965	2.50	5.00	10.00
54126	Don't Mess with Bill/Anything You Wanna Do	1965	2.50	5.00	10.00
54131	You're the One/Paper Boy	1966	2.50	5.00	10.00
54143	The Hunter Gets Captured by the Game/I Think I Can Change You	1967	2.50	5.00	10.00
54150	When You're Young and In Love/The Day You Take One, You Have to Take the Other	1967	2.50	5.00	10.00
54158	My Baby Must Be a Magician/I Need Someone	1967	2.50	5.00	10.00
54166	Here I Am Baby/Keep Off, No Trespassing	1968	2.50	5.00	10.00
54171	Destination: Anywhere/What's So Easy for Two Is So Hard for One	1968	2.50	5.00	10.00
54177	I'm Gonna Hold On Long As I Can/Don't Make Hurting Me a Habit	1968	2.50	5.00	10.00
54186	That's How Heartaches Are Made/Rainy Mourning	1969	2.50	5.00	10.00
54198	Marionette/After All	1970	2.00	4.00	8.00
54213	A Breath Taking Guy/You're the One for Me Baby	1972	2.00	4.00	8.00

TOPPS/MOTOWN

Number	Title (A Side/B Side)	Yr	VG	VG+	NM
12	Please Mr. Postman	1967	18.75	37.50	75.00
—Cardboard record					

Albums

MOTOWN

Number	Title (A Side/B Side)	Yr	VG	VG+	NM
M5-180V1	Greatest Hits	1981	2.50	5.00	10.00
—Reissue of Tamla 253					
M7-827 [(2)]	Anthology	1975	3.75	7.50	15.00
5266 ML	Please Mr. Postman	1982	2.50	5.00	10.00
—Reissue of Tamla 228					

TAMLA

Number	Title (A Side/B Side)	Yr	VG	VG+	NM
T-228 [M]	Please Mr. Postman	1961	150.00	300.00	600.00
—White label					
T-228 [M]	Please Mr. Postman	1963	75.00	150.00	300.00
—Yellow label with globes logo					
T-229 [M]	Smash Hits of 62'	1962	600.00	900.00	1200.
—Title as listed on front cover; large black "M" with song titles in circles					
T-229 [M]	The Marveletts Sing	1962	125.00	250.00	500.00
—Title as listed on front cover (misspelled); all-black cover with white circles					
T-229 [M]	The Marveletts Sing	1963	62.50	125.00	250.00
—Yellow label with side-by-side globes logo					
T-231 [M]	Playboy	1962	125.00	250.00	500.00
—Yellow label with overlapping record and globe logo					
T-231 [M]	Playboy	1962	150.00	300.00	600.00
—White label					
T-231 [M]	Playboy	1963	62.50	125.00	250.00
—Yellow label with side-by-side globes logo					
T-237 [M]	The Marvelous Marvelettes	1963	37.50	75.00	150.00
T-243 [M]	Recorded Live On Stage	1963	20.00	40.00	80.00
T-253 [M]	Greatest Hits	1966	7.50	15.00	30.00
—Yellow cover					
T-253 [M]	Greatest Hits	1967	6.25	12.50	25.00
—Green cover					
TS-253 [S]	Greatest Hits	1966	10.00	20.00	40.00
—Yellow cover					
TS-253 [S]	Greatest Hits	1967	5.00	10.00	20.00
—Green cover					
T-274 [M]	The Marveletttes	1967	7.50	15.00	30.00
TS-274 [S]	The Marveletttes	1967	5.00	10.00	20.00
T-286 [M]	Sophisticated Soul	1968	10.00	20.00	40.00
TS-286 [S]	Sophisticated Soul	1968	5.00	10.00	20.00
TS-288	In Full Bloom	1969	3.75	7.50	15.00
TS-305	Return of the Marvelettes	1970	3.75	7.50	15.00

MARVELLOS, THE (1)

45s

CHA CHA

Number	Title (A Side/B Side)	Yr	VG	VG+	NM
756	Come Back My Love/Boyee Yoing	1963	7.50	15.00	30.00

STEPHENY

Number	Title (A Side/B Side)	Yr	VG	VG+	NM
1818	Come Back My Love/Boyee Yoing	1958	50.00	100.00	200.00

MARVELLOS, THE (2)

45s

EXODUS

Number	Title (A Side/B Side)	Yr	VG	VG+	NM
6214	Salty Sam/She Told Me Lies	1962	50.00	100.00	200.00
6216	I Ask of You/Hip Enough	1962	30.00	60.00	120.00

REPRISE

Number	Title (A Side/B Side)	Yr	VG	VG+	NM
20088	Salty Sam/She Told Me Lies	1962	7.50	15.00	30.00

MARVELLOS, THE (3)

45s

LOMA

Number	Title (A Side/B Side)	Yr	VG	VG+	NM
2045	Something's Burning/We Go Together	1966	3.00	6.00	12.00
2061	You're Such a Sweet Thing/Why Do You Want to Hurt the One You Love	1966	3.00	6.00	12.00

MODERN

Number	Title (A Side/B Side)	Yr	VG	VG+	NM
1054	Down in the City/In the Sunshine	1967	2.50	5.00	10.00

WARNER BROS.

Number	Title (A Side/B Side)	Yr	VG	VG+	NM
7011	Don't Play with My Heart/Let Me Keep You Satisfied	1967	2.50	5.00	10.00
7054	Piece of Silk/Yes I Do	1967	2.50	5.00	10.00

MARVELLOS, THE (U)

Could be group (1); it's doubtful that these could be either of the other two.

45s

MARVELLO

Number	Title (A Side/B Side)	Yr	VG	VG+	NM
5005	Red Hot Momma/I Need a Girl	1955	75.00	150.00	300.00

THERON

Number	Title (A Side/B Side)	Yr	VG	VG+	NM
117	You're the Dream/Calypso Mama	1957	100.00	200.00	400.00

MARVELOWS, THE

45s

ABC

Number	Title (A Side/B Side)	Yr	VG	VG+	NM
10820	Fade Away/You've Been Going to Sally	1966	2.50	5.00	10.00

Number	Title (A Side/B Side)	Yr	VG	VG+	NM
11011	In the Morning/Talkin' 'Bout Ya, Baby	1967	2.00	4.00	8.00
—As "The Mighty Marvelows"					
11073	I'm So Confused/I'm Without a Girl	1968	2.00	4.00	8.00
—As "The Mighty Marvelows"					
11139	Hey, Hey Girl/Wait, Be Cool	1968	2.00	4.00	8.00
—As "The Mighty Marvelows"					
11189	You're Breaking My Heart/This Town's Too Much	1969	2.00	4.00	8.00
—As "The Mighty Marvelows"					
ABC-PARAMOUNT					
10613	A Friend/Hey, Hey Baby	1965	2.50	5.00	10.00
10629	I Do/My Heart	1965	3.75	7.50	15.00
10708	Shim Sham/Your Little Sister	1965	2.50	5.00	10.00
10756	Do It/I've Got My Eyes on You	1965	2.50	5.00	10.00
Albums					
ABC					
S-643	The Mighty Marvelows	1968	7.50	15.00	30.00

MARVELS, THE (1)

Early version of THE DUBS.

Number	Title (A Side/B Side)	Yr	VG	VG+	NM
45s					
ABC-PARAMOUNT					
9771	I Won't Have You Breaking My Heart/Jump Rock and Roll	1956	150.00	300.00	600.00

MARVELS, THE (2)

Number	Title (A Side/B Side)	Yr	VG	VG+	NM
45s					
LAURIE					
3106	I Shed So Many Tears/So Young, So Sweet	1958	17.50	35.00	70.00
—Also released as "The Marvells"					

MARVELS, THE (3)

Number	Title (A Side/B Side)	Yr	VG	VG+	NM
45s					
MUN-RAB					
1008	Just Another Fool/You Crack Me Up	1959	375.00	750.00	1500.

MARVELS, THE (U)

May be group (2).

Number	Title (A Side/B Side)	Yr	VG	VG+	NM
45s					
WINN					
1916	For Sentimental Reasons/Come Back	1961	50.00	100.00	200.00

MARVIN AND JOHNNY

Number	Title (A Side/B Side)	Yr	VG	VG+	NM
45s					
ALADDIN					
3371	Yak Yak/Pretty Eyes	1957	7.50	15.00	30.00
3408	You're in My Heart/Smack Smack	1958	7.50	15.00	30.00
3439	It's Christmas/The Valley of Love	1958	7.50	15.00	30.00
FELSTED					
8681	Hot Biscuits and Gravy/Tired of Being Alone	1963	3.00	6.00	12.00
JAMIE					
1188	Once Upon a Time/Tick Tock	1961	3.00	6.00	12.00
LIBERTY					
1394	It's Christmas/It's Christmas Time	1980	—	2.50	5.00
—B-side by the Five Keys					
MODERN					
933	Tick Tock/Cherry Pie	1954	18.75	37.50	75.00
941	Sugar/Kiss Me	1954	12.50	25.00	50.00
946	Little Honey/Honey Girl	1955	12.50	25.00	50.00
949	Ko Ko Mo/Sometimes I Wonder	1955	10.00	20.00	40.00
952	I Love You, Yes I Do/Baby Won't You Marry Me	1955	10.00	20.00	40.00
959	Butler Ball/Sugar Mama	1955	10.00	20.00	40.00
968	Will You Love Me/Sweet Dreams	1956	7.50	15.00	30.00
974	Ain't That Right/Let Me Know	1956	7.50	15.00	30.00
SPECIALTY					
479	Baby Doll/I'm Not a Fool	1953	15.00	30.00	60.00
479	Baby Doll/I'm Not a Fool	1953	25.00	50.00	100.00
—Red vinyl					
488	Jo Jo/How Long Has She Been Gone	1954	15.00	30.00	60.00
498	School of Love/Boy Loves Girl	1954	15.00	30.00	60.00
530	Day In — Day Out/Flip	1954	15.00	30.00	60.00
554	Ding Dong Baby/Mamo Mamo	1955	12.50	25.00	50.00
SWINGIN'					
641	I'm Tired of Being Alone/Baby You Don't Know	1962	3.00	6.00	12.00
645	Pretty One/Second Helping of Cherry Pie	1963	3.00	6.00	12.00
Albums					
CROWN					
CST-381 [R]	Marvin and Johnny	1963	3.00	6.00	12.00
CLP-5381 [M]	Marvin and Johnny	1963	12.50	25.00	50.00

MARVIN AND THE CHIRPS

Number	Title (A Side/B Side)	Yr	VG	VG+	NM
45s					
TIP TOP					
202	I'll Miss You This Christmas/Sixteen Tons	1958	50.00	100.00	200.00

MARX, THE

Number	Title (A Side/B Side)	Yr	VG	VG+	NM
45s					
CHANTE					
1002	One Minute More/You Are My Love	19??	50.00	100.00	200.00
DAHLIA					
1002	One Minute More/You Are My Love	19??	25.00	50.00	100.00

MARY BUTTERWORTH

Number	Title (A Side/B Side)	Yr	VG	VG+	NM
Albums					
CUSTOM FIDELITY					
2092	Mary Butterworth	1969	75.00	150.00	300.00

MARYLANDERS, THE

Number	Title (A Side/B Side)	Yr	VG	VG+	NM
45s					
JUBILEE					
5079	I'm a Sentimental Fool/Sittin' By the River	1952	100.00	200.00	400.00
5091	Make Me Thrill Again/Please Love Me	1952	100.00	200.00	400.00
5114	Fried Chicken/Good Old 99	1953	100.00	200.00	400.00
—Red vinyl					
5114	Fried Chicken/Good Old 99	1953	75.00	150.00	300.00

MASCOTS, THE (1)

Number	Title (A Side/B Side)	Yr	VG	VG+	NM
45s					
ABC					
11152	Baby, You're So Wrong/Moreen	1968	2.00	4.00	8.00

MASCOTS, THE (2)

Number	Title (A Side/B Side)	Yr	VG	VG+	NM
45s					
BLAST					
206	Once Upon a Love/Hey Little Angel	1963	10.00	20.00	40.00
—Red label					
206	Once Upon a Love/Hey Little Angel	1963	5.00	10.00	20.00
—White label					
MERMAID					
107	Bluebirds Over the Mountain/Timberlands	1962	20.00	40.00	80.00

MASCOTS, THE (3)

Later recorded as THE O'JAYS.

Number	Title (A Side/B Side)	Yr	VG	VG+	NM
45s					
KING					
5377	The Story of My Heart/Do the Wiggle	1960	25.00	50.00	100.00
5435	Lonely Rain/That's the Way I Feel	1960	15.00	30.00	60.00

MASCOTS, THE (4)

Number	Title (A Side/B Side)	Yr	VG	VG+	NM
45s					
MGM					
12027	Relax-Ay-Voo/The Others I Like	1955	5.00	10.00	20.00
12107	Nobody's Arms/Little Mustard Seed	1955	5.00	10.00	20.00
12236	Who Put the Devil in Evelyn's Eyes/Java Jive	1956	5.00	10.00	20.00

MASCOTS, THE (U)

If this is any of the above groups, it's most likely group (1).

Number	Title (A Side/B Side)	Yr	VG	VG+	NM
45s					
RUMBLE					
4197	I Want Love/Waited So Long	196?	5.00	10.00	20.00

MASEKELA, HUGH

Number	Title (A Side/B Side)	Yr	VG	VG+	NM
12-Inch Singles					
JIVE					
9194	Don't Go Lose It Baby (3 versions)	1984	2.00	4.00	8.00
9361	Lady (Remix)/Lady (LP Version)//Coal Train (Live 17:16)	1985	2.50	5.00	10.00
WARNER BROS.					
20634	Bring Him Back Home (Extended) (Instrumental)/ Serengeti	1987	2.00	4.00	8.00
20684	Bring Him Back Home (Extended) (Live)/Stimela (Live)	1987	2.00	4.00	8.00
45s					
A&M					
2107	Foreign Natives/Mama Way	1979	—	2.00	4.00
—With Herb Alpert					
BLUE THUMB					
244	Languta/Rekpete	1973	—	2.50	5.00
255	Been Such a Long Time Gone/Jungle Jim	1974	—	2.00	4.00
260	African Secret Society/Jungle Jim	1974	—	2.00	4.00
CASABLANCA					
848	Excuse Me Please/The Boy's Doin' It	1975	—	2.00	4.00
857	For the Love of You/Witch Doctor	1976	—	2.00	4.00
861	A Person Is a Sometime Thing/Mama	1976	—	2.00	4.00
862	Dance/(B-side unknown)	1976	—	2.00	4.00
879	Hi-Life/Toejam	1977	—	2.00	4.00
CHISA					
003	Chisa/What Is Wrong with Groovin'	1970	—	3.00	6.00
8009	You Keep Me Hangin' On/Make Me a Potion	1971	—	3.00	6.00
8014	Dyambo/Shebeen	1971	—	3.00	6.00
HORIZON					
115	Skokiaan/African Summer	1978	—	2.00	4.00
—With Herb Alpert					
116	Lobo/African Summer	1978	—	2.00	4.00
—With Herb Alpert					
JIVE					
9198	Don't Go Lose It Baby/(Instrumental)	1984	—	—	3.00
9360	Lady/Cool Train	1985	—	—	3.00
MERCURY					
72853	Emavungwani (Green Home)/U-Dwi (Smallpox)	1968	—	3.00	6.00
MGM					
CS3-5 [DJ]	Celebrity Scene: Hugh Masekela	1966	12.50	25.00	50.00
—Box set of five singles (13643-13647). Price includes box, all 5 singles, jukebox title strips, bio. Records are sometimes found by themselves, so they are also listed separately.					
13601	Along Comes Mary/Little Star	1966	—	3.00	6.00
13643 [DJ]	California Dreamin'/U-Dwi	1966	2.00	4.00	8.00
13644 [DJ]	Norwegian Wood/Cantaloupe Island	1966	2.00	4.00	8.00
13645 [DJ]	She's Comin' My Way/Unhlanhla	1966	2.00	4.00	8.00
13646 [DJ]	Along Comes Mary/Little Star	1966	2.00	4.00	8.00
13647 [DJ]	If I Needed Someone/From Me to You	1966	2.00	4.00	8.00
13901	Norwegian Wood/Sound of Silence	1968	—	3.00	6.00
UNI					
55024	Baby, Baby, Baby/Lily the Fox	1967	—	3.00	6.00
55037	Up-Up and Away/Son of the Ice Bag	1967	—	3.00	6.00
55049	There Are Seeds to Sow/Ha Lese Le Di Khana	1968	—	3.00	6.00
55066	Grazing in the Grass/Bajabula Bounce	1968	—	3.00	6.00
55085	Puffin' On Down the Track/Do Me So Lo, So So	1968	—	3.00	6.00
55102	Riot/Mace and Grenades	1968	—	3.00	6.00
55116	A Long Ways from Home/Home Boy	1969	—	3.00	6.00
55130	10,000 Miles to Memphis/Gettin' It On	1969	—	3.00	6.00
55165	Where Has All the Grass Grown/I Haven't Slept	1969	—	3.00	6.00
WARNER BROS.					
28419	Bring Him Back Home/Serengeti	1987	—	—	3.00

Number	Title (A Side/B Side)	Yr	VG	VG+	NM
Albums					
ABC IMPULSE!					
IA-9343 [(2)]	African Connection	1978	3.00	6.00	12.00
BLUE THUMB					
BT-62	Introducing Hedzoleh Sounds	1972	2.50	5.00	10.00
BT-6003	Home Is Where the Music Is	1973	2.50	5.00	10.00
BT-6015	I Am Not Afraid	1974	2.50	5.00	10.00
CASABLANCA					
NBLP 7017	The Boy's Doin' It	1975	2.50	5.00	10.00
NBLP 7023	Colonial Man	1976	2.50	5.00	10.00
NBLP 7036	Melody Maker	1977	2.50	5.00	10.00
NBLP 7079	You Told Your Mama	1978	2.50	5.00	10.00
CHISA					
CS-803	Reconstruction	1970	3.00	6.00	12.00
CS-808	Union of South Africa	1971	3.00	6.00	12.00
JIVE					
JL-8210	Techno Bush	1984	2.50	5.00	10.00
JL-8382	Waiting for the Rain	1985	2.50	5.00	10.00
MERCURY					
MG-20797 [M]	The Trumpet of Hugh Masekela	1963	3.75	7.50	15.00
SR-60797 [S]	The Trumpet of Hugh Masekela	1963	5.00	10.00	20.00
SR-61109	Grr	1969	3.00	6.00	12.00
MGM					
GAS-116	Hugh Masekela (Golden Archive Series)	1970	3.00	6.00	12.00
E-4372 [M]	The Americanization of Ooga Booga	1966	3.00	6.00	12.00
SE-4372 [S]	The Americanization of Ooga Booga	1966	3.75	7.50	15.00
E-4415 [M]	Hugh Masekela's Next Album	1966	3.00	6.00	12.00
SE-4415 [S]	Hugh Masekela's Next Album	1966	3.75	7.50	15.00
NOVUS					
3070-1-R	Uptownship	1990	3.00	6.00	12.00
UNI					
3010 [M]	Hugh Masekela's Latest	1967	3.75	7.50	15.00
3015 [M]	Hugh Masekela Is Alive and Well at the Whisky	1967	5.00	10.00	20.00
73010 [S]	Hugh Masekela's Latest	1967	3.00	6.00	12.00
73015 [S]	Hugh Masekela Is Alive and Well at the Whisky	1967	3.00	6.00	12.00
73028	The Promise of a Future	1968	3.00	6.00	12.00
73041	Masekela	1969	3.00	6.00	12.00
73051	Masekela — Vol. 2	1970	3.00	6.00	12.00
VERVE					
V6-8651 [(2)]	24 Karat Hits	1968	3.75	7.50	15.00
WARNER BROS.					
25566	Tomorrow	1987	2.50	5.00	10.00

MASH, THE

Number	Title (A Side/B Side)	Yr	VG	VG+	NM
45s					
COLUMBIA					
45130	Suicide Is Painless/M*A*S*H March	1970	3.00	6.00	12.00
45130	Song from M*A*S*H/M*A*S*H March	1970	2.00	4.00	8.00
—Alternate A-side title					

MASHMAKHAN

Early version of APRIL WINE.

Number	Title (A Side/B Side)	Yr	VG	VG+	NM
45s					
EPIC					
10634	As the Years Go By/The Days When We Are Free	1970	—	3.00	6.00
JAMIE					
1418	One Night Stand/Dance a Little Step	1969	2.00	4.00	8.00
Albums					
EPIC					
E 30235	Mashmakhan	1970	3.00	6.00	12.00
E 30813	The Family	1971	3.00	6.00	12.00

MASKED MARAUDERS, THE

Fictional supergroup from a Rolling Stone magazine album review, which noted the presence of Bob Dylan, Mick Jagger, John Lennon and Paul McCartney. The below, recorded using the bogus review as a guide, was actually THE CLEANLINESS AND GODLINESS SKIFFLE BAND.

Number	Title (A Side/B Side)	Yr	VG	VG+	NM
45s					
DEITY					
0870	I Can't Get No Nookie/Cow Pie	1969	3.75	7.50	15.00
Albums					
DEITY					
RS 6378	The Masked Marauders	1969	5.00	10.00	20.00

MASON, BARBARA

Number	Title (A Side/B Side)	Yr	VG	VG+	NM
12-Inch Singles					
WEST END					
22164	Another Man (4 versions)	1983	—	3.00	6.00
WMOT					
02237	Let Me Give You Love/(Instrumental)	1981	2.00	4.00	8.00
45s					
ARCTIC					
102	Girls Have Feelings Too/Come to Me	1964	3.00	6.00	12.00
105	Yes I'm Ready/Keep Him	1965	5.00	10.00	20.00
108	Sad, Sad Girl/Come to Me	1965	3.00	6.00	12.00
112	You Got What It Takes/If You Don't (Love Me, Tell Me So)	1965	3.00	6.00	12.00
116	Don't Ever Want to Lose Your Love/Is It Me	1965	3.00	6.00	12.00
120	I Need Love/Bobby Is My Baby	1966	2.50	5.00	10.00
126	Hello Baby/Poor Girl I'm in Trouble	1966	2.50	5.00	10.00
134	You Can Depend on Me/Game of Love	1967	2.00	4.00	8.00
137	Oh, How It Hurts/Ain't Got Nobody	1967	2.00	4.00	8.00
140	Dedicated to the One I Love/Half a Love	1968	2.00	4.00	8.00
142	Half a Love/(I Can Feel Your Love) Slipping Away	1968	2.00	4.00	8.00
146	Don't Ever Go Away/I'm No Good for You	1968	2.00	4.00	8.00
148	Take It Easy/You Never Loved Me	1969	2.00	4.00	8.00
154	You Better Stop It/Happy Girl	1969	2.00	4.00	8.00
BUDDAH					
249	The Pow Pow Song (Sorry Sorry Baby)/Your Old Flame	1971	—	3.00	6.00
296	Bed and Board/Yes It's You	1972	—	2.50	5.00
319	Woman and Man/Who Will You Hurt Next	1972	—	2.50	5.00
331	Give Me Your Love/You Can Be with the One You Don't Love	1972	—	2.50	5.00
355	Yes I'm Ready/Who Will You Hurt Next	1973	—	2.50	5.00
375	Child of Tomorrow/Out of This World	1973	—	2.50	5.00
395	Caught in the Middle/Give Him Up	1973	—	2.50	5.00
405	World War III/I Miss You Gordon	1974	—	2.50	5.00
424	Our Day Will Come/Half Sister, Half Brother	1974	—	2.50	5.00
441	From His Woman to You/When You Wake Up in Georgia	1974	—	2.50	5.00
459	Shackin' Up/One Man Between Us	1975	—	2.50	5.00
481	Make It Last/We Got Each Other	1975	—	2.50	5.00
—With the Futures					
481 [PS]	Make It Last/We Got Each Other	1975	2.00	4.00	8.00
CRUSADER					
111	Dedicated to You/Trouble Child	1965	2.50	5.00	10.00
NATIONAL GENERAL					
005	Raindrops Keep Fallin' on My Head/If You Knew Him Like I Do	1970	—	3.00	6.00
PRELUDE					
71103	I Am Your Woman, She Is Your Wife/Take Me Tonight	1978	—	2.50	5.00
71111	Darling Come Back Home Soon/It Was You Boy	1978	—	2.50	5.00
WEST END					
1264	Another Man (Vocal) (Short)/Another Man (Instrumental)	1984	—	2.00	4.00
WMOT					
02506	She's Got the Papers (But I've Got the Man)/(Instrumental)	1981	—	2.00	4.00
5352	I'll Never Love the Same Way Twice/(B-side unknown)	1980	—	2.00	4.00
70077	On and Off/You're All Inside of Me	1981	—	2.00	4.00
Albums					
ARCTIC					
ALP-1000 [M]	Yes, I'm Ready	1965	7.50	15.00	30.00
ALPS-1000 [P]	Yes, I'm Ready	1965	12.50	25.00	50.00
ALPS-1004	Oh, How It Hurts	1968	7.50	15.00	30.00
BUDDAH					
BDS-5117	Give Me Your Love	1972	3.00	6.00	12.00
BDS-5140	Lady Love	1973	3.00	6.00	12.00
BDS-5610	Transition	1974	3.00	6.00	12.00
BDS-5628	Love's the Thing	1975	3.00	6.00	12.00
NATIONAL GENERAL					
2001	If You Knew Him Like I Do	1970	7.50	15.00	30.00

MASON, BARBARA, AND BUNNY SIGLER

Also see each artist's individual listings.

Number	Title (A Side/B Side)	Yr	VG	VG+	NM
12-Inch Singles					
CURTOM					
PRO-A-689 [DJ]	Locked in This Position (10:05)/Love Song (6:14)	1977	3.75	7.50	15.00
Albums					
CURTOM					
CU 5014	Locked in This Position	1977	2.50	5.00	10.00

MASON, BONNIE JO

See CHER.

MASON, DAVE

Also see DAVE MASON AND CASS ELLIOT; TRAFFIC.

Number	Title (A Side/B Side)	Yr	VG	VG+	NM
12-Inch Singles					
COLUMBIA					
ASF 308 [DJ]	So High (same on both sides)	1977	3.00	6.00	12.00
MCA					
L33-17468 [DJ]	Dreams I Dream (same on both sides)	1987	—	3.00	6.00
—With Phoebe Snow					
L33-17541 [DJ]	Two Hearts (same on both sides)	1988	—	3.00	6.00
45s					
BLUE THUMB					
112	World and Changes/Can't Stop Worrying	1970	—	3.00	6.00
114	Only You Know and I Know/Sad and Deep As You	1970	—	3.00	6.00
205	A Heartache, a Shadow, a Lifetime/Can't Stop Worrying	1972	—	3.00	6.00
209	To Be Free/Pearly Queen	1972	—	3.00	6.00
276	Only You Know and I Know/Sad and Deep As You	1975	—	2.50	5.00
7117	Satin and Red Velvet Woman/Shouldn't Have Took More Than You Gave	1971	—	3.00	6.00
7122	Just a Song/Waitin' on You	1971	—	3.00	6.00
COLUMBIA					
10074	Bring it On Home to Me/Harmony and Melody	1974	—	2.50	5.00
10104	Every Woman/Relationships	1975	—	2.50	5.00
10162	Show Me Some Affection/Get a Hold on Love	1975	—	2.50	5.00
10246	Long Lost Friend/Split Coconut	1975	—	2.50	5.00
10469	All Along the Watchtower/Sad and Deep As You	1976	—	2.50	5.00
10509	So High (Rock Me Baby and Roll Me Away)/You Just Have to Wait Now	1977	—	2.50	5.00
10575	We Just Disagree/Mystic Traveler	1977	—	2.50	5.00
10662	Let it Go, Let It Flow/Takin' the Time to Find	1978	—	2.50	5.00
10749	Will You Still Love Me Tomorrow/Mystic Traveler	1978	—	2.50	5.00
10819	Warm Desire/Don't It Make You Wonder	1978	—	2.50	5.00
11289	Save Me/Tryin' to Get Back to You	1980	—	2.00	4.00
45947	Baby... Please/Side-Tracked	1973	—	2.50	5.00
MCA					
53205	Dreams I Dream/Fighting for Love	1987	—	2.00	4.00
—A-side with Phoebe Snow					
Albums					
BLUE THUMB					
BTS-19	All Together	1970	50.00	100.00	200.00
—Erroneous pressing of "Alone Together"					
BTS-19	Alone Together	1970	5.00	10.00	20.00
—Originals on multicolored vinyl					
BTS-19	Alone Together	1975	3.00	6.00	12.00
—Multicolor label with "ABC" logo					
BTS-34	Headkeeper	1972	3.75	7.50	15.00

Number	Title (A Side/B Side)	Yr	VG	VG+	NM
BTS-54	Dave Mason Is Alive!	1973	3.75	7.50	15.00
ABCD-880	Dave Mason At His Best	1975	2.50	5.00	10.00
BT-6013	The Best of Dave Mason	1974	2.50	5.00	10.00
BT-6032	Very Best of Dave Mason	1978	2.50	5.00	10.00
BTS-8819	Alone Together	1971	12.50	25.00	50.00
—Capitol-distributed black vinyl reissue					
CHUMLEY					
00101	Some Assembly Required	1987	2.50	5.00	10.00
COLUMBIA					
CQ 31721 [Q]	It's Like You Never Left	1973	4.50	9.00	18.00
KC 31721	It's Like You Never Left	1973	2.50	5.00	10.00
PC 31721	It's Like You Never Left	197?	2.00	4.00	8.00
—Reissue with new prefix					
PC 33096	Dave Mason	1974	2.50	5.00	10.00
—No bar code on cover					
PC 33096	Dave Mason	198?	2.00	4.00	8.00
—Budget-line reissue with bar code					
PCQ 33096 [Q]	Dave Mason	1974	4.50	9.00	18.00
PC 33698	Split Coconut	1975	2.50	5.00	10.00
PCQ 33698 [Q]	Split Coconut	1975	4.50	9.00	18.00
PG 34174 [(2)]	Certified Live	1976	3.00	6.00	12.00
PC 34680	Let It Flow	1977	2.50	5.00	10.00
—No bar code on cover					
PC 34680	Let It Flow	198?	2.00	4.00	8.00
—Budget-line reissue with bar code					
JC 35285	Mariposa de Oro	1978	2.50	5.00	10.00
JC 36144	Old Crest on a New Wave	1980	2.50	5.00	10.00
FC 37089	The Best of Dave Mason	1981	2.50	5.00	10.00
PC 37089	The Best of Dave Mason	1983	2.00	4.00	8.00
—Budget-line reissue					
MCA					
712	Headkeeper	198?	2.00	4.00	8.00
—Reissue of Blue Thumb 34					
713	Dave Mason Is Alive	198?	2.00	4.00	8.00
—Reissue of Blue Thumb 54					
714	Dave Mason At His Best	198?	2.00	4.00	8.00
—Reissue of Blue Thumb 880					
715	Very Best of Dave Mason	198?	2.00	4.00	8.00
—Reissue of Blue Thumb 6032					
800	The Best of Dave Mason	1981	2.00	4.00	8.00
—Reissue of Blue Thumb 6013					
11319	Alone Together	1995	5.00	10.00	20.00
—"Heavy Vinyl" gatefold reissue					
27035	Alone Together	198?	2.00	4.00	8.00
—Reissue of Blue Thumb 19					
42086	Two Hearts	1988	2.50	5.00	10.00

MASON, DAVE, AND CASS ELLIOT

45s

Number	Title (A Side/B Side)	Yr	VG	VG+	NM
ABC DUNHILL					
4266	Something to Make You Happy/Next to You	1971	—	3.00	6.00
4271	Walking to the Point/Too Much Truth, Too Much Love	1971	—	3.00	6.00

Albums

Number	Title (A Side/B Side)	Yr	VG	VG+	NM
BLUE THUMB					
BTS-8825	Dave Mason and Cass Elliot	1971	5.00	10.00	20.00

MASON, EULIS

45s

Number	Title (A Side/B Side)	Yr	VG	VG+	NM
BELLA					
20	Carol Lee/Rockin' Santa Claus	1959	10.00	20.00	40.00
—B-side by the Martels					

MASON, JACKIE

45s

Number	Title (A Side/B Side)	Yr	VG	VG+	NM
VERVE					
10289	Don't Blame the Bossa Nova/I Gave My Love	1963	3.00	6.00	12.00

Albums

Number	Title (A Side/B Side)	Yr	VG	VG+	NM
VERVE					
V-15033 [M]	I'm the Greatest Comedian in the World Only Nobody Knows It Yet	1962	5.00	10.00	20.00
V-15034 [M]	I Want to Leave You with the Words of a Great Comedian	1963	5.00	10.00	20.00
V-15045 [M]	Great Moments in Comedy	1964	5.00	10.00	20.00
WARNER BROS.					
25603	The World According to Me!	1987	2.50	5.00	10.00

MASON PROFFIT

45s

Number	Title (A Side/B Side)	Yr	VG	VG+	NM
AMPEX					
11048	Hope/Jewel	1971	—	3.00	6.00
HAPPY TIGER					
545	Voice of Change/A Rectangle Picture	1970	—	3.00	6.00
552	Two Hangmen/Sweet Lady of Love	1970	—	3.00	6.00
570	Hard Luck Woman/Good Friend of Mary's	1971	—	3.00	6.00
WARNER BROS.					
7709	I Saw the Light/Lilly	1973	—	2.50	5.00

Albums

Number	Title (A Side/B Side)	Yr	VG	VG+	NM
AMPEX					
A-10138	Last Night I Had the Strangest Dream	1971	3.00	6.00	12.00
HAPPY TIGER					
HT-1009	Wanted! Mason Proffit	1970	3.75	7.50	15.00
HT-1019	Movin' Toward Happiness	1971	3.75	7.50	15.00
WARNER BROS.					
BS 2657	Rockfish Crossing	1972	2.50	5.00	10.00
BS 2704	Bareback Rider	1973	2.50	5.00	10.00
2WS 2746 [(2)]	Come and Gone	1974	3.00	6.00	12.00

MASONICS, THE

45s

Number	Title (A Side/B Side)	Yr	VG	VG+	NM
INTERPHON					
7714	Mariner II/Call It a Day	1965	2.50	5.00	10.00

MASTER-TONES, THE

45s

Number	Title (A Side/B Side)	Yr	VG	VG+	NM
BRUCE					
111	What'll You Do/Tell Me	1954	125.00	250.00	500.00
—Black vinyl, "New York 19, N.Y." address					
111	What'll You Do/Tell Me	1954	75.00	150.00	300.00
—Blue vinyl					
111	What'll You Do/Tell Me	1962	12.50	25.00	50.00
—Black vinyl, "New York, N.Y." address					

MASTERETTES, THE

45s

Number	Title (A Side/B Side)	Yr	VG	VG+	NM
LE SAGE					
716	Never Ever/Follow the Leader	1961	37.50	75.00	150.00

MASTERS, JOHNNY; MASTRO, JOHNNY

See JOHNNY MAESTRO.

MASTERS, KEN

45s

Number	Title (A Side/B Side)	Yr	VG	VG+	NM
DECCA					
31084	Too Late/Parting Hour	1960	5.00	10.00	20.00

MATADORS, THE (1)

45s

Number	Title (A Side/B Side)	Yr	VG	VG+	NM
CHART MAKER					
404	Let Me Dream/Wiggle Wobble	1966	37.50	75.00	150.00
FORBES					
230	Let Me Dream/Wiggle Wobble	1966	6.25	12.50	25.00

MATADORS, THE (2)

45s

Number	Title (A Side/B Side)	Yr	VG	VG+	NM
COLPIX					
698	Ace of Hearts/Perfidia	1963	6.25	12.50	25.00
718	I've Gotta Drive/La Corrida	1963	12.50	25.00	50.00
—A-side is a Jan and Dean track with a new spoken introduction					
741	C'mon, Let Yourself Go (Part 1)/C'mon, Let Yourself Go (Part 2)	1964	6.25	12.50	25.00

MATADORS, THE (3)

45s

Number	Title (A Side/B Side)	Yr	VG	VG+	NM
KEITH					
6502	If You Left Me Today/It Ain't Nothin' But Rock 'N' Roll	1962	10.00	20.00	40.00
6504	You'd Be Crying, Too/My Foolish Heart	1963	20.00	40.00	80.00

MATADORS, THE (4)

45s

Number	Title (A Side/B Side)	Yr	VG	VG+	NM
SUE					
700	Pennies from Heaven/Vengeance	1957	30.00	60.00	120.00
701	Be Good to Me/Have Mercy Baby	1957	20.00	40.00	80.00

MATADORS, THE (U)

Could be group (2) or (3).

45s

Number	Title (A Side/B Side)	Yr	VG	VG+	NM
JAMIE					
1226	Listen/So Near	1962	5.00	10.00	20.00

MATHERS, JERRY

Better known as "The Beaver."

45s

Number	Title (A Side/B Side)	Yr	VG	VG+	NM
ATLANTIC					
2156	Don'tcha Cry/Wind-Up Toy	1962	5.00	10.00	20.00
2156 [PS]	Don'tcha Cry/Wind-Up Toy	1962	10.00	20.00	40.00

MATHIS, BOBBY, AND THE SEVILLES

45s

Number	Title (A Side/B Side)	Yr	VG	VG+	NM
SIOUX					
51860	Girl in the Drugstore/Going to the City	1960	37.50	75.00	150.00

MATHIS, JOHNNY

12-Inch Singles

Number	Title (A Side/B Side)	Yr	VG	VG+	NM
COLUMBIA					
CAS 1400 [DJ]	Daydreamin' (same on both sides)	1988	2.50	5.00	10.00
CAS 1805 [DJ]	In the Still of the Night (same on both sides)	1989	2.50	5.00	10.00
—With Take 6					
AS 1867 [DJ]	Simple/(Instrumental)	1984	—	3.50	7.00
05034	Simple/(Instrumental)	1984	—	3.00	6.00
07837	Begin the Beguine/Simple	198?	—	3.00	6.00
—"Mixed Masters" reissue					
CAS 8322 [DJ]	Let Your Heart Remember/(Dub Mix)	199?	2.50	5.00	10.00
11002	Begin the Beguine/Gone, Gone, Gone	1979	2.50	5.00	10.00

45s

Number	Title (A Side/B Side)	Yr	VG	VG+	NM
COLUMBIA					
(no #) [DJ]	Columbia Records Presents Johnny Mathis — Take 2	1957	7.50	15.00	30.00
—Promo-only gatefold sleeve containing white-label promos of 40784 and 40851					
SS-7 [S]	The Best of Everything/The Theme from "A Summer Place"	1960	3.75	7.50	15.00
—B-side by Percy Faith; "Stereo Seven" single, small hole, plays at 33 1/3 rpm					
AS 93 [DJ]	The Heart of a Woman (same on both sides)	1974	2.50	5.00	10.00
—Promo release for the Helena Rubenstein cosmetics firm					
AS 93 [PS]	Helena Rubenstein Presents Johnny Mathis for Courant	1974	3.75	7.50	15.00
—Promo sleeve with above single					
AE7 1148 [DJ]	Christmas Is/Sleigh Ride	1977	2.00	4.00	8.00
AE7 1148 [PS]	Christmas Is/Sleigh Ride	1977	3.00	6.00	12.00
—Above single and sleeve were the 1977 Christmas Seals record					
02194	Nothing Between Us But Love/Deep Purple	1981	—	—	3.00
03222	When the Lovin' Goes Out of the Lovin'/Warm	1982	—	—	3.00

Number	Title (A Side/B Side)	Yr	VG	VG+	NM
04468	Simple/Lead Me to Your Love	1984	—	—	3.00
04856	Right From the Heart/Hold On	1985	—	—	3.00
05588	Just One Touch/I Need You (The Journey)	1985	—	—	3.00
06561	Where Can I Find Christmas?/It's Beginning to Look a Lot Like Christmas	1986	—	2.00	4.00
07797	I'm on the Outside Looking In/Just Like You	1988	—	—	3.00
08524	Daydreamin'/Love Brought Us Here Tonight	1988	—	—	3.00
10080	Sail On White Moon/The Heart of a Woman	1974	—	2.50	5.00
10112	I'm Stone in Love with You/Foolish	1975	—	2.50	5.00
10175	The Greatest Gift/You're As Right As Rain	1975	—	2.50	5.00
10250	Stardust/What I Did for Love	1975	—	2.50	5.00
10291	One Day in Your Life/Midnight Blue	1976	—	2.50	5.00
10350	Yellow Roses on Her Gown/Every Time You Touch Me (I Get High)	1976	—	2.50	5.00
10404	Do Me Wrong, But Do Me/Send In the Clowns	1976	—	2.50	5.00
10447	When a Child Is Born/Turn the Lights Down	1976	—	2.50	5.00
10496	Loving You, Losing You/World of Laughter	1977	—	2.50	5.00
10574	Arianne/99 Miles from L.A.	1977	—	2.50	5.00
10611	Hold Me, Thrill Me, Kiss Me/The Most Beautiful Girl	1977	—	2.50	5.00
10640	When a Child Is Born/Every Time You Touch Me (I Get High)	1977	—	2.50	5.00
10902	The Last Time I Felt Like This/As Time Goes By	1979	—	2.00	4.00
—A-side with Jane Olivor					
11001	Begin the Beguine/Gone, Gone, Gone	1979	—	2.00	4.00
11091	No One Else But the One You Love/To the Ends of the Earth	1979	—	2.00	4.00
—A-side with Stephanie Lawrence					
11158	Christmas in the City of the Angels/The Very First Christmas Day	1979	—	2.50	5.00
11313	Different Kinda Different/The Lights of Rio	1980	—	2.00	4.00
—A-side with Paulette					
11409	When a Child Is Born/The Lord's Prayer	1980	—	2.00	4.00
—With Gladys Knight and the Pips					
30355 [S]	Someone/Very Much in Love	1959	5.00	10.00	20.00
—"Stereo Seven" single, small hole, plays at 33 1/3 rpm					
30410 [S]	Small World/You Are Everything to Me	1959	5.00	10.00	20.00
—"Stereo Seven" single, small hole, plays at 33 1/3 rpm					
30483 [S]	Misty/The Story of Our Love	1959	5.00	10.00	20.00
—"Stereo Seven" single, small hole, plays at 33 1/3 rpm					
30583 [S]	The Best of Everything/Cherie	1959	5.00	10.00	20.00
—"Stereo Seven" single, small hole, plays at 33 1/3 rpm					
30598 [S]	Heavenly/Hello, Young Lovers	1959	3.75	7.50	15.00
—"Stereo Seven" single, small hole, plays at 33 1/3 rpm					
30599 [S]	Misty/Stranger in Paradise	1959	3.75	7.50	15.00
—"Stereo Seven" single, small hole, plays at 33 1/3 rpm					
30600 [S]	Tonight/Maria	1959	3.75	7.50	15.00
—"Stereo Seven" single, small hole, plays at 33 1/3 rpm					
30601 [S]	Secret Love/And This Is My Beloved	1959	3.75	7.50	15.00
—"Stereo Seven" single, small hole, plays at 33 1/3 rpm					
30684 [S]	Maria/Hey Love	1960	3.75	7.50	15.00
—"Stereo Seven" single, small hole, plays at 33 1/3 rpm					
30764 [S]	My Love for You/Oh That Feeling	1960	3.75	7.50	15.00
—"Stereo Seven" single, small hole, plays at 33 1/3 rpm					
30828 [S]	Everything's Coming Up Roses/I Wish I Were in Love Again	1960	3.00	6.00	12.00
—Part of "JS7-9"; "Stereo Seven" single, small hole, plays at 33 1/3 rpm					
30829 [S]	You Do Something To Me/Let's Misbehave	1960	3.00	6.00	12.00
—Part of "JS7-9"; "Stereo Seven" single, small hole, plays at 33 1/3 rpm					
30830 [S]	I Could Have Danced All Night/A Cock-Eyed Optimist	1960	3.00	6.00	12.00
—Part of "JS7-9"; "Stereo Seven" single, small hole, plays at 33 1/3 rpm					
30831 [S]	I Just Found Out About Love/Let's Do It	1960	3.00	6.00	12.00
—Part of "JS7-9"; "Stereo Seven" single, small hole, plays at 33 1/3 rpm					
30832 [S]	I Am in Love/Love Eyes	1960	3.00	6.00	12.00
—Part of "JS7-9"; "Stereo Seven" single, small hole, plays at 33 1/3 rpm					
30866 [S]	How to Handle a Woman/While You're Young	1960	3.75	7.50	15.00
—"Stereo Seven" single, small hole, plays at 33 1/3 rpm					
30980 [S]	You Set My Heart to Music/Jenny	1961	3.75	7.50	15.00
—"Stereo Seven" single, small hole, plays at 33 1/3 rpm					
31048 [S]	Laurie, My Love/Should I Wait	1961	3.75	7.50	15.00
—"Stereo Seven" single, small hole, plays at 33 1/3 rpm					
31238 [S]	Christmas Eve/My Kind of Christmas	1961	6.25	12.50	25.00
—"Stereo Seven" single, small hole, plays at 33 1/3 rpm					
31261 [S]	Sweet Thursday/One Look	1962	5.00	10.00	20.00
—"Stereo Seven" single, small hole, plays at 33 1/3 rpm					
31344 [S]	Live It Up/Just Friends	1962	3.00	6.00	12.00
—Part of "JS7-47"; "Stereo Seven" single, small hole, plays at 33 1/3 rpm					
31345 [S]	Why Not/On a Cold and Rainy Day	1962	3.00	6.00	12.00
—Part of "JS7-47"; "Stereo Seven" single, small hole, plays at 33 1/3 rpm					
31346 [S]	I Won't Dance/Johnny One Note	1962	3.00	6.00	12.00
—Part of "JS7-47"; "Stereo Seven" single, small hole, plays at 33 1/3 rpm					
31347 [S]	Crazy in the Heart/Too Much Too Soon	1962	3.00	6.00	12.00
—Part of "JS7-47"; "Stereo Seven" single, small hole, plays at 33 1/3 rpm					
31348 [S]	Hey Look Me Over/Love	1962	3.00	6.00	12.00
—Part of "JS7-47"; "Stereo Seven" single, small hole, plays at 33 1/3 rpm					
31420 [S]	Marianna/Unaccustomed As I Am	1962	5.00	10.00	20.00
—"Stereo Seven" single, small hole, plays at 33 1/3 rpm					
31509 [S]	That's the Way It Is/I'll Never Be Lonely Again	1962	5.00	10.00	20.00
—"Stereo Seven" single, small hole, plays at 33 1/3 rpm					
31582 [S]	Gina/I Love Her That's Why	1962	5.00	10.00	20.00
—"Stereo Seven" single, small hole, plays at 33 1/3 rpm					
31666 [S]	What Will Mary Say/Quiet Girl	1963	6.25	12.50	25.00
—"Stereo Seven" single, small hole, plays at 33 1/3 rpm					
31666 [S]	What Will My Mary Say/Quiet Girl	1963	6.25	12.50	25.00
—"Stereo Seven" single, small hole, plays at 33 1/3 rpm; revised A-side title					
31731 [S]	Rapture/Love Me As Though There Were No Tomorrow	1963	3.00	6.00	12.00
—Part of "JS7-78"; "Stereo Seven" single, small hole, plays at 33 1/3 rpm					
31732 [S]	Moments Like This/You've Come Home	1963	3.00	6.00	12.00
—Part of "JS7-78"; "Stereo Seven" single, small hole, plays at 33 1/3 rpm					
31733 [S]	Here I'll Stay/My Darling, My Darling	1963	3.00	6.00	12.00
—Part of "JS7-78"; "Stereo Seven" single, small hole, plays at 33 1/3 rpm					
31734 [S]	Stars Fell on Alabama/I Was Telling Her About You	1963	3.00	6.00	12.00
—Part of "JS7-78"; "Stereo Seven" single, small hole, plays at 33 1/3 rpm					

Number	Title (A Side/B Side)	Yr	VG	VG+	NM
31735 [S]	Lost in Loveliness/Stella by Starlight	1963	3.00	6.00	12.00
—Part of "JS7-78"; "Stereo Seven" single, small hole, plays at 33 1/3 rpm					
31799 [S]	Every Step of the Way/No Man Can Stand Alone	1963	3.75	7.50	15.00
—"Stereo Seven" single, small hole, plays at 33 1/3 rpm					
31836 [S]	Sooner or Later/In Wisconsin	1963	3.75	7.50	15.00
—"Stereo Seven" single, small hole, plays at 33 1/3 rpm					
31916 [S]	I'll Search My Heart/All the Sad Young Men	1963	3.75	7.50	15.00
—"Stereo Seven" single, small hole, plays at 33 1/3 rpm					
33001	It's Not for Me to Say/Chances Are	196?	—	3.00	6.00
—Red label					
33001	It's Not for Me to Say/Chances Are	198?	—	—	3.00
—Gray label					
3-33001	It's Not for Me to Say/Chances Are	196?	3.75	7.50	15.00
—"Hall of Fame Series"; "Columbia Single 33"; small hole					
33042	Maria/Misty	196?	—	3.00	6.00
—Red label					
33042	Maria/Misty	198?	—	—	3.00
—Gray label					
33048	Wonderful, Wonderful/The Twelfth of Never	196?	—	3.00	6.00
—Red label					
33048	Wonderful, Wonderful/The Twelfth of Never	198?	—	—	3.00
—Gray label					
33056	Small World/A Certain Smile	196?	—	3.00	6.00
—Red label					
33056	Small World/A Certain Smile	198?	—	—	3.00
—Gray label					
33142	Venus/Gina	196?	—	3.00	6.00
—Red label					
33142	Venus/Gina	198?	—	—	3.00
—Gray label					
33174	I'll Never Fall in Love Again/A Time for Us	197?	—	2.00	4.00
—Red label					
33174	I'll Never Fall in Love Again/A Time for Us	198?	—	—	3.00
—Gray label					
33226	What Will My Mary Say/Call Me	197?	—	2.00	4.00
—Red label					
33226	What Will My Mary Say/Call Me	198?	—	—	3.00
—Gray label					
33253	Show and Tell/Soul and Inspiration-Just Once in My Life	197?	—	2.00	4.00
—Red label					
33253	Show and Tell/Soul and Inspiration-Just Once in My Life	198?	—	—	3.00
—Gray label					
33264	I'm Coming Home/I'm Stone in Love with You	197?	—	2.00	4.00
—Red label					
33264	I'm Coming Home/I'm Stone in Love with You	198?	—	—	3.00
—Gray label					
JZSP 39330 [DJ]	In Other Words (Complete Version)/In Other Words (Short Version)	1956	6.25	12.50	25.00
—Promo only, possibly his first single. Came with a "Columbia Records Introduces" sleeve, the presence of which doubles the value					
40784	Wonderful! Wonderful!/When Sunny Gets Blue	1956	3.00	6.00	12.00
40851	It's Not for Me to Say/Warm and Tender	1957	3.00	6.00	12.00
40993	Chances Are/The Twelfth of Never	1957	2.50	5.00	10.00
40993 [PS]	Chances Are/The Twelfth of Never	1957	5.00	10.00	20.00
41060	No Love (But Your Love)/Wild Is the Wind	1957	2.50	5.00	10.00
41060 [PS]	No Love (But Your Love)/Wild Is the Wind	1957	3.75	7.50	15.00
41082	Come to Me/When I Am With You	1957	2.50	5.00	10.00
41152	All the Time/Teacher, Teacher	1958	2.50	5.00	10.00
41193	A Certain Smile/Let It Rain	1958	2.50	5.00	10.00
41193 [PS]	A Certain Smile/Let It Rain	1958	3.75	7.50	15.00
41253	Call Me/Stairway to the Sea	1958	2.50	5.00	10.00
41253 [PS]	Call Me/Stairway to the Sea	1958	3.75	7.50	15.00
41304	Let's Love/You Are Beautiful	1958	2.50	5.00	10.00
41355	Someone/Very Much in Love	1959	2.50	5.00	10.00
41410	Small World/You Are Everything to Me	1959	2.50	5.00	10.00
41483	Misty/The Story of Our Love	1959	2.50	5.00	10.00
41483 [PS]	Misty/The Story of Our Love	1959	3.75	7.50	15.00
41491	The Best of Everything/Cherie	1959	2.50	5.00	10.00
41491 [PS]	The Best of Everything/Cherie	1959	3.75	7.50	15.00
41583	Starbright/All Is Well	1960	2.00	4.00	8.00
41583 [PS]	Starbright/All Is Well	1960	3.00	6.00	12.00
41684	Maria/Hey Love	1960	2.00	4.00	8.00
—Reissued in 1961 with the same catalog number					
41764	My Love for You/Oh That Feeling	1960	2.00	4.00	8.00
3-41764	My Love for You/Oh That Feeling	1960	3.75	7.50	15.00
—"Columbia Single 33"; small hole					
41866	How to Handle a Woman/While You're Young	1960	2.00	4.00	8.00
41866 [PS]	How to Handle a Woman/While You're Young	1960	3.00	6.00	12.00
3-41866	How to Handle a Woman/While You're Young	1960	3.75	7.50	15.00
—"Columbia Single 33"; small hole					
41980	You Set My Heart to Music/Jenny	1961	2.00	4.00	8.00
41980 [PS]	You Set My Heart to Music/Jenny	1961	3.00	6.00	12.00
3-41980	You Set My Heart to Music/Jenny	1961	3.75	7.50	15.00
—"Columbia Single 33"; small hole					
42005	Should I Wait/Oh How I Try	1961	—	—	—
—Unreleased?					
3-42005	Should I Wait/Oh How I Try	1961	—	—	—
—Unreleased?					
42048	Laurie My Love/Should I Wait (Or Should I Run to Her)	1961	2.00	4.00	8.00
42048 [PS]	Laurie My Love/Should I Wait (Or Should I Run to Her)	1961	3.00	6.00	12.00
3-42048	Laurie My Love/Should I Wait (Or Should I Run to Her)	1961	3.75	7.50	15.00
—"Columbia Single 33"; small hole					
42156	Wasn't the Summer Short/There You Are	1961	2.00	4.00	8.00
42156 [PS]	Wasn't the Summer Short/There You Are	1961	3.00	6.00	12.00
3-42156	Wasn't the Summer Short/There You Are	1961	3.75	7.50	15.00
—"Columbia Single 33"; small hole					
42238	My Kind of Christmas/Christmas Eve	1961	3.00	6.00	12.00
42238 [PS]	My Kind of Christmas/Christmas Eve	1961	5.00	10.00	20.00
3-42238	My Kind of Christmas/Christmas Eve	1961	5.00	10.00	20.00
—"Columbia Single 33"; small hole					
42261	Sweet Thursday/One Look	1962	2.00	4.00	8.00

Number	Title (A Side/B Side)	Yr	VG	VG+	NM
42261 [PS]	Sweet Thursday/One Look	1962	3.00	6.00	12.00
3-42261	Sweet Thursday/One Look	1962	3.75	7.50	15.00
—"Columbia Single 33"; small hole					
42420	Marianna/Unaccustomed As I Am	1962	2.00	4.00	8.00
42420 [PS]	Marianna/Unaccustomed As I Am	1962	3.00	6.00	12.00
3-42420	Marianna/Unaccustomed As I Am	1962	3.75	7.50	15.00
—"Columbia Single 33"; small hole					
42509	That's the Way It Is/I'll Never Be Lonely Again	1962	2.00	4.00	8.00
42509 [PS]	That's the Way It Is/I'll Never Be Lonely Again	1962	2.50	5.00	10.00
3-42509	That's the Way It Is/I'll Never Be Lonely Again	1962	3.75	7.50	15.00
—"Columbia Single 33"; small hole					
42582	Gina/I Love Her That's Why	1962	2.00	4.00	8.00
42582 [DJ]	Gina (same on both sides)	1962	5.00	10.00	20.00
—Promo only on red vinyl					
42582 [PS]	Gina/I Love Her That's Why	1962	2.50	5.00	10.00
3-42582	Gina/I Love Her That's Why	1962	3.75	7.50	15.00
—"Columbia Single 33"; small hole					
42666	What Will Mary Say/Quiet Girl	1963	2.50	5.00	10.00
42666	What Will My Mary Say/Quiet Girl	1963	2.00	4.00	8.00
—Revised A-side title					
42666 [DJ]	What Will My Mary Say (same on both sides)	1963	5.00	10.00	20.00
—Promo only on red vinyl					
42666 [PS]	What Will Mary Say/Quiet Girl	1963	3.00	6.00	12.00
3-42666	What Will Mary Say/Quiet Girl	1963	5.00	10.00	20.00
—"Columbia Single 33"; small hole					
3-42666	What Will My Mary Say/Quiet Girl	1963	3.75	7.50	15.00
—"Columbia Single 33"; small hole; revised A-side title					
42799	Every Step of the Way/No Man Can Stand Alone	1963	2.00	4.00	8.00
42799 [PS]	Every Step of the Way/No Man Can Stand Alone	1963	2.50	5.00	10.00
3-42799	Every Step of the Way/No Man Can Stand Alone	1963	5.00	10.00	20.00
—"Columbia Single 33"; small hole					
42836	Sooner or Later/In Wisconsin	1963	2.00	4.00	8.00
3-42836	Sooner or Later/In Wisconsin	1963	5.00	10.00	20.00
—"Columbia Single 33"; small hole					
42916	I'll Search My Heart/All the Sad Young Men	1963	2.00	4.00	8.00
42916 [DJ]	I'll Search My Heart (same on both sides)	1963	5.00	10.00	20.00
—Promo only on red vinyl					
44266	Misty Roses/Don't Talk to Me	1967	—	2.50	5.00
44357	Among the First to Know/Long Winter Nights	1967	—	2.50	5.00
44517	Venus/Don't Go Breakin' My Heart	1968	—	2.50	5.00
44637	You Make Me Think About You/Night Dreams	1968	—	2.50	5.00
44728	The End of the World/The 59th Street Bridge Song (Feelin' Groovy)	1968	—	2.50	5.00
44837	I'll Never Fall in Love Again/Whoever You Are, I Love You	1969	—	2.50	5.00
44915	Love Theme from Romeo and Juliet (A Time for Us)/The World I Threw Away	1969	—	2.50	5.00
JZSP 44991 [DJ]	The Christmas Song (Merry Christmas to You)/What Child Is This?	1958	5.00	10.00	20.00
45022	Midnight Cowboy/We	1969	—	2.50	5.00
45035	Give Me Your Love for Christmas/Calypso Noel	1969	—	3.00	6.00
45035 [PS]	Give Me Your Love for Christmas/Calypso Noel	1969	2.00	4.00	8.00
45100 [DJ]	Give Me Your Love for Christmas/Calypso Noel	1969	2.00	4.00	8.00
45100 [PS]	Give Me Your Love for Christmas/Calypso Noel	1969	2.50	5.00	10.00
—The above sleeve and record were the 1969 Christmas Seals promo					
45104	For All We Know/Odds and Ends	1970	—	2.50	5.00
45183	The Last Time I Saw Her/Wherefore and Why	1970	—	2.50	5.00
45223	Darling Lili/Pieces of Dreams	1970	—	2.50	5.00
45263	Until It's Time for You to Go/Evil Ways	1970	—	2.50	5.00
JZSP 45265 [DJ]	An Open Fire/I Concentrate on You	1959	5.00	10.00	20.00
45281	Christmas Is/Sign of the Dove	1970	—	2.50	5.00
45323	I Was There/Ten Times Forever More	1971	—	2.50	5.00
45371	Evie/Think About Things	1971	—	2.50	5.00
45415	Long Ago and Far Away/For All We Know	1971	—	2.50	5.00
45470	How Can You Mend a Broken Heart/If We Only Have Love	1971	—	2.50	5.00
45513	Christmas Is/Sign of the Dove	1971	—	2.50	5.00
45559	If We Only Have Love/This Way, Mary	1972	—	2.50	5.00
45635	Make It Easy on Yourself/Sometimes	1972	—	2.50	5.00
45729	Soul and Inspiration-Just Once in My Life/I	1972	—	2.50	5.00
45777	Walking Tall (Theme)/Take Good Care of Her	1973	—	2.50	5.00
45835	Show and Tell/Happy (Theme from Lady Sings the Blues)	1973	—	2.50	5.00
45908	I'm Coming Home/Stop, Look, and Listen to Your Heart	1973	—	2.50	5.00
45975	Life Is a Song Worth Singing/I Just Wanted to Be Me	1973	—	2.50	5.00
46048	I'm Stone in Love with You/Sweet Child	1974	—	2.50	5.00
JZSP 55369 [DJ]	Maria/Tonight	1959	5.00	10.00	20.00
69092	In the Still of the Night/True Love Ways	1989	—	2.00	4.00
—A-side with Take 6					
MERCURY					
DJ-72 [DJ]	Chim Chim Cheree (same on both sides?)	1964	3.75	7.50	15.00
72184	Come Back/Your Teenage Dreams	1963	—	3.00	6.00
72184 [PS]	Come Back/Your Teenage Dreams	1963	2.50	5.00	10.00
72217	The Little Drummer Boy/Have Reindeer, Will Travel	1963	2.50	5.00	10.00
72217 [PS]	The Little Drummer Boy/Have Reindeer, Will Travel	1963	5.00	10.00	20.00
72229	Bye Bye Barbara/A Great Night for Cryin'	1964	—	3.00	6.00
72229 [PS]	Bye Bye Barbara/A Great Night for Cryin'	1964	2.50	5.00	10.00
72263	No More/The Fall of Love	1964	—	3.00	6.00
72287	Taste of Tears/White Roses from a Blue Valentine	1964	—	3.00	6.00
72339	Listen Lonely Girl/All I Wanted	1964	—	3.00	6.00
72339 [PS]	Listen Lonely Girl/All I Wanted	1964	2.50	5.00	10.00
72432	Dianacita/Take the Time	1965	—	3.00	6.00
72432 [PS]	Dianacita/Take the Time	1965	2.50	5.00	10.00
72464	Mirage/The Sweetheart Tree	1965	—	3.00	6.00
72464 [PS]	Mirage/The Sweetheart Tree	1965	2.50	5.00	10.00
72493	On a Clear Day You Can See Forever/Come Back to Me	1965	—	3.00	6.00
72539	Moment to Moment/Glass Mountain	1966	—	3.00	6.00
72568	The Shadow of Your Smile (Love Theme from "The Sandpiper")/The Sweetheart Tree	1966	—	3.00	6.00
72610	The Impossible Dream/So Nice	1966	—	3.00	6.00
72610 [PS]	The Impossible Dream/So Nice	1966	2.50	5.00	10.00
72653	Saturday Sunshine/Two Tickets and a Candy Heart	1967	—	3.00	6.00
72653 [PS]	Saturday Sunshine/Two Tickets and a Candy Heart	1967	2.50	5.00	10.00

7-Inch Extended Plays

COLUMBIA

Number	Title (A Side/B Side)	Yr	VG	VG+	NM
B-2129	*It's Not for Me to Say/Warm and Tender/Wonderful, Wonderful/Babalu	1957	3.75	7.50	15.00
B-2129 [PS]	Songs from "Lizzie" and Other Favorites	1957	3.75	7.50	15.00
B-2143	*Come to Me/Wild Is the Wind/No Love/When I Am with You	1957	3.75	7.50	15.00
B-2143 [PS]	Johnny Mathis Sings	1957	3.75	7.50	15.00
B-2537	The Twelfth of Never/Chances Are//Wonderful, Wonderful/It's Not for Me to Say	1959	3.00	6.00	12.00
B-2537 [PS]	Johnny Mathis (Hall of Fame Series)	1959	3.00	6.00	12.00
B-2626	*Call Me/A Certain Smile/All the Time/When Sunny Gets Blue	195?	3.00	6.00	12.00
B-2626 [PS]	Johnny Mathis (Hall of Fame Series)	195?	3.00	6.00	12.00
B-2640	*Come to Me/Wild Is the Wind/Someone/You Are Beautiful	195?	3.00	6.00	12.00
B-2640 [PS]	Johnny Mathis (Hall of Fame Series)	195?	3.00	6.00	12.00
B-8871	*Autumn in Rome/Love, Your Magic Spell Is Everywhere/Cabin in the Sky/In Other Words	1957	3.75	7.50	15.00
B-8871 [PS]	Johnny Mathis, Vol. 1	1957	3.75	7.50	15.00
B-8872	*Caravan/Star Eyes/It Might As Well Be Spring/Street of Dreams	1957	3.75	7.50	15.00
B-8872 [PS]	Johnny Mathis, Vol. 2	1957	3.75	7.50	15.00
B-8873	*Easy to Love/Prelude to a Kiss/Babalu/Angel Eyes	1957	3.75	7.50	15.00
B-8873 [PS]	Johnny Mathis, Vol. 3	1957	3.75	7.50	15.00
B-10281	*Will I Find My Love Today/Looking at You/Let Me Love You/All Through the Night	1957	3.00	6.00	12.00
B-10281 [PS]	Will I Find My Love Today	1957	3.00	6.00	12.00
B-10281 [PS]	Looking at You	1957	3.00	6.00	12.00
—Same contents, different title					
B-10282	*It Could Happen to You/That Old Black Magic/Too Close for Comfort/In the Wee Small Hours of the Morning	1957	3.00	6.00	12.00
B-10282 [PS]	Too Close for Comfort	1957	3.00	6.00	12.00
B-10283	*Year After Year/Early Autumn/You Stepped Out of a Dream/Day In, Day Out	1957	3.00	6.00	12.00
B-10283 [PS]	Day In, Day Out	1957	3.00	6.00	12.00
B-10781	Warm/A Handful of Stars//My One and Only Love/While We're Young	1958	3.00	6.00	12.00
B-10781 [PS]	Warm, Vol. 1	1958	3.00	6.00	12.00
B-10782	*By Myself/I've Grown Accustomed to Her Face/Baby, Baby, Baby/What'll I Do	1958	3.00	6.00	12.00
B-10782 [PS]	Warm, Vol. 2	1958	3.00	6.00	12.00
B-10783	*I'm Glad There Is You/The Lovely Things You Do/There Goes My Heart/Then I'll Be Tired of You	1958	3.00	6.00	12.00
B-10783 [PS]	Warm, Vol. 3	1958	3.00	6.00	12.00
B-11191	*Good Night, Dear Lord/I Heard a Forest Praying/Deep River/Swing Low, Sweet Chariot	1958	2.50	5.00	10.00
B-11191 [PS]	Good Night, Dear Lord	1958	2.50	5.00	10.00
B-11192	*Eli Eli/Kol Nidre/Where Can I Go?/One God	1958	2.50	5.00	10.00
B-11192 [PS]	Eli Eli	1958	2.50	5.00	10.00
B-11193	*Ave Maria (Bach-Gounod)/The Rosary/May the Good Lord Bless and Keep You/Ave Maria (Schubert)	1958	2.50	5.00	10.00
B-11193 [PS]	Ave Maria	1958	2.50	5.00	10.00
B-11651	To Be in Love/You'd Be So Nice to Come Home To//It's De-Lovely/I've Got the World on a String	1958	3.00	6.00	12.00
B-11651 [PS]	Swing Softly, Vol. 1	1958	3.00	6.00	12.00
B-11652	*Sweet Lorraine/Can't Get Out of This Mood/You Hit the Spot/Get Me to the Church on Time	1958	3.00	6.00	12.00
B-11652 [PS]	Swing Softly, Vol. 2	1958	3.00	6.00	12.00
B-11653	*Love Walked In/Easy to Say/This Heart of Mine/Like Someone in Love	1958	3.00	6.00	12.00
B-11653 [PS]	Swing Softly, Vol. 3	1958	3.00	6.00	12.00
B-11951	Winter Wonderland/Blue Christmas//White Christmas/Sleigh Ride	1958	3.00	6.00	12.00
B-11951 [PS]	Merry Christmas, Vol. 1	1958	3.00	6.00	12.00
B-11952	I'll Be Home for Christmas/Oh Holy Night//The Christmas Song/Silver Bells	1958	3.00	6.00	12.00
B-11952 [PS]	Merry Christmas, Vol. 2	1958	3.00	6.00	12.00
B-11953	The First Noel/It Came Upon a Midnight Clear//What Child Is This?/Silent Night, Holy Night	1958	3.00	6.00	12.00
B-11953 [PS]	Merry Christmas, Vol. 3	1958	3.00	6.00	12.00
B-12701	*Open Fire/Please Be Kind/Bye Bye Blackbird/Tenderly	1959	2.50	5.00	10.00
B-12701 [PS]	Open Fire, Two Guitars, Vol. 1	1959	2.50	5.00	10.00
B-12702	*Embraceable You/My Funny Valentine/I'll Be Seeing You/I'm Just a Boy in Love	1959	2.50	5.00	10.00
B-12702 [PS]	Open Fire, Two Guitars, Vol. 2	1959	2.50	5.00	10.00
B-12703	*I Concentrate on You/You'll Never Know/When I Fall in Love/In the Still of the Night	1959	2.50	5.00	10.00
B-12703 [PS]	Open Fire, Two Guitars, Vol. 3	1959	2.50	5.00	10.00
B-13511	*Heavenly/Misty/Hello, Young Lovers/I'll Be Easy to Find	1959	2.50	5.00	10.00
B-13511 [PS]	Heavenly, Vol. 1	1959	2.50	5.00	10.00
B-13512	*Something I Dreamed Last Night/Moonlight Becomes You/They Say It's Wonderful/More Than You Know	1959	2.50	5.00	10.00
B-13512 [PS]	Heavenly, Vol. 2	1959	2.50	5.00	10.00
B-13513	A Lovely Way to Spend an Evening/That's All//A Ride on a Rainbow/Stranger in Paradise	1959	2.50	5.00	10.00
B-13513 [PS]	Heavenly, Vol. 3	1959	2.50	5.00	10.00
B-14221	Secret Love/Where Are You//Maria/Where Do You Think You're Going	1959	2.50	5.00	10.00
B-14221 [PS]	Faithfully, Vol. 1	1959	2.50	5.00	10.00
B-14222	*Faithfully/One Starry Night/Nobody Knows/You Better Go Now	1959	2.50	5.00	10.00
B-14222 [PS]	Faithfully, Vol. 2	1959	2.50	5.00	10.00

Number	Title (A Side/B Side)	Yr	VG	VG+	NM
B-14223	And This Is My Beloved/Tonight//Follow Me/Blue Gardenia	1959	2.50	5.00	10.00
B-14223 [PS]	Faithfully, Vol. 3	1959	2.50	5.00	10.00
B-15261	Goodnight My Love/There's No You//Once/I'm So Lost	1960	2.50	5.00	10.00
B-15261 [PS]	Johnny's Mood, Vol. 1	1960	2.50	5.00	10.00
B-15262	*Corner to Corner/The Folks Who Live on the Hill/ I'm in the Mood for Love/Stay Warm	1960	2.50	5.00	10.00
B-15262 [PS]	Johnny's Mood, Vol. 2	1960	2.50	5.00	10.00
B-15263	*I'm Gonna Laugh You Right Out of My Life/How High the Moon/April in Paris/In Return	1960	2.50	5.00	10.00
B-15263 [PS]	Johnny's Mood, Vol. 3	1960	2.50	5.00	10.00
Albums					
COLUMBIA					
GP 2 [(2)]	Warm/Open Fire, Two Guitars	1969	3.75	7.50	15.00
C2L 17 [(2) M]	The Rhythms and Ballads of Broadway	1960	6.25	12.50	25.00
—Red and black label with six "eye" logos					
C2L 17 [(2) M]	The Rhythms and Ballads of Broadway	1962	5.00	10.00	20.00
—Red label with either "Guaranteed High Fidelity" or "360 Sound Mono"					
C2L 34 [(2) M]	The Great Years	1964	3.75	7.50	15.00
C2S 803 [(2) S]	The Rhythms and Ballads of Broadway	1960	7.50	15.00	30.00
—Red and black label with six "eye" logos					
C2S 803 [(2) S]	The Rhythms and Ballads of Broadway	1962	6.25	12.50	25.00
—Red "360 Sound" label					
C2S 834 [(2) S]	The GreatYears	1964	5.00	10.00	20.00
—Red "360 Sound" label					
CL 887 [M]	Johnny Mathis	1957	12.50	25.00	50.00
CS 1005	Raindrops Keep Fallin' on My Head	1970	3.00	6.00	12.00
CL 1028 [M]	Wonderful Wonderful	1957	7.50	15.00	30.00
—Red and black label with six "eye" logos					
CL 1028 [M]	Wonderful Wonderful	1962	3.75	7.50	15.00
—Red label with either "Guaranteed High Fidelity" or "360 Sound Mono"					
CL 1078 [M]	Warm	1957	7.50	15.00	30.00
—Red and black label with six "eye" logos					
CL 1078 [M]	Warm	1962	3.75	7.50	15.00
—Red label with either "Guaranteed High Fidelity" or "360 Sound Mono"					
CL 1119 [M]	Good Night, Dear Lord	1958	7.50	15.00	30.00
—Red and black label with six "eye" logos					
CL 1119 [M]	Good Night, Dear Lord	1962	3.75	7.50	15.00
—Red label with either "Guaranteed High Fidelity" or "360 Sound Mono"					
CL 1133 [M]	Johnny's Greatest Hits	1958	7.50	15.00	30.00
—Red and black label with six "eye" logos					
CL 1133 [M]	Johnny's Greatest Hits	1962	3.75	7.50	15.00
—Red label with either "Guaranteed High Fidelity" or "360 Sound Mono"					
CL 1165 [M]	Swing Softly	1958	7.50	15.00	30.00
—Red and black label with six "eye" logos					
CL 1165 [M]	Swing Softly	1962	3.75	7.50	15.00
—Red label with either "Guaranteed High Fidelity" or "360 Sound Mono"					
CL 1195 [M]	Merry Christmas	1958	10.00	20.00	40.00
—Original cover has Johnny standing, holding skis and poles					
CL 1195 [M]	Merry Christmas	196?	7.50	15.00	30.00
—Second cover has Johnny sitting, with skis and poles in snow					
CL 1270 [M]	Open Fire, Two Guitars	1959	7.50	15.00	30.00
—Red and black label with six "eye" logos					
CL 1270 [M]	Open Fire, Two Guitars	1962	3.75	7.50	15.00
—Red label with either "Guaranteed High Fidelity" or "360 Sound Mono"					
CL 1344 [M]	More Johnny's Greatest Hits	1959	6.25	12.50	25.00
—Red and black label with six "eye" logos					
CL 1344 [M]	More Johnny's Greatest Hits	1962	3.75	7.50	15.00
—Red label with either "Guaranteed High Fidelity" or "360 Sound Mono"					
CL 1351 [M]	Heavenly	1959	5.00	10.00	20.00
—Red and black label with six "eye" logos					
CL 1351 [M]	Heavenly	1962	3.75	7.50	15.00
—Red label with either "Guaranteed High Fidelity" or "360 Sound Mono"					
CL 1422 [M]	Faithfully	1959	5.00	10.00	20.00
—Red and black label with six "eye" logos					
CL 1422 [M]	Faithfully	1962	3.75	7.50	15.00
—Red label with either "Guaranteed High Fidelity" or "360 Sound Mono"					
CL 1526 [M]	Johnny's Mood	1960	5.00	10.00	20.00
—Red and black label with six "eye" logos					
CL 1526 [M]	Johnny's Mood	1962	3.75	7.50	15.00
—Red label with either "Guaranteed High Fidelity" or "360 Sound Mono"					
CL 1623 [M]	I'll Buy You a Star	1961	3.75	7.50	15.00
—Red and black label with six "eye" logos					
CL 1623 [M]	I'll Buy You a Star	1962	3.00	6.00	12.00
—Red label with either "Guaranteed High Fidelity" or "360 Sound Mono"					
CL 1644 [M]	Portrait of Johnny	1961	3.75	7.50	15.00
—Red and black label with six "eye" logos; add 1/3 if portrait is there					
CL 1644 [M]	Portrait of Johnny	1962	3.00	6.00	12.00
—Red label with either "Guaranteed High Fidelity" or "360 Sound Mono"					
CL 1711 [M]	Live It Up!	1962	3.75	7.50	15.00
—Red and black label with six "eye" logos					
CL 1711 [M]	Live It Up!	1962	3.00	6.00	12.00
—Red label with either "Guaranteed High Fidelity" or "360 Sound Mono"					
CL 1915 [M]	Rapture	1962	3.00	6.00	12.00
CL 2016 [M]	Johnny's Newest Hits	1963	3.00	6.00	12.00
CL 2044 [M]	Johnny	1963	3.00	6.00	12.00
CL 2098 [M]	Romantically	1963	3.00	6.00	12.00
CL 2143 [M]	I'll Search My Heart and Other Great Hits	1964	3.00	6.00	12.00
CL 2223 [M]	The Ballads of Broadway	1964	3.00	6.00	12.00
CL 2224 [M]	The Rhythms of Broadway	1964	3.00	6.00	12.00
CL 2726 [M]	Up, Up and Away	1967	3.75	7.50	15.00
CS 8012 [S]	Good Night, Dear Lord	1958	10.00	20.00	40.00
—Red and black label with six "eye" logos					
CS 8012 [S]	Good Night, Dear Lord	1962	5.00	10.00	20.00
—Red "360 Sound" label					
CS 8021 [S]	Merry Christmas	1959	6.25	12.50	25.00
—Same as CL 1195, but in stereo; cover 1					
CS 8021 [S]	Merry Christmas	196?	5.00	10.00	20.00
—Same as CL 1195, but in stereo; cover 2					
CS 8039 [S]	Warm	1958	10.00	20.00	40.00
—Red and black label with six "eye" logos					
CS 8039 [S]	Warm	1962	5.00	10.00	20.00
—Red "360 Sound" label					
CS 8056 [S]	Open Fire, Two Guitars	1959	10.00	20.00	40.00
—Red and black label with six "eye" logos					

Number	Title (A Side/B Side)	Yr	VG	VG+	NM
CS 8056 [S]	Open Fire, Two Guitars	1962	5.00	10.00	20.00
—Red "360 Sound" label					
CS 8150 [S]	More Johnny's Greatest Hits	1959	7.50	15.00	30.00
—Red and black label with six "eye" logos					
CS 8150 [S]	More Johnny's Greatest Hits	1962	5.00	10.00	20.00
—Red "360 Sound" label					
CS 8150 [S]	More Johnny's Greatest Hits	1971	2.50	5.00	10.00
—Orange label					
PC 8150 [S]	More Johnny's Greatest Hits	198?	—	3.00	6.00
—Reissue with new prefix					
CS 8152 [S]	Heavenly	1959	7.50	15.00	30.00
—Red and black label with six "eye" logos					
CS 8152 [S]	Heavenly	1962	5.00	10.00	20.00
—Red "360 Sound" label					
CS 8152 [S]	Heavenly	1971	2.50	5.00	10.00
—Orange label					
PC 8152 [S]	Heavenly	198?	—	3.00	6.00
—Reissue with new prefix					
CS 8219 [S]	Faithfully	1959	6.25	12.50	25.00
—Red and black label with six "eye" logos					
CS 8219 [S]	Faithfully	1962	5.00	10.00	20.00
—Red "360 Sound" label					
CS 8326 [S]	Johnny's Mood	1960	6.25	12.50	25.00
—Red and black label with six "eye" logos					
CS 8326 [S]	Johnny's Mood	1962	5.00	10.00	20.00
—Red "360 Sound" label					
CS 8423 [S]	I'll Buy You a Star	1961	5.00	10.00	20.00
—Red and black label with six "eye" logos					
CS 8423 [S]	I'll Buy You a Star	1962	3.75	7.50	15.00
—Red "360 Sound" label					
CS 8444 [S]	Portrait of Johnny	1961	5.00	10.00	20.00
—Red and black label with six "eye" logos; add 1/3 if portrait is there					
CS 8444 [S]	Portrait of Johnny	1962	3.75	7.50	15.00
—Red "360 Sound" label					
CS 8511 [S]	Live It Up!	1962	5.00	10.00	20.00
—Red and black label with six "eye" logos; add 1/3 if portrait is there					
CS 8511 [S]	Live It Up!	1962	3.75	7.50	15.00
—Red "360 Sound" label					
CS 8634 [R]	Johnny's Greatest Hits	1963	3.00	6.00	12.00
CS 8715 [S]	Rapture	1962	3.75	7.50	15.00
—Red "360 Sound" label					
CS 8816 [S]	Johnny's Newest Hits	1963	3.75	7.50	15.00
—Red "360 Sound" label					
CS 8844 [S]	Johnny	1963	3.75	7.50	15.00
—Red "360 Sound" label					
CS 8898 [S]	Romantically	1963	3.75	7.50	15.00
—Red "360 Sound" label					
CS 8943 [S]	I'll Search My Heart and Other Great Hits	1964	3.75	7.50	15.00
—Red "360 Sound" label					
CS 9023 [S]	The Ballads of Broadway	1964	3.75	7.50	15.00
—Red "360 Sound" label					
CS 9024 [S]	The Ballads of Broadway	1964	3.75	7.50	15.00
—Red "360 Sound" label					
CS 9046 [R]	Wonderful Wonderful	1964	3.00	6.00	12.00
CS 9526 [S]	Up, Up and Away	1967	3.75	7.50	15.00
CS 9637	Love Is Blue	1968	3.75	7.50	15.00
CS 9705	Those Were the Days	1968	3.75	7.50	15.00
CS 9871	People	1969	3.75	7.50	15.00
CS 9872	The Impossible Dream	1969	3.75	7.50	15.00
—Red "360 Sound" label					
CS 9872	The Impossible Dream	1971	2.50	5.00	10.00
—Orange label					
PC 9872	The Impossible Dream	198?	—	3.00	6.00
—Reissue with new prefix					
CS 9909	Love Theme from "Romeo and Juliet"	1969	3.75	7.50	15.00
—Red "360 Sound" label					
CS 9909	Love Theme from "Romeo and Juliet"	1971	2.50	5.00	10.00
—Orange label					
PC 9909	Love Theme from "Romeo and Juliet"	198?	—	3.00	6.00
—Reissue with new prefix					
CS 9923	Give Me Your Love for Christmas	1969	3.00	6.00	12.00
LE 10196	Christmas with Johnny Mathis	1976	2.50	5.00	10.00
—Reissue of Harmony KH 30684 with same contents					
C 30210	Close to You	1970	3.00	6.00	12.00
G 30350 [(2)]	Johnny Mathis Sings the Music of Bacharach & Kaempfert	1970	3.75	7.50	15.00
C 30499	Love Story	1971	3.00	6.00	12.00
PC 30499	Love Story	198?	2.00	4.00	8.00
—Budget-line reissue					
C 30740	You've Got a Friend	1971	3.00	6.00	12.00
CQ 30740 [Q]	You've Got a Friend	1972	5.00	10.00	20.00
PC 30740	You've Got a Friend	198?	2.00	4.00	8.00
—Budget-line reissue					
2CQ 30979 [(2) Q]	Johnny Mathis in Person	1972	6.25	12.50	25.00
KG 30979 [(2)]	Johnny Mathis In Person	1972	3.75	7.50	15.00
CQ 31342 [Q]	The First Time Ever (I Saw Your Face)	1972	5.00	10.00	20.00
KC 31342	The First Time Ever (I Saw Your Face)	1972	3.00	6.00	12.00
PC 31342	The First Time Ever (I Saw Your Face)	198?	2.00	4.00	8.00
—Budget-line reissue					
KG 31345 [(2)]	Johnny Mathis' All-Time Greatest Hits	1972	3.75	7.50	15.00
CQ 31626 [Q]	Song Sung Blue	1972	5.00	10.00	20.00
KC 31626	Song Sung Blue	1972	3.00	6.00	12.00
CQ 32114 [Q]	Me and Mrs. Jones	1973	4.50	9.00	18.00
KC 32114	Me and Mrs. Jones	1973	2.50	5.00	10.00
KC 32258	Killing Me Softly with Her Song	1973	2.50	5.00	10.00
CQ 32435 [Q]	I'm Coming Home	1973	4.50	9.00	18.00
KC 32435	I'm Coming Home	1973	2.50	5.00	10.00
PC 32435	I'm Coming Home	198?	2.00	4.00	8.00
—Budget-line reissue					
C 32963	What'll I Do	1974	2.50	5.00	10.00
KC 33251	The Heart of a Woman	1974	2.50	5.00	10.00
PC 33420	When Will I See You Again	1975	2.50	5.00	10.00
CG 33621 [(2)]	Heavenly/Faithfully	1975	3.00	6.00	12.00
PC 33887	Feelings	1975	2.50	5.00	10.00
PC 34117	I Only Have Eyes for You	1976	2.50	5.00	10.00
PC 34441	Mathis Is...	1977	2.50	5.00	10.00

Number	Title (A Side/B Side)	Yr	VG	VG+	NM
PC 34667	Johnny Mathis' Greatest Hits	1977	2.50	5.00	10.00
PC 34872	Hold Me, Thrill Me, Kiss Me	1977	2.50	5.00	10.00
PC 35259	You Light Up My Life	1986	2.00	4.00	8.00
—Budget-line reissue					
JC 35359	You Light Up My Life	1978	2.50	5.00	10.00
C 35578	Romantically	1978	2.00	4.00	8.00
JC 35649	The Best Days of My Life	1979	2.50	5.00	10.00
PC 35649	The Best Days of My Life	1985	2.00	4.00	8.00
—Budget-line reissue					
JC 36216	Mathis Magic	1979	2.50	5.00	10.00
JC 36505	Different Kinda Different	1980	2.50	5.00	10.00
JC 36871	The Best of Johnny Mathis 1975-1980	1980	2.50	5.00	10.00
C2X 37440 [(2)]	The First 25 Years — The Silver Anniversary Album	1981	3.00	6.00	12.00
FC 37748	Friends in Love	1982	2.50	5.00	10.00
3C 38306	Christmas with Johnny Mathis	1982	2.00	4.00	8.00
—Reissue of Columbia LE 10196 with same contents					
FC 38699	Johnny Mathis Live	1983	2.50	5.00	10.00
FC 38718	A Special Part of Me	1984	2.50	5.00	10.00
PC 39468	For Christmas	1984	2.00	4.00	8.00
FC 39601	Right from the Heart	1985	2.50	5.00	10.00
FC 40372	The Hollywood Musicals	1986	2.50	5.00	10.00
—With Henry Mancini					
FC 40447	Christmas Eve with Johnny Mathis	1986	2.50	5.00	10.00
OC 44156	Once in a While	1988	2.50	5.00	10.00
OC 44336	In the Still of the Night	1989	3.00	6.00	12.00
COLUMBIA MUSICAL TREASURY					
6P 6030 [(6)]	The Johnny Mathis Treasury	197?	7.50	15.00	30.00
COLUMBIA SPECIAL PRODUCTS					
C 10896	Merry Christmas	1972	3.00	6.00	12.00
—Reissue					
P3 11837 [(3)]	Romantically, Johnny Mathis	197?	6.25	12.50	25.00
P6 14628 [(6)]	Misty Memories: The Complete Johnny Mathis Treasury	197?	7.50	15.00	30.00
—Maunfactured for Candelite Music					
P 14658	Holidays at the Fireside	197?	5.00	10.00	20.00
—Bonus album with box set 14628					
P 14908	The Heart of Johnny Mathis	197?	3.75	7.50	15.00
—Bonus album with box set 14628					
P4 14971 [(4)]	Johnny	197?	6.25	12.50	25.00
HARMONY					
KH 30017	Johnny Mathis	1970	2.50	5.00	10.00
KH 30684	Christmas with Johnny Mathis	1971	3.00	6.00	12.00
—Reissue of Mercury SR 60837 with two fewer tracks thus:					
KH 31935	Something for Everyone	1973	2.50	5.00	10.00
MERCURY					
MG 20837 [M]	Sounds of Christmas	1963	3.00	6.00	12.00
MG-20890 [M]	Tender Is the Night	1964	3.00	6.00	12.00
MG-20913 [M]	The Wonderful World of Make Believe	1964	3.00	6.00	12.00
MG-20942 [M]	This Is Love	1964	3.00	6.00	12.00
MG-20988 [M]	Johnny Mathis Ole	1965	3.00	6.00	12.00
MG-20991 [M]	Love Is Everything	1965	3.00	6.00	12.00
MG-21041 [M]	The Sweetheart Tree	1965	3.00	6.00	12.00
MG-21073 [M]	The Shadow of Your Smile	1966	3.00	6.00	12.00
MG-21093 [M]	So Nice	1966	3.00	6.00	12.00
MG-21107 [M]	Johnny Mathis Sings	1967	3.75	7.50	15.00
SR 60837 [S]	Sounds of Christmas	1963	3.75	7.50	15.00
SR-60890 [S]	Tender Is the Night	1964	3.75	7.50	15.00
SR-60913 [S]	The Wonderful World of Make Believe	1964	3.75	7.50	15.00
SR-60942 [S]	This Is Love	1964	3.75	7.50	15.00
SR-60988 [S]	Johnny Mathis Ole	1965	3.75	7.50	15.00
SR-60991 [S]	Love Is Everything	1965	3.75	7.50	15.00
SR-61041 [S]	The Sweetheart Tree	1965	3.75	7.50	15.00
SR-61073 [S]	The Shadow of Your Smile	1966	3.75	7.50	15.00
SR-61093 [S]	So Nice	1966	3.75	7.50	15.00
SR-61107 [S]	Johnny Mathis Sings	1967	3.75	7.50	15.00
MOBILE FIDELITY					
1-171	Heavenly	1985	6.25	12.50	25.00
—Audiophile vinyl					
READER'S DIGEST					
RB4-097 [(6)]	His Greatest Hits and Finest Performances	198?	6.25	12.50	25.00

MATHIS, JOHNNY/DENIECE WILLIAMS

Also see each artist's individual listings.

45s

Number	Title (A Side/B Side)	Yr	VG	VG+	NM
COLUMBIA					
04379	Love Won't Let Me Wait/Lead Me to Your Love	1984	—	—	3.00
10693	Too Much, Too Little, Too Late/Emotion	1978	—	2.50	5.00
10693	Too Much, Too Little, Too Late/I Wrote a Symphony on My Guitar	1978	2.50	5.00	10.00
—B-side by Johnny Mathis solo					
10772	You're All I Need to Get By/You're a Special Part of My Life	1978	—	2.50	5.00
10772 [PS]	You're All I Need to Get By	1978	2.50	5.00	10.00
—Sleeve is promo only					
10826	That's What Friends Are For/I Just Can't Get Over You	1978	—	2.50	5.00
33360	Too Much, Too Little, Too Late/You're All I Need to Get By	198?	—	2.00	4.00
—Red label					
33360	Too Much, Too Little, Too Late/You're All I Need to Get By	198?	—	—	3.00
—Gray label					

Albums

Number	Title (A Side/B Side)	Yr	VG	VG+	NM
COLUMBIA					
JC 35435	That's What Friends Are For	1978	2.50	5.00	10.00
PC 35435	That's What Friends Are For	198?	2.00	4.00	8.00
—Budget-line reissue					

MATHIS BROTHERS, THE

See DEAN AND MARK; THE NEWBEATS.

MATTHEWS, FAT MAN

45s

Number	Title (A Side/B Side)	Yr	VG	VG+	NM
BAYOU					
016	I'm Thankful/Goin' Down	1952	37.50	75.00	150.00
IMPERIAL					
5211	When Boy Meets Girl/Later Baby	1952	1000.	1500.	2000.
5235	Down the Line/You Know It	1953	25.00	50.00	100.00

MATTHEWS, IAN

Also see MATTHEWS' SOUTHERN COMFORT.

45s

Number	Title (A Side/B Side)	Yr	VG	VG+	NM
COLUMBIA					
10374	Brown Eyed Girl/Steamboat	1976	—	2.50	5.00
10553	Tigers Will Survive/Times	1977	—	2.50	5.00
ELEKTRA					
45851	These Days/Same Old Man	1973	—	2.50	5.00
45871	Seven Bridges Road/You Fell Through My Mind	1973	—	2.50	5.00
45892	Dirty Work/A Wailing Goodbye	1974	—	2.50	5.00
MUSHROOM					
7039	Shake It/Stealin' Home	1978	—	2.00	4.00
7040	Give Me an Inch/Let There Be Blues	1979	—	2.00	4.00
7041	Don't Hang Up Your Dancing Shoes/Slip Away	1979	—	2.00	4.00
7045	Anna/You Don't See Me	1980	—	2.00	4.00
VERTIGO					
101	If You Saw Through My Eyes/Hearts	1971	—	3.00	6.00
102	Reno, Nevada/Desert Inn	1971	—	3.00	6.00
103	Da Doo Ron Ron/House of Un-American Blues Activity Dream	1972	—	3.00	6.00
105	Tigers Will Survive/Hope You Know	1972	—	3.00	6.00

Albums

Number	Title (A Side/B Side)	Yr	VG	VG+	NM
COLUMBIA					
PC 34102	Go for Broke	1976	2.50	5.00	10.00
PC 34671	Hit and Run	1977	2.50	5.00	10.00
ELEKTRA					
EKS-75051	Valley Hi	1973	3.00	6.00	12.00
EKS-75078	Some Days You Eat the Bear	1974	3.00	6.00	12.00
MUSHROOM					
MRS-5012	Stealin' Home	1978	2.50	5.00	10.00
MRS-5014	Siamese Friends	1979	2.50	5.00	10.00
RSO					
RS-1-3092	A Spot of Interference	1980	2.50	5.00	10.00
VERTIGO					
VEL-1002	If You Saw Thro' My Eyes	1971	3.00	6.00	12.00
VEL-1010	Tigers Will Survive	1972	3.00	6.00	12.00
WINDHAM HILL					
WD-1070	Walking a Changing Line: The Songs of Jules Shear	1987	2.50	5.00	10.00

MATTHEWS' SOUTHERN COMFORT

45s

Number	Title (A Side/B Side)	Yr	VG	VG+	NM
DECCA					
32664	Colorado Springs Eternal/The Watch	1970	—	2.50	5.00
—With Ian Matthews					
32774	Woodstock/Ballad of Obray Ramsey	1971	—	3.00	6.00
32845	Mare, Take Me Home/Brand New Tennessee Waltz	1971	—	2.50	5.00
32874	Tell Me Why/To Love	1971	—	2.50	5.00

Albums

Number	Title (A Side/B Side)	Yr	VG	VG+	NM
DECCA					
DL 75191	Matthews' Southern Comfort	1970	3.00	6.00	12.00
DL 75242	Second Spring	1970	3.00	6.00	12.00
DL 75264	Later That Same Year	1971	3.00	6.00	12.00
PICKWICK					
SPC-3698	Later That Same Year	197?	2.00	4.00	8.00

MATTY, JAY

45s

Number	Title (A Side/B Side)	Yr	VG	VG+	NM
ERA					
3008	Janie My Lover/Tall Tale	1959	3.75	7.50	15.00
LUTE					
6021	Merry Twist Mas/Teenage Monster	1961	5.00	10.00	20.00

MAUDS, THE

45s

Number	Title (A Side/B Side)	Yr	VG	VG+	NM
DUNWICH					
160	Hold On/C'mon and Move	1967	3.00	6.00	12.00
MERCURY					
72694	Hold On/C'mon and Move	1967	2.00	4.00	8.00
72720	When Something Is Wrong (With My Baby)/You Make Me Feel So Bad	1967	2.00	4.00	8.00
72760	He Will Break Your Heart/You Must Believe Me	1967	2.00	4.00	8.00
72832	Forever Gone/Soul Drippin'	1968	2.00	4.00	8.00
72877	Only Love Can Save You/Sergeant Sunshine	1968	2.00	4.00	8.00
72919	Brother Chickie/Satisfy My Hunger	1969	2.00	4.00	8.00
RCA VICTOR					
74-0377	Forget It, I've Got It/A Man Without a Dream	1970	—	3.00	6.00

Albums

Number	Title (A Side/B Side)	Yr	VG	VG+	NM
MERCURY					
MG-21135 [M]	The Mauds Hold On	1967	5.00	10.00	20.00
SR-61135 [S]	The Mauds Hold On	1967	6.25	12.50	25.00

MAURIAT, PAUL

45s

Number	Title (A Side/B Side)	Yr	VG	VG+	NM
MGM					
14378	Love Theme from "The Godfather"/Butterfly	1972	—	2.00	4.00
PHILIPS					
40348	I Know a Place/I Tried and I Tried	1966	—	3.00	6.00

Number	Title (A Side/B Side)	Yr	VG	VG+	NM
40426	You Don't Have to Say You Love Me/Kiss Tomorrow Goodbye	1967	—	3.00	6.00
40440	Black Is Black/Reach Out I'll Be There	1967	—	3.00	6.00
40462	This Is My Song/Puppet on a String	1967	—	3.00	6.00
40495	Love Is Blue/Alone in the World	1967	—	3.00	6.00
40495	Love Is Blue/Sunny	1967	—	3.00	6.00
40530	Love in Every Room/The English Nightingale	1968	—	3.00	6.00
40530 [PS]	Love in Every Room/The English Nightingale	1968	2.50	5.00	10.00
40550	San Francisco (Be Sure to Wear Flowers in Your Hair)/I Waited for You	1968	—	3.00	6.00
40574	Chitty Chitty Bang Bang/Come Un Carcon	1968	—	3.00	6.00
40594	Hey Jude/Those Were the Days	1969	—	2.50	5.00
40595	Sweet Charity/Irresistible	1969	—	2.50	5.00
40642	Get Back/Goodbye	1969	—	2.50	5.00
40647	Je T'Aime…Moi Non Plus/I Want to Love	1969	—	2.50	5.00
40683	Gone Is Love/She Is a Little Bit Sweeter	1970	—	2.50	5.00
40700	Etude in the Form of Rhythm and Blues/El Condor Pasa	1971	—	2.50	5.00
40707	Valerie's Theme/To Be the One You Love	1971	—	2.50	5.00
VERVE					
10682	Apres Toi (Come What May)/Theme from "A Summer Place"	1972	—	2.00	4.00
Albums					
FANTASY					
8380	Paris by Night	1968	3.00	6.00	12.00
8389	Joyeux Noel	1968	3.00	6.00	12.00
8394	Latin Style	1969	3.00	6.00	12.00
MERCURY					
SRM-1-3746	Overseas	1978	2.50	5.00	10.00
MGM					
SE-4838	Love Theme from "The Godfather"	1972	2.50	5.00	10.00
M3G-4999	Have You Never Been Mellow	1975	2.50	5.00	10.00
PHILIPS					
PHM 200197 [M]	Listen Too	1965	3.00	6.00	12.00
PHM 200215 [M]	Of Vodka and Caviar	1966	3.00	6.00	12.00
PHM 200226 [M]	More Mauriat	1967	3.75	7.50	15.00
PHM 200248 [M]	Blooming Hits	1967	5.00	10.00	20.00
PHM 200255 [M]	The Christmas Album	1967	5.00	10.00	20.00
PHS 600197 [S]	Listen Too	1965	3.75	7.50	15.00
PHS 600215 [S]	Of Vodka and Caviar	1966	3.75	7.50	15.00
PHS 600226 [S]	More Mauriat	1967	3.75	7.50	15.00
PHS 600248 [S]	Blooming Hits	1967	3.75	7.50	15.00
—Original copies have no "blurb" for "Love Is Blue" on front cover					
PHS 600248 [S]	Blooming Hits	1968	3.00	6.00	12.00
—With blurb for "Love Is Blue" on front cover					
PHS 600255 [S]	The Christmas Album	1967	3.75	7.50	15.00
PHS 600270	Mauriat Magic	1968	3.75	7.50	15.00
PHS 600280	Prevailing Airs	1968	3.75	7.50	15.00
PHS 600292	Doing My Thing	1969	3.75	7.50	15.00
PHS 600299	The Soul of Paul Mauriat	1969	3.75	7.50	15.00
PHS 600320	L-O-V-E	1969	3.75	7.50	15.00
PHS 600337	Midnight Cowboy/Let the Sunshine In	1970	3.00	6.00	12.00
PHS 600345	Gone Is Love	1970	3.00	6.00	12.00
PHS 600352	El Condor Pasa	1970	3.00	6.00	12.00
VERVE					
V6-5087	Theme from "A Summer Place"	1973	2.50	5.00	10.00

MAXIMILLIAN

Organist/keyboard player on DEL SHANNON's biggest hit records of the early 1960s.

Number	Title (A Side/B Side)	Yr	VG	VG+	NM
45s					
BIG TOP					
3068	The Wanderer/The Snake	1961	5.00	10.00	20.00
3095	The Twistin' Ghost/The Breeze and I-Peter Gunn Theme	1961	5.00	10.00	20.00
CUB					
9046	Gee Baby, You're the Utmost/Blowing My Brains Out (Over You)	1959	6.25	12.50	25.00
Albums					
ABC					
S-696	Maximillian	1969	10.00	20.00	40.00

MAXWELL, HOLLY

Number	Title (A Side/B Side)	Yr	VG	VG+	NM
45s					
CONSTELLATION					
152	One Thin Dime/It's Impossible	1965	6.25	12.50	25.00
162	Let Him Go for Himself/Only When You're Lonely	1965	6.25	12.50	25.00
CURTOM					
1942	No One Else/Suffer	1969	3.00	6.00	12.00

MAXWELL, ROBERT

Number	Title (A Side/B Side)	Yr	VG	VG+	NM
45s					
DECCA					
25622	Shangri-La/That Old Black Magic	1964	2.00	4.00	8.00
25637	Peg o' My Heart/Little Dipper	1964	—	3.00	6.00
25671	A Summer Song/Summertime	1965	—	3.00	6.00
31668	One O'Clock Jump/Rosebud	1964	—	3.00	6.00
31734	April in Portugal/The Right to Love	1965	—	3.00	6.00
31839	Song of the Nairobi Trio/Theme from "Morituri"	1965	—	3.00	6.00
MERCURY					
5773	Chinatown, My Chinatown/Shuffle Off to Buffalo	1952	3.75	7.50	15.00
—As "Bobby Maxwell"					
5844	Limehouse Blues/Plink, Plank, Plunk	1952	3.75	7.50	15.00
70033	Shangri-La/Mary Lou	1953	5.00	10.00	20.00
—As "Bobby Maxwell"					
70159	Hindustan/Bobble, Bobble, Bobble	1953	3.75	7.50	15.00
70177	Rose Marie/Ebb Tide	1953	3.75	7.50	15.00
MGM					
12215	The Nearness of You/Midnight Breeze	1956	3.00	6.00	12.00
12254	Spaghetti Rag/Can't Keep Running	1956	3.00	6.00	12.00
12293	Hot Tamale/Freckles	1956	3.00	6.00	12.00
12351	Injury Music for Football Games/Cumana	1956	3.00	6.00	12.00
12410	Song of the Nairobi Trio/Accidental Slip on an Oriental Rug	1957	3.00	6.00	12.00
12488	Mary Lou/Open Your Mouth and Sing	1957	3.00	6.00	12.00
12546	I've Told Every Little Star/Come Follow Me Baby	1957	3.00	6.00	12.00
ROULETTE					
4148	Little Dipper/Mexican Hop	1959	2.50	5.00	10.00
4180	Pink Parfait/Flower of Budapest	1959	2.50	5.00	10.00
4241	The Man with the Monocle/Ver Boten Liebe	1960	2.50	5.00	10.00
4338	Bazaar in Barcelona/Little Dipper	1961	2.50	5.00	10.00
—Roulette titles as "Mickey Mozart"					
Albums					
COMMAND					
33-913 [M]	Anytime	1967	3.75	7.50	15.00
SD 913 [S]	Anytime	1967	3.00	6.00	12.00
DECCA					
DL 4421 [M]	Shangri-La	1964	3.00	6.00	12.00
DL 4563 [M]	Peg o' My Heart	1964	3.00	6.00	12.00
DL 4609 [M]	Songs for All Seasons	1965	3.00	6.00	12.00
DL 4723 [M]	Let's Get Away from It All	1966	3.00	6.00	12.00
DL 74421 [S]	Shangri-La	1964	3.75	7.50	15.00
DL 74563 [S]	Peg o' My Heart	1964	3.75	7.50	15.00
DL 74609 [S]	Songs for All Seasons	1965	3.75	7.50	15.00
DL 74723 [S]	Let's Get Away from It All	1966	3.75	7.50	15.00
MGM					
E-4246 [M]	The Very Best of Robert Maxwell	1964	3.00	6.00	12.00
SE-4246 [S]	The Very Best of Robert Maxwell	1964	3.75	7.50	15.00

MAY BLITZ

Number	Title (A Side/B Side)	Yr	VG	VG+	NM
Albums					
PARAMOUNT					
PAS-5020	May Blitz	1970	5.00	10.00	20.00

MAYALL, JOHN

Number	Title (A Side/B Side)	Yr	VG	VG+	NM
12-Inch Singles					
ISLAND					
PR 2490 [DJ]	The Last Time (same on both sides)	1988	2.00	4.00	8.00
PR 2595 [DJ]	Fascinatin' Lover/Interview (22:33)	1989	3.00	6.00	12.00
45s					
ABC					
12216	Sunshine/Turn Me Loose	1976	—	2.50	5.00
BLUE THUMB					
264	Step in the Sun/Al Goldstein Blues	1975	—	2.50	5.00
IMMEDIATE					
502	Telephone Blues/I'm Your Witch Doctor	1967	2.00	4.00	8.00
LONDON					
20016	Key to Love/Parchman Farm	1966	2.50	5.00	10.00
20024	All Your Love/Hideaway	1966	2.50	5.00	10.00
20035	Oh, Pretty Woman/Suspicions	1967	2.00	4.00	8.00
20037	Jenny/Picture on the Wall	1967	2.00	4.00	8.00
20039	Broken Wings/Sonny Boy Blue	1967	2.00	4.00	8.00
20042	Living Alone/Walking on Sunset	1968	2.00	4.00	8.00
POLYDOR					
14004	Don't Waste My Time/Don't Pick a Flower	1969	—	3.00	6.00
14010	Room to Move/Saw Mill Gulch Road	1969	—	3.00	6.00
14051	Nature's Disappearing/My Pretty Girl	1970	—	3.00	6.00
14117	Nobody Cares/Play the Harp	1972	—	3.00	6.00
14151	Moving On/Keep Our Country Green	1972	—	3.00	6.00
14243	The 1974 Gasoline Blues/Brand New Band	1974	—	3.00	6.00
14253	Let Me Give/Passing Through	1974	—	3.00	6.00
Albums					
ABC					
D-926	Notice to Appear	1975	2.50	5.00	10.00
D-958	A Banquet in Blues	1976	2.50	5.00	10.00
D-992	Lots of People	1977	2.50	5.00	10.00
D-1039	A Hard Core Package	1977	2.50	5.00	10.00
D-1086	Last of the British Blues	1978	2.50	5.00	10.00
ACCORD					
SN-7209	Roadshow Blues Band	1982	2.50	5.00	10.00
BLUE THUMB					
BTS-6019	New Year, New Band, New Company	1975	2.50	5.00	10.00
DECAL					
LIK-1	Some of My Best Friends Are Blues	1986	2.50	5.00	10.00
DJM					
23	The Bottom Line	1979	2.50	5.00	10.00
29	No More Interviews	1979	2.50	5.00	10.00
GNP CRESCENDO					
2184	Behind the Iron Curtain	1986	2.50	5.00	10.00
ISLAND					
91005	Chicago Line	1988	2.50	5.00	10.00
842795-1	A Sense of Place	1990	3.00	6.00	12.00
LONDON					
PS 492 [S]	Blues Breakers with Eric Clapton	1966	10.00	20.00	40.00
PS 502 [S]	A Hard Road	1967	5.00	10.00	20.00
PS 529 [S]	Crusade	1967	5.00	10.00	20.00
PS 534	The Blues Alone	1968	3.75	7.50	15.00
PS 537	Bare Wires	1968	3.75	7.50	15.00
PS 543	Raw Blues	1968	3.75	7.50	15.00
PS 545	Blues from Laurel Canyon	1969	3.75	7.50	15.00
PS 562	Looking Back	1969	3.75	7.50	15.00
PS 570	The Diary of a Band	1970	3.00	6.00	12.00
PS 589	Live in Europe	1971	3.00	6.00	12.00
2PS 600 [(2)]	Through the Years	1971	3.00	6.00	12.00
2PS 618 [(2)]	Down the Line	1973	2.50	5.00	10.00
LL 3492 [M]	Blues Breakers with Eric Clapton	1966	7.50	15.00	30.00
LL 3502 [M]	A Hard Road	1967	5.00	10.00	20.00
LL 3529 [M]	Crusade	1967	5.00	10.00	20.00
LC-50009	Blues Breakers with Eric Clapton	1977	2.50	5.00	10.00
—Reissue of London PS 492					
800086-1	Blues Breakers with Eric Clapton	1983	2.00	4.00	8.00
—Reissue of London 50009					
820320-1	Primal Solos	1985	2.00	4.00	8.00

Number	Title (A Side/B Side)	Yr	VG	VG+	NM
820331-1	Looking Back	1985	2.00	4.00	8.00
—Reissue of London PS 562					
820342-1	Raw Blues	1985	2.00	4.00	8.00
—Reissue of London PS 543					
MCA					
716	Last of the British Blues	1980	2.00	4.00	8.00
—Reissue of ABC 1086					
795	Hard Core	1980	2.00	4.00	8.00
—Reissue of ABC 1039					
MOBILE FIDELITY					
1-183	Blues Breakers Featuring Eric Clapton	1985	10.00	20.00	40.00
—Audiophile vinyl					
1-246	The Blues Alone	1996	7.50	15.00	30.00
—Audiophile vinyl					
POLYDOR					
25-3002 [(2)]	Back to the Roots	1971	3.00	6.00	12.00
PD2-3005 [(2)]	Ten Years Are Gone	1973	3.00	6.00	12.00
PD2-3006 [(2)]	The Best of John Mayall	1973	3.00	6.00	12.00
24-4004	The Turning Point	1970	2.50	5.00	10.00
24-4010	Empty Rooms	1970	2.50	5.00	10.00
24-4022	U.S.A. Union	1970	2.50	5.00	10.00
PD-5012	Memories	1971	2.50	5.00	10.00
PD-5027	Jazz-Blues Fusion	1972	2.50	5.00	10.00
PD-5036	Moving On	1972	2.50	5.00	10.00
PD-6030	The Latest Edition	1974	3.00	6.00	12.00
823305-1	The Turning Point	1985	2.00	4.00	8.00
—Reissue of Polydor 24-4004					
837127-1	Archive to the Eighties	1988	2.00	4.00	8.00

MAYE, LEE

Also recorded as "Arthur Lee Maye."

45s

Number	Title (A Side/B Side)	Yr	VG	VG+	NM
ABC					
11028	If You Leave Me/The Greatest Love I've Ever Known	1967	2.00	4.00	8.00
BUDDAH					
141	He'll Have to Go/Jus' Lookin'	1969	—	3.00	6.00
CASH					
1063	Will You Be Mine/Honey Honey	1958	37.50	75.00	150.00
1065	All I Want Is Someone to Love/Pounding	1958	30.00	60.00	120.00
DIG					
124	This Is the Night for Love/(B-side unknown)	1956	62.50	125.00	250.00
133	A Fool's Prayer/(B-side unknown)	1957	37.50	75.00	150.00
FLIP					
330	Hey Pretty Baby/'Cause You're Mine Alone	1958	20.00	40.00	80.00
—As "Arthur Lee Maye"					
IMPERIAL					
5790	Will You Be Mine/Honey Honey	1961	5.00	10.00	20.00
JAMIE					
1272	Who Made You What You Are/Loving Fool	1964	2.50	5.00	10.00
1276	How's the World Treating You/Loving Fool	1964	2.50	5.00	10.00
1284	Only a Dream/The Breaks of Life	1964	2.50	5.00	10.00
1287	Even a Nobody/Who Made You What You Are	1964	2.50	5.00	10.00
1295	(Don't Pretend) Just Lay It on the Line/Careless Hands	1965	2.00	4.00	8.00
—With Barbara Lynn					
LENOX					
5566	Half Way (Out of Love with You)/I Can't Please You	1963	3.00	6.00	12.00
MODERN					
944	Set My Heart Free/I Wanna Love	1954	150.00	300.00	600.00
—As "Arthur Lee Maye and the Crowns"					
RPM					
424	Truly/Oochie Pachie	1955	50.00	100.00	200.00
—As "Arthur Lee Maye and the Crowns"					
429	Loop De Loop/Love Me Always	1955	30.00	60.00	120.00
—As "Arthur Lee Maye"					
438	Do the Bop/Please Don't Leave Me	1955	37.50	75.00	150.00
—As "Arthur Lee Maye and the Crowns"					
SPECIALTY					
573	Gloria/Oo-Rooba-Lee	1956	15.00	30.00	60.00
—As "Arthur Lee Maye and the Crowns"					
TOWER					
243	When My Heart Hurts No More/At the Party	1966	2.00	4.00	8.00

MAYER, NATHANIEL

45s

Number	Title (A Side/B Side)	Yr	VG	VG+	NM
FORTUNE					
449	Village of Love/I Want a Woman	1962	6.25	12.50	25.00
487	Hurting Love/Leave Me Alone	1962	7.50	15.00	30.00
—Fortune 449 and 487 were part of the United Artists numbering system					
542	My Last Dance with You/My Little Darling	1962	5.00	10.00	20.00
545	Village of Love/I Want a Woman	1962	5.00	10.00	20.00
547	Hurting Love/Leave Me Alone	1962	5.00	10.00	20.00
550	Mr. Santa Claus/(B-side unknown)	1962	7.50	15.00	30.00
550	Work It Out/Well, I've Got News	1962	3.75	7.50	15.00
554	I Had a Dream/I'm Not Gonna Cry	1963	3.75	7.50	15.00
557	Going Back to the Village of Love/My Last Dance with You	1963	3.75	7.50	15.00
562	The Place I Know/Don't Come Back	196?	3.75	7.50	15.00
563	Village of Love/I Want a Woman	196?	3.00	6.00	12.00
567	From Now On/I Want Love and Affection	196?	3.00	6.00	12.00

Albums

Number	Title (A Side/B Side)	Yr	VG	VG+	NM
FORTUNE					
8014 [M]	Goin' Back to the Village of Love	1964	75.00	150.00	300.00
—Light blue label					
8014 [M]	Goin' Back to the Village of Love	196?	37.50	75.00	150.00
—Purple label					
8014 [M]	Goin' Back to the Village of Love	196?	15.00	30.00	60.00
—Yellow label					
8014 [M]	Goin' Back to the Village of Love	197?	3.75	7.50	15.00
—Bluish purple label, with much more flexible vinyl than earlier pressings					

MAYFIELD, CURTIS

Also see THE IMPRESSIONS.

12-Inch Singles

Number	Title (A Side/B Side)	Yr	VG	VG+	NM
CAPITOL					
V-15602	Superfly 1990 (6 versions)	1990	2.00	4.00	8.00
—With Ice-T					
CURTOM					
12-PO-22 [DJ]	I Mo Git U Sucka/He's a Fly Guy	198?	2.50	5.00	10.00
12-PO-52 [DJ]	Got to Be Real/On and On	198?	2.50	5.00	10.00
RSO/CURTOM					
1016 [DJ]	Tell Me, Tell Me (7:16)//Heartbeat/Over the Hump	1979	2.50	5.00	10.00

45s

Number	Title (A Side/B Side)	Yr	VG	VG+	NM
ARISTA					
9806	He's a Flyguy/(Instrumental)	1989	—	—	2.00
9806 [PS]	He's a Flyguy/(Instrumental)	1989	—	—	3.00
—With Fishbone					
BOARDWALK					
NB7-11-122	She Don't Let Nobody (But Me)/You Get All My Love	1981	—	2.00	4.00
NB7-11-132	Toot An'Toot An'Toot/Come Free Your People	1981	—	2.00	4.00
NB7-11-155	Hey Baby (Give It All to Me)/Summer Hot	1982	—	2.00	4.00
NB7-11-169	Dirty Laundry/Nobody But You	1982	—	2.00	4.00
COLUMBIA					
10147	Stash That Butt, Sucker/Zanzibar	1975	—	2.50	5.00
CRC					
001	Baby It's You/(B-side unknown)	1985	—	3.00	6.00
CURTOM					
0105	So in Love/Hard Times	1975	—	2.50	5.00
0118	Only You Babe/Love to the People	1976	—	2.50	5.00
0122	Party Night/P.S. I Love You	1976	—	2.50	5.00
0125	Show Me Love/Just Want to Be with You	1977	—	2.50	5.00
0131	Do Do Wap Is Strong in Here/Need Someone to Love	1977	—	2.50	5.00
0135	You Are, You Are/Get a Little Bit (Give, Get, Take and Have)	1978	—	2.50	5.00
0135 [PS]	You Are, You Are/Get a Little Bit (Give, Get, Take and Have)	1978	—	3.00	6.00
0141	Do It All Night/Party Party	1978	—	2.50	5.00
0142	In Love, In Love, In Love/Keeps Me Loving You	1978	—	2.50	5.00
1955	(Don't Worry) If There's a Hell Below We're All Going to Go/The Makings of You	1970	—	3.00	6.00
1960	Beautiful Brother of Mine/Give It Up	1971	—	3.00	6.00
1963	Mighty Mighty (Spade and Whitey)/(B-side unknown)	1971	—	3.00	6.00
1966	Get Down/We're a Winner	1971	—	3.00	6.00
1968	We Got to Have Peace/We're a Winner	1972	—	3.00	6.00
1968 [PS]	We Got to Have Peace/We're a Winner	1972	2.00	4.00	8.00
1972	Beautiful Brother of Mine/Love to Keep You In My Mind	1972	—	3.00	6.00
1974	Move On Up/Underground	1972	—	3.00	6.00
1975	Freddie's Dead (Theme from "Superfly")/Underground	1972	—	3.00	6.00
1978	Superfly/Underground	1972	—	3.00	6.00
1978 [PS]	Superfly/Underground	1972	2.00	4.00	8.00
1987	Future Shock/The Other Side of Town	1973	—	3.00	6.00
1991	If I Were Only a Child Again/Think	1973	—	3.00	6.00
1993	Can't Say Nothin'/Future Song	1973	—	3.00	6.00
1999	Kung Fu/Right On for the Darkness	1974	—	3.00	6.00
1999 [PS]	Kung Fu/Right On for the Darkness	1974	2.00	4.00	8.00
2005	Sweet Exorcist/Suffer	1974	—	3.00	6.00
2006	Mother's Son/Love Me	1974	—	3.00	6.00
RSO/CURTOM					
919	This Year/(Instrumental)	1979	—	2.50	5.00
941	You're So Good to Me/Between You, Babe, and Me	1979	—	2.50	5.00
—With Linda Clifford					
1029	Love's Sweet Sensation/(Instrumental)	1980	—	2.50	5.00
—With Linda Clifford					
1036	Love Me, Love Me Now/It's Alright	1980	—	2.50	5.00
1046	Tripping Out/Never Stop Loving	1980	—	2.50	5.00

Albums

Number	Title (A Side/B Side)	Yr	VG	VG+	NM
BOARDWALK					
NB1-33239	Love Is the Place	1981	2.50	5.00	10.00
NB1-33256	Honesty	1982	2.50	5.00	10.00
CRC					
2001	We Come in Peace with a Message of Love	1985	3.00	6.00	12.00
CURTOM					
CUR-2003	There's No Place Like America Today	198?	2.00	4.00	8.00
—Reissue of 5001					
CUR-2005	Something to Believe In	198?	2.00	4.00	8.00
—Reissue of RSO 3077					
CUR-2008	Take It to the Street	198?	2.50	5.00	10.00
CUR-2901 [(2)]	Live in Europe	198?	3.00	6.00	12.00
CUR-2902 [(2)]	Greatest Hits of All Time (Classic Collection)	198?	3.00	6.00	12.00
CU 5001	There's No Place Like America Today	1975	3.00	6.00	12.00
CU 5007	Give, Get, Take and Have	1976	3.00	6.00	12.00
CU 5013	Never Say You Can't Survive	1977	3.00	6.00	12.00
CUK 5022	Do It All Night	1978	3.00	6.00	12.00
CRS-8005	Curtis	1970	3.75	7.50	15.00
CRS-8008 [(2)]	Curtis/Live!	1971	5.00	10.00	20.00
CRS-8009	Roots	1971	3.75	7.50	15.00
CRS-8014	Superfly	1972	5.00	10.00	20.00
CRS-8015	Back to the World	1973	3.75	7.50	15.00
CRS-8018	Curtis in Chicago	1973	3.75	7.50	15.00
CRS-8601	Sweet Exorcist	1974	3.00	6.00	12.00
CRS-8604	Got to Find a Way	1974	3.00	6.00	12.00
RSO					
RS-1-3053	Heartbeat	1979	2.50	5.00	10.00
RS-1-3077	Something to Believe In	1980	2.50	5.00	10.00

MAYFIELD, PERCY

45s

Number	Title (A Side/B Side)	Yr	VG	VG+	NM
ATLANTIC					
3207	I Don't Want to Be President/Nothin' Stays the Same Forever	1974	—	2.50	5.00
BRUNSWICK					
55390	Walking on a Tightrope/P.M. Blues	1968	2.00	4.00	8.00
CHESS					
1599	Double Dealing/Are You Out There	1955	15.00	30.00	60.00
IMPERIAL					
5577	One Love/My Reward	1959	3.75	7.50	15.00
5620	My Heart Is a Prisoner/My Memories	1959	3.75	7.50	15.00
KING					
4480	Two Years of Torture/Half Awake	1951	15.00	30.00	60.00
RCA VICTOR					
74-0307	To Live the Past/Lying Woman (Not Trustworthy)	1970	—	3.00	6.00
74-0348	A Highway Is Like a Woman/You Wear Your Hair Too Long	1970	—	3.00	6.00
74-0379	Daddy Wants You to Come Home/Weakness Is a Thing Called Man	1970	—	3.00	6.00
74-0462	The Flirt/California Blues	1971	—	3.00	6.00
SPECIALTY					
375	Please Send Me Someone to Love/Strange Things Happening	1950	20.00	40.00	80.00
390	Lost Love/Life Is Suicide	1951	15.00	30.00	60.00
400	What a Fool I Was/Nightless Lover	1951	15.00	30.00	60.00
408	Prayin' For Your Return/My Blues	1951	15.00	30.00	60.00
416	Cry Baby/Hopeless	1952	10.00	20.00	40.00
425	The Big Question/The Hurt Is On	1952	10.00	20.00	40.00
432	Louisiana/Two Hearts Are Greater Than One	1952	10.00	20.00	40.00
439	Lonesome Highway/My Heart	1952	10.00	20.00	40.00
460	Lost Mind/Lonely One	1953	10.00	20.00	40.00
—Black vinyl					
460	Lost Mind/Lonely One	1953	20.00	40.00	80.00
—Colored vinyl					
473	The Bachelor Blues/How Deep Is the Well	1953	10.00	20.00	40.00
—Black vinyl					
473	The Bachelor Blues/How Deep Is the Well	1953	20.00	40.00	80.00
—Colored vinyl					
485	I Need Love So Bad/Loose Lips	1954	10.00	20.00	40.00
499	You Don't Exist No More/Sugar Mama, Peach Papa	1954	10.00	20.00	40.00
537	My Heart Is Cryin'/You Were Lyin' to Me	1954	10.00	20.00	40.00
544	Baby You're Rich/The Voice Within	1955	7.50	15.00	30.00
607	Diggin' the Moonglow/Please Believe Me	1956	7.50	15.00	30.00
690	When Did You Leave Heaven/What Must I Do	1960	5.00	10.00	20.00
723	Lost Mind/River's Invitation	1973	—	3.00	6.00
TANGERINE					
923	Never No More/I Reached for a Tear	1962	3.00	6.00	12.00
927	Never Say Now/Life Is Suicide	1963	2.50	5.00	10.00
931	River's Invitation/Baby Please	1963	2.50	5.00	10.00
934	The Hunt Is On/Cookin' in Style	1963	2.50	5.00	10.00
935	You Don't Exist No More/Memory Pain	1964	2.50	5.00	10.00
941	Stranger in My Own Home Town/Maybe It's Because of Love	1964	2.50	5.00	10.00
950	Fading Love/Stand By	1965	2.00	4.00	8.00
957	Give Me Time to Explain/My Jug and I	1965	2.00	4.00	8.00
966	It's Time to Make a Change/We Both Must Cry	1966	2.00	4.00	8.00
973	My Love/My Bottle Is My Companion	1966	2.00	4.00	8.00
977	As Long As You're Mine/Ha Ha in the Daytime	1967	2.00	4.00	8.00
979	Don't Start Lyin' to Me/Pretty Eyed Baby	1967	2.00	4.00	8.00

Albums

Number	Title	Yr	VG	VG+	NM
BRUNSWICK					
BL 754145	Walking on a Tightrope	1968	5.00	10.00	20.00
INTERMEDIA					
QS-5010	Please Send Me Someone to Love	198?	2.50	5.00	10.00
RCA VICTOR					
LSP-4269	Percy Mayfield Sings Percy Mayfield	1970	3.75	7.50	15.00
LSP-4444	Weakness Is a Thing Called Man	1970	3.75	7.50	15.00
LSP-4558	Blues And Then Some	1971	3.75	7.50	15.00
SPECIALTY					
SPS-2126	The Best of Percy Mayfield	1970	5.00	10.00	20.00
SP-7001	Poet of the Blues	1990	3.75	7.50	15.00
TANGERINE					
TRC-1505 [M]	My Jug and I	1966	5.00	10.00	20.00
TRCS-1505 [S]	My Jug and I	1966	6.25	12.50	25.00
TRC-1510 [M]	Bought Blues	1967	5.00	10.00	20.00
TRCS-1510 [S]	Bought Blues	1967	6.25	12.50	25.00

MAYO, FRANKIE, AND THE FALCONS

45s

Number	Title (A Side/B Side)	Yr	VG	VG+	NM
RCA VICTOR					
47-7076	Stepping Stone/Jigsaw Puzzle	1957	6.25	12.50	25.00

MAYPOLE

Albums

Number	Title	Yr	VG	VG+	NM
COLOSSUS					
CS-1007	Maypole	1971	15.00	30.00	60.00

MAYS, WILLIE

45s

Number	Title (A Side/B Side)	Yr	VG	VG+	NM
DUKE					
350	My Sad Heart/If You Love Me	1962	2.50	5.00	10.00
418	My Sad Heart/If You Love Me	1967	2.00	4.00	8.00
EPIC					
9066	Say Hey (The Willie Mays Song)/Out of the Bushes	1954	6.25	12.50	25.00
—With the Treniers					

MC5

45s

Number	Title (A Side/B Side)	Yr	VG	VG+	NM
A-SQUARE					
333	Looking at You/Borderline	1967	20.00	40.00	80.00
—500 copies of this record were pressed					
333 [PS]	Looking at You/Borderline	1967	10.00	20.00	40.00
ALIVE/TOTAL ENERGY					
NER 3012	Looking at You/Borderline	1998	—	—	2.00
—30th anniversary reissue					
NER 3012 [PS]	Looking at You/Borderline	1998	—	—	2.00
AMG					
1000 [DJ]	I Can Only Give You Everything (same on both sides)	1966	12.50	25.00	50.00
1001	I Can Only Give You Everything/One of the Guys	1969	12.50	25.00	50.00
—Yellow label					
1001	I Can Only Give You Everything/I Just Don't Know	1969	12.50	25.00	50.00
—Black label					
ATLANTIC					
2678	Tonight/Looking at You	1969	3.75	7.50	15.00
2724	The American Ruse/Shakin' Street	1970	3.75	7.50	15.00
ELEKTRA					
MC5-1 [DJ]	Kick Out the Jams/Motor City Is Burning	1968	17.50	35.00	70.00
—Distributed free at Fillmore East concert 12/12/68; A-side is an alternate take					
45648	Kick Out the Jams/Motor City Is Burning	1969	5.00	10.00	20.00

Albums

Number	Title	Yr	VG	VG+	NM
ALIVE					
0005 [10]	Power Trip	1994	—	3.00	6.00
0008 [10]	Ice Pick Slim/Mad Like Eldridge Cleaver	1994	—	3.00	6.00
ATLANTIC					
SD 8247	Back in the U.S.A.	1970	12.50	25.00	50.00
SD 8285	High Time	1971	12.50	25.00	50.00
ELEKTRA					
EKS-74042	Kick Out the Jams	1969	12.50	25.00	50.00
—Gatefold cover with John Sinclair liner notes in center spread; brownish label					
EKS-74042	Kick Out the Jams	1969	5.00	10.00	20.00
—All other editions					
TOTAL ENERGY					
2001 [10]	The American Ruse	1994	—	3.00	6.00

MCCALL, C.W.

45s

Number	Title (A Side/B Side)	Yr	VG	VG+	NM
AMERICAN GRAMAPHONE					
351	Old Home Filler-Up An' Keep On-a-Truckin' Café/Old 30	1974	3.75	7.50	15.00
MGM					
14738	Old Home Filler-Up An' Keep On-a-Truckin' Café/Old 30	1974	—	2.00	4.00
14764	Wolf Creek Pass/Sloan	1974	—	2.00	4.00
14801	Classified/I've Trucked All Over This Land	1975	—	2.00	4.00
14825	Black Bear Road/Four Wheel Drive	1975	—	2.00	4.00
14839	Convoy/Long Lonesome Road	1975	—	2.50	5.00
POLYDOR					
14310	There Won't Be No Country Music (There Won't Be No Rock 'n' Roll)/Green River	1976	—	2.00	4.00
14331	Crispy Critters/Jackson Hole	1976	—	2.00	4.00
14352	Four Wheel Cowboy/Aurora Borealis	1976	—	2.00	4.00
14365	'Round the World with the Rubber Duck/Night Rider	1976	—	2.00	4.00
14377	Audubon/Ratchetjaw	1977	—	2.00	4.00
14420	Roses for Mama/Columbine	1977	—	2.00	4.00
14445	Sing Silent Night/Old Glory	1977	—	2.50	5.00
14458	Old Glory/Watch the Wildwood Flowers	1978	—	2.00	4.00
14527	Outlaws and Lone Star Beer/Silver Cloud Breakdown	1978	—	2.00	4.00
14550	Milton/The Little Things in Life	1979	—	2.00	4.00

Albums

Number	Title	Yr	VG	VG+	NM
MGM					
M3G-4989	Wolf Creek Pass	1975	2.50	5.00	10.00
M3G-5008	Black Bear Road	1975	2.50	5.00	10.00
POLYDOR					
PD-1-6069	Wilderness	1976	2.50	5.00	10.00
PD-1-6094	Rubber Duck	1977	2.50	5.00	10.00
PD-1-6125	Roses for Mama	1978	2.50	5.00	10.00
PD-1-6156	Greatest Hits	1978	2.50	5.00	10.00
PD-1-6190	C.W. McCall & Co.	1979	2.50	5.00	10.00
825793-1	Greatest Hits	198?	2.00	4.00	8.00
—Reissue of 6156					

MCCALLUM, DAVID

45s

Number	Title (A Side/B Side)	Yr	VG	VG+	NM
CAPITOL					
5571	My Carousel/Communications	1966	2.00	4.00	8.00
5571 [PS]	My Carousel/Communications	1966	3.00	6.00	12.00
5721	Three Bites of the Apple/House on Breckinridge Lane	1966	2.00	4.00	8.00
5721 [PS]	Three Bites of the Apple/House on Breckinridge Lane	1966	3.00	6.00	12.00
5802	A Man and a Woman/House of Mirrors	1966	2.00	4.00	8.00

Albums

Number	Title	Yr	VG	VG+	NM
CAPITOL					
ST 2432 [S]	Music — A Part of Me	1966	3.75	7.50	15.00
T 2432 [M]	Music — A Part of Me	1966	3.00	6.00	12.00
ST 2498 [S]	Music: A Bit More of Me	1966	3.75	7.50	15.00
T 2498 [M]	Music: A Bit More of Me	1966	3.00	6.00	12.00
ST 2651 [S]	Music: It's Happening Now	1967	3.75	7.50	15.00
T 2651 [M]	Music: It's Happening Now	1967	3.75	7.50	15.00
ST 2748 [S]	McCallum	1967	3.75	7.50	15.00
T 2748 [M]	McCallum	1967	3.75	7.50	15.00

MCCANN, LES

Also see ROBERTA FLACK.

12-Inch Singles

Number	Title (A Side/B Side)	Yr	VG	VG+	NM
A&M					
SP-17042 [DJ]	Just the Way You Are (6:31) (same on both sides)	1978	3.00	6.00	12.00

45s

Number	Title (A Side/B Side)	Yr	VG	VG+	NM
ATLANTIC					
2615	With These Hands/Burnin' Coal	1969	—	3.00	6.00
2713	What I Call Soul/Comment	1970	—	3.00	6.00
2918	What's Going On (Part 1)/What's Going On (Part 2)	1972	—	2.50	5.00
3253	When It's Over/Someday We'll Meet Again	1975	—	2.50	5.00
3312	Us/Well, Cuss Me Daddy	1976	—	2.50	5.00
A&M					
2081	Just the Way You Are/How Can You (Live Without Love)	1978	—	2.00	4.00
LIMELIGHT					
3060	But Not Really/Jack V. Schwartz	1965	2.00	4.00	8.00
3066	Green Green Rocky Road/Great City	1965	2.00	4.00	8.00
3077	All/Bucket O' Grease	1967	2.00	4.00	8.00
3078	Caper of the Golden Bulls/Loves of July	1967	2.00	4.00	8.00
3081	The Shout (Part 1)/The Shout (Part 2)	1967	2.00	4.00	8.00
PACIFIC JAZZ					
306	C Jam Blues/The Shout	1960	3.00	6.00	12.00
309	Truth/Little Girl from Casper	1961	3.00	6.00	12.00
311	Fish This Week/Vacushna	1961	3.00	6.00	12.00
317	I Am in Love/Big Jim	1961	3.00	6.00	12.00
318	Gone Up and Get That Church (Part 1)/Gone Up and Get That Church (Part 2)	1961	3.00	6.00	12.00
329	Sweet Georgia Brown/I Cried for You	1961	3.00	6.00	12.00
335	Next Spring/Wonder Why	1962	3.00	6.00	12.00
341	Twist Cha Cha/Little 3/4 for God & Co.	1962	3.00	6.00	12.00
350	Shampoo/Kathleen's Theme	1963	3.00	6.00	12.00
820	They Can't Take That Away from Me/Little Girl from Casper	1960	3.00	6.00	12.00
WORLD PACIFIC					
387	The Gospel Truth/Send It On Down to Me	1963	2.50	5.00	10.00
389	Bye and Bye/Get That Soul	1963	2.50	5.00	10.00
404	Back at the Chicken Shack/Sack o' Woe	1964	2.50	5.00	10.00
406	Bluesette/Spanish Castles	1964	2.50	5.00	10.00
411	Big City/Route 66	1964	2.50	5.00	10.00
418	It Had Better Be Tonight/Que Rico	1964	2.50	5.00	10.00
422	Basuto Baby/McCanna	1965	2.50	5.00	10.00
88133	The Shout/Spanish Onions	1966	2.00	4.00	8.00

Albums

Number	Title (A Side/B Side)	Yr	VG	VG+	NM
ABC IMPULSE!					
AS-9329	The Music Lets Me Be	1977	2.50	5.00	10.00
AS-9333	Live at the Roxy	1978	2.50	5.00	10.00
ATLANTIC					
SD 2-312 [(2)]	Live at Montreux	1974	3.75	7.50	15.00
SD 1516	Much Les	1969	3.75	7.50	15.00
SD 1547	Comment	1970	3.75	7.50	15.00
SD 1603	Invitation to Openness	1972	3.00	6.00	12.00
SD 1619	Talk to the People	1972	3.00	6.00	12.00
SD 1646	Layers	1973	3.00	6.00	12.00
SD 1666	Another Beginning	1974	3.00	6.00	12.00
SD 1679	Hustle to Survive	1975	3.00	6.00	12.00
SD 1690	River High, River Low	1976	3.00	6.00	12.00
A&M					
SP-4718	The Man	1978	2.50	5.00	10.00
SP-4780	Tall, Dark and Handsome	1979	2.50	5.00	10.00
JAM					
012	The Longer You Wait	1984	2.50	5.00	10.00
LIMELIGHT					
LM-82016 [M]	But Not Really	1965	3.75	7.50	15.00
LM-82025 [M]	Poo Boo	1965	3.75	7.50	15.00
LM-82031 [M]	Beaux J. Pooboo	1966	3.75	7.50	15.00
LM-82036 [M]	Live at Shelly's Manne-Hole	1966	3.75	7.50	15.00
LM-82041 [M]	Les McCann Plays the Hits	1966	3.75	7.50	15.00
LM-82043 [M]	Bucket O' Grease	1967	5.00	10.00	20.00
LM-82046 [M]	Live at the Bohemian Caverns, Washington, D.C.	1967	5.00	10.00	20.00
LS-86016 [S]	But Not Really	1965	5.00	10.00	20.00
LS-86025 [S]	Poo Boo	1965	5.00	10.00	20.00
LS-86031 [S]	Beaux J. Pooboo	1966	5.00	10.00	20.00
LS-86036 [S]	Live at Shelly's Manne-Hole	1966	5.00	10.00	20.00
LS-86041 [S]	Les McCann Plays the Hits	1966	5.00	10.00	20.00
LS-86043 [S]	Bucket O' Grease	1967	3.75	7.50	15.00
LS-86046 [S]	Live at the Bohemian Caverns, Washington, D.C.	1967	3.75	7.50	15.00
PACIFIC JAZZ					
PJ-2 [M]	The Truth	1960	6.25	12.50	25.00
ST-2 [S]	The Truth	1960	7.50	15.00	30.00
PJ-7 [M]	The Shout	1960	6.25	12.50	25.00
ST-7 [S]	The Shout	1960	7.50	15.00	30.00
PJ-16 [M]	Les McCann in San Francisco	1961	6.25	12.50	25.00
ST-16 [S]	Les McCann in San Francisco	1961	7.50	15.00	30.00
PJ-25 [M]	Pretty Lady	1961	5.00	10.00	20.00
ST-25 [S]	Pretty Lady	1961	6.25	12.50	25.00
PJ-31 [M]	Les McCann Sings	1961	5.00	10.00	20.00
ST-31 [S]	Les McCann Sings	1961	6.25	12.50	25.00
PJ-45 [M]	Les McCann in New York	1962	5.00	10.00	20.00
ST-45 [S]	Les McCann in New York	1962	6.25	12.50	25.00
PJ-56 [M]	On Time	1962	10.00	20.00	40.00
—Yellow vinyl					
PJ-56 [M]	On Time	1962	5.00	10.00	20.00
—Black vinyl					
ST-56 [S]	On Time	1962	12.50	25.00	50.00
—Yellow vinyl					
ST-56 [S]	On Time	1962	6.25	12.50	25.00
—Black vinyl					
PJ-63 [M]	Shampoo	1962	3.75	7.50	15.00
ST-63 [S]	Shampoo	1962	5.00	10.00	20.00
PJ-69 [M]	The Gospel Truth	1963	3.75	7.50	15.00
ST-69 [S]	The Gospel Truth	1963	5.00	10.00	20.00
PJ-78 [M]	Soul Hits	1963	3.75	7.50	15.00
ST-78 [S]	Soul Hits	1963	5.00	10.00	20.00
PJ-81 [M]	Jazz Waltz	1964	3.75	7.50	15.00
ST-81 [S]	Jazz Waltz	1964	5.00	10.00	20.00
PJ-84 [M]	McCanna	1964	3.75	7.50	15.00
ST-84 [S]	McCanna	1964	5.00	10.00	20.00
PJ-91 [M]	McCann/Wilson	1965	3.75	7.50	15.00
—With Gerald Wilson					
ST-91 [S]	McCann/Wilson	1965	5.00	10.00	20.00
—With Gerald Wilson					
LN-10077	Les McCann In San Francisco	1980	2.00	4.00	8.00
—Budget-line reissue					
LN-10078	Les McCann In New York	1980	2.00	4.00	8.00
—Budget-line reissue					
LN-10079	Soul Hits	1980	2.00	4.00	8.00
—Budget-line reissue					
LN-10083	The Shout	1980	2.00	4.00	8.00
—Budget-line reissue					
PJ-10097 [M]	Spanish Onions	1966	3.75	7.50	15.00
PJ-10107 [M]	A Bag of Gold	1966	3.75	7.50	15.00
ST-20097 [S]	Spanish Onions	1966	5.00	10.00	20.00
ST-20107 [S]	A Bag of Gold	1966	5.00	10.00	20.00
STONE					
1906	Butterfly	1988	2.50	5.00	10.00
SUNSET					
SUS-5214	Django	1969	2.50	5.00	10.00
SUS-5296	Unlimited	1970	2.50	5.00	10.00
WORLD PACIFIC					
ST-20166	More Or Les McCann	1969	3.75	7.50	15.00
ST-20173	New from the Big City	1970	3.75	7.50	15.00

MCCANN, LES, AND EDDIE HARRIS

Also see each artist's individual listings.

45s

Number	Title (A Side/B Side)	Yr	VG	VG+	NM
ATLANTIC					
2694	Compared to What/Cold Duck	1969	—	3.00	6.00
5109	Universal Prisoner/Set Us Free	1971	—	3.00	6.00

Albums

Number	Title (A Side/B Side)	Yr	VG	VG+	NM
ATLANTIC					
SD 1537	Swiss Movement	1969	3.75	7.50	15.00
SD 1583	Second Movement	1971	3.75	7.50	15.00

MCCARTNEY, LINDA

See PAUL McCARTNEY; SUZY AND THE RED STRIPES.

MCCARTNEY, PAUL

Includes duets with Linda McCartney plus his work with Wings. Also see THE BEATLES; MICHAEL JACKSON AND PAUL McCARTNEY.

12-Inch Singles

Number	Title (A Side/B Side)	Yr	VG	VG+	NM
ATLANTIC					
PR 388 [DJ]	Every Night/Lucille	1981	62.50	125.00	250.00
CAPITOL					
SPRO-8574 [DJ]	Maybe I'm Amazed (mono/stereo)	1976	20.00	40.00	80.00
SPRO-9556 [DJ]	Spies Like Us (4:40)/Spies Like Us (3:46)	1985	7.50	15.00	30.00
SPRO-9763 [DJ]	Press (same on both sides)	1986	5.00	10.00	20.00
SPRO-9797 [DJ]	Angry (same on both sides)	1986	6.25	12.50	25.00
SPRO-9861 [DJ]	Stranglehold (same on both sides)	1986	6.25	12.50	25.00
SPRO-9928 [DJ]	Pretty Little Head (same on both sides)	1986	12.50	25.00	50.00
V-15212	Spies Like Us (Party Mix)/(Alternative Mix)//(DJ Version)/My Carnival	1985	5.00	10.00	20.00
—"MPL" correct on label					
V-15212	Spies Like Us (Party Mix)/(Alternative Mix)//(DJ Version)/My Carnival	1985	3.75	7.50	15.00
—"MLP" on label instead of "MPL"					
V-15235	Press (Video Mix)/It's Not True//Hanglide/Press (Dub Mix)	1986	3.00	6.00	12.00
V-15499	Ou Est Le Soleil//Ou Est Le Soleil (Tub Dub Mix)/(Instrumental)	1989	3.00	6.00	12.00
COLUMBIA					
AS 775 [DJ]	Coming Up/Coming Up (Live at Glasgow)	1980	15.00	30.00	60.00
—Red label					
AS 775 [DJ]	Coming Up/Coming Up (Live at Glasgow)	1980	12.50	25.00	50.00
—White label					
AS 1444 [DJ]	Ebony and Ivory//Ballroom Dancing/The Pound Is Sinking	1982	7.50	15.00	30.00
AS 1758 [DJ]	Say Say Say (same on both sides)	1983	3.00	6.00	12.00
—With Michael Jackson					
AS 1940 [DJ]	No More Lonely Nights (Ballad) (same on both sides)	1984	5.00	10.00	20.00
AS 1990 [DJ]	No More Lonely Nights (Special Dance Mix) (same on both sides)	1984	5.00	10.00	20.00
03019	Take It Away//I'll Give You a Ring/Dress Me Up as a Robber	1982	3.00	6.00	12.00
05077	No More Lonely Nights (Playout Version)//Silly Love Songs/No More Lonely Nights (Ballad)	1984	3.00	6.00	12.00
05077	No More Lonely Nights (Special Dance Mix)//Silly Love Songs/No More Lonely Nights (Ballad)	1984	7.50	15.00	30.00
10940	Goodnight Tonight (7:25)/Daytime Nighttime Suffering	1979	2.50	5.00	10.00
—Generic white cover, no picture cover or sticker					
10940	Goodnight Tonight (7:25)/Daytime Nighttime Suffering	1979	20.00	40.00	80.00
—Generic white cover with large blue and white sticker					
10940	Goodnight Tonight (7:25)/Daytime Nighttime Suffering	1979	3.75	7.50	15.00
—With picture cover					
10940 [DJ]	Goodnight Tonight (7:25)/Goodnight Tonight (4:18)	1979	6.25	12.50	25.00
8C8 39927-S1	No More Lonely Nights (2 versions)/Silly Love Songs	1984	5.00	10.00	20.00
—Picture disc					

Number	Title (A Side/B Side)	Yr	VG	VG+	NM
45s					
APPLE					
1829	Another Day/Oh Woman, Oh Why	1971	3.00	6.00	12.00
—With star on A-side label					
1829	Another Day/Oh Woman, Oh Why	1971	2.00	4.00	8.00
1837	Uncle Albert/Admiral Halsey//Too Many People	1971	3.75	7.50	15.00
—Paul and Linda McCartney; with "Pual" misspelling on producer credit					
1837	Uncle Albert/Admiral Halsey//Too Many People	1971	2.00	4.00	8.00
—Paul and Linda McCartney; with no misspelling					
1837	Uncle Albert/Admiral Halsey//Too Many People	1971	12.50	25.00	50.00
—Paul and Linda McCartney; with unsliced apple on B-side label					
1837	Uncle Albert/Admiral Halsey//Too Many People	1975	7.50	15.00	30.00
—Paul and Linda McCartney; with "All rights reserved" on label					
1847	Give Ireland Back to the Irish/Give Ireland Back to the Irish (Version)	1972	2.50	5.00	10.00
—Wings					
1847 [PS]	Give Ireland Back to the Irish/Give Ireland Back to the Irish (Version)	1972	7.50	15.00	30.00
—Wings; title sleeve with large center hole					
1851	Mary Had a Little Lamb/Little Woman Love	1972	2.50	5.00	10.00
—Wings					
1851 [DJ]	Mary Had a Little Lamb/Little Woman Love	1972	75.00	150.00	300.00
—White label promo, lists artist as Paul McCartney					
1851 [PS]	Mary Had a Little Lamb/Little Woman Love	1972	6.25	12.50	25.00
—Wings; without "Little Woman Love" on sleeve					
1851 [PS]	Mary Had a Little Lamb/Little Woman Love	1972	10.00	20.00	40.00
—Wings; with "Little Woman Love" on sleeve					
1857	Hi Hi Hi/C Moon	1972	2.50	5.00	10.00
—Wings; red label					
1861	My Love/The Mess	1973	2.00	4.00	8.00
—Paul McCartney and Wings; custom "Red Rose Speedway" label					
1861 [DJ]	My Love/The Mess	1973	50.00	100.00	200.00
—Paul McCartney and Wings; white label					
1863	Live and Let Die/I Lie Around	1973	2.00	4.00	8.00
—Wings					
1869	Helen Wheels/Country Dreamer	1973	2.00	4.00	8.00
—Paul McCartney and Wings					
1871	Jet/Mamunia	1974	2.50	5.00	10.00
—Paul McCartney and Wings					
1871	Jet/Mamunia	1974	25.00	50.00	100.00
—Paul McCartney and Wings; A-side incorrectly listed as playing for 2:49					
1871	Jet/Let Me Roll It	1974	2.00	4.00	8.00
—Paul McCartney and Wings					
P-1871 [DJ]	Jet (Edited Mono)/Jet (Stereo)	1974	12.50	25.00	50.00
—Paul McCartney and Wings					
1873	Band on the Run/Nineteen Hundred and Eighty-Five	1974	2.00	4.00	8.00
—Paul McCartney and Wings					
P-1873 [DJ]	Band on the Run (Edited Mono)/Band on the Run (Full-length Stereo)	1974	10.00	20.00	40.00
—Paul McCartney and Wings					
P-1873 [DJ]	Band on the Run (mono/stereo, both edits)	1974	25.00	50.00	100.00
—Paul McCartney and Wings					
1875	Junior's Farm/Sally G	1974	2.00	4.00	8.00
—Paul McCartney and Wings					
1875	Junior's Farm/Sally G	1975	20.00	40.00	80.00
—Paul McCartney and Wings; with "All Rights Reserved" on label					
P-1875 [DJ]	Junior's Farm (Edited Mono)/Junior's Farm (Full-length Stereo)	1974	12.50	25.00	50.00
—Paul McCartney and Wings					
P-1875 [DJ]	Sally G (mono/stereo)	1974	20.00	40.00	80.00
—Paul McCartney and Wings					
PRO-6193/4 [DJ]	Another Day/Oh Woman, Oh Why	1971	20.00	40.00	80.00
PRO-6786 [DJ]	Helen Wheels (mono/stereo)	1973	12.50	25.00	50.00
—Paul McCartney and Wings					
PRO-6787 [DJ]	Country Dreamer (mono/stereo)	1973	100.00	200.00	400.00
—Paul McCartney and Wings					
CAPITOL					
(no #) [DJ]	Figure of Eight (same on both sides)	1989	25.00	50.00	100.00
—Test pressings with blank label; most known copies come in a Capitol sleeve					
1829	Another Day/Oh Woman, Oh Why	1976	3.75	7.50	15.00
—Black label					
1837	Uncle Albert/Admiral Halsey//Too Many People	1976	3.75	7.50	15.00
—Black label					
1847	Give Ireland Back to the Irish/Give Ireland Back to the Irish	1976	5.00	10.00	20.00
—Wings; black label					
1851	Mary Had a Little Lamb/Little Woman Love	1976	3.00	6.00	12.00
—Wings; black label					
1857	Hi Hi Hi/C Moon	1976	3.75	7.50	15.00
—Wings; black label					
1861	My Love/The Mess	1976	5.00	10.00	20.00
—Paul McCartney and Wings; black label; "The Mess" plays too fast					
1861	My Love/The Mess	1976	5.00	10.00	20.00
—Paul McCartney and Wings; black label; "The Mess" plays normally					
1863	Live and Let Die/I Lie Around	1976	3.00	6.00	12.00
—Wings; black label					
1869	Helen Wheels/Country Dreamer	1976	3.75	7.50	15.00
—Paul McCartney and Wings; black label					
1871	Jet/Let Me Roll It	1976	3.75	7.50	15.00
—Paul McCartney and Wings; black label					
1873	Band on the Run/Nineteen Hundred and Eighty-Five	1976	3.75	7.50	15.00
—Paul McCartney and Wings; black label					
1875	Junior's Farm/Sally G	1976	3.75	7.50	15.00
—Paul McCartney and Wings; black label					
4091	Listen to What the Man Said/Love in Song	1975	—	2.50	5.00
4091 [PS]	Listen to What the Man Said/Love in Song	1975	3.00	6.00	12.00
—Wings					
4145	Letting Go/You Gave Me the Answer	1975	—	2.50	5.00
—Wings					
4175	Venus and Mars Rock Show/Magneto and Titanium Man	1975	—	2.50	5.00
—Wings					
4256	Silly Love Songs/Cook of the House	1976	2.00	4.00	8.00
—Wings; black label					
4256	Silly Love Songs/Cook of the House	1976	—	2.00	4.00
—Wings; "Speed of Sound" label (more common version)					
4293	Let 'Em In/Beware My Love	1976	—	3.00	6.00
—Wings; black label (more common version)					
4293	Let 'Em In/Beware My Love	1976	—	2.00	4.00
—Wings; "Speed of Sound" label					
4385	Maybe I'm Amazed/Soily	1976	—	2.00	4.00
—Wings; custom label (more common version)					
4385	Maybe I'm Amazed/Soily	1976	5.00	10.00	20.00
—Wings; black label					
4504	Girls' School/Mull of Kintyre	1977	—	2.50	5.00
—Wings; black label (more common version)					
4504	Girls' School/Mull of Kintyre	1978	30.00	60.00	120.00
—Wings; purple label, label has reeded edge					
4504 [PS]	Girls' School/Mull of Kintyre	1977	3.00	6.00	12.00
—Wings					
4559	With a Little Luck/Backwards Traveller-Cuff Link	1978	—	2.00	4.00
—Wings					
4594	I've Had Enough/Deliver Your Children	1978	—	2.00	4.00
—Wings					
4625	London Town/I'm Carrying	1978	—	2.00	4.00
—Wings					
B-5537	Spies Like Us/My Carnival	1985	—	—	3.00
B-5537 [PS]	Spies Like Us/My Carnival	1985	—	3.00	6.00
B-5597	Press/It's Not True	1986	—	2.50	5.00
B-5597 [PS]	Press/It's Not True	1986	—	2.50	5.00
B-5636	Stranglehold/Angry	1986	—	2.50	5.00
B-5636 [PS]	Stranglehold/Angry	1986	—	2.50	5.00
B-5672	Only Love Remains/Tough on a Tightrope	1987	—	2.50	5.00
B-5672 [PS]	Only Love Remains/Tough on a Tightrope	1987	—	2.50	5.00
S7-17318	Off the Ground/Cosmically Conscious	1993	—	3.00	6.00
—White vinyl standard issue					
S7-17318	Off the Ground/Cosmically Conscious	1993	—	3.00	6.00
—Black vinyl "error" issue					
S7-17319	Biker Like an Icon/Things We Said Today	1993	—	3.00	6.00
—Black vinyl "error" issue					
S7-17319	Biker Like an Icon/Things We Said Today	1993	—	3.00	6.00
—White vinyl standard issue					
S7-17489	C'mon People/Down to the River	1993	2.00	4.00	8.00
—All copies on white vinyl					
S7-17643	Wonderful Christmastime/Rudolph, the Red-Nosed Reggae	1993	—	3.00	6.00
—Paul McCartney & Wings; red vinyl					
B-44367	My Brave Face/Flying to My Home	1989	2.50	5.00	10.00
—Version 1: Both title and artist in block print, time of A-side is "3:17"					
B-44367	My Brave Face/Flying to My Home	1989	2.00	4.00	8.00
—Version 2: Artist in custom print, title in block print, time of A-side is "3:17"					
B-44367	My Brave Face/Flying to My Home	1989	—	2.50	5.00
—Version 3: Same as Version 2, time of A-side is "3:16"					
B-44367 [PS]	My Brave Face/Flying to My Home	1989	—	2.50	5.00
S7-56946	Hope of Deliverance/Long Leather Coat	1993	—	3.00	6.00
58823	No Other Baby/Try Not to Cry	1999	—	2.00	4.00
7PRO-79700 [DJ]	This One (same on both sides)	1989	100.00	200.00	400.00
—Vinyl is promo only					
COLUMBIA					
02171	Silly Love Songs/Cook of the House	1981	6.25	12.50	25.00
—Wings; despite label information, this has an edited version of A-side					
03018	Take It Away/I'll Give You a Ring	1982	—	—	3.00
03018 [PS]	Take It Away/I'll Give You a Ring	1982	—	—	3.00
03235	Tug of War/Get It	1982	3.00	6.00	12.00
04127	Wonderful Christmastime/Rudolph the Red-Nosed Reggae	1983	7.50	15.00	30.00
—Scarce reissue with B-side in stereo					
04296	So Bad/Pipes of Peace	1983	—	2.50	5.00
04296 [PS]	So Bad/Pipes of Peace	1983	—	2.50	5.00
04581	No More Lonely Nights/No More Lonely Nights (playout version)	1984	—	2.00	4.00
04581	No More Lonely Nights/No More Lonely Nights (Special Dance Version)	1984	10.00	20.00	40.00
04581 [PS]	No More Lonely Nights/No More Lonely Nights (playout version)	1984	7.50	15.00	30.00
—Title print in gray, credit print in white					
04581 [PS]	No More Lonely Nights/No More Lonely Nights (playout version)	1984	—	2.50	5.00
—Title print in white, credit print in gray					
10939	Goodnight Tonight/Daytime Nighttime Suffering	1979	—	3.00	6.00
—Wings					
11020	Getting Closer/Spin It On	1979	—	3.00	6.00
—Wings					
11020 [PS]	Getting Closer/Spin It On	1979	7.50	15.00	30.00
—Title sleeve with large center hole					
11070	Arrow Through Me/Old Siam, Sir	1979	—	3.00	6.00
—Wings					
11162	Wonderful Christmastime/Rudolph the Red-Nosed Reggae	1979	2.50	5.00	10.00
11162 [PS]	Wonderful Christmastime/Rudolph the Red-Nosed Reggae	1979	3.75	7.50	15.00
11263	Coming Up//Coming Up (Live at Glasgow)/Lunch Box-Odd Sox	1980	—	2.00	4.00
11263 [PS]	Coming Up//Coming Up (Live at Glasgow)/Lunch Box-Odd Sox	1980	—	2.50	5.00
11335	Waterfalls/Check My Machine	1980	—	3.00	6.00
11335 [PS]	Waterfalls/Check My Machine	1980	5.00	10.00	20.00
33405	Goodnight Tonight/Getting Closer	1980	2.50	5.00	10.00
—Wings; red label "Hall of Fame" series					
33407	My Love/Maybe I'm Amazed	1980	2.50	5.00	10.00
—Paul McCartney and Wings; red label "Hall of Fame" series					
33407	My Love/Maybe I'm Amazed	1985	7.50	15.00	30.00
—Paul McCartney and Wings; briefly available gray label reissue					
33408	Jet//Uncle Albert/Admiral Halsey	1980	2.50	5.00	10.00
—Paul McCartney and Wings; red label "Hall of Fame" series					
33408	Jet//Uncle Albert/Admiral Halsey	1985	7.50	15.00	30.00
—Paul McCartney and Wings; briefly available gray label reissue					
33409	Band on the Run/Helen Wheels	1980	2.50	5.00	10.00
—Paul McCartney and Wings; red label "Hall of Fame" series					

Number	Title (A Side/B Side)	Yr	VG	VG+	NM
33409	Band on the Run/Helen Wheels	1985	7.50	15.00	30.00
—Paul McCartney and Wings; briefly available gray label reissue					
EMI					
3977	Walking in the Park with Eloise/Bridge on the River Suite	1974	15.00	30.00	60.00
3977 [PS]	Walking in the Park with Eloise/Bridge on the River Suite	1974	20.00	40.00	80.00
—As "The Country Hams"					

Albums

Number	Title	Yr	VG	VG+	NM
APPLE					
SMAS-3363	McCartney	1975	25.00	50.00	100.00
—With "All Rights Reserved" on label					
SMAS-3363	McCartney	197?	5.00	10.00	20.00
—New prefix on label					
STAO-3363	McCartney	1970	6.25	12.50	25.00
—"McCartney" and "Paul McCartney" on separate lines on label; New York addess on back cover					
STAO-3363	McCartney	1970	7.50	15.00	30.00
—"McCartney" and "Paul McCartney" on separate lines on label; California addess on back cover					
STAO-3363	McCartney	1970	20.00	40.00	80.00
—Apple label with small Capitol logo on B-side					
STAO-3363	McCartney	1970	5.00	10.00	20.00
—Only "McCartney" on label; back cover does NOT say "An Abkco managed company"					
STAO-3363	McCartney	1970	6.25	12.50	25.00
—Only "McCartney" on label; back cover says "An Abkco managed company"					
MAS-3375 [M]	Ram	1971	1000.	2000.	4000.
—Credited to "Paul and Linda McCartney"; mono record in stereo cover for radio station use only					
SMAS-3375	Ram	1971	3.75	7.50	15.00
—Credited to "Paul and Linda McCartney"; unsliced apple on one label, sliced apple on other					
SMAS-3375	Ram	1971	7.50	15.00	30.00
—Credited to "Paul and Linda McCartney"; unsliced apple on both labels					
SMAS-3375	Ram	1971	12.50	25.00	50.00
—Credited to "Paul and Linda McCartney"; Apple label with small Capitol logo on B-side					
SMAS-3375	Ram	1975	25.00	50.00	100.00
—Credited to "Paul and Linda McCartney"; with "All Rights Reserved" on label					
SW-3386	Wild Life	1971	3.75	7.50	15.00
—Credited to "Wings"					
SMAL-3409	Red Rose Speedway	1973	5.00	10.00	20.00
—Credited to "Paul McCartney and Wings"; with bound-in booklet					
SO-3415	Band on the Run	1973	5.00	10.00	20.00
—Credited to "Paul McCartney and Wings"; with photo innersleeve and poster					
SPRO-6210 [DJ]	Brung to Ewe By	1971	100.00	200.00	400.00
—Promo-only radio spots for "Ram"; counterfeits have uneven spacing between tracks					
CAPITOL					
SMAS-3363	McCartney	1976	6.25	12.50	25.00
—Black label, "Manufactured by McCartney Music Inc" at top					
SMAS-3363	McCartney	1976	5.00	10.00	20.00
—Black label, "Manufactured by MPL Communications Inc" at top					
SMAS-3375	Ram	1976	7.50	15.00	30.00
—Credited to "Paul and Linda McCartney"; black label, "Manufactured by McCartney Music Inc" at top					
SMAS-3375	Ram	197?	5.00	10.00	20.00
—Credited to "Paul and Linda McCartney"; black label, "Manufactured by MPL Communications Inc" at top					
SMAS-3375	Ram	197?	10.00	20.00	40.00
—Credited to "Paul and Linda McCartney"; black label, "Manufactured by Capitol Records..." on label					
SW-3386	Wild Life	1976	7.50	15.00	30.00
—Credited to "Wings"; black label, "Manufactured by McCartney Music Inc" at top					
SW-3386	Wild Life	197?	5.00	10.00	20.00
—Credited to "Wings"; black label, "Manufactured by MPL Communications Inc" at top					
SMAL-3409	Red Rose Speedway	1976	7.50	15.00	30.00
—Credited to "Paul McCartney and Wings"; black label, "Manufactured by McCartney Music Inc" at top					
SMAL-3409	Red Rose Speedway	197?	6.25	12.50	25.00
—Credited to "Paul McCartney and Wings"; black label, "Manufactured by MPL Communications Inc" at top					
SO-3415	Band on the Run	1975	5.00	10.00	20.00
—Credited to "Paul McCartney and Wings"; custom label with MPL logo					
SO-3415	Band on the Run	197?	12.50	25.00	50.00
—Credited to "Paul McCartney and Wings"; black label, "Manufactured by Capitol Records..."					
SO-3415	Band on the Run	197?	5.00	10.00	20.00
—Credited to "Paul McCartney and Wings"; black label, "Maunfactured by MPL Communications Inc." at top					
SMAS-11419	Venus and Mars	1975	3.75	7.50	15.00
—Credited to "Wings"; with two posters and two stickers					
SW-11525	Wings at the Speed of Sound	1976	2.50	5.00	10.00
—Credited to "Wings"; custom label					
SW-11525 [DJ]	Wings at the Speed of Sound	1976	75.00	150.00	300.00
—Credited to "Wings"; white label advance promo					
SWCO-11593 [(3)]	Wings Over America	1976	6.25	12.50	25.00
—Credited to "Wings"; custom labels with poster					
ST-11642	Thrillington	1977	25.00	50.00	100.00
—Credited to "Percy 'Thrills' Thrillington"; instrumental versions of songs from Ram LP					
SW-11777	London Town	1978	3.75	7.50	15.00
—Credited to "Wings"; custom label with poster					
SEAX-11901 [PD]	Band on the Run	1978	10.00	20.00	40.00
—Credited to "Paul McCartney and Wings"; picture disc					
SOO-11905	Wings Greatest	1978	3.75	7.50	15.00
—Credited to "Wings"; custom label with poster					
SOO-11905 [DJ]	Wings Greatest	1978	100.00	200.00	400.00
—Credited to "Wings"; white label advance promo/test pressing					
PJAS-12475	Press to Play	1986	3.00	6.00	12.00
CLW-48287 [(2)]	All the Best!	1987	5.00	10.00	20.00
C1-56500	Flaming Pie	1997	3.75	7.50	15.00
C1-91653	Flowers in the Dirt	1989	5.00	10.00	20.00
C1-94778 [(3)]	Tripping the Live Fantastic	1990	15.00	30.00	60.00
99176 [(2)]	Band on the Run	1999	10.00	20.00	40.00
—Limited-edition 180-gram reissue with original LP on one record and interviews and "The Making of.." on the second					
C1-595379	Tripping the Live Fantastic — Highlights!	1990	6.25	12.50	25.00
—Released on vinyl only through Columbia House; with U.S. address on back cover					
C1-595379	Tripping the Live Fantastic — Highlights!	1990	6.25	12.50	25.00
—Released on vinyl only through Columbia House; with Canada address on back cover, this was sold in the U.S. by Columbia House					
COLUMBIA					
A2S 821 [(2) DJ]	The McCartney Interview	1980	10.00	20.00	40.00
—Promo-only set; one LP is the entire interview, the other is banded for airplay; white labels with black print; counterfeits have blank white labels					
FC 36057	Back to the Egg	1979	2.50	5.00	10.00
—Credited to "Wings"; custom label					
FC 36057 [DJ]	Back to the Egg	1979	10.00	20.00	40.00
—Credited to "Wings"; "Demonstration -- Not for Sale" on custom label					
PC 36057	Back to the Egg	1984	7.50	15.00	30.00
—Credited to "Wings"; "PC" cover with "FC" label					
PC 36057	Back to the Egg	1984	10.00	20.00	40.00
—Credited to "Wings"; "PC" cover with "PC" label					
JC 36478	McCartney	1979	3.75	7.50	15.00
PC 36478	McCartney	1984	3.75	7.50	15.00
—Budget-line reissue					
JC 36479	Ram	1980	3.75	7.50	15.00
—Credited to "Paul and Linda McCartney"					
PC 36479	Ram	1984	3.75	7.50	15.00
—Credited to "Paul and Linda McCartney"; budget-line reissue					
JC 36480	Wild Life	1980	3.75	7.50	15.00
—Credited to "Wings"					
PC 36480	Wild Life	1982	3.75	7.50	15.00
—Credited to "Wings"; budget-line reissue					
JC 36481	Red Rose Speedway	1980	3.75	7.50	15.00
—Credited to "Paul McCartney and Wings"; flat or glossy cover					
PC 36481	Red Rose Speedway	198?	3.75	7.50	15.00
—Credited to "Paul McCartney and Wings"; not issued with booklet					
JC 36482	Band on the Run	1980	3.75	7.50	15.00
—Credited to "Paul McCartney and Wings"; custom label					
JC 36482	Band on the Run	198?	25.00	50.00	100.00
—Credited to "Paul McCartney and Wings"; white "MPL" logo on lower left front cover					
PC 36482	Band on the Run	198?	5.00	10.00	20.00
—Credited to "Paul McCartney and Wings"; "PC" cover with "JC" label					
PC 36482	Band on the Run	198?	7.50	15.00	30.00
—Credited to "Paul McCartney and Wings"; "PC" cover with "PC" label					
FC 36511	McCartney II	1980	2.50	5.00	10.00
—Add 80% if bonus single of "Coming Up (Live at Glasgow)" (AE7 1204) is with package					
FC 36511 [DJ]	McCartney II	1980	7.50	15.00	30.00
—White label promo					
PC 36511	McCartney II	1984	6.25	12.50	25.00
—"PC" cover with "FC" label					
PC 36511	McCartney II	1984	25.00	50.00	100.00
—"PC" cover with "PC" label					
JC 36801	Venus and Mars	1980	3.75	7.50	15.00
—Credited to "Wings"; with one poster and two stickers					
PC 36801	Venus and Mars	1982	3.75	7.50	15.00
—Credited to "Wings"; budget-line reissue, not issued with inserts					
PC 36987	The McCartney Interview	1980	3.00	6.00	12.00
—Stock release of interview originally intended for promotional use only					
FC 37409	Wings at the Speed of Sound	1981	3.75	7.50	15.00
—Credited to "Wings"; custom label					
PC 37409	Wings at the Speed of Sound	1982	3.75	7.50	15.00
—Credited to "Wings"; regular Columbia label, budget-line reissue					
PC 37462	Tug of War	1984	7.50	15.00	30.00
—Custom label; "PC" cover with "TC" label					
PC 37462	Tug of War	1984	25.00	50.00	100.00
—Regular Columbia label; "PC" cover with "PC" label					
TC 37462	Tug of War	1982	2.50	5.00	10.00
C3X 37990 [(3)]	Wings Over America	1982	12.50	25.00	50.00
—Credited to "Wings"; custom labels, no poster					
QC 39149	Pipes of Peace	1983	3.00	6.00	12.00
SC 39613	Give My Regards to Broad Street	1984	3.75	7.50	15.00
HC 46382	Band on the Run	1981	12.50	25.00	50.00
—Credited to "Paul McCartney and Wings"; half-speed mastered edition					
MPL/PARLOPHONE					
96413	Unplugged (The Official Bootleg)	1991	18.75	37.50	75.00
—No U.S. pressings; "American" copies were U.K. imports with liner notes in Spanish!					
NATIONAL FEATURES CORP.					
2955/6	Band on the Run Radio Interview Special	1973	375.00	750.00	1500.
—Promo-only interview disc					

MCCARTNEY, PAUL, AND STEVIE WONDER

Also see each artist's individual listings.

12-Inch Singles

Number	Title	Yr	VG	VG+	NM
COLUMBIA					
02878	Ebony and Ivory//Rainclouds/Ebony and Ivory (Solo)	1982	3.00	6.00	12.00

45s

Number	Title	Yr	VG	VG+	NM
COLUMBIA					
02860	Ebony and Ivory/Rainclouds	1982	—	2.00	4.00
02860 [PS]	Ebony and Ivory/Rainclouds	1982	—	2.00	4.00

MCCLAY, YUL, AND THE MONDELLOS

See THE MONDELLOS.

MCCORMICK, GAYLE

Also see SMITH.

45s

Number	Title	Yr	VG	VG+	NM
ABC DUNHILL					
4281	Gonna Be Alright Now/Save Me	1971	—	2.50	5.00
4288	It's a Cryin' Shame/If Only You Believe	1971	—	2.50	5.00
4298	You Really Got a Hold on Me/C'est La Vie	1972	—	2.50	5.00
DECCA					
33030	Near You/Take Me Back	1972	—	2.50	5.00
MCA					
40007	Sweet Feelings/Take Me Back	1973	—	2.00	4.00
SHADYBROOK					
45017	Coming In Out of the Rain/Simon Said	1977	2.50	5.00	10.00

Albums

Number	Title	Yr	VG	VG+	NM
ABC DUNHILL					
DS-50109	Gayle McCormick	1971	3.00	6.00	12.00
DECCA					
DL 75364	Flesh and Blood	1972	3.00	6.00	12.00

Number	Title (A Side/B Side)	Yr	VG	VG+	NM
FANTASY					
9467	One More Hour	1974	3.00	6.00	12.00

MCCORMICK, MAUREEN

Also see THE BRADY BUNCH; CHRIS KNIGHT AND MAUREEN McCORMICK.

45s

Number	Title (A Side/B Side)	Yr	VG	VG+	NM
PARAMOUNT					
0292	Love's in the Roses/Harmonize	1974	3.75	7.50	15.00

MCCOY, CHARLIE

45s

Number	Title (A Side/B Side)	Yr	VG	VG+	NM
CADENCE					
1390	Cherry Berry Wine/My Little Woman	1960	2.50	5.00	10.00
1415	I Just Want to Make Love to You/Rooster Blues	1962	2.50	5.00	10.00
MONUMENT					
870	I'm Ready/Harpoon Man	1965	2.00	4.00	8.00
893	Girl (Those Were the Good Old Days)/It's a Man Down There	1965	2.00	4.00	8.00
926	Let Him Go/Screamin', Shoutin', Beggin', Pleadin'	1966	2.00	4.00	8.00
975	Stubborn Kind of Fellow/My Baby's Back Again	1966	2.00	4.00	8.00
998	Cold Cold World/You've Got to Face Life	1967	2.00	4.00	8.00
1076	Gimme Some Lovin'/Boy from England	1968	—	3.00	6.00
1093	Harper Valley P.T.A./Juke	1968	—	3.00	6.00
1938	Blue Christmas/Christmas Cheer	1976	—	—	3.00
—"Golden Series" reissue					
03518	The State of Our Union/Just Doin' Nothin' with You (Is Really Somethin')	1983	—	—	3.00
—With Laney Hicks					
8529	I Started Loving You Again/The Real McCoy	1971	—	2.50	5.00
8546	I'm So Lonesome I Could Cry/Grade A	1972	—	2.50	5.00
8554	I Really Don't Want to Know/Minor, Minor	1972	—	2.50	5.00
8566	Orange Blossom Special/Hangin' On	1973	—	2.50	5.00
8576	Shenandoah/John Henry	1973	—	2.50	5.00
8589	Release Me/Fastest Harp in the South	1973	—	2.50	5.00
8600	Silver Threads and Golden Needles/I Just Can't Stand to See You Cry	1974	—	2.00	4.00
8611	Boogie Woogie (A/K/A T.D.'s Boogie Woogie)/ Keep On Harpin'	1974	—	2.00	4.00
—With Barefoot Jerry					
8625	The Way We Were/I Can't Help It	1974	—	2.00	4.00
8633	Blue Christmas/Christmas Cheer	1974	—	2.50	5.00
8638	Everybody Stand Up and Holler for the Union/ New River Gorge	1975	—	2.00	4.00
8648	I Can Help/Theme from A Summer Place	1975	—	2.00	4.00
—With Lloyd Green					
8650	Please Don't Tell Me How the Story Ends/Juke	1975	—	2.00	4.00
8660	Blues Stay Away from Me/Pots and Pans	1975	—	2.00	4.00
8672	Columbus Stockade Blues/(I Heard That) Lonesome Whistle	1975	—	2.00	4.00
8683	The Star-Spangled Banner/Silver Wings	1976	—	2.00	4.00
8703	Wabash Cannonball/Ode to Billie Joe	1976	—	2.00	4.00
21001	Until the Nights/(B-side unknown)	1981	—	2.00	4.00
—With Laney Smallwood					
45210	Summit Ridge Drive/Play It Again Charlie	1977	—	2.00	4.00
45224	Amazing Grace/Squeezing	1977	—	2.00	4.00
45239	Foggy River/Last Letter	1977	—	2.00	4.00
45258	Fair and Tender Ladies/18th Century Rosewood Clock	1978	—	2.00	4.00
45272	Drifting Lovers/West Virginia Mountain Melody	1978	—	2.00	4.00
45282	Midnight Flyer/Cripple Creek	1979	—	2.00	4.00
45289	Ramblin' Music Man/Red Haired Boy	1979	—	2.00	4.00
45292	Carolina Morning/Appalachian Fever	1979	—	2.00	4.00
45296	Cold, Cold Heart/Station Break	1980	—	2.00	4.00

Albums

Number	Title (A Side/B Side)	Yr	VG	VG+	NM
CMH					
9030 [(2)]	Flat-Picking Spectacular	1984	3.00	6.00	12.00
MONUMENT					
6623	The Real McCoy	1976	2.50	5.00	10.00
—Reissue of 31359					
6624	Charlie McCoy	1976	2.50	5.00	10.00
—Reissue of 31910					
6625	Good Time Charlie	1976	2.50	5.00	10.00
—Reissue of 32215					
6626	The Fastest Harp in the South	1976	2.50	5.00	10.00
—Reissue of 32749					
6627	The Nashville Hit Man	1976	2.50	5.00	10.00
—Reissue of 32922					
6628	Charlie My Boy!	1976	2.50	5.00	10.00
—Reissue of 33384					
6629	Harpin' the Blues	1976	2.50	5.00	10.00
—Reissue of 33802					
6630	Play It Again Charlie	1976	2.50	5.00	10.00
7612	Cookin'	1977	2.50	5.00	10.00
7622	Greatest Hits	1978	2.50	5.00	10.00
7632	Appalachian Fever	1979	2.50	5.00	10.00
SLP-18097	The World of Charlie McCoy	1968	3.75	7.50	15.00
Z 31359	The Real McCoy	1971	3.00	6.00	12.00
KZ 31910	Charlie McCoy	1972	3.00	6.00	12.00
KZ 32215	Good Time Charlie	1973	3.00	6.00	12.00
KZ 32749	The Fastest Harp in the South	1974	3.00	6.00	12.00
KZ 32922	The Nashville Hit Man	1974	3.00	6.00	12.00
PZ 33384	Charlie My Boy!	1975	3.00	6.00	12.00
PZ 33802	Harpin' the Blues	1975	3.00	6.00	12.00
PW 38387	The Greatest Hits of Charlie McCoy	1982	2.00	4.00	8.00

MCCOY, VAN

12-Inch Singles

Number	Title (A Side/B Side)	Yr	VG	VG+	NM
H&L					
2002	Rhythms of the World (10:12)//Soul Cha Cha/ That's the Joint	1976	5.00	10.00	20.00

45s

Number	Title (A Side/B Side)	Yr	VG	VG+	NM
AVCO					
4639	Love Is the Answer/Killing Me Softly	1974	—	2.50	5.00
4648	Boogie Down/Rainy Night in Georgia	1975	—	2.50	5.00
4653	The Hustle/Hey Girl, Come and Get It	1975	—	2.00	4.00
4660	Change with the Times/Goodnight Baby	1975	—	2.00	4.00
COLUMBIA					
43415	Keep Loving Me/Butterfly	1965	3.00	6.00	12.00
43495	Starlight Starbright/This Is the Way We Fall in Love	1965	2.00	4.00	8.00
43694	I Will Wait for You/The House That Love Built	1966	2.00	4.00	8.00
EPIC					
10470	I Started a Joke/Toney's Theme	1969	—	3.50	7.00
H&L					
4667	Night Walk/Love Child	1976	—	2.00	4.00
4670	Party/The Disco Kid	1976	—	2.00	4.00
4677	The Shuffle/That's the Joint	1976	—	2.00	4.00
4682	Soul Cha Cha/Oriental Boogie	1977	—	2.00	4.00
LIBERTY					
55457	Follow Your Heart/Lonely	1962	3.00	6.00	12.00
MCA					
40885	My Favorite Fantasy/You're So Right for Me	1978	—	2.00	4.00
40938	Trying to Make the Best of It/Two Points	1978	—	2.00	4.00
40984	Lonely Dancer/Decisions	1979	—	2.00	4.00
ROCK'N					
101	Mr. D.J./Never Trust a Friend	1961	12.50	25.00	50.00

Albums

Number	Title (A Side/B Side)	Yr	VG	VG+	NM
AVCO					
AV-69002	Love Is the Answer	1974	2.50	5.00	10.00
AV-69006	Disco Baby	1975	2.50	5.00	10.00
AV-69009	The Disco Kid	1975	2.50	5.00	10.00
BUDDAH					
BDS-5103	Soul Improvisations	1971	3.75	7.50	15.00
BDS-5648	From Disco to Love	1975	2.50	5.00	10.00
—Retitled reissue of 5103					
COLUMBIA					
CL 2497 [M]	Night Time Is the Lonely Time	1966	5.00	10.00	20.00
CS 9297 [S]	Night Time Is the Lonely Time	1966	6.25	12.50	25.00
H&L					
HL-69002	Love Is the Answer	1976	2.00	4.00	8.00
—Reissue of Avco 69002					
HL-69006	Disco Baby	1976	2.00	4.00	8.00
—Reissue of Avco 69006					
HL-69009	The Disco Kid	1976	2.00	4.00	8.00
—Reissue of Avco 69009					
HL-69012	The Real McCoy	1976	2.50	5.00	10.00
HL-69014	Rhythms of the World	1976	2.50	5.00	10.00
HL-69016	The Hustle and Best of Van McCoy	1976	2.50	5.00	10.00
HL-69022	Van McCoy and His Magnificent Movie Machine	1977	2.50	5.00	10.00
MCA					
3036	My Favorite Fantasy	1978	2.50	5.00	10.00
3054	A Woman Called Moses	1978	2.50	5.00	10.00
3071	Lovely Dancer	1979	2.50	5.00	10.00

MCCOYS, THE

Also see RICK DERRINGER.

45s

Number	Title (A Side/B Side)	Yr	VG	VG+	NM
BANG					
506	Hang On Sloopy/I Can't Explain It	1965	3.75	7.50	15.00
511	Fever/Sorrow	1965	2.50	5.00	10.00
516	Up and Down/If You Tell a Lie	1966	2.50	5.00	10.00
522	Come On Let's Go/Little People	1966	2.50	5.00	10.00
527	(You Make Me Feel) So Good/Runaway	1966	2.50	5.00	10.00
532	Don't Worry Mother, Your Son's Heart Is Pure/ Ko-Ko	1966	2.50	5.00	10.00
538	I Got to Go Back (And Watch That Little Girl Dance)/Dynamite	1966	2.50	5.00	10.00
543	Beat the Clock/Like You Do to Me	1967	2.50	5.00	10.00
549	I Wonder If She Remembers Me/Say Those Magic Words	1967	2.50	5.00	10.00
MERCURY					
72843	Jesse Brady/Resurrection	1968	2.00	4.00	8.00
72897	Daybreak/Epilogue	1969	2.00	4.00	8.00
72967	Don't Fight It/Rosa Rodriguez	1969	3.75	7.50	15.00
PHILCO-FORD					
HP-6	Fever/Hang On Sloopy	1967	5.00	10.00	20.00
—4-inch plastic "Hip Pocket Record" with color sleeve					
RCA VICTOR					
47-7204	Daddy's Geisha Girl/Our Love Goes On and On	1958	5.00	10.00	20.00
47-7354	Full Grown Cat/Throwing Kisses	1958	6.25	12.50	25.00

Albums

Number	Title (A Side/B Side)	Yr	VG	VG+	NM
BANG					
BLP-212 [M]	Hang On Sloopy	1965	7.50	15.00	30.00
BLPS-212 [S]	Hang On Sloopy	1965	10.00	20.00	40.00
BLP-213 [M]	You Make Me Feel So Good	1966	7.50	15.00	30.00
BLPS-213 [S]	You Make Me Feel So Good	1966	10.00	20.00	40.00
MERCURY					
SR-61163	Infinite McCoys	1968	6.25	12.50	25.00
SR-61207	Human Ball	1969	6.25	12.50	25.00

MCCRACKEN, HUGH

45s

Number	Title (A Side/B Side)	Yr	VG	VG+	NM
CONGRESS					
257	Buzz in My Head/You Blow My Mind	1965	6.25	12.50	25.00
261	Runnin', Runnin'/What I Gotta Do to Satisfy You	1966	6.25	12.50	25.00

MCCRACKLIN, JIMMY

45s

Number	Title (A Side/B Side)	Yr	VG	VG+	NM
ART-TONE					
825	Just Got to Know/The Drag	1961	3.00	6.00	12.00
826	Christmas Time (Part 1)/Christmas Time (Part 2)	1961	3.00	6.00	12.00
827	Shame, Shame, Shame/I'm the One	1962	3.00	6.00	12.00
831	That's No Big Thing/Susie and Pat	1962	3.00	6.00	12.00
CHECKER					
885	The Walk/I'm to Blame	1958	6.25	12.50	25.00

Number	Title (A Side/B Side)	Yr	VG	VG+	NM
893	Everybody Rock/Get Tough	1958	3.75	7.50	15.00
CHESS					
1809	I Know/Later On	1961	2.50	5.00	10.00
1826	One Track Love/Trottin'	1962	2.50	5.00	10.00
HI					
2023	Things I Meant to Say/Here Today and Gone Tomorrow	1960	3.00	6.00	12.00
HOLLYWOOD					
1054	It's All Right/Fare You Well	1955	12.50	25.00	50.00
IMPERIAL					
5892	Bitter Pill/Head Over Flip	1962	2.50	5.00	10.00
5906	I Don't Care/Just Got to Know	1963	2.50	5.00	10.00
5911	Advice/No No	1963	2.50	5.00	10.00
5926	The Bitter and the Sweet/Just Pretending	1963	2.50	5.00	10.00
5955	That's the Way (It Goes)/I'll See It Through	1963	2.50	5.00	10.00
5977	Every Night/The Slightest Idea	1963	2.50	5.00	10.00
5982	Sooner or Later/Looking for a Woman	1963	2.50	5.00	10.00
66010	I Did Wrong/Someone	1964	2.00	4.00	8.00
66035	Just Like It Is/Let's Do It All	1964	2.00	4.00	8.00
66067	Believe in Me/Set Six	1964	2.00	4.00	8.00
66094	Every Night, Every Day/Can't Raise Me	1965	2.00	4.00	8.00
66116	Arkansas (Part 1)/Arkansas (Part 2)	1965	2.00	4.00	8.00
66129	Think/Steppin' Up in Class	1965	2.00	4.00	8.00
66147	My Answer/Beulah	1966	2.00	4.00	8.00
66168	Come On Home (Back Where You Belong)/Something That Belongs to Me	1966	2.00	4.00	8.00
66180	Just Let Me Cry/These Boots Are Made for Walkin'	1966	2.00	4.00	8.00
66207	It's Got to Be Love/Sorry	1966	2.00	4.00	8.00
IRMA					
102	You're the One/I Wanna Make Love to You	1956	7.50	15.00	30.00
103	Take a Chance/Fare Well	1956	7.50	15.00	30.00
107	I'm the One/Savoy's Jump	1957	7.50	15.00	30.00
109	Beer Tavern Girl/Love for You	1957	7.50	15.00	30.00
KENT					
369	I've Got Eyes for You/I'm Gonna Tell Your Mother	1962	2.50	5.00	10.00
LIBERTY					
56198	Believe Me/I Never Thought	1970	—	2.50	5.00
MERCURY					
71412	The Wobble/With Your Love	1959	3.75	7.50	15.00
71516	Let's Do It (The Chicken Scratch)/Georgia Slop	1959	3.75	7.50	15.00
71613	Doomed Lover/By Myself	1960	3.00	6.00	12.00
71666	You Rascal You/No One to Love Me	1960	3.00	6.00	12.00
71747	What's That (Part 1)/The Bridge	1961	3.00	6.00	12.00
71766	No One to Love Me/(B-side unknown)	1961	3.00	6.00	12.00
MINIT					
32018	Let the Door Hit You/This Thing	1967	—	3.00	6.00
32022	Dog (Part 1)/Dog (Part 2)	1967	—	3.00	6.00
32033	Get Together/How You Like Your Love	1967	—	3.00	6.00
32044	Pretty Little Sweet Thing/A & I	1968	—	3.00	6.00
32052	Love, Love, Love/Married Life	1968	—	3.00	6.00
32064	Drown in My Own Tears/What's Going On	1969	—	3.00	6.00
32086	I Had to Get With It/You Ain't Nothin' But a Devil	1969	—	3.00	6.00
32092	Stick to My Mind/I Just Live by the Rules	1970	—	3.00	6.00
MODERN					
926	Blues Blasters' Boogie/The Panic's On	1954	10.00	20.00	40.00
934	Darlin' Share Your Love/Give My Heart a Break	1954	10.00	20.00	40.00
951	Please Forgive Me Baby/Couldn't Be a Dream	1954	10.00	20.00	40.00
967	Gonna Tell Your Mother/That Ain't Right	1955	10.00	20.00	40.00
PEACOCK					
1605	My Days Are Limited/She's Gone	1952	15.00	30.00	60.00
1615	She Felt Too Good/Share and Share Alike	1953	15.00	30.00	60.00
1634	I Cried/The End	1953	15.00	30.00	60.00
1639	The Cheater/My Story	1954	15.00	30.00	60.00
1683	I Need Your Loving/The Swinging Thing	1958	6.25	12.50	25.00
Albums					
CHESS					
LP-1464 [M]	Jimmy McCracklin Sings	1961	30.00	60.00	120.00
CROWN					
CLP-5244 [M]	Twist with Jimmy McCracklin	1962	12.50	25.00	50.00
—Black label, silver "Crown"					
CLP-5244 [M]	Twist with Jimmy McCracklin	1962	6.25	12.50	25.00
—Gray label					
CLP-5244 [M]	Twist with Jimmy McCracklin	196?	3.75	7.50	15.00
—Black label, multi-color "Crown"					
EVEJIM					
EJR-4013	Same Lovin'	198?	3.00	6.00	12.00
IMPERIAL					
LP-9219 [M]	I Just Gotta Know	1964	6.25	12.50	25.00
LP-9285 [M]	Every Night, Every Day	1965	6.25	12.50	25.00
LP-9297 [M]	Think	1965	6.25	12.50	25.00
LP-9306 [M]	My Answer	1966	6.25	12.50	25.00
LP-9316 [M]	The New Soul of Jimmy McCracklin	1966	6.25	12.50	25.00
LP-12219 [S]	I Just Gotta Know	1964	7.50	15.00	30.00
LP-12285 [S]	Every Night, Every Day	1965	7.50	15.00	30.00
LP-12297 [S]	Think	1965	7.50	15.00	30.00
LP-12306 [S]	My Answer	1966	7.50	15.00	30.00
LP-12316 [S]	The New Soul of Jimmy McCracklin	1966	7.50	15.00	30.00
MINIT					
LP-4009 [M]	The Best of Jimmy McCracklin	1967	7.50	15.00	30.00
LP-24009 [S]	The Best of Jimmy McCracklin	1967	6.25	12.50	25.00
LP-24011	Let's Get Together	1968	6.25	12.50	25.00
LP-24017	Stinger Man	1969	6.25	12.50	25.00
STAX					
STS-2047	Yesterday Is Gone	1972	5.00	10.00	20.00
MPS-8506	High on the Blues	1980	2.50	5.00	10.00

MCCRAE, GEORGE

Number	Title (A Side/B Side)	Yr	VG	VG+	NM
12-Inch Singles					
GOLD MOUNTAIN					
81205	Own the Night/Own the Night (Dub)	1984	2.00	4.00	8.00
T.K. DISCO					
22	Love in Motion (5:00)/Givin' Back the Feeling (5:31)	1977	3.00	6.00	12.00
62	Kiss Me (The Way I Like It) (3:42) (5:47)	1977	3.00	6.00	12.00
91	Let's Dance (6:10)/Hey Sexy Dancer	1978	3.00	6.00	12.00
45s					
SOUL CITY					
XW456	Taking It All Off/Please Help Me Find My Baby	1974	—	3.00	6.00
T.K.					
1004	Rock Your Baby (Part 1)/Rock Your Baby (Part 2)	1974	—	2.50	5.00
1006	I Get Lifted/I Can't Leave You Alone	1974	—	2.50	5.00
1011	Look At You/I Need Someone Like You	1975	—	2.50	5.00
1014	I Ain't Lyin'/You Don't Know	1975	—	2.50	5.00
1016	Honey I/Sing a Happy Song	1975	—	2.50	5.00
1021	I'm Gonna Stay with My Baby Tonight/Love in Motion	1977	—	2.50	5.00
1024	Kiss Me (The Way I Like It) Part 1/Kiss Me (The Way I Like It) Part 2	1977	—	2.50	5.00
1029	Let's Dance (People All Over the World)/Let George Do It	1978	—	2.50	5.00
1032	I Want You Around Me/Are You Looking for Love	1979	—	2.50	5.00
1034	Don't You Feel My Love/You Got Me Going Crazy	1979	—	2.50	5.00
UNITED ARTISTS					
50811	Taking It All Off/Please Help Me Find My Baby	1971	2.50	5.00	10.00
Albums					
GOLD MOUNTAIN					
GM 80008	Own the Night	1984	2.50	5.00	10.00
T.K.					
501	Rock Your Baby	1974	2.50	5.00	10.00
602	George McCrae	1975	2.50	5.00	10.00
606	Diamond Touch	1977	2.50	5.00	10.00

MCCRAE, GEORGE AND GWEN

Also see each artist's individual listings.

Number	Title (A Side/B Side)	Yr	VG	VG+	NM
45s					
CAT					
2002	Winners Together or Losers Apart/Homesick Lovesick	1976	—	2.50	5.00
2004	I'll Do the Rockin'/Mechanical Body	1976	—	2.50	5.00
Albums					
CAT					
2606	Together	1976	2.50	5.00	10.00

MCCRAE, GWEN

Number	Title (A Side/B Side)	Yr	VG	VG+	NM
12-Inch Singles					
ATLANTIC					
PR 387 [DJ]	Keep the Fire Burning (same on both sides)	1982	—	3.00	6.00
BLACK JACK					
0021	Do You Know What I Mean (Long Version) (Short Version) (Dub)	1984	2.00	4.00	8.00
45s					
ATLANTIC					
3853	Funky Sensation/Have a Good Time	1981	—	2.00	4.00
3881	Poison/(B-side unknown)	1981	—	2.00	4.00
89910	Keep the Fire Burning/Hang On	1982	—	2.00	4.00
89961	I Need to Be with You/(B-side unknown)	1982	—	2.00	4.00
CAT					
1987	He Keeps Something Groovy Goin' On/Your Love Is Worse Than a Cold Love	1973	—	2.50	5.00
1989	For Your Love/Your Love	1973	—	2.50	5.00
1992	It's Worth the Hurt/90% of Me Is You	1974	—	2.50	5.00
1994	Move Me Baby/He Don't Ever Lose His Groove	1974	—	2.50	5.00
1996	Rockin' Chair/It Keeps On Raining	1975	—	2.50	5.00
1999	Love Insurance/He Keeps Something Groovy Goin' On	1975	—	2.50	5.00
2000	Cradle of Love/Easy Rock	1976	—	2.50	5.00
2005	Damn Right It's Good/Love Without Sex	1976	—	2.50	5.00
2011	Starting All Over Again/At Bedtime	1977	—	2.50	5.00
2014	The Melody of Life/The Joy	197?	—	2.50	5.00
2015	Maybe I'll Find Somebody New/All This Love That I'm Givin'	197?	—	2.50	5.00
COLUMBIA					
45214	Lead Me On/Lay It On Me	1970	—	2.50	5.00
45320	Been So Long/Lay It On Me	1971	—	2.50	5.00
45448	Ain't Nothing You Can Do/Goin' Down the Road Feelin' Bad	1971	—	2.50	5.00
45578	You Were Always on My Mind/He's Not You	1972	—	2.50	5.00
45684	I'm Losing the Feeling/Leave the Driving to Us	1972	—	2.50	5.00
Albums					
ATLANTIC					
80014	On My Way	1982	2.50	5.00	10.00
CAT					
2603	Gwen McCrae	1974	2.50	5.00	10.00
2605	Rockin' Chair	1975	2.50	5.00	10.00
2608	Something So Right	1976	2.50	5.00	10.00

MCCREA, DARLENE

Number	Title (A Side/B Side)	Yr	VG	VG+	NM
45s					
JUBILEE					
5524	I Feel a Little Bit Better/Soulful Feeling	1965	2.50	5.00	10.00
ROULETTE					
4173	You Made a Fool of Me/You	1959	3.00	6.00	12.00
TOWER					
104	Don't Worry Baby/Heart's Not In It	1964	2.50	5.00	10.00

MCCULLERS, MICKEY

Number	Title (A Side/B Side)	Yr	VG	VG+	NM
45s					
TAMLA					
54064	Same Old Story/I'll Cry a Million Tears	1962	10.00	20.00	40.00
V.I.P.					
25009	Same Old Story/Who You Gonna Run To	1964	12.50	25.00	50.00

MCCULLOCH, DANNY

Number	Title (A Side/B Side)	Yr	VG	VG+	NM
45s					
CAPITOL					
2363	Wings of a Man/Orange and Red Beans	1968	2.00	4.00	8.00
2488	Hold On/Hope	1969	2.00	4.00	8.00
Albums					
CAPITOL					
ST-174	Wings of a Man	1969	5.00	10.00	20.00

MCDANIELS, GENE

Number	Title (A Side/B Side)	Yr	VG	VG+	NM
45s					
ATLANTIC					
2805	The Lord Is Back/Tell Me Mr. President	1971	—	3.00	6.00
—As "Eugene McDaniels"					
COLUMBIA					
43800	Something Blue/Cause I Love You So	1966	2.50	5.00	10.00
44010	Touch of Your Lips/Sweet Lover No More	1967	2.50	5.00	10.00
LIBERTY					
55231	In Times Like These/Once Before	1959	3.75	7.50	15.00
55265	The Green Door/Facts of Life	1960	3.75	7.50	15.00
55308	A Hundred Pounds of Clay/Take a Chance on Love	1961	4.00	8.00	16.00
55344	A Tear/She's Come Back	1961	3.75	7.50	15.00
55371	Tower of Strength/The Secret	1961	4.00	8.00	16.00
55405	Chip Chip/Another Tear Falls	1962	3.75	7.50	15.00
55444	Funny/Chapel of Tears	1962	3.75	7.50	15.00
55480	Point of No Return/Warmer Than a Whisper	1962	3.75	7.50	15.00
55510	Spanish Lace/Somebody's Waiting	1962	3.75	7.50	15.00
55541	The Puzzle/Cry Baby Cry	1963	3.00	6.00	12.00
55597	It's a Lonely Town/False Friends	1963	3.00	6.00	12.00
55637	Old Country/Anyone Else	1963	3.00	6.00	12.00
55723	Make Me a Present of You/In Times Like These	1964	3.00	6.00	12.00
55752	Emily/Forgotten Man	1964	3.00	6.00	12.00
55805	A Miracle/Walk with a Winner	1965	2.50	5.00	10.00
55834	Hang On/Will It Last Forever	1965	2.50	5.00	10.00
MGM					
14613	Ol' Heartbreak Top Ten/River	1973	—	2.50	5.00
ODE					
66107	Lady Fair/Natural Juices	1975	—	2.00	4.00
UNITED ARTISTS					
0053	A Hundred Pounds of Clay/Tower of Strength	1973	—	2.00	4.00
—"Silver Spotlight Series" reissue					
0054	Chip Chip/Point of No Return	1973	—	2.00	4.00
—"Silver Spotlight Series" reissue					
Albums					
ATLANTIC					
SD 8259	Outlaw	1970	3.75	7.50	15.00
SD 8281	Headless Heroes	1971	3.75	7.50	15.00
LIBERTY					
LRP-3146 [M]	In Times Like These	1960	7.50	15.00	30.00
LRP-3175 [M]	Sometimes I'm Happy, Sometimes I'm Blue	1960	7.50	15.00	30.00
LRP-3191 [M]	100 Lbs. of Clay!	1961	7.50	15.00	30.00
LRP-3204 [M]	Gene McDaniels Sings Movie Memories	1962	7.50	15.00	30.00
LRP-3215 [M]	Tower of Strength	1962	7.50	15.00	30.00
LRP-3258 [M]	Hit After Hit	1962	7.50	15.00	30.00
LRP-3275 [M]	Spanish Lace	1963	6.25	12.50	25.00
LRP-3311 [M]	The Wonderful World of Gene McDaniels	1963	6.25	12.50	25.00
LST-7146 [S]	In Times Like These	1960	50.00	100.00	200.00
—Blue vinyl					
LST-7146 [S]	In Times Like These	1960	10.00	20.00	40.00
—Black vinyl					
LST-7175 [S]	Sometimes I'm Happy, Sometimes I'm Blue	1960	10.00	20.00	40.00
LST-7191 [S]	100 Lbs. of Clay!	1961	10.00	20.00	40.00
LST-7204 [S]	Gene McDaniels Sings Movie Memories	1962	10.00	20.00	40.00
LST-7215 [S]	Tower of Strength	1962	10.00	20.00	40.00
LST-7258 [S]	Hit After Hit	1962	10.00	20.00	40.00
LST-7275 [S]	Spanish Lace	1963	7.50	15.00	30.00
LST-7311 [S]	The Wonderful World of Gene McDaniels	1963	7.50	15.00	30.00
ODE					
SP-77028	Natural Juices	1975	3.00	6.00	12.00
SUNSET					
SUM-1122 [M]	Facts of Life	1967	3.00	6.00	12.00
SUS-5122 [S]	Facts of Life	1967	3.75	7.50	15.00
UNITED ARTISTS					
UA-LA447-E	The Very Best of Gene McDaniels	1975	2.50	5.00	10.00

MCDEVITT, CHAS., AND HIS SKIFFLE GROUP

Number	Title (A Side/B Side)	Yr	VG	VG+	NM
45s					
CHIC					
1008	Freight Train/The Cotton Song	1957	3.75	7.50	15.00
EPIC					
9244	Face in the Rain/Sporting Life	1957	3.75	7.50	15.00
KAPP					
216	Sing, Sing, Sing/Johnny-O	1958	3.75	7.50	15.00
238	Stack-O-Lee/Real Love	1958	3.75	7.50	15.00

MCDONALD, COUNTRY JOE

See COUNTRY JOE AND THE FISH.

MCDONALD, KATHI

Number	Title (A Side/B Side)	Yr	VG	VG+	NM
45s					
CAPITOL					
3835	Freak Lover/Bogart to Bowie	1974	2.50	5.00	10.00
3880	Heat Wave/Bogart to Bowie	1974	2.50	5.00	10.00
Albums					
CAPITOL					
ST-11224	Insane Asylum	1974	7.50	15.00	30.00

MCDONALD, MICHAEL

Also see THE DOOBIE BROTHERS; THE REGENTS (5).

Number	Title (A Side/B Side)	Yr	VG	VG+	NM
12-Inch Singles					
MCA					
23641	Sweet Freedom (4 versions)	1986	2.00	4.00	8.00
REPRISE					
PRO-A-4395 [DJ]	All We Got (4 versions)	1990	2.50	5.00	10.00
PRO-A-4398 [DJ]	Tear It Up (same on both sides)	1990	2.00	4.00	8.00
PRO-A-6538 [DJ]	Hey Girl (Edit) (LP Version) (Radio Remix)	1993	2.00	4.00	8.00
21734	All We Got (5 versions)/Show Me	1990	2.00	4.00	8.00
WARNER BROS.					
PRO-A-2325 [DJ]	No Lookin' Back (same on both sides)	1985	2.00	4.00	8.00
45s					
BELL					
45182	Dear Me/I Think I Love You Again	1972	2.00	4.00	8.00
—All Bell records as "Mike McDonald"					
45219	Good Old Time Love Song/When I'm Home	1972	2.00	4.00	8.00
45259 [DJ]	Drivin' Wheel/(B-side unknown)	1972	2.00	4.00	8.00
—Stock copy may not exist					
45308 [DJ]	Where Do I Go from Here/(B-side unknown)	1973	2.00	4.00	8.00
—Stock copy may not exist					
MCA					
52857	Sweet Freedom/The Freedom Eights	1986	—	—	3.00
52857 [PS]	Sweet Freedom/The Freedom Eights	1986	—	—	3.00
QWEST					
29394	Yah Mo B There/Come in Da Machine	1983	—	2.00	4.00
—A-side with James Ingram; B-side: James Ingram solo					
RCA VICTOR					
74-0405	God Knows/If You Won't, I Will	1970	3.75	7.50	15.00
—As "Mike McDonald"					
REPRISE					
18469	I Stand for You/East of Eden	1993	—	—	3.00
WARNER BROS.					
28596	Our Love (Theme from "No Mercy")/Don't Let Me Down	1986	—	—	3.00
28847	Lost in the Parade/By Heart	1985	—	2.00	4.00
28960	No Lookin' Back/Don't Let Me Down	1985	—	—	3.00
28960 [PS]	No Lookin' Back/Don't Let Me Down	1985	—	—	3.00
29743	Believe in It/Playin' by the Rules	1983	—	2.00	4.00
29862	I Gotta Try/Believe in It	1982	—	2.00	4.00
29862 [PS]	I Gotta Try/Believe in It	1982	—	2.00	4.00
29933	I Keep Forgettin'/Losin' End	1982	—	2.50	5.00
—First pressing has no subtitle on A-side					
29933	I Keep Forgettin' (Every Time You're Near)/Losin' End	1982	—	2.00	4.00
—Second pressing has subtitle on A-side					
29933 [PS]	I Keep Forgettin'/Losin' End	1982	—	2.50	5.00
—First pressing has no subtitle on A-side					
29933 [PS]	I Keep Forgettin' (Every Time You're Near)/Losin' End	1982	—	2.00	4.00
—Second pressing has subtitle on A-side					
Albums					
MOBILE FIDELITY					
1-149	If That's What It Takes	1985	5.00	10.00	20.00
—Audiophile vinyl					
REPRISE					
25979	Take It to Heart	1990	3.00	6.00	12.00
WARNER BROS.					
23703	If That's What It Takes	1982	2.50	5.00	10.00
25291	No Lookin' Back	1985	2.50	5.00	10.00

MCDOWELL, MISSISSIPPI FRED

Number	Title (A Side/B Side)	Yr	VG	VG+	NM
Albums					
ARHOOLIE					
F-1021 [M]	Delta Blues	1964	12.50	25.00	50.00
F-1027 [M]	Delta Blues, Volume 2	1966	12.50	25.00	50.00
F-1046	Mississippi Fred McDowell and His Blues Boys	1970	7.50	15.00	30.00
F-1068	Keep Your Lamp Trimmed and Burning	1973	5.00	10.00	20.00
CAPITOL					
ST-403	I Do Not Play No Rock and Roll	1970	6.25	12.50	25.00
MILESTONE					
MLP-3003 [M]	Long Way from Home	1966	7.50	15.00	30.00
MLS-93003 [S]	Long Way from Home	1966	10.00	20.00	40.00
SIRE					
SES-97018	Mississippi Fred McDowell in London	1970	7.50	15.00	30.00

MCDUFF, JACK

Number	Title (A Side/B Side)	Yr	VG	VG+	NM
45s					
ATLANTIC					
2402	Can't Get Satisfied (Part 1)/Can't Get Satisfied (Part 2)	1967	—	3.50	7.00
2423	Do It Now/Mush Melon	1967	—	3.50	7.00
5069	A Change Is Gonna Come/Down in the Valley	1966	2.00	4.00	8.00
5075	Tobacco Road/This Bitter Earth	1966	2.00	4.00	8.00
BLUE NOTE					
1953	Theme from Electric Surfboard/Down Home Style	1969	—	3.00	6.00
1957	The Vibrator/Oblighetto	1970	—	3.00	6.00
1958	Hunk-O-Funk/Mystic John	1970	—	3.00	6.00
CADET					
5614	Let My People Go/Ain't It	1968	—	3.00	6.00
5632	Black Is?/Win, Lose or Draw	1969	—	3.00	6.00
5693	Ain't No Sunshine/The Prophet	1972	—	2.50	5.00
PRESTIGE					
169	Brother Jack/Organ Grinder's Swing	1960	3.00	6.00	12.00
184	Yeah Baby (Part 1)/Yeah Baby (Part 2)	196?	3.00	6.00	12.00
199	The Honeydripper (Part 1)/The Honeydripper (Part 2)	196?	3.00	6.00	12.00
211	Goodnight, It's Time to Go/Sanctified Waltz	1961	3.00	6.00	12.00
219	Mellow Gravy (Part 1)/Mellow Gravy (Part 2)	196?	2.50	5.00	10.00
232	He's a Real Gone Guy (Part 1)/He's a Real Gone Guy (Part 2)	196?	2.50	5.00	10.00
246	Screamin'/Somethin'	196?	2.50	5.00	10.00

Number	Title (A Side/B Side)	Yr	VG	VG+	NM
255	Doin' the '68/Kirk's Work	196?	2.50	5.00	10.00
—With Roland Kirk					
265	Sanctified Samba/Whistle While You Work	196?	2.50	5.00	10.00
273	Rock Candy/Real Good'yn	196?	2.50	5.00	10.00
286	Passing Through/Somewhere in the Night	196?	2.50	5.00	10.00
299	Grease Monkey/Wink's Blues	1963	2.00	4.00	8.00
320	Oh, Look at Me Now/Prelude	1964	2.00	4.00	8.00
330	Once in a Lifetime/Rail Heat	196?	2.00	4.00	8.00
344	A Kettle of Fish/Carry Me Home	1964	2.00	4.00	8.00
351	The Girl from Ipanema/Lew's Place	196?	2.00	4.00	8.00
377	Silk 'n' Soul (Part 1)/Silk 'n' Soul (Part 2)	196?	2.00	4.00	8.00
388	Hot Barbecue/Three Day Thang	196?	2.00	4.00	8.00
399	Walk On By/Too Many Fish in the Sea	196?	2.00	4.00	8.00
423	For Those Who Choose/Talkin' 'Bout My Woman	196?	2.00	4.00	8.00
722	Grease Monkey/Rock Candy	197?	—	3.00	6.00

Albums

ATLANTIC

Number	Title	Yr	VG	VG+	NM
1463 [M]	A Change Is Gonna Come	1966	3.75	7.50	15.00
SD 1463 [S]	A Change Is Gonna Come	1966	5.00	10.00	20.00
1472 [M]	Tobacco Road	1967	5.00	10.00	20.00
SD 1472 [S]	Tobacco Road	1967	3.75	7.50	15.00
SD 1498	Double Barreled Soul	1968	3.75	7.50	15.00

BLUE NOTE

Number	Title	Yr	VG	VG+	NM
BST-84322	Down Home Style	1969	3.75	7.50	15.00
BST-84334	Moon Rappin'	1970	3.75	7.50	15.00
BST-84348	To Seek a New Home	1970	3.75	7.50	15.00
BST-84358	Who Knows	1971	3.75	7.50	15.00

CADET

Number	Title	Yr	VG	VG+	NM
LPS-812	Natural Thing	1968	3.75	7.50	15.00
LPS-817	Getting Our Thing Together	1969	3.75	7.50	15.00
LPS-831	Gin and Orange	1970	3.75	7.50	15.00
CH-50024	Check This Out	1973	3.00	6.00	12.00
CH-50051	Fourth Dimension	1974	3.00	6.00	12.00
CH-60017	The Healin' System	1972	3.00	6.00	12.00
CH-60031	Magnetic Feel	1975	3.00	6.00	12.00

CHESS

Number	Title	Yr	VG	VG+	NM
19004	Sophisticated Funk	1976	3.00	6.00	12.00

FANTASY

Number	Title	Yr	VG	VG+	NM
OJC-222	The Honeydripper	198?	2.50	5.00	10.00
—Reissue of Prestige 7199					
OJC-324	Tough 'Duff	1988	2.50	5.00	10.00
—Reissue of Prestige 7185					
OJC-326	Brother Jack Meets the Boss	1988	2.50	5.00	10.00
—Reissue of Prestige 7228					

MUSE

Number	Title	Yr	VG	VG+	NM
MR-5361	The Re-Entry	1989	3.00	6.00	12.00

PRESTIGE

Number	Title	Yr	VG	VG+	NM
PRLP-7174 [M]	Brother Jack	1960	12.50	25.00	50.00
PRLP-7185 [M]	Tough 'Duff	1960	12.50	25.00	50.00
PRLP-7199 [M]	The Honeydripper	1961	12.50	25.00	50.00
PRLP-7220 [M]	Goodnight, It's Time to Go	1961	10.00	20.00	40.00
PRST-7220 [S]	Goodnight, It's Time to Go	1961	10.00	20.00	40.00
PRLP-7228 [M]	Mellow Gravy — Brother Jack Meets the Boss	1962	10.00	20.00	40.00
PRST-7228 [S]	Mellow Gravy — Brother Jack Meets the Boss	1962	10.00	20.00	40.00
PRLP-7259 [M]	Screamin'	1963	10.00	20.00	40.00
PRST-7259 [S]	Screamin'	1963	10.00	20.00	40.00
PRLP-7265 [M]	Somethin' Slick!	1963	10.00	20.00	40.00
PRST-7265 [S]	Somethin' Slick!	1963	10.00	20.00	40.00
PRLP-7274 [M]	Live!	1963	10.00	20.00	40.00
PRST-7274 [S]	Live!	1963	10.00	20.00	40.00
PRLP-7286 [M]	Live! At the Jazz Workshop	1964	10.00	20.00	40.00
PRST-7286 [S]	Live! At the Jazz Workshop	1964	10.00	20.00	40.00
PRLP-7323 [M]	The Dynamic Jack McDuff	1964	10.00	20.00	40.00
PRST-7323 [S]	The Dynamic Jack McDuff	1964	10.00	20.00	40.00
PRLP-7333 [M]	Prelude	1964	6.25	12.50	25.00
PRST-7333 [S]	Prelude	1964	7.50	15.00	30.00
PRLP-7362 [M]	The Concert McDuff Recorded Live!	1965	6.25	12.50	25.00
PRST-7362 [S]	The Concert McDuff Recorded Live!	1965	7.50	15.00	30.00
PRLP-7404 [M]	Silk and Soul	1965	6.25	12.50	25.00
PRST-7404 [S]	Silk and Soul	1965	7.50	15.00	30.00
PRLP-7422 [M]	Hot Barbeque	1966	5.00	10.00	20.00
PRST-7422 [S]	Hot Barbeque	1966	6.25	12.50	25.00
PRLP-7476 [M]	Walk On By	1967	6.25	12.50	25.00
PRST-7476 [S]	Walk On By	1967	5.00	10.00	20.00
PRLP-7481 [M]	Brother Jack McDuff's Greatest Hits	1967	6.25	12.50	25.00
PRST-7481 [S]	Brother Jack McDuff's Greatest Hits	1967	5.00	10.00	20.00
PRLP-7492 [M]	Hallelujah Time!	1967	6.25	12.50	25.00
PRST-7492 [S]	Hallelujah Time!	1967	5.00	10.00	20.00
PRST-7529	The Midnight Sun	1968	5.00	10.00	20.00
PRST-7567	Soul Circle	1968	5.00	10.00	20.00
PRST-7596	Jack McDuff Plays for Beautiful People	1969	5.00	10.00	20.00
PRST-7642	I Got a Woman	1969	5.00	10.00	20.00
PRST-7666	Steppin' Out	1969	5.00	10.00	20.00
PRST-7703	Live! The Best of Brother Jack McDuff	1969	5.00	10.00	20.00
PRST-7771	Best of the Big Soul Band	1970	3.75	7.50	15.00
PRST-7785	Brother Jack	1970	3.75	7.50	15.00
PRST-7814	Tough Duff	1971	3.75	7.50	15.00
PRST-7851	On With It	1973	3.00	6.00	12.00
24013 [(2)]	Rock Candy	1972	3.75	7.50	15.00

MCFADDEN, BOB

45s

BRUNSWICK

Number	Title (A Side/B Side)	Yr	VG	VG+	NM
55120	Frankie and Igor at a Rock and Roll Party/ Children Cross the Bridge	1959	6.25	12.50	25.00
55140	The Mummy/The Beat Generation	1959	6.25	12.50	25.00
—As "Bob and Dor McFadden"					
55140 [PS]	The Mummy/The Beat Generation	1959	10.00	20.00	40.00
—As "Bob and Dor McFadden"					
55156	Bingo/Shake, Rattle and Roll	1959	6.25	12.50	25.00

CORAL

Number	Title (A Side/B Side)	Yr	VG	VG+	NM
62209	Dracula Cha-Cha/Transylvania Polka	1959	7.50	5.00	30.00

Albums

BRUNSWICK

Number	Title	Yr	VG	VG+	NM
BL 54056 [M]	Songs Our Mummy Taught Us	1959	50.00	100.00	200.00
BL 754056 [S]	Songs Our Mummy Taught Us	1959	75.00	150.00	300.00

MCFARLAND, GARY

45s

IMPULSE!

Number	Title (A Side/B Side)	Yr	VG	VG+	NM
250	Winter Samba/Summer's Gone Away	1966	2.00	4.00	8.00

PRESTIGE

Number	Title (A Side/B Side)	Yr	VG	VG+	NM
331	The Dreamer/River Gal	196?	2.50	5.00	10.00

SKYE

Number	Title (A Side/B Side)	Yr	VG	VG+	NM
453	By the Time I Get to Phoenix/Flea Market	1968	—	3.00	6.00
4511	80 Miles an Hour Through Beer-Can Country/(B-side unknown)	1969	—	3.00	6.00
4516	Slaves/(Instrumental)	1970	—	3.00	6.00

VERVE

Number	Title (A Side/B Side)	Yr	VG	VG+	NM
10272	How to Succeed in Business Without Really Trying/I Believe in You	1962	2.50	5.00	10.00
10342	And I Love Her/A Hard Day's Night	1964	2.50	5.00	10.00
10380	Fried Bananas/Wine and Bread	1966	2.50	5.00	10.00

Albums

ABC IMPULSE!

Number	Title	Yr	VG	VG+	NM
AS-46 [S]	Points of Departure	1968	3.00	6.00	12.00
AS-9104 [S]	Tijuana Jazz	1968	3.00	6.00	12.00
AS-9112 [S]	Profiles	1968	3.00	6.00	12.00
AS-9122 [S]	Simpatico	1968	3.00	6.00	12.00

BUDDAH

Number	Title	Yr	VG	VG+	NM
BDS 95001	Butterscotch Rum	1967	3.75	7.50	15.00

COBBLESTONE

Number	Title	Yr	VG	VG+	NM
CST 9019	Requiem	1972	3.75	7.50	15.00

IMPULSE!

Number	Title	Yr	VG	VG+	NM
A-46 [M]	Points of Departure	1963	5.00	10.00	20.00
AS-46 [S]	Points of Departure	1963	6.25	12.50	25.00
A-9104 [M]	Tijuana Jazz	1966	5.00	10.00	20.00
AS-9104 [S]	Tijuana Jazz	1966	6.25	12.50	25.00
A-9112 [M]	Profiles	1966	5.00	10.00	20.00
AS-9112 [S]	Profiles	1966	6.25	12.50	25.00
A-9122 [M]	Simpatico	1966	5.00	10.00	20.00
AS-9122 [S]	Simpatico	1966	6.25	12.50	25.00

SKYE

Number	Title	Yr	VG	VG+	NM
SK-2	Does the Sun Really Shine	1968	3.75	7.50	15.00
SK-8	America the Beautiful	1969	3.75	7.50	15.00
SK-11	Slaves	1970	3.75	7.50	15.00
SK-14	Today	1970	3.75	7.50	15.00

VERVE

Number	Title	Yr	VG	VG+	NM
V-8443 [M]	How to Succeed in Business Without Really Trying	1962	3.75	7.50	15.00
V6-8443 [S]	How to Succeed in Business Without Really Trying	1962	5.00	10.00	20.00
V-8518 [M]	The Gary McFarland Orchestra with Special Guest Soloist Bill Evans	1963	3.75	7.50	15.00
V6-8518 [S]	The Gary McFarland Orchestra with Special Guest Soloist Bill Evans	1963	5.00	10.00	20.00
V-8603 [M]	Soft Samba	1964	3.75	7.50	15.00
V6-8603 [S]	Soft Samba	1964	5.00	10.00	20.00
V-8632 [M]	The "In" Sound	1965	3.75	7.50	15.00
V6-8632 [S]	The "In" Sound	1965	5.00	10.00	20.00
V/V6-8674	Gary McFarland	1965	—	—	—
—Canceled					
V-8682 [M]	Soft Samba Strings	1966	3.75	7.50	15.00
V6-8682 [S]	Soft Samba Strings	1966	5.00	10.00	20.00
V-8738 [M]	Scorpio and Other Signs	1967	5.00	10.00	20.00
V6-8738 [S]	Scorpio and Other Signs	1967	3.75	7.50	15.00
V6-8786	Sympathetic Vibrations	1969	3.75	7.50	15.00

MCGHEE, BROWNIE

45s

DOT

Number	Title (A Side/B Side)	Yr	VG	VG+	NM
1184	Cheatin' and Lyin'/Need Someone to Love	1954	62.50	125.00	250.00

HARLEM

Number	Title (A Side/B Side)	Yr	VG	VG+	NM
2323	Worrying Over You/Christina	1954	15.00	30.00	60.00
2329	My Confession (I Want to Thank You)/Bluebird, Bluebird	1954	15.00	30.00	60.00

JAX

Number	Title (A Side/B Side)	Yr	VG	VG+	NM
302	Smiling and Crying Blues/A Letter to Lightnin' Hopkins	1951	30.00	60.00	120.00
304	I Feel So Good/Key to the Highway	1952	30.00	60.00	120.00
307	Meet You in the Morning/Brownie's Blues	1952	30.00	60.00	120.00
310	Guitar Strangers Blues/Dissatisfied Woman	1952	30.00	60.00	120.00
312	I'm 10,000 Years Old/Cherry Red	1952	30.00	60.00	120.00
322	New Bad Blood Blues/Pawnshop Blues	1953	30.00	60.00	120.00

RED ROBIN

Number	Title (A Side/B Side)	Yr	VG	VG+	NM
111	Don't Dog Your Woman/Daisy	1953	62.50	125.00	250.00

SAVOY

Number	Title (A Side/B Side)	Yr	VG	VG+	NM
835	Diamond Ring/So Much Trouble	1952	7.50	15.00	30.00
872	Tell Me Baby/Bad Nerves	1952	7.50	15.00	30.00
899	Sweet Baby Blues/4 O'Clock in the Morning	1953	7.50	15.00	30.00
1177	I'd Love to Love You/Anna Mae	1955	5.00	10.00	20.00
1185	When It's Love Time/My Fault	1956	5.00	10.00	20.00
1564	Living with the Blues/Be My Friend	1959	3.75	7.50	15.00

Albums

BLUESVILLE

Number	Title	Yr	VG	VG+	NM
BVLP-1042 [M]	Brownie's Blues	1962	20.00	40.00	80.00
—Blue label, silver print					
BVLP-1042 [M]	Brownie's Blues	1964	6.25	12.50	25.00
—Blue label, trident logo at right					

FANTASY

Number	Title	Yr	VG	VG+	NM
OBC-505	Brownie's Blues	198?	3.00	6.00	12.00

FOLKWAYS

Number	Title	Yr	VG	VG+	NM
FP-30 [10]	Brownie McGhee Blues	1951	30.00	60.00	120.00
FA-2030 [10]	Brownie McGhee Blues	1951	25.00	50.00	100.00

Number	Title (A Side/B Side)	Yr	VG	VG+	NM
2421/2 [(2)]	Traditional Blues Vol. 1 and 2	197?	3.75	7.50	15.00
3557	Brownie McGhee Sings the Blues	197?	3.00	6.00	12.00
SAVOY JAZZ					
SJL-1204	Jumpin' the Blues	1989	3.00	6.00	12.00

MCGHEE, BROWNIE, AND SONNY TERRY
See SONNY TERRY AND BROWNIE McGHEE.

MCGHEE, STICK
45s

Number	Title (A Side/B Side)	Yr	VG	VG+	NM
ATLANTIC					
955	Wee Wee Hours (Part 1)/Wee Wee Hours (Part 2)	1952	25.00	50.00	100.00
—Note: Stick McGhee records on Atlantic before 955 are unconfirmed on 45 rpm					
991	New Found Love/Meet You in the Morning	1953	20.00	40.00	80.00
ATLANTIC CLASSICS					
873	Drinkin' Wine Spo-Dee-O-Dee/Blues Mixture (I'd Rather Drink Muddy Water)	1971	5.00	10.00	20.00
HERALD					
553	Money Fever/Sleep-In Job	1960	3.75	7.50	15.00
KING					
4610	Little Things We Used to Do/Head Happy with Wine	1953	25.00	50.00	100.00
4628	Whiskey, Women and Loaded Dice/Blues in My Heart and Tears in My Eyes	1953	25.00	50.00	100.00
4672	Jungle Juice/Dealing from the Bottom	1953	25.00	50.00	100.00
4700	I'm Doin' All This Time/Wiggle Waggin' Woo	1954	25.00	50.00	100.00
4783	Double Crossin' Liquor/Six to Eight	1955	30.00	60.00	120.00
4800	Get Your Mind Out the Gutter/Sad, Bad, Glad	1955	25.00	50.00	100.00
LONDON					
978	You Gotta Have Something on the Ball/(B-side unknown)	1951	62.50	125.00	250.00
SAVOY					
1148	Things Have Changed/Help Me Baby	1955	7.50	15.00	30.00

MCGHEE, STICK, AND JOHN LEE HOOKER
Also see each artist's individual listings.

Albums

Number	Title (A Side/B Side)	Yr	VG	VG+	NM
AUDIO LAB					
AL-1520 [M]	Highway of Blues	1959	87.50	175.00	350.00

MCGILL, JERRY
45s

Number	Title (A Side/B Side)	Yr	VG	VG+	NM
SUN					
326	Love Struck/I Wanna Make Sweet Love	1959	7.50	15.00	30.00

MCGONNIGLE, MEL
45s

Number	Title (A Side/B Side)	Yr	VG	VG+	NM
ROCKET					
101	Rattle Shakin' Mama/I Want You	1958	175.00	350.00	700.00

MCGOVERN, MAUREEN
45s

Number	Title (A Side/B Side)	Yr	VG	VG+	NM
20TH CENTURY					
2010	The Morning After (Song from The Poseidon Adventure)/Midnight Storm	1973	—	2.00	4.00
2051	I Won't Last a Day Without You/Darlene	1973	—	2.00	4.00
2072	Nice to Be Around/If I Wrote You a Song	1974	—	2.00	4.00
2107	Give Me a Reason to Be Gone/Love Knots	1974	—	2.00	4.00
2158	We May Never Love Like This Again/Wherever Love Takes Me	1974	—	2.00	4.00
2213	Even Better Than I Know Myself/All I Want (All I Need)	1975	—	2.00	4.00
2234	Love Songs Are Getting Harder to Sing/Stop Me	1975	—	2.00	4.00
WARNER BROS.					
8750	Can You Read My Mind/You Love Me Too Late	1979	—	2.00	4.00
8835	Different Worlds/Carolina Moon	1979	—	2.00	4.00
49129	Can't Take My Eyes Off You/A Very Special Love	1979	—	2.00	4.00
49177	We Could Have It All/Don't Stop Now	1980	—	2.00	4.00
49525	Bottom Line/Don't Stop Now	1980	—	2.00	4.00

Albums

Number	Title (A Side/B Side)	Yr	VG	VG+	NM
20TH CENTURY					
T-419	The Morning After	1973	3.00	6.00	12.00
T-439	Nice to Be Around	1974	3.00	6.00	12.00
T-474	Academy Award Performances	1975	3.00	6.00	12.00
WARNER BROS.					
BSK 3329	Maureen McGovern	1979	2.50	5.00	10.00

MCGRIFF, JIMMY
12-Inch Singles

Number	Title (A Side/B Side)	Yr	VG	VG+	NM
T.K. DISCO					
79	Sky Hawk/Tailgunner	1976	3.00	6.00	12.00

45s

Number	Title (A Side/B Side)	Yr	VG	VG+	NM
BLUE NOTE					
1968	Black Pearl/Groove Alley	1971	—	2.50	5.00
CAPITOL					
2875	Sugar Sugar/Fat Cakes	1970	—	2.50	5.00
3019	The Bird/Plain Brown Bag	1971	—	2.50	5.00
GROOVE MERCHANT					
1003	Groove Grease/Mr. Lucky	1972	—	2.50	5.00
1006	Theme from Shaft/Let's Stay Together	1972	—	2.50	5.00
1014	Everyday I Have the Blues/It's You I Adore	1973	—	2.50	5.00
1025	If You're Ready (Come Go with Me)/(B-side unknown)	1974	—	2.50	5.00
1029	Main Squeeze/The Sermon	1975	—	2.50	5.00
1033	Stump Juice/The Worm Turns	1976	—	2.50	5.00
JELL					
503	Soul Song Of Christmas (Silent Nite)/Chip! Chip!	1965	2.00	4.00	8.00
MILESTONE					
313	I'm Walkin'/(B-side unknown)	1984	—	2.00	4.00
SOLID STATE					
2501	I Cover the Waterfront/Slow But Sure	1966	2.00	4.00	8.00
2502	Cherry/The Comeback	1966	2.00	4.00	8.00
2510	I Can't Give You Anything But Love, Baby/(I Can't Get No) Satisfaction	1967	2.00	4.00	8.00
2515	Tennessee Waltz/Swingin' Shepherd Blues	1967	2.00	4.00	8.00
2516	Days of Wine and Roses/You Are My Sunshine	1967	2.00	4.00	8.00
2520	I've Got a Woman/Kiko	1968	—	3.00	6.00
2522	Honey/Since You've Been Gone	1968	—	3.00	6.00
2524	The Worm/Keep Loose	1968	—	3.00	6.00
2528	Step One/South Wes	1969	—	3.00	6.00
2531	Charlotte/Trying to Come By	1969	—	3.00	6.00
2534	Back on the Street/Chris Cross	1970	—	3.00	6.00
SUE					
105	Hello Betty/Close Your Eyes	1964	2.00	4.00	8.00
110	All Day Long/When You're Smiling	1964	2.00	4.00	8.00
112	Topkapi/Theme from "The Man with the Golden Arm"	1964	2.00	4.00	8.00
120	Sho 'Nuff/Bilbo	1965	2.00	4.00	8.00
123	Discotheque U.S.A./People	1965	2.00	4.00	8.00
128	Turn Blue/Bump De Bump	1965	2.00	4.00	8.00
770	I've Got a Woman (Part 1)/I've Got a Woman (Part 2)	1962	2.50	5.00	10.00
777	All About My Girl/M.G. Blues	1963	2.00	4.00	8.00
786	The Last Minute (Part 1)/The Last Minute (Part 2)	1963	2.00	4.00	8.00
791	One of Mine/Broadway	1963	2.00	4.00	8.00
802	Lonely Avenue (Part 1)/Lonely Avenue (Part 2)	1963	2.00	4.00	8.00
804	Christmas with McGriff Part 1/Christmas with McGriff Part 2	1963	3.00	6.00	12.00
804	Winter with McGriff Pt. 1/Winter with McGriff Pt. 2	1963	2.50	5.00	10.00
10001	Kiko/Jumpin' at the Woodside	1964	2.00	4.00	8.00
UNITED ARTISTS					
50826	Pretty Baby/I Need Love So Bad	1971	—	2.50	5.00
—With Junior Parker					

Albums

Number	Title (A Side/B Side)	Yr	VG	VG+	NM
BLUE NOTE					
BST-84350	Electric Funk	1970	3.75	7.50	15.00
BST-84364	Something to Listen To	1971	3.75	7.50	15.00
BST-84374	Black Pearl	1971	3.75	7.50	15.00
CAPITOL					
ST-569	Dudes Doin' Business	1970	3.75	7.50	15.00
ST-616	Soul Sugar	1970	3.75	7.50	15.00
COLLECTABLES					
COL-5147	Blues for Mr. Jimmy	198?	2.50	5.00	10.00
GROOVE MERCHANT					
503	Groove Grease	1972	3.75	7.50	15.00
506	Let's Stay Together	1972	3.75	7.50	15.00
509	Fly Dude	1973	3.75	7.50	15.00
520	Come Together	1973	3.00	6.00	12.00
529	If You're Ready Come Go with Me	1974	3.00	6.00	12.00
534	Main Squeeze	1975	3.00	6.00	12.00
2203	Black and Blues	1971	3.75	7.50	15.00
2205	Good Things Don't Happen Every Day	1971	3.75	7.50	15.00
3300 [(2)]	Giants of the Organ In Concert	1974	3.75	7.50	15.00
3309	Stump Juice	1976	3.00	6.00	12.00
3311	Mean Machine	1976	3.00	6.00	12.00
4403 [(2)]	Flyin' Time	197?	3.75	7.50	15.00
JAM					
002	City Lights	1982	3.00	6.00	12.00
005	Movin' Upside the Blues	1983	3.00	6.00	12.00
LRC					
9316	Tailgunner	1977	3.75	7.50	15.00
9320	Outside Looking In	1978	3.75	7.50	15.00
MILESTONE					
M-9116	Countdown	1984	2.50	5.00	10.00
M-9126	Skywalk	1985	2.50	5.00	10.00
M-9135	State of the Art	1986	2.50	5.00	10.00
M-9148	The Starting Five	1987	2.50	5.00	10.00
M-9163	Blue to the 'Bone	1988	2.50	5.00	10.00
QUINTESSENCE					
25061	Soul	1978	3.00	6.00	12.00
SOLID STATE					
SM-17001 [M]	The Big Band of Jimmy McGriff	1966	3.75	7.50	15.00
SM-17002 [M]	A Bag Full of Soul	1966	3.75	7.50	15.00
SM-17006 [M]	Cherry	1967	5.00	10.00	20.00
SS-18001 [S]	The Big Band of Jimmy McGriff	1966	5.00	10.00	20.00
SS-18002 [S]	A Bag Full of Soul	1966	5.00	10.00	20.00
SS-18006 [S]	Cherry	1967	5.00	10.00	20.00
SS-18017	A Bag Full of Blues	1968	5.00	10.00	20.00
SS-18030	I've Got a New Woman	1968	5.00	10.00	20.00
SS-18036	Honey	1968	5.00	10.00	20.00
SS-18045	The Worm	1968	5.00	10.00	20.00
SS-18053	Step I	1969	5.00	10.00	20.00
SS-18060	A Thing to Come By	1969	5.00	10.00	20.00
SS-18063	The Way You Look Tonight	1970	5.00	10.00	20.00
SUE					
LP-1012 [M]	I've Got a Woman	1962	7.50	15.00	30.00
STLP-1012 [S]	I've Got a Woman	1962	10.00	20.00	40.00
LP-1013 [M]	One of Mine	1963	7.50	15.00	30.00
STLP-1013 [S]	One of Mine	1963	10.00	20.00	40.00
LP-1017 [M]	Jimmy McGriff at the Apollo	1963	7.50	15.00	30.00
STLP-1017 [S]	Jimmy McGriff at the Apollo	1963	10.00	20.00	40.00
LP-1018 [M]	Christmas with McGriff	1963	7.50	15.00	30.00
STLP-1018 [S]	Christmas with McGriff	1963	10.00	20.00	40.00
LP-1020 [M]	Jimmy McGriff at the Organ	1963	7.50	15.00	30.00
STLP-1020 [S]	Jimmy McGriff at the Organ	1963	10.00	20.00	40.00
LP-1033 [M]	Topkapi	1964	7.50	15.00	30.00
STLP-1033 [S]	Topkapi	1964	10.00	20.00	40.00
LP-1039 [M]	Blues for Mister Jimmy	1965	7.50	15.00	30.00
STLP-1039 [S]	Blues for Mister Jimmy	1965	10.00	20.00	40.00
LP-1043 [M]	Toast to Greatest Hits	1966	5.00	10.00	20.00
STLP-1043 [S]	Toast to Greatest Hits	1966	6.25	12.50	25.00
SUNSET					
SUS-5264	The Great Jimmy McGriff	1969	2.50	5.00	10.00

Number	Title (A Side/B Side)	Yr	VG	VG+	NM
UNITED ARTISTS					
UAS-5597	Jimmy McGriff and Junior Parker	1972	3.75	7.50	15.00
VEEP					
VP-13515 [M]	Live Where the Action Is	1966	5.00	10.00	20.00
VP-13522 [M]	Greatest Organ Hits	1967	6.25	12.50	25.00
VPS-16515 [S]	Live Where the Action Is	1966	6.25	12.50	25.00
VPS-16522 [S]	Greatest Organ Hits	1967	5.00	10.00	20.00

MCGUINN, ROGER

Also see THE BYRDS.

Number	Title (A Side/B Side)	Yr	VG	VG+	NM
45s					
COLUMBIA					
10019	Gate of Horn/Same Old Sound	1974	—	3.00	6.00
10181	Somebody Loves You/Easy Does It	1975	—	3.00	6.00
10201	Lover of the Bayou/Easy Does It	1975	—	3.00	6.00
10385	Take Me Away/Friend	1976	—	3.00	6.00
10543	American Girl/I'm Not Lonely Anymore	1977	—	3.00	6.00
45931	Draggin'/Time Cube	1973	—	3.00	6.00
Albums					
ARISTA					
AL 8648	Back from Rio	1991	3.75	7.50	15.00
COLUMBIA					
AS 353 [DJ]	The Roger McGuinn Airplay Anthology	1977	7.50	15.00	30.00
—Promo only; also includes Byrds tracks					
KC 31946	Roger McGuinn	1973	3.00	6.00	12.00
KC 32956	Peace On You	1974	3.00	6.00	12.00
PC 33541	Roger McGuinn & Band	1975	3.00	6.00	12.00
PC 34154	Cardiff Rose	1976	3.00	6.00	12.00
PC 34656	Thunderbyrd	1977	3.00	6.00	12.00

MCGUINNESS FLINT

Number	Title (A Side/B Side)	Yr	VG	VG+	NM
45s					
CAPITOL					
3014	When I'm Dead and Gone/Lazy Afternoon	1971	—	3.00	6.00
3139	Rock On/Malt and Barley Blues	1971	—	3.00	6.00
3186	Friends of Mine/Happy Birthday, Ruthy Baby	1971	—	3.00	6.00
Albums					
CAPITOL					
SMAS-625	McGuinness Flint	1971	3.00	6.00	12.00
ST-794	Happy Birthday, Ruthy Baby	1971	3.00	6.00	12.00
SIRE					
SAS-7405	Lo and Behold	1972	3.00	6.00	12.00

MCGUIRE, BARRY

Also see THE NEW CHRISTY MINSTRELS.

Number	Title (A Side/B Side)	Yr	VG	VG+	NM
45s					
DUNHILL					
4009	Eve of Destruction/What Exactly's the Matter with Me	1965	3.00	6.00	12.00
4014	Child of Our Times/Upon a Painted Ocean	1965	2.50	5.00	10.00
4014 [PS]	Child of Our Times/Upon a Painted Ocean	1965	3.75	7.50	15.00
4019	This Precious Time/Don't You Wonder Where It's At	1966	3.00	6.00	12.00
—A-side backing group: The Mamas and The Papas					
4028	Cloudy Summer Afternoon (Raindrops)/I'd Have to Be Outta My Mind	1966	2.50	5.00	10.00
4048	There's Nothing Else on My Mind/Why Not Stop and Dig It	1966	2.50	5.00	10.00
4098	Masters of War/Stop Now and Dig It While You Can	1967	2.00	4.00	8.00
4116	Lollipop Train/Inner-Manipulations	1968	2.00	4.00	8.00
4124	Grasshopper Song/Top o' the Hill	1968	2.50	5.00	10.00
4124 [PS]	Grasshopper Song/Top o' the Hill	1968	3.75	7.50	15.00
HORIZON					
4	One by One/Town and Country	1963	3.00	6.00	12.00
8	Oh, Miss Mary/So Long, Stay Well	1963	3.00	6.00	12.00
MIRA					
205	Greenback Dollar/Oh, Miss Mary	1965	2.50	5.00	10.00
MOSAIC					
1001	The Three/Theme from The Tree	1961	3.00	6.00	12.00
1004	I've Got a Secret/Cindy and Johnny	1962	3.00	6.00	12.00
MYRRH					
119	Love Is/David and Goliath	1973	—	2.50	5.00
ODE					
66010	Old Farm/South of the Border	1970	—	3.00	6.00
SPARROW					
1023	Cosmic Cowboy/What Good Would It Do	197?	—	3.00	6.00
Albums					
ABC DUNHILL					
DS-50033	The World's Last Private Citizen	1968	6.25	12.50	25.00
DUNHILL					
D-50003 [M]	Eve of Destruction	1965	7.50	15.00	30.00
DS-50003 [S]	Eve of Destruction	1965	10.00	20.00	40.00
D-50005 [M]	This Precious Time	1966	6.25	12.50	25.00
DS-50005 [S]	This Precious Time	1966	7.50	15.00	30.00
HORIZON					
ST-1636 [S]	The Barry McGuire Album	1963	10.00	20.00	40.00
WP-1636 [M]	The Barry McGuire Album	1963	7.50	15.00	30.00
MIRA					
LP-3000 [M]	The Barry McGuire Album	1965	5.00	10.00	20.00
—Reissue of Horizon LP					
LPS-3000 [S]	The Barry McGuire Album	1965	6.25	12.50	25.00
—Reissue of Horizon LP					
MYRRH					
MSA-6519	Seeds	1974	3.00	6.00	12.00
MSA-6531	Lighten Up	1975	3.00	6.00	12.00
ODE					
SP-77004	Barry McGuire with the Doctor	1970	3.75	7.50	15.00

MCGUIRE, BARRY, AND BARRY KANE

Number	Title (A Side/B Side)	Yr	VG	VG+	NM
45s					
HORIZON					
354	Another Man/Bull 'Gine Run	1962	3.00	6.00	12.00
Albums					
HORIZON					
SWP-1608 [S]	Barry and Barry: Here and Now!	1962	7.50	15.00	30.00
WP-1608 [M]	Barry and Barry: Here and Now!	1962	6.25	12.50	25.00

MCGUIRE, PHYLLIS

Also see THE McGUIRE SISTERS.

Number	Title (A Side/B Side)	Yr	VG	VG+	NM
45s					
ABC-PARAMOUNT					
10826	My Happiness/Vaya Con Dios	1966	—	3.00	6.00
ORPHEUM					
4502	Just a Little Lovin'/You Don't Have the Heart to Tell Me	1968	—	3.00	6.00
REPRISE					
0310	I Don't Want to Walk Without You/That's Life	1964	—	3.00	6.00
0354	Run to My Arms/Someone Else Is Taking My Place	1965	—	3.00	6.00
Albums					
ABC-PARAMOUNT					
552 [M]	Phyllis McGuire Sings	1966	3.75	7.50	15.00
S-552 [S]	Phyllis McGuire Sings	1966	5.00	10.00	20.00

MCGUIRE SISTERS, THE

Also see PHYLLIS McGUIRE.

Number	Title (A Side/B Side)	Yr	VG	VG+	NM
45s					
ABC-PARAMOUNT					
10776	Grazia/Truer Than You Are	1966	—	3.00	6.00
CORAL					
60917	Picking Sweethearts/One, Two, Three, Four	1953	3.00	6.00	12.00
60969	Miss You/Tootle-Ooh Siana	1953	3.00	6.00	12.00
61002	Hey, Mister Cotton Picker/Where Good Times Are	1954	3.00	6.00	12.00
61073	Are You Looking for a Sweetheart/You'll Never Know Till Monday	1953	3.00	6.00	12.00
61126	Cling to Me/Pine Tree, Pine Over Me	1954	3.00	6.00	12.00
—With Johnny Desmond and Eileen Barton					
61187	Goodnight, Sweetheart, Goodnight/Heavenly Feeling	1954	3.00	6.00	12.00
61239	Uno, Duo, Tre/Lonesome Polecat	1954	3.00	6.00	12.00
61258	Muskrat Ramble/Not as a Stranger	1954	3.00	6.00	12.00
61278	Muskrat Ramble/Lonesome Polecat	1954	3.00	6.00	12.00
61303	Christmas Alphabet/Give Me Your Heart for Christmas	1954	3.00	6.00	12.00
61323	Sincerely/No More	1954	3.00	6.00	12.00
61334	Open Up Your Heart (And Let the Sun Shine In)/Melody of Love	1955	3.00	6.00	12.00
61335	Hearts of Stone/The Naughty Lady of Shady Lane	1955	3.00	6.00	12.00
61369	It May Sound Silly/Doesn't Anybody Love Me?	1955	3.00	6.00	12.00
61423	Something's Gotta Give/Rhythm 'N' Blues (Mama's Got the Rhythm — Papa's Got the Blues)	1955	3.00	6.00	12.00
61494	Give Me Love/Sweet Song of India	1955	3.00	6.00	12.00
61501	He/If You Believe	1955	3.00	6.00	12.00
61531	The Littlest Angel/I'd Like to Trim a Tree with You	1955	3.00	6.00	12.00
61532	My Baby's Got Such Lovin' Ways/(Baby, Baby) Be Good to Me	1955	3.00	6.00	12.00
61587	Missing/Tell Me Now	1956	2.50	5.00	10.00
61627	Picnic/Delilah Jones	1956	2.50	5.00	10.00
61703	Every Day of My Life/Endless	1956	2.50	5.00	10.00
61748	Goodnight My Love, Pleasant Dreams/Mommy	1956	2.50	5.00	10.00
61771	Kid Stuff/Without Him	1957	2.50	5.00	10.00
61798	He's Got Time/Blue Skies	1957	2.50	5.00	10.00
61815	Drownin' in Memories/Please Don't Do That to Me	1957	2.50	5.00	10.00
61842	Rock Bottom/Beginning to Miss You	1957	2.50	5.00	10.00
61856	Around the World in 80 Days/Interlude	1957	2.50	5.00	10.00
61888	Forgive Me/Kiss Them for Me	1957	2.50	5.00	10.00
61911	Santa Claus Is Comin' to Town/Honorable Congratulations	1957	2.50	5.00	10.00
61924	Sugartime/Banana Split	1958	3.00	6.00	12.00
61991	Ding Dong/Since You Went Away to School	1958	2.50	5.00	10.00
62021	Volare (Nel Blu, Dipinto Di Blue)/Do You Love Me Like You Kiss Me	1958	2.50	5.00	10.00
62047	Sweetie Pie/I'll Think of You	1958	2.50	5.00	10.00
62059	May You Always/Achoo Cha Cha	1958	2.50	5.00	10.00
62106	Summer Dreams/Peace	1959	2.50	5.00	10.00
62135	Red River Valley/Compromise	1959	2.50	5.00	10.00
62155	Some of These Days/Have a Nice Weekend	1959	2.50	5.00	10.00
62162	Livin' Dangerously/Lover's Lullaby	1960	2.00	4.00	8.00
62162 [PS]	Livin' Dangerously/Lover's Lullaby	1960	2.50	5.00	10.00
62196	The Unforgiven/I Give Thanks	1960	2.00	4.00	8.00
62216	The Last Dance/Nine O'Clock	1960	2.00	4.00	8.00
62235	To Be Loved/I Don't Know Why	1960	2.00	4.00	8.00
62249	Just for Old Times' Sake/Really Neat	1961	2.00	4.00	8.00
62249 [PS]	Just for Old Times' Sake/Really Neat	1961	2.50	5.00	10.00
62276	Tears on My Pillow/Will There Be Room in the Space Ship	1961	2.00	4.00	8.00
62276 [PS]	Tears on My Pillow/Will There Be Room in the Space Ship	1961	2.50	5.00	10.00
62288	Just Because/I Do, I Do, I Do	1961	2.00	4.00	8.00
62296	I Can Dream, Can't I/I'm Just Taking My Time	1961	2.00	4.00	8.00
62305	Sugartime Twist/More Hearts Are Broken That Way	1962	2.00	4.00	8.00
62333	I Really Don't Want to Know/Mama's Gone, Goodbye	1962	2.00	4.00	8.00
REPRISE					
0256	Now and Forever/Never	1964	—	3.00	6.00
0330	Dear Heart/Candy Heart	1964	—	3.00	6.00
0338	I'll Walk Alone/Ticket to Anywhere	1965	—	3.00	6.00

Number	Title (A Side/B Side)	Yr	VG	VG+	NM
20197	Summertime (The Time for Love)/Cordially Invited	1963	—	3.00	6.00

7-Inch Extended Plays

Number	Title (A Side/B Side)	Yr	VG	VG+	NM
CORAL					
EC 81074	(contents unknown)	195?	3.75	7.50	15.00
EC 81074 [PS]	The Three McGuire Sisters	195?	3.75	7.50	15.00
EC 81082	(contents unknown)	195?	3.75	7.50	15.00
EC 81082 [PS]	Sweethearts on Broadway	195?	3.75	7.50	15.00
EC 81090	(contents unknown)	195?	3.75	7.50	15.00
EC 81090 [PS]	TV Favorites	195?	3.75	7.50	15.00
EC 81098	Melody of Love/Hearts of Stone//Open Up Your Heart/The Naughty Lady of Shady Lane	1955	3.75	7.50	15.00
EC 81098 [PS]	By Request	1955	3.75	7.50	15.00
EC 81127	(contents unknown)	195?	3.00	6.00	12.00
EC 81127 [PS]	'S Wonderful	195?	3.00	6.00	12.00
EC 81145	Sugartime/Banana Split//I Tried/Lullaby of Birdland	1958	3.00	6.00	12.00
EC 81145 [PS]	The McGuire Sisters	1958	3.00	6.00	12.00
EC 81165	(contents unknown)	1958	3.00	6.00	12.00
EC 81165 [PS]	While the Lights Are Low	1958	3.00	6.00	12.00
EC 81184 [M]	(contents unknown)	1959	3.00	6.00	12.00
EC 81184 [PS]	I'll Think of You	1959	3.00	6.00	12.00
EC 81507	(contents unknown)	1959	3.00	6.00	12.00
EC 81507 [PS]	The McGuire Sisters	1959	3.00	6.00	12.00
EC 82022	(contents unknown)	195?	3.00	6.00	12.00
EC 82022 [PS]	Do You Remember When	195?	3.00	6.00	12.00
EC 82031	(contents unknown)	195?	3.00	6.00	12.00
EC 82031 [PS]	Children's Holiday	195?	3.00	6.00	12.00
EC 781184 [PS]	I'll Think of You	1959	5.00	10.00	20.00
EC 781184 [S]	(contents unknown)	1959	5.00	10.00	20.00

Albums

Number	Title (A Side/B Side)	Yr	VG	VG+	NM
ABC-PARAMOUNT					
530 [M]	The McGuire Sisters Today	1966	3.75	7.50	15.00
S-530 [S]	The McGuire Sisters Today	1966	5.00	10.00	20.00
CORAL					
7CXB 6 [(2) P]	The Best of the McGuire Sisters	1965	6.25	12.50	25.00
CXB 6 [(2) M]	The Best of the McGuire Sisters	1965	6.25	12.50	25.00
CRL 56123 [10]	By Request	1955	12.50	25.00	50.00
CRL 57026 [M]	Do You Remember When	1956	10.00	20.00	40.00
CRL 57028 [M]	'S Wonderful	1956	10.00	20.00	40.00
CRL 57033 [M]	He	1956	10.00	20.00	40.00
CRL 57052 [M]	Sincerely	1956	10.00	20.00	40.00
CRL 57097 [M]	Children's Holiday	1956	10.00	20.00	40.00
CRL 57134 [M]	Teenage Party	1957	7.50	15.00	30.00
CRL 57145 [M]	While the Lights Are Low	1957	7.50	15.00	30.00
CRL 57180 [M]	Musical Magic	1957	7.50	15.00	30.00
CRL 57217 [M]	Sugartime	1958	7.50	15.00	30.00
CRL 57225 [M]	Greetings from the McGuire Sisters	1958	7.50	15.00	30.00
CRL 57296 [M]	May You Always	1959	5.00	10.00	20.00
CRL 57303 [M]	In Harmony with Him	1959	6.25	12.50	25.00
CRL 57337 [M]	His and Hers	1960	5.00	10.00	20.00
CRL 57349 [M]	Our Golden Favorites	1961	5.00	10.00	20.00
CRL 57385 [M]	Just for Old Times' Sake	1961	5.00	10.00	20.00
CRL 57398 [M]	Subways Are for Sleeping	1961	3.75	7.50	15.00
CRL 57415 [M]	Songs Everybody Knows	1962	3.75	7.50	15.00
CRL 57443 [M]	Showcase	196?	5.00	10.00	20.00
CRL 757296 [S]	May You Always	1959	7.50	15.00	30.00
CRL 757303 [S]	In Harmony with Him	1959	10.00	20.00	40.00
CRL 757337 [S]	His and Hers	1960	7.50	15.00	30.00
CRL 757349 [R]	Our Golden Favorites	196?	3.00	6.00	12.00
CRL 757385 [S]	Just for Old Times' Sake	1961	7.50	15.00	30.00
CRL 757398 [S]	Subways Are for Sleeping	1961	5.00	10.00	20.00
CRL 757415 [S]	Songs Everybody Knows	1962	5.00	10.00	20.00
CRL 757443 [R]	Showcase	196?	3.00	6.00	12.00
MCA					
4119 [(2)]	The Best of the McGuire Sisters	1978	3.00	6.00	12.00
—Reissue of Coral 6					
VOCALION					
VL 3685 [M]	Children's Holiday	1960	5.00	10.00	20.00
VL 3798 [M]	The McGuire Sisters	1967	3.75	7.50	15.00
VL 73798 [R]	The McGuire Sisters	1967	3.00	6.00	12.00

MCKAY, SCOTTY

45s

Number	Title (A Side/B Side)	Yr	VG	VG+	NM
ACE					
603	Let the Good Times Roll/Little Liza Jane	1960	12.50	25.00	50.00
608	Brown Eyed Handsome Man/Cry Me a River	1960	15.00	30.00	60.00
623	Ole King Cole/Pull Down the Sky	1961	12.50	25.00	50.00
636	I've Got My Eyes on You/Shattered Dreams	1961	10.00	20.00	40.00
652	Olive Learned to Pop-Eye/Shame	1962	10.00	20.00	40.00
8003	Half a Heartache/Little Miss Blue	1962	7.50	15.00	30.00
CLARIDGE					
309	Batman/All Around the World	1966	6.25	12.50	25.00
EVENT					
4295	Rollin' Dynamite/Evenin' Time	1959	12.50	25.00	50.00
HANNA-BARBERA					
495	I'm Gonna Love Ya/Waikiki Beach	1966	6.25	12.50	25.00
LAWN					
102	I've Been Thinkin'/It's a Fun Thing	1960	6.25	12.50	25.00
PARKWAY					
806	Rollin' Dynamite/Evenin' Time	1959	10.00	20.00	40.00
PHILIPS					
40109	Mess Around/Sittin' Down and Cryin'	1963	5.00	10.00	20.00
SAVANNAH SOUND					
501	Here Comes Batman/All Around the World	196?	10.00	20.00	40.00
SWAN					
4049	Little Lump of Sugar/Midnight Cryin' Time	1960	15.00	30.00	60.00
UNI					
55205	High on Life/If You Really Want Me To, I'll Go	1970	3.00	6.00	12.00

MCKENDREE SPRING

45s

Number	Title (A Side/B Side)	Yr	VG	VG+	NM
DECCA					
32510	If the Sun Should Rise/What Will We Do with the Child	1969	—	3.00	6.00
32773	Because It's Time/Oh, Now My Friend	1971	—	3.00	6.00
32961	Down by the River/Flying Dutchmen	1972	—	3.00	6.00
33000	God Bless the Conspiracy/Flying Dutchmen	1972	—	3.00	6.00
MCA					
40024	Underground Railroad/Watch Those Pennies	1973	—	2.50	5.00
PYE					
71023	Easier Things Have Been Done/(B-side unknown)	1975	—	2.50	5.00
71060	Too Young to Feel This Old/I'm Gonna Lose That Game Again	1976	—	2.50	5.00

Albums

Number	Title (A Side/B Side)	Yr	VG	VG+	NM
DECCA					
DL 75104	McKendree Spring	1969	3.75	7.50	15.00
DL 75230	Second Thoughts	1970	3.75	7.50	15.00
DL 75332	McKendree Spring 3	1972	3.75	7.50	15.00
DL 75385	Tracks	1972	3.75	7.50	15.00
MCA					
44	McKendree Spring 3	1973	2.50	5.00	10.00
—Reissue of Decca 75332					
50	Tracks	1973	2.50	5.00	10.00
—Reissue of Decca 75385					
277	McKendree Spring	1973	2.50	5.00	10.00
—Reissue of Decca 75104					
370	Spring Suite	1973	3.00	6.00	12.00
PYE					
12108	Get Me to the Country	1975	3.00	6.00	12.00
12124	Too Young to Feel This Old	1976	3.00	6.00	12.00

MCKENZIE, SCOTT

Also see THE SMOOTHIES.

45s

Number	Title (A Side/B Side)	Yr	VG	VG+	NM
CAPITOL					
5348	All I Want Is You/Look in Your Eyes	1965	2.50	5.00	10.00
5500	There Stands the Glass/Wipe the Tears (From Your Face)	1965	2.50	5.00	10.00
5961	All I Want Is You/Look in Your Eyes	1967	—	3.00	6.00
EPIC					
10124	No, No, No, No, No/I Want to Be Alone	1967	2.00	4.00	8.00
—B-side by McKenzie's Musicians					
ODE					
103	San Francisco "Wear Some Flowers in Your Hair"/What's the Difference	1967	3.75	7.50	15.00
—Original title; also has a different mix (echoey bass drum in bridge) than the later, more common version					
103	San Francisco (Be Sure to Wear Flowers in Your Hair)/What's the Difference	1967	2.00	4.00	8.00
—Revised title					
105	Like and Old Time Movie/What's the Difference, Chapter II	1967	—	3.00	6.00
107	Holy Man/What's the Difference, Chapter III	1968	—	3.00	6.00
66012	Going Home Again/Take a Moment	1970	—	2.50	5.00

Albums

Number	Title (A Side/B Side)	Yr	VG	VG+	NM
ODE					
Z12 44002 [S]	The Voice of Scott McKenzie	1967	6.25	12.50	25.00
SP-77007	Stained Glass Morning	1970	3.75	7.50	15.00

MCKINLEYS, THE

45s

Number	Title (A Side/B Side)	Yr	VG	VG+	NM
SWAN					
4185	A Million Miles Away/Someone Cares for Me	1964	3.75	7.50	15.00

MCKUEN, ROD

45s

Number	Title (A Side/B Side)	Yr	VG	VG+	NM
A&M					
712	Hi Lonesome/Ballad of Hollywood	1963	2.50	5.00	10.00
BUDDAH					
372	Cycles/I Have Loved You	1973	—	2.00	4.00
401	Seasons in the Sun/(B-side unknown)	1974	—	2.00	4.00
BUENA VISTA					
482	Pastures Green/Scandalous John	1971	—	2.50	5.00
DECCA					
30660	Two Brothers/Jump Up	1958	3.75	7.50	15.00
30840	Lonesome Boy/Time's A-Gettin' Hard	1959	3.75	7.50	15.00
30902	Sure/Take It Like a Man	1959	3.75	7.50	15.00
HORIZON					
3	Advice to Folk Singers/There's a Hoot Tonight	1963	2.50	5.00	10.00
JUBILEE					
5420	Oliver Twist Meets the Duke of Oil/Steel Men	1962	3.00	6.00	12.00
KAPP					
366	In a Lonely Place/Marie, Marie	1961	3.00	6.00	12.00
LIBERTY					
55019	Rock Island Line/Head Like a Rock	1956	3.00	6.00	12.00
55034	Happy Is a Boy Named Me/Repeat After Me	1956	3.00	6.00	12.00
RCA VICTOR					
47-8613	Summer in My Eye/So Many Others	1965	2.00	4.00	8.00
47-8772	So Long, San Francisco/Some Trust in Chariots	1965	2.00	4.00	8.00
47-9139	The Ever Constant Sea/Baby Be My Love	1967	2.00	4.00	8.00
47-9376	Listen to the Warm/A Cat Named Sloopy	1967	2.00	4.00	8.00
47-9478	The Importance of the Rose/The Single Man	1968	2.00	4.00	8.00
SPIRAL					
1407	Oliver Twist/Celebrity Twist	1962	3.75	7.50	15.00
STANYAN					
34	Simple Christmas/A Hand To Hold At Christmas	1974	—	2.50	5.00
—B-side by Glenn Yarbrough					
WARNER BROS.					
7243	Seasons in the Sun/To Watch the Trains	1968	—	3.00	6.00

Number	Title (A Side/B Side)	Yr	VG	VG+	NM
7259	Ivy That Clings to the Wall/Kaleidoscope	1969	—	3.00	6.00
7274	Boat Ride/I'll Catch the Sun	1969	—	3.00	6.00
7288	Look Away/Trashy	1969	—	3.00	6.00
7332	The Things Men Do/The Time It Takes to Love You	1969	—	3.00	6.00
7346	Bring Her a Rose/Mister Kelly-Kelly and Me	1969	—	3.00	6.00
7389	I Think It's Going to Rain Today/London	1970	—	2.50	5.00
7420	My Mother's Eyes/Soldiers Want to Be Heroes	1970	—	2.50	5.00
7454	Champion Charlie Brown/Something for Snoopy	1971	—	3.00	6.00
7533	Hit 'Em in the Head with Love/Soldiers Want to Be Heroes	1971	—	2.50	5.00
7542	The Carols of Christmas/So My Sheep May Safely Graze	1971	—	2.50	5.00
7542 [PS]	The Carols of Christmas/So My Sheep May Safely Graze	1971	—	3.00	6.00
7620	Time to Sing My Song/Minute-Thirty-Second Waltz	1972	—	2.50	5.00
7699	Good for Nothin' Bill/The World I Used to Know	1973	—	2.00	4.00
Albums					
BUDDAH					
BDS-5138	Cycles	197?	3.00	6.00	12.00
CAPITOL					
ST 2079 [S]	Rod McKuen Sings Rod McKuen	1964	5.00	10.00	20.00
T 2079 [M]	Rod McKuen Sings Rod McKuen	1964	3.75	7.50	15.00
ST 2838	Love Movement	1968	3.75	7.50	15.00
DECCA					
DL 4969 [M]	Very Warm	1968	5.00	10.00	20.00
DL 8882 [M]	Anywhere I Wander	1958	5.00	10.00	20.00
DL 8946 [M]	Alone After Dark	1959	5.00	10.00	20.00
DL 74969 [S]	Very Warm	1968	3.75	7.50	15.00
DL 78882 [S]	Anywhere I Wander	1958	7.50	15.00	30.00
DL 78946 [S]	Alone After Dark	1959	7.50	15.00	30.00
EPIC					
BN 26370	In Search of Eros	1968	3.75	7.50	15.00
EVEREST					
3208	Desire Has No Special Time	1968	3.75	7.50	15.00
3267	Life Is	197?	3.75	7.50	15.00
HIFI					
R 407 [M]	Time of Desire	1958	5.00	10.00	20.00
SR 407 [S]	Time of Desire	1958	6.25	12.50	25.00
R 419 [M]	Beatsville	1960	5.00	10.00	20.00
SR 419 [S]	Beatsville	1960	6.25	12.50	25.00
HORIZON					
ST-1612 [S]	New Sounds in Folk Music	1963	6.25	12.50	25.00
WP-1612 [M]	New Sounds in Folk Music	1963	5.00	10.00	20.00
IN					
1003 [M]	Seasons in the Sun	1964	5.00	10.00	20.00
S-1003 [S]	Seasons in the Sun	1964	6.25	12.50	25.00
JUBILEE					
J-5013 [M]	Mr. Oliver Twist	1962	5.00	10.00	20.00
SJ-5013 [S]	Mr. Oliver Twist	1962	6.25	12.50	25.00
KAPP					
KL-1538 [M]	In a Lonely Place	1967	5.00	10.00	20.00
KS-3538 [S]	In a Lonely Place	1967	3.75	7.50	15.00
LIBERTY					
LRP-3011 [M]	Lazy Afternoon	1956	10.00	20.00	40.00
RCA VICTOR					
LPM-3424 [M]	Rod McKuen Sings His Own	1965	3.75	7.50	15.00
LSP-3424 [S]	Rod McKuen Sings His Own	1965	5.00	10.00	20.00
LPM-3508 [M]	The Loner	1966	3.75	7.50	15.00
LSP-3508 [S]	The Loner	1966	5.00	10.00	20.00
LPM-3635 [M]	Other Kinds of Songs	1966	3.75	7.50	15.00
LSP-3635 [S]	Other Kinds of Songs	1966	5.00	10.00	20.00
LPM-3786 [M]	Through European Windows	1967	5.00	10.00	20.00
LSP-3786 [S]	Through European Windows	1967	3.75	7.50	15.00
LPM-3863 [M]	Listen to the Warm	1967	5.00	10.00	20.00
LSP-3863 [S]	Listen to the Warm	1967	3.75	7.50	15.00
LSP-4010	A Single Man	1968	3.75	7.50	15.00
LSP-4127	The Best of Rod McKuen	1969	3.75	7.50	15.00
STANYAN					
STS-001	In Concert	197?	3.75	7.50	15.00
—Originals are numbered, limited editions					
STS-003	Seasons in the Sun	197?	3.75	7.50	15.00
1894 [(2)]	Pastorale	197?	3.00	6.00	12.00
2560	Rod McKuen's Greatest Hits 2	197?	2.50	5.00	10.00
2688	Rod McKuen's Greatest Hits, Vol. 4	197?	2.50	5.00	10.00
4010	A Single Man	197?	2.50	5.00	10.00
5004	Seasons in the Sun Vol. 2	197?	3.00	6.00	12.00
5005	Blessings in Shades of Green	1970	3.00	6.00	12.00
5006	Folk Album	1970	3.00	6.00	12.00
5009	Love's Been Good to Me	1970	3.00	6.00	12.00
5010	A Boy Named Charlie Brown	1970	3.75	7.50	15.00
5016 [(2)]	Live in London!	1971	3.75	7.50	15.00
5020	Try Rod McKuen in Your Own Home	197?	3.00	6.00	12.00
5022	Rod McKuen Sings Jacques Brel	197?	3.00	6.00	12.00
5025	Rod	197?	3.00	6.00	12.00
5031	Rod McKuen's Greatest Hits, Vol. 3	197?	3.00	6.00	12.00
5032	Have a Nice Day	1973	3.00	6.00	12.00
5040	Evening in Vienna	1972	3.00	6.00	12.00
5042	Rod McKuen Grand Tour, Vol. 3	1972	3.00	6.00	12.00
5046 [(2)]	Seasons in the Sun Vols. 1 and 2	197?	3.75	7.50	15.00
5047	Pastures Green	197?	3.00	6.00	12.00
5048 [(2)]	Listen to the Warm	197?	3.75	7.50	15.00
5051 [(2)]	Amsterdam Concert	1972	3.75	7.50	15.00
5072	A Portrait of Rod McKuen	1972	3.00	6.00	12.00
5075	Live at the Sydney Opera House	197?	3.00	6.00	12.00
9001	Concerto No. 1 for Four Harpsichords and Orchestra	197?	3.00	6.00	12.00
9005	Symphony No. 1: "All Men Love Something"	197?	3.00	6.00	12.00
9006	Concerto No. 2 for Guitar and Orchestra; Five Pieces	197?	3.00	6.00	12.00
9008	Piano Variations	197?	3.00	6.00	12.00
9010	McKuen Conducts McKuen	1972	3.00	6.00	12.00
9012	Concerto No. 3 for Piano and Orchestra	1972	3.00	6.00	12.00
9015	Seascapes; Plains of My Country	197?	3.00	6.00	12.00
10009	Concerto No. 1; Four Statements	197?	3.00	6.00	12.00
SUNSET					
SUS-5273	In the Beginning	1970	2.50	5.00	10.00
TRADITION					
2063 [M]	A San Francisco Hippie Trip	1967	6.25	12.50	25.00
WARNER BROS.					
WS 1722	Beautiful Strangers	1968	3.75	7.50	15.00
WS 1758	Lonesome Cities	1968	3.75	7.50	15.00
WS 1772	Greatest Hits of Rod McKuen	1969	3.75	7.50	15.00
2WS 1794 [(2)]	Rod McKuen at Carnegie Hall	1969	5.00	10.00	20.00
WS 1837	New Ballads	1970	3.00	6.00	12.00
2WS 1894 [(2)]	Pastorale	1971	3.75	7.50	15.00
2WS 1947 [(2)]	Rod McKuen Grand Tour	1971	3.75	7.50	15.00
BS 2560	Rod McKuen's Greatest Hits 2	1970	3.00	6.00	12.00
BS 2638	Odyssey	1973	3.00	6.00	12.00
BS 2688	Rod McKuen's Greatest Hits, Vol. 4	1973	3.00	6.00	12.00
2WS 2731 [(2)]	Back to Carnegie Hall	1973	3.75	7.50	15.00
BS 2785	Seasons in the Sun	1974	3.00	6.00	12.00
BS 2817	Alone	1974	3.00	6.00	12.00
BS 2931	McKuen Country	1976	2.50	5.00	10.00
ST-92042	Greatest Hits of Rod McKuen	1969	5.00	10.00	20.00
—Capitol Record Club edition					

MCKUEN, ROD; TAK SHINDO; JULIE MEREDITH

Number	Title (A Side/B Side)	Yr	VG	VG+	NM
Albums					
IMPERIAL					
LP-9092 [M]	The Yellow Unicorn	1960	10.00	20.00	40.00
LP-12036 [S]	The Yellow Unicorn	1960	12.50	25.00	50.00

MCLAIN, DENNY

Number	Title (A Side/B Side)	Yr	VG	VG+	NM
45s					
CAPITOL					
2282	Extra Innings/Lonely Is the Name	1968	3.00	6.00	12.00
Albums					
CAPITOL					
ST-204	Denny McLain In Las Vegas	1969	6.25	12.50	25.00
ST 2881	Denny McLain at the Organ	1968	6.25	12.50	25.00

MCLAUGHLIN, JOHN

Also see MAHAVISHNU ORCHESTRA.

Number	Title (A Side/B Side)	Yr	VG	VG+	NM
Albums					
CELLULOID					
CEL-5010	Devotion	198?	2.00	4.00	8.00
—Reissue of Douglas 31568					
COLUMBIA					
PC 34162	Shakti with John McLaughlin	1976	2.50	5.00	10.00
PC 34372	A Handful of Secrets	1977	2.50	5.00	10.00
JC 34980	Natural Elements	1977	2.50	5.00	10.00
JC 35326	Electric Guitarist	1978	2.50	5.00	10.00
JC 35785	Electric Dreams	1979	2.50	5.00	10.00
JC 36355	The Best of John McLaughlin	1980	2.50	5.00	10.00
FC 37152	Friday Night in San Francisco	1981	2.50	5.00	10.00
—With Al DiMeola and Paco De Lucia					
FC 38645	Passion, Grace & Fire	1983	2.50	5.00	10.00
—With Al DiMeola and Paco De Lucia					
DOUGLAS					
4	Devotion	1970	3.75	7.50	15.00
KZ 30766	My Goals Beyond	1971	3.00	6.00	12.00
KZ 31568	Devotion	1972	3.00	6.00	12.00
—Reissue of 4					
DOUGLAS CASABLANCA					
6003	My Goals Beyond	1976	2.50	5.00	10.00
—Reissue of Douglas 30766					
ELEKTRA/MUSICIAN					
60031	My Goals Beyond	1982	2.50	5.00	10.00
—Reissue of Douglas 30766					
POLYDOR					
5510	Extrapolation	1969	3.75	7.50	15.00
PD-6074	Extrapolation	1972	3.00	6.00	12.00
—Reissue of 5510					
RYKO ANALOGUE					
RALP-0051	My Goals Beyond	1987	5.00	10.00	20.00
—Clear vinyl reissue					
WARNER BROS.					
BSK 3619	Belo Horizonte	1981	2.50	5.00	10.00
23723	Music Spoken Here	1982	2.50	5.00	10.00
25190	Mahavishnu	1985	2.50	5.00	10.00

MCLAWLER, SARAH

Number	Title (A Side/B Side)	Yr	VG	VG+	NM
45s					
KING					
4549	Please Try to Love Me/Ready, Willing, and Able	1952	25.00	50.00	100.00
4561	Romance in the Dark/I'm Just Another One	1952	25.00	50.00	100.00
VEE JAY					
199	Babe in the Woods/Flamingo	1956	7.50	15.00	30.00
239	Snowfall/Relax Miss Frisky	1957	7.50	15.00	30.00
—With Richard Otto					

MCLEAN, DON

Number	Title (A Side/B Side)	Yr	VG	VG+	NM
45s					
ARISTA					
0284	Prime Time/The Statue	1977	—	2.00	4.00
0379	It Doesn't Matter Anymore/If We Try	1978	—	2.00	4.00
CAPITOL					
B-44098	Perfect Love/Can't Blame the Train	1987	—	—	3.00
B-44186	Love in the Heart/Every Day's a Miracle	1988	—	—	3.00
B-44258	Eventually/It's Not Your Fault	1988	—	—	3.00
EMI					
9100	American Pie/Vincent	1992	2.00	4.00	8.00
—Scarce reissue with entire 8:30 version of "American Pie" on one side					

Number	Title (A Side/B Side)	Yr	VG	VG+	NM
EMI AMERICA					
8375	He's Got You/To Have and To Hold	1987	—	—	3.00
43025	Superman's Ghost/(B-side unknown)	1987	—	—	3.00
MEDIARTS					
108	And I Love You So/Castles in the Air	1970	2.50	5.00	10.00
MILLENNIUM					
YB-11799	Crying/Genesis (In the Beginning)	1980	—	2.00	4.00
YB-11803	Lloras "Crying"/Genesis (In the Beginning)	1981	—	—	—
—Unreleased					
YB-11804	Since I Don't Have You/Your Cheating Heart	1981	—	2.00	4.00
YB-11809	It's Just the Sun/Words and Music	1981	—	2.00	4.00
YB-11819	Castles in the Air/Crazy Eyes	1981	—	2.00	4.00
YB-13106	Jerusalem/Left for Dead on the Road of Love	1982	—	2.00	4.00
GB-13477	Crying/Since I Don't Have You	1983	—	—	3.00
—Gold Standard Series					
UNITED ARTISTS					
XW206	If We Try/The More You Pay	1973	—	2.00	4.00
XW363	Fool's Paradise/Happy Trails	1973	—	2.00	4.00
XW519	Vincent/Dreidel	1974	—	2.00	4.00
—Reissue					
XW520	American Pie (Part 1)/American Pie (Part 2)	1974	—	2.00	4.00
—Reissue					
XW541	Sitting on Top of the World/Mule Skinner Blues	1974	—	2.00	4.00
XW579	Homeless Brothers/La La Love You	1974	—	2.00	4.00
XW614	Wonderful Baby/Birthday Song	1975	—	2.00	4.00
50796	And I Love You So/Castles in the Air	1971	—	3.00	6.00
50856	American Pie/Empty Chairs	1971	—	—	—
—Unreleased?					
50856	American Pie — Part 1/American Pie — Part 2	1971	—	2.50	5.00
50856 [DJ]	American Pie (mono/stereo)	1971	2.00	4.00	8.00
—With a different edit than the Part 1/Part 2 stock copy					
50856 [PS]	American Pie	1971	2.50	5.00	10.00
—Comes with both promos and stock copies					
50887	Vincent/Castles in the Air	1972	—	2.50	5.00
50887 [PS]	Vincent/Castles in the Air	1972	2.50	5.00	10.00
51100	Dreidel/Bronco Bill's Lament	1973	—	2.00	4.00
Albums					
ARISTA					
AL 4149	Prime Time	1978	2.50	5.00	10.00
CAPITOL					
C1-48080	Love Tracks	1988	2.50	5.00	10.00
CASABLANCA					
NBLP 7173	Chain Lightning	1979	—	—	—
—Canceled					
EMI AMERICA					
ST-17255	Don McLean's Greatest Hits, Then and Now	1987	2.50	5.00	10.00
LIBERTY					
LN-10037	American Pie	1980	2.00	4.00	8.00
—Reissue of United Artists 5535					
LN-10157	Tapestry	1982	2.00	4.00	8.00
—Reissue of United Artists 5522					
LN-10211	Homeless Brother	198?	2.00	4.00	8.00
—Reissue of United Artists 315					
MEDIARTS					
41-4	Tapestry	1970	5.00	10.00	20.00
MILLENNIUM					
BXL1-7756	Chain Lightning	1981	2.50	5.00	10.00
BXL1-7762	Believers	1981	2.50	5.00	10.00
UNITED ARTISTS					
UA-LA161-F	Playin' Favorites	1973	3.00	6.00	12.00
UA-LA315-G	Homeless Brother	1974	3.00	6.00	12.00
UA-LA652-H2 [(2)]	Solo	1976	3.75	7.50	15.00
UAS-5522	Tapestry	1971	3.00	6.00	12.00
—Reissue of Mediarts LP					
UAS-5535	American Pie	1971	3.00	6.00	12.00
UAS-5651	Don McLean	1972	3.00	6.00	12.00

MCLOLLIE, OSCAR

Number	Title (A Side/B Side)	Yr	VG	VG+	NM
45s					
CLASS					
206	Here I Am/Say	1957	3.75	7.50	15.00
228	Hey Girl — Hey Boy/Let Me Know Let Me Know	1958	3.75	7.50	15.00
—With Jeanette Baker					
238	Let's Get Together/Rock-a-Cha	1958	3.75	7.50	15.00
—With Jeanette Baker					
243	Convicted/My Heart Speaks	1959	3.75	7.50	15.00
265	The Honey Jump/Call It Love	1960	3.75	7.50	15.00
503	Rain/Casino	1956	5.00	10.00	20.00
MERCURY					
70964	Blue Velvet/The Penalty	1956	6.25	12.50	25.00
MODERN					
902	The Honey Jump (Part 1)/The Honey Jump (Part 2)	1952	15.00	30.00	60.00
915	Be Cool My Heart/All the Oil in Texas	1952	12.50	25.00	50.00
920	Falling in Love with You/Lolly Pop	1953	12.50	25.00	50.00
938	Hot Banana/Wiggle Toe	1954	10.00	20.00	40.00
943	God Gave Us Christmas/Dig That Crazy Santa Claus	1954	10.00	20.00	40.00
950	Pretty Girl/Hey Lolly Lolly	1955	10.00	20.00	40.00
955	Pagliacci (With a Broken Heart)/Eternal Love	1955	10.00	20.00	40.00
970	Roll, Hot Rod, Roll/Convicted	1955	10.00	20.00	40.00
976	God Gave Us Christmas/(B-side unknown)	1955	7.50	15.00	30.00
WING					
90083	God's Green Earth/Got Your Love in My Heart	1956	6.25	12.50	25.00
Albums					
CROWN					
CLP-5016 [M]	Oscar McLollie and His Honey Jumpers	1956	100.00	200.00	400.00
—Opinions differ as to whether this LP actually exists. Value is probably conservative.					

MCLUHAN

Number	Title (A Side/B Side)	Yr	VG	VG+	NM
Albums					
BRUNSWICK					
BL 754177	Anomaly	1972	5.00	10.00	20.00

MCLUHAN, MARSHALL

Number	Title (A Side/B Side)	Yr	VG	VG+	NM
Albums					
COLUMBIA					
CL 2701 [M]	The Medium Is the Message	1967	6.25	12.50	25.00
CS 9501 [S]	The Medium Is the Message	1967	6.25	12.50	25.00

MCMANUS, ROSS

Number	Title (A Side/B Side)	Yr	VG	VG+	NM
45s					
IMPERIAL					
66042	Patsy Girl/I'm the Greatest	1964	3.00	6.00	12.00

MCNABB, CECIL

Number	Title (A Side/B Side)	Yr	VG	VG+	NM
45s					
KING					
5116	Clock Tickin' Rhythm/Nothing Like This	1958	62.50	125.00	250.00

MCNAIR, BARBARA

Number	Title (A Side/B Side)	Yr	VG	VG+	NM
45s					
AUDIO FIDELITY					
153	Love Has a Way/(B-side unknown)	1969	2.50	5.00	10.00
162	After St. Francis/I Can Tell	1969	2.50	5.00	10.00
CORAL					
61923	Till There Was You/Bobby	1958	6.25	12.50	25.00
61972	He's Got the Whole World in His Hands/Flipped Over You	1958	7.50	15.00	30.00
61996	Indiscreet/Waltz Me Around	1958	6.25	12.50	25.00
62020	Too Late This Spring/See If I Care	1958	6.25	12.50	25.00
62071	Goin' Steady with the Moon/I Feel a Feeling	1959	6.25	12.50	25.00
62116	Lover's Prayer/Old Devil Moon	1959	6.25	12.50	25.00
KC					
109	Cross Over the Bridge/Gloryland	1962	12.50	25.00	50.00
112	A Little Bird Told Me/Nobody Rings My Bell	1963	10.00	20.00	40.00
MOTOWN					
1087	Touch of Time/You're Gonna Love My Baby	1965	6.25	12.50	25.00
1099	What a Day/Everything Is Good About You	1966	6.25	12.50	25.00
1106	Here I Am Baby/My World Is Empty Without You	1966	6.25	12.50	25.00
1112	Steal Away Tonight/For Once in My Life	1967	125.00	250.00	500.00
1123	Where Would I Be Without You/For Once in My Life	1968	6.25	12.50	25.00
1133	You Could Never Love Him/Fancy Passes	1968	6.25	12.50	25.00
SIGNATURE					
12024	He's a King/Murray, What's Your Hurry	1960	5.00	10.00	20.00
12033	All About Love/You Done Me Wrong	1960	5.00	10.00	20.00
12049	Kansas City/Love Talk	1960	5.00	10.00	20.00
WARNER BROS.					
5633	Wanted Me/It Was Never Like This	1965	7.50	15.00	30.00
Albums					
AUDIO FIDELITY					
AFSD-6222	More Today Than Yesterday	1969	5.00	10.00	20.00
MOTOWN					
644 [M]	Where I Am	1966	12.50	25.00	50.00
S-644 [S]	Where I Am	1966	15.00	30.00	60.00
S-680	The Real Barbara McNair	1969	7.50	15.00	30.00
SIGNATURE					
SM 1042 [M]	Love Talk	1960	10.00	20.00	40.00
SS 1042 [S]	Love Talk	1960	12.50	25.00	50.00
WARNER BROS.					
W 1541 [M]	I Enjoy Being a Girl	1964	6.25	12.50	25.00
WS 1541 [S]	I Enjoy Being a Girl	1964	7.50	15.00	30.00
W 1570 [M]	The Livin' End	1964	6.25	12.50	25.00
WS 1570 [S]	The Livin' End	1964	7.50	15.00	30.00

MCNAUGHTON, BYRON, AND HIS ALL NEWS ORCHESTRA

Number	Title (A Side/B Side)	Yr	VG	VG+	NM
45s					
JAMIE					
1427	Right from the Shark's Jaws (The Jaws Interview)/Jaws Jam	1975	2.50	5.00	10.00

MCNEELY, BIG JAY

Number	Title (A Side/B Side)	Yr	VG	VG+	NM
45s					
BAYOU					
014	Hometown Jamboree/Teenage Hop	1953	20.00	40.00	80.00
018	Catastrophe/Calamity	1953	20.00	40.00	80.00
FEDERAL					
12102	The Goof/Big Jay Shuffle	1952	10.00	20.00	40.00
12111	Just Crazy/Penthouse Serenade	1952	10.00	20.00	40.00
12141	Nervous Man, Nervous/Rock Candy	1953	10.00	20.00	40.00
12151	3-D/Texas Turkey	1953	10.00	20.00	40.00
12168	Mule Walk/Ice Water	1954	10.00	20.00	40.00
12179	Hot Cinders/Whipped Cream	1954	10.00	20.00	40.00
12186	Let's Work/Hard Tack	1954	10.00	20.00	40.00
12191	Beachcomber/Strip Tease Swing	1954	10.00	20.00	40.00
IMPERIAL					
5219	Deacon's Express/Jet Fury	1953	12.50	25.00	50.00
—Note: Earlier Big Jay McNeely releases on Imperial are unknown on 45 rpm					
SAVOY					
1143	Deacon Hop/The Hucklebuck	1955	7.50	15.00	30.00
—With Paul Williams					
SWINGIN'					
614	There Is Something on Your Mind/Back...Shack...Track	1959	6.25	12.50	25.00
618	I Got the Message/Psycho Serenade	1959	3.75	7.50	15.00
622	Minnie/My Darling Dear	1960	3.75	7.50	15.00
627	I Love You, Oh Darling/Oh, What a Fool	1960	3.75	7.50	15.00
629	After Midnight/Before Midnight	1961	3.75	7.50	15.00
637	Without a Love/The Squat	1962	3.75	7.50	15.00
VEE JAY					
142	Big Jay's Hop/Three Blind Mice	1955	10.00	20.00	40.00
212	Jay's Rock/The Convention	1956	15.00	30.00	60.00
—B-side by the Delegates					

Number	Title (A Side/B Side)	Yr	VG	VG+	NM
WARNER BROS.					
5401	You Don't Have to Go/Big Jay's Count	1963	3.00	6.00	12.00

7-Inch Extended Plays

Number	Title (A Side/B Side)	Yr	VG	VG+	NM
FEDERAL					
246	(contents unknown)	1953	75.00	150.00	300.00
246 [PS]	Go! Go! Go! With Big Jay McNeely	1953	75.00	150.00	300.00
301	(contents unknown)	1954	50.00	100.00	200.00
301 [PS]	Big Jay McNeely, Volume 2	1954	50.00	100.00	200.00
332	(contents unknown)	1954	50.00	100.00	200.00
332 [PS]	Wild Man of the Saxophone	1954	50.00	100.00	200.00
373	(contents unknown)	1955	25.00	50.00	100.00
373 [PS]	Just Crazy	1955	25.00	50.00	100.00

Albums

Number	Title (A Side/B Side)	Yr	VG	VG+	NM
COLLECTABLES					
COL-5133	Golden Classics	198?	2.50	5.00	10.00
FEDERAL					
295-96 [10]	Big Jay McNeely	1954	750.00	1500.	3000.
395-530 [M]	Big Jay McNeely in 3-D	1956	200.00	400.00	800.00
KING					
650 [M]	Big Jay McNeely in 3-D	1959	125.00	250.00	500.00
SAVOY					
MG-15045 [10]	A Rhythm and Blues Concert	1955	1000.	1500.	2000.
WARNER BROS.					
W 1533 [M]	Big Jay McNeely	1963	20.00	40.00	80.00
WS 1533 [S]	Big Jay McNeely	1963	25.00	50.00	100.00

MCPHATTER, CLYDE

Also see THE DRIFTERS.

45s

Number	Title (A Side/B Side)	Yr	VG	VG+	NM
AMY					
941	Everybody's Somebody's Fool/I Belong to You	1965	3.75	7.50	15.00
950	Little Bit of Sunshine/Everybody Loves a Good Time	1966	3.00	6.00	12.00
968	A Shot of Rhythm and Blues/I'm Not Going to Work Today	1966	3.00	6.00	12.00
975	Sweet and Innocent/Lavender Lace	1967	3.00	6.00	12.00
993	I Dreamt I Died/Lonely People Can't Afford to Cry	1967	3.00	6.00	12.00
ATLANTIC					
1070	Everybody's Laughing/Hot Ziggity	1955	7.50	15.00	30.00
1077	Love Has Joined Us Together/I Gotta Have You	1955	7.50	15.00	30.00
—With Ruth Brown					
1081	Seven Days/I'm Not Worthy	1956	7.50	15.00	30.00
1092	Treasure of Love/When You're Sincere	1956	10.00	20.00	40.00
1106	Thirty Days/I'm Lonely Tonight	1956	7.50	15.00	30.00
1117	Without Love (There Is Nothing)/I Make Believe	1956	7.50	15.00	30.00
1133	No Matter What/Just to Hold My Hand	1957	6.25	12.50	25.00
1149	Long Lonely Nights/Heartaches	1957	6.25	12.50	25.00
1158	You'll Be There/Rock and Cry	1957	6.25	12.50	25.00
1170	That's Enough for Me/No Love Like Her Love	1958	6.25	12.50	25.00
1185	Come What May/Let Me Know	1958	6.25	12.50	25.00
1199	A Lover's Question/I Can't Stand Up Long	1958	6.25	12.50	25.00
2018	Lovey Dovey/My Island of Dreams	1959	5.00	10.00	20.00
2028	Since You've Been Gone/Try, Try Baby	1959	5.00	10.00	20.00
—B-side actually the "old" Drifters (uncredited)					
2038	You Went Back on Your Word/There You Go	1959	5.00	10.00	20.00
—B-side actually the "old" Drifters (uncredited)					
2049	Just Give Me a Ring/Don't Dog Me	1960	5.00	10.00	20.00
—B-side actually the "old" Drifters (uncredited)					
2060	Deep Sea Ball/Let the Boogie-Woogie Roll	1960	5.00	10.00	20.00
—B-side actually the "old" Drifters (uncredited)					
2082	If I Didn't Love You Like I Do/Go! Yes Go!	1960	5.00	10.00	20.00
—B-side actually the "old" Drifters (uncredited)					
DECCA					
32719	Book of Memories/I'll Belong to You	1970	2.00	4.00	8.00
32753	Why Can't We Get Together/Mixed-Up Cup	1970	2.00	4.00	8.00
DERAM					
85032	Thank You Love/Only a Fool	1968	2.50	5.00	10.00
85039	Baby You've Got It/Baby I Could Be So Good at Loving You	1969	2.50	5.00	10.00
MERCURY					
71660	Ta Ta/I Ain't Givin' Up Nothin'	1960	3.75	7.50	15.00
71692	I Just Want to Love You/You're for Me	1960	3.75	7.50	15.00
71692 [PS]	I Just Want to Love You/You're for Me	1960	7.50	15.00	30.00
71740	One More Chance/Before I Fall in Love Again	1960	3.75	7.50	15.00
71740 [PS]	One More Chance/Before I Fall in Love Again	1960	7.50	15.00	30.00
71783	Tomorrow Is a-Comin'/I'll Love You Till the Cows Come Home	1961	3.75	7.50	15.00
71783 [PS]	Tomorrow Is a-Comin'/I'll Love You Till the Cows Come Home	1961	7.50	15.00	30.00
71809	A Whole Heap o'Love/You're Movin' Me	1961	3.75	7.50	15.00
71809 [PS]	A Whole Heap o'Love/You're Movin' Me	1961	7.50	15.00	30.00
71841	I Never Knew/Happiness	1961	3.75	7.50	15.00
71841 [PS]	I Never Knew/Happiness	1961	6.25	12.50	25.00
71868	Same Time, Same Place/Your Second Choice	1961	3.75	7.50	15.00
71868 [PS]	Same Time, Same Place/Your Second Choice	1961	7.50	15.00	30.00
71941	Lover Please/Let's Forget About the Past	1962	5.00	10.00	20.00
71941 [PS]	Lover Please/Let's Forget About the Past	1962	10.00	20.00	40.00
71987	Little Bitty Pretty One/Next to Me	1962	3.75	7.50	15.00
71987 [PS]	Little Bitty Pretty One/Next to Me	1962	10.00	20.00	40.00
72025	Maybe/I Do Believe	1962	3.75	7.50	15.00
72025 [PS]	Maybe/I Do Believe	1962	7.50	15.00	30.00
72051	The Best Man Cried/Stop	1962	3.75	7.50	15.00
72051 [PS]	The Best Man Cried/Stop	1962	7.50	15.00	30.00
72166	So Close to Being in Love/From One to One	1963	3.75	7.50	15.00
72166 [PS]	So Close to Being in Love/From One to One	1963	7.50	15.00	30.00
72220	Deep in the Heart of Harlem/Happy Good Times	1963	3.75	7.50	15.00
72220 [PS]	Deep in the Heart of Harlem/Happy Good Times	1963	7.50	15.00	30.00
72253	Second Window, Second Floor/In My Tenement	1964	3.75	7.50	15.00
72317	Lucille/Baby, Baby	1964	3.75	7.50	15.00
72407	Crying Won't Help You Now/I Found My Love	1965	3.75	7.50	15.00
72407 [PS]	Crying Won't Help You Now/I Found My Love	1965	7.50	15.00	30.00
MGM					
12780	I Told Myself a Lie/The Masquerade Is Over	1959	5.00	10.00	20.00
12816	Twice As Nice/Where Did I Make My Mistake	1959	5.00	10.00	20.00
12843 [M]	Let's Try Again/Bless You	1959	5.00	10.00	20.00
12877	Think Me a Kiss/When the Right Time Comes Along	1960	5.00	10.00	20.00
12949	One Right After Another/This Is Not Goodbye	1960	5.00	10.00	20.00
12988	The Glory of Love/Take a Step	1961	5.00	10.00	20.00
SK-50134 [S]	Let's Try Again/Bless You	1959	10.00	20.00	40.00

7-Inch Extended Plays

Number	Title (A Side/B Side)	Yr	VG	VG+	NM
ATLANTIC					
584	*Without Love (There Is Nothing)/Thirty Days/I Make Believe/Treasure of Love	1958	62.50	125.00	250.00
584 [PS]	Clyde McPhatter	1958	62.50	125.00	250.00
605	(contents unknown)	1958	62.50	125.00	250.00
605 [PS]	Rock with Clyde McPhatter	1958	62.50	125.00	250.00
618	A Lover's Question/I Can't Stand Up Alone//Lovey Dovey/My Island of Dreams	1959	62.50	125.00	250.00
618 [PS]	Clyde McPhatter	1959	62.50	125.00	250.00

Albums

Number	Title (A Side/B Side)	Yr	VG	VG+	NM
ALLEGIANCE					
AV-5029	The Pretty One	198?	2.50	5.00	10.00
ATLANTIC					
8024 [M]	Love Ballads	1958	125.00	250.00	500.00
—Black label					
8024 [M]	Love Ballads	1960	50.00	100.00	200.00
—Brown and purple label					
8024 [M]	Love Ballads	1960	100.00	200.00	400.00
—White "bullseye" label					
8031 [M]	Clyde	1959	125.00	250.00	500.00
—Black label					
8031 [M]	Clyde	1960	100.00	200.00	400.00
—White "bullseye" label					
8031 [M]	Clyde	1960	50.00	100.00	200.00
—Brown and purple label					
8077 [M]	The Best of Clyde McPhatter	1963	50.00	100.00	200.00
DECCA					
DL 75231	Welcome Home	1970	6.25	12.50	25.00
MERCURY					
MG-20597 [M]	Ta Ta	1960	12.50	25.00	50.00
MG-20655 [M]	Golden Blues Hits	1961	12.50	25.00	50.00
MG-20711 [M]	Lover Please	1962	12.50	25.00	50.00
MG-20750 [M]	Rhythm and Soul	1962	12.50	25.00	50.00
MG-20783 [M]	Clyde McPhatter's Greatest Hits	1963	7.50	15.00	30.00
MG-20902 [M]	Songs of the Big City	1964	7.50	15.00	30.00
MG-20915 [M]	Live at the Apollo	1964	7.50	15.00	30.00
SR-60262 [S]	Ta Ta	1960	17.50	35.00	70.00
SR-60655 [S]	Golden Blues Hits	1961	17.50	35.00	70.00
SR-60711 [S]	Lover Please	1962	17.50	35.00	70.00
SR-60750 [S]	Rhythm and Soul	1962	17.50	35.00	70.00
SR-60783 [S]	Clyde McPhatter's Greatest Hits	1963	10.00	20.00	40.00
SR-60902 [S]	Songs of the Big City	1964	10.00	20.00	40.00
SR-60915 [S]	Live at the Apollo	1964	10.00	20.00	40.00
MGM					
E-3775 [M]	Let's Start Over Again	1959	37.50	75.00	150.00
SE-3775 [S]	Let's Start Over Again	1959	50.00	100.00	200.00
E-3866 [M]	Clyde McPhatter's Greatest Hits	1960	17.50	35.00	70.00
SE-3866 [S]	Clyde McPhatter's Greatest Hits	1960	20.00	40.00	80.00
WING					
MGW-12224 [M]	May I Sing for You?	1962	6.25	12.50	25.00
SRW-16224 [S]	May I Sing for You?	1962	7.50	15.00	30.00

MCRAE, CARMEN

45s

Number	Title (A Side/B Side)	Yr	VG	VG+	NM
ATLANTIC					
2421	For Once in My Life/Got to Get You Into My Life	1967	—	3.00	6.00
2485	Elusive Butterfly/I'm Always Drunk in San Francisco	1968	—	3.00	6.00
2581	Gloomy Sunday/My Heart Reminds Me	1968	—	3.00	6.00
2691	I Love You More Than You'll Ever Know/Just a Dream Ago	1969	—	2.50	5.00
2736	I Want You/Just a Little Lovin'	1970	—	2.50	5.00
2776	Carry That Weight/Goodbye Joe	1971	—	2.50	5.00
2807	Silent Spring/I Love the Life I Lead	1971	—	2.50	5.00
BETHLEHEM					
11009	If I'm Lucky/Tip Toe Gently	1958	3.00	6.00	12.00
COLUMBIA					
42292	Take Five/Easy As You Go	1962	2.50	5.00	10.00
42376	How Does the Wine Taste/Nightlife	1962	2.50	5.00	10.00
42642	Am I Going Out of Your Mind/Baby, Baby	1962	2.50	5.00	10.00
DECCA					
29324	Ooh (What'cha Doin' to Me)/If I'm Lucky	1954	3.75	7.50	15.00
29398	Keep Me in Mind/They All Laughed	1954	3.75	7.50	15.00
29472	Whatever Lola Wants/Am I the One to Blame	1955	3.00	6.00	12.00
29555	Get Set/You Don't Have to Tell Me	1955	3.00	6.00	12.00
29620	I Go for You/A Fine Romance	1955	3.00	6.00	12.00
—With Sammy Davis, Jr.					
29675	Love Is Here to Stay/This Will Make You Laugh	1955	3.00	6.00	12.00
29749	The Next Time It Happens/Come On, Come In	1955	3.00	6.00	12.00
29793	Come Down to Earth, Mr. Smith/I Guess I'll Dress for the Blues	1956	3.00	6.00	12.00
29890	Star Eyes/Tonight He's Out to Break Another Heart	1956	3.00	6.00	12.00
29949	You Don't Know Me/Never Loved Him Anyhow	1956	3.00	6.00	12.00
30004	Skyliner/If You Should Leave Me	1956	3.00	6.00	12.00
30075	I'm Putting All My Eggs in One Basket/Namely You	1956	3.00	6.00	12.00
30112	The Party's Over/I'm a Dreamer, Aren't We All	1956	3.00	6.00	12.00
30274	How Many Stars Have to Shine/It's Like Gettin' a Donkey	1957	3.00	6.00	12.00
30468	Rich Man, Poor Man/Coax Me	1957	3.00	6.00	12.00
30540	Passing Fancy/As I Love You	1958	3.00	6.00	12.00
30618	Invitation/Lo and Behold	1958	3.00	6.00	12.00
30667	So Nice to Be Wrong/Moon Ray	1958	3.00	6.00	12.00
30727	I Love the Ground You Walk On/I'll Love You	1958	3.00	6.00	12.00

Number	Title (A Side/B Side)	Yr	VG	VG+	NM
GROOVE MERCHANT					
1018	It Takes a Whole Lot of Human Feeling/Straighten Up and Fly Right	1973	—	2.50	5.00
1022	The Good Life/How Could I Settle for Less	1973	—	2.50	5.00
KAPP					
259	Which Way Is Love/Play for Keeps	1959	2.50	5.00	10.00
290	Talk to Me/Show Me the Way	1959	2.50	5.00	10.00
302	The More I See You/Don't Cry Joe	1959	2.50	5.00	10.00
327	Big Town/What Has She Got	1960	2.50	5.00	10.00
MAINSTREAM					
613	Haven't We Met?/Life Is Just a Bowl of Cherries	1965	2.00	4.00	8.00
630	Go and Buy Yourself a Dream/(B-side unknown)	1965	2.00	4.00	8.00
650	Alfie/Modesty	1966	2.00	4.00	8.00
7-Inch Extended Plays					
DECCA					
ED 2341	(contents unknown)	1956	3.00	6.00	12.00
ED 2341 [PS]	Torchy! Part 1	1956	3.00	6.00	12.00
ED 2342	(contents unknown)	1956	3.00	6.00	12.00
ED 2342 [PS]	Torchy! Part 2	1956	3.00	6.00	12.00
ED 2343	(contents unknown)	1956	3.00	6.00	12.00
ED 2343 [PS]	Torchy! Part 3	1956	3.00	6.00	12.00
Albums					
ACCORD					
SN-7152	Love Songs	1981	2.50	5.00	10.00
ATLANTIC					
SD 2-904 [(2)]	The Great American Songbook	1971	5.00	10.00	20.00
SD 1568	Just a Little Lovin'	1971	3.00	6.00	12.00
8143 [M]	For Once in My Life	1967	5.00	10.00	20.00
SD 8143 [S]	For Once in My Life	1967	3.75	7.50	15.00
SD 8165	Portrait	1968	3.75	7.50	15.00
SD 8200	The Sound of Silence	1968	3.75	7.50	15.00
BAINBRIDGE					
6221	The Sound of Silence	198?	2.50	5.00	10.00
BETHLEHEM					
BCP-1023 [10]	Carmen McRae	1955	25.00	50.00	100.00
BLUE NOTE					
BN-LA462-G	I Am Music	1975	3.00	6.00	12.00
BN-LA635-G	Can't Hide Love	1976	3.00	6.00	12.00
BN-LA709-H2 [(2)]	The Great Music Hall	1977	3.75	7.50	15.00
LWB-709 [(2)]	The Great Music Hall	1981	3.00	6.00	12.00
—Reissue of BN-LA709-H2					
BUDDAH					
B2D-6501 [(2)]	I'm Coming Home Again	1979	3.75	7.50	15.00
CATALYST					
7904	As Time Goes By	197?	3.00	6.00	12.00
COLUMBIA					
CL 1730 [M]	Lover Man	1962	5.00	10.00	20.00
CL 1943 [M]	Something Wonderful	1962	5.00	10.00	20.00
CS 8530 [S]	Lover Man	1962	6.25	12.50	25.00
CS 8743 [S]	Something Wonderful	1962	6.25	12.50	25.00
CONCORD JAZZ					
CJ-128	Two for the Road	1980	2.50	5.00	10.00
CJ-235	You're Looking at Me: A Collection of Nat King Cole Songs	1984	2.50	5.00	10.00
CJ-342	Fine and Mellow	1988	2.50	5.00	10.00
DECCA					
DL 8173 [M]	By Special Request	1955	12.50	25.00	50.00
—Black label, silver print					
DL 8173 [M]	By Special Request	1960	5.00	10.00	20.00
—Black label with color bars					
DL 8267 [M]	Torchy!	1956	12.50	25.00	50.00
—Black label, silver print					
DL 8267 [M]	Torchy!	1960	5.00	10.00	20.00
—Black label with color bars					
DL 8347 [M]	Blue Moon	1957	12.50	25.00	50.00
—Black label, silver print					
DL 8347 [M]	Blue Moon	1960	5.00	10.00	20.00
—Black label with color bars					
DL 8583 [M]	After Glow	1957	12.50	25.00	50.00
—Black label, silver print					
DL 8583 [M]	After Glow	1960	5.00	10.00	20.00
—Black label with color bars					
DL 8662 [M]	Mad About the Man	1958	12.50	25.00	50.00
—Black label, silver print					
DL 8662 [M]	Mad About the Man	1960	5.00	10.00	20.00
—Black label with color bars					
DL 8738 [M]	Carmen for Cool Ones	1958	12.50	25.00	50.00
—Black label, silver print					
DL 8738 [M]	Carmen for Cool Ones	1960	5.00	10.00	20.00
—Black label with color bars					
DL 8815 [M]	Birds of a Feather	1959	12.50	25.00	50.00
—Black label, silver print					
DL 8815 [M]	Birds of a Feather	1960	5.00	10.00	20.00
—Black label with color bars					
FOCUS					
FL-334 [M]	Bittersweet	1964	3.75	7.50	15.00
FS-334 [S]	Bittersweet	1964	5.00	10.00	20.00
GROOVE MERCHANT					
522	A Whole Lot of Human Feeling	1973	3.00	6.00	12.00
531	Ms. Jazz	1974	3.00	6.00	12.00
4401 [(2)]	Velvet Soul	197?	3.75	7.50	15.00
HARMONY					
HL 7452 [M]	Yesterdays	1968	5.00	10.00	20.00
HS 11252 [S]	Yesterdays	1968	3.00	6.00	12.00
KH 32177	Carmen McRae Sings Billie Holiday	1972	2.50	5.00	10.00
JAZZ MAN					
5004	Carmen McRae and the Kenny Clarke/Francy Boland Big Band	198?	2.50	5.00	10.00
KAPP					
KL-1117 [M]	Book of Ballads	1958	6.25	12.50	25.00
KL-1135 [M]	When You're Away	1959	6.25	12.50	25.00
KL-1169 [M]	Something to Swing About	1960	6.25	12.50	25.00
KL-1541 [M]	This Is Carmen McRae	1967	5.00	10.00	20.00
KS-3000 [S]	Book of Ballads	1958	7.50	15.00	30.00
KS-3018 [S]	When You're Away	1959	7.50	15.00	30.00
KS-3053 [S]	Something to Swing About	1960	7.50	15.00	30.00
KS-3541 [S]	This Is Carmen McRae	1967	3.75	7.50	15.00
MAINSTREAM					
309	Carmen McRae	1971	3.00	6.00	12.00
338	Carmen's Gold	1972	3.00	6.00	12.00
352	Carmen McRae In Person	1972	3.00	6.00	12.00
387	I Want You	1972	3.00	6.00	12.00
403	Live and Doin' It	1974	3.00	6.00	12.00
800 [(2)]	Alive!	1974	3.75	7.50	15.00
S-6028 [S]	Second to None	1965	5.00	10.00	20.00
S-6044 [S]	Haven't We Met?	1965	5.00	10.00	20.00
S-6065 [S]	Woman Talk	1966	5.00	10.00	20.00
S-6084 [S]	Alfie	1966	5.00	10.00	20.00
S-6091 [S]	In Person/San Francisco	1967	3.75	7.50	15.00
S-6110	Live & Wailin'	1968	3.75	7.50	15.00
56028 [M]	Second to None	1965	3.75	7.50	15.00
56044 [M]	Haven't We Met?	1965	3.75	7.50	15.00
56065 [M]	Woman Talk	1966	3.75	7.50	15.00
56084 [M]	Alfie	1966	3.75	7.50	15.00
56091 [M]	In Person/San Francisco	1967	5.00	10.00	20.00
MCA					
4111 [(2)]	The Greatest of Carmen McRae	197?	3.00	6.00	12.00
NOVUS					
3086-1-N	Carmen Sings Monk	1990	3.00	6.00	12.00
PAUSA					
9003	Can't Hide Love	198?	2.50	5.00	10.00
QUINTESSENCE					
25021	Ms. Jazz	1978	2.50	5.00	10.00
—Reissue of Groove Merchant 531					
STANYAN					
10115	Mad About the Man	197?	3.00	6.00	12.00
TEMPONIC					
29562	Carmen	1972	3.00	6.00	12.00
TIME					
S-2104 [S]	Live at Sugar Hill	1960	6.25	12.50	25.00
52104 [M]	Live at Sugar Hill	1960	5.00	10.00	20.00
VOCALION					
VL 3697 [M]	Carmen McRae	1963	3.75	7.50	15.00
VL 73828	My Foolish Heart	1969	3.00	6.00	12.00

MCVIE, CHRISTINE

Also see CHICKEN SHACK; FLEETWOOD MAC.

Number	Title (A Side/B Side)	Yr	VG	VG+	NM
45s					
EPIC					
10536	I'd Rather Go Blind/Get Like You Used to Be	1969	3.00	6.00	12.00
—As "Christine Perfect"					
SIRE					
732	I'd Rather Go Blind/Close to Me	1976	2.00	4.00	8.00
WARNER BROS.					
GWB 0488	Got a Hold on Me/Love Will Show Us How	1986	—	—	3.00
—"Back to Back Hits" series					
29160	I'm the One/The Challenge	1984	—	—	3.00
29313	Love Will Show Us How/The Challenge	1984	—	—	3.00
29313 [PS]	Love Will Show Us How/The Challenge	1984	—	—	3.00
29372	Got a Hold on Me/Who's Dreaming This Dream	1984	—	—	3.00
29372 [PS]	Got a Hold on Me/Who's Dreaming This Dream	1984	—	—	3.00
Albums					
SIRE					
SR 6022	The Legendary Christine Perfect Album	1978	2.50	5.00	10.00
—Reissue with Warner Bros. distribution					
SASD-7522	The Legendary Christine Perfect Album	1976	3.75	7.50	15.00
—Original with ABC distribution					
WARNER BROS.					
25059	Christine McVie	1984	2.00	4.00	8.00
25059 [DJ]	Christine McVie	1984	3.75	7.50	15.00
—Promo on Quiex II vinyl					

MCWILLIAMS, DAVID

Number	Title (A Side/B Side)	Yr	VG	VG+	NM
45s					
COLUMBIA					
4-43793	Blue Eyes/God and My Country	1966	3.00	6.00	12.00
KAPP					
896	Days of Pearly Spencer/There's No Lock Upon My Door	1968	2.50	5.00	10.00
952	This Side of Heaven/Can I Get There by Candlelight?	1968	2.00	4.00	8.00
Albums					
KAPP					
KS-3547	Days of Pearly Spencer	1968	6.25	12.50	25.00

ME AND THEM

Number	Title (A Side/B Side)	Yr	VG	VG+	NM
45s					
U.S. SONGS					
601	Everything I Do Is Wrong/Show You Mean It Too	1964	3.75	7.50	15.00

ME & YOU

Number	Title (A Side/B Side)	Yr	VG	VG+	NM
45s					
PARKWAY					
121	Let the World In/I've Got My Time Baby	1966	5.00	10.00	20.00

MEADER, VAUGHN

Number	Title (A Side/B Side)	Yr	VG	VG+	NM
45s					
VERVE					
10309	St. Nick Visits the White House/'Twas the Night Before Christmas	1963	5.00	10.00	20.00
Albums					
CADENCE					
CLP 3060 [M]	The First Family	1962	3.75	7.50	15.00
CLP 3065 [M]	The First Family, Volume Two	1963	5.00	10.00	20.00

Number	Title (A Side/B Side)	Yr	VG	VG+	NM
CLP 25065 [S]	The First Family, Volume Two	1963	7.50	15.00	30.00
KAMA SUTRA					
KSBS-2038	The Second Coming	1971	3.75	7.50	15.00
LAURIE					
LLP-2035 [M]	Take That!	1966	3.75	7.50	15.00
VERVE					
V-15042 [M]	Have Some Nuts	1964	3.75	7.50	15.00
V6-15042 [S]	Have Some Nuts	1964	5.00	10.00	20.00
V-15050 [M]	If the Shoe Fits	1965	3.75	7.50	15.00

MEADOW

Supposedly, Laura Branigan was in this group.

45s

Number	Title (A Side/B Side)	Yr	VG	VG+	NM
PARAMOUNT					
0187	Here I Am/Something Borrowed, Something Blue	1973	2.00	4.00	8.00
0208	Cane and Able/Something Borrowed, Something Blue	1973	2.00	4.00	8.00

Albums

Number	Title (A Side/B Side)	Yr	VG	VG+	NM
PARAMOUNT					
PAS-6066	The Friend Ship	1973	5.00	10.00	20.00

MEADOWLARKS, THE

See DON JULIAN AND THE MEADOWLARKS.

MEAT LOAF

Also see STONEY AND MEATLOAF.

12-Inch Singles

Number	Title (A Side/B Side)	Yr	VG	VG+	NM
ATLANTIC					
PR 966 [DJ]	Getting Away with Murder (same on both sides)	1986	2.00	4.00	8.00
PR 997 [DJ]	Rock and Roll Mercenaries (same on both sides)	1986	2.00	4.00	8.00
CLEVELAND INT'L.					
AS 1277 [DJ]	I'm Gonna Love Her for Both of Us/Peel Out	1981	2.00	4.00	8.00
EPIC					
AS 477 [DJ]	Paradise by the Dashboard Light (7:55)//same (6:58 with play-by-play)/same (6:58 without play-by-play)	1978	5.00	10.00	20.00
—With "Bat Out of Hell" picture cover					
RCA					
JD-14050 [DJ]	(Give Me the Future with a) Modern Girl (LP Version) (7" Version)	1984	2.50	5.00	10.00
JW-14141 [DJ]	Surf's Up (LP Version)//Surf's Up (Edit)/Bad Attitude	1984	3.75	7.50	15.00

45s

Number	Title (A Side/B Side)	Yr	VG	VG+	NM
ATLANTIC					
89303	Rock 'N' Roll Mercenary/Execution Day	1987	—	—	3.00
—A-side with John Parr					
89340	Getting Away with Murder/Rock 'N' Roll Hero	1986	—	—	3.00
CLEVELAND INT'L.					
02490	I'm Gonna Love Her for Both of Us/Peel Out	1981	—	2.00	4.00
02607	Read 'Em and Weep/Peel Out	1981	—	2.00	4.00
04028	The Razor's Edge/You Never Can Be Too Sure About the Girl	1983	—	2.00	4.00
EPIC					
50467	You Took the Words Right Out of My Mouth/For Crying Out Loud	1977	2.00	4.00	8.00
50513	Two Out of Three Ain't Bad (3:50)/For Crying Out Loud	1978	—	2.50	5.00
50513	Two Out of Three Ain't Bad (5:12)/For Crying Out Loud	1978	—	3.00	6.00
50588	Paradise by the Dashboard Light/"Bat" Overture	1978	—	2.50	5.00
50634	You Took the Words Right Out of My Mouth/ Paradise by the Dashboard Light	1978	—	2.50	5.00
MCA					
54626	I'd Do Anything for Love (But I Won't Do That) (Single Edit)/I'd Do Anything for Love (But I Won't Do That) (Edit)	1993	—	2.00	4.00
54757	Rock and Roll Dreams Come Through/I'd Do Anything for Love (But I Won't Do That) (Live)	1993	—	2.00	4.00
54848	Objects in the Rear View Mirror May Appear Closer Than They Are/Two Out of Three Ain't Bad (Live)	1994	—	2.00	4.00
RCA					
PB-14101	(Give Me the Future with a) Modern Girl/Sailor to a Siren	1985	—	—	3.00
PB-14149	Surf's Up/Jumpin' the Sun	1985	—	—	3.00
RSO					
407	More Than You Deserve/Presence of the Lord	1974	3.00	6.00	12.00

Albums

Number	Title (A Side/B Side)	Yr	VG	VG+	NM
ATLANTIC					
81698	Blind Before I Stop	1986	2.00	4.00	8.00
CLEVELAND INT'L.					
FE 36007	Dead Ringer	1981	2.00	4.00	8.00
PE 36007	Dead Ringer	198?	—	3.00	6.00
—Budget-line reissue					
EPIC					
E99 34974 [PD]	Bat Out of Hell	1978	5.00	10.00	20.00
JE 34974	Bat Out of Hell	1979	2.00	4.00	8.00
—Dark blue label					
PE 34974	Bat Out of Hell	1977	2.50	5.00	10.00
—Orange label; originals do not have bar code on back cover					
PE 34974	Bat Out of Hell	1985	—	3.00	6.00
—Dark blue label; bar code on cover					
FE 38444	Midnight at the Lost and Found	1983	2.00	4.00	8.00
HE 44974	Bat Out of Hell	1981	10.00	20.00	40.00
—Half-speed mastered edition					
RCA VICTOR					
AFL1-5451	Bad Attitude	1985	2.00	4.00	8.00

MEDALLIONS, THE (1)

45s

Number	Title (A Side/B Side)	Yr	VG	VG+	NM
DOOTO					
419	For Better or For Worse/I Wonder, Wonder, Wonder	1957	7.50	15.00	30.00
—As "Vernon Green and the Medallions"					
425	A Lover's Prayer/Unseen	1957	7.50	15.00	30.00
—As "Vernon Green and the Medallions"					
446	Magic Mountain/59 Volvo	1959	6.25	12.50	25.00
—As "Vernon Green and the Medallions"					
454	Behind the Door/Rocket Ship	1959	6.25	12.50	25.00
—As "Vernon Green and the Medallions"					
DOOTONE					
347	The Letter/Buick 59	1955	50.00	100.00	200.00
—Red label					
347	The Letter/Buick 59	1955	15.00	30.00	60.00
—Black label					
357	The Telegram/Coupe de Ville Baby	1955	15.00	30.00	60.00
—Maroon label					
357	The Telegram/Coupe de Ville Baby	1955	37.50	75.00	150.00
—Blue label					
364	Edna/Speeding	1955	15.00	30.00	60.00
373	My Pretty Baby/I'll Never Love Again	1955	15.00	30.00	60.00
—As "Johnny Twovoice and the Medallions"					
379	Dear Darling/Don't Shoot Baby	1955	17.50	35.00	70.00
393	I Want a Love/Dance and Swing	1956	12.50	25.00	50.00
400	Shedding Tears for You/Push Button Automobile	1956	15.00	30.00	60.00
—As "Vernon Green and the Medallions"					
407	My Mary Lou/Did You Have Fun	1956	15.00	30.00	60.00
—As "Vernon Green and the Medallions"					
479	Can You Talk/You Don't Know	1964	3.75	7.50	15.00
MINIT					
32034	Look at Me, Look at Me/Am I Ever Gonna See My Baby	1968	5.00	10.00	20.00
—As "Vernon Green and the Medallions"					
PAN WORLD					
71	Dear Ann/Shimmy Shimmy Shake	1962	12.50	25.00	50.00
—As "Vernon Green and the Medallions"					

7-Inch Extended Plays

Number	Title (A Side/B Side)	Yr	VG	VG+	NM
DOOTONE					
202	(contents unknown)	1958	25.00	50.00	100.00
202 [PS]	Rhythm and Blues	1958	37.50	75.00	150.00

MEDALLIONS, THE (2)

45s

Number	Title (A Side/B Side)	Yr	VG	VG+	NM
ESSEX					
901	I Know/Laki-Lani	1955	100.00	200.00	400.00

MEDALLIONS, THE (3)

45s

Number	Title (A Side/B Side)	Yr	VG	VG+	NM
LENOX					
5556	You Are Irresistible/Why Do You Look at Me	1962	6.25	12.50	25.00

MEDALLIONS, THE (4)

45s

Number	Title (A Side/B Side)	Yr	VG	VG+	NM
SINGULAR					
1002	A Broken Heart/Lolo Baby	1957	12.50	25.00	50.00
SULTAN					
4004	Love That Girl/Carachi	1959	20.00	40.00	80.00

MEDALLIONS, THE (U)

Could be group (1), (3) or (4), or a totally different group.

45s

Number	Title (A Side/B Side)	Yr	VG	VG+	NM
SARG					
191	I Love You True/My Baby's Gone	1961	10.00	20.00	40.00
194	Lovin' Time/Home Town	1961	10.00	20.00	40.00

MEDIUM

Albums

Number	Title (A Side/B Side)	Yr	VG	VG+	NM
GAMMA					
GS-503	Medium	196?	25.00	50.00	100.00

MEDLEY, BILL

Also see THE RIGHTEOUS BROTHERS.

45s

Number	Title (A Side/B Side)	Yr	VG	VG+	NM
A&M					
1285	A Song for You/We've Only Just Begun	1971	—	2.50	5.00
1309	You've Lost That Lovin' Feeling/We've Only Just Begun	1971	—	2.50	5.00
1311	A Song for You/We've Only Just Begun	1971	—	2.00	4.00
1336	Help Me Make It Through the Night/Hung on You	1972	—	2.00	4.00
1350	Freedom for the Stallion/Damn Good Friend	1972	—	2.00	4.00
1371	A Simple Man/Missing You Too Long	1972	—	2.00	4.00
1434	Put a Little Love Away/It's Not Easy	1973	—	2.00	4.00
COLUMBIA					
07938	He Ain't Heavy, He's My Brother/The Bridge	1988	—	—	3.00
—B-side by Georgio Moroder					
CURB					
10542	Most of All You/I'm Gonna Be Strong	1989	—	—	3.00
76890	Don't Let Go/Since I Don't Have You	1990	—	—	3.00
—B-side by Ronnie McDowell					
ELEKTRA					
69281	Rude Awakening/Leave Love Behind	1989	—	—	3.00
—B-side by Jonathan Elias					
LIBERTY					
1402	Don't Know Much/Woman	1981	—	2.00	4.00
1412	Stay the Night/Grandma and Grandpa	1981	—	2.00	4.00
MCA					
53443	Brown Eyed Woman/You've Lost That Lovin' Feelin'	1988	—	—	3.00

Number	Title (A Side/B Side)	Yr	VG	VG+	NM
MGM					
13931	I Can't Make It Alone/One Day Girl	1968	2.00	4.00	8.00
13959	Brown Eyed Woman/Let the Good Times Roll	1968	2.00	4.00	8.00
14000	Peace Brother Peace/Winter Won't Come This Year	1968	2.00	4.00	8.00
14025	Something's So Wrong/This Is a Love Song	1969	2.00	4.00	8.00
14081	Reaching Back/Someone Is Standing Outside	1969	2.00	4.00	8.00
14099	Evie/Let Me Love Again	1969	2.00	4.00	8.00
14119	Hold On, I'm Comin'/Makin' My Way	1970	—	3.00	6.00
14145	Nobody Knows/Something's So Wrong	1970	—	3.00	6.00
14179	Gone/What Have You Got to Lose	1970	—	3.00	6.00
14202	Wasn't It Easy/Gone	1970	—	3.00	6.00
PARAMOUNT					
0089	Swing Low, Sweet Chariot/(B-side unknown)	1971	—	3.00	6.00
PLANET					
YB-13317	Right Here and Now/The Best of My Life	1982	—	2.00	4.00
YB-13425	I'm No Angel/I Need You in My Life	1983	—	—	3.00
YB-13474	For You/I Need You in My Life	1983	—	—	3.00
RCA					
5224-7-RX	(I've Had) The Time of My Life/Love Is Strange	1987	—	—	3.00
—A-side: With Jennifer Warnes; B-side by Mickey and Sylvia					
5224-7-RX [PS]	(I've Had) The Time of My Life/Love Is Strange	1987	—	2.00	4.00
—A-side: With Jennifer Warnes; B-side by Mickey and Sylvia					
PB-13692	I've Got Dreams to Remember/Till Your Memory's Gone	1983	—	—	3.00
PB-13753	I Still Do/I've Got Dreams to Remember	1984	—	—	3.00
PB-13851	Turn It Loose/I've Always Got the Heart to Sing the Blues	1984	—	—	3.00
PB-13962	She Keeps Me in One Piece/Old Friend	1984	—	—	—
—Unreleased					
PB-14021	Is There Anything I Can Do/Old Friend	1985	—	—	3.00
PB-14081	Women in Love/Stand Up	1985	—	—	3.00
REPRISE					
0413	I Surrender to Your Touch/Leavin' Town	1965	3.75	7.50	15.00
UNITED ARTISTS					
XW1256	Lay a Little Lovin' On Me/Wasn't That You Last Night	1978	—	2.00	4.00
XW1270	Statue of a Fool/Wasn't That You Last Night	1978	—	2.00	4.00
1349	Hello Rock & Roll/Still a Fool	1980	—	2.00	4.00
VERVE					
10569	That Lucky Old Sun/My Darling Clementine	1967	2.50	5.00	10.00

Albums

Number	Title (A Side/B Side)	Yr	VG	VG+	NM
A&M					
SP-3505	A Song for You	1971	3.00	6.00	12.00
SP-3517	Smile	1972	3.00	6.00	12.00
LIBERTY					
LT-1097	Sweet Thunder	1981	2.00	4.00	8.00
—Reissue of United Artists 1097					
MGM					
SE-4583	Bill Medley 100%	1968	5.00	10.00	20.00
SE-4603	Soft and Soulful	1969	5.00	10.00	20.00
SE-4640	Someone Is Standing Outside	1969	5.00	10.00	20.00
SE-4702	Nobody Knows	1970	3.75	7.50	15.00
SE-4741	Gone	1970	3.75	7.50	15.00
RCA VICTOR					
BXL1-4434	Right Here and Now	1982	2.50	5.00	10.00
CPL1-5352	Still Hung Up on You	1984	2.50	5.00	10.00
MHL1-8519 [EP]	I Still Do	1985	2.00	4.00	8.00
UNITED ARTISTS					
UA-LA929-H	Lay a Little Lovin' on Me	1978	2.50	5.00	10.00
LT-1097	Sweet Thunder	1980	2.50	5.00	10.00

MEEK, JOE

45s

Number	Title (A Side/B Side)	Yr	VG	VG+	NM
LONDON					
9634	Kennedy March/Theme of Freedom	1964	5.00	10.00	20.00

MEGATRONS, THE

45s

Number	Title (A Side/B Side)	Yr	VG	VG+	NM
ACOUSTICON					
101	Velvet Waters/The Merry Piper	1959	3.75	7.50	15.00
AUDICON					
101	Velvet Waters/The Merry Piper	1959	3.00	6.00	12.00
104	Whispering Winds/Tootie Flutie	1960	2.50	5.00	10.00
107	Dance of the Silhouettes/Ranchero	1960	2.50	5.00	10.00
110	Julienne/By the Waters of the Minnetonka	1960	2.50	5.00	10.00
LAURIE					
3291	Velvet Waters/The Merry Piper	1965	2.00	4.00	8.00
3310	A Love That Will Last Forever/The Detroit Sound	1965	2.00	4.00	8.00

MEL AND TIM

45s

Number	Title (A Side/B Side)	Yr	VG	VG+	NM
BAMBOO					
106	I've Got Puredee/(Instrumental)	1969	—	3.00	6.00
107	Backfield in Motion/Do It Right Baby	1969	2.00	4.00	8.00
—White label, not a promo					
107	Backfield in Motion/Do It Right Baby	1969	—	3.00	6.00
—Multicolor label					
109	Good Guys Only Win in the Movies/I Found That I Was Wrong	1970	—	3.00	6.00
112	Feeling Bad/I've Got Puredee	1970	—	3.00	6.00
114	Mail Call Time/Forget It, I've Got It	1970	—	3.00	6.00
116	We've Got a Groove to Move On/Never on Time	1970	—	3.00	6.00
118	I'm the One/Put An Extra Plus to Your Love	1971	—	3.00	6.00
STAX					
0127	Starting All Over Again/It Hurts to Want It So Bad	1972	—	2.50	5.00
0154	I May Not Be What You Want/Too Much Wheelin' and Dealin'	1973	—	2.50	5.00
0160	Heaven Knows/Don't Mess with My Money, My Honey, Oh My Woman	1973	—	2.50	5.00
0202	Those Little Things That Count/The Same Folks	1974	—	2.50	5.00
0224	Forever and a Day/That's the Way I Want to Live My Life	1974	—	2.50	5.00

Albums

Number	Title (A Side/B Side)	Yr	VG	VG+	NM
BAMBOO					
BMS-8001	Good Guys Only Win in the Movies	1970	6.25	12.50	25.00
STAX					
STS-3007	Starting All Over Again	1972	5.00	10.00	20.00
STS-5501	Mel and Tim	1974	5.00	10.00	20.00

MEL-O-DOTS, THE

45s

Number	Title (A Side/B Side)	Yr	VG	VG+	NM
APOLLO					
1192	One More Time/Just How Long	1952	750.00	1500.	3000.

MELA, DENNY

45s

Number	Title (A Side/B Side)	Yr	VG	VG+	NM
PARKWAY					
802	Forget My Past/Blondie	1959	3.75	7.50	15.00

MELANIE

45s

Number	Title (A Side/B Side)	Yr	VG	VG+	NM
AMHERST					
300	Who's Been Sleeping in My Bed (Edited)/Who's Been Sleeping in My Bed	1985	—	2.00	4.00
ATLANTIC					
3380	If I Needed You/Cyclone	1977	—	2.50	5.00
BLANCHE					
1	Imaginary Heroes/Detroit or Buffalo	1982	—	2.00	4.00
110	When You're Dead and Gone/Detroit or Buffalo	1982	—	2.00	4.00
BUDDAH					
113	Bo Bo's Party/I'm Back in Town	1969	—	3.00	6.00
135	Beautiful People/Any Guy	1969	—	3.00	6.00
161 [DJ]	Take Me Home (mono/stereo)	1970	—	3.00	6.00
—May be promo only					
167	Lay Down (Candles in the Rain)/Candles in the Rain	1970	—	3.00	6.00
167 [PS]	Lay Down (Candles in the Rain)/Candles in the Rain	1970	2.00	4.00	8.00
186	Peace Will Come (According to Plan)/Close to It All	1970	—	2.50	5.00
186	Peace Will Come (According to Plan)/Stop (I Don't Want to Hear It Anymore)	1970	—	2.50	5.00
186 [PS]	Peace Will Come (According to Plan)/Stop (I Don't Want to Hear It Anymore)	1970	—	3.00	6.00
202	Ruby Tuesday/Merry Christmas	1970	—	2.50	5.00
224	We Don't Know Where We're Going/The Good Book	1971	—	2.50	5.00
268	The Nickel Song/What Have They Done to My Song Ma	1971	—	2.50	5.00
268 [PS]	The Nickel Song/What Have They Done to My Song Ma	1971	—	3.00	6.00
304	I'm Back in Town/Johnny Boy	1972	—	2.50	5.00
COLUMBIA					
44349	My Beautiful People/God's Only Daughter	1967	2.50	5.00	10.00
44349 [PS]	My Beautiful People/God's Only Daughter	1967	5.00	10.00	20.00
44524	Garden in the City/Why Didn't My Mother Tell Me	1968	2.50	5.00	10.00
44524 [PS]	Garden in the City/Why Didn't My Mother Tell Me	1968	5.00	10.00	20.00
GORDIAN					
1947	Rag Doll/(B-side unknown)	1985	—	2.00	4.00
MIDSONG INT'L.					
40858	I'd Rather Leave While I'm in Love/Record People	1978	—	2.50	5.00
40903	Knock on Wood/Record People	1978	—	2.50	5.00
NEIGHBORHOOD					
4201	Brand New Key/Some Say (I Got Devil)	1971	—	3.00	6.00
—White label (not a promo)					
4201	Brand New Key/Some Say (I Got Devil)	1971	—	2.50	5.00
—Multicolor label					
4202	Ring the Living Bell/Railroad	1972	—	2.00	4.00
4202 [PS]	Ring the Living Bell/Railroad	1972	—	2.50	5.00
4204	Steppin'/Someday I'll Be a Farmer	1972	—	2.00	4.00
4207	Together Alone/Center of the Circle	1972	—	2.00	4.00
4207 [PS]	Together Alone/Center of the Circle	1972	—	2.50	5.00
4209	Stoneground Woman/Do You Believe	1972	—	2.00	4.00
4210	Bitter Bad/Do You Believe	1973	—	2.00	4.00
4212	Seeds/Some Say (I Got Devil)	1973	—	2.00	4.00
4213	Will You Love Me Tomorrow/Here I Am	1973	—	2.00	4.00
4213 [PS]	Will You Love Me Tomorrow/Here I Am	1973	—	2.50	5.00
4214	Love to Love Again/Fine and Feather	1974	—	2.00	4.00
4215	Lover's Cross/Holding Out	1974	—	2.00	4.00
10000	You're Not a Bad Ghost, Just an Old Song/Eyes of Man	1975	—	2.00	4.00
10001	Sweet Misery/Record Machine	1975	—	2.00	4.00
PORTRAIT					
51001	One More Try/Apathy	1981	—	2.00	4.00
STORK					
(no #)	Timothy Scott Bogart	1970	3.00	6.00	12.00
—One-sided promo of "Christopher Robin" to celebrate the birth of Neil Bogart's son					
TOMATO					
10007	Running After Love/Holding Out	1979	—	2.50	5.00
WORLD UNITED					
1947	Oh Boy/Brand New Key	1978	—	2.50	5.00

7-Inch Extended Plays

Number	Title (A Side/B Side)	Yr	VG	VG+	NM
BUDDAH					
SP 2 [DJ]	Merry Christmas/Christopher Robin//I'm Back In Town/I Really Loved Harold	1971	2.50	5.00	10.00
SP 2 [PS]	I'm Back in Town	1971	2.50	5.00	10.00

Albums

Number	Title (A Side/B Side)	Yr	VG	VG+	NM
ABC					
D-879	From the Beginning	1975	2.50	5.00	10.00
ACCORD					
SN-7109	What Have They Done to My Song Ma	1981	2.50	5.00	10.00
SN-7191	Beautiful People	1982	2.50	5.00	10.00

Number	Title (A Side/B Side)	Yr	VG	VG+	NM
AMHERST					
AMH-3302	Am I Real or What	1985	2.50	5.00	10.00
ATLANTIC					
SD 18190	Photograph	1976	2.50	5.00	10.00
BLANCHE					
BL 6177	Arabesque	1982	2.50	5.00	10.00
BUDDAH					
BDS-5024	Born to Be	1969	3.75	7.50	15.00
BDS-5041	Melanie	1969	3.75	7.50	15.00
BDS-5060	Candles in the Rain	1970	3.75	7.50	15.00
BDS-5066	Leftover Wine	1970	3.75	7.50	15.00
BDS-5074	My First Album	1971	3.00	6.00	12.00
BDS-5095	Garden in the City	1971	3.00	6.00	12.00
BDS-5132	Please Love Me	1973	3.00	6.00	12.00
B2D-5664 [(2)]	The Best...Melanie	197?	3.75	7.50	15.00
BDS-95000	The Good Book	1971	3.75	7.50	15.00
BDS-95005 [(2)]	Four Sides of Melanie	1972	3.75	7.50	15.00
MIDSONG					
MCA-3033	Phonogenic: Not Just Another Pretty Face	1978	2.50	5.00	10.00
NEIGHBORHOOD					
3000	As I See It Now	1974	3.00	6.00	12.00
3001	Sunsets and Other Beginnings	1975	3.00	6.00	12.00
47001	Gather Me	1971	3.00	6.00	12.00
47005	Stoneground Words	1972	3.00	6.00	12.00
48001	Madrugada	1974	3.00	6.00	12.00
49001 [(2)]	Melanie at Carnegie Hall	1973	3.75	7.50	15.00
PICKWICK					
SPC-3317	Try the Real Thing	197?	2.50	5.00	10.00
TOMATO					
TOM-2-9003 [(2)]	Ballroom Streets	1979	3.00	6.00	12.00

MELCHER, TERRY

Also see BRUCE AND TERRY.

Number	Title (A Side/B Side)	Yr	VG	VG+	NM
45s					
COLUMBIA					
42427	I Waited Too Long/That's All I Want	1962	5.00	10.00	20.00
—As "Terry Day"					
42427 [PS]	I Waited Too Long/That's All I Want	1962	10.00	20.00	40.00
—As "Terry Day"					
42678	Be a Soldier/I Love You Betty	1963	5.00	10.00	20.00
—As "Terry Day"					
42678 [PS]	Be a Soldier/I Love You Betty	1963	10.00	20.00	40.00
RCA VICTOR					
PB-10587	Fire in a Rainstorm/So Right Tonight	1976	2.50	5.00	10.00
Albums					
REPRISE					
MS 2185	Terry Melcher	1974	3.75	7.50	15.00

MELLO-HARPS, THE

Number	Title (A Side/B Side)	Yr	VG	VG+	NM
45s					
CASINO					
104	Gumma Gumma/No Good	1959	15.00	30.00	60.00
DO-RE-MI					
203	Love Is a Vow/Valerie	1956	4000.	6000.	8000.
TIN PAN ALLEY					
145/6	I Love Only You/Ain't Got the Money	1955	100.00	200.00	400.00
157/8	What Good Are My Dreams/Gone	1956	150.00	300.00	600.00
159	I Couldn't Believe/My Bleeding Heart	1956	150.00	300.00	600.00

MELLO-KINGS, THE

Number	Title (A Side/B Side)	Yr	VG	VG+	NM
45s					
HERALD					
502	Tonite Tonite/Do Baby Do	1957	125.00	250.00	500.00
—First pressing credits "The Mellotones"					
502	Tonite Tonite/Do Baby Do	1957	12.50	25.00	50.00
—Label corrected to "The Mello-Kings"; script print inside flag					
502	Tonite Tonite/Do Baby Do	1961	6.50	12.50	25.00
—Reissue; block print inside flag					
507	Chapel on the Hill/Sassafras	1957	7.50	15.00	30.00
511	Baby Tell Me Why Why Why/The Only Girl I'll Ever Know	1958	7.50	15.00	30.00
518	Valerie/She's Real Cool	1958	7.50	15.00	30.00
536	Chip Chip/Running to You	1959	7.50	15.00	30.00
—Both sides play as labeled					
536	Chip Chip/Running to You	1959	37.50	75.00	150.00
—Mispressing; plays "Rockin' at the Bandstand"/"Down in Cuba" by the Royal Holidays					
548	Our Love Is Beautiful/Dear Mr. Jock	1960	6.25	12.50	25.00
554	Kid Stuff/I Promise	1960	6.25	12.50	25.00
561	Penny/Till There Were None	1961	6.25	12.50	25.00
567	Love at First Sight/She's Real Cool	1961	6.25	12.50	25.00
LESCAY					
3009	Walk Softly/But You Lied	1962	7.50	15.00	30.00
7-Inch Extended Plays					
HERALD					
451	(contents unknown)	1957	75.00	150.00	300.00
451	(contents unknown)	1960	50.00	100.00	200.00
451 [PS]	The Fabulous Mello-Kings	1957	100.00	200.00	400.00
451 [PS]	The Fabulous Mello-Kings	1960	50.00	100.00	200.00
Albums					
COLLECTABLES					
COL-5020	Greatest Hits	198?	2.50	5.00	10.00
HERALD					
H-1013 [M]	Tonight-Tonight	1960	125.00	250.00	500.00
—Yellow label					
H-1013 [M]	Tonight-Tonight	196?	62.50	125.00	250.00
—Multi-color label					
RELIC					
LP-5035	Greatest Hits	198?	3.00	6.00	12.00

MELLO-MOODS, THE

Number	Title (A Side/B Side)	Yr	VG	VG+	NM
45s					
GAMBLE					
2512	Stop Taking My Love for Granted/Inspirational Pleasure	1972	2.50	5.00	10.00
HAMILTON					
143	I'm Lost/I Woke Up This Morning	1953	25.00	50.00	100.00
PRESTIGE					
799	Call on Me/I Tried and Tried and Tried	1953	175.00	350.00	700.00
856	I'm Lost/I Woke Up This Morning	1953	175.00	350.00	700.00
ROBIN					
104	I Couldn't Sleep a Wink Last Night/And You Just Can't Go Through Life Alone	1952	750.00	1500.	3000.
105	Where Are You (Now That I Need You)/How Could You	1952	1250.	2500.	5000.

MELLO-TONES, THE

More than one group.

Number	Title (A Side/B Side)	Yr	VG	VG+	NM
45s					
COLUMBIA					
6-900 (?)	When The Rain Gates Unfold/What Are They Doing in Heaven	1950	100.00	200.00	400.00
—Probably originally released on Columbia's short-lived special numbering system for 7-inch records					
39051	When The Rain Gates Unfold/What Are They Doing in Heaven	1950	75.00	150.00	300.00
39215	Looking for a City/Flysing Saucers	1951	75.00	150.00	300.00
DECCA					
48318	Winos on Parade/Man Loves Woman	1954	100.00	200.00	400.00
48319	I'm Just Another One in Love with You/I'm Gonna Get	1954	100.00	200.00	400.00
FASCINATION					
1001	Rosie Lee/I'll Never Fall in Love Again	1957	37.50	75.00	150.00
GEE					
1037	Rosie Lee/I'll Never Fall in Love Again	1957	10.00	20.00	40.00
1040	Ca-Sandra/Rattle Shake Roll	1957	10.00	20.00	40.00
OKEH					
6828	Rough and Rocky Road/Cool by the River Banks	1951	75.00	150.00	300.00

MELLOW DROPS, THE

Number	Title (A Side/B Side)	Yr	VG	VG+	NM
45s					
IMPERIAL					
5324	When I Grow Too Old to Dream/The Crazy Song	1955	50.00	100.00	200.00

MELLOWLARKS, THE

Number	Title (A Side/B Side)	Yr	VG	VG+	NM
45s					
ARGO					
5285	Sing a Silly Sing Song/Farewell to You, My Nancy	1958	6.25	12.50	25.00

MELLOWS, THE

Number	Title (A Side/B Side)	Yr	VG	VG+	NM
45s					
CANDLELIGHT					
1011	Moon of Silver/You're Gone	1956	37.50	75.00	150.00
1012	Farewell Farewell/No More Loneliness	1956	37.50	75.00	150.00
CELESTE					
3002	Lucky Guy/My Darling	1956	30.00	60.00	120.00
3004	I'm Yours/Sweet Lorraine	1956	150.00	300.00	600.00
JAY DEE					
793	How Sentimental Can I Be/Nothin' to Do	1954	50.00	100.00	200.00
797	Smoke from Your Cigarette/Pretty Baby	1954	62.50	125.00	250.00
801	I Was a Fool to Let You Go/I Still Care	1955	50.00	100.00	200.00
807	Yesterday's Memories/Loveable Lilly	1955	37.50	75.00	150.00

MELO GENTS, THE

Number	Title (A Side/B Side)	Yr	VG	VG+	NM
45s					
WARNER BROS.					
5056	Baby Be Mine/Get Off My Back	1959	12.50	25.00	50.00

MELODEARS, THE

Number	Title (A Side/B Side)	Yr	VG	VG+	NM
45s					
GONE					
5033	Summer Romance/Charock	1958	3.75	7.50	15.00
5040	It's Love Because/They Don't Say	1958	3.75	7.50	15.00

MELODY MAKERS, THE

Number	Title (A Side/B Side)	Yr	VG	VG+	NM
45s					
HOLLIS					
1001	Carolina Moon/Let's Make Love Worthwhile	1957	25.00	50.00	100.00
1002	The Nearnes of You/Gotta Go	1957	37.50	75.00	150.00

MELVIN, HAROLD, AND THE BLUE NOTES

Also see THE BLUE NOTES (1).

Number	Title (A Side/B Side)	Yr	VG	VG+	NM
12-Inch Singles					
PHILLY WORLD					
PR 751 [DJ]	Today's Your Lucky Day (6:20) (7:07)	1984	2.00	4.00	8.00
SOURCE					
13950	Prayin' (5:56)/Your Love Is Takin' Me on a Journey (5:55)	1979	3.00	6.00	12.00
45s					
ABC					
12240	Reaching for the World/Stay Together	1976	—	2.50	5.00
12268	After You Love Me, Why Do You Leave Me/Big Singing Star	1977	—	2.50	5.00
—With Sharon Paige					
12327	Baby, You Got My Nose Open/Try to Live a Day	1978	—	2.50	5.00
12368	Power of Love/Now Is the Time	1978	—	2.50	5.00
ARCTIC					
135	Go Away/What Can a Man Do	1967	2.50	5.00	10.00
LANDA					
703	Get Out (And Let Me Cry)/You May Not Love Me	1964	4.00	8.00	16.00
—As "The Blue Notes"					

Number	Title (A Side/B Side)	Yr	VG	VG+	NM
MCA					
41291	Tonight's the Night/If You're Looking for Someone to Love	1980	—	2.00	4.00
—With Sharon Paige					
51190	Hang On In There/If You Love Me, Really Love Me	1982	—	2.00	4.00
PHILADELPHIA INT'L.					
3516	I Miss You (Part I)/I Miss You (Part II)	1972	—	2.50	5.00
3520	If You Don't Know Me By Now/Let Me Into Your World	1972	—	2.50	5.00
3525	Yesterday I Had the Blues/Ebony Woman	1973	—	2.50	5.00
3525 [PS]	Yesterday I Had the Blues/Ebony Woman	1973	—	3.00	6.00
3533	The Love I Lost (Part 1)/The Love I Lost (Part 2)	1973	—	2.50	5.00
3543	Satisfaction Guaranteed (Or Take Your Love Back)/I'm Weak for You	1974	—	2.50	5.00
3552	Where Are All My Friends/Let It Be You	1974	—	2.50	5.00
3562	Bad Luck (Part 1)/Bad Luck (Part 2)	1975	—	2.50	5.00
3569	Hope That We Can Be Together Soon/Be for Real	1975	—	2.50	5.00
—With Sharon Paige					
3579	Wake Up Everybody (Part 1)/Wake Up Everybody (Part 2)	1975	—	2.50	5.00
3588	Tell the World How I Feel About 'Cha Baby/You Know How to Make Me Feel So Good	1976	—	2.50	5.00
PHILLY WORLD					
99709	I Really Love You/I Can't Let Go	1984	—	2.00	4.00
99735	Today's Your Lucky Day (Long)/Today's Your Lucky Day (Short)	1984	—	2.00	4.00
99761	Don't Give Me Up/(Instrumental)	1984	—	2.00	4.00
SOURCE					
41156	Prayin' (Part 1)/Prayin' (Part 2)	1979	—	2.00	4.00
41157	Tonight's the Night/Your Love Is Taking Me on a Journey	1979	—	2.00	4.00
41231	I Should Be Your Lover (Part 1)/I Should Be Your Lover (Part 2)	1980	—	2.00	4.00

Albums

Number	Title	Yr	VG	VG+	NM
ABC					
AB-969	Reaching for the World	1977	2.50	5.00	10.00
AB-1041	Now Is the Time	1978	2.50	5.00	10.00
MCA					
5261	All Things Happen in Time	1981	2.50	5.00	10.00
PHILADELPHIA INT'L.					
KZ 31648	Harold Melvin and the Blue Notes	1972	3.00	6.00	12.00
KZ 32407	Black & Blue	1973	3.00	6.00	12.00
ZQ 32407 [Q]	Black & Blue	1973	5.00	10.00	20.00
PZ 33148	To Be True	1975	3.00	6.00	12.00
PZ 33808	Wake Up Everybody	1975	3.00	6.00	12.00
PZQ 33808 [Q]	Wake Up Everybody	1975	5.00	10.00	20.00
PZ 34232	Collector's Item — All Their Greatest Hits!	1976	3.00	6.00	12.00
PHILLY WORLD					
90187	Talk It Up (Tell Everybody)	1985	2.50	5.00	10.00
SOURCE					
3197	The Blue Album	1980	2.50	5.00	10.00

MEMORIES, THE

45s

Number	Title (A Side/B Side)	Yr	VG	VG+	NM
WAY-LIN					
101	Love Bells/I Promise	1959	100.00	200.00	400.00

MEMPHIS MINNIE

45s

Number	Title (A Side/B Side)	Yr	VG	VG+	NM
CHECKER					
771	Broken Heart/Me and My Chauffeur	1953	1000.	2000.	3000.
J.O.B.					
1101	Kissing in the Dark/World of Trouble	1952	250.00	500.00	1000.

MENDES, SERGIO

Includes Brasil '66, '77, '86, '88, etc.

12-Inch Singles

Number	Title (A Side/B Side)	Yr	VG	VG+	NM
A&M					
12103	Dance Attack (Club Mix)/Dance Attack (Dub)	1984	—	3.00	6.00
12195	Nonstop (Remix)/(Instrumental)	1986	—	3.00	6.00
ELEKTRA					
ED 5602 [DJ]	What Is This?/Fanfarra	1992	2.00	4.00	8.00

45s

Number	Title (A Side/B Side)	Yr	VG	VG+	NM
ATLANTIC					
2472	I Say a Little Prayer/Comin' Home Baby	1968	—	3.00	6.00
2502	My Favorite Things/Tempo Feliz	1968	—	3.00	6.00
5056	All My Loving/The Telephone Song	1967	—	3.00	6.00
5076	The Great Arrival/Monday, Monday	1969	—	3.00	6.00
A&M					
807	Mas Que nada/The Joker	1966	—	3.00	6.00
814	Day Tripper/Slow Hot Wind	1966	—	3.00	6.00
825	Constant Rain (Chove Chuva)	1966	—	3.00	6.00
836	For Me/Gente	1967	—	3.00	6.00
853	Night and Day/Cinnamon and Clove	1967	—	2.50	5.00
872	Watch What Happens/The Frog	1967	—	2.50	5.00
910	Look Around/With a Little Help from My Friends	1968	—	2.50	5.00
924	The Look of Love/Like a Lover	1968	—	2.50	5.00
924 [PS]	The Look of Love/Like a Lover	1968	2.00	4.00	8.00
961	The Fool on the Hill/So Many Stars	1968	—	2.50	5.00
961 [PS]	The Fool on the Hill/So Many Stars	1968	2.00	4.00	8.00
986	Scarborough Fair/Canto Triste	1968	—	2.50	5.00
986 [PS]	Scarborough Fair/Canto Triste	1968	2.00	4.00	8.00
1049	Pretty World/Fiesta	1969	—	2.50	5.00
1049 [PS]	Pretty World/Fiesta	1969	—	3.00	6.00
1073	(Sittin' On) The Dock of the Bay/Song of No Regrets	1969	—	2.50	5.00
1073 [PS]	(Sittin' On) The Dock of the Bay/Song of No Regrets	1969	—	3.00	6.00
1132	Wichita Lineman/Ye Me Le	1969	—	2.50	5.00
1164	Norwegian Wood/Masquerade	1970	—	2.00	4.00
1209	For What It's Worth/Vira Mundo	1970	—	2.00	4.00
1226	Chelsea Morning/Where Are You Coming From	1970	—	2.00	4.00
1245	Lost in Paradise/Righteous Life	1971	—	2.00	4.00
1257	Aza Branca/Sometimes in Winter	1971	—	2.00	4.00
1279	Zanzibar/So Many People	1971	—	2.00	4.00
1313	After Midnight/Morro Velho	1971	—	2.00	4.00
1346	After Sunrise/The Grab	1972	—	2.00	4.00
2429	Summer Love/Life in the Movies	1982	—	2.00	4.00
2540	Never Gonna Let You Go/Carnival	1983	—	—	3.00
2563	Rainbow's End/Carnival	1983	—	—	3.00
2623	Olympia/Carnival	1984	—	—	3.00
2623 [PS]	Olympia/Carnival	1984	—	2.00	4.00
2639	Alibis/Confetti	1984	—	—	3.00
2662	Let's Give a Little More This Time/Confetti	1984	—	—	3.00
2672	Real Life/Confetti	1984	—	—	3.00
2706	Let's Give a Little More This Time/Confetti	1985	—	—	3.00
2859	Non-Stop/Flower of Bahia (Flor de Bahia)	1986	—	—	3.00
2875	Take This Love/Your Smile	1986	—	—	3.00
2917	What Do We Mean to Each Other/Flower of Bahia (Flor de Bahia)	1987	—	—	3.00
BELL					
45335	Love Music/Walk the Way You Walk	1973	—	2.00	4.00
45372	Where Is the Love/Hey, Look at the Sun	1973	—	2.00	4.00
45410	Put a Little Love Away/They Look at the Sun	1973	—	2.50	5.00
ELEKTRA					
45235	If I Ever Lose This Heaven/You Been Away Too Long	1975	—	2.00	4.00
45249	The Trouble With Hello Is Goodbye/Davy	1975	—	2.00	4.00
45283	Someday We'll All Be Free/Emerio	1975	—	2.00	4.00
45310	Sunny Day/Tell Me in a Whisper	1976	—	2.00	4.00
45360	Home Cooking/Real Thing	1976	—	2.00	4.00
45405	Love Me Tomorrow/Peninsula	1977	—	2.00	4.00
45416	The Real Thing/Peninsula	1977	—	2.00	4.00
45453	Love City/Peninsula	1978	—	2.00	4.00
45494	Midnight Lovers/Misturada	1978	—	2.00	4.00
45512	Waters of March/Misturada	1978	—	2.00	4.00
46064	Summer Dream/Lonely Woman	1979	—	2.00	4.00
46567	I'll Tell You/Lonely Woman	1979	—	2.00	4.00
46618	Let It Go/Magic Lady	1980	—	2.00	4.00

Albums

Number	Title	Yr	VG	VG+	NM
ATLANTIC					
1434 [M]	The Swinger from Rio	1965	3.75	7.50	15.00
SD 1434 [S]	The Swinger from Rio	1965	5.00	10.00	20.00
1466 [M]	Great Arrival	1966	3.75	7.50	15.00
SD 1466 [S]	Great Arrival	1966	5.00	10.00	20.00
1480 [M]	The Beat of Brazil	1967	5.00	10.00	20.00
SD 1480 [S]	The Beat of Brazil	1967	3.75	7.50	15.00
8112 [M]	Sergio Mendes In Person at the El Matador	1967	5.00	10.00	20.00
SD 8112 [S]	Sergio Mendes In Person at the El Matador	1967	3.75	7.50	15.00
SD 8177	Sergio Mendes' Favorite Things	1968	5.00	10.00	20.00
A&M					
LP-116 [M]	Sergio Mendes and Brasil '66	1966	3.00	6.00	12.00
LP-122 [M]	Equinox	1967	3.75	7.50	15.00
SP-3108	Fool on the Hill	198?	2.00	4.00	8.00
—Budget-line reissue					
SP-3258	Greatest Hits	198?	2.00	4.00	8.00
—Budget-line reissue					
SP-3522 [(2)]	The Sergio Mendes Foursider	1973	3.75	7.50	15.00
SP-4116 [S]	Sergio Mendes and Brasil '66	1966	3.75	7.50	15.00
SP-4122 [S]	Equinox	1967	3.75	7.50	15.00
SP-4137	Look Around	1968	3.75	7.50	15.00
SP-4160	Fool on the Hill	1968	3.75	7.50	15.00
SP-4197	Crystal Illusions	1969	3.75	7.50	15.00
SP-4236	Ye-Me-Le	1969	3.75	7.50	15.00
SP-4252	Greatest Hits	1970	3.75	7.50	15.00
SP-4284	Stillness	1970	3.75	7.50	15.00
SP-4315	Pais Tropical	1971	3.00	6.00	12.00
SP-4353	Primal Roots	1972	3.00	6.00	12.00
SP-4937	Sergio Mendes	1983	2.50	5.00	10.00
SP-4984	Confetti	1984	2.50	5.00	10.00
SP-5135	Sergio Mendes and Brasil '86	1986	2.50	5.00	10.00
SP-5250	Arara	1989	3.00	6.00	12.00
SP-6012 [(2)]	The Sergio Mendes Foursider	198?	2.50	5.00	10.00
—Budget-line reissue					
BELL					
1119	Love Music	1973	2.50	5.00	10.00
1305	Vintage 74	1974	2.50	5.00	10.00
CAPITOL					
ST 2294 [S]	In a Brazilian Bag	1965	15.00	30.00	60.00
T 2294 [M]	In a Brazilian Bag	1965	12.50	25.00	50.00
ELEKTRA					
6E-134	Sergio Mendes and Brasil '88	1978	2.50	5.00	10.00
6E-214	Magic Lady	1980	2.50	5.00	10.00
7E-1027	Sergio Mendes	1975	2.50	5.00	10.00
EQ-1027 [Q]	Sergio Mendes	1975	3.75	7.50	15.00
7E-1055	Homecooking	1976	2.50	5.00	10.00
7E-1102	Sergio Mendes and the New Brasil '77	1977	2.50	5.00	10.00
MOBILE FIDELITY					
1-118	Sergio Mendes and Brasil '66	1984	12.50	25.00	50.00
—Audiophile vinyl					
PHILIPS					
PHM 200263 [M]	Quiet Nights	1968	5.00	10.00	20.00
PHS 600263 [S]	Quiet Nights	1968	3.75	7.50	15.00
PICKWICK					
SPC-3149	So Nice	1972	2.50	5.00	10.00
TOWER					
ST 5052 [S]	In a Brazilian Bag	1966	12.50	25.00	50.00
—Reissue of Capitol 2294					
T 5052 [M]	In a Brazilian Bag	1966	10.00	20.00	40.00
—Reissue of Capitol 2294					

MEPHISTOPHELES

45s

Number	Title (A Side/B Side)	Yr	VG	VG+	NM
REPRISE					
0832	Cricket Song/Take a Jet	1969	3.00	6.00	12.00

Number	Title (A Side/B Side)	Yr	VG	VG+	NM
Albums					
REPRISE					
RS 6355	In Frustration I Hear Singing	1969	10.00	20.00	40.00

MERCED BLUE NOTES, THE

Number	Title (A Side/B Side)	Yr	VG	VG+	NM
45s					
ACCENT					
1069	Rufus/Your Tender Lips	1961	10.00	20.00	40.00
GALAXY					
738	Rufus Jr./Thumping	1965	7.50	15.00	30.00
744	Mama Rufus/Bad Bad Whiskey	1965	7.50	15.00	30.00
SOUL					
35007	Do the Pig/Thumping	1965	250.00	500.00	1000.
TRI-PHI					
1011	Midnight Sessions (Part 1)/Midnight Sessions (Part 2)	1962	12.50	25.00	50.00
1023	Whole Lotta Nothin'/Fragile	1963	10.00	20.00	40.00

MERCER, JOHNNY

Number	Title (A Side/B Side)	Yr	VG	VG+	NM
45s					
CAPITOL					
54-582	Baby It's Cold Outside/I Never Heard You Say	1949	7.50	15.00	30.00
—With Margaret Whiting					
F853	Jamboree Jones/Dixieland Band	1950	5.00	10.00	20.00
F982	She's Shimmyun on the Beach Again/At the Jazzland Ball	1950	5.00	10.00	20.00
F1261	Jingle Bells/Santa Claus Is Comin' to Town	1950	3.75	7.50	15.00
F1285	Winter Wonderland/Goofus	1950	3.75	7.50	15.00
F1618	One for My Baby/St. Louis Blues	1951	3.75	7.50	15.00
—Reissue of material first isued on 78					
F1641	Sugar Blues/Goofus	1951	3.75	7.50	15.00
—Reissue of material first isued on 78					
F2248	The Glow-Worm/New Ashmolean	1952	3.75	7.50	15.00
F15512	Candy/Ac-Cent-Tchu-Ate the Positive	1950	3.75	7.50	15.00
F15513	G.I. Jive/I Lost My Sugar in Salt Lake City	1950	3.75	7.50	15.00
F15514	On the Atchison, Topeka and the Santa Fe/Strip Polka	1950	3.75	7.50	15.00
—The above three comprise CCF-214; all are reissues of hits that charted from 1942-45					
Albums					
CAPITOL					
H 210 [10]	Music of Jerome Kern	1950	20.00	40.00	80.00
H 214 [10]	Johnny Mercer Sings	1950	20.00	40.00	80.00
T 907 [M]	Ac-Cent-Tchu-Ate the Positive	1957	12.50	25.00	50.00
JUPITER					
JLP-1001 [M]	Johnny Mercer Sings Just for Fun	1956	12.50	25.00	50.00

MERCER, WILL

Number	Title (A Side/B Side)	Yr	VG	VG+	NM
45s					
CONSTELLATION					
109	Penny Candy/Willowy Billowy Land	1963	3.75	7.50	15.00
SUN					
329	You're Just My Kind/Ballad of St. Mark's	1959	6.25	12.50	25.00

MERCHANTS OF DREAM, THE

Number	Title (A Side/B Side)	Yr	VG	VG+	NM
45s					
A&M					
989	Sing Me Life/Dorothy the Fairy Queen	1968	2.50	5.00	10.00
Albums					
A&M					
SP-4149	Strange Night Voyage	1969	6.25	12.50	25.00

MERCURY, FREDDIE

Also see QUEEN.

Number	Title (A Side/B Side)	Yr	VG	VG+	NM
12-Inch Singles					
COLUMBIA					
AS 1928 [DJ]	Love Kills (same on both sides)	1984	2.50	5.00	10.00
05314	Living on My Own (Extended Version) (7" Version)	1985	2.00	4.00	8.00
45s					
ANTHEM					
104	I Can Hear Music/Going Back	1973	25.00	50.00	100.00
—As "Larry Lurex"; A-side matrix number on label is "A-0009-REMIX"					
104	I Can Hear Music/Going Back	1973	37.50	75.00	150.00
—As "Larry Lurex"; A-side matrix number on label is "A-0009"					
CAPITOL					
B-5696	The Great Pretender/Exercises in Free Love	1987	—	—	3.00
B-5696 [PS]	The Great Pretender/Exercises in Free Love	1987	—	2.00	4.00
COLUMBIA					
04606	Love Kills/Rotwang's Party (Robot Dance)	1984	—	2.00	4.00
—Lead singer of Queen					
04606 [PS]	Love Kills/Rotwang's Party (Robot Dance)	1984	—	2.00	4.00
04869	I Was Born to Love You/.Stop All the Fighting	1985	—	2.00	4.00
04869 [PS]	I Was Born to Love You/.Stop All the Fighting	1985	—	2.00	4.00
05455	Living on My Own/She Blows Hot and Cold	1985	—	2.00	4.00
Albums					
COLUMBIA					
FC 40071	Mr. Bad Guy	1985	3.00	6.00	12.00

MERCY

Number	Title (A Side/B Side)	Yr	VG	VG+	NM
45s					
SUNDI					
6811	Love (Can Make You Happy)/Fire Ball	1969	2.00	4.00	8.00
WARNER BROS.					
7291	Love Can Make You Happy/Happy As Can Be, La La La	1969	3.75	7.50	15.00
—Pressed in U.S. for export only; A-side is a re-recording of the hit on Sundi					
7297	Forever/The Morning's Come	1969	—	3.00	6.00
7331	Hello Baby/Heard You Went Away	1969	—	3.00	6.00
Albums					
SUNDI					
SRLP-803	The Mercy & Love (Can Make You Happy)	1969	5.00	10.00	20.00
—Has the original version of the title song plus filler instrumentals					
WARNER BROS.					
WS 1799	Love (Can Make You Happy)	1969	3.75	7.50	15.00
—"Love (Can Make You Happy)" was re-recorded for this LP					

MERKIN

Number	Title (A Side/B Side)	Yr	VG	VG+	NM
Albums					
WINDI					
1004/5	Music from Merkin	1972	100.00	200.00	400.00

MERMAIDS, THE

See THE MURMAIDS.

MERRI-MEN, THE

Another group containing former members of BILL HALEY AND HIS COMETS.

Number	Title (A Side/B Side)	Yr	VG	VG+	NM
45s					
APT					
25051	Big Daddy/St, Louis Blues	1960	6.25	12.50	25.00

MERRY ELVES, THE

Number	Title (A Side/B Side)	Yr	VG	VG+	NM
45s					
ARGUS					
250	Rock & Roll Around the Christmas Tree/I Love Christmas	1964	2.50	5.00	10.00

MERRY-GO-ROUND, THE

Also see EMMITT RHODES.

Number	Title (A Side/B Side)	Yr	VG	VG+	NM
45s					
A&M					
834	Live/Time Will Show the Wiser	1967	2.50	5.00	10.00
857	Gonna Fight the World/We're in Love	1967	2.50	5.00	10.00
863	You're a Very Lovely Woman/Where Have You Been All My Life	1967	2.50	5.00	10.00
886	Had to Run Around/She Laughed Loud	1967	2.50	5.00	10.00
920	Missing You/Listen, Listen	1968	2.50	5.00	10.00
957	Highway/'Til the Day After	1968	2.50	5.00	10.00
Albums					
A&M					
LP-132 [M]	The Merry-Go-Round	1967	10.00	20.00	40.00
SP-4132 [S]	The Merry-Go-Round	1967	7.50	15.00	30.00
RHINO					
RNLP 126	The Best of the Merry-Go-Round	1985	2.50	5.00	10.00

MERRYWEATHER, NEIL

Number	Title (A Side/B Side)	Yr	VG	VG+	NM
45s					
CAPITOL					
2537	Curiosity/Feeling of Freedom	1969	2.00	4.00	8.00
MERCURY					
73619	Hollywood Boulevard/High Altitude Hide and Seek	1974	—	2.50	5.00
Albums					
CAPITOL					
SKAO-220	Merryweather	1969	3.75	7.50	15.00
STBB-278 [(2)]	Word of Mouth	1969	5.00	10.00	20.00
KENT					
KST-546	Neil Merryweather and the Boers	197?	3.75	7.50	15.00
MERCURY					
SRM-1-1007	Space Rangers	1974	3.00	6.00	12.00
SRM-1-1024	Kryptonite	1975	3.00	6.00	12.00

MERRYWEATHER AND CAREY

Number	Title (A Side/B Side)	Yr	VG	VG+	NM
45s					
RCA VICTOR					
74-0429	Shop Around/If I Were You	1971	—	3.00	6.00
Albums					
RCA VICTOR					
LSP-4442	Ivar Avenue Reunion	1970	3.75	7.50	15.00
LSP-4485	Vacuum Cleaner	1971	3.75	7.50	15.00

MERSEY LADS, THE

Number	Title (A Side/B Side)	Yr	VG	VG+	NM
45s					
MGM					
13481	Johnny No Love/What 'Cha Gonna Do Baby	1966	3.75	7.50	15.00

MERSEYBEATS, THE

Number	Title (A Side/B Side)	Yr	VG	VG+	NM
45s					
FONTANA					
1513	It Would Take a Long Time/Don't Let It Happen to Us	1965	3.75	7.50	15.00
1532	I Love You, Yes I Do/See Me Back	1965	3.75	7.50	15.00
1882	Mr. Moonlight/I Think of You	1964	3.75	7.50	15.00
1905	Don't Turn Around/Really Mystified	1964	3.75	7.50	15.00
1950	See Me Back/Last Night	1964	3.75	7.50	15.00
Albums					
ARC INTERNATIONAL					
834 [M]	England's Best Sellers	1964	10.00	20.00	40.00

MERSEYBOYS, THE

Number	Title (A Side/B Side)	Yr	VG	VG+	NM
Albums					
VEE JAY					
VJ-1101 [M]	15 Greatest Songs of the Beatles	1964	25.00	50.00	100.00
VJS-1101 [S]	15 Greatest Songs of the Beatles	1964	37.50	75.00	150.00

Number	Title (A Side/B Side)	Yr	VG	VG+	NM
MERSEYS, THE					
45s					
MERCURY					
72582	Sorrow/Some Other Day	1966	5.00	10.00	20.00
MESHEL, BILLY					
45s					
OLD TOWN					
1181	My Little Angel/Tiger and the 71st Street Sharks	1965	3.00	6.00	12.00
PROBE					
459	I Say Hello When I'm Leaving/(It Ain't Easy Being) Shirley Newman's Boyfriend	1969	2.50	5.00	10.00
462	Today Has Been Cancelled/That's What Sends Him to the Bowery	1969	2.50	5.00	10.00
Albums					
PROBE					
CPLP-4502	The Love Songs of A. Wilbur Meshel	1969	5.00	10.00	20.00
MESMERIZING EYE, THE					
Albums					
SMASH					
MGS-27090 [M]	Psychedelia — A Musical Light Show	1967	12.50	25.00	50.00
SRS-67090 [S]	Psychedelia — A Musical Light Show	1967	15.00	30.00	60.00
MESSENGERS, THE (1)					
Milwaukee-based rock group.					
45s					
RARE EARTH					
5032	That's the Way a Woman Is/In the Jungle	1971	—	2.50	5.00
SOUL					
35037	Window Shopping/California Soul	1967	2.50	5.00	10.00
U.S.A.					
866	Midnight Hour/Hard Hard Year	1967	3.75	7.50	15.00
—As "The Messengers"					
866	Midnight Hour/Up 'Til Now	1967	3.00	6.00	12.00
—As "Michael and the Messengers"					
874	Romeo and Juliet/Lies	1967	3.75	7.50	15.00
—As "Michael and the Messengers"					
Albums					
RARE EARTH					
RS-509	The Messengers	1969	5.00	10.00	20.00
MESSENGERS, THE (2)					
45s					
ERA					
3143	Let Me Be Your Man/You've Got Me Cryin'	1964	3.00	6.00	12.00
MESSENGERS, THE (3)					
British group.					
45s					
MGM					
13293	I'm Stealin' Back/This Little Light of Mine	1964	3.00	6.00	12.00
13346	When Did You Leave Heaven/More Pretty Girls Than One	1965	3.00	6.00	12.00
MESSENGERS, THE (4)					
Chicago group; after THE MESSENGERS (1) changed record labels, this group recorded as "Michael and the Messengers" on U.S.A.					
45s					
U.S.A.					
889	Run and Hide/She Was the Girl	1967	2.00	4.00	8.00
—As "Michael and the Messengers"					
897	Gotta Take It Easy/I Need Her Here	1968	2.00	4.00	8.00
—As "Michael and the Messengers"					
MESSINA, JIM					
Also see BUFFALO SPRINGFIELD; LOGGINS AND MESSINA; POCO.					
45s					
AUDIO FIDELITY					
098	The Breeze and I/Straight Man	1964	7.50	15.00	30.00
COLUMBIA					
11094	New and Different Way/(Is This) Lovin' You Lady	1979	—	2.00	4.00
11182	Do You Want to Dance/Seeing You (For the First Time)	1980	—	2.00	4.00
FEATURE					
101	Panther Pounce/Tiger Tail	1964	7.50	15.00	30.00
ULTIMA					
705	Drag Bike Boogie/A-Rab	1964	7.50	15.00	30.00
VIV					
1000	Side Track/Sherrie	1965	6.25	12.50	25.00
WARNER BROS.					
29278	Big Tease/The Island	1984	—	2.00	4.00
29457	Forever My Love/One More Mile	1983	—	2.00	4.00
49784	Move Into Your Heart/Stay the Night	1981	—	2.00	4.00
—With Pauline Wilson					
49839	It's All Right Here/Move Into Your Heart	1981	—	2.00	4.00
Albums					
AUDIO FIDELITY					
DFM-3037 [M]	The Dragsters	1964	20.00	40.00	80.00
DFS-7037 [S]	The Dragsters	1964	25.00	50.00	100.00
COLUMBIA					
JC 36141	Oasis	1979	2.50	5.00	10.00
THIMBLE					
TLP-3	Jim Messina	197?	3.75	7.50	15.00
WARNER BROS.					
BSK 3559	Messina	1981	2.50	5.00	10.00
BSK 3559 [DJ]	Messina	1981	5.00	10.00	20.00
—Promo-only version on Quiex II vinyl					
23825	One More Mile	1983	2.50	5.00	10.00
METERS, THE					
Also see AARON NEVILLE.					
45s					
JOSIE					
1001	Sophisticated Cissy/Sehorn's Farm	1968	2.50	5.00	10.00
1005	Cissy Strut/Here Comes the Meter Man	1969	2.50	5.00	10.00
1008	Ease Back/Ann	1969	2.50	5.00	10.00
1013	Dry Spell/Look-Ka Py Py	1969	2.50	5.00	10.00
1015	Look-Ka Py Py/This Is My Last Affair	1970	2.50	5.00	10.00
1018	Chicken Strut/Hey! Last Minute	1970	2.50	5.00	10.00
1021	Hand Clapping Song/Joog	1970	2.50	5.00	10.00
1024	A Message from the Meters/Zony Mash	1970	2.50	5.00	10.00
1026	Stretch Your Rubber Band/Groovy Lady	1971	2.50	5.00	10.00
1029	(The World Is a Bit Under the Weather) Doodle-Oop/I Need More Time	1971	2.50	5.00	10.00
1031	Good Old Funky Music/Sassy Lady	1971	2.50	5.00	10.00
REPRISE					
1086	Do the Dirt/Smiling	1972	2.00	4.00	8.00
1106	Cabbage Alley/The Flower Song	1972	2.00	4.00	8.00
1135	Chug Chug Chug-A-Lug (Part 1)/Chug Chug Chug-A-Lug (Part 2)	1972	2.00	4.00	8.00
1307	Hey Pocky A-Way/Africa	1974	—	3.00	6.00
1314	People Say/Loving You Is On My Mind	1974	—	3.00	6.00
1338	Running Fast/They All Ask'd for You	1975	—	3.00	6.00
1357	Disco Is the Thing Today/Mister Moon	1976	—	3.00	6.00
1372	Trick Bag/Find Yourself	1976	—	3.00	6.00
WARNER BROS.					
8434	Be My Lady/No More Okey Doke	1977	—	2.50	5.00
Albums					
JOSIE					
JOS-4010	The Meters	1969	17.50	35.00	70.00
JOS-4011	Look-Ka Py Py	1970	17.50	35.00	70.00
JOS-4012	Struttin'	1070	17.50	35.00	70.00
REPRISE					
MS 2076	Cabbage Alley	1972	17.50	35.00	70.00
MS 2200	Rejuvenation	1974	12.50	25.00	50.00
MS 2228	Fire on the Bayou	1975	12.50	25.00	50.00
MS 2252	Trick Bag	1976	12.50	25.00	50.00
ROUNDER					
2103	Look-Ka Py Py	1990	5.00	10.00	20.00
—Reissue of Josie 4011					
2104	Good Old Funky Music	1990	5.00	10.00	20.00
VIRGO					
12002	The Best of the Meters	1972	12.50	25.00	50.00
WARNER BROS.					
BS 3042	New Directions	1977	12.50	25.00	50.00
METRONOMES, THE (1)					
45s					
CADENCE					
1310	I Love My Girl/I'm Gonna Get Me a Girl Somehow	1957	25.00	50.00	100.00
1339	How Much I Love You/Dear Don	1957	30.00	60.00	120.00
METRONOMES, THE (2)					
45s					
CHALLENGE					
9157	Hot Time/Tears, Tears, Tears	1962	3.75	7.50	15.00
MAUREEN					
1000	My Dearest Darling/The Chickie-Goo	1962	12.50	25.00	50.00
METRONOMES, THE (U)					
Could be completely different groups.					
Albums					
STRAND					
SL-1057 [M]	The Fabulous Metronomes Sing the Standard Hits	1962	7.50	15.00	30.00
SLS-1057 [S]	The Fabulous Metronomes Sing the Standard Hits	1962	10.00	20.00	40.00
WYNNE					
106 [M]	And Now... The Metronomes	1960	30.00	60.00	120.00
METROS, THE (1)					
45s					
1-2-3					
1720	If You Can Feel/The Dampness from Your Kiss	1969	2.50	5.00	10.00
RCA VICTOR					
47-8994	Sweetest One/Time Changes Things	1966	3.75	7.50	15.00
47-9159	Since I Found My Baby/No Baby	1967	20.00	40.00	80.00
47-9331	Let's Groove/The Replacer	1967	6.25	12.50	25.00
Albums					
RCA VICTOR					
LPM-3776 [M]	Sweetest One	1967	20.00	40.00	80.00
LSP-3776 [S]	Sweetest One	1967	25.00	50.00	100.00
METROS, THE (2)					
45s					
JUST					
1502	All of My Life/Lookin'	1959	100.00	200.00	400.00
METROTONES, THE					
45s					
COLUMBIA					
40420	A-Ting-a-Ling/Tonight	1955	5.00	10.00	20.00
40486	Write Me Baby/Even Though	1955	5.00	10.00	20.00
RESERVE					
116	Please Come Back/Skitter Skatter	1957	62.50	125.00	250.00
7-Inch Extended Plays					
COLUMBIA					
B-2026	(contents unknown)	1955	5.00	10.00	20.00
B-2026 [PS]	Tops in Rock and Roll, Vol. 1	1955	5.00	10.00	20.00

Number	Title (A Side/B Side)	Yr	VG	VG+	NM
B-2027	(contents unknown)	1955	5.00	10.00	20.00
B-2027 [PS]	Tops in Rock and Roll, Vol. 2	1955	5.00	10.00	20.00
Albums					
COLUMBIA					
CL 6341 [10]	Tops in Rock and Roll	1955	62.50	125.00	250.00

MFSB

Number	Title (A Side/B Side)	Yr	VG	VG+	NM
45s					
PHILADELPHIA INT'L.					
3528	Family Affair/Layin' Low	1973	—	2.50	5.00
3540	TSOP (The Sound of Philadelphia)/Something for Nothing	1974	—	2.50	5.00
3547	Love Is the Message/My One and Only Love	1974	—	2.50	5.00
3567	Sexy/Human Machine	1975	—	2.50	5.00
3576	T.L.C. (Tender Lovin' Care)/Love Has No Time or Place	1975	—	2.50	5.00
3578	The Zip/My Mood	1975	—	2.50	5.00
3583	Smile Happy/When Your Love Is Gone	1976	—	2.50	5.00
3589	Philadelphia Freedom/South Philly	1976	—	2.50	5.00
3600	Summertime And I'm Feelin' Mellow/Hot Summer Nights	1976	—	2.50	5.00
3607	We Got the Time/(B-side unknown)	1976	—	2.50	5.00
3626	I'm On Your Side/Picnic in the Park	1977	—	2.50	5.00
3641	K-Jee/My Mood	1978	—	2.50	5.00
3650	Use Ta Be My Guy/Redwood Beach	1978	—	2.50	5.00
3663	Let's Party Down/To Be in Love	1978	—	2.50	5.00
3668	Dance with Me Tonight/Is It Something I Said	1979	—	2.50	5.00
TSOP					
02022	Mysteries of the World/Thank You Miss Scott	1981	—	2.00	4.00
4797	Manhattan Skyline/Metamorphosis	1980	—	2.00	4.00
Albums					
PHILADELPHIA INT'L.					
KZ 32046	MFSB	1973	2.50	5.00	10.00
KZ 32707	Love Is the Message	1974	2.50	5.00	10.00
ZQ 32707 [Q]	Love Is the Message	1974	4.50	9.00	18.00
PZ 33158	Universal Love	1975	2.50	5.00	10.00
PZ 33845	Philadelphia Freedom	1975	2.50	5.00	10.00
PZQ 33845 [Q]	Philadelphia Freedom	1975	4.50	9.00	18.00
PZ 34238	Summertime	1976	2.50	5.00	10.00
PZ 34658	The End of Phase One	1977	2.50	5.00	10.00
JZ 35516	The Gamble-Huff Orchestra	1978	2.50	5.00	10.00
TSOP					
JZ 36405	Mysteries of the World	1980	2.50	5.00	10.00

MICHAEL AND THE MESSENGERS

See THE MESSENGERS (1); THE MESSENGERS (4).

MICHAELS, LEE

Number	Title (A Side/B Side)	Yr	VG	VG+	NM
45s					
A&M					
911	Sounding the Sleep/Love	1968	—	3.00	6.00
912	Tomorrow/Sounding the Sleep	1968	—	3.00	6.00
942	If I Lose You/My Friends	1968	—	3.00	6.00
1048	Goodbye, Goodbye/The War	1969	—	2.50	5.00
1095	Heighty Ho/Want My Baby	1969	—	2.50	5.00
1219	Uummmm My Lady/What Now America	1970	—	2.50	5.00
1262	Do You Know What I Mean/Keep the Circle Turning	1971	—	2.50	5.00
1303	Can I Get a Witness/You Are What You Do	1971	—	2.00	4.00
1326	Hold On to Freedom/Own Special Way	1972	—	2.00	4.00
1448	Rock Me Baby/Heighty Ho	1973	—	2.00	4.00
COLUMBIA					
45874	Same Old Song/Rock and Roll Community	1973	—	2.50	5.00
Albums					
A&M					
SP-3158	Lee Michaels	198?	2.00	4.00	8.00
—Budget-line reissue					
SP-3518	Live	1973	3.75	7.50	15.00
SP-4140	Carnival of Life	1968	10.00	20.00	40.00
SP-4152	Recital	1968	5.00	10.00	20.00
SP-4199	Lee Michaels	1969	3.75	7.50	15.00
SP-4249	Barrel	1970	3.75	7.50	15.00
SP-4302	5th	1971	3.75	7.50	15.00
SP-4336	Space and First Takes	1972	3.75	7.50	15.00
COLUMBIA					
CQ 32275 [Q]	Nice Day for Something	1973	5.00	10.00	20.00
KC 32275	Nice Day for Something	1973	3.00	6.00	12.00
KC 32846	Tailface	1974	3.00	6.00	12.00

MICHAELS, MARILYN

Number	Title (A Side/B Side)	Yr	VG	VG+	NM
45s					
RCA VICTOR					
47-7771	Tell Tommy I Miss Him/Everyone Was There But You	1960	5.00	10.00	20.00
47-7831	Past the Age of Innocence/Danny	1961	3.75	7.50	15.00

MICKEY AND KITTY

MICKEY BAKER (ex-MICKEY AND SYLVIA) and Kitty Noble.

Number	Title (A Side/B Side)	Yr	VG	VG+	NM
45s					
ATLANTIC					
2024	Ooh-Sha-Lala/The Kid Brother	1959	3.75	7.50	15.00
2036	First Love/St. Louis Blues	1959	3.75	7.50	15.00
2046	My Reverie/Buttercup	1959	3.75	7.50	15.00

MICKEY AND SYLVIA

Also see MICKEY BAKER; SYLVIA (1).

Number	Title (A Side/B Side)	Yr	VG	VG+	NM
45s					
ALL PLATINUM					
2307	Lovedrops/Because You Do It to Me	1969	—	3.00	6.00
2310	Anytime/Souling with Mickey and Sylvia	1969	—	3.00	6.00
CAT					
102	Fine Love/Speedy Life	1954	10.00	20.00	40.00
—As "Little" Sylvia Vanderpool and Mickey Baker					
GROOVE					
0164	No Good Lover/Walkin' in the Rain	1956	7.50	15.00	30.00
0175	Love Is Strange/I'm Going Home	1956	7.50	15.00	30.00
KING					
5737	Baby, Let's Dance/Oh Yea, Ah Ah	1963	3.00	6.00	12.00
6006	Love Is Strange/Darling	1965	2.50	5.00	10.00
RAINBOW					
316	I'm So Glad/Se De Boom Run Dun	1955	7.50	15.00	30.00
318	Forever and a Day/Ride, Sally, Ride	1955	7.50	15.00	30.00
RCA					
5224-7-RX	Love Is Strange/(I've Had) The Time of My Life	1987	—	—	3.00
—B-side by Bill Medley and Jennifer Warnes					
RCA VICTOR					
APAO-0080	Love Is Strange/Dearest	1973	—	3.00	6.00
37-7877	Love Is the Only Thing/Love Lesson	1961	12.50	25.00	50.00
—"Compact Single 33" (small hole, plays at LP speed)					
47-7403	To the Valley/Oh Yeah! Uh-Huh	1958	5.00	10.00	20.00
47-7774 [M]	Sweeter As the Days Go By/Mommy Out De Light	1960	3.75	7.50	15.00
47-7811 [M]	What Would I Do/This Is My Story	1960	5.00	10.00	20.00
47-7877	Love Is the Only Thing/Love Lesson	1961	3.75	7.50	15.00
47-8517	Let's Shake Some More/Gypsy	1965	3.00	6.00	12.00
47-8582	Fallin' in Love/From the Beginning of Time	1965	3.00	6.00	12.00
61-7774 [S]	Sweeter As the Days Go By/Mommy Out De Light	1960	10.00	20.00	40.00
—"Living Stereo" (large hole, plays at 45 rpm)					
61-7811 [S]	What Would I Do/This Is My Story	1960	10.00	20.00	40.00
—"Living Stereo" (large hole, plays at 45 rpm)					
STANG					
5004	Rocky Raccoon/Souling with Mickey and Sylvia	1969	2.00	4.00	8.00
5047	Baby You're So Fine/Anytime You Want To	1973	—	3.00	6.00
VIK					
0252	Love Is Strange/I'm Going Home	1957	7.50	15.00	30.00
0267	There Oughta Be a Law/Dearest	1957	6.25	12.50	25.00
0280	Two Shadows on Your Window/Love Will Make You Fail in School	1957	6.25	12.50	25.00
0290	Love Is a Treasure/Let's Have a Picnic	1957	6.25	12.50	25.00
0297	There'll Be No Backin' Out/Where Is My Honey	1957	6.25	12.50	25.00
0324	Rock and Stroll Room/Bewildered	1958	5.00	10.00	20.00
0334	It's You I Love/True, True Love	1958	5.00	10.00	20.00
WILLOW					
23000	Baby, You're So Fine/Lovedrops	1961	3.75	7.50	15.00
23002	Darling (I Miss You So)/I'm Guilty	1961	3.75	7.50	15.00
23004	Since I Fell for You/He Gave Me Everything	1962	3.75	7.50	15.00
23006	Love Is Strange/Walking in the Rain	1962	3.75	7.50	15.00
7-Inch Extended Plays					
GROOVE					
018	(contents unknown)	1957	37.50	75.00	150.00
018 [PS]	Mickey and Sylvia	1957	37.50	75.00	150.00
VIK					
262	(contents unknown)	1957	20.00	40.00	80.00
262 [PS]	Love Is Strange	1957	20.00	40.00	80.00
Albums					
RCA CAMDEN					
CAL-863 [M]	Love Is Strange	1965	12.50	25.00	50.00
CAS-863(e) [R]	Love Is Strange	1965	7.50	15.00	30.00
RCA VICTOR					
APM1-0327	Do It Again	1973	3.00	6.00	12.00
VIK					
LX-1102 [M]	New Sounds	1957	100.00	200.00	400.00

MIDDLE OF THE ROAD

Number	Title (A Side/B Side)	Yr	VG	VG+	NM
45s					
RCA VICTOR					
74-0407	Chirpy Chirpy Cheep Cheep/Rainin' 'N Painin'	1970	—	2.50	5.00
74-0539	Tweedle Dee, Tweedle Dum/Give It Time	1971	—	2.00	4.00
74-0612	Soley Soley/To Remind Me	1971	—	2.00	4.00
74-0732	On This Land/Talk of All the U.S.A.	1972	—	2.00	4.00
Albums					
RCA VICTOR					
LSP-4674	Acceleration	1972	3.00	6.00	12.00

MIDDLETON, TONY

Also see THE WILLOWS.

Number	Title (A Side/B Side)	Yr	VG	VG+	NM
45s					
ABC-PARAMOUNT					
10695	You Spoiled My Reputation/If I Could Write a Song	1965	7.50	15.00	30.00
ALFA					
113	My Home Town/Please Take Me	1962	3.00	6.00	12.00
ALTO					
2001	Untouchable/I Need You	1960	3.00	6.00	12.00
A&M					
1084	Angela/Keep On Dancing	1969	5.00	10.00	20.00
1124	Harlem Lady/Sound of Goodbye	1969	3.75	7.50	15.00
BIG TOP					
3037	Unchained Melody/Sweet Baby of Mine	1960	7.50	15.00	30.00
ELDORADO					
508	First Taste of Love/Only My Heart	1957	7.50	15.00	30.00
GONE					
5015	Let's Fall in Love/Say Yeah	1957	15.00	30.00	60.00
MALA					
544	Out of This World/My Baby Likes to Boogaloo	1966	6.25	12.50	25.00
MGM					
13493	Don't Ever Leave Me/To the Ends of the Earth	1966	10.00	20.00	40.00
MR. G					
811	Let Me Down Easy (Part 1)/Let Me Down Easy (Part 2)	1968	3.00	6.00	12.00
815	Good Morning World/(B-side unknown)	1968	3.00	6.00	12.00

Number	Title (A Side/B Side)	Yr	VG	VG+	NM
PHILIPS					
40151	I Need You Tonight/Send Me Away	1963	3.00	6.00	12.00
40184	Too Hot to Handle/I Just Couldn't Help Myself	1964	3.00	6.00	12.00
ROULETTE					
4345	Is It This or Is It That/I'm Gonna Try Love One More Time	1961	6.25	12.50	25.00
ROYAL FLUSH					
102	Lady Fingers/A Garden in the Ghetto	1976	—	3.00	6.00
SAXONY					
104	I'm On My Way/(B-side unknown)	1958	12.50	25.00	50.00
SCEPTER					
12290	Border Song (Holy Moses)/Silliest People	1970	2.50	5.00	10.00
TOY					
3803	Rock and Roll Lullaby/Sittin' in the Sunshine	1972	2.00	4.00	8.00
TRIUMPH					
600	Count Your Blessings (See What Love Has Done)/I Just Want Somebody	1959	6.25	12.50	25.00
605	The Universe/Blackjack	1959	6.25	12.50	25.00
UNITED ARTISTS					
410	Drifting/Memories Are Made of This	1962	3.75	7.50	15.00

MIDLER, BETTE

12-Inch Singles

Number	Title (A Side/B Side)	Yr	VG	VG+	NM
ATLANTIC					
DSKO 187 [DJ]	Married Men (7:58) (5:32)	1979	3.00	6.00	12.00
218 [DJ]	Big Noise from Winnetka (same on both sides)	1979	2.50	5.00	10.00
548 [DJ]	Favorite Waste of Time/Only in Miami	1983	2.50	5.00	10.00
578 [DJ]	Beast of Burden (same on both sides)	1983	2.50	5.00	10.00
1655 [DJ]	Moonlight Dancing (3 versions)	1990	—	2.50	5.00
DK 4800	Married Men/Bang You're Dead	1979	3.00	6.00	12.00

45s

Number	Title (A Side/B Side)	Yr	VG	VG+	NM
ATLANTIC					
2928	Do You Want to Dance/Superstar	1972	—	2.50	5.00
2964	Boogie Woogie Bugle Boy/Delta Dawn	1973	—	2.50	5.00
2980	Friends/Chapel of Love	1973	—	2.50	5.00
3004	In the Mood/Drinking Again	1974	—	2.50	5.00
3319	Stranger in the Night/Somedi It Vendredi	1976	—	2.00	4.00
3325	Old Cape Cod/Tragedy	1976	—	2.00	4.00
3379	Let Me Just Follow Behind/You're Movin' Out Today	1976	—	2.00	4.00
3431	Storybook Children/Empty Bed Blues	1977	—	2.00	4.00
3475	Paradise/Red	1978	—	2.00	4.00
3582	Married Men/Bang, You're Dead	1979	—	2.00	4.00
3616	Hang On In There Baby/Cradle Days	1979	—	2.00	4.00
3628	Rain/Big Noise from Winnetka	1979	—	2.00	4.00
3643	When a Man Loves a Woman/Love Me with a Feeling	1980	—	2.00	4.00
3656	The Rose/Stay with Me	1980	—	2.00	4.00
3656 [PS]	The Rose/Stay with Me	1980	—	2.50	5.00
3771	My Mother's Eyes/Chapel of Love	1980	—	2.00	4.00
87572	Every Road Leads Back to You/I Remember You-Dixie's Dream	1991	—	—	3.00
87820	From a Distance/One More Round	1990	—	2.00	4.00
87825	Night and Day/The Girl Is On to You	1990	—	—	3.00
88972	Wind Beneath My Wings/Oh Industry	1989	—	—	3.00
88972 [PS]	Wind Beneath My Wings/Oh Industry	1989	—	2.50	5.00
88976	Under the Boardwalk/The Friendship Theme	1989	—	—	3.00
88976	Under the Boardwalk/Otto Titsling	1989	—	2.00	4.00
89712	Beast of Burden/Come Back Jimmy Dean	1984	—	—	3.00
89761	Favorite Waste of Time/(B-side unknown)	1983	—	—	3.00
89789	All I Need to Know/My Eye on You	1983	—	—	3.00
89789 [PS]	All I Need to Know/My Eye on You	1983	—	2.00	4.00

Albums

Number	Title (A Side/B Side)	Yr	VG	VG+	NM
ATLANTIC					
QD 7238 [Q]	The Divine Miss M	1973	4.50	9.00	18.00
SD 7238	The Divine Miss M	1972	2.50	5.00	10.00
SD 7270	Bette Midler	1973	2.50	5.00	10.00
SD 2-9000 [(2)]	Live! At Last	1977	3.00	6.00	12.00
SD 16004	Thighs and Whispers	1979	2.50	5.00	10.00
SD 16010	The Rose	1979	2.50	5.00	10.00
SD 16022	Divine Madness	1980	2.50	5.00	10.00
SD 18155	Songs for the New Depression	1976	2.50	5.00	10.00
SD 19155	Broken Blossom	1977	2.50	5.00	10.00
80070	No Frills	1983	2.50	5.00	10.00
81291	Mud Will Be Flung Tonight	1985	2.50	5.00	10.00
81933	Beaches	1988	2.50	5.00	10.00
82129	Some People's Lives	1990	3.00	6.00	12.00

MIDNIGHT ANGELS, THE

45s

Number	Title (A Side/B Side)	Yr	VG	VG+	NM
APEX					
77073	I'm Sufferin'/In the Moonlight	1967	7.50	15.00	30.00
77073 [PS]	I'm Sufferin'/In the Moonlight	1967	10.00	20.00	40.00

MIDNIGHT STRING QUARTET

45s

Number	Title (A Side/B Side)	Yr	VG	VG+	NM
VIVA					
606	You Don't Have to Say You Love Me/The Lonely Bull	1966	—	3.00	6.00
616	Prophesy of Love/I Hear a Smyphony	1967	—	3.00	6.00
622	The Little Drummer Boy/Silent Night	1967	—	3.00	6.00
628	Midnight Memories/Classical Gas	1968	—	3.00	6.00

Albums

Number	Title (A Side/B Side)	Yr	VG	VG+	NM
VIVA					
2571 [(2)]	Best of the Midnight String Quartet	1971	3.00	6.00	12.00
V-6001 [M]	Rhapsodies for Young Lovers	1966	3.00	6.00	12.00
VS-6001 [S]	Rhapsodies for Young Lovers	1966	2.50	5.00	10.00
V-6004 [M]	Spanish Rhapsodies for Young Lovers	1967	3.00	6.00	12.00
V-6008 [M]	Rhapsodies for Young Lovers, Volume Two	1967	3.00	6.00	12.00
V-6010 [M]	Christmas Rhapsodies for Young Lovers	1967	3.75	7.50	15.00
V-6013 [M]	Love Rhapsodies	1968	3.75	7.50	15.00
V-36004 [S]	Spanish Rhapsodies for Young Lovers	1967	2.50	5.00	10.00
V-36008 [S]	Rhapsodies for Young Lovers, Volume Two	1967	2.50	5.00	10.00
V-36010 [S]	Christmas Rhapsodies for Young Lovers	1967	2.50	5.00	10.00
V-36013 [S]	Love Rhapsodies	1968	2.50	5.00	10.00
V-36015	The Look of Love and Other Rhapsodies for Young Lovers	1968	2.50	5.00	10.00
V-36022	Rhapsodies for Young Lovers, Volume Three	1969	2.50	5.00	10.00
V-36024	Chamber Music for Young Lovers	1969	2.50	5.00	10.00

MIDNIGHTERS, THE

Also see HANK BALLARD AND THE MIDNIGHTERS; THE ROYALS (1).

45s

Number	Title (A Side/B Side)	Yr	VG	VG+	NM
FEDERAL					
12169	Work With Me Annie/Until I Die	1954	25.00	50.00	100.00
—Silver top label; as " The Midnighters (Formerly Known As the Royals)"					
12169	Work With Me Annie/Until I Die	1954	10.00	20.00	40.00
—All-green label; as "The Midnighters (Formerly Known As the Royals)"					
12177	Give It Up/That Woman	1954	20.00	40.00	80.00
—As "The Midnighters Formerly the Royals"					
12185	Sexy Ways/Don't Say Your Last Goodbye	1954	20.00	40.00	80.00
—As "The Midnighters Formerly the Royals"					
12195	Annie Had a Baby/She's the One	1954	15.00	30.00	60.00
12200	Annie's Aunt Fanny/Crazy Loving	1954	15.00	30.00	60.00
12202	Tell Them/Stingy Little Thing	1954	15.00	30.00	60.00
12205	She's the One/Moonrise	1955	15.00	30.00	60.00
12210	Ashamed of Myself/Ring-a-Ling-Ling	1955	15.00	30.00	60.00
12220	Why Are We Apart/Switchie, Witchie, Titchie	1955	15.00	30.00	60.00
12224	Henry's Got Flat Feet (Can't Dance No More)/Whatsoever You Do	1955	15.00	30.00	60.00
12227	It's Love Baby (24 Hours a Day)/Looka Here	1955	15.00	30.00	60.00
12230	Give It Up/That Woman	1955	15.00	30.00	60.00
12240	Rock and Roll Wedding/That House on the Hill	1955	15.00	30.00	60.00
12243	Don't Change Your Pretty Ways/We'll Never Meet Again	1955	15.00	30.00	60.00
12251	Partners for Life/Sweet Mama, Do Right	1956	15.00	30.00	60.00
12260	Rock Granny Roll/Open Up the Back Door	1956	15.00	30.00	60.00
12270	Tore Up Over You/Early One Morning	1956	12.50	25.00	50.00
12285	I'll Be Home Some Day/Come On and Get It	1957	12.50	25.00	50.00
12288	Let Me Hold Your Hand/Oh Bah Baby	1957	12.50	25.00	50.00
12293	E Basta Cosi/In the Doorway Crying	1957	12.50	25.00	50.00
12299	Oh, So Happy/Is Your Love for Real	1957	10.00	20.00	40.00
12305	Let 'Em Roll/What Made You Change Your Mind	1957	10.00	20.00	40.00
12317	Stay By My Side/Daddy's Little Baby	1958	10.00	20.00	40.00
12339	Baby Please/Ow-Wow-Oo-Wee	1958	10.00	20.00	40.00

7-Inch Extended Plays

Number	Title (A Side/B Side)	Yr	VG	VG+	NM
FEDERAL					
333	Work with Me Annie/Moonrise//Sexy Ways/Get It	1955	75.00	150.00	300.00
—Green label, silver top					
333	Work with Me Annie/Moonrise//Sexy Ways/Get It	1955	37.50	75.00	150.00
—All-green label					
333 [PS]	The Midnighters Sing Their Greatest Hits	1955	50.00	100.00	200.00
—Pink cover					
333 [PS]	The Midnighters Sing Their Greatest Hits	1955	50.00	100.00	200.00
—Purple cover					

Albums

Number	Title (A Side/B Side)	Yr	VG	VG+	NM
FEDERAL					
295-90 [10]	Their Greatest Hits	1954	4000.	6000.	8000.
541 [M]	Their Greatest Hits	1955	375.00	750.00	1500.
—Red cover					
541 [M]	Their Greatest Hits	1955	250.00	500.00	1000.
—Yellow cover					
581 [M]	The Midnighters, Volume 2	1955	300.00	600.00	1200.
KING					
541 [M]	Their Greatest Jukebox Hits	1958	100.00	200.00	400.00
—Crownless black label, "King" is two inches wide on label					
541 [M]	Their Greatest Jukebox Hits	196?	75.00	150.00	300.00
—Crownless black label, "King" is three inches wide on label. Above two have a girl on the cover.					
541 [M]	Their Greatest Jukebox Hits	196?	50.00	100.00	200.00
—Reissue with Hank Ballard on cover					
581 [M]	The Midnighters, Volume 2	1958	75.00	150.00	300.00
—Crownless black label, "King" is two inches wide on label					
581 [M]	The Midnighters, Volume 2	196?	50.00	100.00	200.00
—Crownless black label, "King" is three inches wide on label					

MIDNIGHTERS, THE (2)

45s

Number	Title (A Side/B Side)	Yr	VG	VG+	NM
20TH FOX					
182	The Road Home/Taco	1960	3.00	6.00	12.00

MIGHTY AVENGERS, THE

45s

Number	Title (A Side/B Side)	Yr	VG	VG+	NM
PRESS					
9746	Blue Turns to Grey/I'm Lost Without You	1965	2.50	5.00	10.00

MIGHTY BABY

Albums

Number	Title (A Side/B Side)	Yr	VG	VG+	NM
HEAD					
LPS-025	Mighty Baby	1969	15.00	30.00	60.00

MIGHTY CLOUDS OF JOY

12-Inch Singles

Number	Title (A Side/B Side)	Yr	VG	VG+	NM
EPIC					
50693	Joy in These Changing Times/(Instrumental)	1979	3.00	6.00	12.00

45s

Number	Title (A Side/B Side)	Yr	VG	VG+	NM
ABC					
12164	Mighty High/Touch My Soul	1976	—	2.00	4.00
12196	You Are So Beautiful/Everything Is All	1976	—	2.00	4.00
12241	There's Love in the World (Tell the Lonely People)/(B-side unknown)	1976	—	2.00	4.00
12281	God Is Not Dead/Music Is My Way of Life	1977	—	2.00	4.00
12322	Look on the Bright Side/(B-side unknown)	1978	—	2.00	4.00
ABC DUNHILL					
15012	Time/(B-side unknown)	1974	—	2.50	5.00

Number	Title (A Side/B Side)	Yr	VG	VG+	NM
15025	Mighty Cloud of Joy/Everything Is Going Up	1974	—	2.50	5.00
EPIC					
50690	Joy in These Changing Times/We're Gonna Have a Good Time	1979	—	2.00	4.00
50691	I've Been in the Storm Too Long/We're Blessed	1979	—	2.00	4.00
50788	I Get a Blessing Every Day/Rainy Day Friend	1979	—	2.00	4.00
50875	What a Difference You've Made in My Life/We're Blessed	1980	—	2.00	4.00
MYRRH					
241	Glow Love/(B-side unknown)	1982	—	2.00	4.00
PEACOCK					
1823	Jesus Lead Us Safely/Ain't Got Long Here	1961	3.00	6.00	12.00
1839	I'll Be Alright/My Religion	1961	3.00	6.00	12.00
1857	Time Has Changed/I Love Jesus	1962	2.50	5.00	10.00
1869	Family Circle/None But the Righteous	1962	2.50	5.00	10.00
1895	Glory Hallelujah/Lord Hold My Hand	1962	2.50	5.00	10.00
1896	Nearer to Thee/You'll Never Know	1962	2.50	5.00	10.00
3025	I'll Go (Part 1)/I'll Go (Part 2)	1964	2.50	5.00	10.00
3050	A Friend in Jesus/Two Wings	1965	2.50	5.00	10.00
3064	He's Able/Swing Low	1965	2.50	5.00	10.00
3077	See How They Done My Lord/Look for Me in Heaven	1966	2.50	5.00	10.00
3080	Nobody Can Turn Me Around/Touch Me Lord	1966	2.50	5.00	10.00
3099	I'm Glad About It/Let Jesus Lead You	1966	2.50	5.00	10.00
3132	Somewhere Around God's Throne/The Holy Ghost	1967	2.00	4.00	8.00
3144	Pray for Me/Call Him Up	1968	2.00	4.00	8.00
3167	How Far Have I Strayed/Just to Behold His Face	1969	2.00	4.00	8.00
3175	In This World Alone/Why Do Men Treat the Lord	1970	2.00	4.00	8.00
3189	Heavy Load/I'll Be Alright Someday	1972	—	3.00	6.00
Albums					
ABC					
D-899	Kickin'	1975	2.50	5.00	10.00
D-986	The Truth Is the Power	1976	2.50	5.00	10.00
D-1038	Live and Direct	1977	2.50	5.00	10.00
ABC DUNHILL					
DSX-50177	It's Time	1974	2.50	5.00	10.00
HOB					
288	"Live" Zion Songs	196?	3.75	7.50	15.00
KING					
SG3-1107	Out Talking to Yourself	1970	3.75	7.50	15.00
MCA					
1091 [(2)]	The Very Best of Mighty Clouds of Joy	198?	2.50	5.00	10.00
28008	Family Circle	198?	2.00	4.00	8.00
—Reissue of Peacock 114					
28012	The Bright Side	198?	2.00	4.00	8.00
—Reissue of Peacock 121					
28017	Mighty Clouds of Joy At the Music Hall	198?	2.00	4.00	8.00
—Reissue of Peacock 134					
28019	The Best of Mighty Clouds of Joy	198?	2.00	4.00	8.00
—Reissue of Peacock 136					
28025	The Untouchables	198?	2.00	4.00	8.00
—Reissue of Peacock 151					
28028	Songs of Rev. Julius Cheeks and the Nightingales	198?	2.00	4.00	8.00
—Reissue of Peacock 163					
28030	God Bless America	198?	2.00	4.00	8.00
—Reissue of Peacock 170					
28032	Live at the Apollo	198?	2.00	4.00	8.00
—Reissue of Peacock 173					
28040	The Best of Mighty Clouds of Joy — Volume 2	198?	2.00	4.00	8.00
MYRRH					
MSB-6663	Cloudburst	1980	2.50	5.00	10.00
MSB-6681	The Truth Is the Power	1981	2.50	5.00	10.00
MSB-6694	Miracle Man	1982	2.50	5.00	10.00
MSB-6712	Request Line	1983	2.50	5.00	10.00
WR-8121	Mighty Clouds Alive	1984	2.50	5.00	10.00
WR-8122	Sing and Shout	1984	2.50	5.00	10.00
PEACOCK					
114	Family Circle	196?	5.00	10.00	20.00
121	The Bright Side	196?	5.00	10.00	20.00
134	Mighty Clouds of Joy At the Music Hall	196?	5.00	10.00	20.00
136	The Best of Mighty Clouds of Joy	196?	5.00	10.00	20.00
151	The Untouchables	196?	5.00	10.00	20.00
161	Out Talking to Yourself	196?	5.00	10.00	20.00
163	Songs of Rev. Julius Cheeks and the Nightingales	196?	5.00	10.00	20.00
170	God Bless America	1971	3.75	7.50	15.00
173	Live at the Apollo	1972	3.75	7.50	15.00
PRIORITY					
RV 37707	Changing Times	1982	2.50	5.00	10.00

MIGHTY MARVELOWS, THE

See THE MARVELOWS.

MIGIL FIVE, THE

Number	Title (A Side/B Side)	Yr	VG	VG+	NM
45s					
CAMEO					
316	Mockin' Bird Hill/Long Ago (And Far Away)	1964	2.50	5.00	10.00
HICKORY					
1292	Your Cheatin' Heart/Boys and Girls	1965	2.50	5.00	10.00
1334	I'm in Love Again/One Hundred Years	1965	2.50	5.00	10.00
MERCURY					
72301	Near You/Don't Wanna Go On Shaking	1964	2.50	5.00	10.00

MIKE AND THE JAYS

Number	Title (A Side/B Side)	Yr	VG	VG+	NM
45s					
DOYL					
1001	My Only Girl/Dingle Dangle Doll	1960	20.00	40.00	80.00

MIKE AND THE MODIFIERS

Number	Title (A Side/B Side)	Yr	VG	VG+	NM
45s					
GORDY					
7006	I Found Myself a Brand New Baby/It's Too Bad	1962	15.00	30.00	60.00

MIKE AND THE UTOPIANS

Number	Title (A Side/B Side)	Yr	VG	VG+	NM
45s					
CEE JAY					
574	Erlene/I Wish	1958	75.00	150.00	300.00
574	Erlene/I Found a Penny	1958	37.50	75.00	150.00

MIKE, JOHN AND BILL

"Mike" is MICHAEL NESMITH, later of THE MONKEES.

Number	Title (A Side/B Side)	Yr	VG	VG+	NM
45s					
OMNIBUS					
239	How Can You Kiss Me/Just a Little Love	1963	50.00	100.00	200.00

MILANO, BOBBY

Number	Title (A Side/B Side)	Yr	VG	VG+	NM
45s					
CAPITOL					
F-3012	A King or a Slave/If You Cared	1955	5.00	10.00	20.00
CHALLENGE					
59005	Life Begins at 4 O'Clock/Double Talking Baby	1958	25.00	50.00	100.00
TIME					
1019	Ruby/Do I Love You	1960	5.00	10.00	20.00
WARNER BROS.					
5027	Water Under the Bridge/My Yiddishe Momma	1959	3.00	6.00	12.00

MILBURN, AMOS

Number	Title (A Side/B Side)	Yr	VG	VG+	NM
45s					
ALADDIN					
3014	Chicken Shack Boogie/It Took a Long, Long Time	1950	50.00	100.00	200.00
—78 originally released in 1948					
3018	Bewildered/A and M Blues	1950	30.00	60.00	120.00
—78 originally released in 1948					
3068	Bad, Bad Whiskey/I'm Going to Tell My Mama	1950	125.00	250.00	500.00
—Note: Amos Milburn singles on Aladdin before 3068 are unconfirmed on 45 rpm except those listed					
3080	Let's Rock a While/Tears, Tears, Tears	1951	20.00	40.00	80.00
3090	Everybody Clap Hands/That Was Your Last Mistake	1951	20.00	40.00	80.00
3093	Ain't Nothin' Shaking/Just One More Drink	1951	20.00	40.00	80.00
3105	She's Gone Again/Boogie Woogie	1951	20.00	40.00	80.00
3124	Thinking and Drinking/Trouble in Mind	1952	20.00	40.00	80.00
3125	Flying Home/Put Something in My Hand	1952	20.00	40.00	80.00
3133	I Won't Be Your Fool Anymore/Roll Mr. Jelly	1952	20.00	40.00	80.00
3146	Button Your Lip/Everything I Do Is Wrong	1952	20.00	40.00	80.00
3150	Kiss Me Again/Greyhound	1952	20.00	40.00	80.00
3159	Rock, Rock, Rock/Boo Hoo	1953	15.00	30.00	60.00
3164	Let Me Go Home, Whiskey/Three Times a Fool	1953	15.00	30.00	60.00
3168	Long, Long Day/Please Mr. Johnson	1953	15.00	30.00	60.00
3197	One Scotch, One Bourbon, One Beer/What Can I Do	1953	25.00	50.00	100.00
3218	Good, Good Whiskey/Let's Have a Party	1954	20.00	40.00	80.00
3226	How Could You Hurt Me So/Rocky Mountain	1954	15.00	30.00	60.00
3240	Milk and Water/I'm Still a Fool for You	1954	15.00	30.00	60.00
3248	Glory of Love/Baby, Baby All the Time	1954	15.00	30.00	60.00
3253	Vicious, Vicious Vodka/I Done Done It	1954	15.00	30.00	60.00
3269	That's It/One, Two, Three Everybody	1954	15.00	30.00	60.00
3281	Why Don't You Do Right/I Love You Anyway	1955	10.00	20.00	40.00
3293	All Is Well/My Happiness Depends on You	1955	10.00	20.00	40.00
3306	House Party/I Guess I'll Go	1955	10.00	20.00	40.00
3320	French Fried Potatoes and Ketchup/I Need Someone	1956	10.00	20.00	40.00
3332	Chicken Shack Boogie/Juice, Juice, Juice	1956	10.00	20.00	40.00
3340	Girl of My Dreams/Everyday of the Week	1956	10.00	20.00	40.00
3363	Rum and Coca-Cola/Soft Pollow	1957	7.50	15.00	30.00
3370	Greyhound/Dear Angel	1957	7.50	15.00	30.00
3383	Thinking of You Baby/If I Could Be with You	1957	7.50	15.00	30.00
IMPERIAL					
5831	I'm Still a Fool for You/Rocky Mountain	1962	3.00	6.00	12.00
KING					
5405	Christmas (Comes But Once a Year)/Please Come Home for Christmas	1960	3.00	6.00	12.00
—B-side by Charles Brown					
5464	I Wanna Go Back Home/My Little Baby	1961	3.00	6.00	12.00
—With Charles Brown					
5483	My Sweet Baby's Love/Heartaches That Make You Cry	1961	3.00	6.00	12.00
5529	Movin' Time/The Hammer	1961	3.00	6.00	12.00
6095	Whiz O Shoo Pepi/Same Old Thing	1967	2.50	5.00	10.00
MOTOWN					
1038	I'll Make It Up to You Somehow/My Baby Gave Me Another Chance	1963	7.50	15.00	30.00
1046	My Daily Prayer/(B-side unknown)	1963	7.50	15.00	30.00
UNITED ARTISTS					
0149	Chicken Shack Boogie/Revitalized	1973	—	2.00	4.00
—"Silver Spotlight Series" reissue					
Albums					
ALADDIN					
LP-704 [10]	Rockin' the Boogie	1955	200.00	4000.	8000.
—Red vinyl, blue cover					
LP-704 [10]	Rockin' the Boogie	1955	1000.	2000.	4000.
—Black vinyl					
LP-810 [M]	Rockin' the Boogie	1958	—	—	—
—Canceled					
IMPERIAL					
LP-9176 [M]	Million Sellers	1962	125.00	250.00	500.00
MOTOWN					
608 [M]	The Return of Amos Milburn, "The" Blues Boss	1963	225.00	450.00	900.00
SCORE					
LP-4012 [M]	Let's Have a Party	1957	200.00	400.00	800.00
LP-4035 [M]	Amos Milburn Sings the Blues	1958	—	—	—
—Canceled					

MILBURN, AMOS/WYNONIE HARRIS/ETC.

Albums

ALADDIN

Number	Title (A Side/B Side)	Yr	VG	VG+	NM
LP-703 [10]	Party After Hours	1955	2000.	4000.	8000.
—Red vinyl, blue cover					
LP-703 [10]	Party After Hours	1955	1000.	2000.	4000.
—Black vinyl					

MILES, BUDDY

45s

ATLANTIC

Number	Title (A Side/B Side)	Yr	VG	VG+	NM
3852 [DJ]	Can You Hold Me (same on both sides)	1981	—	2.00	4.00
—May be promo only					
4006 [DJ]	Sunshine of Your Love (same on both sides)	1982	—	2.00	4.00
—May be promo only					

CASABLANCA

Number	Title (A Side/B Side)	Yr	VG	VG+	NM
839	Rockin' and Rollin' on the Streets of Hollywood/Livin' in the Right Space	1975	—	2.00	4.00
849	Nasty Disposition/Do It to Me	1975	—	2.00	4.00
859	Reuben "The Hurricane"/Where You Gonna Run To Lady	1976	—	2.00	4.00

COLUMBIA

Number	Title (A Side/B Side)	Yr	VG	VG+	NM
10030	Pain/We Get Love	1974	—	2.50	5.00
10089	Pull Yourself Together/I'm Just a Kiss Away	1975	—	2.50	5.00
45826	Love Affair/Life Is What You Make It	1973	—	2.50	5.00
45876	Elvira/Hear No Evil	1973	—	2.50	5.00
45969	Crazy Love/Thinking of You	1973	—	2.50	5.00

MERCURY

Number	Title (A Side/B Side)	Yr	VG	VG+	NM
72860	The Train (Part 1)/The Train (Part 2)	1968	2.00	4.00	8.00
72903	This Lady/'69 Freedom Special	1969	2.00	4.00	8.00
72945	Memphis Train/My Chant	1969	—	3.00	6.00
73008	Them Changes/Spot on the Wall	1970	—	3.00	6.00
73086	Down By the River/Hearts Delight	1970	—	3.00	6.00
73119	Dreams/Your Feeling Is Mine	1970	—	3.00	6.00
73159	We Got to Live Together (Part 1)/We Got to Live Together (Part 2)	1970	—	3.00	6.00
73170	Runaway Child/(B-side unknown)	1970	—	3.00	6.00
73205	Wholesale Love/That's the Way Life Is	1971	—	2.50	5.00
73238	Them Changes/The Way I Feel Tonight	1971	—	2.50	5.00
73261	Give Away None of My Love/Take It Off Him and Put It On Me	1972	—	2.50	5.00
73277	Life Is What You Make It (Part 1)/Life Is What You Make It (Part 2)	1972	—	2.50	5.00

Albums

ATLANTIC

Number	Title (A Side/B Side)	Yr	VG	VG+	NM
SD 2-4000 [(2)]	Sneak Attack	1982	3.00	6.00	12.00

CASABLANCA

Number	Title (A Side/B Side)	Yr	VG	VG+	NM
NBLP 7019	More Miles Per Gallon	1975	2.50	5.00	10.00
NBLP 7024	Bicentennial Gathering of the Tribes	1976	2.50	5.00	10.00

COLUMBIA

Number	Title (A Side/B Side)	Yr	VG	VG+	NM
CQ 32048 [Q]	Chapter VII	1973	5.00	10.00	20.00
KC 32048	Chapter VII	1973	3.00	6.00	12.00
CQ 32694 [Q]	Booger Bear	1973	5.00	10.00	20.00
KC 32694	Booger Bear	1973	3.00	6.00	12.00
KC 33089	All the Faces	1974	3.00	6.00	12.00

MERCURY

Number	Title (A Side/B Side)	Yr	VG	VG+	NM
SRM-1-608	A Message to the People	1971	3.75	7.50	15.00
SRM-2-7500 [(2)]	Buddy Miles Live	1971	3.75	7.50	15.00
SR-61196	Expressway to Your Skull	1968	5.00	10.00	20.00
SR-61222	Electric Church	1969	5.00	10.00	20.00
SR-61280	Them Changes	1970	3.75	7.50	15.00
SR-61313	We Got to Live Together	1970	3.75	7.50	15.00

MILES, GARRY

45s

LIBERTY

Number	Title (A Side/B Side)	Yr	VG	VG+	NM
55261	Look for a Star/Afraid of Love	1960	3.75	7.50	15.00
55261 [PS]	Look for a Star/Afraid of Love	1960	7.50	15.00	30.00
55279	Wishing Well/Dream Girl	1960	3.00	6.00	12.00
55596	Candy/Do the Bug	1963	3.00	6.00	12.00
55685	What Kind of Girl Are You/What's New	1964	2.50	5.00	10.00
55714	Here Goes a Fool/Ecstasy	1964	2.50	5.00	10.00
55738	How Are Things in Paradise/Please Take the Time	1964	2.50	5.00	10.00

UNITED ARTISTS

Number	Title (A Side/B Side)	Yr	VG	VG+	NM
0099	Look for a Star/Look for a Star	1973	—	2.50	5.00
—"Silver Spotlight Series" reissue; B-side by Garry Mills					

7-Inch Extended Plays

LIBERTY

Number	Title (A Side/B Side)	Yr	VG	VG+	NM
LSX-1005	Look for a Star/Wishing Well//I Miss You So/Afraid of Love	1960	12.50	25.00	50.00
LSX-1005 [PS]	Look for a Star	1960	12.50	25.00	50.00

MILES, LENNY

45s

GROOVE

Number	Title (A Side/B Side)	Yr	VG	VG+	NM
58-0001	Stay with Me/Hercules	1963	2.50	5.00	10.00
58-0010	I Wouldn't Be Here/Mind Your Own Biz	1963	2.50	5.00	10.00

SCEPTER

Number	Title (A Side/B Side)	Yr	VG	VG+	NM
1212	Don't Believe Him Donna/Invisible	1960	3.00	6.00	12.00
1218	I Know Love/In Between Tears	1961	3.00	6.00	12.00

MILKWOOD (1)

Albums

A&M

Number	Title (A Side/B Side)	Yr	VG	VG+	NM
SP-4226	Under Milkwood	1969	75.00	150.00	300.00

MILKWOOD (2)

Albums

PARAMOUNT

Number	Title (A Side/B Side)	Yr	VG	VG+	NM
PAS-6046	How's the Weather?	1973	10.00	20.00	40.00

MILKWOOD TAPESTRY

Albums

METROMEDIA

Number	Title (A Side/B Side)	Yr	VG	VG+	NM
MD-1007	Milkwood Tapestry	1969	12.50	25.00	50.00

MILLARD & DYCE

Albums

KAYMAR

Number	Title (A Side/B Side)	Yr	VG	VG+	NM
KS-7-265	Open	1973	15.00	30.00	60.00

MILLENNIUM

45s

COLUMBIA

Number	Title (A Side/B Side)	Yr	VG	VG+	NM
4-44546	I Just Want to Be Your Friend/It's You	1968	2.50	5.00	10.00
4-44607	5 A.M./Prelude	1968	2.50	5.00	10.00

MILLER, BOBBY

45s

CONSTELLATION

Number	Title (A Side/B Side)	Yr	VG	VG+	NM
103	The Big Question/I Don't Believe You	1963	5.00	10.00	20.00
111	The Big Question/Uncle Willie Time	1963	5.00	10.00	20.00
116	Whoa (She's All Mine)/Take It in Stride	1964	5.00	10.00	20.00
127	This Is My Dance/Simon Says	1964	5.00	10.00	20.00
134	I'm For the Girls/Love Take the Case	1964	7.50	15.00	30.00

MILLER, CHUCK

45s

CAPITOL

Number	Title (A Side/B Side)	Yr	VG	VG+	NM
F2613	Am I to Blame/Count Your Blessings	1953	5.00	10.00	20.00
F2700	The Pucker-Nut Free/After All	1954	5.00	10.00	20.00
F2766	Idaho Red/The Joker (In the Card Game of Life)	1954	5.00	10.00	20.00
—With Dave Cavanaugh					
F2841	Hopahula Boogie/I'll Know My Love	1954	5.00	10.00	20.00
F3187	No Baby Like You/Rouge River Valley	1955	3.75	7.50	15.00

MERCURY

Number	Title (A Side/B Side)	Yr	VG	VG+	NM
70627	The House of Blue Lights/Can't Help Wonderin'	1955	5.00	10.00	20.00
70697	Hawk Eye/Something to Live For	1955	3.75	7.50	15.00
70767	Boogie Along/Lookout Mountain	1955	3.75	7.50	15.00
70842	Bright Red Convertible/Baltimore Jones	1956	3.75	7.50	15.00
70942	Vim Vam Vamoose/Cool It Baby!	1956	3.75	7.50	15.00
71001	The Auctioneer/Baby Doll	1956	3.75	7.50	15.00
71056	Me Head in De Barrel/Good Mornin' Darlin'	1957	3.00	6.00	12.00
71118	Rang Tang Ding Dong/Bye Bye Love	1957	3.00	6.00	12.00
71173	Plaything/After Yesterday	1957	3.00	6.00	12.00
71308	Down the Road Apiece/Mad About Her Blues	1958	3.00	6.00	12.00

Albums

MERCURY

Number	Title (A Side/B Side)	Yr	VG	VG+	NM
MG-20195 [M]	After Hours	1956	20.00	40.00	80.00

MILLER, CLINT

45s

ABC-PARAMOUNT

Number	Title (A Side/B Side)	Yr	VG	VG+	NM
9878	Bertha Lou/Doggone It Baby, I'm in Love	1957	12.50	25.00	50.00
9938	Polka Dotted Poliwampus/Teenage Dance	1958	7.50	15.00	30.00
9938 [PS]	Polka Dotted Poliwampus/Teenage Dance	1958	15.00	30.00	60.00
9979	A Lover's Prayer/No, Never, My Love	1958	5.00	10.00	20.00

BIG TOP

Number	Title (A Side/B Side)	Yr	VG	VG+	NM
3013	Lonely Traveler/You Must Have Read My Mind	1959	5.00	10.00	20.00

HEADLINE

Number	Title (A Side/B Side)	Yr	VG	VG+	NM
1010	Silly Billy Boy/Do You Remember	1960	12.50	25.00	50.00
1011	London Town/Till the End of the World Rolls Around	1961	7.50	15.00	30.00
1013	I Still Write Your Name in the Sand/The Girl with a Ribbon in Her Hand	1961	7.50	15.00	30.00

LENOX

Number	Title (A Side/B Side)	Yr	VG	VG+	NM
5557	Forget Me Nots/Drummer Boy of Shiloh	1962	3.00	6.00	12.00
5574	Bridge Across the River/Crabs Walk Sideways	1963	3.00	6.00	12.00

MILLER, DREW, AND THE BEL-AIRES

45s

MGM

Number	Title (A Side/B Side)	Yr	VG	VG+	NM
11627	When Christmas Angels Sing/Mystery Trail	1953	5.00	10.00	20.00

MILLER, GLENN

Not included are later incarnations of the Glenn Miller Orchestra without Glenn Miller.

45s

20TH FOX

Number	Title (A Side/B Side)	Yr	VG	VG+	NM
122	Boom Shot/You Say the Sweetest Things	1959	2.50	5.00	10.00

RCA VICTOR

Number	Title (A Side/B Side)	Yr	VG	VG+	NM
27-0026	Chattanooga Choo Choo/(I've Got a Gal in) Kalamazoo	1951	3.75	7.50	15.00
—Silver label, red print					
27-0152	On Army Team/Anchors Aweigh	195?	3.75	7.50	15.00
—Silver label, red print; part of WPT 39					
27-0155	Vilia/I Dream of Jeanie with the Light Brown Hair	195?	3.75	7.50	15.00
—Silver label, red print					
47-2852	American Patrol/Song of the Volga Boatmen	1949	5.00	10.00	20.00
—Aqua label					
47-2852	American Patrol/Song of the Volga Boatmen	1951	3.75	7.50	15.00
—Black label, outline of dog at right					
47-2853	In the Mood/Little Brown Jug	1949	5.00	10.00	20.00
—Aqua label					
47-2853	In the Mood/Little Brown Jug	1951	3.75	7.50	15.00
—Black label, outline of dog at right					
47-2854	Star Dust/Pennsylvania Six-Five Thousand	1949	5.00	10.00	20.00
—Aqua label					
47-2854	Star Dust/Pennsylvania Six-Five Thousand	1951	3.75	7.50	15.00
—Black label, outline of dog at right					
47-2858	A String of Pearls/Chattanooga Choo Choo	1949	5.00	10.00	20.00
47-2877	Bugle Call Rag/Runnin' Wild	1949	5.00	10.00	20.00
47-4086	In the Mood/A String of Pearls	1951	3.75	7.50	15.00

Number	Title (A Side/B Side)	Yr	VG	VG+	NM
447-0026	Holiday for Strings/Flyin' Home	195?	3.75	7.50	15.00
447-0027	Farewell Blues/Stormy Weather	195?	3.75	7.50	15.00
447-0028	St. Louis Blues March/In an Eighteenth Century Drawing Room	195?	3.75	7.50	15.00
447-0030	My Blue Heaven/Begin the Beguine	195?	3.75	7.50	15.00
447-0031	Little Brown Jug/Adios	195?	3.75	7.50	15.00
447-0032	Alice Blue Gown/My Isle of Golden Dreams	195?	3.75	7.50	15.00
447-0033	American Patrol/Song of the Volga Boatmen	195?	3.00	6.00	12.00
447-0034	Anvil Chorus/By the Waters of the Minnetonka	195?	3.75	7.50	15.00
447-0035	Perfidia/At Last	195?	3.75	7.50	15.00
447-0036	Beautiful Ohio/Missouri Waltz	195?	3.75	7.50	15.00
447-0037	Blue Evening/Serenade in Blue	195?	3.75	7.50	15.00
447-0038	Runnin' Wild/Bugle Call Rag	195?	3.75	7.50	15.00
447-0039	Chattanooga Choo Choo/(I've Got a Gal in) Kalamazoo	195?	3.00	6.00	12.00
447-0040	Danny Boy/Ida! Sweet As Apple Cider	195?	3.75	7.50	15.00
447-0041	Elmer's Tune/Johnson Rag	195?	3.75	7.50	15.00
447-0042	Pavanne/Don't Sit Under the Apple Tree (With Anyone Else But Me)	195?	3.75	7.50	15.00
447-0043	In the Mood/A String of Pearls	195?	3.00	6.00	12.00
447-0044	That Old Black Magic/Juke Box Saturday Night	195?	3.75	7.50	15.00
447-0045	Sunrise Serenade/Moonlight Serenade	195?	3.75	7.50	15.00
447-0046	Pennsylvania Six-Five Thousand/Moonlight Cocktail	195?	3.75	7.50	15.00
447-0047	Star Dust/Tuxedo Junction	195?	3.75	7.50	15.00
UNITED STATES ARMY					
HO7H-1760/1 [DJ]	In the Mood/American Patrol	1958	10.00	20.00	40.00
—Promo-only "Recruiting Service" record; white label with red and blue print					
7-Inch Extended Plays					
EPIC					
EG-7012	Time on My Hands/I Got Rhythm//Sleepy Time Gal/Sold American	195?	5.00	10.00	20.00
EG-7012 [PS]	(title unknown)	195?	5.00	10.00	20.00
RCA VICTOR					
SPD 18 [PS]	(title unknown)	1956	37.50	75.00	150.00
—Includes 10 records (599-9105 through 599-9114) plus box and booklet insert					
947-0024	(contents unknown)	195?	5.00	10.00	20.00
—One record of 2-EP set EPBT 3025					
947-0025	(contents unknown)	195?	5.00	10.00	20.00
—One record of 2-EP set EPBT 3025					
947-0026	Anchors Aweigh/My Buddy//I Got Rhythm/I Dream of Jeanie with the Light Brown Hair	195?	5.00	10.00	20.00
—Silver label, red print; one record of 2-EP set EPBT 3026					
947-0027	Vilia/Limehouse Blues//On the Alamo/On Army Team	195?	5.00	10.00	20.00
—Silver label, red print; one record of 2-EP set EPBT 3026					
947-0136	Moonlight Serenade/American Patrol//Pennsylvania Six-Five Thousand/In the Mood	1954	5.00	10.00	20.00
—Silver label, red print; part of 2-EP set EPBT 3057					
947-0137	Tuxedo Junction/St. Louis Blues//String of Pearls/Little Brown Jug	1954	5.00	10.00	20.00
—Silver label, red print; part of 2-EP set EPBT 3057					
EPA 148	*In the Mood/Little Brown Jug/American Patrol/Song of the Volga Boatmen	195?	3.75	7.50	15.00
EPA 148 [PS]	Glenn Miller: An Album of Outstanding Arrangements	195?	3.75	7.50	15.00
947-0178	Along the Santa Fe Trail/Swingin' at the Seance//I'll Never Smile Again/V for Victory Hop	1954	2.50	5.00	10.00
—Side 1 and 30 of 15-EP set EPOT 6701					
947-0179	In a Sentimental Mood/Frenesi//Dancing in a Dream/Sophisticated Lady	1954	2.50	5.00	10.00
—Side 2 and 29 of 15-EP set EPOT 6701					
947-0180	Isn't That Just Like Love/I Dreamt I Dwelt in Harlem//On the Alamo/April in Paris	1954	2.50	5.00	10.00
—Side 3 and 28 of 15-EP set EPOT 6701					
947-0181	You Walk By/Are You Jumpin' Jack?//How Deep Is the Ocean/Measure for Measure	1954	2.50	5.00	10.00
—Side 4 and 27 of 15-EP set EPOT 6701					
947-0182	A Million Dreams Ago/Daisy Mae//Let's Have Another Cup of Coffee/The Rhumba Jumps	1954	2.50	5.00	10.00
—Side 5 and 26 of 15-EP set EPOT 6701					
947-0183	Falling Leaves/Crosstown//Anchors Aweigh/Body and Soul	1954	2.50	5.00	10.00
—Side 6 and 25 of 15-EP set EPOT 6701					
947-0184	At Sundown/My Last Goodbye//So Little Time/Down South Camp Meetin'	1954	2.50	5.00	10.00
—Side 7 and 24 of 15-EP set EPOT 6701					
947-0185	Hallelujah/I'm Sorry for Myself//A Stone's Throw from Heaven/Humoresque	1954	2.50	5.00	10.00
—Side 8 and 23 of 15-EP set EPOT 6701					
947-0186	The Hour of Parting/The Jumpin' Jive//Doin' the Jive/This Can't Be Love	1954	2.50	5.00	10.00
—Side 9 and 22 of 15-EP set EPOT 6701					
947-0187	Twilight Interlude/And the Angels Sing//Daddy/Deep in the Heart of Texas	1954	2.50	5.00	10.00
—Side 10 and 21 of 15-EP set EPOT 6701					
947-0188	Sunrise Serenade/Blue Orchids//I Don't Want to Walk Without You/Limehouse Blues	1954	2.50	5.00	10.00
—Side 11 and 20 of 15-EP set EPOT 6701					
947-0189	We Can Live on Love/Pagan Love Song//Georgia on My Mind/Be Happy	1954	2.50	5.00	10.00
—Side 12 and 19 of 15-EP set EPOT 6701					
947-0190	We've Come a Long Way Together/Get Out of Town//Indian Summer/Tiger Rag	1954	2.50	5.00	10.00
—Side 13 and 18 of 15-EP set EPOT 6701					
947-0191	Blue Skies/Heaven Can Wait//After All/St. Louis Blues	1954	2.50	5.00	10.00
—Side 14 and 17 of 15-EP set EPOT 6701					
947-0192	Bluebirds in the Moonlight/I Want to Be Happy//My Heart Belongs to Daddy/Deep Purple	1954	2.50	5.00	10.00
—Side 15 and 16 of 15-EP set EPOT 6701					
EPAT 401	Chattanooga Choo Choo/Kalamazoo//Juke Box Saturday Night/That Old Black Magic	195?	5.00	10.00	20.00
EPAT 401 [PS]	(title unknown)	195?	5.00	10.00	20.00
EPAT 426	April Played the Fiddle/Blue Rain//Vagabond Dreams/The Story of a Starry Night	1954	5.00	10.00	20.00
—Silver label, red print					
EPAT 426 [PS]	Ah! Spring	1954	5.00	10.00	20.00
EPAT 427	The Nearness of You/To You//Moonlight Becomes You/Faithful to You	1954	5.00	10.00	20.00
—Silver label, red print					
EPAT 427 [PS]	The Nearness of You	1954	5.00	10.00	20.00
EPAT 428	The Spirit Is Willing/Long Tall Mama//Rainbow Rhapsody/Take the "A" Train	1954	5.00	10.00	20.00
—Silver label, red print					
EPAT 428 [PS]	The Spirit Is Willing	1954	5.00	10.00	20.00
EPAT 429	At Last/Blue Evening//Delilah/Elmer's Tune	1954	5.00	10.00	20.00
—Silver label, red print					
EPAT 429 [PS]	Elmer's Tune	1954	5.00	10.00	20.00
EPAT 430	Moonlight Cocktail/Perfidia//Serenade in Blue/It Happened in Hawaii	1954	5.00	10.00	20.00
—Silver label, red print					
EPAT 430 [PS]	Moonlight Cocktail	1954	5.00	10.00	20.00
EPA 727	Beautiful Ohio/Adios//Serenade in Blue/Bugle Call Rag	1956	3.75	7.50	15.00
EPA 727 [PS]	This Is Glenn Miller	1956	3.75	7.50	15.00
547-1100	Moonlight Serenade/Running Wild/Londonderry Air (Danny Boy)//One O'Clock Jump	1957	3.75	7.50	15.00
—"Side 1" and "Side 6" of EPC 1506					
547-1101	Stairway to the Stars/To You/Little Brown Jug//Jim Jam Jump/For Jones/Hold Tight	1957	3.75	7.50	15.00
—"Side 2" and "Side 5" of EPC 1506					
547-1102	In the Mood/Sunrise Serenade//Bugle Call Rag/Moonlight Serenade	1957	3.75	7.50	15.00
—"Side 3" and "Side 4" of EPC 1506					
EPA 1-1494	*Star Dust/A Lovely Way to Spend an Evening/Long Ago and Far Away/My Ideal	1957	3.00	6.00	12.00
EPA 1-1494 [PS]	Marvelous Miller Moods, Vol. 1	1957	3.00	6.00	12.00
EPC-1506 [PS]	The Glenn Miller Carnegie Hall Concert	1957	3.75	7.50	15.00
—Cover for 3-EP set (547-1100, 547-1101, 547-1102)					
EPBT 3025 [PS]	Glenn Miller Concert	195?	5.00	10.00	20.00
—Cover for 2-EP set (947-0024, 947-0025)					
EPBT 3026 [PS]	Glenn Miller Concert, Vol. 2	195?	5.00	10.00	20.00
—Cover for 2-EP set (947-0026, 947-0027)					
EPBT 3057 [PS]	Selections from the Film "The Glenn Miller Story"	1954	5.00	10.00	20.00
—Cover for 2-EP set (947-0136, 947-0137)					
E3CW-3349/50 [DJ]	Highlights from the Great Glenn Miller Limited Edition 1953	1953	12.50	25.00	50.00
—Promo-only sampler from the limited box sets					
EPA 5035	Make Believe Ballroom Time/I Guess I'll Have to Dream the Rest//Juke Box Saturday Night/It Happened in Sun Valley	1958	3.00	6.00	12.00
EPA 5035 [PS]	(title unknown)	1958	3.00	6.00	12.00
EPA 5049	Serenade in Blue/Little Brown Jug//Don't Sit Under the Apple Tree (With Anyone Else But Me)/Pennsylvania Six-Five Thousand	1958	3.00	6.00	12.00
EPA 5049 [PS]	Serenade in Blue	1958	3.00	6.00	12.00
EPA 5081	Chattanooga Choo Choo/American Patrol//Tuxedo Junction/(I've Got a Gal in) Kalamazoo	1958	3.00	6.00	12.00
EPA 5081 [PS]	Chattanooga Choo Choo	1958	3.00	6.00	12.00
EPOT 6701 [(15)]	Glenn Miller and His Orchestra — Limited Edition, Volume Two	1954	50.00	100.00	200.00
—With 15 records (947-0178 through 947-0192), gold loose-leaf folder and numbered booklet					
599-9103	Moonlight Serenade/Perfidia//Love with a Capital "You"/Down for the Count	1956	3.00	6.00	12.00
—Side 1 and 20 of 10-EP set SPD 18; pink label					
599-9103	Moonlight Serenade/Perfidia//Love with a Capital "You"/Down for the Count	1956	3.00	6.00	12.00
—Side 1 and 20 of 10-EP set SPD 18; gray label					
599-9104	Just a Little Bit South of North Carolina/My Devotion/Weekend of a Private Secretary//Always in My Heart/Introduction to a Waltz/Make Believe	1956	3.00	6.00	12.00
—Side 2 and 19 of 10-EP set SPD 18; pink label					
599-9104	Just a Little Bit South of North Carolina/My Devotion/Weekend of a Private Secretary//Always in My Heart/Introduction to a Waltz/Make Believe	1956	3.00	6.00	12.00
—Side 2 and 19 of 10-EP set SPD 18; gray label					
599-9105	Japanese Sandman-What's the Matter with Me-Let's Dance-Blue Room-Bugle Call Rag-Naughty Sweetie Blues//My Melancholy Baby-Moon Love-Stomping at the Savoy-Blue Moon-The Lamplighter's Serenade-Under a Blanket of Blue	1956	3.00	6.00	12.00
—Side 3 and 18 of 10-EP set SPD 18; pink label					
599-9105	Japanese Sandman-What's the Matter with Me-Let's Dance-Blue Room-Bugle Call Rag-Naughty Sweetie Blues//My Melancholy Baby-Moon Love-Stomping at the Savoy-Blue Moon-The Lamplighter's Serenade-Under a Blanket of Blue	1956	3.00	6.00	12.00
—Side 3 and 18 of 10-EP set SPD 18; gray label					
599-9106	On a Little Street in Singapore/Fools Rush In/The Hop//Ida/Fresh As a Daisy/Careless	1956	3.00	6.00	12.00
—Side 4 and 17 of 10-EP set SPD 18; pink label					
599-9106	On a Little Street in Singapore/Fools Rush In/The Hop//Ida/Fresh As a Daisy/Careless	1956	3.00	6.00	12.00
—Side 4 and 17 of 10-EP set SPD 18; gray label					
599-9107	I Guess I'll Have to Change My Plan/Twenty-Four Robbers/Lady Be Good//Wishing Will Make it So/Say Si Si/Mister Meadowlark	1956	3.00	6.00	12.00
—Side 5 and 16 of 10-EP set SPD 18; pink label					
599-9107	I Guess I'll Have to Change My Plan/Twenty-Four Robbers/Lady Be Good//Wishing Will Make it So/Say Si Si/Mister Meadowlark	1956	3.00	6.00	12.00
—Side 5 and 16 of 10-EP set SPD 18; gray label					

Number	Title (A Side/B Side)	Yr	VG	VG+	NM
599-9108	Moon Over Miami-A Million Dreams Ago-Aloha-Baby Me-Rainbow Rhapsody//Boulder Buff/Sweet Eloise/Caribbean Clipper	1956	3.00	6.00	12.00

—Side 6 and 15 of 10-EP set SPD 18; pink label

Number	Title (A Side/B Side)	Yr	VG	VG+	NM
599-9108	Moon Over Miami-A Million Dreams Ago-Aloha-Baby Me-Rainbow Rhapsody//Boulder Buff/Sweet Eloise/Caribbean Clipper	1956	3.00	6.00	12.00

—Side 6 and 15 of 10-EP set SPD 18; gray label

Number	Title (A Side/B Side)	Yr	VG	VG+	NM
599-9109	My Darling-Blueberry Hill-I Can't Get Started-Don't Sit Under the Apple Tree-There'll Be Some Changes Made//Here We Go Again/Imagination/Angel Child	1956	3.00	6.00	12.00

—Side 7 and 14 of 10-EP set SPD 18; pink label

Number	Title (A Side/B Side)	Yr	VG	VG+	NM
599-9109	My Darling-Blueberry Hill-I Can't Get Started-Don't Sit Under the Apple Tree-There'll Be Some Changes Made//Here We Go Again/Imagination/Angel Child	1956	3.00	6.00	12.00

—Side 7 and 14 of 10-EP set SPD 18; gray label

Number	Title (A Side/B Side)	Yr	VG	VG+	NM
599-9110	Chattanooga Choo Choo/American Patrol/Oh So Good//Rhapsody in Blue/Rug Cutter's Swing/King Porter Stomp	1956	3.00	6.00	12.00

—Side 8 and 13 of 10-EP set SPD 18; pink label

Number	Title (A Side/B Side)	Yr	VG	VG+	NM
599-9110	Chattanooga Choo Choo/American Patrol/Oh So Good//Rhapsody in Blue/Rug Cutter's Swing/King Porter Stomp	1956	3.00	6.00	12.00

—Side 8 and 13 of 10-EP set SPD 18; gray label

Number	Title (A Side/B Side)	Yr	VG	VG+	NM
599-9111	Devil May Care/Sleepy Town Train/One O'Clock Jump//Sun Valley Jump/String of Pearls/Flagwaver	1956	3.00	6.00	12.00

—Side 9 and 12 of 10-EP set SPD 18; pink label

Number	Title (A Side/B Side)	Yr	VG	VG+	NM
599-9111	Devil May Care/Sleepy Town Train/One O'Clock Jump//Sun Valley Jump/String of Pearls/Flagwaver	1956	3.00	6.00	12.00

—Side 9 and 12 of 10-EP set SPD 18; gray label

Number	Title (A Side/B Side)	Yr	VG	VG+	NM
599-9112	Sliphorn Jive/Little Brown Jug/Farewell Blues//It Must Be Jelly/Chip Off the Old Block/Glen Island Special	1956	3.00	6.00	12.00

—Side 10 and 11 of 10-EP set SPD 18; pink label

Number	Title (A Side/B Side)	Yr	VG	VG+	NM
599-9112	Sliphorn Jive/Little Brown Jug/Farewell Blues//It Must Be Jelly/Chip Off the Old Block/Glen Island Special	1956	3.00	6.00	12.00

—Side 10 and 11 of 10-EP set SPD 18; gray label

Albums

20TH CENTURY

Number	Title (A Side/B Side)	Yr	VG	VG+	NM
T2-904 [(2)]	Remember Glenn	197?	3.75	7.50	15.00

20TH CENTURY FOX

Number	Title (A Side/B Side)	Yr	VG	VG+	NM
TFM-3159 [M]	This Is Glenn Miller and His Greatest Orchestra, Volume 1	1964	3.75	7.50	15.00
TFM-3160 [M]	This Is Glenn Miller and His Greatest Orchestra, Volume 2	1964	3.75	7.50	15.00
TFS-4159 [R]	This Is Glenn Miller and His Greatest Orchestra, Volume 1	1964	2.50	5.00	10.00
TFS-4160 [R]	This Is Glenn Miller and His Greatest Orchestra, Volume 2	1964	2.50	5.00	10.00

20TH FOX

Number	Title (A Side/B Side)	Yr	VG	VG+	NM
TCF-100-2 [(2) M]	Glenn Miller and His Orchestra Original Film Sound Tracks	1958	7.50	15.00	30.00
TCF-100-2S [(2) R]	Glenn Miller and His Orchestra Original Film Sound Tracks	1961	5.00	10.00	20.00
FOX 3020 [M]	Glenn Miller's Original Film Soundtracks, Volume 1	1958	5.00	10.00	20.00

—Half of 101

Number	Title (A Side/B Side)	Yr	VG	VG+	NM
FOX 3021 [M]	Glenn Miller's Original Film Soundtracks, Volume 2	1958	5.00	10.00	20.00

—Half of 101

BLUEBIRD

Number	Title (A Side/B Side)	Yr	VG	VG+	NM
AXM2-5512 [(2)]	The Complete Glenn Miller Volume 1, 1938-39	1975	3.00	6.00	12.00
AXM2-5514 [(2)]	The Complete Glenn Miller Volume 2, 1939	1975	3.00	6.00	12.00
AXM2-5534 [(2)]	The Complete Glenn Miller Volume 3, 1939-40	197?	3.00	6.00	12.00
AXM2-5558 [(2)]	The Complete Glenn Miller Volume 4, 1940	197?	3.00	6.00	12.00
AXM2-5565 [(2)]	The Complete Glenn Miller Volume 5, 1940	197?	3.00	6.00	12.00
AXM2-5569 [(2)]	The Complete Glenn Miller Volume 6, 1940-41	197?	3.00	6.00	12.00
AXM2-5570 [(2)]	The Complete Glenn Miller Volume 7, 1941	197?	3.00	6.00	12.00
AXM2-5571 [(2)]	The Complete Glenn Miller Volume 8, 1941-42	197?	3.00	6.00	12.00
AXM2-5574 [(2)]	The Complete Glenn Miller Volume 9, 1939-42	197?	3.00	6.00	12.00
6360-1-RB	Maj. Glenn Miller and the Army Air Force Band	1987	2.50	5.00	10.00
9785-1-RB [(4)]	The Popular Recordings 1938-1942	1989	6.25	12.50	25.00

EPIC

Number	Title (A Side/B Side)	Yr	VG	VG+	NM
LA 16002 [M]	Glenn Miller	1960	5.00	10.00	20.00

HARMONY

Number	Title (A Side/B Side)	Yr	VG	VG+	NM
HS 11393 [R]	Collector's Choice	1970	3.00	6.00	12.00

INTERMEDIA

Number	Title (A Side/B Side)	Yr	VG	VG+	NM
QS-5045	A String of Pearls	198?	2.00	4.00	8.00

KOALA

Number	Title (A Side/B Side)	Yr	VG	VG+	NM
AW 14186	Chattanooga Choo Choo	1979	3.00	6.00	12.00

MERCURY

Number	Title (A Side/B Side)	Yr	VG	VG+	NM
826635-1 [(2)]	Glenn Miller In Hollywood	1986	3.00	6.00	12.00

—Reissue of material formerly on 20th Century

MOVIETONE

Number	Title (A Side/B Side)	Yr	VG	VG+	NM
MTM-1003 [M]	Glenn Miller's Shindig	1965	3.75	7.50	15.00
MTS-72003 [R]	Glenn Miller's Shindig	1965	2.50	5.00	10.00
MTS-72018 [R]	The Glenn Miller Years	1967	3.00	6.00	12.00

PAIR

Number	Title (A Side/B Side)	Yr	VG	VG+	NM
PDL2-1003 [(2)]	Original Recordings, Volume 1	1986	3.00	6.00	12.00
PDL2-1036 [(2)]	Original Recordings, Volume 2	1986	3.00	6.00	12.00

RCA

Number	Title (A Side/B Side)	Yr	VG	VG+	NM
7648-1-R	Pure Gold	1988	—	3.00	6.00
7652-1-R	The Best of Glenn Miller	1988	—	3.00	6.00

RCA CAMDEN

Number	Title (A Side/B Side)	Yr	VG	VG+	NM
ACL2-0168 [(2)]	A String of Pearls	1973	3.00	6.00	12.00
ACL-0503	This Time the Dream's On Me	1974	2.00	4.00	8.00
CAL-751 [M]	The Great Glenn Miller	1963	3.75	7.50	15.00
CAS-751(e) [R]	The Great Glenn Miller	1963	3.00	6.00	12.00
CAL-829 [M]	The Original Recordings	1964	3.75	7.50	15.00
CAS-829(e) [R]	The Original Recordings	1964	3.00	6.00	12.00
CAL-2128 [M]	The Nearness of You and Others	1967	3.75	7.50	15.00
CAS-2128 [R]	The Nearness of You and Others	1967	3.00	6.00	12.00
CAS-2267	The One and Only Glenn Miller	1968	2.50	5.00	10.00
CXS-9004 [(2)]	Sunrise Serenade	197?	3.00	6.00	12.00

RCA VICTOR

Number	Title (A Side/B Side)	Yr	VG	VG+	NM
LPT-16 [10]	Glenn Miller Concert — Volume 1	1951	15.00	30.00	60.00
LPT-30 [10]	Glenn Miller Concert — Volume 2	1951	15.00	30.00	60.00
LPT-31 [10]	Glenn Miller	1951	15.00	30.00	60.00
PR-114 [M]	Glenn Miller Originals	1962	5.00	10.00	20.00

—Promotional item for Salada Foods Inc.

Number	Title (A Side/B Side)	Yr	VG	VG+	NM
PRM-181 [M]	Moonlight Serenade	196?	3.75	7.50	15.00
CPM2-0693 [(2)]	A Legendary Performer	1974	3.00	6.00	12.00
ANL1-0974	Pure Gold	1975	2.00	4.00	8.00
LOP-1005 [M]	The Marvelous Miller Medleys	1955	10.00	20.00	40.00
LPT-1016 [M]	Juke Box Saturday Night	1955	10.00	20.00	40.00
LPT-1031 [M]	The Nearness of You	1955	10.00	20.00	40.00
ANL1-1139	The Chesterfield Broadcasts, Volume 1	1975	2.00	4.00	8.00
LPM-1189 [M]	The Sound of Glenn Miller	1956	10.00	20.00	40.00
LPM-1190 [M]	This Is Glenn Miller	1956	10.00	20.00	40.00
AFL1-1192	Selections from "The Glenn Miller Story" and Other Hits	1977	2.00	4.00	8.00
LPM-1192 [M]	Selections from "The Glenn Miller Story" and Other Hits	1956	10.00	20.00	40.00
LSP-1192 [R]	Selections from "The Glenn Miller Story" and Other Hits	196?	3.75	7.50	15.00
LPM-1193 [M]	Glenn Miller Concert	1956	10.00	20.00	40.00
LPM-1494 [M]	Marvelous Miller Moods	1957	10.00	20.00	40.00
LPM-1506 [M]	The Glenn Miller Carnegie Hall Concert	1957	10.00	20.00	40.00
LPM-1973 [M]	The Marvelous Miller Medleys	1959	7.50	15.00	30.00
LSP-1973 [R]	The Marvelous Miller Medleys	196?	3.75	7.50	15.00
CPL1-2080	A Legendary Performer, Volume 2	1976	2.50	5.00	10.00
CPL1-2495	A Legendary Performer, Volume 3	1977	2.50	5.00	10.00
LPM-2767 [M]	Glenn Miller On the Air Volume 1	1963	3.75	7.50	15.00
LSP-2767 [R]	Glenn Miller On the Air Volume 1	1963	2.50	5.00	10.00
LPM-2768 [M]	Glenn Miller On the Air Volume 2	1963	3.75	7.50	15.00
LSP-2768 [R]	Glenn Miller On the Air Volume 2	1963	2.50	5.00	10.00
LPM-2769 [M]	Glenn Miller On the Air Volume 3	1963	3.75	7.50	15.00
LSP-2769 [R]	Glenn Miller On the Air Volume 3	1963	2.50	5.00	10.00
AFL1-2825	The Best of Glenn Miller Volume 3	1978	2.00	4.00	8.00
LPT-3001 [10]	Glenn Miller Concert — Volume 3	195?	15.00	30.00	60.00
LPT-3002 [10]	This Is Glenn Miller	195?	15.00	30.00	60.00
LPT-3036 [10]	This Is Glenn Miller — Volume 2	195?	15.00	30.00	60.00
LPT-3057 [10]	Selections from the Film "The Glenn Miller Story"	1954	15.00	30.00	60.00
LPT-3067 [10]	Sunrise Serenade	1954	15.00	30.00	60.00
LPM-3377 [M]	The Best of Glenn Miller	1965	3.75	7.50	15.00
LSP-3377 [R]	The Best of Glenn Miller	1965	2.50	5.00	10.00
LPM-3564 [M]	The Best of Glenn Miller Volume 2	1966	3.75	7.50	15.00
LSP-3564 [R]	The Best of Glenn Miller Volume 2	1966	2.50	5.00	10.00
LPM-3657 [M]	Blue Moonlight	1966	3.75	7.50	15.00
LSP-3657 [R]	Blue Moonlight	1966	2.50	5.00	10.00
AYL1-3666	Pure Gold	1980	—	3.00	6.00
AYL1-3759	Selections from "The Glenn Miller Story" and Other Hits	1981	—	3.00	6.00
AYL1-3809	The Best of Glenn Miller Volume 2	1981	—	3.00	6.00
AYL1-3810	The Best of Glenn Miller Volume 3	1981	—	3.00	6.00
AYL1-3871	The Best of Glenn Miller	1981	—	3.00	6.00
LPM-3873 [M]	The Chesterfield Broadcasts, Volume 1	1967	3.75	7.50	15.00
LSP-3873 [R]	The Chesterfield Broadcasts, Volume 1	1967	2.50	5.00	10.00
LSP-3981 [R]	The Chesterfield Broadcasts, Volume 2	1968	3.00	6.00	12.00
LSP-4125 [R]	The Best of Glenn Miller Volume 3	1969	3.00	6.00	12.00
VPM-6019 [(2)]	Glenn Miller: A Memorial 1944-1969	1969	3.75	7.50	15.00
VPM-6080 [(2)]	This Is Glenn Miller's Army Air Force Band	1972	3.75	7.50	15.00
LPM-6100 [(3) M]	For the Very First Time...	195?	12.50	25.00	50.00

—Black "Long Play" labels in leatherette spiral-bound binder

Number	Title (A Side/B Side)	Yr	VG	VG+	NM
LPM-6101 [(3) M]	Glenn Miller On the Air	1963	10.00	20.00	40.00
LSP-6101 [(3) R]	Glenn Miller On the Air	1963	6.25	12.50	25.00
LPT-6700 [(5) M]	Glenn Miller and His Orchestra Limited Edition	1953	37.50	75.00	150.00

—Silver labels with red print in leatherette spiral-bound binder

Number	Title (A Side/B Side)	Yr	VG	VG+	NM
LPT-6700 [(5) M]	Glenn Miller and His Orchestra Limited Edition — Second Pressing	195?	15.00	30.00	60.00

—Black "Long Play" labels in leatherette spiral-bound binder

Number	Title (A Side/B Side)	Yr	VG	VG+	NM
LPT-6701 [(5) M]	Glenn Miller and His Orchestra Limited Edition Volume Two	1954	30.00	60.00	120.00

—Black "Long Play" labels in leatherette spiral-bound binder

Number	Title (A Side/B Side)	Yr	VG	VG+	NM
LPT-6701 [(5) M]	Glenn Miller and His Orchestra Limited Edition Volume Two — Second Pressing	195?	15.00	30.00	60.00

—Black "Long Play" labels in leatherette spiral-bound binder; identified as "Second Pressing" throughout

Number	Title (A Side/B Side)	Yr	VG	VG+	NM
LPT-6702 [(4) M]	Glenn Miller Army Air Force Band	1955	30.00	60.00	120.00

—Black "Long Play" labels in leatherette spiral-bound binder

Number	Title (A Side/B Side)	Yr	VG	VG+	NM
LPT-6702 [(4) M]	Glenn Miller Army Air Force Band	195?	15.00	30.00	60.00

—Same as above, but in box rather than in binder

MILLER, HAL, AND THE RAYS

"The Rays" actually are the future FOUR SEASONS.

45s

AMY

Number	Title (A Side/B Side)	Yr	VG	VG+	NM
909	I Still Care/On My Own Two Feet	1964	25.00	50.00	100.00
920	A Blessing in Disguise/Cry Like the Rain	1965	20.00	40.00	80.00

TOPIX

Number	Title (A Side/B Side)	Yr	VG	VG+	NM
6003	An Angel Cried/Faith, Hope, Dreams	1961	10.00	20.00	40.00

MILLER, JODY

45s

CAPITOL

Number	Title (A Side/B Side)	Yr	VG	VG+	NM
2005	To Sir, With Love/Only When You're Lonely	1967	2.00	4.00	8.00
2066	I Knew You Well/I'm Into Lookin' for Someone to Love Me	1967	2.00	4.00	8.00
2187	It's My Time/Over the Edge	1968	2.00	4.00	8.00
2290	Long Black Limousine/Back in the Race	1968	2.00	4.00	8.00
2398	All the Crying in the World/Bon Soir Cher	1969	—	3.00	6.00
2558	Times to Come/My Daddy's Thousand Dollars	1969	—	3.00	6.00
5090	He Walks Like a Man/Looking at the World Through a Tear	1963	2.50	5.00	10.00

Number	Title (A Side/B Side)	Yr	VG	VG+	NM
5162	They Call My Guy a Tiger/Wonderful Round of Indifference	1964	2.50	5.00	10.00
5192	In My Room/Fever	1964	2.50	5.00	10.00
5269	My Baby's Gone/Warm Is the Love	1964	2.50	5.00	10.00
5298	This Is the Life/Look for Small Pleasures	1964	2.50	5.00	10.00
5353	Be My Man/Never Let Him Go	1965	2.50	5.00	10.00
5402	Queen of the House/The Greatest Actor	1965	2.00	4.00	8.00
5429	Silver Threads and Golden Needles/Melody for Robin	1965	2.00	4.00	8.00
5429 [PS]	Silver Threads and Golden Needles/Melody for Robin	1965	3.00	6.00	12.00
5483	Home of the Brave/This Is the Life	1965	2.00	4.00	8.00
5483 [PS]	Home of the Brave/This Is the Life	1965	3.00	6.00	12.00
5541	Magic Town/A Lonely Queen	1965	2.00	4.00	8.00
5594	We're Gonna Let the Good Times Roll/I Don't Care	1966	2.00	4.00	8.00
5671	I Remember Mama/Something in My Eye	1966	2.00	4.00	8.00
5743	Things/Quite a Long, Long Time	1966	2.00	4.00	8.00
5768	If You Were a Carpenter/Let Me Walk with You	1966	2.00	4.00	8.00
5846	Crazy/How Do You Say Goodbye	1967	2.00	4.00	8.00
5911	Shutters and Boards/Kiss Me	1967	2.00	4.00	8.00

EPIC

Number	Title (A Side/B Side)	Yr	VG	VG+	NM
10641	Look at Mine/Safe in These Lovin' Arms of Mine	1970	—	3.00	6.00
10692	If You Think I Love You Now (I've Just Started)/Looking Out My Back Door	1970	—	3.00	6.00
10734	He's So Fine/You're Number Two	1971	—	3.00	6.00
10785	Baby I'm Yours/Good Lovin'	1971	—	3.00	6.00
10835	Be My Baby/Your Love's Been a Long Time Comin'	1972	—	2.50	5.00
10878	There's a Party Goin' On/Love's the Answer	1972	—	2.50	5.00
10916	To Know Him Is to Love Him/Make Me Your Kind of Woman	1972	—	2.50	5.00
10960	Good News/Soul Song	1973	—	2.50	5.00
11016	Darling, You Can Always Come Back Home/We'll Sing Our Song Together	1973	—	2.50	5.00
11056	The House of the Rising Sun/In the Name of Love	1973	—	2.50	5.00
11076	Silent Night, Lonely Night/(B-side unknown)	1973	—	3.00	6.00
11094	Reflections/One More Chance	1974	—	2.50	5.00
11134	Natural Woman/Jimmy's Roses	1974	—	2.50	5.00
50042	Country Girl/Safe in These Lovin' Arms of Mine	1974	—	2.00	4.00
50079	The Best in Me/I'm Alright 'Til I See	1975	—	2.00	4.00
50117	Don't Take It Away/Long, Long Time	1975	—	2.00	4.00
50158	Will You Love Me Tomorrow/Love, You Never Had It So Good	1975	—	2.00	4.00
50203	Ashes of Love/She Calls Me Baby	1976	—	2.00	4.00
50304	When the New Wears Off Our Love/Silver and Gold	1976	—	2.00	4.00
50360	Spread a Little Love Around/Montana Cowboy	1977	—	2.00	4.00
50432	Another Lonely Night/All Night Long	1977	—	2.00	4.00
50512	Soft Lights and Slow Sexy Music/Home	1978	—	2.00	4.00
50568	(I Wanna) Love My Life Away/I'm Gonna Write a Song	1978	—	2.00	4.00
50612	Kiss Away/Hold Me, Thrill Me, Kiss Me	1978	—	2.00	4.00
50673	I'm Gonna Make You Mine/I Don't Want Nobody (To Lead Me On)	1979	—	2.00	4.00
50734	Lay a Little Lovin' On Me/Crazy on You	1979	—	2.00	4.00

Albums

CAPITOL

Number	Title	Yr	VG	VG+	NM
ST 1913 [S]	Wednesday's Child Is Full of Woe	1963	10.00	20.00	40.00
T 1913 [M]	Wednesday's Child Is Full of Woe	1963	7.50	15.00	30.00
ST 2349 [S]	Queen of the House	1965	5.00	10.00	20.00
T 2349 [M]	Queen of the House	1965	3.75	7.50	15.00
ST 2412 [S]	Home of the Brave	1965	5.00	10.00	20.00
T 2412 [M]	Home of the Brave	1965	3.75	7.50	15.00
ST 2446 [S]	Jody Miller Sings the Great Hits of Buck Owens	1966	5.00	10.00	20.00
T 2446 [M]	Jody Miller Sings the Great Hits of Buck Owens	1966	3.75	7.50	15.00
ST 2996	The Nashville Sound of Jody Miller	1968	3.75	7.50	15.00
ST-11169	The Best of Jody Miller	1973	3.00	6.00	12.00

EPIC

Number	Title	Yr	VG	VG+	NM
E 30282	Look at Mine	1971	3.00	6.00	12.00
E 30659	He's So Fine	1971	3.00	6.00	12.00
KE 31706	There's a Party Goin' On	1972	3.00	6.00	12.00
KE 32386	Good News!	1973	3.00	6.00	12.00
KE 32569	House of the Rising Sun	1974	3.00	6.00	12.00
KE 33349	Country Girl	1975	3.00	6.00	12.00
KE 33934	Will You Love Me Tomorrow?	1976	3.00	6.00	12.00
PE 34446	Here's Jody	1977	3.00	6.00	12.00

MILLER, JODY, AND JOHNNY PAYCHECK

Also see each artist's individual listings.

45s

EPIC

Number	Title (A Side/B Side)	Yr	VG	VG+	NM
5-10863	Let's All Go Down to the River/In the Garden	1972	—	3.50	7.00

MILLER, MICKEY

Albums

FOLKWAYS

Number	Title	Yr	VG	VG+	NM
FA-2393 [M]	American Folk Songs	1959	7.50	15.00	30.00

MILLER, MITCH

45s

COLUMBIA

Number	Title (A Side/B Side)	Yr	VG	VG+	NM
B-315 [PS]	Mmmmitch!	1952	2.50	5.00	10.00
—Box for 4-record set					
1-706	Tzena, Tzena, Tzena/The Sleigh	1950	6.25	12.50	25.00
—Microgroove 33 1/3 rpm 7-inch single					
6-706	Tzena, Tzena, Tzena/The Sleigh	1950	5.00	10.00	20.00
1-780 (?)	In My Arms/Au Revoir Again	1950	6.25	12.50	25.00
—Microgroove 33 1/3 rpm 7-inch single					
6-780 (?)	In My Arms/Au Revoir Again	1950	5.00	10.00	20.00
1-790 (?)	Autumn Leaves/Song of Delilah	1950	6.25	12.50	25.00
—Microgroove 33 1/3 rpm 7-inch single					
6-790 (?)	Autumn Leaves/Song of Delilah	1950	5.00	10.00	20.00
S7 30441 [S]	Goodnight Irene/On Top of Old Smoky	1960	2.50	5.00	10.00
—"Stereo Seven" 33 1/3 single, small hole					
31020 [S]	titles unknown	1961	2.50	5.00	10.00
31021 [S]	titles unknown	1961	2.50	5.00	10.00
31022 [S]	titles unknown	1961	2.50	5.00	10.00
31023 [S]	titles unknown	1961	2.50	5.00	10.00
31024 [S]	titles unknown	1961	2.50	5.00	10.00
31079 [S]	titles unknown	1961	2.50	5.00	10.00
31080 [S]	titles unknown	1961	2.50	5.00	10.00
31081 [S]	titles unknown	1961	2.50	5.00	10.00
31082 [S]	titles unknown	1961	2.50	5.00	10.00
31083 [S]	titles unknown	1961	2.50	5.00	10.00
31364 [S]	titles unknown	1962	2.50	5.00	10.00
31365 [S]	titles unknown	1962	2.50	5.00	10.00
31366 [S]	titles unknown	1962	2.50	5.00	10.00
31367 [S]	titles unknown	1962	2.50	5.00	10.00
31368 [S]	titles unknown	1962	2.50	5.00	10.00
31565 [S]	titles unknown	1962	2.50	5.00	10.00
31566 [S]	titles unknown	1962	2.50	5.00	10.00
31567 [S]	titles unknown	1962	2.50	5.00	10.00
31568 [S]	titles unknown	1962	2.50	5.00	10.00
31569 [S]	titles unknown	1962	2.50	5.00	10.00
—Anyone who can fill in these gaps -- the above 20 all are Columbia "Stereo 7" singles -- please let us know.					
39053	The Sea of the Moon/Smile, Smile, Smile	1950	3.75	7.50	15.00
39300	Cider Night/By the Moonlight	1951	3.75	7.50	15.00
39617	Greensleeves/Love Makes the World Go Round	1951	3.75	7.50	15.00
39679	Kalamazoo to Timbuktu/Sing Our Song	1952	3.00	6.00	12.00
39727	Serenade for Horns/Horn Belt Boogie	1952	3.00	6.00	12.00
39742	Cuban Nightingale/Bunk House Boogie	1952	3.00	6.00	12.00
39832	Kalamazoo to Timbuktu/Keep Me in Mind	1952	2.50	5.00	10.00
39833	The Sea of the Moon/Greensleeves	1952	2.50	5.00	10.00
39834	Tzena, Tzena, Tzena/Autumn Leaves	1952	2.50	5.00	10.00
39835	Au Revoir Again/Song of Delilah	1952	2.50	5.00	10.00
—The above four comprise box set B-315					
39851	Meet Mister Callaghan/How Strange	1952	3.00	6.00	12.00
39875	Zulu Warrior/Johnny Goggabie	1952	3.00	6.00	12.00
39901	Without My Love/Just Dreaming	1952	3.00	6.00	12.00
39982	Oriental Polka/Tira Lira Madeira	1953	3.00	6.00	12.00
40100	Under Paris Skies/Farewell	1953	3.00	6.00	12.00
40244	Frou! Frou!/Sail! Sail! Sail!	1954	3.00	6.00	12.00
40261	Napoleon/Monday Serenade	1954	3.00	6.00	12.00
40302	Sabrina/Wooden Shoes and Happy Hearts	1954	3.00	6.00	12.00
40409	Follow Me/The Singing Lesson	1955	2.50	5.00	10.00
40493	Theme from "I Am a Camera"/On Honolulu Bay	1955	2.50	5.00	10.00
40540	The Yellow Rose of Texas/Blackberry Winter	1955	2.50	5.00	10.00
40575	The Bonnie Blue Gal/Bel Sante	1955	2.50	5.00	10.00
40635	Lisbon Antigua (In Old Lisbon)/Willy Can	1956	2.50	5.00	10.00
40655	Madeira/Bolero Gaucho	1956	2.50	5.00	10.00
40683	That Girl/St. Lawrence River	1956	2.50	5.00	10.00
40715	The President on the Dollar/Trapeze	1956	2.50	5.00	10.00
40730	Theme Song from "Song for a Summer Night" (Vocal)/(Instrumental)	1956	2.50	5.00	10.00
40750	Jubilation T. Cornpone/War and Peace	1956	2.50	5.00	10.00
40772	Song of the Sparrow/(Instrumental)	1956	2.50	5.00	10.00
40831	A Very Special Love (Song for the Ninth Day)/Song for the Ninth Day (A Very Special Love)	1957	2.50	5.00	10.00
40871	Just How Much I Love You/(Instrumental)	1957	2.50	5.00	10.00
40947	Java/Who Will Kiss Your Ruby Lips	1957	2.50	5.00	10.00
40999	Whistle Stop/The Bowery Grenadiers	1957	2.50	5.00	10.00
41066	March from the River Kwai and Coloney Bogey/Hey Little Baby	1957	2.50	5.00	10.00
41128	Ginny, My Joy/Bonnie Eloise	1958	2.00	4.00	8.00
41203	Rockabye in Birdland/The Key to Your Heart	1958	2.00	4.00	8.00
41235	Bluebell/It Seems Like Only Yesterday	1958	2.00	4.00	8.00
41301	Lover's Gold/Moonlight and Roses	1958	2.00	4.00	8.00
41317	The Children's Marching Song/Carolina in the Morning	1959	2.00	4.00	8.00
41317 [PS]	The Children's Marching Song/Carolina in the Morning	1959	3.00	6.00	12.00
41375	Holiday for Lovers/This Here Goat	1959	2.00	4.00	8.00
41424	Join the Cavalry/Hey Betty Martin	1959	2.00	4.00	8.00
41499	Do-Re-Mi/Alouette March	1959	2.00	4.00	8.00
41499 [PS]	Do-Re-Mi/Alouette March	1959	3.00	6.00	12.00
41616	Sing Along/Pink Polemoniums	1960	2.00	4.00	8.00
41716	Silly Little Tune/Walkin' Down to Washington	1960	2.00	4.00	8.00
41789	The Zasu Zasu Tree/Sing-Song Girl	1960	2.00	4.00	8.00
41814	Must Be Santa/Christmas Spirit	1960	2.50	5.00	10.00
41941	Tunes of Glory/Shlub-a-Dubba-Due	1961	2.00	4.00	8.00
41988	The Whiffenpoof Song/Sweet Adeline/Let Me Call You Sweetheart	1961	2.00	4.00	8.00
41989	Shine On Harvest Moon/For Me and My Gal/My Wild Irish Rose/When Irish Eyes Are Smiling	1961	2.00	4.00	8.00
41990	There Is a Tavern in the Town/Show Me the Way to Go Home/That Old Gang of Mine	1961	2.00	4.00	8.00
41991	The Prisoner's Song/Where Do You Work/Yes! We Have No Bananas	1961	2.00	4.00	8.00
41992	Poor Butterfly/I'm Looking Over a Four-Leaf Clover	1961	2.00	4.00	8.00
42016	The Guns of Navarone/Bye Bye Blackbird	1961	2.00	4.00	8.00
42210	Sleigh Ride/The Christmas Song	1961	2.00	4.00	8.00
42211	Rudolph the Red-Nosed Reindeer/The Twelve Days of Christmas	1961	2.00	4.00	8.00
42212	Jingle Bells/White Christmas	1961	2.00	4.00	8.00
42213	Silent Night, Holy Night/Deck The Halls With Boughs Of Holly	1961	2.00	4.00	8.00
42214	God Rest Ye Merry Gentlemen/O Come, All Ye Faithful	1961	2.00	4.00	8.00
42215	Aura Lee/The Fog and the Grog	1961	2.00	4.00	8.00
42240	Must Be Santa/Be a Santa	1961	2.00	4.00	8.00
3-42240	Must Be Santa/Be a Santa	1961	3.00	6.00	12.00
—"Columbia Single 33"; small hole					
42305	Happy Whistlin' Blues/(Instrumental)	1962	—	3.00	6.00
42397	Jeepers Creepers/Swanee	1962	—	3.00	6.00
42398	We're In the Money/Chinatown, My Chinatown	1962	—	3.00	6.00
42399	Ain't We Got Fun/You're An Old Smoothie	1962	—	3.00	6.00

Number	Title (A Side/B Side)	Yr	VG	VG+	NM
42400	I Wanna Be Happy/Tea for Two	1962	—	3.00	6.00
42401	Black Bottom/Bidin' My Time	1962	—	3.00	6.00
42484	Rosa Linda/Sweet Evelina	1962	—	3.00	6.00
42585	The Longest Day/(Instrumental)	1962	—	3.00	6.00
42797	The House Is Haunted/It's a Darn Good Thing	1963	—	3.00	6.00
42813	The Great Escape March/Shenandoah	1963	—	3.00	6.00
42914	Pine Cones and Holly Berries/Whispering Hope	1963	2.00	4.00	8.00
42914 [PS]	Pine Cones and Holly Berries/Whispering Hope	1963	2.50	5.00	10.00
43053	Whip Out Your Ukulele/Song for a Summer Night	1964	—	3.00	6.00
43149	Youngblood Hawk Theme/(Instrumental)	1964	—	3.00	6.00
43247	To Be with You/Major Dundee March	1965	—	3.00	6.00
50033	Autumn Leaves/(B-side unknown)	1955	2.50	5.00	10.00
—Early "Hall of Fame Series" reissue, this charted with this number in 1955					
DECCA					
25701	Red Wing/Get Me to the Church On Time	1965	—	3.00	6.00
31883	Ballad from Vietnam/That's All for Now	1965	—	3.00	6.00
31934	Into Each Life Some Rain Must Fall/He Who Hesitates Is Lost	1966	—	3.00	6.00
DIAMOND					
251	Dear World/One Person	1968	—	2.50	5.00
UNITED ARTISTS					
50260	Soft Is the Sparrow/Waking Up Son	1968	—	2.50	5.00

7-Inch Extended Plays

Number	Title (A Side/B Side)	Yr	VG	VG+	NM
COLUMBIA					
C 7791	The Blizzard Song/Frosty The Snow Man//Let It Snow/Sleigh Ride	1966	—	3.00	6.00
C 7791 [PS]	Singin' Up a Blizzard	1966	2.00	4.00	8.00
—Free with a 6-pack of Fresca (sleeve is designed to slip over the neck of a bottle)					
B-11601	*That Old Gang of Mine/Down by the Old Mill Stream/You Are My Sunshine/By the Light of the Silvery Moon	1958	2.00	4.00	8.00
B-11601 [PS]	Sing Along with Mitch, Vol. 1	1958	2.00	4.00	8.00
B-11602	(contents unknown)	1958	2.00	4.00	8.00
B-11602 [PS]	Sing Along with Mitch, Vol. 2	1958	2.00	4.00	8.00
B-11603	(contents unknown)	1958	2.00	4.00	8.00
B-11603 [PS]	Sing Along with Mitch, Vol. 3	1958	2.00	4.00	8.00
B-12051	*Joy to the World/We Three Kings of Orient Are/Hark! The Herald Angels Sing/It Came Upon a Midnight Clear	1958	2.00	4.00	8.00
B-12051 [PS]	Christmas Sing Along with Mitch	1958	2.00	4.00	8.00
B-12431	*Pretty Baby-Be My Little Baby Bumble Bee/Moonlight and Roses/Sweet Adeline-Let Me Call You Sweetheart/The Whiffenpoof Song	1958	2.00	4.00	8.00
B-12431 [PS]	More Sing Along with Mitch, Vol. 1	1958	2.00	4.00	8.00
B-12432	(contents unknown)	1958	2.00	4.00	8.00
B-12432 [PS]	More Sing Along with Mitch, Vol. 2	1958	2.00	4.00	8.00
B-12433	(contents unknown)	1958	2.00	4.00	8.00
B-12433 [PS]	More Sing Along with Mitch, Vol. 3	1958	2.00	4.00	8.00
B-12831	*In a Shanty in Old Shanty Town/Smiles/Beer Barrel Polka/Hinky Dinky Parlez-Vous - She'll Be Coming 'Round the Mountain	1959	2.00	4.00	8.00
B-12831 [PS]	Still More! Sing Along with Mitch	1959	2.00	4.00	8.00
B-13161	On Top of Old Smokey/Medley: Camptown Races-Oh, Susanna//Down in the Valley/Blue Tail Fly	1960	2.00	4.00	8.00
B-13161 [PS]	Folk Songs Sing Along with Mitch, Vol. I	1960	2.00	4.00	8.00
B-13162	(contents unknown)	1960	2.00	4.00	8.00
B-13162 [PS]	Folk Songs Sing Along with Mitch, Vol. II	1960	2.00	4.00	8.00
B-13163	(contents unknown)	1960	2.00	4.00	8.00
B-13163 [PS]	Folk Songs Sing Along with Mitch, Vol. III	1960	2.00	4.00	8.00
B-13311	*I Love You Truly/Meet Me Tonight in Dreamland/The Sweetest Story Ever Told/I Wonder Who's Kissing Her Now	1960	2.00	4.00	8.00
B-13311 [PS]	Party Sing Along with Mitch, Volume 1	1960	2.00	4.00	8.00
B-13312	(contents unknown)	1960	2.00	4.00	8.00
B-13312 [PS]	Party Sing Along with Mitch, Volume 2	1960	2.00	4.00	8.00
B-13313	(contents unknown)	1960	2.00	4.00	8.00
B-13313 [PS]	Party Sing Along with Mitch, Volume 3	1960	2.00	4.00	8.00
B-13891	*Polly Wolly Doodle-Wait for the Wagon-The Old Gray Mare/Juanita-Sweet Genevieve/Drink to Me Only with Thine Eyes-Vive L'Amour/Drunk Last Night	1960	2.00	4.00	8.00
B-13891 [PS]	Fireside Sing Along with Mitch, Vol. 1	1960	2.00	4.00	8.00
B-13892	(contents unknown)	1960	2.00	4.00	8.00
B-13892 [PS]	Fireside Sing Along with Mitch, Vol. 2	1960	2.00	4.00	8.00
B-13893	(contents unknown)	1960	2.00	4.00	8.00
B-13893 [PS]	Fireside Sing Along with Mitch, Vol. 3	1960	2.00	4.00	8.00

Albums

Number	Title (A Side/B Side)	Yr	VG	VG+	NM
ATLANTIC					
SD 8277	Peace Sing Along with Mitch	1970	3.00	6.00	12.00
COLUMBIA					
CL 601 [M]	Mmmmitch!	1954	5.00	10.00	20.00
—Maroon label, gold print					
CL 779 [M]	It's So Peaceful in the Country	1956	5.00	10.00	20.00
—Red and black label with 6 "eye" logos					
CL 1102 [M]	Mitch's Marches	1957	3.75	7.50	15.00
CL 1160 [M]	Sing Along with Mitch	1958	3.75	7.50	15.00
CL 1205 [M]	Christmas Sing Along with Mitch	1958	3.75	7.50	15.00
—Originals have gatefold cover with eight detachable lyric sheets inside					
CL 1243 [M]	More Sing Along with Mitch	1958	3.75	7.50	15.00
CL 1283 [M]	Still More! Sing Along with Mitch	1959	3.75	7.50	15.00
CL 1316 [M]	Folk Songs Sing Along with Mitch	1959	3.75	7.50	15.00
CL 1331 [M]	Party Sing Along with Mitch	1959	3.75	7.50	15.00
CL 1389 [M]	Fireside Sing Along with Mitch	1959	3.75	7.50	15.00
CL 1414 [M]	Saturday Night Sing Along with Mitch	1960	3.00	6.00	12.00
CL 1457 [M]	Sentimental Sing Along with Mitch	1960	3.00	6.00	12.00
CL 1475 [M]	March Along with Mitch	1960	3.00	6.00	12.00
CL 1542 [M]	Memories Sing Along with Mitch	1960	3.00	6.00	12.00
CL 1544 [M]	Mitch's Greatest Hits	1961	3.00	6.00	12.00
CL 1568 [M]	Happy Times! Sing Along with Mitch	1961	3.00	6.00	12.00
CL 1628 [M]	TV Sing Along with Mitch	1961	3.00	6.00	12.00
CL 1671 [M]	Your Request Sing Along with Mitch	1961	3.00	6.00	12.00
CL 1701 [M]	Holiday Sing Along with Mitch	1961	3.00	6.00	12.00
CL 1727 [M]	Rhythm Sing Along with Mitch	1962	3.00	6.00	12.00
CL 1773 [M]	Family Sing Along with Mitch	1962	3.00	6.00	12.00
CL 1864 [M]	Night Time Sing Along with Mitch	1963	3.00	6.00	12.00
CL 2063 [M]	Hymn Sing Along with Mitch	1963	3.00	6.00	12.00
CS 8004	Sing Along with Mitch	1963	3.00	6.00	12.00
—Red label					
CS 8004	Sing Along with Mitch	1970	2.00	4.00	8.00
—Orange label					
CS 8004 [S]	Sing Along with Mitch	1959	5.00	10.00	20.00
—Red and black label with 6 "eye" logos					
PC 8004	Sing Along with Mitch	198?	—	3.00	6.00
—Reissue with new prefix					
CS 8027 [S]	Christmas Sing Along with Mitch	1959	5.00	10.00	20.00
—Originals have gatefold cover with eight detachable lyric sheets inside					
CS 8043 [S]	More Sing Along with Mitch	1959	5.00	10.00	20.00
CS 8099 [S]	Still More! Sing Along with Mitch	1959	5.00	10.00	20.00
CS 8118 [S]	Folk Songs Sing Along with Mitch	1959	5.00	10.00	20.00
CS 8138 [S]	Party Sing Along with Mitch	1959	5.00	10.00	20.00
CS 8184 [S]	Fireside Sing Along with Mitch	1959	5.00	10.00	20.00
CS 8211 [S]	Saturday Night Sing Along with Mitch	1960	3.75	7.50	15.00
CS 8251 [S]	Sentimental Sing Along with Mitch	1960	3.75	7.50	15.00
CS 8342 [S]	Memories Sing Along with Mitch	1960	3.75	7.50	15.00
CS 8368 [S]	Happy Times! Sing Along with Mitch	1961	3.75	7.50	15.00
CS 8428 [S]	TV Sing Along with Mitch	1961	3.75	7.50	15.00
CS 8471 [S]	Your Request Sing Along with Mitch	1961	3.75	7.50	15.00
CS 8501 [S]	Holiday Sing Along with Mitch	1961	3.75	7.50	15.00
CS 8527 [S]	Rhythm Sing Along with Mitch	1962	3.75	7.50	15.00
CS 8573 [S]	Family Sing Along with Mitch	1962	3.75	7.50	15.00
CS 8638 [R]	Mitch's Greatest Hits	1963	2.50	5.00	10.00
CS 8664 [S]	Night Time Sing Along with Mitch	1963	3.75	7.50	15.00
CS 8863 [S]	Hymn Sing Along with Mitch	1963	3.75	7.50	15.00
G 30250 [(2)]	34 All Time Great Sing Along Selections	1970	3.00	6.00	12.00
3C 39297	Holiday Sing Along with Mitch	1984	2.00	4.00	8.00
PC 39298	Christmas Sing Along with Mitch	1984	2.00	4.00	8.00
DECCA					
DL 4777 [M]	Dance and Sing Along with Mitch	1966	2.50	5.00	10.00
DL 74777 [S]	Dance and Sing Along with Mitch	1966	3.00	6.00	12.00
HARMONY					
HL 7404 [M]	March Along with Mitch	1967	2.50	5.00	10.00
HS 11204 [S]	March Along with Mitch	1967	3.00	6.00	12.00
HS 11241	Fireside Sing Along with Mitch	1968	2.50	5.00	10.00
HS 11242	Memories Sing Along with Mitch	1968	2.50	5.00	10.00
HS 11273	Everybody Sing Along with Mitch	1968	2.50	5.00	10.00
HS 11354	Night Time Sing Along with Mitch	1970	2.50	5.00	10.00

MILLER, MRS.

45s

Number	Title (A Side/B Side)	Yr	VG	VG+	NM
AMARET					
101	Up, Up and Away/Green Thumb	1969	2.00	4.00	8.00
114	I've Gotta Be Me/Renaissance of Smut	1970	2.00	4.00	8.00
CAPITOL					
5640	Downtown/A Lover's Concerto	1966	2.50	5.00	10.00

Albums

Number	Title (A Side/B Side)	Yr	VG	VG+	NM
AMARET					
5000	Mrs. Miller Does Her Thing	1969	5.00	10.00	20.00
CAPITOL					
ST 2494 [S]	Mrs. Miller's Greatest Hits	1966	7.50	15.00	30.00
T 2494 [M]	Mrs. Miller's Greatest Hits	1966	6.25	12.50	25.00
ST 2579 [S]	Will Success Spoil Mrs. Miller?	1966	7.50	15.00	30.00
T 2579 [M]	Will Success Spoil Mrs. Miller?	1966	6.25	12.50	25.00
ST 2734 [S]	The Country Soul of Mrs. Miller	1967	6.25	12.50	25.00
T 2734 [M]	The Country Soul of Mrs. Miller	1967	6.25	12.50	25.00

MILLER, NED

45s

Number	Title (A Side/B Side)	Yr	VG	VG+	NM
CAPITOL					
2074	Endless/Only a Fool	1968	—	3.00	6.00
4607	My Heart Waits at the Door/Cold Gray Bars	1961	3.00	6.00	12.00
4652	Dark Moon/Go On Back, You Fool	1961	3.00	6.00	12.00
5431	Whistle Walkin'/Two Voices, Two Shadows, Two Faces	1965	2.00	4.00	8.00
5502	Fall of the King/Down the Street	1965	2.00	4.00	8.00
5568	Lovin' Pains/If the World Turned Into Ashes	1965	2.00	4.00	8.00
5661	Right Behind These Lips/Summer Roses	1966	2.00	4.00	8.00
5742	Lorraine/Teardrop Lane	1966	2.00	4.00	8.00
5868	The Hobo/Echo of the Pines	1967	2.00	4.00	8.00
DOT					
15601	From a Jack to a King/Parade of Broken Hearts	1957	10.00	20.00	40.00
15651	Turn Back/Lights in the Street	1957	3.75	7.50	15.00
FABOR					
114	From a Jack to a King/Parade of Broken Hearts	1962	3.00	6.00	12.00
116	One Among the Many/Man Behind the Gun	1963	2.50	5.00	10.00
121	Another Fool Like Me/Magic Moon	1963	2.50	5.00	10.00
125	Big Love/Sunday Morning Tears	1964	2.50	5.00	10.00
128	Invisible Tears/Old Restless Ocean	1964	2.50	5.00	10.00
137	Do What You Do Do Well/Dusty Guitar	1964	2.00	4.00	8.00
139	What I Know/Lights in the Street	1965	2.00	4.00	8.00
JACKPOT					
48020	Girl from the Second World/Ring the Bell for Johnny	1960	3.00	6.00	12.00
—With Jan Howard					
REPUBLIC					
1404	Autumn Winds/My Last Go-Round	1969	—	2.50	5.00
1410	Breakin'/Just Walkin' in the Rain	1970	—	2.50	5.00
1411	The Lover's Song/Cold Gray Bars	1970	—	2.50	5.00
1416	Back to Oklahoma/I Hang My Head and Cry	1970	—	2.50	5.00

Albums

Number	Title (A Side/B Side)	Yr	VG	VG+	NM
CAPITOL					
ST 2330 [S]	Ned Miller Sings the Songs of Ned Miller	1965	6.25	12.50	25.00
T 2330 [M]	Ned Miller Sings the Songs of Ned Miller	1965	5.00	10.00	20.00
ST 2414 [S]	The Best of Ned Miller	1966	5.00	10.00	20.00
T 2414 [M]	The Best of Ned Miller	1966	3.75	7.50	15.00
ST 2586 [S]	Teardrop Lane	1967	5.00	10.00	20.00
T 2586 [M]	Teardrop Lane	1967	5.00	10.00	20.00
ST 2914	In the Name of Love	1968	3.75	7.50	15.00

Number	Title (A Side/B Side)	Yr	VG	VG+	NM
FABOR					
FLP-1001 [M]	From a Jack to a King	1963	10.00	20.00	40.00
—Black vinyl					
FLP-1001 [M]	From a Jack to a King	1963	25.00	50.00	100.00
—Colored vinyl					

MILLER, ROGER

45s

Number	Title (A Side/B Side)	Yr	VG	VG+	NM
20TH CENTURY					
2421	The Hat/Pleasing the Crowd	1979	—	2.00	4.00
BUENA VISTA					
493	Whistle Stop/Not in Nottingham	1973	—	2.50	5.00
493 [PS]	Whistle Stop/Not in Nottingham	1973	—	2.50	5.00
COLUMBIA					
02681	Old Friends/When a House Is Not a Home	1982	—	2.00	4.00
—Roger Miller/Willie Nelson/Ray Price					
10052	Our Love/Yester Waltz	1974	—	2.50	5.00
10107	I Love a Rodeo/Lovin' You Is Always on My Mind	1975	—	2.50	5.00
45873	Open Up Your Heart/Qua La Linta	1973	—	2.50	5.00
45948	I Believe in the Sunrise/Shannon's Song	1973	—	2.50	5.00
46000	Whistle Stop/The 4th of July	1974	—	2.50	5.00
DECCA					
30838	Wrong Kind of Girl/A Man Like Me	1959	3.75	7.50	15.00
30953	Sweet Ramona/Jason Fleming	1959	3.75	7.50	15.00
ELEKTRA					
47192	Everyone Gets Crazy Now and Then/Aladam Bama	1981	—	2.00	4.00
MCA					
52663	River in the Rain/Hand for the Hog	1985	—	—	3.00
52855	Some Hearts Get All the Breaks/Arkansas	1986	—	—	3.00
MERCURY					
71212	Poor Little John/My Fellow	1957	6.25	12.50	25.00
73102	South/Don't We All Have the Right	1970	—	2.50	5.00
73190	Tomorrow Night in Baltimore/A Million Years or So	1971	—	2.50	5.00
73230	Loving Her Was Easier (Than Anything I'll Ever Do Again)/Que La Linta	1971	—	2.50	5.00
73268	We Found It in Each Other's Arms/Sunny Side of My Life	1972	—	2.50	5.00
73321	Rings for Sale/Conversations	1972	—	2.50	5.00
73354	Hoppy's Gone/I Jumped from Uncle Harvey's Plane	1972	—	2.50	5.00
MUSICOR					
1102	Can't Stop Loving You/You're Forgetting Me	1965	2.50	5.00	10.00
RCA VICTOR					
47-7776	Footprints in the Snow/You Don't Want My Love	1960	3.75	7.50	15.00
47-7878	When Two Worlds Collide/Every Which-A-Way	1961	3.75	7.50	15.00
47-7958	Burma Shave/Fair Swiss Maiden	1961	3.75	7.50	15.00
47-8028	Sorry, Willie/Hitch-Hiker	1962	3.00	6.00	12.00
47-8091	Trouble on the Turnpike/Hey Little Star	1962	3.00	6.00	12.00
47-8175	Lock, Stock and Teardrops/I Know Who It Is	1963	3.00	6.00	12.00
47-8651	If You Want Me To/Hey Little Star	1965	2.50	5.00	10.00
SMASH					
1876	Less and Less/Got Two Again	1964	3.00	6.00	12.00
1881	Dang Me/Got Two Again	1964	2.50	5.00	10.00
1881 [PS]	Dang Me/Got Two Again	1964	3.75	7.50	15.00
—Red sleeve					
1881 [PS]	Dang Me/Got Two Again	1964	5.00	10.00	20.00
—Yellow sleeve					
1926	Chug-a-Lug/Reincarnation	1964	2.50	5.00	10.00
1947	Do-Wacka-Do/Love Is Not for Me	1964	2.50	5.00	10.00
1947 [PS]	Do-Wacka-Do/Love Is Not for Me	1964	3.75	7.50	15.00
1965	King of the Road/Atta Boy Girl	1965	3.00	6.00	12.00
1983	Engine, Engine #9/The Last Word in Lonesome Is Me	1965	2.00	4.00	8.00
1994	One Dyin' and a-Buryin'/It Happened Just That Way	1965	2.00	4.00	8.00
1994 [PS]	One Dyin' and a-Buryin'/It Happened Just That Way	1965	3.75	7.50	15.00
1998	Kansas City Star/Guess I'll Pack Up My Heart (And Go Home)	1965	2.00	4.00	8.00
2010	England Swings/Good Old Days	1965	2.00	4.00	8.00
2024	Husbands and Wives/I've Been a Long Time Leavin'	1966	2.00	4.00	8.00
2043	You Can't Roller Skate in a Buffalo Herd/Train of Life	1966	2.00	4.00	8.00
2055	My Uncle Used to Love Me But She Died/You're My Kingdom	1966	2.00	4.00	8.00
2066	Heartbreak Hotel/Less and Less	1966	2.00	4.00	8.00
2081	Walkin' in the Sunshine/Home	1967	2.00	4.00	8.00
2121	The Ballad of Waterhole #3 (Code of the West)/Rainbow Valley	1967	2.00	4.00	8.00
2121 [PS]	The Ballad of Waterhole #3 (Code of the West)/Rainbow Valley	1967	3.75	7.50	15.00
2130	Old Toy Trains/Silent Night	1967	2.50	5.00	10.00
2130 [PS]	Old Toy Trains/Silent Night	1967	3.00	6.00	12.00
2148	Little Green Apples/Our Little Love	1968	2.00	4.00	8.00
2148 [PS]	Little Green Apples/Our Little Love	1968	3.00	6.00	12.00
2183	What I'd Give (To Be the Wind)/Toliver	1968	2.00	4.00	8.00
2197	Vance/Little Children Run and Play	1968	2.00	4.00	8.00
2230	Me and Bobby McGee/I'm Gonna Teach My Heart to Bend (Instead of Break)	1969	—	3.00	6.00
2246	Where Have All the Average People Gone/Boeing Boeing 707	1969	—	3.00	6.00
2258	The Tom Green County Fair/I Know Who It Is	1970	—	3.00	6.00
STARDAY					
356	Can't Stop Loving You/You're Forgetting Me	1958	5.00	10.00	20.00
718	Playboy/Poor Little John	1965	2.50	5.00	10.00
7029	Under Your Spell Again/I Ain't Never	197?	—	2.50	5.00
7032	Country Girl/Jimmy Brown, The Newsboy	197?	—	2.50	5.00
7038	Tip of My Fingers/I Wish I Could Fall in Love Today	197?	—	2.50	5.00
WINDSONG					
CB-11072	Baby Me Baby/Dark Side of the Moon	1977	—	2.00	4.00
CB-11166	Oklahoma Woman/There's Nobody Like You	1977	—	2.00	4.00

Albums

Number	Title (A Side/B Side)	Yr	VG	VG+	NM
20TH CENTURY					
T-592	Making a Name for Myself	1979	3.00	6.00	12.00
COLUMBIA					
KC 32449	Dear Folks Sorry I Haven't Written Lately	1973	3.75	7.50	15.00
HILLTOP					
6109	King of the Road	197?	2.50	5.00	10.00
6131	Little Green Apples	197?	2.50	5.00	10.00
MCA					
5722	Roger Miller	1986	2.50	5.00	10.00
MERCURY					
SR-61297	A Trip in the Country	1970	3.75	7.50	15.00
SR-61361	The Best of Roger Miller	1971	3.75	7.50	15.00
826261-1	Golden Hits	198?	2.00	4.00	8.00
—Reissue of Smash 67073					
NASHVILLE					
2046	The Amazing Roger Miller	196?	3.00	6.00	12.00
PICKWICK					
PTP-2057 [(2)]	King High	1973	3.00	6.00	12.00
SPC-3226	Engine #9	197?	2.50	5.00	10.00
RCA CAMDEN					
CAL-851 [M]	Roger Miller	1964	3.00	6.00	12.00
CAS-851 [S]	Roger Miller	1964	3.75	7.50	15.00
CAL-903 [M]	The One and Only Roger Miller	1965	3.00	6.00	12.00
CAS-903 [S]	The One and Only Roger Miller	1965	3.75	7.50	15.00
SMASH					
MGS-27049 [M]	Roger and Out	1964	3.75	7.50	15.00
MGS-27049 [M]	Dang Me/Chug-a-Lug	196?	3.00	6.00	12.00
—Retitled version of "Roger and Out"					
MGS-27061 [M]	The Return of Roger Miller	1965	3.75	7.50	15.00
MGS-27068 [M]	The 3rd Time Around	1965	3.75	7.50	15.00
MGS-27073 [M]	Golden Hits	1965	3.75	7.50	15.00
MGS-27075 [M]	Words and Music	1966	3.75	7.50	15.00
MGS-27092 [M]	Walkin' in the Sunshine	1967	5.00	10.00	20.00
MGS-27096 [M]	Waterhole #3	1967	6.25	12.50	25.00
SRS-67049 [S]	Roger and Out	1964	5.00	10.00	20.00
SRS-67049 [S]	Dang Me/Chug-a-Lug	196?	3.75	7.50	15.00
—Retitled version of "Roger and Out"					
SRS-67061 [S]	The Return of Roger Miller	1965	5.00	10.00	20.00
SRS-67068 [S]	The 3rd Time Around	1965	5.00	10.00	20.00
SRS-67073 [S]	Golden Hits	1965	5.00	10.00	20.00
SRS-67075 [S]	Words and Music	1966	5.00	10.00	20.00
SRS-67092 [S]	Walkin' in the Sunshine	1967	5.00	10.00	20.00
SRS-67096 [S]	Waterhole #3	1967	5.00	10.00	20.00
SRS-67103	A Tender Look at Love	1968	5.00	10.00	20.00
SRS-67123	Roger Miller	1969	5.00	10.00	20.00
SRS-67129	Roger Miller 1970	1970	5.00	10.00	20.00
STARDAY					
SLP-318 [M]	Wild Child Roger Miller	1965	7.50	15.00	30.00
SLP-318 [M]	The Country Side of Roger Miller	196?	6.25	12.50	25.00
—Retitled version of "Wild Child"					
3011	Painted Poetry	1978	2.50	5.00	10.00
WINDSONG					
BHL1-2337	Off the Wall	1977	3.00	6.00	12.00

MILLER, STEVE, BAND

Also see THE GOLDBERG-MILLER BLUES BAND; BOZ SCAGGS.

12-Inch Singles

Number	Title (A Side/B Side)	Yr	VG	VG+	NM
CAPITOL					
8613	Shangri-La (Extended)//Shangri-La (Dub)/Abracadabra	1984	2.50	5.00	10.00
SPRO 9008/10 [DJ]	True Fine Love/Dance, Dance, Dance	1976	3.75	7.50	15.00
SPRO 9252/3 [DJ]	Shangri-La (Extended) (7" Version) (Dub Version)	1984	2.00	4.00	8.00
SPRO-9992 [DJ]	I Wanna Be Loved (same on both sides)	1986	2.50	5.00	10.00
—Promo only on blue vinyl					
V-15270	I Want to Make the World Turn Around (3 versions)/Slinky	1986	—	3.00	6.00

45s

Number	Title (A Side/B Side)	Yr	VG	VG+	NM
CAPITOL					
2156	Roll With It/Sittin' in Circles	1968	3.00	6.00	12.00
2156 [PS]	Roll With It/Sittin' in Circles	1968	6.25	12.50	25.00
2287	Living in the U.S.A./Quicksilver Girl	1968	3.00	6.00	12.00
2447	Rock Love/(B-side unknown)	1969	2.50	5.00	10.00
2520	My Dark Hour/Song for Our Ancestors	1969	2.00	4.00	8.00
2638	Don't Let Nobody Turn You Around/Little Girl	1969	2.00	4.00	8.00
2878	Going to the Country/Never Kill Another Man	1970	—	3.00	6.00
2945	Going to Mexico/Steve Miller's Midnight Tango	1970	—	3.00	6.00
3228	Rock Love/Let Me Serve You	1971	—	3.00	6.00
3344	Fandango/Love's Riddle	1972	—	3.00	6.00
3732	The Joker/Something to Believe In	1973	—	2.50	5.00
3837	Your Cash Ain't Nothin' But Trash/Evil	1974	—	2.50	5.00
3884	Living in the U.S.A./Kow Kow Calqulator	1974	—	2.50	5.00
4260	Take the Money and Run/Sweet Maree	1976	—	2.00	4.00
4323	Rock'n Me/Shu Ba Du Da Ma Ma Ma Ma	1976	—	2.00	4.00
4323	Rockin' Me/Living in the U.S.A.	1976	—	2.50	5.00
4372	Fly Like an Eagle/Lovin' Cup	1976	—	2.00	4.00
4424	Jet Airliner/Babes in the Wood	1977	—	2.00	4.00
4466	Jungle Love/Wish Upon a Star	1977	—	2.00	4.00
4496	Swingtown/Winter Time	1977	—	2.00	4.00
A-5068	Heart Like a Wheel/True Fine Love	1981	—	—	3.00
A-5068 [PS]	Heart Like a Wheel/True Fine Love	1981	—	2.00	4.00
A-5086	Circle of Love/(B-side unknown)	1982	—	—	3.00
B-5126	Abracadabra/Live It Up	1982	—	2.00	4.00
B-5126	Abracadabra/Baby Wanna Dance	1982	—	—	3.00
B-5126 [PS]	Abracadabra	1982	—	2.00	4.00
—Same sleeve has been found with record of either B-side					
B-5162	Cool Magic/Young Girl's Heart	1982	—	—	3.00
B-5162 [PS]	Cool Magic/Young Girl's Heart	1982	—	2.00	4.00
B-5194	Live It Up/Heart Like a Wheel	1982	—	—	3.00
B-5223	Buffalo's Serenade/Living in the U.S.A.	1983	—	—	3.00
B-5407	Shangri-La/Circle of Love	1984	—	—	3.00

Number	Title (A Side/B Side)	Yr	VG	VG+	NM
B-5407 [PS]	Shangri-La/Circle of Love	1984	—	—	3.00
B-5442	Get On Home/Bongo Bongo	1985	—	—	3.00
B-5442 [PS]	Get On Home/Bongo Bongo	1985	—	—	3.00
B-5476	Italian X-Rays/Who Do You Love	1985	—	—	3.00
B-5646	I Want to Make the World Turn Around/Slinky	1986	—	—	3.00
B-5646 [PS]	I Want to Make the World Turn Around/Slinky	1986	—	—	3.00
B-5671	Nobody But You Baby/Maelstrom	1987	—	—	3.00
B-5704	I Wanna Be Loved/I Wanna Be Loved	1987	—	—	3.00
B-5704 [PS]	I Wanna Be Loved/I Wanna Be Loved	1987	—	—	3.00
B-44222	Ya Ya/Filthy McNasty	1988	—	—	3.00
B-44222 [PS]	Ya Ya/Filthy McNasty	1988	—	—	3.00
Albums					
CAPITOL					
ST-184	Brave New World	1969	5.00	10.00	20.00
—Black label with colorband					
ST-184	Brave New World	1970	3.75	7.50	15.00
—Green label					
ST-331	Your Saving Grace	1969	3.75	7.50	15.00
ST-436	Number 5	1970	3.75	7.50	15.00
STBB-717 [(2)]	Children of the Future/Living in the U.S.A.	1971	3.75	7.50	15.00
—Repackage of 2920 and 2984 (with new title for the latter)					
SW-748	Rock Love	1971	3.75	7.50	15.00
SKAO 2920	Children of the Future	1968	6.25	12.50	25.00
—Black label with colorband					
SKAO 2920	Children of the Future	1970	3.75	7.50	15.00
—Green label					
ST 2984	Sailor	1968	6.25	12.50	25.00
—Black label with colorband					
ST 2984	Sailor	1970	3.75	7.50	15.00
—Green label					
SMAS-11022	Recall the Beginning...A Journey from Eden	1972	3.75	7.50	15.00
SVBB-11114 [(2)]	Anthology	1972	3.75	7.50	15.00
SMAS-11235	The Joker	1973	2.50	5.00	10.00
ST-11497	Fly Like an Eagle	1976	2.50	5.00	10.00
SO-11630	Book of Dreams	1977	2.50	5.00	10.00
SOO-11872	Greatest Hits 1974-1978	1978	2.50	5.00	10.00
SOO-11872 [DJ]	Greatest Hits 1974-1978	1978	7.50	15.00	30.00
—Promo only on blue vinyl					
SEAX-11903 [PD]	Book of Dreams	1978	3.75	7.50	15.00
ST-12121	Circle of Love	1981	2.50	5.00	10.00
ST-12216	Abracadabra	1982	2.50	5.00	10.00
ST-12263	Steve Miller Live	1983	2.50	5.00	10.00
SJ-12339	Italian X-Rays	1985	2.50	5.00	10.00
PJ-12445	Living in the 20th Century	1987	2.50	5.00	10.00
SN-16078	Brave New World	1980	2.00	4.00	8.00
SN-16079	Your Saving Grace	1980	2.00	4.00	8.00
SN-16262	Children of the Future	1982	2.00	4.00	8.00
SN-16263	Sailor	1982	2.00	4.00	8.00
SN-16321	Greatest Hits 1974-1978	1984	2.00	4.00	8.00
SN-16323	Book of Dreams	1984	2.00	4.00	8.00
SN-16339	Fly Like an Eagle	1984	2.00	4.00	8.00
SN-16357	Circle of Love	1985	2.00	4.00	8.00
21185	Fly Like an Eagle	1999	5.00	10.00	20.00
—Limited-edition reissue on 180-gram vinyl					
C1-48303	Born 2 B Blue	1988	2.50	5.00	10.00
R 223186 [(2)]	Anthology	197?	3.75	7.50	15.00
—RCA Music Service edition					
MOBILE FIDELITY					
1-021	Fly Like an Eagle	1979	10.00	20.00	40.00
—Audiophile vinyl					

MILLER, STEVE, BAND/QUICKSILVER MESSENGER SERVICE/THE BAND

Number	Title (A Side/B Side)	Yr	VG	VG+	NM
Albums					
CAPITOL					
STCR-288 [(3)]	Sailor/Quicksilver Messenger Service/Music from Big Pink	1969	10.00	20.00	40.00
—Special 3-LP box set combining these three LPs, also listed separately in each group's listing, in one package					

MILLER SISTERS, THE

Number	Title (A Side/B Side)	Yr	VG	VG+	NM
45s					
ACME					
111	Let's Start Anew/The Flip Skip	1957	12.50	25.00	50.00
717	You Made Me a Promise/Crazy Billboard Song	1957	10.00	20.00	40.00
721	Let's Start Anew/The Flip Skip	1958	10.00	20.00	40.00
EMBER					
1004	Guess Who/How Am I to Know	1956	7.50	15.00	30.00
FLIP					
504	Someday You Will Pay/I Knew You Would	1955	50.00	100.00	200.00
GLODIS					
1003	Pop Your Finger/You Got to Reap What You Sow	1961	3.75	7.50	15.00
GMC					
10006	I'm Telling It Like It Is/Until You Come Home I'll Walk Alone	1967	2.50	5.00	10.00
HERALD					
455	Hippity Ha/Until You're Mine	1955	12.50	25.00	50.00
527	Hippity Ha/Until You're Mine	1958	5.00	10.00	20.00
HULL					
718	Please Don't Leave/Do You Wanna Go	1956	10.00	20.00	40.00
736	Just Wait and See/Black Pepper	1960	6.25	12.50	25.00
—B-side by Leo Price and Band					
750	Roll Back the Rug (And Twist)/Don't You Forget	1962	6.25	12.50	25.00
752	I Cried All Night/Hully Gully Reel	1962	5.00	10.00	20.00
MILLER					
1140	Oh Lover/Remember That	1960	5.00	10.00	20.00
1141	Pony Dance/Give Me Some Old Fashioned Love	1960	5.00	10.00	20.00
1143	Please Mr. D.J./(B-side unknown)	1960	5.00	10.00	20.00
ONYX					
507	Sugar Candy/My Own	1957	12.50	25.00	50.00
RAYNA					
5001	I Miss You So/Dance Little Sister	1962	3.75	7.50	15.00
5004	Oh Why/Walk On	1962	3.75	7.50	15.00
RIVERSIDE					
4535	Dance Close/Tell Him	1962	5.00	10.00	20.00
ROULETTE					
4491	Baby Your Baby/Silly Girl	1963	3.00	6.00	12.00
STARDUST					
3001	Feel Good/Cooncha	1964	2.50	5.00	10.00
SUN					
230	There's No Right Way to Do Me Wrong/You Can Tell Me	1956	12.50	25.00	50.00
255	Finders Keepers/Ten Cats Down	1956	12.50	25.00	50.00
504	Someday You Will Pay/I Knew You Would	1955	37.50	75.00	150.00
YORKTOWN					
75	Looking Over My Life/Si Senor	1965	2.50	5.00	10.00

MILLINDER, LUCKY

Number	Title (A Side/B Side)	Yr	VG	VG+	NM
45s					
KING					
4449	Chew Tobacco Rag/Georgia Rose	1951	15.00	30.00	60.00
4453	I'm Waiting Just for You/Bongo Boogie	1951	15.00	30.00	60.00
4476	The Grape Vine/No One Else Could Be	1951	15.00	30.00	60.00
4496	The Right Kind of Love/It's Been a Long, Long Time	1951	15.00	30.00	60.00
4534	Ram-Bunk-Shush/Loaded with Love	1952	15.00	30.00	60.00
4545	When I Have You My Love/Please Be Careful	1952	25.00	50.00	100.00
4557	Lord Knows I Tried/Heavy Sugar	1952	25.00	50.00	100.00
4571	Backslider's Ball/Please Be Careful	1952	25.00	50.00	100.00
4792	It's a Sad, Sad Feeling/Ow	1955	20.00	40.00	80.00
—With the Admirals					
4803	Goody Good Love/I'm Here, Love	1955	7.50	15.00	30.00
5240	Heavy Sugar/Honeydripper	1959	3.00	6.00	12.00
RCA VICTOR					
47-2961	Tomorrow/I Ain't Got Nothin' to Lose	1949	12.50	25.00	50.00
47-3005	Awful Natural/In the Middle of the Night	1949	12.50	25.00	50.00
47-3128	I'll Never Be Free/Journey's End	1949	12.50	25.00	50.00
50-0054	D Natural Blues/Little Girl, Don't Cry	1949	15.00	30.00	60.00
—Gray label, orange vinyl					
50-0088	Let It Be/(B-side unknown)	1950	12.50	25.00	50.00
WARWICK					
582	Big Fat Mama/Slide My Trombone	1960	3.00	6.00	12.00

MILLS, GARRY

Number	Title (A Side/B Side)	Yr	VG	VG+	NM
45s					
IMPERIAL					
5674	Look for a Star — Part 1/Look for a Star — Part 2	1960	3.75	7.50	15.00
LONDON					
9504	I'll Step Down/Treasure Island	1962	3.75	7.50	15.00
TOP RANK					
2071	Top Teen Baby/Don't Forget	1960	3.75	7.50	15.00
UNITED ARTISTS					
0099	Look for a Star/Look for a Star	1973	—	2.50	5.00
—"Silver Spotlight Series" reissue; B-side by Gary Miles					

MILLS, HAYLEY

Number	Title (A Side/B Side)	Yr	VG	VG+	NM
45s					
BUENA VISTA					
385	Let's Get Together/Cobbler, Cobbler	1961	3.00	6.00	12.00
385 [PS]	Let's Get Together/Cobbler, Cobbler	1961	6.25	12.50	25.00
395	Johnny Jingo/Jeepers Creepers	1962	2.50	5.00	10.00
395 [PS]	Johnny Jingo/Jeepers Creepers	1962	6.25	12.50	25.00
401	Side by Side/Ching Ching and a Ring Ding Ding	1962	2.50	5.00	10.00
401 [PS]	Side by Side/Ching Ching and a Ring Ding Ding	1962	6.25	12.50	25.00
408	Castaway/Sweet River	1962	2.50	5.00	10.00
408 [PS]	Castaway/Sweet River	1962	6.25	12.50	25.00
409	Let's Climb/Enjoy It	1962	2.50	5.00	10.00
—With Maurice Chevalier					
409 [PS]	Let's Climb/Enjoy It	1962	6.25	12.50	25.00
420	Flitterin'/Beautiful Beulah	1963	2.50	5.00	10.00
—With Eddie Hodges					
420 [PS]	Flitterin'/Beautiful Beulah	1963	6.25	12.50	25.00
MAINSTREAM					
656	Gypsy Girl/Younger Than Seventeen	1966	2.00	4.00	8.00
Albums					
BUENA VISTA					
BV-3311 [M]	Let's Get Together	1962	6.25	12.50	25.00
STER-3311 [S]	Let's Get Together	1962	10.00	20.00	40.00

MILLS BROTHERS, THE

Number	Title (A Side/B Side)	Yr	VG	VG+	NM
45s					
DECCA					
23930	You Always Hurt the One You Love/Till Then	1950	5.00	10.00	20.00
—Reissue of 78 from 1944; black label with lines on either side of "Decca"					
23930	You Always Hurt the One You Love/Till Then	1955	3.00	6.00	12.00
—Black label with star under "Decca"					
23930	You Always Hurt the One You Love/Till Then	1960	2.00	4.00	8.00
—Black label with color bar					
24756	If I Had My Way/Sweet Genevieve	1950	5.00	10.00	20.00
24872	Daddy's Little Girl/If I Live to Be a Hundred	1950	5.00	10.00	20.00
25046	Lazy River/Cielito Lindo	1950	5.00	10.00	20.00
25516	Across the Alley from the Alamo/Don't Be a Baby, Baby	1961	2.00	4.00	8.00
27157	Paper Doll/I'll Be Around	1950	5.00	10.00	20.00
—Reissue of 78 from 1943; black label with lines on either side of "Decca"					
27157	Paper Doll/I'll Be Around	1955	3.00	6.00	12.00
—Black label with star under "Decca"					
27157	Paper Doll/I'll Be Around	1960	2.00	4.00	8.00
—Black label with color bar					
27184	A Star for Everyone/I'm Afraid to Love You	1950	5.00	10.00	20.00
27236	Daddy's Little Boy/I Still Love You	1950	5.00	10.00	20.00
27253	Nevertheless (I'm in Love with You)/Thirsty for Your Kisses	1950	5.00	10.00	20.00
27267	Funny Feelin'/I Don't Mind Being Alone	1950	5.00	10.00	20.00

Number	Title (A Side/B Side)	Yr	VG	VG+	NM
27400	Around the World/You Don't Have to Drop a Heart to Break It	1951	3.75	7.50	15.00
27447	Please Don't Talk About Me When I'm Gone/You Know You Belong to Someone Else	1951	3.75	7.50	15.00
—With Tommy Dorsey					
27579	Mister and Mississippi/Wonderful, Wasn't It	1951	3.75	7.50	15.00
27615	Love Me/Who Knows Love	1951	3.75	7.50	15.00
27683	Lord Ups an' Downs/A Cottage with a Prayer	1951	5.00	10.00	20.00
27762	I Ran All the Way Home/Get Her Off My Hands	1951	3.75	7.50	15.00
27889	Be My Life's Companion/Love Lies	1951	3.75	7.50	15.00
28021	High and Dry/You're Not Worth My Tears	1952	3.75	7.50	15.00
28180	Pretty As a Picture/When You Come Back to Me	1952	3.75	7.50	15.00
28309	Just When We're Falling in Love/Blue and Sentimental	1952	3.75	7.50	15.00
28384	The Glow-Worm/After All	1952	3.75	7.50	15.00
28458	Lazy River/Wish Me Good Luck, Amigo	1952	3.75	7.50	15.00
28459	Someone Loved Someone/A Shoulder to Weep On	1952	3.75	7.50	15.00
28586	Twice As Much/I Want Someone to Care For	1953	3.00	6.00	12.00
28670	Say Si Si/I'm With You	1953	3.00	6.00	12.00
28736	Pretty Butterfly/Don't Let Me Dream	1953	3.00	6.00	12.00
28818	Who Put the Devil in Evelyn's Eyes/Beware	1953	3.00	6.00	12.00
28945	The Jones Boy/She Was Five and He Was Ten	1953	3.00	6.00	12.00
29019	I Had to Call You Up to Say I'm Sorry/You Didn't Want Me When You Had Me	1954	3.00	6.00	12.00
29115	A Carnival in Venice/Go In and Out the Window	1954	3.00	6.00	12.00
29185	How Blue/Why Do I Keep Lovin' You	1954	3.00	6.00	12.00
29276	You're Nobody 'Til Somebody Loves You/Every Second of Every Day	1954	3.00	6.00	12.00
29382	Paper Valentine/The Urge	1954	3.00	6.00	12.00
29496	Opus One/There You Are	1955	3.00	6.00	12.00
29511	Smack Dab in the Middle/Kiss Me and Kill Me with Love	1955	3.00	6.00	12.00
29564	Daddy's Little Girl/Daddy's Little Boy	1955	3.00	6.00	12.00
29686	Suddenly There's a Valley/Gum Drop	1955	3.00	6.00	12.00
29754	I Believe in Santa Claus/You Don't Have to Be a Santa Claus	1955	3.00	6.00	12.00
29781	All the Way 'Round the World/I've Changed My Mind a Thousand Times	1956	2.50	5.00	10.00
29853	Dream of You/In a Mellow Tone	1956	2.50	5.00	10.00
29897	Standing on the Corner/King Porter Stomp	1956	2.50	5.00	10.00
30024	Don't Get Caught (Short on Love)/That's Right	1956	2.50	5.00	10.00
30136	That's All I Need/Tell Me More	1956	2.50	5.00	10.00
30224	In De Banana Tree/Knocked-Out Nightingale	1957	2.50	5.00	10.00
30299	Queen of the Senior Prom/My Troubled Mind	1957	2.50	5.00	10.00
30430	Two Minute Tango/Change for a Penny	1957	2.50	5.00	10.00
30546	The Barbershop Quartet/You Only Told Me Half	1958	2.50	5.00	10.00
DOT					
15695	Get a Job/I Found a Million Dollar Baby	1958	3.75	7.50	15.00
15827	Me and My Shadow/Music, Maestro, Please	1958	2.50	5.00	10.00
15858	Yellow Bird/Baby Clementine	1958	2.00	4.00	8.00
15909	You Can't Be True Dear/Beaver	1959	2.50	5.00	10.00
15950	Lullaby in Ragtime/Te Quiero	1959	2.50	5.00	10.00
15987	You Always Hurt the One You Love/(B-side unknown)	1959	2.50	5.00	10.00
16037	Paper Doll/The Glow-Worm	1960	2.00	4.00	8.00
16049	I Miss You So/Oh Ma Ma	1960	2.00	4.00	8.00
16091	Highways Are Happy Ways/I Got You	1960	2.00	4.00	8.00
16234	Yellow Bird/Baby Clementine	1961	2.00	4.00	8.00
16258	I'll Take Care of Your Cares/Ballerina	1961	2.00	4.00	8.00
16360	I Found the Only Girl for Me/Queen of the Senior Prom	1961	2.00	4.00	8.00
16432	Tonight You Belong to Me/You Broke the Only Heart That Ever Loved You	1963	—	3.50	7.00
16451	The End of the World/Big City	1963	—	3.50	7.00
16579	Don't Blame Me/It Hurts Me More Than It Hurts You	1964	—	3.50	7.00
16703	Welcome Home/Chum Chum Chittilum Chum	1965	—	3.50	7.00
16733	Bye Bye Blackbird/Chum Chum Chittilum Chum	1965	—	3.50	7.00
16972	Smack Dab in the Middle/Honeysuckle Rose Blues Bossa Nova	1967	—	3.00	6.00
17041	Cab Driver/Fortuosity	1967	—	3.00	6.00
17096	My Shy Violet/Flower Road	1968	—	3.00	6.00
17162	The Ol' Race Track/But for Love	1968	—	3.00	6.00
17198	Dream/Jimtown Road	1969	—	3.00	6.00
17235	A Guy on the Go/What Have I Done for Her Lately	1969	—	3.00	6.00
17285	I'll Never Forgive Myself/Up to Maggie Jones	1969	—	3.00	6.00
17321	It Ain't No Big Thing/Help Yourself to Some Tomorrow	1969	—	3.00	6.00
PARAMOUNT					
0046	Smile Away Every Rainy Day/Between Winston-Salem and Nashville, Tennessee	1970	—	2.50	5.00
0095	Happy Songs of Love/I'm Sorry I Answered the Phone	1971	—	2.50	5.00
0117	L-O-V-E/Strollin'	1971	—	2.50	5.00
0147	Come Summer/Sally Sunshine	1972	—	2.50	5.00
0181	There's No Life on the Moon/A Donut and a Dream	1972	—	2.50	5.00
RANWOOD					
961	Truck Stop/He Gives Me Love	1973	—	2.00	4.00
1003	Tiger Rag/On a Chinese Honeymoon	1974	—	2.00	4.00
1020	You Are My Sunshine/Between Winston-Salem and Nashville, Tennessee	1974	—	2.00	4.00
1040	El Paso/Till Then	197?	—	2.00	4.00
1042	Daisies Never Tell/Sawdust Heart	197?	—	2.00	4.00
1054	Coney Island Washboard/Nevertheless	197?	—	2.00	4.00
7-Inch Extended Plays					
DECCA					
ED 2010	Lazy River/I'm Afraid to Love You//Blue and Sentimental/I've Got My Love to Keep Me Warm	195?	3.75	7.50	15.00
ED 2010 [PS]	The Mills Brothers, Volume 1	195?	3.75	7.50	15.00
ED 2044	*Caravan/Solitude/It Don't Mean a Thing/Georgia on My Mind	195?	3.75	7.50	15.00
ED 2044 [PS]	The Mills Brothers, Vol. 2	195?	3.75	7.50	15.00
ED 2742	Daddy's Little Girl/Daddy's Little Boy//You're Nobody 'Til Somebody Loves You/Queen of the Senior Prom	195?	3.00	6.00	12.00
ED 2742 [PS]	The Mills Brothers	195?	3.00	6.00	12.00
DOT					
DEP-1087	Glow Worm/Lazy River//Till Then/Paper Doll	195?	2.50	5.00	10.00
DEP-1087 [PS]	Great Hits	195?	2.50	5.00	10.00
Albums					
ABC					
1027 [(2)]	The Best of the Mills Brothers, Volume 2	1978	3.00	6.00	12.00
4004	16 Great Performances	1975	2.50	5.00	10.00
ARCHIVE OF FOLK AND JAZZ					
300	The Mills Brothers	197?	2.50	5.00	10.00
328	The Mills Brothers, Volume 2	197?	2.50	5.00	10.00
DECCA					
DXB 193 [(2) M]	The Best of the Mills Brothers	1965	5.00	10.00	20.00
DL 4084 [M]	Our Golden Favorites	1960	5.00	10.00	20.00
DL 5050 [10]	Barber Shop Ballads	1950	12.50	25.00	50.00
DL 5051 [10]	Barber Shop Ballads	1950	12.50	25.00	50.00
DL 5102 [10]	Souvenir Album	1950	12.50	25.00	50.00
DL 5337 [10]	Wonderful Words	1951	12.50	25.00	50.00
DL 5506 [10]	Meet the Mills Brothers	1954	12.50	25.00	50.00
DL 5516 [10]	Four Boys and a Guitar	1954	12.50	25.00	50.00
DXSB 7193 [(2) R]	The Best of the Mills Brothers	1965	3.75	7.50	15.00
DL 8148 [M]	Souvenir Album	1955	7.50	15.00	30.00
DL 8209 [M]	Singin' and Swingin'	1956	7.50	15.00	30.00
DL 8219 [M]	Memory Lane	1956	7.50	15.00	30.00
DL 8491 [M]	One Dozen Roses	1957	7.50	15.00	30.00
DL 8664 [M]	The Mills Brothers in Hi-Fi	1958	7.50	15.00	30.00
DL 8827 [M]	Glow with the Mills Brothers	1958	7.50	15.00	30.00
DL 8890 [M]	Barber Shop Harmony	1959	7.50	15.00	30.00
DL 8892 [M]	Harmonizin' with the Mills Brothers	1959	7.50	15.00	30.00
DL 74084 [R]	Our Golden Favorites	196?	3.00	6.00	12.00
DL 75174 [R]	Golden Favorites, Volume 2	1970	2.50	5.00	10.00
DOT					
DLP-3103 [M]	Mmmm, The Mills Brothers	1958	5.00	10.00	20.00
DLP-3157 [M]	The Mills Brothers' Great Hits	1958	5.00	10.00	20.00
DLP-3208 [M]	Great Barbershop Hits	1959	5.00	10.00	20.00
DLP-3232 [M]	Merry Christmas	1959	5.00	10.00	20.00
DLP-3237 [M]	The Mills Brothers Sing	1960	5.00	10.00	20.00
DLP-3308 [M]	The Mills Brothers' Great Hits, Volume 2	1960	3.75	7.50	15.00
DLP-3338 [M]	Yellow Bird	1960	3.75	7.50	15.00
DLP-3363 [M]	San Antonio Rose	1961	3.75	7.50	15.00
DLP-3368 [M]	Great Hawaiian Hits	1961	3.75	7.50	15.00
DLP-3465 [M]	Beer Barrel Polka and Other Hits	1962	3.00	6.00	12.00
DLP-3508 [M]	The End of the World	1963	3.00	6.00	12.00
DLP-3565 [M]	Gems by the Mills Brothers	1964	3.00	6.00	12.00
DLP-3568 [M]	Hymns We Love	1964	3.00	6.00	12.00
DLP-3592 [M]	Say Si Si and Other Great Latin Hits	1964	3.00	6.00	12.00
DLP-3652 [M]	Ten Years of Hits 1954-1964	1965	3.00	6.00	12.00
DLP-3699 [M]	These Are the Mills Brothers	1966	3.00	6.00	12.00
DLP-3744 [M]	That Country Feeling	1966	3.00	6.00	12.00
DL-3766 [M]	The Mills Brothers Today	1966	3.00	6.00	12.00
DLP-3783 [M]	The Mills Brothers Live	1967	3.75	7.50	15.00
DLP-25103 [S]	Mmmm, The Mills Brothers	1958	7.50	15.00	30.00
DLP-25157 [S]	The Mills Brothers' Great Hits	1958	7.50	15.00	30.00
—Black vinyl					
DLP-25157 [S]	The Mills Brothers' Great Hits	195?	15.00	30.00	60.00
—Blue vinyl					
DLP-25208 [S]	Great Barbershop Hits	1959	7.50	15.00	30.00
DLP-25232 [S]	Merry Christmas	1959	7.50	15.00	30.00
—Same as above, but in stereo; with cursive "Dot" logo					
DLP-25232 [S]	Merry Christmas	1968	3.00	6.00	12.00
—With "Dot"/"Paramount" logo					
DLP-25237 [S]	The Mills Brothers Sing	1960	7.50	15.00	30.00
DLP-25308 [S]	The Mills Brothers' Great Hits, Volume 2	1960	5.00	10.00	20.00
DLP-25338 [S]	Yellow Bird	1960	5.00	10.00	20.00
DLP-25363 [S]	San Antonio Rose	1961	5.00	10.00	20.00
DLP-25368 [S]	Great Hawaiian Hits	1961	5.00	10.00	20.00
DLP-25465 [S]	Beer Barrel Polka and Other Hits	1962	3.75	7.50	15.00
DLP-25508 [S]	The End of the World	1963	3.75	7.50	15.00
DLP-25565 [S]	Gems by the Mills Brothers	1964	3.75	7.50	15.00
DLP-25568 [S]	Hymns We Love	1964	3.75	7.50	15.00
DLP-25592 [S]	Say Si Si and Other Great Latin Hits	1964	3.75	7.50	15.00
DLP-25652 [S]	Ten Years of Hits 1954-1964	1965	3.75	7.50	15.00
DLP-25699 [S]	These Are the Mills Brothers	1966	3.75	7.50	15.00
DLP-25744 [S]	That Country Feeling	1966	3.75	7.50	15.00
DLP-25766 [S]	The Mills Brothers Today	1966	3.75	7.50	15.00
DLP-25783 [S]	The Mills Brothers Live	1967	3.75	7.50	15.00
DLP-25809	Fortuosity	1968	3.75	7.50	15.00
DLP-25872	My Shy Violet	1968	3.75	7.50	15.00
DLP-25927	Dream	1969	3.75	7.50	15.00
DLP-25960	The Mills Brothers In Motion	1970	3.75	7.50	15.00
GNP CRESCENDO					
GNP-9106	Four Boys and a Guitar	197?	2.50	5.00	10.00
HAMILTON					
HL-116 [M]	The Mills Brothers Sing for You	1964	3.00	6.00	12.00
HS-12116 [S]	The Mills Brothers Sing for You	1964	3.00	6.00	12.00
MARK 56					
709	Original Radio Broadcasts	197?	2.50	5.00	10.00
MCA					
132	Golden Favorites, Volume 2	1973	2.50	5.00	10.00
188	Old Golden Favorites	1973	2.50	5.00	10.00
717	16 Great Performances	1980	2.00	4.00	8.00
4039 [(2)]	The Best of the Mills Brothers	197?	3.00	6.00	12.00
15029	Merry Christmas	198?	2.50	5.00	10.00
27083	The Mills Brothers Great Hits	1980	2.00	4.00	8.00
28116	Were You There	198?	2.00	4.00	8.00
MCA SPECIAL MARKETS					
MSM2-35067 [(2)]	Classic Mills Brothers	198?	2.50	5.00	10.00
PARAMOUNT					
PAS-1010	The Best of the Mills Brothers	1973	3.00	6.00	12.00
PAS-1027 [(2)]	The Best of the Mills Brothers, Volume 2	1974	3.75	7.50	15.00
PAS-5025	No Turnin' Back	1971	3.00	6.00	12.00

Number	Title (A Side/B Side)	Yr	VG	VG+	NM
PAS-6024	What a Wonderful World	1972	3.00	6.00	12.00
PAS-6038	A Donut and a Dream	1973	3.00	6.00	12.00
PICKWICK					
SPC-1025	Merry Christmas	1979	2.50	5.00	10.00
—Reissue of Dot album with one fewer track					
2008	Songs You Remember	197?	2.50	5.00	10.00
2030	The Mills Brothers	1973	2.50	5.00	10.00
SPC-3076	14 Karat Gold	196?	2.50	5.00	10.00
SPC-3107	Anytime	197?	2.50	5.00	10.00
SPC-3137	Dream a Little Dream	197?	2.50	5.00	10.00
SPC-3158	Till We Meet Again	197?	2.50	5.00	10.00
SPC-3220	Cab Driver	197?	2.50	5.00	10.00
RANWOOD					
7035 [(2)]	22 Great Hits	1985	2.50	5.00	10.00
8123	Cab Driver	197?	2.50	5.00	10.00
8133	The Mills Brothers Story	197?	2.50	5.00	10.00
8139	Country's Greatest Hits	197?	2.50	5.00	10.00
8152	50th Anniversary	197?	2.50	5.00	10.00
8198	Command Performance	198?	2.00	4.00	8.00
SONGBIRD					
255	Hymns We Love	197?	2.50	5.00	10.00
SUNNYVALE					
1023	Timeless	1978	2.50	5.00	10.00
VOCALION					
VL 3607 [M]	In a Mellow Tone	196?	3.00	6.00	12.00
VL 73607 [R]	In a Mellow Tone	196?	2.50	5.00	10.00
VL 73859 [R]	Such Sweet Singing	1969	2.50	5.00	10.00

MILLS BROTHERS, THE, AND LOUIS ARMSTRONG

See ARMSTRONG, LOUIS, AND THE MILLS BROTHERS.

MILSAP, RONNIE

12-Inch Singles

Number	Title (A Side/B Side)	Yr	VG	VG+	NM
RCA					
JD-11683 [DJ]	Get It Up/Hi-Heel Sneakers	1979	5.00	10.00	20.00
—Promo only on green vinyl					

45s

Number	Title (A Side/B Side)	Yr	VG	VG+	NM
BOBLO					
524	Make Love Sweet/(B-side unknown)	1977	—	2.50	5.00
CAPITOL NASHVILLE					
S7-18909	The Christmas Song/Till the Season Comes 'Round Again	1995	—	—	3.00
CHIPS					
2889	Loving You Is a Natural Thing/So Hung Up on Sylvia	1970	2.00	4.00	8.00
2987	A Rose by Any Other Name (Is Still a Rose)/ Sermonette	1970	2.00	4.00	8.00
FESTIVAL					
5002	Wishing You Were Here/Your Tears Leave Me Cold	1977	—	2.50	5.00
LIBERTY					
S7-17595	True Believer/These Foolish Things (Remind Me of You)	1993	—	2.00	4.00
—Red vinyl					
S7-17640	I'm Playing for You/Better Off with the Blues	1993	—	2.00	4.00
PACEMAKER					
245	Wishing You Were Here/A Loving Background	1967	2.00	4.00	8.00
RCA					
2509-7-R	Are You Loving Me Like I'm Loving You/Back to the Grindstone	1990	—	—	3.00
2848-7-R	Since I Don't Have You/I Ain't Gonna Cry No More	1991	—	—	3.00
5033-7-R	How Do I Turn You On/Don't Take It Tonight	1986	—	—	3.00
5049-7-R	Only One Night of the Year/It's Just Not Christmas (If I Can't Spend It With You)	1986	—	—	3.00
5169-7-R	Snap Your Fingers/This Time Last Year	1987	—	—	3.00
5209-7-R	Make No Mistake, She's Mine/You're My Love	1987	—	—	3.00
—With Kenny Rogers					
5259-7-R	Where Do the Nights Go/If You Don't Want Me To	1987	—	—	3.00
5351-7-R	Christmas Medley: Carol of the Bells/O Come, O Come Emmanuel/Silent Night/Joy to the World/ /I'll Be Home for Christmas	1987	—	—	3.00
6896-7-R	Old Folks/Earthquake	1988	—	—	3.00
—A-side: With Mike Reid					
8389-7-R	Button Off My Shirt/One Night	1988	—	—	3.00
8746-7-R	Don't You Ever Get Tired (Of Hurtin' Me)/I Never Expected to See You	1988	—	—	3.00
8868-7-R	Houston Solution/If You Don't Want Me To	1989	—	—	3.00
9027-7-R	A Woman in Love/Starting Today	1989	—	—	3.00
9071-7-R	I'll Be Home for Christrmas/We're Here to Love	1989	—	—	3.00
9120-7-R	Stranger Things Have Happened/Southern Roots	1989	—	—	3.00
PB-10843	Let My Love Be Your Pillow/Busy Makin' Plans	1976	—	2.00	4.00
GB-10931	(I'm a) Stand By My Woman Man/What Goes On When the Sun Goes Down	1977	—	2.00	4.00
—Gold Standard Series					
PB-10976	It Was Almost Like a Song/It Don't Hurt to Dream	1977	—	2.00	4.00
PB-11146	What a Difference You've Made in My Life/Selfish	1977	—	2.00	4.00
PB-11270	Only One Live in My Life/Back on My Mind Again	1978	—	2.00	4.00
PB-11333	Let My Love Be Your Pillow/Busy Makin' Plans	1978	—	2.00	4.00
PB-11369	Let's Take the Long Way Around the World/Not Trying to Forget	1978	—	2.00	4.00
PB-11421	Back on My Mind Again/Santa Barbara	1978	—	2.00	4.00
GB-11496	It Was Almost Like a Song/Only One Love in My Life	1979	—	2.00	4.00
—Gold Standard Series					
PB-11553	Nobody Likes Sad Songs/Just Because It Feels Good	1979	—	2.00	4.00
PB-11695	In No Time at All/Get It Up	1979	—	2.00	4.00
PB-11909	Why Don't You Spend the Night/Heads I Go, Hearts I Stay	1980	—	2.00	4.00
PB-11952	My Heart/Silent Night (After the Fight)	1980	—	2.00	4.00
GB-11987	What a Difference You've Made in My Life/Let's Take the Long Way Around the World	1980	—	2.00	4.00
—Gold Standard Series					
GB-11994	Back on My Mind Again/Nobody Likes Sad Songs	1980	—	2.00	4.00
—Gold Standard Series					
PB-12006	Cowboys and Clowns/Misery Loves Company	1980	—	2.00	4.00
PB-12006 [PS]	Cowboys and Clowns/Misery Loves Company	1980	—	2.50	5.00
PB-12084	Smoky Mountain Rain/Crystal Fallin' Rain	1980	—	2.00	4.00
PB-12194	Am I Losing You/He'll Have to Go	1981	—	2.00	4.00
PB-12264	(There's) No Gettin' Over Me/I Live My Whole Life at Night	1981	—	2.00	4.00
GB-12314	Why Don't You Spend the Night/Smoky Mountain Rain	1981	—	—	3.00
—Gold Standard Series					
GB-12315	My Heart/Silent Night (After the Fight)	1981	—	—	3.00
—Gold Standard Series					
PB-12342	I Wouldn't Have Missed It For the World/It Happens Every Time (I Think of You)	1981	—	2.00	4.00
PB-13216	Any Day Now/It's Just a Room	1982	—	2.00	4.00
PB-13286	He Got You/I Love New Orleans Music	1982	—	2.00	4.00
PB-13362	Inside/Carolina Dreams	1982	—	2.00	4.00
PB-13470	Stranger in My House/Is It Over	1983	—	2.00	4.00
GB-13491	(There's) No Gettin' Over Me/I Wouldn't Have Missed It for the World	1983	—	—	3.00
—Gold Standard Series					
PB-13564	Don't You Know How Much I Love You/Feelings Change	1983	—	2.00	4.00
PB-13658	Show Her/Watch Out for the Other Guy	1983	—	2.00	4.00
PB-13665	It's Christmas/We're Here to Love	1983	—	2.00	4.00
GB-13784	Don't You Know How Much I Love You/Show Her	1984	—	—	3.00
—Gold Standard Series					
GB-13785	Any Day Now/Stranger in My House	1984	—	—	3.00
—Gold Standard Series					
PB-13805	Still Losing You/I'll Take Care of You	1984	—	—	3.00
PB-13847	She Loves My Car/Prisoner of the Highway	1984	—	—	3.00
JD-13869 [DJ]	She Loves My Car/(Instrumental)	1984	2.00	4.00	8.00
PB-13955	She's Always in Love/I Might Have Said	1984	—	—	—
—Unreleased					
PB-14034	She Keeps the Home Fires Burning/Is It Over	1985	—	—	3.00
PB-14135	Lost in the Fifties Tonight (In the Still of the Night)/ I Might Have Said	1985	—	2.00	4.00
PB-14135 [PS]	Lost in the Fifties Tonight (In the Still of the Night)/ I Might Have Said	1985	—	2.00	4.00
PB-14286	Happy Happy Birthday Baby/I'll Take Care of You	1986	—	—	3.00
GB-14349	Lost in the Fifties Tonight (In the Still of the Night)/ She Keeps the Home Fires Burning	1986	—	—	3.00
—Gold Standard Series					
PB-14365	In Love/Old Fashioned Girl Like You	1986	—	—	3.00
62104	Turn That Radio On/Old Habits Are Hard to Break	1991	—	—	3.00
62217	All Is Fair in Love and War/Back to the Grindstone	1992	—	—	3.00
62332	L.A. to the Moon/When the Hurt Comes Down	1992	—	—	3.00
62370	Still Losing You/If You Really Don't Want Me	1992	—	—	3.00
RCA VICTOR					
APBO-0097	That Girl Who Waits on Tables/You're Drivin' Me Out of My Mind	1973	—	3.00	6.00
APBO-0237	Pure Love/Love the Second Time Around	1974	—	3.00	6.00
APBO-0313	Please Don't Tell Me How the Story Ends/Streets of Gold	1974	—	3.00	6.00
PB-10112	(I'd Be) A Legend in My Time/The Biggest Lie	1974	—	2.50	5.00
GB-10167	That Girl Who Waits on Tables/I Hate You	1975	—	2.00	4.00
—Gold Standard Series					
PB-10228	Too Late to Worry, Too Blue to Cry/Country Cookin'	1975	—	2.50	5.00
PB-10335	Daydreams About Night Things/Play Born to Lose	1975	—	2.50	5.00
PB-10420	Just In Case/Remember to Remind Me (I'm Leaving)	1975	—	2.50	5.00
GB-10500	Please Don't Tell Me How the Story Ends/Streets of Gold	1975	—	2.00	4.00
—Gold Standard Series					
GB-10501	Too Late to Worry, Too Blue to Cry/Country Cookin'	1975	—	2.00	4.00
—Gold Standard Series					
GB-10502	(I'd Be) A Legend in My Time/The Biggest Lie	1975	—	2.00	4.00
—Gold Standard Series					
GB-10503	Pure Love/Love the Second Time Around	1975	—	2.00	4.00
—Gold Standard Series					
PB-10593	What Goes On When the Sun Goes Down/Love Takes a Long Time to Die	1976	—	2.50	5.00
GB-10672	Daydreams About Night Things/Just in Case	1976	—	2.00	4.00
—Gold Standard Series					
PB-10724	(I'm a) Stand By My Woman Man/Lovers, Friends and Strangers	1976	—	2.50	5.00
74-0969	I Hate You/(All Together Now) Let's Fall Apart	1973	—	3.00	6.00
SCEPTER					
12109	Let's Go Get Stoned/Never Had It So Good	1965	3.00	6.00	12.00
12127	A Thousand Miles from Nowhere/When It Comes to My Baby	1966	3.00	6.00	12.00
12145	The End of the World/I Saw Pity in the Face of a Friend	1966	3.00	6.00	12.00
12161	When the Boys Talk About the Girls/Ain't No Sole in These Old Shoes	1966	3.00	6.00	12.00
12161	When the Boys Talk About the Girls/Another Branch from the Old Branch	1966	3.00	6.00	12.00
12206	House of the Rising Sun/I Can't Tell a Lie	1967	2.50	5.00	10.00
12228	Do What You Gotta Do/Mr. Mailman	1968	2.00	4.00	8.00
12246	Nothing Is As Good As It Used to Be/Denver	1969	2.00	4.00	8.00
12272	What's Your Game/Love Will Never Pass Us By	1970	2.00	4.00	8.00
VIRGIN					
58853	Time, Love and Money/Livin' on Love	2000	—	—	3.00
WARNER BROS.					
5405	Total Disaster/It Went to Your Head	1963	3.75	7.50	15.00
7540	Sunday Rain/Why	1971	—	3.00	6.00
7629	Magic Me Again/Me and You, You and Me	1972	—	3.00	6.00

Number	Title (A Side/B Side)	Yr	VG	VG+	NM
8127	She Even Woke Me Up to Say Goodbye/Loving You's a Natural Thing	1975	—	2.00	4.00
8160	A Rose by Any Other Name/Please Don't Tell Me How the Story Ends	1975	—	2.00	4.00
8218	Crying/Why	1976	—	2.00	4.00
Albums					
PAIR					
PDL2-1031 [(2)]	Believe It!	1986	3.00	6.00	12.00
PDL2-1105 [(2)]	Back on My Mind Again	1986	3.00	6.00	12.00
PICKWICK					
JS-6179	Plain and Simple	197?	2.50	5.00	10.00
RCA					
9588-1-R	Stranger Things Have Happened	1989	2.50	5.00	10.00
R 183710	Back to the Grindstone	1991	5.00	10.00	20.00
—Only released on vinyl through BMG Direct Marketing					
RCA VICTOR					
APL1-0338	Where My Heart Is	1973	5.00	10.00	20.00
APD1-0500 [Q]	Pure Love	1974	5.00	10.00	20.00
APL1-0500	Pure Love	1974	3.75	7.50	15.00
APD1-0846 [Q]	A Legend in My Time	1975	5.00	10.00	20.00
APL1-0846	A Legend in My Time	1975	3.75	7.50	15.00
APL1-1223	Night Things	1975	3.75	7.50	15.00
APL1-1666	20-20 Vision	1976	3.00	6.00	12.00
APL1-2043	Ronnie Milsap Live	1976	3.00	6.00	12.00
AFL1-2439	It Was Almost Like a Song	1977	3.00	6.00	12.00
AFL1-2780	Only One Love in My Life	1978	3.00	6.00	12.00
AHL1-3346	Images	1979	3.00	6.00	12.00
AHL1-3563	Milsap Magic	1980	2.50	5.00	10.00
AYL1-3760	Where My Heart Is	1980	2.00	4.00	8.00
—"Best Buy Series" reissue					
AHL1-3772	Greatest Hits	1980	2.50	5.00	10.00
AYL1-3899	Pure Love	1981	2.00	4.00	8.00
—"Best Buy Series" reissue					
AAL1-3932	Out Where the Bright Lights Are Glowing	1981	2.50	5.00	10.00
AHL1-4060	There's No Gettin' Over Me	1981	2.50	5.00	10.00
AYL1-4171	Images	1981	2.00	4.00	8.00
—"Best Buy Series" reissue					
AYL1-4255	Ronnie Milsap Live	1982	2.00	4.00	8.00
—"Best Buy Series" reissue					
AHL1-4311	Inside Ronnie Milsap	1982	2.50	5.00	10.00
AHL1-4670	Keyed Up	1983	2.50	5.00	10.00
AHL1-5016	One More Try for Love	1984	2.50	5.00	10.00
AYL1-5139	It Was Almost Like a Song	1984	2.00	4.00	8.00
—"Best Buy Series" reissue					
AYL1-5140	There's No Gettin' Over Me	1984	2.00	4.00	8.00
—"Best Buy Series" reissue					
AYL1-5142	Inside Ronnie Milsap	1984	2.00	4.00	8.00
—"Best Buy Series" reissue					
AHL1-5425	Greatest Hits, Vol. 2	1985	2.50	5.00	10.00
AYL1-5435	Keyed Up	1985	2.00	4.00	8.00
—"Best Buy Series" reissue					
5624-1-R	Christmas with Ronnie Milsap	1986	2.50	5.00	10.00
6425-1-R	Heart and Soul	1987	2.50	5.00	10.00
CPL1-7166	Collector's Series	1986	2.00	4.00	8.00
AHL1-7194	Lost in the Fifties Tonight	1986	2.50	5.00	10.00
7618-1-R	Heart and Soul	1988	2.00	4.00	8.00
—Reissue of 6245					
WARNER BROS.					
WS 1934	Ronnie Milsap	1971	5.00	10.00	20.00
BS 2870	A Rose By Any Other Name	1975	3.75	7.50	15.00

MIMMS, GARNET, AND THE ENCHANTERS

Includes Garnet Mimms credited alone. Also see THE ENCHANTERS (2).

Number	Title (A Side/B Side)	Yr	VG	VG+	NM
45s					
ARISTA					
0239	What It Is (Part 1)/What It Is (Part 2)	1977	—	2.00	4.00
0289	Johnny Perter/Tail Snatcher	1977	—	2.00	4.00
0332	Right Here in the Palm of My Hand/Tail Snatcher	1978	—	2.00	4.00
GSF					
6874	Another Place/Stop and Check Yourself	1972	—	3.00	6.00
6887	I'll Keep On Loving/Somebody, Someplace	1972	—	3.00	6.00
UNITED ARTISTS					
0109	Cry Baby/For Your Precious Love	1973	—	2.00	4.00
—"Silver Spotlight Series" reissue					
629	Cry Baby/Don't Change Your Heart	1963	3.75	7.50	15.00
658	Baby Don't You Weep/For Your Precious Love	1963	3.00	6.00	12.00
658 [PS]	Baby Don't You Weep/For Your Precious Love	1963	15.00	30.00	60.00
694	Tell Me Baby/Anytime You Want Me	1964	3.00	6.00	12.00
715	One Girl/A Quiet Place	1964	3.00	6.00	12.00
773	One Woman Man/Look Away	1964	3.00	6.00	12.00
796	A Little Bit of Soap/I'll Make It Up to You	1964	3.00	6.00	12.00
848	So Close/It Was Easier to Hurt Her	1965	3.00	6.00	12.00
868	Welcome Home/The Adventures of Moll Flanders	1965	3.00	6.00	12.00
887	Everytime/That Goes to Show You	1965	3.00	6.00	12.00
951	Looking for You/More Than a Miracle	1965	3.00	6.00	12.00
995	Prove It to Me/I'll Take Good Care of You	1966	3.00	6.00	12.00
50058	My Baby/Keep On Smilin'	1966	—	—	—
—Unreleased					
VEEP					
1232	Thinkin'/It's Been Such a Long Time Comin'	1966	2.00	4.00	8.00
1234	My Baby/Keep On Smilin'	1966	2.00	4.00	8.00
1252	All About Love/The Truth Hurts	1967	2.00	4.00	8.00
VERVE					
10596	Stop and Think It Over/I Can Hear My Baby Crying	1968	2.00	4.00	8.00
10624	Can You Top This/We Can Find That Love	1968	2.00	4.00	8.00
10642	Take Me/Happy Landing	1969	2.00	4.00	8.00
10650	Sad Song/Get It While You Can	1970	2.00	4.00	8.00
Albums					
ARISTA					
AL 4153	Garnet Mimms Has It All	1978	3.00	6.00	12.00
UNITED ARTISTS					
UAL 3305 [M]	Cry Baby and 11 Other Hits	1963	20.00	40.00	80.00
UAL 3396 [M]	As Long As I Have You	1964	12.50	25.00	50.00
UAL 3498 [M]	I'll Take Good Care of You	1966	12.50	25.00	50.00
UAS 6305 [S]	Cry Baby and 11 Other Hits	1963	25.00	50.00	100.00
UAS 6396 [S]	As Long As I Have You	1964	17.50	35.00	70.00
UAS 6498 [S]	I'll Take Good Care of You	1966	17.50	35.00	70.00

MIND EXPANDERS, THE

Number	Title (A Side/B Side)	Yr	VG	VG+	NM
Albums					
DOT					
DLP-3773 [M]	What's Happening	1967	25.00	50.00	100.00
DLP-25773 [S]	What's Happening	1967	20.00	40.00	80.00

MIND GARAGE, THE

Number	Title (A Side/B Side)	Yr	VG	VG+	NM
45s					
RCA VICTOR					
47-9755	There Was a Time/What's Behind Those Eyes	1969	2.00	4.00	8.00
47-9812	Jailhouse Rock/Tobacco Road	1969	2.00	4.00	8.00
Albums					
RCA VICTOR					
LSP-4218	The Mind Garage	1969	5.00	10.00	20.00
LSP-4319	The Mind Garage Again!	1970	5.00	10.00	20.00

MINDBENDERS, THE

Also see WAYNE FONTANA AND THE MINDBENDERS.

Number	Title (A Side/B Side)	Yr	VG	VG+	NM
45s					
FONTANA					
1541	A Groovy Kind of Love/Love Is Good	1966	3.00	6.00	12.00
1555	Ashes to Ashes/Don't Know About Love	1966	2.00	4.00	8.00
1571	I Want Her, She Wants Me/Morning After	1967	2.00	4.00	8.00
1595	It's Getting Harder All the Time/Off and Running	1967	2.00	4.00	8.00
1620	Yellow Brick Road/Blessed Are the Lonely	1968	2.00	4.00	8.00
1628	Uncle Joe the Ice Cream Man/The Man Who Loved Trees	1968	2.00	4.00	8.00
Albums					
FONTANA					
MGF-27554 [M]	A Groovy Kind of Love	1966	7.50	15.00	30.00
—With "Don't Cry No More"					
MGF-27554 [M]	A Groovy Kind of Love	1966	6.25	12.50	25.00
—With "Ashes to Ashes"					
SRF-67554 [R]	A Groovy Kind of Love	1966	6.25	12.50	25.00
—With "Don't Cry No More"					
SRF-67554 [R]	A Groovy Kind of Love	1966	5.00	10.00	20.00
—With "Ashes to Ashes"					

MINEO, SAL

Number	Title (A Side/B Side)	Yr	VG	VG+	NM
45s					
DECCA					
31692	Why Don't You Love Me/A Girl Across the Way	1964	3.00	6.00	12.00
EPIC					
9216	Start Movin' (In My Direction)/Love Affair	1957	6.25	12.50	25.00
9216 [PS]	Start Movin' (In My Direction)/Love Affair	1957	10.00	20.00	40.00
9227	Lasting Love/You Shouldn't Do That	1957	5.00	10.00	20.00
9227 [PS]	Lasting Love/You Shouldn't Do That	1957	7.50	15.00	30.00
9246	Party Time/The Words That I Whisper	1957	5.00	10.00	20.00
9246 [PS]	Party Time/The Words That I Whisper	1957	7.50	15.00	30.00
9260	Little Pigeon/Cuttin' In	1958	5.00	10.00	20.00
9260 [PS]	Little Pigeon/Cuttin' In	1958	—	—	—
—Rumored to exist, but without conclusive evidence, we will delete this from future editions					
9271	Seven Steps to Love/A Couple of Crazy Kids	1958	5.00	10.00	20.00
9287	Baby Face/Souvenirs of Summertime	1958	5.00	10.00	20.00
9327	Young As We Are/Make Believe Baby	1959	5.00	10.00	20.00
9327 [PS]	Young As We Are/Make Believe Baby	1959	7.50	15.00	30.00
9345	I'll Never Be Myself Again/The Words That I Whisper	1959	5.00	10.00	20.00
FONTANA					
1504	Save the Last Dance for Me/Take Me Back	1965	3.00	6.00	12.00
7-Inch Extended Plays					
EPIC					
EG-7187	(contents unknown)	1958	12.50	25.00	50.00
EG-7187 [PS]	Sal Mineo	1958	12.50	25.00	50.00
EG-7194	(contents unknown)	1958	10.00	20.00	40.00
EG-7194 [PS]	Sal	1958	10.00	20.00	40.00
EG-7195	(contents unknown)	1958	10.00	20.00	40.00
EG-7195 [PS]	Sal	1958	10.00	20.00	40.00
EG-7204	(contents unknown)	1959	12.50	25.00	50.00
EG-7204 [PS]	Souvenirs of Summertime	1959	12.50	25.00	50.00
ZTEP 27283/4	Too Young/Start Movin'//Baby Face/Little Pigeon	195?	15.00	30.00	60.00
—Special item for Scotch cellophane tape					
ZTEP 27283/4 [PS]	(title unknown)	195?	20.00	40.00	80.00
Albums					
EPIC					
LN 3405 [M]	Sal	1958	37.50	75.00	150.00

MINNELLI, LIZA

Also see JUDY GARLAND AND LIZA MINNELLI.

Number	Title (A Side/B Side)	Yr	VG	VG+	NM
12-Inch Singles					
EPIC					
68858	Losing MyMind (4 versions)	1989	2.50	5.00	10.00
73166	Love Pains (5 versions)	1989	2.50	5.00	10.00
45s					
A&M					
915	Married/You Better Sit Down Kids//Waiting for My Friends	1968	—	3.00	6.00
1018	Raggedy Ann and Raggedy Andy/Frank Mills	1969	—	3.00	6.00
1173	Come Saturday Morning/Wherefore and Why	1970	—	3.00	6.00
1244	(I Wonder Where My) Easy Rider's Gone/The Man I Love	1971	—	3.00	6.00
CADENCE					
1436	What Do You Think I Am/You Are For Living	1963	3.00	6.00	12.00
CAPITOL					
4994	One Summer Love/How Much Do I Love You	1963	2.50	5.00	10.00
5103	Day Dreaming/His Woman	1964	2.50	5.00	10.00
5473	Did I Hurt Your Feelings/Imprevu	1965	2.00	4.00	8.00

Number	Title (A Side/B Side)	Yr	VG	VG+	NM
5761	I Who Have Nothing/Middle of the Street	1966	2.00	4.00	8.00
COLUMBIA					
10178	All That Jazz/My Own Best Friend	1975	—	2.00	4.00
45715	Ring Them Bells/It Was a Good Time	1972	—	2.50	5.00
45746	The Singer/Mr. Emery Won't Be Home	1972	—	2.50	5.00
45846	Don't Let Me Be Lonely Tonight/Mr. Emery Won't Be Home	1973	—	2.50	5.00
45995	Harbour/More Than I Like You	1974	—	2.50	5.00
EPIC					
73011	Losing My Mind/Tonight Is Forever	1989	—	2.50	5.00
UNITED ARTISTS					
XW1014	Theme from "New York, New York"/Hazy	1977	—	2.50	5.00

Albums

Number	Title (A Side/B Side)	Yr	VG	VG+	NM
A&M					
SP-3524 [(2)]	Liza Minnelli Foursider	1973	3.75	7.50	15.00
SP-4141	Liza Minnelli	1968	3.75	7.50	15.00
SP-4164	Come Saturday Morning	1969	3.75	7.50	15.00
SP-4272	New Feelin'	1970	3.75	7.50	15.00
SP-4345	Live at the Olympia	1971	3.75	7.50	15.00
SP-6013 [(2)]	Liza Minnelli Foursider	198?	2.50	5.00	10.00
—Reissue of 3524					
CAPITOL					
ST 2174 [S]	Liza! Liza!	1964	6.25	12.50	25.00
T 2174 [M]	Liza! Liza!	1964	5.00	10.00	20.00
SM-2271	It Amazes Me	1976	2.50	5.00	10.00
—Reissue with new prefix					
ST 2271 [S]	It Amazes Me	1965	6.25	12.50	25.00
T 2271 [M]	It Amazes Me	1965	5.00	10.00	20.00
ST 2448 [S]	There Is a Time	1966	6.25	12.50	25.00
T 2448 [M]	There Is a Time	1966	5.00	10.00	20.00
SM-11080	Maybe This Time	197?	2.50	5.00	10.00
—Reissue with new prefix					
ST-11080	Maybe This Time	1972	3.00	6.00	12.00
SM-11803	There Is a Time	1978	2.50	5.00	10.00
—Reissue of ST 2448					
COLUMBIA					
KC 31762	Liza with a "Z"	1972	3.75	7.50	15.00
PC 31762	Liza with a "Z"	198?	2.00	4.00	8.00
—Budget-line reissue					
CQ 32149 [Q]	Liza Minnelli The Singer	1973	5.00	10.00	20.00
KC 32149	Liza Minnelli The Singer	1973	3.75	7.50	15.00
PC 32149	Liza Minnelli The Singer	198?	2.00	4.00	8.00
—Budget-line reissue					
PC 32854	Live at the Winter Garden	1974	3.75	7.50	15.00
PC 34887	Tropical Nights	1977	3.00	6.00	12.00
EPIC					
OE 45098	Results	1989	3.75	7.50	15.00
TELARC					
15502 [(2)]	Liza Minnelli at Carnegie Hall	1987	3.75	7.50	15.00

MINORBOPS, THE

45s

Number	Title (A Side/B Side)	Yr	VG	VG+	NM
LAMP					
2012	Need You Tonight/Want You for My Own	1957	62.50	125.00	250.00

MINT JULEPS, THE

45s

Number	Title (A Side/B Side)	Yr	VG	VG+	NM
HERALD					
481	Bells of Love/Vip-a-Dip	1956	25.00	50.00	100.00
—With script logo inside flag					
481	Bells of Love/Vip-a-Dip	1956	6.25	12.50	25.00
—With block logo inside flag					

MINT TATTOO

45s

Number	Title (A Side/B Side)	Yr	VG	VG+	NM
DOT					
17242	Mark of the Beast/When Talking About You	1969	2.50	5.00	10.00

Albums

Number	Title (A Side/B Side)	Yr	VG	VG+	NM
DOT					
DLP-25918	Mint Tattoo	1969	7.50	15.00	30.00

MINTS, THE

See KEN COPELAND.

MINUTE MEN, THE

45s

Number	Title (A Side/B Side)	Yr	VG	VG+	NM
ARGO					
5469	Please Keep the Beatles in England/My Love Is Gone	1964	3.75	7.50	15.00

MIRABAI

45s

Number	Title (A Side/B Side)	Yr	VG	VG+	NM
ATLANTIC					
3300	Cosmic Overload/To Be Young	1975	—	2.50	5.00

Albums

Number	Title (A Side/B Side)	Yr	VG	VG+	NM
ATLANTIC					
SD 18144	Mirabai	1975	2.50	5.00	10.00

MIRACLES, THE

Includes records as "Smokey Robinson and the Miracles." Also see SMOKEY ROBINSON.

12-Inch Singles

Number	Title (A Side/B Side)	Yr	VG	VG+	NM
COLUMBIA					
AS 283 [DJ]	Sing for Brotherhood (same on both sides)	1976	3.75	7.50	15.00
10515	Women (Make the World Go 'Round)/Spy for Brotherhood	1977	3.00	6.00	12.00

45s

Number	Title (A Side/B Side)	Yr	VG	VG+	NM
CHESS					
1734	Bad Girl/I Love Your Baby	1959	15.00	30.00	60.00
—Blue label with vertical Chess logo (original)					
1734	Bad Girl/I Love Your Baby	1963	6.25	12.50	25.00
—Black label					
1734	Bad Girl/I Love Your Baby	1966	5.00	10.00	20.00
—Blue label with "Chess" at top					
1768	I Need a Change/All I Want (Is You)	1960	10.00	20.00	40.00
COLUMBIA					
10464	Spy for Brotherhood/The Bird Must Fly Away	1976	—	2.50	5.00
10517	Women (Make the World Go 'Round)/I Can Touch the Sky	1977	—	2.50	5.00
10706	Mean Machine/The Magic of Your Eyes (Laura's Eyes)	1978	—	2.50	5.00
END					
1016	Got a Job/My Mama Done Told Me	1958	15.00	30.00	60.00
1029	Money/I Cry	1958	12.50	25.00	50.00
—Mostly gray-white label, no mention of Roulette Records					
1029	Money/I Cry	1958	10.00	20.00	40.00
—Multicolor label with "A Division of Roulette Records Inc." on label					
1084	Money/I Cry	1961	6.25	12.50	25.00
MOTOWN					
G 1/G 2	Bad Girl/I Love Your Baby	1959	1250.	1875.	2500.
TLX-2207	Bad Girl/I Love Your Baby	1959	1250.	1875.	2500.
STANDARD GROOVE					
13090 [DJ]	I Care About Detroit	1968	50.00	100.00	200.00
—With Tamla globe logo on label					
13090 [DJ]	I Care About Detroit	1968	37.50	75.00	150.00
—With no Tamla logo on label					
TAMLA					
EX-009 [DJ]	The Christmas Song/Christmas Everyday	1963	50.00	100.00	200.00
54028	The Feeling Is So Fine/You Can Depend On Me	1960	125.00	250.00	500.00
—With alternate take of B-side; matrix number followed by "A" in trail-off wax					
54028	The Feeling Is So Fine/You Can Depend On Me	1960	100.00	200.00	400.00
54028	Way Over There/Depend On Me	1960	15.00	30.00	60.00
—With overdubbed strings on A-side					
54028	Way Over There/Depend on Me	1960	37.50	75.00	150.00
—No strings on A-side recording					
54034	Shop Around/Who's Lovin' You	1960	45.00	90.00	180.00
—Original take, withdrawn shortly after release. In trail-off wax is "H55518A."					
54034	Shop Around/Who's Lovin' You	1960	7.50	15.00	30.00
—Hit take. In trail-off wax is "L-1." Horizontal lines label.					
54034	Shop Around/Who's Lovin' You	1960	3.00	6.00	12.00
—Hit take. In trail-off wax is "L-1." Globe label.					
54036	Ain't It Baby/The Only One I Love	1961	37.50	75.00	150.00
54044	Mighty Good Lovin'/Broken Hearted	1961	12.50	25.00	50.00
54044 [PS]	Mighty Good Lovin'/Broken Hearted	1961	37.50	75.00	150.00
54048	Everybody's Gotta Pay Some Dues/I Can't Believe	1961	12.50	25.00	50.00
54048	You Gotta Pay Some Dues/I Can't Believe	1961	25.00	50.00	100.00
—Alternate A-side title					
54048 [PS]	Everybody's Gotta Pay Some Dues/I Can't Believe	1961	50.00	100.00	200.00
54053	What's So Good About Good-By/I've Been Good to You	1962	7.50	15.00	30.00
54053 [PS]	What's So Good About Good-By/I've Been Good to You	1962	30.00	60.00	120.00
54059	I'll Try Something New/You Never Miss a Good Thing	1962	5.00	10.00	20.00
54059 [PS]	I'll Try Something New/You Never Miss a Good Thing	1962	30.00	60.00	120.00
54069	Way Over There/If Your Mother Only Knew	1962	5.00	10.00	20.00
54073	You've Really Got a Hold on Me/Happy Landing	1962	5.00	10.00	20.00
54078	A Love She Can Count On/I Can Take a Hint	1963	5.00	10.00	20.00
54083	Mickey's Monkey/Whatever Makes You Happy	1963	5.00	10.00	20.00
54089	I Gotta Dance to Keep from Crying/Such Is Love, Such Is Life	1963	3.75	7.50	15.00
54092	(You Can't Let the Boy Overpower) The Man in You/Heartbreak Road	1964	3.75	7.50	15.00
54098	I Like It Like That/You're So Fine and Sweet	1964	3.75	7.50	15.00
54098 [PS]	I Like It Like That/You're So Fine and Sweet	1964	30.00	60.00	120.00
54102	That's What Love Is Made Of/Would I Love You	1964	3.75	7.50	15.00
54109	Come On Do the Jerk/Baby Don't You Go	1964	3.75	7.50	15.00
54113	Ooo Baby Baby/All That's Good	1965	3.75	7.50	15.00
54118	The Tracks of My Tears/A Fork in the Road	1965	3.75	7.50	15.00
54123	My Girl Has Gone/Since You Won My Heart	1965	3.75	7.50	15.00
54127	Going to A-Go-Go/Choosey Beggar	1965	3.75	7.50	15.00
54127 [PS]	Going to A-Go-Go/Choosey Beggar	1965	25.00	50.00	100.00
54134	Whole Lot of Shakin' in My Heart (Since I Met You)/Oh Be My Lover	1966	2.50	5.00	10.00
54140	Come 'Round Here — I'm the One You Need/Save Me	1966	2.50	5.00	10.00
54140 [PS]	Come 'Round Here — I'm the One You Need/Save Me	1966	25.00	50.00	100.00
54145	The Love I Saw in You Was Just a Mirage/Come Spy with Me	1967	2.00	4.00	8.00
—Starting here, through Tamla 54225, as "Smokey Robinson and the Miracles"					
54152	More Love/Swept for You Baby	1967	2.00	4.00	8.00
54159	I Second That Emotion/You Must Be Love	1967	2.00	4.00	8.00
54162	If You Can Want/When the Words from Your Heart Get Caught Up in Your Throat	1968	2.00	4.00	8.00
—"Tamla" in box on label					
54162	If You Can Want/When the Words from Your Heart Get Caught Up in Your Throat	1968	3.75	7.50	15.00
—"Tamla" in globe on label					
54167	Yester Love/Much Better Off	1968	2.00	4.00	8.00
54172	Special Occasion/Give Her Up	1968	2.00	4.00	8.00
54178	Baby, Baby Don't Cry/Your Mother's Only Daughter	1968	2.00	4.00	8.00
54183	Here I Go Again/Doggone Right	1969	2.00	4.00	8.00
54184	Abraham, Martin, and John/Much Better Off	1969	2.00	4.00	8.00
54189	Point It Out/Darling Dear	1969	2.00	4.00	8.00
54194	Who's Gonna Take the Blame/I Gotta Thing For You	1970	2.00	4.00	8.00
54199	The Tears of a Clown/Promise Me	1970	—	3.00	6.00
54205	I Don't Blame You at All/That Girl	1971	—	3.00	6.00
54206	Crazy About the La La La/Oh Baby Baby I Love You	1971	—	3.00	6.00
54211	Satisfaction/Flower Girl	1971	—	3.00	6.00

Number	Title (A Side/B Side)	Yr	VG	VG+	NM
54220	We've Come Too Far to End It Now/When Sundown Comes	1972	—	3.00	6.00
54225	I Can't Stand to See You Cry/With Your Love Came	1972	—	3.00	6.00
54237	Don't Let It End (Til You Let It Begin)/Wigs and Lashes	1973	—	2.50	5.00
—Starting here, name reverts to The Miracles					
54240	Give Me Just Another Day/I Wanna Be with You	1973	—	2.50	5.00
54248	Do It Baby/I Wanna Be with You	1974	—	2.50	5.00
54256	Don't Cha Love It/Up Again	1974	—	2.50	5.00
54259	You Are Love/Gemini	1975	—	2.50	5.00
54262	Love Machine (Part 1)/Love Machine (Part 2)	1975	—	2.50	5.00
54268	Night Life/Smog	1976	—	2.50	5.00
TOPPS/MOTOWN					
11	Shop Around	1967	18.75	37.50	75.00
—Cardboard record					
Albums					
COLUMBIA					
PC 34460	Love Crazy	1977	3.00	6.00	12.00
PCQ 34460 [Q]	Love Crazy	1977	5.00	10.00	20.00
JC 34910	The Miracles	1978	3.00	6.00	12.00
MOTOWN					
M5-133V1	Do It Baby	1981	2.00	4.00	8.00
—Reissue of Tamla 334					
M5-136V1	Away We a Go-Go	1981	2.00	4.00	8.00
—Reissue of Tamla 271					
M5-156V1	The Tears of a Clown	1981	2.00	4.00	8.00
—Reissue of Tamla 276					
M5-160V1	Hi, We're the Miracles	1981	2.00	4.00	8.00
—Reissue of Tamla 220					
M5-210V1	Greatest Hits, Vol. 2	1981	2.00	4.00	8.00
—Reissue of Tamla 280					
M5-217V1	Doin' Mickey's Monkey	1981	2.00	4.00	8.00
—Reissue of Tamla 245					
M5-220V1	Recorded Live On Stage	1981	2.00	4.00	8.00
—Reissue of Tamla 241					
M8-238M2 [(2)]	Greatest Hits from the Beginning	1982	3.00	6.00	12.00
—Reissue of Tamla 254					
793 [(3)]	Smokey Robinson and the Miracles Anthology	1974	5.00	10.00	20.00
5253 ML	The Season for Miracles	1982	2.00	4.00	8.00
—Reissue of Tamla 307					
5254 ML	Christmas with the Miracles	1982	2.00	4.00	8.00
—Reissue of Tamla 236					
TAMLA					
T 220 [M]	Hi We're the Miracles	1961	150.00	300.00	600.00
—White label					
T 223 [M]	Cookin' with the Miracles	1962	200.00	400.00	800.00
—White label					
T 230 [M]	I'll Try Something New	1962	150.00	300.00	600.00
—White label					
T 236 [M]	Christmas with the Miracles	1963	75.00	150.00	300.00
—Originals have two globes on the top of the label					
T 238 [M]	The Fabulous Miracles	1963	75.00	150.00	300.00
T 238 [M]	You've Really Got a Hold on Me	1963	50.00	100.00	200.00
—Retitled version of "The Fabulous Miracles"					
T 241 [M]	The Miracles On Stage	1963	50.00	100.00	200.00
T 245 [M]	Doin' Mickey's Monkey	1963	50.00	100.00	200.00
TS 245 [S]	Doin' Mickey's Monkey	1963	75.00	150.00	300.00
T 254 [(2) M]	Greatest Hits from the Beginning	1965	12.50	25.00	50.00
TS 254 [(2) P]	Greatest Hits from the Beginning	1965	10.00	20.00	40.00
T 267 [M]	Going to a Go-Go	1966	7.50	15.00	30.00
TS 267 [S]	Going to a Go-Go	1966	10.00	20.00	40.00
T 271 [M]	Away We a Go-Go	1966	6.25	12.50	25.00
TS 271 [S]	Away We a Go-Go	1966	7.50	15.00	30.00
T 276 [M]	Make It Happen	1967	6.25	12.50	25.00
TS 276 [S]	Make It Happen	1967	7.50	15.00	30.00
TS 276 [S]	The Tears of a Clown	1970	3.75	7.50	15.00
—Retitled version of "Make It Happen"					
TS 280	Greatest Hits, Vol. 2	1968	6.25	12.50	25.00
TS 289	Live!	1969	5.00	10.00	20.00
TS 290	Special Occasion	1968	5.00	10.00	20.00
TS 295	Time Out for Smokey Robinson & the Miracles	1969	5.00	10.00	20.00
TS 297	Four in Blue	1969	5.00	10.00	20.00
TS 301	What Love Has...Joined Together	1970	3.75	7.50	15.00
TS 306	A Pocket Full of Miracles	1970	3.75	7.50	15.00
T 307	The Season for Miracles	1970	3.75	7.50	15.00
TS 312	One Dozen Roses	1971	3.75	7.50	15.00
TS 318	Flying High Together	1972	3.75	7.50	15.00
TS 320 [(2)]	1957-1972	1972	5.00	10.00	20.00
T 325F	Renaissance	1973	3.00	6.00	12.00
T6-334	Do It Baby	1974	3.00	6.00	12.00
T6-336	Don't Cha Love It	1975	3.00	6.00	12.00
T6-339	City of Angels	1975	3.00	6.00	12.00
T6-344	The Power of Music	1976	3.00	6.00	12.00
T7-357	Greatest Hits	1977	3.00	6.00	12.00

MIRACLES, THE (2)

No relation to the more famous group above.

Number	Title (A Side/B Side)	Yr	VG	VG+	NM
45s					
BATON					
210	A Lover's Chant/Come Home with Me	1955	37.50	75.00	150.00
CASH					
1008	You're An Angel/A Gal Named Jo	1955	50.00	100.00	200.00

MIRANDA, BOB

Of THE HAPPENINGS.

Number	Title (A Side/B Side)	Yr	VG	VG+	NM
45s					
B.T. PUPPY					
544	Girl on a Swing/When I Lock My Door	1968	2.50	5.00	10.00
JUBILEE					
5709	Everybody Is a Star/Evergreen	1971	2.00	4.00	8.00

MIRETTES, THE

Also see THE IKETTES.

Number	Title (A Side/B Side)	Yr	VG	VG+	NM
45s					
MINIT					
32045	Help Wanted/Play Fair	1968	2.50	5.00	10.00
MIRWOOD					
5514	He's Alright with Me/Your Kind Ain't No Good	1966	3.00	6.00	12.00
5531	He's Alright with Me/Now That I Found You Baby	1967	2.50	5.00	10.00
REVUE					
11004	In the Midnight Hour/To Love Somebody	1968	2.50	5.00	10.00
11017	Take Me for a Little While/Real Thing	1968	2.00	4.00	8.00
11029	First Love/I'm a Whole New Thing	1968	2.00	4.00	8.00
UNI					
55110	Stand By Your Man/If Everybody'd Help Somebody	1969	—	3.00	6.00
55126	Heart Full of Gladness/You Ain't Trying to Cross Over	1969	—	3.00	6.00
55147	Whirlpool/You Ain't Trying to Cross Over	1969	—	3.00	6.00
55161	Rap Run It On Down/Sweet Soul Sister	1969	—	3.00	6.00
—A-side: Nate Turner and the Mirettes; B-side: Venetta Fields and the Mirettes					
Albums					
REVUE					
RS-7205	In the Midnight Hour	1968	3.75	7.50	15.00
UNI					
73062	Whirlpool	1969	3.75	7.50	15.00

MISFITS, THE

More than one group. The punk band is outside the scope of this book and is not included.

Number	Title (A Side/B Side)	Yr	VG	VG+	NM
45s					
ARIES					
3	Midnight Star/I Don't Know	1961	50.00	100.00	200.00
BLANK					
A 101	Cough Cool/She	1977	50.00	100.00	200.00
—500 copies were pressed					
A 101 [PS]	Cough Cool/She	1977	50.00	100.00	200.00
HUSH					
105	Give Me Your Heart/My Mother-in-Law	1960	100.00	200.00	400.00
IMPERIAL					
66054	This Little Piggy (I'm a Hog for You)/Lost Love	1964	6.25	12.50	25.00
JOEY					
117	Naughty Rooster/Chicago Confidential	1961	3.00	6.00	12.00
SOUND STAGE 7					
2538	It's Up to You/Skiing Time	1965	6.25	12.50	25.00
TROY					
227	The Uncle Willie/Big Bad Wolf	196?	6.25	12.50	25.00

MR. CLEAN

Number	Title (A Side/B Side)	Yr	VG	VG+	NM
45s					
ORIGINAL SOUND					
40	Mr. Clean/Jessie Lee	1964	37.50	75.00	150.00
—Written, produced and performed on by Frank Zappa					

MR. GASSER AND THE WEIRDOS

Number	Title (A Side/B Side)	Yr	VG	VG+	NM
Albums					
CAPITOL					
ST 2010 [S]	Hot Rod Hootenanny	1963	30.00	60.00	120.00
T 2010 [M]	Hot Rod Hootenanny	1963	25.00	50.00	100.00
ST 2057 [S]	Rods n' Ratfinks	1963	30.00	60.00	120.00
—Add 25% if ratfink decal is enclosed					
T 2057 [M]	Rods n' Ratfinks	1963	25.00	50.00	100.00
—Add 25% if ratfink decal is enclosed					
ST 2114 [S]	Surfink!	1964	50.00	100.00	200.00
—With bonus single in pocket on cover: "Santa Barbara"/"Midnight Run" by the Super Stocks					
ST 2114 [S]	Surfink!	1964	37.50	75.00	150.00
—Without bonus single					
T 2114 [M]	Surfink!	1964	37.50	75.00	150.00
—With bonus single in pocket on cover: "Santa Barbara"/"Midnight Run" by the Super Stocks					
T 2114 [M]	Surfink!	1964	25.00	50.00	100.00
—Without bonus single					

MR. LUCKY AND THE GAMBLERS

Number	Title (A Side/B Side)	Yr	VG	VG+	NM
45s					
DOT					
16930	Take a Look at Me/I Told You (Once Before)	1966	5.00	10.00	20.00
PANORAMA					
37	Take a Look at Me/I Told You (Once Before)	1966	5.00	10.00	20.00
52	Alice Designs/You Don't Need Me	1967	3.75	7.50	15.00
UNITED INT'L.					
1001	New Orleans/Searching	1965	5.00	10.00	20.00
4404	Koko Joe/I Told You (Once Before)	1966	5.00	10.00	20.00

MR. SHORT STUFF

Number	Title (A Side/B Side)	Yr	VG	VG+	NM
Albums					
SPIVEY					
1005	Mr. Short Stuff	196?	5.00	10.00	20.00

MR. SOUL BOWL

Number	Title (A Side/B Side)	Yr	VG	VG+	NM
45s					
ATLANTIC					
2823	Answer to the Want Ads/H-L-I-C	1971	—	3.00	6.00

MITCHELL, BILLY

Number	Title (A Side/B Side)	Yr	VG	VG+	NM
45s					
ATLANTIC					
933	My Love, My Desire/Pack Up All Your Bags	1951	75.00	150.00	300.00
950	If I Had Known/Verna Lee	1951	50.00	100.00	200.00
954	Let's Have a Ball Tonight/Someday You'll Be Sorry	1952	50.00	100.00	200.00
974	Ghost Train/Bald Headed Woman	1952	50.00	100.00	200.00
—With Joe Morris					

Number	Title (A Side/B Side)	Yr	VG	VG+	NM
CALLA					
165	Oh Happy Day/The Chokin' Kind	1969	2.00	4.00	8.00
167	Too Busy Thinking 'Bout My Baby/Crystal Blue Persuasion	1969	2.00	4.00	8.00
IMPERIAL					
5520	Satellite Be-Bop/Pickin' on the Wrong Chicken	1958	5.00	10.00	20.00
JUBILEE					
5400	Short Skirts/You Know I Do	1961	3.75	7.50	15.00
UNITED ARTISTS					
235	Call to Me (I'll Be Here)/Where	1960	3.75	7.50	15.00
WARWICK					
501	It Doesn't Matter to Me/Stop a Little While	1959	3.75	7.50	15.00

MITCHELL, BOBBY

45s

Number	Title (A Side/B Side)	Yr	VG	VG+	NM
IMPERIAL					
5236	I'm Cryin'/Rack 'Em Back	1953	50.00	100.00	200.00
5250	One Friday Morning/Four-Eleven-Forty-Four	1953	50.00	100.00	200.00
5270	Baby's Gone/Sister Lucy	1954	30.00	60.00	120.00
5282	Angel Child/School Boy Blues	1954	30.00	60.00	120.00
5295	The Wedding Bells Are Ringing/Meant for Me	1954	30.00	60.00	120.00
5309	I'm a Young Man/She Couldn't Be Found	1954	30.00	60.00	120.00
5326	I Wish I Knew/Nothing Sweet As You	1955	20.00	40.00	80.00
5346	I Cried/I'm in Love	1955	15.00	30.00	60.00
5378	Try Rock and Roll/No, No, No	1956	12.50	25.00	50.00
5392	Goin' Round in Circles/I Try So Hard	1956	12.50	25.00	50.00
5412	You Are My Angel/I've Got My Fingers Crossed	1956	12.50	25.00	50.00
5440	You Always Hurt the One You Love/I Would Like to Know	1957	10.00	20.00	40.00
5475	I'm Gonna Be a Wheel Someday/You Better Go Home	1957	12.50	25.00	50.00
5511	I Love to Hold You/64 Hours	1958	10.00	20.00	40.00
5558	Hearts of Fire/You're Going to Be Sorry	1959	10.00	20.00	40.00
5882	My Southern Bell/When First We Met	1962	3.00	6.00	12.00
5923	I Don't Want to Be a Wheel No More/I Got to Call That Number	1963	3.00	6.00	12.00
RON					
337	Sand Me Your Picture/You're Doing Me Wrong	1961	3.00	6.00	12.00
342	Mama Don't Allow/There's Only One of You	1961	3.00	6.00	12.00

MITCHELL, CHAD

Also see THE CHAD MITCHELL TRIO.

45s

Number	Title (A Side/B Side)	Yr	VG	VG+	NM
AMY					
11043	For What It's Worth/Follow	1968	—	2.50	5.00
11054	The Bus Song/What's That Got to Do with Me	1969	—	2.50	5.00
WARNER BROS.					
5880	Quiet Room/Violets of Dawn	1966	—	3.00	6.00
7043	Suzanne/Marieka	1967	—	3.00	6.00

Albums

Number	Title (A Side/B Side)	Yr	VG	VG+	NM
BELL					
6028	Chad	1969	3.75	7.50	15.00
WARNER BROS.					
W 1667 [M]	Chad Mitchell Himself	1966	3.75	7.50	15.00
WS 1667 [S]	Chad Mitchell Himself	1966	5.00	10.00	20.00
W 1706 [M]	A Feeling of Love	1967	5.00	10.00	20.00
WS 1706 [S]	A Feeling of Love	1967	3.75	7.50	15.00

MITCHELL, CHAD, TRIO

45s

Number	Title (A Side/B Side)	Yr	VG	VG+	NM
COLPIX					
133	Sally Ann/Vaya Con Dios	1959	3.00	6.00	12.00
136	Up On the Mountain/Walkin' on the Green Grasses	1959	3.00	6.00	12.00
144	I Do Adore Her/The Gallows Tree	1960	3.00	6.00	12.00
154	The Ballad of Herbie Spear/Pretty Saro	1960	3.00	6.00	12.00
157	Devil Road/Paddy West	1960	3.00	6.00	12.00
610	Six Men/I'm Going Home	1961	2.50	5.00	10.00
—B-side by Eugene Lamarr					
KAPP					
439	Lizzie Borden/Super Skier	1961	3.00	6.00	12.00
439 [PS]	Lizzie Borden/Super Skier	1961	5.00	10.00	20.00
457	John Birch Society/Golden Vanity	1962	2.50	5.00	10.00
481	Alberta/Come Along Home	1962	2.50	5.00	10.00
485	You Can Tell the World/Hello, Susan Brown	1962	2.50	5.00	10.00
510	Blowing in the Wind/Adios, Mi Corazon	1963	2.50	5.00	10.00
518	Green Grow the Lilacs/Leave Me If You Want To	1963	2.50	5.00	10.00
MAY					
116	The Ballad of Herbie Spear/Sally Ann	1962	2.50	5.00	10.00
MERCURY					
72197	The Marvelous Toy/Bonny Streets of Fyve-10	1963	2.50	5.00	10.00
72197 [PS]	The Marvelous Toy/Bonny Streets of Fyve-10	1963	3.75	7.50	15.00
72234	The Tarrier's Song/Tell Old Billy	1964	2.00	4.00	8.00
72234 [PS]	The Tarrier's Song/Tell Old Billy	1964	3.75	7.50	15.00
72257	What Did You Learn in School Today/Barry's Boys	1964	2.00	4.00	8.00

Albums

Number	Title (A Side/B Side)	Yr	VG	VG+	NM
COLPIX					
CP-411 [M]	The Chad Mitchell Trio	1961	5.00	10.00	20.00
SCP-411 [S]	The Chad Mitchell Trio	1961	7.50	15.00	30.00
CP-463 [M]	Everybody's Listening	1964	5.00	10.00	20.00
SCP-463 [S]	Everybody's Listening	1964	7.50	15.00	30.00
KAPP					
KL-1262 [M]	Mighty Day on Campus	1962	5.00	10.00	20.00
KL-1281 [M]	The Chad Mitchell Trio at the Bitter End	1962	5.00	10.00	20.00
KL-1313 [M]	Blowin' in the Wind	1963	5.00	10.00	20.00
KL-1334 [M]	The Best of Chad Mitchell Trio	1963	5.00	10.00	20.00
KS-3262 [S]	Mighty Day on Campus	1962	6.25	12.50	25.00
KS-3281 [S]	The Chad Mitchell Trio at the Bitter End	1962	6.25	12.50	25.00
KS-3313 [S]	Blowin' in the Wind	1963	6.25	12.50	25.00
KS-3334 [S]	The Best of Chad Mitchell Trio	1963	6.25	12.50	25.00

Number	Title (A Side/B Side)	Yr	VG	VG+	NM
MERCURY					
MG-20838 [M]	Singin' Our Mind	1963	3.75	7.50	15.00
MG-20891 [M]	Reflecting	1964	3.75	7.50	15.00
SR-60838 [S]	Singin' Our Mind	1963	5.00	10.00	20.00
SR-60891 [S]	Reflecting	1964	5.00	10.00	20.00

MITCHELL, GUY

45s

Number	Title (A Side/B Side)	Yr	VG	VG+	NM
CHALICE					
711	My Angel/Bit of Love	1963	7.50	15.00	30.00
711	My Angel/Mr. Hobo	1963	7.50	15.00	30.00
712	Take Your Time/(B-side unknown)	1963	7.50	15.00	30.00
713	Your Imagination/(B-side unknown)	1963	7.50	15.00	30.00
COLUMBIA					
1-640 (?)	Giddy Up/Where in the World	1950	7.50	15.00	30.00
—Microgroove 33 1/3 rpm 7-inch single					
1-680 (?)	Me and My Imagination/To Me You're a Song	1950	7.50	15.00	30.00
—Microgroove 33 1/3 rpm 7-inch single					
1-760 (?)	Angels Cry/You're Not in My Arms Tonight	1950	7.50	15.00	30.00
—Microgroove 33 1/3 rpm 7-inch single					
6-760 (?)	Angels Cry/You're Not in My Arms Tonight	1950	6.25	12.50	25.00
1-918	My Heart Cries for You/The Roving Kind	1950	7.50	15.00	30.00
—Microgroove 33 1/3 rpm 7-inch single					
6-918	My Heart Cries for You/The Roving Kind	1950	6.25	12.50	25.00
39067	My Heart Cries for You/The Roving Kind	1950	3.75	7.50	15.00
39190	Sparrow in the Tree Top/Christopher Columbus	1951	3.70	7.50	15.00
3-39190	Sparrow in the Tree Top/Christopher Columbus	1951	7.50	15.00	30.00
—Microgroove 33 1/3 rpm 7-inch single					
39331	Unless/A Beggar in Love	1951	3.75	7.50	15.00
39415	My Truly, Truly Fair/Who Knows Love	1951	3.75	7.50	15.00
39512	Belle, Belle, My Liberty Belle/Sweetheart of Yesterday	1951	3.75	7.50	15.00
39595	There's Always Room at Our House/I Can't Help It (If I'm Still in Love with You)	1951	3.75	7.50	15.00
39639	Wimmin'/We Don't Live in a Castle	1952	5.00	10.00	20.00
39663	Pittsburgh, Pennsylvania/Doll with a Sawdust Heart	1952	3.75	7.50	15.00
39753	The Day of Jubilo/You'll Never Be Mine	1952	5.00	10.00	20.00
39822	Feet Up (Pat Him on the Po-Po)/Jenny Kissed Me	1952	3.75	7.50	15.00
39879	('Cause I Love You) That's-a Why/Train of Love	1952	3.75	7.50	15.00
—With Mindy Carson					
39886	Don't Rob Another Man's Castle/Why Should I Go Home	1952	3.75	7.50	15.00
39909	She Wears Red Feathers/Pretty Little Blackeyed Susie	1952	3.75	7.50	15.00
39950	I Want You for a Sunbeam/So Am I	1953	3.00	6.00	12.00
39992	There's Nothing As Sweet As My Baby/Tell Us Where the Good Times Are	1953	3.00	6.00	12.00
—With Mindy Carson					
40008	Hannah Lee/Look at That Girl	1953	3.00	6.00	12.00
40035	Cloud Lucky Seven/Chicka-Boom	1953	3.00	6.00	12.00
40077	Sippin' Soda/Strollin' Blues	1953	3.00	6.00	12.00
40128	Got a Hole in My Sweater/The Cuff of My Shirt	1953	3.00	6.00	12.00
40175	Tear Down the Mountains/A Dime and a Dollar	1954	3.00	6.00	12.00
40240	There Once Was a Man/My Heaven on Earth	1954	3.00	6.00	12.00
40278	What Am I Doin' in Kansas City/You've Ruined Me	1954	3.00	6.00	12.00
40389	I Met the Cutest Little Eyeful (At the Eiffel Tower)/Gee But You Gotta Come Home	1954	3.00	6.00	12.00
40468	Nobody Home/Zoo Baby	1955	2.50	5.00	10.00
40507	Otto's Gotta Go (Otto Drives Me Crazy)/Man Overboard	1955	3.00	6.00	12.00
40531	Let Us Be Sweethearts Again/Too Late	1955	2.50	5.00	10.00
40560	When Binky Blows/Belonging	1955	2.50	5.00	10.00
40631	Ninety Nine Years (Dead or Alive)/Perfume, Candy and Flowers	1955	2.50	5.00	10.00
40672	Solo/Green Grows the Grass	1956	2.50	5.00	10.00
40700	Give Me a Carriage with Eight White Horses/I Used to Hate Ya	1956	2.50	5.00	10.00
40724	Finders Keepers/I'd Like to Say a Few Words About Texas	1956	2.50	5.00	10.00
40769	Singing the Blues/Crazy with Love	1956	2.50	5.00	10.00
40769 [PS]	Singing the Blues/Crazy with Love	1956	5.00	10.00	20.00
40820	Knee Deep in the Blues/Take Me Back Baby	1957	2.50	5.00	10.00
40820 [PS]	Knee Deep in the Blues/Take Me Back Baby	1957	3.75	7.50	15.00
40877	Rock-a-Billy/Hoot Owl	1957	2.50	5.00	10.00
40877 [PS]	Rock-a-Billy/Hoot Owl	1957	3.75	7.50	15.00
40940	Sweet Stuff/In the Middle of a Dark, Dark Night	1957	2.50	5.00	10.00
40987	A Cure for the Blues/Call Rosie on the Phone	1957	2.50	5.00	10.00
41033	C'mon Let's Go/The Unbeliever	1957	2.50	5.00	10.00
41075	One Way Street/The Lord Made a Peanut	1957	2.50	5.00	10.00
41146	Hey, Madame/Till We're Engaged	1958	2.00	4.00	8.00
41177	Hangin' Around/Honey Brown Eyes	1958	2.00	4.00	8.00
41215	Let It Shine, Let It Shine/Butterfly Doll	1958	2.00	4.00	8.00
41274	My Heart Cries for You/Under the Rainbow	1958	2.00	4.00	8.00
41311	Guilty Heart/Half As Much	1958	2.00	4.00	8.00
41359	Alias Jesse James/Pride o' Dixie	1959	2.00	4.00	8.00
41397	Loosen Up, Lucy/I'm Gonna Leave You Now	1959	2.00	4.00	8.00
41476	Heartaches By the Number/Two	1959	2.50	5.00	10.00
41476 [PS]	Heartaches By the Number/Two	1959	3.75	7.50	15.00
41576	The Same Old Me/Build Up My Gallows High	1960	2.00	4.00	8.00
41653	Symphony of Spring/Cry Hurtin' Heart	1960	2.00	4.00	8.00
41725	My Shoes Keep Walking Back to You/Silver Moon Upon the Golden Sands	1960	2.00	4.00	8.00
41853	Sunshine Guitar/Ridin' Around in the Rain	1960	2.00	4.00	8.00
41853 [PS]	Sunshine Guitar/Ridin' Around in the Rain	1960	3.00	6.00	12.00
41970	Follow Me/Your Goodnight Kiss	1961	2.00	4.00	8.00
42143	Divorce/I'll Just Pretend	1961	2.00	4.00	8.00
42231	Soft Rain/Big Big Chance	1961	2.00	4.00	8.00
JOY					
264	Rusty Old Halo/Charlie's Shoes	1962	2.00	4.00	8.00
270	Go Tiger Go/If You Ever Go Away	1962	2.00	4.00	8.00
273	Have I Told You Lately That I Love You/Blue Violet	1963	2.00	4.00	8.00

Number	Title (A Side/B Side)	Yr	VG	VG+	NM
REPRISE					
0477	Best Thing That Ever Happened to Me/If I Had My Life to Live Over	1966	—	3.00	6.00
0513	Run to the Door/Foreign Love Affair	1966	—	3.00	6.00
STARDAY					
819	Traveling Shoes/Every Night Is a Lifetime	1967	—	3.00	6.00
828	Alabam/Irene Good-By	1968	—	3.00	6.00
846	Frisco Line/Singing the Blues	1968	—	3.00	6.00
866	Get It Over/Just Wish You'd Change Your Mind	1969	—	3.00	6.00
878	Smokey Blue Eyes/Heartaches by the Number	1969	—	3.00	6.00

7-Inch Extended Plays

Number	Title (A Side/B Side)	Yr	VG	VG+	NM
COLUMBIA					
B-1585	My Truly, Truly Fair/The Roving Kind//Sparrow in the Treetop/My Heart Cries for You	195?	5.00	10.00	20.00
B-1585 [PS]	Guy Mitchell Spotlite	195?	5.00	10.00	20.00
B-2502	*My Heart Cries for You/The Roving Kind/My Truly, Truly Fair/Pittsburgh, Pennsylvania	1957	3.00	6.00	12.00
B-2502 [PS]	Guy Mitchell (Hall of Fame Series)	1957	3.00	6.00	12.00

Albums

Number	Title (A Side/B Side)	Yr	VG	VG+	NM
COLUMBIA					
CL 1211 [M]	Guy in Love	1958	10.00	20.00	40.00
CL 1226 [M]	Guy's Greatest Hits	1959	12.50	25.00	50.00
—Red and black label with six "eye" logos					
CL 1226 [M]	Guy's Greatest Hits	1962	7.50	15.00	30.00
—"Guaranteed High Fidelity" on red label					
CL 1226 [M]	Guy's Greatest Hits	1965	5.00	10.00	20.00
—"360 Sound Mono" on red label					
CL 1552 [M]	Sunshine Guitar	1960	7.50	15.00	30.00
CL 6231 [10]	Open Spaces	1953	17.50	35.00	70.00
CS 8011 [S]	Guy in Love	1959	12.50	25.00	50.00
CS 8352 [S]	Sunshine Guitar	1960	10.00	20.00	40.00
KING					
644 [M]	Sincerely Yours	1959	75.00	150.00	300.00
NASHVILLE					
2074	Heartaches	1970	3.00	6.00	12.00
STARDAY					
412	Traveling Shoes	1968	5.00	10.00	20.00
432	Singin' Up a Storm	1969	5.00	10.00	20.00

MITCHELL, GUY, AND ROSEMARY CLOONEY

Also see each artist's individual listings.

45s

Number	Title (A Side/B Side)	Yr	VG	VG+	NM
COLUMBIA					
39052	You're Just in Love/Marrying for Love	1950	3.75	7.50	15.00

MITCHELL, JONI

12-Inch Singles

Number	Title (A Side/B Side)	Yr	VG	VG+	NM
GEFFEN					
PRO-A-2386 [DJ]	Good Friends (same on both sides)	1985	—	3.00	6.00
PRO-A-2441 [DJ]	Shiny Toys (same on both sides)	1986	—	3.00	6.00
PRO-A-3018 [DJ]	Snakes and Ladders (same on both sides)	1988	—	3.00	6.00
PRO-A-3116 [DJ]	My Secret Place (Edit Version) (LP Version)	1988	—	3.00	6.00

45s

Number	Title (A Side/B Side)	Yr	VG	VG+	NM
ASYLUM					
11010	You Turn Me On, I'm a Radio/Urge for Going	1972	—	2.50	5.00
11029	Raised on Robbery/Court and Spark	1973	—	2.50	5.00
11034	Help Me/Just Like This Train	1974	—	2.50	5.00
11041	Free Man in Paris/People's Parties	1974	—	2.50	5.00
45221	Big Yellow Taxi/Rainy Night House	1974	—	2.00	4.00
45244	Jericho/Carey	1975	—	2.00	4.00
45298	In France They Kiss on Main Street/Boho Dance	1976	—	2.00	4.00
45377	Coyote/Blue Motel Room	1976	—	2.00	4.00
45467	Dreamland/Jericho	1978	—	2.00	4.00
46506	The Dry Cleaner from Des Moines/God Must Be a Boogie Man	1979	—	2.00	4.00
47038	Why Do Fools Fall in Love/Black Crow	1980	—	2.00	4.00
GEFFEN					
27887	My Secret Place/Lakota	1988	—	2.00	4.00
28675	Shiny Toys/Three Great Stimulants	1986	—	2.00	4.00
28840	Good Friends/Smokin' Empty (Try Another)	1985	—	2.00	4.00
28840 [PS]	Good Friends/Smokin' Empty (Try Another)	1985	—	2.50	5.00
29757	Underneath the Streetlight/Be Cool	1983	—	2.00	4.00
29849	(You're So Square) Baby I Don't Care/Love	1982	—	2.00	4.00
29849 [PS]	(You're So Square) Baby I Don't Care/Love	1982	—	2.50	5.00
REPRISE					
0694	I Had a King/Night in the City	1968	2.00	4.00	8.00
0906	Big Yellow Taxi/Woodstock	1970	2.00	4.00	8.00
1029	Carey/This Flight Tonight	1971	2.00	4.00	8.00
1049	Case of You/California	1971	—	3.00	6.00
1154	Both Sides Now/Chelsea Morning	1972	—	2.50	5.00
—"Back to Back Hits" series					
1155	Big Yellow Taxi/Carey	1972	—	2.50	5.00
—"Back to Back Hits" series					

Albums

Number	Title (A Side/B Side)	Yr	VG	VG+	NM
ASYLUM					
AB-202	Miles of Aisles	1974	2.50	5.00	10.00
5E-505	Mingus	1979	2.50	5.00	10.00
BB-701 [(2)]	Don Juan's Reckless Daughter	1977	3.00	6.00	12.00
BB-704 [(2)]	Shadows and Light	1980	3.00	6.00	12.00
7E-1001	Court and Spark	1974	2.50	5.00	10.00
EQ-1001 [Q]	Court and Spark	1974	5.00	10.00	20.00
7E-1051	The Hissing of Summer Lawns	1975	2.50	5.00	10.00
EQ-1051 [Q]	The Hissing of Summer Lawns	1975	5.00	10.00	20.00
7E-1087	Hejira	1976	2.50	5.00	10.00
SD 5057	For the Roses	1972	2.50	5.00	10.00
DCC COMPACT CLASSICS					
LPZ-2044	Court and Spark	1997	6.25	12.50	25.00
—Audiophile vinyl					
LPZ-2069	Blue	2000	6.25	12.50	25.00
—Audiophile vinyl; originally scheduled for early 1999 issue, but not released until summer 2000					
GEFFEN					
PRO-A-1081 [DJ]	Wild Things Run Fast Sampler	1982	3.00	6.00	12.00
—Promo-only 4-song EP					
GHS 2019	Wild Things Run Fast	1982	2.00	4.00	8.00
GHS 24074	Dog Eat Dog	1985	2.00	4.00	8.00
GHS 24172	Chalk Mark in a Rain Storm	1988	2.00	4.00	8.00
GEF 24302	Night Ride Home	1991	3.75	7.50	15.00
NAUTILUS					
NR-11	Court and Spark	1980	12.50	25.00	50.00
—Audiophile vinyl					
REPRISE					
MS 2038	Blue	1970	3.75	7.50	15.00
R 6293 [M]	Joni Mitchell	1968	10.00	20.00	40.00
—White label promo; evidently, no stock copies were issued in mono					
RS 6293	Joni Mitchell	1970	3.00	6.00	12.00
—With only "r:" logo on all-orange (tan) label					
RS 6293 [S]	Joni Mitchell	1968	5.00	10.00	20.00
—With "W7" and "r:" logos on two-tone orange label					
RS 6341	Clouds	1969	5.00	10.00	20.00
—With "W7" and "r:" logos on two-tone orange label					
RS 6341	Clouds	1970	3.00	6.00	12.00
—With only "r:" logo on all-orange (tan) label					
RS 6376	Ladies of the Canyon	1970	5.00	10.00	20.00
—With "W7" and "r:" logos on two-tone orange label					
RS 6376	Ladies of the Canyon	1970	3.00	6.00	12.00
—With only "r:" logo on all-orange (tan) label					

MITCHELL, LEE

45s

Number	Title (A Side/B Side)	Yr	VG	VG+	NM
PHILLIPS INT'L.					
3530	The Frog/A Little Bird Told Me	1958	3.75	7.50	15.00
SHARP					
0862	Rootie Tootie Baby/Who's That Big Man	1959	75.00	150.00	300.00

MITCHELL, MARLON

45s

Number	Title (A Side/B Side)	Yr	VG	VG+	NM
VENA					
100	Ice Cold Baby/Bermuda Shorts	1957	30.00	60.00	120.00

MITCHELL, ROSE

45s

Number	Title (A Side/B Side)	Yr	VG	VG+	NM
IMPERIAL					
5243	Slipping In/I'm Searching	1953	15.00	30.00	60.00
5260	Live My Life/Baby Please Don't Go	1954	15.00	30.00	60.00

MITCHELL, STAN

45s

Number	Title (A Side/B Side)	Yr	VG	VG+	NM
GONE					
5106	Devil in Disguise/Lovin' Man	1961	7.50	15.00	30.00

MITCHELL, WILLIE

45s

Number	Title (A Side/B Side)	Yr	VG	VG+	NM
HI					
2044	The Crawl (Part 1)/The Crawl (Part 2)	1962	2.50	5.00	10.00
2053	Drippin'/Buddy Bear	1962	2.50	5.00	10.00
2058	Easy Now/Sunrise Serenade	1962	2.50	5.00	10.00
2066	Percolatin'/Empty Rooms	1963	2.50	5.00	10.00
2075	20-75/Secret Home	1964	2.00	4.00	8.00
2083	Percolatin'/Check Me	1964	2.00	4.00	8.00
2091	Buster Browne/Woodchopper's Ball	1965	2.00	4.00	8.00
2097	That Driving Beat/Everything Is Gonna Be Alright	1965	2.00	4.00	8.00
2103	Bad Eye/Sugar T	1966	—	3.00	6.00
2112	Mercy/Sticks and Stones	1966	—	3.00	6.00
2119	Misty/Barefootin'	1967	—	3.00	6.00
2125	Au Shucks/Slippin' and Slidin'	1967	—	3.00	6.00
2132	Lucky/Ooh Baby, You Turn Me On	1967	—	3.00	6.00
2140	Soul Serenade/Mercy, Mercy, Mercy	1968	—	3.00	6.00
2147	Prayer Meetin'/Run Daddy	1968	—	3.00	6.00
2151	Up-Hard/Beale Street Mood	1968	—	3.00	6.00
2151	Up-Hard/Red Light	1968	—	3.00	6.00
2154	30-60-90/Take Five	1969	—	3.00	6.00
2158	Young People/Kitten Korner	1969	—	3.00	6.00
2167	My Babe/Teenie's Dream	1969	—	3.00	6.00
2175	Six to Go/Robin's Nest	1970	—	2.50	5.00
2181	Wade in the Water/Tails Out	1970	—	2.50	5.00
2190	Too Sweet/Restless	1971	—	2.50	5.00
2196	Breaking Point/Roadhouse	1971	—	2.50	5.00
2237	Last Tango in Paris/Six to Go	1973	—	2.00	4.00
HOME OF THE BLUES					
111	Thirty-Five Thirty/Yvonne	1960	3.00	6.00	12.00
119	One Mint Julep/I've Got a Right	1961	3.00	6.00	12.00
123	I Like It/Willie's House Party	1961	3.00	6.00	12.00

Albums

Number	Title (A Side/B Side)	Yr	VG	VG+	NM
BEARSVILLE					
BRK 3520	... Listen ... Dance	1980	2.50	5.00	10.00
HI					
8002	Willie Mitchell Live	1977	2.50	5.00	10.00
HL-32010 [M]	Sunrise Serenade	1963	10.00	20.00	40.00
SHL-32010 [S]	Sunrise Serenade	1963	6.25	12.50	25.00
HL-32021 [M]	Hold It	1964	6.25	12.50	25.00
SHL-32021 [S]	Hold It	1964	7.50	15.00	30.00
HL-32026 [M]	It's Dance Time	1965	6.25	12.50	25.00
HL-32029 [M]	Driving Beat	1966	6.25	12.50	25.00
SHL-32029 [S]	Driving Beat	1966	7.50	15.00	30.00
HL-32034 [M]	The Hit Sound of Willie Mitchell	1967	7.50	15.00	30.00
SHL-32034 [S]	The Hit Sound of Willie Mitchell	1967	6.25	12.50	25.00
SHL-32036 [S]	It's Dance Time	1965	7.50	15.00	30.00
HL-32039 [M]	Ooh Baby, You Turn Me On	1967	7.50	15.00	30.00
SHL-32039 [S]	Ooh Baby, You Turn Me On	1967	6.25	12.50	25.00
SHL-32042	Willie Mitchell Live	1968	6.25	12.50	25.00
SHL-32045	Solid Soul	1968	6.25	12.50	25.00
SHL-32048	On Top	1969	6.25	12.50	25.00
SHL-32050	Soul Bag	1969	6.25	12.50	25.00

(Top left) "I dig the Mamas and the Papas," sang Peter, Paul and Mary. It's hard not to dig cool promotional picture sleeves, either, such as this one for the semi-autobiographical "Creeque Alley." (Top right) Here's the rarely-seen promotional edition of the MC5's proto-punk anthem "Kick Out the Jams." This 45, which was only given out at a December 12, 1968, appearance at the Fillmore East, has a different version of the song than the one that appeared on the later stock 45s. (Bottom left) The very first release on the Motown label was "Bad Girl" by the Miracles. At the time, the new label's distribution was poor, so when the song became a hit in Detroit, the song was leased to the Chess label for national release. (Bottom right) Guy Mitchell is best-known for his middle-of-the-road hits on Columbia in the 1950s, most notably the country covers "Singing the Blues" and "Heartaches By the Number." But before that, he was a country singer on the King label, which repackaged some of his pre-Columbian material in this rare album.

Number	Title (A Side/B Side)	Yr	VG	VG+	NM
SHL-32056	The Many Moods of Willie Mitchell	1970	6.25	12.50	25.00
SHL-32058	Robin's Nest	1970	6.25	12.50	25.00
SHL-32068/9 [(2)]	The Best of Willie Mitchell	1971	7.50	15.00	30.00

MITCHELL TRIO, THE

Records issued after JOHN DENVER replaced CHAD MITCHELL in THE CHAD MITCHELL TRIO.

Number	Title (A Side/B Side)	Yr	VG	VG+	NM
45s					
MERCURY					
72340	I Can't Help But Wonder/Stewball and Griselda	1964	2.00	4.00	8.00
72340 [PS]	I Can't Help But Wonder/Stewball and Griselda	1964	3.75	7.50	15.00
72400	You Were On My Mind/My Name Is Morgan	1965	2.00	4.00	8.00
72518	That's the Way It's Gonna Be/Violets of Dawn	1966	2.00	4.00	8.00
72544	Your Friendly, Liberal, Neighborhood Ku Klux Klan/Violets of Dawn	1966	2.00	4.00	8.00
72591	Dark Shadows and Empty Hallways/Stay with Me	1966	2.00	4.00	8.00
REPRISE					
0588	Leaving on a Jet Plane/Baby, That's Where It Is	1967	—	3.00	6.00
0630	She Loves You/Like to Deal with the Ladies	1967	—	3.00	6.00
Albums					
MERCURY					
MG-20944 [M]	The Slightly Irreverent Mitchell Trio	1964	3.75	7.50	15.00
MG-20992 [M]	Typical American Boys	1965	3.75	7.50	15.00
MG-21049 [M]	That's the Way It's Gonna Be	1965	3.75	7.50	15.00
MG-21067 [M]	Violets of Dawn	1966	3.75	7.50	15.00
SR-60944 [S]	The Slightly Irreverent Mitchell Trio	1964	5.00	10.00	20.00
SR-60992 [S]	Typical American Boys	1965	5.00	10.00	20.00
SR-61049 [S]	That's the Way It's Gonna Be	1965	5.00	10.00	20.00
SR-61067 [S]	Violets of Dawn	1966	5.00	10.00	20.00
REPRISE					
R-6258 [M]	Alive	1967	5.00	10.00	20.00
RS-6258 [S]	Alive	1967	3.75	7.50	15.00

MITCHUM, ROBERT

Number	Title (A Side/B Side)	Yr	VG	VG+	NM
45s					
CAPITOL					
F3672	What Is This Generation Coming To/Mama Looka Boo Boo	1957	3.75	7.50	15.00
3986	The Ballad of Thunder Road/My Honey's Lovin' Arms	1962	2.00	4.00	8.00
—Orange and yellow swirl label, no "F" prefix					
3986	The Ballad of Thunder Road/My Honey's Lovin' Arms	1969	—	3.00	6.00
—Red and orange "target" label					
3986	The Ballad of Thunder Road/My Honey's Lovin' Arms	1973	—	2.00	4.00
—Orange label, "Capitol" at bottom					
F3986	The Ballad of Thunder Road/My Honey's Lovin' Arms	1958	3.75	7.50	15.00
—Purple label with "F" prefix					
F3986 [PS]	The Ballad of Thunder Road/My Honey's Lovin' Arms	1958	6.25	12.50	25.00
COLUMBIA					
03483	The Ballad of Thunder Road/That Little Ole Wine Drinker Me	1983	—	2.50	5.00
MONUMENT					
1006	Little Old Wine Drinker Me/Walker's Woods	1967	—	3.50	7.00
1025	You Deserve Each Other/That Man Right There	1967	—	3.50	7.00
Albums					
CAPITOL					
T 853 [M]	Calypso — Is Like So...	1957	25.00	50.00	100.00
MONUMENT					
MLP-8066 [M]	That Man, Robert Mitchum, Sings	1967	6.25	12.50	25.00
SLP-18066 [S]	That Man, Robert Mitchum, Sings	1967	6.25	12.50	25.00

MIXTURES, THE (1)

Number	Title (A Side/B Side)	Yr	VG	VG+	NM
45s					
LINDA					
104	Rainbow Stomp (Part 1)/Rainbow Stomp (Part 2)	1962	2.50	5.00	10.00
106	Jawbone/It's Gonna Work Out Fine	1962	2.50	5.00	10.00
108	Olive Oyl/Canadian Sunset	1963	2.50	5.00	10.00
109	Tiki/Poochum	1963	2.50	5.00	10.00
113	Chinese Checkers/Dig These Blues	1963	2.50	5.00	10.00
115	Sen-Say-Shun/The Last Minute	1964	2.50	5.00	10.00
Albums					
LINDA					
3301 [M]	Stompin' at the Rainbow	1962	25.00	50.00	100.00

MIXTURES, THE (2)

Number	Title (A Side/B Side)	Yr	VG	VG+	NM
45s					
SIRE					
350	The Pushbike Song/Who Loves Ya	1971	—	3.00	6.00

MIZELL, HANK

Number	Title (A Side/B Side)	Yr	VG	VG+	NM
45s					
AMAZON					
711	Jungle Rock/Then I'm In Your Arms	1963	12.50	25.00	50.00
EKO					
506	Jungle Rock/Then I'm In Your Arms	1958	150.00	300.00	600.00
—Issued as "Jim Bobo" on A-side and "Jim Bobo and Hank Mizell" on B-side					
KING					
5236	Jungle Rock/Then I'm In Your Arms	1959	75.00	150.00	300.00

MOB, THE (1)

Number	Title (A Side/B Side)	Yr	VG	VG+	NM
45s					
COLOSSUS					
130	I Dig Everything About You/Love Had a Hold on Me	1970	—	3.00	6.00
134	Give It to Me/I'd Like to See More of You	1971	—	3.00	6.00
134 [PS]	Give It to Me/I'd Like to See More of You	1971	2.00	4.00	8.00
145	Money/Once a Man, Twice a Child	1971	—	3.00	6.00
MGM					
14406	Feel Like Dancin'/You Give Me the Strength	1972	—	3.00	6.00
Albums					
COLOSSUS					
CS-1006	The Mob	1971	5.00	10.00	20.00
MGM					
SE-4839	The Mob	1972	3.75	7.50	15.00

MOB, THE (U)

These may or may not be group (1).

Number	Title (A Side/B Side)	Yr	VG	VG+	NM
45s					
MERCURY					
72791	Disappear/I Wish You'd Leave Me Alone	1968	2.00	4.00	8.00
PRIVATE STOCK					
45016	Rock and Roller/(B-side unknown)	1975	—	2.50	5.00
45031	Hot Music/I Can't Stop This Love Song	1975	—	2.50	5.00
45053	All the Dudes Are Dancing/(B-side unknown)	1975	—	2.50	5.00
45084	Don't Let It Get You Down/(B-side unknown)	1976	—	2.50	5.00
45159	Love Connection/(B-side unknown)	1977	—	2.50	5.00
Albums					
PRIVATE STOCK					
PS-2005	The Mob	1975	3.00	6.00	12.00

MOBY GRAPE

Also see ALEXANDER "SKIP" SPENCE.

Number	Title (A Side/B Side)	Yr	VG	VG+	NM
45s					
COLUMBIA					
44170	Changes/Fall on You	1967	2.00	4.00	8.00
44170 [PS]	Changes/Fall on You	1967	5.00	10.00	20.00
44171	Sitting by the Window/Indifference	1967	2.00	4.00	8.00
44171 [PS]	Sitting by the Window/Indifference	1967	5.00	10.00	20.00
44172	8:05/Mister Blues	1967	2.00	4.00	8.00
44172 [PS]	8:05/Mister Blues	1967	5.00	10.00	20.00
44173	Omaha/Someday	1967	2.00	4.00	8.00
44173 [PS]	Omaha/Someday	1967	5.00	10.00	20.00
44174	Hey Grandma/Come in the Morning	1967	2.00	4.00	8.00
44174 [PS]	Hey Grandma/Come in the Morning	1967	5.00	10.00	20.00
44567	Can't Be So Bad/Bitter Wind	1968	—	3.00	6.00
44789	If You Can't Learn From My Mistakes/Trucking Man	1969	—	3.00	6.00
44885	Ooh Mama Ooh/It's a Beautiful Day Today	1969	—	3.00	6.00
JZSP 118972 [DJ]	Omaha/8:05	1967	3.00	6.00	12.00
—Yellow label promo; "Rush Reservice"					
REPRISE					
1040	Gypsy Wedding/Apocalypse	1971	—	2.50	5.00
1055	Goin' Down to Texas/About Time	1971	—	2.50	5.00
1096	Gone Fishin'/Gypsy Wedding	1972	—	2.50	5.00
Albums					
COLUMBIA					
MGS 1	Grape Jam	1968	5.00	10.00	20.00
CXS 3 [(2)]	Wow/Grape Jam	1968	7.50	15.00	30.00
—Joint release of the two albums under one cover					
CXS 3 [(2)]	Wow/Grape Jam	1971	3.75	7.50	15.00
—Orange labels					
2698/9498	Moby Grape Poster	1967	3.75	7.50	15.00
—Poster has Don Stephenson "giving the finger" on his washboard					
2698/9498	Moby Grape Poster	1967	2.00	4.00	8.00
—Poster has offending finger airbrushed out					
CL 2698 [M]	Moby Grape	1967	10.00	20.00	40.00
—Cover has Don Stephenson "giving the finger" on his washboard					
CL 2698 [M]	Moby Grape	1967	5.00	10.00	20.00
—Cover has offending finger airbrushed out					
CS 9498	Moby Grape	1971	3.00	6.00	12.00
—Orange label; with poster					
CS 9498 [S]	Moby Grape	1967	10.00	20.00	40.00
—Cover has Don Stephenson "giving the finger" on his washboard					
CS 9498 [S]	Moby Grape	1967	5.00	10.00	20.00
—Cover has offending finger airbrushed out					
CS 9613	Wow	1968	5.00	10.00	20.00
CS 9696	Moby Grape '69	1969	5.00	10.00	20.00
CS 9912	Truly Fine Citizen	1969	5.00	10.00	20.00
C 31098	Great Grape	1972	3.75	7.50	15.00
ESCAPE					
ESA 1	Live Grape	1978	3.75	7.50	15.00
HARMONY					
KH 30392	Omaha	1971	3.75	7.50	15.00
REPRISE					
RS 6460	20 Granite Creek	1971	5.00	10.00	20.00

MOCEDADES

Number	Title (A Side/B Side)	Yr	VG	VG+	NM
45s					
TARA					
100	Eres Tu (Touch the Wind)/Touch the Wind (Eres Tu)	1973	—	2.50	5.00
105	Dime Senor/I Ask the Lord	1974	—	2.00	4.00
Albums					
TARA					
53000	Eres Tu "Touch the Wind"	1974	3.00	6.00	12.00

MOCKINGBIRDS, THE

With GRAHAM GOULDMAN and Kevin Godley, later of 10CC.

Number	Title (A Side/B Side)	Yr	VG	VG+	NM
45s					
ABC-PARAMOUNT					
10653	That's How/I Never Should Have Kissed You	1965	3.75	7.50	15.00

MOD AND THE ROCKERS

Number	Title (A Side/B Side)	Yr	VG	VG+	NM
Albums					
JUSTICE					
JLP-153	Mod and the Rockers Now!	1967	100.00	200.00	400.00

MODELS, THE
45s
MGM

Number	Title (A Side/B Side)	Yr	VG	VG+	NM
13775	Bend Me, Shape Me/In a World of Pretty Faces	1967	5.00	10.00	20.00

MODUGNO, DOMENICO
45s
DECCA

Number	Title (A Side/B Side)	Yr	VG	VG+	NM
30677	Nel Blu Dipinto Di Blu (Volare)/Mariti in Citta	1958	3.00	6.00	12.00
30747	Stay Here with Me/Io	1958	2.50	5.00	10.00
30777	Coma Prima/Strada 'Nfosa	1958	2.50	5.00	10.00
30845	Piove (Ciao, Ciao Bambino)/Farfalle	1959	2.50	5.00	10.00
30950	The Bandit/Lunga Notte	1959	2.50	5.00	10.00
31071	Olympia/O Solo Mio	1960	2.00	4.00	8.00
31171	Ciao Ciao Bambino/Si, Si, Si	1960	2.00	4.00	8.00
31359	La Novia/Se Dio Vorra	1962	2.00	4.00	8.00
31401	Addio...Addio/Lupi E Percorelle	1962	2.00	4.00	8.00
31718	Tu Si' 'Na Casa Grande/Tu Si O' Mare	1964	—	3.00	6.00

JUBILEE

Number	Title (A Side/B Side)	Yr	VG	VG+	NM
5064	A Sicilian in Paris/The Little Rascal/The Man and the Mountain/Cute Face	1951	—	—	—
5339	La Petit Reveil/Cavudduzzu	1958	2.50	5.00	10.00

MGM

Number	Title (A Side/B Side)	Yr	VG	VG+	NM
13487	Dio, Come Ti Amo (English Version)/Dio, Come Ti Amo (Italian Version)	1966	—	3.00	6.00

RCA VICTOR

Number	Title (A Side/B Side)	Yr	VG	VG+	NM
47-7321	Musetto/Io Mammeta E Tu	1958	2.50	5.00	10.00
47-9502	Meraviglioso (Part 1)/Meraviglioso (Part 2)	1968	—	2.50	5.00
48-1022	Love Is Like the Wind/How Did You	1972	—	2.00	4.00

7-Inch Extended Plays
DECCA

Number	Title (A Side/B Side)	Yr	VG	VG+	NM
ED 2633	*Nel Blu Dipinto Di Blu (Volare)/Mariti in Citta/A Pizza C' 'A Pummarola/Ventu D'Estati	1958	3.75	7.50	15.00
ED 2633 [PS]	Nel Blu Dipinto Di Blu (Volare) and Other Italian Favorites	1958	3.75	7.50	15.00

Albums
DECCA

Number	Title (A Side/B Side)	Yr	VG	VG+	NM
DL 4133 [M]	Viva Italia	1961	7.50	15.00	30.00
DL 8808 [M]	Nel Blu Dipinto Di Blu (Volare) and Other Italian Favorites	1958	12.50	25.00	50.00
DL 8853 [M]	Encore	1959	10.00	20.00	40.00

MOGEN DAVID AND THE GRAPES OF WRATH
45s
CHA CHA

Number	Title (A Side/B Side)	Yr	VG	VG+	NM
757	Little Girl Gone/Go Away Girl	1967	2000.	3000.	4000.

MOJO MEN, THE
45s
AUTUMN

Number	Title (A Side/B Side)	Yr	VG	VG+	NM
11	Mama's Little Baby/Off the Hook	1965	3.75	7.50	15.00
19	Dance with Me/The Loneliest Boy in Town	1965	3.75	7.50	15.00
27	She's My Baby/Fire in My Heart	1966	3.75	7.50	15.00

GRT

Number	Title (A Side/B Side)	Yr	VG	VG+	NM
5	Flower of Love/I Can't Let Go	1969	2.50	5.00	10.00
8	Candle to Burn/Make You at Home	1969	2.50	5.00	10.00
16	Everyday Love/There Goes My Mind	1969	2.50	5.00	10.00

REPRISE

Number	Title (A Side/B Side)	Yr	VG	VG+	NM
0486	She's My Baby/Do the Hanky Panky	1966	5.00	10.00	20.00
0539	Sit Down, I Think I Love You/Don't Leave Me Crying Like Before	1966	2.50	5.00	10.00
0580	Me About You/When You're in Love	1967	2.50	5.00	10.00
0617	Whatever Happened to Happy/Make You at Home	1967	2.50	5.00	10.00
0661	Not Too Old to Start Crying/New York City	1968	2.50	5.00	10.00
0689	Should I Cry/You to Me	1968	2.50	5.00	10.00
0707	Sit Down, I Think I Love You/Me About You	1968	—	3.00	6.00
—"Back to Back Hits" series					
0759	Don't Be Cruel/Let It Be Him	1968	2.50	5.00	10.00

TIDE

Number	Title (A Side/B Side)	Yr	VG	VG+	NM
2000	Surfin' Fat Man/Paula	1964	10.00	20.00	40.00

Albums
GRT

Number	Title (A Side/B Side)	Yr	VG	VG+	NM
10003	Mojo Magic	1969	6.25	12.50	25.00

MOJOS, THE
45s
PARROT

Number	Title (A Side/B Side)	Yr	VG	VG+	NM
9707	Seven Daffodils/Nothin' at All	1964	2.50	5.00	10.00
45001	Everything's Alright/Give Your Loving to Me	1964	3.00	6.00	12.00
45002	Why Not Tonight/Don't Do It Anymore	1964	3.00	6.00	12.00

MOLES, GENE
45s
CHALLENGE

Number	Title (A Side/B Side)	Yr	VG	VG+	NM
59249	Burning Rubber/Twin Pipes	1964	6.25	12.50	25.00

GARPAX

Number	Title (A Side/B Side)	Yr	VG	VG+	NM
44176	Kaha Huna (Goddess of Surfing)/Maria (The Wind)	1963	6.25	12.50	25.00

MOLLERN, RONNIE
45s
KING

Number	Title (A Side/B Side)	Yr	VG	VG+	NM
5365	Rockin' Up/Fat Mama	1960	37.50	75.00	150.00

MOLOCH
Albums
ENTERPRISE

Number	Title (A Side/B Side)	Yr	VG	VG+	NM
ENS-1002	Moloch	1969	5.00	10.00	20.00

MOM'S APPLE PIE
45s
BROWN BAG

Number	Title (A Side/B Side)	Yr	VG	VG+	NM
XW192	Love Plays a Song/Can You Help Me	1973	2.50	5.00	10.00

Albums
BROWN BAG

Number	Title (A Side/B Side)	Yr	VG	VG+	NM
BB-LA073-F	Mom's Apple Pie #2	1973	3.75	7.50	15.00
14200	Mom's Apple Pie	1972	5.00	10.00	20.00
—With vulva showing in the apple pie					
14200	Mom's Apple Pie	1972	5.00	10.00	20.00
—With barbed wire wall covering the former opening. This is much rarer than the first version, though less sought-after					

MOM & DADS, THE
45s
GNP CRESCENDO

Number	Title (A Side/B Side)	Yr	VG	VG+	NM
439	The Rangers Waltz/Quentin's E Flat Boogie	1971	—	2.50	5.00
451	In the Blue Canadian Rockies/Blue Skirt Waltz	1972	—	2.50	5.00
455	Amazing Grace/Rippling River Waltz	1972	—	2.50	5.00
460	Jingle Bell Rock/Auld Lang Syne	1972	—	2.50	5.00
461	Angry/Anniversary Waltz	1973	—	2.00	4.00
466	The Waltz You Saved for Me/When the Saints Go Marching In	1973	—	2.00	4.00
472	Somewhere My Love/My Happiness	1973	—	2.00	4.00
478	My Blue Heaven/Your Cheatin' Heart	1974	—	2.00	4.00
485	Maiden's Prayer/Wabash Cannonball	1974	—	2.00	4.00
496	Kentucky Waltz/(B-side unknown)	1975	—	2.00	4.00
803	Silver Bells/Bill Bailey	1975	—	2.00	4.00

Albums
GNP CRESCENDO

Number	Title (A Side/B Side)	Yr	VG	VG+	NM
GNP-2061	The Rangers Waltz	1971	2.50	5.00	10.00
GNP-2063	In the Blue Canadian Rockies	1972	2.50	5.00	10.00
GNP-2065	Souvenirs	1972	2.50	5.00	10.00
GNP-2068	Again!	1973	2.50	5.00	10.00
GNP-2072	Reminiscing	1973	2.50	5.00	10.00
GNP-2078	Dance with the Mom & Dads	1974	2.50	5.00	10.00
GNP-2082	The Mom & Dads Play Your Favorite Hymns	1974	2.50	5.00	10.00
GNP-2084	Love Is a Beautiful Song	1974	2.50	5.00	10.00
GNP-2087	The Best of the Mom & Dads	1975	2.50	5.00	10.00
GNP-2092	Dream	1975	2.50	5.00	10.00
GNP-2096	Memories	1976	2.50	5.00	10.00
GNP-2102	Summertime	1976	2.50	5.00	10.00
GNP-2106	Down the River of Golden Dreams	1977	2.50	5.00	10.00
GNP-2108	Whispering Hope	1977	2.50	5.00	10.00
GNP-2110	One Dozen Roses	1977	2.50	5.00	10.00
GNP-2117	Gratefully Yours	1978	2.50	5.00	10.00
2GNP-2123 [(2)]	Golden Country	1979	3.00	6.00	12.00
GNP-2125	Love Letters in the Sand	1979	2.50	5.00	10.00
2GNP-2129 [(2)]	The Very Best of the Mom & Dads	1980	3.00	6.00	12.00
GNP-2130	Blue Hawaii	1980	2.50	5.00	10.00
GNP-2136	To Mom & Dad With Love from the Mom & Dads	1980	2.50	5.00	10.00
GNP-2139	Waltz Across Texas	1981	2.50	5.00	10.00
GNP-2150	Good Night Sweetheart	1985	2.00	4.00	8.00
GNP-2173	20 Favorite Waltzes	1986	2.00	4.00	8.00
GNP-2189	Red Sails in the Sunset	1987	2.00	4.00	8.00

MOMENTS, THE
R&B trio. For legal reasons, their records on EMI America, EMI Manhattan, Panoramic and Polydor were issued under the name "Ray, Goodman and Brown."

45s
ALL PLATINUM

Number	Title (A Side/B Side)	Yr	VG	VG+	NM
2350	Sho Nuff Boogie (Part 1)/Sho Nuff Boogie (Part 2)	1974	—	2.50	5.00
—With Sylvia					

EMI AMERICA

Number	Title (A Side/B Side)	Yr	VG	VG+	NM
8365	Take It to the Limit/(Instrumental)	1986	—	—	3.00
8365 [PS]	Take It to the Limit/(Instrumental)	1986	—	—	3.00
8378	Celebrate Our Love/(Instrumental)	1987	—	—	3.00
8378 [PS]	Celebrate Our Love/(Instrumental)	1987	—	—	3.00
43022	Tonight (Baby)/Good Love	1987	—	—	3.00

EMI MANHATTAN

Number	Title (A Side/B Side)	Yr	VG	VG+	NM
50155	Where Did You Get That Body, (Baby)?/Where Are You Now	1988	—	—	3.00
50155 [PS]	Where Did You Get That Body, (Baby)?/Where Are You Now	1988	—	—	3.00

PANORAMIC

Number	Title (A Side/B Side)	Yr	VG	VG+	NM
201	Who's Gonna Make the First Move/Look Like Lovers	1984	—	2.00	4.00

POLYDOR

Number	Title (A Side/B Side)	Yr	VG	VG+	NM
2033	Special Lady/Deja Vu	1979	—	2.50	5.00
2077	Inside of You/Treat Her Right	1980	—	2.00	4.00
2116	My Prayer/The Way It Should Be	1980	—	2.00	4.00
2135	Happy Anniversary/You	1980	—	2.00	4.00
2159	Shoestrings/Me	1981	—	2.00	4.00
2191	How Can Love Be So Right (Yet So Wrong)/Each Time Is Like the First Time	1981	—	2.00	4.00
2203	Stay/Good Ole Days	1982	—	2.00	4.00
2208	Till the Right One Comes Along/Heaven in the Rain	1982	—	2.00	4.00
2222	Gambled on Your Love/Pool of Love	1982	—	2.00	4.00
2227	After All/Love Minus One	1982	—	2.00	4.00
810056-7	Special Lady/My Prayer	1983	—	—	3.00
—Reissue					

STANG

Number	Title (A Side/B Side)	Yr	VG	VG+	NM
5000	Not on the Outside/Understanding	1968	2.00	4.00	8.00
5003	Sunday/Everybody Loves My Baby	1969	—	3.00	6.00
5005	I Do/Pocketful of Heartbreaks	1969	—	3.00	6.00
5008	I'm So Lost/Where	1969	—	3.00	6.00
5009	Lovely Way She Loves/I've Got to Keep On Loving, Love	1969	—	3.00	6.00
5012	Love on a Two-Way Street/I Won't Do Anything	1970	2.00	4.00	8.00
5016	If I Didn't Care/You Make Me Feel Good	1970	—	3.00	6.00
5017	All I Have/The Hurt's On Me	1970	—	3.00	6.00
5020	I Can't Help It/To You with Love	1971	—	3.00	6.00

Number	Title (A Side/B Side)	Yr	VG	VG+	NM
5024	That's How It Feels/That's How It Feels (Long)	1971	—	3.00	6.00
5031	Lucky Me/I Lost One Bird in the Hand (Reaching Out for Two in the Bush)	1971	—	3.00	6.00
5033	To You with Love/Key to My Happiness	1971	—	3.00	6.00
5036	Thanks a Lot/I Lost One Bird in the Hand (Reaching Out for Two in the Bush)	1972	—	3.00	6.00
5041	Just Because He Wants to Make Love (Doesn't Mean He Loves You)/So This Is Our Goodbye	1972	—	3.00	6.00
5045	My Thing/Thanks a Lot	1972	—	3.00	6.00
5048	Girl I'm Gonna Miss You/I Think So	1973	—	2.50	5.00
5050	Gotta Find a Way/Sweeter As the Days Go By	1973	—	2.50	5.00
5052	Sexy Mama/Where Can I Find Her	1973	—	3.00	6.00
5054	Sweet Sweet Lady/Next Time I See You	1974	—	2.50	5.00
5056	What's Your Name/Mama I Miss You	1974	—	2.50	5.00
5057	Girls (Part 1)/Girls (Part 2)	1974	—	2.50	5.00
—With the Whatnauts					
5060	Look at Me (I'm in Love)/You've Come a Long Way	1975	—	2.50	5.00
5064	Got to Get to Know You/I Feel So Bad	1975	—	2.50	5.00
5066	Nine Times/When the Morning Comes	1976	—	2.50	5.00
5068	With You/The Next Time I See You	1976	—	2.50	5.00
5071	We Don't Cry Out Loud/Come In Girl	1977	—	2.50	5.00
5073	I Don't Wanna Go/Oh I Could Have Loved You	1977	—	2.50	5.00
5075	I Could Have Loved You/Jack in the Box	1978	—	2.50	5.00
5076	Rain in My Backyard/Disco Man	1978	—	2.50	5.00
SUGAR HILL					
758	Baby Let's Rap Now (Part 1)/Baby Let's Rap Now (Part 2)	1980	—	2.50	5.00
769	Record Breakin' Love Affair/(B-side unknown)	1981	—	2.50	5.00
Albums					
CHESS					
CH2-92517 [(2)]	Greatest Hits	198?	3.00	6.00	12.00
POLYDOR					
PD-1-6240	Ray, Goodman & Brown	1979	2.50	5.00	10.00
PD-1-6299	Ray, Goodman & Brown II	1980	2.50	5.00	10.00
PD-1-6341	Stay	1981	2.50	5.00	10.00
STANG					
ST-1000	Not On the Outside, But On the Inside Strong	1969	7.50	15.00	30.00
ST-1002	The Moments On Top	1970	7.50	15.00	30.00
ST-1003	A Moment with the Moments	1970	7.50	15.00	30.00
ST-1004	Moments Greatest Hits	1971	5.00	10.00	20.00
ST-1006	The Moments Live at the New York State Womans Prison	1971	6.25	12.50	25.00
ST-1009	The Other Side of the Moments	1972	6.25	12.50	25.00
ST-1015	Live at the Miss Black America Pageant	1972	5.00	10.00	20.00
ST-1019	The Best of the Moments	1975	3.75	7.50	15.00
ST-1022	My Thing	1973	3.75	7.50	15.00
ST-1023	The Sexy Moments	1974	3.75	7.50	15.00
ST-1026	Look at Me	1975	3.75	7.50	15.00
ST-1030	Moments With You	1976	3.75	7.50	15.00
2ST-1033 [(2)]	Greatest Hits	1977	5.00	10.00	20.00
ST-1034	Sharp	1978	3.75	7.50	15.00

MOMENTS, THE (2)

California studio group.

Number	Title (A Side/B Side)	Yr	VG	VG+	NM
45s					
ERA					
3099	Walk Right In/(Instrumental)	1963	2.50	5.00	10.00
3104	Homework/Big Bound Wheel	1963	2.50	5.00	10.00
3114	Surfin' Train/Mamu Zey	1963	3.00	6.00	12.00
3128	In the Phonograph Booth/Blues at Sandy Cove	1964	2.50	5.00	10.00

MOMENTS, THE (3)

Steve Marriott, later of SMALL FACES and HUMBLE PIE, was in this group.

Number	Title (A Side/B Side)	Yr	VG	VG+	NM
45s					
WORLD ARTISTS					
1032	You Really Got Me/Money, Money	1964	2.50	5.00	10.00

MONARCHS, THE (1)

Number	Title (A Side/B Side)	Yr	VG	VG+	NM
45s					
MONUMENT					
03484	Look Homeward, Angel/This Old Heart	1983	—	2.50	5.00
SOUND STAGE 7					
2502	This Old Heart/'Til I Hear It From You	1963	3.00	6.00	12.00
2516	Look Homeward, Angel/What Made You Change Your Mind	1964	3.00	6.00	12.00
2530	Climb Every Mountain/Take Me Home	1964	3.00	6.00	12.00

MONARCHS, THE (2)

Number	Title (A Side/B Side)	Yr	VG	VG+	NM
45s					
DOT					
15228	Gravy/Caravan Mambo	1954	10.00	20.00	40.00

MONARCHS, THE (3)

Number	Title (A Side/B Side)	Yr	VG	VG+	NM
45s					
MELBA					
101	Pretty Little Girl/In My Younger Days	1956	20.00	40.00	80.00
NEIL					
101	Pretty Little Girl/In My Younger Days	1956	37.50	75.00	150.00
103	Always Be Faithful/How Are You	1956	30.00	60.00	120.00

MONARCHS, THE (U)

Some of these could be by the above groups.

Number	Title (A Side/B Side)	Yr	VG	VG+	NM
45s					
LIBAN					
1002	Love You That's Why/Coming Home	1959	500.00	1000.	2000.
WING					
90040	Angels in the Sky/Wanna Go Home	1955	20.00	40.00	80.00
YUCCA					
172	Forever Lost/Cuckoo	1964	12.50	25.00	50.00
ZONE					
1067	Friday Night/El Bandito	1963	3.75	7.50	15.00

MONDAY BLUES

Number	Title (A Side/B Side)	Yr	VG	VG+	NM
45s					
VAULT					
963	Be My Baby/Do I Love You	1970	2.00	4.00	8.00
Albums					
VAULT					
133	The Phil Spector Song Book	1970	5.00	10.00	20.00

MONDAY MORNING QUARTERBACK, THE

Number	Title (A Side/B Side)	Yr	VG	VG+	NM
45s					
WARNER BROS					
7664 [PS]	The 12 Days of Christmas (The Game Plan to Beat Miami)/Santa Claus Medley	1972	3.75	7.50	15.00
WARNER BROS.					
7664	The 12 Days of Christmas (The Game Plan to Beat Miami)/Santa Claus Medley	1972	2.50	5.00	10.00

MONDELLOS, THE

Number	Title (A Side/B Side)	Yr	VG	VG+	NM
45s					
RHYTHM					
102	Come Back Home/100 Years from Today	1956	50.00	100.00	200.00
—As "Alice Jean and the Mondellos"					
105	Over the Rainbow/Never Leave Me Alone	1956	37.50	75.00	150.00
—As "Yul McClay and the Mondellos"					
106	That's What I Call Love/Daylight Saving Time	1956	37.50	75.00	150.00
109	Hard to Please/Happiness Street	1957	37.50	75.00	150.00
114	My Heart/That's What I Call Love	1957	37.50	75.00	150.00
—As "Rudy Lambert and the Mondellos"					
128	That Old Feeling/Sunday Kind of Love	1957	37.50	75.00	150.00
—As "Rudy Lambert and the Mondellos"					

MONEY, ZOOT

Number	Title (A Side/B Side)	Yr	VG	VG+	NM
45s					
EPIC					
10077	Big Time Operator/Zoot's Sermon	1966	2.50	5.00	10.00
Albums					
EPIC					
LN 24241 [M]	All Happening Zoot Money's Big Roll Band at Klooks Kleek	1966	5.00	10.00	20.00

MONITORS, THE (1)

Number	Title (A Side/B Side)	Yr	VG	VG+	NM
45s					
SOUL					
35049	Step by Step (Hand in Hand)/Time Is Passing By	1968	3.75	7.50	15.00
V.I.P.					
25028	Say You/All for Someone	1965	5.00	10.00	20.00
25032	Greetings (This Is Uncle Sam)/Number One in Your Heart	1965	5.00	10.00	20.00
25039	Since I Lost You Girl/Don't Put Off Till Tomorrow What You Can Do Today	1966	5.00	10.00	20.00
25046	Bring Back the Love/The Further You Look, The Less You See	1967	5.00	10.00	20.00
25049	Step by Step (Hand in Hand)/Time Is Passing By	1968	12.50	25.00	50.00
Albums					
SOUL					
SS-714	Greetings, We're the Monitors	1969	15.00	30.00	60.00

MONITORS, THE (2)

Number	Title (A Side/B Side)	Yr	VG	VG+	NM
45s					
ALADDIN					
3309	Tonight's the Night/Candy Coated Kisses	1955	25.00	50.00	100.00

MONITORS, THE (U)

Some of these may be groups (1) or (2).

Number	Title (A Side/B Side)	Yr	VG	VG+	NM
45s					
BUDDAH					
278	Fence Around Your Heart/Have You Seen Her	1972	—	2.50	5.00
CIRCUS					
219	A Boyfriend's Prayer/Nita	1957	37.50	75.00	150.00
SPECIALTY					
595	Our Schooldays/I've Got a Dream	1957	20.00	40.00	80.00
622	Closer to Heaven/Rock 'N' Roll Forever	1957	50.00	100.00	200.00
636	Mamma Linda/Hop Scotch	1958	15.00	30.00	60.00

MONK, THELONIOUS

Number	Title (A Side/B Side)	Yr	VG	VG+	NM
45s					
BLUE NOTE					
542	Thelonious/Suburban Eyes	195?	5.00	10.00	20.00
543	Round About Midnight/Well You Needn't	195?	5.00	10.00	20.00
547	Evonce/Off Minor	195?	5.00	10.00	20.00
548	In Walked Bud/Epistrophy	195?	5.00	10.00	20.00
549	Evidence/Ruby My Dear	195?	5.00	10.00	20.00
1565	Monk's Mood/Who Knows	195?	3.75	7.50	15.00
1575	April in Paris/Nice Work	195?	3.75	7.50	15.00
1589	Straight No Chaser/Four in One	195?	3.75	7.50	15.00
1590	Criss Cross/Ebonel	195?	3.75	7.50	15.00
1602	Skippy/Let's Cool One	195?	3.75	7.50	15.00
1603	Carolina Moon/Hornin' In	195?	3.75	7.50	15.00
1664	'Round Midnight/In Walked Bud	195?	3.75	7.50	15.00
COLUMBIA					
42825	Bye-Ya/Hackensack	1963	2.50	5.00	10.00
44780	Just a Glance at Love/Consecutive Seconds	1969	—	3.00	6.00
PRESTIGE					
162	Blue Monk/Bye-Ya	196?	2.50	5.00	10.00
795	Sweet and Lovely/Bye-Ya	195?	3.00	6.00	12.00
838	These Foolish Things/Trinkle Tinkle	195?	3.00	6.00	12.00
850	Monk's Dream/Little Rootie Tootie	195?	3.00	6.00	12.00
RIVERSIDE					
421	Coming on the Hudson/(B-side unknown)	195?	3.00	6.00	12.00
434	Blue Monk/(B-side unknown)	195?	3.00	6.00	12.00

Number	Title (A Side/B Side)	Yr	VG	VG+	NM
Albums					
ANALOGUE PRODUCTIONS					
AP-37 [(7)]	The Riverside Tenor Sessions	1999	62.50	125.00	250.00
ARCHIVE OF FOLK AND JAZZ					
336	Piano Solos	198?	2.50	5.00	10.00
BANDSTAND					
BDLP-1505	Blue Monk	1992	3.00	6.00	12.00
BDLP-1516	April in Paris	1992	3.00	6.00	12.00
BLACK LION					
152	Something in Blue	1972	3.00	6.00	12.00
197	The Man I Love	1973	3.00	6.00	12.00
BLUE NOTE					
BN-LA579-H2 [(2)]	The Complete Genius	1976	3.75	7.50	15.00
LWB-579 [(2)]	The Complete Genius	1981	3.00	6.00	12.00
—Reissue of BN-LA579-H2					
BLP-1510 [M]	Genius of Modern Music, Vol. 1	1956	50.00	100.00	200.00
—"Deep groove" version (deep indentation under label on both sides)					
BLP-1510 [M]	Genius of Modern Music, Vol. 1	1956	37.50	75.00	150.00
—Regular edition, Lexington Ave. address on label					
BLP-1510 [M]	Genius of Modern Music, Vol. 1	1963	6.25	12.50	25.00
—"New York, USA" address on label					
BLP-1511 [M]	Genius of Modern Music, Vol. 2	1956	50.00	100.00	200.00
—"Deep groove" version (deep indentation under label on both sides)					
BLP-1511 [M]	Genius of Modern Music, Vol. 2	1956	37.50	75.00	150.00
—Regular edition, Lexington Ave. address on label					
BLP-1511 [M]	Genius of Modern Music, Vol. 2	1963	6.25	12.50	25.00
—"New York, USA" address on label					
BLP-5002 [10]	Genius of Modern Music, Vol. 1	1952	100.00	200.00	400.00
BLP-5009 [10]	Genius of Modern Music, Vol. 2	1952	100.00	200.00	400.00
BLP-81510 [R]	Genius of Modern Music, Vol. 1	1968	2.50	5.00	10.00
BST-81510	Genius of Modern Music, Vol. 1	1985	2.50	5.00	10.00
—"The Finest in Jazz Since 1939" reissue					
BLP-81511 [R]	Genius of Modern Music, Vol. 2	1968	2.50	5.00	10.00
BST-81511	Genius of Modern Music, Vol. 2	1985	2.50	5.00	10.00
—"The Finest in Jazz Since 1939" reissue					
COLUMBIA					
CL 1965 [M]	Monk's Dream	1963	5.00	10.00	20.00
CL 2038 [M]	Criss-Cross	1963	5.00	10.00	20.00
CL 2164 [M]	Monk Big Band and Quartet In Concert	1964	5.00	10.00	20.00
CL 2184 [M]	It's Monk's Time	1964	5.00	10.00	20.00
CL 2291 [M]	Monk	1965	5.00	10.00	20.00
CL 2349 [M]	Solo Monk	1965	5.00	10.00	20.00
CL 2416 [M]	Misterioso	1966	5.00	10.00	20.00
CL 2651 [M]	Straight No Chaser	1967	7.50	15.00	50.00
CS 8765 [S]	Monk's Dream	1963	6.25	12.50	25.00
CS 8838 [S]	Criss-Cross	1963	6.25	12.50	25.00
CS 8964 [S]	Monk Big Band and Quartet In Concert	1964	6.25	12.50	25.00
CS 8984 [S]	It's Monk's Time	1964	6.25	12.50	25.00
CS 9091 [S]	Monk	1965	6.25	12.50	25.00
CS 9149	Solo Monk	1971	3.00	6.00	12.00
—Orange label					
CS 9149 [S]	Solo Monk	1965	6.25	12.50	25.00
—Red "360 Sound" label					
PC 9149	Solo Monk	198?	2.00	4.00	8.00
—Reissue with new prefix					
CS 9216 [S]	Misterioso	1966	6.25	12.50	25.00
CS 9451	Straight No Chaser	1971	3.00	6.00	12.00
—Orange label					
CS 9451 [S]	Straight No Chaser	1967	5.00	10.00	20.00
—Red "360 Sound" label					
PC 9451	Straight No Chaser	198?	2.00	4.00	8.00
—Reissue with new prefix					
CS 9632	Underground	1968	5.00	10.00	20.00
—Red "360 Sound" label					
CS 9632	Underground	1971	3.00	6.00	12.00
—Orange label					
PC 9632	Underground	198?	2.00	4.00	8.00
—Reissue with new prefix					
CS 9775	Greatest Hits	1969	3.75	7.50	15.00
—Red "360 Sound" label					
CS 9775	Greatest Hits	1971	3.00	6.00	12.00
—Orange label					
PC 9775	Greatest Hits	198?	2.00	4.00	8.00
—Reissue with new prefix					
CS 9806	Monk's Blues	1969	5.00	10.00	20.00
—Red "360 Sound" label					
CS 9806	Monk's Blues	1971	3.00	6.00	12.00
—Orange label					
PC 9806	Monk's Blues	198?	2.00	4.00	8.00
—Reissue with new prefix					
KG 32892 [(2)]	Who's Afraid of the Big Band Monk	1974	3.75	7.50	15.00
JG 35720 [(2)]	Always Know	1979	3.75	7.50	15.00
C2 38030 [(2)]	Live at the It Club	1983	3.00	6.00	12.00
C2 38269 [(2)]	Live at the Jazz Workshop	1983	3.00	6.00	12.00
C2 38510 [(2)]	The Tokyo Concerts	1984	3.00	6.00	12.00
COLUMBIA JAZZ MASTERPIECES					
CJ 40785	Underground	1987	2.50	5.00	10.00
CJ 40786	Monk's Dream	1987	2.50	5.00	10.00
CJ 44297	The Composer	1988	2.50	5.00	10.00
COLUMBIA MUSICAL TREASURY					
DS 338	Monk's Miracles	1967	6.25	12.50	25.00
—Columbia Record Club exclusive					
FANTASY					
OJC-010	Thelonious Monk Trio	198?	2.50	5.00	10.00
OJC-016	Monk	198?	2.50	5.00	10.00
OJC-024	Thelonious Monk Plays Duke Ellington	198?	2.50	5.00	10.00
OJC-026	Brilliant Corners	198?	2.50	5.00	10.00
OJC-059	Thelonious Monk/Sonny Rollins	198?	2.50	5.00	10.00
OJC-064	The Unique Thelonious Monk	198?	2.50	5.00	10.00
OJC-084	Monk's Music	198?	2.50	5.00	10.00
OJC-103	Thelonious in Action	198?	2.50	5.00	10.00
OJC-135	Thelonious Monk at Town Hall	198?	2.50	5.00	10.00
OJC-206	Misterioso	1985	2.50	5.00	10.00
OJC-231	Alone in San Francisco	1987	2.50	5.00	10.00
OJC-254	Thelonious Himself	1987	2.50	5.00	10.00
OJC-301	Mulligan Meets Monk	1988	2.50	5.00	10.00
OJC-305	Thelonious Monk at the Blackhawk	1988	2.50	5.00	10.00
OJC-362	5 By Monk By 5	1988	2.50	5.00	10.00
OJC-488	Monk in Italy	1991	2.50	5.00	10.00
GATEWAY					
7023	Monk's Music	197?	3.00	6.00	12.00
GNP CRESCENDO					
9008 [(2)]	Thelonious Monk	197?	3.75	7.50	15.00
JAZZ MAN					
5017	Something in Blue	198?	2.50	5.00	10.00
MILESTONE					
9115	Evidence	198?	2.50	5.00	10.00
9124	Blues Five Spot	198?	2.50	5.00	10.00
47004 [(2)]	Pure Monk	1972	3.75	7.50	15.00
47023 [(2)]	Brilliance	197?	3.75	7.50	15.00
47033 [(2)]	Thelonious Monk In Person	197?	3.75	7.50	15.00
47043 [(2)]	Thelonious Monk at the Five Spot	1978	3.75	7.50	15.00
47052 [(2)]	The Riverside Trios	1980	3.75	7.50	15.00
47060 [(2)]	April in Paris/Live	198?	3.75	7.50	15.00
47064 [(2)]	Memorial Album	1982	3.00	6.00	12.00
47067 [(2)]	'Round Midnight	198?	3.00	6.00	12.00
MOSAIC					
M4-101 [(4)]	The Complete Blue Note Recordings of Thelonious Monk	198?	25.00	50.00	100.00
MR4-112 [(4)]	The Complete Black Lion and Vogue Recordings	199?	20.00	40.00	80.00
PICCADILLY					
3521	Monkisms	198?	2.50	5.00	10.00
PRESTIGE					
PRLP-142 [10]	Thelonious Monk Trio	1953	50.00	100.00	200.00
PRLP-166 [10]	Thelonious Monk Quintet with Sonny Rollins and Julius Watkins	1953	50.00	100.00	200.00
PRLP-180 [10]	Thelonious Monk Quintet	1954	50.00	100.00	200.00
PRLP-189 [10]	Thelonious Monk Trio	1954	50.00	100.00	200.00
PRLP-7027 [M]	Thelonious Monk	1956	25.00	50.00	100.00
—Reissue of 142 and 189 on one 12-inch record					
PRLP-7053 [M]	Monk	1956	25.00	50.00	100.00
—Reissue of 150					
PRLP-7075 [M]	Thelonious Monk/Sonny Rollins	1957	25.00	50.00	100.00
—Reissue of 166					
PRLP-7159 [M]	Monk's Moods	1959	18.75	37.50	75.00
—Reissue of 7027					
PRLP-7169 [M]	Work	1959	18.75	37.50	75.00
—Reissue of 7075					
PRLP-7245 [M]	We See	1962	18.75	37.50	75.00
—Reissue of 7053					
PRLP-7363 [M]	The Golden Monk	1965	7.50	5.00	30.00
—Reissue of 7245					
PRST-7363 [R]	The Golden Monk	1965	3.75	7.50	15.00
PRLP-7508 [M]	The High Priest	1967	7.50	15.00	30.00
—Reissue of 7159					
PRST-7508 [R]	The High Priest	1967	3.75	7.50	15.00
PRST-7656	The Genius	1969	3.00	6.00	12.00
PRST-7751	Reflections, Volume 1	1970	3.00	6.00	12.00
PRST-7848	Blue Monk, Volume 2	197?	3.00	6.00	12.00
24006 [(2)]	Thelonious Monk	1971	3.75	7.50	15.00
RIVERSIDE					
R-022 [(22)]	The Complete Riverside Recordings	1987	100.00	200.00	400.00
RLP 12-201 [M]	Thelonious Monk Plays Duke Ellington	1955	100.00	200.00	400.00
—White label with blue print					
RLP 12-201 [M]	Thelonious Monk Plays Duke Ellington	1958	10.00	20.00	40.00
—Blue label with reel and microphone logo					
RLP 12-209 [M]	The Unique Thelonious Monk	1956	25.00	50.00	100.00
—White label with blue print					
RLP 12-209 [M]	The Unique Thelonious Monk	1958	10.00	20.00	40.00
—Blue label with reel and microphone logo					
RLP 12-226 [M]	Brilliant Corners	1957	25.00	50.00	100.00
—White label with blue print					
RLP 12-226 [M]	Brilliant Corners	1958	10.00	20.00	40.00
—Blue label with reel and microphone logo					
RLP 12-235 [M]	Thelonious Himself	1957	25.00	50.00	100.00
—White label with blue print					
RLP 12-235 [M]	Thelonious Himself	1958	10.00	20.00	40.00
—Blue label with reel and microphone logo					
RLP 12-242 [M]	Monk's Music	1957	25.00	50.00	100.00
—White label with blue print					
RLP 12-242 [M]	Monk's Music	1958	10.00	20.00	40.00
—Blue label with reel and microphone logo					
RLP 12-247 [M]	Mulligan Meets Monk	1957	25.00	50.00	100.00
—White label with blue print					
RLP 12-247 [M]	Mulligan Meets Monk	1958	10.00	20.00	40.00
—Blue label with reel and microphone logo					
RLP 12-262 [M]	Thelonious in Action Recorded at the Five Spot Café, New York, With Johnny Griffn	1958	10.00	20.00	40.00
RLP 12-279 [M]	Misterioso	1958	10.00	20.00	40.00
RLP 12-300 [M]	The Thelonious Monk Orchestra at Town Hall	1959	10.00	20.00	40.00
RLP 12-305 [M]	5 By Monk By 5	1959	10.00	20.00	40.00
RLP 12-312 [M]	Thelonious Alone in San Francisco	1959	10.00	20.00	40.00
RLP 12-323 [M]	Thelonious Monk Quartet Plus Two at the Blackhawk	1960	10.00	20.00	40.00
RLP-421 [M]	Thelonious Monk's Greatest Hits	1962	5.00	10.00	20.00
RLP-443 [M]	Thelonious Monk in Italy	1963	5.00	10.00	20.00
RLP-460/1 [(2) M]	April in Paris	1963	10.00	20.00	40.00
RLP-483 [M]	The Thelonious Monk Story, Volume 1	1965	5.00	10.00	20.00
RLP-484 [M]	The Thelonious Monk Story, Volume 2	1965	5.00	10.00	20.00
RLP-491 [M]	Monk in France	1965	5.00	10.00	20.00
RLP 1101 [S]	Monk's Music	1959	10.00	20.00	40.00
—Black label with reel and microphone logo					
RLP 1106 [S]	Mulligan Meets Monk	1959	10.00	20.00	40.00
—Black label with reel and microphone logo					
RLP 1133 [S]	Misterioso	1958	12.50	25.00	50.00
RLP 1138 [S]	The Thelonious Monk Orchestra at Town Hall	1959	12.50	25.00	50.00
RLP 1150 [S]	5 By Monk By 5	1959	12.50	25.00	50.00
RLP 1158 [S]	Thelonious Alone in San Francisco	1959	12.50	25.00	50.00
RLP 1171 [S]	Thelonious Monk Quartet Plus Two at the Blackhawk	1960	12.50	25.00	50.00

Number	Title (A Side/B Side)	Yr	VG	VG+	NM
RLP 1190 [S]	Thelonious in Action Recorded at the Five Spot Café, New York, With Johnny Griffn	1960	12.50	25.00	50.00
RM-3000 [M]	Mighty Monk	1967	5.00	10.00	20.00
RS-3000 [S]	Mighty Monk	1967	3.75	7.50	15.00
RM-3004 [M]	Monk's Music	1967	5.00	10.00	20.00
RS-3004 [S]	Monk's Music	1967	3.75	7.50	15.00
RS-3009 [R]	CT Meets Monk	1968	3.00	6.00	12.00
RS-3015 [R]	Monk Plays Duke	1968	3.00	6.00	12.00
RS-3020X [(2) R]	Two Hours with Thelonious Monk	1969	3.75	7.50	15.00
RS-3037	Best of Thelonious Monk	1969	3.00	6.00	12.00
RS-3047	Panorama!	1970	3.00	6.00	12.00
6039 [M]	Thelonious Monk Plays Duke Ellington	197?	3.00	6.00	12.00
6053 [M]	Thelonious Himself	197?	3.00	6.00	12.00
6068 [M]	The Unique Thelonious Monk	197?	3.00	6.00	12.00
6086	5 By Monk By 5	197?	3.00	6.00	12.00
6102	Thelonious in Action	197?	3.00	6.00	12.00
6107	Meet Thelonious Monk and Gerry Mulligan	197?	3.00	6.00	12.00
6119	Misterioso	197?	3.00	6.00	12.00
6163	Alone in San Francisco	198?	3.00	6.00	12.00
6183	Thelonious Monk at Town Hall	198?	3.00	6.00	12.00
6198	Thelonious Monk at the Blackhawk	198?	3.00	6.00	12.00
6207	Monk's Music	1983	2.50	5.00	10.00
RS-9421 [S]	Thelonious Monk's Greatest Hits	1962	6.25	12.50	25.00
RS-9443 [S]	Monk in Italy	1963	6.25	12.50	25.00
RS-9460/1 [(2) S]	April in Paris	1963	12.50	25.00	250.00
RS-9483 [S]	The Thelonious Monk Story, Volume 1	1965	6.25	12.50	25.00
RS-9484 [S]	The Thelonious Monk Story, Volume 2	1965	6.25	12.50	25.00
RS-9491 [S]	Monk in France	1965	6.25	12.50	25.00
TRIP					
5022	Pure Monk	1974	2.50	5.00	10.00
XANADU					
202	Live at the Village Gate	1985	2.50	5.00	10.00

MONK, THELONIOUS, AND JOHN COLTRANE

Also see each artist's individual listings.

Albums

Number	Title (A Side/B Side)	Yr	VG	VG+	NM
FANTASY					
OJC-039	Thelonious Monk with John Coltrane	198?	2.50	5.00	10.00
JAZZLAND					
JLP-46 [M]	Thelonious Monk with John Coltrane	1961	10.00	20.00	40.00
JLP-946 [S]	Thelonious Monk with John Coltrane	1961	12.50	25.00	50.00
MILESTONE					
47011 [(2)]	Monk/Trane	1973	3.75	7.50	15.00
RIVERSIDE					
RLP-490 [M]	Thelonious Monk with John Coltrane	1965	6.25	12.50	25.00
—Reissue of Jazzland 46					
RS-9490 [S]	Thelonious Monk with John Coltrane	1965	7.50	15.00	30.00
—Reissue of Jazzland 946					

MONKEES, THE

Also see DOLENZ, JONES & TORK; DOLENZ, JONES, BOYCE & HART; MICKEY DOLENZ; DAVY JONES; MICHAEL NESMITH.

12-Inch Singles

Number	Title (A Side/B Side)	Yr	VG	VG+	NM
ARISTA					
9518	That Was Then, This Is Now/(Theme from) The Monkees	1986	2.00	4.00	8.00

45s

Number	Title (A Side/B Side)	Yr	VG	VG+	NM
ARISTA					
0201	Daydream Believer/Monkee's Theme	1976	2.50	5.00	10.00
9505	That Was Then, This Is Now/(Theme from) The Monkees	1986	2.50	5.00	10.00
—First pressings list both sides' artist as "The Monkees"					
9505	That Was Then, This Is Now/(Theme from) The Monkees	1986	—	—	3.00
—With A-side artist listed as " Mickey Dolenz and Peter Tork (of the Monkees)"					
9505 [PS]	That Was Then, This Is Now/(Theme from) The Monkees	1986	2.50	5.00	10.00
—Without "By Mickey Dolenz and Peter Tork (of the Monkees)" on sleeve					
9505 [PS]	That Was Then, This Is Now/(Theme from) The Monkees	1986	—	—	3.00
—With "By Mickey Dolenz and Peter Tork (of the Monkees)" on sleeve					
9532	Daydream Believer/Randy Scouse Git	1986	—	2.00	4.00
9532 [PS]	Daydream Believer/Randy Scouse Git	1986	—	2.00	4.00
COLGEMS					
66-1001	Last Train to Clarksville/Take a Giant Step	1966	3.75	7.50	15.00
66-1001 [PS]	Last Train to Clarksville/Take a Giant Step	1966	7.50	15.00	30.00
—Version 1: Black & white photo, no red strip at bottom					
66-1001 [PS]	Last Train to Clarksville/Take a Giant Step	1966	6.25	12.50	25.00
—Version 2: Black & white photo, red strip at bottom with "Ask For The Monkees LP Album" in white					
66-1001 [PS]	Last Train to Clarksville/Take a Giant Step	1966	5.00	10.00	20.00
—Version 3: Color photo, light blue strip at bottom of each side. Side 1 type reads "Ask For The Monkees LP Album"; Side 2 has "Write To Monkees"					
66-1002	I'm a Believer/(I'm Not Your) Steppin' Stone	1966	3.75	7.50	15.00
66-1002 [PS]	I'm a Believer/(I'm Not Your) Steppin' Stone	1966	7.50	15.00	30.00
66-1003	A Little Bit Me, A Little Bit You/She Hangs Out	1967	—	—	—
—Unreleased					
66-1003 [PS]	A Little Bit Me, A Little Bit You/She Hangs Out	1967	250.00	500.00	1000.
—Though the record does not exist, this picture sleeve does. It uses the same photo that appears on the "Pleasant Valley Sunday" sleeve.					
66-1004	A Little Bit Me, A Little Bit You/The Girl I Knew Somewhere	1967	3.75	7.50	15.00
66-1007	Pleasant Valley Sunday/Words	1967	3.75	7.50	15.00
66-1007 [PS]	Pleasant Valley Sunday/Words	1967	7.50	15.00	30.00
66-1012	Daydream Believer/Goin' Down	1967	3.75	7.50	15.00
66-1012 [PS]	Daydream Believer/Goin' Down	1967	7.50	15.00	30.00
66-1019	Valleri/Tapioca Tundra	1968	2.50	5.00	10.00
66-1023	D.W. Washburn/It's Nice to Be with You	1968	2.50	5.00	10.00
66-1023 [PS]	D.W. Washburn/It's Nice to Be with You	1968	7.50	15.00	30.00
66-1031	Porpoise Song/As We Go Along	1968	2.50	5.00	10.00
66-1031 [PS]	Porpoise Song/As We Go Along	1968	5.00	10.00	20.00
66-5000	Tear Drop City/A Man Without a Dream	1969	2.50	5.00	10.00
66-5000 [PS]	Tear Drop City/A Man Without a Dream	1969	6.25	12.50	25.00
66-5004	Listen to the Band/Someday Man	1969	2.50	5.00	10.00
66-5004 [PS]	Listen to the Band/Someday Man	1969	6.25	12.50	25.00
—"Listen to the Band" listed first					
66-5004 [PS]	Someday Man/Listen to the Band	1969	5.00	10.00	20.00
—"Someday Man" listed first					
66-5005	Good Clean Fun/Mommy and Daddy	1969	3.75	7.50	15.00
66-5005 [PS]	Good Clean Fun/Mommy and Daddy	1969	6.25	12.50	25.00
66-5011	Oh My My/I Love You Better	1970	3.75	7.50	15.00
66-5011 [PS]	Oh My My/I Love You Better	1970	7.50	15.00	30.00
RHINO					
74408	Heart and Soul/M.G.B.G.T.	1987	—	—	3.00
—Black vinyl					
74408	Heart and Soul/M.G.B.G.T.	1987	2.50	5.00	10.00
—Pink vinyl					
74408 [PS]	Heart and Soul/M.G.B.G.T.	1987	—	2.00	4.00
74410	Every Step of the Way/(I'll) Love You Forever	1987	—	—	3.00
74410 [PS]	Every Step of the Way/(I'll) Love You Forever	1987	—	2.00	4.00

7-Inch Extended Plays

Number	Title (A Side/B Side)	Yr	VG	VG+	NM
COLGEMS					
CGLP-101 [DJ]	Theme from The Monkees/I Wanna Be Free/Take a Giant Step//Last Train to Clarksville/Saturday's Child/Tomorrow's Gonna Be Another Day	1966	37.50	75.00	150.00
—Jukebox mini-LP, small hole, plays at 33 1/3 rpm					
CGLP-101 [PS]	The Monkees	1966	37.50	75.00	150.00

Albums

Number	Title (A Side/B Side)	Yr	VG	VG+	NM
ARISTA					
AL 4089	The Monkees' Greatest Hits	1976	3.00	6.00	12.00
—Reissue of Bell LP					
AL8-8313	The Monkees' Greatest Hits	198?	2.00	4.00	8.00
—Reissue of Arista 4089					
AL-8524	The Monkees	1988	3.00	6.00	12.00
AL-8525	More of the Monkees	1988	3.00	6.00	12.00
AL-9432	Then & Now…The Best of the Monkees	1986	3.00	6.00	12.00
BELL					
6081	Re-Focus	1972	7.50	15.00	30.00
COLGEMS					
COM-101 [M]	The Monkees	1966	6.25	12.50	25.00
—First pressing: Side 1, Song 5 listed as "Papa Jean's Blues"					
COM-101 [M]	The Monkees	1966	5.00	10.00	20.00
—Second pressing: Side 1, Song 5 listed as "Papa Gene's Blues" (RE after number on upper right back cover)					
COS-101 [S]	The Monkees	1966	6.25	12.50	25.00
—First pressing: Side 1, Song 5 listed as "Papa Jean's Blues"					
COS-101 [S]	The Monkees	1966	5.00	10.00	20.00
—Second pressing: Side 1, Song 5 listed as "Papa Gene's Blues" (RE after number on upper right back cover)					
COM-102 [M]	More of the Monkees	1966	5.00	10.00	20.00
COS-102 [S]	More of the Monkees	1966	5.00	10.00	20.00
COM-103 [M]	The Monkees' Headquarters	1967	5.00	10.00	20.00
—First pressing: Back cover, center bottom photo is of two of the LP's producers					
COM-103 [M]	The Monkees' Headquarters	1967	7.50	15.00	30.00
—Second pressing: Back cover, center bottom photo is of producers plus the Monkees with beards; "RE" on upper right back cover					
COS-103 [S]	The Monkees' Headquarters	1967	5.00	10.00	20.00
—First pressing: Back cover, center bottom photo is of two of the LP's producers					
COS-103 [S]	The Monkees' Headquarters	1967	7.50	15.00	30.00
—Second pressing: Back cover, center bottom photo is of producers plus the Monkees with beards; "RE" on upper right back cover					
COM-104 [M]	Pisces, Aquarius, Capricorn & Jones Ltd.	1967	10.00	20.00	40.00
COS-104 [S]	Pisces, Aquarius, Capricorn & Jones Ltd.	1967	5.00	10.00	20.00
COM-109 [M]	The Birds, the Bees & the Monkees	1968	25.00	50.00	100.00
COS-109 [S]	The Birds, the Bees & the Monkees	1968	5.00	10.00	20.00
COS-113	Instant Replay	1969	10.00	20.00	40.00
COS-115	The Monkees Greatest Hits	1969	10.00	20.00	40.00
COS-117	The Monkees Present	1969	12.50	25.00	50.00
COS-119	Changes	1970	20.00	40.00	80.00
PRS-329	The Monkees' Golden Hits	1971	25.00	50.00	100.00
—RCA Special Products edition					
SCOS-1001 [(2)]	A Barrel Full of Monkees	1971	18.75	37.50	75.00
COSO-5008	Head	1968	12.50	25.00	50.00
FSH					
71110	Live, 20th Anniversary Tour	1987	5.00	10.00	20.00
—Live album sold at tour stops					
LAURIE HOUSE					
LH-8009	The Monkees	1974	5.00	10.00	20.00
—TV mail-order offer					
PAIR					
ARPDL2-1109 [(2)]	Hit Factory	1986	5.00	10.00	20.00
RCA SPECIAL PRODUCTS					
DPL2-0188 [(2)]	The Monkees	1976	6.25	12.50	25.00
—TV mail-order offer					
RHINO					
RNLP-113	Monkee Flips	1984	3.00	6.00	12.00
RNLP-144	The Birds, the Bees and the Monkees	1985	3.00	6.00	12.00
RNLP-145	Head	1985	3.00	6.00	12.00
RNLP-146	Instant Replay	1985	3.00	6.00	12.00
RNLP-147	The Monkees Present	1985	3.00	6.00	12.00
RNLP-701 [PD]	Monkee Business	1982	3.75	7.50	15.00
RNLP-70139	Live 1967	1987	3.00	6.00	12.00
RNLP-70140	The Monkees	1986	3.00	6.00	12.00
RNLP-70141	Pisces, Aquarius, Capricorn & Jones Ltd.	1986	3.00	6.00	12.00
RNLP-70142	More of the Monkees	1986	3.00	6.00	12.00
RNLP-70143	The Monkees' Headquarters	1986	3.00	6.00	12.00
RNLP-70148	Changes	1986	3.00	6.00	12.00
RNLP-70150	Missing Links	1987	3.00	6.00	12.00
RNIN-70706	Pool It!	1987	2.50	5.00	10.00
SILHOUETTE					
SM-10012 [PD]	Tails of the Monkees	1983	3.75	7.50	15.00
SILVER EAGLE					
SE-1048 [(2)]	The Best of the Monkees	1986	3.75	7.50	15.00
—TV mail-order offer					
SUNDAZED					
LP 5045	The Monkees	1996	2.50	5.00	10.00
LP 5046	More of the Monkees	1996	2.50	5.00	10.00

Number	Title (A Side/B Side)	Yr	VG	VG+	NM
LP 5047	The Monkees Headquarters	1996	2.50	5.00	10.00
LP 5048	Pisces, Aquarius, Capricorn & Jones Ltd.	1996	2.50	5.00	10.00
LP 5049	The Birds, the Bees, and the Monkees	1996	2.50	5.00	10.00
—All of the above are on colored vinyl with bonus tracks and posters					

MONORAYS, THE
More than one group?

Number	Title (A Side/B Side)	Yr	VG	VG+	NM
45s					
20TH CENTURY FOX					
594	You're No Good/Love	1965	12.50	25.00	50.00
ASTRA					
1018	Face in the Crowd/Step Right Up	196?	3.75	7.50	15.00
—Yellow vinyl					
RED ROCKET					
476	Guardian Angel/Five Minutes to Love You	1959	10.00	20.00	40.00
TAMMY					
1005	Guardian Angel/Five Minutes to Love You	1959	50.00	100.00	200.00

MONOTONES, THE (1)
Male vocal group from New Jersey.

Number	Title (A Side/B Side)	Yr	VG	VG+	NM
45s					
ARGO					
5290	Book of Love/You Never Loved Me	1958	7.50	15.00	30.00
5301	Tom Foolery/Zombi	1958	7.50	15.00	30.00
5321	The Legend of Sleepy Hollow/Soft Shadows	1958	7.50	15.00	30.00
5339	Tell It to the Judge/Fools Will Be Fools	1959	12.50	25.00	50.00
HULL					
735	Reading the Book of Love/Dream	1960	12.50	25.00	50.00
743	Daddy's Home, But Momma's Gone/Tattle Tale	1961	12.50	25.00	50.00
MASCOT					
124	Book of Love/You Never Loved Me	1957	200.00	400.00	800.00

MONOTONES, THE (2)
British group.

Number	Title (A Side/B Side)	Yr	VG	VG+	NM
45s					
HICKORY					
1250	Is It Right/What Would You Do	1964	5.00	10.00	20.00
1306	When Will I Be Loved/If You Can't Give Me All	1965	5.00	10.00	20.00

MONOTONES, THE (U)
Could be group (2); it's doubtful that it's group (1).

Number	Title (A Side/B Side)	Yr	VG	VG+	NM
45s					
ABC-PARAMOUNT					
10796	Crystal Ball/A Thousand Faces	1966	5.00	10.00	20.00

MONRO, MATT

Number	Title (A Side/B Side)	Yr	VG	VG+	NM
45s					
CAPITOL					
2058	Only the Night Wind Knows/Fourth Blue Monday	1967	—	3.00	6.00
2103	Don't Answer Me/Pretty Polly	1968	—	2.50	5.00
2207	Yours Alone/The Music Played	1968	—	2.50	5.00
2318	Alguien Canto/De Repente Un Dea	1968	—	2.50	5.00
2390	Real Live Girl/When Joanna Loved Me	1969	—	2.50	5.00
2455	Love Song/Try to Remember	1969	—	2.50	5.00
2509	People/Southern Star	1969	—	2.50	5.00
2588	On Days Like These/Lily M'Lady	1969	—	2.50	5.00
2879	He Ain't Heavy, He's My Brother/We're Gonna Change the World	1970	—	2.00	4.00
3274	This Way Mary/Wish Now Was Then	1972	—	2.00	4.00
5623	Born Free/Other People	1966	—	3.00	6.00
5669	Honey on the Vine/Merci, Cherie	1966	—	3.00	6.00
5823	Wednesday's Child/The Lady Smiles	1967	—	3.00	6.00
5947	These Years/What to Do	1967	—	3.00	6.00
LIBERTY					
55449	Softly, As I Leave You/Is There Anything I Can Do	1962	2.50	5.00	10.00
55573	The Girl I Love/Leave Me Now	1963	2.00	4.00	8.00
55682	From Russia with Love/Here and Now	1964	2.00	4.00	8.00
55725	Softly, As I Leave You/I Love You Too	1964	2.00	4.00	8.00
55745	Walk Away/April Fool	1964	2.00	4.00	8.00
55763	For Mama/Going Places	1965	2.00	4.00	8.00
55786	Without You/Start Living	1965	2.00	4.00	8.00
55847	Yesterday/Just Yesterday	1965	2.00	4.00	8.00
55863	Beyond the Hill/Till Then My Love	1966	—	3.00	6.00
UNITED ARTISTS					
XW521	Softly, As I Leave You/Walk Away	1974	—	2.00	4.00
—Reissue					
WARWICK					
624	Portrait of My Love/You're the Top of My Parade	1961	2.50	5.00	10.00
636	My Kind of Girl/This Time	1961	3.00	6.00	12.00
669	Why Not Now/Love Is the Same Anywhere	1961	2.50	5.00	10.00
Albums					
CAPITOL					
SKAO-152	Best of Matt Monro	1969	2.50	5.00	10.00
ST 2540 [S]	This Is the Life	1966	3.75	7.50	15.00
T 2540 [M]	This Is the Life	1966	3.00	6.00	12.00
ST 2608 [S]	Here's To My Lady	1966	3.75	7.50	15.00
T 2608 [M]	Here's To My Lady	1966	3.00	6.00	12.00
ST 2683 [S]	Invitation to Broadway	1967	3.75	7.50	15.00
T 2683 [M]	Invitation to Broadway	1967	3.00	6.00	12.00
ST 2730 [S]	Invitation to the Movies/Born Free	1967	3.00	6.00	12.00
T 2730 [M]	Invitation to the Movies/Born Free	1967	3.75	7.50	15.00
ST 2801 [S]	These Years	1968	3.00	6.00	12.00
T 2801 [M]	These Years	1968	3.75	7.50	15.00
LIBERTY					
LRP-3240 [M]	Matt Monro	1962	3.75	7.50	15.00
LRP-3256 [M]	From Hollywood With Love	1962	3.75	7.50	15.00
LRP-3402 [M]	Walk Away	1965	3.00	6.00	12.00
LRP-3423 [M]	All My Loving	1965	3.00	6.00	12.00
LRP-3437 [M]	Yesterday	1966	3.00	6.00	12.00
LRP-3459 [M]	Matt Monro's Best	1966	3.00	6.00	12.00
LST-7240 [S]	Matt Monro	1962	5.00	10.00	20.00
LST-7256 [S]	From Hollywood With Love	1962	5.00	10.00	20.00
LST-7402 [S]	Walk Away	1965	3.75	7.50	15.00
LST-7423 [S]	All My Loving	1965	3.75	7.50	15.00
LST-7437 [S]	Yesterday	1966	3.75	7.50	15.00
LST-7459 [S]	Matt Monro's Best	1966	3.75	7.50	15.00
LONDON					
LL 1611 [M]	Blue and Sentimental	1957	7.50	15.00	30.00
PICKWICK					
SPC-3147	This Is All I Ask	197?	2.50	5.00	10.00
WARWICK					
W 2045 [M]	My Kind of Girl	1961	7.50	15.00	30.00
WST 2045 [S]	My Kind of Girl	1961	12.50	25.00	50.00

MONROE, MARILYN

Number	Title (A Side/B Side)	Yr	VG	VG+	NM
45s					
20TH FOX					
311	River of No Return/One Silver Dollar	1962	5.00	10.00	20.00
311 [PS]	River of No Return/One Silver Dollar	1962	20.00	40.00	80.00
RCA VICTOR					
47-5745	River of No Return/I'm Gonna File My Claim	1954	12.50	25.00	50.00
47-5745 [DJ]	River of No Return/I'm Gonna File My Claim	1954	30.00	60.00	120.00
—Promo only with Marilyn Monroe's picture on label					
47-5745 [PS]	River of No Return/I'm Gonna File My Claim	1954	30.00	60.00	120.00
47-6033	Heat Wave/After You Get What You Want	1955	7.50	15.00	30.00
47-6033 [PS]	Heat Wave/After You Get What You Want	1955	30.00	60.00	120.00
UNITED ARTISTS					
161	I Wanna Be Loved By You/I'm Through with Love	1959	5.00	10.00	20.00
Albums					
20TH CENTURY					
T-901	Remember Marilyn	1973	6.25	12.50	25.00
20TH FOX					
FXG-5000 [M]	Marilyn	1962	37.50	75.00	150.00
F/SXG-5000	Marilyn Bonus Photo	1962	12.50	25.00	50.00
SXG-5000 [R]	Marilyn	1962	25.00	50.00	100.00
ASCOT					
AM-13008 [M]	Marilyn Monroe	1963	10.00	20.00	40.00
AS-16008 [S]	Marilyn Monroe	1963	12.50	25.00	50.00
MOVIETONE					
1016 [M]	The Unforgettable Marilyn Monroe	1967	6.25	12.50	25.00
72016 [R]	The Unforgettable Marilyn Monroe	1967	5.00	10.00	20.00
SANDY HOOK					
SH-2013 [PD]	Rare Recordings 1948-1962	1980	6.25	12.50	25.00
STET					
DS-15005	Never Before and Never Again	1980	3.75	7.50	15.00

MONROE, VAUGHN

Number	Title (A Side/B Side)	Yr	VG	VG+	NM
45s					
DOT					
16434	There! I've Said It Again/I Really Love You	1963	—	3.00	6.00
16482	Pee Wee Valley/Valley Forge	1963	—	3.00	6.00
16536	Desert Flower/Ballad of Shadow Mountain	1963	—	3.00	6.00
JUBILEE					
5412	Bye Bye Blackbird/One Hour Before the Posse	1961	2.00	4.00	8.00
MGM					
12968	Learn to Ski by Mail/Song of the Skier	1960	2.00	4.00	8.00
RCA VICTOR					
47-2791	Memory Lane/Memories	1949	3.75	7.50	15.00
47-2792	Just a Memory/Memories of You	1949	3.75	7.50	15.00
47-2793	Thanks for the Memory/Remember	1949	3.75	7.50	15.00
47-2794	Easy to Remember/Roses for Remembrance	1949	3.75	7.50	15.00
47-2799	Racing with the Moon/Tchaikovsky Piano Concerto No. 1	1949	3.75	7.50	15.00
—B-side by Freddie Martin; part of a various artists 4-record box set					
47-2804	I've Got a Pocketful of Dreams/Did You Ever See a Dream Walking	1949	5.00	10.00	20.00
47-2830	It's Only a Paper Moon/Moonlight and Roses	1949	3.75	7.50	15.00
47-2831	Moon of Manakoora/Moonglow	1949	3.75	7.50	15.00
47-2832	Racing with the Moon/Moon Over Miami	1949	3.75	7.50	15.00
—The above three comprise a box set					
47-2833	Drifting and Dreaming/I'll See You in My Dreams	1949	3.75	7.50	15.00
47-2834	Meet Me Tonight in Dreamland/My Isle of Golden Dreams	1949	3.75	7.50	15.00
47-2835	Dream/My Dreams Are Getting Better All the Time	1949	3.75	7.50	15.00
—The above three comprise a box set					
47-2883	Anniversary Song/Something Special	1949	3.75	7.50	15.00
47-2884	Because/Oh, Promise Me	1949	3.75	7.50	15.00
47-2885	The Whiffenpoof Song/Without a Song	1949	3.75	7.50	15.00
—The above three comprise a box set					
47-2889	Red Roses for a Blue Lady/Melancholy Minstrel	1949	5.00	10.00	20.00
47-2902	Riders in the Sky (A Cowboy Legend)/Single Saddle	1949	6.25	12.50	25.00
47-2934	Telephone No Ring/It Looked So Good in De Window	1949	5.00	10.00	20.00
47-2944	Look for the Silver Lining/Kiss in the Night	1949	3.75	7.50	15.00
47-2945	Shine On Harvest Moon/Who	1949	3.75	7.50	15.00
47-2946	Time on My Hands/Avalon	1949	3.75	7.50	15.00
47-2986	Someday (You'll Want Me to Want You)/And It Still Goes	1949	5.00	10.00	20.00
47-3018	That Lucky Old Sun (Just Rolls Around Heaven All Day)/Make Believe	1949	5.00	10.00	20.00
47-3031	My Hot Tamale Want Chilly On Me/Gee, It's Tough to Be a Skunk	1949	5.00	10.00	20.00
47-3042	Vieni Su (Say You Love Me Too)/Blue for a Boy, Pink for a Girl	1949	5.00	10.00	20.00
47-3068	Sonny Boy/I Only Have Eyes for You	1949	5.00	10.00	20.00
47-3070	The Jolly Old Man in the Bright Red Suit/Auld Lang Syne	1949	5.00	10.00	20.00
47-3106	Mule Train/Singing My Way Back Home	1949	5.00	10.00	20.00
47-3112	So This Is Love/There's No One Here But Me	1949	5.00	10.00	20.00
47-3143	Bamboo/A Little Golden Cross	1949	5.00	10.00	20.00
47-3162	Toyland/Ah! Sweet Mystery of Life	1949	3.75	7.50	15.00
47-3163	Kiss Me/Indian Summer	1949	3.75	7.50	15.00

Number	Title (A Side/B Side)	Yr	VG	VG+	NM
47-3164	Gypsy Love Song/I'm Falling in Love with Someone	1949	3.75	7.50	15.00
47-3257	Ballerina/The Stars Will Remember	1949	5.00	10.00	20.00
47-3711	Over and Over/It's Easter Time	1950	3.75	7.50	15.00
47-3773	Thanks, Mr. Florist/Tell Her You Love Her	1950	3.75	7.50	15.00
47-3806	Our Very Own/Violins from Nowhere	1950	3.75	7.50	15.00
47-3810	The Phantom Stagecoach/Gonna Ride 'n' Ride	1950	3.00	6.00	12.00
47-3811	While I'm Smokin' My Last Cigarette/No Range to Ride Anymore	1950	3.00	6.00	12.00
47-3812	The Pony Express/Rounded Up in Glory	1950	3.00	6.00	12.00
—The above three comprise a box set					
47-3818	The Phantom Stagecoach/Mexicali Trail	1950	3.75	7.50	15.00
47-3880	The Beer That I Left on the Bar/Why Fight the Feeling	1950	3.75	7.50	15.00
47-3907	This Is My Country/The Great American Dream	1950	3.75	7.50	15.00
47-3915	Frosty the Snowman/Could Be	1950	3.75	7.50	15.00
47-3929	Dream a Little Dream of Me/Dream Awhile	1950	3.75	7.50	15.00
47-3942	A Marshmallow World/Snowy White Snow and Jingle Bells	1950	3.75	7.50	15.00
47-4007	The Night Is Young/From This Moment On	1950	3.75	7.50	15.00
47-4059	Faithful/They're Playing Our Song	1951	3.75	7.50	15.00
47-4074	You Are the One/Strawberry Moon	1951	3.75	7.50	15.00
47-4113	Sound Off (The Duckworth Chant)/Oh Marry, Marry Me	1951	3.75	7.50	15.00
47-4114	On Top of Old Smoky/Shall We Dance	1951	3.75	7.50	15.00
47-4138	Where or When/The Most Beautiful Girl in the World	1951	3.75	7.50	15.00
47-4146	Old Soldiers Never Die/Love and Devotion	1951	3.75	7.50	15.00
47-4171	So in Love/I Concentrate on You	1951	3.00	6.00	12.00
47-4172	I Get a Kick Out of You/Easy to Love	1951	3.00	6.00	12.00
47-4173	Don't Fence Me In/What Is This Thing Called Love	1951	3.00	6.00	12.00
47-4180	Dark Is the Night/Wonder Why	1951	3.75	7.50	15.00
47-4194	Red Sails in the Sunset/Everlasting	1951	3.75	7.50	15.00
47-4218	Laura Lee/Got Her Off My Hands	1951	3.75	7.50	15.00
47-4271	Meanderin'/They Call the Wind Maria	1951	3.75	7.50	15.00
47-4299	Frosty the Snowman/The Jolly Old Man in the Bright Red Suit	1951	3.75	7.50	15.00
47-4375	Charmaine/Once	1951	3.75	7.50	15.00
47-4403	Tenderly/I Like It, I Like It	1951	3.75	7.50	15.00
47-4479	Mountain Laurel/Ooh What You Did	1952	3.00	6.00	12.00
47-4611	Lady Love/Idaho State Fair	1952	3.00	6.00	12.00
47-4638	Marionette/California Rose	1952	3.00	6.00	12.00
47-4726	On Top of Old Smoky/Ballerina	1952	2.50	5.00	10.00
47-4727	Riders in the Sky (A Cowboy Legend)/Red Roses for a Blue Lady	1952	2.50	5.00	10.00
47-4760	Do You Care/Faith	1952	3.00	6.00	12.00
47-4838	Man on the Misty Mountain/When My Love Comes Back to Me	1952	3.00	6.00	12.00
47-4850	Learn to Lose/Dancing Girl	1952	3.00	6.00	12.00
47-4941	Hound Dog/A Man Don't Life Who Can Die Alone	1952	3.75	7.50	15.00
47-4942	A Man's Best Friend Is His Horse/You'll Never Get Away	1952	3.00	6.00	12.00
47-5007	Voters on Parade/Man on Misty Mountain	1952	3.00	6.00	12.00
47-5030	Yours/I	1952	3.00	6.00	12.00
47-5145	Small World/Lonely Eyes	1953	3.00	6.00	12.00
47-5236	Co-Ed/Don't Build Your Dreams Too High	1953	3.00	6.00	12.00
47-5286	Ruby/Less Than Tomorrow	1953	3.00	6.00	12.00
47-5329	Don't You Care/My Good Girl	1953	3.00	6.00	12.00
47-5490	I Know for Sure/Fiesta	1953	3.00	6.00	12.00
47-5536	Redwood Smoke/Guessing	1953	3.00	6.00	12.00
47-5608	Always, Always in My Dreams/Talkin' to a Sparrow	1954	2.50	5.00	10.00
47-5767	They Were Doin' the Mambo/Mister Sandman	1954	2.50	5.00	10.00
47-5851	Julie's Rainbow/Lila	1954	2.50	5.00	10.00
47-5943	Butterscotch Hop/Goodnight Mrs. Jones	1954	2.50	5.00	10.00
47-5970	The Holy Bible/The Ten Commandments	1954	3.00	6.00	12.00
47-6002	What a Diff'rence a Day Made/The Main Event	1955	2.50	5.00	10.00
47-6118	Roses and Revolvers/I Turned It Down	1955	2.50	5.00	10.00
47-6216	The Moon Was Yellow/You Could Hear a Pin Drop	1955	2.50	5.00	10.00
47-6260	Black Denim Trousers and Motorcycle Boots/All By Myself	1955	2.50	5.00	10.00
47-6358	Don't Go to Strangers/Steel Guitar	1955	2.50	5.00	10.00
47-6501	The Rock 'n' Roll Express/There She Goes	1956	3.00	6.00	12.00
47-6619	In the Middle of the House/Rollin' Heart	1956	2.50	5.00	10.00
47-6895	The Ride Back!/Away Out West	1957	2.50	5.00	10.00
47-6895 [PS]	The Ride Back!/Away Out West	1957	3.75	7.50	15.00
47-7019	Tomorrow, Tomorrow/Miss You	1957	2.50	5.00	10.00
47-7093	The Best Dream of All/Stargazer	1957	2.50	5.00	10.00
47-7193	There's No Piano in This House/Somebody Else Is Taking My Place	1958	2.50	5.00	10.00
47-7345	Ghost Train/Ten Chaperones	1958	2.50	5.00	10.00
47-7443	The Clown/There! I've Said It Again	1959	2.00	4.00	8.00
47-7495	The Battle of New Orleans/Hercules	1959	2.00	4.00	8.00
447-0200	Riders in the Sky/Racing with the Moon	195?	2.50	5.00	10.00
—Black label, dog on top					
UNITED ARTISTS					
214	Love Me Forever/Ballerina	1960	2.00	4.00	8.00
254	Reveille/The Locket	1960	—	—	—
—Canceled					
7-Inch Extended Plays					
RCA VICTOR					
EPA-450	Blue Tail Fly/Billy Boy, Billy Boy//Skip to My Lou/Shoot the Buffalo	195?	5.00	10.00	20.00
EPA-450 [PS]	Blue Tail Fly and Other Folk Favorites	195?	5.00	10.00	20.00
Albums					
DOT					
DLP-3419 [M]	Surfer's Stomp	1962	7.50	15.00	30.00
DLP-3431 [M]	His Greatest Hits	1962	3.00	6.00	12.00
DLP-3470 [M]	Great Themes of Famous Bands and Famous Singers	1962	3.00	6.00	12.00
DLP-3548 [M]	Great Gospels — Great Hymns	1963	3.00	6.00	12.00
DLP-3584 [M]	His Greatest Hits, Volume 2	1964	3.00	6.00	12.00
DLP-25419 [S]	Surfer's Stomp	1962	10.00	20.00	40.00
DLP-25431 [S]	His Greatest Hits	1962	3.75	7.50	15.00
DLP-25470 [S]	Great Themes of Famous Bands and Famous Singers	1962	3.75	7.50	15.00
DLP-25548 [S]	Great Gospels — Great Hymns	1963	3.75	7.50	15.00
DLP-25584 [S]	His Greatest Hits, Volume 2	1964	3.75	7.50	15.00
HAMILTON					
HLP-137 [M]	Racing with the Moon	1965	2.50	5.00	10.00
HLP-12137 [S]	Racing with the Moon	1965	3.00	6.00	12.00
RCA CAMDEN					
CAL-329 [M]	Dance with Me	1956	5.00	10.00	20.00
CAL-354 [M]	Dreamland Special	1956	5.00	10.00	20.00
RCA VICTOR					
LPM-13 [10]	Vaughn Monroe Plays Victor Herbert for Dancing	1952	10.00	20.00	40.00
ANL1-1140	The Best of Vaughn Monroe	1976	2.00	4.00	8.00
LPM-1493 [M]	House Party	1957	7.50	15.00	30.00
LPM-1799 [M]	There I Sing, Swing It Again	1958	5.00	10.00	20.00
LSP-1799 [S]	There I Sing, Swing It Again	1958	7.50	15.00	30.00
LPM-3048 [10]	Vaughn Monroe's Caravan	1952	10.00	20.00	40.00
LPM-3817 [M]	The Best of Vaughn Monroe	1967	5.00	10.00	20.00
LSP-3817 [R]	The Best of Vaughn Monroe	1967	3.00	6.00	12.00
VPM-6073 [(2)]	This Is Vaughn Monroe	197?	3.75	7.50	15.00

MONTAGE

45s

Number	Title (A Side/B Side)	Yr	VG	VG+	NM
LAURIE					
3438	I Shall Call Her Mary/An Audience with Miss Priscilla Gray	1968	2.00	4.00	8.00
3453	Wake Up Jimmy/Tinsel and Ivy	1968	2.00	4.00	8.00
Albums					
LAURIE					
SLP-2049	Montage	1969	5.00	10.00	20.00

MONTCLAIRS, THE (1)

45s

Number	Title (A Side/B Side)	Yr	VG	VG+	NM
PAULA					
345	Is This for Real/All I Really Care About Is You	1971	—	2.50	5.00
363	Dreaming Out of Season/I Just Can't Get Away	1972	—	2.50	5.00
375	Beggin' Is Hard to Do/Unwanted Love	1973	—	2.50	5.00
381	Make Up for Lost Time/How Can One Man Live	1973	—	2.50	5.00
382	I Need You More Than Ever/Prelude to a Heartbreak	1973	—	2.50	5.00
390	I'm Calling You/Hung Up on Your Love	1973	—	2.50	5.00
409	Baby, You Know I'm Gonna Miss You (Part 1)/Baby, You Know I'm Gonna Miss You (Part 2)	1974	—	2.50	5.00

MONTCLAIRS, THE (2)

45s

Number	Title (A Side/B Side)	Yr	VG	VG+	NM
ABC-PARAMOUNT					
10463	I Believe (In Your Love)/No Baby	1963	3.75	7.50	15.00

MONTCLAIRS, THE (3)

45s

Number	Title (A Side/B Side)	Yr	VG	VG+	NM
AUDICON					
111	Goodnight, Well, It's Time to Go/A Broken Promise	1961	7.50	15.00	30.00

MONTCLAIRS, THE (4)

45s

Number	Title (A Side/B Side)	Yr	VG	VG+	NM
HI-Q					
5001	Golden Angel/Don Juan	1957	75.00	150.00	300.00
PREMIUM					
404	Give Me a Chance/My Every Dream	1956	100.00	200.00	400.00
SONIC					
104	All I Want Is Love/I've Heard About You	1956	200.00	400.00	800.00

MONTCLAIRS, THE (U)

Some of these could be group (2) or (3).

45s

Number	Title (A Side/B Side)	Yr	VG	VG+	NM
SUNBURST					
106	Wait for Me/Happy Feet Time	1965	3.00	6.00	12.00
115	Poopsie/Sore Feet	1965	3.00	6.00	12.00
UNITED INT'L.					
1007	Lisa/Tap Tap Daisy	1963	6.25	12.50	25.00
1013	Young Wings Can Fly/Come On and Hold Me	1964	5.00	10.00	20.00
WICKWIRE					
13009	It's Gonna Work Out Fine/If You Need Me	196?	3.00	6.00	12.00

MONTE, LOU

45s

Number	Title (A Side/B Side)	Yr	VG	VG+	NM
GWP					
530	I Really Don't Want to Know/I Have an Angel in Heaven	1972	—	2.50	5.00
LAURIE					
3643	Paul Revere's Ride/Jerusalem, Jerusalem	1976	—	2.00	4.00
3652	Crabs Walk Sideways/Nicolena	1977	—	2.00	4.00
RCA VICTOR					
47-5382	Jealous of You/Angelina	1953	3.00	6.00	12.00
47-5496	Baby Cried/One Moment More	1953	3.00	6.00	12.00
47-5611	Darktown Strutters Ball/I Know How You Feel	1954	3.75	7.50	15.00
47-5691	Somewhere There Is Someone/Won't You Forgive Me	1954	3.00	6.00	12.00
47-5778	Veras Veranda/Chain Reaction	1954	3.00	6.00	12.00
47-5832	Italian Hucklebuck/Just Like Before	1954	3.00	6.00	12.00
47-5883	When I Hold You in My Arms/In My Dreams	1954	3.00	6.00	12.00
47-5963	Cat's Whiskers/Roulette	1954	3.00	6.00	12.00
47-5993	How Important Can It Be/Truly Yours	1955	2.50	5.00	10.00
47-6072	The Italian Wallflower/Dreamboat	1955	2.50	5.00	10.00
47-6133	Bella Notte/With You Beside Me	1955	2.50	5.00	10.00
47-6246	King of the River/Yaller Yaller Gold	1955	2.50	5.00	10.00
47-6287	Tombolee-Tombola/Rosina	1955	2.50	5.00	10.00
47-6320	Santo Natale/Italian Jingle Bells	1955	3.00	6.00	12.00
47-6403	Nina, the Queen of the Teeners/Pony Tail	1956	2.50	5.00	10.00

Number	Title (A Side/B Side)	Yr	VG	VG+	NM
47-6522	If I Knew You Were Comin' I'd've Baked a Cake/Ask Your Heart	1956	2.50	5.00	10.00
47-6704	Elvis Presley for President/If I Were a Millionaire	1956	7.50	15.00	30.00
47-6769	Roman Guitar/Some Cloud Above	1956	2.50	5.00	10.00
47-6848	Calypso Italiano/Someone Else Is Taking You Home	1957	2.50	5.00	10.00
47-6951	The Wife/Musica Bella	1957	2.50	5.00	10.00
47-7061	Ha! Ha! Ha!/Round and Round in My Heart	1957	2.50	5.00	10.00
47-7160	Lazy Mary/Angelique	1958	2.50	5.00	10.00
47-7265	Eh, Marie, Eh, Marie/The Shiek of Araby	1958	2.00	4.00	8.00
47-7346	Marianne/Strada 'Nfosa	1958	2.00	4.00	8.00
47-7423	Where Do You Work, Marie/Skinny Lena	1958	2.00	4.00	8.00
47-7467	The Italian Cowboy Song/Pizza Boy U.S.A.	1959	2.00	4.00	8.00
47-7523	The Angel in the Fountain/Sole Per Te (Only for You)	1959	2.00	4.00	8.00
47-7554	Pistol Packin' Mama/Have Another	1959	2.00	4.00	8.00
47-7641	Santa Nicola/All Because It's Christmas	1959	3.00	6.00	12.00
47-7689	Remember This Cumba/Guardo Che Luna	1960	2.00	4.00	8.00
47-8716	Mama Get the Hammer (There's a Fly on Papa's Head)/Six O'Clock Supper	1965	—	3.00	6.00
47-8754	Paul Revere's Horse (Ba-Cha-Ca-Loop)/Oh Lonesome Me	1965	—	3.00	6.00
47-8831	Cheech the Cat/Makin' Whoopee	1966	—	3.00	6.00
47-9021	Oh How I Miss You Tonight/Seventeen	1966	—	3.00	6.00
47-9216	When You Get What You Want/There'll Be Some Changes Made	1967	—	3.00	6.00
47-9328	Digga Digga Baby/A Girl, A Girl	1967	—	3.00	6.00
47-9405	I Don't Play with Matches Anymore/All for the Kids	1967	—	3.00	6.00
REGALIA					
6600	Goombar Custer's Last Stand/Tattooed Susie	1969	—	3.00	6.00
REPRISE					
0241	Down Little Doggie/La Luna Si Vuola Sposane	1963	—	3.00	6.00
0267	A Baby Cried/The Rooster and the Hen	1964	—	3.00	6.00
0284	Hello Dolly/Jungle Louie	1964	—	3.00	6.00
0302	You're So Bella, Isabella/Too Fat Polka	1964	—	3.00	6.00
0326	I Want to Hold Your Hand/My Parson's Across the Way	1964	2.00	4.00	8.00
0352	The Mixed-Up Bull from Palermo/I Know How You Feel	1965	—	3.00	6.00
0384	Don't Wish Your Heartbreak on Me/No, No, Don't Cry, My Love	1965	—	3.00	6.00
0724	Pepino the Italian Mouse/What Did Washington Say (When He Crossed the Delaware)	1968	—	2.00	4.00
—"Back to Back Hits" series					
20015	A Good Man Is Hard to Find/Sixteen Tons	1961	2.50	5.00	10.00
20037	Oh Mein Papa (Oh Mio Papa)/Tici Ti Tici To Tici Ti	1961	2.50	5.00	10.00
20044	Twist Italiano/Oh Tessie	1962	2.50	5.00	10.00
20085	Please Mr. Columbus (Turn the Ship Around)/Addio, Addio (Good-Bye)	1962	2.50	5.00	10.00
20106	Pepino the Italian Mouse/What Did Washington Say (When He Crossed the Delaware)	1962	2.00	4.00	8.00
20106 [PS]	Pepino the Italian Mouse/What Did Washington Say (When He Crossed the Delaware)	1962	3.00	6.00	12.00
20146	Pepino's Friend Pasqual (The Italian Pussy-Cat)/I Like You, You Like Me, Eh, Paisan?	1963	2.00	4.00	8.00
20146 [PS]	Pepino's Friend Pasqual (The Italian Pussy-Cat)/I Like You, You Like Me, Eh, Paisan?	1963	3.00	6.00	12.00
20171	Limbo Italiano/Bossa Nova Italiano	1963	2.00	4.00	8.00
20193	You're So Smart, You're So Smart Eh Papa/Paulucci	1963	2.00	4.00	8.00
20219	Hootenanny Italian Style/Who Stole My Provolone	1963	2.00	4.00	8.00
ROULETTE					
4253	The Darktown Strutter's Ball/Half a Love	1960	2.00	4.00	8.00
4266	Bim Bam Bu/Oh, Oh, Rosie	1960	2.00	4.00	8.00
4294	The Huckle-Buck/Always You	1960	2.00	4.00	8.00
4308	Christmas at Our House/Dominick the Donkey	1960	3.00	6.00	12.00
4366	The Sheriff of Sicily/Katareena	1961	2.00	4.00	8.00
Albums					
RCA CAMDEN					
CAL-455 [M]	Here's Lou Monte	195?	3.00	6.00	12.00
RCA VICTOR					
LPM-1651 [M]	Lou Monte Sings for You	1957	6.25	12.50	25.00
LPM-1877 [M]	Songs for Pizza Lovers	1958	6.25	12.50	25.00
LPM-1976 [M]	Italian House Party	1959	5.00	10.00	20.00
LSP-1976 [S]	Italian House Party	1959	6.25	12.50	25.00
LPM-3672 [M]	The Best of Lou Monte	1966	3.75	7.50	15.00
LSP-3672 [S]	The Best of Lou Monte	1966	3.00	6.00	12.00
LPM-3705 [M]	Good Time Songs	1967	3.75	7.50	15.00
LSP-3705 [S]	Good Time Songs	1967	3.00	6.00	12.00
REPRISE					
R-6005 [M]	Great Italian-American Hits	1961	5.00	10.00	20.00
R9-6005 [S]	Great Italian-American Hits	1961	6.25	12.50	25.00
R-6014 [M]	Live in Person	1961	5.00	10.00	20.00
R9-6014 [S]	Live in Person	1961	6.25	12.50	25.00
R-6058 [M]	Pepino The Italian Mouse & Other Italian Fun Songs	1962	5.00	10.00	20.00
R9-6058 [S]	Pepino The Italian Mouse & Other Italian Fun Songs	1962	6.25	12.50	25.00
R-6099 [M]	More Italian Fun Songs	1963	5.00	10.00	20.00
R9-6099 [S]	More Italian Fun Songs	1963	6.25	12.50	25.00
R-6118 [M]	The Golden Hits of Lou Monte	1964	3.75	7.50	15.00
RS-6118 [S]	The Golden Hits of Lou Monte	1964	5.00	10.00	20.00
ROULETTE					
R-25126 [M]	Italiano U.S.A.	1960	5.00	10.00	20.00
SR-25126 [S]	Italiano U.S.A.	1960	6.25	12.50	25.00
R-25257 [M]	The Magic World of Italy	1963	3.75	7.50	15.00
SR-25257 [S]	The Magic World of Italy	1963	5.00	10.00	20.00

MONTENEGRO, HUGO

45s

Number	Title (A Side/B Side)	Yr	VG	VG+	NM
20TH FOX					
133	April Showers/La Primavera	1959	2.50	5.00	10.00
161	St. Louis Blues/Vaya Con Dios	1959	2.50	5.00	10.00
GWP					
520	Lay Lady Lay/Blowin' in the Wind	1970	—	2.50	5.00
RCA VICTOR					
PB-10059	Living for the City/You Are the Sunshine of My Life	1974	—	2.00	4.00
PB-10153	Love Said Goodbye/Shoo-Be-Doo-Be-Doo-Da-Day	1975	—	2.00	4.00
47-8369	Theme from The Long Ships/Good Neighbor Sam	1964	—	3.00	6.00
47-8522	Candy's Theme/Polly	1965	—	3.00	6.00
47-8707	Theme from "Bunny Lake Is Missing"/Space Safari	1965	—	3.00	6.00
47-8747	Our Man Flint/Judith	1965	—	3.00	6.00
47-8847	Theme from "The Man from U.N.C.L.E."/Solo Busanova	1966	2.50	5.00	10.00
47-9050	Theme from The Professionals/Jeannie	1966	—	3.00	6.00
47-9074	Hurry Sundown/Charlie's Trip	1967	—	3.00	6.00
47-9224	For a Few Dollars More/The Gentle Rain	1967	—	3.00	6.00
47-9423	The Good, the Bad and The Ugly/March with Hope	1967	2.00	4.00	8.00
47-9554	Hang 'Em High/Tomorrow;'s Love	1968	—	3.00	6.00
47-9638	Theme from "The Fox"/There's Got to Be a Better Way	1968	—	3.00	6.00
47-9712	Tony's Theme/Good Vibrations	1969	—	3.00	6.00
74-0160	Lady in Cement/Happy Together	1969	—	2.50	5.00
74-0302	Viva Max March/Don't Turn Back	1969	—	2.50	5.00
—With Al Hirt					
74-0515	Come Again/Lordy	1971	—	2.50	5.00
74-0607	Peace Train/Mammy Blue	1971	—	2.50	5.00
74-0690	Love Theme from "The Godfather"/Movin' On	1972	—	2.50	5.00
74-0875	Lost Horizon/Learn to Say Goodbye	1973	—	2.50	5.00
74-0954	Tara's Theme/Porcupine Pie	1973	—	2.50	5.00
TIME					
1035	I Ain't Down Yet/If I Knew	1961	2.00	4.00	8.00
1040	The Young Savages/Majorca	1961	2.00	4.00	8.00
1043	Little Dutch Boy/Verdeales	1961	2.00	4.00	8.00
1048	Tarantella Twist/Nenella Bella	1962	2.00	4.00	8.00
1052	Palm Canyon Drive/Dark Eyes	1962	2.00	4.00	8.00
1058	Sherry/Get Off the Moon	1962	2.00	4.00	8.00
1062	Swanee River Boogie/Hot Crawfish	1963	2.00	4.00	8.00
1064	How the West Was Won/To Kill a Mockingbird	1963	2.50	5.00	10.00
—B-side by Dom Sebeskey					
1065	Have I Told You Lately/Mom and Dad's Waltz	1963	2.00	4.00	8.00
1079	Be My Love/I Concentrate on You	1964	2.00	4.00	8.00
Albums					
20TH CENTURY FOX					
S-4204	Lady in Cement	1968	5.00	10.00	20.00
20TH FOX					
3018 [M]	The 20th Century Strings, Volume 1	1959	5.00	10.00	20.00
BAINBRIDGE					
1002	American Musical Theatre, Volume 1 (1924-1935)	198?	2.00	4.00	8.00
1003	American Musical Theatre, Volume 2 (1935-1945)	198?	2.00	4.00	8.00
1004	American Musical Theatre, Volume 3 (1946-1952)	198?	2.00	4.00	8.00
1005	American Musical Theatre, Volume 4 (1953-1960)	198?	2.00	4.00	8.00
1009	Big Band Boogie	198?	2.00	4.00	8.00
1021	Camelot	198?	2.00	4.00	8.00
1028	Hugo Montenegro Plays the Movies	198?	2.00	4.00	8.00
GWP					
2003	The Dawn of Dylan	1971	3.75	7.50	15.00
MAINSTREAM					
S-6101 [S]	Camelot	1967	3.00	6.00	12.00
56101 [M]	Camelot	1967	3.75	7.50	15.00
RCA CAMDEN					
CAL-729 [M]	In a Sentimental Mood	196?	3.00	6.00	12.00
CAS-729 [S]	In a Sentimental Mood	196?	3.00	6.00	12.00
CAS-2309	Hawaiian Wedding Song	1969	2.50	5.00	10.00
RCA VICTOR					
ARD1-0001	Love Theme from "The Godfather"	1972	3.00	6.00	12.00
APD1-0025 [Q]	Scenes and Themes	1973	5.00	10.00	20.00
APL1-0413	Hugo in Wonderland	1974	3.00	6.00	12.00
APD1-1024 [Q]	Rocket Man	1975	5.00	10.00	20.00
APL1-1024	Rocket Man	1975	3.00	6.00	12.00
ANL1-1094	Music from A Fistful of Dollars & For a Few Dollars More & The Good, The Bad and The Ugly	1975	2.50	5.00	10.00
ANL1-2348	The Neil Diamond Songbook	1977	2.50	5.00	10.00
LPM-3540 [M]	Come Spy with Me	1966	3.00	6.00	12.00
LSP-3540 [S]	Come Spy with Me	1966	3.75	7.50	15.00
LPM-3927 [M]	Music from A Fistful of Dollars & For a Few Dollars More & The Good, The Bad and The Ugly	1968	5.00	10.00	20.00
LSP-3927 [S]	Music from A Fistful of Dollars & For a Few Dollars More & The Good, The Bad and The Ugly	1968	3.75	7.50	15.00
LSP-4022	Hang 'Em High	1968	3.75	7.50	15.00
LSP-4104	Good Vibrations	1969	3.75	7.50	15.00
LSP-4170	Moog Power	1969	5.00	10.00	20.00
LSP-4273	Colours of Love	1970	3.00	6.00	12.00
AFL1-4361	The Best of Hugo Montenegro	1977	2.50	5.00	10.00
LSP-4361	The Best of Hugo Montenegro	1970	3.00	6.00	12.00
LSP-4537	People...One to One	1971	3.00	6.00	12.00
LSP-4631	Mammy Blue	1971	3.00	6.00	12.00
VPS-6036 [(2)]	This Is Hugo Montenegro	1971	3.75	7.50	15.00
TIME					
S-2018 [S]	Cha Chas for Dancing	196?	5.00	10.00	20.00
S-2020 [S]	Boogie Woogie and Bongos	196?	5.00	10.00	20.00
S-2030 [S]	Arriba	196?	5.00	10.00	20.00
S-2035 [S]	American Musical Theatre, Volume 1 (1924-1935)	196?	3.75	7.50	15.00
S-2036 [S]	American Musical Theatre, Volume 2 (1935-1945)	196?	3.75	7.50	15.00
S-2037 [S]	American Musical Theatre, Volume 3 (1946-1952)	1961	3.75	7.50	15.00

Number	Title (A Side/B Side)	Yr	VG	VG+	NM
S-2038 [S]	American Musical Theatre, Volume 4 (1953-1960)	1961	3.75	7.50	15.00
S-2044 [S]	Great Songs from Motion Pictures Vol. 1 (1927-1937)	1961	3.75	7.50	15.00
S-2045 [S]	Great Songs from Motion Pictures Vol. 2 (1938-1944)	1961	3.75	7.50	15.00
S-2046 [S]	Great Songs from Motion Pictures Vol. 3 (1945-1960)	1961	3.75	7.50	15.00
S-2051 [S]	Montenegro in Italy	196?	3.75	7.50	15.00
52018 [M]	Cha Chas for Dancing	196?	3.75	7.50	15.00
52020 [M]	Boogie Woogie and Bongos	196?	3.75	7.50	15.00
52030 [M]	Arriba	196?	3.75	7.50	15.00
52035 [M]	American Musical Theatre, Volume 1 (1924-1935)	196?	3.00	6.00	12.00
52036 [M]	American Musical Theatre, Volume 2 (1935-1945)	196?	3.00	6.00	12.00
52037 [M]	American Musical Theatre, Volume 3 (1946-1952)	1961	3.00	6.00	12.00
52038 [M]	American Musical Theatre, Volume 4 (1953-1960)	1961	3.00	6.00	12.00
52044 [M]	Great Songs from Motion Pictures Vol. 1 (1927-1937)	1961	3.00	6.00	12.00
52045 [M]	Great Songs from Motion Pictures Vol. 2 (1938-1944)	1961	3.00	6.00	12.00
52046 [M]	Great Songs from Motion Pictures Vol. 3 (1945-1960)	1961	3.00	6.00	12.00
52051 [M]	Montenegro in Italy	196?	3.00	6.00	12.00
VIK					
LX-1089 [M]	Loves of My Life	1957	6.25	12.50	25.00
LX-1106 [M]	Ellington Fantasy	1957	6.25	12.50	25.00

MONTEREYS, THE

More than one group.

45s

Number	Title (A Side/B Side)	Yr	VG	VG+	NM
ARWIN					
130	Goodbye My Love/It Hurts Me So	1961	10.00	20.00	40.00
BLAST					
219	Face in the Crowd/Step Right Up	1965	100.00	200.00	400.00
DOMINION					
1019	First Kiss/Just One More Kiss	1964	10.00	20.00	40.00
EASTWEST					
121	I'll Love You Again/The American Teens	1958	6.25	12.50	25.00
GNP CRESCENDO					
314	For Sentimental Reasons/I Still Love You	1964	6.25	12.50	25.00
IMPALA					
213	Without a Girl/So Deep	1959	30.00	60.00	120.00
MAJOR					
1009	A Crowded Room/You Said That You Loved Me	1959	17.50	35.00	70.00
PRINCE					
5060	Rita/Billy Bud	1960	3.75	7.50	15.00
ROSE					
109	You're the Girl for Me/Ape Shape	1958	25.00	50.00	100.00
SATURN					
1002	My Girl/With You	1956	10.00	20.00	40.00
TRANS AMERICAN					
1000/1	Darlin' Send Me a Letter/Late Darlin'	1960	150.00	300.00	600.00

MONTEZ, CHRIS

45s

Number	Title (A Side/B Side)	Yr	VG	VG+	NM
A&M					
780	Call Me/Go Head On	1965	2.00	4.00	8.00
796	The More I See You/You, I Love You	1966	2.50	5.00	10.00
810	There Will Never Be Another You/You Can Hurt the One You Love	1966	2.00	4.00	8.00
822	Keep Talkin'/Time After Time	1966	2.00	4.00	8.00
839	Because of You/Elena	1967	2.00	4.00	8.00
852	Just Friends/Twiggy	1967	—	3.00	6.00
855	Foollin' Around/Dindi (Jin-Jee)	1967	—	3.00	6.00
906	Once in a While/The Face I Love	1968	—	3.00	6.00
958	Love Is Here to Stay/Nothing to Hide	1968	—	3.00	6.00
985	Where Are You Now/Watch What Happens	1968	—	3.00	6.00
JAMIE					
1410	Let's Dance/Somebody Loves You	1973	—	2.50	5.00
MONOGRAM					
500	All You Had to Do (Was Tell Me)/Love Me	1962	3.00	6.00	12.00
505	Let's Dance/You're the One	1962	5.00	10.00	20.00
507	Some Kinda Fun/Tell Me	1962	3.00	6.00	12.00
508	Rockin' Blues/(Let's Do the) Limbo	1963	3.75	7.50	15.00
513	In An English Towne/My Baby Loves to Dance	1963	3.00	6.00	12.00
516	No, No, No/Monkey Fever	1963	3.00	6.00	12.00
517	You're the One/All You Had to Do Was Tell Me	1964	3.00	6.00	12.00
—With Kathy Young					
520	It Takes Two/To Shoot the Curl	1964	3.00	6.00	12.00
—With Kathy Young					
522	(It's Not) Puppy Love/He's Been Leading You On	1964	3.00	6.00	12.00
PARAMOUNT					
0109	We Can Make the World a Whole Lot Brighter/The End of the Line	1971	—	2.50	5.00

Albums

Number	Title (A Side/B Side)	Yr	VG	VG+	NM
A&M					
LP-115 [M]	The More I See You/Call Me	1966	5.00	10.00	20.00
LP-120 [M]	Time After Time	1966	3.75	7.50	15.00
LP-128 [M]	Foolin' Around	1967	3.75	7.50	15.00
LP-157 [M]	Watch What Happens	1967	3.75	7.50	15.00
ST-4115 [S]	The More I See You/Call Me	1966	6.25	12.50	25.00
SP-4120 [S]	Time After Time	1966	5.00	10.00	20.00
SP-4128 [S]	Foolin' Around	1967	5.00	10.00	20.00
SP-4157 [S]	Watch What Happens	1967	5.00	10.00	20.00
MONOGRAM					
M-100 [M]	Let's Dance and Have Some Kinda' Fun!!!	1963	100.00	200.00	400.00

MONTGOMERY, BOB

45s

Number	Title (A Side/B Side)	Yr	VG	VG+	NM
BRUNSWICK					
55157	Because I Love You/Taste of the Blues	1959	10.00	20.00	40.00

MONTGOMERY, CHRISTOPHER

45s

Number	Title (A Side/B Side)	Yr	VG	VG+	NM
DOLTON					
84	My Paradise/Giants of Bombora	1963	7.50	15.00	30.00

MONTGOMERY, JACK

45s

Number	Title (A Side/B Side)	Yr	VG	VG+	NM
SCEPTER					
12152	Do You Believe It/My Dearly Beloved	1966	12.50	25.00	50.00

MONTGOMERY, TAMMY

Later known as TAMMI TERRELL.

45s

Number	Title (A Side/B Side)	Yr	VG	VG+	NM
CHECKER					
1072	If I Would Marry You/This Time Tomorrow	1964	10.00	20.00	40.00
—Maroon label					
1072	If I Would Marry You/This Time Tomorrow	1964	6.25	12.50	25.00
—Mostly blue label with red and black checkers					
SCEPTER					
1224	If You See Bill/It's Mine	1961	15.00	30.00	60.00
TRY ME					
28001	I Cried/If You Don't Think	1962	7.50	15.00	30.00
—As "Tana Montgomery"					
WAND					
123	Voice of Experience/Wancha To Be Sure	1962	7.50	15.00	30.00

MONTGOMERY, WES

45s

Number	Title (A Side/B Side)	Yr	VG	VG+	NM
A&M					
865	A Day in the Life (Part 1)/A Day in the Life (Part 2)	1967	2.00	4.00	8.00
883	Windy/Watch What Happens	1967	2.00	4.00	8.00
916	Goin' On to Detroit/Wind Song	1968	2.00	4.00	8.00
940	Georgia on My Mind/I Say a Little Prayer	1968	2.00	4.00	8.00
1008	Where Have All the Flowers Gone/Fly Me to the Moon	1968	2.00	4.00	8.00
1187	The Joker/Trust in Me	1970	—	3.00	6.00
PACIFIC JAZZ					
301	Summertime/Fingerpickin'	1960	3.00	6.00	12.00
RIVERSIDE					
431	Yesterdays/(B-side unknown)	1961	3.00	6.00	12.00
441	Airegan/Mr. Walker	196?	3.00	6.00	12.00
459	Movin' Along/Tune Up	196?	3.00	6.00	12.00
475	Full House/Cariba	196?	3.00	6.00	12.00
VERVE					
CS?-5 [(5)]	Celebrity Scene: Wes Montgomery	1966	15.00	30.00	60.00
—Box set of five singles (10440-10444). Price includes box, all 5 singles, jukebox title strips, bio. Records are sometimes found by themselves, so they are also listed separately.					
10373	Love Theme from "The Sandpiper"/Bumpin'	1965	2.00	4.00	8.00
10384	Goin' Out of My Head/Boss City	1966	2.00	4.00	8.00
10432	Tequila/Bumpin' On Sunset	1966	2.00	4.00	8.00
10440 [DJ]	Goin' Out of My Head/Tequila	1966	2.50	5.00	10.00
10441 [DJ]	Bumpin' (Part 1)/Bumpin' (Part 2)	1966	2.50	5.00	10.00
10442 [DJ]	Bumpin' on Sunset (Part 1)/Bumpin' on Sunset (Part 2)	1966	2.50	5.00	10.00
10443 [DJ]	Phoenix Love Theme/Caravan	1966	2.50	5.00	10.00
10444 [DJ]	Love Theme from "The Sandpiper"/Quiet Thing	1966	2.50	5.00	10.00
10489	California Dreaming/Mr. Walker	1967	2.00	4.00	8.00

Albums

Number	Title (A Side/B Side)	Yr	VG	VG+	NM
ACCORD					
SN-7170	The Classic Sound of Wes Montgomery	1981	2.50	5.00	10.00
A&M					
LP-2001 [M]	A Day in the Life	1967	5.00	10.00	20.00
SP-3001 [S]	A Day in the Life	1967	3.75	7.50	15.00
SP9-3001	A Day in the Life	1985	3.75	7.50	15.00
—Audiophile reissue					
SP-3006	Down Here on the Ground	1968	3.75	7.50	15.00
SP9-3006	Down Here on the Ground	1985	3.75	7.50	15.00
—Audiophile reissue					
SP-3012	Road Song	1968	3.75	7.50	15.00
SP9-3012	Road Song	198?	3.75	7.50	15.00
—Audiophile reissue					
SP-4247	Greatest Hits	1970	3.75	7.50	15.00
BLUE NOTE					
BN-LA531-H2 [(2)]	Beginnings	1976	3.75	7.50	15.00
LWB-531 [(2)]	Beginnings	1981	3.00	6.00	12.00
—Reissue of BN-LA531-H2					
DCC COMPACT CLASSICS					
LPZ-2014	Goin' Out of My Head	1996	6.25	12.50	25.00
—Audiophile vinyl					
FANTASY					
OJC-034	New Concepts in Jazz Guitar	198?	2.50	5.00	10.00
OJC-036	The Incredible Jazz Guitar of Wes Montgomery	198?	2.50	5.00	10.00
OJC-089	Movin' Along	198?	2.50	5.00	10.00
OJC-106	Full House	198?	2.50	5.00	10.00
OJC-144	Portrait of Wes	198?	2.50	5.00	10.00
OJC-233	So Much Guitar!	198?	2.50	5.00	10.00
OJC-261	Boss Guitar	1987	2.50	5.00	10.00
OJC-368	Fusion! Wes Montgomery with Strings	198?	2.50	5.00	10.00
OJC-489	Guitar on the Go	1991	3.00	6.00	12.00
MGM					
GAS-120	Wes Montgomery (Golden Archive Series)	1970	3.75	7.50	15.00
MILESTONE					
9110	Encores	1983	2.50	5.00	10.00
47003 [(2)]	While We're Young	1972	3.75	7.50	15.00
47013 [(2)]	Wes Montgomery and Friends	1973	3.75	7.50	15.00
47030 [(2)]	Pretty Blue	197?	3.00	6.00	12.00
47040 [(2)]	Movin'	197?	3.00	6.00	12.00

Number	Title (A Side/B Side)	Yr	VG	VG+	NM
47051 [(2)]	Groove Brothers	1979	3.00	6.00	12.00
47057 [(2)]	Yesterdays	198?	3.00	6.00	12.00
47065 [(2)]	The Alternative	198?	3.00	6.00	12.00

MOBILE FIDELITY

Number	Title (A Side/B Side)	Yr	VG	VG+	NM
MFSL-508	Bumpin'	198?	7.50	15.00	30.00

—Audiophile vinyl

PACIFIC JAZZ

Number	Title (A Side/B Side)	Yr	VG	VG+	NM
PJ-5 [M]	Montgomeryland	1960	7.50	15.00	30.00
ST-5 [S]	Montgomeryland	1960	10.00	20.00	40.00
PJ-10104 [M]	Easy Groove	1966	3.75	7.50	15.00
PJ-10130 [M]	Kismet	1967	5.00	10.00	20.00
ST-20104 [S]	Easy Groove	1966	5.00	10.00	20.00
ST-20130 [S]	Kismet	1967	3.75	7.50	15.00
ST-20137	Portrait of Wes Montgomery	1968	3.75	7.50	15.00

PICCADILLY

Number	Title (A Side/B Side)	Yr	VG	VG+	NM
3584	Jazz Guitar	198?	2.50	5.00	10.00

RIVERSIDE

Number	Title (A Side/B Side)	Yr	VG	VG+	NM
RLP 12-310 [M]	New Concepts in Jazz Guitar	1959	7.50	15.00	30.00
RLP 12-320 [M]	The Incredible Jazz Guitar of Wes Montgomery	1960	7.50	15.00	30.00
RLP-342 [M]	Movin' Along	1960	6.25	12.50	25.00
RLP-382 [M]	So Much Guitar!	1961	6.25	12.50	25.00
RLP-434 [M]	Full House	1962	7.50	15.00	30.00
RLP-459 [M]	Boss Guitar	1963	5.00	10.00	20.00
RLP-472 [M]	Fusion! Wes Montgomery with Strings	1964	5.00	10.00	20.00
RLP-492 [M]	Portrait of Wes	1965	3.75	7.50	15.00
RLP-494 [M]	Guitar on the Go	1965	3.75	7.50	15.00
RLP 1156 [S]	New Concepts in Jazz Guitar	1959	7.50	15.00	30.00
RLP 1169 [S]	The Incredible Jazz Guitar of Wes Montgomery	1960	7.50	15.00	30.00
RM-3002 [M]	In the Wee Small Hours	1967	3.75	7.50	15.00
—Reissue of 472					
RS-3002 [S]	In the Wee Small Hours	1967	3.00	6.00	12.00
—Reissue of 9472					
RS-3012	This Is Wes Montgomery	1968	3.00	6.00	12.00
—Reissue of 9459					
RS-3014	'Round Midnight	1968	3.00	6.00	12.00
—Reissue of 1156					
RS-3036	March 6, 1925-June 15, 1968	1968	3.00	6.00	12.00
RS-3039	The Best of Wes Montgomery	1968	3.00	6.00	12.00
RS-3046	Panorama	1969	3.00	6.00	12.00
6046	The Incredible Jazz Guitar of Wes Montgomery	197?	2.50	5.00	10.00
6069	Full House	197?	2.50	5.00	10.00
6080	The Dynamic New Jazz Sound of Wes Montgomery	197?	2.50	5.00	10.00
6100	So Much Guitar!	197?	2.50	5.00	10.00
6111	Boss Guitar	197?	2.50	5.00	10.00
6168	Guitar on the Go	198?	2.50	5.00	10.00
6199	Movin' Along	198?	2.50	5.00	10.00
6202	Portrait of Wes	198?	2.50	5.00	10.00
6210	Fusion! Wes Montgomery with Strings	198?	2.50	5.00	10.00
RS-9342 [S]	Movin' Along	1960	6.25	12.50	25.00
RS-9382 [S]	So Much Guitar!	1961	6.25	12.50	25.00
RS-9434 [S]	Full House	1962	7.50	15.00	30.00
RS-9459 [S]	Boss Guitar	1963	6.25	12.50	25.00
RS-9472 [S]	Fusion! Wes Montgomery with Strings	1964	6.25	12.50	25.00
RS-9492 [S]	Portrait of Wes	1965	5.00	10.00	20.00
RS-9494 [S]	Guitar on the Go	1965	5.00	10.00	20.00

VERVE

Number	Title (A Side/B Side)	Yr	VG	VG+	NM
VE-2-2513 [(2)]	Small Group Recording	197?	3.75	7.50	15.00
V-8610 [M]	Movin' Wes	1965	3.75	7.50	15.00
V6-8610 [S]	Movin' Wes	1965	5.00	10.00	20.00
V-8625 [M]	Bumpin'	1965	3.75	7.50	15.00
V6-8625 [S]	Bumpin'	1965	5.00	10.00	20.00
V-8642 [M]	Goin' Out of My Head	1966	3.75	7.50	15.00
V6-8642 [S]	Goin' Out of My Head	1966	5.00	10.00	20.00
V-8653 [M]	Tequila	1966	3.75	7.50	15.00
V6-8653 [S]	Tequila	1966	5.00	10.00	20.00
V-8672 [M]	California Dreaming	1967	5.00	10.00	20.00
V6-8672 [S]	California Dreaming	1967	3.75	7.50	15.00
V-8714 [M]	The Best of Wes Montgomery	1967	5.00	10.00	20.00
V6-8714 [S]	The Best of Wes Montgomery	1967	3.75	7.50	15.00
V6-8757	The Best of Wes Montgomery, Vol. 2	1968	3.75	7.50	15.00
V6-8765	Willow Weep for Me	1969	3.75	7.50	15.00
V6-8796	Eulogy	1970	3.75	7.50	15.00
V6-8804	Just Walkin'	1971	3.00	6.00	12.00
V6-8813 [(2)]	The History of Wes Montgomery	1972	3.75	7.50	15.00
V3HB-8839 [(2)]	Return Engagement	1974	3.75	7.50	15.00

MONTGOMERYS, THE

45s

AMY

Number	Title (A Side/B Side)	Yr	VG	VG+	NM
883	Promise of Love/Gotta Make a Hit Record	1963	62.50	125.00	250.00

MONTROSE

45s

WARNER BROS.

Number	Title (A Side/B Side)	Yr	VG	VG+	NM
7776	Rock the Nation/One Thing on My Mind	1974	—	2.50	5.00
7814	Make It Last/Space Station No. 5	1974	—	2.50	5.00
8063	The Dreamer/Paper Money	1975	—	2.50	5.00
8080	Connection/We're Going Home	1975	—	2.50	5.00
8172	Clown Woman/Matriarch	1976	—	2.50	5.00
8281	Music Man/Tuft-Sedge	1976	—	2.50	5.00
8351	Let's Go/(B-side unknown)	1977	—	2.50	5.00

Albums

ENIGMA

Number	Title (A Side/B Side)	Yr	VG	VG+	NM
ST-73264	Mean	1987	2.50	5.00	10.00
D1-73323	Speed of Sound	1988	2.50	5.00	10.00

WARNER BROS.

Number	Title (A Side/B Side)	Yr	VG	VG+	NM
BS 2740	Montrose	1974	3.00	6.00	12.00
BS 2823	Paper Money	1974	3.00	6.00	12.00
BS 2892	Warner Bros. Presents Montrose!	1975	3.00	6.00	12.00
BS 2963	Jump On It	1976	3.00	6.00	12.00
BSK 3106	Montrose	1978	2.00	4.00	8.00

—Reissue of 2740

MONTY PYTHON

45s

ARISTA

Number	Title (A Side/B Side)	Yr	VG	VG+	NM
0130	The Single/(B-side unknown)	1975	2.00	4.00	8.00
0578	They Won't Play This Song on the Radio/Sit on My Face-Farewell to John Denver	1980	2.00	4.00	8.00

WARNER BROS.

Number	Title (A Side/B Side)	Yr	VG	VG+	NM
49112	Always Look on the Bright Side of Life/Brian	1979	2.50	5.00	10.00

Albums

ARISTA

Number	Title (A Side/B Side)	Yr	VG	VG+	NM
SP-101 [DJ]	Monty Python's Contractural Obligation Sampler	1980	7.50	15.00	30.00
—One side is censored, the other is uncensored					
AL 4039	Matching Tie & Handkerchief	1975	5.00	10.00	20.00
—Side 2 is "trick tracked," with two different routines depending on where you place the needle at the start					
AL 4050	The Album of the Soundtrack of the Trailer of the Film of "Monty Python and the Holy Grail"	1975	5.00	10.00	20.00
AL 4073	Monty Python Live! At City Center	1976	5.00	10.00	20.00
AL 8296	The Monty Python Instant Record Collection	198?	2.00	4.00	8.00
—Reissue					
AL 8343	Monty Python's Contractual Obligation Album	198?	2.00	4.00	8.00
—Reissue					
AL 8353	Monty Python Live! At City Center	198?	2.00	4.00	8.00
—Reissue					
AL 8355	The Album of the Soundtrack of the Trailer of the Film of "Monty Python and the Holy Grail"	198?	2.00	4.00	8.00
—Reissue					
AL 8357	Matching Tie and Handkerchief	198?	2.00	4.00	8.00
—Reissue; we don't know whether Side 2 maintains the trick groove on this issue					
AB 9536	Monty Python's Contractual Obligation Album	1980	5.00	10.00	20.00
AB 9580	The Monty Python Instant Record Collection	1981	3.75	7.50	15.00

BUDDAH

Number	Title (A Side/B Side)	Yr	VG	VG+	NM
BDS 5656 [(2)]	The Worst of Monty Python	1976	5.00	10.00	20.00

—Repackage of the two Charisma LPs

CHARISMA

Number	Title (A Side/B Side)	Yr	VG	VG+	NM
CAS 1049	Another Monty Python Record	1972	6.25	12.50	25.00
CAS 1063	Monty Python's Previous Record	1972	6.25	12.50	25.00

MCA

Number	Title (A Side/B Side)	Yr	VG	VG+	NM
6121	Monty Python and the Meaning of Life	1983	3.00	6.00	12.00

PYE

Number	Title (A Side/B Side)	Yr	VG	VG+	NM
12116	Monty Python's Flying Circus	1975	5.00	10.00	20.00

VIRGIN

Number	Title (A Side/B Side)	Yr	VG	VG+	NM
90865 [(2)]	The Final Rip Off	1988	5.00	10.00	20.00

WARNER BROS.

Number	Title (A Side/B Side)	Yr	VG	VG+	NM
BSK 3396	Life of Brian	1979	3.75	7.50	15.00

MOODS, THE (1)

45s

BANG

Number	Title (A Side/B Side)	Yr	VG	VG+	NM
555	Gotta Figure Out/Genuine Jade	1968	2.00	4.00	8.00

WAND

Number	Title (A Side/B Side)	Yr	VG	VG+	NM
11224	Rainmaker/Lady Rain	1970	2.00	4.00	8.00

MOODS, THE (2)

45s

KOOL

Number	Title (A Side/B Side)	Yr	VG	VG+	NM
1024	High School Days/The Broken Hip	1964	2.50	5.00	10.00
1028	Oop-Sy-Do/Stay with Me	1965	2.50	5.00	10.00
1032	Only the Young/(B-side unknown)	1965	2.50	5.00	10.00

MOODS, THE (3)

45s

SARG

Number	Title (A Side/B Side)	Yr	VG	VG+	NM
162	Little Alice/Lady of the Sea	1959	20.00	40.00	80.00
176	Easy Going/Duck Walk	1959	10.00	20.00	40.00
179	Let Me Have Your Love/Broke Up	1959	12.50	25.00	50.00
184	Rockin' Santa Claus/Teenager's Past	1959	10.00	20.00	40.00
185	On the Move/Teenager's Past	1960	10.00	20.00	40.00

MOODY BLUES, THE

Also see GRAEME EDGE; JUSTIN HAYWARD; DENNY LAINE; RAY THOMAS.

12-Inch Singles

POLYDOR

Number	Title (A Side/B Side)	Yr	VG	VG+	NM
431 [DJ]	The Other Side of Life (Edit) (LP Version)	1986	2.00	4.00	8.00
449 [DJ]	Running Out of Love (same on both sides)	1986	2.00	4.00	8.00

THRESHOLD

Number	Title (A Side/B Side)	Yr	VG	VG+	NM
174 [DJ]	Gemini Dream (same on both sides)	1981	2.00	4.00	8.00
224 [DJ]	Sitting at the Wheel (Edit) (LP Version)	1983	2.00	4.00	8.00

45s

DERAM

Number	Title (A Side/B Side)	Yr	VG	VG+	NM
85023	Nights in White Satin/Cities	1968	2.50	5.00	10.00
—Composer of "Nights in White Satin" listed as "Redwave"					
85023	Nights in White Satin/Cities	1968	2.00	4.00	8.00
—Composer of "Nights in White Satin" listed as "Justin Hayward"					
85028	Tuesday Afternoon (Forever Afternoon)/Another Morning	1968	2.00	4.00	8.00
85033	Ride My See-Saw/Voices in the Sky	1968	2.00	4.00	8.00
85044	Never Comes the Day/So Deep Within You	1969	2.00	4.00	8.00

LONDON

Number	Title (A Side/B Side)	Yr	VG	VG+	NM
270	Steppin' in a Slide Zone/I'll Be Level with You	1978	—	2.00	4.00
273	Driftwood/I'm Your Man	1978	—	2.50	5.00
1005	This Is My House (But Nobody Calls)/Boulevard de la Madelaine	1967	3.00	6.00	12.00
9726	Go Now!/Lose Your Money	1965	5.00	10.00	20.00
—White, purple and blue label					
9726	Go Now!/Lose Your Money	1965	3.00	6.00	12.00
—Blue swirl label, "London" in white					
9726	Go Now!/Lose Your Money	1965	2.00	4.00	8.00
—Blue swirl label, "London" in black					
9726V [DJ]	Go Now!/It's Easy Child	1965	5.00	10.00	20.00

—Orange and brown swirl label; may be promo only

Number	Title (A Side/B Side)	Yr	VG	VG+	NM
9764	From the Bottom of My Heart (I Love You)/And My Baby's Gone	1965	3.75	7.50	15.00
9799	Ev'ry Day/You Don't	1965	3.75	7.50	15.00
9810	Stop!/Bye Bye Bird	1966	3.75	7.50	15.00
20030	Fly Me High/I Really Haven't Got the Time	1967	3.00	6.00	12.00

POLYDOR

Number	Title (A Side/B Side)	Yr	VG	VG+	NM
870990-7	No More Lies/River of Endless Love	1988	—	—	3.00
870990-7 [PS]	No More Lies/River of Endless Love	1988	—	—	3.00
871270-7	Al Fin Voy a Encontrarte (I Know You're Out There Somewhere — Spanish Version)/I Know You're Out There Somewhere	1989	—	2.50	5.00
883906-7	Your Wildest Dreams/Talkin' Talkin'	1986	—	—	3.00
883906-7 [PS]	Your Wildest Dreams/Talkin' Talkin'	1986	—	—	3.00
885201-7	The Other Side of Life/The Spirit	1986	—	2.50	5.00
—Blue vinyl					
885201-7 [PS]	The Other Side of Life/The Spirit	1986	—	2.50	5.00
—Special sleeve for blue vinyl version					
885212-7	The Other Side of Life/The Spirit	1986	—	—	3.00
885212-7 [PS]	The Other Side of Life/The Spirit	1986	—	—	3.00
887600-7	I Know You're Out There Somewhere/Miracle	1988	—	—	3.00
887600-7 [PS]	I Know You're Out There Somewhere/Miracle	1988	—	—	3.00
887815-7	Here Comes the Weekend/River of Endless Love	1988	—	—	3.00

THRESHOLD

Number	Title (A Side/B Side)	Yr	VG	VG+	NM
601	Gemini Dream/Painted Smile	1981	—	2.00	4.00
602	The Voice/22,000 Days	1981	—	2.00	4.00
602 [PS]	The Voice/22,000 Days	1981	—	3.00	6.00
603	Talking Out of Turn/Veteran Cosmic Rocker	1981	—	2.00	4.00
604	Sitting at the Wheel/Going Nowhere	1983	—	2.00	4.00
604 [PS]	Sitting at the Wheel/Going Nowhere	1983	—	3.00	6.00
605	Blue World/Sorry	1983	—	2.00	4.00
606	Running Water/Under My Feet	1983	—	2.00	4.00
67004	Question/Candle of Life	1970	—	3.00	6.00
67006	The Story in Your Eyes/Melancholy Man	1971	—	3.00	6.00
67006 [PS]	The Story in Your Eyes/Melancholy Man	1971	3.00	6.00	12.00
67009	Isn't Life Strange/After You Came	1972	—	2.50	5.00
67012	I'm Just a Singer (In a Rock and Roll Band)/For My Lady	1973	—	2.50	5.00

Albums

COMPLEAT

Number	Title (A Side/B Side)	Yr	VG	VG+	NM
672008 [(2)]	Early Blues	1985	3.75	7.50	15.00
—Reissue of London 1964-66 material					

DERAM

Number	Title (A Side/B Side)	Yr	VG	VG+	NM
DE 16012 [M]	Days of Future Passed	1968	62.50	125.00	250.00
DES 18012 [S]	Days of Future Passed	1968	5.00	10.00	20.00
DES 18017	In Search of the Lost Chord	1968	5.00	10.00	20.00
—Originals have gatefold covers					
DES 18025	On the Threshold of a Dream	1969	5.00	10.00	20.00
—Originals have gatefold covers and lyric booklet					
DES 18051 [R]	In the Beginning	1971	5.00	10.00	20.00
820006-1 [S]	Days of Future Passed	1985	2.00	4.00	8.00
820168-1	In Search of the Lost Chord	1985	2.00	4.00	8.00
820170-1	On the Threshold of a Dream	1985	2.00	4.00	8.00

LONDON

Number	Title (A Side/B Side)	Yr	VG	VG+	NM
PS 428 [R]	Go Now — The Moody Blues #1	1965	10.00	20.00	40.00
PS 690/1 [(2)]	Caught Live + 5	1977	3.00	6.00	12.00
PS 708	Octave	1978	2.50	5.00	10.00
PS 708 [DJ]	Octave	1978	7.50	15.00	30.00
—Promo only on blue vinyl					
LL 3428 [M]	Go Now — The Moody Blues #1	1965	12.50	25.00	50.00
820161-1 [(2)]	Caught Live + 5	1985	2.00	4.00	8.00
820329-1	Octave	1986	2.00	4.00	8.00

MOBILE FIDELITY

Number	Title (A Side/B Side)	Yr	VG	VG+	NM
1-042	Days of Future Passed	1980	15.00	30.00	60.00
—Audiophile vinyl					
1-151	Seventh Sojourn	1984	17.50	35.00	70.00
—Audiophile vinyl					
1-215	On the Threshold of a Dream	1994	6.25	12.50	25.00
—Audiophile vinyl					
1-232	Every Good Boy Deserves Favour	1995	6.25	12.50	25.00
—Audiophile vinyl					
1-253	To Our Children's Children's Children	1996	15.00	30.00	60.00
—Audiophile vinyl					

NAUTILUS

Number	Title (A Side/B Side)	Yr	VG	VG+	NM
NR-21	On the Threshold of a Dream	1981	15.00	30.00	60.00
—Audiophile vinyl					
NR-21	On the Threshold of a Dream	1981	12.50	25.00	50.00
—Audiophile vinyl; DBX-encoded version					

POLYDOR

Number	Title (A Side/B Side)	Yr	VG	VG+	NM
829 179-1	The Other Side of Life	1986	2.50	5.00	10.00
835 756-1	Sur La Mer	1988	3.00	6.00	12.00
840 659-1	Greatest Hits (1967-1988)	1989	3.75	7.50	15.00

THRESHOLD

Number	Title (A Side/B Side)	Yr	VG	VG+	NM
THS 1	To Our Children's Children's Children	1969	3.75	7.50	15.00
—White label with purple logo; gatefold cover					
THS 1	To Our Children's Children's Children	197?	2.50	5.00	10.00
—Blue label; no gatefold					
THS 3	A Question of Balance	1970	3.75	7.50	15.00
—White label with purple logo; gatefold cover					
THS 3	A Question of Balance	197?	2.50	5.00	10.00
—Blue label; no gatefold					
THS 5	Every Good Boy Deserves Favour	1971	3.75	7.50	15.00
—White label with purple logo; gatefold cover					
THS 5	Every Good Boy Deserves Favour	197?	2.50	5.00	10.00
—Blue label; no gatefold					
THS 7	Seventh Sojourn	1972	3.75	7.50	15.00
—White label with purple logo; gatefold cover					
THS 7	Seventh Sojourn	197?	2.50	5.00	10.00
—Blue label; no gatefold					
THS 12/13 [(2)]	This Is the Moody Blues	1974	3.75	7.50	15.00
THX-100 [DJ]	Special Interview Kit	1971	37.50	75.00	150.00
—Includes script					
TRL-2901	Long Distance Voyager	1981	2.50	5.00	10.00
TRL-2902	The Present	1982	2.50	5.00	10.00
SMAS-93329	A Question of Balance	1971	5.00	10.00	20.00
—Capitol Record Club edition					
810119-1	The Present	1983	2.00	4.00	8.00
820007-1 [(2)]	This Is the Moody Blues	1985	2.00	4.00	8.00
820105-1	Long Distance Voyager	1985	2.00	4.00	8.00
820155-1	Voices in the Sky: The Best of the Moody Blues	1985	2.50	5.00	10.00
820159-1	Seventh Sojourn	1985	2.00	4.00	8.00
820160-1	Every Good Boy Deserves Favour	1985	2.00	4.00	8.00
820211-1	A Question of Balance	1985	2.00	4.00	8.00

MOOG MACHINE, THE

Albums

COLUMBIA

Number	Title (A Side/B Side)	Yr	VG	VG+	NM
CS 9921	Switched-On Rock	1969	5.00	10.00	20.00
CS 9959	Christmas Becomes Electric	1969	5.00	10.00	20.00

MOON, KEITH

Also see THE WHO.

45s

TRACK

Number	Title (A Side/B Side)	Yr	VG	VG+	NM
40316	Teenage Idol/Don't Worry Baby	1974	3.75	7.50	15.00
40387	Solid Gold/Move Over Ms. L.	1975	3.75	7.50	15.00
40435	In My Life/Crazy Like a Fox	1975	3.75	7.50	15.00

Albums

TRACK/MCA

Number	Title (A Side/B Side)	Yr	VG	VG+	NM
2136	Two Sides of the Moon	1975	10.00	20.00	40.00

MOON, THE

With David Marks, ex-BEACH BOYS.

45s

IMPERIAL

Number	Title (A Side/B Side)	Yr	VG	VG+	NM
66285	Mothers and Fathers/Someday Girl	1968	7.50	15.00	30.00
66330	Faces/John Automaton	1968	6.25	12.50	25.00
66415	Not to Know/Pirate	1969	6.25	12.50	25.00

Albums

IMPERIAL

Number	Title (A Side/B Side)	Yr	VG	VG+	NM
LP-12381	Without Earth	1968	10.00	20.00	40.00
LP-12444	The Moon	1969	10.00	20.00	40.00

MOON BEAMS, THE

45s

GRATE

Number	Title (A Side/B Side)	Yr	VG	VG+	NM
100	A Lover's Plea/Don't Go Away	1959	37.50	75.00	150.00

MOONGLOWS, THE

Also see HARVEY.

45s

BIG P

Number	Title (A Side/B Side)	Yr	VG	VG+	NM
101	Sincerely '72/You've Chosen Me	1972	2.50	5.00	10.00

CHAMPAGNE

Number	Title (A Side/B Side)	Yr	VG	VG+	NM
7500	I Just Can't Tell No Lie/I've Been Your Dog (Ever Since I've Been Your Man)	1952	375.00	750.00	1500.

CHANCE

Number	Title (A Side/B Side)	Yr	VG	VG+	NM
1147	Baby Please/Whistle My Love	1953	250.00	500.00	1000.
—Black vinyl					
1147	Baby Please/Whistle My Love	1953	1500.	2250.	3000.
—Red vinyl					
1150	Just a Lonely Christmas/Hey, Santa Claus	1953	1500.	2250.	3000.
—Red vinyl (this may not exist legitimately on black vinyl)					
1152	Secret Love/Real Gone Mama	1954	375.00	750.00	1500.
—Silver and blue label					
1152	Secret Love/Real Gone Mama	1954	250.00	500.00	1000.
—Yellow and black label					
1156	I Was Wrong/Ooh Rockin' Daddy	1954	150.00	300.00	600.00
—Yellow and black label					
1156	I Was Wrong/Ooh Rockin' Daddy	1954	150.00	300.00	600.00
—Black and white label					
1161	My Gal/219 Train	1954	2500.	3750.	5000.

CHESS

Number	Title (A Side/B Side)	Yr	VG	VG+	NM
1581	Sincerely/Tempting	1954	15.00	30.00	60.00
—Blue label, silver top					
1589	Most of All/She's Gone	1955	15.00	30.00	60.00
—Blue label, silver top					
1598	Foolish Me/Slow Down	1955	15.00	30.00	60.00
—Blue label, silver top					
1605	Starlite/In Love	1955	15.00	30.00	60.00
—Blue label, silver top					
1611	In My Diary/Lover, Love Me	1955	15.00	30.00	60.00
—Blue label, silver top					
1619	We Go Together/Chickie Um Bah	1956	12.50	25.00	50.00
—Blue label, silver top					
1629	See Saw/When I'm With You	1956	12.50	25.00	50.00
—Blue label, silver top					
1646	Over and Over Again/I Knew from the Start	1957	15.00	30.00	60.00
—With slower version of A-side; "8189A" in the run-off area					
1646	Over and Over Again/I Knew from the Start	1957	12.50	25.00	50.00
—With normal version of A-side; blue label, silver top					
1651	I'm Afraid the Masquerade Is Over/Don't Say Goodbye	1957	12.50	25.00	50.00
—Blue label, silver top					
1661	Please Send Me Someone to Love/Mr. Engineer (Bring Her Back to Me)	1957	12.50	25.00	50.00
—Blue label, silver top					
1669	The Beating of My Heart/Confess It to Your Heart	1957	12.50	25.00	50.00
—In general, for the above singles, the blue label with vertical "Chess" versions are 60% of the above values; yellow early-1960s label versions and black mid-1960s versions are 40% of above; and blue late-1960s versions, with "Chess" on top, are about 20%					
1681	Too Late/Here I Am	1958	7.50	15.00	30.00
1689	In the Middle of the Night/Soda Pop	1958	7.50	15.00	30.00
1701	This Love/Sweeter Than Words	1958	7.50	15.00	30.00
1705	Ten Commandments of Love/Mean Old Blues	1958	7.50	15.00	30.00
—As "Harvey and the Moonglows"					
1717	Love Is a River/I'll Never Stop Wanting You	1959	6.25	12.50	25.00
1738	Mama Loocie/Unemployment	1959	6.25	12.50	25.00
—As "Harvey and the Moonglows"					

Number	Title (A Side/B Side)	Yr	VG	VG+	NM
1770	Beatnick/Junior	1960	6.25	12.50	25.00
1811	Blue Velvet/Penny Arcade	1962	6.25	12.50	25.00
—As "Bobby Lester and the Moonglows"					
CRIMSON					
1003	My Imagination/Gee	1964	5.00	10.00	20.00
LOST NITE					
275	Just a Lonely Christmas/Baby Please	196?	3.00	6.00	12.00
—Reissue					
MELLO					
69	Just a Lonely Christmas/Hey, Santa Claus	19??	2.00	4.00	8.00
—Reissue					
RCA VICTOR					
74-0759	Sincerely/I Was Wrong	1972	—	2.50	5.00
74-0839	When I'm With You/You've Chosen Me	1972	—	2.50	5.00
VEE JAY					
423	Secret Love/Real Gone Mama	1962	6.25	12.50	25.00

7-Inch Extended Plays

Number	Title (A Side/B Side)	Yr	VG	VG+	NM
CHESS					
5122	(contents unknown)	1959	62.50	125.00	250.00
5122 [PS]	Look! It's the Moonglows	1959	62.50	125.00	250.00
5123	True Love/Penny Arcade//I'll Stop Waiting/Sweeter Than Words	1959	62.50	125.00	250.00
5123 [PS]	Look! It's the Moonglows, Vol. 2	1959	62.50	125.00	250.00

Albums

Number	Title (A Side/B Side)	Yr	VG	VG+	NM
CHESS					
LP 1430 [M]	Look! It's the Moonglows	1959	125.00	250.00	500.00
LP 1471 [M]	The Best of Bobby Lester & the Moonglows	1962	75.00	150.00	300.00
—Black label					
LP 1471 [M]	The Best of Bobby Lester & the Moonglows	1966	12.50	25.00	50.00
—Blue, fading to white label					
CH-9111	Their Greatest Sides	1986	3.00	6.00	12.00
CH-9193	Look! It's the Moonglows	1987	3.00	6.00	12.00
—Reissue of 1430					
CONSTELLATION					
C-2 [M]	Collectors Showcase — The Moonglows	1964	25.00	50.00	100.00
—Light blue lettering					
C-2 [M]	Collectors Showcase — The Moonglows	1964	12.50	25.00	50.00
—Dark blue lettering					
LOST-NITE					
LP-23 [10]	The Moonglows	1981	3.00	6.00	12.00
RCA VICTOR					
LSP-4722	The Return of the Moonglows	1972	3.75	7.50	15.00

MOORE, BOB

45s

Number	Title (A Side/B Side)	Yr	VG	VG+	NM
HICKORY					
1357	Only the Lonely/Skokiaan	1965	—	3.00	6.00
1372	Hell's Angels/I Can't Stop Loving You	1966	—	3.00	6.00
1407	Spanish Eyes/Elephant Rock	1966	—	3.00	6.00
1426	Acapulco/Parade of the Matadors	1966	—	3.00	6.00
1437	A White Sport Coat/Amigo No. 1	1967	—	3.00	6.00
1480	The Fastest Guitar Alive/The River	1967	—	3.00	6.00
1521	You Sit Around All Day/Amigo No. 1	1968	—	3.00	6.00
MONUMENT					
406	Theme from My Three Sons/Mais Oui	1959	3.75	7.50	15.00
437	Theme from My Three Sons/Mais Oui	1961	2.50	5.00	10.00
446	Mexico/Hot Spot	1961	2.00	4.00	8.00
457	Auf Wiederseh'n Marlene/Ooh La La	1962	2.00	4.00	8.00
800	Flea Circus/Autumn Souvenirs	1962	2.00	4.00	8.00
814	Kentucky/Flowers of Florence	1963	2.00	4.00	8.00
834	Cologne/Hooten Trumpet	1964	2.00	4.00	8.00

Albums

Number	Title (A Side/B Side)	Yr	VG	VG+	NM
HICKORY					
LP-131 [M]	Viva Bob Moore	1965	3.75	7.50	15.00
LPS-131 [S]	Viva Bob Moore	1965	5.00	10.00	20.00
MONUMENT					
MLP-4005 [M]	Mexico and Other Great Hits!	1961	5.00	10.00	20.00
SLP-4005 [S]	Mexico and Other Great Hits!	1961	6.25	12.50	25.00
MLP-8008 [M]	Mexico	1967	3.00	6.00	12.00
SLP-18008 [S]	Mexico	1967	3.75	7.50	15.00

MOORE, BOBBY, AND THE RHYTHM ACES

45s

Number	Title (A Side/B Side)	Yr	VG	VG+	NM
CHECKER					
1129	Searching for My Love/Hey Mr. D.J.	1966	3.75	7.50	15.00
—Maroon label, vertical "Checker"					
1129	Searching for My Love/Hey Mr. D.J.	1966	2.50	5.00	10.00
—Blue label					
1156	Try My Love Again/Go Ahead and Burn Baby	1966	2.50	5.00	10.00
1180	Reaching Out/Chained to Your Heart	1967	2.50	5.00	10.00

Albums

Number	Title (A Side/B Side)	Yr	VG	VG+	NM
CHECKER					
LP-3000 [M]	Searching for My Love	1966	7.50	15.00	30.00
LPS-3000 [R]	Searching for My Love	1966	5.00	10.00	20.00

MOORE, DUDLEY

Albums

Number	Title (A Side/B Side)	Yr	VG	VG+	NM
ATLANTIC					
1403 [M]	Beyond the Fringe and All That Jazz	1963	6.25	12.50	25.00
SD 1403 [S]	Beyond the Fringe and All That Jazz	1963	7.50	15.00	30.00
LONDON					
PS 558	Dudley Moore Trio	1969	6.25	12.50	25.00

MOORE, HARV

45s

Number	Title (A Side/B Side)	Yr	VG	VG+	NM
AMERICAN ARTS					
20	Interview of the Fab Four/I Feel So Fine	1964	75.00	150.00	300.00

MOORE, JACKIE

12-Inch Singles

Number	Title (A Side/B Side)	Yr	VG	VG+	NM
COLUMBIA					
10994	This Time Baby/Let's Go Somewhere and Make Love	1979	2.50	5.00	10.00
11136	How's Your Love Life Baby/(Instrumental)	1979	2.50	5.00	10.00
11293	With Your Love/Helpless	1980	2.50	5.00	10.00
DIVA					
004	This Old Heart of Mine (4 versions)	198?	2.00	4.00	8.00
SUNNYVIEW					
421	Love Is the Answer (4:23) (6:03)	1985	—	3.00	6.00

45s

Number	Title (A Side/B Side)	Yr	VG	VG+	NM
ATLANTIC					
2681	Precious Precious/Will Power	1969	—	2.50	5.00
2798	Sometimes It's Got to Rain (In Your Love Life)/Wonderful Marvelous	1971	—	2.50	5.00
2830	Time/Cover Me	1971	—	2.50	5.00
2861	Darling Baby/Something in a Love	1972	—	2.50	5.00
2902	It Ain't Who You Know/They Tell Me of an Uncloudy Day	1972	—	2.50	5.00
2956	Sweet Charlie Babe/If	1973	—	2.50	5.00
2989	Both Ends Against the Middle/Clean Up Your Own Yard	1973	—	2.50	5.00
CATAWBA					
1010	Holding Back/(B-side unknown)	1983	—	2.00	4.00
COLUMBIA					
04599	This Time Baby/Let's Go Somewhere and Make Love	1984	—	—	3.00
10779	Personally/Ain't No Trouble Like Love Trouble	1978	—	2.00	4.00
10993	This Time Baby/Let's Go Somewhere and Make Love	1979	—	2.00	4.00
11140	How's Your Love Life Baby/Do Ya Got What It Takes	1979	—	2.00	4.00
11288	Helpless/With Your Love	1980	—	2.00	4.00
11363	Love Won't Let Me Wait/With Your Love	1980	—	2.00	4.00
KAYVETTE					
5122	Make Me Feel Like a Woman/Singin' Funky Music Turns Me On	1975	—	2.50	5.00
5124	Puttin' It Down to You/Never Is Forever	1975	—	2.50	5.00
5125	It's Harder to Leave/(B-side unknown)	1976	—	2.50	5.00
5127	Disco Body (Shake It to the East, Shake It to the West)/Tired of Hiding	1976	—	2.50	5.00
5129	Make Me Yours/Somebody Loves You	1977	—	2.50	5.00
5139	Heart Be Still/Singin' Funky Music Turns Me On	1981	—	2.00	4.00
5140	Who's Next/Singin' Funky Music Turns Me On	1981	—	2.00	4.00
SHOUT					
232	Dear John/Here I Am	1968	2.00	4.00	8.00
239	Why Don't You Call on Me/(B-side unknown)	1968	2.00	4.00	8.00

Albums

Number	Title (A Side/B Side)	Yr	VG	VG+	NM
ATLANTIC					
SD 7285	Sweet Charlie Babe	1973	3.75	7.50	15.00
COLUMBIA					
JC 35991	On My Way	1979	2.50	5.00	10.00
JC 36455	With Your Love	1980	2.50	5.00	10.00
KAYVETTE					
801	Make Me Feel Like a Woman	1975	3.75	7.50	15.00

MOORE, LATTIE

45s

Number	Title (A Side/B Side)	Yr	VG	VG+	NM
ARC					
8005	Juke Joint Johnny/Pretty Woman Blues	1952	37.50	75.00	150.00
KING					
4955	100,000 Women Can't Be Wrong/Lonesome Man Blues	1956	12.50	25.00	50.00
5370	Cajun Doll/Mine Again	1960	10.00	20.00	40.00
5413	Driving Nails/Drunk Again	1960	3.75	7.50	15.00
5526	Sundown and Sorrow/If the Good Lord's Willing	1961	3.75	7.50	15.00
5685	I Told You So/Heaven All Around Me	1962	3.75	7.50	15.00
5723	Out of Control/Just About Then	1963	3.00	6.00	12.00
5762	Honky Tonk Heaven/Lonesome Man Blues	1963	3.00	6.00	12.00
SPEED					
101	Juke Joint Johnny/(B-side unknown)	1952	50.00	100.00	200.00
STARDAY					
403	You Never Looked Sweeter/Why Did You Lie to Me	1958	6.25	12.50	25.00
441	Too Hot to Handle/Just a-Waitin'	1959	6.25	12.50	25.00

Albums

Number	Title (A Side/B Side)	Yr	VG	VG+	NM
AUDIO LAB					
AL-1555 [M]	The Best of Lattie Moore	1960	50.00	100.00	200.00
AL-1573 [M]	Country Side	1962	37.50	75.00	150.00
DERBYTOWN					
102 [M]	Lattie Moore	196?	10.00	20.00	40.00

MOORE, MELBA

12-Inch Singles

Number	Title (A Side/B Side)	Yr	VG	VG+	NM
CAPITOL					
8543	Mind Up Tonight (Extended) (Instrumental)	1982	—	3.00	6.00
8586	Love Me Right (Extended) (Instrumental)	1983	—	3.00	6.00
8627	Read My Lips/Got to Have Your Love	1985	2.00	4.00	8.00
8647	When You Love Me Like This/Winner (Instrumental Edit)	1985	—	3.00	6.00
SPRO-9335/6 [DJ]	Read My Lips (Special Mix) (Single Version)	1985	—	3.00	6.00
SPRO-9381/2 [DJ]	Read My Lips (Remix) (Extended Version)	1985	—	3.00	6.00
SPRO-9446/7 [DJ]	When You Love Me Like This (Club Mix) (Monster Groove Mix)	1985	2.00	4.00	8.00
SPRO-9500 [DJ]	I Can't Believe (It's Over) (Extended Version) (Edit Version)	1985	2.00	4.00	8.00
SPRO-9717 [DJ]	Love the One I'm With (5:44) (same on both sides)	1986	—	3.00	6.00
SPRO-9776 [DJ]	Love the One I'm With (3 versions)	1986	—	3.00	6.00
SPRO-9858/9980 [DJ]	Falling (Single Version) (LP Version)	1986	2.00	4.00	8.00
V-15236	Love the One I'm With (5:44)/Don't Go Away	1986	—	3.00	6.00

Number	Title (A Side/B Side)	Yr	VG	VG+	NM
V-15256	A Little Bit More (4:54) (4:15)/When We Touch	1986	—	3.00	6.00
—With Freddie Jackson					
V-15280	It's Been So Long (2 versions)/Don't Go Away	1987	—	3.00	6.00
V-15426	Love and Kisses (3 versions)/I'm in Love	1988	—	3.00	6.00
V-15561	Do You Really Want My Love (4 versions)	1990	—	3.00	6.00
EMI AMERICA					
SPRO-9817 [DJ]	Love's Comin' At Ya (7" Version) (LP Version)	1981	2.00	4.00	8.00
EPIC					
AS 660 [DJ]	Miss Thing (same on both sides)	1979	2.00	4.00	8.00
50665	Pick Me Up, I'll Dance/(Instrumental)	1979	3.00	6.00	12.00
50771	Miss Thing/Need Love	1979	3.00	6.00	12.00
50807	Hot and Tasty/Night People	1979	3.00	6.00	12.00

45s

Number	Title (A Side/B Side)	Yr	VG	VG+	NM
BUDDAH					
452	I Am His Lady/If I Lose You	1975	—	2.50	5.00
469	Natural Part of Everything/Must Be Dues	1975	—	2.50	5.00
496	Starting to Fall/Must Be Dues	1975	—	2.50	5.00
—With Jo Ellen Cohn					
519	This Is It/Stay Awhile	1976	—	2.50	5.00
519 [PS]	This Is It/Stay Awhile	1976	2.00	4.00	8.00
535	Lean On Me/One Less Morning	1976	—	2.50	5.00
562	The Way You Make Me Feel/So Many Mountains	1977	—	2.50	5.00
568	The Long and Winding Road/Ain't No Love Lost	1977	—	2.50	5.00
572	My Sensitive, Passionate Man/The Greatest Feeling	1977	—	2.50	5.00
589	Standing Right Here/Living Free	1977	—	2.50	5.00
596	I Don't Know No One Else to Turn To/Just Another Link	1978	—	2.50	5.00
CAPITOL					
B-5180	Mind Up Tonight/(Instrumental)	1982	—	—	3.00
B-5208	Underlove/(Instrumental)	1983	—	—	3.00
B-5288	Keepin' My Lover Satisfied/(Instrumental)	1983	—	—	3.00
B-5288 [PS]	Keepin' My Lover Satisfied/(Instrumental)	1983	—	2.00	4.00
B-5308	Livin' for Your Love/Got to Have Your Love	1984	—	—	3.00
B-5308 [PS]	Livin' for Your Love/Got to Have Your Love	1984	—	2.00	4.00
B-5343	Love Me Right/Never Say Never	1984	—	—	3.00
B-5343 [PS]	Love Me Right/Never Say Never	1984	—	2.00	4.00
B-5415	(Can't Take Half) All of You/Let Me Be Yours	1984	—	—	3.00
—With Lillo Thomas					
B-5415 [PS]	(Can't Take Half) All of You/Let Me Be Yours	1984	—	2.00	4.00
B-5437	Read My Lips/Got to Have Your Love	1985	—	—	3.00
B-5437 [PS]	Read My Lips/Got to Have Your Love	1985	—	2.00	4.00
B-5484	When You Love Me Like This/Winner	1985	—	—	3.00
B-5484 [PS]	When You Love Me Like This/Winner	1985	—	2.00	4.00
B-5520	I Can't Believe It (It's Over)/King of No Heart	1985	—	—	3.00
B-5577	Love the One I'm With (A Lot of Love)/Don't Go Away	1986	—	—	3.00
—With Kashif					
B-5577 [PS]	Love the One I'm With (A Lot of Love)/Don't Go Away	1986	—	—	3.00
B-5632	A Little Bit More/When We Touch	1986	—	—	3.00
—A-side with Freddie Jackson					
B-5651	Falling/(B-side unknown)	1986	—	—	3.00
B-5681	It's Been So Long/Don't Go Away	1987	—	—	3.00
B-5681 [PS]	It's Been So Long/Don't Go Away	1987	—	—	3.00
B-44012	I'm Not Gonna Let You Go/Dreams	1987	—	—	3.00
B-44012 [PS]	I'm Not Gonna Let You Go/Dreams	1987	—	—	3.00
B-44148	I Can't Complain/There I Go Falling in Love Again	1988	—	—	3.00
—A-side with Freddie Jackson					
B-44148 [PS]	I Can't Complain/There I Go Falling in Love Again	1988	—	—	3.00
B-44195	I'm in Love/Stay	1988	—	—	3.00
—With Kashif					
B-44195 [PS]	I'm in Love/Stay	1988	—	—	3.00
B-44265	Love and Kisses/I'm in Love	1988	—	—	3.00
EMI AMERICA					
8092	Take My Love/Just You, Just Me	1981	—	2.00	4.00
8104	Let's Stand Together/What a Woman Needs	1981	—	2.00	4.00
8114	Piece of the Rock/(Instrumental)	1982	—	2.00	4.00
8126	Love's Comin' At Ya/(Instrumental)	1982	—	2.00	4.00
EPIC					
50600	You Stepped Into My Life/There's No Other Like You	1978	—	2.00	4.00
50663	Pick Me Up, I'll Dance/Where Did You Ever Go	1979	—	2.00	4.00
50762	Miss Thing/Need Love	1979	—	2.00	4.00
50805	Hot and Tasty/Night People	1979	—	2.00	4.00
50909	Everything So Good About You/Next to You	1980	—	2.00	4.00
50954	Rest Inside My Love/Something on My Mind	1980	—	2.00	4.00
MERCURY					
72942	I Messed Up a Good Thing/I'll Do It All Over Again	1969	2.00	4.00	8.00
72989	We're Living to Give (Each Other)/(B-side unknown)	1969	2.00	4.00	8.00
73040	Time and Love/(B-side unknown)	1970	2.00	4.00	8.00
73072	I Got Love/I Love Making Love to You	1970	2.00	4.00	8.00
73134	Look What You're Doing to the Man/Patience Is Rewarded	1970	2.00	4.00	8.00
73183	If I Had a Million/Loving You Comes So Easy	1971	2.00	4.00	8.00
73217	He Ain't Heavy, He's My Brother/Take Up a Course in Happiness	1971	2.00	4.00	8.00
73289	Love Letters/I Ain't Got to Love Nobody Else	1972	2.00	4.00	8.00
MUSICOR					
1189	Does Love Believe in Me/Don't Cry, Sing Along with the Music	1966	2.50	5.00	10.00

Albums

Number	Title (A Side/B Side)	Yr	VG	VG+	NM
ACCORD					
SN-7129	Sweet Melba	1981	2.50	5.00	10.00
BUDDAH					
BDS-5629	Peach Melba	1975	2.50	5.00	10.00
BDS-5657	This Is It	1976	2.50	5.00	10.00
BDS-5677	Melba	1976	2.50	5.00	10.00
BDS-5695	Portrait of Melba Moore	1977	2.50	5.00	10.00
BDS-5720	Dancin' with Melba	1979	2.50	5.00	10.00
CAPITOL					
ST-12243	The Other Side of the Rainbow	1982	2.50	5.00	10.00
ST-12305	Never Say Never	1983	2.50	5.00	10.00
ST-12382	Read My Lips	1985	2.50	5.00	10.00
ST-12471	A Lot of Love	1986	2.50	5.00	10.00
C1-92355	Soul Exposed	1990	3.00	6.00	12.00
EMI AMERICA					
ST-17060	What a Woman Needs	1981	2.50	5.00	10.00
EPIC					
JE 35507	Melba	1978	2.50	5.00	10.00
JE 36128	Burn	1979	2.50	5.00	10.00
JE 36412	Closer	1980	2.50	5.00	10.00
MERCURY					
SRM-1-622	Live!	1972	3.00	6.00	12.00
SR-61255	Living to Give	1970	3.75	7.50	15.00
SR-61287	I Got Love	1970	3.75	7.50	15.00
SR-61321	Look What You're Doing to the Man	1971	3.75	7.50	15.00

MOORE, MELVIN

45s

Number	Title (A Side/B Side)	Yr	VG	VG+	NM
KING					
4539	Possessed/Hold Me, Kiss Me, Squeeze Me	1952	25.00	50.00	100.00

MOORE, RUDY

45s

Number	Title (A Side/B Side)	Yr	VG	VG+	NM
FEDERAL					
12253	My Little Angel/I'm Mad with You	1956	12.50	25.00	50.00
12259	The Buggy Ride/Ring-a-Ling-Dong	1956	12.50	25.00	50.00
12276	Step It Up and Go/Let Me Come Home	1956	25.00	50.00	100.00
12280	Bobbie Dobbie/I'll Be Home to See You Tomorrow Night	1956	12.50	25.00	50.00

MOORE, SAM

Also see SAM AND DAVE.

45s

Number	Title (A Side/B Side)	Yr	VG	VG+	NM
ATLANTIC					
2762	Give You Plenty Lovin'/Tennessee Waltz	1970	—	3.00	6.00
2791	Keep On Sockin' It To Me/Stop	1971	—	3.00	6.00
2814	Shop Around/If I Should Lose Your Love	1971	—	3.00	6.00

MOORE, SCOTTY

Original guitarist in ELVIS PRESLEY's backup band.

45s

Number	Title (A Side/B Side)	Yr	VG	VG+	NM
FERNWOOD					
107	Have Guitar Will Travel/Rest	1958	7.50	15.00	30.00

Albums

Number	Title (A Side/B Side)	Yr	VG	VG+	NM
EPIC					
LN 24103 [M]	The Guitar That Changed the World	1964	20.00	40.00	80.00
BN 26103 [S]	The Guitar That Changed the World	1964	25.00	50.00	100.00
GUINNESS					
GNS-36038	What's Left	1977	3.75	7.50	15.00

MOORE, TIM

45s

Number	Title (A Side/B Side)	Yr	VG	VG+	NM
A SMALL RECORD COMPANY					
0601	Second Avenue/(B-side unknown)	1974	2.50	5.00	10.00
ABC DUNHILL					
4337	Fool Like You/Thinking About You	1973	—	2.50	5.00
ASYLUM					
45208	Second Avenue/Aviation Man	1974	—	2.00	4.00
45214	Charmer/I'll Be Your Time	1974	—	2.00	4.00
45214 [PS]	Charmer/I'll Be Your Time	1974	—	3.00	6.00
45265	If Somebody Needs It/Sweet Navel Lightning	1975	—	2.00	4.00
45276	Rock and Roll Love Letter/Sweet Navel Lightning	1975	—	2.00	4.00
45287	Lay Down the Line to Me/Sweet Navel Lightning	1975	—	2.00	4.00
45394	In the Middle/Strengthen My Love	1977	—	2.00	4.00
45427	Second Avenue/Strengthen My Love	1977	—	2.00	4.00
46047	Fallen Angel/Crisis in the Finyard	1979	—	2.00	4.00

Albums

Number	Title (A Side/B Side)	Yr	VG	VG+	NM
A SMALL RECORD COMPANY					
SRS-10001	Tim Moore	1974	7.50	15.00	30.00
ABC DUNHILL					
DSX-50132	Of Woodstock and Other Places	1973	3.00	6.00	12.00
ASYLUM					
6E-179	High Contrast	1979	2.50	5.00	10.00
7E-1019	Tim Moore	1974	2.50	5.00	10.00
7E-1042	Behind the Eyes	1975	2.50	5.00	10.00
7E-1088	White Shadows	1977	2.50	5.00	10.00
ELEKTRA					
60463	Flash Forward	1985	2.50	5.00	10.00

MORGAN, JANE

45s

Number	Title (A Side/B Side)	Yr	VG	VG+	NM
ABC					
10969	Somebody Someplace/This Is My World Without You	1967	—	3.00	6.00
11002	Him's a Dope/I Promise You	1967	—	3.00	6.00
11024	The Marvelous Toy/Smile	1967	—	3.00	6.00
11034	Masquerade/Smile	1968	—	2.50	5.00
11054	My Funny Valentine/A Child	1968	—	2.50	5.00
11092	Look What You've Done to Me/There's Nothing Else in My Mind	1968	—	2.50	5.00
COLPIX					
713	Does Goodnight Mean Goodbye/Bless 'Em All	1963	2.00	4.00	8.00
713 [PS]	Does Goodnight Mean Goodbye/Bless 'Em All	1963	3.00	6.00	12.00
727	Frum Russia with Love/The Song from Moulin Rouge (Where Is Your Heart)	1964	2.00	4.00	8.00
734	C'est Si Bon/Once Upon a Summertime	1964	2.00	4.00	8.00
754	Dominique/Funny World	1964	2.00	4.00	8.00
755	The Poor People of Paris/Funny World	1964	2.00	4.00	8.00
761	After the Fall/Oh, How I Lie	1965	2.00	4.00	8.00
EPIC					
9819	Maybe/Walking the Streets in the Rain	1965	2.00	4.00	8.00
9847	Side by Side/Till I Waltz Again with You	1965	2.00	4.00	8.00

Number	Title (A Side/B Side)	Yr	VG	VG+	NM
9881	Little Hands/Everyone Come to My Party	1965	2.00	4.00	8.00
10012	I Will Wait for You/Love Me True	1966	—	3.00	6.00
10032	Kiss Away/1-2-3	1966	—	3.00	6.00
10058	Elusive Butterfly/Good Lovin'	1966	—	3.00	6.00
10113	Kiss Tomorrow Goodbye/Now and Forever	1966	—	3.00	6.00
10159	The Three Bells/I Want to Be with You	1967	—	3.00	6.00
KAPP					
KJB-14	Fascination/The Day the Rains Came	196?	—	3.00	6.00
—"Winners Circle Series" reissue					
KJB-14 [PS]	Fascination/The Day the Rains Came	196?	2.50	5.00	10.00
104	Baseball, Baseball/Fairweather Friends	1954	3.75	7.50	15.00
111	I Try to Forget You/Why Don't They Leave Us Alone	1955	3.00	6.00	12.00
115	Flyin' High/Give Me Your World	1955	3.00	6.00	12.00
121	In Paree/Take Me Away	1955	3.00	6.00	12.00
140	Let's Go Steady/Take Care	1956	3.00	6.00	12.00
148	La Ronde/Midnight Blues	1956	3.00	6.00	12.00
161	Two Different Worlds/Nights in Verona	1956	2.50	5.00	10.00
—With Roger Williams					
172	Come Home, Come Home, Come Home/From the First Hello to Our Last Goodbye	1957	2.50	5.00	10.00
185	It's Not for Me to Say/Around the World	1957	2.50	5.00	10.00
191	Fascination/(Instrumental)	1957	2.50	5.00	10.00
191 [PS]	Fascination/(Instrumental)	1957	5.00	10.00	20.00
200	It's Been a Long, Long Time/I'm New at the Game of Romance	1957	2.50	5.00	10.00
214	Only One Love/I've Got Bells on My Heart	1958	2.50	5.00	10.00
221	Enchanted Island/Once More, My Love, Once More	1958	2.50	5.00	10.00
235	The Day the Rains Came/The Day the Rains Came (French Version)	1958	2.50	5.00	10.00
236	You'll Never Walk Alone/I May Never Pass This Way Again	1958	2.50	5.00	10.00
253	To Love and Be Loved/If Only I Could Live My Life Again	1958	2.50	5.00	10.00
264	To Each His Own/Love Is Like Champagne	1959	2.50	5.00	10.00
284	With Open Arms/I Can't Begin to Tell You	1959	2.50	5.00	10.00
284 [PS]	With Open Arms/I Can't Begin to Tell You	1959	3.75	7.50	15.00
304	I'm in Love/Was It Day, Was It Night	1959	2.50	5.00	10.00
305	Happy Anniversary/C'est La Vie, C'est L'Amour	1959	2.50	5.00	10.00
305 [PS]	Happy Anniversary/C'est La Vie, C'est L'Amour	1959	3.75	7.50	15.00
317	The Bells of St. Mary's/Ballad of Lady Jane	1960	2.50	5.00	10.00
332	I Am a Heart/Romantica	1960	2.50	5.00	10.00
351	Lord and Master/Where's the Boy (I Never Met)	1960	2.50	5.00	10.00
358	The Angry Sea/Somebody	1960	2.50	5.00	10.00
369	Jerusalem/Jerusalem (French Version)	1961	2.00	4.00	8.00
390	Love Makes the World Go 'Round/He Makes Me Feel I'm Lonely	1961	2.00	4.00	8.00
418	It Takes Love/Homesick for New England	1961	2.00	4.00	8.00
431	Moon River/Blue Hawaii	1961	2.00	4.00	8.00
450	What Now My Love/Forever My Love	1962	2.00	4.00	8.00
478	Ask Me to Dance/Waiting for Charlie to Come Home	1962	2.00	4.00	8.00
RCA VICTOR					
47-9727	Congratulations, I Guess/All of My Laughter	1969	—	2.50	5.00
47-9839	A Girl Named Johnny Cash/Charley	1970	—	2.50	5.00
47-9901	First Day/I'm Only a Woman	1970	—	2.50	5.00
74-0153	Marry Me, Marry Me/Three Rest Stops	1969	—	2.50	5.00
74-0194	Traces/Where Do I Go	1969	—	2.50	5.00
74-0316	He Gives Me Love/He's Never Too Busy	1970	—	2.50	5.00
74-0395	Jamie Boy/Things of Life	1970	—	2.50	5.00
7-Inch Extended Plays					
EPIC					
5-26166 [PS]	In My Style	1965	2.50	5.00	10.00
5-26166 [S]	I'm Sorry/You Belong to Me/Downtown//Fascination/Why Don't You Believe Me/We'll Sing in the Sunshine	1965	2.50	5.00	10.00
—33 1/3 rpm, small hole, "For Jukebox Use Only"					
KAPP					
KE-758	The Day the Rains Came/Volare//It's All in the Game/Everybody Loves a Lover	1958	3.75	7.50	15.00
KE-758 [PS]	Jane Morgan	1958	3.75	7.50	15.00
Albums					
ABC					
S-638	The Happening	1968	3.00	6.00	12.00
COLPIX					
CP 497 [M]	The Jane Morgan Album	1966	3.75	7.50	15.00
SCP 497 [S]	The Jane Morgan Album	1966	5.00	10.00	20.00
EPIC					
LN 24166 [M]	In My Style	1965	3.00	6.00	12.00
LN 24190 [M]	Today's Hits...Tomorrow's Golden Favorites	1966	3.00	6.00	12.00
LN 24211 [M]	Fresh Flavor	1966	3.00	6.00	12.00
LN 24247 [M]	Kiss Tomorrow Goodbye	1967	3.75	7.50	15.00
BN 26166 [S]	In My Style	1965	3.75	7.50	15.00
BN 26190 [S]	Today's Hits...Tomorrow's Golden Favorites	1966	3.75	7.50	15.00
BN 26211 [S]	Fresh Flavor	1966	3.75	7.50	15.00
BN 26247 [S]	Kiss Tomorrow Goodbye	1967	3.00	6.00	12.00
HARMONY					
HS 11398	Sounds of Silence	1970	2.50	5.00	10.00
KAPP					
KJM-1 [DJ]	Radio Station Sampler	196?	—	—	—
—Promo only, gatefold cover					
KL-1023 [M]	Jane Morgan	1956	7.50	15.00	30.00
KL-1066 [M]	Fascination	1957	7.50	15.00	30.00
KL-1080 [M]	All the Way	1958	7.50	15.00	30.00
KL-1089S [S]	Something Old, New, Borrowed, Blue	1958	10.00	20.00	40.00
KL-1089 [M]	Something Old, New, Borrowed, Blue	1958	7.50	15.00	30.00
KL-1093 [M]	Jane Morgan	1958	7.50	15.00	30.00
KL-1105S [S]	The Day the Rains Came	1958	10.00	20.00	40.00
KL-1105 [M]	The Day the Rains Came	1958	7.50	15.00	30.00
KL-1129 [M]	Jane in Spain	1959	6.25	12.50	25.00
KL-1170 [M]	Jane Morgan Time	1959	5.00	10.00	20.00
KL-1191 [M]	Ballads of Lady Jane	1960	3.75	7.50	15.00
KL-1239 [M]	Second Time Around	1961	3.75	7.50	15.00

Number	Title (A Side/B Side)	Yr	VG	VG+	NM
KL-1246 [M]	The Great Golden Hits	1961	3.75	7.50	15.00
KL-1247 [M]	Big Hits from Broadway	1961	3.75	7.50	15.00
KL-1250 [M]	Love Makes the World Go 'Round	1961	3.75	7.50	15.00
KL-1268 [M]	Jane Morgan at the Cocoanut Grove	1962	3.75	7.50	15.00
KL-1275 [M]	More Golden Hits	1962	3.75	7.50	15.00
KL-1296 [M]	What Now My Love	1962	3.75	7.50	15.00
KL-1329 [M]	Jane Morgan's Greatest Hits	1963	3.00	6.00	12.00
KS-3001 [S]	Broadway in Stereo	1959	7.50	15.00	30.00
KS-3014 [S]	Jane in Spain	1959	7.50	15.00	30.00
KS-3017 [S]	Fascination	1959	7.50	15.00	30.00
KS-3054 [S]	Jane Morgan Time	1959	6.25	12.50	25.00
KS-3066 [S]	Fascination	1962	5.00	10.00	20.00
KS-3191 [S]	Ballads of Lady Jane	1960	5.00	10.00	20.00
KS-3239 [S]	Second Time Around	1961	5.00	10.00	20.00
KS-3246 [S]	The Great Golden Hits	1961	5.00	10.00	20.00
KS-3247 [S]	Big Hits from Broadway	1961	5.00	10.00	20.00
KS-3250 [S]	Love Makes the World Go 'Round	1961	5.00	10.00	20.00
KS-3268 [S]	Jane Morgan at the Cocoanut Grove	1962	5.00	10.00	20.00
KS-3275 [S]	More Golden Hits	1962	5.00	10.00	20.00
KS-3296 [S]	What Now My Love	1962	5.00	10.00	20.00
KS-3329 [S]	Jane Morgan's Greatest Hits	1963	3.75	7.50	15.00
UXL-5006 [(2) M]	Great Songs from the Great Shows of the Century	195?	10.00	20.00	40.00
MCA					
537	Jane Morgan's Greatest Hits	197?	2.50	5.00	10.00
RCA VICTOR					
LSP-4171	Traces of Love	1969	3.00	6.00	12.00
LSP-4322	Jane Morgan in Nashville	1970	3.00	6.00	12.00

MORGAN, LEE

Number	Title (A Side/B Side)	Yr	VG	VG+	NM
45s					
BLUE NOTE					
1661	Gaza Strip/Reggie of Chester	195?	3.00	6.00	12.00
1692	A Night in Tunisia, Part 1/A Night in Tunisia, Part 2	1957	3.00	6.00	12.00
1911	The Sidewinder, Part 1/The Sidewinder, Part 2	1964	2.00	4.00	8.00
1918	The Rumproller, Part 1/The Rumproller, Part 2	1966	2.00	4.00	8.00
1930	Cornbread, Part 1/Cornbread, Part 2	1967	2.00	4.00	8.00
1947	Hey Chico/Sweet Honey Bee	1968	2.00	4.00	8.00
1951	Midnight Cowboy/Popi	1969	2.00	4.00	8.00
VEE JAY					
360	I'm a Fool to Want You/Terrible "T"	1960	3.00	6.00	12.00
401	Expoobedient/Just in Time	1961	3.00	6.00	12.00
Albums					
BLUE NOTE					
BN-LA224-G	Memorial Album	1974	3.75	7.50	15.00
BN-LA582-J2 [(2)]	Procrastinator	1977	3.75	7.50	15.00
LT-987	Sonic Boom	1979	3.00	6.00	12.00
LT-1031	Taru	1980	3.00	6.00	12.00
LT-1058	Tom Cat	1980	3.00	6.00	12.00
LT-1091	Infinity	1981	3.00	6.00	12.00
BLP-1538 [M]	Lee Morgan Indeed!	1957	62.50	125.00	250.00
—"Deep groove" version (deep indentation under label on both sides)					
BLP-1538 [M]	Lee Morgan Indeed!	1957	50.00	100.00	200.00
—Regular edition, Lexington Ave. address on label					
BLP-1538 [M]	Lee Morgan Indeed!	1963	6.25	12.50	25.00
—"New York, USA" address on label					
BLP-1541 [M]	Lee Morgan, Volume 2	1957	62.50	125.00	250.00
—"Deep groove" version (deep indentation under label on both sides)					
BLP-1541 [M]	Lee Morgan, Volume 2	1957	50.00	100.00	200.00
—Regular edition, Lexington Ave. address on label					
BLP-1541 [M]	Lee Morgan, Volume 2	1963	6.25	12.50	25.00
—"New York, USA" address on label					
BLP-1557 [M]	Lee Morgan, Volume 3	1957	37.50	75.00	150.00
—"Deep groove" version (deep indentation under label on both sides)					
BLP-1557 [M]	Lee Morgan, Volume 3	1957	25.00	50.00	100.00
—Regular edition, W. 63rd St. address on label					
BLP-1557 [M]	Lee Morgan, Volume 3	1963	6.25	12.50	25.00
—"New York, USA" address on label					
BLP-1575 [M]	City Lights	1958	37.50	75.00	150.00
—"Deep groove" version (deep indentation under label on both sides)					
BLP-1575 [M]	City Lights	1958	25.00	50.00	100.00
—Regular edition, W. 63rd St. address on label					
BLP-1575 [M]	City Lights	1963	6.25	12.50	25.00
—"New York, USA" address on label					
BST-1575 [S]	City Lights	1959	25.00	50.00	100.00
—"Deep groove" version (deep indentation under label on both sides)					
BST-1575 [S]	City Lights	1959	20.00	40.00	80.00
—Regular edition, W. 63rd St. address on label					
BST-1575 [S]	City Lights	1963	5.00	10.00	20.00
—"New York, USA" address on label					
BLP-1578 [M]	The Cooker	1958	37.50	75.00	150.00
—"Deep groove" version (deep indentation under label on both sides)					
BLP-1578 [M]	The Cooker	1958	25.00	50.00	100.00
—Regular edition, W. 63rd St. address on label					
BLP-1578 [M]	The Cooker	1963	6.25	12.50	25.00
—"New York, USA" address on label					
BST-1578 [S]	The Cooker	1959	25.00	50.00	100.00
—"Deep groove" version (deep indentation under label on both sides)					
BST-1578 [S]	The Cooker	1959	20.00	40.00	80.00
—Regular edition, W. 63rd St. address on label					
BST-1578 [S]	The Cooker	1963	5.00	10.00	20.00
—"New York, USA" address on label					
BLP-1590 [M]	Candy	1958	37.50	75.00	150.00
—"Deep groove" version (deep indentation under label on both sides)					
BLP-1590 [M]	Candy	1958	25.00	50.00	100.00
—Regular edition, W. 63rd St. address on label					
BLP-1590 [M]	Candy	1963	6.25	12.50	25.00
—"New York, USA" address on label					
BST-1590 [S]	Candy	1959	25.00	50.00	100.00
—"Deep groove" version (deep indentation under label on both sides)					
BST-1590 [S]	Candy	1959	20.00	40.00	80.00
—Regular edition, W. 63rd St. address on label					
BST-1590 [S]	Candy	1963	5.00	10.00	20.00
—"New York, USA" address on label					
BLP-4034 [M]	Lee-Way	1960	30.00	60.00	120.00
—"Deep groove" version (deep indentation under label on both sides)					

Number	Title (A Side/B Side)	Yr	VG	VG+	NM
BLP-4034 [M]	Lee-Way	1960	20.00	40.00	80.00
—Regular edition, W. 63rd St. address on label					
BLP-4034 [M]	Lee-Way	1963	6.25	12.50	25.00
—"New York, USA" address on label					
BLP-4157 [M]	The Sidewinder	1964	7.50	15.00	30.00
BLP-4169 [M]	Search for the New Land	1965	7.50	15.00	30.00
BLP-4199 [M]	The Rumproller	1966	7.50	15.00	30.00
BLP-4212 [M]	The Gigolo	1966	7.50	15.00	30.00
BLP-4222 [M]	Cornbread	1967	7.50	15.00	30.00
BLP-4243 [M]	Delightfulee Morgan	1967	10.00	20.00	40.00
LN-10075	The Sidewinder	1981	2.50	5.00	10.00
—Budget-line reissue					
B1-32089	Lee-Way	1995	3.75	7.50	15.00
B1-33579	The Procrastinator	1995	3.75	7.50	15.00
B1-46137	The Sidewinder	1997	3.75	7.50	15.00
BST-81578 [S]	The Cooker	1968	3.00	6.00	12.00
—"A Division of Liberty Records" on label					
BST-84034 [S]	Lee-Way	1960	12.50	25.00	50.00
—Regular edition, W. 63rd St. address on label					
BST-84034 [S]	Lee-Way	1963	5.00	10.00	20.00
—"New York, USA" address on label					
BST-84034 [S]	Lee-Way	1968	3.00	6.00	12.00
—"A Division of Liberty Records" on label					
BST-84157	The Sidewinder	1985	2.50	5.00	10.00
—"The Finest in Jazz Since 1939" reissue					
BST-84157 [S]	The Sidewinder	1964	10.00	20.00	40.00
—"New York, USA" address on label					
BST-84157 [S]	The Sidewinder	1968	3.00	6.00	12.00
—"A Division of Liberty Records" on label					
BST-84169 [S]	Search for the New Land	1965	10.00	20.00	40.00
—"New York, USA" address on label					
BST-84169 [S]	Search for the New Land	1968	3.00	6.00	12.00
—"A Division of Liberty Records" on label					
BST-84199 [S]	The Rumproller	1966	10.00	20.00	40.00
—"New York, USA" address on label					
BST-84199 [S]	The Rumproller	1968	3.00	6.00	12.00
—"A Division of Liberty Records" on label					
BST-84212	The Gigolo	1986	2.50	5.00	10.00
—"The Finest in Jazz Since 1939" reissue					
BST-84212 [S]	The Gigolo	1966	10.00	20.00	40.00
—"New York, USA" address on label					
BST-84212 [S]	The Gigolo	1968	3.00	6.00	12.00
—"A Division of Liberty Records" on label					
BST-84222 [S]	Cornbread	1967	10.00	20.00	40.00
—"New York, USA" address on label					
BST-84222 [S]	Cornbread	1968	3.00	6.00	12.00
—"A Division of Liberty Records" on label					
BST-84243	Delightfulee Morgan	198?	2.50	5.00	10.00
—"The Finest in Jazz Since 1939" reissue					
BST-84243 [S]	Delightfulee Morgan	1967	7.50	15.00	30.00
—"New York, USA" address on label					
BST-84243 [S]	Delightfulee Morgan	1968	3.00	6.00	12.00
—"A Division of Liberty Records" on label					
BST-84289	Caramba!	1969	6.25	12.50	25.00
BST-84312	Charisma	1969	6.25	12.50	25.00
BST-84335	The Sixth Sense	1969	6.25	12.50	25.00
BST-84426	The Rajah	1984	2.50	5.00	10.00
BST-84901 [(2)]	Lee Morgan	1972	5.00	10.00	20.00
BST-89906 [(2)]	Lee Morgan at the Lighthouse	1970	6.25	12.50	25.00
B1-91138	The Best of Lee Morgan	1988	3.00	6.00	12.00
FANTASY					
OJC-310	Take Twelve	198?	2.50	5.00	10.00
GNP CRESCENDO					
GNP-2079 [(2)]	Lee Morgan	1973	5.00	10.00	20.00
JAZZLAND					
JLP-80 [M]	Take Twelve	1962	7.50	15.00	30.00
JLP-980 [S]	Take Twelve	1962	10.00	20.00	40.00
MOSAIC					
MQ6-162 [(6)]	The Complete Blue Note Lee Morgan Fifties Sessions	199?	25.00	50.00	100.00
PRESTIGE					
2510	Take Twelve	198?	2.50	5.00	10.00
SAVOY					
MG-12091 [M]	Introducing Lee Morgan	1956	50.00	100.00	200.00
SUNSET					
SUS-5269	All the Way	1969	3.00	6.00	12.00
TRADITION					
2079	Genius	1969	3.00	6.00	12.00
TRIP					
5003 [(2)]	Two Sides of Lee Morgan	1974	3.75	7.50	15.00
5020	Speedball	1974	3.00	6.00	12.00
5029	One of a Kind	1974	3.00	6.00	12.00
5037	A Date with Lee	1974	3.00	6.00	12.00
5041 [(2)]	Live Sessions	1975	3.75	7.50	15.00
VEE JAY					
VJ-2508 [M]	Lee Morgan Quintet	1965	7.50	15.00	30.00
VJS-2508 [S]	Lee Morgan Quintet	1965	10.00	20.00	40.00
LP-3007 [M]	Here's Lee Morgan	1960	7.50	15.00	30.00
SR-3007 [S]	Here's Lee Morgan	1960	10.00	20.00	40.00
VJS-3007	Here's Lee Morgan	1986	3.00	6.00	12.00
—Reissue on reactivated label					
LP-3015 [M]	Expoobident	1960	7.50	15.00	30.00
SR-3015 [S]	Expoobident	1960	10.00	20.00	40.00
E-4000	Lee Morgan 1938-1972	198?	3.00	6.00	12.00

MORGAN, LOUMELL

45s

Number	Title (A Side/B Side)	Yr	VG	VG+	NM
ATLANTIC					
953	Charmaine/Jock-O-Mo	1952	50.00	100.00	200.00

MORGAN TWINS, THE

45s

Number	Title (A Side/B Side)	Yr	VG	VG+	NM
RCA VICTOR					
47-7300	TV Hop/This Feeling's Bound to Be Love	1958	6.25	12.50	25.00
47-7373	Let's Get Goin'/While It Lasted	1958	6.25	12.50	25.00

MORGEN

Number	Title (A Side/B Side)	Yr	VG	VG+	NM
45s					
PROBE					
474	Of Dreams/She's the Nighttime	1969	5.00	10.00	20.00
Albums					
PROBE					
CPLP-4507	Morgen	1969	37.50	75.00	150.00

MORLEY, COZY

Number	Title (A Side/B Side)	Yr	VG	VG+	NM
45s					
ABC-PARAMOUNT					
9811	I Love My Girl/Why Don't You Fall in Love	1957	6.25	12.50	25.00

MORLY GREY

Number	Title (A Side/B Side)	Yr	VG	VG+	NM
Albums					
STARSHINE					
69000	The Only Truth	1969	50.00	100.00	200.00

MORNING DEW, THE

Number	Title (A Side/B Side)	Yr	VG	VG+	NM
Albums					
ROULETTE					
SR-42049	The Morning Dew	1970	75.00	150.00	300.00

MORNING GLORY

Number	Title (A Side/B Side)	Yr	VG	VG+	NM
45s					
FONTANA					
1613	Need Someone/I See a Light	1968	2.50	5.00	10.00
Albums					
FONTANA					
SRF-67573	Two Suns Worth	1968	6.25	12.50	25.00

MORNINGLORY

Number	Title (A Side/B Side)	Yr	VG	VG+	NM
Albums					
TOYA					
STLP-003	Growing	1972	10.00	20.00	40.00

MORRIS, JOE

Number	Title (A Side/B Side)	Yr	VG	VG+	NM
45s					
ATLANTIC					
914	Any Time, Any Place, Any Where/Come Back Daddy Daddy	1950	125.00	250.00	500.00
—With Laura Tate...Atlantic's earliest number on 45. Morris had numerous 78s on Atlantic before 914, which are not listed here.					
985	I'm Goin' to Leave You/That's What Makes My Baby Fat	1953	25.00	50.00	100.00
1160	Going, Going, Gone/Sinner Woman	1957	5.00	10.00	20.00
HERALD					
420	Travelin' Man/No, It Can't Be Done	1954	10.00	20.00	40.00
—Black vinyl					
420	Travelin' Man/No, It Can't Be Done	1954	20.00	40.00	80.00
—Red vinyl					
446	Be Careful/Way Down Yonder	1955	7.50	15.00	30.00

MORRISON, VAN

Number	Title (A Side/B Side)	Yr	VG	VG+	NM
12-Inch Singles					
MERCURY					
447 [DJ]	Got to Go Back (same on both sides)	1986	—	3.00	6.00
WARNER BROS.					
PRO-A-755 [DJ]	Wavelength (6:07) (3:57)	1978	3.75	7.50	15.00
PRO-A-911 [DJ]	Summertime in England (Edit)/Haunts	1980	2.50	5.00	10.00
45s					
BANG					
545	Brown Eyed Girl/Goodbye, Baby	1967	3.00	6.00	12.00
552	Chick-a-Boom/Ro Ro Rosey	1967	2.50	5.00	10.00
585	Spanish Rose/Midnight Special	1971	2.00	4.00	8.00
MERCURY					
880669-7	Haunts of Ancient Peace/Tore Down A La Rimbaud	1985	—	2.00	4.00
884841-7	Ivory Tower/New Kind of Man	1986	—	2.00	4.00
PHILCO-FORD					
HP-16	Brown Eyed Girl/Midnight Special	1968	5.00	10.00	20.00
—4-inch plastic "Hip Pocket Record" with color sleeve					
POINTBLANK					
38655	Precious Time/Jackie Wilson Said (I'm in Heaven When You Smile) (Live)	1999	—	2.00	4.00
WARNER BROS.					
7383	Come Running/Crazy Love	1970	—	3.00	6.00
7434	Domino/Sweet Janine	1970	—	3.00	6.00
7462	Blue Money/Sweet Thing	1971	—	3.00	6.00
7488	Call Me Up in Dreamland/Street Choir	1971	—	3.00	6.00
7518	Wild Night/When That Evening Sun Goes Down	1971	—	3.00	6.00
7543	Tupelo Honey/Starting a New Life	1971	—	3.00	6.00
7573	Straight to My Heart Like a Cannonball/Old Old Woodstock	1972	—	2.50	5.00
7616	Jackie Wilson Said (I'm in Heaven When You Smile)/You've Got the Power	1972	—	2.50	5.00
7638	Redwood Tree/Saint Dominic's Preview	1972	—	2.50	5.00
7665	Gypsy/Saint Dominic's Preview	1972	—	2.50	5.00
7706	Warm Love/I Will Be There	1973	—	2.50	5.00
7744	Green/Wild Children	1973	—	2.50	5.00
7786	Gloria/(B-side unknown)	1973	—	2.50	5.00
7797	Ain't Nothin' You Can Do/Wild Children	1974	—	2.50	5.00
8029	Bulbs/Cul-De-Sac	1974	—	2.50	5.00
8411	Joyous Sound/Mechanical Bliss	1977	—	2.50	5.00
8450	Moondance/Cold Wind in August	1977	—	2.50	5.00
8661	Wavelength/Checkin' It Out	1978	—	2.50	5.00
8743	Lifetimes/Natalia	1979	—	2.00	4.00
8805	Checkin' It Out/Kingdom Hall	1979	—	2.00	4.00
49086	Rolling Hills/Bright Side of the Road	1979	—	2.00	4.00

Number	Title (A Side/B Side)	Yr	VG	VG+	NM
49162	Full Force Gale/You Make Me Feel So Free	1980	—	2.00	4.00
50031	Scandinavia/Cleaning Windows	1982	—	2.00	4.00

Albums

BANG

Number	Title (A Side/B Side)	Yr	VG	VG+	NM
BLB-218 [M]	Blowin' Your Mind	1968	12.50	25.00	50.00
—With the censored "Brown Eyed Girl" lyric, "Laughin' and a-runnin', hey hey, behind the stadium with you," part of which was spliced in from another part of the song. This has been confirmed to exist in mono.					
BLBS-218 [S]	Blowin' Your Mind	1968	5.00	10.00	20.00
—With the censored "Brown Eyed Girl" lyric, "Laughin' and a-runnin', hey hey, behind the stadium with you," part of which was spliced in from another part of the song!					
BLP-218 [M]	Blowin' Your Mind	1967	7.50	15.00	30.00
—With the true "Brown Eyed Girl" lyric, "Makin' love in the green grass behind the stadium with you."					
BLPS-218 [S]	Blowin' Your Mind	1967	10.00	20.00	40.00
—With the true "Brown Eyed Girl" lyric, "Makin' love in the green grass behind the stadium with you."					
BLPS-222	The Best of Van Morrison	1970	3.75	7.50	15.00
BLPS-400	T.B. Sheets	1973	5.00	10.00	20.00

DIRECT DISK

Number	Title (A Side/B Side)	Yr	VG	VG+	NM
SD-16604	Moondance	1981	25.00	50.00	100.00
—Audiophile vinyl					

MERCURY

Number	Title (A Side/B Side)	Yr	VG	VG+	NM
818336-1	Live at the Grand Opera House, Belfast	1985	2.50	5.00	10.00
822895-1	A Sense of Wonder	1985	2.00	4.00	8.00
830077-1	No Guru, No Method, No Teacher	1986	2.00	4.00	8.00
832585-1	Poetic Champions Compose	1987	2.00	4.00	8.00
834496-1	Irish Heartbeat	1988	2.00	4.00	8.00
—With the Chieftains					
839262-1	Avalon Sunset	1989	2.50	5.00	10.00
841970-1	The Best of Van Morrison	1990	3.75	7.50	15.00
847100-1	Enlightenment	1990	3.75	7.50	15.00

WARNER BROS.

Number	Title (A Side/B Side)	Yr	VG	VG+	NM
WBMS-102 [DJ]	Live at the Roxy	1978	12.50	25.00	50.00
WS 1768	Astral Weeks	1968	6.25	12.50	25.00
—With "W7" logo on green label					
WS 1768	Astral Weeks	1970	3.00	6.00	12.00
—With "WB" logo on green label					
WS 1768	Astral Weeks	1973	2.50	5.00	10.00
—"Burbank" palm-tree label					
WS 1768	Astral Weeks	1979	2.00	4.00	8.00
—Later white or tan label					
WS 1835	Moondance	1969	5.00	10.00	20.00
—With "W7" logo on green label					
WS 1835	Moondance	1970	3.00	6.00	12.00
—With "WB" logo on green label					
WS 1835	Moondance	1973	2.50	5.00	10.00
—"Burbank" palm-tree label					
WS 1885	His Band and the Street Choir	1970	3.75	7.50	15.00
—With "WB" logo on green label					
WS 1885	His Band and the Street Choir	1973	2.50	5.00	10.00
—"Burbank" palm-tree label					
WS 1885	His Band and the Street Choir	1979	2.00	4.00	8.00
—Later white or tan label					
WS 1950	Tupelo Honey	1971	3.75	7.50	15.00
—With "WB" logo on green label, plus poster					
WS 1950	Tupelo Honey	1973	2.50	5.00	10.00
—"Burbank" palm-tree label					
WS 1950	Tupelo Honey	1979	2.00	4.00	8.00
—Later white or tan label					
WS 2633	Saint Dominic's Preview	1972	3.75	7.50	15.00
—With "WB" logo on green label					
WS 2633	Saint Dominic's Preview	1973	2.50	5.00	10.00
—"Burbank" palm-tree label					
WS 2633	Saint Dominic's Preview	1979	2.00	4.00	8.00
—Later white or tan label					
BS 2712	Hard Nose the Highway	1973	3.00	6.00	12.00
—"Burbank" palm-tree label					
BS 2712	Hard Nose the Highway	1979	2.00	4.00	8.00
—Later white or tan label					
2BS 2760 [(2)]	It's Too Late to Stop Now	1974	3.75	7.50	15.00
—"Burbank" palm-tree labels					
2BS 2760 [(2)]	It's Too Late to Stop Now	1979	2.00	4.00	8.00
—Later white or tan label					
BS 2805	Veedon Fleece	1974	3.00	6.00	12.00
—"Burbank" palm-tree labels					
BS 2805	Veedon Fleece	1979	2.00	4.00	8.00
—Later white or tan label					
BS 2987	A Period of Transition	1977	3.00	6.00	12.00
—"Burbank" palm-tree labels					
BS 2987	A Period of Transition	1979	2.00	4.00	8.00
—Later white or tan label					
BSK 3103	Moondance	1977	2.50	5.00	10.00
—Reissue with new number; "Burbank" palm-tree label					
BSK 3103	Moondance	1979	2.00	4.00	8.00
—Later white or tan label					
BSK 3212	Wavelength	1978	3.00	6.00	12.00
HS 3390	Into the Music	1979	3.00	6.00	12.00
BSK 3462	Common One	1980	3.00	6.00	12.00
BSK 3652	Beautiful Vision	1981	3.00	6.00	12.00
23802	Inarticulate Speech of the Heart	1983	3.00	6.00	12.00

MORTIMER

45s

PHILIPS

Number	Title (A Side/B Side)	Yr	VG	VG+	NM
40524	Dedicated Music Man/To Understand Someone	1968	2.00	4.00	8.00
40524 [PS]	Dedicated Music Man/To Understand Someone	1968	3.00	6.00	12.00
40567	Ingenue's Theme/Slicker Beauty Hints	1968	2.00	4.00	8.00

Albums

PHILIPS

Number	Title (A Side/B Side)	Yr	VG	VG+	NM
PHS 600267	Mortimer	1969	6.25	12.50	25.00

MOSBY, JOHNNY AND JONIE

45s

CAPITOL

Number	Title (A Side/B Side)	Yr	VG	VG+	NM
2087	Mr. and Mrs. John Smith/Hello There Stranger	1968	—	3.00	6.00
2179	Our Golden Wedding Day/Two Dollar Honeymoon Room	1968	—	3.00	6.00
2258	Come In the Back Door (Go 'Round, Go 'Round)/You Be the Mama, I'll Be the Papa	1968	—	3.00	6.00
2384	Just Hold My Hand/Walkin' Papers	1969	—	3.00	6.00
2505	Hold Me, Thrill Me, Kiss Me/Comparing Him with You	1969	—	3.00	6.00
2608	I'll Never Be Free/Pattern of Our Lives	1969	—	3.00	6.00
2730	Third World/You Go Back to Your World (I'll Go Back to Mine)	1970	—	2.50	5.00
2796	I'm Leavin' It Up to You/If It's Left Up to Me	1970	—	2.50	5.00
2865	My Happiness/Let Your Sun Shine on Me	1970	—	2.50	5.00
2978	A Little of Me, A Little of You/Someone to Take My Place	1970	—	2.50	5.00
3039	Oh, Love of Mine/Closing Time Till Dawn	1971	—	2.50	5.00
3141	Let's Get This Show on the Road/Souvenirs of Love	1971	—	2.50	5.00
3219	Just One More Time/Meet Me Tonight	1971	—	2.50	5.00
3277	Music to My Ears/I'll Say It Again	1972	—	2.50	5.00
5980	Make a Left and Then a Right/Take Back the World	1967	—	3.00	6.00

CHALLENGE

Number	Title (A Side/B Side)	Yr	VG	VG+	NM
59088	He Wouldn't Take Me Home to Meet His Mother/Hard Luck and Misery	1960	3.75	7.50	15.00

COLUMBIA

Number	Title (A Side/B Side)	Yr	VG	VG+	NM
42668	Don't Call Me from a Honky Tonk/Wrong Side of Town	1963	2.50	5.00	10.00
42841	Trouble in My Arms/Who's Been Cheatin' Who	1963	2.50	5.00	10.00
43005	Keep Those Cards and Letters Coming In/Take Me Home	1964	2.50	5.00	10.00
43100	How the Other Half Lives/Stolen Paradise	1964	2.50	5.00	10.00
43218	Strawberry Wine/Wrong Company	1965	2.00	4.00	8.00
43344	The High Cost of Loving/The Home She's Tearing Down	1965	2.00	4.00	8.00
43631	Heartbreak U.S.A./Identity	1966	2.00	4.00	8.00

TOPPA

Number	Title (A Side/B Side)	Yr	VG	VG+	NM
1034	Unreceived, Address Unknown/A Cup of Coffee	1961	3.75	7.50	15.00
1039	Making Believe/Ain't You Ever	1961	3.75	7.50	15.00
1047	Dear Okie/You Can't Hurt Me Anymore	1962	3.75	7.50	15.00

Albums

CAPITOL

Number	Title (A Side/B Side)	Yr	VG	VG+	NM
ST-170	Just Hold My Hand	1969	3.75	7.50	15.00
ST-286	Hold Me	1969	3.75	7.50	15.00
ST-414	I'll Never Be Free	1970	3.75	7.50	15.00
ST-556	My Happiness	1970	3.75	7.50	15.00
ST-737	Oh, Love of Mine	1971	3.75	7.50	15.00
ST 2903	Make a Left and Then a Right	1968	3.75	7.50	15.00

COLUMBIA

Number	Title (A Side/B Side)	Yr	VG	VG+	NM
CL 2297 [M]	Mr. & Mrs. Country Music	1965	3.75	7.50	15.00
CS 9097 [S]	Mr. & Mrs. Country Music	1965	5.00	10.00	20.00

HARMONY

Number	Title (A Side/B Side)	Yr	VG	VG+	NM
HS 11389	Mr. & Mrs. Country Music	1970	2.50	5.00	10.00

STARDAY

Number	Title (A Side/B Side)	Yr	VG	VG+	NM
328 [M]	The New Sweethearts of Country Music	1965	7.50	15.00	30.00

MOSES, JOHNNY

45s

IMPERIAL

Number	Title (A Side/B Side)	Yr	VG	VG+	NM
5329	You're Torturing Me/Do You Love Me? Do You?	1955	10.00	20.00	40.00

MOSLEY, BOB

Albums

REPRISE

Number	Title (A Side/B Side)	Yr	VG	VG+	NM
MS 2068	Bob Mosley	1972	5.00	10.00	20.00

MOSS, ROY

45s

FASCINATION

Number	Title (A Side/B Side)	Yr	VG	VG+	NM
1002	Wiggle Walkin' Baby/(B-side unknown)	1957	50.00	100.00	200.00

MERCURY

Number	Title (A Side/B Side)	Yr	VG	VG+	NM
70770	You're My Big Baby Now/You Nearly Lost Your Mind	1955	50.00	100.00	200.00
70858	Corinne, Corinna/You Don't Know My Mind	1956	50.00	100.00	200.00

MOST, MICKIE

45s

LAWN

Number	Title (A Side/B Side)	Yr	VG	VG+	NM
236	Sea Cruise/It's a Little Bit Hot	1964	5.00	10.00	20.00

MOTHER EARTH

Also see TRACY NELSON.

45s

MERCURY

Number	Title (A Side/B Side)	Yr	VG	VG+	NM
72878	Down So Long/Goodbye Nelda Greeby	1968	2.00	4.00	8.00
72909	Mother Earth/I Did My Part	1969	2.00	4.00	8.00
72943	Painted Girls and Wine/Your Time's Comin'	1969	2.00	4.00	8.00

REPRISE

Number	Title (A Side/B Side)	Yr	VG	VG+	NM
1019	Soul of Sadness/Temptation Took Control of Me and I Fell	1971	—	3.00	6.00
1041	I'll Be Long Gone/Bring Me Home	1971	—	3.00	6.00

UNITED ARTISTS

Number	Title (A Side/B Side)	Yr	VG	VG+	NM
50303	Revolution/Stranger in My Own Home	1968	2.50	5.00	10.00

Albums

MERCURY

Number	Title (A Side/B Side)	Yr	VG	VG+	NM
SR-61194	Living with the Animals	1968	6.25	12.50	25.00
SR-61226	Make a Joyful Noise	1969	5.00	10.00	20.00
SR-61230	Tracy Nelson Country	1969	5.00	10.00	20.00
SR-61270	Satisfied	1970	5.00	10.00	20.00

REPRISE

Number	Title (A Side/B Side)	Yr	VG	VG+	NM
MS 2054	Tracy Nelson/Mother Earth	1972	3.75	7.50	15.00
RS 6431	Bring Me Home	1971	3.75	7.50	15.00

Number	Title (A Side/B Side)	Yr	VG	VG+	NM

MOTHERLODE

45s

BUDDAH

Number	Title (A Side/B Side)	Yr	VG	VG+	NM
131	When I Die/Hard Life	1969	2.00	4.00	8.00
144	What Does It Take (To Win Your Love)/Memories of a Broken Promise	1969	—	3.00	6.00
185	I'm So Glad You're You, Not Me/Whippoorwill	1970	—	3.00	6.00

Albums

BUDDAH

Number	Title (A Side/B Side)	Yr	VG	VG+	NM
BDS-5046	When I Die	1969	3.75	7.50	15.00
BDS-5108	Tapped Out	1970	3.75	7.50	15.00

MOTHERS OF INVENTION, THE

See FRANK ZAPPA.

MOTIONS, THE (1)

45s

ABC-PARAMOUNT

Number	Title (A Side/B Side)	Yr	VG	VG+	NM
10529	Big Chief/Where Is Your Heart	1964	3.00	6.00	12.00

CONGRESS

Number	Title (A Side/B Side)	Yr	VG	VG+	NM
237	It's Gone/I've Got Money	1965	3.00	6.00	12.00

MERCURY

Number	Title (A Side/B Side)	Yr	VG	VG+	NM
72297	Beatle Drums/Long Hair	1964	6.25	12.50	25.00
72368	I Can Dance/Land Beyond the Moon	1964	5.00	10.00	20.00
72413	Bumble Bee '65/Motions	1965	5.00	10.00	20.00

MOTIONS, THE (2)

45s

LAURIE

Number	Title (A Side/B Side)	Yr	VG	VG+	NM
3112	Make Me a Love/Mr. Night	1961	30.00	60.00	120.00

MOTIONS, THE (3)

45s

PHILIPS

Number	Title (A Side/B Side)	Yr	VG	VG+	NM
40624	Freedom/What's Your Name	1969	2.00	4.00	8.00

Albums

PHILIPS

Number	Title (A Side/B Side)	Yr	VG	VG+	NM
PHS 600317	Electric Baby	1969	5.00	10.00	20.00

MOTT THE HOOPLE

Also see IAN HUNTER.

45s

ATLANTIC

Number	Title (A Side/B Side)	Yr	VG	VG+	NM
2749	Rock and Roll Queen/Backsliding Fearlessly	1970	2.00	4.00	8.00

COLUMBIA

Number	Title (A Side/B Side)	Yr	VG	VG+	NM
10091	All the Young Dudes/Rose	1975	—	2.50	5.00
45673	All the Young Dudes/One of the Boys	1972	—	3.00	6.00
—A-side has altered lyrics from LP version to avoid British airplay ban on brand names; matrix number in dead wax ends in "1" plus a letter					
45673	All the Young Dudes/One of the Boys	1972	2.00	4.00	8.00
—A-side is the LP version with "Marks and Sparks"; matrix number ends in the number "2" plus a letter					
45673 [PS]	All the Young Dudes/One of the Boys	1972	5.00	10.00	20.00
45754	One of the Boys/Sucker	1973	—	2.50	5.00
45784	Sweet Jane/Jerkin' Crocus	1973	—	2.50	5.00
45882	Honaloochie Boogie/Rose	1973	—	2.50	5.00
45920	All the Way from Memphis/I Wish I Was Your Mother	1973	—	2.50	5.00
46035	The Golden Age of Rock 'N' Roll/Rest in Peace	1974	—	2.50	5.00
46076	Roll Away the Stone/Looking Glass	1974	—	2.50	5.00
74712	All the Young Dudes/Hanoloochie Boogie	1992	—	—	3.00
—Reissue					

Albums

ATLANTIC

Number	Title (A Side/B Side)	Yr	VG	VG+	NM
SD 7297	Rock and Roll Queen	1974	5.00	10.00	20.00
SD 8258	Mott the Hoople	1970	5.00	10.00	20.00
—With "1841 Broadway" address and no mention of Warner Communications on label					
SD 8258	Mott the Hoople	198?	2.00	4.00	8.00
—With Warner Communications "W" logo on label					
SD 8272	Mad Shadows	1970	5.00	10.00	20.00
SD 8284	Wildlife	1971	5.00	10.00	20.00
SD 8304	Brain Capers	1972	5.00	10.00	20.00

COLUMBIA

Number	Title (A Side/B Side)	Yr	VG	VG+	NM
KC 31750	All the Young Dudes	1972	3.75	7.50	15.00
PC 31750	All the Young Dudes	198?	2.00	4.00	8.00
—Budget-line reissue					
KC 32425	Mott	1973	3.75	7.50	15.00
PC 32425	Mott	198?	2.00	4.00	8.00
—Budget-line reissue					
PC 32871	The Hoople	1974	3.75	7.50	15.00
PCQ 32871 [Q]	The Hoople	1974	6.25	12.50	25.00
PC 33282	Mott the Hoople Live	1974	3.75	7.50	15.00
—No bar code on cover					
PC 33282	Mott the Hoople Live	198?	2.00	4.00	8.00
—Reissue with bar code on cover					
PC 33705	Drive On	1975	3.75	7.50	15.00
PC 34236	Shouting and Pointing	1976	3.75	7.50	15.00
PC 34368	Mott the Hoople's Greatest Hits	1976	3.00	6.00	12.00
—No bar code on cover					
PC 34368	Mott the Hoople's Greatest Hits	198?	2.00	4.00	8.00
—Reissue with bar code on cover					

MOTTOLA, TONY

45s

COMMAND

Number	Title (A Side/B Side)	Yr	VG	VG+	NM
4024	Nina/Tra Vegila E Sonno	1962	2.00	4.00	8.00
4058	Michelle/Boulevard of Broken Dreams	1964	2.00	4.00	8.00
4076	Brasilia/Sabor A Mi	1965	2.00	4.00	8.00

PROJECT 3

Number	Title (A Side/B Side)	Yr	VG	VG+	NM
1303	The Gang That Sang Heart of My Heart/Georgia on My Mind	1967	—	3.00	6.00
1318	Call Me/The World of Your Embrace	1967	—	3.00	6.00
1323	Spanish Harlem/I Love, I Live, I Love	1968	—	3.00	6.00
1329	Somethin' Stupid/Lush and Lovely	1968	—	3.00	6.00
1337	Love in Every Room/This Guy's in Love with You	1968	—	3.00	6.00
1352	I've Gotta Be Me/Guitar Underground	1969	—	2.50	5.00
1355	I'll Never Fall in Love Again/Those Were the Days	1969	—	2.50	5.00
1378	Something/Chewy Chewy Gum Gum	1970	—	2.50	5.00
1381	Tequila/Bluesette	1970	—	2.50	5.00
1402	It's Too Late/(B-side unknown)	1971	—	2.00	4.00
1413	Love/I Don't Know How to Love Him	1971	—	2.00	4.00
1430	Classical Gas/Galloping Guitars	197?	—	2.00	4.00
1431	Sugar Blues/Chicken A La Spring	197?	—	2.00	4.00
1437	Jelly Bean/One	197?	—	2.00	4.00
1438	Nadia's Theme/I Love My Wife	1976	—	2.00	4.00

Albums

ABC

Number	Title (A Side/B Side)	Yr	VG	VG+	NM
S-738	16 Great Performances	1972	2.50	5.00	10.00
X-770	Mister Guitar	1973	2.50	5.00	10.00

COMMAND

Number	Title (A Side/B Side)	Yr	VG	VG+	NM
33-807 [M]	Mr. Big	1961	3.00	6.00	12.00
SD 807 [S]	Mr. Big	1961	3.75	7.50	15.00
33-816 [M]	Roman Guitar	1962	3.00	6.00	12.00
SD 816 [S]	Roman Guitar	1962	3.75	7.50	15.00
33-823 [M]	Country and Western Folk Songs	1962	3.00	6.00	12.00
SD 823 [S]	Country and Western Folk Songs	1962	3.75	7.50	15.00
33-828 [M]	String Band Strum-Along	1962	3.00	6.00	12.00
SD 828 [S]	String Band Strum-Along	1962	3.75	7.50	15.00
33-836 [M]	Roman Guitar, Volume Two	1962	3.00	6.00	12.00
SD 836 [S]	Roman Guitar, Volume Two	1962	3.75	7.50	15.00
33-841 [M]	Spanish Guitar	1963	3.00	6.00	12.00
SD 841 [S]	Spanish Guitar	1963	3.75	7.50	15.00
33-847 [M]	Romantic Guitar	1963	3.00	6.00	12.00
SD 847 [S]	Romantic Guitar	1963	3.75	7.50	15.00
33-864 [M]	Sentimental Guitar	1964	3.00	6.00	12.00
SD 864 [S]	Sentimental Guitar	1964	3.75	7.50	15.00
33-877 [M]	Guitar — Paris	1964	3.00	6.00	12.00
SD 877 [S]	Guitar — Paris	1964	3.75	7.50	15.00
33-885 [M]	Command Performance	1965	3.00	6.00	12.00
SD 885 [S]	Command Performance	1965	3.75	7.50	15.00
33-889 [M]	Love Songs — Mexico/S.A.	1965	3.00	6.00	12.00
SD 889 [S]	Love Songs — Mexico/S.A.	1965	3.75	7.50	15.00
33-900 [M]	Amor — Mexico/S.A.	1966	3.00	6.00	12.00
SD 900 [S]	Amor — Mexico/S.A.	1966	3.75	7.50	15.00
33-908 [M]	Guitar — U.S.A.	1967	3.75	7.50	15.00
SD 908 [S]	Guitar — U.S.A.	1967	3.00	6.00	12.00
QD-40001 [Q]	Guitar — Paris	1972	5.00	10.00	20.00

PICKWICK

Number	Title (A Side/B Side)	Yr	VG	VG+	NM
SPC-3610	Spanish Guitar	1978	2.00	4.00	8.00

PROJECT 3

Number	Title (A Side/B Side)	Yr	VG	VG+	NM
PR-5003	Heart and Soul	1967	3.00	6.00	12.00
PR-5010	A Latin Love-In	1967	3.00	6.00	12.00
PR4C-5010 [Q]	A Latin Love-In	1973	4.50	9.00	18.00
PR-5020	Lush, Latin & Lovely	1968	3.00	6.00	12.00
PR4C-5020 [Q]	Lush, Latin & Lovely	1973	4.50	9.00	18.00
PR-5025	Warm, Wild & Wonderful	1968	3.00	6.00	12.00
PR4C-5025 [Q]	Warm, Wild & Wonderful	1973	4.50	9.00	18.00
PR-5032	Roma Oggi/Rome Today	1969	3.00	6.00	12.00
PR4C-5032 [Q]	Roma Oggi/Rome Today	1973	4.50	9.00	18.00
PR-5035	Tony Mottola Joins the Guitar Underground	1969	3.00	6.00	12.00
PR-5041	The Tony Touch	1970	3.00	6.00	12.00
PR4C-5041 [Q]	The Tony Touch	1973	4.50	9.00	18.00
PR-5044	Tony Mottola's Guitar Factory	1970	3.00	6.00	12.00
PR-5050	Close to You	1971	3.00	6.00	12.00
PR-5058	Warm Feelings	1971	3.00	6.00	12.00
PR-5062	Superstar Guitar	1972	3.00	6.00	12.00
PR4C-5062 [Q]	Superstar Guitar	1973	3.75	7.50	15.00
PR-5069	Tony and Strings	1973	3.00	6.00	12.00
PR4C-5069 [Q]	Tony and Strings	1973	4.50	9.00	18.00
PR-5074	Two Guitars	1974	2.50	5.00	10.00
PR4C-5078 [Q]	Tony Mottola with the Quad Guitars	1974	3.75	7.50	15.00
PR-5082	Tony Mottola with the Brass Menagerie	1974	3.00	6.00	12.00
PR-5094	I Only Have Eyes for You	197?	2.50	5.00	10.00
PR-5101	Goin' Out of My Head	197?	2.50	5.00	10.00
PR-6007/8 [(2)]	Favorite Things: The Best of Tony Mottola	1975	3.75	7.50	15.00
PR-6025/6 [(2)]	Feelings	198?	3.00	6.00	12.00
PR-6031/2 [(2)]	The Best of Tony Mottola	198?	3.00	6.00	12.00

MOULTRY, MARY

45s

KING

Number	Title (A Side/B Side)	Yr	VG	VG+	NM
6038	Last Year's Senior Prom/They're Trying to Tear Us Apart	1966	7.50	15.00	30.00

MOUNT RUSHMORE

45s

DOT

Number	Title (A Side/B Side)	Yr	VG	VG+	NM
17158	Stone Free/She's So Good to Me	1968	2.00	4.00	8.00

Albums

DOT

Number	Title (A Side/B Side)	Yr	VG	VG+	NM
DLP-25898	High on Mount Rushmore	1968	5.00	10.00	20.00
DLP-25934	Mount Rushmore '69	1969	5.00	10.00	20.00

MOUNTAIN

Also see FELIX PAPPALARDI; LESLIE WEST; WEST, BRUCE AND LAING.

45s

COLUMBIA

Number	Title (A Side/B Side)	Yr	VG	VG+	NM
74711	Mississippi Queen/The Animal Trainer and the Toad	1992	—	—	3.00
—Reissue					

WINDFALL

Number	Title (A Side/B Side)	Yr	VG	VG+	NM
532	Mississippi Queen/The Laird	1970	—	3.00	6.00
533	For Yasgur's Farm/To My Friend	1970	—	2.50	5.00
534	The Animal Trainer and the Toad/Tired Angels	1971	—	2.50	5.00

Number	Title (A Side/B Side)	Yr	VG	VG+	NM
535	Silver Paper/Travelin' in the Dark	1971	—	2.50	5.00
536	Roll Over Beethoven/Crossroader	1971	—	2.50	5.00
537	Waiting to Take You Away/(B-side unknown)	1972	—	2.50	5.00
Albums					
COLUMBIA					
CQ 32079 [Q]	The Best of Mountain	1973	5.00	10.00	20.00
KC 32079	The Best of Mountain	1973	3.00	6.00	12.00
PC 32079	The Best of Mountain	198?	2.00	4.00	8.00
—Budget-line reissue					
CG 32818 [(2)]	Twin Peaks	1974	3.75	7.50	15.00
PG 32818 [(2)]	Twin Peaks	198?	2.50	5.00	10.00
—Budget-line reissue					
CQ 33008 [Q]	Avalanche	1974	5.00	10.00	20.00
KC 33008	Avalanche	1974	3.00	6.00	12.00
PC 33008	Avalanche	197?	2.00	4.00	8.00
—Budget-line reissue					
SCOTTI BROTHERS					
FZ 40006	Go for Your Life	1985	2.50	5.00	10.00
WINDFALL					
4501	Mountain Climbing!	1970	3.75	7.50	15.00
5500	Nantucket Sleighride	1971	3.75	7.50	15.00
—Deduct 20% if inserts are missing					
5501	Flowers of Evil	1971	3.75	7.50	15.00
5502	Mountain Live (The Road Goes Ever On)	1972	3.75	7.50	15.00

MOUNTAIN BUS

Number	Title (A Side/B Side)	Yr	VG	VG+	NM
Albums					
GOOD					
101	Sundance	1971	37.50	75.00	150.00

MOURNING REIGN, THE

Number	Title (A Side/B Side)	Yr	VG	VG+	NM
45s					
CONTOUR					
601	Evil Hearted You/Get Out of My Life, Woman	1967	6.25	12.50	25.00
LINK					
1	Satisfaction Guaranteed/Our Fate	1966	7.50	15.00	30.00
1 [PS]	Satisfaction Guaranteed/Our Fate	1966	150.00	300.00	600.00
2	Evil Hearted You/Get Out of My Life, Woman	1966	7.50	15.00	30.00
7-Inch Extended Plays					
SUNDAZED					
SEP 115	*Satisfaction Guaranteed/Our Fate/Light Switch/ Cut Back	199?	—	—	2.00
SEP 115 [PS]	The Mourning Reign	199?	—	—	2.00
Albums					
BEAT ROCKET					
BR 102	The Mourning Reign	1999	3.00	6.00	12.00

MOUSE AND THE TRAPS

Number	Title (A Side/B Side)	Yr	VG	VG+	NM
45s					
CAPITOL					
2460	Streets of a Dusty Town/Mouse	1969	2.50	5.00	10.00
FRATERNITY					
956	A Public Execution/All for You	1966	5.00	10.00	20.00
966	Mad of Sugar/I Am the One	1966	3.75	7.50	15.00
971	Would You Believe/Like I Know You Do	1966	3.75	7.50	15.00
973	Promises, Promises/Do the Best You Can	1966	3.75	7.50	15.00
989	Ya Ya/Cryin' Inside	1967	3.75	7.50	15.00
1000	Beg, Borrow, and Steal/L.O.V.E. Love	1967	3.75	7.50	15.00
1005	Sometimes You Just Can't Win/Cryin' Inside	1968	3.75	7.50	15.00
1005 [PS]	Sometimes You Just Can't Win/Cryin' Inside	1968	20.00	40.00	80.00
1011	I Satisfy/Good Times	1968	3.75	7.50	15.00
1015	Look at the Sun/Requiem for Sarah	1968	3.75	7.50	15.00
SMUDGE					
0703	Bottom Line/Gypsy Girl	1981	3.00	6.00	12.00

MOUTH AND MACNEIL

Number	Title (A Side/B Side)	Yr	VG	VG+	NM
45s					
PHILIPS					
40715	How Do You Do?/Land of Milk and Honey	1972	—	2.50	5.00
—Light blue label					
40715	How Do You Do?/Land of Milk and Honey	1972	—	2.00	4.00
—Dark blue label					
40717	Why Did You, Why?/Hey, You Love	1972	—	2.00	4.00
40721	Sing Along/Hello	1973	—	2.00	4.00
40724	You-Kou-La-La-Lou-Pi/Let Your Life Lead by Love	1973	—	2.00	4.00
TARA					
110	I See a Star/My Friends	1974	—	2.00	4.00
Albums					
PHILIPS					
PHS 700000	How Do You Do?	1972	3.00	6.00	12.00
PHS 700003	Mouth & MacNeil II	1973	3.00	6.00	12.00

MOVE, THE

Also see ELECTRIC LIGHT ORCHESTRA; ROY WOOD.

Number	Title (A Side/B Side)	Yr	VG	VG+	NM
45s					
A&M					
884	Flowers in the Rain/(Here We Go Round the) Lemon Tree	1967	3.00	6.00	12.00
914	Walk Upon the Water/Fire Brigade	1968	3.75	7.50	15.00
966	Yellow Rainbow/Something	1968	3.00	6.00	12.00
1020	Blackberry Way/Something	1969	3.00	6.00	12.00
1119	This Time Tomorrow/Curly	1969	3.00	6.00	12.00
1197	Brontosaurus/Lightning Never Strikes Twice	1970	3.00	6.00	12.00
1239	When Alice Comes Back to the Farm/What?	1971	3.00	6.00	12.00
1546	Zing Went the Strings of My Heart/Wild Tiger Woman	1974	2.50	5.00	10.00
CAPITOL					
3126	Tonight/Don't Mess Me Up	1971	5.00	10.00	20.00
—Stock copies have been confirmed					
DERAM					
7504	The Disturbance/Night of Fear	1967	3.75	7.50	15.00
7506	I Can Hear the Grass Grow/Wave the Flag and Stop the Train	1967	3.75	7.50	15.00
MGM					
14332 [DJ]	Chinatown/Down by the Bay	1971	5.00	10.00	20.00
—Evidently not released as stock copy					
UNITED ARTISTS					
XW202	Tonight/My Marge	1973	—	3.00	6.00
50876	Chinatown/Down on the Bay	1972	2.00	4.00	8.00
50928	Do Ya/California Man	1972	2.00	4.00	8.00
Albums					
A&M					
SP-3181	Shazam	1982	2.50	5.00	10.00
—Budget-line reissue of 4259					
SP-3625 [(2)]	Best of the Move/First Move	1974	3.75	7.50	15.00
SP-4259	Shazam	1969	7.50	15.00	30.00
CAPITOL					
ST-658	Looking On	1971	5.00	10.00	20.00
ST-811	Message from the Country	1971	5.00	10.00	20.00
UNITED ARTISTS					
UAS-5666	Split Ends	1972	3.75	7.50	15.00

MOVING SIDEWALKS, THE

With Billy Gibbons, later of ZZ TOP.

Number	Title (A Side/B Side)	Yr	VG	VG+	NM
45s					
TANTARA					
3101	99th Floor/What Are You Going to Do	1967	10.00	20.00	40.00
3103	I Want to Hold Your Hand/Joe Blues	1968	10.00	20.00	40.00
3113	Flashback/(B-side unknown)	1969	7.50	15.00	30.00
WAND					
1156	99th Floor/What Are You Going to Do	1967	6.25	12.50	25.00
1167	Need Me/Every Night a New Surprise	1968	6.25	12.50	25.00
Albums					
TANTARA					
6919	Flash	1968	75.00	150.00	300.00

MOZART, MICKEY

See ROBERT MAXWELL.

MRS. MILLS

Number	Title (A Side/B Side)	Yr	VG	VG+	NM
45s					
CAPITOL					
4758	Bobbikins/Popcorn	1962	3.00	6.00	12.00
Albums					
LIBERTY					
LRP-3359 [M]	My Mother — The Ragtime Piano Player	1964	3.00	6.00	12.00
LST-7359 [S]	My Mother — The Ragtime Piano Player	1964	3.75	7.50	15.00

MUDCRUTCH

Early Tom Petty and the Heartbreakers.

Number	Title (A Side/B Side)	Yr	VG	VG+	NM
45s					
PEPPER					
9449	Up in Mississippi/Cause Is Understood	1971	100.00	200.00	400.00
SHELTER					
40357	Depot Street/Wild Eyes	1975	7.50	15.00	30.00

MUDLARKS, THE

Number	Title (A Side/B Side)	Yr	VG	VG+	NM
45s					
ROULETTE					
4143	Love Game/My Grandfather's Clock	1959	3.00	6.00	12.00

MUDSLINGER, ROGER

Number	Title (A Side/B Side)	Yr	VG	VG+	NM
45s					
RED BIRD					
10-013	The Election Year 1964 (Part 1)/The Election Year 1964 (Part 2)	1964	5.00	10.00	20.00

MUEHLEISEN, MAURY

Lead guitarist for JIM CROCE on most, if not all, of his hits.

Number	Title (A Side/B Side)	Yr	VG	VG+	NM
45s					
CAPITOL					
3076	I Have No Time/Just a Passing Thing	1971	—	3.00	6.00

MUGWUMPS, THE

Also see DENNY DOHERTY; CASS ELLIOT; ZALMAN YANOVSKY.

Number	Title (A Side/B Side)	Yr	VG	VG+	NM
45s					
SIDEWALK					
900	Bald Headed Woman/Jug Band Music	1966	6.25	12.50	25.00
909	Season of the Witch/My Gal	1967	5.00	10.00	20.00
WARNER BROS.					
5471	I'll Remember Tonight/I Don't Wanna Know	1964	3.75	7.50	15.00
7018	Searchin'/Here It Is, Another Day	1967	2.50	5.00	10.00
Albums					
WARNER BROS.					
W 1697 [M]	The Mugwumps	1967	6.25	12.50	25.00
WS 1697 [S]	The Mugwumps	1967	7.50	15.00	30.00

MULBERRY FRUIT BAND, THE

Number	Title (A Side/B Side)	Yr	VG	VG+	NM
45s					
BUDDAH					
1	Yes, We Have No Bananas/The Audition	1967	3.00	6.00	12.00

MULDAUR, GEOFF

Number	Title (A Side/B Side)	Yr	VG	VG+	NM
Albums					
FOLKLORE					
FRLP-14004 [M]	Sleepy Man Blues	1964	7.50	15.00	30.00
FRST-14004 [S]	Sleepy Man Blues	1964	10.00	20.00	40.00

PRESTIGE

Number	Title (A Side/B Side)	Yr	VG	VG+	NM
PRST-7727	Sleepy Man Blues	1969	5.00	10.00	20.00

—Reissue of Folklore LP

MULDAUR, GEOFF & MARIA

45s

REPRISE

Number	Title (A Side/B Side)	Yr	VG	VG+	NM
0807	Open Up Your Soul/Sittin' Alone in the Moonlight	1969	2.00	4.00	8.00

Albums

CARTHAGE

Number	Title (A Side/B Side)	Yr	VG	VG+	NM
CGLP-4428	Pottery Pie	198?	2.50	5.00	10.00

REPRISE

Number	Title (A Side/B Side)	Yr	VG	VG+	NM
MS 2073	Sweet Potatoes	1972	3.00	6.00	12.00

MULDAUR, MARIA

45s

REPRISE

Number	Title (A Side/B Side)	Yr	VG	VG+	NM
1183	Midnight at the Oasis/Any Old Time	1973	—	2.50	5.00
1319	I'm a Woman/Cool River	1974	—	2.00	4.00
1331	Oh Papa/Gringo de Mexico	1975	—	2.00	4.00
1352	Sad Eyes/Wild Bird	1976	—	2.00	4.00
1362	Sweet Harmony/Jon the Generator	1976	—	2.00	4.00

WARNER BROS.

Number	Title (A Side/B Side)	Yr	VG	VG+	NM
8580	Make Love to the Music/I'll Keep My Light in My Window	1978	—	2.00	4.00
49058	Dancin' in the Street/Birds Fly South (When Winter Comes)	1979	—	2.00	4.00
49131	Fall in Love Again/Love Is Everything	1979	—	2.00	4.00

Albums

MYRRH

Number	Title (A Side/B Side)	Yr	VG	VG+	NM
MSB-6685	There Is a Love	1984	2.50	5.00	10.00

REPRISE

Number	Title (A Side/B Side)	Yr	VG	VG+	NM
MS 2148	Maria Muldaur	1973	3.00	6.00	12.00
MS 2194	Waitress in a Donut Shop	1974	3.00	6.00	12.00
MS 2235	Sweet Harmony	1976	3.00	6.00	12.00

TAKOMA

Number	Title (A Side/B Side)	Yr	VG	VG+	NM
7084	Gospel Nights	1980	2.50	5.00	10.00

TUDOR

Number	Title (A Side/B Side)	Yr	VG	VG+	NM
109902	Sweet & Sour	1983	2.50	5.00	10.00

WARNER BROS.

Number	Title (A Side/B Side)	Yr	VG	VG+	NM
BSK 3162	Southern Winds	1978	2.50	5.00	10.00
BSK 3305	Open Your Eyes	1979	2.50	5.00	10.00

MULL, MARTIN

45s

ABC

Number	Title (A Side/B Side)	Yr	VG	VG+	NM
12251	Boogie Man/Bombed Away	1977	—	2.50	5.00
12304	Humming Song/Get Up, Get Down	1977	—	2.50	5.00

CAPRICORN

Number	Title (A Side/B Side)	Yr	VG	VG+	NM
0019	Dueling Tubas/2001 Polkas	1973	2.00	4.00	8.00
0024	In the Eyes of My Dog (Part 1)/In the Eyes of My Dog (Part 2)	1973	2.00	4.00	8.00
0037	Santafly/Santa Doesn't Cop Out On Dope	1973	3.00	6.00	12.00
0241	Do the Dog/Thousands of Girls	1975	2.00	4.00	8.00
0282	Santafly/Santa Doesn't Cop Out On Dope	1977	2.50	5.00	10.00

ELEKTRA

Number	Title (A Side/B Side)	Yr	VG	VG+	NM
46056	The Fruit Song/Pig in a Blanket	1979	—	2.50	5.00
46057	Bernie Don't Disco/Bun and Run Part 1 and 3	1979	—	2.50	5.00

Albums

ABC

Number	Title (A Side/B Side)	Yr	VG	VG+	NM
AB-997	I'm Everyone I've Ever Loved	1977	2.50	5.00	10.00
AA-1064	Sex and Violins	1978	2.50	5.00	10.00

CAPRICORN

Number	Title (A Side/B Side)	Yr	VG	VG+	NM
CP 0106	Martin Mull	1972	3.00	6.00	12.00
CP 0117	Martin Mull and His Fabulous Furniture	1973	3.00	6.00	12.00
CP 0126	Normal	1974	3.00	6.00	12.00
CP 0155	Days of Wine and Neurosis	1975	3.00	6.00	12.00
CP 0195	No Hits Four Errors	1977	2.50	5.00	10.00

ELEKTRA

Number	Title (A Side/B Side)	Yr	VG	VG+	NM
6E-200	Near Perfect	1979	2.50	5.00	10.00

MCA

Number	Title (A Side/B Side)	Yr	VG	VG+	NM
795	I'm Everyone I've Ever Loved	1980	2.00	4.00	8.00

—Reissue of ABC 997

MULTIPLICATION ROCK (SOUNDTRACK)

45s

CAPITOL

Number	Title (A Side/B Side)	Yr	VG	VG+	NM
3693	Naughty Number Nine/I Got Six	1973	3.75	7.50	15.00

Albums

CAPITOL

Number	Title (A Side/B Side)	Yr	VG	VG+	NM
SJA-11174	Multiplication Rock	1973	10.00	20.00	40.00

MUNGO JERRY

45s

BELL

Number	Title (A Side/B Side)	Yr	VG	VG+	NM
45123	Lady Rose/Little Louis	1971	—	2.00	4.00
45383	Alright, Alright, Alright/Little Miss Hipshake	1973	—	2.00	4.00
45427	Wild Love/Glad I'm a Rocker	1973	—	2.00	4.00
45451	Long Legged Woman Dressed in Black/Gonna Bop Till I Drop	1974	—	2.00	4.00

JANUS

Number	Title (A Side/B Side)	Yr	VG	VG+	NM
125	In the Summertime/Mighty Man	1970	—	3.00	6.00
128	Johnny B. Badde/My Friend	1970	—	2.50	5.00
148	Baby Jump/The Man Beside the Piano	1971	—	2.50	5.00

PYE

Number	Title (A Side/B Side)	Yr	VG	VG+	NM
65003	You Don't Have to Be in the Army/O'Reilly	1972	—	2.00	4.00
65009	Going Back Home/Open Up	1972	—	2.00	4.00
71032	In the Summertime/(B-side unknown)	1975	—	2.00	4.00

Albums

JANUS

Number	Title (A Side/B Side)	Yr	VG	VG+	NM
JLS-3027	Memoirs of a Stockbroker	1972	3.75	7.50	15.00
JXS-7000	Mungo Jerry	1970	3.75	7.50	15.00

MUNSTERS, THE

45s

DECCA

Number	Title (A Side/B Side)	Yr	VG	VG+	NM
31670	Munster Creep/Make It Go Away	1964	5.00	10.00	20.00

Albums

DECCA

Number	Title (A Side/B Side)	Yr	VG	VG+	NM
DL 4588 [M]	The Munsters	1964	25.00	50.00	100.00
DL 74588 [S]	The Munsters	1964	37.50	75.00	150.00

MURMAIDS, THE

45s

CHATTAHOOCHIE

Number	Title (A Side/B Side)	Yr	VG	VG+	NM
628	Popsicles and Icicles/Blue Dress	1963	5.00	10.00	20.00
628	Popsicles and Icicles/Huntington Flats	1963	3.75	7.50	15.00
628	Popsicles and Icicles/Bunny Stomp	1963	3.75	7.50	15.00
628	Popsicles and Icicles/Comedy and Tragedy	1963	3.75	7.50	15.00
636	Heartbreak Ahead/He's Good to Me	1964	2.50	5.00	10.00
641	Wild and Wonderful/Bull Talk	1964	2.50	5.00	10.00
668	Stuffed Animals/Little White Lies	1965	2.50	5.00	10.00
711	Little Boys/Go Away	1966	2.50	5.00	10.00

LIBERTY

Number	Title (A Side/B Side)	Yr	VG	VG+	NM
56069	Paper Sun/Song Through Perception	1968	—	—	—
—Unreleased					
56078	Paper Sun/Song Through Perception	1968	2.50	5.00	10.00

Albums

CHATTAHOOCHEE

Number	Title (A Side/B Side)	Yr	VG	VG+	NM
CHLP-628 [M]	The Mermaids Resurface!	1981	7.50	15.00	30.00

MURPHEY, MICHAEL

Also includes records as "Michael Martin Murphey."

45s

A&M

Number	Title (A Side/B Side)	Yr	VG	VG+	NM
1368	Geronimo's Cadillac/Boy from the Country	1972	—	2.50	5.00
1368 [PS]	Geronimo's Cadillac/Boy from the Country	1972	—	3.00	6.00
1447	Cosmic Cowboy/Temperature Train	1973	—	2.50	5.00
1459	Calico Silver/Blessing in Disguise	1973	—	2.50	5.00
1712	Geronimo's Cadillac/Blessing in Disguise	1975	—	2.00	4.00

EMI AMERICA

Number	Title (A Side/B Side)	Yr	VG	VG+	NM
8243	What She Wants/Still Taking Chances	1984	—	—	3.00
8265	Carolina in the Pines/Cherokee Fiddle	1985	—	—	3.00

EPIC

Number	Title (A Side/B Side)	Yr	VG	VG+	NM
02075	Take It As It Comes/Hard Country	1981	—	2.00	4.00
—With Katy Moffatt					
11130	Holy Roller/Rye By-The-Sea	1974	—	2.00	4.00
11130 [PS]	Holy Roller/Rye By-The-Sea	1974	—	3.00	6.00
50014	You Can Only Say So Much/Fort Worth, I Love You	1974	—	2.00	4.00
50084	Wildfire/Night Thunder	1975	—	2.50	5.00
50131	Carolina in the Pines/Without My Lady There	1975	—	2.00	4.00
50184	Mansion on the Hill/Renegade	1976	—	2.00	4.00
50214	Rhythm of the Road/Swans Against the Sun	1976	—	2.00	4.00
50319	Cherokee Fiddler/Running Wide Open	1976	—	2.00	4.00
50369	Changing Woman/A North Wind and a New Moon	1977	—	2.00	4.00
50540	Nothing Is Your Own/Song Day	1978	—	2.00	4.00
50572	Paradise Tonight/Song Dog	1978	—	2.00	4.00
50686	Lightning/Chain Gang	1979	—	2.00	4.00
50739	South Coast/Backsliders Wine	1979	—	2.00	4.00

LIBERTY

Number	Title (A Side/B Side)	Yr	VG	VG+	NM
1455	Lost River/The Two-Step Is Easy	1982	—	—	3.00
1466	What's Forever For/Crystal	1982	—	—	3.00
1486	Still Taking Chances/Lost River	1982	—	—	3.00
1494	Crystal/Love Affairs	1983	—	—	3.00
1505	The Heart Never Lies/Don't Count the Rainy Days	1983	—	—	3.00
1514	Will It Be Love by Morning/Goodbye Money Mountain	1983	—	—	3.00
1517	Disenchanted/Sacred Heart	1984	—	—	3.00
—Starting here, as "Michael Martin Murphey"					
1523	Radio Land/The Heart Never Lies	1984	—	—	3.00

WARNER BROS

Number	Title (A Side/B Side)	Yr	VG	VG+	NM
PRO-S-2869 [DJ]	Colorado Christmas/The Cowboy's Christmas Ball	1987	—	3.00	6.00

—B-side by Nitty Gritty Dirt Band

WARNER BROS.

Number	Title (A Side/B Side)	Yr	VG	VG+	NM
7-18321	Big Iron/Cowboy Logic	1993	—	2.00	4.00
18928	I Don't Do Floors/I'm Gonna Miss You Girl	1992	—	—	3.00
19290	What Am I Doin' Here/Where Do Cowboys Go When They Die-Reincarnation	1991	—	—	3.00
19412	Let the Cowboy Dance/Red River Valley	1991	—	—	3.00
19724	Cowboy Logic/Spanish Is the Lovin' Tongue	1990	—	—	3.00
22666	Route 66/Juke Box	1990	—	—	3.00
22765	Family Tree/Wood Smoke in the Wind	1989	—	—	3.00
22970	Never Givin' Up on Love/Desperation Road	1989	—	—	3.00
27668	From the Word Go/Vanishing Breed	1989	—	—	3.00
27810	Pilgrims on the Way (Matthew's Song)/Still Got the Fire	1988	—	—	3.00
27947	Talkin' to the Wrong Man/What Am I Doin' Hangin' 'Round	1988	—	—	3.00
28168	I'm Gonna Miss You, Girl/Running Blood	1987	—	—	3.00
28370	A Long Line of Love/Worlds Apart	1987	—	—	3.00
28471	A Face in the Crowd/You're History	1987	—	—	3.00
—With Holly Dunn					
28598	Fiddlin' Man/Ghost Town (Messages from the Ghost Ranch)	1986	—	—	3.00
28694	Rollin' Nowhere/Face-2-Face with the Night	1986	—	—	3.00
28797	Tonight We Ride/Santa Fe Cantina	1986	—	—	3.00

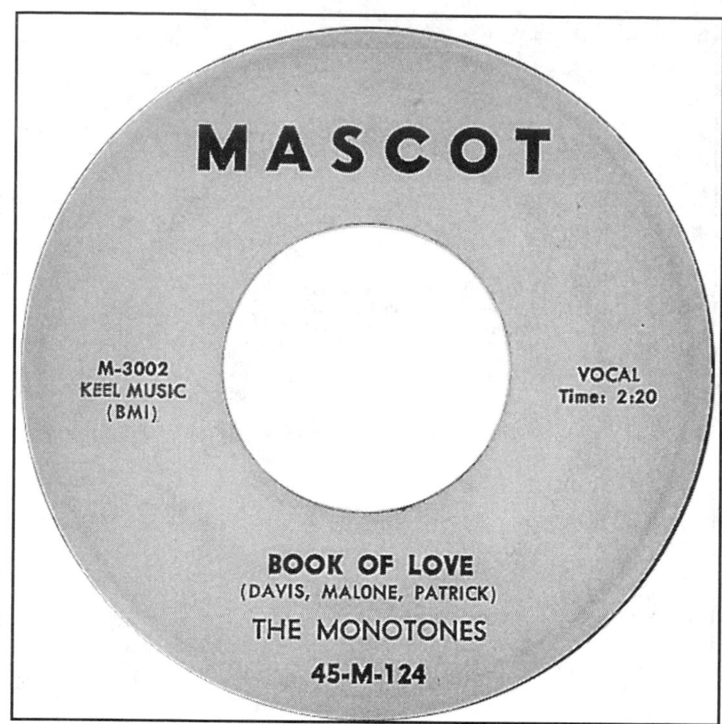

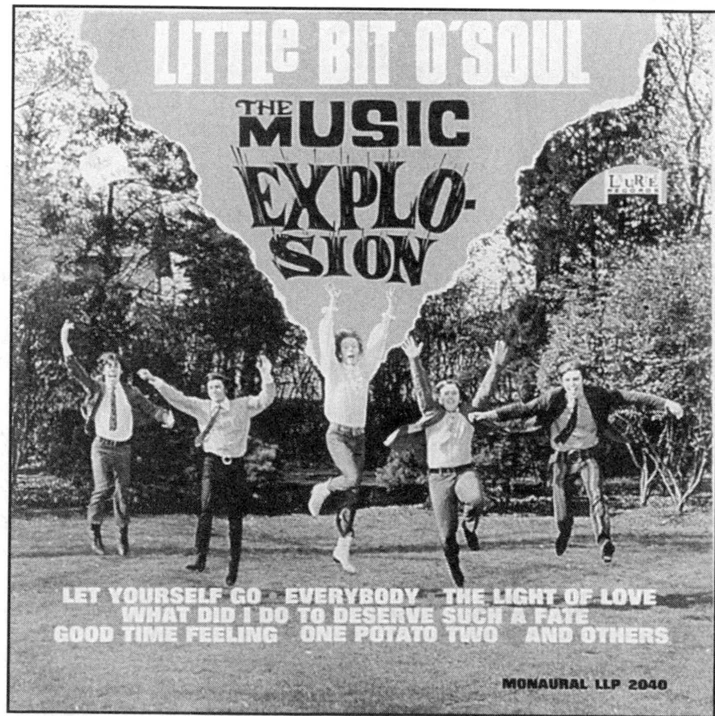

(Top left) The Monotones' biggest hit, "Book of Love," was a hit on the Argo label. But the hard-to-find original was on the tiny Mascot label. (Top right) RCA Victor was the label that invented the 45 rpm record. By mid-1949, almost all of its current material was available on the new format, including the Number One hit of the entire year, Vaughn Monroe's rendition of "Riders In the Sky." His deep-voiced version remains the standard against which other renditions — and there have been many — are measured. (Bottom left) Though often considered to be a manufactured group, there was a real Music Explosion from Mansfield, Ohio. This was their only album, built around the hit song "Little Bit o' Soul." (Bottom right) Tough to find, especially in stereo, is the debut album by the Music Machine, *Turn On the Music Machine*.

Number	Title (A Side/B Side)	Yr	VG	VG+	NM
Albums					
A&M					
SP-3134	Geronimo's Cadillac	198?	2.00	4.00	8.00
—Budget-line reissue					
SP-3137	Cosmic Cowboy Souvenir	198?	2.00	4.00	8.00
—Budget-line reissue					
SP-4358	Geronimo's Cadillac	1972	3.00	6.00	12.00
SP-4388	Cosmic Cowboy Souvenir	1973	3.00	6.00	12.00
EMI AMERICA					
LN-10310	The Heart Never Lies	1986	2.00	4.00	8.00
—Budget-line reissue					
ST-17143	The Best of Michael Martin Murphey	1984	2.50	5.00	10.00
EPIC					
KE 32835	Michael Murphey	1974	3.00	6.00	12.00
KE 33290	Blue Sky — Night Thunder	1975	2.50	5.00	10.00
PE 33290	Blue Sky — Night Thunder	197?	2.00	4.00	8.00
—Reissue with new prefix & dark blue label					
PE 33851	Swans Against the Sun	1975	2.50	5.00	10.00
PEQ 33851 [Q]	Swans Against the Sun	1975	4.00	8.00	16.00
PE 34220	Flowing Free Forever	1976	2.50	5.00	10.00
JE 35013	Lonewolf	1978	2.50	5.00	10.00
JE 35742	Peaks, Valleys, Honky-Tonks & Alleys	1979	2.50	5.00	10.00
LIBERTY					
LT-51120	Michael Martin Murphey	1982	2.50	5.00	10.00
LT-51150	The Heart Never Lies	1983	2.50	5.00	10.00
WARNER BROS.					
25369	Tonight We Ride	1986	2.50	5.00	10.00
25500	Americana	1987	2.50	5.00	10.00
25644	River of Time	1988	2.50	5.00	10.00
25894	Land of Enchantment	1989	3.00	6.00	12.00

MURPHY, KEITH, AND THE DAZE

Number	Title (A Side/B Side)	Yr	VG	VG+	NM
45s					
KING					
6171	Dirty Ol' Sam/Slightly Reminiscent of Her	1968	25.00	50.00	100.00

MURRAY, ANNE

Number	Title (A Side/B Side)	Yr	VG	VG+	NM
45s					
CAPITOL					
2738	Snowbird/Just Bidin' My Time	1970	—	3.00	6.00
2988	Sing High — Sing Low/Days of the Looking Glass	1970	—	2.50	5.00
3059	A Stranger in My Place/Sycamore Slick	1971	—	2.50	5.00
3082	Put Your Hand in the Hand/It Takes Time	1971	—	2.50	5.00
3159	Talk It Over in the Morning/Head Above the Water	1971	—	2.50	5.00
3260	Cotton Jenny/Destiny	1972	—	2.50	5.00
3352	Bobbie's Song for Jesus/You Can't Have a Hand on Me	1972	—	2.50	5.00
3481	Danny's Song/Drown Me	1972	—	2.00	4.00
3600	What About Me/Let Sunshine Have Its Day	1973	—	2.00	4.00
3648	Send a Little Love My Way/Head Above the Water	1973	—	2.00	4.00
3776	Love Song/You Can't Go Back	1973	—	2.00	4.00
3867	You Won't See Me/He Thinks I Still Care	1974	—	2.50	5.00
3955	Just One Look/Son of a Rotten Gambler	1974	—	2.00	4.00
4000	Day Tripper/Lullaby	1974	—	2.00	4.00
4025	Uproar/Lift Your Hearts to the Sun	1975	—	2.00	4.00
4072	A Stranger in My Place/Dream Lover	1975	—	2.00	4.00
4142	Sunday Sunrise/Out on the Road Again	1975	—	2.00	4.00
4207	The Call/Lady Bug	1976	—	2.00	4.00
4265	Golden Oldie/Together	1976	—	2.00	4.00
4329	Things/Caress Me Pretty Music	1976	—	2.00	4.00
4375	Sunday School to Broadway/Dancin' All Night Long	1976	—	2.00	4.00
4402	Canterbury Song/Shilo Song	1977	—	2.00	4.00
—With Gene MacLellan					
4527	Walk Right Back/A Million More	1978	—	2.00	4.00
4574	You Needed Me/I Still Wish the Very Best for You	1978	—	2.00	4.00
4675	I Just Fall in Love Again/Just to Feel This Love from You	1979	—	2.00	4.00
4675 [PS]	I Just Fall in Love Again/Just to Feel This Love from You	1979	—	2.50	5.00
4716	Shadows in the Moonlight/Yucatan Cafe	1979	—	2.00	4.00
4773	Broken Hearted Me/Why Don't You Stick Around	1979	—	2.00	4.00
4813	Daydream Believer/Do You Think of Me	1979	—	2.00	4.00
4848	Lucky Me/Somebody's Waiting	1980	—	2.00	4.00
4878	I'm Happy Just to Dance with You/What's Forever For	1980	—	2.00	4.00
4920	Could I Have This Dance/Somebody's Waiting	1980	—	2.00	4.00
4920 [PS]	Could I Have This Dance/Somebody's Waiting	1980	—	2.50	5.00
4987	Blessed Are the Believers/Only Love	1981	—	2.00	4.00
4987 [PS]	Blessed Are the Believers/Only Love	1981	—	2.50	5.00
A-5013	We Don't Have to Hold Out/Call Me with the News	1981	—	2.00	4.00
A-5023	It's All I Can Do/If a Heart Must Be Broken	1981	—	2.00	4.00
A-5083	Another Sleepless Night/It Should Have Been Easy	1982	—	2.00	4.00
B-5145	Hey! Baby!/Song for the Mira	1982	—	—	3.00
B-5183	Somebody's Always Saying Goodbye/That'll Keep Me Dreamin'	1982	—	—	3.00
B-5264	A Little Good News/I'm Not Afraid Anymore	1983	—	—	3.00
B-5264 [PS]	A Little Good News/I'm Not Afraid Anymore	1983	—	2.50	5.00
B-5305	That's Not the Way (It's S'posed to Be)/The More We Try	1983	—	—	3.00
B-5344	Just Another Woman in Love/Heart Stealer	1984	—	—	3.00
B-5384	Let Your Heart Do the Talking/I Don't Think I'm Ready for You	1984	—	—	3.00
B-5401	Nobody Loves Me Like You Do/Love You Out of Your Mind	1984	—	—	3.00
—A-side: With Dave Loggins					
B-5436	Time Don't Run Out on Me/Let Your Heart Do the Talking	1985	—	—	3.00
B-5472	I Don't Think I'm Ready for You/Take Good Care of My Baby	1985	—	—	3.00
B-5472 [PS]	I Don't Think I'm Ready for You/Take Good Care of My Baby	1985	—	2.00	4.00
B-5536	Go Tell It On the Mountain/O Holy Night	1985	—	2.00	4.00
B-5536 [PS]	Go Tell It On the Mountain/O Holy Night	1985	—	2.50	5.00
B-5547	Now and Forever (You and Me)/I Don't Wanna Spend Another Night Without You	1986	—	—	3.00
B-5547 [PS]	Now and Forever (You and Me)/I Don't Wanna Spend Another Night Without You	1986	—	2.00	4.00
B-5576	Who's Leaving Who/Reach for Me	1986	—	—	3.00
B-5610	My Life's a Dance/Call Us Fools	1986	—	—	3.00
B-5655	On and On/Gotcha	1986	—	—	3.00
SPRO-9723 [DJ]	Christmas Medley: Silver Bells/I'll Be Home for Christmas/Winter Wonderland (same on both sides)	1981	2.00	4.00	8.00
B-44005	Are You Still in Love with Me/Give Me Your Love	1987	—	—	3.00
B-44053	Anyone Can Do the Heartbreak/Without You	1987	—	—	3.00
B-44134	Perfect Strangers/It Happens All the Time	1988	—	—	3.00
—With Doug Mallory					
B-44219	Flying On Your Own/Slow All Night	1988	—	—	3.00
B-44272	Slow Passin' Time/Flying on Your Own	1989	—	—	3.00
B-44341	Who But You/You Make Me Curious	1989	—	—	3.00
B-44432	If I Ever Fall in Love Again/Just Another Woman in Love	1989	—	—	3.00
—A-side: With Kenny Rogers					
B-44495	I'd Fall in Love Tonight/Now and Forever (You and Me)	1989	—	—	3.00
SBK					
S7-18912	Winter Wonderland/The Little Drummer Boy	1995	—	—	3.00
Albums					
CAPITOL					
ST-579	Snowbird	1970	3.00	6.00	12.00
ST-667	Anne Murray	1971	3.00	6.00	12.00
ST-821	Talk It Over in the Morning	1971	3.00	6.00	12.00
ST-11024	Annie	1972	2.50	5.00	10.00
ST-11172	Danny's Song	1973	2.50	5.00	10.00
ST-11266	Love Song	1974	2.50	5.00	10.00
ST-11324	Country	1974	2.50	5.00	10.00
ST-11354	Highly Prized Possession	1974	2.50	5.00	10.00
ST-11433	Together	1975	2.50	5.00	10.00
ST-11559	Keeping in Touch	1976	2.50	5.00	10.00
ST-11743	Let's Keep It That Way	1978	2.50	5.00	10.00
SW-11849	New Kind of Feeling	1979	2.50	5.00	10.00
SOO-12012	I'll Always Love You	1979	2.50	5.00	10.00
ST-12039	A Country Collection	1980	2.50	5.00	10.00
SOO-12064	Somebody's Waiting	1980	2.50	5.00	10.00
SOO-12110	Anne Murray's Greatest Hits	1980	2.50	5.00	10.00
SOO-12144	Where Do You Go When You Dream	1981	2.50	5.00	10.00
ST-12225	The Hottest Night of the Year	1982	2.50	5.00	10.00
ST-12301	A Little Good News	1983	2.50	5.00	10.00
SJ-12363	Heart Over Mind	1984	2.50	5.00	10.00
SJ-12466	Something to Talk About	1986	2.50	5.00	10.00
PJ-12562	Harmony	1987	2.50	5.00	10.00
SN-16080	Talk It Over in the Morning	1980	2.00	4.00	8.00
—Budget-line reissue					
SN-16081	Highly Prized Possession	1980	2.00	4.00	8.00
—Budget-line reissue					
SN-16082	Keeping in Touch	1980	2.00	4.00	8.00
—Budget-line reissue					
SN-16211	Danny's Song	1981	2.00	4.00	8.00
—Budget-line reissue					
SN-16212	Love Song	1981	2.00	4.00	8.00
—Budget-line reissue					
SN-16213	Country	1981	2.00	4.00	8.00
—Budget-line reissue					
SN-16232	Christmas Wishes	1981	2.50	5.00	10.00
—Original issue was on the budget-line series					
SN-16233	There's a Hippo in My Tub	1981	2.50	5.00	10.00
—Original issue was on the budget-line series					
SN-16282	Together	1982	2.00	4.00	8.00
—Budget-line reissue					
SN-16283	New Kind of Feeling	1982	2.00	4.00	8.00
—Budget-line reissue					
SN-16338	A Country Collection	198?	2.00	4.00	8.00
—Budget-line reissue					
SN-16341	Let's Keep It That Way	198?	2.00	4.00	8.00
—Budget-line reissue					
C1-48764	As I Am	1988	2.50	5.00	10.00
C1-90886	Christmas	1987	2.00	4.00	8.00
C1-92072	Greatest Hits Volume II	1989	3.00	6.00	12.00
CAPITOL NASHVILLE					
R 173232	You Will	1990	5.00	10.00	20.00
—Only released on vinyl through BMG Direct Marketing					
PICKWICK					
SPC-3350	What About Me	197?	2.00	4.00	8.00

MURRAY, ANNE, AND GLEN CAMPBELL

Also see each artist's individual listings.

Number	Title (A Side/B Side)	Yr	VG	VG+	NM
45s					
CAPITOL					
3200	I Say a Little Prayer-By the Time I Get to Phoenix/All Through the Night	1971	—	2.50	5.00
3287	United We Stand/Ease Your Pain	1972	—	2.50	5.00
Albums					
CAPITOL					
SW-869	Anne Murray/Glen Campbell	1971	3.00	6.00	12.00
SN-16144	Anne Murray/Glen Campbell	1980	2.00	4.00	8.00
—Budget-line reissue					

MURRAY, JACK

Number	Title (A Side/B Side)	Yr	VG	VG+	NM
45s					
LAURIE					
3199	Surfin' with Me/What Do You Think of Me Baby	1963	3.75	7.50	15.00

MURRAY, RAY, AND THE DYNAMICS

Number	Title (A Side/B Side)	Yr	VG	VG+	NM
45s					
ARBO					
222	With All My Love/Baby, What You Want Me to Do	1960	25.00	50.00	100.00

MURRAY THE "K"

Also see VARIOUS ARTISTS COLLECTIONS.

Number	Title (A Side/B Side)	Yr	VG	VG+	NM
45s					
BRS					
1/2	Murray the "K" and The Beatles As It Happened	1964	10.00	20.00	40.00
1/2 [PS]	Murray the "K" and The Beatles As It Happened	1964	30.00	60.00	120.00
IBC					
F4KM-0082/3	Murray the "K" and The Beatles As It Happened	1976	2.50	5.00	10.00
F4KM-0082/3 [PS]	Murray the "K" and The Beatles As It Happened	1976	2.50	5.00	10.00
RED BIRD					
10-045	It's What's Happening, Baby/Sins of a Family	1966	3.75	7.50	15.00

MUSIC ASYLUM, THE

Number	Title (A Side/B Side)	Yr	VG	VG+	NM
45s					
ASCOT					
2238	Yesterday's Children/I Need Someone (The Painter)	1967	2.50	5.00	10.00
Albums					
UNITED ARTISTS					
UAS-6778	Commit Thyself	1970	5.00	10.00	20.00

MUSIC COMPANY, THE

Number	Title (A Side/B Side)	Yr	VG	VG+	NM
Albums					
CRESTVIEW					
CRS-3057	Hard and Heavy	196?	6.25	12.50	25.00
MIRWOOD					
M-7002 [M]	Rubber Soul Jazz	1966	5.00	10.00	20.00
MS-7002 [S]	Rubber Soul Jazz	1966	6.25	12.50	25.00

MUSIC EXPLOSION, THE

Number	Title (A Side/B Side)	Yr	VG	VG+	NM
45s					
ATTACK					
1404	The Little Black Egg/Stay By My Side	1966	6.25	12.50	25.00
LAURIE					
3380	Little Bit O'Soul/I See the Light	1967	3.00	6.00	12.00
3400	Can't Stop Now/Sunshine Games	1967	2.00	4.00	8.00
3414	We Gotta Go Home/Hearts and Flowers	1967	2.00	4.00	8.00
3429	What You Want/Road Runner	1968	2.00	4.00	8.00
3440	Where Are We Going/Flash	1968	2.00	4.00	8.00
3454	Yes Sir/Dazzling	1968	2.00	4.00	8.00
3466	Jack in the Box/Rewind	1968	2.00	4.00	8.00
3479	What's Your Name/Call Me Anything	1969	2.00	4.00	8.00
3500	The Little Black Egg/Stay By My Side	1969	2.00	4.00	8.00
Albums					
LAURIE					
LLP-2040 [M]	Little Bit O'Soul	1967	5.00	10.00	20.00
SLLP-2040 [S]	Little Bit O'Soul	1967	6.25	12.50	25.00

MUSIC MACHINE, THE

Also see T.S. BONNIWELL.

Number	Title (A Side/B Side)	Yr	VG	VG+	NM
45s					
BELL					
764	Mother Nature—Father Earth/Advise and Consent	1969	2.00	4.00	8.00
ORIGINAL SOUND					
(no #)	The Music Machine	1967	2.50	5.00	10.00
—Custom sleeve, large center hole, not assigned to any one record, with pictures of band members on front and ads for "Oldies But Goodies" LPs on back					
61	Talk Talk/Come On In	1966	3.00	6.00	12.00
67	The People in Me/Masculine Institution	1967	2.50	5.00	10.00
71	Double Yellow Line/Absolutely Positive	1967	2.50	5.00	10.00
75	I've Loved You/The Eagle Never Hunts the Fly	1967	2.50	5.00	10.00
82	Hey Joe/Wrong	1968	2.50	5.00	10.00
SUNDAZED					
131	Point of No Return/King Mixer	199?	—	—	2.00
131 [PS]	Point of No Return/King Mixer	199?	—	—	2.00
WARNER BROS.					
7093	Bottom of the Soul/Astrologically Incompatible	1968	2.00	4.00	8.00
7093 [PS]	Bottom of the Soul/Astrologically Incompatible	1968	3.75	7.50	15.00
7199	To the Light/You'll Love Me Again	1968	2.00	4.00	8.00
Albums					
ORIGINAL SOUND					
5015 [M]	(Turn On) The Music Machine	1966	10.00	20.00	40.00
8875 [S]	(Turn On) The Music Machine	1966	12.50	25.00	50.00
WARNER BROS.					
W 1732 [M]	Bonniwell's Music Machine	1967	6.25	12.50	25.00
WS 1732 [S]	Bonniwell's Music Machine	1967	10.00	20.00	40.00

MYDDLE CLASS, THE

Number	Title (A Side/B Side)	Yr	VG	VG+	NM
45s					
BUDDAH					
150	I Happen to Love You/Don't Let Me Sleep Too Long	1969	2.50	5.00	10.00
TOMORROW					
912	Don't Look Back/Wind Chimes Laughter	1966	5.00	10.00	20.00
7501	Gates of Eden/Free As the Wind	1966	5.00	10.00	20.00
7503	I Happen to Love You/Don't Let Me Sleep Too Long	1966	6.25	12.50	25.00

MYLES, BILLY

Number	Title (A Side/B Side)	Yr	VG	VG+	NM
45s					
DOT					
15809	King of Clowns/So In Need of You	1958	5.00	10.00	20.00
EMBER					
1026	The Joker (That's What They Call Me)/Honey Bee	1957	7.50	15.00	30.00
1040	Price of Your Love/I'm Too Sentimental	1958	6.25	12.50	25.00
1046	I'm Gonna Walk/Price of Your Love	1958	6.25	12.50	25.00
KING					
5395	Dance Little Girlie/Two Empty Arms	1960	3.75	7.50	15.00

MYSTERY TOUR, THE

Number	Title (A Side/B Side)	Yr	VG	VG+	NM
45s					
MGM					
14097	The Ballad of Paul/The Ballad of Paul (Follow the Bouncing Ball)	1969	6.25	12.50	25.00

MYSTIC ASTROLOGICAL CRYSTAL BAND, THE

Number	Title (A Side/B Side)	Yr	VG	VG+	NM
45s					
CAROLE					
1004	Flowers Never Cry/(B-side unknown)	1967	6.25	12.50	25.00
Albums					
CAROLE					
8001 [M]	Mystic Astrological Crystal Band	1967	6.25	12.50	25.00
S-8001 [S]	Mystic Astrological Crystal Band	1967	7.50	15.00	30.00
S-8003	Clip Out, Put On Book	1968	7.50	15.00	30.00

MYSTIC MOODS ORCHESTRA, THE

Number	Title (A Side/B Side)	Yr	VG	VG+	NM
45s					
PHILIPS					
40366	Fire Island/A Dream	1966	—	3.00	6.00
40419	Theme from "The Sand Pebbles"/Wednesday's Child	1966	—	3.00	6.00
40581	Medley: Sounds of Silence-Canticle-Scarborough Fair/Homeward Bound	1969	—	2.50	5.00
40623	Early Morning Rain/Lalena	1969	—	2.50	5.00
40659	Love Token/Green, Green Grass of Home	1970	—	2.50	5.00
40696	Love Grows (Where My Rosemary Goes)/Early in the Morning	1971	—	2.00	4.00
SOUNDBIRD					
5002	Honeytrippin'/Midnight Snack	197?	—	2.00	4.00
WARNER BROS.					
7686	Awakening/Cosmic Sea	1973	—	2.00	4.00
7743	Astral Trip/Drifting Thought	1973	—	2.00	4.00
7817	Your Place or Mine/Any Way You Want It	1974	—	2.00	4.00
Albums					
BAINBRIDGE					
6201	More Than Music	1982	—	3.00	6.00
6202	Moods for a Stormy Night	1982	—	3.00	6.00
—Reissue of Sound Bird 7504					
6203	Mexico!	1982	—	3.00	6.00
6204	Nightide	1982	—	3.00	6.00
—Reissue of Sound Bird 7502					
6205	One Stormy Night	1982	—	3.00	6.00
—Reissue of Sound Bird 7501					
6206	Emotions	1982	—	3.00	6.00
—Reissue of Sound Bird 7505					
6207	Love Token	1982	—	3.00	6.00
6208	Stormy Weekend	1982	—	3.00	6.00
—Reissue of Sound Bird 7506					
6209	Highway One	1982	—	3.00	6.00
6210	English Muffins	1982	—	3.00	6.00
6211	Country Lovin' Folk	1982	—	3.00	6.00
—Reissue of Sound Bird 8512					
6212	Extensions	1982	—	3.00	6.00
6215	Erogenous	1982	—	3.00	6.00
—Reissue of Sound Bird 7509					
6216	Another Stormy Night	1983	2.00	4.00	8.00
6219	Summer Moods	1985	2.00	4.00	8.00
MOBILE FIDELITY					
1-001	Emotions	1979	6.25	12.50	25.00
—Audiophile vinyl					
1-002	Cosmic Forces	1979	6.25	12.50	25.00
—Audiophile vinyl					
1-003	Stormy Weekend	1979	6.25	12.50	25.00
—Audiophile vinyl					
PHILIPS					
PHM 200205 [M]	One Stormy Night	1966	3.00	6.00	12.00
PHM 200213 [M]	Nightide	1966	3.00	6.00	12.00
PHM 200231 [M]	More Than Music	1967	3.75	7.50	15.00
PHM 200250 [M]	Mexican Trip	1967	3.75	7.50	15.00
PHM 200260 [M]	The Mystic Moods of Love	1968	3.75	7.50	15.00
PHS 600205 [S]	One Stormy Night	1966	3.75	7.50	15.00
PHS 600213 [S]	Nightide	1966	3.75	7.50	15.00
PHS 600231 [S]	More Than Music	1967	3.00	6.00	12.00
PHS 600250 [S]	Mexican Trip	1967	3.00	6.00	12.00
PHS 600260 [S]	The Mystic Moods of Love	1968	3.00	6.00	12.00
PHS 600277	Emotions	1968	3.00	6.00	12.00
PHS 600301	Extensions	1969	3.00	6.00	12.00
PHS 600321	Love Token	1969	3.00	6.00	12.00
PHS 600342	Stormy Weekend	1970	3.00	6.00	12.00
PHS 600349	English Muffins	1970	3.00	6.00	12.00
PHS 600351	Country Lovin' Folk	1971	3.00	6.00	12.00
SOUND BIRD					
7501	One Stormy Night	1975	2.00	4.00	8.00
—Reissue of Warner Bros. 2594					
7502	Nightide	1975	2.00	4.00	8.00
—Reissue of Warner Bros. 2593					
7503	Man and...	1975	2.00	4.00	8.00
7504	Moods for a Stormy Night	1975	2.00	4.00	8.00
7505	Emotions	1975	2.00	4.00	8.00
7506	Stormy Weekend	1975	2.00	4.00	8.00
—Reissue of Warner Bros. 2596					
7507	Touch	1975	2.00	4.00	8.00
SQ 7507 [Q]	Touch	1975	3.00	6.00	12.00
7508	Love the One You're With	1975	2.00	4.00	8.00
—Reissue of Warner Bros. 2577					
SQ 7508 [Q]	Love the One You're With	1975	3.00	6.00	12.00
—Reissue of Warner Bros. BS4 2577					
7509	Erogenous	1975	2.00	4.00	8.00
—Reissue of Warner Bros. 2786					
SQ 7509 [Q]	Erogenous	1975	3.00	6.00	12.00
—Reissue of Warner Bros. BS4 2786					
7510	Being with You	1976	2.50	5.00	10.00

Number	Title (A Side/B Side)	Yr	VG	VG+	NM
SQ 7510 [Q]	Being with You	1976	4.00	8.00	16.00
8503	Misty	1978	2.00	4.00	8.00
8505	Midnight	1978	2.00	4.00	8.00
8508	Alone Together	1978	2.00	4.00	8.00
8510	Being with You	1978	2.00	4.00	8.00
—Reissue of Sound Bird 7510					
8511	Cosmic Forces	1978	2.00	4.00	8.00
8512	Country Lovin' Folk	1978	2.00	4.00	8.00
8514	Simple	1978	2.00	4.00	8.00
WARNER BROS.					
BS 2577	Love the One You're With	1972	3.00	6.00	12.00
BS4 2577 [Q]	Love the One You're With	1974	4.00	8.00	16.00
BS 2593	Nightide	1972	2.50	5.00	10.00
—Reissue of Philips 600-213					
BS 2594	One Stormy Night	1972	2.50	5.00	10.00
—Reissue of Philips 600-205					
BS 2595	Love Token	1972	2.50	5.00	10.00
—Reissue of Philips 600-321					
BS 2596	Stormy Weekend	1972	2.50	5.00	10.00
—Reissue of Philips 600-342					
BS 2597	Emotions	1972	2.50	5.00	10.00
—Reissue of Philips 600-277					
BS 2598	The Mystic Moods of Love	1972	2.50	5.00	10.00
—Reissue of Philips 600-260					
BS 2648	Highway One	1973	3.00	6.00	12.00
BS4 2648 [Q]	Highway One	1974	4.00	8.00	16.00
BS 2690	Awakening	1973	3.00	6.00	12.00
BS4 2690 [Q]	Awakening	1974	4.00	8.00	16.00
BS 2745	Clear Light	1974	3.00	6.00	12.00
BS4 2745 [Q]	Clear Light	1974	4.00	8.00	16.00
BS 2786	Erogenous	1974	2.50	5.00	10.00
BS4 2786 [Q]	Erogenous	1974	4.00	8.00	16.00

MYSTIC NUMBER NATIONAL BANK, THE

Albums

Number	Title (A Side/B Side)	Yr	VG	VG+	NM
PROBE					
CPLP-4501	The Mystic Number National Bank	1969	5.00	10.00	20.00

MYSTIC SIVA

Albums

Number	Title (A Side/B Side)	Yr	VG	VG+	NM
VO					
19713	Mystic Siva	1971	250.00	500.00	1000.

MYSTICS, THE

45s

Number	Title (A Side/B Side)	Yr	VG	VG+	NM
AMBIENT SOUND					
02871	Now That Summer Is Here/Prayer to An Angel	1982	—	2.50	5.00
BLACK CAT					
101	Snoopy/Ooh Poo Pah Doo	1966	10.00	20.00	40.00
CONSTELLATION					
138	She's Got Everything/Just a Loser	1964	3.00	6.00	12.00
DOT					
16862	Now and For Always/Didn't We Have a Good Time	1966	2.50	5.00	10.00
KING					
5678	Mashed Potatoes With Me/The Hoppy Hop	1962	3.75	7.50	15.00
5735	The Jumpin' Bean/Just For Your Love	1963	3.75	7.50	15.00
LAURIE					
3028 [M]	Hushabye/Adam and Eve	1959	7.50	15.00	30.00
S-3028 [S]	Hushabye/Adam and Eve	1959	30.00	60.00	120.00
3038	Don't Take the Stars/So Tenderly	1959	6.25	12.50	25.00
3047	All Through the Night/To Think of You Again	1960	6.25	12.50	25.00
3058	White Cliffs of Dover/Blue Star	1960	6.25	12.50	25.00
3086	Star Crossed Lovers/Goodbye Mr. Blue	1961	6.25	12.50	25.00
3104	Sunday Kind of Love/Darling I Know How	1961	7.50	15.00	30.00
NOLTA					
353	The Fox/Dan	1963	3.75	7.50	15.00

Albums

Number	Title (A Side/B Side)	Yr	VG	VG+	NM
AMBIENT SOUND					
FZ 37716	Crazy for You	1982	2.50	5.00	10.00
COLLECTABLES					
COL-5043	16 Golden Classics	198?	2.50	5.00	10.00

N

NABAY

45s

IMPACT

Number	Title (A Side/B Side)	Yr	VG	VG+	NM
1032	Believe It or Not/(Instrumental)	1967	100.00	200.00	400.00

NABORS, JIM

45s

COLUMBIA

Number	Title (A Side/B Side)	Yr	VG	VG+	NM
AE 1028 [DJ]	Ave Maria/How Great Thou Art	1971	—	3.00	6.00
10035	That's What Friends Are For/Lena the Queen of the Honky-Tonk Angels	1974	—	2.00	4.00
43395	Shazam!/Old Blue	1965	3.00	6.00	12.00
43553	Love Me with All Your Heart/Rock-a-Bye	1966	2.00	4.00	8.00
43751	You Don't Know Me/You're Gonna Hear from Me	1966	2.00	4.00	8.00
44114	You Know You Don't Want Me/It Hurts to Say Goodbye	1967	—	3.00	6.00
44241	You Don't Have to Say You Love Me/Time After Time	1967	—	3.00	6.00
44359	White Christmas/In A Humble Place	1967	—	3.00	6.00
44462	The Impossible Dream/Time After Time	1968	—	3.00	6.00
44537	To Give (The Reason I Live)/I Must Have Been Out of My Mind	1968	—	3.00	6.00
44965	It's My Life/Young Hearts	1969	—	3.00	6.00
45053	O Holy Night/I Was a King at Jesus' Birth	1969	—	3.00	6.00
45126	Tomorrow Never Comes/It's My Life	1970	—	2.50	5.00
45126 [PS]	Tomorrow Never Comes/It's My Life	1970	2.00	4.00	8.00
45271	I'll Begin Again/Louisiana Lady	1970	—	2.50	5.00
45321	God Bless America/The Star-Spangled Banner	1971	—	2.50	5.00
45636	(At) The End (Of a Rainbow)/It Won't Hurt to Try It	1972	—	2.50	5.00
45932	Oh Babe, What Would You Say/Cardboards, Crayons and Clay	1973	—	2.50	5.00

RANWOOD

Number	Title (A Side/B Side)	Yr	VG	VG+	NM
1081	Always Leave 'Em Laughing/Sing Me a Love Song	1977	—	2.00	4.00

ROULETTE

Number	Title (A Side/B Side)	Yr	VG	VG+	NM
4105	There's No Tomorrow/I'm Working	1958	6.25	12.50	25.00

—As "Jimmy Nabors"

Albums

CAPITOL SPECIAL MARKETS

Number	Title (A Side/B Side)	Yr	VG	VG+	NM
SL-8136	20 All-Time Favorites	1977	2.50	5.00	10.00

COLUMBIA

Number	Title (A Side/B Side)	Yr	VG	VG+	NM
CS 1020	The Jim Nabors Hour	1970	3.00	6.00	12.00
CL 2368 [M]	Shazam! (Gomer Pyle, U.S.M.C.)	1965	5.00	10.00	20.00
CL 2558 [M]	Jim Nabors Sings Love Me with All Your Heart	1966	3.00	6.00	12.00
CL 2665 [M]	Jim Nabors By Request	1967	3.00	6.00	12.00
CL 2703 [M]	The Things I Love	1967	3.00	6.00	12.00
CL 2731 [M]	Jim Nabors' Christmas Album	1967	3.00	6.00	12.00
CS 9168 [S]	Shazam! (Gomer Pyle, U.S.M.C.)	1965	6.25	12.50	25.00
CS 9358 [S]	Jim Nabors Sings Love Me with All Your Heart	1966	3.75	7.50	15.00
CS 9465 [S]	Jim Nabors By Request	1967	3.75	7.50	15.00
CS 9503 [S]	The Things I Love	1967	3.75	7.50	15.00
CS 9531	Jim Nabors' Christmas Album	1970	2.50	5.00	10.00
—Later editions with orange label					
CS 9531 [S]	Jim Nabors' Christmas Album	1967	3.00	6.00	12.00
—Originals with "360 Sound" label					
CS 9620	Kiss Me Goodbye	1968	3.00	6.00	12.00
CS 9716	The Lord's Prayer and Other Sacred Songs	1968	3.00	6.00	12.00
PC 9716	The Lord's Prayer	1979	2.00	4.00	8.00
—Budget-line reissue					
CS 9817	Galveston	1969	3.00	6.00	12.00
C 30129	Everything Is Beautiful	1970	3.00	6.00	12.00
C 30449	For the Good Times/The Jim Nabors Hour	1971	3.00	6.00	12.00
3C 30671	How Great Thou Art	198?	2.00	4.00	8.00
—Budget-line reissue					
C 30671	How Great Thou Art	1971	3.00	6.00	12.00
C 30810	Help Me Make It Through the Night	1971	3.00	6.00	12.00
KC 31336	The Way of Love	1972	3.00	6.00	12.00
KG 31591 [(2)]	Great Love Songs	1972	3.75	7.50	15.00
PG 31591 [(2)]	Great Love Songs	198?	2.50	5.00	10.00
—Budget-line reissue					
C 31630	Merry Christmas	1972	2.50	5.00	10.00
KG 31973 [(2)]	The World of Jim Nabors	1972	3.75	7.50	15.00
PG 31973 [(2)]	The World of Jim Nabors	1979	2.50	5.00	10.00
—Budget-line reissue					
KC 32377	The Twelfth of Never	1972	3.00	6.00	12.00
KC 32909	Peace in the Valley	1973	3.00	6.00	12.00
PC 32909	Peace in the Valley	1979	2.00	4.00	8.00
—Budget-line reissue					
KC 32950	It's My Life	1973	3.00	6.00	12.00
KC 33401	A Very Special Love Song	1974	3.00	6.00	12.00
PC 33401	A Very Special Love Song	1979	2.00	4.00	8.00
—Budget-line reissue					
CG 33618 [(2)]	The Lord's Prayer/How Great Thou Art	1975	3.75	7.50	15.00

COLUMBIA SPECIAL PRODUCTS

Number	Title (A Side/B Side)	Yr	VG	VG+	NM
P 13507	Somewhere My Love	1977	2.50	5.00	10.00

HARMONY

Number	Title (A Side/B Side)	Yr	VG	VG+	NM
KH 30398	More	1971	2.50	5.00	10.00

PAIR

Number	Title (A Side/B Side)	Yr	VG	VG+	NM
PDL2-1077 [(2)]	The Very Special Warmth of Jim Nabors	1986	3.00	6.00	12.00
PDL2-1097 [(2)]	On the Country Side	1986	3.00	6.00	12.00

RANWOOD

Number	Title (A Side/B Side)	Yr	VG	VG+	NM
R-7017 [(2)]	22 Great Hymn and Country Favorites	1984	3.00	6.00	12.00
R-8157	Old Time Religion	1976	2.50	5.00	10.00
R-8164	Town & Country	1976	2.50	5.00	10.00
R-8176	Sincerely	1977	2.50	5.00	10.00
R-8178	I See God	1977	2.50	5.00	10.00

REALM

Number	Title (A Side/B Side)	Yr	VG	VG+	NM
1V-8170	Christmas with Jim Nabors	1982	2.00	4.00	8.00

NADER, RICHARD

See VARIOUS ARTISTS COLLECTIONS.

NAGLE, RON

Albums

WARNER BROS.

Number	Title (A Side/B Side)	Yr	VG	VG+	NM
WS 1902	Bad Rice	1970	5.00	10.00	20.00

NAPOLEON XIV

45s

WARNER BROS.

Number	Title (A Side/B Side)	Yr	VG	VG+	NM
5831	They're Coming to Take Me Away, Ha-Haaa!/ !Aaah-Ah, Yawa Em Ekat ot Gnimoc Er'yeht	1966	3.00	6.00	12.00
5853	I'm in Love with My Little Red Tricycle/Doin' the Napoleon	1966	2.50	5.00	10.00
7726	They're Coming to Take Me Away, Ha-Haaa!/ !Aaah-Ah, Yawa Em Ekat ot Gnimoc Er'yeht	1973	2.00	4.00	8.00

Albums

RHINO

Number	Title (A Side/B Side)	Yr	VG	VG+	NM
RNLP 816	They're Coming to Take Me Away, Ha-Haaa!	1985	3.00	6.00	12.00

WARNER BROS.

Number	Title (A Side/B Side)	Yr	VG	VG+	NM
W 1661 [M]	They're Coming to Take Me Away, Ha-Haaa!	1966	15.00	30.00	60.00
WS 1661 [S]	They're Coming to Take Me Away, Ha-Haaa!	1966	25.00	50.00	100.00

NARZ, JACK

Albums

DOT

Number	Title (A Side/B Side)	Yr	VG	VG+	NM
DLP-3244 [M]	Sing the Folk Hits with Jack Narz	1960	6.25	12.50	25.00
DLP-25244 [S]	Sing the Folk Hits with Jack Narz	1960	7.50	15.00	30.00

NASH, GRAHAM

Also see CROSBY, STILLS AND NASH; CROSBY, STILLS, NASH & YOUNG; THE HOLLIES.

45s

ATLANTIC

Number	Title (A Side/B Side)	Yr	VG	VG+	NM
2804	Chicago/Simple Man	1971	—	3.00	6.00
2827	Military Madness/Sleep Song	1971	—	2.50	5.00
2840	Used to Be a King/Wounded Bird	1971	—	2.50	5.00
2990	Prison Song/Hey You (Looking at the Moon)	1973	—	2.50	5.00
89373	Chippin' Away/Newday	1986	—	—	3.00
89396	Sad Eyes/Newday	1986	—	—	3.00
89434	Innocent Eyes/I Got a Rock	1986	—	—	3.00
89434 [PS]	Innocent Eyes/I Got a Rock	1986	—	2.00	4.00

CAPITOL

Number	Title (A Side/B Side)	Yr	VG	VG+	NM
4812	In the 80's/T.V. Guide	1979	—	2.00	4.00
4849	Helicopter Song/Out on the Island	1980	—	2.00	4.00
4879	Earth and Sky/Magical Child	1980	—	2.00	4.00

Albums

ATLANTIC

Number	Title (A Side/B Side)	Yr	VG	VG+	NM
SD 7204	Songs for Beginners	1971	3.00	6.00	12.00
SD 7288	Wild Tales	1974	2.50	5.00	10.00
81633	Innocent Eyes	1986	2.00	4.00	8.00

CAPITOL

Number	Title (A Side/B Side)	Yr	VG	VG+	NM
SWAK-12014	Earth & Sky	1980	2.50	5.00	10.00

NASH, GRAHAM, AND DAVID CROSBY

Also see each artist's individual listings.

45s

ABC

Number	Title (A Side/B Side)	Yr	VG	VG+	NM
12140	Carry Me/Mama Lion	1975	—	2.00	4.00
12165	Bittersweet/Take the Money and Run	1976	—	2.00	4.00
12185	Love Workout/Bittersweet	1976	—	2.00	4.00
12199	Out of the Darkness/Broken Bird	1976	—	2.00	4.00
12217	Foolish Man/Spotlight	1976	—	2.00	4.00

ATLANTIC

Number	Title (A Side/B Side)	Yr	VG	VG+	NM
2873	Immigration Man/Whole Cloth	1972	—	2.50	5.00
2892	Southbound Train/The Wall Song	1972	—	2.50	5.00

Albums

ABC

Number	Title (A Side/B Side)	Yr	VG	VG+	NM
D-902	Wind on the Water	1975	2.50	5.00	10.00
D-956	Whistling Down the Wire	1976	2.50	5.00	10.00
AA-1042	Crosby/Nash — Live	1977	2.50	5.00	10.00
AA-1102	The Best of Crosby/Nash	1978	2.50	5.00	10.00

ATLANTIC

Number	Title (A Side/B Side)	Yr	VG	VG+	NM
SD 7220	Graham Nash/David Crosby	1972	3.00	6.00	12.00

MCA

Number	Title (A Side/B Side)	Yr	VG	VG+	NM
37007	Wind on the Water	198?	2.00	4.00	8.00
—Reissue of ABC 902					
37008	The Best of Crosby/Nash	198?	2.00	4.00	8.00
—Reissue of ABC 1102					

NASH, JOHNNY

Also see PAUL ANKA/GEORGE HAMILTON IV/JOHNNY NASH.

45s

ABC-PARAMOUNT

Number	Title (A Side/B Side)	Yr	VG	VG+	NM
9743	Out of Town/A Teenager Sings the Blues	1956	5.00	10.00	20.00
9844	The Ladder of Love/I'll Walk Alone	1957	5.00	10.00	20.00
9874	A Very Special Love/Won't You Let Me Share My Love with You	1957	5.00	10.00	20.00
9894	My Pledge to You/It's So Easy to Say	1958	5.00	10.00	20.00
9927	Please Don't Go/I Lost My Love Last Night	1958	5.00	10.00	20.00
9942	Truly Love/You're Looking at Me	1958	5.00	10.00	20.00
9960	Almost in Your Arms/Midnight Moonlight	1958	5.00	10.00	20.00
9989	Roots of Heaven/Walk with Faith in Your Heart	1958	5.00	10.00	20.00
9996	As Time Goes By/The Voice of Love	1959	5.00	10.00	20.00
9996 [PS]	As Time Goes By/The Voice of Love	1959	10.00	20.00	40.00
10026	And the Angels Sing/Baby, Baby, Baby	1959	5.00	10.00	20.00
10046	Take a Giant Step/But Not for Me	1959	5.00	10.00	20.00
10060	The Wish/Too Proud	1959	5.00	10.00	20.00
10076	A Place in the Sun/Goodbye	1960	3.75	7.50	15.00
10095	Never My Love/(You've Got the) Love I Love	1960	3.75	7.50	15.00
10112	Let the Rest of the World Go By/Music of Love	1960	3.75	7.50	15.00

Number	Title (A Side/B Side)	Yr	VG	VG+	NM
10137	(Looks Like) The End of the World/We Kissed	1960	3.75	7.50	15.00
10160	Kisses/Somebody	1960	3.75	7.50	15.00
10181	World of Tears/Some of Your Lovin'	1961	3.00	6.00	12.00
10205	I Need Someone to Stand By/A House on the Hill	1961	3.00	6.00	12.00
10212	A Thousand Miles Away/I Need Someone to Stand By Me	1961	3.00	6.00	12.00
10230	I'm Counting on You/I Lost My Baby	1961	3.00	6.00	12.00
10251	Too Much Love/Love's Young Dream	1961	3.00	6.00	12.00
ARGO					
5471	Talk to Me/Love Ain't Nothin'	1964	2.00	4.00	8.00
5479	Then You Can Tell Me Goodbye/Always	1964	2.00	4.00	8.00
5492	Spring Is Here/Strange Feeling	1965	2.00	4.00	8.00
5501	Teardrops in the Rain/I Know What I Want	1965	2.00	4.00	8.00
ATLANTIC					
2344	Big City/Somewhere	1966	2.00	4.00	8.00
CADET					
5528	Teardrops in the Rain/Get Myself Together	1966	5.00	10.00	20.00
EPIC					
10873	Stir It Up/Cream Puff	1972	—	3.50	7.00
10902	I Can See Clearly Now/How Good It Is	1972	—	3.00	6.00
10949	Stir It Up/Ooh Baby You've Been Good to Me	1973	—	3.00	6.00
11003	My Merry-Go-Round/We're Trying to Get Back to You	1973	—	2.50	5.00
11034	Ooh What a Feeling/Yellow House	1973	—	2.50	5.00
11070	Loving You/Gonna Open Up My Heart Again	1973	—	2.50	5.00
50021	You Can't Go Halfway/The Very First Time	1974	—	2.50	5.00
50051	Beautiful Baby/Celebrate Life	1974	—	2.50	5.00
50091	Good Vibrations/The Very First Time	1975	—	2.50	5.00
50138	Tears on My Pillow (I Can't Take It)/Beautiful Baby	1975	—	2.50	5.00
50219	(What a) Wonderful World/Rock It Baby (We've Got a Date)	1976	—	2.50	5.00
50386	Back in Time/That Woman	1977	—	2.00	4.00
50737	Closer/Mr. Sea	1979	—	2.00	4.00
50821	You're the One/Don't Forget	1980	—	2.00	4.00
GROOVE					
58-0018	Helpless/I've Got a Lot to Offer, Darling	1963	2.50	5.00	10.00
58-0018 [PS]	Helpless/I've Got a Lot to Offer, Darling	1963	7.50	15.00	30.00
58-0021	Deep in the Heart of Harlem/What Kind of Love Is This	1963	10.00	20.00	40.00
58-0021 [PS]	Deep in the Heart of Harlem/What Kind of Love Is This	1963	12.50	25.00	50.00
58-0026	It's No Good for Me/Town of Lonely Hearts	1963	2.50	5.00	10.00
58-0030	I'm Leaving/Oh Mary Don't You Weep	1964	2.50	5.00	10.00
JAD					
207	Hold Me Tight/Cupid	1968	2.00	4.00	8.00
—Mostly light green label with purple trim					
209	You Got Soul/Don't Cry	1968	2.00	4.00	8.00
214	Lovey Dovey/You Got Soul	1969	—	3.00	6.00
215	Sweet Charity/People in Love	1969	—	3.00	6.00
218	Love and Peace/People in Love	1969	—	3.00	6.00
220	Cupid/Hold Me Tight	1969	—	3.00	6.00
223	What a Groovy Feeling/You Got Soul (Part 1)	1970	—	3.00	6.00
JANUS					
136	Falling In and Out of Love/You've Got to Change Your Ways	1970	—	3.00	6.00
JODA					
102	Let's Move and Groove (Together)/ Understanding	1965	2.50	5.00	10.00
105	One More Time/Got to Find Her	1965	2.50	5.00	10.00
106	Somewhere/Big City	1966	2.50	5.00	10.00
MGM					
13637	Amen/Perfumed Flower	1966	2.00	4.00	8.00
13683	Good Goodness/You Never Know	1967	2.00	4.00	8.00
13805	Stormy/(I'm So) Glad You're My Baby	1967	2.00	4.00	8.00
WARNER BROS.					
5270	Don't Take Your Love Away/Moment of Weakness	1962	3.00	6.00	12.00
5301	Ol' Man River/My Dear Little Sweetheart	1962	3.00	6.00	12.00
5336	Cigarettes, Whiskey and Wild, Wild Women/I'm Movin' On	1963	3.00	6.00	12.00

Albums

Number	Title (A Side/B Side)	Yr	VG	VG+	NM
ABC-PARAMOUNT					
244 [M]	Johnny Nash	1958	7.50	15.00	30.00
S-244 [S]	Johnny Nash	1959	10.00	20.00	40.00
276 [M]	Quiet Hour	1959	7.50	15.00	30.00
S-276 [S]	Quiet Hour	1959	10.00	20.00	40.00
299 [M]	I Got Rhythm	1959	7.50	15.00	30.00
S-299 [S]	I Got Rhythm	1959	10.00	20.00	40.00
344 [M]	Let's Get Lost	1960	7.50	15.00	30.00
S-344 [S]	Let's Get Lost	1960	10.00	20.00	40.00
383 [M]	Studio Time	1961	7.50	15.00	30.00
S-383 [S]	Studio Time	1961	10.00	20.00	40.00
ARGO					
LP-4038 [M]	Composer's Choice	1964	5.00	10.00	20.00
LPS-4038 [S]	Composer's Choice	1964	6.25	12.50	25.00
EPIC					
KE 31607	I Can See Clearly Now	1972	3.75	7.50	15.00
—Yellow label					
KE 31607	I Can See Clearly Now	1973	3.00	6.00	12.00
—Orange label					
KE 32158	My Merry-Go-Round	1973	3.75	7.50	15.00
PE 32828	Celebrate Life	1974	3.75	7.50	15.00
JAD					
JS-1001	Prince of Peace	1969	6.25	12.50	25.00
JS-1006	Folk Soul	1970	6.25	12.50	25.00
JS-1207	Hold Me Tight	1968	7.50	15.00	30.00

NASHVILLE GUITARS, THE

Albums

Number	Title (A Side/B Side)	Yr	VG	VG+	NM
MONUMENT					
MLP-8058 [M]	The Nashville Guitars	1966	3.75	7.50	15.00
SLP-18058 [S]	The Nashville Guitars	1966	5.00	10.00	20.00

NASHVILLE TEENS, THE

45s

Number	Title (A Side/B Side)	Yr	VG	VG+	NM
LONDON					
9689	Tobacco Road/I Like It Like That	1964	3.75	7.50	15.00
9712	T.N.T./Google Eyes	1964	3.00	6.00	12.00
9736	Devil-in-Law/Find My Way Back Home	1965	3.00	6.00	12.00
MGM					
13357	Little Bird/Whatcha Gonna Do	1965	2.50	5.00	10.00
13406	I Know How It Feels to Be Loved/Soon Forgotten	1965	2.50	5.00	10.00
13483	The Hard Way/Upside Down	1966	2.50	5.00	10.00
13678	That's My Woman/Words	1967	2.50	5.00	10.00
UNITED ARTISTS					
50880	Tennessee Woman/Ella James	1972	5.00	10.00	20.00

Albums

Number	Title (A Side/B Side)	Yr	VG	VG+	NM
LONDON					
PS 407 [R]	Tobacco Road	1964	20.00	40.00	80.00
LL 3407 [M]	Tobacco Road	1964	25.00	50.00	100.00

NATIONAL GALLERY, THE

Albums

Number	Title (A Side/B Side)	Yr	VG	VG+	NM
PHILIPS					
PHS 600266	The National Gallery (Performing Musical Interpretations of the Paintings of Paul Klee)	1968	7.50	15.00	30.00

NATIONAL LAMPOON

Also see MELISSA MANCHESTER.

45s

Number	Title (A Side/B Side)	Yr	VG	VG+	NM
BLUE THUMB					
218	Deteriorata/Thise Fabulous Sixties	1972	2.00	4.00	8.00
233	Pizza Man/Lemmings Lament	1974	2.00	4.00	8.00
240	The Watergate Tapes/The Silent Majority	1973	2.00	4.00	8.00
LABEL 21					
202	What Were You Expecting — Rock 'n Roll?/(B-side unknown)	197?	—	3.00	6.00
202 [PS]	What Were You Expecting — Rock 'n Roll?/(B-side unknown)	197?	2.50	5.00	10.00

Albums

Number	Title (A Side/B Side)	Yr	VG	VG+	NM
BANANA					
BTS 38	Radio Dinner	1972	3.75	7.50	15.00
BTS 6006	Lemmings	1973	3.75	7.50	15.00
BTS 6008	Missing White House Tapes	1974	3.75	7.50	15.00
EPIC					
PE 33410	Gold Turkey	1974	3.00	6.00	12.00
—Orange label					
PE 33410	Gold Turkey	1979	2.00	4.00	8.00
—Dark blue label					
PE 33956	Goodbye Pop	1975	3.00	6.00	12.00
—Orange label					
PE 33956	Goodbye Pop	1979	2.00	4.00	8.00
—Dark blue label					
LABEL 21					
IMP-2001	That's Not Funny, That's Sick!	1978	2.50	5.00	10.00
PIC-2001 [PD]	That's Not Funny, That's Sick!	1978	5.00	10.00	20.00
IMP-2002	The White Album	1979	2.50	5.00	10.00
MCA					
27023	Lemmings	198?	2.00	4.00	8.00
27024	Radio Dinner	198?	2.00	4.00	8.00
PASSPORT					
PB 6018	Sex, Drugs, Rock and Roll and the End of the World	1982	2.50	5.00	10.00
VISA					
2001	That's Not Funny, That's Sick!	198?	2.00	4.00	8.00
2002	The White Album	198?	2.00	4.00	8.00
7008	Greatest Hits of the National Lampoon	1978	3.00	6.00	12.00

NATIVE BOYS, THE

45s

Number	Title (A Side/B Side)	Yr	VG	VG+	NM
COMBO					
113	Strange Love/Cherrlyn	1956	15.00	30.00	60.00
115	Tears/When I Met You	1956	17.50	35.00	70.00
119	Laughing Love/Valley of Lovers	1956	17.50	35.00	70.00
120	Oh Let Me Dream/I've Got a Feeling	1956	15.00	30.00	60.00
MODERN					
939	Native Girl/It Won't Take Long	1954	100.00	200.00	400.00

NATURAL FOUR, THE

45s

Number	Title (A Side/B Side)	Yr	VG	VG+	NM
ABC					
11205	Why Should We Stop Now/You Did This for Me	1969	2.00	4.00	8.00
11236	Same Thing in Mind/The Situation Needs No Explanation	1969	3.00	6.00	12.00
11253	Hurt/I Thought You Were Mine	1969	6.25	12.50	25.00
11257	Message from a Black Man/Stepping On Up	1970	3.00	6.00	12.00
CURTOM					
0101	Heaven Right Here on Earth/While We're Away	1975	—	2.50	5.00
0104	Love's So Wonderful/What's Happening Here	1975	—	2.50	5.00
0114	It's the Music/It's the Music (Disco Version)	1976	—	2.50	5.00
0119	Free/Nothing Beats a Failure (But a Try)	1976	—	2.50	5.00
1981	Things Will Be Better Tomorrow/Eddie, You Should Know Better	1973	—	2.50	5.00
1984	Try Love Again/Eddie, You Should Know Better	1973	—	2.50	5.00
1990	Can This Be Real/Try Love Again	1973	—	2.50	5.00
1995	Love That Really Counts/Love's Society	1974	—	2.50	5.00
2000	You Bring Out the Best in Me/You Can't Keep Running Away	1974	—	2.50	5.00

Albums

Number	Title (A Side/B Side)	Yr	VG	VG+	NM
CURTOM					
CU 5004	Heaven Right Here on Earth	1975	5.00	10.00	20.00
CRT-8600	The Natural Four	1974	5.00	10.00	20.00

Number	Title (A Side/B Side)	Yr	VG	VG+	NM

NATURALS, THE (1)

45s

Number	Title (A Side/B Side)	Yr	VG	VG+	NM
CALLA					
181	I Can't Share You/Young Generation	1972	—	3.00	6.00
MOTOWN					
1208	Good Things/Where Was I When Love Came By	1972	—	3.00	6.00
SHOUT					
307	Color Him Father/Crystal Blue Persuasion	197?	—	3.00	6.00
310	Cold Day in Hell/(B-side unknown)	197?	—	3.00	6.00

NATURALS, THE (2)

45s

Number	Title (A Side/B Side)	Yr	VG	VG+	NM
BEACON					
462	You Give Me So Much/What a Shape I'm In	1958	10.00	20.00	40.00

NATURALS, THE (3)

45s

Number	Title (A Side/B Side)	Yr	VG	VG+	NM
CHATTAHOOCHIE					
633	Just in Case You Change Your Mind/Why Don't They Understand	1963	3.00	6.00	12.00

NATURALS, THE (4)

45s

Number	Title (A Side/B Side)	Yr	VG	VG+	NM
ERA					
1089	The Mummy/Don't Send Me Away	1959	3.75	7.50	15.00

NATURALS, THE (5)

Also see THE FOUR NATURALS.

45s

Number	Title (A Side/B Side)	Yr	VG	VG+	NM
HUNT					
325	Blue Moon/How Strange	1959	3.75	7.50	15.00
RED TOP					
113	Blue Moon/How Strange	1959	7.50	15.00	30.00

NATURALS, THE (6)

British group.

45s

Number	Title (A Side/B Side)	Yr	VG	VG+	NM
LIBERTY					
55741	I Should Have Known Better/Didn't I	1964	3.00	6.00	12.00
55758	It Was You/Look at Me Now	1964	3.00	6.00	12.00

NATURALS, THE (7)

45s

Number	Title (A Side/B Side)	Yr	VG	VG+	NM
MGM					
12576	Patti Ann/Missing	1957	3.00	6.00	12.00
12576 [PS]	Patti Ann/Missing	1957	5.00	10.00	20.00

NATURALS, THE (8)

45s

Number	Title (A Side/B Side)	Yr	VG	VG+	NM
SMASH					
1925	Different Girls/Hey Fellas	1964	3.00	6.00	12.00

NATURALS, THE (U)

We're not sure if this is a ninth different group.

45s

Number	Title (A Side/B Side)	Yr	VG	VG+	NM
20TH CENTURY FOX					
545	Caravan/Whole Lotta Rockin'	1964	3.00	6.00	12.00

NATURE BOY & FRIENDS

45s

Number	Title (A Side/B Side)	Yr	VG	VG+	NM
BERTRAM INT'L.					
255	Surfer John/John John	1964	10.00	20.00	40.00

NAZARETH

45s

Number	Title (A Side/B Side)	Yr	VG	VG+	NM
A&M					
1453	Broken Down Angel/Hard Living	1973	—	2.50	5.00
1469	Bad Bad Boy/Razamanaz	1973	—	2.50	5.00
1511	Go Down Fighting/This Flight Tonight	1974	—	2.50	5.00
1548	Sunshine/This Flight Tonight	1974	—	2.50	5.00
1671	Love Hurts/Hair of the Dog	1975	—	2.00	4.00
1671 [PS]	Love Hurts/Hair of the Dog	1975	—	3.00	6.00
1854	Loretta/Lift the Lid	1976	—	2.00	4.00
1895	I Want To (Do Everything for You)/I Don't Want to Go On Without You	1976	—	2.00	4.00
1936	Somebody to Roll/This Flight Tonight	1976	—	2.00	4.00
2009	Kentucky Fried Blues/Shot Me Down	1978	—	2.00	4.00
2029	Gone Dead Train/Kentucky Fried Blues	1978	—	2.00	4.00
2116	Expect No Mercy/May the Sunshine	1979	—	2.00	4.00
2130	Whatever You Want Babe/Expect No Mercy	1979	—	2.00	4.00
2158	Star/Expect No Mercy	1979	—	2.00	4.00
2219	Holiday/Ship of Dreams	1980	—	2.00	4.00
2237	Hearts Grown Cold/Ship of Dreams	1980	—	2.00	4.00
2324	Dressed to Kill/Pop the Silo	1981	—	2.00	4.00
2378	Juicy Lucy/Morning Dew	1981	—	2.00	4.00
2389	Hair of the Dog/Holiday	1982	—	2.00	4.00
2421	Love Leads to Madness/Take the Rap	1982	—	2.00	4.00
2444	Dream On/Take the Rap	1982	—	2.00	4.00
WARNER BROS.					
7599	Dear John/Morning Dew	1972	2.00	4.00	8.00

Albums

Number	Title (A Side/B Side)	Yr	VG	VG+	NM
A&M					
SP-3109	Close Enough for Rock 'N' Roll	1981	2.00	4.00	8.00
—Budget-line reissue					
SP-3168	Exercises	1982	2.00	4.00	8.00
—Reissue of Warner Bros. 2639					
SP-3169	Nazareth	1982	2.00	4.00	8.00
—Reissue of Warner Bros. 2615					
SP-3225	Hair of the Dog	1984	2.00	4.00	8.00
—Budget-line reissue					
SP-3226	Hot Tracks	1984	2.00	4.00	8.00
—Budget-line reissue					
SP-3609	Loud 'N' Proud	1974	2.50	5.00	10.00
SP-3641	Rampant	1974	2.50	5.00	10.00
SP-4396	Razamanaz	1973	3.75	7.50	15.00
—First edition with brown label					
SP-4396	Razamanaz	1974	2.50	5.00	10.00
SP-4511	Hair of the Dog	1975	2.50	5.00	10.00
SP-4562	Close Enough for Rock 'N' Roll	1976	2.50	5.00	10.00
SP-4610	Play 'N' the Game	1976	2.50	5.00	10.00
SP-4643	Hot Tracks	1977	2.50	5.00	10.00
SP-4666	Expect No Mercy	1977	2.50	5.00	10.00
SP-4741	No Mean City	1979	2.50	5.00	10.00
SP-4799	Malice in Wonderland	1980	2.50	5.00	10.00
SP-4844	The Fool Circle	1981	2.50	5.00	10.00
SP-4901	2XS	1982	2.50	5.00	10.00
SP-6703 [(2)]	'Snaz	1981	3.00	6.00	12.00
MCA					
5458	Sound Elixir	1983	2.50	5.00	10.00
WARNER BROS.					
BS 2615	Nazareth	1972	5.00	10.00	20.00
BS 2639	Exercises	1972	5.00	10.00	20.00

NAZZ (1)

Also see TODD RUNDGREN.

45s

Number	Title (A Side/B Side)	Yr	VG	VG+	NM
SGC					
001	Hello It's Me/Open My Eyes	1969	5.00	10.00	20.00
—First pressing: Light yellow label, no horizontal lines on label					
001	Hello It's Me/Open My Eyes	1969	3.00	6.00	12.00
—Second pressing: Darker yellow label with horizontal lines					
001	Hello It's Me/Open My Eyes	1969	2.00	4.00	8.00
—Third printing: Mostly green label with some yellow. Red vinyl copies on any label are bootlegs.					
001 [PS]	Hello It's Me/Open My Eyes	1969	5.00	10.00	20.00
—Legitimate sleeves are paper, not cardboard					
006	Not Wrong Long/Under the Ice	1969	3.00	6.00	12.00
006 [PS]	Not Wrong Long/Under the Ice	1969	5.00	10.00	20.00
009	Magic Me/Some People	1970	3.00	6.00	12.00
009	Magic Me/Kicks	1970	6.25	12.50	25.00

Albums

Number	Title (A Side/B Side)	Yr	VG	VG+	NM
RHINO					
RNLP 109	Nazz	1984	2.50	5.00	10.00
RNLP 110	Nazz Nazz	1984	2.50	5.00	10.00
RNLP 111	Nazz III	1984	2.50	5.00	10.00
RNLP 116	The Best of Nazz	1984	2.50	5.00	10.00
R1 70116	The Best of Nazz	1987	2.00	4.00	8.00
SGC					
SD 5001	Nazz	1968	10.00	20.00	40.00
5002 [DJ]	Nazz Nazz	1969	20.00	40.00	80.00
—Promo-only mono pressing on red vinyl					
SD 5002	Nazz Nazz	1969	10.00	20.00	40.00
—Red vinyl					
SD 5002	Nazz Nazz	1969	20.00	40.00	80.00
—Black vinyl					
SD 5004	Nazz III	1970	10.00	20.00	40.00

NAZZ (2)

Early ALICE COOPER.

45s

Number	Title (A Side/B Side)	Yr	VG	VG+	NM
VERY					
001	Lay Down and Die, Goodbye/Wonder Who's Loving Her Now	1967	1000.	1500.	2000.
—Warning! Reproductions of this record were made in the 1990s with white promo labels and picture sleeves. They are NOT the real thing.					

NEAL, JERRY

45s

Number	Title (A Side/B Side)	Yr	VG	VG+	NM
DOT					
15810	I Hates Rabbits/Scratchin'	1958	20.00	40.00	80.00
—With Eddie Cochran on guitar on B-side					

NED AND GARY

45s

Number	Title (A Side/B Side)	Yr	VG	VG+	NM
LIBERTY					
55160	Lovin'/I Bust My Seams	1958	15.00	30.00	60.00

NED AND NELDA

FRANK ZAPPA and Ray Collins.

45s

Number	Title (A Side/B Side)	Yr	VG	VG+	NM
VIGAH					
002	Hey Nelda/Surf Along	1963	37.50	75.00	150.00

NEELY, SAM

45s

Number	Title (A Side/B Side)	Yr	VG	VG+	NM
A&M					
1523	Come a Little Bit Closer/Sadie Take a Lover	1974	—	2.00	4.00
1612	You Can Have Her/It's a Fine Morning	1974	—	2.00	4.00
1651	I Fought the Law/Guitar Man	1974	—	2.00	4.00
1694	Sanctuary/Cajun Man	1975	—	2.00	4.00
CAPITOL					
3358	Blue Time/Cry Me a Song	1972	—	3.00	6.00
3381	Loving You Just Crossed My Mind/Everyday Is the Same As Today	1972	—	2.50	5.00
3510	Rosalie/Try to Reason Why	1973	—	2.50	5.00
3586	Blue Time/Kiss the Morning Sunshine	1973	—	2.50	5.00
ELEKTRA					
45419	Sail Away/My Lover and My Friend	1977	—	2.00	4.00
45484	Your Love Is In Good Hands/Things That Lovers Do	1978	—	2.00	4.00
MCA					
52194	The Party's Over (Everybody's Gone)/What Do I Tell My Heart	1983	—	—	3.00

Number	Title (A Side/B Side)	Yr	VG	VG+	NM
52226	When You Leave That Way You Can Never Go Back/Music Made Me Do It	1983	—	—	3.00
52269	Let's Fall in Love Again Tonight/You're No Ordinary Memory	1983	—	—	3.00
52323	Old Photographs/Somebody's Leaving	1983	—	—	3.00
Albums					
A&M					
SP-3626	Sam Neely	1974	3.00	6.00	12.00
CAPITOL					
ST-873	Long Road to Texas	1972	3.75	7.50	15.00
ST-11097	Loving You Just Crossed My Mind	1972	3.00	6.00	12.00
—Reissued version of ST-873					
SMAS-11143	Sam Neely — 2	1973	3.00	6.00	12.00

NEIGHB'RHOOD CHILDREN

Number	Title (A Side/B Side)	Yr	VG	VG+	NM
45s					
ACTA					
813	Maintain/Just No Way	1967	5.00	10.00	20.00
—As "Neighborhood"					
823	Happy Child/Please Leave Me Alone	1968	3.75	7.50	15.00
828	Behold the Lilies/I Want Action	1968	5.00	10.00	20.00
DOT					
17238	On Our Way/Woman Thing	1969	3.75	7.50	15.00
NAM					
2014	Dancing in the Street/(B-side unknown)	196?	3.75	7.50	15.00
Albums					
ACTA					
8005 [M]	The Neighb'rhood Children	1968	20.00	40.00	80.00
38005 [S]	The Neighb'rhood Children	1968	25.00	50.00	100.00

NEIGHBORHOOD, THE

Number	Title (A Side/B Side)	Yr	VG	VG+	NM
45s					
BIG TREE					
102	Big Yellow Taxi/You Could Be Born Again	1970	—	2.50	5.00
—Originals have white labels					
102	Big Yellow Taxi/You Could Be Born Again	1970	—	2.00	4.00
—Later pressings have red and yellow labels					
106	Laugh/Now's the Time for Love	1970	—	2.50	5.00
Albums					
BIG TREE					
2001	Debut	1970	3.75	7.50	15.00

NEIGHBORHOOD KIDS, THE

Number	Title (A Side/B Side)	Yr	VG	VG+	NM
45s					
BRUNSWICK					
55466	The Christmas Party of the Eighth Reindeer/Christmas Is for Everyone	1971	2.00	4.00	8.00

NEIL, FRED

Also see VINCE MARTIN AND FRED NEIL.

Number	Title (A Side/B Side)	Yr	VG	VG+	NM
45s					
BRUNSWICK					
55117	Listen Kitten/Take Me Back Again	1959	7.50	15.00	30.00
—As "Freddie Neil"					
CAPITOL					
2047	The Dolphins/I've Got a Secret	1967	7.50	15.00	30.00
2091	Felicity/Please Send Me Someone to Love	1968	7.50	15.00	30.00
2256	Everybody's Talkin'/That's the Bag I'm In	1968	7.50	15.00	30.00
2604	Everybody's Talkin'/Badi-Da	1969	6.25	12.50	25.00
EPIC					
5-9334	Love's Funny/Secret, Secret	1959	5.00	10.00	20.00
5-9403	Slippin' Around/You Don't Have to Be a Baby to Cry	1960	5.00	10.00	20.00
5-9435	Four Chaplains/The Rainbow and the Rose	1961	5.00	10.00	20.00
LOOK					
1002	You Ain't Treatin' Me Right/(B-side unknown)	1958	15.00	30.00	60.00
—As "Freddie Neil"					
Albums					
CAPITOL					
ST-294	Everybody's Talkin'	1969	6.25	12.50	25.00
ST 2665 [S]	Fred Neil	1966	10.00	20.00	40.00
—With color photo on back					
ST 2665 [S]	Fred Neil	1967	7.50	15.00	30.00
—With black & white photo on back					
T 2665 [M]	Fred Neil	1966	7.50	15.00	30.00
ST 2862 [S]	Fred Neil Sessions	1968	7.50	15.00	30.00
T 2862 [M]	Fred Neil Sessions	1968	10.00	20.00	40.00
ELEKTRA					
EKL-293 [M]	Bleecker and MacDougal	1965	7.50	15.00	30.00
EKS-7293 [S]	Bleecker and MacDougal	1965	10.00	20.00	40.00
EKS-74073	Little Bit of Rain	1970	5.00	10.00	20.00
—Reissue of 7293					

NEIL AND JACK

NEIL DIAMOND and Jack Parker.

Number	Title (A Side/B Side)	Yr	VG	VG+	NM
45s					
DUEL					
508	What Will I Do/You Are My Love at Last	1962	100.00	200.00	400.00
517	I'm Afraid/Till You've Tried Love	1962	100.00	200.00	400.00

NEKTAR

Number	Title (A Side/B Side)	Yr	VG	VG+	NM
45s					
PASSPORT					
7902	Remember the Future/Confusion	1974	—	3.00	6.00
7904	Astral Man/Nelly the Elephant	1975	—	2.50	5.00
Albums					
PASSPORT					
98002	Remember the Future	1974	3.00	6.00	12.00
98005	Down to Earth	1975	3.00	6.00	12.00
98011	Recycled	1976	2.50	5.00	10.00
98017	A Tab in the Ocean	1976	2.50	5.00	10.00

Number	Title (A Side/B Side)	Yr	VG	VG+	NM
POLYDOR					
PD-1-6115	Magic Is a Child	1977	2.50	5.00	10.00
VISA					
9001 [(2)]	Thru the Ears	1979	3.00	6.00	12.00

NELSON, KATHY

Number	Title (A Side/B Side)	Yr	VG	VG+	NM
45s					
LIBERTY					
55115	Santa Dear/Gimmie a Little Kiss, Will Ya Huh?	1957	5.00	10.00	20.00

NELSON, RICKY

Includes records as "Rick Nelson."

Number	Title (A Side/B Side)	Yr	VG	VG+	NM
45s					
CAPITOL					
4962	Almost Saturday Night/The Loser Babe Is You	1981	—	2.50	5.00
4974	Call It What You Want/It Hasn't Happened Yet	1981	—	2.50	5.00
4988	Believe What You Say/The Loser Babe Is You	1981	—	2.50	5.00
B-5178	No Fair Falling in Love/Give 'Em My Number	1982	—	2.50	5.00
DECCA					
31475	You Don't Love Me Anymore (And I Can Tell)/I Got a Woman	1963	3.75	7.50	15.00
31475 [PS]	You Don't Love Me Anymore (And I Can Tell)/I Got a Woman	1963	7.50	15.00	30.00
31495	String Along/Gypsy Woman	1963	3.75	7.50	15.00
31495 [PS]	String Along/Gypsy Woman	1963	7.50	15.00	30.00
31533	Fools Rush In/Down Home	1963	3.75	7.50	15.00
31533 [PS]	Fools Rush In/Down Home	1963	7.50	15.00	30.00
31574	For You/That's All She Wrote	1963	3.75	7.50	15.00
31574 [PS]	For You/That's All She Wrote	1963	7.50	15.00	30.00
31612	The Very Thought of You/I Wonder (If Your Love Will Ever Belong to Me)	1964	3.00	6.00	12.00
31612 [PS]	The Very Thought of You/I Wonder (If Your Love Will Ever Belong to Me)	1964	7.50	15.00	30.00
31656	There's Nothing I Can Say/Lonely Corner	1964	3.00	6.00	12.00
31656 [PS]	There's Nothing I Can Say/Lonely Corner	1964	7.50	15.00	30.00
31703	A Happy Guy/Don't Breathe a Word	1964	3.00	6.00	12.00
31703 [PS]	A Happy Guy/Don't Breathe a Word	1964	7.50	15.00	30.00
31756	Mean Old World/When the Chips Are Down	1965	3.00	6.00	12.00
31756 [PS]	Mean Old World/When the Chips Are Down	1965	7.50	15.00	30.00
31800	Yesterday's Love/Come Out Dancin'	1965	3.00	6.00	12.00
31845	Love and Kisses/Say You Love Me	1965	3.00	6.00	12.00
31900	Your Kind of Lovin'/Fire Breathin' Dragon	1966	3.00	6.00	12.00
31900 [PS]	Your Kind of Lovin'/Fire Breathin' Dragon	1966	20.00	40.00	80.00
31956	Louisiana Man/You Jsut Can't Quit	1966	3.00	6.00	12.00
31956 [PS]	Louisiana Man/You Jsut Can't Quit	1966	15.00	30.00	60.00
32026	Alone/Things You Gave Me	1966	3.00	6.00	12.00
32026 [PS]	Alone/Things You Gave Me	1966	20.00	40.00	80.00
32055	They Don't Give Medals (To Yesterday's Heroes)/Take a Broken Heart	1966	3.00	6.00	12.00
32120	Take a City Bride/I'm Called Lonely	1967	2.50	5.00	10.00
32120 [PS]	Take a City Bride/I'm Called Lonely	1967	15.00	30.00	60.00
32176	Moonshine/Suzanne on a Sunday Morning	1967	2.50	5.00	10.00
32222	Dream Weaver/Baby Close Your Eyes	1967	2.50	5.00	10.00
32284	Don't Blame It on Your Wife/Promenade in Green	1968	2.50	5.00	10.00
32298	Barefoot Boy/Don't Make Promises	1968	2.50	5.00	10.00
32550	She Belongs to Me/Promises	1969	2.00	4.00	8.00
32635	Easy to Be Free/Come On In	1970	2.00	4.00	8.00
32635 [PS]	Easy to Be Free/Come On In	1970	3.75	7.50	15.00
32676	I Shall Be Released/If You Gotta Go, Go Now	1970	2.00	4.00	8.00
32711	Look at Mary/We Got Such a Long Way to Go	1970	2.00	4.00	8.00
32739	How Long/Down Along the Bayou Country	1970	2.00	4.00	8.00
32779	Life/California	1971	2.00	4.00	8.00
32860	Thank You Lord/Sing Me a Song	1971	2.00	4.00	8.00
32906	Love Minus Zero-No Limit/Gypsy Pilot	1971	2.00	4.00	8.00
32980	Garden Party/So Long Mama	1972	2.50	5.00	10.00
34193/7 [PS]	Envelope, bonus photo and intact jukebox title strips for above 5 singles	1963	25.00	50.00	100.00
34193 [S]	Gypsy Woman/For Your Sweet Love	1963	25.00	50.00	100.00
34194 [S]	Pick Up the Pieces/Every Time I See You Smilin'	1963	25.00	50.00	100.00
34195 [S]	One Boy Too Late/Everytime I Think About You	1963	25.00	50.00	100.00
34196 [S]	Let's Talk the Whole Thing Over/I Got a Woman	1963	25.00	50.00	100.00
34197 [S]	I Will Follow You/What Comes Next	1963	25.00	50.00	100.00
—34193-34197 are 33 1/3 rpm, small hole jukebox singles. The set came with a package, priced separately.					
EPIC					
06066	Dream Lover/Rave On	1986	—	2.00	4.00
06066 [PS]	Dream Lover/Rave On	1986	—	2.00	4.00
50458	It's Another Day/You Can't Dance	1977	—	2.50	5.00
50501	Gimme A Little Sign/Something You Can't Buy	1978	—	2.50	5.00
50674	Dream Lover/That Ain't the Way Love's Supposed to Be	1979	—	2.50	5.00
IMPERIAL					
5463	Be-Bop Baby/Have I Told You Lately That I Love You	1957	12.50	25.00	50.00
—Red label					
5463	Be-Bop Baby/Have I Told You Lately That I Love You	1957	6.25	12.50	25.00
—Black label					
5463 [PS]	Be-Bop Baby/Have I Told You Lately That I Love You	1957	20.00	40.00	80.00
5483	Stood Up/Waitin' in School	1957	10.00	20.00	40.00
—Red label					
5483	Stood Up/Waitin' in School	1957	6.25	12.50	25.00
—Black label					
5483 [PS]	Stood Up/Waitin' in School	1957	17.50	35.00	70.00
5503	Believe What You Say/My Bucket's Got a Hole in It	1958	7.50	15.00	30.00
5503 [PS]	Believe What You Say/My Bucket's Got a Hole in It	1958	17.50	35.00	70.00
5528	Poor Little Fool/Don't Leave Me This Way	1958	7.50	15.00	30.00
5545	Lonesome Town/I Got a Feeling	1958	7.50	15.00	30.00
5545	Lonesome Town/I Got a Feeling	1958	150.00	300.00	600.00
—Red vinyl					
5545 [PS]	Lonesome Town/I Got a Feeling	1958	17.50	35.00	70.00

Number	Title (A Side/B Side)	Yr	VG	VG+	NM
5565	Never Be Anyone Else But You/It's Late	1959	6.25	12.50	25.00
—Black label					
5565	Never Be Anyone Else But You/It's Late	1959	10.00	20.00	40.00
—Red label					
5565 [PS]	Never Be Anyone Else But You/It's Late	1959	20.00	40.00	80.00
5595	Just a Little Too Much/Sweeter Than You	1959	6.25	12.50	25.00
5595 [PS]	Just a Little Too Much/Sweeter Than You	1959	17.50	35.00	70.00
5614	I Wanna Be Loved/Mighty Good	1959	6.25	12.50	25.00
5614 [PS]	I Wanna Be Loved/Mighty Good	1959	17.50	35.00	70.00
5663	Young Emotions/Right By My Side	1960	6.25	12.50	25.00
5663 [PS]	Young Emotions/Right By My Side	1960	17.50	35.00	70.00
5685	I'm Not Afraid/Yes Sir, That's My Baby	1960	6.25	12.50	25.00
5685 [PS]	I'm Not Afraid/Yes Sir, That's My Baby	1960	17.50	35.00	70.00
5707	You Are the Only One/Milk Cow Blues	1960	6.25	12.50	25.00
5707 [PS]	You Are the Only One/Milk Cow Blues	1960	17.50	35.00	70.00
5741	Travelin' Man/Hello Mary Lou	1961	6.25	12.50	25.00
5741	Travelin' Man/Hello Mary Lou	1961	200.00	400.00	800.00
—Red vinyl					
5741 [PS]	Travelin' Man/Hello Mary Lou	1961	17.50	35.00	70.00
5770	A Wonder Like You/Everlovin'	1961	5.00	10.00	20.00
—Starting here, Imperial singles by "Rick Nelson"					
5770 [PS]	A Wonder Like You/Everlovin'	1961	10.00	20.00	40.00
5805	Young World/Summertime	1962	5.00	10.00	20.00
5805 [PS]	Young World/Summertime	1962	10.00	20.00	40.00
5864	Teen Age Idol/I've Got My Eyes on You	1962	5.00	10.00	20.00
5864 [PS]	Teen Age Idol/I've Got My Eyes on You	1962	10.00	20.00	40.00
5901	It's Up to You/I Need You	1962	5.00	10.00	20.00
5901 [PS]	It's Up to You/I Need You	1962	10.00	20.00	40.00
5910	That's All/I'm in Love Again	1963	6.25	12.50	25.00
5935	Old Enough to Love/If You Can't Rock Me	1963	5.00	10.00	20.00
5935 [PS]	Old Enough to Love/If You Can't Rock Me	1963	10.00	20.00	40.00
5958	A Long Vacation/Mad Mad World	1963	5.00	10.00	20.00
5958	A Long Vacation/Mad Mad World	1963	75.00	150.00	300.00
—Red vinyl					
5985	Time After Time/There's Not a Minute	1963	5.00	10.00	20.00
66004	Today's Teardrops/Thank You Darlin'	1963	3.75	7.50	15.00
66004 [PS]	Today's Teardrops/Thank You Darlin'	1963	10.00	20.00	40.00
66017	Congratulations/One Minute to One	1964	3.75	7.50	15.00
66039	Everybody But Me/Lucky Star	1964	3.75	7.50	15.00

MCA

Number	Title (A Side/B Side)	Yr	VG	VG+	NM
40001	Palace Guard/A Flower Opens Gently By	1973	—	3.00	6.00
40130	Evil Woman Child/Lifestream	1973	—	3.00	6.00
40187	Windfall/Legacy	1974	—	3.00	6.00
40214	One Night Stand/Lifestream	1974	—	3.00	6.00
40392	Louisiana Belle/Try (Try to Fall in Love)	1975	—	3.00	6.00
40458	Rock and Roll Lady/Fadeaway	1975	—	3.00	6.00
52781	You Know What I Mean/Don't Leave Me This Way	1986	—	2.50	5.00
52781 [PS]	You Know What I Mean/Don't Leave Me This Way	1986	—	2.50	5.00

UNITED ARTISTS

Number	Title (A Side/B Side)	Yr	VG	VG+	NM
0071	Be-Bop Baby/Stood Up	1973	—	2.50	5.00
0072	Lonesome Town/It's Up to You	1973	—	2.50	5.00
0073	Poor Little Fool/My Bucket's Got a Hole in It	1973	—	2.50	5.00
0074	Travelin' Man/Believe What You Say	1973	—	2.50	5.00
0075	Teen Age Idol/Young Emotions	1973	—	2.50	5.00
0076	Never Be Anyone Else But You/That's All	1973	—	2.50	5.00
0077	Young World/It's Late	1973	—	2.50	5.00
0078	Just a Little Too Much/Waitin' in School	1973	—	2.50	5.00
0079	Hello Mary Lou/Sweeter Than You	1973	—	2.50	5.00
0080	A Wonder Like You/Everlovin'	1973	—	2.50	5.00
—0071 through 0080 are "Silver Spotlight Series" reissues					

VERVE

Number	Title (A Side/B Side)	Yr	VG	VG+	NM
10047	I'm Walkin'/A Teenager's Romance	1957	12.50	25.00	50.00
—Orange and yellow label					
10047	I'm Walkin'/A Teenager's Romance	1957	10.00	20.00	40.00
—Black and white label					
10070	You're My One and Only Love/Honey Rock	1957	10.00	20.00	40.00
—B-side by Barney Kessel					

7-Inch Extended Plays

DECCA

Number	Title (A Side/B Side)	Yr	VG	VG+	NM
ED 2760	I Will Follow You/Pick Up the Pieces//One Boy Too Late/Let's Talk the Whole Thing Over	1963	37.50	75.00	150.00
ED 2760 [PS]	One Boy Too Late	1963	37.50	75.00	150.00
7-34319 [PS]	Best Always	1965	7.50	15.00	30.00
—With title strips					
7-34319 [S]	I'm Not Ready for You Yet/Lonely Corner/Mean Old World//I Know a Place/It's Beginning to Hurt/When the Chips Are Down	1965	7.50	15.00	30.00
—33 1/3 rpm, small hole jukebox edition					

IMPERIAL

Number	Title (A Side/B Side)	Yr	VG	VG+	NM
IMP 153	Be-Bop Baby/Have I Told You Lately That I Love You//Honeycomb/Boppin' the Blues	1957	12.50	25.00	50.00
IMP 153 [PS]	Ricky (Honeycomb)	1957	12.50	25.00	50.00
IMP 154	Teenage Doll/If You Can't Rock Me//Whole Lotta Shakin' Goin' On/Baby I'm Sorry	1957	12.50	25.00	50.00
IMP 154 [PS]	Ricky, Volume 2	1957	12.50	25.00	50.00
IMP 155	Your True Love/True Love//Am I Blue/I'm Confessin'	1957	12.50	25.00	50.00
IMP 155 [PS]	Ricky (True Love)	1957	12.50	25.00	50.00
IMP 156	Shirley Lee/There's Good Rockin' Tonight//Someday/I'm Feelin' Sorry	1958	12.50	25.00	50.00
IMP 156 [PS]	Ricky Nelson (Someday)	1958	12.50	25.00	50.00
IMP 157	Down the Line/Don't Leave Me This Way//I'm in Love Again/My Babe	1958	12.50	25.00	50.00
IMP 157 [PS]	Ricky Nelson (Down the Line)	1958	12.50	25.00	50.00
IMP 158	Unchained Melody/I'll Walk Alone//There Goes My Baby/Poor Little Fool	1958	12.50	25.00	50.00
IMP 158 [PS]	Ricky Nelson (Unchained Melody)	1958	12.50	25.00	50.00
IMP 159	Be True to Me/One of These Mornings//Lonesome Town/It's Late	1959	12.50	25.00	50.00
IMP 159 [PS]	Ricky Sings Again (Be True to Me)	1959	12.50	25.00	50.00
IMP 160	Restless Kid/It's All in the Game//Believe What You Say/You Tear Me Up	1959	12.50	25.00	50.00
IMP 160 [PS]	Ricky Sings Again (Restless Kid)	1959	12.50	25.00	50.00
IMP 161	Old Enough to Love/Tryin' to Get to You//Never Be Anyone Else But You/I Can't Help It	1959	12.50	25.00	50.00
IMP 161 [PS]	Ricky Sings Again (Old Enough to Love)	1959	12.50	25.00	50.00
IMP 162	You'll Never Know What You're Missin'/I've Been Thinkin'//So Long/You're So Fine	1959	12.50	25.00	50.00
IMP 162 [PS]	Songs by Ricky (You'll Never Know What You're Missin')	1959	12.50	25.00	50.00
IMP 163	One Minute To One/Blood from a Stone//Half Breed/Just a Little Too Much	1959	12.50	25.00	50.00
IMP 163 [PS]	Songs by Ricky (One Minute to One)	1959	12.50	25.00	50.00
IMP 164	Don't Leave Me/That's All//Sweeter Than You/A Long Vacation	1959	12.50	25.00	50.00
IMP 164 [PS]	Songs by Ricky (Don't Leave Me)	1959	12.50	25.00	50.00
IMP 165	Glory Train/I Bowed My Head in Shame//March with the Band of the Lord/If You Believe It	1959	25.00	50.00	100.00
IMP 165 [PS]	Ricky Sings Spirituals	1959	25.00	50.00	100.00
LP 4-2232 [PS]	Million Sellers	1964	20.00	40.00	80.00
LP 4-2232 [S]	Travelin' Man/Never Be Anyone Else But You/It's Late//Young Emotions/Hello Mary Lou/Yes Sir, That's My Baby	1964	20.00	40.00	80.00
—33 1/3 rpm, small hole, jukebox edition					

VERVE

Number	Title (A Side/B Side)	Yr	VG	VG+	NM
5048	I'm Walkin'/A Teenager's Romance//You're My One and Only Love/Honey Rock	1957	37.50	75.00	150.00
5048 [PS]	Ricky	1957	50.00	100.00	200.00

Albums

CAPITOL

Number	Title	Yr	VG	VG+	NM
SOO-12109	Playing to Win	1981	2.50	5.00	10.00

DECCA

Number	Title	Yr	VG	VG+	NM
DL 4419 [M]	For Your Sweet Love	1963	7.50	15.00	30.00
DL 4479 [M]	Rick Nelson Sings "For You"	1963	7.50	15.00	30.00
DL 4559 [M]	The Very Thought of You	1964	7.50	15.00	30.00
DL 4608 [M]	Spotlight on Rick	1964	7.50	15.00	30.00
DL 4660 [M]	Best Always	1965	7.50	15.00	30.00
DL 4678 [M]	Love and Kisses	1965	7.50	15.00	30.00
DL 4779 [M]	Bright Lights and Country Music	1966	6.25	12.50	25.00
DL 4827 [M]	Country Fever	1967	6.25	12.50	25.00
DL 4944 [M]	Another Side of Rick	1967	6.25	12.50	25.00
DL 5014 [M]	Perspective	1968	12.50	25.00	50.00
—Mono copies are promo only					
DL 74419 [S]	For Your Sweet Love	1963	10.00	2.00	40.00
DL 74479 [S]	Rick Nelson Sings "For You"	1963	10.00	20.00	40.00
DL 74559 [S]	The Very Thought of You	1964	10.00	20.00	40.00
DL 74608 [S]	Spotlight on Rick	1964	10.00	20.00	40.00
DL 74660 [S]	Best Always	1965	10.00	20.00	40.00
DL 74678 [S]	Love and Kisses	1965	10.00	20.00	40.00
DL 74779 [S]	Bright Lights and Country Music	1966	7.50	15.00	30.00
DL 74827 [S]	Country Fever	1967	7.50	15.00	30.00
DL 74944 [S]	Another Side of Rick	1967	7.50	15.00	30.00
DL 75014 [S]	Perspective	1968	7.50	15.00	30.00
DL 75162	Rick Nelson In Concert	1970	6.25	12.50	25.00
DL 75236	Rick Sings Nelson	1970	6.25	12.50	25.00
—Deduct 20 percent if poster is missing					
DL 75297	Rudy the Fifth	1971	6.25	12.50	25.00
DL 75391	Garden Party	1972	6.25	12.50	25.00

EPIC

Number	Title	Yr	VG	VG+	NM
JE 34420	Intakes	1977	3.00	6.00	12.00
FE 40388	The Memphis Sessions	1986	2.50	5.00	10.00

EPIC/NU-DISK

Number	Title	Yr	VG	VG+	NM
3E 36868 [10]	Four You	1981	3.00	6.00	12.00

IMPERIAL

Number	Title	Yr	VG	VG+	NM
LP 9048 [M]	Ricky	1957	25.00	50.00	100.00
—Black label with stars					
LP 9048 [M]	Ricky	1964	6.25	12.50	25.00
—Black label with pink and white at left					
LP 9048 [M]	Ricky	1966	5.00	10.00	20.00
—Black label with green and white at left					
LP 9050 [M]	Ricky Nelson	1958	25.00	50.00	100.00
—Black label with stars					
LP 9050 [M]	Ricky Nelson	1964	6.25	12.50	25.00
—Black label with pink and white at left					
LP 9050 [M]	Ricky Nelson	1966	5.00	10.00	20.00
—Black label with green and white at left					
LP 9061 [M]	Ricky Sings Again	1959	25.00	50.00	100.00
—Black label with stars					
LP 9061 [M]	Ricky Sings Again	1964	6.25	12.50	25.00
—Black label with pink and white at left					
LP 9061 [M]	Ricky Sings Again	1966	5.00	10.00	20.00
—Black label with green and white at left					
LP 9082 [M]	Songs by Ricky	1959	18.75	37.50	75.00
—Black label with stars					
LP 9082 [M]	Songs by Ricky	1964	6.25	12.50	25.00
—Black label with pink and white at left					
LP 9082 [M]	Songs by Ricky	1966	5.00	10.00	20.00
—Black label with green and white at left					
LP 9122 [M]	More Songs by Ricky	1960	18.75	37.50	75.00
—Black label with stars					
LP 9122 [M]	More Songs by Ricky	1964	6.25	12.50	25.00
—Black label with pink and white at left					
LP 9122 [M]	More Songs by Ricky	1966	5.00	10.00	20.00
—Black label with green and white at left					
LP 9152 [M]	Rick Is 21	1961	10.00	20.00	40.00
—Black label with stars					
LP 9152 [M]	Rick Is 21	1964	6.25	12.50	25.00
—Black label with pink and white at left					
LP 9152 [M]	Rick Is 21	1966	5.00	10.00	20.00
—Black label with green and white at left					
LP 9167 [M]	Album Seven by Rick	1962	10.00	20.00	40.00
—Black label with stars					
LP 9167 [M]	Album Seven by Rick	1964	6.25	12.50	25.00
—Black label with pink and white at left					
LP 9167 [M]	Album Seven by Rick	1966	5.00	10.00	20.00
—Black label with green and white at left					
LP 9218 [M]	Best Sellers by Rick Nelson	1963	10.00	20.00	40.00
—Black label with stars					
LP 9218 [M]	Best Sellers by Rick Nelson	1964	6.25	12.50	25.00
—Black label with pink and white at left					

Number	Title (A Side/B Side)	Yr	VG	VG+	NM
LP 9218 [M]	Best Sellers by Rick Nelson	1966	5.00	10.00	20.00
—Black label with green and white at left					
LP 9223 [M]	It's Up to You	1963	10.00	20.00	40.00
—Black label with stars					
LP 9223 [M]	It's Up to You	1964	6.25	12.50	25.00
—Black label with pink and white at left					
LP 9223 [M]	It's Up to You	1966	5.00	10.00	20.00
—Black label with green and white at left					
LP 9232 [M]	Million Sellers	1963	10.00	20.00	40.00
—Black label with stars					
LP 9232 [M]	Million Sellers	1964	6.25	12.50	25.00
—Black label with pink and white at left					
LP 9232 [M]	Million Sellers	1966	5.00	10.00	20.00
—Black label with green and white at left					
LP 9244 [M]	A Long Vacation	1963	10.00	20.00	40.00
—Black label with stars					
LP 9244 [M]	A Long Vacation	1964	6.25	12.50	25.00
—Black label with pink and white at left					
LP 9244 [M]	A Long Vacation	1966	5.00	10.00	20.00
—Black label with green and white at left					
LP 9251 [M]	Rick Nelson Sings for You	1964	10.00	20.00	40.00
—Black label with stars					
LP 9251 [M]	Rick Nelson Sings for You	1964	6.25	12.50	25.00
—Black label with pink and white at left					
LP 9251 [M]	Rick Nelson Sings for You	1966	5.00	10.00	20.00
—Black label with green and white at left					
LP 12030 [S]	Songs by Ricky	1959	50.00	100.00	200.00
—Black label with silver print					
LP 12030 [S]	Songs by Ricky	1964	10.00	20.00	40.00
—Black label with pink and white at left					
LP 12030 [S]	Songs by Ricky	1966	6.25	12.50	25.00
—Black label with green and white at left					
LP 12059 [DJ]	More Songs by Ricky	1960	250.00	500.00	1000.
—Promo copy on blue vinyl. Add 20 percent for enclosed poster.					
LP 12059 [S]	More Songs by Ricky	1960	25.00	50.00	100.00
—Black label with silver print					
LP 12059 [S]	More Songs by Ricky	1964	10.00	20.00	40.00
—Black label with pink and white at left					
LP 12059 [S]	More Songs by Ricky	1966	6.25	12.50	25.00
—Black label with green and white at left					
LP 12071 [S]	Rick Is 21	1961	25.00	50.00	100.00
—Black label with silver print					
LP 12071 [S]	Rick Is 21	1964	10.00	20.00	40.00
—Black label with pink and white at left					
LP 12071 [S]	Rick Is 21	1966	6.25	12.50	25.00
—Black label with green and white at left					
LP 12082 [S]	Album Seven by Rick	1962	25.00	50.00	100.00
—Black label with silver print					
LP 12082 [S]	Album Seven by Rick	1964	10.00	20.00	40.00
—Black label with pink and white at left					
LP 12082 [S]	Album Seven by Rick	1966	6.25	12.50	25.00
—Black label with green and white at left					
LP 12090 [S]	Ricky Sings Again	1962	37.50	75.00	150.00
—Black label with silver print					
LP 12090 [S]	Ricky Sings Again	1964	10.00	20.00	40.00
—Black label with pink and white at left					
LP 12090 [S]	Ricky Sings Again	1966	6.25	12.50	25.00
—Black label with green and white at left					
LP 12218 [R]	Best Sellers	1964	5.00	10.00	20.00
—Black label with pink and white at left					
LP 12218 [R]	Best Sellers	1966	3.75	7.50	15.00
—Black label with green and white at left					
LP 12232 [R]	Million Sellers	1964	5.00	10.00	20.00
—Black label with pink and white at left					
LP 12232 [R]	Million Sellers	1966	3.75	7.50	15.00
—Black label with green and white at left					
LP 12244 [R]	A Long Vacation	1964	5.00	10.00	20.00
—Black label with pink and white at left					
LP 12244 [R]	A Long Vacation	1966	3.75	7.50	15.00
—Black label with green and white at left					
LP 12251 [R]	Rick Nelson Sings for You	1964	6.25	12.50	25.00
—Black label with silver print					
LP 12251 [R]	Rick Nelson Sings for You	1964	5.00	10.00	20.00
—Black label with pink and white at left					
LP 12251 [R]	Rick Nelson Sings for You	1966	3.75	7.50	15.00
—Black label with green and white at left					
LP 12392 [R]	Ricky	1968	3.75	7.50	15.00
—Rechanneled reissue of 9048					
LP 12393 [R]	Ricky Nelson	1968	3.75	7.50	15.00
—Rechanneled reissue of 9050					
LIBERTY					
LM-1004	Ricky	1981	2.00	4.00	8.00
—Reissue of United Artists 1004					
LXB-9960 [(2)]	Legendary Masters	198?	3.00	6.00	12.00
—Reissue of United Artists 9960					
LN-10134	Ricky Sings Again	1982	2.50	5.00	10.00
—Reissue of Imperial 12090					
LN-10205	Souvenirs	1983	2.00	4.00	8.00
LN-10253	Teen Age Idol	1984	2.00	4.00	8.00
LN-10305	Ricky Nelson	1986	2.00	4.00	8.00
—Another reissue					
LM-51004	Ricky	1983	2.00	4.00	8.00
—Reissue of Liberty 1004					
MCA					
3	Rick Nelson In Concert	1973	3.00	6.00	12.00
—Reissue of Decca 75162					
20	Rick Sings Nelson	1973	3.00	6.00	12.00
—Reissue of Decca 75236					
37	Rudy the Fifth	1973	3.00	6.00	12.00
—Reissue of Decca 75297					
62	Garden Party	1973	3.00	6.00	12.00
—Reissue of Decca 75391					
383	Windfall	1974	3.75	7.50	15.00
1517	The Decca Years	1982	2.00	4.00	8.00
2-4004 [(2)]	Rick Nelson Country	1973	3.75	7.50	15.00
6163	All My Best	1986	2.50	5.00	10.00
RHINO					
RNLP 215	Greatest Hits	1985	3.00	6.00	12.00
RNDF 259 [PD]	Greatest Hits	1985	3.75	7.50	15.00
R1-70215	Greatest Hits	1987	2.50	5.00	10.00
R1-71114	Live 1983-1985	1989	3.00	6.00	12.00
SUNSET					
SUM-1118 [M]	Ricky Nelson	1966	3.75	7.50	15.00
SUS-5118 [P]	Ricky Nelson	1966	5.00	10.00	20.00
SUS-5205	I Need You	1968	3.75	7.50	15.00
TIME-LIFE					
SRNR 31 [(2)]	Rick Nelson: 1957-1972	1989	3.75	7.50	15.00
UNITED ARTISTS					
UA-LA330-E	The Very Best of Rick Nelson	1974	3.00	6.00	12.00
LM-1004	Ricky	1980	2.50	5.00	10.00
—Reissue of Imperial 9048					
UAS-9960 [(2)]	Legendary Masters	1971	6.25	12.50	25.00
VERVE					
V 2083 [M]	Teen Time	1957	125.00	250.00	500.00
—Has three Ricky Nelson songs plus tracks by four others; usually treated as Rick's LP because of his prominence on the cover					

NELSON, SANDY

Also see THE GAMBLERS.

45s

Number	Title (A Side/B Side)	Yr	VG	VG+	NM
IMPERIAL					
5630	Drum Party/Big Noise from Winnetka	1959	3.00	6.00	12.00
5648	Party Time/The Wiggle	1960	3.00	6.00	12.00
5672	Bouncy/Lost Dreams	1960	3.00	6.00	12.00
5708	Cool Operator/Jive Talk	1960	3.00	6.00	12.00
5745	Big Noise from the Jungle/Get With It	1961	3.00	6.00	12.00
5775	Let There Be Drums/Quite a Beat	1961	3.75	7.50	15.00
5809	Drums Are My Beat/The Birth of the Beat	1962	3.00	6.00	12.00
5829	Drummin' Up a Storm/Drum Stomp	1962	3.00	6.00	12.00
5860	All Night Long/Rompin' and Stompin'	1962	3.00	6.00	12.00
5870	And Then There Were Drums/Live It Up	1962	3.00	6.00	12.00
5884	Teenage House Party/Day Train	1962	3.00	6.00	12.00
5904	Be-Bop Baby/Let the Four Winds Blow	1962	3.00	6.00	12.00
5932	Ooh Poo Pah Doo/Feel So Good	1963	3.00	6.00	12.00
5940	You Name It/Alexis	1963	3.00	6.00	12.00
5965	Here We Go Again/Just Bill	1963	3.00	6.00	12.00
5988	Caravan/Sandy	1963	3.00	6.00	12.00
66019	Drum Shack/Kitty's Theme	1964	2.50	5.00	10.00
66034	Castle Rock/You Don't Say	1964	2.50	5.00	10.00
66060	Teen Beat '65/Kitty's Theme	1964	3.00	6.00	12.00
66093	Chop Chop/Reach for a Star	1965	2.50	5.00	10.00
66107	Land of 1000 Dances/Let There Be Drums	1965	2.50	5.00	10.00
66127	Drums A-Go-Go/Caesar	1965	2.50	5.00	10.00
66146	A Lover's Concerto/Treat Her Right	1965	2.50	5.00	10.00
66193	Rock It To 'Em J.B./The Charge	1966	2.50	5.00	10.00
66209	Let's Go Trippin'/Pipeline	1966	3.00	6.00	12.00
66246	The Drums Go On/Lawdy Miss Clawdy	1967	2.50	5.00	10.00
66253	Peter Gunn/You Got Me Hummin'	1967	2.50	5.00	10.00
66284	Alligator Boogaloo/Midnight Magic	1968	2.50	5.00	10.00
66350	Rebirth of the Beat/Lion in Winter	1969	2.50	5.00	10.00
66375	Manhattan Spiritual/The Stripper	1969	2.50	5.00	10.00
66402	Let There Be Drums and Brass/Leap Frog	1969	2.50	5.00	10.00
ORIGINAL SOUND					
5	Teen Beat/Big Jump	1959	6.25	12.50	25.00
UNITED ARTISTS					
0082	Teen Beat/Let There Be Drums	1973	—	2.50	5.00
—"Silver Spotlight Series" reissue					
XW383	You Are the Sunshine of My Life/Dance with the Devil	1974	2.50	5.00	10.00
50830	Sapporo '72	1971	—	—	—
—Unreleased					
VEEBLETRONICS					
1	Drum Tunnel/Boogie #5	198?	—	2.50	5.00
2	Hunk of Drums/Witch Hunt	198?	—	2.50	5.00
3	A Drum Is a Woman/Boogie #5	198?	—	2.50	5.00

Albums

Number	Title (A Side/B Side)	Yr	VG	VG+	NM
IMPERIAL					
LP 9105 [M]	Sandy Nelson Plays Teen Beat	1960	7.50	15.00	30.00
LP 9136 [M]	He's a Drummer Boy	1961	7.50	15.00	30.00
LP 9159 [M]	Let There Be Drums	1962	7.50	15.00	30.00
LP 9168 [M]	Drums Are My Beat!	1962	5.00	10.00	20.00
LP 9189 [M]	Drummin' Up a Storm	1962	5.00	10.00	20.00
LP 9202 [M]	Golden Hits	1962	5.00	10.00	20.00
LP 9203 [M]	Country Style	1962	5.00	10.00	20.00
LP 9203 [M]	On the Wild Side	1966	3.75	7.50	15.00
—Same LP as above, but new title on cover					
LP 9204 [M]	Compelling Percussion	1962	5.00	10.00	20.00
LP 9215 [M]	Teenage House Party	1963	5.00	10.00	20.00
LP 9224 [M]	The Best of the Beats	1963	3.75	7.50	15.00
LP 9237 [M]	Beat That Drum	1963	3.75	7.50	15.00
LP 9249 [M]	Sandy Nelson Plays	1963	3.75	7.50	15.00
LP 9258 [M]	Be True to Your School	1964	3.75	7.50	15.00
LP 9272 [M]	Live! In Las Vegas	1964	5.00	10.00	20.00
LP 9278 [M]	Teen Beat '65	1965	3.75	7.50	15.00
LP 9283 [M]	Drum Discotheque	1965	3.75	7.50	15.00
LP 9287 [M]	Drums A Go-Go	1965	3.75	7.50	15.00
LP 9298 [M]	Boss Beat	1965	3.75	7.50	15.00
LP 9305 [M]	"In" Beat	1966	3.75	7.50	15.00
LP 9314 [M]	Super Drums	1966	3.75	7.50	15.00
LP 9329 [M]	Beat That #!!@* Drum	1966	3.00	6.00	12.00
LP 9340 [M]	Cheetah Beat	1967	3.00	6.00	12.00
LP 9345 [M]	The Beat Goes On	1967	3.00	6.00	12.00
LP 9362 [M]	Soul Drums	1967	3.75	7.50	15.00
LP 12044 [S]	Sandy Nelson Plays Teen Beat	1960	10.00	20.00	40.00
LP 12080 [R]	Let There Be Drums	1962	6.25	12.50	25.00
LP 12083 [S]	Drums Are My Beat!	1962	6.25	12.50	25.00
LP 12089 [R]	He's a Drummer Boy	1962	6.25	12.50	25.00
LP 12189 [S]	Drummin' Up a Storm	1962	6.25	12.50	25.00
LP 12202 [P]	Golden Hits	1962	6.25	12.50	25.00
LP 12203 [S]	Country Style	1962	6.25	12.50	25.00

Number	Title (A Side/B Side)	Yr	VG	VG+	NM
LP 12203 [S]	On the Wild Side	1966	5.00	10.00	20.00
—Same LP as above, but new title on cover					
LP 12204 [S]	Compelling Percussion	1962	6.25	12.50	25.00
LP 12215 [S]	Teenage House Party	1963	6.25	12.50	25.00
LP 12224 [S]	The Best of the Beats	1963	5.00	10.00	20.00
LP 12237 [S]	Beat That Drum	1963	5.00	10.00	20.00
LP 12249 [S]	Sandy Nelson Plays	1963	5.00	10.00	20.00
LP 12258 [S]	Be True to Your School	1964	5.00	10.00	20.00
LP 12272 [R]	Live! In Las Vegas	1964	3.75	7.50	15.00
LP 12278 [S]	Teen Beat '65	1965	5.00	10.00	20.00
LP 12283 [S]	Drum Discotheque	1965	5.00	10.00	20.00
LP 12287 [S]	Drums A Go-Go	1965	5.00	10.00	20.00
LP 12298 [S]	Boss Beat	1965	5.00	10.00	20.00
LP 12305 [S]	"In" Beat	1966	5.00	10.00	20.00
LP 12314 [S]	Super Drums	1966	5.00	10.00	20.00
LP 12329 [S]	Beat That #!!@* Drum	1966	3.75	7.50	15.00
LP 12340 [S]	Cheetah Beat	1967	3.75	7.50	15.00
LP 12345 [S]	The Beat Goes On	1967	3.75	7.50	15.00
LP 12362 [S]	Soul Drums	1967	3.00	6.00	12.00
LP 12367	Boogaloo Beat	1968	3.00	6.00	12.00
LP 12400	Rock and Roll Revival	1968	3.00	6.00	12.00
LP 12424	Rebirth of the Beat	1969	3.00	6.00	12.00
LP 12439	Manhattan Spiritual	1969	3.00	6.00	12.00
LP 12451	Groovy	1970	3.00	6.00	12.00
LIBERTY					
LN-10172	The Very Best of Sandy Nelson	1982	2.00	4.00	8.00
LN-10209	Collectors' Gems, Vol. 2	1983	2.00	4.00	8.00
SUNSET					
SUM-1114 [M]	Walking Beat	1966	2.50	5.00	10.00
SUM-1166 [M]	Teen Drums	1967	2.50	5.00	10.00
SUS-5114 [S]	Walking Beat	1966	3.00	6.00	12.00
SUS-5166 [S]	Teen Drums	1967	3.00	6.00	12.00
SUS-5224	And There Were Drums (Drums and More Drums)	1968	2.50	5.00	10.00
SUS-5261	Heavy Drums	1969	2.50	5.00	10.00
SUS-5201	Sandy Nelson Plays Fats Domino Hits	1970	2.50	5.00	10.00
UNITED ARTISTS					
UA-LA440-E	The Very Best of Sandy Nelson	1975	3.00	6.00	12.00

NELSON, TERI, GROUP

45s

Number	Title (A Side/B Side)	Yr	VG	VG+	NM
KAMA SUTRA					
245	Sweet Talkin' Willie/Back Side	1968	2.50	5.00	10.00

NELSON, TRACY

Also see MOTHER EARTH; TRACY AND WILLIE NELSON.

45s

Number	Title (A Side/B Side)	Yr	VG	VG+	NM
ATLANTIC					
3235	It Takes a Lot to Laugh, It Takes a Train to Cry/Lean On Me	1975	—	2.50	5.00
CAPITOL					
4442	Sad Situation/Let's Get Down to the Truth	1977	—	2.00	4.00
—With Larry Ballard					
MCA					
40479	Sweet Soul Music/Nothing I Can't Handle	1975	—	2.00	4.00
MERCURY					
72995	Sad Situation/Stay As Sweet As You Are	1970	2.00	4.00	8.00

Albums

Number	Title (A Side/B Side)	Yr	VG	VG+	NM
ADELPHI					
4119	Doin' It My Way	1981	2.50	5.00	10.00
ATLANTIC					
SD 7310	Tracy Nelson	1974	3.00	6.00	12.00
COLUMBIA					
KC 31759	Poor Man's Paradise	1973	3.00	6.00	12.00
FLYING FISH					
FF-052	Homemade Songs	1978	2.50	5.00	10.00
FF-209	Come See About Me	1980	2.50	5.00	10.00
MCA					
494	Sweet Soul Music	1975	3.00	6.00	12.00
2203	Time Is On My Side	1976	3.00	6.00	12.00
PRESTIGE					
PRLP 7393 [M]	Deep Are the Roots	1965	6.25	12.50	25.00
PRST 7393 [S]	Deep Are the Roots	1965	7.50	15.00	30.00
PRST 7726	Deep Are the Roots	1969	3.75	7.50	15.00

NELSON, TRACY AND WILLIE

Also see each artist's individual listings.

45s

Number	Title (A Side/B Side)	Yr	VG	VG+	NM
ATLANTIC					
4028	After the Fire Is Gone/Whiskey River	1976	—	2.50	5.00

NELSON, WILLIE

Includes many duets not listed separately below. Also see HANK COCHRAN; DANNY DAVIS; MERLE HAGGARD; WAYLON JENNINGS; WAYLON AND WILLIE.

45s

Number	Title (A Side/B Side)	Yr	VG	VG+	NM
AMERICAN GOLD					
7601	Night Life/Rainy Day Blues	1976	—	2.50	5.00
ATLANTIC					
2968	Shotgun Willie/Sad Songs and Waltzes	1973	—	2.50	5.00
2979	Devil in a Sleepin' Bag/Stay All Night	1973	—	2.50	5.00
3008	Heaven and Hell/I Still Can't Believe You're Gone	1974	—	2.50	5.00
3020	Phases and Stages/Bloody Mary Morning	1974	—	2.50	5.00
3228	Sister's Coming Home/Pick Up the Tempo	1974	—	2.50	5.00
3334	Heaven and Hell/I Still Can't Believe You're Gone	1976	—	2.50	5.00
BELLAIRE					
107	Night Life/Rainy Day Blues	1963	7.50	15.00	30.00
107	Night Life/Rainy Day Blues	1963	15.00	30.00	60.00
—Colored vinyl					
5000	Night Life '76/Man with the Blues	1976	—	2.50	5.00
BETTY					
5702	What a Way to Love/Misery Mansion	1964	5.00	10.00	20.00
5703	Man with the Blues/The Storm Has Just Begun	1964	5.00	10.00	20.00
CHALLENGE					
59280	I'm Talking About Love/I'm in Love with a Dancing Girl Working at Metropole	1965	3.75	7.50	15.00
COLUMBIA					
AE7 1182 [DJ]	White Christmas/Blue Christmas	1979	6.25	12.50	25.00
—Green vinyl					
AE7 1183 [DJ]	Pretty Paper/Rudolph the Red-Nosed Reindeer	1979	6.25	12.50	25.00
—Red vinyl					
AE7 1775 [DJ]	Pretty Paper/White Christmas	1982	—	3.00	6.00
02000	Mona Lisa/Twinkle, Twinkle Little Star	1981	—	2.00	4.00
02166	On the Road Again/September Song	1981	—	—	3.00
—Reissue					
02187	I'm Gonna Sit Right Down and Write Myself a Letter/Over the Rainbow	1981	—	2.00	4.00
02558	Heartaches of a Fool/Uncloudy Day	1981	—	2.00	4.00
02741	Always on My Mind/The Party's Over	1982	—	2.00	4.00
03073	Let It Be Me/Permanently Lonely	1982	—	2.00	4.00
03123	Angel Flying Too Close to the Ground/Mona Lisa	1982	—	—	3.00
—Reissue					
03124	Heartache of a Fool/Midnight Rider	1982	—	—	3.00
—Reissue					
03385	Last Thing I Needed First Thing This Morning/Old Fords and a Natural Stone	1982	—	2.00	4.00
03476	Pretty Paper/White Christmas	1982	—	2.50	5.00
03674	Beer Barrel Polka/Little Old Fashioned Karma	1983	—	2.00	4.00
03965	Why Do I Have to Choose/Would You Lay with Me (In a Field of Stone)	1983	—	2.00	4.00
04217	To All the Girls I've Loved Before/I Don't Want to Wake You	1984	—	—	3.00
—Julio Iglesias & Willie Nelson; B-side by Julio Iglesias solo					
04217 [PS]	To All the Girls I've Loved Before/I Don't Want to Wake You	1984	—	2.50	5.00
—Julio Iglesias & Willie Nelson; first sleeve has artists' names in both capital and small letters					
04217 [PS]	To All the Girls I've Loved Before/I Don't Want to Wake You	1984	—	2.00	4.00
—Julio Iglesias & Willie Nelson; second sleeve has artists' names in all capital letters					
04263	Without a Song/I Can't Begin to Tell You	1983	—	—	3.00
04495	As Time Goes By/You'll Never Know	1984	6.25	12.50	25.00
—Willie Nelson and Julio Iglesias; withdrawn immediately upon release					
04495 [PS]	As Time Goes By/You'll Never Know	1984	6.25	12.50	25.00
—Willie Nelson and Julio Iglesias; withdrawn immediately upon release					
04568	City of New Orleans/Why Are You Pickin' On Me	1984	—	—	3.00
04568 [PS]	City of New Orleans/Why Are You Pickin' On Me	1984	—	2.00	4.00
04715	Seven Spanish Angels/Who Cares	1984	—	—	3.00
—A-side: Ray Charles and Willie Nelson; B-side: Ray Charles and Janie Frickie					
04847	Forgiving You Was Easy/You Wouldn't Cross the Street (To Say Goodbye)	1985	—	—	3.00
04881	Highwayman/The Human Condition	1985	—	—	3.00
—A-side: Willie Nelson/Waylon Jennings/Johnny Cash/Kris Kristofferson; B-side: Nelson, Cash					
04881 [PS]	Highwayman/The Human Condition	1985	—	2.00	4.00
—A-side: Willie Nelson/Waylon Jennings/Johnny Cash/Kris Kristofferson; B-side: Nelson, Cash					
05594	Desperadoes Waiting for a Train/The Twentieth Century Is Almost Over	1985	—	—	3.00
—A-side: Willie Nelson/Waylon Jennings/Johnny Cash/Kris Kristofferson; B-side: Nelson, Cash					
05597	Me and Paul/I Let My Mind Wander	1985	—	—	3.00
05677	Slow Movin' Outlaw/They All Went to Mexico	1985	—	—	3.00
—A-side with Lacy J. Dalton; B-side with Carlos Santana					
05749	I Told a Lie to My Heart/Slow Movin' Outlaw	1986	—	—	3.00
—A-side with Hank Williams, Jr.; B-side: with Lacy J. Dalton					
05834	Living in the Promiseland/Bach Minuet in G	1986	—	—	3.00
06227	I've Already Cheated on You/Take My Advice	1986	—	—	3.00
—A-side with David Allan Coe; B-side: Coe solo					
06246	I'm Not Trying to Forget You/I've Got the Craziest Feeling	1986	—	—	3.00
06530	Partners After All/Home Away from Home	1986	—	—	3.00
07007	Heart of Gold/So Much Like My Dad	1987	—	—	3.00
07202	Island in the Sun/There Is No Easy Way (But There Is a Way)	1987	—	—	3.00
07636	Nobody There But Me/Wake Me When It's Over	1987	—	—	3.00
08044	Spanish Eyes/Ole Buttermilk Sky	1988	—	—	3.00
—With Julio Iglesias					
08395	Living in the Promiseland/Forgiving You Was Easy	1988	—	—	3.00
—Reissue					
08406	Highwayman/Desperadoes Waiting for a Train	1988	—	—	3.00
—Waylon Jennings/Willie Nelson/Johnny Cash/Kris Kristofferson; reissue					
08541	Twilight Time/Ac-Cent-Tchu-Ate the Positive	1989	—	—	3.00
10176	Blue Eyes Cryin' in the Rain/Bandera	1975	—	2.50	5.00
10275	Remember Me/Time of the Preacher	1975	—	2.50	5.00
10327	I'd Have to Be Crazy/Amazing Grace	1976	—	2.50	5.00
10383	If You've Got the Money, I've Got the Time/The Sound in Your Mind	1976	—	2.50	5.00
10453	Uncloudy Day/Precious Memories	1976	—	2.50	5.00
10480	Lily Dale/Please Don't Leave Me	1976	—	2.50	5.00
—With Darrell McCall					
10588	I Love You a Thousand Ways/Mom and Dad's Waltz	1977	—	2.50	5.00
10644	Something to Brag About/Anybody's Darlin' (Anybody But Mine)	1977	—	2.50	5.00
—With Mary Kay Place					
10704	Georgia on My Mind/On the Sunny Side of the Street	1978	—	2.50	5.00
10784	Blue Skies/Moonlight in Vermont	1978	—	2.50	5.00
10834	All of Me/Unchained Melody	1978	—	2.50	5.00
10877	Whiskey River/Under the Double Eagle	1978	—	2.50	5.00
10929	September Song/Don't Get Around Much Anymore	1979	—	2.00	4.00
11126	Help Me Make It Through the Night/The Pilgrim: Chapter 33	1979	—	2.00	4.00
11186	My Heroes Have Always Been Cowboys/Rising Star (Love Theme)	1980	—	2.00	4.00
11257	Midnight Rider/Do You Think You're a Cowboy	1980	—	2.00	4.00
11351	On the Road Again/Jumpin' Cotton-Eyed Joe	1980	—	2.00	4.00
—B-side by Johnny Gimble					
11418	Angel Flying Too Close to the Ground/I Guess I've Come to Live Here in Your Eyes	1981	—	2.00	4.00

Number	Title (A Side/B Side)	Yr	VG	VG+	NM
68923	Nothing I Can Do About It Now/If I Were a Painting	1989	—	—	3.00
73015	There You Are/Spirit	1989	—	—	3.00
73233	Silver Stallion/America Remains	1990	—	—	3.00
—Waylon Jennings/Willie Nelson/Johnny Cash/Kris Kristofferson					
73249	The Highway/Spirit	1990	—	—	3.00
73374	Is the Better Part Over/Mr. Record Man	1990	—	—	3.00
73381	Born and Raised in Black and White/Texas	1990	—	—	3.00
—The Highwaymen (Waylon Jennings/Willie Nelson/Johnny Cash/Kris Kristofferson)					
73518	It Ain't Necessarily So/I Never Cared for You	1990	—	—	3.00
73572	American Remains/Texas	1990	—	—	3.00
—The Highwaymen (Waylon Jennings/Willie Nelson/Johnny Cash/Kris Kristofferson)					
73655	The Piper Came Today/(I Don't Have a Reason) To Go to California Anymore	1991	—	—	3.00
73749	Ten with a Two/You Decide	1991	—	—	3.00
77184	Still Is Still Moving to Me/Valentine	1993	—	—	3.00
D					
1084	Man with the Blues/The Storm Has Just Begun	1959	7.50	15.00	30.00
1131	What a Way to Love/Misery Mansion	1960	7.50	15.00	30.00
ISLAND					
572414-7	The Maker/I Never Cared for You	1998	—	—	3.00
LIBERTY					
S7-18486	It Is What It Is/The Devil's Right Hand	1995	—	—	3.00
—By The Highwaymen					
S7-18584	One After 909/Yesterday	1995	—	—	3.00
—B-side by Billy Dean					
55155	Susie/No Dough	1958	6.25	12.50	25.00
55386	Mr. Record Man/The Part Where I Cry	1961	5.00	10.00	20.00
55403	Willingly/Chain of Love	1962	3.75	7.50	15.00
—A-side with Shirley Collie					
55439	Touch Me/Where My House Lives	1962	3.75	7.50	15.00
55468	You Dream About Me/Is This My Destiny	1962	3.75	7.50	15.00
—A-side with Shirley Collie					
55494	Wake Me When It's Over/There's Gonna Be Love in My House	1962	3.75	7.50	15.00
55532	Half a Man/The Last Letter	1963	3.00	6.00	12.00
55591	Take My Word/Feed It a Memory	1963	3.00	6.00	12.00
55638	How Long Is Forever/You Took My Happy Away	1963	3.00	6.00	12.00
55661	Am I Blue/There'll Be No Teardrops Tonight	1964	2.50	5.00	10.00
55697	River Boy/Opportunity to Cry	1964	2.50	5.00	10.00
56143	Right or Wrong/I Hope So	1969	—	3.00	6.00
LONE STAR					
703	The End of Understanding/Will You Remember Mine	1978	—	2.50	5.00
MONUMENT					
855	I Never Cared for You/You Left Me	1964	3.75	7.50	15.00
03408	Everything Is Beautiful (In Its Own Way)/Put It Off Until Tomorrow	1982	—	2.00	4.00
—A-side: Willie Nelson and Dolly Parton; B-side: Dolly Parton and Kris Kristofferson					
03781	You're Gonna Love Yourself (In the Morning)/ What Do You Think About Lovin'	1983	—	2.00	4.00
—A-side: Willie Nelson and Brenda Lee; B-side: Dolly Parton and Brenda Lee					
PARADISE					
629	Wabash Cannonball/Tennessee Waltz	1984	—	2.00	4.00
—A-side with Hank Wilson (a.k.a. Leon Russell); B-side by Wilson solo					
RCA					
PB-10969	I'm a Memory/It Should Be Easier Now	1977	—	2.50	5.00
—With Darrell McCall					
PB-11061	You Ought to Hear Me Cry/One in a Row	1977	—	2.50	5.00
PB-11235	If You Can Touch Her at All/Rainy Day Blues	1978	—	2.50	5.00
PB-11465	Sweet Memories/Little Things	1979	—	2.50	5.00
PB-11673	Crazy Arms/Hurricane Shirley	1979	—	2.50	5.00
—B-side by Bobby Bare					
GB-11995	Sweet Memories/If You Can Touch Her At All	1980	—	—	3.00
—Gold Standard Series					
PB-12254	Good Times/Where Do You Stand	1981	—	2.00	4.00
PB-12254 [PS]	Good Times/Where Do You Stand	1981	—	2.50	5.00
PB-12328	Mountain Dew/Laying My Burdens Down	1981	—	2.00	4.00
RCA VICTOR					
PB-10429	I'm a Memory/Fire and Rain	1975	—	2.50	5.00
PB-10461	Pretty Paper/What a Merry Christmas This Could Be	1975	2.00	4.00	8.00
PB-10591	Summer of Roses/I Gotta Get Drunk	1976	—	2.50	5.00
47-8484	Pretty Paper/What a Merry Christmas This Could Be	1964	3.75	7.50	15.00
47-8519	She's Not for You/Permanently Lonely	1965	3.00	6.00	12.00
47-8594	Healing Hands of Time/One Day at a Time	1965	3.00	6.00	12.00
47-8682	I Just Can't Let You Say Goodbye/And So Will You, My Love	1965	3.00	6.00	12.00
47-8801	Columbus Stockade Blues/He Sits at My Table	1966	3.00	6.00	12.00
47-8852	I'm Still Not Over You/I Love You Because	1966	3.00	6.00	12.00
47-8933	One in a Row/San Antonio Rose	1966	3.00	6.00	12.00
47-9029	Pretty Paper/What a Merry Christmas This Could Be	1966	3.00	6.00	12.00
47-9100	The Party's Over/Make Way for a Better Man	1967	2.50	5.00	10.00
47-9202	Blackjack County Chain/Some Other World	1967	2.50	5.00	10.00
47-9324	San Antonio/To Make a Long Story Short	1967	2.50	5.00	10.00
47-9427	Little Things/I'll Stay Around	1968	2.50	5.00	10.00
47-9536	Good Times/Don't You Ever Get Tired	1968	2.50	5.00	10.00
47-9605	Johnny One Time/She's Still Gone	1968	2.50	5.00	10.00
47-9684	Bring Me Sunshine/Don't Say Love or Nothing	1968	2.50	5.00	10.00
47-9778	Pretty Paper/What a Merry Christmas This Could Be	1969	—	—	—
—Unreleased					
47-9798	Who Do I Know in Dallas/Once More with Feeling	1969	2.00	4.00	8.00
47-9903	Laying My Burdens Down/Truth Number One	1970	2.00	4.00	8.00
47-9931	Pretty Paper/What a Merry Christmas This Could Be	1970	2.00	4.00	8.00
47-9951	I'm a Memory/I'm So Lonesome I Could Cry	1971	—	3.00	6.00
47-9984	Kneel at the Feet of Jesus/What Can You Do to Me Now	1971	—	3.00	6.00
74-0162	Jimmy's Road/Natural to Be Gone	1969	2.00	4.00	8.00
74-0542	Yesterday's Wine/Me and Paul	1971	—	3.00	6.00
74-0635	A Moment Isn't Very Long/Words Don't Fit the Picture	1972	—	3.00	6.00
74-0816	Mountain Dew/Phases, Stages, Circles, Cycles, and Scenes	1972	—	3.00	6.00
SARG					
260	A Storm Has Just Begun/When I Sang My Last Hillbilly Song	196?	12.50	25.00	50.00
—Some sources say this came out in 1955, but that doesn't coincide with this label's history					
SONGBIRD					
41313	Family Bible/In God's Eyes	1980	—	2.00	4.00
UNITED ARTISTS					
641	Night Life/Rainy Day Blues	1963	3.75	7.50	15.00
XW771	The Last Letter/There Goes a Man	1976	—	2.50	5.00
XW1165	Hello Walls/The Last Letter	1978	—	2.50	5.00
XW1254	There'll Be Teardrops Tonight/Blue Must Be the Color of the Blues	1978	—	2.50	5.00
WILLIE NELSON					
628	No Place for Me/The Lumberjack	1957	75.00	150.00	300.00

Albums

Number	Title	Yr	VG	VG+	NM
ALLEGIANCE					
AV-5005	Willie or Won't He	1983	2.50	5.00	10.00
AV-5010	Wild & Willie	1983	2.50	5.00	10.00
ATLANTIC					
SD 7262	Shotgun Willie	1973	5.00	10.00	20.00
SD 7291	Phases and Stages	1974	5.00	10.00	20.00
COLUMBIA					
PC 33482	Red Headed Stranger	1975	3.75	7.50	15.00
—No bar code on back cover					
PC 33482	Red Headed Stranger	1979	2.00	4.00	8.00
—With bar code on back cover; budget-line reissue					
PC 34092	The Sound in Your Mind	1976	3.00	6.00	12.00
—No bar code on back cover					
PC 34092	The Sound in Your Mind	1979	2.00	4.00	8.00
—With bar code on back cover; budget-line reissue					
PC 34112	The Troublemaker	1976	3.00	6.00	12.00
—No bar code on back cover					
PC 34112	The Troublemaker	1979	2.00	4.00	8.00
—With bar code on back cover; budget-line reissue					
JC 34695	To Lefty From Willie	1977	3.00	6.00	12.00
PC 34695	To Lefty From Willie	1979	2.00	4.00	8.00
—Budget-line reissue					
JC 35305	Stardust	1978	2.50	5.00	10.00
KC2 35642 [(2)]	Willie and Family Live	1978	3.75	7.50	15.00
JC 36188	Willie Nelson Sings Kristofferson	1979	2.50	5.00	10.00
PC 36188	Willie Nelson Sings Kristofferson	1980	2.00	4.00	8.00
—Budget-line reissue					
JC 36189	Pretty Paper	1979	2.50	5.00	10.00
JS 36327	The Electric Horseman	1979	2.50	5.00	10.00
—Side 2 by Dave Grusin					
S2 36752 [(2)]	Honeysuckle Rose	1980	3.00	6.00	12.00
—Over half of the LP is by Willie					
FC 36883	Somewhere Over the Rainbow	1981	2.50	5.00	10.00
KC2 37542 [(2)]	Willie Nelson's Greatest Hits (& Some That Will Be)	1981	3.00	6.00	12.00
FC 37951	Always on My Mind	1982	2.50	5.00	10.00
PC 37951	Always on My Mind	1984	2.00	4.00	8.00
—Budget-line reissue					
PC 38248	Tougher Than Leather	1984	2.00	4.00	8.00
—Budget-line reissue					
QC 38248	Tougher Than Leather	1983	2.50	5.00	10.00
CX 38250 [(10)]	Willie Nelson	1983	30.00	60.00	120.00
FC 39110	Without a Song	1983	2.50	5.00	10.00
PC 39110	Without a Song	1984	2.00	4.00	8.00
—Budget-line reissue					
FC 39145	City of New Orleans	1984	2.50	5.00	10.00
PC 39145	City of New Orleans	1985	2.00	4.00	8.00
—Budget-line reissue					
FC 39363	Angel Eyes	1984	2.50	5.00	10.00
PC 39363	Angel Eyes	1985	2.00	4.00	8.00
—Budget-line reissue					
FC 39894	Partners	1986	2.50	5.00	10.00
PC 39894	Partners	1987	2.00	4.00	8.00
—Budget-line reissue					
9C9 39943 [PD]	Always on My Mind	1985	5.00	10.00	20.00
FC 39990	Half Nelson	1985	2.50	5.00	10.00
—Duets with 10 different artists					
PC 39990	Half Nelson	1986	2.00	4.00	8.00
—Budget-line reissue					
FC 40008	Me and Paul	1985	2.50	5.00	10.00
PC 40008	Me and Paul	1986	2.00	4.00	8.00
—Budget-line reissue					
FC 40327	The Promiseland	1986	2.50	5.00	10.00
FC 40487	Island in the Sea	1987	2.50	5.00	10.00
HC 43482	Red Headed Stranger	1982	10.00	20.00	40.00
—Half-speed mastered edition					
FC 44431	What a Wonderful World	1988	2.50	5.00	10.00
FC 45046	A Horse Called Music	1989	2.50	5.00	10.00
HC 45305	Stardust	1981	17.50	35.00	70.00
—Half-speed mastered edition					
HC 47951	Always on My Mind	1982	12.50	25.00	50.00
—Half-speed mastered edition					
HC 48248	Tougher Than Leather	1983	12.50	25.00	50.00
—Half-speed mastered edition					
HEARTLAND					
HL 1038/9 [(2)]	The Best of Willie Nelson	1987	3.75	7.50	15.00
LIBERTY					
LRP-3239 [M]	...And Then I Wrote	1962	10.00	20.00	40.00
LRP-3308 [M]	Here's Willie Nelson	1963	10.00	20.00	40.00
LST-7239 [S]	...And Then I Wrote	1962	12.50	25.00	50.00
LST-7308 [S]	Here's Willie Nelson	1963	12.50	25.00	50.00
LN-10013	Country Willie	1980	2.00	4.00	8.00
—Budget-line reissue					
LN-10118	The Best of Willie Nelson	1982	2.00	4.00	8.00
—Budget-line reissue					
PAIR					
PDL2-1007 [(2)]	Country Winners	1986	3.00	6.00	12.00

Number	Title (A Side/B Side)	Yr	VG	VG+	NM
PDL2-1032 [(2)]	Once More with Feeling	1986	3.00	6.00	12.00
PDL2-1114 [(2)]	Good Hearted Woman	1986	3.00	6.00	12.00
PICKWICK					
ACL1-0326	Country Winners	1976	2.00	4.00	8.00
ACL1-0705	Spotlight on Willie Nelson	1976	2.00	4.00	8.00
SPC-3584	Hello Walls	197?	2.50	5.00	10.00
ACL1-7018	Columbus Stockade Blues	1976	2.00	4.00	8.00
RCA CAMDEN					
ACL1-0326	Country Winners	1973	3.00	6.00	12.00
ACL1-705	Spotlight on Willie Nelson	1974	3.00	6.00	12.00
CAS-2444	Columbus Stockade Blues	1970	3.75	7.50	15.00
ACL1-7018	Columbus Stockade Blues	1975	2.50	5.00	10.00
RCA VICTOR					
ANL1-1102	Yesterday's Wine	1975	2.50	5.00	10.00
APL1-1234	What Can You Do to Me Now	1975	3.00	6.00	12.00
APL1-1487	Willie Nelson Live	1976	3.00	6.00	12.00
APL1-2210	Before His Time	1977	2.50	5.00	10.00
AHL1-3243	Sweet Memories	1979	2.50	5.00	10.00
LPM-3418 [M]	Country Willie — His Own Songs	1965	5.00	10.00	20.00
LSP-3418 [S]	Country Willie — His Own Songs	1965	6.25	12.50	25.00
LPM-3528 [M]	Country Favorites, Willie Nelson Style	1966	5.00	10.00	20.00
LSP-3528 [S]	Country Favorites, Willie Nelson Style	1966	6.25	12.50	25.00
AHL1-3549	Danny Davis & Willie Nelson with the Nashville Brass	1980	2.50	5.00	10.00
LPM-3659 [M]	Country Music Concert	1966	5.00	10.00	20.00
LSP-3659 [S]	Country Music Concert	1966	6.25	12.50	25.00
AYL1-3671	Before His Time	1980	2.00	4.00	8.00
—"Best Buy Series" reissue					
LPM-3748 [M]	Make Way for Willie Nelson	1967	5.00	10.00	20.00
LSP-3748 [S]	Make Way for Willie Nelson	1967	6.25	12.50	25.00
AYL1-3800	Yesterday's Wine	1980	2.00	4.00	8.00
—"Best Buy Series" reissue					
LPM-3858 [M]	The Party's Over and Other Great Willie Nelson Songs	1967	6.25	12.50	25.00
LSP-3858 [S]	The Party's Over and Other Great Willie Nelson Songs	1967	5.00	10.00	20.00
LPM-3937 [M]	Texas in My Soul	1968	25.00	50.00	100.00
LSP-3937 [S]	Texas in My Soul	1968	5.00	10.00	20.00
AYL1-3958	What Can You Do to Me Now	1981	2.00	4.00	8.00
—"Best Buy Series" reissue					
AHL1-4045	The Minstrel Man	1981	2.50	5.00	10.00
LSP-4057	Good Times	1968	5.00	10.00	20.00
LSP-4111	My Own Peculiar Way	1969	5.00	10.00	20.00
AYL1-4165	Willie Nelson Live	1981	2.00	4.00	8.00
—"Best Buy Series" reissue					
LSP-4294	Both Sides Now	1970	5.00	10.00	20.00
AYL1-4300	Sweet Memories	1982	2.00	4.00	8.00
—"Best Buy Series" reissue					
LSP-4404	Laying My Burdens Down	1970	5.00	10.00	20.00
AHL1-4420	The Best of Willie Nelson	1982	2.50	5.00	10.00
LSP-4489	Willie Nelson & Family	1971	5.00	10.00	20.00
LSP-4568	Yesterday's Wine	1971	5.00	10.00	20.00
LSP-4653	The Picture	1972	5.00	10.00	20.00
LSP-4760	The Willie Way	1972	5.00	10.00	20.00
AHL1-4819	My Own Way	1983	2.50	5.00	10.00
AYL1-5143	The Best of Willie Nelson	1984	2.00	4.00	8.00
—"Best Buy Series" reissue					
CPL1-5174	Don't You Ever Get Tired of Hurting Me	1984	2.50	5.00	10.00
AYL1-5438	My Own Way	1985	2.00	4.00	8.00
—"Best Buy Series" reissue					
AHL1-5470	Collector's Series	1985	2.50	5.00	10.00
CPL1-7158	Willie	1986	2.50	5.00	10.00
SONGBIRD					
3258	Family Bible	1980	2.50	5.00	10.00
SUNSET					
SUM-1138 [M]	Hello Walls	1966	3.75	7.50	15.00
SUS-5138 [S]	Hello Walls	1966	5.00	10.00	20.00
TAKOMA					
TAK-7104	The Legend Begins	1983	2.50	5.00	10.00
TIME-LIFE					
P 16946 [(3)]	Country and Western Classics	1983	5.00	10.00	20.00
UNITED ARTISTS					
UA-LA086-E	The Best of Willie Nelson	1973	3.75	7.50	15.00
—Reissue of Liberty tracks					
UA-LA410-G	Country Willie	1975	3.75	7.50	15.00
UA-LA574-H2 [(2)]	Texas Country	1975	4.50	9.00	18.00
UA-LA930-G	There'll Be No Teardrops Tonight	1978	3.75	7.50	15.00

NELSON, WILLIE, AND KRIS KRISTOFFERSON

Also see each artist's individual listings.

Number	Title (A Side/B Side)	Yr	VG	VG+	NM
45s					
COLUMBIA					
38-04652	How Do You Feel About Foolin' Around/Eye of the Storm	1984	—	—	3.00
Albums					
COLUMBIA					
FC 39531	Music from Songwriter	1984	2.50	5.00	10.00

NELSON, WILLIE, AND ROGER MILLER

Also see each artist's individual listings.

Number	Title (A Side/B Side)	Yr	VG	VG+	NM
45s					
COLUMBIA					
02681	Old Friends/When a House Is Not a Home	1982	—	2.00	4.00
—With Ray Price					
Albums					
COLUMBIA					
FC 38013	Old Friends	1982	2.50	5.00	10.00
PC 38013	Old Friends	198?	2.00	4.00	8.00
—Budget-line reissue					

NELSON, WILLIE, AND WEBB PIERCE

Number	Title (A Side/B Side)	Yr	VG	VG+	NM
45s					
COLUMBIA					
03231	In the Jailhouse Now/Back Street Affair	1982	—	2.00	4.00
Albums					
COLUMBIA					
FC 38095	In the Jailhouse Now	1982	2.50	5.00	10.00
PC 38095	In the Jailhouse Now	198?	2.00	4.00	8.00
—Budget-line reissue					

NELSON, WILLIE, AND RAY PRICE

Also see each artist's individual listings.

Number	Title (A Side/B Side)	Yr	VG	VG+	NM
45s					
COLUMBIA					
11329	Faded Love/This Cold World with You	1980	—	2.00	4.00
11405	Don't You Ever Get Tired (Of Loving Me)/Funny How Time Slips Away	1980	—	2.00	4.00
Albums					
COLUMBIA					
JC 36476	San Antonio Rose	1980	2.50	5.00	10.00
PC 36476	San Antonio Rose	198?	2.00	4.00	8.00
—Budget-line reissue					

NELSON, WILLIE, AND LEON RUSSELL

Also see each artist's individual listings.

Number	Title (A Side/B Side)	Yr	VG	VG+	NM
45s					
COLUMBIA					
11023	Heartbreak Hotel/Sioux City Sue	1979	—	2.00	4.00
11119	Trouble in Mind/One for My Baby (And One More for the Road)	1979	—	2.00	4.00
Albums					
COLUMBIA					
KC2 36064 [(2)]	One for the Road	1979	3.75	7.50	15.00

NELSON, WILLIE, AND HANK SNOW

Number	Title (A Side/B Side)	Yr	VG	VG+	NM
Albums					
COLUMBIA					
FC 39977	Brand on My Heart	1984	2.50	5.00	10.00
PC 39977	Brand on My Heart	1985	2.00	4.00	8.00
—Budget-line reissue					

NELSON, WILLIE, AND FARON YOUNG

Number	Title (A Side/B Side)	Yr	VG	VG+	NM
Albums					
COLUMBIA					
FC 39484	Funny How Time Slips Away	1984	2.50	5.00	10.00
PC 39484	Funny How Time Slips Away	1985	2.00	4.00	8.00
—Budget-line reissue					

NEON PHILHARMONIC, THE

Number	Title (A Side/B Side)	Yr	VG	VG+	NM
45s					
MCA					
40518	So Glad You're a Woman/Making Out the Best You Can	1976	—	2.50	5.00
TRX					
5039	Annie Poor/Love Will Find a Way	1972	—	2.50	5.00
WARNER BROS.					
7261	Morning Girl/Brilliant Colors	1969	2.00	4.00	8.00
7311	No One Is Going to Hurt You/You Lied	1969	—	3.00	6.00
7355	Clouds/Snow	1969	—	3.00	6.00
7380	Don't Know the Way Around Soul/Highty-Ho, Princess	1970	—	3.00	6.00
7419	Flowers for Your Pillow/To Be Continued	1970	—	3.00	6.00
7457	Something to Believe In/A Little Love	1971	—	3.00	6.00
7497	Gotta Feeling in My Bones/Keep the Faith in Me	1971	—	3.00	6.00
Albums					
WARNER BROS.					
WS 1769	The Moth Confesses	1968	6.25	12.50	25.00
WS 1804	The Neon Philharmonic	1969	3.75	7.50	15.00

NEONS, THE (1)

Number	Title (A Side/B Side)	Yr	VG	VG+	NM
45s					
CHALLENGE					
9147	Magic Moment/Fat Girls	1962	25.00	50.00	100.00
59147	Magic Moment/Fat Girls	1962	12.50	25.00	50.00

NEONS, THE (2)

Number	Title (A Side/B Side)	Yr	VG	VG+	NM
45s					
GONE					
5090	Angel Face/Golden Dreams	1960	10.00	20.00	40.00
TETRA					
4444	Angel Face/Kiss Me Quickly	1956	20.00	40.00	80.00
4449	Road of Romance/My Chickadee	1957	20.00	40.00	80.00
VINTAGE					
1016	Honey Bun/Golden Dreams	1974	—	2.50	5.00

NEONS, THE (3)

Number	Title (A Side/B Side)	Yr	VG	VG+	NM
45s					
WALDON					
1001	My Lover/Tucson	1961	175.00	350.00	700.00

NEP-TUNES, THE

Number	Title (A Side/B Side)	Yr	VG	VG+	NM
Albums					
FAMILY					
FLP-152 [M]	Surfer's Holiday	1963	50.00	100.00	200.00
SFLP-152 [S]	Surfer's Holiday	1963	75.00	150.00	300.00

NEPTUNES, THE

Several different groups.

45s

Number	Title (A Side/B Side)	Yr	VG	VG+	NM
CHECKER					
967	She'll Understand/So Little Time	1960	3.00	6.00	12.00
GEM					
100	Turn Around/(B-side unknown)	196?	6.25	12.50	25.00
GLORY					
269	Fraidy Cat/As Long As	1959	5.00	10.00	20.00
INSTANT					
3255	Make a Memory/House of Heartaches	1963	6.25	12.50	25.00
PAYSON					
101/2	If You Care/She Went That-a-Way	1958	5.00	10.00	20.00
RCA VICTOR					
47-7931	Curiosity Killed the Cat/This Is Love	1961	3.00	6.00	12.00
VICTORIA					
102	I'm Coming Home/I Don't Cry Anymore	1964	6.25	12.50	25.00
WARNER BROS.					
5453	Shame Girl/I've Got Plans	1964	3.00	6.00	12.00

NERO, FRANCES

45s

Number	Title (A Side/B Side)	Yr	VG	VG+	NM
SOUL					
35020	Keep On Lovin' Me/Fight Off Fire with Fire	1966	12.50	25.00	50.00

NERO, PETER

45s

Number	Title (A Side/B Side)	Yr	VG	VG+	NM
ARIOLA AMERICA					
7635	There'll Be Time/Always Lovely Times	1976	—	2.00	4.00
7650	Tara's Theme/Always Lovely Times	1976	—	2.00	4.00
ARISTA					
0112	Emmanuelle/Soul Ballet	1975	—	2.00	4.00
0125	Theme from "The Young and the Restless"/Superstition	1975	—	2.00	4.00
COLUMBIA					
44846	Soulful Strut/For Once in My Life	1969	—	2.50	5.00
44934	Be-In/Theme from Picasso Summer	1969	—	2.50	5.00
45077	Come Saturday Morning/Maybe Tomorrow	1970	—	2.00	4.00
45167	Company/Raindrops Keep Fallin' on My Head	1970	—	2.00	4.00
45198	The Great Hits of Summer Medley/Something	1970	—	2.00	4.00
45279	Theme from "Love Story"/El Condor Pasa	1970	—	2.00	4.00
45399	Theme from "Summer of '42"/Theme from "Jesus Christ Superstar"	1971	—	2.00	4.00
45544	Brian's Song/Just for Her	1972	—	2.00	4.00
45651	Love Theme from "The Godfather"/A Love That Never Ends	1972	—	2.00	4.00
45731	Ben (Theme from "Ben")/His World	1972	—	2.00	4.00
45756	Lady Sings the Blues/Love Is Waiting	1973	—	2.00	4.00
45756 [PS]	Lady Sings the Blues/Love Is Waiting	1973	—	2.50	5.00
45825	Theme from "Baxter"/Love Is Waiting	1973	—	2.00	4.00
45959	The Morning After/Daydream	1973	—	2.00	4.00
RCA VICTOR					
47-7932	Maria/On the Street Where You Live	1961	2.00	4.00	8.00
47-7956	Theme from "Summer and Smoke"/Maria	1961	2.00	4.00	8.00
47-7956 [PS]	Theme from "Summer and Smoke"/Maria	1961	3.00	6.00	12.00
47-8161	Space Flight/It's a Darn Good Thing	1963	2.00	4.00	8.00
47-8322	Sunday in New York/More in Love	1964	—	3.00	6.00
47-8503	Theme from "36 Hours"/If You've Got a Heart	1965	—	3.00	6.00
47-8620	Ship of Fools/Why Did I Choose You	1965	—	3.00	6.00
47-8715	Thunderball/Theme from "The Spy Who Came In from the Cold"	1965	—	3.00	6.00
47-8892	Born Free/Who's Afraid	1966	—	3.00	6.00
47-9125	Theme from The Quiller Memorandum/Amy's Theme	1967	—	3.00	6.00
47-9247	Guantanamera/Xochimilco	1967	—	3.00	6.00
47-9429	Theme from The Fox/Who Will Answer	1968	—	3.00	6.00
47-9556	Elvira/A Heart Without Love	1968	—	3.00	6.00

Albums

Number	Title (A Side/B Side)	Yr	VG	VG+	NM
ARISTA					
AL 4034	Disco, Dance and Love Themes	1976	2.50	5.00	10.00
BAINBRIDGE					
BT-6268	The Sounds of Love	1987	2.50	5.00	10.00
COLUMBIA					
CS 1009	I'll Never Fall in Love Again	1970	2.50	5.00	10.00
CS 9800	I've Gotta Be Me	1969	3.00	6.00	12.00
C 30586	Love Story	1971	2.50	5.00	10.00
KC 31105	Summer of '42	1971	2.50	5.00	10.00
KC 31335	The First Time Ever (I Saw Your Face)	1972	2.50	5.00	10.00
C2 31982 [(2)]	The World of Peter Nero	1972	3.00	6.00	12.00
KC 32689	Say, Has Anybody Seen My Sweet Gypsy Rose	1973	2.50	5.00	10.00
PC 33136	Greatest Hits	1974	2.50	5.00	10.00
CONCORD JAZZ					
CJ-48	Peter Nero Now	1978	2.50	5.00	10.00
CJ-48	Now	1978	2.50	5.00	10.00
CRYSTAL CLEAR					
6001	The Wiz	198?	5.00	10.00	20.00
—Direct-to-disc recording					
MODE					
LP-117 [M]	Bernie Nerow Trio	1957	20.00	40.00	80.00
—As "Bernie Nerow"					
PREMIER					
PM-2011 [M]	Just For You	1963	5.00	10.00	20.00
PS-2011 [R]	Just For You	1963	3.00	6.00	12.00
RCA CAMDEN					
CAL-2139 [M]	Peter Nero Plays Born Free and Others	1967	3.75	7.50	15.00
CAS-2139 [S]	Peter Nero Plays Born Free and Others	1967	3.00	6.00	12.00
CAL-2228 [M]	If Ever I Would Leave You	1968	3.75	7.50	15.00
CAS-2228 [S]	If Ever I Would Leave You	1968	3.00	6.00	12.00
RCA VICTOR					
PRM-241 [M]	Tender Is the Night	1967	3.75	7.50	15.00
PRS-241 [S]	Tender Is the Night	1967	5.00	10.00	20.00
—Special-products release					
ADL1-0284 [(2)]	Music Festival of Hits	1973	3.00	6.00	12.00
LPM-2334 [M]	Piano Forte	1961	3.75	7.50	15.00
LSP-2334 [S]	Piano Forte	1961	5.00	10.00	20.00
LPM-2383 [M]	New Piano in Town	1961	3.75	7.50	15.00
LSP-2383 [S]	New Piano in Town	1961	5.00	10.00	20.00
LPM-2484 [M]	Young and Warm and Wonderful	1962	3.75	7.50	15.00
LSP-2484 [S]	Young and Warm and Wonderful	1962	5.00	10.00	20.00
LPM-2536 [M]	For the Nero-Minded	1962	3.75	7.50	15.00
LSP-2536 [S]	For the Nero-Minded	1962	5.00	10.00	20.00
LPM-2618 [M]	The Colorful Peter Nero	1963	3.75	7.50	15.00
LSP-2618 [S]	The Colorful Peter Nero	1963	5.00	10.00	20.00
LPM-2638 [M]	Hail the Conquering Nero	1963	3.75	7.50	15.00
LSP-2638 [S]	Hail the Conquering Nero	1963	5.00	10.00	20.00
LPM-2710 [M]	Peter Nero in Person	1963	3.75	7.50	15.00
LSP-2710 [S]	Peter Nero in Person	1963	5.00	10.00	20.00
LPM-2827 [M]	Sunday in New York	1964	3.75	7.50	15.00
LSP-2827 [S]	Sunday in New York	1964	5.00	10.00	20.00
LPM-2853 [M]	Reflections	1964	3.75	7.50	15.00
LSP-2853 [S]	Reflections	1964	5.00	10.00	20.00
LPM-2935 [M]	Songs You Won't Forget	1964	3.75	7.50	15.00
LSP-2935 [S]	Songs You Won't Forget	1964	5.00	10.00	20.00
LPM-2978 [M]	The Best of Peter Nero	1965	3.75	7.50	15.00
LSP-2978 [S]	The Best of Peter Nero	1965	5.00	10.00	20.00
LPM-3313 [M]	Career Girls	1965	3.75	7.50	15.00
LSP-3313 [S]	Career Girls	1965	5.00	10.00	20.00
LPM-3496 [M]	The Screen Scene	1966	3.00	6.00	12.00
LSP-3496 [S]	The Screen Scene	1966	3.75	7.50	15.00
LPM-3550 [M]	Peter Nero — Up Close	1966	3.00	6.00	12.00
LSP-3550 [S]	Peter Nero — Up Close	1966	3.75	7.50	15.00
LPM-3610 [M]	Peter Nero On Tour	1966	3.00	6.00	12.00
LSP-3610 [S]	Peter Nero On Tour	1966	3.75	7.50	15.00
LPM-3720 [M]	Plays a Salute to Herb Alpert and the Tijuana Brass	1967	3.75	7.50	15.00
LSP-3720 [S]	Plays a Salute to Herb Alpert and the Tijuana Brass	1967	3.00	6.00	12.00
LPM-3814 [M]	Xochimilico	1967	3.75	7.50	15.00
LSP-3814 [S]	Xochimilico	1967	3.00	6.00	12.00
LPM-3871 [M]	Nero-ing In on the Hits	1968	3.75	7.50	15.00
LSP-3871 [S]	Nero-ing In on the Hits	1968	3.00	6.00	12.00
LPM-3936 [M]	Peter Nero Plays Love Is Blue and Ten Other Great Songs	1968	3.75	7.50	15.00
LSP-3936 [S]	Peter Nero Plays Love Is Blue and Ten Other Great Songs	1968	3.00	6.00	12.00
LSP-4072	Impressions (Great Songs of Burt Bacharach and Hal David)	1968	3.00	6.00	12.00
LSP-4205	Love Trip	1969	3.00	6.00	12.00

NERVOUS NORVUS

45s

Number	Title (A Side/B Side)	Yr	VG	VG+	NM
DOT					
15470	Transfusion/Dig	1956	12.50	25.00	50.00
—Originals have maroon labels					
15470	Transfusion/Dig	1956	7.50	15.00	30.00
—Second pressings have black labels					
15485	Ape Call/Wild Dog of Kentucky	1956	7.50	15.00	30.00
—Originals have maroon labels					
15485	Ape Call/Wild Dog of Kentucky	1956	5.00	10.00	20.00
—Second pressings have black labels					
15500	The Fang/The Bullfrog	1956	7.50	15.00	30.00
—Originals have maroon labels					
15500	The Fang/The Bullfrog	1956	5.00	10.00	20.00
—Second pressings have black labels					
16765	Transfusion/Ape Call	1965	3.00	6.00	12.00
EMBEE					
117	I Like Girls/Stone Age Woo	1959	5.00	10.00	20.00

NESMITH, MICHAEL

Also see MIKE, JOHN AND BILL; THE MONKEES.

45s

Number	Title (A Side/B Side)	Yr	VG	VG+	NM
COLPIX					
787	The New Recruit/A Journey	1965	37.50	75.00	150.00
—As "Michael Blessing"					
792	Until It's Time for You to Go/What's the Trouble, Officer	1965	37.50	75.00	150.00
—As "Michael Blessing"					
EDAN					
1001	Just a Little Love/Curson Terrace	1965	30.00	60.00	120.00
PACIFIC ARTS					
084	Life, the Unsuspecting Captive/Rio	1977	2.00	4.00	8.00
101	Roll with the Flow/I've Just Begun to Care	1978	—	3.00	6.00
104	Casablanca Moonlight/Rio	1978	—	3.00	6.00
104 [PS]	Casablanca Moonlight/Rio	1978	3.00	6.00	12.00
106	Magic (This Night Is Magic)/Dance	1979	—	3.00	6.00
108	Cruisin'/Horserace	1979	—	3.00	6.00
6373	Life, the Unsuspecting Captive/Rio	1976	2.50	5.00	10.00
6398	Navajo Trail/Love's First Kiss	1976	2.50	5.00	10.00
RCA VICTOR					
47-9853	Rose City Chimes/Little Red Rider	1970	2.50	5.00	10.00
74-0368	Joanne/One Rose	1970	3.00	6.00	12.00
74-0399	Silver Moon/Lady of the Valley	1970	2.50	5.00	10.00
74-0453	Nevada Fighter/Here I Am	1971	2.00	4.00	8.00
74-0453 [PS]	Nevada Fighter/Here I Am	1971	5.00	10.00	20.00
74-0491	Tumbling Tumbleweeds/Texas Morning	1971	2.00	4.00	8.00
74-0540	Only Bound/Propinquity	1971	2.00	4.00	8.00
74-0629	Lazy Lady/Mama Rocker	1971	2.00	4.00	8.00
74-0804	Roll with the Flow/Keep On	1972	2.00	4.00	8.00

Albums

Number	Title (A Side/B Side)	Yr	VG	VG+	NM
PACIFIC ARTS					
(no #) [DJ]	The Michael Nesmith Radio Special	1979	10.00	20.00	40.00
11-101A	The Prison	1975	12.50	25.00	50.00
—Boxed set with booklet					

Number	Title (A Side/B Side)	Yr	VG	VG+	NM
7-101	The Prison	197?	5.00	10.00	20.00
—Standard cover					
7-106	Compilation	1976	5.00	10.00	20.00
7-107	From a Radio Engine to the Photon Wing	1977	5.00	10.00	20.00
7-116	And the Hits Just Keep On Comin'	1978	5.00	10.00	20.00
—Reissue of RCA 4695					
7-117	Pretty Much Your Standard Ranch Stash	1978	5.00	10.00	20.00
—Reissue of RCA APL1-0164					
7-118	Live at the Palais	1978	5.00	10.00	20.00
7-130	Infinite Rider on the Big Dogma	1979	5.00	10.00	20.00
RCA VICTOR					
APL1-0164	Pretty Much Your Standard Ranch Stash	1973	6.25	12.50	25.00
LSP-4371	Magnetic South	1970	7.50	15.00	30.00
LSP-4415	Loose Salute	1970	7.50	15.00	30.00
LSP-4497	Nevada Fighter	1971	6.25	12.50	25.00
LSP-4563	Tantamount to Treason	1971	6.25	12.50	25.00
LSP-4695	And the Hits Just Keep On Comin'	1972	6.25	12.50	25.00
RHINO					
R1-70168	The Newer Stuff	1989	3.00	6.00	12.00

NETHERWORLD

Albums

Number	Title (A Side/B Side)	Yr	VG	VG+	NM
R.E.M.					
4441	Netherworld	196?	15.00	30.00	60.00

NEUMAN, ALFRED E., AND THE FURSHLUGGINER FIVE

45s

Number	Title (A Side/B Side)	Yr	VG	VG+	NM
ABC-PARAMOUNT					
10013	What — Me Worry?/Potrzebie	1959	10.00	20.00	40.00
10013 [PS]	What — Me Worry?/Potrzebie	1959	15.00	30.00	60.00

NEVILLE, AARON

Also see THE METERS; LINDA RONSTADT.

45s

Number	Title (A Side/B Side)	Yr	VG	VG+	NM
A&M					
31458 0312 7	The Grand Tour/Don't Take Away My Heaven	1993	—	2.00	4.00
31458 0442 7	Please Come Home for Christmas/Louisiana Christmas Day	1993	—	2.50	5.00
31458 1112 7	For the Good Times/Crying in the Chapel	1995	—	2.00	4.00
75021 1563 7	Everybody Plays the Fool/House on a Hill	1991	—	2.00	4.00
BELL					
746	You Can Give, But You Can't Take/Where Is My Baby	1968	2.00	4.00	8.00
781	Speak to Me/You Don't Love Me Anymore	1969	2.00	4.00	8.00
834	All These Things/She's On My Mind	1969	2.00	4.00	8.00
MERCURY					
73310	Baby I'm-a Want You/Mojo Hannah	1972	—	3.00	6.00
73387	Hercules/Going Home	1973	—	3.00	6.00
MINIT					
612	Over You/Every Day	1960	3.75	7.50	15.00
—As "Arron Neville"					
618	Show Me the Way/Get Out of My Life	1960	3.00	6.00	12.00
624	Don't Cry/Reality	1961	3.00	6.00	12.00
631	Let's Live/I Found Another Love	1961	3.00	6.00	12.00
639	How Many Times/I'm Waitin' at the Station	1962	3.00	6.00	12.00
650	Humdinger/Sweet Little Mama	1962	3.00	6.00	12.00
657	Wrong Number/How Could I Help But Love You	1963	3.00	6.00	12.00
PAR-LO					
101	Tell It Like It Is/Why Worry	1966	5.00	10.00	20.00
—Black and white label					
101	Tell It Like It Is/Why Worry	1966	6.25	12.50	25.00
—Turquoise label, silver print					
103	She Took You for a Ride/Space Man	1967	2.00	4.00	8.00
POLYDOR					
14426	Greatest Love/Performance	1977	—	2.00	4.00
WHO DAT?					
VPAG-4476/7	Who Dat? (The History of the Saints)/(Extended Version)	1987	2.00	4.00	8.00
Albums					
MINIT					
LP 24007 [R]	Like It 'Tis	1967	7.50	15.00	30.00
LP 40007 [M]	Like It 'Tis	1967	10.00	20.00	40.00
PAR-LO					
1 [M]	Tell It Like It Is	1967	20.00	40.00	80.00
1 [S]	Tell It Like It Is	1967	50.00	100.00	200.00

NEVILLE, AARON, AND TRISHA YEARWOOD

45s

Number	Title (A Side/B Side)	Yr	VG	VG+	NM
MCA					
54836	I Fall to Pieces/(Instrumental)	1994	—	2.00	4.00

NEW BIRTH, THE

Also see LOVE, PEACE AND HAPPINESS; THE NITE-LITERS.

45s

Number	Title (A Side/B Side)	Yr	VG	VG+	NM
ARIOLA AMERICA					
7760	I Love You/Fastest Gun	1979	—	2.00	4.00
BUDDAH					
464	Granddaddy (Part 1)/Granddaddy (Part 2)	1975	—	2.00	4.00
470	Dream Merchant/Why Did It	1975	—	2.00	4.00
RCA VICTOR					
APBO-0003	Until It's Time for You to Go/You Are What I'm All About	1973	—	2.50	5.00
APBO-0185	It's Been a Long Time/Keep On Doin' It	1973	—	2.50	5.00
APBO-0265	Wildflower/Got to Get a Knutt	1974	—	2.50	5.00
PB-10017	I Wash My Hands of the Whole Damn Deal Part 1/Part 2	1974	—	2.50	5.00
PB-10110	Comin' From All Sides/Patiently	1974	—	2.50	5.00
PB-10242	Do It Again/Pretty Music	1975	—	2.50	5.00
74-0400	What'll I Do/One Way Bus	1970	—	3.00	6.00
74-0520	It's Impossible/Honeybee	1971	—	2.50	5.00
74-0657	Unh Song/Two Kinds of People	1972	—	2.50	5.00
74-0774	Come Back in My Life (Part 1)/Come Back in My Life (Part 2)	1972	—	2.50	5.00
74-0912	I Can Understand It/Oh Baby, I Love the Way	1973	—	2.50	5.00
WARNER BROS.					
8217	The Long and Winding Road/Hurry Hurry	1976	—	2.00	4.00
8256	Fallin' in Love — Part I/Fallin' in Love — Part II	1976	—	2.00	4.00
8292	We Are All God's Children — Part I/We Are All God's Children — Part II	1976	—	2.00	4.00
8422	Deeper/Deeper (Part 2)	1977	—	2.00	4.00
8499	The Mighty Army/Hurry Hurry	1977	—	2.00	4.00
8536	How Will I Live/Squeezing Too Much Living	1978	—	2.00	4.00
Albums					
ARIOLA AMERICA					
SW-50062	Platinum City	1979	2.50	5.00	10.00
BUDDAH					
BDS-5636	Blind Baby	1975	2.50	5.00	10.00
COLLECTABLES					
COL-5100	Golden Classics	1988	2.50	5.00	10.00
RCA VICTOR					
APD1-0285 [Q]	It's Been a Long Time	1974	5.00	10.00	20.00
APL1-0285	It's Been a Long Time	1974	2.50	5.00	10.00
APL1-0494	Comin' From All Ends	1974	2.50	5.00	10.00
APL1-1021	The Best of the New Birth	1975	2.50	5.00	10.00
ANL1-2145	Birth Day	1977	2.50	5.00	10.00
—Reissue of 4797					
AFL1-4411	I'm Back	1982	2.50	5.00	10.00
LSP-4450	The New Birth	1970	3.75	7.50	15.00
LSP-4526	Ain't No Big Thing, But It's Growing	1971	3.75	7.50	15.00
LSP-4697	Coming Together	1972	3.75	7.50	15.00
LSP-4797	Birth Day	1973	3.00	6.00	12.00
WARNER BROS.					
BS 2953	Love Potion	1976	2.50	5.00	10.00
BSK 3071	Behold the Mighty Army	1977	2.50	5.00	10.00

NEW CHRISTY MINSTRELS, THE

Also see BARRY McGUIRE; KENNY ROGERS.

45s

Number	Title (A Side/B Side)	Yr	VG	VG+	NM
COLUMBIA					
42592	This Land Is Your Land/Don't Cry, Suzanne	1962	2.50	5.00	10.00
42592 [PS]	This Land Is Your Land/Don't Cry, Suzanne	1962	3.75	7.50	15.00
42673	Denver/Liza Lee	1963	2.50	5.00	10.00
42805	Green, Green/The Banjo	1963	2.50	5.00	10.00
42887	Saturday Night/The Wheeler-Dealers	1963	2.50	5.00	10.00
43000	Today/Miss Katy Cruel	1964	2.00	4.00	8.00
43092	Silly Ol' Summertime/The Far Side of the Hill	1964	2.00	4.00	8.00
43137	Same Ol' Huckleberry Finn/The Ol' Riverboat	1964	2.00	4.00	8.00
43178	Down the Road I Go/Gotta Get a-Goin'	1964	2.00	4.00	8.00
43215	Chim Chim Cheree/They Gotta Quit Kickin' My Dog Around	1965	2.00	4.00	8.00
43281	The River/Se Paingi, Se Ridi	1965	2.00	4.00	8.00
43347	Jim 'n' I, Him 'n' I, Flying in the Gemini/A Little Bit of Happiness	1965	2.00	4.00	8.00
43470	Born to Be Free/Everybody Loves Saturday Night	1965	2.00	4.00	8.00
43533	Dance My Troubles Away (Zorba's Dance)/There But for Fortune	1966	—	3.00	6.00
43644	If I Could Start My Life Again/The Music of the World a-Turnin'	1966	—	3.00	6.00
43822	A Corner in the Sun/Beautiful, Beautiful World	1966	—	3.00	6.00
43940	We Need a Little Christmas/Oh Holy Night	1966	2.50	5.00	10.00
43961	It Should Have Been You/Sleep Comes Easy	1967	—	3.00	6.00
44176	I'll Coat Your Mind with Honey/Night and Day	1967	—	3.00	6.00
44355	The Clown/No Matter What People	1967	—	3.00	6.00
44528	Ballad for Americans/Gallant Men	1968	—	2.50	5.00
44577	Alice's Restaurant/Summertime Love	1968	—	2.50	5.00
JZSP 116417/8 [DJ]	We Need a Little Christmas/Sleigh Ride	1966	3.00	6.00	12.00
—Yellow label					
JZSP 116417/8 [DJ]	We Need a Little Christmas/Sleigh Ride	1966	3.00	6.00	12.00
—White label					
GREGAR					
71-0102	You Need Someone to Love/South American Getaway	1970	—	2.00	4.00
71-0106	Brother/I Still Do	1970	—	2.00	4.00
71-0109	You Are Always On My Mind/Where Are You Then	1971	—	2.00	4.00
71-0114	The Age of Not Believing/Love It Along	1972	—	2.00	4.00
Albums					
COLUMBIA					
CL 1872 [M]	The New Christy Minstrels	1962	5.00	10.00	20.00
CL 1941 [M]	The New Christy Minstrels In Person	1963	5.00	10.00	20.00
CL 2017 [M]	Tall Tales! Legends & Nonsense	1963	5.00	10.00	20.00
CL 2055 [M]	Ramblin' Feturing Green, Green	1963	5.00	10.00	20.00
CL 2096 [M]	Merry Christmas	1963	5.00	10.00	20.00
CL 2159 [M]	Today	1964	5.00	10.00	20.00
CL 2187 [M]	Land of Giants	1964	5.00	10.00	20.00
CL 2280 [M]	The Quiet Sides of the New Christy Minstrels	1965	5.00	10.00	20.00
CL 2303 [M]	Cowboys and Indians	1965	5.00	10.00	20.00
CL 2369 [M]	Chim Chim Cher-ee	1965	5.00	10.00	20.00
CL 2384 [M]	The Wandering Minstrels	1965	5.00	10.00	20.00
CL 2479 [M]	Greatest Hits	1966	5.00	10.00	20.00
CL 2531 [M]	In Italy...In Italian	1966	5.00	10.00	20.00
CL 2542 [M]	New Kick	1967	5.00	10.00	20.00
CL 2556 [M]	Christmas with the Christies	1966	5.00	10.00	20.00
CS 8672 [S]	The New Christy Minstrels	1962	6.25	12.50	25.00
CS 8741 [S]	The New Christy Minstrels In Person	1963	6.25	12.50	25.00
CS 8817 [S]	Tall Tales! Legends & Nonsense	1963	6.25	12.50	25.00
CS 8855 [S]	Ramblin' Feturing Green, Green	1963	6.25	12.50	25.00
CS 8896 [S]	Merry Christmas	1963	6.25	12.50	25.00
CS 8959 [S]	Today	1964	6.25	12.50	25.00
CS 8987 [S]	Land of Giants	1964	6.25	12.50	25.00
CS 9080 [S]	The Quiet Sides of the New Christy Minstrels	1965	6.25	12.50	25.00
CS 9103 [S]	Cowboys and Indians	1965	6.25	12.50	25.00
CS 9169 [S]	Chim Chim Cher-ee	1965	6.25	12.50	25.00
CS 9184 [S]	The Wandering Minstrels	1965	6.25	12.50	25.00
CS 9279 [S]	Greatest Hits	1966	6.25	12.50	25.00

Number	Title (A Side/B Side)	Yr	VG	VG+	NM
CS 9331 [S]	In Italy...In Italian	1966	6.25	12.50	25.00
CS 9342 [S]	New Kick	1967	6.25	12.50	25.00
CS 9356 [S]	Christmas with the Christies	1966	6.25	12.50	25.00
CS 9616	On Tour Through Motortown	1968	5.00	10.00	20.00
CS 9709	Chitty Chitty Bang Bang	1969	5.00	10.00	20.00
GREGAR					
102	You Need Someone to Love	1970	3.75	7.50	15.00

NEW COLONY SIX, THE

45s

Number	Title (A Side/B Side)	Yr	VG	VG+	NM
CENTAUR					
1201	I Confess/Dawn Is Breaking	1966	3.75	7.50	15.00
1202	I Like Awake/At the River's Edge	1966	3.75	7.50	15.00
MCA					
40215	Never Be Lonely/Long Time to Be Alone	1974	6.25	12.50	25.00
40288	I Really Don't Want to Go/Run	1974	7.50	15.00	30.00
MERCURY					
72737	Treat Her Groovy/Rap-a-Tap	1967	2.50	5.00	10.00
—Orange and red swirl label					
72737	Treat Her Groovy/Rap-a-Tap	1967	3.00	6.00	12.00
—Red label with "Mercury" logo in all capital letters					
72737 [PS]	Treat Her Groovy/Rap-a-Tap	1967	3.75	7.50	15.00
72775	I Will Always Think About You/Hold Me with Your Eyes	1968	2.50	5.00	10.00
—Orange and red swirl label					
72775	I Will Always Think About You/Hold Me with Your Eyes	1968	3.00	6.00	12.00
—Red label with "Mercury" logo in all capital letters					
72817	Can't You See Me Cry/Summertime's Another Name for Love	1968	2.00	4.00	8.00
72817 [PS]	Can't You See Me Cry/Summertime's Another Name for Love	1968	3.75	7.50	15.00
72858	Things I'd Like to Say/Come and Give Your Love to Me	1968	2.50	5.00	10.00
—Red label with "Mercury" logo in an oval					
72858	Things I'd Like to Say/Come and Give Your Love to Me	1968	3.00	6.00	12.00
—Orange and red swirl label					
72920	I Could Never Lie to You/Just Feel Worse	1969	2.00	4.00	8.00
72961	I Want You to Know/Free	1969	2.00	4.00	8.00
73004	Barbara, I Love You/Prairie Grey	1970	2.00	4.00	8.00
73063	People and Me/Ride the Wicked Wind	1970	3.75	7.50	15.00
73093	Close Your Eyes Little Girl/Love, That's the Best I Can Do	1970	5.00	10.00	20.00
—Promo copies go for less					
SENTAR					
1203	Cadillac/Sunshine	1966	3.75	7.50	15.00
1204	(Ballad of the) Wingbat Marmaduke/Power of Love	1966	3.75	7.50	15.00
1205	Love You So Much/Let Me Love You	1967	3.75	7.50	15.00
1206	You're Gonna Be Mine/Woman	1967	3.75	7.50	15.00
1207	I'm Just Waiting Anticipating for Her to Show Up/Hello Lonely	1967	3.75	7.50	15.00
SENTAUR					
1202	I Like Awake/At the River's Edge	1966	5.00	10.00	20.00
—Reissue of Centaur 1202, but harder to find					
SUNLIGHT					
1001	Roll On/If You Could See	1971	—	3.00	6.00
1004	Long Time to Be Alone/Never Be Lonely	1971	—	3.00	6.00
1005	Someone, Sometime/Come On Down	1972	2.00	4.00	8.00
TWILIGHT					
1004	Long Time to Be Alone/Never Be Lonely	1973	—	—	—
—The existence of this record as a US pressing has not been confirmed					

Albums

Number	Title (A Side/B Side)	Yr	VG	VG+	NM
MERCURY					
SR-61165	Revelations	1968	7.50	15.00	30.00
SR-61228	Attacking a Straw Man	1969	7.50	15.00	30.00
SENTAR					
LP-101 [M]	Breakthrough	1966	125.00	250.00	500.00
SST-3001 [S]	Colonization	1967	15.00	30.00	60.00
ST-3001 [M]	Colonization	1967	12.50	25.00	50.00
SUNDAZED					
LP 5007	At the River's Edge	1995	2.50	5.00	10.00

NEW DAWN, THE

45s

Number	Title (A Side/B Side)	Yr	VG	VG+	NM
GARLAND					
2020	Why Did You Go/Tears	1970	6.25	12.50	25.00
IMPERIAL					
66397	Melody Fair/Sometimes in the Morning	1969	2.00	4.00	8.00
MAINSTREAM					
652	If I Can't Have Your Love/Loser	1966	6.25	12.50	25.00
664	Slave of Desire/Funny Feeling	1966	6.25	12.50	25.00
RCA VICTOR					
47-9569	Listen to the Music/Someday	1968	2.00	4.00	8.00

Albums

Number	Title (A Side/B Side)	Yr	VG	VG+	NM
HOOT					
GR 704569	There's a New Dawn	1970	250.00	500.00	1000.

NEW HOPE

See THE KIT KATS.

NEW KINGSTON TRIO, THE

See THE KINGSTON TRIO.

NEW MARKETTS, THE

See THE MARKETTS.

NEW MIX, THE

Albums

Number	Title (A Side/B Side)	Yr	VG	VG+	NM
UNITED ARTISTS					
UAS-6678	The New Mix	1968	5.00	10.00	20.00

NEW RENAISSANCE SOCIETY, THE

Albums

Number	Title (A Side/B Side)	Yr	VG	VG+	NM
HANNA-BARBERA					
HLP-9504 [M]	Baroque n' Stones	1966	5.00	10.00	20.00
HST-9504 [S]	Baroque n' Stones	1966	6.25	12.50	25.00

NEW RIDERS OF THE PURPLE SAGE

JERRY GARCIA was briefly in this group.

45s

Number	Title (A Side/B Side)	Yr	VG	VG+	NM
A&M					
2327	Fly Right/Night for Making Love	1981	—	2.00	4.00
2352	Full Moon at Midnite/No Other Love	1981	—	2.00	4.00
COLUMBIA					
10067	You Angel You/Parson Brown	1974	—	2.50	5.00
45469	Louisiana Lady/The Last Lonely Eagle	1971	—	3.00	6.00
45526	Garden of Eden/I Don't Know You	1972	—	2.50	5.00
45607	I Don't Need No Doctor/Runnin' Back to You	1972	—	2.50	5.00
45682	Rainbow/Dim Lights, Thick Smoke	1972	—	2.50	5.00
45763	Groupie/She's No Angel	1973	—	2.50	5.00
45976	Panama Red/Cement, Clay, and Glass	1973	—	3.00	6.00
MCA					
40564	Don't Put Her Down/Fifteen Days Under the Hood	1976	—	2.00	4.00
40591	Dead Flowers/She's Looking Better Every Beer	1976	—	2.00	4.00
40686	Red Hot Women and Ice Cold Beer/Love Has Strange Ways	1977	—	2.00	4.00
40715	(Just) Another Night in Reno/Home Grown	1977	—	2.00	4.00

Albums

Number	Title (A Side/B Side)	Yr	VG	VG+	NM
A&M					
SP-4818	Feelin' All Right	1981	2.50	5.00	10.00
COLUMBIA					
KC 30888	New Riders of the Purple Sage	1971	3.75	7.50	15.00
PC 30888	New Riders of the Purple Sage	1979	2.00	4.00	8.00
—Budget-line reissue					
KC 31284	Powerglide	1972	3.75	7.50	15.00
PC 31284	Powerglide	1979	2.00	4.00	8.00
—Budget-line reissue					
KC 31930	Gypsy Cowboy	1972	3.75	7.50	15.00
PC 31930	Gypsy Cowboy	1979	2.00	4.00	8.00
—Budget-line reissue					
CQ 32450 [Q]	The Adventures of Panama Red	1974	5.00	10.00	20.00
KC 32450	The Adventures of Panama Red	1973	3.75	7.50	15.00
PC 32450	The Adventures of Panama Red	1979	2.00	4.00	8.00
—Budget-line reissue					
PC 32870	Home, Home on the Road	1974	3.75	7.50	15.00
—Originals have no bar code					
PC 33145	Brujo	1974	3.75	7.50	15.00
—Originals have no bar code					
PC 33688	Oh, What a Mighty Time	1975	3.75	7.50	15.00
—Originals have no bar code					
PC 34367	The Best of New Riders of the Purple Sage	1976	3.00	6.00	12.00
—Originals have no bar code					
PC 34367	The Best of New Riders of the Purple Sage	1979	2.00	4.00	8.00
—Budget-line reissue with bar code					
MCA					
632	Marin County Line	1980	2.00	4.00	8.00
—Reissue of 2307					
2196	New Riders	1976	3.00	6.00	12.00
2248	Who Are These Guys	1977	3.00	6.00	12.00
2307	Marin County Line	1977	3.00	6.00	12.00
RELIX					
RRLP-2024	Before Time Began	1986	2.00	4.00	8.00
RRLP-2025	Vintage NRPS	1987	2.00	4.00	8.00

NEW SEEKERS, THE

45s

Number	Title (A Side/B Side)	Yr	VG	VG+	NM
COCA-COLA					
(no #) [DJ]	Buy the World a Coke//Bring a Little Sunshine/It's the Real Thing	1971	3.00	6.00	12.00
—All three songs are Coca-Coca jingles. The A-side became "I'd Like to Teach the World to Sing"					
COLUMBIA					
10559	You Never Can Tell/Give Me Love Your Way	1977	—	2.50	5.00
ELEKTRA					
45699	Look What They've Done to My Song, Ma/It's a Beautiful Day	1970	—	3.00	6.00
45710	Beautiful People/When There's No Love Left	1970	—	2.50	5.00
45719	The Nickel Song/Cincinnati	1971	—	2.50	5.00
45734	Never Ending Song of Love/All Right My Love	1971	—	—	—
—Unreleased					
45747	Tonight/Sweet Louise	1971	—	2.50	5.00
45762	I'd Like to Teach the World to Sing/Boom Town	1971	—	3.00	6.00
45780	Beg, Steal or Borrow/Mystic Queen	1972	—	2.50	5.00
45787	Circles/I Can Say You're Beautiful	1972	—	2.50	5.00
45805	Dance, Dance, Dance/I Can Say You're Beautiful	1972	—	2.50	5.00
MGM					
14586	The Greatest Song I've Ever Heard/Woman Grows	1973	—	2.50	5.00
14683	Reach Out I'll Be There/You Won't Find Another Fool Like Me	1973	—	2.50	5.00
14691	Song for You and Me/You Won't Find Another Fool Like Me	1974	—	2.50	5.00
VERVE					
10698	Come Softly to Me/Unwithered Rose	1972	—	2.50	5.00
10698 [PS]	Come Softly to Me/Unwithered Rose	1972	—	2.50	5.00
10709	Pinball Wizard-See Me, Feel Me/Come Softly to Me	1973	—	2.50	5.00

Albums

Number	Title (A Side/B Side)	Yr	VG	VG+	NM
ELEKTRA					
EQ-5051 [Q]	The Best of the New Seekers	1973	5.00	10.00	20.00
EKS-74088	Beautiful People	1971	3.00	6.00	12.00
EKS-74108	New Colours	1971	3.00	6.00	12.00
EKS-74115	We'd Like to Teach the World to Sing	1971	3.00	6.00	12.00
EKS-75034	Circles	1972	3.00	6.00	12.00

Number	Title (A Side/B Side)	Yr	VG	VG+	NM
EKS-75051	The Best of the New Seekers	1973	3.00	6.00	12.00
MGM VERVE					
V 5090	Come Softly to Me	1972	2.50	5.00	10.00
V 5095	The History of the New Seekers	1973	2.50	5.00	10.00
V 5098	Pinball Wizards	1973	2.50	5.00	10.00

NEW THINGS, THE

45s

Number	Title (A Side/B Side)	Yr	VG	VG+	NM
ACCENT					
1228	Dumbo/I Want You Back	1967	10.00	20.00	40.00

NEW TWEEDY BROTHERS, THE

Number	Title (A Side/B Side)	Yr	VG	VG+	NM
45s					
DOT					
16910	Good Time Car/Terms of You Love Me	1966	10.00	20.00	40.00
Albums					
RIDON					
234	The New Tweedy Brothers	1968	500.00	1000.	2000.
—With oversized hexagonal cover designed to look like a sugar cube					
234	The New Tweedy Brothers	1968	100.00	200.00	400.00
—With plain white cover					

NEW VAUDEVILLE BAND, THE

Number	Title (A Side/B Side)	Yr	VG	VG+	NM
45s					
FONTANA					
1562	Winchester Cathedral/Wait for Me Baby	1966	2.00	4.00	8.00
1573	Peek-A-Boo/Amy	1967	—	3.00	6.00
1589	Finchley Central/Sadie Moonshine	1967	—	3.00	6.00
1589 [PS]	Finchley Central/Sadie Moonshine	1967	2.50	5.00	10.00
1598	Green Street Green/Fourteen Lovely Women	1967	—	3.00	6.00
1612	Bonnie and Clyde/Anniversary Song	1968	—	3.00	6.00
Albums					
FONTANA					
MGF-27560 [M]	Winchester Cathedral	1966	3.75	7.50	15.00
—With "Whatever Happened to Phyllis Puke" and "Diana Goodbye"					
MGF-27560 [M]	Winchester Cathedral	1966	3.00	6.00	12.00
—With "Oh, Donna Clara"					
MGF-27688 [M]	The New Vaudeville Band on Tour	1967	3.00	6.00	12.00
SRF-67560 [P]	Winchester Cathedral	1966	3.75	7.50	15.00
—With "Whatever Happened to Phyllis Puke" and "Diana Goodbye"					
SRF-67560 [P]	Winchester Cathedral	1966	3.00	6.00	12.00
—With "Oh, Donna Clara"					
SRF-67688 [P]	The New Vaudeville Band on Tour	1967	3.00	6.00	12.00

NEW WAVE, THE

Number	Title (A Side/B Side)	Yr	VG	VG+	NM
45s					
CANTERBURY					
503	Where Do We Go from Here/Not from You	1967	2.50	5.00	10.00
512	Little Dreams/Autre Fois	1967	2.50	5.00	10.00
Albums					
CANTERBURY					
CLPS-1501	The New Wave	1967	6.25	12.50	25.00

NEW YORK CITY

Number	Title (A Side/B Side)	Yr	VG	VG+	NM
45s					
CHELSEA					
BCBO-0025	Make Me Twice the Man/Uncle James	1973	—	2.50	5.00
78-0113	I'm Doin' Fine Now/Ain't It So	1973	—	2.50	5.00
BCBO-0150	Quick, Fast, In a Hurry/Set the Record Straight	1973	—	2.50	5.00
3000	Happiness Is/Darling Take Me Back	1974	—	2.50	5.00
3008	Love Is What You Make It/Do You Remember Yesterday	1974	—	2.50	5.00
3010	Got to Get You Back In My Life/Reach Out	1975	—	2.50	5.00
3031	Can't Survive Without My Sweets/Take My Hand	1975	—	2.50	5.00
Albums					
CHELSEA					
BCL1-0198	I'm Doin' Fine Now	1973	3.75	7.50	15.00
CHL 500	Soulful Road	1974	3.75	7.50	15.00
CHL 514	The Best of New York City	1977	3.00	6.00	12.00

NEW YORK DOLLS

Number	Title (A Side/B Side)	Yr	VG	VG+	NM
45s					
MERCURY					
DJ-378 [DJ]	Trash (mono/stereo)	1973	3.75	7.50	15.00
DJ-378 [PS]	Trash (mono/stereo)	1973	18.75	37.50	75.00
—Promo-only numbered sleeve					
DJ-387 [DJ]	Personality Crisis (mono/stereo)	1973	3.75	7.50	15.00
73414	Trash/Personality Crisis	1973	15.00	30.00	60.00
73414 [PS]	Trash/Personality Crisis	1973	3.75	7.50	15.00
73478	Stranded in the Jungle/Who Are the Mystery Girls	1974	3.75	7.50	15.00
73615	Puss 'N' Boots/Showmen	1974	5.00	10.00	20.00
Albums					
MERCURY					
SRM-1-675	New York Dolls	1973	10.00	20.00	40.00
SRM-1-1001	In Too Much Too Soon	1974	10.00	20.00	40.00
826094-1	Night of the Living Dolls	1985	3.00	6.00	12.00

NEW YORK ROCK ENSEMBLE, THE

Includes records as "The New York Rock and Roll Ensemble."

Number	Title (A Side/B Side)	Yr	VG	VG+	NM
45s					
ATCO					
6467	Biji/Biji Rock	1967	2.50	5.00	10.00
6501	Kiss Her Once/Suddenly	1967	2.50	5.00	10.00
6584	The Thing to Do/Pick Up in the Morning	1968	2.50	5.00	10.00
6671	Wait Until Tomorrow/The Brandenburg	1969	2.50	5.00	10.00
COLUMBIA					
45242	Running Down the Highway/Law and Order	1970	—	2.50	5.00
45288	The King Is Dead/Beside You	1970	—	2.50	5.00
45367	Fields of Joy/Ride, Ride My Lady	1971	—	2.50	5.00
45574	Roll Over/A Whiter Shade of Pale	1972	—	2.50	5.00
Albums					
ATCO					
SD 33-240	The New York Rock 'n' Roll Ensemble	1968	3.75	7.50	15.00
SD 33-294	Faithful Friends	1969	3.75	7.50	15.00
SD 33-312	Reflections	1970	3.75	7.50	15.00
COLUMBIA					
C 30033	Roll Over	1970	3.75	7.50	15.00
KC 31317	Freedomburger	1972	3.75	7.50	15.00

NEW YORK SOUNDS, THE

Number	Title (A Side/B Side)	Yr	VG	VG+	NM
45s					
RED BIRD					
10-060	Drag Street/Good Lovin'	1966	5.00	10.00	20.00

NEW YORKERS, THE (1)

With FRED PARRIS of THE FIVE SATINS.

Number	Title (A Side/B Side)	Yr	VG	VG+	NM
45s					
WALL					
547	Miss Fine/Dream a Little Dream	1961	7.50	15.00	30.00
548	Tears in My Eyes/A Little Bit	1961	7.50	15.00	30.00

NEW YORKERS, THE (2)

Early version of THE HUDSON BROTHERS.

Number	Title (A Side/B Side)	Yr	VG	VG+	NM
45s					
DECCA					
32569	I Guess the Lord Must Be in New York City/Do Wah Diddy	1969	2.50	5.00	10.00
JERDEN					
906	Adrienne/Ice Cream World	1968	3.00	6.00	12.00
908	Land of Ur/Michael Glover	1969	3.00	6.00	12.00
SCEPTER					
12190	You're Not My Girl/When I'm Gone	1967	3.75	7.50	15.00
12199	Mr. Kirby/Seeds of Spring	1967	3.75	7.50	15.00
12207	Again/Show Me the Way to Love	1968	3.00	6.00	12.00
WARNER BROS.					
7318	Lonely/There'll Come a Time	1969	2.50	5.00	10.00

NEW YORKERS, THE (3)

Number	Title (A Side/B Side)	Yr	VG	VG+	NM
45s					
TAC-FUL					
101	You Should Have Told Me/Don't Want to Be Your Fool	1964	12.50	25.00	50.00

NEW YORKERS FIVE, THE

Number	Title (A Side/B Side)	Yr	VG	VG+	NM
45s					
DANICE					
801	Gloria My Darling/Cha Cha Baby	1955	100.00	200.00	400.00

NEWBAG, JOHNNY

Number	Title (A Side/B Side)	Yr	VG	VG+	NM
45s					
ATLANTIC					
2355	The Poorer the Man (The Higher His Love)/Got to Get You Back	1966	3.00	6.00	12.00
PORT					
3008	Sweet Thing/Little Samson	1965	6.25	12.50	25.00

NEWBEATS, THE

Also see DEAN AND MARC.

Number	Title (A Side/B Side)	Yr	VG	VG+	NM
45s					
BUDDAH					
390	The Way You Do the Things You Do/Does Your Body Need Lovin'	1973	2.00	4.00	8.00
HICKORY					
326	Bread and Butter/Tough Little Buggy	1974	—	3.00	6.00
1269	Bread and Butter/Tough Little Buggy	1964	3.75	7.50	15.00
1282	Everything's All Right/Pink Dally Rue	1964	3.00	6.00	12.00
1290	Break Away (From That Boy)/Hey-O Daddy-O	1965	2.50	5.00	10.00
1305	(The Bees Are For the Birds) The Birds Are For the Bees/Better Watch Your Step	1965	2.50	5.00	10.00
1320	Little Child/I Can't Hear You No More	1965	2.50	5.00	10.00
1332	Run, Baby, Run (Back Into My Arms)/Mean Wooly Willie	1965	3.00	6.00	12.00
1366	Shake Hands (And Come Out Crying)/Too Sweet to Be Forgotten	1966	2.50	5.00	10.00
1387	Short on Love/Crying My Heart Out	1966	2.00	4.00	8.00
1408	Bird Dog/Evil Eva	1966	2.00	4.00	8.00
1422	My Yesterday Love/Patent on Love	1966	2.00	4.00	8.00
1436	So Fine/Top Secret	1967	2.00	4.00	8.00
1467	Hide the Moon/It's Really Goodbye	1967	2.00	4.00	8.00
1485	Don't Turn Me Loose/You and Me and Happiness	1967	2.00	4.00	8.00
1496	Bad Dreams/Swinger	1968	2.00	4.00	8.00
1510	I've Been a Long Time Loving You/Michelle de Ann	1968	2.00	4.00	8.00
1522	Ain't That Lovin' You/The Girls and the Boys	1968	2.00	4.00	8.00
1539	Great Balls of Fire/Thou Shalt Not Steal	1969	2.00	4.00	8.00
1552	Groovin' (Out on Life)/Bread and Butter	1969	2.50	5.00	10.00
1562	Laura (What's He Got That I Ain't Got)/Break Away (From That Boy)	1970	—	3.00	6.00
1569	I'm a Teardrop/She Won't Hang Her Love (Out on the Line)	1970	—	3.00	6.00
1600	Am I Not My Brother's Keeper/Run, Baby, Run (Back Into My Arms)	1971	2.50	5.00	10.00
1624	Oh, Pretty Woman/Remember Love	1972	2.50	5.00	10.00
1637	Love Gets Sweeter/Eveything's All Right	1972	2.50	5.00	10.00
PLAYBOY					
6013	I Believe I'm in Love with You/I Know (You Don't Want Me No More)	1974	—	3.00	6.00
Albums					
HICKORY					
LPM 120 [M]	Bread and Butter	1964	12.50	25.00	50.00
LPS 120 [S]	Bread and Butter	1964	37.50	75.00	150.00

Number	Title (A Side/B Side)	Yr	VG	VG+	NM
LPM 122 [M]	Big Beat Sounds by the Newbeats	1965	12.50	25.00	50.00
LPS 122 [S]	Big Beat Sounds by the Newbeats	1965	25.00	50.00	100.00
LPM 128 [M]	Run Baby Run	1965	12.50	25.00	50.00
LPS 128 [S]	Run Baby Run	1965	25.00	50.00	100.00
DT 90701 [R]	Bread and Butter	1965	37.50	75.00	150.00
—Capitol Record Club edition					
ST 90701 [S]	Bread and Butter	1965	50.00	100.00	200.00
—Capitol Record Club edition					
T 90701 [M]	Bread and Butter	1965	37.50	75.00	150.00
—Capitol Record Club edition					

NEWBURY, MICKEY

45s

Number	Title (A Side/B Side)	Yr	VG	VG+	NM
ABC HICKORY					
54006	Hand Me Another of Those/Leavin' Kentucky	1977	—	2.50	5.00
54015	Makes Me Wonder If I Ever Said Goodbye/ Shenandoah	1977	—	2.50	5.00
54025	Gone to Alabama/Westphalia Texas Blues	1978	—	2.50	5.00
54034	It Don't Matter Anymore/Wish I Was	1978	—	2.50	5.00
54042	Looking for the Sunshine/A Weed Is a Weed	1979	—	2.50	5.00
AIRBORNE					
10005	An American Trilogy/San Francisco Mabel Joy	1988	—	2.50	5.00
ELEKTRA					
45206	You Only Live Once (In a While)/Baby's Not Home	1974	—	2.50	5.00
45238	Lovers/Good Night	1975	—	2.50	5.00
45256	Sail Away/If You Ever Get to Houston	1975	—	2.50	5.00
45329	An American Trilogy/Sunshine	1976	—	2.50	5.00
45750	An American Trilogy/San Francisco Mable Joy	1971	2.50	5.00	10.00
45771	Mobile Blue/Frisco Depot	1972	—	3.00	6.00
45789	How I Love Them Old Songs/Remember the Good	1972	—	3.00	6.00
45840	Heaven Help the Child/Good Morning Dear	1973	—	2.50	5.00
45853	Sunshine/Song for Susan	1973	—	2.50	5.00
45889	If I Could Be/Love Look	1974	—	2.50	5.00
HICKORY					
1312	Lonely Place/Well I Did (Last Night)	1965	2.50	5.00	10.00
1344	There Is a Time to Die/Travelin' Man	1965	2.50	5.00	10.00
1370	Anyway You Want Me/(It May Not Take) Too Much	1966	2.50	5.00	10.00
1419	After the Rains/Baby Just Said Goodbye	1966	2.50	5.00	10.00
1463	Dreamin' in the Rain/Leavin' Makes the Rain Come Down	1967	2.50	5.00	10.00
1673	America the Beautiful/Freedom	1980	—	2.50	5.00
MCA					
41032	Blue Sky Shinin'/Darlin' Take Care of Yourself	1979	—	2.50	5.00
MERCURY					
72975	Ten Tottle Tommy/San Francisco Mable Joy	1969	—	3.50	7.00
73036	Sunshine/Sad Satin Rhyme	1970	—	3.50	7.00
RCA VICTOR					
47-9570	Weeping Annaleah/Are My Thoughts with You	1968	2.00	4.00	8.00
47-9632	Got Down on Saturday/Sweet Memories	1968	2.00	4.00	8.00
47-9690	Organized Noise/The Queen	1968	2.00	4.00	8.00

Albums

Number	Title (A Side/B Side)	Yr	VG	VG+	NM
ABC HICKORY					
HA-44002	Rusty Tracks	1977	2.50	5.00	10.00
HA-44011	Eye on the Sparrow	1978	2.50	5.00	10.00
HB-44017	The Sailor	1979	2.50	5.00	10.00
ELEKTRA					
7E-1007	I Came to Hear the Music	1974	2.50	5.00	10.00
7E-1030	Lovers	1975	2.50	5.00	10.00
EQ-4107 [Q]	'Frisco Mabel Joy	1974	5.00	10.00	20.00
EKS-74107	'Frisco Mabel Joy	1971	2.50	5.00	10.00
EKS-75055	Heaven Help the Child	1973	2.50	5.00	10.00
MCA					
802	Rusty Tracks	198?	2.00	4.00	8.00
—Reissue					
803	Eye on the Sparrow	198?	2.00	4.00	8.00
—Reissue					
804	The Sailor	198?	2.00	4.00	8.00
—Reissue					
945	Sweet Memories	1885	2.50	5.00	10.00
MERCURY					
SR 61236	Looks Like Rain	1969	3.75	7.50	15.00
RCA VICTOR					
LSP-4043	Harlequin Melodies	1968	3.75	7.50	15.00

NEWHART, BOB

Albums

Number	Title (A Side/B Side)	Yr	VG	VG+	NM
HARMONY					
HS 11344	The Very Funny Bob Newhart	196?	3.00	6.00	12.00
MURRAY HILL					
OP 2529 [(2)]	The Best of the Button-Down Mind	197?	5.00	10.00	20.00
WARNER BROS.					
W 1379 [M]	The Button-Down Mind of Bob Newhart	1960	7.50	15.00	30.00
WS 1379 [S]	The Button-Down Mind of Bob Newhart	1960	6.25	12.50	25.00
W 1393 [M]	The Button-Down Mind Strikes Back!	1960	7.50	15.00	30.00
WS 1393 [S]	The Button-Down Mind Strikes Back!	1960	6.25	12.50	25.00
2N 1399 [(2) M]	The Bob Newhart Deluxe Edition	1961	12.50	25.00	50.00
2NS 1399 [(2) S]	The Bob Newhart Deluxe Edition	1961	10.00	20.00	40.00
W 1417 [M]	Behind the Button-Down Mind of Bob Newhart	1961	6.25	12.50	25.00
WS 1417 [S]	Behind the Button-Down Mind of Bob Newhart	1961	5.00	10.00	20.00
W 1467 [M]	The Button-Down Mind on TV	1962	6.25	12.50	25.00
WS 1467 [S]	The Button-Down Mind on TV	1962	5.00	10.00	20.00
W 1517 [M]	Bob Newhart Faces Bob Newhart (Faces Bob Newhart)	1964	6.25	12.50	25.00
W 1588 [M]	The Windmills Are Weakening	1965	7.50	15.00	30.00
W 1672 [M]	The Best of Bob Newhart	1966	7.50	15.00	30.00
WS 1672 [S]	The Best of Bob Newhart	1966	6.25	12.50	25.00
—Gold label					
WS 1672 [S]	The Best of Bob Newhart	1968	5.00	10.00	20.00
—Green "W7" label					
WS 1672 [S]	The Best of Bob Newhart	1970	3.75	7.50	15.00
—Green "WB" label					
WS 1672 [S]	The Best of Bob Newhart	1973	3.00	6.00	12.00
—"Burbank" palm-trees label					
WS 1672 [S]	The Best of Bob Newhart	1979	2.00	4.00	8.00
—White or tan label					
W 1717 [M]	This Is It	1967	7.50	15.00	30.00

NEWLEY, ANTHONY

45s

Number	Title (A Side/B Side)	Yr	VG	VG+	NM
ACAPELLA					
778	Tribute/Lament for a Hero	1964	3.00	6.00	12.00
KAPP					
984	I'm All I Need/When You Gotta Go	1969	—	3.00	6.00
LONDON					
1871	I've Waited So Long/Sat'day Night Rock-a-Boogie	1959	3.00	6.00	12.00
1882	My Blue Angel/Idle Rock	1959	2.50	5.00	10.00
1918	Do You Mind/Girls Were Made to Love and Kiss	1960	2.50	5.00	10.00
1929	If She Should Come to You/A Lifetime of Happiness	1960	2.50	5.00	10.00
1972	And the Heavens Cried/Lonely Boy and Pretty Girl	1961	2.50	5.00	10.00
5201	There's No Such Thing/She's Just Another Girl	1963	2.50	5.00	10.00
5202	I Saw Her Standing There/I Love Everything About Her	1963	5.00	10.00	20.00
—One of the first cover versions of a Beatles song to be released in the U.S.					
5205	Father of Girls/Young Only Yesterday	1963	2.50	5.00	10.00
9501	Gone with the Wind/Pop Goes the Weasel	1961	2.50	5.00	10.00
9512	When Your Lover Has Gone/Yes, We Have No Bananas	1961	2.50	5.00	10.00
9518	What Now My Love/Why	1961	2.50	5.00	10.00
9531	Deep River/Letters to My Love	1962	2.50	5.00	10.00
9546	What Kind of Fool Am I/Gonna Build a Mountain	1962	3.00	6.00	12.00
MGM					
14220	Pure Imagination/Love Story (Where Do I Begin)	1971	—	2.50	5.00
14252	The Candy Man/Pure Imagination	1971	—	2.50	5.00
14307	Cheer Up Charlie/Pop Goes the Weasel	1971	—	2.50	5.00
14479	A Fool Who Dared to Dream/Ain't It Funny	1973	—	2.00	4.00
14627	Good Old Bad Old Days/Ain't It Funny	1973	—	2.00	4.00
14724	If I Were Free/Long Live Hope	1974	—	2.00	4.00
RCA VICTOR					
47-8485	Who Can I Turn To/The Joker	1964	2.00	4.00	8.00
47-8785	Is There a Way Back to Your Arms/Why Can't You Try to Didgeridoo	1966	2.00	4.00	8.00
47-9310	I Think I Love You/Something in Your Smile	1967	2.00	4.00	8.00
UNITED ARTISTS					
XW825	Shelby/Teach the Children	1976	—	2.00	4.00
XW1012	The Hollywood Seven/Lunch with a Friend	1977	—	2.00	4.00
WARNER BROS.					
7174	Sweet November/Sara's Theme	1968	—	3.00	6.00
—B-side by Michel Legrand					

Albums

Number	Title (A Side/B Side)	Yr	VG	VG+	NM
LONDON					
PS 244 [S]	Tony	1962	6.25	12.50	25.00
PS 461 [S]	Genius	1966	3.75	7.50	15.00
LL 3156 [M]	Love Is a Now and Then Thing	1960	5.00	10.00	20.00
LL 3252 [M]	Tony	1962	3.75	7.50	15.00
LL 3262 [M]	This Is Tony Newley	1962	3.75	7.50	15.00
LL 3461 [M]	Genius	1966	3.00	6.00	12.00
RCA VICTOR					
LPM-2925 [M]	In My Solitude	1964	3.75	7.50	15.00
LSP-2925 [S]	In My Solitude	1964	5.00	10.00	20.00
LPM-3347 [M]	Who Can I Turn To	1965	3.00	6.00	12.00
LSP-3347 [S]	Who Can I Turn To	1965	3.75	7.50	15.00
LPM-3614 [M]	Newly Recorded	1966	3.00	6.00	12.00
LSP-3614 [S]	Newly Recorded	1966	3.75	7.50	15.00
LPM-3839 [M]	Doctor Dolittle	1967	3.00	6.00	12.00
LSP-3839 [S]	Doctor Dolittle	1967	3.75	7.50	15.00
LSP-4163	The Best of Anthony Newley	1969	3.00	6.00	12.00

NEWLYWEDS, THE

45s

Number	Title (A Side/B Side)	Yr	VG	VG+	NM
HOMOGENIZED SOUL					
601	Love Walked Out/The Quarrel	1961	1500.	2250.	3000.

NEWMAN, RANDY

12-Inch Singles

Number	Title (A Side/B Side)	Yr	VG	VG+	NM
WARNER BROS.					
PRO-A-860 [DJ]	Political Science/Spys	1979	2.00	4.00	8.00

45s

Number	Title (A Side/B Side)	Yr	VG	VG+	NM
DOT					
16411	Golden Gridiron Boy/Country Boy	1962	12.50	25.00	50.00
—May be promo only					
REPRISE					
0692	I Think It's Going to Rain Today/The Beehive State	1968	3.75	7.50	15.00
0771	Last Night I Had a Dream/I Think He's Hiding	1968	6.25	12.50	25.00
—May be promo only					
0917	Have You Seen My Baby/Hold On	1970	3.75	7.50	15.00
0945	Gone Dead Train/Harry Flowers	1970	3.75	7.50	15.00
1102	Sail Away/Political Science	1972	—	3.00	6.00
1123	You Can Leave Your Hat On/Memo to My Son	1972	—	3.00	6.00
1324	Guilty/Naked Man	1975	—	2.50	5.00
1387	Louisiana 1927/Marie	1977	—	2.50	5.00
22798	I'd Love to See You Smile/End Title (I'd Love to See You Smile)	1989	—	—	3.00
27709	It's Money That Matters/Roll with the Punches	1988	—	—	3.00
27709 [PS]	It's Money That Matters/Roll with the Punches	1988	—	—	3.00
27856	Falling in Love/Bad News from Home	1989	—	—	3.00
WARNER BROS.					
8492	Short People/Old Man on the Farm	1977	—	2.50	5.00
8550	Baltimore/You Can't Fool the Fat Man	1978	—	2.00	4.00
8630	Rider in the Rain/Sigmund Freud's Impersonation of Albert Einstein in America	1978	—	2.00	4.00

Number	Title (A Side/B Side)	Yr	VG	VG+	NM
29241	The Natural/The Natural (Final Game)	1984	—	2.00	4.00
29687	I Love L.A./Song for the Dead	1983	—	2.00	4.00
29803	The Blues/The Same Girl	1983	—	2.00	4.00
—A-side: With Paul Simon					
29803 [PS]	The Blues/The Same Girl	1983	—	2.00	4.00
49088	It's Money That I Love/Ghosts	1979	—	2.00	4.00
49149	Half a Man/The Story of a Rock and Roll Band	1979	—	2.00	4.00
49223	Spies/Political Science (Let's Drop the Big One)	1980	—	2.00	4.00

Albums

REPRISE

Number	Title (A Side/B Side)	Yr	VG	VG+	NM
MS 2064	Sail Away	1972	3.75	7.50	15.00
—With no song titles listed on back					
MS 2064	Sail Away	1972	2.50	5.00	10.00
—With song titles listed on back					
MS 2193	Good Old Boys	1974	2.50	5.00	10.00
MS4 2193 [Q]	Good Old Boys	1974	3.75	7.50	15.00
RS 6286	Randy Newman	1968	5.00	10.00	20.00
—Cover with Randy standing in the clouds					
RS 6286	Randy Newman	1968	3.75	7.50	15.00
—Cover with close-up of Randy's face; "W7" and "r:" logos on two-tone orange label					
RS 6286	Randy Newman	1970	3.00	6.00	12.00
—With only "r:" logo on all-orange (tan) label					
RS 6373	12 Songs	1970	3.75	7.50	15.00
—With "W7" and "r:" logos on two-tone orange label					
RS 6373	12 Songs	1970	2.50	5.00	10.00
—With only "r:" logo on all-orange (tan) label					
RS 6459	Randy Newman/Live	1971	2.50	5.00	10.00
25773	Land of Dreams	1988	2.50	5.00	10.00

WARNER BROS.

Number	Title (A Side/B Side)	Yr	VG	VG+	NM
BSK 3079	Little Criminals	1977	2.50	5.00	10.00
HS 3346	Born Again	1979	2.50	5.00	10.00
23755	Trouble in Paradise	1983	2.50	5.00	10.00

NEWMAN, TED

45s

RCA VICTOR

Number	Title (A Side/B Side)	Yr	VG	VG+	NM
47-7197	It's Hot in Here/Why Did You Break My Heart	1958	3.75	7.50	15.00
47-7251	Hey Little Freshman/Brigette	1958	3.75	7.50	15.00

REV

Number	Title (A Side/B Side)	Yr	VG	VG+	NM
3505	Plaything/Unlucky Me	1957	5.00	10.00	20.00
3511	I Double Dare You/None of Your Tears	1957	3.75	7.50	15.00

NEWPORTS, THE (1)

45s

CRYSTAL BALL

Number	Title (A Side/B Side)	Yr	VG	VG+	NM
129	Jingle Bells/My Juanita	1979	2.00	4.00	8.00

GUYDEN

Number	Title (A Side/B Side)	Yr	VG	VG+	NM
2067	If I Could Tonight/A Fellow Needs a Girl	1962	7.50	15.00	30.00
2116	Tears/Disillusioned Love	1964	7.50	15.00	30.00

NEWPORTS, THE (2)

45s

KENT

Number	Title (A Side/B Side)	Yr	VG	VG+	NM
380	The Wonder of Love/Dixie Women	1962	7.50	15.00	30.00

NEWPORTS, THE (3)

45s

LAURIE

Number	Title (A Side/B Side)	Yr	VG	VG+	NM
3327	The Trouble Is You/I Want You	1966	6.25	12.50	25.00

NEWPORTS, THE (U)

May be group (3), may be completely different.

45s

PARROT

Number	Title (A Side/B Side)	Yr	VG	VG+	NM
45008	Party Night/Listen to Your Big Brother	1966	3.75	7.50	15.00

NEWTON, JUICE

45s

CAPITOL

Number	Title (A Side/B Side)	Yr	VG	VG+	NM
4499	Come to Me/Save a Heart	1977	—	3.00	6.00
4552	It's a Heartache/Wouldn't Mind the Rain	1978	—	3.00	6.00
4611	Hey Baby/It's Not Impossible	1978	—	3.00	6.00
4679	Let's Keep It That Way/Tell My Baby Goodbye	1979	—	2.50	5.00
4714	Lay Back in the Arms of Someone/It's Not Impossible	1979	—	2.50	5.00
4768	Any Way That You Want Me/A Dream Never Dies	1979	—	2.50	5.00
4793	Until Tonight/Lay Back in the Arms of Someone	1979	—	2.50	5.00
4818	Sunshine/Go Easy on Me	1980	—	2.00	4.00
4856	You Fill My Life/Tear It Up	1980	—	2.00	4.00
4976	Angel of the Morning/Headin' for a Heartache	1981	—	—	3.00
4976 [PS]	Angel of the Morning/Headin' for a Heartache	1981	—	2.00	4.00
4997	Queen of Hearts/River of Love	1981	—	—	3.00
4997 [PS]	Queen of Hearts/River of Love	1981	—	2.00	4.00
A-5046	The Sweetest Thing (I've Ever Known)/Ride 'Em Cowboy	1981	—	—	3.00
A-5046 [PS]	The Sweetest Thing (I've Ever Known)/Ride 'Em Cowboy	1981	—	2.00	4.00
B-5120	Love's Been a Little Bit Hard on Me/Ever True	1982	—	—	3.00
B-5120 [PS]	Love's Been a Little Bit Hard on Me/Ever True	1982	—	2.00	4.00
B-5148	Break It to Me Gently/Adios Mi Corazon	1982	—	—	3.00
B-5148 [PS]	Break It to Me Gently/Adios Mi Corazon	1982	—	2.00	4.00
B-5192	Heart of the Night/Love Sail Away	1982	—	—	3.00
B-5192 [PS]	Heart of the Night/Love Sail Away	1982	—	2.00	4.00
B-5265	Tell Her No/Stranger at My Door	1983	—	—	3.00
B-5265 [PS]	Tell Her No/Stranger at My Door	1983	—	2.00	4.00
B-5289	Dirty Looks/20 Years Ago	1983	—	—	3.00
B-5289 [PS]	Dirty Looks/20 Years Ago	1983	—	2.00	4.00
B-5379	Ride 'Em Cowboy/Love Sail Away	1984	—	—	3.00

RCA

Number	Title (A Side/B Side)	Yr	VG	VG+	NM
5068-7-R	What Can I Do with My Heart/Let Your Woman Take Care of You	1986	—	—	3.00
5170-7-R	First Time Caller/Til You Cry	1987	—	—	3.00
5283-7-R	Tell Me True/If I Didn't Love You	1987	—	—	3.00
8815-7-R	When Love Comes Around the Bend/(B-side unknown)	1989	—	—	3.00
PB-10828	If I Ever/Bye, Bye Baby	1976	2.00	4.00	8.00
PB-13823	A Little Love/Waiting for the Sun	1984	—	—	3.00
PB-13823 [PS]	A Little Love/Waiting for the Sun	1984	—	2.00	4.00
PB-13863	Can't Wait All Night/Restless Heart	1984	—	—	3.00
PB-13863 [PS]	Can't Wait All Night/Restless Heart	1984	—	2.00	4.00
PB-13907	Restless Heart/Eye of a Hurricane	1984	—	—	3.00
PB-14139	You Make Me Want to Make You Mine/Waiting for the Sun	1985	—	—	3.00
PB-14139 [PS]	You Make Me Want to Make You Mine/Waiting for the Sun	1985	—	2.00	4.00
PB-14199	Hurt/Eye of a Hurricane	1985	—	—	3.00
PB-14295	Old Flame/One Touch	1986	—	—	3.00
GB-14355	Hurt/You Make Me Want to Make You Mine	1986	—	—	3.00
PB-14377	Both to Each Other (Friends and Lovers)/A World Without Love	1986	—	—	3.00
—With Eddie Rabbitt					
PB-14377 [PS]	Both to Each Other (Friends and Lovers)/A World Without Love	1986	—	2.50	5.00
PB-14417	Cheap Love/Old Flame	1986	—	—	3.00

RCA VICTOR

Number	Title (A Side/B Side)	Yr	VG	VG+	NM
PB-10354	Catwillow River/It's High Time	1975	2.00	4.00	8.00
—With Silver Spur					
PB-10412	The Sweetest Thing (I've Ever Known)/The Shelter of Your Love	1975	2.00	4.00	8.00
—With Silver Spur					
PB-10538	Love Is a Word/The Sweetest Thing (I've Ever Known)	1976	2.00	4.00	8.00
—With Silver Spur					

Albums

CAPITOL

Number	Title (A Side/B Side)	Yr	VG	VG+	NM
ST-11682	Come to Me	1977	3.75	7.50	15.00
ST-11811	Well-Kept Secret	1978	3.75	7.50	15.00
ST-12000	Take Heart	1980	3.75	7.50	15.00
ST-12136	Juice	1981	2.50	5.00	10.00
ST-12210	Quiet Lies	1982	2.50	5.00	10.00
ST-12294	Dirty Looks	1983	2.50	5.00	10.00
SJ-12353	Greatest Hits	1984	2.50	5.00	10.00
SN-16242	Come to Me	1982	2.00	4.00	8.00
—Budget-line reissue					
SN-16243	Well-Kept Secret	1982	2.00	4.00	8.00
—Budget-line reissue					
SN-16244	Take Heart	1982	2.00	4.00	8.00
—Budget-line reissue					
SN-16313	Juice	1984	2.00	4.00	8.00
—Budget-line reissue					
SN-16314	Quiet Lies	1984	2.00	4.00	8.00
—Budget-line reissue					
SN-16356	Dirty Looks	1985	2.00	4.00	8.00
—Budget-line reissue					
SN-16471	Greatest Hits	1987	2.00	4.00	8.00
—Budget-line reissue					

RCA

Number	Title (A Side/B Side)	Yr	VG	VG+	NM
5646-1-R	Old Flame	1986	2.50	5.00	10.00
—Reissue of 5493 with slightly different lineup					
6371-1-R	Emotion	1987	2.50	5.00	10.00
8376-1-R	Ain't Gonna Cry	1989	2.50	5.00	10.00

RCA VICTOR

Number	Title (A Side/B Side)	Yr	VG	VG+	NM
APL1-1004	Juice Newton and Silver Spur	1975	5.00	10.00	20.00
APL1-1722	After Dust Settled	1977	3.75	7.50	15.00
AYL1-4037	Juice Newton and Silver Spur	1982	2.00	4.00	8.00
—"Best Buy Series" reissue					
AYL1-4038	After Dust Settled	1982	2.00	4.00	8.00
—"Best Buy Series" reissue					
AFL1-4995	Can't Wait All Night	1984	2.50	5.00	10.00
AFL1-5493	Old Flame	1985	3.00	6.00	12.00

NEWTON, WAYNE

Also see THE NEWTON BROTHERS.

45s

20TH CENTURY

Number	Title (A Side/B Side)	Yr	VG	VG+	NM
2393	Hold Me Like You Never Had Me/Housewife	1978	—	2.00	4.00

ARIES II

Number	Title (A Side/B Side)	Yr	VG	VG+	NM
101	You Stepped Into My Life/She Believes in Me	1979	—	2.00	4.00
108	Years/Rhythm Rhapsody	1980	—	2.00	4.00

CAPITOL

Number	Title (A Side/B Side)	Yr	VG	VG+	NM
2016	Love of the Common People/It's Still Loving You	1967	—	3.00	6.00
2917	Up Here in a Tree/Fallin'	1970	—	2.50	5.00
2980	For the Good Times/Little Dreamer	1970	—	2.50	5.00
3044	Apartment 21/Me and Bobby McGee	1971	—	2.50	5.00
3118	Remember the Good Times/Good Morning Dear	1971	—	2.50	5.00
3189	I Ain't That Easy to Love/Leavin' Ya Going My Way	1971	—	2.50	5.00
3241	Just a Memory/Higher Ground	1971	—	2.50	5.00
4920	Heart! (I Hear You Beating)/So Long Lucy	1963	2.50	5.00	10.00
4989	Danke Schoen/Better Now Than Later	1963	3.00	6.00	12.00
5058	Shirl Girl/Someone's Ahead of You	1963	2.50	5.00	10.00
5124	Dream Baby (How Long Must I Dream)/I'm Looking Over a Four-Leaf Clover	1964	2.50	5.00	10.00
5171	Bill Bailey/When the Saints Go Marching In	1964	2.50	5.00	10.00
5203	Only You/Too Late to Meet	1964	2.50	5.00	10.00
5338	Comin' On Too Strong/Lookin' Through a Tear	1965	6.24	12.50	25.00
—Bruce Johnston and Terry Melcher help out on this record					
5366	Red Roses for a Blue Lady/One More Memory	1965	2.00	4.00	8.00
5419	I'll Be With You in Apple Blossom Time/Laura Lee	1965	2.00	4.00	8.00
5470	Summer Wind/I'll Be Standing By	1965	2.00	4.00	8.00
5514	Keep the Lovin' Feelin'/Remember When	1965	2.00	4.00	8.00
5553	A Little Bit of Heaven/Some Sunday Morning	1965	2.00	4.00	8.00
5578	You Just Don't Know/After the Laughter	1966	2.00	4.00	8.00
5643	Somebody to Love/Stagecoach to Cheyenne	1966	2.00	4.00	8.00
5692	Excuse Me/How Loud a Sound	1966	2.00	4.00	8.00
5754	The Games That Lovers Play/Half a World Away	1966	2.00	4.00	8.00

Number	Title (A Side/B Side)	Yr	VG	VG+	NM
5793	Happy Is Gone/How D'Ya Talk to a Girl	1966	2.00	4.00	8.00
5842	If I Only Had a Song to Sing/Sunny Day Girl	1967	—	3.00	6.00
5954	Dream Street Rose/Summer Colors	1967	—	3.00	6.00
5993	Through the Eyes of Love/Just a Memory	1967	—	3.00	6.00
CHALLENGE					
59228	I Want to Mean Everything to You/I Still Love You	1964	2.50	5.00	10.00
59238	The Little White Cloud That Cried/Calorie Date	1964	2.50	5.00	10.00
59238	The Little White Cloud That Cried/Born When You Kissed Me	1964	2.50	5.00	10.00
CHELSEA					
BCBO-0091	May the Road Rise to Meet You/Pour Me a Little More Wine	1973	—	2.00	4.00
78-0100	Daddy Don't You Walk So Fast/Echo Valley 2-6809	1972	—	3.00	6.00
—White label (not a promo)					
78-0100	Daddy Don't You Walk So Fast/Echo Valley 2-6809	1972	—	2.50	5.00
—Mostly pink label					
78-0105	Can't You Hear the Song?/You Don't Have to Ask	1972	—	2.00	4.00
78-0109	Anthem/Fool	1972	—	2.00	4.00
78-0116	Just Yesterday/While We're Still Young	1973	—	2.00	4.00
78-0124	Help Me Help You/We Didn't Know the Time of Day	1973	—	2.00	4.00
3003	Lay Lady Lay/Walking in the Sand	1974	—	2.00	4.00
3018	All Alone Am I/You Don't Have to Ask	1975	—	2.00	4.00
3028	Run to Me/Lady Lonely	1975	—	2.00	4.00
3041	The Hungry Years/In Dreams	1976	—	2.00	4.00
3058	It Could Have Been a Wonderful Christmas/Jingle Bell Hustle	1976	—	2.50	5.00
CURB					
10520	Cowboy's Christmas/(B-side unknown)	1988	—	—	3.00
10559	While the Feeling's Good/Our Wedding Band	1989	—	—	3.00
—A-side with Tammy Wynette					
GEORGE					
7777	The Little White Cloud That Cried/(B-side unknown)	1962	5.00	10.00	20.00
MGM					
13891	All the Time/Like Everything Else	1968	—	2.50	5.00
13936	Remembering/Angelica	1968	—	2.50	5.00
13955	Dreams of the Everyday Housewife/The Tip of My Fingers	1968	—	2.50	5.00
13993	Silence Says/Town and Country	1968	—	2.50	5.00
14014	I Just Can't Help Believin'/Husbands and Wives	1968	—	2.50	5.00
14019	Christmas Prayer/Santa Claus Is Comin' to Town	1968	—	2.50	5.00
14046	Everything's in Love Today/The Silence Says	1969	—	2.50	5.00
14083	New York City/For the First Time	1969	—	2.50	5.00
14098	It's Such a Lonely Time of the Year/The Country	1969	—	2.50	5.00
14430	With Pen in Hand/Town and Country	1972	—	2.00	4.00
RCA VICTOR					
AMBO-0126	Daddy Don't You Walk So Fast/Fool	1973	—	2.00	4.00
—Gold Standard Series reissue					
WARNER BROS.					
8415	I Want You with Me/Midnight Sun	1977	—	2.00	4.00
7-Inch Extended Plays					
ARIES II					
102	White Christmas/It's the Season//I'll Be Home for Christmas/Blue Snow at Christmas	1979	—	2.00	4.00
Albums					
20TH CENTURY					
T-576	Change of Heart	1979	2.50	5.00	10.00
ARIES II					
WY 201	Wayne Newton Christmas	1979	2.50	5.00	10.00
CAPITOL					
SKAO-137	The Best of Wayne Newton, Volume 2	1968	3.75	7.50	15.00
STBB-487 [(2)]	Merry Christmas to You	1970	3.75	7.50	15.00
ST 1973 [S]	Danke Schoen	1963	5.00	10.00	20.00
T 1973 [M]	Danke Schoen	1963	3.75	7.50	15.00
ST 2029 [S]	Wayne Newton In Person	1964	5.00	10.00	20.00
T 2029 [M]	Wayne Newton In Person	1964	3.75	7.50	15.00
ST 2130 [S]	Wayne Newton Sings Hit Songs	1964	5.00	10.00	20.00
T 2130 [M]	Wayne Newton Sings Hit Songs	1964	3.75	7.50	15.00
SM-2335	Red Roses for a Blue Lady	197?	2.50	5.00	10.00
—Reissue					
ST 2335 [S]	Red Roses for a Blue Lady	1965	5.00	10.00	20.00
T 2335 [M]	Red Roses for a Blue Lady	1965	3.75	7.50	15.00
ST 2389 [S]	Summer Wind	1965	5.00	10.00	20.00
T 2389 [M]	Summer Wind	1965	3.75	7.50	15.00
ST 2445 [S]	Wayne Newton — Now!	1966	5.00	10.00	20.00
T 2445 [M]	Wayne Newton — Now!	1966	3.75	7.50	15.00
SM-2563	The Old Rugged Cross	197?	2.50	5.00	10.00
—Reissue					
ST 2563 [S]	The Old Rugged Cross	1966	5.00	10.00	20.00
T 2563 [M]	The Old Rugged Cross	1966	3.75	7.50	15.00
ST 2588 [S]	Songs for a Merry Christmas	1966	3.75	7.50	15.00
T 2588 [M]	Songs for a Merry Christmas	1966	3.00	6.00	12.00
ST 2635 [S]	It's Only the Good Times	1967	5.00	10.00	20.00
T 2635 [M]	It's Only the Good Times	1967	3.75	7.50	15.00
ST 2714 [S]	Song of the Year...Wayne Newton Style	1967	3.75	7.50	15.00
T 2714 [M]	Song of the Year...Wayne Newton Style	1967	5.00	10.00	20.00
ST 2797 [S]	The Best of Wayne Newton	1967	3.75	7.50	15.00
T 2797 [M]	The Best of Wayne Newton	1967	5.00	10.00	20.00
ST 2832 [S]	God Is Alive	1968	3.75	7.50	15.00
T 2832 [M]	God Is Alive	1968	5.00	10.00	20.00
ST 2847 [S]	Wayne Newton — The Greatest	1968	3.75	7.50	15.00
T 2847 [M]	Wayne Newton — The Greatest	1968	5.00	10.00	20.00
SM-11972	Danke Schoen	1979	2.50	5.00	10.00
—Reissue					
SN-16083	The Best of Wayne Newton	1980	2.00	4.00	8.00
—Budget-line reissue					
CAPITOL PICKWICK SERIES					
PC-3455 [M]	Somewhere My Love	196?	2.50	5.00	10.00
SPC-3455 [S]	Somewhere My Love	196?	2.50	5.00	10.00
PC-3459 [M]	Everybody Loves Somebody	196?	2.50	5.00	10.00
SPC-3459 [S]	Everybody Loves Somebody	196?	2.50	5.00	10.00
PC-3461 [M]	Michelle	196?	2.50	5.00	10.00
SPC-3461 [S]	Michelle	196?	2.50	5.00	10.00
PC-3464 [M]	Wow! Wayne Newton Live	196?	2.50	5.00	10.00
SPC-3464 [S]	Wow! Wayne Newton Live	196?	2.50	5.00	10.00
CHELSEA					
BCL1-0367	Pour Me a Little More Wine	1973	3.00	6.00	12.00
CHL-504	The Best of Wayne Newton Live	1974	2.50	5.00	10.00
CHL-507	Midnight Idol	1975	2.50	5.00	10.00
CHL-512	Tomorrow	1976	2.50	5.00	10.00
CHL-513	Daddy Don't You Walk So Fast	1976	2.50	5.00	10.00
—Reissue of 1001					
CHE 1001	Daddy Don't You Walk So Fast	1972	3.00	6.00	12.00
CHE 1003	Can't You Hear the Song?	1972	3.00	6.00	12.00
CHE 1006	While We're Still Young	1973	3.00	6.00	12.00
MGM					
E-4523 [M]	Walking on New Grass	1968	5.00	10.00	20.00
SE-4523 [S]	Walking on New Grass	1968	3.00	6.00	12.00
E-4549 [M]	One More Time	1968	5.00	10.00	20.00
SE-4549 [S]	One More Time	1968	3.00	6.00	12.00
SE-4593	Christmas Isn't Christmas Without You	1968	3.00	6.00	12.00
SE-4594	Dreams of the Everyday Housewife/Town and Country	1969	3.00	6.00	12.00

NEWTON BROTHERS, THE

With WAYNE NEWTON.

Number	Title (A Side/B Side)	Yr	VG	VG+	NM
45s					
CAPITOL					
F-4236	The Real Thing/I Spy	1959	20.00	40.00	80.00

NEWTON-JOHN, OLIVIA

Number	Title (A Side/B Side)	Yr	VG	VG+	NM
12-Inch Singles					
MCA					
23606	Toughen Up (Dance Remix) (Instrumental)	1986	2.00	4.00	8.00
23890	The Rumour (4 versions)	1988	2.00	4.00	8.00
45s					
ATLANTIC					
89420	The Best of Me/Sage	1986	—	—	3.00
—With David Foster					
89420 [PS]	The Best of Me/Sage	1986	—	—	3.00
MCA					
40043	Take Me Home, Country Roads/Sail Into Tomorrow	1973	—	—	—
—Unreleased?					
40043 [DJ]	Take Me Home, Country Roads (mono/stereo)	1973	5.00	10.00	20.00
40101	Let Me Be There/Maybe Then I'll Think of You	1973	—	2.50	5.00
40209	If You Love Me (Let Me Know)/Brotherly Love	1974	—	2.50	5.00
40280	I Honestly Love You/Home Ain't Home Anymore	1974	—	2.50	5.00
40349	Have You Never Been Mellow/Water Under the Bridge	1974	—	2.50	5.00
40418	Please Mr. Please/And In the Morning	1975	—	2.50	5.00
40418 [PS]	Please Mr. Please/And In the Morning	1975	2.50	5.00	10.00
40459	Something Better to Do/He's My Rock	1975	—	2.50	5.00
40459 [PS]	Something Better to Do/He's My Rock	1975	—	3.00	6.00
40495	Let It Shine/He Ain't Heavy, He's My Brother	1975	—	2.50	5.00
40525	Come On Over/Small Talk and Pride	1976	—	2.00	4.00
40600	Don't Stop Believin'/Greensleeves	1976	—	2.00	4.00
—A-side not a Christmas song					
40600 [PS]	Don't Stop Believin'/Greensleeves	1976	—	2.50	5.00
40642	Every Face Tells a Story/Love You Hold the Key	1976	—	2.00	4.00
40670	Sam/I'll Bet You a Kangaroo	1976	—	2.00	4.00
40737	Making a Good Thing Better/I Think I'll Say Goodbye	1977	—	2.00	4.00
40811	I Honestly Love You/Don't Cry for Me Argentina	1977	—	2.50	5.00
40811 [PS]	I Honestly Love You/Don't Cry for Me Argentina	1977	2.50	5.00	10.00
40975	A Little More Love/Borrowed Time	1978	—	2.00	4.00
40975 [PS]	A Little More Love/Borrowed Time	1978	—	2.50	5.00
41009	Deeper Than the Night/Please Don't Keep Me Waiting	1979	—	2.00	4.00
41074	Totally Hot/Dancing Round and Round	1979	—	2.00	4.00
41074 [PS]	Totally Hot/Dancing Round and Round	1979	—	2.50	5.00
41247	Magic/Fool Country	1980	—	2.50	5.00
—Custom pink "Xanadu" label					
41247	Magic/Fool Country	1980	—	2.00	4.00
—Standard blue rainbow label					
41247 [PS]	Magic/Fool Country	1980	—	2.50	5.00
41286	Xanadu/Whenever You're Away from Me	1980	—	2.00	4.00
—A-side with Electric Light Orchestra; B-side with Gene Kelly. Persistent rumors claim existence of a U.S. picture sleeve for this record, but we've never seen one.					
41287	Suddenly/You Made Me Love You	1980	—	2.50	5.00
—A-side with Cliff Richard					
51007	Suddenly/You Made Me Love You	1980	—	2.00	4.00
—A-side with Cliff Richard					
51007 [PS]	Suddenly/You Made Me Love You	1980	—	2.50	5.00
51182	Physical/The Promise (The Dolphin Song)	1981	—	—	3.00
51182 [PS]	Physical/The Promise (The Dolphin Song)	1981	—	2.00	4.00
52000	Make a Move on Me/Falling	1982	—	—	3.00
52000 [PS]	Make a Move on Me/Falling	1982	—	2.50	5.00
52069	Landslide/Recovery	1982	—	—	3.00
52069 [PS]	Landslide/Recovery	1982	—	2.00	4.00
52100	Heart Attack/Strangers Touch	1982	—	—	3.00
52100 [PS]	Heart Attack/Strangers Touch	1982	—	—	3.00
52155	Tied Up/Silvery Rain	1983	—	—	3.00
52155 [PS]	Tied Up/Silvery Rain	1983	—	—	3.00
52284	Twist of Fate/Take a Chance	1983	—	—	3.00
52284 [PS]	Twist of Fate/Take a Chance	1983	—	—	3.00
52341	Livin' in Desperate Times/Landslide	1984	—	—	3.00
52341 [PS]	Livin' in Desperate Times/Landslide	1984	—	—	3.00
52686	Soul Kiss/Electric	1985	—	—	3.00
52686 [PS]	Soul Kiss/Electric	1985	—	—	3.00
52757	Toughen Up/Driving Music	1986	—	—	3.00
52757 [PS]	Toughen Up/Driving Music	1986	—	—	3.00
53294	The Rumour/Winter Angel	1988	—	—	3.00
53294 [PS]	The Rumour/Winter Angel	1988	—	—	3.00
53438	Can't We Talk It Over in Bed/Get Out	1988	—	—	3.00

Number	Title (A Side/B Side)	Yr	VG	VG+	NM
72053	I Honestly Love You/I Honestly Love You (Remix)	1998	—	—	3.00
—New recordings					
MCA NASHVILLE					
72074	Back with a Heart/Under My Skin	1998	—	—	3.00
RSO					
903	Hopelessly Devoted to You/Love Is a Many-Splendored Thing	1978	—	2.00	4.00
UNI					
55281	If Not for You/The Biggest Clown	1971	2.50	5.00	10.00
55304	Banks of the Ohio/It's So Hard to Say Goodbye	1971	2.00	4.00	8.00
55317	What Is Life/I'm a Small and Lonely Light	1972	2.00	4.00	8.00
55348	Just a Little Too Much/My Old Man's Gotta Gun	1972	3.00	6.00	12.00
Albums					
GEFFEN					
GHS 24257	Warm and Tender	1989	3.00	6.00	12.00
MCA					
389	Let Me Be There	1973	3.75	7.50	15.00
411	If You Love Me Let Me Know	1974	3.75	7.50	15.00
—Originals have incorrect song title: "I Love You, I Honestly Love You"					
411	If You Love Me Let Me Know	1974	2.50	5.00	10.00
—With corrected song title: "I Honestly Love You"					
2133	Have You Never Been Mellow	1975	2.50	5.00	10.00
2148	Clearly Love	1975	2.50	5.00	10.00
2186	Come On Over	1976	2.50	5.00	10.00
2223	Don't Stop Believin'	1976	2.50	5.00	10.00
2280	Making a Good Thing Better	1977	2.50	5.00	10.00
3012	Let Me Be There	1977	2.00	4.00	8.00
—Reissue					
3013	If You Love Me Let Me Know	1977	2.00	4.00	8.00
—Reissue					
3014	Have You Never Been Mellow	1977	2.00	4.00	8.00
—Reissue					
3015	Clearly Love	1977	2.00	4.00	8.00
—Reissue					
3016	Come On Over	1977	2.00	4.00	8.00
—Reissue					
3017	Don't Stop Believin'	1977	2.00	4.00	8.00
—Reissue					
3018	Making a Good Thing Better	1977	2.00	4.00	8.00
—Reissue					
3028	Olivia Newton-John's Greatest Hits	1977	2.50	5.00	10.00
3067	Totally Hot	1978	2.50	5.00	10.00
5229	Physical	1981	2.00	4.00	8.00
5347	Olivia's Greatest Hits, Vol. 2	1982	2.00	4.00	8.00
6151	Soul Kiss	1985	2.00	4.00	8.00
6245	The Rumour	1988	2.00	4.00	8.00
16011	Physical	1982	6.25	12.50	25.00
—Audiophile edition					
37061	Clearly Love	1980	2.00	4.00	8.00
—Reissue					
37062	Come On Over	1980	2.00	4.00	8.00
—Reissue					
37063	Don't Stop Believin'	1980	2.00	4.00	8.00
—Reissue					
37123	Totally Hot	1981	2.00	4.00	8.00
—Reissue					
MOBILE FIDELITY					
1-040	Totally Hot	1980	5.00	15.00	20.00
—Audiophile vinyl					
UNI					
73117	If Not for You	1971	20.00	40.00	80.00

NEXT MORNING, THE

Number	Title (A Side/B Side)	Yr	VG	VG+	NM
Albums					
CALLA					
SC-2002	The Next Morning	1972	25.00	50.00	100.00

NIC NACS, THE

Number	Title (A Side/B Side)	Yr	VG	VG+	NM
45s					
RPM					
342	Gonna Have a Merry Christmas/Found Me a Sugar Daddy	1951	50.00	100.00	200.00

NICE, THE

Keith Emerson, later of EMERSON, LAKE AND PALMER, was in this group.

Number	Title (A Side/B Side)	Yr	VG	VG+	NM
45s					
IMMEDIATE					
5004	Azrial (Angel of Death)/Thoughts of Emerlist Davjack	1968	3.00	6.00	12.00
5008	America/Diamnd Hard Apples of the Moon	1968	3.00	6.00	12.00
MERCURY					
73114	Country Pie/(B-side unknown)	1970	2.00	4.00	8.00
73272	Country Pie-Brandenburg Concerto No. 6 (Part 1)/Finale-5th Bridge	1972	—	3.00	6.00
Albums					
COLUMBIA SPECIAL PRODUCTS					
P 11633	Thoughts of Emerlist Davjack	1973	3.00	6.00	12.00
P 11634	Ars Longa Vita Brevis	1973	3.00	6.00	12.00
P 11635	The Nice	1973	3.00	6.00	12.00
IMMEDIATE					
Z12 52004	Thoughts of Emerlist Davjack	1968	5.00	10.00	20.00
Z12-52020	Ars Longa Vita Brevis	1969	5.00	10.00	20.00
Z12-52022	The Nice	1969	3.75	7.50	15.00
MERCURY					
SRM-2-6500 [(2)]	Keith Emerson with The Nice	1972	3.75	7.50	15.00
SR 61295	Five Bridges	1970	3.00	6.00	12.00
SR 61324	Elegy	1971	3.00	6.00	12.00
SIRE					
SASH-3710 [(2)]	The Vintage Years	1975	3.75	7.50	15.00

NICHOLAS, PAUL

Number	Title (A Side/B Side)	Yr	VG	VG+	NM
45s					
COLUMBIA					
46050	D.J. Saturday Night/Lovely Lady	1974	—	2.50	5.00
RSO					
851	Reggae Like It Used to Be/Heat of the Night	1976	—	2.00	4.00
878	Heaven on the 7th Floor/Do You Want My Love	1977	—	2.00	4.00
887	On the Strip/Beauty Queen	1978	—	2.00	4.00
Albums					
RSO					
RS-1-3028	Paul Nicholas	1977	3.00	6.00	12.00

NICHOLS, MIKE, AND ELAINE MAY

Number	Title (A Side/B Side)	Yr	VG	VG+	NM
Albums					
MERCURY					
SRM-2-628 [(2)]	Retrospect	1972	5.00	10.00	20.00
OCM 2200 [M]	An Evening with Mike Nichols and Elaine May	1961	7.50	15.00	30.00
OCS 6200 [S]	An Evening with Mike Nichols and Elaine May	1961	10.00	20.00	40.00
MG 20376 [M]	Improvisations to Music	1959	7.50	15.00	30.00
MG 20680 [M]	Nichols and May Examine Doctors	1962	6.25	12.50	25.00
MG 20997 [M]	The Best of Nichols and May	1965	5.00	10.00	20.00
SR 60040 [S]	Improvisations to Music	1959	10.00	20.00	40.00
SR 60680 [S]	Nichols and May Examine Doctors	1962	7.50	15.00	30.00
SR 60997 [S]	The Best of Nichols and May	1965	6.25	12.50	25.00

NICHOLS, NICHELLE

Number	Title (A Side/B Side)	Yr	VG	VG+	NM
Albums					
EPIC					
BN 26351	Down to Earth	1968	10.00	20.00	40.00

NICK AND THE JAGUARS

Number	Title (A Side/B Side)	Yr	VG	VG+	NM
45s					
TAMLA					
5501F	Ich-I-Bon #1/Cool and Crazy	1960	75.00	150.00	300.00

NICK AND THE NACKS

Number	Title (A Side/B Side)	Yr	VG	VG+	NM
45s					
BARRY					
108	The Night/That Old Black Magic	1964	100.00	200.00	400.00

NICK AND THE STINGRAYS

Number	Title (A Side/B Side)	Yr	VG	VG+	NM
45s					
MILL-MONT					
1628	You Are So Beautiful/Broken Hearted Baby	196?	50.00	100.00	200.00

NICKEL BAG, THE

Number	Title (A Side/B Side)	Yr	VG	VG+	NM
Albums					
KAMA SUTRA					
KLPS-8066	Doing Their Love Thing	1968	6.25	12.50	25.00

NICKIE AND THE NITELITES

With Nick Massi, later of THE FOUR SEASONS.

Number	Title (A Side/B Side)	Yr	VG	VG+	NM
45s					
BRUNSWICK					
55155	I'm Lonely/Tell Me You Care	1959	25.00	50.00	100.00

NICKY AND THE NOBLES

Number	Title (A Side/B Side)	Yr	VG	VG+	NM
45s					
END					
1021	Schoolhouse Rock/A Way to Tell Her	1958	12.50	25.00	50.00
1098	School Bells/School Day Crush	1961	6.25	12.50	25.00
GONE					
5039	School Bells/School Day Crush	1958	15.00	30.00	60.00
—Black label					
5039	School Bells/School Day Crush	1958	6.25	12.50	25.00
—Multicolor label					
5039	School Bells/School Days	1958	25.00	50.00	100.00
—With B-side title variation					

NICO

Also see THE VELVET UNDERGROUND.

Number	Title (A Side/B Side)	Yr	VG	VG+	NM
Albums					
ELEKTRA					
EKS-74029	The Marble Index	1968	6.25	12.50	25.00
ISLAND					
ILPS-9311	The End	1975	3.75	7.50	15.00
PVC					
8938	Camera Obscura	198?	3.00	6.00	12.00
REPRISE					
RS 6424	Desert Shore	1970	5.00	10.00	20.00
VERVE					
V-5032 [M]	Chelsea Girl	1967	7.50	15.00	30.00
V6-5032 [S]	Chelsea Girl	1967	10.00	20.00	40.00

NICOL, JIMMY

His 15 minutes of fame were from his brief stint filling in for an ailing Ringo Starr on a 1964 Beatles tour.

Number	Title (A Side/B Side)	Yr	VG	VG+	NM
45s					
ARGO					
5464	Night Train/Humpty Dumpty	1964	—	—	—
—Unreleased					
MAR MAR					
313	Night Train/Humpty Dumpty	1965	37.50	75.00	150.00
PARROT					
9752	Sweet Clementine/Roaring Blue	1965	6.25	12.50	25.00

NIGHT WATCH, THE

45s

Number	Title (A Side/B Side)	Yr	VG	VG+	NM
ABC					
10862	Closed Time/Lips to Your Heart	1966	6.25	12.50	25.00

NIGHTCRAWLERS, THE

45s

Number	Title (A Side/B Side)	Yr	VG	VG+	NM
KAPP					
KE-110	The Little Black Egg/You're Running Wild	1966	2.50	5.00	10.00
709	The Little Black Egg/You're Running Wild	1965	3.75	7.50	15.00
746	A Basket of Flowers/Washboard	1966	3.75	7.50	15.00
826	My Butterfly/Today I'm Happy	1967	7.50	15.00	30.00
LEE					
101	Cry/Marie	1964	15.00	30.00	60.00
1012	The Little Black Egg/You're Running Wild	1965	12.50	25.00	50.00
MARLIN					
1904	A Basket of Flowers/Washboard	1966	5.00	10.00	20.00

Albums

Number	Title (A Side/B Side)	Yr	VG	VG+	NM
KAPP					
KL-1520 [M]	The Little Black Egg	1967	15.00	30.00	60.00
KS-3520 [S]	The Little Black Egg	1967	10.00	20.00	40.00

NIGHTHAWK, ROBERT

45s

Number	Title (A Side/B Side)	Yr	VG	VG+	NM
STATES					
131	The Moon Is Rising/Maggie Campbell	1954	75.00	150.00	300.00

NILSSON

Also see THE FOTO-FI FOUR; THE RIC-A-SHAYS.

45s

Number	Title (A Side/B Side)	Yr	VG	VG+	NM
CRUSADER					
103	Baa Baa Black Sheep/Baa Baa Black Sheep (Part 2)	1964	7.50	15.00	30.00
—As "Bo Pete"					
MUSICOR					
6308	Please Mr. Music Man/Foolish Clock	1977	—	2.00	4.00
POLYDOR					
881177-7	Silver Horse/Loneliness	1984	—	2.00	4.00
RCA					
PB-10759	Just One Look-Baby I'm Yours/That Is All	1976	—	2.00	4.00
—With Lynda Lawrence					
PB-11059	Perfect Day/Who Done It	1977	—	2.00	4.00
PB-11059 [PS]	Perfect Day/Who Done It	1977	—	2.50	5.00
PB-11144	All I Think About Is You/I Never Thought I'd Get This Lonely	1977	—	2.00	4.00
PB-11193	Ain't It Kinda Wonderful/I'm Bringing a Red, Red Rose	1978	—	2.00	4.00
PB-11318	Spaceman/Me and My Arrow	1978	—	2.00	4.00
RCA VICTOR					
APBO-0039	As Time Goes By/Lullabye in Ragtime	1973	—	3.00	6.00
APBO-0246	Daybreak/Down	1974	—	2.00	4.00
APBO-0246 [PS]	Daybreak/Down	1974	—	3.00	6.00
SP-45-304 [DJ]	Jump Into the Fire (mono/stereo)	1972	2.50	5.00	10.00
—Promo-only number					
PB-10001	Many Rivers to Cross/Don't Forget Me	1974	2.00	4.00	8.00
PB-10078	Subterranean Homesick Blues/Mucho Mungo	1974	2.00	4.00	8.00
PB-10130	Remember (Christmas)/The Lottery Song	1974	—	2.00	4.00
PB-10139	Loop De Loop/Don't Forget Me	1974	—	2.00	4.00
PB-10183	Kojak Columbo/Turn Out the Light	1975	—	2.00	4.00
PB-10183 [PS]	Kojak Columbo/Turn Out the Light	1975	—	2.50	5.00
PB-10634	Sail Away/Moonshine Bandit	1976	—	2.00	4.00
47-9206	Without Her/Freckles	1967	2.00	4.00	8.00
47-9298	You Can't Do That/Ten Little Indians	1967	2.50	5.00	10.00
47-9383	River Deep Mountain High/She Sang Hymns Out of Tune	1967	2.00	4.00	8.00
47-9442	One/Sister Marie	1968	2.00	4.00	8.00
47-9544	Everybody's Talkin'/Don't Leave Me	1968	3.00	6.00	12.00
47-9675	Rainmaker/I Will Take You There	1968	2.00	4.00	8.00
74-0161	Everybody's Talkin'/Rainmaker	1969	2.50	5.00	10.00
74-0207	Maybe/Marchin' Down Broadway	1969	2.00	4.00	8.00
74-0261	I Guess the Lord Must Be in New York City/Maybe	1969	2.00	4.00	8.00
74-0310	I'll Be Home/Waiting	1970	—	3.00	6.00
74-0336	Caroline/Yellow Man	1970	—	3.00	6.00
74-0362	Down to the Valley/Buy My Album	1970	—	3.00	6.00
74-0443	Me and My Arrow/Are You Sleeping	1971	—	3.00	6.00
74-0524	Without Her/Good Old Desk	1971	—	3.00	6.00
74-0604	Without You/Gotta Get Up	1971	—	2.50	5.00
74-0673	Jump Into the Fire/The Moonbeam Song	1972	—	2.50	5.00
74-0718	Coconut/Down	1972	—	2.50	5.00
74-0788	Spaceman/Turn On Your Radio	1972	—	2.50	5.00
74-0855	Remember (Christmas)/The Lottery Song	1972	—	2.50	5.00
TOWER					
103	Sixteen Tons/I'm Gonna Lose My Mind	1964	3.75	7.50	15.00
136	You Can't Take Your Love Away from Me/Born in Grenada	1965	3.75	7.50	15.00
244	She's Yours/Growing Up	1966	3.75	7.50	15.00
518	Good Time/Growin' Up	1969	3.75	7.50	15.00
TRY					
501	Do You Wanna/Groovy Little Suzie	1964	10.00	20.00	40.00
—As "Bo Pete"					

Albums

Number	Title (A Side/B Side)	Yr	VG	VG+	NM
MUSICOR					
MS-2505 [S]	Early Times	1970	3.75	7.50	15.00
PICKWICK					
SPC-3321	Rock 'N' Roll	1977	2.50	5.00	10.00
RAPPLE					
ABL1-0220	Son of Dracula	1974	3.00	6.00	12.00
RCA VICTOR					
(no #) [M]	The True One	1967	50.00	100.00	200.00
—Boxed set with mono copy of RCA Victor 3874, two photos, button, poster, sticker, bios					
APL1-0097	A Little Touch of Schmilsson in the Night	1973	3.00	6.00	12.00
APD1-0319 [Q]	Nilsson Schmilsson	1974	5.00	10.00	20.00
SPS-33-567 [DJ]	Scatalogue	197?	25.00	50.00	100.00
APD1-0570 [Q]	Pussy Cats	1974	7.50	15.00	30.00
CPL1-0570	Pussy Cats	1974	5.00	10.00	20.00
APD1-0817 [Q]	Duit On Mon Dei	1975	5.00	10.00	20.00
APL1-0817	Duit On Mon Dei	1975	3.00	6.00	12.00
LSPX-1003	The Point!	1971	3.00	6.00	12.00
APD1-1031 [Q]	Sandman	1976	5.00	10.00	20.00
APL1-1031	Sandman	1976	3.00	6.00	12.00
APL1-1119	That's the Way It Is	1976	3.00	6.00	12.00
AFL1-2276	Knnillssonn	1977	3.00	6.00	12.00
AFL1-2798	Greatest Hits	1978	3.00	6.00	12.00
ANL1-3464	Nilsson Schmilsson	1979	2.00	4.00	8.00
AYL1-3761	A Little Touch of Schmilsson in the Night	1980	2.00	4.00	8.00
—"Best Buy Series" reissue					
AYL1-3811	The Point!	1980	2.00	4.00	8.00
—"Best Buy Series" reissue					
AYL1-3812	Son of Schmilsson	1980	2.00	4.00	8.00
—"Best Buy Series" reissue					
LPM-3874 [M]	Pandemonium Shadow Show	1967	10.00	20.00	40.00
LSP-3874 [S]	Pandemonium Shadow Show	1967	5.00	10.00	20.00
—"Stereo" on black label					
LPM-3956 [M]	Aerial Ballet	1968	12.50	25.00	50.00
LSP-3956 [S]	Aerial Ballet	1968	5.00	10.00	20.00
—"Stereo" on black label					
LSP-3956 [S]	Aerial Ballet	1969	3.75	7.50	15.00
—Orange label, non-flexible vinyl					
LSP-4197	Harry	1969	3.75	7.50	15.00
—Orange label, non-flexible vinyl					
LSP-4289	Nilsson Sings Newman	1970	3.00	6.00	12.00
—Orange label, non-flexible vinyl					
LSP-4417	The Point!	1971	2.50	5.00	10.00
—Reissue of LSPX-1003					
LSP-4515	Nilsson Schmillson	1971	3.00	6.00	12.00
LSP-4543	Aerial Pandemonium Ballet	1971	3.00	6.00	12.00
—Collection of tracks from 3874 and 3956, remixed with, in some cases, new vocals					
LSP-4717	Son of Schmilsson	1972	3.00	6.00	12.00
—With custom black "Victor" label					
TOWER					
ST 5095 [S]	Spotlight on Nilsson	1967	5.00	10.00	20.00
T 5095 [M]	Spotlight on Nilsson	1967	5.00	10.00	20.00
DT 5165 [R]	Spotlight on Nilsson	1969	3.75	7.50	15.00

NIMBLE, JACK B. AND THE QUICKS

45s

Number	Title (A Side/B Side)	Yr	VG	VG+	NM
DEL RIO					
2303/4	Like Keyed/Babes in Toyland	1962	6.25	12.50	25.00
2305	Nut Rocker/Never on Sunday	1962	7.50	15.00	30.00
DOT					
16319	Nut Rocker/Never on Sunday	1962	3.75	7.50	15.00

NIMOY, LEONARD

45s

Number	Title (A Side/B Side)	Yr	VG	VG+	NM
DOT					
17028	The Ballad of Bilbo Baggins/Cotton Candy	1967	3.75	7.50	15.00
17038	Theme from "Star Trek"/Visit to a Sad Planet	1967	5.00	10.00	20.00
17125	I'd Love Making Love to You/Please Don't Try to Change My Mind	1968	3.75	7.50	15.00
17175	Consilium/Here We Go 'Round Again	1968	3.75	7.50	15.00
17330	The Sun Will Rise/Time to Get It Together	1969	3.75	7.50	15.00

Albums

Number	Title (A Side/B Side)	Yr	VG	VG+	NM
CAEDMON					
TC-1466	The Martian Chronicles	1976	7.50	15.00	30.00
TC-1479	The Illustrated Man	1976	7.50	15.00	30.00
TC-1520	War of the Worlds	1977	7.50	15.00	30.00
TC-1526	Green Hills of Earth	1977	7.50	15.00	30.00
DOT					
DLP 3794 [M]	Mr. Spock's Music from Outer Space	1967	12.50	25.00	50.00
DLP 3835 [M]	Two Sides of Leonard Nimoy	1968	12.50	25.00	50.00
DLP 25794 [S]	Mr. Spock's Music from Outer Space	1967	20.00	40.00	80.00
DLP 25835 [S]	Two Sides of Leonard Nimoy	1968	20.00	40.00	80.00
DLP 25883	The Way I Feel	1968	15.00	30.00	60.00
DLP 25910	The Touch of Leonard Nimoy	1969	15.00	30.00	60.00
DLP 25966	The New World of Leonard Nimoy	1969	15.00	30.00	60.00
JRT					
(# unknown)	The Mysterious Golem	1982	10.00	20.00	40.00
PARAMOUNT					
PAS-1030 [(2)]	Outer Space/Inner Mind	1970	12.50	25.00	50.00
PICKWICK					
SPC-3199	Space Odyssey	197?	12.50	25.00	50.00
SEARS					
SPS-491	Leonard Nimoy	196?	20.00	40.00	80.00

1910 FRUITGUM COMPANY

Also see KASENETZ-KATZ SINGING ORCHESTRAL CIRCUS.

45s

Number	Title (A Side/B Side)	Yr	VG	VG+	NM
ATTACK					
10293	Lawdy, Lawdy/The Clock	1970	3.00	6.00	12.00
BUDDAH					
24	Simon Says/Reflections from the Looking Glass	1968	2.50	5.00	10.00
39	May I Take a Giant Step (Into Your Heart)/(Poor Old) Mr. Jensen	1968	2.00	4.00	8.00
54	1,2,3, Red Light/Sticky, Sticky	1968	2.50	5.00	10.00
71	Goody Goody Gumdrops/Candy Kisses	1968	2.00	4.00	8.00
91	Indian Giver/Pow Wow	1969	2.50	5.00	10.00
114	Special Delivery/No Good Annie	1969	2.00	4.00	8.00
130	The Train/Eternal Light	1969	2.00	4.00	8.00
146	When We Get Married/Baby Sweet	1969	2.00	4.00	8.00
SUPER K					
115	Go Away/The Track	1970	3.00	6.00	12.00

Albums

Number	Title (A Side/B Side)	Yr	VG	VG+	NM
BUDDAH					
BDS-5010	Simon Says	1968	6.25	12.50	25.00
BDS-5022	1,2,3 Red Light	1968	6.25	12.50	25.00

Number	Title (A Side/B Side)	Yr	VG	VG+	NM
BDS-5027	Goody, Goody Gumdrops	1969	6.25	12.50	25.00
BDS-5036	Indian Giver	1969	6.25	12.50	25.00
BDS-5043	Hard Ride	1969	6.25	12.50	25.00
BDS-5057	Juiciest Fruitgum	1970	6.25	12.50	25.00

NINO AND THE EBB TIDES

Number	Title (A Side/B Side)	Yr	VG	VG+	NM
45s					
ACME					
720	Franny Franny/Darling I'll Love Only You	1958	75.00	150.00	300.00
MADISON					
162	Those Oldies But Goodies (Remind Me of You)/ Don't Run Away	1961	10.00	20.00	40.00
166	Juke Box Saturday Night/(Someday) I'll Fall in Love	1961	7.50	15.00	30.00
MALA					
480	Automatic Reaction/Linda Lou Garrett Like 24 Karat	1964	5.00	10.00	20.00
MARCO					
105	Little Miss Blue/Someday	1961	12.50	25.00	50.00
MR. PEACOCK					
102	Wished I Was Home/Happy Guy	1961	6.25	12.50	25.00
117	Lovin' Time/Stamps, Baby, Stamps	1962	6.25	12.50	25.00
MR. PEEKE					
123	Tonight I'll Be Lonely/Nursery Rhymes	1963	6.25	12.50	25.00
RECORTE					
405	Puppy Love/You Make Me Rock 'N' Roll	1958	12.50	25.00	50.00
408	The Real Meaning of Christmas/Two Purple Shadows in the Snow	1958	75.00	150.00	300.00
409	I'm Confessin'/Tell the World I Do	1959	12.50	25.00	50.00
413	Don't Look Around/I Love Girls	1959	25.00	50.00	100.00

NIRVANA

Number	Title (A Side/B Side)	Yr	VG	VG+	NM
45s					
BELL					
715	We Can Help You/Pentecost Hotel	1968	2.50	5.00	10.00
730	You Are Just the One/Girl in the Park	1968	2.50	5.00	10.00
739	Trapeze/The Touchables	1968	2.50	5.00	10.00
Albums					
BELL					
6015	The Story of Simon Simopath	1968	6.25	12.50	25.00
6024	All of Us	1969	6.25	12.50	25.00
METROMEDIA					
MD-1018	Nirvana	1970	6.25	12.50	25.00

NITE-LITERS, THE

Also see LOVE, PEACE AND HAPPINESS; THE NEW BIRTH.

Number	Title (A Side/B Side)	Yr	VG	VG+	NM
45s					
RCA VICTOR					
APBO-0244	Pe-Foul/Serenade for a Jive Turkey	1974	—	2.50	5.00
74-0374	Con-Funk-Shun/Down and Dirty	1970	—	3.00	6.00
74-0461	K-Jee/Tanga Boo Gonk	1971	—	2.50	5.00
74-0591	Afro-Strut/(We've Got to) Pull Together	1971	—	2.50	5.00
74-0714	Cherish Every Precious Moment/I've Got Dreams to Remember	1972	—	2.50	5.00
74-0812	Funky-Doo/Do the Granny	1972	—	2.50	5.00
Albums					
RCA VICTOR					
LSP-4493	Morning, Noon & The Nite-Liters	1971	3.75	7.50	15.00
LSP-4580	Instrumental Directions	1972	3.75	7.50	15.00

NITE RIDERS, THE

Possibly two different groups.

Number	Title (A Side/B Side)	Yr	VG	VG+	NM
45s					
MGM					
12487	Sippin' Coffee/Tank Town	1957	7.50	15.00	30.00
TEEN					
116	Starlight and You/I Know You're In There	1955	10.00	20.00	40.00
118	Got Me a Six-Button Benny/Don't Hang Up the Phone	1955	10.00	20.00	40.00
120	When a Man Cries/Waiting in the Schoolroom	1955	10.00	20.00	40.00

NITE ROCKERS, THE

Number	Title (A Side/B Side)	Yr	VG	VG+	NM
45s					
RCA VICTOR					
47-7323	Nite Rock/Oh! Baby	1958	7.50	15.00	30.00

NITTY GRITTY DIRT BAND

Includes The Dirt Band. Also see JOHN DENVER.

Number	Title (A Side/B Side)	Yr	VG	VG+	NM
45s					
DECCA					
55206	Maybe Baby/Crying, Waiting, Hoping	1996	—	—	3.00
—B-side by Marty Stuart and Steve Earle					
LIBERTY					
1389	High School Yearbook/Too Good to Be True	1980	—	2.00	4.00
—As "The Dirt Band"					
1398	Nazamas Nuestra Magic (Make a Little Magic)/ Jas' Moon	1981	—	2.00	4.00
—As "The Dirt Band"					
1429	Fire in the Sky/EZ Slow	1981	—	2.00	4.00
—As "The Dirt Band"					
1449	Badlands/Jealousy	1982	—	2.00	4.00
—As "The Dirt Band"					
1467	Too Close for Comfort/Circular Man	1982	—	2.00	4.00
—As "The Dirt Band"					
1499	Let's Go/Shot Full of Love	1983	—	2.00	4.00
1507	Mary Anne/Dance Little Jean	1983	—	2.00	4.00
1513	Colorado Christmas/Mr. Bojangles	1983	—	3.00	6.00
55948	Buy for Me the Rain/Candy Man	1967	2.50	5.00	10.00
55982	The Teddy Bear's Picnic/Truly Right	1967	2.00	4.00	8.00
55982 [PS]	The Teddy Bear's Picnic/Truly Right	1967	3.75	7.50	15.00
56054	These Days/Collegiana	1968	2.00	4.00	8.00
56134	Some of Shelley's Blues/Yukon Railroad	1969	—	3.00	6.00
56159	Rave On/The Cure	1970	—	3.00	6.00
56197	Mr. Bojangles/Mr. Bojangles (Prelude: Uncle Charlie and His Dog Teddy)	1970	—	3.00	6.00
56197	Mr. Bojangles (Prelude: Uncle Charlie and His Dog Teddy)/Spanish Fandango	1970	2.00	4.00	8.00
S7-57766	I Fought the Law/Mr. Bojangles	1992	—	2.00	4.00
MCA					
53795	One Step Over the Line/Riding Along	1990	—	—	3.00
—A-side: With Roseanne Cash; B-side: With Emmylou Harris					
53964	The Rest of the Dream/Snowballs	1990	—	—	3.00
55182	You Believed in Me/Atlanta Reel '96	1996	—	—	3.00
—A-side by Karla Bonoff and the Nitty Gritty Dirt Band; B-side by Michael Omartian					
79013	From Small Things (Big Things One Day Come)/ Blues Berry Hill	1990	—	—	3.00
79075	You Make Life Good Again/Snowballs	1990	—	—	3.00
UNITED ARTISTS					
0061	Mr. Bojangles/Buy for Me the Rain	1973	—	2.00	4.00
—"Silver Spotlight Series" reissue					
XW177	Will the Circle Be Unbroken/Honky Tonkin'	1973	—	2.50	5.00
XW247	Grand Ole Opry Song/Orange Blossom Special	1973	—	2.50	5.00
XW263	Cosmic Cowboy (Part 1)/Cosmic Cowboy (Part 2)	1973	—	2.50	5.00
XW321	Tennessee Stud/Way Down Town	1973	—	2.50	5.00
—With Doc Watson					
XW544	The Battle of New Orleans/Mountain Whipporwill	1974	—	2.50	5.00
XW544 [PS]	The Battle of New Orleans/Mountain Whipporwill	1974	—	3.00	6.00
XW655	(All I Have to Do Is) Dream/Raleigh-Durham Reel	1975	—	2.50	5.00
XW741	Mother of Love/The Moon Just Turned Blue	1975	—	2.50	5.00
XW830	Cosmic Cowboy/Stars and Stripes Forever	1976	—	2.00	4.00
—As "The Dirt Band"					
XW889	Jamaica Lady/Bayou Jubilee-Sally Was a Goodun	1976	—	2.00	4.00
—As "The Dirt Band"					
XW936	Buy for Me the Rain/Mother Earth (Provides for Me)	1976	—	2.00	4.00
—As "The Dirt Band"					
XW1164	Orange Blossom Special/Will the Circle Be Unbroken	1978	—	2.00	4.00
XW1228	Wild Nights/In for the Night	1978	—	2.00	4.00
—As "The Dirt Band"					
XW1268	For a Little While/On the Loose	1978	—	2.00	4.00
—As "The Dirt Band"					
1312	In Her Eyes/Jas' Moon	1979	—	2.00	4.00
—As "The Dirt Band"					
1330	An American Dream/Take Me Back	1979	—	2.50	5.00
—As "The Dirt Band"					
1356	Make a Little Magic/Jas' Moon	1980	—	2.00	4.00
—As "The Dirt Band"					
1378	Badlands/Too Good to Be True	1980	—	2.00	4.00
—As "The Dirt Band"					
50769	House at Pooh Corner/Travelin' Mood	1971	—	3.00	6.00
50769 [PS]	House at Pooh Corner/Travelin' Mood	1971	2.00	4.00	8.00
50817	The Cure/Some of Shelly's Blues	1971	—	3.00	6.00
50849	Precious Jewel/I Saw the Light	1971	—	3.00	6.00
—With Roy Acuff					
50861	I Saw the Light/Sixteen Tracks	1971	—	3.00	6.00
50890	Jambalaya (On the Bayou)/Hoping to Say	1972	—	3.00	6.00
50890 [PS]	Jambalaya (On the Bayou)/Hoping to Say	1972	2.00	4.00	8.00
50921	Baltimore/Fish Song	1972	—	3.00	6.00
50965	Honky Tonkin'/Jamaica	1972	—	3.00	6.00
UNIVERSAL					
UVL-66009	Turn of the Century/Blueberry Hill	1989	—	—	3.00
UVL-66023	When It's Gone/I'm Sittin' on Top of the World	1989	—	2.00	4.00
WARNER BROS					
PRO-S-2869 [DJ]	Colorado Christmas/The Cowboy's Christmas Ball	1987	—	3.00	6.00
—B-side by Michael Martin Murphey					
WARNER BROS.					
27679	Down That Road Tonight/A Lot Like Me	1989	—	—	3.00
27750	I've Been Lookin'/Must Be Love	1988	—	—	3.00
27940	Workin' Man/Brass Sky	1988	—	—	3.00
28173	Oh What a Love/America, My Sweetheart	1987	—	—	3.00
28311	Fishin' in the Dark/Keepin' the Road Hot	1987	—	—	3.00
28443	Baby's Got a Hold on Me/Oleanna	1987	—	—	3.00
28547	Cadillac Ranch/Fire in the Sky	1986	—	—	3.00
28690	Stand a Little Rain/Miner's Night Out	1986	—	—	3.00
28780	Partners, Brothers and Friends/Redneck Riviera	1986	—	—	3.00
28897	Home Again in My Heart/Telluride	1985	—	2.00	4.00
29027	Modern Day Romance/Queen of the Road	1985	—	2.00	4.00
29099	High Horse/Must Be Love	1985	—	2.00	4.00
29203	I Love Only You/Face on the Cutting Room Floor	1984	—	2.00	4.00
29282	Long Hard Road (The Sharecropper's Dream)/ Video Tape	1984	—	2.00	4.00
Albums					
LIBERTY					
LWB-184 [(2)]	Stars and Stripes Forever	1981	2.50	5.00	10.00
LKCL-670 [(3)]	Dirt, Silver and Gold	1981	3.00	6.00	12.00
LO-974	An American Dream	1981	2.00	4.00	8.00
LT-1042	Make a Little Magic	1981	2.00	4.00	8.00
LRP-3501 [M]	The Nitty Gritty Dirt Band	1967	6.25	12.50	25.00
LRP-3516 [M]	Ricochet	1967	6.25	12.50	25.00
LMAS-5553	All the Good Times	1981	2.00	4.00	8.00
LST-7501 [S]	The Nitty Gritty Dirt Band	1967	7.50	15.00	30.00
LST-7516 [S]	Ricochet	1967	7.50	15.00	30.00
LST-7540	Rare Junk	1968	6.25	12.50	25.00
LST-7611	Alive	1969	6.25	12.50	25.00
LST-7642	Uncle Charlie and His Dog Teddy	1970	6.25	12.50	25.00
—Standard issue of LP					
LST-7642 [DJ]	Uncle Charlie and His Dog Teddy	1970	30.00	60.00	120.00
—Leatherette promo pack with LP, two other discs, photos, booklet					
LTAO-7642	Uncle Charlie and His Dog Teddy	1981	2.00	4.00	8.00
LT-51146	Let's Go	1982	2.50	5.00	10.00
LWCL-51158 [(3)]	Will the Circle Be Unbroken	1986	3.75	7.50	15.00
MCA					
6407	The Rest of the Dream	1990	3.00	6.00	12.00

Number	Title (A Side/B Side)	Yr	VG	VG+	NM
UNITED ARTISTS					
UA-LA184-J2 [(2)]	Stars and Stripes Forever	1974	3.75	7.50	15.00
UA-LA469-G	Dream	1975	3.00	6.00	12.00
UA-LA670-L3 [(3)]	Dirt, Silver and Gold	1976	5.00	10.00	20.00
UA-LA830-H	The Chicken Chronicles	1978	2.50	5.00	10.00
UA-LA854-H	The Dirt Band	1978	2.50	5.00	10.00
UA-LA974-H	An American Dream	1979	2.50	5.00	10.00
LT-1042	Make a Little Magic	1980	2.50	5.00	10.00
LW-1106	Jealousy	1981	2.50	5.00	10.00
UAS-5553	All the Good Times	1972	3.75	7.50	15.00
UAS-9801 [(3)]	Will the Circle Be Unbroken	1972	7.50	15.00	30.00
UNIVERSAL					
UVL2-12500 [(2)]	Will the Circle Be Unbroken, Volume Two	1989	5.00	10.00	20.00
WARNER BROS.					
25113	Plain Dirt Fashion	1984	2.00	4.00	8.00
25304	Partners, Brothers and Friends	1985	2.00	4.00	8.00
25382	Twenty Years of Dirt: The Best of the Nitty Gritty Dirt Band	1986	2.00	4.00	8.00
25573	Hold On	1987	2.00	4.00	8.00
25722	Workin' Band	1988	2.00	4.00	8.00
25830	More Great Dirt: The Best of the Nitty Gritty Dirt Band, Vol. 2	1989	2.50	5.00	10.00

NITZINGER

45s

Number	Title (A Side/B Side)	Yr	VG	VG+	NM
20TH CENTURY					
2311	Yellow Dog/Are You With Me	1976	—	2.00	4.00
CAPITOL					
3359	Earth Eater/One Foot in History	1973	—	2.50	5.00

Albums

Number	Title (A Side/B Side)	Yr	VG	VG+	NM
20TH CENTURY					
T-518	Live Better Electrically	1976	3.00	6.00	12.00
CAPITOL					
SMAS-11091	Nitzinger	1972	3.75	7.50	15.00
SMAS-11122	One Foot in History	1973	3.75	7.50	15.00

NITZSCHE, JACK

45s

Number	Title (A Side/B Side)	Yr	VG	VG+	NM
FANTASY					
760	One Flew Over the Cuckoo's Next/The Last Dance	1976	—	3.00	6.00
760 [PS]	One Flew Over the Cuckoo's Next/The Last Dance	1976	2.50	5.00	10.00
—Jack Nicholson is pictured on the sleeve					
MCA					
40897	Coke Machine/Hard Workin' Man	1978	—	2.00	4.00
REPRISE					
0262	The Last Race/Man with the Golden Arm	1964	5.00	10.00	20.00
0285	Theme from The Long Ships/Zapata	1964	5.00	10.00	20.00
0337	The Green Grass of Texas/Night Walker	1965	5.00	10.00	20.00
0364	Senorita from Detroit/Puerto Vallarta	1965	5.00	10.00	20.00
20202	The Lonely Surfer/Song for a Summer Night	1963	7.50	15.00	30.00
20202 [PS]	The Lonely Surfer/Song for a Summer Night	1963	25.00	50.00	100.00
20225	Rumble/Theme for a Broken Heart	1963	5.00	10.00	20.00

Albums

Number	Title (A Side/B Side)	Yr	VG	VG+	NM
REPRISE					
MS 2092	St. Giles Cripplegate	1972	5.00	10.00	20.00
R 6101 [M]	The Lonely Surfer	1963	25.00	50.00	100.00
RS 6101 [S]	The Lonely Surfer	1963	50.00	100.00	200.00
—Pink, gold and green label					
RS 6101 [S]	The Lonely Surfer	197?	5.00	10.00	20.00
—With only "r:" logo on all-orange (tan) label					
R 6115 [M]	Dance to the Hits of the Beatles	1964	12.50	25.00	50.00
RS 6115 [S]	Dance to the Hits of the Beatles	1964	15.00	30.00	60.00
R 6200 [M]	Chopin '66	1966	6.25	12.50	25.00
RS 6200 [S]	Chopin '66	1966	7.50	15.00	30.00

NIX, DON

45s

Number	Title (A Side/B Side)	Yr	VG	VG+	NM
CREAM					
7604	A Demain (Until Tomorrow)/A Demain (Until Tomorrow) (Edited Version)	1976	—	2.00	4.00
7608	Rollin' in My Dreams/(B-side unknown)	1976	—	2.00	4.00
ELEKTRA					
45746	Olena/Riding the Blues	1971	—	2.50	5.00
45776	Going Down/She Don't Want a Lover, She Just Needs a Friend	1972	—	2.50	5.00
ENTERPRISE					
9067	Black Cat Moan/The Train Don't Stop Here No More	1973	—	2.50	5.00
9083	She's a Friend of Mine/When I Lay My Burden Down	1973	—	2.50	5.00

Albums

Number	Title (A Side/B Side)	Yr	VG	VG+	NM
CREAM					
1001	Gone Too Long	1979	2.50	5.00	10.00
ELEKTRA					
EKS-74101	Living by the Days	1971	3.00	6.00	12.00
ENTERPRISE					
ENS-1032	Hobos, Heroes and Street Corner Clowns	1974	3.00	6.00	12.00

NIX, WILLIE

45s

Number	Title (A Side/B Side)	Yr	VG	VG+	NM
CHANCE					
1163	Nervous Wreck/No More Love	1954	750.00	1500.	3000.
SABRE					
104	All By Myself/Just Can't Stay	1953	500.00	1000.	2000.

NO NAMES, THE

45s

Number	Title (A Side/B Side)	Yr	VG	VG+	NM
GUYDEN					
2114	Love/Jam	1964	12.50	25.00	50.00

NOBELLS, THE

45s

Number	Title (A Side/B Side)	Yr	VG	VG+	NM
MAR					
101	Searchin' for My Love/Crying Over You	1962	25.00	50.00	100.00

NOBLES, CLIFF

45s

Number	Title (A Side/B Side)	Yr	VG	VG+	NM
ATLANTIC					
2352	My Love Is Getting Stronger/Too Fond of You	1966	2.00	4.00	8.00
2380	Your Love Is All I Need/Everybody Is Weak for Somebody	1967	2.00	4.00	8.00
JAMIE					
1406	The Horse/If You Don't	1972	—	3.00	6.00
MOON SHOT					
6710	Pony the Horse/Little Claudie	1969	2.00	4.00	8.00
PHIL-L.A. OF SOUL					
310	The More I Do for You Baby/This Love Will Last	1968	2.00	4.00	8.00
313	The Horse/Love Is All Right	1968	2.50	5.00	10.00
318	Horse Fever/Judge Baby, I'm Back	1968	2.00	4.00	8.00
324	Switch It On/Burning Desire	1969	2.00	4.00	8.00
329	The Camel/Goin' Away	1969	2.00	4.00	8.00
ROULETTE					
7142	This Feeling of Loneliness/We Got Our Thing Together	1973	—	3.00	6.00

Albums

Number	Title (A Side/B Side)	Yr	VG	VG+	NM
MOON SHOT					
601	Pony the Horse	1969	10.00	20.00	40.00
PHIL-L.A. OF SOUL					
4001	The Horse	1968	15.00	30.00	60.00

NOBLES, THE (1)

45s

Number	Title (A Side/B Side)	Yr	VG	VG+	NM
ABC-PARAMOUNT					
9984	Till the End of Time/Standing Loose	1958	6.25	12.50	25.00
10012	Just for Me/To Me	1959	6.25	12.50	25.00

NOBLES, THE (2)

45s

Number	Title (A Side/B Side)	Yr	VG	VG+	NM
KLIK					
305	Poor Rock and Roll/Ting-a-Ling	1958	50.00	100.00	200.00
TIMES SQUARE					
1	Poor Rock and Roll/Ting-a-Ling	1963	7.50	15.00	30.00
—Blue vinyl					
1	Poor Rock and Roll/Ting-a-Ling	1963	6.25	12.50	25.00
—Green vinyl					
12	Crime Doesn't Pay/Darkness	1963	5.00	10.00	20.00
—All copies on blue vinyl					
33	Why Be a Fool/The Search	1964	5.00	10.00	20.00

NOBLES, THE (3)

45s

Number	Title (A Side/B Side)	Yr	VG	VG+	NM
SELBON					
1005	Black Widow/Jaguar	1963	10.00	20.00	40.00

NOBLES, THE (4)

45s

Number	Title (A Side/B Side)	Yr	VG	VG+	NM
STACY					
926	Serenade/You Ain't Right	1962	10.00	20.00	40.00

NOBLES, THE (5)

45s

Number	Title (A Side/B Side)	Yr	VG	VG+	NM
U.S.A.					
788	Marlene/That Special One	1965	6.25	12.50	25.00

NOBLES, THE (U)

45s

Number	Title (A Side/B Side)	Yr	VG	VG+	NM
TEE GEE					
101	Oops Oh Lawdy/Stop Crying	1958	12.50	25.00	50.00

NOCTURNES, THE

45s

Number	Title (A Side/B Side)	Yr	VG	VG+	NM
CARLSON INT'L					
4105	My Christmas Star/(B-side unknown)	1964	15.00	30.00	60.00

NODAENS, THE

With Dave Nowlen, formerly of THE SURVIVORS.

45s

Number	Title (A Side/B Side)	Yr	VG	VG+	NM
GOLD					
1001	Beach Girl/Gypsy	196?	20.00	40.00	80.00

NOEL, SID

45s

Number	Title (A Side/B Side)	Yr	VG	VG+	NM
ALADDIN					
3331	The Flying Saucer (Part 1)/The Flying Saucer (Part 2)	1956	10.00	20.00	40.00
—Cover version of the Buchanan and Goodman break-in record					

NOLAN, FRANKIE

45s

Number	Title (A Side/B Side)	Yr	VG	VG+	NM
ABC-PARAMOUNT					
10231	I Still Care/(I Wish It Were) Summer All Year Round	1961	10.00	20.00	40.00
—Frankie Valli also appears on this record					

NOLAND, TERRY

45s

Number	Title (A Side/B Side)	Yr	VG	VG+	NM
APT					
25065	There Goes a Girl/Long Gone Baby	1962	3.75	7.50	15.00

Number	Title (A Side/B Side)	Yr	VG	VG+	NM
BRUNSWICK					
55010	Hypnotized/Ten Little Women	1957	7.50	15.00	30.00
55036	Patti Baby/Don't Do Me This Way	1957	7.50	15.00	30.00
55054	Puppy Love/Oh Baby, Look at Me	1958	7.50	15.00	30.00
55069	Crazy Dream/Everyone But One	1958	7.50	15.00	30.00
55092	There Was a Fungus Among Us/Sugar Drop	1958	10.00	20.00	40.00
55122	Guess I'm Gonna Fall/Teenage Teardrops	1959	7.50	15.00	30.00
CORAL					
62274	There Was a Fungus Among Us/Sugar Drop	1961	5.00	10.00	20.00
Albums					
BRUNSWICK					
BL 54041 [M]	Terry Noland	1958	150.00	300.00	600.00
—Buddy Holly plays guitar					

NON-CONFORMISTS, THE

Number	Title (A Side/B Side)	Yr	VG	VG+	NM
45s					
SCEPTER					
12184	Two-Legged Big Eyed Yellow Haired Crying Canary/Bird Walk	1967	7.50	15.00	30.00

NOONE, PETER

Also see HERMAN'S HERMITS.

Number	Title (A Side/B Side)	Yr	VG	VG+	NM
45s					
BELL					
45131	Oh You Pretty Thing/Because You're There	1971	12.50	25.00	50.00
—Allegedly features David Bowie on A-side piano					
45266	Should I/(B-side unknown)	1972	2.00	4.00	8.00
CASABLANCA					
0017	Meet Me at the Corner Down at Joe's Cafe/(Blame It)On the Pony Express	1974	—	2.50	5.00
0106	Meet Me at the Corner Down at Joe's Cafe/(Blame It)On the Pony Express	1974	—	2.00	4.00
802	Meet Me at the Corner Down at Joe's Cafe/(Blame It)On the Pony Express	1974	—	2.00	4.00
823	Something Old, Something New/(B-side unknown)	1975	—	2.00	4.00
JOHNSTON					
02838	(I Don't Wanna Love You But) You Got Me Anyway/I'm One of the Glory Boys	1982	—	2.00	4.00
PHILIPS					
40730	All SIng Together/Getting Over You	1974	—	2.50	5.00
Albums					
JOHNSTON					
ARZ 37369	One of the Glory Boys	1982	2.50	5.00	10.00

NORMAN, GENE, AND THE ROCKIN' ROCKETS

Number	Title (A Side/B Side)	Yr	VG	VG+	NM
45s					
SNAG					
101	Snaggle Tooth Ann/Long Gone Night Train	1958	250.00	500.00	1000.

NORMAN, LARRY

A founding father of Christian rock. Also see PEOPLE.

Number	Title (A Side/B Side)	Yr	VG	VG+	NM
45s					
CAPITOL					
2766	Sweet Sweet Song of Salvation/Walking Backwards Down the Stairs	1970	5.00	10.00	20.00
MGM					
14351	Righteous Rocker, Holy Rocker/Peace, Pollution, Revolution	1972	3.75	7.50	15.00
14676	Christmas Time/The Same Old Story	1973	3.75	7.50	15.00
14703	Nightmare/Baroquen Spirits	1974	3.75	7.50	15.00
SOLID ROCK					
202	Christmas Time/The Christmas Song	1976	2.00	4.00	8.00
VERVE					
10718	I've Got to Learn to Live Without You/Readers Digest	1973	5.00	10.00	20.00
10720	I've Got to Learn to Live Without You/The Outlaw	1973	5.00	10.00	20.00
Albums					
AB					
777	Streams of White Light Into Darkened Corners	1977	6.25	12.50	25.00
CAPITOL					
ST-446	Upon This Rock	1970	7.50	15.00	30.00
IMPACT					
3121	Upon This Rock	197?	5.00	10.00	20.00
MGM					
SE-4942	So Long Ago the Garden	1974	10.00	20.00	40.00
ONE WAY					
900	Bootleg	1972	7.50	15.00	30.00
—Regular cover					
4847	Bootleg	1972	10.00	20.00	40.00
—Gatefold cover					
7397	Street Level	1971	7.50	15.00	30.00
PHYDEAUX					
ARF-777-6	Almost So Long Ago the Garden	1984	3.00	6.00	12.00
BONE-777-6	Almost So Long Ago the Garden	1981	3.75	7.50	15.00
SOLID ROCK					
2001	In Another Land	1976	3.75	7.50	15.00
2007	Something New Under the Son	1981	3.75	7.50	15.00
STREET LEVEL					
ROCK-888-5	Only Visiting This Planet	1978	3.75	7.50	15.00
—Gatefold cover					
ROCK-888-5	Only Visiting This Planet	1978	3.00	6.00	12.00
—Regular cover					
VERVE					
V6-5092	Only Visiting This Planet	1973	7.50	15.00	30.00
—Tri-fold cover					
V6-5092	Only Visiting This Planet	1973	10.00	20.00	40.00
—Gatefold cover					

NORMANAIRES, THE

Number	Title (A Side/B Side)	Yr	VG	VG+	NM
45s					
MGM					
11622	My Greatest Sin/Wrap It Up	1953	20.00	40.00	80.00

NORRIS, CHARLES

Number	Title (A Side/B Side)	Yr	VG	VG+	NM
45s					
ATLANTIC					
994	Messin' Up/Let Me Know	1953	15.00	30.00	60.00

NORTH, FREDDIE

Number	Title (A Side/B Side)	Yr	VG	VG+	NM
Albums					
MANKIND					
204	Friend	1971	3.00	6.00	12.00

NORTH, JAY

Number	Title (A Side/B Side)	Yr	VG	VG+	NM
45s					
KEM					
2756	The Cat And The Christmas Tree/Christmas For Tommy	1960	3.75	7.50	15.00
Albums					
KEM					
27	Look Who's Singing!	1960	25.00	50.00	100.00

NORTHERN LIGHTS, THE

With Bjorn Ulvaeus, later of ABBA.

Number	Title (A Side/B Side)	Yr	VG	VG+	NM
45s					
UNITED ARTISTS					
991	Time to Move Along/No Time	1966	5.00	10.00	20.00

NOSY PARKER

Number	Title (A Side/B Side)	Yr	VG	VG+	NM
Albums					
(NO LABEL)					
(no #)	Nosy Parker	1975	62.50	125.00	250.00

NOTE-TORIALS, THE

Number	Title (A Side/B Side)	Yr	VG	VG+	NM
45s					
IMPALA					
201	Valerie/Loved and Lost	1958	250.00	500.00	1000.
SUNBEAM					
119	Valerie/Loved and Lost	1958	50.00	100.00	200.00

NOTES, THE

Number	Title (A Side/B Side)	Yr	VG	VG+	NM
45s					
CAPITOL					
F3332	Don't Leave Me Now/Cha Jezebel	1956	75.00	150.00	300.00
MGM					
12338	Trust in Me/Round and Round	1956	50.00	100.00	200.00
SARG					
177	Little Girl/G.I. Blues	1959	12.50	25.00	50.00

NOVA LOCAL, THE

Number	Title (A Side/B Side)	Yr	VG	VG+	NM
45s					
DECCA					
32138	Games/If You Only Had the Time	1967	5.00	10.00	20.00
32194	Other Girls/John Knight's Body (I Wanna Get Out)	1967	5.00	10.00	20.00
Albums					
DECCA					
DL 74977	Nova 1	1968	17.50	35.00	70.00

NOVAS, THE

Number	Title (A Side/B Side)	Yr	VG	VG+	NM
45s					
PARROT					
45005	The Crusher/Take 7	1964	20.00	40.00	80.00
TWIN TOWN					
713	Novas Coaster/On the Road Again	1965	10.00	20.00	40.00

NOVELLS, THE

Number	Title (A Side/B Side)	Yr	VG	VG+	NM
Albums					
MOTHER'S					
MLPS-73	A Happening	1968	12.50	25.00	50.00

NRBQ

Number	Title (A Side/B Side)	Yr	VG	VG+	NM
45s					
BEARSVILLE					
29588	Rain at the Drive-In/Shackaroo	1983	—	2.50	5.00
BUTTON					
037	Froggy Went a-Courtin'/Bless Your Beautiful Hide	1975	12.50	25.00	50.00
COLUMBIA					
44865	Stomp/I Didn't Know Myself	1969	—	3.00	6.00
44937	C'mon Everybody/Rocket No. 9	1969	—	3.00	6.00
45019	Sure to Fall (In Love With You)/Down in My Heart	1969	—	3.00	6.00
KAMA SUTRA					
544	Howard Johnson's Got His Hojo Workin'/Do You Feel It	1972	—	3.00	6.00
549	Only You/Magnet	1972	—	3.00	6.00
575	C'mon If You're Comin'/RC Cola and a Moon Pie	1973	—	3.00	6.00
586	Get That Gasoline Blues/Mona	1974	—	3.00	6.00
MERCURY					
73991	Green Lights/I Love Her, She Loves Me	1978	—	2.50	5.00
RED ROOSTER					
1001	Ridin' in My Car/Do the Bump	1977	2.50	5.00	10.00
1002	I Got a Rocket in My Pocket/Tapdancin' Bats	1977	—	3.00	6.00
1002 [PS]	I Got a Rocket in My Pocket/Tapdancin' Bats	1977	2.50	5.00	10.00
1006	Christmas Wish/Jolly Old St. Nicholas	1978	2.50	5.00	10.00
1006 [PS]	Christmas Wish/Jolly Old St. Nicholas	1978	2.50	5.00	10.00

Number	Title (A Side/B Side)	Yr	VG	VG+	NM
ROUNDER					
1010	Captain Lou!/Boardin' House Pie	1982	—	2.00	4.00
1010 [PS]	Captain Lou!/Boardin' House Pie	1982	—	2.00	4.00
4521	Hot Biscuits and Sweet Marie/She Don't Look Good	1979	—	2.50	5.00
4522	Get That Gasoline Blues/Wacky Tobacky	1979	—	2.50	5.00
4525	Christmas Wish/Jolly Old St. Nicholas	1979	—	2.50	5.00
4525 [PS]	Christmas Wish/Jolly Old St. Nicholas	1979	—	3.00	6.00
4531	Me and the Boys/People	1980	—	2.50	5.00
4531 [PS]	Me and the Boys/People	1980	2.50	5.00	10.00
4539	Never Take the Place of You/Captain Lou Albano for Tiddlywinks	1980	—	2.50	5.00
4556	Things to Do/I Can't Stop Loving You Now	1985	—	2.00	4.00
—With Skeeter Davis					
SCEPTER					
12322	Sho' Need Love/Don't Talk About My Music1	1971	12.50	25.00	50.00
—As "The Dickens"					
SELECT-O-HIT					
022	Sourpuss/Rumors	1974	12.50	25.00	50.00
VIRGIN					
99130	If I Don't Have You/Boozoo, That's Who	1989	—	2.00	4.00
99161 [DJ]	Wild Weekend/This Love Is True	1989	—	2.00	4.00
7-Inch Extended Plays					
RED ROOSTER					
EP-1	Christmas Wish/Here Comes Santa Claus//God Rest Ye Merry Gentlemen/Message from the North Pole	1979	3.75	7.50	15.00
—Called "Merry Christmas from NRBQ"; not issued with cover					
Albums					
ANNUIT COEPTIS					
1001/2 [(2)]	Scraps/Workshop	1976	5.00	10.00	20.00
—Reissue of Kama Sutra LPs					
BEARSVILLE					
23817	Grooves in Orbit	1983	2.50	5.00	10.00
COLUMBIA					
CS 9858	NRBQ	1969	6.25	12.50	25.00
—"360 Sound Stereo" label					
CS 9858	NRBQ	1970	3.00	6.00	12.00
—Orange label					
PC 9858	NRBQ	198?	2.00	4.00	8.00
—Budget-line reissue					
KAMA SUTRA					
KSBS-2045	Scraps	1972	7.50	15.00	30.00
KSBS-2065	Workshop	1973	10.00	20.00	40.00
MERCURY					
SRM-1-3712	NRBQ at Yankee Stadium	1978	3.75	7.50	15.00
824462-1	NRBQ at Yankee Stadlum	1984	2.50	5.00	10.00
—Reissue					
RED ROOSTER					
101	All Hopped Up	1977	3.75	7.50	15.00
ROUNDER					
EP-2501 [EP]	Christmas Wish	1985	3.00	6.00	12.00
3029	All Hopped Up	1979	3.00	6.00	12.00
3030	Kick Me Hard	1979	3.00	6.00	12.00
3048	Tiddlywinks	1980	3.00	6.00	12.00
3055	Scraps	1982	2.50	5.00	10.00
3066	Tapdancin' Bats	1983	2.50	5.00	10.00
3090	RC Cola & a Moon Pie	1987	2.50	5.00	10.00
3098	Lou and the Q	1986	2.50	5.00	10.00
—With pro wrestler Captain Lou Albano					
3108	God Bless Us All	1988	2.50	5.00	10.00
3109	Live! Diggin' Uncle Q	1988	2.50	5.00	10.00
VIRGIN					
91291	Wild Weekend	1989	2.50	5.00	10.00

NU-TONES, THE

Number	Title (A Side/B Side)	Yr	VG	VG+	NM
45s					
COMBO					
127	At Midnight/Beans 'N' Greens	1957	37.50	75.00	150.00
HOLLYWOOD STAR					
798	Annie Kicked the Bucket/Believe	1955	2000.	4000.	8000.
798	You're No Barking Dog/Believe	1955	150.00	300.00	600.00

NU TORNADOS, THE

Number	Title (A Side/B Side)	Yr	VG	VG+	NM
45s					
CARLTON					
492	Philadelphia, U.S.A./Magic Record	1959	6.25	12.50	25.00
497	The "Ole Mummers" Strut/Let's Have a Party	1959	5.00	10.00	20.00
FELSTED					
8577	Cry Baby Cry/Keep a Flower Growing in Your Heart	1959	5.00	10.00	20.00

NUGENT, TED

Also see THE AMBOY DUKES.

Number	Title (A Side/B Side)	Yr	VG	VG+	NM
45s					
ATLANTIC					
89436	Little Miss Dangerous/Angry Young Man	1986	—	—	3.00
89442	High Heels in Motion/Angry Young Man	1986	—	—	3.00
89661	Lean Mean R&R Machine/(Where Do You) Draw the Line	1984	—	—	3.00
89705 [DJ]	Tied Up in Love (same on both sides)	1984	—	2.00	4.00
—May be promo only					
89978	No, No, No/Habitual Offender	1982	—	—	3.00
89998	Bound and Gagged/Habitual Offender	1982	—	—	3.00
89998 [PS]	Bound and Gagged/Habitual Offender	1982	—	2.50	5.00
EPIC					
01046	Land of a Thousand Dances/The TNT Overture	1981	—	2.00	4.00
50172	Motor City Madness/Where Have You Been All My Life	1975	—	2.50	5.00
50197	Hey Baby/Stormtroopin'	1976	—	2.50	5.00
50301	Dog Eat Dog/Light My Way	1976	—	2.50	5.00
50363	Free-for-All/Street Rags	1977	—	2.00	4.00
50425	Cat Scratch Fever/Wang Dang Sweet Poontang	1977	—	2.50	5.00
50493	Death by Misadventure/Home Bound	1977	—	2.00	4.00
50533	Yank Me, Crank Me/Cat Scratch Fever	1978	—	2.00	4.00
50648	Need You Bad/I Got the Feelin'	1979	—	2.00	4.00
50713	Bite Down Hard/I Want to Tell You	1979	—	2.00	4.00
50907	Wango Tango/Scream Dream	1980	—	2.00	4.00
Albums					
ATLANTIC					
SD 19365	Nugent	1982	2.50	5.00	10.00
80125	Penetrator	1984	2.50	5.00	10.00
81632	Little Miss Dangerous	1986	2.50	5.00	10.00
81812	If You Can't Lick 'Em...Lick 'Em	1988	2.50	5.00	10.00
EPIC					
AS99-607 [PD]	State of Shock	1979	10.00	20.00	40.00
—Promo-only picture disc					
PE 33692	Ted Nugent	1975	3.00	6.00	12.00
—Orange label					
PE 33692	Ted Nugent	1979	2.00	4.00	8.00
—Reissue with dark blue label and bar code					
PE 34121	Free-for-All	1976	3.00	6.00	12.00
—Orange label					
PE 34121	Free-for-All	1979	2.00	4.00	8.00
—Reissue with dark blue label and bar code					
PEQ 34121 [Q]	Free-for-All	1976	5.00	10.00	20.00
JE 34700	Cat Scratch Fever	1977	3.00	6.00	12.00
—Orange label					
PE 34700	Cat Scratch Fever	198?	2.00	4.00	8.00
—Reissue with dark blue label and bar code					
KE2 35069 [(2)]	Double Live Gonzo!	1978	3.75	7.50	15.00
—Orange labels					
JE 35551	Weekend Warriors	1978	3.00	6.00	12.00
—Orange label					
PE 35551	Weekend Warriors	198?	2.00	4.00	8.00
—Reissue with dark blue label and bar code					
FE 36000	State of Shock	1979	2.50	5.00	10.00
PE 36000	State of Shock	198?	2.00	4.00	8.00
—Budget-line reissue					
FE 36404	Scream Dream	1980	2.50	5.00	10.00
FE 37084	Intensities in 10 Cities	1981	2.50	5.00	10.00
PE 37084	Intensities in 10 Cities	198?	2.00	4.00	8.00
—Budget-line reissue					
FE 37667	Great Gonzos! The Best of Ted Nugent	1981	2.50	5.00	10.00
PE 37667	Great Gonzos! The Best of Ted Nugent	198?	2.00	4.00	8.00
—Budget-line reissue					

NUGGETS, THE (1)

Number	Title (A Side/B Side)	Yr	VG	VG+	NM
45s					
CAPITOL					
F-2989	So Help Me I Love You/Quirl Up in My Arms	1954	5.00	10.00	20.00
F-3052	Anxious Heart/Shtiggy Boom	1955	3.75	7.50	15.00

NUGGETS, THE (2)

Number	Title (A Side/B Side)	Yr	VG	VG+	NM
45s					
RCA VICTOR					
47-7930	Before We Say Goodnight/Angel on the Dance Floor	1961	7.50	5.00	30.00
47-8031	Just a Friend/Cat Snapper	1962	3.75	7.50	15.00

NUMBERS, THE

Number	Title (A Side/B Side)	Yr	VG	VG+	NM
45s					
BONNEVILLE					
101	Big Red/My Pillow	1962	50.00	100.00	200.00
DORE					
641	Big Red/My Pillow	1962	12.50	25.00	50.00

NUTMEGS, THE

Number	Title (A Side/B Side)	Yr	VG	VG+	NM
45s					
BABY GRAND					
800	Story Untold '72/Tell Me	1972	2.00	4.00	8.00
HERALD					
452	Story Untold/Make Me Lose My Mind	1955	17.50	35.00	70.00
459	Ship of Love/Rock Me	1955	10.00	20.00	40.00
466	Whispering Sorrows/Betty Lou	1955	12.50	25.00	50.00
475	Key to the Kingdom (Of Your Heart)/Gift O' Gabbin' Woman	1956	12.50	25.00	50.00
492	Love So True/Comin' Home	1956	10.00	20.00	40.00
538	My Sweet Dream/My Story	1959	10.00	20.00	40.00
574	Rip Van Winkle/Crazy 'Bout You	1962	6.25	12.50	25.00
NIGHTRAIN					
905	Shifting Sands/Take Me and Make Me	1973	2.00	4.00	8.00
TEL					
1014	A Dream of Love/Someone, Somewhere (Help Me)	1960	25.00	50.00	100.00
TIMES SQUARE					
6	Let Me Tell You/Hello	1963	6.25	12.50	25.00
—Blue vinyl					
14	The Way Love Should Be/Wide Hoop Skirts	1963	5.00	10.00	20.00
19	Down to Earth/Coo Coo Cuddle Coo	1963	5.00	10.00	20.00
—B-side by the Admirations					
22	Why Must We Go to School/Ink Dries Quicker Than Tears	1963	5.00	10.00	20.00
—B-side by the Volumes					
27	Down in Mexico/My Sweet Dreams	1964	5.00	10.00	20.00
103	You're Crying/Wa-Do-Wa	1964	5.00	10.00	20.00
7-Inch Extended Plays					
HERALD					
452	*Story Untold/Betty Lou/Comin' Home/Whispering Sorrows	1960	25.00	50.00	100.00
452 [PS]	Story Untold	1960	30.00	60.00	120.00
Albums					
COLLECTABLES					
COL-5018	Greatest Hits	198?	2.50	5.00	10.00

Number	Title (A Side/B Side)	Yr	VG	VG+	NM
QUICKSILVER					
QS-1001	Shoo-Wop-a-Doo-Wop	198?	2.50	5.00	10.00
RELIC					
LP-5002	The Nutmegs Featuring Leroy Griffin	198?	2.50	5.00	10.00
LP-5011	Greatest Hits (1955-1959)	198?	2.50	5.00	10.00
NUTTY SQUIRRELS, THE					
45s					
COLUMBIA					
41818	Please Don't Take Our Tree for Christmas/Nutty Noel	1960	5.00	10.00	20.00
41818 [PS]	Please Don't Take Our Tree for Christmas/Nutty Noel	1960	10.00	20.00	40.00
HANOVER					
4540	Uh! Oh! (Part 1)/Uh! Oh! (Part 2)	1959	6.25	12.50	25.00
4540 [PS]	Uh! Oh! (Part 1)/Uh! Oh! (Part 2)	1959	12.50	25.00	50.00
4551	Eager Beaver/Zowee	1960	5.00	10.00	20.00
RCA VICTOR					
47-8287	Hello Again/Bluesette	1963	3.75	7.50	15.00
Albums					
COLUMBIA					
CL 1589 [M]	Bird Watching	1961	7.50	15.00	30.00
CS 8389 [S]	Bird Watching	1961	10.00	20.00	40.00
HANOVER					
HML-8014 [M]	The Nutty Squirrels	1960	12.50	25.00	50.00
MGM					
E-4272 [M]	A Hard Day's Night	1964	6.25	12.50	25.00
SE-4272 [S]	A Hard Day's Night	1964	7.50	15.00	30.00
NYRO, LAURA					
45s					
COLUMBIA					
44531	Sweet Blindness/Eli's Comin'	1968	2.00	4.00	8.00
44786	Once It Was Alright (Farmer Joe)/Lu	1969	—	3.00	6.00
45041	Time and Love/A Man Who Sends Me Home	1969	—	3.00	6.00
45089	Save the Country/New York Tendaberry	1970	—	3.00	6.00
45230	Up On the Roof/Captain Saint Lucifer	1970	—	3.00	6.00
45298	When I Was a Freeport and You Were the Main Drag/Been On a Train	1971	—	3.00	6.00
VERVE FOLKWAYS					
5024	Wedding Bell Blues/Stoney End	1966	2.50	5.00	10.00
5038	Billie's Blues/Goodbye Joe	1967	2.50	5.00	10.00
5051	And When I Die/Flim Flam Man	1967	2.50	5.00	10.00
VERVE FORECAST					
5095	Stoney End/Flim Flam Man	1968	2.00	4.00	8.00
5104	And When I Die/I Never Meant to Hurt You	1969	2.00	4.00	8.00

Number	Title (A Side/B Side)	Yr	VG	VG+	NM
5112	Goodbye Joe/I Never Meant to Hurt You	1969	2.00	4.00	8.00
Albums					
COLUMBIA					
CL 2826 [M]	Eli and the Thirteenth Confession	1968	10.00	20.00	40.00
CS 9626	Eli and the Thirteenth Confession	1970	2.50	5.00	10.00
—Orange label					
CS 9626 [S]	Eli and the Thirteenth Confession	1968	3.75	7.50	15.00
—"360 Sound Stereo" label					
PC 9626	Eli and the Thirteenth Confession	198?	2.00	4.00	8.00
—Budget-line reissue					
CS 9737	New York Tendaberry	1969	3.75	7.50	15.00
—"360 Sound Stereo" label					
CS 9737	New York Tendaberry	1970	2.50	5.00	10.00
—Orange label					
PC 9737	New York Tendaberry	198?	2.00	4.00	8.00
—Budget-line reissue					
KC 30259	Christmas and the Beads of Sweat	1970	3.75	7.50	15.00
—"360 Sound Stereo" label					
KC 30259	Christmas and the Beads of Sweat	1970	2.50	5.00	10.00
—Orange label					
PC 30259	Christmas and the Beads of Sweat	198?	2.00	4.00	8.00
—Budget-line reissue					
KC 30987	Gonna Take a Miracle	1971	3.75	7.50	15.00
PC 30987	Gonna Take a Miracle	197?	2.00	4.00	8.00
—Budget-line reissue					
KC 31410	The First Songs	1973	3.75	7.50	15.00
—Reissue of Verve Forecast 3020					
PC 31410	The First Songs	197?	2.00	4.00	8.00
—Budget-line reissue					
PC 33912	Smile	1976	3.00	6.00	12.00
—No bar code on cover					
PC2 34331 [(2) DJ]	Season of Lights...Laura Nyro in Concert	1977	12.50	25.00	50.00
—Promo only in plain cardboard jacket; this LP was edited to one LP for release					
JC 34786	Season of Lights...Laura Nyro in Concert	1977	3.00	6.00	12.00
—Edited version of above					
JC 35449	Nested	1978	3.00	6.00	12.00
PC 35449	Nested	198?	2.00	4.00	8.00
—Budget-line reissue					
FC 39215	Mother's Spiritual	1984	2.50	5.00	10.00
VERVE FOLKWAYS					
FT-3020 [M]	Laura Nyro — More Than a New Discovery	1967	7.50	15.00	30.00
FTS-3020 [S]	Laura Nyro — More Than a New Discovery	1967	7.50	15.00	30.00
VERVE FORECAST					
FTS-3020 [S]	Laura Nyro — More Than a New Discovery	1967	5.00	10.00	20.00
FTS-3029	Laura Nyro	1968	—	—	—
—Canceled					
ST 93036	Laura Nyro — More Than a New Discovery	1968	6.25	12.50	25.00
—Capitol Record Club edition					

O

O'BRIAN, HUGH

7-Inch Extended Plays

Number	Title (A Side/B Side)	Yr	VG	VG+	NM
ABC-PARAMOUNT					
A-203	(contents unknown)	1957	5.00	10.00	20.00
A-203 [PS]	Hugh O'Brian (TV's Wyatt Earp) Sings, Vol. I	1957	5.00	10.00	20.00
B-203	(contents unknown)	1957	5.00	10.00	20.00
B-203 [PS]	Hugh O'Brian (TV's Wyatt Earp) Sings, Vol. II	1957	5.00	10.00	20.00
C-203	Don't Move/Timothy//I'm Walkin' Away/Down in the Meadow	1957	5.00	10.00	20.00
C-203 [PS]	Hugh O'Brian (TV's Wyatt Earp) Sings, Vol. III	1957	5.00	10.00	20.00

Albums

Number	Title (A Side/B Side)	Yr	VG	VG+	NM
ABC-PARAMOUNT					
ABC-203 [M]	TV's Wyatt Earp Sings	1957	15.00	30.00	60.00

O'BRIEN, RHYS

45s

Number	Title (A Side/B Side)	Yr	VG	VG+	NM
MGM					
13862	The Word Called Love/Christmas Morning	1967	2.00	4.00	8.00

O'BRIEN, TIMMY

45s

Number	Title (A Side/B Side)	Yr	VG	VG+	NM
RASON					
1001	Just In Time For Christmas/I Been A Good Boy	1959	3.00	6.00	12.00

O'CONNOR, CARROLL

Albums

Number	Title (A Side/B Side)	Yr	VG	VG+	NM
AUDIO FIDELITY					
AFSD-6727	Carroll O'Connor Sings for Old P.F.A.R.T.S.	1976	6.25	12.50	25.00
A&M					
SP-4340	Remembering You	1972	3.00	6.00	12.00
SP-4340	Remembering You	1972	6.25	12.50	25.00

O'CONNOR, CARROLL, AND JEAN STAPLETON

45s

Number	Title (A Side/B Side)	Yr	VG	VG+	NM
ATLANTIC					
2847	Those Were the Days/Those Were the Days	1971	—	2.50	5.00
2847 [PS]	Those Were the Days/Those Were the Days	1971	2.00	4.00	8.00

O'DELL, KENNY

45s

Number	Title (A Side/B Side)	Yr	VG	VG+	NM
CAPRICORN					
0020	Rock and Roll Man/Ain't Gonna Study No More	1973	—	2.50	5.00
0038	You Bet Your Sweet. Sweet Love/Let's Go Find Some Country Music	1973	—	2.50	5.00
0203	I Take It On Home/I'll Find Another Way	1974	—	2.00	4.00
0219	Soulful Woman/Let's Get On the Road	1975	—	2.00	4.00
0233	My Honky Tonk Ways/Behind Closed Doors	1975	—	2.00	4.00
0247	Together This Christmas/I Can't Think When You're Doing That to Me	1975	—	2.00	4.00
0301	Let's Shake Hands and Come Out Lovin'/We Might Be All Night	1978	—	2.00	4.00
0309	As Long As I Can Wake Up in Your Arms/Soulful Woman	1978	—	2.00	4.00
0317	Medicine Woman/Who Do I Know in Denver	1979	—	2.00	4.00
EPIC					
10693	If I Was a Rambler/High on Life	1971	—	2.50	5.00
10730	I Was a Loser (But Now I've Got You)/Jubal	1971	—	2.50	5.00
10791	I Was a Loser (But Now I've Got You)/Jubal	1971	—	2.50	5.00
KAPP					
2169	Two for the Road/Why Don't We Go Somewhere and Love	1972	—	2.50	5.00
2178	Lizzie and the Rainman/Homecoming Queen	1972	—	2.50	5.00
MAR-KAY					
3696	Old Time Lovin'/Take Another Look	1966	2.50	5.00	10.00
VEGAS					
718	Beautiful People/Flower Girl	1967	2.00	4.00	8.00
722	Springfield Plane/I'm Gonna Take It	1968	—	3.00	6.00
724	Happy with You/Couldn't Love You	1968	—	3.00	6.00
WHITE WHALE					
319	No Obligation/(B-side unknown)	1969	—	3.00	6.00
331	Groovy Relationship/(B-side unknown)	1969	—	3.00	6.00

Albums

Number	Title (A Side/B Side)	Yr	VG	VG+	NM
CAPRICORN					
CP 0140	Kenny O'Dell	1974	3.00	6.00	12.00
CP 0211	Let's Shake Hands and Come Out Lovin'	1978	3.00	6.00	12.00
VEGAS					
401	Beautiful People	1968	6.25	12.50	25.00

O'HENRY, LENNY

45s

Number	Title (A Side/B Side)	Yr	VG	VG+	NM
ABC-PARAMOUNT					
10222	Billy the Continental Kid/Cheated Heart	1961	3.75	7.50	15.00
10272	Goin' to a Party/Touch of You	1961	3.75	7.50	15.00
ATCO					
6291	Across the Street/Saturday Angel	1964	3.00	6.00	12.00
6312	Sweet Young Love/Savin' All My Love	1964	3.00	6.00	12.00
6525	Across the Street/Saturday Angel	1967	2.00	4.00	8.00
SMASH					
1800	Burning Memories/Mr. Moonlight	1963	3.00	6.00	12.00

O'JAYS, THE

12-Inch Singles

Number	Title (A Side/B Side)	Yr	VG	VG+	NM
EMI					
SPRO-04305/20 [DJ]	Have You Had Your Love Today (2 versions)/ Lovin' You	1989	2.00	4.00	8.00
4853/4 [DJ]	Merry Christmas Baby/The Christmas Song	1991	2.00	4.00	8.00
56127	Have You Had Your Love Today (4 versions)	1989	—	3.00	6.00
PHILADELPHIA INT'L.					
3708	Sing a Happy Song (5:00)/Get On Out and Party (5:02)	1979	3.00	6.00	12.00
05000	Extraordinary Girl/(Instrumental)	1984	—	3.00	6.00
56049	Don't Take Your Love Away (3 versions)/I Just Want Somebody to Love Me	1987	—	3.00	6.00

45s

Number	Title (A Side/B Side)	Yr	VG	VG+	NM
APOLLO					
759	Miracles/Can't Take It	1961	7.50	15.00	30.00
ASTROSCOPE					
106	Wisdom of a Child/Peace	1974	2.00	4.00	8.00
110	Peace/Don't You Know a True Love (When You See Her)	1974	2.00	4.00	8.00
BELL					
691	I'll Be Sweeter Tomorrow (Than I Was Today)/I Dig Your Act	1967	2.50	5.00	10.00
704	Look Over Your Shoulder/I'm So Glad I Found You	1968	2.50	5.00	10.00
737	The Choice/Going, Going, Gone	1968	2.50	5.00	10.00
749	I Miss You/Now That I Found You	1968	2.50	5.00	10.00
770	Don't You Know a True Love/That's All Right	1969	2.00	4.00	8.00
45378	Look Over Your Shoulder/Four for the Price of One	1973	—	2.50	5.00
EMI					
S7-17491	Somebody Else Will/Decisions	1993	—	2.00	4.00
S7-18914	Have Yourself a Merry Little Christmas/I Can Hardly Wait 'Til Christmas	1995	—	—	3.00
50180	Have You Had Your Love Today/The Pot Can't Call the Kettle Black	1989	—	—	3.00
50212	Out of My Mind (Radio Mix)/Out of My Mind (Soul 2 Mix)	1989	—	—	3.00
IMPERIAL					
5942	How Does It Feel/Crack Up Laughing	1963	3.75	7.50	15.00
5976	Lonely Drifter/That's Enough	1963	2.50	5.00	10.00
66007	Stand Tall/The Storm Is Over	1963	2.50	5.00	10.00
66025	I'll Never Stop Loving You/My Dearest Beloved	1964	2.50	5.00	10.00
66037	You're on Top/Lovely Dee	1964	2.50	5.00	10.00
66076	Girl Machine/Oh How You Hurt Me	1964	2.50	5.00	10.00
66102	Lipstick Traces/Think It Over, Baby	1965	2.50	5.00	10.00
66121	Whip It On Me Baby/I've Cried My Last Tear	1965	2.50	5.00	10.00
66131	You're the One (You're the Only One)/Let It All Come Out	1965	2.50	5.00	10.00
66145	I'll Never Let You Go/It Won't Hurt	1965	2.50	5.00	10.00
66162	I'll Never Forget You/Pretty Words	1966	10.00	20.00	40.00
66177	No Time for You/It's a Blowin' Wind	1966	2.50	5.00	10.00
66197	Friday Night/Stand In for Love	1966	2.50	5.00	10.00
66200	Lonely Drifter/That's Enough	1966	2.50	5.00	10.00
LITTLE STAR					
124	How Does It Feel/Crack Up Laughing	1963	6.25	12.50	25.00
125	Dream Girl/Joey St. Vincent	1963	6.25	12.50	25.00
1401	Now He's Home/Just to Be with You	1962	6.25	12.50	25.00
MINIT					
32015	Hold On/Working on Your Case	1967	2.50	5.00	10.00
NEPTUNE					
12	One Night Affair/There's Someone (Waiting Back Home)	1969	2.00	4.00	8.00
18	Branded Bad/You're the Best Thing Since Candy	1969	2.00	4.00	8.00
20	Christmas Ain't Christmas New Year's Ain't New Year's Without the One You Love/There's Someone Waiting	1969	2.50	5.00	10.00
22	Deeper (In Love with You)/I've Got the Groove	1970	2.00	4.00	8.00
31	Looky Looky (Look at Me Girl)/Let Me in Your World	1970	2.00	4.00	8.00
33	Christmas Ain't Christmas New Year's Ain't New Year's Without the One You Love/Just Can't Get Enough	1970	2.00	4.00	8.00
PHILADELPHIA INT'L.					
02096	Forever Mine/Girl, Don't Let It Get You Down	1981	—	—	3.00
—Reissue					
02834	Don't Walk Away Mad/I Just Want to Satisfy	1982	—	2.00	4.00
02982	One by One/My Favorite Person	1982	—	2.00	4.00
03009	Out in the Real World/Your Body's Here with Me	1982	—	2.00	4.00
3517	Back Stabbers/Sunshine	1972	—	2.50	5.00
3522	992 Arguments/Listen to the Clock on the Wall	1972	—	2.50	5.00
3524	Love Train/Who Am I	1973	—	2.50	5.00
3531	Time to Get Down/Shiftless, Shady, Jealous Kind of People	1973	—	2.50	5.00
3535	Put Your Hands Together/You Got Your Hooks in Me	1973	—	2.50	5.00
3537	Christmas Ain't Christmas New Year's Ain't New Year's Without the One You Love/Just Can't Get Enough	1973	—	3.00	6.00
3544	For the Love of Money/People Keep Tellin' Me	1974	—	2.50	5.00
3558	Sunshine (Part 1)/Sunshine (Part 2)	1974	—	2.50	5.00
3565	Give the People What They Want/What Am I Waiting For	1975	—	2.50	5.00
3573	Let Me Make Love to You/Survival	1975	—	2.50	5.00
3577	I Love Music (Part 1)/I Love Music (Part 2)	1975	—	2.50	5.00
3581	Christmas Ain't Christmas New Year's Ain't New Year's Without the One You Love/Just Can't Get Enough	1975	—	2.50	5.00
3587	Livin' for the Weekend/Stairway to Heaven	1976	—	2.50	5.00
3596	Family Reunion/Unity	1976	—	2.50	5.00
3601	Message in Our Music/She's Only a Woman	1976	—	2.50	5.00
3610	Darlin' Darlin' Baby (Sweet, Tender, Love)/A Prayer	1976	—	2.50	5.00
3631	Work On Me/Let's Spend Some Time Together	1977	—	2.50	5.00
3642	Use Ta Be My Girl/This Time Baby	1978	—	2.50	5.00
3652	Brandy/Take Me to the Stars	1978	—	2.50	5.00
3666	Cry Together/Strokety Stroke	1978	—	2.50	5.00
3707	Sing a Happy Song/One in a Million (Girl)	1979	—	2.50	5.00
3726	I Want You Here with Me/Get On Out and Party	1979	—	2.50	5.00
3727	Forever Mine/Get On Out and Party	1979	—	2.50	5.00

Number	Title (A Side/B Side)	Yr	VG	VG+	NM
03892	A Letter to My Friends/I Can't Stand the Pain	1983	—	2.00	4.00
04069	Put Our Heads Together/Nice and Easy	1983	—	2.00	4.00
04437	I Really Need You Now/Extraordinary Girl	1984	—	2.00	4.00
04535	Let Me Show You (How Much I Really Love You)/ Love You Direct	1984	—	2.00	4.00
50013	Just Another Lonely Night/What Good Are These Arms of Mine	1985	—	—	3.00
50021	What a Woman/I Love America	1985	—	—	3.00
50067	Don't Take Your Love Away/I Just Want Somebody to Love Me	1987	—	—	3.00
50084	Lovin' You/Don't Let the Dream Get Along	1987	—	—	3.00
50104	Let Me Touch You/Undercover Lover	1987	—	—	3.00
50122	I Just Want Someone to Love Me/Lovin' You	1988	—	—	3.00
SARU					
1220	Shattered Man/La De Da (Means I'm Out to Get You)	1971	—	3.00	6.00
TSOP					
3771	Christmas Ain't Christmas New Year's Ain't New Year's Without the One You Love/Just Can't Get Enough	1980	—	2.00	4.00
4790	Girl, Don't Let It Get You Down/You're the Girl of My Dreams	1980	—	2.00	4.00
4791	Once Is Not Enough/To Prove I Love You	1980	—	2.00	4.00
70050	You Won't Fall/You'll Never Know (All There Is to Know 'Bout Love)	1981	—	—	—

Albums

Number	Title	Yr	VG	VG+	NM
BELL					
6014	Back on Top	1968	5.00	10.00	20.00
6082	The O'Jays	1973	3.00	6.00	12.00
EMI					
E1-90921	Serious	1989	2.50	5.00	10.00
E1-93390	Emotionally Yours	1991	3.75	7.50	15.00
E1-96420	Home for Christmas	1991	3.75	7.50	15.00
IMPERIAL					
LP 9290 [M]	Comin' Through	1965	10.00	20.00	40.00
LP 12290 [S]	Comin' Through	1965	12.50	25.00	50.00
KORY					
1006	The O'Jays	1977	2.50	5.00	10.00
LIBERTY					
LN-10119	Greatest Hits	1980	2.00	4.00	8.00
—Budget-line reissue of Imperial material					
MINIT					
LP-24008 [S]	Soul Sounds	1967	12.50	25.00	50.00
LP-40008 [M]	Soul Sounds	1967	10.00	20.00	40.00
NEPTUNE					
202	The O'Jays in Philadelphia	1969	7.50	15.00	30.00
PHILADELPHIA INT'L.					
ASZ 140 [DJ]	Everything You Always Wanted to Hear by the O'Jays But Were Afraid to Ask For	1975	3.75	7.50	15.00
KZ 31712	Back Stabbers	1972	3.00	6.00	12.00
KZ 32120	The O'Jays in Philadelphia	1973	3.00	6.00	12.00
—Reissue of Neptune LP					
KZ 32408	Ship Ahoy	1973	2.50	5.00	10.00
PZ 32408	Ship Ahoy	198?	2.00	4.00	8.00
—Budget-line reissue					
PZQ 32408 [Q]	Ship Ahoy	1974	3.75	7.50	15.00
KZ 32953	The O'Jays Live in London	1974	2.50	5.00	10.00
PZQ 32953 [Q]	The O'Jays Live in London	1974	3.75	7.50	15.00
PZ 33150	Survival	1975	2.50	5.00	10.00
PZ 33807	Family Reunion	1975	2.50	5.00	10.00
—No bar code on back cover					
PZ 33807	Family Reunion	198?	2.00	4.00	8.00
—Budget-line reissue with bar code					
PZQ 33807 [Q]	Family Reunion	1975	3.75	7.50	15.00
PZ 34245	Message in the Music	1976	2.50	5.00	10.00
PZ 34684	Travelin' at the Speed of Thought	1977	2.50	5.00	10.00
PZG 35024 [(2)]	The O'Jays: Collector's Items	1978	3.00	6.00	12.00
Z2 35024 [(2)]	The O'Jays: Collector's Items	198?	2.50	5.00	10.00
—Reissue					
JZ 35355	So Full of Love	1978	2.50	5.00	10.00
PZ 35355	So Full of Love	198?	2.00	4.00	8.00
—Budget-line reissue					
FZ 36027	Identify Yourself	1979	2.50	5.00	10.00
FZ 37999	My Favorite Person	1982	2.50	5.00	10.00
FZ 38518	When Will I See You Again	1983	2.50	5.00	10.00
PZ 38518	When Will I See You Again	1985	2.00	4.00	8.00
—Budget-line reissue					
FZ 39251	Greatest Hits	1984	2.50	5.00	10.00
53015	Love Fever	1985	2.50	5.00	10.00
53036	Let Me Touch You	1987	2.50	5.00	10.00
SUNSET					
SUS-5222	Full of Soul	1968	3.75	7.50	15.00
—Reissue of Imperial LP					
TSOP					
FZ 36416	The Year 2000	1980	2.50	5.00	10.00
UNITED ARTISTS					
UAS-5655	The O'Jays Greatest Hits	1972	3.00	6.00	12.00

O'KAYSIONS, THE

45s

Number	Title	Yr	VG	VG+	NM
ABC					
11094	Girl Watcher/Deal Me In	1968	2.00	4.00	8.00
11153	Love Machine/Dedicated to the One I Love	1968	—	3.00	6.00
11207	Twenty-Four Hours from Tulsa/Colors	1969	—	3.00	6.00
COTILLION					
44089	Happiness/Watch Out Girl	1970	—	2.50	5.00
44134	Life and Things/Travelin' Life	1971	—	2.50	5.00
NORTH STATE					
1001	Girl Watcher/Deal Me In	1968	25.00	50.00	100.00

Albums

Number	Title	Yr	VG	VG+	NM
ABC					
S-664	Girl Watcher	1968	10.00	20.00	40.00

O'KEEFE, DANNY

45s

Number	Title (A Side/B Side)	Yr	VG	VG+	NM
ATLANTIC					
2978	Angel, Spread Your Wings/Mad Ruth the Babe	1973	—	2.50	5.00
3267	The Delta Queen/Quits	1975	—	2.50	5.00
JERDEN					
806	Don't Wake Me in the Morning/That Old Sweet Song	1966	2.50	5.00	10.00
PICCADILLY					
228	Don't Wake Me in the Morning/That Old Sweet Song	1967	2.00	4.00	8.00
237	Today One Day Later/Baby	1967	2.00	4.00	8.00
SIGNPOST					
70004	Good Time Charlie's Got the Blues/The Valentine Pieces	1972	—	3.00	6.00
70012	The Road/I'm Sober Now	1972	—	2.50	5.00
WARNER BROS.					
8435	You Look Just Like a Girl Again/On Discovering a Missing Person	1977	—	2.50	5.00
8489	The Runaway/Just Jones	1977	—	2.50	5.00

Albums

Number	Title	Yr	VG	VG+	NM
ATLANTIC					
SD 7264	Breezy Stories	1973	3.00	6.00	12.00
SD 18125	So Long, Harry Truman	1975	3.00	6.00	12.00
COTILLION					
SD 9036	Danny O'Keefe	1971	3.75	7.50	15.00
FIRST AMERICAN					
7700	The Seattle Tapes	1977	3.00	6.00	12.00
7721	The Seattle Tapes, Volume 2	1979	3.00	6.00	12.00
PANORAMA					
105	Introducing Danny O'Keefe	1966	10.00	20.00	40.00
SIGNPOST					
SD 8404	O'Keefe	1972	3.00	6.00	12.00
WARNER BROS.					
PRO 760 [DJ]	The O'Keefe File	1977	3.75	7.50	15.00
BS 3050	American Roulette	1977	2.50	5.00	10.00
BSK 3314	Global Blues	1978	2.50	5.00	10.00

O'KEEFE, JOHNNY

45s

Number	Title	Yr	VG	VG+	NM
BRUNSWICK					
55067	Real Wild Child/Shake Baby Shake	1958	50.00	100.00	200.00
LIBERTY					
55223	She's My Baby/Own True Self	1959	10.00	20.00	40.00
55228	She's My Baby/It's Too Late	1959	7.50	15.00	30.00
55228 [PS]	She's My Baby/It's Too Late	1959	12.50	25.00	50.00
55262	Come On and Take My Hand/Don't You Know Little Baby	1960	10.00	20.00	40.00
MR. PEACOCK					
111	I'm Counting on You/The Steady Game	1962	10.00	20.00	40.00
SIMS					
337	So Why/Cryin' Is the One Thing I Do Very Well	1968	2.00	4.00	8.00

O'KEEFE, PAUL

45s

Number	Title	Yr	VG	VG+	NM
EVEREST					
19322	(Santa Claus) What Would You Like for Christmas?/A Baby in a Basket	1959	3.00	6.00	12.00
19322 [PS]	(Santa Claus) What Would You Like for Christmas?/A Baby in a Basket	1959	3.75	7.50	15.00

O'SULLIVAN, GILBERT

45s

Number	Title	Yr	VG	VG+	NM
EPIC					
50415	You Got Me Going/Call On Me	1977	—	2.00	4.00
50967	What's in a Kiss/Down, Down, Down	1981	—	2.00	4.00
MAM					
3602	Nothing Rhymed/Everybody Knows	1971	—	3.00	6.00
3607	Underneath the Blanket Go/(B-side unknown)	1971	—	3.00	6.00
3613	We Will/I Didn't Know What to Do	1971	—	3.00	6.00
3617	No Matter How I Try/If I Don't Get You Back	1972	—	2.50	5.00
3619	Alone Again (Naturally)/Save It	1972	—	3.00	6.00
3626	Clair/Ooh Wakka Doo Wakka Day	1972	—	2.50	5.00
3626 [PS]	Clair/Ooh Wakka Doo Wakka Day	1972	—	3.00	6.00
3628	Out of the Question/Everybody Knows	1973	—	2.50	5.00
3629	Get Down/A Very Extraordinary Sort of Girl	1973	—	2.50	5.00
3633	Ooh Baby/Good Company	1973	—	2.00	4.00
3636	Happiness Is Me and You/Breakfast, Dinner and Tea	1974	—	2.00	4.00
3641	A Woman's Place/Too Bad	1974	—	2.00	4.00
3642	You Are You/To Cut a Long Story Short	1974	—	2.00	4.00
3643	Marriage Machine/Tell Me Why	1975	—	2.00	4.00
3644	I Don't Love You But I Think I Like You/That's a Fact	1975	—	2.00	4.00
3645	Christmas Song/Just As You Are	1975	—	2.50	5.00

Albums

Number	Title	Yr	VG	VG+	NM
EPIC					
JE 37013	Off Centre	1981	2.50	5.00	10.00
MAM					
4	Gilbert O'Sullivan — Himself	1972	3.75	7.50	15.00
5	Back to Front	1972	3.75	7.50	15.00
7	I'm a Writer, Not a Fighter	1973	3.75	7.50	15.00
10	Stranger in My Own Backyard	1974	3.75	7.50	15.00

OAK RIDGE BOYS, THE

45s

Number	Title	Yr	VG	VG+	NM
ABC					
12350	I'll Be True to You/Old Time Family Bluegrass Band	1978	—	2.00	4.00
12397	Cryin' Again/I Can Love You	1978	—	2.00	4.00
12434	Come On In/Morning Glory Do	1978	—	2.00	4.00

Number	Title (A Side/B Side)	Yr	VG	VG+	NM
12463	Sail Away/Only One	1979	—	2.00	4.00
ABC/DOT					
17710	Y'All Come Back Saloon/Emmylou	1977	—	2.00	4.00
17732	You're the One/Morning Glory Do	1977	—	2.00	4.00
CADENCE					
1362	The Mocking Bird/The House of the Lord	1959	6.25	12.50	25.00
—As "The Oak Ridge Quartet"					
CAPITOL					
F2181	A Mother's Prayer/My Lord's Gonna Move This Wicked Race	1952	7.50	15.00	30.00
F2182	Give Me That Old Time Religion/No Tears in Heaven	1952	7.50	15.00	30.00
F2183	Her Mansion Is Higher Than Mine/I've Found a Hidin' Place	1952	7.50	15.00	30.00
—The above three as "The Oak Ridge Quartet"					
CAPITOL NASHVILLE					
S7-19345	Blue Christmas/I Still Believe in Christmas	1996	—	—	3.00
—B-side by Billy Dean					
COLUMBIA					
10083	Rhythm Guitar/There Must Be a Better Way	1975	—	2.50	5.00
10226	Heaven Bound/Look Away Mama	1975	—	2.50	5.00
10320	Where the Soul Never Dies/No Earthly Good	1976	—	2.50	5.00
10349	Family Reunion/Don't Be Late	1976	—	2.50	5.00
10419	All Our Favorite Songs/Whoever Finds This, I Love You	1976	—	2.50	5.00
11009	Rhythm Guitar/All Our Favorite Songs	1979	—	2.00	4.00
46001	He's Gonna Shine on Me/Put Your Arms Around Me, Blessed Jesus	1974	—	2.50	5.00
46044	Loves Me Like a Rock/He	1974	—	2.50	5.00
HEARTWARMING					
5067	How Much Farther Can We Go/(B-side unknown)	197?	2.00	4.00	8.00
5094	Talk About the Good Times/Get Together	197?	2.00	4.00	8.00
5103	Jesus Christ, What a Man/God Is Beautiful	197?	2.00	4.00	8.00
5119	The Flowers Kissed the Shoes/(B-side unknown)	197?	2.00	4.00	8.00
MCA					
S45-1154 [DJ]	Santa's Song/Happy Christmas Eve	1982	3.00	6.00	12.00
S45-1250 [DJ]	Thank God for Kids/Jesus Is Born Today	1982	3.00	6.00	12.00
12463	Sail Away/Only One	1979	—	—	3.00
S45-17233 [DJ]	When You Give It Away/The Voices Of Rejoicing Love	1986	3.75	7.50	15.00
—Promo only on green vinyl					
S45-17450 [DJ]	There's A New Kid In Town/From a Distance	1986	2.50	5.00	10.00
—B-side by Nanci Griffith					
41078	Dream On/Sometimes the Rain Won't Let Me Sleep	1979	—	2.00	4.00
41154	Leaving Louisiana in the Broad Daylight/I Gotta Get Over This	1979	—	2.00	4.00
41217	Trying to Love Two Women/Hold On 'Til Sunday	1980	—	2.00	4.00
41280	Love Takes Two/Heart of Mine	1980	—	2.00	4.00
51022	Ready to Take My Chances/Beautiful You	1980	—	2.00	4.00
51084	Elvira/A Woman Like You	1981	—	2.00	4.00
51169	Fancy Free/How Long Has It Been	1981	—	2.00	4.00
51231	Bobbie Sue/Live In Love	1982	—	2.00	4.00
52006	Bobbie Sue/Live In Love	1982	—	2.00	4.00
52065	So Fine/I Wish You Were Here	1982	—	2.00	4.00
52095	Back in Your Arms Again/I Wish I Could Have Turned My Head	1982	—	2.00	4.00
52145	Thank God for Kids/Christmas Is Paintin' the Town	1982	—	2.00	4.00
52179	American Made/The Cure for My Broken Heart	1983	—	2.00	4.00
52224	Love Song/Heart on the Line	1983	—	2.00	4.00
52288	Ozark Mountain Jubilee/Down Deep Inside	1983	—	2.00	4.00
52342	I Guess It Never Hurts to Hurt Sometimes/Through My Eyes	1984	—	—	3.00
52419	Everyday/Ain't No Cure for the Rock 'N' Roll	1984	—	—	3.00
52488	Make My Life with You/Break My Mind	1984	—	—	3.00
52556	Little Things/Secret of Love	1985	—	—	3.00
52646	Touch a Hand, Make a Friend/Only One I Love	1985	—	—	3.00
52722	Come On In (You Did the Best You Could Do)/Roll Tennessee River	1985	—	—	3.00
52722 [PS]	Come On In (You Did the Best You Could Do)/Roll Tennessee River	1985	—	2.00	4.00
52801	Juliet/Everybody Wins	1986	—	—	3.00
52873	You Made a Rock Out of a Rolling Stone/Hidin' Place	1986	—	—	3.00
53010	It Takes a Little Rain (To Make Love Grow)/Looking for Love	1987	—	—	3.00
53023	This Crazy Love/Where the Fast Lane Ends	1987	—	—	3.00
53175	Time In/A Little More Coal on the Fire	1987	—	—	3.00
53272	True Heart/Love Without Mercy	1988	—	—	3.00
53381	Gonna Take a Lot of River/Private Lives	1988	—	—	3.00
53460	Bridges and Walls/Never Together (But Close Sometimes)	1988	—	—	3.00
53625	Beyond Those Years/Too Many Heartaches	1989	—	—	3.00
53705	An American Family/Too Many Heartaches	1989	—	—	3.00
53757	No Matter How High/Bed of Roses	1989	—	—	3.00
79006	Baby, You'll Be My Baby/Cajun Girl	1990	—	—	3.00
RCA					
2665-7-R	Soul and Inspiration/(B-side unknown)	1990	—	2.00	4.00
2779-7-R	Lucky Moon/Walkin' After Midnight	1991	—	2.00	4.00
62013	Change My Mind/Our Love Is Here to Stay	1991	—	2.00	4.00
62099	Baby On Board/When It Comes to You	1991	—	2.00	4.00
62228	Fall/Wait Until You're Back in My Arms Again	1992	—	2.00	4.00
WARNER BROS.					
5359	This Ole House/Early in the Morning	1963	5.00	10.00	20.00

Albums

Number	Title	Yr	VG	VG+	NM
ABC					
AA-1065	Room Service	1978	2.50	5.00	10.00
AA-1135	Have Arrived	1979	3.00	6.00	12.00
ABC/DOT					
DA-2093	Y'all Come Back Saloon	1977	2.50	5.00	10.00
ACCORD					
SN-7138	Spiritual Jubilee	198?	2.50	5.00	10.00
SN-7159	Spiritual Jubilee — Volume 2	198?	2.50	5.00	10.00
SN-7199	Spiritual Jubilee — Volume 3	198?	2.50	5.00	10.00
CADENCE					
CLP-3019 [M]	The Oak Ridge Quartet	1958	15.00	30.00	60.00
CANAAN					
9625	Together	1966	5.00	10.00	20.00
—With the Harvesters					
COLUMBIA					
KC 32742	The Oak Ridge Boys	1974	3.00	6.00	12.00
PC 32742	The Oak Ridge Boys	197?	2.00	4.00	8.00
—Reissue					
KC 33057	Sky High	1975	3.00	6.00	12.00
PC 33057	Sky High	197?	2.00	4.00	8.00
—Reissue					
KC 33935	Old Fashioned, Down Home, Hand Clappin', Foot Stompin', Southern Style, Gospel Quartet Music	1976	3.00	6.00	12.00
PC 35202	The Best of the Oak Ridge Boys	1978	2.50	5.00	10.00
PC 37711	Old Fashoned Gospel Quartet Music	1984	2.00	4.00	8.00
FC 37737	All Our Favorite Songs	1981	2.50	5.00	10.00
PC 38467	Smoky Mountain Gospel	1984	2.00	4.00	8.00
HEARTWARMING					
HWS 3036	Thanks	1971	3.75	7.50	15.00
HWS 3091	International	1971	3.75	7.50	15.00
HWS 3159	The Light	1972	3.75	7.50	15.00
INTERMEDIA					
QS-5012	Glory Train	198?	2.50	5.00	10.00
LIBERTY					
LN-10046	The Oak Ridge Boys at Their Best	1981	2.00	4.00	8.00
MCA					
AA-1135	Have Arrived	1979	2.50	5.00	10.00
L33-2-1276 [(2) DJ]	"Step On Out" World Premiere	1985	6.25	12.50	25.00
—Promo-only interview and music LP with no script or cover					
1446	Deliver	1985	2.00	4.00	8.00
—Budget-line reissue					
1447	American Made	1985	2.00	4.00	8.00
—Budget-line reissue					
3220	Together	1980	2.50	5.00	10.00
5150	Greatest Hits	1980	2.50	5.00	10.00
5209	Fancy Free	1981	2.50	5.00	10.00
5294	Bobbie Sue	1982	2.50	5.00	10.00
5365	Christmas	1982	2.50	5.00	10.00
5390	American Made	1983	2.50	5.00	10.00
5455	Deliver	1983	2.50	5.00	10.00
5496	Greatest Hits 2	1984	2.50	5.00	10.00
5555	Step On Out	1985	2.50	5.00	10.00
5714	Seasons	1986	2.50	5.00	10.00
5799	Christmas Again	1986	2.50	5.00	10.00
5945	Where the Fast Lane Ends	1987	2.50	5.00	10.00
37153	Room Service	198?	2.00	4.00	8.00
—Budget-line reissue					
37221	Have Arrived	1984	2.00	4.00	8.00
—Budget-line reissue					
37222	Y'all Come Back Saloon	1984	2.00	4.00	8.00
—Budget-line reissue					
37223	Together	1984	2.00	4.00	8.00
—Budget-line reissue					
42036	Heartbeat	1987	2.50	5.00	10.00
42205	Monongahela	1988	2.50	5.00	10.00
42311	American Dreams	1989	2.50	5.00	10.00
NASHVILLE					
2086	Higher Power	1970	3.75	7.50	15.00
POWER PAK					
716	The Oak Ridge Boys	197?	2.50	5.00	10.00
PRIORITY					
PU 37711	Old Fashoned Gospel Quartet Music	1981	2.50	5.00	10.00
PU 38467	Smoky Mountain Gospel	1983	2.50	5.00	10.00
RCA					
R 164223	Unstoppable	1991	3.75	7.50	15.00
—Only released on vinyl through BMG Direct Marketing					
SKYLITE					
RLP-6020 [M]	The Oak Ridge Boys Sing for You	1964	5.00	10.00	20.00
SRLP-6020 [S]	The Oak Ridge Boys Sing for You	1964	6.25	12.50	25.00
RLP-6030 [M]	I Wouldn't Take Nothing for My Journey Now	1965	5.00	10.00	20.00
SRLP-6030 [S]	I Wouldn't Take Nothing for My Journey Now	1965	6.25	12.50	25.00
RLP-6040 [M]	The Solid Gospel Sound of the Oak Ridge Boys	1966	5.00	10.00	20.00
SRLP-6040 [S]	The Solid Gospel Sound of the Oak Ridge Boys	1966	6.25	12.50	25.00
RLP-6045 [M]	River of Love	1967	5.00	10.00	20.00
SRLP-6045 [S]	River of Love	1967	6.25	12.50	25.00
STARDAY					
SLP-356 [M]	The Sensational Oak Ridge Boys	1965	6.25	12.50	25.00
UNITED ARTISTS					
UAL 3554 [M]	The Oak Ridge Boys at Their Best	1966	5.00	10.00	20.00
UAS 6554 [S]	The Oak Ridge Boys at Their Best	1966	6.25	12.50	25.00
LN-10046	The Oak Ridge Boys at Their Best	1979	2.50	5.00	10.00
WARNER BROS.					
W 1497 [M]	With Sounds of Nashville	1963	5.00	10.00	20.00
WS 1497 [S]	With Sounds of Nashville	1963	6.25	12.50	25.00
W 1521 [M]	Folk-Minded Spirituals for Spiritual-Minded Folks	1963	5.00	10.00	20.00
WS 1521 [S]	Folk-Minded Spirituals for Spiritual-Minded Folks	1963	6.25	12.50	25.00

OBOLER, ARCH

Albums

Number	Title	Yr	VG	VG+	NM
CAPITOL					
ST 1763 [S]	Drop Dead! An Exercise in Horror	1962	7.50	15.00	30.00
T 1763 [M]	Drop Dead! An Exercise in Horror	1962	6.25	12.50	25.00

OBSESSIONS, THE

45s

Number	Title (A Side/B Side)	Yr	VG	VG+	NM
ACCENT					
1182	Love Always/A Fool	1964	50.00	100.00	200.00

OCEAN

Number	Title (A Side/B Side)	Yr	VG	VG+	NM
45s					
KAMA SUTRA					
519	Put Your Hand in the Hand/Tear Down the Fences	1971	—	2.50	5.00
525	Deep Enough for Me/No Other Woman	1971	—	2.00	4.00
529	We Got a Dream/Will the Circle Be Unbroken	1971	—	2.00	4.00
556	One More Chance/Will the Circle Be Unbroken	1972	—	2.00	4.00
Albums					
KAMA SUTRA					
KSBS-2033	Put Your Hand in the Hand	1971	3.00	6.00	12.00
KSBS-2064	Give Tomorrow's Children One More Chance	1972	3.00	6.00	12.00

OCHS, PHIL

Number	Title (A Side/B Side)	Yr	VG	VG+	NM
45s					
A&M					
881	Flower Lady/Cross My Heart	1967	2.50	5.00	10.00
891	Outside of a Small Circle of Friends/Miranda	1967	2.50	5.00	10.00
932	The War Is Over/The Harder They Fall	1968	2.00	4.00	8.00
1070	My Life/The World Began in Eden and Ended in Los Angeles	1969	2.00	4.00	8.00
1180	My Kingdom for a Car/One Way Ticket Home	1970	2.00	4.00	8.00
1509	Here's to the State of Richard Nixon/Power and Glory	1974	2.00	4.00	8.00
Albums					
A&M					
LP-133 [M]	Pleasures of the Harbor	1967	6.25	12.50	25.00
SP-3125	Phil Ochs Greatest Hits	198?	2.00	4.00	8.00
—Budget-line reissue					
SP-4133 [S]	Pleasures of the Harbor	1967	5.00	10.00	20.00
SP-4148	Tape from California	1968	5.00	10.00	20.00
SP-4181	Rehearsals for Retirement	1969	5.00	10.00	20.00
SP-4253	Phil Ochs Greatest Hits	1970	5.00	10.00	20.00
SP-6511 [(2)]	Chords of Fame	1976	5.00	10.00	20.00
(# unknown)	Gunfight at Carnegie Hall	197?	5.00	10.00	20.00
CARTHAGE					
CGLP-4422	I Ain't Marching Anymore	198?	2.50	5.00	10.00
CGLP-4427	All the News That's Fit to Sing	198?	2.50	5.00	10.00
ELEKTRA					
EKL-269 [M]	All the News That's Fit to Sing	1964	7.50	15.00	30.00
—Gold label with "guitar player" logo					
EKL-269 [M]	All the News That's Fit to Sing	1966	5.00	10.00	20.00
—Gold label with stylized "E" logo					
EKL-287 [M]	I Ain't Marching Anymore	1965	7.50	15.00	30.00
—Gold label with "guitar player" logo					
EKL-287 [M]	I Ain't Marching Anymore	1966	5.00	10.00	20.00
—Gold label with stylized "E" logo					
EKL-310 [M]	Phil Ochs in Concert	1966	5.00	10.00	20.00
EKS-7269 [S]	All the News That's Fit to Sing	1964	10.00	20.00	40.00
—Gold label with "guitar player" logo					
EKS-7269 [S]	All the News That's Fit to Sing	1966	6.25	12.50	25.00
—Gold label with stylized "E" logo					
EKS-7287 [S]	I Ain't Marching Anymore	1965	10.00	20.00	40.00
—Gold label with "guitar player" logo					
EKS-7287 [S]	I Ain't Marching Anymore	1966	6.25	12.50	25.00
—Gold label with stylized "E" logo					
EKS-7310 [S]	Phil Ochs in Concert	1966	6.25	12.50	25.00
FOLKWAYS					
FB-5320	Phil Ochs Sings Songs for Broadside (#10)	197?	3.00	6.00	12.00
FB-5321	Phil Ochs Interviews	197?	3.00	6.00	12.00
FD-5362	Broadside Tapes 1 (#14)	1979	3.00	6.00	12.00
PICKWICK					
SPC-3707	Rehearsals for Retirement	197?	2.50	5.00	10.00
RHINO					
RNLP-70080	A Toast to Those Who Are Gone	1986	2.50	5.00	10.00
SMITHSONIAN/FOLKWAYS					
SF-40008	Broadside Tapes 1 (#14)	1989	3.00	6.00	12.00

OCTAVES, THE

Number	Title (A Side/B Side)	Yr	VG	VG+	NM
45s					
VAL					
1001	You're Too Young/Mambo Carolyn	1958	18.75	37.50	75.00

OCTOBER COUNTRY

Number	Title (A Side/B Side)	Yr	VG	VG+	NM
45s					
EPIC					
5-10252	October Country/Baby What I Mean	1967	2.50	5.00	10.00
5-10320	My Girlfriend Is a Witch/I Just Don't Know	1968	2.50	5.00	10.00
Albums					
EPIC					
BN 26381	October Country	1968	5.00	10.00	20.00

ODA

Number	Title (A Side/B Side)	Yr	VG	VG+	NM
Albums					
LOUD					
A 0011	Oda	1973	50.00	100.00	200.00

ODDIS, RAY

Number	Title (A Side/B Side)	Yr	VG	VG+	NM
45s					
V.I.P.					
25012	Happy Ghoul Tide/Ray the Newspaper Boy	1964	5.00	10.00	20.00

ODDS AND ENDS

Number	Title (A Side/B Side)	Yr	VG	VG+	NM
45s					
RED BIRD					
10-083	Before You Go (Hey Little Girl)/Never Learn	1967	3.00	6.00	12.00

ODETTA

Number	Title (A Side/B Side)	Yr	VG	VG+	NM
45s					
ABC DUNHILL					
4213	Ballad of Easy Rider/Visa Versa	1969	—	3.00	6.00
POLYDOR					
14045	Take Me to the Pilot/Hit or Miss	1970	—	2.50	5.00
RCA VICTOR					
47-8262	Got My Mind on Freedom/It's a Mighty World	1963	2.50	5.00	10.00
RIVERSIDE					
4524	Make Me a Pallet on Your Floor/Oh, My Babe	1962	2.50	5.00	10.00
VANGUARD					
35007	Motherless Children/The Ox-Driver Song	1959	3.00	6.00	12.00
VERVE FOLKWAYS					
5030	Until It's Time for You to Go/Clown Town	1966	2.00	4.00	8.00
VERVE FORECAST					
5087	Peace and Harmony/Until It's Time for You to Go	1968	—	3.00	6.00
Albums					
ALCAZAR					
ALC-104	Christmas Spirituals	198?	2.50	5.00	10.00
ARCHIVE OF FOLK & JAZZ					
273	Odetta	197?	3.00	6.00	12.00
FANTASY					
3-15 [10]	Odetta and Larry	1955	12.50	25.00	50.00
OBC-509	Odetta and the Blues	198?	2.50	5.00	10.00
—Reissue of Riverside LP					
F-3252 [M]	Odetta and Larry	1957	12.50	25.00	50.00
—Dark red vinyl					
F-3252 [M]	Odetta and Larry	1958	7.50	15.00	30.00
F-8345	Odetta and Larry	1963	3.00	6.00	12.00
—Reissue of 3252					
RCA VICTOR					
LPM-2573 [M]	Sometimes I Feel Like Crying	1962	5.00	10.00	20.00
LSP-2573 [S]	Sometimes I Feel Like Crying	1962	6.25	12.50	25.00
LPM-2643 [M]	Odetta Sings Folk Songs	1963	5.00	10.00	20.00
LSP-2643 [S]	Odetta Sings Folk Songs	1963	6.25	12.50	25.00
LPM-2792 [M]	It's a Mighty World	1964	3.75	7.50	15.00
LSP-2792 [S]	It's a Mighty World	1964	5.00	10.00	20.00
LPM-3324 [M]	Odetta Sings Dylan	1965	3.75	7.50	15.00
LSP-3324 [S]	Odetta Sings Dylan	1965	5.00	10.00	20.00
LPM-3457 [M]	Odetta in Japan	1965	3.75	7.50	15.00
LSP-3457 [S]	Odetta in Japan	1965	5.00	10.00	20.00
RIVERSIDE					
RLP-417 [M]	Odetta and the Blues	1962	6.25	12.50	25.00
RS-9417 [S]	Odetta and the Blues	1962	7.50	15.00	30.00
ROSE QUARTZ					
RQ-101	Movin' It On	1987	2.50	5.00	10.00
TRADITION					
TRP-1010 [M]	Odetta Sings Ballads and Blues	1957	7.50	15.00	30.00
TRP-1025 [M]	Odetta at the Gate of Horn	1958	7.50	15.00	30.00
TRP-1052 [M]	The Best of Odetta	1967	5.00	10.00	20.00
TRS-2052 [R]	The Best of Odetta	1967	3.75	7.50	15.00
VANGUARD					
VSD-43/44 [(2)]	Essential Odetta	1973	3.75	7.50	15.00
VSD-2046 [S]	My Eyes Have Seen	1960	6.25	12.50	25.00
VSD-2057 [S]	Ballads for Americans	1960	6.25	12.50	25.00
VSD-2072 [S]	Odetta at Carnegie Hall	1961	6.25	12.50	25.00
VSD-2079 [S]	Christmas Spirituals	1961	6.25	12.50	25.00
VSD-2109 [S]	Odetta at Town Hall	1962	6.25	12.50	25.00
VSD-2153 [S]	One Grain of Sand	1963	6.25	12.50	25.00
VRS-3003 [M]	Odetta at Carnegie Hall	1967	3.75	7.50	15.00
VRS-9059 [M]	My Eyes Have Seen	1960	5.00	10.00	20.00
VRS-9066 [M]	Ballads for Americans	1960	5.00	10.00	20.00
VRS-9076 [M]	Odetta at Carnegie Hall	1961	5.00	10.00	20.00
VRS-9079 [M]	Christmas Spirituals	1961	5.00	10.00	20.00
VRS-9103 [M]	Odetta at Town Hall	1962	5.00	10.00	20.00
VRS-9137 [M]	One Grain of Sand	1963	5.00	10.00	20.00
VSD-73003 [S]	Odetta at Carnegie Hall	1967	5.00	10.00	20.00

OFF KEYS, THE

Number	Title (A Side/B Side)	Yr	VG	VG+	NM
45s					
ROWE					
003	Our Wedding Day/Singing Bells	1962	25.00	50.00	100.00
TECHNICHORD					
1001	Our Wedding Day/Singing Bells	1962	12.50	25.00	50.00
—Glossy red label					
1001	Our Wedding Day/Singing Bells	1962	6.25	12.50	25.00
—Flat maroon label					

OGNIR AND THE NIGHT PEOPLE

Number	Title (A Side/B Side)	Yr	VG	VG+	NM
45s					
SAMRON					
102	I Found a New Love/All My Heart	1965	10.00	20.00	40.00
WARNER BROS.					
5687	I Found a New Love/All My Heart	1965	6.25	12.50	25.00

OHIO EXPRESS, THE

Also see THE RARE BREED.

Number	Title (A Side/B Side)	Yr	VG	VG+	NM
45s					
BUDDAH					
38	Yummy Yummy Yummy/Zig Zag	1968	2.50	5.00	10.00
56	Down at Lulu's/She's Not Coming Home	1968	2.00	4.00	8.00
70	Chewy Chewy/Firebird	1968	2.50	5.00	10.00
92	Sweeter Than Sugar/Bitter Than Lemon	1969	2.00	4.00	8.00
102	Mercy/Roll It Up	1969	2.00	4.00	8.00
117	Pinch Me (Baby, Convince Me)/Peanuts	1969	2.00	4.00	8.00
129	Sausalito (Is the Place to Go)/Make Love Not War	1969	2.00	4.00	8.00
—With Graham Gouldman, later of 10CC, on lead vocal					
147	Cowboy Convention/The Race (That Took Place)	1970	2.00	4.00	8.00
160	Love Equals Love/Peanuts	1970	2.00	4.00	8.00
386	Wham Bam/Slow and Steady	1973	3.75	7.50	15.00
—As "Ohio Ltd."					

Number	Title (A Side/B Side)	Yr	VG	VG+	NM
CAMEO					
483	Beg, Borrow and Steal/Maybe	1967	3.00	6.00	12.00
2001	Try It/Soul Struttin'	1967	3.00	6.00	12.00
SUPER K					
114	Hot Dog/Ooh La La	1970	2.50	5.00	10.00
Albums					
BUDDAH					
BDS 5018	The Ohio Express	1968	5.00	10.00	20.00
BDS 5026	Chewy, Chewy	1969	5.00	10.00	20.00
BDS 5037	Mercy	1969	5.00	10.00	20.00
BDS 5058	The Very Best of the Ohio Express	1970	5.00	10.00	20.00
CAMEO					
C 20000 [M]	Beg, Borrow and Steal	1967	7.50	15.00	30.00
CS 20000 [S]	Beg, Borrow and Steal	1967	10.00	20.00	40.00

OHIO PLAYERS, THE

Also see THE OHIO UNTOUCHABLES.

Number	Title (A Side/B Side)	Yr	VG	VG+	NM
12-Inch Singles					
AIR CITY					
A-402	Sight for Sore Eyes/(Instrumental)	1984	—	3.00	6.00
ARISTA					
SP-46 [DJ]	Everybody Up (9:32) (3:57)	1979	2.00	4.00	8.00
MERCURY					
MK-43 [DJ]	Magic Trick/Good Luck Charm	1976	3.75	7.50	15.00
TRACK					
58813	Sweat (3 versions)/Rock the House	1988	—	3.00	6.00
45s					
AIR CITY					
402	Sight for Sore Eyes/(B-side unknown)	1984	—	2.00	4.00
402 [PS]	Sight for Sore Eyes/(B-side unknown)	1984	—	2.00	4.00
ARISTA					
0408	Everybody Up/Take De Funk Off, Fly	1979	—	2.00	4.00
0440	Don't Say Goodbye/Say It	1979	—	2.00	4.00
BOARDWALK					
NB7-11-133	Star of the Party/I Better Take a Coffee Break	1981	—	2.00	4.00
02063	Skinny/Call Me	1981	—	2.00	4.00
5708	Try a Little Tenderness/Try to Be a Man	1981	—	2.00	4.00
CAPITOL					
2385	Bad Bargain/Here Today and Gone Tomorrow	1969	2.50	5.00	10.00
2523	Find Someone to Love/Over the Rainbow	1969	2.50	5.00	10.00
COMPASS					
7015	Tresspassin'/You Don't Mean It	1967	3.00	6.00	12.00
7018	It's a Crying Shame/I've Got to Hold On	1968	3.00	6.00	12.00
MERCURY					
73480	Jive Turkey (Part 1)/Streakin' Cheek to Cheek	1974	—	2.50	5.00
73609	Skin Tight/Heaven Must Be Like This	1974	—	2.50	5.00
73643	Fire/Together	1974	—	2.50	5.00
73675	I Want to Be Free/Smoke	1975	—	2.50	5.00
73713	Sweet Sticky Thing/Alone	1975	—	2.50	5.00
73734	Love Rollercoaster/It's All Over	1975	—	2.50	5.00
73753	Happy Holidays (Part 1)/Happy Holidays (Part 2)	1975	—	3.00	6.00
73775	Fopp/Let's Love	1976	—	2.50	5.00
73814	Who'd She Coo?/Bi-Centennial	1976	—	2.50	5.00
73860	Far East Mississippi/Only a Child Can Love	1976	—	2.50	5.00
73881	Feel the Beat (Everybody Disco)/Contradiction	1976	—	2.50	5.00
73913	Body Vibes/Don't Fight My Love	1977	—	2.50	5.00
73932	O-H-I-O/Can You Still Love Me	1977	—	2.50	5.00
73956	Merry Go Round/Angel	1977	—	2.50	5.00
73974	Good Luck Charm (Part 1)/Good Luck Charm (Part 2)	1977	—	2.50	5.00
73983	Magic Trick/Mr. Mean	1978	—	2.50	5.00
74014	Funk-O-Nots/Sleepwalkin'	1978	—	2.50	5.00
74031	Time Slips Away/Nott Enuff	1978	—	2.50	5.00
TANGERINE					
978	Neighbors/A Thing Called Love	1967	3.00	6.00	12.00
TRACK					
58812	Let's Play (From Now On)/(B-side unknown)	1988	—	—	3.00
58815	Sweat/Rock the House	1988	—	—	3.00
WESTBOUND					
188	Pain (Part 1)/Pain (Part 2)	1971	—	3.00	6.00
204	Pleasure/I Wanna Hear from You	1972	—	3.00	6.00
208	Walt's First Trip/Varce Is Love	1972	—	3.00	6.00
214	Funky Worm/Paint Me	1973	—	3.00	6.00
216	Ecstasy/Not So Sad and Lonely	1973	—	3.00	6.00
228	Sleep Talk/Food Stamps Y'All	1974	—	3.00	6.00
5018	Rattlesnake/Gone Forever	1976	—	3.00	6.00
Albums					
ACCORD					
SN-7102	Young and Ready	1981	2.00	4.00	8.00
ARISTA					
AB 4226	Everybody Up	1979	2.00	4.00	8.00
BOARDWALK					
FW 37090	Tenderness	1981	2.00	4.00	8.00
CAPITOL					
ST-192	Observations in Time	1969	12.50	25.00	50.00
ST-11291	The Ohio Players	1974	3.00	6.00	12.00
—Reissue of 192					
MERCURY					
SRM-1-705	Skin Tight	1974	3.00	6.00	12.00
—Red label					
SRM-1-705	Skin Tight	1974	2.50	5.00	10.00
—Chicago skyline label					
SRM-1-1013	Fire	1974	2.50	5.00	10.00
SRM-1-1038	Honey	1975	2.50	5.00	10.00
SRM-1-1088	Contradiction	1976	2.50	5.00	10.00
SRM-1-1122	Ohio Players Gold	1976	2.50	5.00	10.00
SRM-1-3701	Angel	1977	2.50	5.00	10.00
SRM-1-3707	Mr. Mean	1977	2.50	5.00	10.00
SRM-1-3730	Jass-Ay-Lay-Dee	1978	2.50	5.00	10.00
824461-1	Ohio Players Gold	198?	2.00	4.00	8.00
—Reissue of 1122					
TRIP					
8029	First Impression	1972	3.00	6.00	12.00
UNITED ARTISTS					
UA-LA502-E	The Very Best of The Ohio Players	1975	3.00	6.00	12.00
WESTBOUND					
211	Rattlesnake	1975	3.00	6.00	12.00
219	Pain	1976	3.00	6.00	12.00
220	Pleasure	1976	3.00	6.00	12.00
222	Ecstasy	1976	3.00	6.00	12.00
1003	Climax	1974	3.75	7.50	15.00
1005	Ohio Players Greatest Hits	1975	3.75	7.50	15.00
2015	Pain	1972	5.00	10.00	20.00
2017	Pleasure	1973	5.00	10.00	20.00
2021	Ecstasy	1973	5.00	10.00	20.00

OHIO UNTOUCHABLES, THE

Early version of THE OHIO PLAYERS.

Number	Title (A Side/B Side)	Yr	VG	VG+	NM
45s					
LUPINE					
109	She's My Heart's Desire/What to Do	1962	12.50	25.00	50.00
110	Love Is Amazing/Forgive Me Darling	1962	12.50	25.00	50.00
116/7	I'm Tired/Uptown	1962	10.00	20.00	40.00
1009	She's My Heart's Desire/What to Do	1964	5.00	10.00	20.00
1010	Love Is Amazing/Forgive Me Darling	1964	5.00	10.00	20.00
1011	I'm Tired/Uptown	1964	3.75	7.50	15.00

OKLAHOMA WRANGLERS, THE

Number	Title (A Side/B Side)	Yr	VG	VG+	NM
45s					
RCA VICTOR					
47-4376	Unhappy New Year/Savannah River Rag	1951	3.75	7.50	15.00

OLA AND THE JANGLERS

Number	Title (A Side/B Side)	Yr	VG	VG+	NM
45s					
GNP CRESCENDO					
423	Let's Dance/Strolling Along	1969	2.00	4.00	8.00
427	What a Way to Die/That's Why I Cry	1969	2.00	4.00	8.00
432	California Sun/Baby, Baby, Baby	1970	2.00	4.00	8.00
LONDON					
20034	Eeny Meeny Miney Moe/I Can Wait	1967	2.50	5.00	10.00
Albums					
GNP CRESCENDO					
GNPS-2050	Let's Dance/What a Way to Die	1969	5.00	10.00	20.00

OLD & IN THE WAY

JERRY GARCIA heads a bluegrass band!

Number	Title (A Side/B Side)	Yr	VG	VG+	NM
Albums					
ROUND					
RX-103	Old & In the Way	1975	6.25	12.50	25.00
SUGAR HILL					
SH-3746	Old & In the Way	1987	2.50	5.00	10.00
—Reissue of Round LP					

OLDFIELD, MIKE

Number	Title (A Side/B Side)	Yr	VG	VG+	NM
12-Inch Singles					
REPRISE					
40749	The Bell-Sentinel Restructure (5 versions)	1992	2.50	5.00	10.00
45s					
VIRGIN					
9505	Theme from Ommadawn/On Horseback	1975	—	2.50	5.00
9510	Algiers/Portsmouth	1975	—	2.50	5.00
55100	Tubular Bells (Now the Original Theme from the Movie "The Exorcist")/Tubular Bells	1973	—	3.00	6.00
99402	Magic Touch/Wind Chimes Part 1	1987	—	2.00	4.00
99402 [PS]	Magic Touch/Wind Chimes Part 1	1987	—	2.00	4.00
VIRGIN/EPIC					
02877	Mount Teidi/Family Man	1982	—	2.50	5.00
Albums					
VIRGIN					
QR 13-105 [Q]	Tubular Bells	1974	6.25	12.50	25.00
VR 13-105	Tubular Bells	1973	3.75	7.50	15.00
VR 13-109	Hergest Ridge	1974	3.00	6.00	12.00
VR 13-109 [DJ]	Hergest Ridge	1974	5.00	10.00	20.00
—Banded for airplay					
VR 13-113	The Orchestral Tubular Bells	1975	3.00	6.00	12.00
SD 13135	Tubular Bells	1979	2.50	5.00	10.00
—Reissue of 34116					
SD 13143 [(2)]	Airborn	1980	3.75	7.50	15.00
PZ 33913	Ommadawn	1975	3.00	6.00	12.00
PZQ 33913 [Q]	Ommadawn	1975	6.25	12.50	25.00
PZ 34116	Tubular Bells	1976	3.00	6.00	12.00
—Reissue of 13-105 (no bar code)					
90589	Tubular Bells	1987	2.00	4.00	8.00
—Reissue of Virgin/Epic 33913					
90590	Hergest Ridge	1987	2.00	4.00	8.00
—Reissue of Virgin International 2013					
90591	The Killing Fields	1987	2.50	5.00	10.00
90645	Islands	1988	2.50	5.00	10.00
90894	The Orchestral Tubular Bells	1989	2.50	5.00	10.00
—Reissue of 13-115					
91270	Earth Moving	1990	3.00	6.00	12.00
VIRGIN INTERNATIONAL					
VI-2013	Hergest Ridge	1979	2.50	5.00	10.00
—Reissue of 13-109					
VI-2043	Ommadawn	1979	2.50	5.00	10.00
—Reissue of 33913					
VIRGIN/EPIC					
PE 34116	Tubular Bells	1982	2.00	4.00	8.00
—Reissue of 13135 (with bar code)					
FW 37358	QE2	1981	2.50	5.00	10.00
ARE 37983	Five Miles Out	1982	2.50	5.00	10.00
HE 44116	Tubular Bells	1982	7.50	15.00	30.00
—Half-speed mastered edition					

OLDHAM, ANDREW

Number	Title (A Side/B Side)	Yr	VG	VG+	NM
45s					
PARROT					
9684	Theme from The Dick Van Dyke Show/I'd Like to See Me on the "B" Side	1964	7.50	15.00	30.00
9745	I Get Around/Save It For Me	1965	7.50	15.00	30.00
Albums					
LONDON					
PS 457 [S]	The Rolling Stones Songbook	1965	37.50	75.00	150.00
LL 3457 [M]	The Rolling Stones Songbook	1965	25.00	50.00	100.00
PARROT					
PA 61003 [M]	East Meets West	1965	20.00	40.00	80.00
PAS 71003 [S]	East Meets West	1965	25.00	50.00	100.00

OLIVA, TONY

Number	Title (A Side/B Side)	Yr	VG	VG+	NM
Albums					
KUBANY					
SD-600	My Favorite Music	1966	7.50	15.00	30.00

OLIVER

Number	Title (A Side/B Side)	Yr	VG	VG+	NM
45s					
CREWE					
334	Jean/The Arrangement	1969	2.00	4.00	8.00
334 [PS]	Jean/The Arrangement	1969	3.75	7.50	15.00
337	Sunday Mornin'/Let Me Kiss You with a Dream	1969	—	3.00	6.00
341	Angelica/Anna	1970	—	3.00	6.00
346	I Can Remember/Where There's a Heartache There Must Be a Heart	1970	—	3.00	6.00
JUBILEE					
5659	Good Morning Starshine/Can't You See	1969	2.00	4.00	8.00
MCA					
52063	Don't Take Your Love Away/Everybody Wants to Be the Boss	1982	—	—	3.00
52113	I Want Your Love, I Need Your Love/Make Up Your Mind	1982	—	—	3.00
PARAMOUNT					
0198	Everybody I Love You/I Am Reaching	1973	—	2.00	4.00
UNITED ARTISTS					
0130	Good Morning Starshine/Jean	1973	—	2.00	4.00
—"Silver Spotlight Series" reissue					
50735	Sweet Kindness/Light the Way	1970	—	2.50	5.00
50750	Dedicated to the One I Love/Light the Way	1971	—	—	—
—Unreleased					
50762	Early Morning Rain/Catch Me If You Can	1971	—	2.50	5.00
50814	Walkin' Down the Line/Firelight	1971	—	2.50	5.00
50862	Why You Been Gone So Long/Please	1971	—	2.50	5.00
Albums					
CREWE					
1333	Good Morning Starshine	1969	3.75	7.50	15.00
1344	Oliver Again	1970	3.75	7.50	15.00
UNITED ARTISTS					
UAS-5511	Prisms	1971	3.75	7.50	15.00

OLIVER AND THE TWISTERS

Number	Title (A Side/B Side)	Yr	VG	VG+	NM
45s					
COLPIX					
615	Mother Goose Twist/Locomotion Twist	1961	3.00	6.00	12.00
615 [PS]	Mother Goose Twist/Locomotion Twist	1961	6.25	12.50	25.00
Albums					
COLPIX					
CP-423 [M]	Look Who's Twistin' Everybody	1961	10.00	20.00	40.00

OLIVERS, THE

Number	Title (A Side/B Side)	Yr	VG	VG+	NM
45s					
PHALANX					
1022	Bleecker Street/I Saw What You Did	1967	15.00	30.00	60.00
RCA VICTOR					
47-9113	Bleecker Street/I Saw What You Did	1967	5.00	10.00	20.00

OLLIE AND THE NIGHTINGALES

Number	Title (A Side/B Side)	Yr	VG	VG+	NM
45s					
STAX					
0014	You're Leaving Me/Showered with Love	1968	—	3.00	6.00
0027	The Mellow Way You Treat Your Man/Don't Do What I Did	1969	—	3.00	6.00
0045	I've Got a Feeling/You'll Never Do Wrong	1969	—	3.00	6.00
0065	I'll Be Your Anything/Bracing Myself for the Fall	1970	—	3.00	6.00
245	I Got a Sure Thing/Girl You Have My Heart Singing	1968	2.00	4.00	8.00
Albums					
STAX					
STS-2021	Ollie and the Nightingales	1969	12.50	25.00	50.00

OLSEN, DOROTHY

Number	Title (A Side/B Side)	Yr	VG	VG+	NM
45s					
RCA VICTOR					
47-7654	The Christmas Spirit/Little Donkey	1959	3.75	7.50	15.00

OLSSON, NIGEL

Drummer in ELTON JOHN's band.

Number	Title (A Side/B Side)	Yr	VG	VG+	NM
12-Inch Singles					
BANG					
4801	Little Bit of Soap (5:28)/Cassey Blue-Au Revoir (6:24)	1979	3.75	7.50	15.00
45s					
BANG					
740	Dancin' Shoes/Living in a Fantasy	1978	—	2.50	5.00
4800	Little Bit of Soap/Thinking of You	1979	—	2.00	4.00
4803	All It Takes/Part of the Chosen Few	1979	—	2.00	4.00
COLUMBIA					
10733	Rainy Day/Right or Wrong	1978	—	2.50	5.00
ROCKET					
40337	Only One Woman/In Good Time	1974	—	2.50	5.00
40455	Songs I Sing/Something Lacking in Me	1975	—	2.50	5.00
40491	A Girl Like You/Girl, We've Got to Keep On	1975	—	2.50	5.00
UNI					
55291	Some Sweet Day/Weirdhouse	1971	—	3.00	6.00
—As "Nigel Olsson's Drum Orchestra"					
55308	And I Know in My Heart/Sunshine Looks Like Rain	1971	—	3.00	6.00
Albums					
BANG					
JZ 35792	Nigel	1979	2.50	5.00	10.00
JZ 36491	Changing Tides	1980	2.50	5.00	10.00
ROCKET					
L33-1962 [DJ]	Drummers Can Sing Too!	1975	5.00	10.00	20.00
—Promo-only interview album					
PIG-2158	Nigel Olsson	1975	3.00	6.00	12.00
UNI					
73113	Nigel Olsson's Drum Orchestra	1971	3.75	7.50	15.00

OLYMPIC RUNNERS

PETE WINGFIELD was in this group.

Number	Title (A Side/B Side)	Yr	VG	VG+	NM
45s					
LONDON					
202	Do It Over/Put the Music Where Your Mouth Is	1974	—	2.50	5.00
216	Grab It/Let Your Fingers Do the Talking	1974	—	2.50	5.00
217	Sproutin' Out/Be My Main Squeeze	1975	—	2.50	5.00
219	Drag It Over Here/Mac B. Coolie	1975	—	2.50	5.00
227	Dump the Bump/Exit City	1976	—	2.50	5.00
233	Party Time Is Here to Stay/'Til the Sun Comes Up	1976	—	2.50	5.00
247	Say WhatYou Wanna But It Sure Is Funny/It's Only Love	1976	—	2.50	5.00
261	Keep It Up/The Kool Gent	1977	—	2.50	5.00
POLYDOR					
2008	Onya/The Bitch	1979	—	2.00	4.00
2030	God Bless You/The Bitch	1979	—	2.00	4.00
Albums					
LONDON					
PS 653	Put the Music Where Your Mouth Is	1974	3.75	7.50	15.00
PS 658	Out in Front	1975	3.75	7.50	15.00
PS 668	Don't Let Up	1975	3.75	7.50	15.00
PS 678	Hot to Trot	1977	3.75	7.50	15.00
POLYDOR					
PD-1-6196	Dancealot	1979	3.00	6.00	12.00

OLYMPICS, THE

Also see THE CHALLENGERS (3); WALTER WARD AND THE CHALLENGERS.

Number	Title (A Side/B Side)	Yr	VG	VG+	NM
45s					
ARVEE					
562	(Baby) Hully Gully/Private Eye	1959	6.25	12.50	25.00
595	Big Boy Pete/The Slop	1960	6.25	12.50	25.00
5006	Shimmy Like Kate/Workin' Hard	1960	5.00	10.00	20.00
5020	Dance by the Light of the Moon/Dodge City	1960	5.00	10.00	20.00
5023	Little Pedro/The Bullfight	1961	5.00	10.00	20.00
5031	Stay Where You Are/Dooley	1961	10.00	20.00	40.00
5044	Mash Them 'Taters/The Stomp	1961	5.00	10.00	20.00
5051	Everybody Likes to Cha Cha Cha/The Twist	1962	3.75	7.50	15.00
5056	Baby It's Hot/The Scotch	1962	3.75	7.50	15.00
5073	What'd I Say (Part 1)/What'd I Say (Part 2)	1963	3.75	7.50	15.00
6501	Big Boy Pete '65/Stay Where You Are	1965	3.00	6.00	12.00
DEMON					
1508	Western Movies/Well!	1958	7.50	15.00	30.00
1512	Dance with the Teacher/Everybody Needs Love	1958	6.25	12.50	25.00
1514	Your Love/The Chicken	1959	6.25	12.50	25.00
DUO DISC					
104	The Boogler (Part 1)/The Boogler (Part 2)	1964	3.00	6.00	12.00
105	Return of Big Boy Pete/Return of the Watusi	1964	3.00	6.00	12.00
JUBILEE					
5674	The Cartoon Song/Things That Make Me Laugh	1969	2.00	4.00	8.00
LOMA					
2010	I'm Comin' Home/Rainin' in My Heart	1965	2.50	5.00	10.00
2013	Good Lovin'/Olympic Shuffle	1965	2.50	5.00	10.00
2017	Baby I'm Yours/No More Will I Cry	1965	2.50	5.00	10.00
MGM					
14505	Worm in Your Wheatgerm/The Apartment	1973	—	2.50	5.00
MIRWOOD					
5504	We Go Together (Pretty Baby)/Secret Agents	1966	2.00	4.00	8.00
5513	Mine Exclusively/Secret Agents	1966	2.00	4.00	8.00
5523	Baby Do the Philly Dog/Western Movies	1966	2.00	4.00	8.00
5525	The Bounce/The Duck	1966	2.00	4.00	8.00
5529	The Same Old Thing/I'll Do a Little Bit More	1967	2.00	4.00	8.00
5533	Big Boy Pete/(Baby) Hully Gully	1967	2.00	4.00	8.00
PARKWAY					
6003	Lookin' for a Love/Good Things	1968	2.00	4.00	8.00
TITAN					
1718	The Chicken/Cool Short	1961	6.25	12.50	25.00
TRI DISC					
105	Return of Big Boy Pete/Return of the Watusi	1962	3.75	7.50	15.00
106	The Bounce/Fireworks	1963	3.75	7.50	15.00
107	Dancin' Holiday/Do the Slauson Shuffle	1963	3.75	7.50	15.00
110	Bounce Again/A New Dancin' Partner	1963	3.75	7.50	15.00
112	The Broken Hip/So Goodbye	1963	3.75	7.50	15.00
WARNER BROS.					
7369	Girl, You're My Kind of People/Please, Please, Please	1970	—	3.00	6.00
7-Inch Extended Plays					
ARVEE					
423	(contents unknown)	1960	50.00	100.00	200.00
423 [PS]	Doin' the Hully Gully	1960	50.00	100.00	200.00

Number	Title (A Side/B Side)	Yr	VG	VG+	NM
Albums					
ARVEE					
A-423 [M]	Doin' the Hully Gully	1960	40.00	80.00	160.00
A-424 [M]	Dance by the Light of the Moon	1961	30.00	60.00	120.00
A-429 [M]	Party Time	1961	30.00	60.00	120.00
EVEREST					
4109	The Olympics	1981	2.50	5.00	10.00
MIRWOOD					
M-7003 [M]	Something Old, Something New	1966	10.00	20.00	40.00
MS-7003 [S]	Something Old, Something New	1966	12.50	25.00	50.00
POST					
8000	The Olympics Sing	196?	6.25	12.50	25.00
RHINO					
RNDF-207	The Official Record Album of the Olympics	1983	3.00	6.00	12.00
TRI-DISC					
1001 [M]	Do the Bounce	1963	20.00	40.00	80.00

OMEGAS, THE (1)

Number	Title (A Side/B Side)	Yr	VG	VG+	NM
45s					
DECCA					
31008	When You Touch Me/Froze	1959	5.00	10.00	20.00
31094	So How Come (No One Loves Me)/Study Hall	1960	5.00	10.00	20.00
31138	Falling in Love/No One Will Ever Know	1960	5.00	10.00	20.00
GROOVE					
4	I Wanna Go Home/Midnight Run	1961	3.75	7.50	15.00

OMEGAS, THE (2)

Number	Title (A Side/B Side)	Yr	VG	VG+	NM
45s					
UNITED ARTISTS					
50247	I Can't Believe/Mr. Yates	1968	7.50	15.00	30.00

OMNIBUS

Number	Title (A Side/B Side)	Yr	VG	VG+	NM
45s					
UNITED ARTISTS					
50631	It's All in Your Heart/The Man Song	1970	2.00	4.00	8.00
Albums					
UNITED ARTISTS					
UAS-6743	Omnibus	1970	10.00	20.00	40.00

ONCOMERS, THE

Number	Title (A Side/B Side)	Yr	VG	VG+	NM
45s					
GATEWAY CUSTOM					
103	Every Day Now/You Let Me Down	196?	10.00	20.00	40.00

100 PROOF AGED IN SOUL

Number	Title (A Side/B Side)	Yr	VG	VG+	NM
45s					
HOT WAX					
6904	Too Many Cooks (Spoil the Soup)/Not Enough Love to Satisfy	1969	3.00	6.00	12.00
—First pressings as "Aged in Soul"					
6904	Too Many Cooks (Spoil the Soup)/Not Enough Love to Satisfy	1969	—	3.00	6.00
—Later pressings as "100 Proof Aged in Soul"					
7004	Somebody's Been Sleeping/I've Come to Save You	1970	—	3.00	6.00
7009	One Man's Leftovers (Is Another Man's Feast)/If I Could See the Light in the Window	1970	—	3.00	6.00
7104	Driveway/Love Is Sweeter	1971	—	3.00	6.00
7108	90 Day Freeze (On Her Love)/Not Enough Love to Satisfy	1971	—	3.00	6.00
7202	Everything Good Is Bad/I'd Rather Fight Than Switch	1972	—	3.00	6.00
7206	Don't Scratch/If I Could See the Light in the Window	1972	—	3.00	6.00
7211	Nothing Sweeter Than Love/Since You've Been Gone	1972	—	3.00	6.00
Albums					
HOT WAX					
704	Somebody's Been Sleeping in My Bed	1970	3.75	7.50	15.00
712	100 Proof Aged in Soul	1971	3.75	7.50	15.00

ONO, YOKO

Also see JOHN LENNON.

Number	Title (A Side/B Side)	Yr	VG	VG+	NM
12-Inch Singles					
GEFFEN					
PRO-A-934 [DJ]	Walking on Thin Ice (3:23)/Walking on Thin Ice (5:58)	1981	3.75	7.50	15.00
PRO-A-975 [DJ]	No, No, No (same on both sides)	1981	2.50	5.00	10.00
POLYDOR					
192 [DJ]	My Man/Let the Tears Dry	1982	—	3.00	6.00
810575-1	Never Say Goodbye/(B-side unknown)	1983	2.00	4.00	8.00
883455-1	Hell in Paradise (3 versions)	1985	—	3.00	6.00
883872-1 [DJ]	Walking on Thin Ice (Remix)/Cape Clear (2 versions)	1986	3.00	6.00	12.00
45s					
APPLE					
GM/OYB-1 [DJ]	Greenfield Morning/Open Your Box	1971	200.00	400.00	800.00
—Exactly six copies made for the personal use of Yoko Ono.					
1839	Mrs. Lennon/Midsummer New York	1971	—	3.50	7.00
—As "Yoko Ono/Plastic Ono Band"					
1853	Now or Never/Move On Fast	1972	—	3.50	7.00
1853 [PS]	Now or Never/Move On Fast	1972	2.00	4.00	8.00
1859	Death of Samantha/Yang Yang	1973	—	3.50	7.00
1867	Woman Power/Men, Men, Men	1973	—	3.50	7.00
CAPITOL					
S7-18550	Never Say Goodbye/We're All Water	1995	—	—	3.00
GEFFEN					
PRO-S-935 [DJ]	Walking on Thin Ice (3:23)/Walking on Thin Ice (5:58)	1981	2.50	5.00	10.00
49683	Walking on Thin Ice/It Happened	1981	—	2.00	4.00
49683 [PS]	Walking on Thin Ice/It Happened	1981	—	2.00	4.00
—Includes picture sleeve and lyric insert					
49802	No, No, No/Will You Touch Me	1981	—	2.00	4.00
49802 [PS]	No, No, No/Will You Touch Me	1981	—	2.00	4.00
49849	Goodbye Sadness/I Don't Know Why	1981	—	2.00	4.00
POLYDOR					
2224	My Man/Let the Tears Dry	1982	—	—	3.00
2224 [PS]	My Man/Let the Tears Dry	1982	—	—	3.00
883455-7	Hell in Paradise/(Instrumental)	1985	—	—	3.00
883455-7 [PS]	Hell in Paradise/(Instrumental)	1985	—	—	3.00
Albums					
APPLE					
SW-3373	Yoko Ono Plastic Ono Band	1970	5.00	10.00	20.00
SVBB-3380 [(2)]	Fly	1971	6.50	12.50	25.00
SVBB-3399 [(2)]	Approximately Infinite Universe	1973	6.25	12.50	25.00
SW-3412	Feeling the Space	1973	5.00	10.00	20.00
CAPITOL					
(# unknown) [DJ]	Rising Mixes	1996	3.00	6.00	12.00
—Promo-only vinyl EP of six remixes from the CD "Rising"					
GEFFEN					
GHS 2004	Season of Glass	1981	3.00	6.00	12.00
POLYDOR					
PD1-6364	It's Alright (I See Rainbows)	1982	2.50	5.00	10.00
823289-1	It's Alright (I See Rainbows)	1984	2.00	4.00	8.00
—Reissue					
827530-1	Starpeace	1985	3.00	6.00	12.00

OPALS, THE (1)

Number	Title (A Side/B Side)	Yr	VG	VG+	NM
45s					
APOLLO					
462	My Heart's Desire/Oh But She Did	1954	50.00	100.00	200.00
—Original with flat (non-glossy) label					
462	My Heart's Desire/Oh But She Did	1958	10.00	20.00	40.00
—Reissue with glossy label					

OPALS, THE (2)

Number	Title (A Side/B Side)	Yr	VG	VG+	NM
45s					
BELTONE					
2025	Love/Two-Sided Love	1962	6.25	12.50	25.00

OPALS, THE (3)

Number	Title (A Side/B Side)	Yr	VG	VG+	NM
45s					
OKEH					
7188	Does It Matter/Tender Lover	1964	6.25	12.50	25.00
7202	You Can't Hurt Me No More/Rhythm	1964	6.25	12.50	25.00
7224	I'm So Afraid/Restless Lover	1965	6.25	12.50	25.00

OPALS, THE (U)

May be group (3); could be a different group.

Number	Title (A Side/B Side)	Yr	VG	VG+	NM
45s					
LAURIE					
3288	No, No, Never Again/Just Like a Little Bitty Baby	1965	3.00	6.00	12.00

ORANG UTAN

Number	Title (A Side/B Side)	Yr	VG	VG+	NM
Albums					
BELL					
6054	Orang Utan	1971	10.00	20.00	40.00

ORANGE COLORED SKY

Number	Title (A Side/B Side)	Yr	VG	VG+	NM
45s					
UNI					
55088	Orange Colored Sky/The Shadow of Summer	1968	3.00	6.00	12.00
55115	Happiness Is/Another Sky	1969	3.00	6.00	12.00
55156	The Sun and I/Sweet Potato	1969	3.00	6.00	12.00
Albums					
UNI					
73031	Orange Colored Sky	1968	12.50	25.00	50.00

ORANGE WEDGE

Number	Title (A Side/B Side)	Yr	VG	VG+	NM
Albums					
(NO LABEL)					
(no #)	No One Left But Me	1975	75.00	150.00	300.00
(no #)	Wedge	1975	75.00	150.00	300.00

ORBISON, ROY

Number	Title (A Side/B Side)	Yr	VG	VG+	NM
12-Inch Singles					
VIRGIN					
PR 2593 [DJ]	You Got It (same on both sides)	1989	2.50	5.00	10.00
PR 2667 [DJ]	She's a Mystery to Me (same on both sides)	1989	2.50	5.00	10.00
45s					
ASYLUM					
46048	Tears/Easy Way Out	1979	—	2.50	5.00
46541	Poor Baby/Lay It Down	1979	—	2.50	5.00
ERIC					
7101	Pretty Paper/Oh Pretty Woman	197?	—	2.00	4.00
JE-WEL					
101	Ooby Dooby/Tryin' to Get to You	1956	1500.	2750.	4000.
—As "The Teen Kings"; with "Vocal: Roy Orbison" credit (spelled correctly)					
101	Ooby Dooby/Tryin' to Get to You	1956	1500.	2750.	4000.
—As "The Teen Kings"; with "Vocal: Roy Oribson" credit (spelled incorrectly)					
MERCURY					
73610	Sweet Mama Blue/Heartache	1974	2.00	4.00	8.00
73652	Hung Up onYou/Spanish Nights	1975	—	3.00	6.00
73705	It's Lonely/Still	1975	—	3.00	6.00
MGM					
CS9-5	Celebrity Scene: Roy Orbison	1967	25.00	50.00	100.00
—Box set of five singles (13756-13760). Price includes box, all 5 singles, jukebox title strips, bio. Records are sometimes found by themselves, so they are also listed separately.					
13386	Ride Away/Wonderin'	1965	2.50	5.00	10.00
13386 [PS]	Ride Away/Wonderin'	1965	5.00	10.00	20.00

Number	Title (A Side/B Side)	Yr	VG	VG+	NM
13410	Crawling Back/If You Can't Say Something Nice	1965	2.50	5.00	10.00
13410 [PS]	Crawling Back/If You Can't Say Something Nice	1965	5.00	10.00	20.00
13446	Breakin' Up Is Breakin' My Heart/Wait	1966	2.50	5.00	10.00
13446 [PS]	Breakin' Up Is Breakin' My Heart/Wait	1966	5.00	10.00	20.00
13498	Twinkle Toes/Where Is Tomorrow	1966	2.50	5.00	10.00
13498 [PS]	Twinkle Toes/Where Is Tomorrow	1966	5.00	10.00	20.00
13549	Too Soon to Know/You'll Never Be Sixteen Again	1966	2.50	5.00	10.00
13549 [PS]	Too Soon to Know/You'll Never Be Sixteen Again	1966	5.00	10.00	20.00
13634	Communication Breakdown/Going Back to Gloria	1966	2.50	5.00	10.00
13685	So Good/Memories	1967	2.50	5.00	10.00
13756	Ride Away/Crawlin' Back	1967	3.75	7.50	15.00
—Part of Celebrity Scene CS9-5					
13757	Breakin' Up Is Breakin' My Heart/Too Soon to Know	1967	3.75	7.50	15.00
—Part of Celebrity Scene CS9-5					
13758	Twinkle Toes/Where Is Tomorrow?	1967	3.75	7.50	15.00
—Part of Celebrity Scene CS9-5					
13759	Sweet Dreams/Going Back to Gloria	1967	3.75	7.50	15.00
—Part of Celebrity Scene CS9-5					
13760	You'll Never Be Sixteen Again/There Won't Be Many Coming Home	1967	3.75	7.50	15.00
—Part of Celebrity Scene CS9-5					
13764	Cry Softly Lonely One/Pistolero	1967	2.50	5.00	10.00
13764 [PS]	Cry Softly Lonely One/Pistolero	1967	5.00	10.00	20.00
13817	She/Here Comes the Rain Baby	1967	2.50	5.00	10.00
13889	Shy Away/Born to Be Loved by You	1968	2.50	5.00	10.00
13950	Flowers/Walk On	1968	2.50	5.00	10.00
13991	Heartache/Sugar Man	1968	2.50	5.00	10.00
14039	Southbound Jericho Parkway/My Friend	1969	2.50	5.00	10.00
14079	Penny Arcade/Tennessee Own My Soul	1969	2.50	5.00	10.00
14105	How Do You Start Over/She Cheats on Me	1970	2.50	5.00	10.00
14121	So Young/If I Had a Woman Like You	1970	2.50	5.00	10.00
14293	Close Again/Last Night	1971	2.50	5.00	10.00
14358	Changes/God Loves You	1972	2.50	5.00	10.00
14413	Remember the Good/Harlem Woman	1972	2.50	5.00	10.00
14413	Remember the Good/If Only for a While	1972	2.50	5.00	10.00
14441	I Can Read Between the Lines/Memphis, Tennessee	1972	2.50	5.00	10.00
14552	Rain Rain (Coming Down)/Sooner or Later	1973	2.50	5.00	10.00
14626	I Wanna Live/You Lay So Easy on My Mind	1973	2.50	5.00	10.00
MONUMENT					
409	Paper Boy/With the Bug	1959	20.00	40.00	80.00
—White label with vertical lines					
412	Uptown/Pretty One	1959	7.50	15.00	30.00
421	Only the Lonely (Know the Way I Feel)/Here Comes That Song Again	1960	6.25	12.50	25.00
425	Blue Angel/Today's Teardrops	1960	5.00	10.00	20.00
433	I'm Hurtin'/I Can't Stop Loving You	1960	5.00	10.00	20.00
433 [PS]	I'm Hurtin'/I Can't Stop Loving You	1960	30.00	60.00	120.00
438	Running Scared/Love Hurts	1961	5.00	10.00	20.00
438 [PS]	Running Scared/Love Hurts	1961	10.00	20.00	40.00
447	Crying/Candy Man	1961	5.00	10.00	20.00
447 [PS]	Crying/Candy Man	1961	10.00	20.00	40.00
456	Dream Baby (How Long Must I Dream)/The Actress	1962	5.00	10.00	20.00
456 [PS]	Dream Baby (How Long Must I Dream)/The Actress	1962	10.00	20.00	40.00
461	The Crowd/Mama	1962	5.00	10.00	20.00
461 [PS]	The Crowd/Mama	1962	10.00	20.00	40.00
467	Leah/Workin' for the Man	1962	5.00	10.00	20.00
467 [PS]	Leah/Workin' for the Man	1962	10.00	20.00	40.00
806	In Dreams/Shahdaroba	1963	5.00	10.00	20.00
806 [PS]	In Dreams/Shahdaroba	1963	10.00	20.00	40.00
815	Falling/Distant Drums	1963	5.00	10.00	20.00
815 [PS]	Falling/Distant Drums	1963	12.50	25.00	50.00
824	Mean Woman Blues/Blue Bayou	1963	5.00	10.00	20.00
830	Pretty Paper/Beautiful Dreamer	1963	5.00	10.00	20.00
837	It's Over/Indian Wedding	1964	5.00	10.00	20.00
837 [PS]	It's Over/Indian Wedding	1964	10.00	20.00	40.00
851	Pretty Woman/Yo Te Amo Maria	1964	7.50	15.00	30.00
—Original title					
851	Oh Pretty Woman/Yo Te Amo Maria	1964	5.00	10.00	20.00
—Revised title					
873	Goodnight/Only with You	1965	3.75	7.50	15.00
891	(Say) You're My Girl/Sleepy Hollow	1965	3.75	7.50	15.00
906	Let the Good Times Roll/Distant Drums	1965	3.75	7.50	15.00
939	Lana/Our Summer Song	1966	3.75	7.50	15.00
1936	Pretty Paper/Beautiful Dreamer	1976	—	2.00	4.00
8690	Belinda/All These Chains	1976	—	2.50	5.00
45200	(I'm a) Southern Man/Born to Love Me	1976	—	2.50	5.00
45215	Drifting Away/Under Suspicion	1977	—	2.50	5.00
RCA VICTOR					
47-7381	Sweet and Innocent/Seems to Me	1958	10.00	20.00	40.00
47-7447	Almost Eighteen/Julie	1959	10.00	20.00	40.00
SUN					
242	Ooby Dooby/Go! Go! Go!	1956	25.00	50.00	100.00
251	Rockhouse/You're My Baby	1956	15.00	30.00	60.00
265	Devil Doll/Sweet and Easy to Love	1957	20.00	40.00	80.00
284	Chicken Hearted/I Like Love	1958	12.50	25.00	50.00
353	Devil Doll/Sweet and Easy to Love	1960	62.50	125.00	250.00
VIRGIN					
99159	Oh Pretty Woman/Claudette	1989	—	—	3.00
99159 [PS]	Oh Pretty Woman/Claudette	1989	—	—	3.00
99202	California Blue/In Dreams	1989	—	—	3.00
99202 [PS]	California Blue/In Dreams	1989	—	—	3.00
99227	She's a Mystery to Me/Dream Baby	1989	—	—	3.00
99227 [PS]	She's a Mystery to Me/Dream Baby	1989	—	—	3.00
99245	You Got It/The Only One	1989	—	—	3.00
99245 [PS]	You Got It/The Only One	1989	—	—	3.00
99388	Crying/Falling	1988	—	—	3.00
—A-side: With k.d. lang					
99388 [PS]	Crying/Falling	1988	—	—	3.00
99434	In Dreams/Leah	1987	—	—	3.00
99434 [PS]	In Dreams/Leah	1987	—	2.00	4.00

Number	Title (A Side/B Side)	Yr	VG	VG+	NM
WARNER BROS.					
49262	That Lovin' You Feeling Again/Lola	1980	—	2.50	5.00
—A-side: With Emmylou Harris; B-side by Craig Hundley					
Albums					
ACCORD					
SN-7150	Ooby Dooby	1981	2.00	4.00	8.00
ASYLUM					
6E-198	Laminar Flow	1979	3.00	6.00	12.00
BUCKBOARD					
5-1015	Roy Orbison's Golden Hits	197?	2.50	5.00	10.00
CANDELITE					
P2 12946 [(2)]	The Living Legend of Roy Orbison	1976	3.75	7.50	15.00
DESIGN					
DLP-164 [M]	Orbiting with Roy Orbison	196?	3.75	7.50	15.00
DLPS-164 [R]	Orbiting with Roy Orbison	196?	2.50	5.00	10.00
HALLMARK					
SHM-824	The Exciting Roy Orbison	197?	2.00	4.00	8.00
HITS UNLIMITED					
233-0	My Spell on You	1982	2.00	4.00	8.00
MERCURY					
SRM-1-1045	I'm Still in Love with You	1975	3.00	6.00	12.00
MGM					
E-4308 [M]	There Is Only One Roy Orbison	1965	6.25	12.50	25.00
SE-4308 [S]	There Is Only One Roy Orbison	1965	8.75	17.50	35.00
E-4322 [M]	The Orbison Way	1965	6.25	12.50	25.00
SE-4322 [S]	The Orbison Way	1965	8.75	17.50	35.00
E-4379 [M]	The Classic Roy Orbison	1966	6.25	12.50	25.00
SE-4379 [S]	The Classic Roy Orbison	1966	8.75	17.50	35.00
E-4424 [M]	Roy Orbison Sings Don Gibson	1967	6.25	12.50	25.00
SE-4424 [S]	Roy Orbison Sings Don Gibson	1967	8.75	17.50	35.00
E-4514 [M]	Cry Softly, Lonely One	1967	6.25	12.50	25.00
SE-4514 [S]	Cry Softly, Lonely One	1967	8.75	17.50	35.00
SE-4636	The Many Moods of Roy Orbison	1969	6.25	12.50	25.00
SE-4659	The Great Songs of Roy Orbison	1970	6.25	12.50	25.00
SE-4683	Hank Williams the Roy Orbison Way	1970	6.25	12.50	25.00
SE-4835	Roy Orbison Sings	1972	3.75	7.50	15.00
SE-4867	Memphis	1972	3.75	7.50	15.00
SE-4934	Milestones	1973	3.75	7.50	15.00
ST 90454 [S]	There Is Only One Roy Orbison	1965	10.00	20.00	40.00
—Capitol Record Club edition					
T 90454 [M]	There Is Only One Roy Orbison	1965	10.00	20.00	40.00
—Capitol Record Club edition					
ST-90631 [S]	The Orbison Way	1965	8.75	17.50	35.00
—Capitol Record Club edition					
T-90631 [M]	The Orbison Way	1965	8.75	17.50	35.00
—Capitol Record Club edition					
ST-90928 [S]	The Classic Roy Orbison	1966	8.75	17.50	35.00
—Capitol Record Club edition					
T-90928 [M]	The Classic Roy Orbison	1966	8.75	17.50	35.00
—Capitol Record Club edition					
ST-91173 [S]	Roy Orbison Sings Don Gibson	1967	8.75	17.50	35.00
—Capitol Record Club edition					
T-91173 [M]	Roy Orbison Sings Don Gibson	1967	8.75	17.50	35.00
—Capitol Record Club edition					
MONUMENT					
M-4002 [M]	Lonely and Blue	1961	37.50	75.00	150.00
M-4007 [M]	Crying	1962	30.00	60.00	120.00
M-4009 [M]	Roy Orbison's Greatest Hits	1962	12.50	25.00	50.00
MC-6619	Roy Orbison's Greatest Hits	1977	3.00	6.00	12.00
MC-6620	In Dreams	1977	3.00	6.00	12.00
MC-6621	More of Roy Orbison's Greatest Hits	1977	3.00	6.00	12.00
MC-6622	The Very Best of Roy Orbison	1977	3.00	6.00	12.00
MG-7600	Regeneration	1976	3.75	7.50	15.00
MLP-8000 [M]	Roy Orbison's Greatest Hits	1963	7.50	15.00	30.00
MLP-8003 [M]	In Dreams	1963	12.50	25.00	50.00
—White and rainbow label					
MLP-8003 [M]	In Dreams	1964	7.50	15.00	30.00
—Green and gold label					
MLP-8023 [M]	Early Orbison	1964	7.50	15.00	30.00
MLP-8024 [M]	More of Roy Orbison's Greatest Hits	1964	7.50	15.00	30.00
MLP-8035 [M]	Orbisongs	1965	6.25	12.50	25.00
MLP-8045 [M]	The Very Best of Roy Orbison	1966	6.25	12.50	25.00
MP-8600 [(2)]	The All-Time Greatest Hits of Roy Orbison	1977	4.00	8.00	16.00
SM-14002 [S]	Lonely and Blue	1961	150.00	300.00	600.00
SM-14007 [S]	Crying	1962	150.00	300.00	600.00
SM-14009 [S]	Roy Orbison's Greatest Hits	1962	20.00	40.00	80.00
SLP-18000 [S]	Roy Orbison's Greatest Hits	1963	10.00	20.00	40.00
SLP-18003 [S]	In Dreams	1963	25.00	50.00	100.00
—White and rainbow label					
SLP-18003 [S]	In Dreams	1964	12.50	25.00	50.00
—Green and gold label					
SLP-18023 [S]	Early Orbison	1964	12.50	25.00	50.00
SLP-18024 [S]	More of Roy Orbison's Greatest Hits	1964	10.00	20.00	40.00
SLP-18035 [S]	Orbisongs	1965	8.75	17.50	35.00
SLP-18045 [P]	The Very Best of Roy Orbison	1966	8.75	17.50	35.00
—"It's Over" is rechanneled					
KZG 31484 [(2)]	The All-Time Greatest Hits of Roy Orbison	1972	6.25	12.50	25.00
KWG 38384 [(2)]	The All-Time Greatest Hits of Roy Orbison	1982	2.50	5.00	10.00
RHINO					
R1 70711	The Classic Roy Orbison	1989	3.00	6.00	12.00
R1 70916	The Sun Years	1989	3.75	7.50	15.00
R1 71493 [(2)]	For the Lonely: A Roy Orbison Anthology	1988	3.00	6.00	12.00
SUN					
113	The Original Sun Sound of Roy Orbison	1969	3.00	6.00	12.00
SLP-1260 [M]	Roy Orbison at the Rockhouse	1961	150.00	300.00	600.00
TIME-LIFE					
SRNR 34 [(2)]	Roy Orbison 1960-1965	1990	5.00	10.00	20.00
—Box set in "The Rock 'n' Roll Era" series					
TRIP					
TLX-8505	The Best of Roy Orbison	197?	2.00	4.00	8.00
VIRGIN					
90604 [(2)]	In Dreams: The Greatest Hits	1987	3.00	6.00	12.00
—Re-recordings of his original hits					
91058	Mystery Girl	1989	2.50	5.00	10.00

Number	Title (A Side/B Side)	Yr	VG	VG+	NM
91295	A Black and White Night	1990	3.75	7.50	15.00

ORBITS, THE
More than one group.

Number	Title (A Side/B Side)	Yr	VG	VG+	NM
45s					
ARGO					
5286	Who Are You/Mr. Bad Luck	1958	10.00	20.00	40.00
DOOTO					
601	Tell Me Baby/Two Crazy Scientists	196?	5.00	10.00	20.00
FLAIR-X					
5000	Message of Love/I Really Do	1956	7.50	15.00	30.00
NU-KAT					
116/7	Knock Her Down/My Love	1959	7.50	15.00	30.00

ORCHIDS, THE (1)

Number	Title (A Side/B Side)	Yr	VG	VG+	NM
45s					
COLUMBIA					
42913	That Boy Is Messin' Up My Mind/Harlem Tango	1963	5.00	10.00	20.00
43066	Tell Me a Story/From Bad to Worse	1964	5.00	10.00	20.00
43175	Christmas Is the Time to Be With Your Baby/It Doesn't Matter	1964	5.00	10.00	20.00

ORCHIDS, THE (2)

Number	Title (A Side/B Side)	Yr	VG	VG+	NM
45s					
HARLOW					
101	I Don't Think You Missed Me/We're in Love	1962	5.00	10.00	20.00

ORCHIDS, THE (3)

Number	Title (A Side/B Side)	Yr	VG	VG+	NM
45s					
KING					
4661	Oh Why/All Night Baby	1953	100.00	200.00	400.00
4663	I've Been a Fool from the Start/Beginning to Miss You	1953	100.00	200.00	400.00
PARROT					
815	Newly Wed/You're Everything to Me	1955	100.00	200.00	400.00
819	I Can't Refuse/You Said You Loved Me	1955	62.50	125.00	250.00

ORCHIDS, THE (U)
Some of these could be group (1) or (2).

Number	Title (A Side/B Side)	Yr	VG	VG+	NM
45s					
ROULETTE					
4412	Pony Walk/Good Time Stomp	1962	5.00	10.00	20.00
4633	Good Good Time/Love Is What You Make It	1965	3.00	6.00	12.00
UNITED ARTISTS					
375	You'll Never Know/Say Yes	1961	5.00	10.00	20.00
WALL					
549	Soft Shadows/Good Gully	1961	5.00	10.00	20.00
Albums					
ROULETTE					
R-25169 [M]	Twistin' at the Roundtable	1962	5.00	10.00	20.00
SR-25169 [S]	Twistin' at the Roundtable	1962	6.25	12.50	25.00

ORGAN GRINDERS, THE

Number	Title (A Side/B Side)	Yr	VG	VG+	NM
45s					
SMASH					
2242	Babylon/Precious Time	1969	2.50	5.00	10.00
Albums					
MERCURY					
SR-61282	Out of the Egg	1970	7.50	15.00	30.00

ORIENT EXPRESS, THE

Number	Title (A Side/B Side)	Yr	VG	VG+	NM
Albums					
MAINSTREAN					
S-6117	The Orient Express	1969	20.00	40.00	80.00

ORIENTS, THE

Number	Title (A Side/B Side)	Yr	VG	VG+	NM
45s					
LAURIE					
3232	Queen of the Angels/Shouldn't I	1964	10.00	20.00	40.00

ORIGINAL CADILLACS, THE
See THE CADILLACS.

ORIGINAL CASTE, THE

Number	Title (A Side/B Side)	Yr	VG	VG+	NM
45s					
DOT					
17071	Just Like Tom Thumb's Blues/I Can't Make It Anymore	1968	3.75	7.50	15.00
17138	Snakes and Ladders/I'm So Much in Love	1968	3.75	7.50	15.00
T-A					
186	One Tin Soldier/Live for Tomorrow	1969	3.00	6.00	12.00
186 [PS]	One Tin Soldier/Live for Tomorrow	1969	3.00	6.00	12.00
192	Mr. Monday/Highway	1970	2.50	5.00	10.00
197	Nothing Can Touch Me/Country Song	1970	2.50	5.00	10.00
204	Sweet Chicago/Ain't That Tellin' You People	1970	2.50	5.00	10.00
211	Sault Ste. Marie/When Love Is Near	1971	2.50	5.00	10.00
Albums					
T-A					
5003	One Tin Soldier	1970	3.75	7.50	15.00

ORIGINAL CASUALS, THE

Number	Title (A Side/B Side)	Yr	VG	VG+	NM
45s					
BACK BEAT					
503	So Tough/I Love My Darling	1958	10.00	20.00	40.00
—Original pressings by "The Casuals"					
503	So Tough/I Love My Darling	1958	6.25	12.50	25.00
510	Ju-Judy/Don't Pass Me By	1958	6.25	12.50	25.00
514	Three Kisses Past Midnight/It's Been a Long Time	1958	6.25	12.50	25.00

ORIGINAL LAST POETS, THE
See THE LAST POETS.

ORIGINAL SURFARIS, THE
See THE SURFARIS (2).

ORIGINAL TWISTERS, THE

Number	Title (A Side/B Side)	Yr	VG	VG+	NM
Albums					
WING					
MGW-12217 [M]	Come On and Twist	1962	5.00	10.00	20.00
SRW-16217 [S]	Come On and Twist	1962	6.25	12.50	25.00

ORIGINALS, THE (1)

Number	Title (A Side/B Side)	Yr	VG	VG+	NM
12-Inch Singles					
FANTASY					
118	Blue Moon (8:27)/While the Cat's Away (7:34)	1979	3.00	6.00	12.00
45s					
FANTASY					
820	Take This Love/Ladies (We Need You)	1978	—	2.50	5.00
847	Blue Moon/Ladies (We Need You)	1979	—	2.50	5.00
856	J-E-A-L-O-U-S (Means I Love You)/Jezebel (You've Got Me Under Your Spell)	1979	—	2.50	5.00
MOTOWN					
PR-1 [DJ]	Young Train (same on both sides?)	1973	50.00	100.00	200.00
1355	Good Lovin' Is Just a Dime Away/Nothing Can Take the Place (Of Your Love)	1975	—	3.00	6.00
1370	50 Years/Financial Affair	1975	—	3.00	6.00
1379	Everybody's Got to Do Something/(Instrumental)	1975	—	3.00	6.00
PHASE II					
02061	Baby I'm for Real/Share Your Love with Me	1981	—	2.00	4.00
02147	The Magic Is You/Let Me Dance	1981	—	2.00	4.00
02724	Baby I'm for Real/The Magic Is You	1982	—	2.00	4.00
—As "Hank Dixon and the Originals"					
5653	Waitin' on a Letter-Mr. Postman/(B-side unknown)	1981	—	2.50	5.00
SOUL					
35029	Goodnight Irene/Need Your Loving (Want It Back)	1967	3.00	6.00	12.00
35056	We've Got a Way Out Love/You're the One	1969	3.00	6.00	12.00
35061	Green Grow the Lilacs/You're the One	1969	3.00	6.00	12.00
35066	Baby I'm for Real/The Moment of Truth	1969	2.00	4.00	8.00
35069	The Bells/I'll Wait for You	1970	2.00	4.00	8.00
35074	We Can Make It Baby/I Like Your Style	1970	2.00	4.00	8.00
35074	We Can Make It/I Like Your Style	1970	3.00	6.00	12.00
35079	God Bless Whoever Sent You/Desperate Young Man	1970	2.00	4.00	8.00
35085	Keep Me/A Man Without Love	1971	—	3.00	6.00
35093	I'm Someone Who Cares/Once I Have You	1972	—	3.00	6.00
35102	Be My Love/Endlessly Love	1973	—	3.00	6.00
35109	First Lady (Sweet Mother's Love)/There's a Chance When You Love, You Love	1973	—	3.00	6.00
35112	Supernatural Voodoo Woman (Part 1)/Supernatural Voodoo Woman (Part 2)	1974	—	3.00	6.00
35113	Game Called Love/Ooh You Put a Spell on Me	1974	—	3.00	6.00
35115	You're My Only World/So Near (And Yet So Far)	1974	—	3.00	6.00
35117	Touch/Ooh You Put a Spell on Me	1975	—	3.00	6.00
35119	Down to Love Town/Just to Be Closer to You	1976	—	3.00	6.00
35121 [DJ]	Call On Your Six Million Dollar Man (mono/stereo)	1977	—	3.00	6.00
Albums					
FANTASY					
F-9546	Another Time, Another Place	1978	2.50	5.00	10.00
F-9577	Come Away with Me	1979	2.50	5.00	10.00
MOTOWN					
M5-110V	Motown Superstar Series, Vol. 10	1982	2.50	5.00	10.00
M7-826	California Sunset	1975	3.75	7.50	15.00
SOUL					
SS-716	Baby I'm for Real	1969	10.00	20.00	40.00
SS-724	Portrait of the Originals	1970	6.25	12.50	25.00
SS-729	Naturally Together	1971	6.25	12.50	25.00
SS-734	Definitions	1971	5.00	10.00	20.00
SS-740	The Game Called…	1973	3.75	7.50	15.00
SS-743	California Sunset	1974	—	—	—
—Unreleased					
S7-746	Communique	1976	3.75	7.50	15.00
S7-749	Down to Love Town	1977	3.75	7.50	15.00

ORIGINALS, THE (2)

Number	Title (A Side/B Side)	Yr	VG	VG+	NM
45s					
DIAMOND					
102	At Times Like These/Gimme a Little Kiss, Will Ya, Huh?	1961	10.00	20.00	40.00
116	Summer Schoo/You and I	1962	10.00	20.00	40.00

ORIGINALS, THE (3)
CHUCK RIO was in this group.

Number	Title (A Side/B Side)	Yr	VG	VG+	NM
45s					
JACKPOT					
48007	The Whip/The Blue Kat	1959	7.50	15.00	30.00
48012	Anna/Sleepless Nights	1959	7.50	15.00	30.00

ORIGINALS, THE (4)
TONY ALLEN was in this group.

Number	Title (A Side/B Side)	Yr	VG	VG+	NM
45s					
ORIGINAL SOUND					
10	Wishing Star/Let Me Hear You Say Yeah	1960	7.50	15.00	30.00
13	Little Lonely Girl/I Still Love You	1960	5.00	10.00	20.00
—As "Tony Allen and the Originals"					

ORIOLES, THE

Also see SONNY TIL.

45s

Number	Title (A Side/B Side)	Yr	VG	VG+	NM
ABNER					
1016	Sugar Girl/Didn't I Say	1958	15.00	30.00	60.00
CHARLIE PARKER					
211	Secret Love/The Wobble	1962	5.00	10.00	20.00
212	In the Chapel in the Moonlight/Hey! Little Woman	1962	5.00	10.00	20.00
213	Back to the Chapel Again/(It's Gonna Be a) Lonely Christmas	1962	5.00	10.00	20.00
214	What Are You Doing New Year's Eve/Don't Mess Around with My Love	1962	5.00	10.00	20.00
215	It's Too Soon to Know/I Miss You So	1963	3.75	7.50	15.00
216	Write and Tell Me Why/Don't Tell Her What Happens to Me	1963	3.75	7.50	15.00
219	I Miss You So/Hey! Little Woman	1963	3.75	7.50	15.00
HARLEM SOUND					
1001	Lonely Christmas/What Are You Doing New Year's Eve	19??	—	2.50	5.00
JUBILEE					
5000	It's Too Soon to Know/Barbara Lee	1951	1000.	2000.	4000.
5005	Tell Me So/Deacon Jones	1951	500.00	1000.	2000.
5016	So Much/Forgive and Forget	1951	500.00	1000.	2000.
5017	What Are You Doing New Year's Eve/Lonely Christmas	1951	200.00	400.00	800.00
5017 [PS]	What Are You Doing New Year's Eve/Lonely Christmas	1954	250.00	500.00	1000.
5025	At Night/Every Dog-Gone Time	1951	250.00	500.00	1000.
5040	I Cross My Fingers/Can't Seem to Laugh Anymore	1951	500.00	1000.	2000.
5045	Oh Holy Night/The Lord's Prayer	1951	150.00	300.00	600.00
—Original on blue label					
5045	Oh Holy Night/The Lord's Prayer	196?	6.25	12.50	25.00
—Reissue on black label					
5045 [PS]	Oh Holy Night/The Lord's Prayer	1954	150.00	300.00	600.00
5051	I Miss You So/You Are My First Love	1951	1000.	1500.	2000.
—Red vinyl					
5051	I Miss You So/You Are My First Love	1951	200.00	400.00	800.00
5055	Pal of Mine/Happy Go Lucky Local Blues	1951	200.00	400.00	800.00
5061	I'm Just a Fool in Love/Hold Me, Squeeze Me	1951	200.00	400.00	800.00
5065	Baby, Please Don't Go/Don't Tell Her What's Happened to Me	1951	1000.	1500.	2000.
—Red vinyl					
5065	Baby, Please Don't Go/Don't Tell Her What's Happened to Me	1951	150.00	300.00	600.00
5071	When You're Not Around/How Blind Can You Be	1952	150.00	300.00	600.00
5074	Trust in Me/Shrimp Boats	1952	125.00	250.00	500.00
5076	Proud of You/You Never Cared for Me	1952	125.00	250.00	500.00
5082	It's All Over Because We're Through/Waiting	1952	125.00	250.00	500.00
5084	Barfly/Getting Tired, Tired, Tired	1952	100.00	200.00	400.00
5092	Don't Cry Baby/See See Rider	1952	375.00	750.00	1500.
—Red vinyl					
5092	Don't Cry Baby/See See Rider	1952	100.00	200.00	400.00
5102	You Belong to Me/I Don't Want to Take a Chance	1952	125.00	250.00	500.00
5107	I Miss You So/Till Then	1952	375.00	750.00	1500.
—Red vinyl					
5107	I Miss You So/Till Then	1952	100.00	200.00	400.00
5107	I Miss You So/Till Then	1963	6.25	12.50	25.00
—Reissue, credited to "Sonny Til and the Orioles"					
5108	Teardrops on My Pillow/Hold Me, Thrill Me, Kiss Me	1953	375.00	750.00	1500.
—Red vinyl					
5108	Teardrops on My Pillow/Hold Me, Thrill Me, Kiss Me	1953	100.00	200.00	400.00
5115	Bad Little Girl/Dem Days	1953	100.00	200.00	400.00
5120	I Cover the Waterfront/One More Time	1953	300.00	600.00	1200.
—Red vinyl					
5120	I Cover the Waterfront/One More Time	1953	100.00	200.00	400.00
5122	Crying in the Chapel/Don't You Think I Ought to Know	1953	20.00	40.00	80.00
5127	In the Mission of St. Augustine/Write and Tell Me Why	1953	12.50	25.00	50.00
5134	There's No One But You/Rose of Calvary	1954	12.50	25.00	50.00
5137	Secret Love/Don't Go to Strangers	1954	12.50	25.00	50.00
5143	Maybe You'll Be There/Drowining Every Hope I Ever Had	1954	20.00	40.00	80.00
5154	In the Chapel in the Moonlight/Thank the Lord, Thank the Lord	1954	12.50	25.00	50.00
5161	If You Believe/Longing	1954	12.50	25.00	50.00
5172	Runaround/Count Your Blessings Instead of Sheep	1954	12.50	25.00	50.00
5177	I Love You Mostly/Fair Exchange	1955	10.00	20.00	40.00
5189	I Need You Baby/The Good Lord Will Smile	1955	10.00	20.00	40.00
5221	Please Sing My Blues Tonight/Moody Over You	1955	10.00	20.00	40.00
5231	Angel/Don't Go to Strangers	1956	15.00	30.00	60.00
5363	Tell Me So/At Night	1959	3.75	7.50	15.00
—As "Sonny Til and the Orioles"					
5384	Come On Home/The First of Summer	1960	3.75	7.50	15.00
—As "Sonny Til and the Orioles"					
6001	Crying in the Chapel/Forgive and Forget	1959	3.75	7.50	15.00
—As "Sonny Til and the Orioles"					
LANA					
109	What Are You Doing New Year's Eve/Crying in the Chapel	196?	—	3.00	6.00
VEE JAY					
196	I Just Got Lucky/Happy 'Til the Letter	1956	7.50	15.00	30.00
228	For All We Know/Never Leave Me Baby	1956	7.50	15.00	30.00
244	Sugar Girl/Didn't I Say	1957	10.00	20.00	40.00
VIRGO					
6017	What Are You Doing New Year's Eve/Crying in the Chapel	1972	—	2.00	4.00

7-Inch Extended Plays

Number	Title (A Side/B Side)	Yr	VG	VG+	NM
JUBILEE					
5000	Too Soon to Know/Forgive and Forget//Tell Me So/At Night	1954	250.00	500.00	1000.
5000 [PS]	The Orioles Sing	1954	250.00	500.00	1000.

Albums

Number	Title (A Side/B Side)	Yr	VG	VG+	NM
BIG A					
LP-2001	The Orioles' Greatest All-Time Hits	1969	7.50	15.00	30.00
CHARLIE PARKER					
PLP-816S [S]	Modern Sounds of the Orioles	1962	25.00	50.00	100.00
PLP-816 [M]	Modern Sounds of the Orioles	1962	20.00	40.00	80.00
COLLECTABLES					
COL-5014	Sonny Til and the Orioles' Greatest Hits	198?	3.00	6.00	12.00
MURRAY HILL					
M 61234 [(5)]	For Collectors Only	1983	10.00	20.00	40.00

ORION

Also see JIMMY ELLIS.

45s

Number	Title (A Side/B Side)	Yr	VG	VG+	NM
KRISTAL					
2292/2308	I'm Saving Up My Pennies/I'm Starting Over	1985	—	2.00	4.00
2338	100 Pounds of Clay/Because He Lived	1986	—	2.00	4.00
RADIOACTIVE					
18772-1 [DJ]	Unchained Melody (same on both sides)	1987	—	2.50	5.00
STARGEM					
2465 [DJ]	Only a Woman Like You (same on both sides)	1990	—	2.50	5.00
2469	I Want You, I Need You, I Love You/Plastic Saddle	1990	—	2.50	5.00
2502	Love It Back Together/If That Isn't Love	1990	—	2.50	5.00
—Red vinyl					
2502 [PS]	Love It Back Together/If That Isn't Love	1990	—	2.50	5.00
SUN					
1142	Honey/Ebony Eyes	1979	—	2.00	4.00
1147	Before the Next Teardrop Falls/Washing Machine	1979	—	2.00	4.00
1148	Remember Bethlehem/Silent Night	1979	—	2.00	4.00
1148 [DJ]	Remember Bethlehem (same on both sides)	1979	2.50	5.00	10.00
—Yellow vinyl promo					
1151	Be-Bop-a-Lula/The Breakup	1980	—	2.00	4.00
—A-side with Jerry Lee Lewis; B-side with Charlie Rich					
1152	It Ain't No Mystery/Stranger in My Place	1980	—	2.00	4.00
1152 [DJ]	It Ain't No Mystery (same on both sides)	1980	2.50	5.00	10.00
—Yellow vinyl promo					
1153	Texas Tea/Faded Love	1980	—	2.00	4.00
1153 [DJ]	Texas Tea (same on both sides)	1980	2.50	5.00	10.00
—Yellow vinyl promo					
1156	Am I That Easy to Forget/Crazy Arms	1980	—	2.00	4.00
1156 [DJ]	Am I That Easy to Forget (same on both sides)	1980	2.50	5.00	10.00
—Yellow vinyl promo					
1159	Rockabilly Rebel/Memphis Sun	1980	—	2.00	4.00
1159 [DJ]	Rockabilly Rebel (same on both sides)	1980	2.50	5.00	10.00
—Yellow vinyl promo					
1162	Crazy Little Thing Called Love/Matchbox	1981	—	2.00	4.00
1165	Born/If I Can't Have You	1981	—	2.00	4.00
1165 [DJ]	Born (same on both sides)	1981	2.50	5.00	10.00
—Yellow vinyl promo					
1170	Some You Win, Some You Lose/Ain't No Good	1981	—	2.00	4.00
1170 [DJ]	Some You Win, Some You Lose (same on both sides)	1981	2.50	5.00	10.00
—Yellow vinyl promo					
1172	Baby Please Say Yes/Feelings	1982	—	2.00	4.00
1175	Honky Tonk Heaven/Morning, Noon and Night	1982	—	2.00	4.00
1175 [DJ]	Honky Tonk Heaven (same on both sides)	1982	2.50	5.00	10.00
—Yellow vinyl promo					
1178	That Old-Time Feelin'/Morning, Noon and Night	1982	—	—	—
—According to Sun International, this record was never released.					

7-Inch Extended Plays

Number	Title (A Side/B Side)	Yr	VG	VG+	NM
SUN					
1152 [DJ]	Stranger in My Place Greetings: Wedding Anniversary/Good Music/Great Station//Favorite Station/Best Music/Birthday	1981	10.00	20.00	40.00
—Came with insert but no cover					

Albums

Number	Title (A Side/B Side)	Yr	VG	VG+	NM
SUN					
1012	Orion Reborn	1978	7.50	15.00	30.00
—White cover, also known as the "coffin cover"					
1012	Orion Reborn	1978	2.50	5.00	10.00
—Blue cover					
1017	Sunrise	1979	2.50	5.00	10.00
1019	Orion Country	1980	2.50	5.00	10.00
1021	Rockabilly	1981	2.50	5.00	10.00
1025	Glory	1982	2.50	5.00	10.00
1028	Fresh	1983	2.50	5.00	10.00

ORION, P.J., AND THE MAGNATES

Albums

Number	Title (A Side/B Side)	Yr	VG	VG+	NM
MAGNATE					
122459	P.J. Orion and the Magnates	196?	37.50	75.00	150.00

ORLANDO, TONY

Also see BERTELL DACHE; DAWN (1).

12-Inch Singles

Number	Title (A Side/B Side)	Yr	VG	VG+	NM
CASABLANCA					
20158	They're Playing Our Song (8:06)	1979	2.50	5.00	10.00
—B-side is blank					

45s

Number	Title (A Side/B Side)	Yr	VG	VG+	NM
ATCO					
6376	Think Before You Act/She Loves Me (For What I Am)	1965	2.50	5.00	10.00
CAMEO					
471	Sweet Sweet/Manuelito (Little Manuel	1967	2.50	5.00	10.00
CASABLANCA					
967	They're Playing Our Song (Medley)/Moonlight	1979	—	2.00	4.00
991	Sweets for My Sweet/High Steppin'	1979	—	2.00	4.00

Number	Title (A Side/B Side)	Yr	VG	VG+	NM
2229	San Pedros Children/High Steppin'	1979	—	2.00	4.00
2249	Pullin' Together/She Always Knew	1980	—	2.00	4.00
EPIC					
9441	Halfway to Paradise/Lonely Tomorrows	1961	3.75	7.50	15.00
9441 [PS]	Halfway to Paradise/Lonely Tomorrows	1961	6.25	12.50	25.00
9452	Bless You/Am I the Guy	1961	3.75	7.50	15.00
9452 [PS]	Bless You/Am I the Guy	1961	6.25	12.50	25.00
9476	Hapy Times (Are Here to Stay)/Lonely Am I	1961	3.00	6.00	12.00
9476 [PS]	Hapy Times (Are Here to Stay)/Lonely Am I	1961	6.25	12.50	25.00
9491	My Baby's a Starnger/Talkin' About You	1962	3.00	6.00	12.00
9491 [PS]	My Baby's a Starnger/Talkin' About You	1962	6.25	12.50	25.00
9502	I'd Never Find Another You/Love on Your Lips	1962	3.00	6.00	12.00
9519	At the Edge of Tears/Chills	1962	3.00	6.00	12.00
9519 [PS]	At the Edge of Tears/Chills	1962	6.25	12.50	25.00
9562	Beautiful Dreamer/The Loneliest	1962	2.50	5.00	10.00
9570	Joanie/Shirley	1963	2.50	5.00	10.00
9622	I'll Be There/What Am I Gonna Do	1963	2.50	5.00	10.00
9668	She Doesn't Know It/Tell Me What I Can Do	1964	2.50	5.00	10.00
9715	To Wait for Love/Accept It	1964	2.50	5.00	10.00
Albums					
CASABLANCA					
NBLP 7153	I Got Rhythm	1979	2.50	5.00	10.00
NBLP 7209	Living for the Music	1980	2.50	5.00	10.00
EPIC					
BN 611 [S]	Bless You and 11 Other Great Hits	1961	10.00	20.00	40.00
LN 3808 [M]	Bless You and 11 Other Great Hits	1961	7.50	15.00	30.00
BG 33785 [(2)]	Before Dawn	1975	3.75	7.50	15.00

ORLANDO, TONY (2)
This is not by the same singer as the rest.

Number	Title (A Side/B Side)	Yr	VG	VG+	NM
45s					
MILO					
101	Ding Dong/You and Only You	1959	25.00	50.00	100.00
—Not the same Tony Orlando					

ORLANDO, TONY, AND DAWN
See DAWN (1).

ORLEANS

Number	Title (A Side/B Side)	Yr	VG	VG+	NM
12-Inch Singles					
INFINITY					
L33-1004 [DJ]	Love Takes Time (same on both sides)	1979	2.00	4.00	8.00
45s					
ABC					
11408	Please Be There/Mountains	1973	—	2.50	5.00
11420	If/Stoned	1974	—	2.50	5.00
ASYLUM					
45243	Let There Be Music/Give One Heart	1975	—	2.00	4.00
45261	Dance with Me/Ending of a Song	1975	—	2.50	5.00
45336	Still the One/Siam Sam	1976	—	2.50	5.00
—Clouds label					
45336	Still the One/Siam Sam	1976	—	2.50	5.00
—Dark blue cloudless label					
45375	Reach/Sweet Destiny	1976	—	2.00	4.00
45391	The Bum/Spring Fever	1977	—	2.00	4.00
45447	Business As Usual/Time Passes On	1977	—	2.00	4.00
ATLANTIC AMERICA					
99981	One of a Kind/Beatin' Around the Bush	1982	—	2.00	4.00
INFINITY					
50006	Love Takes Time/Isn't It Easy	1979	—	2.00	4.00
50017	Don't Throw Our Love Away/The Flame and the Moth	1979	—	2.00	4.00
50036	Forever/Keep On Rollin'	1979	—	2.00	4.00
MCA					
41228	Change Your Mind/When Are You Coming Home	1980	—	2.00	4.00
41283	No Ordinary Lady/Dukie's Tune	1980	—	2.00	4.00
52862	Lady Liberty/On Hold	1986	—	—	3.00
52909	Grown-Up Children/On Hold	1986	—	—	3.00
52963	You're Mine/Language of Love	1986	—	—	3.00
Albums					
ABC					
ABCX-795	Orleans	1973	3.75	7.50	15.00
AA-1058	Before the Dance	1977	2.50	5.00	10.00
ASYLUM					
7E-1029	Let There Be Music	1975	2.50	5.00	10.00
7E-1070	Waking and Dreaming	1976	2.50	5.00	10.00
INFINITY					
INF-9006	Forever	1979	2.50	5.00	10.00
MCA					
5110	Orleans	1980	2.50	5.00	10.00
5767	Grown Up Children	1986	2.00	4.00	8.00
RADIO					
90012	One of a Kind	1982	2.50	5.00	10.00

ORLONS, THE

Number	Title (A Side/B Side)	Yr	VG	VG+	NM
45s					
ABC					
10894	Everything/Keep Your Hands Off My Baby	1967	2.50	5.00	10.00
10948	Kissin' Time/Once Upon a Time	1967	2.50	5.00	10.00
CALLA					
113	Spinnin' Top/Anyone Who Had a Heart	1966	2.50	5.00	10.00
CAMEO					
105 [DJ]	Big Girls Don't Cry/Pop Pop Pop-Pie	1962	10.00	20.00	40.00
—Yellow label, black print, promo only					
198	I'll Be True/Heart Darling Angel	1961	12.50	25.00	50.00
211	Mr. 21/Please Let It Be Me	1961	12.50	25.00	50.00
218	The Wah-Watusi/Holiday Hill	1962	5.00	10.00	20.00
231	Don't Hang Up/The Conservative	1962	5.00	10.00	20.00
231 [PS]	Don't Hang Up/The Conservative	1962	10.00	20.00	40.00
243	South Street/Those Terrible Boots	1963	5.00	10.00	20.00
243 [PS]	South Street/Those Terrible Boots	1963	10.00	20.00	40.00
257	Not Me/My Best Friend	1963	5.00	10.00	20.00
257 [PS]	Not Me/My Best Friend	1963	7.50	15.00	30.00
273	Cross Fire!/It's No Big Thing	1963	5.00	10.00	20.00
273 [PS]	Cross Fire!/It's No Big Thing	1963	7.50	15.00	30.00
287	Bon-Doo-Wah/Don't Throw Your Love Away	1963	3.75	7.50	15.00
287 [PS]	Bon-Doo-Wah/Don't Throw Your Love Away	1963	7.50	15.00	30.00
295	Shimmy Shimmy/Everything Nice	1964	3.75	7.50	15.00
295 [PS]	Shimmy Shimmy/Everything Nice	1964	6.25	12.50	25.00
319	Rules of Love/Heartbreak Hotel	1964	3.75	7.50	15.00
319 [PS]	Rules of Love/Heartbreak Hotel	1964	6.25	12.50	25.00
332	Knock! Knock! (Who's There)/Goin' Places	1964	3.75	7.50	15.00
332 [PS]	Knock! Knock! (Who's There)/Goin' Places	1964	6.25	12.50	25.00
346	I Ain't Coming Back/Envy (In My Eyes)	1965	3.00	6.00	12.00
352	Come On Down Baby/I Ain't Coming Back	1965	3.00	6.00	12.00
372	Don't You Want My Lovin'/I Can't Take It	1965	3.00	6.00	12.00
384	No Love But Your Love/Envy (In My Eyes)	1965	10.00	20.00	40.00
Albums					
CAMEO					
C 1020 [M]	The Wah-Watusi	1962	15.00	30.00	60.00
C 1033 [M]	All the Hits by the Orlons	1962	15.00	30.00	60.00
C 1041 [M]	South Street	1963	15.00	30.00	60.00
C 1054 [M]	Not Me	1963	12.50	25.00	50.00
C 1061 [M]	The Orlons' Biggest Hits	1964	12.50	25.00	50.00
C 1073 [M]	Down Memory Lane with the Orlons	1964	12.50	25.00	50.00

ORLONS, THE / THE DOVELLS
Also see each artist's individual listings.

Number	Title (A Side/B Side)	Yr	VG	VG+	NM
Albums					
CAMEO					
C 1067 [M]	Golden Hits of the Orlons and the Dovells	1964	12.50	25.00	50.00

ORPHAN EGG

Number	Title (A Side/B Side)	Yr	VG	VG+	NM
Albums					
CAROLE					
CARS-8004	Orphan Egg	1968	10.00	20.00	40.00

ORPHANS, THE

Number	Title (A Side/B Side)	Yr	VG	VG+	NM
45s					
EPIC					
10288	There's No Flowers in My Garden/One Spoken Word	1968	2.50	5.00	10.00
10348	This Is the Time/Deserted	1968	2.50	5.00	10.00

ORPHEUS

Number	Title (A Side/B Side)	Yr	VG	VG+	NM
45s					
BELL					
45128	Big Green Pearl/Sweet Life	1971	—	2.50	5.00
MGM					
13882	Can't Find the Time/Lesley's Girl	1967	2.50	5.00	10.00
—Originals have black labels					
13882	Can't Find the Time/Lesley's Girl	1969	—	3.00	6.00
—Reissues (same number) have blue and gold labels					
13947	I've Never Seen Love Like This/Congress Alley	1968	—	3.00	6.00
14022	Brown Arms in Houston/I Can Make the Sun Rise	1969	—	3.00	6.00
14022 [PS]	Brown Arms in Houston/I Can Make the Sun Rise	1969	2.50	5.00	10.00
14139	Joyful/By the Size of My Shoes	1970	—	3.00	6.00
RED BIRD					
10-041	My Life/Music Minus Orpheus	1965	3.75	7.50	15.00
Albums					
MGM					
E-4524 [M]	Orpheus	1968	6.25	12.50	25.00
SE-4524 [S]	Orpheus	1968	5.00	10.00	20.00
SE-4569	Ascending	1968	5.00	10.00	20.00
SE-4599	Joyful	1969	5.00	10.00	20.00

ORR, J.D.

Number	Title (A Side/B Side)	Yr	VG	VG+	NM
45s					
SUMMIT					
105	Hula-Hoop Boogie/Lonesome Hearted Blues	1958	100.00	200.00	400.00

ORSI, PHIL, AND THE LITTLE KINGS

Number	Title (A Side/B Side)	Yr	VG	VG+	NM
45s					
LUCKY					
1009	Come On Everybody/Oh My Darling	1963	18.75	37.50	75.00
1015	Don't You Just Know It/(B-side unknown)	1964	6.25	12.50	25.00
U.S.A.					
837	Stay/Whoever He May Be	1965	6.25	12.50	25.00
841	Sorry (I Ran All the Way Home)/Whoever He May Be	1965	6.25	12.50	25.00

OSBORNE, ARTHUR

Number	Title (A Side/B Side)	Yr	VG	VG+	NM
45s					
BRUNSWICK					
55068	Hey Ruby/Don't Give Me Heartaches	1958	15.00	30.00	60.00

OSBORNE, KELL, AND THE CHICKS

Number	Title (A Side/B Side)	Yr	VG	VG+	NM
45s					
CLASS					
302	Little Chick-A-Dee/Do You Mind	1962	3.75	7.50	15.00
LOMA					
2023	That's What's Happening/You Can't Outsmart a Woman	1965	2.50	5.00	10.00
TITANIC					
5008	Quicksand/Lonely Boy Song	1963	25.00	50.00	100.00
TREY					
3006	The Bells of St. Mary's/That's Alright, Baby	1960	6.25	12.50	25.00

OSBORNE BROTHERS, THE

45s

Number	Title (A Side/B Side)	Yr	VG	VG+	NM
CMH					
1522	Shackles and Chains/(B-side unknown)	1979	—	2.00	4.00
—With Mac Wiseman					
1524	I Can Hear Kentucky Calling Me/(B-side unknown)	1980	—	2.00	4.00
DECCA					
31546	Take This Hammer/Don't Even Look at Me	1963	2.00	4.00	8.00
31595	Bluegrass Express/Cuckoo Bird	1964	2.00	4.00	8.00
31655	Charlie Cotton/This Heart of Mine	1964	2.00	4.00	8.00
31751	Hey, Hey, Bartender/Me and My Old Banjo	1965	2.00	4.00	8.00
31823	Lonesome Day/I'll Be Alright Tomorrow	1965	2.00	4.00	8.00
31886	Up This Hill and Down/Memories	1965	2.00	4.00	8.00
31977	Hard Times/A World of Unwanted	1966	2.00	4.00	8.00
32052	The Kind of Woman I Got/One Tear	1966	2.00	4.00	8.00
32137	Roll Muddy River/Making Plans	1967	2.00	4.00	8.00
32242	Rocky Top/My Favorite Memory	1967	2.00	4.00	8.00
32325	Cut the Cornbread, Mama/If I Could Count on You	1968	2.00	4.00	8.00
32382	Son of a Sawmill Man/That Was Yesterday	1968	2.00	4.00	8.00
32451	Working Man/World of Forgotten	1969	2.00	4.00	8.00
32516	Tennessee Hound Dog/Thanks for All the Yesterdays	1969	2.00	4.00	8.00
32598	Ruby, Are You Mad/Sempre	1969	2.00	4.00	8.00
32680	Listen to the Rain/Midnight Angel	1970	2.00	4.00	8.00
32746	My Old Kentucky Home (Turpentine and Dandelion Wine)/No Good Son of a Gun	1970	2.00	4.00	8.00
32794	Georgia Pineywoods/Searching for Yesterday	1971	2.00	4.00	8.00
32864	Muddy Bottom/Beneath Still Waters	1971	2.00	4.00	8.00
32908	Take Me Home, Country Roads/Tears Are No Stranger	1971	2.00	4.00	8.00
32942	Windy City/Shelly's Winter Love	1972	2.00	4.00	8.00
32979	Miss You Mississippi/Today I Started Loving You Again	1972	2.00	4.00	8.00
33028	Midnight Flyer/Tears Will Kiss the Morning Dew	1972	2.00	4.00	8.00
55274	Rocky Top (Radio Mix)/Rocky Top (Original Version)	1996	—	2.00	4.00
MCA					
40028	Lizzie Lou/Tears	1973	—	2.00	4.00
40113	Blue Heartache/You're Heavy on My Mind	1973	—	2.00	4.00
40169	Sled Ridin'/Fastest Grass Alive	1973	—	2.00	4.00
40226	Bluegrass Melodies/The Seventh of December	1974	—	2.00	4.00
40346	El Rancho/A Heartache Looking for a Home	1974	—	2.00	4.00
40509	Don't Let Smokey Mountain Smoke Get In Your Eyes/Born a Ramblin' Man	1976	—	2.00	4.00
MGM					
12308	My Aching Heart/Ruby Are You Mad	1956	3.75	7.50	15.00
—With Red Allen					
12383	Whu Dun It/Teardrops in My Eyes	1956	3.75	7.50	15.00
—With Red Allen					
12420	Ho Honey Ho/Down in the Willow Garden	1957	3.00	6.00	12.00
—With Red Allen					
12527	Della Mae/Wild Mountain Honey	1957	3.00	6.00	12.00
—With Red Allen					
12583	Once More/She's No Angel	1957	3.00	6.00	12.00
—With Red Allen					
12633	My Destiny/If You Don't Somebody Else Will	1958	3.00	6.00	12.00
—With Red Allen					
12689	Love Pains/It Hurts to Know	1958	3.00	6.00	12.00
—With Red Allen					
12762	I Love You Only/Give This Message to Your Heart	1959	3.00	6.00	12.00
12805	Lost Highway/You'll Never Know	1959	3.00	6.00	12.00
12839	Sweethearts Again/There's a Woman Behind Every Man	1959	3.00	6.00	12.00
12930	Blame Me/Lonely, Lonely Me	1960	2.50	5.00	10.00
12970	At the First Fall of Snow/Fair and Tender Ladies	1960	2.50	5.00	10.00
13045	Black Sheep Returned to the Fold/Each Season Changes You	1961	2.50	5.00	10.00
13073	Five Days of Heaven/It Ain't Gonna Rain No Mo'	1962	2.50	5.00	10.00
13098	Banjo Boys/Poor Old Cora	1962	2.50	5.00	10.00
13126	Mule Skinner Blues/Lovey Told Me Goodbye	1963	2.50	5.00	10.00
RCA					
PB-13097	Rocky Top/Old Flames Can't Hold a Candle to You	1982	—	2.00	4.00

Albums

Number	Title (A Side/B Side)	Yr	VG	VG+	NM
CMH					
4501	Greatest Bluegrass Hits, Vol. 1	198?	3.00	6.00	12.00
6206	#1	197?	3.00	6.00	12.00
6231	Bluegrass Concerto	197?	3.00	6.00	12.00
6244	Kentucky Calling Me	1980	3.00	6.00	12.00
6256	Bobby and His Mandolin	1981	3.00	6.00	12.00
9008 [(2)]	From Rocky Top to Muddy Bottom	1977	3.75	7.50	15.00
9011 [(2)]	Bluegrass Collection	1978	3.75	7.50	15.00
9016 [(2)]	The Essential Bluegrass Album	1979	3.75	7.50	15.00
—With MacWiseman					
DECCA					
DL 4602 [M]	Voices in the Bluegrass	1965	3.75	7.50	15.00
DL 4767 [M]	Up This Hill and Down	1966	3.75	7.50	15.00
DL 4903 [M]	Modern Sounds of Bluegrass Music	1967	3.75	7.50	15.00
DL 4993 [M]	Yesterday, Today and The Osborne Brothers	1968	6.25	12.50	25.00
DL 74602 [S]	Voices in the Bluegrass	1965	5.00	10.00	20.00
DL 74767 [S]	Up This Hill and Down	1966	5.00	10.00	20.00
DL 74903 [S]	Modern Sounds of Bluegrass Music	1967	5.00	10.00	20.00
DL 74993 [S]	Yesterday, Today and The Osborne Brothers	1968	5.00	10.00	20.00
DL 75079	Favorite Hymns by the Osborne Brothers	1969	5.00	10.00	20.00
DL 75128	Up to Date and Down to Earth	1969	5.00	10.00	20.00
DL 75204	Ru-Beeeee	1970	5.00	10.00	20.00
DL 75271	The Osborne Brothers	1971	3.75	7.50	15.00
DL 75321	Country Roads	1971	3.75	7.50	15.00
DL 75356	Bobby & Sonny	1972	3.75	7.50	15.00
MCA					
105	Voices in the Bluegrass	1973	3.00	6.00	12.00
—Reissue of Decca 74602					
119	Yesterday, Today and The Osborne Brothers	1973	3.00	6.00	12.00
—Reissue of Decca 74993					
125	Favorite Hymns by the Osborne Brothers	1973	3.00	6.00	12.00
—Reissue of Decca 75079					
135	Ru-Beeeee	1973	3.00	6.00	12.00
—Reissue of Decca 75204					
4086 [(2)]	The Best of the Osborne Brothers	1974	3.75	7.50	15.00
MGM					
GAS 140	The Osborne Brothers (Golden Archives Series)	1970	5.00	10.00	20.00
E-3734 [M]	Country Pickin' and Hillside Singin'	1959	12.50	25.00	50.00
E-4018 [M]	Bluegrass Music	1962	6.25	12.50	25.00
SE-4018 [S]	Bluegrass Music	1962	7.50	15.00	30.00
E-4090 [M]	Bluegrass Instrumentals	1962	6.25	12.50	25.00
SE-4090 [S]	Bluegrass Instrumentals	1962	7.50	15.00	30.00
E-4149 [M]	Cuttin' Grass	1963	6.25	12.50	25.00
SE-4149 [S]	Cuttin' Grass	1963	7.50	15.00	30.00
RCA VICTOR					
AHL1-4324	Bluegrass Spectacular	1982	2.50	5.00	10.00
AYL1-5436	Bluegrass Spectacular	1985	2.00	4.00	8.00
—"Best Buy Series" reissue					
ROUNDER					
SS-03	The Osborne Brothers with Red Allen	1981	3.00	6.00	12.00
SS-04	The Osborne Brothers	198?	3.00	6.00	12.00
SUGAR HILL					
SH-3740	Some Things I Want to Sing About	1984	2.50	5.00	10.00
SH-3754	Once More, Vol. 1	1986	2.50	5.00	10.00
SH-3758	Once More, Vol. 2	1987	2.50	5.00	10.00
SH-3764	Singing, Shouting Praises	1988	2.50	5.00	10.00

OSHINS, MILT

45s

Number	Title (A Side/B Side)	Yr	VG	VG+	NM
PELVIS					
169	All About Elvis/All About Elvis (Part 2)	1956	18.75	37.50	75.00

OSIBISA

45s

Number	Title (A Side/B Side)	Yr	VG	VG+	NM
DECCA					
32920	Woyaya/Music for Gong Gong	1972	—	2.50	5.00
32957	Move On/Survival	1972	—	2.50	5.00
32994	Ana-Bo/Wango Wango	1972	—	2.50	5.00
ISLAND					
053	Sunshine Day/Bum to Bum	1976	—	2.00	4.00
064	Dance the Body Music/Right Now	1976	—	2.00	4.00
080	The Coffee Song/The Warrior	1977	—	2.00	4.00
WARNER BROS.					
7770	Adwoa/Fire	1974	—	2.50	5.00
8031	Rokoto/Who's Got the Paper	1974	—	2.50	5.00

Albums

Number	Title (A Side/B Side)	Yr	VG	VG+	NM
ANTILLES					
7051	Welcome Home	1978	2.50	5.00	10.00
7058	Ojah Awake	1978	2.50	5.00	10.00
BUDDAH					
BDS-5136	Super Fly T.N.T.	1973	7.50	15.00	30.00
DECCA					
DL 75285	Osibisa	1971	3.75	7.50	15.00
DL 75327	Woyaya	1972	3.75	7.50	15.00
DL 75368	Heads	1972	3.75	7.50	15.00
ISLAND					
ILPS 9355	Welcome Home	1976	2.50	5.00	10.00
ILPS 9411	Ojah Awake	1977	2.50	5.00	10.00
MCA					
32	Osibisa	1973	2.50	5.00	10.00
—Reissue of Decca 75285					
43	Woyaya	1973	2.50	5.00	10.00
—Reissue of Decca 75327					
WARNER BROS.					
BS 2732	Happy Children	1973	2.50	5.00	10.00
BS 2802	Osibirock	1974	2.50	5.00	10.00

OSMOND, DONNY

Also see DONNY AND MARIE OSMOND; THE OSMONDS.

12-Inch Singles

Number	Title (A Side/B Side)	Yr	VG	VG+	NM
CAPITOL					
V-15505	Hold On (5 versions)	1989	—	3.00	6.00
V-15642	My Love Is a Fire (3 versions)	1990	—	3.00	6.00
SPRO-79419 [DJ]	My Love Is a Fire (3 versions)	1990	2.00	4.00	8.00

45s

Number	Title (A Side/B Side)	Yr	VG	VG+	NM
CAPITOL					
B-44369	Soldier of Love/My Secret Touch	1989	—	—	3.00
B-44369 [PS]	Soldier of Love/My Secret Touch	1989	—	2.50	5.00
B-44379	Sacred Emotion/Groove	1989	—	—	3.00
7PRO-79608 [DJ]	Sacred Emotion (same on both sides)	1989	—	2.50	5.00
7PRO-79608 [PS]	Sacred Emotion (same on both sides)	1989	—	2.50	5.00
—Picture sleeve appears to have been released only with promo copies					
7PRO-79683 [DJ]	Hold On (same on both sides)	1989	—	2.50	5.00
—Vinyl is promo only					
7PRO-79913 [DJ]	I'll Be Good to You (same on both sides)	1990	—	2.50	5.00
—Vinyl is promo only					
MGM					
14227	Sweet and Innocent/Flirtin'	1971	—	3.00	6.00
14227 [PS]	Sweet and Innocent/Flirtin'	1971	2.00	4.00	8.00
14285	Go Away Little Girl/Time to Ride	1971	—	3.00	6.00
14285	Go Away Little Girl/The Wild Rover (Time to Ride)	1971	—	2.50	5.00
—Altered B-side title					
14322	Hey Girl/I Knew You When	1971	—	3.00	6.00
14367	Puppy Love/Let My People Go	1972	—	3.00	6.00
14407	Too Young/Love Me	1972	—	3.00	6.00
14424	Lonely Boy/Why	1972	—	3.00	6.00
14503	The Twelfth of Never/Life Is Just What You Make It	1973	—	2.50	5.00
14503 [PS]	The Twelfth of Never/Life Is Just What You Make It	1973	2.00	4.00	8.00

Number	Title (A Side/B Side)	Yr	VG	VG+	NM
14583	A Million to One/Young Love	1973	—	2.50	5.00
14677	Are You Lonesome Tonight/When I Fall in Love	1973	—	2.50	5.00
14781	I Have a Dream/I'm Dyin'	1975	—	2.00	4.00
POLYDOR					
14320	C'mon Marianne/Ol' Man Auctioneer	1976	—	2.00	4.00
14417	You Got Me Dangling on a String/I'm Sorry	1977	—	2.00	4.00
Albums					
CAPITOL					
C1-92354	Donny Osmond	1989	3.00	6.00	12.00
C1-94051	Eyes Don't Lie	1990	3.00	6.00	12.00
MGM					
SE-4782	The Donny Osmond Album	1971	3.00	6.00	12.00
SE-4797	To You with Love, Donny	1971	2.50	5.00	10.00
SE-4820	Portrait of Donny	1972	2.50	5.00	10.00
SE-4854	Too Young	1972	2.50	5.00	10.00
SE-4872	My Best to You	1972	2.50	5.00	10.00
SE-4886	Alone Together	1973	2.50	5.00	10.00
M3G-4930	A Time for Us	1973	2.50	5.00	10.00
M3G-4978	Donny	1974	2.50	5.00	10.00
POLYDOR					
PD-1-6067	Disco Train	1976	2.00	4.00	8.00
PD-1-6109	Donald Clark Osmond	1977	2.00	4.00	8.00

OSMOND, DONNY AND MARIE

Also see DONNY OSMOND; MARIE OSMOND; THE OSMONDS.

Number	Title (A Side/B Side)	Yr	VG	VG+	NM
45s					
MGM					
14735	I'm Leaving It (All) Up to You/The Umbrella Song	1974	—	2.50	5.00
14765	Morning Side of the Mountain/One of Those Days	1974	—	2.00	4.00
14807	Make the World Go Away/Living on My Suspicion	1975	—	2.00	4.00
14840	Deep Purple/Take Me Back Again	1975	—	2.00	4.00
POLYDOR					
14363	Ain't Nothin' Like the Real Thing/Sing	1976	—	2.00	4.00
14439	(You're My) Soul and Inspiration/Now We're Together	1977	—	2.00	4.00
14456	Baby, I'm Sold on You/Sure Would Be Nice	1978	—	2.00	4.00
14474	May Tomorrow Be a Perfect Day/I Want to Give You My Everything	1978	—	2.00	4.00
14510	On the Shelf/Certified Honey	1978	—	2.00	4.00
Albums					
MGM					
M3G-4968	I'm Leaving It All Up to You	1974	2.50	5.00	10.00
M3G-4996	Make the World Go Away	1975	2.50	5.00	10.00
POLYDOR					
PD-1-6068	Donny & Marie — Featuring Songs from Their Television Show	1976	2.00	4.00	8.00
PD-1-6083	Donny & Marie — New Season	1976	2.00	4.00	8.00
PD-1-6127	Winning Combination	1978	2.00	4.00	8.00
PD-1-6169	Goin' Coconuts	1978	2.00	4.00	8.00

OSMOND, JIMMY

Youngest of the first generation of singing Osmonds.

Number	Title (A Side/B Side)	Yr	VG	VG+	NM
45s					
MERCURY					
74005	Life Is Just What You Make It/Theme from "The Great Brain"	1978	—	2.00	4.00
MGM					
14199	Santa, No Chimney/I Hope You Have a Merry Christmas	1970	—	3.00	6.00
14328	If Santa Were My Daddy/Silent Night	1971	—	3.00	6.00
—As "Little Jimmy Osmond"					
14328 [PS]	If Santa Were My Daddy/Silent Night	1971	2.00	4.00	8.00
14376	Long Haired Lover from Liverpool/Mother of Mine	1972	—	2.50	5.00
14468	Tweedlee Dee/Mama'd Know What to Do	1972	—	2.50	5.00
14687	I'm Gonna Knock on Your Door/Give Me a Good Old Mammy Song	1973	—	2.50	5.00
14770	Yes Virginia, There Is a Santa Claus/If Santa Were My Daddy	1974	—	3.00	6.00
14771	Don't You Remember/Little Arrows	1974	—	2.50	5.00
Albums					
MGM					
SE-4855	Killer Joe	1972	2.50	5.00	10.00

OSMOND, MARIE

Also see DONNY AND MARIE OSMOND.

Number	Title (A Side/B Side)	Yr	VG	VG+	NM
45s					
CAPITOL					
B-5445	Until I Fall in Love Again/I Don't Want to Go Too Far	1985	—	—	3.00
B-5478	Meet Me in Montana/What Do Lonely People Do	1985	—	—	3.00
—With Dan Seals					
B-5478 [PS]	Meet Me in Montana/What Do Lonely People Do	1985	—	2.00	4.00
B-5521	There's No Stopping Your Heart/Blue Sky Shinin'	1985	—	—	3.00
B-5563	Read My Lips/That Old Devil Moon	1986	—	—	3.00
B-5613	You're Still New to Me/New Love	1986	—	—	3.00
—With Paul Davis					
B-5613 [PS]	You're Still New to Me/New Love	1986	—	2.00	4.00
B-5663	I Only Wanted You/We're Gonna Need a Love Song	1986	—	—	3.00
B-5703	Everybody's Crazy 'Bout My Baby/Making Music	1987	—	—	3.00
B-44044	Cry Just a Little/More Than Dancing	1987	—	—	3.00
B-44176	Without a Trace/Baby's Blue Eyes	1988	—	—	3.00
B-44215	Sweet Life/My Home Town Boy	1988	—	—	3.00
—A-side: With Paul Davis					
B-44269	I'm in Love and He's in Dallas/My Home Town Boy	1989	—	—	3.00
B-44412	Steppin' Stone/What Would You Do About Me If You Were Me	1989	—	—	3.00
7PRO-79808 [DJ]	Slowly But Surely (same on both sides)	1989	—	2.50	5.00
—Vinyl is promo only					
7PRO-(# unk) [DJ]	Let Me Be the First (same on both sides)	1990	—	2.50	5.00
—Vinyl is promo only					
CURB					
76840	Like a Hurricane/I'll Be Faithful to You	1990	—	2.00	4.00
76851	Paper Roses/Think with Your Heart	1990	—	2.00	4.00
ELEKTRA					
69882	I'm Learning/Look Who's Getting Over Who	1982	—	2.00	4.00
69995	Back to Believing Again/Look Who's Getting Over Who	1982	—	2.00	4.00
MGM					
14609	Paper Roses/Least of All You	1973	—	2.50	5.00
14609 [PS]	Paper Roses/Least of All You	1973	2.00	4.00	8.00
14694	My Little Corner of the World/It's Just the Other Way Around	1974	—	2.00	4.00
14786	Who's Sorry Now/This I Promise You	1975	—	2.00	4.00
POLYDOR					
14333	"A" My Name Is Alice/Weeping Willow	1976	—	2.00	4.00
14385	This Is the Way That I Feel/Play the Music Loud	1977	—	2.00	4.00
14385 [PS]	This Is the Way That I Feel/Play the Music Loud	1977	—	2.50	5.00
14405	Cry, Baby, Cry/Please Tell Him I Said Hello	1977	—	2.00	4.00
RCA					
PB-13680	Who's Counting/'Til the Best Comes Along	1983	—	2.00	4.00
Albums					
CAPITOL					
ST-12414	There's No Stopping Your Heart	1985	2.00	4.00	8.00
ST-12516	I Only Wanted You	1986	2.00	4.00	8.00
C1-48968	All in Love	1988	2.00	4.00	8.00
C1-91781	Steppin' Stone	1989	2.50	5.00	10.00
MGM					
SE-4910	Paper Roses	1973	3.00	6.00	12.00
M3G-4944	In My Little Corner of the World	1974	3.00	6.00	12.00
M3G-4979	Who's Sorry Now	1975	3.00	6.00	12.00
POLYDOR					
PD-1-6099	This Is the Way That I Feel	1977	2.00	4.00	8.00

OSMONDS, THE

Includes records as "The Osmond Brothers." (Most of these were pre-1970, before Donny was a member of the group.) Also see DONNY OSMOND.

Number	Title (A Side/B Side)	Yr	VG	VG+	NM
45s					
BARNABY					
2002	Mary Elizabeth/Speak Like a Child	1968	2.50	5.00	10.00
2004	I've Got Loving on My Mind/Mollie-"A"	1968	2.50	5.00	10.00
2005	Taking a Chance on Love/Groove With What You Got	1969	2.50	5.00	10.00
ELEKTRA					
47438	I Think About Your Lovin'/Working Man's Blues	1982	—	2.00	4.00
69883	Never Ending Song of Love/You'll Be Seeing Me	1982	—	2.00	4.00
69969	It's Like Falling in Love/Your Leaving Was the Last Thing on My Mind	1982	—	2.00	4.00
EMI AMERICA					
8298	Baby When Your Heart Breaks Down/Love Burning Down	1985	—	—	3.00
8313	Baby Wants/Lovin' Proof	1986	—	—	3.00
8325	You Look Like the One I Love/It's Only a Heartache	1986	—	—	3.00
8360	Looking for Suzanne/Back in Your Arms	1986	—	—	3.00
43033	Slow Ride/Heartbreak Radio	1987	—	—	3.00
MERCURY					
74056	Love on the Line/You're Mine	1979	—	2.00	4.00
74079	Emily/Rainin'	1979	—	2.00	4.00
MGM					
13162	Be My Little Baby Bumble Bee/I Wouldn't Trade the Silver in My Mother's Hair	1963	3.75	7.50	15.00
13174	Theme from "The Travels of Jamie McPheeters"/Aura Lee	1963	3.75	7.50	15.00
13174 [PS]	Theme from "The Travels of Jamie McPheeters"/Aura Lee	1963	7.50	15.00	30.00
13281	Mr. Sandman/My Mom	1964	5.00	10.00	20.00
13281 [PS]	Mr. Sandman/My Mom	1964	12.50	25.00	50.00
14159	Movin' Along/Open Up Your Heart	1970	2.00	4.00	8.00
14193	One Bad Apple/He Ain't Heavy, He's My Brother	1970	—	3.00	6.00
14259	Double Lovin'/Chilly Winds	1971	—	3.00	6.00
14295	Yo-Yo/Keep on My Side	1971	—	3.00	6.00
14324	Down by the Lazy River/He's the Light of the World	1971	—	3.00	6.00
14405	Hold Her Tight/Love Is	1972	—	2.50	5.00
14450	Crazy Horses/That's My Girl	1972	—	2.50	5.00
14562	Goin' Home/Are You Up There	1973	—	2.50	5.00
14617	Let Me In/One Way Ticket to Anywhere	1973	—	2.50	5.00
14617 [PS]	Let Me In/One Way Ticket to Anywhere	1973	2.00	4.00	8.00
14746	Love Me for a Reason/Fever	1974	—	2.50	5.00
14791	The Proud One/The Last Day Is Coming	1975	—	2.50	5.00
14831	Thank You/I'm Still Gonna Need You	1975	—	2.50	5.00
14831 [PS]	Thank You/I'm Still Gonna Need You	1975	—	3.00	6.00
POLYDOR					
14348	Check It Out/I Can't Live a Dream	1976	—	2.00	4.00
UNI					
55015	I Can't Stop/Flower Music	1967	2.50	5.00	10.00
55276	I Can't Stop/Flower Music	1971	—	3.00	6.00
WARNER BROS.					
28982	Any Time/(B-side unknown)	1985	—	—	3.00
29312	If Every Man Had a Woman Like You/Come Back to Me	1984	—	2.00	4.00
29387	Where Does An Angel Go When She Cries/One More for Lovers	1984	—	2.00	4.00
29594	She's Ready for Someone to Love Her/You Make the Long Road Shorter with Your Love	1983	—	2.00	4.00
Albums					
ELEKTRA					
60180	The Osmond Brothers	1982	2.50	5.00	10.00
MERCURY					
SRM-1-3766	Steppin' Out	1979	2.50	5.00	10.00

Number	Title (A Side/B Side)	Yr	VG	VG+	NM
METRO					
M 543 [M]	We Sing You a Merry Christmas	1965	3.75	7.50	15.00
—Reissue of 4187 with one track missing and remaining contents rearranged					
MS 543 [S]	We Sing You a Merry Christmas	1965	5.00	10.00	20.00
MGM					
PM-7 [M]	The Travels of Jaimie McPheeters	1963	12.50	25.00	50.00
—Side 1: Dialogue from TV show; Side 2: Osmond Brothers tracks. AC Spark Plugs promo.					
PM-9 [M]	We Sing You a Merry Christmas	1963	10.00	20.00	40.00
—Special-products issue for AC Spark Plug dealers					
E-4146 [M]	Songs We Sang on the Andy Williams Show	1963	6.25	12.50	25.00
SE-4146 [S]	Songs We Sang on the Andy Williams Show	1963	7.50	15.00	30.00
—As "The Osmond Brothers"					
E-4187 [M]	We Sing You a Merry Christmas	1963	6.25	12.50	25.00
—As "The Osmond Brothers"					
SE-4187 [S]	We Sing You a Merry Christmas	1963	7.50	15.00	30.00
E-4235 [M]	The Osmond Brothers Sing the All-Time Hymn Favorites	1964	5.00	10.00	20.00
SE-4235 [S]	The Osmond Brothers Sing the All-Time Hymn Favorites	1964	6.25	12.50	25.00
E-4291 [M]	The New Sound of the Osmond Brothers	1965	5.00	10.00	20.00
SE-4291 [S]	The New Sound of the Osmond Brothers	1965	6.25	12.50	25.00
SE-4724	Osmonds	1971	3.00	6.00	12.00
SE-4770	Homemade	1971	3.00	6.00	12.00
SE-4796	Phase-III	1972	3.00	6.00	12.00
SE-4826 [(2)]	The Osmonds "Live"	1972	3.75	7.50	15.00
SE-4851	Crazy Horses	1972	3.00	6.00	12.00
SE-4902	The Plan	1973	2.50	5.00	10.00
M3G-4939	Love Me for a Reason	1974	2.50	5.00	10.00
M3G-4993	The Proud One	1975	2.50	5.00	10.00
MG-2-5012 [(2)]	Around the World — Live in Concert	1975	3.00	6.00	12.00
ST 90403 [S]	The New Sound of the Osmond Brothers	1965	10.00	20.00	40.00
—Capitol Record Club edition					
T 90403 [M]	The New Sound of the Osmond Brothers	1965	10.00	20.00	40.00
—Capitol Record Club edition					
POLYDOR					
PD-1-6077	Brainstorm	1976	2.50	5.00	10.00
PD-2-8001 [(2)]	The Osmond Christmas Album	1976	3.75	7.50	15.00
—Includes group, solo and duet recordings (The Osmonds unless indicated)					
PD-2-9005	The Osmonds Greatest Hits	1977	3.00	6.00	12.00
WARNER BROS.					
25070	One Way Rider	1983	2.00	4.00	8.00

OSWALD, LEE HARVEY

Number	Title (A Side/B Side)	Yr	VG	VG+	NM
Albums					
EYEWITNESS					
1002	Lee Harvey Oswald Speaks	1967	20.00	40.00	80.00
INCA					
1001	Oswald: Self Portrait in Red	1965	25.00	50.00	100.00
KEY					
880	The President's Assassin Speaks	1964	25.00	50.00	100.00

OTHER HALF, THE (1)

Number	Title (A Side/B Side)	Yr	VG	VG+	NM
45s					
ACTA					
801	Flight of the Dragon Lady/Wonderful Day	1967	5.00	10.00	20.00
806	I Need You/No Doubt About It	1967	5.00	10.00	20.00
819	What Can I Do for You/Bad Day	1968	3.75	7.50	15.00
825	Morning Fire/Ozlee Eaves Drop	1968	3.75	7.50	15.00
GNP CRESCENDO					
378	I've Come So Far/Mr. Pharmacist	1966	5.00	10.00	20.00
Albums					
ACTA					
38004	The Other Half	1968	25.00	50.00	100.00

OTHER HALF, THE (2)

Number	Title (A Side/B Side)	Yr	VG	VG+	NM
Albums					
7/2					
(no #)	The Other Half	1966	375.00	750.00	1500.
—Album has been counterfeited, but those records are translucent when held to a light, originals are not					

OTHER ONES, THE

Number	Title (A Side/B Side)	Yr	VG	VG+	NM
45s					
ABC-PARAMOUNT					
10793	Stop/Dreaming Out Loud	1966	3.00	6.00	12.00

OTHER TIKIS, THE

See THE TIKIS.

OTHERS, THE (1)

British group.

Number	Title (A Side/B Side)	Yr	VG	VG+	NM
45s					
FONTANA					
1944	Oh Yeah!/I'm Taking Her Home	1964	7.50	15.00	30.00

OTHERS, THE (2)

Number	Title (A Side/B Side)	Yr	VG	VG+	NM
45s					
MERCURY					
72602	Revenge/I'm in Need	1966	7.50	15.00	30.00

OTHERS, THE (U)

Number	Title (A Side/B Side)	Yr	VG	VG+	NM
45s					
RCA VICTOR					
47-8669	I Can't Stand This Love, Goodbye/Until I Heard It From You	1965	7.50	15.00	30.00
47-8776	Lonely Street/(I Remember) The First Time I Saw You	1965	3.75	7.50	15.00

OTIS, JOHNNY

Number	Title (A Side/B Side)	Yr	VG	VG+	NM
45s					
ATLANTIC					
2409	Keep the Faith — Part I/Keep the Faith — Part II	1967	3.00	6.00	12.00
CAPITOL					
F3799/3802	The Johnny Otis Show	1957	100.00	200.00	400.00
—Four-record set with four-pocket cover. Price is for entire set. Records alone are valued separately below.					
F3799	Can't You Hear Me Callin'/My Ding-a-Ling	1957	12.50	25.00	50.00
F3800	Ma, He's Makin' Eyes at Me/In the Dark	1957	12.50	25.00	50.00
F3801	Stay with Me/Tell Me So	1957	12.50	25.00	50.00
F3802	It's Too Soon to Know/Star of Love	1957	12.50	25.00	50.00
F3852	Bye Bye Baby/Good Golly	1957	6.25	12.50	25.00
F3889	Well, Well, Well/You Just Kissed Me Goodbye	1958	6.25	12.50	25.00
F3966	Willie and the Hand Jive/Ring-a-Ling	1958	7.50	15.00	30.00
F4060	Willie Did the Cha Cha/Crazy Country Hop	1958	6.25	12.50	25.00
F4156	My Dear/You	1959	5.00	10.00	20.00
F4168 [M]	Castin' My Spell/Telephone Baby	1959	5.00	10.00	20.00
F4168 [S]	Castin' My Spell/Telephone Baby	1959	12.50	25.00	50.00
F4226	Three Girls Named Molly (Doin' the Hully Gully)/I'll Do the Same for You	1959	5.00	10.00	20.00
F4260	Let the Sun Shine in My Life/Baby, Just You	1959	5.00	10.00	20.00
4326	Mumblin' Mosie/Hey Baby, Don't You Know	1960	3.75	7.50	15.00
DIG					
119	Hey! Hey! Hey! Hey!/Let the Sunshine in My Heart	1956	7.50	15.00	30.00
122	The Midnite Creeper (Part 1)/The Midnite Creeper (Part 2)	1956	7.50	15.00	30.00
132	My Eyes Are Full of Tears/Turtle Dove	1957	7.50	15.00	30.00
134	Wa Wa (Part 1)/Wa Wa (Part 2)	1957	7.50	15.00	30.00
139	Stop, Look and Love Me/The Night Is Young	1957	7.50	15.00	30.00
ELDO					
106	The New Bo Diddley/The Jelly Roll	1960	3.75	7.50	15.00
152	Keep the Faith (Part 1)/Keep the Faith (Part 2)	1968	2.00	4.00	8.00
153	Long Distance/Banana Peels	1968	2.00	4.00	8.00
EPIC					
10606	You Can Depend on Me/The Watts Breakaway	1970	—	3.00	6.00
10757	Willie and the Hand Jive/Goin' Back to L.A.	1971	—	3.00	6.00
—With Delmar Evans					
HAWK SOUND					
1003	Jaws/Good to the Last Drop	1975	—	2.50	5.00
KENT					
506	Country Girl/Bye Bye Baby	1969	2.00	4.00	8.00
4521	Shuggie's Blues/Cool Ade	1969	2.00	4.00	8.00
KING					
5581	Hand Jive One More Time/Baby I Got News for You	1961	3.75	7.50	15.00
5606	She's All Right/It Must Be Love	1962	3.75	7.50	15.00
5634	Queen of the Twist/I Know My Love Is True	1962	3.75	7.50	15.00
5690	The Hey Hey Hey Song/Early in the Morning Blues	1962	3.75	7.50	15.00
5707	Somebody Call the Station/Yes	1963	3.00	6.00	12.00
5790	Bye, Bye Baby/The Hash	1963	3.00	6.00	12.00
MERCURY					
8263	Oopy Doo/Stardust	1952	12.50	25.00	50.00
8273	One-Nighter Blues/Goomp Blues	1952	12.50	25.00	50.00
8289	Call Operator 210/Baby Baby Blues	1952	12.50	25.00	50.00
8295	Gypsy Blues/The Candle's Burning Low	1952	12.50	25.00	50.00
70038	Why Don't You Believe Me/Wishing Well	1953	12.50	25.00	50.00
70050	Love Bug Boogie/Brown Skin Butterball	1953	12.50	25.00	50.00
OKEH					
7332	Watts Breakaway/You Can Depend On Me	1969	—	3.00	6.00
PEACOCK					
1625	Young Girl/Rock Me Baby	1953	20.00	40.00	80.00
1636	Shake It/I Won't Be Your Fool No More	1954	12.50	25.00	50.00
1648	Sittin' Here Drinkin'/You Got Me Crying	1955	12.50	25.00	50.00
1675	Butter Ball/Dandy's Boogie	1957	12.50	25.00	50.00
SAVOY					
731	Double Crossing Blues/Ain't Nothin' Shakin'	1950	30.00	60.00	120.00
731	Double Crossing Blues/Back Alley Blues	1950	25.00	50.00	100.00
—B-side by the Beale Street Gang					
750	Cupid Boogie/Just Can't Get Free	1950	15.00	30.00	60.00
764	Wedding Blues/Far Away Blues (Xmas Blues)	1950	15.00	30.00	60.00
766	Rockin' Blues/My Heart Tells Me	1950	15.00	30.00	60.00
777	Gee Baby/Mambo Boogie	1951	12.50	25.00	50.00
780	Doggin' Blues/Living and Loving You	1951	12.50	25.00	50.00
787	I Dream/Hangover Blues	1951	12.50	25.00	50.00
788	All Nite Long/New Love	1951	12.50	25.00	50.00
812	Warning Blues/I'll Ask My Heart	1951	12.50	25.00	50.00
815	Harlem Nocturne/Midnight in the Barrelhouse	1951	12.50	25.00	50.00
824	Get Together Blues/Chittlin' Switch	1951	12.50	25.00	50.00
855	It Ain't the Beauty/Gonna Take a Train	1952	12.50	25.00	50.00
7-Inch Extended Plays					
CAPITOL					
EAP 1-940	Hum Ding a Ling/It's Too Soon to Know//Stay with Me/Ma (He's Makin' Eyes at Me)	1958	37.50	75.00	150.00
EAP 1-940 [PS]	The Johnny Otis Show	1958	37.50	75.00	150.00
Albums					
ALLIGATOR					
AL-4726	The New Johnny Otis Show	1982	2.50	5.00	10.00
CAPITOL					
T 940 [M]	The Johnny Otis Show	1958	62.50	125.00	250.00
C1-92858 [(2)]	The Capitol Years	1989	3.75	7.50	15.00
DIG					
104 [M]	Rock and Roll Hit Parade, Volume 1	1957	300.00	600.00	900.00
—Gold cover with thick cardboard and thick vinyl records. Counterfeits have noticeably thinner vinyl.					
104 [M]	Rock and Roll Hit Parade, Volume 1	1958	150.00	300.00	600.00
—Yellow cover with thick cardboard and thick vinyl records. Counterfeits have noticeably thinner vinyl.					
EPIC					
BN 26524	Cuttin' Up	1970	6.25	12.50	25.00
EG 30473 [(2)]	The Johnny Otis Show Live at Monterey	1971	7.50	15.00	30.00
KENT					
KST-534	Cold Shot	1968	6.25	12.50	25.00

Number	Title (A Side/B Side)	Yr	VG	VG+	NM
SAVOY					
SJL-2230 [(2)]	The Original Johnny Otis Show	1978	3.75	7.50	15.00
SJL-2252 [(2)]	The Original Johnny Otis Show, Vol. 2	1980	3.75	7.50	15.00

OTIS, SHUGGIE

45s

Number	Title (A Side/B Side)	Yr	VG	VG+	NM
EPIC					
10603	Hurricane/Jennie Lee	1970	—	3.00	6.00
10798	Strawberry Letter 23/Ice Cold Daydream	1971	2.00	4.00	8.00
10978	Purple (Part 1)/Purple (Part 2)	1973	—	3.00	6.00
50054	Inspiration Information/Aht Uh Mi Hed	1975	—	3.00	6.00

Albums

Number	Title (A Side/B Side)	Yr	VG	VG+	NM
EPIC					
BN 26511	Here Comes Shuggie Otis	1970	3.75	7.50	15.00
KE 30752	Freedom Flight	1971	3.75	7.50	15.00
PE 33059	Inspiration Information	1975	3.75	7.50	15.00

OTIS AND CARLA

45s

Number	Title (A Side/B Side)	Yr	VG	VG+	NM
ATCO					
6665	When Something Is Wrong with My Baby/Ooh Carla, Ooh Otis	1968	2.50	5.00	10.00
STAX					
216	Tramp/Tell It Like It Is	1967	2.50	5.00	10.00
228	Knock on Wood/Let Me Be Good to You	1967	2.50	5.00	10.00
244	Lovey Dovey/New Year's Resolution	1968	2.50	5.00	10.00

Albums

Number	Title (A Side/B Side)	Yr	VG	VG+	NM
STAX					
ST-716 [M]	King and Queen	1967	8.75	17.50	35.00
STS-716 [S]	King and Queen	1967	12.50	25.00	50.00

OUR GANG

45s

Number	Title (A Side/B Side)	Yr	VG	VG+	NM
BR'ER BIRD					
001	Summertime Summertime/Theme from Leon's Garage	1966	50.00	100.00	200.00

OUTLAW BLUES BAND, THE

Albums

Number	Title (A Side/B Side)	Yr	VG	VG+	NM
BLUESWAY					
BLS-6020	Breakin' In	1969	6.25	12.50	25.00
BLS-6021	The Outlaw Blues Band	1968	6.25	12.50	25.00

OUTLAWS

"Southern rock" band; few, if any, of their releases used the word "The" before their name.

45s

Number	Title (A Side/B Side)	Yr	VG	VG+	NM
ARISTA					
0150	There Goes Another Love Song/Keep Prayin'	1975	—	2.00	4.00
0188	Breaker-Breaker/South Carolina	1976	—	2.00	4.00
0213	Green Grass and High Tides/Prisoner	1976	—	2.50	5.00
0258	Hurry Sundown/So Afraid	1977	—	2.00	4.00
0282	Hearin' My Heart Talkin'/Holiday	1977	—	2.00	4.00
0338	Green Grass and High Tides/Holiday	1978	—	2.00	4.00
0378	Take It Anyway You Want It/Cry Some More	1978	—	2.00	4.00
0397	You Are the Show/If Dreams Came True	1979	—	2.00	4.00
0582	(Ghost) Riders in the Sky/Devil's Road	1981	—	2.00	4.00
0597	Wishing Well/I Can't Stop Loving You	1981	—	2.00	4.00
0678	Running/(B-side unknown)	1982	—	2.00	4.00
PASHA					
06550	Saved by the Bell/One Last Ride	1987	—	—	3.00

Albums

Number	Title (A Side/B Side)	Yr	VG	VG+	NM
ARISTA					
AL 4042	Outlaws	1975	2.50	5.00	10.00
AL 4070	Lady in Waiting	1976	2.50	5.00	10.00
AL 4135	Hurry Sundown	1977	2.50	5.00	10.00
AB 4205	Playin' to Win	1978	2.50	5.00	10.00
A2L 8114 [(2)]	Bring It Back Alive	198?	2.50	5.00	10.00
—Second reissue					
A2L 8300 [(2)]	Bring It Back Alive	1978	3.00	6.00	12.00
AL 8301	Outlaws	198?	2.00	4.00	8.00
—Reissue					
AL 8319	Greatest Hits of the Outlaws/High Tides Forever	198?	2.00	4.00	8.00
—Reissue					
AL 8369	Hurry Sundown	198?	2.00	4.00	8.00
—Reissue					
A2L 8608 [(2)]	Bring It Back Alive	198?	2.50	5.00	10.00
—Reissue					
AL 9507	In the Eye of the Storm	1979	2.50	5.00	10.00
AL 9542	Ghost Riders	1980	2.50	5.00	10.00
AL 9584	Los Hombres Malo	1982	2.50	5.00	10.00
AL 9614	Greatest Hits of the Outlaws/High Tides Forever	1982	2.50	5.00	10.00
DIRECT DISC					
SD 16617	Outlaws	198?	12.50	25.00	50.00
—Audiophile vinyl					
PAIR					
PDL2-1050 [(2)]	The Outlaws	1986	3.00	6.00	12.00
PASHA					
BFZ 40512	Soldiers of Fortune	1986	2.00	4.00	8.00

OUTLAWS, THE (2)

45s

Number	Title (A Side/B Side)	Yr	VG	VG+	NM
CRUSADE					
92765	Chains/(B-side unknown)	1965	7.50	15.00	30.00

OUTLAWS, THE (3)

45s

Number	Title (A Side/B Side)	Yr	VG	VG+	NM
DOT					
16512	Hold-Up/Somethin' Else	1963	10.00	20.00	40.00

OUTLAWS, THE (U)

Could be group (2); could be a completely different group.

45s

Number	Title (A Side/B Side)	Yr	VG	VG+	NM
SMASH					
2025	Don't Cry/Only for You	1966	3.00	6.00	12.00

OUTSIDERS, THE

Lead singer Sonny Geraci later sang with CLIMAX.

45s

Number	Title (A Side/B Side)	Yr	VG	VG+	NM
BELL					
904	Changes/Lost in My World	1970	—	3.00	6.00
CAPITOL					
2055	Little Bit of Lovin'/I Will Love You	1967	2.00	4.00	8.00
2216	Oh How It Hurts/We Ain't Gonna Make It	1968	2.00	4.00	8.00
5573	Time Won't Let Me/Was It Really Real	1966	3.00	6.00	12.00
5646	Girl in Love/What Makes You So Bad	1966	2.50	5.00	10.00
5646 [PS]	Girl in Love/What Makes You So Bad	1966	5.00	10.00	20.00
5701	Respectable/Lost in My World	1966	2.50	5.00	10.00
5759	Help Me Girl/You Gotta Look	1966	2.50	5.00	10.00
5759 [PS]	Help Me Girl/You Gotta Look	1966	5.00	10.00	20.00
5843	I'll Give You Time/I'm Not Trying to Hurt You	1967	2.00	4.00	8.00
5843 [PS]	I'll Give You Time/I'm Not Trying to Hurt You	1967	5.00	10.00	20.00
5892	I Just Can't See You Anymore/Gotta Leave Us Alone	1967	2.00	4.00	8.00
5955	I'll See You in Summertime/And Now You Want My Sympathy	1967	2.00	4.00	8.00
ELLEN					
503	Rickity-Boom-Bal-Aye/The Bird Rattle	196?	3.75	7.50	15.00
KAPP					
2104	Tinker, Tailor/Oh You're Not So Pretty	1970	—	3.00	6.00

Albums

Number	Title (A Side/B Side)	Yr	VG	VG+	NM
CAPITOL					
ST 2501 [S]	Time Won't Lert Me	1966	7.50	15.00	30.00
T 2501 [M]	Time Won't Lert Me	1966	6.25	12.50	25.00
ST 2558 [S]	The Outsiders Album #2	1966	7.50	15.00	30.00
T 2568 [M]	The Outsiders Album #2	1966	6.25	12.50	25.00
ST 2636 [S]	In	1967	6.25	12.50	25.00
T 2636 [M]	In	1967	7.50	15.00	30.00
ST 2745 [S]	Happening "Live!"	1967	6.25	12.50	25.00
T 2745 [M]	Happening "Live!"	1967	7.50	15.00	30.00
RHINO					
RNLP-70132	The Best of the Outsiders (1965-1968)	1986	2.50	5.00	10.00

OUTSIDERS, THE (U)

Probably not the same group as above.

45s

Number	Title (A Side/B Side)	Yr	VG	VG+	NM
KARATE					
505	The Guy with the Long Liverpool Hair/Outsider	1964	5.00	10.00	20.00

OVATIONS, THE (1)

R&B vocal group. In essence this is two versions of the same group; the later records featured former members of OLLIE AND THE NIGHTINGALES.

45s

Number	Title (A Side/B Side)	Yr	VG	VG+	NM
GOLDWAX					
110	Pretty Little Angel/Won't You Call	1964	3.75	7.50	15.00
113	It's Wonderful to Be in Love/Dance Party	1965	3.75	7.50	15.00
117	I'm Living Good/Recipe for Love	1965	3.75	7.50	15.00
300	Don't Cry/I Need a Lot of Loving	1966	3.75	7.50	15.00
306	I Believe I'll Go Back Home/Qualifications	1966	3.75	7.50	15.00
314	Me and My Imagination/They Say	1967	3.75	7.50	15.00
322	I've Gotta Go/Kiss My Troubles and Blues Away	1967	3.75	7.50	15.00
341	Happiness/Rockin' Chair	1969	3.75	7.50	15.00
342	You Had Your Choice/I'm Living Good	1969	3.75	7.50	15.00
MGM					
14623	"Having a Party" Medley/Just Too Good to Be True	1973	2.00	4.00	8.00
14705	I'm in Love/Don't Say You Love Me	1974	2.00	4.00	8.00
—As "Louis Williams and the Ovations"					
SOUNDS OF MEMPHIS					
708	Touching Me/Don't Break Your Promise	1972	2.00	4.00	8.00
712	Hooked on a Feeling/Take It From One Who Knows	1972	2.00	4.00	8.00
717	One in a Million/So Nice to Be Loved by You	1973	2.00	4.00	8.00

Albums

Number	Title (A Side/B Side)	Yr	VG	VG+	NM
MGM					
SE-4945	Having a Party	1973	3.75	7.50	15.00
SOUNDS OF MEMPHIS					
7001	Hooked on a Feeling	1972	5.00	10.00	20.00

OVATIONS, THE (2)

45s

Number	Title (A Side/B Side)	Yr	VG	VG+	NM
ANDIE					
5017	My Lullaby/Whole Wide World	1960	10.00	20.00	40.00
BARRY					
101	My Lullaby/The Day We Fell in Love	1961	10.00	20.00	40.00
EPIC					
9470	Oh, What a Day/Real True Love	1961	10.00	20.00	40.00

OVATIONS, THE (3)

45s

Number	Title (A Side/B Side)	Yr	VG	VG+	NM
CAPITOL					
5082	I Don't Wanna Cry/Loneliness Never Entered My Mind	1963	7.50	15.00	30.00

OVATIONS, THE (U)

Each of these could be by one of the above groups.

45s

Number	Title (A Side/B Side)	Yr	VG	VG+	NM
HAWK					
153	I Still Love You/Runaround	1963	50.00	100.00	200.00

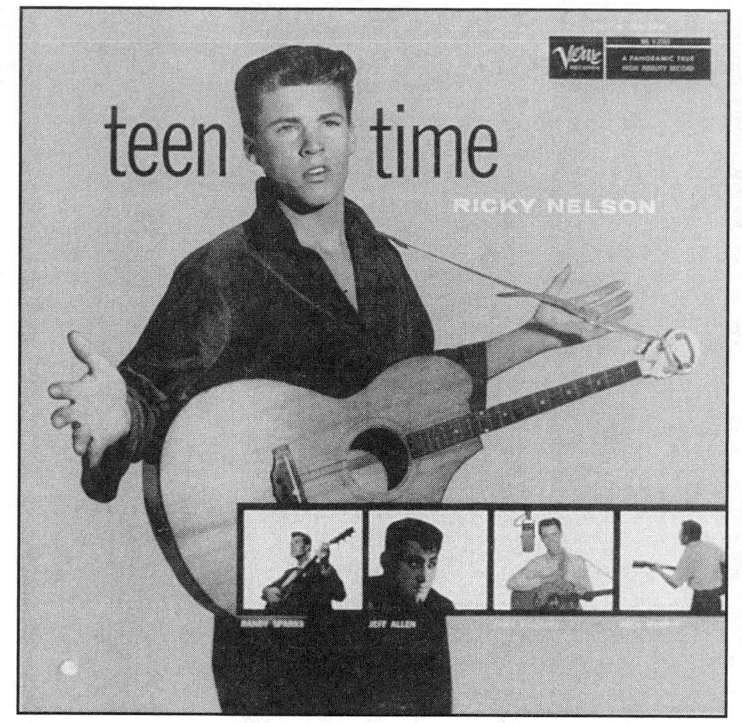

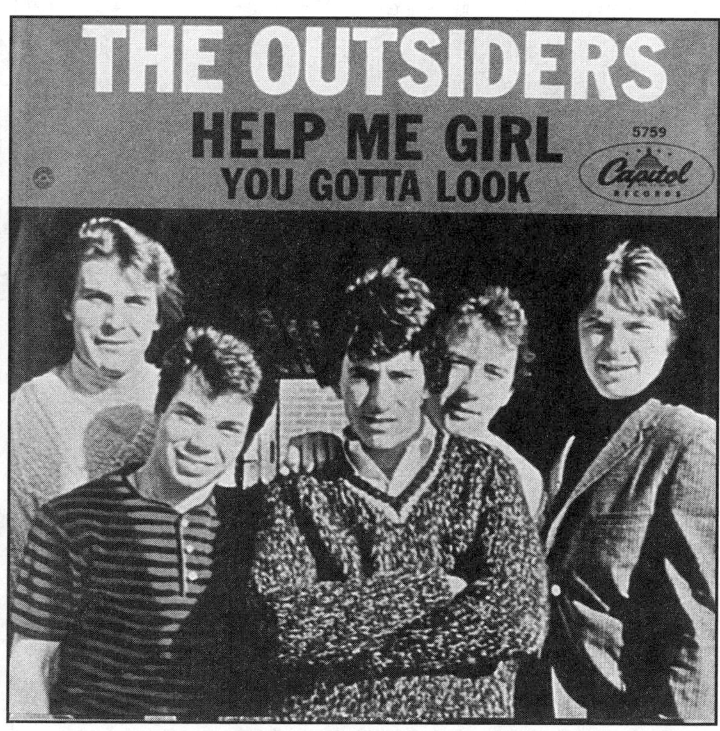

(Top left) Ricky Nelson transcended the status of teen idol and is well regarded for his music today. By far his most collectible album is this one, which appeared on the more jazz-oriented Verve label in 1957. As he had only recorded three songs for the label, the rest of this album was rounded out by tracks by other musicians including future New Christy Minstrel Randy Sparks. (Top right) In the wake of the release of her first greatest-hits album, Olivia Newton-John's first chart-topping single, "I Honestly Love You," was reissued in late 1976 with a new number, B-side and this picture sleeve. (Bottom left) Roy Orbinson's first Monument album, *Lonely and Blue*, is a three-figure album in either mono (pictured) or stereo. The stereo is especially well-regarded among audiophiles as a fine example of early stereo rock. (Bottom right) The last of four chart hits for the Outsiders was "Help Me Girl" in late 1966. It was issued with this nice picture sleeve.

JOSIE

Number	Title (A Side/B Side)	Yr	VG	VG+	NM
916	Who Needs Love/Remembering	1964	6.25	12.50	25.00

OVERLANDERS, THE

45s

HICKORY

Number	Title (A Side/B Side)	Yr	VG	VG+	NM
1258	Yesterday's Gone/Gone the Rainbow	1964	3.00	6.00	12.00
1275	Movin'/Don't It Make You Feel Good	1964	3.00	6.00	12.00
1295	January/Leaves Are Falling	1965	3.00	6.00	12.00
1327	Rainbow/Take the Bucket to the Well	1965	3.00	6.00	12.00
1362	Michelle/Cradle of Love	1965	3.00	6.00	12.00
1384	My Life/Girl from Indiana	1966	3.00	6.00	12.00
1427	Shanghai Rooster/Leaves Are Falling	1966	3.00	6.00	12.00

MERCURY

Number	Title (A Side/B Side)	Yr	VG	VG+	NM
72165	Call of the Wild/Summer Skies and Golden Sands	1963	3.75	7.50	15.00

OWEN, MACK

45s

SUN

Number	Title (A Side/B Side)	Yr	VG	VG+	NM
336	Walkin' and Talkin'/Somebody Like You	1960	5.00	10.00	20.00

OWEN-B

Albums

MUS-I-COL

Number	Title (A Side/B Side)	Yr	VG	VG+	NM
101209	Owen-B	1970	15.00	30.00	60.00

OWENS, BUCK

45s

CAPITOL

Number	Title (A Side/B Side)	Yr	VG	VG+	NM
2001	It Takes People Like You (To Make People Like Me)/You Left Her Lonely Too Long	1967	2.00	4.00	8.00
2001 [PS]	It Takes People Like You (To Make People Like Me)/You Left Her Lonely Too Long	1967	3.00	6.00	12.00
2080	How Long Will My Baby Be Gone/Everybody Needs Somebody	1968	2.00	4.00	8.00
2080 [PS]	How Long Will My Baby Be Gone/Everybody Needs Somebody	1968	3.00	6.00	12.00
2142	Sweet Rosie Jones/Happy Times Are Here Again	1968	2.00	4.00	8.00
2142 [PS]	Sweet Rosie Jones/Happy Times Are Here Again	1968	3.00	6.00	12.00
2237	Let the World Keep On a-Turnin'/I'll Love You Forever and Ever	1968	2.00	4.00	8.00
2237 [PS]	Let the World Keep On a-Turnin'/I'll Love You Forever and Ever	1968	3.00	6.00	12.00
—As "Buck Owens and Buddy Alan and the Buckaroos"					
2300	I've Got You on My Mind Again/That's All Right with Me (If It's All Right with You)	1968	2.00	4.00	8.00
2300 [PS]	I've Got You on My Mind Again/That's All Right with Me (If It's All Right with You)	1968	3.00	6.00	12.00
2328	Christmas Shopping/One of Everything You Got	1968	2.00	4.00	8.00
2330	Turkish Holiday/Things I Saw Happening at the Fountain	1968	2.00	4.00	8.00
2377	Who's Gonna Mow Your Grass/There's Gotta Be Some Chances Made	1969	2.00	4.00	8.00
2377 [PS]	Who's Gonna Mow Your Grass/There's Gotta Be Some Chances Made	1969	3.00	6.00	12.00
2485	Johnny B. Goode/Maybe If I Close My Eyes (It'll Go Away)	1969	2.00	4.00	8.00
2485 [PS]	Johnny B. Goode/Maybe If I Close My Eyes (It'll Go Away)	1969	3.00	6.00	12.00
2570	Tall Dark Stranger/Sing That Kind of Song	1969	2.00	4.00	8.00
2570 [PS]	Tall Dark Stranger/Sing That Kind of Song	1969	3.00	6.00	12.00
2646	Big in Vegas/White Satin Bed	1969	2.00	4.00	8.00
2646 [PS]	Big in Vegas/White Satin Bed	1969	3.00	6.00	12.00
2783	The Kansas City Song/I'd Love to Be Your Man	1970	2.00	4.00	8.00
2783 [PS]	The Kansas City Song/I'd Love to Be Your Man	1970	2.50	5.00	10.00
2947	I Wouldn't Live in New York City (If They Gave Me the Whole Dang Town)/No Milk and Honey in Baltimore	1970	2.00	4.00	8.00
2947 [PS]	I Wouldn't Live in New York City (If They Gave Me the Whole Dang Town)/No Milk and Honey in Baltimore	1970	2.50	5.00	10.00
2962	Buckaroo/Okie from Muskogee	1970	3.00	6.00	12.00
—As "Buck Owens' Bakersfield Brass"					
3011	Act Naturally/My Heart Skips a Beat	1971	3.00	6.00	12.00
—As "Buck Owens' Bakersfield Brass"					
3023	Bridge Over Troubled Water/(I'm Goin') Home	1971	—	3.00	6.00
3023 [PS]	Bridge Over Troubled Water/(I'm Goin') Home	1971	2.50	5.00	10.00
3066	Cajun Brass/Waitin' in Your Welfare Line	1971	2.50	5.00	10.00
—As "Buck Owens' Bakersfield Brass"					
3096	Ruby (Are You Mad)/Heartbreak Mountain	1971	—	3.00	6.00
3164	Rollin' in My Sweet Baby's Arms/Corn Likker	1971	—	3.00	6.00
3164 [PS]	Rollin' in My Sweet Baby's Arms/Corn Likker	1971	2.50	5.00	10.00
3215	Too Old to Cut the Mustard/Wham Bam	1971	—	3.00	6.00
—As "Buck and Buddy"					
3215 [PS]	Too Old to Cut the Mustard/Wham Bam	1971	2.50	5.00	10.00
3262	I'll Still Be Waiting for You/Full Time Daddy	1972	—	3.00	6.00
3314	Made in Japan/Black Texas Dirt	1972	—	3.00	6.00
3429	You Ain't Gonna Have Ol' Buck to Kick Around No More/I Love You So Much It Hurts	1972	—	3.00	6.00
3504	In the Palm of Your Hand/Get Out of Town Before Sundown	1972	—	3.00	6.00
3563	Ain't It Amazing, Gracie/The Good Old Days	1973	—	3.00	6.00
3688	Arms Full of Empty/Songwriter's Lament	1973	—	3.00	6.00
3769	Big Game Hunter/That Loving Feeling	1973	—	3.00	6.00
F3824	Come Back/I Know What It Means	1957	5.00	10.00	20.00
3841	On the Cover of the Music City News/Stony Mountain, West Virginia	1974	—	3.00	6.00
3907	(It's a) Monsters' Holiday/Great Expectations	1974	—	3.00	6.00
F3957	Sweet Thing/I Only Know That I Love You So	1957	5.00	10.00	20.00
3976	Great Expectations/Let the Fun Begin	1974	—	3.00	6.00
4043	41st Street Lonely Hearts Club/Weekend Daddy	1975	—	3.00	6.00
F4090	I'll Take a Chance on Loving You/Walk the Floor	1958	5.00	10.00	20.00
4138	The Battle of New Orleans/Run Him to the Roundhouse Nellie	1975	—	3.00	6.00
F4172	Second Fiddle/Everlasting Love	1959	5.00	10.00	20.00
4181	Meanwhile Back at the Ranch/Country Singer's Prayer	1976	—	3.00	6.00
F4245	Under Your Spell Again/Tired of Livin'	1959	5.00	10.00	20.00
4337	Above and Beyond/Till These Dreams Come True	1960	3.75	7.50	15.00
4412	Excuse Me (I Think I've Got a Heartache)/I've Got a Right to Know	1960	3.75	7.50	15.00
4496	Foolin' Around/High As the Mountains	1961	3.75	7.50	15.00
4602	Under the Influence of Love/Bad Dreams	1961	3.75	7.50	15.00
4679	Nobody's Fool But Yours/Mirror Mirror on the Wall	1962	3.75	7.50	15.00
4765	Save the Last Dance for Me/King of Fools	1962	3.75	7.50	15.00
4826	Kickin' Our Hearts Around/I Can't Stop (My Lovin' You)	1962	3.75	7.50	15.00
4872	You're for Me/House Down the Block	1962	3.75	7.50	15.00
4937	Act Naturally/Over and Over Again	1963	3.75	7.50	15.00
5025	Love's Gonna Live Here/Getting Used to Losing You	1963	3.00	6.00	12.00
5136	My Heart Skips a Beat/Together Again	1964	3.00	6.00	12.00
5240	I Don't Care (Just As Long As You Love Me)/Don't Let Her Know	1964	3.00	6.00	12.00
5336	I've Got a Tiger by the Tail/Cryin' Time	1965	2.50	5.00	10.00
5336 [PS]	I've Got a Tiger by the Tail/Cryin' Time	1965	3.75	7.50	15.00
5410	Before You Go/No One But You	1965	2.50	5.00	10.00
5410 [PS]	Before You Go/No One But You	1965	3.75	7.50	15.00
5465	Only You (Can Break My Heart)/Gonna Have Love	1965	2.50	5.00	10.00
5465 [PS]	Only You (Can Break My Heart)/Gonna Have Love	1965	3.75	7.50	15.00
5517	Buckaroo/If You Want a Love	1965	2.50	5.00	10.00
5537	Santa Looked a Lot Like Daddy/All I Want for Christmas Dear Is You	1965	2.50	5.00	10.00
5537	Santa Looked A Lot Like Daddy/All I Want For Christmas Dear Is You	1973	—	2.00	4.00
—Orange label, "Capitol" at bottom					
5537 [PS]	Santa Looked a Lot Like Daddy/All I Want for Christmas Dear Is You	1965	3.75	7.50	15.00
5566	Waitin' in Your Welfare Line/In the Palm of Your Hand	1965	2.50	5.00	10.00
5647	Think of Me/Heart of Glass	1966	2.50	5.00	10.00
5647 [PS]	Think of Me/Heart of Glass	1966	3.75	7.50	15.00
5705	Open Up Your Heart/No More Me and You	1966	2.50	5.00	10.00
5705 [PS]	Open Up Your Heart/No More Me and You	1966	3.75	7.50	15.00
5811	Where Does the Good Times Go/The Way That I Love You	1967	2.00	4.00	8.00
5811 [PS]	Where Does the Good Times Go/The Way That I Love You	1967	3.00	6.00	12.00
5865	Sam's Place/Don't Ever Tell Me Goodbye	1967	2.00	4.00	8.00
5865 [PS]	Sam's Place/Don't Ever Tell Me Goodbye	1967	3.00	6.00	12.00
5942	Your Tender Loving Care/What a Liar I Am	1967	2.00	4.00	8.00
5942 [PS]	Your Tender Loving Care/What a Liar I Am	1967	3.00	6.00	12.00
B-44248	Hot Dog/Second Fiddle	1988	—	2.00	4.00
B-44248 [PS]	Hot Dog/Second Fiddle	1988	—	2.50	5.00
B-44295	A-11/Sweethearts in Heaven	1989	—	2.00	4.00
B-44356	Put a Quarter in the Jukebox/Don't Let Her Know	1989	—	2.00	4.00
B-44409	Act Naturally/The Key's in the Mailbox	1989	3.75	7.50	15.00
—A-side with Ringo Starr					
7PRO-79805 [DJ]	Gonna Have Love (same on both sides)	1989	2.50	5.00	10.00
—Vinyl is promo only					

DIXIE

Number	Title (A Side/B Side)	Yr	VG	VG+	NM
505	Hot Dog/Rhythm and Booze	1956	100.00	200.00	400.00
—As "Corky Jones"					

PEP

Number	Title (A Side/B Side)	Yr	VG	VG+	NM
105	It Don't Show on Me/Down on the Corner of Love	1956	12.50	25.00	50.00
106	The House Down the Block/Right After the Dance	1956	12.50	25.00	50.00
107	Hot Dog/Rhythm and Booze	1956	62.50	125.00	250.00
—As "Corky Jones"					
109	There Goes My Love/Sweethearts in Heaven	1957	12.50	25.00	50.00

REPRISE

Number	Title (A Side/B Side)	Yr	VG	VG+	NM
27964	Streets of Bakersfield/One More Name	1988	—	—	3.00
—With Dwight Yoakam					
27964 [PS]	Streets of Bakersfield/One More Name	1988	—	2.00	4.00

STARDAY

Number	Title (A Side/B Side)	Yr	VG	VG+	NM
588	Down on the Corner of Love/Right After the Dance	1962	3.75	7.50	15.00
7010	Sweethearts in Heaven/Down on the Corner of Love	196?	—	2.50	5.00
8004	Sweethearts in Heaven/Down on the Corner of Love	197?	—	2.00	4.00

WARNER BROS.

Number	Title (A Side/B Side)	Yr	VG	VG+	NM
8223	Hollywood Waltz/Rain on Your Parade	1976	—	2.50	5.00
8255	California Okie/Child Support	1976	—	2.50	5.00
8316	World Famous Holiday Inn/He Don't Deserve You Anymore	1977	2.50	5.00	10.00
8316	World Famous Paradise Inn/He Don't Deserve You Anymore	1977	—	2.50	5.00
8395	It's Been a Long, Long Time/Rain on Your Parade	1977	—	2.50	5.00
8433	Our Old Mansion/How Come My God Don't Bark	1977	—	2.50	5.00
8486	Let the Good Times Roll/Texas Tornado	1977	—	2.50	5.00
8614	Nights Are Forever Without You/When I Need You	1978	—	2.00	4.00
8701	Do You Wanna Make Love/Seasons of My Heart	1978	—	2.00	4.00
8830	Play Together Again Again/He Don't Deserve You Anymore	1979	—	2.00	4.00
—A-side with Emmylou Harris					
49046	Hangin' In and Hangin' On/Sweet Molly Brown's	1979	—	2.00	4.00
49118	Let Jesse Rob the Train/Victim of Life's Circumstances	1979	—	2.00	4.00
49200	Love Is a Warm Cowboy/I Don't Want to Live in San Francisco	1980	—	2.00	4.00
49278	Moonlight and Magnolia/Nickels and Dimes	1980	—	2.00	4.00
49651	Without You/Love Don't Make the Bars	1981	—	2.00	4.00

7-Inch Extended Plays

CAPITOL

Number	Title (A Side/B Side)	Yr	VG	VG+	NM
R-5446	Memphis/Let the Bad Times Roll On//Fallin' for You/If You Fall Out of Love	1965	3.75	7.50	15.00
R-5446 [PS]	4-By Buck Owens	1965	6.25	12.50	25.00

Albums

CAPITOL

Number	Title (A Side/B Side)	Yr	VG	VG+	NM
ST-131	I've Got You on My Mind Again	1969	5.00	10.00	20.00
SKAO-145	The Best of Buck Owens, Volume 3	1969	5.00	10.00	20.00
ST-194	Anywhere U.S.A.	1969	5.00	10.00	20.00
ST-212	Tall Dark Stranger	1969	5.00	10.00	20.00
ST-232	Buck Owens in London	1969	5.00	10.00	20.00
SWBB-257 [(2)]	Close-Up	1969	5.00	10.00	20.00
—Reissue of "Together Again" and "No One But You"					
ST-439	Your Mother's Prayer	1970	5.00	10.00	20.00
ST-476	The Kansas City Song	1970	5.00	10.00	20.00
STBB-486 [(2)]	A Merry "Hee Haw" Christmas	1970	6.25	12.50	25.00
STCL-574 [(3)]	Buck Owens	1970	10.00	20.00	40.00
ST-628	I Wouldn't Live in New York City	1970	5.00	10.00	20.00
ST-685	Bridge Over Troubled Water	1971	3.75	7.50	15.00
ST 1482 [S]	Buck Owens Sings Harlan Howard	1961	12.50	25.00	50.00
T 1482 [M]	Buck Owens Sings Harlan Howard	1961	10.00	20.00	40.00
DT 1489 [R]	Under Your Spell Again	1968	6.25	12.50	25.00
T 1489 [M]	Under Your Spell Again	1961	10.00	20.00	40.00
ST 1777 [S]	You're for Me	1962	12.50	25.00	50.00
T 1777 [M]	You're for Me	1962	10.00	20.00	40.00
ST 1879 [S]	On the Bandstand	1963	12.50	25.00	50.00
T 1879 [M]	On the Bandstand	1963	10.00	20.00	40.00
ST 1989 [S]	Buck Owens Sings Tommy Collins	1963	12.50	25.00	50.00
T 1989 [M]	Buck Owens Sings Tommy Collins	1963	10.00	20.00	40.00
ST 2105 [S]	The Best of Buck Owens	1964	7.50	15.00	30.00
T 2105 [M]	The Best of Buck Owens	1964	6.25	12.50	25.00
ST 2135 [S]	Together Again/My Heart Skips a Beat	1964	7.50	15.00	30.00
T 2135 [M]	Together Again/My Heart Skips a Beat	1964	6.25	12.50	25.00
ST 2186 [S]	I Don't Care	1964	7.50	15.00	30.00
T 2186 [M]	I Don't Care	1964	6.25	12.50	25.00
ST 2283 [S]	I've Got a Tiger by the Tail	1965	7.50	15.00	30.00
T 2283 [M]	I've Got a Tiger by the Tail	1965	6.25	12.50	25.00
ST 2353 [S]	Before You Go	1965	7.50	15.00	30.00
T 2353 [M]	Before You Go	1965	6.25	12.50	25.00
ST 2367 [S]	The Instrumental Hits of Buck Owens & the Buckaroos	1965	7.50	15.00	30.00
T 2367 [M]	The Instrumental Hits of Buck Owens & the Buckaroos	1965	6.25	12.50	25.00
ST 2396 [S]	Christmas with Buck Owens and His Buckaroos	1965	7.50	15.00	30.00
T 2396 [M]	Christmas with Buck Owens and His Buckaroos	1965	5.00	10.00	20.00
ST 2443 [S]	Roll Out the Red Carpet for Buck Owens & The Buckaroos	1966	6.25	12.50	25.00
T 2443 [M]	Roll Out the Red Carpet for Buck Owens & The Buckaroos	1966	5.00	10.00	20.00
ST 2497 [S]	Dust on Mother's Bible	1966	6.25	12.50	25.00
T 2497 [M]	Dust on Mother's Bible	1966	5.00	10.00	20.00
ST 2556 [S]	Carnegie Hall Concert	1966	6.25	12.50	25.00
T 2556 [M]	Carnegie Hall Concert	1966	5.00	10.00	20.00
ST 2640 [S]	Open Up Your Heart	1967	6.25	12.50	25.00
T 2640 [M]	Open Up Your Heart	1967	5.00	10.00	20.00
ST 2715 [S]	Buck Owens and His Buckaroos in Japan	1967	6.25	12.50	25.00
T 2715 [M]	Buck Owens and His Buckaroos in Japan	1967	5.00	10.00	20.00
ST 2760 [S]	Your Tender Loving Care	1967	6.25	12.50	25.00
T 2760 [M]	Your Tender Loving Care	1967	6.25	12.50	25.00
ST 2841 [S]	It Takes People Like You to Make People Like Me	1968	6.25	12.50	25.00
T 2841 [M]	It Takes People Like You to Make People Like Me	1968	10.00	20.00	40.00
ST 2897	The Best of Buck Owens, Vol. 2	1968	6.25	12.50	25.00
ST 2902	A Night on the Town	1968	6.25	12.50	25.00
ST 2962	Sweet Rosie Jones	1968	6.25	12.50	25.00
ST 2977	Christmas Shopping	1968	6.25	12.50	25.00
SPRO 2980/1 [DJ]	Minute Masters	1966	12.50	25.00	50.00
—Promo-only excerpts of 24 songs					
ST 2994	Buck Owens, The Guitar Player	1968	6.25	12.50	25.00
ST-11105	Live at the White House	1972	3.75	7.50	15.00
ST-11136	In the Palm of Your Hand	1973	3.75	7.50	15.00
SMAS-11180	Ain't It Amazing, Gracie	1973	3.75	7.50	15.00
ST-11222	Arms Full of Empty	1972	3.75	7.50	15.00
ST-11332	Monster's Holiday	1974	3.75	7.50	15.00
ST-11390	Weekend Daddy	1974	3.75	7.50	15.00
ST-11471	The Best of Buck Owens, Volume 6	1976	3.75	7.50	15.00
C1-91132	Hot Dog!	1988	3.00	6.00	12.00
C1-92893	Act Naturally	1989	3.75	7.50	15.00

COUNTRY MUSIC FOUNDATION

Number	Title (A Side/B Side)	Yr	VG	VG+	NM
CMF-012	Live at Carnegie Hall	198?	3.00	6.00	12.00

LABREA

Number	Title (A Side/B Side)	Yr	VG	VG+	NM
1017 [M]	Buck Owens	1961	25.00	50.00	100.00
8017 [S]	Buck Owens	1961	37.50	75.00	150.00

STARDAY

Number	Title (A Side/B Side)	Yr	VG	VG+	NM
SLP-172	The Fabulous Country Music Sound of Buck Owens	1962	12.50	25.00	50.00
SLP-324	Coutnry Hit Maker #1	1964	6.25	12.50	25.00

WARNER BROS.

Number	Title (A Side/B Side)	Yr	VG	VG+	NM
BS 2952	Buck 'Em	1976	3.00	6.00	12.00
BS 3087	Our Old Mansion	1977	3.00	6.00	12.00

OWENS, BUCK, AND ROSE MADDOX

45s

CAPITOL

Number	Title (A Side/B Side)	Yr	VG	VG+	NM
4550	Mental Cruelty/Loose Talk	1961	3.75	7.50	15.00
4992	We're the Talk of the Town/Sweethearts in Heaven	1963	3.75	7.50	15.00

OWENS, BUCK, AND SUSAN RAYE

45s

CAPITOL

Number	Title (A Side/B Side)	Yr	VG	VG+	NM
2731	We're Gonna Get Together/Everybody Needs Somebody	1970	2.00	4.00	8.00
2731 [PS]	We're Gonna Get Together/Everybody Needs Somebody	1970	2.50	5.00	10.00
2791	Togetherness/Fallin' for You	1970	2.00	4.00	8.00
2791 [PS]	Togetherness/Fallin' for You	1970	2.50	5.00	10.00
2871	The Great White Horse/Your Tender Loving Care	1970	2.00	4.00	8.00
2871 [PS]	The Great White Horse/Your Tender Loving Care	1970	2.50	5.00	10.00
3225	Santa's Gonna Come in a Stagecoach/One of Everything You Got	1971	2.00	4.00	8.00
3368	Looking Back to See/Cryin' Time	1972	—	3.00	6.00
3368 [PS]	Looking Back to See/Cryin' Time	1972	2.50	5.00	10.00
3601	The Good Old Days (Are Here Again)/When You Get to Heaven (I'll Be There)	1973	—	3.00	6.00
4100	Love Is Strange/Sweethearts in Heaven	1975	—	3.00	6.00

Albums

CAPITOL

Number	Title (A Side/B Side)	Yr	VG	VG+	NM
ST-448	We're Gonna Get Together	1970	5.00	10.00	20.00
ST-558	Great White Horse	1970	3.75	7.50	15.00
ST-837	Merry Christmas from Buck Owens and Susan Raye	1971	3.75	7.50	15.00
ST-11084	The Best of Buck Owens and Susan Raye	1972	3.75	7.50	15.00
ST-11207	The Good Old Days (Are Here Again)	1973	3.75	7.50	15.00

OWENS BROTHERS, THE

45s

ABC-PARAMOUNT

Number	Title (A Side/B Side)	Yr	VG	VG+	NM
9775	Night Train/Don't Cry	1956	10.00	20.00	40.00
—Also released on Sheraton by the Four Chaps.					

OXFORD CIRCLE, THE

45s

WORLD UNITED

Number	Title (A Side/B Side)	Yr	VG	VG+	NM
002	Mind Destruction/Foolsih Woman	196?	12.50	25.00	50.00

OXFORD CIRCUS, THE

45s

ZIG ZAG

Number	Title (A Side/B Side)	Yr	VG	VG+	NM
101	Tracy/4th Street Carnival	1967	10.00	20.00	40.00

OZ KNOZZ

Albums

OZONE

Number	Title (A Side/B Side)	Yr	VG	VG+	NM
O2-1000	Ruff Mix	1975	125.00	250.00	500.00

OZARK MOUNTAIN DAREDEVILS

45s

A&M

Number	Title (A Side/B Side)	Yr	VG	VG+	NM
1477	Country Girl/Within Without	1973	—	2.50	5.00
1515	If You Wanna Get to Heaven/Spaceship Orion	1974	—	2.50	5.00
1623	Look Away/It Probably Always Will	1974	—	2.00	4.00
1654	Jackie Blue/Better Days	1974	—	2.00	4.00
1654 [PS]	Jackie Blue/Better Days	1974	—	3.00	6.00
1709	Colorado Song/Thin Ice	1975	—	2.00	4.00
1772	If I Only Knew/Dreams	1975	—	2.00	4.00
1808	Keep On Churnin'/Time Warp	1976	—	2.00	4.00
1809	Dreams/You Make It Right	1976	—	2.00	4.00
1842	Journey to the Center of Your Heart/Chicken Train Stomp	1976	—	2.00	4.00
1880	Noah (Let It Rain)/Red Plum	1976	—	2.00	4.00
1888	You Know Like I Know/Arroyo	1976	—	2.00	4.00
1888 [PS]	You Know Like I Know/Arroyo	1976	—	3.00	6.00
1989	Crazy Lovin'/Stinghead	1977	—	2.00	4.00
2016	Following (The Way That I Feel)/Snowbound	1978	—	2.00	4.00

COLUMBIA

Number	Title (A Side/B Side)	Yr	VG	VG+	NM
11247	Take You Tonight/Runnin' Out	1980	—	2.00	4.00
11357	Oh Darlin'/Sailin' Around the World	1980	—	2.00	4.00

Albums

A&M

Number	Title (A Side/B Side)	Yr	VG	VG+	NM
SP-3110	The Ozark Mountain Daredevils	198?	2.00	4.00	8.00
—Budget-line reissue					
SP-3192	It'll Shine When It Shines	198?	2.00	4.00	8.00
—Budget-line reissue					
SP-3202	The Best of Ozark Mountain Daredevils	1982	2.50	5.00	10.00
SP-3654	It'll Shine When It Shines	1974	3.00	6.00	12.00
SP-4411	The Ozark Mountain Daredevils	1973	3.00	6.00	12.00
SP-4549	The Car Over the Lake Album	1975	3.00	6.00	12.00
SP-4601	Men from Earth	1976	3.00	6.00	12.00
SP-4662	Don't Look Down	1977	3.00	6.00	12.00
SP-6006 [(2)]	It's Alive	1978	3.75	7.50	15.00

COLUMBIA

Number	Title (A Side/B Side)	Yr	VG	VG+	NM
JC 36375	Ozark Mountain Daredevils	1980	2.50	5.00	10.00

SOUNDS GREAT

Number	Title (A Side/B Side)	Yr	VG	VG+	NM
SG-5004	The Lost Cabin Sessions	1985	2.50	5.00	10.00

P

P.F.M.

45s

Number	Title (A Side/B Side)	Yr	VG	VG+	NM
MANTICORE					
2002	Celebration/(B-side unknown)	1973	—	3.00	6.00
7003	Mr. Nine Til Five/Celebration	1974	—	2.50	5.00

Albums

Number	Title (A Side/B Side)	Yr	VG	VG+	NM
ASYLUM					
7E-1071	Chocolate Kings	1976	2.50	5.00	10.00
7E-1101	Jet Lag	1977	2.50	5.00	10.00
MANTICORE					
MA6-502	P.F.M. 'Cook'	1974	3.00	6.00	12.00
MC 66668	Photos of Ghosts	1973	3.00	6.00	12.00
MC 66673	The World Became the World	1974	3.00	6.00	12.00

P.J.

45s

Number	Title (A Side/B Side)	Yr	VG	VG+	NM
TAMLA					
54215	T.L.C./It Takes a Man to Teach a Woman How to Love	1972	6.25	12.50	25.00
V.I.P.					
25062	It Takes a Man to Teach a Woman How to Love/ The Best Years of My Life	1970	10.00	20.00	40.00

PABLO CRUISE

12-Inch Singles

Number	Title (A Side/B Side)	Yr	VG	VG+	NM
A&M					
SP-17050 [DJ]	Don't Want to Live Without It (Disco Version) (same on both sides)	1978	2.50	5.00	10.00
SP-17105 [DJ]	I Want You Tonight (LP Version)/I Want You Tonight (Edit)	1979	2.00	4.00	8.00
SP-17161 [DJ]	Cool Love/This Time	1981	2.00	4.00	8.00
SP-17244 [DJ]	Will You, Won't You (LP Version)/Will You, Won't You (Edit)	1983	2.00	4.00	8.00

45s

Number	Title (A Side/B Side)	Yr	VG	VG+	NM
A&M					
1695	Island Woman/Denny	1975	—	2.50	5.00
1742	What Does It Take/In My Own Quiet Way	1975	—	2.50	5.00
1815	(I Think) It's Finally Over/Look to the Sky	1976	—	2.50	5.00
1834	Don't Believe It/Look to the Sky	1976	—	2.50	5.00
1876	Crystal/Look to the Sky	1976	—	2.50	5.00
1910	A Place in the Sun/El Verano	1977	—	2.50	5.00
1920	Whatcha Gonna Do?/Atlanta June	1977	—	2.00	4.00
1920 [PS]	Whatcha Gonna Do?/Atlanta June	1977	—	3.00	6.00
1976	A Place in the Sun/El Verano	1977	—	2.00	4.00
1999	Atlanta June/Never Had a Love	1977	—	2.00	4.00
2048	Love Will Find a Way/Always Be Together	1978	—	2.00	4.00
2048 [PS]	Love Will Find a Way/Always Be Together	1978	—	2.50	5.00
2076	Don't Want to Live Without It/Raging Fire	1978	—	2.00	4.00
2112	I Go to Rio/Raging Fire	1979	—	2.00	4.00
2195	I Want You Tonight/Family Man	1979	—	2.00	4.00
2217 [DJ]	Part of the Game (mono/stereo)	1980	—	2.50	5.00
—No stock copies known					
2349	Cool Love/Jenny	1981	—	2.00	4.00
2373	Slip Away/That's When	1981	—	2.00	4.00
2373 [PS]	Slip Away/That's When	1981	—	2.00	4.00
2570	Another World/Will You, Won't You	1983	—	—	3.00

Albums

Number	Title (A Side/B Side)	Yr	VG	VG+	NM
A&M					
SP-3111	Pablo Cruise	198?	2.00	4.00	8.00
—Budget-line reissue of 4528					
SP-3198	Worlds Away	198?	2.00	4.00	8.00
—Budget-line reissue of 4697					
SP-3236	A Place in the Sun	198?	2.00	4.00	8.00
—Budget-line reissue of 4625					
SP-3712	Part of the Game	1979	2.50	5.00	10.00
SP-3726	Reflector	1981	2.50	5.00	10.00
SP-4528	Pablo Cruise	1975	2.50	5.00	10.00
SP-4575	Lifeline	1976	2.50	5.00	10.00
SP-4625	A Place in the Sun	1977	2.50	5.00	10.00
SP-4697	Worlds Away	1978	2.50	5.00	10.00
SP-4909	Out of Our Hands	1983	2.50	5.00	10.00
MOBILE FIDELITY					
1-029	A Place in the Sun	1979	5.00	10.00	20.00
—Audiophile vinyl					
NAUTILUS					
NR-6	Lifeline	1980	5.00	10.00	20.00
—Audiophile vinyl					
NR-28	Worlds Away	1981	5.00	10.00	20.00
—Audiophile vinyl					

PACERS, THE

More than one group.

45s

Number	Title (A Side/B Side)	Yr	VG	VG+	NM
CALICO					
101/2	I Found a Dream/I Wanna Dance with You	1958	7.50	15.00	30.00
CORAL					
62398	Sassy Sue/You Got Me Bugged	1964	2.50	5.00	10.00
GUYDEN					
2064	How Sweet/No Wonder	1962	375.00	750.00	1500.
RAZORBACK					
103	Fright Street/Sooie	1958	6.25	12.50	25.00
108	Confound It/Skeeter Dape	1960	6.25	12.50	25.00
112	Don't Get Around Much/Sad Sad	1962	6.25	12.50	25.00
115	West Memphis/Dollar, Two Ninety-Eight	1963	6.25	12.50	25.00
118	Tennessee Stud/Beautiful Debbie	1964	5.00	10.00	20.00
123	The Pit/Pace Setter	1965	5.00	10.00	20.00
125	Batman/Gotham City	1966	5.00	10.00	20.00
137	Short Squashed Texan/Sock It To 'Em Soobey	1967	5.00	10.00	20.00

Albums

Number	Title (A Side/B Side)	Yr	VG	VG+	NM
RAZORBACK					
121 [M]	You Asked For It	1965	25.00	50.00	100.00

PACIFIC DRIFT

Albums

Number	Title (A Side/B Side)	Yr	VG	VG+	NM
DERAM					
DES 18040	Feelin' Free	1970	5.00	10.00	20.00

PACIFIC GAS & ELECTRIC

45s

Number	Title (A Side/B Side)	Yr	VG	VG+	NM
COLUMBIA					
45009	Redneck/Bluebuster	1969	—	3.00	6.00
45158	Are You Ready?/Staggolee	1970	—	3.00	6.00
—Available with at least three different label variations, all equal in value					
45221	Elvira/Father Come On Home	1970	—	2.50	5.00
45304	The Time Has Come/Death Row No. 172	1971	—	2.50	5.00
45444	One More River to Cross/Rocky Roller's Lament	1971	—	2.50	5.00
45519	Thank God for You Baby/See the Monkey Run	1971	—	2.50	5.00
45621	Heat Wave/We Did What We Could	1972	—	2.50	5.00
POWER					
1701	Wade in the Water/Live Love	1969	2.50	5.00	10.00

Albums

Number	Title (A Side/B Side)	Yr	VG	VG+	NM
ABC DUNHILL					
DSX-50157	Pacific Gas and Electric Starring Charlie Allen	1974	3.00	6.00	12.00
BRIGHT ORANGE					
701	Get It On	1968	10.00	20.00	40.00
COLUMBIA					
CS 1017	Are You Ready	1970	3.75	7.50	15.00
—"360 Sound" label					
CS 1017	Are You Ready	1970	3.00	6.00	12.00
—Orange label					
CS 9900	Pacific Gas and Electric	1969	3.75	7.50	15.00
—"360 Sound" label					
CS 9900	Pacific Gas and Electric	1970	3.00	6.00	12.00
—Orange label					
C 30362	PG&E	1971	3.00	6.00	12.00
C 32019	The Best of Pacific Gas & Electric	1972	3.00	6.00	12.00
POWER					
701	Get It On	1969	6.25	12.50	25.00

PACKARDS, THE

45s

Number	Title (A Side/B Side)	Yr	VG	VG+	NM
PARADISE					
105	Dream of Love/Ding Dong	1956	100.00	200.00	400.00
PLA-BAC					
106	Ladise/My Doctor of Love	1956	500.00	1000.	2000.

PADDY, KLAUS AND GIBSON

45s

Number	Title (A Side/B Side)	Yr	VG	VG+	NM
CHESS					
1956	No Good Without You Baby/Rejected	1966	2.00	4.00	8.00

PAGE, GENE

12-Inch Singles

Number	Title (A Side/B Side)	Yr	VG	VG+	NM
ARISTA					
SP-13 [DJ]	Close Encounters of the Third Kind (6:00) (3:38)	1978	2.50	5.00	10.00
ATLANTIC					
DSKO 69 [DJ]	Wild Cherry (6:00) (same on both sides)	1976	3.00	6.00	12.00

45s

Number	Title (A Side/B Side)	Yr	VG	VG+	NM
ARISTA					
0302	Close Encounters of the Third Kind/When You Wish Upon a Star	1978	—	2.50	5.00
0322	Theme from "Star Trek"/Sho Like to Ride on a Star	1978	—	2.50	5.00
0337	Moonglow-Love Theme/Beyond the Hole in Space	1978	—	2.50	5.00
0492	Love Starts After Dark/I Wanna Dance	1980	—	2.00	4.00
0516	Put a Little Love in Your Lovin'/With You in the Night	1980	—	2.00	4.00
ATLANTIC					
3247	All My Dreams Are Coming True/Cream Corner	1975	—	2.50	5.00
3322	Wild Cherry/Fantasy Woman	1976	—	2.50	5.00
3338	Into My Thing/Organ Grinder	1976	—	2.50	5.00

Albums

Number	Title (A Side/B Side)	Yr	VG	VG+	NM
ARISTA					
AL 4174	Close Encounters	1978	2.50	5.00	10.00
AL 4262	Love Starts After Dark	1980	2.50	5.00	10.00
ATLANTIC					
SD 18111	Hot City	1974	3.00	6.00	12.00
SD 18161	Lovelock!	1975	3.00	6.00	12.00

PAGE, HOT LIPS

45s

Number	Title (A Side/B Side)	Yr	VG	VG+	NM
KING					
1404	Cadillac Song/Ain't Nothing Wrong	1954	25.00	50.00	100.00
4584	Last Call for Alcohol/Old Parie	1952	75.00	150.00	300.00
4594	I Bongo You/Ruby	1953	50.00	100.00	200.00
4616	Jungle King/What Shall I Do	1953	37.50	75.00	150.00
RCA VICTOR					
50-0120	Let Me In/That's the One for Me	1951	25.00	50.00	100.00
50-0129	Strike While the Iron's Hot/I Wanna Ride Like the Cowboys Do	1951	25.00	50.00	100.00

Albums

Number	Title (A Side/B Side)	Yr	VG	VG+	NM
CONTINENTAL					
16007 [M]	Hot and Cozy	1962	7.50	15.00	30.00
ONYX					
207	After Hours	197?	3.00	6.00	12.00
XANADU					
107	Trumpet at Minton's	197?	3.00	6.00	12.00

PAGE, LARRY, ORCHESTRA

45s

CALLA

Number	Title (A Side/B Side)	Yr	VG	VG+	NM
126	Jo Jo/Waltzing to Jazz	1966	3.00	6.00	12.00
144	Girl on a Swing/The Last Waltz	1967	2.50	5.00	10.00

LONDON

Number	Title (A Side/B Side)	Yr	VG	VG+	NM
259	I'm Hooked on You/Erotic Soul	1977	—	2.00	4.00

PAGE ONE

Number	Title (A Side/B Side)	Yr	VG	VG+	NM
21010	Hey Jude/Those Were the Days	1969	2.00	4.00	8.00
21018	Promises, Promises/Wichita Lineman	1969	2.00	4.00	8.00

Albums

RHINO

Number	Title (A Side/B Side)	Yr	VG	VG+	NM
RNLP-058	Kinky Music	1984	2.50	5.00	10.00
RNDF-257 [PD]	Kinky Music	1984	3.00	6.00	12.00

PAGE, PATTI

Also see FRANKIE LAINE.

45s

AVCO

Number	Title (A Side/B Side)	Yr	VG	VG+	NM
603	I May Not Be Lovin' You/Whoever Finds This, I Love You	1974	—	2.00	4.00
607	Pour Your Lovin' on Me/Big Wind from Dallas	1975	—	2.00	4.00
613	Less Than the Song/Did He Ask About Me	1975	—	2.00	4.00

COLUMBIA

Number	Title (A Side/B Side)	Yr	VG	VG+	NM
42671	Pretty Boy Lonely/Just a Simple Melody	1963	2.00	4.00	8.00
42791	Say Wonderful Things/I Knew I Would See Him Again	1963	2.00	4.00	8.00
42857	Nobody/Maybe He'll Come Back to Me	1963	2.00	4.00	8.00
42963	I Adore You/I Wonder, I Wonder, I Wonder	1964	—	3.00	6.00
43019	Drive-In Movie/I'd Rather Be Sorry	1964	—	3.00	6.00
43078	Drina (Little Soldier Boy)/Promises	1964	—	3.00	6.00
43183	Don't You Pass Me By/Days of the Waltz	1964	—	3.00	6.00
43251	Hush, Hush, Sweet Charlotte/Longing to Hold You Again	1965	2.00	4.00	8.00
43345	You Can't Be True, Dear/Who's Gonna Shoe My Pretty Little Feet	1965	—	3.00	6.00
43447	Happy Birthday, Jesus (A Child's Prayer)/ Christmas Bells	1965	2.00	4.00	8.00
43447 [PS]	Happy Birthday, Jesus (A Child's Prayer)/ Christmas Bells	1965	2.50	5.00	10.00
43517	Till You Come Back to Me/Custody	1966	—	3.00	6.00
43647	Can I Trust You?/In This Day and Age	1966	—	3.00	6.00
43761	It's the World Outside/Detour	1966	—	3.00	6.00
43794	Almost Persuaded/It's the World Outside	1966	—	3.00	6.00
43909	The Wishing Doll/Music and Memories	1966	—	3.00	6.00
43990	Wish Me a Rainbow/This Is the Sunday	1967	—	2.50	5.00
44115	Walkin' — Just Walkin'/Same Old You	1967	—	2.50	5.00
44242	What's She Got That I Ain't Got (Darlin')/Pretty Bluebird	1967	—	2.50	5.00
44257	All the Time/Pretty Bluebird	1967	—	2.50	5.00
44353	Gentle on My Mind/Excuse Me	1967	—	2.50	5.00
44556	Little Green Apples/This House	1968	—	2.50	5.00
44666	Stand By Your Man/Red Summer Roses	1968	—	2.50	5.00
44778	A Mighty Fortress Is Our Love/The Love Song	1969	—	2.50	5.00
44989	Boy from the Country/You Don't Need a Heart	1969	—	2.50	5.00
45059	Pickin' Up the Pieces/Tied Down	1969	—	2.50	5.00
45159	I Wish I Had a Mommy Like You/He'll Never Take the Place of You	1970	—	2.50	5.00
JZSP 111907/8 [DJ]	Happy Birthday, Jesus (A Child's Prayer)/ Christmas Bells	1965	2.50	5.00	10.00
—Green vinyl					
JZSP 111907/8 [DJ]	Happy Birthday, Jesus (A Child's Prayer)/ Christmas Bells	1965	2.00	4.00	8.00
—Black vinyl					

EPIC

Number	Title (A Side/B Side)	Yr	VG	VG+	NM
11032	Love Lives Again/I Can't Sit Still	1973	—	2.00	4.00
11072	You're Gonna Hurt Me/Mama Take Me Home	1973	—	2.00	4.00
11109	Someone Came to See Me/One Final Stand	1974	—	2.00	4.00

MERCURY

Number	Title (A Side/B Side)	Yr	VG	VG+	NM
505	Confess/Money, Marbles and Chalk	1950	7.50	15.00	30.00
—Reissue of her first hit from 1948					
5396	I Don't Care If the Sun Don't Shine/I'm Gonna Paper All My Walls with Your Love Letters	1950	5.00	10.00	20.00
5455	All My Love (Bolero)/Roses Remind Me of You	1950	5.00	10.00	20.00
5463	Back in Your Own Backyard/Right Kind of Love	1950	5.00	10.00	20.00
5511	Confess/That Old Feeling	1950	5.00	10.00	20.00
5512	All My Love (Bolero)/Back in Your Own Backyard	1950	5.00	10.00	20.00
5521	So in Love/Why Can't You Behave	1950	5.00	10.00	20.00
5534	The Tennessee Waltz/Boogie Woogie Santa Claus	1950	5.00	10.00	20.00
5534	The Tennessee Waltz/Long, Long Ago	1951	3.75	7.50	15.00
5571	Would I Love You (Love You, Love You)/ Sentimental Music	1951	3.75	7.50	15.00
5579	Down the Trail of Achin' Hearts/Ever True Ever More	1951	3.75	7.50	15.00
5592	Tag-a-Long/Soft and Tenderly	1951	5.00	10.00	20.00
—With Rex Allen					
5595	Mockin' Bird Hill/I Love You Because	1951	3.75	7.50	15.00
5645	Mister and Mississippi/These Things I Offer You	1951	3.75	7.50	15.00
—Black vinyl					
5645	Mister and Mississippi/These Things I Offer You	1951	10.00	20.00	40.00
—Red vinyl					
5682	Detour/Who's Gonna Shoe My Pretty Little Feet	1951	3.75	7.50	15.00
5706	And So to Sleep Again/One Sweet Letter	1951	3.75	7.50	15.00
5707	Whispering/Cabaret	1951	3.75	7.50	15.00
5715	That's All I Ask of You/I'm Glad You're Happy with Someone Else	1951	3.75	7.50	15.00
5729	Boogie Woogie Santa Claus/Christmas Bells	1951	3.75	7.50	15.00
5730	Jingle Bells/Christmas Choir	1951	3.75	7.50	15.00
5731	Santa Claus Is Coming to Town/Silent Night	1951	3.75	7.50	15.00
5732	White Christmas/The Christmas Song	1951	3.75	7.50	15.00
—The above four comprise a box set					
5751	Down in the Valley/I Want to Be a Cowboy's Sweetheart	1951	3.75	7.50	15.00
5772	Come What May/Retreat (Cries My Heart)	1952	3.75	7.50	15.00
5816	Whispering Winds/Love Where You Are	1952	3.75	7.50	15.00
5867	Once in Awhile/I'm Glad You're Happy with Someone Else	1952	3.75	7.50	15.00
5895	Release Me/Wedding Bells Will Soon Be Ringing	1952	3.75	7.50	15.00
—With Rusty Draper					
5899	I Went to Your Wedding/You Belong to Me	1952	3.75	7.50	15.00
70025	Why Don't You Believe Me/Conquest	1952	3.75	7.50	15.00
70070	The Doggie in the Window/My Jealous Eyes	1953	3.75	7.50	15.00
70127	Do What You Do to Me/Now That I'm in Love	1953	3.75	7.50	15.00
70137	Tell Me Why/Big Mamou	1953	3.75	7.50	15.00
—With Rusty Draper					
70183	Butterflies/This Is My Song	1953	3.75	7.50	15.00
70190	Arfie, the Doggie in the Window/Arfie Goes to School	1953	5.00	10.00	20.00
70222	Father, Father/The Lord's Prayer	1953	5.00	10.00	20.00
70230	My World Is You/Milwaukee Polka	1953	3.75	7.50	15.00
70260	Changing Partners/Where Did My Snowman Go	1953	3.75	7.50	15.00
70295	Changing Partners/Don't Get Around Much Anymore	1954	3.75	7.50	15.00
70302	Cross Over the Bridge/My Restless Lover	1954	3.75	7.50	15.00
70380	Steam Heat/Lonely Days	1954	3.75	7.50	15.00
70416	What a Dream/I Cried	1954	3.75	7.50	15.00
70458	The Mama Doll Song/I Can't Tell a Waltz from a Tango	1954	3.75	7.50	15.00
70506	Pretty Snowflakes/I Wanna Go Dancing with Willie	1954	3.75	7.50	15.00
70511	Let Me Go, Lover!/Hocus Pocus	1954	3.75	7.50	15.00
70528	Everlovin'/You Too Can Be a Dreamer	1955	3.00	6.00	12.00
70532	I Got It Bad/Don't Get Around Much Anymore	1955	3.00	6.00	12.00
70579	Little Crazy Quilt/Keep Me in Mind	1955	3.00	6.00	12.00
70607	Near to You/I Love to Dance with You	1955	3.00	6.00	12.00
70657	Piddily Patter Patter/Every Day	1955	3.00	6.00	12.00
70713	Croce di Oro (Cross of Gold)/Search My Heart	1955	3.00	6.00	12.00
70766	Go On with the Wedding/The Voice Inside	1956	3.00	6.00	12.00
70820	Too Young to Go Steady/My First Formal Gown	1956	3.00	6.00	12.00
70878	Allegheny Moon/The Strangest Romance	1956	3.00	6.00	12.00
70971	Mama from the Train/Every Time (I Feel His Spirit)	1956	3.00	6.00	12.00
71015	Repeat After Me/Learnin' My Latin	1956	3.00	6.00	12.00
71059	A Poor Man's Roses (Or a Rich Man's Gold)/The Wall	1957	2.50	5.00	10.00
71101	Old Cape Cod/Wondering	1957	2.50	5.00	10.00
71177	No One to Cry To/Money, Marbles and Chalk	1957	2.50	5.00	10.00
71189	I'll Remember Today/My How the Time Goes By	1957	2.50	5.00	10.00
71247	Belonging to Someone/Bring Up Together	1957	2.50	5.00	10.00
71294	Another Time, Another Place/These Worldly Wonders	1958	2.50	5.00	10.00
71331	Left Right Out of Your Heart (Hi Lee Hi Lo Hi Lup Up Up)/Longing to Hold You Again	1958	2.50	5.00	10.00
71355	Fibbin'/You Will Find Your Love (In Paris)	1958	2.50	5.00	10.00
71355 [PS]	Fibbin'/You Will Find Your Love (In Paris)	1958	5.00	10.00	20.00
71400	Trust in Me/Under the Sun Valley Moon	1958	2.50	5.00	10.00
71428	The Walls Have Ears/My Promise	1959	2.50	5.00	10.00
71469	With My Eyes Wide Open I'm Dreaming/My Mother's Eyes	1959	2.50	5.00	10.00
71510	Goodbye Charlie/Because Him Is a Baby	1959	2.50	5.00	10.00
71555	The Sound of Music/Little Donkey	1959	2.50	5.00	10.00
71597	Two Thousand, Two Hundred, Twenty-Three Miles/Promise Me, Thomas	1960	2.00	4.00	8.00
71639	One of Us (Will Weep Tonight)/What Will My Future Be	1960	2.00	4.00	8.00
71639 [PS]	One of Us (Will Weep Tonight)/What Will My Future Be	1960	3.75	7.50	15.00
71695	I Wish I'd Never Been Born/I Need You	1960	2.00	4.00	8.00
71695 [PS]	I Wish I'd Never Been Born/I Need You	1960	3.75	7.50	15.00
71745	Don't Read the Letter/That's All I Need to Know	1960	2.00	4.00	8.00
71745 [PS]	Don't Read the Letter/That's All I Need to Know	1960	3.75	7.50	15.00
71792	A City Girl Stole My Country Boy/Dondi	1961	2.00	4.00	8.00
71792 [PS]	A City Girl Stole My Country Boy/Dondi	1961	3.75	7.50	15.00
71823	You'll Answer to Me/Mom and Dad's Waltz	1961	2.00	4.00	8.00
71823 [PS]	You'll Answer to Me/Mom and Dad's Waltz	1961	3.75	7.50	15.00
71870	Broken Heart and a Pillow Filled with Tears/Dark Moon	1961	2.00	4.00	8.00
71870 [PS]	Broken Heart and a Pillow Filled with Tears/Dark Moon	1961	3.75	7.50	15.00
71906	Go On Home/Too Late to Cry	1961	2.00	4.00	8.00
71906 [PS]	Go On Home/Too Late to Cry	1961	3.75	7.50	15.00
71950	Most People Get Married/You Don't Know Me	1962	2.00	4.00	8.00
71950 [PS]	Most People Get Married/You Don't Know Me	1962	3.00	6.00	12.00
72013	The Boys' Night Out/Three Fools	1962	2.00	4.00	8.00
72013 [PS]	The Boys' Night Out/Three Fools	1962	3.00	6.00	12.00
72044	Everytime I Hear Your Name/Let's Cry Together	1962	2.00	4.00	8.00
72078	High on the Hill of Hope/By a Long Shot	1963	2.00	4.00	8.00
72123	I'm Walkin'/Invitation to the Blues	1963	2.00	4.00	8.00
73162	Give Him Love/Wish I Could Take That Little Boy Home	1970	—	2.50	5.00
73199	Make Me Your Kind of Woman/I Wish I Was a Little Boy Again	1971	—	2.50	5.00
73222	I'd Rather Be Sorry/Words	1971	—	2.50	5.00
73249	Think Again/A Woman Left Lonely	1971	—	2.50	5.00
73280	Jody and the Kid/Things We Care About	1972	—	2.50	5.00
73306	Come What May/Love Is a Friend of Mine	1972	—	2.50	5.00

PLANTATION

Number	Title (A Side/B Side)	Yr	VG	VG+	NM
197	No Aces/Everytime You Touch Me	1981	—	2.00	4.00
199	Wasn't It Good/Detour	1981	—	2.00	4.00
201	On the Inside/A Poor Man's Roses	1981	—	2.00	4.00
208	My Man Friday/Tennessee Waltz	1982	—	2.00	4.00
212	Barbara's Daughter/(B-side unknown)	1982	—	2.00	4.00

7-Inch Extended Plays

MERCURY

Number	Title (A Side/B Side)	Yr	VG	VG+	NM
EP-1-3008	The Tennessee Waltz/And So to Sleep Again// Come What May/Down the Trail of Aching Hearts	195?	3.00	6.00	12.00
EP-1-3008 [PS]	Tennessee Waltz	195?	3.00	6.00	12.00

Number	Title (A Side/B Side)	Yr	VG	VG+	NM
EP-1-3038	The Christmas Song/The First Noel//Christmas Choir/Christmas Bells	1956	3.00	6.00	12.00
EP-1-3038 [PS]	Christmas with Patti Page	1956	3.00	6.00	12.00
Albums					
ACCORD					
SN-7206	Special Thoughts	1982	2.50	5.00	10.00
COLUMBIA					
CL 2049 [M]	Say Wonderful Things	1963	3.75	7.50	15.00
CL 2132 [M]	Love After Midnight	1964	3.75	7.50	15.00
CL 2353 [M]	Hush, Hush, Sweet Charlotte	1965	3.75	7.50	15.00
CL 2414 [M]	Christmas with Patti Page	1965	3.00	6.00	12.00
CL 2505 [M]	America's Favorite Hymns	1966	3.00	6.00	12.00
CL 2526 [M]	Patti Page's Greatest Hits	1966	3.00	6.00	12.00
CL 2761 [M]	Today My Way	1967	5.00	10.00	20.00
CS 8849 [S]	Say Wonderful Things	1963	5.00	10.00	20.00
CS 8932 [S]	Love After Midnight	1964	5.00	10.00	20.00
CS 9153 [S]	Hush, Hush, Sweet Charlotte	1965	5.00	10.00	20.00
CS 9214 [S]	Christmas with Patti Page	1965	3.75	7.50	15.00
CS 9305 [S]	America's Favorite Hymns	1966	3.75	7.50	15.00
CS 9326	Patti Page's Greatest Hits	1970	2.50	5.00	10.00
—Orange label					
CS 9326 [S]	Patti Page's Greatest Hits	1966	3.75	7.50	15.00
—"360 Sound" label					
PC 9326	Patti Page's Greatest Hits	198?	2.00	4.00	8.00
—Budget-line reissue					
CS 9561 [S]	Today My Way	1967	3.75	7.50	15.00
CS 9666	Gentle on My Mind	1968	3.75	7.50	15.00
CS 9999	Honey Come Back	1970	3.00	6.00	12.00
EMARCY					
MG-36074 [M]	In the Land of Hi-Fi	1956	12.50	25.00	50.00
MG-36116 [M]	The East Side	1957	12.50	25.00	50.00
MG-36136 [M]	The West Side	1957	12.50	25.00	50.00
SR-60013 [S]	The West Side	1959	12.50	25.00	50.00
SR-60014 [S]	The East Side	1959	12.50	25.00	50.00
SR-80000 [S]	In the Land of Hi-Fi	1959	12.50	25.00	50.00
HARMONY					
HS 11381	Stand By Your Man	1970	2.50	5.00	10.00
KH 30407	Green, Green Grass of Home	1971	2.50	5.00	10.00
MERCURY					
PKW-118 [(2)]	The Most	1969	3.75	7.50	15.00
MG-20076 [M]	Romance on the Range	1955	7.50	15.00	30.00
MG 20093 [M]	Christmas with Patti Page	1956	7.50	15.00	30.00
MG-20095 [M]	Page I	1955	7.50	15.00	30.00
MG-20096 [M]	Page II	1955	7.50	15.00	30.00
MG-20097 [M]	Page III	1955	7.50	15.00	30.00
MG-20098 [M]	You Go to My Head	1955	7.50	15.00	30.00
MG-20099 [M]	Music for Two in Love	1955	7.50	15.00	30.00
MG-20100 [M]	The Voice of Patti Page	1955	7.50	15.00	30.00
MG-20101 [M]	Page IV	1955	7.50	15.00	30.00
MG-20102 [M]	This Is My Song	1955	7.50	15.00	30.00
MG-20226 [M]	Manhattan Tower	1956	7.50	15.00	30.00
MG-20318 [M]	The Waltz Queen	1957	7.50	15.00	30.00
MG-20387 [M]	Let's Get Away From it All	1957	7.50	15.00	30.00
MG-20388 [M]	I've Heard That Song Before	1957	7.50	15.00	30.00
MG-20398 [M]	Patti Page On Camera	1958	7.50	15.00	30.00
MG-20405 [M]	Indiscretion	1959	7.50	15.00	30.00
MG-20406 [M]	I'll Remember April	1959	7.50	15.00	30.00
MG-20417 [M]	Three Little Words	1960	7.50	15.00	30.00
MG-20495 [M]	Patti Page's Golden Hits	1960	7.50	15.00	30.00
MG-20573 [M]	Just a Closer Walk with Thee	1960	7.50	15.00	30.00
MG-20599 [M]	Patti Page Sings and Stars In "Elmer Gantry"	1960	6.25	12.50	25.00
MG-20615 [M]	Country & Western Golden Hits	1961	5.00	10.00	20.00
MG-20689 [M]	Go On Home	1962	5.00	10.00	20.00
MG-20712 [M]	Golden Hits of the Boys	1962	5.00	10.00	20.00
MG-20758 [M]	Patti Page On Stage	1963	5.00	10.00	20.00
MG-20794 [M]	Patti Page's Golden Hits, Volume 2	1963	5.00	10.00	20.00
MG-20819 [M]	The Singing Rage	1963	5.00	10.00	20.00
MG-20909 [M]	Blue Dream Street	1964	5.00	10.00	20.00
MG-20952 [M]	The Nearness of You	1965	3.75	7.50	15.00
MG-25059 [10]	Songs	1950	10.00	20.00	40.00
MG-25101 [10]	Folksong Favorites	1951	10.00	20.00	40.00
MG-25109 [10]	Christmas	1951	10.00	20.00	40.00
MG-25154 [10]	Tennessee Waltz	1952	10.00	20.00	40.00
MG-25185 [10]	Patti Sings for Romance	1954	10.00	20.00	40.00
MG-25187 [10]	Song Souvenirs	1954	10.00	20.00	40.00
MG-25196 [10]	Just Patti	1954	10.00	20.00	40.00
MG-25197 [10]	Patti's Songs	1954	10.00	20.00	40.00
MG-25209 [10]	And I Thought About You	1954	10.00	20.00	40.00
MG-25210 [10]	So Many Memories	1954	10.00	20.00	40.00
SR-60010 [S]	Let's Get Away From it All	1959	10.00	20.00	40.00
SR-60011 [S]	I've Heard That Song Before	1959	10.00	20.00	40.00
SR-60025 [S]	Patti Page On Camera	1959	10.00	20.00	40.00
SR-60037 [S]	Three Little Words	1960	10.00	20.00	40.00
SR-60049 [S]	The Waltz Queen	1959	10.00	20.00	40.00
SR-60059 [S]	Indiscretion	1959	10.00	20.00	40.00
SR-60081 [S]	I'll Remember April	1959	10.00	20.00	40.00
SR-60233 [S]	Just a Closer Walk with Thee	1960	10.00	20.00	40.00
SR-60260 [S]	Patti Page Sings and Stars In "Elmer Gantry"	1960	7.50	15.00	30.00
SR-60495 [S]	Patti Page's Golden Hits	196?	6.25	12.50	25.00
SR-60615 [S]	Country & Western Golden Hits	1961	6.25	12.50	25.00
SR-60689 [S]	Go On Home	1962	6.25	12.50	25.00
SR-60712 [S]	Golden Hits of the Boys	1962	6.25	12.50	25.00
SR-60758 [S]	Patti Page On Stage	1963	6.25	12.50	25.00
SR-60794 [S]	Patti Page's Golden Hits, Volume 2	1963	6.25	12.50	25.00
SR-60819 [S]	The Singing Rage	1963	6.25	12.50	25.00
SR-60909 [S]	Blue Dream Street	1964	6.25	12.50	25.00
SR-60952 [S]	The Nearness of You	1965	5.00	10.00	20.00
SR-61344	I'd Rather Be Sorry	1971	3.00	6.00	12.00
822740-1	Christmas with Patti Page	1987	2.50	5.00	10.00
—Reissue					
PLANTATION					
548	Aces	1981	2.50	5.00	10.00
WING					
MGW 12121 [M]	The Waltz Queen	196?	3.00	6.00	12.00
MGW 12174 [M]	Christmas with Patti Page	196?	5.00	10.00	20.00
—Same contents and order as Mercury 20093					
MGW 12250 [M]	Let's Get Away From It All	196?	3.00	6.00	12.00
SRW 16121 [S]	The Waltz Queen	196?	3.75	7.50	15.00
SRW 16250 [S]	Let's Get Away From It All	196?	3.75	7.50	15.00

PAGE, PATTI, AND TOM T. HALL

Also see each artist's individual listings.

Number	Title (A Side/B Side)	Yr	VG	VG+	NM
45s					
MERCURY					
73347	Hello We're Lonely/We're Not Getting Older	1972	—	2.50	5.00

PAGE BOYS, THE

Probably more than one group.

Number	Title (A Side/B Side)	Yr	VG	VG+	NM
45s					
ABC-PARAMOUNT					
10323	Lonely Sea/Road of Life	1962	2.50	5.00	10.00
BIG B					
1017	Santa's Snowdeer/White Wonderland	19??	2.00	4.00	8.00
DECCA					
31505	If Tears Could Speak/Ole Buttermilk Skies	1963	3.00	6.00	12.00
HAMILTON					
50025	Barracuda/Peter Gunn	1960	3.00	6.00	12.00
PREP					
117	Waiting/This I Give to You	1957	6.25	12.50	25.00

PAGENTS, THE

Number	Title (A Side/B Side)	Yr	VG	VG+	NM
45s					
BAMBOO					
525	Pa-Cha/Sad and Lonely	1963	12.50	25.00	50.00
ERA					
3119	Enchanted/The Big Daddy	1963	7.50	15.00	30.00
3124	Glenda/Shake	1964	7.50	15.00	30.00
3134	Pa-Cha/Sad and Lonely	1964	6.25	12.50	25.00
IKE					
631	Enchanted Surf/The Big Daddy	1963	25.00	50.00	100.00

PAIGE, HAL

Number	Title (A Side/B Side)	Yr	VG	VG+	NM
45s					
ATLANTIC					
996	Drive It Home/Break of Day Blues	1953	37.50	75.00	150.00
1032	Big Foot May/Please Say You Do	1954	37.50	75.00	150.00
CHECKER					
873	Don't Have to Cry No More/Pour the Corn	1957	5.00	10.00	20.00
FURY					
1002	Don't Have to Cry No More/Pour the Corn	1957	20.00	40.00	80.00
1024	After Hours Blues/Going Back to My Home Town	1959	5.00	10.00	20.00
J&S					
1601	Thunderbird/Sugar Bare	1957	7.50	15.00	30.00

PAIR, THE

Number	Title (A Side/B Side)	Yr	VG	VG+	NM
45s					
LIBERTY					
55820	Get Up Off It Baby/Donna Lee	1965	—	—	—
—Canceled					
55910	Run for Your Life/Girl, I Think I Love You	1966	2.00	4.00	8.00
Albums					
LIBERTY					
LRP-3410 [M]	The Pair Live! At the Ice House	1965	5.00	10.00	20.00
LRP-3440 [M]	The Pair Extraordinaire	1966	3.75	7.50	15.00
LRP-3461 [M]	"In"-Citement	1966	3.75	7.50	15.00
LRP-3504 [M]	It's a Wonderful World	1967	3.75	7.50	15.00
LST-7410 [S]	The Pair Live! At the Ice House	1965	6.25	12.50	25.00
LST-7440 [S]	The Pair Extraordinaire	1966	5.00	10.00	20.00
LST-7461 [S]	"In"-Citement	1966	5.00	10.00	20.00
LST-7504 [S]	It's a Wonderful World	1967	5.00	10.00	20.00

PAISLEYS, THE

Number	Title (A Side/B Side)	Yr	VG	VG+	NM
Albums					
AUDIO CITY					
70	Cosmic Mind at Play	1970	50.00	100.00	200.00

PALACE GUARD, THE

Number	Title (A Side/B Side)	Yr	VG	VG+	NM
45s					
ORANGE EMPIRE					
331	All Night Long/Playgirl	1965	3.75	7.50	15.00
332	A Girl You Can Depend On/If You Need Me	1965	3.75	7.50	15.00
400	Falling Sugar/Oh Blue	1965	3.75	7.50	15.00
PARKWAY					
111	Saturday's Child/Party Lights	1966	3.00	6.00	12.00
124	Calliope/Creed	1966	3.00	6.00	12.00
VERVE					
10410	Falling Sugar/Oh Blue	1966	2.50	5.00	10.00

PALANCE, JACK

Number	Title (A Side/B Side)	Yr	VG	VG+	NM
Albums					
WARNER BROS.					
WS 1865	Palance	1970	7.50	15.00	30.00

PALISADES, THE

More than one group.

Number	Title (A Side/B Side)	Yr	VG	VG+	NM
45s					
CALICO					
113	Close Your Eyes/I Can't Quit	1960	5.00	10.00	20.00
CHAIRMAN					
4401	Heaven Is Being with You/Make the Night a Little Longer	1963	6.25	12.50	25.00
—With Carole King					

DEBRA

Number	Title (A Side/B Side)	Yr	VG	VG+	NM
1003	Chapel Bells/She Can't Stop Dancing	1963	37.50	75.00	150.00

—Also released credited to "The Magics"

DORE

Number	Title (A Side/B Side)	Yr	VG	VG+	NM
609	Hometown Girl/Oh My Love	1961	3.75	7.50	15.00

LEADER

Number	Title (A Side/B Side)	Yr	VG	VG+	NM
806	Dear Joan/The Shrine	1960	5.00	10.00	20.00

MEDIEVAL

Number	Title (A Side/B Side)	Yr	VG	VG+	NM
205	This Is the Night/Relic Rock	1962	5.00	10.00	20.00

PALM BEACH BAND BOYS, THE

45s

RCA VICTOR

Number	Title (A Side/B Side)	Yr	VG	VG+	NM
47-9003	Bend It/Gypsy Caravan	1966	—	3.00	6.00
47-9026	I'm Gonna Sit Right Down and Write Myself a Letter/I Don't Want to Set the World on Fire	1966	—	3.00	6.00
47-9207	More and More/Fernanda's Theme	1967	—	3.00	6.00

Albums

RCA VICTOR

Number	Title (A Side/B Side)	Yr	VG	VG+	NM
LPM-3734 [M]	Winchester Cathedral	1966	3.00	6.00	12.00
LSP-3734 [S]	Winchester Cathedral	1966	2.50	5.00	10.00
LPM-3808 [M]	The Palm Beach Band Boys Strike Again	1967	3.75	7.50	15.00
LSP-3808 [S]	The Palm Beach Band Boys Strike Again	1967	2.50	5.00	10.00

PALMER, BRUCE

Albums

VERVE FORECAST

Number	Title (A Side/B Side)	Yr	VG	VG+	NM
FTS-3086	The Cycle Is Complete	1970	5.00	10.00	20.00

PALMER, ROBERT

12-Inch Singles

EMI

Number	Title (A Side/B Side)	Yr	VG	VG+	NM
SPRO 4739/45 [DJ]	Mercy Mercy Me (The Ecology)-I Want You (4 versions)	1991	2.00	4.00	8.00
V-56140	Tell Me I'm Not Dreaming (5 versions)	1989	—	3.00	6.00

EMI MANHATTAN

Number	Title (A Side/B Side)	Yr	VG	VG+	NM
SPRO 04074 [DJ]	Simply Irresistible (same on both sides)	1988	—	3.00	6.00
SPRO 04192 [DJ]	More Than Ever (LP Version)/More Than Ever (Live)	1988	—	3.00	6.00
56113	Early in the Morning (3 versions)/Disturbing Behavior	1988	—	3.00	6.00

ISLAND

Number	Title (A Side/B Side)	Yr	VG	VG+	NM
PR 635 [DJ]	You Are in My System (6:06) (2:57)	1983	—	3.00	6.00
PR 678 [DJ]	Pride (3 versions)	1983	2.00	4.00	8.00
PR 791 [DJ]	Discipline of Love (6:44) (3:20)	1985	—	3.00	6.00
PR 827 [DJ]	Addicted to Love (6:01) (same on both sides)	1986	2.00	4.00	8.00
PR 879 [DJ]	Hyperactive (same on both sides)	1986	—	3.00	6.00
PR 891 [DJ]	I Didn't Mean to Turn You On (same on both sides)	1986	—	3.00	6.00
PRO-A-906 [DJ]	Johnny and Mary	1980	2.00	4.00	8.00

—B-side is blank

Number	Title (A Side/B Side)	Yr	VG	VG+	NM
PRO-A-922 [DJ]	Looking for Clues (same on both sides)	1980	2.00	4.00	8.00
PR 969 [DJ]	I Didn't Mean to Turn You On (3 versions)/Addicted to Love	1986	2.50	5.00	10.00
2236 [DJ]	Sweet Lies (same on both sides)	1988	—	3.00	6.00
96804	I Didn't Mean to Turn You On (3 versions)/Addicted to Love	1986	2.00	4.00	8.00
96840	Discipline of Love//Woke Up Laughing/Dance for Me	1985	—	3.00	6.00
96984	Pride (Remix)/Pride (Dub)	1983	2.00	4.00	8.00

45s

EMI

Number	Title (A Side/B Side)	Yr	VG	VG+	NM
7PRO-04311 [DJ]	Tell Me I'm Not Dreaming/Tell Me I'm Not Dreaming (12" Edit)	1989	—	2.50	5.00

—Vinyl is promo only

Number	Title (A Side/B Side)	Yr	VG	VG+	NM
S7-18129	Know By Now/In the Stars	1994	—	—	3.00
50183	She Makes My Day/Casting a Spell	1989	—	—	3.00
50183 [PS]	She Makes My Day/Casting a Spell	1989	—	—	3.00

EMI MANHATTAN

Number	Title (A Side/B Side)	Yr	VG	VG+	NM
50133	Simply Irresistible/Nova	1988	—	—	3.00
50133 [PS]	Simply Irresistible/Nova	1988	—	—	3.00
50157	Early in the Morning/Disturbing Behavior	1988	—	—	3.00
50157 [PS]	Early in the Morning/Disturbing Behavior	1988	—	—	3.00

ISLAND

Number	Title (A Side/B Side)	Yr	VG	VG+	NM
006	Sneakin' Sally Through the Alley/Epidemic	1974	—	2.50	5.00
015	Get Ta Steppin'/Get Right On Down	1975	—	2.50	5.00
042	Which One of Us Is the Fool/Get Outside	1975	—	2.50	5.00
049	Pressure Drop/Give Me an Inch Girl	1976	—	2.50	5.00
075	Man Smart, Woman Smarter/Keep in Touch	1976	—	2.50	5.00
081	One Last Look/Some People Can Do What They Want	1977	—	2.50	5.00
100	Every Kinda People/How Much Fun	1978	—	2.00	4.00
105	You Overwhelm Me/Come Over	1978	—	2.00	4.00
8697	Where Can It Go/You're Gonna Get What's Coming	1978	—	2.00	4.00
49016	Bad Case of Loving You (Doctor, Doctor)/Love Can Run Faster	1979	—	2.00	4.00
49094	In Walks Love Again/Jealous	1979	—	2.00	4.00
49137	Can We Still Be Friends/Remember to Remember	1979	—	2.00	4.00
49554	Style Kills/Johnny and Mary	1980	—	2.00	4.00
49620	Looking for Clues/Woke Up Laughing	1980	—	2.00	4.00
50042	Some Guys Have All the Luck/Too Good to Be True	1982	—	2.00	4.00
99139	Bad Case of Loving You/Sweet Lies	1989	—	—	3.00
99139 [PS]	Bad Case of Loving You/Sweet Lies	1989	—	2.00	4.00
99377	Sweet Lies/Want You More	1988	—	—	3.00
99377 [PS]	Sweet Lies/Want You More	1988	—	—	3.00
99537	I Didn't Mean to Turn You On/Get It Through Your Heart	1986	—	—	3.00
99537 [PS]	I Didn't Mean to Turn You On/Get It Through Your Heart	1986	—	—	3.00
99545	Hyperactive/Woke Up Laughing	1986	—	—	3.00
99570	Addicted to Love/Let's Fall in Love Tonight	1986	—	—	3.00
99570 [PS]	Addicted to Love/Let's Fall in Love Tonight	1986	—	2.00	4.00

—First version: Close-up photo of Robert Palmer

Number	Title (A Side/B Side)	Yr	VG	VG+	NM
99570 [PS]	Addicted to Love/Let's Fall in Love Tonight	1986	—	2.00	4.00

—Second version: Photo of "models" band from video

Number	Title (A Side/B Side)	Yr	VG	VG+	NM
99597	Discipline of Love (Why Did You Do It)/Dance for Me	1985	—	—	3.00
99597 [PS]	Discipline of Love (Why Did You Do It)/Dance for Me	1985	—	—	3.00
99835	Pride/(B-side unknown)	1983	—	—	3.00
99835 [PS]	Pride/(B-side unknown)	1983	—	2.00	4.00
99866	You Are In My System/Deadline	1983	—	—	3.00
99866 [PS]	You Are In My System/Deadline	1983	—	—	3.00

MCA

Number	Title (A Side/B Side)	Yr	VG	VG+	NM
52643	All Around the World/It's Not Difficult	1985	—	—	3.00

Albums

EMI MANHATTAN

Number	Title (A Side/B Side)	Yr	VG	VG+	NM
E1-48057	Heavy Nova	1988	2.50	5.00	10.00

ISLAND

Number	Title (A Side/B Side)	Yr	VG	VG+	NM
PRO-819 [DJ]	Secrets	1979	7.50	15.00	30.00

—Promo-only picture disc

Number	Title (A Side/B Side)	Yr	VG	VG+	NM
ILPS 9294	Sneakin' Sally Through the Alley	1975	3.00	6.00	12.00
ILPS 9372	Pressure Drop	1976	3.00	6.00	12.00
ILPS 9420	Some People Can Do What They Like	1977	3.00	6.00	12.00
ILPS 9476	Double Fun	1978	3.00	6.00	12.00

—Original copies of the above four albums were NOT distributed by Warner Bros.

Number	Title (A Side/B Side)	Yr	VG	VG+	NM
ILPS 9544	Secrets	1979	2.50	5.00	10.00
ILPS 9595	Clues	1980	2.50	5.00	10.00
ILPS 9665	Maybe It's Live	1982	2.50	5.00	10.00
90065	Pride	1983	2.50	5.00	10.00
90086	Sneakin' Sally Through the Alley	1984	2.00	4.00	8.00
90087	Pressure Drop	1984	2.00	4.00	8.00
90089	Secrets	1984	2.00	4.00	8.00
90471	Riptide	1985	2.50	5.00	10.00
90493	Clues	1986	2.00	4.00	8.00
90494	Double Fun	1986	2.00	4.00	8.00
91318	Addictions Volume I	1989	3.00	6.00	12.00

—Original pressing available only for a short time

Number	Title (A Side/B Side)	Yr	VG	VG+	NM
842301-1	Addictions Volume I	1990	2.50	5.00	10.00

WARNER BROS.

Number	Title (A Side/B Side)	Yr	VG	VG+	NM
WBMS-111 [DJ]	Live in Boston	1979	7.50	15.00	30.00

—Part of "The Warner Bros. Music Show"

PALS, THE

45s

GUYDEN

Number	Title (A Side/B Side)	Yr	VG	VG+	NM
2019	My Baby Likes to Rock/Summer Is Here	1959	5.00	10.00	20.00

TURF

Number	Title (A Side/B Side)	Yr	VG	VG+	NM
1000	My Baby Likes to Rock/Summer Is Here	1958	10.00	20.00	40.00

PANDIT, KORLA

45s

FANTASY

Number	Title (A Side/B Side)	Yr	VG	VG+	NM
545	Turkish Dance/Brazilian Brion	195?	3.75	7.50	15.00

VITA

Number	Title (A Side/B Side)	Yr	VG	VG+	NM
V-1	White Christmas/Merry Christmas	195?	3.75	7.50	15.00
V-2	Ave Maria/Bist Du Bi Mir	195?	3.75	7.50	15.00
V-3	Adeste Fideles//Jesu Bambino/Silent Night	195?	3.75	7.50	15.00
V-4	Joy to the World/Hark! The Herald Angels Sing	195?	3.75	7.50	15.00
220	Remembering/(B-side unknown)	195?	5.00	10.00	20.00

Albums

FANTASY

Number	Title (A Side/B Side)	Yr	VG	VG+	NM
3272 [M] —Red vinyl	Music of the Exotic East	1958	10.00	20.00	40.00
3272 [M] —Black vinyl	Music of the Exotic East	1958	6.25	12.50	25.00
3284 [M] —Red vinyl	Latin Holiday	1959	10.00	20.00	40.00
3284 [M] —Black vinyl	Latin Holiday	1959	6.25	12.50	25.00
3286 [M] —Red vinyl	Korla Pandit at the Pipe Organ	1959	10.00	20.00	40.00
3286 [M] —Black vinyl	Korla Pandit at the Pipe Organ	1959	6.25	12.50	25.00
3288 [M] —Red vinyl	Tropical Magic	1959	10.00	20.00	40.00
3288 [M] —Black vinyl	Tropical Magic	1959	6.25	12.50	25.00
3293 [M] —Red vinyl	Speak to Me of Love	1959	10.00	20.00	40.00
3293 [M] —Black vinyl	Speak to Me of Love	1959	6.25	12.50	25.00
3304 [M] —Red vinyl	Korla Pandit in Concert	1960	10.00	20.00	40.00
3304 [M] —Black vinyl	Korla Pandit in Concert	1960	6.25	12.50	25.00
3320 [M] —Red vinyl	Music of Mystery and Romance	1961	10.00	20.00	40.00
3320 [M] —Black vinyl	Music of Mystery and Romance	1961	6.25	12.50	25.00
3327 [M] —Red vinyl	Love Letters	1961	10.00	20.00	40.00
3327 [M] —Black vinyl	Love Letters	1961	6.25	12.50	25.00
3329 [M] —Red vinyl	Hypnotique	1961	10.00	20.00	40.00
3329 [M] —Black vinyl	Hypnotique	1961	6.25	12.50	25.00
3334 [M] —Red vinyl	Music of Hollywood	1962	10.00	20.00	40.00
3334 [M] —Black vinyl	Music of Hollywood	1962	6.25	12.50	25.00
3342 [M] —Red vinyl	Music for Meditation	1962	10.00	20.00	40.00

Number	Title (A Side/B Side)	Yr	VG	VG+	NM
3342 [M]	Music for Meditation	1962	6.25	12.50	25.00
—Black vinyl					
3347 [M]	Korla Pandit in Paris	1962	6.25	12.50	25.00
3350 [M]	Christmas with Korla Pandit	1962	10.00	20.00	40.00
—Red vinyl					
3350 [M]	Christmas with Korla Pandit	1962	6.25	12.00	25.00
—Black vinyl					
8013 [S]	Music of the Exotic East	1960	12.50	25.00	50.00
—Blue vinyl					
8013 [S]	Music of the Exotic East	1960	7.50	15.00	30.00
—Black vinyl					
8018 [S]	Korla Pandit at the Pipe Organ	1960	12.50	25.00	50.00
—Blue vinyl					
8018 [S]	Korla Pandit at the Pipe Organ	1960	7.50	15.00	30.00
—Black vinyl					
8027 [S]	Latin Holiday	1960	12.50	25.00	50.00
—Blue vinyl					
8027 [S]	Latin Holiday	1960	7.50	15.00	30.00
—Black vinyl					
8034 [S]	Tropical Magic	1960	12.50	25.00	50.00
—Blue vinyl					
8034 [S]	Tropical Magic	1960	7.50	15.00	30.00
—Black vinyl					
8039 [S]	Speak to Me of Love	1960	12.50	25.00	50.00
—Blue vinyl					
8039 [S]	Speak to Me of Love	1960	7.50	15.00	30.00
—Black vinyl					
8049 [S]	Korla Pandit in Concert	1960	12.50	25.00	50.00
—Blue vinyl					
8049 [S]	Korla Pandit in Concert	1960	7.50	15.00	30.00
—Black vinyl					
8061 [S]	Music of Mystery and Romance	1961	12.50	25.00	50.00
—Blue vinyl					
8061 [S]	Music of Mystery and Romance	1961	7.50	15.00	30.00
—Black vinyl					
8070 [S]	Love Letters	1961	12.50	25.00	50.00
—Blue vinyl					
8070 [S]	Love Letters	1961	7.50	15.00	30.00
—Black vinyl					
8075 [S]	Hypnotique	1961	12.50	25.00	50.00
—Blue vinyl					
8075 [S]	Hypnotique	1961	7.50	15.00	30.00
—Black vinyl					
8086 [S]	Music of Hollywood	1962	12.50	25.00	50.00
—Blue vinyl					
8086 [S]	Music of Hollywood	1962	7.50	15.00	30.00
—Black vinyl					
8342 [S]	Music for Meditation	1962	12.50	25.00	50.00
—Blue vinyl					
8342 [S]	Music for Meditation	1962	7.50	15.00	30.00
—Black vinyl					
8347 [S]	Korla Pandit in Paris	1962	7.50	15.00	30.00
8350 [S]	Christmas with Korla Pandit	1962	12.50	25.00	50.00
—Blue vinyl					
8350 [S]	Christmas with Korla Pandit	1962	7.50	15.00	30.00
—Black vinyl					
NATIONAL CUSTOM					
NCR 12-574	Fantastique!	196?	7.50	15.00	30.00
SYMPATHY FOR THE RECORD INDUSTRY					
SFTRI 387	Exotica 2000	1996	3.00	6.00	12.00
VITA					
VLP-14 [10]	Rememb'ring with Korla Pandit	195?	20.00	40.00	80.00

PANICS, THE

Number	Title (A Side/B Side)	Yr	VG	VG+	NM
45s					
ABC-PARAMOUNT					
10072	Heartaches/You're Driving Me Crazy	1959	3.75	7.50	15.00
CHANCELLOR					
1109	Panicsville/Bony Moronie	1962	3.75	7.50	15.00
1127	Skinnie Minnie Olive Oil/Voodoo Walk	1962	3.75	7.50	15.00
PHILIPS					
40230	The Kangaroo/It Ain't What You Got	1964	3.00	6.00	12.00
SWAN					
4247	Beans/Show Her You Care	1966	3.00	6.00	12.00
Albums					
CHANCELLOR					
CHL-5026 [M]	Panicsville	1962	7.50	15.00	30.00
CHLS-5026 [S]	Panicsville	1962	10.00	20.00	40.00
PHILIPS					
PHM 200159 [M]	Discotheque Dance Party	1964	3.75	7.50	15.00
PHS 600159 [S]	Discotheque Dance Party	1964	5.00	10.00	20.00

PAPA DOO RUN RUN

With BRUCE JOHNSTON.

Number	Title (A Side/B Side)	Yr	VG	VG+	NM
45s					
BLUE PACIFIC					
1-001	Lady Love/Slow Down	197?	—	2.00	4.00
1-001 [PS]	Lady Love/Slow Down	197?	—	2.00	4.00
EQUINOX					
PB-10404	Disney Girls/Be True to Your School	1975	2.50	5.00	10.00
Albums					
TELARC					
70501	California Project	1985	2.50	5.00	10.00

PAPER DOLLS, THE

Number	Title (A Side/B Side)	Yr	VG	VG+	NM
45s					
MGM					
13766	'Cause I Love You/You're the Boy I Want to Marry	1967	3.00	6.00	12.00
UNI					
55104	Someday/Any Old Time You're Lonely and Sad	1969	2.50	5.00	10.00
WARNER BROS.					
7191	All the Time in the World/Something Here in My Heart (Keeps a-Tellin' Me No)	1968	2.50	5.00	10.00

PAPER GARDEN, THE

Number	Title (A Side/B Side)	Yr	VG	VG+	NM
Albums					
MUSICOR					
MS-(# unknown)	The Paper Garden	1968	10.00	20.00	40.00

PAPER LACE

Number	Title (A Side/B Side)	Yr	VG	VG+	NM
45s					
BANG					
700	Martha/You Can't Touch Me	1972	—	2.50	5.00
704	Ragamuffin Man/Elsie	1973	—	2.50	5.00
711	Ragamuffin Man/Elsie	1974	—	—	—
—Canceled					
MERCURY					
73479	Billy, Don't Be a Hero/Celia	1974	—	3.00	6.00
73492	The Night Chicago Died/Can You Get It When You Want It	1974	—	3.00	6.00
—Red label					
73492	The Night Chicago Died/Can You Get It When You Want It	1974	—	2.00	4.00
—Chicago skyline label					
73620	The Black-Eyed Boys/Jean	1974	—	2.00	4.00
73694	So What If I Am/Himalayan Lullaby	1975	—	2.00	4.00
Albums					
MERCURY					
SRM-1-1008	Paper Lace	1974	3.00	6.00	12.00

PAPPALARDI, FELIX

Also see MOUNTAIN.

Number	Title (A Side/B Side)	Yr	VG	VG+	NM
45s					
COLUMBIA					
43773	Love Someday/You Lie to Me	1966	6.25	12.50	25.00
Albums					
A&M					
SP-4586	Creation	1976	2.50	5.00	10.00
SP-4729	Don't Worry Me	1979	2.50	5.00	10.00

PARADE, THE

Number	Title (A Side/B Side)	Yr	VG	VG+	NM
45s					
A&M					
841	Sunshine Girl/This Old Melody	1967	2.50	5.00	10.00
867	She's Got the Magic/Welcome, You're in Love	1967	—	3.00	6.00
887	Frog Prince/Hallelujah Rocket	1967	—	3.00	6.00
904	I Can See Love/Radio Song	1968	—	3.00	6.00
950	A.C.-D.C./She Sleeps Alone	1968	—	3.00	6.00
970	Laughing Lady/Hallelujah Rocket	1968	—	3.00	6.00

PARADONS, THE

Number	Title (A Side/B Side)	Yr	VG	VG+	NM
45s					
MILESTONE					
2003	Diamonds and Pearls/I Want Love	1960	12.50	25.00	50.00
—Maroon label					
2003	Diamonds and Pearls/I Want Love	1960	7.50	15.00	30.00
—Red label					
2003	Diamonds and Pearls/I Want Love	1960	5.00	10.00	20.00
—Green label					
2005	Bells Ring/Please Tell Me	1960	7.50	15.00	30.00
2015	I Had a Dream/Never, Never	1962	10.00	20.00	40.00
TUFFEST					
102	Never Again/This Is Love	1961	37.50	75.00	150.00
WARNER BROS.					
5186	Take All of Me/So Fine, So Fine, So Fine	1960	5.00	10.00	20.00

PARAGONS, THE

Number	Title (A Side/B Side)	Yr	VG	VG+	NM
45s					
BUDDAH					
478	Oh Lovin' You/Con Me	1975	—	3.00	6.00
MUSIC CLEF					
3001/2	Time After Time/Baby, Take My Hand	1963	5.00	10.00	20.00
MUSICRAFT					
1102	Wedding Bells/Blue Velvet	1960	6.25	12.50	25.00
TAP					
500	If/Hey Baby	1961	12.50	25.00	50.00
503	In the Midst of the Night/Begin the Beguine	1961	10.00	20.00	40.00
504	These Are the Things I Love/If You Love Me	1961	10.00	20.00	40.00
TIMES SQUARE					
9	So You Will Know/Don't Cry Baby	1963	5.00	10.00	20.00
WINLEY					
215	Hey Little School Girl/Florence	1957	12.50	25.00	50.00
220	Let's Start All Over Again/Stick With Me Baby	1957	12.50	25.00	50.00
223	Two Hearts Are Better Than One/Give Me Love	1958	10.00	20.00	40.00
227	The Vows of Love/Twilight	1958	10.00	20.00	40.00
227	The Wows of Love/Twilight	1958	250.00	500.00	1000.
—With misspelled A-side title					
228	Don't Cry Baby/So You Will Know	1958	10.00	20.00	40.00
236	Darling, I Love You/Doll Baby	1959	10.00	20.00	40.00
240	So You Will Know/Doll Baby	1959	7.50	15.00	30.00
250	Kneel and Pray/Just a Moment	1961	7.50	15.00	30.00
Albums					
COLLECTABLES					
COL-5035	The Best of the Paragons	198?	2.50	5.00	10.00
LOST-NITE					
LLP-4 [10]	The Paragons	1981	2.50	5.00	10.00
—Red vinyl					

PARAGONS, THE & THE HARPTONES

Albums

Number	Title (A Side/B Side)	Yr	VG	VG+	NM
MUSICTONE					
M-8001 [M]	The Paragons vs. the Harptones	1964	10.00	20.00	40.00

PARAGONS, THE & THE JESTERS

Albums

Number	Title (A Side/B Side)	Yr	VG	VG+	NM
JOSIE					
4008 [M]	The Paragons Meet the Jesters	1962	50.00	100.00	200.00
JUBILEE					
JLP-1098 [M]	The Paragons Meet the Jesters	1959	75.00	150.00	300.00
—Blue label, black vinyl					
JLP-1098 [M]	The Paragons Meet the Jesters	1959	750.00	1125.	1500.
—Multi-color splash vinyl					
JLP-1098 [M]	The Paragons Meet the Jesters	196?	37.50	75.00	150.00
—Flat black label					
JLP-1098 [M]	The Paragons Meet the Jesters	196?	15.00	30.00	60.00
—Black label with multi-color logo					
WINLEY					
LP-6003 [M]	War! The Jesters vs. the Paragons	195?	125.00	250.00	500.00

PARAGONS, THE (2)

Not the same group as the others.

45s

Number	Title (A Side/B Side)	Yr	VG	VG+	NM
CENTURY CUSTOM					
19317	Surf Drums/Sunday Morning	196?	15.00	30.00	60.00
—B-side by the Samohi Serenaders					

PARAKEETS, THE (1)

45s

Number	Title (A Side/B Side)	Yr	VG	VG+	NM
BIG TOP					
3130	I Love You Like I Do/I Want You Right Now	1962	5.00	10.00	20.00
JUBILEE					
5407	Come Back/Shangri-La	1961	6.25	12.50	25.00

PARAKEETS, THE (2)

45s

Number	Title (A Side/B Side)	Yr	VG	VG+	NM
GEM					
218	Give Me Time/I'm Losing My Mind Over You	1954	100.00	200.00	400.00

PARAMOR, NORRIE

45s

Number	Title (A Side/B Side)	Yr	VG	VG+	NM
CAPITOL					
F3629	Every Street's a Boulevard/Magic Banjo	1957	2.50	5.00	10.00
F3714	Taurus Tango/Gemini Waltz	1957	2.50	5.00	10.00
F4266	Waltzing Matilda/Barcelona	1959	2.50	5.00	10.00
ESSEX					
337	Callahan's Monkey/Melodia	1953	3.75	7.50	15.00
356	Wedding Day/Luxembourg Polka	1954	3.00	6.00	12.00

Albums

Number	Title (A Side/B Side)	Yr	VG	VG+	NM
CAPITOL					
ST 2071 [S]	In London...In Love Again	1964	3.75	7.50	15.00
T 2071 [M]	In London...In Love Again	1964	3.00	6.00	12.00
ST 2357 [S]	Warm and Willing	1965	3.75	7.50	15.00
T 2357 [M]	Warm and Willing	1965	3.00	6.00	12.00
ST 2526 [S]	In Tokyo — In Love	1966	3.75	7.50	15.00
T 2526 [M]	In Tokyo — In Love	1966	3.00	6.00	12.00
ST 10025 [S]	In London...In Love	196?	3.75	7.50	15.00
T 10025 [M]	In London...In Love	196?	3.00	6.00	12.00
T 10052 [M]	London After Dark	196?	3.00	6.00	12.00
T 10130 [M]	Norrie Paramor's Moods	196?	3.00	6.00	12.00
ST 10212 [S]	Autumn	196?	3.75	7.50	15.00
T 10212 [M]	Autumn	196?	3.00	6.00	12.00
ST 10238 [S]	Amor Amor	196?	3.75	7.50	15.00
T 10238 [M]	Amor Amor	196?	3.00	6.00	12.00
POLYDOR					
24-6006	Love at First Sight	1970	2.50	5.00	10.00

PARAMOUNTS, THE (1)

45s

Number	Title (A Side/B Side)	Yr	VG	VG+	NM
CARLTON					
524	Girl Friend/Trying	1960	10.00	20.00	40.00

PARAMOUNTS, THE (2)

45s

Number	Title (A Side/B Side)	Yr	VG	VG+	NM
CENTAUR					
103	When I Dream/Where's Carolyn Tonight	1963	15.00	30.00	60.00

PARAMOUNTS, THE (3)

ROBERT KNIGHT was in this group.

45s

Number	Title (A Side/B Side)	Yr	VG	VG+	NM
DOT					
16175	Why Do You Have to Go/Congratulations	1961	6.25	12.50	25.00
16201	When You Dance/Year 17	1961	6.25	12.50	25.00

PARAMOUNTS, THE (4)

British group; an early incarnation of PROCOL HARUM.

45s

Number	Title (A Side/B Side)	Yr	VG	VG+	NM
LIVERPOOL SOUND					
903	Poison Ivy/I Feel Good All Over	1964	12.50	25.00	50.00

PARAMOUNTS, THE (U)

Could be any of the above groups except (4), or they could be entirely different.

45s

Number	Title (A Side/B Side)	Yr	VG	VG+	NM
COMBO					
156	Take My Heart/Thunderbird Baby	1960	30.00	60.00	120.00
FLEETWOOD					
1014	I Know You'll Be My Love/Christopher Columbus	1960	25.00	50.00	100.00
LAURIE					
3201	Just to Be with You/One More for the Road	1963	7.50	15.00	30.00
MAGNUM					
722	Time Will Bring a Change/Under Your Spell	1964	7.50	15.00	30.00
MERCURY					
72429	Girl with the Big Black Boots/I Won't Share Your Love	1965	3.00	6.00	12.00

PARAMOURS, THE

BIL MEDLEY and BOBBY HATFIELD, later THE RIGHTEOUS BROTHERS.

45s

Number	Title (A Side/B Side)	Yr	VG	VG+	NM
MOONGLOW					
214	That's All I Want Tonight/There She Goes	1962	5.00	10.00	20.00
214	That's All I Want Tonight/There She Goes	1962	10.00	20.00	40.00
—Red vinyl					
SMASH					
1701	That's the Way We Love/Prison Break	1961	5.00	10.00	20.00
1718	Cutie Cutie/Miss Social Climber	1961	5.00	10.00	20.00

PARFAYS, THE

45s

Number	Title (A Side/B Side)	Yr	VG	VG+	NM
FONTANA					
1526	You've Got a Good Thing Goin' Boy/In the Beginning	1965	7.50	15.00	30.00

PARIS

With Bob Welch, ex-FLEETWOOD MAC.

45s

Number	Title (A Side/B Side)	Yr	VG	VG+	NM
CAPITOL					
4356	Blue Robin/Big Towne, 2061	1976	—	2.50	5.00

Albums

Number	Title (A Side/B Side)	Yr	VG	VG+	NM
CAPITOL					
ST-11464	Paris	1975	3.00	6.00	12.00
ST-11560	Big Towne, 2061	1976	3.00	6.00	12.00

PARIS, FREDDIE

No relation to FRED PARRIS.

45s

Number	Title (A Side/B Side)	Yr	VG	VG+	NM
RCA VICTOR					
47-9232	Take Me As I Am/It's Okay to Cry Now	1967	2.50	5.00	10.00
47-9358	Little Things Can Make a Woman Cry/Face It, Boy, It's Over	1967	2.50	5.00	10.00
47-9571	There She Goes/Young Hearts, Young Hands	1968	5.00	10.00	20.00

Albums

Number	Title (A Side/B Side)	Yr	VG	VG+	NM
RCA VICTOR					
LSP-4064	Lovin' Mood	1968	5.00	10.00	20.00

PARIS BROTHERS, THE

45s

Number	Title (A Side/B Side)	Yr	VG	VG+	NM
BRUNSWICK					
55132	This Is It/Our Love Is Here to Stay	1959	7.50	15.00	30.00
CORAL					
62220	Funny Feeling/(B-side unknown)	1959	5.00	10.00	20.00

PARIS PILOT

Albums

Number	Title (A Side/B Side)	Yr	VG	VG+	NM
HIP					
7004	Paris Pilot	1970	6.25	12.50	25.00

PARIS SISTERS, THE

45s

Number	Title (A Side/B Side)	Yr	VG	VG+	NM
CAPITOL					
2081	Golden Days/Greener Days	1968	2.00	4.00	8.00
CAVALIER					
828	Christmas in My Home Town/Man with the Mistletoe Moustache	197?	—	3.00	6.00
DECCA					
29372	Ooh La La/Whose Arms Are You Missing	1954	6.25	12.50	25.00
29488	Baby, Honey, Baby/Huckleberry Pie	1955	6.25	12.50	25.00
29527	His and Hers/Truly Do	1955	6.25	12.50	25.00
—With Gary Crosby					
29574	The Know How/I Wanna	1955	6.25	12.50	25.00
29744	Lover Boy/Oh Yes You Do	1955	6.25	12.50	25.00
29891	I Love You Dear/Mistaken	1956	6.25	12.50	25.00
29970	Daughter! Daughter!/So Much — So Very Much	1956	6.25	12.50	25.00
30554	Don't Tell Anybody/Mind Reader	1958	5.00	10.00	20.00
GNP CRESCENDO					
410	Stand Naked Clown/Ugliest Girl in Town	1968	2.00	4.00	8.00
GREGMARK					
2	Be My Boy/I'll Be Crying Tomorrow	1961	5.00	10.00	20.00
6	I Love How You Love Me/All Through the Night	1961	6.25	12.50	25.00
10	He Knows I Love Him Too Much/Lonely Girl's Prayer	1962	5.00	10.00	20.00
12	Let Me Be the One/What Am I to Do	1962	5.00	10.00	20.00
13	Yes I Love You/Once Upon a While Ago	1962	5.00	10.00	20.00
—All the Gregmark records were Phil Spector productions					
IMPERIAL					
5465	Old Enough to Cry/Tell Me More	1957	5.00	10.00	20.00
5487	Some Day/My Original Love	1958	5.00	10.00	20.00
MERCURY					
72320	Once Upon a Time/When I Fall in Love	1964	2.50	5.00	10.00
72320 [PS]	Once Upon a Time/When I Fall in Love	1964	5.00	10.00	20.00
72468	Always Waitin'/Why Do I Take It from You	1965	2.50	5.00	10.00
72468 [PS]	Always Waitin'/Why Do I Take It from You	1965	5.00	10.00	20.00
MGM					
13236	Dream Lover/Lonely Girl	1964	3.75	7.50	15.00
13236 [PS]	Dream Lover/Lonely Girl	1964	6.25	12.50	25.00
REPRISE					
0440	Sincerely/Too Good to Be True	1965	2.50	5.00	10.00
0472	I'm Me/You	1966	2.50	5.00	10.00
0511	It's My Party/My Good Friend	1966	2.50	5.00	10.00

Number	Title (A Side/B Side)	Yr	VG	VG+	NM
0548	Some of Your Lovin'/Long After Tonight Is All Over	1967	2.50	5.00	10.00
Albums					
REPRISE					
R-6259 [M]	Everything Under the Sun	1967	10.00	20.00	40.00
RS-6359 [S]	Everything Under the Sun	1967	15.00	30.00	60.00
SIDEWALK					
DT 5906 [R]	Golden Hits of the Paris Sisters	1967	7.50	15.00	30.00
T 5906 [M]	Golden Hits of the Paris Sisters	1967	12.50	25.00	50.00
UNIFILMS					
505 [M]	The Paris Sisters Sing Songs from Glass House	1966	10.00	20.00	40.00
S-505 [S]	The Paris Sisters Sing Songs from Glass House	1966	12.50	25.00	50.00

PARISH HALL

Number	Title (A Side/B Side)	Yr	VG	VG+	NM
Albums					
FANTASY					
8398	Parish Hall	1969	5.00	10.00	20.00

PARKER, CHARLIE

Number	Title (A Side/B Side)	Yr	VG	VG+	NM
45s					
CLEF					
89129	Cosmic Rays/Kim	1955	6.25	12.50	25.00
89138	I Remember You/Chi Chi	1955	6.25	12.50	25.00
89144	I Hear Music/Laird Baird	1955	6.25	12.50	25.00
Albums					
AMERICAN RECORDING SOCIETY					
G-441 [M]	Now's the Time	1957	12.50	25.00	50.00
ARCHIVE OF FOLK AND JAZZ					
214	Charlie Parker	1969	3.00	6.00	12.00
232	Charlie Parker, Volume 2	1970	2.50	5.00	10.00
254	Charlie Parker, Vol. 3	197?	2.50	5.00	10.00
295	Charlie Parker, Vol. 4	197?	2.50	5.00	10.00
315	Charlie Parker, Vol. 5	197?	2.50	5.00	10.00
BARONET					
B-105 [M]	A Handful of Modern Jazz	1962	5.00	10.00	20.00
BS-105 [R]	A Handful of Modern Jazz	1962	3.00	6.00	12.00
B-107 [M]	The Early Bird	1962	5.00	10.00	20.00
BS-107 [R]	The Early Bird	1962	3.00	6.00	12.00
BIRDLAND					
425 [10]	A Night at Carnegie Hall	1956	75.00	150.00	300.00
BLUE NOTE					
BT-85108	Charlie Parker at Storyville	198?	3.00	6.00	12.00
BLUE RIBBON					
8011 [M]	The Early Bird	1962	5.00	10.00	20.00
S-8011 [R]	The Early Bird	1962	3.00	6.00	12.00
CHARLIE PARKER					
PLP-401 [M]	Bird Is Free	1961	10.00	20.00	40.00
PLP-404 [M]	The Happy Bird	1961	10.00	20.00	40.00
PLP-406 [M]	Charlie Parker	1961	10.00	20.00	40.00
PLP-407 [M]	Bird Symbols	1961	10.00	20.00	40.00
PLP-408 [M]	Once There Was Bird	1961	10.00	20.00	40.00
CP-2-502 [(2) M]	Live at Rockland Palace, September 26, 1952	1961	12.50	25.00	50.00
CP-513 [M]	Charlie Parker Plus Strings	196?	10.00	20.00	40.00
PLP-701 [(3)]	Historical Masterpieces	196?	15.00	30.00	60.00
CLEF					
MGC-101 [10]	Charlie Parker with Strings	1958	—	—	—
—Canceled					
MGC-157 [10]	Charlie Parker	1954	100.00	200.00	400.00
MGC-501 [10]	Charlie Parker with Strings	1954	100.00	200.00	400.00
—Reissue of Mercury 501					
MGC-509 [10]	Charlie Parker with Strings, No. 2	1954	100.00	200.00	400.00
—Reissue of Mercury 509					
MGC-512 [10]	Bird and Diz	1954	100.00	200.00	400.00
—Reissue of Mercury 512					
MGC-513 [10]	South of the Border	1954	100.00	200.00	400.00
—Reissue of Mercury 513					
MGC-609 [M]	Charlie Parker Big Band	1954	100.00	200.00	400.00
MGC-646 [M]	The Magnificent Charlie Parker	1955	100.00	200.00	400.00
MGC-675 [M]	Charlie Parker with Strings	1955	100.00	200.00	400.00
MGC-725 [M]	Night and Day	1956	30.00	60.00	120.00
COLUMBIA					
C2 34808 [(2)]	One Night in Birdland	198?	3.00	6.00	12.00
—Reissue with new prefix					
JG 34808 [(2)]	One Night in Birdland	1977	3.75	7.50	15.00
JC 34831	Summit Meeting	1977	3.00	6.00	12.00
JC 34832	Bird with Strings Live	1977	3.00	6.00	12.00
CONCERT HALL JAZZ					
1004 [10]	The Fabulous Bird	1955	15.00	30.00	60.00
1017 [10]	The Art of Charlie Parker, Vol. 2	1955	15.00	30.00	60.00
CONTINENTAL					
16004 [M]	Bird Lives	1962	10.00	20.00	40.00
DEBUT					
DEB-611 [M]	Bird on 52nd Street	196?	12.50	25.00	50.00
DIAL					
LP-1 [M]	The Bird Blows the Blues	1949	1000.	2000.	4000.
—Mail-order offer					
LP-201 [10]	Charlie Parker Quintet	1949	200.00	400.00	800.00
LP-202 [10]	Charlie Parker Quintet	1949	200.00	400.00	800.00
LP-203 [10]	Charlie Parker	1949	200.00	400.00	800.00
LP-207 [10]	Charlie Parker Sextet	1949	200.00	400.00	800.00
LP-901 [M]	The Bird Blows the Blues	1950	150.00	300.00	600.00
LP-904 [M]	Alternate Masters	1951	150.00	300.00	600.00
LP-905 [M]	Alternate Masters	1951	150.00	300.00	600.00
ELEKTRA/MUSICIAN					
60019	One Night in Washington	1982	2.50	5.00	10.00
FANTASY					
OJC-041	Bird at St. Nick's	198?	2.50	5.00	10.00
OJC-044	Jazz at Massey Hall	198?	2.50	5.00	10.00
OJC-114	Bird on 52nd St.	198?	2.50	5.00	10.00
6011 [M]	Bird on 52nd St.	1964	7.50	15.00	30.00
6012 [M]	Bird at St. Nick's	1964	7.50	15.00	30.00
86011 [R]	Bird on 52nd St.	1964	3.75	7.50	15.00
86012 [R]	Bird at St. Nick's	1964	3.75	7.50	15.00
HALL OF FAME					
617	Giants of Jazz	197?	2.50	5.00	10.00
620	Takin' Off	197?	2.50	5.00	10.00
JAZZ WORKSHOP					
JWS-500 [M]	Bird at St. Nick's	1958	30.00	60.00	120.00
JWS-501 [M]	Bird on 52nd Street	1958	30.00	60.00	120.00
JAZZTONE					
J-1204 [M]	Giants of Modern Jazz	1955	12.50	25.00	50.00
J-1214 [M]	The Fabulous Bird	1955	12.50	25.00	50.00
J-1240 [M]	The Saxes of Stan Getz and Charlie Parker	1957	12.50	25.00	50.00
J-(# unknown) [M]	The Art of Charlie Parker, Vol. 2	1955	12.50	25.00	50.00
LES JAZZ COOL					
101 [M]	Les Jazz Cool, Volume 1	1960	12.50	25.00	50.00
102 [M]	Les Jazz Cool, Volume 2	1960	12.50	25.00	50.00
103 [M]	Les Jazz Cool, Volume 3	1960	12.50	25.00	50.00
MERCURY					
MGC-101 [10]	Charlie Parker with Strings	1950	125.00	250.00	500.00
—Reissue of 35010					
MGC-109 [10]	Charlie Parker with Strings, Volume 2	1950	125.00	250.00	500.00
MGC-501 [10]	Charlie Parker with Strings	1951	125.00	250.00	500.00
—Reissue of 101 with new number					
MGC-509 [10]	Charlie Parker with Strings, Volume 2	1952	125.00	250.00	500.00
—Reissue of 109 with new number					
MGC-512 [10]	Bird and Diz	1952	125.00	250.00	500.00
MGC-513 [10]	South of the Border	1952	125.00	250.00	500.00
MG-35010 [10]	Charlie Parker with Strings	1950	150.00	300.00	600.00
MGM					
M3G-4949	Archetypes	1974	3.00	6.00	12.00
MOSAIC					
129 [(10)]	The Complete Dean Benedetti Recordings of Charlie Parker	199?	25.00	50.00	100.00
ONYX					
221	First Recordings with Jay McShann	197?	3.00	6.00	12.00
PHOENIX					
10	New Bird	197?	2.50	5.00	10.00
12	New Bird, Vol. 2	197?	2.50	5.00	10.00
17	Yardbird in Lotusland	197?	2.50	5.00	10.00
PICKWICK					
PC-3054 [M]	Yardbird	196?	3.00	6.00	12.00
SPC-3054 [R]	Yardbird	196?	2.50	5.00	10.00
PRESTIGE					
24009 [(2)]	Charlie Parker	197?	3.75	7.50	15.00
24024 [(2)]	Parker/Powell/Mingus/Roach	197?	3.75	7.50	15.00
ROOST					
LP-2210 [M]	All Star Sextet	1958	30.00	60.00	120.00
LP-2257 [M]	The World of Charlie Parker	1963	10.00	20.00	40.00
SAVOY					
MG-9000 [10]	Charlie Parker	1950	125.00	250.00	500.00
MG-9001 [10]	Charlie Parker, Volume 2	1951	125.00	250.00	500.00
MG-9010 [10]	Charlie Parker, Volume 3	1952	125.00	250.00	500.00
MG-9011 [10]	Charlie Parker, Volume 4	1952	125.00	250.00	500.00
MG-12000 [M]	Charlie Parker Memorial	1955	25.00	50.00	100.00
MG-12001 [M]	The Immortal Charlie Parker	1955	25.00	50.00	100.00
MG-12009 [M]	Charlie Parker Memorial, Volume 2	1955	25.00	50.00	100.00
MG-12014 [M]	The Genius of Charlie Parker	1955	25.00	50.00	100.00
MG-12079 [M]	The Charlie Parker Story	1956	25.00	50.00	100.00
MG-12138 [M]	Bird's Night	1960	10.00	20.00	40.00
MG-12152 [M]	An Evening at Home with the Bird	196?	10.00	20.00	40.00
MG-12179 [M]	The "Bird" Returns	196?	7.50	15.00	30.00
MG-12186 [M]	Newly Discovered Sides by the Immortal Charlie Parker	1966	7.50	15.00	30.00
SAVOY JAZZ					
SJL-1107	Encores	197?	3.00	6.00	12.00
SJL-1108	Bird at the Roost	197?	3.00	6.00	12.00
SJL-1129	Encores, Vol. 2	198?	2.50	5.00	10.00
SJL-1132	One Night in Chicago	198?	2.50	5.00	10.00
SJL-1173	Bird at the Roost, Vol. 3	1987	2.50	5.00	10.00
SJL-1208	Original Bird: The Best on Savoy	198?	2.50	5.00	10.00
SJL-2201 [(2)]	Bird: The Savoy Recordings	197?	3.75	7.50	15.00
SJL-2259 [(2)]	Bird at the Roost: The Complete Royal Roost Performances, Vol. 1	198?	3.75	7.50	15.00
SJL-2260 [(2)]	Bird at the Roost: The Complete Royal Roost Performances, Vol. 2	1986	3.75	7.50	15.00
SJL-5500 [(5)]	The Complete Savoy Studio Sessions	197?	7.50	15.00	30.00
SPOTLITE					
101	Charlie Parker on Dial, Vol. 1	197?	2.50	5.00	10.00
102	Charlie Parker on Dial, Vol. 2	197?	2.50	5.00	10.00
103	Charlie Parker on Dial, Vol. 3	197?	2.50	5.00	10.00
104	Charlie Parker on Dial, Vol. 4	197?	2.50	5.00	10.00
105	Charlie Parker on Dial, Vol. 5	197?	2.50	5.00	10.00
106	Charlie Parker on Dial, Vol. 6	197?	2.50	5.00	10.00
STASH					
ST-260	Birth of the Bebop	1986	2.50	5.00	10.00
ST-280	The Bird You Never Heard	1988	2.50	5.00	10.00
TRIP					
5035 [(2)]	The Master	197?	3.00	6.00	12.00
5039 [(2)]	Birdology	197?	3.75	7.50	15.00
VERVE					
VSP-23 [M]	Bird Wings	1966	5.00	10.00	20.00
VSPS-23 [R]	Bird Wings	1966	3.00	6.00	12.00
UMV-2029	Now's the Time	198?	2.50	5.00	10.00
UMV-2030	Swedish Schnapps	198?	2.50	5.00	10.00
VE-2-2501 [(2)]	The Verve Years 1948-50	197?	3.75	7.50	15.00
VE-2-2508 [(2)]	Charlie Parker Sides	197?	3.75	7.50	15.00
VE-2-2512 [(2)]	The Verve Years 1950-51	197?	3.75	7.50	15.00
VE-2-2523 [(2)]	The Verve Years 1952-54	197?	3.75	7.50	15.00
UMV-2562	Charlie Parker with Strings	198?	2.50	5.00	10.00
UMV-2617	Jazz Perennial	198?	2.50	5.00	10.00
MGV-8000 [M]	The Charlie Parker Story, Volume 1	1957	20.00	40.00	80.00
V-8000 [M]	The Charlie Parker Story, Volume 1	1961	6.25	12.50	25.00
V6-8000 [R]	The Charlie Parker Story, Volume 1	196?	3.00	6.00	12.00
MGV-8001 [M]	The Charlie Parker Story, Volume 2	1957	20.00	40.00	80.00

Number	Title (A Side/B Side)	Yr	VG	VG+	NM
V-8001 [M]	The Charlie Parker Story, Volume 2	1961	6.25	12.50	25.00
V6-8001 [R]	The Charlie Parker Story, Volume 2	196?	3.00	6.00	12.00
MGV-8002 [M]	The Charlie Parker Story, Volume 3	1957	20.00	40.00	80.00
V-8002 [M]	The Charlie Parker Story, Volume 3	1961	6.25	12.50	25.00
V6-8002 [R]	The Charlie Parker Story, Volume 3	196?	3.00	6.00	12.00
MGV-8003 [M]	Night and Day (The Genius of Charlie Parker #1)	1957	20.00	40.00	80.00
V-8003 [M]	Night and Day (The Genius of Charlie Parker #1)	1961	6.25	12.50	25.00
V6-8003 [R]	Night and Day (The Genius of Charlie Parker #1)	196?	3.00	6.00	12.00
MGV-8004 [M]	April in Paris (The Genius of Charlie Parker #2)	1957	20.00	40.00	80.00
V-8004 [M]	April in Paris (The Genius of Charlie Parker #2)	1961	6.25	12.50	25.00
V6-8004 [R]	April in Paris (The Genius of Charlie Parker #2)	196?	3.00	6.00	12.00
MGV-8005 [M]	Now's the Time (The Genius of Charlie Parker #3)	1957	20.00	40.00	80.00
V-8005 [M]	Now's the Time (The Genius of Charlie Parker #3)	1961	6.25	12.50	25.00
V6-8005 [R]	Now's the Time (The Genius of Charlie Parker #3)	196?	3.00	6.00	12.00
MGV-8006 [M]	Bird and Diz (The Genius of Charlie Parker #4)	1957	20.00	40.00	80.00
V-8006 [M]	Bird and Diz (The Genius of Charlie Parker #4)	1961	6.25	12.50	25.00
V6-8006 [R]	Bird and Diz (The Genius of Charlie Parker #4)	196?	3.00	6.00	12.00
MGV-8007 [M]	Charlie Parker Plays Cole Porter (The Genius of Charlie Parker #5)	1957	20.00	40.00	80.00
V-8007 [M]	Charlie Parker Plays Cole Porter (The Genius of Charlie Parker #5)	1961	6.25	12.50	25.00
V6-8007 [R]	Charlie Parker Plays Cole Porter (The Genius of Charlie Parker #5)	196?	3.00	6.00	12.00
MGV-8008 [M]	Fiesta (The Genius of Charlie Parker #6)	1957	20.00	40.00	80.00
V-8008 [M]	Fiesta (The Genius of Charlie Parker #6)	1961	6.25	12.50	25.00
V6-8008 [R]	Fiesta (The Genius of Charlie Parker #6)	196?	3.00	6.00	12.00
MGV-8009 [M]	Jazz Perennial (The Genius of Charlie Parker #7)	1957	20.00	40.00	80.00
V-8009 [M]	Jazz Perennial (The Genius of Charlie Parker #7)	1961	6.25	12.50	25.00
V6-8009 [R]	Jazz Perennial (The Genius of Charlie Parker #7)	196?	3.00	6.00	12.00
MGV-8010 [M]	Swedish Schnapps (The Genius of Charlie Parker #8)	1957	20.00	40.00	80.00
V-8010 [M]	Swedish Schnapps (The Genius of Charlie Parker #8)	1961	6.25	12.50	25.00
V6-8010 [R]	Swedish Schnapps (The Genius of Charlie Parker #8)	196?	3.00	6.00	12.00
MGV-8100-3 [(3) M]	The Charlie Parker Story	1957	37.50	75.00	150.00
—Combines 8000, 8001 and 8002 in a box set					
V-8100-3 [(3) M]	The Charlie Parker Story	1961	15.00	30.00	60.00
—Combines 8000, 8001 and 8002 in a box set					
V-8409 [M]	The Essential Charlie Parker	1961	6.25	12.50	25.00
V6-8409 [R]	The Essential Charlie Parker	196?	3.00	6.00	12.00
V6-8787 [R]	Bird Set	1969	3.75	7.50	15.00
V3HB-8840 [(2)]	Return Engagement	197?	3.75	7.50	15.00
817442-1	Bird on Verve, Vol. 1: Charlie Parker with Strings	1985	2.50	5.00	10.00
817443-1	Bird on Verve, Vol. 2: Bird and Diz	1985	2.50	5.00	10.00
817444-1	Bird on Verve, Vol. 3: More Charlie Parker with Strings	1985	2.50	5.00	10.00
817445-1	Bird on Verve, Vol. 4: Afro-Cuban Jazz	1985	2.50	5.00	10.00
817446-1	Bird on Verve, Vol. 5: Charlie Parker	1985	2.50	5.00	10.00
817447-1	Bird on Verve, Vol. 6: South of the Border	1985	2.50	5.00	10.00
817448-1	Bird on Verve, Vol. 7: Big Band	1985	2.50	5.00	10.00
817449-1	Bird on Verve, Vol. 8: Charlie Parker in Hi-Fi	1985	2.50	5.00	10.00
823250-1	The Cole Porter Songbook	1986	2.50	5.00	10.00
833564-1	Charlie Parker Sides	198?	2.50	5.00	10.00
837176-1	Bird: The Original Recordings of Charlie Parker	1987	2.50	5.00	10.00
VOGUE					
LAE-12002 [M]	Memorial Album	1955	37.50	75.00	150.00
WARNER BROS.					
6BS 3159 [(6)]	The Complete Dial Recordings	1977	20.00	40.00	80.00
—Limited edition of 4,000 box sets					
2WB 3198 [(2)]	The Very Best of Bird	1977	5.00	10.00	20.00
ZIM					
1001	Lullaby in Rhythm	197?	3.00	6.00	12.00
1003	At the Pershing Ballroom, Chicago, 1950	197?	3.00	6.00	12.00
1006	Apartment Jam	197?	3.00	6.00	12.00

PARKER, CHARLIE/STAN GETZ/WARDELL GRAY

Albums

Number	Title (A Side/B Side)	Yr	VG	VG+	NM
DESIGN					
DLP-183 [M]	Charlie Parker/Stan Getz/Wardell Gray	196?	3.75	7.50	15.00

PARKER, CHARLIE; DIZZY GILLESPIE; RED NORVO

Albums

Number	Title (A Side/B Side)	Yr	VG	VG+	NM
DIAL					
LP-903 [M]	Fabulous Jam Session	1951	150.00	300.00	600.00

PARKER, CHARLIE/DIZZY GILLESPIE/BUD POWELL/MAX ROACH

Albums

Number	Title (A Side/B Side)	Yr	VG	VG+	NM
SAVOY					
MG-9034 [10]	Bird, Diz, Bud, Max	1953	150.00	300.00	600.00

PARKER, CHARLIE/COLEMAN HAWKINS/GEORGIE AULD

Albums

Number	Title (A Side/B Side)	Yr	VG	VG+	NM
JAM					
5006	Unearthed Masters, Vol. 1	198?	2.50	5.00	10.00

PARKER, JUNIOR

Also includes records as "Little Junior Parker."

45s

Number	Title (A Side/B Side)	Yr	VG	VG+	NM
BLUE ROCK					
4064	I Got Money/Lover to Friend	1968	2.00	4.00	8.00
4067	Reconsider Baby/Lovin' Man on Your Hands	1968	2.00	4.00	8.00
4080	Ain't Gon' Be No Cuttin' Loose/I'm So Satisfied	1969	2.00	4.00	8.00
4088	Easy Lovin'/You Can't Keep a Good Woman Down	1969	2.00	4.00	8.00
CAPITOL					
2857	The Outside Man/Darling, Depend on Me	1970	—	3.00	6.00
2997	Drownin' on Dry Land/River's Invitation	1970	—	3.00	6.00
DUKE					
120	Dirty Friend Blues/Can't Understand	1954	15.00	30.00	60.00
127	Please Baby Please/Sittin', Drinkin' and Thinkin'	1954	15.00	30.00	60.00
137	Backtracking/I Wanna Ramble	1954	17.50	35.00	70.00
147	Driving Me/There Better Not Be No Feel	1956	12.50	25.00	50.00
157	Mother-in-Law Blues/That's My Baby	1956	12.50	25.00	50.00
164	Next Time You See Me/My Dolly Bee	1957	7.50	15.00	30.00
168	That's Alright/Pretty Baby	1957	7.50	15.00	30.00
177	Peaches/Pretty Little Doll	1957	7.50	15.00	30.00
184	Wondering/Sitting and Thinking	1958	6.25	12.50	25.00
193	Barefoot Rock/What Did I Do	1958	6.25	12.50	25.00
301	Sweet Home Chicago/Sometimes	1959	5.00	10.00	20.00
306	Five Long Years/I'm Holding On	1959	5.00	10.00	20.00
309	Stranded/Blue Letter	1959	5.00	10.00	20.00
315	Dangerous Woman/Belinda Marie	1960	3.75	7.50	15.00
317	The Next Time/You're On My Mind	1960	3.75	7.50	15.00
326	I'll Learn to Love Again/That's Just Alright	1960	3.75	7.50	15.00
330	Stand By Me/I'll Forget About You	1960	3.75	7.50	15.00
335	Driving Wheel/Seven Days	1961	6.25	12.50	25.00
341	In the Dark/How Long Can This Go On	1961	3.00	6.00	12.00
345	Annie Get Your Yo-Yo/Mary Jo	1961	3.00	6.00	12.00
351	I Feel Alright Again/Sweeter As the Days Go By	1962	3.00	6.00	12.00
357	Foxy Devil/Someone Somewhere	1962	3.00	6.00	12.00
362	It's a Pity/Last Night	1963	3.00	6.00	12.00
364	If You Don't Love Me/I Can't Forget About You	1963	3.00	6.00	12.00
367	The Tables Have Turned/Yonders Wall	1963	3.00	6.00	12.00
371	Strange Things Happening/I'm Gonna Stop	1964	3.00	6.00	12.00
376	Things I Used to Do/That's Why I'm Always Crying	1964	3.00	6.00	12.00
384	I'm in Love/Jivin' Woman	1964	3.00	6.00	12.00
389	Crying for My Baby/Guess You Don't Know (The Golden Rule)	1965	3.00	6.00	12.00
394	These Kind of Blues (Part 1)/These Kind of Blues (Part 2)	1966	3.00	6.00	12.00
398	Walking the Floor Over You/Goodbye Little Girl	1966	3.00	6.00	12.00
406	Get Away Blues/Why Do You Make Me Cry	1966	3.00	6.00	12.00
413	Man or Mouse/Wait for Another Day	1966	3.00	6.00	12.00
MERCURY					
72620	Baby Please/Just Like a Fish	1966	2.50	5.00	10.00
72651	You Can Make It If You Care/Ooh Wee Baby, That's the Way You Make Me Feel	1967	2.50	5.00	10.00
72672	Country Girl/Sometimes I Wonder	1967	2.50	5.00	10.00
72699	I Can't Put My Finger On It/If I Had Your Love	1967	2.50	5.00	10.00
72733	Hurtin' Inside/What a Fool I Was	1967	2.50	5.00	10.00
72793	It Must Be Love/Your Love's All Over	1968	2.00	4.00	8.00
MINIT					
32080	Worried Life Blues/Let the Good Times Roll	1969	—	3.00	6.00
SUN					
187	Feelin' Good/Fussin' and Fightin' Blues	1953	100.00	200.00	400.00
—As "Little Junior's Blue Flames"					
192	Mystery Train/Love My Baby	1954	75.00	150.00	300.00
—As "Little Junior's Blue Flames"					

Albums

Number	Title (A Side/B Side)	Yr	VG	VG+	NM
ABC					
AC-30010	The ABC Collection	1976	3.75	7.50	15.00
ABC DUKE					
DLP-76	Driving Wheel	1974	3.75	7.50	15.00
DLP-83	The Best of Junior Parker	1974	3.75	7.50	15.00
BLUE ROCK					
SRB-64004	Honey-Drippin' Blues	1969	3.75	7.50	15.00
BLUESWAY					
BLS-6066	Sometime Tomorrow	1973	3.75	7.50	15.00
CAPITOL					
ST-564	Outside Man	1970	3.75	7.50	15.00
DUKE					
DLP-76 [M]	Driving Wheel	1962	37.50	75.00	150.00
—With Cadillac on front cover					
DLP-76 [M]	Driving Wheel	196?	25.00	50.00	100.00
—With Wagon Wheel on front cover					
DLP-83 [M]	The Best of Junior Parker	1967	12.50	25.00	50.00
DLPS-83 [P]	The Best of Junior Parker	1967	10.00	20.00	40.00
GROOVE MERCHANT					
513	Love Ain't Nothin'	1974	3.75	7.50	15.00
MCA					
27046	The Best of Junior Parker	1980	2.50	5.00	10.00
MERCURY					
MG-21101 [M]	Like It Is	1967	7.50	15.00	30.00
SR-61101 [S]	Like It Is	1967	6.25	12.50	25.00
MINIT					
24024	Blues Man	1969	6.25	12.50	25.00
UNITED ARTISTS					
UAS-6823	I Tell Stories Sad and True	1971	3.75	7.50	15.00

PARKER, JUNIOR, AND BOBBY BLAND

Also see each artist's individual listings.

Albums

Number	Title (A Side/B Side)	Yr	VG	VG+	NM
ABC DUKE					
DLP-72	Blues Consolidated	1974	3.75	7.50	15.00
DUKE					
DLP-72 [M]	Blues Consolidated	1961	37.50	75.00	150.00

PARKER, JUNIOR, AND JIMMY MCGRIFF

Also see each artist's individual listings.

Albums

Number	Title (A Side/B Side)	Yr	VG	VG+	NM
CAPITOL					
ST-569	Dudes Doin' Business	1971	3.75	7.50	15.00
UNITED ARTISTS					
UAS-6814	100 Proof Black Magic	1971	3.75	7.50	15.00

PARKER, ROBERT

45s

Number	Title (A Side/B Side)	Yr	VG	VG+	NM
IMPERIAL					
5842	Mash Potatoes All Night Long/Twistin' Out of Space	1962	3.00	6.00	12.00
5889	You're Lookin' Good/Little Things Mean a Lot	1962	3.00	6.00	12.00
5916	Please Forgive Me/You Got It	1963	3.00	6.00	12.00

Number	Title (A Side/B Side)	Yr	VG	VG+	NM
ISLAND					
044	Give Me the Country Side of Life/It's Hard But It's Fair	1975	—	2.00	4.00
074	A Little Bit Something/Better Luck in the Summer	1976	—	2.00	4.00
NOLA					
721	Barefootin'/Let's Go Baby (Where the Action Is)	1966	5.00	10.00	20.00
724	Ring Around the Hoses/She's Coming Home	1966	3.00	6.00	12.00
726	Happy Feet/The Scratch	1966	3.00	6.00	12.00
729	Tip Toe/Soul Kind of Loving	1966	3.00	6.00	12.00
730	A Letter To Santa/C.C. Rider	1966	3.00	6.00	12.00
733	Yak Yak Yak/Secret Agents	1967	3.00	6.00	12.00
735	Everybody's Hip-Hugging/Foxy Mama	1967	3.00	6.00	12.00
738	I Caught You in a Lie/Holdin' Out	1967	3.00	6.00	12.00
RON					
327	All Nite Long (Part 1)/All Nite Long (Part 2)	1959	3.75	7.50	15.00
331	Walkin'/Across the Track	1960	3.75	7.50	15.00
SILVER FOX					
12	You Shakin' Things Up/You See Me	1969	—	3.00	6.00
Albums					
NOLA					
LP-1001 [M]	Barefootin'	1966	7.50	15.00	30.00

PARKS, GINO

45s

Number	Title (A Side/B Side)	Yr	VG	VG+	NM
CRAZY HORSE					
1303	Nerves of Steel/Help Me Somebody	1968	7.50	15.00	30.00
FORTUNE					
528	Last Night I Cried/Just Go	1957	20.00	40.00	80.00
GOLDEN WORLD					
32	My Sophisticated Lady/Talkin' About My Baby	1966	5.00	10.00	20.00
MIRACLE					
3	Don't Say Bye Bye/(B-side unknown)	1960	200.00	400.00	800.00
TAMLA					
54042	That's No Lie/Same Thing	1961	15.00	30.00	60.00
54066	For This I Thank You/Fire	1962	15.00	30.00	60.00

PARKS, MICHAEL

45s

Number	Title (A Side/B Side)	Yr	VG	VG+	NM
MGM					
14092	Tie Me to Your Apron Strings Again/Won't You Ride in My Little Red Wagon	1969	—	2.50	5.00
14104	Long Lonesome Highway/Mountain High	1970	—	3.00	6.00
14154	Sally/Save a Little, Spend a Little	1970	—	2.50	5.00
14363	Won't You Ride in My Little Red Wagon/Big "T" Water	1972	—	2.50	5.00
VERVE					
10653	Drownin' on Dry Land/River's Invitation	1971	—	2.50	5.00
Albums					
FIRST AMERICAN					
7781	You Don't Know Me	1983	2.50	5.00	10.00
MGM					
SE-4646	Closing the Gap	1969	3.75	7.50	15.00
SE-4662	Long Lonesome Highway	1970	3.75	7.50	15.00
SE-4717	Blue	1970	3.75	7.50	15.00
SE-4784	The Best of Michael Parks	1971	3.75	7.50	15.00
VERVE					
V6-5079	Lost and Found	1971	3.75	7.50	15.00

PARKS, RAY

45s

Number	Title (A Side/B Side)	Yr	VG	VG+	NM
CAPITOL					
F3580	You're Gonna Have to Bawl, That's All/Just a-Hangin' Around	1956	17.50	35.00	70.00

PARKS, VAN DYKE

45s

Number	Title (A Side/B Side)	Yr	VG	VG+	NM
MGM					
13441	Do What You Wanta/Number Nine	1966	3.00	6.00	12.00
13570	Come to the Sunshine/Farther Along	1966	3.00	6.00	12.00
WARNER BROS.					
7026	Donovan's Colors Part 1/Part 2	1967	3.00	6.00	12.00
—As "George Washington Brown"					
7409	On the Rolling Sea When Jesus Speaks to Me/The Eagle and Me	1970	2.50	5.00	10.00
7609	Occapella/Ode to Tobago	1972	—	3.00	6.00
7632	Riverboat/John Jones	1972	—	3.00	6.00
Albums					
WARNER BROS.					
WS 1727	Song Cycle	1968	6.25	12.50	25.00
—Gold label					
WS 1727	Song Cycle	1968	3.75	7.50	15.00
—Green label with "W7" box logo					
WS 1727	Song Cycle	1970	3.00	6.00	12.00
—Green label with "WB" shield logo					
BS 2589	Discover America	1972	3.00	6.00	12.00
BS 2878	Clang of the Yankee Reaper	1975	3.00	6.00	12.00
23829	Jump!	1984	3.00	6.00	12.00
25968	Tokyo Rose	1989	3.00	6.00	12.00

PARLETTES, THE

45s

Number	Title (A Side/B Side)	Yr	VG	VG+	NM
JUBILEE					
5467	Tonight I Met An Angel/Because We're Very Young	1964	3.00	6.00	12.00

PARLIAMENT

Also see GEORGE CLINTON; FUNKADELIC; THE PARLIAMENTS.

12-Inch Singles

Number	Title (A Side/B Side)	Yr	VG	VG+	NM
CASABLANCA					
NBD 20113	Flash Light (10:31)	1977	10.00	20.00	40.00
—B-side is blank					
NBD 20208	Theme from The Black Hole/Big Bang Theory	1979	5.00	10.00	20.00
—Both songs on same side; B-side is blank					
876585-1	Flash Light (10:31)/P-Funk (Wants to Get Funked Up) (7:34)	198?	2.50	5.00	10.00
—"Timepieces" reissue					

45s

Number	Title (A Side/B Side)	Yr	VG	VG+	NM
CASABLANCA					
0003	The Goose (Part 1)/The Goose (Part 2)	1974	—	3.00	6.00
0013	Up for the Down Stroke/Presence of a Brain	1974	—	3.00	6.00
0104	Up for the Down Stroke/Presence of a Brain	1974	—	2.50	5.00
803	Up for the Down Stroke/Presence of a Brain	1974	—	2.50	5.00
811	Testify/I Can Move You	1974	—	2.50	5.00
831	Chocolate City/Chocolate City (Part 2)	1975	—	2.50	5.00
843	Ride On/Big Footin'	1975	—	2.50	5.00
852	P. Funk (Wants to Get Funked Up)/Night of the Tempasaurus Peoples	1976	—	2.50	5.00
856	Tear the Roof Off the Sucker (Give Up the Funk)/P-Funk	1976	—	2.50	5.00
—Blue label					
856	Tear the Roof Off the Sucker (Give Up the Funk)/P-Funk	1976	—	2.00	4.00
—Tan label					
864	Star Child (Mothership Connection)/Supergroovealistic	1976	—	2.50	5.00
871	Do That Stuff/Handcuffs	1976	—	2.50	5.00
875	Dr. Funkenstein/Children of Production	1977	—	2.50	5.00
892	Fantasy Is Reality/The Landing (Of the Mothership)	1977	—	2.50	5.00
900	Bop Gun (Endangered Species)/I've Been Watchin' You	1977	—	2.50	5.00
909	Flash Light/Swing Down, Sweet Chariot	1978	—	2.50	5.00
921	Funkentelechy/Funkentelechy (Part 2)	1978	—	2.50	5.00
950	Aqua Boogie (A Psychoalphadiscobetabioaquadoloop)/(You're a Fish and I'm a) Water Sign	1978	—	2.50	5.00
950 [PS]	Aqua Boogie (A Psychoalphadiscobetabioaquadoloop)/(You're a Fish and I'm a) Water Sign	1978	2.50	5.00	10.00
976	Rumpofsteelskin/Liquid Sunshine	1979	—	2.50	5.00
2222	Party People/Party People (Part 2)	1979	—	2.50	5.00
2235	Theme from The Black Hole/(You're a Fish and I'm a) Water Sign	1980	—	2.50	5.00
2250	The Big Bang Theory/The Big Bang Theory (Part 2)	1980	—	2.50	5.00
2317	Agony of DeFeet/The Freeze	1980	—	2.50	5.00
2330	Crush It/Body Language	1981	—	2.50	5.00
INVICTUS					
9077	I Call My Baby Pussy Cat/Little Ole Country Boy	1970	2.50	5.00	10.00
9091	Red Hot Mama/Little Ole Country Boy	1971	2.50	5.00	10.00
9095	Breakdown/Little Ole Country Boy	1971	2.50	5.00	10.00
9123	Come In Out of the Rain/Little Ole Country Boy	1972	2.00	4.00	8.00
Albums					
CASABLANCA					
NBLP 7002	Up for the Down Stroke	1974	10.00	20.00	40.00
NBLP 7014	Chocolate City	1975	10.00	20.00	40.00
NBLP 7022	Mothership Connection	1976	7.50	15.00	30.00
NBLP 7034	The Clones of Dr. Funkenstein	1976	7.50	15.00	30.00
NBLP 7053 [(2)]	Parliament Live/P. Funk Earth Tour	1977	10.00	20.00	40.00
NBLP 7084	Funkentelechy vs. the Placebo Syndrome	1977	7.50	15.00	30.00
NBLP 7125	Motor-Booty Affair	1978	7.50	15.00	30.00
NBPIX 7125 [PD]	Motor-Booty Affair	1978	10.00	20.00	40.00
NBLP 7195	Gloryhallastoopid (Or Pin the Tale on the Funky)	1979	7.50	15.00	30.00
NBLP 7249	Trombipulation	1980	7.50	15.00	30.00
NBLP 9003	Up for the Down Stroke	1974	12.50	25.00	50.00
—Original pressing, distributed by Warner Bros.					
822637-1	Greatest Hits	1984	3.75	7.50	15.00
824501-1	Funkentelechy vs. the Placebo Syndrome	1985	3.75	7.50	15.00
824502-1	Mothership Connection	1985	3.75	7.50	15.00
INVICTUS					
ST-7302	Osmium	1970	25.00	50.00	100.00

PARLIAMENTS, THE

All of the below are probably the same group, a Detriot-based R&B group led by GEORGE CLINTON that evolved into PARLIAMENT and FUNKADELIC.

45s

Number	Title (A Side/B Side)	Yr	VG	VG+	NM
APT					
25036	Poor Willie/Party Boys	1959	10.00	20.00	40.00
ATCO					
6675	A New Day Begins/I'll Wait	1969	5.00	10.00	20.00
FLIPP					
100/1	Lonely Island/You Make Me Wanna Cry	1960	10.00	20.00	40.00
—Red label					
100/1	Lonely Island/You Make Me Wanna Cry	1960	7.50	15.00	30.00
—Yellow label					
GOLDEN WORLD					
46	Heart Trouble/That Was My Girl	1966	12.50	25.00	50.00
LEN					
101	Don't Need You Anymore/Honey, Take Me Home with You	1958	20.00	40.00	80.00
REVILOT					
207	(I Wanna) Testify/I Can Feel the Ice Melting	1967	3.75	7.50	15.00
211	All Your Goodies Are Gone (The Loser's Seat)/Don't Be Sore at Me	1967	3.75	7.50	15.00
214	Little Man/The Goose (That Laid the Golden Egg)	1968	3.75	7.50	15.00
217	Look at What I Almost Missed/What You Been Growing	1968	3.75	7.50	15.00
223	Good Old Music/Time	1968	3.75	7.50	15.00

Number	Title (A Side/B Side)	Yr	VG	VG+	NM
228	A New Day Begins/I'll Wait	1968	7.50	15.00	30.00
SYMBOL					
917	You're Cute/I'll Get You Yet	1962	6.25	12.50	25.00
U.S.A.					
719	My Only Love/To Be Alone	1961	5.00	10.00	20.00

PARRIS, FRED

Not to be confused with FREDDIE PARIS. Also see THE CHAMPLAINS; THE CHEROKEES (5); THE FIVE SATINS; THE NEW YORKERS (1).

45s

Number	Title (A Side/B Side)	Yr	VG	VG+	NM
ATCO					
6439	Land of the Broken Hearts/Bring It Home to Daddy	1966	2.50	5.00	10.00
BIRTH					
101	Dark at the Top of My Heart/Benediction	196?	2.00	4.00	8.00
CHECKER					
1108	No Use in Crying/Walk a Little Faster	1965	2.50	5.00	10.00
GREEN SEA					
106	Blushing Bride/Giving My Love to You	1966	2.50	5.00	10.00
107	I'll Be Hangin' On/I Can Really Satisfy	1966	2.50	5.00	10.00
MAMA SADIE					
1001	In the Still of the Nite "67"/Heck No	1967	2.50	5.00	10.00

PARROTS, THE (1)

45s

Number	Title (A Side/B Side)	Yr	VG	VG+	NM
CHECKER					
772	Don't Leave Me/Weep, Weep, Weep	1953	125.00	250.00	500.00

PARROTS, THE (2)

45s

Number	Title (A Side/B Side)	Yr	VG	VG+	NM
MALA					
558	They All Got Carried Away/Hey, Put the Clock Back on the Wall	1967	3.00	6.00	12.00

PARSONS, BILL

Also see BOBBY BARE.

45s

Number	Title (A Side/B Side)	Yr	VG	VG+	NM
FRATERNITY					
835	The All American Boy/Rubber Dolly	1959	10.00	20.00	40.00
—This record is actually by Bobby Bare miscredited					
838	Educated Rock and Roll/Carefree Wanderer	1959	7.50	15.00	30.00
STARDAY					
526	Hod Rod Volkswagen/Guitar Blues	1960	7.50	15.00	30.00
544	The Price We Pay for Livin'/A-Waitin'	1960	5.00	10.00	20.00

PARSONS, GRAM

Also see THE BYRDS; THE FLYING BURRITO BROTHERS; THE INTERNATIONAL SUBMARINE BAND.

45s

Number	Title (A Side/B Side)	Yr	VG	VG+	NM
REPRISE					
1139	That's All It Took/She	1972	—	3.00	6.00
1192	Love Hurts/In My Hour of Darkness	1974	—	3.00	6.00
SIERRA					
104	Medley (Bony Moronie/40 Days/Almost Grown)/ /Conversations/Hot Burrito #1	1982	—	2.50	5.00
—Second song on side 2 by Gene Parsons					
104 [PS]	Gram Parsons and the Fallen Angels	1982	—	2.50	5.00
105	Love Hurts/The New Soft Shoe	1982	—	2.50	5.00
WARNER BROS.					
50013	Return of the Grievous Angel/Hearts on Fire	1982	—	2.50	5.00

Albums

Number	Title (A Side/B Side)	Yr	VG	VG+	NM
REPRISE					
MS 2123	G.P.	1973	3.75	7.50	15.00
MS 2171	Grievous Angel	1974	3.75	7.50	15.00
SIERRA					
SP-1963	Early Years, Volume 1 (1963-65)	198?	2.00	4.00	8.00
—Reissue of 8702					
GP-1973	Gram Parsons and the Fallen Angels Live '73	1982	2.50	5.00	10.00
8702	Early Years, Volume 1 (1963-65)	1979	2.50	5.00	10.00

PARTON, DOLLY

Also see KENNY ROGERS AND DOLLY PARTON; PORTER WAGONER AND DOLLY PARTON.

12-Inch Singles

Number	Title (A Side/B Side)	Yr	VG	VG+	NM
RCA					
JD-11425	Baby I'm Burning/I'm Falling in Love	1978	2.50	5.00	10.00
PD-13545	Potential New Boyfriend (Long)/(Short) (Instrumental)	1983	2.00	4.00	8.00
PW-13545 [DJ]	Potential New Boyfriend (Long Version)/ (Instrumental) (Short Version)	1983	2.50	5.00	10.00
JD-13712 [DJ]	Save the Last Dance for Me (Long)/(Short) (Instrumental)	1984	2.50	5.00	10.00
PW-13712 [DJ]	Save the Last Dance for Me (Long Version)/ (Instrumetnal) (Short Version)	1983	2.00	4.00	8.00
RCA VICTOR					
PD-11425	Baby I'm Burnin'/I Wanna Fall in Love	1978	3.00	6.00	12.00
—Pink vinyl					

45s

Number	Title (A Side/B Side)	Yr	VG	VG+	NM
COLUMBIA					
07665	The River Unbroken/More Than I Can Say	1988	—	—	3.00
07665 [PS]	The River Unbroken/More Than I Can Say	1988	—	—	3.00
07727	I Know You by Heart/Could I Have Your Autograph	1988	—	—	3.00
—With Smokey Robinson					
07727 [PS]	I Know You by Heart/Could I Have Your Autograph	1988	—	—	3.00
07995	Make Love Mine/Two Lovers	1988	—	—	3.00
68760	Why'd You Come In Here Lookin' Like That/Wait Til I Get You Home	1989	—	—	3.00
69040	Yellow Roses/Wait Til I Get You Home	1989	—	—	3.00
73200	He's Alive/What Is It We Love	1990	—	—	3.00
73226	Time for Me to Fly/The Moon, the Stars, and Me	1990	—	—	3.00
73341	White Limozeen/The Moon, the Stars, and Me	1990	—	—	3.00
73498	Slow Healin' Heart/Take Me Back to the Country	1990	—	—	3.00
73711	Rockin' Years/What a Heartache	1991	—	—	3.00
—A-side with Ricky Van Shelton					
73826	Silver and Gold/Runaway Feelin'	1991	—	—	3.00
74011	Eagle When She Flies/Wildest Dreams	1991	—	—	3.00
74183	The Best Woman Wins/Country Road	1992	—	—	3.00
—A-side with Lorrie Morgan					
74876	Romeo/The High and the Mighty	1993	—	—	3.00
—A-side: "Dolly Parton and Friends"					
74954	More Where That Came From/I'll Make Your Bed	1993	—	—	3.00
77083	Full Circle/What Will Baby Be	1993	—	—	3.00
77294	Silver Threads and Golden Needles/Let Her Fly	1993	—	—	3.00
—Dolly Parton/Tammy Wynette/Loretta Lynn					
77723	To Daddy/PMS Blues	1994	—	—	3.00
78079	I Will Always Love You/Speakin' of the Devil	1995	—	—	3.00
—A-side: "With Special Guest Vince Gill"					
DECCA					
72061	Honky Tonk Songs/Paradise Road	1998	—	—	3.00
72080	The Salt in My Tears/Hungry Again	1998	—	—	3.00
GOLD BAND					
1086	Puppy Love/Girl Left Alone	1959	250.00	500.00	1000.
MERCURY					
71982	It's Sure Gonna Hurt/The Love You Gave	1962	75.00	150.00	300.00
MONUMENT					
869	I Wasted My Tears/What Do You Think About Lovin'	1965	3.75	7.50	15.00
897	Old Enough to Know Better (Too Young to Resist)/Happy, Happy Birthday Baby	1965	3.75	7.50	15.00
913	Busy Signal/I Took Him for Granted	1965	3.75	7.50	15.00
922	Control Yourself/Don't Drop Out	1966	3.75	7.50	15.00
948	Little Things/I'll Put It Off Until Tomorrow	1966	3.75	7.50	15.00
982	Dumb Blonde/The Giving and the Taking	1967	2.50	5.00	10.00
1007	Something Fishy/I've Lived My Life	1967	2.50	5.00	10.00
1032	Why, Why, Why/I Couldn't Wait Forever	1967	2.50	5.00	10.00
1047	I'm Not Worth the Tears/Ping Pong	1968	2.00	4.00	8.00
03408	Everything Is Beautiful (In Its Own Way)/Put It Off Until Tomorrow	1982	—	2.00	4.00
—A-side with Willie Nelson; B-side with Kris Kristofferson					
03781	What Do You Think About Lovin'/You're Gonna Love Yourself (In the Morning)	1983	—	2.00	4.00
—A-side: Dolly Parton and Brenda Lee; B-side: Willie Nelson and Brenda Lee					
RCA					
5001-7-R	Do I Ever Cross Your Mind/We Had It All	1986	—	—	3.00
PB-10935	Light of a Clear Blue Morning/There	1977	—	2.00	4.00
PB-11123	Here You Come Again/Me and Little Andy	1977	—	2.00	4.00
PB-11240	Two Doors Down/It's All Wrong, But It's All Right	1978	—	2.00	4.00
JB-11296 [DJ]	Heartbreaker (same on both sides)	1978	2.50	5.00	10.00
—Promo only on red vinyl					
PB-11296	Heartbreaker/Sure Thing	1978	—	2.00	4.00
JB-11420 [DJ]	Baby I'm Burning (same on both sides)	1978	2.50	5.00	10.00
—Promo only on red vinyl					
PB-11420	Baby I'm Burning/I Really Got the Feeling	1978	—	2.00	4.00
GB-11505	Here You Come Again/Two Doors Down	1979	—	—	3.00
—Gold Standard Series					
PB-11577	You're the Only One/Down	1979	—	2.00	4.00
JB-11705 [DJ]	Great Balls of Fire (same on both sides)	1979	2.50	5.00	10.00
—Promo only on red vinyl					
PB-11705	Sweet Summer Lovin'/Great Balls of Fire	1979	—	2.00	4.00
PB-11926	Starting Over Again/Sweet Agony	1980	—	2.00	4.00
GB-11993	Baby I'm Burnin'/Heartbreaker	1980	—	—	3.00
—Gold Standard Series					
PB-12040	Old Flames Can't Hold a Candle to You/I Knew You When	1980	—	2.00	4.00
PB-12133	9 to 5/Odd Jobs	1980	—	2.00	4.00
PB-12133 [PS]	9 to 5/Odd Jobs	1980	—	2.50	5.00
PB-12200	But You Know I Love You/Poor Folks' Town	1981	—	2.00	4.00
PB-12282	The House of the Rising Sun/Working Girl	1981	—	2.00	4.00
GB-12316	9 to 5/Old Flames Can't Hold a Candle to You	1981	—	—	3.00
—Gold Standard Series					
PB-13057	Single Women/Barbara on Your Mind	1982	—	2.00	4.00
PB-13234	Heartbreak Express/Act Like a Fool	1982	—	2.00	4.00
PB-13260	I Will Always Love You/Do I Ever Cross Your Mind	1982	—	2.00	4.00
—A-side is the same song, but a different recording than that on APBO-0234					
PB-13260 [PS]	I Will Always Love You/Do I Ever Cross Your Mind	1982	—	2.50	5.00
PB-13361	Hard Candy Christmas/Me and Little Andy	1982	—	2.00	4.00
PB-13514	Potential New Boyfriend/One of Those Days	1983	—	—	3.00
PB-13619	Tennessee Homesick Blues/Butterflies	1984	—	—	3.00
PB-13703	Save the Last Dance for Me/Elusive Butterfly	1983	—	—	3.00
PB-13756	The Great Pretender/Downtown	1984	—	—	3.00
PB-13756 [PS]	The Great Pretender/Downtown	1984	—	—	3.00
PB-13856	Sweet Lovin' Friends/Too Much Water	1984	—	—	—
—Unreleased					
PB-13883	Sweet Lovin' Friends/God Won't Get You	1984	—	—	3.00
—With Sylvester Stallone					
JK-13944 [DJ]	Medley: Winter Wonderland/Sleigh Ride (same on both sides)	1984	—	2.00	4.00
PB-13944	Medley: Winter Wonderland-Sleigh Ride/The Christmas Song	1984	—	—	3.00
—B-side by Kenny Rogers					
PB-13987	Don't Call It Love/We Got Too Much	1985	—	—	3.00
GB-14070	Tennessee Homesick Blues/Hard Candy Christmas	1985	—	—	3.00
—Gold Standard Series					
PB-14218	Think About Love/Come Back to Me	1985	—	—	3.00
PB-14297	Tie Our Love (In a Double Knot)/I Hope You're Never Happy	1986	—	—	3.00
GB-14346	Don't Call It Love/Real Love	1986	—	—	3.00
—Gold Standard Series					
RCA VICTOR					
APBO-0145	Jolene/Love, You're So Beautiful Tonight	1973	—	2.50	5.00
APBO-0234	I Will Always Love You/Lonely Comin' Down	1974	—	2.50	5.00
PB-10031	Love Is Like a Butterfly/Sacred Memories	1974	—	2.00	4.00
PB-10164	The Bargain Store/I'll Never Forget	1975	—	2.00	4.00

Number	Title (A Side/B Side)	Yr	VG	VG+	NM
GB-10165	Jolene/My Tennessee Mountain Home	1975	—	—	3.00
—Gold Standard Series					
PB-10310	The Seeker/Love with Feeling	1975	—	2.00	4.00
PB-10396	We Used To/My Heart Started Breaking	1975	—	2.00	4.00
GB-10504	Love Is Like a Butterfly/Sacred Memories	1975	—	—	3.00
—Gold Standard Series					
GB-10505	I Will Always Love You/Lovely Comin' Down	1975	—	—	3.00
—Gold Standard Series					
PB-10564	Hey, Lucky Lady/Most of All, Why	1976	—	2.00	4.00
GB-10676	The Bargain Store/The Seeker	1976	—	—	3.00
—Gold Standard Series					
PB-10730	All I Can Do/Falling Out of Love with Me	1976	—	2.00	4.00
47-9548	Just Because I'm a Woman/I Wish I Felt This Way at Home	1968	2.00	4.00	8.00
47-9657	In the Good Old Days (When Times Were Bad)/Try Being Lonely	1968	2.00	4.00	8.00
47-9784	Daddy Come and Get Me/Chas	1969	—	3.00	6.00
47-9863	Mule Skinner Blues/More Than Their Share	1970	—	3.00	6.00
47-9928	Joshua/I'm Doing This for Your Sake	1970	—	3.00	6.00
47-9971	Comin' For to Carry Me Home/Golden Streets of Glory	1971	—	3.00	6.00
47-9999	My Blue Tears/The Mystery of the Mystery	1971	—	3.00	6.00
74-0132	Daddy/He's a Go-Getter	1969	—	3.00	6.00
74-0192	In the Ghetto/Bridge	1969	—	3.00	6.00
74-0243	My Blue Ridge Mountain Boy/'Til Death Do Us Part	1969	—	3.00	6.00
74-0538	Coat of Many Colors/Here I Am	1971	—	3.00	6.00
74-0538 [PS]	Coat of Many Colors/Here I Am	1971	2.50	5.00	10.00
74-0662	Touch Your Woman/Mission Chapel Memories	1972	—	2.50	5.00
74-0757	Washday Blues/Just As Good As Gone	1972	—	2.50	5.00
74-0797	Lord, Hold My Hand/When I Sing for Him	1972	—	2.50	5.00
74-0868	My Tennessee Mountain Home/Better Part of Life	1973	—	2.50	5.00
74-0950	Traveling Man/I Remember	1973	—	2.50	5.00

RISING TIDE

Number	Title (A Side/B Side)	Yr	VG	VG+	NM
56041	Just When I Needed You Most/For the Good Times	1996	—	—	3.00

Albums

COLUMBIA

Number	Title (A Side/B Side)	Yr	VG	VG+	NM
FC 40968	Rainbow	1987	2.50	5.00	10.00
FC 44384	White Limozeen	1989	3.00	6.00	12.00
C 46882	Eagle When She Flies	1991	5.00	10.00	20.00
—Available on vinyl only through Columbia House					

MONUMENT

Number	Title (A Side/B Side)	Yr	VG	VG+	NM
7623	In the Beginning	197?	3.00	6.00	12.00
MLP-8085 [M]	Hello, I'm Dolly	1967	7.50	15.00	30.00
SLP-18085 [S]	Hello, I'm Dolly	1967	10.00	20.00	40.00
SLP-18136	As Long As I Love	1970	5.00	10.00	20.00
KZG 31913 [(2)]	The World of Dolly	1972	5.00	10.00	20.00
KZG 33876 [(2)]	Hello, I'm Dolly	1975	5.00	10.00	20.00

PAIR

Number	Title (A Side/B Side)	Yr	VG	VG+	NM
PDL2-1009 [(2)]	Just the Way I Am	1986	3.00	6.00	12.00
PDL2-1116 [(2)]	Portrait	1986	3.00	6.00	12.00

RCA

Number	Title (A Side/B Side)	Yr	VG	VG+	NM
5706-1-R	The Best of Dolly Parton, Vol. 3	1987	2.50	5.00	10.00
6497-1-R	The Best There Is	1987	2.50	5.00	10.00

RCA CAMDEN

Number	Title (A Side/B Side)	Yr	VG	VG+	NM
ACL1-0307	Mine	1973	2.50	5.00	10.00
CAS-2583	Just the Way I Am	1972	2.50	5.00	10.00

RCA VICTOR

Number	Title (A Side/B Side)	Yr	VG	VG+	NM
APD1-0033 [Q]	My Tennessee Mountain Home	1973	5.00	10.00	20.00
APL1-0033	My Tennessee Mountain Home	1973	3.00	6.00	12.00
APL1-0286	Bubbling Over	1973	3.00	6.00	12.00
APL1-0473	Jolene	1974	3.00	6.00	12.00
APL1-0712	Love Is Like a Butterfly	1974	3.00	6.00	12.00
APL1-0950	The Bargain Store	1975	3.00	6.00	12.00
APL1-1117	The Best of Dolly Parton	1975	3.00	6.00	12.00
APL1-1221	Dolly	1975	3.00	6.00	12.00
APL1-1665	All I Can Do	1976	3.00	6.00	12.00
APL1-2188	New Harvest...First Gathering	1977	3.00	6.00	12.00
DJL1-2314 [DJ]	Personal Music Dialogue with Dolly Parton	1976	6.25	12.50	25.00
AFL1-2544	Here You Come Again	1977	3.00	6.00	12.00
AFL1-2797	Heartbreaker	1978	3.00	6.00	12.00
AHL1-3361	Great Balls of Fire	1979	3.00	6.00	12.00
AHL1-3546	Dolly Dolly Dolly	1980	3.00	6.00	12.00
AYL1-3665	Heartbreaker	1980	2.00	4.00	8.00
—"Best Buy Series" reissue					
AYL1-3764	My Tennessee Mountain Home	1980	2.00	4.00	8.00
—"Best Buy Series" reissue					
AHL1-3852	9 to 5 and Odd Jobs	1980	3.00	6.00	12.00
AYL1-3898	Jolene	1981	2.00	4.00	8.00
—"Best Buy Series" reissue					
LPM-3949 [M]	Just Because I'm a Woman	1968	25.00	50.00	100.00
LSP-3949 [S]	Just Because I'm a Woman	1968	7.50	15.00	30.00
—"Stereo" on black label					
LSP-3949 [S]	Just Because I'm a Woman	1968	5.00	10.00	20.00
—Orange label					
AYL1-3980	New Harvest	1981	2.00	4.00	8.00
—"Best Buy Series" reissue					
LSP-4099	In the Good Old Days	1969	5.00	10.00	20.00
LSP-4188	My Blue Ridge Mountain Boy	1969	5.00	10.00	20.00
LSP-4288	The Fairest of Them All	1970	5.00	10.00	20.00
AHL1-4289	Heartbreak Express	1982	3.00	6.00	12.00
LSP-4387	A Real Live Dolly	1970	6.25	12.50	25.00
—Four songs feature Porter Wagoner					
LSP-4398	Golden Streets of Glory	1971	5.00	10.00	20.00
AHL1-4422	Greatest Hits	1982	2.50	5.00	10.00
—Contains one Christmas song:					
AHL1-4422	Greatest Hits	1982	3.00	6.00	12.00
LSP-4449	The Best of Dolly Parton	1970	5.00	10.00	20.00
LSP-4507	Joshua	1971	5.00	10.00	20.00
LSP-4603	Coat of Many Colors	1971	5.00	10.00	20.00
LSP-4686	Touch Your Woman	1972	5.00	10.00	20.00
AHL1-4691	Burlap & Satin	1983	2.50	5.00	10.00
LSP-4752	My Favorite Song Writer: Porter Wagoner	1972	5.00	10.00	20.00
LSP-4762	Dolly Parton Sings	1972	3.75	7.50	15.00
AYL1-4829	Here You Come Again	1984	2.00	4.00	8.00
—"Best Buy Series" reissue					
AYL1-4830	9 to 5 and Odd Jobs	1984	2.00	4.00	8.00
—"Best Buy Series" reissue					
AHL1-4940	The Great Pretender	1984	2.50	5.00	10.00
AYL1-5146	The Best of Dolly Parton	1984	2.00	4.00	8.00
—"Best Buy Series" reissue					
AHL1-5414	Real Love	1985	2.50	5.00	10.00
AYL1-5437	Burlap & Satin	1985	2.00	4.00	8.00
—"Best Buy Series" reissue					
AHL1-5471	Collector's Series	1985	2.50	5.00	10.00
AHL1-9508	Think About Love	1986	2.50	5.00	10.00

PARTON, DOLLY/GEORGE JONES

Albums

STARDAY

Number	Title (A Side/B Side)	Yr	VG	VG+	NM
LP 429 [P]	Dolly Parton and George Jones	1968	10.00	20.00	40.00
—One side of Dolly in stereo, one side of "Possum" in rechanneled stereo					

PARTON, DOLLY/FAYE TUCKER

Albums

SOMERSET

Number	Title (A Side/B Side)	Yr	VG	VG+	NM
S-9700 [M]	Hits Made Famous by Country Queens	1963	6.25	12.50	25.00
SF-19700 [S]	Hits Made Famous by Country Queens	1963	7.50	15.00	30.00
—Dolly Parton sings songs made famous by Kitty Wells					
SF-29400	Dolly Parton Sings Country Oldies	1968	3.75	7.50	15.00

TIME

Number	Title (A Side/B Side)	Yr	VG	VG+	NM
2108	Country & Western Soul	1963	10.00	20.00	40.00

PARTRIDGE FAMILY, THE

Also see DANNY BONADUCE; DAVID CASSIDY.

45s

BELL

Number	Title (A Side/B Side)	Yr	VG	VG+	NM
910	I Think I Love You/Somebody Wants to Love You	1970	—	2.50	5.00
910 [PS]	I Think I Love You/Somebody Wants to Love You	1970	—	3.00	6.00
963	Doesn't Somebody Want to Be Wanted/You Are Always on My Mind	1971	—	2.50	5.00
963 [PS]	Doesn't Somebody Want to Be Wanted/You Are Always on My Mind	1971	—	3.00	6.00
996	I'll Meet You Halfway/Morning Rider on the Road	1971	—	2.50	5.00
45130	I Woke Up in Love This Morning/Twenty-Four Hours a Day	1971	—	2.50	5.00
45160	It's One of Those Nights (Yes Love)/One Night Stand	1971	—	2.50	5.00
45200	Am I Losing You/If You Ever Go	1972	—	2.00	4.00
45235	Breaking Up Is Hard to Do/I'm Here, You're Here	1972	—	2.00	4.00
45301	Looking Through the Eyes of Love/Storybook Love	1972	—	2.00	4.00
45336	Friend and a Lover/Something's Wrong	1973	—	2.00	4.00
45414	Lookin' for a Good Time/Money Money	1973	—	2.00	4.00
45414 [PS]	Lookin' for a Good Time/Money Money	1973	2.00	4.00	8.00

Albums

BELL

Number	Title (A Side/B Side)	Yr	VG	VG+	NM
1107	The Partridge Family At Home with Their Greatest Hits	1972	5.00	10.00	20.00
1111	The Partridge Family Notebook	1972	6.25	12.50	25.00
1122	Crossword Puzzle	1973	7.50	15.00	30.00
1137	Bulletin Board	1973	12.50	25.00	50.00
1319 [(2)]	The World of the Partridge Family	1974	10.00	20.00	40.00
6050	The Partridge Family Album	1970	5.00	10.00	20.00
6050	The Partridge Family Album Bonus Photo	1970	2.50	5.00	10.00
6059	Up to Date	1971	5.00	10.00	20.00
6059	Up to Date Book Cover	1971	2.50	5.00	10.00
6064	The Partridge Family Sound Magazine	1971	5.00	10.00	20.00
6066	A Partridge Family Christmas Card	1971	6.25	12.50	25.00
—With attached Christmas card					
6066	A Partridge Family Christmas Card	1971	3.75	7.50	15.00
—Without Christmas card					
6066	A Partridge Family Christmas Card	1971	10.00	20.00	40.00
—With Christmas card printed on the cover (later pressing)					
6072	The Partridge Family Shopping Bag	1972	5.00	10.00	20.00
6072	The Partridge Family Shopping Bag Bonus Shopping Bag	1972	2.50	5.00	10.00

LAURIE HOUSE

Number	Title (A Side/B Side)	Yr	VG	VG+	NM
H-8014 [(2)]	The Partridge Family	197?	12.50	25.00	50.00

PASSIONS, THE (1)

45s

ABC-PARAMOUNT

Number	Title (A Side/B Side)	Yr	VG	VG+	NM
10436	The Bully/The Empty Seat	1963	6.25	12.50	25.00

AUDICON

Number	Title (A Side/B Side)	Yr	VG	VG+	NM
102	Just to Be with You/Oh Melancholy Me	1959	10.00	20.00	40.00
105	I Only Want You/This Is My Love	1960	7.50	15.00	30.00
—Red label					
105	I Only Want You/This Is My Love	1960	5.00	10.00	20.00
—Red, black and white label					
106	Gloria/Jungle Drums	1960	7.50	15.00	30.00
108	Beautiful Dreamer/One Look Is All It Took	1960	7.50	15.00	30.00
112	Made for Lovers/You Don't Have Me Anymore	1961	10.00	20.00	40.00

DIAMOND

Number	Title (A Side/B Side)	Yr	VG	VG+	NM
146	Sixteen Candles/The Third Floor	1963	10.00	20.00	40.00

JUBILEE

Number	Title (A Side/B Side)	Yr	VG	VG+	NM
5406	Lonely Road/One Look Is All It Took	1961	5.00	10.00	20.00

OCTAVIA

Number	Title (A Side/B Side)	Yr	VG	VG+	NM
8005	Aphrodite/I've Gotta Know	1962	200.00	400.00	800.00

PASSIONS, THE (2)

45s

BACK BEAT

Number	Title (A Side/B Side)	Yr	VG	VG+	NM
573	Baby I Do/Man About Town	1966	2.50	5.00	10.00

TOWER

Number	Title (A Side/B Side)	Yr	VG	VG+	NM
424	Without a Warning/Just Like a Rolling Seal	1968	2.00	4.00	8.00

Number	Title (A Side/B Side)	Yr	VG	VG+	NM
443	I Can See My Way Through/Just Another Reason	1968	2.00	4.00	8.00
443	I Can See My Way Through/Without a Warning	1968	2.00	4.00	8.00
474	Just Like a Rolling Stone/Just Another	1969	2.00	4.00	8.00
485	Hijacked/Hijacked	1969	2.00	4.00	8.00

PASSIONS, THE (3)

45s

Number	Title (A Side/B Side)	Yr	VG	VG+	NM
CAPITOL					
F-3963	Jackie Brown/My Aching Heart	1958	7.50	15.00	30.00
ERA					
1063	Jackie Brown/My Aching Heart	1957	10.00	20.00	40.00

PASSIONS, THE (U)

Could be group (1) or (3), or a completely different group.

45s

Number	Title (A Side/B Side)	Yr	VG	VG+	NM
DORE					
505	Nervous About Sally/Tango of Love	1958	7.50	15.00	30.00
TOPAZ					
1317	It Ain't Fair/I'm So Afraid	196?	2.50	5.00	10.00

PASSPORT

45s

Number	Title (A Side/B Side)	Yr	VG	VG+	NM
ATCO					
7054	Ju-Ju Man/(B-side unknown)	1976	—	2.00	4.00
ATLANTIC					
3487	Loco-Motive/Mandrake	1978	—	2.00	4.00

Albums

Number	Title (A Side/B Side)	Yr	VG	VG+	NM
ATCO					
SD 36-107	Cross-Collateral	1975	3.00	6.00	12.00
SD 36-132	Infinity Machine	1976	3.00	6.00	12.00
SD 36-149	Iguacu	1977	3.00	6.00	12.00
SD 7042	Looking Through	1974	3.75	7.50	15.00
ATLANTIC					
SD 18162	Doldinger Jubilee '75	1976	3.00	6.00	12.00
SD 19177	Sky Blue	1978	2.50	5.00	10.00
SD 19233	Garden of Eden	1979	2.50	5.00	10.00
SD 19265	Oceanliner	1980	2.50	5.00	10.00
SD 19304	Blue Tattoo	1981	2.50	5.00	10.00
80034	Earthborn	1982	2.50	5.00	10.00
80144	Man in the Mirror	1983	2.50	5.00	10.00
81251	Running in Real Time	1985	2.50	5.00	10.00
81727	Heavy Nights	1986	2.50	5.00	10.00
81937	Talk Back	1989	2.50	5.00	10.00

PASTEL SIX, THE

45s

Number	Title (A Side/B Side)	Yr	VG	VG+	NM
CHATTAHOOCHIE					
696	I Can't Dance/Red River Quetzal	1966	2.50	5.00	10.00
DOWNEY					
101	Twitchin'/Wino Stomp	1962	7.50	15.00	30.00
101	Twitchin'/Open House at the Cinder	1962	7.50	15.00	30.00
102	Braum's Nightmare/Open House at the Cinder	1962	6.25	12.50	25.00
ZEN					
102	The Cinnamon Cinder (It's a Very Nice Dance)/ Bandido	1962	6.25	12.50	25.00
105	Sing Along Song/The Strange Ghost	1963	6.25	12.50	25.00
108	The Milkshake/Parchman Farm	1963	6.25	12.50	25.00
111	Miss Sue/Baby Please Don't Go	1963	6.25	12.50	25.00

Albums

Number	Title (A Side/B Side)	Yr	VG	VG+	NM
ZEN					
1001 [M]	The Cinnamon Cinder	1963	25.00	50.00	100.00

PASTELS, THE

45s

Number	Title (A Side/B Side)	Yr	VG	VG+	NM
ARGO					
5287	Been So Long/My One and Only Dream	1958	6.25	12.50	25.00
5297	You Don't Love Me Anymore/Let's Go to the Rock 'N' Roll Ball	1958	7.50	15.00	30.00
5314	So Far Away/Don't Knock	1958	6.25	12.50	25.00
ARK					
298	Jungle Run/K-Nif	196?	12.50	25.00	50.00
JUBILEE					
5495	First Star/Tokyo Melody	1965	3.00	6.00	12.00
MASCOT					
123	Been So Long/My One and Only Dream	1957	75.00	150.00	300.00
UNITED					
196	Put Your Arms Around Me/Boom De De Boom	1957	20.00	40.00	80.00

PATIENCE AND PRUDENCE

45s

Number	Title (A Side/B Side)	Yr	VG	VG+	NM
CHATATHOOCHIE					
665	Tonight You Belong to Me (New Version)/How Can I Tell Him	1965	2.50	5.00	10.00
LIBERTY					
55022	Tonight You Belong to Me/A Smile and a Ribbon	1956	7.50	15.00	30.00
55040	Gonna Get Along Without Ya Now/The Money Tree	1956	6.25	12.50	25.00
55058	Dreamer's Bay/We Can't Sing Rhythm and Blues	1957	6.25	12.50	25.00
55084	You Tattletale/Very Nice in Bali Bali	1957	6.25	12.50	25.00
55084 [PS]	You Tattletale/Very Nice in Bali Bali	1957	12.50	25.00	50.00
55107	Witchcraft/Over Here	1957	6.25	12.50	25.00
55125	Heavenly Angel/Little Wheel	1958	6.25	12.50	25.00
55154	All I Do Is Dream of You/Your Careless Love	1958	6.25	12.50	25.00
55169	Golly Oh Gee/Tom Thumb's Tune	1958	6.25	12.50	25.00
55207	Should I/Whisper Whisper	1959	3.75	7.50	15.00
—With Mike Clifford					
UNITED ARTISTS					
0012	Tonight You Belong to Me/Gonna Get Along Without You Now	1973	—	2.50	5.00
—"Silver Spotlight Series" reissue					

PATRICK, MILT

45s

Number	Title (A Side/B Side)	Yr	VG	VG+	NM
CAPITOL					
4634	Up to My Ears in Tears/When I Met You	1961	2.50	5.00	10.00
DEMON					
1518	A Fountain of Love/You Are My Inspiration	1959	3.00	6.00	12.00
EVEREST					
2014	I Don't Think I Wanna Do It/No Fool Like an Old Fool	1963	2.00	4.00	8.00
TERRI-ANN					
101	Merry Twistmas/Just A Doggone Dream	1962	2.50	5.00	10.00

PATRON SAINTS, THE

Albums

Number	Title (A Side/B Side)	Yr	VG	VG+	NM
PATRON SAINT					
JT-1001	Fohhob Bohob	1997	6.25	12.50	25.00
—Authorized reissue with bonus 7-inch single; numbered edition of 500					
(NO LABEL)					
JT-1001	Fohhob Bohob	1969	1000.	2000.	3000.
—100 copies were pressed					

PATTERSON, MIKE, AND THE FUGITIVES

45s

Number	Title (A Side/B Side)	Yr	VG	VG+	NM
IMPERIAL					
66083	Cookin' Beans/Jerky	1965	3.00	6.00	12.00
66118	Don't You Just Know It/Righteous Theme	1965	3.00	6.00	12.00

PATTO

Also see SPOOKY TOOTH.

45s

Number	Title (A Side/B Side)	Yr	VG	VG+	NM
ISLAND					
1208	Mummy/Singing the Blues on Reds	1972	—	3.00	6.00

Albums

Number	Title (A Side/B Side)	Yr	VG	VG+	NM
ISLAND					
SW-9322	Roll 'Em, Smoke 'Em, Put Another Line Out	1972	7.50	15.00	30.00
VERTIGO					
VEL-1001	Patto	1971	3.75	7.50	15.00
VEL-1008	Hold Your Fire	1972	3.75	7.50	15.00

PATTON, JIMMY

45s

Number	Title (A Side/B Side)	Yr	VG	VG+	NM
SAGE AND SAND					
261	Call Me/Forty-Nine Women	1958	30.00	60.00	120.00
282	Ocean Full of Tears/Twinklin' Teardrops	1959	10.00	20.00	40.00
SIMS					
103	Careful/Guilty	1955	12.50	25.00	50.00
—With Ann Jones					
104	Teenage Haert/Jalopy	1955	12.50	25.00	50.00
105	Ocean of Tears/I Don't Want It	1955	12.50	25.00	50.00
117	Okie's in the Pokie/Lonely Nights	1960	50.00	100.00	200.00
256	Can't Shake the Blues/(B-side unknown)	1965	3.00	6.00	12.00

Albums

Number	Title (A Side/B Side)	Yr	VG	VG+	NM
MOON					
101 [M]	Make Room for the Blues	1966	10.00	20.00	40.00
SIMS					
127 [M]	Blue Darlin'	1965	10.00	20.00	40.00
SOURDOUGH					
127 [M]	Blue Darlin'	1965	12.50	25.00	50.00
STEREOPHONIC					
LP-1002 [S]	Take 30 Minutes with Jimmy Patton	196?	30.00	60.00	120.00

PATTY AND THE EMBLEMS

45s

Number	Title (A Side/B Side)	Yr	VG	VG+	NM
CONGRESS					
263	Easy Come, Easy Go/It's the Little Things	1966	5.00	10.00	20.00
HERALD					
590	Mixed-Up, Shook-Up, Girl/Ordinary Guy	1964	5.00	10.00	20.00
593	The Sound of Music Makes Me Want to Dance/ You Took Advantage of a Good Thing	1964	3.75	7.50	15.00
595	And We Danced/You Can't Get Away from Me	1964	3.75	7.50	15.00
KAPP					
791	Let Him Go Little Heart/Try It, You Won't Forget It	1966	5.00	10.00	20.00
850	Please Don't Ever Leave Me/All My Tomorrows Are Gone	1967	5.00	10.00	20.00
870	I'll Cry Later/One Man Woman	1967	5.00	10.00	20.00
897	I'm Gonna Love You a Long, Long Time/My Heart's So Full of You	1968	3.75	7.50	15.00

PATTY FLABBIE'S COUGHED ENGINE

45s

Number	Title (A Side/B Side)	Yr	VG	VG+	NM
DIAMOND					
252	Billy Got a Goat/Tin Can Eater	1968	6.25	12.50	25.00

PAUL

See RAY HILDEBRAND.

PAUL, BILLY

12-Inch Singles

Number	Title (A Side/B Side)	Yr	VG	VG+	NM
PHILADELPHIA INT'L.					
3678	Bring the Family Back (5:53)/It's Critical (6:33)	1979	3.00	6.00	12.00
3706	False Faces (6:52)/(B-side unknown)	1979	3.00	6.00	12.00

45s

Number	Title (A Side/B Side)	Yr	VG	VG+	NM
GAMBLE					
232	Somewhere/Bluesette	1968	3.00	6.00	12.00
JUBILEE					
5081	That's Why I Dream/Why Am I	1952	7.50	15.00	30.00
5086	You Didn't Know/The Stars Are Mine	1952	7.50	15.00	30.00
NEPTUNE					
30	Mrs. Robinson/Let's Fall in Love All Over	1970	2.50	5.00	10.00

PHILADELPHIA INT'L.

Number	Title (A Side/B Side)	Yr	VG	VG+	NM
3120	Jesus Boy (You Only Look Like a Man)/Love Buddies	1980	—	2.50	5.00
3509	Love Buddies/Magic Carpet Ride	1971	—	3.00	6.00
3515	This Is Your Life/I Wish It Were Yesterday	1972	—	3.00	6.00
3521	Me and Mrs. Jones/Your Song	1972	—	2.50	5.00
3526	Am I Black Enough for You/I'm Gonna Make It This Time	1973	—	2.50	5.00
3538	Thanks for Saving My Life/I Was Married	1974	—	2.50	5.00
3551	Be Truthful to Me/I Wish It Was Yesterday	1974	—	2.50	5.00
3563	Billy's Back Home/I've Got So Much to Live For	1975	—	2.50	5.00
3572	When It's Your Turn to Go/July, July, July, July	1975	—	2.50	5.00
3584	Let's Make a Baby/My Head's On Straight	1976	—	2.50	5.00
3593	People Power/I Want Cha Baby	1976	—	2.50	5.00
3613	How Good Is Your Game/I Think I'll Stay Home Today	1977	—	2.50	5.00
3621	Let 'Em In/We All Got a Mission	1977	—	2.50	5.00
3630	I Trust You/Love Won't Come Easy	1977	—	2.50	5.00
3635	Only the Strong Survive/Where I Belong	1977	—	2.50	5.00
3639	Everybody's Breakin' Up/Sooner or Later	1978	—	2.50	5.00
3645	One Man's Junk/Don't Give Up on Love	1978	—	2.50	5.00
3676	Bring the Family Back/It's Critical	1979	—	2.50	5.00
3699	False Faces/I Gotta Put This Life Down	1979	—	2.50	5.00
3736	You're My Sweetness/(B-side unknown)	1979	—	2.50	5.00

Albums

Number	Title	Yr	VG	VG+	NM
GAMBLE					
SG-5002	Feeling Good at the Cadillac Club	1968	7.50	15.00	30.00
ICHIBAN					
ICH-1025	Wide Open	198?	2.50	5.00	10.00
NEPTUNE					
201	Ebony Woman	1970	5.00	10.00	20.00
PHILADELPHIA INT'L.					
Z 30580	Going East	1971	3.00	6.00	12.00
KZ 31793	360 Degrees of Billy Paul	1972	3.00	6.00	12.00
ZQ 31793 [Q]	360 Degrees of Billy Paul	1972	5.00	10.00	20.00
KZ 32118	Ebony Woman	1973	3.00	6.00	12.00
—Reissue of Neptune LP					
KZ 32119	Feeling Good at the Cadillac Club	1973	3.00	6.00	12.00
—Reissue of Gamble LP					
KZ 32409	War of the Gods	1973	2.50	5.00	10.00
ZQ 32409 [Q]	War of the Gods	1973	5.00	10.00	20.00
KZ 32952	Live in Europe	1974	2.50	5.00	10.00
ZQ 32952 [Q]	Live in Europe	1974	5.00	10.00	20.00
PZ 33157	Got My Head On Straight	1975	2.50	5.00	10.00
PZ 33843	When Love Is New	1975	2.50	5.00	10.00
PZ 34389	Let 'Em In	1976	2.50	5.00	10.00
PZ 34923	Only the Strong Survive	1977	2.50	5.00	10.00
JZ 35756	First Class	1979	2.50	5.00	10.00
Z2 36314 [(2)]	The Best of Billy Paul	1980	3.75	7.50	15.00
TOTAL EXPERIENCE					
TEL8-5711	Lately	1985	2.50	5.00	10.00

PAUL, BUNNY

45s

Number	Title (A Side/B Side)	Yr	VG	VG+	NM
BRUNSWICK					
55003	Poor Joe/Buzz Me	1957	3.75	7.50	15.00
55022	Breedle-Lump-Bump/The One You Love	1957	3.75	7.50	15.00
DOT					
15107	Magic Guitar/Never Let Me Go	1953	6.25	12.50	25.00
ESSEX					
344	New Love/You'll Never Leave My Side	1954	25.00	50.00	100.00
352	Such a Night/I'm Gonna Have Some Fun	1954	15.00	30.00	60.00
359	Lovey Dovey/Answer the Call	1954	15.00	30.00	60.00
364	Honey Love/I'll Never Tell	1954	25.00	50.00	100.00
371	You Are Always in My Heart/You Came a Long Way from St. Louis	1954	15.00	30.00	60.00
385	Brown Jug/Pam-Poo-Dey	1955	15.00	30.00	60.00
GORDY					
7017	We're Only Young Once/I'm Hooked	1963	5.00	10.00	20.00
POINT					
5	Sweet Talk/History	1956	10.00	20.00	40.00
ROULETTE					
4186	Such a Night/A Million Miles from Nowhere	1959	3.75	7.50	15.00

PAUL, LES

See note under LES PAUL AND MARY FORD.

45s

Number	Title (A Side/B Side)	Yr	VG	VG+	NM
DECCA					
27903	Blue Skies/Dark Eyes	1951	3.75	7.50	15.00
29013	Steel Guitar Rag/Guitar Boogie	1954	3.75	7.50	15.00
LONDON					
120	Los Angeles/The System	1969	—	3.00	6.00

Albums

Number	Title	Yr	VG	VG+	NM
CAPITOL					
N-16286	Early Les Paul	1982	2.00	4.00	8.00
DECCA					
DL-5018 [10]	Hawaiian Paradise	1949	25.00	50.00	100.00
DL-5376 [10]	Galloping Guitars	1952	25.00	50.00	100.00
DL 8589 [M]	More of Les	1957	10.00	20.00	40.00
GLENDALE					
6014	The Les Paul Trio	198?	2.50	5.00	10.00
LONDON					
50016	Multi-Trackin'	1979	3.00	6.00	12.00
LONDON PHASE 4					
SP-44101	Les Paul Now!	1968	3.75	7.50	15.00
VOCALION					
VL 3849 [M]	The Guitar Artistry of Les Paul	196?	3.00	6.00	12.00
VL 73849 [R]	The Guitar Artistry of Les Paul	196?	2.50	5.00	10.00

PAUL, LES, AND MARY FORD

Included in the Capitol listings are LES PAUL solo works. Some of these appear on B-sides of duet hits.

45s

Number	Title (A Side/B Side)	Yr	VG	VG+	NM
CAPITOL					
F1014	Nola/Jealous	1950	5.00	10.00	20.00
F1088	Dry My Tears/Cryin'	1950	5.00	10.00	20.00
F1192	Goofus/Sugar Sweet	1950	5.00	10.00	20.00
F1316	Tennessee Waltz/Little Rock Getaway	1950	5.00	10.00	20.00
F1373	Mockin' Bird Hill/Chicken Reel	1951	5.00	10.00	20.00
F1451	How High the Moon/Walkin' Whistlin' Blues	1951	6.25	12.50	25.00
F1592	Josephine/I Wish I Had Never Seen Sunshine	1951	3.75	7.50	15.00
F1621	Nola/Jealous	1951	3.00	6.00	12.00
—Reissue					
F1675	How High the Moon/Josephine	195?	3.00	6.00	12.00
—Reissue					
F1676	Tennessee Waltz/Mockin' Bird Hill	195?	3.00	6.00	12.00
—Reissue					
F1690	Meet Mister Callaghan/My Baby's Comin' Home	195?	3.00	6.00	12.00
—Reissue					
F1748	The World Is Waiting for the Sunrise/Whispering	1951	3.75	7.50	15.00
F1825	Just One More Chance/Jazz Me Blues	1951	3.75	7.50	15.00
F1881	Jingle Bells/Silent Night	1951	3.75	7.50	15.00
F1920	Tiger Rag/It's a Lonesome Old Town	1951	3.75	7.50	15.00
F2080	I'm Confessin' (That I Love You)/Carioca	1952	3.75	7.50	15.00
F2123	Smoke Rings/In the Good Old Summertime	1952	3.75	7.50	15.00
F2193	Meet Mister Callaghan/Take Me in Your Arms and Hold Me	1952	3.75	7.50	15.00
F2265	My Baby's Coming Home/Lady of Spain	1952	3.75	7.50	15.00
F2316	Bye Bye Blues/Mammy's Boogie	1953	3.75	7.50	15.00
F2400	I'm Sitting on Top of the World/Sleep	1953	3.75	7.50	15.00
F2486	Vaya Con Dios (May God Be With You)/Johnny (Is the Boy for Me)	1953	3.75	7.50	15.00
F2614	Don'cha Hear Them Bells/The Kangaroo	1953	3.75	7.50	15.00
F2617	Jungle Bells (Dingo-Dango-Day)/White Chirstmas	1953	3.75	7.50	15.00
F2735	I Really Don't Want to Know/South	1954	3.00	6.00	12.00
F2839	I'm a Fool to Care/Auctioneer	1954	3.00	6.00	12.00
F2928	Whither Thou Goest/Mandolino	1954	3.00	6.00	12.00
F3015	Someday Sweetheart/Song in Blue	1955	3.00	6.00	12.00
F3108	No Letter Today/Genuine Love	1955	3.00	6.00	12.00
F3165	Hummingbird/Goodbye My Love	1955	3.00	6.00	12.00
F3248	Amukiriki (The Lord Willing)/Magic Melody	1955	3.00	6.00	12.00
F3301	Texas Lady/Alabamy Bound	1955	3.00	6.00	12.00
F3302	Rudolph the Red-Nosed Reindeer/Santa Claus Is Comin' to Town	1955	3.00	6.00	12.00
F3329	Moritat (Theme from Threepenny Opera)/Nuevo Laredo	1956	2.50	5.00	10.00
F3389	Say the Words I Love to Hear/Send Me Some Money	1956	2.50	5.00	10.00
F3444	Cimarron/San Antonio Rose	1956	2.50	5.00	10.00
F3570	Blow the Smoke Away/Running Wild	1956	2.50	5.00	10.00
F3612	Cinco Robles (Five Oaks)/Ro-Ro-Robinson	1957	2.50	5.00	10.00
F3725	Tuxedos and Flowers/Hummin' and Waltzin'	1957	2.50	5.00	10.00
F3776	I Don't Want You No More/Strollin' Blues	1957	2.50	5.00	10.00
F3825	A Pair of Fools/Fire	1957	2.50	5.00	10.00
F3858	Goodnight My Someone/The Night of the Fourth	1957	2.50	5.00	10.00
F3934	More and More Each Day/A Small Island	1958	2.50	5.00	10.00
COLUMBIA					
31385 [S]	'Deed I Do/Makin' Whoopee!	1962	3.00	6.00	12.00
—"Stereo Seven" jukebox single, part of set JS7-52					
31386 [S]	A Cottage for Sale/Chasing Shadows	1962	3.00	6.00	12.00
—"Stereo Seven" jukebox single, part of set JS7-52					
31387 [S]	It's Been a Long, Long Time/After You've Gone	1962	3.00	6.00	12.00
—"Stereo Seven" jukebox single, part of set JS7-52					
31388 [S]	Am I Blue/You Brought a New Kind of Love to Me	1962	3.00	6.00	12.00
—"Stereo Seven" jukebox single, part of set JS7-52					
31389 [S]	(titles unknown)	1962	3.00	6.00	12.00
—"Stereo Seven" jukebox single, part of set JS7-52					
41222	Put a Ring on My Finger/Fantasy	1958	2.50	5.00	10.00
41222 [PS]	Put a Ring on My Finger/Fantasy	1958	3.75	7.50	15.00
41278	Jealous Heart/Big Eyed Gal	1958	2.50	5.00	10.00
41350	All I Need Is You/At the Save-a-Penny Super Store	1959	2.50	5.00	10.00
41592	The Poor People of Paris/All Night Long	1960	2.00	4.00	8.00
41660	Wonderful Rain/Take a Warning	1960	2.00	4.00	8.00
41994	Jura (I Swear I Love You)/It's Been a Long, Long Time	1961	2.00	4.00	8.00
41994 [PS]	Jura (I Swear I Love You)/It's Been a Long, Long Time	1961	3.00	6.00	12.00
42179	It's Too Late/Mountain Railroad	1961	2.00	4.00	8.00
42241	Goodnight Irene/Lonely Guitar	1961	2.00	4.00	8.00
42241 [PS]	Goodnight Irene/Lonely Guitar	1961	3.00	6.00	12.00
42419	Your Cheatin' Heart/Another Town, Another Time	1962	2.00	4.00	8.00
42419 [PS]	Your Cheatin' Heart/Another Town, Another Time	1962	3.00	6.00	12.00
42602	Playing Make Believe/I Just Don't Understand	1962	2.00	4.00	8.00
42602 [PS]	Playing Make Believe/I Just Don't Understand	1962	3.00	6.00	12.00
42754	Gentle Is Your Love/Move Along Baby (Don't Waste My Time)	1963	2.00	4.00	8.00
42754 [PS]	Gentle Is Your Love/Move Along Baby (Don't Waste My Time)	1963	3.00	6.00	12.00

7-Inch Extended Plays

Number	Title	Yr	VG	VG+	NM
CAPITOL					
EAP 1-416	How High the Moon//Josephine//Mockin' Bird Hill/Whispering	195?	5.00	10.00	20.00
EAP 1-416 [PS]	The Hit Makers, Volume 1	195?	5.00	10.00	20.00
EAP 2-416	(contents unknown)	195?	5.00	10.00	20.00
EAP 2-416 [PS]	The Hit Makers, Volume 2	195?	5.00	10.00	20.00
EAP 3-416	(contents unknown)	195?	5.00	10.00	20.00
EAP 3-416 [PS]	The Hit Makers, Volume 3	195?	5.00	10.00	20.00
EAP 1-495	Vaya Con Dios (May God Be With You)/Sleep//Lady of Spain/My Baby's Comin' Home	195?	5.00	10.00	20.00
EAP 1-495 [PS]	Vaya Con Dios	195?	5.00	10.00	20.00
EAP 1-540	I'm Sitting on Top of the World/South//Smoke Rings/Jazz Me Blues	195?	5.00	10.00	20.00

Number	Title (A Side/B Side)	Yr	VG	VG+	NM
EAP 1-540 [PS]	Sitting on Top of the World	195?	5.00	10.00	20.00
EAP 1-543	Jingle Bells/White Christmas//Santa Claus Is Comin' to Town/Silent Night	195?	5.00	10.00	20.00
EAP 1-543 [PS]	Christmas Cheer	195?	5.00	10.00	20.00
EAP 1-554	I'm a Fool to Care/I Really Don't Want to Know//Auctioneer/It's a Lonesome Old Town	1956	3.75	7.50	15.00
EAP 1-554 [PS]	I'm a Fool to Care	1956	3.75	7.50	15.00
EAP 1-559	Whither Thou Goest/Nola//Take Me in Your Arms and Hold Me/Mandolino	1955	5.00	10.00	20.00
EAP 1-559 [PS]	Whither Thou Goest	1955	5.00	10.00	20.00
EAP 1-577	(contents unknown)	195?	3.75	7.50	15.00
EAP 1-577 [PS]	Les & Mary, Volume 1	195?	3.75	7.50	15.00
EAP 2-577	(contents unknown)	195?	3.75	7.50	15.00
EAP 2-577 [PS]	Les & Mary, Volume 2	195?	3.75	7.50	15.00
EAP 3-577	(contents unknown)	195?	3.75	7.50	15.00
EAP 3-577 [PS]	Les & Mary, Volume 3	195?	3.75	7.50	15.00
EAP 1-599	(contents unknown)	195?	3.75	7.50	15.00
EAP 1-599 [PS]	Whither Thou Goest	195?	3.75	7.50	15.00
EAP 1-695	(contents unknown)	195?	3.75	7.50	15.00
EAP 1-695 [PS]	Songs for Today	195?	3.75	7.50	15.00
EAP 1-802	(contents unknown)	1956	3.75	7.50	15.00
EAP 1-802 [PS]	Time to Dream, Volume 1	1956	3.75	7.50	15.00
EAP 2-802	(contents unknown)	1956	3.75	7.50	15.00
EAP 2-802 [PS]	Time to Dream, Volume 2	1956	3.75	7.50	15.00
EAP 3-802	(contents unknown)	1956	3.75	7.50	15.00
EAP 3-802 [PS]	Time to Dream, Volume 3	1956	3.75	7.50	15.00
EAP 1-9121	Mister Sandman/That's What I Like//I Need You Now/The Things I Didn't Do	1955	3.75	7.50	15.00
EAP 1-9121 [PS]	Les Paul and Mary Ford	1955	3.75	7.50	15.00
Albums					
CAPITOL					
H 226 [10]	The New Sound, Volume 1	1950	20.00	40.00	80.00
T 226 [M]	The New Sound, Volume 1	1955	12.50	25.00	50.00
H 286 [10]	The New Sound, Volume 2	1951	20.00	40.00	80.00
SM-286	The New Sound, Volume 2	197?	2.50	5.00	10.00
T 286 [M]	The New Sound, Volume 2	1955	12.50	25.00	50.00
H 356 [10]	Bye Bye Blues	1952	20.00	40.00	80.00
T 356 [M]	Bye Bye Blues	1955	12.50	25.00	50.00
H 416 [10]	The Hit Makers	1953	20.00	40.00	80.00
T 416 [M]	The Hit Makers	1955	12.50	25.00	50.00
H 577 [10]	Les and Mary	1955	20.00	40.00	80.00
W 577 [M]	Les and Mary	1955	12.50	25.00	50.00
T 802 [M]	Time to Dream	1956	12.50	25.00	50.00
DT 1476 [R]	The Hits of Les and Mary	1960	5.00	10.00	20.00
T 1476 [M]	The Hits of Les and Mary	1960	6.25	12.50	25.00
SM-11308	The World Is Still Waiting for the Sunrise	197?	2.50	5.00	10.00
—Reissue with new prefix					
ST-11308	The World Is Still Waiting for the Sunrise	1974	3.00	6.00	12.00
COLUMBIA					
CL 1276 [M]	Lover's Luau	1959	5.00	10.00	20.00
CL 1688 [M]	Warm and Wonderful	1962	5.00	10.00	20.00
CL 1821 [M]	Bouquet of Roses	1962	5.00	10.00	20.00
CL 1928 [M]	Swingin' South	1963	3.75	7.50	15.00
CS 8488 [S]	Warm and Wonderful	1962	6.25	12.50	25.00
CS 8621 [S]	Bouquet of Roses	1962	6.25	12.50	25.00
CS 8728 [S]	Swingin' South	1963	5.00	10.00	20.00
HARMONY					
HL 7333 [M]	The Fabulous Les Paul and Mary Ford	1965	3.00	6.00	12.00
HS 11133 [S]	The Fabulous Les Paul and Mary Ford	1965	3.00	6.00	12.00
PICKWICK					
SPC-3122	Brazil	197?	2.50	5.00	10.00

PAUL, LOUIS

Number	Title (A Side/B Side)	Yr	VG	VG+	NM
45s					
ENTERPRISE					
9056	Gotta Get Away/With a Little Bit of Love	1972	—	3.00	6.00
9060	It's Christmas Time/Santa Claus Is on His Way Again	1972	—	3.00	6.00
9077	Merry-Go-Round/Mister Crystal	1973	—	3.00	6.00
9094	I Like Rock and Roll/My Dream	1974	—	3.00	6.00
Albums					
ENTERPRISE					
ENS-1034	Reflections of the Way It Really Is	1971	3.75	7.50	15.00

PAUL AND PAULA

Also see RAY HILDEBRAND; JILL JACKSON.

Number	Title (A Side/B Side)	Yr	VG	VG+	NM
45s					
LE CAM					
99	The Beginning of Love/All I Want Is You	1963	5.00	10.00	20.00
305	From the Top of the World/All I Want Is You	197?	—	2.00	4.00
—As "Jill and Ray"					
315	Hey Paula ('77 Disco)/(Instrumental)	1977	—	2.00	4.00
321	Hey Paula/Paula (My Love)	1978	—	2.00	4.00
—Reissued in 1982 with the same catalog number					
354	Hey Paula/Elmer's Tune	198?	—	2.00	4.00
979	Hey Paula/Bobbie Is the One	1962	12.50	25.00	50.00
—As "Jill and Ray"					
PHILIPS					
40084	Hey Paula/Bobby Is the One	1962	3.75	7.50	15.00
40096	Young Lovers/Ba-Hey-Be	1963	3.00	6.00	12.00
40096 [PS]	Young Lovers/Ba-Hey-Be	1963	5.00	10.00	20.00
40114	First Quarrel/School Is Thru	1963	3.00	6.00	12.00
40114 [PS]	First Quarrel/School Is Thru	1963	5.00	10.00	20.00
40130	Something Old, Something New/Flipped Over You	1963	3.00	6.00	12.00
40142	First Day Back at School/A Perfect Pair	1963	3.00	6.00	12.00
40158	Holiday for Teens/Holiday Hootenanny	1963	3.00	6.00	12.00
40168	We'll Never Break Up for Good/Crazy Little Things	1964	2.50	5.00	10.00
40209	The Young Years/Darlin'	1964	2.50	5.00	10.00
40234	No Other Baby/Too Dark to See	1964	2.50	5.00	10.00
40268	True Love/Any Way You Want Me	1965	2.00	4.00	8.00
40296	Dear Paula/All the Love	1965	2.00	4.00	8.00
40352	All I Want Is You/The Beginning of Love	1966	2.50	5.00	10.00
UNI					
55052	All These Things/Wedding	1968	2.00	4.00	8.00
UNITED ARTISTS					
50712	Moments Like These/Mrs. Bean	1970	—	3.00	6.00
Albums					
PHILIPS					
PHM 200078 [M]	Paul and Paula Sing for Young Lovers	1963	7.50	15.00	30.00
PHM 200089 [M]	We Go Together	1963	7.50	15.00	30.00
PHM 200101 [M]	Holiday for Teens	1963	7.50	15.00	30.00
PHS 600078 [S]	Paul and Paula Sing for Young Lovers	1963	10.00	20.00	40.00
PHS 600089 [S]	We Go Together	1963	10.00	20.00	40.00
PHS 600101 [S]	Holiday for Teens	1963	10.00	20.00	40.00

PAULA, MARLENA

Number	Title (A Side/B Side)	Yr	VG	VG+	NM
45s					
REGENT					
7506	I Wanna Spend Christmas with Elvis/Once More It's Christmas	1956	12.50	25.00	50.00

PAULSON, BUTCH

Number	Title (A Side/B Side)	Yr	VG	VG+	NM
45s					
VIRGELLE					
708	Man from Mars/My Own Brother	195?	25.00	50.00	100.00
718	Candy Lou/Today Was Blue Tomorrow	195?	12.50	25.00	50.00

PAULSON, PAT

Number	Title (A Side/B Side)	Yr	VG	VG+	NM
Albums					
RUBICON/MERCURY					
SR 61179	Pat Paulson for President	1968	5.00	10.00	20.00
SR 61251	Live at the Ice House	1970	3.75	7.50	15.00

PAUPERS, THE

Number	Title (A Side/B Side)	Yr	VG	VG+	NM
45s					
VERVE FOLKWAYS					
5033	Copper Penny/If I Call You by Some Other Name	1966	2.50	5.00	10.00
5043	Let Me Be/Simple Deed	1967	2.50	5.00	10.00
VERVE FORECAST					
5056	One Rainy Day/Tudor Impressions	1967	2.50	5.00	10.00
5062	Magic People/Black Thank You Package	1967	2.50	5.00	10.00
5074	Think I Care/White Song	1967	2.50	5.00	10.00
5094	Another Man's Hair on My Razor/Cairo Hotel	1968	2.50	5.00	10.00
Albums					
VERVE FORECAST					
FT-3026 [M]	Magic People	1967	5.00	10.00	20.00
FTS-3026 [S]	Magic People	1967	5.00	10.00	20.00
FTS-3051	Ellis Island	1968	3.75	7.50	15.00

PAVLOV'S DOG

Number	Title (A Side/B Side)	Yr	VG	VG+	NM
45s					
ABC					
12086	Episode/Julia	1975	2.50	5.00	10.00
Albums					
ABC					
D-866	Pampered Menial	1975	6.25	12.50	25.00
COLUMBIA					
PC 33552	Pampered Menial	1976	3.00	6.00	12.00
—Reissue of ABC album					
PC 33964	At the Sound of the Bell	1976	3.00	6.00	12.00

PAVONE, RITA

Number	Title (A Side/B Side)	Yr	VG	VG+	NM
45s					
POLYDOR					
15011	'Til Tomorrow/Try It and See	1970	—	3.00	6.00
RCA VICTOR					
47-8212	Cuore/Ballo del Mattone	1963	2.00	4.00	8.00
47-8365	Remember Me/Just One More	1964	2.00	4.00	8.00
47-8365 [PS]	Remember Me/Just One More	1964	2.50	5.00	10.00
47-8420	Wait for Me/It's Not Easy	1964	2.00	4.00	8.00
47-8420 [PS]	Wait for Me/It's Not Easy	1964	2.50	5.00	10.00
47-8538	I Don't Wanna Be Hurt/Eyes of Mine	1965	2.00	4.00	8.00
47-8612	Oh My Mama/Right Now	1965	2.00	4.00	8.00
Albums					
RCA VICTOR					
LPM-2900 [M]	Rita Pavone	1964	3.75	7.50	15.00
LSP-2900 [S]	Rita Pavone	1964	5.00	10.00	20.00
LPM-2996 [M]	Small Wonder	1965	3.75	7.50	15.00
LSP-2996 [S]	Small Wonder	1965	5.00	10.00	20.00

PAXTON, GARY

Also see THE HOLLYWOOD ARGYLES; THE PLEDGES; SKIP AND FLIP.

Number	Title (A Side/B Side)	Yr	VG	VG+	NM
45s					
CAPITOL					
5467	My Heart Won't Let My Lips Say Goodbye/It's My Way (Of Lovin' You)	1965	3.75	7.50	15.00
5707	Goin' Through the Motions/You Got to Do the Best You Can	1966	3.75	7.50	15.00
5975	Mother-in-Law/Miles and Cities	1967	3.75	7.50	15.00
FELSTED					
8691	Sweet Senorita from Santa Fe/Kansas City	1964	5.00	10.00	20.00
GARPAX					
44172	It Had to Be You/We're Going Back Together	1963	5.00	10.00	20.00
44177	The Scavenger/How to Be a Fool (In Six Easy Lessons)	1963	5.00	10.00	20.00
44180	Two Duel Bump Camel Named Robert E. Lee/Your Past Is Back Again	1964	5.00	10.00	20.00
LIBERTY					
55407	Teen Age Crush/It's So Funny I Could Cry	1962	5.00	10.00	20.00
55485	Stop Twistin' Baby/Alley Oop Was a Two Dab Man	1962	5.00	10.00	20.00
55584	Spooky Movies (Part 1)/Spooky Movies (Part 2)	1963	5.00	10.00	20.00

Number	Title (A Side/B Side)	Yr	VG	VG+	NM
LONDON					
5208	Super Torque/Cute Little Coly	1964	5.00	10.00	20.00
LUTE					
5801	You're Ruinin' My Gladness/The Way I See It	1960	5.00	10.00	20.00
MGM					
14306	Carin' for Karen/Out on a Limb	1971	—	3.00	6.00
14362	Rocky Top/Parchman Farm	1972	—	3.00	6.00
PAX					
2406	The Big A/The Big M	197?	—	3.00	6.00
—Red vinyl					
PRIVATE STOCK					
45007	The Clone Affair/(B-side unknown)	1975	—	2.50	5.00
RCA VICTOR					
APBO-0081	It's Hard to Be a Rock and Roll Star When You're Old and Fat/White Tornado Alias Gary S. Paxton	1973	—	2.50	5.00
PB-10449	Too Far Gone (To Care What You Do to Me)/ Freedom Lives in a Country Song	1975	—	2.50	5.00
74-0916	Shadow of Your Memory/This Little Light of Mine	1973	—	2.50	5.00
Albums					
NEW PAX					
NP-33005	The Astonishing, Outrageous, Amazing, Incredible, Unbelievably Different World of Gary S. Paxton	1976	3.00	6.00	12.00
NP-33033	More from the Astonishing, Outrageous, Amazing, Incredible, Unbelievable World of Gary S. Paxton	1977	3.00	6.00	12.00
NP-33048	The Gospel According to Gary S.	1979	3.00	6.00	12.00
NP-33080	(Some of) The Best of Gary S. Paxton (So Far)	1980	3.00	6.00	12.00
PAX					
R-2406	Terminally Weird but Godly Right/Anchored in the Rock of Ages	1978	3.00	6.00	12.00
R-2411	Gary Sanford Paxton	1979	3.00	6.00	12.00

PAXTON, TOM

45s

Number	Title (A Side/B Side)	Yr	VG	VG+	NM
ELEKTRA					
45667	Crazy John/Things I Notice Now	1969	—	3.00	6.00
45674	Jimmy Newman/Forest Lawn	1970	—	3.00	6.00
45703	Whose Garden Was This/Annie's Going to Sing Her Song	1970	—	3.00	6.00
REPRISE					
1110	Peace Will Come (According to Plan)/Jesus Christ S.R.O.	1972	—	2.50	5.00
VANGUARD					
35206	The Death of Stephen Biko/Anita O.J.	1977	—	2.50	5.00
Albums					
ELEKTRA					
EKL-277 [M]	Ramblin' Boy	1964	5.00	10.00	20.00
EKL-298 [M]	Ain't That News	1965	5.00	10.00	20.00
EKL-317 [M]	Outward Bound	1966	5.00	10.00	20.00
7E-2003 [(2)]	The Compleat Tom Paxton	1971	5.00	10.00	20.00
EKS-7277 [S]	Ramblin' Boy	1964	6.25	12.50	25.00
EKS-7298 [S]	Ain't That News	1965	6.25	12.50	25.00
EKS-7317 [S]	Outward Bound	1966	6.25	12.50	25.00
EKS-74019	Morning Again	1968	5.00	10.00	20.00
EKS-74043	The Things I Notice Now	1969	3.75	7.50	15.00
EKS-74066	Tom Paxton 6	1970	3.75	7.50	15.00
FLYING FISH					
FF-280	Even a Gray Day	1983	2.50	5.00	10.00
FF-356	One Million Lawyers...And Other Disasters	1986	2.50	5.00	10.00
FF-408	The Marvellous Toy and Other Gallimaufry	1987	2.50	5.00	10.00
FF-414	And Loving You	1987	2.50	5.00	10.00
FF-486	Politics	199?	3.00	6.00	12.00
FF-519	The Very Best of Tom Paxton	199?	3.00	6.00	12.00
GASLIGHT					
GV-116 [M]	I'm the Man Who Built the Bridges	1962	20.00	40.00	80.00
HOGEYE					
004	Bulletin...We Interrupt This Record	198?	2.50	5.00	10.00
MOUNTAIN RAILROAD					
52792	Up and Up	1980	3.00	6.00	12.00
52796	The Paxton Report	198?	3.00	6.00	12.00
PRIVATE STOCK					
PS-2002	Something in My Life	1975	3.00	6.00	12.00
REPRISE					
MS 2096	Peace Will Come	1972	3.75	7.50	15.00
MS 2144	New Songs for Old Friends	1973	3.75	7.50	15.00
RS 6443	How Come the Sun	1971	3.75	7.50	15.00
VANGUARD					
VSD-79395	New Songs from the Briarpatch	1977	3.00	6.00	12.00
VSD-79411	Heroes	1978	3.00	6.00	12.00

PAYCHECK, JOHNNY

45s

Number	Title (A Side/B Side)	Yr	VG	VG+	NM
AMI					
1322	I Never Got Over You/Ole Pay Ain't Checked Out Yet	1984	—	2.50	5.00
1323	You're Every Step I Take/I Can't Stop Drinking	1985	—	2.50	5.00
1327	Everything Is Changing/Palimony	1985	—	2.50	5.00
CERTRON					
10003	Forever Ended Yesterday/It's For Sure I Can't Go On	1970	2.00	4.00	8.00
DAMASCUS					
2001	Scars/(B-side unknown)	1989	—	3.00	6.00
DECCA					
9-30763	On This Mountaintop/It's Been a Long, Long Time for Me	1958	7.50	15.00	30.00
—A-side as "Donny Young and Roger Miller"; B-side as "Donny Young"					
9-30881	The Old Man and the River/Pictures Can't Talk Back	1959	6.25	12.50	25.00
—As "Donny Young"					
31077	Shakin' the Blues/Miracle of Love	1960	10.00	20.00	40.00
—As "Donny Young"					
31283	Go Ring the Bells/I Guess I Had It Coming	1961	6.25	12.50	25.00
—As "Donny Young"					
DESPERADO					
1001	Out of Beer/Oklahoma Lady	1988	—	3.00	6.00
EPIC					
19-02144	Yesterday's News (Just Hit Home Today)/ Someone Told My Story	1981	—	2.00	4.00
14-02684	The Highlight of '81/Sharon Rae	1982	—	2.00	4.00
14-02817	No Way Out/We've All Gone Crazy	1982	—	2.00	4.00
14-03052	D.O.A. (Drunk On Arrival)/Gonna Get Right (And Do Something Wrong)	1982	—	2.00	4.00
5-10783	She's All I Got/You Touched	1971	—	3.50	7.00
5-10836	Someone to Give My Love To/Love Sure Is Beautiful	1972	—	3.50	7.00
5-10876	Love Is a Good Thing/High on the Thought of You	1972	—	3.50	7.00
5-10912	Somebody Loves Me/Without You	1972	—	3.50	7.00
5-10947	Something About You I Love/Your Love Is the Key to It All	1973	—	3.00	6.00
5-10999	Mr. Lovemaker/Once You've Had the Best	1973	—	3.00	6.00
5-11046	Song and Dance Man/Love Is a Strange and Wonderful Thing	1973	—	3.00	6.00
5-11090	My Part of Forever/If Love Gets Any Better	1974	—	3.00	6.00
5-11142	Keep On Lovin' Me/The Ballad of Thunder Road	1974	—	3.00	6.00
8-50040	For a Minute There/She's All I Live For	1974	—	3.00	6.00
8-50073	Loving You Beats All I've Ever Seen/Touch of the Master's Hand	1975	—	3.00	6.00
8-50111	I Didn't Love Her Anymore/Loving Her Is All I Thought It Would Be	1975	—	3.00	6.00
8-50146	All-American Man/The Fool Strikes Again	1975	—	3.00	6.00
8-50193	The Feminine Touch/Rhythm Guitar	1976	—	3.00	6.00
8-50215	Gone at Last/Live with Me	1976	—	3.00	6.00
8-50249	11 Months and 29 Days/Live with Me (Till I Can Learn to Live Again)	1976	—	3.00	6.00
8-50291	I Can See Me Lovin' You Again/I Sleep with Her Memory Every Night	1976	—	3.00	6.00
8-50334	Slide Off of Your Satin Sheets/That's What the Outlaws in Texas Want to Hear	1977	—	3.00	6.00
8-50391	I'm the Only Hell (Mama Ever Raised)/She's Still Lookin' Good	1977	—	3.00	6.00
8-50469	Take This Job and Shove It/Colorado Kool-Aid	1977	2.00	4.00	8.00
8-50539	Georgia in a Jug/Me and the I.R.S.	1978	—	3.00	6.00
8-50621	Friend, Lover, Wife/Leave It to Me	1978	—	3.00	6.00
8-50655	The Outlaw's Prayer/Armed and Crazy	1979	—	3.00	6.00
9-50777	(Stay Away From) The Cocaine Train/Billy Bardo	1979	—	2.50	5.00
9-50818	Drinkin' and Drivin'/Just Makin' Love Don't Make It Love	1979	—	2.50	5.00
9-50863	Fifteen Beers/Who Was That Man Who Beat Me So	1980	—	2.50	5.00
9-50923	In Memory of a Memory/New York Town	1980	—	2.50	5.00
HILLTOP					
3002	Don't Start Countin' on Me/I'd Rather Be Your Fool	1964	5.00	10.00	20.00
3006	For Those Who Think Young/The Girl They Talk About	1965	3.75	7.50	15.00
3007	A-11/Where (In the World)	1965	3.75	7.50	15.00
3009	Heartbreak Tennessee/Help Me Hank, I'm Fallin'	1966	3.75	7.50	15.00
3015	I'm Barely Hangin' On to Me/The Real Mr. Heartache	1966	3.75	7.50	15.00
LITTLE DARLIN'					
008	The Lovin' Machine/Pride Covered Ears	1966	2.50	5.00	10.00
0011	The Ballad of the Green Berets/A Dying Hero	1966	2.50	5.00	10.00
0014	Right Back Where We Parted/The Way Things Were Going	1966	2.50	5.00	10.00
—With Micki Evans					
0016	Motel Time Again/If You Should Come Back Today	1966	2.50	5.00	10.00
0020	Jukebox Charlie/Something in Your World	1967	2.50	5.00	10.00
0032	The Cave/Then Love Dies	1967	2.50	5.00	10.00
0035	Don't Monkey with Another Monkey's Monkey/ You'll Recover in Time	1967	2.50	5.00	10.00
0042	(It Won't Be Long) And I'll Be Hating You/Fools Hall of Fame	1968	2.50	5.00	10.00
0043	The Old Year Is Gone/According to the Bible	1968	2.50	5.00	10.00
0046	My Heart Keeps Running to You/Yesterday, Today and Tomorrow	1968	2.50	5.00	10.00
0052	If I'm Gonna Sink/The Loser	1968	2.50	5.00	10.00
0055	Jingle Bells/The Old Year Is Gone	1968	2.50	5.00	10.00
0057	My World of Memories/(B-side unknown)	1969	2.50	5.00	10.00
0060	Wherever You Are/I Can't Promise You Won't Get Lonely	1969	2.50	5.00	10.00
0072	Wildfire/Basin Street Mama	1969	2.50	5.00	10.00
7804	It Won't Be Long/If I'm Gonna Sink (Might As Well Go to the Bottom)	1978	—	3.00	6.00
7808	Down on the Corner at a Bar Named Kelly's/ Something He'll Have to Learn	1978	—	3.00	6.00
7810	I'll Place My Order Early/The Old Year Is Gone	1978	—	3.00	6.00
7918	California Dreams/The Loser	1979	—	3.00	6.00
7923	Gentle on My Mind/Everything You Touch Turns to Hurt	1979	—	3.00	6.00
MERCURY					
71900	On Second Thought/One Day a Week	1962	5.00	10.00	20.00
—As "Donny Young"					
71981	Not Much I Don't/I'd Come Back to Me	1962	5.00	10.00	20.00
—As "Donny Young"					
884720-7	Old Violin/Comin' Home to Baby	1986	—	2.00	4.00
888088-7	Don't Bury Me 'Til I'm Ready/Ex-Wives and Lovers	1986	—	2.00	4.00
888341-7	Come to Me/Ragtime Redneck	1987	—	2.00	4.00
888651-7	I Grow Old Too Fast (And Smart Too Slow)/ Caught Between a Rock and a Soft Place	1987	—	2.00	4.00
888925-7	Modern Times/She Don't Love Me All the Time	1987	—	2.00	4.00
TODD					
1098	Don't You Get Lonesome Without Me/I'm Glad to Have Her Back Again	1964	5.00	10.00	20.00
—As "Donny Young"					

Number	Title (A Side/B Side)	Yr	VG	VG+	NM
Albums					
ACCORD					
SN-7173	Extra Special	1981	2.50	5.00	10.00
ALLEGIANCE					
AV-435	I Don't Need to Know That Right Now	198?	2.00	4.00	8.00
CERTRON					
7002	Johnny Paycheck Again	1970	3.75	7.50	15.00
EPIC					
E 31141	She's All I Got	1971	3.00	6.00	12.00
KE 31449	Someone to Give My Love To	1972	3.00	6.00	12.00
KE 31702	Somebody Loves Me	1972	3.00	6.00	12.00
KE 32387	Something About You I Love	1973	3.00	6.00	12.00
KE 32570	Song and Dance Man	1973	3.00	6.00	12.00
KE 33091	Greatest Hits	1974	2.50	5.00	10.00
PE 33091	Greatest Hits	198?	2.00	4.00	8.00
—Budget-line reissue					
KE 33354	Loving You	1975	2.50	5.00	10.00
KE 33943	11 Months and 29 Days	1975	2.50	5.00	10.00
PE 34693	Slide Off of Your Satin Sheets	1976	2.50	5.00	10.00
KE 35045	Take This Job and Shove It	1977	2.50	5.00	10.00
PE 35045	Take This Job and Shove It	198?	2.00	4.00	8.00
—Budget-line reissue					
KE 35444	Armed and Crazy	1978	2.50	5.00	10.00
KE 35623	Greatest Hits, Volume 2	1978	2.50	5.00	10.00
PE 35623	Greatest Hits, Volume 2	198?	2.00	4.00	8.00
—Budget-line reissue					
JE 36200	Everybody's Got a Family — Meet Mine	1979	2.50	5.00	10.00
JE 36496	New York Town	1980	2.50	5.00	10.00
FE 36761	Mr. Hag Told My Story	1981	2.50	5.00	10.00
PE 36761	Mr. Hag Told My Story	1981	2.00	4.00	8.00
—Budget-line reissue					
FE 37345	Encore	1981	2.50	5.00	10.00
PE 37345	Encore	198?	2.00	4.00	8.00
—Budget-line reissue					
FE 37933	Lovers and Losers	1982	2.50	5.00	10.00
FE 38322	Johnny Paycheck's Biggest Hits	1983	2.50	5.00	10.00
PE 39943	John Austin Paycheck	1984	2.00	4.00	8.00
INTERMEDIA					
QS-5018	Back On the Job	198?	2.00	4.00	8.00
LITTLE DARLIN'					
LD-4001 [M]	Johnny Paycheck at Carnegie Hall	1966	5.00	10.00	20.00
LD-4003 [M]	The Lovin' Machine	1966	5.00	10.00	20.00
LD-4004 [M]	Gospeltime in My Fashion	1967	5.00	10.00	20.00
LD-4006 [M]	Johnny Paycheck Sings Jukebox Charlie	1967	6.25	12.50	25.00
SLD-8001 [S]	Johnny Paycheck at Carnegie Hall	1966	6.25	12.50	25.00
SLD-8003 [S]	The Lovin' Machine	1966	6.25	12.50	25.00
SLD-8004 [S]	Gospeltime in My Fashion	1967	6.25	12.50	25.00
SLD-8006 [S]	Johnny Paycheck Sings Jukebox Charlie	1967	6.25	12.50	25.00
SLD-8010	Country Soul	1968	6.25	12.50	25.00
SLD-8012	Johnny Paycheck's Greatest Hits	1968	6.25	12.50	25.00
SLD-8023	Wherever You Are	1969	6.25	12.50	25.00
MERCURY					
830404-1	Modern Times	1987	2.50	5.00	10.00
POWER PAK					
284	Johnny Paycheck At His Best	197?	2.00	4.00	8.00

PAYCHECK, JOHNNY, AND MERLE HAGGARD

Also see each artist's individual listings.

Number	Title (A Side/B Side)	Yr	VG	VG+	NM
45s					
EPIC					
19-51012	I Can't Hold Myself in Line/Carolyn	1981	—	2.00	4.00

PAYNE, FREDA

Number	Title (A Side/B Side)	Yr	VG	VG+	NM
12-Inch Singles					
CAPITOL					
8509	I'll Do Anything for You (7:40)/(Instrumental)	1978	3.00	6.00	12.00
SPRO-8922/3 [DJ]	Happy Days Are Here Again-Happy Music/I'll Do Anything for You	1978	3.75	7.50	15.00
SPRO-9219 [DJ]	Red Hot (7:01) (same on both sides)	1979	2.50	5.00	10.00
SUTRA					
SUD 009	In Motion (5:35)/(Instrumental)	1982	3.75	7.50	15.00
45s					
ABC					
12079	Shadows on the Wall/I Get Carried Away	1975	—	2.50	5.00
12139	Lost in Love/You	1975	—	2.50	5.00
ABC-PARAMOUNT					
10366	Desafinado/He Who Laughs Last	1962	5.00	10.00	20.00
10437	Pretty Baby/Grin and Bear It	1963	5.00	10.00	20.00
ABC DUNHILL					
15018	It's Yours to Have/Run for Life	1974	—	2.50	5.00
CAPITOL					
4383	I Can't Live on a Memory/I Get High (On Your Memory)	1976	—	2.50	5.00
4431	Baby, You've Got What It Takes/Bring Back the Joy	1977	—	2.50	5.00
4494	Love Magnet/Loving You Means So Much to Me	1977	—	2.50	5.00
4537	Feed Me Your Love/Stares and Whispers	1978	—	2.50	5.00
4631	Happy Days Are Here Again-Happy Music (Dance the Night Away)/Falling in Love	1978	—	2.50	5.00
4695	I'll Do Anything for You (Part 1)/I'll Do Anything for You (Part 2)	1979	—	2.50	5.00
4775	Red Hot/Longest Night	1979	—	2.50	5.00
4805	Can't Wait/Longest Night	1979	—	2.50	5.00
IMPULSE!					
221	It's Time/Sweet September	1963	5.00	10.00	20.00
INVICTUS					
1255	Two Wrongs Don't Make a Right/We've Gotta Find a Way Back to Love	1973	—	3.00	6.00
1257	For No Reason/Mother Misery's Favorite Child	1973	—	3.00	6.00
9073	The Unhooked Generation/Easiest Way to Fall	1969	—	3.00	6.00
9075	Band of Gold/Easiest Way to Fall	1970	—	3.00	6.00
9080	Deeper and Deeper/The Unhooked Genration	1970	—	3.00	6.00
9085	Cherish What Is Dear to You (While It Is Near to You)/They Don't Owe Me a Thing	1971	—	3.00	6.00
9085 [PS]	Cherish What Is Dear to You (While It Is Near to You)/They Don't Owe Me a Thing	1971	2.50	5.00	10.00
9092	Bring the Boys Home/I Shall Not Be Moved	1971	—	3.00	6.00
9100	You Brought the Joy/Suddenly It's Yesterday	1971	—	3.00	6.00
9109	I'm Not Getting Any Better/The Road We Didn't Take	1972	—	3.00	6.00
9128	She's in My Life/Through the Memory of My Mind	1972	—	3.00	6.00
MGM					
13509	You've Lost That Lovin' Feelin'/Sad Sad September	1966	5.00	10.00	20.00
SUTRA					
117	In Motion/(Instrumental)	1982	—	2.50	5.00
Albums					
ABC					
D-901	Out of Payne Comes Love	1976	3.00	6.00	12.00
ABC DUNHILL					
DSX-50176	Payne and Pleasure	1974	3.75	7.50	15.00
ABC IMPULSE!					
AS-53 [S]	After the Lights Go Down Low...And Much More	1968	3.75	7.50	15.00
CAPITOL					
ST-11700	Stares and Whispers	1977	3.00	6.00	12.00
ST-11864	Supernatural	1978	3.00	6.00	12.00
ST-12003	Hot	1979	3.00	6.00	12.00
IMPULSE!					
A-53 [M]	After the Lights Go Down Low...And Much More	1964	7.50	15.00	30.00
AS-53 [S]	After the Lights Go Down Low...And Much More	1964	10.00	20.00	40.00
INVICTUS					
ST-7301	Band of Gold	1970	3.75	7.50	15.00
SMAS-7307	Contact	1971	3.75	7.50	15.00
ST-9804	The Best of Freda Payne	1972	3.75	7.50	15.00
Z 32493	Reaching Out	1973	3.75	7.50	15.00
MGM					
GAS-128	Freda Payne (Golden Archive Series)	1970	3.75	7.50	15.00
E-4370 [M]	How Do You Say I Don't Love You Anymore	1966	5.00	10.00	20.00
SE-4370 [S]	How Do You Say I Don't Love You Anymore	1966	6.25	12.50	25.00

PEACE, JOE

Number	Title (A Side/B Side)	Yr	VG	VG+	NM
Albums					
RITE					
29917	Finding Peace	1972	50.00	100.00	200.00

PEACHEROOS, THE

Number	Title (A Side/B Side)	Yr	VG	VG+	NM
45s					
EXCELLO					
2044	Be-Bop Baby/Everyday My Love Is True	1954	100.00	200.00	400.00

PEACHES AND HERB

Herb Fame with at least three different female singers who were "Peaches."

Number	Title (A Side/B Side)	Yr	VG	VG+	NM
12-Inch Singles					
POLYDOR					
PRO 165 [DJ]	Freeway (6:03) (same on both sides)	1981	3.00	6.00	12.00
45s					
COLUMBIA					
03872	Remember/Come to Me	1983	—	2.00	4.00
04081	In My World/Keep On Smiling	1983	—	2.00	4.00
45386	The Sound of Silence/The Two of Us	1971	—	2.50	5.00
45554	God Save This World/I Can't Forget the One I Love	1972	—	2.50	5.00
DATE					
1523	Let's Fall in Love/We're In This Thing Together	1966	2.50	5.00	10.00
1549	Close Your Eyes/I Will Watch Over You	1967	2.50	5.00	10.00
1549 [PS]	Close Your Eyes/I Will Watch Over You	1967	3.75	7.50	15.00
1555	Cupid-Venus/Darling, How Long	1967	3.75	7.50	15.00
1563	For Your Love/I Need Your Love So Desperately	1967	2.50	5.00	10.00
1563 [PS]	For Your Love/I Need Your Love So Desperately	1967	3.75	7.50	15.00
1574	Love Is Strange/It's True I Love You	1967	2.50	5.00	10.00
1574 [PS]	Love Is Strange/It's True I Love You	1967	3.75	7.50	15.00
1586	Two Little Kids/We've Got to Love One Another	1967	2.00	4.00	8.00
1592	The Ten Commandments of Love/What a Lovely Way (To Say Goodnight)	1968	2.00	4.00	8.00
1603	United/Thank You	1968	2.00	4.00	8.00
1603 [PS]	United/Thank You	1968	3.75	7.50	15.00
1623	Let's Make a Promise/Me and You	1968	2.00	4.00	8.00
1623 [PS]	Let's Make a Promise/Me and You	1968	3.75	7.50	15.00
1633	We've Got to Love One Another/So True	1968	2.50	5.00	10.00
1637	When He Touches Me (Nothing Else Matters)/Thank You	1969	2.00	4.00	8.00
1649	Let Me Be the One/I Need Your Love So Desperately	1969	2.00	4.00	8.00
1655	Cupid/Darling, How Long	1969	2.00	4.00	8.00
1669	It's Just a Game, Love/Satisfy My Hunger	1970	2.00	4.00	8.00
1676	Soothe Me with Your Love/We're So Much in Love	1970	2.00	4.00	8.00
MCA					
40701	We're Still Together/Love Is Here Beside Us	1977	—	2.50	5.00
40782	It Will Never Be the Same Again/I'm Counting on You	1977	—	2.50	5.00
MERCURY					
73350	Keep It Coming/I'm a-Hurtin' Inside	1973	—	2.50	5.00
73388	Can't It Wait/Thank Heaven for You	1973	—	2.50	5.00
POLYDOR					
2031	Roller-Skatin' Mate (Part 1)/Roller-Skatin' Mate (Part 2)	1979	—	2.00	4.00
2053	I Pledge My Love/(I Want Us) Back Together	1980	—	2.00	4.00
2115	Funtime (Part 1)/Funtime (Part 2)	1980	—	2.00	4.00
2140	One Child of Love/Hearsay	1980	—	2.00	4.00
2157	Surrender/Love Stealers	1981	—	2.00	4.00
2178	Freeway/Pickin' Up the Pieces	1981	—	2.00	4.00
2187	Bluer Than Blue/Go with the Flow	1981	—	2.00	4.00
14514	Shake Your Groove Thing/All Your Love (Get It Here)	1978	—	2.00	4.00

Number	Title (A Side/B Side)	Yr	VG	VG+	NM
14547	Reunited/Easy as Pie	1979	—	2.00	4.00
14577	We've Got Love/Four's a Traffic Jam	1979	—	2.00	4.00
Albums					
COLUMBIA					
FC 38746	Remember	1983	2.50	5.00	10.00
DATE					
TEM 3004 [M]	Let's Fall in Love	1967	5.00	10.00	20.00
TEM 3005 [M]	For Your Love	1967	6.25	12.50	25.00
TEM 3007 [M]	Golden Duets	1968	7.50	15.00	30.00
TES 4004 [S]	Let's Fall in Love	1967	6.25	12.50	25.00
TES 4005 [S]	For Your Love	1967	5.00	10.00	20.00
TES 4007 [S]	Golden Duets	1968	5.00	10.00	20.00
TES 4012	Peaches and Herb's Greatest Hits	1968	5.00	10.00	20.00
EPIC					
E 36089	Love Is Strange	1979	2.50	5.00	10.00
—Reissue of Date material					
JE 36099	Peaches and Herb's Greatest Hits	1979	2.50	5.00	10.00
—Reissue of Date 4012					
MCA					
2261	Peaches and Herb	1977	3.00	6.00	12.00
POLYDOR					
PD-1-6172	2 Hot!	1978	2.50	5.00	10.00
PD-1-6239	Twice the Fire	1979	2.50	5.00	10.00
PD-1-6298	Worth the Wait	1980	2.50	5.00	10.00
PD-1-6332	Sayin' Something!	1981	2.50	5.00	10.00

PEANUT BUTTER CONSPIRACY, THE

Number	Title (A Side/B Side)	Yr	VG	VG+	NM
45s					
CHALLENGE					
500	Back in L.A./Have a Little Faith	1969	2.00	4.00	8.00
500 [PS]	Back in L.A./Have a Little Faith	1969	12.50	25.00	50.00
COLUMBIA					
43985	It's a Happening Thing/Twice Is Life	1967	2.50	5.00	10.00
44063	Then Came Love/Dark on You Now	1967	2.00	4.00	8.00
44356	Turn On a Friend (To the Good Life)/Captain Sandwich	1967	2.00	4.00	8.00
44667	I'm a Fool/It's So Hard	1968	2.00	4.00	8.00
VAULT					
933	Time Is After You/Floating Dream	1966	3.75	7.50	15.00
Albums					
CHALLENGE					
2000	For Children of All Ages	1969	7.50	15.00	30.00
COLUMBIA					
CL 2654 [M]	The Peanut Butter Conspiracy Is Spreading	1967	7.50	15.00	30.00
CL 2790 [M]	The Great Conspiracy	1968	10.00	20.00	40.00
CS 9454 [S]	The Peanut Butter Conspiracy Is Spreading	1967	7.50	15.00	30.00
CS 9590 [S]	The Great Conspiracy	1968	7.50	15.00	30.00

PEARLS, THE (1)

Number	Title (A Side/B Side)	Yr	VG	VG+	NM
45s					
AMBER					
2003	I Cried/It Must Be Love	1961	125.00	250.00	500.00
—Originals have matrix muber stamped into trail-off wax					

PEARLS, THE (2)

Number	Title (A Side/B Side)	Yr	VG	VG+	NM
45s					
ATCO					
6057	Shadows of Love/Yum Yummy	1956	7.50	15.00	30.00
6066	Bells of Love/Come On Home	1956	10.00	20.00	40.00
ON THE SQUARE					
320	Band of Angels/Ugly Face	1959	5.00	10.00	20.00
ONYX					
503	Let's You and I Go Steady/Zippidy Zippidy Zoom	1956	15.00	30.00	60.00
506	My Oh My/Tree in the Meadow	1956	37.50	75.00	150.00
510	Your Cheatin' Heart/I Sure Need You	1957	15.00	30.00	60.00
511	Ice Cream Baby/Yuz-a-Ma-Tuz	1957	15.00	30.00	60.00
516	The Wheel of Love/It's Love, Love, Love	1957	30.00	60.00	120.00

PEARLS, THE (3)

Number	Title (A Side/B Side)	Yr	VG	VG+	NM
45s					
BELL					
45342	You Came, You Saw, You Conquered/(B-side unknown)	1973	—	2.50	5.00

PEARLS, THE (4)

Number	Title (A Side/B Side)	Yr	VG	VG+	NM
45s					
WARNER BROS.					
5300	Happy Over You/If I Had a Choice	1962	5.00	10.00	20.00

PEARLS BEFORE SWINE

Number	Title (A Side/B Side)	Yr	VG	VG+	NM
45s					
ESP-DISK'					
4554	Morning Song/Drop Out	1967	10.00	20.00	40.00
4575	Images of April/There Was a Man	1968	10.00	20.00	40.00
4576	I Saw the World/(B-side unknown)	1968	10.00	20.00	40.00
REPRISE					
0873	If You Don't Want To/These Things Too	1969	3.00	6.00	12.00
0916	God Save the Child/Rocket Man	1970	3.00	6.00	12.00
0949	The Jeweler/Rocket Man	1970	3.00	6.00	12.00
Albums					
ADELPHI					
4111 [(2)]	The Best of Pearls Before Swine	198?	3.75	7.50	15.00
ESP-DISK					
1054	One Nation Under Ground Bonus Poster	1967	6.25	12.50	25.00
1054 [M]	One Nation Under Ground	1967	12.50	25.00	50.00
1054 [S]	One Nation Under Ground	1967	12.50	25.00	50.00
—Sepia-tone cover with white border					
1054 [S]	One Nation Under Ground	1967	12.50	25.00	50.00
—Sepia-tone cover with no border					
1054 [S]	One Nation Under Ground	1967	12.50	25.00	50.00
—Black and white cover					
1054 [S]	One Nation Under Ground	1968	7.50	15.00	30.00
—Full-color cover					
1075	Balaklava	1968	10.00	20.00	40.00
REPRISE					
RS 6364	These Things Too	1969	7.50	15.00	30.00
RS 6405	The Use of Ashes	1970	7.50	15.00	30.00
RS 6442	City of Gold	1971	10.00	20.00	40.00
RS 6467	Beautiful Lies You Could Live In	1971	10.00	20.00	40.00

PEARSON, DUKE

Number	Title (A Side/B Side)	Yr	VG	VG+	NM
45s					
BLUE NOTE					
1754	Black Coffee/Gate City	1960	2.50	5.00	10.00
1755	Taboo/Like Somebody in Love	1960	2.50	5.00	10.00
1931	Ready Rudy/Sweet Honey Bee	1966	2.00	4.00	8.00
Albums					
ATLANTIC					
3002 [M]	Honeybuns	196?	3.75	7.50	15.00
SD 3002 [S]	Honeybuns	196?	3.75	7.50	15.00
SD 3005	Prairie Dog	196?	3.75	7.50	15.00
BLUE NOTE					
BN-LA317-G	It Could Only Happen with You	1974	3.75	7.50	15.00
BLP-4022 [M]	Profile — Duke Pearson	1959	30.00	60.00	120.00
—"Deep groove" version (deep indentation under label on both sides)					
BLP-4022 [M]	Profile — Duke Pearson	1959	20.00	40.00	80.00
—Regular version with W. 63rd St. address on label					
BLP-4022 [M]	Profile — Duke Pearson	1963	6.25	12.50	25.00
—With New York, USA address on label					
BLP-4035 [M]	Tender Feelin's	1960	30.00	60.00	120.00
—"Deep groove" version (deep indentation under label on both sides)					
BLP-4035 [M]	Tender Feelin's	1960	20.00	40.00	80.00
—Regular version with W. 63rd St. address on label					
BLP-4035 [M]	Tender Feelin's	1963	6.25	12.50	25.00
—With New York, USA address on label					
BLP-4191 [M]	Wahoo!	1965	7.50	15.00	30.00
BLP-4252 [M]	Sweet Honey Bee	1966	7.50	15.00	30.00
B1-28269	The Right Touch	1994	3.00	6.00	12.00
—Reissue of 84267					
B1-35220	I Don't Care Who Knows It	1996	3.00	6.00	12.00
BST-84022 [S]	Profile — Duke Pearson	1959	15.00	30.00	60.00
—With W. 63rd St. address on label					
BST-84022 [S]	Profile — Duke Pearson	1963	5.00	10.00	20.00
—With New York, USA address on label					
BST-84022 [S]	Profile — Duke Pearson	1967	3.00	6.00	12.00
—With "A Division of Liberty Records" on label					
BST-84035 [S]	Tender Feelin's	1960	15.00	30.00	60.00
—With W. 63rd St. address on label					
BST-84035 [S]	Tender Feelin's	1963	5.00	10.00	20.00
—With New York, USA address on label					
BST-84035 [S]	Tender Feelin's	1967	3.00	6.00	12.00
—With "A Division of Liberty Records" on label					
B1-84191	Wahoo!	1986	3.00	6.00	12.00
—"The Finest in Jazz Since 1939" reissue					
BST-84191 [S]	Wahoo!	1965	7.50	15.00	30.00
—With New York, USA address on label					
BST-84191 [S]	Wahoo!	1967	3.00	6.00	12.00
—With "A Division of Liberty Records" on label					
BST-84252 [S]	Sweet Honey Bee	1966	7.50	15.00	30.00
—With New York, USA address on label					
BST-84252 [S]	Sweet Honey Bee	1967	3.00	6.00	12.00
—With "A Division of Liberty Records" on label					
BST-84267	The Right Touch	1968	6.25	12.50	25.00
BST-84276	Introducing Duke Pearson's Big Band	1968	6.25	12.50	25.00
BST-84293	The Phantom	1969	6.25	12.50	25.00
BST-84308	Now Hear This	1969	6.25	12.50	25.00
BST-84323	Merry Ole Soul	1970	5.00	10.00	20.00
BST-84344	How Insensitive	1970	5.00	10.00	20.00
B1-89792	Sweet Honey Bee	1993	3.00	6.00	12.00
—Reissue of 84252					
JAZZTIME					
33-02 [M]	Hush!	1962	10.00	20.00	40.00
PRESTIGE					
PRST-7729	Dedication	1970	3.75	7.50	15.00

PEBBLES AND BAMM BAMM

Number	Title (A Side/B Side)	Yr	VG	VG+	NM
45s					
HANNA-BARBERA					
449	Open Up Your Heart/The Lord Is Counting on You	1965	6.25	12.50	25.00
449 [PS]	Open Up Your Heart/The Lord Is Counting on You	1965	12.50	25.00	50.00
484	The World Is Full of Toys/Daddy	1966	6.25	12.50	25.00
7-Inch Extended Plays					
HANNA-BARBERA					
CS 7044	Little Drummer Boy/We Three Kings//Silent Night/It Came Upon a Midnight Clear	1965	12.50	25.00	50.00
CS 7044 [PS]	We Wish You a Merry Christmas	1965	25.00	50.00	100.00
Albums					
HANNA-BARBERA					
HLP-2033 [M]	Pebbles and Bamm-Bamm Sing Songs of Christmas	1965	30.00	60.00	120.00
HLP-2040 [M]	On the Good Ship Lollipop	1966	25.00	50.00	100.00

PEDICIN, MIKE

Number	Title (A Side/B Side)	Yr	VG	VG+	NM
45s					
20TH CENTURY					
5006	My Heart Is Breaking/I'll Always Love You Some	195?	7.50	15.00	30.00
5009	Kiss, Kiss, Kiss/Love Every Moment	195?	7.50	15.00	30.00
5012	Never Mind/M-m-Boy	195?	7.50	15.00	30.00
5019	I've Got a Feeling It's Love/Is That What You Call Love	195?	7.50	15.00	30.00
5021	Disc Jockey's Boogie/Tiger Rag	195?	7.50	15.00	30.00
5023	It's My Heart to Give/Kiss Me Before You Say Goodbye	195?	7.50	15.00	30.00
5027	Shake a Hand/When We Meet	195?	10.00	20.00	40.00

Number	Title (A Side/B Side)	Yr	VG	VG+	NM
5029	Not Somebody Else Just Me/Sweet Georgia Brown	195?	7.50	15.00	30.00
ABC-PARAMOUNT					
10303	Gotta Twist/When the Cats Come Twistin' In	1962	3.00	6.00	12.00
APOLLO					
534	Hey Pop, Give Me the Keys/St. James Infirmary	1959	10.00	20.00	40.00
CAMEO					
125	Shake a Hand/The Dickie Doo	1957	6.25	12.50	25.00
FEDERAL					
12417	Burnt Toast/You Gotta Go, You Gotta Go	1961	3.75	7.50	15.00
MALVERN					
101	The Dickie Doo/(B-side unknown)	1957	7.50	15.00	30.00
RCA VICTOR					
47-6043	I'm Hip/I Wanna Hug You, Kiss You, Squeeze You	1955	6.25	12.50	25.00
47-6051	Mambo Rock/D-E-V-I-L	1955	6.25	12.50	25.00
47-6150	Fe-Fi-Fo-Fum/The Hot Barcarolle	1955	6.25	12.50	25.00
47-6235	You Gotta Go/The Banjo Rock	1955	6.25	12.50	25.00
47-6285	Jackpot/When the Cats Come Marching In	1955	6.25	12.50	25.00
47-6369	The Large, Large House/Hotter Than a Pistol	1955	6.25	12.50	25.00
47-6546	The Beat/Save Us, Preacher Davis	1956	6.25	12.50	25.00
47-6676	Teenage Fairy Tales/Close All the Doors	1956	6.25	12.50	25.00
47-6847	The Hucklebuck/Calypso Rock	1957	6.25	12.50	25.00
Albums					
APOLLO					
LP-484 [M]	Musical Medicine	1957	37.50	75.00	150.00

PEDRICK, BOBBY, JR.

See ROBERT JOHN.

PEEBLES, ANN

Number	Title (A Side/B Side)	Yr	VG	VG+	NM
12-Inch Singles					
HI					
78510	I Didn't Take Your Man/(B-side unknown)	1978	3.00	6.00	12.00
45s					
HI					
2157	Walk Away/I Can't Let You Go	1969	—	3.00	6.00
2165	Give Me Some Credit/Solid Foundation	1969	—	3.00	6.00
2173	Generation Gap Between Us/I'll Get Along	1970	—	3.00	6.00
2178	Part Time Love/I Still Love You	1970	—	3.00	6.00
2186	I Pity the Fool/Heartaches, Heartaches	1971	—	3.00	6.00
2198	Slipped, Tripped and Fell in Love/99 Lbs.	1971	—	3.00	6.00
2205	Breaking Up Somebody's Home/Troubles, Heartaches and Sadness	1972	—	3.00	6.00
2219	Somebody's On Your Case/I've Been There Before	1972	—	3.00	6.00
2232	I'm Gonna Tear Your Playhouse Down/One Way Street	1973	—	3.00	6.00
2248	I Can't Stand the Rain/I've Been There Before	1973	—	3.00	6.00
2265	(You Keep Me) Hangin' On/Heartaches, Heartaches	1974	—	3.00	6.00
2271	Do I Need You/Love Vibration	1974	—	3.00	6.00
2278	Until You Came Into My Life/Put Yourself in My Place	1974	—	3.00	6.00
2284	Beware/You Got to Feed the Fire	1975	—	3.00	6.00
2294	Come to Mama/I'm Leaving You	1975	—	3.00	6.00
2302	Dr. Love Power/I Still Love You	1976	—	3.00	6.00
2309	I Don't Lend My Man/I Need Somebody	1976	—	3.00	6.00
2320	Fill This World with Love/It Was Jealousy	1976	—	3.00	6.00
77502	If This Is Heaven/Sailing	1977	—	2.50	5.00
78509	Old Man with Young Ideas/A Good Day for Lovin'	1978	—	2.50	5.00
78518	I Didn't Take Your Man/Being Here with You	1978	—	2.50	5.00
79528	If You've Got the Time (I've Got the Love)/Let Your Lovelight Shine	1979	—	2.50	5.00
80533	I'd Rather Leave While I'm in Love/Heartaches	1980	—	2.50	5.00
81534	Mon Belle-Amour/(B-side unknown)	1981	—	2.50	5.00
Albums					
HI					
HLP-6002	If This Is Heaven	1977	3.00	6.00	12.00
HLP-6007	The Handwriting Is On the Wall	1978	3.00	6.00	12.00
HLP-8005	Part Time Love	197?	3.00	6.00	12.00
—Reissue of 32059					
HLP-8009	Straight from the Heart	197?	3.00	6.00	12.00
—Reissue of 32065					
SHL-32059	Part Time Love	1971	5.00	10.00	20.00
SHL-32065	Straight from the Heart	1972	5.00	10.00	20.00
XSHL-32079	I Can't Stand the Rain	1974	5.00	10.00	20.00
SHL-32091	Tellin' It	1975	5.00	10.00	20.00

PEEL, DAVID

Number	Title (A Side/B Side)	Yr	VG	VG+	NM
45s					
APPLE					
PRO-6498/9 [DJ]	F Is Not a Dirty Word/The Ballad of New York City	1972	30.00	60.00	120.00
PRO-6545/6 [DJ]	Hippie from New York City/The Ballad of New York City	1972	30.00	60.00	120.00
ORANGE					
1001	Bring Back the Beatles/Imagine	1977	2.50	5.00	10.00
Albums					
APPLE					
SW-3391	The Pope Smokes Dope	1972	18.75	37.50	75.00
ELEKTRA					
EKS-74032	Have a Marijuana	1968	10.00	20.00	40.00
EKS-74069	The American Revolution	1970	7.50	15.00	30.00

PEELS, THE

Number	Title (A Side/B Side)	Yr	VG	VG+	NM
45s					
KARATE					
522	Juanita Banana/Fun	1966	3.00	6.00	12.00
527	Scrooey Mooey/Time Marches On	1966	2.00	4.00	8.00
533	Juanita Banana II/Rosita Tomato	1966	2.50	5.00	10.00
Albums					
KARATE					
5402 [M]	Juanita Banana	1966	20.00	40.00	80.00

PEEPS, THE

Number	Title (A Side/B Side)	Yr	VG	VG+	NM
45s					
PHILIPS					
40315	Now Is the Time/Got Plenty of Love	1965	2.50	5.00	10.00

PEIL, DANNY, AND THE APOLLOS

Number	Title (A Side/B Side)	Yr	VG	VG+	NM
45s					
REYNARD					
602	Jingle Jump/Flip Side	1964	3.75	7.50	15.00

PEJOE, MORRIS

Number	Title (A Side/B Side)	Yr	VG	VG+	NM
45s					
CHECKER					
766	Tired of Crying Over You/Gonna Buy Me a Telephone	1953	125.00	250.00	500.00
—Black vinyl					
766	Tired of Crying Over You/Gonna Buy Me a Telephone	1953	1500.	2250.	3000.
—Red vinyl					
781	Can't Get Along/It'll Plumb Get It	1953	100.00	200.00	400.00
—Black vinyl					
781	Can't Get Along/It'll Plumb Get It	1953	250.00	500.00	1000.
—Red vinyl					
VEE JAY					
148	You're Gonna Need Me/Hurt My Feelings	1955	15.00	30.00	60.00

PELICANS, THE

Number	Title (A Side/B Side)	Yr	VG	VG+	NM
45s					
IMPERIAL					
5307	Chimes/Ain't Gonna Do It	1954	250.00	500.00	1000.
PARROT					
793	White Cliffs of Dover/Aurelia	1954	750.00	1500.	3000.
793	White Cliffs of Dover/Aurelia	1954	3000.	4500.	6000.
—Red vinyl					

PENDARVIS, TRACY

Number	Title (A Side/B Side)	Yr	VG	VG+	NM
45s					
SUN					
335	A Thousand Guitars/Is It Too Late	1960	5.00	10.00	20.00
345	Is It Me/South Bound Line	1960	6.25	12.50	25.00
359	Eternally/Belle of the Swanee	1961	5.00	10.00	20.00

PENDLETONS, THE

Number	Title (A Side/B Side)	Yr	VG	VG+	NM
45s					
DOT					
16511	Board Party/Barefoot Adventure	1963	25.00	50.00	100.00
RENDEZVOUS					
194	The Waddle/Itchy Bon Mash	1962	10.00	20.00	40.00

PENETRATIONS, THE

Number	Title (A Side/B Side)	Yr	VG	VG+	NM
45s					
ICON					
1002	Bring 'Em In/Fackin' Out	196?	15.00	30.00	60.00
—Blue vinyl					
1002	Bring 'Em Back Alive/Fackin' Out	196?	7.50	15.00	30.00
—Black vinyl; note slightly different A-side title					

PENGUINS, THE

Number	Title (A Side/B Side)	Yr	VG	VG+	NM
45s					
ATLANTIC					
1132	Pledge of Love/I Knew I'd Fall in Love	1957	7.50	15.00	30.00
DOOTO					
348	Earth Angel/Hey Senorita	1959	5.00	10.00	20.00
—Reissue on altered label name and yellow label					
428	That's How Much I Need You/Be My Lovin' Baby	1957	10.00	20.00	40.00
432	Sweet Love/Let Me Make Up Your Mind	1958	7.50	15.00	30.00
435	Do Not Pretend/If You're Mine	1958	7.50	15.00	30.00
DOOTONE					
345	No There Ain't No News Today/When I Am Gone	1954	75.00	150.00	300.00
—B-side by Dootsie Williams Orchestra					
348	Earth Angel/Hey Senorita	1954	37.50	75.00	150.00
—First pressings on glossy red labels					
348	Earth Angel/Hey Senorita	1955	12.50	25.00	50.00
—Maroon label					
348	Earth Angel/Hey Senorita	1955	10.00	20.00	40.00
—Blue label					
348	Earth Angel/Hey Senorita	1955	7.50	15.00	30.00
—Black label					
353	Love Will Make Your Mind Go Wild/Ookey Ook	1954	17.50	35.00	70.00
—First pressings on glossy red label					
353	Love Will Make Your Mind Go Wild/Ookey Ook	1955	12.50	25.00	50.00
—Maroon label					
353	Love Will Make Your Mind Go Wild/Ookey Ook	1955	10.00	20.00	40.00
—Blue label					
353	Love Will Make Your Mind Go Wild/Ookey Ook	1955	7.50	15.00	30.00
—Black label					
362	Baby, Let's Make Some Love/Kiss a Fool Goodbye	1955	12.50	25.00	50.00
ELDO					
119	Universal Twist/To Keep Our Love	1962	5.00	10.00	20.00
GLENVILLE					
101	Earth Angel/Hey Senorita	197?	—	3.00	6.00
—Reissue					
MERCURY					
70610	Don't Do It/Be Mine or Be a Fool	1955	12.50	25.00	50.00
—Black vinyl					

Number	Title (A Side/B Side)	Yr	VG	VG+	NM
70610	Don't Do It/Be Mine or Be a Fool	1955	50.00	100.00	200.00
—Red vinyl					
70654	Walkin' Down Broadway/It Only Happens with You	1955	12.50	25.00	50.00
70703	Promises, Promises, Promises/The Devil That I See	1955	12.50	25.00	50.00
70762	A Christmas Prayer/Jingle Jangle	1955	20.00	40.00	80.00
70799	My Troubles Are Not At an End/She's Gone, Gone	1956	12.50	25.00	50.00
—Maroon label					
70799	My Troubles Are Not At an End/She's Gone, Gone	1956	6.25	12.50	25.00
—Black label					
70943	Earth Angel/Ice	1956	10.00	20.00	40.00
—Not the same recording as the hit on Dootone					
71033	Cool Baby Cool/Will You Be Mine	1957	10.00	20.00	40.00
ORIGINAL SOUND					
27	Memories of El Monte/Be Mine	1963	25.00	50.00	100.00
—Black and red label					
27	Memories of El Monte/Be Mine	1963	12.50	25.00	50.00
—Black and silver label; A-side written by Frank Zappa					
54	Heavenly Angel/Big Bobo's Party Train	1965	6.25	12.50	25.00
SUN STATE					
001	Believe Me/The Pony Rock	1962	6.25	12.50	25.00
WING					
90076	Dealer of Dreams/Peace of Mind	1956	7.50	15.00	30.00
7-Inch Extended Plays					
DOOTO					
241	(contents unknown)	1959	30.00	60.00	120.00
241 [PS]	The Cool, Cool Penguins Vol. 1	1959	30.00	60.00	120.00
243	(contents unknown)	1959	30.00	60.00	120.00
243 [PS]	The Cool, Cool Penguins, Vol. 2	1959	30.00	60.00	120.00
244	(contents unknown)	1959	30.00	60.00	120.00
244 [PS]	The Cool, Cool Penguins, Vol. 3	1959	30.00	60.00	120.00
DOOTONE					
201	(contents unknown)	1955	62.50	125.00	250.00
201 [PS]	The Penguins	1955	62.50	125.00	250.00
—Issued in "Dootone" jacket rather than custom jacket					
Albums					
COLLECTABLES					
COL-5045	Golden Classics	198?	2.50	5.00	10.00
DOOTO					
DTL-204 [M]	The Best Vocal Groups...Rhythm and Blues	1959	50.00	100.00	200.00
—Reissue of Dootone 204; blue and yellow label					
DTL-204 [M]	The Best Vocal Groups...Rhythm and Blues	196?	25.00	50.00	100.00
—Black label with gold/orange/blue ring. This is NOT a counterfeit.					
DTL-242 [M]	The Cool, Cool Penguins	1959	175.00	350.00	700.00
—Red and yellow label					
DTL-242 [M]	The Cool, Cool Penguins	1959	175.00	350.00	700.00
—Blue and yellow label					
DTL-242 [M]	The Cool, Cool Penguins	196?	50.00	100.00	200.00
—Black label with gold/orange/blue ring. This is NOT a counterfeit.					
DOOTONE					
DTL-204 [M]	The Best Vocal Groups...Rhythm and Blues	1957	375.00	750.00	1500.
—Also includes tracks by the Medallions, Don Julian and the Meadowlarks, and the Dootones. Flat maroon label.					
DTL-204 [M]	The Best Vocal Groups...Rhythm and Blues	195?	125.00	250.00	500.00
—As above; glossy maroon label					

PENN, LITTLE "LAMBSIE"

Number	Title (A Side/B Side)	Yr	VG	VG+	NM
45s					
ATCO					
6082	I Wanna Spend Christmas With Elvis/Painted Lips and Pigtails	1956	12.50	25.00	50.00

PENN, WILLIAM, AND THE QUAKERS

Number	Title (A Side/B Side)	Yr	VG	VG+	NM
45s					
DUANE					
104	Coming Up My Way/Care Free	196?	10.00	20.00	40.00
HUSH					
230	Little Girl/Somebody's Dum Dum	196?	12.50	25.00	50.00
MELRON					
5013	California Sun/No More Love	1966	12.50	25.00	50.00
5024	Santa Needs Ear Muffs on His Nose/Philly	1966	15.00	30.00	60.00
5024	Santa Needs Ear Muffs on His Nose/Sweet Caroline	1966	15.00	30.00	60.00
THUNDERBIRD					
502	Blow My Mind/Swami	1966	10.00	20.00	40.00
—As the "William Penn Fyve"					
TWILIGHT					
410	Ghost of the Monks/Goodbye My Love	1967	7.50	15.00	30.00
UPTOWN					
745	Chrome Dome Wheeler Dealer/Scrapped	1967	10.00	20.00	40.00

PENNANTS, THE

Number	Title (A Side/B Side)	Yr	VG	VG+	NM
45s					
WORLD					
102	Don't Go/Workin' Man	1961	25.00	50.00	100.00

PENNER, DICK

Number	Title (A Side/B Side)	Yr	VG	VG+	NM
45s					
SUN					
282	Cindy Lou/Your Honey Love	1958	12.50	25.00	50.00

PENNSYLVANIA PLAYERS, THE

See DICKIE GOODMAN.

PENNY AND JEAN

Number	Title (A Side/B Side)	Yr	VG	VG+	NM
45s					
RCA VICTOR					
47-7844	I Forgot More Than You'll Ever Know/How Come I'm Crying Now?	1961	3.00	6.00	12.00
Albums					
RCA VICTOR					
LPM-2244 [M]	Two for the Road	1961	5.00	10.00	20.00
LSP-2244 [S]	Two for the Road	1961	6.25	12.50	25.00

PENNY AND THE OVERTONES

Number	Title (A Side/B Side)	Yr	VG	VG+	NM
45s					
RIM					
2021	What Made You Forget/(B-side unknown)	1958	25.00	50.00	100.00

PENTANGLE, THE

Number	Title (A Side/B Side)	Yr	VG	VG+	NM
45s					
REPRISE					
PRO 391 [DJ]	Light Flight/Sally Go 'Round the Roses	1969	2.50	5.00	10.00
0784	Let No Man Steal Your Throne/Way Behind the Sun	1968	2.00	4.00	8.00
0843	I Saw an Angel/Once I Had a Sweetheart	1969	2.00	4.00	8.00
Albums					
GREEN LINNET					
SIF-3048	So Early in the Spring	1990	3.00	6.00	12.00
REPRISE					
MS 2100	Solomon's Seal	1972	3.75	7.50	15.00
RS 6315	The Pentangle	1968	5.00	10.00	20.00
—With "W7" and "r:" logos on two-tone orange label					
RS 6315	The Pentangle	1970	3.75	7.50	15.00
—With only "r:" logo on all-orange (tan) label					
2RS 6334 [(2)]	Sweet Child	1969	6.25	12.50	25.00
—With "W7" and "r:" logos on two-tone orange label					
2RS 6334 [(2)]	Sweet Child	1970	4.50	9.00	18.00
—With only "r:" logo on all-orange (tan) label					
RS 6372	Basket of Light	1969	5.00	10.00	20.00
—With "W7" and "r:" logos on two-tone orange label					
RS 6372	Basket of Light	1970	3.75	7.50	15.00
—With only "r:" logo on all-orange (tan) label					
RS 6430	Cruel Sister	1971	3.75	7.50	15.00
RS 6463	Reflection	1971	3.75	7.50	15.00
SHANACHIE					
79066	A Maid That's Deep in Love	198?	2.50	5.00	10.00
VARRICK					
VR-017	Open the Door	1985	2.50	5.00	10.00
VR-026	In the Round	1986	2.50	5.00	10.00

PEOPLE

Also see LARRY NORMAN.

Number	Title (A Side/B Side)	Yr	VG	VG+	NM
45s					
CAPITOL					
2078	I Love You/Somebody Tell Me My Name	1968	3.00	6.00	12.00
2251	Apple Cider/Ashes of Me	1968	2.50	5.00	10.00
2499	Turnin' Me In/Ulla	1969	2.50	5.00	10.00
5920	Organ Grinder/Riding High	1967	2.50	5.00	10.00
PARAMOUNT					
0005	Love Will Take Us Higher and Higher/Livin' It Up	1969	—	3.00	6.00
0011	Sunshine Lady/Crosstown Bus	1969	—	3.00	6.00
0019	For What It's Worth/Maple Street	1970	—	3.00	6.00
0028	One Chain Don't Make No Prison/Keep It Alive	1970	—	3.00	6.00
POLYDOR					
14087	Chant for Peace/I Don't Carry No Guns	1971	—	3.00	6.00
ZEBRA					
102	Come Back Beatles (same on both sides)	1978	2.50	5.00	10.00
Albums					
CAPITOL					
ST-151	Both Sides of People	1969	10.00	20.00	40.00
ST 2924	I Love You	1968	10.00	20.00	40.00
PARAMOUNT					
PAS-5013	There Are People	1970	5.00	10.00	20.00

PEOPLE'S CHOICE

Number	Title (A Side/B Side)	Yr	VG	VG+	NM
45s					
CASABLANCA					
2322	My Feet Won't Move, But My Shoes Did the Boogie/You Ought to Be Dancin'	1980	—	2.00	4.00
PALMER					
5020	Easy to Be True/Savin' My Love for You	1967	62.50	125.00	250.00
PHIL-L.A. OF SOUL					
349	I Likes to Do It/Big Ladies Man	1971	—	3.00	6.00
352	Wootie-T-Woo/'Cause That's the Way I Know	1971	—	3.00	6.00
356	Magic/Oh How I Love It	1972	—	3.00	6.00
358	Let Me Do My Thing/On a Cloudy Day	1972	—	3.00	6.00
PHILADELPHIA INT'L.					
3649	Turn Me Loose/Soft and Tender	1978	—	2.00	4.00
3658	Rough-Ride/Stay with Me	1978	—	2.00	4.00
PHILIPS					
40653	Keep On Holding On/Just Look What You've Done	1969	3.00	6.00	12.00
TSOP					
4751	Love Shot/The Big Hurt	1973	—	2.50	5.00
4759	Party Is a Groovy Thing/Asking for Trouble	1974	—	2.50	5.00
4769	Do It Any Way You Wanna/The Big Hurt	1975	—	2.50	5.00
4773	Nursery Rhymes (Part 1)/Nursery Rhymes (Part 2)	1975	—	2.50	5.00
4781	Here We Go Again/Mickey D's	1976	—	2.50	5.00
4782	Movin' In All Directions/Mellow Hood	1976	—	2.50	5.00
4784	Cold Blooded & Down-Right Funky/Jam, Jam, Jam (All Night Long)	1976	—	2.50	5.00
4786	If You Gonna Do It (Put Your Mind To It) (Part I)/If You Gonna Do It (Put Your Mind To It) (Part II)	1977	—	2.50	5.00
Albums					
PHILADELPHIA INT'L.					
JZ 35363	Turn Me Loose	1978	2.50	5.00	10.00
TSOP					
KZ 33154	Boogie Down U.S.A.	1975	2.50	5.00	10.00

Number	Title (A Side/B Side)	Yr	VG	VG+	NM
PZ 34124	We Got the Rhythm	1976	2.50	5.00	10.00

PEPE AND THE ASTROS

45s

Number	Title (A Side/B Side)	Yr	VG	VG+	NM
SWAMI					
553/4	Judy My Love/Now, Ain't That a Shame	1961	12.50	25.00	50.00

PEPPERMINT RAINBOW, THE

45s

Number	Title (A Side/B Side)	Yr	VG	VG+	NM
DECCA					
32316	Pink Lemonade/Walking in Different Circles	1968	2.00	4.00	8.00
32410	Will You Be Staying After Sunday/And I'll Be There	1968	2.50	5.00	10.00
32498	Don't Wake Me Up in the Morning, Michael/Rosemary	1969	2.00	4.00	8.00
32498 [PS]	Don't Wake Me Up in the Morning, Michael/Rosemary	1969	3.00	6.00	12.00
32562	You're the Sound of Love/Jamais	1969	2.00	4.00	8.00
32601	Good Morning Means Goodbye/Don't Love Me Unless It's Forever	1969	2.00	4.00	8.00

Albums

Number	Title (A Side/B Side)	Yr	VG	VG+	NM
DECCA					
DL 75129	Will You Be Staying After Sunday	1969	5.00	10.00	20.00

PEPPERMINT TROLLEY COMPANY, THE

45s

Number	Title (A Side/B Side)	Yr	VG	VG+	NM
ACTA					
807	She's the Kind of Girl/Little Miss Sunshine	1967	2.00	4.00	8.00
809	It's a Lazy Summer Day/Blue Eyes	1967	2.00	4.00	8.00
815	Baby You Come Rollin' Across My Mind/9 O'Clock Business Man	1968	2.50	5.00	10.00
829	Trust/I Remember Long Along	1968	2.00	4.00	8.00
834	The Last Thing on My Mind/Memphis City Letter	1969	2.00	4.00	8.00
835	Spinnin' 'n' Whirlin' Around/New York City	1969	2.00	4.00	8.00
VALIANT					
752	Lollipop Train/Bored to Tears	1966	3.75	7.50	15.00

Albums

Number	Title (A Side/B Side)	Yr	VG	VG+	NM
ACTA					
38007	The Peppermint Trolley Company	1968	6.25	12.50	25.00

PEPS, THE

See THE FABULOUS PEPS.

PERENNIALS, THE

45s

Number	Title (A Side/B Side)	Yr	VG	VG+	NM
BALL					
1016	My Big Mistake/I'm Yours 'Til the End	1963	100.00	200.00	400.00

PERFECT, CHRISTINE

See CHRISTINE McVIE.

PERFIDIANS, THE

45s

Number	Title (A Side/B Side)	Yr	VG	VG+	NM
HUSKY					
1	La Paz/Whiplash	1962	20.00	40.00	80.00
—Red vinyl					
1	La Paz/Whiplash	1962	10.00	20.00	40.00
—Black vinyl					

PERHACS, LINDA

Albums

Number	Title (A Side/B Side)	Yr	VG	VG+	NM
KAPP					
KS-3636	Parallelograms	1970	50.00	100.00	200.00

PERKINS, CARL

45s

Number	Title (A Side/B Side)	Yr	VG	VG+	NM
COLUMBIA					
41131	Pink Pedal Pushers/Jive After Five	1958	7.50	15.00	30.00
41131 [PS]	Pink Pedal Pushers/Jive After Five	1958	30.00	60.00	120.00
41207	Levi Jacket/Pop, Let Me Have the Car	1958	6.25	12.50	25.00
41296	Y-O-U/This Life I Live	1958	6.25	12.50	25.00
41379	Pointed Toe Shoes/Highway of Love	1959	6.25	12.50	25.00
41449	One Ticket to Loneliness/I Don't See Me in Your Eyes Anymore	1959	6.25	12.50	25.00
41651	L-O-V-E-V-I-L-L-E/Too Much for a Man to Understand	1960	6.25	12.50	25.00
41825	Honey, 'Cause I Love You/Just for You	1960	6.25	12.50	25.00
42061	Anyway the Wind Blows/The Unhappy Girls	1961	6.25	12.50	25.00
42403	Hollywood City/Forget Me Next Time Around	1962	—	—	—
—Unreleased?					
42405	Hollywood City/The Fool I Used to Be	1962	6.25	12.50	25.00
42405 [PS]	Hollywood City/The Fool I Used to Be	1962	30.00	60.00	120.00
42514	Sister Twister/Hambone	1962	6.25	12.50	25.00
42514 [PS]	Sister Twister/Hambone	1962	100.00	200.00	400.00
42753	I Just Got Back from There/Forget Me Next Time Around	1963	6.25	12.50	25.00
44723	Restless/1143	1968	2.00	4.00	8.00
44883	For Your Love/Four Letter Word	1969	2.00	4.00	8.00
44993	C.C. Rider/Soul Beat	1969	2.00	4.00	8.00
45107	All Mama's Children/Step Aside	1970	2.00	4.00	8.00
—With NRBQ					
45132	State of Confusion/My Son, My Son	1970	—	3.00	6.00
45253	What Every Little Boy Ought to Know/Just As Long	1970	—	2.50	5.00
45347	Me Without You/Red Headed Woman	1971	—	2.50	5.00
45466	Cotton Top/About All I Can Give You Is My Love	1971	—	2.50	5.00
45582	High on Love/Take Me Back to Memphis	1972	—	2.50	5.00
45694	Someday/The Trip	1972	—	2.50	5.00
DECCA					
31548	Help Me Find My Baby/For a Little While	1963	3.75	7.50	15.00
31591	After Sundown/I Wouldn't Have Told You	1964	3.75	7.50	15.00
31709	The Monkeyshine/Let My Baby Be	1964	3.75	7.50	15.00
31786	One of These Days/Mama of My Song	1965	3.75	7.50	15.00
DOLLIE					
505	Country Boy's Dream/If I Could Come Back	1966	3.00	6.00	12.00
508	Shine, Shine, Shine/Almost Love	1967	3.00	6.00	12.00
512	Without You/You Can Take the Boy Out of the Country	1967	3.00	6.00	12.00
514	My Old Home Town/Back to Tennessee	1967	3.00	6.00	12.00
516	It's You/Lake County Cotton Country	1968	3.00	6.00	12.00
FLIP					
501	Movie Magg/Turn Around	1955	250.00	500.00	1000.
JET					
5054	Blue Suede Shoes/Rock Around the World	1979	—	2.00	4.00
MERCURY					
55009	The E.P. Express/Big Bad Blues	1977	—	2.00	4.00
73425	(Let's Get) Dixiefried/One More Loser Goin' Home	1973	—	3.00	6.00
73489	Ruby, Don't Take Your Love to Town/Sing My Song	1974	—	2.50	5.00
73653	You'll Always Be a Lady to Me/Low Class	1974	—	2.50	5.00
73690	The E.P. Express/Big Bad Blues	1975	—	2.50	5.00
73993	Help Me Dream/You Tore My Heaven All to Hell	1973	—	3.00	6.00
MMI					
1016	Don't Get Off Gettin' It On/Georgia Court Room	1977	—	2.00	4.00
1019	Standing in the Need of Love/Georgia Court Room	1977	—	2.00	4.00
MUSIC MILL					
1007	Born to Boogie/Take Me Back	1976	—	2.00	4.00
SMASH					
884760-7	Birth of Rock and Roll/Rock and Roll (Fais-Do-Do)	1986	—	2.00	4.00
—B-side with Jerry Lee Lewis, Roy Orbison and Johnny Cash					
884760-7 [PS]	Birth of Rock and Roll/Rock and Roll (Fais-Do-Do)	1986	—	2.00	4.00
—B-side with Jerry Lee Lewis, Roy Orbison and Johnny Cash					
884934-7	Sixteen Candles/Rock & Roll (Fais-Do-Do)	1986	—	2.00	4.00
—B-side with Jerry Lee Lewis, Roy Orbison and Johnny Cash; A-side by Jerry Lee Lewis					
888142-7	Class of '55/We Remember the King	1987	—	2.00	4.00
—B-side with Jerry Lee Lewis, Roy Orbison and Johnny Cash					
SUEDE					
101	I Don't Want to Fall in Love Again/We Did It in '54	1978	—	2.00	4.00
102	Rock-a-Billy Fever/Till You Get Through with Me	1978	—	2.00	4.00
6777	Little Teardrops/Green Grass of Home	1977	—	2.00	4.00
SUN					
224	Gone, Gone, Gone/Let the Jukebox Keep On Playing	1955	25.00	50.00	100.00
234	Blue Suede Shoes/Honey Don't	1956	15.00	30.00	60.00
235	Sure to Fall/Tennessee	1956	—	—	—
—Unreleased					
243	Boppin' the Blues/All Mama's Children	1956	10.00	20.00	40.00
249	Dixie Fried/I'm Sorry, I'm Not Sorry	1956	7.50	15.00	30.00
261	Matchbox/Your True Love	1957	7.50	15.00	30.00
274	That's Right/Forever Yours	1957	7.50	15.00	30.00
287	Glad All Over/Lend Me Your Comb	1958	7.50	15.00	30.00
UNIVERSAL					
UVL-66002	Charlene/Love Makes Dreams Come True	1989	—	2.00	4.00
UVL-66019	Hambone/Love Makes Dreams Come True	1989	—	2.00	4.00

7-Inch Extended Plays

Number	Title (A Side/B Side)	Yr	VG	VG+	NM
COLUMBIA					
B-12341	(contents unknown)	1958	50.00	100.00	200.00
B-12341 [PS]	Whole Lotta Shakin'	1958	50.00	100.00	200.00
SUN					
EPA-115	Blue Suede Shoes/Movie Magg//Sure to Fall/Gone, Gone, Gone	1958	100.00	200.00	400.00
EPA-115 [PS]	Carl Perkins	1958	100.00	200.00	400.00

Albums

Number	Title (A Side/B Side)	Yr	VG	VG+	NM
ACCORD					
SN-7169	Presenting Carl Perkins	1982	2.50	5.00	10.00
ALBUM GLOBE					
8118	Country Soul	1980	2.50	5.00	10.00
9037	Goin' Back to Memphis	1980	2.50	5.00	10.00
ALLEGIANCE					
AV-5001	The Heart and Soul of Carl Perkins	198?	2.50	5.00	10.00
BULLDOG					
BDL-2034	Twenty Golden Pieces	198?	2.50	5.00	10.00
COLUMBIA					
CL 1234 [DJ]	Whole Lotta Shakin'	1958	200.00	400.00	800.00
—White label promo					
CL 1234 [M]	Whole Lotta Shakin'	1958	100.00	200.00	400.00
CS 9833	Carl Perkins' Greatest Hits	1969	6.25	12.50	25.00
—Red "360 Sound Stereo" label					
CS 9931	Carl Perkins On Top	1969	6.25	12.50	25.00
—Red "360 Sound Stereo" label					
CS 9981	Boppin' the Blues	1970	6.25	12.50	25.00
—Red "360 Sound Stereo" label					
CS 9981	Boppin' the Blues	1970	3.00	6.00	12.00
—Orange label					
PC 9981	Boppin' the Blues	198?	2.00	4.00	8.00
—Budget-line reissue					
LE 10117	Carl Perkins' Greatest Hits	1974	3.00	6.00	12.00
—"Limited Edition" brown label					
FC 37961	The Survivors	1982	2.50	5.00	10.00
—With Johnny Cash and Jerry Lee Lewis					
PC 37961	The Survivors	198?	2.00	4.00	8.00
—Budget-line reissue					
DESIGN					
DLP-611 [M]	Tennessee	1963	7.50	15.00	30.00
SDLP-611 [R]	Tennessee	1963	5.00	10.00	20.00
DOLLIE					
4001	Country Boy's Dream	1967	7.50	15.00	30.00
ST-91428	Country Boy's Dream	1967	10.00	20.00	40.00
—Capitol Record Club edition					
HARMONY					
HS 11385	Carl Perkins	1970	3.75	7.50	15.00

Number	Title (A Side/B Side)	Yr	VG	VG+	NM
KH 31179	Brown Eyed Handsome Man	1971	3.00	6.00	12.00
KH 31792	Greatest Hits	1972	3.00	6.00	12.00
HILLTOP					
6103	Matchbox	197?	3.00	6.00	12.00
JET					
JT LA856-H	Ol' Blue Suede's Back	1978	3.75	7.50	15.00
JZ 35604	Ol' Blue Suede's Back	1978	2.50	5.00	10.00
KOALA					
AW 14164	Country Soul	198?	2.50	5.00	10.00
MCA DOT					
39035	Carl Perkins	1985	2.50	5.00	10.00
MERCURY					
SRM-1-691	My Kind of Country	1973	3.00	6.00	12.00
RHINO					
RNLP-70221	Original Sun Greatest Hits (1955-1957)	1986	3.00	6.00	12.00
ROUNDER					
SS-27	Honky Tonk Gal: Rare and Unissued Sun Masters	1989	3.00	6.00	12.00
SMASH					
830002-1	Class of '55	1986	3.00	6.00	12.00
—With Jerry Lee Lewis, Roy Orbison and Johnny Cash					
SUEDE					
002	Live at Austin City Limits	1981	2.50	5.00	10.00
SUN					
LP-111	Original Golden Hits	1969	3.00	6.00	12.00
LP-112	Blue Suede Shoes	1969	3.00	6.00	12.00
SLP-1225 [M]	The Dance Album of Carl Perkins	1957	300.00	600.00	1200.
SLP-1225 [M]	Teen Beat — The Best of Carl Perkins	1961	125.00	250.00	500.00
—Reissue with new title					
SUNNYVALE					
9330803	The Sun Story, Vol. 3	1977	3.00	6.00	12.00
TRIP					
TLP-8503 [(2)]	The Best of Carl Perkins	1974	3.00	6.00	12.00
UNIVERSAL					
76001	Born to Rock	1989	3.75	7.50	15.00

PERKINS, LAURA LEE

45s

Number	Title (A Side/B Side)	Yr	VG	VG+	NM
IMPERIAL					
5493	Kiss Me Baby/I Just Don't Like This Kind of Lovin'	1958	10.00	20.00	40.00
5507	Don't Wait Up/Oh La Baby	1958	10.00	20.00	40.00

PERKINS, ROY

45s

Number	Title (A Side/B Side)	Yr	VG	VG+	NM
MELADEE					
111	Bye Bye Baby/You're on My Mind	1958	25.00	50.00	100.00
112	You're Gone/Here Am I	1958	150.00	300.00	600.00
MERCURY					
71278	Drop Top/That's What the Mailman Had to Say	1958	10.00	20.00	40.00

PERKINS, TONY

45s

Number	Title (A Side/B Side)	Yr	VG	VG+	NM
EPIC					
9165	If You'll Be Mine/A Little Love Can Go a Long Way	1956	5.00	10.00	20.00
—As "Anthony Perkins"					
9181	Friendly Persuasion/If You Were the Only Girl	1956	5.00	10.00	20.00
—As "Anthony Perkins"					
9201	A Fool in Love/Melody for Lovers	1957	5.00	10.00	20.00
—As "Anthony Perkins"					
RCA VICTOR					
47-7020	Moon-Light Swim/First Romance	1957	3.00	6.00	12.00
47-7078	When School Starts Again/Rocket to the Moon	1957	3.00	6.00	12.00
47-7155	Indian Giver/Just Being of Age	1958	3.00	6.00	12.00
47-7155 [PS]	Indian Giver/Just Being of Age	1958	6.25	12.50	25.00
47-7244	The Prettiest Girl in School/No, No, No	1958	3.00	6.00	12.00
47-7295	Moonlight Swim/She Used to Be My Girl	1958	3.00	6.00	12.00
47-7415	Treasure Island/Gonna Get Some Lovin'	1958	3.00	6.00	12.00

Albums

Number	Title (A Side/B Side)	Yr	VG	VG+	NM
EPIC					
LN 3394 [M]	Tony Perkins	1957	12.50	25.00	50.00
RCA VICTOR					
LPM-1679 [M]	From My Heart	1958	10.00	20.00	40.00
LSP-1679 [S]	From My Heart	1958	15.00	30.00	60.00
LPM-1853 [M]	On a Rainy Afternoon	1958	10.00	20.00	40.00
LSP-1853 [S]	On a Rainy Afternoon	1958	15.00	30.00	60.00

PERPETUAL MOTION

45s

Number	Title (A Side/B Side)	Yr	VG	VG+	NM
DIAL					
4078	Neckin' Don't Make It/Get Ready	1968	3.00	6.00	12.00

PERRINE, PEP

Albums

Number	Title (A Side/B Side)	Yr	VG	VG+	NM
HIDEOUT					
1003 [M]	Pep Perrine Live and In Person	196?	30.00	60.00	120.00

PERSIANS, THE (1)

45s

Number	Title (A Side/B Side)	Yr	VG	VG+	NM
ABC					
11087	Too Much Pride/That's If You Want Me To	1968	2.00	4.00	8.00
11145	I Only Have Eyes for You/The Sun's Gotta Shine in Your Heart	1968	2.00	4.00	8.00
CAPITOL					
3230	Your Love/Keep On Moving	1971	—	3.00	6.00
3333	I Want to Go Home/Baby Come Back Home	1972	—	3.00	6.00
3414	Give Me a Little Tune/I Won't Cry for You Anymore	1972	—	3.00	6.00
GWP					
509	I Don't Know How (To Fall Out of Love)/Here It Comes	1969	—	3.50	7.00
GWP'S GRAPEVINE					
201	Detour/(B-side unknown)	1970	—	3.50	7.00

PERSIANS, THE (2)

45s

Number	Title (A Side/B Side)	Yr	VG	VG+	NM
GOLDEN EAGLE					
1813	Love Me Tonight/Gee What a Girl	1962	6.25	12.50	25.00
GOLDISC					
1	Teardrops Are Falling/Vault of Memories	1963	15.00	30.00	60.00
17	Let's Monkey Again/When You Said Let's Get Married	1963	7.50	15.00	30.00
MUSIC WORLD					
102	Let's Monkey Again/When You Said Let's Get Married	1963	3.00	6.00	12.00
PAGEANT					
601	Get a Hold of Yourself/The Steady Kind	1963	3.75	7.50	15.00
RSVP					
114	Tears of Love/Dance Now	1962	7.50	15.00	30.00
RTO					
100	Sunday Kind of Love/When We Get Married	1963	3.75	7.50	15.00

PERSONALITIES, THE

45s

Number	Title (A Side/B Side)	Yr	VG	VG+	NM
SAFARI					
1002	Woe Woe Baby/Yours to Command	1957	50.00	100.00	200.00
—With giraffe on label					
1002	Woe Woe Baby/Yours to Command	1957	12.50	25.00	50.00
—No giraffe on label					

PERSUADERS, THE

More than one group?

45s

Number	Title (A Side/B Side)	Yr	VG	VG+	NM
ATCO					
6822	Thin Line Between Love and Hate/Thigh Spy	1971	2.50	5.00	10.00
6919	Bad, Bold and Beautiful Girl/Please Stay	1973	—	3.50	7.00
6943	Some Guys Have All the Luck/Love Attack	1973	2.00	4.00	8.00
6956	Best Thing That Ever Happened to Me/The Way She Is	1974	—	3.50	7.00
6964	All Strung Out on You/Once in a Lifetime Thing	1974	—	3.50	7.00
7012	I've Been Through This Before/Stay with Me	1975	—	3.50	7.00
BUM BUM					
701	Miserlou/World of Wonder	196?	7.50	15.00	30.00
CALLA					
3006	I Need Love/Sure Shot	1977	—	3.00	6.00
3007	Trying to Love Two Women/Quickest Way Out	1977	—	3.00	6.00
CARLTON					
568	Arabella/Viva El Matador	1962	3.75	7.50	15.00
SATURN					
404	Surfing Strip/Hanging Ten	1963	7.50	15.00	30.00
405	Caught in the Soup/Gremmie Bread	1963	7.50	15.00	30.00
WIN OR LOSE					
220	Love Gonna Pack Up (And Walk Out)/You Musta Put Something In Your Love	1971	2.00	4.00	8.00
222	If This Is What You Call Love (I Don't Want No Part of It)/Thanks for Loving Me	1972	2.00	4.00	8.00
225	Peace in the Valley of Love/What Is the Definition of Love	1972	2.00	4.00	8.00
WINLEY					
235	Tears/What Could It Be	1959	37.50	75.00	150.00

Albums

Number	Title (A Side/B Side)	Yr	VG	VG+	NM
ATCO					
SD 7021	The Persuaders	1973	5.00	10.00	20.00
SD 7046	Best Thing That Ever Happened to Me	1974	5.00	10.00	20.00
CALLA					
PZ 34802	It's All About Love	1977	3.75	7.50	15.00
COLLECTABLES					
COL-5139	Thin Line Between Love and Hate (Golden Classics)	198?	2.50	5.00	10.00
SATURN					
SAT-5000 [M]	Surfer's Nightmare	1963	75.00	150.00	300.00
SATS-5000 [S]	Surfer's Nightmare	1963	100.00	200.00	400.00
WIN OR LOSE					
SD 33-387	Thin Line Between Love and Hate	1972	6.25	12.50	25.00

PERSUASIONS, THE

45s

Number	Title (A Side/B Side)	Yr	VG	VG+	NM
A&M					
1531	I Really Got It Bad for You/We're All Goin' Home	1974	—	3.00	6.00
1631	With This Ring/Somewhere to Lay My Head	1974	—	3.00	6.00
1658	I Just Want to Sing with My Friends/Somewhere to Lay My Head	1975	—	3.00	6.00
1698	One Thing on My Mind/Darlin'	1975	—	3.00	6.00
CAPITOL					
3162	Let It Be/It's You That I Need	1971	2.00	4.00	8.00
3242	Don't Know Why I Love You/Tempts Jam	1971	2.00	4.00	8.00
3317	People Get Ready/Buffalo Soldier	1972	2.00	4.00	8.00
3425	The Ten Commandments of Love/Good Times	1972	2.00	4.00	8.00
3492	Three Angels (Part 1)/Three Angels (Part 2)	1972	2.00	4.00	8.00
ELEKTRA					
45396	Papa-Oom-Mow-Mow/Women and Drinkin'	1977	—	2.50	5.00
MCA					
40080	Good Old Accapella/You Must Believe in Me	1973	—	3.00	6.00
40118	Chapel of Love/Love You Most of All	1973	—	3.00	6.00
REPRISE					
0977	Since I Fell for You/Without a Song	1970	2.00	4.00	8.00
TOWER					
146	Try Me/I'll Go Crazy	1965	2.50	5.00	10.00
197	Big Brother/Deep Down Love	1966	2.50	5.00	10.00

Number	Title (A Side/B Side)	Yr	VG	VG+	NM
Albums					
A&M					
SP-3635	More Than Before	1974	3.00	6.00	12.00
SP-3656	I Just Want to Sing with My Friends	1974	3.00	6.00	12.00
CAPITOL					
SM-791	We Came to Play	197?	2.50	5.00	10.00
—Reissue with new prefix					
ST-791	We Came to Play	1971	6.25	12.50	25.00
ST-872	Street Corner Symphony	1972	6.25	12.50	25.00
ST-11101	Spread the Word	1972	6.25	12.50	25.00
CATAMOUNT					
905	Stardust	197?	10.00	20.00	40.00
ELEKTRA					
7E-1099	Chirpin'	1977	3.00	6.00	12.00
FLYING FISH					
FF-093	Comin' At Ya	1979	3.00	6.00	12.00
MCA					
326	We Still Ain't Got No Band	1973	3.75	7.50	15.00
REPRISE					
RS 6394	Acapella	1970	7.50	15.00	30.00
ROUNDER					
3053	Good News	1981	2.50	5.00	10.00
3083	No Frills	1984	2.50	5.00	10.00

PETER AND GORDON

Also see GORDON WALLER.

Number	Title (A Side/B Side)	Yr	VG	VG+	NM
45s					
CAPITOL					
2071	Greener Days/Never Ever	1968	2.50	5.00	10.00
2214	You've Had Better Times/Sipping My Wine	1968	2.50	5.00	10.00
2544	I Can Remember (But Not Too Long Ago)/Hard Time, Rainy Day	1969	2.50	5.00	10.00
5175	A World Without Love/If I Were You	1964	3.00	6.00	12.00
5211	Nobody I Know/You Don't Have to Tell Me	1964	3.00	6.00	12.00
5211 [PS]	Nobody I Know/You Don't Have to Tell Me	1964	4.00	8.00	16.00
5272	I Don't Want to See You Again/I Would Buy You Presents	1964	3.00	6.00	12.00
5272 [PS]	I Don't Want to See You Again/I Would Buy You Presents	1964	4.00	8.00	16.00
5335	I Go to Pieces/Love Me, Baby	1965	3.00	6.00	12.00
5335 [PS]	I Go to Pieces/Love Me, Baby	1965	4.00	8.00	16.00
5406	True Love Ways/If You Wish	1965	3.00	6.00	12.00
5406 [PS]	True Love Ways/If You Wish	1965	4.00	8.00	16.00
5461	To Know You Is to Love You/I Told You So	1965	2.50	5.00	10.00
5461 [PS]	To Know You Is to Love You/I Told You So	1965	3.75	7.50	15.00
5532	Don't Pity Me/Crying in the Rain	1965	2.50	5.00	10.00
5579	Woman/Wrong from the Start	1966	3.00	6.00	12.00
—A-side composer listed as "Bernard Webb"					
5579	Woman/Wrong from the Start	1966	2.50	5.00	10.00
—A-side composer listed as "A. Smith"					
5650	There's No Living Without Your Loving/Stranger with a Black Dove	1966	2.50	5.00	10.00
5650 [PS]	There's No Living Without Your Loving/Stranger with a Black Dove	1966	3.75	7.50	15.00
5684	To Show I Love You/Start Trying Someone Else	1966	2.50	5.00	10.00
5684 [PS]	To Show I Love You/Start Trying Someone Else	1966	3.75	7.50	15.00
5740	Lady Godiva/Morning's Calling	1966	2.50	5.00	10.00
5740	Lady Godiva/The House I Live In	1966	3.75	7.50	15.00
5808	Knight in Rusty Armour/Flower Lady	1966	2.50	5.00	10.00
5808 [PS]	Knight in Rusty Armour/Flower Lady	1966	3.75	7.50	15.00
5864	Sunday for Tea/Hurtin' Is Lovin'	1967	2.50	5.00	10.00
5864 [PS]	Sunday for Tea/Hurtin' Is Lovin'	1967	3.75	7.50	15.00
5919	The Jokers/Red Cream and Velvet	1967	2.50	5.00	10.00
CAPITOL CREATIVE PRODUCTS					
51 [DJ]	Wrong from the Start/You've Lost That Lovin' Feelin'	1966	3.00	6.00	12.00
—B-side by the Lettermen					
CAPITOL STARLINE					
6076	A World Without Love/Nobody I Know	1965	2.00	4.00	8.00
—Green swirl label original					
6103	I Go to Pieces/Love Me Baby	1966	2.00	4.00	8.00
—Green swirl label original					
6104	There's No Living Without Your Loving/Stranger with a Black Dove	1966	2.00	4.00	8.00
—Green swirl label original					
6155	I Don't Want to See You Again/Woman	197?	—	3.00	6.00
—Red and white "bullseye" label original					
6156	Lady Godiva/You've Had Better Times	197?	—	3.00	6.00
—Red and white "bullseye" label original					
Albums					
CAPITOL					
ST 2115 [S]	A World Without Love	1964	6.25	12.50	25.00
T 2115 [M]	A World Without Love	1964	5.00	10.00	20.00
ST 2220 [S]	I Don't Want to See You Again	1964	6.25	12.50	25.00
T 2220 [M]	I Don't Want to See You Again	1964	5.00	10.00	20.00
ST 2324 [S]	I Go to Pieces	1965	6.25	12.50	25.00
T 2324 [M]	I Go to Pieces	1965	5.00	10.00	20.00
ST 2368 [S]	True Love Ways	1965	6.25	12.50	25.00
T 2368 [M]	True Love Ways	1965	5.00	10.00	20.00
ST 2430 [S]	Peter and Gordon Sing the Hits of Nashville	1966	6.25	12.50	25.00
T 2430 [M]	Peter and Gordon Sing the Hits of Nashville	1966	5.00	10.00	20.00
ST 2477 [P]	Woman	1966	6.25	12.50	25.00
—"Woman" is rechanneled					
T 2477 [M]	Woman	1966	5.00	10.00	20.00
ST 2549 [P]	The Best of Peter and Gordon	1966	4.50	9.00	18.00
—Black label with colorband; "Woman" is rechanneled					
ST 2549 [P]	The Best of Peter and Gordon	1967	3.75	7.50	15.00
—"Starline" label					
T 2549 [M]	The Best of Peter and Gordon	1966	3.75	7.50	15.00
—Black label with colorband					
T 2549 [M]	The Best of Peter and Gordon	1967	3.00	6.00	12.00
—"Starline" label					
ST 2664 [S]	Lady Godiva	1967	5.00	10.00	20.00
T 2664 [M]	Lady Godiva	1967	3.75	7.50	15.00
ST 2729 [S]	Knight in Rusty Armour	1967	5.00	10.00	20.00
T 2729 [M]	Knight in Rusty Armour	1967	3.75	7.50	15.00
ST 2747 [S]	In London for Tea	1967	5.00	10.00	20.00
T 2747 [M]	In London for Tea	1967	3.75	7.50	15.00
ST 2882 [S]	Hot, Cold and Custard	1968	6.25	12.50	25.00
SN-16084 [S]	The Best of Peter and Gordon	1979	2.00	4.00	8.00

PETER, PAUL AND MARY

Also see PAUL STOOKEY; MARY TRAVERS; PETER YARROW.

Number	Title (A Side/B Side)	Yr	VG	VG+	NM
45s					
WARNER BROS.					
(no #)	A-Soalin' (mono/stereo)	196?	3.00	6.00	12.00
—Green custom label					
(no #) [PS]	A-Soalin' (mono/stereo)	196?	5.00	10.00	20.00
—Illustrated book with lyrics					
PRO 149 [DJ]	Morning Train/(B-side unknown)	1963	3.75	7.50	15.00
—Promo-only 7-inch 33 1/3 rpm record with small hole					
5274	Lemon Tree/Early in the Morning	1962	2.50	5.00	10.00
5296	If I Had a Hammer/Gone the Rainbow	1962	2.50	5.00	10.00
5325	Big Boat/Tiny Sparrow	1962	2.50	5.00	10.00
5325 [PS]	Big Boat/Tiny Sparrow	1962	5.00	10.00	20.00
5334	Settle Down (Goin' Down That Highway)/500 Miles	1963	2.50	5.00	10.00
5348	Puff/Pretty Mary	1963	3.00	6.00	12.00
—First pressings have no subtitle on A-side					
5348	Puff (The Magic Dragon)/Pretty Mary	1963	2.50	5.00	10.00
—Later pressings add subtitle					
5368	Blowin' in the Wind/Flora	1963	2.50	5.00	10.00
5385	Don't Think Twice, It's All Right/Autumn to May	1963	2.50	5.00	10.00
5399	Stewball/The Cruel War	1963	2.50	5.00	10.00
5402	A-Soalin'/High-A-Bye	1963	3.00	6.00	12.00
5402 [PS]	A-Soalin'/High-A-Bye	1963	5.00	10.00	20.00
5418	Tell It on the Mountain/Old Coat	1964	2.50	5.00	10.00
5442	Oh, Rock My Soul (Part 1)/Oh, Rock My Soul (Part 2)	1964	2.50	5.00	10.00
5496	For Lovin' Me/Monday Morning	1965	2.00	4.00	8.00
5625	When the Ship Comes In/The Times They Are a-Changin'	1965	2.00	4.00	8.00
5659	Early Morning Rain/The Rising of the Moon	1965	2.00	4.00	8.00
5809	The Cruel War/Mon Vrai Destin	1966	2.00	4.00	8.00
5842	Hurry Sundown/Sometime Lover	1966	—	—	—
—Unreleased?					
5849	The Other Side of This Life/Sometime Lover	1966	2.00	4.00	8.00
5883	For Baby (For Bobbie)/Hurry Sundown	1967	2.00	4.00	8.00
7067	I Dig Rock and Roll Music/The Great Mandella (The Wheel of Life)	1967	2.50	5.00	10.00
7092	Too Much of Nothing/The House Song	1967	2.00	4.00	8.00
7232	Yesterday's Tomorrow/Love City (Postcards to Duluth)	1968	2.00	4.00	8.00
7279	Day Is Done/Make Believe Town	1969	2.00	4.00	8.00
7340	Leaving on a Jet Plane/The House Song	1969	2.50	5.00	10.00
7359	Christmas Dinner/The Marvelous Toy	1969	2.50	5.00	10.00
8684	Like the First Time/Best of Friends	1978	—	2.00	4.00
8728	Forever Young/Best of Friends	1978	—	2.00	4.00
(NO LABEL)					
(no #) [DJ]	Eugene McCarthy for President	1968	6.25	12.50	25.00
Albums					
GOLD CASTLE					
D1-71301	No Easy Walk to Freedom	1988	2.50	5.00	10.00
—Reissue of 171001					
D1-71316	A Holiday Celebration	1988	2.50	5.00	10.00
R 164086	A Holiday Celebration	1988	3.00	6.00	12.00
—Same as above, except BMG Direct Marketing edition					
171001	No Easy Walk to Freedom	1987	3.00	6.00	12.00
WARNER BROS.					
W 1449 [M]	Peter, Paul and Mary	1962	5.00	10.00	20.00
WS 1449 [S]	Peter, Paul and Mary	1962	6.25	12.50	25.00
—Gold label					
WS 1449 [S]	Peter, Paul and Mary	1968	3.00	6.00	12.00
—Green "W7" label					
WS 1449 [S]	Peter, Paul and Mary	1970	2.50	5.00	10.00
—Any later Warner Bros. label (green "WB", palm trees, white label)					
W 1473 [M]	(Moving)	1963	5.00	10.00	20.00
WS 1473 [S]	(Moving)	1963	6.25	12.50	25.00
—Gold label					
WS 1473 [S]	(Moving)	1968	2.50	5.00	10.00
—Any later Warner Bros. label (green "W7", green "WB", palm trees, white label)					
W 1507 [M]	In the Wind	1963	5.00	10.00	20.00
WS 1507 [S]	In the Wind	1963	6.25	12.50	25.00
—Gold label					
WS 1507 [S]	In the Wind	1968	2.50	5.00	10.00
—Any later Warner Bros. label					
2W 1555 [(2) M]	Peter, Paul and Mary In Concert	1964	6.25	12.50	25.00
2WS 1555 [(2) S]	Peter, Paul and Mary In Concert	1964	7.50	15.00	30.00
—Gold labels					
2WS 1555 [(2) S]	Peter, Paul and Mary In Concert	1968	3.00	6.00	12.00
—Any later Warner Bros. label					
W 1589 [M]	A Song Will Rise	1965	5.00	10.00	20.00
WS 1589 [S]	A Song Will Rise	1965	6.25	12.50	25.00
—Gold label					
WS 1589 [S]	A Song Will Rise	1968	2.50	5.00	10.00
—Any later Warner Bros. label					
W 1615 [M]	See What Tomorrow Brings	1965	5.00	10.00	20.00
WS 1615 [S]	See What Tomorrow Brings	1965	6.25	12.50	25.00
—Gold label					
WS 1615 [S]	See What Tomorrow Brings	1968	2.50	5.00	10.00
—Any later Warner Bros. label					
W 1648 [M]	Peter, Paul and Mary Album	1966	5.00	10.00	20.00
WS 1648 [S]	Peter, Paul and Mary Album	1966	6.25	12.50	25.00
—Gold label					
WS 1648 [S]	Peter, Paul and Mary Album	1968	2.50	5.00	10.00
—Any later Warner Bros. label					
W 1700 [M]	Album 1700	1967	6.25	12.50	25.00
WS 1700 [S]	Album 1700	1967	6.25	12.50	25.00
—Gold label					

Number	Title (A Side/B Side)	Yr	VG	VG+	NM
WS 1700 [S]	Album 1700	1968	3.00	6.00	12.00
—Green "W7" label					
WS 1700 [S]	Album 1700	1970	2.50	5.00	10.00
—Any later Warner Bros. label					
WS 1751	Late Again	1968	3.75	7.50	15.00
—Green "W7" label					
WS 1751	Late Again	1970	2.50	5.00	10.00
—Any later Warner Bros. label					
WS 1785	Peter, Paul and Mommy	1969	3.75	7.50	15.00
—Green "W7" label					
WS 1785	Peter, Paul and Mommy	1970	2.50	5.00	10.00
—Any later Warner Bros. label					
BS 2552	(Ten) Years Together — The Best of Peter, Paul and Mary	1970	3.75	7.50	15.00
—Green "WB" label					
BS 2552	(Ten) Years Together — The Best of Peter, Paul and Mary	1973	3.00	6.00	12.00
—"Burbank" palm-trees label					
BSK 3105	(Ten) Years Together — The Best of Peter, Paul and Mary	1977	2.50	5.00	10.00
—"Burbank" palm-trees label					
BSK 3105	(Ten) Years Together — The Best of Peter, Paul and Mary	1979	2.00	4.00	8.00
—White or tan label					
BSK 3231	Reunion	1978	2.50	5.00	10.00

PETERSEN, PAUL

Also see JAMES DARREN/SHELLEY FABARES/PAUL PETERSEN.

45s

Number	Title (A Side/B Side)	Yr	VG	VG+	NM
COLPIX					
620	She Can't Find Her Keys/Very Likely	1962	3.75	7.50	15.00
620 [PS]	She Can't Find Her Keys/Very Likely	1962	7.50	15.00	30.00
—Sleeve spells his last name "Peterson" in error					
631	What Did They Do Before Rock and Roll/Very Unlikely	1962	5.00	10.00	20.00
—With Shelly Fabares					
631 [PS]	What Did They Do Before Rock and Roll/Very Unlikely	1962	20.00	40.00	80.00
632	Keep Your Love Locked (Deep in Your Heart)/Be Everything to Anyone You Love	1962	3.00	6.00	12.00
632 [PS]	Keep Your Love Locked (Deep in Your Heart)/Be Everything to Anyone You Love	1962	7.50	15.00	30.00
649	Lollipops and Roses/Please Mr. Sun	1962	3.00	6.00	12.00
663	My Dad/Little Boy Sad	1962	3.75	7.50	15.00
663 [PS]	My Dad/Little Boy Sad	1962	7.50	15.00	30.00
676	Amy/Goody Goody	1963	3.00	6.00	12.00
676	Amy/I Only Have Eyes for You	1963	3.00	6.00	12.00
697	Girls in the Summertime/Mama, Your Little Boy Fell	1963	3.00	6.00	12.00
707	The Cheer Leader/Polka Dots and Moonbeams	1963	3.00	6.00	12.00
720	She Rides with Me/Poorest Boy in Town	1964	20.00	40.00	80.00
—A-side produced by Brian Wilson					
730	Where Is She/Hey There Beautiful	1964	3.00	6.00	12.00
763	Happy/Little Dreamer	1965	3.00	6.00	12.00
785	The Ring/You Don't Need Money	1965	3.00	6.00	12.00
MOTOWN					
1108	Chained/Don't Let It Happen	1967	5.00	10.00	20.00
1129	A Little Bit for Sandy/Your Love's Got Me Runnin'	1968	5.00	10.00	20.00

Albums

Number	Title (A Side/B Side)	Yr	VG	VG+	NM
COLPIX					
CP-429 [M]	Lollipops and Roses	1962	12.50	25.00	50.00
SCP-429 [S]	Lollipops and Roses	1962	15.00	30.00	60.00
CP-442 [M]	My Dad	1963	12.50	25.00	50.00
SCP-442 [S]	My Dad	1963	15.00	30.00	60.00

PETERSON, EARL

45s

Number	Title (A Side/B Side)	Yr	VG	VG+	NM
COLUMBIA					
21364	Boogie Blues/Believe Me	1955	12.50	25.00	50.00
21406	Be Careful of the Heart You're Going to Break/I'm Not Buying Baby	1955	12.50	25.00	50.00
21467	I Ain't Gonna Fall in Love/I'll Live My Life Alone	1955	12.50	25.00	50.00
21540	You Gotta Be My Baby/World of Make Believe	1956	10.00	20.00	40.00
SUN					
197	Boogie Blues/In the Dark	1954	125.00	250.00	500.00

PETERSON, OSCAR

45s

Number	Title (A Side/B Side)	Yr	VG	VG+	NM
CLEF					
89076	I Was Doing All Right/Oh, Lady Be Good	1953	3.75	7.50	15.00
89077	Begin the Beguine/Let's Do It	1953	3.75	7.50	15.00
89078	Cheek to Cheek/I've Got My Love to Keep Me Warm	1953	3.75	7.50	15.00
89079	Sophisticated Lady/Cottontail	1953	3.75	7.50	15.00
89093	Autumn in New York/I Hear Music	1954	3.75	7.50	15.00
89106	One for My Baby/Polka Dots and Moonbeams	1954	3.75	7.50	15.00
89113	It's Easy to Remember/Pooper	1954	3.75	7.50	15.00
89124	Unforgettable/Angel Eyes	1954	3.75	7.50	15.00
89130	Nuages/Dark Eyes	1955	3.00	6.00	12.00
89139	Pettiford's Tune/(B-side unknown)	1955	3.00	6.00	12.00
89148	Soft Winds/Sweet Lorraine	1955	3.00	6.00	12.00
LIMELIGHT					
3056	March Past/Place St. Henri	1965	2.00	4.00	8.00
3062	Lover's Promenade/The Smudge	1965	2.00	4.00	8.00
3072	Straighten Up and Fly Right/When My Sugar Walks Down the Street	1966	2.00	4.00	8.00
MERCURY					
8917	Debut/Tenderly	1950	6.25	12.50	25.00
8921	Lover Come Back to Me/They Didn't Believe Me	1950	5.00	10.00	20.00
8922	Where or When/Oscar's Blues	1950	5.00	10.00	20.00
8923	All the Things You Are/Three O'Clock in the Morning	1950	5.00	10.00	20.00
8926	Little White Lies/Lover	1951	5.00	10.00	20.00
8930	Exactly Like You/Robin's Nest	1951	5.00	10.00	20.00
8933	Get Happy/Jumping with Symphony Sid	1951	5.00	10.00	20.00
8940	Squatty Roo/Salute to Garne	1951	5.00	10.00	20.00
8943	How High the Moon/Nameless	1951	5.00	10.00	20.00
8952	What's New/I Get a Kick Out of You	1951	5.00	10.00	20.00
8959	Love for Sale/Until the Real Thing Comes Along	1952	5.00	10.00	20.00
8976	Rough Ridin'/But Not for Me	1952	5.00	10.00	20.00
8999	Just One of Those Things/Willow Weep for Me	1952	5.00	10.00	20.00
72342	Incoherent Blues/Mumbles	1964	2.00	4.00	8.00
89006	You Go to My Head/You Turn the Tables on Me	1952	3.75	7.50	15.00
89007	I Can't Get Started/Small Hotel	1952	3.75	7.50	15.00
89008	East of the Moon (West of the Sun)/These Foolish Things	1952	3.75	7.50	15.00
89009	Blue Moon/They Can't Take That Away from Me	1952	3.75	7.50	15.00
89038	The Man I Love/It Ain't Necessarily So	1953	3.75	7.50	15.00
89039	Blue Skies/Isn't This a Lovely Day	1953	3.75	7.50	15.00
89040	In the Still of the Night/What Is This Thing Called Love	1953	3.75	7.50	15.00
89041	Prelude to a Kiss/John Hardy's Wife	1953	3.75	7.50	15.00
89062	I Can't Give You Anything But Love, Baby/Spring Is Here	1953	3.75	7.50	15.00
PRESTIGE					
711	Sandy's Blues (Part 1)/Sandy's Blues (Part 2)	1969	—	3.00	6.00
727	Girl Talk/On a Clear Day	1969	—	3.00	6.00
VERVE					
10056	Soft Sands/Echoes	1957	3.00	6.00	12.00
10073	Why, Oh Why/I've Never Left Your Arms	1957	3.00	6.00	12.00
10084	Song to the Stars/Chanel	1957	3.00	6.00	12.00
10145	Bye Bye Blackbird/Golden Striker	1958	3.00	6.00	12.00
10192	On the Street Where You Live/I Could Have Danced All Night	1959	3.00	6.00	12.00
10207	Gentleman Jimmy/'Til Tomorrow	1960	2.50	5.00	10.00
10268	Billy Boy/Yours Is My Heart Alone	1962	2.50	5.00	10.00
10292	This Could Be the Start of Something Big/Gravy Waltz	1963	2.50	5.00	10.00
10302	Hallelujah Time/Hymn to Freedom	1963	2.50	5.00	10.00
10320	Someday My Prince Will Come/Come Sunday	1964	2.00	4.00	8.00
10354	People/Quiet Nights of Quiet Stars	1965	2.00	4.00	8.00

Albums

Number	Title (A Side/B Side)	Yr	VG	VG+	NM
AMERICAN RECORDING SOCIETY					
G-415 [M]	An Oscar for Peterson	1957	10.00	20.00	40.00
G-438 [M]	Oscar Peterson Trio at Newport	1957	10.00	20.00	40.00
BASF					
20713	Motions and Emotions	1972	3.00	6.00	12.00
20723	Hello Herbie	1972	3.00	6.00	12.00
20734	Tristeza on Piano	1972	3.00	6.00	12.00
20868	Walking the Line	1973	3.00	6.00	12.00
20905	In Tune	1973	3.00	6.00	12.00
20908	Reunion Blues	1973	3.00	6.00	12.00
21281	Great Connection	1974	3.00	6.00	12.00
25101 [(2)]	Exclusively for My Friends	1972	3.75	7.50	15.00
25156 [(2)]	In a Mellow Mood	1973	3.75	7.50	15.00
CLEF					
MGC-106 [10]	Oscar Peterson Piano Solos	1951	25.00	50.00	100.00
—Reissue of Mercury 25024					
MGC-107 [10]	Oscar Peterson at Carnegie Hall	1951	25.00	50.00	100.00
MGC-110 [10]	Oscar Peterson Collates	1952	25.00	50.00	100.00
MGC-116 [10]	The Oscar Peterson Quartet	1952	25.00	50.00	100.00
MGC-119 [10]	Oscar Peterson Plays Pretty	1952	25.00	50.00	100.00
MGC-127 [10]	Oscar Peterson Collates No. 2	1953	20.00	40.00	80.00
MGC-145 [10]	Oscar Peterson Sings	1954	20.00	40.00	80.00
MGC-155 [10]	Oscar Peterson Plays Pretty No. 2	1954	20.00	40.00	80.00
MGC-168 [10]	The Oscar Peterson Quartet No. 2	1954	20.00	40.00	80.00
MGC-603 [M]	Oscar Peterson Plays Cole Porter	1953	15.00	30.00	60.00
MGC-604 [M]	Oscar Peterson Plays Irving Berlin	1953	15.00	30.00	60.00
MGC-605 [M]	Oscar Peterson Plays George Gershwin	1953	15.00	30.00	60.00
MGC-606 [M]	Oscar Peterson Plays Duke Ellington	1953	15.00	30.00	60.00
MGC-623 [M]	Oscar Peterson Plays Jerome Kern	1954	12.50	25.00	50.00
MGC-624 [M]	Oscar Peterson Plays Richard Rodgers	1954	12.50	25.00	50.00
MGC-625 [M]	Oscar Peterson Plays Vincent Youmans	1954	12.50	25.00	50.00
MGC-648 [M]	Oscar Peterson Plays Harry Warren	1955	12.50	25.00	50.00
MGC-649 [M]	Oscar Peterson Plays Harold Arlen	1955	12.50	25.00	50.00
MGC-650 [M]	Oscar Peterson Plays Jimmy McHugh	1955	12.50	25.00	50.00
MGC-688 [M]	The Oscar Peterson Quartet	1956	12.50	25.00	50.00
—Reissue of 116					
MGC-694 [M]	Recital by Oscar Peterson	1956	12.50	25.00	50.00
MGC-695 [M]	Nostalgic Memories by Oscar Peterson	1956	12.50	25.00	50.00
MGC-696 [M]	Tenderly — Music by Oscar Peterson	1956	12.50	25.00	50.00
MGC-697 [M]	Keyboard Music by Oscar Peterson	1956	12.50	25.00	50.00
MGC-698 [M]	An Evening with the Oscar Peterson Duo/Quartet	1956	12.50	25.00	50.00
MGC-708 [M]	Oscar Peterson Plays Count Basie	1956	12.50	25.00	50.00
MGC-751 [M]	The Oscar Peterson Trio at the Stratford Shakespearean Festival, Volume 1	1955	—	—	—
—Canceled					
MGC-752 [M]	The Oscar Peterson Trio at the Stratford Shakespearean Festival, Volume 2	1955	—	—	—
—Canceled					
DCC COMPACT CLASSICS					
LPZ-2021	West Side Story	1996	6.25	12.50	25.00
—Audiophile vinyl					
EMARCY					
405 [(2)]	Oscar Peterson Trio Transition	1976	3.75	7.50	15.00
FANTASY					
OJC-378	Oscar Peterson Jam — Montreux '77	1989	2.50	5.00	10.00
OJC-383	Oscar Peterson and the Bassists — Montreux '77	1989	2.50	5.00	10.00
OJC-498	Skol	1991	2.50	5.00	10.00
OJC-603	Trumpet Summit Meets the Oscar Peterson Big Four	1991	2.50	5.00	10.00
OJC-627	The Good Life	1991	2.50	5.00	10.00
LIMELIGHT					
LM-82010 [M]	Canadiana Suite	1965	3.75	7.50	15.00
LM-82023 [M]	Eloquence	1965	3.75	7.50	15.00
LM-82029 [M]	With Respect to Nat	1966	3.75	7.50	15.00
LM-82039 [M]	Blues Etude	1966	3.75	7.50	15.00
LM-82044 [M]	Soul Espanol	1967	5.00	10.00	20.00
LS-86010 [S]	Canadiana Suite	1965	5.00	10.00	20.00

Number	Title (A Side/B Side)	Yr	VG	VG+	NM
LS-86023 [S]	Eloquence	1965	5.00	10.00	20.00
LS-86029 [S]	With Respect to Nat	1966	5.00	10.00	20.00
LS-86039 [S]	Blues Etude	1966	3.75	7.50	15.00
LS-86044 [S]	Soul Espanol	1967	3.75	7.50	15.00
MERCURY					
MGC-106 [10]	Oscar Peterson Piano Solos	1951	30.00	60.00	120.00
MGC-107 [10]	Oscar Peterson at Carnegie Hall	1951	30.00	60.00	120.00
MGC-110 [10]	Oscar Peterson Collates	1952	30.00	60.00	120.00
MGC-116 [10]	The Oscar Peterson Quartet	1952	30.00	60.00	120.00
MGC-119 [10]	Oscar Peterson Plays Pretty	1952	30.00	60.00	120.00
MGC-603 [M]	Oscar Peterson Plays Cole Porter	1953	25.00	50.00	100.00
MGC-604 [M]	Oscar Peterson Plays Irving Berlin	1953	25.00	50.00	100.00
MGC-605 [M]	Oscar Peterson Plays George Gershwin	1953	25.00	50.00	100.00
MGC-606 [M]	Oscar Peterson Plays Duke Ellington	1953	25.00	50.00	100.00
MG-20975 [M]	Oscar Peterson Trio + One	1964	6.25	12.50	25.00
MG-25024 [10]	Oscar Peterson Piano Solos	1950	37.50	75.00	150.00
SR-60975 [S]	Oscar Peterson Trio + One	1964	7.50	15.00	30.00
MGM					
GAS-133	Oscar Peterson (Golden Archive Series)	1970	3.00	6.00	12.00
MOBILE FIDELITY					
1-243	Very Tall	1995	5.00	10.00	20.00
—Audiophile vinyl					
PABLO					
2310701	The Trio	1975	3.00	6.00	12.00
2310739	Oscar Peterson and Roy Eldridge	1976	3.00	6.00	12.00
2310740	Oscar Peterson and Dizzy Gillespie	1976	3.00	6.00	12.00
2310741	Oscar Peterson and Harry Edison	1976	3.00	6.00	12.00
2310742	Oscar Peterson and Clark Terry	1976	3.00	6.00	12.00
2310743	Oscar Peterson and Jon Faddis	1976	3.00	6.00	12.00
2310747	Montreux '75	1976	3.00	6.00	12.00
2310779	Porgy and Bess	1976	3.00	6.00	12.00
2310796	Giants	1977	3.00	6.00	12.00
2310817	Jousts	1979	3.00	6.00	12.00
2310895	History of An Artist, Volume 2	1983	3.00	6.00	12.00
2310918	If You Could See Me Now	1987	2.50	5.00	10.00
2310927	Oscar Peterson + Harry Edison + Eddie "Cleanhead" Vinson	1988	2.50	5.00	10.00
2310940	Live	1990	2.50	5.00	10.00
2625702 [(2)]	History of An Artist	1975	3.75	7.50	15.00
2625705 [(2)]	A Salle Pleyel	1975	3.75	7.50	15.00
2625711 [(2)]	Oscar Peterson in Russia	1976	3.00	6.00	12.00
2640101 [(2)]	Freedom Songbook	1983	3.75	7.50	15.00
PABLO LIVE					
2308208	Oscar Peterson Jam — Montreux '77	1977	3.00	6.00	12.00
2308213	Oscar Peterson and the Bassists — Montreux '77	1978	3.00	6.00	12.00
2308224	Digital at Montreux	1980	3.00	6.00	12.00
2308231	Nigerian Marketplace	1982	3.00	6.00	12.00
2308232	Skol	1982	3.00	6.00	12.00
2308241	The Good Life	1983	3.00	6.00	12.00
2620111 [(2)]	The London Concert	1979	3.75	7.50	15.00
2620112 [(2)]	The Paris Concert	1979	3.75	7.50	15.00
2620115 [(2)]	Live at the Northsea Jazz Festival, 1980	1981	3.75	7.50	15.00
PABLO TODAY					
2312108	Night Child	1979	3.00	6.00	12.00
2312129	A Royal Wedding Suite	198?	3.00	6.00	12.00
2312135	The Personal Touch	1982	3.00	6.00	12.00
2313103	Silent Partner	1980	3.00	6.00	12.00
PAUSA					
7044	Mellow Wood	1979	2.50	5.00	10.00
7059	Action	1980	2.50	5.00	10.00
7064	Girl Talk	1980	2.50	5.00	10.00
7069	My Favorite Instrument	1980	2.50	5.00	10.00
7073	In Tune	1980	2.50	5.00	10.00
7080	The Way I Really Play	1981	2.50	5.00	10.00
7099	Reunion Blues	1981	2.50	5.00	10.00
7102	Motions and Emotions	1982	2.50	5.00	10.00
7113	Great Connection	1983	2.50	5.00	10.00
7124	Tristeza on Piano	1983	2.50	5.00	10.00
7135	Another Day	1983	2.50	5.00	10.00
PRESTIGE					
PRST-7595	Soul-O!	1968	3.75	7.50	15.00
PRST-7620	The Great Oscar Peterson on Prestige!	1969	3.75	7.50	15.00
PRST-7649	Oscar Peterson Plays for Lovers	1969	3.75	7.50	15.00
PRST-7690	Easy Walker	1969	3.75	7.50	15.00
RCA VICTOR					
LPT-3006 [10]	This Is Oscar Peterson	1952	30.00	60.00	120.00
TRIP					
5560	Eloquence	197?	2.50	5.00	10.00
VERVE					
VSP-11 [M]	Stage Right	1966	3.00	6.00	12.00
VSPS-11 [S]	Stage Right	1966	3.75	7.50	15.00
MGV-2002 [M]	In a Romantic Mood — Oscar Peterson with Strings	1956	10.00	20.00	40.00
V-2002 [M]	In a Romantic Mood — Oscar Peterson with Strings	1961	5.00	10.00	20.00
MGV-2004 [M]	Pastel Moods by Oscar Peterson	1956	10.00	20.00	40.00
V-2004 [M]	Pastel Moods by Oscar Peterson	1961	5.00	10.00	20.00
MGV-2012 [M]	Romance — The Vocal Styling of Oscar Peterson	1956	10.00	20.00	40.00
—Reissue of Clef 145					
V-2012 [M]	Romance — The Vocal Styling of Oscar Peterson	1961	5.00	10.00	20.00
MGV-2044 [M]	Recital by Oscar Peterson	1957	10.00	20.00	40.00
—Reissue of Clef 694					
V-2044 [M]	Recital by Oscar Peterson	1961	5.00	10.00	20.00
MGV-2045 [M]	Nostalgic Memories by Oscar Peterson	1957	10.00	20.00	40.00
—Reissue of Clef 695					
V-2045 [M]	Nostalgic Memories by Oscar Peterson	1961	5.00	10.00	20.00
MGV-2046 [M]	Tenderly — Music by Oscar Peterson	1957	10.00	20.00	40.00
—Reissue of Clef 696					
V-2046 [M]	Tenderly — Music by Oscar Peterson	1961	5.00	10.00	20.00
MGV-2047 [M]	Keyboard Music by Oscar Peterson	1957	10.00	20.00	40.00
—Reissue of Clef 697					
V-2047 [M]	Keyboard Music by Oscar Peterson	1961	5.00	10.00	20.00
MGV-2048 [M]	An Evening with Oscar Peterson	1957	10.00	20.00	40.00
—Reissue of Clef 698					

Number	Title (A Side/B Side)	Yr	VG	VG+	NM
V-2048 [M]	An Evening with Oscar Peterson	1961	5.00	10.00	20.00
MGV-2052 [M]	Oscar Peterson Plays the Cole Porter Songbook	1957	10.00	20.00	40.00
—Reissue of Clef 603					
V-2052 [M]	Oscar Peterson Plays the Cole Porter Songbook	1961	5.00	10.00	20.00
V6-2052 [S]	Oscar Peterson Plays the Cole Porter Songbook	1961	3.75	7.50	15.00
—Reissue of 6083					
MGV-2053 [M]	Oscar Peterson Plays the Irving Berlin Songbook	1957	10.00	20.00	40.00
—Reissue of Clef 604					
V-2053 [M]	Oscar Peterson Plays the Irving Berlin Songbook	1961	5.00	10.00	20.00
V6-2053 [S]	Oscar Peterson Plays the Irving Berlin Songbook	1961	3.75	7.50	15.00
—Reissue of 6084					
MGV-2054 [M]	Oscar Peterson Plays the George Gershwin Songbook	1957	10.00	20.00	40.00
—Reissue of Clef 605					
V-2054 [M]	Oscar Peterson Plays the George Gershwin Songbook	1961	5.00	10.00	20.00
V6-2054 [S]	Oscar Peterson Plays the George Gershwin Songbook	1961	3.75	7.50	15.00
—Reissue of 6085					
MGV-2055 [M]	Oscar Peterson Plays the Duke Ellington Songbook	1957	10.00	20.00	40.00
—Reissue of Clef 606					
V-2055 [M]	Oscar Peterson Plays the Duke Ellington Songbook	1961	5.00	10.00	20.00
V6-2055 [S]	Oscar Peterson Plays the Duke Ellington Songbook	1961	3.75	7.50	15.00
—Reissue of 6086					
MGV-2056 [M]	Oscar Peterson Plays the Jerome Kern Songbook	1957	10.00	20.00	40.00
—Reissue of Clef 623					
V-2056 [M]	Oscar Peterson Plays the Jerome Kern Songbook	1961	5.00	10.00	20.00
V6-2056 [S]	Oscar Peterson Plays the Jerome Kern Songbook	1961	3.75	7.50	15.00
—Reissue of 6087					
MGV-2057 [M]	Oscar Peterson Plays the Richard Rodgers Songbook	1957	10.00	20.00	40.00
—Reissue of Clef 624					
V-2057 [M]	Oscar Peterson Plays the Richard Rodgers Songbook	1961	5.00	10.00	20.00
V6-2057 [S]	Oscar Peterson Plays the Richard Rodgers Songbook	1961	3.75	7.50	15.00
—Reissue of 6088					
MGV-2058 [M]	Oscar Peterson Plays the Vincent Youmans Songbook	1957	—	—	—
—Reissue planned but canceled					
MGV-2059 [M]	Oscar Peterson Plays the Harry Warren Songbook	1957	10.00	20.00	40.00
—Reissue of Clef 648					
V-2059 [M]	Oscar Peterson Plays the Harry Warren Songbook	1961	5.00	10.00	20.00
V6-2059 [S]	Oscar Peterson Plays the Harry Warren Songbook	1961	3.75	7.50	15.00
—Reissue of 6090					
MGV-2060 [M]	Oscar Peterson Plays the Harold Arlen Songbook	1957	10.00	20.00	40.00
—Reissue of Clef 649					
V-2060 [M]	Oscar Peterson Plays the Harold Arlen Songbook	1961	5.00	10.00	20.00
V6-2060 [S]	Oscar Peterson Plays the Harold Arlen Songbook	1961	3.75	7.50	15.00
—Reissue of 6091					
MGV-2061 [M]	Oscar Peterson Plays the Jimmy McHugh Songbook	1957	10.00	20.00	40.00
—Reissue of Clef 650					
V-2061 [M]	Oscar Peterson Plays the Jimmy McHugh Songbook	1961	5.00	10.00	20.00
V6-2061 [S]	Oscar Peterson Plays the Jimmy McHugh Songbook	1961	3.75	7.50	15.00
—Reissue of 6092					
MGV-2079 [M]	Soft Sands	1957	10.00	20.00	40.00
V-2079 [M]	Soft Sands	1961	5.00	10.00	20.00
MGV-2119 [M]	Oscar Peterson Plays "My Fair Lady"	1958	10.00	20.00	40.00
V-2119 [M]	Oscar Peterson Plays "My Fair Lady"	1961	5.00	10.00	20.00
V6-2119 [S]	Oscar Peterson Plays "My Fair Lady"	1961	3.75	7.50	15.00
—Reissue of 6060					
MGV-2156 [M]	The Oscar Peterson Trio with David Rose	1958	—	—	—
—Canceled					
UMV-2502	Oscar Peterson at the Stratford Shakespearean Festival	198?	2.50	5.00	10.00
UMV-2626	Oscar Peterson at the Concertgebouw	198?	2.50	5.00	10.00
MGVS-6036 [S]	A Night on the Town	1960	—	—	—
—Canceled					
MGVS-6060 [S]	Oscar Peterson Plays "My Fair Lady"	1960	7.50	15.00	30.00
MGVS-6069 [S]	The Oscar Peterson Trio with the Modern Jazz Quartet at the Opera House	1960	7.50	15.00	30.00
MGVS-6071 [S]	Songs for a Swingin' Affair — A Jazz Portrait of Sinatra	1960	10.00	20.00	40.00
MGVS-6083 [S]	Oscar Peterson Plays the Cole Porter Songbook	1960	7.50	15.00	30.00
MGVS-6084 [S]	Oscar Peterson Plays the Irving Berlin Songbook	1960	7.50	15.00	30.00
MGVS-6085 [S]	Oscar Peterson Plays the George Gershwin Songbook	1960	7.50	15.00	30.00
MGVS-6086 [S]	Oscar Peterson Plays the Duke Ellington Songbook	1960	7.50	15.00	30.00
MGVS-6087 [S]	Oscar Peterson Plays the Jerome Kern Songbook	1960	7.50	15.00	30.00
MGVS-6088 [S]	Oscar Peterson Plays the Richard Rodgers Songbook	1960	7.50	15.00	30.00
MGVS-6089 [S]	Oscar Peterson Plays the Vincent Youmans Songbook	1960	—	—	—
—Canceled					
MGVS-6090 [S]	Oscar Peterson Plays the Harry Warren Songbook	1960	7.50	15.00	30.00
MGVS-6091 [S]	Oscar Peterson Plays the Harold Arlen Songbook	1960	7.50	15.00	30.00
MGVS-6092 [S]	Oscar Peterson Plays the Jimmy McHugh Songbook	1960	7.50	15.00	30.00
MGVS-6098 [S]	Porgy and Bess	1960	—	—	—
—Canceled					

Number	Title (A Side/B Side)	Yr	VG	VG+	NM
MGVS-6116 [S]	The Jazz Soul of Oscar Peterson	1960	—	—	—
—Canceled					
MGVS-6119 [S]	Swinging Brass with the Oscar Peterson Trio	1960	7.50	15.00	30.00
MGVS-6134 [S]	The Music from "Fiorello!"	1960	—	—	—
—Canceled					
MGV-8024 [M]	The Oscar Peterson Trio at the Stratford Shakespearean Festival	1957	10.00	20.00	40.00
V-8024 [M]	The Oscar Peterson Trio at the Stratford Shakespearean Festival	1961	5.00	10.00	20.00
MGV-8072 [M]	The Oscar Peterson Quartet No. 1	1957	10.00	20.00	40.00
V-8072 [M]	The Oscar Peterson Quartet No. 1	1961	5.00	10.00	20.00
MGV-8078 [M]	Recital by Oscar Peterson	1957	—	—	—
—Canceled					
MGV-8079 [M]	Nostalgic Memories by Oscar Peterson	1957	—	—	—
—Canceled					
MGV-8080 [M]	Tenderly — Music by Oscar Peterson	1957	—	—	—
—Canceled					
MGV-8081 [M]	Keyboard Music by Oscar Peterson	1957	—	—	—
—Canceled					
MGV-8082 [M]	An Evening with Oscar Peterson	1957	—	—	—
—Canceled					
MGV-8092 [M]	Oscar Peterson Plays Count Basie	1957	10.00	20.00	40.00
—Reissue of Clef 708					
V-8092 [M]	Oscar Peterson Plays Count Basie	1961	5.00	10.00	20.00
MGV-8239 [M]	The Oscar Peterson Trio with Sonny Stitt, Roy Eldredge and Jo Jones at Newport	1958	10.00	20.00	40.00
V-8239 [M]	The Oscar Peterson Trio with Sonny Stitt, Roy Eldredge and Jo Jones at Newport	1961	5.00	10.00	20.00
MGV-8268 [M]	The Oscar Peterson Trio at the Concertgebouw	1958	10.00	20.00	40.00
V-8268 [M]	The Oscar Peterson Trio at the Concertgebouw	1961	5.00	10.00	20.00
MGV-8269 [M]	The Oscar Peterson Trio with the Modern Jazz Quartet at the Opera House	1958	10.00	20.00	40.00
V-8269 [M]	The Oscar Peterson Trio with the Modern Jazz Quartet at the Opera House	1961	5.00	10.00	20.00
V6-8269 [S]	The Oscar Peterson Trio with the Modern Jazz Quartet at the Opera House	1961	3.75	7.50	15.00
—Reissue of 6069					
MGV-8287 [M]	A Night on the Town	1958	10.00	20.00	40.00
V-8287 [M]	A Night on the Town	1961	5.00	10.00	20.00
MGV-8334 [M]	Songs for a Swingin' Affair — A Jazz Portrait of Sinatra	1959	12.50	25.00	50.00
V-8334 [M]	Songs for a Swingin' Affair — A Jazz Portrait of Sinatra	1961	5.00	10.00	20.00
V6-8334 [S]	Songs for a Swingin' Affair — A Jazz Portrait of Sinatra	1961	3.75	7.50	15.00
—Reissue of 6071					
MGV-8340 [M]	Porgy and Bess	1959	10.00	20.00	40.00
V-8340 [M]	Porgy and Bess	1961	5.00	10.00	20.00
V6-8340 [S]	Porgy and Bess	1961	3.75	7.50	15.00
MGV-8351 [M]	The Jazz Soul of Oscar Peterson	1959	10.00	20.00	40.00
V-8351 [M]	The Jazz Soul of Oscar Peterson	1961	5.00	10.00	20.00
MGV-8364 [M]	Swinging Brass with the Oscar Peterson Trio	1959	10.00	20.00	40.00
V-8364 [M]	Swinging Brass with the Oscar Peterson Trio	1961	5.00	10.00	20.00
V6-8364 [S]	Swinging Brass with the Oscar Peterson Trio	1961	3.75	7.50	15.00
—Reissue of 6119					
MGV-8366 [M]	The Music from "Fiorello!"	1960	10.00	20.00	40.00
V-8366 [M]	The Music from "Fiorello!"	1961	5.00	10.00	20.00
MGV-8368 [M]	The Oscar Peterson Trio at J.A.T.P.	1960	10.00	20.00	40.00
V-8368 [M]	The Oscar Peterson Trio at J.A.T.P.	1961	5.00	10.00	20.00
MGV-8399 [M]	Carnival	1960	—	—	—
—Canceled					
V-8420 [M]	The Trio — Live from Chicago	1961	6.25	12.50	25.00
V6-8420 [S]	The Trio — Live from Chicago	1961	7.50	15.00	30.00
V-8429 [M]	Very Tall	1962	6.25	12.50	25.00
V6-8429 [S]	Very Tall	1962	7.50	15.00	30.00
V-8454 [M]	West Side Story	1962	6.25	12.50	25.00
V6-8454 [S]	West Side Story	1962	7.50	15.00	30.00
V-8476 [M]	Bursting Out with the All Star Big Band!	1962	6.25	12.50	25.00
V6-8476 [S]	Bursting Out with the All Star Big Band!	1962	7.50	15.00	30.00
V-8480 [M]	The Sound of the Trio	1962	6.25	12.50	25.00
V6-8480 [S]	The Sound of the Trio	1962	7.50	15.00	30.00
V-8482 [M]	The Modern Jazz Quartet and the Oscar Petereson Trio at the Opera House	1962	5.00	10.00	20.00
—Reissue of 8269					
V6-8482 [S]	The Modern Jazz Quartet and the Oscar Petereson Trio at the Opera House	1962	5.00	10.00	20.00
—Reissue of 8269					
V-8516 [M]	Affinity	1963	6.25	12.50	25.00
V6-8516 [S]	Affinity	1963	7.50	15.00	30.00
V-8538 [M]	Night Train	1963	6.25	12.50	25.00
V6-8538 [S]	Night Train	1963	7.50	15.00	30.00
V-8562 [M]	The Oscar Peterson Trio with Nelson Riddle	1963	6.25	12.50	25.00
V6-8562 [S]	The Oscar Peterson Trio with Nelson Riddle	1963	7.50	15.00	30.00
V-8581 [M]	Oscar Peterson Plays "My Fair Lady"	1964	3.75	7.50	15.00
V6-8581 [S]	Oscar Peterson Plays "My Fair Lady"	1964	5.00	10.00	20.00
V-8591 [M]	The Oscar Peterson Trio Plays	1964	3.75	7.50	15.00
V6-8591 [S]	The Oscar Peterson Trio Plays	1964	5.00	10.00	20.00
V-8606 [M]	We Get Requests	1965	3.75	7.50	15.00
V6-8606 [S]	We Get Requests	1965	5.00	10.00	20.00
V-8660 [M]	Put On a Happy Face	1966	3.75	7.50	15.00
V6-8660 [S]	Put On a Happy Face	1966	5.00	10.00	20.00
V-8681 [M]	Something Warm	1966	3.75	7.50	15.00
V6-8681 [S]	Something Warm	1966	5.00	10.00	20.00
V-8700 [M]	Thoroughly Modern '20s	1967	3.75	7.50	15.00
V6-8700 [S]	Thoroughly Modern '20s	1967	3.75	7.50	15.00
V-8740 [M]	Night Train, Volume 2	1967	5.00	10.00	20.00
V6-8740 [S]	Night Train, Volume 2	1967	3.75	7.50	15.00
V6-8775	Oscars — Oscar Peterson Plays the Academy Awards	1969	3.75	7.50	15.00
V6-8810 [(2)]	The Oscar Peterson Collection	1972	3.75	7.50	15.00
V3G-8828	The Newport Years	1974	3.00	6.00	12.00
V3HB-8842 [(2)]	Return Engagement	1975	3.75	7.50	15.00
810047-1	We Get Requests	1986	2.50	5.00	10.00
821289-1	Motions and Emotions	1984	2.50	5.00	10.00
—Reissue					
821663-1	Travelin' On	1985	2.50	5.00	10.00
821849-1	Tracks	1985	2.50	5.00	10.00
821987-1	Oscar Peterson Plays the Cole Porter Songbook	1986	2.50	5.00	10.00
—Reissue of 2053					
823249-1	Oscar Peterson Plays the George Gershwin Songbook	1985	2.50	5.00	10.00
—Reissue of 2054					
825099-1	The Oscar Peterson Trio Set	1985	2.50	5.00	10.00
825769-1	Songs for a Swingin' Affair — A Jazz Portrait of Sinatra	1985	2.50	5.00	10.00
—Reissue of 8334					
825865-1	Oscar Peterson Plays the Jerome Kern Songbook	1985	2.50	5.00	10.00
—Reissue of 2056					
WING					
SRW 16351	Canadiana Suite	1969	3.00	6.00	12.00

PETERSON, OSCAR, AND STEPHANE GRAPPELLI

Albums

Number	Title (A Side/B Side)	Yr	VG	VG+	NM
JAZZ MAN					
5054	Time After Time	1983	3.00	6.00	12.00
PABLO					
2310907	Violins No End	198?	3.00	6.00	12.00
—With Stuff Smith					
PRESTIGE					
24041 [(2)]	Oscar Peterson Featuring Stephane Grappelli	1974	3.75	7.50	15.00

PETERSON, OSCAR, AND MILT JACKSON

Albums

Number	Title (A Side/B Side)	Yr	VG	VG+	NM
PABLO					
2310881	Two of the Few	1983	3.00	6.00	12.00

PETERSON, OSCAR/GERRY MULLIGAN

Albums

Number	Title (A Side/B Side)	Yr	VG	VG+	NM
VERVE					
V-8559 [M]	The Oscar Peterson Trio and the Gerry Mulligan Four at Newport	1963	6.25	12.50	25.00
V6-8559 [S]	The Oscar Peterson Trio and the Gerry Mulligan Four at Newport	1963	7.50	15.00	30.00

PETERSON, RAY

45s

Number	Title (A Side/B Side)	Yr	VG	VG+	NM
CLOUD 9					
134	Nobody But Me/(B-side unknown)	1975	—	2.50	5.00
DECCA					
32861	Stamp Out Loneliness/There's a Better Way	1971	—	2.50	5.00
DUNES					
2002	Corrina, Corinna/Be My Girl	1960	6.25	12.50	25.00
—Produced by Phil Spector					
2002 [PS]	Corrina, Corinna/Be My Girl	1960	15.00	30.00	60.00
2004	Sweet Little Kathy/You Didn't Care	1961	3.75	7.50	15.00
2006	Missing You/You Thrill Me	1961	3.75	7.50	15.00
2009	I Could Have Loved You So Well/Why Don't You Write Me	1961	5.00	10.00	20.00
—Produced by Phil Spector					
2013	You Know Me Much Too Well/You Didn't Care	1962	3.75	7.50	15.00
2018	If Only Tomorrow/You Didn't Care	1962	3.75	7.50	15.00
2019	Is It Wrong/Slowly	1963	3.75	7.50	15.00
2022	A Love to Remember/I'm Not Jimmy	1963	3.75	7.50	15.00
2024	Where Are You/Deep Are the Roots	1963	3.75	7.50	15.00
2025	Give Us Your Blessing/Without Love (There Is Nothing)	1963	3.75	7.50	15.00
2027	I Forgot What It Was Like/Be My Girl	1963	3.75	7.50	15.00
2030	Promises/Sweet Little Kathy	1963	3.75	7.50	15.00
MGM					
13269	If You Were Here/Oh No	1964	2.50	5.00	10.00
13269 [PS]	If You Were Here/Oh No	1964	3.75	7.50	15.00
13299	Across the Street (Is a Million Miles Away)/When I Stop Dreaming	1964	2.50	5.00	10.00
13330	Unchained Melody/That's All	1965	2.00	4.00	8.00
13336	A House Without WIndows/Wish I Could Say No to You	1965	2.00	4.00	8.00
13388	I'm Only Human/One Lonesome Rose	1965	2.00	4.00	8.00
13436	Love Hurts/Everybody	1966	2.00	4.00	8.00
13508	Amanda/I'm Gonna Change Everything	1966	2.00	4.00	8.00
13564	Just One Smile/The Whole World's Goin' Crazy	1966	2.00	4.00	8.00
RCA					
GB-11758	Tell Laura I Love Her/The Wonder of You	1979	—	—	3.00
—Gold Standard Series					
RCA VICTOR					
37-7845	My Blue Angel/I'm Tired	1961	12.50	25.00	50.00
—"Compact Single 33" (small hole, plays at LP speed)					
47-7087	Fever/We're Old Enough to Cry	1957	6.25	12.50	25.00
47-7165	Let's Try Romance/Shirley Purley	1958	5.00	10.00	20.00
47-7255	Suddenly/Tall Light	1958	5.00	10.00	20.00
47-7303	Patricia/The Blue-Eyed Baby	1958	5.00	10.00	20.00
47-7336	Dream Way/I'll Always Want You Near	1958	5.00	10.00	20.00
47-7404	Richer Than I/Love Is a Woman	1958	5.00	10.00	20.00
47-7513	The Wonder of You/I'm Gone	1959	6.25	12.50	25.00
47-7578	My Blue Angel/Come and Get It	1959	5.00	10.00	20.00
47-7635	Goodnight My Love (Pleasant Dreams)/Till Then	1959	5.00	10.00	20.00
47-7635 [PS]	Goodnight My Love (Pleasant Dreams)/Till Then	1959	7.50	15.00	30.00
47-7703	Answer Me, My Love/What Do You Want to Make Those Eyes At Me For	1960	5.00	10.00	20.00
47-7745	Tell Laura I Love Her/Wedding Days	1960	6.25	12.50	25.00
47-7779	Teenage Heartache/I'll Always Want You Near	1960	5.00	10.00	20.00
47-7845	My Blue Angel/I'm Tired	1961	5.00	10.00	20.00
47-8333	The Wonder of You/Goodnight My Love	1964	2.50	5.00	10.00
61-7578 [S]	My Blue Angel/Come and Get It	1959	20.00	40.00	80.00
—"Living Stereo" (large hole, plays at 45 rpm)					
61-7745 [S]	Tell Laura I Love Her/Wedding Days	1960	25.00	50.00	100.00
—"Living Stereo" (large hole, plays at 45 rpm)					
REPRISE					
0811	Love Rules the World/Together	1969	2.00	4.00	8.00

Number	Title (A Side/B Side)	Yr	VG	VG+	NM
UNI					
55249	Love the Understanding Way/Oklahoma City Rimes	1970	2.00	4.00	8.00
55268	Tell Laura I Love Her/To Wait for Love	1971	—	3.00	6.00
55275	Fever/Changes	1971	—	3.00	6.00
7-Inch Extended Plays					
RCA VICTOR					
EPA-4367	(contents unknown)	1960	30.00	60.00	120.00
EPA-4367 [PS]	Tell Laura I Love Her	1960	30.00	60.00	120.00
Albums					
DECCA					
DL 75307	Ray Peterson Country	1971	5.00	10.00	20.00
MGM					
E-4250 [M]	The Very Best of Ray Peterson	1964	6.25	12.50	25.00
SE-4250 [S]	The Very Best of Ray Peterson	1964	7.50	15.00	30.00
E-4277 [M]	The Other Side of Ray Peterson	1965	6.25	12.50	25.00
SE-4277 [S]	The Other Side of Ray Peterson	1965	7.50	15.00	30.00
RCA CAMDEN					
CAL-2119 [M]	Goodnight My Love	1966	3.00	6.00	12.00
CAS-2119 [S]	Goodnight My Love	1966	3.00	6.00	12.00
RCA VICTOR					
LPM-2297 [M]	Tell Laura I Love Her	1960	25.00	50.00	100.00
LSP-2297 [S]	Tell Laura I Love Her	1960	37.50	75.00	150.00
UNI					
73078	The Best of Ray Peterson	1969	5.00	10.00	20.00

PETRIFIED FOREST, THE

Number	Title (A Side/B Side)	Yr	VG	VG+	NM
45s					
FONTANA					
1596	So Mystifying/She's the Only Thing That's Kept Me Going	1967	3.75	7.50	15.00

PETTICOATS, THE (1)

Number	Title (A Side/B Side)	Yr	VG	VG+	NM
45s					
CHALLENGE					
9211	Surfin' Sally/Why Does Billy Play in Your Yard	1963	6.25	12.50	25.00

PETTICOATS, THE (2)

Number	Title (A Side/B Side)	Yr	VG	VG+	NM
45s					
DOT					
16052	By the Light of the Silvery Moon/Troubadour	1960	5.00	10.00	20.00
16155	For Sentimental Reasons/Cincinnati	1960	5.00	10.00	20.00

PETTICOATS, THE (3)

Number	Title (A Side/B Side)	Yr	VG	VG+	NM
45s					
PREP					
125	I Ain't Gonna Do It No More/Manhattan Mountains	1957	5.00	10.00	20.00
UNIQUE					
344	The Motorboat Song/The First One	1956	5.00	10.00	20.00
363	High Heels/I'll Go Along with You	1956	5.00	10.00	20.00

PETTY, NORMAN, TRIO

Also see THE PICKS.

Number	Title (A Side/B Side)	Yr	VG	VG+	NM
45s					
ABC-PARAMOUNT					
9787	Almost Paradise/It's Been a Long, Long Time	1957	3.00	6.00	12.00
COLUMBIA					
40929	The First Kiss/(Instrumental)	1957	3.00	6.00	12.00
41039	Moondreams/Toy Boy	1957	25.00	50.00	100.00
—With Buddy Holly on guitar					
JARO					
77027	Ditty Dum/Bring Your Heart	1960	3.00	6.00	12.00
"X"					
0040	Mood Indigo/Petty's Little Polka	1954	3.00	6.00	12.00
0071	On the Alamo/Echo Polka	1954	3.00	6.00	12.00
0104	I Wonder Why/Three Little Kisses	1955	3.00	6.00	12.00
0130	Oh! You Pretty Woman/Hey! Good Lookin'	1955	3.00	6.00	12.00
0167	Solitude/When It's Darkness on the Delta	1955	3.00	6.00	12.00
7-Inch Extended Plays					
COLUMBIA					
B-10921	(contents unknown)	1958	25.00	50.00	100.00
B-10921 [PS]	Moondreams	1958	25.00	50.00	100.00
"X"					
EXA-82	(contents unknown)	1955	5.00	10.00	20.00
EXA-82 [PS]	The Norman Petty Trio In Full Fidelity	1955	5.00	10.00	20.00
Albums					
COLUMBIA					
CL 1092 [M]	Moondreams	1958	37.50	75.00	150.00
TOP RANK					
R-639 [M]	Petty for Your Thoughts	1960	7.50	15.00	30.00
RS-639 [S]	Petty for Your Thoughts	1960	10.00	20.00	40.00
VIK					
LX-1073 [M]	Corsage	1957	17.50	35.00	70.00

PHAETONS, THE

Number	Title (A Side/B Side)	Yr	VG	VG+	NM
45s					
HI-Q					
5012	Fling/Homemade	1959	5.00	10.00	20.00
SAHARA					
102	I'm So Lonely/Road of Blues	1963	5.00	10.00	20.00
103	The Beatle Walk/Frantic	1964	12.50	25.00	50.00
—B-side by the Premiers					
VIN					
1015	I Love My Baby/As You Know	1959	15.00	30.00	60.00
WARNER BROS.					
7082	She Came Like the Rain/Three Weeks, Four Days and Fifteen Hours	1967	2.50	5.00	10.00
7205	Leave It to Me/You'd Better Come Home	1968	2.50	5.00	10.00

PHANTOM, THE (1)

Number	Title (A Side/B Side)	Yr	VG	VG+	NM
45s					
CAPITOL					
3857	Calm Before the Storm/Black Magic, White Magic	1974	3.00	6.00	12.00
HIDEOUT					
1080	Calm Before the Storm/Black Magic, White Magic	1974	5.00	10.00	20.00
Albums					
CAPITOL					
ST-11313	The Phantom's Divine Comedy, Part One	1974	15.00	30.00	60.00

PHANTOM, THE (2)

Number	Title (A Side/B Side)	Yr	VG	VG+	NM
45s					
DOT					
16056	Love Me/Whisper Your Love	1960	37.50	75.00	150.00
16056 [PS]	Love Me/Whisper Your Love	1960	75.00	150.00	300.00

PHAPHNER

Number	Title (A Side/B Side)	Yr	VG	VG+	NM
45s					
DRAGON					
1001	Overdrive/(B-side unknown)	1971	50.00	100.00	200.00
Albums					
DRAGON					
LP-101	Overdrive	1971	1000.	2000.	3000.

PHELPS, JAMES

Number	Title (A Side/B Side)	Yr	VG	VG+	NM
45s					
ARGO					
5499	Love Is a Five-Letter Word/I'll Do the Best I Can	1965	2.00	4.00	8.00
5509	La De Da, I'm a Fool in Love/Wasting Time	1965	2.00	4.00	8.00
CADET					
5534	Oh, What a Feeling/Action	1966	2.00	4.00	8.00
FONTANA					
1581	Don't Be a Cry Baby/Walking the Floor Over You	1967	—	3.00	6.00
1600	Fabulous One/The Wrong Number	1967	—	3.00	6.00
PARAMOUNT					
0136	My Lover's Prayer/Check Yourself	1971	—	2.50	5.00

PHILBIN, REGIS

Number	Title (A Side/B Side)	Yr	VG	VG+	NM
Albums					
MERCURY					
SR-61169	It's Time for Regis!	1968	6.25	12.50	25.00

PHILIP AND STEPHAN

P.F. SLOAN and STEVE BARRI, again.

Number	Title (A Side/B Side)	Yr	VG	VG+	NM
45s					
INTERPHON					
7711	Meet Me Tonight Little Girl/When You're Near, You're So Far Away	1964	3.75	7.50	15.00

PHILIPS, TERRY

Number	Title (A Side/B Side)	Yr	VG	VG+	NM
45s					
CORAL					
62247	Fear/Find a Horseshoe	1961	3.75	7.50	15.00
UNITED ARTISTS					
351	My Foolish Ways/Hands of a Fool	1961	20.00	40.00	80.00

PHILLIPS, CHARLIE

Number	Title (A Side/B Side)	Yr	VG	VG+	NM
45s					
COLUMBIA					
42289	I Guess I'll Never Learn/Now That It's Over	1962	2.50	5.00	10.00
42526	Cancel the Call/You're Moving Away	1962	2.50	5.00	10.00
42691	No One to Love/'Til Sunday	1963	2.50	5.00	10.00
42851	Later Tonight/This Is the House	1963	2.50	5.00	10.00
43014	Street of Loneliness/Please Help Me Believe	1964	2.50	5.00	10.00
CORAL					
61970	Be My Bride/Too Many Tears	1958	6.25	12.50	25.00
REPRISE					
0581	Be Careful, Go Easy, Go Slow/Souvenirs of Sorrow	1967	2.00	4.00	8.00

PHILLIPS, ESTHER

Includes records as "Little Esther" and "Little Esther Phillips."

Number	Title (A Side/B Side)	Yr	VG	VG+	NM
12-Inch Singles					
MERCURY					
90 [DJ]	Oo-Oop-Oo-Oop (Long Version)/Oo-Oop-Oo-Oop (Edit)	1979	3.00	6.00	12.00
101 [DJ]	Our Day Will Come (same on both sides)	1979	3.00	6.00	12.00
WINNING					
1002	Turn Me Out (4:39) (5:51)	1983	2.50	5.00	10.00
45s					
ATLANTIC					
2223	Hello Walls/Double Crossing Blues	1964	3.75	7.50	15.00
—With Jimmy Ricks					
2229	No Headstone on My Grave/Mo Jo Hannah	1964	3.75	7.50	15.00
2251	It's Too Soon to Know/You're the Reason I'm Living	1964	3.75	7.50	15.00
2265	Half a Heart/Some Things You Never Get Used To	1964	3.75	7.50	15.00
2281	And I Love Him/Shangri-La	1965	3.00	6.00	12.00
2294	Moonglow & Theme from Picnic/Makin' Whoopee	1965	3.00	6.00	12.00
2304	Let Me Know When It's Over/I Saw Me	1965	3.00	6.00	12.00
2324	Just Say Goodbye/I Could Have Told You	1966	3.00	6.00	12.00
2335	When a Woman Loves a Man/Ups and Downs	1966	3.00	6.00	12.00
2360	Somebody Else Is Taking My Place/When Love Comes to the Human Race	1966	3.00	6.00	12.00
2370	Fever/Try Me	1966	3.00	6.00	12.00
2411	Release Me/Don't Feel Rained	1967	2.50	5.00	10.00
2417	I'm Sorry/Cheater Man	1967	2.50	5.00	10.00
2745	Brand New Day/Set Me Free	1970	—	3.00	6.00

Number	Title (A Side/B Side)	Yr	VG	VG+	NM
2775	Crazy Love/All God Has Is Us	1970	—	3.00	6.00
2783	Catch Me I'm Falling/Woman Will Do Wrong	1971	—	3.00	6.00
2800	Cry Me a River Blues/I'm Getting 'Long Alright	1971	—	3.00	6.00
DECCA					
28804	If You Want Me/Talkin' All Out of My Head	1953	10.00	20.00	40.00
48305	Please Don't Send Me/Stop Crying	1953	10.00	20.00	40.00
48314	Sit Back Down/He's a No Good Man	1954	15.00	30.00	60.00
FEDERAL					
12023	I'm a Bad, Bad Girl/Don't Make a Fool Out of Me	1951	20.00	40.00	80.00
12036	Heart to Heart/Looking for a Man to Satisfy My Soul	1951	125.00	250.00	500.00
—With the Dominoes					
12042	Cryin' and Singin' the Blues/Tell Him That I Need Him	1951	20.00	40.00	80.00
12055	Ring-a-Ding-Doo/The Crying Blues	1952	17.50	35.00	70.00
12063	Summertime/The Storm	1952	17.50	35.00	70.00
12065	Better Beware/I'll Be There	1952	17.50	35.00	70.00
12078	Aged and Mellow/Bring My Lovin' Back to Me	1952	17.50	35.00	70.00
12090	Somebody New/Ramblin' Blues	1952	17.50	35.00	70.00
12100	Saturday Night Daddy/Mainliner	1952	75.00	150.00	300.00
—With Bobby Nunn					
12108	Last Laugh Blues/Flesh, Blood and Bones	1952	17.50	35.00	70.00
—With Little Willie Littlefield					
12115	Hollerin' and Screamin'/Turn the Lamp Down Low	1953	17.50	35.00	70.00
—With Little Willie Littlefield					
12122	You Took My Love Too Fast/Street Lights	1953	75.00	150.00	300.00
—With Bobby Nunn					
12126	Hound Dog/Sweet Lips	1953	17.50	35.00	70.00
12142	Cherry Wine/Love Oh Love	1953	17.50	35.00	70.00
KUDU					
904	Home Is Where the Hatred Is/Til My Back Ain't Got No Bone	1972	—	2.50	5.00
906	Baby I'm for Real/That's All Right with Me	1972	—	2.50	5.00
910	I've Never Found a Man (To Love Me Like You Do)/Cherry Red	1972	—	2.50	5.00
915	Use Me/Let Me in Your Life	1973	—	2.50	5.00
917	Justified/Too Many Roads	1973	—	2.50	5.00
921	Such a Night/Can't Trust Your Neighbor	1974	—	2.50	5.00
922	Disposable Society/(B-side unknown)	1974	—	2.50	5.00
925	What a Difference a Day Makes/Turn Around, Look at Me	1975	—	2.50	5.00
929	For All We Know/Fever	1976	—	2.50	5.00
936	Boy I Really Tied One On/Magic's in the Air	1976	—	2.50	5.00
938	Higher and Higher/All the Way Down	1976	—	2.50	5.00
LENOX					
5555	Release Me/Don't Feel Rained On	1962	7.50	15.00	30.00
5560	Ain't That Easy to Forget/I Really Don't Want to Know	1963	5.00	10.00	20.00
5565	You Never Miss Your Water (Till the Well Runs Dry)/If You Want It (I Got It)	1963	5.00	10.00	20.00
—As "Little Esther Phillips and Big Al Downing"					
5570	Why Should We Try Anymore/While It Lasted	1963	5.00	10.00	20.00
5575	Don't Let Me Go/Why Was I Born	1963	5.00	10.00	20.00
5577	A Lover's Hymn/God Bless the Child Who's Got His Own	1963	5.00	10.00	20.00
MERCURY					
73967	Love Addict/I've Never Been a Woman Before	1977	—	2.00	4.00
74030	There You Go Again (There She Goes Again)/Stormy Weather	1978	—	2.00	4.00
74060	Oo-Oop-Oo-Oop/I'll Close My Eyes	1979	—	2.00	4.00
74077	Our Day Will Come/Mr. Melody	1979	—	2.00	4.00
ROULETTE					
7031	Too Late to Worry, Too Blue to Cry/I'm in the Mood for Love	1969	—	3.50	7.00
7049	Tonight I'll Be Staying Here with You/Sweet Dreams	1969	—	3.50	7.00
7059	Nobody But You/Too Much of a Man	1969	—	3.50	7.00
SAVOY					
1193	You Can Bet Your Life/'Tain't Whatcha Say It's Whatcha Do	1956	6.25	12.50	25.00
1516	Longing in My Heart/If It's News to Me	1957	5.00	10.00	20.00
1563	It's So Good/Do You Ever Think of Me	1959	3.75	7.50	15.00
WARWICK					
610	Gee Baby/Wild Child	1961	3.75	7.50	15.00
WINNING					
1001	Turn Me Out/(B-side unknown)	1983	—	2.50	5.00
Albums					
ATLANTIC					
SD 1565	Burnin'	1970	6.25	12.50	25.00
SD 1680	Confessin' the Blues	1975	3.75	7.50	15.00
8102 [M]	And I Love Him	1965	12.50	25.00	50.00
—Cover has a pink Cupid on it					
8102 [M]	And I Love Him	1966	7.50	15.00	30.00
—Cover has a black photo on it					
SD 8102 [S]	And I Love Him	1965	20.00	40.00	80.00
—Cover has a pink Cupid on it					
SD 8102 [S]	And I Love Him	1966	10.00	20.00	40.00
—Cover has a black photo on it					
8122 [M]	Esther	1966	7.50	15.00	30.00
SD 8122 [S]	Esther	1966	10.00	20.00	40.00
8130 [M]	The Country Side of Esther Phillips	1966	7.50	15.00	30.00
SD 8130 [S]	The Country Side of Esther Phillips	1966	10.00	20.00	40.00
90670	Confessin' the Blues	1987	2.50	5.00	10.00
—Reissue of 1680					
CBS ASSOCIATED					
PZ 40710	What a Diff'rence a Day Makes	1987	2.00	4.00	8.00
—Reissue of Kudu 23					
PZ 40935	From a Whisper to a Scream	1988	2.00	4.00	8.00
—Reissue of Kudu 05					
KING					
622 [M]	Memory Lane	1959	1000.	2000.	4000.
KUDU					
05	From a Whisper to a Scream	1972	3.00	6.00	12.00
09	Alone Again, Naturally	1972	3.00	6.00	12.00
14	Black-Eyed Blues	1973	3.00	6.00	12.00
18	Performance	1974	3.00	6.00	12.00
23	What a Diff'rence a Day Makes	1975	3.00	6.00	12.00
28	For All We Know	1976	3.00	6.00	12.00
31	Capricorn Princess	1976	3.00	6.00	12.00
LENOX					
227 [M]	Release Me	1962	25.00	50.00	100.00
S-227 [S]	Release Me	1962	50.00	100.00	200.00
MERCURY					
SRM-1-1187	You've Come a Long Way, Baby	1977	2.50	5.00	10.00
SRM-1-3733	All About Esther Phillips	1978	2.50	5.00	10.00
SRM-1-3769	Here's Esther — Are You Ready?	1979	2.50	5.00	10.00
SRM-1-4005	A Good Black Is Hard to Crack	1981	2.50	5.00	10.00
MUSE					
MR-5302	A Way to Say Goodbye	1986	3.00	6.00	12.00
SAVOY JAZZ					
SJL-2258	The Complete Savoy Recordings	1984	2.50	5.00	10.00

PHILLIPS, GENE

Number	Title (A Side/B Side)	Yr	VG	VG+	NM
Albums					
CROWN					
CLP-5375 [M]	Gene Phillips and the Rockers	1963	7.50	15.00	30.00

PHILLIPS, JOHN

Also see THE JOURNEYMEN; THE MAMAS AND THE PAPAS; THE SMOOTHIES.

Number	Title (A Side/B Side)	Yr	VG	VG+	NM
45s					
ABC DUNHILL					
4236	Mississippi/April Anne	1970	—	3.00	6.00
ATCO					
6960	Green-Eyed Lady/Lion	1974	—	3.00	6.00
COLUMBIA					
45737	Cup of Tea/Revolution on Vacation	1972	—	2.50	5.00
Albums					
ABC DUNHILL					
DS-50077	John Phillips (John the Wolfking of L.A.)	1970	3.75	7.50	15.00

PHILLIPS, MICHELLE

Also see THE MAMAS AND THE PAPAS.

Number	Title (A Side/B Side)	Yr	VG	VG+	NM
45s					
A&M					
1740	There She Goes/Aloha Louie	1975	—	2.50	5.00
1824	No Love Today/Aloha Louie	1976	—	2.00	4.00
1824 [PS]	No Love Today/Aloha Louie	1976	—	3.00	6.00
1996	The Aching Kind/Lady of Fantasy	1977	—	2.50	5.00
2021	There She Goes/Victim of Romance	1978	—	2.50	5.00
Albums					
A&M					
SP-4651	Victim of Romance	1977	3.75	7.50	15.00

PHILLIPS, PHIL

Number	Title (A Side/B Side)	Yr	VG	VG+	NM
45s					
KHOURY'S					
711	Sea of Love/Juella	1959	375.00	750.00	1500.
MERCURY					
10021 [S]	Take This Heart/Verdie Mae	1959	12.50	25.00	50.00
71465	Sea of Love/Juella	1959	6.25	12.50	25.00
71531 [M]	Take This Heart/Verdie Mae	1959	5.00	10.00	20.00
71550	Providing/Don't Leave Me	1960	5.00	10.00	20.00
71611	What Will I Tell My Heart/Your True Love Once More	1960	5.00	10.00	20.00
71649	Stormy Weather/Don't Cry Baby	1960	5.00	10.00	20.00
71657	Come BackMy Darling/Nobody Knows-Nobody Cares	1960	5.00	10.00	20.00

PHILLIPS, SHAWN

Number	Title (A Side/B Side)	Yr	VG	VG+	NM
45s					
ASCOT					
2152	The New Frankie and Johnny Song/Cloudy Summer Afternoon	1964	3.00	6.00	12.00
A&M					
1238	A Christmas Song/Lovely Lady	1970	2.50	5.00	10.00
1238 [PS]	A Christmas Song/Lovely Lady	1970	2.50	5.00	10.00
1402	We/"L" Ballade	1972	—	2.50	5.00
1405	Lost Horizon/Landscape	1973	—	2.50	5.00
1435	Anella/Hey Miss Lonely	1973	—	2.50	5.00
1482	Dream Queen/Bright White	1973	—	2.50	5.00
1507	All the Kings and Castles/Salty Tears	1974	—	2.50	5.00
1750	Do You Wonder/Summer Vignette	1975	—	2.50	5.00
Albums					
A&M					
SP-3128	Second Contribution	198?	2.00	4.00	8.00
—Budget-line reissue					
SP-3135	Faces	198?	2.00	4.00	8.00
—Budget-line reissue					
SP-3662	Furthermore	1974	3.00	6.00	12.00
SP-4241	Contribution	1970	3.75	7.50	15.00
SP-4282	Second Contribution	1971	3.75	7.50	15.00
SP-4324	Collaboration	1972	3.75	7.50	15.00
SP-4363	Faces	1972	3.00	6.00	12.00
SP-4402	Bright White	1973	3.00	6.00	12.00
SP-4539	Do You Wonder	1975	3.00	6.00	12.00
SP-4582	Rumpelstiltskin's Resolve	1976	3.00	6.00	12.00
SP-4650	Spaced	1977	3.00	6.00	12.00
CHAMELEON					
D1-74764	Beyond Here Be Dragons	1988	2.50	5.00	10.00
RCA VICTOR					
AFL1-3028	Transcendence	1978	2.50	5.00	10.00
AYL1-3873	Transcendence	1981	2.00	4.00	8.00
—"Best Buy Series" reissue					

PHILOSOPHERS, THE

Albums

Number	Title (A Side/B Side)	Yr	VG	VG+	NM
PHILO					
1001	After Sundown	1969	37.50	75.00	150.00

PHLUPH

45s

Number	Title (A Side/B Side)	Yr	VG	VG+	NM
VERVE					
10564	Another Day/Doctor Mind	1967	3.75	7.50	15.00

Albums

Number	Title (A Side/B Side)	Yr	VG	VG+	NM
VERVE					
V6-5054	Phluph	1968	7.50	15.00	30.00

PIANO RED

Also see DR. FEELGOOD AND THE INTERNS.

45s

Number	Title (A Side/B Side)	Yr	VG	VG+	NM
CHECKER					
911	Get Up Mare/So Worried	1958	7.50	15.00	30.00
GROOVE					
0023	Decatur Street Blues/Big Rock Joe from Kokomo	1954	7.50	15.00	30.00
0101	Pay It No Mind/Jump, Man, Jump	1955	7.50	15.00	30.00
0118	Six O'Clock Bounce/Goodbye	1955	7.50	15.00	30.00
0126	Red's Blues/Gordy's Rock	1955	7.50	15.00	30.00
0136	Jumpin' with Daddy/She Knocks Me Out	1956	7.50	15.00	30.00
0145	I'm Nobody's Fool/That's My Desire	1956	7.50	15.00	30.00
0169	Woo-Ee/You Were Mine for Awhile	1956	7.50	15.00	30.00
JAX					
1000	This Old World/I Feel Good	1959	3.75	7.50	15.00
1006	Guitar Walk/I've Been Walkin'	1959	3.75	7.50	15.00
KING					
6330	I Want a Bowlegged Woman/Underground Atlanta	1970	—	2.50	5.00
RCA VICTOR					
47-4265	Diggin' the Boogie/Let's Have a Good Time Tonight	1951	15.00	30.00	60.00
47-4380	Hey Good Lookin'/It Makes No Difference Now	1951	15.00	30.00	60.00
47-4524	Bouncin' with Red/Count the Days I'm Gone	1952	15.00	30.00	60.00
47-4766	She Walks Right In/Sales Tax Boogie	1952	15.00	30.00	60.00
47-4957	Yoo Doopee Doo/Daybreak	1952	15.00	30.00	60.00
47-5101	I'm Gonna Rock Some More/Everybody's Boogie	1952	12.50	25.00	50.00
47-5224	She's Dynamite/I'm Gonna Tell Everybody	1953	10.00	20.00	40.00
47-5337	Decatur Street Boogie/Your Mouth's Got a Hole In It	1953	10.00	20.00	40.00
47-5544	Right and Read, Taxi, Taxi 6963	1953	10.00	20.00	40.00
47-6856	Wild Fire/Rock Baby	1957	5.00	10.00	20.00
47-6953	Peachtree Parade/Please Don't Talk About Me	1957	5.00	10.00	20.00
47-7065	South/Coo Cha	1957	5.00	10.00	20.00
47-7217	Comin' On/One Glimpse of Heaven	1958	5.00	10.00	20.00
50-0099	Rockin' with Red/Red's Boogie	1950	37.50	75.00	150.00
—Gray label, orange vinyl					
50-0106	The Wrong Yo-Yo/My Gal Jo	1951	15.00	30.00	60.00
50-0118	Jumpin' the Boogie/Just Right Bounce	1951	15.00	30.00	60.00
50-0130	Layin' the Boogie/Baby What's Wrong	1951	15.00	30.00	60.00

7-Inch Extended Plays

Number	Title (A Side/B Side)	Yr	VG	VG+	NM
GROOVE					
EGA-3	(contents unknown)	1956	25.00	50.00	100.00
EGA-3 [PS]	Jump, Man, Jump	1956	25.00	50.00	100.00
EGA-26	(contents unknown)	1956	15.00	30.00	60.00
EGA-26 [PS]	Piano Red In Concert, Vol. 1	1956	15.00	30.00	60.00
EGA-27	(contents unknown)	1956	15.00	30.00	60.00
EGA-27 [PS]	Piano Red In Concert, Vol. 2	1956	15.00	30.00	60.00
EGA-28	(contents unknown)	1956	15.00	30.00	60.00
EGA-28 [PS]	Piano Red In Concert, Vol. 3	1956	15.00	30.00	60.00
RCA VICTOR					
EPA-587	(contents unknown)	1954	25.00	50.00	100.00
EPA-587 [PS]	Rockin' with Red	1954	25.00	50.00	100.00
EPA-5091	(contents unknown)	1959	25.00	50.00	100.00
—Maroon label					
EPA-5091	(contents unknown)	1959	12.50	25.00	50.00
—Black label					
EPA-5091 [PS]	Rockin' with Red	1959	12.50	25.00	50.00

Albums

Number	Title (A Side/B Side)	Yr	VG	VG+	NM
ARHOOLIE					
1064	William Perryman (Alone with Piano)	197?	3.00	6.00	12.00
EUPHONIC					
1212	Percussive Piano	198?	2.50	5.00	10.00
GROOVE					
LG-1001 [M]	Jump Man, Jump	1956	—	—	—
—The existence of this LP has not been confirmed					
LG-1002 [M]	Piano Red in Concert	1956	150.00	300.00	600.00
KING					
KS-1117	Happiness Is Piano Red	1970	5.00	10.00	20.00
RCA CAMDEN					
ACL1-0547	Rockin' with Red	1974	3.00	6.00	12.00
SOUTHLAND					
8	Willie Perryman-Piano Red-Dr. Feelgood	1983	3.75	7.50	15.00

PICKETT, BOBBY "BORIS"

45s

Number	Title (A Side/B Side)	Yr	VG	VG+	NM
ANTHEM					
205	Monster Concert/Am I	1973	—	3.00	6.00
CAPITOL					
5063	Simon the Sensible Surfer/Simon Says So What	1963	6.25	12.50	25.00
GARPAX					
P-1	Monster Mash/Monster's Mash Party	1962	7.50	15.00	30.00
—Orange label, first release of 44167?					
724	I'm Down to My Last Heartbreak/I Can't Stop	1962	6.25	12.50	25.00
44167	Monster Mash/Monster's Mash Party	1962	6.25	12.50	25.00
44167 [PS]	Monster Mash/Monster's Mash Party	1962	15.00	30.00	60.00
44171	Monster's Holiday/Monster's Motion	1962	6.25	12.50	25.00
44171 [PS]	Monster's Holiday/Monster's Motion	1962	10.00	20.00	40.00
44175	Graduation Day/The Humpty Dumpty	1963	6.25	12.50	25.00
44175 [PS]	Graduation Day/The Humpty Dumpty	1963	10.00	20.00	40.00
44185	Blood Bank Blues/Me and My Mummy	1965	6.25	12.50	25.00
METROMEDIA					
BMBO-0089	Me and My Mummy/It's Not the Same Without You	1973	2.50	5.00	10.00
—B-side by Pickett and Payne					
PARROT					
348	Monster Mash/Monster's Mash Party	1970	2.50	5.00	10.00
—Reissued in 1973 with the same number and label design					
366	Monster's Holiday/Monster Minuet	1971	2.50	5.00	10.00
PIZZERIA					
1	Star Drek/Mangy Old Sidewinder	1977	2.00	5.00	10.00
—With Peter Ferrara; originals are autographed on the label by both					
POLYDOR					
14361	King Kong (Your Song)/Disco Kong	1976	—	2.50	5.00
—With Peter Ferrara					
RCA VICTOR					
47-8312	Smoke! Smoke! Smoke! (That Cigarette)/Gotta Leave This Town	1964	3.75	7.50	15.00
47-8459	The Werewolf Watusi/Monster Swim	1964	3.75	7.50	15.00
WHITE WHALE					
363	Monster Man Jam/Am I	1970	6.25	12.50	25.00
—B-side by Bobby and Joan Pickett					
365	Monster Concert/(B-side unknown)	1970	6.25	12.50	25.00

Albums

Number	Title (A Side/B Side)	Yr	VG	VG+	NM
GARPAX					
GPX 57001 [M]	The Original Monster Mash	1962	37.50	75.00	150.00
SGP 67001 [S]	The Original Monster Mash	1962	62.50	125.00	250.00
PARROT					
XPAS 71063 [R]	The Original Monster Mash	1973	6.25	12.50	25.00
—Reissue of Garpax LP with four tracks deleted and one added					

PICKETT, WILSON

Also see THE FALCONS.

12-Inch Singles

Number	Title (A Side/B Side)	Yr	VG	VG+	NM
MOTOWN					
217	Land of a Thousand Dances (4 versions)/Just Let Her Know	1987	2.00	4.00	8.00

45s

Number	Title (A Side/B Side)	Yr	VG	VG+	NM
ATLANTIC					
2233	I'm Gonna Cry/For Better or Worse	1964	3.75	7.50	15.00
2271	Come Home Baby/Take a Little Love	1965	3.75	7.50	15.00
2289	In the Midnight Hour/I'm Not Tired	1965	3.75	7.50	15.00
2306	Don't Fight It/It's All Over	1965	3.75	7.50	15.00
2320	634-5789 (Soulsville, U.S.A.)/That's a Man's Way	1966	3.75	7.50	15.00
2334	Ninety-Nine and a Half (Won't Do)/Danger Zone	1966	3.75	7.50	15.00
2348	Land of 1000 Dances/You're So Fine	1966	3.75	7.50	15.00
2365	Mustang Sally/Three Time Loser	1966	3.75	7.50	15.00
2381	Eveybody Needs Somebody to Love/Nothing You Can Do	1967	3.00	6.00	12.00
2394	I Found a Love — Part I/I Found a Love — Part II	1967	3.00	6.00	12.00
2412	Soul Dance Number Three/You Can't Stand Alone	1967	3.00	6.00	12.00
2430	Funky Broadway/I'm Sorry About That	1967	3.00	6.00	12.00
2448	Stag-O-Lee/I'm In Love	1967	3.00	6.00	12.00
2484	Jealous Love/I've Come a Long Way	1968	2.50	5.00	10.00
2504	She's Lookin' Good/We've Got to Have Love	1968	2.50	5.00	10.00
2528	I'm a Midnight Mover/Deborah	1968	2.50	5.00	10.00
2558	I Found a True Love/For Better or Worse	1968	2.50	5.00	10.00
2575	A Man and a Half/People Make the World (What It Is)	1968	2.50	5.00	10.00
2591	Hey Jude/Search Your Heart	1968	2.50	5.00	10.00
2611	Mini-Skirt Minnie/Back in Your Arms	1969	2.00	4.00	8.00
2631	Born to Be Wild/Toe Hold	1969	2.00	4.00	8.00
2648	Hey Joe/Night Owl	1969	2.00	4.00	8.00
2682	You Keep Me Hangin' On/Now You See Me, Now You Don't	1969	2.00	4.00	8.00
2722	Sugar, Sugar/Cole, Cooke, and Redding	1970	2.00	4.00	8.00
2753	She Said Yes/It's Still Good	1970	—	3.00	6.00
2765	Engine Number Nine/International Playboy	1970	—	3.00	6.00
2781	Don't Let the Green Grass Fool You/Ain't No Doubt About It	1971	—	3.00	6.00
2797	Don't Knock My Love (Part 1)/Don't Knock My Love (Part 2)	1971	—	3.00	6.00
2824	Call My Name, I'll Be There/Woman Let Me Down Home	1971	—	3.00	6.00
2852	Fire and Water/Pledging My Love	1971	—	3.00	6.00
2878	Funk Factory/One Step Away	1972	—	3.00	6.00
2909	Mama Told Me Not to Come/Covering the Same Old Ground	1972	—	3.00	6.00
2961	Come Right Here/International Playboy	1973	—	3.00	6.00
BIG TREE					
16121	Who Turned You On/Dance You Down	1978	—	2.50	5.00
16129	Groovin'/Time to Let the Sun Shine In	1978	—	2.50	5.00
CORREC-TONE					
501	Let Me Be Your Boy/My Heart Belongs to You	1962	15.00	30.00	60.00
CUB					
9113	Let Me Be Your Boy/My Heart Belongs to You	1962	7.50	15.00	30.00
DOUBLE L					
713	If You Need Me/Baby Call on Me	1963	5.00	10.00	20.00
717	It's Too Late/I'm Gonna Love You	1963	5.00	10.00	20.00
724	I'm Down to My Last Heartbreak/I Can't Stop	1963	3.75	7.50	15.00
EMI AMERICA					
8027	I Want You/Love of My Life	1979	—	2.50	5.00
8034	Live with Me/Granny	1980	—	2.50	5.00
8070	Ain't Gonna Give You No More/Don't Underestimate the Power of Love	1981	—	2.50	5.00
8082	Back on the Right Track/It's You	1981	—	2.50	5.00
ERVA					
318	Love Dagger/Time to Let the Sun Shine on Me	1977	—	2.50	5.00
MOTOWN					
1898	Don't Turn Away/Can't Stop Now	1987	—	2.00	4.00

Number	Title (A Side/B Side)	Yr	VG	VG+	NM
1916	In the Midnight Hour/Just Let Her Know	1987	—	2.00	4.00
1938	Love Never Let Me Down/Just Let Her Know	1988	—	2.00	4.00
53407	Love Never Let Me Down/Just Let Her Know	1988	—	2.00	4.00
PHILCO-FORD					
HP-11	Land of a 1000 Dances/Midnight Hour	1967	3.75	7.50	15.00
—4-inch plastic "Hip Pocket Record" with color sleeve					
RCA VICTOR					
APBO-0049	Take a Closer Look at the Woman You're With/Two Woman and a Wife	1973	—	3.00	6.00
APBO-0174	Soft Soul Boogie Woogie/Take That Pollution Out of Your Throat	1973	—	3.00	6.00
APBO-0309	Take Your Pleasure Where You FInd It/What Good Is a Lie	1974	—	3.00	6.00
PB-10067	I Was Too Nice/Isn't That So	1974	—	3.00	6.00
74-0908	Mr. Magic Man/I Sho' Love You	1973	—	3.00	6.00
VERVE					
10378	Let Me Be Your Boy/My Heart Belongs to You	1966	5.00	10.00	20.00
WICKED					
8101	The Best Part of a Man/How Will I Ever Know	1975	—	3.00	6.00
8102	Love Will Keep Us Together/It's Gonna Be Good	1976	—	3.00	6.00

7-Inch Extended Plays

Number	Title (A Side/B Side)	Yr	VG	VG+	NM
ATLANTIC					
SD 8129 [DJ]	Something You Got/Barefootin'/Land of 1000 Dances//In the Midnight Hour/Ninety-Nine and a Half (Won't Do)/I'm Drifting	1966	3.75	7.50	15.00
—Jukebox mini-LP, small hole, plays at 33 1/3 rpm					
SD 8129 [PS]	The Exciting Wilson Pickett	1966	3.75	7.50	15.00

Albums

Number	Title (A Side/B Side)	Yr	VG	VG+	NM
ATLANTIC					
SD 2-501 [(2)]	Wilson Pickett's Greatest Hits	1973	5.00	10.00	20.00
8114 [M]	In the Midnight Hour	1965	10.00	20.00	40.00
SD 8114 [R]	In the Midnight Hour	1965	7.50	15.00	30.00
8129 [M]	The Exciting Wilson Pickett	1966	10.00	20.00	40.00
SD 8129 [R]	The Exciting Wilson Pickett	1966	7.50	15.00	30.00
8136 [M]	The Wicked Pickett	1967	10.00	20.00	40.00
SD 8136 [R]	The Wicked Pickett	1967	7.50	15.00	30.00
8145 [M]	The Sound of Wilson Pickett	1967	10.00	20.00	40.00
SD 8145 [P]	The Sound of Wilson Pickett	1967	10.00	20.00	40.00
8151 [M]	The Best of Wilson Pickett	1967	10.00	20.00	40.00
SD 8151 [R]	The Best of Wilson Pickett	1967	5.00	10.00	20.00
SD 8175	I'm in Love	1968	6.25	12.50	25.00
SD 8183	The Midnight Mover	1968	6.25	12.50	25.00
SD 8215	Hey Jude	1969	5.00	10.00	20.00
SD 8250	Right On	1970	5.00	10.00	20.00
SD 8270	Wilson Pickett in Philadelphia	1970	5.00	10.00	20.00
SD 8290	The Best of Wilson Pickett, Vol. II	1971	3.75	7.50	15.00
SD 8300	Don't Knock My Love	1971	3.75	7.50	15.00
81283	The Best of Wilson Pickett	1985	2.50	5.00	10.00
BIG TREE					
SD 76011	Funky Situation	1978	3.00	6.00	12.00
DOUBLE-L					
DL-2300 [M]	It's Too Late	1963	12.50	25.00	50.00
SDL-8300 [S]	It's Too Late	1963	17.50	35.00	70.00
EMI AMERICA					
SW-17019	I Want You	1979	3.00	6.00	12.00
SW-17043	Right Track	1981	3.00	6.00	12.00
MOTOWN					
6244 ML	American Soul Man	1987	2.50	5.00	10.00
RCA VICTOR					
APL1-0312	Miz Lena's Boy	1973	3.75	7.50	15.00
APL1-0495	Pickett in the Pocket	1974	3.75	7.50	15.00
APL1-0856	Join Me and Let's Be Free	1975	3.75	7.50	15.00
ANL1-2149	Join Me and Let's Be Free	1977	2.50	5.00	10.00
—Reissue					
LSP-4858	Mr. Magic Man	1973	3.75	7.50	15.00
TRIP					
8010	Wickedness	1972	2.50	5.00	10.00
WAND					
WD-672 [M]	Great Wilson Pickett Hits	1966	7.50	15.00	30.00
WDS-672 [R]	Great Wilson Pickett Hits	1966	5.00	10.00	20.00
WICKED					
9001	Chocolate Mountain	1976	6.25	12.50	25.00

PICKS, THE

Also see NORMAN PETTY TRIO.

45s

Number	Title (A Side/B Side)	Yr	VG	VG+	NM
COLUMBIA					
41096	Moondreams/Look to the Future	1958	12.50	25.00	50.00

PICKWICKS, THE

45s

Number	Title (A Side/B Side)	Yr	VG	VG+	NM
PARROT					
9679	Apple Blossom Time/I Don't Want to Tell You Again	1964	3.75	7.50	15.00
WARNER BROS.					
5492	Little by Little/I Took My Baby Home	1965	3.75	7.50	15.00

PILOT (1)

45s

Number	Title (A Side/B Side)	Yr	VG	VG+	NM
ARISTA					
AS 0259	One Good Reason Why/Get Up and Go	1977	—	2.00	4.00
EMI					
3992	Magic/Just Let Me Be	1974	—	2.50	5.00
4135	Don't Speak Loudly/Just a Smile	1975	—	2.00	4.00
4202	January/Do Me Good	1975	—	2.00	4.00
4305	Canada/Mover	1976	—	2.00	4.00

Albums

Number	Title (A Side/B Side)	Yr	VG	VG+	NM
EMI					
ST-11368	Pilot	1975	2.50	5.00	10.00
ST-11488	January	1976	2.50	5.00	10.00

PILOT (2)

45s

Number	Title (A Side/B Side)	Yr	VG	VG+	NM
RCA VICTOR					
74-0770	Rider/Miss Sandy	1972	—	3.00	6.00

Albums

Number	Title (A Side/B Side)	Yr	VG	VG+	NM
RCA VICTOR					
LSP-4730	Pilot	1972	3.00	6.00	12.00
LSP-4825	Point of View	1973	5.00	10.00	20.00

PING PONGS, THE

45s

Number	Title (A Side/B Side)	Yr	VG	VG+	NM
CUB					
9062	Big Ben/In the Chapel in the Moonlight	1960	5.00	10.00	20.00
UNITED ARTISTS					
236	Zyzzle/Summer Reverie	1960	5.00	10.00	20.00

PINK CLOUD, THE

45s

Number	Title (A Side/B Side)	Yr	VG	VG+	NM
TOWER					
376	Midnight Sun (Vocal)/Midnight Sun (Instrumental)	1967	5.00	10.00	20.00

PINK FLOYD

Also see SYD BARRETT.

12-Inch Singles

Number	Title (A Side/B Side)	Yr	VG	VG+	NM
COLUMBIA					
AS 777 [DJ]	Run Like Hell/Don't Leave Me Now	1980	5.00	10.00	20.00
AS 1334 [DJ]	Money/Another Brick in the Wall, Part 2	1981	6.25	12.50	25.00
—Pink vinyl					
AS 1541 [DJ]	When the Tigers Broke Free/Bring the Boys Back Home	1982	3.00	6.00	12.00
AS 1635 [DJ]	Your Possible Pasts/The Final Cut	1982	3.00	6.00	12.00
CAS 2775 [DJ]	Learning to Fly (Edit)/Learning to Fly (LP)	1987	3.00	6.00	12.00
CAS 2878 [DJ]	On the Turning Away (7" Edit)/On the Turning Away (Live)	1987	3.00	6.00	12.00

45s

Number	Title (A Side/B Side)	Yr	VG	VG+	NM
COLUMBIA					
AE7 1653 [DJ]	Not Now John (Obscured Version) (same on both sides)	1983	2.50	5.00	10.00
AE7 1653 [PS]	Not Now John (Obscured Version) (same on both sides)	1983	2.50	5.00	10.00
02165	Run Like Hell/Comfortably Numb	1981	—	—	3.00
—Reissue					
03118	Another Brick in the Wall, Part 2/One of My Turns	1982	—	—	3.00
—Reissue					
03142	When the Tigers Broke Free/Bring the Boys Back Home	1982	—	2.00	4.00
03142 [PS]	When the Tigers Broke Free/Bring the Boys Back Home	1982	—	2.50	5.00
—Fold-open cardboard sleeve					
X18-03176	When the Tigers Broke Free/Bring the Boys Back Home	1982	2.50	5.00	10.00
X18-03176 [PS]	When the Tigers Broke Free/Bring the Boys Back Home	1982	2.50	5.00	10.00
—Fold-open cardboard sleeve					
03905	Not Now John (Obscured Version)/The Heroes Return	1983	—	2.00	4.00
03905 [PS]	Not Now John (Obscured Version)/The Heroes Return	1983	—	2.50	5.00
07363	Learning to Fly/Terminal Frost	1987	—	2.00	4.00
07363 [PS]	Learning to Fly/Terminal Frost	1987	—	2.00	4.00
07660	On the Turning Away/Run Like Hell	1987	—	2.00	4.00
07660 [PS]	On the Turning Away/Run Like Hell	1987	—	2.00	4.00
10248	Have a Cigar/Welcome to the Machine	1975	3.00	6.00	12.00
11187	Another Brick in the Wall (Part 2)/One of My Turns	1980	—	2.50	5.00
—Custom "wall" label					
11187	Another Brick in the Wall (Part 2)/One of My Turns	1980	—	2.00	4.00
—Regular Columbia orange label					
11187 [PS]	Another Brick in the Wall (Part 2)/One of My Turns	1980	2.00	4.00	8.00
11265	Run Like Hell/Don't Leave Me Now	1980	—	2.00	4.00
11311	Comfortably Numb/Hey You	1980	—	2.00	4.00
77493	Take It Back/Astronomy Domine (Live)	1994	—	2.00	4.00
HARVEST					
3240	Fearless/One of These Days	1971	5.00	10.00	20.00
3391	Stay/Free Four	1972	5.00	10.00	20.00
3609	Money/Any Colour You Like	1973	3.75	7.50	15.00
P-3609 [DJ]	Money (Edited Mono)/Money (Edited Stereo)	1973	5.00	10.00	20.00
3832	Time/Us and Them	1974	5.00	10.00	20.00
SPRO-6669 [DJ]	Money (Censored Edited Mono)/Money (Censored Edited Stereo)	1973	3.75	7.50	15.00
—This promo was sent to radio stations with a frantic note telling them to disregard the first promo					
TOWER					
333	Arnold Layne/Candy and a Currant Bun	1967	50.00	100.00	200.00
333 [PS]	Arnold Layne/Candy and a Currant Bun	1967	175.00	350.00	700.00
—Only issued with promotional copies					
356	See Emily Play/Scarecrow	1967	50.00	100.00	200.00
356 [PS]	See Emily Play/Scarecrow	1967	175.00	350.00	700.00
—Title sleeve; only issued with some promotional copies					
356 [PS]	See Emily Play/Scarecrow	1967	200.00	400.00	800.00
—Photo sleeve; only issued with some promotional copies					
378	The Gnome/Flaming	1967	37.50	75.00	150.00
426	It Would Be So Nice/Julia Dream	1968	62.50	125.00	250.00
440	Let There Be More Light/Remember a Day	1968	75.00	150.00	300.00

Albums

Number	Title (A Side/B Side)	Yr	VG	VG+	NM
CAPITOL					
SPRO-8116/7 [DJ]	Pink Floyd Tour '75	1975	20.00	40.00	80.00
SEAX-11902 [PD]	The Dark Side of the Moon	1978	7.50	15.00	30.00
ST-12276	Works	1983	2.50	5.00	10.00
SN-16230	More	1982	2.00	4.00	8.00
—Budget-line reissue					
SN-16234	Relics	1982	2.00	4.00	8.00
—Budget-line reissue					

Number	Title (A Side/B Side)	Yr	VG	VG+	NM
SN-16330	Obscured by Clouds	1985	2.00	4.00	8.00
—Budget-line reissue					
SN-16337	Atom Heart Mother	1985	2.00	4.00	8.00
—Budget-line reissue					
COLUMBIA					
AP-1 [DJ]	Animals	1977	37.50	75.00	150.00
—White cover, with the song "Pigs" edited for airplay					
AS 736 [DJ]	Off the Wall	1979	37.50	75.00	150.00
—Sampler from 2-LP set					
AS 1636 [DJ]	The Final Cut	1983	6.25	12.50	25.00
—White label, record banded for airplay					
HC 33453	Wish You Were Here	1981	15.00	30.00	60.00
—Half-speed mastered edition (original)					
PC 33453	Wish You Were Here	1975	3.00	6.00	12.00
—Standard copy (no blue wraparound) without bar code					
PC 33453	Wish You Were Here	1975	6.25	12.50	25.00
—Original copies had a blue wraparound with title/artist sticker. Most buyers threw this out upon opening the LP!					
PC 33453 [DJ]	Wish You Were Here	1975	75.00	150.00	300.00
—Blue cover with photo and title on jacket; unbanded record					
PC 33453 [DJ]	Wish You Were Here	1975	62.50	125.00	250.00
—White cover, "Special DJ Copy"; banded for airplay					
PCQ 33453 [Q]	Wish You Were Here	1975	50.00	100.00	200.00
JC 33474	Animals	1977	2.50	5.00	10.00
JC 33474 [DJ]	Animals	1977	25.00	50.00	100.00
—"Demonstration Not for Sale" on label; also has insert					
PC2 36183 [(2)]	The Wall	1979	3.75	7.50	15.00
PC 37680	A Collection of Great Dance Songs	198?	2.00	4.00	8.00
—Budget-line reissue					
TC 37680	A Collection of Great Dance Songs	1981	2.50	5.00	10.00
QC 38243	The Final Cut	1983	2.50	5.00	10.00
OC 40599	A Momentary Lapse of Reason	1987	2.50	5.00	10.00
HC 43453	Wish You Were Here	1982	10.00	20.00	40.00
—Half-speed mastered edition (reissue)					
PC2 44484 [(2)]	Delicate Sound of Thunder	1988	5.00	10.00	20.00
HC2 46183 [(2)]	The Wall	1983	62.50	125.00	250.00
—Half-speed mastered edition					
HC 47680	A Collection of Great Dance Songs	1982	12.50	25.00	50.00
—Half-speed mastered edition					
C 64200	The Division Bell	1994	5.00	10.00	20.00
—U.S. pressings on blue vinyl					
EMI					
32700 [(4)]	Pulse	1995	15.00	30.00	60.00
—Pressed in U.K. for U.S. release; box set with 12x12 hardback book; identical to British pressings except for American bar code (67065) on shrink wrap					
HARVEST					
SKAO-382	Atom Heart Mother	1970	6.25	12.50	25.00
—Without title on front cover					
SKAO-382	Atom Heart Mother	197?	3.75	7.50	15.00
—With title on front cover					
STBB-388 [(2)]	Ummagumma	1969	10.00	20.00	40.00
—With the soundtrack LP from "Gigi" leaning against wall on front cover					
STBB-388 [(2)]	Ummagumma	1970	5.00	10.00	20.00
—With white LP cover leaning against wall on front cover					
SW-759	Relics	1971	3.75	7.50	15.00
SMAS-832	Meddle	1971	3.75	7.50	15.00
ST-11078	Obscured by Clouds	1972	3.75	7.50	15.00
SMAS-11163	The Dark Side of the Moon	1973	6.25	12.50	25.00
—With poster and two stickers					
SMAS-11163	The Dark Side of the Moon	1973	3.00	6.00	12.00
—With no inserts					
ST-11198	More	1973	3.00	6.00	12.00
—Reissue of Tower 5169					
SABB-11257 [(2)]	A Nice Pair	1973	3.75	7.50	15.00
MOBILE FIDELITY					
1-017	The Dark Side of the Moon	1980	12.50	25.00	50.00
—Audiophile vinyl					
MFQR-017	The Dark Side of the Moon	1982	75.00	150.00	300.00
—Audiophile vinyl; "Ultra High Quality Recording" in box					
1-190	Meddle	1987	12.50	25.00	50.00
—Audiophile vinyl					
1-202	Atom Heart Mother	1994	7.50	15.00	30.00
—Audiophile vinyl					
TOWER					
ST 5093 [S]	Pink Floyd (The Piper at the Gates of Dawn)	1967	20.00	40.00	80.00
—Orange label					
ST 5093 [S]	Pink Floyd (The Piper at the Gates of Dawn)	1968	10.00	20.00	40.00
—Multi-color striped label					
T 5093 [M]	Pink Floyd (The Piper at the Gates of Dawn)	1967	62.50	125.00	250.00
ST 5131	A Saucerful of Secrets	1968	20.00	40.00	80.00
—Orange label					
ST 5131	A Saucerful of Secrets	1968	10.00	20.00	40.00
—Multi-color striped label					
ST 5169	More	1968	12.50	25.00	50.00

PINKERTON'S ASSORTED COLOURS

45s

Number	Title (A Side/B Side)	Yr	VG	VG+	NM
LONDON					
9820	Mirror, Mirror/She Don't Care	1966	5.00	10.00	20.00
PARROT					
40001	Don't Stop Loving Me Baby/Will You	1966	5.00	10.00	20.00

PINKNEY, BILL

Also see THE DRIFTERS.

45s

Number	Title (A Side/B Side)	Yr	VG	VG+	NM
FONTANA					
1956	Don't Call Me/I Do the Jerk	1964	3.00	6.00	12.00
GAME					
394	Ol' Man River/Millionaire	196?	12.50	25.00	50.00
PHILLIPS INT'L.					
3524	After the Hop/Sally's Got a Sister	1958	5.00	10.00	20.00
—As "Bill Pinky"					
VEEP					
1264	I Found Some Lovin'/The Masquerade Is Over	1967	2.50	5.00	10.00

PIPES, THE (1)

45s

Number	Title (A Side/B Side)	Yr	VG	VG+	NM
CARLTON					
575	Teamwork/Soon I Will Be Done	1962	5.00	10.00	20.00

PIPES, THE (2)

45s

Number	Title (A Side/B Side)	Yr	VG	VG+	NM
DOOTO					
388	Be Fair/Let Me Give You Money	1958	6.25	12.50	25.00
401	You Are An Angel/I Love the Life I Live	1958	6.25	12.50	25.00
DOOTONE					
388	Be Fair/Let Me Give You Money	1956	75.00	150.00	300.00
401	You Are An Angel/I Love the Life I Live	1956	75.00	150.00	300.00

PIPKINS, THE

45s

Number	Title (A Side/B Side)	Yr	VG	VG+	NM
CAPITOL					
2819	Gimme Dat Ding/To Love You	1970	—	3.00	6.00
2874	Sugra and Spice-Are You Cookin' Goose/Yakety Yak	1970	—	2.50	5.00

Albums

Number	Title (A Side/B Side)	Yr	VG	VG+	NM
CAPITOL					
ST-483	Gimme Dat Ding	1970	6.25	12.50	25.00

PIPS, THE

See GLADYS KNIGHT AND THE PIPS.

PIPSQUEEKS, THE

45s

Number	Title (A Side/B Side)	Yr	VG	VG+	NM
WARNER BROS.					
5878	Santa's Little Helpers/Santa's Magic Flute	1966	2.50	5.00	10.00

PIRANHAS, THE

Albums

Number	Title (A Side/B Side)	Yr	VG	VG+	NM
CUSTOM FIDELITY					
1452	Somethin' Fishy	1969	37.50	75.00	150.00

PIRATES, THE

Early version of THE TEMPTATIONS.

45s

Number	Title (A Side/B Side)	Yr	VG	VG+	NM
MEL-O-DY					
105	Mind Over Matter (I'm Gonna Make You Mine)/ I'll Love You Till I Die	1962	25.00	50.00	100.00

PISTILLI, GENE

Also see CASHMAN, PISTILLI & WEST; MANHATTAN TRANSFER.

45s

Number	Title (A Side/B Side)	Yr	VG	VG+	NM
ATCO					
6850	Benn Down So Long It Looks Like Up to Me/Lettin' Down an Old Friend	1971	—	2.50	5.00
CAPITOL					
2627	Mr. Bojangles/Ruby Tuesday	1969	—	2.50	5.00

PITNEY, GENE

45s

Number	Title (A Side/B Side)	Yr	VG	VG+	NM
BLAZE					
351	Going Back to My Love/Cradle of My Arms	1958	7.50	15.00	30.00
—As "Billy Bryan"					
EPIC					
50332	Dedication AKA This Song I Want to Dedicate to You/Sandman	1977	—	2.50	5.00
50461	It's Over, It's Over/Walkin' in the Sun	1977	—	2.50	5.00
FESTIVAL					
25002	Please Come Back/I'll Find You	1960	7.50	15.00	30.00
MUSICOR					
1002	(I Wanna) Love My Life Away/I Laughed So Hard I Cried	1960	3.75	7.50	15.00
1002 [PS]	(I Wanna) Love My Life Away/I Laughed So Hard I Cried	1960	10.00	20.00	40.00
1006	Louisiana Mama/Take Me Tonight	1961	3.75	7.50	15.00
1006 [PS]	Louisiana Mama/Take Me Tonight	1961	7.50	15.00	30.00
1009	Town Without Pity/Air Mail Special Delivery	1961	3.75	7.50	15.00
1011	Every Breath I Take/Mr. Moon, Mr. Cupid and I	1961	5.00	10.00	20.00
—Produced by Phil Spector					
1011 [PS]	Every Breath I Take/Mr. Moon, Mr. Cupid and I	1961	6.25	12.50	25.00
1020	(The Man Who Shot) Liberty Valance/Take It Like a Man	1962	3.75	7.50	15.00
1022	Only Love Can Break a Heart/If I Didn't Have a Dime	1962	3.75	7.50	15.00
1026	Half Heaven-Half Heartache/Tower Tall	1962	3.75	7.50	15.00
1028	Mecca/Teardrop by Teardrop	1963	3.75	7.50	15.00
1028 [PS]	Mecca/Teardrop by Teardrop	1963	5.00	10.00	20.00
1032	True Love Never Runs Smooth/Donna Means Heartbreak	1963	3.75	7.50	15.00
1034	Twenty-Four Hours from Tulsa/Lonely Night Dream	1963	3.75	7.50	15.00
1034 [PS]	Twenty-Four Hours from Tulsa/Lonely Night Dream	1963	5.00	10.00	20.00
1036	That Girl Belongs to Yesterday/Who Needs It	1964	5.00	10.00	20.00
—A-side written by Mick Jagger and Keith Richards and produced by Andrew Oldham					
1036 [PS]	That Girl Belongs to Yesterday/Who Needs It	1964	6.25	12.50	25.00
1038	Yesterday's Hero/Cornflower Blue	1964	3.75	7.50	15.00
1039	I'm Gonna Find Myself a Girl/Lips Are Redder	1964	—	—	—
—Unreleased?					
1040	It Hurts to Be in Love/Hawaii	1964	3.75	7.50	15.00
1040 [PS]	It Hurts to Be in Love/Hawaii	1964	5.00	10.00	20.00
1045	I'm Gonna Be Strong/Aladdin's Lamp	1964	5.00	10.00	20.00
1045	I'm Gonna Be Strong/E Se Domani	1964	3.75	7.50	15.00
1045 [PS]	I'm Gonna Be Strong/E Se Domani	1964	5.00	10.00	20.00
1065	Amici Miri/I Tuoi Anni Piu Belli	1965	—	—	—
—Unreleased?					

Number	Title (A Side/B Side)	Yr	VG	VG+	NM
1070	I Must Be Seeing Things/Marianne	1965	3.00	6.00	12.00
1070 [PS]	I Must Be Seeing Things/Marianne	1965	3.75	7.50	15.00
1093	Last Chance to Turn Around/Save Your Love	1965	3.00	6.00	12.00
1103	Looking Through the Eyes of Love/There's No Living Without Your Loving	1965	3.00	6.00	12.00
1130	Princess in Rags/Amore Mio	1965	3.00	6.00	12.00
1150	Me Voy Para El Compo/Hojas Muertas	1966	—	—	—
—Unreleased?					
1155	Lei Mi Aspetta/Nessuno Mi Puo' Guidcare	1966	3.75	7.50	15.00
1171	Backstage/Blue Color	1966	2.50	5.00	10.00
1171 [PS]	Backstage/Blue Color	1966	3.75	7.50	15.00
1200	(In the) Cold Light of Day/The Boss' Daughter	1966	2.50	5.00	10.00
1200 [PS]	(In the) Cold Light of Day/The Boss' Daughter	1966	3.75	7.50	15.00
1219	Just One Smile/Innamorato	1966	2.50	5.00	10.00
1233	For Me, This Is Happy/I'm Gonna Listen to Me	1967	2.50	5.00	10.00
1235	Don't Mean to Be a Preacher/Animal Crackers (In Cellophane Boxes)	1967	2.50	5.00	10.00
1245	Tremblin'/Where Did the Magic Go	1967	2.50	5.00	10.00
1252	Somethin' Gotten Hold of My Heart/Building Up My Dream World	1967	2.50	5.00	10.00
1299	The More I Saw of Her/Won't Take Long	1968	2.00	4.00	8.00
1306	She's a Heartbreaker/Conquistador	1968	2.50	5.00	10.00
1308	Somewhere in the Country/Lonely Drifter	1968	2.00	4.00	8.00
1331	Billy, You're My Friend/She Believes in Me	1968	2.00	4.00	8.00
1331	Billy, You're My Friend/Lonely Drifter	1968	2.00	4.00	8.00
1331 [PS]	Billy, You're My Friend/Lonely Drifter	1968	3.00	6.00	12.00
1348	Baby, You're My Kind of Woman/Hate	1969	2.00	4.00	8.00
1358	Maria Elena/The French Horn	1969	2.00	4.00	8.00
1361	Playing Games of Love/California	1969	2.00	4.00	8.00
1384	She Lets Her Hair Down (Early in the Morning)/I Remember	1969	2.00	4.00	8.00
1394	All the Young Women/I Remember	1970	—	3.00	6.00
1405	A Street Called Hope/Think of Us	1970	—	3.00	6.00
1419	Shady Lady/Billy, You're My Friend	1970	—	3.00	6.00
1439	Higher and Higher/Beautiful Sounds	1971	—	3.00	6.00
1442	A Thousand Arms (Five Hundred Hearts)/Gene, Are You There?	1971	—	3.00	6.00
1453	I Just Can't Help Myself/Beautiful Sounds	1972	—	3.00	6.00
1461	Summertime Dreaming/A Thousand Arms (Five Hundred Hearts)	1972	—	3.00	6.00
1474	Shady Lady/Run, Run Roadrunner	1973	—	3.00	6.00

Albums

MUSIC DISC

Number	Title (A Side/B Side)	Yr	VG	VG+	NM
MDS 1003	The Man Who Shot Liberty Valance	1969	3.00	6.00	12.00
MDS 1005	Town Without Pity	1969	3.00	6.00	12.00
MDS 1006	America's Greatest Country Songs	1969	3.00	6.00	12.00
MDS 1008	Twenty Four Hours from Tulsa	1969	3.00	6.00	12.00
MDS 1014	Baby, I Need Your Lovin'	1969	3.00	6.00	12.00

MUSICOR

Number	Title (A Side/B Side)	Yr	VG	VG+	NM
MM-2001 [M]	The Many Sides of Gene Pitney	1962	12.50	25.00	50.00
—Brown label					
MM-2001 [M]	The Many Sides of Gene Pitney	1963	6.25	12.50	25.00
—Black label					
MM-2003 [M]	Only Love Can Break a Heart	1962	10.00	20.00	40.00
—Brown label					
MM-2003 [M]	Only Love Can Break a Heart	1963	6.25	12.50	25.00
—Black label					
MM-2004 [M]	Gene Pitney Sings Just for You	1963	7.50	15.00	30.00
MM-2005 [M]	World-Wide Winners	1963	7.50	15.00	30.00
MM-2006 [M]	Blue Gene	1963	7.50	15.00	30.00
MM-2007 [M]	The Fair Young Ladies of Folkland	1964	7.50	15.00	30.00
MM-2008 [M]	Gene Pitney's Big Sixteen	1964	7.50	15.00	30.00
MM-2015 [M]	Gene Italiano	1964	6.25	12.50	25.00
MM-2019 [M]	It Hurts to Be in Love	1964	6.25	12.50	25.00
MM-2043 [M]	Gene Pitney's More Big Sixteen	1965	6.25	12.50	25.00
MM-2056 [M]	I Must Be Seeing Things	1965	6.25	12.50	25.00
MM-2069 [M]	Looking Through the Eyes of Love	1965	6.25	12.50	25.00
MM-2072 [M]	Gene Pitney En Espanol	1965	6.25	12.50	25.00
MM-2085 [M]	Big Sixteen, Vol. 3	1966	5.00	10.00	20.00
MM-2095 [M]	Backstage I'm Lonely	1966	5.00	10.00	20.00
MM-2100 [M]	Messumo Mi Puo Giudicare	1966	5.00	10.00	20.00
MM-2101 [M]	The Gene Pitney Show	1966	5.00	10.00	20.00
MM-2102 [M]	Greatest Hits of All Times	1966	5.00	10.00	20.00
MM-2104 [M]	The Country Side of Gene Pitney	1967	5.00	10.00	20.00
MM-2108 [M]	Young and Warm and Wonderful	1967	5.00	10.00	20.00
MM-2117 [M]	Just One Smile	1967	5.00	10.00	20.00
MM-2134 [M]	Golden Greats	1967	6.25	12.50	25.00
MS-3001 [R]	The Many Sides of Gene Pitney	1962	7.50	15.00	30.00
—Brown label					
MS-3001 [R]	The Many Sides of Gene Pitney	1963	5.00	10.00	20.00
—Black label					
MS-3003 [S]	Only Love Can Break a Heart	1962	12.50	25.00	50.00
—Brown label					
MS-3003 [S]	Only Love Can Break a Heart	1963	7.50	15.00	30.00
—Black label					
MS-3004 [S]	Gene Pitney Sings Just for You	1963	10.00	20.00	40.00
MS-3005 [P]	World-Wide Winners	1963	10.00	20.00	40.00
MS-3006 [S]	Blue Gene	1963	10.00	20.00	40.00
MS-3007 [S]	The Fair Young Ladies of Folkland	1964	10.00	20.00	40.00
MS-3008 [P]	Gene Pitney's Big Sixteen	1964	10.00	20.00	40.00
MS-3015 [S]	Gene Italiano	1964	7.50	15.00	30.00
MS-3019 [P]	It Hurts to Be in Love	1964	7.50	15.00	30.00
MS-3043 [P]	Gene Pitney's More Big Sixteen	1965	7.50	15.00	30.00
MS-3056 [S]	I Must Be Seeing Things	1965	7.50	15.00	30.00
MS-3069 [S]	Looking Through the Eyes of Love	1965	7.50	15.00	30.00
MS-3072 [S]	Gene Pitney En Espanol	1965	7.50	15.00	30.00
MS-3085 [S]	Big Sixteen, Vol. 3	1966	6.25	12.50	25.00
MS-3095 [S]	Backstage I'm Lonely	1966	6.25	12.50	25.00
MS-3100 [S]	Messumo Mi Puo Giudicare	1966	6.25	12.50	25.00
MS-3101 [S]	The Gene Pitney Show	1966	6.25	12.50	25.00
MS-3102 [P]	Greatest Hits of All Times	1966	6.25	12.50	25.00
MS-3104 [S]	The Country Side of Gene Pitney	1967	6.25	12.50	25.00
MS-3108 [S]	Young and Warm and Wonderful	1967	6.25	12.50	25.00
MS-3117 [S]	Just One Smile	1967	6.25	12.50	25.00
MS-3134 [S]	Golden Greats	1967	5.00	10.00	20.00
M2-3148 [(2) M]	The Gene Pitney Story	1968	10.00	20.00	40.00
—Mono is promo only					
M2S-3148 [(2) S]	The Gene Pitney Story	1968	6.25	12.50	25.00
—Add 40% if bonus photo is enclosed					
MS-3161	Gene Pitney Sings Burt Bacharach	1968	5.00	10.00	20.00
MS-3164	She's a Heartbreaker	1968	5.00	10.00	20.00
MS-3174	The Greatest Hits of Gene Pitney	1969	5.00	10.00	20.00
MS-3183	Gene Pitney Sings the Platters' Golden Platters	1970	3.75	7.50	15.00
MS-3193	Gene Pitney Super Star	1971	3.75	7.50	15.00
MS-3206	Ten Years After	1971	3.75	7.50	15.00
MS-3233	Golden Hour	1972	3.75	7.50	15.00

RHINO

Number	Title (A Side/B Side)	Yr	VG	VG+	NM
RNDA-1102 [(2)]	Anthology (1961-1968)	1984	3.00	6.00	12.00

SPRINGBOARD

Number	Title (A Side/B Side)	Yr	VG	VG+	NM
SPB-4057	Gene Pitney	1975	2.50	5.00	10.00

PITNEY, GENE, AND GEORGE JONES

Also see each artist's individual listings.

45s

MUSICOR

Number	Title (A Side/B Side)	Yr	VG	VG+	NM
1066	I've Got Five Dollars and It's Saturday Night/Wreck on the Highway	1965	3.00	6.00	12.00
1071	I've Got a New Heartache/My Shoes Keep Walking Back to You	1965	—	—	—
—Unreleased?					
1097	I'm a Fool to Care/Louisiana Man	1965	3.00	6.00	12.00
1097 [PS]	I'm a Fool to Care/Louisiana Man	1965	3.75	7.50	15.00
1115	Your Old Standby/Big Job	1965	3.00	6.00	12.00
1115 [PS]	Your Old Standby/Big Job	1965	3.75	7.50	15.00
1165	Y'All Come/That's All It Took	1966	2.50	5.00	10.00

Albums

MUSICOR

Number	Title (A Side/B Side)	Yr	VG	VG+	NM
MM-2044 [M]	For the First Time! Two Great Singers Together: George Jones and Gene Pitney	1965	6.25	12.50	25.00
MM-2065 [M]	It's Country Time Again	1965	6.25	12.50	25.00
MS-3044 [S]	For the First Time! Two Great Singers Together: George Jones and Gene Pitney	1965	7.50	15.00	30.00
MS-3065 [S]	It's Country Time Again	1965	7.50	15.00	30.00

PITNEY, GENE, AND MELBA MONTGOMERY

45s

MUSICOR

Number	Title (A Side/B Side)	Yr	VG	VG+	NM
1135	Baby, Ain't That Fine/Everybody Knows But You and Me	1965	3.00	6.00	12.00
1173	King and Queen/Being Together	1966	2.50	5.00	10.00

Albums

MUSICOR

Number	Title (A Side/B Side)	Yr	VG	VG+	NM
MM-2077 [M]	Being Together	1966	6.25	12.50	25.00
MS-3077 [S]	Being Together	1966	7.50	15.00	30.00

PITTMAN, BARBARA

45s

PHILLIPS INT'L.

Number	Title (A Side/B Side)	Yr	VG	VG+	NM
3518	Two Young Fools in Love/I'm Getting Better All the Time	1957	10.00	20.00	40.00
3527	Cold, Cold Heart/Everlasting Love	1958	10.00	20.00	40.00
3553	Handsome Man/The Eleventh Commandment	1960	5.00	10.00	20.00

SUN

Number	Title (A Side/B Side)	Yr	VG	VG+	NM
253	I Need a Man/No Matter Who's to Blame	1956	37.50	75.00	150.00

PITTS, GLORIA JEAN

45s

IMPERIAL

Number	Title (A Side/B Side)	Yr	VG	VG+	NM
5406	I Don't Stand No Quittin'/Things You Should Know	1956	12.50	25.00	50.00

PIXIES THREE, THE

45s

MERCURY

Number	Title (A Side/B Side)	Yr	VG	VG+	NM
72130	Birthday Party/Our Love	1963	3.75	7.50	15.00
72130 [PS]	Birthday Party/Our Love	1963	6.25	12.50	25.00
72208	Cold, Cold Winter/442 Glenwood Avenue	1963	3.75	7.50	15.00
72208 [PS]	Cold, Cold Winter/442 Glenwood Avenue	1963	6.25	12.50	25.00
72250	Gee/After the Party	1964	3.75	7.50	15.00
72250 [PS]	Gee/After the Party	1964	7.50	15.00	30.00
72288	It's Summertime U.S.A./The Hootch	1964	3.75	7.50	15.00
72288 [PS]	It's Summertime U.S.A./The Hootch	1964	6.25	12.50	25.00
72331	Love Walked In/Orphan Boy	1964	3.75	7.50	15.00
72357	Love Me, Love Me/Your Way	1964	3.75	7.50	15.00

Albums

MERCURY

Number	Title (A Side/B Side)	Yr	VG	VG+	NM
MG-20912 [M]	Party with the Pixies Three	1964	37.50	75.00	150.00
SR-60912 [S]	Party with the Pixies Three	1964	50.00	100.00	200.00

PLAIDS, THE

45s

DARL

Number	Title (A Side/B Side)	Yr	VG	VG+	NM
1001	Keeper of My Heart/I Sing for You	1956	5.00	10.00	20.00

ERA

Number	Title (A Side/B Side)	Yr	VG	VG+	NM
3002	Around the Corner/He Stole Flo	1959	5.00	10.00	20.00

LIBERTY

Number	Title (A Side/B Side)	Yr	VG	VG+	NM
55167	Hungry for Your Love/Chit-Chat	1958	100.00	200.00	400.00

NASCO

Number	Title (A Side/B Side)	Yr	VG	VG+	NM
6011	Till the End of the Dance/My Pretty Baby	1958	5.00	10.00	20.00

PLANETS, THE (1)

45s

ALJON

Number	Title (A Side/B Side)	Yr	VG	VG+	NM
1244	Be Sure/Once Upon a Lifetime	1962	75.00	150.00	300.00

Number	Title (A Side/B Side)	Yr	VG	VG+	NM

PLANETS, THE (2)

45s

Number	Title (A Side/B Side)	Yr	VG	VG+	NM
ERA					
1038	Never Again/Stand There Mountain	1957	12.50	25.00	50.00
1049	Be Sure/Wild Leaves	1957	12.50	25.00	50.00
NU-CLEAR					
7422	I Need You So/Sharin' Lockers	1959	15.00	30.00	60.00

PLANETS, THE (3)

45s

Number	Title (A Side/B Side)	Yr	VG	VG+	NM
ROULETTE					
4551	You Are My Sunshine/Mr. Moon	1964	3.75	7.50	15.00

PLANT LIFE

45s

Number	Title (A Side/B Side)	Yr	VG	VG+	NM
DATE					
1572	Flower Girl/Say It Over Again	1967	2.50	5.00	10.00

PLANT & SEE

45s

Number	Title (A Side/B Side)	Yr	VG	VG+	NM
WHITE WHALE					
309	Henrietta/Put Out the Fire	1969	3.00	6.00	12.00

Albums

Number	Title (A Side/B Side)	Yr	VG	VG+	NM
WHITE WHALE					
WWS-7120	Plant & See	1969	6.25	12.50	25.00

PLANTS, THE

45s

Number	Title (A Side/B Side)	Yr	VG	VG+	NM
J&S					
248/9	I Searched the Seven Seas/I Took a Trip Way Over the Sea	1956	100.00	200.00	400.00
1602	Dear, I Swear/It's You	1957	100.00	200.00	400.00
—Address under label name					
1602	Dear, I Swear/It's You	1957	10.00	20.00	40.00
—No address under label name					

PLASTER CASTERS, THE

Albums

Number	Title (A Side/B Side)	Yr	VG	VG+	NM
BLUESTIME					
BTS-9001	The Plaster Casters Blues Band	1969	12.50	25.00	50.00

PLASTIC COW, THE

45s

Number	Title (A Side/B Side)	Yr	VG	VG+	NM
DOT					
17284	The Plastic Cow/Medicine Man	1969	2.50	5.00	10.00
17300	Lady Jane/One Many, One Vault	1969	2.50	5.00	10.00

Albums

Number	Title (A Side/B Side)	Yr	VG	VG+	NM
DOT					
DLP 25961	The Plastic Cow Goes Moooooog	1969	5.00	10.00	20.00

PLASTIC ONO BAND

See JOHN LENNON; YOKO ONO.

PLATTERS, THE

More than one group has used this name over the years, but all are related. Also see TONY WILLIAMS.

45s

Number	Title (A Side/B Side)	Yr	VG	VG+	NM
ANTLER					
3000/1	I Do It All the Time/Shake What Your Mama Gave You	1982	—	3.00	6.00
AVALANCHE					
XW224	Sunday with You/If the World Loved	1973	2.00	4.00	8.00
—As "The Buck Ram Platters"					
ENTREE					
107	Won't You Be My Friend/Run While It's Dark	1965	2.00	4.00	8.00
—As "The Platters 1965"					
FEDERAL					
12153	Give Thanks/Hey Now	1953	100.00	200.00	400.00
—As "Tony Williams and the Platters"					
12164	I'll Cry When You're Gone/I Need You All the Time	1954	250.00	500.00	1000.
12181	Roses of Picardy/Beer Barrel Polka	1954	75.00	150.00	300.00
12188	Tell the World/Love All Night	1954	50.00	100.00	200.00
12198	Voo-Vee-Ah-Bee/Shake It Up Mambo	1954	50.00	100.00	200.00
12204	Maggie Doesn't Work Here Anymore/Take Me Back, Take Me Back	1955	50.00	100.00	200.00
12244	Only You (And You Alone)/You Made Me Cry	1955	75.00	150.00	300.00
12250	Tell the World/I Need You All the Time	1956	30.00	60.00	120.00
12271	Give Thanks/I Need You All the Time	1956	20.00	40.00	80.00
MERCURY					
10001 [S]	Smoke Gets In Your Eyes/No Matter What You Are	1959	12.50	25.00	50.00
10007 [S]	Remember When/Love of a Lifetime	1959	10.00	20.00	40.00
70633	Only You (And You Alone)/Bark, Battle and Ball	1955	12.50	25.00	50.00
—Earliest pressings have pink labels					
70633	Only You (And You Alone)/Bark, Battle and Ball	1955	10.00	20.00	40.00
—Black label					
70753	The Great Pretender/I'm Just a Dancing Partner	1955	10.00	20.00	40.00
—Maroon label					
70753	The Great Pretender/I'm Just a Dancing Partner	1955	5.00	10.00	20.00
—Black label					
70819	(You've Got) The Magic Touch/Winner Take All	1956	10.00	20.00	40.00
—Maroon label					
70819	(You've Got) The Magic Touch/Winner Take All	1956	5.00	10.00	20.00
—Black label					
70893	My Prayer/Heaven on Earth	1956	10.00	20.00	40.00
—Maroon label					
70893	My Prayer/Heaven on Earth	1956	5.00	10.00	20.00
—Black label					
70948	You'll Never Never Know/It Isn't Right	1956	7.50	15.00	30.00
—Maroon label					
70948	You'll Never Never Know/It Isn't Right	1956	5.00	10.00	20.00
—Black label					
71011	One in a Million/On My Word of Honor	1956	7.50	15.00	30.00
71032	I'm Sorry/He's Mine	1957	7.50	15.00	30.00
—Maroon label					
71032	I'm Sorry/He's Mine	1957	5.00	10.00	20.00
—Black label					
71093	My Dream/I Wanna	1957	7.50	15.00	30.00
—Maroon label					
71093	My Dream/I Wanna	1957	5.00	10.00	20.00
—Black label					
71184	Only Because/The Mystery of You	1957	6.25	12.50	25.00
71246	Helpless/Indifferent	1957	6.25	12.50	25.00
71289	Twilight Time/Out of My Mind	1958	6.25	12.50	25.00
71320	You're Making a Mistake/My Old Flame	1958	6.25	12.50	25.00
71353	I Wish/It's Raining Outside	1958	6.25	12.50	25.00
—Black label					
71353	I Wish/It's Raining Outside	1958	7.50	15.00	30.00
—Blue label					
71383	Smoke Gets In Your Eyes/No Matter What You Are	1958	6.25	12.50	25.00
—Black label					
71383	Smoke Gets In Your Eyes/No Matter What You Are	1958	7.50	15.00	30.00
—Blue label					
71427	Enchanted/The Sound and the Fury	1959	5.00	10.00	20.00
71467 [M]	Remember When/Love of a Lifetime	1959	5.00	10.00	20.00
71502	Where/Wish It Were Me	1959	5.00	10.00	20.00
71538	My Secret/What Does It Matter	1959	5.00	10.00	20.00
71563	Harbor Lights/Sleepy Lagoon	1960	5.00	10.00	20.00
71563 [PS]	Harbor Lights/Sleepy Lagoon	1960	10.00	20.00	40.00
71624	Ebb Tide/(I'll Be With You) In Apple Blossom Time	1960	5.00	10.00	20.00
71656	Red Sails in the Sunset/Sad River	1960	5.00	10.00	20.00
71656 [PS]	Red Sails in the Sunset/Sad River	1960	7.50	15.00	30.00
71697	To Each His Own/Down the River of Golden Dreams	1960	5.00	10.00	20.00
71697 [PS]	To Each His Own/Down the River of Golden Dreams	1960	7.50	15.00	30.00
71749	If I Didn't Care/True Lover	1961	3.75	7.50	15.00
71749 [PS]	If I Didn't Care/True Lover	1961	7.50	15.00	30.00
71791	Trees/Immortal Love	1961	3.75	7.50	15.00
71791 [PS]	Trees/Immortal Love	1961	7.50	15.00	30.00
71847	I'll Never Smile Again/You Don't Say	1961	3.75	7.50	15.00
71847 [PS]	I'll Never Smile Again/You Don't Say	1961	7.50	15.00	30.00
71904	Song for the Lonely/You'll Never Know	1961	3.75	7.50	15.00
71921	It's Magic/Reaching for a Star	1962	3.75	7.50	15.00
71921 [PS]	It's Magic/Reaching for a Star	1962	7.50	15.00	30.00
71986	More Than You Know/Every Little Moment	1962	3.00	6.00	12.00
72060	Memories/Heartbreak	1962	3.00	6.00	12.00
72107	Once in a While/I'll See You in My Dreams	1963	2.50	5.00	10.00
72129	Strangers/Here Comes Heaven Again	1963	2.50	5.00	10.00
72194	Viva Ju Joy/Quando Caliente El Sol	1963	2.50	5.00	10.00
72242	Java Jive/Michael Row the Boat Ashore	1964	2.50	5.00	10.00
72305	Sincerely/P.S. I Love You	1964	2.50	5.00	10.00
72359	Love Me Tender/Little Things Mean a Lot	1964	2.50	5.00	10.00
76160	Platterama Medley/Red Sails in the Sunset	1982	—	3.00	6.00
MUSICOR					
1166	I Love You 1000 Times/Don't Hear, Speak, See No Evil	1966	2.00	4.00	8.00
1195	Alone in the Light (Without You)/Devri	1966	2.00	4.00	8.00
1211	I'll Be Home/(You've Got) The Magic Touch	1966	2.00	4.00	8.00
1229	With This Ring/If I Had a Love	1967	2.50	5.00	10.00
1251	Washed Ashore (On a Lonely Island in the Sea)/What Name Shall I Give You, My Love	1967	2.00	4.00	8.00
1251	Washed Ashore (On a Lonely Island in the Sea)/One in a Million	1967	2.00	4.00	8.00
1262	On Top of My Mind/Shing-a-Ling-a-Loo	1967	2.00	4.00	8.00
1275	Sweet, Sweet Lovin'/Sonata	1967	2.00	4.00	8.00
1288	Love Must Go On/How Beautiful Our Love Is	1968	2.00	4.00	8.00
1302	So Many Tears/Think Before You Walk Away	1968	2.00	4.00	8.00
1322	Hard to Get a Thing Called Love/Why	1968	2.00	4.00	8.00
1341	Fear of Loving You/Sonata	1968	2.00	4.00	8.00
1443	Be My Love/Sweet Sweet Lovin'	1971	2.00	4.00	8.00
OWL					
320	Sixteen Tons/Are You Sincere	1973	2.00	4.00	8.00
RAM					
1002	Only You/Here Comes the Boogie Man	1977	2.00	4.00	8.00
1004/5	My Ship Is Coming In/Guilty	1977	2.00	4.00	8.00
4852	Personality/Who's Sorry Now	1978	2.00	4.00	8.00

7-Inch Extended Plays

Number	Title (A Side/B Side)	Yr	VG	VG+	NM
FEDERAL					
378	(contents unknown)	1956	100.00	200.00	400.00
378 [PS]	The Platters Sing for Only You	1956	100.00	200.00	400.00
KING					
378	(contents unknown)	1956	37.50	75.00	150.00
378 [PS]	The Platters	1956	37.50	75.00	150.00
—Reissue of Federal EP					
651	(contents unknown)	1956	40.00	80.00	160.00
—"Federal" 651 is a counterfeit; all originals are on King					
651 [PS]	The Platters	1956	40.00	80.00	160.00
MERCURY					
EP 1-3336	(contents unknown)	1957	10.00	20.00	40.00
EP 1-3336 [PS]	The Platters	1957	10.00	20.00	40.00
EP 1-3343	Heart of Stone/I'd Climb the Highest Mountain//September in the Rain/You've Changed	1957	10.00	20.00	40.00
EP 1-3343 [PS]	The Platters (Part 1)	1957	10.00	20.00	40.00
EP 1-3344	I'll Get By/I'll Give You My Word//In the Still of the Night/Wagon Wheels	1957	10.00	20.00	40.00
EP 1-3344 [PS]	The Platters (Part 2)	1957	10.00	20.00	40.00
EP 1-3345	Take Me in Your Arms/You Can Depend on Me//Temptation/I Don't Know Why	1957	10.00	20.00	40.00
EP 1-3345 [PS]	The Platters (Part 3)	1957	10.00	20.00	40.00
EP 1-3353	(contents unknown)	1958	10.00	20.00	40.00
EP 1-3353 [PS]	The Flying Platters (Part 1)	1958	10.00	20.00	40.00
EP 1-3354	(contents unknown)	1958	10.00	20.00	40.00

Number	Title (A Side/B Side)	Yr	VG	VG+	NM
EP 1-3354 [PS]	The Flying Platters (Part 2)	1958	10.00	20.00	40.00
EP 1-3355	Mean to Me/Oh Promise Me//Time and Tide/Don't Forget	1958	10.00	20.00	40.00
EP 1-3355 [PS]	The Flying Platters	1958	10.00	20.00	40.00
EP 1-3393	(contents unknown)	1958	10.00	20.00	40.00
EP 1-3393 [PS]	Twilight Time	1958	10.00	20.00	40.00

Albums

CANDELITE MUSIC

Number	Title (A Side/B Side)	Yr	VG	VG+	NM
CMI 1000 [(5)]	The 50 Golden Hits of the Platters	197?	10.00	20.00	40.00

COLUMBIA SPECIAL PRODUCTS

Number	Title (A Side/B Side)	Yr	VG	VG+	NM
P 11834 [S]	Christmas with the Platters	1973	3.75	7.50	15.00

—Reissue of Mercury SR-60841 with fewer tracks

FEDERAL

Number	Title (A Side/B Side)	Yr	VG	VG+	NM
549 [M]	The Platters	1957	400.00	800.00	1600.

KING

Number	Title (A Side/B Side)	Yr	VG	VG+	NM
651 [M]	The Platters	1959	200.00	400.00	800.00
KLP-651 [M]	The Platters	1987	2.50	5.00	10.00
—Reissue with "Highland Records" on label					
5002	19 Hits of the Platters	197?	3.00	6.00	12.00

MERCURY

Number	Title (A Side/B Side)	Yr	VG	VG+	NM
SRM-1-4050	Platterama	1982	2.50	5.00	10.00
MG-20146 [M]	The Platters	1956	25.00	50.00	100.00
MG-20216 [M]	The Platters, Volume Two	1956	25.00	50.00	100.00
MG-20298 [M]	The Flying Platters	1957	25.00	50.00	100.00
MG-20366 [M]	The Flying Platters Around the World	1958	7.50	15.00	30.00
MG-20410 [M]	Remember When?	1959	7.50	15.00	30.00
MG-20472 [M]	Encore of Golden Hits	1960	7.50	15.00	30.00
MG-20481 [M]	Reflections	1960	6.25	12.50	25.00
MG-20589 [M]	Life Is Just a Bowl of Cherries	1960	6.25	12.50	25.00
MG-20591 [M]	More Encore of Golden Hits	1960	6.25	12.50	25.00
MG-20613 [M]	Encore of Broadway Golden Hits	1961	5.00	10.00	20.00
MG-20669 [M]	Song for the Lonely	1962	5.00	10.00	20.00
MG-20759 [M]	Moonlight Memories	1963	5.00	10.00	20.00
MG-20782 [M]	The Platters Present All-Time Movie Hits	1963	5.00	10.00	20.00
MG-20808 [M]	The Platters Sing Latino	1963	5.00	10.00	20.00
MG-20841 [M]	Christmas with the Platters	1963	7.50	15.00	30.00
MG-20893 [M]	Encore of Golden Hits of the Groups	1964	5.00	10.00	20.00
MG-20933 [M]	10th Anniversary Album	1964	5.00	10.00	20.00
MG-20983 [M]	The New Soul of the Platters	1965	3.75	7.50	15.00
SR-60043 [S]	The Flying Platters Around the World	1959	12.50	25.00	50.00
SR-60087 [S]	Remember When?	1959	12.50	25.00	50.00
SR-60160 [S]	Reflections	1960	7.50	15.00	30.00
SR-60243 [P]	Encore of Golden Hits	1960	10.00	20.00	40.00
SR-60245 [S]	Life Is Just a Bowl of Cherries	1960	7.50	15.00	30.00
SR-60252 [S]	More Encore of Golden Hits	1960	7.50	15.00	30.00
SR-60613 [S]	Encore of Broadway Golden Hits	1961	6.25	12.50	25.00
SR-60669 [S]	Song for the Lonely	1962	6.25	12.50	25.00
SR-60759 [S]	Moonlight Memories	1963	6.25	12.50	25.00
SR-60782 [S]	The Platters Present All-Time Movie Hits	1963	6.25	12.50	25.00
SR-60808 [S]	The Platters Sing Latino	1963	6.25	12.50	25.00
SR-60841 [S]	Christmas with the Platters	1963	10.00	20.00	40.00
—Same as above, but in stereo					
SR-60893 [S]	Encore of Golden Hits of the Groups	1964	6.25	12.50	25.00
SR-60933 [S]	10th Anniversary Album	1964	6.25	12.50	25.00
SR-60983 [S]	The New Soul of the Platters	1965	5.00	10.00	20.00
828246-1	More Encore of Golden Hits	198?	2.00	4.00	8.00
—Reissue					
828254-1	Encore of Golden Hits	198?	2.00	4.00	8.00
—Reissue					

MUSIC DISC

Number	Title (A Side/B Side)	Yr	VG	VG+	NM
MDS-1002	Only You	1969	3.00	6.00	12.00

MUSICOR

Number	Title (A Side/B Side)	Yr	VG	VG+	NM
MM-2091 [M]	I Love You 1,000 Times	1966	3.75	7.50	15.00
MM-2111 [M]	The Platters Have the Magic Touch	1966	3.75	7.50	15.00
MM-2125 [M]	Going Back to Detroit	1967	3.75	7.50	15.00
MM-2141 [M]	New Golden Hits of the Platters	1967	5.00	10.00	20.00
MS-3091 [S]	I Love You 1,000 Times	1966	5.00	10.00	20.00
MS-3111 [S]	The Platters Have the Magic Touch	1966	5.00	10.00	20.00
MS-3125 [S]	Going Back to Detroit	1967	3.75	7.50	15.00
MS-3141 [S]	New Golden Hits of the Platters	1967	3.75	7.50	15.00
MS-3156	Sweet, Sweet Lovin'	1968	3.75	7.50	15.00
MS-3171	I Get the Sweetest Feeling	1968	3.75	7.50	15.00
MS-3185	Singing the Great Hits Our Way	1969	3.75	7.50	15.00
MS-3231	Golden Hour	1973	3.00	6.00	12.00
MS-3254	The Golden Hits of the Platters	1973	3.00	6.00	12.00

PICKWICK

Number	Title (A Side/B Side)	Yr	VG	VG+	NM
PTP-2083 [(2)]	Only You	1973	3.00	6.00	12.00
SPC-3236	Super Hits	197?	2.50	5.00	10.00

RHINO

Number	Title (A Side/B Side)	Yr	VG	VG+	NM
RNFP-71495 [(2)]	Anthology (1955-1967)	1986	3.00	6.00	12.00

SPRINGBOARD

Number	Title (A Side/B Side)	Yr	VG	VG+	NM
SPB-4059	The Platters	197?	2.50	5.00	10.00

WING

Number	Title (A Side/B Side)	Yr	VG	VG+	NM
MGW-12112 [M]	Encores!	1959	7.50	15.00	30.00
—With liner notes on back cover					
MGW-12112 [M]	Encores!	196?	3.75	7.50	15.00
—With photos of other Wing LPs on back cover					
MGW-12226 [M]	Flying Platters	1963	3.00	6.00	12.00
MGW-12272 [M]	Reflections	1964	3.00	6.00	12.00
MGW-12346 [M]	10th Anniversary Album	196?	3.00	6.00	12.00
SRW-16112 [R]	Encores!	196?	3.00	6.00	12.00
SRW-16226 [S]	Flying Platters	1963	3.00	6.00	12.00
SRW-16272 [S]	Reflections	1964	3.00	6.00	12.00
SRW-16346 [S]	10th Anniversary Album	196?	3.00	6.00	12.00

PLAYBOYS, THE (1)

The only of the many Playboys groups to have a national hit (other than Gary Lewis' or John Fred's bands).

45s

CAMEO

Number	Title (A Side/B Side)	Yr	VG	VG+	NM
142	Over the Weekend/Double Talk	1958	5.00	10.00	20.00

MARTINIQUE

Number	Title (A Side/B Side)	Yr	VG	VG+	NM
101	Over the Weekend/Double Talk	1958	12.50	25.00	50.00
400	Please Forgive Me/Sing Along	1959	10.00	20.00	40.00

PLAYBOYS, THE (2)

45s

ABC-PARAMOUNT

Number	Title (A Side/B Side)	Yr	VG	VG+	NM
10070	You're All I See/Memories	1959	5.00	10.00	20.00

PLAYBOYS, THE (3)

45s

ACE

Number	Title (A Side/B Side)	Yr	VG	VG+	NM
670	Gotta Feelin'/How Could You Forget	1963	3.00	6.00	12.00

PLAYBOYS, THE (4)

45s

CAT

Number	Title (A Side/B Side)	Yr	VG	VG+	NM
108	Tell Me/Rock, Moan and Cry	1954	12.50	25.00	50.00
115	Good Golly Miss Molly/Honey Run	1955	12.50	25.00	50.00

PLAYBOYS, THE (5)

45s

CATALINA

Number	Title (A Side/B Side)	Yr	VG	VG+	NM
1069	Shortnin' Bread/Cheater Stomp	1964	7.50	15.00	30.00

PLAYBOYS, THE (6)

45s

TETRA

Number	Title (A Side/B Side)	Yr	VG	VG+	NM
4447	One Question/So Good	1956	37.50	75.00	150.00

PLAYBOYS, THE (U)

Many of these could be by the above groups; many probably are not.

45s

CHANCELLOR

Number	Title (A Side/B Side)	Yr	VG	VG+	NM
1074	Boston Hop/What'd I Say	1961	3.75	7.50	15.00
—B-side by the Cousins					
1106	Duck Walk/If I Had My Way	1962	3.75	7.50	15.00

COTTON

Number	Title (A Side/B Side)	Yr	VG	VG+	NM
1008	Careful with My Heart/Girl of My Dreams	1962	6.25	12.50	25.00

DOLTON

Number	Title (A Side/B Side)	Yr	VG	VG+	NM
8	Party Ice/Icy Fingers	1959	5.00	10.00	20.00

HEARTBEAT

Number	Title (A Side/B Side)	Yr	VG	VG+	NM
60	Harlem Nocturne/Blue Moon	1963	5.00	10.00	20.00

IMPERIAL

Number	Title (A Side/B Side)	Yr	VG	VG+	NM
5586	Sweet Talk/Crazy Daisy	1959	5.00	10.00	20.00

LEGATO

Number	Title (A Side/B Side)	Yr	VG	VG+	NM
101	Mope De Mope/The Night Before Christmas	1963	7.50	15.00	30.00

MERCURY

Number	Title (A Side/B Side)	Yr	VG	VG+	NM
71228	Why Do I Love You, Why Do I Care/Don't Do Me Wrong	1957	6.25	12.50	25.00

RIK

Number	Title (A Side/B Side)	Yr	VG	VG+	NM
572	Jungle Fever/Shotgun	1959	6.25	12.50	25.00

SOUVENIR

Number	Title (A Side/B Side)	Yr	VG	VG+	NM
1001	Believe It or Not/Hawaiian War Chant	1959	3.75	7.50	15.00

TITAN

Number	Title (A Side/B Side)	Yr	VG	VG+	NM
1732	The Scramble/Cat Walk	1963	5.00	10.00	20.00

ZIPP

Number	Title (A Side/B Side)	Yr	VG	VG+	NM
101	Sweet Talk/Crazy Daisy	1959	10.00	20.00	40.00

PLAYMATES, THE

45s

ABC-PARAMOUNT

Number	Title (A Side/B Side)	Yr	VG	VG+	NM
10422	"A" My Name Is Alice/Just a Little Bit	1963	2.50	5.00	10.00
10468	She Never Looked Better/But Not Through Tears	1963	2.50	5.00	10.00
10492	I Cross My Fingers/I'll Never Get Over You	1963	2.50	5.00	10.00
10522	Guy Behind the Wheel/One Guy Left on the Corner	1964	2.50	5.00	10.00

BELL

Number	Title (A Side/B Side)	Yr	VG	VG+	NM
45149	Foundation of Love/Davenu	1971	—	3.00	6.00

COLPIX

Number	Title (A Side/B Side)	Yr	VG	VG+	NM
760	Fiddler on the Roof/Piece of the Sky	1964	2.00	4.00	8.00
769	One by One the Roses Died/Spanish Perfume	1965	2.00	4.00	8.00

CONGRESS

Number	Title (A Side/B Side)	Yr	VG	VG+	NM
245	Ballad of Stanley the Lifeguard/Should I Ask Someone Else to Tell Her	1965	2.00	4.00	8.00

RAINBOW

Number	Title (A Side/B Side)	Yr	VG	VG+	NM
360	Nickelodeon Rag/I Have Only Myself to Blame	1956	7.50	15.00	30.00

ROULETTE

Number	Title (A Side/B Side)	Yr	VG	VG+	NM
4003	Barefoot Girl/Pretty Woman	1957	3.75	7.50	15.00
4022	Darling It's Wonderful/Magic Shoes	1957	3.75	7.50	15.00
4022	Darling It's Wonderful/Island Girl	1957	3.75	7.50	15.00
4037	Jo-Ann/You Can't Stop Me from Dreaming	1957	6.25	12.50	25.00
4056	Let's Be Lovers/Give Me Another Chance	1958	3.75	7.50	15.00
4072	Don't Go Home/Can't You Get It Through Your Head	1958	3.75	7.50	15.00
4100	The Day I Died/While the Record Goes Around	1958	3.75	7.50	15.00
4115	Beep Beep/Your Love	1958	6.25	12.50	25.00
4136	Star Love/The Thing-A-Ma-Jig	1959	3.00	6.00	12.00
4160	What Is Love/I Am	1959	3.00	6.00	12.00
4200	First Love/A-Ciu-E	1959	3.00	6.00	12.00
4211	On the Beach/The Song Everybody's Singing	1959	3.00	6.00	12.00
4227	Second Chance/These Things I Offer You	1960	3.00	6.00	12.00
4252	Parade of Pretty Girls/Our Wedding Day	1960	3.00	6.00	12.00
4276	Wait for Me/Eyes of Angel	1960	3.00	6.00	12.00
4322	Little Mis Stuck-Up/Real Life	1961	3.00	6.00	12.00
4370	Tell Me What She Said/Cowboys Never Cry	1961	3.00	6.00	12.00
4393	Wimoweh/One Little Kiss	1961	3.00	6.00	12.00
4417	A Rose and a Star/Bachelor Flat	1962	2.50	5.00	10.00
4432	Keep Your Hands in Your Pocket/The Cop on the Beat	1962	2.50	5.00	10.00
4464	What a Funny Way to Show It/Petticoats Fly	1962	2.50	5.00	10.00

Number	Title (A Side/B Side)	Yr	VG	VG+	NM
Albums					
FORUM					
F-9012 [M]	At Play with the Playmates	196?	3.00	6.00	12.00
SF-9012 [S]	At Play with the Playmates	196?	3.75	7.50	15.00
F-9021 [M]	Broadway Show Stoppers	196?	3.00	6.00	12.00
SF-9021 [S]	Broadway Show Stoppers	196?	3.75	7.50	15.00
F-16001 [M]	The Playmates Visit West of the Indies	1960	3.75	7.50	15.00
SF-16001 [S]	The Playmates Visit West of the Indies	1960	5.00	10.00	20.00
ROULETTE					
R-25001 [M]	Calypso	1957	6.25	12.50	25.00
R-25043 [M]	At Play with the Playmates	1958	6.25	12.50	25.00
SR-25043 [S]	At Play with the Playmates	1958	7.50	15.00	30.00
R-25059 [M]	Rock and Roll Record Hop	1959	5.00	10.00	20.00
SR-25059 [S]	Rock and Roll Record Hop	1959	6.25	12.50	25.00
R-25068 [M]	Cuttin' Capers	1960	5.00	10.00	20.00
SR-25068 [S]	Cuttin' Capers	1960	6.25	12.50	25.00
R-25084 [M]	Broadway Show Stoppers	1961	5.00	10.00	20.00
SR-25084 [S]	Broadway Show Stoppers	1961	6.25	12.50	25.00

PLEASE, BOBBY

Number	Title (A Side/B Side)	Yr	VG	VG+	NM
45s					
IMPERIAL					
5508	I'm Girl Crazy/My Tummy Flip	1958	3.75	7.50	15.00
JAMIE					
1118	The Monster/The Switch	1959	3.75	7.50	15.00

PLEASURE FAIR, THE

With Robb Royer, later of BREAD.

Number	Title (A Side/B Side)	Yr	VG	VG+	NM
45s					
UNI					
55016	Morning Glory Days/Fade In, Fade Out	1967	2.00	4.00	8.00
55078	Today/I'm Gonna Hafta Let You Go	1968	2.00	4.00	8.00
Albums					
UNI					
3008 [M]	The Pleasure Fair	1967	5.00	10.00	20.00
73008 [S]	The Pleasure Fair	1967	5.00	10.00	20.00

PLEASURE SEEKERS

SUZI QUATRO was in this group.

Number	Title (A Side/B Side)	Yr	VG	VG+	NM
45s					
CAPITOL					
2050	(Theme from) Valley of the Dolls/If You Climb on the Tiger's Back	1967	5.00	10.00	20.00
HIDEOUT					
1006	Never Thought You'd Leave Me/What a Way to Die	1967	25.00	50.00	100.00
MERCURY					
72800	Good Kind of Hurt/Light of Love	1968	6.25	12.50	25.00

PLEBS, THE

Number	Title (A Side/B Side)	Yr	VG	VG+	NM
45s					
MGM					
13320	Bad Blood/Babe I'm Gonna Leave You	1965	3.00	6.00	12.00

PLEDGES, THE

Actually Clyde Battin and GARY PAXTON, who recorded as SKIP AND FLIP.

Number	Title (A Side/B Side)	Yr	VG	VG+	NM
45s					
REV					
3517	Betty Jean/Her Bermuda Shorts	1958	6.25	12.50	25.00

PLUM NELLY

Number	Title (A Side/B Side)	Yr	VG	VG+	NM
Albums					
CAPITOL					
ST-692	Deceptive Lines	1971	5.00	10.00	20.00

PLUMB, EVE

"Jan Brady" of THE BRADY BUNCH.

Number	Title (A Side/B Side)	Yr	VG	VG+	NM
45s					
RCA VICTOR					
74-0409	How Will It Be/Fortune Cookie Song	1970	3.75	7.50	15.00
74-0409 [PS]	How Will It Be/Fortune Cookie Song	1970	5.00	10.00	20.00

PLUMMER, DAVE, AND THE PLUNGERS

Number	Title (A Side/B Side)	Yr	VG	VG+	NM
45s					
MAYBROOK					
320	Surfin' Monster/King of the Road	196?	10.00	20.00	40.00

POCO

Also see JIM MESSINA.

Number	Title (A Side/B Side)	Yr	VG	VG+	NM
12-Inch Singles					
MCA					
2314 [DJ]	Under the Gun (same on both sides)	1980	2.00	4.00	8.00
RCA					
9039-1-RAB [DJ]	Call It Love (Edit)/Call It Love (LP)	1989	—	3.00	6.00
45s					
ABC					
12126	Keep On Tryin'/Georgia, Bind My Ties	1975	—	2.50	5.00
12159	Makin' Love/Flyin' Solo	1976	—	2.50	5.00
12204	Rose of Cimarron/Tulsa Turnaround	1976	—	2.50	5.00
12295	Indian Summer/Me and You	1977	—	2.50	5.00
12439	Crazy Love/Barbados	1978	—	2.50	5.00
ATLANTIC					
89629 [DJ]	Save a Corner of Your Heart (same on both sides)	1984	—	—	3.00
—May be promo only					
89650	This Old Flame/The Storm	1984	—	—	3.00
89674	Days Gone By/Daylight	1984	—	—	3.00
89851 [DJ]	Break of Hearts (same on both sides)	1983	—	—	3.00
—May be promo only					
89919	Shoot for the Moon/The Midnight Rodeo	1982	—	—	3.00
89970	Ghostown/High Sierra	1982	—	—	3.00
89970 [PS]	Ghostown/High Sierra	1982	—	2.00	4.00
EPIC					
10501	Pickin' Up the Pieces/First Love	1969	2.50	5.00	10.00
10543	My Kind of Love/Hard Luck	1969	2.50	5.00	10.00
10636	You Better Think Twice/Anyway, Bye Bye	1970	2.00	4.00	8.00
10714	C'Mon/I Guess You Made It	1971	2.00	4.00	8.00
10804	Just for Me and You/Ol' Forgiver	1971	2.00	4.00	8.00
10816	You Are the One/Railroad Days	1971	2.00	4.00	8.00
10890	Good Feeling to Know/Early Times	1972	—	3.00	6.00
10958	I Can See Everything/Go and Say Goodbye	1973	—	3.00	6.00
11055	Here We Go Again/Fools Gold	1973	—	3.00	6.00
11092	Magnolia/Blue Water	1974	—	3.00	6.00
11141	Rocky Mountain Breakdown/Faith in the Families	1974	—	3.00	6.00
50076	Bitter Blue/High and Dry	1975	—	3.00	6.00
MCA					
41023	Heart of the Night/Last Goodbye	1979	—	2.00	4.00
41103	Legend/Indian Summer	1979	—	2.00	4.00
41269	Under the Gun/Reputation	1980	—	2.00	4.00
41269 [PS]	Under the Gun/Reputation	1980	—	3.00	6.00
41326	Midnight Rain/Fool's Paradise	1980	—	2.00	4.00
51034	Everlasting Kind/Friends in the Distance	1980	—	2.00	4.00
51172	Down on the River Again/Widowmaker	1981	—	2.00	4.00
52001	Seas of Heartbreals/Feudin'	1982	—	2.00	4.00
RCA					
9038-7-R	Call It Love/Lovin' You Every Minute	1989	—	—	3.00
9038-7-R [PS]	Call It Love/Lovin' You Every Minute	1989	—	—	3.00
9131-7-R	Nothin' to Hide/If It Wasn't for You	1989	—	—	3.00
9131-7-R [PS]	Nothin' to Hide/If It Wasn't for You	1989	—	—	3.00
Albums					
ABC					
D-890	Head Over Heels	1975	2.50	5.00	10.00
D-946	Rose of Cimarron	1976	2.50	5.00	10.00
D-989	Indian Summer	1977	2.50	5.00	10.00
AA-1099	Legend	1978	3.00	6.00	12.00
ATLANTIC					
80008	Ghost Town	1982	2.50	5.00	10.00
80148	Inamorata	1984	2.50	5.00	10.00
EPIC					
BN 26460	Pickin' Up the Pieces	1969	3.75	7.50	15.00
—Yellow label					
BN 26460	Pickin' Up the Pieces	1973	2.50	5.00	10.00
—Orange label					
BN 26522	Poco	1970	3.75	7.50	15.00
—Yellow label					
BN 26522	Poco	1973	2.50	5.00	10.00
—Orange label					
EQ 30209 [Q]	Deliverin'	1972	5.00	10.00	20.00
KE 30209	Deliverin'	1971	3.75	7.50	15.00
—Yellow label					
KE 30209	Deliverin'	1973	2.50	5.00	10.00
—Orange label					
E 30753	From the Inside	1973	2.50	5.00	10.00
—Reissue with new prefix					
KE 30753	From the Inside	1971	3.75	7.50	15.00
—Yellow label					
KE 30753	From the Inside	1973	2.50	5.00	10.00
—Orange label					
KE 31601	A Good Feelin' to Know	1972	3.75	7.50	15.00
—Yellow label					
KE 31601	A Good Feelin' to Know	1973	2.50	5.00	10.00
—Orange label					
PE 31601	A Good Feelin' to Know	198?	2.00	4.00	8.00
—Budget-line reissue					
EQ 32354 [Q]	Crazy Eyes	1973	5.00	10.00	20.00
KE 32354	Crazy Eyes	1973	3.00	6.00	12.00
—Orange label					
PE 32354	Crazy Eyes	1979	2.00	4.00	8.00
—Blue label					
EQ 32895 [Q]	Seven	1974	5.00	10.00	20.00
KE 32895	Seven	1974	3.00	6.00	12.00
—Orange label					
PCQ 33192 [Q]	Cantamos	1974	5.00	10.00	20.00
PE 33192	Cantamos	1974	3.00	6.00	12.00
—Orange label					
PE 33336	Live	1976	3.00	6.00	12.00
—Orange label					
PEG 33537 [(2)]	The Very Best of Poco	1975	3.75	7.50	15.00
—Orange labels					
JE 36210	The Songs of Paul Cotton	1980	2.50	5.00	10.00
JE 36211	The Songs of Richie Furay	1980	2.50	5.00	10.00
MCA					
AA-1099	Legend	1979	2.50	5.00	10.00
—Reissue of ABC 1099					
5132	Under the Gun	1980	2.50	5.00	10.00
5227	Blue and Gray	1981	2.50	5.00	10.00
5288	Cowboys & Englishmen	1982	2.50	5.00	10.00
5363	Backtracks	1983	2.50	5.00	10.00
37009	Head Over Heels	1980	2.00	4.00	8.00
—Budget-line reissue					
37010	Rose of Cimarron	1980	2.00	4.00	8.00
—Budget-line reissue					
37011	Indian Summer	1980	2.00	4.00	8.00
—Budget-line reissue					
37117	Legend	1981	2.00	4.00	8.00
—Budget-line reissue					
37160	Under the Gun	198?	2.00	4.00	8.00
—Budget-line reissue					
MOBILE FIDELITY					
1-020	Legend	1979	5.00	10.00	20.00
—Audiophile vinyl					
RCA					
9694-1-R	Legacy	1989	2.50	5.00	10.00

POETS, THE (1)

45s

Number	Title (A Side/B Side)	Yr	VG	VG+	NM
SYMBOL					
214	She Blew a Good Thing/Out to Lunch	1966	3.75	7.50	15.00
216	So Young (And So Innocent)/A Sure Thing	1966	3.00	6.00	12.00
219	I'm Particular/I've Only Two Hearts	1966	3.00	6.00	12.00
VEEP					
1286	The Hustler/Soul Brothers Holiday	1968	5.00	10.00	20.00

POETS, THE (2)

British group.

45s

Number	Title (A Side/B Side)	Yr	VG	VG+	NM
DYNO VOX					
201	Now We're Thru/There Are Some	1965	2.50	5.00	10.00

POETS, THE (3)

45s

Number	Title (A Side/B Side)	Yr	VG	VG+	NM
FLASH					
129	Vowels of Love/Dead	1958	50.00	100.00	200.00
—Black label					
129	Vowels of Love/Dead	1958	15.00	30.00	60.00
—Maroon label					

POETS, THE (4)

45s

Number	Title (A Side/B Side)	Yr	VG	VG+	NM
IMPERIAL					
5664	Honey Chile/I'm in Love	1960	3.75	7.50	15.00

POETS, THE (U)

These could be group (1) or (2).

45s

Number	Title (A Side/B Side)	Yr	VG	VG+	NM
CHAIRMAN					
4408	Coffee House/Number One (More Time)	1963	3.00	6.00	12.00
RED BIRD					
10-046	Merry Christmas Baby/I'm Stuck on You	1965	3.00	6.00	12.00

POINDEXTER, DON, AND THE STARLITE WRANGLERS

45s

Number	Title (A Side/B Side)	Yr	VG	VG+	NM
SUN					
202	Now She Cares No More for Me/My Kind of Love	1954	500.00	1000.	2000.

POINTER SISTERS, THE

12-Inch Singles

Number	Title (A Side/B Side)	Yr	VG	VG+	NM
COLUMBIA					
07883	Power of Persuasion (3 versions)	1988	—	3.00	6.00
MCA					
23769	Be There (4 versions)	1987	—	3.00	6.00
MOTOWN					
4661	Friend's Advice (Don't Take It) (3 versions)	1990	—	3.00	6.00
L33-17922 [DJ]	Friend's Advice (Don't Take It) (5 versions)	1990	2.00	4.00	8.00
PLANET					
11403 [DJ]	Happiness (same on both sides)	1979	2.00	4.00	8.00
11406 [DJ]	Come and Get Your Love/Dirty Work/Echoes of Love/Hypnotized	1979	3.00	6.00	12.00
11407 [DJ]	Fire/Happiness	1979	3.00	6.00	12.00
—Red vinyl					
JD-13328 [DJ]	I'm So Excited	1982	2.50	5.00	10.00
—One-sided promo					
YD-13429	I'm So Excited/If You Wanna Get Back My Love	1983	2.50	5.00	10.00
YD-13721	Automatic (4:48) (6:06)	1984	2.00	4.00	8.00
YD-13781	Jump (For My Love) (6:24)/(Instrumental)/Heartbeat	1984	2.00	4.00	8.00
JR-13858 [DJ]	I'm So Excited (same on both sides)	1984	2.50	5.00	10.00
YD-13952	Neutron Dance (4:59)/Telegraph Your Love	1984	2.00	4.00	8.00
YD-14042	Baby Come and Get It (7:14)/Operator	1985	2.00	4.00	8.00
RCA					
5774-1-RDAC [DJ]	Goldmine (2 versions)/Sexual Power	1986	—	3.00	6.00
6491-1-RDAC [DJ]	Mercury Rising (3 versions)	1986	—	3.00	6.00
6865-1-RD	He Turned Me Out (4 versions)	1988	—	3.00	6.00
PD-14127	Dare Me (Long) (Instrumental)/I'll Be There	1985	—	3.00	6.00
PD-14196	Twist My Arm (Dance Mix)/(Instrumental)/Easy Persuasion	1985	2.00	4.00	8.00
PD-14225	Freedom (4:18) (6:21)	1985	—	3.00	6.00

45s

Number	Title (A Side/B Side)	Yr	VG	VG+	NM
ATLANTIC					
2845	Don't Try to Take the Fifth/Tulsa County	1971	5.00	10.00	20.00
2893	Destination No More Heartaches/Send Him Back	1972	5.00	10.00	20.00
BLUE THUMB					
229	Yes We Can Can/Jada	1973	—	3.00	6.00
243	Wang Dang Doodle/Cloudburst	1973	—	3.00	6.00
248	Steam Heat/Shaky Flat Blues	1974	—	3.00	6.00
254	Fairytale/Love In Them Thar Hills	1974	2.50	5.00	10.00
—First pressing has a gray to white label and no reference to ABC					
254	Fairytale/Love In Them Thar Hills	1974	—	2.50	5.00
—Second pressing has a multicolor label with ABC logo					
262	Live Your Life Before You Die/Shaky Flat Blues	1975	—	2.50	5.00
265	How Long (Betcha' Got a Chick on the Side)/Easy Days	1975	—	2.50	5.00
268	Going Down Slowly/Sleeping Alone	1975	—	2.50	5.00
271	You Gotta Believe/Shaky Flat Blues	1976	—	2.50	5.00
275	Having a Party/Lonely Gal	1977	—	2.50	5.00
277	I Need a Man/I'll Get By Without You	1978	—	2.50	5.00
COLUMBIA					
08015	Power of Persuasion/(Instrumental)	1988	—	—	3.00
08015 [PS]	Power of Persuasion/(Instrumental)	1988	—	—	3.00
MCA					
53120	Be There/(Instrumental)	1987	—	—	3.00
53120 [PS]	Be There/(Instrumental)	1987	—	—	3.00
MOTOWN					
902	Friends' Advice (Don't Take It)/Friends' Advice (Don't Take It) (Dub)	1990	—	2.00	4.00
PLANET					
YB-13254	American Music/I Want to Do It with You	1982	—	2.00	4.00
YB-13327	I'm So Excited/Nothing But a Heartache (Live)	1982	—	2.00	4.00
YB-13430	If You Wanna Get Back Your Lady/I'm So Excited	1983	—	2.00	4.00
GB-13485	American Music/I'm So Excited	1983	—	—	3.00
—Gold Standard Series					
YB-13639	I Need You/If You Wanna Get Back Your Lady	1983	—	2.00	4.00
YB-13730	Automatic/Nightline	1984	—	2.00	4.00
YB-13780	Jump (For My Love)/Heart Beat	1984	—	2.00	4.00
GB-13795	I Need You/If You Wanna Get Back Your Lady	1984	—	—	3.00
—Gold Standard Series					
YB-13857	I'm So Excited/Dance Electric	1984	—	2.00	4.00
YB-13951	Neutron Dance/Telegraph Your Love	1984	—	2.00	4.00
YB-14041	Baby Come and Get It/Operator	1985	—	2.00	4.00
YB-14041 [PS]	Baby Come and Get It/Operator	1985	—	2.00	4.00
GB-14072	Jump (For My Love)/Automatic	1985	—	—	3.00
—Gold Standard Series					
GB-14076	Fire/He's So Shy	1985	—	—	3.00
—Gold Standard Series					
GB-14077	Slow Hand/Should I Do It	1985	—	—	3.00
—Gold Standard Series					
45901	Fire/Love Is Like a Rolling Stone	1978	—	2.00	4.00
45901 [PS]	Fire/Love Is Like a Rolling Stone	1978	—	3.00	6.00
45902	Happiness/Too Late	1979	—	2.00	4.00
45906	Blind Faith/The Shape I'm In	1979	—	2.00	4.00
47916	He's So Shy/Movin' On	1980	—	2.00	4.00
47918	Es Tan Timido/Cosas Especiales	1980	—	3.00	6.00
47920	Could I Be Dreaming/Evil	1980	—	2.00	4.00
47925	Where Did the Time Go/Special Things	1981	—	2.00	4.00
47929	Slow Hand/Holdin' Out for Love	1981	—	2.00	4.00
47937	What a Surprise/Fall in Love Again	1981	—	2.00	4.00
47945	Sweet Lover Man/Got to Find Love	1981	—	2.00	4.00
47960	Should I Do It/We're Gonna Make It	1982	—	2.00	4.00
RCA					
5062-7-R	Goldmine/Sexual Power	1986	—	—	3.00
5062-7-R [PS]	Goldmine/Sexual Power	1986	—	—	3.00
5112-7-R	All I Know Is the Way I Feel/Translation	1987	—	—	3.00
5230-7-R	Mercury Rising/Say the Word	1987	—	—	3.00
6865-7-R	He Turned Me Out/Translation	1988	—	—	3.00
6865-7-R [PS]	He Turned Me Out/Translation	1988	—	—	3.00
8378-7-R	I'm in Love/Uh-Oh	1988	—	—	3.00
PB-14126	Dare Me/I'll Be There	1985	—	—	3.00
PB-14126 [PS]	Dare Me/I'll Be There	1985	—	—	3.00
PB-14197	Twist My Arm/Easy Persuasion	1986	—	—	3.00
PB-14197 [PS]	Twist My Arm/Easy Persuasion	1986	—	—	3.00
PB-14224	Freedom/Telegraph Your Love	1985	—	—	3.00
PB-14224 [PS]	Freedom/Telegraph Your Love	1985	—	—	3.00
GB-14354	Neutron Dance/Baby Come and Get It	1986	—	—	3.00
—Gold Standard Series					
SBK					
S7-17637	Don't Walk Away/Tell It to My Heart	1993	—	2.00	4.00

Albums

Number	Title (A Side/B Side)	Yr	VG	VG+	NM
BLUE THUMB					
BTS-48	The Pointer Sisters	1973	3.00	6.00	12.00
BTS-6009	That's a Plenty	1974	3.00	6.00	12.00
BTS-6021	Steppin	1975	3.00	6.00	12.00
BTS-6023	Having a Party	1977	3.00	6.00	12.00
BTS-6026 [(2)]	The Best of the Pointer Sisters	1976	3.75	7.50	15.00
BTS-8002 [(2)]	Live at the Opera House	1974	3.75	7.50	15.00
MCA					
3275	Retrospect	1981	2.50	5.00	10.00
—Reissue of Blue Thumb material					
MOTOWN					
6287 ML	Right Rhythm	1990	3.00	6.00	12.00
PLANET					
P-1	Energy	1978	2.50	5.00	10.00
P-9	Special Things	1980	2.50	5.00	10.00
P-18	Black and White	1981	2.50	5.00	10.00
BXL1-4355	So Excited!	1982	2.50	5.00	10.00
BEL1-4705A	Break Out	1984	2.00	4.00	8.00
—Reissue has "I'm So Excited" plus a remix of "Jump (For My Love)"					
BXL1-4705	Break Out	1983	2.50	5.00	10.00
—Original does not have "I'm So Excited"					
P-9003	Priority	1979	2.50	5.00	10.00
60203	Pointer Sisters' Greatest Hits	1982	2.50	5.00	10.00
RCA					
5609-1-R	Hot Together	1986	2.50	5.00	10.00
6562-1-R	Serious Slammin'	1988	2.50	5.00	10.00
RCA VICTOR					
AYL1-5088	Special Things	1985	2.00	4.00	8.00
—Budget-line reissue					
AYL1-5089	Priority	1985	2.00	4.00	8.00
—Budget-line reissue					
AYL1-5091	Energy	1985	2.00	4.00	8.00
—Budget-line reissue					
AYL1-5092	Black and White	1985	2.00	4.00	8.00
—Budget-line reissue					
AJL1-5487	Contact	1985	2.50	5.00	10.00

POITIER, SIDNEY

Albums

Number	Title (A Side/B Side)	Yr	VG	VG+	NM
WARNER BROS.					
W 1561 [M]	Poitier Meets Plato	1965	6.25	12.50	25.00
WS 1561 [S]	Poitier Meets Plato	1965	7.50	15.00	30.00

POLLUTION

45s

Number	Title (A Side/B Side)	Yr	VG	VG+	NM
CAPITOL					
2458	Getting Together/Angela Jerome	1969	2.50	5.00	10.00
PROPHECY					
55001	Do You Really Have a Heart/(B-side unknown)	1971	2.00	4.00	8.00
55003	The River/(B-side unknown)	1972	2.00	4.00	8.00

Number	Title (A Side/B Side)	Yr	VG	VG+	NM
Albums					
CAPITOL					
ST-205	Heir: Pollution	1969	5.00	10.00	20.00
PROPHECY					
SD 6051	Pollution	1971	5.00	10.00	20.00
SD 6067	Pollution II	1972	5.00	10.00	20.00

POLNAREFF, MICHEL

Number	Title (A Side/B Side)	Yr	VG	VG+	NM
45s					
4 CORNERS OF THE WORLD					
141	Time Will Tell/Under What Star Was I Born	1967	3.75	7.50	15.00
ATLANTIC					
3314	Since I Saw You/If You Only Believe	1976	—	2.50	5.00
3330	Lipstick (Part 1)/Lipstick (Part 2)	1976	—	2.50	5.00
KAPP					
786	Love Me, Please Love Me/No, No, No, No, No	1966	2.00	4.00	8.00
Albums					
4 CORNERS OF THE WORLD					
FCL-4240 [M]	French Rock-Blues	1967	3.00	6.00	12.00
FCS-4240 [S]	French Rock-Blues	1967	3.75	7.50	15.00
ATLANTIC					
SD 18153	Michel Polnareff	1976	2.50	5.00	10.00

PONI-TAILS, THE

Number	Title (A Side/B Side)	Yr	VG	VG+	NM
45s					
ABC-PARAMOUNT					
9846	Wild Eyes and Tender Lips/It's Just My Luck to Be Fifteen	1957	5.00	10.00	20.00
9934	Born Too Late/Come On Joey Dance With Me	1958	6.25	12.50	25.00
9969	Close Friends/Seven Minutes in Heaven	1958	5.00	10.00	20.00
9995	Early to Bed/Father Time	1959	5.00	10.00	20.00
10027	Moody/Ooh-Pah Polka	1959	5.00	10.00	20.00
10047	I'll Be Seeing You/I'll Keep Tryin'	1959	5.00	10.00	20.00
10077	Before We Say Goodnight/Come Be My Love	1960	5.00	10.00	20.00
10114	Who, When and Why/Oh My, You	1960	5.00	10.00	20.00
MARC					
1001	Can I Be Sure/Still in Your Teens	1957	6.25	12.50	25.00
POINT					
8	Your Wild Heart/Que La Bozena	1957	6.25	12.50	25.00

PONTY, JEAN-LUC

Number	Title (A Side/B Side)	Yr	VG	VG+	NM
12-Inch Singles					
ATLANTIC					
PR 420 [DJ]	As (3:15) (5:45)	1982	—	3.00	6.00
PR 524 [DJ]	Far from Beaten Paths (3:50) (5:58)	1983	—	3.00	6.00
PR 801 [DJ]	Open Mind (Edit) (Extended)	1984	—	3.00	6.00
PR 809 [DJ]	Infinite Pursuit (same on both sides)	1985	—	3.00	6.00
45s					
ATLANTIC					
3368	New Country/Renaissance	1976	—	2.50	5.00
3523	Cosmic Messenger/The Art of Happiness	1978	—	2.50	5.00
3778	Demagomania/(B-side unknown)	1980	—	2.00	4.00
4009	As/Rhythms of Hope	1982	—	2.00	4.00
89787	Far from Beaten Paths/(B-side unknown)	1983	—	2.00	4.00
Albums					
ATLANTIC					
SD 16020	Civilized Evil	1980	2.50	5.00	10.00
SD 18138	Upon the Wings of Music	1975	2.50	5.00	10.00
SD 18163	Aurora	1976	2.50	5.00	10.00
SD 18195	Imaginary Voyage	1976	2.50	5.00	10.00
SD 19110	Enigmatic Ocean	1977	2.50	5.00	10.00
SD 19136	Imaginary Voyage	1978	2.00	4.00	8.00
—Reissue of 18195					
SD 19158	Aurora	1978	2.00	4.00	8.00
—Reissue of 18163					
SD 19189	Cosmic Messenger	1978	2.50	5.00	10.00
SD 19229	Jean-Luc Ponty: Live	1979	2.50	5.00	10.00
SD 19253	A Taste for Passion	1979	2.50	5.00	10.00
SD 19333	Mystical Adventures	1982	2.50	5.00	10.00
80098	Individual Choice	1983	2.00	4.00	8.00
80185	Open Mind	1984	2.00	4.00	8.00
81276	Fables	1985	2.00	4.00	8.00
BASF					
20645	Sunday Walk	1972	3.00	6.00	12.00
21288	Open Strings	1973	3.00	6.00	12.00
BLUE NOTE					
BN-LA632-H2 [(2)]	Cantaloupe Island	1976	3.75	7.50	15.00
LWB-632 [(2)]	Cantaloupe Island	1981	3.00	6.00	12.00
—Reissue of BN-LA632-H2					
LN-1102	Live at Donte's	1981	2.50	5.00	10.00
COLUMBIA					
FC 40983	The Gift of Time	1987	2.00	4.00	8.00
FC 45252	Storytelling	1989	3.00	6.00	12.00
DIRECT DISC					
SD-16603	Cosmic Messenger	1980	7.50	15.00	30.00
—Audiophile vinyl					
INNER CITY					
1003	Live at Montreux	197?	2.50	5.00	10.00
1005	Jean-Luc Ponty and Stephane Grappelli	197?	2.50	5.00	10.00
PACIFIC JAZZ					
ST-20156	Electric Connection	1969	3.75	7.50	15.00
ST-20168	The Jean-Luc Ponty Experience	1969	3.75	7.50	15.00
ST-20172	King Kong — Jean-Luc Ponty Plays the Music of Frank Zappa	1970	6.25	12.50	25.00
PAUSA					
7014	Jean-Luc Ponty Meets Giorgio Gaslini	1979	2.50	5.00	10.00
7033	Sunday Walk	1980	2.50	5.00	10.00
—Reissue of BASF 20645					
7065	Open Strings	1980	2.50	5.00	10.00
—Reissue of BASF 21288					
9001	The Jean-Luc Ponty Experience	1982	2.50	5.00	10.00
PRESTIGE					
PRST-7676	Critic's Choice	1969	3.75	7.50	15.00
WORLD PACIFIC					
ST-20134	More Than Meets the Ear	1969	3.75	7.50	15.00

POOBAH

Number	Title (A Side/B Side)	Yr	VG	VG+	NM
Albums					
A.E.I.					
A-LP-1	U.S. Rock	1976	62.50	125.00	250.00
PEPPERMINT					
PP-1180	Steamroller	1979	37.50	75.00	150.00
RITE					
(no #)	Let Me In	1972	150.00	300.00	600.00

POOH AND THE HEFFALUMPS

Number	Title (A Side/B Side)	Yr	VG	VG+	NM
45s					
LAURIE					
3281	Lady Godiva/Rooty Toot	1965	3.00	6.00	12.00

POOLE, BRIAN

Also see BRIAN POOLE AND THE TREMELOES.

Number	Title (A Side/B Side)	Yr	VG	VG+	NM
45s					
DATE					
1539	Everything I Touch Turns to Tears/I Need Her Tonight	1966	2.50	5.00	10.00

POOLE, BRIAN, AND THE TREMELOES

Also see BRIAN POOLE; THE TREMELOES.

Number	Title (A Side/B Side)	Yr	VG	VG+	NM
45s					
AUDIO FIDELITY					
112	I Go Crazy/Love Me Baby	1965	2.50	5.00	10.00
121	Good Lovin'/Could It Be You	1966	2.50	5.00	10.00
LONDON					
9600	Keep On Dancing/Blue	1963	3.75	7.50	15.00
9625	Do You Love Me/Why Can't You Love Me	1964	3.75	7.50	15.00
MONUMENT					
840	Candy Man/I Can Dream	1964	3.00	6.00	12.00
846	Someone, Someone/(Meet Me) Where We Used to Meet	1964	3.00	6.00	12.00
882	After a While/Don't Cry	1965	3.00	6.00	12.00
Albums					
AUDIO FIDELITY					
AFLP 2151 [M]	Brian Poole Is Here	1966	12.50	25.00	50.00
AFSD 2151 [R]	Brian Poole Is Here	1966	10.00	20.00	40.00
AFLP 2177 [M]	The Tremeloes Are Here	1967	10.00	20.00	40.00
—Reissue of above album with new title					
AFSD 2177 [R]	The Tremeloes Are Here	1967	7.50	15.00	30.00
—Reissue of above album with new title					

POPCORN AND THE MOHAWKS

Number	Title (A Side/B Side)	Yr	VG	VG+	NM
45s					
MOTOWN					
1002	Custer's Last Man/Shimmy Gully	1960	15.00	30.00	60.00

POPCORN BLIZZARD, THE

Number	Title (A Side/B Side)	Yr	VG	VG+	NM
45s					
DE-LITE					
516	Good Thing Going/My Suzanne	1969	5.00	10.00	20.00
522	Good Good Day/I Just Saw a Face	1969	5.00	10.00	20.00
Albums					
DE-LITE					
DE-2004	Explode!	1969	10.00	20.00	40.00

POPE, RAYMOND, AND THE LOVETONES

Number	Title (A Side/B Side)	Yr	VG	VG+	NM
45s					
SQUALOR					
1313	I Love Nadine/Star	1962	37.50	75.00	150.00

POPE JOHN XXIII

Number	Title (A Side/B Side)	Yr	VG	VG+	NM
Albums					
MERCURY					
200 [M]	Pope John XXIII	1963	3.75	7.50	15.00
—Tribute album released after his death					

POPPIES, THE

Dorothy Moore of "Misty Blue" fame was in this group.

Number	Title (A Side/B Side)	Yr	VG	VG+	NM
45s					
EPIC					
9893	I Wonder Why/Lullaby of Love	1966	2.50	5.00	10.00
10019	He's Ready/He's Got Real Love	1966	2.50	5.00	10.00
10019 [PS]	He's Ready/He's Got Real Love	1966	5.00	10.00	20.00
10059	Do It with Soul/He Means So Much to Me	1966	3.00	6.00	12.00
10086	There's a Pain in My Heart/My Love and I	1966	6.25	12.50	25.00
TUFF					
372	Johnny Don't Cry/(Instrumental)	1964	3.75	7.50	15.00
Albums					
EPIC					
LN 24200 [M]	Lullaby of Love	1966	10.00	20.00	40.00
BN 26200 [S]	Lullaby of Love	1966	12.50	25.00	50.00

POPPY FAMILY, THE

Also see TERRY JACKS.

Number	Title (A Side/B Side)	Yr	VG	VG+	NM
45s					
LONDON					
129	Which Way You Goin' Billy/Endless Sleep	1970	—	3.00	6.00
139	That's When I Went Wrong/Shadows on My Wall	1970	—	2.50	5.00
148	I Was Wondering/Where Evil Grows	1971	—	2.50	5.00
164	No Good to Cry/I'll See You There	1971	—	2.50	5.00
172	Good Friends/Tryin'	1972	—	2.50	5.00

Number	Title (A Side/B Side)	Yr	VG	VG+	NM
Albums					
LONDON					
PS 574	Which Way You Goin' Billy?	1970	3.75	7.50	15.00
PS 599	Seeds	1971	3.75	7.50	15.00

POPSICLES, THE (1)

Number	Title (A Side/B Side)	Yr	VG	VG+	NM
45s					
GNP CRESCENDO					
336	I Don't Want to Be Your Baby Anymore/Baby I Miss You	1965	2.50	5.00	10.00

POPSICLES, THE (2)

Number	Title (A Side/B Side)	Yr	VG	VG+	NM
45s					
KNIGHT					
2002	Thumb Print/This Is the End	1958	10.00	20.00	40.00

POPULAIRES, THE

Number	Title (A Side/B Side)	Yr	VG	VG+	NM
45s					
MARVELLO					
5001	Island of Paradise/I Lost My Heart	1957	50.00	100.00	200.00

PORCELAIN BEARMEAT

Number	Title (A Side/B Side)	Yr	VG	VG+	NM
Albums					
DILL PICKLE					
3468	Free Love, Free Sex, Free Music	1971	5.00	10.00	20.00

PORTER, DAVID

Number	Title (A Side/B Side)	Yr	VG	VG+	NM
45s					
ENTERPRISE					
9014	Can't See You When I Want To/One Part, Two Parts	1970	—	3.00	6.00
9049	Ain't That Loving You (For More Reasons Than One)/Baby I'm-a Want You	1972	—	2.50	5.00
—With Isaac Hayes					
9050	I'm Afraid the Masquerade Is Over/Sloopy	1972	—	2.50	5.00
9055	Wanna Be Your Somebody/When the Chips Are Down	1972	—	2.50	5.00
9071	As Long As You're the One Somebody in the World/When You Have to Sneak	1973	—	2.50	5.00
9090	Falling Out, Falling In/I Got You and I'm Glad	1973	—	2.50	5.00
STAX					
163	Can't See You When I Want To/Win You Over	1965	5.00	10.00	20.00
Albums					
ENTERPRISE					
ENS-1009	Gritty, Groovy, & Gettin' It	1970	5.00	10.00	20.00
ENS-1012	David Porter...Into a Real Thing	1971	5.00	10.00	20.00
ENS-1019	Victim of the Joke?	1972	5.00	10.00	20.00
ENS-1026	Sweat and Love	1973	5.00	10.00	20.00

PORTER, ROYCE

Number	Title (A Side/B Side)	Yr	VG	VG+	NM
45s					
D					
1026	Lookin'/I Still Belong to You	1958	25.00	50.00	100.00
LOOK					
1001	Yes I Do/(B-side unknown)	1957	62.50	125.00	250.00
MERCURY					
71314	Good Time/Beach of Love	1958	25.00	50.00	100.00

PORTRAITS, THE (1)

Number	Title (A Side/B Side)	Yr	VG	VG+	NM
45s					
CAPITOL					
F-4181	Close to You/Easy Cash	1959	7.50	15.00	30.00

PORTRAITS, THE (2)

Number	Title (A Side/B Side)	Yr	VG	VG+	NM
45s					
SIDEWALK					
928	A Million to One/Let's Tell the World	1967	3.75	7.50	15.00
935	Over the Rainbow/Runaround Girl	1968	5.00	10.00	20.00

PORTRAITS, THE (3)

Number	Title (A Side/B Side)	Yr	VG	VG+	NM
45s					
TRI-DISC					
109	We're Gonna Party/Three Blind Mice	1963	3.75	7.50	15.00

PORTRAITS, THE (U)

Could be group (1) or (3).

Number	Title (A Side/B Side)	Yr	VG	VG+	NM
45s					
RCA VICTOR					
47-7900	Yo-Yo Girl/My Big Brother's Friend	1961	3.75	7.50	15.00

POSEY, SANDY

Number	Title (A Side/B Side)	Yr	VG	VG+	NM
45s					
AUDIOGRAPH					
449	Can't Get Used to Sleeping Without You/(B-side unknown)	1983	—	2.00	4.00
COLUMBIA					
45360	Losing Out on You/You Say Beautiful Things to Me	1971	—	2.50	5.00
45458	Bring Him Safely Home To Me/A Man in Need of Love	1971	—	2.50	5.00
45596	Why Don't We Go Somewhere and Love/Together	1972	—	2.50	5.00
45703	Happy Happy Birthday Baby/Thank the Lord for New York City	1972	—	2.50	5.00
45828	Don't/Thank the Lord for New York City	1973	—	2.50	5.00
45828	Don't/Thank the Lord for New York City	1973	—	2.50	5.00
MGM					
13501	Born a Woman/Caution to the Wind	1967	2.00	4.00	8.00
13612	Single Girl/Blue Is My Best Color	1966	2.00	4.00	8.00
13612 [PS]	Single Girl/Blue Is My Best Color	1966	3.00	6.00	12.00
13702	What a Woman in Love Won't Do/Shattered	1967	2.00	4.00	8.00
13744	I Take It Back/The Boy I Love	1967	2.00	4.00	8.00
13744 [PS]	I Take It Back/The Boy I Love	1967	3.00	6.00	12.00
13824	Are You Never Coming Home/I Can Show You How to Live	1967	2.00	4.00	8.00
13892	Silly Girl, Silly Boy/Something I'll Remember	1968	—	3.00	6.00
13967	Ways of the World/Wonderful World of Summer	1968	—	3.00	6.00
14006	All Hung Up in Your Green Eyes/Your Conception of Love	1968	—	3.00	6.00
MONUMENT					
8698	Trying to Live Without You Kind of Days/Why Do We Carry On	1976	—	2.50	5.00
WARNER BROS.					
8289	It's Midnight (Do You Know Where Your Baby Is)/Long Distance Kissing	1976	—	2.00	4.00
8540	Born to Be with You/It's Not Too Late	1978	—	2.00	4.00
8610	Love, Love, Love-Chapel of Love/I Believe in Love	1978	—	2.00	4.00
8731	Love Is Sometimes Easy/I Believe in Love	1979	—	2.00	4.00
8852	Try Home/Love Is Sometimes Easy	1979	—	2.00	4.00
49104	Black Is the Night/Best Things in My Life	1979	—	2.00	4.00
Albums					
COLUMBIA					
KC 31594	Why Don't We Go Somewhere and Love	1972	3.00	6.00	12.00
MGM					
GAS-125	Sandy Posey (Golden Archive Series)	1970	3.75	7.50	15.00
E-4418 [M]	Born a Woman	1966	3.75	7.50	15.00
SE-4418 [S]	Born a Woman	1966	5.00	10.00	20.00
E-4455 [M]	Single Girl	1967	5.00	10.00	20.00
SE-4455 [S]	Single Girl	1967	5.00	10.00	20.00
E-4480 [M]	I Take It Back	1967	5.00	10.00	20.00
SE-4480 [S]	I Take It Back	1967	5.00	10.00	20.00
E-4509 [M]	The Best of Sandy Posey	1967	6.25	12.50	25.00
SE-4509 [S]	The Best of Sandy Posey	1967	5.00	10.00	20.00
E-4525 [M]	Looking at You	1968	6.25	12.50	25.00
SE-4525 [S]	Looking at You	1968	3.75	7.50	15.00
ST-91110	Single Girl	1967	6.25	12.50	25.00
—Capitol Record Club issue					

POSEY, SANDY/ SKEETER DAVIS

Also see each artist's individual listings.

Number	Title (A Side/B Side)	Yr	VG	VG+	NM
Albums					
GUSTO					
0005	The Best of Sandy Posey/Skeeter Davis	198?	2.00	4.00	8.00

POSITIVELY 13 O'CLOCK

Number	Title (A Side/B Side)	Yr	VG	VG+	NM
45s					
HANNA-BARBERA					
500	Psychotic Reaction/13 O'Clock Theme for Psychotics	1966	10.00	20.00	40.00

POSSESSIONS, THE

Number	Title (A Side/B Side)	Yr	VG	VG+	NM
45s					
BRITTON					
1003	No More Love/You and Your Lies	1964	10.00	20.00	40.00
1003	No More Love/You and Your Lies	1964	17.50	35.00	70.00
—Blue vinyl					
PARKWAY					
930	No More Love/You and Your Lies	1964	5.00	10.00	20.00

POSSUM

Possibly two different groups.

Number	Title (A Side/B Side)	Yr	VG	VG+	NM
45s					
HIGHLAND					
10	The Cockroach That Ate Cincinnati/Chula Vista	1966	3.75	7.50	15.00
Albums					
CAPITOL					
ST-648	Possum	1970	3.00	6.00	12.00

POSSUM HUNTERS, THE

Number	Title (A Side/B Side)	Yr	VG	VG+	NM
Albums					
TAKOMA					
C-1010	Death on Lee Highway	1970	5.00	10.00	20.00

POST, MIKE

Number	Title (A Side/B Side)	Yr	VG	VG+	NM
45s					
BELL					
45155	Nicholas and Alexandra's Theme/Kotch	1971	—	2.50	5.00
ELEKTRA					
47186	The Theme from Hill Street Blues/Aaron's Tune	1981	—	2.00	4.00
47186 [PS]	The Theme from Hill Street Blues/Aaron's Tune	1981	—	2.00	4.00
47400	Theme from Magnum, P.I./Gumbus Bed	1982	—	2.00	4.00
47400 [PS]	Theme from Magnum, P.I./Gumbus Bed	1982	—	2.00	4.00
47477	School's Out/Aaron's Tune	1982	—	2.00	4.00
EPIC					
50325	Theme from "Baa Baa Black Sheep"/Southbound	1976	—	2.00	4.00
MGM					
14772	The Rockford Files/Dixie Lullabye	1974	—	2.50	5.00
14829	Manhattan Spiritual/Lay Back Lafayette	1975	—	2.00	4.00
MUSIC FACTORY					
419	Harper Valley P.T.A./Walking to San Francisco	1968	2.00	4.00	8.00
POLYDOR					
887145-7	Theme from "L.A. Law"/Jenny's Ayre	1987	—	2.00	4.00
REPRISE					
0406	For My Home/Long Time Alone	1965	2.50	5.00	10.00
0468	Hard Times/Louisiana Man	1966	2.50	5.00	10.00
WARNER BROS.					
7357	Bubble Gum Breakthrough/Not a Blade of Grass	1969	2.00	4.00	8.00
Albums					
ELEKTRA					
60028 [EP]	Television Theme Songs	1982	2.00	4.00	8.00

Number	Title (A Side/B Side)	Yr	VG	VG+	NM
MGM					
M3G-5005	Railhead Overture	1975	2.50	5.00	10.00
POLYDOR					
833985-1	Theme from L.A. Law and Otherwise	1987	2.00	4.00	8.00
RCA VICTOR					
AFL1-5415	Mike Post	1985	2.50	5.00	10.00

POSTA, ADRIENNE

45s

Number	Title (A Side/B Side)	Yr	VG	VG+	NM
LONDON					
9782	When a Girl Really Loves You/Winds That Bloe	1966	2.50	5.00	10.00

POTLIQUOR

45s

Number	Title (A Side/B Side)	Yr	VG	VG+	NM
CAPITOL					
4795	Misery/Oh So Long	1979	—	2.00	4.00
4819	Boy Oh Boy/Red Stick	1980	—	2.00	4.00
JANUS					
139	Down the River Boogie/Riverboat	1970	—	2.50	5.00
179	Cheer/Chattanooga	1972	—	2.50	5.00
186	Beyond the River Jordan/(B-side unknown)	1972	—	2.50	5.00
195	Waitin' for Me at the River/(B-side unknown)	1972	—	2.50	5.00

Albums

Number	Title (A Side/B Side)	Yr	VG	VG+	NM
CAPITOL					
ST-11998	Potliquor	1979	2.50	5.00	10.00
JANUS					
JLS-3002	Potliquor	1970	3.75	7.50	15.00
JLS-3033	Levee Blues	1972	3.75	7.50	15.00
JLS-3036	Louisiana Rock and Roll	1973	3.75	7.50	15.00

POWDER PUFFS, THE

45s

Number	Title (A Side/B Side)	Yr	VG	VG+	NM
IMPERIAL					
66014	(You Can't Take) My Boyfriend's Woody/Woody Wagon	1964	6.25	12.50	25.00

POWELL, ADAM CLAYTON

Albums

Number	Title (A Side/B Side)	Yr	VG	VG+	NM
JUBILEE					
JGM 2062 [M]	Keep the Faith, Baby!	1967	3.75	7.50	15.00

POWELL, AUSTIN

45s

Number	Title (A Side/B Side)	Yr	VG	VG+	NM
ATLANTIC					
968	Wrong Again/What More Can I Ask	1952	50.00	100.00	200.00
DECCA					
48206	All This Can't Be True/Some Other Spring	1951	20.00	40.00	80.00

POWELL, CHRIS, AND THE FIVE BLUE FLAMES

45s

Number	Title (A Side/B Side)	Yr	VG	VG+	NM
COLUMBIA					
39272	Country Girl Blues/Man with a Horn	1951	37.50	75.00	150.00
39407	My Love Has Gone/In the Cool of the Evening	1951	125.00	250.00	500.00
GRAND					
108	Sweet Sue Mambo/Uh Uh Baby	1953	12.50	25.00	50.00
112	Secret Love Mambo/I Love Paris Mambo	1954	12.50	25.00	50.00
116	Dinah/Song of the Vagabond	1954	12.50	25.00	50.00
120	Mr. Sandman/Mambo Gunch	1954	12.50	25.00	50.00
124	Anniversary Waltz/Sweet Georgia Brown	1955	10.00	20.00	40.00
127	Mandolin Mambo/The Whiffenpoof Song	1955	10.00	20.00	40.00
GROOVE					
0105	Break It Up/Love Ya Like Crazy	1955	5.00	10.00	20.00
0111	Unchained Melody/Something's Gotta Give	1955	5.00	10.00	20.00
0128	Goodbye Little Girl/Chinatown	1955	5.00	10.00	20.00
0144	Moritat/The Poor People of Paris	1956	5.00	10.00	20.00
OKEH					
6818	The Masquerade Is Over/Talkin'	1951	75.00	150.00	300.00
6850	October Twilight/That's Right	1952	25.00	50.00	100.00
6875	Ida Red/Darn That Dream	1952	25.00	50.00	100.00
6900	Blue Boy/I Come from Jamaica	1952	25.00	50.00	100.00

POWELL, JIMMY

45s

Number	Title (A Side/B Side)	Yr	VG	VG+	NM
DECCA					
32685	Stranger on a Train/Sugar Man	1970	—	3.00	6.00
LONDON					
9545	I Love You/Dance Her By Me (One More Time)	1962	2.50	5.00	10.00

POWELL, SANDY

45s

Number	Title (A Side/B Side)	Yr	VG	VG+	NM
HERALD					
557	Bon Bon/Pistol-Packin' Mama	1961	25.00	50.00	100.00
IMPALA					
211	Bon Bon/Pistol-Packin' Mama	1961	75.00	150.00	300.00
SINGULAR					
714	My Jimmie/Next Thing to Paradise	1958	6.25	12.50	25.00

POWER, DUFFY

45s

Number	Title (A Side/B Side)	Yr	VG	VG+	NM
EPIC					
10650	Hellhound/Hummingbird	1970	—	3.00	6.00
VEEP					
1204	Where Am I/I Don't Care	1964	3.00	6.00	12.00

Albums

Number	Title (A Side/B Side)	Yr	VG	VG+	NM
GSF					
1005	Duffy Power	1973	2.50	5.00	10.00

POWERS, JETT

See P.J. PROBY.

POWERS, JOEY

45s

Number	Title (A Side/B Side)	Yr	VG	VG+	NM
AMY					
892	Midnight Mary/Where Do You Want the World Delivered	1963	3.00	6.00	12.00
898	Billy Old Buddy/In the Morning Gloria	1964	2.50	5.00	10.00
903	Love Is a Season/You Comb Her Hair	1964	2.50	5.00	10.00
914	Tears Keep Falling/Where Did the Summer Go	1964	2.50	5.00	10.00
986	Gimmie Gimmie/Baila Maria	1967	2.00	4.00	8.00
MGM					
13421	I Love You/Leave Me Alone	1965	2.00	4.00	8.00
RCA VICTOR					
47-8039	Two Tickets and a Candy Heart/Jenny, Won't You Walk Up?	1962	2.50	5.00	10.00
47-8119	Don't Envy Me/Me, Myself and I	1962	2.50	5.00	10.00
47-9790	Hard to Be Without You/You're in a Bad Way	1969	—	2.50	5.00
—As "Joey Powers' Flower"					
74-0326	Land of the Midnight Sun/So Sing the Children on the Avenue	1970	—	2.50	5.00
—As "Joey Powers' Flower"					

Albums

Number	Title (A Side/B Side)	Yr	VG	VG+	NM
AMY					
8001 [M]	Midnight Mary	1964	7.50	15.00	30.00

POWERS, JOHNNY

45s

Number	Title (A Side/B Side)	Yr	VG	VG+	NM
FORTUNE					
199	Honey Let's Go (To a Rock and Roll Show)/Your Love	1955	50.00	100.00	200.00
FOX					
916	Rock Rock/Long Blonde Hair, Red Rose Lips	1957	125.00	250.00	500.00
HI-Q					
5044	Rock the Universe/Honey Let's Go (To a Rock and Roll Show)	1958	25.00	50.00	100.00
SUN					
327	With Your Love, With Your Kiss/Be Mine, All Mine	1959	12.50	25.00	50.00
TRIODEX					
103	A Teenage Prayer/A Young Boy's Heart	1960	6.25	12.50	25.00

POWERS OF BLUE, THE

45s

Number	Title (A Side/B Side)	Yr	VG	VG+	NM
MTA					
113	Good Lovin'/(I Can't Get No) Satisfaction	1966	2.50	5.00	10.00
118	Cool Jerk/You Blow My Mind	1967	2.00	4.00	8.00

Albums

Number	Title (A Side/B Side)	Yr	VG	VG+	NM
MTA					
1002 [M]	Flipout	1967	7.50	15.00	30.00
5002 [S]	Flipout	1967	7.50	15.00	30.00

POZO-SECO SINGERS, THE

DON WILLIAMS was in this group.

45s

Number	Title (A Side/B Side)	Yr	VG	VG+	NM
CERTRON					
10006	Apartment #9/Comin' Apart	1970	—	2.50	5.00
10020	Strawberry Fields & Something/There's Never Been a Time	1970	—	2.50	5.00
10033	Bringing It Down to Me/He's a Friend of Mine	1971	—	2.50	5.00
COLUMBIA					
43437	Time/Down the Road I Go	1965	2.00	4.00	8.00
43646	I'll Be Gone/It Ain't Worth the Lonely Road Back	1966	2.00	4.00	8.00
43784	I Can Make It With You/Come a Little Bit Closer	1966	2.00	4.00	8.00
43927	Look What You've Done/Almost Persuaded	1966	2.00	4.00	8.00
44041	I Believed It All/Excuse Me Dear Martha	1967	2.00	4.00	8.00
44168	It's All Right/Morning Dew	1967	2.00	4.00	8.00
44263	Louisiana Man/Tomorrow Proper	1967	2.00	4.00	8.00
44598	Gotta Come Up with Something/The Renegade	1968	—	3.00	6.00
44690	Good Morning Today/Remember Suzie	1968	—	3.00	6.00
44841	Leavin'/Creole Woman	1969	—	3.00	6.00
44979	Woman in Love/God Save the Children	1969	—	3.00	6.00
—As "Susan Taylor and Pozo Seco"					
44980	Morning Mama Memories/The Proper Mrs. Brown	1969	2.50	5.00	10.00
—As "Don Williams and Pozo Seco"; his first "solo" credit					
45065	High on Life/Till You Hear Your Mama Call	1970	—	3.00	6.00
EDMARK					
10017	Time/Down the Road I Go	1965	5.00	10.00	20.00

Albums

Number	Title (A Side/B Side)	Yr	VG	VG+	NM
CERTRON					
CS-7007	Spend Some Time with Me	1970	3.75	7.50	15.00
COLUMBIA					
CL 2515 [M]	Time/I'll Be Gone	1966	3.75	7.50	15.00
CL 2600 [M]	I Can Make It with You	1967	5.00	10.00	20.00
CS 9315 [S]	Time/I'll Be Gone	1966	5.00	10.00	20.00
CS 9400 [S]	I Can Make It with You	1967	3.75	7.50	15.00
CS 9656	Shades of Time	1968	3.75	7.50	15.00
POWER PAK					
285	The Pozo-Seco Singers with Don Williams	198?	2.50	5.00	10.00

PRADO, PEREZ

45s

Number	Title (A Side/B Side)	Yr	VG	VG+	NM
RCA VICTOR					
47-3782	El Mambo/Mambo #5	1950	5.00	10.00	20.00
47-3873	Chattanoogie Shoe Shine Boy/More Mambo Jambo	1950	3.75	7.50	15.00
47-3917	Mambo #8/Babarabatiri	1950	3.75	7.50	15.00
47-3918	Pachito E-Che/Mambo #5	1950	3.75	7.50	15.00
47-3988	Cuban Mambo/Mambo del Papelero	1950	3.75	7.50	15.00
47-4196	Syncopated Clock Mambo/Broadway Mambo	1951	3.75	7.50	15.00

Number	Title (A Side/B Side)	Yr	VG	VG+	NM
47-4319	C'est Si Bon Mambo/In a Little Spanish Town Mambo	1951	3.75	7.50	15.00
47-5281	A La Billy May/Beautiful	1953	3.00	6.00	12.00
47-5367	Anna/Silvana Mangano	1953	3.00	6.00	12.00
47-5738	Such a Night/Ballin' the Jack	1954	3.00	6.00	12.00
47-5820	St. Louis Blues Mambo/Tomcat Mambo	1954	3.00	6.00	12.00
47-5839	Skokiaan/The High and the Mighty	1954	3.00	6.00	12.00
47-5892	Marilyn Monroe Mambo/Steam Heat Mambo	1954	6.25	12.50	25.00
47-5965	Cherry Pink and Apple Blossom White/Rhythm Sticks	1954	3.00	6.00	12.00
47-6085	Mood Indigo/Back Bay Shuffle (Mambo)	1955	2.50	5.00	10.00
47-6122	Whatever Lola Wants/Dilo (Mambo)	1955	2.50	5.00	10.00
47-6214	Crazy, Crazy/Monitor Mambo	1955	2.50	5.00	10.00
47-6277	Pretty Doll/La Macarena	1955	2.50	5.00	10.00
47-6375	Red River Valley Mambo/Black Horse Mambo	1955	2.50	5.00	10.00
47-6477	The Story of Love/Tomorrow I Will Live	1956	2.50	5.00	10.00
47-6538	Cuban Rock/Hawaiian War Chant	1956	3.00	6.00	12.00
47-6684	Petticoats of Portugal/Bandido	1956	2.50	5.00	10.00
47-6752	Bongo Bash/Donna	1956	2.50	5.00	10.00
47-6776	Hawaiian Cha Cha Cha/Mambo Japanese	1956	2.50	5.00	10.00
47-6882	Rum and Coca-Cola/Cose, Cose, Cose	1957	2.50	5.00	10.00
47-6960	Calypso Man/Cucara Cha Cha Cha	1957	2.50	5.00	10.00
47-7120	A Lo Loco/Kilindini Dance	1957	2.50	5.00	10.00
47-7245	Patricia/Why Wait	1958	2.50	5.00	10.00
47-7337	Guaglione/Paris	1958	2.00	4.00	8.00
47-7456	The Millionaire/Catalania	1959	2.00	4.00	8.00
47-7630	Clap Hands/Divina	1959	2.00	4.00	8.00
47-7768	Oh, Oh, Rosie/Rockambo Baby	1960	2.00	4.00	8.00
47-7826	Julie Is Her Name/Be True to Me	1960	2.00	4.00	8.00
47-7873	Teresita La Chunga/Ritmo De Chunga	1961	2.00	4.00	8.00
47-7963	Arrivederci Roma/Moliendo Café	1961	2.00	4.00	8.00
47-8006	Patricia Twist/Ti-Pi-Tin Twist	1962	2.00	4.00	8.00
47-8077	La Raggaza (The Girl)/Via Veneto	1962	2.00	4.00	8.00
47-8204	Katanga/Teresita	1963	2.00	4.00	8.00
47-8259	Natalia Dengue/El Dengue	1963	2.00	4.00	8.00
47-8356	Caravan/Papa Mi	1964	2.00	4.00	8.00
61-8520 [S]	You're Driving Me Crazy! (What Did I Do?)/Taking a Chance on Love	1960	6.25	12.50	25.00
—"Living Stereo" (large hole, plays at 45 rpm)					
UNITED ARTISTS					
765	The Girl with the Green Eyes/Woman of Straw	1964	2.00	4.00	8.00

7-Inch Extended Plays

Number	Title (A Side/B Side)	Yr	VG	VG+	NM
RCA VICTOR					
LPC-114	Cherry Pink and Apple Blossom White/Mambo No. 5//In a Little Spanish Town/Patricia	1961	3.00	6.00	12.00
—"Compact 33 Double" with small hole					
LPC-114 [PS]	Big Hits by Prado	1961	3.00	6.00	12.00

Albums

Number	Title	Yr	VG	VG+	NM
RCA CAMDEN					
CAL-409 [M]	Mambo Happy!	1957	5.00	10.00	20.00
CAL-547 [M]	Latino!	1960	5.00	10.00	20.00
RCA VICTOR					
LPM-21 [10]	Perez Prado Plays Mucho Mambo for Dancing	1951	15.00	30.00	60.00
LPM-1075 [M]	Mambo Mania	1955	10.00	20.00	40.00
LPM-1101 [M]	Voodoo Suite (and Six All-Time Greats)	1955	10.00	20.00	40.00
LPM-1196 [M]	Mambo by the King	1956	10.00	20.00	40.00
LPM-1257 [M]	Havana 3 A.M.	1956	10.00	20.00	40.00
LPM-1459 [M]	Latin Satin	1957	10.00	20.00	40.00
LPM-1556 [M]	"Prez"	1958	7.50	15.00	30.00
LSP-1556 [S]	"Prez"	1959	10.00	20.00	40.00
LPM-1883 [M]	Dilo (Ugh!)	1958	7.50	15.00	30.00
LSP-1883 [S]	Dilo (Ugh!)	1959	10.00	20.00	40.00
ANL1-1941	Pure Gold	1975	2.50	5.00	10.00
LPM-2028 [M]	Pops and Prado	1959	7.50	15.00	30.00
LSP-2028 [S]	Pops and Prado	1959	10.00	20.00	40.00
LPM-2104 [M]	Big Hits by Prado	1959	7.50	15.00	30.00
LSP-2104 [S]	Big Hits by Prado	1959	10.00	20.00	40.00
LPM-2133 [M]	A Touch of Tabasco	1960	5.00	10.00	20.00
LSP-2133 [S]	A Touch of Tabasco	1960	7.50	15.00	30.00
LPM-2308 [M]	Rockambo	1961	5.00	10.00	20.00
LSP-2308 [S]	Rockambo	1961	7.50	15.00	30.00
LPM-2379 [M]	The New Dance La Chunga	1961	5.00	10.00	20.00
LSP-2379 [S]	The New Dance La Chunga	1961	7.50	15.00	30.00
LPM-2524 [M]	The Twist Goes Latin	1962	5.00	10.00	20.00
LSP-2524 [S]	The Twist Goes Latin	1962	7.50	15.00	30.00
LPM-2571 [M]	Exotic Suite	1962	5.00	10.00	20.00
LSP-2571 [S]	Exotic Suite	1962	7.50	15.00	30.00
LPM-2610 [M]	Our Man in Latin America	1963	5.00	10.00	20.00
LSP-2610 [S]	Our Man in Latin America	1963	7.50	15.00	30.00
LPM-3108 [10]	Mambo by the King	1953	15.00	30.00	60.00
LPM-3330 [M]	Dance Latino	1965	3.75	7.50	15.00
LSP-3330 [S]	Dance Latino	1965	5.00	10.00	20.00
LPM-3732 [M]	The Best of Perez Prado	1967	5.00	10.00	20.00
LSP-3732 [S]	The Best of Perez Prado	1967	3.75	7.50	15.00
VPS-6066 [(2)]	This Is Perez Prado	1972	3.75	7.50	15.00
UNITED ARTISTS					
LS-61032	Estas Si Viven (The Living End)	196?	3.75	7.50	15.00

PRATT, ANDY

45s

Number	Title (A Side/B Side)	Yr	VG	VG+	NM
COLUMBIA					
45804	Avenging Annie/So Fine (It's Frightening)	1973	—	2.50	5.00
NEMPEROR					
007	If You Could See Yourself (Through My Eyes)/(B-side unknown)	1976	—	2.00	4.00
008	Some Things Go On Forever/That's When Miracles Occur	1976	—	2.00	4.00
013	All I Want Is You/(B-side unknown)	1977	—	2.00	4.00

Albums

Number	Title	Yr	VG	VG+	NM
COLUMBIA					
KC 31722	Andy Pratt	1973	2.50	5.00	10.00
NEMPEROR					
SD 438	Resolution	1976	2.50	5.00	10.00
SD 443	Shiver in the Night	1977	2.50	5.00	10.00
POLYDOR					
24-4015	Records Are Like Life	1970	3.00	6.00	12.00

PRATT & MCCLAIN

45s

Number	Title (A Side/B Side)	Yr	VG	VG+	NM
ABC DUNHILL					
4387	Spirit of Love/When My Ship Comes In	1974	—	2.50	5.00
15004	Turn, Turn, Turn/Here I Am	1974	—	2.50	5.00
15024	We've Lost the Magic/When My Ship Comes In	1974	—	2.50	5.00
REPRISE					
1351	Happy Days/Cruisin' with the Fonz	1976	—	2.50	5.00
1367	Devil with a Blue Dress/Tonight We're Gonna Fall in Love	1976	—	2.00	4.00
1367	One Way or the Other/Tonight We're Gonna Fall in Love	1976	—	—	—
—Canceled?					
1373	Whachersign/Who Needs It	1976	—	2.00	4.00

Albums

Number	Title	Yr	VG	VG+	NM
ABC DUNHILL					
DSX-50164	Pratt-McClain	1974	3.00	6.00	12.00
REPRISE					
MS 2250	Pratt & McClain Featuring "Happy Days"	1976	2.50	5.00	10.00

PREACHERS, THE

45s

Number	Title (A Side/B Side)	Yr	VG	VG+	NM
CHALLENGE					
501	Vitamin L.O.V.E./Till the Dawn	1969	3.00	6.00	12.00
MOONGLOW					
240	Who Do You Love/Chicken Poppa	1965	6.25	12.50	25.00
5006	Pain and Sorrow/Stay Out of My World	1965	5.00	10.00	20.00

PRECISIONS, THE (1)

45s

Number	Title (A Side/B Side)	Yr	VG	VG+	NM
ATCO					
6643	Don't Double (With Trouble)/Into My Life	1969	3.00	6.00	12.00
6669	New York City/You're the Best (That Ever Did It)	1969	3.00	6.00	12.00
D-TOWN					
1033	My Lover Come Back/I Wanna Tell My Baby	1965	50.00	100.00	200.00
1055	Mexican Love Song/You're Sweet	1965	6.25	12.50	25.00
DREW					
1001	Such Misery/Lover's Plea	1967	6.25	12.50	25.00
1002	Why Girl/What I Want	1967	3.75	7.50	15.00
1003	If This Is Love (I'd Rather Be Lonely)/You'll Soon Be Gone	1967	6.25	12.50	25.00
1004	Instant Heartbreak/Dream Girl	1968	3.75	7.50	15.00
1005	A Place/Never Let Her Go	1968	3.75	7.50	15.00

PRECISIONS, THE (2)

45s

Number	Title (A Side/B Side)	Yr	VG	VG+	NM
HIGHLAND					
300	Eight Reasons Why I Love You/(B-side unknown)	1962	100.00	200.00	400.00

PRECISIONS, THE (U)

May be group (2); could be someone else.

45s

Number	Title (A Side/B Side)	Yr	VG	VG+	NM
RAYNA					
1001	White Christmas/Silent Night	19??	25.00	50.00	100.00

PRELUDE

45s

Number	Title (A Side/B Side)	Yr	VG	VG+	NM
ISLAND					
IXPI 1 [DJ]	Christmas Message (same on both sides)	1974	2.50	5.00	10.00
002	After the Goldrush/Johnson Boy	1974	—	3.00	6.00
018	Fly/Lady from a Small Town	1975	—	2.50	5.00
PYE					
71045	For a Dancer/Best of a Bad Time	1975	—	2.50	5.00

Albums

Number	Title	Yr	VG	VG+	NM
ISLAND					
ILPS 9282	After the Gold Rush	1974	3.00	6.00	12.00
PYE					
12120	Owlcreek Incident	1975	3.00	6.00	12.00
12139	Back Into the Light	1976	3.00	6.00	12.00

PRELUDES, THE (1)

45s

Number	Title (A Side/B Side)	Yr	VG	VG+	NM
ARLISS					
1004	Lorraine/Oh Please, Genie	1961	20.00	40.00	80.00
OCTAVIA					
8008	A Place for You (In My Heart)/That Would Be So Good	1962	10.00	20.00	40.00

PRELUDES, THE (2)

45s

Number	Title (A Side/B Side)	Yr	VG	VG+	NM
CUB					
9005	Kingdom of Love/Vanishing Angel	1958	37.50	75.00	150.00

PRELUDES, THE (3)

45s

Number	Title (A Side/B Side)	Yr	VG	VG+	NM
EMPIRE					
103	Don't Fall in Love Too Soon/I Want Your Arms Around Me (All the Time)	1956	25.00	50.00	100.00

PRELUDES FIVE, THE

45s

Number	Title (A Side/B Side)	Yr	VG	VG+	NM
PIK					
231	Starlight/Don't You Know Love?	1961	6.25	12.50	25.00

PREMEERS, THE

45s

Number	Title (A Side/B Side)	Yr	VG	VG+	NM
HERALD					
577	Diary of Our Love/Gee Oh Gee	1963	7.50	15.00	30.00

PREMIATA FORNERIA MARCONI

See P.F.M.

PREMIERS, THE (1)

45s

Number	Title (A Side/B Side)	Yr	VG	VG+	NM
FARO					
615	Farmer John/Duffy's Blues	1964	7.50	15.00	30.00
621	Get Your Baby/Little Ways	1965	3.00	6.00	12.00
624	Come On and Dance/Get On the Plane	1966	3.00	6.00	12.00
627	Ring Around My Rosie (Part 1)/Ring Around My Rosie (Part 2)	1967	3.00	6.00	12.00
WARNER BROS.					
5443	Farmer John/Duffy's Blues	1964	3.75	7.50	15.00
5464	Annie Oakley/Blues for Arlene	1964	3.00	6.00	12.00

Albums

Number	Title (A Side/B Side)	Yr	VG	VG+	NM
WARNER BROS.					
W 1565 [M]	Farmer John	1964	10.00	20.00	40.00
WS 1565 [S]	Farmer John	1964	12.50	25.00	50.00

PREMIERS, THE (2)

45s

Number	Title (A Side/B Side)	Yr	VG	VG+	NM
ALERT					
706	Jolene/Oh, Theresa	1959	25.00	50.00	100.00
FURY					
1029	I Pray/Pigtails, Eyes Are Blue	1960	10.00	20.00	40.00
RUST					
5032	Falling Star/She Gives Me Fever	1961	25.00	50.00	100.00

PREMIERS, THE (3)

45s

Number	Title (A Side/B Side)	Yr	VG	VG+	NM
CINDY					
3008	China Doll/Life Is Grand	1958	20.00	40.00	80.00
DIG					
106	New Moon/Baby	1956	37.50	75.00	150.00
113	My Darling/Have a Heart	1956	62.50	125.00	250.00
FORTUNE					
527	When You Are in Love/The Trap of Love	1956	20.00	40.00	80.00
GONE					
5009	Is It a Dream/Valerie	1957	125.00	250.00	500.00
—With correct track on side 1					
5009	Is It a Dream/Valerie	1957	50.00	100.00	200.00
—With "Let Me Share Your Dream" by The Deltas (Gone 5010) on Side 1 by mistake					
RCA VICTOR					
47-6958	Run Along Baby/Hey Miss Fancy	1957	20.00	40.00	80.00

PREMIERS, THE (4)

45s

Number	Title (A Side/B Side)	Yr	VG	VG+	NM
KING					
6061	She's Always There/I'm Better Off Now	1966	5.00	10.00	20.00
STAX					
177	Make It Me/You Make a Strong Girl Weak	1965	7.50	15.00	30.00

PREMIERS, THE (5)

45s

Number	Title (A Side/B Side)	Yr	VG	VG+	NM
MINK					
21	Tonight/I Think I Love You	1959	25.00	50.00	100.00
PARKWAY					
807	Tonight/I Think I Love You	1959	5.00	10.00	20.00

PREMIERS, THE (6)

45s

Number	Title (A Side/B Side)	Yr	VG	VG+	NM
NU-PHI					
367/8	Cruisin'/(B-side unknown)	1959	7.50	15.00	30.00
701	Firewater/Younger Than You	1960	7.50	15.00	30.00

PREMIERS, THE (U)

Could be one of the above groups; could be a completely different group.

45s

Number	Title (A Side/B Side)	Yr	VG	VG+	NM
BOND					
5803/4	Hop and Skip/Uh-Huh	1958	5.00	10.00	20.00

PRESENT, THE

45s

Number	Title (A Side/B Side)	Yr	VG	VG+	NM
PHILIPS					
40466	I Know/Many's the Slip Twixt the Cup and the Lip	1966	7.50	15.00	30.00

PRESIDENTS, THE (1)

45s

Number	Title (A Side/B Side)	Yr	VG	VG+	NM
SUSSEX					
200	For You/Gotta Keep Movin'	1970	—	3.50	7.00
207	5-10-15-20 (25-30 Years of Love)/I'm Still Dancing	1970	2.00	4.00	8.00
212	Triangle of Love (Hey Diddle Diddle)/Sweet Magic	1971	—	3.50	7.00
217	The Sweetest Thing This Side of Heaven/It's All Over Now	1971	—	3.50	7.00

Albums

Number	Title (A Side/B Side)	Yr	VG	VG+	NM
SUSSEX					
SXBX-7005	5-10-15-20 (25-30 Years of Love)	1970	6.25	12.50	25.00

PRESIDENTS, THE (2)

Not the same as group (1). The Sussex group's success forced this group to change its name, as reflected in the label credit on their final DeLuxe 45.

45s

Number	Title (A Side/B Side)	Yr	VG	VG+	NM
DELUXE					
113	Gold Walk/I Want My Baby	1969	2.00	4.00	8.00
120	Snoopy/Stinky	1969	2.00	4.00	8.00
127	Which Way/Peter Rabbit	1970	2.00	4.00	8.00
134	Lover's Psalm/Our Meeting	1971	—	3.00	6.00
—As "The President's Band"					

PRESIDENTS, THE (3)

45s

Number	Title (A Side/B Side)	Yr	VG	VG+	NM
MERCURY					
72016	Pots 'n' Pans/The Toasts	1962	5.00	10.00	20.00

PRESIDENTS, THE (U)

The Hollywood record could be group (1) or (2); the Warner Bros. record could be group (3).

45s

Number	Title (A Side/B Side)	Yr	VG	VG+	NM
HOLLYWOOD					
1137	Shoeshine (Part 1)/Shoeshine (Part 2)	1968	2.50	5.00	10.00
WARNER BROS.					
5240	Hot Toddy March/I Do Love You (Do I Love You)	1961	3.75	7.50	15.00

PRESLEY, ELVIS

12-Inch Singles

Number	Title (A Side/B Side)	Yr	VG	VG+	NM
RCA					
EP-0517 [DJ]	Little Sister/Rip It Up	1983	25.00	50.00	100.00

45s

Number	Title (A Side/B Side)	Yr	VG	VG+	NM
COLLECTABLES					
COL-4500	Good Rockin' Tonight/I Don't Care If the Sun Don't Shine	1986	—	—	3.00
—Black vinyl					
COL-4500	Good Rockin' Tonight/I Don't Care If the Sun Don't Shine	1992	—	2.00	4.00
—Gold vinyl					
COL-4501	You're a Heartbreaker/Milkcow Blues Boogie	1986	—	—	3.00
—Black vinyl					
COL-4501	You're a Heartbreaker/Milkcow Blues Boogie	1992	—	2.00	4.00
—Gold vinyl					
COL-4502	Baby Let's Play House/I'm Left, You're Right, She's Gone	1986	—	—	3.00
—Black vinyl					
COL-4502	Baby Let's Play House/I'm Left, You're Right, She's Gone	1992	—	2.00	4.00
—Gold vinyl					
COL-4503	I Got a Woman/I'm Counting on You	1986	—	—	3.00
—Black vinyl					
COL-4503	I Got a Woman/I'm Counting on You	1992	—	2.00	4.00
—Gold vinyl					
COL-4504	I'll Never Let You Go (Little Darlin')/I'm Gonna Sit Right Down and Cry (Over You)	1986	—	—	3.00
—Black vinyl					
COL-4504	I'll Never Let You Go (Little Darlin')/I'm Gonna Sit Right Down and Cry (Over You)	1992	—	2.00	4.00
—Gold vinyl					
COL-4505	Tryin' to Get to You/I Love You Because	1986	—	—	3.00
—Black vinyl					
COL-4505	Tryin' to Get to You/I Love You Because	1992	—	2.00	4.00
—Gold vinyl					
COL-4506	Money Honey/One-Sided Love Affair	1986	—	—	3.00
—Black vinyl					
COL-4506	Money Honey/One-Sided Love Affair	1992	—	2.00	4.00
—Gold vinyl					
COL-4507	Too Much/Playing for Keeps	1986	—	—	3.00
—Black vinyl					
COL-4507	Too Much/Playing for Keeps	1992	—	2.00	4.00
—Gold vinyl					
COL-4508	A Big Hunk o'Love/My Wish Came True	1986	—	—	3.00
—Black vinyl					
COL-4508	A Big Hunk o'Love/My Wish Came True	1992	—	2.00	4.00
—Gold vinyl					
COL-4509	Stuck on You/Fame and Fortune	1986	—	—	3.00
—Black vinyl					
COL-4509	Stuck on You/Fame and Fortune	1992	—	2.00	4.00
—Gold vinyl					
COL-4510	I Feel So Bad/Wild in the Country	1986	—	—	3.00
—Black vinyl					
COL-4510	I Feel So Bad/Wild in the Country	1992	—	2.00	4.00
—Gold vinyl					
COL-4511	She's Not You/Jailhouse Rock	1986	—	—	3.00
—Black vinyl					
COL-4511	She's Not You/Jailhouse Rock	1992	—	2.00	4.00
—Gold vinyl					
COL-4512	One Broken Heart for Sale/Devil in Disguise	1986	—	—	3.00
—Black vinyl					
COL-4512	One Broken Heart for Sale/Devil in Disguise	1992	—	2.00	4.00
—Gold vinyl					
COL-4513	Bossa Nova Baby/Such a Night	1986	—	—	3.00
—Black vinyl					
COL-4513	Bossa Nova Baby/Such a Night	1992	—	2.00	4.00
—Gold vinyl					
COL-4514	Love Me/Flaming Star	1986	—	—	3.00
—Black vinyl					
COL-4514	Love Me/Flaming Star	1992	—	2.00	4.00
—Gold vinyl					
COL-4515	Follow That Dream/When My Blue Moon Turns to Gold Again	1986	—	—	3.00
—Black vinyl					
COL-4515	Follow That Dream/When My Blue Moon Turns to Gold Again	1992	—	2.00	4.00
—Gold vinyl					

Number	Title (A Side/B Side)	Yr	VG	VG+	NM
COL-4516	Frankie and Johnny/Love Letters	1986	—	—	3.00
—Black vinyl					
COL-4516	Frankie and Johnny/Love Letters	1992	—	2.00	4.00
—Gold vinyl					
COL-4517	U.S. Male/Until It's Time for You to Go	1986	—	—	3.00
—Black vinyl					
COL-4517	U.S. Male/Until It's Time for You to Go	1992	—	2.00	4.00
—Gold vinyl					
COL-4518	Old Shep/You'll Never Walk Alone	1986	—	—	3.00
—Black vinyl					
COL-4518	Old Shep/You'll Never Walk Alone	1992	—	2.00	4.00
—Gold vinyl					
COL-4519	Poor Boy/An American Trilogy	1986	—	—	3.00
—Black vinyl					
COL-4519	Poor Boy/An American Trilogy	1992	—	2.00	4.00
—Gold vinyl					
COL-4520	How Great Thou Art/His Hand in Mine	1986	—	—	3.00
—Black vinyl					
COL-4520	How Great Thou Art/His Hand in Mine	1992	—	2.00	4.00
—Gold vinyl					
COL-4521	Big Boss Man/Paralyzed	1986	—	—	3.00
—Black vinyl					
COL-4521	Big Boss Man/Paralyzed	1992	—	2.00	4.00
—Gold vinyl					
COL-4522	Fools Fall in Love/Blue Suede Shoes	1986	—	—	3.00
—Black vinyl					
COL-4522	Fools Fall in Love/Blue Suede Shoes	1992	—	2.00	4.00
—Gold vinyl					
COL-4564	The Elvis Medley/Always on My Mind	1986	—	—	3.00
COL-4738	Ask Me/The Girl of My Best Friend	1997	—	—	3.00
COL-4743	Girls! Girls! Girls!/Ain't That Loving You Baby	1997	—	—	3.00
COL-4744	It's Only Love/Beyond the Reef	1997	—	—	3.00
04764	Witchcraft/Spinout	1997	—	—	3.00
80000	(Now and Then There's) A Fool Such As I/I Need Your Love Tonight	1997	—	2.00	4.00
—Gray marbled vinyl					
80001	Separate Ways/Always On My Mind	1997	—	2.00	4.00
—Gray marbled vinyl					
80002	An American Trilogy/Until It's Time for You to Go	1997	—	2.00	4.00
—Gray marbled vinyl					
80003	Crying in the Chapel/I Believe in the Man in the Sky	1997	—	2.00	4.00
—Gray marbled vinyl					
80004	Don't/I Beg of You	1997	—	2.00	4.00
—Gray marbled vinyl					
80005	Don't Cry Daddy/Rubberneckin'	1997	—	2.00	4.00
—Gray marbled vinyl					
80006	Good Luck Charm/Anything That's Part of You	1997	—	2.00	4.00
—Gray marbled vinyl					
80007	Guitar Man/Hi-Heel Sneakers	1997	—	2.00	4.00
—Gray marbled vinyl					
80008	Hard Headed Woman/Don't Ask Me Why	1997	—	2.00	4.00
—Gray marbled vinyl					
80009	Heartbreak Hotel/I Was the One	1997	—	2.00	4.00
—Gray marbled vinyl					
80010	Mystery Train/I Forgot to Remember to Forget	1997	—	2.00	4.00
—Gray marbled vinyl					
80011	One Night/I Got Stung	1997	—	2.00	4.00
—Gray marbled vinyl					
80012	I Really Don't Want to Know/There Goes My Everything	1997	—	2.00	4.00
—Gray marbled vinyl					
80013	I Want You, I Need You, I Love You/My Baby Left Me	1997	—	2.00	4.00
—Gray marbled vinyl					
80014	If I Can Dream/Edge of Reality	1997	—	2.00	4.00
—Gray marbled vinyl					
80015	Kentucky Rain/My Little Friend	1997	—	2.00	4.00
—Gray marbled vinyl					
80016	Kiss Me Quick/Suspicion	1997	—	2.00	4.00
—Gray marbled vinyl					
80017	Kissin' Cousins/It Hurts Me	1997	—	2.00	4.00
—Gray marbled vinyl					
80018	Marie's the Name His Latest Flame/Little Sister	1997	—	2.00	4.00
—Gray marbled vinyl					
80019	(Let Me Be You) Teddy Bear/Loving You	1997	—	2.00	4.00
—Gray marbled vinyl					
80020	The Wonder of You/Mama Liked the Roses	1997	—	2.00	4.00
—Gray marbled vinyl					
80021	Memories/Charro	1997	—	2.00	4.00
—Gray marbled vinyl					
80022	My Boy/Thinking About You	1997	—	2.00	4.00
—Gray marbled vinyl					
80023	Way Down/My Way	1997	—	2.00	4.00
—Gray marbled vinyl					
80024	Patch It Up/You Don't Have to Say You Love Me	1997	—	2.00	4.00
—Gray marbled vinyl					
80025	Surrender/Lonely Man	1997	—	2.00	4.00
—Gray marbled vinyl					
80026	That's All Right/Blue Moon of Kentucky	1997	—	2.00	4.00
—Gray marbled vinyl					
80027	Wear My Ring Around Your Neck/Doncha' Think It's Time	1997	—	2.00	4.00
—Gray marbled vinyl					
80028	Puppet on a String/Wooden Heart	1997	—	2.00	4.00
—Gray marbled vinyl					

RCA

Number	Title (A Side/B Side)	Yr	VG	VG+	NM
DME1-1803R	King of the Whole Wide World/King Creole	1997	3.75	7.50	15.00
—Red vinyl, marked as a promotional copy (about 3,000 pressed)					
DME1-1803	King of the Whole Wide World/King Creole	1997	2.00	4.00	8.00
—Gold vinyl (about 7,000 pressed)					
DME1-1803 [DJ]	King of the Whole Wide World/King Creole	1997	100.00	200.00	400.00
—Test pressings of above on green, blue, white and clear vinyl. Value is for any of them.					
DME1-1803 [PS]	King of the Whole Wide World/King Creole	1997	2.00	4.00	8.00
—Same picture sleeve with either edition					
8760-7-R	Heartbreak Hotel/Heartbreak Hotel	1988	—	2.50	5.00
—B-side by David Keith					
8760-7-R [PS]	Heartbreak Hotel/Heartbreak Hotel	1988	—	3.00	6.00
—"Pink Cadillac" sleeve					
8760-7-R [PS]	Heartbreak Hotel/Heartbreak Hotel	1988	20.00	40.00	80.00
—Promo-only sleeve of RCA executive Butch Waugh dressed as Elvis					
GB-10485	Take Good Care of Her/I've Got a Thing About You, Baby	1977	—	2.00	4.00
—Gold Standard Series; black label					
GB-10486	Separate Ways/Always on My Mind	1977	—	2.00	4.00
—Gold Standard Series; black label					
GB-10487	T-R-O-U-B-L-E/Mr. Songman	1977	—	2.00	4.00
—Gold Standard Series; black label					
GB-10488	Promised Land/It's Midnight	1977	—	2.00	4.00
—Gold Standard Series; black label					
GB-10489	My Boy/Thinking About You	1977	—	2.00	4.00
—Gold Standard Series; black label					
PB-10601	Hurt/For the Heart	1976	25.00	50.00	100.00
—Second pressings (very rare) on the 1976-88 "dog near top" black label					
JB-10857 [DJ]	Moody Blue/She Thinks I Still Care	1976	250.00	500.00	1000.
—Colored vinyl pressings exist in five different colors -- red, white, gold, blue green. Value is for any of them.					
PB-10857	Moody Blue/She Thinks I Still Care	1976	—	2.50	5.00
PB-10857 [PS]	Moody Blue/She Thinks I Still Care	1976	2.50	5.00	10.00
JH-10951 [DJ]	Let Me Be There (mono/stereo)	1977	50.00	100.00	200.00
—Promo only					
PB-10998	Way Down/Pledging My Love	1977	—	2.50	5.00
PB-10998 [PS]	Way Down/Pledging My Love	1977	2.50	5.00	10.00
PB-11099	Hound Dog/Don't Be Cruel	1977	—	2.00	4.00
PB-11099 [PS]	Hound Dog/Don't Be Cruel	1977	—	2.00	4.00
—From boxes "15 Golden Records, 30 Golden Hits" and "20 Golden Hits in Full Color Sleeves"					
PB-11100	In the Ghetto/Any Day Now	1977	—	2.00	4.00
PB-11100 [PS]	In the Ghetto/Any Day Now	1977	—	2.00	4.00
—From boxes "15 Golden Records, 30 Golden Hits" and "20 Golden Hits in Full Color Sleeves"					
PB-11101	Jailhouse Rock/Treat Me Nice	1977	—	2.00	4.00
PB-11101 [PS]	Jailhouse Rock/Treat Me Nice	1977	—	2.00	4.00
—From box "15 Golden Records, 30 Golden Hits"					
PB-11102	Can't Help Falling in Love/Rock-a-Hula Baby	1977	—	2.00	4.00
PB-11102 [PS]	Can't Help Falling in Love/Rock-a-Hula Baby	1977	—	2.00	4.00
—From boxes "15 Golden Records, 30 Golden Hits" and "20 Golden Hits in Full Color Sleeves"					
PB-11103	Suspicious Minds/You'll Think of Me	1977	—	2.00	4.00
PB-11103 [PS]	Suspicious Minds/You'll Think of Me	1977	—	2.00	4.00
—From box "15 Golden Records, 30 Golden Hits"					
PB-11104	Are You Lonesome To-Night?/I Gotta Know	1977	—	2.00	4.00
PB-11104 [PS]	Are You Lonesome To-Night?/I Gotta Know	1977	—	2.00	4.00
—From boxes "15 Golden Records, 30 Golden Hits" and "20 Golden Hits in Full Color Sleeves"					
PB-11105	Heartbreak Hotel/I Was the One	1977	—	2.00	4.00
PB-11105 [PS]	Heartbreak Hotel/I Was the One	1977	—	2.00	4.00
—From boxes "15 Golden Records, 30 Golden Hits" and "20 Golden Hits in Full Color Sleeves"					
PB-11106	All Shook Up/That's When Your Heartaches Begin	1977	—	2.00	4.00
PB-11106 [PS]	All Shook Up/That's When Your Heartaches Begin	1977	—	2.00	4.00
—From boxes "15 Golden Records, 30 Golden Hits" and "20 Golden Hits in Full Color Sleeves"					
PB-11107	Blue Suede Shoes/Tutti Frutti	1977	—	2.00	4.00
PB-11107 [PS]	Blue Suede Shoes/Tutti Frutti	1977	—	2.00	4.00
—From boxes "15 Golden Records, 30 Golden Hits" and "20 Golden Hits in Full Color Sleeves"					
PB-11108	Love Me Tender/Any Way You Want Me (That's How I Will Be)	1977	—	2.00	4.00
PB-11108 [PS]	Love Me Tender/Any Way You Want Me (That's How I Will Be)	1977	—	2.00	4.00
—From boxes "15 Golden Records, 30 Golden Hits" and "20 Golden Hits in Full Color Sleeves"					
PB-11109	(Let Me Be Your) Teddy Bear/Loving You	1977	—	2.00	4.00
PB-11109 [PS]	(Let Me Be Your) Teddy Bear/Loving You	1977	—	2.00	4.00
—From boxes "15 Golden Records, 30 Golden Hits" and "20 Golden Hits in Full Color Sleeves"					
PB-11110	It's Now or Never/A Mess of Blues	1977	—	2.00	4.00
PB-11110 [PS]	It's Now or Never/A Mess of Blues	1977	—	2.00	4.00
—From box "15 Golden Records, 30 Golden Hits"					
PB-11111	Return to Sender/Where Do You Come From	1977	—	2.00	4.00
PB-11111 [PS]	Return to Sender/Where Do You Come From	1977	—	2.00	4.00
—From boxes "15 Golden Records, 30 Golden Hits" and "20 Golden Hits in Full Color Sleeves"					
PB-11112	One Night/I Got Stung	1977	—	2.00	4.00
PB-11112 [PS]	One Night/I Got Stung	1977	—	2.00	4.00
—From box "15 Golden Records, 30 Golden Hits"					
PB-11113	Crying in the Chapel/I Believe in the Man in the Sky	1977	—	2.00	4.00
PB-11113 [PS]	Crying in the Chapel/I Believe in the Man in the Sky	1977	—	2.00	4.00
—From box "15 Golden Records, 30 Golden Hits"					
PB-11165	My Way/America	1977	—	2.50	5.00
PB-11165	My Way/America the Beautiful	1977	5.00	10.00	20.00
PB-11165 [PS]	My Way/America	1977	2.50	5.00	10.00
PB-11165 [PS]	My Way/America the Beautiful	1977	6.25	12.50	25.00
PB-11212	Unchained Melody/Softly, As I Leave You	1978	2.50	5.00	10.00
—Erroneously states "Vocal Accompaniment by Sherrill Nielsen" on "Unchained Melody" side					
PB-11212	Unchained Melody/Softly, As I Leave You	1978	—	2.50	5.00
—No credit to Sherrill Nielsen on the "Unchained Melody" side					
PB-11212 [PS]	Unchained Melody/Softly, As I Leave You	1978	2.50	5.00	10.00
PP-11301	15 Golden Records, 30 Golden Hits	1977	15.00	30.00	60.00
—Includes 15 records (11099-11113) and outer box					
PB-11320	(Let Me Be Your) Teddy Bear/Puppet on a String	1978	—	2.50	5.00
PB-11320 [PS]	(Let Me Be Your) Teddy Bear/Puppet on a String	1978	2.50	5.00	10.00
GB-11326	Moody Blue/For the Heart	1978	—	2.00	4.00
—Gold Standard Series					
PP-11340	20 Golden Hits in Full Color Sleeves	1977	20.00	40.00	80.00
—Includes 10 records (11099, 11100, 11102, 11104-11109, 11111) and outer box					
GB-11504	Way Down/My Way	1979	—	2.00	4.00
—Gold Standard Series					
PB-11533	Are You Sincere/Solitaire	1979	—	2.50	5.00
PB-11533 [PS]	Are You Sincere/Solitaire	1979	2.50	5.00	10.00
PB-11679	There's a Honky Tonk Angel (Who Will Take Me Back In)/I Got a Feelin' in My Body	1979	3.75	7.50	15.00
—Has full production credits (background vocals, strings) listed in error on both sides					
PB-11679	There's a Honky Tonk Angel (Who Will Take Me Back In)/I Got a Feelin' in My Body	1979	—	2.50	5.00
—Has production credits removed; only producers are listed					

Number	Title (A Side/B Side)	Yr	VG	VG+	NM
PB-11679 [PS]	There's a Honky Tonk Angel (Who Will Take Me Back In)/I Got a Feelin' in My Body	1979	2.50	5.00	10.00
GB-11988	Unchained Melody/Are You Sincere	1980	—	2.00	4.00
—Gold Standard Series					
JH-12158 [DJ]	Guitar Man (mono/stereo)	1981	75.00	150.00	300.00
—Promo only on red vinyl					
PB-12158	Guitar Man/Faded Love	1981	—	2.50	5.00
PB-12158 [PS]	Guitar Man/Faded Love	1981	2.50	5.00	10.00
JB-12205 [DJ]	Lovin' Arms/You Asked Me To	1981	75.00	150.00	300.00
—Promo only on green vinyl					
PB-12205	Lovin' Arms/You Asked Me To	1981	—	3.00	6.00
—Not issued with picture sleeve (bootlegs exist)					
PB-13058	There Goes My Everything/You'll Never Walk Alone	1982	—	2.50	5.00
PB-13058 [PS]	There Goes My Everything/You'll Never Walk Alone	1982	2.50	5.00	10.00
GB-13275	Suspicious Minds/You'll Think of Me	1982	—	2.00	4.00
—Gold Standard Series					
JH-13302	The Impossible Dream (The Quest)/An American Trilogy	1982	25.00	50.00	100.00
JH-13302 [PS]	The Impossible Dream (The Quest)/An American Trilogy	1982	25.00	50.00	100.00
—Promo only, distributed to visitors to Elvis' birthplace in Tupelo, Mississippi, in 1982.					
JB-13351 [DJ]	The Elvis Medley (Long Version)/The Elvis Medley (Short Version)	1982	75.00	150.00	300.00
—Promo only on gold vinyl					
PB-13351	The Elvis Medley/Always on My Mind	1982	—	2.50	5.00
PB-13351 [PS]	The Elvis Medley/Always on My Mind	1982	2.50	5.00	10.00
JB-13500 [DJ]	I Was the One/Wear My Ring Around Your Neck	1983	75.00	150.00	300.00
—Promo only on gold vinyl					
PB-13500	I Was the One/Wear My Ring Around Your Neck	1983	—	2.50	5.00
PB-13500 [PS]	I Was the One/Wear My Ring Around Your Neck	1983	2.50	5.00	10.00
JB-13547 [DJ]	Little Sister/Paralyzed	1983	75.00	150.00	300.00
—Promo only on blue vinyl					
PB-13547	Little Sister/Paralyzed	1983	—	2.50	5.00
PB-13547 [PS]	Little Sister/Paralyzed	1983	2.50	5.00	10.00
JB-13875 [DJ]	Baby Let's Play House/Hound Dog	1984	50.00	100.00	200.00
—Gold vinyl, custom label					
PB-13875	Baby Let's Play House/Hound Dog	1984	10.00	20.00	40.00
—Gold vinyl, custom label					
PB-13875 [PS]	Baby Let's Play House/Hound Dog	1984	10.00	20.00	40.00
PB-13885	Blue Suede Shoes/Tutti Frutti	1984	—	2.00	4.00
—From box "Elvis' Greatest Hits, Golden Singles, Volume 1"; gold vinyl					
PB-13885 [PS]	Blue Suede Shoes/Tutti Frutti	1984	—	2.00	4.00
PB-13886	Don't Be Cruel/Hound Dog	1984	—	2.00	4.00
—From box "Elvis' Greatest Hits, Golden Singles, Volume 1"; gold vinyl					
PB-13886 [PS]	Don't Be Cruel/Hound Dog	1984	—	2.00	4.00
PB-13887	I Want You, I Need You, I Love You/Love Me	1984	—	2.00	4.00
—From box "Elvis' Greatest Hits, Golden Singles, Volume 1"; gold vinyl					
PB-13887 [PS]	I Want You, I Need You, I Love You/Love Me	1984	—	2.00	4.00
PB-13888	All Shook Up/(Let Me Be Your) Teddy Bear	1984	—	2.00	4.00
—From box "Elvis' Greatest Hits, Golden Singles, Volume 1"; gold vinyl					
PB-13888 [PS]	All Shook Up/(Let Me Be Your) Teddy Bear	1984	—	2.00	4.00
PB-13889	It's Now or Never/Surrender	1984	—	2.00	4.00
—From box "Elvis' Greatest Hits, Golden Singles, Volume 1"; gold vinyl					
PB-13889 [PS]	It's Now or Never/Surrender	1984	—	2.00	4.00
PB-13890	In the Ghetto/If I Can Dream	1984	—	2.00	4.00
—From box "Elvis' Greatest Hits, Golden Singles, Volume 1"; gold vinyl					
PB-13890 [PS]	In the Ghetto/If I Can Dream	1984	—	2.00	4.00
PB-13891	That's All Right/Blue Moon of Kentucky	1984	—	2.00	4.00
—From box "Elvis' Greatest Hits, Golden Singles, Volume 2"; gold vinyl					
PB-13891 [PS]	That's All Right/Blue Moon of Kentucky	1984	—	2.00	4.00
PB-13892	Heartbreak Hotel/Jailhouse Rock	1984	—	2.00	4.00
—From box "Elvis' Greatest Hits, Golden Singles, Volume 2"; gold vinyl					
PB-13892 [PS]	Heartbreak Hotel/Jailhouse Rock	1984	—	2.00	4.00
PB-13893	Love Me Tender/Loving You	1984	—	2.00	4.00
—From box "Elvis' Greatest Hits, Golden Singles, Volume 2"; gold vinyl					
PB-13893 [PS]	Love Me Tender/Loving You	1984	—	2.00	4.00
PB-13894	(Marie's the Name) His Latest Flame/Little Sister	1984	—	2.00	4.00
—From box "Elvis' Greatest Hits, Golden Singles, Volume 2"; gold vinyl					
PB-13894 [PS]	(Marie's the Name) His Latest Flame/Little Sister	1984	—	2.00	4.00
PB-13895	Are You Lonesome Tonight/Can't Help Falling in Love	1984	—	2.00	4.00
—From box "Elvis' Greatest Hits, Golden Singles, Volume 2"; gold vinyl					
PB-13895 [PS]	Are You Lonesome Tonight/Can't Help Falling in Love	1984	—	2.00	4.00
PB-13896	Suspicious Minds/Burning Love	1984	—	2.00	4.00
—From box "Elvis' Greatest Hits, Golden Singles, Volume 2"; gold vinyl					
PB-13896 [PS]	Suspicious Minds/Burning Love	1984	—	2.00	4.00
PB-13897	Elvis' Greatest Hits, Golden Singles, Volume 1	1984	3.75	7.50	15.00
—Box set of six 45s with sleeves (13885-13890) with box					
PB-13898	Elvis' Greatest Hits, Golden Singles, Volume 2	1984	3.75	7.50	15.00
—Box set of six 45s with sleeves (13891-13896) with box					
PB-13929	Blue Suede Shoes/Promised Land	1984	3.75	7.50	15.00
—Blue vinyl; incorrect label -- "Blue Suede Shoes" side says "Stereo" and "Promised Land" side says "Mono"					
PB-13929	Blue Suede Shoes/Promised Land	1984	3.00	6.00	12.00
—Blue vinyl; correct label -- "Blue Suede Shoes" side says "Mono" and "Promised Land" side says "Stereo"					
PB-13929 [PS]	Blue Suede Shoes/Promised Land	1984	2.50	5.00	10.00
PB-14090	Always on My Mind/My Boy	1985	2.50	5.00	10.00
—Purple vinyl					
PB-14090 [PS]	Always on My Mind/My Boy	1985	2.50	5.00	10.00
PB-14237	Merry Christmas Baby/Santa Claus Is Back in Town	1985	3.75	7.50	15.00
—"Elvis 50th Anniversary" label					
PB-14237	Merry Christmas Baby/Santa Claus Is Back in Town	1985	—	2.50	5.00
—Normal black RCA label					
PB-14237	Merry Christmas Baby/Santa Claus Is Back in Town	1985	3.75	7.50	15.00
—Green vinyl					
PB-14237 [PS]	Merry Christmas Baby/Santa Claus Is Back in Town	1985	3.00	6.00	12.00
62402	Don't Be Cruel/Ain't That Lovin' You Baby (Fast Version)	1992	—	2.50	5.00
62402 [PS]	Don't Be Cruel/Ain't That Lovin' You Baby (Fast Version)	1992	—	2.50	5.00
—Generic white sleeve with "Elvis -- The King of Rock 'n' Roll" sticker					
62403	Blue Christmas/Love Me Tender	1992	—	2.50	5.00
62403 [PS]	Blue Christmas/Love Me Tender	1992	—	2.50	5.00
—Generic white sleeve with "Elvis -- The King of Rock 'n' Roll" sticker					
62411	Silver Bells (Unreleased Version)/Silver Bells	1993	—	2.50	5.00
62449	Heartbreak Hotel/Hound Dog	1992	—	2.50	5.00
64476	Heartbreak Hotel/I Was the One//Heartbreak Hotel (Alternate Take 5)/I Was the One (Alternate Take 2)	1996	—	—	3.00
64476 [PS]	Heartbreak Hotel/I Was the One//Heartbreak Hotel (Alternate Take 5)/I Was the One (Alternate Take 2)	1996	—	—	3.00
447-0600	I Forgot to Remember to Forget/Mystery Train	1977	—	2.00	4.00
—Note: All RCA releases with a "447" prefix are from the Gold Standard Series and are black label, dog near top					
447-0601	That's All Right/Blue Moon of Kentucky	1977	—	2.00	4.00
447-0602	Good Rockin' Tonight/I Don't Care If the Sun Don't Shine	1977	—	2.00	4.00
447-0603	Milkcow Blues Boogie/You're a Heartbreaker	1977	—	2.00	4.00
447-0604	Baby Let's Play House/I'm Left, You're Right, She's Gone	1977	—	2.00	4.00
447-0605	Heartbreak Hotel/I Was the One	1977	—	2.00	4.00
447-0607	I Want You, I Need You, I Love You/My Baby Left Me	1977	—	2.00	4.00
447-0608	Hound Dog/Don't Be Cruel	1977	—	2.00	4.00
447-0609	Blue Suede Shoes/Tutti Frutti	1977	—	2.00	4.00
447-0613	Blue Moon/Just Because	1977	—	2.00	4.00
447-0614	Money Honey/One-Sided Love Affair	1977	—	2.00	4.00
447-0615	Lawdy Miss Clawdy/Shake, Rattle, and Roll	1977	—	2.00	4.00
447-0616	Love Me Tender/Anyway You Want Me (That's How I Will Be)	1977	—	2.00	4.00
447-0617	Too Much/Playing for Keeps	1977	—	2.00	4.00
447-0618	All Shook Up/That's When Your Heartaches Begin	1977	—	2.00	4.00
447-0619	Jailhouse Rock/Treat Me Nice	1977	—	2.00	4.00
447-0620	(Let Me Be Your) Teddy Bear/Loving You	1977	—	2.00	4.00
447-0621	Don't/I Beg of You	1977	—	2.00	4.00
447-0622	Wear My Ring Around Your Neck/Don'tcha Think It's Time	1977	—	2.00	4.00
447-0623	Hard Headed Woman/Don't Ask Me Why	1977	—	2.00	4.00
447-0624	One Night/I Got Stung	1977	—	2.00	4.00
447-0625	(Now and Then There's) A Fool Such As I/I Need Your Love Tonight	1977	—	2.00	4.00
447-0626	A Big Hunk o'Love/My Wish Came True	1977	—	2.00	4.00
447-0627	Stuck on You/Fame and Fortune	1977	—	2.00	4.00
447-0628	It's Now or Never/A Mess of Blues	1977	—	2.00	4.00
447-0629	Are You Lonesome To-Night?/I Gotta Know	1977	—	2.00	4.00
447-0630	Surrender/Lonely Man	1977	—	2.00	4.00
447-0631	I Feel So Bad/Wild in the Country	1977	—	2.00	4.00
447-0634	(Marie's the Name) His Latest Flame/Little Sister	1977	—	2.00	4.00
447-0635	Can't Help Falling in Love/Rock-a-Hula Baby	1977	—	2.00	4.00
447-0636	Good Luck Charm/Anything That's Part of You	1977	—	2.00	4.00
447-0637	She's Not You/Just Tell Her Jim Said Hello	1977	—	2.00	4.00
447-0638	Return to Sender/Where Do You Come From	1977	—	2.00	4.00
447-0639	Kiss Me Quick/Suspicion	1977	—	2.00	4.00
447-0640	One Broken Heart for Sale/They Remind Me Too Much of You	1977	—	2.00	4.00
447-0641	(You're the) Devil in Disguise/Please Don't Drag That String Around	1977	—	2.00	4.00
447-0642	Bossa Nova Baby/Witchcraft	1977	—	2.00	4.00
447-0643	Crying in the Chapel/I Believe in the Man in the Sky	1977	—	2.00	4.00
447-0644	Kissin' Cousins/It Hurts Me	1977	—	2.00	4.00
447-0645	Such a Night/Never Ending	1977	—	2.00	4.00
447-0646	Viva Las Vegas/What'd I Say	1977	—	2.00	4.00
447-0647	Blue Christmas/Santa Claus Is Back in Town	1977	—	2.00	4.00
447-0647 [PS]	Blue Christmas/Santa Claus Is Back in Town	1977	2.50	5.00	10.00
—Does not mention "Gold Standard Series" on sleeve					
447-0648	Do the Clam/You'll Be Gone	1977	—	2.00	4.00
447-0649	Ain't That Loving You Baby/Ask Me	1977	—	2.00	4.00
447-0650	Puppet on a String/Wooden Heart	1977	—	2.00	4.00
447-0651	Joshua Fit the Battle/Known Only to Him	1977	—	2.00	4.00
447-0653	(Such An) Easy Question/It Feels So Right	1977	—	2.00	4.00
447-0654	I'm Yours/(It's a) Long, Lonely Highway	1977	—	2.00	4.00
447-0655	Tell Me Why/Blue River	1977	—	2.00	4.00
447-0656	Frankie and Johnny/Please Don't Stop Loving Me	1977	—	2.00	4.00
447-0657	Love Letters/Come What May	1977	—	2.00	4.00
447-0658	Spinout/All That I Do	1977	—	2.00	4.00
447-0659	Indescribably Blue/Fools Fall in Love	1977	—	2.00	4.00
447-0661	There's Always Me/Judy	1977	—	2.00	4.00
447-0662	Big Boss Man/You Don't Know Me	1977	—	2.00	4.00
447-0663	Guitar Man/High Heel Sneakers	1977	—	2.00	4.00
447-0664	U.S. Male/Stay Away	1977	—	2.50	5.00
447-0665	You'll Never Walk Alone/We Call on Him	1977	—	2.00	4.00
447-0666	Let Yourself Go/Your Time Hasn't Come Yet, Baby	1977	—	2.00	4.00
447-0667	A Little Less Conversation/Almost in Love	1977	—	2.00	4.00
447-0668	If I Can Dream/Edge of Reality	1977	—	2.00	4.00
447-0669	Memories/Charro	1977	—	2.00	4.00
447-0670	How Great Thou Art/His Hand in Mine	1977	—	2.00	4.00
447-0671	In the Ghetto/Any Day Now	1977	—	2.00	4.00
447-0672	Clean Up Your Own Back Yard/The Fair Is Moving On	1977	—	2.00	4.00
447-0673	Suspicious Minds/You'll Think of Me	1977	—	2.00	4.00
447-0674	Don't Cry Daddy/Rubberneckin'	1977	—	2.00	4.00
447-0675	Kentucky Rain/My Little Friend	1977	—	2.00	4.00
447-0676	The Wonder of You/Mama Liked the Roses	1977	—	2.00	4.00
447-0677	I've Lost You/The Next Step Is Love	1977	—	2.00	4.00
447-0678	You Don't Have to Say You Love Me/Patch It Up	1977	—	2.00	4.00
447-0679	I Really Don't Want to Know/There Goes My Everything	1977	—	2.00	4.00
447-0680	Where Did They Go, Lord/Rags to Riches	1977	—	2.00	4.00
447-0681	If Every Day Was Like Christmas/How Would You Like to Be	1977	—	2.00	4.00

Number	Title (A Side/B Side)	Yr	VG	VG+	NM
447-0682	Life/Only Believe	1977	—	2.00	4.00
447-0683	I'm Leavin'/Heart of Rome	1977	—	2.00	4.00
447-0684	It's Only Love/The Sound of Your Cry	1977	—	2.00	4.00
447-0685	An American Trilogy/Until It's Time for You to Go	1977	—	2.00	4.00
RCA VICTOR					
CR-15 [DJ]	Old Shep	1956	250.00	500.00	1000.
—One-sided promo					
SP-45-76 [DJ]	Don't/Wear My Ring Around Your Neck	1960	200.00	400.00	800.00
SP-45-76 [PS]	Don't/Wear My Ring Around Your Neck	1960	1000.	1500.	2000.
APBO-0088	Raised on Rock/For Ol' Times Sake	1973	—	3.00	6.00
APBO-0088 [PS]	Raised on Rock/For Ol' Times Sake	1973	3.75	7.50	15.00
4-834-115 [DJ]	I'll Be Back	1966	4000.	6000.	8000.
—One-sided promo with designation "For Special Academy Consideration Only"					
SP-45-118 [DJ]	King of the Whole Wide World/Home Is Where the Heart Is	1962	50.00	100.00	200.00
SP-45-118 [PS]	King of the Whole Wide World/Home Is Where the Heart Is	1962	75.00	150.00	300.00
SP-45-139 [DJ]	Roustabout/One Track Heart	1964	75.00	150.00	300.00
SP-45-162 [DJ]	How Great Thou Art/So High	1967	37.50	75.00	150.00
SP-45-162 [PS]	How Great Thou Art/So High	1967	50.00	100.00	200.00
APBO-0196	Take Good Care of Her/I've Got a Thing About You, Baby	1973	—	3.00	6.00
APBO-0196 [PS]	Take Good Care of Her/I've Got a Thing About You, Baby	1973	3.75	7.50	15.00
APBO-0280	If You Talk in Your Sleep/Help Me	1974	3.00	6.00	12.00
—On label, the title "If You Talk in Your Sleep" is all on one line					
APBO-0280	If You Talk in Your Sleep/Help Me	1974	—	3.00	6.00
—On label, the title "If You Talk" is on one line and "In Your Sleep" is on another line					
APBO-0280 [PS]	If You Talk in Your Sleep/Help Me	1974	3.75	7.50	15.00
HO7W-0808 [DJ]	Blue Christmas (same on both sides)	1957	375.00	750.00	1500.
PB-10074	Promised Land/It's Midnight	1974	—	2.50	5.00
—Orange label (available at the same time as gray label)					
PB-10074	Promised Land/It's Midnight	1974	—	2.50	5.00
—Gray label (available at the same time as orange label)					
PB-10074	Promised Land/It's Midnight	1975	6.25	12.50	25.00
—Tan label (reissue)					
PB-10074 [PS]	Promised Land/It's Midnight	1975	2.50	5.00	10.00
GB-10156	Burning Love/Steamroller Blues	1975	2.00	4.00	8.00
—Gold Standard Series; red label					
GB-10156	Burning Love/Steamroller Blues	1977	—	2.00	4.00
—Gold Standard Series; black label					
GB-10157	Raised on Rock/If You Talk in Your Sleep	1975	2.00	4.00	8.00
—Gold Standard Series; red label					
GB-10157	Raised on Rock/If You Talk in Your Sleep	1977	—	2.00	4.00
—Gold Standard Series; black label					
PB-10191	My Boy/Thinking About You	1975	—	2.50	5.00
—Orange label					
PB-10191	My Boy/Thinking About You	1975	—	2.50	5.00
—Tan label					
PB-10191 [PS]	My Boy/Thinking About You	1975	2.50	5.00	10.00
PB-10278	T-R-O-U-B-L-E/Mr. Songman	1975	—	2.50	5.00
—Orange label					
PB-10278	T-R-O-U-B-L-E/Mr. Songman	1975	25.00	50.00	100.00
—Gray label					
PB-10278	T-R-O-U-B-L-E/Mr. Songman	1975	2.50	5.00	10.00
—Tan label					
PB-10278 [PS]	T-R-O-U-B-L-E/Mr. Songman	1975	2.50	5.00	10.00
PB-10401	Bringing It Back/Pieces of My Life	1975	50.00	100.00	200.00
—Orange label					
PB-10401	Bringing It Back/Pieces of My Life	1975	—	2.50	5.00
—Tan label					
PB-10401 [PS]	Bringing It Back/Pieces of My Life	1975	2.50	5.00	10.00
GB-10485	Take Good Care of Her/I've Got a Thing About You, Baby	1975	2.00	4.00	8.00
—Gold Standard Series; red label					
GB-10486	Separate Ways/Always on My Mind	1975	2.00	4.00	8.00
—Gold Standard Series; red label					
GB-10487	T-R-O-U-B-L-E/Mr. Songman	1975	2.00	4.00	8.00
—Gold Standard Series; red label					
GB-10488	Promised Land/It's Midnight	1975	2.00	4.00	8.00
—Gold Standard Series; red label					
GB-10489	My Boy/Thinking About You	1975	2.00	4.00	8.00
—Gold Standard Series; red label					
PB-10601	Hurt/For the Heart	1976	—	2.50	5.00
—Originals on tan labels					
PB-10601 [PS]	Hurt/For the Heart	1976	2.50	5.00	10.00
37-7850	Surrender/Lonely Man	1961	150.00	300.00	600.00
—"Compact Single 33" (small hole, plays at LP speed)					
37-7850 [PS]	Surrender/Lonely Man	1961	250.00	500.00	1000.
—Special picture sleeve for above record					
37-7880	I Feel So Bad/Wild in the Country	1961	250.00	500.00	1000.
—"Compact Single 33" (small hole, plays at LP speed)					
37-7880 [PS]	I Feel So Bad/Wild in the Country	1961	300.00	600.00	1200.
—Special picture sleeve for above record					
37-7908	(Marie's the Name) His Latest Flame/Little Sister	1961	375.00	750.00	1500.
—"Compact Single 33" (small hole, plays at LP speed)					
37-7908 [PS]	(Marie's the Name) His Latest Flame/Little Sister	1961	1000.	1500.	2000.
—Special picture sleeve for above record					
37-7908 [PS]	(Marie's the Name) His Latest Flame/Little Sister	1961	1125.	1688.	2250.
—Special picture sleeve for above record; says "Stereo-Orthophonic" on sleeve in error					
37-7968	Can't Help Falling in Love/Rock-a-Hula Baby	1961	1000.	1500.	2000.
—"Compact Single 33" (small hole, plays at LP speed)					
37-7968 [PS]	Can't Help Falling in Love/Rock-a-Hula Baby	1961	2000.	3000.	4000.
—Special picture sleeve for above record					
37-7992	Good Luck Charm/Anything That's Part of You	1962	1250.	1875.	2500.
—"Compact Single 33" (small hole, plays at LP speed)					
37-7992 [PS]	Good Luck Charm/Anything That's Part of You	1962	2500.	3750.	5000.
—Special picture sleeve for above record					
47-6357	I Forgot to Remember to Forget/Mystery Train	1955	15.00	30.00	60.00
—No horizontal line on label					
47-6357	I Forgot to Remember to Forget/Mystery Train	1955	15.00	30.00	60.00
—With horizontal line on label					
47-6380	That's All Right/Blue Moon of Kentucky	1955	15.00	30.00	60.00
—No horizontal line on label					
47-6380	That's All Right/Blue Moon of Kentucky	1955	15.00	30.00	60.00
—With horizontal line on label					
47-6381	Good Rockin' Tonight/I Don't Care If the Sun Don't Shine	1955	15.00	30.00	60.00
—No horizontal line on label					
47-6381	Good Rockin' Tonight/I Don't Care If the Sun Don't Shine	1955	15.00	30.00	60.00
—With horizontal line on label					
47-6382	Milkcow Blues Boogie/You're a Heartbreaker	1955	15.00	30.00	60.00
—No horizontal line on label					
47-6382	Milkcow Blues Boogie/You're a Heartbreaker	1955	15.00	30.00	60.00
—With horizontal line on label					
47-6383	Baby Let's Play House/I'm Left, You're Right, She's Gone	1955	15.00	30.00	60.00
—No horizontal line on label					
47-6383	Baby Let's Play House/I'm Left, You're Right, She's Gone	1955	15.00	30.00	60.00
—With horizontal line on label					
47-6420	Heartbreak Hotel/I Was the One	1956	10.00	20.00	40.00
—No horizontal line on label					
47-6420	Heartbreak Hotel/I Was the One	1956	10.00	20.00	40.00
—With horizontal line on label					
47-6540	I Want You, I Need You, I Love You/My Baby Left Me	1956	10.00	20.00	40.00
—No horizontal line on label					
47-6540	I Want You, I Need You, I Love You/My Baby Left Me	1956	10.00	20.00	40.00
—With horizontal line on label					
47-6540 [PS]	This Is His Life: Elvis Presley	1956	300.00	600.00	1200.
—Promo-only sleeve issued with above single; no stock picture sleeve was issued					
47-6604	Don't Be Cruel/Hound Dog	1956	7.50	15.00	30.00
—No horizontal line on label					
47-6604	Don't Be Cruel/Hound Dog	1956	7.50	15.00	30.00
—With horizontal line on label					
47-6604 [PS]	Don't Be Cruel/Hound Dog	1956	50.00	100.00	200.00
—"Don't Be Cruel" listed on top of "Hound Dog!"					
47-6604 [PS]	Don't Be Cruel/Hound Dog	1956	30.00	60.00	120.00
—"Hound Dog!" listed on top of "Don't Be Cruel"					
47-6636	Blue Suede Shoes/Tutti Frutti	1956	20.00	40.00	80.00
—No horizontal line on label					
47-6636	Blue Suede Shoes/Tutti Frutti	1956	20.00	40.00	80.00
—With horizontal line on label					
47-6637	I Got a Woman/I'm Countin' On You	1956	20.00	40.00	80.00
—No horizontal line on label					
47-6637	I Got a Woman/I'm Countin' On You	1956	20.00	40.00	80.00
—With horizontal line on label					
47-6638	I'm Gonna Sit Right Down and Cry (Over You)/I'll Never Let You Go (Little Darlin')	1956	17.50	35.00	70.00
—No horizontal line on label					
47-6638	I'm Gonna Sit Right Down and Cry (Over You)/I'll Never Let You Go (Little Darlin')	1956	17.50	35.00	70.00
—With horizontal line on label					
47-6639	Tryin' to Get to You/I Love You Because	1956	17.50	35.00	70.00
—No horizontal line on label					
47-6639	Tryin' to Get to You/I Love You Because	1956	17.50	35.00	70.00
—With horizontal line on label					
47-6640	Blue Moon/Just Because	1956	15.00	30.00	60.00
—No horizontal line on label					
47-6640	Blue Moon/Just Because	1956	15.00	30.00	60.00
—With horizontal line on label					
47-6641	Money Honey/One-Sided Love Affair	1956	12.50	25.00	50.00
—No horizontal line on label					
47-6641	Money Honey/One-Sided Love Affair	1956	12.50	25.00	50.00
—With horizontal line on label					
47-6642	Lawdy Miss Clawdy/Shake, Rattle, and Roll	1956	10.00	20.00	40.00
—No horizontal line on label					
47-6642	Lawdy Miss Clawdy/Shake, Rattle, and Roll	1956	50.00	100.00	200.00
—With horizontal line on label, but with no dog					
47-6642	Lawdy Miss Clawdy/Shake, Rattle, and Roll	1956	10.00	20.00	40.00
—With horizontal line on label, dog on label as usual					
47-6643	Love Me Tender/Anyway You Want Me (That's How I Will Be)	1956	7.50	15.00	30.00
—With horizontal line on label					
47-6643	Love Me Tender/Anyway You Want Me (That's How I Will Be)	1956	10.00	20.00	40.00
—No reference to the movie "Love Me Tender" on label					
47-6643	Love Me Tender/Anyway You Want Me (That's How I Will Be)	1956	7.50	15.00	30.00
—No horizontal line on label					
47-6643 [PS]	Love Me Tender/Anyway You Want Me (That's How I Will Be)	1956	45.00	90.00	180.00
—Black and white sleeve					
47-6643 [PS]	Love Me Tender/Anyway You Want Me (That's How I Will Be)	1956	18.75	37.50	75.00
—Black and green sleeve					
47-6643 [PS]	Love Me Tender/Anyway You Want Me (That's How I Will Be)	1956	10.00	20.00	40.00
—Black and dark pink sleeve					
47-6643 [PS]	Love Me Tender/Anyway You Want Me (That's How I Will Be)	1956	7.50	15.00	30.00
—Black and light pink sleeve					
47-6800	Too Much/Playing for Keeps	1957	7.50	15.00	30.00
—No horizontal line on label					
47-6800	Too Much/Playing for Keeps	1957	50.00	100.00	200.00
—With horizontal line on label, but with no dog					
47-6800	Too Much/Playing for Keeps	1957	7.50	15.00	30.00
—With horizontal line on label, dog on label as normal					
47-6800 [PS]	Too Much/Playing for Keeps	1957	22.50	45.00	90.00
47-6870	All Shook Up/That's When Your Heartaches Begin	1957	7.50	15.00	30.00
—No horizontal line on label					
47-6870	All Shook Up/That's When Your Heartaches Begin	1957	7.50	15.00	30.00
—With horizontal line on label					
47-6870 [PS]	All Shook Up/That's When Your Heartaches Begin	1957	22.50	45.00	90.00
47-7000	(Let Me Be Your) Teddy Bear/Loving You	1957	10.00	20.00	40.00
—Label says "Let Me Be Your TEDDY BEAR" (no parentheses)					

Number	Title (A Side/B Side)	Yr	VG	VG+	NM
47-7000	(Let Me Be Your) Teddy Bear/Loving You	1957	7.50	15.00	30.00
—Parentheses around "Let Me Be Your", no horizontal line on label					
47-7000	(Let Me Be Your) Teddy Bear/Loving You	1957	7.50	15.00	30.00
—Parentheses around "Let Me Be Your", with horizontal line on label					
47-7000 [PS]	(Let Me Be Your) Teddy Bear/Loving You	1957	30.00	60.00	120.00
47-7035	Jailhouse Rock/Treat Me Nice	1957	7.50	15.00	30.00
—No horizontal line on label					
47-7035	Jailhouse Rock/Treat Me Nice	1957	7.50	15.00	30.00
—With horizontal line on label					
47-7035 [PS]	Jailhouse Rock/Treat Me Nice	1957	25.00	50.00	100.00
47-7150	Don't/I Beg of You	1958	6.25	12.50	25.00
—No horizontal line on label					
47-7150	Don't/I Beg of You	1958	6.25	12.50	25.00
—With horizontal line on label					
47-7150 [PS]	Don't/I Beg of You	1958	22.50	45.00	90.00
47-7240	Wear My Ring Around Your Neck/Don'tcha Think It's Time	1958	6.25	12.50	25.00
47-7240 [PS]	Wear My Ring Around Your Neck/Don'tcha Think It's Time	1958	22.50	45.00	90.00
47-7280	Hard Headed Woman/Don't Ask Me Why	1958	6.25	12.50	25.00
47-7280 [PS]	Hard Headed Woman/Don't Ask Me Why	1958	17.50	35.00	70.00
47-7410	One Night/I Got Stung	1958	6.25	12.50	25.00
47-7410 [PS]	One Night/I Got Stung	1958	17.50	35.00	70.00
47-7506	(Now and Then There's) A Fool Such As I/I Need Your Love Tonight	1959	6.25	12.50	25.00
47-7506 [PS]	(Now and Then There's) A Fool Such As I/I Need Your Love Tonight	1959	250.00	500.00	1000.
—Sleeve promotes the "Elvis Sails" EP					
47-7506 [PS]	(Now and Then There's) A Fool Such As I/I Need Your Love Tonight	1959	15.00	30.00	60.00
—Sleeve lists Elvis' EPs and Gold Standard singles					
47-7600	A Big Hunk o'Love/My Wish Came True	1959	6.25	12.50	25.00
47-7600 [PS]	A Big Hunk o'Love/My Wish Came True	1959	17.50	35.00	70.00
47-7740	Stuck on You/Fame and Fortune	1960	5.00	10.00	20.00
47-7740 [PS]	Stuck on You/Fame and Fortune	1960	15.00	30.00	60.00
47-7777	It's Now or Never/A Mess of Blues	1960	250.00	500.00	1000.
—An early mispress is missing the piano part on the A-side. Has the number "L2WW-0100-3S" or "L2WW-0100-4S" in trail-off wax.					
47-7777	It's Now or Never/A Mess of Blues	1960	5.00	10.00	20.00
—All other pressings with overdubbed piano					
47-7777 [PS]	It's Now or Never/A Mess of Blues	1960	15.00	30.00	60.00
47-7810	Are You Lonesome To-Night?/I Gotta Know	1960	5.00	10.00	20.00
47-7810 [PS]	Are You Lonesome To-Night?/I Gotta Know	1960	15.00	30.00	60.00
47-7850	Surrender/Lonely Man	1961	5.00	10.00	20.00
47-7850 [PS]	Surrender/Lonely Man	1961	15.00	30.00	60.00
47-7880	I Feel So Bad/Wild in the Country	1961	5.00	10.00	20.00
47-7880 [PS]	I Feel So Bad/Wild in the Country	1961	12.50	25.00	50.00
47-7908	(Marie's the Name) His Latest Flame/Little Sister	1961	5.00	10.00	20.00
—All copies of this record actually read "Marie's the Name HIS LATEST FLAME" (no parentheses)					
47-7908 [PS]	(Marie's the Name) His Latest Flame/Little Sister	1961	12.50	25.00	50.00
47-7968	Can't Help Falling in Love/Rock-a-Hula Baby	1961	5.00	10.00	20.00
47-7968 [PS]	Can't Help Falling in Love/Rock-a-Hula Baby	1961	10.00	20.00	40.00
47-7992	Good Luck Charm/Anything That's Part of You	1962	5.00	10.00	20.00
47-7992 [PS]	Good Luck Charm/Anything That's Part of You	1962	10.00	20.00	40.00
—Titles in blue and pink letters					
47-7992 [PS]	Good Luck Charm/Anything That's Part of You	1962	10.00	20.00	40.00
—Titles in rust and lavender letters					
47-8041	She's Not You/Just Tell Her Jim Said Hello	1962	5.00	10.00	20.00
47-8041 [PS]	She's Not You/Just Tell Her Jim Said Hello	1962	10.00	20.00	40.00
47-8100	Return to Sender/Where Do You Come From	1962	5.00	10.00	20.00
47-8100 [PS]	Return to Sender/Where Do You Come From	1962	10.00	20.00	40.00
47-8134	One Broken Heart for Sale/They Remind Me Too Much of You	1963	3.00	6.00	12.00
47-8134 [PS]	One Broken Heart for Sale/They Remind Me Too Much of You	1963	7.50	15.00	30.00
47-8188	(You're the) Devil in Disguise/Please Don't Drag That String Along	1963	50.00	100.00	200.00
—First pressing with incorrect B-side title					
47-8188	(You're the) Devil in Disguise/Please Don't Drag That String Around	1963	3.00	6.00	12.00
—Second pressing with correct B-side title					
47-8188 [PS]	(You're the) Devil in Disguise/Please Don't Drag That String Around	1963	7.50	15.00	30.00
—All sleeves have correct B-side title					
47-8243	Bossa Nova Baby/Witchcraft	1963	3.00	6.00	12.00
47-8243 [PS]	Bossa Nova Baby/Witchcraft	1963	7.50	15.00	30.00
—"Coming Soon" on sleeve					
47-8243 [PS]	Bossa Nova Baby/Witchcraft	1963	7.50	15.00	30.00
—"Ask For" on sleeve					
47-8243 [PS]	Bossa Nova Baby/Witchcraft	1963	7.50	15.00	30.00
—No reference to another album on sleeve					
47-8307	Kissin' Cousins/It Hurts Me	1964	3.00	6.00	12.00
47-8307 [PS]	Kissin' Cousins/It Hurts Me	1964	6.25	12.50	25.00
47-8360	Viva Las Vegas/What'd I Say	1964	3.00	6.00	12.00
47-8360 [PS]	Viva Las Vegas/What'd I Say	1964	6.25	12.50	25.00
—"Coming Soon" on sleeve					
47-8360 [PS]	Viva Las Vegas/What'd I Say	1964	12.50	25.00	50.00
—"Ask For" on sleeve					
47-8400	Such a Night/Never Ending	1964	3.00	6.00	12.00
47-8400 [DJ]	Such a Night/Never Ending	1964	2500.	3750.	5000.
—An inexplicably rare regular white label promo					
47-8400 [PS]	Such a Night/Never Ending	1964	6.25	12.50	25.00
47-8440	Ain't That Loving You Baby/Ask Me	1964	2.50	5.00	10.00
47-8440 [PS]	Ain't That Loving You Baby/Ask Me	1964	6.25	12.50	25.00
—"Coming Soon" on sleeve					
47-8440 [PS]	Ain't That Loving You Baby/Ask Me	1964	6.25	12.50	25.00
—"Ask For" on sleeve					
47-8500	Do the Clam/You'll Be Gone	1965	2.50	5.00	10.00
47-8500 [PS]	Do the Clam/You'll Be Gone	1965	6.25	12.50	25.00
47-8585	(Such An) Easy Question/It Feels So Right	1965	2.50	5.00	10.00
47-8585 [PS]	(Such An) Easy Question/It Feels So Right	1965	6.25	12.50	25.00
—"Coming Soon" on sleeve					
47-8585 [PS]	(Such An) Easy Question/It Feels So Right	1965	6.25	12.50	25.00
—"Ask For" on sleeve					
47-8657	I'm Yours/(It's a) Long, Lonely Highway	1965	2.50	5.00	10.00
47-8657 [PS]	I'm Yours/(It's a) Long, Lonely Highway	1965	6.25	12.50	25.00
47-8740	Tell Me Why/Blue River	1965	2.50	5.00	10.00
47-8740 [PS]	Tell Me Why/Blue River	1965	6.25	12.50	25.00
47-8780	Frankie and Johnny/Please Don't Stop Loving Me	1966	2.50	5.00	10.00
47-8780 [PS]	Frankie and Johnny/Please Don't Stop Loving Me	1966	6.25	12.50	25.00
47-8870	Love Letters/Come What May	1966	2.50	5.00	10.00
47-8870 [PS]	Love Letters/Come What May	1966	6.25	12.50	25.00
—"Coming Soon" on sleeve					
47-8870 [PS]	Love Letters/Come What May	1966	6.25	12.50	25.00
—"Ask For" on sleeve					
47-8941	Spinout/All That I Do	1966	2.50	5.00	10.00
47-8941 [PS]	Spinout/All That I Do	1966	6.25	12.50	25.00
—"Watch For" on sleeve					
47-8941 [PS]	Spinout/All That I Do	1966	6.25	12.50	25.00
—"Ask For" on sleeve					
47-8950	If Every Day Was Like Christmas/How Would You Like to Be	1966	5.00	10.00	20.00
47-8950 [PS]	If Every Day Was Like Christmas/How Would You Like to Be	1966	10.00	20.00	40.00
47-9056	Indescribably Blue/Fools Fall in Love	1966	2.50	5.00	10.00
47-9056 [PS]	Indescribably Blue/Fools Fall in Love	1966	6.25	12.50	25.00
47-9115	Long Legged Girl (With the Short Dress On)/That's Someone You Never Forget	1967	2.50	5.00	10.00
47-9115 [PS]	Long Legged Girl (With the Short Dress On)/That's Someone You Never Forget	1967	6.25	12.50	25.00
—"Coming Soon" on sleeve					
47-9115 [PS]	Long Legged Girl (With the Short Dress On)/That's Someone You Never Forget	1967	6.25	12.50	25.00
—"Ask For" on sleeve					
47-9287	There's Always Me/Judy	1967	2.50	5.00	10.00
47-9287 [PS]	There's Always Me/Judy	1967	6.25	12.50	25.00
47-9341	Big Boss Man/You Don't Know Me	1967	2.50	5.00	10.00
47-9341 [PS]	Big Boss Man/You Don't Know Me	1967	6.25	12.50	25.00
47-9425	Guitar Man/High Heel Sneakers	1968	2.50	5.00	10.00
47-9425 [PS]	Guitar Man/High Heel Sneakers	1968	6.25	12.50	25.00
—"Coming Soon" on sleeve					
47-9425 [PS]	Guitar Man/High Heel Sneakers	1968	6.25	12.50	25.00
—"Ask For" on sleeve					
47-9465	U.S. Male/Stay Away	1968	2.50	5.00	10.00
47-9465 [PS]	U.S. Male/Stay Away	1968	6.25	12.50	25.00
47-9547	Let Yourself Go/Your Time Hasn't Come Yet, Baby	1968	2.50	5.00	10.00
47-9547 [PS]	Let Yourself Go/Your Time Hasn't Come Yet, Baby	1968	6.25	12.50	25.00
—"Coming Soon" on sleeve					
47-9547 [PS]	Let Yourself Go/Your Time Hasn't Come Yet, Baby	1968	6.25	12.50	25.00
—"Ask For" on sleeve					
47-9600	You'll Never Walk Alone/We Call on Him	1968	3.00	6.00	12.00
47-9600 [PS]	You'll Never Walk Alone/We Call on Him	1968	25.00	50.00	100.00
47-9610	A Little Less Conversation/Almost in Love	1968	2.50	5.00	10.00
47-9610 [PS]	A Little Less Conversation/Almost in Love	1968	6.25	12.50	25.00
47-9670	If I Can Dream/Edge of Reality	1968	2.00	4.00	8.00
—First Elvis single on orange label					
47-9670 [PS]	If I Can Dream/Edge of Reality	1968	5.00	10.00	20.00
—Mentions his NBC-TV special on sleeve					
47-9670 [PS]	If I Can Dream/Edge of Reality	1968	5.00	10.00	20.00
—Does not mention his NBC-TV special on sleeve					
47-9731	Memories/Charro	1969	2.00	4.00	8.00
47-9731 [PS]	Memories/Charro	1969	5.00	10.00	20.00
47-9741	In the Ghetto/Any Day Now	1969	2.00	4.00	8.00
47-9741 [PS]	In the Ghetto/Any Day Now	1969	5.00	10.00	20.00
—"Coming Soon" on sleeve					
47-9741 [PS]	In the Ghetto/Any Day Now	1969	5.00	10.00	20.00
—"Ask For" on sleeve					
47-9747	Clean Up Your Own Back Yard/The Fair Is Moving On	1969	2.00	4.00	8.00
47-9747 [PS]	Clean Up Your Own Back Yard/The Fair Is Moving On	1969	5.00	10.00	20.00
47-9764	Suspicious Minds/You'll Think of Me	1969	2.00	4.00	8.00
47-9764 [PS]	Suspicious Minds/You'll Think of Me	1969	5.00	10.00	20.00
47-9768	Don't Cry Daddy/Rubberneckin'	1969	2.00	4.00	8.00
47-9768 [PS]	Don't Cry Daddy/Rubberneckin'	1969	3.75	7.50	15.00
47-9791	Kentucky Rain/My Little Friend	1969	2.00	4.00	8.00
47-9791 [PS]	Kentucky Rain/My Little Friend	1969	3.75	7.50	15.00
47-9835	The Wonder of You/Mama Liked the Roses	1970	2.00	4.00	8.00
47-9835 [PS]	The Wonder of You/Mama Liked the Roses	1970	3.75	7.50	15.00
47-9873	I've Lost You/The Next Step Is Love	1970	—	3.00	6.00
47-9873 [PS]	I've Lost You/The Next Step Is Love	1970	3.75	7.50	15.00
47-9916	You Don't Have to Say You Love Me/Patch It Up	1970	—	3.00	6.00
47-9916 [PS]	You Don't Have to Say You Love Me/Patch It Up	1970	3.75	7.50	15.00
47-9960	I Really Don't Want to Know/There Goes My Everything	1971	—	3.00	6.00
47-9960 [PS]	I Really Don't Want to Know/There Goes My Everything	1971	3.75	7.50	15.00
—"Coming Soon" on sleeve					
47-9960 [PS]	I Really Don't Want to Know/There Goes My Everything	1971	3.75	7.50	15.00
—"Ask For" on sleeve					
47-9980	Where Did They Go, Lord/Rags to Riches	1971	—	3.00	6.00
47-9980 [PS]	Where Did They Go, Lord/Rags to Riches	1971	5.00	10.00	20.00
47-9985	Life/Only Believe	1971	—	3.00	6.00
47-9985 [PS]	Life/Only Believe	1971	7.50	15.00	30.00
47-9998	I'm Leavin'/Heart of Rome	1971	—	3.00	6.00
47-9998 [PS]	I'm Leavin'/Heart of Rome	1971	5.00	10.00	20.00
48-1017	It's Only Love/The Sound of Your Cry	1971	—	3.00	6.00
48-1017 [PS]	It's Only Love/The Sound of Your Cry	1971	3.75	7.50	15.00
61-7740 [S]	Stuck on You/Fame and Fortune	1960	100.00	200.00	400.00
—"Living Stereo" (large hole, plays at 45 rpm)					
61-7777 [S]	It's Now or Never/A Mess of Blues	1960	100.00	200.00	400.00
—"Living Stereo" (large hole, plays at 45 rpm)					
61-7810 [S]	Are You Lonesome To-Night?/I Gotta Know	1960	150.00	300.00	600.00
—"Living Stereo" (large hole, plays at 45 rpm)					
61-7850 [S]	Surrender/Lonely Man	1961	200.00	400.00	800.00
—"Living Stereo" (large hole, plays at 45 rpm)					
68-7850 [S]	Surrender/Lonely Man	1961	1000.	1500.	2000.
—"Compact Stereo 33" in "Living Stereo"					

Number	Title (A Side/B Side)	Yr	VG	VG+	NM
74-0130	How Great Thou Art/His Hand in Mine	1969	6.25	12.50	25.00
74-0130 [PS]	How Great Thou Art/His Hand in Mine	1969	37.50	75.00	150.00
74-0572	Merry Christmas Baby/O Come All Ye Faithful	1971	3.75	7.50	15.00
74-0572 [PS]	Merry Christmas Baby/O Come All Ye Faithful	1971	10.00	20.00	40.00
74-0619	Until It's Time for You to Go/We Can Make the Morning	1971	—	3.00	6.00
74-0619 [PS]	Until It's Time for You to Go/We Can Make the Morning	1971	3.75	7.50	15.00
74-0651	He Touched Me/The Bosom of Abraham	1972	37.50	75.00	150.00
—"He Touched Me" actually plays at about 35 rpm in error. A-side has "AWKS-1277" stamped in trail-off wax.					
74-0651	He Touched Me/The Bosom of Abraham	1972	2.00	4.00	8.00
—"He Touched Me" plays correctly. A-side has "APKS-1277" stamped in trail-off wax.					
74-0651 [PS]	He Touched Me/The Bosom of Abraham	1972	30.00	60.00	120.00
74-0672	An American Trilogy/The First Time Ever I Saw Your Face	1972	5.00	10.00	20.00
74-0672 [PS]	An American Trilogy/The First Time Ever I Saw Your Face	1972	10.00	20.00	40.00
74-0769	Burning Love/It's a Matter of Time	1972	—	3.00	6.00
—Originals have orange labels					
74-0769	Burning Love/It's a Matter of Time	1974	37.50	75.00	150.00
—Very rare reissues have gray labels					
74-0769 [PS]	Burning Love/It's a Matter of Time	1972	3.75	7.50	15.00
74-0815	Separate Ways/Always on My Mind	1972	—	3.00	6.00
74-0815 [PS]	Separate Ways/Always on My Mind	1972	3.75	7.50	15.00
74-0910	Steamroller Blues/Fool	1973	—	3.00	6.00
74-0910 [PS]	Steamroller Blues/Fool	1973	3.75	7.50	15.00
447-0600	I Forgot to Remember to Forget/Mystery Train	1959	3.75	7.50	15.00
—Note: All RCA Victor releases with a "447" prefix are from the Gold Standard Series. Black label, dog on top					
447-0600	I Forgot to Remember to Forget/Mystery Train	1965	2.50	5.00	10.00
—Black label, dog on left					
447-0600	I Forgot to Remember to Forget/Mystery Train	1969	6.25	12.50	25.00
—Orange label					
447-0600	I Forgot to Remember to Forget/Mystery Train	1970	2.00	4.00	8.00
—Red label					
447-0601	That's All Right/Blue Moon of Kentucky	1959	3.75	7.50	15.00
—Black label, dog on top					
447-0601	That's All Right/Blue Moon of Kentucky	1965	2.50	5.00	10.00
—Black label, dog on left					
447-0601	That's All Right/Blue Moon of Kentucky	1969	2.00	4.00	8.00
—Red label; B-side artist credit is misspelled "Elvis Presely"					
447-0601 [DJ]	That's All Right/Blue Moon of Kentucky	1964	25.00	50.00	100.00
447-0601 [PS]	That's All Right/Blue Moon of Kentucky	1964	50.00	100.00	200.00
447-0602	Good Rockin' Tonight/I Don't Care If the Sun Don't Shine	1959	3.75	7.50	15.00
—Black label, dog on top					
447-0602	Good Rockin' Tonight/I Don't Care If the Sun Don't Shine	1965	2.50	5.00	10.00
—Black label, dog on left					
447-0602	Good Rockin' Tonight/I Don't Care If the Sun Don't Shine	1970	2.00	4.00	8.00
—Red label					
447-0602 [DJ]	Good Rockin' Tonight/I Don't Care If the Sun Don't Shine	1964	25.00	50.00	100.00
447-0602 [PS]	Good Rockin' Tonight/I Don't Care If the Sun Don't Shine	1964	50.00	100.00	200.00
447-0603	Milkcow Blues Boogie/You're a Heartbreaker	1959	3.75	7.50	15.00
—Black label, dog on top					
447-0603	Milkcow Blues Boogie/You're a Heartbreaker	1965	2.50	5.00	10.00
—Black label, dog on left					
447-0603	Milkcow Blues Boogie/You're a Heartbreaker	1969	6.25	12.50	25.00
—Orange label					
447-0603	Milkcow Blues Boogie/You're a Heartbreaker	1970	2.00	4.00	8.00
—Red label					
447-0604	Baby Let's Play House/I'm Left, You're Right, She's Gone	1959	3.75	7.50	15.00
—Black label, dog on top					
447-0604	Baby Let's Play House/I'm Left, You're Right, She's Gone	1965	2.50	5.00	10.00
—Black label, dog on left					
447-0604	Baby Let's Play House/I'm Left, You're Right, She's Gone	1970	2.00	4.00	8.00
—Red label					
447-0605	Heartbreak Hotel/I Was the One	1959	3.75	7.50	15.00
—Black label, dog on top					
447-0605	Heartbreak Hotel/I Was the One	1965	2.50	5.00	10.00
—Black label, dog on left					
447-0605	Heartbreak Hotel/I Was the One	1969	6.25	12.50	25.00
—Orange label					
447-0605	Heartbreak Hotel/I Was the One	1970	2.00	4.00	8.00
—Red label					
447-0605 [DJ]	Heartbreak Hotel/I Was the One	1964	25.00	50.00	100.00
447-0605 [PS]	Heartbreak Hotel/I Was the One	1964	50.00	100.00	200.00
447-0607	I Want You, I Need You, I Love You/My Baby Left Me	1959	3.75	7.50	15.00
—Black label, dog on top					
447-0607	I Want You, I Need You, I Love You/My Baby Left Me	1965	2.50	5.00	10.00
—Black label, dog on left					
447-0607	I Want You, I Need You, I Love You/My Baby Left Me	1969	6.25	12.50	25.00
—Orange label					
447-0607	I Want You, I Need You, I Love You/My Baby Left Me	1970	2.00	4.00	8.00
—Red label					
447-0608	Hound Dog/Don't Be Cruel	1959	3.75	7.50	15.00
—Black label, dog on top					
447-0608	Hound Dog/Don't Be Cruel	1965	2.50	5.00	10.00
—Black label, dog on left					
447-0608	Hound Dog/Don't Be Cruel	1969	6.25	12.50	25.00
—Orange label					
447-0608	Hound Dog/Don't Be Cruel	1970	2.00	4.00	8.00
—Red label					
447-0608 [DJ]	Hound Dog/Don't Be Cruel	1964	25.00	50.00	100.00
447-0608 [PS]	Hound Dog/Don't Be Cruel	1964	50.00	100.00	200.00
447-0609	Blue Suede Shoes/Tutti Frutti	1959	3.75	7.50	15.00
—Black label, dog on top					
447-0609	Blue Suede Shoes/Tutti Frutti	1965	2.50	5.00	10.00
—Black label, dog on left					
447-0609	Blue Suede Shoes/Tutti Frutti	1969	6.25	12.50	25.00
—Orange label					
447-0609	Blue Suede Shoes/Tutti Frutti	1970	2.00	4.00	8.00
—Red label					
447-0610	I Got a Woman/I'm Countin' On You	1959	3.75	7.50	15.00
—Black label, dog on top					
447-0611	I'm Gonna Sit Right Down and Cry (Over You)/I'll Never Let You Go (Little Darlin')	1959	3.75	7.50	15.00
—Black label, dog on top					
447-0612	Tryin' to Get to You/I Love You Because	1959	3.75	7.50	15.00
—Black label, dog on top					
447-0613	Blue Moon/Just Because	1959	3.75	7.50	15.00
—Black label, dog on top					
447-0613	Blue Moon/Just Because	1965	2.50	5.00	10.00
—Black label, dog on left					
447-0613	Blue Moon/Just Because	1969	6.25	12.50	25.00
—Orange label					
447-0613	Blue Moon/Just Because	1970	2.00	4.00	8.00
—Red label					
447-0614	Money Honey/One-Sided Love Affair	1959	3.75	7.50	15.00
—Black label, dog on top					
447-0614	Money Honey/One-Sided Love Affair	1965	2.50	5.00	10.00
—Black label, dog on left					
447-0614	Money Honey/One-Sided Love Affair	1969	6.25	12.50	25.00
—Orange label					
447-0614	Money Honey/One-Sided Love Affair	1970	2.00	4.00	8.00
—Red label					
447-0615	Lawdy Miss Clawdy/Shake, Rattle, and Roll	1959	3.75	7.50	15.00
—Black label, dog on top					
447-0615	Lawdy Miss Clawdy/Shake, Rattle, and Roll	1965	2.50	5.00	10.00
—Black label, dog on left					
447-0615	Lawdy Miss Clawdy/Shake, Rattle, and Roll	1969	6.25	12.50	25.00
—Orange label					
447-0615	Lawdy Miss Clawdy/Shake, Rattle, and Roll	1970	2.00	4.00	8.00
—Red label					
447-0616	Love Me Tender/Anyway You Want Me (That's How I Will Be)	1959	3.75	7.50	15.00
—Black label, dog on top					
447-0616	Love Me Tender/Anyway You Want Me (That's How I Will Be)	1965	2.50	5.00	10.00
—Black label, dog on left					
447-0616	Love Me Tender/Anyway You Want Me (That's How I Will Be)	1969	6.25	12.50	25.00
—Orange label					
447-0616	Love Me Tender/Anyway You Want Me (That's How I Will Be)	1970	2.00	4.00	8.00
—Red label					
447-0617	Too Much/Playing for Keeps	1959	3.75	7.50	15.00
—Black label, dog on top					
447-0617	Too Much/Playing for Keeps	1965	2.50	5.00	10.00
—Black label, dog on left					
447-0617	Too Much/Playing for Keeps	1969	6.25	12.50	25.00
—Orange label					
447-0617	Too Much/Playing for Keeps	1970	2.00	4.00	8.00
—Red label					
447-0618	All Shook Up/That's When Your Heartaches Begin	1959	3.75	7.50	15.00
—Black label, dog on top					
447-0618	All Shook Up/That's When Your Heartaches Begin	1965	2.50	5.00	10.00
—Black label, dog on left					
447-0618	All Shook Up/That's When Your Heartaches Begin	1969	6.25	12.50	25.00
—Orange label					
447-0618	All Shook Up/That's When Your Heartaches Begin	1970	2.00	4.00	8.00
—Red label					
447-0618 [DJ]	All Shook Up/That's When Your Heartaches Begin	1964	25.00	50.00	100.00
447-0618 [PS]	All Shook Up/That's When Your Heartaches Begin	1964	50.00	100.00	200.00
447-0619	Jailhouse Rock/Treat Me Nice	1959	3.75	7.50	15.00
—Black label, dog on top					
447-0619	Jailhouse Rock/Treat Me Nice	1965	2.50	5.00	10.00
—Black label, dog on left					
447-0619	Jailhouse Rock/Treat Me Nice	1969	6.25	12.50	25.00
—Orange label					
447-0619	Jailhouse Rock/Treat Me Nice	1970	2.00	4.00	8.00
—Red label					
447-0620	(Let Me Be Your) Teddy Bear/Loving You	1959	3.75	7.50	15.00
—Black label, dog on top					
447-0620	(Let Me Be Your) Teddy Bear/Loving You	1965	2.50	5.00	10.00
—Black label, dog on left					
447-0620	(Let Me Be Your) Teddy Bear/Loving You	1969	6.25	12.50	25.00
—Orange label					
447-0620	(Let Me Be Your) Teddy Bear/Loving You	1970	2.00	4.00	8.00
—Red label					
447-0621	Don't/I Beg of You	1961	3.00	6.00	12.00
—Black label, dog on top					
447-0621	Don't/I Beg of You	1965	2.50	5.00	10.00
—Black label, dog on left					
447-0621	Don't/I Beg of You	1969	6.25	12.50	25.00
—Orange label					
447-0621	Don't/I Beg of You	1970	2.00	4.00	8.00
—Red label					
447-0622	Wear My Ring Around Your Neck/Don'tcha Think It's Time	1961	3.00	6.00	12.00
—Black label, dog on top					
447-0622	Wear My Ring Around Your Neck/Don'tcha Think It's Time	1965	2.50	5.00	10.00
—Black label, dog on left					

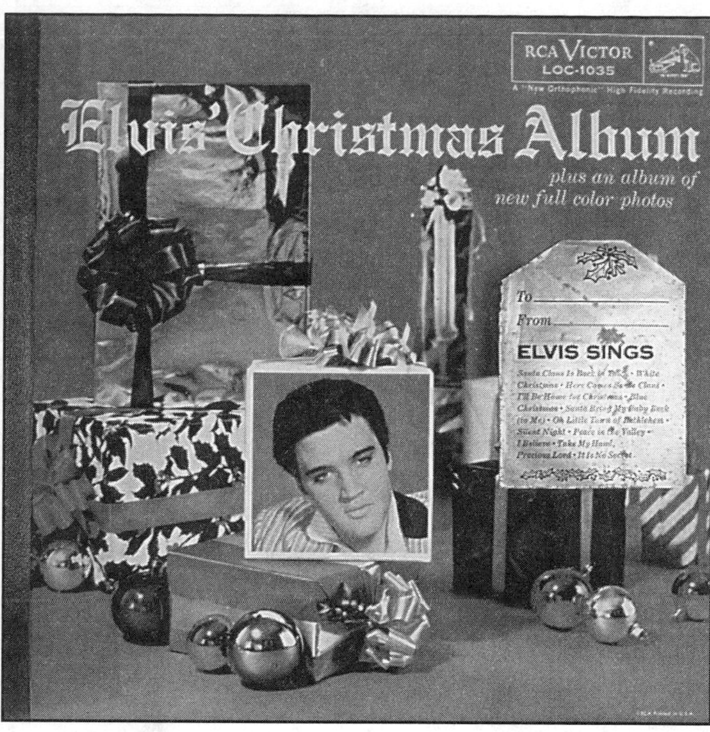

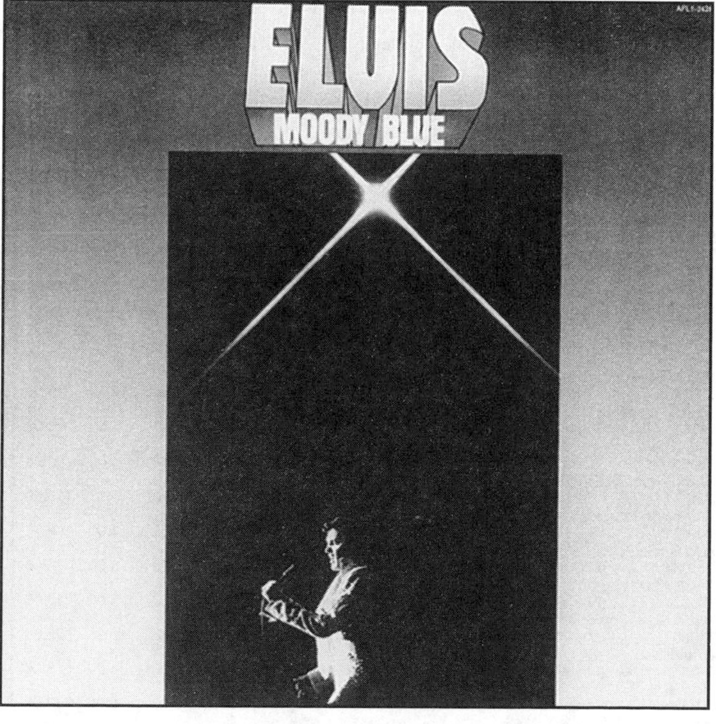

Elvis Presley rules the collecting roost. His records are more avidly collected worldwide than anyone else's, with only the Beatles in competition. (Top left) The last, and perhaps greatest, of Elvis' Sun singles was "Mystery Train." It's the most common of the original Suns, but even so, a near-mint copy fetches in four figures. (Top right) Of Elvis' regular commercially issued albums, the first edition of *Elvis' Christmas Album* is the rarest. It comes with a lavish gatefold and a bound-in booklet — and was only available like that during the Christmas season of 1957. A year later, it was replaced with a simpler package and completely different cover design. (Bottom left) One of RCA's failed attempts to replace its own invention, the 45 rpm single, was with the Compact 33. It marketed these to a disinterested public, often with unique picture sleeves. By far the most sought after of these rare pressings, which have a "37" prefix, are the Elvis ones. Here's the picture sleeve for the first of them, "Surrender." (Bottom right) Many people with the *Moody Blue* album on blue vinyl think they have a true collectible. But the blue vinyl version is so common that only the uninformed will pay more than $8-$10 for a sealed copy. Copies on black vinyl, however, go for hundreds.

Number	Title (A Side/B Side)	Yr	VG	VG+	NM
447-0622	Wear My Ring Around Your Neck/Don'tcha Think It's Time	1969	6.25	12.50	25.00
—Orange label					
447-0622	Wear My Ring Around Your Neck/Don'tcha Think It's Time	1970	2.00	4.00	8.00
—Red label					
447-0623	Hard Headed Woman/Don't Ask Me Why	1961	3.75	7.50	15.00
—Black label, dog on top					
447-0623	Hard Headed Woman/Don't Ask Me Why	1965	2.50	5.00	10.00
—Black label, dog on left					
447-0623	Hard Headed Woman/Don't Ask Me Why	1969	6.25	12.50	25.00
—Orange label					
447-0623	Hard Headed Woman/Don't Ask Me Why	1970	2.00	4.00	8.00
—Red label					
447-0624	One Night/I Got Stung	1961	3.00	6.00	12.00
—Black label, dog on top					
447-0624	One Night/I Got Stung	1965	2.50	5.00	10.00
—Black label, dog on left					
447-0624	One Night/I Got Stung	1969	6.25	12.50	25.00
—Orange label					
447-0624	One Night/I Got Stung	1970	2.00	4.00	8.00
—Red label					
447-0625	(Now and Then There's) A Fool Such As I/I Need Your Love Tonight	1961	3.75	7.50	15.00
—Black label, dog on top					
447-0625	(Now and Then There's) A Fool Such As I/I Need Your Love Tonight	1965	2.50	5.00	10.00
—Black label, dog on left					
447-0625	(Now and Then There's) A Fool Such As I/I Need Your Love Tonight	1969	6.25	12.50	25.00
—Orange label					
447-0625	(Now and Then There's) A Fool Such As I/I Need Your Love Tonight	1970	2.00	4.00	8.00
—Red label					
447-0626	A Big Hunk o'Love/My Wish Came True	1962	3.75	7.50	15.00
—Black label, dog on top					
447-0626	A Big Hunk o'Love/My Wish Came True	1965	2.50	5.00	10.00
—Black label, dog on left					
447-0626	A Big Hunk o'Love/My Wish Came True	1969	6.25	12.50	25.00
—Orange label					
447-0626	A Big Hunk o'Love/My Wish Came True	1970	2.00	4.00	8.00
—Red label					
447-0627	Stuck on You/Fame and Fortune	1962	3.00	6.00	12.00
—Black label, dog on top					
447-0627	Stuck on You/Fame and Fortune	1965	2.50	5.00	10.00
—Black label, dog on left					
447-0627	Stuck on You/Fame and Fortune	1969	6.25	12.50	25.00
—Orange label					
447-0627	Stuck on You/Fame and Fortune	1970	2.00	4.00	8.00
—Red label					
447-0628	It's Now or Never/A Mess of Blues	1962	3.00	6.00	12.00
—Black label, dog on top					
447-0628	It's Now or Never/A Mess of Blues	1965	2.50	5.00	10.00
—Black label, dog on left					
447-0628	It's Now or Never/A Mess of Blues	1969	6.25	12.50	25.00
—Orange label					
447-0628	It's Now or Never/A Mess of Blues	1970	2.00	4.00	8.00
—Red label					
447-0629	Are You Lonesome To-Night?/I Gotta Know	1962	3.75	7.50	15.00
—Black label, dog on top					
447-0629	Are You Lonesome To-Night?/I Gotta Know	1965	2.50	5.00	10.00
—Black label, dog on left					
447-0629	Are You Lonesome To-Night?/I Gotta Know	1969	6.25	12.50	25.00
—Orange label					
447-0629	Are You Lonesome To-Night?/I Gotta Know	1970	2.00	4.00	8.00
—Red label					
447-0630	Surrender/Lonely Man	1962	6.25	12.50	25.00
—Black label, dog on top					
447-0630	Surrender/Lonely Man	1965	2.50	5.00	10.00
—Black label, dog on left					
447-0630	Surrender/Lonely Man	1969	6.25	12.50	25.00
—Orange label					
447-0630	Surrender/Lonely Man	1970	2.00	4.00	8.00
—Red label					
447-0631	I Feel So Bad/Wild in the Country	1962	3.00	6.00	12.00
—Black label, dog on top					
447-0631	I Feel So Bad/Wild in the Country	1965	2.50	5.00	10.00
—Black label, dog on left					
447-0631	I Feel So Bad/Wild in the Country	1970	2.00	4.00	8.00
—Red label					
447-0634	(Marie's the Name) His Latest Flame/Little Sister	1962	3.00	6.00	12.00
—Black label, dog on top					
447-0634	(Marie's the Name) His Latest Flame/Little Sister	1965	2.50	5.00	10.00
—Black label, dog on left					
447-0634	(Marie's the Name) His Latest Flame/Little Sister	1969	6.25	12.50	25.00
—Orange label					
447-0634	(Marie's the Name) His Latest Flame/Little Sister	1970	2.00	4.00	8.00
—Red label					
447-0635	Can't Help Falling in Love/Rock-a-Hula Baby	1962	3.00	6.00	12.00
—Black label, dog on top					
447-0635	Can't Help Falling in Love/Rock-a-Hula Baby	1965	2.50	5.00	10.00
—Black label, dog on left					
447-0635	Can't Help Falling in Love/Rock-a-Hula Baby	1969	6.25	12.50	25.00
—Orange label					
447-0635	Can't Help Falling in Love/Rock-a-Hula Baby	1970	2.00	4.00	8.00
—Red label					
447-0636	Good Luck Charm/Anything That's Part of You	1962	3.00	6.00	12.00
—Black label, dog on top					
447-0636	Good Luck Charm/Anything That's Part of You	1965	2.50	5.00	10.00
—Black label, dog on left					
447-0636	Good Luck Charm/Anything That's Part of You	1969	6.25	12.50	25.00
—Orange label					
447-0636	Good Luck Charm/Anything That's Part of You	1970	2.00	4.00	8.00
—Red label					
447-0637	She's Not You/Just Tell Her Jim Said Hello	1963	3.00	6.00	12.00
—Black label, dog on top					
447-0637	She's Not You/Just Tell Her Jim Said Hello	1965	2.50	5.00	10.00
—Black label, dog on left					
447-0637	She's Not You/Just Tell Her Jim Said Hello	1969	6.25	12.50	25.00
—Orange label					
447-0637	She's Not You/Just Tell Her Jim Said Hello	1970	2.00	4.00	8.00
—Red label					
447-0638	Return to Sender/Where Do You Come From	1963	3.00	6.00	12.00
—Black label, dog on top					
447-0638	Return to Sender/Where Do You Come From	1965	2.50	5.00	10.00
—Black label, dog on left					
447-0638	Return to Sender/Where Do You Come From	1969	6.25	12.50	25.00
—Orange label					
447-0638	Return to Sender/Where Do You Come From	1970	2.00	4.00	8.00
—Red label					
447-0639	Kiss Me Quick/Suspicion	1964	2.50	5.00	10.00
—Black label, dog on top					
447-0639	Kiss Me Quick/Suspicion	1969	6.25	12.50	25.00
—Orange label					
447-0639	Kiss Me Quick/Suspicion	1970	2.00	4.00	8.00
—Red label					
447-0639 [PS]	Kiss Me Quick/Suspicion	1964	10.00	20.00	40.00
447-0640	One Broken Heart for Sale/They Remind Me Too Much of You	1964	6.25	12.50	25.00
—Black label, dog on top					
447-0640	One Broken Heart for Sale/They Remind Me Too Much of You	1965	2.50	5.00	10.00
—Black label, dog on left					
447-0640	One Broken Heart for Sale/They Remind Me Too Much of You	1969	6.25	12.50	25.00
—Orange label					
447-0640	One Broken Heart for Sale/They Remind Me Too Much of You	1970	2.00	4.00	8.00
—Red label					
447-0641	(You're the) Devil in Disguise/Please Don't Drag That String Around	1964	6.25	12.50	25.00
—Black label, dog on top					
447-0641	(You're the) Devil in Disguise/Please Don't Drag That String Around	1965	2.50	5.00	10.00
—Black label, dog on left					
447-0641	(You're the) Devil in Disguise/Please Don't Drag That String Around	1970	2.00	4.00	8.00
—Red label					
447-0642	Bossa Nova Baby/Witchcraft	1964	6.25	12.50	25.00
—Black label, dog on top					
447-0642	Bossa Nova Baby/Witchcraft	1965	2.50	5.00	10.00
—Black label, dog on left					
447-0642	Bossa Nova Baby/Witchcraft	1969	6.25	12.50	25.00
—Orange label					
447-0642	Bossa Nova Baby/Witchcraft	1970	2.00	4.00	8.00
—Red label					
447-0643	Crying in the Chapel/I Believe in the Man in the Sky	1965	2.50	5.00	10.00
—Black label, dog on left					
447-0643	Crying in the Chapel/I Believe in the Man in the Sky	1970	2.00	4.00	8.00
—Red label					
447-0643 [PS]	Crying in the Chapel/I Believe in the Man in the Sky	1965	7.50	15.00	30.00
447-0644	Kissin' Cousins/It Hurts Me	1965	2.50	5.00	10.00
—Black label, dog on left					
447-0644	Kissin' Cousins/It Hurts Me	1969	6.25	12.50	25.00
—Orange label					
447-0644	Kissin' Cousins/It Hurts Me	1970	2.00	4.00	8.00
—Red label					
447-0645	Such a Night/Never Ending	1965	10.00	20.00	40.00
—Black label, dog on top					
447-0645	Such a Night/Never Ending	1965	2.50	5.00	10.00
—Black label, dog on left					
447-0645	Such a Night/Never Ending	1969	6.25	12.50	25.00
—Orange label					
447-0645	Such a Night/Never Ending	1970	2.00	4.00	8.00
—Red label					
447-0646	Viva Las Vegas/What'd I Say	1965	6.25	12.50	25.00
—Black label, dog on top					
447-0646	Viva Las Vegas/What'd I Say	1965	2.50	5.00	10.00
—Black label, dog on left					
447-0646	Viva Las Vegas/What'd I Say	1969	6.25	12.50	25.00
—Orange label					
447-0646	Viva Las Vegas/What'd I Say	1970	2.00	4.00	8.00
—Red label					
447-0647	Blue Christmas/Santa Claus Is Back in Town	1965	3.00	6.00	12.00
—Black label, dog on side					
447-0647	Blue Christmas/Santa Claus Is Back in Town	1969	6.25	12.50	25.00
—Orange label					
447-0647	Blue Christmas/Santa Claus Is Back in Town	1970	2.00	4.00	8.00
—Red label					
447-0647 [PS]	Blue Christmas/Santa Claus Is Back in Town	1965	7.50	15.00	30.00
—Has "Gold Standard Series" on sleeve					
447-0648	Do the Clam/You'll Be Gone	1965	2.50	5.00	10.00
—Black label, dog on left					
447-0648	Do the Clam/You'll Be Gone	1970	2.50	5.00	10.00
—Red label					
447-0649	Ain't That Loving You Baby/Ask Me	1965	2.50	5.00	10.00
—Black label, dog on left					
447-0649	Ain't That Loving You Baby/Ask Me	1970	2.00	4.00	8.00
—Red label					
447-0650	Puppet on a String/Wooden Heart	1965	2.50	5.00	10.00
—Black label, dog on left					
447-0650	Puppet on a String/Wooden Heart	1970	2.00	4.00	8.00
—Red label					
447-0650 [PS]	Puppet on a String/Wooden Heart	1965	7.50	15.00	30.00
447-0651	Joshua Fit the Battle/Known Only to Him	1966	3.75	7.50	15.00
—Black label, dog on left					
447-0651	Joshua Fit the Battle/Known Only to Him	1970	2.00	4.00	8.00
—Red label					
447-0651 [PS]	Joshua Fit the Battle/Known Only to Him	1966	50.00	100.00	200.00

Number	Title (A Side/B Side)	Yr	VG	VG+	NM
447-0652	Milky White Way/Swing Down Sweet Chariot	1966	3.75	7.50	15.00
—Black label, dog on left					
447-0652	Milky White Way/Swing Down Sweet Chariot	1970	2.00	4.00	8.00
—Red label					
447-0652 [PS]	Milky White Way/Swing Down Sweet Chariot	1966	50.00	100.00	200.00
447-0653	(Such An) Easy Question/It Feels So Right	1966	2.50	5.00	10.00
—Black label, dog on left					
447-0653	(Such An) Easy Question/It Feels So Right	1970	2.00	4.00	8.00
—Red label					
447-0654	I'm Yours/(It's a) Long, Lonely Highway	1966	2.50	5.00	10.00
—Black label, dog on left					
447-0654	I'm Yours/(It's a) Long, Lonely Highway	1970	2.00	4.00	8.00
—Red label					
447-0655	Tell Me Why/Blue River	1968	2.50	5.00	10.00
—Black label, dog on left					
447-0655	Tell Me Why/Blue River	1970	2.00	4.00	8.00
—Red label					
447-0656	Frankie and Johnny/Please Don't Stop Loving Me	1968	2.50	5.00	10.00
—Black label, dog on left					
447-0656	Frankie and Johnny/Please Don't Stop Loving Me	1969	6.25	12.50	25.00
—Orange label					
447-0656	Frankie and Johnny/Please Don't Stop Loving Me	1970	2.00	4.00	8.00
—Red label					
447-0657	Love Letters/Come What May	1968	2.50	5.00	10.00
—Black label, dog on left					
447-0657	Love Letters/Come What May	1970	2.00	4.00	8.00
—Red label					
447-0658	Spinout/All That I Do	1968	2.50	5.00	10.00
—Black label, dog on left					
447-0658	Spinout/All That I Do	1970	2.00	4.00	8.00
—Red label					
447-0659	Indescribably Blue/Fools Fall in Love	1969	6.25	12.50	25.00
—Orange label					
447-0659	Indescribably Blue/Fools Fall in Love	1970	2.00	4.00	8.00
—Red label					
447-0660	Long Legged Girl (With the Short Dress On)/ That's Someone You Never Forget	1970	10.00	20.00	40.00
447-0661	There's Always Me/Judy	1970	3.75	7.50	15.00
447-0662	Big Boss Man/You Don't Know Me	1970	2.50	5.00	10.00
447-0663	Guitar Man/High Heel Sneakers	1970	2.00	4.00	8.00
447-0664	U.S. Male/Stay Away	1970	2.00	4.00	8.00
447-0665	You'll Never Walk Alone/We Call on Him	1970	2.50	5.00	10.00
447-0666	Let Yourself Go/Your Time Hasn't Come Yet, Baby	1970	2.00	4.00	8.00
447-0667	A Little Less Conversation/Almost in Love	1970	2.00	4.00	8.00
447-0668	If I Can Dream/Edge of Reality	1970	2.00	4.00	8.00
447-0669	Memories/Charro	1970	2.00	4.00	8.00
447-0670	How Great Thou Art/His Hand in Mine	1970	2.50	5.00	10.00
447-0671	In the Ghetto/Any Day Now	1970	2.00	4.00	8.00
447-0672	Clean Up Your Own Back Yard/The Fair Is Moving On	1970	2.00	4.00	8.00
447-0673	Suspicious Minds/You'll Think of Me	1970	2.00	4.00	8.00
447-0674	Don't Cry Daddy/Rubberneckin'	1970	2.00	4.00	8.00
447-0675	Kentucky Rain/My Little Friend	1971	2.00	4.00	8.00
447-0676	The Wonder of You/Mama Liked the Roses	1971	2.00	4.00	8.00
447-0677	I've Lost You/The Next Step Is Love	1971	2.00	4.00	8.00
447-0678	You Don't Have to Say You Love Me/Patch It Up	1972	2.00	4.00	8.00
447-0679	I Really Don't Want to Know/There Goes My Everything	1972	2.00	4.00	8.00
447-0680	Where Did They Go, Lord/Rags to Riches	1972	2.00	4.00	8.00
447-0681	If Every Day Was Like Christmas/How Would You Like to Be	1972	2.00	4.00	8.00
447-0682	Life/Only Believe	1972	2.50	5.00	8.00
447-0683	I'm Leavin'/Heart of Rome	1972	2.00	4.00	8.00
447-0684	It's Only Love/The Sound of Your Cry	1972	2.00	4.00	8.00
447-0685	An American Trilogy/Until It's Time for You to Go	1973	2.00	4.00	8.00
447-0720	Blue Christmas/Wooden Heart	1964	3.75	7.50	15.00
447-0720 [PS]	Blue Christmas/Wooden Heart	1964	15.00	30.00	60.00

SUN

Number	Title (A Side/B Side)	Yr	VG	VG+	NM
209	That's All Right/Blue Moon of Kentucky	1954	2000.	4000.	6000.
—A mint copy of this has sold for over $17,000, but so far that is an aberration					
210	Good Rockin' Tonight/I Don't Care If the Sun Don't Shine	1954	1500.	2500.	3500.
215	Milkcow Blues Boogie/You're a Heartbreaker	1955	2000.	3500.	5000.
217	Baby Let's Play House/I'm Left, You're Right, She's Gone	1955	1000.	2000.	3000.
223	I Forgot to Remember to Forget/Mystery Train	1955	625.00	1250.	2500.

7-Inch Extended Plays

RCA VICTOR

Number	Title (A Side/B Side)	Yr	VG	VG+	NM
SPD-22 [PS]	Elvis Presley	1956	100.00	200.00	400.00
—Bonus given to buyers of a Victrola					
SPD-22 [(2)]	Elvis Presley	1956	100.00	200.00	400.00
—Value is for both discs together					
SPD-23 [PS]	Elvis Presley	1956	1000.	2000.	3000.
—Bonus given to buyers of a more expensive Victrola					
SPD-23 [(3)]	Elvis Presley	1956	1000.	2000.	3000.
—Value is for all three discs together					
SPA-7-37 [DJ]	Perfect for Parties	1956	15.00	30.00	60.00
—Without horizontal line on label					
SPA-7-37 [DJ]	Perfect for Parties	1956	15.00	30.00	60.00
—With horizontal line on label					
SPA-7-37 [PS]	Perfect for Parties	1956	15.00	30.00	60.00
LPC-126	Flaming Star/Summer Kisses, Winter Tears//Are You Lonesome To-Night?/It's Now or Never	1961	10.00	20.00	40.00
—"Compact 33 Double" with small hole					
LPC-126 [PS]	Elvis By Request	1961	10.00	20.00	40.00
EPA-747	Blue Suede Shoes/Tutti Frutti//I Got a Woman/ Just Because	1956	12.50	25.00	50.00
—Without horizontal line on label					
EPA-747	Blue Suede Shoes/Tutti Frutti//I Got a Woman/ Just Because	1956	12.50	25.00	50.00
—With horizontal line on label					
EPA-747	Blue Suede Shoes/Tutti Frutti//I Got a Woman/ Just Because	1956	50.00	100.00	200.00
—With horizontal line on label, but with no dog					
EPA-747	Blue Suede Shoes/Tutti Frutti//I Got a Woman/ Just Because	1956	50.00	100.00	200.00
—With incorrect label on Side 1 that lists, as song 3, "I'm Gonna Sit Right Down and Cry (Over You)," which does not appear on this record. Known copies of this version do not have horizontal line on label.					
EPA-747	Blue Suede Shoes/Tutti Frutti//I Got a Woman/ Just Because	1965	7.50	15.00	30.00
—Black label, dog on left					
EPA-747	Blue Suede Shoes/Tutti Frutti//I Got a Woman/ Just Because	1969	20.00	40.00	80.00
—Orange label					
EPA-747 [PS]	Elvis Presley	1956	250.00	500.00	1000.
—Temporary envelope sleeve with dark blue print, "Blue Suede Shoes by Elvis Presley" in big letters					
EPA-747 [PS]	Elvis Presley	1956	150.00	300.00	600.00
—Temporary envelope sleeve with black print, "Blue Suede Shoes by Elvis Presley" in big letters					
EPA-747 [PS]	Elvis Presley	1956	12.50	25.00	50.00
—Five different back covers exist, all with titles on front cover; any are of equal value					
EPA-747 [PS]	Elvis Presley	1965	7.50	15.00	30.00
—No titles at top of front cover					
EPA-821	Heartbreak Hotel/I Was the One//Money Honey/ I Forgot to Remember to Forget	1956	12.50	25.00	50.00
—Without horizontal line on label					
EPA-821	Heartbreak Hotel/I Was the One//Money Honey/ I Forgot to Remember to Forget	1956	12.50	25.00	50.00
—With horizontal line on label					
EPA-821	Heartbreak Hotel/I Was the One//Money Honey/ I Forgot to Remember to Forget	1956	50.00	100.00	200.00
—With horizontal line on label, but with no dog					
EPA-821	Heartbreak Hotel/I Was the One//Money Honey/ I Forgot to Remember to Forget	1965	7.50	15.00	30.00
—Black label, dog on left					
EPA-821	Heartbreak Hotel/I Was the One//Money Honey/ I Forgot to Remember to Forget	1969	20.00	40.00	80.00
—Orange label					
EPA-821 [PS]	Heartbreak Hotel	1956	12.50	25.00	50.00
EPA-830	Shake, Rattle and Roll/I Love You Because//Blue Moon/Lawdy, Miss Clawdy	1956	12.50	25.00	50.00
—Without horizontal line on label					
EPA-830	Shake, Rattle and Roll/I Love You Because//Blue Moon/Lawdy, Miss Clawdy	1956	12.50	25.00	50.00
—With horizontal line on label					
EPA-830	Shake, Rattle and Roll/I Love You Because//Blue Moon/Lawdy, Miss Clawdy	1956	50.00	100.00	200.00
—With horizontal line on label, but with no dog					
EPA-830	Shake, Rattle and Roll/I Love You Because//Blue Moon/Lawdy, Miss Clawdy	1965	7.50	15.00	30.00
—Black label, dog on left					
EPA-830	Shake, Rattle and Roll/I Love You Because//Blue Moon/Lawdy, Miss Clawdy	1969	20.00	40.00	80.00
—Orange label					
EPA-830 [PS]	Elvis Presley	1956	12.50	25.00	50.00
EPA-940	Don't Be Cruel/I Want You, I Need You, I Love You//Hound Dog/My Baby Left Me	1956	12.50	25.00	50.00
—Without horizontal line on label					
EPA-940	Don't Be Cruel/I Want You, I Need You, I Love You//Hound Dog/My Baby Left Me	1956	12.50	25.00	50.00
—With horizontal line on label					
EPA-940	Don't Be Cruel/I Want You, I Need You, I Love You//Hound Dog/My Baby Left Me	1956	50.00	100.00	200.00
—With horizontal line on label, but with no dog					
EPA-940 [PS]	The Real Elvis	1956	12.50	25.00	50.00
EPA-965	Anyway You Want Me (That's How I Will Be)/I'm Left, You're Right, She's Gone//I Don't Care If the Sun Don't Shine/Mystery Train	1956	10.00	20.00	40.00
—Without horizontal line on label					
EPA-965	Anyway You Want Me (That's How I Will Be)/I'm Left, You're Right, She's Gone//I Don't Care If the Sun Don't Shine/Mystery Train	1956	10.00	20.00	40.00
—With horizontal line on label					
EPA-965	Anyway You Want Me (That's How I Will Be)/I'm Left, You're Right, She's Gone//I Don't Care If the Sun Don't Shine/Mystery Train	1956	50.00	100.00	200.00
—With horizontal line on label, but with no dog					
EPA-965	Anyway You Want Me (That's How I Will Be)/I'm Left, You're Right, She's Gone//I Don't Care If the Sun Don't Shine/Mystery Train	1965	7.50	15.00	30.00
—Black label, dog on left					
EPA-965	Anyway You Want Me (That's How I Will Be)/I'm Left, You're Right, She's Gone//I Don't Care If the Sun Don't Shine/Mystery Train	1969	20.00	40.00	80.00
—Orange label					
EPA-965 [PS]	Anyway You Want Me	1956	12.50	25.00	50.00
—With song titles and catalog number on front					
EPA-965 [PS]	Anyway You Want Me	196?	10.00	20.00	40.00
—Without song titles and catalog number on front					
EPA-992	Rip It Up/Love Me//When My Blue Moon Turns to Gold Again/Paralyzed	1956	10.00	20.00	40.00
—Without horizontal line on label					
EPA-992	Rip It Up/Love Me//When My Blue Moon Turns to Gold Again/Paralyzed	1956	10.00	20.00	40.00
—With horizontal line on label					
EPA-992	Rip It Up/Love Me//When My Blue Moon Turns to Gold Again/Paralyzed	1956	50.00	100.00	200.00
—With horizontal line on label; bot with no dog					
EPA-992	Rip It Up/Love Me//When My Blue Moon Turns to Gold Again/Paralyzed	1965	7.50	15.00	30.00
—Black label, dog on left					
EPA-992	Rip It Up/Love Me//When My Blue Moon Turns to Gold Again/Paralyzed	1969	20.00	40.00	80.00
—Orange label					
EPA-992 [PS]	Elvis (Volume 1)	1956	12.50	25.00	50.00
EPA-993	So Glad You're Mine/Old Shep//Ready Teddy/ Anyplace Is Paradise	1956	10.00	20.00	40.00
—Without horizontal line on label					

Number	Title (A Side/B Side)	Yr	VG	VG+	NM
EPA-993	So Glad You're Mine/Old Shep//Ready Teddy/ Anyplace Is Paradise	1956	10.00	20.00	40.00
—With horizontal line on label					
EPA-993	So Glad You're Mine/Old Shep//Ready Teddy/ Anyplace Is Paradise	1956	50.00	100.00	200.00
—With horizontal line on label, but with no dog					
EPA-993	So Glad You're Mine/Old Shep//Ready Teddy/ Anyplace Is Paradise	1965	7.50	15.00	30.00
—Black label, dog on left					
EPA-993	So Glad You're Mine/Old Shep//Ready Teddy/ Anyplace Is Paradise	1969	20.00	40.00	80.00
—Orange label					
EPA-993 [PS]	Elvis (Volume 2)	1956	12.50	25.00	50.00
—Titles at top of front cover					
EPA-993 [PS]	Elvis (Volume 2)	1965	7.50	15.00	30.00
—No titles at top of front cover					
EPA-994	Long Tall Sally/First in Line//How Do You Think I Feel/How's the World Treating You	1956	12.50	25.00	50.00
—Without horizontal line on label					
EPA-994	Long Tall Sally/First in Line//How Do You Think I Feel/How's the World Treating You	1956	12.50	25.00	50.00
—With horizontal line on label					
EPA-994	Long Tall Sally/First in Line//How Do You Think I Feel/How's the World Treating You	1956	50.00	100.00	200.00
—With horizontal line on label, but with no dog					
EPA-994	Long Tall Sally/First in Line//How Do You Think I Feel/How's the World Treating You	1965	7.50	15.00	30.00
—Black label, dog on left					
EPA-994	Long Tall Sally/First in Line//How Do You Think I Feel/How's the World Treating You	1969	20.00	40.00	80.00
—Orange label					
EPA-994 [PS]	Strictly Elvis (Elvis, Vol. 3)	1956	12.50	25.00	50.00
—With titles listed on front cover					
EPA-994 [PS]	Strictly Elvis (Elvis, Vol. 3)	1965	7.50	15.00	30.00
—No titles listed on front cover					
EPB-1254 [PS]	Elvis Presley	1956	50.00	100.00	200.00
—Three different back covers exist hyping other non-Elvis RCA Victor releases; any are of equal value					
EPB-1254 [PS]	Elvis Presley	1956	37.50	75.00	150.00
—With no hype of other non-Elvis releases on back					
EPB-1254 [PS]	Elvis Presley... the most talked-about new personality in the last ten years of recorded music	1956	375.00	750.00	1500.
EPB-1254 [(2)]	Elvis Presley	1956	50.00	100.00	200.00
—Without horizontal line on label; eight songs on two discs; value is for both discs together					
EPB-1254 [(2)]	Elvis Presley	1956	50.00	100.00	200.00
—With horizontal line on label; eight songs on two discs; value is for both discs together					
EPB-1254 [(2)]	Elvis Presley	1956	375.00	750.00	1500.
—Two records have three songs on each side (12 total), as opposed to the two of the standard release					
EPA-1-1515	Loving You/Party//(Let Me Be Your) Teddy Bear/ True Love	1957	10.00	20.00	40.00
—Without horizontal line on label					
EPA-1-1515	Loving You/Party//(Let Me Be Your) Teddy Bear/ True Love	1957	10.00	20.00	40.00
—With horizontal line on label					
EPA-1-1515	Loving You/Party//(Let Me Be Your) Teddy Bear/ True Love	1965	7.50	15.00	30.00
—Black label, dog on left					
EPA-1-1515	Loving You/Party//(Let Me Be Your) Teddy Bear/ True Love	1969	20.00	40.00	80.00
—Orange label					
EPA-1-1515 [PS]	Loving You, Vol. I	1957	10.00	20.00	40.00
EPA-2-1515	Lonesome Cowboy/Hot Dog//Mean Woman Blues/Got a Lot of Livin' to Do	1957	10.00	20.00	40.00
—Without horizontal line on label					
EPA-2-1515	Lonesome Cowboy/Hot Dog//Mean Woman Blues/Got a Lot of Livin' to Do	1957	10.00	20.00	40.00
—With horizontal line on label					
EPA-2-1515	Lonesome Cowboy/Hot Dog//Mean Woman Blues/Got a Lot of Livin' to Do	1965	7.50	15.00	30.00
—Black label, dog on left					
EPA-2-1515	Lonesome Cowboy/Hot Dog//Mean Woman Blues/Got a Lot of Livin' to Do	1969	20.00	40.00	80.00
—Orange label					
EPA-2-1515 [PS]	Loving You, Vol. II	1957	10.00	20.00	40.00
—With song titles on top of front cover					
EPA-2-1515 [PS]	Loving You, Vol. II	1965	7.50	15.00	30.00
—No song titles on top of front cover					
EPA-4006	Love Me Tender/Let Me//Poor Boy/We're Gonna Move	1956	12.50	25.00	50.00
—Without horizontal line on label					
EPA-4006	Love Me Tender/Let Me//Poor Boy/We're Gonna Move	1956	12.50	25.00	50.00
—With horizontal line on label					
EPA-4006	Love Me Tender/Let Me//Poor Boy/We're Gonna Move	1956	50.00	100.00	200.00
—With horizontal line on label, but with no dog					
EPA-4006	Love Me Tender/Let Me//Poor Boy/We're Gonna Move	1965	7.50	15.00	30.00
—Black label, dog on left					
EPA-4006	Love Me Tender/Let Me//Poor Boy/We're Gonna Move	1969	20.00	40.00	80.00
—Orange label					
EPA-4006 [PS]	Love Me Tender	1956	12.50	25.00	50.00
—With song titles on top of front cover					
EPA-4006 [PS]	Love Me Tender	1965	7.50	15.00	30.00
—No song titles on top of front cover					
EPA-4041	I Need You So/Have I Told You Lately//Blueberry Hill/Is It So Strange	1957	12.50	25.00	50.00
—Without horizontal line on label					
EPA-4041	I Need You So/Have I Told You Lately//Blueberry Hill/Is It So Strange	1957	12.50	25.00	50.00
—With horizontal line on label					
EPA-4041	I Need You So/Have I Told You Lately//Blueberry Hill/Is It So Strange	1957	50.00	100.00	200.00
—With horizontal line on label, but with no dog					
EPA-4041	I Need You So/Have I Told You Lately//Blueberry Hill/Is It So Strange	1965	7.50	15.00	30.00
—Black label, dog on left					
EPA-4041	I Need You So/Have I Told You Lately//Blueberry Hill/Is It So Strange	1969	20.00	40.00	80.00
—Orange label					
EPA-4041 [PS]	Just for You (Elvis Presley)	1957	12.50	25.00	50.00
EPA-4054	(There'll Be) Peace in the Valley (For Me)/It Is No Secret (What God Can Do)//I Believe/Take My Hand, Precious Lord	1957	10.00	20.00	40.00
—Without horizontal line on label					
EPA-4054	(There'll Be) Peace in the Valley (For Me)/It Is No Secret (What God Can Do)//I Believe/Take My Hand, Precious Lord	1957	10.00	20.00	40.00
—With horizontal line on label					
EPA-4054 [PS]	Peace in the Valley	1957	10.00	20.00	40.00
EPA-4108	Santa Bring My Baby Back (To Me)/Blue Christmas//Santa Claus Is Back in Town/I'll Be Home for Christmas	1957	10.00	20.00	40.00
—Black label, dog on top					
EPA-4108	Santa Bring My Baby Back (To Me)/Blue Christmas//Santa Claus Is Back in Town/I'll Be Home for Christmas	1965	7.50	15.00	30.00
—Black label, dog on left					
EPA-4108	Santa Bring My Baby Back (To Me)/Blue Christmas//Santa Claus Is Back in Town/I'll Be Home for Christmas	1969	20.00	40.00	80.00
—Orange label					
EPA-4108 [PS]	Elvis Sings Christmas Songs	1957	10.00	20.00	40.00
EPA-4114	Jailhouse Rock/Young and Beautiful//I Want to Be Free/Don't Leave Me Now//(You're So Square) Baby I Don't Care	1957	10.00	20.00	40.00
—Black label, dog on top					
EPA-4114	Jailhouse Rock/Young and Beautiful//I Want to Be Free/Don't Leave Me Now//(You're So Square) Baby I Don't Care	1965	7.50	15.00	30.00
—Black label, dog on left					
EPA-4114	Jailhouse Rock/Young and Beautiful//I Want to Be Free/Don't Leave Me Now//(You're So Square) Baby I Don't Care	1969	20.00	40.00	80.00
—Orange label					
EPA-4114 [PS]	Jailhouse Rock	1957	10.00	20.00	40.00
EPA-4319	King Creole/New Orleans//As Long As I Have You/Lover Doll	1958	10.00	20.00	40.00
EPA-4319 [PS]	King Creole	1958	12.50	25.00	50.00
—With copyright notice on front cover					
EPA-4319 [PS]	King Creole	1958	10.00	20.00	40.00
—Without copyright notice on front cover					
EPA-4321	Trouble/Young Dreams//Crawfish/Dixieland Rock	1958	10.00	20.00	40.00
—Black label, dog on top					
EPA-4321	Trouble/Young Dreams//Crawfish/Dixieland Rock	1965	7.50	15.00	30.00
—Black label, dog on left					
EPA-4321	Trouble/Young Dreams//Crawfish/Dixieland Rock	1969	20.00	40.00	80.00
—Orange label					
EPA-4321 [PS]	King Creole, Vol. 2	1958	10.00	20.00	40.00
EPA-4325	Press Interview with Elvis Presley//Elvis Presley's Newsreel Interview/Pat Hernon Interviews Elvis...	1958	20.00	40.00	80.00
EPA-4325 [PS]	Elvis Sails	1958	20.00	40.00	80.00
—With 1959 calendar and a hole to make it suitable for hanging					
EPA-4340	White Christmas/Here Comes Santa Claus//Oh Little Town of Bethlehem/Silent Night	1958	17.50	35.00	70.00
—Black label, dog on top					
EPA-4340	White Christmas/Here Comes Santa Claus//Oh Little Town of Bethlehem/Silent Night	1965	10.00	20.00	40.00
—Black label, dog on left					
EPA-4340	White Christmas/Here Comes Santa Claus//Oh Little Town of Bethlehem/Silent Night	1969	10.00	40.00	80.00
—Orange label					
EPA-4340 [PS]	Christmas with Elvis	1958	20.00	40.00	80.00
—With copyright notice and "Printed in U.S.A." at lower right					
EPA-4340 [PS]	Christmas with Elvis	1965	10.00	20.00	40.00
—Without copyright notice and "Printed in U.S.A." at lower right					
EPA-4368	Follow That Dream/Angel//What a Wonderful Life/I'm Not the Marrying Kind	1962	7.50	15.00	30.00
—Black label, dog on top, no playing times on label					
EPA-4368	Follow That Dream/Angel//What a Wonderful Life/I'm Not the Marrying Kind	1962	10.00	20.00	40.00
—Black label, dog on top, with playing times on label					
EPA-4368	Follow That Dream/Angel//What a Wonderful Life/I'm Not the Marrying Kind	1965	6.25	12.50	25.00
—Black label, dog on left					
EPA-4368	Follow That Dream/Angel//What a Wonderful Life/I'm Not the Marrying Kind	1969	20.00	40.00	80.00
—Orange label					
EPA-4368 [PS]	Follow That Dream	1962	37.50	75.00	150.00
—Paper sleeve with "Coin Operator -- DJ Prevue" at top; print is in red					
EPA-4368 [PS]	Follow That Dream	1962	10.00	20.00	40.00
—Incorrect playing times on back cover; "Follow That Dream" is listed as 1:35 but is actually 1:38, and two others are wrong also					
EPA-4368 [PS]	Follow That Dream	1965	6.25	12.50	25.00
—Correct playing times on back cover					
EPA-4371	King of the Whole Wide World/This Is Living/ Riding the Rainbow//Home Is Where the Heart Is/I Got Lucky/A Whistling Tune	1962	10.00	20.00	40.00
—Black label, dog on top					
EPA-4371	King of the Whole Wide World/This Is Living/ Riding the Rainbow//Home Is Where the Heart Is/I Got Lucky/A Whistling Tune	1965	7.50	15.00	30.00
—Black label, dog on left					

Number	Title (A Side/B Side)	Yr	VG	VG+	NM
EPA-4371	King of the Whole Wide World/This Is Living/ Riding the Rainbow//Home Is Where the Heart Is/I Got Lucky/A Whistling Tune	1969	20.00	40.00	80.00
—Orange label					
EPA-4371 [PS]	Kid Galahad	1962	10.00	20.00	40.00
EPA-4382	If You Think I Don't Need You/I Need Somebody to Lean On//C'mon Everybody/Today, Tomorrow and Forever	1964	10.00	20.00	40.00
—Black label, dog on top					
EPA-4382	If You Think I Don't Need You/I Need Somebody to Lean On//C'mon Everybody/Today, Tomorrow and Forever	1965	7.50	15.00	30.00
—Black label, dog on left					
EPA-4382	If You Think I Don't Need You/I Need Somebody to Lean On//C'mon Everybody/Today, Tomorrow and Forever	1969	20.00	40.00	80.00
—Orange label					
EPA-4382 [PS]	Viva Las Vegas	1964	10.00	20.00	40.00
EPA-4383	I Feel That I've Known You Forever/Slowly But Surely//Night Rider/Dirty Feeling	1965	7.50	15.00	30.00
—Black label, dog on left					
EPA-4383	I Feel That I've Known You Forever/Slowly But Surely//Night Rider/Dirty Feeling	1969	20.00	40.00	80.00
—Orange label					
EPA-4383 [PS]	Tickle Me	1965	7.50	15.00	30.00
—"Coming Soon" on front cover					
EPA-4383 [PS]	Tickle Me	1965	7.50	15.00	30.00
—"Ask For" on front cover					
EPA-4383 [PS]	Tickle Me	1969	8.75	17.50	35.00
—No blurb for new album on front cover					
EPA-4387	Easy Come, Easy Go/The Love Machine/Yoga Is As Yoga Does//You Gotta Shop/Sing You Children/I'll Take Love	1967	7.50	15.00	30.00
—All copies appear to be black label, dog on left					
EPA-4387 [PS]	Easy Come, Easy Go	1967	7.50	15.00	30.00
EPA-5088	Hard Headed Woman/Good Rockin' Tonight// Don't/I Beg of You	1959	15.00	30.00	60.00
—Black label, dog on top					
EPA-5088	Hard Headed Woman/Good Rockin' Tonight// Don't/I Beg of You	1959	100.00	200.00	400.00
—Maroon label					
EPA-5088	Hard Headed Woman/Good Rockin' Tonight// Don't/I Beg of You	1965	7.50	15.00	30.00
—Black label, dog on left					
EPA-5088	Hard Headed Woman/Good Rockin' Tonight// Don't/I Beg of You	1969	20.00	40.00	80.00
—Orange label					
EPA-5088 [PS]	A Touch of Gold	1959	15.00	30.00	60.00
EPA-5101	Wear My Ring Around Your Neck/Treat Me Nice //One Night/That's All Right	1959	15.00	30.00	60.00
—Black label, dog on top					
EPA-5101	Wear My Ring Around Your Neck/Treat Me Nice //One Night/That's All Right	1959	100.00	200.00	400.00
—Maroon label					
EPA-5101	Wear My Ring Around Your Neck/Treat Me Nice //One Night/That's All Right	1965	7.50	15.00	30.00
—Black label, dog on left					
EPA-5101	Wear My Ring Around Your Neck/Treat Me Nice //One Night/That's All Right	1969	20.00	40.00	80.00
—Orange label					
EPA-5101 [PS]	A Touch of Gold, Volume II	1959	15.00	30.00	60.00
EPA-5120	Don't Be Cruel/I Want You, I Need You, I Love You//Hound Dog/My Baby Left Me	1959	15.00	30.00	60.00
—Black label, dog on top					
EPA-5120	Don't Be Cruel/I Want You, I Need You, I Love You//Hound Dog/My Baby Left Me	1959	150.00	300.00	600.00
—Maroon label					
EPA-5120	Don't Be Cruel/I Want You, I Need You, I Love You//Hound Dog/My Baby Left Me	1965	6.25	12.50	25.00
—Black label, dog on left					
EPA-5120	Don't Be Cruel/I Want You, I Need You, I Love You//Hound Dog/My Baby Left Me	1969	20.00	40.00	80.00
—Orange label					
EPA-5120 [PS]	The Real Elvis	1959	15.00	30.00	60.00
EPA-5121	(There'll Be) Peace in the Valley (For Me)/It Is No Secret (What God Can Do)//I Believe/Take My Hand, Precious Lord	1959	7.50	15.00	30.00
—Black label, dog on top					
EPA-5121	(There'll Be) Peace in the Valley (For Me)/It Is No Secret (What God Can Do)//I Believe/Take My Hand, Precious Lord	1959	100.00	200.00	400.00
—Maroon label					
EPA-5121	(There'll Be) Peace in the Valley (For Me)/It Is No Secret (What God Can Do)//I Believe/Take My Hand, Precious Lord	1965	6.25	12.50	25.00
—Black label, dog on left					
EPA-5121	(There'll Be) Peace in the Valley (For Me)/It Is No Secret (What God Can Do)//I Believe/Take My Hand, Precious Lord	1969	20.00	40.00	80.00
—Orange label					
EPA-5121 [PS]	Peace in the Valley	1959	10.00	20.00	40.00
—Three slightly different cover variations with no difference in value					
EPA-5122	King Creole/New Orleans//As Long As I Have You/Lover Doll	1959	7.50	15.00	30.00
—Black label, dog on top					
EPA-5122	King Creole/New Orleans//As Long As I Have You/Lover Doll	1959	1000.	1500.	2000.
—Maroon label					
EPA-5122	King Creole/New Orleans//As Long As I Have You/Lover Doll	1965	6.25	12.50	25.00
—Black label, dog on left					
EPA-5122	King Creole/New Orleans//As Long As I Have You/Lover Doll	1969	20.00	40.00	80.00
—Orange label					
EPA-5122 [PS]	King Creole	1959	10.00	20.00	40.00
—With "Gold Standard Series" on front cover					

Number	Title (A Side/B Side)	Yr	VG	VG+	NM
EPA-5122 [PS]	King Creole	1965	7.50	15.00	30.00
—Without "Gold Standard Series" on front cover					
EPA-5141	All Shook Up/Don't Ask Me Why//Too Much/Blue Moon of Kentucky	1959	17.50	35.00	70.00
—Black label, dog on top					
EPA-5141	All Shook Up/Don't Ask Me Why//Too Much/Blue Moon of Kentucky	1959	100.00	200.00	400.00
—Maroon label					
EPA-5141	All Shook Up/Don't Ask Me Why//Too Much/Blue Moon of Kentucky	1959	7.50	15.00	30.00
—Black label, dog on left					
EPA-5141	All Shook Up/Don't Ask Me Why//Too Much/Blue Moon of Kentucky	1959	20.00	40.00	80.00
—Orange label					
EPA-5141 [PS]	A Touch of Gold, Volume 3	1959	17.50	35.00	70.00
EPA-5157	Press Interview with Elvis Presley//Elvis Presley's Newsreel Interview/Pat Hernon Interviews Elvis...	1965	7.50	15.00	30.00
—Black label, dog on top					
EPA-5157	Press Interview with Elvis Presley//Elvis Presley's Newsreel Interview/Pat Hernon Interviews Elvis...	1969	20.00	40.00	80.00
—Orange label					
EPA-5157 [PS]	Elvis Sails	1965	7.50	15.00	30.00
G8-MW-8705 [DJ]	TV Guide Presents Elvis Presley	1956	300.00	600.00	1200.
—Blue label, locked grooves (needle has to be lifted to play each of the four excerpts)					
Albums					
BOXCAR					
(no #)	Having Fun with Elvis on Stage	1974	37.50	75.00	150.00
—All-talking record sold at Elvis concerts in 1974					
DCC COMPACT CLASSICS					
LPZ-2037 [S]	Elvis Is Back!	1997	6.25	12.50	25.00
—Audiophile vinyl					
LPZ-2040 [(2)]	24 Karat Hits!	1997	7.50	15.00	30.00
—Audiophile vinyl					
FOTOPLAY					
FSP-1001 [PD]	To Elvis: Love Still Burning	1978	6.25	12.50	25.00
—Tribute-song picture disc of Elvis; in plastic bag with 11x11 insert					
FSP-1001 [PD]	To Elvis: Love Still Burning	1978	7.50	15.00	30.00
—In white cardboard cover with black printing					
FSP-1001 [PD]	To Elvis: Love Still Burning	1978	3.75	7.50	15.00
—In black cardboard cover with white printing					
GOLDEN EDITIONS					
KING-1	The First Year (Elvis, Scotty and Bill)	1979	3.75	7.50	15.00
GEL-101	The First Year (Elvis, Scotty and Bill)	1979	5.00	10.00	20.00
GREAT NORTHWEST					
GV-2004	The King Speaks (February 1961, Memphis, Tennessee)	1977	2.50	5.00	10.00
—Label says this is on "Green Valley" while sleeve says "Great Northwest"					
GNW-4005	The Elvis Tapes	1977	3.00	6.00	12.00
GNW-4006	The King Speaks (February 1961, Memphis, Tennessee)	1977	2.00	4.00	8.00
—Both label and sleeve say this is on "Great Northwest"					
GREEN VALLEY					
GV-2001/3 [(2)]	Elvis (Speaks to You)	1978	7.50	15.00	30.00
—Elvis interviews plus tracks by the Jordanaires					
GV-2001	Elvis Exclusive Live Press Conference (Memphis, Tennessee, February 1961)	1977	10.00	20.00	40.00
—Issued with two slightly different covers					
GUSTO					
SD-995	Interviews with Elvis (Canada 1957)	1978	10.00	20.00	40.00
—Reissue of Great Northwest album					
HALW					
HALW-0001	The First Years	1978	7.50	15.00	30.00
—With stamped, limited edition number					
HALW-0001	The First Years	1978	5.00	10.00	20.00
—Without limited edition number					
K-TEL					
NU 9900	Love Songs	1981	5.00	10.00	20.00
LOUISIANA HAYRIDE					
LH-3061	Beginning Years	1984	5.00	10.00	20.00
—With booklet and facsimile contract					
MARVENCO					
101	Beginning (1954-1955)	1988	3.75	7.50	15.00
—Pink vinyl with booklet and facsimile contract					
MOBILE FIDELITY					
1-059	From Elvis in Memphis	1982	12.50	25.00	50.00
—Audiophile vinyl					
MUSIC WORKS					
PB-3601	The First Live Recordings	1984	3.75	7.50	15.00
PB-3602	The Hillbilly Cat	1984	3.75	7.50	15.00
OAK					
1003	Vintage 1955 Elvis	1990	15.00	30.00	60.00
PAIR					
PDL2-1010 [(2)]	Double Dynamite	1982	5.00	10.00	20.00
PDL2-1037 [(2)]	Remembering	1983	7.50	15.00	30.00
PDL2-1185 [(2)]	Elvis Aron Presley Forever	1988	5.00	10.00	20.00
PICKWICK					
(no #) [(7)]	The Pickwick Pack (unofficial title)	1978	15.00	30.00	60.00
—Seven Pickwick albums in special package and cardboard wrapper; one of the LPs is Elvis' Christmas Album					
(no #) [(7)]	The Pickwick Pack (unofficial title)	1979	15.00	30.00	60.00
—Seven Pickwick albums in special package and cardboard wrapper; one of the LPs is Frankie and Johnny					
CAS-2304	Elvis Sings Flaming Star	1976	2.50	5.00	10.00
CAS-2408	Let's Be Friends	1975	2.50	5.00	10.00
CAL-2428 [M]	Elvis' Christmas Album	1975	3.00	6.00	12.00
—Same contents as RCA Camden LP; no Christmas trim on border					
CAL-2428 [M]	Elvis' Christmas Album	1976	2.50	5.00	10.00
—Same as above, but with Christmas trim on cover border					
CAS-2440	Almost in Love	1975	2.50	5.00	10.00
CAL-2472	You'll Never Walk Alone	1975	2.50	5.00	10.00
CAL-2518	C'mon Everybody	1975	2.50	5.00	10.00
CAS-2533	I Got Lucky	1975	2.50	5.00	10.00

Number	Title (A Side/B Side)	Yr	VG	VG+	NM
CAS-2567	Elvis Sings Hits from His Movies, Volume 1	1975	2.50	5.00	10.00
CAS-2595	Burning Love And Hits from His Movies, Vol. 2	1975	3.00	6.00	12.00
—First cover contains a notice about the upcoming "Aloha from Hawaii" show					
CAS-2595	Burning Love And Hits from His Movies, Vol. 2	1976	2.00	4.00	8.00
—Reissue deletes the "Aloha from Hawaii" notice					
CAS-2611	Separate Ways	1975	2.50	5.00	10.00
DL2-5001 [(2)]	Double Dynamite	1975	6.25	12.50	25.00
ACL-7007	Frankie and Johnny	1976	2.50	5.00	10.00
ACL-7064	Mahalo from Elvis	1978	5.00	10.00	20.00
PREMORE					
PL-589	Early Elvis (1954-1956 Live at the Louisiana Hayride)	1989	7.50	15.00	30.00
RCA					
2023-1-R	The Million Dollar Quartet	1990	3.00	6.00	12.00
—With Jerry Lee Lewis, Carl Perkins, and perhaps Johnny Cash					
2227-1-R	The Great Performances	1990	10.00	20.00	40.00
3114-1-R [(3)]	Collectors Gold	1991	—	—	—
—Rumored to exist on US vinyl, but unconfirmed					
5600-1-R	Return of the Rocker	1986	5.00	10.00	20.00
6221-1-R [(2)]	The Memphis Record	1987	7.50	15.00	30.00
6313-1-R	Elvis Talks!	1987	7.50	15.00	30.00
6382-1-R	The Number One Hits	1987	7.50	15.00	30.00
6383-1-R [(2)]	The Top Ten Hits	1987	7.50	15.00	30.00
6414-1-R [(2)]	The Complete Sun Sessions	1987	7.50	15.00	30.00
6738-1-R	Essential Elvis: The First Movies	1988	6.25	12.50	25.00
6985-1-R	The Alternate Aloha	1988	5.00	10.00	20.00
8468-1-R	Elvis in Nashville (1956-1971)	1988	10.00	20.00	40.00
9586-1-R	Elvis Gospel 1957-1971 (Known Only to Him)	1989	10.00	20.00	40.00
9589-1-R	Essential Elvis, Vol. 2 (Stereo '57)	1989	6.25	12.50	25.00
07863-67642-1	Elvis' Golden Records	1997	7.50	15.00	30.00
—Reissue for the Tower Records chain with 6 bonus tracks					
07863-67643-1	Elvis' Gold Records Volume 2 — 50,000,000 Elvis Fans Can't Be Wrong	1997	7.50	15.00	30.00
—Reissue for the Tower Records chain with 10 bonus tracks					
RCA CAMDEN					
CAS-2304	Elvis Sings Flaming Star	1969	7.50	15.00	30.00
CAS-2408	Let's Be Friends	1970	7.50	15.00	30.00
CAL-2428 [M]	Elvis' Christmas Album	1970	7.50	15.00	30.00
—Blue label, non-flexible vinyl					
CAL-2428 [M]	Elvis' Christmas Album	1971	3.00	6.00	12.00
—Blue label, flexible vinyl					
CAS-2440	Almost in Love	1970	10.00	20.00	40.00
—Last song on Side 2 is "Stay Away, Joe"					
CAS-2440	Almost in Love	1973	6.25	12.50	25.00
—Last song on Side 2 is "Stay Away"					
CAL-2472	You'll Never Walk Alone	1974	7.50	15.00	30.00
CALX-2472	You'll Never Walk Alone	1971	3.75	7.50	15.00
CAL-2518	C'mon Everybody	1971	5.00	10.00	20.00
CAL-2533	I Got Lucky	1971	6.25	12.50	25.00
CAS-2567	Elvis Sings Hits from His Movies, Volume 1	1972	5.00	10.00	20.00
CAS-2595	Burning Love And Hits from His Movies, Vol. 2	1972	6.25	12.50	25.00
—With star on front cover advertising a bonus photo, the presence of which doubles the value of this LP					
CAS-2595	Burning Love And Hits from His Movies, Vol. 2	1972	2.50	5.00	10.00
—No star on cover, no bonus photo					
CAS-2611	Separate Ways	1973	7.50	15.00	30.00
RCA SPECIAL PRODUCTS					
DPL2-0056(e) [(2)]	Elvis	1973	12.50	25.00	50.00
—Mustard labels					
DPL2-0056(e) [(2)]	Elvis	1973	6.25	12.50	25.00
—Blue labels					
DPL2-0056(e) [(2)]	Elvis Commemorative Album	1978	20.00	40.00	80.00
—Reissue of "Elvis" (same number) with new title and gold vinyl					
DPL2-0168 [(2)]	Elvis in Hollywood	1976	15.00	30.00	60.00
—Blue labels; with 20-page booklet					
DML5-0263 [(5)]	The Elvis Story	1977	15.00	30.00	60.00
—Available through Candelite Music via mail order					
DML1-0264	His Songs of Inspiration	1977	3.75	7.50	15.00
DPL5-0347 [(5)]	Memories of Elvis (A Lasting Tribute to the King of Rock 'N' Roll)	1978	20.00	40.00	80.00
DML1-0348	The Greatest Show on Earth	1978	3.75	7.50	15.00
DML6-0412 [(6)]	The Legendary Recordings of Elvis Presley	1979	25.00	50.00	100.00
DML1-0413	The Greatest Moments in Music	1980	3.75	7.50	15.00
DML1-0437	Rock 'N Roll Forever	1981	3.75	7.50	15.00
DVL1-0461	The Legendary Magic of Elvis Presley	1980	3.75	7.50	15.00
DML3-0632 [(3)]	The Elvis Presley Collection	1984	20.00	40.00	80.00
—Available through Candelite Music via mail order					
DPL1-0647	Elvis Country	1984	7.50	15.00	30.00
DVM1-0704	Elvis (One Night with You)	1984	15.00	30.00	60.00
—With poster (deduct 25% if missing)					
SVL3-0710 [(3)]	50 Years — 50 Hits	1985	7.50	15.00	30.00
DVL2-0728 [(2)]	His Songs of Faith and Inspiration	1986	12.50	25.00	50.00
SVL2-0824 [(2)]	Good Rockin' Tonight	1988	5.00	10.00	20.00
CAL-2428 [M]	Elvis' Christmas Album	1986	7.50	15.00	30.00
—Reissue for The Special Music Company					
RCA VICTOR					
(no #)	International Hotel, Las Vegas Nevada, Presents Elvis, 1969	1969	1250.	1875.	2500.
—Gift box to guests at Elvis' July 31-Aug, 1, 1969 shows. Includes LPM-4088 and LSP-4155; press release; 1969 catalog; three photos; and thank-you note from Elvis and the Colonel. Most of the value is for the box.					
(no #)	International Hotel, Las Vegas Nevada, Presents Elvis, 1970	1970	1250.	1875.	2500.
—Gift box to guests at Elvis' Jan. 28, 1970 show. Includes LSP-6020 and 47-9791; press release; 1970 catalog; photo; booklet; and dinner menu. Most of the value is for the box.					
PRS-279	Singer Presents Elvis Singing Flaming Star and Others	1968	25.00	50.00	100.00
—Sold only at Singer sewing machine dealers; reissued on RCA Camden 2304					
APL1-0283	Elvis	1973	12.50	25.00	50.00
CPL1-0341	A Legendary Performer, Volume 1	1974	6.25	12.50	25.00
—Includes booklet (deduct 40% if missing); with die-cut hole in front cover					
CPL1-0341	A Legendary Performer, Volume 1	1986	3.75	7.50	15.00
—No die-cut hole in cover and no booklet					
APL1-0388	Raised on Rock/For Ol' Times Sake	1973	7.50	15.00	30.00
—Orange label					

Number	Title (A Side/B Side)	Yr	VG	VG+	NM
APL1-0388	Raised on Rock/For Ol' Times Sake	1975	7.50	15.00	30.00
—Tan label					
APL1-0388	Raised on Rock/For Ol' Times Sake	1977	3.00	6.00	12.00
—Black label, dog near top					
SP-33-461 [DJ]	Special Palm Sunday Programming	1967	175.00	350.00	700.00
—White label promo. Add 25% for cue sheet.					
AFL1-0475	Good Times	1977	3.00	6.00	12.00
—Black label, dog near top; includes copies with sticker wrapped around spine with new number					
CPL1-0475	Good Times	1974	12.50	25.00	50.00
—Orange label					
CPL1-0475	Good Times	1976	3.00	6.00	12.00
—Black label, dog near top					
SPS-33-571 [DJ]	Elvis As Recorded at Madison Square Garden	1972	75.00	150.00	300.00
—"Radio Station Banded Special Version"; came in plain white cover with stickers					
AFL1-0606	Elvis Recorded Live on Stage in Memphis	1977	3.00	6.00	12.00
—Black label, dog near top; includes copies with sticker wrapped around spine with new number					
APD1-0606 [Q]	Elvis Recorded Live on Stage in Memphis	1974	50.00	100.00	200.00
—"RCA QuadraDisc" labels					
CPL1-0606	Elvis Recorded Live on Stage in Memphis	1974	6.25	12.50	25.00
—Orange label					
CPL1-0606	Elvis Recorded Live on Stage in Memphis	1975	6.25	12.50	25.00
—Tan label					
DJL1-0606 [DJ]	Elvis Recorded Live on Stage in Memphis	1974	75.00	150.00	300.00
—Special banded version for radio airplay					
AFM1-0818	Having Fun with Elvis on Stage	1977	6.25	12.50	25.00
—Black label, dog near top					
CPM1-0818	Having Fun with Elvis on Stage	1974	7.50	15.00	30.00
—Commercial issue of Boxcar LP; orange label					
CPM1-0818	Having Fun with Elvis on Stage	1975	5.00	10.00	20.00
—Tan label					
DJM1-0835 [DJ]	Elvis Presley Interview Record: An Audio Self-Portrait	1984	20.00	40.00	80.00
—Promotional item for "50th Anniversary" series; later issued as RCA 6313-1-R					
AFL1-0873	Promised Land	1977	3.75	7.50	15.00
—Black label, dog near top					
APD1-0873 [Q]	Promised Land	1975	50.00	100.00	200.00
—"RCA QuadraDisc" label					
APD1-0873 [Q]	Promised Land	1977	30.00	60.00	120.00
—Black label, dog near top; quadraphonic reissue					
APL1-0873	Promised Land	1975	15.00	30.00	60.00
—Orange label					
APL1-0873	Promised Land	1975	5.00	10.00	20.00
—Tan label					
ANL1-0971(e)	Pure Gold	1975	3.75	7.50	15.00
—Orange label					
ANL1-0971(e)	Pure Gold	1976	3.00	6.00	12.00
—Yellow label					
LOC-1035 [M]	Elvis' Christmas Album	1957	125.00	250.00	500.00
—Gatefold cover; title printed in gold on LP spine; includes bound-in booklet but not sticker					
LOC-1035 [M]	Elvis' Christmas Album	1957	125.00	250.00	500.00
—Gatefold cover; title printed in silver on LP spine; includes bound-in booklet but not sticker					
LOC-1035 [M]	Elvis' Christmas Album	1957	7500.	11250.	15000.
—Red vinyl; unique					
LOC-1035 [M]	Elvis' Christmas Album Sticker	1957	37.50	75.00	150.00
—Gold sticker with "To________" and "From________" blanks					
AFL1-1039	Elvis Today	1977	3.00	6.00	12.00
—Black label, dog near top; includes copies with sticker wrapped around spine with new number					
APD1-1039 [Q]	Elvis Today	1975	50.00	100.00	200.00
—"RCA QuadraDisc" labels					
APD1-1039 [Q]	Elvis Today	1977	37.50	75.00	150.00
—Black label, dog near top; quadraphonic reissue					
APL1-1039	Elvis Today	1975	15.00	30.00	60.00
—Orange label					
APL1-1039	Elvis Today	1975	7.50	15.00	30.00
—Tan label					
AFL1-1254(e) [R]	Elvis Presley	1977	3.00	6.00	12.00
—Black label, dog near top; includes copies with sticker wrapped around spine with new number					
LPM-1254 [M]	Elvis Presley	1956	125.00	250.00	500.00
—Version 1: "Long Play" on label; "Elvis" in pale pink, "Presley" in pale green on cover; pale green logo box in upper right front cover					
LPM-1254 [M]	Elvis Presley	1956	100.00	200.00	400.00
—Version 2: "Long Play" on label; "Elvis" in pale pink, "Presley" in neon green on cover; neon green logo box in upper right front cover					
LPM-1254 [M]	Elvis Presley	1956	62.50	125.00	250.00
—Version 3: "Long Play" on label; "Elvis" in pale pink, "Presley" in neon green on cover; black logo box in upper right front cover					
LPM-1254 [M]	Elvis Presley	1958	50.00	100.00	200.00
—Version 4: "Long Play" on label; "Elvis" in neon pink, almost red, "Presley" in neon green on cover; black logo box in upper right front cover					
LPM-1254 [M]	Elvis Presley	1963	30.00	60.00	120.00
—"Mono" on label; cover photo is slightly left of center, otherwise same as Version 4 above					
LPM-1254 [M]	Elvis Presley	1964	15.00	30.00	60.00
—"Monaural" on label					
LSP-1254(e) [R]	Elvis Presley	1962	50.00	100.00	200.00
—"Stereo Electronically Reprocessed" and silver "RCA Victor" on label					
LSP-1254(e) [R]	Elvis Presley	1965	10.00	20.00	40.00
—"Stereo Electronically Reprocessed" and white "RCA Victor" on label					
LSP-1254(e) [R]	Elvis Presley	1968	7.50	15.00	30.00
—Orange label, non-flexible vinyl					
LSP-1254(e) [R]	Elvis Presley	1975	3.75	7.50	15.00
—Tan label					
LSP-1254(e) [R]	Elvis Presley	1976	3.00	6.00	12.00
—Black label, dog near top					
ANL1-1319 [S]	His Hand in Mine	1976	3.75	7.50	15.00
—Reissue with more tightly cropped photo of Elvis on front cover					
CPL1-1349	A Legendary Performer, Volume 2	1976	7.50	15.00	30.00
—Includes booklet (deduct 40% if missing); with die-cut hole in front cover					
CPL1-1349	A Legendary Performer, Volume 2	1976	15.00	30.00	60.00
—Without false starts and outtakes of "Such a Night" and "Cane and a High Starched Collar," which are supposed to be there. End of matrix number may be "31."					
CPL1-1349	A Legendary Performer, Volume 2	1986	3.75	7.50	15.00
—No die-cut hole in cover and no booklet					
AFL1-1382(e) [R]	Elvis	1977	3.00	6.00	12.00
—Black label, dog near top; includes copies with sticker wrapped around spine with new number					

Number	Title (A Side/B Side)	Yr	VG	VG+	NM
LPM-1382 [M]	Elvis	1956	75.00	150.00	300.00
—Back cover has ads for other albums. At least 11 different variations of this are known, all of equal value.					
LPM-1382 [M]	Elvis	1956	75.00	150.00	300.00
—Back cover has no ads for other albums. "Long Play" on label.					
LPM-1382 [M]	Elvis	1956	200.00	400.00	800.00
—With alternate take of "Old Shep" on side 2. Matrix number ends in "15S," "17S" or "19S," but should be played for positive ID. On alternate take, Elvis sings "he grew old AND his eyes were growing dim" (no AND on standard press)					
LPM-1382 [M]	Elvis	1956	100.00	200.00	400.00
—With tracks listed on labels as "Band 1" through "Band 6"					
LPM-1382 [M]	Elvis	1963	20.00	40.00	80.00
—"Mono" on label					
LPM-1382 [M]	Elvis	1965	15.00	30.00	60.00
—"Monaural" on label					
LSP-1382(e) [R]	Elvis	1962	50.00	100.00	200.00
—"Stereo Electronically Reprocessed" and silver "RCA Victor" on label					
LSP-1382(e) [R]	Elvis	1964	12.50	25.00	50.00
—"Stereo Electronically Reprocessed" and white "RCA Victor" on label					
LSP-1382(e) [R]	Elvis	1968	7.50	15.00	30.00
—Orange label, non-flexible vinyl					
LSP-1382(e) [R]	Elvis	1971	5.00	10.00	20.00
—Orange label, flexible vinyl					
LSP-1382(e) [R]	Elvis	1975	3.75	7.50	15.00
—Tan label					
LSP-1382(e) [R]	Elvis	1976	3.00	6.00	12.00
—Black label, dog near top					
AFL1-1506	From Elvis Presley Boulevard, Memphis, Tennessee	1977	3.00	6.00	12.00
—Black label, dog near top; with sticker wrapped around spine with new number (old number still on label)					
AFL1-1506	From Elvis Presley Boulevard, Memphis, Tennessee	1977	2.50	5.00	10.00
—Black label, dog near top; new number is on cover and label					
APL1-1506	From Elvis Presley Boulevard, Memphis, Tennessee	1976	7.50	15.00	30.00
—Tan label					
AFL1-1515(e) [R]	Loving You	1977	3.00	6.00	12.00
—Black label, dog near top; includes copies with sticker wrapped around spine with new number					
LPM-1515 [M]	Loving You	1957	75.00	150.00	300.00
—"Long Play" on label					
LPM-1515 [M]	Loving You	1963	25.00	50.00	100.00
—"Mono" on label					
LPM-1515 [M]	Loving You	1964	12.50	25.00	50.00
—"Monaural" on label					
LSP-1515(e) [R]	Loving You	1962	37.50	75.00	150.00
—"Stereo Electronically Reprocessed" and silver "RCA Victor" on label					
LSP-1515(e) [R]	Loving You	1964	12.50	25.00	50.00
—"Stereo Electronically Reprocessed" and white "RCA Victor" on label					
LSP-1515(e) [R]	Loving You	1968	10.00	20.00	40.00
—Orange label, non-flexible vinyl					
LSP-1515(e) [R]	Loving You	1971	5.00	10.00	20.00
—Orange label, flexible vinyl					
LSP-1515(e) [R]	Loving You	1975	5.00	10.00	20.00
—Tan label					
LSP-1515(e) [R]	Loving You	1976	3.00	6.00	12.00
—Black label, dog near top					
AFM1-1675	The Sun Sessions	1977	3.75	7.50	15.00
—Black label, dog near top; includes copies with sticker wrapped around spine with new number					
APM1-1675	The Sun Sessions	1976	5.00	10.00	20.00
—Tan label					
APM1-1675	The Sun Sessions	1976	3.00	6.00	12.00
—Black label, dog near top					
AFL1-1707(e) [R]	Elvis' Golden Records	1977	3.00	6.00	12.00
—Black label, dog near top; includes copies with sticker wrapped around spine with new number					
AQL1-1707(e) [R]	Elvis' Golden Records	1979	2.50	5.00	10.00
—Another reissue with new prefix					
LPM-1707 [M]	Elvis' Golden Records	1958	62.50	125.00	250.00
—Title on cover in light blue letters; no song titles listed on front cover					
LPM-1707 [M]	Elvis' Golden Records	1958	37.50	75.00	150.00
—Title on cover in light blue letters; no song titles listed on front cover; "RE" on back cover					
LPM-1707 [M]	Elvis' Golden Records	1963	15.00	30.00	60.00
—"Mono" on label; title on cover in white letters; song titles added to front cover					
LPM-1707 [M]	Elvis' Golden Records	1964	10.00	20.00	40.00
—"Monaural" on label; "RE2" on back cover					
LSP-1707(e) [R]	Elvis' Golden Records	1962	50.00	100.00	200.00
—"Stereo Electronically Reprocessed" and silver "RCA Victor" on label					
LSP-1707(e) [R]	Elvis' Golden Records	1964	12.50	25.00	50.00
—"Stereo Electronically Reprocessed" and white "RCA Victor" on label					
LSP-1707(e) [R]	Elvis' Golden Records	1968	7.50	15.00	30.00
—Orange label, non-flexible vinyl					
LSP-1707(e) [R]	Elvis' Golden Records	1971	5.00	10.00	20.00
—Orange label, flexible vinyl					
LSP-1707(e) [R]	Elvis' Golden Records	1975	5.00	10.00	20.00
—Tan label					
LSP-1707(e) [R]	Elvis' Golden Records	1976	3.00	6.00	12.00
—Black label, dog near top					
AFL1-1884(e) [R]	King Creole	1977	3.00	6.00	12.00
—Black label, dog near top; includes copies with sticker wrapped around spine with new number					
LPM-1884 [M]	King Creole	1958	50.00	100.00	200.00
—"Long Play" on label; contrary to some other sources, this was NOT issued with a bonus photo					
LPM-1884 [M]	King Creole	1963	20.00	40.00	80.00
—"Mono" on label					
LPM-1884 [M]	King Creole	1964	15.00	30.00	60.00
—"Monaural" on label					
LSP-1884(e) [R]	King Creole	1962	37.50	75.00	150.00
—"Stereo Electronically Reprocessed" and silver "RCA Victor" on label					
LSP-1884(e) [R]	King Creole	1964	15.00	30.00	60.00
—"Stereo Electronically Reprocessed" and white "RCA Victor" on label					
LSP-1884(e) [R]	King Creole	1968	10.00	20.00	40.00
—Orange label, non-flexible vinyl					
LSP-1884(e) [R]	King Creole	1971	5.00	10.00	20.00
—Orange label, flexible vinyl					
LSP-1884(e) [R]	King Creole	1975	5.00	10.00	20.00
—Tan label					
LSP-1884(e) [R]	King Creole	1976	3.00	6.00	12.00
—Black label, dog near top					
ANL1-1936	Elvis Sings the Wonderful World of Christmas	1975	3.75	7.50	15.00
—New number; same contents as LSP-4579. Orange label.					
ANL1-1936	Elvis Sings the Wonderful World of Christmas	1976	3.00	6.00	12.00
—Tan label					
ANL1-1936	Elvis Sings the Wonderful World of Christmas	1977	2.50	5.00	10.00
—Black label, dog near top					
LPM-1951 [M]	Elvis' Christmas Album	1958	37.50	75.00	150.00
—Same contents as LOC-1035, but with non-gatefold blue cover; "Long Play" at bottom of label					
LPM-1951 [M]	Elvis' Christmas Album	1963	17.50	35.00	70.00
—"Mono" at bottom of label: "RE" on lower left front cover (photos on back were altered)					
LPM-1951 [M]	Elvis' Christmas Album	1964	10.00	20.00	40.00
—"Monaural" at bottom of label; "RE" on lower left front cover					
LSP-1951(e) [R]	Elvis' Christmas Album	1964	12.50	25.00	50.00
—Black label, dog on top; "Stereo Electronically Reprocessed" at bottom of label					
LSP-1951(e) [R]	Elvis' Christmas Album	1968	15.00	30.00	60.00
—Orange label, non-flexible vinyl					
AFL1-1990(e) [R]	For LP Fans Only	1977	3.00	6.00	12.00
—Black label, dog near top; includes copies with sticker wrapped around spine with new number					
LPM-1990 [M]	For LP Fans Only	1959	62.50	125.00	250.00
—"Long Play" on label					
LPM-1990 [M]	For LP Fans Only	1963	20.00	40.00	80.00
—"Mono" on label					
LPM-1990 [M]	For LP Fans Only	1964	12.50	25.00	50.00
—"Monaural" on label					
LSP-1990(e) [R]	For LP Fans Only	1965	75.00	150.00	300.00
—"Stereo Electronically Reprocessed" on label; error cover with same photo on both front and back					
LSP-1990(e) [R]	For LP Fans Only	1965	12.50	25.00	50.00
—"Stereo Electronically Reprocessed" on label; normal cover with different front and back cover photos					
LSP-1990(e) [R]	For LP Fans Only	1968	7.50	15.00	30.00
—Orange label, non-flexible vinyl					
LSP-1990(e) [R]	For LP Fans Only	1975	5.00	10.00	20.00
—Tan label					
LSP-1990(e) [R]	For LP Fans Only	1976	3.00	6.00	12.00
—Black label, dog near top					
AFL1-2011(e) [R]	A Date with Elvis	1977	3.00	6.00	12.00
—Black label, dog near top; includes copies with sticker wrapped around spine with new number					
LPM-2011 [M]	A Date with Elvis	1959	100.00	200.00	400.00
—"Long Play" on label; gatefold cover, no sticker on cover					
LPM-2011 [M]	A Date with Elvis	1959	125.00	250.00	500.00
—"Long Play" on label; gatefold cover, with sticker on cover					
LPM-2011 [M]	A Date with Elvis	1963	25.00	50.00	100.00
—"Mono" on label; no gatefold cover					
LPM-2011 [M]	A Date with Elvis	1965	12.50	25.00	50.00
—"Monaural" on label					
LSP-2011(e) [R]	A Date with Elvis	1965	12.50	25.00	50.00
—Black label, "Stereo Electronically Reprocessed" on label					
LSP-2011(e) [R]	A Date with Elvis	1968	7.50	15.00	30.00
—Orange label, non-flexible vinyl					
LSP-2011(e) [R]	A Date with Elvis	1971	5.00	10.00	20.00
—Orange label, flexible vinyl					
LSP-2011(e) [R]	A Date with Elvis	1975	5.00	10.00	20.00
—Tan label					
LSP-2011(e) [R]	A Date with Elvis	1977	3.00	6.00	12.00
—Black label, dog near top					
AFL1-2075(e) [R]	Elvis' Gold Records Volume 2 — 50,000,000 Elvis Fans Can't Be Wrong	1977	3.00	6.00	12.00
—Black label, dog near top; includes copies with sticker wrapped around spine with new number					
LPM-2075 [M]	Elvis' Gold Records Volume 2 — 50,000,000 Elvis Fans Can't Be Wrong	1960	50.00	100.00	200.00
—"Long Play" on label; "Magic Millions" on upper right front cover with RCA Victor logo					
LPM-2075 [M]	Elvis' Gold Records Volume 2 — 50,000,000 Elvis Fans Can't Be Wrong	1963	20.00	40.00	80.00
—"Mono" on label; "RE" on lower right front cover					
LPM-2075 [M]	Elvis' Gold Records Volume 2 — 50,000,000 Elvis Fans Can't Be Wrong	1964	12.50	25.00	50.00
—"Monaural" on label; label has words "50,000,000 Elvis Presley Fans Can't Be Wrong"					
LPM-2075 [M]	Elvis' Gold Records Volume 2 — 50,000,000 Elvis Fans Can't Be Wrong	1964	12.50	25.00	50.00
—"Monaural" on label; label only has "Elvis' Gold Records - Vol. 2"					
LSP-2075(e) [R]	Elvis' Gold Records Volume 2 — 50,000,000 Elvis Fans Can't Be Wrong	1962	37.50	75.00	150.00
—"Stereo Electronically Reprocessed" on label; label has words "50,000,000 Elvis Presley Fans Can't Be Wrong"					
LSP-2075(e) [R]	Elvis' Gold Records Volume 2 — 50,000,000 Elvis Fans Can't Be Wrong	1964	12.50	25.00	50.00
—"Stereo Electronically Reprocessed" and white "RCA Victor" on label					
LSP-2075(e) [R]	Elvis' Gold Records Volume 2 — 50,000,000 Elvis Fans Can't Be Wrong	1968	7.50	15.00	30.00
—Orange label, non-flexible vinyl					
LSP-2075(e) [R]	Elvis' Gold Records Volume 2 — 50,000,000 Elvis Fans Can't Be Wrong	1971	5.00	10.00	20.00
—Orange label, flexible vinyl					
LSP-2075(e) [R]	Elvis' Gold Records Volume 2 — 50,000,000 Elvis Fans Can't Be Wrong	1975	5.00	10.00	20.00
—Tan label					
LSP-2075(e) [R]	Elvis' Gold Records Volume 2 — 50,000,000 Elvis Fans Can't Be Wrong	1976	3.00	6.00	12.00
—Black label, dog near top					
AFL1-2231 [S]	Elvis Is Back!	1977	3.00	6.00	12.00
—Black label, dog near top; includes copies with sticker wrapped around spine with new number					
LPM-2231 [M]	Elvis Is Back!	1960	37.50	75.00	150.00
—With sticker attached to front cover. Side 2, Song 4 is listed as "The Girl Next Door."					
LPM-2231 [M]	Elvis Is Back!	1960	37.50	75.00	150.00
—With sticker attached to front cover. Side 2, Song 4 is listed as "The Girl Next Door Went a-Walking."					
LPM-2231 [M]	Elvis Is Back!	1960	50.00	100.00	200.00
—With no sticker attached to front cover. Side 2, Song 4 is listed as "The Girl Next Door."					
LPM-2231 [M]	Elvis Is Back!	1960	50.00	100.00	200.00
—With no sticker attached to front cover. Side 2, Song 4 is listed as "The Girl Next Door Went a-Walking."					
LPM-2231 [M]	Elvis Is Back!	1963	15.00	30.00	60.00
—"Mono" on label; song titles printed on front cover					

Number	Title (A Side/B Side)	Yr	VG	VG+	NM
LPM-2231 [M]	Elvis Is Back!	1964	15.00	30.00	60.00
—"Monaural" on label					
LSP-2231 [S]	Elvis Is Back!	1960	75.00	150.00	300.00
—"Living Stereo" on label; with sticker attached to front cover. Side 2, Song 4 is listed as "The Girl Next Door."					
LSP-2231 [S]	Elvis Is Back!	1960	75.00	150.00	300.00
—"Living Stereo" on label; with sticker attached to front cover. Side 2, Song 4 is listed as "The Girl Next Door Went a-Walking."					
LSP-2231 [S]	Elvis Is Back!	1960	75.00	150.00	300.00
—"Living Stereo" on label; with no sticker attached to front cover. Side 2, Song 4 is listed as "The Girl Next Door."					
LSP-2231 [S]	Elvis Is Back!	1960	75.00	150.00	300.00
—"Living Stereo" on label; with no sticker attached to front cover. Side 2, Song 4 is listed as "The Girl Next Door Went a-Walking."					
LSP-2231 [S]	Elvis Is Back!	1964	15.00	30.00	60.00
—"Stereo" on label; song titles printed on front cover					
LSP-2231 [S]	Elvis Is Back!	1968	10.00	20.00	40.00
—Orange label, non-flexible vinyl					
LSP-2231 [S]	Elvis Is Back!	1975	5.00	10.00	20.00
—Tan label					
LSP-2231 [S]	Elvis Is Back!	1976	3.75	7.50	15.00
—Black label, dog on top					
AFL1-2256 [S]	G.I. Blues	1977	3.00	6.00	12.00
—Black label, dog near top; includes copies with sticker wrapped around spine with new number					
LPM-2256 [M]	G.I. Blues	1960	125.00	250.00	500.00
—"Long Play" on label; with sticker on front cover advertising the presence of "Wooden Heart"					
LPM-2256 [M]	G.I. Blues	1960	30.00	60.00	120.00
—"Long Play" on label; with no sticker on front cover					
LPM-2256 [M]	G.I. Blues	1963	25.00	50.00	100.00
—"Mono" on label					
LPM-2256 [M]	G.I. Blues	1964	12.50	25.00	50.00
—"Monaural" on label					
LSP-2256 [S]	G.I. Blues	1960	150.00	300.00	600.00
—"Living Stereo" on label; with sticker on front cover advertising the presence of "Wooden Heart"					
LSP-2256 [S]	G.I. Blues	1960	25.00	50.00	100.00
—"Living Stereo" on label; with no sticker on front cover					
LSP-2256 [S]	G.I. Blues	1964	12.50	25.00	50.00
—"Stereo" on black label					
LSP-2256 [S]	G.I. Blues	1968	10.00	20.00	40.00
—Orange label, non-flexible vinyl					
LSP-2256 [S]	G.I. Blues	1971	5.00	10.00	20.00
—Orange label, flexible vinyl					
LSP-2256 [S]	G.I. Blues	1975	6.25	12.50	25.00
—Tan label					
LSP-2256 [S]	G.I. Blues	1976	3.00	6.00	12.00
—Black label, dog near top					
AFL1-2274	Welcome to My World	1977	3.00	6.00	12.00
—Black label, dog near top; includes copies with sticker wrapped around spine with new number					
APL1-2274	Welcome to My World	1977	5.00	10.00	20.00
—Black label, dog near top					
AQL1-2274	Welcome to My World	1979	2.50	5.00	10.00
—Black label, dog near top; includes copies with sticker wrapped around spine with new number					
LPM-2328 [M]	His Hand in Mine	1960	30.00	60.00	120.00
—"Long Play" on label					
LPM-2328 [M]	His Hand in Mine	1963	15.00	30.00	60.00
—"Mono" on label					
LPM-2328 [M]	His Hand in Mine	1964	12.50	25.00	50.00
—"Monaural" on label					
LSP-2328 [S]	His Hand in Mine	1960	50.00	100.00	200.00
—"Living Stereo" on label					
LSP-2328 [S]	His Hand in Mine	1964	150.00	300.00	600.00
—"Stereo" and silver "RCA Victor" on black label					
LSP-2328 [S]	His Hand in Mine	1964	25.00	50.00	100.00
—"Stereo" and white "RCA Victor" on black label					
LSP-2328 [S]	His Hand in Mine	1968	12.50	25.00	50.00
—Orange label, non-flexible vinyl					
LSP-2328 [S]	His Hand in Mine	1975	5.00	10.00	20.00
—Tan label					
LSP-2328 [S]	His Hand in Mine	197?	5.00	10.00	20.00
—Orange label, flexible vinyl					
AHL1-2347	Greatest Hits, Volume One	1981	6.25	12.50	25.00
—With embossed cover					
AHL1-2347	Greatest Hits, Volume One	1983	3.75	7.50	15.00
—Without embossed cover					
AFL1-2370 [S]	Something for Everybody	1977	3.00	6.00	12.00
—Black label, dog near top; includes copies with sticker wrapped around spine with new number					
LPM-2370 [M]	Something for Everybody	1961	30.00	60.00	120.00
—"Long Play" on label; back cover advertises RCA Compact 33 singles and doubles					
LPM-2370 [M]	Something for Everybody	1963	20.00	40.00	80.00
—"Mono" on label; back cover advertises "Viva Las Vegas" EP					
LPM-2370 [M]	Something for Everybody	1964	12.50	25.00	50.00
—"Monaural" on label; back cover advertises "Viva Las Vegas" EP					
LSP-2370 [S]	Something for Everybody	1961	50.00	100.00	200.00
—"Living Stereo" on label; back cover advertises RCA Compact 33 singles and doubles					
LSP-2370 [S]	Something for Everybody	1963	25.00	50.00	100.00
—"Stereo" and silver "RCA Victor" on black label; back cover advertises Elvis' Christmas Album and His Hand in Mine LPs and "Viva Las Vegas" EP					
LSP-2370 [S]	Something for Everybody	1964	12.50	25.00	50.00
—"Stereo" and white "RCA Victor" on black label; back cover advertises "Viva Las Vegas" EP					
LSP-2370 [S]	Something for Everybody	1968	10.00	20.00	40.00
—Orange label, non-flexible vinyl; final back cover change advertises Elvis (NBC-TV Special), Elvis' Christmas Album and His Hand in Mine LPs					
LSP-2370 [S]	Something for Everybody	1971	5.00	10.00	20.00
—Orange label, flexible vinyl					
LSP-2370 [S]	Something for Everybody	1975	5.00	10.00	20.00
—Tan label					
LSP-2370 [S]	Something for Everybody	1976	3.00	6.00	12.00
—Black label, dog near top					
AFL1-2426 [S]	Blue Hawaii	1977	3.00	6.00	12.00
—Black label, dog near top; with sticker wrapped around spine with new number					
LPM-2426 [M]	Blue Hawaii	1961	25.00	50.00	100.00
—"Long Play" on label; with sticker on cover advertising the presence of "Can't Help Falling in Love" and "Rock-a-Hula Baby"					
LPM-2426 [M]	Blue Hawaii	1962	15.00	30.00	60.00
—"Long Play" on label; no sticker on front cover					
LPM-2426 [M]	Blue Hawaii	1963	12.50	25.00	50.00
—"Mono" on label					

Number	Title (A Side/B Side)	Yr	VG	VG+	NM
LPM-2426 [M]	Blue Hawaii	1964	10.00	20.00	40.00
—"Monaural" on label					
LSP-2426 [S]	Blue Hawaii	1961	37.50	75.00	150.00
—"Living Stereo" on label and upper right front cover; with sticker on cover advertising the presence of "Can't Help Falling in Love" and "Rock-a-Hula Baby"					
LSP-2426 [S]	Blue Hawaii	1962	20.00	40.00	80.00
—"Living Stereo" on label and upper right front cover; no sticker on front cover					
LSP-2426 [S]	Blue Hawaii	1964	12.50	25.00	50.00
—"Stereo" on label; "Victor Stereo" on upper right front cover					
LSP-2426 [S]	Blue Hawaii	1968	10.00	20.00	40.00
—Orange label, non-flexible vinyl					
LSP-2426 [S]	Blue Hawaii	1971	50.00	10.00	20.00
—Orange label, flexible vinyl					
LSP-2426 [S]	Blue Hawaii	1975	50.00	10.00	20.00
—Tan label					
LSP-2426 [S]	Blue Hawaii	1977	3.00	6.00	12.00
—Black label, dog near top					
LSP-2426 [S]	Blue Hawaii	197?	250.00	500.00	1000.
—One-of-a-kind blue vinyl pressing with black label, dog near top					
AFK1-2428	Moody Blue	1977	1500.	2250.	3000.
—Alternate cover slick (never put on an actual cover), with the words "Moody Blue" inside the large word "Elvis." See any late-1970s Elvis inner sleeve for a black and white photo of the scrapped cover.					
AFL1-2428	Moody Blue	1977	2.50	5.00	10.00
—Blue vinyl					
AFL1-2428	Moody Blue	1977	50.00	100.00	200.00
—Black vinyl					
AFL1-2428 [DJ]	Moody Blue	1977	500.00	1000.	2000.
—Experimental colored vinyl pressings (with no cover), any color or combination except blue or black					
AQL1-2428	Moody Blue	1979	6.25	12.50	25.00
—Reissue with new prefix					
AFL1-2523 [S]	Pot Luck with Elvis	1977	3.00	6.00	12.00
—Black label, dog near top; includes copies with sticker wrapped around spine with new number					
LPM-2523 [M]	Pot Luck with Elvis	1962	25.00	50.00	100.00
—"Long Play" on label					
LPM-2523 [M]	Pot Luck with Elvis	1964	30.00	60.00	120.00
—"Monaural" on label					
LSP-2523 [S]	Pot Luck with Elvis	1962	37.50	75.00	150.00
—"Living Stereo" on label					
LSP-2523 [S]	Pot Luck with Elvis	1964	15.00	30.00	60.00
—"Stereo" on black label					
LSP-2523 [S]	Pot Luck with Elvis	1968	10.00	20.00	40.00
—Orange label, non-flexible vinyl					
LSP-2523 [S]	Pot Luck with Elvis	1975	5.00	10.00	20.00
—Tan label					
LSP-2523 [S]	Pot Luck with Elvis	1976	3.00	6.00	12.00
—Black label, dog near top					
CPD2-2542 [(2) Q]	Aloha from Hawaii Via Satellite	1975	6.25	12.50	25.00
—Reissue with new number; orange labels					
CPD2-2542 [(2) Q]	Aloha from Hawaii Via Satellite	1975	5.00	10.00	20.00
—Reissue with new number; tan labels					
CPD2-2542 [(2) Q]	Aloha from Hawaii Via Satellite	1977	5.00	10.00	20.00
—Black labels, dog near top					
CPL2-2542 [(2) Q]	Aloha from Hawaii Via Satellite	1984	3.00	6.00	12.00
—New prefix; single-pocket instead of gatefold jacket					
APL1-2558 [S]	Harum Scarum	1977	3.00	6.00	12.00
—Black label, dog near top					
APL1-2560 [S]	Spinout	1977	3.00	6.00	12.00
—Black label, dog near top					
APL1-2564 [S]	Double Trouble	1977	3.00	6.00	12.00
—Black label, dog near top; includes copies with sticker wrapped around spine with new number					
APL1-2565	Clambake	1977	3.00	6.00	12.00
APL1-2568 [S]	It Happened at the World's Fair	1977	3.00	6.00	12.00
APL2-2587 [(2)]	Elvis in Concert	1977	6.25	12.50	25.00
CPL2-2587 [(2)]	Elvis in Concert	1982	10.00	20.00	40.00
AFL1-2621 [S]	Girls! Girls! Girls!	1977	3.00	6.00	12.00
—Black label, dog near top; includes copies with sticker wrapped around spine with new number					
LPM-2621 [M]	Girls! Girls! Girls!	1962	20.00	40.00	80.00
—"Long Play" on label					
LPM-2621 [M]	Girls! Girls! Girls!	1963	15.00	30.00	60.00
—"Mono" on label					
LPM-2621 [M]	Girls! Girls! Girls!	1964	10.00	20.00	40.00
—"Monaural" on label					
LPM/LSP-2621	Girls! Girls! Girls! Bonus 1963 Calendar	1962	37.50	75.00	150.00
—With listing of other Elvis records on back					
LSP-2621 [S]	Girls! Girls! Girls!	1962	37.50	75.00	150.00
—"Living Stereo" on label					
LSP-2621 [S]	Girls! Girls! Girls!	1964	15.00	30.00	60.00
—"Stereo" on black label					
LSP-2621 [S]	Girls! Girls! Girls!	1968	10.00	20.00	40.00
—Orange label, non-flexible vinyl					
LSP-2621 [S]	Girls! Girls! Girls!	1971	5.00	10.00	20.00
—Orange label, flexible vinyl					
LSP-2621 [S]	Girls! Girls! Girls!	1975	6.25	12.50	25.00
—Tan label					
LSP-2621 [S]	Girls! Girls! Girls!	1976	3.00	6.00	12.00
—Black label, dog near top					
CPD2-2642 [(2) Q]	Aloha from Hawaii Via Satellite	1975	7.50	15.00	30.00
—Orange labels					
CPD2-2642 [(2) Q]	Aloha from Hawaii Via Satellite	1977	20.00	40.00	80.00
—Black labels, dog near top					
LPM-2697 [M]	It Happened at the World's Fair	1963	30.00	60.00	120.00
LPM/LSP-2697	It Happened at the World's Fair Photo	1963	62.50	125.00	250.00
LSP-2697 [S]	It Happened at the World's Fair	1963	50.00	100.00	200.00
—"Stereo" and silver "RCA Victor" on black label					
LSP-2697 [S]	It Happened at the World's Fair	1964	20.00	40.00	80.00
—"Stereo" and white "RCA Victor" on black label					
AFL1-2756 [S]	Fun in Acapulco	1977	3.00	6.00	12.00
—Black label, dog near top; includes copies with sticker wrapped around spine with new number					
LPM-2756 [M]	Fun in Acapulco	1963	20.00	40.00	80.00
—"Mono" on label					
LPM-2756 [M]	Fun in Acapulco	1964	12.50	25.00	50.00
—"Monaural" on label					
LSP-2756 [S]	Fun in Acapulco	1963	25.00	50.00	100.00
—"Stereo" and silver "RCA Victor" on black label					
LSP-2756 [S]	Fun in Acapulco	1964	15.00	30.00	60.00
—"Stereo" and white "RCA Victor" on black label					

Number	Title (A Side/B Side)	Yr	VG	VG+	NM
LSP-2756 [S]	Fun in Acapulco	1968	10.00	20.00	40.00
—Orange label, non-flexible vinyl					
LSP-2756 [S]	Fun in Acapulco	1975	6.25	12.50	25.00
—Tan label					
LSP-2756 [S]	Fun in Acapulco	1976	3.00	6.00	12.00
—Black label, dog near top					
AFL1-2765 [S]	Elvis' Golden Records, Volume 3	1977	3.00	6.00	12.00
—Black label, dog near top; includes copies with sticker wrapped around spine with new number					
LPM-2765 [M]	Elvis' Golden Records, Volume 3	1963	25.00	50.00	100.00
—"Mono" on label					
LPM-2765 [M]	Elvis' Golden Records, Volume 3	1964	15.00	30.00	60.00
—"Monaural" on label					
LSP-2765 [S]	Elvis' Golden Records, Volume 3	1963	37.50	75.00	150.00
—"Stereo" and silver "RCA Victor" on black label					
LSP-2765 [S]	Elvis' Golden Records, Volume 3	1964	12.50	25.00	50.00
—"Stereo" and white "RCA Victor" on black label					
LSP-2765 [S]	Elvis' Golden Records, Volume 3	1968	10.00	20.00	40.00
—Orange label, non-flexible vinyl					
LSP-2765 [S]	Elvis' Golden Records, Volume 3	1975	5.00	10.00	20.00
—Tan label					
LSP-2765 [S]	Elvis' Golden Records, Volume 3	1976	3.00	6.00	12.00
—Black label, dog near top					
AFL1-2772	He Walks Beside Me	1978	6.25	12.50	25.00
—Includes 20-page photo booklet					
AFL1-2894 [S]	Kissin' Cousins	1977	3.00	6.00	12.00
—Black label, dog near top; includes copies with sticker wrapped around spine with new number					
LPM-2894 [M]	Kissin' Cousins	1964	20.00	40.00	80.00
—"Mono" on label; front cover has a small black and white photo of six cast members in lower right					
LPM-2894 [M]	Kissin' Cousins	1964	50.00	100.00	200.00
—"Mono" on label; front cover does NOT have black and white photo in lower right					
LPM-2894 [M]	Kissin' Cousins	1964	25.00	50.00	100.00
—"Monaural" on label; front cover has a small black and white photo of six cast members in lower right					
LPM-2894 [M]	Kissin' Cousins	1964	50.00	100.00	200.00
—"Monaural" on label, front cover does NOT have black and white photo in lower right					
LSP-2894 [S]	Kissin' Cousins	1964	30.00	60.00	120.00
—"Stereo" and silver "RCA Victor" on black label; front cover has a small black and white photo of six cast members in lower right					
LSP-2894 [S]	Kissin' Cousins	1964	50.00	100.00	200.00
—"Stereo" and silver "RCA Victor" on black label; front cover does NOT have black and white photo in lower right					
LSP-2894 [S]	Kissin' Cousins	1964	15.00	30.00	60.00
—"Stereo" and white "RCA Victor" on black label; all front covers have the cast photo in lower right					
LSP-2894 [S]	Kissin' Cousins	1968	10.00	20.00	40.00
—Orange label, non-flexible vinyl					
LSP-2894 [S]	Kissin' Cousins	1971	5.00	10.00	20.00
—Orange label, flexible vinyl					
LSP-2894 [S]	Kissin' Cousins	1975	6.25	12.50	25.00
—Tan label					
LSP-2894 [S]	Kissin' Cousins	1976	3.00	6.00	12.00
—Black label, dog near top					
LSP-2894 [S]	Kissin' Cousins	1976	375.00	750.00	1500.
—Black label, dog near top; blue vinyl					
CPL1-2901	Elvis Sings for Children and Grownups Too!	1978	5.00	10.00	20.00
—With two slits for removable greeting card on back cover (card should be with package)					
CPL1-2901	Elvis Sings for Children and Grownups Too!	1978	2.50	5.00	10.00
—With greeting card graphic printed on back cover, and no slits on back cover					
AFL1-2999 [S]	Roustabout	1977	3.00	6.00	12.00
—Black label, dog near top; includes copies with sticker wrapped around spine with new number					
LPM-2999 [M]	Roustabout	1964	25.00	50.00	100.00
—"Mono" on label					
LPM-2999 [M]	Roustabout	1965	15.00	30.00	60.00
—"Monaural" on label					
LSP-2999 [S]	Roustabout	1964	150.00	300.00	600.00
—"Stereo" and silver "RCA Victor" on black label					
LSP-2999 [S]	Roustabout	1964	15.00	30.00	60.00
—"Stereo" and white "RCA Victor" on black label					
LSP-2999 [S]	Roustabout	1968	10.00	20.00	40.00
—Orange label, non-flexible vinyl					
LSP-2999 [S]	Roustabout	1971	5.00	10.00	20.00
—Orange label, flexible vinyl					
LSP-2999 [S]	Roustabout	1975	5.00	10.00	20.00
—Tan label					
LSP-2999 [S]	Roustabout	1976	3.00	6.00	12.00
—Black label, dog near top					
CPL1-3078 [PD]	A Legendary Performer, Volume 3	1978	6.25	12.50	25.00
—Picture disc applied to blue vinyl LP; with booklet (deduct 40% if missing)					
CPL1-3082	A Legendary Performer, Volume 3	1978	6.25	12.50	25.00
—Includes booklet (deduct 40% if missing); with die-cut hole in front cover					
CPL1-3082	A Legendary Performer, Volume 3	1986	2.00	4.00	8.00
—No die-cut hole in cover and no booklet					
AQL1-3279	Our Memories of Elvis	1979	5.00	10.00	20.00
AFL1-3338 [S]	Girl Happy	1977	3.00	6.00	12.00
—Black label, dog near top; includes copies with sticker wrapped around spine with new number					
LPM-3338 [M]	Girl Happy	1965	15.00	30.00	60.00
LSP-3338 [S]	Girl Happy	1965	15.00	30.00	60.00
—"Stereo" on black label					
LSP-3338 [S]	Girl Happy	1968	10.00	20.00	40.00
—Orange label, non-flexible vinyl					
LSP-3338 [S]	Girl Happy	1971	5.00	10.00	20.00
—Orange label, flexible vinyl					
LSP-3338 [S]	Girl Happy	1975	6.25	12.50	25.00
—Tan label					
LSP-3338 [S]	Girl Happy	1976	3.00	6.00	12.00
—Black label, dog near top					
AQL1-3448	Our Memories of Elvis, Volume 2	1979	5.00	10.00	20.00
AFL1-3450 [P]	Elvis for Everyone	1977	3.00	6.00	12.00
—Black label, dog near top; includes copies with sticker wrapped around spine with new number					
LPM-3450 [M]	Elvis for Everyone	1965	15.00	30.00	60.00
LSP-3450 [P]	Elvis for Everyone	1965	15.00	30.00	60.00
—Black label, "Stereo" on label					
LSP-3450 [P]	Elvis for Everyone	1968	10.00	20.00	40.00
—Orange label, non-flexible vinyl					
LSP-3450 [P]	Elvis for Everyone	1971	5.00	10.00	20.00
—Orange label, flexible vinyl					
LSP-3450 [P]	Elvis for Everyone	1975	5.00	10.00	20.00
—Tan label					
LSP-3450 [P]	Elvis for Everyone	1976	3.00	6.00	12.00
—Black label, dog near top					
DJL1-3455 [DJ]	Pure Elvis	1979	150.00	300.00	600.00
—Promo-only item for Our Memories of Elvis, Volume 2; contains original version of five songs on one side, "unsweetened" versions of same songs on the other					
LPM-3468 [M]	Harum Scarum	1965	15.00	30.00	60.00
LPM/LSP-3468	Harum Scarum Bonus Photo	1965	15.00	30.00	60.00
LSP-3468 [S]	Harum Scarum	1965	15.00	30.00	60.00
—"Stereo" on black label					
LPM-3553 [M]	Frankie and Johnny	1966	15.00	30.00	60.00
LPM/LSP-3553	Frankie and Johnny Bonus Print	1966	15.00	30.00	60.00
LSP-3553 [S]	Frankie and Johnny	1966	15.00	30.00	60.00
—"Stereo" on black label					
AFL1-3643 [S]	Paradise, Hawaiian Style	1977	3.00	6.00	12.00
—Black label, dog near top; includes copies with sticker wrapped around spine with new number					
LPM-3643 [M]	Paradise, Hawaiian Style	1966	15.00	30.00	60.00
LSP-3643 [S]	Paradise, Hawaiian Style	1966	15.00	30.00	60.00
—"Stereo" on black label					
LSP-3643 [S]	Paradise, Hawaiian Style	1968	10.00	20.00	40.00
—Orange label, non-flexible vinyl					
LSP-3643 [S]	Paradise, Hawaiian Style	1971	5.00	10.00	20.00
—Orange label, flexible vinyl					
LSP-3643 [S]	Paradise, Hawaiian Style	1975	3.75	7.50	15.00
—Tan label					
LSP-3643 [S]	Paradise, Hawaiian Style	1976	3.00	6.00	12.00
—Black label, dog near top					
AYL1-3683 [S]	Blue Hawaii	1980	2.50	5.00	10.00
—"Best Buy Series" reissue					
AYL1-3684 [S]	Spinout	1980	2.00	4.00	8.00
—"Best Buy Series" reissue					
CPL8-3699 [(8)]	Elvis Aron Presley	1980	25.00	50.00	100.00
—Box set; regular issue with booklet					
CPL8-3699 [(8)]	Elvis Aron Presley	1980	62.50	125.00	250.00
—Box set; "Reviewer Series" edition (will be identified as such on the cover)					
LPM-3702 [M]	Spinout	1966	15.00	30.00	60.00
LPM/LSP-3702	Spinout Bonus Photo	1966	15.00	30.00	60.00
LSP-3702 [S]	Spinout	1966	15.00	30.00	60.00
—"Stereo" on black label					
DJL1-3729 [DJ]	Elvis Aron Presley (Excerpts)	1980	30.00	60.00	120.00
—Promo-only excerpts of songs from box set					
AYL1-3732	Pure Gold	1980	2.00	4.00	8.00
—"Best Buy Series" reissue					
AYL1-3733 [R]	King Creole	1980	2.00	4.00	8.00
—"Best Buy Series" reissue; includes copies with sticker wrapped around spine with new number					
AYL1-3734 [S]	Harum Scarum	1980	2.00	4.00	8.00
—"Best Buy Series" reissue					
AYL1-3735 [S]	G.I. Blues	1980	2.00	4.00	8.00
—"Best Buy Series" reissue					
AFL1-3758 [S]	How Great Thou Art	1977	3.00	6.00	12.00
—Black label, dog near top; includes copies with sticker wrapped around spine with new number					
AQL1-3758 [S]	How Great Thou Art	1979	2.50	5.00	10.00
—Reissue with new prefix					
LPM-3758 [M]	How Great Thou Art	1967	15.00	30.00	60.00
—"Mono Dynagroove" on label					
LSP-3758 [S]	How Great Thou Art	1967	15.00	30.00	60.00
—"Stereo Dynagroove" on black label					
LSP-3758 [S]	How Great Thou Art	1968	10.00	20.00	40.00
—Orange label, non-flexible vinyl					
LSP-3758 [S]	How Great Thou Art	1971	6.25	12.50	25.00
—Orange label, flexible vinyl					
LSP-3758 [S]	How Great Thou Art	1975	5.00	10.00	20.00
—Tan label					
LSP-3758 [S]	How Great Thou Art	1976	3.00	6.00	12.00
—Black label, dog near top					
DJL1-3781 [DJ]	Elvis Aron Presley (Selections)	1980	30.00	60.00	120.00
—Promo-only complete versions of songs from box set					
LPM-3787 [M]	Double Trouble	1967	15.00	30.00	60.00
—With bonus photo announcement on cover					
LPM-3787 [M]	Double Trouble	1967	20.00	40.00	80.00
—With no bonus photo announcement on cover					
LPM/LSP-3787	Double Trouble Bonus Photo	1967	12.50	25.00	50.00
LSP-3787 [S]	Double Trouble	1967	15.00	30.00	60.00
—With bonus photo announcement on cover					
LSP-3787 [S]	Double Trouble	1967	17.50	35.00	70.00
—With no bonus photo announcement on cover; black label "Stereo"					
LSP-3787 [S]	Double Trouble	1968	10.00	20.00	40.00
—Orange label, non-flexible vinyl					
LSP-3787 [S]	Double Trouble	1975	5.00	10.00	20.00
—Tan label					
LSP-3787 [S]	Double Trouble	1977	3.00	6.00	12.00
—Black label, dog near top					
AYL1-3892	Elvis in Person at the International Hotel, Las Vegas, Nevada	1981	2.00	4.00	8.00
—"Best Buy Series" reissue					
AYM1-3893	The Sun Sessions	1981	2.00	4.00	8.00
—"Best Buy Series" reissue; includes copies with sticker wrapped around spine with new number					
LPM-3893 [M]	Clambake	1967	62.50	125.00	250.00
LPM/LSP-3893	Clambake Bonus Photo	1967	12.50	25.00	50.00
LSP-3893 [S]	Clambake	1967	15.00	30.00	60.00
AYM1-3894	Elvis (NBC-TV Special)	1981	2.00	4.00	8.00
—"Best Buy Series" reissue					
AAL1-3917	Guitar Man	1981	7.50	15.00	30.00
AFL1-3921 [P]	Elvis' Gold Records, Volume 4	1976	3.75	7.50	15.00
—Tan label with new prefix					
AFL1-3921 [P]	Elvis' Gold Records, Volume 4	1977	3.00	6.00	12.00
—Black label, dog near top; includes copies with sticker wrapped around spine with new number					
LPM-3921 [M]	Elvis' Gold Records, Volume 4	1968	500.00	1000.	2000.
—"Monaural" on label					
LSP-3921 [P]	Elvis' Gold Records, Volume 4	1968	12.50	25.00	50.00
—"Stereo" and white "RCA Victor" on black label					
LSP-3921 [P]	Elvis' Gold Records, Volume 4	1968	10.00	20.00	40.00
—Orange label, non-flexible vinyl					
LSP-3921 [P]	Elvis' Gold Records, Volume 4	1975	6.25	12.50	25.00
—Tan label					

Number	Title (A Side/B Side)	Yr	VG	VG+	NM
LSP-3921 [P]	Elvis' Gold Records, Volume 4	1976	3.00	6.00	12.00
—Black label, dog near top					
LSP-3921 [P]	Elvis' Gold Records, Volume 4	197?	5.00	10.00	20.00
—Orange label, flexible vinyl					
AYL1-3935 [S]	His Hand in Mine	1981	2.00	4.00	8.00
—"Best Buy Series" reissue; includes copies with sticker wrapped around spine with new number					
AYL1-3956	Elvis Country ("I'm 10,000 Years Old")	1981	2.00	4.00	8.00
—"Best Buy Series" reissue					
AFL1-3989 [S]	Speedway	1977	3.00	6.00	12.00
—Black label, dog near top; includes copies with sticker wrapped around spine with new number					
LPM-3989 [M]	Speedway	1968	500.00	1000.	2000.
LPM/LSP-3989	Speedway Bonus Photo	1968	12.50	25.00	50.00
LSP-3989 [S]	Speedway	1968	15.00	30.00	60.00
—"Stereo" on black label					
LSP-3989 [S]	Speedway	1968	10.00	20.00	40.00
—Orange label, non-flexible vinyl					
LSP-3989 [S]	Speedway	1971	5.00	10.00	20.00
—Orange label, flexible vinyl					
LSP-3989 [S]	Speedway	1975	5.00	10.00	20.00
—Tan label					
LSP-3989 [S]	Speedway	1976	3.00	6.00	12.00
—Black label, dog near top					
CPL2-4031 [(2)]	This Is Elvis	1980	3.75	7.50	15.00
AFM1-4088	Elvis (NBC-TV Special)	1977	3.00	6.00	12.00
—Black label, dog near top; includes copies with sticker wrapped around spine with new number					
LPM-4088	Elvis (NBC-TV Special)	1968	10.00	20.00	40.00
—Orange label, non-flexible vinyl					
LPM-4088	Elvis (NBC-TV Special)	1971	7.50	15.00	30.00
—Orange label, flexible vinyl					
LPM-4088	Elvis (NBC-TV Special)	1975	5.00	10.00	20.00
—Tan label					
LPM-4088	Elvis (NBC-TV Special)	1976	3.75	7.50	15.00
—Black label, dog near top					
AYL1-4114	That's the Way It Is	1981	2.00	4.00	8.00
—"Best Buy Series" reissue; includes copies with sticker wrapped around spine with new number					
AYL1-4115 [S]	Kissin' Cousins	1981	2.00	4.00	8.00
—"Best Buy Series" reissue; includes copies with sticker wrapped around spine with new number					
AYL1-4116 [S]	Something for Everybody	1981	2.00	4.00	8.00
—"Best Buy Series" reissue; includes copies with sticker wrapped around spine with new number					
AFL1-4155	From Elvis in Memphis	1977	3.00	6.00	12.00
—Black label, dog near top; includes copies with sticker wrapped around spine with new number					
LSP-4155	From Elvis in Memphis	1969	10.00	20.00	40.00
—Orange label, non-flexible vinyl					
LSP-4155	From Elvis in Memphis Bonus Photo	1969	10.00	20.00	40.00
LSP-4155	From Elvis in Memphis	1971	7.50	15.00	30.00
—Orange label, flexible vinyl					
LSP-4155	From Elvis in Memphis	1975	6.25	12.50	25.00
—Tan label					
LSP-4155	From Elvis in Memphis	1976	3.75	7.50	15.00
—Black label, dog near top					
AYL1-4232 [P]	Elvis for Everyone	1982	2.00	4.00	8.00
—"Best Buy Series" reissue					
AFL1-4362	On Stage February, 1970	1977	3.00	6.00	12.00
—Black label, dog near top; includes copies with sticker wrapped around spine with new number					
AQL1-4362	On Stage February, 1970	1983	2.00	4.00	8.00
—Reissue with some cover changes					
LSP-4362	On Stage February, 1970	1970	10.00	20.00	40.00
—Orange label, non-flexible vinyl					
LSP-4362	On Stage February, 1970	1971	6.25	12.50	25.00
—Orange label, flexible vinyl					
LSP-4362	On Stage February, 1970	1975	6.25	12.50	25.00
—Tan label					
LSP-4362	On Stage February, 1970	1976	7.50	15.00	30.00
—Black label, dog near top					
CPL1-4395	Memories of Christmas	1982	3.75	7.50	15.00
—With greeting card (deduct 1/3 if missing)					
AFL1-4428	Elvis in Person at the International Hotel, Las Vegas, Nevada	1977	3.00	6.00	12.00
—Black label, dog near top; includes copies with sticker wrapped around spine with new number					
LSP-4428	Elvis in Person at the International Hotel, Las Vegas, Nevada	1970	12.50	25.00	50.00
—Orange label, non-flexible vinyl					
LSP-4428	Elvis in Person at the International Hotel, Las Vegas, Nevada	1971	10.00	20.00	40.00
—Orange label, flexible vinyl					
LSP-4428	Elvis in Person at the International Hotel, Las Vegas, Nevada	1975	6.25	12.50	25.00
—Tan label					
LSP-4428	Elvis in Person at the International Hotel, Las Vegas, Nevada	1976	3.75	7.50	15.00
—Black label, dog near top					
AFL1-4429	Back in Memphis	1977	3.00	6.00	12.00
—Black label, dog near top; with sticker wrapped around spine with new number					
LSP-4429	Back in Memphis	1970	10.00	20.00	40.00
—Orange label, non-flexible vinyl					
LSP-4429	Back in Memphis	1971	7.50	15.00	30.00
—Orange label, flexible vinyl					
LSP-4429	Back in Memphis	1975	6.25	12.50	25.00
—Tan label					
LSP-4429	Back in Memphis	1977	3.75	7.50	15.00
—Black label, dog near top					
AFL1-4445	That's the Way It Is	1977	3.00	6.00	12.00
—Black label, dog near top; includes copies with sticker wrapped around spine with new number					
LSP-4445	That's the Way It Is	1970	20.00	40.00	80.00
—Orange label, non-flexible vinyl					
LSP-4445	That's the Way It Is	1971	6.25	12.50	25.00
—Orange label, flexible vinyl					
LSP-4445	That's the Way It Is	1975	5.00	10.00	20.00
—Tan label					
LSP-4445	That's the Way It Is	1976	3.75	7.50	15.00
—Black label, dog near top					
AFL1-4460	Elvis Country ("I'm 10,000 Years Old")	1977	3.00	6.00	12.00
—Black label, dog near top; includes copies with sticker wrapped around spine with new number					
LSP-4460	Elvis Country ("I'm 10,000 Years Old")	1971	10.00	20.00	40.00
—Orange label, non-flexible vinyl					
LSP-4460	Elvis Country ("I'm 10,000 Years Old")	1971	6.25	12.50	25.00
—Orange label, flexible vinyl					
LSP-4460	Elvis Country ("I'm 10,000 Years Old") Bonus Photo	1971	3.75	7.50	15.00
—Available in either orange-label pressing					
LSP-4460	Elvis Country ("I'm 10,000 Years Old")	1975	6.25	12.50	25.00
—Tan label					
LSP-4460	Elvis Country ("I'm 10,000 Years Old")	1976	3.75	7.50	15.00
—Black label, dog near top					
LSP-4460	Elvis Country ("I'm 10,000 Years Old")	197?	500.00	1000.	2000.
—Green vinyl; black label, dog near top					
AFL1-4530	Love Letters from Elvis	1977	3.00	6.00	12.00
—Black label, dog near top; includes copies with sticker wrapped around spine with new number					
AHL1-4530	The Elvis Medley	1982	3.00	6.00	12.00
LSP-4530	Love Letters from Elvis	1971	10.00	20.00	40.00
—Orange label; "Love Letters from" on one line of cover, "Elvis" on a second line					
LSP-4530	Love Letters from Elvis	1971	7.50	15.00	30.00
—Orange label; "Love Letters" on one line of cover; "from" on a second line, "Elvis" on a third line					
LSP-4530	Love Letters from Elvis	1975	7.50	15.00	30.00
—Tan label; "Love Letters from" on one line of cover, "Elvis" on a second line					
LSP-4530	Love Letters from Elvis	1975	6.25	12.50	25.00
—Tan label; "Love Letters" on one line of cover; "from" on a second line, "Elvis" on a third line					
LSP-4530	Love Letters from Elvis	1976	5.00	10.00	20.00
—Black label, dog near top					
LSP-4579	Elvis Sings the Wonderful World of Christmas	1971	7.50	15.00	30.00
—Orange label. Bonus postcard is priced separately					
LSP-4579	Elvis Sings the Wonderful World of Christmas Postcard	1971	5.00	10.00	20.00
AFL1-4671	Elvis Now	1977	3.00	6.00	12.00
—Black label, dog near top; includes copies with sticker wrapped around spine with new number					
LSP-4671	Elvis Now	1972	7.50	15.00	30.00
—Orange label					
LSP-4671	Elvis Now	1975	6.25	12.50	25.00
—Tan label					
LSP-4671	Elvis Now	1976	3.75	7.50	15.00
—Black label, dog near top					
LSP-4671 [DJ]	Elvis Now	1972	25.00	50.00	100.00
—Orange label; with white timing sticker on front cover					
AHL1-4678	I Was the One	1983	2.50	5.00	10.00
AFL1-4690	He Touched Me	1977	3.00	6.00	12.00
—Black label, dog near top; includes copies with sticker wrapped around spine with new number					
LSP-4690	He Touched Me	1972	10.00	20.00	40.00
—Orange label					
LSP-4690	He Touched Me	1975	5.00	10.00	20.00
—Tan label					
LSP-4690	He Touched Me	1976	3.75	7.50	15.00
—Black label, dog near top					
LSP-4690 [DJ]	He Touched Me	1972	25.00	50.00	100.00
—Orange label; with white timing sticker on front cover					
AFL1-4776	Elvis As Recorded at Madison Square Garden	1977	3.00	6.00	12.00
—Black label, dog near top; includes copies with sticker wrapped around spine with new number					
AQL1-4776	Elvis As Recorded at Madison Square Garden	1980	2.00	4.00	8.00
—Another reissue with new prefix					
LSP-4776	Elvis As Recorded at Madison Square Garden	1972	7.50	15.00	30.00
—Orange label					
LSP-4776	Elvis As Recorded at Madison Square Garden	1975	5.00	10.00	20.00
—Tan label					
LSP-4776	Elvis As Recorded at Madison Square Garden	1976	3.75	7.50	15.00
—Black label, dog near top					
LSP-4776 [DJ]	Elvis As Recorded at Madison Square Garden	1972	25.00	50.00	100.00
—Orange label; with white timing sticker on front cover					
CPL1-4848	A Legendary Performer, Volume 4	1983	7.50	15.00	30.00
—Includes booklet (deduct 40% if missing); with die-cut hole in front cover					
CPL1-4848	A Legendary Performer, Volume 4	1986	5.00	10.00	20.00
—No die-cut hole in cover					
AFL1-4941	Elvis' Gold Records, Volume 5	1984	2.50	5.00	10.00
CPM6-5172 [(6)]	A Golden Celebration	1984	25.00	50.00	100.00
AFM1-5182	Rocker	1984	5.00	10.00	20.00
AFM1-5196 [M]	Elvis' Golden Records	1984	5.00	10.00	20.00
—50th Anniversary reissue in mono with banner					
AFM1-5197 [M]	Elvis' Gold Records Volume 2—50,000,000 Elvis Fans Can't Be Wrong	1984	5.00	10.00	20.00
—50th Anniversary reissue in mono with banner					
AFM1-5198 [M]	Elvis Presley	1984	5.00	10.00	20.00
—50th Anniversary reissue in mono with banner					
AFM1-5199 [M]	Elvis	1984	5.00	10.00	20.00
—50th Anniversary reissue in mono with banner					
AFL1-5353	A Valentine Gift for You	1985	5.00	10.00	20.00
—Red vinyl					
AFL1-5353	A Valentine Gift for You	1985	2.50	5.00	10.00
—Black vinyl					
AFL1-5418	Reconsider Baby	1985	5.00	10.00	20.00
—All copies on blue vinyl					
AFL1-5430	Always on My Mind	1985	5.00	10.00	20.00
—All copies on purple vinyl					
AFM1-5486 [M]	Elvis' Christmas Album	1985	5.00	10.00	20.00
—Same as LOC-1035; green vinyl with booklet					
AFM1-5486 [M]	Elvis' Christmas Album	1985	3.75	7.50	15.00
—Same as LOC-1035; black vinyl with booklet					
UNRM-5697/8 [DJ]	Special Christmas Programming	1967	300.00	600.00	1200.
—White label promo. Add 25% for script.					
LSP-6020	From Memphis to Vegas/From Vegas to Memphis Bonus Photos	1969	12.50	25.00	50.00
—Four different photos came with LP, but no more than two per set. Value is for any two different of the four photos.					
LSP-6020 [(2)]	From Memphis to Vegas/From Vegas to Memphis	1969	25.00	50.00	100.00
—Orange labels, non-flexible vinyl; with composers of "Words" correctly listed as Barry, Robin and Maurice Gibb					
LSP-6020 [(2)]	From Memphis to Vegas/From Vegas to Memphis	1969	37.50	75.00	150.00
—Orange labels, non-flexible vinyl; with composers of "Words" incorrectly listed as Tommy Boyce and Bobby Hart					
LSP-6020 [(2)]	From Memphis to Vegas/From Vegas to Memphis	1971	10.00	20.00	40.00
—Orange labels, flexible vinyl					

Number	Title (A Side/B Side)	Yr	VG	VG+	NM
LSP-6020 [(2)]	From Memphis to Vegas/From Vegas to Memphis Bonus Photos	1975	7.50	15.00	30.00
—Tan labels					
LSP-6020 [(2)]	From Memphis to Vegas/From Vegas to Memphis Bonus Photos	1976	5.00	10.00	20.00
—Black label, dog near top					
VPSX-6089 [(2) DJ]	Aloha from Hawaii Via Satellite	1973	500.00	1000.	2000.
—Orange or dark orange label; with white timing sticker on front cover					
VPSX-6089 [(2) Q]	Aloha from Hawaii Via Satellite	1973	25.00	50.00	100.00
—Dark orange labels, "QuadraDisc" on top, "RCA" on bottom					
VPSX-6089 [(2) Q]	Aloha from Hawaii Via Satellite	1973	2500.	3750.	5000.
—Stokely-Van Camp employee version with Saturn-shaped sticker on front cover with "Chicken of the Sea" and mermaid					
VPSX-6089 [(2) Q]	Aloha from Hawaii Via Satellite	1973	10.00	20.00	40.00
—Lighter orange labels, "RCA" on side					
LPM-6401	Worldwide 50 Gold Award Hits, Vol. 1 Photo Book	1970	10.00	20.00	40.00
—Two different books have been found in this LP box; price is for either					
LPM-6401 [(4)]	Worldwide 50 Gold Award Hits, Vol. 1	1970	20.00	40.00	80.00
—Orange labels, non-flexible vinyl; with blurb for photo book on cover					
LPM-6401 [(4)]	Worldwide 50 Gold Award Hits, Vol. 1	1970	20.00	40.00	80.00
—Orange labels, flexible vinyl; with blurb for photo book on cover					
LPM-6401 [(4)]	Worldwide 50 Gold Award Hits, Vol. 1	1975	10.00	20.00	40.00
—Tan labels					
LPM-6401 [(4)]	Worldwide 50 Gold Award Hits, Vol. 1	1977	7.50	15.00	30.00
—Black labels, dog near top					
LPM-6402	The Other Sides: Worldwide 50 Gold Award Hits, Vol. 2 Poster	1971	6.25	12.50	25.00
LPM-6402	The Other Sides: Worldwide 50 Gold Award Hits, Vol. 2 Swatch and Envelope	1971	6.25	12.50	25.00
LPM-6402 [(4)]	The Other Sides: Worldwide 50 Gold Award Hits, Vol. 2	1971	17.50	35.00	70.00
—Orange labels, flexible vinyl; with blurb for inserts on cover					
LPM-6402 [(4)]	The Other Sides: Worldwide 50 Gold Award Hits, Vol. 2	1975	7.50	15.00	30.00
—Tan labels					
LPM-6402 [(4)]	The Other Sides: Worldwide 50 Gold Award Hits, Vol. 2	1977	5.00	10.00	20.00
—Black labels, dog near top					
KKL1-7065	A Canadian Tribute	1978	5.00	10.00	20.00
—Gold vinyl, embossed cover					
R 213690 [(2)]	Worldwide Gold Award Hits, Parts 1 & 2	1974	30.00	60.00	120.00
—RCA Record Club version; one label is orange, the other is tan (orange label on both records is unknown)					
R 213690 [(2)]	Worldwide Gold Award Hits, Parts 1 & 2	1974	10.00	20.00	40.00
—RCA Record Club version; tan labels					
R 213690 [(2)]	Worldwide Gold Award Hits, Parts 1 & 2	1977	6.25	12.50	25.00
—RCA Record Club version; black labels, dog near top					
R 213736 [(2) S]	Aloha from Hawaii Via Satellite	1973	17.50	35.00	70.00
—RCA Record Club edition in stereo instead of quadraphonic; orange labels					
R 213736 [(2) S]	Aloha from Hawaii Via Satellite	1975	15.00	30.00	60.00
—RCA Record Club edition in stereo instead of quadraphonic; tan labels					
R 213736 [(2) S]	Aloha from Hawaii Via Satellite	1977	7.50	5.00	30.00
—RCA Record Club edition in stereo instead of quadraphonic; black labels, dog near top					
R 214657 [(2)]	Worldwide Gold Award Hits, Parts 3 & 4	1978	5.00	10.00	20.00
—RCA Record Club version; black labels, dog near top					
R 233299(e) [(2)]	Country Classics	1980	10.00	20.00	40.00
—RCA Music Service exclusive					
R 234340 [(2)]	From Elvis with Love	1978	10.00	20.00	40.00
—RCA Music Service exclusive					
R 244047 [(2)]	The Legendary Concert Performances	1978	10.00	20.00	40.00
—RCA Music Service exclusive					
R 244069 [(2)]	Country Memories	1978	10.00	20.00	40.00
—RCA Music Service exclusive					
READER'S DIGEST					
010/A [(7)]	His Greatest Hits	1983	15.00	30.00	60.00
—Yellow box					
010/A [(7)]	His Greatest Hits	1990	10.00	20.00	40.00
—White box					
RD-10/A [(8)]	His Greatest Hits	1979	100.00	200.00	400.00
—White box					
RBA-072/D	Great Hits of 1956-57	1987	5.00	10.00	20.00
RD4A-181/D	Elvis Sings Inspirational Favorites	1983	5.00	10.00	20.00
RB4-191/A [(7)]	The Legend Lives On	1986	15.00	30.00	60.00
RDA-242/D	Elvis Sings Country Favorites	1984	15.00	30.00	60.00
SHOW-LAND					
LP-2001	The First of Elvis	1979	25.00	50.00	100.00
SILHOUETTE					
10001/2 [(2)]	Personally Elvis	1979	7.50	15.00	30.00
—Interview records; no music					
SUN					
1001	The Sun Years — Interviews and Memories	1977	6.25	12.50	25.00
—With "Memphis, Tennessee" on label					
1001	The Sun Years — Interviews and Memories	1977	2.00	4.00	8.00
—With "Nashville, U.S.A." on label; white cover with brown print					
1001	The Sun Years — Interviews and Memories	1977	3.75	7.50	15.00
—With "Nashville, U.S.A." on label; dark yellow cover with brown print					
TIME-LIFE					
STL-106 [(2)]	Elvis Presley: 1954-1961	1986	7.50	15.00	30.00
STW-106	Country Music	1981	5.00	10.00	20.00
STL-126 [(2)]	Elvis the King: 1954-1965	1989	20.00	40.00	80.00

PRESTON, BILLY

12-Inch Singles

Number	Title (A Side/B Side)	Yr	VG	VG+	NM
MEGATONE					
124	And Dance (5:41)/Kick It (5:46)	1984	—	3.00	6.00
MOTOWN					
PR-64 [DJ]	Give It Up Hot/Sock-It, Rocket	1979	3.00	6.00	12.00
4570	Since I Held You Close (3 versions)/It Don't Get Better Than This	1986	—	3.00	6.00

45s

Number	Title (A Side/B Side)	Yr	VG	VG+	NM
APPLE					
1808	That's the Way God Planned It/What About You	1969	2.00	4.00	8.00
1808	That's the Way God Planned It/What About You	1972	2.00	4.00	8.00
—With "Mono" on both sides of record and reference to LP					
1808 [PS]	That's the Way God Planned It/What About You	1969	2.50	5.00	10.00
P-1808/PRO 6555 [DJ]	That's the Way God Planned It (Parts 1 & 2) (mono/stereo)	1969	15.00	30.00	60.00
1814	Everything's All Right/I Want to Thank You	1969	2.00	4.00	8.00
1817	All That I've Got (I'm Gonna Give It to You)/As I Get Older	1970	2.00	4.00	8.00
1817 [PS]	All That I've Got (I'm Gonna Give It to You)/As I Get Older	1970	3.75	7.50	15.00
1826	My Sweet Lord/Little Girl	1970	2.00	4.00	8.00
1826	My Sweet Lord/Little Girl	1970	3.00	6.00	12.00
—With star on A-side label					
APPLE/AMERICOM					
1808P/M-433	That's the Way God Planned It (Edit)/What About You	1969	100.00	200.00	400.00
—Four-inch flexi-disc sold from vending machines					
A&M					
1320	Outa-Space/I Wrote a Simple Song	1972	—	2.50	5.00
1340	Should Have Known Better/The Bus	1972	—	2.50	5.00
1380	Slaughter/God Loves You	1972	—	2.50	5.00
1380 [PS]	Slaughter/God Loves You	1972	—	3.00	6.00
1411	Will It Go Round in Circles/Blackbird	1973	—	2.00	4.00
1463	Space Race/We're Gonna Make It	1973	—	2.00	4.00
1463 [PS]	Space Race/We're Gonna Make It	1973	—	3.00	6.00
1492	You're So Unique/How Long Has the Train Been Gone	1973	—	2.00	4.00
1536	Creature Feature/My Soul Is a Witness	1974	—	2.00	4.00
1544	Nothing from Nothing/My Soul Is a Witness	1974	—	2.00	4.00
1544 [PS]	Nothing from Nothing/My Soul Is a Witness	1974	—	3.00	6.00
1644	Struttin'/You Are So Beautiful	1974	—	2.00	4.00
1735	Fancy Lady/Song of Joy	1975	—	2.00	4.00
1735 [PS]	Fancy Lady/Song of Joy	1975	—	3.00	6.00
1768	Do It While You Can/Song of Joy	1975	—	2.00	4.00
1892	Do What You Want/I've Got the Spirit	1976	—	2.00	4.00
1925	Girl/Ecstasy	1977	—	2.00	4.00
1954	Wide Stride/When You Are Mine	1977	—	2.00	4.00
1980	A Whole New Thing/Wide Stride	1977	—	2.00	4.00
2012	I Really Miss You/Attitudes	1978	—	2.00	4.00
2071	Get Back/Space Race	1978	—	2.00	4.00
CAPITOL					
2309	Hey Brother (Part 1)/Hey Brother (Part 2)	1968	2.00	4.00	8.00
5611	The Girl's Got "It"/The Night	1966	2.00	4.00	8.00
5660	In the Midnight Hour/Advice	1966	2.00	4.00	8.00
5730	Sunny/Let the Music Play	1966	2.00	4.00	8.00
5797	Phony Friends/Can't She Tell	1966	2.00	4.00	8.00
MGM					
14001	The Split/It's Just a Love Game	1968	2.00	4.00	8.00
MOTOWN					
1470	It Will Come In Time/All I Wanted Was You	1979	—	2.00	4.00
1505	Sock-It Rocket/Hope	1981	—	2.00	4.00
1511	A Change Is Gonna Come/You	1981	—	2.00	4.00
1625	I'm Never Gonna Say Goodbye/Love You So	1982	—	2.00	4.00
VEE JAY					
646	Don't Let the Sun Catch You Cryin'/(B-side unknown)	1965	—	—	—
—Canceled?					
653	Don't Let the Sun Catch You Cryin'/Billy's Bag	1965	2.50	5.00	10.00
692	Log Cabin/Drown in My Own Tears	1965	2.50	5.00	10.00

Albums

Number	Title (A Side/B Side)	Yr	VG	VG+	NM
APPLE					
ST-3359	That's the Way God Planned It	1969	12.50	25.00	50.00
—Cover has close-up of Billy Preston					
ST-3359	That's the Way God Planned It	1972	5.00	10.00	20.00
—Cover has multiple images of Billy Preston					
ST-3370	Encouraging Words	1970	5.00	10.00	20.00
A&M					
SP-3205	The Best of Billy Preston	1982	2.50	5.00	10.00
SP-3507	I Wrote a Simple Song	1971	3.00	6.00	12.00
SP-3516	Music Is My Life	1972	3.00	6.00	12.00
SP-3526	Everybody Likes Some Kind of Music	1973	3.00	6.00	12.00
SP-3637	Live European Tour	1974	3.00	6.00	12.00
SP-3645	The Kids & Me	1974	3.00	6.00	12.00
SP-4532	It's My Pleasure	1975	3.00	6.00	12.00
SP-4587	Billy Preston	1976	3.00	6.00	12.00
SP-4657	It's a Whole New Thing	1977	3.00	6.00	12.00
BUDDAH					
BDS-7502	Billy Preston	1969	3.75	7.50	15.00
CAPITOL					
ST 2532 [S]	Wildest Organ in Town!	1966	10.00	20.00	40.00
T 2532 [M]	Wildest Organ in Town!	1966	7.50	15.00	30.00
DT 2607 [R]	Club Meetin'	1967	5.00	10.00	20.00
T 2607 [M]	Club Meetin'	1967	7.50	15.00	30.00
DERBY					
LPM-701 [M]	16 Year Old Soul	1963	62.50	125.00	250.00
EXODUS					
304 [M]	Early Hits of 1965	1965	6.25	12.50	25.00
GNP CRESCENDO					
GNPS-2071 [(2)]	Soul'd Out	1973	3.75	7.50	15.00
MCA					
28037	Gospel Soul	198?	2.00	4.00	8.00
—Reissue of Peacock LP					
MOTOWN					
M7-925	Late at Night	1980	2.50	5.00	10.00
M8-941	The Way I Am	1981	2.50	5.00	10.00
M7-958	Billy Preston & Syreeta	1981	2.50	5.00	10.00
6020 ML	Pressin' On	1982	2.50	5.00	10.00
MYRRH					
6605	Behold	1978	2.50	5.00	10.00
6607	Universal Love	1979	2.50	5.00	10.00
PEACOCK					
179	Gospel Soul	197?	3.00	6.00	12.00
PICKWICK					
SPC-3315	Organ Transplant	197?	2.50	5.00	10.00
VEE JAY					
LP-1123 [M]	The Most Exciting Organ Ever	1965	7.50	15.00	30.00

Number	Title (A Side/B Side)	Yr	VG	VG+	NM
LPS-1123 [S]	The Most Exciting Organ Ever	1965	12.50	25.00	50.00
LP-1142 [M]	Greatest Hits	1966	7.50	15.00	30.00
LPS-1142 [S]	Greatest Hits	1966	12.50	25.00	50.00

PRESTON, BILLY, AND SYREETA

Also see each artist's individual listings.

45s

Number	Title (A Side/B Side)	Yr	VG	VG+	NM
MOTOWN					
1460	With You I'm Born Again/Go For It	1979	—	2.50	5.00
1477	With You I'm Born Again/All I Wanted Was You	1979	—	2.00	4.00
1520	Searchin'/Hey You	1981	—	2.00	4.00
1522	Just for You (Put the Boogie in Your Body)/Hey You	1981	—	2.00	4.00
TAMLA					
54312	Dance For Me Children/One More Time for Love	1980	—	2.00	4.00
54319	Please Stay/Signed, Sealed, Delivered (I'm Yours)	1980	—	2.00	4.00

PRESTON, JOHNNY

45s

Number	Title (A Side/B Side)	Yr	VG	VG+	NM
ABC					
11085	I'm Only Human/There's No One Like You	1968	2.50	5.00	10.00
11187	Kick the Can/I've Just Been Wasting My Time	1969	2.50	5.00	10.00
HALLWAY					
1201	All Around the World/Just Plain Hurt	1964	3.75	7.50	15.00
1204	Willie and the Hand Jive/I've Got My Eyes on You	1964	3.75	7.50	15.00
1927	Running Bear '65/Dedicated to the One I Love	1965	3.75	7.50	15.00
IMPERIAL					
5924	This Little Bitty Tear/The Day the World Stood Still	1963	2.50	5.00	10.00
5947	I've Got My Eyes on You/I Couldn't Take It Again	1963	2.50	5.00	10.00
MERCURY					
10027 [S]	Cradle of Love/City of Tears	1960	12.50	25.00	50.00
10036 [S]	Feel So Fine/I'm Starting to Go Steady	1960	15.00	30.00	60.00
71474	Running Bear/My Heart Knows	1959	6.25	12.50	25.00
71598 [M]	Cradle of Love/City of Tears	1960	5.00	10.00	20.00
71598 [PS]	Cradle of Love/City of Tears	1960	7.50	15.00	30.00
71651 [M]	Feel So Fine/I'm Starting to Go Steady	1960	5.00	10.00	20.00
71651 [PS]	Feel So Fine/I'm Starting to Go Steady	1960	7.50	15.00	30.00
71691	Charming Billy/Up in the Air	1960	5.00	10.00	20.00
71728	New Baby for Christmas/(I Want a) Rock and Roll Guitar	1960	5.00	10.00	20.00
71761	Leave My Kitten Alone/Token of Love	1961	5.00	10.00	20.00
71761 [PS]	Leave My Kitten Alone/Token of Love	1961	7.50	15.00	30.00
71803	I Feel Good/Willy Walk	1961	5.00	10.00	20.00
71865	Let Them Talk/She Once Belonged to Me	1961	5.00	10.00	20.00
71908	Free Me/Kissin' Tree	1961	5.00	10.00	20.00
71908 [PS]	Free Me/Kissin' Tree	1961	7.50	15.00	30.00
71951	Let's Leave It That Way/Broken Hearts Anonymous	1962	3.75	7.50	15.00
72049	Let the Big Boss Man (Pull You Through)/The Day After Forever	1962	3.75	7.50	15.00
TCF HALL					
101	Running Bear '65/Dedicated to the One I Love	1965	2.50	5.00	10.00
110	Sounds Like Trouble/You Can Make It If You Try	1965	3.75	7.50	15.00
120	I'm Askin' Forgiveness/Good Good Lovin'	1965	2.50	5.00	10.00

Albums

Number	Title (A Side/B Side)	Yr	VG	VG+	NM
MERCURY					
MG-20592 [M]	Running Bear	1960	25.00	50.00	100.00
MG-20609 [M]	Come Rock with Me	1960	25.00	50.00	100.00
SR-60250 [S]	Running Bear	1960	37.50	75.00	150.00
—Black label					
SR-60250 [S]	Running Bear	1981	3.00	6.00	12.00
—Reissue on Chicago skyline label					
SR-60609 [S]	Come Rock with Me	1960	37.50	75.00	150.00
WING					
MGW-12246 [M]	Running Bear	1963	5.00	10.00	20.00
SRW-16246 [S]	Running Bear	1963	6.25	12.50	25.00

PRESTON, MIKE

45s

Number	Title (A Side/B Side)	Yr	VG	VG+	NM
LONDON					
1834	A House, a Car and a Wedding Ring/My Lucky Love	1958	3.00	6.00	12.00
1865	Girl Without a Heart/In Surabaya	1959	2.50	5.00	10.00
1903	'Till Tomorrow/An Ordinary Couple	1960	2.50	5.00	10.00
1981	Girl Without a Heart/Marry Me	1960	2.50	5.00	10.00
9601	Careless Love/Little Grain of Sand	1963	2.50	5.00	10.00

PRESTON, TERRY

See FERLIN HUSKY.

PRETENDERS, THE (1)

Also see JIMMY JONES.

45s

Number	Title (A Side/B Side)	Yr	VG	VG+	NM
APT					
25026	Blue and Lonely/Daddy Needs Baby	1959	125.00	250.00	500.00
CENTRAL					
2605	Blue and Lonely/Daddy Needs Baby	1958	375.00	750.00	1500.

PRETENDERS, THE (2)

45s

Number	Title (A Side/B Side)	Yr	VG	VG+	NM
BETHLEHEM					
3050	The Day You Are Mine/Ding Dong Bells	1962	50.00	100.00	200.00

PRETENDERS, THE (3)

45s

Number	Title (A Side/B Side)	Yr	VG	VG+	NM
CHATTAHOOCHIE					
685	Pepita's Theme/Tijuana Taxi	1965	5.00	10.00	20.00

PRETENDERS, THE (U)

The Rama and Whirlin' Disc records could be by group (1). None of these, or any of the above, are by the group fronted by Chrissie Hynde; they are outside the scope of this book.

45s

Number	Title (A Side/B Side)	Yr	VG	VG+	NM
POWER-MARTIN					
1001	Smile/I'm So Happy	1961	25.00	50.00	100.00
RAMA					
198	Possessive Love/I've Got to Have You Baby	1956	30.00	60.00	120.00
WHIRLIN' DISC					
106	Close Your Eyes/Part-Time Sweetheart	1957	62.50	125.00	250.00

PRETTY BOY

See DON COVAY.

PRETTY THINGS, THE

45s

Number	Title (A Side/B Side)	Yr	VG	VG+	NM
FONTANA					
1508	I Can Never Say/Honey, I Need	1965	3.75	7.50	15.00
1518	Cry to Me/I Can Never Say	1965	3.75	7.50	15.00
1518	Cry to Me/Judgment Day	1965	3.75	7.50	15.00
1540	Midnight to Six Man/Can't Stand Pain	1966	3.75	7.50	15.00
1550	Come See Me/Judgment Day	1966	3.75	7.50	15.00
1550	Come See Me/Progress	1966	3.75	7.50	15.00
1916	Big Boss Man/Rosalyn	1964	3.75	7.50	15.00
1941	Don't Bring Me Down/We'll Be Together	1964	3.75	7.50	15.00
LAURIE					
3458	Talkin' About the Good Times/Walking Through My Dreams	1968	7.50	15.00	30.00
NORTON					
PT 109	All Light Up/Pretty Beat	1999	—	2.00	4.00
—Red vinyl, small hole, called "The Pretty Things U.S. Tour 45"					
RARE EARTH					
5005	Private Sorrow/Balloon Burning	1969	3.75	7.50	15.00
SWAN SONG					
70104	Come Home Momma/Joey	1975	—	2.50	5.00
70107	It Isn't Rock & Roll/Remember That Boy	1975	—	2.50	5.00

7-Inch Extended Plays

Number	Title (A Side/B Side)	Yr	VG	VG+	NM
NORTON					
EP-501	Rosalyn/Judgement Day//Roadrunner/Don't Bring Me Down	1999	—	—	2.00
EP-501 [PS]	Rosalyn	1999	—	—	2.00
EP-502	Big City/I Can Never Say//Get Yourself Home/Honey I Need	1999	—	—	2.00
EP-502 [PS]	Big City	1999	—	—	2.00
EP-503	You Don't Believe Me/Buzz the Jerk//You'll Never Do It Baby/Come See Me	1999	—	—	2.00
EP-503 [PS]	Buzz the Jerk	1999	—	—	2.00
EP-504	Midnight to Six Man/Can't Stand the Pain//LSD/Me Needing You	1999	—	—	2.00
EP-504 [PS]	Midnight to Six Man	1999	—	—	2.00
EP-505	A House in the Country/Progress//Tripping/Photographer	1999	—	—	2.00
EP-505 [PS]	A House in the Country	1999	—	—	2.00

Albums

Number	Title (A Side/B Side)	Yr	VG	VG+	NM
BIG BEAT					
WIK-24	Live at Heartbreak Hotel	1985	2.50	5.00	10.00
FONTANA					
MGF-27544 [M]	The Pretty Things	1965	20.00	40.00	80.00
SRF-67544 [P]	The Pretty Things	1965	20.00	40.00	80.00
RARE EARTH					
RS 506	S.F. Sorrow	1969	12.50	25.00	50.00
—Original covers are rounded at top					
RS 506	S.F. Sorrow	1969	5.00	10.00	20.00
—Later copies are standard in shape					
RS 515	Parachute	1970	5.00	10.00	20.00
R 549R2 [(2)]	Real Pretty	1976	3.75	7.50	15.00
—The two prior Rare Earth albums in one package					
SIRE					
SASH-3713 [(2)]	The Vintage Years	1976	3.75	7.50	15.00
SWAN SONG					
SS 8411	Silk Torpedo	1975	2.50	5.00	10.00
SS 8414	Savage Eye	1976	2.50	5.00	10.00
WARNER BROS.					
BS 2680	Freeway Madness	1973	2.50	5.00	10.00
BSK 3466	Cross Talk	1980	2.50	5.00	10.00

PREVIN, ANDRE

45s

Number	Title (A Side/B Side)	Yr	VG	VG+	NM
COLUMBIA					
30833 [S]	(titles unknown)	1960	2.50	5.00	10.00
30834 [S]	(titles unknown)	1960	2.50	5.00	10.00
30835 [S]	(titles unknown)	1960	2.50	5.00	10.00
30836 [S]	(titles unknown)	1960	2.50	5.00	10.00
30837 [S]	(titles unknown)	1960	2.50	5.00	10.00
31074 [S]	(titles unknown)	1961	2.50	5.00	10.00
31075 [S]	(titles unknown)	1961	2.50	5.00	10.00
31076 [S]	(titles unknown)	1961	2.50	5.00	10.00
31077 [S]	(titles unknown)	1961	2.50	5.00	10.00
31078 [S]	(titles unknown)	1961	2.50	5.00	10.00
31540 [S]	(titles unknown)	1962	2.50	5.00	10.00
31541 [S]	(titles unknown)	1962	2.50	5.00	10.00
31542 [S]	(titles unknown)	1962	2.50	5.00	10.00
31543 [S]	(titles unknown)	1962	2.50	5.00	10.00
31544 [S]	(titles unknown)	1962	2.50	5.00	10.00
—Anyone who can fill in these gaps -- the above 15 all are Columbia "Stereo 7" singles -- please let us know.					
41683	Love Me or Leave Me/Like Love	1960	2.00	4.00	8.00
42596	Song from "Two for the Seesaw"/Song from "Long Day's Journey Into Night"	1962	2.00	4.00	8.00
43136	Goodbye, Charlie/Kiss Me, Stupid	1964	2.00	4.00	8.00

Number	Title (A Side/B Side)	Yr	VG	VG+	NM
JZSP 55071/0 [DJ]	God Rest Ye Merry, Gentlemen/Let No Walls Divide	1961	3.00	6.00	12.00
—B-side by Doris Day					
DECCA					
25529	Moonlight Becomes You/Let's Fall in Love	1961	2.00	4.00	8.00
MGM					
12792	Like Young/Young Man's Lament	1959	2.50	5.00	10.00
12840	Young and Tender/Too Young to Be True	1959	2.50	5.00	10.00
RCA VICTOR					
47-2764	But Not for Me/Hallelujah	1949	3.75	7.50	15.00
47-2765	My Shining Hour/This Can't Be Love	1949	3.75	7.50	15.00
47-2766	Mad About the Boy/Just One of Those Things	1949	3.75	7.50	15.00
47-2767	I Didn't Know What Time It Was/Should I	1949	3.75	7.50	15.00
—The above four comprise a box set					
47-3080	Dardanella/The Gypsy in My Soul	1949	3.75	7.50	15.00
47-3123	Anything Goes/Bewitched, Bothered and Bewildered	1949	3.75	7.50	15.00
47-3124	You're the Top/I'm Old Fashioned	1949	3.75	7.50	15.00
47-3125	Who Cares/Who	1949	3.75	7.50	15.00
—The above three comprise a box set					
47-3263	I Didn't Know What Time It Was/Should I	1949	3.75	7.50	15.00
47-3836	Three Little Words/Thinking of You	1950	3.75	7.50	15.00
47-3837	Who's Sorry Now/All Alone	1950	3.75	7.50	15.00
47-4161	Skylark/You Took Advantage of Me	1951	3.75	7.50	15.00
47-4163	Dearly Beloved/Love Is Just Around the Corner	1951	3.75	7.50	15.00
47-4351	Lullaby of Broadway/I Only Have Eyes for You	1951	3.00	6.00	12.00
47-4352	This Head of Mine/September in the Rain	1951	3.00	6.00	12.00
47-4353	This Heart of Mine/I Know Why and So Do You	1951	3.00	6.00	12.00
47-4354	I'll String Along/Jeepers Creepers	1951	3.00	6.00	12.00
—The above four comprise a box set					
47-4780	The Story of a Piano (Part 1)/Romance, Op. 28, No. 2	1952	3.00	6.00	12.00
47-4781	The Story of a Piano (Part 2)/Valse Brilliance in A Minor	1952	3.00	6.00	12.00
47-4782	The Story of a Piano (Part 3)/Traumere Op. 15	1952	3.00	6.00	12.00
47-4783	The Story of a Piano (Part 4)/Adagio Cantabile	1952	3.00	6.00	12.00
—The above four comprise a box set					
47-9122	Theme from Hotel/The Bad Guys	1967	—	3.00	6.00
UNITED ARTISTS					
50080	Bad Guys/Waltz of the Fortune Cookie	1966	—	3.00	6.00

Albums

Number	Title (A Side/B Side)	Yr	VG	VG+	NM
ANGEL					
DS-37780	A Different Kind of Blues	1981	2.50	5.00	10.00
DS-37799	It's a Breeze	1982	2.50	5.00	10.00
ARCHIVE OF FOLK AND JAZZ					
247	Early Years	1970	2.50	5.00	10.00
COLUMBIA					
CL 1437 [M]	Like Love	1960	3.75	7.50	15.00
—Red and black label with six "eye" logos					
CL 1437 [M]	Like Love	1963	3.00	6.00	12.00
—Red label with "Guaranteed High Fidelity" or "360 Sound Mono" at bottom					
CL 1495 [M]	Rhapsody in Blue	1960	3.75	7.50	15.00
—Red and black label with six "eye" logos					
CL 1495 [M]	Rhapsody in Blue	1963	3.00	6.00	12.00
—Red label with "Guaranteed High Fidelity" or "360 Sound Mono" at bottom					
CL 1530 [M]	Give My Regards to Broadway	1960	5.00	10.00	20.00
—Red and black label with six "eye" logos					
CL 1530 [M]	Give My Regards to Broadway	1963	3.00	6.00	12.00
—Red label with "Guaranteed High Fidelity" or "360 Sound Mono" at bottom					
CL 1569 [M]	Camelot	1961	5.00	10.00	20.00
—Red and black label with six "eye" logos					
CL 1569 [M]	Camelot	1963	3.00	6.00	12.00
—Red label with "Guaranteed High Fidelity" or "360 Sound Mono" at bottom					
CL 1595 [M]	Thinking of You	1961	5.00	10.00	20.00
—Red and black label with six "eye" logos					
CL 1595 [M]	Thinking of You	1963	3.00	6.00	12.00
—Red label with "Guaranteed High Fidelity" or "360 Sound Mono" at bottom					
CL 1649 [M]	A Touch of Elegance	1961	5.00	10.00	20.00
—Red and black label with six "eye" logos					
CL 1741 [M]	Mack the Knife and Other Kurt Weill Music	1962	5.00	10.00	20.00
—Red and black label with six "eye" logos					
CL 1741 [M]	Mack the Knife and Other Kurt Weill Music	1963	3.00	6.00	12.00
—Red label with "Guaranteed High Fidelity" or "360 Sound Mono" at bottom					
CL 1786 [M]	Faraway Part of Town	1962	5.00	10.00	20.00
—Red and black label with six "eye" logos					
CL 1786 [M]	Faraway Part of Town	1963	3.00	6.00	12.00
—Red label with "Guaranteed High Fidelity" or "360 Sound Mono" at bottom					
CL 1888 [M]	The Light Fantastic	1962	5.00	10.00	20.00
—Red and black label with six "eye" logos					
CL 1888 [M]	The Light Fantastic	1963	3.00	6.00	12.00
—Red label with "Guaranteed High Fidelity" or "360 Sound Mono" at bottom					
CL 2034 [M]	Andre Previn in Hollywood	1963	3.75	7.50	15.00
—Red label with "Guaranteed High Fidelity" at bottom					
CL 2034 [M]	Andre Previn in Hollywood	1966	3.00	6.00	12.00
—Red label with "360 Sound Mono" at bottom					
CL 2114 [M]	The Soft and Swinging Music of Jimmy McHugh	1964	3.75	7.50	15.00
—Red label with "Guaranteed High Fidelity" at bottom					
CL 2114 [M]	The Soft and Swinging Music of Jimmy McHugh	1966	3.00	6.00	12.00
—Red label with "360 Sound Mono" at bottom					
CL 2195 [M]	My Fair Lady	1964	3.75	7.50	15.00
—Red label with "Guaranteed High Fidelity" at bottom					
CL 2195 [M]	My Fair Lady	1966	3.00	6.00	12.00
—Red label with "360 Sound Mono" at bottom					
CL 2294 [M]	Popular Previn	1965	3.75	7.50	15.00
—Red label with "Guaranteed High Fidelity" at bottom					
CL 2294 [M]	Popular Previn	1966	3.00	6.00	12.00
—Red label with "360 Sound Mono" at bottom					
CS 8233 [S]	Like Love	1960	5.00	10.00	20.00
—Red and black label with six "eye" logos					
CS 8233 [S]	Like Love	1963	3.75	7.50	15.00
—Red label with "360 Sound Stereo" at bottom					
CS 8286 [S]	Rhapsody in Blue	1960	5.00	10.00	20.00
—Red and black label with six "eye" logos					
CS 8286 [S]	Rhapsody in Blue	1963	3.75	7.50	15.00
—Red label with "360 Sound Stereo" at bottom					
CS 8330 [S]	Give My Regards to Broadway	1960	6.25	12.50	25.00
—Red and black label with six "eye" logos					
CS 8330 [S]	Give My Regards to Broadway	1960	3.75	7.50	15.00
—Red label with "360 Sound Stereo" at bottom					
CS 8369 [S]	Camelot	1961	6.25	12.50	25.00
—Red and black label with six "eye" logos					
CS 8369 [S]	Camelot	1963	3.75	7.50	15.00
—Red label with "360 Sound Stereo" at bottom					
CS 8395 [S]	Thinking of You	1961	6.25	12.50	25.00
—Red and black label with six "eye" logos					
CS 8395 [S]	Thinking of You	1963	3.75	7.50	15.00
—Red label with "360 Sound Stereo" at bottom					
CS 8541 [S]	Mack the Knife and Other Kurt Weill Music	1962	6.25	12.50	25.00
—Red and black label with six "eye" logos					
CS 8541 [S]	Mack the Knife and Other Kurt Weill Music	1962	3.75	7.50	15.00
—Red label with "360 Sound Stereo" at bottom					
CS 8586 [S]	Faraway Part of Town	1962	6.25	12.50	25.00
—Red and black label with six "eye" logos					
CS 8586 [S]	Faraway Part of Town	1963	3.75	7.50	15.00
—Red label with "360 Sound Stereo" at bottom					
CS 8649 [S]	A Touch of Elegance	1961	6.25	12.50	25.00
—Red and black label with six "eye" logos					
CS 8688 [S]	The Light Fantastic	1962	6.25	12.50	25.00
—Red and black label with six "eye" logos					
CS 8688 [S]	The Light Fantastic	1963	3.75	7.50	15.00
—Red label with "360 Sound Stereo" at bottom					
CS 8834 [S]	Andre Previn in Hollywood	1963	5.00	10.00	20.00
—Red label with "360 Sound Stereo" in black at bottom					
CS 8834 [S]	Andre Previn in Hollywood	1966	3.75	7.50	15.00
—Red label with "360 Sound Stereo" in white at bottom					
CS 8914 [S]	The Soft and Swinging Music of Jimmy McHugh	1964	5.00	10.00	20.00
—Red label with "360 Sound Stereo" in black at bottom					
CS 8914 [S]	The Soft and Swinging Music of Jimmy McHugh	1966	3.75	7.50	15.00
—Red label with "360 Sound Stereo" in white at bottom					
CS 8995 [S]	My Fair Lady	1964	5.00	10.00	20.00
—Red label with "360 Sound Stereo" in black at bottom					
CS 8995 [S]	My Fair Lady	1966	3.75	7.50	15.00
—Red label with "360 Sound Stereo" in white at bottom					
CS 9094 [S]	Popular Previn	1965	5.00	10.00	20.00
—Red label with "360 Sound Stereo" in black at bottom					
CS 9094 [S]	Popular Previn	1966	3.75	7.50	15.00
—Red label with "360 Sound Stereo" in white at bottom					
CONTEMPORARY					
C-3543 [M]	Pal Joey	1957	12.50	25.00	50.00
C-3548 [M]	Gigi	1958	12.50	25.00	50.00
M-3558 [M]	Andre Previn Plays Vernon Duke	1959	12.50	25.00	50.00
M-3567 [M]	Andre Previn Plays Jerome Kern	1959	12.50	25.00	50.00
M-3570 [M]	Jazz Trio, King Size	1959	12.50	25.00	50.00
M-3572 [M]	West Side Story	1960	10.00	20.00	40.00
M-3575 [M]	Like Previn	1960	10.00	20.00	40.00
M-3586 [M]	Andre Previn Plays Harold Arlen	1960	10.00	20.00	40.00
S-7543 [S]	Pal Joey	1959	10.00	20.00	40.00
S-7548 [S]	Gigi	1959	10.00	20.00	40.00
S-7558 [S]	Andre Previn Plays Vernon Duke	1959	10.00	20.00	40.00
S-7567 [S]	Andre Previn Plays Jerome Kern	1959	10.00	20.00	40.00
S-7570 [S]	Jazz Trio, King Size	1959	10.00	20.00	40.00
S-7572 [S]	West Side Story	1960	7.50	15.00	30.00
S-7575 [S]	Like Previn	1960	7.50	15.00	30.00
S-7586 [S]	Andre Previn Plays Harold Arlen	1960	7.50	15.00	30.00
CORONET					
170	Featuring Andre Previn	196?	3.00	6.00	12.00
181	The Magic Sounds of Andre Previn	196?	3.00	6.00	12.00
DECCA					
DL 4115 [M]	Andre Previn Plays Pretty	1961	3.00	6.00	12.00
DL 4350 [M]	But Beautiful	1963	3.00	6.00	12.00
DL 8131 [M]	Let's Get Away From It All	1955	10.00	20.00	40.00
DL 8341 [M]	Hollywood at Midnight	1957	10.00	20.00	40.00
DL 74115 [S]	Andre Previn Plays Pretty	1961	3.75	7.50	15.00
DL 74350 [S]	But Beautiful	1963	3.75	7.50	15.00
FANTASY					
OJC-157	Double Play!	198?	2.50	5.00	10.00
—Reissue of Contemporary 7011					
OJC-170	Like Previn	198?	2.50	5.00	10.00
—Reissue of Contemporary 7575					
OJC-422	West Side Story	1990	2.50	5.00	10.00
OJC-637	Pal Joey	1991	3.00	6.00	12.00
GUEST STAR					
1436	Piano Greats	196?	3.00	6.00	12.00
HARMONY					
HL 7348 [M]	Misty	1965	3.00	6.00	12.00
HL 7407 [M]	Starlight Piano	196?	3.00	6.00	12.00
HL 7429 [M]	Camelot	1967	3.00	6.00	12.00
HS 11148 [S]	Misty	1965	3.00	6.00	12.00
HS 11207 [S]	Starlight Piano	196?	3.00	6.00	12.00
HS 11229 [S]	Camelot	1967	3.00	6.00	12.00
JAZZ ODYSSEY					
32160260	Mack the Knife and Other Kurt Weill Music	196?	3.00	6.00	12.00
—Reissue of Columbia 8541					
MGM					
E-3716 [M]	Secret Songs for Young Lovers	1959	5.00	10.00	20.00
SE-3716 [S]	Secret Songs for Young Lovers	1959	6.25	12.50	25.00
E-3811 [M]	Like Blue	1960	5.00	10.00	20.00
SE-3811 [S]	Like Blue	1960	6.25	12.50	25.00
E-4186 [M]	Andre Previn—Composer, Conductor, Arranger, Pianist	1964	3.75	7.50	15.00
SE-4186 [S]	Andre Previn—Composer, Conductor, Arranger, Pianist	1964	5.00	10.00	20.00
MOBILE FIDELITY					
1-095	West Side Story	1982	6.25	12.50	25.00
—Audiophile vinyl					
MONARCH					
203 [10]	All Star Jazz	1952	20.00	40.00	80.00
204 [10]	Andre Previn Plays Duke	1952	20.00	40.00	80.00

Number	Title (A Side/B Side)	Yr	VG	VG+	NM
PRI					
3026 [S]	The World's Most Honored Pianist	1962	6.25	12.50	25.00
—Issued on yellow vinyl					
RCA CAMDEN					
CAL-792 [M]	Love Walked In	1964	3.00	6.00	12.00
CAS-792 [R]	Love Walked In	1964	2.50	5.00	10.00
RCA VICTOR					
LPM-1011 [M]	Gershwin	1955	10.00	20.00	40.00
LPM-1356 [M]	Three Little Words	1957	10.00	20.00	40.00
ANL1-2805	Pure Gold	1978	2.50	5.00	10.00
LPT-3002 [10]	Andre Previn Plays Harry Warren	1952	20.00	40.00	80.00
LPM-3491 [M]	Andre Previn Plays Music of the Young Hollywood Composers	1966	3.00	6.00	12.00
LSP-3491 [S]	Andre Previn Plays Music of the Young Hollywood Composers	1966	3.75	7.50	15.00
LPM-3551 [M]	Andre Previn with Voices	1966	3.00	6.00	12.00
LSP-3551 [S]	Andre Previn with Voices	1966	3.75	7.50	15.00
LPM-3806 [M]	All Alone	1967	3.75	7.50	15.00
LSP-3806 [S]	All Alone	1967	3.00	6.00	12.00
SPRINGBOARD					
SPB-4053	After Dark	197?	2.50	5.00	10.00
STEREO RECORDS					
S-7004 [S]	Pal Joey	1958	12.50	25.00	50.00
S-7020 [S]	Gigi	1958	12.50	25.00	50.00
VERVE					
V-8565 [M]	The Essential Andre Previn	1963	3.00	6.00	12.00
V6-8565 [S]	The Essential Andre Previn	1963	3.75	7.50	15.00

PREVIN, ANDRE; HERB ELLIS; SHELLY MANNE; RAY BROWN

Albums

Number	Title (A Side/B Side)	Yr	VG	VG+	NM
COLUMBIA					
CL 2018 [M]	Four to Go	1963	3.75	7.50	15.00
CS 8818 [S]	Four to Go	1963	5.00	10.00	20.00

PREVIN, ANDRE, AND RUSS FREEMAN

Albums

Number	Title (A Side/B Side)	Yr	VG	VG+	NM
CONTEMPORARY					
C-3537 [M]	Double Play!	1957	12.50	25.00	50.00
S-7011 [S]	Double Play!	1959	10.00	20.00	40.00
STEREO RECORDS					
S-7011 [S]	Double Play!	1958	12.50	25.00	50.00

PRICE, ALAN

Also see THE ANIMALS.

45s

Number	Title (A Side/B Side)	Yr	VG	VG+	NM
COTILLION					
44044	Falling in Love Again/Sly Sadie	1969	—	3.00	6.00
EPIC					
04319	I Don't Feel No Pain No More (Time and Tide)/Rowf and Snitter Run to Sea	1984	—	2.00	4.00
JET					
XW1119	I Wanna Dance/Just for You	1978	—	2.00	4.00
5056	This Is Your Lucky Day/Mama Don't Go Home	1979	—	2.00	4.00
PARROT					
3001	I Put a Spell on You/Iechyd-Da	1966	2.50	5.00	10.00
3007	Hi-Lili, Hi-Lo/Take Me Home	1966	2.50	5.00	10.00
3009	Tickle Me/Simon Smith and His Amazing Dancing Bears	1966	2.50	5.00	10.00
3013	Who Cares/The House That Jack Built	1967	2.00	4.00	8.00
3014	Shame/Don't Do That Again	1967	2.00	4.00	8.00
3019	Not Born to Follow/To Ramona	1968	2.00	4.00	8.00
WARNER BROS.					
7717	Poor People/O Lucky Man	1973	—	2.50	5.00

Albums

Number	Title (A Side/B Side)	Yr	VG	VG+	NM
ACCORD					
SJA-7904	It's Priceless	1982	2.50	5.00	10.00
JET					
JT-LA809-H	Alan Price	1977	2.50	5.00	10.00
JZ 35710	Lucky Day	1979	2.50	5.00	10.00
NJZ 36510	Rising Sun	1980	2.50	5.00	10.00
PARROT					
PAS 71018 [P]	The Price Is Right	1968	7.50	15.00	30.00
TOWNHOUSE					
SN-7126	House of the Rising Sun	1981	2.50	5.00	10.00
WARNER BROS.					
BS 2710	O Lucky Man	1973	3.00	6.00	12.00
BS 2783	Between Today and Yesterday	1974	3.00	6.00	12.00

PRICE, LLOYD

45s

Number	Title (A Side/B Side)	Yr	VG	VG+	NM
ABC					
1237	Stagger Lee/Personality	1969	—	3.00	6.00
—"Golden Treasure Chest" reissue; contains the "samitized" version of "Stagger Lee" with Mr. Lee and Billy arguing over a woman					
11016	Personality/Just Because	1967	2.00	4.00	8.00
ABC-PARAMOUNT					
9792	Just Because/Why	1957	5.00	10.00	20.00
9972 [M]	Stagger Lee/You Need Love	1958	5.00	10.00	20.00
—Most, if not all, copies contain the "raunchy" version of "Stagger Lee" with Mr. Lee and Billy playing cards					
S-9972 [S]	Stagger Lee/You Need Love	1958	10.00	20.00	40.00
9997 [M]	Where Were You (On Our Wedding Day)?/Is It Really Love	1959	5.00	10.00	20.00
S-9997 [S]	Where Were You (On Our Wedding Day)?/Is It Really Love	1959	10.00	20.00	40.00
10018 [M]	Personality/Have You Ever Had the Blues	1959	5.00	10.00	20.00
10018 [M]	(You've Got) Personality/Have You Ever Had the Blues	1959	5.00	10.00	20.00
—Note longer title					
S-10018 [S]	Personality/Have You Ever Had the Blues	1959	12.50	25.00	50.00
10032 [M]	I'm Gonna Get Married/Three Little Pigs	1959	5.00	10.00	20.00
S-10032 [S]	I'm Gonna Get Married/Three Little Pigs	1959	12.50	25.00	50.00
10062	Come Into My Heart/Won't Cha Come Home	1959	3.75	7.50	15.00
S-10062 [S]	Come Into My Heart/Won't Cha Come Home	1959	12.50	25.00	50.00
10075	Lady Luck/Never Let Me Go	1960	3.75	7.50	15.00
10102	No If's — No And's/For Love	1960	3.75	7.50	15.00
10123	Question/If I Look a Little Blue	1960	3.75	7.50	15.00
10139	Just Call Me (And I'll Understand)/Who Could've Told You	1960	3.75	7.50	15.00
10162	(You Better) Know What You're Doin'/That's Why Tears Come and Go	1960	3.75	7.50	15.00
10177	Boo Hoo/I Made You Cry	1961	3.75	7.50	15.00
10197	One Hundred Percent/Say I'm the One	1961	3.75	7.50	15.00
10206	String of Pearls/Chantilly Lace	1961	3.75	7.50	15.00
10221	Mary and Man-O/I Ain't Givin' Up Nothin'	1961	3.75	7.50	15.00
10229	Talk to Me/I Cover the Waterfront	1961	3.75	7.50	15.00
10288	Be a Leader/'Nother Fairy Tale	1962	3.75	7.50	15.00
10299	Twistin' the Blues/Pop Eye's Irresistable You	1962	3.75	7.50	15.00
10342	Counterfeit Friends/Your Picture	1962	3.75	7.50	15.00
10372	Under Your Spell Again/Happy Birthday Mama	1962	3.75	7.50	15.00
10412	Who's Sorry Now/Hello Bill	1963	3.75	7.50	15.00
DOUBLE-L					
714	Pistol Packin' Mama/Tennessee Waltz	1963	2.50	5.00	10.00
722	Misty/Cry On	1963	2.50	5.00	10.00
728	Merry Christmas Mama/Auld Lang Syne	1963	3.00	6.00	12.00
729	Billie Baby/Try a Little Bit of Tenderness	1964	2.50	5.00	10.00
729 [PS]	Billie Baby/Try a Little Bit of Tenderness	1964	6.25	12.50	25.00
730	I'll Be a Fool for You/You're Nobody Till Somebody Loves You	1964	2.50	5.00	10.00
736	Go On Little Girl/You're Reading Me	1965	2.50	5.00	10.00
739	Every Night/Peeping and Hiding	1966	2.50	5.00	10.00
740	Send Me Some Loving/Somewhere Along the Way	1966	2.50	5.00	10.00
GSF					
6882	Sing a Song/(B-side unknown)	1972	—	3.00	6.00
6894	Love Music/Just for Baby	1973	—	3.00	6.00
6904	Trying to Slip (Away)/They Get Down	1973	—	3.00	6.00
HURD					
82	Misty '66/Saturday Night	1966	2.00	4.00	8.00
JAD					
208	Luv, Luv, Luv/Take All	1968	2.00	4.00	8.00
212	Don't Stop Now/The Truth	1968	2.00	4.00	8.00
KRC					
301	Lonely Chair/The Chicken and the Bop	1957	12.50	25.00	50.00
303	Hello Little Girl/Georgianna	1957	6.25	12.50	25.00
305	How Many Times/To Love and Be Loved	1957	6.25	12.50	25.00
587	Just Because/Why	1957	20.00	40.00	80.00
5000	No Limit to Love/Such a Mess	195?	6.25	12.50	25.00
5002	Gonna Let You Come Back Home/Down by the River	195?	6.25	12.50	25.00
LPG					
111	What Did You Do with My Love/Love Music	1976	—	3.00	6.00
LUDIX					
4747	Feelin' Good/Cupid's Bandwagon	197?	—	3.00	6.00
MONUMENT					
856	Don't Cry/I Love You, I Just Love You	1964	2.50	5.00	10.00
865	Amen/I'd Fight the World	1964	2.50	5.00	10.00
877	Oh, Lady Luck/Woman	1965	2.50	5.00	10.00
887	If I Had My Life to Live Over/Two for Love	1965	2.50	5.00	10.00
PARAMOUNT					
0168	In the Eyes of God/The Legend of Nigger Charley	1972	—	3.00	6.00
REPRISE					
0499	I Won't Cry Anymore/The Man Who Took the Valise Off the Floor at Grand Central Station at Noon	1966	2.00	4.00	8.00
SCEPTER					
12310	Hooked on a Feeling/If You Really Love Him	1971	—	3.00	6.00
12327	Mr. and Mrs. Untrue/Natural SInner	1971	—	3.00	6.00
SPECIALTY					
428	Lawdy Miss Clawdy/Mailman Blues	1952	62.50	125.00	250.00
428	Lawdy Miss Clawdy/Mailman Blues	1952	375.00	750.00	1500.
—Red vinyl					
440	Oooh-Oooh-Oooh/Restless Heart	1952	25.00	50.00	100.00
452	Ain't It a Shame?/Tell Me Pretty Baby	1953	25.00	50.00	100.00
452	Ain't It a Shame?/Tell Me Pretty Baby	1953	50.00	100.00	200.00
—Red vinyl					
457	What's the Matter Now/So Long	1953	25.00	50.00	100.00
457	What's the Matter Now/So Long	1953	50.00	100.00	200.00
—Red vinyl					
463	Where You At?/Baby Don't Turn Your Back on Me	1953	25.00	50.00	100.00
463	Where You At?/Baby Don't Turn Your Back on Me	1953	50.00	100.00	200.00
—Red vinyl					
471	I Wish Your Picture Was You/Frog Legs	1953	25.00	50.00	100.00
483	Let Me Come Home, Baby/Too Late for Tears	1954	20.00	40.00	80.00
483	Let Me Come Home, Baby/Too Late for Tears	1954	50.00	100.00	200.00
—Red vinyl					
494	Walkin' the Track/Jimmie Lee	1954	20.00	40.00	80.00
535	Oo-Ee Baby/Chee-Koo Baby	1954	10.00	20.00	40.00
540	Trying to Find Someone to Love/Lord, Lord, Amen!	1955	10.00	20.00	40.00
571	Woe Ho Ho/I Yi Yi Gomen-a-Sai (I'm Sorry)	1956	10.00	20.00	40.00
578	Country Boy Rock/Rock 'N' Dance	1956	12.50	25.00	50.00
582	Forgive Me, Clawdy/I'm Glad	1956	7.50	15.00	30.00
602	Baby Please Come Home/Breaking My Heart (All Over Again)	1957	7.50	15.00	30.00
661	Lawdy Miss Clawdy/Mailman Blues	1959	5.00	10.00	20.00
TURNTABLE					
501	I Understand/The Grass Will Sing (For You)	1969	2.00	4.00	8.00
502	I Heard It Through the Grapevine/It's Your Thing	1969	2.00	4.00	8.00
506	Bad Conditions/The Truth	1969	2.00	4.00	8.00
509	Lawdy Miss Clawdy/Little Volcano	1969	2.00	4.00	8.00

7-Inch Extended Plays

Number	Title (A Side/B Side)	Yr	VG	VG+	NM
ABC-PARAMOUNT					
277	(contents unknown)	1959	25.00	50.00	100.00
277 [PS]	The Exciting Lloyd Price	1959	25.00	50.00	100.00
315	(contents unknown)	1960	25.00	50.00	100.00

Number	Title (A Side/B Side)	Yr	VG	VG+	NM
315 [PS]	Mr. Personality Sings the Blues	1960	25.00	50.00	100.00
A-324	Lady Luck/Personality//Stagger Lee/I'm Gonna Get Married	1960	25.00	50.00	100.00
A-324 [PS]	Mr. Personality's Big Hits	1960	25.00	50.00	100.00
Albums					
ABC					
S-297	Mr. Personality	1967	3.75	7.50	15.00
—Reissue on revised label					
S-324 [R]	Mr. Personality's Big 15	1968	3.75	7.50	15.00
—Reissue on revised label					
X-763	16 Greatest Hits	1972	3.75	7.50	15.00
AC-30006	The ABC Collection	1976	3.75	7.50	15.00
ABC-PARAMOUNT					
277 [M]	The Exciting Lloyd Price	1959	10.00	20.00	40.00
S-277 [S]	The Exciting Lloyd Price	1959	20.00	40.00	80.00
297 [M]	Mr. Personality	1959	10.00	20.00	40.00
S-297 [S]	Mr. Personality	1959	20.00	40.00	80.00
315 [M]	Mr. Personality Sings the Blues	1960	10.00	20.00	40.00
S-315 [S]	Mr. Personality Sings the Blues	1960	20.00	40.00	80.00
324 [M]	Mr. Personality's Big 15	1960	10.00	20.00	40.00
346 [M]	The Fantastic Lloyd Price	1960	10.00	20.00	40.00
S-346 [R]	The Fantastic Lloyd Price	196?	6.25	12.50	25.00
366 [M]	Lloyd Price Sings the Million Sellers	1961	10.00	20.00	40.00
S-366 [S]	Lloyd Price Sings the Million Sellers	1961	12.50	25.00	50.00
382 [M]	Cookin' with Lloyd Price	1961	10.00	20.00	40.00
S-382 [S]	Cookin' with Lloyd Price	1961	12.50	25.00	50.00
DOUBLE-L					
DL-2301 [M]	The Lloyd Price Orchestra	1963	6.25	12.50	25.00
DL-2303 [M]	Misty	1963	6.25	12.50	25.00
SDL-8301 [S]	The Lloyd Price Orchestra	1963	10.00	20.00	40.00
SDL-8303 [S]	Misty	1963	10.00	20.00	40.00
GRAND PRIX					
422 [M]	Mr. Rhythm and Blues	196?	3.00	6.00	12.00
S-422 [R]	Mr. Rhythm and Blues	196?	2.50	5.00	10.00
GUEST STAR					
G-1910 [M]	Come to Me	196?	3.00	6.00	12.00
GS-1910 [R]	Come to Me	196?	2.50	5.00	10.00
JAD					
1002	Lloyd Price Now	1969	6.25	12.50	25.00
LPG					
001	Music...Music	1976	2.50	5.00	10.00
MCA					
1503	Greatest Hits	1982	2.00	4.00	8.00
MONUMENT					
MLP-8032 [M]	Lloyd Swings for Sammy	1965	6.25	12.50	25.00
SLP-18032 [S]	Lloyd Swings for Sammy	1965	10.00	20.00	40.00
PICKWICK					
SPC-3518	Big Hits	197?	2.00	4.00	8.00
SCEPTER					
CTN-18006	The Best of Lloyd Price	1972	2.50	5.00	10.00
SPECIALTY					
SP-2105	Lloyd Price	198?	3.00	6.00	12.00
—1980s reissue					
SP-2105 [M]	Lloyd Price	1959	45.00	90.00	180.00
TRIP					
TOP 16-5	16 Greatest Hits	1976	2.50	5.00	10.00
TURNTABLE					
5001	Lloyd Price Now	197?	3.75	7.50	15.00
UPFRONT					
UPF-126	Misty	197?	3.00	6.00	12.00

PRICE, RAY

Also see WILLIE NELSON.

45s

Number	Title (A Side/B Side)	Yr	VG	VG+	NM
ABC					
12095	Farthest Thing from My Mind/All That Keeps Me Going	1975	—	2.00	4.00
ABC DOT					
17588	Say I Do/I'll Still Love You	1975	—	2.00	4.00
17616	That's All She Wrote/I Didn't Feel Nothing	1976	—	2.00	4.00
17637	To Make a Long Story Short/We're Getting There	1976	—	2.00	4.00
17666	A Mansion on the Hill/Hey, Good Lookin'	1976	—	2.00	4.00
17690	Different Kind of Flower/Don't Let the Stars Get in Your Eyes	1977	—	2.00	4.00
17718	Born to Love Me/The Only Way to Say Good Morning	1977	—	2.00	4.00
COLUMBIA					
10006	Like a First Time Thing/You Are the Song	1974	—	2.50	5.00
10150	If You Ever Change Your Mind/Just Enough to Make Me Stay	1975	—	2.00	4.00
10503	Help Me/Nobody Wins	1977	—	2.00	4.00
10631	Born to Love Me/I'm Sorry for the Hateful Things I Did	1977	—	2.00	4.00
20810	You've Got My Troubles Now/If You're Ever Lonely Darling	1951	7.50	15.00	30.00
20833	I Saw My Castles Fall Today/Hey Lala	1951	7.50	15.00	30.00
20863	Heart Aching Blues/Till Death Do Us Part	1951	7.50	15.00	30.00
20883	I Made a Mistake and I'm Sorry/Weary Blues	1952	6.25	12.50	25.00
20913	Talk to Your Heart/I've Got to Hurry, Hurry, Hurry	1952	6.25	12.50	25.00
20943	Hot Diggity Dog/I've Got to Hurry, Hurry, Hurry	1952	5.00	10.00	20.00
—With Jimmy Dickens					
20963	Road of No Return/I Know I'll Never Win Your Love Again	1952	5.00	10.00	20.00
21015	I Can't Escape from You/Won't You Please Be Mine	1952	5.00	10.00	20.00
21025	Don't Let the Stars Get In Your Eyes/I Lost the Only Love I Know	1952	5.00	10.00	20.00
21053	You're Under Arrest/My Old Scrapbook	1953	5.00	10.00	20.00
21089	Price for Loving You/That's What I Got for Loving You	1953	5.00	10.00	20.00
21117	Cold Shoulder/You Weren't Ashamed to Kiss Me	1953	5.00	10.00	20.00
21149	Wrong Side of Town/Who Stole That Train	1953	5.00	10.00	20.00
21214	I'll Be There (If You Ever Want Me)/Release Me	1954	5.00	10.00	20.00
21249	Much Too Young to Die/I Love You So Much	1954	5.00	10.00	20.00
21299	I Could Love You More/What If He Don't Love You	1954	5.00	10.00	20.00
21315	If You Don't, Somebody Else Will/Oh Yes Darling	1954	5.00	10.00	20.00
21354	One Broken Heart/I'm Alone Because I Love You	1955	3.75	7.50	15.00
21402	Sweet Little Miss Blue Eyes/Let Me Talk to You	1955	3.75	7.50	15.00
21404	A Man Called Peter/Call the Lord and He'll Be There	1955	5.00	10.00	20.00
21442	I Can't Go On Like This/I Don't Want It on My Conscience	1955	3.75	7.50	15.00
21474	Run Boy/You Never Will Be True	1955	3.75	7.50	15.00
21510	Crazy Arms/You Done Me Wrong	1956	3.75	7.50	15.00
21562	I've Got a New Heartache/Wasted Words	1956	3.75	7.50	15.00
31428 [S]	(titles unknown)	1962	3.75	7.50	15.00
31429 [S]	(titles unknown)	1962	3.75	7.50	15.00
31430 [S]	(titles unknown)	1962	3.75	7.50	15.00
31431 [S]	(titles unknown)	1962	3.75	7.50	15.00
31432 [S]	(titles unknown)	1962	3.75	7.50	15.00
—Anyone who can fill in these gaps -- the above 5 all are Columbia "Stereo 7" singles -- please let us know.					
40889	I'll Be There (When You Get Lonely)/Please Don't Leave Me	1957	3.75	7.50	15.00
40951	My Shoes Keep Walking Back to You/Don't Do This to Me	1957	3.75	7.50	15.00
41105	Curtain in the Window/It's All Your Fault	1958	3.00	6.00	12.00
41191	City Lights/Invitation to the Blues	1958	3.00	6.00	12.00
41309	That's What It's Like to Be Lonesome/Kissing Your Picture	1958	3.00	6.00	12.00
41374	Heartaches By the Number/Wall of Tears	1959	3.00	6.00	12.00
41477	The Same Old Me/Under Your Spell Again	1959	3.00	6.00	12.00
41590	One More Time/Who'll Be the First	1960	3.00	6.00	12.00
41767	I Wish I Could Fall in Love Today/I Can't Run Away from Myself	1960	3.00	6.00	12.00
41947	Heart Over Mind/The Twenty-Fourth Hour	1961	2.50	5.00	10.00
42132	Soft Rain/Here We Are Again	1961	2.50	5.00	10.00
42310	I've Just Destroyed the World (I'm Living In)/Big Shoes	1962	2.50	5.00	10.00
42518	Pride/I'm Walking Slow	1962	2.50	5.00	10.00
42658	Walk Me to the Door/You Took Her Off My Hands (Now Please Take Her Off My Mind)	1963	2.50	5.00	10.00
42827	Make the World Go Away/Night Life	1963	2.50	5.00	10.00
42971	Burning Memories/That's All That Matters	1964	2.50	5.00	10.00
43086	Please Talk to My Heart/I Don't Know Why	1964	2.50	5.00	10.00
43162	A Thing Called Sadness/Here Comes My Baby Back Again	1964	2.50	5.00	10.00
43264	The Other Woman/Tearful Earful	1965	2.00	4.00	8.00
43427	Don't You Ever Get Tired of Hurting Me/Unloved, Unwanted	1965	2.00	4.00	8.00
43560	A Way to Survive/I'm Not Crazy Yet	1966	2.00	4.00	8.00
43795	Touch My Heart/It Should Be Easier Now	1966	2.00	4.00	8.00
44042	Danny Boy/I'll Let My Mind Wander	1967	2.00	4.00	8.00
44042 [PS]	Danny Boy/I'll Let My Mind Wander	1967	3.00	6.00	12.00
44195	I'm Still Not Over You/Crazy	1967	2.00	4.00	8.00
44374	Take Me As I Am (Or Let Me Go)/In the Summer of My Life	1967	2.00	4.00	8.00
44505	I've Been There Before/Night Life	1968	2.00	4.00	8.00
44628	She Wears My Ring/Goin' Away	1968	2.00	4.00	8.00
44747	Set Me Free/Trouble	1969	—	3.00	6.00
44761	Sweetheart of the Year/How Can I Write on Paper (What I Feel in My Heart)	1969	—	3.00	6.00
44931	Raining in My Heart/I Know Love	1969	—	3.00	6.00
45005	April's Fool/Make It Rain	1969	—	3.00	6.00
45046	Jingle Bells/Happy Birthday to You, Our Lord	1969	—	3.00	6.00
45095	You Wouldn't Know Love/Everybody Wants to Get to Heaven	1970	—	3.00	6.00
45178	For the Good Times/Grazin' in Greener Pastures	1970	—	3.00	6.00
45329	I Won't Mention It Again/Kiss the World Goodbye	1971	—	2.50	5.00
45425	I'd Rather Be Sorry/When I Loved Her	1971	—	2.50	5.00
45583	The Lonesomest Lonesome/That's What Leaving's About	1972	—	2.50	5.00
45724	She's Got to Be a Saint/Oh Lonesome Me	1972	—	2.50	5.00
45889	You're the Best Thing That Ever Happened to Me/What Kind of Love Is This	1973	—	2.50	5.00
46015	Storms of Troubled Times/Some Things Never Change	1974	—	2.50	5.00
DIMENSION					
1018	Getting Over You Again/Circle Driveway	1981	—	2.00	4.00
1021	It Don't Hurt Me Half As Bad/She's the Right Kind of Woman (Loving the Wrong Kind of Man)	1981	—	2.00	4.00
1024	Diamonds in the Stars/Grazing in Greener Pastures	1981	—	2.00	4.00
1031	Forty and Fadin'/Something to Forget You By	1982	—	2.00	4.00
1035	Will Till Those Bridges Are Gone/Angel in My Heart (Devil in My Mind)	1982	—	2.00	4.00
1038	Somewhere in Texas/Getting Down and Getting High	1982	—	2.00	4.00
MONUMENT					
45267	Feet/Let's Make a Nice Memory (Today)	1978	—	2.00	4.00
45277	There's Always Me/If It All the Same to You (I'll Be Leaving in the Morning)	1979	—	2.00	4.00
45283	That's the Only Way to Say Good Morning/All the Good Things Are Gone	1979	—	2.00	4.00
45290	Misty Morning Rain/We Can't Build a Fire in the Rain	1979	—	2.00	4.00
MYRRH					
146	Like Old Times Again/My First Day Without Her	1974	—	2.50	5.00
150	Roses and Love Songs/The Closest Thing to Love	1975	—	2.50	5.00
STEP ONE					
341	(She Got a Hold of Me Where It Hurts) She Won't Let Go/Memories to Burn	1985	—	2.00	4.00
344	I'm Not Leaving (I'm Just Getting Out of Your Way)/Why Don't Love Just Go Away	1985	—	2.00	4.00
350	Five Fingers/Lonely Like a Rose	1985	—	2.00	4.00
352	You're Nobody Till Somebody Loves You/I'm In the Mood for Love	1986	—	2.00	4.00

Number	Title (A Side/B Side)	Yr	VG	VG+	NM
355	All the Way/Bummin' Around	1986	—	2.00	4.00
361	Please Don't Talk About Me When I'm Gone/For the Good Times	1986	—	2.00	4.00
366	When You Gave Your Love to Me/Forty and Fadin'	1986	—	2.00	4.00
370	Sentimental Journey/Better Class of Loser	1987	—	2.00	4.00
378	Just Enough Love/Why Don't Love Just Go Away	1987	—	2.00	4.00
381	For Christmas/With Christmas Near	1987	—	2.00	4.00
383	Big Ole Teardrops/The Season for Missing You	1988	—	2.00	4.00
388	Don't the Morning Always Come Too Soon/All You Have to Do Is Come Back	1988	—	2.00	4.00
393	I'd Do It All Over Again/Wind Beneath My Wings	1988	—	2.00	4.00
410	Love Me Down to Size/(B-side unknown)	1989	—	2.00	4.00
436	Memories That Last/A Whole Lot of You	1991	—	2.00	4.00
—With Faron Young					
VIVA					
29147	What Am I Gonna Do Without You/You've Been Leaving Me for Years	1984	—	—	3.00
29217	Better Class of Loser/Everytime I Sing a Love Song	1984	—	—	3.00
29277	A New Place to Begin/Everyone Gets Crazy Now and Then	1984	—	—	3.00
WARNER BROS.					
29543	Scotch and Soda/I Love You Eyes	1983	—	—	3.00
29691	Willie, Write Me a Song/I Love You Eyes	1983	—	—	3.00
29830	One Fiddle, Two Fiddle/San Antonio Rose	1982	—	—	3.00

7-Inch Extended Plays

Number	Title (A Side/B Side)	Yr	VG	VG+	NM
COLUMBIA					
B-1786	(contents unknown)	195?	7.50	15.00	30.00
B-1786 [PS]	Ray Price	195?	7.50	15.00	30.00
B-2809	*I'll Be There/Release Me/Don't Let the Stars Get In Your Eyes/I Lost the Only Love I Knew	195?	3.75	7.50	15.00
B-2809 [PS]	Ray Price (Hall of Fame Series)	195?	3.75	7.50	15.00
B-2812	The Last Letter/My Shoes Keep Walking Back to You//Crazy Arms/I'm Alone Because I Love You	195?	3.75	7.50	15.00
B-2812 [PS]	Ray Price (Hall of Fame Series)	195?	3.75	7.50	15.00

Albums

Number	Title	Yr	VG	VG+	NM
ABC DOT					
DO-2037	Say I Do	1975	3.00	6.00	12.00
DO-2053	Rainbows and Tears	1976	3.00	6.00	12.00
DO-2073	Reunited	1977	3.00	6.00	12.00
COLUMBIA					
GP 28 [(2)]	The World of Ray Price	1970	3.75	7.50	15.00
CL 1015 [M]	Ray Price Sings Heart Songs	1957	12.50	25.00	50.00
CL 1148 [M]	Talk to Your Heart	1958	10.00	20.00	40.00
CL 1494 [M]	Faith	1960	7.50	15.00	30.00
CL 1566 [M]	Ray Price's Greatest Hits	1961	7.50	15.00	30.00
CL 1756 [M]	San Antonio Rose	1962	5.00	10.00	20.00
CL 1971 [M]	Night Life	1963	3.75	7.50	15.00
CL 2189 [M]	Love Life	1964	3.75	7.50	15.00
CL 2289 [M]	Burning Memories	1965	3.75	7.50	15.00
CL 2339 [M]	Western Strings	1965	5.00	10.00	20.00
CL 2382 [M]	The Other Woman	1965	3.75	7.50	15.00
CL 2528 [M]	Another Bridge to Burn	1966	3.75	7.50	15.00
CL 2606 [M]	Touch My Heart	1967	5.00	10.00	20.00
CL 2670 [M]	Ray Price's Greatest Hits, Volume 2	1967	5.00	10.00	20.00
CL 2677 [M]	Danny Boy	1967	5.00	10.00	20.00
CL 2806 [M]	Take Me As I Am	1968	7.50	15.00	30.00
CS 8285 [S]	Faith	1960	10.00	20.00	40.00
CS 8556 [S]	San Antonio Rose	1962	7.50	15.00	30.00
CS 8771 [S]	Night Life	1963	5.00	10.00	20.00
CS 8866 [R]	Ray Price's Greatest Hits	1964	3.00	6.00	12.00
PC 8866	Ray Price's Greatest Hits	198?	2.00	4.00	8.00
—Reissue with new prefix					
CS 8989 [S]	Love Life	1964	5.00	10.00	20.00
CS 9089 [S]	Burning Memories	1965	5.00	10.00	20.00
CS 9139 [S]	Western Strings	1965	6.25	12.50	25.00
CS 9182 [S]	The Other Woman	1965	5.00	10.00	20.00
CS 9328 [S]	Another Bridge to Burn	1966	5.00	10.00	20.00
CS 9406 [S]	Touch My Heart	1967	3.75	7.50	15.00
CS 9470 [S]	Ray Price's Greatest Hits, Volume 2	1967	3.75	7.50	15.00
CS 9477 [S]	Danny Boy	1967	3.75	7.50	15.00
CS 9606 [S]	Take Me As I Am	1968	3.75	7.50	15.00
CS 9733	She Wears My Ring	1968	3.75	7.50	15.00
CS 9822	Sweetheart of the Year	1969	3.75	7.50	15.00
CS 9861	Ray Price's Christmas Album	1969	3.75	7.50	15.00
CS 9918	You Wouldn't Know Love	1970	3.75	7.50	15.00
C 30106	For the Good Times	1970	3.00	6.00	12.00
CQ 30106 [Q]	For the Good Times	1972	5.00	10.00	20.00
C 30510	I Won't Mention It Again	1971	3.00	6.00	12.00
CG 30878 [(2)]	Welcome to My World	1971	3.75	7.50	15.00
KG 31364 [(2)]	Ray Price's All-Time Greatest Hits	1972	3.75	7.50	15.00
KC 31546	The Lonesomest Lonesome	1972	3.00	6.00	12.00
KC 32033	She's Got to Be a Saint	1973	3.00	6.00	12.00
PC 32033	She's Got to Be a Saint	197?	2.00	4.00	8.00
—Reissue with new prefix					
KC 32777	You're the Best Thing That Ever Happened to Me	1973	3.00	6.00	12.00
PC 32777	You're the Best Thing That Ever Happened to Me	197?	2.00	4.00	8.00
—Reissue with new prefix					
PC 33560	If You Change Your Mind	1975	3.00	6.00	12.00
CG 33633 [(2)]	For the Good Times/I Won't Mention It Again	1975	3.75	7.50	15.00
—Reissue of two LPs in one package					
PC 34160	The Best of Ray Price	1976	3.00	6.00	12.00
PC 34710	Help Me	1977	3.00	6.00	12.00
JC 37061	A Tribute to Willie and Kris	1982	2.50	5.00	10.00
HARMONY					
HL 7372 [M]	Collectors' Choice	196?	3.00	6.00	12.00
HL 7440 [M]	Born to Lose	1967	3.00	6.00	12.00
HS 11172 [R]	Collectors' Choice	196?	3.00	6.00	12.00
HS 11240 [S]	Born to Lose	1967	3.00	6.00	12.00
HS 11373	I Fall to Pieces	1969	2.50	5.00	10.00
KH 30272	Make the World Go Away	1970	2.50	5.00	10.00
MONUMENT					
7633	Always Me	1979	2.50	5.00	10.00
MYRRH					
6532	This Time, Lord	1975	3.00	6.00	12.00
PAIR					
PDL2-1044 [(2)]	Happens to Be the Best	1986	3.00	6.00	12.00
PDL2-1044 [(2)]	Ray Price Happens to Be the Best!	1986	3.00	6.00	12.00
PDL2-1096 [(2)]	Priceless	1986	3.00	6.00	12.00
ROUNDER					
SS-22	The Honky Tonk Years	1986	2.50	5.00	10.00
WORD					
8723	Precious Memories	197?	3.00	6.00	12.00
8780	How Great Thou Art	1978	3.00	6.00	12.00

PRIDE

Albums

Number	Title	Yr	VG	VG+	NM
WARNER BROS.					
WS 1848	Pride	1970	6.25	12.50	25.00

PRIDE, CHARLEY

Includes releases as "Country Charley Pride."

45s

Number	Title (A Side/B Side)	Yr	VG	VG+	NM
16TH AVENUE					
70400	Have I Got Some Blues for You/Ever Knowin'	1987	—	2.00	4.00
70402	If You Still Want a Fool Around/You Took Me There	1987	—	2.00	4.00
70408	Shouldn't It Be Easier Than This/Look in Your Mirror	1987	—	2.00	4.00
70414	I'm Gonna Love Her on the Radio/Shouldn't It Be Easier Than This	1988	—	2.00	4.00
70420	Where Was I/A Whole Lotta Lovin' (Goes a Long, Long Way)	1988	—	2.00	4.00
70425	White Houses/Shouldn't It Be Easier Than This	1989	—	2.00	4.00
70429	The More I Do/(B-side unknown)	1989	—	2.00	4.00
70435	Amy's Eyes/(B-side unknown)	1989	—	2.00	4.00
70440	Woody Woman/(B-side unknown)	1990	—	2.50	5.00
RCA					
2723-7-R	The Easy Part's Over/The Right to Do Wrong	1990	—	—	3.00
—"Gold Standard Series" reissue					
PB-10757	A Whole Lotta Things to Sing About/The Hardest Part of Livin's Lovin' Me	1976	—	2.00	4.00
PB-10875	She's Just An Old Love Turned Memory/Country Music	1977	—	2.00	4.00
PB-10975	I'll Be Leaving Alone/We Need Lovin'	1977	—	2.00	4.00
PB-11086	More to Me/Heaven Watches Over Fools Like Me	1977	—	2.00	4.00
PB-11201	Someone Loves You Honey/Days of Our Lives	1978	—	2.00	4.00
PB-11287	When I Stop Leaving (I'll Be Gone)/I Can See the Lovin' in Your Eyes	1978	—	2.00	4.00
GB-11331	My Eyes Can Only See As Far As You/A Whole Lotta Things to Sing About	1978	—	—	3.00
—"Gold Standard Series" reissue					
PB-11391	Burgers and Fries/Nothing's Prettier Than Rose Is	1978	—	2.00	4.00
PB-11477	Where Do I Put Her Memory/The Best in the World	1979	—	2.00	4.00
GB-11498	Someone Loves You Honey/When I Stop Leaving (I'll Be Gone)	1979	—	—	3.00
—"Gold Standard Series" reissue					
PB-11655	You're My Jamaica/Let Me Have a Chance to Love You	1979	—	2.00	4.00
PB-11736	Dallas Cowboys/When I Stop Leaving	1979	3.00	6.00	12.00
—Special blue and silver label edition					
PB-11736	Dallas Cowboys/When I Stop Leaving	1979	—	3.00	6.00
—Regular black-label edition					
PB-11751	Missin' You/Heartbreak Mountain	1979	—	2.00	4.00
PB-11912	Honky Tonk Blues/I'm So Lonesome I Could Cry	1980	—	—	3.00
GB-11992	Burgers and Fries/Where Do I Put Her Memory	1980	—	—	3.00
—"Gold Standard Series" reissue					
PB-12002	You Win Again/There's a Little Bit of Hank in Me	1980	—	—	3.00
PB-12100	You Almost Slipped My Mind/Ghost Written Love Letters	1980	—	—	3.00
PB-12178	Roll On Mississippi/Fall Back on Me	1981	—	—	3.00
PB-12294	Never Been So Loved (In All My Life)/I Call Her My Girl	1981	—	—	3.00
GB-12371	Honky Tonk Blues/You Win Again	1981	—	—	3.00
—"Gold Standard Series" reissue					
PB-13014	Mountain of Love/Love Is a Shadow	1981	—	—	3.00
PB-13096	I Don't Think She's in Love Anymore/Oh What a Beautiful Love Song	1982	—	—	3.00
PB-13293	You're So Good When You're Bad/I Haven't Loved This Way in Years	1982	—	—	3.00
PB-13359	Let It Snow, Let It Snow, Let It Snow/Peace on Earth	1982	—	2.50	5.00
—B-side by Razzy Bailey					
PB-13397	Why Baby Why/It's So Good to Be Together	1982	—	—	3.00
PB-13451	More and More/Radio Heroes	1983	—	—	3.00
PB-13542	Night Games/I Could Let Her Get Close to Me	1983	—	—	3.00
PB-13648	Ev'ry Heart Should Have One/Lovin' It Up (Livin' It Down)	1983	—	—	3.00
PB-13667	Let It Snow, Let It Snow, Let It Snow/O Holy Night	1983	—	2.00	4.00
PB-13732	The Late Show/Love on a Blue Rainy Day	1984	—	2.00	4.00
JK-13754	Stagger Lee (same on both sides)	1984	2.50	5.00	10.00
—Promo on red vinyl					
PB-13821	The Power of Love/Ellie	1984	—	—	3.00
PB-13936	Missin' Mississippi/Falling in Love Again	1984	—	—	3.00
PB-14045	Down on the Farm/Now and Then	1985	—	—	3.00
PB-14134	Let a Little Love Come In/Night Games	1985	—	—	3.00
PB-14265	The Best There Is/The Tumbleweed and the Rose	1986	—	—	3.00
PB-14296	Love on a Blue Rainy Day/I Used It All on You	1986	—	—	3.00
RCA VICTOR					
APBO-0073	Amazing Love/Blue Ridge Mountains Turnin' Green	1973	—	2.50	5.00
AMBO-0128	A Shoulder to Cry On/Don't Fight the Feelings of Love	1973	—	2.00	4.00
—"Gold Standard Series" reissue					
APBO-0257	We Could/Love Put a Song in My Heart	1974	—	2.50	5.00

Number	Title (A Side/B Side)	Yr	VG	VG+	NM
PB-10030	Mississippi Cotton Picking Delta Town/Merry-Go-Round	1974	—	2.00	4.00
PB-10126	Then Who Am I/Completely Helpless	1974	—	2.00	4.00
PB-10236	I Ain't All Bad/Hard Times Will Be the Best Times	1975	—	2.00	4.00
PB-10344	Hope You're Feelin' Me (Like I'm Feelin' You)/Searching for the Morning Sun	1975	—	2.00	4.00
PB-10455	The Happiness of Having You/Right Back Missing You Again	1975	—	2.00	4.00
GB-10507	Then Who Am I/Completely Helpless	1975	—	—	3.00
—"Gold Standard Series" reissue					
GB-10508	Mississippi Cotton Picking Delta Town/Merry-Go-Round	1975	—	—	3.00
—"Gold Standard Series" reissue					
GB-10509	Amazing Love/Blue Ridge Mountains Turning Green	1975	—	—	3.00
—"Gold Standard Series" reissue					
PB-10592	My Eyes Can Only See As Far As You/Oklahoma Morning	1976	—	2.00	4.00
PB-10643	In Jesus' Name I Pray/I Don't Deserve a Mansion	1976	—	3.00	6.00
GB-10674	I Ain't All Bad/Hope You're Feelin' Me (Like I'm Feelin' You)	1976	—	2.00	4.00
—"Gold Standard Series" reissue					
47-9000	Just Between You and Me/Detroit City	1966	3.00	6.00	12.00
47-9162	I Know One/The Best Banjo Picker	1967	3.00	6.00	12.00
47-9281	Does My Ring Hurt Your Finger/The Spell of the Freight Train	1967	3.00	6.00	12.00
—Above three labeled as "Country Charley Pride"					
47-9403	The Day the World Stood Still/Gone, On the Other Hand	1967	2.00	4.00	8.00
47-9514	The Easy Part's Over/Right to Do Wrong	1968	2.00	4.00	8.00
47-9622	Let the Chips Fall/She Made Me Go	1968	2.00	4.00	8.00
47-9716	Kaw-Liga/Little Folks	1969	2.00	4.00	8.00
47-9777	Wings of a Dove/They Stood in Silent Prayer	1969	3.00	6.00	12.00
47-9806	Is Anybody Goin' to San Antone/Things Are Looking Up	1970	—	3.00	6.00
47-9855	Wonder Could I Live There Anymore/Piroque Joe	1970	—	3.00	6.00
47-9902	I Can't Believe That You've Stopped Loving Me/Time	1970	—	3.00	6.00
47-9933	Christmas in My Home Town/Santa and the Kids	1970	2.00	4.00	8.00
47-9952	I'd Rather Love You/You Don't Belong	1971	—	3.00	6.00
47-9974	Let Me Live/Did You Think to Pray	1971	2.00	4.00	8.00
47-9996	I'm Just Me/A Place for the Lonesome	1971	—	3.00	6.00
74-0167	All I Have to Offer You (Is Me)/Brand New Bed of Roses	1969	2.00	4.00	8.00
74-0265	(I'm So) Afraid of Losing You Again/Good Chance of Tear-Fall Tonight	1969	2.00	4.00	8.00
74-0550	Kiss an Angel Good Mornin'/No One Could Ever Take Me from You	1971	—	3.00	6.00
74-0624	All His Children/You'll Still Be the One	1972	—	2.50	5.00
74-0707	It's Gonna Take a Little Bit Longer/You're Wanting Me to Stop Loving You	1972	—	2.50	5.00
74-0707 [PS]	It's Gonna Take a Little Bit Longer/You're Wanting Me to Stop Loving You	1972	2.00	4.00	8.00
74-0802	She's Too Good to Be True/She's That Kind	1972	—	2.50	5.00
74-0884	A Shoulder to Cry On/I'm Learning to Love Her	1973	—	2.50	5.00
74-0942	Don't Fight the Feelings of Love/Tennessee Girl	1973	—	2.50	5.00
447-0935	Christmas In My Home Town/Santa and the Kids	1972	—	2.00	4.00
—Gold Standard Series					

Albums

16TH AVENUE

Number	Title (A Side/B Side)	Yr	VG	VG+	NM
ST-70550	After All This Time	1987	3.00	6.00	12.00
D1-70551	I'm Gonna Love Her on the Radio	1988	3.00	6.00	12.00
D1-70554	Moody Woman	1989	3.00	6.00	12.00

PAIR

Number	Title (A Side/B Side)	Yr	VG	VG+	NM
PDL2-1023 [(2)]	Country in My Soul	1986	3.00	6.00	12.00

RCA CAMDEN

Number	Title (A Side/B Side)	Yr	VG	VG+	NM
CAS-2584	The Incomparable Charley Pride	1972	3.75	7.50	15.00

RCA VICTOR

Number	Title (A Side/B Side)	Yr	VG	VG+	NM
APD1-0217 [Q]	Sweet Country	1973	6.25	12.50	25.00
APL1-0217	Sweet Country	1973	3.75	7.50	15.00
APL1-0315	Charley Pride Presents the Pridesmen	1973	3.75	7.50	15.00
APD1-0397 [Q]	Amazing Love	1974	6.25	12.50	25.00
APL1-0397	Amazing Love	1974	3.75	7.50	15.00
APL1-0534	Country Feelin'	1974	3.75	7.50	15.00
APD1-0757 [Q]	Pride of America	1974	6.25	12.50	25.00
APL1-0757	Pride of America	1974	3.75	7.50	15.00
ANL1-0996	Charley Pride — In Person	1975	2.50	5.00	10.00
—Reissue of LSP-4094					
APD1-1038 [Q]	Charley	1975	6.25	12.50	25.00
APL1-1038	Charley	1975	3.75	7.50	15.00
ANL1-1214	I'm Just Me	1975	2.50	5.00	10.00
—Reissue of LSP-4560					
APD1-1241 [Q]	The Happiness of Having You	1975	6.25	12.50	25.00
APL1-1241	The Happiness of Having You	1975	3.75	7.50	15.00
APD1-1359 [Q]	Sunday Morning with Charley Pride	1976	6.25	12.50	25.00
APL1-1359	Sunday Morning with Charley Pride	1976	3.75	7.50	15.00
ANL1-1934	Christmas in My Home Town	1976	2.00	4.00	8.00
—Reissue of LSP-4406					
APL1-2023	The Best of Charley Pride, Vol. III	1976	3.00	6.00	12.00
APL1-2261	She's Just an Old Love Turned Memory	1977	3.00	6.00	12.00
AHL1-2478	Someone Loves You Honey	1978	3.00	6.00	12.00
AHL1-2963	Burgers and Fries	1978	3.00	6.00	12.00
AHL1-3441	You're My Jamaica	1979	3.00	6.00	12.00
AHL1-3548	There's a Little Bit of Hank in Me	1980	3.00	6.00	12.00
LPM-3645 [M]	Country Charley Pride	1966	6.25	12.50	25.00
LSP-3645 [S]	Country Charley Pride	1966	7.50	15.00	30.00
AYL1-3676	Someone Loves You Honey	1980	2.00	4.00	8.00
—"Best Buy Series" reissue					
AYL1-3740	Sunday Morning with Charley Pride	1980	2.00	4.00	8.00
—"Best Buy Series" reissue					
LPM-3775 [M]	The Pride of Country Music	1967	6.25	12.50	25.00
LSP-3775 [S]	The Pride of Country Music	1967	5.00	10.00	20.00
AYL1-3874	I'm Just Me	1981	2.00	4.00	8.00
—"Best Buy Series" reissue					
LPM-3895 [M]	The Country Way	1967	6.25	12.50	25.00
LSP-3895 [S]	The Country Way	1967	5.00	10.00	20.00
AHL1-3905	Roll On Mississippi	1981	2.50	5.00	10.00
AYL1-3943	The Happiness of Having You	1981	2.00	4.00	8.00
—"Best Buy Series" reissue					
LPM-3952 [M]	Make Mine Country	1968	15.00	30.00	60.00
LSP-3952 [S]	Make Mine Country	1968	5.00	10.00	20.00
LSP-4041	Songs of Pride — Charley, That Is	1968	5.00	10.00	20.00
AYL1-4074	Amazing Love	1981	2.00	4.00	8.00
—"Best Buy Series" reissue					
LSP-4094	Charley Pride — In Person	1969	5.00	10.00	20.00
AHL1-4151	Greatest Hits	1981	2.50	5.00	10.00
LSP-4153	The Sensational Charley Pride	1969	5.00	10.00	20.00
AYL1-4166	She's Just an Old Love Turned Memory	1981	2.00	4.00	8.00
—"Best Buy Series" reissue					
AHL1-4223	The Best of Charley Pride	198?	2.50	5.00	10.00
—Reissue of LSP-4223					
LSP-4223	The Best of Charley Pride	1969	5.00	10.00	20.00
AYL1-4252	Burgers and Fries	1982	2.00	4.00	8.00
—"Best Buy Series" reissue					
AHL1-4287	Charley Pride Sings Everybody's Choice	1982	2.50	5.00	10.00
LSP-4290	Just Plain Charley	1970	5.00	10.00	20.00
LSP-4367	Charley Pride's 10th Album	1970	5.00	10.00	20.00
LSP-4406	Christmas in My Home Town	1970	5.00	10.00	20.00
LSP-4468	From Me to You	1971	5.00	10.00	20.00
LSP-4513	Did You Think to Pray	1971	5.00	10.00	20.00
AHL1-4524	Charley Pride Live	1983	2.50	5.00	10.00
LSP-4560	I'm Just Me	1971	5.00	10.00	20.00
LSP-4617	Charley Pride Sings Heart Songs	1971	5.00	10.00	20.00
AHL1-4662	Country Classics	1983	2.50	5.00	10.00
AHL1-4682	The Best of Charley Pride, Volume 2	198?	2.50	5.00	10.00
—Reissue of LSP-4682					
LSP-4682	The Best of Charley Pride, Volume 2	1972	5.00	10.00	20.00
LSP-4742	A Sunshiny Day with Charley Pride	1972	5.00	10.00	20.00
AHL1-4822	Night Games	1983	2.50	5.00	10.00
AYL1-4831	There's a Little Bit of Hank in Me	1983	2.00	4.00	8.00
—"Best Buy Series" reissue					
LSP-4837	Songs of Love by Charley Pride	1973	3.75	7.50	15.00
AHL1-5031	The Power of Love	1984	2.50	5.00	10.00
AYL1-5147	Greatest Hits	1984	2.00	4.00	8.00
—"Best Buy Series" reissue					
AYL1-5148	The Best of Charley Pride	1984	2.00	4.00	8.00
—"Best Buy Series" reissue					
AHL1-5426	Greatest Hits, Volume 2	1985	2.50	5.00	10.00
AHL1-5851	Back to the Country	1986	2.50	5.00	10.00
CPL1-7049	Collector's Series	1985	2.50	5.00	10.00
AHL1-7174	The Best There Is	1986	2.50	5.00	10.00

READER'S DIGEST

Number	Title (A Side/B Side)	Yr	VG	VG+	NM
(# unknown) [(6)]	Charley Pride's Country	1979	10.00	20.00	40.00

TIME-LIFE

Number	Title (A Side/B Side)	Yr	VG	VG+	NM
STW-101	Country Music	1981	3.00	6.00	12.00

PRIESMAN, MAGEL

45s

SUN

Number	Title (A Side/B Side)	Yr	VG	VG+	NM
294	Memories of You/I Feel So Blue	1958	6.25	12.50	25.00

PRIMA, LOUIS

45s

ABC

Number	Title (A Side/B Side)	Yr	VG	VG+	NM
11093	Almost Persuaded/Waitin' in Your Welfare Line	1968	—	3.00	6.00
11122	Joanna/You Can't Take the Country Out of the Boy	1968	—	3.00	6.00
11166	Flooby Dooby Doo/I Never Opened My Eyes	1969	—	3.00	6.00
12047	Time Heals Everything/When Hazel Comes in the Room	1974	—	2.00	4.00

BRUNSWICK

Number	Title (A Side/B Side)	Yr	VG	VG+	NM
55485	I Left My Heart in San Francisco/I Never Promised You a Rose Garden	1972	—	3.00	6.00

BUENA VISTA

Number	Title (A Side/B Side)	Yr	VG	VG+	NM
446	Jolly Holiday/Supercalifragilisticexpialidocious	1965	3.75	7.50	15.00
—With Gia Maione					
454	Santa, How Come Your Eyes Are Green When Last Year They Were Blue/Senor Santa Claus	1966	3.00	6.00	12.00

CAPITOL

Number	Title (A Side/B Side)	Yr	VG	VG+	NM
F3566	A Banana Spilt for My Baby/Five Months, Two Weeks, Two Days	1956	3.00	6.00	12.00
—With Sam Butera					
F3615	Whistle Stop/Be Mine	1957	3.00	6.00	12.00
—With Sam Butera					
F3667	Midnight Melody/The Wild Ones	1957	3.00	6.00	12.00
—With Sam Butera					
F3856	Beep Beep/Buona Sera	1957	3.00	6.00	12.00
4732	Twist All Night/Everybody Knows	1962	2.50	5.00	10.00
4805	Big Daddy/Ooh, Look What You've Done to Me	1962	2.50	5.00	10.00
—With Gia Maione					
58572	Jump, Jive, An' Wail/Just a Gigolo-I Ain't Got Nobody (Medley)	1998	—	—	3.00
58804	Buona Sera/Oh Marie	1999	—	—	3.00

COLUMBIA

Number	Title (A Side/B Side)	Yr	VG	VG+	NM
39614	Shake Hands with Santa/Eleanor	1951	5.00	10.00	20.00
39692	Basta/Ooh Dah Dilly Dah	1952	5.00	10.00	20.00
39735	The Bigger the Figure/Boney Bones	1952	5.00	10.00	20.00
39823	Chili Sauce/One Mint Julep	1952	5.00	10.00	20.00
39969	Oh Marie/Luigi	1953	5.00	10.00	20.00
40015	Paul Revere/It's As Good As New	1953	5.00	10.00	20.00
40064	Barncale Bill the Sailor/Shepherd Boy	1953	5.00	10.00	20.00

DECCA

Number	Title (A Side/B Side)	Yr	VG	VG+	NM
29162	Paper Doll/The Dummy Song	1954	3.75	7.50	15.00

DOT

Number	Title (A Side/B Side)	Yr	VG	VG+	NM
15978	Confessin'/Night and Day	1959	2.50	5.00	10.00
16009	Hey Ba-Ba-Re-Bop/My Cucuzza	1959	2.50	5.00	10.00
16060	When My Baby Smiles at Me/Paradise	1960	2.50	5.00	10.00
16108	Don't You Know/Brooklyn Bridge	1960	2.50	5.00	10.00
16151	Wonderland by Night/Ol' Man Moses	1960	2.50	5.00	10.00

Number	Title (A Side/B Side)	Yr	VG	VG+	NM
16193	Enchantment/Chapel by the Sea	1961	2.50	5.00	10.00
16211	My Prayer/You Can Depend on Me	1961	2.50	5.00	10.00
16273	Mod Indigo/Come Back to Sorrento	1961	2.50	5.00	10.00
16301	Continental Twist/Oh Ma Ma Twist	1962	2.50	5.00	10.00
16401	Josephine, Please No Lean on the Bell/Brooklyn Bridge	1962	2.50	5.00	10.00
HANNA-BARBERA					
467	I'm Gonna Sit Right Down and Write Myself a Letter/Civilization (Bongo, Bongo, Bongo)	1966	2.50	5.00	10.00
KAMA SUTRA					
213	Jug Band Music/Bald-Headed Girl	1966	2.00	4.00	8.00
MERCURY					
5386	Over the Rainbow/Tears on My Tie	1950	7.50	15.00	30.00
—Note: Earlier Louis Prima 45s on Mercury may exist.					
5406	Francis, the Talking Mule/A Good Time Was Had By All	1950	7.50	15.00	30.00
5451	Here, Pretty Kitty/Buona Sera	1950	7.50	15.00	30.00
RCA VICTOR					
47-2960	Five Foot Two, Eyes of Blue/For Mari-Yooten	1949	5.00	10.00	20.00
ROBIN HOOD					
101	Oh Babe!/Piccolina Lena	1950	7.50	15.00	30.00
SAVOY					
1111	Robin Hood/Brooklyn Boogie	1953	5.00	10.00	20.00
UNITED ARTISTS					
50175	Illya Darling/I Believe in You	1967	—	3.00	6.00
50200	My Cup Runneth Over/Cabaret	1967	—	3.00	6.00
50223	The Impossible Dream/Poor Old Marat	1967	—	3.00	6.00
7-Inch Extended Plays					
CAPITOL					
EAP 1-908	*On the Sunny Side of the Street/Exactly Like You/Robin Hood/Oh Babe	1957	3.75	7.50	15.00
EAP 1-908 [PS]	The Wildest Show at Tahoe, Part 1	1957	3.75	7.50	15.00
EAP 2-908	(contents unknown)	1957	3.75	7.50	15.00
EAP 2-908 [PS]	The Wildest Show at Tahoe, Part 2	1957	3.75	7.50	15.00
Albums					
CAPITOL					
T 755 [M]	The Wildest	1956	12.50	25.00	50.00
T 836 [M]	Call of the Wildest	1957	12.50	25.00	50.00
T 908 [M]	The Wildest Show at Tahoe	1957	12.50	25.00	50.00
T 1010 [M]	Las Vegas Prima Style	1958	12.50	25.00	50.00
T 1132 [M]	Strictly Prima	1959	7.50	15.00	30.00
ST 1723 [S]	The Wildest Comes Home	1962	7.50	15.00	30.00
T 1723 [M]	The Wildest Comes Home	1962	6.25	12.50	25.00
ST 1797 [S]	Lake Tahoe Prima Style	1962	7.50	15.00	30.00
T 1797 [M]	Lake Tahoe Prima Style	1962	6.25	12.50	25.00
COLUMBIA					
CL 1206 [M]	Breakin' It Up	1959	10.00	20.00	40.00
DOT					
DLP-3262 [M]	His Greatest Hits	1960	6.25	12.50	25.00
DLP-3264 [M]	Pretty Music Prima Style	1960	6.25	12.50	25.00
DLP-3272 [M]	The Wildest Clan	1960	6.25	12.50	25.00
DLP-3352 [M]	Wonderland by Night	1960	6.25	12.50	25.00
DLP-3385 [M]	Blue Moon	1961	6.25	12.50	25.00
DLP-3392 [M]	Return of the Wildest!	1961	6.25	12.50	25.00
DLP-3410 [M]	Doin' the Twist	1961	6.25	12.50	25.00
DLP-25262 [S]	His Greatest Hits	1960	7.50	15.00	30.00
DLP-25264 [S]	Pretty Music Prima Style	1960	7.50	15.00	30.00
DLP-25272 [S]	The Wildest Clan	1960	7.50	15.00	30.00
DLP-25352 [S]	Wonderland by Night	1960	7.50	15.00	30.00
DLP-25385 [S]	Blue Moon	1961	7.50	15.00	30.00
DLP-25392 [S]	Return of the Wildest!	1961	7.50	15.00	30.00
DLP-25410 [S]	Doin' the Twist	1961	7.50	15.00	30.00
MERCURY					
MG-25142 [10]	Louis Prima Plays	1953	20.00	40.00	80.00
RONDO-LETTE					
A-9 [M]	Louis Prima in All His Moods	1959	7.50	15.00	30.00
A-25 [M]	Louis Prima Entertains	1959	7.50	15.00	30.00
SAVOY JAZZ					
SJL-2264 [(2)]	Play Pretty for the People	198?	3.00	6.00	12.00
TOPS					
9759 [M]	Italian Favorites	195?	3.75	7.50	15.00

PRIMA, LOUIS, AND KEELY SMITH

Also see each artist's individual listings.

Number	Title (A Side/B Side)	Yr	VG	VG+	NM
45s					
CAPITOL					
F4063	That Old Black Magic/You Are My Love	1958	3.00	6.00	12.00
F4140	I've Got You Under My Skin/Don't Take Your Love from Me	1959	2.50	5.00	10.00
DOT					
15956	Bei Mir Bist Du Schoen/I Don't Know Why	1959	2.50	5.00	10.00
16042	Nyot! Nyot! Nyot! (The Pussycat Song)/Moshiya	1960	2.50	5.00	10.00
16192	Begin the Beguine/Surprise Package	1961	2.50	5.00	10.00
16221	Mustapha/The Shepard Man	1961	2.50	5.00	10.00
16249	Because of You/Absent Minded Lover	1961	2.50	5.00	10.00
TOD					
123	Oh Babe!/(B-side unknown)	196?	2.00	4.00	8.00
Albums					
CAPITOL					
T 1160 [M]	Hey Boy! Hey Girl!	1959	12.50	25.00	50.00
SM-1531	The Hits of Louis and Keely	197?	2.50	5.00	10.00
—Reissue with new prefix					
ST 1531 [S]	The Hits of Louis and Keely	1961	7.50	15.00	30.00
T 1531 [M]	The Hits of Louis and Keely	1961	6.25	12.50	25.00
CORONET					
121 [M]	Louis Prima Digs Keely Smith	196?	3.75	7.50	15.00
DOT					
DLP-3210 [M]	Louis and Keely!	1959	7.50	15.00	30.00
DLP-3263 [M]	Together	1960	6.25	12.50	25.00
DLP-3266 [M]	Louis and Keely on Stage	1960	6.25	12.50	25.00
DLP-25210 [S]	Louis and Keely!	1959	10.00	20.00	40.00
DLP-25263 [S]	Together	1960	7.50	15.00	30.00
DLP-25266 [S]	Louis and Keely on Stage	1960	7.50	15.00	30.00
RHINO					
RNLP-70225	Zooma Zooma: The Best of Louis Prima Featuring Keely Smith	1986	2.50	5.00	10.00
SPIN-O-RAMA					
74 [M]	Box of Oldies	196?	3.75	7.50	15.00

PRIMETTES, THE

Early version of THE SUPREMES.

Number	Title (A Side/B Side)	Yr	VG	VG+	NM
45s					
LUPINE					
120	Tears of Sorrow/Pretty	1962	75.00	150.00	300.00

PRIMITIVES, THE (1)

Number	Title (A Side/B Side)	Yr	VG	VG+	NM
45s					
PARKWAY					
940	Help Me/Let Them Fall	1965	5.00	10.00	20.00

PRIMITIVES, THE (2)

LOU REED was in this group.

Number	Title (A Side/B Side)	Yr	VG	VG+	NM
45s					
PICKWICK					
1001	The Ostrich/Sneaky Pete	1964	75.00	150.00	300.00

PRINCE, BOBBY

Number	Title (A Side/B Side)	Yr	VG	VG+	NM
45s					
CHANCE					
1128	Tell Me Why, Why, Why/I Want to Hold You	1953	125.00	250.00	500.00
1158	Better Think It Over/If You Only Knew	1954	100.00	200.00	400.00
EXCELLO					
2039	Too Many Keys/Please Give Me Your Love	1954	20.00	40.00	80.00

PRINCE BUSTER

Number	Title (A Side/B Side)	Yr	VG	VG+	NM
45s					
AMY					
906	Everybody Ska/30 Pieces of Silver	1964	3.75	7.50	15.00
ATLANTIC					
2231	Don't Make Me Cry/That Lucky Old Sun	1964	3.75	7.50	15.00
PHILIPS					
40427	Ten Commandments/Don't Make Me Cry	1967	3.00	6.00	12.00
RCA VICTOR					
47-9114	Ten Commandments from Woman to Man/Ain't That Saying a Lot	1967	3.00	6.00	12.00
Albums					
RCA VICTOR					
LPM-3792 [M]	Ten Commandments	1967	6.25	12.50	25.00
LSP-3792 [S]	Ten Commandments	1967	7.50	15.00	30.00

PRINE, JOHN

Number	Title (A Side/B Side)	Yr	VG	VG+	NM
45s					
ASYLUM					
45509	Fish and Whistle/Sabu Visits the Twin Cities Alone	1978	—	2.00	4.00
45550	There She Goes/That's the Way That the World Goes 'Round	1978	—	2.00	4.00
46562	Ubangi Stomp/Automobile	1979	—	2.00	4.00
ATLANTIC					
2815	Sam Stone/Blue Umbrella	1971	—	2.50	5.00
2857	Quiet Man/Illegal Smile	1972	—	2.50	5.00
2925	Clocks and Spoons/Everybody	1972	—	2.50	5.00
3013	Grandpa Was a Carpenter/Onomatopoeia	1974	—	2.00	4.00
3218	Quiet Man/Illegal Smile	1974	—	2.00	4.00
3276	Middle Man/Saddle in the Rain	1975	—	2.00	4.00
3297	Common Sense/Come Back to Us Barbara Lewis, Harre Krishna, Beauregard	1975	—	2.00	4.00
OH BOY					
001	I Saw Mommy Kissing Santa Claus/Silver Bells	198?	2.50	5.00	10.00
—Red vinyl					
001 [PS]	I Saw Mommy Kissing Santa Claus/Silver Bells	198?	3.00	6.00	12.00
Albums					
ASYLUM					
6E-139	Bruised Orange	1978	3.00	6.00	12.00
6E-222	Pink Cadillac	1979	3.00	6.00	12.00
6E-286	Storm Windows	1980	3.00	6.00	12.00
ATLANTIC					
SD 7240	Diamonds in the Rough	1972	3.00	6.00	12.00
SD 7274	Sweet Revenge	1973	3.00	6.00	12.00
SD 8296	John Prine	1971	3.00	6.00	12.00
SD 18127	Common Sense	1975	3.00	6.00	12.00
SD 18202	Prime Prine — The Best of John Prine	1976	3.00	6.00	12.00
SD 19156	John Prine	1978	2.50	5.00	10.00
—Reissue of 8296					
OH BOY					
002	Aimless Love	198?	2.50	5.00	10.00
003	German Afternoons	198?	2.50	5.00	10.00
005 [(2)]	John Prine Live	1986	3.75	7.50	15.00

PRISONAIRES, THE

Number	Title (A Side/B Side)	Yr	VG	VG+	NM
45s					
SUN					
186	Just Walking in the Rain/Baby Please	1953	125.00	250.00	500.00
186	Just Walking in the Rain/Baby Please	1953	2500.	3750.	5000.
—Red vinyl					
189	Softly and Tenderly/My God Is Real	1953	175.00	350.00	700.00
191	A Prisoner's Prayer/I Know	1953	125.00	250.00	500.00
207	There Is Love in You/What'll You Do Next	1954	5000.	8500.	12000.

THE PINK FLOYD

See Emily Play

tower

356

Everything is a matter of timing. This record was released almost one year ago in England and made Top 5. Tower released it here at the same time. No action.

"Now is the time to release 'See Emily Play.'"

That's what we have been hearing from many of the country's top P.D.'s and D.J.'s, as well as several music reviewers.

We hope they're right. We're re-releasing the record.

Will you play it?

(Top left) To most people, the Penguins were a one-hit wonder — the sublime "Earth Angel" in early 1955. But they hung around long enough to make a pretty good-sized body of work, including four EPs. Here's one of them, Volume 3 of *The Cool, Cool Penguins*. (Top right) Tower Records (the label, not the chain) believed that "See Emily Play," the second American Pink Floyd single, could be a hit, so they re-serviced radio stations with this sleeve, known as the "title sleeve." Alas, the song failed again, and a collectible was born. (Bottom left) Before the Platters had dozens of his on Mercury, they recorded for the Federal label. Years later, King, Federal's parent company, issued this album. A reissue of an even rarer album on Federal, this contains the original, pre-hit version of "Only You." (Bottom right) The Prisonaires were indeed prisoners in the Tennessee State Penitentiary in Nashville. Johnny Bragg formed the group there and co-wrote their best-known song, "Just Walkin' In the Rain." It later was a big hit for Johnnie Ray.

PROBY, P.J.

45s

Number	Title (A Side/B Side)	Yr	VG	VG+	NM
BETA					
1008	Loud Perfume/(B-side unknown)	1958	50.00	100.00	200.00
—As "Jett Powers"					
DESIGN					
811	Go Girl Go/(B-side unknown)	1957	75.00	150.00	300.00
—As "Jett Powers"					
IMPERIAL					
66079	Rocking Pneumonia/Just Call, I'll Be There	1964	3.75	7.50	15.00
66084	Somewhere/Just Like Him	1965	—	—	—
—Unreleased					
LIBERTY					
55367	There Stands the One/Try to Forget Her	1961	3.75	7.50	15.00
55505	The Other Side of Town/Watch Me Walk Away	1962	3.75	7.50	15.00
55588	So Do I/I Can't Take It Like You Can	1963	3.75	7.50	15.00
55757	Somewhere/Just Like Him	1964	3.00	6.00	12.00
55777	Rocking Pneumonia/I Apologize	1965	3.00	6.00	12.00
55791	Stagger Lee/Mission Bell	1965	3.00	6.00	12.00
55806	That Means a Lot/Let the Water Run Down	1965	3.75	7.50	15.00
—The A-side is a Lennon-McCartney song; the Beatles' own version was not released until 1996					
55850	Good Things Are Coming My Way/Maria	1965	3.00	6.00	12.00
55875	My Prayer/Wicked Woman	1966	3.00	6.00	12.00
55915	I Can't Make It Alone/If I Ruled the World	1966	3.00	6.00	12.00
55915 [PS]	I Can't Make It Alone/If I Ruled the World	1966	3.75	7.50	15.00
55936	Niki-Hoeky/Good Things Are Coming My Way	1966	2.50	5.00	10.00
55974	Work with Me Annie/You Can't Come Home Again (If You Leave Me Now)	1967	2.50	5.00	10.00
55974 [PS]	Work with Me Annie/You Can't Come Home Again (If You Leave Me Now)	1967	3.75	7.50	15.00
55989	Butterfly High/Just Holding On	1967	2.50	5.00	10.00
56031	It's Your Day Today/I Apologize	1968	2.00	4.00	8.00
56051	What's Wrong with My World/Turn Her Away	1968	2.00	4.00	8.00
LONDON					
9648	Hold Me/The Tip of My Fingers	1964	3.75	7.50	15.00
9688	Hold Me/The Tip of My Fingers	1964	3.75	7.50	15.00
9705	Sweet and Tender Romance/Together	1964	3.75	7.50	15.00
SURFSIDE					
714	You Got Me Crying/I Need Love	1965	5.00	10.00	20.00
UNITED ARTISTS					
0070	Niki-Hoeky/Let the Water Run Down	1973	—	2.00	4.00
—"Silver Spotlight Series" reissue					

Albums

Number	Title	Yr	VG	VG+	NM
LIBERTY					
LRP-3406 [M]	Somewhere/Go Go P.J. Proby	1965	5.00	10.00	20.00
LRP-3421 [M]	P.J. Proby	1965	5.00	10.00	20.00
LRP-3497 [M]	Enigma	1967	5.00	10.00	20.00
LRP-3515 [M]	Phenomenon	1967	5.00	10.00	20.00
LST-7406 [S]	Somewhere/Go Go P.J. Proby	1965	6.25	12.50	25.00
LST-7421 [S]	P.J. Proby	1965	6.25	12.50	25.00
LST-7497 [S]	Enigma	1967	6.25	12.50	25.00
LST-7515 [S]	Phenomenon	1967	6.25	12.50	25.00
LST-7561	What's Wrong with My World?	1968	6.25	12.50	25.00

PROCESSION

45s

Number	Title (A Side/B Side)	Yr	VG	VG+	NM
SMASH					
2225	Adelaide, Adelaide/One Day in Every Week	1969	2.00	4.00	8.00
2239	Every American Citizen/You-Me	1969	2.00	4.00	8.00

Albums

Number	Title	Yr	VG	VG+	NM
SMASH					
SRS-67122	Procession	1969	5.00	10.00	20.00

PROCOL HARUM

Also see THE PARAMOUNTS (4); ROBIN TROWER.

45s

Number	Title (A Side/B Side)	Yr	VG	VG+	NM
A&M					
885	Homburg/Good Captain Clack	1967	3.00	6.00	12.00
927	In the Wee Small Hours of Sixpence/Quite Rightly So	1968	3.00	6.00	12.00
1069	A Salty Dog/Long Gone Geek	1969	2.00	4.00	8.00
1111	The Devil Came from Kansas/Boredom	1969	2.00	4.00	8.00
1218	Whiskey Train/About to Die	1970	—	3.00	6.00
1264	Power Failure/Broken Barricades	1971	—	3.00	6.00
1287	Song for a Dreamer/Simple Sister	1971	—	3.00	6.00
1287 [PS]	Song for a Dreamer/Simple Sister	1971	2.50	5.00	10.00
1347	Conquistador/A Salty Dog	1972	—	2.50	5.00
1347 [PS]	Conquistador/A Salty Dog	1972	2.00	4.00	8.00
1389	A Whiter Shade of Pale/Lime Street Blues	1972	—	2.50	5.00
1389 [PS]	A Whiter Shade of Pale/Lime Street Blues	1972	—	2.50	5.00
CHRYSALIS					
2011 [DJ]	Bringing Home the Bacon (mono/stereo)	1973	2.00	4.00	8.00
—May be promo only					
2013	Grand Hotel/Fires	1973	—	2.50	5.00
2013 [PS]	Grand Hotel/Fires	1973	2.50	5.00	10.00
2032	Nothing But the Truth/Drunk Again	1973	—	2.50	5.00
2109	Pandora's Box/Piper's Tune	1975	—	2.50	5.00
DERAM					
7507	A Whiter Shade of Pale/Lime Street Blues	1967	3.75	7.50	15.00
WARNER BROS.					
CRS 2115	Wizard Man/Something Magic	1977	—	3.00	6.00
—Warner Bros. label with Chrysalis number; possible factory mispress?					

Albums

Number	Title	Yr	VG	VG+	NM
A&M					
SP-3123	A Salty Dog	1979	2.00	4.00	8.00
—Reissue of 4179					
SP-3259	The Best of Procol Harum	198?	2.00	4.00	8.00
—Reissue of 4401					
SP-4151	Shine On Brightly	1968	6.25	12.50	25.00
SP-4179	A Salty Dog	1969	3.75	7.50	15.00
SP-4261	Home	1970	3.00	6.00	12.00
SP-4294	Broken Barricades	1971	3.00	6.00	12.00
SP-4335	Procol Harum Live in Concert with the Edmonton Symphony Orchestra	1972	3.00	6.00	12.00
SP-4373	A Whiter Shade of Pale	1972	3.00	6.00	12.00
—Reissue of Deram 18008 with one more track					
SP-4401	The Best of Procol Harum	1973	3.00	6.00	12.00
SP-8503 [DJ]	Procol Harum Lives	197?	75.00	150.00	300.00
—Promo-only box set with press kit, photos, keychain and interview LP					
SP-8503 [DJ]	Procol Harum Lives	197?	12.50	25.00	50.00
—Interview LP alone					
CHRYSALIS					
CHR 1037	Grand Hotel	1973	3.00	6.00	12.00
—Green label with "3300 Warner Blvd." address					
CHR 1037	Grand Hotel	1977	2.50	5.00	10.00
—Blue label with New York address					
CHR 1058	Exotic Birds and Fruit	1974	3.00	6.00	12.00
—Green label with "3300 Warner Blvd." address					
CHR 1058	Exotic Birds and Fruit	1977	2.50	5.00	10.00
—Blue label with New York address					
CHR 1080	Procol's Ninth	1975	3.00	6.00	12.00
—Green label with "3300 Warner Blvd." address					
CHR 1080	Procol's Ninth	1977	2.50	5.00	10.00
—Blue label with New York address					
CHR 1130	Something Magic	1977	2.50	5.00	10.00
PV 41037	Grand Hotel	1985	2.00	4.00	8.00
PV 41058	Exotic Birds and Fruit	1985	2.00	4.00	8.00
PV 41080	Procol's Ninth	1985	2.00	4.00	8.00
DERAM					
DE 16008 [M]	Procol Harum	1967	20.00	40.00	80.00
DE/S 16008/18008	Procol Harum Poster	1967	6.25	12.50	25.00
DES 18008 [R]	Procol Harum	1967	10.00	20.00	40.00

PROCTOR, BILLY

45s

Number	Title (A Side/B Side)	Yr	VG	VG+	NM
EPIC					
50160	(I'm Gonna) Chop Down That Oak Tree/Keeping Up with the Joneses	1975	—	2.50	5.00
SOUL					
35099	What Is Black/I Can Take It All	1972	5.00	10.00	20.00

PROFESSOR MORRISON'S LOLLIPOP

45s

Number	Title (A Side/B Side)	Yr	VG	VG+	NM
WHITE WHALE					
275	Gypsy Lady/You Got the Love	1968	2.50	5.00	10.00
288	Angela/Duba Duba Doo	1968	2.50	5.00	10.00
293	Oo Poo Pah Susie/You Can Take It	1969	2.50	5.00	10.00

PROFFITT, RANDY, AND THE BEACHCOMBERS

45s

Number	Title (A Side/B Side)	Yr	VG	VG+	NM
BETT-COE					
103	Check That Baby Out One Time/Young Love in Spring	196?	12.50	25.00	50.00

PROFILES, THE (1)

45s

Number	Title (A Side/B Side)	Yr	VG	VG+	NM
BAMBOO					
104	Got to Be Love (Something Stupid)/You Don't Care About Me	1969	2.00	4.00	8.00
108	Be Careful/I Still Love You	1969	2.00	4.00	8.00
115	A Little Misunderstanding/Got to Be Love	1970	2.00	4.00	8.00
DUO					
7449	If I Didn't Love You/(B-side unknown)	1968	2.50	5.00	10.00

PROFILES, THE (2)

45s

Number	Title (A Side/B Side)	Yr	VG	VG+	NM
GAIT					
1444	Never/Right By Her Side	1962	50.00	100.00	200.00

PROGRESSIVES, THE

45s

Number	Title (A Side/B Side)	Yr	VG	VG+	NM
DOT					
16514	Hot Cinders/Man of Mystery	1963	5.00	10.00	20.00

PROVINE, DOROTHY

45s

Number	Title (A Side/B Side)	Yr	VG	VG+	NM
WARNER BROS.					
5202	Bye Bye Blackbird/Crazy Words-Crazy Tune	1961	3.00	6.00	12.00
5249	The Whisper Song/Don't Bring Lulu	1961	3.00	6.00	12.00

Albums

Number	Title	Yr	VG	VG+	NM
WARNER BROS.					
W 1394 [M]	The Roaring 20's	1961	5.00	10.00	20.00
WS 1394 [S]	The Roaring 20's	1961	6.25	12.50	25.00
W 1419 [M]	The Vamp of the Roaring 20's	1961	5.00	10.00	20.00
WS 1419 [S]	The Vamp of the Roaring 20's	1961	6.25	12.50	25.00

PROW, JIMMY LEE

45s

Number	Title (A Side/B Side)	Yr	VG	VG+	NM
KING					
4929	Shopping List/You Tell Her, I Stutter	1956	7.50	15.00	30.00

PRUETT, JEANNE

45s

Number	Title (A Side/B Side)	Yr	VG	VG+	NM
AUDIOGRAPH					
454	Love Me/Safely in the Arms of Jesus	1983	—	2.50	5.00
—A-side with Marty Robbins					
467	Lady of the Eighties/(B-side unknown)	1983	—	2.00	4.00
477	We Came So Close/(B-side unknown)	1983	—	2.00	4.00
483	Star-Studded Nights/Wild Side of Life	1984	—	2.00	4.00
DECCA					
32383	One Woman Man/One Day Ahead of My Tears	1968	2.00	4.00	8.00
32435	Make Me Feel Like a Woman Again/Don't Hold Your Breath	1969	2.00	4.00	8.00

Number	Title (A Side/B Side)	Yr	VG	VG+	NM
32614	It Ain't Fair That It Ain't Right/At the Sight of You	1970	—	3.00	6.00
32703	King Size Bed/One Day Ahead of My Tears	1970	—	3.00	6.00
32857	Hold On to My Unchanging Love/He's Calling Me Baby Again	1971	—	3.00	6.00
32929	Love Me/I'm Out Looking for You	1972	—	3.00	6.00
32977	Call On Me/Stay on His Mind	1972	—	3.00	6.00
33013	I Forgot More Than You'll Ever Know (About Him)/ Don't Hold Your Breath	1972	—	3.00	6.00
IBC					
0002	Please Sing Satin Sheets for Me/(B-side unknown)	1979	—	2.00	4.00
0005	Back to Back/(B-side unknown)	1979	—	2.00	4.00
0008	Temporarily Yours/(B-side unknown)	1980	—	2.00	4.00
00010	It's Too Late/(B-side unknown)	1980	—	2.00	4.00
MCA					
40015	Satin Sheets/Sweet Sweetheart	1973	—	3.00	6.00
40116	I'm Your Woman/Your Memory's Comin' On	1973	—	2.00	4.00
40207	You Don't Need to Move a Mountain/Hopefully	1974	—	2.00	4.00
40284	Welcome to the Sunshine (Sweet Baby Jane)/ What My Thoughts Do All the Time	1974	—	2.00	4.00
40340	Just Like Your Daddy/One More Time	1974	—	2.00	4.00
40395	Honey on His Hands/One of These Days	1975	—	2.00	4.00
40440	A Poor Man's Woman/Momma Let Me Find Shelter (In Your Sweet Woman's Arms)	1975	—	2.00	4.00
40490	My Baby's Gone/But Not Today	1975	—	2.00	4.00
40527	Driftin' Too Far Away/Sweet Sorrow	1976	—	2.00	4.00
40569	It Doesn't Hurt to Ask/If I'm Not Girl Enough to Hold You	1976	—	2.00	4.00
40605	I've Taken/Sweet and Warm and Right	1976	—	2.00	4.00
40678	I'm Living a Lie/My First Pay Day	1977	—	2.00	4.00
40723	She's Still All Over You/Fancy Place to Cry	1977	—	2.00	4.00
MERCURY					
55017	I'm a Woman/Midnight Exchange	1978	—	2.00	4.00
55034	I Guess I'm Not That Good at Being Bad/Where Do You Draw the Line	1978	—	2.00	4.00
MSR					
1956	Rented Room/(B-side unknown)	1987	—	2.00	4.00
PAID					
118	Sad Ole Shade of Gray/When I Stop Dreaming	1981	—	2.00	4.00
136	I Ought to Feel Guilty/Who'll Turn Out the Lights (In Your World)	1981	—	2.00	4.00
RCA VICTOR					
47-8157	Another Heart to Break/Just a Little After Heartaches	1963	3.75	7.50	15.00
47-8232	Little Black Book/The Things I Don't Know	1963	3.75	7.50	15.00
47-8297	As a Matter of Fact/Sing Me a Song I Can Cry By	1963	3.75	7.50	15.00

Albums

Number	Title	Yr	VG	VG+	NM
ALLEGIANCE					
AV-5028	Stand By Your Man	1984	2.50	5.00	10.00
DECCA					
DL 75320	Love Me	1972	3.75	7.50	15.00
DOT/MCA					
39031	Jeanne Pruett	1985	2.50	5.00	10.00
MCA					
338	Satin Sheets	1973	3.00	6.00	12.00
388	Jeanne Pruett	1974	3.00	6.00	12.00
479	Honey on His Hands	1975	3.00	6.00	12.00
503	Love Me	1975	3.00	6.00	12.00
—Reissue of Decca LP					

PRYOR, RICHARD

Albums

Number	Title	Yr	VG	VG+	NM
AUDIOFIDELITY					
349 [PD]	Richard Pryor Live	198?	3.75	7.50	15.00
DOVE					
RS 6325	Richard Pryor	1968	5.00	10.00	20.00
LAFF					
A 146	Craps: After Hours	1971	3.00	6.00	12.00
A 170	Pryor Goes Foxx Hunting	197?	3.00	6.00	12.00
A 184	Down 'N' Dirty	197?	3.00	6.00	12.00
A 196	Are You Serious???	1977	3.00	6.00	12.00
A 198	Who Me? I'm Not Him	1977	3.00	6.00	12.00
A 200	Black Ben	1978	2.50	5.00	10.00
A 202	Wizard of Comedy	1978	2.50	5.00	10.00
A 206	Outrageous	1979	2.50	5.00	10.00
A 209	Insane	1980	2.50	5.00	10.00
A 212	Holy Smoke	1980	2.50	5.00	10.00
A 216	Rev. Du Rite	1981	2.50	5.00	10.00
A 221	The Very Best of Richard Pryor	1982	2.50	5.00	10.00
226	Blackjack	198?	2.00	4.00	8.00
—Reissue of 146					
227	Show Biz	198?	2.00	4.00	8.00
—Reissue of 200					
279	Richard Pryor Live	198?	2.00	4.00	8.00
(# unknown)	Supernigger	198?	2.00	4.00	8.00
PARTEE					
2404	That Nigger's Crazy	1974	3.00	6.00	12.00
REPRISE					
MS 2227	Is It Something I Said?	1975	3.00	6.00	12.00
MSK 2285	Is It Something I Said?	1977	2.50	5.00	10.00
—Reissue of 2227					
MSK 2287	That Nigger's Crazy	1977	2.50	5.00	10.00
—Reissue of Partee LP					
RS 6325	Richard Pryor	197?	3.00	6.00	12.00
—Reissue of Dove LP					
TIGER LILY					
TL 14023	L.A. Jail	1977	3.00	6.00	12.00
WARNER BROS.					
BS 2960	Bicentennial Nigger	1976	3.00	6.00	12.00
BSK 3057	Richard Pryor's Greatest Hits	1977	2.50	5.00	10.00
BSK 3114	Bicentennial Nigger	1977	2.50	5.00	10.00
—Reissue of 2960					
2BSK 3364 [(2)]	Wanted	1978	3.00	6.00	12.00
BSK 3660	Richard Pryor Live on the Sunset Strip	1982	2.50	5.00	10.00
23981	Richard Pryor: Here and Now	1983	2.50	5.00	10.00

PRYOR, SNOOKY

45s

Number	Title (A Side/B Side)	Yr	VG	VG+	NM
J.O.B.					
1014	Cryin' Shame/Eight, Nine, Ten	1953	100.00	200.00	400.00
1126	Uncle Sam, Don't Take My Man/Boogie Twist	1963	50.00	100.00	200.00
PARROT					
807	Crosstown Blues/I Want You for Myself	1954	375.00	750.00	1500.
—Black vinyl					
807	Crosstown Blues/I Want You for Myself	1954	625.00	1250.	2500.
—Red vinyl					
VEE JAY					
215	Judgment Day/Someone to Love Me	1956	30.00	60.00	120.00

PRYSOCK, ARTHUR

45s

Number	Title (A Side/B Side)	Yr	VG	VG+	NM
BETHLEHEM					
3100	The Girls I Never Kissed/Funny World	1972	—	3.00	6.00
DECCA					
25684	When Day Is Done/What Will I Tell My Heart	1965	2.00	4.00	8.00
27722	Blue Velvet/Morning Side Of the Mountain	1951	3.75	7.50	15.00
27769	Sin/The Love of a Gypsy	1951	3.75	7.50	15.00
27871	A Man Ain't Supposed to Cry/I Didn't Sleep a Wink Last Night	1951	3.75	7.50	15.00
27967	Wheel of Fortune/'Til the Stars Fall in the Ocean	1952	3.75	7.50	15.00
27978	I Hear a Rhapsody/Am I to Blame	1952	3.75	7.50	15.00
28270	School of Love/Sentimental Fool	1952	3.75	7.50	15.00
28700	I'd Give Anything/This Is the Time	1953	3.75	7.50	15.00
28867	My Mood/Temptation	1953	3.75	7.50	15.00
28950	Nobody Cares/Jean	1953	3.75	7.50	15.00
29118	Baby Don't You Cry/My Last Goodbye	1954	3.75	7.50	15.00
31710	Wheel of Fortune/I Cover the Waterfront	1964	2.00	4.00	8.00
31775	Baby, Don't You Cry/I Didn't Sleep a Wink Last Night	1965	2.00	4.00	8.00
GUSTO					
9023	Today I Started Loving You Again/It Ain't No Big Thing	1979	—	2.00	4.00
KING					
6243	Soul Soliloquy/(I Wanna Go) Where the Soul Trees Grow	1969	—	3.00	6.00
6271	The 23rd Psalm/I Believe	1969	—	3.00	6.00
6276	Save Your Love for Me/If I Were Young Again	1969	—	3.00	6.00
6279	Go Ahead and Fly/How Do I Tell Her	1969	—	3.00	6.00
6307	Have a Good Time/Frisco Line	1970	—	3.00	6.00
6315	Lord, Is That Me/My Home Is Not a Home Without You	1970	—	3.00	6.00
6353	Cry/Unforgettable	1971	—	3.00	6.00
6354	It Ain't No Big Thing/Big Blue Diamonds	1971	—	3.00	6.00
6364	Precious Memories/Just a Closer Walk with Thee	1971	—	3.00	6.00
MCA					
40943	Here's to Good Friends/All I Can Do Is Cry	1978	2.00	4.00	8.00
—The song that became the "Tonight, let it be Lowenbrau" commercial					
MERCURY					
70352	Take Care of Yourself/I'll Never Let You Cry	1954	3.75	7.50	15.00
70414	This I Know/If You Don't, Somebody Will	1954	3.75	7.50	15.00
70502	Show Me How to Mambo/I'm in Heaven Tonight	1954	3.75	7.50	15.00
70599	I Have Lied/Morning, Noon and Night	1955	3.75	7.50	15.00
OLD TOWN					
100	In the Rain/Thank Heaven for You	1973	—	2.50	5.00
103	Color My World/Good Morning News	1974	—	2.50	5.00
106	Hurt So Bad/Love Makes It Right	1974	—	2.50	5.00
108	I Wantcha Baby/One Broken Heart	1975	—	2.50	5.00
1000	When Love Is New/All I Need Is You	1976	—	2.50	5.00
1001	I Wantcha Baby/One Broken Heart	1977	—	2.50	5.00
1002	You Can Do It/You Can Do It (Part 2)	1977	—	2.50	5.00
1003	Since I Fell for You/Between Hello and Goodbye	1978	—	2.50	5.00
1055	I Love You So/The Greatest Gift	1958	3.00	6.00	12.00
1060	I Just Want to Make Love to You/Keep a Light in the Window	1958	3.00	6.00	12.00
1073	I Worry About You/My Faith	1959	3.00	6.00	12.00
1079	The Very Thought of You/If Ever I Should Fall in Love	1960	2.50	5.00	10.00
1087	This Is My Love/Do You Believe	1960	2.50	5.00	10.00
1092	Good Rockin' Tonight/My Everything	1960	2.50	5.00	10.00
1101	This Time/I Wonder Where Our Love Has Gone	1961	2.50	5.00	10.00
1106	One More Time/Speak to Me	1961	2.50	5.00	10.00
1115	April in Paris/When I Fall in Love	1962	2.50	5.00	10.00
1125	Where Can I Go/Pianissimo	1962	2.50	5.00	10.00
1132	Our Love Will Last/Come and See This Old Fool	1963	2.50	5.00	10.00
1138	My Special Prayer/You Can't Come In	1963	2.50	5.00	10.00
1144	There Will Never Be Another You/Crawdad	1963	2.50	5.00	10.00
1146	Stella by Starlight/My Wish	1963	2.50	5.00	10.00
1155	Ebb Tide/Are You Ready for a Laugh	1964	2.00	4.00	8.00
1163	Close Your Eyes/My Everlasting Love	1964	2.00	4.00	8.00
1170	Fly Me to the Moon/Without the One You Love	1964	2.00	4.00	8.00
1174	Full Moon and Empty Arms/You Always Hurt the One You Love	1964	2.00	4.00	8.00
1177	Teardrops in the Rain/I'm Crossing Over	1965	2.00	4.00	8.00
1183	It's Too Late, Baby Too Late/Who Can I Turn To	1965	2.00	4.00	8.00
1185	Open Up Your Heart/Only a Fool Breaks His Own Heart	1965	2.00	4.00	8.00
1188	Again/I Got the Blues So Bad	1965	2.00	4.00	8.00
1191	My Funny Valentine/House by the Side of the Road	1966	2.00	4.00	8.00
1196	Because/Let It Be Me	1966	2.00	4.00	8.00
VERVE					
10470	You Don't Have to Say You Love Me/10,000 Kisses, 10,000 Hugs	1966	—	3.00	6.00
10515	Love Me/She's a Woman	1967	—	3.00	6.00
10544	Before You Break My Heart/Goodbye, So Long	1967	—	3.00	6.00
10574	A Working Man's Prayer/No More in Life	1967	—	3.00	6.00
10592	Madam/No Sun Today	1968	—	3.00	6.00

Number	Title (A Side/B Side)	Yr	VG	VG+	NM
10620	I Must Be Doing Something Right/Young Runaways	1968	—	3.00	6.00
10633	My Special Prayer/Pretty Girl	1969	—	3.00	6.00
Albums					
DECCA					
DL 4581 [M]	Strictly Sentimental	1965	3.75	7.50	15.00
DL 4628 [M]	Showcase	1965	3.75	7.50	15.00
DL 74581 [S]	Strictly Sentimental	1965	5.00	10.00	20.00
DL 74628 [S]	Showcase	1965	5.00	10.00	20.00
KING					
KS-1064	The Country Side of Arthur Prysock	1969	3.00	6.00	12.00
KS-1066	Where the Soul Trees Go	1970	3.00	6.00	12.00
KS-1067	The Lord Is My Shepherd	1970	3.00	6.00	12.00
KS-1088	Fly My Love	1970	3.00	6.00	12.00
KS-1134	Unforgettable	1971	3.00	6.00	12.00
MCA					
3061	Here's To Good Friends	1978	2.50	5.00	10.00
MGM					
GAS-134	Arthur Prysock (Golden Archive Series)	1970	3.00	6.00	12.00
SE-4694	Arthur Prysock	1970	3.00	6.00	12.00
MILESTONE					
M-9139	A Rockin' Good Way	1986	2.50	5.00	10.00
M-9146	This Guy's in Love with You	1987	2.50	5.00	10.00
M-9157	Today's Love Songs, Tomorrow's Blues	1988	2.50	5.00	10.00
OLD TOWN					
12-001	Arthur Prysock '74	1973	3.00	6.00	12.00
12-002	Love Makes It Right	1974	3.00	6.00	12.00
12-004	All My Life	1976	3.00	6.00	12.00
LP-102 [M]	I Worry About You	1962	12.50	25.00	50.00
LP-2004 [M]	Arthur Prysock Sings Only for You	1962	12.50	25.00	50.00
LP-2005 [M]	Coast to Coast	1963	10.00	20.00	40.00
LP-2006 [M]	A Portrait of Arthur Prysock	1963	10.00	20.00	40.00
LP-2007 [M]	Everlasting Songs for Everlasting Lovers	1964	10.00	20.00	40.00
LP-2008 [M]	Intimately Yours	1964	10.00	20.00	40.00
LP-2009 [M]	A Double Header with Arthur Prysock	1965	10.00	20.00	40.00
LP-2010 [M]	In a Mood	1965	10.00	20.00	40.00
T-90604 [M]	A Portrait of Arthur Prysock	1965	10.00	20.00	40.00
—Capitol Record Club edition					
POLYDOR					
PD-2-8901 [(2)]	Silk and Satin	1977	3.75	7.50	15.00
VERVE					
V6-650 [(2)]	24 Karat Hits	1969	3.75	7.50	15.00
V-5009 [M]	Art and Soul	1966	3.00	6.00	12.00
V6-5009 [S]	Art and Soul	1966	3.75	7.50	15.00
V-5011 [M]	The Best of Arthur Prysock	1967	3.00	6.00	12.00
V6-5011 [S]	The Best of Arthur Prysock	1967	3.75	7.50	15.00
V-5012 [M]	A Portrait of Arthur Prysock	1967	3.75	7.50	15.00
V6-5012 [S]	A Portrait of Arthur Prysock	1967	3.75	7.50	15.00
V-5014 [M]	Mister Prysock	1967	3.75	7.50	15.00
V6-5014 [S]	Mister Prysock	1967	3.75	7.50	15.00
V-5029 [M]	Love Me	1968	3.75	7.50	15.00
V6-5029 [S]	Love Me	1968	3.00	6.00	12.00
V6-5038	The Best of Arthur Prysock, Volume 2	1968	3.00	6.00	12.00
V6-5048	To Love or Not to Love	1968	3.00	6.00	12.00
V6-5059	I Must Be Doing Something Right	1968	3.00	6.00	12.00
V6-5070	This Is My Beloved	1969	3.00	6.00	12.00

PRYSOCK, ARTHUR/COUNT BASIE

Also see each artist's individual listings.

Number	Title (A Side/B Side)	Yr	VG	VG+	NM
Albums					
VERVE					
V-8646 [M]	Arthur Prysock/Count Basie	1966	3.75	7.50	15.00
V6-8646 [S]	Arthur Prysock/Count Basie	1966	5.00	10.00	20.00
827011-1	Arthur Prysock/Count Basie	1985	2.00	4.00	8.00
—Reissue					

PRYSOCK, RED

Number	Title (A Side/B Side)	Yr	VG	VG+	NM
45s					
CHESS					
2042	I Heard It Through the Grapevine/Groovy Sax	1968	2.00	4.00	8.00
KING					
5595	Hand Clapping One More Time/Smokestack	1962	2.50	5.00	10.00
5644	Quick as a Flash/Old Folks	1962	2.50	5.00	10.00
5669	Harem Girl/Ride Away	1962	2.50	5.00	10.00
5704	Here We Go Again/Can't Sit Down	1963	2.50	5.00	10.00
MERCURY					
70367	Jump Red Jump/Body and Soul	1954	5.00	10.00	20.00
70419	Happy Feet/Blow Your Horn	1954	5.00	10.00	20.00
70460	Hey There/Fats' Place	1954	5.00	10.00	20.00
70540	Rock 'n' Roll/Little Jamie	1955	5.00	10.00	20.00
70602	The Zonked/Horn Blows	1955	5.00	10.00	20.00
70674	Hand Clappin'/Shoe String	1955	5.00	10.00	20.00
70698	Jumbo/Hand Clappin'	1955	5.00	10.00	20.00
70733	Finger Tips/Short Circuit	1955	5.00	10.00	20.00
70787	Zip/Red Speaks	1956	3.75	7.50	15.00
70918	Rock and Roll Party/Rock and Roll Mambo	1956	3.75	7.50	15.00
70985	Teen-Age Rock/Paquino Walk	1956	3.75	7.50	15.00
71054	Head Snappin'/Pog Wog	1957	3.75	7.50	15.00
71175	Rooster Walk/Two Point Eight	1957	3.75	7.50	15.00
71214	What's the Word, Thunderbird/Satellite	1957	3.75	7.50	15.00
71358	Billie's Blues/Willow Weep for Me	1958	3.00	6.00	12.00
71411	Margie/Chop Suey	1959	3.00	6.00	12.00
71476	Riffin' with Red/And the Angels Sing	1959	3.00	6.00	12.00
71573	Deep Purple/Offshore	1960	3.00	6.00	12.00
71735	More Handclappin'/Twistin' 'n' Bendin'	1960	3.00	6.00	12.00
71786	Charleston Twist/Bony Maronie	1961	3.00	6.00	12.00
RED ROBIN					
107	Wiggles/Crying My Heart Out	1952	30.00	60.00	120.00
117	Hard Rock/Jump for George	1953	25.00	50.00	100.00
139	Jackpot/The Hammer	1956	20.00	40.00	80.00
Albums					
MERCURY					
MG-20088 [M]	Rock 'n Roll	1955	50.00	100.00	200.00
MG-20211 [M]	Fruit Boots	1957	30.00	60.00	120.00
MG-20307 [M]	The Beat	1957	20.00	40.00	80.00
MG-20512 [M]	Swing Softly Red	1958	12.50	25.00	50.00
SR-60188 [S]	Swing Softly Red	1959	20.00	40.00	80.00
WING					
MGW-12007 [M]	Fruit Boots	1959	10.00	20.00	40.00
—Originals have liner notes on back cover					
MGW-12007 [M]	Fruit Boots	196?	5.00	10.00	20.00
—Reissues have other LPs listed on back cover					
SRW-16007 [R]	Fruit Boots	196?	3.00	6.00	12.00

PUCKETT, GARY, AND THE UNION GAP

Includes Gary Puckett solo and records credited to "The Union Gap Featuring Gary Puckett."

Number	Title (A Side/B Side)	Yr	VG	VG+	NM
45s					
COLUMBIA					
44297	Woman, Woman/Don't Make Promises	1967	2.00	4.00	8.00
44297 [PS]	Woman, Woman/Don't Make Promises	1967	3.00	6.00	12.00
—As "The Union Gap"					
44450	Young Girl/I'm Losing You	1968	2.00	4.00	8.00
44450 [PS]	Young Girl/I'm Losing You	1968	3.00	6.00	12.00
—As "The Union Gap"					
44547	Lady Willpower/Daylight Strangers	1968	2.00	4.00	8.00
44547 [PS]	Lady Willpower/Daylight Strangers	1968	3.00	6.00	12.00
—As "The Union Gap"					
44644	Over You/If the Day Would Come	1968	—	3.00	6.00
44644 [PS]	Over You/If the Day Would Come	1968	3.00	6.00	12.00
44788	Don't Give In to Him/Could I	1969	—	3.00	6.00
44967	This Girl Is a Woman Now/His Other Woman	1969	—	3.00	6.00
45097	Let's Give Adam and Eve Another Chance/The Beggar	1970	—	3.00	6.00
45097 [PS]	Let's Give Adam and Eve Another Chance/The Beggar	1970	2.00	4.00	8.00
45249	I Just Don't Know What to Do With Myself/All That Matters	1970	—	2.50	5.00
45303	Keep the Customer Satisfied/No One Really Knows	1971	—	2.50	5.00
45358	Life Has Its Little Ups and Downs/Shimmering Eyes	1971	—	2.50	5.00
45438	Hello Morning/Gentle Woman	1971	—	2.50	5.00
45509	Hello Morning/I Can't Hold On	1971	—	2.50	5.00
45678	Bless the Child/Leavin' in the Morning	1972	—	2.50	5.00
Albums					
COLUMBIA					
CS 1042	Gary Puckett and the Union Gap's Greatest Hits	1970	5.00	10.00	20.00
CS 9612	Woman, Woman	1968	5.00	10.00	20.00
—As "The Union Gap Featuring Gary Puckett"					
CS 9664	Young Girl	1968	5.00	10.00	20.00
CS 9715	Incredible	1968	5.00	10.00	20.00
CS 9935	The New Gary Puckett and the Union Gap Album	1969	5.00	10.00	20.00
C 30862	The Gary Puckett Album	1971	3.75	7.50	15.00
HARMONY					
KH 31184	Lady Willpower	1972	2.50	5.00	10.00

PUFNSTUF

Number	Title (A Side/B Side)	Yr	VG	VG+	NM
45s					
DECCA					
32702	Pufnstuf/Nonsense	1970	3.75	7.50	15.00

PUGSLEY MUNION

Number	Title (A Side/B Side)	Yr	VG	VG+	NM
Albums					
J&S					
SLP-001	Just Like You	1969	25.00	50.00	100.00

PULLEN, DWIGHT

Number	Title (A Side/B Side)	Yr	VG	VG+	NM
45s					
CARLTON					
455	Sunglasses After Dark/Teenage Bug	1958	75.00	150.00	300.00
SAGE AND SAND					
279	By You, By the Bayou/It's Over With	1959	7.50	15.00	30.00
283	I Live a Lifetime Last Night/You'll Get Yours Some Day	1959	7.50	15.00	30.00

PUMPKIN

Number	Title (A Side/B Side)	Yr	VG	VG+	NM
45s					
BRUNSWICK					
55004	Half Past Seventeen/Boom Boom	1957	10.00	20.00	40.00

PURE LOVE AND PLEASURE

Number	Title (A Side/B Side)	Yr	VG	VG+	NM
45s					
ABC DUNHILL					
4232	All in My Mind/What Cha Gonna Do	1970	2.00	4.00	8.00
Albums					
ABC DUNHILL					
DS-50076	A Record of Pure Love and Pleasure	1970	3.75	7.50	15.00

PURE PRAIRIE LEAGUE

Number	Title (A Side/B Side)	Yr	VG	VG+	NM
45s					
CASABLANCA					
2266	Let Me Love You Tonight/Janny Lou	1980	—	2.00	4.00
2294	I'm Almost Ready/You're My True Love	1980	—	2.00	4.00
2319	I Can't Stop the Feelin'/A Lifetime of Nightime	1980	—	2.00	4.00
2332	Still Right Here in My Heart/Don't Keep Me Hangin'	1981	—	2.00	4.00
2337	You're Mine Tonight.Do You Love Me Truly, Julie	1981	—	2.00	4.00
RCA					
PB-10829	Dance/Help Yourself	1976	—	2.00	4.00
PB-10880	All the Way/Fade Away	1977	—	2.00	4.00
PB-11148	The Sun Shone Lightly/Lucille Crawfield	1977	—	2.00	4.00
PB-11260	Working in the Coal Mine/Bad Cream	1978	—	2.00	4.00
PB-11282	Love Will Grow/Slim Pickin's	1978	—	2.00	4.00
PB-11678	Can't Hold Back/Restless Woman	1979	—	2.00	4.00

Number	Title (A Side/B Side)	Yr	VG	VG+	NM
RCA VICTOR					
PB-10184	Amie/Memories	1975	—	2.50	5.00
PB-10302	Two-Lane Highway/Sister's Keeper	1975	—	2.00	4.00
PB-10382	Just Can't Believe It/Kentucky Moonshine	1975	—	2.00	4.00
GB-10490	Amie/Memories	1975	—	—	3.00
—Gold Standard Series					
PB-10580	Long Cold Winter/The Sun Shone Brightly	1976	—	2.00	4.00
PB-10679	That'll Be the Day/I Can Only Dream of You	1976	—	2.00	4.00
48-1028	Tears/You're Between Me	1972	—	3.00	6.00
74-0742	Woman/She Darked the Sun	1972	—	3.00	6.00
74-0794	Early Morning Riser/Angel #9	1972	—	3.00	6.00
Albums					
CASABLANCA					
NBLP-7212	Firin' Up	1980	2.50	5.00	10.00
NBLP-7255	Something in the Night	1981	2.50	5.00	10.00
PAIR					
PDL2-1034 [(2)]	Home on the Range	1986	3.00	6.00	12.00
RCA VICTOR					
APD1-0933 [Q]	Two Lane Highway	1975	5.00	10.00	20.00
APL1-0933	Two Lane Highway	1975	3.00	6.00	12.00
APD1-1247 [Q]	If The Shoe Fits	1976	5.00	10.00	20.00
APL1-1247	If The Shoe Fits	1976	3.00	6.00	12.00
APL1-1924	Dance	1976	3.00	6.00	12.00
CPL2-2404 [(2)]	Live!! Takin' the Stage	1977	3.75	7.50	15.00
AFL1-2590	Just Fly	1978	3.00	6.00	12.00
AFL1-3335	Can't Hold Back	1979	3.00	6.00	12.00
AYL1-3669	Two Lane Highway	1980	2.00	4.00	8.00
—"Best Buy Series" reissue					
AYL1-3717	If the Shoe Fits	1981	2.00	4.00	8.00
—"Best Buy Series" reissue					
AYL1-3718	Just Fly	1981	2.00	4.00	8.00
—"Best Buy Series" reissue					
AYL1-3719	Pure Prairie League	1981	2.00	4.00	8.00
—"Best Buy Series" reissue					
AYL1-3723	Dance	1981	2.00	4.00	8.00
—"Best Buy Series" reissue					
AFL1-4650	Pure Prairie League	1977	2.50	5.00	10.00
—Reissue of LSP-4650					
LSP-4650	Pure Prairie League	1972	3.00	6.00	12.00
AYL1-4656	Bustin' Out	1984	2.00	4.00	8.00
—"Best Buy Series" reissue					
AFL1-4769	Bustin' Out	1977	2.50	5.00	10.00
—Reissue of LSP-4769					
LSP-4769	Bustin' Out	1972	3.00	6.00	12.00

PURIFY, JAMES AND BOBBY

Number	Title (A Side/B Side)	Yr	VG	VG+	NM
45s					
BELL					
648	I'm Your Puppet/So Many Reasons	1966	3.75	7.50	15.00
660	Wish You Didn't Have to Go/You Can't Keep a Good Man Down	1967	2.00	4.00	8.00
669	Shake a Tail Feather/Goodness Gracious	1967	3.00	6.00	12.00
680	I Take What I Want/Sixteen Tons	1967	2.00	4.00	8.00
685	Let Love Come Between Us/I Don't Want to Have to Go	1967	2.00	4.00	8.00
700	Do Unto Me/Everybody Needs Somebody	1967	2.00	4.00	8.00
721	I Can Remember/I Was Born to Lose Out	1968	2.00	4.00	8.00
735	Help Yourself (To All of My Lovin')/Last Piece of Love	1968	2.00	4.00	8.00
751	Untie Me/We're Finally Gonna Make It	1968	2.00	4.00	8.00
774	I Don't Know What It Is You Got/Section C	1969	2.00	4.00	8.00
CASABLANCA					
812	Do Your Thing/Why Love	1974	—	2.50	5.00
827	Man Can't Be a Man Without a Woman/You and Me Together Forever	1975	—	2.50	5.00
830	All the Love I Got/(B-side unknown)	1975	—	2.50	5.00
MERCURY					
73767	I'm Your Puppet/Lay Me Down Easy	1976	—	2.50	5.00
73806	Morning Glory/Turning Back the Pages	1976	—	2.50	5.00
73884	I Ain't Got to Love Nobody Else/What's Better Than Love	1977	—	2.50	5.00
73893	Get Closer/What's Better Than Love	1977	—	2.50	5.00
PHILCO-FORD					
HP-28	I'm Your Puppet/Goodnight Gracious	1968	3.75	7.50	15.00
—4-inch plastic "Hip Pocket Record" with color sleeve					
SPHERE SOUND					
77004	I'm Your Puppet/Everybody Needs Somebody	196?	2.00	4.00	8.00
Albums					
BELL					
6003 [M]	James and Bobby Purify	1966	6.25	12.50	25.00
S-6003 [S]	James and Bobby Purify	1966	7.50	15.00	30.00
6010 [M]	The Pure Sound of the Purifys	1967	6.25	12.50	25.00
S-6010 [S]	The Pure Sound of the Purifys	1967	7.50	15.00	30.00
MERCURY					
SRM-1-1134	The Purify Brothers	1977	3.00	6.00	12.00

PURIM, FLORA

Number	Title (A Side/B Side)	Yr	VG	VG+	NM
45s					
MILESTONE					
301	Casa Forte/Search for Peace	1975	—	2.50	5.00
303	Open Your Eyes, You Can Fly/Andei (I Walked)	1976	—	2.50	5.00
WARNER BROS.					
8392	Angels/Fairy Tale Song	1977	—	2.50	5.00
8650	Everyday, Everynight/Walking Away	1978	—	2.50	5.00
Albums					
FANTASY					
OJC-315	Butterfly Dreams	1988	2.00	4.00	8.00
—Reissue of Milestone 9052					
OJC-619	Stories to Tell	1991	2.00	4.00	8.00
—Reissue of Milestone 9058					
MILESTONE					
9052	Butterfly Dreams	1974	2.50	5.00	10.00
9058	Stories to Tell	1975	2.50	5.00	10.00
9065	Open Your Eyes You Can Fly	1976	2.50	5.00	10.00
9070	500 Miles High	1976	2.50	5.00	10.00
9077	Encounter	1977	2.50	5.00	10.00
9081	That's What She Said	1978	2.50	5.00	10.00
9095	Love Reborn	1980	2.50	5.00	10.00
VENTURE					
90995	The Midnight Sun	1988	2.50	5.00	10.00
WARNER BROS.					
BS 2985	Nothing Will Be As It Was...Tomorrow	1977	2.50	5.00	10.00
BSK 3168	Everyday, Everynight	1978	2.50	5.00	10.00
BSK 3344	Carry On	1979	2.50	5.00	10.00

PURIM, FLORA, AND AIRTO

Number	Title (A Side/B Side)	Yr	VG	VG+	NM
Albums					
CROSSOVER					
CR-5001	The Magicians	1988	2.00	4.00	8.00
CR-5003	The Sun Is Out	1989	2.50	5.00	10.00
GEORGE WEIN COLLECTION					
GW-3007	Humble People	1986	2.00	4.00	8.00

PURPLE GANG, THE

Number	Title (A Side/B Side)	Yr	VG	VG+	NM
Albums					
SIRE					
SES 97006	The Purple Gang Strikes	1969	5.00	10.00	20.00

PURPLE IMAGE

Number	Title (A Side/B Side)	Yr	VG	VG+	NM
Albums					
MAP CITY					
3015	Purple Image	1971	12.50	25.00	50.00

PURSELL, BILL

Number	Title (A Side/B Side)	Yr	VG	VG+	NM
45s					
COLUMBIA					
42619	Our Winter Love/A Wound Can't Erase	1962	2.00	4.00	8.00
42780	Loved/Stranger	1963	—	3.00	6.00
42832	Pride/Farewell to Adra	1963	—	3.00	6.00
42876	Dark Alley/Autumn Magic	1963	—	3.00	6.00
42970	The Theme from Captain Newman/Remember Me (I'm the One Who Loves You)	1964	—	3.00	6.00
43090	Crying/I'll Never Be Free	1964	—	3.00	6.00
43255	Madrilena/Remembered Love	1965	—	3.00	6.00
43380	You've Lost That Lovin' Feelin'/Quiet Nights of Quiet Stars	1965	—	3.00	6.00
43593	Love Theme from Superman/Soul Shall It Be	1966	2.50	5.00	10.00
DOT					
17217	Geary Street/Winter Waves	1969	—	2.50	5.00
Albums					
COLUMBIA					
CL 1992 [M]	Our Winter Love	1963	3.75	7.50	15.00
CL 2077 [M]	Chasing a Dream	1964	3.75	7.50	15.00
CL 2421 [M]	Remembered Love	1965	3.75	7.50	15.00
CS 8792 [S]	Our Winter Love	1963	5.00	10.00	20.00
CS 8877 [S]	Chasing a Dream	1964	5.00	10.00	20.00
CS 9221 [S]	Remembered Love	1965	5.00	10.00	20.00

PUZZLE

Number	Title (A Side/B Side)	Yr	VG	VG+	NM
45s					
ABC					
11181	Hey Medusa/Make the Children Happy	1969	2.00	4.00	8.00
Albums					
ABC					
ABCS-671	Puzzle	1969	5.00	10.00	20.00

PYRAMIDS, THE

More than one group.

Number	Title (A Side/B Side)	Yr	VG	VG+	NM
45s					
BEST					
1	Pyramid's Stomp/Paul	1963	7.50	15.00	30.00
102	Penetration/Here Comes Marsha	1963	10.00	20.00	40.00
13001	Pyramid's Stomp/Paul	1963	5.00	10.00	20.00
13002	Penetration/Here Comes Marsha	1964	5.00	10.00	20.00
—No mention of London Records on label					
13002	Penetration/Here Comes Marsha	1964	3.75	7.50	15.00
—With "Dist. by London" or similar wording on label					
13002 [PS]	Penetration/Here Comes Marsha	1964	10.00	20.00	40.00
—Red sleeve					
13002 [PS]	Penetration/Here Comes Marsha	1964	10.00	20.00	40.00
—Black sleeve					
CEDWICKE					
13005	Midnight Run/Custom Caravan	1964	10.00	20.00	40.00
13006	Contact/Pressure	1964	10.00	20.00	40.00
CUB					
9112	I'm the Playboy/Cryin'	1962	5.00	10.00	20.00
DAVIS					
453	At Any Cost/Okay, Baby!	1956	12.50	25.00	50.00
457	Why Did You Go/Before It's Too Late	1957	12.50	25.00	50.00
FEDERAL					
12233	Deep in My Heart for You/And I Need You	1955	100.00	200.00	400.00
HOLLYWOOD					
1047	Someday/Bow Wow	1955	125.00	250.00	500.00
RCA VICTOR					
47-7556	Long Long Time/Oh No You Won't (Oh Yes You Will)	1959	3.75	7.50	15.00
SHELL					
304	Ankle Bracelet/Hot Dog Dooly Wah	1961	6.25	12.50	25.00
—As "The Original Pyramids"					
711	Ankle Bracelet/Hot Dog Dooly Wah	1958	12.50	25.00	50.00
SONBERT					
82861	I'm the Playboy/Cryin'	1962	10.00	20.00	40.00
VEE JAY					
489	What Is Love/Shakin' Fit	1963	6.25	12.50	25.00

Number	Title (A Side/B Side)	Yr	VG	VG+	NM
Albums					
BEST					
LPM-1001 [M]	The Original Penetration! And Other Favorites	1964	62.50	125.00	250.00
—Original issue with "Walkin' the Dog"					
BR 16501 [M]	The Original Penetration! And Other Favorites	1964	50.00	100.00	200.00
—Reissue with "Road Runnah"					
BS 36501 [R]	The Original Penetration! And Other Favorites	1964	30.00	60.00	120.00
SUNDAZED					
LP-5012	Penetration! The Best of the Pyramids	1995	2.50	5.00	10.00

PYTHON LEE JACKSON

With ROD STEWART on vocals.

Number	Title (A Side/B Side)	Yr	VG	VG+	NM
45s					
GNP CRESCENDO					
449	In a Broken Dream/Doin' Fine	1972	—	3.00	6.00
449	In a Broken Dream/Turn the Music Down	1972	—	3.00	6.00
462	Cloud Nine/Rod's Blues	1973	—	3.00	6.00
Albums					
GNP CRESCENDO					
GNPS-2066	In a Broken Dream	1972	3.75	7.50	15.00

Q

QUADRANGLE, THE

45s

Number	Title (A Side/B Side)	Yr	VG	VG+	NM
PHILIPS					
40408	She's Too Familiar Now/No More Time	1966	7.50	15.00	30.00

QUADRELLS, THE

45s

Number	Title (A Side/B Side)	Yr	VG	VG+	NM
WHIRLIN' DISC					
103	What Can the Matter Be/Come to Me	1957	17.50	35.00	70.00

QUADS, THE

45s

Number	Title (A Side/B Side)	Yr	VG	VG+	NM
VAULT					
907	Surfin' Hearse/Little Queenie	1963	10.00	20.00	40.00

QUAILS, THE (1)

See BILL ROBINSON AND THE QUAILS.

QUAILS, THE (2)

45s

Number	Title (A Side/B Side)	Yr	VG	VG+	NM
HARVEY					
116	My Love/Never Felt Like This Before	1961	12.50	25.00	50.00
120	I Thought/Over the Hump	1963	12.50	25.00	50.00

QUAITE, CHRISTINE

45s

Number	Title (A Side/B Side)	Yr	VG	VG+	NM
WORLD ARTISTS					
1022	Tell Me Mamma/In the Middle of the Floor	1964	3.00	6.00	12.00
1028	Mr. Stuck Up/Will You Be the Same Tomorrow	1964	3.00	6.00	12.00

QUAKER CITY BOYS, THE

45s

Number	Title (A Side/B Side)	Yr	VG	VG+	NM
SWAN					
4023	Teasin'/Won't Ya Come Out Mary Ann	1958	3.00	6.00	12.00
4026	Everywhere You Go/Love Me Tonight	1959	2.50	5.00	10.00
4045	Goodbye 50's, Hello 60's/You Call Everybody Darlin'	1959	2.50	5.00	10.00

QUARTER NOTES, THE (1)

45s

Number	Title (A Side/B Side)	Yr	VG	VG+	NM
BISON					
757	Frantic Flip/Canadian Sunset	1960	7.50	15.00	30.00
IMPERIAL					
5647	Frantic Flip/Canadian Sunset	1960	3.75	7.50	15.00
WIZZ					
715	Record Hop Blues/Suki-Yaki-Rocki	1959	6.25	12.50	25.00

QUARTER NOTES, THE (2)

45s

Number	Title (A Side/B Side)	Yr	VG	VG+	NM
BOOM					
60018	Hey Little Girl/I've Been Loved	1966	3.75	7.50	15.00

QUARTER NOTES, THE (3)

45s

Number	Title (A Side/B Side)	Yr	VG	VG+	NM
DELUXE					
6116	Loneliness/Come De Nite	1957	6.25	12.50	25.00
6129	My Fantasy/Ten Minutes to Midnight	1957	6.25	12.50	25.00

QUARTER NOTES, THE (U)

Some of these could be group (1) or (3).

45s

Number	Title (A Side/B Side)	Yr	VG	VG+	NM
DOT					
15685	Please Come Home/Like You Bug Me	1958	6.25	12.50	25.00
GUYDEN					
2083	Pretty Pretty Eyes/I Don't Wanna Go Home	1963	5.00	10.00	20.00
RCA VICTOR					
47-7327	The Interview/Punkanilla	1958	3.75	7.50	15.00

QUARTERMASS

Albums

Number	Title (A Side/B Side)	Yr	VG	VG+	NM
HARVEST					
SKAO-314	Quartermass	1970	7.50	15.00	30.00

QUATRO, SUZI

Also see THE PLEASURE SEEKERS.

45s

Number	Title (A Side/B Side)	Yr	VG	VG+	NM
ARISTA					
0106	Your Mama Won't Like Me/Peter Peter	1975	—	2.50	5.00
BELL					
45401	48 Crash/Little Bitch Blue	1973	—	2.50	5.00
45416	Can the Can/48 Crash	1973	—	2.50	5.00
45477	All Shook Up/Glycerine Queen	1974	—	2.50	5.00
45609	Devil Gate Drive/In the Morning	1974	—	2.50	5.00
45615	Keep a-Knockin'/Cat Size	1974	—	2.50	5.00
BIG TREE					
16053	Can the Can/Don't Mess Around	1975	—	2.50	5.00
DREAMLAND					
104	Rock Hard/State of Mind	1980	—	2.00	4.00
104 [PS]	Rock Hard/State of Mind	1980	—	2.00	4.00
107	Lipstick/Woman Cry	1980	—	2.00	4.00
RAK					
4512	Brain Confusion (For All the Lonely People)/Rolling Stone	1972	2.50	5.00	10.00
RSO					
917	Stumblin' In/A Stranger to Paradise	1979	—	2.00	4.00
—With Chris Norman (lead singer of Smokie)					
929	If You Can't Give Me Love/Non-Citizen	1979	—	2.00	4.00
1001	I've Never Been in Love/Space Cadets	1979	—	2.00	4.00
1014	Starlight Lady/She's in Love with You	1979	—	2.00	4.00

Albums

Number	Title (A Side/B Side)	Yr	VG	VG+	NM
ARISTA					
AL 4035	Your Mama Won't Like Me	1975	3.00	6.00	12.00
BELL					
1302	Suzi Quatro	1974	3.75	7.50	15.00
1313	Quatro	1974	3.75	7.50	15.00
DREAMLAND					
DL-1-5006	Rock Hard	1980	2.50	5.00	10.00
RSO					
RS-1-3044	If You Knew Suzi…	1979	2.50	5.00	10.00
RS-1-3064	Suzi...And Other Four Letter Words	1980	2.50	5.00	10.00

QUATTLEBAUM, DOUG

45s

Number	Title (A Side/B Side)	Yr	VG	VG+	NM
GOTHAM					
519	Don't Be Funny Baby/Lizzie Lou	1953	25.00	50.00	100.00

Albums

Number	Title (A Side/B Side)	Yr	VG	VG+	NM
BLUESVILLE					
BVLP-1065 [M]	Softee Man Blues	1963	15.00	30.00	60.00
—Blue label, silver print					
BVLP-1065 [M]	Softee Man Blues	1964	5.00	10.00	20.00
—Blue label, trident logo at right					

QUEEN

Also see FREDDIE MERCURY.

12-Inch Singles

Number	Title (A Side/B Side)	Yr	VG	VG+	NM
CAPITOL					
SPRO-9714/5 [DJ]	A Kind of Magic (4:30) (6:30)	1986	3.75	7.50	15.00
V-15210	One Vision (Extended Version)/Blurred Vision	1985	3.75	7.50	15.00
V-15260	Pain Is So Close to Pleasure (2 versions)/Don't Lose Your Head	1986	3.75	7.50	15.00
ELEKTRA					
AS 11461 [DJ]	Another One Bites the Dust (same on both sides)	1980	3.75	7.50	15.00
AS 11481 [DJ]	Flash's Theme AKA Flash (same on both sides)	1980	3.75	7.50	15.00

45s

Number	Title (A Side/B Side)	Yr	VG	VG+	NM
CAPITOL					
B-5317	Radio Ga Ga/I Go Crazy	1984	—	2.00	4.00
B-5317 [PS]	Radio Ga Ga/I Go Crazy	1984	—	2.00	4.00
B-5350	I Want to Break Free/Machines (Or Back to Humans)	1984	—	2.00	4.00
B-5350 [PS]	I Want to Break Free/Machines (Or Back to Humans)	1984	—	2.50	5.00
—With Freddie Mercury in center					
B-5350 [PS]	I Want to Break Free/Machines (Or Back to Humans)	1984	—	2.50	5.00
—With Brian May in center					
B-5350 [PS]	I Want to Break Free/Machines (Or Back to Humans)	1984	—	2.50	5.00
—With Roger Taylor in center					
B-5350 [PS]	I Want to Break Free/Machines (Or Back to Humans)	1984	—	2.50	5.00
—With John Deacon in center					
B-5372	It's a Hard Life/Is This the World We Created?	1984	—	2.50	5.00
B-5372 [PS]	It's a Hard Life/Is This the World We Created?	1984	—	2.50	5.00
B-5424	Hammer to Fall/Tear It Up	1984	—	2.50	5.00
B-5424 [PS]	Hammer to Fall/Tear It Up	1984	—	2.50	5.00
B-5530	One Vision/Blurred Vision	1985	—	2.00	4.00
B-5530 [PS]	One Vision/Blurred Vision	1985	—	2.00	4.00
B-5568	Princes of the Universe/A Dozen Red Roses for My Darling	1985	—	2.00	4.00
B-5568 [PS]	Princes of the Universe/A Dozen Red Roses for My Darling	1985	—	2.00	4.00
B-5590	A Kind of Magic/A Dozen Red Roses for My Darling	1986	—	2.00	4.00
B-5590 [PS]	A Kind of Magic/A Dozen Red Roses for My Darling	1986	—	2.00	4.00
B-5633	Pain Is So Close to Pleasure/Don't Lose Your Head	1986	—	2.00	4.00
B-5633 [PS]	Pain Is So Close to Pleasure/Don't Lose Your Head	1986	—	2.00	4.00
7PRO-9114 [DJ]	I Want to Break Free	1984	—	—	—
7PRO-9114 [DJ]	I Want to Break Free	1984	3.00	6.00	12.00
—No song title or name of group on label					
7PRO-9546/7 [DJ]	One Vision (4:00)/One Vision (3:46)	1985	3.00	6.00	12.00
B-44372	I Want It All/Hang On In There	1989	—	2.50	5.00
B-44372 [PS]	I Want It All/Hang On In There	1989	—	2.50	5.00
7PRO-79685 [DJ]	Breakthru (same on both sides)	1989	3.00	6.00	12.00
—Vinyl is promo only					
ELEKTRA					
45226	Killer Queen/Flick of the Wrist	1975	2.00	4.00	8.00
45268	Keep Yourself Alive//Lily of the Valley/God Save the Queen	1975	2.00	4.00	8.00
45297	Bohemian Rhapsody/I'm in Love with My Car	1975	2.00	4.00	8.00
—Butterfly label					
45297	Bohemian Rhapsody/I'm in Love with My Car	1976	2.50	5.00	10.00
—Red label, much scarcer than butterfly label					
45318	You're My Best Friend/'39	1976	—	3.00	6.00
—Butterfly label					
45318	You're My Best Friend/'39	1976	2.50	5.00	10.00
—Red label, much scarcer than butterfly label					
45362	Somebody to Love/White Man	1976	—	3.00	6.00
—Butterfly label					
45362	Somebody to Love/White Man	1976	2.50	5.00	10.00
—Red label, much scarcer than butterfly label					
45385	Tie Your Mother Down/Drowse	1977	—	3.00	6.00
45412	Long Way/You and I	1977	2.00	4.00	8.00
45441	We Are the Champions/We Will Rock You	1977	—	3.00	6.00

Number	Title (A Side/B Side)	Yr	VG	VG+	NM
45441 [PS]	We Are the Champions/We Will Rock You	1977	2.50	5.00	10.00
45478	It's Late/Sheer Heart Attack	1978	—	3.00	6.00
45478 [PS]	It's Late/Sheer Heart Attack	1978	2.50	5.00	10.00
45541	Bicycle Race/Fat Bottomed Girls	1978	—	3.00	6.00
45541 [PS]	Bicycle Race/Fat Bottomed Girls	1978	3.00	6.00	12.00
45863	Keep Yourself Alive/Son and Daughter	1973	3.75	7.50	15.00
45884	Liar/Doing All Right	1974	3.00	6.00	12.00
45891	Seven Seas of Rhye/See What a Fool I've Been	1974	3.00	6.00	12.00
46008	Don't Stop Me Now/More of That Jazz	1979	—	3.00	6.00
46039	Jealousy/Fun It	1979	—	3.00	6.00
46532	We Will Rock You (Live)/Let Me Entertain You	1979	2.00	4.00	8.00
46579	Crazy Little Thing Called Love/Spread Your Wings	1979	—	2.00	4.00
46652	Play the Game/A Human Body	1980	—	2.00	4.00
46652 [PS]	Play the Game/A Human Body	1980	—	2.50	5.00
47031	Another One Bites the Dust/Don't Try Suicide	1980	—	2.00	4.00
47086	Need Your Loving Tonight/Rock It (prime jive)	1980	—	2.00	4.00
47092	Flash's Theme AKA Flash/Football Fight	1980	—	2.00	4.00
47092 [PS]	Flash's Theme AKA Flash/Football Fight	1980	—	2.50	5.00
47235	Under Pressure/Soul Brother	1981	—	2.00	4.00
—A-side with David Bowie					
47235 [PS]	Under Pressure/Soul Brother	1981	—	3.00	6.00
47452	Body Language/Life Is Real (Song for Lennon)	1981	—	2.00	4.00
—Most copies of this did not come with picture sleeves					
47452 [PS]	Body Language/Life Is Real (Song for Lennon)	1981	3.75	7.50	15.00
—Nude bodies sleeve					
47452 [PS]	Body Language/Life Is Real (Song for Lennon)	1981	2.50	5.00	10.00
—All-white sleeve					
69941	Back Chat/Staying Power	1982	—	2.00	4.00
69941 [PS]	Back Chat/Staying Power	1982	—	2.50	5.00
69981	Calling All Girls/Put Out the Fire	1981	—	2.00	4.00
69981 [PS]	Calling All Girls/Put Out the Fire	1981	—	2.50	5.00
HOLLYWOOD					
64725	We Are the Champions/These Are the Days of Our Lives	1992	—	2.00	4.00
64794	Bohemian Rhapsody/The Show Must Go On	1992	—	2.00	4.00

Albums

Number	Title	Yr	VG	VG+	NM
CAPITOL					
ST-12322	The Works	1984	2.50	5.00	10.00
SMAS-12476	A Kind of Magic	1986	2.50	5.00	10.00
C1-92357	The Miracle	1989	3.75	7.50	15.00
ELEKTRA					
6E-101	A Day at the Races	1977	2.50	5.00	10.00
—Butterfly, red, or red/black labels					
6E-112	News of the World	1977	2.50	5.00	10.00
6E-112 [DJ]	News of the World	1977	37.50	75.00	150.00
—White label promo with oversize cover and press kit					
6E-166	Jazz	1978	3.00	6.00	12.00
—With poster of the nude bicycle race					
6E-166	Jazz	1978	2.00	4.00	8.00
—Without poster of the nude bicycle race. Some copies had a sticker on the shrink wrap with an address at which the poster was available free.					
5E-513	The Game	1980	3.75	7.50	15.00
—With shiny, mirrorlike cover					
5E-513	The Game	1980	2.50	5.00	10.00
—With dull gray cover					
5E-564	Queen's Greatest Hits	1981	3.00	6.00	12.00
BB-702 [(2)]	Live Killers	1979	3.00	6.00	12.00
7E-1026	Sheer Heart Attack	1974	2.50	5.00	10.00
—Butterfly, red, or red/black labels					
7E-1026 [DJ]	Sheer Heart Attack	1974	12.50	25.00	50.00
—White label promo					
7E-1053	A Night at the Opera	1975	2.50	5.00	10.00
—Butterfly, red, or red/black labels					
EQ-5064 [Q]	Queen	1973	10.00	20.00	40.00
60128	Hot Space	1982	2.50	5.00	10.00
EKS-75064	Queen	1973	7.50	15.00	30.00
—With "Queen" gold-embossed on the cover					
EKS-75064	Queen	1973	2.50	5.00	10.00
—With "Queen" printed on the cover; butterfly, red, or red/black labels					
EKS-75064 [DJ]	Queen	1973	12.50	25.00	50.00
—White label promo					
EKS-75082	Queen II	1974	2.50	5.00	10.00
—Butterfly, red, or red/black labels					
EKS-75082 [DJ]	Queen II	1974	12.50	25.00	50.00
—White label promo					
HOLLYWOOD					
ED-62005 [PD]	Queen at the BBC	1995	25.00	50.00	100.00
—Promo-only picture disc (no U.S. stock vinyl)					
62017	Made in Heaven	1996	5.00	10.00	20.00
—Imported from Europe; the only distinguishing mark to make this a U.S. version is the Hollywood bar code, which was stuck to the shrink wrap					
MOBILE FIDELITY					
1-067	A Night at the Opera	1980	20.00	40.00	80.00
—Audiophile vinyl					
1-211	The Game	1995	7.50	15.00	30.00
—Audiophile vinyl					
1-256	A Day at the Races	1996	12.50	25.00	50.00
—Audiophile vinyl					

QUEEN, THE

45s

Number	Title	Yr	VG	VG+	NM
MERCURY					
71389	Honky Tonky/Somewhere Along the Line	1958	5.00	10.00	20.00

QUEEN'S NECTORINE MACHINE, THE

45s

Number	Title	Yr	VG	VG+	NM
ABC					
11172	I Got Trouble/Gypsy Lady	1969	3.75	7.50	15.00

Albums

Number	Title	Yr	VG	VG+	NM
ABC					
S-666	The Mystical Powers of Roving Tarot Gamble	1969	10.00	20.00	40.00

? (QUESTION MARK) AND THE MYSTERIANS

45s

Number	Title (A Side/B Side)	Yr	VG	VG+	NM
ABKCO					
4020	96 Tears/Can't Get Enough of You, Baby	1973	3.00	6.00	12.00
—Reissue; contains full-length version of A-side (Cameo single is edited)					
4033	I Need Somebody/Girl (You Captivate Me)	1973	3.00	6.00	12.00
—Reissue					
CAMEO					
428	96 Tears/Midnight Hour	1966	5.00	10.00	20.00
441	I Need Somebody/"8" Teen	1966	3.75	7.50	15.00
467	Can't Get Enough of You, Baby/Smokes	1967	3.75	7.50	15.00
479	Girl (You Captivate Me)/Got To	1967	3.75	7.50	15.00
496	Do Something to Me/Love Me, Baby	1967	3.75	7.50	15.00
CAPITOL					
2162	Make You Mine/I Love You, Baby (Like Nobody's Business)	1968	5.00	10.00	20.00
CHICORY					
410	Talk Is Cheap/She Goes to Church on Sunday	1968	7.50	15.00	30.00
COLLECTABLES					
4050	96 Tears/Midnight Hour	1997	—	2.00	4.00
—Yellow-orange vinyl; new recordings by the original group					
LUV					
159	Funky Lady/Hot N' Groovin'	1975	3.75	7.50	15.00
PA-GO-GO					
102	96 Tears/Midnight Hour	1965	175.00	350.00	700.00
SUPER K					
102	Hang In/Sha La La	1969	3.75	7.50	15.00
TANGERINE					
989	Ain't It a Shame/Turn Around Baby (Don't Ever Look Back)	1970	3.75	7.50	15.00

Albums

Number	Title	Yr	VG	VG+	NM
CAMEO					
C-2004 [M]	96 Tears	1966	25.00	50.00	100.00
CS-2004 [P]	96 Tears	1966	20.00	40.00	80.00
C-2006 [M]	Action	1967	37.50	75.00	150.00
CS-2006 [P]	Action	1967	25.00	50.00	100.00
COLLECTABLES					
COL 2004	Featuring 96 Tears	1997	3.00	6.00	12.00
—Re-recorded tracks; orange vinyl					

QUICK, THE

Featuring ERIC CARMEN.

45s

Number	Title	Yr	VG	VG+	NM
EPIC					
10516	Ain't Nothing Gonna Stop Me/Southern Comfort	1969	6.25	12.50	25.00

QUICKLY, TOMMY

45s

Number	Title	Yr	VG	VG+	NM
LIBERTY					
55732	It's As Simple As That/You Might As Well Forget Him	1964	2.50	5.00	10.00
55753	Wild Side of Life/Forget the Other Guy	1964	2.50	5.00	10.00

QUICKSILVER MESSENGER SERVICE

Includes records as "Quicksilver." Also see DINO VALENTI.

45s

Number	Title	Yr	VG	VG+	NM
CAPITOL					
2194	Pride of Man/Dino's Song	1968	3.00	6.00	12.00
2320	Stand By Me/Bears	1968	3.00	6.00	12.00
2557	Who Do You Love/Which Do You Love	1969	3.00	6.00	12.00
2670	Words Can't Say/Holy Holy	1969	3.00	6.00	12.00
2800	Shady Grove/Three or Four Feet from Home	1970	2.50	5.00	10.00
2920	Fresh Air/Freeway Flyer	1970	2.50	5.00	10.00
3046	Good Old Rock and Roll/What About Me	1971	2.00	4.00	8.00
3233	Hope/I Found Love	1971	2.00	4.00	8.00
3349	Doin' Time in the U.S.A./Changes	1972	2.00	4.00	8.00
3417	Fresh Air/Freeway Flyer	1972	2.00	4.00	8.00
4206	Gypsy Lights/Witches' Moon	1976	—	3.00	6.00

Albums

Number	Title	Yr	VG	VG+	NM
CAPITOL					
ST-120	Happy Trails	1969	7.50	15.00	30.00
—Black label with colorband					
ST-120	Happy Trails	1973	3.00	6.00	12.00
—Orange label					
SKAO-391	Shady Grove	1969	6.25	12.50	25.00
—Lime green label					
SKAO-391	Shady Grove	1973	3.00	6.00	12.00
—Orange label					
SMAS-498	Just for Love	1970	6.25	12.50	25.00
—Lime green label					
SMAS-498	Just for Love	1973	3.00	6.00	12.00
—Orange label					
SMAS-630	What About Me	1970	6.25	12.50	25.00
—Lime green label					
SMAS-630	What About Me	1973	3.00	6.00	12.00
—Orange label					
SW-819	Quicksilver	1971	6.25	12.50	25.00
—Red label with stylized "C" at top					
SW-819	Quicksilver	1973	3.00	6.00	12.00
—Orange label					
ST-2904	Quicksilver Messenger Service	1969	5.00	10.00	20.00
—Lime green or red label					
ST-2904	Quicksilver Messenger Service	1973	3.00	6.00	12.00
—Orange label					
ST 2904	Quicksilver Messenger Service	1968	10.00	210.00	40.00
—Black label with colorband; glossy black cover with red and silver foil-like printing					
SMAS-11002	Comin' Thru	1972	3.75	7.50	15.00
SVBB-11165 [(2)]	Anthology	1973	5.00	10.00	20.00
ST-11462	Solid Silver	1975	3.75	7.50	15.00
SM-11820	Solid Silver	1978	2.50	5.00	10.00
ST-12496	Peace By Piece	1986	2.50	5.00	10.00

Number	Title (A Side/B Side)	Yr	VG	VG+	NM
SN-16089	Quicksilver Messenger Service	1980	2.00	4.00	8.00
—Budget-line reissue					
SN-16090	Happy Trails	1980	2.00	4.00	8.00
—Budget-line reissue					
SN-16091	Quicksilver	1980	2.00	4.00	8.00
—Budget-line reissue					
SN-16092	What About Me	1980	2.00	4.00	8.00
—Budget-line reissue					
SN-16093	Just for Love	1980	2.00	4.00	8.00
—Budget-line reissue					
SN-16094	Shady Grove	1980	2.00	4.00	8.00
—Budget-line reissue					

QUILL
Albums
COTILLION

Number	Title (A Side/B Side)	Yr	VG	VG+	NM
SD 9017	Quill	1970	5.00	10.00	20.00

QUIN-TONES, THE
45s
HUNT

Number	Title (A Side/B Side)	Yr	VG	VG+	NM
321	Down the Aisle of Love/Please Dear	1958	12.50	25.00	50.00
322	There'll Be No Sorrow/What Am I to Do	1958	15.00	30.00	60.00
RED TOP					
108	Down the Aisle of Love/Please Dear	1958	30.00	60.00	120.00
—Red label					
108	Down the Aisle of Love/Please Dear	1958	10.00	20.00	40.00
116	Heavenly Father/I Watch the Stars	1959	25.00	50.00	100.00

QUINN, CAROLE
45s
MGM

Number	Title (A Side/B Side)	Yr	VG	VG+	NM
K-13265	Good Boy Gone Bad/What's So Sweet About Sweet Sixteen	1964	2.50	5.00	10.00
K-13326	Do Those Little Things/I'll Do It for You	1965	2.50	5.00	10.00

QUINTEROS, EDDIE
45s
BRENT

Number	Title (A Side/B Side)	Yr	VG	VG+	NM
7009	Come Dance with Me/Vivian	1960	7.50	15.00	30.00
7012	Please Don't Go/Lookin' for My Baby	1960	8.75	17.50	35.00
7014	Slow Down Sandy/Lindy Lou	1960	12.50	25.00	50.00

QUINTESSENCE
Albums
ISLAND

Number	Title (A Side/B Side)	Yr	VG	VG+	NM
SMAS-9301	Quintessence	1971	6.25	12.50	25.00
SW-9305	Dive Deep	1971	6.25	12.50	25.00

QUINTET, THE
Albums
UNITED ARTISTS

Number	Title (A Side/B Side)	Yr	VG	VG+	NM
UAS-5514	Future Tense	1971	3.75	7.50	15.00
UAS-5599	The Quintet	1972	3.75	7.50	15.00

QUINTONES, THE (1)
45s
CHESS

Number	Title (A Side/B Side)	Yr	VG	VG+	NM
1685	I Try So Hard/Ding Dong	1957	10.00	20.00	40.00

QUINTONES, THE (2)
45s
GEE

Number	Title (A Side/B Side)	Yr	VG	VG+	NM
1009	I'm Willing/Strange As It Seems	1956	250.00	500.00	1000.

QUINTONES, THE (3)
45s
PHILLIPS INT'L.

Number	Title (A Side/B Side)	Yr	VG	VG+	NM
3586	Times Sho' Gettin' Ruff/Softie	1963	5.00	10.00	20.00

QUINTONES, THE (U)
45s
JORDAN

Number	Title (A Side/B Side)	Yr	VG	VG+	NM
1601	The Lonely Telephone/Just a Little Loving	196?	75.00	150.00	300.00
PARK					
111/2	South Sea Island/More Than a Notion	1957	100.00	200.00	400.00

QUIVER
Also see SUTHERLAND BROTHERS AND QUIVER.
Albums
WARNER BROS.

Number	Title (A Side/B Side)	Yr	VG	VG+	NM
WS 1939	Quiver	1971	3.75	7.50	15.00
BS 2630	Gone in the Morning	1972	3.75	7.50	15.00

QUOTATIONS, THE
Several different groups.
45s
ADMIRAL

Number	Title (A Side/B Side)	Yr	VG	VG+	NM
753	In the Night/Oh No, I Still Love Her	1964	5.00	10.00	20.00
DEVENUS					
107	It Can Happen to You/You Don't Have to Worry	1968	3.00	6.00	12.00
DOWNSTAIRS					
1003	Night/Why Do You Do Me Like You Do	1970	2.00	4.00	8.00
IMPERIAL					
66338	Havin' a Good Time/Can I Have Someone	1968	2.50	5.00	10.00
66368	Havin' a Good Time (With My Baby)/Can I Have Someone (For Once)	1969	2.50	5.00	10.00
LIBERTY					
55527	Listen, My Children, And You Shall Hear/Speak Softly and Carry a Big Horn	1962	6.25	12.50	25.00
VERVE					
10245	Imagination/Ala-Men-Say	1961	7.50	15.00	30.00
10252	This Love of Mine/We'll Reach Heaven Together	1962	7.50	15.00	30.00
10261	See You in September/Sumemrtime Goodbye	1962	12.50	25.00	50.00

R

R.P.S.

Albums

MARS

Number	Title (A Side/B Side)	Yr	VG	VG+	NM
(# unknown)	R.P.S.	197?	20.00	40.00	80.00

RABBITT, EDDIE

45s

Number	Title (A Side/B Side)	Yr	VG	VG+	NM
20TH FOX					
474	Six Nights and Seven Days/Next to the Note	1964	5.00	10.00	20.00
CAPITOL					
NR-44527	On Second Thought/Only One Love in My Life	1990	—	2.00	4.00
—This may exist only as cassette, but we've put it in just in case					
NR-44538	Runnin' with the Wind/Feel Like a Stranger	1990	—	—	3.00
CAPITOL NASHVILLE					
S7-19347	Rockin' Around the Christmas Tree/Have Yourself a Merry Little Christmas	1996	—	—	3.00
DATE					
1599	The Bed/Holding On	1968	3.00	6.00	12.00
ELEKTRA					
378 [DJ]	Song of Ireland (same on both sides)	1978	3.75	7.50	15.00
—Promo only on green vinyl; small center hole					
45237	Forgive and Forget/Pure Love	1975	—	2.50	5.00
45269	I Should Have Married You/Sweet Janine	1975	—	2.50	5.00
45301	Drinkin' My Baby (Off My Mind)/When I Was Young	1976	—	2.50	5.00
45315	Rocky Mountian Music/Do You Right Tonight	1976	—	2.50	5.00
—Butterfly label; most, if not all, copies misspell "Mountain" as above					
45315	Rocky Mountian Music/Do You Right Tonight	1976	—	3.00	6.00
—Red label; most, if not all, copies misspell "Mountain" as above					
45357	Two Dollars in the Jukebox/Don't Wanna Make Love	1976	—	2.50	5.00
—Butterfly label					
45357	Two Dollars in the Jukebox/Don't Wanna Make Love	1976	—	3.00	6.00
—Red label					
45381	Could You Love a Poor Boy, Dolly/There's Someone She Lies To (To Lie Here with Me)	1977	—	3.00	6.00
45390	I Can't Help Myself/She Loves Me Like She Means It	1977	—	2.00	4.00
45418	We Can't Go On Living Like This/We Made Love Beautiful	1977	—	2.00	4.00
45461	Hearts on Fire/Girl on My Mind	1978	—	2.00	4.00
45488	You Don't Love Me Anymore/Caroline	1978	—	2.00	4.00
45531	I Just Want to Love You/Crossin' the Mississippi	1978	—	2.00	4.00
45554	Every Which Way But Loose/Under the Double Eagle	1978	—	2.00	4.00
45895	You Get to Me/Que Pasa	1974	—	2.50	5.00
46053	Suspicions/I Don't Want to Make Love (With Anyone But You)	1979	—	2.00	4.00
46558	Pour Me Another Tequila/I Will Never Let You Go	1979	—	2.00	4.00
46613	Gone Too Far/Loveline	1980	—	2.00	4.00
46656	Drivin' My Life Away/Pretty Lady	1980	—	2.00	4.00
47066	I Love a Rainy Night/Short Road to Love	1980	—	2.00	4.00
47174	Step By Step/My Only Wish	1981	—	2.00	4.00
47174 [PS]	Step By Step/My Only Wish	1981	—	3.00	6.00
47239	Someone Could Lose a Heart Tonight/Nobody Loves Me Like My Baby	1981	—	2.00	4.00
47435	I Don't Know Where to Start/Skip-A-Beat	1982	—	2.00	4.00
69936	You and I/All My Life, All My Love	1982	—	2.00	4.00
—A-side: With Crystal Gayle					
RCA					
5012-7-R	Gotta Have You/Singing in the Subway	1986	—	—	3.00
5093-7-R	When We Make Love/(B-side unknown)	1987	—	—	3.00
5238-7-R	Wanna Dance with You/Gotta Have You	1987	—	—	3.00
8306-7-R	The Wanderer/Workin' Out	1988	—	—	3.00
8716-7-R	We Must Be Doing Something Right/He's a Cheater	1988	—	—	3.00
8819-7-R	That's Why I Fell in Love with You/She's An Old Cadillac	1988	—	—	3.00
PB-14192	A World Without Love/1-2-3, You Really Got a Hold on Me (The Wrestling Song)	1985	—	—	3.00
PB-14317	Repetitive Love/Letter from Home	1986	—	—	3.00
PB-14377	Both to Each Other (Friends and Lovers)/A World Without Love	1986	—	—	3.00
—With Juice Newton					
PB-14377 [PS]	Both to Each Other (Friends and Lovers)/A World Without Love	1986	—	2.50	5.00
UNIVERSAL					
UVL-66025	On Second Thought/Only One Love in My Life	1989	—	2.00	4.00
WARNER BROS.					
28976	She's Comin' Back to Say Goodbye/Dial That Telephone	1985	—	2.00	4.00
29089	Warning Sign/Go to Sleep, Big Bertha	1985	—	2.00	4.00
29186	The Best Year of My Life/Over There	1984	—	2.00	4.00
29279	B-B-B-Burnin' Up with Love/747	1984	—	2.00	4.00
29431	Nothing Like Falling in Love/Gone Too Far	1983	—	2.00	4.00
29512	Our Love Will Survive/You Put the Beat in My Heart	1983	—	2.00	4.00
29712	You Can't Run from Love/You Got Me Now	1983	—	2.00	4.00

Albums

Number	Title (A Side/B Side)	Yr	VG	VG+	NM
ELEKTRA					
CM-3	Eddie Rabbitt	1975	3.75	7.50	15.00
6E-127	Variations	1978	3.00	6.00	12.00
6E-181	Loveline	1979	2.50	5.00	10.00
6E-235	The Best of Eddie Rabbitt	1979	2.50	5.00	10.00
6E-276	Horizon	1980	2.50	5.00	10.00
5E-532	Step By Step	1981	2.50	5.00	10.00
7E-1065	Rocky Mountain Music	1976	3.75	7.50	15.00
—Butterfly label					
7E-1065	Rocky Mountain Music	198?	2.00	4.00	8.00
—Red label					
7E-1105	Rabbitt	1977	3.75	7.50	15.00
—Butterfly label					
7E-1105	Rabbitt	198?	2.00	4.00	8.00
—Red label					
60160	Radio Romance	1982	2.50	5.00	10.00
RCA					
6373-1-R	I Wanna Dance with You	1988	2.00	4.00	8.00
RCA VICTOR					
AHL1-7041	Rabbitt Trax	1986	2.00	4.00	8.00
WARNER BROS.					
6E-127	Variations	1983	2.00	4.00	8.00
—Reissue of Elektra LP					
6E-181	Loveline	1983	2.00	4.00	8.00
—Reissue of Elektra LP					
6E-235	The Best of Eddie Rabbitt	1983	2.00	4.00	8.00
—Reissue of Elektra LP					
6E-276	Horizon	1983	2.00	4.00	8.00
—Reissue of Elektra LP					
5E-532	Step by Step	1983	2.00	4.00	8.00
—Reissue of Elektra LP					
7E-1065	Rocky Mountain Music	1983	2.00	4.00	8.00
—Reissue of Elektra LP					
23925	Greatest Hits, Volume II	1983	2.50	5.00	10.00
25251	The Best Year of My Life	1984	2.50	5.00	10.00
25278	#1's	1985	2.50	5.00	10.00
60160	Radio Romance	1983	2.00	4.00	8.00
—Reissue of Elektra LP					

RABBLE, THE

Albums

ROULETTE

Number	Title (A Side/B Side)	Yr	VG	VG+	NM
SR-42010	The Rabble	1968	37.50	75.00	150.00

RABIN, MIKE, AND THE DEMONS

Also see FREDDIE AND THE DREAMERS.

45s

TOWER

Number	Title (A Side/B Side)	Yr	VG	VG+	NM
109	Head Over Heels/I'm Leaving You	1964	3.75	7.50	15.00

RACE MARBLES, THE

45s

TOWER

Number	Title (A Side/B Side)	Yr	VG	VG+	NM
194	Like a Dribbling Fram/Someday	1965	7.50	15.00	30.00

RACHEL AND THE REVOLVERS

45s

DOT

Number	Title (A Side/B Side)	Yr	VG	VG+	NM
16392	The Revo-Lution/Number One	1962	125.00	250.00	500.00
—Produced by Brian Wilson					

RACKET SQUAD, THE

45s

JUBILEE

Number	Title (A Side/B Side)	Yr	VG	VG+	NM
5591	Hung Up/Higher Than High	1967	7.50	15.00	30.00
5601	Little Red Wagon/(Just Like) Romeo and Juliet	1967	5.00	10.00	20.00
5613	The Loser/No Fair at All	1968	5.00	10.00	20.00
5623	Let's Dance to the Beat of My Heart/Higher Than High	1968	5.00	10.00	20.00
5628	That's How Much I Love My Baby/(B-side unknown)	1968	5.00	10.00	20.00
5638	Suburban Life/The Loser	1968	5.00	10.00	20.00
5657	I'll Never Forget Your Love/(B-side unknown)	1969	5.00	10.00	20.00
5682	In Your Arms/(B-side unknown)	1969	7.50	15.00	30.00
5694	Roller Coaster Ride/Coal Town	1970	7.50	15.00	30.00

Albums

JUBILEE

Number	Title (A Side/B Side)	Yr	VG	VG+	NM
JGS-8015	The Racket Squad	1968	10.00	20.00	40.00
JGS-8026	Corners of Your Mind	1969	10.00	20.00	40.00

RADHA KRISHNA TEMPLE

45s

APPLE

Number	Title (A Side/B Side)	Yr	VG	VG+	NM
1810	Hare Krishna Mantra/Prayer to the Spiritual Masters	1969	2.00	4.00	8.00
1810 [PS]	Hare Krishna Mantra/Prayer to the Spiritual Masters	1969	100.00	200.00	400.00
—Only one copy is known to exist. The price is highly speculative.					
1821	Govinda/Govinda Jai Jai	1970	2.00	4.00	8.00
1821	Govinda/Govinda Jai Jai	1970	2.50	5.00	10.00
—With Capitol logo on B-side label bottom					
1821 [PS]	Govinda/Govinda Jai Jai	1970	2.50	5.00	10.00
PRO-5013/4 [DJ]	Govinda/Govinda Jai Jai	1970	6.25	12.50	25.00
—With an edit of the A-side					
SPRO-5067/8 [DJ]	Govinda (Edit)/Govinda	1970	10.00	20.00	40.00

Albums

APPLE

Number	Title (A Side/B Side)	Yr	VG	VG+	NM
SKAO-3376	The Radha Krishna Temple	1971	5.00	10.00	20.00

RADIANTS, THE

45s

Number	Title (A Side/B Side)	Yr	VG	VG+	NM
ABC					
12394	I Need a Vacation/Just Like You	1978	—	2.50	5.00
CHESS					
1832	Father Knows Best/One Day I'll SHow You	1962	3.75	7.50	15.00
1849	Please Don't Leave Me/Heartbreak Society	1963	3.75	7.50	15.00
1872	I'm in Love/Shy Guy	1963	3.75	7.50	15.00
1887	Noble the Bargain Man/I Got to Dance to Keep My Baby	1964	3.75	7.50	15.00
1904	Voice Your Choice/If I Only Had You	1964	3.00	6.00	12.00
1925	It Ain't No Big Thing/I Got a Girl	1965	3.00	6.00	12.00

Number	Title (A Side/B Side)	Yr	VG	VG+	NM
1939	Whole Lot of Love/Tomorrow	1965	3.00	6.00	12.00
1954	I Want to Thank You, Baby/Baby You've Got It	1966	3.00	6.00	12.00
—As "Maurice and the Radiants"					
1986	(Don't It Make You) Feel Kind of Bad/Anything You Do Is Alright	1967	3.00	6.00	12.00
2021	Don't Take Your Love/The Clown Is Clever	1967	3.00	6.00	12.00
2037	Hold On/I'm Glad I'm the Loser	1968	3.00	6.00	12.00
2057	Tears of a Clown/I'm Just a Man	1968	3.00	6.00	12.00
2066	Choo Choo/Ida Mae Foster	1969	2.50	5.00	10.00
2078	Book of Love/Another Mule Is Kicking In Your Stall	1969	2.50	5.00	10.00
2083	I'm So Glad I'm the Loser/Shadow of a Doubt	1970	2.50	5.00	10.00
TWINIGHT					
153	My Sunshine Girl/Don't Wanna Face the Truth	1971	2.00	4.00	8.00

RAE, CHARLOTTE

Albums

Number	Title (A Side/B Side)	Yr	VG	VG+	NM
VANGUARD					
VRS-9004 [M]	Songs I Taught My Mother	1956	10.00	20.00	40.00

RAELETTS, THE

Backing vocalists for RAY CHARLES.

45s

Number	Title (A Side/B Side)	Yr	VG	VG+	NM
TANGERINE					
972	One Hurt Deserves Another/One Room Paradise	1967	2.00	4.00	8.00
976	Into Something Fine/Lover's Blues	1967	2.00	4.00	8.00
984	I'm Gett'n Long Alright/All I Need Is His Love	1968	2.00	4.00	8.00
986	I Want to Thank You/It's Almost Here	1968	2.00	4.00	8.00
1006	I Want To (Do Everything for You)/Keep It to Yourself	1970	2.00	4.00	8.00
1014	Bad Water/That Goes to Show You	1970	2.00	4.00	8.00
1017	Here I Go Again/Leave My Man Alone	1971	2.00	4.00	8.00
1024	Come Get It, I Got It/Try a Little Kindness	197?	2.00	4.00	8.00
1029	You Must Be Doing Alright/You Have a Way with Me	197?	2.00	4.00	8.00
1031	Many Rivers to Cross/If You Wanna Keep Him	197?	2.00	4.00	8.00

Albums

Number	Title (A Side/B Side)	Yr	VG	VG+	NM
TANGERINE					
TRCS-1515	Yesterday, Today, Tomorrow	1972	3.75	7.50	15.00

RAFFERTY, GERRY

Also see THE HUMBLEBUMS; STEALERS WHEEL

45s

Number	Title (A Side/B Side)	Yr	VG	VG+	NM
BLUE THUMB					
231	Can I Have My Money Back/Sign on the Dotted Line	1973	2.00	4.00	8.00
LIBERTY					
1482	Good Intentions/Standing at the Gates	1982	—	2.00	4.00
SIGNPOST					
70001	Make You, Break You/Mary Skeffington	1972	2.50	5.00	10.00
UNITED ARTISTS					
XW1098	Mattie's Rag/City to City	1977	—	2.50	5.00
XW1192	Baker Street/Big Change in the Weather	1978	2.00	4.00	8.00
—Mispress with the full-length album version of "Baker Street" on A-side There is no "E" in the trail-off wax.					
XW1192	Baker Street/Big Change in the Weather	1978	—	2.00	4.00
—Regular press with the edited, slightly sped-up version of "Baker Street" on A-side					
XW1233	Right Down the Line/Waiting for the Day	1978	—	2.00	4.00
XW1233 [PS]	Right Down the Line/Waiting for the Day	1978	—	2.50	5.00
XW1266	Home and Dry/Mattie's Rag	1978	—	2.00	4.00
XW1298	Days Gone Down (Still Got That Light in Your Eyes)/Why Won't You Talk to Me	1979	—	2.00	4.00
1316	Get It Right Next Time/It's Gonna Be a Long Night	1979	—	2.00	4.00
1366	The Royal Mile/In Transit	1980	—	2.00	4.00

Albums

Number	Title (A Side/B Side)	Yr	VG	VG+	NM
ABC/BLUE THUMB					
6031	Can I Have My Money Back?	1978	3.00	6.00	12.00
BLUE THUMB					
BT-58	Can I Have My Money Back?	1973	5.00	10.00	20.00
LIBERTY					
LO-840	City to City	1981	2.00	4.00	8.00
—Reissue of United Artists 840					
LOO-958	Night and Day	1981	2.00	4.00	8.00
—Reissue of United Artists 958					
LOO-1039	Snakes and Ladders	1981	2.00	4.00	8.00
—Reissue of United Artists 1039					
LT-51132	Sleepwalking	1982	2.50	5.00	10.00
MOBILE FIDELITY					
1-058	City to City	1980	10.00	20.00	40.00
—Audiophile vinyl					
POLYDOR					
835449-1	North and South	1988	2.50	5.00	10.00
UNITED ARTISTS					
UA-LA840-H	City to City	1978	2.50	5.00	10.00
UA-LA958-I	Night and Day	1979	2.50	5.00	10.00
LOO-1039	Snakes and Ladders	1980	2.50	5.00	10.00
VISA					
7006	Gerry Rafferty	1978	2.50	5.00	10.00
—Reissue of Blue Thumb material					

RAG DOLLS, THE

45s

Number	Title (A Side/B Side)	Yr	VG	VG+	NM
MALA					
493	Dusty/Hey Hoagy	1964	2.50	5.00	10.00
499	Baby's Gone/We Almost Made It	1965	2.50	5.00	10.00
506	Little Girl Tears/Put a Ring on My Finger	1965	2.50	5.00	10.00
PARKWAY					
921	Society Girl/Ragen (Society Girl Bossa Nova)	1964	3.00	6.00	12.00

RAGLAND, LOU

45s

Number	Title (A Side/B Side)	Yr	VG	VG+	NM
AMY					
988	Travel Alone/Big Wheel	1967	50.00	100.00	200.00

RAIDERS, THE (1)

See PAUL REVERE AND THE RAIDERS.

RAIDERS, THE (2)

45s

Number	Title (A Side/B Side)	Yr	VG	VG+	NM
ANDEX					
4015	Yoo Hoo/Hocus Pocus	1958	30.00	60.00	120.00
ATCO					
6125	Raiders from Outer Space/The Castle of Love	1958	20.00	40.00	80.00
BRUNSWICK					
55090	Walking Through the Jungle/My Steady Girl	1958	10.00	20.00	40.00

RAIDERS, THE (3)

45s

Number	Title (A Side/B Side)	Yr	VG	VG+	NM
LIBERTY					
55393	Dardanella/What Time Is It	1961	7.50	15.00	30.00

Albums

Number	Title (A Side/B Side)	Yr	VG	VG+	NM
LIBERTY					
LRP-3225 [M]	Twistin' the Country Classics	1962	6.25	12.50	25.00
LST-7225 [S]	Twistin' the Country Classics	1962	7.50	15.00	30.00

RAIDERS, THE (4)

45s

Number	Title (A Side/B Side)	Yr	VG	VG+	NM
SPRING-DALE					
102	Raiders' Rhythm/Tall Texas Women	1964	12.50	25.00	50.00

RAIDERS, THE (5)

45s

Number	Title (A Side/B Side)	Yr	VG	VG+	NM
VAN					
00262	Stick Shift/Skipping Around	1962	12.50	25.00	50.00
00663	On a Straight Away/It's Motivation	1963	5.00	10.00	20.00
00763	Supercharger/Cruisin' Low	1963	5.00	10.00	20.00
01064	Raisin' Cain/Repetition	1964	5.00	10.00	20.00
VEE JAY					
504	Stick Shift/Skipping Around	1963	5.00	10.00	20.00

RAIN

At least two different groups.

45s

Number	Title (A Side/B Side)	Yr	VG	VG+	NM
A.P.I.					
336	Outta My Life/E.S.P.	1967	10.00	20.00	40.00
337	Substitute/Hear You Cry	1967	10.00	20.00	40.00
LONDON					
107	Outta My Life/E.S.P.	1967	6.25	12.50	25.00
111	Substitute/Hear You Cry	1967	7.50	15.00	30.00
MGM					
13622	Take It Away/City Lovin'	1966	6.25	12.50	25.00
PARAMOUNT					
0087	Show Me the Road Home/Funky Junky Blues	1971	5.00	10.00	20.00

Albums

Number	Title (A Side/B Side)	Yr	VG	VG+	NM
PROJECT 3					
PR 5072 SD	New Rock Group	1972	6.25	12.50	25.00
WHAZOO					
USR-3049	Live Christmas Night	1969	37.50	75.00	150.00
—Issued with no cover					

RAINBO

Sissy Spacek is on this record.

45s

Number	Title (A Side/B Side)	Yr	VG	VG+	NM
ROULETTE					
7030	John You Went Too Far This Time/C'mon Teach Me to Live	1969	5.00	10.00	20.00

RAINBOW

45s

Number	Title (A Side/B Side)	Yr	VG	VG+	NM
MERCURY					
76146	Stone Cold/Rock Fever	1982	—	2.00	4.00
76146 [PS]	Stone Cold/Rock Fever	1982	—	2.50	5.00
815660-7	Street of Dreams/Anybody There	1983	—	2.00	4.00
815660-7 [PS]	Street of Dreams/Anybody There	1983	—	2.00	4.00
POLYDOR					
2014	Since You Been Gone/Bad Girls	1979	—	2.00	4.00
2163	I Surrender/Vielleicht Das Nachster Leit	1981	—	2.00	4.00
14290	Snake Charmer/Man on the Silver Mountain	1975	—	3.00	6.00
—As "Blackmore's Rainbow"					
14481	Long Live Rock 'n Roll/Sensitive to Light	1978	—	2.00	4.00

Albums

Number	Title (A Side/B Side)	Yr	VG	VG+	NM
MERCURY					
SRM-1-4041	Straight Between the Eyes	1982	2.50	5.00	10.00
815305-1	Bent Out of Shape	1983	2.50	5.00	10.00
827987-1 [(2)]	Finyl Vinyl	1986	3.00	6.00	12.00
OYSTER					
OY-1-1601	Rainbow Rising	1976	3.00	6.00	12.00
OY-2-1801 [(2)]	On Stage	1977	3.75	7.50	15.00
OY-6049	Ritchie Blackmore's R-A-I-N-B-O-W	1975	3.00	6.00	12.00
POLYDOR					
PX-1-502 [EP]	Jealous Lover	1981	2.00	4.00	8.00
PD-1-6143	Long Live Rock 'n' Roll	1978	2.50	5.00	10.00
PD-1-6221	Down to Earth	1979	2.50	5.00	10.00
PD-1-6316	Difficult to Cure	1981	2.50	5.00	10.00
823655-1	Rainbow Rising	1985	2.00	4.00	8.00
—Reissue					
823656-1 [(2)]	On Stage	1985	2.50	5.00	10.00
—Reissue					

Number	Title (A Side/B Side)	Yr	VG	VG+	NM
823705-1	Down to Earth	1985	2.00	4.00	8.00
—Reissue					
825089-1	Ritchie Blackmore's R-A-I-N-B-O-W	1985	2.00	4.00	8.00
—Reissue					
825090-1	Long Live Rock 'n' Roll	1985	2.00	4.00	8.00
—Reissue					
825383-1	Difficult to Cure	1985	2.00	4.00	8.00
—Reissue					
881516-1 [EP]	Jealous Lover	1985	—	3.00	6.00
—Reissue					

RAINBOW (2)

Albums

Number	Title (A Side/B Side)	Yr	VG	VG+	NM
GNP CRESCENDO					
GNPS-2049	After the Storm	1969	6.25	12.50	25.00

RAINBOW PRESS, THE

45s

Number	Title (A Side/B Side)	Yr	VG	VG+	NM
MR. G					
817	There's a War On/Better Way	1968	3.75	7.50	15.00
821	Great White Whale/The Last Platoon	1969	3.75	7.50	15.00

Albums

Number	Title (A Side/B Side)	Yr	VG	VG+	NM
MR. G					
9003	There's a War On	1968	7.50	15.00	30.00
9004	Sunday Funnies	1969	7.50	15.00	30.00

RAINBOW PROMISE, THE

Albums

Number	Title (A Side/B Side)	Yr	VG	VG+	NM
NEW WINE					
LPS-251-01	The Rainbow Promise	1970	75.00	150.00	300.00

RAINBOWS, THE (1)

45s

Number	Title (A Side/B Side)	Yr	VG	VG+	NM
ARGYLE					
1012	Shirley/Stay	1962	6.25	12.50	25.00
FIRE					
1012	Mary Lee/Evening	1960	5.00	10.00	20.00
PILGRIM					
703	Mary Lee/Evening	1956	12.50	25.00	50.00
711	Shirley/Stay	1956	50.00	100.00	200.00
RAMA					
209	Minnie/They Say	1956	150.00	300.00	600.00
RED ROBIN					
134	Mary Lee/Evening	1955	150.00	300.00	600.00
—Note: Red Robin 141 is a bootleg					

RAINBOWS, THE (2)

45s

Number	Title (A Side/B Side)	Yr	VG	VG+	NM
DAVE					
908	I Know/Only a Picture	1963	7.50	15.00	30.00
909	It Wouldn't Be Right/Family Monkey	1963	7.50	15.00	30.00

RAINBOWS, THE (3)

45s

Number	Title (A Side/B Side)	Yr	VG	VG+	NM
DOT					
16612	My Ringo/He's Hooked on J's	1964	3.75	7.50	15.00
16920	Color of Love/Down the Block	1966	2.50	5.00	10.00

RAINBOWS, THE (4)

45s

Number	Title (A Side/B Side)	Yr	VG	VG+	NM
EPIC					
9900	Balla Balla/Ju Ju Hand	1966	2.50	5.00	10.00
JAMIE					
1339	Balla Balla/Ju Ju Hand	1967	2.00	4.00	8.00

RAINBOWS, THE (U)

Some of these could be by groups (2), (3) or (4).

45s

Number	Title (A Side/B Side)	Yr	VG	VG+	NM
GRAMO					
5508	Till Tomorrow/Mama, Take Your Daughter Back	196?	5.00	10.00	20.00
MERCURY					
72068	Gonna Go Down/Dreamwalk	1962	3.75	7.50	15.00
MGM					
13058	Old Man's Twist/Straight Ahead	1962	5.00	10.00	20.00
RONNIE					
202	The Christmas Song/Love Me	19??	2.50	5.00	10.00
—B-side by the Mellow Moods					

RAINDROPS, THE (1)

JEFF BARRY and ELLIE GREENWICH.

45s

Number	Title (A Side/B Side)	Yr	VG	VG+	NM
JUBILEE					
5444	What a Guy/It's So Wonderful	1963	5.00	10.00	20.00
5455	The Kind of Boy You Can't Forget/Even Though You Can't Dance	1963	6.25	12.50	25.00
5466	That Boy John/Hanky Panky	1963	6.25	12.50	25.00
5469	Book of Love/I Won't Cry	1964	5.00	10.00	20.00
5475	Let;s Go Together/You Got What I Like	1964	5.00	10.00	20.00
5487	One More Tear/Another Boy Like Mine	1964	5.00	10.00	20.00
5497	Don't Let Go/My Mama Don't Like Him	1965	5.00	10.00	20.00

Albums

Number	Title (A Side/B Side)	Yr	VG	VG+	NM
JUBILEE					
JGM-5023 [M]	The Raindrops	1963	37.50	75.00	150.00
JGS-5023 [S]	The Raindrops	1963	75.00	150.00	300.00

RAINDROPS, THE (2)

45s

Number	Title (A Side/B Side)	Yr	VG	VG+	NM
CAPITOL					
F-4136	Rockababy Rock/Rain	1959	7.50	15.00	30.00

RAINDROPS, THE (3)

45s

Number	Title (A Side/B Side)	Yr	VG	VG+	NM
CORSAIR					
104	Maybe/Love Is Like a Mountain	1960	20.00	40.00	80.00
DORE					
561	Maybe/Love Is Like a Mountain	1960	6.25	12.50	25.00

RAINDROPS, THE (4)

45s

Number	Title (A Side/B Side)	Yr	VG	VG+	NM
IMPERIAL					
5785	I Remember in the Still of the Night/Sweet Song	1961	7.50	15.00	30.00

RAINDROPS, THE (5)

45s

Number	Title (A Side/B Side)	Yr	VG	VG+	NM
SPIN-IT					
104	(I Found) Heaven in Love/I Prayed for Gold	1956	50.00	100.00	200.00
106	Little One/Rockin' on the Farm	1956	50.00	100.00	200.00

RAINDROPS, THE (U)

Not sure which group this is.

45s

Number	Title (A Side/B Side)	Yr	VG	VG+	NM
HAMILTON					
50021	Oh Why/Without Love, Love, Love	1960	5.00	10.00	20.00

RAINY DAYS, THE

45s

Number	Title (A Side/B Side)	Yr	VG	VG+	NM
JUBILEE					
5517	He Was a Friend of Mine/Don't Want No Fool	1965	3.00	6.00	12.00
PANIK					
7542	Turn on Your Lovelight/Go On and Cry	1966	6.25	12.50	25.00
7566	I Can Only Give You Anything/(B-side unknown)	1966	6.25	12.50	25.00

RAINY DAZE, THE

45s

Number	Title (A Side/B Side)	Yr	VG	VG+	NM
CHICORY					
404	That Acapulco Gold/In My Mind Lives a Forest	1967	3.75	7.50	15.00
UNI					
55002	That Acapulco Gold/In My Mind Lives a Forest	1967	2.50	5.00	10.00
55011	Discount City/Good Morning, Mr. Smith	1967	2.50	5.00	10.00
55026	Stop Sign/Blood of Oblivion	1967	2.50	5.00	10.00
WHITE WHALE					
279	My Door Is Always Open/Make Me Laugh	1968	2.50	5.00	10.00

Albums

Number	Title (A Side/B Side)	Yr	VG	VG+	NM
UNI					
3002 [M]	That Acapulco Gold	1967	5.00	10.00	20.00
73002 [S]	That Acapulco Gold	1967	6.25	12.50	25.00

RAITT, BONNIE

12-Inch Singles

Number	Title (A Side/B Side)	Yr	VG	VG+	NM
WARNER BROS.					
PRO-A-1030 [DJ]	Me and the Boys (same on both sides)	1982	3.00	6.00	12.00
PRO-A-2536 [DJ]	No Way to Treat a Lady (same on both sides)	1986	—	3.00	6.00
PRO-A-2613 [DJ]	Who But a Fool (same on both sides)	1986	—	3.00	6.00
PRO-A-2655 [DJ]	Crimes of Passion (same on both sides)	1986	—	3.00	6.00

45s

Number	Title (A Side/B Side)	Yr	VG	VG+	NM
ARISTA					
12795	You Got It/Feeling of Falling	1995	—	—	3.00
A&M					
1249	Baby Mine/Mickey Mouse March	1988	—	2.00	4.00
—A-side with Was (Not Was); B-side by Aaron Neville					
1249 [PS]	Baby Mine/Mickey Mouse March	1988	—	2.00	4.00
CAPITOL					
S7-17818	Love Sneakin' Up on You/Hell to Pay	1994	—	—	3.00
S7-18039	You/Feeling of Falling	1994	—	2.00	4.00
—Red vinyl					
S7-18299	Storm Warning/Longing in Their Hearts	1995	—	—	3.00
B-44364	Nick of Time/The Road's My Middle Name	1989	—	2.00	4.00
B-44365	Thing Called Love/The Road's My Middle Name	1989	—	2.00	4.00
B-44365 [PS]	Thing Called Love/The Road's My Middle Name	1989	—	2.00	4.00
NR-44729	I Can't Make You Love Me/Come to Me	1991	—	2.00	4.00
—White label, but not a promo					
S7-56799	All at Once/Come to Me	1992	—	2.00	4.00
S7-57698	Not the Only One/All at Once	1992	—	2.00	4.00
S7-57741	I Can't Make You Love Me/Something to Talk About	1992	—	2.00	4.00
S7-57879	Good Man, Good Woman/Nick of Time	1992	—	2.00	4.00
—A-side: Duet with Delbert McClinton					
58844	The Fundamental Things/Cold, Cold, Cold	2000	—	—	3.00
7PRO-79940 [DJ]	Have a Heart (same on both sides)	1990	2.00	4.00	8.00
—Vinyl is promo only					
FULL MOON					
49612	Once in a Lifetime/You're Only Lonely	1980	—	2.00	4.00
—B-side by J.D. Souther					
FULL MOON/ASYLUM					
47033	Don't It Make You Wanna Dance/Orange Blossom Special	1980	—	2.50	5.00
—B-side by Gilley's Urban Cowboy Band					
47033 [PS]	Don't It Make You Wanna Dance/Orange Blossom Special	1980	—	3.00	6.00
REPRISE					
1370	When You Touch Me This Way/Since I've Been With You Babe	1976	—	2.50	5.00
—By Geoff Muldaur and Bonnie Raitt					
WARNER BROS.					
7554	Bluebird/Women Be Wise	1972	2.00	4.00	8.00
7645	Too Long at the Fair/Under the Falling Sky	1972	2.00	4.00	8.00
7758	Everybody's Cryin' Mercy/You've Been in Love Too Long	1973	—	3.00	6.00
8044	I Got Plenty/You Got to Be Ready for Love	1974	—	3.00	6.00
8166	Good Enough/My First Night Alone Without You	1975	—	3.00	6.00
8189	Run Like a Thief/Walk Out the Front Door	1976	—	2.50	5.00

Number	Title (A Side/B Side)	Yr	VG	VG+	NM
8382	Runaway/Louise	1977	—	2.50	5.00
8430	Two Lives/Three Time Loser	1977	—	2.50	5.00
8485	Gamblin' Man/About to Make Me Leave Home	1977	—	2.50	5.00
28450	Crimes of Passion/Stand Up to the Night	1987	—	2.00	4.00
28615	No Way to Treat a Lady/Stand Up to the Night	1986	—	2.00	4.00
29992	River of Tears/Me and the Boys	1982	—	2.00	4.00
49116	You're Gonna Get What's Comin'/The Glow	1979	—	2.00	4.00
49116 [PS]	You're Gonna Get What's Comin'/The Glow	1979	2.00	4.00	8.00
49185	Wild for You Baby/(I Could Have Been Your) Best Old Friend	1980	—	2.00	4.00
50022	Can't Get Enough/Keep This Heart in Mind	1982	—	2.00	4.00

Albums

CAPITOL

Number	Title (A Side/B Side)	Yr	VG	VG+	NM
C1-91268	Nick of Time	1989	3.00	6.00	12.00
C1-96111	Luck of the Draw	1991	3.75	7.50	15.00

DCC COMPACT CLASSICS

Number	Title (A Side/B Side)	Yr	VG	VG+	NM
LPZ-2025	Nick of Time	1996	5.00	10.00	20.00
—Audiophile vinyl					
LPZ-2031	Luck of the Draw	1997	5.00	10.00	20.00
—Audiophile vinyl					

WARNER BROS.

Number	Title (A Side/B Side)	Yr	VG	VG+	NM
WS 1953	Bonnie Raitt	1971	3.75	7.50	15.00
—Green "WB" label					
WS 1953	Bonnie Raitt	1973	3.00	6.00	12.00
—"Burbank" palm trees label					
WS 1953	Bonnie Raitt	1979	2.00	4.00	8.00
—White or tan label					
BS 2643	Give It Up	1972	3.75	7.50	15.00
—Green "WB" label					
BS 2643	Give It Up	1973	3.00	6.00	12.00
—"Burbank" palm trees label					
BS 2643	Give It Up	1979	2.00	4.00	8.00
—White or tan label					
BS 2729	Takin' My Timo	1973	3.00	6.00	12.00
—"Burbank" palm trees label					
BS 2729	Takin' My Time	1979	2.00	4.00	8.00
—White or tan label					
BS 2818	Streetlights	1974	3.00	6.00	12.00
—"Burbank" palm trees label					
BS 2818	Streetlights	1979	2.00	4.00	8.00
—White or tan label					
BS 2864	Home Plate	1975	3.00	6.00	12.00
—"Burbank" palm trees label					
BS 2864	Home Plate	1979	2.00	4.00	8.00
—White or tan label					
BS 2990	Sweet Forgiveness	1977	3.00	6.00	12.00
—"Burbank" palm trees label					
BS 2990	Sweet Forgiveness	1979	2.00	4.00	8.00
—White or tan label					
HS 3369	The Glow	1979	3.00	6.00	12.00
BSK 3630	Green Light	1982	3.00	6.00	12.00
25486	Nine Lives	1986	2.50	5.00	10.00

RAJAHS, THE

45s

KLIK

Number	Title (A Side/B Side)	Yr	VG	VG+	NM
7805	I Fell in Love/Shifting Sands	1957	75.00	150.00	300.00

RALLY PACKS, THE

STEVE BARRI and P.F. SLOAN with JAN AND DEAN.

45s

IMPERIAL

Number	Title (A Side/B Side)	Yr	VG	VG+	NM
66036	Move Out Little Mustang/Bucket Seats	1964	15.00	30.00	60.00

RAM

45s

POLYDOR

Number	Title (A Side/B Side)	Yr	VG	VG+	NM
14099	The Want in You/Mother's Day Song	1971	2.00	4.00	8.00

Albums

POLYDOR

Number	Title (A Side/B Side)	Yr	VG	VG+	NM
24-5013	Where (In Conclusion)	1972	6.25	12.50	25.00

RAMAL, BILL

45s

20TH CENTURY FOX

Number	Title (A Side/B Side)	Yr	VG	VG+	NM
432	Exodus/Theme from "Dr. No"	1963	2.50	5.00	10.00

MGM

Number	Title (A Side/B Side)	Yr	VG	VG+	NM
13123	Hard Times/Sax Fifth Ave.	1963	2.50	5.00	10.00

RAMATAM

45s

ATLANTIC

Number	Title (A Side/B Side)	Yr	VG	VG+	NM
2916	Changing Days/Wild Like Wind	1972	—	2.50	5.00

Albums

ATLANTIC

Number	Title (A Side/B Side)	Yr	VG	VG+	NM
SD 7236	Ramatam	1972	3.75	7.50	15.00
SD 7261	In April Came the Dawning of the Red Suns	1973	3.75	7.50	15.00

RAMBEAU, EDDIE

45s

20TH CENTURY FOX

Number	Title (A Side/B Side)	Yr	VG	VG+	NM
491	Come Closer/She's Smilin' at Me	1964	2.50	5.00	10.00

BELL

Number	Title (A Side/B Side)	Yr	VG	VG+	NM
847	Who Will Buy-Where Is Love/Solitary Man	1969	—	3.00	6.00
873	Don't Leave Me/Solitary Man	1970	—	3.00	6.00

DYNO VOICE

Number	Title (A Side/B Side)	Yr	VG	VG+	NM
204	Concrete and Clay/Don't Believe Him	1965	2.50	5.00	10.00
207	I Just Need Your Love/My Name Is Mud	1965	2.00	4.00	8.00
211	The Train/Yesterday's Newspapers	1966	2.00	4.00	8.00
217	I Just Need Your Love/I'm the Sky	1966	2.00	4.00	8.00
221	I Miss You/Thinkin' About You Baby	1966	2.00	4.00	8.00
225	The Clock/If I Were You	1966	2.00	4.00	8.00

SWAN

Number	Title (A Side/B Side)	Yr	VG	VG+	NM
4077	Skin Divin'/Toni	1961	2.50	5.00	10.00
4105	My Four Leaf Clover/Anyone Want More Flowers	1962	2.50	5.00	10.00
4112	Summertime Guy/Last Night Was My Last Night with You	1962	2.50	5.00	10.00
4145	Lover's Medley/The Car Hop and the Hard Top	1963	2.50	5.00	10.00

Albums

DYNO VOICE

Number	Title (A Side/B Side)	Yr	VG	VG+	NM
9001 [M]	Concrete and Clay	1965	5.00	10.00	20.00
DS-9001 [S]	Concrete and Clay	1965	6.25	12.50	25.00

RAMBLERS, THE (1)

45s

ADDIT

Number	Title (A Side/B Side)	Yr	VG	VG+	NM
1257	Rambling/Devil Train	1960	7.50	15.00	30.00

RAMBLERS, THE (2)

45s

ALMONT

Number	Title (A Side/B Side)	Yr	VG	VG+	NM
311	Father Sebastian/Barbara (I Loved You)	1964	6.25	12.50	25.00
313	School Girl/Birdland Baby	1964	5.00	10.00	20.00
315	Surfin' Santa/Silly Little Boy	1964	6.25	12.50	25.00

RAMBLERS, THE (3)

45s

FEDERAL

Number	Title (A Side/B Side)	Yr	VG	VG+	NM
12286	Don't You Know?/The Heaven and Earth	1957	37.50	75.00	150.00

RAMBLERS, THE (4)

45s

JAX

Number	Title (A Side/B Side)	Yr	VG	VG+	NM
319	Search My Heart/50-50 Love	1953	125.00	250.00	500.00
—Red vinyl					

RAMBLERS, THE (5)

45s

MGM

Number	Title (A Side/B Side)	Yr	VG	VG+	NM
11850	Vadunt-Un-Va-Da Song (Oui Oui Baby)/Please Bring Yourself Back Home	1954	75.00	150.00	300.00
55006	Bad Girl/Rickey-Do, Rickey-Do	1955	37.50	75.00	150.00

RAMBLERS, THE (6)

45s

TRUMPET

Number	Title (A Side/B Side)	Yr	VG	VG+	NM
102	Come On Back/So Sad	1963	100.00	200.00	400.00

RAMBLERS, THE (U)

Some of these could be by some of the above groups.

45s

IMPACT

Number	Title (A Side/B Side)	Yr	VG	VG+	NM
10	Yaba Daba Ah Doo/Funny Papers	1961	6.25	12.50	25.00

RCA VICTOR

Number	Title (A Side/B Side)	Yr	VG	VG+	NM
47-5240	Mama He Treats Your Daughter Mean/And the Bull Walked Around Olay	1953	100.00	200.00	400.00

SIDEWINDER

Number	Title (A Side/B Side)	Yr	VG	VG+	NM
101	Ticonderoga/Mozart Stomp	1964	10.00	20.00	40.00

RAMISTELLA, JOHNNY

See JOHNNY RIVERS.

RAMRODS

45s

AMY

Number	Title (A Side/B Side)	Yr	VG	VG+	NM
813	(Ghost) Riders in the Sky/Zig Zag	1961	6.25	12.50	25.00
817	Loch Lomond Rock/Take Me Back to My Boots and Saddle	1961	5.00	10.00	20.00
846	War Cry/Boing!	1962	5.00	10.00	20.00

QUEEN

Number	Title (A Side/B Side)	Yr	VG	VG+	NM
240145	Slee-Zee/Slouchee	1962	5.00	10.00	20.00

R&H

Number	Title (A Side/B Side)	Yr	VG	VG+	NM
1001	Moonlight Surf/Night Ride	1963	12.50	25.00	50.00

RAMS, THE

45s

FLAIR

Number	Title (A Side/B Side)	Yr	VG	VG+	NM
1066	Sweet Thing/Rock Bottom	1955	37.50	75.00	150.00

RAN-DELLS, THE

45s

CHAIRMAN

Number	Title (A Side/B Side)	Yr	VG	VG+	NM
4403	Martian Hop/Forgive Me, Darling (I Have Lied)	1963	5.00	10.00	20.00
4403 [PS]	Martian Hop/Forgive Me, Darling (I Have Lied)	1963	12.50	25.00	50.00
4407	Sound of the Sun/Come On and Love Me	1964	3.75	7.50	15.00

R.S.V.P.

Number	Title (A Side/B Side)	Yr	VG	VG+	NM
1104	Beyond the Stars/Wintertime	1964	3.75	7.50	15.00

RANCHEROS, THE

45s

DOT

Number	Title (A Side/B Side)	Yr	VG	VG+	NM
16572	Linda's Tune/Little Linda	1964	6.25	12.50	25.00

LONNIE

Number	Title (A Side/B Side)	Yr	VG	VG+	NM
5005	Linda's Tune/Little Linda	1963	12.50	25.00	50.00

RANDAZZO, TEDDY

Also see THE THREE CHUCKLES.

45s

ABC-PARAMOUNT

Number	Title (A Side/B Side)	Yr	VG	VG+	NM
9998	Papito/You Are Always in My Heart	1959	3.00	6.00	12.00
10014	Laughing on the Outside/Awkward Age	1959	3.00	6.00	12.00

Number	Title (A Side/B Side)	Yr	VG	VG+	NM
10043	Lies/I'm On a Merry-Go Round	1959	3.00	6.00	12.00
10068	How I Need You/You Don't Care Anymore	1959	3.00	6.00	12.00
10088	The Way of a Clown/Cherie	1960	3.00	6.00	12.00
10103	The Way of a Clown (Italian)/Cherie	1960	3.75	7.50	15.00
10127	But You Broke My Heart/Misery	1960	3.00	6.00	12.00
10131	Journey of Love/Misery	1960	3.00	6.00	12.00
10193	Happy Ending/But You Broke My Heart	1961	2.50	5.00	10.00
10228	Broken Bell/Let the Sunshine In	1961	2.50	5.00	10.00
10247	Don't Go Away/One More Chance	1961	2.50	5.00	10.00
10287	Mother Goose Twist/It's a Pity to Say Goodbye	1961	2.50	5.00	10.00
10312	Teenage Senorita/Blue Hawaii Moon	1962	2.50	5.00	10.00
10350	Dance to the Locomotion/Cotton Fields	1962	2.50	5.00	10.00
10377	Echoes/It Wasn't a Dream	1962	2.50	5.00	10.00
COLPIX					
662	Big Wide World/Be Sure My Love	1962	3.00	6.00	12.00
684	Dear Heart/Just Hold My Hand	1963	2.50	5.00	10.00
DCP					
1003	Pretty Blue Eyes/Doo Dah	1964	2.00	4.00	8.00
1108	Less Than Tomorrow/Lost Without You	1964	2.00	4.00	8.00
1134	You Don't Need a Heart/As Long As I Live	1965	2.00	4.00	8.00
1153	You're Not That Girl Anymore/Soul	1966	2.00	4.00	8.00
MGM					
13448	Lara's Theme/The Old and the New	1966	2.00	4.00	8.00
13449	Theme from "A Patch of Blue"/The Old and the New	1966	2.00	4.00	8.00
13511	Watch What Happens/Per Un Pugno Di Dollari	1966	2.00	4.00	8.00
13635	Mechanical Man/Sweet and Sour	1966	2.00	4.00	8.00
13648	I'm Losing You/Trick or Treat	1966	2.00	4.00	8.00
13682	A Fistful of Dollars/Take Me Back	1967	2.00	4.00	8.00
VERVE FOLKWAYS					
5050	A World Without Love/Just One More Time	1967	2.00	4.00	8.00
VIK					
0277	Next Stop Paradise/How Could You Know?	1957	3.00	6.00	12.00
0289	Kiddio/I Was the Last One to Know	1957	3.00	6.00	12.00
0310	I'll Never Smile Again/Red Ruby Lips	1957	3.00	6.00	12.00
0319	Dutch Treat/To Belong	1958	3.00	6.00	12.00
0330	Little Serenade/Be My Kitten, Little Chicken	1958	3.75	7.50	15.00
Albums					
ABC-PARAMOUNT					
352 [M]	Journey to Love	1961	7.50	15.00	30.00
S-352 [S]	Journey to Love	1961	10.00	20.00	40.00
421 [M]	Teddy Randazzo Twists	1962	7.50	15.00	30.00
S-421 [S]	Teddy Randazzo Twists	1962	10.00	20.00	40.00
COLPIX					
CP-445 [M]	Big Wide World	1963	7.50	15.00	30.00
SCP-445 [S]	Big Wide World	1963	10.00	20.00	40.00
VIK					
LX-1121 [M]	I'm Confessin'	1958	50.00	100.00	200.00

RANDELL, BUDDY

45s

Number	Title (A Side/B Side)	Yr	VG	VG+	NM
UNI					
55209	Be My Baby/Randi Randi	1970	—	3.00	6.00

RANDELL, LYNNE

45s

Number	Title (A Side/B Side)	Yr	VG	VG+	NM
ABC					
11112	Open Letter/Right to Cry	1968	5.00	10.00	20.00
EPIC					
10147	Stranger in My Arms/Ciao Baby	1967	7.50	15.00	30.00
10197	I Need You Boy/That's a Hoe-Down	1967	7.50	15.00	30.00

RANDOLPH, BARBARA

45s

Number	Title (A Side/B Side)	Yr	VG	VG+	NM
SOUL					
35038	I Got a Feeling/You Got Me Hurtin' All Over	1967	5.00	10.00	20.00
35050	Can I Get a Witness/You Got Me Hurtin' All Over	1968	5.00	10.00	20.00

RANDOLPH, BOOTS

45s

Number	Title (A Side/B Side)	Yr	VG	VG+	NM
MONUMENT					
443	Fancy Dan/Hey, Daddy Daddy	1961	2.50	5.00	10.00
460	Bluebird of Happiness/Keep a Light in Your Window Tonight	1962	2.50	5.00	10.00
804	Yakety Sax/I Really Don't Want to Know	1963	2.50	5.00	10.00
821	Lonely Street/Windy and Warm	1963	2.00	4.00	8.00
835	Hey, Mr. Sax Man/Baby, Go to Sleep	1964	2.00	4.00	8.00
852	Mickey's Tune/I'll Take You Home Again, Kathleen	1964	2.00	4.00	8.00
884	King of the Road/Theme from a Dream	1965	2.00	4.00	8.00
928	These Boots Are Made for Walking/Honey in Your Heart	1966	2.00	4.00	8.00
950	Yodeling Sax/Miss You	1966	2.00	4.00	8.00
976	The Shadow of Your Smile/I'll Just Walk Away	1966	2.00	4.00	8.00
1009	Temptation/You've Lost That Lovin' Feelin'	1967	—	3.00	6.00
1038	Love Letters/Big Daddy	1967	—	3.00	6.00
1056	Wonderland by Night/Fred	1968	—	3.00	6.00
1081	Gentle on My Mind/Jackson	1968	—	3.00	6.00
1125	Games People Play/By the Time I Get to Phoenix	1969	—	3.00	6.00
1165	Hey Jude/Down Yonder	1969	—	3.00	6.00
1176	Sleigh Ride/White Christmas	1969	2.00	4.00	8.00
1199	Spanish Harlem/Anna	1970	—	2.50	5.00
1219	Sunday Morning Coming Down/Those Were the Days	1970	—	2.50	5.00
1226	Proud Mary/Without Love (There Is Nothing)	1970	—	2.50	5.00
1233	Take a Letter Maria/See See Rider	1970	—	2.50	5.00
1937	Sleigh Ride/White Christmas	1976	—	2.00	4.00
—Golden Series					
8500	My Sweet Lord/(B-side unknown)	1971	—	2.50	5.00
8534	Lookin'/Alligator Annie	1972	—	2.00	4.00
8541	Lonesome Ladies/Mountain Minuet	1972	—	2.00	4.00
8552	Love Theme from "The Godfather"/Rocky Top	1972	—	2.00	4.00
8588	Marie/Sentimental Journey	1973	—	2.00	4.00
8616	Behind Closed Doors/Old Joe Clarke	1974	—	2.00	4.00
8632	Sleigh Ride/White Christmas	1974	—	2.50	5.00
8634	Sanford & Son Theme/Ebb Tide	1974	—	2.50	5.00
45209	Honky Tonk/Memphis	1977	—	2.00	4.00
45227	Jive Talkin'/Blueberry Hill	1977	—	2.00	4.00
45263	You Light Up My Life/Movin' On Up	1978	—	2.00	4.00
45294	I Write the Songs/Motherland-Oluwa	1980	—	2.00	4.00
RCA VICTOR					
47-7278	Difficult/I'm Getting Your Message Baby	1958	3.75	7.50	15.00
—As "Randy Randolph"					
47-7395	Yakety Sax/Percolator	1958	5.00	10.00	20.00
—As "Randy Randolph"					
47-7515	Blue Guitar/Greenback Dollar	1959	3.00	6.00	12.00
—As "Randy Randolph"					
47-7611	Temptation/Sweet Talk	1959	3.00	6.00	12.00
47-7721	Red Light/La Golondrina	1960	3.00	6.00	12.00
47-7835	Bog Daddy/Bongo Band	1961	3.00	6.00	12.00
7-Inch Extended Plays					
MONUMENT					
SMN-361 [DJ]	Sleigh Ride/Rudolph the Red-Nosed Reindeer//White Christmas/I'll Be Home for Christmas	1969	5.00	10.00	20.00
Albums					
MONUMENT					
6600	Boots Randolph's Yakety Sax	197?	2.50	5.00	10.00
—Reissue of 18002					
6601	Hip Boots	197?	2.50	5.00	10.00
—Reissue of 18015					
6602	Boots Randolph Plays More Yakety Sax	197?	2.50	5.00	10.00
—Reissue of 18037					
6603	The Fantastic Boots Randolph	197?	2.50	5.00	10.00
—Reissue of 18042					
6604	Boots with Strings	197?	2.50	5.00	10.00
—Reissue of 18066					
6605	Sax-Sational	197?	2.50	5.00	10.00
—Reissue of 18079					
6606	Boots Randolph with the Knightsbridge Strings & Voices	197?	2.50	5.00	10.00
—Reissue of 18082					
6607	Sunday Sax	197?	2.50	5.00	10.00
—Reissue of 18092					
6608	The Sound of Boots	197?	2.50	5.00	10.00
—Reissue of 18099					
6609	...With Love/The Seductive Sax of Boots Randolph	197?	2.50	5.00	10.00
—Reissue of 18111					
6610	Boots and Stockings	197?	2.50	5.00	10.00
—Reissue of 18127					
6611	Yakety Revisited	197?	2.50	5.00	10.00
—Reissue of 18128					
6612	Hit Boots 1970	197?	2.50	5.00	10.00
—Reissue of 18144					
6613	Boots with Brass	197?	2.50	5.00	10.00
—Reissue of 18147					
6614	Homer Louis Randolph, III	197?	2.50	5.00	10.00
—Reissue of 30678					
6615	Boots Randolph Plays the Great Hits of Today	197?	2.50	5.00	10.00
—Reissue of 31908					
6616	Sentimental Journey	197?	2.50	5.00	10.00
—Reissue of 32292					
6617	Country Boots	197?	2.50	5.00	10.00
—Reissue of 32912					
6618	Cool Boots	197?	2.50	5.00	10.00
—Reissue of 33803					
7602	Greatest Hits	1977	2.50	5.00	10.00
7611	Sax Appeal	1977	2.50	5.00	10.00
7627	Put a Little Sax	1978	2.50	5.00	10.00
MLP-8002 [M]	Boots Randolph's Yakety Sax	1963	5.00	10.00	20.00
MLP-8015 [M]	Hip Boots	1964	3.75	7.50	15.00
MLP-8029 [M]	12 Monstrous Sax Hits	1965	3.75	7.50	15.00
MLP-8037 [M]	Boots Randolph Plays More Yakety Sax	1965	3.75	7.50	15.00
MLP-8042 [M]	The Fantastic Boots Randolph	1966	3.75	7.50	15.00
MLP-8066 [M]	Boots with Strings	1966	3.75	7.50	15.00
MLP-8079 [M]	Sax-Sational	1967	5.00	10.00	20.00
MLP-8082 [M]	Boots Randolph with the Knightsbridge Strings & Voices	1967	5.00	10.00	20.00
8604 [(2)]	Party Boots	197?	3.00	6.00	12.00
—Reissue of 34082					
SLP-18002 [S]	Boots Randolph's Yakety Sax	1963	6.25	12.50	25.00
SLP-18015 [S]	Hip Boots	1964	5.00	10.00	20.00
SLP-18029 [S]	12 Monstrous Sax Hits	1965	5.00	10.00	20.00
SLP-18037 [S]	Boots Randolph Plays More Yakety Sax	1965	5.00	10.00	20.00
SLP-18042 [S]	The Fantastic Boots Randolph	1966	5.00	10.00	20.00
SLP-18066 [S]	Boots with Strings	1966	5.00	10.00	20.00
SLP-18079 [S]	Sax-Sational	1967	3.75	7.50	15.00
SLP-18082 [S]	Boots Randolph with the Knightsbridge Strings & Voices	1967	3.75	7.50	15.00
SLP-18092	Sunday Sax	1968	5.00	10.00	20.00
SLP-18099	The Sound of Boots	1968	5.00	10.00	20.00
SLP-18111	...With Love/The Seductive Sax of Boots Randolph	1969	3.75	7.50	15.00
SLP 18127	Boots and Stockings	1969	3.75	7.50	15.00
SLP-18128	Yakety Revisited	1969	3.75	7.50	15.00
SLP-18144	Hit Boots 1970	1970	3.75	7.50	15.00
SLP-18147	Boots with Brass	1970	3.75	7.50	15.00
Z 30678	Homer Louis Randolph, III	1971	3.00	6.00	12.00
Z2 30964 [(2)]	The World of Boots Randolph	1971	3.75	7.50	15.00
KZ 31908	Boots Randolph Plays the Great Hits of Today	1972	3.00	6.00	12.00
KZ 32292	Sentimental Journey	1973	3.00	6.00	12.00
KZ 32912	Country Boots	1974	3.00	6.00	12.00
KZ 33803	Cool Boots	1975	3.00	6.00	12.00
Z2 34082 [(2)]	Party Boots	1976	3.75	7.50	15.00
PW 38388	Greatest Hits	1983	2.50	5.00	10.00
JW 38396	Dedication	1983	2.50	5.00	10.00
RCA CAMDEN					
CAL-825 [M]	Yakin' Sax Man	1964	3.75	7.50	15.00

Number	Title (A Side/B Side)	Yr	VG	VG+	NM
CAS-825 [S]	Yakin' Sax Man	1964	3.75	7.50	15.00
CAL-865 [M]	Sweet Talk	1965	3.75	7.50	15.00
CAS-865 [R]	Sweet Talk	1965	3.00	6.00	12.00
ACL-9003 [(2)]	Yakety Sax	1972	3.00	6.00	12.00
RCA VICTOR					
LPM-2165 [M]	Yakety Sax	1960	10.00	20.00	40.00
LSP-2165 [S]	Yakety Sax	1960	12.50	25.00	50.00

RANDY AND THE RADIANTS

45s

Number	Title (A Side/B Side)	Yr	VG	VG+	NM
SUN					
395	The Mountain's High/Peek-a-Boo	1965	6.25	12.50	25.00
398	My Way of Thinking/Truth from My Eyes	1966	6.25	12.50	25.00

RANDY AND THE RAINBOWS

45s

Number	Title (A Side/B Side)	Yr	VG	VG+	NM
AMBIENT SOUND					
02872	Debbie/Try the Impossible	1982	—	2.50	5.00
B.T. PUPPY					
535	I'll Be Seeing You/Oh to Get Away	1967	2.50	5.00	10.00
MIKE					
4001	Lovely Lies/I'll Forget Her Tomorrow	1966	3.00	6.00	12.00
4004	Quarter to Three/He's a Fugitive	1966	3.00	6.00	12.00
4008	Bonnie's Part of Town/Can It Be	1966	3.00	6.00	12.00
RUST					
5059	Denise/Come Back	1963	7.50	15.00	30.00
—Blue label					
5059	Denise/Come Back	1963	5.00	10.00	20.00
—Mostly white label					
5073	She's My Angel/Why Do Kids Grow Up	1964	3.75	7.50	15.00
5080	Happy Teenager/Dry Your Eyes	1964	3.75	7.50	15.00
5091	Little Star/Sharin'	1964	3.75	7.50	15.00
5101	Joy Ride/Little Hot Rod Suzie	1965	3.75	7.50	15.00

Albums

Number	Title (A Side/B Side)	Yr	VG	VG+	NM
AMBIENT SOUND					
ASR-601	Remember	1985	3.00	6.00	12.00
FZ 37715	C'mon, Let's Go	1982	3.00	6.00	12.00

RANGERS, THE

45s

Number	Title (A Side/B Side)	Yr	VG	VG+	NM
CHALLENGE					
59229	Snow Skiing/Mogul Monster	1964	5.00	10.00	20.00
59239	Justine/Reputation	1964	5.00	10.00	20.00
FTP					
404	Four on the Floor/Riders in the Sky	1961	7.50	15.00	30.00

RANGLIN, ERNEST

45s

Number	Title (A Side/B Side)	Yr	VG	VG+	NM
STUDIO					
1	Surfing (Part 1)/Surfing (Part 2)	196?	12.50	25.00	50.00

RANK, KEN

45s

Number	Title (A Side/B Side)	Yr	VG	VG+	NM
FENTON					
2194	Twin City Saucer/Ken's Thing	1968	7.50	15.00	30.00

RANKIN, KENNY

45s

Number	Title (A Side/B Side)	Yr	VG	VG+	NM
ABC-PARAMOUNT					
10268	Funny That's Love/Go Home Little Girl	1961	3.00	6.00	12.00
—As "Ken Rankin"					
ATLANTIC					
3663	Regrets/(B-side unknown)	1980	—	2.00	4.00
COLUMBIA					
42881	Soft Guitar/Baby Goodbye	1963	2.50	5.00	10.00
43036	Where Did My Little Girl Go/U.S. Mail	1964	2.50	5.00	10.00
43885	Haven't We Met/In the Name of Love	1966	2.50	5.00	10.00
DECCA					
30485	Saturday After the Game/I'll Be Waiting	1957	5.00	10.00	20.00
30691	My Popular Baby/You Be the Judge	1958	3.75	7.50	15.00
30852	Cindy Loo/Catch Love	1959	3.75	7.50	15.00
30954	I Cry By Night/Have Pity Miss Kitty	1959	3.75	7.50	15.00
31054	What Do You Want to Make Those Eyes at Me For/Tonight I'm Speaking Love	1960	3.00	6.00	12.00
31124	Casey Jones/It Started in Naples	1960	3.00	6.00	12.00
31162	Sure As You're Born/Teasin' Heart	1960	3.00	6.00	12.00
LITTLE DAVID					
725	String Man/Comin' Down	1972	—	2.50	5.00
726	Peaceful/Sometimes	1973	—	2.50	5.00
727	Why Do Fools Fall in Love/(B-side unknown)	1973	—	2.50	5.00
728	Penny Lane/Killed a Cat	1974	—	2.50	5.00
729	Catfish/Silver Morning	1975	—	2.50	5.00
732	Sunday Kind of Love/Inside	1975	—	2.50	5.00
733	Creepin'/Lost Up in Loving You	1976	—	2.50	5.00
735	On and On/Through the Eyes of the Eagle	1977	—	2.50	5.00
737	When Sunny Gets Blue/I Love You	1977	—	2.50	5.00
8072	Penny Lane/Killed a Cat	1975	—	2.50	5.00
8093	Catfish/Silver Morning	1975	—	2.50	5.00
MERCURY					
72768	Peaceful/The Dolphin	1968	2.00	4.00	8.00
72768 [PS]	Peaceful/The Dolphin	1968	3.00	6.00	12.00
72956	Minuet/Peaceful	1969	2.00	4.00	8.00

Albums

Number	Title (A Side/B Side)	Yr	VG	VG+	NM
ATLANTIC					
SD 19271	After the Roses	1980	2.50	5.00	10.00
LITTLE DAVID					
LD 1003	Like a Seed	1972	2.50	5.00	10.00
LD 1009	Inside	1975	2.50	5.00	10.00
LD 1013	The Kenny Rankin Album	1977	2.50	5.00	10.00
SD 3000	Silver Morning	1974	2.50	5.00	10.00
90131	Silver Morning	1984	2.00	4.00	8.00
—Reissue of 3000					
MERCURY					
MG-21141 [M]	Mind Dusters	1967	3.75	7.50	15.00
SR-61141 [S]	Mind Dusters	1967	3.00	6.00	12.00
SR-61240	Family	1969	3.00	6.00	12.00

RARE BIRD

45s

Number	Title (A Side/B Side)	Yr	VG	VG+	NM
ABC					
11284	Hammerhead/What You Want to Know	1970	—	3.00	6.00
POLYDOR					
15079	Birdman (Part 1)/Birdman (Part 2)	1973	—	2.50	5.00
15081	The Darkest Hour/Hey Man	1973	—	2.50	5.00
15087	Somebody's Watching (Part 1)/Somebody's Watching (Part 2)	1974	—	2.50	5.00
15093	Body and Soul/(B-side unassigned)	1974	—	—	—
—Canceled					
PROBE					
477	Sympathy/Beautiful Scarlet	1970	2.00	4.00	8.00

Albums

Number	Title (A Side/B Side)	Yr	VG	VG+	NM
ABC					
X-715	As Your Mind Flies	1972	3.75	7.50	15.00
POLYDOR					
PD 5530	Epic Forest	1973	3.75	7.50	15.00
PD 6502	Somebody's Watching	1974	3.75	7.50	15.00
PD 6506	Born Again	1974	3.75	7.50	15.00
PROBE					
4514	Rare Bird	1970	6.25	12.50	25.00

RARE BREED, THE

Later known as THE OHIO EXPRESS.

45s

Number	Title (A Side/B Side)	Yr	VG	VG+	NM
ATTACK					
1401	Beg, Borrow and Steal/Jeri's Theme	1966	7.50	15.00	30.00
1403	Come and Take a Ride in My Boat/Take Me to This World of Yours	1966	5.00	10.00	20.00

RARE EARTH

45s

Number	Title (A Side/B Side)	Yr	VG	VG+	NM
PRODIGAL					
0637	Crazy Love/Is Your Teacher Cool	1977	—	2.50	5.00
0640	Warm Ride/Would You Like to Come Along	1978	—	2.50	5.00
0643	I Can Feel My Love Risin'/S.O.S. (Stop Her On Sight)	1978	—	2.50	5.00
RARE EARTH					
960/961 [DJ]	What'd I Say (stereo/mono)	1972	6.25	12.50	25.00
—Blue vinyl, promo only, white label					
5010	Generation (Light of the Sky)/Magic Key	1969	3.00	6.00	12.00
5012	Get Ready/Magic Key	1970	—	3.00	6.00
5017	(I Know) I'm Losing You/When Joanie Smiles	1970	—	3.00	6.00
5021	Born to Wander/Here Comes the Night	1970	—	3.00	6.00
5031	I Just Want to Celebrate/The Seed	1971	—	3.00	6.00
5031 [PS]	I Just Want to Celebrate/The Seed	1971	2.50	5.00	10.00
5038	Hey Big Brother/Under God's Light	1971	—	3.00	6.00
5043	What'd I Say/Nice to Be with You	1972	—	3.00	6.00
5048	Good Time Sally/Love Shines Down	1972	—	3.00	6.00
5052	We're Gonna Have a Good Time/Would You Like to Come Along	1973	—	3.00	6.00
5053	Ma/(Instrumental)	1973	—	3.00	6.00
5054	Hum Along and Dance/Come with Me	1973	—	3.00	6.00
5056	Big John Is My Name/Ma	1974	—	3.00	6.00
5057	Chained/Fresh from the Can	1974	—	3.00	6.00
5058	It Makes You Happy (But It Ain't Gonna Last Too Long)/Boogie with Me Children	1975	—	3.00	6.00
5059	Let Me Be Your Sunshine/Keep Me Out of the Storm	1976	—	3.00	6.00
5060	Midnight Lady/Walking Shtick	1976	—	3.00	6.00
RCA					
PB-13076	Howzabout Some Love/Let Me Take You Out	1982	—	—	—
—Unreleased					
VERVE					
10622	Stop-Where Did Our Love Go/Mother's Oats	1968	3.00	6.00	12.00

Albums

Number	Title (A Side/B Side)	Yr	VG	VG+	NM
MOTOWN					
M5-116V1	Motown Superstar Series, Vol. 16	1981	2.50	5.00	10.00
M5-202V1	Ecology	1981	2.00	4.00	8.00
5229 ML	Get Ready	1982	2.00	4.00	8.00
PRODIGAL					
P6-10019	Rare Earth	1977	2.50	5.00	10.00
P7-10025	Band Together	1978	2.50	5.00	10.00
P7-10027	Grand Slam	1979	2.50	5.00	10.00
RARE EARTH					
RS 507	Get Ready	1969	7.50	15.00	30.00
—Original cover has a rounded top					
RS 507	Get Ready	1970	3.00	6.00	12.00
—Regular square cover					
RS 510	Generation	1970	—	—	—
—Canceled					
RS 514	Ecology	1970	3.75	7.50	15.00
RS 520	One World	1971	3.75	7.50	15.00
R 534 [(2)]	Rare Earth in Concert	1971	3.75	7.50	15.00
R 543	Willie Remembers	1972	3.00	6.00	12.00
R6-546	Ma	1973	3.00	6.00	12.00
R6-548	Back to Earth	1975	3.00	6.00	12.00
R7-550	Midnight Lady	1976	3.00	6.00	12.00
VERVE					
V6-5066	Dreams/Answers	1968	12.50	25.00	50.00

RASCALS, THE

Includes "The Young Rascals." Also see FELIX CAVALIERE; GENE CORNISH; FELIX AND THE ESCORTS.

45s

ATLANTIC

Number	Title (A Side/B Side)	Yr	VG	VG+	NM
2312	I Ain't Gonna Eat Out My Heart Anymore/Slow Down	1965	3.75	7.50	15.00
—From here through Atlantic 2463, as "The Young Rascals"					
2321	Good Lovin'/Mustang Sally	1966	3.75	7.50	15.00
2338	You Better Run/Love Is a Beautiful Thing	1966	2.50	5.00	10.00
2338 [PS]	You Better Run/Love Is a Beautiful Thing	1966	5.00	10.00	20.00
2353	Come On Up/What Is the Reason	1966	2.50	5.00	10.00
2377	I've Been Lonely Too Long/If You Knew	1967	2.50	5.00	10.00
2377 [PS]	I've Been Lonely Too Long/If You Knew	1967	5.00	10.00	20.00
2401	Groovin'/Sueno	1967	2.00	4.00	8.00
2401 [PS]	Groovin'/Sueno	1967	5.00	10.00	20.00
2424	A Girl Like You/It's Love	1967	2.00	4.00	8.00
2424 [PS]	A Girl Like You/It's Love	1967	5.00	10.00	20.00
2428	Groovin' (Spanish)/Groovin' (Italian)	1967	5.00	10.00	20.00
2438	How Can I Be Sure/I'm So Happy Now	1967	2.00	4.00	8.00
2463	It's Wonderful/Of Course	1967	2.00	4.00	8.00
2493	A Beautiful Morning/Rainy Day	1968	—	3.00	6.00
—First record as "The Rascals"					
2493 [PS]	A Beautiful Morning/Rainy Day	1968	5.00	10.00	20.00
2537	People Got to Be Free/My World	1968	—	3.00	6.00
2537 [PS]	People Got to Be Free/My World	1968	3.00	6.00	12.00
2584	A Ray of Hope/Any Dance'll Do	1968	—	3.00	6.00
2584 [PS]	A Ray of Hope/Any Dance'll Do	1968	3.00	6.00	12.00
2599	Heaven/Baby I'm Blue	1969	—	3.00	6.00
2634	See/Away Away	1969	—	3.00	6.00
2634 [PS]	See/Away Away	1969	3.00	6.00	12.00
2664	Carry Me Back/Real Thing	1969	—	3.00	6.00
2664 [PS]	Carry Me Back/Real Thing	1969	3.00	6.00	12.00
2695	Hold On/I Believe	1969	—	3.00	6.00
2695 [PS]	Hold On/I Believe	1969	3.00	6.00	12.00
2743	Glory Glory/You Don't Know	1970	—	3.00	6.00
2743 [PS]	Glory Glory/You Don't Know	1970	3.00	6.00	12.00
2773	Right On/Almost Home	1970	—	3.00	6.00

COLUMBIA

Number	Title (A Side/B Side)	Yr	VG	VG+	NM
45400	Love Me/Happy Song	1971	—	3.00	6.00
45491	Lucky Day/Love Letter	1971	—	3.00	6.00
45568	Brother Tree/Saga of New York	1972	—	3.00	6.00
45600	Echoes/Hummin' Song	1972	—	3.00	6.00
45649	Jungle Walk/Saga of New York	1972	2.50	5.00	10.00

PHILCO

Number	Title (A Side/B Side)	Yr	VG	VG+	NM
HP-18	A Girl Like You/I've Been Lonely Too Long	1967	3.75	7.50	15.00
—4-inch plastic "Hip Pocket Record" with color sleeve					

Albums

ATLANTIC

Number	Title	Yr	VG	VG+	NM
ST-137 [DJ]	Freedom Suite Sampler	1969	12.50	25.00	50.00
SD 2-901 [(2)]	Freedom Suite	1969	5.00	10.00	20.00
8123 [M]	The Young Rascals	1966	7.50	15.00	30.00
SD 8123 [S]	The Young Rascals	1966	10.00	20.00	40.00
—Green and blue label					
SD 8123 [S]	The Young Rascals	1966	12.50	25.00	50.00
—Purple and green label					
SD 8123 [S]	The Young Rascals	1969	3.00	6.00	12.00
—Red and green label					
8134 [M]	Collections	1967	6.25	12.50	25.00
SD 8134 [S]	Collections	1967	7.50	15.00	30.00
—Green and blue label					
SD 8134 [S]	Collections	1969	3.00	6.00	12.00
—Red and green label					
8148 [M]	Groovin'	1967	6.25	12.50	25.00
SD 8148 [S]	Groovin'	1967	7.50	15.00	30.00
—Green and blue label					
SD 8148 [S]	Groovin'	1969	3.00	6.00	12.00
—Red and green label					
8169 [M]	Once Upon a Dream	1968	10.00	20.00	40.00
SD 8169 [S]	Once Upon a Dream	1968	6.25	12.50	25.00
—Green and blue label					
SD 8169 [S]	Once Upon a Dream	1969	3.00	6.00	12.00
—Red and green label					
8190 [M]	Time Peace/The Rascals' Greatest Hits	1968	12.50	25.00	50.00
—Mono is promo only					
SD 8190 [S]	Time Peace/The Rascals' Greatest Hits	1968	6.25	12.50	25.00
—Green and blue label					
SD 8190 [S]	Time Peace/The Rascals' Greatest Hits	1968	3.75	7.50	15.00
—Purple and gold label					
SD 8190 [S]	Time Peace/The Rascals' Greatest Hits	1969	3.00	6.00	12.00
—Red and green label					
SD 8246	See	1969	3.75	7.50	15.00
SD 8276	Search and Nearness	1970	3.75	7.50	15.00

COLUMBIA

Number	Title	Yr	VG	VG+	NM
G 30462 [(2)]	Peaceful World	1971	3.75	7.50	15.00
KC 31103	The Island of Real	1972	3.00	6.00	12.00

PAIR

Number	Title	Yr	VG	VG+	NM
PDL2-1106 [(2)]	Rock and Roll Treasures	1986	3.75	7.50	15.00

RHINO

Number	Title	Yr	VG	VG+	NM
RNLP 70237	The Young Rascals	1988	2.50	5.00	10.00
RNLP 70238	Collections	1988	2.50	5.00	10.00
RNLP 70239	Groovin'	1988	2.50	5.00	10.00
R1-70240	Once Upon a Dream	1988	2.50	5.00	10.00
R1-70241	Freedom Suite	1988	2.50	5.00	10.00
R1-70242	Searching for Ecstasy: The Rest of the Rascals 1969-1972	1988	2.50	5.00	10.00

WARNER SPECIAL PRODUCTS

Number	Title	Yr	VG	VG+	NM
SP-2502 [(2)]	24 Greatest Hits	1971	5.00	10.00	20.00

WES FARRELL

Number	Title	Yr	VG	VG+	NM
PFT-1002 [DJ]	Songs from the Rascals	197?	6.25	12.50	25.00
—Promo-only publisher's demo					

RASPBERRIES

Also see ERIC CARMEN; THE CHOIR.

45s

CAPITOL

Number	Title (A Side/B Side)	Yr	VG	VG+	NM
3280	Don't Want to Say Goodbye/Rock and Roll Mama	1972	2.00	4.00	8.00
3280 [PS]	Don't Want to Say Goodbye/Rock and Roll Mama	1972	6.25	12.50	25.00
3348	Go All the Way/With You in My Life	1972	—	3.00	6.00
3473	I Wanna Be with You/Goin' Nowhere Tonight	1972	—	3.00	6.00
3546	Let's Pretend/Every Way I Can	1973	—	3.00	6.00
3546 [PS]	Let's Pretend/Every Way I Can	1973	3.00	6.00	12.00
3610	Tonight/Had to Get Over a Heartbreak	1973	—	3.00	6.00
3765	I'm a Rocker/Money Down	1973	—	3.00	6.00
3826	Don't Want to Say Goodbye/Ecstasy	1974	—	3.00	6.00
3885	Drivin' Around/Might As Well	1974	—	3.00	6.00
3946	Overnight Sensation (Hit Record)/Hands on You	1974	—	3.00	6.00
4001	The Party's Over/Cruisin' Music	1974	—	3.00	6.00

Albums

CAPITOL

Number	Title	Yr	VG	VG+	NM
SK-11036	Raspberries	1972	7.50	15.00	30.00
—Originals have red labels and a "scratch 'n' sniff" cover, the smell of which fades over time					
ST-11036	Raspberries	1973	5.00	10.00	20.00
—Orange label, "Capitol" at bottom					
ST-11123	Fresh	1972	5.00	10.00	20.00
SMAS-11220	Side 3	1973	5.00	10.00	20.00
—With cover cut in the shape of a basket of raspberries					
ST-11329	Starting Over	1974	5.00	10.00	20.00
ST-11524	Raspberries' Best Featuring Eric Carmen	1976	3.75	7.50	15.00
SN-16095	Raspberries' Best Featuring Eric Carmen	1979	2.50	5.00	10.00

RATCHELL

45s

DECCA

Number	Title (A Side/B Side)	Yr	VG	VG+	NM
32893	Lazy Lady/Problems	1971	—	3.00	6.00
32958	Julie My Woman/Out of Hand	1972	—	2.50	5.00
32981	Peace of Mind/My My	1972	—	2.50	5.00

Albums

DECCA

Number	Title	Yr	VG	VG+	NM
DL 75330	Ratchell	1972	3.75	7.50	15.00
DL 75365	Ratchell 2	1972	3.75	7.50	15.00

RATIONALS, THE

45s

A-SQUARE

Number	Title (A Side/B Side)	Yr	VG	VG+	NM
101	Look What You're Doin'/Gave My Love	1966	6.25	12.50	25.00
103	Feelin' Lost/Little Girls Cry	1966	5.00	10.00	20.00
104/3	Leavin' Here/Feelin' Lost	1966	6.25	12.50	25.00
104	Leavin' Here/Respect	1966	7.50	15.00	30.00
—This is the original issue of this single					
107	I Need You/Out in the Streets	1968	5.00	10.00	20.00
402	I Need You/Get the Picture	1967	6.25	12.50	25.00
—B-side by SRC (Scott Richard Case)					

CAMEO

Number	Title (A Side/B Side)	Yr	VG	VG+	NM
437	Respect/Feelin' Lost	1966	3.00	6.00	12.00
455	Hold On Baby/Sing	1967	3.75	7.50	15.00
481	Leavin' Here/Not Like It Is	1967	3.75	7.50	15.00

CAPITOL

Number	Title (A Side/B Side)	Yr	VG	VG+	NM
2124	I Need You/Out in the Streets	1968	3.00	6.00	12.00

CREWE

Number	Title (A Side/B Side)	Yr	VG	VG+	NM
360	Handbags and Gladrags/Guitar Army	1969	2.50	5.00	10.00

DANBY'S

Number	Title (A Side/B Side)	Yr	VG	VG+	NM
(no #)	Turn On/Irrational	1966	12.50	25.00	50.00
—Made for Danby's clothiers					

GENESIS

Number	Title (A Side/B Side)	Yr	VG	VG+	NM
1	Guitar Army/Sunset	1969	3.75	7.50	15.00

Albums

CREWE

Number	Title	Yr	VG	VG+	NM
CR-1334	The Rationals	1969	10.00	20.00	40.00

RATS, THE

45s

LAURIE

Number	Title (A Side/B Side)	Yr	VG	VG+	NM
3276	Spoonful/I've Got My Eyes on You Baby	1964	3.00	6.00	12.00

RUST

Number	Title (A Side/B Side)	Yr	VG	VG+	NM
TR-2	Spoonful/I've Got My Eyes on You Baby	1965	3.75	7.50	15.00

RATTLES, THE

Also see THE SEARCHERS.

45s

LONDON

Number	Title (A Side/B Side)	Yr	VG	VG+	NM
1037	Devil's on the Loose/I Know You Don't Know	1972	—	2.50	5.00
1047	Devil's Sun/Why Do I Care	1973	—	2.50	5.00

MERCURY

Number	Title (A Side/B Side)	Yr	VG	VG+	NM
72403	Shame, Shame, Shame/Someone Who Is Just Like You	1965	3.00	6.00	12.00
72554	Sha La La La Lee/Dance	1966	3.00	6.00	12.00

PROBE

Number	Title (A Side/B Side)	Yr	VG	VG+	NM
480	The Witch/Geraldine	1970	2.00	4.00	8.00

Albums

MERCURY

Number	Title	Yr	VG	VG+	NM
MG 21127 [M]	The Rattles' Greatest Hits	1967	20.00	40.00	80.00
SR 61127 [R]	The Rattles' Greatest Hits	1967	12.50	25.00	50.00

RAVEN, PAUL

See GARY GLITTER.

RAVENAIRS, THE

45s

ALGONQUIN

Number	Title (A Side/B Side)	Yr	VG	VG+	NM
718	A Night to Remember/Together Forever	1958	25.00	50.00	100.00
—Originally released as "The Rivieras"					

RAVENS, THE

Also see JIMMY RICKS.

45s

Number	Title (A Side/B Side)	Yr	VG	VG+	NM
ARGO					
5255	Kneel and Pray/I Can't Believe	1956	10.00	20.00	40.00
5261	A Simple Prayer/Water Boy	1956	20.00	40.00	80.00
5276	That'll Be the Day/Dear One	1957	7.50	15.00	30.00
5284	Here Is My Heart/Lazy Mule	1957	7.50	15.00	30.00
CHECKER					
871	That'll Be the Day/Dear One	1957	5.00	10.00	20.00
COLUMBIA					
1-903	Don't Look Now/Time Takes Care of Everything	1950	375.00	750.00	1500.
—Microgroove 33 1/3 single					
6-903	Don't Look Now/Time Takes Care of Everything	1950	175.00	350.00	700.00
1-925	My Baby's Gone/I'm So Crazy for Love	1950	375.00	750.00	1500.
—Microgroove 33 1/3 single					
6-925	My Baby's Gone/I'm So Crazy for Love	1950	150.00	300.00	600.00
39112	You Don't Have to Drop a Heart/Midnight Blues	1950	500.00	1000.	2000.
39194	You're Always in My Dreams/Gotta Find My Baby	1951	500.00	1000.	2000.
39408	You Foolish Thing/Honey I Don't Want You	1951	500.00	1000.	2000.
JUBILEE					
5184	Bye Bye Baby Blues/Happy Go Lucky Baby	1955	7.50	15.00	30.00
5203	Green Eyes/The Bells of San Rafael	1955	7.50	15.00	30.00
—As "Jimmy Ricks and the Ravens"					
5217	On Chapel Hill/We'll Raise a Ruckus Tonight	1955	7.50	15.00	30.00
5237	I'll Always Be in Love with You/(Take Me Back To My) Boots and Saddles	1956	7.50	15.00	30.00
—As "Jimmy Ricks and the Ravens"					
MERCURY					
5764	There's No Use Pretending/Wagon Wheels	1951	75.00	150.00	300.00
5800	Begin the Beguine/Looking for My Baby	1952	62.50	125.00	250.00
5853	Why Did You Leave Me/Chloe	1952	62.50	125.00	250.00
8291	Rock Me All Night Long/One Sweet Letter	1952	37.50	75.00	150.00
70060	I'll Be Back/Don't Mention My Name	1953	50.00	100.00	200.00
70119	Come a Little Bit Closer/She's Got to Go	1953	37.50	75.00	150.00
70213	Who'll Be the Fool/Rough Ridin'	1953	37.50	75.00	150.00
70240	Without a Song/Walkin' My Blues Away	1953	37.50	75.00	150.00
70307	September Song/Escortin' Or Courtin'	1954	37.50	75.00	150.00
70330	Going Home/Lonesome Road	1954	37.50	75.00	150.00
70413	I've Got You Under My Skin/Love Is No Dream	1954	62.50	125.00	250.00
—Pink label					
70413	I've Got You Under My Skin/Love Is No Dream	1954	25.00	50.00	100.00
—Black label					
70505	White Christmas/Silent Night	1954	50.00	100.00	200.00
—Pink label					
70505	White Christmas/Silent Night	1954	25.00	50.00	100.00
—Black label					
70554	Ol' Man River/Write Me a Letter	1955	50.00	100.00	200.00
—Pink label					
70554	Ol' Man River/Write Me a Letter	1955	25.00	50.00	100.00
—Black label					
NATIONAL					
9111	Count Every Star/I'm Gonna Paper All My Walls with Your Love	1950	1500.	2250.	3000.
—The only known Ravens single on a National 45; 20 other Ravens singles exist on National 78s					
OKEH					
6825	The Whiffenpoof Song/I Get All My Lovin' on a Saturday Night	1951	125.00	250.00	500.00
6843	That Old Gang of Mine/Everything But You	1951	125.00	250.00	500.00
6888	Mam'selle/Calypso Song	1952	100.00	200.00	400.00
SAVOY					
1540	White Christmas/Silent Night	1958	5.00	10.00	20.00
TOP RANK					
2003	Into the Shadows/The Rising Sun	1959	6.25	12.50	25.00
2016	Solitude/Hole in the Middle of the Moon	1959	6.25	12.50	25.00

7-Inch Extended Plays

Number	Title (A Side/B Side)	Yr	VG	VG+	NM
KING					
310	(contents unknown)	1954	125.00	250.00	500.00
310 [PS]	The Ravens Featuring Jimmy Ricks	1954	125.00	250.00	500.00
RENDITION					
104	(contents unknown)	195?	375.00	750.00	1500.
104 [PS]	Ol' Man River	195?	500.00	1000.	2000.

Albums

Number	Title (A Side/B Side)	Yr	VG	VG+	NM
HARLEM HIT PARADE					
1007	The Ravens	1975	2.50	5.00	10.00
REGENT					
MG-6062 [M]	Write Me a Letter	1957	75.00	150.00	300.00
—Green label					
MG-6062 [M]	Write Me a Letter	195?	37.50	75.00	150.00
—Red label					
SAVOY JAZZ					
SJL-2227 [(2)]	The Greatest Group of Them All	1978	3.00	6.00	12.00

RAW

Albums

Number	Title (A Side/B Side)	Yr	VG	VG+	NM
CORAL					
CRL 757515	Raw Holly	1971	7.50	15.00	30.00

RAW SPITT

45s

Number	Title (A Side/B Side)	Yr	VG	VG+	NM
UNITED ARTISTS					
50813	That Ain't My Wife/Song to Sing	1971	3.00	6.00	12.00

Albums

Number	Title (A Side/B Side)	Yr	VG	VG+	NM
UNITED ARTISTS					
UAS-6795	Maybe You Ain't Black	1971	6.25	12.50	25.00

RAWLS, LOU

12-Inch Singles

Number	Title (A Side/B Side)	Yr	VG	VG+	NM
PHILADELPHIA INT'L.					
3686	Let Me Be Good to You/Lover's Holiday	1979	2.50	5.00	10.00

45s

Number	Title (A Side/B Side)	Yr	VG	VG+	NM
ARISTA					
0103	Baby You Don't Know How Good You Are/Hour Glass	1975	—	3.00	6.00
BELL					
45608	She's Gone/Hour Glass	1974	—	3.00	6.00
45616	Who Can Tell Us Why?/Now You're Coming Back Michelle	1974	—	3.00	6.00
CANDIX					
305	In My Little Black Book/Just Thought You'd Like to Know	1960	5.00	10.00	20.00
312	When We Get Old/Eighty Ways	1961	5.00	10.00	20.00
CAPITOL					
2026	Little Drummer Boy/A Child with a Toy	1967	2.00	4.00	8.00
2084	Evil Woman/My Ancestors	1968	2.00	4.00	8.00
2172	Soul Serenade/You're Good for Me	1968	2.00	4.00	8.00
2252	Down Here on the Ground/I'm Satisfied (The Duffy Theme)	1968	2.00	4.00	8.00
2348	The Split/Why Can't I Speak	1968	2.00	4.00	8.00
2408	It's You/Sweet Charity	1969	2.00	4.00	8.00
2550	Your Good Thing (Is About to End)/Season of the Witch	1969	2.00	4.00	8.00
2668	I Can't Make It Alone/Make the World Go Away	1969	2.00	4.00	8.00
2734	You've Made Me So Very Happy/Let's Burn Down the Cornfield	1970	2.00	4.00	8.00
2856	Bring It On Home/Can You Dig It-Take Me for What I Am	1970	2.00	4.00	8.00
2942	Win Your Love for Me/Coppin' a Plea	1970	2.00	4.00	8.00
4622	That Lucky Old Sun/In My Heart	1961	3.75	7.50	15.00
4669	Nine-Pound Hammer/Above My Head	1961	3.75	7.50	15.00
4695	The Wedding (The Bride)/The Biggest Lover in Town	1962	3.00	6.00	12.00
4743	Trust Me/Please Let Me Be the First to Know	1962	3.00	6.00	12.00
4761	Save Your Love for Me/Trust Me	1962	3.00	6.00	12.00
4803	Stormy Monday/Sweet Lover	1962	3.00	6.00	12.00
—With Les McCann					
5049	Tobacco Road/Blues for Four-String Guitar	1963	3.00	6.00	12.00
5160	The House Next Door/Come On In, Mr. Blues	1964	3.00	6.00	12.00
5227	Love Is Blind/I Fell in Love	1964	3.00	6.00	12.00
5424	Three O'Clock in the Morning/Nothing Really Feels the Same	1965	3.00	6.00	12.00
5505	What'll I Do/Can I Please	1965	3.00	6.00	12.00
5655	The Shadow of Your Smile/Southside Blues	1966	2.50	5.00	10.00
5709	Love Is a Hurtin' Thing/Memory Lane	1966	2.50	5.00	10.00
5790	You Can Bring Me All Your Heartaches/A Woman Who's a Woman	1966	2.50	5.00	10.00
5824	Trouble Down Here Below/The Life That I Lead	1967	2.50	5.00	10.00
5824 [PS]	Trouble Down Here Below/The Life That I Lead	1967	2.50	5.00	10.00
5869	Dead End Street/Yes It Hurts, Doesn't It	1967	2.50	5.00	10.00
5941	Show Business/When Love Goes Wrong	1967	2.50	5.00	10.00
S7-18908	What Are You Doing New Year's Eve?/Have Yourself a Merry Little Christmas	1995	—	—	3.00
EPIC					
02999	Now Is the Time for Love/Will You Kiss Me One More Time	1982	—	2.00	4.00
03299	Together Again/Here Comes Garfield	1982	—	2.00	4.00
—Lou Rawls and Desiree Goyette					
03357	Let Me Show You How/Watch Your Back	1982	—	2.00	4.00
03758	Wind Beneath My Wings/Midnight Sun	1983	—	2.00	4.00
03944	Couple More Years/Upside Down	1983	—	2.00	4.00
04079	The One I Sing My Love Songs To/You Can't Take It With You	1983	—	2.00	4.00
04550	All-Time Lover/When We Were Young	1984	—	2.00	4.00
04677	Close Company/The Lady in My Life	1984	—	2.00	4.00
04773	Close Company/Forever I Do	1985	—	2.00	4.00
05714	Learn to Love Again/Ready or Not	1985	—	2.00	4.00
05831	Are You With Me/(Instrumental)	1986	—	2.00	4.00
05831 [PS]	Are You With Me/(Instrumental)	1986	—	2.00	4.00
06145	Stop Me from Starting This Feeling/Never Entered My Mind	1986	—	2.00	4.00
GAMBLE & HUFF					
310	I Wish You Belonged to Me/(B-side unknown)	1987	—	2.50	5.00
MGM					
14262	A Natural Man/You Can't Hold On	1971	—	3.00	6.00
14349	His Song Shall Be Sung/I'm Waiting	1972	—	3.00	6.00
14428	Politician/Walk On In	1972	—	3.00	6.00
14489	Man of Value/Learning Cup	1973	—	3.00	6.00
14527	Star Spangled Banner/Just a Closer Walk with Thee	1973	—	3.00	6.00
14574	Send for Me/Morning Comes Around	1973	—	3.00	6.00
14652	Dead End Street/Love Is a Hurtin' Thing	1973	—	3.00	6.00
PHILADELPHIA INT'L.					
3102	Ain't That Loving You (For More Reasons Than One)/(B-side unknown)	1980	—	2.50	5.00
3114	I Go Crazy/Be Anything (But Be Mine)	1980	—	2.50	5.00
3592	You'll Never Find Another Love Like Mine/Let's Fall in Love All Over Again	1976	—	2.50	5.00
3604	Groovy People/This Song Will Last Forever	1976	—	2.50	5.00
3623	See You When I Git There/Spring Again	1977	—	2.50	5.00
3634	Lady Love/Not the Staying Kind	1977	—	2.50	5.00
3643	One Life to Live/If I Coulda, Woulda, Shoulda	1978	—	2.50	5.00
3653	There Will Be Love/Unforgettable	1978	—	2.50	5.00
3672	Send In the Clowns/This Song Will Last Forever	1978	—	2.50	5.00
3684	Let Me Be Good to You/Lover's Holiday	1979	—	2.50	5.00
3738	Sit Down and Talk to Me/(B-side unknown)	1979	—	2.50	5.00
70051	Hoochie Coochie Man/You've Lost That Lovin' Feelin'	1981	—	2.50	5.00

Albums

Number	Title (A Side/B Side)	Yr	VG	VG+	NM
ALLEGIANCE					
AV-5016	Trying As Hard As I Can	198?	2.50	5.00	10.00
BELL					
1318	She's Gone	1974	3.00	6.00	12.00

Number	Title (A Side/B Side)	Yr	VG	VG+	NM
BLUE NOTE					
B1-91441	Stormy Monday	1990	3.00	6.00	12.00
—Reissue of Capitol 1714					
B1-91937	At Last	1989	3.00	6.00	12.00
B1-93841	It's Supposed to Be Fun	1990	3.75	7.50	15.00
CAPITOL					
ST-122	The Way It Was	1969	3.75	7.50	15.00
ST-215	The Way It Was — The Way It Is	1969	3.75	7.50	15.00
SWBB-261 [(2)]	Close-Up	1969	5.00	10.00	20.00
—Reissue of 1824 and 2042 in one package					
ST-325	Your Good Thing	1969	3.75	7.50	15.00
ST-427	You've Made Me So Very Happy	1970	3.75	7.50	15.00
ST-479	Bring It On Home	1970	3.75	7.50	15.00
STBB-720 [(2)]	Down Here on the Ground/I'd Rather Drink Muddy Water	1971	5.00	10.00	20.00
SM-1714	Stormy Monday	197?	2.50	5.00	10.00
—Reissue with new prefix					
ST 1714 [S]	Stormy Monday	1962	6.25	12.50	25.00
T 1714 [M]	Stormy Monday	1962	5.00	10.00	20.00
ST 1824 [S]	Black and Blue	1963	6.25	12.50	25.00
T 1824 [M]	Black and Blue	1963	5.00	10.00	20.00
ST 2042 [S]	Tobacco Road	1964	6.25	12.50	25.00
T 2042 [M]	Tobacco Road	1964	5.00	10.00	20.00
ST 2273 [S]	Nobody But Lou	1965	6.25	12.50	25.00
T 2273 [M]	Nobody But Lou	1965	5.00	10.00	20.00
ST 2401 [S]	Lou Rawls and Strings	1965	6.25	12.50	25.00
T 2401 [M]	Lou Rawls and Strings	1965	5.00	10.00	20.00
SM-2459	Lou Rawls Live!	197?	2.50	5.00	10.00
—Reissue with new prefix					
ST 2459 [S]	Lou Rawls Live!	1966	5.00	10.00	20.00
T 2459 [M]	Lou Rawls Live!	1966	3.75	7.50	15.00
SM-2566	Lou Rawls Soulin'	197?	2.50	5.00	10.00
—Reissue with new prefix					
ST 2566 [S]	Lou Rawls Soulin'	1966	5.00	10.00	20.00
T 2566 [M]	Lou Rawls Soulin'	1966	3.75	7.50	15.00
ST 2632 [S]	Lou Rawls Carryin' On!	1966	5.00	10.00	20.00
T 2632 [M]	Lou Rawls Carryin' On!	1966	3.75	7.50	15.00
ST 2713 [S]	Too Much!	1967	3.75	7.50	15.00
T 2713 [M]	Too Much!	1967	5.00	10.00	20.00
ST 2756 [S]	That's Lou	1967	3.75	7.50	15.00
T 2756 [M]	That's Lou	1967	5.00	10.00	20.00
ST 2790 [S]	Merry Christmas, Ho, Ho, Ho	1967	3.00	6.00	12.00
T 2790 [M]	Merry Christmas, Ho, Ho, Ho	1967	3.75	7.50	15.00
ST 2864 [S]	Feelin' Good	1968	3.75	7.50	15.00
T 2864 [M]	Feelin' Good	1968	7.50	15.00	30.00
ST 2927	You're Good for Me	1968	3.75	7.50	15.00
SKAO 2948	The Best of Lou Rawls	1968	3.75	7.50	15.00
SM-2948	The Best of Lou Rawls	197?	2.50	5.00	10.00
—Reissue with new prefix					
SKBB-11585 [(2)]	The Best of Lou Rawls	1976	3.00	6.00	12.00
SN-16096	The Best of Lou Rawls	1980	2.00	4.00	8.00
—Budget-line reissue					
SN-16097	Lou Rawls Live!	1980	2.00	4.00	8.00
—Budget-line reissue					
EPIC					
FE 37448	Now Is the Time	1982	2.50	5.00	10.00
FE 38553	When the Night Comes	1983	2.50	5.00	10.00
FE 39403	Close Company	1984	2.50	5.00	10.00
FE 40210	Love All Your Blues Away	1986	2.50	5.00	10.00
MGM					
SE-4771	Natural Man	1971	3.00	6.00	12.00
SE-4809	Silk & Soul	1972	3.00	6.00	12.00
SE-4861	A Man of Value	1973	3.00	6.00	12.00
SE-4965	Live at the Century Plaza	1974	3.00	6.00	12.00
PHILADELPHIA INT'L.					
PZ 33957	All Things in Time	1976	2.50	5.00	10.00
—No bar code on cover					
PZ 33957	All Things in Time	198?	2.00	4.00	8.00
—With bar code on cover					
PZ 34488	Unmistakably Lou	1977	2.50	5.00	10.00
PZ 34488	Unmistakably Lou	1986	2.00	4.00	8.00
—Budget-line reissue					
JZ 35036	When You Hear Lou, You've Heard It All	1977	2.50	5.00	10.00
PZ2 35517 [(2)]	Lou Rawls Live	1978	3.00	6.00	12.00
JZ 36006	Let Me Be Good to You	1979	2.50	5.00	10.00
PZ 36006	Let Me Be Good to You	198?	2.00	4.00	8.00
—Budget-line reissue					
JZ 36304	Sit Down and Talk to Me	1979	2.50	5.00	10.00
PZ 36304	Sit Down and Talk to Me	198?	2.00	4.00	8.00
—Budget-line reissue					
JZ 36774	Shades of Blue	1980	2.50	5.00	10.00
FZ 39285	Classics	1984	2.50	5.00	10.00
PICKWICK					
SPC-3156	Come On In, Mr. Blues	1971	2.50	5.00	10.00
SPC-3228	Gee Baby	1972	2.50	5.00	10.00
POLYDOR					
PD-1-6086	Naturally	1976	2.50	5.00	10.00

RAY, ALDER

45s

Number	Title (A Side/B Side)	Yr	VG	VG+	NM
LIBERTY					
55715	'Cause I Love Him/A Little Love (Will Go a Long Way)	1964	3.75	7.50	15.00
MINIT					
32005	I Need You Baby/My Heart Is in Danger	1966	2.50	5.00	10.00
REVUE					
11014	Love Will Let You Down/Run, Baby, Run	1968	2.00	4.00	8.00

RAY, DANNY

45s

Number	Title (A Side/B Side)	Yr	VG	VG+	NM
VIN					
1025	Love Me/Gone	1960	25.00	50.00	100.00

RAY, DAVE

Albums

Number	Title (A Side/B Side)	Yr	VG	VG+	NM
ELEKTRA					
EKL-284 [M]	Snaker's Here	1965	5.00	10.00	20.00
EKL-319 [M]	Fine Soft Land	1966	5.00	10.00	20.00
EKS-7284 [S]	Snaker's Here	1965	6.25	12.50	25.00
EKS-7319 [S]	Fine Soft Land	1966	6.25	12.50	25.00

RAY, DIANE

45s

Number	Title (A Side/B Side)	Yr	VG	VG+	NM
MERCURY					
72117	Please Don't Talk to the Lifeguard/That's All I Want from You	1963	3.75	7.50	15.00
72117 [PS]	Please Don't Talk to the Lifeguard/That's All I Want from You	1963	25.00	50.00	100.00
72195	My Summer Love/Where Is the Boy	1963	3.75	7.50	15.00
72195 [PS]	My Summer Love/Where Is the Boy	1963	15.00	30.00	60.00
72223	Snow Man/Just So Bobby Can See	1963	3.75	7.50	15.00
72223 [PS]	Snow Man/Just So Bobby Can See	1963	15.00	30.00	60.00
72248	No Arms Can Ever Hold You/Tied Up with Mary	1964	3.75	7.50	15.00
72276	Happy Happy Birthday Baby/That Boy's Gonna Be Mine	1964	3.75	7.50	15.00

Albums

Number	Title (A Side/B Side)	Yr	VG	VG+	NM
MERCURY					
MG-20903 [M]	The Exciting Years	1964	20.00	40.00	80.00
SR-60903 [S]	The Exciting Years	1964	25.00	50.00	100.00

RAY, JAMES

45s

Number	Title (A Side/B Side)	Yr	VG	VG+	NM
CAPRICE					
110	If You Gotta Make a Fool of Somebody/It's Been a Drag	1961	7.50	15.00	30.00
114	Itty Bitty Pieces/You Remember the Face	1962	6.25	12.50	25.00
117	Things Are Gonna Be Different/A Miracle	1962	6.25	12.50	25.00
CONGRESS					
109	Marie/The Old Man and the Mule	1963	5.00	10.00	20.00
201	Do the Monkey/Put Me in Your Diary	1963	5.00	10.00	20.00
203	The Masquerade Is Over/One by One	1963	5.00	10.00	20.00
218	We Got a Thing Goin' On/On That Day	1964	5.00	10.00	20.00
DYNAMIC SOUND					
503	I've Got My Mind Set on You/Always	1963	10.00	20.00	40.00
—The A-side was remade by George Harrison in 1987 as "Gof My Mind Set on You"					

7-Inch Extended Plays

Number	Title (A Side/B Side)	Yr	VG	VG+	NM
CAPRICE					
1002	(contents unknown)	1962	12.50	25.00	50.00
1002 [PS]	James Ray	1962	12.50	25.00	50.00

Albums

Number	Title (A Side/B Side)	Yr	VG	VG+	NM
CAPRICE					
LP-1002 [M]	James Ray	1962	20.00	40.00	80.00
SLP-1002 [S]	James Ray	1962	30.00	60.00	120.00

RAY, JOHNNIE

Also see DORIS DAY/JOHNNIE RAY.

45s

Number	Title (A Side/B Side)	Yr	VG	VG+	NM
CADENCE					
1387	In the Heart of a Fool/Let's Forget It Now	1960	3.00	6.00	12.00
COLUMBIA					
39636	Please Mr. Sun/Here Am I — Broken Hearted	1952	3.75	7.50	15.00
39659	Cry/Because of You	1952	3.00	6.00	12.00
—B-side by Tony Bennett; early reissue					
39698	What's the Use?/Mountains in Moonlight	1952	3.75	7.50	15.00
39700	Coffee and Cigarettes/Don't Blame Me	1952	3.00	6.00	12.00
39701	Walking My Baby Back Home/Out in the Cold Again	1952	3.00	6.00	12.00
39702	Don't Take Your Love from Me/The Lady Drinks Champagne	1952	3.00	6.00	12.00
39703	All of Me/Give Me Time	1952	3.00	6.00	12.00
—The above four comprise a box set					
39729	What's the Use?/A Guy Is a Guy	1952	2.50	5.00	10.00
—B-side by Doris Day					
39750	Walkin' My Baby Back Home/Give Me Time	1952	3.75	7.50	15.00
39788	All of Me/A Sinner Am I	1952	3.75	7.50	15.00
39814	Gee But I'm Lonesome/Don't Say Love Has Ended	1952	3.75	7.50	15.00
39837	Love Me (Baby Can't You Love Me)/Faith Can Move Mountains	1952	3.75	7.50	15.00
39897	The Thing I Might Have Been/The Commandments of Love	1952	3.75	7.50	15.00
39908	A Touch of God's Hand/I'm Gonna Walk and Talk with the Lord	1952	3.75	7.50	15.00
39939	Mr. Midnight/Oh, What a Sad, Sad Day	1953	3.00	6.00	12.00
39961	Somebody Stole My Gal/Glad Rag Doll	1953	3.00	6.00	12.00
40006	Satisfied/With These Hands	1953	3.00	6.00	12.00
40046	All I Do Is Dream of You/Tell the Lady I Said Goodbye	1953	3.00	6.00	12.00
40090	Please Don't Talk About Me When I'm Gone/An Orchid for the Lady	1953	3.00	6.00	12.00
40154	Why Should I Be Sorry?/You'd Be Surprised	1954	3.00	6.00	12.00
40200	Such a Night/Destiny	1954	3.75	7.50	15.00
40224	Hernando's Hideaway/Hey There	1954	3.00	6.00	12.00
40252	Going-Going-Gone/To Ev'ry Girl-To Ev'ry Boy	1954	3.00	6.00	12.00
40324	Papa Loves Mambo/The Only Girl I'll Ever Love	1954	3.00	6.00	12.00
40391	Alexander's Ragtime Band/If You Believe	1954	3.00	6.00	12.00
40392	As Time Goes By/Nobody's Sweetheart	1954	3.00	6.00	12.00
40435	Parade of Broken Hearts/Paths of Paradise	1955	3.00	6.00	12.00
40471	Flip, Flop and Fly/Thine Eyes Are As the Eyes of a Dove	1955	3.00	6.00	12.00
40528	Song of the Dreamer/I've Got So Many Million Miles	1955	3.00	6.00	12.00
40578	Johnnie's Comin' Home/Love, Love, Love	1955	3.00	6.00	12.00
40613	Who's Sorry Now/A Heart Comes In Handy	1955	3.00	6.00	12.00
40649	Ain't Misbehavin'/Walk Along with Kings	1956	3.00	6.00	12.00
40695	Because I Love You/Goodbye, Au Revoir, Adios	1956	3.00	6.00	12.00

Number	Title (A Side/B Side)	Yr	VG	VG+	NM
40729	Just Walking in the Rain/In the Candlelight	1956	2.50	5.00	10.00
40803	You Don't Owe Me a Thing/Look Homeward, Angel	1956	2.50	5.00	10.00
40893	Yes Tonight, Josephine/No Wedding Today	1957	2.50	5.00	10.00
40942	Build Your Love (On a Strong Foundation)/Street of Memories	1957	2.50	5.00	10.00
41002	Pink Sweater Angel/Texas Tambourine	1957	2.50	5.00	10.00
41069	Miss Me Just a Little/Soliloquy of a Fool	1957	2.50	5.00	10.00
41124	Plant a Little Seed/Strollin' Girl	1958	2.50	5.00	10.00
41162	Endlessly/Lonely for a Letter	1958	2.50	5.00	10.00
41213	Up Until Now/No Regrets	1958	2.50	5.00	10.00
41327	One Man's Love Song Is Another Man's Blues/ When's Your Birthday, Baby	1959	2.50	5.00	10.00
41372	Call Me Yours/Here and Now	1959	2.50	5.00	10.00
41438	I'll Never Fall in Love Again/You're All That I Live For	1959	2.50	5.00	10.00
41528	When It's Springtime in the Rockies/An Ordinary Couple	1959	2.50	5.00	10.00
41626	I'll Make You Mine/Before You	1959	2.50	5.00	10.00
41705	Don't Leave Me Now/Tell Me	1960	2.50	5.00	10.00
DECCA					
31459	After My Laughter Came Tears/Lookout Chattanooga	1963	2.00	4.00	8.00
31507	Lonely Wine/I Can't Stop Crying for You	1963	2.00	4.00	8.00
31601	Can't I/Break My Heartbreak	1964	2.00	4.00	8.00
GROOVE					
58-0044	One Life/Sometime Love	1964	2.00	4.00	8.00
LIBERTY					
55400	I Believe/A Mother's Love	1961	2.50	5.00	10.00
—With Timi Yuro					
55404	A Lover's Question/Nothing Goes Up Without Coming Down	1962	2.00	4.00	8.00
55431	Cry/Scotch and Soda	1962	2.00	4.00	8.00
OKEH					
6809	Whiskey and Gin/Tell the Lady I Said Goodbye	1951	6.25	12.50	25.00
6840	Cry/The Little White Cloud That Cried	1951	5.00	10.00	20.00
UNITED ARTISTS					
341	How Many Nights, How Many Days/I'll Bring Along My Banjo	1961	2.50	5.00	10.00
7-Inch Extended Plays					
COLUMBIA					
B-2536	*Walkin' My Baby Back Home/Somebody Stole My Gal/Nobody's Sweetheart/Please Don't Talk About Me When I'm Gone	195?	5.00	10.00	20.00
B-2536 [PS]	Johnnie Ray (Hall of Fame Series)	195?	5.00	10.00	20.00
B-2566	*Just Walking in the Rain/Please, Mr. Sun/All of Me/Tell the Lady I Said Goodbye	195?	5.00	10.00	20.00
B-2566 [PS]	Johnnie Ray (Hall of Fame Series)	195?	5.00	10.00	20.00
B-9611	Pretty-Eyed Baby/Lotus Blossom//Shake a Hand/I'll Never Be Free	1957	5.00	10.00	20.00
B-9611 [PS]	The Big Beat, Part 1	1957	5.00	10.00	20.00
B-9612	(contents unknown)	1957	5.00	10.00	20.00
B-9612 [PS]	The Big Beat, Part 2	1957	5.00	10.00	20.00
EPIC					
EG-7021	Cry/The Little White Cloud That Cried//Whiskey and Gin/Tell the Lady I Said Goodbye	1957	6.25	12.50	25.00
EG-7021 [PS]	Johnnie Ray's Greatest	1957	6.25	12.50	25.00
Albums					
COLUMBIA					
CL 961 [M]	The Big Beat	1957	12.50	25.00	50.00
CL 1093 [M]	At the Desert Inn in Las Vegas	1957	12.50	25.00	50.00
CL 1225 [M]	'Til Morning	1958	10.00	20.00	40.00
—Red and black label with six "eye" logos					
CL 1225 [M]	'Til Morning	1963	5.00	10.00	20.00
—Red label with either "Guraranteed High Fidelity" or "360 Sound Mono" at bottom					
CL 1227 [M]	Johnnie Ray's Greatest Hits	1958	10.00	20.00	40.00
—Red and black label with 6 "eye" logos					
CL 1227 [M]	Johnnie Ray's Greatest Hits	1962	6.25	12.50	25.00
—"Guaranteed High Fidelity" on label					
CL 1227 [M]	Johnnie Ray's Greatest Hits	1965	3.75	7.50	15.00
—"360 Sound" label					
CL 1385 [M]	On the Trail	1959	10.00	20.00	40.00
CL 2510 [10]	I Cry for You	1955	17.50	35.00	70.00
—"House Party Series" issue					
CL 6199 [10]	Johnnie Ray	1951	20.00	40.00	80.00
CS 8180 [S]	On the Trail	1959	12.50	25.00	50.00
COLUMBIA SPECIAL PRODUCTS					
P 13086	Greatest Hits	197?	2.50	5.00	10.00
EPIC					
LN 1120 [10]	Johnnie Ray	1955	20.00	40.00	80.00
HARMONY					
H 30609	The Best of Johnnie Ray	1971	3.00	6.00	12.00
LIBERTY					
LRP-3221 [M]	Johnnie Ray	1962	5.00	10.00	20.00
LST-7221 [S]	Johnnie Ray	1962	7.50	15.00	30.00
SUNSET					
SUM-1125 [M]	Mr. Cry	196?	3.00	6.00	12.00
SUS-5125 [S]	Mr. Cry	196?	3.00	6.00	12.00

RAY AND THE DARCHAES

45s

Number	Title (A Side/B Side)	Yr	VG	VG+	NM
ALJON					
1249	Carol/Little Girl So Fine	1962	30.00	60.00	120.00
BUZZY					
202	Darling Forever/There Will Always Be	1962	25.00	50.00	100.00

RAY, GOODMAN AND BROWN

See THE MOMENTS.

RAY-O-VACS, THE

45s

Number	Title (A Side/B Side)	Yr	VG	VG+	NM
ATCO					
6085	Party Time/Crying All Alone	1957	6.25	12.50	25.00
DECCA					
48162	Besame Mucho/You Gotta Love My Baby Too	1950	6.25	12.50	25.00
48181	A Kiss in the Dark/Got Two Arms	1950	6.25	12.50	25.00
48197	Goodnight My Love/Take Me Back to My Boots and Saddle	1951	6.25	12.50	25.00
48211	You Can Depend on Me/If You Ever Should Leave Me	1951	6.25	12.50	25.00
48221	My Baby's Gone/Let's	1951	6.25	12.50	25.00
48234	What's Mine Is Mine/I Still Love You Baby	1951	6.25	12.50	25.00
48260	Charmaine/Hands Across the Table	1951	6.25	12.50	25.00
48274	When the Swallows Come Back to Capistrano/ She's a Real Lovin' Baby	1952	6.25	12.50	25.00
JOSIE					
763	Darling/Ridin' High	1954	7.50	15.00	30.00
781	I Still Love You/Daddy	1955	7.50	15.00	30.00
JUBILEE					
5098	What Can I Say/Start Lovin' Me	1952	7.50	15.00	30.00
5124	Outside of Paradise/You Know	1953	7.50	15.00	30.00
KAISER					
384	Crying All Alone/Party Time	1956	7.50	15.00	30.00
389	Wine-O/Hong Kong	1956	7.50	15.00	30.00
SHARP					
103	I'll Always Be in Love with You/Little Boy	1960	5.00	10.00	20.00

RAY-VONS, THE

45s

Number	Title (A Side/B Side)	Yr	VG	VG+	NM
LAURIE					
3248	Judy/Regina	1964	20.00	40.00	80.00

RAYE, SUSAN

Also see BUCK OWENS AND SUSAN RAYE.

45s

Number	Title (A Side/B Side)	Yr	VG	VG+	NM
CAPITOL					
2701	Put a Little Love in Your Heart/I've Carried This Torch Much Too Long	1969	—	3.00	6.00
2833	One Night Stand/She Don't Deserve You Anymore	1970	—	3.00	6.00
2950	Willy Jones/I'll Love You Forever (If You're Sure You'll Want Me Then)	1970	—	3.00	6.00
3035	L.A. International Airport/Merry-Go-Round of Love	1971	—	3.00	6.00
3129	Pitty, Pitty, Patter/I'll Be Gone	1971	—	3.00	6.00
3209	(I've Got a) Happy Heart/How Long Will My Baby Be Gone	1971	—	3.00	6.00
3289	A Song to Sing/Adios, Farewell, Goodbye, Good Luck, So Long	1972	—	2.50	5.00
3327	My Heart Has a Mind of Its Own/You'll Never Miss the Water	1972	—	2.50	5.00
3438	Wheel of Fortune/My Heart Skips a Beat	1972	—	2.50	5.00
3499	Love Sure Feels Good in My Heart/I've Got You on My Mind Again	1972	—	2.50	5.00
3569	Cheating Game/I'll Love You Forever and Ever	1973	—	2.50	5.00
3699	Plastic Trains, Paper Planes/I Won't Be Needing You	1973	—	2.50	5.00
3782	When You Get Back from Nashville/Nobody's Fool But Yours	1973	—	2.50	5.00
3850	Stop the World (And Let Me Off)/Love's Ups and Downs	1974	—	2.00	4.00
3927	You Can Sure See It from Here/I Wish I Was a Butterfly	1974	—	2.00	4.00
3980	Whatcha Gonna Do with a Dog Like That/That Loving Feeling	1974	—	2.00	4.00
4063	Ghost Story/Beginner's Luck	1975	—	2.00	4.00
4197	Honey Toast and Sunshine/Only a Good Love Lasts Forever	1975	—	2.00	4.00
UNITED ARTISTS					
XW870	Ozark Mountain Lullaby/Johnny Sunshine	1976	—	2.00	4.00
XW934	Mr. Heartache/Turn Away	1977	—	2.00	4.00
XW976	Saturday Night to Sunday Quiet/My Hiding Place	1977	—	2.00	4.00
XW1026	It Didn't Have to Be a Diamond/My Hiding Place	1977	—	2.00	4.00
WESTEXAS AMERICA					
1	Put Another Notch in Your Belt/I Just Can't Take the Leaving Anymore	1984	—	2.00	4.00
Albums					
CAPITOL					
ST-543	One Night Stand	1970	3.75	7.50	15.00
ST-736	Willy Jones	1971	3.75	7.50	15.00
ST-807	Pitty, Pitty, Patter	1971	3.75	7.50	15.00
ST-875	(I've Got a) Happy Heart	1972	3.75	7.50	15.00
ST-11055	My Heart Has a Mind of Its Own	1972	3.00	6.00	12.00
ST-11106	Wheel of Fortune	1972	3.00	6.00	12.00
ST-11135	Love Sure Feels Good in My Heart	1973	3.00	6.00	12.00
ST-11179	Cheating Game	1973	3.00	6.00	12.00
ST-11223	Plastic Trains, Paper Planes	1973	3.00	6.00	12.00
ST-11255	Hymns by Susan Raye	1974	3.00	6.00	12.00
ST-11282	The Best of Susan Raye	1974	3.00	6.00	12.00
ST-11333	Singing	1974	3.00	6.00	12.00
ST-11393	Whatch Gonna Do with a Dog Like That	1975	3.00	6.00	12.00
UNITED ARTISTS					
UA-LA764-G	Susan Raye	1977	3.00	6.00	12.00

RAYS, THE

45s

Number	Title (A Side/B Side)	Yr	VG	VG+	NM
AMY					
900	Love Another Girl/Sad Saturday	1964	2.00	4.00	8.00

Number	Title (A Side/B Side)	Yr	VG	VG+	NM
CAMEO					
117	Silhouettes/Daddy Cool	1957	6.25	12.50	25.00
128	Rendezvous/Triangle	1958	7.50	15.00	30.00
133	Rags to Riches/The Man Above	1958	7.50	15.00	30.00
CHESS					
1613	Tippity Top/Moo-Goo-Gai-Pan	1956	6.25	12.50	25.00
1678	How Long Must I Wait/Second Fiddle	1957	6.25	12.50	25.00
UNART					
2001	Souvenirs of Summertime/Elevator Operator	1958	10.00	20.00	40.00
XYZ					
100	My Steady Girl/No One Loves You Like I Do	1957	15.00	30.00	60.00
102	Silhouettes/Daddy Cool	1957	50.00	100.00	200.00
—Gray label					
102	Silhouettes/Daddy Cool	1957	15.00	30.00	60.00
—Blue label					
106	Souvenirs of Summertime/Elevator Operator	1958	12.50	25.00	50.00
600	Why Do You Look the Other Way/Zimbo Lula	1959	12.50	25.00	50.00
605	It's a Cryin' Shame/Mediterranean Moon	1959	10.00	20.00	40.00
607	Magic Moon/Louie Hoo Hoo	1960	10.00	20.00	40.00
—Blue label					
607	Magic Moon/Louie Hoo Hoo	1960	6.25	12.50	25.00
—Red label					
608	Old Devil Moon/Silver Starlight	1960	6.25	12.50	25.00
7-Inch Extended Plays					
CHESS					
5120	(contents unknown)	1958	100.00	200.00	400.00
5120 [PS]	The Rays	1958	100.00	200.00	400.00

RAYS, THE (2)

45s

Number	Title (A Side/B Side)	Yr	VG	VG+	NM
PERRI					
1004	Are You Happy Now/Bright Brown Eyes	1962	7.50	15.00	30.00
—Frankie Valli performed on this record					

RE'VELLS, THE

45s

Number	Title (A Side/B Side)	Yr	VG	VG+	NM
ROMAN PRESS					
201	Let It Please Be You/Love Walked In	1962	25.00	50.00	100.00

RE-VELS, THE

45s

Number	Title (A Side/B Side)	Yr	VG	VG+	NM
ATLAS					
1035	My Lost Love/Love Me, Baby	1954	100.00	200.00	400.00
—As "The Re-Vels Quartette"					
CHESS					
1708	False Alarm/When You Come Back to Me	1958	37.50	75.00	150.00
SOUND					
129	You Lied to Me/Later, Later Baby	1956	37.50	75.00	150.00
135	Dream, My Darlin', Dream/Cha Cha Toni	1956	37.50	75.00	150.00
TEEN					
122	So in Love/It Happened to Me	1955	200.00	400.00	600.00

REAL ORIGINAL BEATLES, THE

Yeah, right.

45s

Number	Title (A Side/B Side)	Yr	VG	VG+	NM
DOT					
16655	The Beatle Story (Part 1)/The Beatle Story (Part 2)	1964	5.00	10.00	20.00

REBECCA AND THE SUNNY BROOK FARMERS

Albums

Number	Title (A Side/B Side)	Yr	VG	VG+	NM
MUSICOR					
MS-3176	Rebecca and the Sunny Brook Farmers	1969	10.00	20.00	40.00

REBELS, THE (1)

See ROCKIN' REBELS.

REBELS, THE (2)

45s

Number	Title (A Side/B Side)	Yr	VG	VG+	NM
KING'S X					
3362	In the Park/In My Heart	1959	250.00	500.00	1000.

REBELS, THE (3)

45s

Number	Title (A Side/B Side)	Yr	VG	VG+	NM
PEACOCK					
1909	The Donkey Step/Just Give Me Your Heart	1962	5.00	10.00	20.00

REBENACK, MAC

See DR. JOHN.

REBIRTH

Albums

Number	Title (A Side/B Side)	Yr	VG	VG+	NM
AVANT GARDE					
AVS-135	Rebirth	1971	12.50	25.00	50.00

REBOUNDS, THE

This is not the group that became the Stampeders, according to a former member of the band.

45s

Number	Title (A Side/B Side)	Yr	VG	VG+	NM
TOWER					
288	Since I Fell for You/I'm Not Your Steppin' Stone	1966	3.75	7.50	15.00

REBS, THE

Albums

Number	Title (A Side/B Side)	Yr	VG	VG+	NM
FREDLO					
6830	1968 A.D. Break Through	1968	100.00	200.00	400.00

RECALLS, THE

45s

Number	Title (A Side/B Side)	Yr	VG	VG+	NM
ARROW					
2002	No Reason/Nobody's Guy	196?	20.00	40.00	80.00

RED CRAYOLA, THE

Albums

Number	Title (A Side/B Side)	Yr	VG	VG+	NM
INTERNATIONAL ARTISTS					
2	Parable of the Arable Land	1979	3.75	7.50	15.00
—Reissue with "Masterfonics" in trail-off wax					
2 [M]	Parable of the Arable Land	1968	25.00	50.00	100.00
2 [S]	Parable of the Arable Land	1968	15.00	30.00	60.00
7	God Bless the Red Crayola	1968	15.00	30.00	60.00
7	God Bless the Red Crayola	1979	3.75	7.50	15.00
—Reissue with "Masterfonics" in trail-off wax					

REDBONE

Also see PAT AND LOLLY VEGAS.

45s

Number	Title (A Side/B Side)	Yr	VG	VG+	NM
EPIC					
10597	Crazy Cajun Cade Walk Band/Night Come Down	1970	—	3.00	6.00
10670	Maggie/New Blue Sermonette	1970	—	3.00	6.00
10712	Who Can Say/Light as a Feather	1971	—	3.00	6.00
10749	The Witch Queen of New Orleans/Chant: 13th Hour	1971	—	3.00	6.00
10839	When You Got Trouble/(B-side unknown)	1972	—	2.50	5.00
10866	One Monkey (Don't Stop No Show)/Message from a Drum	1972	—	2.50	5.00
10910	Already Here/Fais-Do	1972	—	2.50	5.00
10946	Poison Ivy/Condition Your Condition	1973	—	2.50	5.00
10979	We Were All Wounded at Wounded Knee/Speakeasy	1973	—	2.50	5.00
11035	Come and Get Your Love/Your Miserable Face	1973	—	2.50	5.00
11035	Come and Get Your Love/Day to Day Life	1973	—	2.50	5.00
11131	Wovoka/Clouds in My Sunshine	1974	—	2.00	4.00
50015	Suzie Girl/Interstate Highway 101	1974	—	2.00	4.00
50043	One More Time/Blood, Sweat and Tears	1974	—	2.00	4.00
50074	Only You and Rock and Roll/Interstate Highway 101	1975	—	2.00	4.00
50107	Physical Attraction/I've Got to Find the Right Woman	1975	—	2.00	4.00
RCA					
PB-11096	Give Our Love Another Try/Funny Silk	1977	—	2.00	4.00
PB-11182	Checkin' It Out/Funky Silk	1977	—	2.00	4.00
Albums					
EPIC					
EGP 501 [(2)]	Redbone	1970	5.00	10.00	20.00
E 30109	Potlatch	1970	3.75	7.50	15.00
EQ 30815 [Q]	Message from a Drum	1973	5.00	10.00	20.00
KE 30815	Message from a Drum	1972	3.75	7.50	15.00
KE 31598	Already Here	1972	3.75	7.50	15.00
KE 32462	Wovoka	1974	3.75	7.50	15.00
EQ 33053 [Q]	Bearded Dreams Through Turquoise Eyes	1974	5.00	10.00	20.00
KE 33053	Bearded Dreams Through Turquoise Eyes	1974	3.75	7.50	15.00
KEG 33456 [(2)]	Come & Get Your Redbone	1975	5.00	10.00	20.00
RCA VICTOR					
AFL1-2352	Cycles	1977	3.00	6.00	12.00

REDCOATS, THE

Also see STEVE ALAIMO.

45s

Number	Title (A Side/B Side)	Yr	VG	VG+	NM
KITE					
2003	Perkin/Hi Ho	1957	12.50	25.00	50.00
2003	Perkins/Hi Ho	1957	12.50	25.00	50.00
—Note slight variation in A-side title					

REDDING, OTIS

Also see OTIS AND CARLA; THE SHOOTERS.

45s

Number	Title (A Side/B Side)	Yr	VG	VG+	NM
ATCO					
6592	Hard to Handle/Amen	1968	2.50	5.00	10.00
6612	I've Got Dreams to Remember/Nobody's Fault But Mine	1968	2.50	5.00	10.00
6631	White Christmas/Merry Christmas, Baby	1968	2.50	5.00	10.00
6636	Papa's Got a Brand New Bag/Direct Me	1968	2.50	5.00	10.00
6654	A Lover's Question/You Made a Man Out of Me	1969	2.50	5.00	10.00
6677	Love Man/I Can't Turn You Loose	1969	2.50	5.00	10.00
6700	Free Me/Higher and Higher	1969	2.50	5.00	10.00
6723	Look at the Girl/That's a Good Idea	1969	2.50	5.00	10.00
6742	Demonstration/Johnny's Heartbreak	1970	2.00	4.00	8.00
6766	Giving Away None of My Love/Snatch a Little Piece	1970	2.00	4.00	8.00
6802	Try a Little Tenderness/I've Been Loving You Too Long (To Stop Now)	1971	—	3.00	6.00
6907	My Girl/Good to Me	1972	—	2.50	5.00
7069	White Christmas/Merry Christmas, Baby	1976	—	2.50	5.00
7321	White Christmas/Merry Christmas, Baby	1980	—	2.00	4.00
99955	White Christmas/Merry Christmas, Baby	1982	—	2.00	4.00
BETHLEHEM					
3083	Shout Bamalama/Fat Girl	1964	5.00	10.00	20.00
CONFEDERATE					
135	Shout Bamalama/Fat Girl	1962	12.50	25.00	50.00
FINER ARTS					
2016	She's Alright/Tough Enuff	1961	12.50	25.00	50.00
—Originally released on Trans World by "The Shooters"					
KING					
6149	Shout Bamalama/Fat Girl	1968	2.50	5.00	10.00
ORBIT					
135	Shout Bamalama/Fat Girl	1961	75.00	150.00	300.00
PHILCO-FORD					
HP-13	Shake/Fa-Fa-Fa-Fa-Fa	1967	5.00	10.00	20.00
—4-inch plastic "Hip Pocket Record" with color sleeve					
STONE					
209	You Left the Water Running/The Otis Jam	1976	3.00	6.00	12.00
—B-side by the Memphis Studio Band					
VOLT					
103	These Arms of Mine/Hey, Hey Baby	1962	5.00	10.00	20.00

Number	Title (A Side/B Side)	Yr	VG	VG+	NM
109	That's What My Heart Needs/Mary's Little Lamb	1963	5.00	10.00	20.00
112	Pain in My Heart/Something Is Worrying Me	1963	5.00	10.00	20.00
116	Come to Me/Don't Leave Me This Way	1964	3.75	7.50	15.00
117	Security/I Want to Thank You	1964	3.75	7.50	15.00
121	Chained and Bound/Your One and Only Man	1964	3.75	7.50	15.00
124	Mr. Pitiful/That's How Strong My Love Is	1965	3.75	7.50	15.00
126	I've Been Loving You Too Long (To Stop Now)/ I'm Depending on You	1965	3.75	7.50	15.00
128	Respect/Ole Man Trouble	1965	3.75	7.50	15.00
130	I Can't Turn You Loose/Just One More Day	1965	3.75	7.50	15.00
132	Satisfaction/Any Ole Way	1966	3.75	7.50	15.00
136	My Lover's Prayer/Don't Mess with Cupid	1966	3.75	7.50	15.00
138	Fa-Fa-Fa-Fa-Fa (Sad Song)/Good to Me	1966	3.75	7.50	15.00
141	Try a Little Tenderness/I'm Sick Y'All	1966	3.75	7.50	15.00
146	I Love You More Than Words Can Say/Let Me Come On Home	1967	3.00	6.00	12.00
149	Shake/You Don't Miss Your Water	1967	3.00	6.00	12.00
152	Glory of Love/I'm Coming Home	1967	3.00	6.00	12.00
157	(Sittin' On) The Dock of the Bay/Sweet Lorene	1968	3.00	6.00	12.00
—Black and red label					
157	(Sittin' On) The Dock of the Bay/Sweet Lorene	1968	2.50	5.00	10.00
—Multicolor (mostly brown) label					
163	The Happy Song (Dum-Dum)/Open That Door	1968	2.50	5.00	10.00

Albums

ATCO

Number	Title	Yr	VG	VG+	NM
33-161 [M]	Pain in My Heart	1964	62.50	125.00	250.00
SD 33-161 [R]	Pain in My Heart	1968	62.50	125.00	250.00
33-252 [M]	The Immortal Otis Redding	1968	12.50	25.00	50.00
—Mono is white label promo only					
SD 33-252 [S]	The Immortal Otis Redding	1968	3.75	7.50	15.00
SD 33-261	History of Otis Redding	1968	3.75	7.50	15.00
—Reissue of Volt 418					
SD 33-265	Otis Redding In Person at the Whiskey A-Go-Go	1968	3.75	7.50	15.00
SD 33-284	Otis Blue/Otis Redding Sings Soul	1969	3.75	7.50	15.00
—Reissue of Volt 412					
SD 33-285	The Soul Album	1969	3.75	7.50	15.00
—Reissue of Volt 413					
SD 33-286	Otis Redding Live in Europe	1969	3.75	7.50	15.00
—Reissue of Volt 416					
SD 33-287	Complete & Unbelievable...The Otis Redding Dictionary of Soul	1969	3.75	7.50	15.00
—Reissue of Volt 415					
SD 33-288	The Dock of the Bay	1969	3.75	7.50	15.00
—Reissue of Volt 419					
SD 33-289	Love Man	1969	3.75	7.50	15.00
SD 33-333	Tell the Truth	1970	3.75	7.50	15.00
SD 2-801 [(2)]	The Best of Otis Redding	1972	5.00	10.00	20.00

ATLANTIC

Number	Title	Yr	VG	VG+	NM
SD 19346	Recorded Live	198?	2.50	5.00	10.00
81282	The Best of Otis Redding	1985	2.50	5.00	10.00
81762 [(4)]	The Otis Redding Story	1987	7.50	15.00	30.00

PAIR

Number	Title	Yr	VG	VG+	NM
PDL2-1062 [(2)]	The Legend of Otis Redding	1986	3.75	7.50	15.00

VOLT

Number	Title	Yr	VG	VG+	NM
411 [M]	The Great Otis Redding Sings Soul Ballads	1965	22.50	45.00	90.00
S-411 [R]	The Great Otis Redding Sings Soul Ballads	1968	27.50	55.00	110.00
412 [M]	Otis Blue/Otis Redding Sings Soul	1965	10.00	20.00	40.00
S-412 [S]	Otis Blue/Otis Redding Sings Soul	1965	12.50	25.00	50.00
413 [M]	The Soul Album	1966	10.00	20.00	40.00
S-413 [S]	The Soul Album	1966	12.50	25.00	50.00
415 [M]	Complete & Unbelievable...The Otis Redding Dictionary of Soul	1966	10.00	20.00	40.00
S-415 [S]	Complete & Unbelievable...The Otis Redding Dictionary of Soul	1966	12.50	25.00	50.00
416 [M]	Otis Redding Live in Europe	1967	7.50	15.00	30.00
S-416 [S]	Otis Redding Live in Europe	1967	10.00	20.00	40.00
418 [M]	History of Otis Redding	1967	10.00	20.00	40.00
S-418 [S]	History of Otis Redding	1967	7.50	15.00	30.00
S-419	The Dock of the Bay	1968	7.50	15.00	30.00

REDDY, HELEN

45s

CAPITOL

Number	Title (A Side/B Side)	Yr	VG	VG+	NM
3027	I Don't Know How to Love Him/I Believe in Music	1971	—	2.50	5.00
3138	Crazy Love/Best Friend	1971	—	2.50	5.00
3231	No Sad Song/More Than You Could Take	1971	—	2.50	5.00
3350	I Am Woman/More Than You Could Take	1972	—	2.50	5.00
—Red and orange "target" label					
3350	I Am Woman/More Than You Could Take	1972	—	2.00	4.00
—Orange label, "Capitol" at bottom					
3527	Peaceful/What Would They Say	1973	—	2.00	4.00
3645	Delta Dawn/If We Could Still Be Friends	1973	—	2.00	4.00
3768	Leave Me Alone (Ruby Red Dress)/The Old Fashioned Way	1973	—	2.00	4.00
3845	Keep On Singing/You're My Home	1974	—	2.00	4.00
3897	You and Me Against the World/Love Song for Jeffrey	1974	—	2.00	4.00
3972	Angie Baby/I Think I'll Write a Song	1974	—	2.00	4.00
4021	Emotion/I've Been Waiting for You So Long	1974	—	2.00	4.00
4098	You Don't Need a Reason/Long Time Looking	1975	—	2.00	4.00
4108	Bluebird/You Don't Need a Reason	1975	—	2.00	4.00
4128	Ain't No Way to Treat a Lady/Long Time Looking	1975	—	2.00	4.00
4192	Somewhere in the Night/Ten to Eight	1975	—	2.00	4.00
4312	I Can't Hear You No More/Music Is My Life	1976	—	2.00	4.00
4350	You Make It So Easy/Gladiola	1976	—	2.00	4.00
4418	You're My World/Thank You	1977	—	2.00	4.00
4487	The Happy Girls/Laissez Les Bontemps Rouler	1977	—	2.00	4.00
4521	Candle on the Water/Brazzle Dazzle Day	1977	—	2.00	4.00
4521 [PS]	Candle on the Water/Brazzle Dazzle Day	1977	—	3.00	6.00
4555	We'll Sing in the Sunshine/I'd Rather Be Alone	1978	—	2.00	4.00
4582	Ready or Not/If I Ever Had to Say Goodbye to You	1978	—	2.00	4.00
4628	Lady of the Night/Poor Little Fool	1978	—	2.00	4.00
4654	Mama/West Wind Circus	1978	—	2.00	4.00
4712	Make Love to Me/More Than You Could Take	1979	—	2.00	4.00
4786	Trying to Get to You/Let Me Be Your Woman	1979	—	2.00	4.00
4867	Love's Not the Question/Take What You Find	1980	—	2.00	4.00
4918	Way with the Ladies/Killer Barracuda	1980	—	2.00	4.00

FONTANA

Number	Title (A Side/B Side)	Yr	VG	VG+	NM
1611	One Way Ticket/Go	1968	3.75	7.50	15.00

MCA

Number	Title (A Side/B Side)	Yr	VG	VG+	NM
51106	I Can't Say Goodbye to You/Let's Just Stay Home Tonight	1981	—	2.00	4.00
51143	Stars Fell on California/When I Dream	1981	—	2.00	4.00
51186	Theme from "Continental Divide"/When I Dream	1981	—	2.00	4.00
52170	Don't Tell Me Tonight/Yesterday Can't Hurt Me	1983	—	2.00	4.00
52221	Imagination/The Way I Feel	1983	—	2.00	4.00

Albums

CAPITOL

Number	Title	Yr	VG	VG+	NM
ST-762	I Don't Know How to Love Him	1971	3.75	7.50	15.00
ST-857	Helen Reddy	1971	3.75	7.50	15.00
ST-11068	I Am Woman	1972	2.50	5.00	10.00
SMAS-11213	Long Hard Climb	1973	2.50	5.00	10.00
SO-11284	Love Song for Jeffrey	1974	2.50	5.00	10.00
ST-11348	Free and Easy	1974	2.50	5.00	10.00
ST-11418	No Way to Treat a Lady	1975	2.50	5.00	10.00
ST-11467	Helen Reddy's Greatest Hits	1975	2.50	5.00	10.00
—Orange label					
SW-11467	Helen Reddy's Greatest Hits	1978	2.00	4.00	8.00
—Purple label					
ST-11547	Music, Music	1976	2.50	5.00	10.00
SO-11640	Ear Candy	1977	2.50	5.00	10.00
SW-11759	We'll Sing in the Sunshine	1978	2.50	5.00	10.00
SKBO-11873 [(2)]	Live	1979	3.00	6.00	12.00
SO-11949	Reddy	1979	2.50	5.00	10.00
SOO-12068	Take What You Find	1980	2.50	5.00	10.00
SN-16098	Helen Reddy	1980	2.00	4.00	8.00
—Budget-line reissue					
SN-16099	I Am Woman	1980	2.00	4.00	8.00
—Budget-line reissue					
SN-16100	I Don't Know How to Love Him	1980	2.00	4.00	8.00
—Budget-line reissue					
SN-16101	Long Hard Climb	1980	2.00	4.00	8.00
—Budget-line reissue					
SN-16195	Love Song for Jeffrey	198?	2.00	4.00	8.00
—Budget-line reissue					
SN-16196	No Way to Treat a Lady	1980	2.00	4.00	8.00
—Budget-line reissue					
SN-16199	We'll Sing in the Sunshine	1980	2.00	4.00	8.00
—Budget-line reissue					
SN-16200	Reddy	1980	2.00	4.00	8.00
—Budget-line reissue					
SN-16248	Take What You Find	198?	2.00	4.00	8.00
—Budget-line reissue					
SN-16249	Free and Easy	198?	2.00	4.00	8.00
—Budget-line reissue					
SN-16250 [(2)]	Live	198?	2.00	4.00	8.00
—Budget-line reissue					
SN-16333	Helen Reddy's Greatest Hits	1984	—	3.00	6.00
—Budget-line reissue					

MCA

Number	Title	Yr	VG	VG+	NM
5376	Imagination	198?	2.00	4.00	8.00

PAIR

Number	Title	Yr	VG	VG+	NM
PDL2-1066 [(2)]	Lust for Life	1986	3.00	6.00	12.00

REDELL, TEDDY

45s

ATCO

Number	Title (A Side/B Side)	Yr	VG	VG+	NM
6162	Judy/Can't You See	1960	5.00	10.00	20.00

HI

Number	Title (A Side/B Side)	Yr	VG	VG+	NM
2024	Pipeliner/I Want to Hold You	1960	5.00	10.00	20.00

VADEN

Number	Title (A Side/B Side)	Yr	VG	VG+	NM
110	Knockin' on the Backside/Before It Began	1960	30.00	60.00	120.00
115	Goldust/Corrine, Corrina	1960	30.00	60.00	120.00
116	Judy/Can't You See	1960	30.00	60.00	120.00
117	Pipeliner/I Want to Hold You	1960	30.00	60.00	120.00
301	Pipeliner/I Want to Hold You	1961	20.00	40.00	80.00
305	I'll Sail My Ship Alone/Don't Grow Old Alone	1961	20.00	40.00	80.00

REDEYE

45s

PENTAGRAM

Number	Title (A Side/B Side)	Yr	VG	VG+	NM
202	Mississippi State Line/199 Thoughts Too Late	1970	—	3.00	6.00
204	Games/Collections of Yesterday and Now	1970	—	3.00	6.00
206	Red Eye Blues/Making of a Hero	1971	—	3.00	6.00
209	Homebound Feelin'/I'm Going Blind	1971	—	3.00	6.00
213	Mountain Annie/Just a Little More	1971	—	3.00	6.00

Albums

PENTAGRAM

Number	Title	Yr	VG	VG+	NM
PE-10003	Redeye	1970	3.75	7.50	15.00
PR-10006	One Man's Poison	1971	3.75	7.50	15.00

REDJACKS, THE

45s

APT

Number	Title (A Side/B Side)	Yr	VG	VG+	NM
25006	Big Brown Eyes/To Make You Mine	1958	5.00	10.00	20.00

OKLAHOMA

Number	Title (A Side/B Side)	Yr	VG	VG+	NM
5005	Big Brown Eyes/To Make You Mine	1958	12.50	25.00	50.00

REDNOW, EIVETS

See STEVIE WONDER.

REDWOODS, THE

JEFF BARRY was involved with this group.

45s

EPIC

Number	Title (A Side/B Side)	Yr	VG	VG+	NM
9447	Shake, Shake Sherry/The Memory Lingers On	1961	10.00	20.00	40.00
—As "The Flairs"					

Number	Title (A Side/B Side)	Yr	VG	VG+	NM
9447	Shake, Shake Sherry/The Memory Lingers On	1961	7.50	15.00	30.00
—As "The Redwoods"					
9473	Never Take It Away/Unemployment Insurance	1961	7.50	15.00	30.00
9505	Please, Mr. Scientist/Where You Need to Be	1962	10.00	20.00	40.00

REED, DEAN

45s

Number	Title (A Side/B Side)	Yr	VG	VG+	NM
CAPITOL					
F4121	The Search/Annabelle	1959	3.75	7.50	15.00
F4198	A Pair of Scissors/I Kissed a Queen	1959	3.75	7.50	15.00
F4273	Our Summer Romance/I Ain't Got You	1959	3.75	7.50	15.00
4384	Don't Let Her Go/No Wonder	1960	3.75	7.50	15.00
4438	Pistolero/Hummingbird	1960	3.75	7.50	15.00
IMPERIAL					
5733	I Forgot More Than You'll Ever Know/Once Again	1961	3.00	6.00	12.00

REED, JAMES

45s

Number	Title (A Side/B Side)	Yr	VG	VG+	NM
BIG TOWN					
117	Things Ain't What They Used to Be/You Better Hold Me	1954	37.50	75.00	150.00
FLAIR					
1034	My Mama Told Me/This Is the End	1954	50.00	100.00	200.00
1042	Dr. Brown/You Better Hold Me	1954	50.00	100.00	200.00
MONEY					
201	Oh People/My Love Is Real	1954	50.00	100.00	200.00
RHYTHM					
1775	Tin Pan Alley/Biggest Place in Town	1954	125.00	250.00	500.00

REED, JERRY

45s

Number	Title (A Side/B Side)	Yr	VG	VG+	NM
CAPITOL					
F3294	If the Good Lord's Willing and the Creeks Don't Rise/Here I Am	1955	5.00	10.00	20.00
F3381	I'm a Lover, Not a Fighter/Honey Chile	1956	5.00	10.00	20.00
F3429	When I Found You/Mister Whiz	1956	5.00	10.00	20.00
F3504	Just a Romeo/This Great Big Empty Room	1956	5.00	10.00	20.00
F3592	Too Busy Cryin' the Blues/You're Braggin', Boy	1956	5.00	10.00	20.00
F3657	It's High Time/Forever	1957	3.75	7.50	15.00
F3731	Rockin' in Bagdad/Oh Lonely Heart	1957	3.75	7.50	15.00
F3823	In My Own Back Yard/Ba-Bee	1957	3.75	7.50	15.00
F3882	Too Young to Be Blue/Bessie Baby	1958	3.75	7.50	15.00
F3992	How Can I Go On This Way/Your Money Makes You Purty	1958	3.75	7.50	15.00
B-5531	Big Time Fool/What Comes Around	1985	—	—	3.00
B-5556	Country's Alive and Doing Well/Let It Go	1986	—	—	3.00
B-5612	This Missin' You's a Whole Lotta Fun/There Was You	1986	—	—	3.00
B-5660	You Can't Get the Hell Out of Texas/Old Fashioned Heart	1986	—	—	3.00
COLUMBIA					
42047	Love and War (Ain't Much Difference in the Two)/ Love Is the Cause of It All	1961	2.50	5.00	10.00
42183	Hit and Run/Sure Is Blue Out Tonight	1961	2.50	5.00	10.00
42311	Pity the Fool/I've Got Everybody Fooled But Me	1962	2.50	5.00	10.00
42417	I'm Movin' On/Goodnight Irene	1962	2.50	5.00	10.00
42533	Twist-a-Roo/Hully Gully Guitars	1962	2.50	5.00	10.00
42639	Too Old to Cut the Mustard/Overlooked and Underloved	1962	2.50	5.00	10.00
42704	I Want to Be Loved/I'll See You in My Dreams	1963	2.50	5.00	10.00
42808	The Shock/Let's Get Ready for Summer	1963	2.50	5.00	10.00
42863	The Mountain Man/Love Don't Grow on Trees	1963	2.50	5.00	10.00
43052	June Night/Spilled Milk	1964	2.50	5.00	10.00
NRC					
014	Have Blues Will Travel/This Can't Be Happening to Me	1958	3.75	7.50	15.00
032	Just Right/Stone Eternal	1959	3.00	6.00	12.00
5008	Little Lovin' Liza/Soldier's Joy	1959	3.00	6.00	12.00
RCA					
PB-10784	Remembering/Babe	1976	—	2.00	4.00
PB-10893	Semolita/Phantom of the Opry	1977	—	2.00	4.00
PB-11008	With His Pants in His Hand/We Called It Everything Else	1977	—	2.00	4.00
PB-11056	East Bound and Down/(I'm Just A) Redneck in a Rock and Roll Bar	1977	—	2.00	4.00
PB-11164	You Know What/Louisiana Lady	1977	—	2.00	4.00
—With Seidina					
PB-11232	Sweet Love Feelings/You're Gonna Need Someone	1978	—	2.00	4.00
PB-11281	(I Love You) What Can I Say/I Feel for You	1978	—	2.00	4.00
PB-11281	(I Love You) What Can I Say/High Rollin'	1978	—	2.00	4.00
PB-11370	Stars and Stripes Forever/Reedology	1978	—	2.00	4.00
PB-11407	Gimme Back My Blues/Honkin'	1978	—	2.00	4.00
PB-11472	Second-Hand Satin Lady (And a Bargain Basement Boy)/Jiffy Jam	1979	—	2.00	4.00
PB-11638	(Who Was the Man Who Put) The Line in Gasoline/Piece of Cake	1979	—	2.00	4.00
PB-11698	Hot Stuff/Nervous Breakdown	1979	—	2.00	4.00
PB-11764	Sugar Foot Rag/I Wanna Go Back Home to Georgia	1979	—	2.00	4.00
PB-11944	Age/Workin' at the Car Wash Blues	1980	—	2.00	4.00
GB-11986	East Bound and Down/(I'm Just a) Redneck in a Rock and Roll Bar	1980	—	—	3.00
—Gold Standard Series					
PB-12034	The Friendly Family Inn/Bandit	1980	—	2.00	4.00
PB-12083	Texas Bound and Flyin'/Concrete Sailor	1980	—	2.00	4.00
PB-12157	Caffein, Nicotine, Benzedrine (And Wish Me Luck)/If Love's Not Around the House	1981	—	2.00	4.00
PB-12210	The Testimony of Soddy Hoe/Dreaming Fairy Tales	1981	—	2.00	4.00
PB-12253	Good Friends Make Good Lovers/The Devil Went Down to Georgia	1981	—	2.00	4.00
PB-12318	Patches/Stray Dogs and Stray Women	1981	—	2.00	4.00
PB-13081	The Man with the Golden Thumb/East Bound and Down	1982	—	2.00	4.00
PB-13268	She Got the Goldmine (I Got the Shaft)/44	1982	—	2.50	5.00
PB-13355	The Bird/The Hobo	1982	—	2.50	5.00
—As "Jerry Reed and Friends"					
PB-13422	Down on the Corner/Good Times	1983	—	2.00	4.00
PB-13527	Good Ole Boys/She's Ready for Someone to Love Her	1983	—	2.00	4.00
PB-13663	I'm a Slave/Nobody Ever Loved Me	1983	—	2.00	4.00
JK-13666 [DJ]	Christmas Time's a-Coming (same on both sides)	1983	—	2.50	5.00
PB-13666	Christmas Time's a-Coming/The Best I Ever Had	1983	—	2.50	5.00
GB-14069	She Got the Goldmine (I Got the Shaft)/The Bird	1985	—	—	3.00
—Gold Standard Series					
RCA VICTOR					
APBO-0194	The Uptown Poker Club/Honkin'	1973	—	2.50	5.00
APBO-0224	The Crude Oil Blues/Pickie, Pickie, Pickie	1974	—	2.50	5.00
APBO-0273	A Good Woman's Love/Everybody Needs Someone	1974	—	2.50	5.00
PB-10013	You've Got It/Lightning Rod	1974	—	2.50	5.00
PB-10063	Boogie Woogie Rock and Roll/In Between	1974	—	2.50	5.00
PB-10132	Let's Sing Our Song/Grab Bag	1974	—	2.50	5.00
PB-10247	Mind Your Love/Struttin'	1975	—	2.50	5.00
PB-10325	The Telephone/City of New Orleans	1975	—	2.50	5.00
PB-10389	You Got a Lock on Me/Reedology	1975	—	2.50	5.00
GB-10510	Lord, Mr. Ford/Two-Timin'	1975	—	—	3.00
—Gold Standard Series					
PB-10717	Gator/Good for Him	1976	—	2.50	5.00
47-8565	If I Don't Live Up to It/I Feel a Sin Coming On	1965	2.00	4.00	8.00
47-8667	Ain't That Just Like a Fool/Love's Battleground	1965	2.00	4.00	8.00
47-8730	Fighting for the U.S.A./Navy Blues	1965	2.00	4.00	8.00
47-8957	Woman Shy/I Feel for You	1966	2.00	4.00	8.00
47-9152	Guitar Man/It Don't Work That Way	1967	2.50	5.00	10.00
47-9334	Tupelo Mississippi Flash/Wabash Cannonball	1967	2.00	4.00	8.00
47-9493	Remembering/Fine on My Mind	1968	2.00	4.00	8.00
47-9623	Alabama Wild Man/Twelve Bar Midnight	1968	2.00	4.00	8.00
47-9701	Oh, What a Woman/Losing Your Love	1968	2.00	4.00	8.00
47-9794	Turn It Around in Your Mind/Long Gone	1969	—	—	—
—Unreleased					
47-9804	Talk About the Good Times/Alabama Jubilee	1969	—	3.00	6.00
47-9870	Georgia Sunshine/Swinging '69	1970	—	3.00	6.00
47-9890	Tennessee Stud/Cannonball Rag	1970	—	3.00	6.00
—With Chet Atkins					
47-9904	Amos Moses/The Preacher and the Bear	1970	—	3.00	6.00
47-9976	When You're Hot, You're Hot/You've Been Crying Again	1971	—	3.00	6.00
48-1011	Ko Ko Joe/I Feel for You	1971	—	3.00	6.00
74-0124	Blues Land/There's Better Things in Life	1969	—	3.00	6.00
74-0211	Are You From Dixie/A Worried Man	1969	—	3.00	6.00
74-0242	A Thing Called Love/Hallelujah I Love Her So	1969	—	—	—
—Unreleased					
74-0613	Another Puff/Love Man	1971	—	2.50	5.00
74-0667	Smell the Flowers/If It Comes to That	1972	—	2.50	5.00
74-0738	Alabama Wildman/Take It Easy	1972	—	2.50	5.00
74-0775	Nashtownville/Jerry's Breakdown	1972	—	2.50	5.00
—With Chet Atkins					
74-0857	You Took All the Ramblin' Out of Me/I'm Not Playing Games	1972	—	2.50	5.00
74-0960	Lord, Mr. Ford/2-Timin'	1973	—	2.50	5.00

Albums

Number	Title (A Side/B Side)	Yr	VG	VG+	NM
CAPITOL					
ST-12492	Lookin' at You	1986	2.00	4.00	8.00
HARMONY					
H 30574	I'm Movin' On	1971	2.50	5.00	10.00
RCA CAMDEN					
ACL1-0331	Tupelo Mississippi Flash	1973	2.50	5.00	10.00
CAS-2585	Oh What a Woman!	1972	2.50	5.00	10.00
RCA VICTOR					
APD1-0238 [Q]	Lord, Mr. Ford	1973	6.25	12.50	25.00
APL1-0238	Lord, Mr. Ford	1973	3.00	6.00	12.00
APL1-0356	The Uptown Poker Club	1973	3.00	6.00	12.00
APL1-0544	A Good Woman's Love	1974	3.00	6.00	12.00
APL1-1226	Red Hot Picker	1975	3.00	6.00	12.00
ANL1-1345	When You're Hot, You're Hot	1975	2.50	5.00	10.00
—Reissue of 4506					
APL1-1861	Both Barrels	1976	3.00	6.00	12.00
ANL1-2167	Me and Chet	1976	2.50	5.00	10.00
—Reissue of 4707					
AHL1-2346	Jerry Reed Rides Again	1977	3.00	6.00	12.00
AHL1-2516	East Bound and Down	1977	3.00	6.00	12.00
AHL1-2764	Sweet Love Feelings	1978	3.00	6.00	12.00
AHL1-3359	Half Singin' & Half Pickin'	1979	3.00	6.00	12.00
AHL1-3453	Jerry Reed Live!	1979	3.00	6.00	12.00
AHl1-3604	Jerry Reed Sings Jim Croce	1980	3.00	6.00	12.00
AYL1-3677	East Bound and Down	1980	2.00	4.00	8.00
—"Best Buy Series" reissue					
LPM-3756 [M]	The Unbelievable Guitar and Voice of Jerry Reed	1967	6.25	12.50	25.00
LSP-3756 [S]	The Unbelievable Guitar and Voice of Jerry Reed	1967	5.00	10.00	20.00
AHL1-3771	Texas Bound and Flyin'	1980	3.00	6.00	12.00
LPM-3978 [M]	Nashville Underground	1968	12.50	25.00	50.00
LSP-3978 [S]	Nashville Underground	1968	5.00	10.00	20.00
AHL1-4021	Dixie Dreams	1981	3.00	6.00	12.00
LSP-4069	Alabama Wild Man	1968	5.00	10.00	20.00
LSP-4147	Better Things in Life	1969	5.00	10.00	20.00
AYL1-4167	Jerry Reed Live!	1982	2.00	4.00	8.00
—"Best Buy Series" reissue					
LSP-4204	Jerry Reed Explores Guitar Country	1969	5.00	10.00	20.00
LSP-4293	Cookin'	1970	5.00	10.00	20.00
AHL1-4315	The Man with the Golden Thumb	1982	2.50	5.00	10.00
LSP-4391	Georgia Sunshine	1970	5.00	10.00	20.00
AYL1-4394	Texas Bound and Flyin'	1982	2.00	4.00	8.00
—"Best Buy Series" reissue					
LSP-4506	When You're Hot, You're Hot	1971	3.75	7.50	15.00
AHL1-4529	The Bird	1982	2.50	5.00	10.00
LSP-4596	Ko-Ko Joe	1971	3.75	7.50	15.00
LSP-4660	Smell the Flowers	1972	3.75	7.50	15.00

Number	Title (A Side/B Side)	Yr	VG	VG+	NM
AHL1-4692	Ready	1983	2.50	5.00	10.00
LSP-4707	Me and Chet	1972	3.75	7.50	15.00
—With Chet Atkins					
LSP-4729	The Best of Jerry Reed	1972	3.75	7.50	15.00
LSP-4750	Jerry Reed	1972	3.75	7.50	15.00
LSP-4838	Hot A' Mighty!	1973	3.75	7.50	15.00
AYL1-5151	The Bird	1984	2.00	4.00	8.00
—"Best Buy Series" reissue					
AHL1-5176	Greatest Hits	1984	2.50	5.00	10.00
AHL1-5472	Collector's Series	1985	2.50	5.00	10.00

REED, JIMMY

45s

Number	Title (A Side/B Side)	Yr	VG	VG+	NM
ABC					
10887	Got Nowhere to Go/Two Ways to Skin (A Cat)	1966	2.00	4.00	8.00
BLUESWAY					
61003	I Wanna Know/Two Heads Are Better Than One	1967	2.00	4.00	8.00
61006	Don't Press Your Luck Woman/Feel Like I Want to Ramble	1967	2.00	4.00	8.00
61013	Buy Me a Hound Dog/Crazy About Oklahoma	1968	2.00	4.00	8.00
61020	Peepin' and Hidin'/My Baby Told Me	1968	2.00	4.00	8.00
61025	Don't Light My Fire/The Judge Should Know	1969	2.00	4.00	8.00
CANYON					
38	Hard Walkin' Hannah (Part 1)/Hard Walkin' Hannah (Part 2)	196?	2.00	4.00	8.00
CHANCE					
1142	High and Lonesome/Roll and Rhumba	1953	700.00	1400.	2100.
EXODUS					
2005	Knockin' At Your Door/Dedication to Sonny	1966	2.50	5.00	10.00
2008	Cousin Peaches/Crazy 'Bout Oklahoma	1966	2.50	5.00	10.00
RRG					
44001	Christmas Present Blues/Crying Blind	19??	2.00	4.00	8.00
VEE JAY					
100	High and Lonesome/Roll and Rumba	1953	300.00	600.00	1200.
—Red vinyl					
100	High and Lonesome/Roll and Rumba	1953	150.00	300.00	600.00
105	I Found My Baby/Jimmy's Boogie	1953	100.00	200.00	400.00
—Red vinyl					
105	I Found My Baby/Jimmy's Boogie	1953	50.00	100.00	200.00
119	You Don't Have to Go/Boogie in the Dark	1954	75.00	150.00	300.00
—Red vinyl					
119	You Don't Have to Go/Boogie in the Dark	1954	20.00	40.00	80.00
132	Pretty Thing/I'm Gonna Ruin You	1955	25.00	50.00	100.00
153	I Don't Go for That/She Don't Want Me No More	1955	12.50	25.00	50.00
168	Ain't That Lovin' You Baby/Baby, Don't Say That No More	1956	10.00	20.00	40.00
186	Can't Stand to See You Go/Rockin' with Reed	1956	10.00	20.00	40.00
203	I Love You Baby/My First Plea	1956	7.50	15.00	30.00
226	You've Got Me Dizzy/Honey, Don't Let Me Go	1956	7.50	15.00	30.00
237	Honey, Where You Going/Little Rain	1957	7.50	15.00	30.00
248	The Sun Is Shining/Baby, What's On Your Mind	1957	7.50	15.00	30.00
253	Honest I Do/Signals of Love	1957	7.50	15.00	30.00
270	You're Something Else/A String to My Heart	1958	7.50	15.00	30.00
275	You Got Me Crying/Go On to School	1958	7.50	15.00	30.00
287	I Know It's a Sin/Down in Virginia	1958	7.50	15.00	30.00
298	I'm Gonna Get My Baby/Odds and Ends	1958	7.50	15.00	30.00
304	I Told You Baby/Ends and Odds (Instrumental)	1958	7.50	15.00	30.00
314	Take Out Some Insurance/You Know I Love You	1959	7.50	15.00	30.00
326	I Wanna Be Loved/Going to New York	1959	7.50	15.00	30.00
333	Baby What You Want Me to Do/Caress Me, Baby	1959	7.50	15.00	30.00
347	Found Love/Where Can You Be	1960	6.25	12.50	25.00
357	Hush Hush/Going to the River, Part 2	1960	6.25	12.50	25.00
373	Laughing at the Blues/Close Together	1961	6.25	12.50	25.00
380	Big Boss Man/I'm a Love You	1961	6.25	12.50	25.00
398	Bright Lights, Big City/I'm Mr. Luck	1961	6.25	12.50	25.00
425	Aw, Shucks, Hush Your Mouth/Baby, What's Wrong	1962	5.00	10.00	20.00
449	Tell Me You Love Me/Good Lover	1962	5.00	10.00	20.00
459	I'll Change My Style/Too Much	1962	5.00	10.00	20.00
473	Let's Get Together/Oh, John	1962	5.00	10.00	20.00
509	There'll Be a Day/Shame, Shame, Shame	1963	3.75	7.50	15.00
552	Mary Mary/I'm Gonna Help You	1963	3.75	7.50	15.00
570	Outskirts of Town/St. Louis Blues	1963	3.75	7.50	15.00
584	See See Rider/Wee Wee Baby Blues	1964	3.75	7.50	15.00
593	Help Yourself/Heading for a Fall	1964	3.75	7.50	15.00
616	Oh John/Down in Mississippi	1964	3.75	7.50	15.00
622	I'm Going Upside Your Head/The Devil's Shoestring	1964	3.75	7.50	15.00
642	I Wanna Be Loved/A New Leaf	1965	3.75	7.50	15.00
702	I'm the Man Down There/Left Handed Woman	1965	3.75	7.50	15.00
709	Don't Think I'm Through/When Girls Do It	1966	3.75	7.50	15.00

Albums

Number	Title (A Side/B Side)	Yr	VG	VG+	NM
ANTILLES					
7007	Cold Chills	197?	3.75	7.50	15.00
ARCHIVE OF FOLK AND JAZZ					
234	Jimmy Reed	197?	3.00	6.00	12.00
BLUESVILLE					
BLS-6054	I Ain't From Chicago	1973	3.75	7.50	15.00
BLS-6067	The Ultimate Jimmy Reed	1973	3.75	7.50	15.00
BLS-6073 [(2)]	Jimmy Reed at Carnegie Hall	1973	5.00	10.00	20.00
BLUESWAY					
BL-6004 [M]	The New Jimmy Reed Album	1967	5.00	10.00	20.00
BLS-6004 [S]	The New Jimmy Reed Album	1967	5.00	10.00	20.00
BL-6009 [M]	Soulin'	1967	5.00	10.00	20.00
BLS-6009 [S]	Soulin'	1967	5.00	10.00	20.00
BLS-6015	Big Boss Man	1968	5.00	10.00	20.00
BLS-6024	Down in Virginia	1969	5.00	10.00	20.00
BUDDAH					
BDS-4003	The Very Best of Jimmy Reed	1969	3.75	7.50	15.00
—Reissue of Vee Jay 1039					
CHAMELEON					
D1-74762	Bright Lights, Big City	1988	2.50	5.00	10.00
GNP CRESCENDO					
GNPS-10006 [(2)]	The Best of Jimmy Reed	1974	3.75	7.50	15.00
SUNSET					
SUS-5218	Somethin' Else	1968	3.00	6.00	12.00
TRADITION					
2069	Wailin' the Blues	1969	3.00	6.00	12.00
TRIP					
8012 [(2)]	History of Jimmy Reed	1971	3.75	7.50	15.00
VEE JAY					
LP-1004 [M]	I'm Jimmy Reed	1958	55.00	110.00	220.00
—Maroon label					
LP-1004 [M]	I'm Jimmy Reed	1961	20.00	40.00	80.00
—Black label with colorband					
VJLP-1004	I'm Jimmy Reed	198?	2.50	5.00	10.00
—Reissue with glossy labels					
LP-1008 [M]	Rockin' with Reed	1959	50.00	100.00	200.00
—Maroon label					
LP-1008 [M]	Rockin' with Reed	1961	20.00	40.00	80.00
—Black label with colorband					
VJLP-1008	Rockin' with Reed	198?	2.50	5.00	10.00
—Reissue with glossy labels					
LP-1022 [M]	Found Love	1959	50.00	100.00	200.00
—Maroon label					
LP-1022 [M]	Found Love	1961	20.00	40.00	80.00
—Black label with colorband					
LP-1025 [M]	Now Appearing	1960	20.00	40.00	80.00
VJLP-1025	Now Appearing	198?	2.50	5.00	10.00
—Reissue with glossy labels					
2LP-1035 [(2) M]	Jimmy Reed at Carnegie Hall	1961	12.50	25.00	50.00
2SR-1035 [(2) S]	Jimmy Reed at Carnegie Hall	1961	17.50	35.00	70.00
VJLP2-1035 [(2)]	Jimmy Reed at Carnegie Hall	198?	3.00	6.00	12.00
—Reissue with glossy labels					
LP-1039 [M]	The Best of Jimmy Reed	1962	10.00	20.00	40.00
SR-1039 [S]	The Best of Jimmy Reed	1962	15.00	30.00	60.00
VJLP-1039	The Best of Jimmy Reed	198?	2.50	5.00	10.00
—Reissue with glossy labels					
LP-1050 [M]	Just Jimmy Reed	1962	10.00	20.00	40.00
SR-1050 [S]	Just Jimmy Reed	1962	15.00	30.00	60.00
LP-1067 [M]	T'Ain't No Big Thing...But He Is Jimmy Reed	1963	10.00	20.00	40.00
SR-1067 [S]	T'Ain't No Big Thing...But He Is Jimmy Reed	1963	15.00	30.00	60.00
LP-1072 [M]	The Best of the Blues	1963	10.00	20.00	40.00
LP-1073 [M]	The 12 String Guitar Blues	1963	10.00	20.00	40.00
SR-1073 [S]	The 12 String Guitar Blues	1963	37.50	7.50	150.00
LP-1080 [M]	More of the Best of Jimmy Reed	1964	10.00	20.00	40.00
SR-1080 [S]	More of the Best of Jimmy Reed	1964	37.50	75.00	150.00
LP-1095 [M]	Jimmy Reed at Soul City	1964	10.00	20.00	40.00
VJS-1095	Jimmy Reed at Soul City	198?	2.50	5.00	10.00
—Reissue with glossy labels					
VJS-7303	Blues Is My Business	198?	2.50	5.00	10.00
LP-8501 [M]	The Legend, The Man	1965	10.00	20.00	40.00
VJLP-8501	The Legend, The Man	198?	2.50	5.00	10.00
—Reissue with glossy labels					
VJS-8501 [S]	The Legend, The Man	1965	37.50	75.00	150.00

REED, LOU

Also see THE PRMITIVES; THE VELVET UNDERGROUND.

12-Inch Singles

Number	Title (A Side/B Side)	Yr	VG	VG+	NM
ARISTA					
SP-14 [DJ]	Street Hassle (stereo)/Street Hassle (mono)	1978	2.50	5.00	10.00
SP-36 [DJ]	Walk on the Wild Side/Coney Island Baby/Satellite of Love	1978	2.50	5.00	10.00
SP-56 [DJ]	Disco Mystic/I Wanna Boogie with You	1979	2.50	5.00	10.00
SP-84 [DJ]	How Do You Speak to An Angel/Keep Away/The Power of Positive Drinking/Standing on Ceremony	1980	3.75	7.50	15.00
9375 [DJ]	Hot Hips (same on both sides)	1985	2.50	5.00	10.00
ATLANTIC					
819 [DJ]	My Love Is Chemical (same on both sides)	1985	—	3.50	7.00
A&M					
17352 [DJ]	September Song/September Song (7" Version)	1986	—	3.00	6.00
RCA					
5711-1	Original Wrapper (2 versions)/Video Violence (2 versions)	198?	2.00	4.00	8.00
JR-13849 [DJ]	I Love You, Suzanne (same on both sides)	1984	—	3.50	7.00
PD-13928	My Red Joystick (remix) (instrumental)/I Love You Suzanne	1984	2.50	5.00	10.00
PD-14388	No Money Down (Extended)/No Money Down (Dub)/Don't Hurt a Woman	1986	2.00	4.00	8.00
PD-14427	The Original Wrapper (3 mixes)/Video Violence	1986	2.00	4.00	8.00
RCA VICTOR					
JR-14343 [DJ]	No Money Down (same on both sides)	1986	3.00	6.00	12.00
—Gren vinyl					
JR-14420 [DJ]	Video Violence (same on both sides)	1986	2.00	4.00	8.00
SIRE					
PRO-A-3359 [DJ]	Dirty Blvd. (Radio Edit)/Dirty Blvd. (LP Version)	1988	2.00	4.00	8.00

45s

Number	Title (A Side/B Side)	Yr	VG	VG+	NM
ARISTA					
215	I Believe in Love/Senselessly Cruel	1976	—	2.00	4.00
431	City Lights/I Want to Boogie with You	1979	—	2.00	4.00
535	Growing Up in Public/The Power of Positive Drinking	1980	—	2.00	4.00
ATLANTIC					
89468	My Love Is Chemical/People Have Got to Move	1985	—	—	3.00
—B-side by Jenny Burton					
89468 [PS]	My Love Is Chemical/People Have Got to Move	1985	—	—	3.00
A&M					
2781	September Song/Oh Heavenly Salvation	1985	—	2.00	4.00
—B-side by Mark Bingham/Johnny Adams/Aaron Neville					
2883	Soul Man/Sweet Sarah	1986	—	—	3.00
—With Sam Moore					
RCA					
JB-13558	Martial Law/Don't Talk to Me About Work	1983	—	—	3.00
PB-13841	I Love You Suzanne/My Friend George	1984	—	—	3.00

Number	Title (A Side/B Side)	Yr	VG	VG+	NM
PB-14368	No Money Down/Don't Hurt a Woman	1986	—	—	3.00
RCA VICTOR					
APBO-0054	Vicious/Good Night Ladies	1973	—	2.50	5.00
APBO-0172	Lady Day/How Do You Think It Feels	1973	—	2.50	5.00
APBO-0238	Sweet Jane/Lady Day	1974	7.50	15.00	30.00
—Part of U.S. numbering system, but pressed for export.					
PB-10053	Sally Can't Dance/Vicious	1974	—	2.00	4.00
PB-10081	Sally Can't Dance/Ennui	1974	—	2.00	4.00
GB-10162	Walk on the Wild Side/Vicious	1975	—	—	3.00
—Gold Standard Series reissue					
PB-10573	Charley's Girl/Nowhere At All	1976	—	2.00	4.00
PB-10648	Crazy Feeling/Nowhere At All	1976	—	2.00	4.00
74-0727	I Can't Stand It/Going Down	1972	—	3.00	6.00
74-0784	Walk and Talk It/Wild Child	1972	—	3.00	6.00
74-0887	Walk on the Wild Side/Perfect Day	1973	—	3.00	6.00
74-0964	Satellite of Love/Walk and Talk It	1973	—	3.00	6.00
SIRE					
22876	Romeo Had Juliette/Busload of Faith	1989	—	—	3.00
22876 [PS]	Romeo Had Juliette/Busload of Faith	1989	—	—	3.00
Albums					
ARISTA					
AL 4100	Rock and Roll Heart	1976	3.75	7.50	15.00
—Originals on light blue labels					
AL 4169	Street Hassle	1978	3.75	7.50	15.00
AL 4229	The Bells	1979	3.00	6.00	12.00
ALB6-8390	City Lights — Classic Performances by Lou Reed	1985	2.50	5.00	10.00
AL11 8434 [(2)]	Rock and Roll Diary 1967-1980	198?	4.00	8.00	16.00
—Reissue					
AL 8502 [(2)]	Live! Take No Prisoners	1978	4.50	9.00	18.00
A2L 8603 [(2)]	Rock and Roll Diary 1967-1980	1980	4.50	9.00	18.00
AL 9522	Growing Up in Public	1980	3.00	6.00	12.00
R 252506 [(2)]	Rock and Roll Diary 1967-1980	1980	4.50	9.00	18.00
—RCA Music Service edition					
DIRECT DISK					
(no #) [DJ]	The Blue Mask	1982	37.50	75.00	150.00
—Only exists on test pressings; no stock copies made					
RCA VICTOR					
APL1-0207	Berlin	1973	3.00	6.00	12.00
AFL1-0472	Rock & Roll Animal	1977	2.00	4.00	8.00
—Reissue					
APL1-0472	Rock & Roll Animal	1974	3.00	6.00	12.00
AFL1-0611	Sally Can't Dance	1977	2.00	4.00	8.00
—Reissue					
CPL1-0611	Sally Can't Dance	1974	5.00	10.00	20.00
APL1-0915	Coney Island Baby	1976	4.00	8.00	16.00
AFL1-0959	Lou Reed Live	1977	2.00	4.00	8.00
—Reissue					
APL1-0959	Lou Reed Live	1975	3.75	7.50	15.00
APD2-1101 [(2) Q]	Metal Machine Music	1975	37.50	75.00	150.00
CPL2-1101 [(2)]	Metal Machine Music	1975	12.50	25.00	50.00
—Orange or brown label					
AFL1-2001	Walk on the Wild Side	1978	2.00	4.00	8.00
—Reissue					
APL1-2001	Walk on the Wild Side	1977	3.00	6.00	12.00
ANL1-2480	Coney Island Baby	1977	2.00	4.00	8.00
—Reissue					
AYL1-3664	Rock & Roll Animal	1980	2.00	4.00	8.00
—Best Buy Series reissue					
AYL1-3752	Lou Reed Live	1980	2.00	4.00	8.00
—Best Buy Series reissue					
AYL1-3753	Walk on the Wild Side	1980	2.00	4.00	8.00
—Best Buy Series reissue					
AYL1-3806	Transformer	1980	2.00	4.00	8.00
—Best Buy Series reissue					
AYL1-3807	Coney Island Baby	1980	2.00	4.00	8.00
—Best Buy Series reissue					
AFL1-4221	The Blue Mask	1982	2.50	5.00	10.00
DJL1-4266 [DJ]	Special Radio Series, Vol. XVII	1980	6.25	12.50	25.00
—Promo-only with insert					
DJL1-4267	The Blue Mask Interview Album	1982	10.00	20.00	40.00
DJL1-4345 [DJ]	The Blue Mask Sampler	1982	3.00	6.00	12.00
—Three-song EP released to radio					
AYL1-4388	Berlin	1983	2.00	4.00	8.00
—Best Buy Series reissue					
AYL1-4555	Sally Can't Dance	1983	2.00	4.00	8.00
—Best Buy Series reissue					
AFL1-4568	Legendary Hearts	1983	2.50	5.00	10.00
LSP-4701	Lou Reed	1972	5.00	10.00	20.00
AYL1-4780	The Blue Mask	1984	2.00	4.00	8.00
—Best Buy Series reissue					
AFL1-4807	Transformer	1977	2.00	4.00	8.00
—Reissue					
LSP-4807	Transformer	1972	5.00	10.00	20.00
AFL1-4998	New Sensations	1984	2.00	4.00	8.00
AFL1-7190	Mistrial	1986	3.00	6.00	12.00
SIRE					
25829	New York	1989	2.50	5.00	10.00
R 101058	New York	1989	3.00	6.00	12.00
—BMG Music Service edition					

REED, LOU, AND JOHN CALE

Number	Title (A Side/B Side)	Yr	VG	VG+	NM
Albums					
SIRE					
26140	Songs for Drella	1990	2.50	5.00	10.00

REED, TAWNEY

Number	Title (A Side/B Side)	Yr	VG	VG+	NM
45s					
CONGRESS					
270	My Heart Cried/Can't Take It Away	1966	3.00	6.00	12.00
RED BIRD					
10-044	Needle in a Haystack/I Got a Feeling	1965	10.00	20.00	40.00

REED, URSULA

Number	Title (A Side/B Side)	Yr	VG	VG+	NM
45s					
OLD TOWN					
1001	Your're Laffin' "Cause I'm Cryin'/Ursula's Blues	1954	100.00	200.00	400.00

REEDER, BILL

Number	Title (A Side/B Side)	Yr	VG	VG+	NM
45s					
FERNWOOD					
121	You're My Baby/Where Were You Last Night	1960	20.00	40.00	80.00
HI					
2037	Till I Waltz Again with You/There Was a Time	1961	20.00	40.00	80.00
2041	Secret Love/Judy	1961	5.00	10.00	20.00
VOLL					
100	Till I Waltz Again with You/There Was a Time	1961	50.00	100.00	200.00

REEKERS, THE

Number	Title (A Side/B Side)	Yr	VG	VG+	NM
45s					
RY-JAC					
13	Grindin'/Don't Call Me Flyface	1964	12.50	25.00	50.00

REESE, DELLA

Number	Title (A Side/B Side)	Yr	VG	VG+	NM
45s					
ABC					
10815	Stranger on Earth/If It's the Last Thing I Do	1966	2.00	4.00	8.00
10841	It Was a Very Good Year/Solitary Woman	1966	2.00	4.00	8.00
10876	Sunny/That's Life	1966	2.00	4.00	8.00
10931	Soon/Every Other Day	1967	—	3.00	6.00
10962	I Heard You Cried Last Night/On the South Side of Chicago	1967	—	3.00	6.00
11017	Let's Make the Most of a Beautiful Thing/Sorry Baby	1967	—	3.00	6.00
11051	I Gotta Be Me/Never My Love	1968	—	3.00	6.00
ABC-PARAMOUNT					
10691	After Loving You/How Do You Keep from Crying	1965	2.00	4.00	8.00
10721	And That Reminds Me/I Only Want a Buddy, Not a Sweetheart	1965	2.00	4.00	8.00
10759	'T'Ain't Nobody's Bizness If I Do/I Ain't Ready for That	1965	2.00	4.00	8.00
AVCO					
4586	If It Feels Good Do It/Good Lovin' Makes It Right	1972	—	2.50	5.00
AVCO EMBASSY					
4515	Games People Play/Compared to What	1969	—	3.00	6.00
4545	Billy My Love/(B-side unknown)	1970	—	3.00	6.00
4566	The Troublemaker/The Love I've Been Looking For	1971	—	3.00	6.00
CHI-SOUND					
XW978	I'll Be Your Sunshine/Nothing But a True Love	1977	—	2.00	4.00
JUBILEE					
5198	In the Still of the Night/Kiss My Love Goodbye	1955	3.75	7.50	15.00
5214	Time After Time/Fine Sugar	1955	3.75	7.50	15.00
5233	I've Got My Love to Keep Me Warm/Years from Now	1956	3.75	7.50	15.00
5247	Headin' Home/Daybreak Serenade	1956	3.75	7.50	15.00
5251	My Melancholy Baby/One for My Baby	1956	3.75	7.50	15.00
5263	In the Meantime/The More I See You	1956	3.75	7.50	15.00
5278	How About You/How Can You Not Believe	1957	3.75	7.50	15.00
5292	And That Reminds Me/I Cried for You	1957	3.00	6.00	12.00
5307	I Only Want to Love You/By Love Possessed	1957	3.00	6.00	12.00
5317	How Can You Lose (What You Never Had)/If Not for You	1958	3.00	6.00	12.00
5323	I've Got a Feelin' You're Foolin'/C'mon, C'mon	1958	3.00	6.00	12.00
5332	I Wish/You Gotta Love Everybody	1958	3.00	6.00	12.00
5345	Sermonette/Dreams End at Dawn	1958	3.00	6.00	12.00
5346	When I Grow Too Old to Dream/You're Just in Love	1958	3.00	6.00	12.00
—Della Reese and Kirk Stuart					
5369	Time Was/Once Upon a Dream	1959	3.00	6.00	12.00
5375	I Don't Want to Walk Without You/I'm Nobody's Baby	1959	3.00	6.00	12.00
5453	Sermonette/You Gotta Love Somebody	1963	2.50	5.00	10.00
RCA VICTOR					
47-7591	Don't You Know/Soldier Won't You Marry Me	1959	2.50	5.00	10.00
47-7644	Not One Minute More/You're My Love	1959	2.50	5.00	10.00
47-7683	Someday/The Lady Is a Tramp	1960	2.50	5.00	10.00
47-7706	Someday You'll Want Me to Want You/Faraway Boy	1960	2.50	5.00	10.00
47-7750	Everyday/There's No Two Ways About It	1960	2.50	5.00	10.00
47-7750 [PS]	Everyday/There's No Two Ways About It	1960	5.00	10.00	20.00
47-7784	And Now/There's Nothin' Like a Boy	1960	2.50	5.00	10.00
47-7784 [PS]	And Now/There's Nothin' Like a Boy	1960	5.00	10.00	20.00
47-7833	The Most Beautiful Words/You Mean All the World to Me	1961	2.50	5.00	10.00
47-7867	The Touch of Your Lips/Won'cha Come Home, Bill Bailey	1961	2.50	5.00	10.00
47-7884	I Possess/A Far, Far Better Thing	1961	2.50	5.00	10.00
47-7961	One/What Do You Think, Joe	1961	2.50	5.00	10.00
47-7996	Ninety-Nine and a Half Won't Do/You Don't Know How Blessed You Are	1962	2.50	5.00	10.00
47-8021	Rome Adventure/Here's That Rainy Day	1962	2.50	5.00	10.00
47-8070	I Love You So Much It Hurts/Blow Out the Sun	1962	2.50	5.00	10.00
47-8093	As Long As He Needs Me/It Makes No Difference Now	1962	2.50	5.00	10.00
47-8093 [PS]	As Long As He Needs Me/It Makes No Difference Now	1962	3.75	7.50	15.00
47-8145	Be My Love/I Behold You	1963	2.50	5.00	10.00
47-8187	More/Serenade	1963	2.50	5.00	10.00
47-8260	Angel D'Amore/Forbidden Games	1963	2.50	5.00	10.00
47-8337	The Bottom of Old Smokey/A Clock That's Got No Hands	1964	2.00	4.00	8.00
47-8394	If I Didn't Care/Wind in the Willows	1964	2.00	4.00	8.00
48-1018	Ninety-Nine and a Half Won't Do/And Now	1971	—	2.00	4.00
74-0558	You Came a Long Way from St. Louis/Nobody's Sweetheart	1971	—	2.00	4.00

7-Inch Extended Plays

RCA VICTOR

Number	Title (A Side/B Side)	Yr	VG	VG+	NM
EPA-4349	Don't You Know/Soldier, Won't You Marry Me//Not One Minute More/You're My Love	1959	3.75	7.50	15.00
EPA-4349 [PS]	Don't You Know	1959	3.75	7.50	15.00

Albums

ABC

Number	Title (A Side/B Side)	Yr	VG	VG+	NM
569 [M]	Della Reese Live	1966	3.75	7.50	15.00
S-569 [S]	Della Reese Live	1966	5.00	10.00	20.00
589 [M]	One More Time	1967	5.00	10.00	20.00
S-589 [S]	One More Time	1967	3.75	7.50	15.00
612 [M]	Della on Strings of Blue	1967	5.00	10.00	20.00
S-612 [S]	Della on Strings of Blue	1967	3.75	7.50	15.00
S-636	I Gotta Be Me...This Trip Out	1968	3.75	7.50	15.00
AC-30002	The ABC Collection	1976	3.75	7.50	15.00

ABC-PARAMOUNT

Number	Title (A Side/B Side)	Yr	VG	VG+	NM
ABC-524 [M]	C'mon and Hear Della Reese	1965	3.75	7.50	15.00
ABCS-524 [S]	C'mon and Hear Della Reese	1965	5.00	10.00	20.00
ABC-540 [M]	I Like It Like Dat!	1966	3.75	7.50	15.00
ABCS-540 [S]	I Like It Like Dat!	1966	5.00	10.00	20.00

AVCO EMBASSY

Number	Title (A Side/B Side)	Yr	VG	VG+	NM
33004	Black Is Beautiful	1969	3.75	7.50	15.00
33017	Right Now	1970	3.75	7.50	15.00

JAZZ A LA CARTE

Number	Title (A Side/B Side)	Yr	VG	VG+	NM
3	One of a Kind	1978	3.75	7.50	15.00

JUBILEE

Number	Title (A Side/B Side)	Yr	VG	VG+	NM
JLP-1026 [M]	Melancholy Baby	1957	7.50	15.00	30.00
JLP-1071 [M]	A Date with Della Reese at Mr. Kelly's in Chicago	1959	6.25	12.50	25.00
SDJLP-1071 [S]	A Date with Della Reese at Mr. Kelly's in Chicago	1959	7.50	15.00	30.00
JLP-1083 [M]	Amen	1959	6.25	12.50	25.00
SDJLP-1083 [S]	Amen	1959	7.50	15.00	30.00
JLP-1095 [M]	The Story of the Blues	1960	6.25	12.50	25.00
SDJLP-1095 [S]	The Story of the Blues	1960	7.50	15.00	30.00
JLP-1109 [M]	What Do You Know About Love	1960	6.25	12.50	25.00
JLP-1116 [M]	And That Reminds Me	1960	6.25	12.50	25.00
JGM-5002 [M]	The Best of Della Reese	196?	3.75	7.50	15.00
JGS-5002 [S]	The Best of Della Reese	196?	5.00	10.00	20.00

PICKWICK

Number	Title (A Side/B Side)	Yr	VG	VG+	NM
SPC-3058	And That Reminds Me	196?	3.00	6.00	12.00

RCA VICTOR

Number	Title (A Side/B Side)	Yr	VG	VG+	NM
LPM-2157 [M]	Della	1960	5.00	10.00	20.00
LSP-2157 [S]	Della	1960	6.25	12.50	25.00
LPM-2204 [M]	Della by Starlight	1960	5.00	10.00	20.00
LSP-2204 [S]	Della by Starlight	1960	6.25	12.50	25.00
LPM-2280 [M]	Della Della Cha-Cha-Cha	1961	5.00	10.00	20.00
LSP-2280 [S]	Della Della Cha-Cha-Cha	1961	6.25	12.50	25.00
LPM-2391 [M]	Special Delivery	1961	5.00	10.00	20.00
LSP-2391 [S]	Special Delivery	1961	6.25	12.50	25.00
LPM-2419 [M]	The Classic Della	1962	5.00	10.00	20.00
LSP-2419 [S]	The Classic Della	1962	6.25	12.50	25.00
LPM-2568 [M]	Della on Stage	1962	5.00	10.00	20.00
LSP-2568 [S]	Della on Stage	1962	6.25	12.50	25.00
LPM-2711 [M]	Waltz with Me	1963	5.00	10.00	20.00
LSP-2711 [S]	Waltz with Me	1963	6.25	12.50	25.00
LPM-2872 [M]	Della Reese at Basin Street East	1964	5.00	10.00	20.00
LSP-2872 [S]	Della Reese at Basin Street East	1964	6.25	12.50	25.00
LSP-4651	The Best of Della Reese	1972	3.00	6.00	12.00

REEVES, JIM

45s

ABBOTT

Number	Title (A Side/B Side)	Yr	VG	VG+	NM
115	Wagon Load of Love/What Were You Doing Last Nite	1953	6.25	12.50	25.00
115	Wagon Load of Love/What Were You Doing Last Nite	1953	15.00	30.00	60.00
—Red vinyl					
116	Mexican Joe/I Could Cry	1953	15.00	30.00	60.00
—Red vinyl					
116	Mexican Joe/I Could Cry	1953	6.25	12.50	25.00
137	Let Me Love You Just a Little/Butterfly Love	1953	6.25	12.50	25.00
137	Let Me Love You Just a Little/Butterfly Love	1953	15.00	30.00	60.00
—Red vinyl					
143	El Rancho Del Rio/It's Hard to Love Just One	1953	6.25	12.50	25.00
143	El Rancho Del Rio/It's Hard to Love Just One	1953	15.00	30.00	60.00
—Red vinyl					
148	Bimbo/Gypsy Heart	1953	6.25	12.50	25.00
148	Bimbo/Gypsy Heart	1953	15.00	30.00	60.00
—Red vinyl					
160	Echo Bonita/Then I'll Stop Loving You	1954	5.00	10.00	20.00
164	Ramblin' Heart/Beatin' on the Ding Dong	1954	5.00	10.00	20.00
168	Padre of Old San Antone/Mother Went A-Walkin'	1954	5.00	10.00	20.00
170	Penny Candy/I'll Follow You	1954	5.00	10.00	20.00
174	Where Does a Broken Heart Go/The Wilder Your Heart Beats, The Sweeter You Love	1954	5.00	10.00	20.00
180	Drinking Tequila/Red Eyed and Rowdy	1955	5.00	10.00	20.00
182	Give Me One More Kiss/Tahiti	1955	5.00	10.00	20.00
184	Are You the One/How Many	1955	5.00	10.00	20.00
—With Alvadean Coker					
186	Let Me Remember/Hillbilly Waltz	1956	5.00	10.00	20.00

RCA

Number	Title (A Side/B Side)	Yr	VG	VG+	NM
PB-10956	It's Nothin' to Me/I Won't Forget You	1977	—	2.00	4.00
PB-11060	Little Ole Dime/A Letter to My Heart	1977	—	2.00	4.00
PB-11187	You're the Only Good Thing (That's Happened to Me)/When You Are Gone	1978	—	2.00	4.00
PB-11564	Don't Let Me Cross Over/I've Enjoyed As Much of This As I Can Stand	1979	—	2.00	4.00
PB-11737	Oh, How I Miss You Tonight/The Talking Walls	1979	—	2.00	4.00
PB-11946	Take Me in Your Arms and Hold Me/Missing Angel	1980	—	2.00	4.00
—With Deborah Allen (overdubbed)					
PB-12118	There's Always Me/Somewhere Along the Line	1980	—	2.00	4.00
PB-13410	The Jim Reeves Medley/He'll Have to Go	1982	—	2.00	4.00
PB-13693	The Image of Me/Won't Come In While He's There	1983	—	2.00	4.00

RCA VICTOR

Number	Title (A Side/B Side)	Yr	VG	VG+	NM
APBO-0255	I'd Fight the World/What's In It for Me	1974	—	2.00	4.00
EP-10133	He Will/We Thank Thee	1974	—	2.00	4.00
PB-10299	You Belong to Me/Maureen	1975	—	2.00	4.00
PB-10418	You'll Never Know/There's That Smile Again	1975	—	2.00	4.00
GB-10511	Missing You/I'd Fight the World	1975	—	2.00	4.00
—Gold Standard Series					
47-6200	Yonder Comes a Sucker/I'm Hurtin' Inside	1955	5.00	10.00	20.00
47-6274	I've Lived a Lot in My Time/Jimbo Jenkins	1955	5.00	10.00	20.00
47-6401	If You Were Mine/That's a Sad Affair	1956	5.00	10.00	20.00
47-6517	My Lips Are Sealed/Pickin' a Chicken	1956	5.00	10.00	20.00
47-6620	According to My Heart/The Mother of a Honky Tonk Girl	1956	5.00	10.00	20.00
—With Carol Johnson					
47-6625	Bimbo/Penny Candy	1956	5.00	10.00	20.00
47-6626	Mexican Joe/How Many	1956	5.00	10.00	20.00
47-6627	Then I'll Stop Loving You/Drinking Tequila	1956	5.00	10.00	20.00
47-6749	Am I Losing You/Waitin' for a Train	1956	5.00	10.00	20.00
47-6874	Four Walls/I Know and You Know	1957	3.75	7.50	15.00
47-6973	Young Hearts/Two Shadows on Your Window	1957	3.75	7.50	15.00
47-7070	Anna Marie/Everywhere You Go	1957	3.75	7.50	15.00
47-7171	I Love You More/Overnight	1958	3.75	7.50	15.00
47-7266	Blue Boy/Theme of Love (I Love to Say I Love You)	1958	3.75	7.50	15.00
47-7380	Billy Bayou/I'd Like to Be	1958	3.75	7.50	15.00
47-7479	Home/If Heartache Is the Fashion	1959	3.75	7.50	15.00
47-7557	Partners/I'm Beginning to Forget You	1959	3.75	7.50	15.00
47-7643	He'll Have to Go/In a Mansion Stands My Love	1959	3.00	6.00	12.00
47-7756	I'm Gettin' Better/I Know One	1960	3.00	6.00	12.00
47-7756 [PS]	I'm Gettin' Better/I Know One	1960	5.00	10.00	20.00
47-7800	Am I Losing You/I Missed Me	1960	3.00	6.00	12.00
47-7800 [PS]	Am I Losing You/I Missed Me	1960	5.00	10.00	20.00
47-7855	The Blizzard/Danny Boy	1961	3.00	6.00	12.00
47-7905	What Would You Do?/Stand At Your Window	1961	3.00	6.00	12.00
47-7950	Losing Your Love/(How Can I Write on Paper) What I Feel in My Heart	1961	3.00	6.00	12.00
47-8019	Adios Amigos/A Letter to My Heart	1962	2.50	5.00	10.00
47-8080	I'm Gonna Change Everything/Pride Goes Before a Fall	1962	2.50	5.00	10.00
47-8127	Is This Me?/Missing Angel	1963	2.50	5.00	10.00
47-8193	Guilty/Little Ole You	1963	2.50	5.00	10.00
47-8193 [PS]	Guilty/Little Ole You	1963	3.75	7.50	15.00
47-8252	An Old Christmas Card/Senor Santa Claus	1963	3.75	7.50	15.00
47-8252 [PS]	An Old Christmas Card/Senor Santa Claus	1963	10.00	20.00	40.00
47-8289	Welcome to My World/Good Morning Self	1963	2.50	5.00	10.00
47-8324	Love Is No Excuse/Look Who's Talking	1964	2.50	5.00	10.00
—With Dottie West					
47-8383	I Guess I'm Crazy/Not Until the Next Time	1964	2.50	5.00	10.00
47-8461	I Won't Forget You/Highway to Nowhere	1964	2.50	5.00	10.00
47-8508	This Is It/There's That Smile Again	1965	2.00	4.00	8.00
47-8625	Is It Really Over?/Rosa Rio	1965	2.00	4.00	8.00
47-8625 [PS]	Is It Really Over?/Rosa Rio	1965	3.00	6.00	12.00
47-8719	Snowflake/Take My Hand, Precious Lord	1965	2.00	4.00	8.00
47-8789	Distant Drums/Old Tige	1966	2.00	4.00	8.00
47-8902	Blue Side of Lonesome/It Hurts So Much (To See You Go)	1966	2.00	4.00	8.00
47-9057	I Won't Come In While He's There/Maureen	1966	2.00	4.00	8.00
47-9238	The Storm/Trying to Forget	1967	2.00	4.00	8.00
47-9343	I Heard a Heart Break Last Night/Golden Memories and Silver Tears	1967	2.00	4.00	8.00
47-9455	That's When I See the Blues (In Your Pretty Brown Eyes)/I've Lived a Lot in My Time	1968	2.00	4.00	8.00
47-9614	When You Are Gone/How Can I Write on Paper	1968	2.00	4.00	8.00
47-9880	Angels Don't Lie/You Kept Me Awake Last Night	1970	—	3.00	6.00
47-9969	Gypsy Feet/He Will	1971	—	3.00	6.00
74-0135	When Two Worlds Collide/Could I Be Falling in Love	1969	—	3.00	6.00
74-0286	Why Do I Love You (Melody of Love)/Nobody's Fool	1969	—	3.00	6.00
74-0626	The Writing on the Wall/You're Free to Go	1971	—	3.00	6.00
74-0744	Missing You/The Tie That Binds	1972	—	2.50	5.00
74-0859	Blue Christmas/Snowflake	1972	—	2.50	5.00
74-0963	Am I That Easy to Forget/Rosa Rio	1973	—	2.00	4.00
447-0884	An Old Christmas Card/Senor Santa Claus	1972	—	2.00	4.00
—Gold Standard Series					
447-0885	Snowflake/Take My Hand, Precious Lord	1972	—	2.00	4.00
—Gold Standard Series					

7-Inch Extended Plays

RCA VICTOR

Number	Title (A Side/B Side)	Yr	VG	VG+	NM
EPA-4357	*He'll Have to Go/Wishful Thinking/Please Come Home/After Awhile	1960	5.00	10.00	20.00
EPA-4357 [PS]	He'll Have to Go	1960	5.00	10.00	20.00

Albums

ABBOTT

Number	Title (A Side/B Side)	Yr	VG	VG+	NM
LP-5001 [M]	Jim Reeves Sings	1956	1000.	1500.	2000.

COUNTRY MUSIC FOUNDATION

Number	Title (A Side/B Side)	Yr	VG	VG+	NM
CMF-008	Live at the Opry	198?	2.50	5.00	10.00

PAIR

Number	Title (A Side/B Side)	Yr	VG	VG+	NM
PDL2-1002 [(2)]	The Country Side of Jim Reeves	1986	3.00	6.00	12.00

RCA CAMDEN

Number	Title (A Side/B Side)	Yr	VG	VG+	NM
ACL1-0123	Kimberley Jim	1973	3.75	7.50	15.00
CAL-583 [M]	According to My Heart	1960	5.00	10.00	20.00
CAS-583 [R]	According to My Heart	1960	5.00	10.00	20.00
CAL-686 [M]	The Country Side of Jim Reeves	1962	5.00	10.00	20.00
CAS-686 [S]	The Country Side of Jim Reeves	1962	5.00	10.00	20.00
CAL-784 [M]	Good 'N' Country	1963	5.00	10.00	20.00
CAS-784 [S]	Good 'N' Country	1963	5.00	10.00	20.00
CAL-842 [M]	Have I Told You Lately That I Love You?	1964	5.00	10.00	20.00
CAS-842 [S]	Have I Told You Lately That I Love You?	1964	5.00	10.00	20.00
CAS-2532	Young and Country	1971	3.75	7.50	15.00
CAX-9001 [(2)]	Jim Reeves	1972	5.00	10.00	20.00

RCA VICTOR

Number	Title (A Side/B Side)	Yr	VG	VG+	NM
APL1-0039	Am I That Easy to Forget	1973	5.00	10.00	20.00
APL1-0330	Great Moments with Jim Reeves	1973	5.00	10.00	20.00
APL1-0537	I'd Fight the World	1974	5.00	10.00	20.00

Number	Title (A Side/B Side)	Yr	VG	VG+	NM
APL1-0793	The Best of Jim Reeves Sacred Songs	1974	5.00	10.00	20.00
APL1-1037	Songs of Love	1975	5.00	10.00	20.00
APL1-1224	I Love You Because	1976	5.00	10.00	20.00
LPM-1256 [M]	Singing Down the Lane	1956	50.00	100.00	200.00
LPM-1410 [M]	Bimbo	1957	50.00	100.00	200.00
—Reissue of Abbott LP					
LPM-1576 [M]	Jim Reeves	1957	20.00	40.00	80.00
LPM-1685 [M]	Girls I Have Known	1958	15.00	30.00	60.00
CPL1-1891	A Legendary Performer	1976	5.00	10.00	20.00
ANL1-1927	Twelve Songs of Christmas	1976	2.00	4.00	8.00
—Reissue of LSP-2758					
LPM-1950 [M]	God Be With You	1958	10.00	20.00	40.00
LSP-1950 [S]	God Be With You	1958	12.50	25.00	50.00
LPM-2001 [M]	Songs to Warm the Heart	1959	10.00	20.00	40.00
LSP-2001 [S]	Songs to Warm the Heart	1959	12.50	25.00	50.00
LPM-2216 [M]	The Intimate Jim Reeves	1960	7.50	15.00	30.00
LSP-2216 [S]	The Intimate Jim Reeves	1960	10.00	20.00	40.00
LPM-2223 [M]	He'll Have to Go	1960	7.50	15.00	30.00
LSP-2223 [S]	He'll Have to Go	1960	10.00	20.00	40.00
LPM-2284 [M]	Tall Tales and Short Tempers	1961	6.25	12.50	25.00
LSP-2284 [S]	Tall Tales and Short Tempers	1961	7.50	15.00	30.00
APL1-2309	It's Nothin' to Me	1977	3.75	7.50	15.00
LPM-2339 [M]	Talkin' to Your Heart	1961	6.25	12.50	25.00
LSP-2339 [S]	Talkin' to Your Heart	1961	7.50	15.00	30.00
LPM-2487 [M]	A Touch of Velvet	1962	6.25	12.50	25.00
LSP-2487 [S]	A Touch of Velvet	1962	7.50	15.00	30.00
LPM-2552 [M]	We Thank Thee	1962	6.25	12.50	25.00
LSP-2552 [S]	We Thank Thee	1962	7.50	15.00	30.00
LPM-2605 [M]	Gentleman Jim	1963	6.25	12.50	25.00
LSP-2605 [S]	Gentleman Jim	1963	7.50	15.00	30.00
LPM-2704 [M]	The International Jim Reeves	1963	6.25	12.50	25.00
LSP-2704 [S]	The International Jim Reeves	1963	7.50	15.00	30.00
AHL1-2720	Jim Reeves	1978	3.75	7.50	15.00
LPM-2758 [M]	Twelve Songs of Christmas	1963	6.25	12.50	25.00
LSP-2758 [S]	Twelve Songs of Christmas	1963	7.50	15.00	30.00
LPM-2780 [M]	Kimberley Jim	1964	6.25	12.50	25.00
LSP-2780 [S]	Kimberley Jim	1964	7.50	15.00	30.00
LPM-2854 [M]	Moonlight and Roses	1964	6.25	12.50	25.00
LSP-2854 [S]	Moonlight and Roses	1964	7.50	15.00	30.00
LPM-2890 [M]	The Best of Jim Reeves	1964	5.00	10.00	20.00
LSP-2890 [S]	The Best of Jim Reeves	1964	6.25	12.50	25.00
LPM-2968 [M]	The Jim Reeves Way	1965	5.00	10.00	20.00
LSP-2968 [S]	The Jim Reeves Way	1965	6.25	12.50	25.00
ANL1-3014	Pure Gold, Volume 1	1978	3.00	6.00	12.00
AHL1-3271	The Best of Jim Reeves, Volume IV	1979	3.75	7.50	15.00
LPM-3427 [M]	Up Through the Years	1965	5.00	10.00	20.00
LSP-3427 [S]	Up Through the Years	1965	6.25	12.50	25.00
AHL1-3454	Don't Let Me Cross Over	1979	3.75	7.50	15.00
LPM-3482 [M]	The Best of Jim Reeves, Vol. II	1966	5.00	10.00	20.00
LSP-3482 [S]	The Best of Jim Reeves, Vol. II	1966	6.25	12.50	25.00
LPM-3542 [M]	Distant Drums	1966	5.00	10.00	20.00
LSP-3542 [S]	Distant Drums	1966	6.25	12.50	25.00
AYL1-3678	The Best of Jim Reeves	1980	3.00	6.00	12.00
—"Best Buy Series" reissue					
LPM-3709 [M]	Yours Sincerely, Jim Reeves	1966	5.00	10.00	20.00
LSP-3709 [S]	Yours Sincerely, Jim Reeves	1966	6.25	12.50	25.00
AYL1-3765	The Best of Jim Reeves Sacred Songs	1980	2.50	5.00	10.00
—"Best Buy Series" reissue					
LPM-3793 [M]	Blue Side of Lonesome	1967	6.25	12.50	25.00
LSP-3793 [S]	Blue Side of Lonesome	1967	5.00	10.00	20.00
AHL1-3827	There's Always Me	1980	3.00	6.00	12.00
LPM-3903 [M]	My Cathedral	1967	7.50	15.00	30.00
LSP-3903 [S]	My Cathedral	1967	6.25	12.50	25.00
AYL1-3936	Pure Gold, Volume 1	1980	2.50	5.00	10.00
—"Best Buy Series" reissue					
LPM-3987 [M]	A Touch of Sadness	1968	15.00	30.00	60.00
LSP-3987 [S]	A Touch of Sadness	1968	5.00	10.00	20.00
LSP-4062	Jim Reeves On Stage	1968	5.00	10.00	20.00
AYL1-4075	The Best of Jim Reeves, Volume IV	1981	2.50	5.00	10.00
—"Best Buy Series" reissue					
LSP-4112	Jim Reeves and Some Friends	1969	5.00	10.00	20.00
AYL1-4168	The Best of Jim Reeves, Vol. II	1981	2.50	5.00	10.00
—"Best Buy Series" reissue					
LSP-4187	The Best of Jim Reeves Volume III	1969	5.00	10.00	20.00
LSP-4475	Jim Reeves Writes You a Record	1971	5.00	10.00	20.00
LSP-4528	Something Special	1971	5.00	10.00	20.00
AHL1-4531	The Jim Reeves Medley	1983	2.50	5.00	10.00
LSP-4646	My Friend	1972	5.00	10.00	20.00
LSP-4749	Missing You	1972	5.00	10.00	20.00
AYL1-4833	Don't Let Me Cross Over	1983	2.50	5.00	10.00
—"Best Buy Series" reissue					
AYL1-4835	I Love You Because	1983	2.50	5.00	10.00
—"Best Buy Series" reissue					
AYL1-4836	Songs of Love	1983	2.50	5.00	10.00
—"Best Buy Series" reissue					
AYL1-4838	The Best of Jim Reeves Vol. III	1983	2.50	5.00	10.00
—"Best Buy Series" reissue					
AYL1-4839	There's Always Me	1983	2.50	5.00	10.00
—"Best Buy Series" reissue					
AYL1-4840	We Thank Thee	1983	2.50	5.00	10.00
—"Best Buy Series" reissue					
AHL1-4865	A Special Collection	1983	3.00	6.00	12.00
CPL2-5044 [(2)]	Just for You	1984	3.75	7.50	15.00
AHL1-5424	Collector's Series	1985	3.00	6.00	12.00

REEVES, JIM, AND PATSY CLINE

Also see each artist's individual listings. These duets were created electronically; they never actually recorded together.

Number	Title (A Side/B Side)	Yr	VG	VG+	NM
45s					
MCA					
52052	So Wrong/I Fall to Pieces	1982	—	2.00	4.00
RCA					
PB-12346	Have You Ever Been Lonely (Have You Ever Been Blue)/Welcome to My World	1981	—	2.00	4.00
Albums					
MCA					
5319	Remembering Jim Reeves and Patsy Cline	1982	3.75	7.50	15.00
RCA VICTOR					
AHL1-4127	Greatest Hits	1981	3.75	7.50	15.00
AYL1-5152	Greatest Hits	1984	2.50	5.00	10.00
—"Best Buy Series" reissue					

REEVES, MARTHA

Also see MARTHA AND THE VANDELLAS.

Number	Title (A Side/B Side)	Yr	VG	VG+	NM
45s					
ARISTA					
0124	Love Blind/This Time I'll Be Sweeter	1975	—	2.50	5.00
—Also see "Martha and the Vandellas"					
0160	Now That We Found Love/Higher and Higher	1975	—	2.00	4.00
0211	The Rest of My Life/Thank You	1976	—	2.00	4.00
0228	You've Lost That Lovin' Feelin'/Now That We Found Love	1977	—	2.00	4.00
FANTASY					
825	Love Don't Come No Stronger/You're Like Sunshine	1978	—	2.00	4.00
868	Dancin' in the Streets (Skatin' in the Streets)/When You Came	1979	—	2.00	4.00
887	Really Like Your Rap/That's What I Want	1979	—	2.00	4.00
MCA					
40194	Power of Love/Stand By Me	1974	—	2.50	5.00
40274	Stand By Me/Wild Night	1974	—	2.50	5.00
40329	My Man/Facsimile	1974	—	2.50	5.00
Albums					
ARISTA					
AL 4105	The Rest of My Life	1976	3.00	6.00	12.00
FANTASY					
F-9549	We'll Meet Again	1978	3.00	6.00	12.00
F-9591	Gotta Keep Moving	1980	3.00	6.00	12.00
MCA					
414	Martha Reeves	1974	3.00	6.00	12.00

REFLECTIONS, THE (1)

Detroit-based rock group.

Number	Title (A Side/B Side)	Yr	VG	VG+	NM
45s					
ABC					
10794	Like Adam and Eve/Vito's House	1966	6.25	12.50	25.00
10822	You're Gonna Find Out (You Love Me)/Long Cigarette	1966	7.50	15.00	30.00
GOLDEN WORLD					
9	(Just Like) Romeo and Juliet/Can't You Tell By the Look in His Eyes	1964	5.00	10.00	20.00
12	Like Columbus Did/Lonely Girl	1964	3.75	7.50	15.00
15	Oowee Now/Talkin' Bout My Girl	1964	3.75	7.50	15.00
16	Henpecked Guy/Don't Do That to Me	1964	3.75	7.50	15.00
19	You're My Baby/Shabby Little Hut	1964	3.75	7.50	15.00
20	Poor Man's Son/Comin' At You	1965	3.75	7.50	15.00
22	Wheelin' and Dealin'/Deborah Ann	1965	3.75	7.50	15.00
24	June Bride/Out of the Picture	1965	3.75	7.50	15.00
29	Girl in the Candy Store/Your Kind of Love	1965	3.75	7.50	15.00
LANA					
140	(Just Like) Romeo and Juliet/(B-side unknown)	196?	—	3.00	6.00
—Early reissue					
Albums					
GOLDEN WORLD					
300 [M]	(Just Like) Romeo and Juliet	1964	37.50	75.00	150.00

REFLECTIONS, THE (2)

R&B group from New York.

Number	Title (A Side/B Side)	Yr	VG	VG+	NM
45s					
CAPITOL					
4078	Three Steps from True Love/How Could We Let the Love Get Away	1975	—	3.00	6.00
4137	Love on Delivery/One Into One	1975	—	2.50	5.00
4222	Are You Ready (Here I Am)/Day After Day (Night After Night)	1976	—	2.50	5.00
4358	Gift Wrap My Love/She's My Summer Breeze	1976	—	2.50	5.00
RCA					
PB-11408	Boogie City/I'm Gonna Let You Go This Time	1978	—	2.50	5.00

REFLECTIONS, THE (3)

Number	Title (A Side/B Side)	Yr	VG	VG+	NM
45s					
CROSSROADS					
401	I Really Must Know/Maybe Tomorrow	1961	15.00	30.00	60.00
402	Rocket to the Moon/Because of You	1962	20.00	40.00	80.00

REFLECTIONS, THE (U)

These could be either group (1) or (3).

Number	Title (A Side/B Side)	Yr	VG	VG+	NM
45s					
KAY-KO					
1003	Helpless/You Said Goodbye	1963	50.00	100.00	200.00
TIGRE					
602	In the Still of the Night/Tic Toc	1962	10.00	20.00	40.00

REGALS, THE (1)

Number	Title (A Side/B Side)	Yr	VG	VG+	NM
45s					
ALADDIN					
3266	Run Pretty Baby/May the Good Lord Bless and Keep You	1954	30.00	60.00	120.00
ATLANTIC					
1062	I'm So Lonely/Got the Water Boiling	1955	15.00	30.00	60.00
MGM					
11869	There'll Always Be a Christmas/When You're Home with the Ones You Love	1954	10.00	20.00	40.00

Number	Title (A Side/B Side)	Yr	VG	VG+	NM

REGALS, THE (2)

45s

Number	Title (A Side/B Side)	Yr	VG	VG+	NM
LAST CHANCE					
109	See You in the Morning/Yes My Love	1961	2.50	5.00	10.00
LAVENDER					
1452	See You in the Morning/Yes My Love	1960	7.50	15.00	30.00
UNITED ARTISTS					
380	Icy Fingers/Tiger Tears	1961	7.50	15.00	30.00

REGAN, DENISE

45s

Number	Title (A Side/B Side)	Yr	VG	VG+	NM
DEE GEE					
3005	A Date with Santa Claus/Hole in the Stocking	1965	2.50	5.00	10.00
3005 [PS]	A Date with Santa Claus/Hole in the Stocking	1965	5.00	10.00	20.00

REGAN, EDDIE

45s

Number	Title (A Side/B Side)	Yr	VG	VG+	NM
ABC					
10795	Playin' Hide and Seek/Talk About Heartaches	1966	7.50	15.00	30.00

REGAN, RUSS

45s

Number	Title (A Side/B Side)	Yr	VG	VG+	NM
ABC-PARAMOUNT					
9949	Junior, Junior, Junior/I Never Knew	1958	5.00	10.00	20.00
CAPITOL					
F4169	Joan of Love/That's When I Ran	1959	3.00	6.00	12.00
F4280	Adults Only/Just the Two of Us	1959	3.00	6.00	12.00

REGAN, TOMMY

45s

Number	Title (A Side/B Side)	Yr	VG	VG+	NM
COLPIX					
725	I'll Never Stop Loving You/This Time I'm Losing You	1964	25.00	50.00	100.00
TELL STAR					
5001	Santa Twist/(B-side unknown)	1962	3.00	6.00	12.00
WORLD ARTISTS					
1049	I Adore You/9 to 5	1965	3.75	7.50	15.00

REGENTS, THE (1)

45s

Number	Title (A Side/B Side)	Yr	VG	VG+	NM
COUSINS					
1002	Barbara-Ann/I'm So Lonely	1961	300.00	600.00	1200.
GEE					
1065	Barbara-Ann/I'm So Lonely	1961	7.50	15.00	30.00
1071	Runaround/Laura My Darling	1961	6.25	12.50	25.00
1073	Don't Be a Fool/Liar	1961	6.25	12.50	25.00
1075	Lonesome Boy/Oh Baby	1961	6.25	12.50	25.00

Albums

Number	Title (A Side/B Side)	Yr	VG	VG+	NM
GEE					
GLP-706 [M]	Barbara Ann	1961	37.50	75.00	150.00
SGLP-706	Barbara Ann	197?	6.25	12.50	25.00
—Reissue by Publishers Central Bureau (clearly marked as such on cover)					
SGLP-706 [S]	Barbara Ann	1961	62.50	125.00	250.00

REGENTS, THE (2)

45s

Number	Title (A Side/B Side)	Yr	VG	VG+	NM
ARGO					
5268	Isle of Trinidad/Bamboo Tree	1957	6.25	12.50	25.00

REGENTS, THE (3)

45s

Number	Title (A Side/B Side)	Yr	VG	VG+	NM
BLUE CAT					
110	Playmates/Me and You	1965	2.50	5.00	10.00
DOT					
16970	The Russian Spy and I/Bald Headed Woman	1966	2.50	5.00	10.00
PENTHOUSE					
502	Words/Worryin' Kind	1966	2.50	5.00	10.00

REGENTS, THE (4)

45s

Number	Title (A Side/B Side)	Yr	VG	VG+	NM
KAYO					
101	(That's What I Call) A Real Good Time/No Hard Feelings	1960	6.25	12.50	25.00
PEORIA					
8	Summertime Blues/(B-side unknown)	196?	3.75	7.50	15.00

REGENTS, THE (5)

MICHAEL McDONALD, later of THE DOOBIE BROTHERS, was in this group.

45s

Number	Title (A Side/B Side)	Yr	VG	VG+	NM
REPRISE					
0430	She's Got Her Own Way of Lovin'/When I Die, Don't You Cry	1965	7.50	15.00	30.00

REGENTS, THE (U)

Albums

Number	Title (A Side/B Side)	Yr	VG	VG+	NM
CAPITOL					
KAO 2153 [M]	Live at the AM-PM Discotheque	1964	12.50	25.00	50.00
SKAO 2153 [S]	Live at the AM-PM Discotheque	1964	15.00	30.00	60.00

REID, CLARENCE

45s

Number	Title (A Side/B Side)	Yr	VG	VG+	NM
ALSTON					
3717	Baptize Me in Your Love/Whatever It Takes	1975	—	2.50	5.00
3720	Come On With It/Mr. Smith's Wife	1976	—	2.50	5.00
3723	Shake Your Butt/Caution! Love Ahead	1976	—	2.50	5.00
3733	Just Another Guy in the Band/I'm Excited	1977	—	2.50	5.00
3748	You Get Me Up/It's Hell Trying to Get to Heaven	1979	—	2.50	5.00
4572	Fools Are Not Born (They Are Made)/Part-Time Lover	1969	2.00	4.00	8.00
4574	Nobody But You Babe	1969	2.00	4.00	8.00
4578	I'm a Man of My Word/I'm Gonna Tear You a New Heart	1969	2.00	4.00	8.00
4582	I've Been Trying/Don't Look Too Hard	1970	—	3.00	6.00
4584	Chicken Hawk/That's How It Is	1970	—	3.00	6.00
4588	Masterpiece/Down the Road of Love	1970	—	3.00	6.00
4592	Direct Me/You Knock Me Out	1971	—	3.00	6.00
4597	You Got to Fight/Three Is a Crowd	1971	—	3.00	6.00
4598	I Get My Kicks/Gotta Take It Home to Mother	1971	—	3.00	6.00
4602	Love Every Woman You Can/Ten Tons of Dynamite	1971	—	3.00	6.00
4603	Good Old Days/Ten Tons of Dynamite	1972	—	3.00	6.00
4608	I'm Gonna Do Something Good to You/Real Woman	1972	—	3.00	6.00
4613	Ruby/Two People in Love	1972	—	3.00	6.00
4616	Till I Get My Share/With Friends Like These	1973	—	3.00	6.00
4621	Funky Party/Winter Man	1974	—	3.00	6.00
DIAL					
3018	I Got My Shake/There'll Come a Day	1964	3.75	7.50	15.00
4019	I Refuse to Give Up/Somebody Will	1965	3.00	6.00	12.00
4040	Gimmie a Try/Part of Your Love	1966	3.00	6.00	12.00
PHIL-L.A. OF SOUL					
301	Cadillac Annie/Tired Blood	1967	2.50	5.00	10.00
WAND					
1106	Somebody Will/I Refuse to Give Up	1966	6.25	12.50	25.00
1121	I'm Your Yes Man/Your Love Is All the Help I Need	1966	10.00	20.00	40.00

Albums

Number	Title (A Side/B Side)	Yr	VG	VG+	NM
ATCO					
SD 33-307	Dancin' with Nobody But You Babe	1969	7.50	15.00	30.00

REID, MATTHEW

45s

Number	Title (A Side/B Side)	Yr	VG	VG+	NM
ABC-PARAMOUNT					
10259	Jane/Why Start	1961	6.25	12.50	25.00
10305	Tarzan Twist (Bwana Ungava)/Through My Tears	1962	6.25	12.50	25.00
DECCA					
31662	One More Minute/Hurt Me	1964	3.00	6.00	12.00
PHILIPS					
40634	Outward Bound/Hey There Sweet Sue	1969	2.50	5.00	10.00
SCEPTER					
1238	Faded Roses/Tomorrow	1962	6.25	12.50	25.00
TOPIX					
6006	Cry Myself to Sleep/Lollipops Went Out of Style	1961	10.00	20.00	40.00

REID, TERRY

45s

Number	Title (A Side/B Side)	Yr	VG	VG+	NM
ABC					
12209	Ooh Baby (Make Me Feel So Young)/Brace Awakening	1976	—	2.50	5.00
EPIC					
10498	May Fly/Superlungs My Supergirl	1969	2.00	4.00	8.00

Albums

Number	Title (A Side/B Side)	Yr	VG	VG+	NM
ABC					
X-935	Seed of Memory	1976	3.00	6.00	12.00
ATLANTIC					
SD 7259	River	1973	3.00	6.00	12.00
CAPITOL					
SW-11857	Rogue Waves	1978	3.00	6.00	12.00
EPIC					
BN 26427	Bang, Bang You're Terry Reid	1968	3.75	7.50	15.00
BN 26477	Terry Reid	1969	3.75	7.50	15.00

REINER, CARL, AND MEL BROOKS

Albums

Number	Title (A Side/B Side)	Yr	VG	VG+	NM
CAPITOL					
SW 1529 [S]	2000 Years	1961	5.00	10.00	20.00
W 1529 [M]	2000 Years	1961	3.75	7.50	15.00
SW 1618 [S]	2000 and One Years	1961	5.00	10.00	20.00
W 1618 [M]	2000 and One Years	1961	3.75	7.50	15.00
SW 1815 [S]	At the Cannes Film Festival	1962	5.00	10.00	20.00
W 1815 [M]	At the Cannes Film Festival	1962	3.75	7.50	15.00
ST 2981	The Best of the 2000 Year Old Man	1968	3.75	7.50	15.00
WARNER BROS.					
BS 2741	2000 and Thirteen	1973	3.75	7.50	15.00
3XX 2744 [(3)]	The Incomplete Works of Reiner and Brooks	1973	6.25	12.50	25.00
WORLD PACIFIC					
WP-1401 [M]	2000 Years	1960	7.50	15.00	30.00

RELATIVES, THE

45s

Number	Title (A Side/B Side)	Yr	VG	VG+	NM
ALMONT					
306	Never Will I Love You Again/I'm Just Looking for Love	1964	10.00	20.00	40.00
MUSICOR					
1063	Eternally/Hadn't Been for Baby	1965	2.50	5.00	10.00

RELF, KEITH

Lead singer of THE YARDBIRDS. Also see ARMAGEDDON (2); RENAISSANCE.

45s

Number	Title (A Side/B Side)	Yr	VG	VG+	NM
EPIC					
10044	Mr. Zero/Knowing	1966	12.50	25.00	50.00
—Lead singer of The Yardbirds					
10044 [DJ]	Mr. Zero/Knowing	1966	37.50	75.00	150.00
—Promo on red vinyl... Reportedly, two promos were released for this single; the second, a different mix, was accompanied by a note telling the radio people not to play the first one, but to use the second one instead. This has not been confirmed.					
10110	Shapes in My Mind/Blue Sands	1966	12.50	25.00	50.00
10110 [DJ]	Shapes in My Mind (same on both sides)	1966	37.50	75.00	150.00
—Promo on red vinyl					
10110 [PS]	Shapes in My Mind/Blue Sands	1966	25.00	50.00	100.00

Number	Title (A Side/B Side)	Yr	VG	VG+	NM
MCCM					
002	Together Now/All the Falling Angels	1989	—	2.50	5.00
—Purple marbled vinyl					
002 [PS]	Together Now/All the Falling Angels	1989	—	2.50	5.00

RELLA, CINDY

Number	Title (A Side/B Side)	Yr	VG	VG+	NM
45s					
CARLTON					
583	He Don't Love Me Anymore/I Want Him to Come Back Home	1962	3.00	6.00	12.00
601	Phil Will/To Tommy with Love	1964	3.00	6.00	12.00
DRUM BOY					
112	Bring Me A Beatle for Christmas/Cla-wence	1964	3.00	6.00	12.00

REMAINS, THE

Number	Title (A Side/B Side)	Yr	VG	VG+	NM
45s					
EPIC					
9777	You Say You're Sorry/I'm Talking About You	1965	20.00	40.00	80.00
9783	My Babe/Why Do I Cry	1965	20.00	40.00	80.00
9872	But I Ain't Got You/I Can't Get Away from You	1965	20.00	40.00	80.00
10001	Diddy Wah Diddy/Once Before	1966	20.00	40.00	80.00
10001 [DJ]	Diddy Wah Diddy/Once Before	1966	27.50	75.00	150.00
—Promo on red vinyl					
10001 [PS]	To Be Seen and Heard: Diddy Wah Diddy	1966	25.00	50.00	100.00
—Promo-only sleeve					
10060	Don't Look Back/Me Right Now	1966	20.00	40.00	80.00
Albums					
EPIC					
LN 24214 [M]	The Remains	1966	50.00	100.00	200.00
BN 26214 [S]	The Remains	1966	75.00	150.00	300.00
SPOONFED					
SFD-3205	The Remains	1978	3.75	7.50	15.00
—Red vinyl					
SUNDAZED					
SEP 10-162 [10]	The Remains	2000	2.00	4.00	8.00
LP 5015	A Session with the Remains	199?	2.50	5.00	10.00
LP 5055	The Remains	1999	3.00	6.00	12.00

REMINISCENTS, THE

Number	Title (A Side/B Side)	Yr	VG	VG+	NM
45s					
DAY					
1000	Zoom Zoom Zoom/Oh Let Me Dream	1963	12.50	25.00	50.00
—Blue vinyl					
MARCEL					
1000	Cards of Love/Flames	1962	30.00	60.00	120.00

REMUS, EUGENE

Number	Title (A Side/B Side)	Yr	VG	VG+	NM
45s					
MOTOWN					
1001	You Never Miss a Good Thing/Hold Me Tight	1960	150.00	300.00	600.00
1001	You Never Miss a Good Thing/Gotta Have Your Lovin'	1960	125.00	250.00	500.00

RENAISSANCE

Actually two diffferent groups, though treated by collectors as one. The first, on Elektra, featured KEITH RELF and other ex-YARDBIRDS. The later group was that group's spiritual heir, but had all new members.

Number	Title (A Side/B Side)	Yr	VG	VG+	NM
45s					
CAPITOL					
3487	Prologue/Spare Some Love	1972	2.00	4.00	8.00
3715	Carpet of the Sun/Bound for Infinity	1973	2.00	4.00	8.00
I.R.S.					
9904	Remember/Bon Jour Swan Song	1982	—	2.50	5.00
9914	Richard IX/(B-side unknown)	1982	—	2.50	5.00
SIRE					
714	Mother Russia/I Think of You	1974	—	3.00	6.00
728	Carpet of the Sun/Kiev	1976	—	3.00	6.00
740	Midas Man/Captive Heart	1977	—	3.00	6.00
1022	Northern Lights/Opening Out	1978	—	2.50	5.00
1041	Northern Lights/Opening Out	1979	—	2.50	5.00
49041	Forever Changing/Jekyll and Hyde	1979	—	2.50	5.00
Albums					
CAPITOL/SOVEREIGN					
SMAS-11116	Prologue	1972	3.75	7.50	15.00
ST-11216	Ashes Are Burning	1973	3.75	7.50	15.00
SWBC-11871 [(2)]	In the Beginning	1978	3.75	7.50	15.00
—Combines 11116 and 11216 in one package					
ELEKTRA					
EKS-74068	Renaissance	1969	7.50	15.00	30.00
I.R.S.					
SP-70019	Camera Camera	1981	2.50	5.00	10.00
SP-70033	Time Line	1983	2.50	5.00	10.00
MOBILE FIDELITY					
1-099	Scheherazade and Other Stories	1982	12.50	25.00	50.00
—Audiophile vinyl					
SIRE					
SASD-3902 [(2)]	Live at Carnegie Hall	1976	3.75	7.50	15.00
SR 6015	Turn of the Cards	1977	2.50	5.00	10.00
—Reissue of 7502					
SR 6017	Scheherazade and Other Stories	1977	2.50	5.00	10.00
—Reissue of 7510					
SR 6024	Novella	1977	2.50	5.00	10.00
—Reissue of 7526					
2XS 6029 [(2)]	Live at Carnegie Hall	1977	3.00	6.00	12.00
—Reissue of 3902					
SRK 6049	A Song for All Seasons	1978	3.00	6.00	12.00
SRK 6068	Azure d'Or	1979	3.00	6.00	12.00
SAS-7502	Turn of the Cards	1974	3.00	6.00	12.00
SASD-7510	Scheherazade and Other Stories	1975	3.00	6.00	12.00
SASD-7526	Novella	1977	3.00	6.00	12.00

RENAY, DIANE

Number	Title (A Side/B Side)	Yr	VG	VG+	NM
45s					
20TH CENTURY FOX					
456	Navy Blue/Unbelievable Boy	1964	3.75	7.50	15.00
477	Kiss Me Sailor/Soft Spoken Guy	1964	2.50	5.00	10.00
514	Growin' Up Too Fast/Waitin' for Joey	1964	2.50	5.00	10.00
533	It's In Your Tears/Present from Eddie	1964	2.50	5.00	10.00
ATCO					
6240	Falling Star/Little White Lies	1962	3.00	6.00	12.00
6262	Dime a Dozen/Tender	1963	3.00	6.00	12.00
FONTANA					
1679	Hold Me, Thrill Me, Kiss Me/Yesterday	1969	2.50	5.00	10.00
MGM					
13296	Billy Blue Eyes/Watch Out Sally	1964	2.50	5.00	10.00
13335	I Had a Dream/Troublemaker	1965	5.00	10.00	20.00
NEW VOICE					
800	Words/The Company You Keep	1965	2.50	5.00	10.00
803	Cross My Heart, Hope to Die/Happy Birthday, Broken Heart	1965	2.50	5.00	10.00
UNITED ARTISTS					
50048	Dynamite/Please Gypsy	1966	3.75	7.50	15.00
Albums					
20TH CENTURY FOX					
TF-3133 [M]	Navy Blue	1964	20.00	40.00	80.00
TFS-4133 [S]	Navy Blue	1964	37.50	75.00	150.00

RENDEZVOUS

Number	Title (A Side/B Side)	Yr	VG	VG+	NM
45s					
REPRISE					
20089	Congratulations Baby/Faithfully	1962	7.50	15.00	30.00
RUST					
5041	It Breaks My Heart/Take a Break	1961	10.00	20.00	40.00

RENDEZVOUS STOMPERS, THE

Number	Title (A Side/B Side)	Yr	VG	VG+	NM
45s					
DORE					
626	Gremmies Unite/Rock Me Gently	1962	10.00	20.00	40.00

RENE AND RENE

Number	Title (A Side/B Side)	Yr	VG	VG+	NM
45s					
CERTRON					
10011	My Amigo Jose/Good Old Days	1970	—	2.50	5.00
COLUMBIA					
43045	Angelito/Write Me Soon	1964	2.00	4.00	8.00
43045 [PS]	Angelito/Write Me Soon	1964	3.00	6.00	12.00
43163	Please Don't Bother/Undecided	1964	2.00	4.00	8.00
EPIC					
10443	Muchachita/Our Day Will Come	1969	—	2.50	5.00
JOX					
017	Angelito/Write Me Soon	1964	3.00	6.00	12.00
025	Pretty Flowers/Fade Away	1965	2.50	5.00	10.00
032	Chantilly Lace/I'm Not the Only One	1965	2.50	5.00	10.00
041	Little Peanuts/Little Vagabond	1965	2.50	5.00	10.00
050	Loving You Could Hurt Me So/Little Diamonds	1966	2.50	5.00	10.00
WHITE WHALE					
281	Lo Mucho Que Te Quiero/Lloraras	1968	—	3.00	6.00
287	Lo Mucho Que Te Quiero/Mornin'	1968	—	2.50	5.00
298	Las Cosas/You Will Cry	1969	—	2.50	5.00
303	Enchilada Jose/Lloraras	1969	—	2.50	5.00
327	Love Is for the Two of Us/Sally Tosis	1969	—	2.50	5.00
Albums					
WHITE WHALE					
WWS-7119	Lo Mucho Que Te Quiero	1968	3.75	7.50	15.00

RENEGADES, THE (1)

Number	Title (A Side/B Side)	Yr	VG	VG+	NM
45s					
AMERICAN INT'L.					
537	Charge/Geronimo	1959	12.50	25.00	50.00

RENEGADES, THE (2)

Number	Title (A Side/B Side)	Yr	VG	VG+	NM
45s					
CONGRESS					
241	Cadillac/Matelot (Sailor Boy)	1965	7.50	15.00	30.00

RENEGADES, THE (3)

Number	Title (A Side/B Side)	Yr	VG	VG+	NM
45s					
DORSET					
5007	Stolen Angel/Keep Laughin'	1961	12.50	25.00	50.00

RENEGADES, THE (U)

If these are any of the above, they are most likely group (2).

Number	Title (A Side/B Side)	Yr	VG	VG+	NM
45s					
GARLAND					
2036	I'm a Loner/Travelin' Through This Countryside	196?	2.50	5.00	10.00
KARATE					
519	Take a Heart/If It Gets Lonesome	1966	3.75	7.50	15.00

RENO, AL

Number	Title (A Side/B Side)	Yr	VG	VG+	NM
45s					
KAPP					
432	Cheryl/Congratulations	1961	10.00	20.00	40.00

REO SPEEDWAGON

Number	Title (A Side/B Side)	Yr	VG	VG+	NM
12-Inch Singles					
EPIC					
AE 314 [DJ]	Ridin' the Storm Out (mono/stereo)	1977	2.50	5.00	10.00
AE 1489 [DJ]	Keep the Fire Burnin' (same on both sides)	1982	—	3.00	6.00
EAS 2091 [DJ]	Gotta Feel More (3 versions)	1985	2.00	4.00	8.00

45s

EPIC

Number	Title (A Side/B Side)	Yr	VG	VG+	NM
01054	Take It on the Run/Someone Tonight	1981	—	2.00	4.00
02127	Don't Let Him Go/I Wish You Were There	1981	—	2.00	4.00
02127 [PS]	Don't Let Him Go/I Wish You Were There	1981	—	2.50	5.00
02153	Keep On Loving You/Time for Me to Fly	1981	—	—	3.00
—Reissue					
02457	In Your Letter/Shakin' It Loose	1981	—	2.00	4.00
02967	Keep the Fire Burnin'/I'll Follow You	1982	—	2.00	4.00
03175	Sweet Time/Stillness of the Night	1982	—	2.00	4.00
03175 [PS]	Sweet Time/Stillness of the Night	1982	—	2.50	5.00
ENR-03264	Sweet Time	1982	—	2.50	5.00
—One-sided budget release					
03400	Let's Be-Bop/The Key	1982	—	2.00	4.00
03846	Keep the Fire Burnin'/Take It on the Run	1983	—	—	3.00
—Reissue					
03847	In Your Letter/Don't Let Him Go	1983	—	—	3.00
—Reissue					
04659	I Do'Wanna Know/Rock 'N Roll Star	1984	—	—	3.00
04659 [PS]	I Do'Wanna Know/Rock 'N Roll Star	1984	—	2.00	4.00
04713	Can't Fight This Feeling/Break His Spell	1984	—	—	3.00
04713 [PS]	Can't Fight This Feeling/Break His Spell	1984	—	3.00	6.00
04848	One Lonely Night/Wheels Are Turnin'	1985	—	—	3.00
04848 [PS]	One Lonely Night/Wheels Are Turnin'	1985	—	2.00	4.00
05412	Live Every Moment/Gotta Feel More	1985	—	—	3.00
06656	That Ain't Love/Accidents Can Happen	1987	—	—	3.00
06656 [PS]	That Ain't Love/Accidents Can Happen	1987	—	—	3.00
07055	Variety Tonight/Tired of Gettin' Nowhere	1987	—	—	3.00
07055 [PS]	Variety Tonight/Tired of Gettin' Nowhere	1987	—	—	3.00
07255	In My Dreams/Over the Edge	1987	—	—	3.00
07255 [PS]	In My Dreams/Over the Edge	1987	—	—	3.00
07901	Here with Me/Wherever You're Goin' (It's Alright)	1988	—	—	3.00
07901 [PS]	Here with Me/Wherever You're Goin' (It's Alright)	1988	—	—	3.00
08030	I Don't Want to Lose You/On the Road Again	1988	—	—	3.00
10827	Sophisticated Lady/Prison Women	1972	3.00	6.00	12.00
10847	157 Riverside Avenue/Five Men Were Killed Today	1972	3.00	6.00	12.00
10892	Lay Me Down/Gypsy Woman's Passion	1972	3.00	6.00	12.00
10975	Golden Country/Little Queenie	1973	3.00	6.00	12.00
11078	Ridin' the Storm Out/Whiskey Night	1974	3.00	6.00	12.00
11132	Start a New Life/Open Up	1974	2.50	5.00	10.00
50059	Sky Blues/Throw the Chains Away	1975	2.00	4.00	8.00
50120	Out of Control/Running Blind	1975	2.00	4.00	8.00
50180	Reelin'/Headed for a Fall	1975	2.00	4.00	8.00
50254	Tonight/Keep Pushin'	1976	—	3.00	6.00
50288	Flying Turkey Trot/Keep Pushin'	1976	—	3.00	6.00
50367	Ridin' the Storm Out/Being Kind	1977	—	3.00	6.00
50459	Flying Turkey Trot/Keep Pushin'	1977	—	3.00	6.00
50545	Roll with the Changes/Unidentified Flying Tuna Trot	1978	—	2.50	5.00
50582	Time for Me to Fly/Runnin' Blind	1978	—	2.50	5.00
50764	I Need You Tonight/Easy Money	1979	—	2.50	5.00
50790	Only the Strong Survive/Drop It (An Old Disguise)	1979	—	2.50	5.00
50858	Time for Me to Fly/Lightning	1980	—	2.00	4.00
50953	Keep On Loving You/Follow My Heart	1980	—	2.00	4.00
51006	Take It on the Run/Someone Tonight	1981	—	—	—
—Unreleased?					
73499	Live It Up/All Heaven Broke Loose	1990	—	—	3.00
73540	Love Is a Rock/Go for Broke	1990	—	—	3.00

Albums

EPIC

Number	Title (A Side/B Side)	Yr	VG	VG+	NM
E 31089	REO Speedwagon	1972	3.75	7.50	15.00
—Yellow label original					
KE 31089	REO Speedwagon	1973	3.00	6.00	12.00
—Orange label					
PE 31089	REO Speedwagon	1979	2.00	4.00	8.00
—Dark blue label					
KE 31745	R.E.O./T.W.O.	1972	3.75	7.50	15.00
—Yellow label original					
KE 31745	R.E.O./T.W.O.	1973	3.00	6.00	12.00
—Orange label					
PE 31745	R.E.O./T.W.O.	1979	2.00	4.00	8.00
—Dark blue label					
KE 32378	Ridin' the Storm Out	1973	3.00	6.00	12.00
—Orange label					
PE 32378	Ridin' the Storm Out	1979	2.00	4.00	8.00
—Dark blue label					
PE 32948	Lost in a Dream	1974	3.00	6.00	12.00
—Orange label					
PE 32948	Lost in a Dream	1979	2.00	4.00	8.00
—Dark blue label					
PE 33338	This Time We Mean It	1975	3.00	6.00	12.00
—Orange label					
PE 33338	This Time We Mean It	1979	2.00	4.00	8.00
—Dark blue label					
PE 34143	R.E.O.	1976	3.00	6.00	12.00
—Orange label					
PE 34143	R.E.O.	1979	2.00	4.00	8.00
—Dark blue label					
PEG 34494 [(2)]	REO Speedwagon Live/You Get What You Play For	1977	3.75	7.50	15.00
—Orange labels					
PEG 34494 [(2)]	REO Speedwagon Live/You Get What You Play For	1979	3.00	6.00	12.00
—Dark blue labels					
JE 35062	You Can Tune a Piano, But You Can't Tuna Fish	1978	3.00	6.00	12.00
—Orange label; no bar code on back cover					
JE 35062	You Can Tune a Piano, But You Can't Tuna Fish	1978	2.50	5.00	10.00
—Orange label; with bar code on back cover					
JE 35062	You Can Tune a Piano, But You Can't Tuna Fish	1979	2.00	4.00	8.00
—Dark blue label					
PE 35062	You Can Tune a Piano, But You Can't Tuna Fish	198?	2.00	4.00	8.00
FE 35988	Nine Lives	1979	2.50	5.00	10.00
PE 35988	Nine Lives	198?	2.00	4.00	8.00
—Budget-line reissue					
KE2 36444 [(2)]	A Decade of Rock and Roll 1970 to 1980	1980	3.00	6.00	12.00
FE 36844	Hi Infidelity	1980	2.00	4.00	8.00
FE 38100	Good Trouble	1982	2.50	5.00	10.00
PE 38100	Good Trouble	198?	2.00	4.00	8.00
—Budget-line reissue					
QE 39593	Wheels Are Turnin'	1984	2.00	4.00	8.00
FE 40444	Life As We Know It	1987	2.00	4.00	8.00
OE 44202	The Hits	1988	2.50	5.00	10.00
HE 45062	You Can Tune a Piano, But You Can't Tuna Fish	198?	10.00	20.00	40.00
—Half-speed mastered edition					
E 45246	The Earth, a Small Man, His Dog and a Chicken	1990	3.00	6.00	12.00
HE 46844	Hi Infidelity	1982	7.50	15.00	30.00
—Half-speed mastered edition					
HE 48100	Good Trouble	1982	7.50	15.00	30.00
—Half-speed mastered edition					

REPARATA AND THE DELRONS

45s

Number	Title (A Side/B Side)	Yr	VG	VG+	NM
BIG TREE					
114	Just You/There's So Little Time	1971	—	2.50	5.00
KAPP					
989	(That's What Sends Men to) The Bowery/I've Got an Awful Lot of Losing to Do	1969	—	3.00	6.00
2010	San Juan/We're Gonna Hold the Night	1969	—	3.00	6.00
2050	Waking in the Rain/Got Fear of Losing You	1969	—	3.00	6.00
LAURIE					
3252	Your Big Mistake/Leave Us Alone	1964	7.50	15.00	30.00
—As "The Delrons"					
3589	Octopus' Garden/Your Life Is Gone	1972	—	2.50	5.00
—As "Reparata"					
MALA					
573	I Believe/It's Waiting There for You	1967	—	3.00	6.00
589	Captain of Your Ship/Toom Toom Is a Little Boy	1968	3.00	6.00	12.00
12000	Saturday Night Didn't Happen/Panic	1968	—	3.00	6.00
12016	You Can't Change a Young Boy's Mind/Weather Forecast	1968	—	3.00	6.00
12026	Heaven Only Knows/Summer Laughter	1968	—	3.00	6.00
POLYDOR					
14271	Shoes/Song for All	1975	—	2.00	4.00
—As "Reparata"					
14298	Jezebee Lancer the Belly Dancer/We Need You	1975	—	—	—
—Unreleased					
RCA VICTOR					
47-8721	I Can Tell/Take a Look Around You	1965	2.50	5.00	10.00
47-8820	I'm Nobody's Baby Now/The Loneliest Girl in Town	1966	3.75	7.50	15.00
47-8921	Mama's Little Girl/He Don't Want You	1966	2.50	5.00	10.00
47-9123	Boys and Girls/That Kind of Trouble That I Love	1967	2.50	5.00	10.00
47-9185	I Can Hear the Rain/Always Waitin'	1967	2.50	5.00	10.00
WORLD ARTISTS					
1036	Whenever a Teenager Cries/He's My Guy	1964	3.00	6.00	12.00
1051	Tommy/Mama Don't Allow	1965	3.00	6.00	12.00
1057	He's the Greatest/A Summer Thought	1965	3.00	6.00	12.00
1062	The Boy I Love/I Found My Place	1965	3.00	6.00	12.00

Albums

Number	Title (A Side/B Side)	Yr	VG	VG+	NM
AVCO EMBASSY					
AVE-33008	Rock and Roll Revolution	1970	6.25	12.50	25.00
WORLD ARTISTS					
WAM-2006 [M]	Whenever a Teenager Cries	1965	12.50	25.00	50.00
WAS-3006 [S]	Whenever a Teenager Cries	1965	15.00	30.00	60.00

REPRISE REPERTORY THEATRE, THE

Artists who were signed to Reprise Records at the time, including ROSEMARY CLOONEY, BING CROSBY, SAMMY DAVIS, JR., DEAN MARTIN, FRANK SINATRA and JO STAFFORD, perform new versions of famous musicals under this collective name.

Albums

REPRISE

Number	Title (A Side/B Side)	Yr	VG	VG+	NM
F-2015 [M]	Finian's Rainbow	1964	7.50	15.00	30.00
—Gatefold cover					
F-2015 [M]	Finian's Rainbow	196?	5.00	10.00	20.00
—Standard cover					
FS-2015 [S]	Finian's Rainbow	1964	10.00	20.00	40.00
—Gatefold cover					
FS-2015 [S]	Finian's Rainbow	196?	6.25	12.50	25.00
—Standard cover					
F-2016 [M]	Guys and Dolls	1964	7.50	15.00	30.00
—Gatefold cover					
F-2016 [M]	Guys and Dolls	196?	5.00	10.00	20.00
—Standard cover					
FS-2016 [S]	Guys and Dolls	1964	10.00	20.00	40.00
—Gatefold cover					
FS-2016 [S]	Guys and Dolls	196?	6.25	12.50	25.00
—Standard cover					
F-2017 [M]	Kiss Me, Kate	1964	7.50	15.00	30.00
—Gatefold cover					
F-2017 [M]	Kiss Me, Kate	196?	5.00	10.00	20.00
—Standard cover					
FS-2017 [S]	Kiss Me, Kate	1964	10.00	20.00	40.00
—Gatefold cover					
FS-2017 [S]	Kiss Me, Kate	196?	6.25	12.50	25.00
—Standard cover					
F-2018 [M]	South Pacific	1964	7.50	15.00	30.00
—Gatefold cover					
F-2018 [M]	South Pacific	196?	5.00	10.00	20.00
—Standard cover					
FS-2018 [S]	South Pacific	1964	10.00	20.00	40.00
—Gatefold cover					
FS-2018 [S]	South Pacific	196?	6.25	12.50	25.00
—Standard cover					
F-2019 [(4) M]	The Reprise Repertory Theatre	1964	50.00	100.00	200.00
—Box set of all four of the above LPs in gatefold covers					
FS-2019 [(4) S]	The Reprise Repertory Theatre	1964	75.00	150.00	300.00
—Box set of all four of the above LPs in gatefold covers					

RESIDENTS, THE

12-Inch Singles

RALPH

Number	Title (A Side/B Side)	Yr	VG	VG+	NM
RZ 8006-D	Diskomo/Goosebump	1980	5.00	10.00	20.00
—Green vinyl					
RZ 8006-D	Diskomo/Goosebump	1980	2.50	5.00	10.00
RR 8721	Hit the Road Jack (Dance Mix)/Jambalaya-Firefly-The Big Bubble-Cry for the Fire	1987	2.00	4.00	8.00

45s

CRYPTIC

Number	Title (A Side/B Side)	Yr	VG	VG+	NM
RZ-SP-1SP 1	Earth Vs. the Flying Saucers	1986	5.00	10.00	20.00
—Green vinyl, one-sided, bonus with collector's edition of book "The Cryptic Guide to the Residents"					

EVA-TONE

Number	Title (A Side/B Side)	Yr	VG	VG+	NM
10371900-1	Diskomo (Live)	1988	—	2.50	5.00
—Flexi-disc included with April 1988 issue of Reflex					

RALPH

Number	Title (A Side/B Side)	Yr	VG	VG+	NM
RR 0577	Beyond the Valley of A Day in the Life/Flying	1977	37.50	75.00	150.00
RR 0577 [PS]	Beyond the Valley of A Day in the Life/Flying	1977	37.50	75.00	150.00
—Also known as "The Residents Meet the Beatles and The Beatles Meet the Residents"					
RR 0776	Satisfaction/Loser Is Congruent to Weed	1976	37.50	75.00	150.00
RR 0776 [PS]	Satisfaction/Loser Is Congruent to Weed	1976	37.50	75.00	150.00
RR 1272	Fire/Aircraft Damage	1972	25.00	50.00	100.00
—Part of "Santa Dog" two-7" single set					
RR 1272	Lightning/Explosion	1972	25.00	50.00	100.00
—Part of "Santa Dog" two-7" single set					
RR 1272 [PS]	Santa Dog: Fire/Aircraft Damage; Lightning/Explosion	1972	100.00	200.00	400.00
—Signed, intentionally misnumbered sleeve for above two records					
RR 7803	Satisfaction/Loser Is Congruent to Weed	1978	—	2.00	4.00
RR 7803 [PS]	Satisfaction/Loser Is Congruent to Weed	1978	—	2.00	4.00
RR 7812	Santa Dog '78/Fire	1978	5.00	10.00	20.00
RR 7812 [PS]	Santa Dog '78/Fire	1978	5.00	10.00	20.00
RZ 8422	It's a Man's Man's Man's World/Safety Is a Cootie Wootie	1984	2.50	5.00	10.00
—White vinyl picture disc					
RZ 8422	It's a Man's Man's Man's World/Safety Is a Cootie Wootie	1984	—	—	3.00
RZ 8422	It's a Man's Man's Man's World/Safety Is a Cootie Wootie	1984	3.75	7.50	15.00
—White vinyl picture disc; first pressing was mislabeled					
RZ 8422 [PS]	It's a Man's Man's Man's World/Safety Is a Cootie Wootie	1984	—	—	3.00
RZ 8621	Kaw-Liga/Stars and Stripes Forever	1986	2.50	5.00	10.00
—Picture disc					
RZ 8622	Kaw-Liga/Stars and Stripes Forever	1986	2.00	4.00	8.00
—White vinyl					
RZ 8622	Kaw-Liga/Stars and Stripes Forever	1986	—	—	3.00
RZ 8622 [PS]	Kaw-Liga/Stars and Stripes Forever	1986	—	—	3.00
RR 8722	Hit the Road Jack/For Elsie (Excerpt)	1987	—	—	3.00
RR 8722 [PD]	Hit the Road Jack/For Elsie (Excerpt)	1987	2.50	5.00	10.00
—Picture disc					
RR 8722 [PS]	Hit the Road Jack/For Elsie (Excerpt)	1987	—	—	3.00

7-Inch Extended Plays

RALPH

Number	Title (A Side/B Side)	Yr	VG	VG+	NM
WEIRD 1	Babyfingers	1981	5.00	10.00	20.00
—Pink vinyl on labels left over from fan club issue					
WEIRD 1 [PS]	Babyfingers	1981	5.00	10.00	20.00
RR 0377	Babyfingers	1979	18.75	37.50	75.00
RR 0377 [PS]	Babyfingers	1979	18.75	37.50	75.00
RR 1177	Duck Stab	1978	—	2.50	5.00
—Red label					
RR 1177 [PS]	Duck Stab	1978	—	2.50	5.00
—Matte cover					
RR 1177 [PS]	Duck Stab	1978	11.25	22.50	45.00
—Shiny cover					

W.E.I.R.D.

Number	Title (A Side/B Side)	Yr	VG	VG+	NM
WEIRD 1	Babyfingers	1981	5.00	10.00	20.00
—Fan club reissue					
WEIRD 1 [PS]	Babyfingers	1981	5.00	10.00	20.00

Albums

CRYPTIC

Number	Title (A Side/B Side)	Yr	VG	VG+	NM
S-18335 SP-2	For Elsie	1987	18.75	37.50	75.00
—Green vinyl one-sided LP					

ENIGMA

Number	Title (A Side/B Side)	Yr	VG	VG+	NM
73547	The King & Eye	1989	2.50	5.00	10.00

EPISODE

Number	Title (A Side/B Side)	Yr	VG	VG+	NM
ED 21	The Census Taker (Soundtrack)	1985	6.25	12.50	25.00
—Red vinyl					
ED 21	The Census Taker (Soundtrack)	1985	5.00	10.00	20.00

OP

Number	Title (A Side/B Side)	Yr	VG	VG+	NM
011 [DJ]	Freak Show	1991	12.50	25.00	50.00
—Promo-only black vinyl pressing; 400 made					
011 [PD]	Freak Show	1991	3.00	6.00	12.00
—Picture disc					

RALPH

Number	Title (A Side/B Side)	Yr	VG	VG+	NM
Mole Show 001	The Mole Show (The Roxy)	1983	7.50	15.00	30.00
RR 0274	Meet the Residents	1974	50.00	100.00	200.00
—First version: "Meet the Beatles" LP parody cover and "First Edition" on back cover					
RR 0278	Duck Stab	1978	3.00	6.00	12.00
—First version: Green titles box on back					
RR 0278	Duck Stab	1978	2.50	5.00	10.00
—Second version: Yellow titles box on back					
RR 0677	Meet the Residents	1977	5.00	10.00	20.00
—Second version: "She Loves You" picture sleeve parody cover, split "a" Ralph logo					
RR 0677	Meet the Residents	1977	3.75	7.50	15.00
—Third version: same cover as second version, black "a" Ralph logo					
RR 0677	Meet the Residents	1977	2.50	5.00	10.00
—Fourth version: same cover as second version, modified and orange back cover					
RR 1075	The Third Reich 'N' Roll	1976	12.50	25.00	50.00
—First version of 1,000: Liner notes inside, orange carrot					
RR 1075	The Third Reich 'N' Roll	1976	3.75	7.50	15.00
—Second version: Gray carrot, split "a" Ralph logo					
RR 1075	The Third Reich 'N' Roll	1976	3.00	6.00	12.00
—Third version: Orange carrot, black "a" Ralph logo					
RR 1075	The Third Reich 'N' Roll	1976	2.50	5.00	10.00
—Fourth version: Gray carrot, black "a" Ralph logo					
RR 1075	The Third Reich 'N' Roll	1976	375.00	750.00	1500.
—Numbered box set on marbled vinyl, silkscreened cover and lithographs inside					
RR 1075	The Third Reich 'N' Roll	1976	12.50	25.00	50.00
—Censored cover with swastikas obscured, pressed in U.S. for export to Germany					
RR 1174	Not Available	1978	6.25	12.50	25.00
—Purple label, mis-mastered, "Re-1" in trail-off vinyl					
RR 1174	Not Available	1978	3.75	7.50	15.00
—Orange label, remastered, "Re-3" in trail-off vinyl					
RR 1174	Not Available	1978	3.00	6.00	12.00
—Green label, address is "444 Grove"					
RR 1174	Not Available	1978	2.50	5.00	10.00
—Green label, address is "109 Minna"					
RR 1276	Fingerprince	1977	20.00	40.00	80.00
—First version: Dark brown cover, "First Pressing" written on back cover					
RR 1276	Fingerprince	1977	5.00	10.00	20.00
—Second version: Lighter brown cover					
RR 1276	Fingerprince	1977	2.50	5.00	10.00
—Third version: Color cover					
RZ 7707 [PD]	Meet the Residents	1986	6.25	12.50	25.00
—Picture disc, with original cover on one side, replacement cover on other					
DJ 7901 [DJ]	Please Do Not Steal It!	1979	6.25	12.50	25.00
—Promo-only sampler					
ESK 7906	Eskimo	1979	6.25	12.50	25.00
—First version: White vinyl, gatefold cover					
ESK 7906	Eskimo	1979	3.75	7.50	15.00
—Second version: Black vinyl, gatefold					
ESK 7906	Eskimo	1979	2.50	5.00	10.00
—Third version: Black vinyl, standard cover					
RZ 7906 [PD]	Eskimo	1979	7.50	15.00	30.00
—Picture disc					
RZ 8052	The Residents Commercial Album	1980	5.00	10.00	20.00
—First version: Purple Ralph logo, songs listed in wrong order					
RZ 8052	The Residents Commercial Album	1980	3.75	7.50	15.00
—Second version: Corrected song order, green logo					
RZ 8052	The Residents Commercial Album	1980	3.00	6.00	12.00
—Third version: Green vinyl					
RZ 8152	Mark of the Mole	1981	12.50	25.00	50.00
—Signed brown vinyl edition with lyrics					
RZ 8152	Mark of the Mole	1981	2.50	5.00	10.00
RZ 8202	The Tunes of Two Cities	1982	3.00	6.00	12.00
—First edition: "444 Grove Street" address					
RZ 8202	The Tunes of Two Cities	1982	2.50	5.00	10.00
—Second edition: "109 Minna Street" address					
RZ 8252	Intermission	1982	3.50	7.00	14.00
—Red vinyl					
RZ 8252	Intermission	1982	3.00	6.00	12.00
RR 8315	Title in Limbo	1983	3.00	6.00	12.00
—With Renaldo and The Loaf					
RZ 8402	George & James	1984	7.50	15.00	30.00
—First edition: Rejected mix with "Re-1" in trail-off					
RZ 8402	George & James	1984	2.50	5.00	10.00
—Second edition: Approved mix with "Re-5" in trail-off					
RZ 8452	Whatever Happened to Vileness Fats?	1984	12.50	25.00	50.00
—Red vinyl					
RZ 8452	Whatever Happened to Vileness Fats?	1984	3.00	6.00	12.00
RZ 8552	The Big Bubble	1985	12.50	25.00	50.00
—Pink vinyl					
RZ 8552	The Big Bubble	1985	3.00	6.00	12.00
RZ 8602	The Eyeball Show (The 13th Anniversary Show) Live in Japan	1986	5.00	10.00	20.00
—White vinyl					
RZ 8602	The Eyeball Show (The 13th Anniversary Show) Live in Japan	1986	2.50	5.00	10.00
RZ 8652	Stars & Hank Forever	1986	5.00	10.00	20.00
—Blue vinyl					
RZ 8652	Stars & Hank Forever	1986	2.50	5.00	10.00
RR 82761	Fingerprince	1988	3.00	6.00	12.00
—New number, purple vinyl					
RR 82761	Fingerprince	1988	2.50	5.00	10.00
—New number, black vinyl					
RR 87521	Duck Stab	1988	3.00	6.00	12.00
—New number, red vinyl					
RR 87521	Duck Stab	1988	2.50	5.00	10.00
—New number, black vinyl					
RR 88521	Meet the Residents	1988	3.75	7.50	15.00
—Original "Meet the Beatles" parody cover restored, white vinyl					
RR 88521	Meet the Residents	1988	3.00	6.00	12.00
—Original "Meet the Beatles" parody cover restored, black vinyl					

RYKO ANALOGUE

Number	Title (A Side/B Side)	Yr	VG	VG+	NM
RALP-0044-2	God in Three Persons	1988	2.50	5.00	10.00
—2-LP set on clear vinyl					
RALP-0045-2	God in Three Persons Instrumental	1988	2.50	5.00	10.00
—Clear vinyl					

RESTIVO, JOHNNY

45s

20TH FOX

Number	Title (A Side/B Side)	Yr	VG	VG+	NM
260	Sweet Lovin'/Looka Here Now	1961	3.75	7.50	15.00
279	Doctor Love/The Magic Age Is Seventeen	1961	3.75	7.50	15.00
279 [PS]	Doctor Love/The Magic Age Is Seventeen	1961	7.50	15.00	30.00

EPIC

Number	Title (A Side/B Side)	Yr	VG	VG+	NM
9537	My Reputation/You Can't Turn Back the Clock	1962	3.75	7.50	15.00

RCA VICTOR

Number	Title (A Side/B Side)	Yr	VG	VG+	NM
47-7559 [M]	The Shape I'm In/Ya Ya	1959	5.00	10.00	20.00
47-7559 [PS]	The Shape I'm In/Ya Ya	1959	12.50	25.00	50.00
47-7601	Dear Someone/I Like Girls	1959	3.75	7.50	15.00
47-7601 [PS]	Dear Someone/I Like Girls	1959	7.50	15.00	30.00
47-7636	Our Wedding Day/Come Closer	1959	5.00	10.00	20.00
47-7697	High School Play/But I Love You	1960	3.75	7.50	15.00
47-7758	That's Good That's Bad/I Can't Take It	1960	3.75	7.50	15.00
47-7818	Two Crazy Kids/Give Me a Little Whistle (And I'll Be There)	1960	3.75	7.50	15.00

Number	Title (A Side/B Side)	Yr	VG	VG+	NM
61-7559 [S]	The Shape I'm In/Ya Ya	1959	12.50	25.00	50.00
—"Living Stereo" issue with large hole					
Albums					
RCA VICTOR					
LPM-2149 [M]	Oh, Johnny!	1959	15.00	30.00	60.00
LSP-2149 [S]	Oh, Johnny!	1959	25.00	50.00	100.00

RETURN TO FOREVER

Also see CHICK COREA.

Number	Title (A Side/B Side)	Yr	VG	VG+	NM
45s					
COLUMBIA					
10497	Musicmagic/When Love Is New	1977	—	2.00	4.00
POLYDOR					
15067	Spain/Captain Marvel	1973	—	3.00	6.00
—As "Chick Corea and Return to Forever"					
15094	Earth Juice/Beyond the Seventh Galaxy	1974	—	2.50	5.00
—As "Chick Corea and Return to Forever"					
15099	An Excerpt from the First Movement of Heavy Metal/Jungle Waterfall	1975	—	2.50	5.00
—As "Chick Corea and Return to Forever"					
Albums					
COLUMBIA					
PC 34076	Romantic Warrior	1976	2.50	5.00	10.00
—No bar code on cover					
PC 34076	Romantic Warrior	198?	2.00	4.00	8.00
—Reissue with bar code					
PC 34682	Musicmagic	1977	2.50	5.00	10.00
—No bar code on cover					
PC 34682	Musicmagic	1985	2.00	4.00	8.00
—Reissue with bar code					
PCQ 34682 [Q]	Musicmagic	1977	5.00	10.00	20.00
JC 35281	Return to Forever Live	1979	2.50	5.00	10.00
JC 36359	The Best of Return to Forever	1980	2.50	5.00	10.00
PC 36359	The Best of Return to Forever	198?	2.00	4.00	8.00
—Budget-line reissue					
ECM					
1015	Return to Forever	197?	3.75	7.50	15.00
POLYDOR					
PD-5525	Light As A Feather	1973	3.00	6.00	12.00
PD-5536	Hymn of the Seventh Galaxy	1973	3.00	6.00	12.00
PD-6509	Where Have I Known You Before	1974	3.00	6.00	12.00
PD-6512	No Mystery	1975	3.00	6.00	12.00
825336-1	Hymn of the Seventh Galaxy	198?	2.00	4.00	8.00
—Reissue					

REUNION

Number	Title (A Side/B Side)	Yr	VG	VG+	NM
45s					
A&M					
1308	City Song/No Good Alone	1971	—	2.00	4.00
BELL					
45222	Smile (Theme from Modern Times)/Turn Back the Hands of Time (Gotta Have You Back)	1972	—	2.00	4.00
45287	Living Together, Growing Together/Just Say Goodbye	1974	—	2.00	4.00
RCA VICTOR					
PB-10056	Life Is a Rock (But the Radio Rolled Me)/Are You Ready to Believe	1974	—	2.50	5.00
PB-10150	Disco-Tekin/Goodstuff	1975	—	2.00	4.00
PB-10252	They Don't Make 'Em Like That Anymore/Goodstuff	1975	—	2.00	4.00
GB-10491	Life Is a Rock (But the Radio Rolled Me)/Are You Ready to Believe	1975	—	—	3.00
—Gold Standard Series					

REV-LONS, THE

Number	Title (A Side/B Side)	Yr	VG	VG+	NM
45s					
GARPAX					
44168	Boy Trouble/Give Me One More Chance	1962	3.75	7.50	15.00
REPRISE					
0251	After Last Night/It's Gonna Happen Someday	1964	3.00	6.00	12.00
20200	I Can't Forget About You/Love Can't Be a One-Way Deal	1963	3.00	6.00	12.00

REVALONS, THE

Number	Title (A Side/B Side)	Yr	VG	VG+	NM
45s					
PET					
802	Dreams Are for Fools/This Is the Moment	1958	30.00	60.00	120.00

REVELLS, THE

Number	Title (A Side/B Side)	Yr	VG	VG+	NM
Albums					
REPRISE					
R-6160 [M]	The Go Sound of the Slots	1965	37.50	75.00	150.00
RS-6160 [S]	The Go Sound of the Slots	1965	50.00	100.00	200.00

REVELS, THE (1)

Number	Title (A Side/B Side)	Yr	VG	VG+	NM
45s					
NORGOLDE					
103	Dead Man's Stroll/Talking to My Heart	1959	30.00	60.00	120.00
103	Midnight Stroll/Talking to My Heart	1959	6.25	12.50	25.00
—Same A-side as above, but with revised title					
104	Tweedlee Dee/Foo Man Choo	1959	5.00	10.00	20.00

REVELS, THE (2)

Number	Title (A Side/B Side)	Yr	VG	VG+	NM
45s					
CT					
1	Church Key/Vesuvius	1960	25.00	50.00	100.00
DOWNEY					
123	Intoxica/Comanche	1964	6.25	12.50	25.00
IMPACT					
1	Church Key/Vesuvius	1960	6.25	12.50	25.00
—Black vinyl					
1	Church Key/Vesuvius	1960	12.50	25.00	50.00
—Red vinyl					
3	Intoxica/Tequila	1961	6.25	12.50	25.00
7	Comanche/Rampage	1961	6.25	12.50	25.00
—Black vinyl					
7	Comanche/Rampage	1961	12.50	25.00	50.00
—Yellow vinyl					
13	Party Time/Soft Top	1961	6.25	12.50	25.00
22	The Monkey Bird/Revellion	1962	6.25	12.50	25.00
—Black vinyl					
22	The Monkey Bird/Revellion	1962	12.50	25.00	50.00
—Yellow vinyl					
22	Conga Twist/Revellion	1962	6.25	12.50	25.00
—Black vinyl					
22	Conga Twist/Revellion	1962	12.50	25.00	50.00
—Yellow vinyl; Both A-sides of Impact 22 are the same song					
LYNN					
1302	Six Pak/Good Grief	1960	15.00	30.00	60.00
SWINGIN'					
620	Six Pak/Good Grief	1960	10.00	20.00	40.00
WESTCO					
3/4	Party Time/Soft Top	1963	12.50	25.00	50.00
—Red and yellow vinyl					
Albums					
IMPACT					
LPM-1 [M]	Revels on a Rampage	1964	125.00	250.00	500.00
SUNDAZED					
LP 5010	Intoxica! The Best of the Revels	199?	2.50	5.00	10.00

REVELS, THE (3)

Number	Title (A Side/B Side)	Yr	VG	VG+	NM
45s					
DIAMOND					
143	Lots of Luck/Gonna Have Some Fun	1963	3.75	7.50	15.00

REVELS, THE (4)

Number	Title (A Side/B Side)	Yr	VG	VG+	NM
45s					
JAMIE					
1318	True Love/Everybody Can Do the New Dog But Me	1966	2.50	5.00	10.00

REVELS, THE (U)

It's doubtful that any of these are group (2), and they probably aren't group (1), either. Group (3) and (4) are not out of the question, though.

Number	Title (A Side/B Side)	Yr	VG	VG+	NM
45s					
ANDIE					
5077	Please/Two Little Monkeys (In a Banana Tree)	1960	5.00	10.00	20.00
KAPP					
621	Downtown/Dollar Sign	1964	7.50	15.00	30.00
PALETTE					
5074	O How I Love You/I Met My Lost Love	1961	5.00	10.00	20.00

REVENGERS, THE

Number	Title (A Side/B Side)	Yr	VG	VG+	NM
45s					
MGM					
13465	Batman Theme/Back Side Blues	1966	3.00	6.00	12.00
Albums					
METRO					
M-565 [M]	Batman and Other Supermen	1966	7.50	15.00	30.00
MS-565 [S]	Batman and Other Supermen	1966	10.00	20.00	40.00

REVERE, PAUL, AND THE RAIDERS

Includes records as "Raiders" in the early 1970s. Also see MARK LINDSAY; JIM VALLEY; FREDDY WELLER.

Number	Title (A Side/B Side)	Yr	VG	VG+	NM
45s					
20TH CENTURY					
2283	The British Are Coming/Surrender at Appomattox	1976	—	2.50	5.00
—B-side by Susie Allanson					
COLUMBIA					
CSP-262	SS 396/Corvair Baby	1965	6.25	12.50	25.00
CSM-466	SS 396/Camaro	1967	6.25	12.50	25.00
—B-side by The Cyrcle					
CSM-466 [PS]	SS 396/Camaro	1967	12.50	25.00	50.00
—B-side by The Cyrcle					
10126	Gonna Have a Good Time/Your Love (Is the Only Love)	1975	2.50	5.00	10.00
42814	Louie Louie/Night Train	1963	10.00	20.00	40.00
43008	Louie Go Home/Have Love Will Travel	1964	3.75	7.50	15.00
43114	Over You/Swim	1964	3.75	7.50	15.00
43273	Ooh Poo Pah Doo/Sometimes	1965	3.75	7.50	15.00
43375	Steppin' Out/Blue Fox	1965	2.50	5.00	10.00
43375 [DJ]	Steppin' Out (same on both sides)	1965	12.50	25.00	50.00
—Red vinyl promo					
43461	Just Like Me/B.F.R.D.F. Blues	1965	2.50	5.00	10.00
43461 [DJ]	Just Like Me (same on both sides)	1965	12.50	25.00	50.00
—Red vinyl promo					
43556	Kicks/Shake It Up	1966	2.50	5.00	10.00
43556 [DJ]	Kicks (same on both sides)	1966	12.50	25.00	50.00
—Red vinyl promo					
43678	Hungry/There She Goes	1966	2.50	5.00	10.00
43678 [DJ]	Hungry (same on both sides)	1966	12.50	25.00	50.00
—Red vinyl promo					
43678 [PS]	Hungry/There She Goes	1966	5.00	10.00	20.00
43810	The Great Airplane Strike/In My Community	1966	2.50	5.00	10.00
43810 [DJ]	The Great Airplane Strike (same on both sides)	1966	12.50	25.00	50.00
—Red vinyl promo					
43810 [PS]	The Great Airplane Strike/In My Community	1966	3.75	7.50	15.00
43907	Good Thing/Undecided Man	1966	2.50	5.00	10.00
43907 [PS]	Good Thing/Undecided Man	1966	5.00	10.00	20.00
44018	Ups and Downs/Leslie	1967	2.50	5.00	10.00
44018 [PS]	Ups and Downs/Leslie	1967	3.75	7.50	15.00
44094	Him or Me — What's It Gonna Be?/Legend of Paul Revere	1967	2.50	5.00	10.00

Number	Title (A Side/B Side)	Yr	VG	VG+	NM
44094 [PS]	Him or Me—What's It Gonna Be?/Legend of Paul Revere	1967	3.75	7.50	15.00
44227	I Had a Dream/Upon Your Leaving	1967	2.00	4.00	8.00
44227 [PS]	I Had a Dream/Upon Your Leaving	1967	2.50	5.00	10.00
44335	Peace of Mind/Do Unto Others	1967	2.00	4.00	8.00
44335 [PS]	Peace of Mind/Do Unto Others	1967	2.50	5.00	10.00
44444	Too Much Talk/Happening '68	1968	2.00	4.00	8.00
44444 [PS]	Too Much Talk/Happening '68	1968	2.50	5.00	10.00
44553	Don't Take It Too Hard/Observation from Flight 285 (In 3/4 Time)	1968	—	3.00	6.00
44553 [PS]	Don't Take It Too Hard/Observation from Flight 285 (In 3/4 Time)	1968	2.50	5.00	10.00
44655	Cinderella Sunshine/It's Happening	1968	2.00	4.00	8.00
44744	Mr. Sun, Mr. Moon/Without You	1969	—	3.00	6.00
44744 [PS]	Mr. Sun, Mr. Moon/Without You	1969	2.50	5.00	10.00
44854	Let Me/I Don't Know	1969	—	3.00	6.00
44970	We Gotta All Get Together/Frankfort Side Street	1969	—	3.00	6.00
45082	Just Seventeen/Sorceress with Blue Eyes	1970	—	3.00	6.00
—As "Raiders"					
45150	Gone Movin' On/Interlude (To Be Forgotten)	1970	—	3.00	6.00
—As "Raiders"					
45332	Indian Reservation (The Lament of the Cherokee Reservation Indian)/Terry's Tune	1971	2.00	4.00	8.00
—As "Raiders"; red label, black print					
45332	Indian Reservation (The Lament of the Cherokee Reservation Indian)/Terry's Tune	1971	—	3.00	6.00
—As "Raiders"; orange label with "Columbia" background print					
45453	Birds of a Feather/The Turkey	1971	—	3.00	6.00
—As "Raiders"					
45535	Country Wine/It's So Hard Getting Up Today	1972	—	3.00	6.00
—As "Raiders"					
45601	Powder Blue Mercedes Queen/Golden Girls Sometimes	1972	2.00	4.00	8.00
—As "Raiders"					
45688	Song Seller/A Simple Song	1972	2.00	4.00	8.00
—As "Raiders"					
45759	Love Music/Goodbye, No. 9	1973	2.00	4.00	8.00
—As "Raiders"					
45898	All Over You/Seaboard Line Boogie	1973	2.00	4.00	8.00
—As "Raiders"					
DRIVE					
6248	Ain't Nothing Wrong/You're Really Saying Something	1976	—	2.50	5.00
GARDENA					
106	Beatnik Sticks/Orbit (The Spy)	1960	7.50	15.00	30.00
115	Paul Revere's Ride/Unfinished Fifth	1960	10.00	20.00	40.00
116	Like, Long Hair/Sharon	1961	7.50	15.00	30.00
118	Like, Charleston/Midnite Ride	1961	6.25	12.50	25.00
124	All Night Long/Groovey	1962	10.00	20.00	40.00
127	Like, Bluegrass/Leatherneck	1962	10.00	20.00	40.00
131	Shake It Up (Part 1)/Shake It Up (Part 2)	1962	10.00	20.00	40.00
137	Tall Cool One/Road Runner	1963	12.50	25.00	50.00
HITBOUND					
X-2	Jingle Bell Rock/Jingle Bells	1983	3.00	6.00	12.00
—B-side by Mike Love and Dean Torrence					
X-2 [PS]	Jingle Bell Rock/Jingle Bells	1983	5.00	10.00	20.00
—B-side by Mike Love and Dean Torrence					
JERDEN					
807	So Fine/Blues Stay Away	1966	6.25	12.50	25.00
SANDE					
101	Louie Louie/Night Train	1963	62.50	125.00	250.00
Albums					
COLUMBIA					
GP 12	Two All Time Great Selling LPs	1971	5.00	10.00	20.00
—Combines 9395 and 9521 in one package; orange labels					
GP 12 [(2)]	Two All Time Great Selling LPs	1969	6.25	12.50	25.00
—Combines 9395 and 9521 in one package; red labels					
CL 2307 [M]	Here They Come!	1965	7.50	15.00	30.00
—"Guaranteed High Fidelity" on label					
CL 2307 [M]	Here They Come!	1965	5.00	10.00	20.00
—"360 Sound Mono" on label					
CL 2451 [M]	Just Like Us!	1966	6.25	12.50	25.00
CL 2508 [M]	Midnight Ride	1966	6.25	12.50	25.00
CL 2595 [M]	The Spirit of '67	1966	6.25	12.50	25.00
KCL 2662 [M]	Greatest Hits	1967	7.50	15.00	30.00
—Add 20% if booklet is included					
CL 2721 [M]	Revolution!	1967	7.50	15.00	30.00
CL 2755 [M]	A Christmas Present...And Past	1967	15.00	30.00	60.00
CL 2805 [M]	Goin' to Memphis	1968	20.00	40.00	80.00
CS 9107 [S]	Here They Come!	1965	10.00	20.00	40.00
—"360 Sound Stereo" in black on label					
CS 9107 [S]	Here They Come!	1965	6.25	12.50	25.00
—"360 Sound Stereo" in white on label					
CS 9251 [S]	Just Like Us!	1966	7.50	15.00	30.00
CS 9308 [S]	Midnight Ride	1966	7.50	15.00	30.00
CS 9395 [S]	The Spirit of '67	1966	7.50	15.00	30.00
KCS 9462 [S]	Greatest Hits	1967	6.25	12.50	25.00
—Add 20% if booklet is included					
CS 9521 [S]	Revolution!	1967	6.25	12.50	25.00
CS 9555 [S]	A Christmas Present...And Past	1967	6.25	12.50	25.00
CS 9605 [S]	Goin' to Memphis	1968	5.00	10.00	20.00
CS 9665	Something Happening	1968	5.00	10.00	20.00
CS 9753	Hard 'N' Heavy (With Marshmallow)	1969	5.00	10.00	20.00
—Black and white cover					
CS 9753	Hard 'N' Heavy (With Marshmallow)	1969	7.50	15.00	30.00
—Color cover					
CS 9905	Alias Pink Puzz	1969	5.00	10.00	20.00
CS 9964	Collage	1970	5.00	10.00	20.00
C 30386	Greatest Hits, Volume 2	1971	5.00	10.00	20.00
C 30768	Indian Reservation	1971	3.75	7.50	15.00
KC 31106	Country Wine	1972	3.75	7.50	15.00
KG 31464 [(2)]	All-Time Greatest Hits	1972	5.00	10.00	20.00
PC 35593	Greatest Hits	1978	2.50	5.00	10.00
GARDENA					
LP-G-1000 [M]	Like, Long Hair	1961	150.00	300.00	600.00
HARMONY					
H 30089	Paul Revere and the Raiders Featuring Mark Lindsay	1970	3.00	6.00	12.00
KH 30975	Good Thing	1971	3.00	6.00	12.00
KH 31183	Movin' On	1972	3.00	6.00	12.00
JERDEN					
JRL-7004 [M]	Paul Revere and the Raiders In the Beginning	1966	15.00	30.00	60.00
JRS-7004 [R]	Paul Revere and the Raiders In the Beginning	1966	7.50	15.00	30.00
DT-90709 [R]	Paul Revere and the Raiders In the Beginning	1966	12.50	25.00	50.00
—Capitol Record Club edition					
T-90709 [M]	Paul Revere and the Raiders In the Beginning	1966	12.50	25.00	50.00
—Capitol Record Club edition					
PICKWICK					
SPC-3176	Paul Revere and the Raiders	1969	2.50	5.00	10.00
SANDE					
S-1001 [M]	Paul Revere and the Raiders	1963	300.00	600.00	1200.
—Original version with "Sande" and no mention of "Etiquette" in trail-off area					
S-1001 [M]	Paul Revere and the Raiders	1979	6.25	12.50	25.00
—Legitimate reissue with "Sande" and "Etiquette" in trail-off area					
SEARS					
SPS-493	Paul Revere and the Raiders	1969	6.25	12.50	25.00

REVERES, THE (1)

45s

Number	Title (A Side/B Side)	Yr	VG	VG+	NM
GLORY					
272	Leonore/Honeystroller	1958	5.00	10.00	20.00
—B-side by the Honeystrollers					

REVERES, THE (2)

45s

Number	Title (A Side/B Side)	Yr	VG	VG+	NM
JUBILEE					
5463	Beyond the Sea/The Show Must Go On	1963	6.25	12.50	25.00

REVERES, THE (3)

BRUCE JOHNSTON appears on this record.

45s

Number	Title (A Side/B Side)	Yr	VG	VG+	NM
VALIANT					
6041	Big "T"/Me and My Spider	1964	12.50	25.00	50.00

REVLONS, THE

More than one group.

45s

Number	Title (A Side/B Side)	Yr	VG	VG+	NM
CAPITOL					
4739	Dry Your Eyes/She'll Come to Me	1962	7.50	15.00	30.00
PARKWAY					
107	Ya Ya/It Could Happen to You	1966	3.00	6.00	12.00
RAE COX					
105	This Restless Heart/I Promise Love	1961	7.50	15.00	30.00
TIMES SQUARE					
15	Ride Awy/Betty	1963	6.25	12.50	25.00
—B-side by the Centuries					
TOY					
101	What a Love This Is/Did I Make a Mistake	1962	5.00	10.00	20.00

REYNOLDS, JODY

45s

Number	Title (A Side/B Side)	Yr	VG	VG+	NM
BRENT					
7042	Raggedy Ann/The Girl from King Marie	1963	2.50	5.00	10.00
DEMON					
1507	Endless Sleep/Tight Capris	1958	7.50	15.00	30.00
1509	Fire of Love/Daisy Mae	1958	6.25	12.50	25.00
1511	Closin' In/Elope with Me	1958	6.25	12.50	25.00
1515	Golden Idol/Beulah Lee	1959	6.25	12.50	25.00
1519	The Storm/Please Remember	1959	6.25	12.50	25.00
1523	Whipping Post/I Wanna Be with You Tonight	1960	6.25	12.50	25.00
1524	Stone Cold/(The Girl with) The Raven Hair	1960	6.25	12.50	25.00
INDIGO					
127	Tarantula/Thunder	1961	12.50	25.00	50.00
PULSAR					
2419	Endless Sleep/My Baby's Eyes	1969	—	3.00	6.00
SMASH					
1810	Don't Jmp/Stormy	1963	3.00	6.00	12.00
TITAN					
1734	Devil Girl/A Tear for Hesse	1963	3.75	7.50	15.00
1736	Requiem for Love/Stranger in the Mirror	1963	3.75	7.50	15.00
—With Bobbie Gentry					
Albums					
TRU-GEMS					
1002	Endless Sleep	1978	3.00	6.00	12.00

RHINOCEROS

45s

Number	Title (A Side/B Side)	Yr	VG	VG+	NM
ELEKTRA					
45640	You're My Girl/I Will Serenade You	1968	—	3.00	6.00
45647	Apricot Brandy/When You Say You're Sorry	1969	2.00	4.00	8.00
45659	I Need Love/Velvuekus	1969	—	3.00	6.00
45677	Back Door/In a Little Room	1970	—	3.00	6.00
45691	Let's Party/Old Age	1970	—	3.00	6.00
45694	Better Times/It's a Groovy World	1970	—	3.00	6.00
Albums					
ELEKTRA					
EKS-74030	Rhinoceros	1968	6.25	12.50	25.00
EKS-74056	Satin Chickens	1969	5.00	10.00	20.00
EKS-74075	Better Times Are Coming	1970	5.00	10.00	20.00

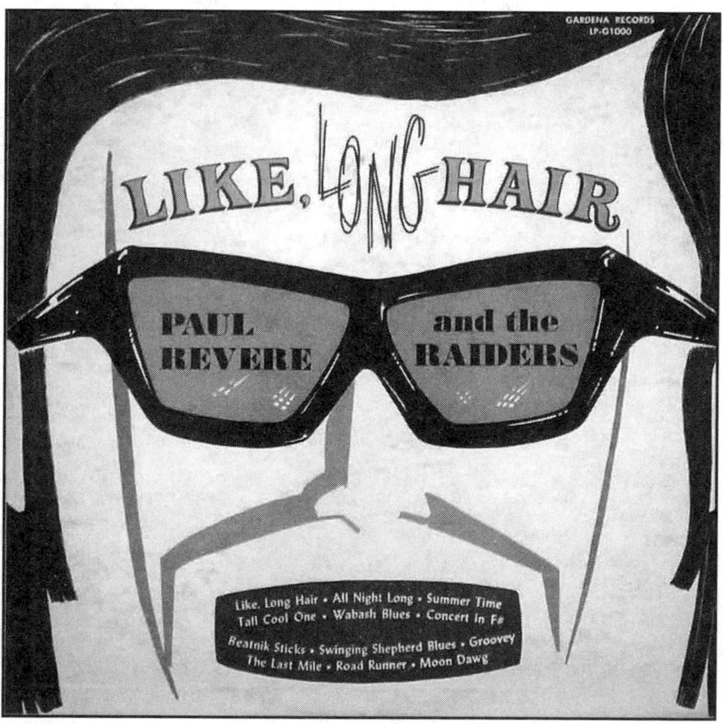

(Top left) "Keep Yourself Alive" was Queen's first single, in 1973. It is quite scarce as a stock copy. The original 45 featured the full-length version of the song; a 1975 issue of the same song, with a different number and flip side, featured an edited version. (Top right) A rare extended-play single is this issue by the Ravens on the Rendition label, a reissue of tracks that had appeared on National. (Bottom left) When the group Renaissance first recorded in 1970, it featured ex-Yardbirds lead singer Keith Relf and his wife Jane. By the time another album by the group came out in the U.S., the band's personnel was 100 percent different. (Bottom right) The first album by Paul Revere and the Raiders, before they became hugely successful on Columbia, was the Gardena release *Like, Long Hair*, based around the hit single of the same name.

RHODES, EMITT
Also see THE MERRY-GO-ROUND.

Number	Title (A Side/B Side)	Yr	VG	VG+	NM
45s					
ABC DUNHILL					
4267	Fresh as a Daisy/You Take the Dark Out of the Night	1970	—	3.00	6.00
4274	Live Till You Die/Promises I've Made	1971	—	2.50	5.00
4280	A Lullaby/With My Face on the Floor	1971	—	2.50	5.00
4295	Really Wanted You/Love Will Stone You	1971	—	2.50	5.00
4303	Take You Far Away/Golden Child of God	1972	—	2.50	5.00
4315	Tame the Lion/Golden Child of God	1972	—	2.50	5.00
A&M					
1254	Till the Day After/You're a Very Lovely Woman	1971	—	3.00	6.00
—As "Emitt Rhodes with the Merry-Go-Round"					
Albums					
ABC DUNHILL					
DS-50089	Emitt Rhodes	1970	3.00	6.00	12.00
DS-50111	Mirror	1971	3.00	6.00	12.00
DS-50122	Farewell to Paradise	1972	3.00	6.00	12.00
A&M					
SP-4254	The American Dream	1970	6.25	12.50	25.00
—Original album contains "You're a Very Lovely Woman" and has Rhodes in front of a paint-covered backdrop on cover					
SP-4254	The American Dream	1971	3.75	7.50	15.00
—Reissue contains "Saturday Night" and a framed photo of Rhodes on cover					

RHODES, SLIM

Number	Title (A Side/B Side)	Yr	VG	VG+	NM
45s					
RHODES					
101	Brothers Frank and Jesse James/(B-side unknown)	195?	12.50	25.00	50.00
SUN					
216	Don't Believe/Uncertain Blues	1955	25.00	50.00	100.00
225	Are You Ashamed of Me/The House of Sin	1955	75.00	150.00	300.00
238	Bad Girl/Gonna Romp and Stomp	1956	25.00	50.00	100.00
256	Do What I Do/Take and Give	1956	12.50	25.00	50.00

RHODES, TODD

Number	Title (A Side/B Side)	Yr	VG	VG+	NM
45s					
KING					
4469	Gin, Gin, Gin/I Shouldn't Cry But I Do	1951	25.00	50.00	100.00
4486	Good Man/Evening Breeze	1951	15.00	30.00	60.00
4509	Your Daddy's Doggin' Around/Red Boy Is Back	1952	15.00	30.00	60.00
4528	Rocket 69/Possessed	1952	12.50	25.00	50.00
4556	Snuff Dipper/Trying	1952	12.50	25.00	50.00
—B-side by La Vern Baker					
4566	Pig Latin Blues/Blue Autumn	1952	12.50	25.00	50.00
4583	Hog Maw and Cabbage Slaw/Must I Cry Again	1952	12.50	25.00	50.00
—B-side by La Vern Baker					
4601	Thunderbolt Boogie/Lost Child	1953	12.50	25.00	50.00
—B-side by La Vern Baker					
4648	Your Mouth Got a Hole In It/Feathers	1953	10.00	20.00	40.00
4666	Let Down Blues/Beet Patch	1953	10.00	20.00	40.00
4736	Silver Sunset/Specks	1954	7.50	15.00	30.00
4755	Chicken Strut/Echoes	1954	7.50	15.00	30.00
Albums					
KING					
295-88 [10]	Todd Rhodes Playing His Greatest Hits	1954	375.00	750.00	1500.
658 [M]	Dance Music	1960	200.00	400.00	800.00

RHYTHM, JOHNNY

Number	Title (A Side/B Side)	Yr	VG	VG+	NM
45s					
MGM					
13043	This Is It/Wouldn't It Be Nice	1961	10.00	20.00	40.00

RHYTHM ACES, THE (1)

Number	Title (A Side/B Side)	Yr	VG	VG+	NM
45s					
ACE					
518	Rock and Roll March/Look What You've Done	1956	10.00	20.00	40.00
—B-side by Bob Douglas					
VEE JAY					
124	I Wonder Why/Get Lost	1954	500.00	1000.	2000.
—Red vinyl					
124	I Wonder Why/Get Lost	1954	50.00	100.00	200.00
—Black vinyl					
138	Whisper to Me/Olly, Olly, Oxsen Free	1955	500.00	1000.	2000.
—Red vinyl					
138	Whisper to Me/Olly, Olly, Oxsen Free	1955	50.00	100.00	200.00
—Black vinyl					
160	That's My Sugar/Flippety Flop	1955	30.00	60.00	120.00

RHYTHM ACES, THE (2)

Number	Title (A Side/B Side)	Yr	VG	VG+	NM
45s					
MARK-X					
8004	Boppin' Sloppin' Baby/Crazy Jealousy	1960	7.50	15.00	30.00

RHYTHM ACES, THE (3)

Number	Title (A Side/B Side)	Yr	VG	VG+	NM
45s					
ROULETTE					
4268	Mohawk Rock/It'll Do	1960	3.75	7.50	15.00
4426	Raunchy Twist/Mockin' Bird Twist	1962	3.75	7.50	15.00
SIOUX					
82260	Allan's Rock/Go Get It	1960	7.50	15.00	30.00
102261	Yahma/What'd I Say Twist	1961	7.50	15.00	30.00
UNIVERSAL ARTISTS					
3160	Mohawk Rock/It'll Do	1960	10.00	20.00	40.00

RHYTHM CADETS, THE

Number	Title (A Side/B Side)	Yr	VG	VG+	NM
45s					
VESTA					
501/2	Dearest Doryce/Rocking Jimmy	1957	200.00	400.00	800.00

RHYTHM HERITAGE

Number	Title (A Side/B Side)	Yr	VG	VG+	NM
45s					
ABC					
12063	Theme from "Young Frankenstein"/I Wouldn't Treat a Dog (The Way You Treated Me)	1975	—	2.50	5.00
12135	Theme from S.W.A.T./I Wouldn't Treat a Dog (The Way You Treated Me)	1975	—	2.50	5.00
—Version 1: With short version of A-side					
12135	Theme from S.W.A.T./I Wouldn't Treat a Dog (The Way You Treated Me)	1975	—	2.00	4.00
—Version 2: With long version of A-side; "RE-1" on label next to matrix number					
12177	Baretta's Theme (Keep Your Eye on the Sparrow)/My Cherie Amour	1976	—	2.00	4.00
12205	Disco-Fied/(It's Time to) Boogie Down	1976	—	2.00	4.00
12243	Gonna Fly Now (Theme from "Rocky")/Last Night on Earth	1976	—	2.00	4.00
12273	Theme from "Starsky and Hutch"/Disco Queen	1977	—	2.00	4.00
12334 [DJ]	Holdin' Out for You Love (mono/stereo)	1978	—	2.00	4.00
—May be promo only					
12378	Language of Love/Sail Away with Me	1978	—	2.00	4.00
Albums					
ABC					
D-934	Disco-Fied	1976	2.50	5.00	10.00
D-987	Last Night on Earth	1977	2.50	5.00	10.00
AA-1037	The Sky's the Limit	1978	2.50	5.00	10.00

RHYTHM MASTERS, THE (1)

Number	Title (A Side/B Side)	Yr	VG	VG+	NM
45s					
ACE					
610	The Devil and His Old Suitcase/Holding My Savior's Hand	1961	5.00	10.00	20.00
Albums					
ACE					
LP-1010 [M]	Hymns and Spirituals	1961	25.00	50.00	100.00

RHYTHM MASTERS, THE (2)

Number	Title (A Side/B Side)	Yr	VG	VG+	NM
45s					
FLIP					
314	Baby We Two/Patricia	1956	75.00	150.00	300.00

RHYTHM ROCKERS (1)

Number	Title (A Side/B Side)	Yr	VG	VG+	NM
45s					
CHALLENGE					
9196	Rendezvous Stomp/The Slide	1963	6.25	12.50	25.00
Albums					
CHALLENGE					
CHL-617 [M]	Soul Surfin'	1963	22.50	45.00	90.00

RHYTHM ROCKERS (2)

Number	Title (A Side/B Side)	Yr	VG	VG+	NM
45s					
SATIN					
921	Oh Boy/We Belong Together	1960	15.00	30.00	60.00
921 [PS]	Oh Boy/We Belong Together	1960	25.00	50.00	100.00

RHYTHM ROCKERS (3)

Number	Title (A Side/B Side)	Yr	VG	VG+	NM
45s					
SUN					
248	Fiddle Bop/Juke Box, Help Me Find My Baby	1956	25.00	50.00	100.00

RHYTHM ROCKERS (U)
These could be by group (1) or (2).

Number	Title (A Side/B Side)	Yr	VG	VG+	NM
45s					
FENTON					
944	Surf Around/Three Strikes	1962	12.50	25.00	50.00
WIPE OUT					
1001	Foot Cruising/Get It On	1962	10.00	20.00	40.00

RHYTHMETTES, THE

Number	Title (A Side/B Side)	Yr	VG	VG+	NM
45s					
BRUNSWICK					
55012	Mind Reader/Mister Love	1957	3.75	7.50	15.00
55050	That's a-Plenty/Till My Baby Comes Home	1958	3.00	6.00	12.00
55083	Elaine/Bow Legged Woman	1958	3.00	6.00	12.00
55097	I'll Be With You in Apple Blossom Time/Page from the Future	1958	3.00	6.00	12.00
CORAL					
62186	High School Lovers/Snow Queen	1960	2.50	5.00	10.00
RCA VICTOR					
47-6089	Only You/Him	1955	5.00	10.00	20.00
47-6244	Show Me the Way/The Bridge of Love	1955	3.75	7.50	15.00
47-6349	Take My Hand, Show Me the Way/I've Got to Know	1955	3.75	7.50	15.00
47-6539	Homin' Pigeon/Boom-Boom	1956	3.75	7.50	15.00
47-6742	Winter Snow/Take a Look in the Mirror	1956	3.75	7.50	15.00

RIA AND THE REASONS

Number	Title (A Side/B Side)	Yr	VG	VG+	NM
45s					
AMY					
888	Memories Linger On/Sorry I Lied	1963	6.25	12.50	25.00
888	Memories Linger On/Sorry I Lied	1963	20.00	40.00	80.00
—Blue vinyl					
RSVP					
1110	He's Not There/She Fell in Love	1965	5.00	10.00	20.00
—As "Ria and the Revellons"					

RIALTOS, THE

Number	Title (A Side/B Side)	Yr	VG	VG+	NM
45s					
CB					
5009	Let Me In/It Hurts	1962	75.00	150.00	300.00

RIBBONS, THE

45s

Number	Title (A Side/B Side)	Yr	VG	VG+	NM
MARSH					
202	Ain't Gonna Kiss Ya/My Baby Said	1963	3.75	7.50	15.00
203	After Last Night/This Is Our Melody	1963	3.00	6.00	12.00
PARKWAY					
912	Meoldie D'Amour/They Played a Sad Song	1964	3.00	6.00	12.00

RIC-A-SHAYS, THE

Harry NILSSON was in this group.

45s

Number	Title (A Side/B Side)	Yr	VG	VG+	NM
LOLA					
002	Groovy/Turn On	1964	6.25	12.50	25.00

RICARDOS, THE

45s

Number	Title (A Side/B Side)	Yr	VG	VG+	NM
STAR-X					
512	Mary's Little Lamb/I Mean Really	1958	40.00	80.00	160.00

RICE, JIMMY

45s

Number	Title (A Side/B Side)	Yr	VG	VG+	NM
RED BIRD					
10-022	The Grass Is Always Greener/Spanish Perfume	1965	5.00	10.00	20.00
10-027	Nobody But You/Or Not at All	1965	5.00	10.00	20.00

RICE, TONY

45s

Number	Title (A Side/B Side)	Yr	VG	VG+	NM
ACTION					
100	My Darling Y-O-U/I Thank You Baby	1961	7.50	15.00	30.00
PRINCETON					
101	Summer's Love/Please Don't	1960	15.00	30.00	60.00
RAE COX					
106	Little School Girl/Blue Bird of Happiness	1961	5.00	10.00	20.00

RICH, BUDDY

45s

Number	Title (A Side/B Side)	Yr	VG	VG+	NM
ARGO					
5384	Makin' Whoopee/Lulu's Back in Town	1961	2.00	4.00	8.00
CLEF					
89066	Sleepyhead/Bugle Call Rag	1953	3.00	6.00	12.00
89094	Let's Fall in Love/Me and My Jaguar	1954	3.00	6.00	12.00
GROOVE MERCHANT					
1031	The Bull/Nik Nik	197?	—	2.00	4.00
MCA					
51116	Fantasy/Listen Here Goes Funky	1981	—	2.00	4.00
PACIFIC JAZZ					
88136	Uptight/Sister Sadie	1966	—	2.50	5.00
88139	Norwegian Wood/Monitor Theme	1967	—	2.50	5.00
88140	The Beat Goes On/Mexicali Rose	1967	—	2.50	5.00
88145	Mercy, Mercy, Mercy/Big Mama Cass	1968	—	3.00	6.00
RCA VICTOR					
PB-10712	Speak No Evil/Sophisticated Lady (She's a Different Lady)	1976	—	2.00	4.00

Albums

Number	Title (A Side/B Side)	Yr	VG	VG+	NM
ARCHIVE OF FOLK AND JAZZ					
260	Buddy Rich	197?	3.75	7.50	15.00
ARGO					
LP-676 [M]	Playtime	1961	7.50	15.00	30.00
LPS-676 [S]	Playtime	1961	10.00	20.00	40.00
EMARCY					
EMS-2-402 [(2)]	Both Sides	1976	3.75	7.50	15.00
66006	Driver	1967	5.00	10.00	20.00
GREAT AMERICAN					
1030	Class of '78	1978	5.00	10.00	20.00
—Direct-to-disc version of Gryphon 781					
GROOVE MERCHANT					
528	The Roar of '74	1974	3.00	6.00	12.00
3301	Very Live at Buddy's Place	1974	3.00	6.00	12.00
3303	The Last Blues Album, Vol. 1	1975	3.00	6.00	12.00
3307	The Big Band Machine	1976	3.00	6.00	12.00
4407 [(2)]	Tuff Dude!	197?	3.75	7.50	15.00
GRYPHON					
781	Class of '78	1978	3.00	6.00	12.00
LIBERTY					
11006	Keep the Customer Satisfied	1970	3.75	7.50	15.00
MCA					
5186	The Buddy Rich Band	1981	2.50	5.00	10.00
MERCURY					
MG-20451 [M]	Richcraft	1959	15.00	30.00	60.00
MG-20461 [M]	The Voice Is Rich	1959	12.50	25.00	50.00
SR-60136 [S]	Richcraft	1959	17.50	35.00	70.00
SR-60144 [S]	The Voice Is Rich	1959	15.00	30.00	60.00
NORGRAN					
MGN-26 [10]	Buddy Rich Swingin'	1954	30.00	60.00	120.00
MGN-1031 [M]	Sing and Swing with Buddy Rich	1955	20.00	40.00	80.00
MGN-1052 [M]	The Swingin' Buddy Rich	1955	15.00	30.00	60.00
—Reissue of 26					
MGN-1078 [M]	The Wailing Buddy Rich	1956	15.00	30.00	60.00
MGN-1088 [M]	This One's for Basie	1956	15.00	30.00	60.00
PACIFIC JAZZ					
LN-10089	Swingin' New Big Band	1981	2.00	4.00	8.00
—Budget-line reissue					
LN-10090	Big Swing Face	1981	2.00	4.00	8.00
—Budget-line reissue					
PJ-10113 [M]	Swingin' New Big Band	1966	6.25	12.50	25.00
PJ-10117 [M]	Big Swing Face	1967	6.25	12.50	25.00
ST-20113 [S]	Swingin' New Big Band	1966	5.00	10.00	20.00
ST-20117 [S]	Big Swing Face	1967	5.00	10.00	20.00
ST-20126	A New One	1968	5.00	10.00	20.00
PAUSA					
9004	Buddy & Soul	1983	2.50	5.00	10.00
QUINTESSENCE					
25051	Mr. Drums	1978	3.00	6.00	12.00
RCA VICTOR					
ANL1-1090	A Different Drummer	1975	2.50	5.00	10.00
—Reissue of 4593					
APL1-1503	Speak No Evil	1976	3.00	6.00	12.00
CPL2-2273 [(2)]	Buddy Rich Plays & Plays & Plays	1977	3.75	7.50	15.00
LSP-4593	A Different Drummer	1971	3.00	6.00	12.00
AFL1-4666	Rich in London	1977	2.50	5.00	10.00
—Reissue with new prefix					
LSP-4666	Rich in London	1972	3.00	6.00	12.00
AFL1-4802	Stick It	1977	2.50	5.00	10.00
—Reissue with new prefix					
LSP-4802	Stick It	1972	3.00	6.00	12.00
UNITED ARTISTS					
UXS-86 [(2)]	Buddy Rich Superpak	1972	3.75	7.50	15.00
VERVE					
VSP-40 [M]	Buddy Rich at J.A.T.P.	1966	3.75	7.50	15.00
VSPS-40 [R]	Buddy Rich at J.A.T.P.	1966	3.00	6.00	12.00
MGV-2009 [M]	Buddy Rich Sings Johnny Mercer	1956	15.00	30.00	60.00
V-2009 [M]	Buddy Rich Sings Johnny Mercer	1961	5.00	10.00	20.00
MGV-2075 [M]	Buddy Rich Just Sings	1957	15.00	30.00	60.00
V-2075 [M]	Buddy Rich Just Sings	1961	5.00	10.00	20.00
MGV-8142 [M]	The Swingin' Buddy Rich	1957	12.50	25.00	50.00
—Reissue of Norgran 1052					
V-8142 [M]	The Swingin' Buddy Rich	1961	5.00	10.00	20.00
MGV-8168 [M]	The Wailing Buddy Rich	1957	12.50	25.00	50.00
—Reissue of Norgran 1078					
V-8168 [M]	The Wailing Buddy Rich	1961	5.00	10.00	20.00
MGV-8176 [M]	This One's for Basie	1957	12.50	25.00	50.00
—Reissue of Norgran 1086					
V-8176 [M]	This One's for Basie	1961	5.00	10.00	20.00
MGV-8285 [M]	Buddy Rich in Miami	1958	15.00	30.00	60.00
V-8285 [M]	Buddy Rich in Miami	1961	5.00	10.00	20.00
V-8425 [M]	Blues Caravan	1962	6.25	12.50	25.00
V6-8425 [S]	Blues Caravan	1962	7.50	15.00	30.00
V-8471 [M]	Burnin' Beat	1962	6.25	12.50	25.00
V6-8471 [S]	Burnin' Beat	1962	7.50	15.00	30.00
V-8484 [M]	Drum Battle: Gene Krupa vs. Buddy Rich	1962	6.25	12.50	25.00
V6-8484 [S]	Drum Battle: Gene Krupa vs. Buddy Rich	1962	7.50	15.00	30.00
V-8712 [M]	Big Band Shout	1967	5.00	10.00	20.00
V6-8712 [S]	Big Band Shout	1967	3.75	7.50	15.00
V6-8778	Super Rich	1969	3.75	7.50	15.00
V6-8824 [(2)]	Monster	1973	3.75	7.50	15.00
WHO'S WHO IN JAZZ					
21006	Lionel Hampton Presents Buddy Rich	1978	3.00	6.00	12.00
WORLD PACIFIC					
WPS-20113	The Buddy Rich Big Band	1968	3.75	7.50	15.00
WPS-20133	Mercy, Mercy	1968	3.75	7.50	15.00
WPS-20158	Buddy & Soul	1969	3.75	7.50	15.00
WPS-20169	The Best of Buddy Rich	1970	3.75	7.50	15.00

RICH, BUDDY, AND SWEETS EDISON

Albums

Number	Title (A Side/B Side)	Yr	VG	VG+	NM
NORGRAN					
MGN-1038 [M]	Buddy Rich and Sweets Edison	1955	20.00	40.00	80.00
VERVE					
MGV-8129 [M]	Buddy and Sweets	1957	12.50	25.00	50.00
—Reissue of Norgran 1038					
V-8129 [M]	Buddy and Sweets	1961	5.00	10.00	20.00

RICH, BUDDY, AND MAX ROACH

Albums

Number	Title (A Side/B Side)	Yr	VG	VG+	NM
MERCURY					
MG-20448 [M]	Rich Versus Roach	1959	15.00	30.00	60.00
SR-60133 [S]	Rich Versus Roach	1959	17.50	35.00	70.00

RICH, CHARLIE

45s

Number	Title (A Side/B Side)	Yr	VG	VG+	NM
ELEKTRA					
45553	I'll Wake You Up When I Get Home/Salty Dog Blues	1978	—	2.00	4.00
47047	A Man Just Doesn't Know What a Woman Goes Through/Marie	1980	—	2.00	4.00
47104	Are We Dreamin' the Same Dream/Angelina	1981	—	2.00	4.00
EPIC					
02058	You Made It Beautiful/How Good It Used to Be	1981	—	2.00	4.00
03165	Try a Little Tenderness/As Time Goes By	1982	—	2.00	4.00
10287	Set Me Free/I'll Just Go Away	1968	—	3.00	6.00
10358	Raggedy Ann/Nothing in the World	1968	—	3.00	6.00
10492	Life's Little Ups and Downs/It Takes Time	1969	—	3.00	6.00
10585	July 12, 1939/I'm Flying to Nashville Tonight	1970	—	3.00	6.00
10662	Nice 'N' Easy/I Can't Even Drink It Away	1970	—	3.00	6.00
10745	A Woman Left Lonely/Have a Heart	1971	—	2.50	5.00
10809	A Part of Your Life/A Sunday Kind of Woman	1971	—	2.50	5.00
10867	I Take It On Home/Peace on You	1972	—	2.50	5.00
10950	Behind Closed Doors/A Sunday Kind of Woman	1973	—	2.50	5.00
—Originals have yellow labels					
10950	Behind Closed Doors/A Sunday Kind of Woman	1973	—	2.00	4.00
—Repressings have orange labels					
11040	The Most Beautiful Girl/I Feel Like Going Home	1973	—	2.00	4.00
11091	A Very Special Love Song/I Can't Even Drink It Away	1974	—	2.00	4.00
20006	I Love My Friend/Why Oh Why	1974	—	2.00	4.00
50064	My Elusive Dreams/Whatever Happened	1975	—	2.00	4.00
50103	Every Time You Touch Me (I Get High)/Pass On By	1975	—	2.00	4.00
50142	All Over Me/You & I	1975	—	2.00	4.00
50182	Since I Fell for You/She	1975	—	2.00	4.00
50222	America the Beautiful (1976)/Down By the Riverside	1976	—	2.00	4.00

Number	Title (A Side/B Side)	Yr	VG	VG+	NM
50268	Road Song/The Grass Is Always Greener	1976	—	2.00	4.00
50328	Easy Look/My Lady	1976	—	2.00	4.00
50392	Rollin' with the Flow/To Sing a Love Song	1977	—	2.00	4.00
50562	Beautiful Woman/Everybody Wrote That Song for Me	1978	—	2.00	4.00
50616	On My Knees/Mellow Melody	1978	—	2.00	4.00
50701	Spanish Eyes/I Do My Swingin' at Home	1979	—	2.00	4.00
50869	Even a Fool Would Let Go/Pretty People	1980	—	2.00	4.00
GROOVE					
58-0020	The Grass Is Always Greener/She Loved Everybody But Me	1963	3.75	7.50	15.00
58-0020 [PS]	The Grass Is Always Greener/She Loved Everybody But Me	1963	7.50	15.00	30.00
58-0025	Big Boss Man/Let Me Go My Merry Way	1963	3.75	7.50	15.00
58-0032	Lady Love/Why, Oh Why	1964	3.75	7.50	15.00
58-0035	The Ways of a Woman in Love/My Mountain Dew	1964	3.75	7.50	15.00
58-0041	Nice 'N' Easy/Turn Around and Face Me	1964	3.75	7.50	15.00
HI					
2116	Love Is After Me/Pass On By	1966	2.50	5.00	10.00
2123	My Heart Would Know/Nobody's Lonesome for Me	1967	2.50	5.00	10.00
2134	Hurry Up Freight Train/Only Me	1967	2.50	5.00	10.00
MERCURY					
73466	I Washed My Hands in Muddy Water/No Home	1974	—	2.50	5.00
73498	A Field of Yellow Daisies/Party Girl	1974	—	2.50	5.00
73646	Something Just Came Over Me/Best Years	1974	—	2.50	5.00
PHILLIPS INT'L.					
3532	Whirlwind/Philadelphia Baby	1959	6.25	12.50	25.00
3542	Rebound/Big Man	1959	6.25	12.50	25.00
3552	Lonely Weekends/Everything I Do Is Wrong	1960	6.25	12.50	25.00
3560	School Days/Gonna Be Waiting	1960	6.25	12.50	25.00
3562	On My Knees/Stay	1960	6.25	12.50	25.00
3566	Who Will the Next Fool Be/Caught in the Middle	1961	6.25	12.50	25.00
3572	Just a Little Sweet/It's Too Late	1962	5.00	10.00	20.00
3576	Easy Money/Midnight Blues	1962	5.00	10.00	20.00
3582	Sittin' and Thinkin'/Finally Found Out	1962	5.00	10.00	20.00
3584	There's Another Place I Can't Go/I Need Your Love	1963	5.00	10.00	20.00
RCA					
PB-10859	My Mountain Dew/Nice 'N Easy	1976	—	2.00	4.00
PB-10966	Nice 'N Easy/It's All Over Now	1977	—	2.00	4.00
RCA VICTOR					
APBO-0195	There Won't Be Anymore/It's All Over Now	1973	—	2.50	5.00
APBO-0260	I Don't See Me in Your Eyes Anymore/No Room to Dance	1974	—	2.00	4.00
PB-10062	She Called Me Baby/$10 and a Clean White Shirt	1974	—	2.00	4.00
GB-10159	There Won't Be Anymore/Tomorrow Night	1975	—	—	3.00
—Gold Standard Series					
PB-10256	It's All Over Now/Big Jack	1975	—	2.00	4.00
PB-10458	Not Everybody Knows/I've Got You Under My Skin	1975	—	2.00	4.00
GB-10512	She Called Me Baby/$10 And a Clean White Shirt	1975	—	—	3.00
—Gold Standard Series					
47-8468	It's All Over Now/Too Many Teardrops	1964	3.75	7.50	15.00
47-8536	There Won't Be Anymore/Gentleman Jim	1965	5.00	10.00	20.00
47-8817	Nice 'N' Easy/Ol' Man River	1966	3.00	6.00	12.00
74-0983	Tomorrow Night/The Ways of a Woman in Love	1973	—	2.00	4.00
SMASH					
1993	Mohair Sam/I Washed My Hands in Muddy Water	1965	5.00	10.00	20.00
2012	Dance of Love/I Can't Go On	1965	3.75	7.50	15.00
2022	Hawg Jaw/Something Just Came Over Me	1966	3.75	7.50	15.00
2038	No Home/Tears a-Go-Go	1966	3.75	7.50	15.00
2060	That's the Way/When My Baby Comes Home	1966	3.75	7.50	15.00
SUN					
1110	Who Will the Next Fool Be/Stay	1970	—	2.50	5.00
1151	The Breakup/Be-Bop-a-Lula	1980	—	2.00	4.00
—B-side by Jerry Lee Lewis; both sides are duets with Orion					
UNITED ARTISTS					
XW1193	Puttin' In Overtime at Home/Ghost of Another Man	1978	—	2.00	4.00
XW1223	I Still Believe in Love/Wishful Thinking	1978	—	2.00	4.00
XW1269	The Fool Strikes Again/I Loved You All the Way	1978	—	2.00	4.00
XW1280	I Lost My Head/She Knows Just How to Touch Me	1979	—	2.00	4.00
XW1307	Life Goes On/Standing Tall	1979	—	2.00	4.00
1325	You're Gonna Love Yourself in the Morning/Top of the Stairs	1979	—	2.00	4.00
1340	I'd Build a Bridge/All You Ever Have to Do Is Touch Me	1980	—	2.00	4.00

Albums

Number	Title (A Side/B Side)	Yr	VG	VG+	NM
BUCKBOARD					
1019	The Entertainer	197?	2.50	5.00	10.00
ELEKTRA					
6E-301	Once a Drifter	1981	2.50	5.00	10.00
EPIC					
AS 50 [DJ]	Charlie Rich	1973	7.50	15.00	30.00
—Promo-only compilation					
AS 139 [DJ]	Everything You Always Wanted to Hear by Charlie Rich But Were Afraid to Ask For	1976	6.25	12.50	25.00
—Promo-only sampler					
BN 26376	Set Me Free	1968	5.00	10.00	20.00
BN 26516	The Fabulous Charlie Rich	1970	5.00	10.00	20.00
E 30214	Boss Man	1970	5.00	10.00	20.00
CQ 31933 [Q]	The Best of Charlie Rich	1972	5.00	10.00	20.00
KE 31933	The Best of Charlie Rich	1972	3.75	7.50	15.00
—Yellow label					
KE 31933	The Best of Charlie Rich	1973	3.00	6.00	12.00
—Orange label					
CQ 32247 [Q]	Behind Closed Doors	1973	5.00	10.00	20.00
KE 32247	Behind Closed Doors	1973	3.00	6.00	12.00
PE 32247	Behind Closed Doors	197?	2.00	4.00	8.00
—Reissue					
PE 32531	Very Special Love Songs	1974	3.00	6.00	12.00
PEQ 32531 [Q]	Very Special Love Songs	1974	5.00	10.00	20.00
PE 33250	The Silver Fox	1974	3.00	6.00	12.00
PEQ 33250 [Q]	The Silver Fox	1974	5.00	10.00	20.00
PE 33455	Every Time You Touch Me (I Get High)	1975	3.00	6.00	12.00
PEQ 33455 [Q]	Every Time You Touch Me (I Get High)	1975	5.00	10.00	20.00
PE 33545	Silver Linings	1976	2.50	5.00	10.00
PE 34240	Greatest Hits	1976	2.50	5.00	10.00
—Without bar code on cover					
PE 34240	Greatest Hits	1979	2.00	4.00	8.00
—With bar code on cover					
PE 34444	Take Me	1977	2.50	5.00	10.00
PE 34444	Take Me	1977	2.50	5.00	10.00
PE 34891	Rollin' with the Flow	1977	2.50	5.00	10.00
JE 35394	Classic Rich, Vol. 1	1978	2.50	5.00	10.00
JE 35624	Classic Rich, Vol. 2	1978	2.50	5.00	10.00
GROOVE					
GM-1000 [M]	Charlie Rich	1964	37.50	75.00	150.00
GS-1000 [S]	Charlie Rich	1964	75.00	150.00	300.00
HARMONY					
KH 32166	I Do My Swingin' at Home	1973	3.00	6.00	12.00
HI					
8006	I'm So Lonesome I Could Cry	197?	3.00	6.00	12.00
8006	I'm So Lonesome I Could Cry	198?	2.00	4.00	8.00
—Reissue of Hi 32084					
HL 12037 [M]	Charlie Rich Sings Country and Western	1967	7.50	15.00	30.00
SHL 32037 [S]	Charlie Rich Sings Country and Western	1967	5.00	10.00	20.00
SHL 32084	Charlie Rich Sings the Songs of Hank Williams & Others	1974	3.00	6.00	12.00
—Reissue of 32037					
HILLTOP					
6139	Lonely Weekends	197?	2.50	5.00	10.00
6149	Songs for Beautiful Girls	1974	2.50	5.00	10.00
6160	Entertainer of the Year	197?	2.50	5.00	10.00
MERCURY					
SRM-2-7505 [(2)]	Fully Realized	1974	3.75	7.50	15.00
PHILLIPS INTERNATIONAL					
PLP-1970 [M]	Lonely Weekends	1960	150.00	300.00	600.00
PICKWICK					
ACL-7001	Too Many Teardrops	1975	2.50	5.00	10.00
POWER PAK					
PO-241	There Won't Be Anymore	197?	2.50	5.00	10.00
PO-245	Arkansas Traveler	197?	2.50	5.00	10.00
PO-252	The Silver Fox	197?	2.50	5.00	10.00
QUICKSILVER					
QS-1005	Midnight Blue	198?	3.00	6.00	12.00
RCA CAMDEN					
CAS-2417	The Versatile and Talented Charlie Rich	1970	2.50	5.00	10.00
RCA VICTOR					
APL1-0258	Tomorrow Night	1973	3.00	6.00	12.00
APL1-0433	There Won't Be Anymore	1974	3.00	6.00	12.00
APL1-0686	She Called Me Baby	1974	3.00	6.00	12.00
APL1-0857	Greatest Hits	1975	3.00	6.00	12.00
APL1-1242	Now Everybody Knows	1975	3.00	6.00	12.00
ANL1-1542	Tomorrow Night	1976	2.50	5.00	10.00
—Reissue					
APL1-2260	Big Boss Man/My Mountain Dew	1977	3.00	6.00	12.00
ANL1-2424	She Called Me Baby	1977	2.50	5.00	10.00
—Reissue of APL1-0686					
LPM-3352 [M]	That's Rich	1965	10.00	20.00	40.00
LSP-3352 [S]	That's Rich	1965	12.50	25.00	50.00
LPM-3537 [M]	Big Boss Man	1966	10.00	20.00	40.00
LSP-3557 [S]	Big Boss Man	1966	12.50	25.00	50.00
AHL1-5496	Collector's Series	1985	2.00	4.00	8.00
SMASH					
MGS-27070 [M]	The Many New Sides of Charlie Rich	1965	7.50	15.00	30.00
MGS-27078 [M]	The Best Years	1966	7.50	15.00	30.00
SRS-67070 [S]	The Many New Sides of Charlie Rich	1965	10.00	20.00	40.00
SRS-67070 [S]	The Best Years	1966	10.00	20.00	40.00
SUN					
LP 110	Lonely Weekend	1970	3.00	6.00	12.00
LP 123	A Time for Tears	1971	3.00	6.00	12.00
LP 132	The Early Years	1974	3.00	6.00	12.00
LP 133	The Memphis Sound of Charlie Rich	1974	3.00	6.00	12.00
LP 134	Golden Treasures	1974	3.00	6.00	12.00
LP 135	Sun's Best of Charlie Rich	1974	3.00	6.00	12.00
1003	20 Golden Hits	1979	2.50	5.00	10.00
—Gold vinyl					
1007	The Original Charlie Rich	1979	2.50	5.00	10.00
SUNNYVALE					
9330	The Sun Story Vol. 2	1977	2.50	5.00	10.00
TIME-LIFE					
STW 115	Country Music	1981	3.00	6.00	12.00
TRIP					
TLP-8502 [(2)]	The Best of Charlie Rich	1974	3.00	6.00	12.00
UNITED ARTISTS					
UA-LA876-H	I Still Believe in Love	1978	3.00	6.00	12.00
UA-H	The Fool Strikes Again	1978	2.50	5.00	10.00
WING					
SRW-16375	A Lonely Weekend	1969	3.00	6.00	12.00

RICH, DAVE

45s

Number	Title (A Side/B Side)	Yr	VG	VG+	NM
RCA VICTOR					
47-6327	I Forgot/I Think I'm Gonna Die	1955	7.50	15.00	30.00
47-6435	I'm Glad/Darling, I'm Lonesome	1956	7.50	15.00	30.00
47-6595	Your Pretty Blue Eyes/Ain't It Fine	1956	10.00	20.00	40.00
47-6687	I'm Sorry, Goodbye/I Love 'Em All	1956	7.50	15.00	30.00
47-6753	Lonely Street/Didn't Work Out, Did It	1956	7.50	15.00	30.00
47-6824	Tuggin' on My Heart Strings/Our Last Night Together	1957	7.50	15.00	30.00
47-6926	The Key to My Heart/Red Sweater	1957	7.50	15.00	30.00
47-7045	Chicken House/I've Learned	1957	7.50	15.00	30.00
47-7141	School Blues/I've Thought It Over	1958	7.50	15.00	30.00
47-7247	City Lights/Burn On Love Fire	1958	7.50	15.00	30.00
47-7334	Rosie Let's Get Cozy/Sunshine in My Heart	1958	7.50	15.00	30.00

Number	Title (A Side/B Side)	Yr	VG	VG+	NM
STOP					
122	When I've Learned/I Don't Need Nobody Else	196?	2.00	4.00	8.00
132	I Never Gave Up/On the Battlefield	196?	2.00	4.00	8.00
171	I Believe/Peace On Earth Begins Today	196?	2.00	4.00	8.00
Albums					
STOP					
10007	Soul Brother	196?	7.50	15.00	30.00

RICHARD, CLIFF

Also see THE SHADOWS.

Number	Title (A Side/B Side)	Yr	VG	VG+	NM
45s					
ABC-PARAMOUNT					
10042	Living Doll/Apron Strings	1959	6.25	12.50	25.00
10066	Travellin' Light/Dynamite	1959	5.00	10.00	20.00
10093	Voice in the Wilderness/Don't Be Mad at Me	1960	5.00	10.00	20.00
10109	Fall in Love with You/Choppin' 'N' Changin'	1960	5.00	10.00	20.00
10136	Please Don't Tease/Where Is My Heart	1960	5.00	10.00	20.00
10175	Catch Me, I'm Falling/"D" in Love	1961	5.00	10.00	20.00
10195	Theme for a Dream/Mumblin' Mosie	1961	10.00	20.00	40.00
BIG TOP					
3101	The Young Ones/We Say Yeah	1962	5.00	10.00	20.00
CAPITOL					
F4096	Move It/High Class Baby	1958	10.00	20.00	40.00
F4154	Livin' Lovin' Doll/Steady with You	1959	10.00	20.00	40.00
DOT					
16399	Wonderful to Be Young/Got a Funny Feeling	1962	5.00	10.00	20.00
EMI					
S7-19767	Mistletoe and Wine/Have Yourself a Merry Little Christmas	1997	—	2.00	4.00
EMI AMERICA					
8025	We Don't Talk Anymore/Count Me Out	1979	—	2.00	4.00
8035	Carrie/Language of Love	1980	—	2.00	4.00
8057	Dreaming/Dynamite	1980	—	2.50	5.00
—Green label					
8057	Dreaming/Dynamite	1980	—	2.00	4.00
—Gray label					
8068	A Little in Love/Everyman	1980	—	2.00	4.00
8076	Give a Little Bit More/Keep Lookin'	1981	—	2.00	4.00
8076 [PS]	Give a Little Bit More/Keep Lookin'	1981	—	2.50	5.00
8095	Wired for Sound/Hold On	1981	—	2.00	4.00
8103	Daddy's Home/Summer Rain	1982	—	2.00	4.00
8135	The Only Way Out/Be in My Heart	1982	—	2.00	4.00
8149	Little Town/Be in My Heart	1982	—	2.00	4.00
8180	Never Say Die (Give a Little Bit More)/Front Page	1983	—	2.00	4.00
8193	Donna/Ocean Deep	1984	—	2.00	4.00
EPIC					
9597	Lucky Lips/Next Time	1963	5.00	10.00	20.00
9597 [PS]	Lucky Lips/Next Time	1963	6.25	12.50	25.00
9633	It's All in the Game/I'm Looking Out the Window	1963	5.00	10.00	20.00
9633 [PS]	It's All in the Game/I'm Looking Out the Window	1963	—	—	—
—Rumored to exist, but without conclusive evidence, we will delete this from future editions					
9670	I'm the Lonely One/I Only Have Eyes for You	1964	5.00	10.00	20.00
9670 [PS]	I'm the Lonely One/I Only Have Eyes for You	1964	6.25	12.50	25.00
9691	Bachelor Boy/True, True Lovin'	1964	5.00	10.00	20.00
9737	I Don't Wanna Love You/Look in My Eyes Maria	1964	3.75	7.50	15.00
9757	Again/The Minute You're Gone	1965	3.75	7.50	15.00
9810	I Could Easily Fall (In Love with You)/On My Word	1965	3.75	7.50	15.00
9839	The Twelfth of Never/Paradise Lost	1965	3.75	7.50	15.00
9866	Wind Me Up (and Let Me Go)/Eye of a Needle	1965	3.75	7.50	15.00
10018	Blue Turns to Grey/I'll Walk Alone	1966	3.75	7.50	15.00
10070	Visions/Quando, Quando, Quando	1966	3.75	7.50	15.00
10101	Time Drags By/The La La La Song	1966	3.75	7.50	15.00
10178	It's All Over/Heartbeat	1967	3.75	7.50	15.00
MONUMENT					
1211	Goodbye Sam, Hello Samantha/You Never Can Tell	1970	—	3.00	6.00
1229	I Ain't Got Time Anymore/Morning Comes Too Soon	1970	—	3.00	6.00
POLYDOR					
885336-7	All I Ask of You/Phantom of the Opera Overture, Act 2	1987	—	—	3.00
—With Sarah Brightman					
885336-7 [PS]	All I Ask of You/Phantom of the Opera Overture, Act 2	1987	—	—	3.00
ROCKET					
YB-11463	Green Light/Needing a Friend	1979	—	2.00	4.00
40531	Miss You Nights/Love Enough	1976	—	2.00	4.00
40574	Devil Woman/Love On (Shine On)	1976	—	2.50	5.00
40652	Junior Cowboy/I Can't Ask for Anymore Than You	1976	—	2.00	4.00
40724	Don't Turn the Light Out/Nothing Left for Me to Say	1977	—	2.00	4.00
40771	You've Got Me Wondering/Try a Smile	1977	—	2.00	4.00
SIRE					
703	Living in Harmony/Jesus	1973	—	2.50	5.00
707	Power to All Our Friends/Come Back Billie Joe	1973	—	2.50	5.00
STRIPED HORSE					
7008	My Pretty One/Love Ya	1988	—	—	3.00
7008 [PS]	My Pretty One/Love Ya	1988	—	—	3.00
7011	Some People/Love Ya	1988	—	—	3.00
7011 [PS]	Some People/Love Ya	1988	—	—	3.00
UNI					
55061	All My Love/Our Story Book	1968	2.50	5.00	10.00
55069	Congratulations/High 'N' Dry	1968	2.50	5.00	10.00
55145	The Day I Met Marie/Sweet Little Jesus Boy	1969	3.00	6.00	12.00
WARNER BROS.					
7344	Throw Down a Line/Reflections	1969	2.00	4.00	8.00
—A-side by Cliff and Hank (Marvin)					
Albums					
ABC-PARAMOUNT					
321 [M]	Cliff Sings	1960	20.00	40.00	80.00
S-321 [S]	Cliff Sings	1960	25.00	50.00	100.00
391 [M]	Listen to Cliff	1961	20.00	40.00	80.00
S-391 [S]	Listen to Cliff	1961	25.00	50.00	100.00
EMI AMERICA					
SN-16220	Green Light	1981	2.00	4.00	8.00
SN-16221	I'm Nearly Famous	1981	2.00	4.00	8.00
SN-16253	Every Face Tells a Story	1981	2.00	4.00	8.00
SW-17018	We Don't Talk Anymore	1979	2.50	5.00	10.00
SW-17039	I'm No Hero	1980	2.50	5.00	10.00
SW-17059	Wired for Sound	1981	2.50	5.00	10.00
ST-17081	Now You See Me, Now You Don't	1982	2.50	5.00	10.00
ST-17105	Give a Little Bit More	1983	2.50	5.00	10.00
EPIC					
LN 24063 [M]	Summer Holiday	1963	10.00	20.00	40.00
LN 24089 [M]	It's All in the Game	1964	7.50	15.00	30.00
LN 24115 [M]	Cliff Richard in Spain	1965	7.50	15.00	30.00
BN 26063 [S]	Summer Holiday	1963	12.50	25.00	50.00
BN 26089 [S]	It's All in the Game	1964	10.00	20.00	40.00
BN 26115 [S]	Cliff Richard in Spain	1965	10.00	20.00	40.00
ROCKET					
PIG-2210	I'm Nearly Famous	1976	3.00	6.00	12.00
PIG-2268	Every Face Tells a Story	1977	3.00	6.00	12.00
BXL1-2958	Green Light	1978	3.00	6.00	12.00
WORD					
WR-8306	Walking in the Light	1985	3.00	6.00	12.00

RICHARD AND THE YOUNG LIONS

Number	Title (A Side/B Side)	Yr	VG	VG+	NM
45s					
PHILIPS					
40381	Open Up Your Door/Once Upon Your Smile	1966	2.50	5.00	10.00
40381 [PS]	Open Up Your Door/Once Upon Your Smile	1966	5.00	10.00	20.00
40414	Nasty/Lost and Found	1966	2.00	4.00	8.00
40438	To Have and to Hold/You Can Make It	1967	2.00	4.00	8.00

RICHARDSON, JAPE

See THE BIG BOPPER.

RICHARDSON, RUDI

Number	Title (A Side/B Side)	Yr	VG	VG+	NM
45s					
SUN					
271	Fools Hall of Fame/Why Should I Cry	1957	7.50	15.00	30.00

RICHARDSON, WARREN S., JR.

Number	Title (A Side/B Side)	Yr	VG	VG+	NM
Albums					
COTILLION					
SD 9013	Warren S. Richardson, Jr.	1970	7.50	15.00	30.00

RICHIE, LITTLE JOE

See LITTLE JOE.

RICHIE AND THE ROYALS

Number	Title (A Side/B Side)	Yr	VG	VG+	NM
45s					
GOLDEN CREST					
573	Be My Girl/We're Strollin'	1962	12.50	25.00	50.00
RELLO					
1	And When I'm Near You/Goody Goody	1961	20.00	40.00	80.00
3	Be My Girl/We're Strollin'	1962	50.00	100.00	200.00

RICHIE AND THE SAXONS

Number	Title (A Side/B Side)	Yr	VG	VG+	NM
45s					
TIP					
1020	Bottom of the Barrel/Easy Now	196?	12.50	25.00	50.00

RICHMAN, JONATHAN, AND THE MODERN LOVERS

Number	Title (A Side/B Side)	Yr	VG	VG+	NM
45s					
BESERKLEY					
5701	Roadrunner/Friday on My Mind	1975	2.50	5.00	10.00
—B-side by Earth Quake					
5701 [PS]	Roadrunner/Friday on My Mind	1975	2.50	5.00	10.00
5743	New England/Here Come the Martians	1976	2.50	5.00	10.00
5743 [PS]	New England/Here Come the Martians	1976	2.50	5.00	10.00
Albums					
BESERKLEY					
BZ-0048	Jonathan Richman and the Modern Lovers	1976	7.50	15.00	30.00
—Distributed by GRT					
JBZ 0048	Jonathan Richman and the Modern Lovers	1976	6.25	12.50	25.00
—Distributed by Playboy/CBS					
BZ-0050	The Modern Lovers	1976	7.50	15.00	30.00
—Distributed by GRT					
JBZ 0050	The Modern Lovers	1978	6.25	12.50	25.00
—Distributed by Playboy/CBS					
BZ-0053	Rock 'N' Roll with the Modern Lovers	1977	4.50	9.00	18.00
—Distributed by Janus/GRT					
JBZ 0055	Modern Lovers "Live"	1978	3.50	7.00	14.00
—Distributed by Playboy/CBS					
JBZ 0060	Back in Your Life	1979	2.50	5.00	10.00
—Distributed by Playboy/CBS					
10060	Back in Your Life	1980	3.00	6.00	12.00
—Reissue -- change in distributing label to Elektra					
PZ 34800	Rock 'N' Roll with the Modern Lovers	1977	3.50	7.00	14.00
—Distributed by Playboy/CBS					
BOMP!					
4021	The Original Modern Lovers	1981	5.00	10.00	20.00
—Same album as Mohawk releasse					
HOME OF THE HITS					
HH-1910	The Modern Lovers	1975	12.50	25.00	50.00
MOHAWK					
SCALP 0002	The Original Modern Lovers	1981	6.25	12.50	25.00
RHINO					
RNLP 70091	The Modern Lovers	1986	3.00	6.00	12.00
—Reissue					
RNLP 70092	Jonathan Richman and the Modern Lovers	1986	3.00	6.00	12.00
—Reissue					
RNLP 70093	Rock 'N' Roll with the Modern Lovers	1986	3.00	6.00	12.00
—Reissue					

Number	Title (A Side/B Side)	Yr	VG	VG+	NM
RNLP 70094 —*Reissue*	Modern Lovers "Live"	1986	3.00	6.00	12.00
RNLP 70095 —*Reissue*	Back in Your Life	1986	3.00	6.00	12.00
ROUNDER					
9014	Modern Lovers '88	1988	3.00	6.00	12.00
9021	Jonathan Richman	1989	3.00	6.00	12.00
9024	Jonathan Goes Country	1990	3.00	6.00	12.00
SIRE					
23939	Jonathan Sings!	1983	3.00	6.00	12.00

RICHY, PAUL

Number	Title (A Side/B Side)	Yr	VG	VG+	NM
45s					
SUN					
338	The Legend of the Big Steeple/Broken Hearted Willie	1960	5.00	10.00	20.00

RICK AND DONNA

Number	Title (A Side/B Side)	Yr	VG	VG+	NM
45s					
A&M					
710	I'm a Losing Guy/Wedding Bells Will Ring	1963	3.00	6.00	12.00
TOWER					
112	A.B.C./What Good Is Love	1965	2.50	5.00	10.00

RICK AND THE KEENS

Number	Title (A Side/B Side)	Yr	VG	VG+	NM
45s					
AUSTIN					
303	Peanuts/I'll Be Home	1961	12.50	25.00	50.00
JAMIE					
1219	Your Turn ot Cry/Tender Years	1962	5.00	10.00	20.00
LE CAM					
133	Darla/Someone New	1964	7.50	15.00	30.00
721	Peanuts/I'll Be Home	1961	12.50	25.00	50.00
SMASH					
1705	Peanuts/I'll Be Home	1961	5.00	10.00	20.00
1722	Maybe/Popcorn	1961	5.00	10.00	20.00
TOLLIE					
9016	Darla/Someone New	1964	5.00	10.00	20.00

RICK AND THE MASTERS

Number	Title (A Side/B Side)	Yr	VG	VG+	NM
45s					
CAMEO					
226	Flame of Love/Here Come Nancy	1962	12.50	25.00	50.00
247	Let It Please Be You/I Don't Want Your Love	1963	12.50	25.00	50.00
HARAL					
776	Bewitched, Bothered and Bewildered/A Kissin' Friend	1962	15.00	30.00	60.00
TABA					
101	Flame of Love/Here Come Nancy	1962	37.50	75.00	150.00

RICK AND THE RANDELLS

Number	Title (A Side/B Side)	Yr	VG	VG+	NM
45s					
ABC-PARAMOUNT					
10055	Let It Be You/Honey Doll	1959	10.00	20.00	40.00

RICK AND THE RAVENS

With RAY MANZAREK, later of THE DOORS.

Number	Title (A Side/B Side)	Yr	VG	VG+	NM
45s					
AURA					
4506	Henrietta/Just for Me	1965	15.00	30.00	60.00
4511	Soul Train/Geraldine	1965	12.50	25.00	50.00
POSAE					
101	Big Bucket "T"/Rampage	196?	20.00	40.00	80.00

RICK, ROBIN & HIM

Number	Title (A Side/B Side)	Yr	VG	VG+	NM
45s					
V.I.P.					
25035	Three Choruses of Despair/Cause You Know Me	1965	6.25	12.50	25.00

RICKIE AND THE HALLMARKS

Number	Title (A Side/B Side)	Yr	VG	VG+	NM
45s					
AMY					
877	Wherever You Are/Joanie Don't You Cry	1963	10.00	20.00	40.00

RICKLES, DON

Number	Title (A Side/B Side)	Yr	VG	VG+	NM
Albums					
WARNER BROS.					
WS 1745	Hello Dummy!	1968	3.75	7.50	15.00
WS 1779	Don Rickles Speaks!	1969	3.75	7.50	15.00

RICKS, JIMMY

Also see THE RAVENS.

Number	Title (A Side/B Side)	Yr	VG	VG+	NM
45s					
ARNOLD					
1011	Canadian Sunset/Change of Heart	1961	3.75	7.50	15.00
ATCO					
6220	Daddy Rolling Stone/Homesick	1962	5.00	10.00	20.00
ATLANTIC					
2246	Trouble in Mind/Romance in the Dark	1964	3.75	7.50	15.00
BATON					
236	I'm a Fool to Want You/Bad Man of Missouri	1957	10.00	20.00	40.00
DECCA					
30443	What Have I Done/Lazy Mule	1957	6.25	12.50	25.00
FELSTED					
8560	Secret Love/If It Didn't Hurt So Much	1959	6.25	12.50	25.00
8582	Leaning On Your Love/Here Come the Tears Again	1959	6.25	12.50	25.00
FURY					
1070	I Wonder/Let Me Down Easy	1962	5.00	10.00	20.00
JOSIE					
796	She's Fine, She's Mine/The Unbeliever	1956	10.00	20.00	40.00
JUBILEE					
5559	Lonely Man/If You Ever Loved Someone	1967	3.00	6.00	12.00
5561	Wigglin' and Gigglin'/Long, Long Arm of Love	1967	3.00	6.00	12.00
5579	Don't Go to Strangers/Lonely Man	1967	3.00	6.00	12.00
5608	It's All in the Game/Baby Don't Leave Me	1967	3.00	6.00	12.00
5619	Snap Your Fingers/Wigglin' and Gigglin'	1968	3.00	6.00	12.00
MAINSTREAM					
625	Girl of My Dreams/Glow Worm	1965	3.75	7.50	15.00
MERCURY					
8296	Love Is the Thing/Too Soon	1952	20.00	40.00	80.00
PARIS					
504	Do You Promise/The Sugar Man Song	1957	7.50	15.00	30.00
SIGNATURE					
12040	I Needed Your Love/Timber	1960	5.00	10.00	20.00
12051	The Christmas Song/Love Is the Thing	1960	5.00	10.00	20.00
Albums					
JUBILEE					
JGS-8021	Tell Her You Love Her	1969	12.50	25.00	50.00
MAINSTREAM					
S-6050 [S]	Vibrations	1965	15.00	30.00	60.00
56050 [M]	Vibrations	1965	12.50	25.00	50.00
SIGNATURE					
SM-1032 [M]	Jimmy Ricks	1961	75.00	150.00	300.00
SM-1032 [M-DJ]	Jimmy Ricks	1961	50.00	100.00	200.00

RICKY AND THE VACELS

Number	Title (A Side/B Side)	Yr	VG	VG+	NM
45s					
EXPRESS					
711	Lorraine/Bubble Gum	1962	7.50	15.00	30.00
FARGO					
1050	His Girl/Don't Want Your Love No More	1963	7.50	15.00	30.00
1050 —*Blue vinyl*	His Girl/Don't Want Your Love No More	1963	20.00	40.00	80.00

RICO AND THE RAVENS

Number	Title (A Side/B Side)	Yr	VG	VG+	NM
45s					
AUTUMN					
6	Don't You Know/In My Heart	1965	3.75	7.50	15.00
RALLY					
1601	Don't You Know/In My Heart	1965	10.00	20.00	40.00

RIDGLEY, TOMMY

Number	Title (A Side/B Side)	Yr	VG	VG+	NM
45s					
ATLANTIC					
1009	Ooh Lawdy My Baby/I'm Gonna Cross That River	1953	15.00	30.00	60.00
1039	Jam Up/Wish I Had Never	1954	10.00	20.00	40.00
2136	Jam Up Twist/Wish I Had Never	1962	3.75	7.50	15.00
DECCA					
48226	Anything But Love/Once in a Lifetime	1951	20.00	40.00	80.00
HERALD					
501	When I Meet My Girl/Whatcha Gonna Do	1957	5.00	10.00	20.00
508	Baby Do Liddle/Just a Memory	1957	5.00	10.00	20.00
513	Come back Baby/Woncha Gone	1958	5.00	10.00	20.00
526	Mairzy Doats and Dozy Doats/I've Heard That Story Before	1958	5.00	10.00	20.00
537	I'll Be True/Girl Across the Street	1959	5.00	10.00	20.00
540	Tina/How I Feel	1959	5.00	10.00	20.00
IMPERIAL					
5198	I Live My Life/Lavinia	1952	37.50	75.00	150.00
5203	Looped/Junie Mae	1952	37.50	75.00	150.00
5214	Monkey Man/Nobody Cares	1953	37.50	75.00	150.00
5223	Good Times/A Day Is Coming	1953	37.50	75.00	150.00
RIC					
968	Is It True/Let's Try and Talk It Over	1959	3.75	7.50	15.00
973	Do You Remember/Please Hurry Home	1960	3.75	7.50	15.00
978	Double Eye Whammy/Should I Ever Love Again	1961	3.75	7.50	15.00
982	Three Times/The Only Girl for Me	1961	3.75	7.50	15.00
984	The Girl from Kooka Monga/In the Same Old Way	1961	3.75	7.50	15.00
990	My Ordinary Girl/She's Got What It Takes	1962	3.00	6.00	12.00
993	Heavenly/I Love You Yes I Do	1963	3.00	6.00	12.00
994	Honest I Do/I've Heard That Story Before	1963	3.00	6.00	12.00
RONN					
36	It's the Same Old Way/I'm Not the Same Person	1969	2.50	5.00	10.00
WHITE CLIFFS					
260	Hey Little Chick/Did You Tell Him	1967	2.50	5.00	10.00

RIFFS, THE

Number	Title (A Side/B Side)	Yr	VG	VG+	NM
45s					
JAMIE					
1296	Tell Her/I Been Thinkin'	1965	3.00	6.00	12.00
OLD TOWN					
1179	Tell Tale Friends/Why Are the Nights So Cold	1965	12.50	25.00	50.00
SUNNY					
22	Little Girl/Why Are the Nights So Cold	1964	50.00	100.00	200.00

RIG

Number	Title (A Side/B Side)	Yr	VG	VG+	NM
45s					
CAPITOL					
2855	Quiet Lady/Sister Liza Bookman	1970	3.00	6.00	12.00
Albums					
CAPITOL					
ST-473	Rig	1970	5.00	10.00	20.00

RIGHTEOUS BROTHERS, THE

Also see BOBBY HATFIELD; BILL MEDLEY; THE PARAMOURS; PHIL SPECTOR.

Number	Title (A Side/B Side)	Yr	VG	VG+	NM
45s					
HAVEN					
800	Hold On to What You Got/Let Me Make the Music	1976	—	2.00	4.00

Number	Title (A Side/B Side)	Yr	VG	VG+	NM
7002	Rock and Roll Heaven/I Just Wanna Be Me	1974	—	2.50	5.00
7004	Give It to the People/Love Is Not a Dirty Word	1974	—	2.00	4.00
7006	Dream On/Dr. Rock and Roll	1974	—	2.00	4.00
7011	High Blood Pressure/Never Say I Love You	1975	—	2.00	4.00
7014	Young Blood/Substitute	1975	—	2.00	4.00

MOONGLOW

Number	Title (A Side/B Side)	Yr	VG	VG+	NM
215	Little Latin Lupe Lu/I'm So Lonely	1963	5.00	10.00	20.00
215 [DJ]	Little Latin Lupe Lu (same on both sides)	1963	12.50	25.00	50.00
—Red vinyl promo					
221	Gotta Tell You How I Feel/If You're Lying, You'll Be Crying	1963	5.00	10.00	20.00
223	My Babe/Fee-Fi-Fidily-I-Oh	1963	5.00	10.00	20.00
224	Ko Ko Joe/B-Flat Blues	1963	5.00	10.00	20.00
231	Try to Find Another Man/I Still Love You	1964	5.00	10.00	20.00
234	Bring Your Love to Me/If You're Lying, You'll Be Crying	1964	5.00	10.00	20.00
235	This Little Girl of Mine/If You're Lying, You'll Be Crying	1964	3.75	7.50	15.00
238	Bring Your Love to Me/Fannie Mae	1965	3.75	7.50	15.00
239	You Can Have Her/Love or Magic	1965	3.75	7.50	15.00
242	Justine/In That Great Gettin' Up Morning	1965	3.75	7.50	15.00
243	For Your Love/Gotta Tell You How I Feel	1965	3.75	7.50	15.00
244	Georgia on My Mind/My Tears Will Go Away	1966	3.75	7.50	15.00
245	I Need a Girl/Bring Your Love to Me	1966	3.75	7.50	15.00

PHILLES

Number	Title (A Side/B Side)	Yr	VG	VG+	NM
124	You've Lost That Lovin' Feelin'/There's a Woman	1964	3.75	7.50	15.00
127	Just Once in My Life/The Blues	1965	3.75	7.50	15.00
127 [PS]	Just Once in My Life/The Blues	1965	7.50	15.00	30.00
129	Unchained Melody/Hung on You	1965	3.75	7.50	15.00
130	Ebb Tide/(I Love You) For Sentimental Reasons	1965	3.75	7.50	15.00
130 [PS]	Ebb Tide/(I Love You) For Sentimental Reasons	1965	7.50	15.00	30.00
132	The White Cliffs of Dover/She's Mine, All Mine	1966	5.00	10.00	20.00

VERVE

Number	Title (A Side/B Side)	Yr	VG	VG+	NM
CS8-5	Celebrity Scene: The Righteous Brothers	1967	15.00	30.00	60.00
—Box set of five singles (10520-10524). Price includes box, all 5 singles, jukebox title strips, bio. Records are sometimes found by themselves, so they are also listed separately.					
10383	(You're My) Soul and Inspiration/B Side Blues	1966	3.75	7.50	15.00
10383 [PS]	(You're My) Soul and Inspiration/B Side Blues	1966	7.50	15.00	30.00
10403	Rat Race/Green Onions	1966	3.75	7.50	15.00
10406	He/He Will Break Your Heart	1966	2.50	5.00	10.00
10406 [PS]	He/He Will Break Your Heart	1966	5.00	10.00	20.00
10430	Go Ahead and Cry/Things Didn't Go Your Way	1966	2.50	5.00	10.00
10449	On This Side of Goodbye/A Man Without a Dream	1966	2.50	5.00	10.00
10479	Along Came Jones/Jimmy's Blues	1967	2.00	4.00	8.00
10507	Melancholy Music Man/Don't Give Up on Me	1967	2.00	4.00	8.00
10520	(You're My) Soul and Inspiration/Go Ahead and Cry	1967	2.50	5.00	10.00
10521	Hold On, I'm Coming/He Will Break Your Heart	1967	2.50	5.00	10.00
10522	Melancholy Music Man/I Believe	1967	2.50	5.00	10.00
10523	I (Who Have Nothing)/Island in the Sun	1967	2.50	5.00	10.00
10524	My Girl/Something You Got	1967	2.50	5.00	10.00
10551	Stranded in the Middle of No Place/Been So Nice	1967	2.00	4.00	8.00
10551 [PS]	Stranded in the Middle of No Place/Been So Nice	1967	3.75	7.50	15.00
10577	Here I Am/So Many Lonely Nights Ahead	1968	2.00	4.00	8.00
10637	Let the Good Times Roll/You've Lost That Lovin' Feelin'	1968	2.00	4.00	8.00
10648	And the Party Goes On/Woman, Man Needs Ya	1968	2.00	4.00	8.00
10649	Good N' Nuff/Po' Folks	1968	2.00	4.00	8.00
871882-7	Unchained Melody/Hung on You	1989	—	2.00	4.00

Albums

HAVEN

Number	Title	Yr	VG	VG+	NM
ST-9201	Give It to the People	1974	3.75	7.50	15.00
ST-9203	Sons of Mrs. Righteous	1975	3.75	7.50	15.00

MGM

Number	Title	Yr	VG	VG+	NM
GAS-102	The Righteous Brothers (Golden Archive Series)	1970	3.75	7.50	15.00
SE-4885	The History of the Righteous Brothers	1973	3.75	7.50	15.00

MOONGLOW

Number	Title	Yr	VG	VG+	NM
MLP-1001 [M]	Right Now!	1963	10.00	20.00	40.00
MSP-1001 [S]	Right Now!	1963	15.00	30.00	60.00
MLP-1002 [M]	Some Blue-Eyed Soul	1964	10.00	20.00	40.00
MSP-1002 [S]	Some Blue-Eyed Soul	1964	15.00	30.00	60.00
MLP-1003 [M]	This Is New!	1965	10.00	20.00	40.00
MSP-1003 [S]	This Is New!	1965	15.00	30.00	60.00
MLP-1004 [M]	The Best of the Righteous Brothers	1966	6.25	12.50	25.00
MSP-1004 [S]	The Best of the Righteous Brothers	1966	7.50	15.00	30.00

PHILLES

Number	Title	Yr	VG	VG+	NM
PHLP-4007 [M]	You've Lost That Lovin' Feelin'	1964	6.25	12.50	25.00
PHLPS-4007 [S]	You've Lost That Lovin' Feelin'	1964	10.00	20.00	40.00
PHLP-4008 [M]	Just Once in My Life	1965	6.25	12.50	25.00
PHLPS-4008 [S]	Just Once in My Life	1965	10.00	20.00	40.00
PHLP-4009 [M]	Back to Back	1965	6.25	12.50	25.00
PHLPS-4009 [S]	Back to Back	1965	10.00	20.00	40.00
ST-90692 [S]	You've Lost That Lovin' Feelin'	1965	12.50	25.00	50.00
—Capitol Record Club edition					
T-90692 [M]	You've Lost That Lovin' Feelin'	1965	12.50	25.00	50.00
—Capitol Record Club edition					

RHINO

Number	Title	Yr	VG	VG+	NM
R1-71488 [(2)]	Anthology	1989	3.75	7.50	15.00

VERVE

Number	Title	Yr	VG	VG+	NM
V-5001 [M]	Soul and Inspiration	1966	5.00	10.00	20.00
V6-5001 [S]	Soul and Inspiration	1966	6.25	12.50	25.00
V-5004 [M]	Go Ahead and Cry	1966	5.00	10.00	20.00
V6-5004 [S]	Go Ahead and Cry	1966	6.25	12.50	25.00
V-5010 [M]	Sayin' Somethin'	1967	5.00	10.00	20.00
V6-5010 [S]	Sayin' Somethin'	1967	6.25	12.50	25.00
V-5020 [M]	Greatest Hits	1967	6.25	12.50	25.00
V6-5020 [S]	Greatest Hits	1967	5.00	10.00	20.00
V-5031 [M]	Souled Out	1967	7.50	15.00	30.00
V6-5031 [S]	Souled Out	1967	5.00	10.00	20.00
V6-5051	Standards	1968	5.00	10.00	20.00
V6-5058	One for the Road	1968	7.50	15.00	30.00
—With The Blossoms credited on the back cover					
V6-5058	One for the Road	1968	5.00	10.00	20.00
—Without The Blossoms credited on the back cover					
V6-5071	Greatest Hits, Vol. 2	1969	5.00	10.00	20.00
V6-5076	Re-Birth	1970	5.00	10.00	20.00
ST-91057 [S]	Sayin' Somethin'	1967	6.25	12.50	25.00
—Capitol Record Club edition					
823662-1	Greatest Hits	198?	2.50	5.00	10.00

RILEY, BILLY LEE

45s

Number	Title (A Side/B Side)	Yr	VG	VG+	NM
ATLANTIC					
2525	Sittin' and a Waitin'/Happy Man	1968	2.00	4.00	8.00
BRUNSWICK					
55085	Rockin' on the Moon/Is That All to the Ball	1958	50.00	100.00	200.00
ENTRANCE					
7508	I Got a Thing About You Baby/You Don't Love Me	1972	—	2.50	5.00
GNP CRESCENDO					
371	Gonna Find a Cave/That's the Bag I'm In	1966	2.50	5.00	10.00
377	The Way I Feel/St. James Infirmary	1966	2.50	5.00	10.00
HIP					
8006	Family Portrait/Going Back to Memphis	1968	2.00	4.00	8.00
8011	Show Me Your Soul/Midnight Hour	1968	2.00	4.00	8.00
HOME OF THE BLUES					
233	Flip, Flop, and Fly/Teenage Letter	1961	7.50	15.00	30.00
MERCURY					
72314	Bo Diddley/Memphis	1964	3.75	7.50	15.00
72385	Mojo Workout/Charlene	1965	3.00	6.00	12.00
MOJO					
1933	Southern Soul/Midnight Hour	1967	2.50	5.00	10.00
SUN					
245	Trouble Bound/Rock with Me, Baby	1956	30.00	60.00	120.00
260	Flying Saucers Rock and Roll/I Want You Baby	1957	25.00	50.00	100.00
277	Red Hot/Pearly Lee	1957	15.00	30.00	60.00
289	Baby Please Don't Go/Wouldn't You Know	1958	12.50	25.00	50.00
313	Down by the Riverside/No Name Girl	1959	6.25	12.50	25.00
322	One More Time/Got the Water Bollin'	1959	12.50	25.00	50.00
1100	Kay/Looking for Her Heart	1969	—	3.00	6.00
1105	Pilot Town L.A./Workin' on the River	1969	—	3.00	6.00
1116	Tallahassee/Old Home Place	1970	—	2.50	5.00

Albums

Number	Title	Yr	VG	VG+	NM
GNP CRESCENDO					
GNP-2020 [M]	Billy Lee Riley	1966	3.75	7.50	15.00
GNPS-2020 [S]	Billy Lee Riley	1966	5.00	10.00	20.00
MERCURY					
MG-20958 [M]	The Whiskey A-Go-Go Presents Billy Lee Riley	1964	5.00	10.00	20.00
MG-20965 [M]	Big Harmonica Special	1964	5.00	10.00	20.00
MG-20974 [M]	Beatlemania Harmonica	1965	5.00	10.00	20.00
SR-60958 [S]	The Whiskey A-Go-Go Presents Billy Lee Riley	1964	6.25	12.50	25.00
SR-60965 [S]	Big Harmonica Special	1964	6.25	12.50	25.00
SR-60974 [S]	Beatlemania Harmonica	1965	6.25	12.50	25.00

RILEY, BOB

45s

Number	Title (A Side/B Side)	Yr	VG	VG+	NM
CORAL					
62125	I Think It's a Shame/Blue Guitar Waltz	1959	5.00	10.00	20.00
DOT					
15625	Baby Sittin'/Without Your Love	1957	6.25	12.50	25.00
MGM					
12612	Wanda Jean/The Midnight Line	1958	37.50	75.00	150.00

RILEY, JEANNIE C.

45s

Number	Title (A Side/B Side)	Yr	VG	VG+	NM
CAPITOL					
2378	The Price I Pay to Stay/How Can Anything So Right Be So Wrong	1969	—	2.50	5.00
2449	I Don't Know What I'm Doing Here/You've Got Me Singing Nursery Rhymes	1969	—	2.50	5.00
LITTLE DARLIN'					
0031	What About Them/You Write the Music	1967	3.75	7.50	15.00
—As "Jean Riley"					
0048	I Don't Know What I'm Doing Here/I'll Be a Woman of the World	1968	—	3.00	6.00
MCA					
52018	From Harper Valley to the Mountain/I Don't Have to Die to Get Into Heaven	1982	—	—	3.00
MERCURY					
73616	Plain Vanilla/Country Girl	1974	—	2.00	4.00
MGM					
14310	Houston Blues/How Hard I'm Trying	1971	—	2.00	4.00
14341	Give Myself a Party/Why You Been Gone So Long	1972	—	2.00	4.00
14382	Good Morning Country Rain/This Is for You	1972	—	2.00	4.00
14427	One Night/Without You	1972	—	2.00	4.00
14495	When Love Has Gone Away/Thou Shalt Not Kill	1973	—	2.00	4.00
14554	Hush/Not Looking Back	1973	—	2.00	4.00
14666	Another Football Year/Mother America	1973	—	2.00	4.00
14696	Missouri/Sing Jeannie Sing	1974	—	2.00	4.00
PLANTATION					
3	Harper Valley P.T.A./Yesterday All Day Long Today	1968	2.00	4.00	8.00
—Yellow label					
3	Harper Valley P.T.A./Yesterday All Day Long Today	1968	—	3.00	6.00
—Green and white label					
7	The Girl Most Likely/My Scrapbook	1968	—	2.50	5.00
16	There Never Was a Time/Back to School	1969	—	2.50	5.00
22	The Rib/I'm the Woman	1969	—	2.50	5.00
29	The Back Side of Dallas/Things Go Better with Love	1969	—	2.50	5.00
44	Country Girl/We Were Raised on Love	1970	—	2.50	5.00
59	Duty Not Desire/Holdin' On	1970	—	2.50	5.00
65	My Man/The Generation Gap	1970	—	2.50	5.00
72	Oh, Singer/I'll Take What's Left of You	1971	—	2.50	5.00
75	Good Enough to Be Your Wife/Light Your Light	1971	—	2.50	5.00
79	Roses and Thorns/Shed Me No Tears	1971	—	2.50	5.00

Number	Title (A Side/B Side)	Yr	VG	VG+	NM
96	The Lion's Club/Tell the Truth and Shame the Devil	1972		2.50	5.00
93	If You Could Read My Mind/Will the Real Jesus Please Stand Up	1972	—	2.50	5.00
173	Harper Valley P.T.A. (Soundtrack Version)/I've Done a Lot of Living Since Then	1979	—	3.00	6.00
WARNER BROS.					
8226	The Best I've Ever Had/Thank You for Forgiving	1976	—	2.00	4.00
8290	Pure Gold/Take Time	1976	—	2.00	4.00
Albums					
ALLEGIANCE					
AV-5026	Tears, Joys and Memories	198?	2.50	5.00	10.00
CAPITOL					
ST-177	The Songs of Jeannie C. Riley	1969	3.75	7.50	15.00
MGM					
SE-4805	Give Myself a Party	1972	3.00	6.00	12.00
SE-4849	Down to Earth	1973	3.00	6.00	12.00
SE-4891	When Love Has Gone Away	1973	3.00	6.00	12.00
SE-4909	Just Jeannie C. Riley	1973	3.00	6.00	12.00
PICKWICK					
6098	The Girl Most Likely	197?	2.50	5.00	10.00
6119	The World of Country	197?	2.50	5.00	10.00
PLANTATION					
PLP 1	Harper Valley P.T.A.	1968	5.00	10.00	20.00
PLP 2	Yearbooks and Yesterdays	1969	3.75	7.50	15.00
PLP 3	Things Go Better with Love	1969	3.75	7.50	15.00
PLP 8	Country Girl	1970	3.75	7.50	15.00
PLP 11	The Generation Gap	1970	3.75	7.50	15.00
PLP 13	Jeannie C. Riley's Greatest Hits	1971	3.75	7.50	15.00
PLP 16	Jeannie	1971	3.75	7.50	15.00
508	Country Queens	197?	3.00	6.00	12.00
POWER PAK					
250	Country Gold	197?	2.50	5.00	10.00

RINCON SURFSIDE BAND, THE

Another creation of P.F. SLOAN and STEVE BARRI.

Number	Title (A Side/B Side)	Yr	VG	VG+	NM
Albums					
DUNHILL					
D 50001 [M]	Surfing Songbook	1965	50.00	100.00	200.00
DS 50001 [S]	Surfing Songbook	1965	75.00	150.00	300.00

RINGO, JIMMY

Number	Title (A Side/B Side)	Yr	VG	VG+	NM
45s					
DOT					
15787	I Like This Kind of Music/No One Else	1958	7.50	15.00	30.00
15997	I Like This Kind of Music/No One Else	1959	5.00	10.00	20.00

RINKY-DINKS, THE

See BOBBY DARIN.

RIO, BOBBY

Number	Title (A Side/B Side)	Yr	VG	VG+	NM
45s					
ABC-PARAMOUNT					
10656	Boy Meets Girl/Don't Break My Heart and Run Away	1965	3.75	7.50	15.00
LENOX					
5569	Don Diddley/I Got You	1963	3.75	7.50	15.00

RIO, CHUCK

Also see THE CHAMPS; THE ORIGINALS (3).

Number	Title (A Side/B Side)	Yr	VG	VG+	NM
45s					
CHALLENGE					
59019	Bad Boy/Denise	1958	5.00	10.00	20.00
59073	Ramblin' Through Dixie/Akiko	1960	5.00	10.00	20.00
FLAIR					
103	You Don't Have to Be a Baby to Cry/Big Boy	1962	10.00	20.00	40.00
JACKPOT					
48016	Margarita/C'est La Vie	1960	7.50	15.00	30.00
KENT					
308	Bye Bye Baby/No Matter What You Do	1958	5.00	10.00	20.00
SATURN					
402	Kreschendo Stomp/Rock-A-Nova	1962	12.50	25.00	50.00
TEQUILA					
100	Caravan/El Bracero	1961	5.00	10.00	20.00
103	La Cha Cha Twist/If You Were the Only Girl in the World	1961	5.00	10.00	20.00

RIOS, AUGIE

Number	Title (A Side/B Side)	Yr	VG	VG+	NM
45s					
METRO					
20010	Donde Esta Santa Claus?/Ol' Fatso	1958	10.00	20.00	40.00
20016	Run Rattler Run/Hop, Skip and Jump	1959	7.50	15.00	30.00
20027	Trip to the Island/Teacher Walked Out of the Room	1959	7.50	15.00	30.00
MGM					
12966	Feliz Navidades/Gypsy Boy	1960	5.00	10.00	20.00
13292	Donde Esta Santa Claus?/Ol' Fatso	1964	3.00	6.00	12.00
SHELLEY					
181	I've Got a Girl/There's a Girl Down the Way	1963	10.00	20.00	40.00
186	When You Dance/No One	1963	7.50	15.00	30.00
192	Teach Me Tonight/Linda Lou	1964	5.00	10.00	20.00

RIOS, MIGUEL

Number	Title (A Side/B Side)	Yr	VG	VG+	NM
45s					
A&M					
1193	A Song of Joy (Himno A La Alegria)/El Rio	1970	—	2.50	5.00
1193 [PS]	A Song of Joy (Himno A La Alegria)/El Rio	1970	2.00	4.00	8.00
1203	Himno A La Alegria/El Rio	1970	—	3.00	6.00
Albums					
A&M					
SP-4267	A Song of Joy	1970	3.75	7.50	15.00

RIOS, WALDO DE LOS

Number	Title (A Side/B Side)	Yr	VG	VG+	NM
45s					
UNITED ARTISTS					
50772	Mozart Symphony No. 40 in G Minor, K.550, 1st Movement/Ode to Joy	1971	—	2.50	5.00
50821	Serenata #13/Concerto Para Piano	1971	—	2.00	4.00
50871	Elvira Madigan Theme/A Night of Music	1972	—	2.00	4.00
VAULT					
952	Those Were the Days/Aranguez (Mon Amour)	1969	—	2.50	5.00
WARNER BROS.					
8034	Elixir de Amor/Nabucco	1974	—	2.00	4.00
Albums					
UNITED ARTISTS					
UAS-5554	Mozartmania	1972	3.00	6.00	12.00
UAS-6802	Sinfonias	1971	3.00	6.00	12.00
VAULT					
VS-126	International Hits	1969	3.75	7.50	15.00
WARNER BROS.					
BS 2801	Operas	1974	3.00	6.00	12.00

RIOT SQUAD, THE

Number	Title (A Side/B Side)	Yr	VG	VG+	NM
45s					
HANNA-BARBERA					
485	I Take It That We're Through/Working Man	1966	3.00	6.00	12.00
REPRISE					
0457	Cry, Cry, Cry/How Is It Done?	1966	2.50	5.00	10.00
ROULETTE					
4621	Gonna Make You Mine/I Wanna Talk About My Baby	1965	3.00	6.00	12.00

RIP CHORDS, THE

Number	Title (A Side/B Side)	Yr	VG	VG+	NM
45s					
COLUMBIA					
42687	Here I Stand/Karen	1963	3.75	7.50	15.00
42687 [DJ]	Here I Stand (same on both sides)	1963	12.50	25.00	50.00
—Green vinyl promo					
42687 [PS]	Here I Stand (same on both sides)	1963	12.50	25.00	50.00
—Sleeve is promo only					
42812	Gone/She Thinks I Still Care	1963	3.75	7.50	15.00
42812 [DJ]	Gone (same on both sides)	1963	12.50	25.00	50.00
—Blue vinyl promo					
42812 [PS]	Gone (same on both sides)	1963	12.50	25.00	50.00
—Sleeve is promo only					
42921	Hey, Little Cobra/The Queen	1963	5.00	10.00	20.00
42921 [DJ]	Hey, Little Cobra (same on both sides)	1963	12.50	25.00	50.00
—Yellow vinyl promo					
43035	Three Window Coupe/Hot Rod U.S.A.	1964	3.75	7.50	15.00
43035 [DJ]	Three Window Coupe (same on both sides)	1964	12.50	25.00	50.00
—Red vinyl promo					
43093	One Piece Topless Bathing Suit/Wah-Wahini	1964	3.75	7.50	15.00
43221	Don't Be Scared/Bunny Hill	1965	3.75	7.50	15.00
Albums					
COLUMBIA					
CL 2151 [M]	Hey Little Cobra and Other Hot Rod Hits	1964	10.00	20.00	40.00
CL 2216 [M]	Three Window Coupe	1964	12.50	25.00	50.00
CS 8951 [S]	Hey Little Cobra and Other Hot Rod Hits	1964	12.50	25.00	50.00
CS 9016 [S]	Three Window Coupe	1964	17.50	35.00	70.00

RIP-CHORDS, THE

Number	Title (A Side/B Side)	Yr	VG	VG+	NM
45s					
ABCO					
105	I Love You the Most/Let's Do the Razzle Dazzle	1956	150.00	300.00	600.00
—Black vinyl					
105	I Love You the Most/Let's Do the Razzle Dazzle	1956	375.00	750.00	1500.
—Red vinyl					

RIPERTON, MINNIE

Also see ROTARY CONNECTION.

Number	Title (A Side/B Side)	Yr	VG	VG+	NM
45s					
CAPITOL					
4706	Memory Lane/I'm a Woman	1979	—	2.00	4.00
4761	Lover and Friend/Return to Forever	1979	—	2.00	4.00
4902	Here We Go/Return to Forever	1980	—	2.00	4.00
4955	Give Me Time/Island in the Sun	1980	—	2.00	4.00
CHESS					
1980	Lonely Girl/You Gave Me Soul	1966	2.50	5.00	10.00
—As "Andrea Davis"					
EPIC					
11139	Every Time He Comes Around/Reasons	1974	—	2.50	5.00
50020	Edge of a Dream/Seeing You This Way	1974	—	2.50	5.00
50057	Lovin' You/Edge of a Dream	1974	—	2.50	5.00
50128	Don't Let Anyone Bring You Down/Inside My Love	1975	—	2.50	5.00
50155	When It Comes Down To It/Minnie's Lament	1975	—	2.50	5.00
50166	Simple Things/Minnie's Lament	1975	—	2.50	5.00
50190	Adventures in Paradise/When It Comes Down To It	1976	—	2.50	5.00
50337	Stick Together (Part One)/Stick Together (Part Two)	1977	—	2.50	5.00
50351	Young, Willing and Able/Stick Together	1977	—	2.50	5.00
50394	Wouldn't Matter Where You Are	1977	—	2.50	5.00
50427	How Could I Love You More/Young, Willing and Able	1977	—	2.50	5.00
GRT					
42	Oh! By the Way/Le Fleur	1972	—	3.00	6.00
Albums					
ACCORD					
SN-7205	Wistful Memories	1981	2.50	5.00	10.00

Number	Title (A Side/B Side)	Yr	VG	VG+	NM
CAPITOL					
SO-11936	Minnie	1979	2.50	5.00	10.00
SN-12004	Perfect Angel	1979	2.50	5.00	10.00
—Reissue of Epic 32561					
SN-12005	Adventures in Paradise	1979	2.50	5.00	10.00
—Reissue of Epic 33454					
SN-12006	Stay in Love	1979	2.50	5.00	10.00
—Reissue of Epic 34191					
SOO-12097	Love Lives Forever	1980	2.50	5.00	10.00
ST-12189	The Best of Minnie Riperton	1981	2.50	5.00	10.00
SN-16145	Perfect Angel	1980	2.00	4.00	8.00
—Budget-line reissue					
SN-16146	Adventures in Paradise	1980	2.00	4.00	8.00
—Budget-line reissue					
SN-16147	Stay in Love	1980	2.00	4.00	8.00
—Budget-line reissue					
EPIC					
KE 32561	Perfect Angel	1974	3.00	6.00	12.00
PE 33454	Adventures in Paradise	1975	3.00	6.00	12.00
PEQ 33454 [Q]	Adventures in Paradise	1975	5.00	10.00	20.00
PE 34191	Stay in Love	1977	3.00	6.00	12.00
GRT					
30001	Come To My Garden	1970	3.75	7.50	15.00
JANUS					
7011	Come To My Garden	1974	3.00	6.00	12.00
—Reissue of GRT LP					

RIPPLES AND WAVES PLUS MICHAEL, THE

See THE JACKSONS.

RIPPY, RODNEY ALLEN

Number	Title (A Side/B Side)	Yr	VG	VG+	NM
45s					
BELL					
45403	Take Life a Little Easier/World of Love	1973	2.00	4.00	8.00
Albums					
BELL					
1311	Take Life a Little Easier	1974	5.00	10.00	20.00

RISERS, THE

Number	Title (A Side/B Side)	Yr	VG	VG+	NM
Albums					
IMPERIAL					
LP-9269 [M]	She's a Bad Motorcycle	1964	25.00	50.00	100.00
LP-12269 [S]	She's a Bad Motorcycle	1964	37.50	75.00	150.00

RISING STORM, THE

Number	Title (A Side/B Side)	Yr	VG	VG+	NM
Albums					
ARF! ARF!					
007	Alive in Anover Again	1983	30.00	60.00	120.00
REMNANT					
BBA-3571	Calm Before the Rising Storm	1968	600.00	900.00	1200.
STANTON PARK					
001	Calm Before the Rising Storm	1991	5.00	10.00	20.00
—Reissue of Remnant album					

RISING SUNS, THE

Among the members of this group were RY COODER and TAJ MAHAL.

Number	Title (A Side/B Side)	Yr	VG	VG+	NM
45s					
COLUMBIA					
43534	Candy Man/The Devil's Got My Woman	1966	10.00	20.00	40.00

RITA MARIE

Number	Title (A Side/B Side)	Yr	VG	VG+	NM
45s					
SUN					
1106	Lottie's Lament/Trouble	1969	—	2.50	5.00

RITCHIE FAMILY, THE

Number	Title (A Side/B Side)	Yr	VG	VG+	NM
12-Inch Singles					
CASABLANCA					
NBD 20192	Put Your Feet to the Beat (6:58)/Bad Reputation (6:01)	1979	3.75	7.50	15.00
RCA					
PD-13093	I'll Do My Best (For You Baby)/You've Got Me Dancin'	1982	—	3.00	6.00
PD-13551	All Night All Right/Fantasy	1983	—	3.00	6.00
45s					
20TH CENTURY					
2218	Brazil/Hot Trip	1975	—	2.00	4.00
2252	I Want to Dance with You (Dance with Me)/Lady Champagne	1975	—	2.00	4.00
CASABLANCA					
2206	Put Your Feet to the Beat/It's a Man's World	1979	—	2.00	4.00
2259	Give Me a Break/Bad Reputation	1980	—	2.00	4.00
2292	All My Love/I'll Never Be Able to Set You Free	1980	—	2.00	4.00
MARLIN					
3306	The Best Disco in Town/The Best Disco in Town (Part 2)	1976	—	2.00	4.00
3309	Life Is Music/Lady Luck	1977	—	2.00	4.00
3316	Quiet Village/Voodoo	1977	—	2.00	4.00
3323	American Generation/Music Man	1978	—	2.00	4.00
RCA					
PB-13092	I'll Do My Best (For You Baby)/You've Got Me Dancin'	1982	—	—	3.00
PB-13281	Walk with Me/Tonight I Need to Have Your Love	1982	—	—	3.00
PB-13550	All Night All Right/Fantasy	1983	—	—	3.00
Albums					
20TH CENTURY					
T-498	Brazil	1975	2.50	5.00	10.00
CASABLANCA					
NBLP-7166	Bad Reputation	1979	2.50	5.00	10.00
NBLP-7223	Give Me a Break	1980	2.50	5.00	10.00
MARLIN					
2201	Arabian Nights	1976	2.50	5.00	10.00
2203	Life Is Music	1977	2.50	5.00	10.00
2206	African Queens	1977	2.50	5.00	10.00
2215	American Generation	1978	2.50	5.00	10.00
RCA VICTOR					
AFL1-4324	I'll Do My Best	1982	2.50	5.00	10.00
AFL1-4601	All Night, All Night	1983	2.50	5.00	10.00

RITES, THE

Number	Title (A Side/B Side)	Yr	VG	VG+	NM
45s					
DECCA					
32218	Things/Hour Glass	1967	6.25	12.50	25.00

RITES OF SPRING, THE

Number	Title (A Side/B Side)	Yr	VG	VG+	NM
45s					
PARKWAY					
109	Why/Comin' On to Me	1966	7.50	15.00	30.00

RITUALS, THE

Featuring Arnie Ginsburg, formerly of JAN AND ARNIE.

Number	Title (A Side/B Side)	Yr	VG	VG+	NM
45s					
ARWIN					
120	Girl in Zanzibar/Guitarro	1963	7.50	15.00	30.00
127	This Is Paradise/Gone	1964	7.50	15.00	30.00
128	Surfers Rule/Gone	1964	10.00	20.00	40.00

RIVERA, LUCY

Number	Title (A Side/B Side)	Yr	VG	VG+	NM
45s					
END					
1041	Make Me Queen/Ific	1959	5.00	10.00	20.00

RIVERS, JOHNNY

Number	Title (A Side/B Side)	Yr	VG	VG+	NM
45s					
ATLANTIC					
3011	Sitting in Limbo/Artists and Poets	1974	—	2.50	5.00
3028	Six Days on the Road/Artists and Poets	1974	—	2.50	5.00
3230	John Lee Hooker '74/Get It Up for Love	1974	—	2.50	5.00
BIG TREE					
16094	Swayin' to the Music (Slow Dancin')/Outside Help	1977	—	2.00	4.00
16106	Curious Mind (Um, Um, Um, Um, Um, Um)/Ashes and Sand	1977	—	2.00	4.00
CAPITOL					
4850	Long Black Veil/This Could Be the One	1962	3.75	7.50	15.00
4913	If You Want It, I've Got It/My Heart Is In Your Hands	1963	3.75	7.50	15.00
5232	Long Black Veil/Don't Look Now	1964	3.75	7.50	15.00
CHANCELLOR					
1070	I Get So Doggone Lonesome/Knock Three Times	1961	5.00	10.00	20.00
1108	To Be Loved/Too Good to Last	1962	5.00	10.00	20.00
CORAL					
62425	That's My Baby/Your First and Last Love	1964	3.75	7.50	15.00
CUB					
9047	Everyday/Darling Talk to Me	1959	6.25	12.50	25.00
9058	Answer Me My Love/The Customary Thing	1960	5.00	10.00	20.00
DEE DEE					
239	The White Cliffs of Dover/Your First and Last Love	1959	5.00	10.00	20.00
EPIC					
50121	Help Me Rhonda/New Lovers and Old Friends	1975	—	2.50	5.00
—A-side features Brian Wilson on backing vocals					
50150	Can I Change My Mind/John Lee Hooker	1975	—	2.00	4.00
50208	Welcome Home/Outside Help	1976	—	2.00	4.00
50248	Linda Lue/Outside Help	1976	—	2.00	4.00
ERA					
3037	Call Me/Andersonville	1961	5.00	10.00	20.00
GONE					
5026	Baby Come Back/Long Long Walk	1958	10.00	20.00	40.00
GUYDEN					
2003	You're the One/A Hole in the Ground	1958	6.25	12.50	25.00
2110	You're the One/A Hole in the Ground	1964	3.75	7.50	15.00
IMPERIAL					
66032	Memphis/It Wouldn't Happen with Me	1964	3.00	6.00	12.00
66056	Maybelline/Walk Myself On Home	1964	2.50	5.00	10.00
66056 [PS]	Maybelline/Walk Myself On Home	1964	3.75	7.50	15.00
66075	Mountain of Love/Moody River	1964	2.50	5.00	10.00
66087	Midnight Special/Cupid	1965	2.50	5.00	10.00
66112	Seventh Son/Unsquare Dance	1965	2.50	5.00	10.00
66112 [PS]	Seventh Son/Unsquare Dance	1965	3.75	7.50	15.00
66133	Where Have All the Flowers Gone/Love Me While You Can	1965	2.50	5.00	10.00
66144	Under Your Spell Again/Long Time Man	1965	2.50	5.00	10.00
66144 [PS]	Under Your Spell Again/Long Time Man	1965	3.75	7.50	15.00
66159	Secret Agent Man/You Dig	1966	3.00	6.00	12.00
66159 [PS]	Secret Agent Man/You Dig	1966	3.75	7.50	15.00
66175	(I Washed My Hands In) Muddy Water/Roogalator	1966	2.50	5.00	10.00
66205	Poor Side of Town/A Man Can Cry	1966	3.00	6.00	12.00
66205 [PS]	Poor Side of Town/A Man Can Cry	1966	3.75	7.50	15.00
66227	Baby I Need Your Lovin'/Gettin' Ready for Tomorrow	1967	2.50	5.00	10.00
66227 [PS]	Baby I Need Your Lovin'/Gettin' Ready for Tomorrow	1967	3.75	7.50	15.00
66244	The Tracks of My Tears/Rewind Medley	1967	2.50	5.00	10.00
66244 [PS]	The Tracks of My Tears/Rewind Medley	1967	3.75	7.50	15.00
66267	Summer Rain/Memory of the Coming Good	1967	2.50	5.00	10.00
66286	Look To Your Soul/Something's Strange	1968	2.00	4.00	8.00
66286 [PS]	Look To Your Soul/Something's Strange	1968	3.00	6.00	12.00
66314	Everybody's Talkin'/The Way We Live	1968	—	—	—
—Unreleased					
66335	Right Relations/Better Life	1968	2.00	4.00	8.00
66335 [PS]	Right Relations/Better Life	1968	3.00	6.00	12.00
66360	These Are Not My People/Going Back to Big Sur	1969	2.00	4.00	8.00

Number	Title (A Side/B Side)	Yr	VG	VG+	NM
66386	Muddy River/Resurrection	1969	2.00	4.00	8.00
66386 [PS]	Muddy River/Resurrection	1969	3.00	6.00	12.00
66418	One Woman/Ode to John Lee	1969	2.00	4.00	8.00
66448	Into the Mystic/Jesus Is a Soul Man	1970	2.00	4.00	8.00
66453	Fire and Rain/Apple Tree	1970	2.00	4.00	8.00
MCA					
52502	Heartbreak Love/Why Can't We Communicate	1984	—	2.00	4.00
MGM					
13266	Answer Me, My Love/Customary Thing	1964	3.75	7.50	15.00
RIVERAIRE					
1001	Don't Bug Me Baby/Haunting Black Eyes	1959	7.50	15.00	30.00
ROULETTE					
4565	Baby Come Back/Long Long Walk	1964	5.00	10.00	20.00
RSO					
1030	Romance (Give Me a Chance)/Don't Need No Other Now	1980	—	2.00	4.00
1045	China/The Price	1980	—	2.00	4.00
SOUL CITY					
007	Ashes and Sand/Outside Help	1977	—	2.50	5.00
008	Swayin' to the Music (Slow Dancin')/Outside Help	1977	2.00	4.00	8.00
010	Little White Lie/Be My Baby	1980	—	2.50	5.00
014	RSVP/The Price	1982	—	2.50	5.00
SUEDE					
1401	Little Girl/Two by Two	1957	25.00	50.00	100.00
—As "Johnny Ramistella"					
UNITED ARTISTS					
0101	Memphis/Secret Agent Man	1973	—	2.00	4.00
0102	Mountain of Love/Maybellene	1973	—	2.00	4.00
0103	Seventh Son/Midnight Special	1973	—	2.00	4.00
0104	Poor Side of Town/Baby I Need Your Lovin'	1973	—	2.00	4.00
0105	Summer Rain/The Tracks of My Tears	1973	—	2.00	4.00
—0101 through 0105 are "Silver Spotlight Series" reissues					
XW198	Blue Suede Shoes/Stories to a Child	1973	—	2.50	5.00
XW226	Searchin'-So Fine/New York City Dues	1973	—	2.50	5.00
XW310	I'll Feel a Whole Lot Better/Over the Line	1973	—	2.50	5.00
XW522	Rockin' Pneumonia-Boogie Woogie Flu/Blue Suede Shoes	1974	—	2.00	4.00
—Reissue					
XW523	Where Have All the Flowers Gone/(I Washed My Hands in) Muddy Water	1974	—	2.00	4.00
—Reissue					
741	Oh What a Kiss/Knock Three Times	1964	3.00	6.00	12.00
769	Dream Doll/To Be Loved	1964	3.00	6.00	12.00
50778	Sea Cruise/Our Lady of the Well	1971	—	3.00	6.00
50822	Think His Name/Permanent Change	1971	—	3.00	6.00
50948	On the Borderline/Come Home America	1972	—	2.50	5.00
50960	Rockin' Pneumonia-Boogie Woogie Flu/Come Home America	1972	—	3.00	6.00
—On some pressings, the intro of the A-side is not repeated (lasts about 20 seconds)					
50960	Rockin' Pneumonia-Boogie Woogie Flu/Come Home America	1972	—	3.00	6.00
—On most pressings, the intro of the A-side lasts about 35 seconds					
Albums					
ATLANTIC					
SD 7301	The Road	1974	3.00	6.00	12.00
BIG TREE					
BT 76004	Outside Help	1977	3.00	6.00	12.00
CAPITOL					
ST 2161 [S]	The Sensational Johnny Rivers	1964	6.25	12.50	25.00
T 2161 [M]	The Sensational Johnny Rivers	1964	5.00	10.00	20.00
COLUMBIA					
FE 38429	Not a Through Street	1983	2.50	5.00	10.00
PE 38429	Not a Through Street	1985	2.00	4.00	8.00
—Budget-line reissue					
EPIC					
PE 33681	New Lovers and Old Friends	1975	3.00	6.00	12.00
IMPERIAL					
LP-9264 [M]	Johnny Rivers at the Whiskey A-Go-Go	1964	5.00	10.00	20.00
—Black label with pink and white at left					
LP-9264 [M]	Johnny Rivers at the Whiskey A-Go-Go	1966	3.00	6.00	12.00
—Black label with green and white at left					
LP-9274 [M]	Here We A-Go-Go Again!	1964	5.00	10.00	20.00
—Black label with pink and white at left					
LP-9274 [M]	Here We A-Go-Go Again!	1966	3.00	6.00	12.00
—Black label with green and white at left					
LP-9280 [M]	Johnny Rivers In Action!	1965	5.00	10.00	20.00
—Black label with pink and white at left					
LP-9280 [M]	Johnny Rivers In Action!	1966	3.00	6.00	12.00
—Black label with green and white at left					
LP-9284 [M]	Meanwhile Back at the Whiskey a-Go-Go	1965	5.00	10.00	20.00
—Black label with pink and white at left					
LP-9284 [M]	Meanwhile Back at the Whiskey a-Go-Go	1966	3.00	6.00	12.00
—Black label with green and white at left					
LP-9293 [M]	Johnny Rivers Rocks the Folk	1965	5.00	10.00	20.00
—Black label with pink and white at left					
LP-9293 [M]	Johnny Rivers Rocks the Folk	1966	3.00	6.00	12.00
—Black label with green and white at left					
LP-9307 [M]	...And I Know You Wanna Dance	1966	5.00	10.00	20.00
—Black label with pink and white at left					
LP-9307 [M]	...And I Know You Wanna Dance	1966	3.00	6.00	12.00
—Black label with green and white at left					
LP-9324 [M]	Johnny Rivers' Golden Hits	1966	3.75	7.50	15.00
LP-9334 [M]	Changes	1966	3.75	7.50	15.00
LP-9341 [M]	Rewind	1967	5.00	10.00	20.00
LP-12264 [S]	Johnny Rivers at the Whiskey A-Go-Go	1964	6.25	12.50	25.00
—Black label with pink and white at left					
LP-12264 [S]	Johnny Rivers at the Whiskey A-Go-Go	1966	3.75	7.50	15.00
—Black label with green and white at left					
LP-12274 [S]	Here We A-Go-Go Again!	1964	6.25	12.50	25.00
—Black label with pink and white at left					
LP-12274 [S]	Here We A-Go-Go Again!	1966	3.75	7.50	15.00
—Black label with green and white at left					
LP-12280 [S]	Johnny Rivers In Action!	1965	6.25	12.50	25.00
—Black label with pink and white at left					
LP-12280 [S]	Johnny Rivers In Action!	1966	3.75	7.50	15.00
—Black label with green and white at left					
LP-12284 [S]	Meanwhile Back at the Whiskey a-Go-Go	1965	6.25	12.50	25.00
—Black label with pink and white at left					
LP-12284 [S]	Meanwhile Back at the Whiskey a-Go-Go	1966	3.75	7.50	15.00
—Black label with green and white at left					
LP-12293 [S]	Johnny Rivers Rocks the Folk	1965	6.25	12.50	25.00
—Black label with pink and white at left					
LP-12293 [S]	Johnny Rivers Rocks the Folk	1966	3.75	7.50	15.00
—Black label with green and white at left					
LP-12307 [S]	...And I Know You Wanna Dance	1966	6.25	12.50	25.00
—Black label with pink and white at left					
LP-12307 [S]	...And I Know You Wanna Dance	1966	3.75	7.50	15.00
—Black label with green and white at left					
LP-12324 [S]	Johnny Rivers' Golden Hits	1966	5.00	10.00	20.00
LP-12334 [S]	Changes	1966	5.00	10.00	20.00
LP-12341 [S]	Rewind	1967	5.00	10.00	20.00
LP-12372	Realization	1968	5.00	10.00	20.00
LP-12427	A Touch of Gold	1969	5.00	10.00	20.00
LP-16001	Slim Slo Slider	1970	5.00	10.00	20.00
LIBERTY					
LN-10120	The Best of Johnny Rivers	1981	2.00	4.00	8.00
LN-10121	Changes	1981	2.00	4.00	8.00
—Budget-line reissue					
LN-10154	Blue Suede Shoes	1981	2.00	4.00	8.00
—Budget-line reissue					
LO-12324	Johnny Rivers' Golden Hits	198?	2.00	4.00	8.00
—Budget-line reissue					
LW-12427	A Touch of Gold	198?	2.00	4.00	8.00
—Budget-line reissue					
MCA					
917	Greatest Hits	1985	2.50	5.00	10.00
PICKWICK					
PC-3022 [M]	Johnny Rivers	196?	2.50	5.00	10.00
SPC-3022 [S]	Johnny Rivers	196?	3.00	6.00	12.00
RSO					
RS-1-3082	Borrowed Time	1980	2.50	5.00	10.00
SEARS					
SPS-417	Mr. Teenage	196?	6.25	12.50	25.00
SPS-487	Groovin'	1968	6.25	12.50	25.00
SOUL CITY					
SC 1007-1	Greatest Hits	1998	5.00	10.00	20.00
—500 copies, each autographed by Johnny Rivers					
SUNSET					
SUM-1157 [M]	Whiskey A-Go-Go Revisited	1967	3.00	6.00	12.00
SUS-5157 [S]	Whiskey A-Go-Go Revisited	1967	2.50	5.00	10.00
SUS-5251	The Early Years	1969	2.50	5.00	10.00
UNART					
M-20007 [M]	The Great Johnny Rivers	1967	3.00	6.00	12.00
S-21007 [S]	The Great Johnny Rivers	1967	3.00	6.00	12.00
UNITED ARTISTS					
UA-LA075-F	Blue Suede Shoes	1973	3.00	6.00	12.00
USX-93 [(2)]	Johnny Rivers Superpak	1971	5.00	10.00	20.00
UA-LA253-G	The Very Best of Johnny Rivers	1974	3.00	6.00	12.00
UA-LA387-E	The Very Best of Johnny Rivers	1975	3.00	6.00	12.00
UA-LA486-G	Wild Night	1976	3.00	6.00	12.00
UAL-3386 [M]	Go, Johnny, Go	1964	5.00	10.00	20.00
UAS-5532	Home Grown	1971	3.75	7.50	15.00
UAS-5650	L.A. Reggae	1972	3.75	7.50	15.00
UAS-6386 [S]	Go, Johnny, Go	1964	6.25	12.50	25.00
ST-90813 [S]	Go, Johnny, Go	1965	7.50	15.00	30.00
—Capitol Record Club edition					
T-90813 [M]	Go, Johnny, Go	1965	6.25	12.50	25.00
—Capitol Record Club edition					

RIVERS, TONY, AND THE CASTAWAYS

Number	Title (A Side/B Side)	Yr	VG	VG+	NM
45s					
CONSTELLATION					
128	I Love the Way You Walk/I Love You	1964	3.75	7.50	15.00

RIVIERAS, THE (1)

R&B vocal group from northern New Jersey.

Number	Title (A Side/B Side)	Yr	VG	VG+	NM
45s					
COED					
503	Count Every Star/True Love Is Hard to Find	1958	12.50	25.00	50.00
508	Moonlight Serenade/Neither Rain Nor Snow	1959	10.00	20.00	40.00
513	Our Love/True Love Is Hard to Find	1959	7.50	15.00	30.00
513	Our Love/Midnight Flyer	1959	7.50	15.00	30.00
522	Since I Made You Cry/11th Hour Melody	1959	7.50	15.00	30.00
529	Blessing of Love/Moonlight Cocktails	1960	6.25	12.50	25.00
538	My Friend/Great Big Eyes	1960	6.25	12.50	25.00
542	Easy to Remember/Stay in My Heart	1960	6.25	12.50	25.00
551	El Doraado/Refrigerator	1961	6.25	12.50	25.00
592	Moonlight Cocktails/Midnight Flyer	1964	3.75	7.50	15.00
Albums					
POST					
2000	The Rivieras Sing	196?	10.00	20.00	40.00

RIVIERAS, THE (2)

Surf-garage rock band from South Bend, Indiana.

Number	Title (A Side/B Side)	Yr	VG	VG+	NM
45s					
RIVIERA					
1401	California Sun/H.B. Goose Step	1964	5.00	10.00	20.00
1401	California Sun/Played On	1964	10.00	20.00	40.00
—Possibly as few as 1,000 were pressed with this B-side					
1402	Little Donna/Let's Have a Party	1964	3.75	7.50	15.00
1403	Rockin' Robin/Battle Line	1964	3.75	7.50	15.00
1405	Whole Lotta Shakin'/Rip It Up	1965	3.75	7.50	15.00
1405	Whole Lotta Shakin'/Lakeview Lane	1965	5.00	10.00	20.00
1406	Let's Go to Hawaii/Lakeview Lane	1965	3.75	7.50	15.00
1407	Somebody Asked Me/Somebody New	1965	3.75	7.50	15.00
—Credited to the Rivieras, but actually by Bobby Whiteside					
1409	Bug Juice/Never Feel the Pain	1965	5.00	10.00	20.00

Number	Title (A Side/B Side)	Yr	VG	VG+	NM
Albums					
RIVIERA					
701 [M]	Campus Party	1964	62.50	125.00	250.00
U.S.A.					
102 [M]	Let's Have a Party	1964	37.50	75.00	150.00

RIVIERAS, THE (3)

Number	Title (A Side/B Side)	Yr	VG	VG+	NM
45s					
ALGONQUIN					
718	Together Forever/A Night to Remember	1958	50.00	100.00	200.00
—Reissued as "The Ravenairs"					

RIVILEERS, THE

Number	Title (A Side/B Side)	Yr	VG	VG+	NM
45s					
BATON					
200	A Thousand Stars/Hey Chiquita	1953	50.00	100.00	200.00
201	Forever/Darling Farewell	1954	30.00	60.00	120.00
205	Carolyn/Eternal Love	1954	30.00	60.00	120.00
207	(I Love You) For Sentimental Reasons/I Want to See My Baby	1955	15.00	30.00	60.00
209	Little Girl/Don't Ever Leave Me	1955	15.00	30.00	60.00
241	A Thousand Stars/Who Is the Girl	1957	10.00	20.00	40.00

RIVINGTONS, THE

Number	Title (A Side/B Side)	Yr	VG	VG+	NM
45s					
AGC					
5	I Lost the Love/Mind Your Man	1968	2.00	4.00	8.00
A.R.E. AMERICAN					
100	All That Glitters/You Move Me Baby	1964	3.75	7.50	15.00
BATON MASTER					
202	Teach Me Tonight/Reach Our Goal	1967	2.00	4.00	8.00
COLUMBIA					
43581	A Rose Growing in the Ruins/Tend to Business	1966	3.00	6.00	12.00
43772	Yadi Yadi Yum Yum/Yadi Yadi Revisited	1966	3.00	6.00	12.00
J.D.					
122	Don't Hate Your Father (Part 1)/Don't Hate Your Father (Part 2)	1976	—	2.50	5.00
LIBERTY					
1484 [DJ]	Papa-Oom-Mow-Mow (same on both sides)	1982	—	3.00	6.00
—Reissue; promo only					
55427	Papa-Oom-Mow-Mow/Deep Water	1962	6.25	12.50	25.00
55513	Kickapoo Joy Juice/My Reward	1962	3.75	7.50	15.00
55528	Mama-Oom-Mow-Mow/Waiting	1962	3.75	7.50	15.00
55553	The Bird's the Word/I'm Losing My Grip	1963	5.00	10.00	20.00
55585	The Shaky Bird (Part 1)/The Shaky Bird (Part 2)	1963	3.75	7.50	15.00
55610	Little Sally Walker/Cherry	1963	7.50	15.00	30.00
55671	Fairy Tales/Wee Jee Walk	1964	3.75	7.50	15.00
QUAN					
1379	I Don't Want a New Baby/You're Gonna Pay	1967	2.50	5.00	10.00
RCA VICTOR					
74-0301	Pop Your Corn (Part 1)/Pop Your Corn (Part 2)	1969	2.00	4.00	8.00
REPRISE					
0293	I Tried/One Monkey Don't Stop No Show	1964	3.00	6.00	12.00
UNITED ARTISTS					
0096	Papa-Oom-Mow-Mow/The Bird's the Word	1973	—	2.00	4.00
—"Silver Spotlight Series" reissue					
VEE JAY					
634	All That Glitters/You Move Me Baby	1964	3.00	6.00	12.00
649	I Love You Always/Years of Tears	1965	3.00	6.00	12.00
677	The Willy/Just Got to Be Mine	1965	3.00	6.00	12.00
WAND					
11253	Papa-Oom-Mow-Mow/I Don't Want a New Baby	1973	—	2.50	5.00
Albums					
LIBERTY					
LRP-3282 [M]	Doin' the Bird	1963	25.00	50.00	100.00
LST-7282 [S]	Doin' the Bird	1963	50.00	100.00	200.00

ROAD, THE

Number	Title (A Side/B Side)	Yr	VG	VG+	NM
45s					
BLUE ONION					
106	It's So Hard to Find/You Rub Me the Wrong Way	1969	7.50	15.00	30.00
KAMA SUTRA					
256	She's Not There/A Bummer	1968	2.00	4.00	8.00
266	The Grass Looks Greener on the Other Side/In Love	1969	2.00	4.00	8.00
267	Mr. Soul/I Can Only Give You Everything	1969	2.00	4.00	8.00
504	Mr. Soul/The Grass Looks Greener on the Other Side	1970	—	3.00	6.00
531	Alone/If You Ever Needed a Woman	1971	—	3.00	6.00
Albums					
KAMA SUTRA					
KSBS-2012	The Road	1970	3.75	7.50	15.00
—Reissue of 8075					
KSBS-2032 [(2)]	Cognition	1970	5.00	10.00	20.00
KLPS-8075	The Road	1969	5.00	10.00	20.00

ROAD RUNNERS, THE

More than one group. Also see GARY PAXTON.

Number	Title (A Side/B Side)	Yr	VG	VG+	NM
45s					
CHALLENGE					
9197	Dead Man/Pretty Girls	1963	5.00	10.00	20.00
FELSTED					
8692	Quasimoto/Road Runnah	1964	10.00	20.00	40.00
MIRAMAR					
116	Take Me/I'll Make It Up to You	1965	3.75	7.50	15.00
MOROCCO					
001	Goodbye/Tell Her You Love Her	1966	5.00	10.00	20.00
REPRISE					
0418	Take Me/I'll Make It Up to You	1965	3.75	7.50	15.00

Number	Title (A Side/B Side)	Yr	VG	VG+	NM
Albums					
LONDON					
PS 381 [S]	The New Mustang (And Other Hot Rod Hits)	1964	75.00	150.00	300.00
LL 3381 [M]	The New Mustang (And Other Hot Rod Hits)	1964	50.00	100.00	200.00

ROBB, DEE

Later of THE ROBBS.

Number	Title (A Side/B Side)	Yr	VG	VG+	NM
45s					
ARGO					
5439	Bye Bye Baby/The Prom	1963	3.00	6.00	12.00
SCORE					
1006	He's Got the Whole World in His Hands/Say That Thing	1964	3.75	7.50	15.00

ROBBINS, EDDIE

Number	Title (A Side/B Side)	Yr	VG	VG+	NM
45s					
DAVID					
1001	Janice/It Was Fun	196?	6.25	12.50	25.00
DOT					
15702	A Girl Like You/Dear Parents	1958	10.00	20.00	40.00
POWER					
214	A Girl Like You/Dear Parents	1958	30.00	60.00	120.00

ROBBINS, MARTY

Number	Title (A Side/B Side)	Yr	VG	VG+	NM
45s					
AUDIOGRAPH					
454	Love Me/Safely in the Arms of Jesus	1983	—	2.50	5.00
—With Jeanne Pruett; Pruett solo on B-side					
COLUMBIA					
02444	Jumper Cable Man/Good Hearted Woman	1981	—	2.00	4.00
02575	Teardrops on My Heart/Honeycomb	1981	—	2.00	4.00
02854	Lover, Lover/Some Memories Just Won't Die	1982	—	2.00	4.00
03236	Tie Your Dream to Mine/That's All She Wrote	1982	—	2.00	4.00
03789	Change of Heart/Devil in a Cowboy Hat	1983	—	2.00	4.00
03927	Baby That's Love/What If I Said I Love You	1983	—	2.00	4.00
10305	El Paso City/When I'm Gone	1976	—	2.50	5.00
10396	Among My Souvenirs/She's Just a Drifter	1976	—	2.50	5.00
10472	Adios Amigo/Helen	1977	—	2.50	5.00
10536	I Don't Know Why (I Just Do)/Inspiration for a Song	1977	—	2.50	5.00
10629	Don't Let Me Touch You/Tomorrow, Tomorrow, Tomorrow	1977	—	2.50	5.00
10673	Return to Me/More Than Anything, I Miss You	1978	—	2.50	5.00
10821	Please Don't Play a Love Song/Jenny	1978	—	2.50	5.00
10905	Touch Me with Magic/Confused and Lonely	1979	—	2.50	5.00
11016	All Around Cowboy/The Dreamer	1979	—	2.50	5.00
11102	Buenos Dias Argentina/Ballad of a Small Man	1979	—	2.50	5.00
11240	She's Made of Faith/Misery in My Soul	1980	—	2.00	4.00
11291	One Man's Trash (Is Another Man's Treasure)/I Can't Wait Until Tomorrow	1980	—	2.00	4.00
11372	An Occasional Rose/Holding On to You	1980	—	2.00	4.00
11425	Completely Out of Love/Another Cup of Coffee	1981	—	2.00	4.00
20925	Tomorrow You'll Be Gone/Love Me or Leave Me Alone	1952	7.50	15.00	30.00
20965	Crying 'Cause I Love You/I Wish Somebody Loved Me	1952	7.50	15.00	30.00
21022	I'll Go On Alone/You're Breaking My Heart	1952	7.50	15.00	30.00
21032	My Isle of Golden Dreams/Sweet Hawaiian Dream	1952	—	—	—
—Unreleased					
21075	I Couldn't Keep from Crying/After You Leave	1953	7.50	15.00	30.00
21111	A Castle in the Sky/A Half-Way Chance with You	1953	7.50	15.00	30.00
21145	Sing Me Something Sentimental/At the End of Long, Lonely Days	1953	7.50	15.00	30.00
21172	Blesserd Jesus Should I Fall Don't Let Me Lay/Kneel and Let the Lord Take Your Load	1953	7.50	15.00	30.00
21176	Don't Make Me Ashamed/It's a Long, Long Ride	1953	7.50	15.00	30.00
21213	My Isle of Golden Dreams/Aloha Oe	1954	7.50	15.00	30.00
21246	Pretty Words/Your Heart's Turn to Break	1954	7.50	15.00	30.00
21291	Call Me Up (And I'll Come Calling on You)/I'm Too Big to Cry	1954	7.50	15.00	30.00
21324	Time Goes By/It's a Pity What Money Can Do	1954	7.50	15.00	30.00
21351	That's All Right/Gossip	1955	12.50	25.00	50.00
21352	God Understands/Have Thine Own Way, Lord	1955	6.25	12.50	25.00
21388	Daddy Loves You/Pray for Me, Mother of Mine	1955	6.25	12.50	25.00
21414	It Looks Like I'm Just in the Way/I'll Love You Till the Day I Die	1955	6.25	12.50	25.00
21446	Maybellene/This Broken Heart of Mine	1955	12.50	25.00	50.00
21461	Pretty Mama/Don't Let Me Hang Around	1955	12.50	25.00	50.00
21477	Tennessee Toddy/Mean Mama Blues	1955	12.50	25.00	50.00
21508	Singing the Blues/I Can't Quit (I've Gone Too Far)	1956	10.00	20.00	40.00
21525	I'll Know You're Gone/How Long Will It Be	1956	6.25	12.50	25.00
—With Lee Emerson					
21545	Singing the Blues/I Can't Quit (I've Gone Too Far)	1956	7.50	15.00	30.00
30511 [S]	El Paso/Running Gun	1959	7.50	15.00	30.00
—"Stereo Seven" (small hole, plays at 33 1/3 rpm)					
31124 [S]	titles unknown	1961	5.00	10.00	20.00
—"Stereo Seven" single, small hole, plays at 33 1/3 rpm					
31125 [S]	Answer Me My Love/Clara	1961	5.00	10.00	20.00
—"Stereo Seven" single, small hole, plays at 33 1/3 rpm					
31126 [S]	Half As Much/Unchained Melody	1961	5.00	10.00	20.00
—"Stereo Seven" single, small hole, plays at 33 1/3 rpm					
31127 [S]	titles unknown	1961	5.00	10.00	20.00
—"Stereo Seven" single, small hole, plays at 33 1/3 rpm					
31128 [S]	titles unknown	1961	5.00	10.00	20.00
—"Stereo Seven" single, small hole, plays at 33 1/3 rpm					
31747 [S]	titles unknown	1963	5.00	10.00	20.00
—"Stereo Seven" single, small hole, plays at 33 1/3 rpm					
31748 [S]	titles unknown	1963	5.00	10.00	20.00
—"Stereo Seven" single, small hole, plays at 33 1/3 rpm					
31749 [S]	titles unknown	1963	5.00	10.00	20.00
—"Stereo Seven" single, small hole, plays at 33 1/3 rpm					
31750 [S]	Progressive Love/Love Is a Hurting Thing	1963	5.00	10.00	20.00
—"Stereo Seven" single, small hole, plays at 33 1/3 rpm					

Number	Title (A Side/B Side)	Yr	VG	VG+	NM
31751 [S]	Kinda Halfway Feel/The Wine Flowed Freely	1963	5.00	10.00	20.00
—"Stereo Seven" single, small hole, plays at 33 1/3 rpm					
40679	Long Tall Sally/Mr. Teardrop	1956	12.50	25.00	50.00
40706	Respectfully Miss Brooks/You Don't Owe Me a Thing	1956	12.50	25.00	50.00
40815	Knee Deep in the Blues/The Same Two Lips	1957	6.25	12.50	25.00
40864	A White Sport Coat (And a Pink Carnation)/Grown Up Tears	1957	6.25	12.50	25.00
40864 [PS]	A White Sport Coat (And a Pink Carnation)/Grown Up Tears	1957	10.00	20.00	40.00
40868	I Cried Like a Baby/Where D'Ja Go	1957	6.25	12.50	25.00
—With Lee Emerson					
40969	Please Don't Blame Me/Teen-Age Dream	1957	6.25	12.50	25.00
41013	The Story of My Life/Once-a-Week Date	1957	6.25	12.50	25.00
41013 [PS]	The Story of My Life/Once-a-Week Date	1957	10.00	20.00	40.00
41143	Just Married/Stairway of Love	1958	5.00	10.00	20.00
41208	She Was Only Seventeen (He Was One Year More)/Sittin' in a Tree House	1958	5.00	10.00	20.00
41208 [PS]	She Was Only Seventeen (He Was One Year More)/Sittin' in a Tree House	1958	10.00	20.00	40.00
41282	Ain't I the Lucky One/The Last Time I Saw My Heart	1958	5.00	10.00	20.00
41325	The Hanging Tree/The Blues, Country Style	1959	5.00	10.00	20.00
41325 [PS]	The Hanging Tree/The Blues, Country Style	1959	10.00	20.00	40.00
41408	Cap and Gown/Last Night About This Time	1959	5.00	10.00	20.00
41511 [M]	El Paso/Running Gun	1959	5.00	10.00	20.00
41511 [PS]	El Paso/Running Gun	1959	7.50	15.00	30.00
41589	Big Iron/Saddle Tramp	1960	3.75	7.50	15.00
41686	Is There Any Chance/I Told My Heart	1960	3.75	7.50	15.00
41766	Don't Worry/A Time and a Place for Everything	1960	—	—	—
—Unreleased					
41771	Five Brothers/Ride, Cowboy, Ride	1960	3.75	7.50	15.00
41809	Ballad of the Alamo/A Time and a Place for Everything	1960	3.75	7.50	15.00
41809 [PS]	Ballad of the Alamo/A Time and a Place for Everything	1960	7.50	15.00	30.00
41922	Don't Worry/Like All the Other Times	1961	3.75	7.50	15.00
41922 [PS]	Don't Worry/Like All the Other Times	1961	6.25	12.50	25.00
42008	Jimmy Martinez/Ghost Train	1961	3.75	7.50	15.00
42008 [PS]	Jimmy Martinez/Ghost Train	1961	6.25	12.50	25.00
42065	It's Your World/You Told Me So	1961	3.75	7.50	15.00
42065 [PS]	It's Your World/You Told Me So	1961	6.25	12.50	25.00
42246	I Told the Brook/Sometimes I'm Tempted	1961	3.75	7.50	15.00
42246 [PS]	I Told the Brook/Sometimes I'm Tempted	1961	6.25	12.50	25.00
42375	Love Can't Wait/Too Far Gone	1962	3.75	7.50	15.00
42375 [PS]	Love Can't Wait/Too Far Gone	1962	6.25	12.50	25.00
42486	Devil Woman/April Fool's Day	1962	3.75	7.50	15.00
42486 [PS]	Devil Woman/April Fool's Day	1962	6.25	12.50	25.00
42614	Ruby Ann/Won't You Forgive	1962	3.75	7.50	15.00
42614 [PS]	Ruby Ann/Won't You Forgive	1962	6.25	12.50	25.00
42672	Hawaii's Calling Me/Ka-Lu-A	1963	3.00	6.00	12.00
42701	Cigarettes and Coffee Blues/Teenager's Dad	1963	3.00	6.00	12.00
42701 [PS]	Cigarettes and Coffee Blues/Teenager's Dad	1963	6.25	12.50	25.00
42781	No Sign of Loneliness Here/I'm Not Ready Yet	1963	3.00	6.00	12.00
42781 [PS]	No Sign of Loneliness Here/I'm Not Ready Yet	1963	6.25	12.50	25.00
42831	Not So Long Ago/I Hope You Learn a Lot	1963	3.00	6.00	12.00
42890	Begging to You/Over High Mountain	1963	3.00	6.00	12.00
42968	Girl from Spanish Town/Kingston Girl	1964	2.50	5.00	10.00
43049	The Cowboy in the Continental Suit/Man Walks Among Us	1964	2.50	5.00	10.00
43134	One of These Days/Up in the Air	1964	2.50	5.00	10.00
43196	I Eish-Tay-Mah-Su (I Love You)/A Whole Lot Easier	1964	2.50	5.00	10.00
43258	Ribbon of Darkness/Little Robin	1965	2.50	5.00	10.00
43377	Old Red/Matilda	1965	2.00	4.00	8.00
43428	While You're Dancing/Lonely Too Long	1965	2.00	4.00	8.00
43500	Count Me Out/Private Wilson White	1965	2.00	4.00	8.00
43651	Ain't I Right/My Own Native Land	1966	—	—	—
—Unreleased					
43680	The Shoe Goes On the Other Foot Tonight/It Kind of Reminds Me of You	1966	2.00	4.00	8.00
43845	No Tears Milady/Fly Butterfly Fly	1966	2.00	4.00	8.00
43870	Mr. Shorty/Tall Handsome Strangers	1966	2.00	4.00	8.00
44128	Tonight Carmen/Waiting in Reno	1967	—	3.00	6.00
44271	Gardenias in Her Hair/In the Valley of the Rio Grande	1967	—	3.00	6.00
44509	Love Is In the Air/I've Been Leaving Everyday	1968	—	3.00	6.00
44633	I Walk Alone/Lily of the Valley	1968	—	3.00	6.00
44641	It Finally Happened/Big Mouthin' Around	1968	—	3.00	6.00
—By "Marty Robbins Jr. and Sr."					
44739	It's a Sin/I Feel Another Heartache Coming On	1969	—	2.50	5.00
44895	I Can't Say Goodbye/Hello Daily News	1969	—	2.50	5.00
44968	Girl from Spanish Town/Kingston Girl	1969	2.00	4.00	8.00
45024	Camelia/Virginia	1969	—	2.50	5.00
45091	My Woman, My Woman, My Wife/Martha Ellen Jenkins	1970	—	2.50	5.00
45215	Jolie Girl/The City	1970	—	2.50	5.00
45273	Padre/At Times	1970	—	3.00	6.00
45346	Little Spot in Heaven/Wait a Little Longer Please, Jesus	1971	—	3.00	6.00
45377	The Chair/Seventeen Years	1971	—	2.50	5.00
45442	Early Morning Sunshine/Another Day Has Gone By	1971	—	2.50	5.00
45520	The Best Part of Living/Gone with the Wind	1971	—	2.50	5.00
45668	I've Got a Woman's Love/A Little Spot in Heaven	1972	—	2.50	5.00
45775	Laura (What's He Got That I Ain't Got)/It Kind of Reminds Me of You	1973	—	2.50	5.00
DECCA					
33006	This Much a Man/Guess I'll Stand Here Looking Dumb	1972	—	3.50	7.00
MCA					
40012	Franklin, Tennessee/Walking Piece of Heaven	1973	—	2.50	5.00
40067	A Man and a Train/Las Vegas, Nevada	1973	—	2.50	5.00
40134	Love Me/Crawling on My Knees	1973	—	2.50	5.00
40172	I'm Wanting To/Twentieth Century Drifter	1973	—	2.50	5.00
40236	Don't You Think/I Couldn't Believe It Was True	1974	—	2.50	5.00

Number	Title (A Side/B Side)	Yr	VG	VG+	NM
40296	Two-Gun Daddy/Queen of the Big Rodeo	1974	—	2.50	5.00
40342	Life/It Takes Faith	1974	—	2.50	5.00
40425	These Are My Souvenirs/Shotgun Rider	1975	—	2.50	5.00
52197	Two Gun Daddy/Life	1983	—	2.50	5.00
WARNER BROS.					
29847	Honkytonk Man/Shotgun Rag	1982	—	2.00	4.00
—B-side by Johnny Gimble and the Texas Swing Band					
7-Inch Extended Plays					
COLUMBIA					
B-1785	I'll Go On Alone/Crying 'Cause I Love You//I Couldn't Keep from Crying/A Half-Way Chance with You	1953	15.00	30.00	60.00
B-1785 [PS]	Marty Robbins	1953	15.00	30.00	60.00
B-2116	(contents unknown)	1956	12.50	25.00	50.00
B-2116 [PS]	Singing the Blues	1956	12.50	25.00	50.00
B-2134	(contents unknown)	1957	10.00	20.00	40.00
B-2134 [PS]	A White Sport Coat	1957	10.00	20.00	40.00
B-2153	The Letter Edged in Black/The Little Rosewood Casket//The Dream of a Miner's Child/The Convict and the Rose	1957	7.50	15.00	30.00
B-2153 [PS]	Marty Robbins	1957	7.50	15.00	30.00
B-2808	I Couldn't Keep from Crying/Sing Me Something Sentimental//Tennessee Toddy/You Don't Owe Me a Thing	1957	12.50	25.00	50.00
B-2808 [PS]	Marty Robbins	1957	12.50	25.00	50.00
B-2814	(contents unknown)	1958	3.00	6.00	12.00
B-2814 [PS]	Marty Robbins	1958	3.00	6.00	12.00
B-9761	Lovesick Blues/I'm So Lonesome I Could Cry//It's Too Late Now/Rose of Ol' Pawnee	1957	3.75	7.50	15.00
B-9761 [PS]	The Song of Robbins Vol. I	1957	3.75	7.50	15.00
B-9762	I Never Let You Cross My Mind/I Hang My Head and Cry//You Only Want Me When You're Lonely/Moanin' the Blues	1957	3.75	7.50	15.00
B-9762 [PS]	The Song of Robbins Vol. II	1957	3.75	7.50	15.00
B-9763	I'll Step Aside/All the World Is Lonely Now//Bouquet of Roses/Have I Told You Lately That I Love You?	1957	3.75	7.50	15.00
B-9763 [PS]	The Song of Robbins, Vol. III	1957	3.75	7.50	15.00
B-10871	(contents unknown)	1957	3.75	7.50	15.00
B-10871 [PS]	Song of the Islands	1957	3.75	7.50	15.00
B-11891	Kaw-Liga/Waltz of the Wind//Then I Turned and Walked Slowly Away/A House with Everything But Love	1958	3.75	7.50	15.00
B-11891 [PS]	Marty Robbins	1958	3.75	7.50	15.00
B-13491	El Paso/A Hundred and Sixty Acres//They're Hanging Me Tonight/The Strawberry Roan	1959	3.00	6.00	12.00
B-13491 [PS]	Gunfighter Ballads and Trail Songs, Vol. I	1959	3.00	6.00	12.00
B-13492	Big Iron/In the Valley//Running Gun/Utah Carol	1959	3.00	6.00	12.00
B-13492 [PS]	Gunfighter Ballads and Trail Songs, Vol. II	1959	3.00	6.00	12.00
B-13493	Cool Water/The Master's Call//Billy the Kid/The Little Green Valley	1959	3.75	7.50	15.00
B-13493 [PS]	Gunfighter Ballads and Trail Songs, Vol. III	1959	3.75	7.50	15.00
B-14811	(contents unknown)	1960	3.00	6.00	12.00
B-14811 [PS]	More Gunfighter Ballads and Trail Songs, Vol. I	1960	3.00	6.00	12.00
B-14812	(contents unknown)	1960	3.00	6.00	12.00
B-14812 [PS]	More Gunfighter Ballads and Trail Songs, Vol. II	1960	3.00	6.00	12.00
B-14813	(contents unknown)	1960	3.00	6.00	12.00
B-14813 [PS]	More Gunfighter Ballads and Trail Songs, Vol. III	1960	3.00	6.00	12.00
Albums					
ARTCO					
110	The Best of Marty Robbins	1973	10.00	20.00	40.00
COLUMBIA					
GP 15 [(2)]	Marty's Country	1969	6.25	12.50	25.00
CL 976 [M]	The Song of Robbins	1957	25.00	50.00	100.00
—Red and black label with six "eye" logos					
CL 976 [M]	The Song of Robbins	1963	5.00	10.00	20.00
—Red label with "Guaranteed High Fidelity" or "360 Sound Mono"					
CL 1087 [M]	Song of the Islands	1957	30.00	60.00	120.00
—Red and black label with six "eye" logos					
CL 1087 [M]	Song of the Islands	1963	5.00	10.00	20.00
—Red label with "Guaranteed High Fidelity" or "360 Sound Mono"					
CL 1189 [M]	Marty Robbins	1958	20.00	40.00	80.00
—Red and black label with six "eye" logos					
CL 1189 [M]	Marty Robbins	1963	5.00	10.00	20.00
—Red label with "Guaranteed High Fidelity" or "360 Sound Mono"					
CL 1325 [M]	Marty's Greatest Hits	1959	20.00	40.00	80.00
—Red and black label with six "eye" logos					
CL 1325 [M]	Marty's Greatest Hits	1963	5.00	10.00	20.00
—Red label with "Guaranteed High Fidelity" or "360 Sound Mono"					
CL 1349 [M]	Gunfighter Ballads and Trail Songs	1959	7.50	15.00	30.00
—Red and black label with six "eye" logos					
CL 1349 [M]	Gunfighter Ballads and Trail Songs	1963	3.75	7.50	15.00
—Red label with "Guaranteed High Fidelity" or "360 Sound Mono"					
CL 1481 [M]	More Gunfighter Ballads and Trail Songs	1960	7.50	15.00	30.00
—Red and black label with six "eye" logos					
CL 1481 [M]	More Gunfighter Ballads and Trail Songs	1963	3.75	7.50	15.00
—Red label with "Guaranteed High Fidelity" or "360 Sound Mono"					
CL 1635 [M]	More Greatest Hits	1961	6.25	12.50	25.00
—Red and black label with six "eye" logos					
CL 1635 [M]	More Greatest Hits	1963	3.75	7.50	15.00
—Red label with "Guaranteed High Fidelity" or "360 Sound Mono"					
CL 1666 [M]	Just a Little Sentimental	1961	6.25	12.50	25.00
—Red and black label with six "eye" logos					
CL 1666 [M]	Just a Little Sentimental	1963	3.75	7.50	15.00
—Red label with "Guaranteed High Fidelity" or "360 Sound Mono"					
CL 1801 [M]	Marty After Midnight	1962	12.50	25.00	50.00
—Red and black label with six "eye" logos					
CL 1801 [M]	Marty After Midnight	1962	5.00	10.00	20.00
—Red label with "Guaranteed High Fidelity"					
CL 1801 [M]	Marty After Midnight	1965	3.75	7.50	15.00
—Red label with "360 Sound Mono"					
CL 1855 [M]	Portrait of Marty	1962	10.00	20.00	40.00
CL 1855/CS 8655	Portrait of Marty Bonus Photo	1962	7.50	15.00	30.00
CL 1918 [M]	Devil Woman	1962	6.25	12.50	25.00
—Red label with "Guaranteed High Fidelity"					

Number	Title (A Side/B Side)	Yr	VG	VG+	NM
CL 1918 [M]	Devil Woman	1965	3.75	7.50	15.00
—Red label with "360 Sound Mono"					
CL 2040 [M]	Hawaii's Calling Me	1963	6.25	12.50	25.00
—Red label with "Guaranteed High Fidelity"					
CL 2040 [M]	Hawaii's Calling Me	1965	3.75	7.50	15.00
—Red label with "360 Sound Mono"					
CL 2072 [M]	Return of the Gunfighter	1963	5.00	10.00	20.00
—Red label with "Guaranteed High Fidelity"					
CL 2072 [M]	Return of the Gunfighter	1965	3.75	7.50	15.00
—Red label with "360 Sound Mono"					
CL 2176 [M]	Island Woman	1964	7.50	15.00	30.00
—Red label with "Guaranteed High Fidelity"					
CL 2176 [M]	Island Woman	1965	5.00	10.00	20.00
—Red label with "360 Sound Mono"					
CL 2220 [M]	R.F.D.	1964	5.00	10.00	20.00
—Red label with "Guaranteed High Fidelity"					
CL 2220 [M]	R.F.D.	1965	3.75	7.50	15.00
—Red label with "360 Sound Mono"					
CL 2304 [M]	Turn the Lights Down Low	1965	6.25	12.50	25.00
—Red label with "Guaranteed High Fidelity"					
CL 2304 [M]	Turn the Lights Down Low	1965	3.75	7.50	15.00
—Red label with "360 Sound Mono"					
CL 2448 [M]	What God Has Done	1966	3.75	7.50	15.00
CL 2527 [M]	The Drifter	1966	3.75	7.50	15.00
CL 2601 [10]	Rock 'N Roll 'N Robbins	1956	250.00	500.00	1000.
CL 2645 [M]	My Kind of Country	1967	6.25	12.50	25.00
CL 2725 [M]	Tonight Carmen	1967	7.50	15.00	30.00
CL 2735 [M]	Christmas with Marty Robbins	1967	12.50	25.00	50.00
CL 2817 [M]	By the Time I Get to Phoenix	1968	15.00	30.00	60.00
CS 8158 [S]	Gunfighter Ballads and Trail Songs	1959	10.00	20.00	40.00
—Red and black label with six "eye" logos					
CS 8158 [S]	Gunfighter Ballads and Trail Songs	1963	5.00	10.00	20.00
—Red label with "360 Sound Stereo"					
CS 8158 [S]	Gunfighter Ballads and Trail Songs	1971	2.50	5.00	10.00
—Orange label					
PC 8158	Gunfighter Ballads and Trail Songs	198?	2.00	4.00	8.00
—Reissue with new prefix					
CS 8272 [S]	More Gunfighter Ballads and Trail Songs	1960	10.00	20.00	40.00
—Red and black label with six "eye" logos					
CS 8272 [S]	More Gunfighter Ballads and Trail Songs	1963	5.00	10.00	20.00
—Red label with "360 Sound Stereo"					
CS 8272 [S]	More Gunfighter Ballads and Trail Songs	1971	2.50	5.00	10.00
—Orange label					
PC 8272	More Gunfighter Ballads and Trail SongsMore	198?	2.00	4.00	8.00
—Reissue with new prefix					
CS 8435 [S]	More Greatest Hits	1961	7.50	15.00	30.00
—Red and black label with six "eye" logos					
CS 8435 [S]	More Greatest Hits	1963	5.00	10.00	20.00
—Red label with "360 Sound Stereo"					
CS 8435 [S]	More Greatest Hits	1971	2.50	5.00	10.00
—Orange label					
PC 8435	More Greatest Hits	198?	2.00	4.00	8.00
—Reissue with new prefix					
CS 8466 [S]	Just a Little Sentimental	1961	7.50	15.00	30.00
—Red and black label with six "eye" logos					
CS 8466 [S]	Just a Little Sentimental	1963	5.00	10.00	20.00
—Red label with "360 Sound Stereo"					
CS 8601 [S]	Marty After Midnight	1962	20.00	40.00	80.00
—Red and black label with six "eye" logos					
CS 8601 [S]	Marty After Midnight	1962	7.50	15.00	30.00
—Red label with "360 Sound Stereo" in black					
CS 8601 [S]	Marty After Midnight	1965	5.00	10.00	20.00
—Red label with "360 Sound Stereo" in white					
CS 8639 [P]	Marty's Greatest Hits	1962	7.50	15.00	30.00
—Red label with "360 Sound Stereo" in black					
CS 8639 [P]	Marty's Greatest Hits	1965	5.00	10.00	20.00
—Red label with "360 Sound Stereo" in white					
CS 8639 [P]	Marty's Greatest Hits	1970	2.50	5.00	10.00
—Orange label					
PC 8639	Marty's Greatest Hits	198?	2.00	4.00	8.00
—Reissue with new prefix					
CS 8655 [S]	Portrait of Marty	1962	12.50	25.00	50.00
CS 8718 [S]	Devil Woman	1962	7.50	15.00	30.00
—Red label with "360 Sound Stereo" in black					
CS 8718 [S]	Devil Woman	1965	5.00	10.00	20.00
—Red label with "360 Sound Stereo" in white					
CS 8718 [S]	Devil Woman	1970	2.50	5.00	10.00
—Orange label					
CS 8840 [S]	Hawaii's Calling Me	1963	7.50	15.00	30.00
—Red label with "360 Sound Stereo" in black					
CS 8840 [S]	Hawaii's Calling Me	1965	5.00	10.00	20.00
—Red label with "360 Sound Stereo" in white					
CS 8872 [S]	Return of the Gunfighter	1963	6.25	12.50	25.00
—Red label with "360 Sound Stereo" in black					
CS 8872 [S]	Return of the Gunfighter	1965	5.00	10.00	20.00
—Red label with "360 Sound Stereo" in white					
CS 8872 [S]	Return of the Gunfighter	1970	2.50	5.00	10.00
—Orange label					
CS 8976 [S]	Island Woman	1964	10.00	20.00	40.00
—Red label with "360 Sound Stereo" in black					
CS 8976 [S]	Island Woman	1965	7.50	15.00	30.00
—Red label with "360 Sound Stereo" in white					
CS 9020 [S]	R.F.D.	1964	6.25	12.50	25.00
—Red label with "360 Sound Stereo" in black					
CS 9020 [S]	R.F.D.	1965	5.00	10.00	20.00
—Red label with "360 Sound Stereo" in white					
CS 9104 [S]	Turn the Lights Down Low	1965	7.50	15.00	30.00
—Red label with "360 Sound Stereo" in black					
CS 9104 [S]	Turn the Lights Down Low	1965	5.00	10.00	20.00
—Red label with "360 Sound Stereo" in white					
CS 9248 [S]	What God Has Done	1966	5.00	10.00	20.00
—Red "360 Sound" label					
CS 9248 [S]	What God Has Done	1970	2.50	5.00	10.00
—Orange label					
CS 9327 [S]	The Drifter	1966	5.00	10.00	20.00
—Red "360 Sound" label					
CS 9327 [S]	The Drifter	1970	2.50	5.00	10.00
—Orange label					
CS 9421 [R]	The Song of Robbins	1967	3.75	7.50	15.00
—Red "360 Sound" label					
CS 9421 [R]	The Song of Robbins	1970	2.50	5.00	10.00
—Orange label					
CS 9425 [R]	Song of the Islands	1967	3.75	7.50	15.00
CS 9445 [S]	My Kind of Country	1967	5.00	10.00	20.00
CS 9525 [S]	Tonight Carmen	1967	5.00	10.00	20.00
—Red "360 Sound" label					
CS 9525 [S]	Tonight Carmen	1970	2.50	5.00	10.00
—Orange label					
3C 9535	Christmas with Marty Robbins	198?	2.50	5.00	10.00
—Budget-line reissue					
CS 9535 [S]	Christmas with Marty Robbins	1967	7.50	15.00	30.00
CS 9617 [S]	By the Time I Get to Phoenix	1968	5.00	10.00	20.00
CS 9725	I Walk Alone	1968	5.00	10.00	20.00
—Red "360 Sound" label					
CS 9725	I Walk Alone	1970	2.50	5.00	10.00
—Orange label					
CS 9811	It's a Sin	1969	5.00	10.00	20.00
—Red "360 Sound" label					
CS 9811	It's a Sin	1970	2.50	5.00	10.00
—Orange label					
CS 9978	My Woman, My Woman, My Wife	1970	5.00	10.00	20.00
—Red "360 Sound" label					
CS 9978	My Woman, My Woman, My Wife	1970	3.75	7.50	15.00
—Orange label					
PC 30316	El Paso	198?	2.00	4.00	8.00
—Reissue of Harmony 30316					
C 30571	Marty Robbins' Greatest Hits Vol. III	1971	3.75	7.50	15.00
PC 30571	Marty Robbins' Greatest Hits Vol. III	198?	2.00	4.00	8.00
—Budget-line reissue					
CG 30811 [(2)]	The World of Marty Robbins	1971	4.50	9.00	18.00
C 30816	Today	1971	3.75	7.50	15.00
G 30881 [(2)]	The World of Marty Robbins	1971	5.00	10.00	20.00
KC 31341	Bound for Old Mexico (Great Hits from South of the Border)	1973	3.75	7.50	15.00
CG 31361 [(2)]	All Time Greatest Hits	1972	4.50	9.00	18.00
KG 31361 [(2)]	Marty Robbins' All-Time Greatest Hits	1972	5.00	10.00	20.00
KC 31628	I've Got a Woman's Love	1972	3.75	7.50	15.00
KC 32586	Have I Told You Lately That I Love You	1974	3.75	7.50	15.00
KC 33476	No Sign of Loneliness Here	1976	3.00	6.00	12.00
CG 33630 [(2)]	Gunfighter Ballads and Trail Songs/My Woman, My Woman, My Wife	1976	3.75	7.50	15.00
PC 34303	El Paso City	1976	3.00	6.00	12.00
—No bar code on cover					
PC 34306	El Paso City	198?	2.00	4.00	8.00
—With bar code on cover					
PC 34408	Adios Amigo	1977	3.00	6.00	12.00
—No bar code on cover					
PC 34448	Adios Amigo	198?	2.00	4.00	8.00
—With bar code on cover					
KC 35040	Don't Let Me Touch You	1977	3.00	6.00	12.00
JC 35446	The Performer	1979	3.00	6.00	12.00
KC 35629	Greatest Hits Vol. IV	1978	3.00	6.00	12.00
JC 36085	All Around Cowboy	1979	3.00	6.00	12.00
PC 36085	All Around Cowboy	198?	2.00	4.00	8.00
—Budget-line reissue					
JC 36507	With Love	1980	3.00	6.00	12.00
JC 36860	Everything I've Always Wanted	1981	3.00	6.00	12.00
FC 37353	Encore	1981	3.00	6.00	12.00
PC 37353	Encore	198?	2.00	4.00	8.00
—Budget-line reissue					
FC 37541	The Legend	1982	3.00	6.00	12.00
PC 37541	The Legend	1985	2.00	4.00	8.00
—Budget-line reissue					
FC 37995	Come Back to Me	1982	3.00	6.00	12.00
PC 37995	Come Back to Me	198?	2.00	4.00	8.00
—Budget-line reissue					
FC 38309	Biggest Hits	1982	3.00	6.00	12.00
FC 38603	Some Memories Just Won't Die	1983	3.00	6.00	12.00
C2 38870 [(2)]	A Lifetime of Song 1951-1982	1983	3.75	7.50	15.00
KC2 39575 [(2)]	Long, Long Ago	1984	3.75	7.50	15.00
COLUMBIA MUSICAL TREASURY					
P5S 5812 [(5)]	Marty	1972	10.00	20.00	40.00
COLUMBIA RECORD CLUB					
DS 445	Bend in the River	1968	10.00	20.00	40.00
COLUMBIA SPECIAL PRODUCTS					
C 10980 [S]	Christmas with Marty Robbins	1972	3.75	7.50	15.00
—Stereo reissue; "Distributed by Apex Rendezvous, Inc." on back cover					
C 11122	Marty's Greatest Hits	1972	3.00	6.00	12.00
C 11311	By the Time I Get to Phoenix	1972	3.75	7.50	15.00
C 11513	By the Time I Get to Phoenix	1973	3.75	7.50	15.00
P 12416	Marty Robbins' Own Favorites	1974	3.75	7.50	15.00
P 13358	Christmas with Marty Robbins	1976	3.00	6.00	12.00
P 14035	Legendary Music Man	1977	3.00	6.00	12.00
P 14613	The Best of Marty Robbins	1978	2.50	5.00	10.00
P 15594	The Number One Cowboy	1981	2.50	5.00	10.00
P 15812	Marty Robbins' Best	1982	2.50	5.00	10.00
P 16561	Reflections	1982	2.50	5.00	10.00
3P 16578 [(3)]	Classics	1983	5.00	10.00	20.00
P 16914	Country Classics	1983	2.50	5.00	10.00
P 17120	Sincerely	1983	2.50	5.00	10.00
P 17136	Forever Yours	1983	2.50	5.00	10.00
P 17137	That Country Feeling	1983	2.50	5.00	10.00
P 17138	Banquet of Songs	1983	2.50	5.00	10.00
P 17159	The Great Marty Robbins	1983	2.50	5.00	10.00
P 17206	The Legendary Marty Robbins	1983	2.50	5.00	10.00
P 17209	Country Cowboy	1983	2.50	5.00	10.00
P 17367	Song of the Islands	1983	2.50	5.00	10.00
DECCA					
DL 75389	This Much a Man	1972	3.75	7.50	15.00
HARMONY					
HS 11338	Singing the Blues	1969	3.75	7.50	15.00

Number	Title (A Side/B Side)	Yr	VG	VG+	NM
HS 11409	The Story of My Life	1970	3.75	7.50	15.00
KH 30316	El Paso	1971	3.00	6.00	12.00
KH 31257	Marty Robbins Favorites	1972	3.00	6.00	12.00
H 31258	Songs of the Islands	1972	5.00	10.00	20.00
KH 32286	Streets of Laredo	1973	3.00	6.00	12.00
MCA					
61	This Much a Man	1973	3.00	6.00	12.00
—Reissue of Decca LP					
342	Marty Robbins	1973	3.75	7.50	15.00
421	Good'n Country	1974	3.75	7.50	15.00

ROBBINS, MEL

45s

Number	Title (A Side/B Side)	Yr	VG	VG+	NM
ARGO					
5340	Save It/To Know You	1959	25.00	50.00	100.00

ROBBS, THE

Also see DEE ROBB.

45s

Number	Title (A Side/B Side)	Yr	VG	VG+	NM
ABC					
11270	I'll Never Get Enough/It All Comes Back	1970	—	3.00	6.00
ABC DUNHILL					
4208	Write to You/Movin'	1969	2.50	5.00	10.00
4233	Written in the Dust/Last of the Wine	1970	2.00	4.00	8.00
ATLANTIC					
2511	Castles in the Air/I Don't Want to Discuss It	1968	2.50	5.00	10.00
2578	A Good Time Song/Changin' Winds	1968	2.50	5.00	10.00
MERCURY					
72579	Race with the Wind/In a Funny Sort of Way	1966	2.50	5.00	10.00
72616	I Don't Feel Alone/Next Time You Call Me	1966	2.50	5.00	10.00
72641	Bittersweet/End of the Week	1966	2.50	5.00	10.00
72641 [PS]	Bittersweet/End of the Week	1966	3.75	7.50	15.00
72678	Rapid Transit/Cynthia Loves	1967	2.50	5.00	10.00
72730	Girls, Girls/Violets of Dawn	1967	2.50	5.00	10.00

Albums

Number	Title (A Side/B Side)	Yr	VG	VG+	NM
MERCURY					
MG-21130 [M]	The Robbs	1967	10.00	20.00	40.00
SR-61130 [S]	The Robbs	1967	7.50	15.00	30.00

ROBBY AND THE ROBBINS

45s

Number	Title (A Side/B Side)	Yr	VG	VG+	NM
TODD					
1089	Surfer's Life/She Cried	1963	10.00	20.00	40.00

ROBERT AND JOHNNY

45s

Number	Title (A Side/B Side)	Yr	VG	VG+	NM
OLD TOWN					
1021	I Believe You/Train to Paradise	1956	12.50	25.00	50.00
1029	You're Mine/Million Dollar Bills	1956	10.00	20.00	40.00
1038	Don't Do It/Baby Come Home	1957	10.00	20.00	40.00
1043	Broken Hearted Man/Indian Marriage	1957	10.00	20.00	40.00
1047	We Belong Together/In the Rain	1958	12.50	25.00	50.00
1052	I Know/Marry Me	1958	10.00	20.00	40.00
1052	I Believe in You/Marry Me	1958	10.00	20.00	40.00
1058	Eternity with You/I'm Truly, Truly Yours	1958	7.50	15.00	30.00
1065	Give Me the Key to Your Heart/Truly in Love	1959	7.50	15.00	30.00
1068	Dream Girl/Oh My Love	1959	7.50	15.00	30.00
1072	Wear This Ring/Bad Dan	1959	7.50	15.00	30.00
1078	Hear My Heartbeat/Try Me Pretty Baby	1960	6.25	12.50	25.00
1086	We Belong Together/In the Rain	1960	6.25	12.50	25.00
1100	You're Mine/Please Me Please	1961	5.00	10.00	20.00
1108	Togetherness/I Got You	1961	5.00	10.00	20.00
1117	Wear This Ring/Broken Hearted Man	1962	5.00	10.00	20.00
SUE					
792	A Perfect Wife/Brown, Pretty Brown Eyes	1963	6.25	12.50	25.00

ROBERTINO

45s

Number	Title (A Side/B Side)	Yr	VG	VG+	NM
4 CORNERS OF THE WORLD					
101	Santo Natale/Caro Gesu Bambino	1963	2.00	4.00	8.00
KAPP					
416	O Sole Mio/Romantica	1961	2.00	4.00	8.00
445	Ave Maria/Santa Lucia	1962	2.00	4.00	8.00
474	Papa/Parlami D'Amore	1962	2.00	4.00	8.00

Albums

Number	Title (A Side/B Side)	Yr	VG	VG+	NM
KAPP					
KL-1252 [M]	O Sole Mio	1962	3.75	7.50	15.00
KL-1293 [M]	The Young Italian Singing Sensation	1962	3.75	7.50	15.00
KL-1338 [M]	Italia Mia	1963	3.75	7.50	15.00
KL-1471 [M]	The Best of Robertino	1966	3.00	6.00	12.00
KS-3252 [S]	O Sole Mio	1962	5.00	10.00	20.00
KS-3293 [S]	The Young Italian Singing Sensation	1962	5.00	10.00	20.00
KS-3338 [S]	Italia Mia	1963	5.00	10.00	20.00
KS-3471 [S]	The Best of Robertino	1966	3.75	7.50	15.00

ROBERTS, ART

45s

Number	Title (A Side/B Side)	Yr	VG	VG+	NM
IMPERIAL					
5504	Give Her the Ax, Max/Terrible Ivan	1958	6.25	12.50	25.00

ROBERTS, AUSTIN

45s

Number	Title (A Side/B Side)	Yr	VG	VG+	NM
ABC					
11289	Live Is for Living/I Can Make It Better	1971	—	3.00	6.00
ARISTA					
0335	Don't Stop Me Baby/Question of Love	1978	—	2.00	4.00
CHELSEA					
BCBO-0053	Baby Don't You Walk Out on Me/One Word	1973	—	2.00	4.00
78-0101	Something's Wrong wtih Me/My Song	1972	—	2.50	5.00
78-0110	Keep On Singing/Take Away the Sunshine	1973	—	2.50	5.00
78-0123	The Last Thing on My Mind/Losing You Is More Than I Can Stand	1973	—	2.50	5.00
AMBO-0129	Something's Wrong with Me/Keep On Singing	1973	—	2.00	4.00
—Gold Standard Series reissue					
BCBO-0219	Somethin' to Believe In/Nothing Seems the Same When You're Not Here	1974	—	2.00	4.00
PHILIPS					
40560	I'll Smiule/Mary and Me	1968	—	3.00	6.00
40586	Ricky Ticky Ta Ta Ta/No Last Goodbyes	1969	—	3.00	6.00
40638	Runaway-Just a Little (Medley)/Sarah	1969	—	3.00	6.00
40649	Baltimore/Sarah	1969	—	3.00	6.00
40660	One Night Ann/The Other Side	1970	—	3.00	6.00
PRIVATE STOCK					
45020	Rocky/You Got the Power	1975	—	2.00	4.00
45051	Fool/Children of the Rain	1975	—	2.00	4.00
45061	Is There Somethin' Goin' On/Just to Make You Mine	1975	—	2.00	4.00
45080	This Time I'm In It for Love/Susannah	1976	—	2.00	4.00

Albums

Number	Title (A Side/B Side)	Yr	VG	VG+	NM
CHELSEA					
BCL1-0199	The Last Thing on My Mind	1973	3.00	6.00	12.00
CES-1004	Austin Roberts	1972	3.00	6.00	12.00
NEW PAX					
NP-33016	8 Days (A Personal Journey)	1977	3.00	6.00	12.00
PRIVATE STOCK					
PS-5000	Rocky	1975	3.00	6.00	12.00

ROBERTS, DEREK

45s

Number	Title (A Side/B Side)	Yr	VG	VG+	NM
ROULETTE					
4656	There Won't Be Any Snow (Christmas In The Jungle)/A World Without Sunshine	1965	2.50	5.00	10.00

ROBERTS, LANCE

45s

Number	Title (A Side/B Side)	Yr	VG	VG+	NM
SUN					
348	The Good Guy Always Wins/The Time Is Right	1960	5.00	10.00	20.00

ROBERTS, LOU

45s

Number	Title (A Side/B Side)	Yr	VG	VG+	NM
GENIE					
101	Rattle Snake Shake/(B-side unknown)	1965	20.00	40.00	80.00
MGM					
13347	Gettin' Ready/You Fooled Me	1965	7.50	15.00	30.00
13387	Don't Count on Me/Ten to One	1965	6.25	12.50	25.00

ROBERTS, ROCKY, AND THE AIREDALES

45s

Number	Title (A Side/B Side)	Yr	VG	VG+	NM
BRUNSWICK					
55357	Buzz Buzz Buzz/Too Much	1967	2.50	5.00	10.00
55368	Tell Me/Gotta Thing Going	1968	2.50	5.00	10.00

Albums

Number	Title (A Side/B Side)	Yr	VG	VG+	NM
BRUNSWICK					
BL 754133	Rocky Roberts and the Airedales	1968	5.00	10.00	20.00

ROBINS, THE (1)

Vocal group from Los Angeles. Part of the group splintered off and became the core of THE COASTERS.

45s

Number	Title (A Side/B Side)	Yr	VG	VG+	NM
ATCO					
6059	Smokey Joe's Cafe/Just Like a Fool	1956	12.50	25.00	50.00
CROWN					
106	I Made a Vow/Double Crossing Baby	1954	100.00	200.00	400.00
120	Key to My Heart/All I Do Is Rock	1954	75.00	150.00	300.00
KNIGHT					
2001	Quarter to Twelve/Pretty Little Dolly	1958	12.50	25.00	50.00
2008	It's Never Too Late/A Little Bird Told Me	1958	20.00	40.00	80.00
RCA VICTOR					
47-5175	(Now and Then There's) A Fool Such As I/My Heart's the Biggest Fool	1953	125.00	250.00	500.00
47-5271	Oh Why/All Night Baby	1953	100.00	200.00	400.00
47-5434	How Would You Know/Let's Go to the Dance	1953	100.00	200.00	400.00
47-5486	My Baby Done Told Me/I'll Do It	1953	75.00	150.00	300.00
47-5489	Ten Days in Jail/Empty Bottles	1953	50.00	100.00	200.00
47-5564	Get It Off Your Mind/Don't Stop Now	1953	50.00	100.00	200.00
SPARK					
103	Riot in Cell Block #9/Wrap It Up	1954	75.00	150.00	300.00
—Copies on yellow labels are bootlegs					
107	Loop De Loop Mambo/Framed	1954	75.00	150.00	300.00
—Silver top label					
107	Loop De Loop Mambo/Framed	1954	25.00	50.00	100.00
—Red label					
110	If Teardrops Were Kisses/Whadaya Want	1955	75.00	150.00	300.00
—Red label					
110	If Teardrops Were Kisses/Whadaya Want	1955	25.00	50.00	100.00
—Blue label					
113	One Kiss/I Love Paris	1955	75.00	150.00	300.00
116	I Must Be Dreamin'/The Hatchet Man	1955	50.00	100.00	200.00
—Red label					
116	I Must Be Dreamin'/The Hatchet Man	1955	12.50	25.00	50.00
—Yellow label					
122	Smokey Joe's Cafe/Just Like a Fool	1955	87.50	175.00	350.00
WHIPPET					
200	Cherry Lips/Out of the Picture	1956	20.00	40.00	80.00
201	Hurt Me/Merry-Go-Rock	1956	17.50	35.00	70.00
203	That Old Black Magic/Since I First Met You	1956	17.50	35.00	70.00
206	A Fool in Love/All of a Sudden My Heart Sings	1957	17.50	35.00	70.00
208	Every Night/Where's the Fire	1957	17.50	35.00	70.00
211	In My Dreams/Keep Your Mind on Me	1957	17.50	35.00	70.00
212	Snowball/You Wanted Fun	1958	17.50	35.00	70.00

Number	Title (A Side/B Side)	Yr	VG	VG+	NM
Albums					
GNP CRESCENDO					
GNPS-9034	The Best of the Robins	1975	3.75	7.50	15.00
WHIPPET					
WLP-703 [M]	Rock 'n' Roll with the Robins	1958	200.00	400.00	800.00

ROBINS, THE (2)

Number	Title (A Side/B Side)	Yr	VG	VG+	NM
45s					
ARDENT					
106	Batman/Batarang	1966	7.50	15.00	30.00

ROBINS, THE (3)

Number	Title (A Side/B Side)	Yr	VG	VG+	NM
45s					
LAVENDER					
001	The White Cliffs of Dover/How Many More Times	1961	10.00	20.00	40.00
002	Magic of a Dream/Mary Lou Loves to Hootchy Kootchy Koo	1961	10.00	20.00	40.00

ROBINS, THE (4)

Number	Title (A Side/B Side)	Yr	VG	VG+	NM
45s					
NEW HIT					
3010	Johnny/Doing the Popeye	1963	3.75	7.50	15.00
SWEET TAFFY					
400	Johnny/Doing the Popeye	1963	7.50	15.00	30.00

ROBINS, THE (U)

These could be by any of the above, or none of the above.

Number	Title (A Side/B Side)	Yr	VG	VG+	NM
45s					
ARVEE					
5001	Just Like That/Whole Lot of Imagination	1960	6.25	12.50	25.00
5013	Live Wire Suzie/Oh No	1960	6.25	12.50	25.00
DOT					
16510	Blue Grass Blues/Top 40 Blues	1963	3.00	6.00	12.00
GONE					
5101	Baby Love/We Loved	1961	7.50	15.00	30.00
MUSICOR					
1050	Cry Over You/Lucy Watusi	1964	3.75	7.50	15.00

ROBINSON, BILL, AND THE QUAILS

Number	Title (A Side/B Side)	Yr	VG	VG+	NM
45s					
DATE					
1620	Do I Love You/Lay My Head on Your Shoulder	1969	2.50	5.00	10.00
DELUXE					
6030	Lonely Star/Quit Pushin'	1954	50.00	100.00	200.00
6047	I Know She's Gone/Baby Don't Want Me No More	1954	75.00	150.00	300.00
6057	A Little Bit of Love/Somewhere Somebody Cares	1954	50.00	100.00	200.00
6059	Why Do I Wait/Heaven Is the Place	1954	50.00	100.00	200.00
6074	Love of My Life/Oh Sugar	1955	37.50	75.00	150.00
6085	The Things She Used to Do/Pretty Huggin' Baby	1955	17.50	35.00	70.00
—As "The Quails"					

ROBINSON, FLOYD

Number	Title (A Side/B Side)	Yr	VG	VG+	NM
45s					
DOT					
16290	The Art of Making Love/Don't Let Me Fall	1961	3.00	6.00	12.00
16352	I Need You/Show Boat	1961	3.00	6.00	12.00
GROOVE					
58-0040	My Little Martian/Surprise	1964	20.00	40.00	80.00
JAMIE					
1186	Mother Nature/Is There Something I Ought to Know?	1961	3.75	7.50	15.00
RCA VICTOR					
47-7529	Makin' Love/My Girl	1959	5.00	10.00	20.00
47-7637	Tonight You Belong to Me/Let It Be Me	1959	3.75	7.50	15.00
47-7685	Little Sir Echo/Alphabet Song	1960	3.75	7.50	15.00
47-7693	Tattletale/I Believe in Love	1960	6.25	12.50	25.00
47-7736	Boys and Girls/Sonja	1960	3.75	7.50	15.00
47-7789	A Girl Like You/Why Can't It Go On	1960	3.75	7.50	15.00
47-7827	Out of Gas/Magic Lamp	1960	7.50	15.00	30.00
UNITED ARTISTS					
534	Heartaches/I've Got a Sweetheart	1963	3.00	6.00	12.00
986	Sidewalk Surfer/Motorcycle Man	1966	3.75	7.50	15.00
7-Inch Extended Plays					
RCA VICTOR					
EPA-4350	(contents unknown)	1959	12.50	25.00	50.00
EPA-4350 [PS]	Makin' Love	1959	12.50	25.00	50.00
Albums					
RCA VICTOR					
LPM-2162 [M]	Floyd Robinson	1960	20.00	40.00	80.00
LSP-2162 [S]	Floyd Robinson	1960	30.00	60.00	120.00

ROBINSON, FREDDY

Number	Title (A Side/B Side)	Yr	VG	VG+	NM
45s					
CHECKER					
1143	The Creeper/Go Go Girl	1966	2.50	5.00	10.00
LIBERTY					
56214	Carmalita/Stone Stallion	1970	—	3.00	6.00
LIMELIGHT					
3005	Not Like Now/Five Feet of Lovin'	1963	3.00	6.00	12.00
MERCURY					
71270	Be Mine/You and Me	1958	3.00	6.00	12.00
PACIFIC JAZZ					
88152	Before Six/The Coming Atlantis	1969	—	3.00	6.00
88155	Black Fox/The Oogue Boogum Song	1970	—	3.00	6.00
QUEEN					
24005	The Buzzard/The Hawk	196?	2.50	5.00	10.00
Albums					
ENTERPRISE					
ENS-1025	Freddy Robinson at the Drive-In	1972	3.00	6.00	12.00
PACIFIC JAZZ					
ST-20162	The Coming Atlantis	1970	3.75	7.50	15.00
ST-20176	Hot Fun in the Summertime	1971	3.75	7.50	15.00

ROBINSON, JOHNNY

Number	Title (A Side/B Side)	Yr	VG	VG+	NM
45s					
EPIC					
10578	God Is Love/Kansas City	1970	2.50	5.00	10.00
10607	Person to Person/Lady Doctor	1970	2.50	5.00	10.00
MERCURY					
72434	I Gotta Kick the Habit (Part 1)/I Gotta Kick the Habit (Part 2)	1965	5.00	10.00	20.00
OKEH					
7307	Gone But Not Forgotten/I Need Your Love So Bad	1968	25.00	50.00	100.00
7317	Poor Man/When a Man Cries	1968	5.00	10.00	20.00
7328	Green Green Grass of Home/You've Been With Him	1969	5.00	10.00	20.00
Albums					
EPIC					
BN 26528	Memphis High	1970	5.00	10.00	20.00

ROBINSON, MARK

Number	Title (A Side/B Side)	Yr	VG	VG+	NM
45s					
JAMIE					
1103	Pretty Jane/Want Me	1958	6.25	12.50	25.00
TEE GEE					
104	Pretty Jane/Want Me	1958	10.00	20.00	40.00

ROBINSON, SMOKEY

Also see THE MIRACLES; RON AND BILL.

Number	Title (A Side/B Side)	Yr	VG	VG+	NM
12-Inch Singles					
MOTOWN					
00027	Get Ready/(Instrumental)	1979	3.00	6.00	12.00
PR-92 [DJ]	Tell Me Tomorrow/Right in the Middle (vocal) (instrumental)	1982	2.50	5.00	10.00
—B-side by Bettye Lavette					
L33-17828 [DJ]	(It's the) Same Old Love (3 versions)	1990	—	3.00	6.00
L33-18141 [DJ]	Everything You Touch (3 versions)/It's the Same Old Feeling	1990	—	3.00	6.00
50109	Everything You Touch (3 versions)/It's the Same Old Feeling	1990	—	3.50	7.00
TAMLA					
145 [DJ]	And I Don't Love You (7:10)/And I Don't Love You (Dub)	1984	2.00	4.00	8.00
45s					
COLUMBIA					
07727	I Know You by Heart/Could I Have Your Autograph	1988	—	—	3.00
—With Dolly Parton					
MOTOWN					
914	(It's the) Same Old Love/(Instrumental)	1990	—	2.00	4.00
1877	Just to See Her/I'm Gonna Love You Like There's No Tomorrow	1987	—	—	3.00
1877 [PS]	Just to See Her/I'm Gonna Love You Like There's No Tomorrow	1987	2.00	4.00	8.00
1897	One Heartbeat/Love Will Set You Free (Theme from Solarbabies)	1987	—	—	3.00
1897 [PS]	One Heartbeat/Love Will Set You Free (Theme from Solarbabies)	1987	—	3.00	6.00
1911	What's Too Much/I've Made Love to You a Thousand Times	1987	—	—	3.00
1911 [PS]	What's Too Much/I've Made Love to You a Thousand Times	1987	—	2.50	5.00
1925	Love Don't Give No Reason/Hanging On by a Thread	1988	—	—	3.00
1925 [PS]	Love Don't Give No Reason/Hanging On by a Thread	1988	—	2.50	5.00
SBK					
07379	Double Good Everything/Guess What I Got for You	1991	—	2.00	4.00
TAMLA					
1601	Tell Me Tomorrow (Part 1)/Tell Me Tomorrow (Part 2)	1982	—	2.00	4.00
1615	Old Fashioned Love/Destiny	1982	—	2.00	4.00
1630	Are You Still Here/Yes It's You Lady	1982	—	2.00	4.00
1655	I've Made Love to You a Thousand Times/Into Each Rain Some Life Must Fall	1983	—	2.00	4.00
1678	Touch the Sky/All My Life's a Lie	1983	—	2.00	4.00
1684	Blame It on Love/Even Tho'	1983	—	2.00	4.00
—With Barbara Mitchell					
1700	Don't Play Another Love Song/Wouldn't You Like to Know	1983	—	2.00	4.00
1735	And I Don't Love You/Dynamite	1984	—	2.00	4.00
1756	I Can't Find/Gimme What You Want	1984	—	2.00	4.00
1786	First Time on a Ferris Wheel/Train of Thought	1985	—	2.00	4.00
1828	Hold On to Your Love/Train of Thought	1985	—	2.00	4.00
1828 [PS]	Hold On to Your Love/Train of Thought	1985	—	3.00	6.00
1839	Sleepless Nights/Close Encounters of the First Kind	1986	—	2.00	4.00
1839 [PS]	Sleepless Nights/Close Encounters of the First Kind	1986	—	2.50	5.00
1855	Girl I'm Standing There/Because of You (It's the Best It's Ever Been)	1986	—	2.00	4.00
1868	Love Will Set You Free (Theme from Solarbabies) (Parts 1 & 2)	1986	—	2.00	4.00
54233	Sweet Harmony/Want to Know My Mind	1973	—	2.50	5.00
54239	Baby Come Close/A Silent Partner in a Three-Way Love Affair	1973	—	2.50	5.00
54246	It's Her Turn to Live/Just My Soul Responding	1974	—	2.50	5.00
54250	Virgin Man/Fulfill Your Need	1974	—	2.50	5.00
54251	I Am, I Am/The Family Song	1974	—	2.50	5.00
54258	Baby That's Backatcha/Just Passing Through	1975	—	2.50	5.00
54261	The Agony and the Ecstasy/Wedding Song	1975	—	2.50	5.00

Number	Title (A Side/B Side)	Yr	VG	VG+	NM
54265	Quiet Storm/Asleep on My Love	1975	—	2.50	5.00
54267	Open/Coincidentally	1976	—	2.50	5.00
54272	An Old Fashioned Man/(B-side unassigned)	1976	—	—	—
—Unreleased					
54276	An Old Fashioned Man/Just Passing Through	1976	—	2.50	5.00
54279	There Will Come a Day (I'm Gonna Happen to You)/Humming Song	1977	—	2.50	5.00
54284	Vitamin U/Holly	1977	—	2.50	5.00
54288	Theme from Big Time (Part 1)/Theme from Big Time (Part 2)	1977	—	2.50	5.00
54293	Daylight and Darkness/Why You Wanna See My Bad Side	1978	—	2.50	5.00
54296	I'm Loving You Softly/Shoe Soul	1978	—	2.50	5.00
54301	Get Ready/Ever Had a Dream	1979	—	2.00	4.00
54306	Cruisin'/Ever Had a Dream	1979	—	2.00	4.00
54311	Let Me Be the Clock/Travelin' Through	1980	—	2.00	4.00
54313	Heavy on Pride/I Love the Nearness of You	1980	—	2.00	4.00
54318	I Want to Be Your Love/Wine, Women and Song	1980	—	2.00	4.00
54321	Being with You/What's In Your Life for Me	1981	—	2.00	4.00
54325	Aquicontigo/Being with You (Aquicontigo)	1981	—	2.00	4.00
54327	You Are Forever/I Hear the Children Singing	1981	—	2.00	4.00
54332	Who's Sad/Food for Thought	1981	—	2.00	4.00
Albums					
MOTOWN					
M5-118V1	Motown Superstar Series, Vol. 18	1981	2.50	5.00	10.00
M5-134V1	Smokey	1981	2.00	4.00	8.00
—Reissue of Tamla 328					
M5-154V1	Deep in My Soul	1981	2.00	4.00	8.00
—Reissue of Tamla 350					
M5-168V1	Pure Smokey	1981	2.00	4.00	8.00
—Reissue of Tamla 331					
M5-197V1	A Quiet Storm	1981	2.00	4.00	8.00
—Reissue of Tamla 337					
5267ML	Where There;s Smoke	1982	2.00	4.00	8.00
—Reissue of Tamla 366					
5349ML	Being with You	1983	2.00	4.00	8.00
—Reissue of Tamla 375					
MOT-6226	One Heartbeat	1987	2.50	5.00	10.00
MOT-6268	Love, Smokey	1990	3.00	6.00	12.00
TAMLA					
T 328	Smokey	1973	3.00	6.00	12.00
T6-331	Pure Smokey	1974	3.00	6.00	12.00
T6-337	A Quiet Storm	1975	3.00	6.00	12.00
T6-341	Smokey's Family Robinson	1976	3.00	6.00	12.00
T6-350	Deep in My Soul	1977	3.00	6.00	12.00
T7-359	Love Breeze	1978	3.00	6.00	12.00
T9-363 [(2)]	Smokin'	1979	3.75	7.50	15.00
T7-366	Where There's Smoke	1979	2.50	5.00	10.00
T8-367	Warm Thoughts	1980	2.50	5.00	10.00
T8-375	Being with You	1981	2.50	5.00	10.00
6001TL	Yes It's You Lady	1982	2.50	5.00	10.00
6030TL	Touch the Sky	1983	2.50	5.00	10.00
6064TL	Blame It on Love & All the Great Hits	1983	2.50	5.00	10.00
6098TL	Essar	1984	2.50	5.00	10.00
6156TL	Smoke Signals	1986	2.50	5.00	10.00

ROBINSON, SMOKEY, AND THE MIRACLES

See THE MIRACLES.

ROBINSON, VICKI SUE

Number	Title (A Side/B Side)	Yr	VG	VG+	NM
12-Inch Singles					
PRELUDE					
532	Hot Summer Night/(Version)	1981	3.00	6.00	12.00
PROFILE					
7025	To Sir with Love/(Instrumental)	1983	2.00	4.00	8.00
7039	Everlasting Love/(Instrumental)	1983	2.00	4.00	8.00
RCA					
PD-11029	Hold Tight/Falling in Love	1977	3.75	7.50	15.00
PD-11228	Trust in Me (7:03)/Don't Try to Win Me Back Again (6:06)	1978	3.00	6.00	12.00
PD-11442	Nighttime Fantasy (8:15)/Feels So Good It Must Be Wrong	1979	3.00	6.00	12.00
PC-11507	Turn the Beat Around/Hold Tight	1979	3.00	6.00	12.00
PC-11520	Nighttime Fantasy (8:15)/Feels So Good It Must Be Wrong	1980	2.00	4.00	8.00
PD-11721	What's Happening in My Life (5:42)/Movin' On	1979	3.00	6.00	12.00
45s					
PRELUDE					
8038	Hot Summer Nights/(Version)	1981	—	2.00	4.00
PROFILE					
5025	To Sir with Love/(Instrumental)	1983	—	2.00	4.00
5039	Everlasting Love/(Instrumental)	1983	—	2.00	4.00
RCA					
PB-10775	Daylight/Never Gonna Let You Go	1976	—	2.00	4.00
PB-10863	Should I Stay-I Won't Let You Go/When You're Loving Me	1976	—	2.00	4.00
GB-10944	Turn the Beat Around/Daylight	1977	—	—	3.00
—Gold Standard Series					
PB-11028	Falling in Love/Hold Tight	1977	—	2.00	4.00
PB-11227	Trust in Me/Don't Try to Win Me Back Again	1978	—	2.00	4.00
PB-11280	Freeway Song/Half and Half	1978	—	2.00	4.00
PB-11384	Jealousy/We Found Each Other	1978	—	2.00	4.00
PB-11441	Nighttime Fantasy/Feel So Good It Must Be Wrong	1978	—	2.00	4.00
PB-11720	What's Happening in My Life/Movin' On	1979	—	2.00	4.00
RCA VICTOR					
PB-10282	Baby, Now That I've Found You/Thanks a Million	1975	—	2.00	4.00
PB-10435	Never Gonna Let You Go (Part 1)/Never Gonna Let You Go (Part 2)	1975	—	2.00	4.00
PB-10562	Turn the Beat Around/Lack of Respect	1976	—	2.50	5.00
Albums					
RCA VICTOR					
APL1-1256	Never Gonna Let You Go	1976	3.00	6.00	12.00
APL1-1829	Vicki Sue Robinson	1977	3.00	6.00	12.00
AFL1-2294	Half and Half	1978	3.00	6.00	12.00
AYL1-3949	Turn the Beat Around	1981	2.00	4.00	8.00

ROBINSON, WANDA

Number	Title (A Side/B Side)	Yr	VG	VG+	NM
45s					
PERCEPTION					
505	John Harvey's Blues/Final Hour	1971	2.00	4.00	8.00
Albums					
PERCEPTION					
18	Black Ivory	1971	3.00	6.00	12.00

ROCCO, LENNY

Number	Title (A Side/B Side)	Yr	VG	VG+	NM
45s					
DELSEY					
301	Sugar Girl/Rochelle	1961	75.00	150.00	300.00

ROCHELL AND THE CANDLES

Number	Title (A Side/B Side)	Yr	VG	VG+	NM
45s					
CHALLENGE					
9158	Turn Her Down/Each Night	1962	10.00	20.00	40.00
9191	Annie's Not an Orphan Anymore/Let's Run Away and Get Married	1963	5.00	10.00	20.00
SWINGIN'					
623	Once Upon a Time/When My Baby Is Gone	1960	5.00	10.00	20.00
634	So Far Away/Hey, Pretty Baby	1961	5.00	10.00	20.00
640	Peg of My Heart/Squat with Me, Baby	1962	5.00	10.00	20.00
652	Big Boy Pete/A Long Time Ago	1963	5.00	10.00	20.00

ROCK-A-FELLAS, THE

Number	Title (A Side/B Side)	Yr	VG	VG+	NM
45s					
ABC-PARAMOUNT					
9923	Don't Torment Me/Red Lips	1958	5.00	10.00	20.00
DEVERE					
313	Don't Torment Me/Red Lips	1958	12.50	25.00	50.00

ROCK-A-TEENS, THE

Number	Title (A Side/B Side)	Yr	VG	VG+	NM
45s					
DORAN					
3515	Woo Hoo/Untrue	1959	37.50	75.00	150.00
ROULETTE					
4192	Woo Hoo/Untrue	1959	7.50	15.00	30.00
4217	Twangy/Doggone It, Baby	1959	6.25	12.50	25.00
Albums					
ROULETTE					
R-25109 [M]	Woo-Hoo	1960	37.50	75.00	150.00
SR-25109 [S]	Woo-Hoo	1960	62.50	125.00	250.00

ROCK BROTHERS, THE

Number	Title (A Side/B Side)	Yr	VG	VG+	NM
45s					
KING					
4851	Dungaree Doll/Livin' It Up	1955	7.50	15.00	30.00
4882	Oh, Didn't I Ramble/I Gotta Get Back	1956	6.25	12.50	25.00

ROCK GARDEN, THE

Number	Title (A Side/B Side)	Yr	VG	VG+	NM
45s					
B.T. PUPPY					
536	Sweet Pajamas/Perhaps the Joy of Giving	1967	2.50	5.00	10.00

ROCK ISLAND

Number	Title (A Side/B Side)	Yr	VG	VG+	NM
45s					
PROJECT 3					
1382	Babe I'm Gonna Leave You/Hard and Never Easy	1970	2.50	5.00	10.00
Albums					
PROJECT 3					
PR-4005 SD	Rock Island	1970	7.50	15.00	30.00

ROCKA, BILLY

Number	Title (A Side/B Side)	Yr	VG	VG+	NM
45s					
BRUNSWICK					
55049	Listen Pretty Baby/I'm Gonna Sit Right Down and Cry	1958	15.00	30.00	60.00

ROCKAWAYS, THE

Number	Title (A Side/B Side)	Yr	VG	VG+	NM
45s					
RED BIRD					
10-005	Top Down Time/Don't Cry	1964	6.25	12.50	25.00

ROCKERS, THE

Number	Title (A Side/B Side)	Yr	VG	VG+	NM
45s					
CARTER					
3029	Tell Me Why/Count Every Star	1955	200.00	400.00	800.00
FEDERAL					
12267	What Am I to Do/I'll Die in Love with You	1956	50.00	100.00	200.00
12273	Down in the Bottom/Why Don't You Believe Me	1956	25.00	50.00	100.00

ROCKETEERS, THE (1)

Number	Title (A Side/B Side)	Yr	VG	VG+	NM
45s					
GLAD HAMP					
2017	Drag Strip/Summertime	1963	10.00	20.00	40.00

ROCKETEERS, THE (2)

Number	Title (A Side/B Side)	Yr	VG	VG+	NM
45s					
HERALD					
415	Foolish One/Gonna Feed My Baby Poison	1953	175.00	350.00	700.00
—Black vinyl					
415	Foolish One/Gonna Feed My Baby Poison	1953	500.00	1000.	2000.
—Red vinyl					

Number	Title (A Side/B Side)	Yr	VG	VG+	NM
ROCKETEERS, THE (3)					
45s					
MODERN					
999	Talk It Over Baby/Hey Rube	1956	12.50	25.00	50.00
ROCKETEERS, THE (4)					
45s					
M.J.C.					
501	My Reckless Heart/They Turned the Party Out Down at Bessie's House	1958	500.00	1000.	2000.
ROCKETEERS, THE (U)					
45s					
VAL-UE					
102	Rippin' and Rockin'/Downtown	1960	7.50	15.00	30.00
ROCKETONES, THE					
45s					
MELBA					
113	Mexico/I Do	1957	15.00	30.00	60.00
113	Mexico/Dee I	1957	12.50	25.00	50.00
ROCKETS, THE (1)					
45s					
ATLANTIC					
988	Open the Door/Big Leg Mama	1953	25.00	50.00	100.00
ROCKETS, THE (2)					
45s					
COLUMBIA					
41512	Gibraltar Rock/Walkin' Home	1959	6.25	12.50	25.00
ROCKETS, THE (3)					
45s					
MODERN					
992	You Are the First One/Be Lovey Dovey	1956	10.00	20.00	40.00
ROCKETS, THE (4)					
Features three future members of CRAZY HORSE.					
45s					
WHITE WHALE					
270	Hole in My Pocket/Let Me Go	1968	3.75	7.50	15.00
Albums					
WHITE WHALE					
WWS-7116	The Rockets	1968	6.25	12.50	25.00
ROCKETTES, THE					
45s					
PARROT					
789	I Can't Forget/Love Nobody	1954	1000.	2000.	3000.
ROCKIN' BERRIES, THE					
45s					
REPRISE					
0329	He's in Town/Flashbook	1964	3.00	6.00	12.00
0355	What in the World's Come Over You/You Don't Know What to Do	1965	2.50	5.00	10.00
0377	Poor Man's Son/Follow Me	1965	2.50	5.00	10.00
0400	You're My Girl/Brother Bill (Last Clean Shirt)	1965	2.50	5.00	10.00
0442	Doesn't Time Fly/The Water Is Over My Head	1965	2.50	5.00	10.00
ROCKIN' CHAIRS, THE					
45s					
RECORTE					
402	Rockin' Chair Boogie/A Kiss Is a Kiss	1958	25.00	50.00	100.00
404	Please Mary/Come On Baby	1958	12.50	25.00	50.00
412	Memories of Love/(B-side unknown)	1959	12.50	25.00	50.00
ROCKIN' DUKES, THE					
45s					
O.J.					
1007	Angel and a Rose/My Baby Left Me	1957	75.00	150.00	300.00
ROCKIN' KIDS, THE					
45s					
DOT					
15749	Black Stockings/Yea Yea (I'm in the Mood)	1958	7.50	15.00	30.00
ROCKIN' R'S, THE					
45s					
STEPHENY					
1842	Walkin' You to School/Bewitched (Bothered and Bewildered)	1960	6.25	12.50	25.00
TEMPUS					
1507	Nameless/Heat	1959	7.50	15.00	30.00
1515	Mustang/I'm Still in Love with You	1959	7.50	15.00	30.00
7541	Crazy Baby/The Beat	1959	10.00	20.00	40.00
VEE JAY					
334	Mustang/I'm Still in Love with You	1959	5.00	10.00	20.00
346	Hum Bug/The Mix	1960	5.00	10.00	20.00
ROCKIN' RAMRODS, THE					
45s					
BON-BON					
1315	She Lies/The Girl Can't Help It	1964	10.00	20.00	40.00
CLARIDGE					
301	Don't Fool with Fu Manchu/Tears	1965	5.00	10.00	20.00
317	Play It/Got My Mojo Workin'	1966	7.50	15.00	30.00

Number	Title (A Side/B Side)	Yr	VG	VG+	NM
PLYMOUTH					
2961	I Wanna Be Your Man/I'll Be On My Way	1964	7.50	15.00	30.00
2963	Mister Wind/Bright Lit Blue Skies	1966	6.25	12.50	25.00
—As "The Ramrods"					
2965	Flowers in My Mind/Mary, Mary	1967	7.50	15.00	30.00
—As "The Ramrods"					
ROCKIN' REBELS, THE					
Includes records by "The Hot-Toddys" and "The Rebels."					
45s					
CORSICAN					
0056	Rockin' Crickets/Shakin' and Stompin'	1959	10.00	20.00	40.00
—As "The Hot-Toddys"					
ITZY					
8	Wild Weekend/Wild Weekend Cha Cha	1963	5.00	10.00	20.00
MAR-LEE					
0094	Wild Weekend/Wild Weekend Cha Cha	1960	25.00	50.00	100.00
—As "The Rebels"					
0095	Buffalo Blues/Donkey Walk	1961	7.50	15.00	30.00
—As "The Buffalo Rebels"					
0096	Theme from Rebel/Any Way You Want Me	1961	7.50	15.00	30.00
—As "The Buffalo Rebels"					
SHAN-TODD					
0056	Rockin' Crickets/Shakin' and Stompin'	1959	20.00	40.00	80.00
—As "The Hot-Toddys"					
STORK					
3	Bongo Blue Beat/Burn Baby Burn	1964	6.25	12.50	25.00
SWAN					
4125	Wild Weekend/Wild Weekend Cha Cha	1962	10.00	20.00	40.00
—First pressings credit "The Rebels"					
4125	Wild Weekend/Wild Weekend Cha Cha	1962	7.50	15.00	30.00
—Second pressings credit "Rockin' Rebels" and do not have "Don't Drop Out" on the label					
4125	Wild Weekend/Wild Weekend Cha Cha	1963	5.00	10.00	20.00
—Later pressings credit "Rockin' Rebels" and have "Don't Drop Out" on the label					
4140	Rockin' Crickets/Hully Gully Rock	1963	6.25	12.50	25.00
—A-side is the same recording as on Corsican and Shan-Todd					
4150	Another Wild Weekend/Happy Popcorn	1963	6.25	12.50	25.00
4161	Monday Morning/Flibbity Jibbit	1963	6.25	12.50	25.00
4248	Wild Weekend/Dockey Twine	1966	5.00	10.00	20.00
Albums					
SWAN					
SLP-509 [M]	Wild Weekend	1963	50.00	100.00	200.00
ROCKIN' SAINTS, THE					
45s					
DECCA					
30990	Saints Rock/Alright Baby	1959	7.50	15.00	30.00
31144	Cheat on Me, Baby/Half and Half	1960	20.00	40.00	80.00
ROCKIN' SIDNEY					
45s					
EPIC					
34-05430	My Toot Toot/Jalapeno Lena	1985	—	2.00	4.00
GOLDBAND					
1158	Actions Speak Louder Than Words/Lais Per La Patate	196?	3.00	6.00	12.00
1159	My Poor Heart/Something Working Baby	196?	3.00	6.00	12.00
1163	Deedle Didie Da/Life Without Love	196?	2.50	5.00	10.00
1170	Gonna Be Looking/Shed So Many Tears	196?	2.50	5.00	10.00
1177	Corpus Christi/(B-side unknown)	196?	3.00	6.00	12.00
1178	Trust/Put On It	196?	2.50	5.00	10.00
1183	Soul Christmas (Part 1)/Soul Christmas (Part 2)	1966	3.00	6.00	12.00
1186	The Grandpa/Feel Delicious	1967	2.50	5.00	10.00
JIN					
110	My Little Girl/Don't Say Goodbye	1959	12.50	25.00	50.00
141	Walking Out on You/Rocky	1960	7.50	15.00	30.00
156	No Good Woman/You Ain't Nothin' But Fine	1960	7.50	15.00	30.00
164	Send Me Some Lovin'/Past Bedtime	196?	7.50	15.00	30.00
168	No Good Man/If I Could, I Win	196?	7.50	15.00	30.00
170	Don't Let Me Cross Over/You Don't Have to Go	196?	7.50	15.00	30.00
174	Something's Wrong/It Really Is a Hurtin' Thing	196?	7.50	15.00	30.00
177	Ya Ya/Wasted Days and Wasted Nights	196?	7.50	15.00	30.00
MAISON DE SOUL					
1024	My Toot Toot/(B-side unknown)	1985	2.00	4.00	8.00
Albums					
EPIC					
5E 40153 [EP]	My Toot Toot	1985	2.00	4.00	8.00
ZBC					
LP-100	A Holiday Celebration with Rockin' Sidney	1983	3.75	7.50	15.00
ROCKIN' STOCKIN', THE					
45s					
SUN					
350	Rockin' Lang Syne/Yuleville U.S.A.	1960	7.50	15.00	30.00
1960	Rockin' Lang Syne/Yuleville U.S.A.	197?	3.75	7.50	15.00
—Reissue with green and red print on a white label with original Sun logo					
ROCKIN' VICKERS					
45s					
COLUMBIA					
43818	Dandy/I Don't Need Your Love	1966	3.00	6.00	12.00
ROCKING BROTHERS, THE					
45s					
IMPERIAL					
5333	Rock It/Behind the Sun	1955	7.50	15.00	30.00
5341	Blow Torch/Evening Shadows	1955	7.50	15.00	30.00
SAVOY					
1144	Play Boy Hop/The Grinder	1955	12.50	25.00	50.00
WHIPPET					
207	Yeah! Yeah!/Little Mike	1957	5.00	10.00	20.00

ROCKY AND HIS FRIENDS

45s

TOWER

Number	Title (A Side/B Side)	Yr	VG	VG+	NM
178	Riot City/You're Not Wrong	1965	3.00	6.00	12.00

ROCKY FELLERS, THE

45s

DONNA

Number	Title (A Side/B Side)	Yr	VG	VG+	NM
1383	Don't Sit Down/The Beachcomber Song	1963	3.00	6.00	12.00

PARKWAY

Number	Title (A Side/B Side)	Yr	VG	VG+	NM
836	Long Tall Sally/South Pacific Twist	1962	3.00	6.00	12.00

SCEPTER

Number	Title (A Side/B Side)	Yr	VG	VG+	NM
1245	Santa Santa/Great Big World	1962	5.00	10.00	20.00
—A-side is a very early Neil Diamond composition					
1245 [DJ]	Santa Santa/Santa's Grove	1963	3.00	6.00	12.00
—Promo reissue with new B-side. All-white label (no black oval)					
1245 [DJ]	Santa Santa (same on both sides)	196?	2.00	4.00	8.00
—Promo reissue; white label with mid-1960s Scepter Records logo (black oval)					
1246	Killer Joe/Lonely Teardrops	1963	3.75	7.50	15.00
1254	Like the Big Guys Do/Great Big World	1963	3.00	6.00	12.00
1254 [PS]	Like the Big Guys Do/Great Big World	1963	5.00	10.00	20.00
1258	Ching-a-Ling Baby/Hey Little Donkey	1963	3.00	6.00	12.00
1263	Bye Bye Baby/She Makes Me Wanna Dance	1963	3.00	6.00	12.00
1271	My Prayer/Two Guys from Trinidad	1964	3.00	6.00	12.00

VALMOR

Number	Title (A Side/B Side)	Yr	VG	VG+	NM
2004	Opus/Orange Peel	1962	3.75	7.50	15.00

WARNER BROS.

Number	Title (A Side/B Side)	Yr	VG	VG+	NM
5440	(Everybody Wants to Be a) Tiger/Jeannie Memsoh	1964	2.50	5.00	10.00
5459	Better Let Her Go/Nina	1964	2.50	5.00	10.00
5497	Man with the Blue Guitar/Don't Throw My Toys Away	1965	2.50	5.00	10.00
5613	Rented Tuxedo/Two Steps Downstairs in the Basement	1965	2.50	5.00	10.00

Albums

SCEPTER

Number	Title (A Side/B Side)	Yr	VG	VG+	NM
SP-512 [M]	Killer Joe	1964	7.50	15.00	30.00
SPS-512 [S]	Killer Joe	1964	10.00	20.00	40.00

RODGERS, JIMMIE (1)

Legendary country & western singer known as "The Singing Brakeman."

45s

RCA VICTOR

Number	Title (A Side/B Side)	Yr	VG	VG+	NM
47-6092	In the Jailhouse Now No. 2/Peach Pickin' Time Down in Georgia	1955	5.00	10.00	20.00
47-6205	Mule Skinner Blues/Mother, the Queen of My Heart	1955	5.00	10.00	20.00
47-6408	Never No Mo' Blues/Daddy and Home	1955	5.00	10.00	20.00

Albums

RCA VICTOR

Number	Title (A Side/B Side)	Yr	VG	VG+	NM
DPL2-0075 [(2)]	The Legendary Jimmie Rodgers, Vol. 1	1974	10.00	20.00	40.00
—Special-products issue for Country Music Magazine					
ANL1-1209	My Rough and Rowdy Ways	1976	2.50	5.00	10.00
LPM-1232 [M]	Never No Mo' Blues — A Memorial Album	1955	37.50	75.00	150.00
LPM-1640 [M]	Train Whistle Blues	1957	37.50	75.00	150.00
LPM-2112 [M]	My Rough and Rowdy Ways	1960	20.00	40.00	80.00
LPM-2213 [M]	Jimmie the Kid	1961	20.00	40.00	80.00
CPL1-2504	A Legendary Performer	1977	2.50	5.00	10.00
LPM-2531 [M]	Country Music Hall of Fame	1962	20.00	40.00	80.00
LPM-2634 [M]	The Short But Brilliant Life of Jimmie Rodgers	1963	20.00	40.00	80.00
LPM-2865 [M]	My Time Ain't Long	1964	12.50	25.00	50.00
LPM-3037 [10]	Jimmie Rodgers Memorial Album, Volume 1	1952	100.00	200.00	400.00
LPM-3038 [10]	Jimmie Rodgers Memorial Album, Volume 2	1952	100.00	200.00	400.00
LPM-3039 [10]	Jimmie Rodgers Memorial Album, Volume 3	1952	100.00	200.00	400.00
LPM-3073 [10]	Travelin' Blues	1952	100.00	200.00	400.00
AHL1-3315	The Best of the Legendary Jimmie Rodgers	197?	2.00	4.00	8.00
—Reissue with new prefix					
LPM-3315 [M]	The Best of the Legendary Jimmie Rodgers	1965	10.00	20.00	40.00
LSP-3315 [R]	The Best of the Legendary Jimmie Rodgers	1965	5.00	10.00	20.00
VPS-6091(e) [(2)]	This Is Jimmie Rodgers	1971	5.00	10.00	20.00

ROUNDER

Number	Title (A Side/B Side)	Yr	VG	VG+	NM
1056	First Sessions 1927-1928	1990	3.00	6.00	12.00
1057	The Early Years 1928-1929	1990	3.00	6.00	12.00

RODGERS, JIMMIE (2)

Pop-country vocalist, no relation to the above.

45s

A&M

Number	Title (A Side/B Side)	Yr	VG	VG+	NM
842	I'll Say Goodbye/Shadows	1967	—	3.00	6.00
871	Child of Clay/Turnaround	1967	—	3.00	6.00
898	If I Were the Man/What a Strange Town	1967	—	3.00	6.00
902	I Believe It All/You Pass Me By	1968	—	3.00	6.00
930	How Do You Say Goodbye/I Wanna Be Free	1968	—	3.00	6.00
976	Today/The Lovers	1968	—	3.00	6.00
1055	The Windmills of Your Mind/L.A. Break Down (And Take Me Back In)	1969	—	3.00	6.00
1120	Father Paul/Me About You	1969	—	3.00	6.00
1152	Cycles/Tomorrow My Friends	1969	—	3.00	6.00
1213	Troubled Times/The Dum Dum Song	1970	—	2.50	5.00

DOT

Number	Title (A Side/B Side)	Yr	VG	VG+	NM
16378	No One Will Ever Know/Because	1962	2.50	5.00	10.00
16378 [PS]	No One Will Ever Know/Because	1962	3.75	7.50	15.00
16407	Rainbow at Midnight/Rhumba Boogie	1962	2.50	5.00	10.00
16428	I'll Never Stand in Your Way/Afraid	1963	2.50	5.00	10.00
16450	Lonely Tears/A Face in the Crowd	1963	2.50	5.00	10.00
16467	(I Don't Know Why) I Just Do/Load 'Em Up (And Keep a Steppin')	1963	2.50	5.00	10.00
16490	Poor Little Raggedy Ann/I'm Gonna Be the Winner	1963	2.50	5.00	10.00
16527	Two-Ten Six-Eighteen (Doesn't Anybody Know My Name)/The Banana Boat Song	1963	2.50	5.00	10.00
16561	Together/Mama Was a Cotton Picker	1963	2.50	5.00	10.00
16595	The World I Used to Know/I Forgot More Than You'll Ever Know	1964	2.50	5.00	10.00
16653	Water Boy/Someplace Green	1964	2.50	5.00	10.00
16673	Two Tickets/I Forgot More Than You'll Ever Know	1964	2.50	5.00	10.00
16694	(All My Friends Are Gonna Be) Strangers/Bon Soir Mademoiselle	1965	2.00	4.00	8.00
16720	Careless Love/When I'm Right You Don't Remember	1965	2.00	4.00	8.00
16749	Are You Going My Way (Little Beachcomber)/Little Schoolgirl	1965	2.00	4.00	8.00
16781	Bye Bye Love/Hollow Words	1965	2.00	4.00	8.00
16795	The Chipmunk Song (Christmas Don't Be Late)/In the Snow	1965	2.00	4.00	8.00
16826	A Falen Star/Brother, Where Are You	1966	2.00	4.00	8.00
16861	It's Over/Anita, You're Dreaming	1966	2.50	5.00	10.00
16916	Morning Means Tomorrow/New Ideas	1966	2.00	4.00	8.00
16973	Love Me, Please Love Me/Wonderful You	1966	2.00	4.00	8.00
17040	Time/Yours and Mine	1967	2.00	4.00	8.00

EPIC

Number	Title (A Side/B Side)	Yr	VG	VG+	NM
10828	Froggy's Fable/Daylight Lights the Dawning	1972	—	2.50	5.00
10857	Kick the Can/Go On By	1972	—	2.50	5.00

MGM

Number	Title (A Side/B Side)	Yr	VG	VG+	NM
11732	Mama, Don't Cry at My Wedding/You Don't Live Here No More	1954	6.25	12.50	25.00

ROULETTE

Number	Title (A Side/B Side)	Yr	VG	VG+	NM
4015	Honeycomb/Their Hearts Were Full of Spring	1957	5.00	10.00	20.00
4031	Kisses Sweeter Than Wine/Better Loved You'll Never Be	1957	5.00	10.00	20.00
4045	Oh-Oh, I'm Falling in Love Again/The Long Hot Summer	1958	5.00	10.00	20.00
—Red label					
4045	Oh-Oh, I'm Falling in Love Again/The Long Hot Summer	1958	3.75	7.50	15.00
—White label with colored spokes					
4070	Secretly/Make Me a Miracle	1958	5.00	10.00	20.00
4070 [PS]	Secretly/Make Me a Miracle	1958	10.00	20.00	40.00
4090	Are You Really Mine/The Wizard	1958	3.75	7.50	15.00
4090 [PS]	Are You Really Mine/The Wizard	1958	10.00	20.00	40.00
4116	Bimbombey/You Understand Me	1958	3.75	7.50	15.00
4129	I'm Never Gonna Tell/Because You're Young	1959	3.75	7.50	15.00
4158 [M]	Ring-a-Ling-a-Lario/Wonderful You	1959	3.75	7.50	15.00
4158 [PS]	Ring-a-Ling-a-Lario/Wonderful You	1959	6.25	12.50	25.00
SSR-4158 [S]	Ring-a-Ling-a-Lario/Wonderful You	1959	7.50	15.00	30.00
4191	Tucumcari/That Night You Became Seventeen	1959	3.75	7.50	15.00
4205	It's Christmas Once Again/Wistful Willie	1959	5.00	10.00	20.00
4218 [M]	T.L.C. Tender Love and Care/Waltzing Matilda	1960	3.00	6.00	12.00
SSR-4218 [S]	T.L.C. Tender Love and Care/Waltzing Matilda	1960	7.50	15.00	30.00
4234	Just a Closer Walk with Thee/Joshua Fit the Battle of Jericho	1960	3.00	6.00	12.00
4260	The Wreck of the John B/Four Little Girls in Boston	1960	3.00	6.00	12.00
4293	Woman from Liberia/Come Along Julie	1960	3.00	6.00	12.00
4293 [PS]	Woman from Liberia/Come Along Julie	1960	5.00	10.00	20.00
4318	When Love Is Young/The Little Shepherd of Kingdom Come	1960	3.00	6.00	12.00
4349	Everytime My Heart Sings/I'm On My Way	1961	3.00	6.00	12.00
4371	John Brown's Baby/I'm Going Home	1961	3.00	6.00	12.00
4384	A Little Dog Cried/Englidh Country Garden	1961	3.00	6.00	12.00
4439	You Are Everything to Me/Wanderin' Eyes	1962	3.00	6.00	12.00
SSR-8001 [S]	Bo Diddley/Soldier Won't You Marry Me	1959	7.50	15.00	30.00
SSR-8007 [S]	Froggy Went a-Courtin'/Lisa	1959	7.50	15.00	30.00
SSR-8010 [S]	St. James Infirmary/Just a Wearyin' for You	1959	7.50	15.00	30.00

SCRIMSHAW

Number	Title (A Side/B Side)	Yr	VG	VG+	NM
1313	A Good Woman Likes to Drink with the Boys/Dancing on the Moon	1977	—	2.00	4.00
1314	Everytime I Sing a Love Song/Just a Little Time	1978	—	2.00	4.00
1316	When Our Love Began (Cowboys and Indians)/(B-side unknown)	1978	—	2.00	4.00
1318	Secretly/Shovelin' Coal	1978	—	2.00	4.00
1319/20	Easy to Love/Easy	1979	—	2.00	4.00
—With Michele					

7-Inch Extended Plays

ROULETTE

Number	Title (A Side/B Side)	Yr	VG	VG+	NM
EPR-1-303	Woman from Liberia/The Mating Call//Hey Little Baby/Water Boy	1957	12.50	25.00	50.00
EPR-1-303 [PS]	Jimmie Rodgers	1957	12.50	25.00	50.00
EPR-1-312	*Honeycomb/Oh-Oh, I'm Falling in Love Again/The Preacher/Better Loved You'll Never Be	195?	12.50	25.00	50.00
EPR-1-312 [PS]	Jimmie Rodgers Sings	195?	12.50	25.00	50.00
EPR-1-313	*Tammy/The Song from Moulin Rouge/Love Letters in the Sand/Hey There	195?	12.50	25.00	50.00
EPR-1-313 [PS]	The Number One Ballads, Part 1	195?	12.50	25.00	50.00
EPR-1-315	Bo Diddley/Riddle Song//The Fox and the Goose/Black Is the Color	1960	12.50	25.00	50.00
EPR-1-315 [PS]	Jimmie Rodgers Sings Folk Songs, Part I	1960	12.50	25.00	50.00
EPR-1-316	Waltzing Matilda/The Crocodile//Lord Randal/Gotta Lotta Tunes in My Guitar	195?	12.50	25.00	50.00
EPR-1-316 [PS]	Jimmie Rodgers Sings Folk Songs, Part II	195?	12.50	25.00	50.00
EPR-1-317	Soldier, Won't You Marry Me?/Lassie O'Mine//Liza/Froggy Went a-Courtin'	1960	12.50	25.00	50.00
EPR-1-317 [PS]	Jimmie Rodgers Sings Folk Songs, Part III	1960	12.50	25.00	50.00

Albums

ACCORD

Number	Title (A Side/B Side)	Yr	VG	VG+	NM
SN-7198	Honeycomb & Other Hits	198?	2.50	5.00	10.00

A&M

Number	Title (A Side/B Side)	Yr	VG	VG+	NM
SP-130 [M]	Child of Clay	1967	6.25	12.50	25.00
SP-4130 [S]	Child of Clay	1967	3.75	7.50	15.00
SP-4187	Windmills of Your Mind	1969	3.75	7.50	15.00
SP-4242	Troubled Times	1970	3.75	7.50	15.00

DOT

Number	Title (A Side/B Side)	Yr	VG	VG+	NM
DLP-3453 [M]	No One Will Ever Know	1962	3.75	7.50	15.00
DLP-3496 [M]	Jimmie Rodgers Folk Concert	1963	3.75	7.50	15.00
DLP-3502 [M]	My Favorite Hymns	1963	3.75	7.50	15.00
DLP-3525 [M]	Honeycomb & Kisses Sweeter Than Wine	1963	3.75	7.50	15.00

Number	Title (A Side/B Side)	Yr	VG	VG+	NM
DLP-3556 [M]	Town and Country	1964	5.00	10.00	20.00
DLP-3556 [M]	The World I Used to Know	1964	3.75	7.50	15.00
—Retitled version of above					
DLP-3579 [M]	12 Great Hits	1964	3.75	7.50	15.00
DLP-3614 [M]	Deep Purple	1965	3.75	7.50	15.00
DLP 3657 [M]	Christmas with Jimmie	1965	3.00	6.00	12.00
DLP-3687 [M]	The Nashville Sound	1966	3.75	7.50	15.00
DLP-3710 [M]	Country Music 1966	1966	3.75	7.50	15.00
DLP-3717 [M]	It's Over	1966	3.75	7.50	15.00
DLP-3780 [M]	Love Me, Please Love Me	1967	3.75	7.50	15.00
DLP-3815 [M]	Golden Hits/15 Hits of Jimmie Rodgers	1967	5.00	10.00	20.00
DLP-25453 [S]	No One Will Ever Know	1962	5.00	10.00	20.00
DLP-25496 [S]	Jimmie Rodgers Folk Concert	1963	5.00	10.00	20.00
DLP-25502 [S]	My Favorite Hymns	1963	5.00	10.00	20.00
DLP-25525 [S]	Honeycomb & Kisses Sweeter Than Wine	1963	5.00	10.00	20.00
DLP-25556 [S]	Town and Country	1964	6.25	12.50	25.00
DLP-25556 [S]	The World I Used to Know	1964	5.00	10.00	20.00
—Retitled version of above					
DLP-25579 [S]	12 Great Hits	1964	5.00	10.00	20.00
DLP-25614 [S]	Deep Purple	1965	5.00	10.00	20.00
DLP 25657 [S]	Christmas with Jimmie	1965	3.75	7.50	15.00
DLP-25687 [S]	The Nashville Sound	1966	5.00	10.00	20.00
DLP-25710 [S]	Country Music 1966	1966	5.00	10.00	20.00
DLP-25717 [S]	It's Over	1966	5.00	10.00	20.00
DLP-25780 [S]	Love Me, Please Love Me	1967	5.00	10.00	20.00
DLP-25815 [S]	Golden Hits/15 Hits of Jimmie Rodgers	1967	3.75	7.50	15.00
FORUM					
F-9025 [M]	At Home with Jimmie Rodgers: An Evening of Folk Songs	196?	3.00	6.00	12.00
SF-9025 [S]	At Home with Jimmie Rodgers: An Evening of Folk Songs	196?	3.00	6.00	12.00
F-9049 [M]	Just for You	196?	3.00	6.00	12.00
SF-9049 [S]	Just for You	196?	3.00	6.00	12.00
F-9059 [M]	Jimmie Rodgers Sings Folk Songs	196?	3.00	6.00	12.00
SF-9059 [S]	Jimmie Rodgers Sings Folk Songs	196?	3.00	6.00	12.00
HAMILTON					
HL-114 [M]	6 Favorite Hymns and 6 Favorite Folk Ballads	1964	3.00	6.00	12.00
HL-148 [M]	12 Immortal Songs	196?	3.00	6.00	12.00
HS-12114 [S]	6 Favorite Hymns and 6 Favorite Folk Ballads	1964	3.00	6.00	12.00
HS-12148 [S]	12 Immortal Songs	196?	3.00	6.00	12.00
PARAMOUNT					
PAS-2-1042 [(2)]	Honeycomb	1974	3.75	7.50	15.00
PICKWICK					
PC-3040 [M]	Jimmie Rodgers	196?	3.00	6.00	12.00
SPC-3040 [S]	Jimmie Rodgers	196?	3.00	6.00	12.00
SPC-3599	Big Hits	197?	2.50	5.00	10.00
ROULETTE					
R-25020 [M]	Jimmie Rodgers	1957	12.50	25.00	50.00
—Black label					
R-25020 [M]	Jimmie Rodgers	1959	6.25	12.50	25.00
—White label with colored spokes					
R-25033 [M]	Number One Ballads	1958	12.50	25.00	50.00
—Black label					
R-25033 [M]	Number One Ballads	1959	6.25	12.50	25.00
—White label with colored spokes					
R-25042 [M]	Jimmie Rodgers Sings Folk Songs	1958	12.50	25.00	50.00
—Black label					
R-25042 [M]	Jimmie Rodgers Sings Folk Songs	1959	6.25	12.50	25.00
—White label with colored spokes					
R-25057 [M]	His Golden Year	1959	6.25	12.50	25.00
R-25071 [M]	TV Favorites	1959	7.50	15.00	30.00
SR-25071 [S]	TV Favorites	1959	12.50	25.00	50.00
R-25081 [M]	Twilight on the Trail	1959	7.50	15.00	30.00
SR-25081 [S]	Twilight on the Trail	1959	12.50	25.00	50.00
R 25095 [M]	It's Christmas Once Again	1959	7.50	15.00	30.00
SR 25095 [S]	It's Christmas Once Again	1959	12.50	25.00	50.00
R-25103 [M]	When the Spirit Moves You	1960	7.50	15.00	30.00
SR-25103 [S]	When the Spirit Moves You	1960	10.00	20.00	40.00
R-25128 [M]	At Home with Jimmie Rodgers: An Evening of Folk Songs	1960	7.50	15.00	30.00
SR-25128 [S]	At Home with Jimmie Rodgers: An Evening of Folk Songs	1960	10.00	20.00	40.00
R-25150 [M]	The Folk Song World of Jimmie Rodgers	1961	7.50	15.00	30.00
SR-25150 [S]	The Folk Song World of Jimmie Rodgers	1961	10.00	20.00	40.00
R-25160 [M]	The Best of Jimmie Rodgers' Folk Tunes	1961	7.50	15.00	30.00
SR-25160 [S]	The Best of Jimmie Rodgers' Folk Tunes	1961	10.00	20.00	40.00
—Black vinyl					
SR-25160 [S]	The Best of Jimmie Rodgers' Folk Tunes	1961	62.50	125.00	250.00
—Red vinyl					
R-25179 [M]	15 Million Sellers	1962	6.25	12.50	25.00
SR-25179 [P]	15 Million Sellers	1962	7.50	15.00	30.00
R-25199 [M]	Folk Songs	1963	5.00	10.00	20.00
SR-25199 [S]	Folk Songs	1963	6.25	12.50	25.00
SR-42006	Yours Truly	1968	3.75	7.50	15.00

RODRIGUEZ, JOHNNY

45s

Number	Title (A Side/B Side)	Yr	VG	VG+	NM
CAPITOL					
B-44071	I Didn't (Every Chance I Had)/I'm Not That Good at Goodbye	1987	—	2.00	4.00
B-44204	I Wanta Wake Up with You/Someday I'm Gonna Finish Leaving You	1988	—	2.00	4.00
B-44245	You Might Want to Use Me Again/She Loves Austin	1988	—	2.00	4.00
B-44325	No Chance to Dance/Back to Stay	1989	—	2.00	4.00
B-44403	Back to Stay/Someday I'm Gonna Finish Leaving You	1989	—	2.00	4.00
COLUMBIA					
02987	The Most Beautiful Girl/Too Far Gone	1982	—	2.00	4.00
—With Ray Conniff; B-side by Zella Lehr with Ray Conniff					
EPIC					
01033	I Want You Tonight/Your Love Isn't Mine Anymore	1981	—	—	3.00
02411	Trying Not to Love You/Mexico Rain	1981	—	—	3.00
02638	It's Not the Same Old You/Born with the Blues	1981	—	—	3.00
03275	He's Not Entitled to Your Love/Starting All Over Again	1982	—	—	3.00
03598	Foolin'/Because of You	1983	—	—	3.00
03972	How Could I Love Her So Much/Somethin' About a Jukebox	1983	—	—	3.00
04206	Back on Her Mind Again/Eleven Roses	1983	—	—	3.00
04336	Too Late to Go Home/No Memories Hangin' 'Round	1984	—	—	3.00
04460	Let's Leave the Lights On Tonight/What a Movie You'd Make	1984	—	—	3.00
04562	First Time Burned/Hand Me Another of Those	1984	—	—	3.00
04628	Rose of My Heart/Down in the Boondocks	1984	—	—	3.00
04838	Here I Am Again/Full Circle	1985	—	—	3.00
05732	She Don't Cry Like She Used To/Back on Her Mind Again	1985	—	—	3.00
05863	Maxine/Full Circle	1986	—	—	3.00
50671	Down on the Rio Grande/Mexico Holiday	1979	—	2.00	4.00
50735	Fools for Each Other/Street Walker	1979	—	2.00	4.00
50791	I Hate the Way I Love It/Almost Persuaded	1979	—	2.00	4.00
—With Charly McClain					
50808	What'll I Tell Virginia/Whatever Gets Me Through the Night	1979	—	2.00	4.00
50859	Love, Look At Us Now/Where Did It Go	1980	—	2.00	4.00
50932	North of the Border/When She Gets Around to Me	1980	—	2.00	4.00
MERCURY					
55004	Eres Tu/You Put a Hold on Me	1977	—	2.00	4.00
55012	Savin' This Love Song for You/Que Te Quiero	1977	—	2.00	4.00
55020	We Believe in Happy Endings/The Immigrant	1978	—	2.00	4.00
55029	Love Me with All Your Heart (Cuando Caliente El Sol)	1978	—	2.00	4.00
55050	Alibis/Rest Your Love on Me	1978	—	2.00	4.00
73334	Pass Me By (If You're Only Passing Through)/ Jealous Heart	1972	—	2.50	5.00
73368	You Always Come Back (To Hurting Me)/I Wonder Where You Are Tonight	1973	—	2.50	5.00
73416	Ridin' My Thumb to Mexico/Release Me	1973	—	2.50	5.00
73446	That's the Way Love Goes/I Really Don't Want to Know	1973	—	2.50	5.00
73471	Something/Born to Lose	1974	—	2.50	5.00
73493	Dance with Me (Just One More Time)/Faded Love	1974	—	2.50	5.00
—Red label					
73493	Dance with Me (Just One More Time)/Faded Love	1974	—	2.00	4.00
—Chicago skyline label					
73621	We're Over/Oh I Miss You	1974	—	2.00	4.00
73659	I Just Can't Get Her Out of My Mind/Have I Told You Lately	1975	—	2.00	4.00
73682	Just Get Up and Close the Door/Am I That Easy to Forget	1975	—	2.00	4.00
73715	Love Put a Song in My Heart/Steppin' Out on You	1975	—	2.00	4.00
73769	I Couldn't Be Me Without You/Sometimes I Wish I Were You	1976	—	2.00	4.00
73815	I Wonder If I Ever Said Goodbye/Louisiana	1976	—	2.00	4.00
73855	Hillbilly Heart/Commonly Known As the Blues	1976	—	2.00	4.00
73878	Desperado/There'll Always Be Honky-Tonks in Texas	1976	—	2.00	4.00
73914	If Practice Makes Perfect/Hard Times	1977	—	2.00	4.00

Albums

Number	Title (A Side/B Side)	Yr	VG	VG+	NM
CAPITOL					
C1-90040	Gracias	1988	2.50	5.00	10.00
EPIC					
JE 36014	Rodriguez	1979	2.50	5.00	10.00
JE 36274	Through My Eyes	1980	2.50	5.00	10.00
JE 36587	Gypsy	1980	2.50	5.00	10.00
FE 37103	After the Rain	1981	2.50	5.00	10.00
FE 38321	Biggest Hits	1982	2.50	5.00	10.00
FE 38806	For Every Rose	1983	2.50	5.00	10.00
FE 39172	Foolin' with Fire	1984	2.50	5.00	10.00
FE 39583	Full Circle	1985	2.50	5.00	10.00
MERCURY					
SRM-1-686	All I Ever Meant to Do Was Sing	1973	3.75	7.50	15.00
SRM-1-699	My Third Album	1974	3.75	7.50	15.00
SRM-1-1012	Songs About Ladies and Love	1974	3.75	7.50	15.00
SRM-1-1032	Just Get Up and Close the Door	1975	3.75	7.50	15.00
SRM-1-1057	Love Put a Song in My Heart	1975	3.75	7.50	15.00
SRM-1-1078	The Greatest Hits of Johnny Rodriguez	1976	3.75	7.50	15.00
SRM-1-1110	Reflecting	1976	3.00	6.00	12.00
SRM-1-1144	Practice Makes Perfect	1977	3.00	6.00	12.00
SRM-1-5003	Just for You	1977	3.00	6.00	12.00
SRM-1-5011	Love Me with All You Heart	1978	3.00	6.00	12.00
SRM-1-5015	Johnny Rodriguez Was Here	1979	3.00	6.00	12.00
SRM-1-5022	Sketches	1980	3.00	6.00	12.00
SR-61378	Introducing Johnny Rodriguez	1973	3.75	7.50	15.00
826271-1	The Greatest Hits of Johnny Rodriguez	1985	2.00	4.00	8.00
—Reissue					

ROE, TOMMY

45s

Number	Title (A Side/B Side)	Yr	VG	VG+	NM
ABC					
10762	Sweet Pea/Much More Love	1966	2.50	5.00	10.00
—Reissue; this was the common version when this song was a hit; earliest copies have "ABC Records" standing alone (not in a circle)					
10852	Hooray for Hazel/Need Your Love	1966	2.50	5.00	10.00
10888	It's Now Winters Day/Kick Me Charlie	1966	2.00	4.00	8.00
10888 [PS]	It's Now Winters Day/Kick Me Charlie	1966	3.75	7.50	15.00
10908	Sing Along with Me/Night Time	1967	2.00	4.00	8.00
10933	Moon Talk/Sweet Sounds	1967	2.00	4.00	8.00
10945	Little Miss Sunshine/You I Need	1967	2.00	4.00	8.00
10989	Melancholy Mood/Paisley Dreams	1967	2.00	4.00	8.00
11039	Dottie I Like It/Soft Words	1968	2.00	4.00	8.00
11076	An Oldie But a Goodie/Sugar Cane	1968	2.00	4.00	8.00
11140	It's Gonna Hurt Me/Gotta Keep Rolling Along	1968	2.00	4.00	8.00
11164	Dizzy/The You I Need	1969	2.50	5.00	10.00
11211	Heather Honey/Money Is My Pay	1969	—	3.00	6.00
11229	Jack and Jill/Tip Toe Tina	1969	—	3.00	6.00
11247	Jam Up Jelly Tight/Moontalk	1969	2.00	4.00	8.00

Number	Title (A Side/B Side)	Yr	VG	VG+	NM
11247 [PS]	Jam Up Jelly Tight/Moontalk	1969	3.00	6.00	12.00
11258	Stir It Up and Serve It/Fire Fly	1970	—	3.00	6.00
11266	Pearl/A Dollar's Worth of Pennies	1970	—	3.00	6.00
11273	We Can Make Music/Gotta Keep Rolling Along	1970	—	3.00	6.00
11273 [PS]	We Can Make Music/Gotta Keep Rolling Along	1970	—	3.00	6.00
11281	King of Fools/Brush a Little Sunshine	1970	—	3.00	6.00
11287	Little Miss Goodie Two Shoes/Traffic Jam	1971	—	3.00	6.00
11293	King of Fools/Pistol-Legged Mama	1971	—	3.00	6.00
11307	Stagger Lee/Back Streets and Alleys	1971	—	3.00	6.00
ABC-PARAMOUNT					
10329	Sheila/Save Your Kisses	1962	3.75	7.50	15.00
10362	Susie Darlin'/Piddle De Pat	1962	3.00	6.00	12.00
10362 [PS]	Susie Darlin'/Piddle De Pat	1962	6.25	12.50	25.00
10379	Town Crier/Rainbow	1962	3.00	6.00	12.00
10389	Don't Cry Donna/Gonna Take a Chance	1962	3.00	6.00	12.00
10423	The Folk Singer/Count on Me	1963	2.50	5.00	10.00
10454	Kiss and Run/What Makes the Blues	1963	2.50	5.00	10.00
10478	Everybody/Sorry I'm Late, Lisa	1963	3.75	7.50	15.00
10515	Come On/There Will Be Better Years	1964	2.50	5.00	10.00
10543	Carol/Be a Good Little Girl	1964	2.50	5.00	10.00
10555	Dance with Me/Wild Water Skiing Weekend	1964	5.00	10.00	20.00
10579	Oh So Right/I Think I Love You	1964	3.00	6.00	12.00
10604	Party Girl/Oh How I Could Love You	1964	2.50	5.00	10.00
10623	Love Me, Love Me/Diane from Manchester Square	1965	3.00	6.00	12.00
10665	Fourteen Pair of Shoes/Combo Music	1965	2.50	5.00	10.00
10696	The Gunfighter/I'm a Rambler, I'm a Gambler	1965	5.00	10.00	20.00
10706	I Keep Remembering (Things I Forgot)/Wish You Didn't Have to Go	1965	2.50	5.00	10.00
10738	Doesn't Anybody Know My Name/Everytime a Bluebird Cries	1965	2.50	5.00	10.00
10762	Sweet Pea/Much More Love	1966	6.25	12.50	25.00
BGO					
1003	She Do Run Run/(B-side unknown)	1982	2.50	5.00	10.00
JUDD					
1018	Caveman/I Gotta Girl	1960	12.50	25.00	50.00
1022	Sheila/Pretty Girl	1960	37.50	75.00	150.00
MARK IV					
001	Caveman/I Gotta Girl	1960	25.00	50.00	100.00
MCA CURB					
52711	Some Such Foolishness/Barbara Lou	1985	—	2.00	4.00
52778	Radio Romance/Barbara Lou	1986	—	2.00	4.00
MERCURY					
888206-7	Let's Be Fools Like That Again/Barbara Lou	1986	—	—	3.00
888497-7	Back When It Really Mattered/Radio Romance	1987	—	—	3.00
MGM SOUTH					
7001	Mean Little Woman, Rosalie/Skyline	1972	—	2.50	5.00
7008	Sarah My Love/Chewing on Sugar Cane	1972	—	2.50	5.00
7013	Working Class Hero/Sun in My Eyes	1973	—	2.50	5.00
7025	Silver Eyes/Memphis Me	1973	—	3.00	6.00
MONUMENT					
8644	Glitter and Gleam/Bad News	1975	—	2.50	5.00
8662	Snowing Me Under/Rita and Her Band	1975	—	2.50	5.00
8684	Slow Dancing/Burn On Love Light	1976	—	2.50	5.00
8705	Everybody/Energy	1976	—	2.50	5.00
45205	Early in the Morning/Bad News	1976	—	2.50	5.00
45228	Your Love Will See Me Through/Working Class Hero	1977	—	2.50	5.00
TRUMPET					
1401	Caveman/I Gotta Girl	1960	50.00	100.00	200.00
WARNER BROS.					
8660	Dreamin' Again/Love the Way You Love Me Up	1978	—	2.00	4.00
8720	Just Look at Me/Love the Way You Love Me Up	1978	—	2.50	5.00
8800	Massachusetts/Just Look at Me	1979	—	2.50	5.00
49085	You Better Move On/Just Look at Me	1979	—	2.00	4.00
49235	There Is No Sun on Sunset Boulevard/Charlie, I Love Your Wife	1980	—	2.00	4.00
Albums					
ABC					
S-467 [R]	Something for Everybody	1968	12.50	25.00	50.00
—Issued in rechanneled stereo four years after its original release					
594 [M]	It's Now Winters Day	1967	5.00	10.00	20.00
S-594 [S]	It's Now Winters Day	1967	6.25	12.50	25.00
610 [M]	Phantasy	1967	10.00	20.00	40.00
S-610 [S]	Phantasy	1967	10.00	20.00	40.00
S-683	Dizzy	1969	5.00	10.00	20.00
S-700	12 in a Roe/A Collection of Tommy Roe's Greatest Hits	1969	5.00	10.00	20.00
S-714	We Can Make Music	1970	3.75	7.50	15.00
S-732	Beginnings	1971	3.75	7.50	15.00
X-762	16 Greatest Hits	1972	3.75	7.50	15.00
ST-90883 [S]	Sweet Pea	1966	10.00	20.00	40.00
—Capitol Record Club issue					
T-90883 [M]	Sweet Pea	1966	10.00	20.00	40.00
—Capitol Record Club issue					
ABC-PARAMOUNT					
432 [M]	Sheila	1962	10.00	20.00	40.00
S-432 [S]	Sheila	1962	12.50	25.00	50.00
467 [M]	Something for Everybody	1964	7.50	15.00	30.00
575 [M]	Sweet Pea	1966	7.50	51.00	30.00
S-575 [S]	Sweet Pea	1966	10.00	20.00	40.00
ACCORD					
SN-7155	Sheila	1981	2.50	5.00	10.00
MCA					
1519	Collectibles — Greatest Hits	1982	2.00	4.00	8.00
MONUMENT					
7604	Energy	1977	2.50	5.00	10.00
—Reissue of 34182					
7614	Full Bloom	1977	2.50	5.00	10.00
PZ 34182	Energy	1976	3.00	6.00	12.00

ROEMANS, THE

TOMMY ROE's backing group.

Number	Title (A Side/B Side)	Yr	VG	VG+	NM
45s					
ABC					
10814	When the Sun Shines in the Mornin'/Love (That's All I Want)	1966	3.75	7.50	15.00
10871	All the Good Things/Pleasing You Pleases Me	1966	3.75	7.50	15.00
ABC-PARAMOUNT					
10583	Give Me a Chance/Your Friend	1964	5.00	10.00	20.00
10671	Miserlou/Don't	1965	5.00	10.00	20.00
10723	Universal Soldier/Lost Little Girl	1965	5.00	10.00	20.00
10757	Listen to Me/You Make Me Feel Good	1965	5.00	10.00	20.00

ROGER AND THE TRAVELERS

Number	Title (A Side/B Side)	Yr	VG	VG+	NM
45s					
EMBER					
1079	You're Daddy's Little Girl/Just Gonna Be That Way	1961	25.00	50.00	100.00

ROGERS, JIMMY

Number	Title (A Side/B Side)	Yr	VG	VG+	NM
45s					
CHESS					
1506	I Used to Love a Woman/Back Door Friend	1952	50.00	100.00	200.00
—Earlier Jimmy Rogers 45s on Chess are not known to exist					
1519	The Last Time/Out on the Road	1952	50.00	100.00	200.00
1543	Left Me with a Broken Heart/Act Like You Love Me	1953	50.00	100.00	200.00
1574	Chicago Bound/Sloppy Drunk	1954	75.00	150.00	300.00
1616	You're the One/Blues All Day Long	1956	12.50	25.00	50.00
1643	Walking By Myself/If It Ain't Me	1956	12.50	25.00	50.00
1659	One Kiss/I Can't Believe	1957	12.50	25.00	50.00
1687	What Have I Done/Trace of You	1958	10.00	20.00	40.00
1721	Rock This House/My Last Meal	1959	7.50	15.00	30.00

ROGERS, JULIE

Number	Title (A Side/B Side)	Yr	VG	VG+	NM
45s					
MEGA					
0075	Almost Close to You/Where Do You Go	1972	—	2.50	5.00
MERCURY					
72332	The Wedding/Without Your Love	1964	2.50	5.00	10.00
—Black label					
72332	The Wedding/Without Your Love	1964	2.00	4.00	8.00
—Red label					
72380	Like a Child/The Love of a Boy	1965	2.00	4.00	8.00
72380 [PS]	Like a Child/The Love of a Boy	1965	3.00	6.00	12.00
72426	Hawaiian Wedding Song/Turn Around, Look at Me	1965	2.00	4.00	8.00
72535	Another Year, Another Love, Another Heartache/Don't Waste Your Young Years on Him	1966	2.00	4.00	8.00
72646	Climb Ev'ry Mountain/While the Angelus Was Ringing	1966	2.00	4.00	8.00
Albums					
MERCURY					
MG-20981 [M]	Julie Rogers	1965	3.75	7.50	15.00
SR-60981 [S]	Julie Rogers	1965	5.00	10.00	20.00

ROGERS, KENNY

Also see THE BOBBY DOYLE THREE; THE FIRST EDITION; THE NEW CHRISTY MINSTRELS; THE SCHOLARS (1).

Number	Title (A Side/B Side)	Yr	VG	VG+	NM
45s					
CARLTON					
454	That Crazy Feeling/We'll Always Have Each Other	1958	25.00	50.00	100.00
—As "Kenneth Rogers"					
454	That Crazy Feeling/We'll Always Have Each Other	1958	25.00	50.00	100.00
—As "Kenny Rogers"					
468	For You Alone/I've Got a Lot to Learn	1958	15.00	30.00	60.00
KEN-LEE					
102	Jole Blon/Lonely	195?	25.00	50.00	100.00
LIBERTY					
1380	Lady/Sweet Music Man	1980	—	2.00	4.00
1380 [PS]	Lady/Sweet Music Man	1980	—	2.50	5.00
1391	Long Arm of the Law/You Were a Good Friend	1980	—	2.00	4.00
1415	I Don't Need You/Without You in My Life	1981	—	—	3.00
1415 [PS]	I Don't Need You/Without You in My Life	1981	—	2.00	4.00
1430	Share Your Love with Me/Greybeard	1981	—	—	3.00
1430 [PS]	Share Your Love with Me/Greybeard	1981	—	2.00	4.00
1438	Kentucky Homemade Christmas/Carol of the Bells	1981	—	2.50	5.00
1438 [PS]	Kentucky Homemade Christmas/Carol of the Bells	1981	—	3.00	6.00
1441	Blaze of Glory/The Good Life	1981	—	—	3.00
1444	Through the Years/So In Love with You	1981	—	—	3.00
1471	Love Will Turn You Around/I Want a Son	1982	—	—	3.00
1471 [PS]	Love Will Turn You Around/I Want a Son	1982	—	2.50	5.00
1485	A Love Song/Fool in Me	1982	—	—	3.00
1492	We've Got Tonight/You Are So Beautiful	1983	—	—	3.00
—A-side: With Sheena Easton					
1492 [PS]	We've Got Tonight/You Are So Beautiful	1983	—	2.00	4.00
1495	All My Life/The Farther I Go	1983	—	—	3.00
1495 [PS]	All My Life/The Farther I Go	1983	—	2.00	4.00
1503	Scarlet Fever/What I Learned from Loving You	1983	—	—	3.00
1511	Sweet Music Man/You Were a Good Friend	1983	—	—	3.00
1524	A Stranger in My Place/Love Is What We Make It	1985	—	—	3.00
1525	Twentieth Century Fool/It Turns Me Inside Out	1985	—	—	3.00
1526	Abraham, Martin and John/Goodbye Marie	1985	—	—	3.00
4065 [DJ]	Christmas Everyday//Kentucky Homemade Christmas/Carol Of The Bells	198?	—	3.00	6.00
MERCURY					
72545	Here's That Rainy Day/Take Life in Stride	1966	6.25	12.50	25.00

Number	Title (A Side/B Side)	Yr	VG	VG+	NM
RCA					
5016-7-R	They Don't Make Them Like They Used To/Just the Thought of Losing You	1986	—	—	3.00
5016-7-R [PS]	They Don't Make Them Like They Used To/Just the Thought of Losing You	1986	—	—	3.00
5078-7-R	Twenty Years Ago/The Heart of the Matter	1986	—	—	3.00
5209-7-R	Make No Mistake, She's Mine/You're My Love	1987	—	—	3.00
—With Ronnie Milsap					
5258-7-R	I Prefer the Moonlight/We're Doin' Alright	1987	—	—	3.00
6832-7-R	The Factory/One More Day	1987	—	—	3.00
8381-7-R	I Prefer the Moonlight/Make No Mistake, She's Mine	1988	—	—	3.00
—Gold Standard Series; B-side with Ronnie Milsap					
8390-7-R	I Don't Call Him Daddy/We're Doin' Alright	1988	—	—	3.00
PB-13710	This Woman/Buried Treasure	1984	—	—	3.00
PB-13710 [PS]	This Woman/Buried Treasure	1984	—	2.00	4.00
JK-13713 [DJ]	Buried Treasure (same on both sides)	1984	—	2.50	5.00
PB-13774	Eyes That See in the Dark/Hold Me	1984	—	—	3.00
PB-13832	Evening Star/Midsummer Nights	1984	—	—	3.00
PB-13899	What About Me/The Rest of Last Night	1984	—	—	3.00
—With Kim Carnes and James Ingram					
PB-13899 [PS]	What About Me/The Rest of Last Night	1984	—	2.00	4.00
PB-13944	The Christmas Song/Medley: Winter Wonderland-Sleigh Ride	1984	—	2.00	4.00
—B-side by Dolly Parton					
PB-13975	Crazy/The Stranger	1984	—	—	3.00
PB-13975 [PS]	Crazy/The Stranger	1984	—	2.00	4.00
GB-14074	This Woman/What About Me	1985	—	—	3.00
—Gold Standard Series; B-side by Kenny Rogers, Kim Carnes and James Ingram					
PB-14194	Morning Desire/People in Love	1985	—	—	3.00
PB-14194 [PS]	Morning Desire/People in Love	1985	—	2.00	4.00
—Fold-out poster sleeve					
PB-14298	Tomb of the Unknown Love/Our Perfect Song	1986	—	—	3.00
PB-14298 [PS]	Tomb of the Unknown Love/Our Perfect Song	1986	—	2.00	4.00
GB-14353	Crazy/Morning Desire	1986	—	—	3.00
—Gold Standard Series					
PB-14384	The Pride Is Back/Didn't We?	1986	—	2.00	4.00
—A-side: With Nickie Ryder					
PB-14384 [PS]	The Pride Is Back/Didn't We?	1986	—	2.00	4.00
REPRISE					
18835	Bed of Roses/I'll Be There for You	1992	—	—	3.00
18967	Someone Must Feel Like a Fool Tonight/Sunshine	1992	—	—	3.00
19080	If You Want to Find Love/Sunshine	1991	—	—	3.00
19324	Walk Away/What I Did for Love	1991	—	—	3.00
19504	Lay My Body Down/Crazy in Love	1991	—	—	3.00
19972	Maybe/If I Knew Then What I Know Now	1990	—	—	3.00
—A-side: With Holly Dunn; B-side: With Gladys Knight					
22750	Christmas in America/Joy to the World	1989	—	—	3.00
22750 [PS]	Christmas in America/Joy to the World	1989	—	—	3.00
22828	The Vows Go Unbroken (Always True to You)/One Night	1989	—	—	3.00
22853	(Something Inside) So Strong/When You Put Your Heart In It	1989	—	—	3.00
27690	Planet Texas/When You Put Your Heart in It	1988	—	—	3.00
27690 [PS]	Planet Texas/When You Put Your Heart in It	1988	—	—	3.00
27812	When You Put Your Heart In It/(Instrumental)	1988	—	—	3.00
27812 [PS]	When You Put Your Heart In It/(Instrumental)	1988	—	—	3.00
UNITED ARTISTS					
XW746	Love Lifted Me/Home-Made Love	1975	—	2.00	4.00
XW798	There's an Old Man in Our Town/Home-Made Love	1976	—	2.00	4.00
XW812	I Would Like to See You Again/While the Feeling's Good	1976	—	2.00	4.00
XW868	Laura (What's He Got That I Ain't Got)/I Wasn't Mad Enough	1976	—	2.00	4.00
XW929	Lucille/Till I Get It Right	1976	—	2.00	4.00
XW1027	Daytime Friends/We Don't Make Love Anymore	1977	—	2.00	4.00
XW1095	Sweet Music Man/Lying Again	1977	—	2.00	4.00
XW1151	Love Lifted Me/Reuben James	1978	—	2.00	4.00
XW1152	Today I Started Loving You Again/Just Dropped In (To See What Condition My Condition Was In)	1978	—	2.00	4.00
XW1153	Daytime Friends/But You Know I Love You	1978	—	2.00	4.00
XW1154	Lucille/Something's Burning	1978	—	2.00	4.00
XW1155	Sweet Music Man/Ruby, Don't Take Your Love to Town	1978	—	2.00	4.00
—B-sides of the above five singles are re-recordings of First Edition hits paired with early United Artists country hits					
XW1210	Love Or Something Like It/Starting Again	1978	—	2.00	4.00
XW1250	The Gambler/Momma's Waiting	1978	—	2.00	4.00
XW1273	She Believes in Me/Morgana Jones	1979	—	2.00	4.00
XW1273 [PS]	She Believes in Me/Morgana Jones	1979	—	2.50	5.00
1315	You Decorated My Life/One Man's Woman	1979	—	2.00	4.00
1315 [PS]	You Decorated My Life/One Man's Woman	1979	—	2.50	5.00
1327	Coward of the County/I Wanna Make You Smile	1979	—	2.00	4.00
1345	Don't Fall in Love with a Dreamer/Intro: Goin' Home to the Rock-Gideon Tanner	1980	—	2.00	4.00
—A-side: With Kim Carnes					
1345 [PS]	Don't Fall in Love with a Dreamer/Intro: Goin' Home to the Rock-Gideon Tanner	1980	—	2.50	5.00
1359	Love the World Away/Sayin' Goodbye-Requiem	1980	—	2.00	4.00

Albums

Number	Title	Yr	VG	VG+	NM
LIBERTY					
LO-607	Love Lifted Me	1981	2.00	4.00	8.00
—Reissue of United Artists 607					
LO-689	Kenny Rogers	1981	2.00	4.00	8.00
—Reissue of United Artists 689					
LO-754	Daytime Friends	1981	2.00	4.00	8.00
—Reissue of United Artists 754					
LO-835	Ten Years of Gold	1981	2.00	4.00	8.00
—Reissue of United Artists 835					
LO-903	Love Or Something Like It	1981	2.00	4.00	8.00
—Reissue of United Artists 903					
LO-934	The Gambler	1981	2.00	4.00	8.00
—Reissue of United Artists 934					
LOO-979	Kenny	1981	2.00	4.00	8.00
—Reissue of United Artists 979					
LOO-1035	Gideon	1981	2.00	4.00	8.00
—Reissue of United Artists 1035					
LOO-1072	Kenny Rogers' Greatest Hits	1980	2.00	4.00	8.00
LOO-1108	Share Your Love	1981	2.00	4.00	8.00
LN-10207	Love Lifted Me	1984	—	3.00	6.00
—Budget-line reissue					
LN-10208	Kenny Rogers	1983	—	3.00	6.00
—Budget-line reissue					
LN-10240	Christmas	198?	2.00	4.00	8.00
—Reissue of LOO 51115					
LN-10243	Gideon	1984	—	3.00	6.00
—Budget-line reissue					
LN-10245	We've Got Tonight	1984	—	3.00	6.00
—Budget-line reissue					
LN-10246	Love Will Turn You Around	1984	—	3.00	6.00
—Budget-line reissue					
LN-10247	The Gambler	1984	—	3.00	6.00
—Budget-line reissue					
LN-10248	Kenny	1984	—	3.00	6.00
—Budget-line reissue					
LN-10249	Daytime Friends	1984	—	3.00	6.00
—Budget-line reissue					
LN-10250	Love Or Something Like It	1984	—	3.00	6.00
—Budget-line reissue					
LN-10254	Ten Years of Gold	1984	—	3.00	6.00
—Budget-line reissue					
LOO-51115	Christmas	1981	2.50	5.00	10.00
LO-51124	Love Will Turn You Around	1982	2.00	4.00	8.00
LO-51143	We've Got Tonight	1983	2.00	4.00	8.00
LV-51152	Twenty Greatest Hits	1983	2.00	4.00	8.00
LO-51154	Duets	1984	2.00	4.00	8.00
LO-51157	Love Is What We Make It	1985	2.00	4.00	8.00
MOBILE FIDELITY					
1-044	The Gambler	1981	5.00	10.00	20.00
—Audiophile vinyl					
1-049	Kenny Rogers' Greatest Hits	1981	5.00	10.00	20.00
—Audiophile vinyl					
RCA					
5833-1-R	They Don't Make Them Like They Used To	1986	2.00	4.00	8.00
6484-1-R	I Prefer the Moonlight	1987	2.00	4.00	8.00
8371-1-R	Greatest Hits	1988	2.00	4.00	8.00
RCA VICTOR					
AFL1-4697	Eyes That See in the Dark	1983	2.00	4.00	8.00
AJL1-5335	What About Me	1984	2.00	4.00	8.00
AJL1-7023	The Heart of the Matter	1985	2.00	4.00	8.00
REPRISE					
25792	Something Inside So Strong	1989	2.50	5.00	10.00
25973	Christmas in America	1989	3.00	6.00	12.00
R 144593	Love Is Strange	1990	5.00	10.00	20.00
—Only available on vinyl from BMG Direct Marketing					
UNITED ARTISTS					
UA-LA607-G	Love Lifted Me	1976	3.75	7.50	15.00
UA-LA689-G	Kenny Rogers	1976	2.50	5.00	10.00
UA-LA754-G	Daytime Friends	1977	2.50	5.00	10.00
UA-LA835-H	Ten Years of Gold	1978	2.50	5.00	10.00
UA-LA903-H	Love Or Something Like It	1978	2.50	5.00	10.00
UA-LA934-H	The Gambler	1978	2.50	5.00	10.00
LWAK-979	Kenny	1979	2.50	5.00	10.00
LOO-1035	Gideon	1980	2.50	5.00	10.00

ROGERS, KENNY, AND DOLLY PARTON

Also see each artist's individual listings.

12-Inch Singles

Number	Title (A Side/B Side)	Yr	VG	VG+	NM
RCA					
JR-13662 [DJ]	Islands in the Stream (same on both sides)	1983	2.00	4.00	8.00

45s

Number	Title (A Side/B Side)	Yr	VG	VG+	NM
RCA					
5352-7-R	Christmas Without You/I Believe in Santa Claus	1987	—	—	3.00
—B-side by Dolly Parton					
9070-7-R	Christmas Without You/Medley: Winter Wonderland-Sleigh Ride	1989	—	—	3.00
—B-side by Dolly Parton					
PB-13615	Islands in the Stream/I Will Always Love You	1983	—	—	3.00
PB-13615 [PS]	Islands in the Stream/I Will Always Love You	1983	—	2.50	5.00
—Version 1: With "(Duet with Dolly Parton)" in small letters					
PB-13615 [PS]	Islands in the Stream/I Will Always Love You	1983	—	2.00	4.00
—Version 2: With Dolly Parton's name the same size as Kenny Rogers'					
PB-13945	The Greatest Gift of All/White Christmas	1984	—	2.00	4.00
PB-14058	Real Love/I Can't Be True	1985	—	—	3.00
GB-14073	Islands in the Stream/Eyes That See in the Dark	1985	—	—	3.00
—Gold Standard Series; B-side by Kenny Rogers					
PB-14261	Christmas Without You/A Christmas to Remember	1985	—	—	3.00
PB-14261 [PS]	Christmas Without You/A Christmas to Remember	1985	—	2.00	4.00
REPRISE					
19760	Love Is Strange/Walk Away	1990	—	—	3.00

Albums

Number	Title	Yr	VG	VG+	NM
RCA VICTOR					
ASL1-5307	Once Upon a Christmas	1984	2.50	5.00	10.00

ROGERS, KENNY, AND THE FIRST EDITION

See THE FIRST EDITION.

ROGERS, KENNY, AND DOTTIE WEST

Also see each artist's individual listings.

45s

Number	Title (A Side/B Side)	Yr	VG	VG+	NM
LIBERTY					
1516	Baby I'm-a Want You/Together Again	1984	—	—	3.00

Number	Title (A Side/B Side)	Yr	VG	VG+	NM
UNITED ARTISTS					
XW-1137	Every Time Two Fools Collide/We Love Each Other	1978	—	2.00	4.00
XW-1234	Anyone Who Isn't Me Tonight/You and Me	1978	—	2.00	4.00
XW-1276	All I Ever Need Is You/Another Somebody Done Somebody Wrong Song	1979	—	2.00	4.00
XW-1299	Till I Can Make It on My Own/Midnight Flyer	1979	—	2.00	4.00
Albums					
UNITED ARTISTS					
UA-LA864-G	Every Time Two Fools Collide	1978	2.50	5.00	10.00
UA-LA946-H	Classics	1979	2.50	5.00	10.00

ROGERS, MORRIS, AND THE CONTINENTALS

Number	Title (A Side/B Side)	Yr	VG	VG+	NM
45s					
DELTA					
601/2	The Leg/Wonders of Love	1963	50.00	100.00	200.00

ROGERS, TIMMIE

Number	Title (A Side/B Side)	Yr	VG	VG+	NM
45s					
CADET					
5685	Super Soul Brothers/It Rolls Through Everything	1971	—	2.50	5.00
CAMEO					
116	Back to School Again/I've Got a Dog Who Loves Me	1957	7.50	15.00	30.00
131	Take Me to Your Leader/Fla-Ga-La-Pa	1958	6.25	12.50	25.00
CAPITOL					
F2406	Saturday Night/If I Were You, Baby	1953	6.25	12.50	25.00
F2509	Oh Yeah/Nothin' Wrong with Nothin'	1953	6.25	12.50	25.00
EPIC					
9813	If You Can't Smile and Say Yes (Please Don't Cry and Say No)/Chum Goy Tum Toy Fricasee (Soy Soy Soo)	1965	2.00	4.00	8.00
9899	Everybody Wants to Go to Heaven, But Nobody Wants to Die/Too Young to Go Steady	1966	2.00	4.00	8.00
MERCURY					
70451	If I Give My Heart to You/Teedle-Dee Teedle-Dum	1954	10.00	20.00	40.00
PAR-TEE					
1303	Watergate/Snake Hips	1973	—	2.50	5.00
PARKWAY					
814	I Love Ya, I Love Ya, I Love Ya/Tee-Hee	1960	3.75	7.50	15.00
PHILIPS					
40074	Oh Yeah/Fla-Ga-La-Pa	1962	2.50	5.00	10.00
SIGNATURE					
12037	First Proposal/Underwater Cha Cha Cha	1960	3.75	7.50	15.00
Albums					
PHILIPS					
PHM 200088 [M]	If I Were President	1963	5.00	10.00	20.00
PHS 600088 [S]	If I Were President	1963	6.25	12.50	25.00

ROGERS, WELDON

Number	Title (A Side/B Side)	Yr	VG	VG+	NM
45s					
IMPERIAL					
5451	So Long, Good Luck and Goodbye/Trying to Get to You	1957	50.00	100.00	200.00
—B-side is actually The Teen Kings' version rather than Rogers'; by mistake, the wrong recording left Norman Petty's studio for Imperial.					
JE-WEL					
103	Everybody Wants You/This Song's Just for You	1956	250.00	500.00	1000.

ROKES, THE

Number	Title (A Side/B Side)	Yr	VG	VG+	NM
45s					
RCA VICTOR					
47-9199	Let's Live for Today/Change of Papers	1967	3.00	6.00	12.00
47-9546	When the Wind Arises/The Works of Bartholomew	1968	3.00	6.00	12.00
Albums					
RCA VICTOR INTERNATIONAL					
FPM-185 [M]	Che Mondo Strano	1967	20.00	40.00	80.00

ROLLERS, THE

Number	Title (A Side/B Side)	Yr	VG	VG+	NM
45s					
LIBERTY					
55303	Bonneville/Got My Eye on You	1961	5.00	10.00	20.00
55320	The Continental Walk/I Want You So	1961	5.00	10.00	20.00
55357	The Bounce/Teenager's Waltz	1961	5.00	10.00	20.00

ROLLETTES, THE

Number	Title (A Side/B Side)	Yr	VG	VG+	NM
45s					
CLASS					
201	Sad Fool/Wham Bam	1957	10.00	20.00	40.00
203	Kiss Me Benny/More Than You Realize	1957	10.00	20.00	40.00
MELKER					
103	An Understanding/I'm Trying (To Make You Love Me)	1960	500.00	1000.	2000.

ROLLING STONES, THE

Also see BRIAN JONES; RONNIE WOOD; MICK TAYLOR.

Number	Title (A Side/B Side)	Yr	VG	VG+	NM
12-Inch Singles					
ROLLING STONES					
PR 70 [DJ]	Hot Stuff/Crazy Mama	1976	20.00	40.00	80.00
—Black and blue "splash" vinyl (counterfeits have black spots in blue vinyl)					
DSKO 174 [DJ]	Miss You/Hot Stuff	1979	5.00	10.00	20.00
DMD 253 [DJ]	If I Was a Dancer (Dance Pt. II)/Dance (Instrumental)	1981	5.00	10.00	20.00
PR 367 [DJ]	Emotional Rescue (4:18) (5:38)	1980	6.25	12.50	25.00
PR 397 [DJ]	Start Me Up (same on both sides?)	1981	6.25	12.50	25.00
PR 574 [DJ]	She Was Hot/Think I'm Going Mad	1983	6.25	12.50	25.00
PR 685 [DJ]	Undercover of the Night (Remix) (LP Version)	1983	3.75	7.50	15.00
—Yellow label promo					
PR 692 [DJ]	Too Much Blood (same on both sides?)	1983	5.00	10.00	20.00
CAS 1765 [DJ]	Mixed Emotions (Chris Kimsey's 12" Mix)/(LP Version)	1989	5.00	10.00	20.00
CAS 2275 [DJ]	Harlem Shuffle (same on both sides?)	1986	3.00	6.00	12.00
CAS 2340 [DJ]	One Hit (To the Body) (London Mix 7:00) (Edit) (LP Version)	1986	3.75	7.50	15.00
DK 4609	Miss You (8:36)/Far Away Eyes (4:24)	1978	3.00	6.00	12.00
—With custom die-cut sleeve					
DK 4609	Miss You (8:36)/Far Away Eyes (4:24)	1978	2.50	5.00	10.00
—With "Atlantic/Atco Disco" sleeve					
DK 4616	Miss You/Hot Stuff	1979	3.75	7.50	15.00
05365	Harlem Shuffle (NY Mix 6:25)/Harlem Shuffle (London Mix 6:19)	1986	2.50	5.00	10.00
05388	One Hit (To the Body) (London Mix 7:00)//One Hit (To the Body) (Edit)/Fight	1986	2.00	4.00	8.00
73133	Rock and a Hard Place (Dance Mix) (Oh-Oh Hard Dub Mix)//(Michael Brauer Mix) (Bonus Beats Mix)	1989	3.00	6.00	12.00
96902	Too Much Blood (12:33)//Too Much Blood (Dub 8:00)/Too Much Blood (Album 6:25)	1984	3.75	7.50	15.00
96978	Undercover of the Night (6:22)/Feel On Baby (Instrumental)	1983	2.50	5.00	10.00
VIRGIN					
38446	Love Is Strong (6 versions)	1994	2.00	4.00	8.00
38468	You Got Me Rocking (4 versions)/Jump on Top of Me	1995	2.00	4.00	8.00
38626	Saint of Me (Deep Dish Club Mix) (Deep Dish Grunge Dub)//(Todd Terry Extended Remix)/Anyway You Look at It	1998	2.00	4.00	8.00
45s					
ABKCO					
4701	I Don't Know Why/Try a Little Harder	1975	—	2.50	5.00
—With A-side writing credits of "Wonder, Riser, Hunter, Hardaway"					
4701	I Don't Know Why/Try a Little Harder	1975	2.50	5.00	10.00
—With A-side writing credits of "Jagger, Richards, Taylor"					
4701 [DJ]	I Don't Know Why (same on both sides)	1975	5.00	10.00	25.00
4702	Out of Time/Jiving Sister Fanny	1975	—	3.00	6.00
4702 [DJ]	Out of Time/Jiving Sister Fanny	1975	5.00	10.00	25.00
LONDON					
901	Paint It, Black/Stupid Girl	1966	3.75	7.50	15.00
901 [DJ]	Paint It, Black/Stupid Girl	1966	25.00	50.00	75.00
—Orange swirl label					
901 [PS]	Paint It, Black/Stupid Girl	1966	15.00	30.00	60.00
902	Mothers Little Helper/Lady Jane	1966	3.75	7.50	15.00
902 [DJ]	Mothers Little Helper/Lady Jane	1966	25.00	50.00	75.00
—Orange swirl label					
902 [PS]	Mothers Little Helper/Lady Jane	1966	15.00	30.00	60.00
903	Have You Seen Your Mother, Baby, Standing in the Shadow?/Who's Driving My Plane	1966	3.75	7.50	15.00
903 [DJ]	Have You Seen Your Mother, Baby, Standing in the Shadow?/Who's Driving My Plane	1966	25.00	50.00	75.00
—Orange swirl label					
903 [PS]	Have You Seen Your Mother, Baby, Standing in the Shadow?/Who's Driving My Plane	1966	15.00	30.00	60.00
904	Ruby Tuesday/Let's Spend the Night Together	1967	3.75	7.50	15.00
904 [DJ]	Ruby Tuesday/Let's Spend the Night Together	1967	25.00	50.00	75.00
—Orange swirl label					
904 [PS]	Let's Spend the Night Together/Ruby Tuesday	1967	15.00	30.00	60.00
905	Dandelion/We Love You	1967	5.00	10.00	20.00
905 [DJ]	Dandelion/We Love You	1967	25.00	50.00	75.00
—With full-length version of "We Love You"; orange swirl label					
905 [DJ]	Dandelion/We Love You	1967	50.00	100.00	150.00
—With 3:10 edited version of "We Love You"; orange swirl label					
905 [PS]	We Love You/Dandelion	1967	100.00	300.00	600.00
906	She's a Rainbow/2000 Light Years from Home	1967	5.00	10.00	20.00
906 [DJ]	She's a Rainbow/2000 Light Years from Home	1967	25.00	50.00	75.00
—Orange swirl label					
906 [PS]	She's a Rainbow/2000 Light Years from Home	1967	12.50	25.00	50.00
907	In Another Land/The Lantern	1967	6.25	12.50	25.00
—A-side credited to Bill Wyman, though taken from "Their Satanic Majesties Request"					
907 [DJ]	In Another Land/The Lantern	1967	25.00	50.00	75.00
—A-side credited to Bill Wyman; orange swirl label					
907 [PS]	In Another Land/The Lantern	1967	12.00	30.00	75.00
908	Jumpin' Jack Flash/Child of the Moon	1968	3.75	7.50	15.00
908 [DJ]	Jumpin' Jack Flash/Child of the Moon	1968	25.00	50.00	75.00
—Orange swirl label					
908 [PS]	Jumpin' Jack Flash/Child of the Moon	1968	10.00	20.00	40.00
909	Street Fighting Man/No Expectations	1968	5.00	10.00	20.00
909 [DJ]	Street Fighting Man/No Expectations	1968	25.00	50.00	75.00
—Orange swirl label					
909 [PS]	Street Fighting Man/No Expectations	1968	4000.	8000.	10000.
910	Honky Tonk Women/You Can't Always Get What You Want	1969	3.75	7.50	15.00
910 [PS]	Honky Tonk Women/You Can't Always Get What You Want	1969	7.50	15.00	30.00
9641	I Wanna Be Your Man/Stoned	1964	3000.	6000.	9000.
9641 [DJ]	I Wanna Be Your Man/Stoned	1964	300.00	600.00	1000.
—With similar label to stock copy, except in white, black and gray					
9641 [DJ]	I Wanna Be Your Man/Stoned	1964	200.00	500.00	1500.
—White label, black print, script "London" at top					
9657	Not Fade Away/I Wanna Be Your Man	1964	10.00	20.00	40.00
—White, purple and blue label					
9657	Not Fade Away/I Wanna Be Your Man	1964	2.00	4.00	8.00
—Blue swirl label					
9657 [DJ]	Not Fade Away/I Wanna Be Your Man	1964	200.00	400.00	900.00
—With similar label to original stock copy, except in white, black and gray					
9657 [DJ]	Not Fade Away/I Wanna Be Your Man	1964	300.00	600.00	1000.
—White label, black print, script "London" at top					
9657 [PS]	Not Fade Away/I Wanna Be Your Man	1964	75.00	300.00	450.00
9682	Tell Me (You're Coming Back)/I Just Want to Make Love to You	1964	10.00	20.00	40.00
—White, purple and blue label					
9682	Tell Me (You're Coming Back)/I Just Want to Make Love to You	1964	2.50	5.00	10.00
—Blue swirl label					

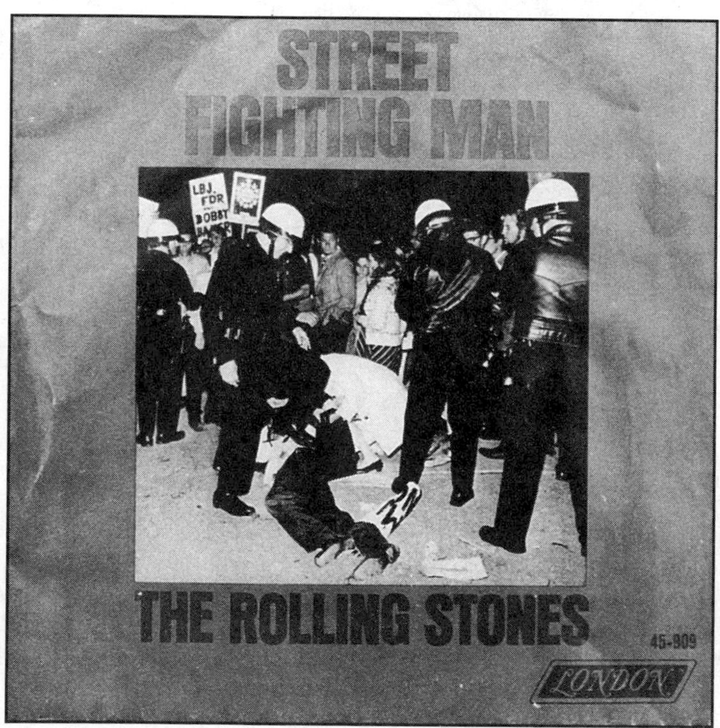

The Rolling Stones have settled into a comfortable No. 3 spot behind Elvis Presley and the Beatles in worldwide record collecting interest. The prices of their rarest items have been rising quickly. (Top left) Their first American 45 had "I Wanna Be Your Man" on the A-side and this innocuous instrumental, "Stoned," on the B-side. This record was immediately pulled from the market and has become prized, especially in its stock copy. (Top right) The original issue of the 1966 compilation *Big Hits (High Tide and Green Grass)* had the title in two lines, as pictured. Most copies have the title spaced over five lines. (Bottom left) The world's most valuable picture sleeve is the cover for "Street Fighting Man." No more than 20 copies are known to exist, and a near-mint one will likely set you back over $10,000. (Bottom right) The 1978 "Beast of Burden" picture sleeve has skyrocketed in value that past several years; we now list it at a cool $2,000. But beware of counterfeits! The listing for this sleeve tells you what to look for.

Number	Title (A Side/B Side)	Yr	VG	VG+	NM
9682 [DJ]	Tell Me (You're Coming Back)/I Just Want to Make Love to You	1964	25.00	50.00	75.00
—Orange swirl label					
9682 [PS]	Tell Me (You're Coming Back)/I Just Want to Make Love to You	1964	50.00	125.00	175.00
9687	It's All Over Now/Good Times, Bad Times	1964	10.00	20.00	40.00
—White, purple and blue label					
9687	It's All Over Now/Good Times Bad Times	1964	2.50	5.00	10.00
—Blue swirl label					
9687 [DJ]	It's All Over Now/Good Times, Bad Times	1964	25.00	50.00	75.00
—Orange swirl label					
9687 [PS]	It's All Over Now/Good Times, Bad Times	1964	50.00	85.00	125.00
9708	Time Is On My Side/Congratulations	1964	7.50	15.00	30.00
—White, purple and blue label					
9708	Time Is On My Side/Congratulations	1964	2.50	5.00	10.00
—Blue swirl label					
9708 [DJ]	Time Is On My Side/Congratulations	1964	25.00	50.00	75.00
—Orange swirl label					
9708 [PS]	Time Is On My Side/Congratulations	1964	25.00	50.00	100.00
9725	Heart of Stone/What a Shame	1964	7.50	15.00	30.00
—White, purple and blue label					
9725	Heart of Stone/What a Shame	1964	2.50	5.00	10.00
—Blue swirl label					
9725 [DJ]	Heart of Stone/What a Shame	1964	25.00	50.00	75.00
—Orange swirl label					
9725 [PS]	Heart of Stone/What a Shame	1964	200.00	400.00	800.00
9741	The Last Time/Play with Fire	1965	2.50	5.00	10.00
—Blue swirl label, "London" in black letters					
9741	The Last Time/Play with Fire	1965	3.75	7.50	15.00
—Blue swirl label, "London" in white letters					
9741	The Last Time/Play with Fire	1965	6.25	12.50	25.00
—White, purple and blue label					
9741 [DJ]	The Last Time/Play with Fire	1965	25.00	50.00	75.00
—Orange swirl label					
9741 [PS]	The Last Time/Play with Fire	1965	37.50	75.00	150.00
9766	(I Can't Get No) Satisfaction/The Under Assistant West Coast Promotion Man	1965	5.00	10.00	20.00
9766 [DJ]	(I Can't Get No) Satisfaction/The Under Assistant West Coast Promotion Man	1965	25.00	50.00	75.00
—Orange swirl label					
9766 [PS]	(I Can't Get No) Satisfaction/The Under Assistant West Coast Promotion Man	1965	100.00	200.00	500.00
5N-9766 [DJ]	(I Can't Get No) Satisfaction/The Under Assistant West Coast Promotion Man	1975	20.00	40.00	60.00
—Promo reissue; orange swirl label					
9792	Get Off of My Cloud/I'm Free	1965	5.00	10.00	20.00
9792 [DJ]	Get Off of My Cloud/I'm Free	1965	25.00	50.00	75.00
—Orange swirl label					
9792 [PS]	Get Off of My Cloud/I'm Free	1965	15.00	30.00	60.00
9808	As Tears Go By/Gotta Get Away	1965	3.75	7.50	15.00
9808 [DJ]	As Tears Go By/Gotta Get Away	1965	25.00	50.00	75.00
—Orange swirl label					
9808 [PS]	As Tears Go By/Gotta Get Away	1965	15.00	30.00	60.00
9823	19th Nervous Breakdown/Sad Day	1966	3.75	7.50	15.00
9823 [DJ]	19th Nervous Breakdown/Sad Day	1966	25.00	50.00	75.00
—Orange swirl label					
9823 [PS]	19th Nervous Breakdown/Sad Day	1966	15.00	30.00	60.00
ROLLING STONES					
PR 228 [DJ]	Time Waits for No One (mono/stereo)	1974	15.00	50.00	75.00
PR 228 [PS]	Time Waits for No One (mono/stereo)	1974	75.00	125.00	175.00
PR 316 [DJ]	Before They Make Me Run (mono/stereo)	1978	6.25	12.50	25.00
PR 316 [PS]	Before They Make Me Run (mono/stereo)	1978	10.00	20.00	50.00
05802	Harlem Shuffle/Had It with You	1986	—	—	3.00
05802 [DJ]	Harlem Shuffle (same on both sides)	1986	5.00	10.00	20.00
05802 [PS]	Harlem Shuffle/Had It with You	1986	—	—	3.00
05802 [PS]	Harlem Shuffle	1986	5.00	10.00	20.00
—"Demonstration Not for Sale" on sleeve, and no B-side listed					
05906	One Hit (To the Body)/Fight	1986	—	—	3.00
05906 [DJ]	One Hit (To the Body) (same on both sides)	1986	5.00	10.00	20.00
05906 [PS]	One Hit (To the Body)/Fight	1986	—	—	3.00
05906 [PS]	One Hit (To the Body)	1986	5.00	10.00	20.00
—"Demonstration Not for Sale" on sleeve, and no B-side listed					
19100	Brown Sugar/Bitch	1971	—	2.50	5.00
19100 [DJ]	Brown Sugar (mono/stereo)	1971	10.00	20.00	30.00
19101	Wild Horses/Sway	1971	—	2.50	5.00
19101 [DJ]	Wild Horses (mono/stereo, both full length)	1971	10.00	20.00	30.00
19101 [DJ]	Wild Horses (long version/short version)	1971	20.00	30.00	50.00
19103	Tumbling Dice/Sweet Black Angel	1972	—	2.50	5.00
19103 [DJ]	Tumbling Dice (mono/stereo)	1972	10.00	20.00	30.00
19104	Happy/All Down the Line	1972	—	2.50	5.00
19104 [DJ]	Happy/All Down the Line	1972	10.00	20.00	30.00
19105	Silver Train/Angie	1973	3.00	6.00	12.00
—With "Silver Train" listed as "Side One" and "Angie" listed as "Side Two"					
19105	Angie/Silver Train	1973	—	2.50	5.00
—With "Angie" listed as "Side One" and "Silver Train" listed as "Side Two", or with no reference at all to "Side One" and "Side Two"					
19105 [DJ]	Angie (mono/stereo)	1973	10.00	20.00	30.00
19109	Doo Doo Doo Doo Doo (Heartbreaker)/Dancing with Mr. D.	1973	—	2.50	5.00
19109 [DJ]	Doo Doo Doo Doo Doo (Heartbreaker) (mono/stereo)	1973	10.00	20.00	30.00
19301	It's Only Rock 'N' Roll (But I Like It)/Through the Lonely Nights	1974	—	2.50	5.00
19301 [DJ]	It's Only Rock 'N' Roll (But I Like It) (Edit/Long Version)	1974	10.00	20.00	30.00
19302	Ain't Too Proud to Beg/Dance Little Sister	1974	—	2.50	5.00
19302 [DJ]	Ain't Too Proud to Beg (mono/stereo)	1974	10.00	20.00	30.00
19304	Fool to Cry/Hot Stuff	1976	—	2.00	4.00
19304	Fool to Cry/Crazy Mama	1976	—	—	—
—Promotional 12-inch singles exist with this coupling, but do U.S. 45s? Please advise.					
19304 [DJ]	Fool to Cry/Hot Stuff	1976	50.00	100.00	200.00
19304 [DJ]	Fool to Cry (same on both sides)	1976	10.00	20.00	30.00
19304 [DJ]	Fool to Cry (long/short versions)	1976	15.00	25.00	35.00
19304 [DJ]	Hot Stuff (same on both sides)	1976	10.00	20.00	30.00
19304 [DJ]	Hot Stuff (long/short versions)	1976	15.00	25.00	35.00
19307	Miss You/Far Away Eyes	1978	—	2.00	4.00
19307 [DJ]	Miss You (same on both sides)	1978	10.00	20.00	30.00
19307 [DJ]	Far Away Eyes (same on both sides)	1978	50.00	100.00	250.00
19307 [PS]	Miss You/Far Away Eyes	1978	—	2.00	4.00
19309	Beast of Burden/When the Whip Comes Down	1978	—	2.00	4.00
19309 [DJ]	Beast of Burden (long/short versions)	1978	10.00	20.00	30.00
19309 [PS]	Beast of Burden/When the Whip Comes Down	1978	1000.	1500.	2000.
—Beware of counterfeits! Original copies have a 1/2-inch inner fold on the inside of the picture sleeve (counterfeits have a much smaller fold). Also, the originals are a light lavender, almost pink, color (counterfeits are a grape or purple color).					
19310	Shattered/Everything Is Turning to Gold	1978	—	2.00	4.00
19310 [DJ]	Shattered (same on both sides)	1978	5.00	10.00	20.00
19310 [PS]	Shattered/Everything Is Turning to Gold	1978	—	3.00	6.00
20001	Emotional Rescue/Down in the Hole	1980	—	2.00	4.00
20001 [DJ]	Emotional Rescue (edit/LP versions)	1980	5.00	10.00	20.00
20001 [PS]	Emotional Rescue/Down in the Hole	1980	—	2.00	4.00
21001	She's So Cold/Send It to Me	1980	—	2.00	4.00
21001 [DJ]	She's So Cold (edit/LP versions)	1980	5.00	10.00	20.00
21001 [PS]	She's So Cold/Send It to Me	1980	—	3.00	6.00
21003	Start Me Up/No Use in Crying	1981	—	2.00	4.00
21003 [DJ]	Start Me Up (same on both sides)	1981	5.00	10.00	20.00
21003 [PS]	Start Me Up/No Use in Crying	1981	—	2.00	4.00
21004	Waiting on a Friend/Little T & A	1981	—	2.00	4.00
21004 [DJ]	Waiting on a Friend (same on both sides)	1981	5.00	10.00	20.00
21004 [PS]	Waiting on a Friend/Little T & A	1981	—	2.00	4.00
21300	Hang Fire/Neighbours	1982	—	2.00	4.00
21300 [DJ]	Hang Fire (same on both sides)	1982	5.00	10.00	20.00
21301	Going to A-Go-Go/Beast of Burden	1982	—	2.00	4.00
21301 [DJ]	Going to A-Go-Go/Beast of Burden	1982	5.00	10.00	20.00
21301 [PS]	Going to A-Go-Go/Beast of Burden	1982	—	2.00	4.00
69008	Mixed Emotions/Fancy Man Blues	1989	—	—	3.00
69008 [DJ]	Mixed Emotions (same on both sides)	1989	10.00	20.00	45.00
73057	Rock and a Hard Place/Cook Cook Blues	1989	—	—	3.00
73093	Almost Hear You Sigh/Break the Spell	1989	—	—	3.00
73742	Highwire/2000 Light Years from Home	1991	—	2.50	5.00
73789	Sexdrive/Undercover of the Night	1991	2.00	4.00	8.00
99724	Too Tough/Miss You	1984	10.00	20.00	40.00
99724 [DJ]	Miss You (same on both sides)	1984	10.00	20.00	30.00
99788	She Was Hot/Think I'm Going Mad	1984	—	—	3.00
99788 [DJ]	She Was Hot (long/short versions)	1984	10.00	20.00	30.00
99788 [PS]	She Was Hot/Think I'm Going Mad	1984	—	—	3.00
99813	Undercover of the Night/All the Way Down	1983	—	—	3.00
99813 [DJ]	Undercover of the Night (same on both sides)	1983	5.00	10.00	20.00
99813 [PS]	Undercover of the Night/All the Way Down	1983	—	—	3.00
99978	Time Is On My Side (Live)/Twenty Flight Rock	1982	—	2.50	5.00
99978 [DJ]	Time Is On My Side (Live) (same on both sides)	1982	5.00	10.00	20.00
99978 [PS]	Time Is On My Side (Live)/Twenty Flight Rock	1982	—	2.50	5.00
VIRGIN					
38446	Love Is Strong//The Storm/Love Is Strong (Teddy Riley Remix)	1994	—	2.50	5.00
38446 [PS]	Love Is Strong//The Storm/Love Is Strong (Teddy Riley Remix)	1994	—	2.50	5.00
38459	Out of Tears//Out of Tears (Bob Clearmountain Remix Edit)/I'm Gonna Drive	1994	—	2.50	5.00
38459 [PS]	Out of Tears//Out of Tears (Bob Clearmountain Remix Edit)/I'm Gonna Drive	1994	—	2.50	5.00
NR-38626	Saint of Me/Anyway You Look At It	1998	—	—	2.00
NR-38626 [PS]	Saint of Me/Anyway You Look At It	1998	—	—	2.00

7-Inch Extended Plays

Number	Title (A Side/B Side)	Yr	VG	VG+	NM
ROLLING STONES					
PR 287 [DJ]	If You Can't Rock Me/Get Off of My Cloud/Brown Sugar//Jumpin' Jack Flash/Hot Stuff	1977	7.50	15.00	30.00
—Large hole; promo-only sampler from "Love You Live"					
PR 287 [PS]	Love You Live	1977	12.50	25.00	50.00

Albums

Number	Title	Yr	VG	VG+	NM
ABKCO					
ANA 1 [P]	Metamorphosis	1975	3.00	6.00	12.00
MPD-1 [DJ]	Songs of the Rolling Stones	1975	175.00	350.00	700.00
—"Band in field" cover					
MPD-1 [DJ]	Songs of the Rolling Stones	1975	1000.	2000.	3000.
—"Rock and Roll Circus" cover					
DVL2-0268 [P (2)]	The Rolling Stones' Greatest Hits	1977	5.00	10.00	20.00
—RCA Special Products mail-order offer					
1218-1 [(4)]	Singles Collection: The London Years	1989	12.50	25.00	50.00
AB-4224	Necrophilia	1973	2000.	4000.	8000.
—Canceled; covers exist. Value is for complete tri-fold cover.					
LONDON					
NP 1 [M]	Big Hits (High Tide and Green Grass)	1966	2000.	4000.	8000.
—With two lines of type on the front cover, all in small letters					
NP 1 [M]	Big Hits (High Tide and Green Grass)	1966	10.00	20.00	40.00
—With five lines of type on the front cover, all in capital letters					
NPS 1 [R]	Big Hits (High Tide and Green Grass)	1966	2.50	5.00	10.00
RSD-1 [DJ]	The Rolling Stones — The Promotional Album	1969	1000.	2000.	3000.
—Not to be confused with imports of this rare promo					
NP 2 [M]	Their Satanic Majesties Request	1967	62.50	125.00	250.00
NPS 2 [S]	Their Satanic Majesties Request	1967	10.00	20.00	40.00
—With 3-D cover					
NPS 2 [S]	Their Satanic Majesties Request	197?	2.00	4.00	8.00
—Without 3-D cover					
NPS 3 [PD]	Through the Past, Darkly (Big Hits Vol. 2)	1969	3000.	4500.	6000.
—Prototype picture discs that used the cover art from "Big Hits (High Tide and Green Grass)" either on one or both sides.					
NPS 3 [S]	Through the Past, Darkly (Big Hits Vol. 2)	1969	2.50	5.00	10.00
—With hexagonal cover					
NPS 3 [S]	Through the Past, Darkly (Big Hits Vol. 2)	197?	5.00	10.00	20.00
—Reissue with regular square cover					
NPS 4 [S]	Let It Bleed	1969	3.75	7.50	15.00
—With poster					
NPS 4 [S]	Let It Bleed	1969	2.50	5.00	10.00
—Without poster					
NPS-4	Let It Bleed	1970	5000.	7500.	10000.
—One-of-a-kind red/yellow/blue/green vinyl (all on the same record!)					
NPS 5 [S]	Get Yer Ya-Ya's Out!	1970	2.50	5.00	10.00
PS 375 [R]	England's Newest Hit Makers — The Rolling Stones	1964	75.00	150.00	300.00
—Dark blue label; lower left-hand corner of cover advertises a bonus photo					

Number	Title (A Side/B Side)	Yr	VG	VG+	NM
PS 375 [R]	England's Newest Hit Makers — The Rolling Stones	1965	6.25	12.50	25.00
—Dark blue label with "London" unboxed at top					
PS 375 [R]	England's Newest Hit Makers — The Rolling Stones	1966	2.50	5.00	10.00
—Dark blue label with "London" boxed at top					
PS 402 [R]	12 x 5	1964	6.25	12.50	25.00
—Dark blue label with "London" unboxed at top					
PS 402 [R]	12 x 5	1965	2.50	5.00	10.00
—Dark blue label with "London" boxed at top					
PS 420 [R]	The Rolling Stones, Now!	1965	6.25	12.50	25.00
—Dark blue label with "London" unboxed at top. Add 20% for complete liner notes (or sticker) on back cover (both columns of type about equal in length).					
PS 420 [R]	The Rolling Stones, Now!	1966	2.50	5.00	10.00
—Dark blue label with "London" boxed at top. Add 20% for censored liner notes (or sticker) on back cover (second column an inch shorter than the first column; "offensive" notes were quietly restored in the 1970s).					
PS 429 [R]	Out of Our Heads	1965	6.25	12.50	25.00
—Dark blue label with "London" unboxed at top					
PS 429 [R]	Out of Our Heads	1965	2.50	5.00	10.00
—Dark blue label with "London" boxed at top					
PS 451 [R-S]	December's Children (and Everybody's)	1965	6.25	12.50	25.00
—Dark blue label with "London" unboxed at top					
PS 451 [R-S]	December's Children (and Everybody's)	1966	2.50	5.00	10.00
—Dark blue label with "London" boxed at top. "Look What You've Done" is in true stereo; all other tracks are rechanneled.					
PS 476 [S]	Aftermath	1966	2.50	5.00	10.00
PS 493 [R-S]	Got Live If You Want It!	1966	2.50	5.00	10.00
—"Fortune Teller" is rechanneled (it's actually an early studio recording with overdubbed crowd noise)					
PS 499 [S]	Between the Buttons	1967	2.50	5.00	10.00
PS 509	Back Behind and In Front	1967	1250.	2500.	5000.
—Prototype cover slick for an unreleased LP; the same number was used for "Flowers"					
PS 509 [M]	Flowers	197?	2.00	4.00	8.00
—Some later "stereo" copies of this LP are actually entirely in mono					
PS 509 [R-S]	Flowers	1967	2.50	5.00	10.00
—"Have You Seen Your Mother, Baby, Standing in the Shadow?" and "Mother's Little Helper" are rechanneled; all others are true stereo					
PS 539	Beggars Banquet	1968	2500.	5000.	10000.
—Original "toilet graffiti" cover slick (not on a cover)					
PS 539 [S]	Beggars Banquet	1968	6.25	12.50	25.00
—With all songs credited to "Jagger-Richard"					
PS 539 [S]	Beggars Banquet	1968	2.50	5.00	10.00
—With "Rev. Wilkins: credited as composer of "Prodigal Son"					
2PS 606/7 [P (2)]	Hot Rocks 1964-1971	1971	250.00	500.00	1000.
—With alternate mixes of "Brown Sugar" and "Wild Horses" unavailable elsewhere. The date "11-5-71" or "11-18-71" is in the Side 4 trail-off area.					
2PS 606/7 [P (2)]	Hot Rocks 1964-1971	1971	5.00	10.00	20.00
—With regular mixes of all tracks. All of Side 1 and "Mothers Little Helper" and "19th Nervous Breakdown" on Side 2 are rechanneled. All of Side 3 and 4 are stereo.					
2PS 626/7 [P (2)]	More Hot Rocks (Big Hits and Fazed Cookies)	1972	5.00	10.00	20.00
—All of Side 4 is rechanneled; stereo content uncertain otherwise					
LL 3375	England's Newest Hit Makers — The Rolling Stones Bonus Photo	1964	50.00	100.00	200.00
LL 3375 [DJ]	England's Newest Hit Makers — The Rolling Stones	1964	750.00	1500.	3000.
—White label promo					
LL 3375 [M]	England's Newest Hit Makers — The Rolling Stones	1964	75.00	150.00	300.00
—Maroon label with "Full Frequency Range Recording" inside horizontal lines that go through the center hole; lower left-hand corner of cover advertises a bonus photo					
LL 3375 [M]	England's Newest Hit Makers — The Rolling Stones	1965	15.00	30.00	60.00
—Maroon label with "London" unboxed at top					
LL 3375 [M]	England's Newest Hit Makers — The Rolling Stones	1966	10.00	20.00	40.00
—Red or maroon label with "London" boxed at top					
LL 3402 [M]	12 x 5	1964	50.00	100.00	200.00
—Maroon label with "London/ffrr" in a box at top					
LL 3402 [M]	12 x 5	1964	15.00	30.00	60.00
—Maroon label with "London" unboxed at top					
LL 3402 [M]	12 x 5	1964	5000.	7500.	10000.
—Maroon label with "London" unboxed at top; possibly unique blue vinyl pressing					
LL 3402 [M]	12 x 5	1965	10.00	20.00	40.00
—Red or maroon label with "London" boxed at top					
LL 3420 [M]	The Rolling Stones, Now!	1965	50.00	100.00	200.00
—Maroon label with "London/ffrr" in a box at top. Add 20% for complete liner notes (or sticker) on back cover (both columns of type about equal in length).					
LL 3420 [M]	The Rolling Stones, Now!	1965	15.00	30.00	60.00
—Maroon label with "London" unboxed at top. Add 20% for complete liner notes (or sticker) on back cover (both columns of type about equal in length).					
LL 3420 [M]	The Rolling Stones, Now!	1966	10.00	20.00	40.00
—Red or maroon label with "London" boxed at top and censored liner notes (second column an inch shorter than the first column)					
LL 3429 [M]	Out of Our Heads	1965	50.00	100.00	200.00
—Maroon label with "London/ffrr" in a box at top					
LL 3429 [M]	Out of Our Heads	1965	10.00	20.00	40.00
—Maroon label with "London" unboxed at top					
LL 3429 [M]	Out of Our Heads	1966	6.25	12.50	25.00
—Red or maroon label with "London" boxed at top					
LL 3451 [M]	December's Children (and Everybody's)	1965	10.00	20.00	40.00
—Maroon label with "London" unboxed at top					
LL 3451 [M]	December's Children (and Everybody's)	1966	6.25	12.50	25.00
—Maroon label with "London" boxed at top					
LL 3476 [M]	Aftermath	1966	10.00	20.00	40.00
LL 3493 [M]	Got Live If You Want It!	1966	10.00	20.00	40.00
LL 3499 [M]	Between the Buttons	1967	10.00	20.00	40.00
LL 3509 [M]	Flowers	1967	12.50	25.00	50.00

LONDON/ABKCO

Number	Title (A Side/B Side)	Yr	VG	VG+	NM
62671 [P (2)]	Hot Rocks 1964-1971	1986	3.75	7.50	15.00
—"Digitally Remastered from Original Master Recording" on cover; red label; same stereo content as original					
62671 [P (2)]	More Hot Rocks (Big Hits and Fazed Cookies)	1986	3.75	7.50	15.00
—"Digitally Remastered from Original Master Recording" on cover; red label					
73751 [M]	England's Newest Hit Makers — The Rolling Stones	1986	2.00	4.00	8.00
—"Digitally Remastered from Original Master Recording" on cover; red label					
74021 [M]	12 x 5	1986	2.00	4.00	8.00
—"Digitally Remastered from Original Master Recording" on cover; red label					
74201 [M]	The Rolling Stones, Now!	1986	2.00	4.00	8.00
—"Digitally Remastered from Original Master Recording" on cover; red label					
74291 [P]	Out of Our Heads	1986	2.00	4.00	8.00
—"Digitally Remastered from Original Master Recording" on cover; red label					
74511 [M]	December's Children (and Everybody's)	1986	2.00	4.00	8.00
—"Digitally Remastered from Original Master Recording" on cover; red label					
74761 [S]	Aftermath	1986	2.00	4.00	8.00
—"Digitally Remastered from Original Master Recording" on cover; red label					
74931 [S]	Got Live If You Want It!	1986	2.00	4.00	8.00
—"Digitally Remastered from Original Master Recording" on cover; red label					
74991 [S]	Between the Buttons	1986	2.00	4.00	8.00
—"Digitally Remastered from Original Master Recording" on cover; red label					
75091 [S]	Flowers	1986	2.00	4.00	8.00
—"Digitally Remastered from Original Master Recording" on cover; red label					
75391 [S]	Beggars Banquet	1986	3.00	6.00	12.00
—"Digitally Remastered from Original Master Recording" on cover; red label; original banned "toilet cover" released for the first time on this reissue					
80011 [M]	Big Hits (High Tide and Green Grass)	1986	2.00	4.00	8.00
—"Digitally Remastered from Original Master Recording" on cover; red label					
80021 [S]	Their Satanic Majesties Request	1986	2.00	4.00	8.00
—"Digitally Remastered from Original Master Recording" on cover; red label					
80031 [S]	Through the Past, Darkly (Big Hits Vol. 2)	1986	2.00	4.00	8.00
—"Digitally Remastered from Original Master Recording" on cover; red label					
80041	Let It Bleed	1986	2.00	4.00	8.00
—"Digitally Remastered from Original Master Recording" on cover; red label					
80051	Get Yer Ya-Ya's Out!	1986	2.00	4.00	8.00
—"Digitally Remastered from Original Master Recording" on cover; red label					

MOBILE FIDELITY

Number	Title (A Side/B Side)	Yr	VG	VG+	NM
RC-1 [(11)]	The Rolling Stones	1984	125.00	250.00	500.00
—London LPs pressed on audiophile vinyl in box					
1-060	Sticky Fingers	1980	12.50	25.00	50.00
—Audiophile vinyl					
1-087	Some Girls	1982	12.50	25.00	50.00
—Audiophile vinyl					

RADIO PULSEBEAT NEWS

Number	Title (A Side/B Side)	Yr	VG	VG+	NM
4	It's Here Luv!!	1965	45.00	90.00	180.00
—Ed Rudy interview album; this has been counterfeited, but originals can be identified thus: Charlie Watts' jacket should be completely black with no white marks; the label is very clear; the vinyl is all black					

ROLLING STONES

Number	Title (A Side/B Side)	Yr	VG	VG+	NM
PR 164 [DJ]	Interview with Mick Jagger by Tom Donahue	1971	50.00	100.00	200.00
—Yellow label					
COC 2-2900 [(2)]	Exile on Main St.	1972	3.75	7.50	15.00
—Original covers have Unipak design -- cover has to be opened to remove the records. Add 33% for sheet of postcards.					
COC 2-2900 [(2)]	Exile on Main St.	1973	3.00	6.00	12.00
—Reissue covers have two pockets, one for each record					
COC 2-9001 [(2)]	Love You Live	1977	3.00	6.00	12.00
COC 16015	Emotional Rescue	1980	3.75	7.50	15.00
—Originally released with a large poster wrapped around the outside of the record jacket					
COC 16015	Emotional Rescue	1980	2.50	5.00	10.00
—Without poster					
COC 16028	Sucking in the Seventies	1981	2.50	5.00	10.00
COC 16052	Tattoo You	1981	2.50	5.00	10.00
COC 39100	Jamming with Edward	1972	3.75	7.50	15.00
—Not an official Stones album, this includes Jagger, Watts and Wyman with Ry Cooder and Nicky Hopkins					
COC 39100 [DJ]	Jamming with Edward	1972	43.75	87.50	175.00
—White label stereo promo					
COC 39100 [M]	Jamming with Edward	1972	62.50	125.00	250.00
—White label mono promo					
COC 39105	Sticky Fingers	1977	2.00	4.00	8.00
—Reissue on Atlantic with photo of zipper only					
COC 39106	Goats Head Soup	1977	2.00	4.00	8.00
—Reissue on Atlantic					
COC 39107	Made in the Shade	1977	2.00	4.00	8.00
—Reissue on Atlantic					
COC 39108	Some Girls	1978	3.75	7.50	15.00
—With all women's faces visible. Nine different color schemes exist for the front cover.					
COC 39108	Some Girls	1978	2.50	5.00	10.00
—With "cover under reconstruction." Nine different color schemes exist for the front cover.					
COC 39113	Still Life (American Concert 1981)	1982	2.50	5.00	10.00
COC 39114 [PD]	Still Life (American Concert 1981)	1982	10.00	20.00	40.00
OC 40250	Dirty Work	1986	2.00	4.00	8.00
—Originals came with red shrink wrap; add 50% if it is still with the package					
FC 40488	Sticky Fingers	1986	2.00	4.00	8.00
—Reissue on CBS with photo of zipper only					
CG2 40489 [(2)]	Exile on Main St.	1986	2.50	5.00	10.00
—Reissue on CBS					
FC 40492	Goats Head Soup	1986	2.00	4.00	8.00
—Reissue on CBS					
FC 40493	It's Only Rock 'n' Roll	1986	2.00	4.00	8.00
—Reissue on CBS					
FC 40494	Made in the Shade	1986	2.00	4.00	8.00
—Reissue on CBS					
FC 40495	Black and Blue	1986	2.00	4.00	8.00
—Reissue on CBS					
CG2 40496 [(2)]	Love You Live	1986	2.50	5.00	10.00
—Reissue on CBS					
FC 40499	Some Girls	1986	2.00	4.00	8.00
—Reissue on CBS					
FC 40500	Emotional Rescue	1986	2.00	4.00	8.00
—Reissue on CBS					
FC 40501	Sucking in the Seventies	1986	2.00	4.00	8.00
—Reissue on CBS					
FC 40502	Tattoo You	1986	2.00	4.00	8.00
—Reissue on CBS					
FC 40503	Still Life (American Concert 1981)	1986	2.00	4.00	8.00
—Reissue on CBS					
FC 40504	Undercover	1986	2.00	4.00	8.00
—Reissue on CBS has no stickers on cover					
FC 40505	Rewind (1971-1984)	1986	2.00	4.00	8.00
—Reissue on CBS					
OC 45333	Steel Wheels	1989	2.50	5.00	10.00

Number	Title (A Side/B Side)	Yr	VG	VG+	NM
C 47456	Flashpoint	1991	5.00	10.00	20.00
COC 59100	Sticky Fingers	1971	2.50	5.00	10.00
—With working zipper					
COC 59100 [DJ]	Sticky Fingers	1971	75.00	150.00	300.00
—White label stereo promo					
COC 59100 [M]	Sticky Fingers	1971	125.00	250.00	500.00
—White label mono promo					
COC 59101	Goats Head Soup	1973	3.75	7.50	15.00
—With bonus photo					
COC 59101	Goats Head Soup	1973	2.50	5.00	10.00
—Without bonus photo					
COC 79101	It's Only Rock 'n' Roll	1974	2.50	5.00	10.00
COC 79102	Made in the Shade	1975	2.50	5.00	10.00
COC 79104	Black and Blue	1976	2.50	5.00	10.00
90120	Undercover	1983	3.00	6.00	12.00
—With stickers intact					
90120	Undercover	1983	2.00	4.00	8.00
—With stickers peeled off					
90176	Rewind (1971-1984)	1984	6.25	12.50	25.00

VIRGIN

Number	Title (A Side/B Side)	Yr	VG	VG+	NM
V 2750 (8 39782 1) [(2)]	Voodoo Lounge	1994	5.00	10.00	20.00
—U.S. versions pressed in U.K., but have UPC code paste-over and blue sticker "Marketed by Caroline"					
V 2801 (8 41040 1) [(2)]	Stripped	1995	3.75	7.50	15.00
—U.S. versions pressed in U.K., but have UPC code paste-over with "Marketed and Distributed by Caroline Records"					
8 44712 1 [(2)]	Bridges to Babylon	1997	3.75	7.50	15.00
—U.S. versions pressed in U.K., but have "Virgin Records America Inc." on back cover					
8 46740 1 [(2)]	No Security	1998	3.75	7.50	15.00
—U.S. versions pressed in U.K., but have "Virgin Records America Inc." on back cover					
47863	Sticky Fingers	1999	6.25	12.50	25.00
—Limited-edition reissue with 180-gram vinyl and original working zipper cover					
47864 [(2)]	Exile on Main St.	1999	12.50	25.00	50.00
—Limited-edition reissue with 180-gram vinyl and all original inserts					
47867	Some Girls	1999	6.25	12.50	25.00
—Limited-edition reissue with 180-gram vinyl and original inserts (except it has the "cover under reconstruction" inner sleeve)					

ROLLINS, SONNY

45s

BLUE NOTE

Number	Title (A Side/B Side)	Yr	VG	VG+	NM
1669	Decision (Part 1)/Decision (Part 2)	1957	3.00	6.00	12.00
1670	Plain Jane (Part 1)/Plain Jane (Part 2)	1957	3.00	6.00	12.00
1687	You Stepped Out of a Dream/Why Don't Ewe	1957	3.00	6.00	12.00
1698	Sonny Moon for Two (Part 1)/Sonny Moonfor Two (Part 2)	1958	3.00	6.00	12.00

IMPULSE!

Number	Title (A Side/B Side)	Yr	VG	VG+	NM
247	Alfie's Theme (Part 1)/Alfie's Theme (Part 2)	1966	2.00	4.00	8.00

MILESTONE

Number	Title (A Side/B Side)	Yr	VG	VG+	NM
305	Isn't She Lovely/Arroz Con Pollo	1977	—	2.50	5.00
307	Harlem Boys/My Ideal	197?	—	2.50	5.00

PRESTIGE

Number	Title (A Side/B Side)	Yr	VG	VG+	NM
108	St. Thomas (Part 1)/St. Thomas (Part 2)	196?	2.50	5.00	10.00
128	They Can't Take That Away from Me/Ee-Ah	196?	2.50	5.00	10.00
173	Mack the Knife/The Stopper	196?	2.50	5.00	10.00
284	Almost Like Being in Love/In a Sentimental Mood	196?	2.50	5.00	10.00
769	Mambo Bounce/This Love of Mine	195?	3.75	7.50	15.00
780	With a Song in My Heart/Shadrack	195?	3.75	7.50	15.00
874	In a Sentimental Mood/Stopper	195?	3.00	6.00	12.00
905	Almost Like Being in Love/No Moe	195?	3.00	6.00	12.00

RCA VICTOR

Number	Title (A Side/B Side)	Yr	VG	VG+	NM
47-8111	If Ever I Would Leave You/Brown Skin Girl	1962	2.00	4.00	8.00

Albums

ABC IMPULSE!

Number	Title (A Side/B Side)	Yr	VG	VG+	NM
AS-91 [S]	Sonny Rollins On Impulse!	1968	3.75	7.50	15.00
AS-9121 [S]	East Broadway Run Down	1968	3.75	7.50	15.00
AS-9236 [(2)]	Reevaluation: The Impulse Years	1973	3.75	7.50	15.00
IA-9349	There Will Never Be Another You	1978	2.50	5.00	10.00

ANALOGUE PRODUCTIONS

Number	Title (A Side/B Side)	Yr	VG	VG+	NM
AP 008	Way Out West	199?	6.25	12.50	25.00
—Audiophile vinly					

ARCHIVE OF FOLK AND JAZZ

Number	Title (A Side/B Side)	Yr	VG	VG+	NM
220 [R]	Sonny Rollins with Guest Artist Thad Jones	1968	2.50	5.00	10.00

BLUE NOTE

Number	Title (A Side/B Side)	Yr	VG	VG+	NM
BN-LA401-H2 [(2)]	Sonny Rollins	1975	3.75	7.50	15.00
BN-LA475-H2 [(2)]	More from the Vanguard	1975	3.75	7.50	15.00
BLP-1542 [M]	Sonny Rollins	1957	50.00	100.00	200.00
—"Deep groove" version (deep indentation under label on both sides)					
BLP-1542 [M]	Sonny Rollins	1957	37.50	75.00	150.00
—Regular version, Lexington Ave. address on label					
BLP-1542 [M]	Sonny Rollins	1963	6.25	12.50	25.00
—With "New York, USA" address on label					
BLP-1558 [M]	Sonny Rollins, Volume 2	1957	30.00	60.00	120.00
—"Deep groove" version (deep indentation under label on both sides)					
BLP-1558 [M]	Sonny Rollins, Volume 2	1957	20.00	40.00	80.00
—Regular version, W. 63rd St. address on label					
BLP-1558 [M]	Sonny Rollins, Volume 2	1963	6.25	12.50	25.00
—With "New York, USA" address on label					
BLP-1581 [M]	A Night at the Village Vanguard	1958	30.00	60.00	120.00
—"Deep groove" version (deep indentation under label on both sides)					
BLP-1581 [M]	A Night at the Village Vanguard	1958	20.00	40.00	80.00
—Regular version, W. 63rd St. address on label					
BLP-1581 [M]	A Night at the Village Vanguard	1963	6.25	12.50	25.00
—With "New York, USA" address on label					
BLP-4001 [M]	Newk's Time	1958	30.00	60.00	120.00
—"Deep groove" version (deep indentation under label on both sides)					
BLP-4001 [M]	Newk's Time	1958	20.00	40.00	80.00
—Regular version, W. 63rd St. address on label					
BLP-4001 [M]	Newk's Time	1963	6.25	12.50	25.00
—With "New York, USA" address on label					
BST-4001 [S]	Newk's Time	1959	20.00	40.00	80.00
—"Deep groove" version (deep indentation under label on both sides)					
BST-4001 [S]	Newk's Time	1959	15.00	30.00	60.00
—Regular version, W. 63rd St. address on label					
BST-4001 [S]	Newk's Time	1963	5.00	10.00	20.00
—With "New York, USA" address on label					
BST-81542 [M]	Sonny Rollins	1985	2.50	5.00	10.00
—"The Finest in Jazz Since 1939" reissue					
BST-81542 [R]	Sonny Rollins	1967	3.00	6.00	12.00
—With "A Division of Liberty Records" on label					
BST-81558 [M]	Sonny Rollins, Volume 2	1985	2.50	5.00	10.00
—"The Finest in Jazz Since 1939" reissue					
BST-81558 [R]	Sonny Rollins, Volume 2	1967	3.00	6.00	12.00
—With "A Division of Liberty Records" on label					
BST-81581 [M]	A Night at the Village Vanguard, Vol. 1	1987	2.50	5.00	10.00
—"The Finest in Jazz Since 1939" reissue					
BST-81581 [R]	A Night at the Village Vanguard	1967	3.00	6.00	12.00
—With "A Division of Liberty Records" on label					
BST-84001 [S]	Newk's Time	1967	3.75	7.50	15.00
—With "A Division of Liberty Records" on label					
BST-84001 [S]	Newk's Time	198?	2.50	5.00	10.00
—"The Finest in Jazz Since 1939" reissue					
B1-93203	The Best of Sonny Rollins	1989	3.00	6.00	12.00

BLUEBIRD

Number	Title (A Side/B Side)	Yr	VG	VG+	NM
5634-1-RB [(2)]	The Quartets Featuring Jim Hall	1986	3.75	7.50	15.00

CONTEMPORARY

Number	Title (A Side/B Side)	Yr	VG	VG+	NM
C-3530 [M]	Way Out West	1957	25.00	50.00	100.00
M-3564 [M]	Sonny Rollins and the Contemporary Leaders	1959	20.00	40.00	80.00
S-7530 [S]	Way Out West	1959	12.50	25.00	50.00
S-7564 [S]	Sonny Rollins and the Contemporary Leaders	1959	12.50	25.00	50.00
C-7651	Alternate Takes	1986	2.50	5.00	10.00

DCC COMPACT CLASSICS

Number	Title (A Side/B Side)	Yr	VG	VG+	NM
LPZ-2008	Saxophone Colossus	1995	6.25	12.50	25.00
—Audiophile vinyl					
LPZ-2022	Tenor Madness	1996	6.25	12.50	25.00
—Audiophile vinyl					

FANTASY

Number	Title (A Side/B Side)	Yr	VG	VG+	NM
OJC-007	Work Time	1982	2.50	5.00	10.00
OJC-011	Sonny Rollins with the Modern Jazz Quartet	1982	2.50	5.00	10.00
OJC-029	The Sound of Sonny	198?	2.50	5.00	10.00
OJC-058	Moving Out	198?	2.50	5.00	10.00
OJC-067	Freedom Suite	198?	2.50	5.00	10.00
OJC-124	Tenor Madness	198?	2.50	5.00	10.00
OJC-214	Sonny Rollins Plays for Bird	198?	2.50	5.00	10.00
OJC-243	Sonny Rollins Plus 4	1987	2.50	5.00	10.00
OJC-291	Saxophone Colossus	198?	2.50	5.00	10.00
OJC-312	The Next Album	1988	2.50	5.00	10.00
OJC-314	Horn Culture	198?	2.50	5.00	10.00
OJC-337	Way Out West	198?	2.50	5.00	10.00
OJC-340	Sonny Rollins and the Contemporary Leaders	198?	2.50	5.00	10.00
OJC-348	Sonny Boy	198?	2.50	5.00	10.00
OJC-468	The Cutting Edge: Montreux 1974	198?	2.50	5.00	10.00
OJC-620	Nucleus	1991	2.50	5.00	10.00

GATEWAY

Number	Title (A Side/B Side)	Yr	VG	VG+	NM
7024	The Sound of Sonny	198?	2.50	5.00	10.00

IMPULSE!

Number	Title (A Side/B Side)	Yr	VG	VG+	NM
A-91 [M]	Sonny Rollins On Impulse!	1966	6.25	12.50	25.00
AS-91 [S]	Sonny Rollins On Impulse!	1966	7.50	15.00	30.00
A-9121 [M]	East Broadway Run Down	1967	7.50	15.00	30.00
AS-9121 [S]	East Broadway Run Down	1967	6.25	12.50	25.00

JAZZLAND

Number	Title (A Side/B Side)	Yr	VG	VG+	NM
JLP-72 [M]	Sonny's Time	1962	10.00	20.00	40.00
JLP-86 [M]	Shadow Waltz	1962	10.00	20.00	40.00
JLP-972 [S]	Sonny's Time	1962	7.50	15.00	30.00
JLP-986 [S]	Shadow Waltz	1962	7.50	15.00	30.00

MCA

Number	Title (A Side/B Side)	Yr	VG	VG+	NM
4127 [(2)]	Great Moments with Sonny Rollins	198?	3.00	6.00	12.00
29054	Sonny Rollins on Impulse!	1980	2.50	5.00	10.00
29055	There Will Never Be Another You	1980	2.50	5.00	10.00

MCA IMPULSE!

Number	Title (A Side/B Side)	Yr	VG	VG+	NM
MCA-5655	Sonny Rollins on Impulse!	1986	2.50	5.00	10.00

METROJAZZ

Number	Title (A Side/B Side)	Yr	VG	VG+	NM
E-1002 [M]	Sonny Rollins and the Big Brass	1958	15.00	30.00	60.00
SE-1002 [S]	Sonny Rollins and the Big Brass	1958	12.50	25.00	50.00
E-1011 [M]	Sonny Rollins at Music Inn	1958	15.00	30.00	60.00
SE-1011 [S]	Sonny Rollins at Music Inn	1958	12.50	25.00	50.00

MILESTONE

Number	Title (A Side/B Side)	Yr	VG	VG+	NM
M-9042	The Next Album	197?	3.00	6.00	12.00
M-9051	Horn Culture	1974	3.00	6.00	12.00
M-9059	The Cutting Edge: Montreux 1974	1975	3.00	6.00	12.00
M-9064	Nucleus	1975	3.00	6.00	12.00
M-9074	The Way I Feel	1976	3.00	6.00	12.00
M-9080	Easy Living	1977	3.00	6.00	12.00
M-9090	Don't Ask	1979	3.00	6.00	12.00
M-9098	Love at First Sight	1980	3.00	6.00	12.00
M-9104	No Problem	1981	2.50	5.00	10.00
M-9108	Reel Life	1982	2.50	5.00	10.00
M-9122	Sunny Days, Starry Nights	1984	2.50	5.00	10.00
M-9150	G-Man	1987	3.00	6.00	12.00
M-9155	Dancing in the Dark	1988	3.00	6.00	12.00
M-9179	Falling in Love with Jazz	1990	3.75	7.50	15.00
47007 [(2)]	Freedom Suite Plus	197?	3.75	7.50	15.00
55005 [(2)]	Don't Stop the Carnival	1977	3.75	7.50	15.00

PRESTIGE

Number	Title (A Side/B Side)	Yr	VG	VG+	NM
PRLP-137 [10]	Sonny Rollins Quartet	1952	75.00	150.00	300.00
PRLP-186 [10]	Sonny Rollins Quartet	1954	62.50	125.00	250.00
PRLP-190 [10]	Sonny Rollins	1954	62.50	125.00	250.00
PRLP-7020 [M]	Work Time	1956	20.00	40.00	80.00
PRLP-7029 [M]	Sonny Rollins with the Modern Jazz Quartet	1956	25.00	50.00	100.00
—Blue cover					
PRLP-7029 [M]	Sonny Rollins with the Modern Jazz Quartet	1956	25.00	50.00	100.00
—Green cover					
PRLP-7029 [M]	Sonny Rollins with the Modern Jazz Quartet	1956	20.00	40.00	80.00
—Yellow cover					
PRLP-7038 [M]	Sonny Rollins Plus 4	1956	20.00	40.00	80.00
PRLP-7047 [M]	Tenor Madness	1956	20.00	40.00	80.00
PRLP-7058 [M]	Moving Out	1956	20.00	40.00	80.00
PRLP-7079 [M]	Saxophone Colossus	1957	20.00	40.00	80.00

Number	Title (A Side/B Side)	Yr	VG	VG+	NM
PRLP-7095 [M]	Rollins Plays for Bird	1957	20.00	40.00	80.00
PRLP-7126 [M]	Tour De Force	1957	20.00	40.00	80.00
PRLP-7207 [M]	Sonny Boy	1961	10.00	20.00	40.00
PRLP-7246 [M]	Work Time	1962	10.00	20.00	40.00
PRST-7246 [R]	Work Time	1962	6.25	12.50	25.00
PRLP-7269 [M]	Sonny and the Stars	1963	10.00	20.00	40.00
PRST-7269 [R]	Sonny and the Stars	1963	6.25	12.50	25.00
PRLP-7326 [M]	Saxophone Colossus	1964	10.00	20.00	40.00
PRST-7326 [R]	Saxophone Colossus	1964	6.25	12.50	25.00
PRLP-7433 [M]	Sonny Rollins Plays Jazz Classics	1967	10.00	20.00	40.00
PRST-7433 [R]	Sonny Rollins Plays Jazz Classics	1967	5.00	10.00	20.00
PRST-7553 [R]	Sonny Rollins Plays for Bird	1968	3.75	7.50	15.00
PRST-7657 [R]	Tenor Madness	1969	3.75	7.50	15.00
PRST-7750	Worktime	1970	3.00	6.00	12.00
PRST-7856	The First Recordings	1972	3.00	6.00	12.00
24004 [(2)]	Sonny Rollins	197?	3.75	7.50	15.00
24050 [(2)]	Saxophone Colossus and More	1974	3.75	7.50	15.00
24082 [(2)]	Taking Care of Business	198?	3.75	7.50	15.00
24096 [(2)]	Vintage Sessions	198?	3.75	7.50	15.00
QUINTESSENCE					
25181	Green Dolphin Street	197?	3.00	6.00	12.00
RCA VICTOR					
AFL1-0859	The Bridge	1977	2.50	5.00	10.00
—Reissue with new prefix					
APL1-0859	The Bridge	1975	3.00	6.00	12.00
—Reissue of LSP-2527					
LPM-2527 [M]	The Bridge	1962	10.00	20.00	40.00
LSP-2527 [S]	The Bridge	1962	17.50	35.00	70.00
LSP-2527 [S]	The Bridge	199?	7.50	15.00	30.00
—Classic Records reissue on audiophile vinyl					
LSP-2527-45 [(4)]	The Bridge	1999	10.00	20.00	40.00
—Classic Records reissue; 4 single-sided LPs that play at 45 rpm					
LPM-2572 [M]	What's New?	1962	7.50	15.00	30.00
LSP-2572 [S]	What's New?	1962	15.00	30.00	60.00
LPM-2612 [M]	Our Man In Jazz	1962	7.50	15.00	30.00
LSP-2612 [S]	Our Man In Jazz	1962	15.00	30.00	60.00
LSP-2612 [S]	Our Man in Jazz	199?	6.25	12.50	25.00
—Classic Records reissue on audiophile vinyl					
LPM-2712 [M]	Sonny Meets Hawk!	1963	7.50	15.00	30.00
LSP-2712 [S]	Sonny Meets Hawk!	1963	15.00	30.00	60.00
LSP-2712 [S]	Sonny Meets Hawk!	199?	6.25	12.50	25.00
—Classic Records reissue on audiophile vinyl					
ANL1-2809	Pure Gold	1978	2.50	5.00	10.00
LPM-2927 [M]	Now's the Time	1964	6.25	12.50	25.00
LSP-2927 [S]	Now's the Time!	1964	7.50	15.00	30.00
LSP-2927 [S]	Now's the Time!	199?	6.25	12.50	25.00
—Classic Records reissue on audiophile vinyl					
LPM-3355 [M]	The Standard Sonny Rollins	1965	6.25	12.50	25.00
LSP-3355 [S]	The Standard Sonny Rollins	1965	7.50	15.00	30.00
RIVERSIDE					
RLP 12-241 [M]	The Sound of Sonny	1957	25.00	50.00	100.00
—White label, blue print					
RLP 12-241 [M]	The Sound of Sonny	1959	12.50	25.00	50.00
—Blue label, microphone logo at top					
RLP-258 [M]	Freedom Suite	1958	20.00	40.00	80.00
RLP-1124 [S]	The Sound of Sonny	1959	12.50	25.00	50.00
RS-3010 [S]	Freedom Suite	1968	3.75	7.50	15.00
6044	Freedom Suite	197?	3.00	6.00	12.00
STEREO RECORDS					
S-7017 [S]	Way Out West	1958	20.00	40.00	80.00
VERVE					
VSP-32 [M]	Tenor Titan	1966	3.75	7.50	15.00
VSPS-32 [S]	Tenor Titan	1966	3.00	6.00	12.00
UMV-2555	Sonny Rollins/Brass, Sonny Rollins/Trio	198?	2.50	5.00	10.00
V-8430 [M]	Sonny Rollins/Brass, Sonny Rollins/Trio	1962	7.50	15.00	30.00
V6-8430 [S]	Sonny Rollins/Brass, Sonny Rollins/Trio	1962	6.25	12.50	25.00

ROLLINS, SONNY; CLIFFORD BROWN; MAX ROACH

Albums

Number	Title (A Side/B Side)	Yr	VG	VG+	NM
PRESTIGE					
PRLP-7291 [M]	Three Giants	1964	10.00	20.00	40.00
PRST-7291 [R]	Three Giants	1964	6.25	12.50	25.00
PRST-7821	Three Giants	1971	3.00	6.00	12.00

ROLLINS, SONNY/JIMMY CLEVELAND

Albums

Number	Title (A Side/B Side)	Yr	VG	VG+	NM
PERIOD					
SPL-1204 [M]	Sonny Rollins Plays/Jimmy Cleveland Plays	1956	25.00	50.00	100.00

ROMAN NUMERALS, THE

45s

Number	Title (A Side/B Side)	Yr	VG	VG+	NM
COLUMBIA					
44314	The Come-On/Matchstick in a Whirlpool	1967	5.00	10.00	20.00
44314 [PS]	The Come-On/Matchstick in a Whirlpool	1967	7.50	15.00	30.00

ROMEOS, THE (1)

Featuring Philly Soul producers KENNY GAMBLE and Leon Huff.

45s

Number	Title (A Side/B Side)	Yr	VG	VG+	NM
MARK II					
101	Precious Memories/Juicy Lucy	1967	3.75	7.50	15.00
103	A Tear and a Smile/Seaching	1967	3.75	7.50	15.00

Albums

Number	Title (A Side/B Side)	Yr	VG	VG+	NM
MARK II					
1001	Precious Memories	1967	6.25	12.50	25.00

ROMEOS, THE (2)

45s

Number	Title (A Side/B Side)	Yr	VG	VG+	NM
AMY					
840	The Tiger's Wide Awake (The Lion Sleeps Tonight)/Hitch-Hikin'	1962	3.75	7.50	15.00

ROMEOS, THE (3)

45s

Number	Title (A Side/B Side)	Yr	VG	VG+	NM
APOLLO					
461	Love Me/I Beg You Please	1954	150.00	300.00	600.00

ROMEOS, THE (4)

45s

Number	Title (A Side/B Side)	Yr	VG	VG+	NM
ATCO					
6107	Moments to Remember You By/Fine, Fine Baby	1958	15.00	30.00	60.00
FOX					
749	Gone, Gone, Get Away/Let's Be Partners	1957	75.00	150.00	300.00
—Cream label					
749	Gone, Gone, Get Away/Let's Be Partners	1957	30.00	60.00	120.00
—Yellow label					
846	Moments to Remember You By/Fine, Fine Baby	1957	125.00	250.00	500.00
—Cream label					
846	Moments to Remember You By/Fine, Fine Baby	1957	30.00	60.00	120.00
—Yellow label					

ROMEOS, THE (5)

45s

Number	Title (A Side/B Side)	Yr	VG	VG+	NM
COLUMBIA					
43074	Baby Stay in Line/Two of the Chosen Few	1964	2.50	5.00	10.00

ROMEOS, THE (U)

If these are any of the above groups, the most likely contenders are groups (1), (2) or (5).

45s

Number	Title (A Side/B Side)	Yr	VG	VG+	NM
FELSTED					
8528	Two Innocent Loves/Love-Mobile	1958	7.50	15.00	30.00
8672	Julie/I'm Gonna Rebuild This World	1963	5.00	10.00	20.00
LOMA					
2028	Mucho Soul/Are You Ready for That	1966	3.00	6.00	12.00
2041	Calypso Chili/Mon Petite Chow	1966	3.00	6.00	12.00

ROMERO, CHAN

45s

Number	Title (A Side/B Side)	Yr	VG	VG+	NM
CHALLENGE					
59285	The Funniest Things/It's Not Fine	1965	3.75	7.50	15.00
DEL-FI					
4119	The Hippy Hippy Shake/If I Had My Way	1959	25.00	50.00	100.00
4126	I Don't Care Now/My Little Rudy	1959	15.00	30.00	60.00
PHILIPS					
40391	Humpy Bumpy/Man Can't Dog a Woman	1966	2.50	5.00	10.00

RON AND BILL

Ron White and Bill "SMOKEY" ROBINSON.

45s

Number	Title (A Side/B Side)	Yr	VG	VG+	NM
ARGO					
5350	It/Don't Say Bye Bye	1959	12.50	25.00	50.00
TAMLA					
54025	It/Don't Say Bye Bye	1960	30.00	60.00	120.00

RON-DELLS, THE

45s

Number	Title (A Side/B Side)	Yr	VG	VG+	NM
ARLEN					
723	I'll Be Gone/Slow Down	1963	3.75	7.50	15.00

RON-DELS, THE

45s

Number	Title (A Side/B Side)	Yr	VG	VG+	NM
BROWNFIELD					
18	If You Really Want Me To, I'll Go/Walk About	1965	6.25	12.50	25.00
SMASH					
1986	If You Really Want Me To, I'll Go/Walk About	1965	2.50	5.00	10.00
2002	She's My Girl/Over	1965	2.00	4.00	8.00
2014	A Picture of You/Lose Your Money	1965	2.00	4.00	8.00

RONDELLS, THE

More than one group.

45s

Number	Title (A Side/B Side)	Yr	VG	VG+	NM
ABC-PARAMOUNT					
10690	Don't Say That You Love Me/Parking in the Ko Ko Mo	1965	3.75	7.50	15.00
CARLTON					
467	Good Good/Dreamy	1958	5.00	10.00	20.00
DOT					
16593	Far Horizons/On the Run	1964	6.25	12.50	25.00
17323	Matilda/Tina	1970	2.50	5.00	10.00
—As "The Ron-Dels"					
SHALIMAR					
104	Matilda/Tina	1963	3.75	7.50	15.00

RONDELS, THE

45s

Number	Title (A Side/B Side)	Yr	VG	VG+	NM
AMY					
825	Back Beat #1/Shades of Green	1961	6.25	12.50	25.00
830	My Prayer/Satan's Theme	1961	6.25	12.50	25.00
839	Caldonia/110 Lbs. of Drums	1962	6.25	12.50	25.00
844	Red Peppers/Flute Salad	1962	6.25	12.50	25.00
857	Meet Us at the Peppermint Lounge/Cover Charge	1962	6.25	12.50	25.00

RONDO, DON

45s

Number	Title (A Side/B Side)	Yr	VG	VG+	NM
ATLANTIC					
2194	Malibu/So Did I	1963	2.00	4.00	8.00
CARLTON					
531	Friends/Hoot an' a Holler	1960	2.00	4.00	8.00
536	Wanderlust/The King of Holiday Island	1960	2.00	4.00	8.00
551	You'll Never Walk Alone/They Were You	1961	2.00	4.00	8.00

Number	Title (A Side/B Side)	Yr	VG	VG+	NM
DECCA					
29738	Evening Star/Beyond the Mighty River	1955	3.00	6.00	12.00
30248	I Offer You My Heart/Evening Star	1957	3.00	6.00	12.00
32561	Statue of a Fool/I'll Be True	1969	—	2.50	5.00
JUBILEE					
5256	Two Different Worlds/He Made You Mine	1956	3.00	6.00	12.00
5270	Don't/The Love I Never Had	1957	3.00	6.00	12.00
5282	To Belong/On Forgotten Street	1957	3.00	6.00	12.00
5288	White Silver Sands/Stars Fell on Alabama	1957	3.00	6.00	12.00
5297	Forsaking All Others/There's Only You	1957	3.00	6.00	12.00
5305	Wanderin' Heart/In Chi-Chi-Chihuahua	1957	2.50	5.00	10.00
5313	Made for Each Other/What a Shame	1958	2.50	5.00	10.00
5319	There Goes My Heart Again/Blonde Bombshell	1958	2.50	5.00	10.00
5320	School Dance/I've Got Bells in My Heart	1958	2.50	5.00	10.00
5325	Dormi, Dormi, Dormi/Her Hair Was Yellow	1958	2.50	5.00	10.00
5334	City Lights/As Long As I Have You	1958	2.50	5.00	10.00
5341	I Could Be a Mountain/Great Adventure	1958	2.50	5.00	10.00
5354	Song from "Geisha Boy"/Gretna Green	1958	2.50	5.00	10.00
5364	My Foolish Heart/Leave Your Trouble on My Lips	1959	2.50	5.00	10.00
5372	You're On My Mind Again/Cuckoo Girl	1959	2.50	5.00	10.00
5381	Because of You/Alone in the World	1960	2.00	4.00	8.00
5421	Two Different Worlds/Blonde Bombshell	1962	2.00	4.00	8.00
5522	Love Me Back/Play the Other Side	1966	—	3.00	6.00
ROULETTE					
4202	Batch of Love/Quiet Girl	1959	2.50	5.00	10.00
4216	Wall to Wall Tears/The Golden Rule	1959	2.50	5.00	10.00
4236	That's My Girl/Even the Heavens Cried	1960	2.50	5.00	10.00
UNITED ARTISTS					
50111	Till the World Knows You're Mine/Is There Room in Your Tomorrow	1967	—	3.00	6.00
50191	Let's Live for Today/Oh Why My Love	1967	—	3.00	6.00
Albums					
JUBILEE					
JLP-1052 [M]	Rondo	195?	5.00	10.00	20.00
JLP-1081 [M]	Have You Met Don Rondo	195?	5.00	10.00	20.00
VOCALION					
VL 73897	Two Different Worlds	1970	3.00	6.00	12.00

RONETTES, THE

Also see RONNIE SPECTOR.

Number	Title (A Side/B Side)	Yr	VG	VG+	NM
45s					
A&M					
1040	You Came, You Saw, You Conquered/Oh, I Love You	1969	4.00	8.00	16.00
BUDDAH					
384	Go Out and Get It/Lover, Lover	1973	5.00	10.00	20.00
—As "Ronnie Spector and the Ronettes"					
408	I Wish I Never Saw the Sunshine/I Wonder What He's Doing	1974	5.00	10.00	20.00
COLPIX					
601	I Want a Boy/Sweet Sixteen	1961	25.00	50.00	100.00
—As "Ronnie and the Relatives"					
646	I'm Gonna Quit While I'm Ahead/I'm On the Wagon	1962	15.00	30.00	60.00
DIMENSION					
1046	He Did It/Recipe for Love	1965	12.50	25.00	50.00
MAY					
111	My Darling Angel/I'm Gonna Quit While I'm Ahead	1961	37.50	75.00	150.00
—As "Ronnie and the Relatives"					
114	Silhouettes/You Bet I Would	1962	12.50	25.00	50.00
138	Memory/Good Girls	1963	12.50	25.00	50.00
PAVILLION					
03333	I Saw Mommy Kissing Santa Claus/Rudolph the Red-Nosed Reindeer	1982	—	2.50	5.00
—B-side by The Crystals					
PHILLES					
116	Be My Baby/Tedesco and Pittman	1963	7.50	15.00	30.00
118	Baby I Love You/Miss Joan and Mr. Sam	1963	7.50	15.00	30.00
120	(The Best Part of) Breakin' Up/Big Red	1964	7.50	15.00	30.00
121	Do I Love You?/Bebe and Susu	1964	7.50	15.00	30.00
123	Walkin' in the Rain/How Does It Feel	1964	10.00	20.00	40.00
123 [PS]	Walkin' in the Rain/How Does It Feel	1964	37.50	75.00	150.00
126	Born to Be Together/Blues for Baby	1965	6.25	12.50	25.00
126 [PS]	Born to Be Together/Blues for Baby	1965	37.50	75.00	150.00
128	Is This What I Get for Loving You?/Oh, I Love You	1965	6.25	12.50	25.00
128 [PS]	Is This What I Get for Loving You?/Oh, I Love You	1965	37.50	75.00	150.00
133	I Can Hear Music/When I Saw You	1966	7.50	15.00	30.00
Albums					
COLPIX					
CLP-486 [M]	The Ronettes Featuring Veronica	1965	50.00	100.00	200.00
—Gold label					
CLP-486 [M]	The Ronettes Featuring Veronica	1965	25.00	50.00	100.00
—Blue label					
CST-486 [S]	The Ronettes Featuring Veronica	1965	75.00	150.00	300.00
—Gold label					
CST-486 [S]	The Ronettes Featuring Veronica	1965	37.50	75.00	150.00
—Blue label					
PHILLES					
PHLP-4006 [M]	Presenting the Fabulous Ronettes Featuring Veronica	1964	200.00	400.00	800.00
—Blue and black label					
PHLP-4006 [M]	Presenting the Fabulous Ronettes Featuring Veronica	1964	100.00	200.00	400.00
—Yellow and red label					
PHLP-ST-4006 [S]	Presenting the Fabulous Ronettes Featuring Veronica	1965	150.00	300.00	600.00
ST-90721 [S]	Presenting the Fabulous Ronettes Featuring Veronica	1965	100.00	200.00	400.00
—Capitol Record Club edition					
T-90721 [M]	Presenting the Fabulous Ronettes Featuring Veronica	1965	62.50	125.00	250.00
—Capitol Record Club edition					

RONNIE AND THE DEL-AIRES

See THE DEL-AIRES.

RONNIE AND THE HI-LITES

Number	Title (A Side/B Side)	Yr	VG	VG+	NM
45s					
ABC-PARAMOUNT					
10685	High School Romance/Too Young	1965	5.00	10.00	20.00
JOY					
260	I Wish That We Were Married/Twistin' and Kissin'	1962	6.25	12.50	25.00
265	Be Kind/Send My Love (Special Delivery)	1962	5.00	10.00	20.00
RAVEN					
8000	Valerie/The Fact of the Matter	1963	5.00	10.00	20.00
WIN					
250	A Slow Dance/What the Next Day May Bring	1963	5.00	10.00	20.00
251	The Fact of the Matter/You Keep Me Guessin'	1963	5.00	10.00	20.00
252	High School Romance/Uptown-Downtown	1963	6.25	12.50	25.00

RONNIE AND THE POMONA CASUALS

Number	Title (A Side/B Side)	Yr	VG	VG+	NM
45s					
DONNA					
1400	Swimming at the Rainbow/Casual Blues	1964	3.00	6.00	12.00
1402	I Wanna Do the Jerk/Sloopy	1965	3.00	6.00	12.00
Albums					
DONNA					
2113 [M]	Everybody Jerk	1965	7.50	15.00	30.00

RONNIE AND THE RELATIVES

RONNIE AND THE ROCKIN' KINGS

Number	Title (A Side/B Side)	Yr	VG	VG+	NM
45s					
RCA VICTOR					
47-7248	Rock and Roll Sal/You Know	1958	10.00	20.00	40.00

RONNY AND THE DAYTONAS

Number	Title (A Side/B Side)	Yr	VG	VG+	NM
45s					
MALA					
481	G.T.O./Hot Rod Baby	1964	6.25	12.50	25.00
490	California Bound/Hey Little Girl	1964	5.00	10.00	20.00
492	Bucket "T"/Little Rail Job	1964	5.00	10.00	20.00
497	Little Scrambler/Teenage Years	1965	5.00	10.00	20.00
503	Beach Boy/No Wheels	1965	6.25	12.50	25.00
513	Sandy/(Instrumental)	1965	5.00	10.00	20.00
525	Goodbye Baby/Somebody to Love Me	1966	5.00	10.00	20.00
531	Antique '32 Studebaker Dictator Coupe/Then the Rains Came	1966	5.00	10.00	20.00
542	I'll Think of Summer/Little Scrambler	1966	3.75	7.50	15.00
RCA VICTOR					
47-8896	All American Girl/Dianne, Dianne	1966	3.00	6.00	12.00
47-8896 [PS]	All American Girl/Dianne, Dianne	1966	6.25	12.50	25.00
47-9022	Winter Weather/Young	1966	3.00	6.00	12.00
47-9107	Walk with the Sun/The Last Letter	1967	3.00	6.00	12.00
47-9253	Brave New World/Hold Onto Your Heart	1968	3.00	6.00	12.00
47-9435	The Girls and the Boys/Alfie	1968	3.00	6.00	12.00
SHOW BIZ					
21207 [DJ]	4-Cast She'll Love Me Again	1968	5.00	10.00	20.00
—One-sided promo					
Albums					
MALA					
4001 [M]	G.T.O.	1964	30.00	60.00	120.00
4002S [S]	Sandy	1966	25.00	50.00	100.00
4002 [M]	Sandy	1966	20.00	40.00	80.00
SUNDAZED					
LP 5050	G.T.O. — Best of the Mala Recordings	199?	2.50	5.00	10.00

RONSON, MICK

Number	Title (A Side/B Side)	Yr	VG	VG+	NM
45s					
RCA VICTOR					
APBO-0212	Love Me Tender/Only After Dark	1974	—	3.00	6.00
APBO-0291	Slaughter on Tenth Avenue/Leave My Heart Alone	1974	—	3.00	6.00
PB-10237	Easy Days/Billy Porter	1975	—	3.00	6.00
7-Inch Extended Plays					
RCA VICTOR					
DJEO-0259 [DJ]	Slaughter on 10th Avenue/Growing Up and I'm Fine//All Cut Up on You/Andy Warhol	1974	3.00	6.00	12.00
—Promo-only EP with B-side by Dana Gillespie					
Albums					
RCA VICTOR					
APL1-0353	Slaughter on 10th Avenue	1974	3.00	6.00	12.00
APL1-0681	Play Don't Worry	1975	3.00	6.00	12.00

RONSTADT, LINDA

Number	Title (A Side/B Side)	Yr	VG	VG+	NM
12-Inch Singles					
ASYLUM					
4935 [DJ]	What's New (same on both sides)	1983	2.00	4.00	8.00
AS 11431 [DJ]	Blue Bayou/Lago Azul	1977	7.50	15.00	30.00
—Blue vinyl					
CAPITOL					
ST-1003 [DJ]	Living Like a Fool (same on both sides)	1977	7.50	15.00	30.00
—Red vinyl; yellow label, "Capitol" in red at bottom					
ST-1003 [DJ]	Living Like a Fool (same on both sides)	1977	10.00	20.00	40.00
—Red vinyl; yellow "SM" label with Capitol tower					
45s					
ASYLUM					
11026	Love Has No Pride/I Can Almost See It	1973	—	2.50	5.00
11032	Silver Threads and Golden Needles/Don't Cry Now	1974	—	2.50	5.00
11039	Desperado/Colorado	1974	—	2.50	5.00
45271	Love Is a Rose/Silver Blue	1975	—	3.00	6.00
45282	Heat Wave/Love Is a Rose	1975	—	2.00	4.00

Number	Title (A Side/B Side)	Yr	VG	VG+	NM
45295	Tracks of My Tears/The Sweetest Gift	1975	—	2.00	4.00
45340	That'll Be the Day/Try Me Again	1976	—	2.00	4.00
—Clouds label					
45340	That'll Be the Day/Try Me Again	1976	—	2.50	5.00
—All-blue label					
45361	Someone to Lay Down Beside Me/Crazy	1976	—	2.00	4.00
45402	Lose Again/Lo Siento Mi Vida	1977	2.00	4.00	8.00
45431	Blue Bayou/Old Paint	1977	—	2.00	4.00
45438	It's So Easy/Lo Siento Mi Vida	1977	—	2.00	4.00
45462	Poor Poor Pitiful Me/Simple Man, Simple Dream	1978	—	2.00	4.00
45464	Lago Azul/Lo Siento Mi Vida	1978	2.00	4.00	8.00
45479	Tumbling Dice/I Never Will Marry	1978	—	2.00	4.00
45519	Back in the U.S.A./White Rhythm and Blues	1978	—	2.00	4.00
45519 [PS]	Back in the U.S.A./White Rhythm and Blues	1978	—	3.00	6.00
45546	Ooh Baby Baby/Blowing Away	1978	—	2.00	4.00
46011	Just One Look/Love Me Tender	1979	—	2.00	4.00
46034	Alison/Mohammed's Radio	1979	—	2.00	4.00
46602	How Do I Make You/Rambler Gambler	1980	—	2.00	4.00
46602 [PS]	How Do I Make You/Rambler Gambler	1980	—	2.50	5.00
46624	Hurt So Bad/Justine	1980	—	2.00	4.00
46654	I Can't Let Go/Look Out for My Love	1980	—	2.00	4.00
69476	(I Love You) For Sentimental Reasons/Straighten Up and Fly Right	1987	—	2.00	4.00
69507	When You Wish Upon a Star/Little Girl Blue	1986	—	2.00	4.00
69507 [PS]	When You Wish Upon a Star/Little Girl Blue	1986	—	2.00	4.00
69653	When I Fall in Love/It Never Entered My Mind	1985	—	2.00	4.00
69671	Lush Life/Skylark	1985	—	2.00	4.00
69725	Someone to Watch Over Me/What'll I Do	1984	—	2.00	4.00
69752	I've Got a Crush on You/Lover Man	1984	—	2.00	4.00
69780	What's New/Crazy He Calls Me	1983	—	2.00	4.00
69838	Easy for You to Say/Mr. Radio	1983	—	2.00	4.00
69853	I Knew You When/Talk to Me of Mendocino	1982	—	2.00	4.00
69853 [PS]	I Knew You When/Talk to Me of Mendocino	1982	—	2.50	5.00
69948	Get Closer/Sometimes You Just Can't Win	1982	—	2.00	4.00
69948 [PS]	Get Closer/Sometimes You Just Can't Win	1982	—	2.50	5.00
CAPITOL					
2438	Dolphins/The Long Way Around	1969	3.00	6.00	12.00
2767	Lovesick Blues/Will You Love Me Tomorrow	1970	2.00	4.00	8.00
2846	Long Long Time/Nobody's	1970	2.00	4.00	8.00
3021	The Long Way Around/(She's a) Very Lovely Woman	1971	—	3.00	6.00
3210	I Fall to Pieces/Can It Be True	1971	—	3.00	6.00
3273	Rock Me on the Water/Crazy Arms	1972	—	3.00	6.00
3990	You're No Good/I Can't Help It (If I'm Still in Love with You)	1974	—	2.00	4.00
4050	When Will I Be Loved/It Doesn't Matter Anymore	1975	—	2.00	4.00
ELEKTRA					
64427	The Waiting/Walk On	1995	—	—	3.00
64987	All My Life/Shattered	1990	—	—	3.00
—With Aaron Neville					
69261	Don't Know Much/Cry Like a Rainstorm	1989	—	—	3.00
—With Aaron Neville					
MCA					
52973	Somewhere Out There/(Instrumental)	1986	—	—	3.00
—With James Ingram					
52973 [PS]	Somewhere Out There/(Instrumental)	1986	—	2.00	4.00
Albums					
ASYLUM					
6E-104	Simple Dreams	1977	2.50	5.00	10.00
6E-106	Greatest Hits	1977	2.50	5.00	10.00
6E-155	Living in the U.S.A.	1978	2.50	5.00	10.00
DP-401 [PD]	Living in the U.S.A.	1978	4.50	9.00	18.00
5E-510	Mad Love	1980	2.50	5.00	10.00
5E-516	Greatest Hits, Volume 2	1980	2.50	5.00	10.00
5E-540	Keeping Out of Mischief	1981	—	—	—
—Canceled					
7E-1045	Prisoner in Disguise	1975	2.50	5.00	10.00
7E-1072	Hasten Down the Wind	1976	2.50	5.00	10.00
—"Clouds" label					
7E-1072	Hasten Down the Wind	1976	3.75	7.50	15.00
—Solid blue label with white stylized "a" at top					
7E-1092	Greatest Hits	1976	3.00	6.00	12.00
SD 5064	Don't Cry Now	1973	2.50	5.00	10.00
60185	Get Closer	1982	2.50	5.00	10.00
60260	What's New	1983	2.50	5.00	10.00
60387	Lush Life	1984	2.50	5.00	10.00
60474	For Sentimental Reasons	1987	2.50	5.00	10.00
60489 [(3)]	'Round Midnight: The Nelson Riddle Sessions	1987	6.25	12.50	25.00
60765	Canciones De Mi Padre	1988	3.00	6.00	12.00
CAPITOL					
ST-208	Hand Sown...Home Grown	1969	5.00	10.00	20.00
—Black label with colorband					
ST-208	Hand Sown...Home Grown	1970	3.75	7.50	15.00
—Green label					
ST-208	Hand Sown...Home Grown	1971	3.00	6.00	12.00
—Red label					
ST-407	Silk Purse	1970	3.75	7.50	15.00
—Green label					
ST-407	Silk Purse	1971	3.00	6.00	12.00
—Red label					
ST-8-0407	Silk Purse	1970	5.00	10.00	20.00
—Capitol Record Club edition					
SMAS-635	Linda Ronstadt	1972	3.00	6.00	12.00
ST-11269	Different Drum	1974	3.00	6.00	12.00
—Also includes Stone Poneys tracks					
ST-11358	Heart Like a Wheel	1974	3.00	6.00	12.00
SW-11358	Heart Like a Wheel	1975	2.50	5.00	10.00
SKBB-11629 [(2)]	A Retrospective	1977	3.75	7.50	15.00
—Also includes Stone Poneys tracks					
SN-16130	Hand Sown...Home Grown	1980	2.00	4.00	8.00
SN-16131	Silk Purse	1980	2.00	4.00	8.00
SN-16132	Linda Ronstadt	1980	2.00	4.00	8.00
SN-16133	Beginnings	1980	2.00	4.00	8.00
SN-16299	Different Drum	198?	2.00	4.00	8.00
—Budget-line reissue					
ELEKTRA					
60872	Cry Like a Rainstorm, Howl Like the Wind	1989	3.00	6.00	12.00
MOBILE FIDELITY					
1-158	What's New	1984	12.50	25.00	50.00
—Audiophile vinyl					
NAUTILUS					
NR-26	Simple Dreams	1982	12.50	25.00	50.00
—Audiophile vinyl					
PAIR					
PDL2-1070 [(2)]	Prime of Life	1986	3.00	6.00	12.00
PDL2-1125 [(2)]	Rockfile	1986	3.00	6.00	12.00

RONSTADT, LINDA, AND THE STONE PONEYS

See STONE PONEYS.

ROOFTOP SINGERS, THE

Number	Title (A Side/B Side)	Yr	VG	VG+	NM
45s					
ATCO					
6526	My Life Is My Own/Kites	1967	—	3.00	6.00
PHILCO-FORD					
HP-37	Walk Right In/Tom Cat	1969	3.75	7.50	15.00
—4-inch plastic "Hip Pocket Record" with color sleeve					
VANGUARD					
35017	Walk Right In/Cool Water	1962	2.50	5.00	10.00
35019	Tom Cat/Shoes	1963	2.00	4.00	8.00
35019 [PS]	Tom Cat/Shoes	1963	3.00	6.00	12.00
35020	Mama Don't Allow/It Don't Mean a Thing	1963	2.00	4.00	8.00
35020 [PS]	Mama Don't Allow/It Don't Mean a Thing	1963	3.00	6.00	12.00
35024	Sail Away Ladies/Twelve String	1964	2.00	4.00	8.00
35029	Rainy Day/Buddy Won't You Roll Down the Line	1964	2.00	4.00	8.00
35034	Ham and Eggs/Somebody Came Home	1965	2.00	4.00	8.00
Albums					
VANGUARD					
VSD-2136 [S]	Walk Right In	1963	5.00	10.00	20.00
VRS-9123 [M]	Walk Right In	1963	3.75	7.50	15.00
VRS-9134 [M]	Good Time	1964	3.75	7.50	15.00
VRS-9190 [M]	Rainy River	1965	3.75	7.50	15.00
VSD-79134 [S]	Good Time	1964	5.00	10.00	20.00
VSD-79190 [S]	Rainy River	1965	5.00	10.00	20.00

ROOMATES, THE

Also see CATHY JEAN AND THE ROOMATES.

Number	Title (A Side/B Side)	Yr	VG	VG+	NM
45s					
BAN					
691	A Place Called Love/Knowing You	1985	—	2.50	5.00
CAMEO					
233	Sunday Kind of Love/A Lovely Way to Spend An Evening	1962	7.50	15.00	30.00
CANADIAN AMERICAN					
166	My Heart/Just for Tonight	1964	10.00	20.00	40.00
PHILIPS					
40105	Gee/Answer Me, My Love	1963	6.25	12.50	25.00
40153	The Nearness of You/Don't Cheat on Me	1963	6.25	12.50	25.00
PROMO					
2211	I Want a Little Girl/Making Believe	196?	5.00	10.00	20.00
—Sources conflict as to date (1960 or 1964)					
VALMOR					
008	Glory of Love/Never Know	1961	5.00	10.00	20.00
010	Band of Gold/O Baby Love	1961	5.00	10.00	20.00
013	My Foolish Heart/My Kisses for Your Thoughts	1962	5.00	10.00	20.00

ROONEY, TEDDY

Number	Title (A Side/B Side)	Yr	VG	VG+	NM
45s					
IMPERIAL					
5644	Bite Your Tongue/After the Dance	1960	10.00	20.00	40.00

ROOSTERS, THE

More than one group.

Number	Title (A Side/B Side)	Yr	VG	VG+	NM
45s					
A&M					
746	Shake a Tail Feather/Rooster Walk	1964	3.00	6.00	12.00
EPIC					
9487	Let's Try Again/Pretty Girl	1962	3.75	7.50	15.00
FELSTED					
8642	Chicken Hop/Fun House	1962	3.75	7.50	15.00
PHILIPS					
40504	Love Machine/I'm Suspectin'	1968	2.50	5.00	10.00
40559	Good Good Lovin'/Home Down Right	1968	2.00	4.00	8.00
SHAR-DEE					
704	Chicken Hop/Fun House	1959	5.00	10.00	20.00

ROSE, BIFF

Number	Title (A Side/B Side)	Yr	VG	VG+	NM
45s					
BUDDAH					
218	The Captain/I Forgot to Tell You	1971	—	2.50	5.00
TETRAGRAMMATON					
1506	What's Gnawing at Me/Molly	1969	—	3.00	6.00
1510	Buzz the Fuzz/Gentle People	1969	—	3.00	6.00
1543	Take Care of My Brother/Myrtle's Files	1970	—	3.00	6.00
Albums					
BUDDAH					
BDS-5069	Ride On!	1970	3.00	6.00	12.00
BDS-5075	The Thorn in Mrs. Rose's Side	1971	3.00	6.00	12.00
—Reissue of Tetragrammaton 103					
BDS-5076	Children of Light	1971	3.00	6.00	12.00
—Reissue of Tetragrammaton 116					
BDS-5078	Half Live at the Bitter End	1971	3.00	6.00	12.00
TETRAGRAMMATON					
T-103	The Thorn in Mrs. Rose's Side	1968	3.75	7.50	15.00
T-116	Children of Light	1969	3.75	7.50	15.00

Number	Title (A Side/B Side)	Yr	VG	VG+	NM
UNITED ARTISTS					
UAS-5594	Uncle Jesus Auntie Christ	1972	3.00	6.00	12.00

ROSE, TIM

45s

Number	Title (A Side/B Side)	Yr	VG	VG+	NM
CAPITOL					
3001	I've Gotta Get a Message to You/Janie Sue	1970	—	3.00	6.00
COLUMBIA					
43563	I'm Bringing It Home/Mother, Father, Where Are You	1966	2.00	4.00	8.00
43648	Hey Joe/The Lonely Blue King	1966	2.00	4.00	8.00
43722	Where Was I/I Gotta Do Things My Way	1966	2.00	4.00	8.00
43958	I'm Gonna Be Strong/I Got a Loneliness	1967	2.00	4.00	8.00
44031	Morning Dew/You're Slipping Away from Me	1967	2.00	4.00	8.00
44387	Long Time Man/Come Away Melinda	1967	2.00	4.00	8.00
44603	Long-Haired Boy/Looking at a Baby	1968	—	3.00	6.00
44792	Angela/Whatcha Gonna Do	1969	—	3.00	6.00
44849	Babe Do You Turn Me On/Roanoke	1969	—	3.00	6.00
PLAYBOY					
50005	It Takes a Little Longer/Ride Your Love Away	1972	—	2.50	5.00
50012	Goin' Down in Hollywood/(B-side unknown)	1972	—	2.50	5.00

Albums

Number	Title (A Side/B Side)	Yr	VG	VG+	NM
CAPITOL					
ST-673	Love, A Kind of Hate Story	1970	3.00	6.00	12.00
COLUMBIA					
CS 9577	Tim Rose	1968	3.00	6.00	12.00
CS 9772	Thru Rose Colored Glasses	1969	3.00	6.00	12.00
PLAYBOY					
P-101	Tim Rose	1972	3.00	6.00	12.00

ROSE GARDEN, THE

45s

Number	Title (A Side/B Side)	Yr	VG	VG+	NM
ATCO					
6510	Next Plane to London/Flower Town	1967	3.00	6.00	12.00
6564	Here's Today/If My World Falls Through	1968	2.50	5.00	10.00

Albums

Number	Title (A Side/B Side)	Yr	VG	VG+	NM
ATCO					
SD 33-225	The Rose Garden	1968	6.25	12.50	25.00

ROSEBUDS, THE (1)

45s

Number	Title (A Side/B Side)	Yr	VG	VG+	NM
GEE					
1033	Dearest Darling/Unconditional Surrender	1957	12.50	25.00	50.00
LANCER					
102	Kiss Me Goodnight/Joey	1959	15.00	30.00	60.00

ROSEBUDS, THE (2)

45s

Number	Title (A Side/B Side)	Yr	VG	VG+	NM
TOWER					
104	Say You'll Be Mine/Mama Said	1964	3.00	6.00	12.00

ROSELLA, CARMELA

45s

Number	Title (A Side/B Side)	Yr	VG	VG+	NM
NANCY					
1004	Oh, It Was Elvis/Where?	1961	10.00	20.00	40.00

ROSELLI, JIMMY

45s

Number	Title (A Side/B Side)	Yr	VG	VG+	NM
LENOX					
5571	Mala Femmina/Her Eyes Shone Like Diamonds	1963	2.00	4.00	8.00
5576	Passione/Satte Vincino A Me	1963	2.00	4.00	8.00
RIC					
138	Yellow and Green Make Blue/Anema E Core	1964	2.00	4.00	8.00
148	Don't Cry Little Girl, Don't Cry/Just Say I Love Her	1965	2.00	4.00	8.00
UNITED ARTISTS					
866	Laugh It Off/Why Don't We Do This More Often	1965	—	3.00	6.00
928	Have You Ever Been Lonely/Rage to Live	1965	—	3.00	6.00
957	New York: My Port of Call/This Is My Kind of Love	1965	—	3.00	6.00
996	I'll Never Let You Cry/I'm Gonna Change Everything	1966	—	3.00	6.00
1659	Buon Natale (Means Merry Christmas To You)/Christmas	1966	—	3.00	6.00
—"Silver Spotlight Series"					
50059	Love Me Love/Lusingame	1966	—	3.00	6.00
50064	This Planet Earth/Who Can Say (Africa Addio)	1966	—	3.00	6.00
50179	There Must Be a Way/I'm Yours to Command	1967	—	3.00	6.00
50217	Walkin' My Baby Back Home/All the Time	1967	—	3.00	6.00
50234	I Don't Want to Walk Without You/Please Believe Me	1967	—	3.00	6.00
50273	Bella/O Surdato 'Enammurato	1968	—	3.00	6.00
50287	Get Out of My Heart/Oh What It Seemed to Be	1968	—	3.00	6.00
50480	My Heart Cries for You/Why Did You Leave Me	1969	—	2.50	5.00
50490	Buona Sera, Mrs. Campbell/I'll Take Care of You	1969	—	2.50	5.00
50496	Buona Sera, Mrs. Campbell (Italian)/Te Purtavo Na Rosa	1969	2.00	4.00	8.00
50546	E Rose Parlano/Senza Mamma E Inamurata	1969	—	2.50	5.00
50624	I'm Coming Home, Los Angeles/Angelina	1970	—	2.50	5.00

Albums

Number	Title (A Side/B Side)	Yr	VG	VG+	NM
UNITED ARTISTS					
UXS-83 [(2)]	Jimmy Roselli Superpak	1972	3.75	7.50	15.00
UAL-3429 [M]	Life & Love Italian Style	1965	3.00	6.00	12.00
UAL-3430 [M]	Mala Femmina	1965	3.00	6.00	12.00
UAL-3438 [M]	The Great Ones!	1965	3.00	6.00	12.00
UAL-3451 [M]	Saloon Songs	1966	3.00	6.00	12.00
UAL-3467 [M]	New York: My Port of Call	1966	3.00	6.00	12.00
UAL 3539 [M]	The Christmas Album	1966	3.00	6.00	12.00
UAL-3544 [M]	The Italian Album	1966	3.00	6.00	12.00
UAL-3564 [M]	Sold Out	1967	3.00	6.00	12.00
UAL-3585 [M]	Saloon Songs, Vol. 2	1967	3.00	6.00	12.00
UAL-3611 [M]	There Must Be a Way	1967	3.75	7.50	15.00
UAS-5641	Simmo 'e Napule	1972	3.00	6.00	12.00
UAS-6429 [S]	Life & Love Italian Style	1965	3.75	7.50	15.00
UAS-6430 [S]	Mala Femmina	1965	3.75	7.50	15.00
UAS-6438 [S]	The Great Ones!	1965	3.75	7.50	15.00
UAS-6451 [S]	Saloon Songs	1966	3.75	7.50	15.00
UAS-6467 [S]	New York: My Port of Call	1966	3.75	7.50	15.00
UAS 6539 [S]	The Christmas Album	1966	3.75	7.50	15.00
UAS-6544 [S]	The Italian Album	1966	3.75	7.50	15.00
UAS-6564 [S]	Sold Out	1967	3.75	7.50	15.00
UAS-6585 [S]	Saloon Songs, Vol. 2	1967	3.75	7.50	15.00
UAS-6611 [S]	There Must Be a Way	1967	3.75	7.50	15.00
UAS-6635	Core Napulitano	1968	3.75	7.50	15.00
UAS-6645	The Best of Jimmy Roselli	1968	3.75	7.50	15.00
UAS-6665	3 A.M.	1968	3.00	6.00	12.00
UAS-6698	Core Spezzato	1969	3.75	7.50	15.00
UAS-6724	Let Me Sing	1969	3.00	6.00	12.00
UAS-6747	It's Been Swell	1970	3.00	6.00	12.00
UAS-6775	I'te Voglio Bene Assale	1970	3.00	6.00	12.00

ROSES, THE

45s

Number	Title (A Side/B Side)	Yr	VG	VG+	NM
DOT					
15816	Almost Paradise/I Kissed An Angel	1958	6.25	12.50	25.00

ROSIE AND THE ORIGINALS

45s

Number	Title (A Side/B Side)	Yr	VG	VG+	NM
BRUNSWICK					
55205	Lonely Blue Nights/We'll Have a Chance	1961	6.25	12.50	25.00
—By "Rosie, formerly with the Originals"					
55212	My Darling Forever/The Time Is Near	1961	6.25	12.50	25.00
—By "Rosie, formerly with the Originals"					
ERA BACK TO BACK HITS					
038	Angel Baby/Bumble Boogie	197?	—	3.00	6.00
—B-side by B. Bumble and the Stingers					
HIGHLAND					
1011	Angel Baby/Give Me Love	1960	6.25	12.50	25.00
1032	Lonely Blue Nights/We'll Have a Chance	196?	6.25	12.50	25.00
—Actually a reissue of Brunswick 55205, but harder to find					

Albums

Number	Title (A Side/B Side)	Yr	VG	VG+	NM
BRUNSWICK					
BL 54102 [M]	Lonely Blue Nights with Rosie	1961	37.50	75.00	150.00
BL 754102 [S]	Lonely Blue Nights with Rosie	1961	50.00	100.00	200.00

ROSS, DIANA

Also see THE SUPREMES.

12-Inch Singles

Number	Title (A Side/B Side)	Yr	VG	VG+	NM
MOTOWN					
00026	The Boss (Remix)/Loving, Living and Giving	1979	3.75	7.50	15.00
PR 42 [DJ]	What You Gave Me (6:06) (same on both sides)	1978	3.75	7.50	15.00
PR 54 [DJ]	It's My House//No One Gets the Prize/The Boss	1979	3.75	7.50	15.00
37463 1008	You're Gonna Love It (6 versions)	1991	2.00	4.00	8.00
37463 1212	The Boss (3 versions)/I'm Coming Out (3 versions)	1994	2.50	5.00	10.00
4632	Love Hangover '89 (3 versions)	1989	—	3.00	6.00
L33-17770 [DJ]	Love Hangover '89 (5 versions)	1989	2.00	4.00	8.00
L33-17827 [DJ]	Workin' Overtime (6 versions)	1989	2.00	4.00	8.00
L33-17909 [DJ]	Paradise (3 versions)	1989	2.00	4.00	8.00
L33-17963 [DJ]	This House (4:20) (5:34)	1989	2.00	4.00	8.00
L33-18048 [DJ]	Bottom Line (4 versions)	1989	—	3.50	7.00
RCA					
6416-1-R	Dirty Looks (3 versions)	1987	2.50	5.00	10.00
PD-13022	Mirror, Mirror/Sweet Nothings	1981	3.00	6.00	12.00
PD-13202	Work That Body/Two Can Make It	1982	3.00	6.00	12.00
PD-13568	Pieces of Ice/(Instrumental)	1983	2.50	5.00	10.00
PD-13625	Up Front/Love or Loneliness	1983	2.50	5.00	10.00
PD-13672	Let's Go Up/Girls	1983	2.50	5.00	10.00
PD-13865	Swept Away/(Instrumental)	1984	2.50	5.00	10.00
JD-14183 [DJ]	Eaten Alive/(Instrumental)	1985	2.00	4.00	8.00
PD-14183	Eaten Alive/(Instrumental)	1985	2.00	4.00	8.00
PD-14245	Chain Reaction (2 versions)	1985	2.00	4.00	8.00
JR-14267 [DJ]	Chain Reaction (6:52) (same on both sides)	1985	2.00	4.00	8.00
PD-14267	Chain Reaction (6:52)/More and More	1985	2.50	5.00	10.00

45s

Number	Title (A Side/B Side)	Yr	VG	VG+	NM
COLUMBIA					
04507	All of You/The Last Time	1984	—	—	3.00
—A-side: Diana Ross and Julio Iglesias; B-side: Iglesias solo					
04507 [PS]	All of You/The Last Time	1984	—	—	3.00
MCA					
40947	Ease On Down the Road/Poppy Girls	1978	—	2.50	5.00
—With Michael Jackson					
40947 [PS]	Ease On Down the Road/Poppy Girls	1978	—	2.50	5.00
—With Michael Jackson					
53448	If We Hold On Together/(Instrumental)	1988	—	—	3.00
53448 [PS]	If We Hold On Together/(Instrumental)	1988	—	—	3.00
MOTOWN					
(no #) [PS]	Diana Ross TV Special 4/8/71	1971	2.00	4.00	8.00
—Special sleeve issued with some Motown (usually Diana Ross) 45s in March and April 1971					
1165	Reach Out and Touch (Somebody's Hand)/Dark Side of the World	1970	—	2.50	5.00
1165 [PS]	Reach Out and Touch (Somebody's Hand)/Dark Side of the World	1970	3.00	6.00	12.00
1169	Ain't No Mountain High Enough/Can't It Wait Until Tomorrow	1970	—	2.50	5.00
1169 [PS]	Ain't No Mountain High Enough/Can't It Wait Until Tomorrow	1970	3.00	6.00	12.00
1176	Remember Me/What About You	1971	—	2.50	5.00
1176 [PS]	Remember Me/What About You	1971	3.00	6.00	12.00
1184	Reach Out I'll Be There/Close to You	1971	—	2.50	5.00
1188	Surrender/I'm a Winner	1971	—	2.50	5.00
1192	I'm Still Waiting/A Simple Thing Like Cry	1971	—	2.50	5.00
1211	Good Morning Heartache/God Bless the Child	1972	—	2.50	5.00
1211 [PS]	Good Morning Heartache/God Bless the Child	1972	2.50	5.00	10.00
1239	Touch Me in the Morning/I Won't Last a Day Without You	1973	—	2.50	5.00

Number	Title (A Side/B Side)	Yr	VG	VG+	NM
1278	Last Time I Saw Him/Save the Children	1973	—	2.50	5.00
1295	Sleepin'/You	1974	—	2.50	5.00
1335	Sorry Doesn't Always Make It Right/Together	1975	—	2.50	5.00
1335 [PS]	Sorry Doesn't Always Make It Right/Together	1975	3.00	6.00	12.00
1377	Do You Know Where You're Going To/No One's Gonna Be a Fool Forever	1975	3.00	6.00	12.00
—Possibly Canadian release only, with different A-side title					
1377	Theme from Mahogany (Do You Know Where You're Going To)/No One's Gonna Be a Fool Forever	1975	—	2.50	5.00
1377 [PS]	Theme from Mahogany (Do You Know Where You're Going To)/No One's Gonna Be a Fool Forever	1975	5.00	10.00	20.00
1387	I Thought It Took a Little Time (But Today I Fell in Love)/After You	1976	—	2.50	5.00
1387 [PS]	I Thought It Took a Little Time (But Today I Fell in Love)/After You	1976	2.50	5.00	10.00
1392	Love Hangover/Kiss Me Now	1976	—	2.50	5.00
1398	One Love in My Lifetime/Smile	1976	—	2.50	5.00
1427	Gettin' Ready for Love/Confide in Me	1977	—	2.50	5.00
1436	Your Love Is So Good for Me/Baby It's Me	1978	—	2.50	5.00
1442	You Got It/Too Shy to Say	1978	—	2.50	5.00
1449 [DJ]	Top of the World (same on both sides)	1978	12.50	25.00	50.00
—Promo only; withdrawn before stock copies were pressed					
1450	Lovin' Livin' and Givin'/Baby It's Me	1978	—	—	—
—Unreleased					
1456	What You Gave Me/Together	1979	—	2.00	4.00
1462	The Boss/I'm in the World	1979	—	2.00	4.00
1471	It's My House/Sparkle	1979	—	2.00	4.00
1491	I'm Coming Out/Give Up	1980	—	2.00	4.00
1494	Upside Down/Friend to Friend	1980	—	2.00	4.00
1496	It's My Turn/Together	1980	—	2.00	4.00
1496 [PS]	It's My Turn/Together	1980	3.00	6.00	12.00
1508	One More Chance/After You	1981	—	2.00	4.00
1513	To Love Again/Crying My Heart Out for You	1981	—	2.00	4.00
1519	Endless Love/(Instrumental)	1981	—	2.00	4.00
—With Lionel Richie					
1531	My Old Piano/Now That You're Gone	1981	—	2.00	4.00
1626	We Can Never Light That Old Flame Again/Old Funky Rolls	1982	—	2.00	4.00
1964	Workin' Overtime/(Instrumental)	1989	—	—	3.00
1964 [PS]	Workin' Overtime/(Instrumental)	1989	—	—	3.00
1998	This House/Paradise	1989	—	—	3.00
2003	Bottom Line/(Instrumental)	1989	—	—	3.00
2139	When You Tell Me That You Love Me/You and I	1991	—	2.00	4.00

RCA

Number	Title (A Side/B Side)	Yr	VG	VG+	NM
5172-7-R	Dirty Looks/So Close	1987	—	—	3.00
5172-7-R [PS]	Dirty Looks/So Close	1987	—	—	3.00
5297-7-R	Tell Me Again/I Am Me	1987	—	—	3.00
5297-7-R [PS]	Tell Me Again/I Am Me	1987	—	—	3.00
PB-12349	Why Do Fools Fall in Love/Think I'm in Love	1981	—	2.00	4.00
JB-13013 [DJ]	Endless Love (Long)/Endless Love (Short)	1981	2.50	5.00	10.00
—Promo only					
PB-13021	Mirror, Mirror/Sweet Nothings	1981	—	2.00	4.00
PB-13201	Work That Body/You Can Make It	1982	—	2.00	4.00
PB-13348	Muscles/I Am Me	1982	—	2.00	4.00
PB-13348 [PS]	Muscles/I Am Me	1982	—	2.00	4.00
PB-13424	So Close/Fool for Your Love	1983	—	2.00	4.00
GB-13479	Why Do Fools Fall in Love/Mirror, Mirror	1983	—	—	3.00
—Gold Standard Series					
PB-13549	Pieces of Ice/Still in Love	1983	—	2.00	4.00
PB-13549 [PS]	Pieces of Ice/Still in Love	1983	—	2.00	4.00
PB-13624	Up Front/Love or Loneliness	1983	—	2.00	4.00
PB-13671	Let's Go Up/Girls	1983	—	2.00	4.00
GB-13798	Muscles/Pieces of Ice	1984	—	—	3.00
—Gold Standard Series					
PB-13864	Swept Away/Fight for It	1984	—	—	3.00
PB-13864 [PS]	Swept Away/Fight for It	1984	—	—	3.00
PB-13966	Missing You/We Are the Children of the World	1984	—	—	3.00
PB-13966 [PS]	Missing You/We Are the Children of the World	1984	—	—	3.00
PB-14032	Telephone/Fool for Your Love	1985	—	—	3.00
PB-14032 [PS]	Telephone/Fool for Your Love	1985	—	—	3.00
PB-14181	Eaten Alive/(Instrumental)	1985	—	—	3.00
PB-14181 [PS]	Eaten Alive/(Instrumental)	1985	—	—	3.00
PB-14244	Chain Reaction/More and More	1985	—	2.00	4.00
PB-14244	Chain Reaction (Remix)/More and More	1986	—	—	3.00
PB-14244 [PS]	Chain Reaction/More and More	1985	—	—	3.00
GB-14342	Missing You/Swept Away	1986	—	—	3.00
—Gold Standard Series					

7-Inch Extended Plays

MOTOWN

Number	Title (A Side/B Side)	Yr	VG	VG+	NM
LLP-133 [DJ]	My Place/Baby It's Love/The Long and Winding Road//How About You/I'm Still Waiting/Everything Is Everything	1971	3.00	6.00	12.00
—Jukebox issue, small hole, plays at 33 1/3 rpm					
LLP-133 [PS]	Everything Is Everything	1971	3.00	6.00	12.00
—Part of "Little LP" series					

Albums

MOTOWN

Number	Title (A Side/B Side)	Yr	VG	VG+	NM
M5-135V1	Diana Ross	1981	2.00	4.00	8.00
—Reissue of 711					
M5-155V1	Diana!	1981	2.00	4.00	8.00
—Reissue of 719					
M5-163V1	Touch Me in the Morning	1981	2.00	4.00	8.00
—Reissue of 772					
M5-169V1	Diana Ross Live at Caesars Palace	1981	2.00	4.00	8.00
—Reissue of 801					
M5-198V1	The Boss	1981	2.00	4.00	8.00
—Reissue of 923					
M5-214V1	Duets with Diana	1981	2.50	5.00	10.00
MS-711	Diana Ross	1970	3.75	7.50	15.00
MS-719	Diana!	1971	3.75	7.50	15.00
MS-723	Surrender	1971	3.75	7.50	15.00
MS-724	Everything Is Everything	1970	3.75	7.50	15.00
M7-758 [(2)]	Lady Sings the Blues	1972	3.75	7.50	15.00
—With booklet; all but four tracks are by Diana Ross					
M 772	Touch Me in the Morning	1973	3.75	7.50	15.00
M7-801	Diana Ross Live at Caesars Palace	1974	3.00	6.00	12.00
M7-812	Last Time I Saw Him	1974	3.00	6.00	12.00
M7-861	Diana Ross	1976	3.00	6.00	12.00
M7-869	Diana Ross' Greatest Hits	1976	3.00	6.00	12.00
M7-877R2 [(2)]	An Evening with Diana Ross	1977	3.75	7.50	15.00
M7-890	Baby It's Me	1977	3.00	6.00	12.00
M7-907	Ross	1978	3.00	6.00	12.00
M7-923M1	The Boss	1979	2.50	5.00	10.00
M8-936	Diana	1980	2.50	5.00	10.00
M8-951	To Love Again	1981	2.50	5.00	10.00
M13-960C2 [(2)]	All the Great Hits	1981	3.00	6.00	12.00
5294 ML	Diana Ross	1983	2.00	4.00	8.00
—Reissue of 861					
6049 ML2 [(2)]	Diana Ross Anthology	1983	3.75	7.50	15.00
MOT-6274	Workin' Overtime	1989	2.50	5.00	10.00
37463-6377-1	The Remixes	1994	3.00	6.00	12.00

NAUTILUS

Number	Title (A Side/B Side)	Yr	VG	VG+	NM
NR-37	Diana	1981	10.00	20.00	40.00
—Audiophile vinyl					

RCA VICTOR

Number	Title (A Side/B Side)	Yr	VG	VG+	NM
AFL1-4153	Why Do Fools Fall in Love	1981	2.50	5.00	10.00
AFL1-4384	Silk Electric	1982	2.50	5.00	10.00
AFL1-4677	Ross	1983	2.00	4.00	8.00
AFL1-5009	Swept Away	1984	2.00	4.00	8.00
AYL1-5162	Why Do Fools Fall in Love	1985	—	3.00	6.00
—"Best Buy Series" reissue					
AFL1-5422	Eaten Alive	1985	2.00	4.00	8.00
6388-1-R	Red Hot Rhythm and Blues	1987	2.00	4.00	8.00

ROSS, DIANA, AND MARVIN GAYE

Also see each artist's individual listings.

45s

MOTOWN

Number	Title (A Side/B Side)	Yr	VG	VG+	NM
1269	My Mistake (Was to Love You)/Include Me in Your Life	1973	—	2.50	5.00
1280	You're a Special Part of Me/I'm Falling in Love with You	1973	—	2.50	5.00
1296	Don't Knock My Love/Just Say Just Say	1974	—	2.50	5.00

Albums

MOTOWN

Number	Title (A Side/B Side)	Yr	VG	VG+	NM
M5-124V1	Diana & Marvin	1981	2.00	4.00	8.00
—Reissue					
M7-803	Diana & Marvin	1973	3.75	7.50	15.00

ROSS, DIANA; MARVIN GAYE; SMOKEY ROBINSON; AND STEVIE WONDER

Also see each artist's individual listings.

45s

MOTOWN

Number	Title (A Side/B Side)	Yr	VG	VG+	NM
1455	Pops, We Love You/(Instrumental)	1979	—	2.00	4.00

ROSS, DIANA, AND THE SUPREMES

See THE SUPREMES.

ROSS, JACKIE

45s

BRUNSWICK

Number	Title (A Side/B Side)	Yr	VG	VG+	NM
55325	Keep Your Chin Up/Love Is Easy to Lose	1967	2.00	4.00	8.00
55361	Mr. Sunshine/Walk on My Side	1968	2.00	4.00	8.00

CAPITOL

Number	Title (A Side/B Side)	Yr	VG	VG+	NM
4308	I Can't Stand to See You Go/Ain't No Fun to Me	1976	—	2.00	4.00

CHESS

Number	Title (A Side/B Side)	Yr	VG	VG+	NM
1903	Selfish One/Everything But Love	1964	2.00	4.00	8.00
1913	I've Got the Skill/Change Your Ways	1964	2.00	4.00	8.00
1915	Haste Makes Waste/Wasting Time	1964	2.00	4.00	8.00
1920	Jerk and Twine/New Lover	1965	2.00	4.00	8.00
1929	You Really Know How to Hurt a Girl/Dynamite Lovin'	1965	2.00	4.00	8.00
1938	Take Me for a Little While/Honey Dear	1965	2.00	4.00	8.00
1940	We Can Do It/Honey Dear	1965	2.00	4.00	8.00

GSF

Number	Title (A Side/B Side)	Yr	VG	VG+	NM
6886	Woman Get Nothing from Love/Do I	1972	—	2.50	5.00
6895	A One Woman Man/Take the Weight Off Me	1973	—	2.50	5.00

MERCURY

Number	Title (A Side/B Side)	Yr	VG	VG+	NM
73041	Angel of the Morning/Showcase	1970	—	3.00	6.00
73185	Glory Be/I Must Give You Time	1971	—	3.00	6.00

SAR

Number	Title (A Side/B Side)	Yr	VG	VG+	NM
129	Hard Times/Hold Me	1962	3.75	7.50	15.00
—As "Jacki Ross"					

SCEPTER

Number	Title (A Side/B Side)	Yr	VG	VG+	NM
12345	The World's in a Hell of a Shape/What Would You Give	1972	—	2.50	5.00

Albums

CHESS

Number	Title (A Side/B Side)	Yr	VG	VG+	NM
LP-1489 [M]	In Full Bloom	1966	7.50	15.00	30.00
LPS-1489 [S]	In Full Bloom	1966	10.00	20.00	40.00

ROSSINI, TONI

45s

SUN

Number	Title (A Side/B Side)	Yr	VG	VG+	NM
349	I Gotta Know/Is It Too Late	1960	5.00	10.00	20.00
366	Well I Ask Ya/Darlena	1961	5.00	10.00	20.00
378	Meet Me After School/Just Around the Corner	1962	5.00	10.00	20.00
380	New Girl in Town/You Made It Sound So Easy	1962	5.00	10.00	20.00
387	Nobody/Moved to Kansas City	1964	5.00	10.00	20.00

ROTARY CONNECTION
Also see MINNIE RIPERTON.

45s

CADET CONCEPT

Number	Title (A Side/B Side)	Yr	VG	VG+	NM
DJ-1 [DJ]	Lady Jane/Amen	1968	3.75	7.50	15.00
7000	Like a Rollin' Stone/Turn Me On	1967	2.50	5.00	10.00
7002	Ruby Tuesday/Soul Man	1968	2.50	5.00	10.00
7007	Paper Castle/Teach Me How to Fly	1968	2.50	5.00	10.00
7008	Aladdin/Magical World	1968	2.50	5.00	10.00
7009	Silent Night Chant/Peace At Least	1968	3.00	6.00	12.00
7014	The Weight/Respect	1969	2.50	5.00	10.00
7018	Want You to Know/Memory Band	1969	2.50	5.00	10.00
7021	Love Me Now/May Our Amens Be True	1970	2.50	5.00	10.00
7027	Stormy Monday Blues/Teach Me How to Fly	1970	2.50	5.00	10.00
7028	Hey Love/If I Sing My Song	1971	2.50	5.00	10.00

—As "New Rotary Connection"

JANUS

Number	Title (A Side/B Side)	Yr	VG	VG+	NM
249	Living Alone/Magical World	1975	—	2.50	5.00

—As "Minnie Riperton and Rotary Connection"

Albums

CADET

Number	Title (A Side/B Side)	Yr	VG	VG+	NM
CS-50006	Hey Love	1971	5.00	10.00	20.00

CADET CONCEPT

Number	Title (A Side/B Side)	Yr	VG	VG+	NM
LPS-312	Rotary Connection	1968	6.25	12.50	25.00
LPS-317	Aladdin	1968	6.25	12.50	25.00
LPS 318	Peace	1969	5.00	10.00	20.00
LPS-322	Songs	1969	6.25	12.50	25.00
LSP-328	Dinner Music	1970	6.25	12.50	25.00

ROTATIONS, THE (1)

45s

FRANTIC

Number	Title (A Side/B Side)	Yr	VG	VG+	NM
200	Put a Nickel on D-9 (Pt. 1)/Put a Nickel on D-9 (Pt. 2)	1965	37.50	75.00	150.00
202	Changed Man/Heartaches	1967	25.00	50.00	100.00

MALA

Number	Title (A Side/B Side)	Yr	VG	VG+	NM
576	Misty Roses/Trying to Make You My Own	1967	7.50	15.00	30.00

ROTATIONS, THE (2)

45s

ORIGINAL SOUND

Number	Title (A Side/B Side)	Yr	VG	VG+	NM
41	The Crusher/Heavies	1964	25.00	50.00	100.00

—Produced by FRANK ZAPPA

ROULETTES, THE
More than one group.

45s

ANGLE

Number	Title (A Side/B Side)	Yr	VG	VG+	NM
1001	Surfer's Charge/Archibald II (Duke of Nothing)	1963	12.50	25.00	50.00

CHAMP

Number	Title (A Side/B Side)	Yr	VG	VG+	NM
102	I See a Star/Come On, Baby	1958	20.00	40.00	80.00

EBB

Number	Title (A Side/B Side)	Yr	VG	VG+	NM
124	The Way You Carry On/You Don't Care Anymore	1957	7.50	15.00	30.00

SCEPTER

Number	Title (A Side/B Side)	Yr	VG	VG+	NM
1204	Hasten Jason/Wouldn't It Be Goin' Steady	1959	150.00	300.00	600.00

UNITED ARTISTS

Number	Title (A Side/B Side)	Yr	VG	VG+	NM
718	Can You Go/Soon You'll Be Leaving Me	1964	2.50	5.00	10.00
990	Long Cigarette/Junk	1966	2.50	5.00	10.00

ROUND, JONATHAN

45s

WESTBOUND

Number	Title (A Side/B Side)	Yr	VG	VG+	NM
186	Don't It Make You Want to Go Home/Train a-Comin'	1971	2.00	4.00	8.00
199	Sympathy for the Devil/Travelin' Mama Blues	1972	2.50	5.00	10.00

Albums

WESTBOUND

Number	Title (A Side/B Side)	Yr	VG	VG+	NM
2009	Jonathan Round *—Round cover*	1971	7.50	15.00	30.00
2009	Jonathan Round *—Square cover*	1972	3.75	7.50	15.00

ROUTERS, THE

45s

MERCURY

Number	Title (A Side/B Side)	Yr	VG	VG+	NM
73418	Superbird/Sack of Woe	1973	—	3.00	6.00

WARNER BROS.

Number	Title (A Side/B Side)	Yr	VG	VG+	NM
5283	Let's Go (pony)/Mashy	1962	3.75	7.50	15.00
5332	Half Time/Make It Snappy	1963	3.00	6.00	12.00
5349	Sting Ray/Snap Happy	1963	3.00	6.00	12.00
5379	A-Ooga/Big Band	1963	3.00	6.00	12.00
5403	Snap, Crackle and Pop/Amoeba	1963	3.00	6.00	12.00
5444	Crack Up/Let's Dance	1964	3.00	6.00	12.00
5467	Stamp and Shake/Ah-Ya	1964	3.00	6.00	12.00
7117	Let's Go (pony)/Mashy	1967	2.50	5.00	10.00

Albums

WARNER BROS.

Number	Title (A Side/B Side)	Yr	VG	VG+	NM
W 1490 [M]	Let's Go! with the Routers	1963	6.25	12.50	25.00
WS 1490 [S]	Let's Go! with the Routers	1963	7.50	15.00	30.00
W 1524 [M]	1963's Great Instrumental Hits	1964	7.50	15.00	30.00
WS 1524 [S]	1963's Great Instrumental Hits	1964	10.00	20.00	40.00
W 1559 [M]	Charge!	1964	6.25	12.50	25.00
WS 1559 [S]	Charge!	1964	7.50	15.00	30.00
W 1595 [M]	Go Go Go with the Chuck Berry Songbook	1965	5.00	10.00	20.00
WS 1595 [S]	Go Go Go with the Chuck Berry Songbook	1965	6.25	12.50	25.00

ROUZAN SISTERS, THE

45s

FRISCO

Number	Title (A Side/B Side)	Yr	VG	VG+	NM
113	Men of War/Dance Every Dance	1965	2.50	5.00	10.00

ROVER BOYS, THE

45s

ABC-PARAMOUNT

Number	Title (A Side/B Side)	Yr	VG	VG+	NM
9659	Come to Me/Love Me Again	1955	3.75	7.50	15.00
9678	My Queen/Sixteen Teens	1956	3.75	7.50	15.00
9700	Graduation Day/I Hear Music	1956	3.75	7.50	15.00
9732	From a School Ring to a Wedding Ring/Young Love	1956	3.75	7.50	15.00
9760	The Piano Tuner/Whoop Doodly Baby	1956	3.75	7.50	15.00
9779	Little Did I Know/Again and Again	1957	3.75	7.50	15.00

CORAL

Number	Title (A Side/B Side)	Yr	VG	VG+	NM
61271	Show Me/You've Got It	1954	5.00	10.00	20.00

DECCA

Number	Title (A Side/B Side)	Yr	VG	VG+	NM
31485	Shalom/I Hear Havana	1963	2.00	4.00	8.00

RCA VICTOR

Number	Title (A Side/B Side)	Yr	VG	VG+	NM
47-7432	Magic Lamp/Little Darlin'	1959	3.00	6.00	12.00
47-7482	Sweet Violets/Julia	1959	3.00	6.00	12.00

UNITED ARTISTS

Number	Title (A Side/B Side)	Yr	VG	VG+	NM
288	Is It Me/Marry Young	1961	2.50	5.00	10.00
331	For Every Boy or Girl/If You Plant a Little Kiss	1961	2.50	5.00	10.00

VIK

Number	Title (A Side/B Side)	Yr	VG	VG+	NM
0283	Soft Sands/My Baby's Steppin' Out	1957	5.00	10.00	20.00
0302	What Can I Do for a Heartache/I Got to You	1957	5.00	10.00	20.00
0313	Blue Willow/You're My Everything	1958	5.00	10.00	20.00
0317	Blind Date/Make Room for Me	1958	5.00	10.00	20.00
0338	S'Agapo/Ask Me Who Loves You	1958	5.00	10.00	20.00

ROVERS, THE (1)

45s

CAPITOL

Number	Title (A Side/B Side)	Yr	VG	VG+	NM
F-3078	Why Oh-h/Ichi-Bon Tami Dachi	1955	12.50	25.00	50.00

MUSIC CITY

Number	Title (A Side/B Side)	Yr	VG	VG+	NM
750	Why Oh-h/Ichi-Bon Tami Dachi *—Black vinyl*	1954	20.00	40.00	80.00
750	Why Oh-h/Ichi-Bon Tami Dachi *—Red vinyl*	1954	62.50	125.00	250.00
780	Salute to Johnny Ace/Jadda *—Black vinyl*	1955	20.00	40.00	80.00
780	Salute to Johnny Ace/Jadda *—Red vinyl*	1955	62.50	125.00	250.00

ROVERS, THE (2)

45s

CHATTAHOOCHIE

Number	Title (A Side/B Side)	Yr	VG	VG+	NM
653	The Web/Can't Be the First	1964	2.50	5.00	10.00

ROVERS, THE (3)

45s

KAPP

Number	Title (A Side/B Side)	Yr	VG	VG+	NM
278	Delia's Gone/I Know Where I'm Goin'	1959	3.00	6.00	12.00

ROVIN' KIND, THE

45s

DUNWICH

Number	Title (A Side/B Side)	Yr	VG	VG+	NM
146	My Generation/Girl	1967	5.00	10.00	20.00
154	She/Didn't Want to Have to Do It	1967	5.00	10.00	20.00

ROULETTE

Number	Title (A Side/B Side)	Yr	VG	VG+	NM
4687	Right on Time/Night People	1966	3.75	7.50	15.00

ROWLES, JOHN

Albums

KAPP

Number	Title (A Side/B Side)	Yr	VG	VG+	NM
KS-3597	Exciting	1969	3.75	7.50	15.00
KS-3637	Cheryl Moana Marie	1971	3.75	7.50	15.00

MCA

Number	Title (A Side/B Side)	Yr	VG	VG+	NM
549	John Rowles	197?	2.50	5.00	10.00

ROXY MUSIC
Also see BRYAN FERRY.

12-Inch Singles

WARNER BROS.

Number	Title (A Side/B Side)	Yr	VG	VG+	NM
PRO-A-1056 [DJ]	Take a Chance with Me (2 versions)/More Than This/Avalon	1982	3.00	6.00	12.00
PRO-A-2033 [DJ]	More Than This/Avalon	1982	2.50	5.00	10.00

45s

ATCO

Number	Title (A Side/B Side)	Yr	VG	VG+	NM
7018	The Thrill of It All/The Application Failed	1975	—	2.00	4.00
7042	Love Is the Drug/Both Ends Burning	1975	—	2.00	4.00
7100	Dance Away/Trash 2	1979	—	2.00	4.00
7204	Angel Eyes/My Little Girl	1979	—	2.00	4.00
7301	Over You/My Only Love	1980	—	2.00	4.00
7310	Oh Yeah (On the Radio)/Rain, Rain, Rain	1980	—	2.00	4.00
7315	In the Midnight Hour/(B-side unknown)	1980	—	2.00	4.00
7329	Jealous Guy/To Turn You On	1981	—	2.00	4.00
7329 [PS]	Jealous Guy/To Turn You On	1981	—	2.00	4.00

ATLANTIC

Number	Title (A Side/B Side)	Yr	VG	VG+	NM
13269	Love Is the Drug/Dance Away *—Oldies Series reissue*	198?	—	—	3.00

REPRISE

Number	Title (A Side/B Side)	Yr	VG	VG+	NM
1124	Virginia Plan/The Numberer	1972	—	2.50	5.00

WARNER BROS.

Number	Title (A Side/B Side)	Yr	VG	VG+	NM
GWB 0316	Do the Strand/Virginia Plain *—"Back to Back Hits" series*	197?	—	—	3.00
7719	Do the Strand/Editions of You	1973	—	2.50	5.00
29912	More Than This/Always Unknowing	1982	—	—	3.00
29978	Take a Chance with Me/India	1982	—	—	3.00
29978 [PS]	Take a Chance with Me/India	1982	—	—	3.00

Albums

ATCO

Number	Title (A Side/B Side)	Yr	VG	VG+	NM
SD 32-102	Flesh + Blood	1980	2.50	5.00	10.00

Number	Title (A Side/B Side)	Yr	VG	VG+	NM
SD 38-103	Greatest Hits	1977	2.50	5.00	10.00
SD 36-106	Country Life	1975	6.25	12.50	25.00
—Original cover shows two semi-naked women on a grassy background					
SD 36-106A	Country Life	1975	2.50	5.00	10.00
—Revised cover deletes women, leaves only the grassy background					
SD 38-114	Manifesto	1979	2.50	5.00	10.00
SD 38-114 [PD]	Manifesto	1979	7.50	15.00	30.00
—Picture disc					
SD 36-127	Siren	1975	2.50	5.00	10.00
—Originals have yellow labels					
SD 36-133	The First Roxy Music Album	1975	3.00	6.00	12.00
—Reissue of Reprise MS 2114; originals have yellow labels					
SD 36-134	For Your Pleasure	1975	3.00	6.00	12.00
—Reissue of Warner Bros. BS 2696; originals have yellow labels					
SD 36-139	Viva! Roxy Music (Live)	1976	2.50	5.00	10.00
—Originals have yellow labels					
SD 7045	Stranded	1974	3.00	6.00	12.00
90122	The Atlantic Years (1973-80)	1983	2.50	5.00	10.00
REPRISE					
MS 2114	Roxy Music	1972	7.50	15.00	30.00
25857 [(2)]	Street Life: 20 Greatest Hits	1989	3.75	7.50	15.00
—By "Bryan Ferry & Roxy Music"					
WARNER BROS.					
BS 2696	For Your Pleasure	1973	6.25	12.50	25.00
23686	Avalon	1982	2.50	5.00	10.00
23808 [EP]	Musique — The High Road	1983	2.00	4.00	8.00

ROY C

45s

Number	Title (A Side/B Side)	Yr	VG	VG+	NM
ALAGA					
1000	In Divorce Court/I Don't Want to Worry	1970	2.50	5.00	10.00
1003	Falling in Love/I Found a Man in My Bed	1970	2.50	5.00	10.00
1005	A Merry Black Christmas/I Don't Want To Worry	1970	2.50	5.00	10.00
1006	Got to Get Enough (Of Your Sweet Love Stuff)/ An Open Letter to the President	1971	2.50	5.00	10.00
1007	I Wasn't There/Those Days Are Gone	1971	2.50	5.00	10.00
1008	I'll Never Leave You Lonely/I'm Gonna Love (Somebody Else's Woman)	1972	2.50	5.00	10.00
1009	Since I Met You Baby/Lonely I Was	1972	2.50	5.00	10.00
—With Linda Caver					
1013	I Caught You in the Act/Back Into My Arms	1973	2.50	5.00	10.00
1014	Since God Made a Woman/We're On the Road to Hell	1973	2.50	5.00	10.00
BLACK HAWK					
12101	Shotgun Wedding/(B-side unknown)	1965	3.00	6.00	12.00
MERCURY					
73391	Don't Blame the Man/I'm Bustin' My Rocks	1973	—	3.00	6.00
73445	She Kept On Walkin'/Back Into My Arms	1973	—	3.00	6.00
73605	Loneliness Has Got a Hold on Me/If I Could Love You Forever	1974	—	2.50	5.00
73672	Love Me Till Tomorrow Comes/Virgin Girl	1975	—	2.50	5.00
73735	My Girl (Reggae)/The Second Time Around	1975	—	2.50	5.00
73780	Every Woman Has a Right/Don't Stop Short of Satisfaction	1976	—	2.50	5.00
73848	You Can't Judge a Man (By the Color of His Skin)/ I Wanna Do It Again	1976	—	2.50	5.00
73981	From the Outside Looking In (He Used to Be My Friend)/After Loving You	1977	—	2.50	5.00
SHOUT					
206	Gone Gone/Stop What You're Doing	1966	2.50	5.00	10.00
UPTOWN					
731	Shotgun Wedding/High School Dropout	1966	2.50	5.00	10.00

Albums

Number	Title (A Side/B Side)	Yr	VG	VG+	NM
MERCURY					
SRM-1-678	Sex and Soul	1974	3.75	7.50	15.00
SRM-1-1056	Nice	1976	3.75	7.50	15.00
SRM-1-1192	More	1978	3.75	7.50	15.00

ROYAL, BILLY JOE

45s

Number	Title (A Side/B Side)	Yr	VG	VG+	NM
ALL WOOD					
401	Wait for Me Baby/If It Wasn't for a Woman	1962	5.00	10.00	20.00
ATLANTIC					
2328	Never in a Hundred Years/We Haven't a Moment to Lose	1966	2.50	5.00	10.00
87770	If the Jukebox Took Teardrops/How Could You	1991	—	2.00	4.00
87867	Ring Where a Ring Used to Be/We Need to Walk	1990	—	2.00	4.00
87933	Searchin' for Some Kind of Clue/This Too Shall Pass	1990	—	2.00	4.00
88815	Till I Can't Take It Anymore/He Don't Know	1990	—	2.00	4.00
ATLANTIC AMERICA					
99217	Love Has No Right/Cross My Heart and Hope to Try	1989	—	—	3.00
99242	Tell It Like It Is/Losing You	1989	—	—	3.00
99295	It Keeps Right On Hurtin'/Let It Rain	1988	—	—	3.00
99364	Out of Sight and On My Mind/She Don't Cry Like She Used To	1988	—	—	3.00
99404	I'll Pin a Note on Your Pillow/A Place for a Heartache	1987	—	—	3.00
99404 [PS]	I'll Pin a Note on Your Pillow/A Place for a Heartache	1987	—	—	3.00
99519	I Miss You Already/Another Endless Night	1986	—	—	3.00
99555	Boardwalk Angel/Out of Sight and On My Mind	1986	—	—	3.00
99599	Burned Like a Rocket/Lonely Loving You	1985	—	—	3.00
COLUMBIA					
43305	Down in the Boondocks/Oh, What a Night	1965	2.50	5.00	10.00
43305 [DJ]	Down in the Boondocks (same on both sides)	1965	10.00	20.00	40.00
—Red vinyl promo					
43390	I Knew You When/Steal Away	1965	2.50	5.00	10.00
43390 [DJ]	I Knew You When (same on both sides)	1965	10.00	20.00	40.00
—Red vinyl promo					
43465	I've Got to Be Somebody/You Make Me Feel Like a Man	1965	2.00	4.00	8.00
43465 [DJ]	I've Got to Be Somebody (same on both sides)	1965	7.50	15.00	30.00
—Red vinyl promo					
43538	It's a Good Time/Don't Wait Up for Me Mama	1966	2.00	4.00	8.00
43622	Heart's Desire/Keep Inside Me	1966	2.00	4.00	8.00
43740	Campfire Girls/Should I Come Back	1966	2.00	4.00	8.00
43883	Yo-Yo/We Tried	1966	2.00	4.00	8.00
44003	Wisdom of a Fool/Everything Turned Blue	1967	2.00	4.00	8.00
44103	These Are Not My People/The Greatest Love	1967	2.00	4.00	8.00
44277	Hush/Watching from the Bandstand	1967	2.00	4.00	8.00
44468	Don't You Be Ashamed (To Call My Name)/Don't You Think It's Time	1968	2.00	4.00	8.00
44574	Storybook Children/Just Between You and Me	1968	2.00	4.00	8.00
44677	Movies in My Mind/Gabriel	1968	—	3.00	6.00
44743	Bed of Roses/The Greatest Love	1969	—	3.00	6.00
44814	Nobody Loves You But Me/Baby I'm Thinking of You	1969	—	2.50	5.00
44902	Cherry Hill Park/Helping Hand	1969	2.00	4.00	8.00
45085	Mama's Song/Me Without You	1970	—	2.50	5.00
45220	Burning a Hole/Every Night	1970	—	2.50	5.00
45289	Tulsa/Pick Up the Pieces	1970	—	2.50	5.00
45406	Poor Little Pearl/Lady Lives to Love	1971	—	2.50	5.00
45495	Colorado Rain/We Go Back	1971	—	2.50	5.00
45557	Later/The Family	1972	—	3.00	6.00
45620	Child of Mine/Natchez Trace	1972	—	3.00	6.00
FAIRLANE					
21009	Never in a Hundred Years/We Haven't a Moment to Lose	1961	7.50	15.00	30.00
21013	Dark Glasses/Perhaps	1962	7.50	15.00	30.00
KAT FAMILY					
01044	(Who is Like You) Sweet America/No Love Like a First Love	1981	—	2.00	4.00
02074	You Really Got a Hold on Me/No Love Like a First Love	1981	—	2.00	4.00
02297	Wasted Time/Outrun the Sun	1981	—	2.00	4.00
MERCURY					
76069	Mr. Kool/Let's Talk It Over	1980	—	2.00	4.00
888680-7	Members Only/Funny Face	1987	—	—	3.00
—A-side with Donna Fargo; B-side by Fargo solo					
MGM SOUTH					
7011	This Magic Moment/Mountain Woman	1973	—	2.50	5.00
7018	Summertime Skies/Look What I Found	1973	—	2.50	5.00
7022	If This Is the Last Time/Perfect Harmony	1973	—	2.50	5.00
7032	Star Again/Sugar Blue	1974	—	2.50	5.00
PLAYER'S					
1	I'm Specialized/Really You	1965	5.00	10.00	20.00
PRIVATE STOCK					
45192	Under the Boardwalk/Precious Time	1978	—	2.50	5.00
45212 [DJ]	Anchors Aweigh (mono/stereo)	1979	—	2.50	5.00
SCEPTER					
12419	All Night Rain/Time Don't Pass By Here	1976	—	2.00	4.00
TOLLIE					
9011	Mama Didn't Raise No Fools/Get Behind Me, Devil	1964	3.75	7.50	15.00

Albums

Number	Title (A Side/B Side)	Yr	VG	VG+	NM
ATLANTIC AMERICA					
90508	Looking Ahead	1986	2.50	5.00	10.00
90658	The Royal Treatment	1987	2.50	5.00	10.00
91064	Tell It Like It Is	1989	2.50	5.00	10.00
COLUMBIA					
CL 2403 [M]	Down in the Boondocks	1965	5.00	10.00	20.00
CL 2781 [M]	Billy Joe Royal	1967	6.25	12.50	25.00
CS 9203 [S]	Down in the Boondocks	1965	6.25	12.50	25.00
CS 9581 [S]	Billy Joe Royal	1967	6.25	12.50	25.00
CS 9974	Cherry Hill Park	1969	6.25	12.50	25.00
KAT FAMILY					
JW 37342	Billy Joe Royal	1982	2.50	5.00	10.00
MERCURY					
SRM-1-3837	Billy Joe Royal	1980	2.50	5.00	10.00

ROYAL DEBS, THE

45s

Number	Title (A Side/B Side)	Yr	VG	VG+	NM
TIFCO					
826	I Do/Jerry	1962	6.25	12.50	25.00

ROYAL DRIFTERS, THE

45s

Number	Title (A Side/B Side)	Yr	VG	VG+	NM
TEEN					
506	S'Why Hard/Little Linda	1959	25.00	50.00	100.00
508	To Each His Own/Da Kind	1959	37.50	75.00	150.00

ROYAL GUARDSMEN, THE

45s

Number	Title (A Side/B Side)	Yr	VG	VG+	NM
LAURIE					
112	Snoopy's Christmas/The Smallest Astronaut	197?	—	2.00	4.00
—B-side by Barry Winslow; reissue					
3359	Baby Let's Wait/Leaving Me	1966	2.50	5.00	10.00
3366	Snoopy vs. the Red Baron/I Needed You	1966	3.00	6.00	12.00
3379	The Return of the Red Baron/Sweetmeats Slide	1967	2.50	5.00	10.00
3391	Airplane Song (My Airplane)/Om	1967	2.00	4.00	8.00
3397	Wednesday/So Right (To Be in Love)	1967	2.00	4.00	8.00
3416	Snoopy's Christmas/It Kinda Looks Like Christmas	1967	2.50	5.00	10.00
3416 [PS]	Snoopy's Christmas/It Kinda Looks Like Christmas	1967	5.00	10.00	20.00
3428	I Say Love/I'm Not Gonna Stay	1968	2.00	4.00	8.00
3451	Snoopy for President/Down Behind the Lines	1968	2.00	4.00	8.00
3461	Baby Let's Wait/Biplane "Evermore"	1968	2.00	4.00	8.00
3461	Baby Let's Wait/So Right (To Be in Love)	1968	2.00	4.00	8.00
3494	Magic Window/Mother, Where's Your Daughter	1969	2.50	5.00	8.00
3590	Snoopy for President/Down Behind the Lines	1972	—	3.00	6.00
3646	Snoopy for President/Sweetmeats Slide	1976	—	2.50	5.00

Number	Title (A Side/B Side)	Yr	VG	VG+	NM
Albums					
HOLIDAY					
HDY 1913	Merry Snoopy's Christmas	1980	2.50	5.00	10.00
—Reissue of Laurie 2042					
LAURIE					
LLP-2038 [M]	Snoopy vs. the Red Baron	1967	5.00	10.00	20.00
SLP-2038 [S]	Snoopy vs. the Red Baron	1967	6.25	12.50	25.00
LLP-2039 [M]	The Return of the Red Baron	1967	5.00	10.00	20.00
SLP-2039 [S]	The Return of the Red Baron	1967	6.25	12.50	25.00
LLP 2042 [M]	Snoopy and His Friends	1967	6.25	12.50	25.00
—With "Merry Snoopy's Christmas" poster still attached to back cover					
LLP 2042 [M]	Snoopy and His Friends	1967	3.75	7.50	15.00
—With "Merry Snoopy's Christmas" poster missing					
SLP 2042 [S]	Snoopy and His Friends	1967	7.50	15.00	30.00
—With "Merry Snoopy's Christmas" poster still attached to back cover					
SLP 2042 [S]	Snoopy and His Friends	1967	5.00	10.00	20.00
—With "Merry Snoopy's Christmas" poster missing					
SLP-2046	Snoopy for President	1968	6.25	12.50	25.00

ROYAL HALOS, THE

Number	Title (A Side/B Side)	Yr	VG	VG+	NM
45s					
ALADDIN					
3460	My Love Is True/Nobody But Me and My Girl	1959	10.00	20.00	40.00

ROYAL HOLIDAYS, THE

Number	Title (A Side/B Side)	Yr	VG	VG+	NM
45s					
CARLTON					
472	Margaret/I'm Sorry	1958	6.25	12.50	25.00
HERALD					
536	Rockin' at the Bandstand/Down in Cuba	1959	37.50	75.00	150.00
—Most, and perhaps all, copies were labeled "Chip Chip"/"Running to You" by the Mello-Kings					
PENTHOUSE					
9357	Margaret/I'm Sorry	1958	37.50	75.00	150.00

ROYAL PLAYBOYS, THE

Number	Title (A Side/B Side)	Yr	VG	VG+	NM
Albums					
WALDORF					
33-136 [10]	Rock and Roll/New Orleans Blues	195?	125.00	250.00	500.00

ROYAL ROBINS, THE

Number	Title (A Side/B Side)	Yr	VG	VG+	NM
45s					
ABC-PARAMOUNT					
10504	Turn Me Loose/Country Fool	1963	7.50	15.00	30.00
10542	How High the Moon/Something You've Got, Baby	1964	7.50	15.00	30.00

ROYAL TEENS, THE

Bob Gaudio, later of THE FOUR SEASONS, was in this group.

Number	Title (A Side/B Side)	Yr	VG	VG+	NM
45s					
ABC-PARAMOUNT					
9882	Short Shorts/Planet Rock	1958	7.50	15.00	30.00
9918	Big Name Button/Sham Rock	1958	6.25	12.50	25.00
9945	Harvey's Got a Girl Friend/Hangin' Around	1958	6.25	12.50	25.00
9955	Open the Door/My Kind of Dream	1958	6.25	12.50	25.00
ALLNEW					
1415	Short Short Twist/Royal Twist	1962	5.00	10.00	20.00
ASTRA					
1012	Mad Gass/Sittin' with My Baby	196?	3.75	7.50	15.00
CAPITOL					
F4261	Believe Me/Little Cricket	1959	7.50	15.00	30.00
4335	The Moon's Not Meant for Lovers/Was It a Dream	1960	7.50	15.00	30.00
4402	With You/It's the Talk of the Town	1960	7.50	15.00	30.00
JUBILEE					
5418	Short Short Twist/Royal Twist	1962	3.75	7.50	15.00
MIGHTY					
111	Leotards/Royal Blues	1959	6.25	12.50	25.00
112	Cave Man/Wounded Heart	1959	7.50	15.00	30.00
200	My Memories of You/Little Trixie	1961	10.00	20.00	40.00
MUSICOR					
1398	Smile a Little Smile for Me/Hey Jude	1969	2.50	5.00	10.00
POWER					
113	Mad Gass/Sittin' with My Baby	1959	10.00	20.00	40.00
215	Short Shorts/Planet Rock	1957	37.50	75.00	150.00
SWAN					
4200	I'll Love You ('Til the End of Time)/(Instrumental)	1965	25.00	50.00	100.00
TCF HALL					
117	Bad Girl/Do the Montoona	1965	3.75	7.50	15.00
Albums					
COLLECTABLES					
COL-5094	Short Shorts: Golden Classics	198?	2.50	5.00	10.00
MUSICOR					
MS-3186	Newies But Oldies	1970	5.00	10.00	20.00
TRU-GEMS					
1001	Short Shorts & Others	1975	5.00	10.00	20.00

ROYAL TONES, THE

Number	Title (A Side/B Side)	Yr	VG	VG+	NM
45s					
TITANIC					
5014	Black Lightnin'/Surfer's Junction	1964	15.00	30.00	60.00

ROYALETTES, THE

Number	Title (A Side/B Side)	Yr	VG	VG+	NM
45s					
CHANCELLOR					
1133	No Big Thing/Yesterday's Lovers	1963	5.00	10.00	20.00
1140	Willie the Wolf/Blue Summer	1963	3.75	7.50	15.00
MGM					
13283	He's Gone/Don't You Cry	1964	3.00	6.00	12.00
13327	Poor Boy/Watch What Happens	1965	3.00	6.00	12.00
13366	It's Gonna Take a Miracle/Out of Sight, Out of Mind	1965	3.75	7.50	15.00
13405	I Want to Meet Him/Never Again	1965	3.00	6.00	12.00
13451	You Bring Me Down/Only When You're Lonely	1966	3.00	6.00	12.00
13507	It's a Big Mistake/It's Better Not to Know	1966	3.00	6.00	12.00
13544	I Don't Want to Be the One/An Affair to Remember	1966	3.00	6.00	12.00
13588	Love Without An End/When Summer's Gone	1966	3.00	6.00	12.00
13627	My Man/Take My Love	1966	3.00	6.00	12.00
ROULETTE					
4768	River of Ters/Something Wonderful	1967	2.50	5.00	10.00
WARNER BROS.					
5439	There He Goes/Come to Me	1964	3.75	7.50	15.00
Albums					
MGM					
E-4332 [M]	It's Gonna Take a Miracle	1965	5.00	10.00	20.00
SE-4332 [S]	It's Gonna Take a Miracle	1965	6.25	12.50	25.00
E-4366 [M]	The Elegant Sound of the Royalettes	1966	5.00	10.00	20.00
SE-4366 [S]	The Elegant Sound of the Royalettes	1966	6.25	12.50	25.00

ROYALS, THE (1)

Later known as THE MIDNIGHTERS. Also see HANK BALLARD AND THE MIDNIGHTERS.

Number	Title (A Side/B Side)	Yr	VG	VG+	NM
45s					
FEDERAL					
12064	Every Beat of My Heart/All Night Long	1952	375.00	750.00	1500.
12064AA	Every Beat of My Heart/All Night Long	1952	1000.	2000.	3000.
—Blue vinyl					
12077	I Know I Love You So/Starting From Tonight	1952	625.00	1250.	2500.
12088	Moonrise/Fifth Street Blues	1952	500.00	1000.	2000.
12088	Moonrise/Fifth Street Blues	1952	1000.	2000.	3000.
—Blue vinyl					
12098	A Love in My Heart/I'll Never Let You Go	1952	250.00	500.00	1000.
12113	Are You Forgetting?/What Did I Do	1952	150.00	300.00	600.00
12121	The Shrine of St. Cecelia/I Feel So Blue	1953	200.00	400.00	800.00
12133	Get It/No It Ain't	1953	50.00	100.00	200.00
12150	Hello Miss Fine/I Feel That-A-Way	1953	50.00	100.00	200.00
12160	That's It/Someone Like You	1953	62.50	125.00	250.00
12169	Work With Me Annie/Until I Die	1954	62.50	125.00	250.00
—Original pressing; for reissues, see "Midnighters, The"					
12177 [DJ]	Give It Up/That Woman	1954	75.00	150.00	300.00
—Evidently, some promos exist crediting The Royals					

ROYALS, THE (2)

Also see CHUCK WILLIS.

Number	Title (A Side/B Side)	Yr	VG	VG+	NM
45s					
OKEH					
6832	If You Love Me/Dreams of You	1951	250.00	500.00	1000.

ROYALS, THE (3)

Number	Title (A Side/B Side)	Yr	VG	VG+	NM
45s					
PENGUIN					
1008	Thunder Wagon/Teen Beat	1959	7.50	15.00	30.00

ROYALS, THE (4)

Number	Title (A Side/B Side)	Yr	VG	VG+	NM
45s					
VAGABOND					
134	Surfin' Lagoon/Wild Safari	1962	12.50	25.00	50.00
444	Christmas Party/White Christmas	1963	12.50	25.00	50.00
—Black vinyl					
444	Christmas Party/White Christmas	1963	25.00	50.00	100.00
—Red vinyl					

ROYALS, THE (5)

This Royals later became The Scooters.

Number	Title (A Side/B Side)	Yr	VG	VG+	NM
45s					
VENUS					
103	Someday We'll Meet Again/I Want You to Be My Mambo Baby	1954	100.00	200.00	400.00

ROYALTONES, THE

Number	Title (A Side/B Side)	Yr	VG	VG+	NM
45s					
GOLDISC					
3004	Short Line/Big Wheel	1960	2.50	5.00	10.00
3011	Flamingo Express/Tacos	1960	2.50	5.00	10.00
3011	Flamingo Express/Secret Love	1960	2.50	5.00	10.00
3016	Butterscotch/Dixie Cup	1961	2.00	4.00	8.00
3017	Royal Whirl/Dixie Rock	1961	2.00	4.00	8.00
3026	Peppermint Twist/Scotch and Soda	1962	2.00	4.00	8.00
3028	Do the Early Bird/Scotch and Soda	1962	2.00	4.00	8.00
JUBILEE					
5338	Poor Boy/Wail!	1958	3.75	7.50	15.00
5362	Seesaw/Little Bo	1959	3.00	6.00	12.00
MALA					
473	Holy Smokes/Our Faded Love	1964	2.00	4.00	8.00
482	El Toro/Lonely World	1964	2.00	4.00	8.00
487	The Yea Yea Song/Misty Sea	1964	2.00	4.00	8.00
OLD TOWN					
1018	Crazy Love/Never Let Me Go	1956	25.00	50.00	100.00
PORT					
70037	Poor Boy/See Saw	1963	3.00	6.00	12.00

ROYCE, EARL, AND THE OLYMPICS

British group; no relation to other Olympics groups.

Number	Title (A Side/B Side)	Yr	VG	VG+	NM
45s					
TOWER					
137	Que Sera Sera Sera/I Really Do	1965	2.00	4.00	8.00

ROZZI, LITTLE SAMMY

Number	Title (A Side/B Side)	Yr	VG	VG+	NM
45s					
PELHAM					
722	Christine/Over the Rainbow	1961	50.00	100.00	200.00

RUBBER BAND, THE (1)

45s

Number	Title (A Side/B Side)	Yr	VG	VG+	NM
ABC					
10849	Plastic Soul/Let's Sail Away	1966	2.50	5.00	10.00
COLUMBIA					
44013	In and Out of My Life/Bring Your Love	1967	2.50	5.00	10.00
REPRISE					
0637	I'm Gonna Make It/Messin' Up the Mind of a Young Girl	1967	2.50	5.00	10.00

RUBBER BAND, THE (2)

45s

Number	Title (A Side/B Side)	Yr	VG	VG+	NM
GRT					
1	Sunshine of Your Love/Deserted Cities of the Heart	1969	—	3.00	6.00

Albums

Number	Title (A Side/B Side)	Yr	VG	VG+	NM
GRT					
10000	Cream Songbook	1969	6.25	12.50	25.00
10007	Hendrix Songbook	1969	6.25	12.50	25.00
10015	Beatles Songbook	1969	6.25	12.50	25.00

RUBBER MEMORY

Albums

Number	Title (A Side/B Side)	Yr	VG	VG+	NM
R.P.C.					
69401	Welcome	196?	250.00	500.00	1000.

RUBEN AND THE JETS

Also see FRANK ZAPPA.

45s

Number	Title (A Side/B Side)	Yr	VG	VG+	NM
MERCURY					
73381	If I Could Be Your Love Again/Wedding Bells	1973	—	3.00	6.00
73411	Charlena/Mah Man Flash	1973	—	3.00	6.00

Albums

Number	Title (A Side/B Side)	Yr	VG	VG+	NM
MERCURY					
SRM-1-659	For Real	1973	3.75	7.50	15.00
SRM-1-694	Con Safos	1974	3.00	6.00	12.00

RUBETTES

45s

Number	Title (A Side/B Side)	Yr	VG	VG+	NM
POLYDOR					
15089	Sugar Baby Love/You Could Have Told Me	1974	—	2.50	5.00
15092	Tonight/Silent Movie Queen	1974	—	2.00	4.00
15102	I Can Do It/If You've Got the Time	1975	—	2.00	4.00
STATE/MCA					
40549	Juke Box Jive/Put a Back Beat to That Music	1976	—	2.00	4.00
40632	Rock Is Dead/Dark Side of the World	1976	—	2.00	4.00

Albums

Number	Title (A Side/B Side)	Yr	VG	VG+	NM
STATE					
MCA-2193	Rubettes	1976	3.00	6.00	12.00

RUBIN

45s

Number	Title (A Side/B Side)	Yr	VG	VG+	NM
KAPP					
869	You've Been Away/Baby, You're My Everything	1967	15.00	30.00	60.00

RUBY AND THE ROMANTICS

45s

Number	Title (A Side/B Side)	Yr	VG	VG+	NM
ABC					
10911	Twilight Time/Una Bella Brazilian Melody	1967	2.50	5.00	10.00
10941	Only Heaven Knows/This Is No Laughing Matter	1967	2.50	5.00	10.00
11065	On a Clear Day You Can See Forever/More Than Yesterday, Less Than Tomorrow	1968	2.50	5.00	10.00
A&M					
1042	Hurting Each Other/Baby, I Could Be So Good at Loving You	1969	2.00	4.00	8.00
KAPP					
501	Our Day Will Come/Moonlight and Music	1963	3.75	7.50	15.00
525	My Summer Love/Sweet Love and Sweet Forgiveness	1963	3.00	6.00	12.00
544	Hey There Lonely Boy/Not a Moment Too Soon	1963	3.00	6.00	12.00
544 [PS]	Hey There Lonely Boy/Not a Moment Too Soon	1963	3.75	7.50	15.00
557	Young Wings Can Fly (Higher Than You Know)/Day Dreaming	1963	3.00	6.00	12.00
557 [PS]	Young Wings Can Fly (Higher Than You Know)/Day Dreaming	1963	3.75	7.50	15.00
578	Our Everlasting Love/Much Better Off Than I've Ever Been	1964	3.00	6.00	12.00
601	Baby Come Home/Every Day's a Holiday	1964	3.00	6.00	12.00
615	When You're Young and In Love/I Cry Alone	1964	3.00	6.00	12.00
646	Does He Really Care for Me/Nevertheless (I'm in Love with You)	1965	3.00	6.00	12.00
665	We'll Meet Again/Your Baby Doesn't Love You Anymore	1965	3.00	6.00	12.00
702	Nobody But My Baby/Imagination	1965	3.00	6.00	12.00
759	We Can Make It/Remember Me	1966	2.50	5.00	10.00
773	Hey There Lonely Boy/Think	1966	2.50	5.00	10.00
839	I Know/We'll Love Again	1967	2.50	5.00	10.00

Albums

Number	Title (A Side/B Side)	Yr	VG	VG+	NM
ABC					
S-638	More Than Yesterday	1968	5.00	10.00	20.00
KAPP					
KL-1323 [M]	Our Day Will Come	1963	7.50	15.00	30.00
KL-1341 [M]	Till Then	1963	6.25	12.50	25.00
KL-1458 [M]	The Greatest Hits Album	1966	5.00	10.00	20.00
KL-1526 [M]	Ruby and the Romantics	1967	6.25	12.50	25.00
KS-3323 [S]	Our Day Will Come	1963	10.00	20.00	40.00
KS-3341 [S]	Till Then	1963	7.50	15.00	30.00
KS-3458 [S]	The Greatest Hits Album	1966	6.25	12.50	25.00
KS-3526 [S]	Ruby and the Romantics	1967	6.25	12.50	25.00
MCA					
541	The Greatest Hits Album	197?	2.50	5.00	10.00
PICKWICK					
SPC-3519	Makin' Out	197?	2.50	5.00	10.00

RUFFIN, DAVID

Also see DARYL HALL AND JOHN OATES; THE TEMPTATIONS.

45s

Number	Title (A Side/B Side)	Yr	VG	VG+	NM
ANNA					
1127	I'm in Love/One of These Days	1961	15.00	30.00	60.00
CHECK MATE					
1003	You Can Get What I Got/Action Speaks Louder Than Words	1961	15.00	30.00	60.00
1010	Mr. Bus Driver — Hurry!/Knock You Out (With Love)	1962	15.00	30.00	60.00
MOTOWN					
1140	My Whole World Ended (The Moment You Left Me)/I've Got to Find Myself a Brand New Baby	1968	—	3.00	6.00
1149	I've Lost Everything I've Ever Loved/We'll Have a Good Thing Going On	1969	—	3.00	6.00
1158	I'm So Glad I Fell for You/I Pray Every Day You Won't Regret Loving Me	1969	—	3.00	6.00
1178	Each Day Is a Lifetime/Don't Stop Loving Me	1971	—	3.00	6.00
1187	You Can Come Right Back to Me/Dinah	1971	—	3.00	6.00
1204	A Day in the Life of a Working Man/A Little More Trust	1972	—	3.00	6.00
1223	Blood Donors Needed/Go On with Your Bad Self	1973	—	3.00	6.00
1259	Common Man/I'm Just a Mortal Man	1973	—	3.00	6.00
1327	Me and Rock and Roll (Are Here to Stay)/Smiling Faces Sometimes	1974	—	3.00	6.00
1332	Take Me Clear from Here/I Just Want to Celebrate	1975	—	—	—
—Unreleased					
1336	Superstar/No Matter Where	1975	—	2.50	5.00
1376	Walk Away from Love/Love Can Be Hazardous to Your Health	1975	—	2.50	5.00
1388	Heavy Love/Love Can Be Hazardous To Your Health	1976	—	2.50	5.00
1393	Everything's Coming Up Love/No Matter Where	1976	—	2.50	5.00
1405	On and Off/Statue of a Fool	1976	—	2.50	5.00
1420	Just Let Me Hold You for a Night/Rode by the Place (Where We Used to Stay)	1977	—	2.50	5.00
1435	You're My Peace of Mind/Rose By the Place (Where We Used to Stay)	1978	—	2.50	5.00
WARNER BROS.					
49030	Sexy Dancer/Break My Heart	1979	—	2.00	4.00
49123	I Get Excited/Chain on the Brain	1979	—	2.00	4.00
49277	Slow Dance/Don't You Go Home	1980	—	2.00	4.00
49577	Still in Love with You/I Wanna Be with You	1980	—	2.00	4.00

Albums

Number	Title (A Side/B Side)	Yr	VG	VG+	NM
MOTOWN					
M5-146V1	My Whole World Ended	1981	2.00	4.00	8.00
—Reissue					
M5-211V1	At His Best	1981	2.00	4.00	8.00
—Reissue					
MS-685	My Whole World Ended	1969	5.00	10.00	20.00
MS-696	Feelin' Good	1969	3.75	7.50	15.00
M 733	David Ruffin	1971	—	—	—
—Canceled					
M-762	David Ruffin	1973	3.00	6.00	12.00
M6-818	Me 'N' Rock 'N' Roll Are Here to Stay	1974	3.00	6.00	12.00
M6-849	Who I Am	1975	3.00	6.00	12.00
M6-866	Everything's Coming Up Love	1976	3.00	6.00	12.00
M6-885	In My Stride	1977	3.00	6.00	12.00
M7-895	At His Best	1978	3.00	6.00	12.00
WARNER BROS.					
BSK 3306	So Soon We Change	1979	2.50	5.00	10.00
BSK 3416	Gentleman Ruffin	1980	2.50	5.00	10.00

RUFFIN, DAVID, AND EDDIE KENDRICK

Also see each artist's individual listings; DARYL HALL AND JOHN OATES; THE TEMPTATIONS.

45s

Number	Title (A Side/B Side)	Yr	VG	VG+	NM
RCA					
5313-7-R	I Couldn't Believe It/Don't Know Why You're Dreamin'	1987	—	—	3.00
6925-7-R	One More for the Lonely Hearts Club/Don't Know Why You're Dreaming	1988	—	—	3.00

RUFFIN, JIMMY

45s

Number	Title (A Side/B Side)	Yr	VG	VG+	NM
CHESS					
2160	Tell Me What You Want/Do You Know Me	1974	—	2.50	5.00
2168	What You See (Ain't Always What You Get)/Boy from Mississippi	1975	—	2.50	5.00
EPIC					
50339	Fallin' in Love with You/Fallin' in Love with You	1977	—	2.50	5.00
50384	Fallin' in Love with You/Fallin' in Love with You	1977	—	2.50	5.00
MIRACLE					
1	Don't Feel Sorry for Me/Heart	1961	50.00	100.00	200.00
RSO					
1021	Hold On to My Love/(Instrumental)	1980	—	2.50	5.00
1042	Night of Love/Searchin'	1980	—	2.50	5.00
SOUL					
35002	Since I've Lost You/I Want Her Love	1964	10.00	20.00	40.00
35016	As Long As There Is L-O-V-E/How Can I Say I'm Sorry	1965	2.50	5.00	10.00
35022	What Becomes of the Brokenhearted/Baby I've Got It	1966	3.75	7.50	15.00
35027	I've Passed This Way Before/Tomorrow's Tears	1966	2.50	5.00	10.00
35032	Gonna Give Her All the Love I've Got/World So Wide (Nowhere to Hide from Your Heart)	1967	2.00	4.00	8.00
35035	Don't You Miss Me A Little Bit Baby/I Want Her Love	1967	2.00	4.00	8.00
35043	I'll Say Forever My Love/Everybody Needs Love	1968	2.00	4.00	8.00

Number	Title (A Side/B Side)	Yr	VG	VG+	NM
35046	Don't Let Him Take Your Love from Me/Lonely, Lonely Man Am I	1968	2.00	4.00	8.00
35053	Sad and Lonesome Feeling/Gonna Keep On Trying Till I Win Your Love	1968	2.00	4.00	8.00
35060	Farewell Is a Lonely Sound/If You Will Let Me, I Know I Can	1969	2.00	4.00	8.00
35077	Maria (You Were the Only One)/Living in a World I Created For Myself	1970	2.00	4.00	8.00
35092	Our Favorite Melody/You Gave Me Love	1972	—	3.00	6.00
Albums					
RSO					
RS-1-3078	Sunrise	1980	2.50	5.00	10.00
SOUL					
704 [M]	Top Ten	1967	12.50	25.00	50.00
—One-color cover					
704 [M]	Top Ten	1967	6.25	12.50	25.00
—Full-color cover					
S-704 [S]	Top Ten	1967	6.25	12.50	25.00
S-708	Ruff'n Ready	1969	6.25	12.50	25.00
SS-727	The Groove Governor	1970	5.00	10.00	20.00

RUFFIN, JIMMY AND DAVID

Also see DAVID RUFFIN; JIMMY RUFFIN.

Number	Title (A Side/B Side)	Yr	VG	VG+	NM
45s					
SOUL					
35076	Stand By Me/Your Love Was Worth Waiting For	1970	—	2.50	5.00
35082	When My Love Hand Comes Do Down/Steppin' On a Dream	1971	—	2.50	5.00
35086	Lo and Behold/The Things We Have to Do	1971	—	2.50	5.00
Albums					
MOTOWN					
M5-108V1	Motown Superstar Series, Vol. 8	1981	2.50	5.00	10.00
SOUL					
SS-728	I Am My Brother's Keeper	1970	5.00	10.00	20.00

RUFUS

Includes records as "Rufus Featuring Chaka Khan" and "Rufus and Chaka." Also see THE AMERICAN BREED.

Number	Title (A Side/B Side)	Yr	VG	VG+	NM
45s					
ABC					
11356	Slip 'N Slide/I Finally Found You	1973	2.00	4.00	8.00
11376	Whoever's Thrilling You (Is Killing Me)/I Finally Found You	1973	—	3.00	6.00
11394	Feel Good/Keep It Coming	1973	—	3.00	6.00
11427	Tell Me Something Good/Smokin' Room	1974	—	3.00	6.00
12010	Tell Me Something Good/Smokin' Room	1974	—	2.50	5.00
12032	You Got the Love/Rags to Rufus	1974	—	2.50	5.00
12066	Once You Get Started/Rufusized	1975	—	2.50	5.00
12099	Please Pardon Me (You Remind Me of a Friend)/Somebody's Watching You	1975	—	2.50	5.00
12149	Sweet Thing/Circles	1975	—	2.50	5.00
12179	Dance Wit' Me/Everybody's Got an Aura	1976	—	2.50	5.00
12197	Jive Talkin'/On Time	1976	—	2.50	5.00
12239	At Midnight (My Love Will Lift You Up)/Better Days	1976	—	2.50	5.00
12269	Holywood/Earth Song	1977	—	2.50	5.00
12296	Everlasting Love/Close the Door	1977	—	2.50	5.00
12349	Stay/My Ship Will Sail	1978	—	2.50	5.00
12390	Blue Love/Turn	1978	—	2.50	5.00
12444	Keep It Together (Declaration of Love)/Red Hot Poker	1979	—	2.50	5.00
EPIC					
10691	Read All About It/Brand New Day	1971	3.00	6.00	12.00
10691 [PS]	Read All About It/Brand New Day	1971	5.00	10.00	20.00
10726	Follow the Lamb/Fire One, Fire Two, Fire Three	1971	3.00	6.00	12.00
MCA					
41025	Ain't Nobody Like You/You're to Blame	1979	—	2.00	4.00
41131	Do You Love What You Feel/Dancin' Mood	1979	—	2.00	4.00
41191	What Am I Missing/Any Love	1980	—	2.00	4.00
41230	I'm Dancing for Your Love/Walk the Rockway	1980	—	2.00	4.00
51070	Tonight We Love/Afterwards	1981	—	2.00	4.00
51125	Party 'Til You're Broke/Hold On to a Friend	1981	—	2.00	4.00
51203	Sharing the Love/We Got the Way	1981	—	2.00	4.00
52002	True Love/Better Together	1982	—	2.00	4.00
WARNER BROS.					
29406	One Million Kisses/Stay	1983	—	2.00	4.00
29555	Ain't Nobody/Sweet Thing	1983	—	2.00	4.00
29675	Blinded by the Boogie/You're Really Out of Line	1983	—	2.00	4.00
29790	Take It to the Hop/Distant Lover	1983	—	2.00	4.00
Albums					
ABC					
X-783	Rufus	1973	2.50	5.00	10.00
X-809	Rags to Rufus	1974	2.50	5.00	10.00
D-837	Rufusized	1974	2.50	5.00	10.00
D-909	Rufus Featuring Chaka Khan	1975	2.50	5.00	10.00
D-975	Ask Rufus	1977	2.50	5.00	10.00
AA-1049	Street Player	1978	2.50	5.00	10.00
AA-1049 [PD]	Street Player	1978	6.25	12.50	25.00
—Promo-only picture disc					
AA-1098	Numbers	1979	2.50	5.00	10.00
AA-1098 [PD]	Numbers	1979	5.00	10.00	20.00
—Promo-only picture disc					
COMMAND					
CQD-40023 [Q]	Rufusized	1974	5.00	10.00	20.00
CQD-40024 [Q]	Rags to Rufus	1974	5.00	10.00	20.00
MCA					
642	Rufus	1980	—	3.00	6.00
—Reissue of ABC 783					
5103	Masterjam	1979	2.50	5.00	10.00
5159	Party 'Til You're Broke	1981	2.50	5.00	10.00
5270	Camouflage	1982	2.50	5.00	10.00
5339	The Very Best of Rufus	1983	2.50	5.00	10.00
37034	Rags to Rufus	1980	—	3.00	6.00
—Reissue of ABC 809					
37035	Rufusized	1980	—	3.00	6.00
—Reissue of ABC 837					
37036	Rufus Featuring Chaka Khan	1980	—	3.00	6.00
—Reissue of ABC 909					
37037	Ask Rufus	1980	—	3.00	6.00
—Reissue of ABC 975					
37038	Street Player	1980	—	3.00	6.00
—Reissue of ABC 1049					
37039	Numbers	1980	—	3.00	6.00
—Reissue of ABC 1098					
37157	Masterjam	198?	—	3.00	6.00
—Reissue of 5103					
WARNER BROS.					
23679 [(2)]	Live: Stompin' at the Savoy	1983	3.00	6.00	12.00
23753	Seal in Red	1984	2.50	5.00	10.00

RUFUS AND CARLA

Also see CARLA THOMAS; RUFUS THOMAS.

Number	Title (A Side/B Side)	Yr	VG	VG+	NM
45s					
ATCO					
6177	Cause I Love You/Deep Down Inside	1960	6.25	12.50	25.00
—As "Carla and Rufus"					
6199	I Didn't Believe/Yeah, Yea-Ah	1961	6.25	12.50	25.00
—As "Rufus and Friend"					
SATELLITE					
102	Cause I Love You/Deep Down Inside	1960	10.00	20.00	40.00
STAX					
151	That's Really Some Good/Night Time Is the Right Time	1964	3.00	6.00	12.00
176	When You Move You Lose/We're Tight	1965	3.00	6.00	12.00
184	Birds and Bees/Never Let You Go	1966	3.00	6.00	12.00
Albums					
STAX					
STX-4124	Chronicle	1979	3.75	7.50	15.00

RUGBYS, THE

Number	Title (A Side/B Side)	Yr	VG	VG+	NM
45s					
AMAZON					
1	You, I/Stay with Me	1969	2.00	4.00	8.00
—Black vinyl					
1 [DJ]	You, I/Stay with Me	1969	5.00	10.00	20.00
—Colored vinyl					
4	The Light/Wendegahl Warlock	1970	2.00	4.00	8.00
6	Rockin' All Over/(B-side unknown)	1970	2.00	4.00	8.00
SMASH					
1997	James Is the Name/'Til the Day I Die	1965	3.00	6.00	12.00
Albums					
AMAZON					
1000	Hot Cargo	1970	5.00	10.00	20.00

RUMBLERS, THE

Number	Title (A Side/B Side)	Yr	VG	VG+	NM
45s					
DOT					
16421	Boss/I Don't Need You No More	1963	3.75	7.50	15.00
16455	Boss Strikes Back/Sorry	1963	3.75	7.50	15.00
16480	Angry Sea (Walmea)/Bugged	1963	3.75	7.50	15.00
16521	It's a Gas/Tootananny	1963	3.75	7.50	15.00
DOWNEY					
103	Boss/I Don't Need You No More	1962	7.50	15.00	30.00
106	Boss Strikes Back/Sorry	1963	7.50	15.00	30.00
107	Angry Sea (Walmea)/Bugged	1963	7.50	15.00	30.00
111	It's a Gas/Tootananny	1963	7.50	15.00	30.00
114	High Octane/Night Scene	1964	6.25	12.50	25.00
119	The Hustler/Riot in Cell Block #9	1964	6.25	12.50	25.00
127	Soulful Jerk/Hey-Did-a-Da-Do	1964	6.25	12.50	25.00
133	Boss Soul/Till Always	1965	6.25	12.50	25.00
HIGHLAND					
1026	Intersection/Stomping Theme	1962	12.50	25.00	50.00
Albums					
DOT					
DLP-3509 [M]	Boss!	1963	12.50	25.00	50.00
DLP-25509 [S]	Boss!	1963	15.00	30.00	60.00
DOWNEY					
DLP-1001 [M]	Boss!	1963	45.00	90.00	180.00
DLPS-1001 [S]	Boss!	1963	62.50	125.00	250.00

RUNAROUNDS, THE

Probably more than one group.

Number	Title (A Side/B Side)	Yr	VG	VG+	NM
45s					
CAPITOL					
5644	Perfect Woman/You're a Drag	1966	6.25	12.50	25.00
COUSINS					
1004	Mashed Potato Mary/I'm All Alone	1964	5.00	10.00	20.00
FELSTED					
8704	Send Her Back/Carrie, You're An Angel	1964	7.50	15.00	30.00
KC					
116	Unbelievable/Hurray for Love	1963	6.25	12.50	25.00
116	Unbelievable/Hurray for Love	1963	10.00	20.00	40.00
—Brown vinyl					
MGM					
13763	My Little Girl/You Lied	1967	3.75	7.50	15.00
PIO					
107	The Nearest Thing to Heaven/Lover's Lane	1961	37.50	75.00	150.00
TARHEEL					
065	Are You Looking for a Sweetheart/Let Them Talk	1963	5.00	10.00	20.00

RUNDGREN, TODD

Also see NAZZ; UTOPIA.

12-Inch Singles

Number	Title (A Side/B Side)	Yr	VG	VG+	NM
FORWARD					
7008 [DJ]	Day Job (LP Version) (Radio Version) (Dub)	1993	3.75	7.50	15.00
WARNER BROS.					
PRO-A-2371 [DJ]	Something to Fall Back On (same on both sides)	1985	2.50	5.00	10.00

45s

Number	Title (A Side/B Side)	Yr	VG	VG+	NM
AMPEX					
31001	We Gotta Get You a Woman/Medley	1970	2.50	5.00	10.00
—As "Runt"					
BEARSVILLE					
0003	I Saw the Light/Marlene	1972	3.00	6.00	12.00
—Blue vinyl					
0003	I Saw the Light/Marlene	1972	3.00	6.00	12.00
0007	Couldn't I Just Tell You/Wolfman Jack	1972	—	3.00	6.00
0009	Hello It's Me/Cold Morning Light	1973	—	3.00	6.00
0020	A Dream Goes On Forever/Heavy Metal Kids	1974	—	3.00	6.00
0030	We Gotta Get You a Woman/I Saw the Light	1973	—	2.00	4.00
—"Back to Back Hits" series					
0301	Breathless/Wolfman Jack	1974	—	3.00	6.00
0304	Real Man/Prana	1975	—	2.50	5.00
0309	Good Vibrations/When I Pray	1976	—	2.50	5.00
0310	Love of the Common Man/Black and White	1976	—	2.50	5.00
0324	Can We Still Be Friends/Determination	1978	—	2.50	5.00
0326	Can We Still Be Friends/Out of Control	1978	—	2.50	5.00
0330	You Cried Wolf/Onomatopoeia	1978	—	2.50	5.00
0335	It Wouldn't Have Made Any Difference/Did You Ever Learn	1979	—	2.50	5.00
29686	Bang the Drum All Day/Chant	1983	—	3.00	6.00
29759	Emperor of the Highway/Hideaway	1983	—	2.00	4.00
31002	Be Nice to Me/Broke Down and Busted	1971	2.00	4.00	8.00
—As "Runt-Todd Rundgren"					
31004	A Long Time, A Long Way to Go/Parole	1971	2.00	4.00	8.00
—As "Runt-Todd Rundgren"					
49696	Time Heals/Tiny Demon	1981	—	2.00	4.00
49771	Compassion/Pulse	1981	—	2.50	5.00
COLUMBIA					
6151	Loving You's a Dirty Job (But Somebody's Gotta Do It)/(B-side unknown)	1986	—	2.00	4.00
—With Bonnie Tyler					
GUARDIAN					
S7-19726	Can We Still Be Friends/I Saw the Light	1997	—	—	3.00
RHINO					
74426	Bang the Drum All Day/Can We Still Be Friends	1987	—	2.00	4.00
WARNER BROS.					
22868	I Love My Life/Parallel Lines	1989	—	—	3.00
28821	Something to Fall Back On/Lockjaw	1986	—	2.00	4.00

Albums

Number	Title	Yr	VG	VG+	NM
AMPEX					
A-10105	Runt	1970	37.50	75.00	150.00
—LP jacket and label list 10 tracks, but the album has 12					
A-10105	Runt	1970	25.00	50.00	100.00
—LP jacket and label list 10 tracks, but the album has 11					
A-10105	Runt	1970	12.50	25.00	50.00
—LP jacket and label list 10 tracks and album actually has 10					
BEARSVILLE					
PRO 524 [DJ]	The Todd Rundgren Radio Show	1972	37.50	75.00	150.00
PRO 597 [DJ]	Ikon/Todd Rundgren Interview	1974	30.00	60.00	120.00
PRO-A-788 [DJ]	Todd Rundgren Radio Sampler	1978	12.50	25.00	50.00
—Highlights of "Back to the Bars" plus interview of Todd by Patti Smith					
BR 2046	Runt	1972	3.75	7.50	15.00
—Another reissue, after switch from Ampex to Warner Bros. distribution					
BR 2047	The Ballad of Todd Rundgren	1972	3.75	7.50	15.00
—Reissue of 10116					
2BX 2066 [(2)]	Something/Anything?	1972	6.25	12.50	25.00
—Regular copy with black vinyl					
2BX 2066 [(2)]	Something/Anything?	1972	100.00	200.00	400.00
—White label with one record on red vinyl and the other on blue vinyl					
BR 2133	A Wizard/A True Star	1973	3.00	6.00	12.00
BRK 3522	Healing	1981	2.50	5.00	10.00
2BR 6952 [(2)]	Todd	1974	3.75	7.50	15.00
BR 6957	Initiation	1975	2.50	5.00	10.00
BR 6963	Faithful	1976	2.50	5.00	10.00
BRK 6981	Hermit of Mink Hollow	1978	2.50	5.00	10.00
2BRX 6986 [(2)]	Back to the Bars	1978	3.00	6.00	12.00
A-10105	Runt	1971	6.25	12.50	25.00
—Reissue with new label					
A-10116	The Ballad of Todd Rundgren	1971	20.00	40.00	80.00
23732	The Ever Popular Tortured Artist Effect	1983	2.50	5.00	10.00
MOBILE FIDELITY					
2-225	Something/Anything?	1995	10.00	20.00	40.00
—Audiophile vinyl					
RHINO					
RNLP 70862	Runt	1987	2.50	5.00	10.00
RNLP 70863	The Ballad of Todd Rundgren	1987	2.50	5.00	10.00
RNLP 70864	A Wizard/A True Star	1987	2.50	5.00	10.00
RNLP 70866	Initiation	1987	2.50	5.00	10.00
RNLP 70868	Faithful	1987	2.50	5.00	10.00
RNLP 70871	Hermit of Mink Hollow	1988	2.50	5.00	10.00
RNLP 70874	Healing	1987	2.50	5.00	10.00
RNLP 70876	The Ever Popular Tortured Artist Effect	1988	2.50	5.00	10.00
RNDA 71107	Something/Anything?	1987	3.00	6.00	12.00
RNDA 71108	Todd	1987	3.00	6.00	12.00
RNDA 71109	Back to the Bars	1987	3.00	6.00	12.00
R1-71491	Anthology (1968-1985)	1989	5.00	10.00	20.00
WARNER BROS.					
25128	A Cappella	1985	2.50	5.00	10.00
25881	Nearly Human	1989	3.75	7.50	15.00

RUSH

12-Inch Singles

Number	Title (A Side/B Side)	Yr	VG	VG+	NM
MERCURY					
382 [DJ]	The Big Money (same on both sides)	1985	3.00	6.00	12.00
532 [DJ]	Force Ten (same on both sides)	1987	3.00	6.00	12.00

45s

Number	Title (A Side/B Side)	Yr	VG	VG+	NM
MERCURY					
73623	Finding My Way/Need Some Love	1974	12.50	25.00	50.00
73623 [DJ]	Finding My Way (mono/stereo)	1974	10.00	20.00	40.00
73647	In the Mood/What You're Doing	1974	6.25	12.50	25.00
73681	Anthem/Fly by Night	1975	2.50	5.00	10.00
73737	Bastille Day/Lakeside Park	1975	2.50	5.00	10.00
73803	Lessons/Twilight Zone	1976	2.50	5.00	10.00
73873	Fly by Night-In the Mood/Something for Nothing	1976	2.50	5.00	10.00
73912	Making Memories/Temples of Syrinx	1977	2.50	5.00	10.00
73958	Closer to the Heart/Madrigal	1977	2.50	5.00	10.00
73990	Anthem/Fly by Night	1978	2.50	5.00	10.00
74051	The Trees/Circumstances	1979	2.50	5.00	10.00
76044	The Spirit of Radio/Circumstances	1980	2.50	5.00	10.00
76060	Entre Nous/Different Strings	1980	2.50	5.00	10.00
76095	Limelight/XYZ	1981	2.50	5.00	10.00
76109	Tom Sawyer/Witch Hunt	1981	2.50	5.00	10.00
76109 [PS]	Tom Sawyer/Witch Hunt	1981	6.25	12.50	25.00
76124	Closer to the Heart/Freewill	1981	2.00	4.00	8.00
76179	New World Man/Vital Signs	1982	2.00	4.00	8.00
76179 [PS]	New World Man/Vital Signs	1982	3.75	7.50	15.00
76196	Countdown/Subdivision	1982	2.50	5.00	10.00
880050-7	Body Electric/Between the Wheels	1984	2.00	4.00	8.00
884191-7	The Big Money/Red Sector A	1985	2.00	4.00	8.00
884191-7 [PS]	The Big Money/Red Sector A	1985	3.75	7.50	15.00
888891-7	Time Stand Still/High Water	1987	—	3.00	6.00
888891-7 [PS]	Time Stand Still/High Water	1987	2.50	5.00	10.00

Albums

Number	Title	Yr	VG	VG+	NM
ATLANTIC					
82040	Presto	1989	5.00	10.00	20.00
MERCURY					
MK-32 [DJ]	Everything Your Listener Ever Wanted to Hear by Rush	1975	25.00	50.00	100.00
MK-185 [DJ]	Rush N Roulette	1981	25.00	50.00	100.00
—Promo-only six-track EP that has six grooves cut in it; the song it plays is based on where you place the stylus					
SRM-1-1011	Rush	1974	2.50	5.00	10.00
SRM-1-1023	Fly by Night	1975	2.50	5.00	10.00
SRM-1-1046	Caress of Steel	1975	2.50	5.00	10.00
SRM-1-1079	2112	1976	2.50	5.00	10.00
SRM-1-1184	A Farewell to Kings	1977	2.50	5.00	10.00
SRP-1-1300 [PD]	Hemispheres	1979	10.00	20.00	40.00
SRM-1-3743	Hemispheres	1978	2.50	5.00	10.00
SRM-1-4001	Permanent Waves	1980	2.50	5.00	10.00
SRM-1-4013	Moving Pictures	1981	2.50	5.00	10.00
SRM-1-4063	Signals	1982	2.50	5.00	10.00
SRM-2-7001 [(2)]	Exit... Stage Left	1981	3.00	6.00	12.00
SRM-2-7508 [(2)]	All the World's a Stage	1976	3.00	6.00	12.00
SRM-3-9200 [(3)]	Archives	1978	5.00	10.00	20.00
818476-1	Grace Under Pressure	1984	2.50	5.00	10.00
822541-1	Rush	1985	2.00	4.00	8.00
—Reissue					
822542-1	Fly by Night	1985	2.00	4.00	8.00
—Reissue					
822543-1	Caress of Steel	1985	2.00	4.00	8.00
—Reissue					
822545-1	2112	1985	2.00	4.00	8.00
—Reissue					
822546-1	A Farewell to Kings	1985	2.00	4.00	8.00
—Reissue					
822547-1	Hemispheres	1985	2.00	4.00	8.00
—Reissue					
822548-1	Permanent Waves	1985	2.00	4.00	8.00
—Reissue					
822549-1	Moving Pictures	1985	2.00	4.00	8.00
—Reissue					
822550-1	Signals	1985	2.00	4.00	8.00
—Reissue					
822551-1 [(2)]	Exit...Stage Left	1985	2.50	5.00	10.00
—Reissue					
822552-1 [(2)]	All the World's a Stage	1985	2.50	5.00	10.00
—Reissue					
822553-1 [(3)]	Archives	1985	3.75	7.50	15.00
—Reissue					
826098-1	Power Windows	1985	2.50	5.00	10.00
832464-1	Hold Your Fire	1987	2.50	5.00	10.00
836346-1 [(2)]	A Show of Hands	1988	3.00	6.00	12.00

RUSH, MERRILEE

45s

Number	Title (A Side/B Side)	Yr	VG	VG+	NM
AGP					
107	Reach Out/Love Street	1969	—	3.00	6.00
112	Your Loving Eyes Are Blind/Everyday Livin' Days	1969	—	3.00	6.00
121	Sign On for the Good Times/Robin McCarver	1969	—	3.00	6.00
126	Angel of the Morning/It's Worth It All	1970	—	3.00	6.00
BELL					
705	Angel of the Morning/Reap What You Sow	1968	2.00	4.00	8.00
738	Sunshine and Roses/That Kind of Woman	1968	2.00	4.00	8.00
SCEPTER					
12329	Child of Mine/Everything Has Got to Be Free	1971	—	3.00	6.00
UNITED ARTISTS					
XW930	Could It Be Love I Found Tonight/Be True to You	1976	—	2.00	4.00
XW993	Save Me/Easy, Soft and Slow	1977	—	2.00	4.00
XW1103	Mama/Rainstorm	1977	—	2.00	4.00
XW1181	Angel of the Morning/Save	1978	—	2.00	4.00

Albums

Number	Title	Yr	VG	VG+	NM
BELL					
6020	Angel of the Morning	1968	5.00	10.00	20.00

Number	Title (A Side/B Side)	Yr	VG	VG+	NM
LIBERTY					
LN-10166	Merilee Rush	1981	2.00	4.00	8.00
—Budget-line reissue					
UNITED ARTISTS					
UA-LA735-G	Merilee Rush	1977	2.50	5.00	10.00

RUSH, TOM

Number	Title (A Side/B Side)	Yr	VG	VG+	NM
45s					
COLUMBIA					
10021	Ladies Love Outlaws/Maggie	1974	—	2.00	4.00
10087	No Regrets/Maggie	1975	—	2.00	4.00
45185	Old Man's Song/Lost My Drivin' Wheel	1970	—	2.50	5.00
45364	Wrong End of the Rainbow/Merrimac County	1971	—	2.50	5.00
45584	Wind on the Water/Mother Earth	1972	—	2.50	5.00
45669	Kids These Days/Seems the Songs	1972	—	2.50	5.00
ELEKTRA					
45604	Who Do You Love/On the Road Again	1966	2.00	4.00	8.00
45607	Sugar Babe/Urge for Going	1967	2.00	4.00	8.00
45630	No Regrets/Shadow Dream Song	1968	—	3.00	6.00
45718	Something in the Way She Moves/Who Do You Love	1971	—	3.00	6.00
PRESTIGE					
289	Diamond Joe/Every Day in the Week	1964	3.00	6.00	12.00
Albums					
COLUMBIA					
CS 9972	Tom Rush	1970	3.75	7.50	15.00
—Red "360 Sound" label					
CS 9972	Tom Rush	1970	3.00	6.00	12.00
—Orange label					
C 30402	Wrong End of the Rainbow	1970	3.00	6.00	12.00
KC 31306	Merrimack County	1972	3.00	6.00	12.00
KC 33054	Ladies Love Outlaws	1974	3.00	6.00	12.00
PC 33907	The Best of Tom Rush	1976	3.00	6.00	12.00
ELEKTRA					
EKL-288 [M]	Tom Rush	1965	3.75	7.50	15.00
EKL-308 [M]	Take a Little Walk with Me	1966	3.75	7.50	15.00
EKS-7288 [S]	Tom Rush	1965	3.75	7.50	15.00
EKS-7308 [S]	Take a Little Walk with Me	1966	3.75	7.50	15.00
EKS-74018	The Circle Game	1968	3.75	7.50	15.00
EKS-74062	Classic Rush	1971	3.75	7.50	15.00
FANTASY					
24709 [(2)]	Tom Rush	1973	3.75	7.50	15.00
—Reissue of Prestige/Folklore recordings					
FOLKLORE					
FRLP-14003 [M]	Got a Mind to Ramble	1964	5.00	10.00	20.00
FRST-14003 [S]	Got a Mind to Ramble	1964	6.25	12.50	25.00
LY CORNU					
SA-70-2	Tom Rush at the Unicorn	1970	5.00	10.00	20.00
PRESTIGE					
PRLP-7374 [M]	Blues — Songs — Ballads	1965	5.00	10.00	20.00
PRST-7374 [S]	Blues — Songs — Ballads	1965	6.25	12.50	25.00
PRST-7536	Got a Mind to Ramble	1968	3.75	7.50	15.00
—Reissue of Folklore LP					

RUSSELL, BOBBY

Number	Title (A Side/B Side)	Yr	VG	VG+	NM
45s					
BUENA VISTA					
473	The Ballad of Smith & Gabriel Jimmy Boy/ Summer Sweet	1969	2.50	5.00	10.00
474	The Ballad of Smith & Gabriel Billyboy/Summer Sweet	1969	2.50	5.00	10.00
COLUMBIA					
45901	Mid American Manufacturing Tycoon/Ships in the Night	1973	—	2.00	4.00
46045	The Night the Lights Went Out in Georgia/Go Chase Your Rainbow	1974	—	2.00	4.00
D					
1115	Not Even Friends/Shackled	1960	3.00	6.00	12.00
—With Sadie Russell					
ELF					
90014	Dusty/I Made You This Way	1968	—	3.00	6.00
90020	1432 Franklin Pike Circle Hero/Let's Talk About Them	1968	—	3.00	6.00
90023	Carlie/Ain't Society Great	1969	—	3.00	6.00
90027	Then She's a Lover/He Wrote a Song	1969	—	3.00	6.00
90031	Better Homes and Gardens/Summer Sweet	1969	—	3.00	6.00
FELSTED					
8520	The Raven/She's Gonna Be Sorry	1958	3.75	7.50	15.00
IMAGE					
1014	Goin' Steady Dream/To the Ones with Broken Hearts	1961	3.00	6.00	12.00
MONUMENT					
899	Once a Day/You Were Mine	1965	2.00	4.00	8.00
929	Friends and Memories/Wish I'd Say That	1966	2.00	4.00	8.00
PRIVATE STOCK					
45046	Little Boxes/(B-side unknown)	1975	—	2.50	5.00
RISING SONS					
700	Bluebird/Tears Tell	1967	2.00	4.00	8.00
UNITED ARTISTS					
50788	Saturday Morning Confusion/Little Ole Song About Love	1971	—	2.50	5.00
50853	Goodbye/It Hurts	1971	—	2.50	5.00
50888	Easy Made for Lovin'/The Bell	1972	—	2.50	5.00
50904	You Babe/Back to Sausalito	1972	—	2.50	5.00
50959	Welcome to the U.S. Army/This Is the Life	1972	—	2.50	5.00
Albums					
ELF					
5500	Words, Music, Laughter & Tears	1969	5.00	10.00	20.00
5501	Unlimited	1970	3.75	7.50	15.00
UNITED ARTISTS					
UAS-5548	Saturday Morning Confusion	1971	3.00	6.00	12.00

RUSSELL, KURT

Number	Title (A Side/B Side)	Yr	VG	VG+	NM
45s					
CAPITOL					
2823	I Believe in Love/It Ain't Gonna Rain Anymore	1970	2.50	5.00	10.00
Albums					
CAPITOL					
SKAO-492	Kurt Russell	1970	7.50	15.00	30.00

RUSSELL, LEE

See LEON RUSSELL.

RUSSELL, LEON

Includes records by his country-western alter ego, "Hank Wilson" and "Hank and Mary Wilson." Also see WILLIE NELSON.

Number	Title (A Side/B Side)	Yr	VG	VG+	NM
45s					
ARK 21					
S7-58714	Daddy Sang Bass/He Stopped Loving Her Today	1998	—	—	3.00
A&M					
734	Cindy/Misty	1964	5.00	10.00	20.00
COLUMBIA					
11023	Heartbreak Hotel/Sioux City Sue	1979	—	2.00	4.00
—With Willie Nelson					
11119	Trouble in Mind/One for My Baby (And One More for the Road)	1979	—	2.00	4.00
—With Willie Nelson					
DOT					
16771	Everybody's Talkin' 'Bout the Young/It's Alright with Me	1965	3.75	7.50	15.00
PARADISE					
628	Good Time Charlie's Got the Blues/(B-side unknown)	1984	—	2.00	4.00
629	Wabash Cannonball/Tennessee Waltz	1984	—	2.00	4.00
—As "Hank Wilson"; A-side with Willie Nelson					
631	Rescue My Heart/Lost Love	1985	—	2.00	4.00
631 [PS]	Rescue My Heart/Lost Love	1985	2.50	5.00	10.00
8208	Rainbow in Your Eyes/Love's Supposed to Be That Way	1976	—	2.00	4.00
—As "Leon and Mary Russell"					
8274	Satisfy You/Windsong	1976	—	2.00	4.00
—As "Leon and Mary Russell"					
8369	Love Crazy/Say You Will	1977	—	2.00	4.00
—As "Leon and Mary Russell"					
8438	Easy Love/Hold On to This Feeling	1977	—	2.00	4.00
—As "Leon and Mary Russell"					
8667	Elvis and Marilyn/Anita Bryant	1978	—	2.50	5.00
8667 [PS]	Elvis and Marilyn/Anita Bryant	1978	—	2.50	5.00
8719	Midnight Lover/From Maine to Mexico	1978	—	2.50	5.00
49662	Over the Rainbow/I've Just Seen a Face	1981	—	2.00	4.00
RCA VICTOR					
47-6884	(I Tasted) Tears on Your Lips/A Catchy Tune	1957	7.50	15.00	30.00
—As "Lee Russell"					
ROULETTE					
4049	Honky Tonk Woman/Rainbow at Midnight	1958	6.25	12.50	25.00
—As "Lee Russell"					
SHELTER					
301	Roll Away the Stone/Hummingbird	1970	—	3.00	6.00
7302	It Takes a Lot to Laugh, It Takes a Train to Cry/ Home Sweet Oklahoma	1970	—	3.00	6.00
7305	A Hard Rain's A-Gonna Fall/Me and Baby Jane	1971	—	3.00	6.00
7316	A Song for You/A Hard Rain's A-Gonna Fall	1971	—	3.00	6.00
7325	Tight Rope/This Masquerade	1972	—	2.50	5.00
7328	Slipping Into Christmas/Christmas in Chicago	1972	—	2.50	5.00
7328 [PS]	Slipping Into Christmas/Christmas In Chicago	1972	6.25	12.50	25.00
7336	Roll in My Sweet Baby's Arms/I'm So Lonesome I Could Cry	1973	—	2.50	5.00
—As "Hank Wilson"					
7337	Queen of the Roller Derby/Roll Away the Stone	1973	—	2.50	5.00
7338	Six Pack to Go/Uncle Pen	1973	—	2.50	5.00
—As "Hank Wilson"					
40210	If I Were a Carpenter/Wild Horses	1974	—	2.00	4.00
40210 [PS]	If I Were a Carpenter/Wild Horses	1974	2.00	4.00	8.00
40277	Time for Love/Leaving Whipporwhill	1974	—	2.00	4.00
40378	Lady Blue/Laying Right Here in Heaven	1975	—	2.00	4.00
40483	Back to the Island/Little Hideaway	1975	—	2.00	4.00
62004	Bluebird/Back to the Island	1976	—	2.00	4.00
65033	Slipping Into Christmas/Christmas in Chicago	1975	—	2.50	5.00
—Reissue of 7328					
Albums					
MCA					
682	Leon Russell	1979	2.00	4.00	8.00
—Reissue of Shelter 52007					
683	Leon Russell and the Shelter People	1979	2.00	4.00	8.00
—Reissue of Shelter 52008					
685	Carney	1979	2.00	4.00	8.00
—Reissue of Shelter 52011					
686	Will O' the Wisp	1979	2.00	4.00	8.00
—Reissue of Shelter 52020					
37114	Best of Leon	1980	2.00	4.00	8.00
—Reissue of Shelter 52004					
PARADISE					
0002	Hank Wilson Vol. II	1984	3.00	6.00	12.00
BS 2943	Wedding Album	1976	3.00	6.00	12.00
—As "Leon and Mary Russell"					
BSK 3066	Make Love to the Music	1977	3.00	6.00	12.00
—As "Leon and Mary Russell"					
BSK 3172	Americana	1978	3.00	6.00	12.00
BSK 3341	Life and Love	1979	3.00	6.00	12.00
BSK 3532	The Live Album	1981	2.50	5.00	10.00
SHELTER					
SHE-1001	Leon Russell	1968	5.00	10.00	20.00
SR 2108	Stop All That Jazz	1974	3.75	7.50	15.00
SR 2118	Leon Russell	1974	3.00	6.00	12.00
—Reissue of 8901					

Number	Title (A Side/B Side)	Yr	VG	VG+	NM
SR 2119	Leon Russell and the Shelter People	1974	3.00	6.00	12.00
—Reissue of 8903					
SR 2121	Carney	1974	3.00	6.00	12.00
—Reissue of 8911					
SR 2138	Will O' the Wisp	1975	3.75	7.50	15.00
SW-8901	Leon Russell	1970	3.75	7.50	15.00
—Early reissue of 1001					
SW-8903	Leon Russell and the Shelter People	1971	3.75	7.50	15.00
SW-8911	Carney	1972	3.75	7.50	15.00
STCO-8917 [(3)]	Leon Live	1973	5.00	10.00	20.00
SW-8923	Hank Wilson's Back, Vol. 1	1973	3.75	7.50	15.00
—As "Hank Wilson"					
52004	Best of Leon	1976	2.50	5.00	10.00
52007	Leon Russell	1977	2.50	5.00	10.00
—Reissue of 2118					
52008	Leon Russell and the Shelter People	1977	2.50	5.00	10.00
—Reissue of 2119					
52011	Carney	1977	2.50	5.00	10.00
—Reissue of 2121					
52014	Hank Wilson's Back, Vol. 1	1977	2.50	5.00	10.00
—Reissue of 8923					
52016	Stop All That Jazz	1977	2.50	5.00	10.00
—Reissue of 2108					
52020	Will O' the Wisp	1977	2.50	5.00	10.00
—Reissue of 2138					

RUSSELL, LEON, AND MARC BENNO

Also see each artist's individual listings.

Number	Title (A Side/B Side)	Yr	VG	VG+	NM
45s					
SHELTER					
7313	Straight Brother/Tryin' to Stay Alive	1971	2.00	4.00	8.00
SMASH					
2186	Soul Food/Welcome to Hollywood	1968	2.00	4.00	8.00
—As "Asylum Choir"					
2204	Indian Style/Icicle Star Tree	1969	2.00	4.00	8.00
—As "Asylum Choir"					
Albums					
MCA					
684	Asylum Choir II	1979	2.00	4.00	8.00
—Reissue of Shelter 52010					
SHELTER					
SR 2120	Asylum Choir II	1974	3.00	6.00	12.00
—Reissue of 8910					
SW-8910	Asylum Choir II	1971	3.75	7.50	15.00
52010	Asylum Choir II	1977	2.50	5.00	10.00
—Reissue of 2120					
SMASH					
SRS-67107	Look Inside	1968	5.00	10.00	20.00
—As "Asylum Choir"					

RUSTIX

Number	Title (A Side/B Side)	Yr	VG	VG+	NM
45s					
RARE EARTH					
5011	Can't You Hear the Music Play/I Guess This Is Goodbye	1969	—	3.00	6.00
5014	Come On People/Free Again	1970	—	3.00	6.00
5034	My Peace of Heaven/Down, Down	1971	—	—	—
—Canceled					
5037	We All End Up in Boxes/Down, Down	1971	—	3.00	6.00
Albums					
RARE EARTH					
RS-508	Bedlam	1969	3.75	7.50	15.00
—Regular cover					
RS-508	Bedlam	1969	7.50	15.00	30.00
—Rounded-top cover					
RS-513	Come On, People	1970	3.00	6.00	12.00

RUSTY AND DOUG

See RUSTY AND DOUG KERSHAW.

RYAN, BARRY

Also see PAUL AND BARRY RYAN.

Number	Title (A Side/B Side)	Yr	VG	VG+	NM
45s					
MGM					
14010	Eloise/Love, I Almost Found You	1968	2.00	4.00	8.00
POLYDOR					
14014	Look to the Right, Look to the Left/Oh For the Love of Me	1970	—	3.00	6.00
14035	Give Me a Sign/Kitsch	1970	—	3.00	6.00
14065	It Is Written/Annabelle	1970	—	—	—
—Canceled					
14108	Can't Let You Go/When I Was a Child	1971	—	3.00	6.00
PRIDE					
1012	Alimony Money Blues/From My Head to My Toe	1972	—	2.50	5.00
1032	Can't Let You Go/L.A. Woman	1973	—	2.50	5.00

RYAN, CATHY

Number	Title (A Side/B Side)	Yr	VG	VG+	NM
45s					
KING					
4848	Come Home/The Cricket, the Dove, and the Goldfish	1955	7.50	15.00	30.00
4890	Only a Dream/High Falutin' Heart	1956	7.50	15.00	30.00
4916	Lazy River/Love You with All My Might	1956	7.50	15.00	30.00

RYAN, PAUL AND BARRY

Also see BARRY RYAN.

Number	Title (A Side/B Side)	Yr	VG	VG+	NM
45s					
MGM					
13442	Don't Bring Me Your Heartaches/To Remind You of Our Love	1966	2.50	5.00	10.00
13472	Have Pity on the Boy/There You Go	1966	2.50	5.00	10.00
13546	Silent Street/'Twas on a Night Like This	1966	2.50	5.00	10.00
13609	Have You Ever Loved Somebody/I'll Tell You Later	1966	2.50	5.00	10.00
13719	Keep It Out of Sight/Who Told You	1967	2.00	4.00	8.00
13911	Madrigal/Pictures of Today	1968	2.00	4.00	8.00

RYDELL, BOBBY

Number	Title (A Side/B Side)	Yr	VG	VG+	NM
45s					
CAMEO					
(no #) [DJ]	Steel Pier	1963	6.25	12.50	25.00
—One-sided "Steel Pier Promotion"					
160	Please Don't Be Mad/Makin' Time	1959	12.50	25.00	50.00
164	All I Want Is You/For You, For You	1959	5.00	10.00	20.00
167	Kissin' Time/You'll Never Tame Me	1959	3.75	7.50	15.00
167 [PS]	Kissin' Time/You'll Never Tame Me	1959	6.25	12.50	25.00
169	We Got Love/I Dig Girls	1959	3.75	7.50	15.00
169 [PS]	We Got Love/I Dig Girls	1959	6.25	12.50	25.00
171	Wild One/Little Bitty Girl	1960	3.75	7.50	15.00
171 [PS]	Wild One/Little Bitty Girl	1960	6.25	12.50	25.00
175	Swingin' School/Ding-a-Ling	1960	3.75	7.50	15.00
175 [PS]	Swingin' School/Ding-a-Ling	1960	6.25	12.50	25.00
179	Volare/I'd Do It Again	1960	3.75	7.50	15.00
179 [PS]	Volare/I'd Do It Again	1960	6.25	12.50	25.00
182	Sway/Groovy Tonight	1961	3.75	7.50	15.00
182 [PS]	Sway/Groovy Tonight	1961	6.25	12.50	25.00
186	Good Time Baby/Cherie	1961	3.75	7.50	15.00
186 [PS]	Good Time Baby/Cherie	1961	6.25	12.50	25.00
190	That Old Black Magic/Don't Be Afraid (To Fall in Love)	1961	3.75	7.50	15.00
190 [PS]	That Old Black Magic/Don't Be Afraid (To Fall in Love)	1961	6.25	12.50	25.00
192	The Fish/The Third House	1961	3.75	7.50	15.00
192 [PS]	The Fish/The Third House	1961	6.25	12.50	25.00
201	I Wanna Thank You/The Door to Paradise	1961	3.75	7.50	15.00
201 [PS]	I Wanna Thank You/The Door to Paradise	1961	6.25	12.50	25.00
209	I've Got Bonnie/Lose Her	1962	3.00	6.00	12.00
209 [PS]	I've Got Bonnie/Lose Her	1962	5.00	10.00	20.00
217	I'll Never Dance Again/Gee It's Wonderful	1962	3.00	6.00	12.00
217 [PS]	I'll Never Dance Again/Gee It's Wonderful	1962	5.00	10.00	20.00
228	The Cha-Cha-Cha/The Best Man Cried	1962	3.75	7.50	15.00
228 [PS]	The Cha-Cha-Cha/The Best Man Cried	1962	6.25	12.50	25.00
242	Butterfly Baby/Love Is Blind	1963	3.75	7.50	15.00
242 [PS]	Butterfly Baby/Love Is Blind	1963	6.25	12.50	25.00
252	Wildwood Days/Will You Be My Baby	1963	3.00	6.00	12.00
252 [PS]	Wildwood Days/Will You Be My Baby	1963	5.00	10.00	20.00
265	Little Queenie/The Woodpecker Song	1963	3.75	7.50	15.00
265 [PS]	Little Queenie/The Woodpecker Song	1963	6.25	12.50	25.00
272	Let's Make Love Tonight/Childhood Sweetheart	1963	3.00	6.00	12.00
272 [PS]	Let's Make Love Tonight/Childhood Sweetheart	1963	5.00	10.00	20.00
280	Forget Him/Love, Love Go Away	1963	3.00	6.00	12.00
280 [PS]	Forget Him/Love, Love Go Away	1963	5.00	10.00	20.00
309	Make Me Forget/Little Girl, You've Had a Busy Day	1964	3.00	6.00	12.00
309 [PS]	Make Me Forget/Little Girl, You've Had a Busy Day	1964	5.00	10.00	20.00
320	A World Without Love/Our Faded Love	1964	3.75	7.50	15.00
320 [PS]	A World Without Love/Our Faded Love	1964	6.25	12.50	25.00
361	Ciao, Ciao Bambino/Voce de la Notte	1965	3.75	7.50	15.00
1070	Forget Him/A Message from Bobby	1963	5.00	10.00	20.00
—Bonus single with Cameo LP C-1070, "Top Hits of 1963"					
CAPITOL					
5305	I Just Can't Say Goodbye/Two Is the Loneliest Number	1964	2.50	5.00	10.00
5305 [PS]	I Just Can't Say Goodbye/Two Is the Loneliest Number	1964	3.75	7.50	15.00
5352	Diana/Stranger in the World	1965	2.50	5.00	10.00
5436	The Joker/Side Show	1965	2.50	5.00	10.00
5513	When I See That Girl of Mine/It Takes Two	1965	2.50	5.00	10.00
5556	Roses in the Snow/A Word for Today	1965	2.50	5.00	10.00
5696	She Was the Girl/Not You	1966	2.50	5.00	10.00
5780	Open for Business As Usual/You Gotta Enjoy Joy	1966	2.50	5.00	10.00
PERCEPTION					
519	California Sunshine/Honey Buns	1973	—	2.50	5.00
552	Everything Seemed Better (When I Was Younger)/Sunday Son	1974	—	2.50	5.00
P.I.P.					
6515	Sway/Feels Good	1976	—	2.50	5.00
6521	You're Not the Only Girl for Me/Give Me Your Answer	1976	—	2.00	4.00
6531	It's Getting Better/The Singles Scene	1976	—	2.00	4.00
RCA VICTOR					
47-9892	Chapel on the Hill/It Must Be Love	1970	—	3.00	6.00
REPRISE					
0656	The Lovin' Thing/It's Getting Better	1968	2.00	4.00	8.00
0684	The River Is Wide/Absence Makes the Heart Grow Fonder	1968	2.00	4.00	8.00
0751	Every Little Bit Hurts/Time and Changes	1968	2.00	4.00	8.00
VEKO					
730/1	Dream Age/Fatty Fatty	1958	30.00	60.00	120.00
VENISE					
201	Fatty, Fatty/Happy Happy	1961	7.50	15.00	30.00
Albums					
CAMEO					
C-1006 [M]	We Got Love	1959	15.00	30.00	60.00
C-1007 [M]	Bobby Sings	1960	12.50	25.00	50.00
C-1009 [M]	Bobby's Biggest Hits	1961	20.00	40.00	80.00
—Original with die-cut cover and textured inner sleeve					
C-1009 [M]	Bobby's Biggest Hits	1961	6.25	12.50	25.00
—Standard cover					
C-1010 [M]	Bobby Rydell Salutes "The Great Ones"	1961	6.25	12.50	25.00
SC-1010 [S]	Bobby Rydell Salutes "The Great Ones"	1961	10.00	20.00	40.00
C-1011 [M]	Rydell at the Copa	1961	6.25	12.50	25.00
SC-1011 [S]	Rydell at the Copa	1961	10.00	20.00	40.00
C-1019 [M]	All the Hits	1962	6.25	12.50	25.00
—Black vinyl					

Number	Title (A Side/B Side)	Yr	VG	VG+	NM
C-1019 [M]	All the Hits	1962	37.50	75.00	150.00
—Red vinyl					
C-1028 [M]	Bobby Rydell's Biggest Hits, Volume 2	1962	6.25	12.50	25.00
C-1040 [M]	All the Hits, Volume 2	1963	6.25	12.50	25.00
SC-1040 [P]	All the Hits, Volume 2	1963	10.00	20.00	40.00
C-1043 [M]	Bye Bye Birdie	1963	6.25	12.50	25.00
C-1055 [M]	Wild (Wood) Days	1963	5.00	10.00	20.00
SC-1055 [S]	Wild (Wood) Days	1963	7.50	15.00	30.00
C-1070 [M]	The Top Hits of 1963	1963	5.00	10.00	20.00
—Came with bonus single, also numbered 1070 (see 45 listing)					
SC-1070 [S]	The Top Hits of 1963	1963	7.50	15.00	30.00
—Came with bonus single, also numbered 1070					
C-1080 [M]	Forget Him	1964	5.00	10.00	20.00
SC-1080 [R]	Forget Him	1964	5.00	10.00	20.00
C-2001 [M]	16 Golden Hits	1965	5.00	10.00	20.00
SC-2001 [R]	16 Golden Hits	1965	5.00	10.00	20.00
CAPITOL					
ST 2281 [S]	Somebody Loves You	1965	5.00	10.00	20.00
T 2281 [M]	Somebody Loves You	1965	3.75	7.50	15.00
P.I.P.					
6818	Born with a Smile	1976	2.50	5.00	10.00
SPIN-O-RAMA					
143 [M]	Starring Bobby Rydell	196?	3.00	6.00	12.00
S-143 [S]	Starring Bobby Rydell	196?	3.00	6.00	12.00
STRAND					
SL-1120 [M]	Bobby Rydell Sings	196?	6.25	12.50	25.00
SLS-1120 [R]	Bobby Rydell Sings	196?	5.00	10.00	20.00
VENISE					
10035 [M]	Twistin'	1962	6.25	12.50	25.00
—Also includes tracks by Barry Norman and Stephen Garrick					

RYDELL, BOBBY/CHUBBY CHECKER

Also see each artist's individual listings.

Number	Title (A Side/B Side)	Yr	VG	VG+	NM
45s					
CAMEO					
12E [DJ]	Chubby Sings Bobby-Bobby Sings Chubby	1962	10.00	20.00	40.00
—B-side blank, promo only					
13E [DJ]	What Are You Doing New Year's Eve?	1962	10.00	20.00	40.00
—B-side blank, promo only					
205	Jingle Bell Rock/Jingle Bell Imitations	1961	3.75	7.50	15.00
205 [PS]	Jingle Bell Rock/Jingle Bell Imitations	1961	6.25	12.50	25.00
214	Teach Me to Twist/Swingin' Together	1962	3.75	7.50	15.00
214 [PS]	Teach Me to Twist/Swingin' Together	1962	6.25	12.50	25.00
Albums					
CAMEO					
C 1013 [M]	Bobby Rydell/Chubby Checker	1961	7.50	15.00	30.00
C-1063 [M]	Chubby Checker and Bobby Rydell	1963	5.00	10.00	20.00

RYDER, MITCH

Also see DETROIT; MITCH RYDER AND THE DETROIT WHEELS.

Number	Title (A Side/B Side)	Yr	VG	VG+	NM
45s					
AVCO EMBASSY					
4550	Jenny Take a Ride/I Never Had It Better	1970	2.50	5.00	10.00
DOT					
17290	I Believe (There Must Be Someone)/Sugar Bee (We Three)	1970	—	3.00	6.00
17325	It's Been a Long, Long, Long Time/Direct Me	1970	—	3.00	6.00
DYNOVOICE					
901	What Now My Love/Blessing in Disguise	1967	2.00	4.00	8.00
905	Personality-Chantilly Lace/I Make a Fool of Myself	1968	2.00	4.00	8.00
916	Lights of the Night/I Need Loving You	1968	2.00	4.00	8.00
934	Baby I Need Your Loving/Ring Your Bell	1969	2.00	4.00	8.00
NEW VOICE					
824	Joy/I'd Rather Go to Jail	1967	2.00	4.00	8.00
826	You Are My Sunshine/Wild Child	1967	2.00	4.00	8.00
828	Come See About Me/A Face in the Crowd	1968	2.00	4.00	8.00
830	Ruby Baby/You Get Your Kicks	1968	2.00	4.00	8.00
RIVA					
213	When You Were Mine/Stand	1983	—	2.50	5.00
Albums					
DYNO VOICE					
1901 [M]	What Now My Love	1967	5.00	10.00	20.00
31901 [S]	What Now My Love	1967	5.00	10.00	20.00
RIVA					
RV 7503	Never Kick a Sleeping Dog	1983	2.50	5.00	10.00
SEEDS & STEMS					
7801	How I Spent My Summer Vacation	1978	3.00	6.00	12.00
7804	Naked But Not Dead	1980	3.00	6.00	12.00

RYDER, MITCH, AND THE DETROIT WHEELS

Also see DETROIT; THE DETROIT WHEELS; BILLY LEE AND THE RIVIERAS; MITCH RYDER.

Number	Title (A Side/B Side)	Yr	VG	VG+	NM
45s					
NEW VOICE					
801	I Need Help/I Hope	1965	2.50	5.00	10.00
806	Jenny Takes a Ride!/Baby Jane (Mo-Mo Jane)	1965	6.25	12.50	25.00
—Note slightly different A-side title					
806	Jenny Take a Ride!/Baby Jane (Mo-Mo Jane)	1965	3.00	6.00	12.00
—Actual A-side title					
808	Little Latin Lupe Lu/I Hope	1966	2.50	5.00	10.00
811	Break Out/I Need Help	1966	2.50	5.00	10.00
814	Takin' All I Can Get/You Get Your Kicks	1966	2.50	5.00	10.00
817	Devil with a Blue Dress On & Good Golly Miss Molly/I Had It Made	1966	3.00	6.00	12.00
820	Sock It To Me — Baby!/I Never Had It Better	1967	6.25	12.50	25.00
—Version 1: With lyric "Feels like a punch," mumbled to the point that it sounds obscene. The copy of this we've seen has a multicolor, concentric circle label, but we can't yet say that ALL copies with this label are this version.					
820	Sock It To Me — Baby!/I Never Had It Better	1967	2.50	5.00	10.00
—Version 2: With lyric "Hits me like a PUNCH!" with no doubt about the last word. The copies of this we've seen have a blue label, both "painted on" and not "painted on," but we can't say yet that ALL copies with that label have this version.					
820 [PS]	Sock It To Me — Baby!/I Never Had It Better	1967	5.00	10.00	20.00
822	Too Many Fish in the Sea & Three Little Fishes/One Grain of Sand	1967	2.50	5.00	10.00
822 [PS]	Too Many Fish in the Sea & Three Little Fishes/One Grain of Sand	1967	5.00	10.00	20.00
PHILCO-FORD					
HP-4	Jenny Take a Ride/Sock It To Me Baby	1967	3.75	7.50	15.00
—4-inch plastic "Hip Pocket Record" with color sleeve					
Albums					
CREWE					
CR-1335	All Mitch Ryder Hits!	1969	3.75	7.50	15.00
—Reissue of New Voice 2004					
NEW VOICE					
2000 [M]	Take a Ride	1966	6.25	12.50	25.00
S-2000 [S]	Take a Ride	1966	7.50	15.00	30.00
2002 [M]	Breakout...!!!	1966	6.25	12.50	25.00
—Without "Devil with a Blue Dress On/Good Golly Miss Molly"					
2002 [M]	Breakout...!!!	1966	5.00	10.00	20.00
—With "Devil with a Blue Dress On/Good Golly Miss Molly"					
S-2002 [S]	Breakout...!!!	1966	7.50	15.00	30.00
—Without "Devil with a Blue Dress On/Good Golly Miss Molly"					
S-2002 [S]	Breakout...!!!	1966	6.25	12.50	25.00
—With "Devil with a Blue Dress On/Good Golly Miss Molly"					
2003 [M]	Sock It To Me!	1967	6.25	12.50	25.00
S-2003 [S]	Sock It To Me!	1967	7.50	15.00	30.00
2004 [M]	All Mitch Ryder Hits!	1967	7.50	15.00	30.00
S-2004 [S]	All Mitch Ryder Hits!	1967	5.00	10.00	20.00
S-2005	Mitch Ryder Sings the Hits	1968	5.00	10.00	20.00
RHINO					
R1-70941	Rev Up: The Best of Mitch Ryder and the Detroit Wheels	1989	3.00	6.00	12.00
VIRGO					
12001	The Best of Mitch Ryder and the Detroit Wheels	1972	3.00	6.00	12.00

S

SA-SHAYS, THE

45s

Number	Title (A Side/B Side)	Yr	VG	VG+	NM
ALFI					
1	Boo Hoo Hoo/You Got Love	1961	6.25	12.50	25.00
ZEN					
110	Boo Hoo Hoo/You Got Love	1961	3.00	6.00	12.00

SABERS, THE

45s

Number	Title (A Side/B Side)	Yr	VG	VG+	NM
BULLSEYE					
101	You Can Depend on Me/Calypso Baby	1955	62.50	125.00	250.00
CAL-WEST					
847	Cool, Cool Christmas/Always and Forever	1955	100.00	200.00	400.00

SABRE, JOHNNY, AND THE PASSIONS

45s

Number	Title (A Side/B Side)	Yr	VG	VG+	NM
ADONIS					
103	Wish It Could Be Me/Dolly in a Toy Shop	1959	50.00	100.00	200.00

SACCO

See LOU CHRISTIE.

SACRED MUSHROOM, THE

Members of this group were later in POCO and PURE PRAIRIE LEAGUE.

Albums

Number	Title (A Side/B Side)	Yr	VG	VG+	NM
PARALLAX					
P-4001	The Sacred Mushroom	1969	37.50	75.00	150.00

SAD SACKS, THE

45s

Number	Title (A Side/B Side)	Yr	VG	VG+	NM
IMPERIAL					
5517	Sack Dresses/Guard Your Heart	1958	3.75	7.50	15.00

SADLER, SSGT. BARRY

45s

Number	Title (A Side/B Side)	Yr	VG	VG+	NM
RCA VICTOR					
47-8739	The Ballad of the Green Berets/Letter from Vietnam	1966	—	3.00	6.00
47-8739 [PS]	The Ballad of the Green Berets/Letter from Vietnam	1966	2.00	4.00	8.00
47-8804	The "A" Team/An Empty Glass	1966	—	3.00	6.00
47-8804 [PS]	The "A" Team/An Empty Glass	1966	2.00	4.00	8.00
47-8966	Not Just Lonely/One Day Nearer Home	1966	—	3.00	6.00
47-9008	I Won't Be Home This Christmas/A Woman Is a Weepin' Willow Tree	1966	2.00	4.00	8.00

Albums

Number	Title (A Side/B Side)	Yr	VG	VG+	NM
RCA VICTOR					
LPM-3547 [M]	Ballads of the Green Berets	1966	3.75	7.50	15.00
LSP-3547 [S]	Ballads of the Green Berets	1966	5.00	10.00	20.00
LPM-3605 [M]	The "A" Team	1966	3.75	7.50	15.00
LSP-3605 [S]	The "A" Team	1966	5.00	10.00	20.00
LPM-3691 [M]	Back Home	1967	5.00	10.00	20.00
LSP-3691 [S]	Back Home	1967	3.75	7.50	15.00

SAFARIS, THE

45s

Number	Title (A Side/B Side)	Yr	VG	VG+	NM
ELDO					
101	Image of a Girl/Four Steps to Love	1960	6.25	12.50	25.00
105	The Girl with the Story in Her Eyes/Summer Nights	1960	6.25	12.50	25.00
110	In the Still of the Night/Shadows	1960	7.50	15.00	30.00
113	Garden of Love/Soldier of Fortune	1961	7.50	15.00	30.00
VALIANT					
6036	Kick Out/Lonely Surf Guitar	1963	7.50	15.00	30.00

SAGES, THE

45s

Number	Title (A Side/B Side)	Yr	VG	VG+	NM
RCA VICTOR					
47-8760	In the Beginning/I'm Not Going to Cry	1965	6.25	12.50	25.00

SAGITTARIUS

45s

Number	Title (A Side/B Side)	Yr	VG	VG+	NM
COLUMBIA					
44163	My World Fell Down/Libra	1967	2.50	5.00	10.00
44289	Hotel Indiscreeet/Virgo	1967	2.50	5.00	10.00
44398	Another Time/Pisces	1967	2.50	5.00	10.00
44503	The Truth Is Not Real/You Know I've Found a Way	1968	2.50	5.00	10.00
44613	Keeper of the Games/I'm Not Living Here	1968	2.50	5.00	10.00
TOGETHER					
105	In My Room/Navajo Girl	1969	2.50	5.00	10.00
122	I Can Still See Your Face/I Guess the Lord Must Be in New York City	1969	2.50	5.00	10.00

Albums

Number	Title (A Side/B Side)	Yr	VG	VG+	NM
COLUMBIA					
CS 9644	Present Tense	1968	7.50	15.00	30.00
TOGETHER					
STT-1002	The Blue Marble	1969	12.50	25.00	50.00
—With two bonus photos; deduct 25 percent if missing					

SAHL, MORT

45s

Number	Title (A Side/B Side)	Yr	VG	VG+	NM
GNP CRESCENDO					
467	Nixon's Odyssey/Watergate	1973	—	2.50	5.00
REPRISE					
20038	About Women (Part 1)/About Women (Part 2)	1961	2.50	5.00	10.00

Albums

Number	Title (A Side/B Side)	Yr	VG	VG+	NM
FANTASY					
7005 [M]	Mort Sahl at Sunset	196?	10.00	20.00	40.00
—Red vinyl					
7005 [M]	Mort Sahl at Sunset	196?	7.50	15.00	30.00
—Black vinyl					
GNP CRESCENDO					
GNPS-2070	Sing a Song of Watergate	1973	3.75	7.50	15.00
MERCURY					
MG-21112 [M]	Anyway...Onward	1967	5.00	10.00	20.00
SR-61112 [S]	Anyway...Onward	1967	5.00	10.00	20.00
REPRISE					
R-5002 [M]	The New Frontier	1961	5.00	10.00	20.00
R9-5002 [S]	The New Frontier	1961	6.25	12.50	25.00
R-5003 [M]	Mort Sahl On Relationships	1961	10.00	20.00	40.00
R9-5003 [S]	Mort Sahl On Relationships	1961	12.50	25.00	50.00
—Joan Collins appears on the cover					
VERVE					
MGV-15002 [M]	The Future Lies Ahead	1959	5.00	10.00	20.00
MGV-15004 [M]	1960: Look Forward in Anger	1959	5.00	10.00	20.00
MGV-15006 [M]	A Way of Life	1960	5.00	10.00	20.00
MGV-15012 [M]	Mort Sahl at the Hungry I	1960	5.00	10.00	20.00
MGVS-15012 [S]	Mort Sahl at the Hungry I	1960	6.25	12.50	25.00
V-15021 [M]	The Next President	1961	5.00	10.00	20.00
V6-15021 [S]	The Next President	1961	6.25	12.50	25.00
V-15049 [M]	Great Moments of Comedy	1965	3.75	7.50	15.00

SAHM, DOUG

Also see SIR DOUGLAS QUINTET.

45s

Number	Title (A Side/B Side)	Yr	VG	VG+	NM
ABC/DOT					
17656	Cowboy Peyton Place/I Love the Way You Love (The Way I Love You)	1976	—	3.00	6.00
17674	Crying Inside Sometimes/I'm Missing You	1976	—	3.00	6.00
ATLANTIC					
2946	Is Anybody Going to San Antone/Don't Turn Around	1973	2.00	4.00	8.00
COBRA					
116	Just a Moment/Sapphire	1961	12.50	25.00	50.00
CRAZY CAJUN					
2004	If You Really Want/Not Tomato Man	1974	—	2.50	5.00
HARLEM					
108	Baby Tell Me/Sapphire	1960	12.50	25.00	50.00
108 [DJ]	Baby Tell Me/Sapphire	1960	25.00	50.00	100.00
—Gold vinyl promo					
113	More and More/Slow Down	1960	12.50	25.00	50.00
MERCURY					
73098	Be Real/I Don't Want to Go Home	1970	5.00	10.00	20.00
—As "Wayne Douglas"					
PERSONALITY					
260	Baby, What's On Your Mind/Crazy, Crazy Feeling	1962	12.50	25.00	50.00
RENNER					
212	Big Hat/Makes No Difference	1961	10.00	20.00	40.00
212 [DJ]	Big Hat/Makes No Difference	1961	25.00	50.00	100.00
—Red vinyl promo					
215	Baby, What's On Your Mind/Crazy, Crazy Feeling	1961	10.00	20.00	40.00
215 [DJ]	Baby, What's On Your Mind/Crazy, Crazy Feeling	1961	25.00	50.00	100.00
—Red vinyl promo					
226	Two Hearts in Love/Just Because	1962	10.00	20.00	40.00
232	Little Angel/Cry	1963	10.00	20.00	40.00
240	Lucky Me/A Year Ago Tonight	1963	10.00	20.00	40.00
247	Mr. Kool/Bill Beatty	1964	12.50	25.00	50.00
SARG					
113	A Real American Joe/Rolling Rolling	1958	25.00	50.00	100.00
—As "Little Doug"					
SATIN					
100	Crazy Daisy/I Can't Believe You Wanna Leave	1959	12.50	25.00	50.00
SOFT					
1031	Cry/Down the Pike	1965	7.50	15.00	30.00
SWINGIN'					
625	Why, Why, Why/If You Ever Need Me	1960	6.25	12.50	25.00
TEAR DROP					
3074	It's a Man Down There/4 A.M.	1966	6.25	12.50	25.00
—As "Him"					
TEARDROP					
3479	Who Were You Thinking Of/Velma	1982	—	2.00	4.00
—With Augie Myers					
3481	I'm Not a Fool Anymore/Don't Fight It	1982	—	2.00	4.00
—With Augie Myers					
WARNER BROS.					
7819	Girls Today/Groover's Paradise	1974	—	2.50	5.00
WARRIOR					
507	Crazy Daisy/If I Ever Need You	1958	20.00	40.00	80.00

Albums

Number	Title (A Side/B Side)	Yr	VG	VG+	NM
ABC DOT					
DO-2057	Texas Rock for Country Rollers	1976	3.75	7.50	15.00
ANTONE'S					
ANT-0008	Juke Box Music	1989	3.00	6.00	12.00
ATLANTIC					
SD 7254	Doug Sahm and Band	1973	3.75	7.50	15.00
MERCURY					
SRM-1-655	Rough Edges	1972	7.50	15.00	30.00
TAKOMA					
TAK-7075	Hell of a Spell	1980	3.00	6.00	12.00
TEARDROP					
TD-5000	The West Side Sound Rolls Again	1982	3.00	6.00	12.00
WARNER BROS.					
BS 2810	Groovers Paradise	1974	5.00	10.00	20.00

SAIGONS, THE
45s
DOOTONE

Number	Title (A Side/B Side)	Yr	VG	VG+	NM
375	You're Heavenly/Honey Gee	1955	100.00	200.00	400.00

SAILCAT
45s
ELEKTRA

Number	Title (A Side/B Side)	Yr	VG	VG+	NM
45782	Motorcycle Mama/Rainbow Road	1972	—	2.50	5.00
45817	Bee Bee Gunn/Baby Ruth	1972	—	2.50	5.00
45844	She Showed Me/Sweet Little Jenny	1973	—	2.50	5.00

Albums
ELEKTRA

Number	Title (A Side/B Side)	Yr	VG	VG+	NM
EKS-75029	Sailcat	1972	3.75	7.50	15.00

SAINT, CATHY
45s
DAISY

Number	Title (A Side/B Side)	Yr	VG	VG+	NM
501	Big Bad World/Mr. Heartbreak	1963	12.50	25.00	50.00

ST. ANTHONY'S FIRE
Albums
ZONK

Number	Title (A Side/B Side)	Yr	VG	VG+	NM
(# unknown)	St. Anthony's Fire	1968	100.00	200.00	400.00

ST. CLOUD, ENDLE
45s
INTERNATIONAL ARTISTS

Number	Title (A Side/B Side)	Yr	VG	VG+	NM
129	Tell Me One More Time/(B-side unknown)	1969	5.00	10.00	20.00
139	She Wears It Like a Badge/Laughter	1970	5.00	10.00	20.00

Albums
INTERNATIONAL ARTISTS

Number	Title (A Side/B Side)	Yr	VG	VG+	NM
IA-12	Thank You All Very Much	1970	15.00	30.00	60.00

ST. JAMES, HOLLY
45s
ABC

Number	Title (A Side/B Side)	Yr	VG	VG+	NM
10996	That's Not Love/Two Good Reasons	1967	15.00	30.00	60.00
11042	Waiting for My Friend/Magic Moments	1968	5.00	10.00	20.00

ST. JOHN, BARRY
45s
GRT

Number	Title (A Side/B Side)	Yr	VG	VG+	NM
2	Cry Like a Baby/Long and Lonely Nights	1969	—	3.00	6.00

ST. JOHN, DICK
Also see DICK AND DEEDEE; SANDY AND DICK.

45s

Number	Title (A Side/B Side)	Yr	VG	VG+	NM
DOT					
17080	Childhood/Lady of the Burning Green-Jade	1968	2.00	4.00	8.00
—Of Dick and Deedee					
17140	Leaving on a Jet Plane/Brand New Season	1968	2.00	4.00	8.00
LIBERTY					
55380	Gonna Stick By You/Sha-Ta	1961	3.00	6.00	12.00
PHILIPS					
40256	Love's a Funny Little Game/Believe Me Baby	1965	2.50	5.00	10.00
40325	Swanee River/You Know What I Mean	1965	2.50	5.00	10.00
POM POM					
4156	Gonna Stick By You/Sha-Ta	1961	6.25	12.50	25.00
ROMA					
1001	Hey, Little Gal/Boogie Man (I Ain't Afraid of You)	1961	3.75	7.50	15.00

ST. JOHN, TAMMY
45s
CONGRESS

Number	Title (A Side/B Side)	Yr	VG	VG+	NM
236	He's the One for Me/I'm Tired Just Lookin' at You	1965	2.50	5.00	10.00
258	Dark Shadows and Empty Hallways/I Mustn't Cry	1965	2.50	5.00	10.00

ST. LOUIS JIMMY
45s

Number	Title (A Side/B Side)	Yr	VG	VG+	NM
DUKE					
110	Drinkin' Woman/Why Work	1953	30.00	60.00	120.00
HERALD					
407	Hard Luck Boogie/Good Book Blues	1953	50.00	100.00	200.00
408	Your Evil Ways/Whiskey Drinkin' Woman	1953	50.00	100.00	200.00
PARROT					
823	Going Down Slow/Murder in the First Degree	1955	50.00	100.00	200.00

Albums
BLUESVILLE

Number	Title (A Side/B Side)	Yr	VG	VG+	NM
BVLP-1028 [M]	Goin' Down Blues	1961	30.00	60.00	120.00
—Blue label, silver print					
BVLP-1028 [M]	Goin' Down Blues	1964	6.25	12.50	25.00
—Blue label, trident logo at right					

ST. LOUIS UNION
45s
PARROT

Number	Title (A Side/B Side)	Yr	VG	VG+	NM
9812	Girl/Respect	1966	2.00	4.00	8.00

ST. PETERS, CRISPIAN
45s
JAMIE

Number	Title (A Side/B Side)	Yr	VG	VG+	NM
1302	At This Moment/You'll Forget Me, Goodbye	1965	3.75	7.50	15.00
1309	At This Moment/No No No	1966	2.50	5.00	10.00
1310	You Were On My Mind/What I'm Gonna Be	1966	2.50	5.00	10.00
1320	The Pied Piper/Sweet Dawn My True Love	1966	3.00	6.00	12.00
1324	Changes/My Little Brown Eyes	1966	2.50	5.00	10.00
1328	Your Ever Changin' Mind/But She's Untrue	1966	2.50	5.00	10.00
1334	Almost Persuaded/You Are Gone	1967	2.50	5.00	10.00
1344	Free Spirit/I'm Always Crying	1967	2.50	5.00	10.00
1359	Please Take Me Back/Look Into My Teardrops	1968	2.00	4.00	8.00

Albums
JAMIE

Number	Title (A Side/B Side)	Yr	VG	VG+	NM
JLPM-3027 [M]	The Pied Piper	1966	12.50	25.00	50.00
JLPS-3027 [R]	The Pied Piper	1966	8.75	17.50	35.00

ST. SHAW, MIKE
45s
REPRISE

Number	Title (A Side/B Side)	Yr	VG	VG+	NM
0273	Take This Hammer/What's That I Hear	1964	2.50	5.00	10.00
0282	Mike's Mid-Nite Special/Summer Skies and Golden Sands	1964	2.50	5.00	10.00
0325	From the Bottom of My Heart/Send Me Some Lovin'	1964	3.00	6.00	12.00

Albums
REPRISE

Number	Title (A Side/B Side)	Yr	VG	VG+	NM
R-6128 [M]	The Mike St. Shaw Trio	1964	5.00	10.00	20.00
RS-6128 [S]	The Mike St. Shaw Trio	1964	6.25	12.50	25.00

SAINT STEVEN
45s
PROBE

Number	Title (A Side/B Side)	Yr	VG	VG+	NM
463	Louisiana Home/Aye Aye Poe Day	1969	5.00	10.00	20.00

Albums
PROBE

Number	Title (A Side/B Side)	Yr	VG	VG+	NM
CPLP-4506	Over the Hills	1969	15.00	30.00	60.00

SAINTE-MARIE, BUFFY
45s

Number	Title (A Side/B Side)	Yr	VG	VG+	NM
ABC					
12183	Starwalker/Free the Lady	1976	—	2.50	5.00
12203	Look at the Facts/(B-side unknown)	1976	—	2.50	5.00
MCA					
40193	Can't Believe the Feeling When You're Gone/Waves	1974	—	2.50	5.00
40216	Sweet Little Vera/Waves	1974	—	2.50	5.00
40286	I Can't Take It No More/Native North American Child: An Odyssey	1974	—	2.50	5.00
40347	Sweet, Fast Hooker Blues/Generation	1975	—	2.50	5.00
40368	Love's Got to Breathe and Fly/Nobody Will Ever Know It's Real But You	1975	—	2.50	5.00
VANGUARD					
35028	Until It's Time for You to Go/The Flower and the Apple Tree	1963	2.50	5.00	10.00
35050	Until It's Time for You to Go/Jusqu'au Jour Ou Tu Partiras	1967	2.00	4.00	8.00
35053	Circle Game/Until It's Time for You to Go	1967	2.00	4.00	8.00
35064	Soulful Shade of Blue/Piney Wood Hills	1968	2.00	4.00	8.00
35072	Better to Find Out for Yourself/Sometimes When I Get to Thinkin'	1968	2.00	4.00	8.00
35075	From the Bottom of My Heart/I'm Gonna Be a Country Girl Again	1969	2.00	4.00	8.00
35091	He's a Keeper of the Fire/Better to Find Out for Yourself	1970	—	3.00	6.00
35108	The Circle Game/Better to Find Out for Yourself	1970	—	3.00	6.00
35116	Soldier Blue/Until It's Time for You to Go	1970	—	3.00	6.00
35127	She Used to Wanna Be a Ballerina/Moratorium	1971	—	3.00	6.00
35135	Helpless/Now You've Been Gone a Long Time	1971	—	3.00	6.00
35143	I'm Gonna Be a Country Girl Again/Piney Wood Hills	1971	—	2.50	5.00
35151	Mister Can't You See/Moonshot	1972	—	2.50	5.00
35156	He's an Indian Cowboy in the Rodeo/Not the Lovin' Kind	1972	—	2.50	5.00
35172	I Wanna Hold Your Hand Forever/Jeremiah	1972	—	2.50	5.00
35180	Soldier Blue/(B-side unknown)	1973	—	2.50	5.00

Albums

Number	Title (A Side/B Side)	Yr	VG	VG+	NM
ABC					
D-929	Sweet America	1976	3.00	6.00	12.00
MCA					
405	Buffy	1974	3.00	6.00	12.00
451	Changing Woman	1975	3.00	6.00	12.00
VANGUARD					
VSD 3/4 [(2)]	The Best of Buffy Sainte-Marie	1970	5.00	10.00	20.00
VSD 33/34 [(2)]	The Best of Buffy Sainte-Marie, Vol. 2	1974	3.75	7.50	15.00
VRS 9142 [M]	It's My Way	1964	3.75	7.50	15.00
VRS 9171 [M]	Many a Mile	1965	3.75	7.50	15.00
VRS 9211 [M]	Little Wheel Spin and Spin	1966	3.75	7.50	15.00
VRS 9250 [M]	Fire & Fire & Candlelight	1967	3.75	7.50	15.00
VMS 73113	The Best of Buffy Sainte-Marie	1985	2.50	5.00	10.00
VSD 79142 [S]	It's My Way	1964	5.00	10.00	20.00
VSD 79171 [S]	Many a Mile	1965	5.00	10.00	20.00
VSD 79211 [S]	Little Wheel Spin and Spin	1966	5.00	10.00	20.00
VSD 79250 [S]	Fire & Fire & Candlelight	1967	5.00	10.00	20.00
VSD 79280	I'm Gonna Be a Country Girl Again	1968	3.75	7.50	15.00
VSD 79300	Illuminations	1969	3.75	7.50	15.00
VSD 79311	She Used to Wanna Be a Ballerina	1971	3.75	7.50	15.00
VSD 79312	Moon Shot	1972	3.75	7.50	15.00
VSD 79330	Quiet Places	1973	3.00	6.00	12.00
VSD 79340	Native Child: Odyssey	1974	3.00	6.00	12.00

SAKAMOTO, KYU
45s
CAPITOL

Number	Title (A Side/B Side)	Yr	VG	VG+	NM
4945	Sukiyaka/Anoko No Namaewa Nantenkana	1963	3.75	7.50	15.00
—First pressing: Misspelled A-side					
4945	Sukiyaki/Anoko No Namaewa Nantenkana	1963	2.50	5.00	10.00
—Second pressing: A-side spelled correctly, subtittled "Music of 'Ue O Muite Aruko' "					
4945	Sukiyaki/Anoko No Namaewa Nantenkana	1963	2.00	4.00	8.00
—Third pressing: A-side spelled correctly with no subtitle					
5016	China Nights (Shina No Yoru)/Benkyo No Cha Cha Cha	1963	2.00	4.00	8.00

Number	Title (A Side/B Side)	Yr	VG	VG+	NM
5080	The Olympics Song/Tankobushi	1963	2.00	4.00	8.00
5262	Sayonara Tokyo/I Like You	1964	2.00	4.00	8.00
EMI					
4150	Why/Elimo	1975	—	2.50	5.00
Albums					
CAPITOL					
DT 10349 [R]	Sukiyaki and Other Japanese Hits	1963	3.75	7.50	15.00
T 10349 [M]	Sukiyaki and Other Japanese Hits	1963	6.25	12.50	25.00

SALAS BROTHERS, THE

45s

FARO

Number	Title (A Side/B Side)	Yr	VG	VG+	NM
614	Leaving You/Darling, Please Bring Your Love	1964	2.50	5.00	10.00
619	The Return of Farmer John/Love Is Strange	1965	2.50	5.00	10.00
625	Donde Este Santa Claus/One Like Mine	1966	2.00	4.00	8.00

SALEM MASS

Albums

SALEM MASS

Number	Title (A Side/B Side)	Yr	VG	VG+	NM
SM-101	Witch Burning	1972	62.50	125.00	250.00

SALEMS, THE

45s

Number	Title (A Side/B Side)	Yr	VG	VG+	NM
EPIC					
9480	Ol' Man River/Maria	1961	3.75	7.50	15.00
MERCURY					
71754	My Precious Love/I'll Still Go On Loving You	1961	3.75	7.50	15.00

SALES, SOUPY

45s

Number	Title (A Side/B Side)	Yr	VG	VG+	NM
ABC-PARAMOUNT					
10646	The Mouse/Pachalafaka	1965	3.00	6.00	12.00
10681	Speedy Gonzales/Hey, Pearl	1965	2.50	5.00	10.00
10747	I'm a Bird Watching Man/Where the Blue Folks Go	1965	2.50	5.00	10.00
BRUNSWICK					
55472	Break Your Back/Tom Jones (Push and Pull)	1972	2.50	5.00	10.00
CAPITOL					
5752	Spanish Flea/That Wasn't No Girl	1966	2.50	5.00	10.00
5766	Backwards Alphabet/Use Your Noggin	1966	2.50	5.00	10.00
MOTOWN					
1141	Muck-Arty Park/Green Grow the Lilacs	1968	10.00	20.00	40.00
REPRISE					
244	Santa Claus Is Surfin' to Town/Santa Claus Is Comin' to Town	1963	7.50	15.00	30.00
0368	Pie in the Face/Soupy Sez	1965	3.75	7.50	15.00
20041	Hippy's Cha Cha Hips/White Fang	1961	3.75	7.50	15.00
20064	Because of Black Tooth/Soupy's Theme	1962	3.75	7.50	15.00
20108	My Baby's Got a Crush on Frankenstein/Doggone Doggie	1962	3.75	7.50	15.00
20189	And That's a Shame/Hilly Billy Ding Dong Choo Choo	1963	3.75	7.50	15.00
Albums					
ABC-PARAMOUNT					
503 [M]	Spy with a Pie	1965	6.25	12.50	25.00
S-503 [S]	Spy with a Pie	1965	7.50	15.00	30.00
517 [M]	Soupy Sales Sez Do the Mouse and Other Teen Hits	1965	6.25	12.50	25.00
S-517 [S]	Soupy Sales Sez Do the Mouse and Other Teen Hits	1965	7.50	15.00	30.00
MCA					
5274	Still Soupy After All These Years	1981	3.00	6.00	12.00
MOTOWN					
MS 686	A Bag of Soup	1969	6.25	12.50	25.00
REPRISE					
R 6010 [M]	The Soupy Sales Show	1961	7.50	15.00	30.00
R9 6010 [S]	The Soupy Sales Show	1961	10.00	20.00	40.00
R 6052 [M]	Up in the Air	1962	7.50	15.00	30.00
R9 6052 [S]	Up in the Air	1962	10.00	20.00	40.00

SALLEE, VICKIE

45s

Number	Title (A Side/B Side)	Yr	VG	VG+	NM
DOT					
16651	Jimmy Darling/Wild Angel	1964	2.50	5.00	10.00
16710	Little Wishing Star/Oh My Love	1965	2.50	5.00	10.00
REPRISE					
20118	There Goes the Lucky One/Your Favorite Lie	1962	3.75	7.50	15.00

SALLYANGIE

Also see MIKE OLDFIELD.

Albums

WARNER BROS.

Number	Title (A Side/B Side)	Yr	VG	VG+	NM
WS 1783	Children of the Sun	1969	3.75	7.50	15.00

SALSOUL ORCHESTRA, THE

12-Inch Singles

Number	Title (A Side/B Side)	Yr	VG	VG+	NM
SALSOUL					
358 [DJ]	Deck the Halls (7:29)/The Salsoul Christmas Suite (7:59)	1981	3.00	6.00	12.00
45s					
SALSOUL					
2002	Salsoul Hustle/Salsoul Hustle (Part 2)	1975	—	2.50	5.00
2004	Tangerine/Salsoul Hustle	1975	—	2.50	5.00
2007	You're Just the Right Size/Chicago Bus Stop (Ooh I Like It)	1976	—	2.50	5.00
2011	Nice 'n' Naasty/Nightcrawler	1976	—	2.50	5.00
2016	My Love Is Free/(B-side unknown)	1976	—	2.50	5.00
2018	Ritzy Mambo/Salsoul: 3001	1977	—	2.50	5.00
2037	Short Shorts/It's a New Day	1977	—	2.50	5.00
2038	Getaway/Magic Bird of Fire	1977	—	2.50	5.00
2052	We Wish You a Merry Christmas/Merry Christmas All	1976	—	2.50	5.00
2052 [PS]	We Wish You a Merry Christmas/Merry Christmas All	1976	—	3.00	6.00
2064	West Side Encounter — West Side Story (Medley)/Evergreen	1978	—	2.00	4.00
2072	Sgt. Pepper's Lonely Hearts Club Band/Ease On Down the Road	1978	—	2.00	4.00
2077	The Little Drummer Boy/Christmas Time	1978	—	2.50	5.00
2086	Somebody to Love/(B-side unknown)	1979	—	2.00	4.00
2093	Street Sense/Sun After the Rain	1979	—	2.00	4.00
2096	How High/Nothing Can Change This Love	1979	—	2.00	4.00
2155	Deck The Halls/The Salsoul Christmas Suite	1981	—	2.00	4.00
7026	Take Some Time Out (For Love)/(B-side unknown)	1982	—	—	3.00
7050	How I Love It So/(B-side unknown)	1983	—	—	3.00
Albums					
SALSOUL					
CA-1001	Christmas Jollies	198?	2.00	4.00	8.00
—Reissue					
CA-1004	Christmas Jollies II	198?	2.00	4.00	8.00
—Reissue					
SZS 5501	The Salsoul Orchestra	1975	2.50	5.00	10.00
SZS 5502	Nice 'n' Naasty	1976	2.50	5.00	10.00
SZS 5507	Christmas Jollies	1976	3.00	6.00	12.00
SZS 5515	Magic Journey	1977	2.50	5.00	10.00
SA-8500	Up the Yellow Brick Road	1978	2.50	5.00	10.00
SA-8508	Greatest Disco Hits/Music for Non-Stop Dancing	1978	2.50	5.00	10.00
SA-8516	Street Sense	1979	2.50	5.00	10.00
SA-8528	How High	1980	2.50	5.00	10.00
SA 8547	Christmas Jollies II	1981	3.00	6.00	12.00
SA-8552	Heat It Up	1982	2.50	5.00	10.00

SALT WATER TAFFY

45s

Number	Title (A Side/B Side)	Yr	VG	VG+	NM
BUDDAH					
37	Finders Keepers/He'll Pay	1968	2.00	4.00	8.00
57	Sticks and Stones/Suddenly I See	1968	2.00	4.00	8.00
METROMEDIA					
220	Summertime Girl/Spend the Sunshine	1971	2.00	4.00	8.00
UNITED ARTISTS					
50691	Summertime Girl/One Hand Washes the Other	1970	2.50	5.00	10.00
Albums					
BUDDAH					
BDS-5021	Finders Keepers	1968	5.00	10.00	20.00

SALVATION

45s

Number	Title (A Side/B Side)	Yr	VG	VG+	NM
ABC					
11025	Love Comes in Funny Packages/Think Twice	1967	2.00	4.00	8.00
UNITED ARTISTS					
50695	Tomorrow Is the First Day of the Rest of Your Life/Someday the Gray Will Come	1970	2.00	4.00	8.00
Albums					
ABC					
S-623	Salvation	1968	5.00	10.00	20.00
S-653	Gypsy Carnival Caravan	1968	5.00	10.00	20.00

SAM AND DAVE

Also see SAM MOORE.

45s

Number	Title (A Side/B Side)	Yr	VG	VG+	NM
ALSTON					
777	Never, Never/Lotta Lovin'	1964	5.00	10.00	20.00
ATLANTIC					
2517	You Don't Know What You Mean to Me/This Is Your World	1968	—	3.00	6.00
2540	Can't You Find Another Way (Of Doing It)/Still Is the Night	1968	—	3.00	6.00
2568	Everybody Got to Believe in Somebody/If I Didn't Have a Girl Like You	1968	—	3.00	6.00
2590	Soul Sister, Brown Sugar/Come On In	1968	—	3.00	6.00
2608	Born Again/Get It	1969	—	3.00	6.00
2668	Holdin' On/Ooh Ooh Ooh	1969	—	3.00	6.00
2714	I'm Not an Indian Giver/Baby-Baby Don't Stop Now	1970	—	3.00	6.00
2728	One Part Love, Two Parts Pain/When You Steal from Me	1970	—	3.00	6.00
2733	When You Steal from Me (You're Only Hurting Yourself)/You Easily Excite Me	1970	—	3.00	6.00
2839	Don't Pull Your Love/Jody Ryder Got Killed	1971	—	3.00	6.00
CONTEMPO					
7004	We Can Work It Out/Why Did You Do It	1977	—	2.50	5.00
MARLIN					
6100	I Need Love/Keep a-Walkin'	1961	10.00	20.00	40.00
6104	No More Pain/My Love Belongs to You	1961	10.00	20.00	40.00
ROULETTE					
4419	I Need Love/Keep a-Walkin'	1962	3.00	6.00	12.00
4445	No More Pain/My Love Belongs to You	1962	3.00	6.00	12.00
4461	She's Alright/It Feels So Nice	1962	3.00	6.00	12.00
4480	It Was So Nice While It Lasted/You Ain't No Big Thing, Baby	1963	3.00	6.00	12.00
4508	If She'll Still Have Me/Listening for My Name	1963	3.00	6.00	12.00
4533	I Found Out/I Got a Thing Going On	1963	3.00	6.00	12.00
4671	It Feels So Nice/It Was So Nice While It Lasted	1966	2.00	4.00	8.00
STAX					
168	Goodnight Baby/A Place Nobody Can Find	1965	3.75	7.50	15.00
175	I Take What I Want/Sweet Home	1965	3.00	6.00	12.00
180	You Don't Know Like I Know/Blame Me (Don't Blame My Heart)	1965	3.00	6.00	12.00
189	Hold On! I'm a-Comin'/I Got Everything I Need	1966	3.75	7.50	15.00
198	Said I Wasn't Gonna Tell Nobody/If You Got the Loving	1966	2.50	5.00	10.00

Number	Title (A Side/B Side)	Yr	VG	VG+	NM
204	You Got Me Hummin'/Sleep Good Tonight	1967	2.50	5.00	10.00
210	When Something Is Wrong with My Baby/Small Portion of Your Love	1967	2.50	5.00	10.00
218	Soothe Me/I Can't Stand Up for Falling Down	1967	2.50	5.00	10.00
231	Soul Man/May I Baby	1967	3.00	6.00	12.00
242	I Thank You/Wrap It Up	1968	3.00	6.00	12.00
UNITED ARTISTS					
XW438	A Little Bit of Good (Cures a Whole Lot of Bad)/Blinded by Love	1974	—	3.00	6.00
XW531	Under the Boardwalk/Give It What You Can	1974	—	3.00	6.00
Albums					
ATLANTIC					
SD 8205	I Thank You	1968	6.25	12.50	25.00
SD 8218	The Best of Sam and Dave	1969	5.00	10.00	20.00
81279	The Best of Sam and Dave	1985	2.50	5.00	10.00
81718	Soul Men	1987	2.50	5.00	10.00
—Reissue of Stax 725					
GUSTO					
0045	Sweet and Funky Gold	197?	2.50	5.00	10.00
ROULETTE					
R-25323 [M]	Sam and Dave	1966	7.50	15.00	30.00
SR-25323 [S]	Sam and Dave	1966	10.00	20.00	40.00
STAX					
ST-708 [M]	Hold On, I'm Comin'	1966	10.00	20.00	40.00
STS-708 [S]	Hold On, I'm Comin'	1966	12.50	25.00	50.00
ST-712 [M]	Double Dynamite	1966	7.50	15.00	30.00
STS-712 [S]	Double Dynamite	1966	10.00	20.00	40.00
ST-725 [M]	Soul Men	1967	7.50	15.00	30.00
STS-725 [S]	Soul Men	1967	10.00	20.00	40.00
UNITED ARTISTS					
UA-LA524-G	Back At 'Cha!	1975	3.00	6.00	12.00

SAM THE SHAM AND THE PHARAOHS

Number	Title (A Side/B Side)	Yr	VG	VG+	NM
45s					
ATLANTIC					
2767	Me and Bobby McGee/Key to the Highway	1970	—	2.50	5.00
—As "Sam Samudio"					
DINGO					
001	Haunted House/How Does a Cheating Woman Feel	1964	50.00	100.00	200.00
FRETONE					
048	Wookie (Part 1)/Wookie (Part 2)	1977	2.50	5.00	10.00
—As "Sam the Sham"					
049	Ain't No Lie/Baby You Got It	1977	2.50	5.00	10.00
—As "Sam the Sham"					
MGM					
13322	Wooly Bully/Ain't Gonna Move	1965	3.75	7.50	15.00
13364	Ju Ju Hand/Big City Lights	1965	3.00	6.00	12.00
13364 [PS]	Ju Ju Hand/Big City Lights	1965	5.00	10.00	20.00
13397	Ring Dang Doo/Don't Try It Again	1965	3.00	6.00	12.00
13397 [PS]	Ring Dang Doo/Don't Try It Again	1965	5.00	10.00	20.00
13452	Red Hot/Long Long Way	1966	3.00	6.00	12.00
13506	Lil' Red Riding Hood/Love Me Like Before	1966	3.75	7.50	15.00
13581	The Hair on My Chinny Chin Chin/(I'm In with the) Out Crowd	1966	3.00	6.00	12.00
13581 [PS]	The Hair on My Chinny Chin Chin/(I'm In with the) Out Crowd	1966	5.00	10.00	20.00
13649	How Do You Catch a Girl/Love You Left Behind	1966	3.00	6.00	12.00
13649 [PS]	How Do You Catch a Girl/Love You Left Behind	1966	5.00	10.00	20.00
13713	Oh That's Good, No That's Bad/Take What You Can Get	1967	2.50	5.00	10.00
13747	Black Sheep/My Day's Gonna Come	1967	2.50	5.00	10.00
13803	Banned in Boston/Money's My Problem	1967	2.50	5.00	10.00
—As "The Sam the Sham Revue"					
13863	Yakety Yak/Let Our Love Light Shine	1967	2.50	5.00	10.00
—As "The Sam the Sham Revue"					
13920	Old Mac Donald Has a Boogaloo Farm/I Never Was No One	1968	2.50	5.00	10.00
13972	I Couldn't Spell !!@!/Down Home Strut	1968	3.75	7.50	15.00
14021	Wolly Bully/Ain't Gonna Move	1968	2.50	5.00	10.00
14642	Fate/Oh Lo	1973	2.50	5.00	10.00
PHILCO-FORD					
HP-3	Ju Ju Hand/Wooly Bully	1967	7.50	15.00	30.00
—4-inch plastic "Hip Pocket Record" with color sleeve					
TUPELO					
2982	Betty and Dupree/Manchild	1963	15.00	30.00	60.00
XL					
905	The Signifyin' Monkey/Juimonos	1964	12.50	25.00	50.00
906	Wooly Bully/Ain't Gonna Move	1965	75.00	150.00	300.00
Albums					
ATLANTIC					
SD 8271	Hard and Heavy	1971	3.75	7.50	15.00
—As "Sam Samudio"					
MGM					
E-4297 [M]	Wooly Bully	1965	7.50	15.00	30.00
SE-4297 [S]	Wooly Bully	1965	10.00	20.00	40.00
E-4317 [M]	Their Second Album	1965	6.25	12.50	25.00
SE-4317 [S]	Their Second Album	1965	7.50	15.00	30.00
E-4347 [M]	On Tour	1966	6.25	12.50	25.00
SE-4347 [S]	On Tour	1966	7.50	15.00	30.00
E-4407 [M]	Lil' Red Riding Hood	1966	6.25	12.50	25.00
SE-4407 [S]	Lil' Red Riding Hood	1966	7.50	15.00	30.00
E-4422 [M]	The Best of Sam the Sham and the Pharoahs	1967	5.00	10.00	20.00
SE-4422 [S]	The Best of Sam the Sham and the Pharoahs	1967	6.25	12.50	25.00
E-4477 [M]	Nefertiti	1967	6.25	12.50	25.00
SE-4477	The Sam The Sham Revue	1968	5.00	10.00	20.00
—Retitled reissue					
SE-4477 [S]	Nefertiti	1967	6.25	12.50	25.00
SE-4526	Ten of Pentacles	1968	5.00	10.00	20.00
ST 90422 [S]	Wooly Bully	1965	12.50	25.00	50.00
—Capitol Record Club edition					
T 90422 [M]	Wooly Bully	1965	10.00	20.00	40.00
—Capitol Record Club edition					
POLYDOR					
827917-1	The Best of Sam the Sham and the Pharoahs	1985	2.50	5.00	10.00
RHINO					
RNLP-122	Pharoahization: The Best of Sam the Sham and the Pharoahs (1965-1967)	1986	2.50	5.00	10.00

SAMMY AND THE DEL-LARKS

Number	Title (A Side/B Side)	Yr	VG	VG+	NM
45s					
EA-JAY					
100	Baby Come On/I Never Will Forget	1961	50.00	100.00	200.00

SAMUDIO, SAM

See SAM THE SHAM AND THE PHARAOHS.

SAN REMO GOLDEN STRINGS

Number	Title (A Side/B Side)	Yr	VG	VG+	NM
45s					
GORDY					
7060	Festival Time/Joy Road	1967	6.25	12.50	25.00
RIC-TIC					
104	Hungry for Love/All Turned On	1965	3.00	6.00	12.00
108	I'm Satisfied/Blueberry Hill	1965	3.00	6.00	12.00
112	Festival Time/Joy Road	1966	3.00	6.00	12.00
116	International Love Theme/Quanto Si Bella	1966	3.00	6.00	12.00
Albums					
GORDY					
G-923 [M]	Hungry for Love	1967	6.25	12.50	25.00
GS-923 [S]	Hungry for Love	1967	7.50	15.00	30.00
GS-928	Swing	1968	5.00	10.00	20.00
RIC-TIC					
901 [M]	Hungry for Love	1966	12.50	25.00	50.00
S-901 [S]	Hungry for Love	1966	15.00	30.00	60.00

SAN SEBASTIAN STRINGS, THE

Number	Title (A Side/B Side)	Yr	VG	VG+	NM
45s					
WARNER BROS.					
7012	Days of the Dancing/Pushing the Clouds Away	1967	—	2.50	5.00
7084	Mud Kids/Tender Earth	1967	—	2.50	5.00
7754	And Every Day Was Christmas/Sunset Colors	1973	—	2.50	5.00
Albums					
STANYAN					
10043	La Mer	1972	2.50	5.00	10.00
WARNER BROS.					
W 1670 [M]	The Sea	1967	3.75	7.50	15.00
WS 1670 [S]	The Sea	1967	3.00	6.00	12.00
W 1705 [M]	The Earth	1967	3.75	7.50	15.00
WS 1705 [S]	The Earth	1967	3.00	6.00	12.00
WS 1720	The Sky	1968	3.00	6.00	12.00
3WS 1730 [(3)]	The Sea, The Earth, The Sky	1968	5.00	10.00	20.00
WS 1764	Home to the Sea	1968	3.00	6.00	12.00
WS 1795	For Lovers	1969	3.00	6.00	12.00
3WS 1827 [(3)]	The Complete Sea	1969	5.00	10.00	20.00
WS 1839	The Soft Sea	1970	3.00	6.00	12.00
BS 2622	Winter	1972	2.50	5.00	10.00
BS 2707	Summer	1973	2.50	5.00	10.00
4WS 2754 [(4)]	Seasons	1973	5.00	10.00	20.00
BS 2768	Bouquet—The Best of the San Sebastian Strings	1974	2.50	5.00	10.00
BS 2837	With Love	1975	2.50	5.00	10.00

SANCHEZ, JOE

Number	Title (A Side/B Side)	Yr	VG	VG+	NM
45s					
IMPERIAL					
66190	Unlucky Me/Our Love Baby Is Running Down	1966	5.00	10.00	20.00

SANDALS, THE

Number	Title (A Side/B Side)	Yr	VG	VG+	NM
45s					
AURA					
4501	School's Out/Wild As the Sea	1964	6.25	12.50	25.00
—As "The Sandells"					
WORLD PACIFIC					
405	Scrambler/Out Front	1964	6.25	12.50	25.00
—As "The Sandells"					
415	Endless Summer/6-Pak	1964	6.25	12.50	25.00
421	All Over Again/Always	1965	3.75	7.50	15.00
77840	Theme from Endless Summer/6-Pak	1966	3.75	7.50	15.00
77852	Tell Us Dylan/Why Should I Cry	1966	3.75	7.50	15.00
77867	Cloudy/House of Painted Glass	1967	3.75	7.50	15.00
Albums					
WORLD PACIFIC					
ST-1818 [S]	Scrambler	1964	25.00	50.00	100.00
—As "The Sandells"; black vinyl					
ST-1818 [S]	Scrambler	1964	62.50	125.00	250.00
—As "The Sandells"; red vinyl					
WP-1818 [M]	Scrambler	1964	20.00	40.00	80.00
—As "The Sandells"					
ST-1832 [S]	The Endless Summer	1966	7.50	15.00	30.00
WP-1832 [M]	The Endless Summer	1966	6.25	12.50	25.00
ST-21884	The Last of the Ski Bums	1969	6.25	12.50	25.00
—With skiers' silhouettes on cover					
ST-21884	The Last of the Ski Bums	1969	6.25	12.50	25.00
—With Volkswagon bus on cover					

SANDERS, BOBBY

Number	Title (A Side/B Side)	Yr	VG	VG+	NM
45s					
KAYBO					
618	It Was You/I'm On My Way	1961	25.00	50.00	100.00
KENT					
382	Maybe I'm Wrong/You've Forgotten Me	1962	75.00	150.00	300.00
PICK-A-HIT					
100	Lover/The Way I Feel	196?	2.50	5.00	10.00

SANDERS, ED

Albums

REPRISE

Number	Title (A Side/B Side)	Yr	VG	VG+	NM
MS 2105	Beer Cans on the Moon	1972	6.25	12.50	25.00
RS-6374	Sanders' Truckstop	1969	6.25	12.50	25.00

SANDERS, PHAROAH

45s

ARISTA

Number	Title (A Side/B Side)	Yr	VG	VG+	NM
0329	As You Are/Pharomba	1978	—	2.50	5.00
0356	Got to Give It Up/(B-side unknown)	1978	—	2.50	5.00

Albums

ABC IMPULSE!

Number	Title (A Side/B Side)	Yr	VG	VG+	NM
A-9138 [M]	Tauhid	1967	7.50	15.00	30.00
AS-9138 [S]	Tauhid	1967	5.00	10.00	20.00
AS-9181	Karma	1969	5.00	10.00	20.00
AS-9190	Jewels of Thought	1970	5.00	10.00	20.00
AS-9199	Summun Bukmun Umyum	1970	5.00	10.00	20.00
AS-9206	Thembi	1971	3.75	7.50	15.00
AQ-9219 [Q]	Black Unity	1974	4.50	9.00	18.00
AS-9219	Black Unity	1972	3.75	7.50	15.00
AQ-9227 [Q]	Live at the East	1974	4.50	9.00	18.00
AS-9227	Live at the East	1973	3.75	7.50	15.00
AS-9229 [(2)]	The Best of Pharoah Sanders	1973	5.00	10.00	20.00
AS-9233	Wisdom Through Music	1973	3.75	7.50	15.00
AQ-9254 [Q]	Village of the Pharoahs	1974	4.50	9.00	18.00
AS-9254	Village of the Pharoahs	1974	3.00	6.00	12.00
AQ-9261 [Q]	Elevation	1974	4.50	9.00	18.00
AS-9261	Elevation	1974	3.00	6.00	12.00
AQ-9280 [Q]	Love in Us All	1975	4.50	9.00	18.00
ASD-9280	Love in Us All	1975	3.00	6.00	12.00

ARISTA

Number	Title (A Side/B Side)	Yr	VG	VG+	NM
AL 4161	Love Will Find a Way	1978	3.00	6.00	12.00

ESP-DISK'

Number	Title (A Side/B Side)	Yr	VG	VG+	NM
1003 [M]	Pharoah's First	1965	6.25	12.50	25.00
S-1003 [S]	Pharoah's First	1965	7.50	15.00	30.00

GRP/IMPULSE!

Number	Title (A Side/B Side)	Yr	VG	VG+	NM
IMP-219	Black Unity	199?	3.75	7.50	15.00
—Reissue on audiophile vinyl					

INDIA NAVIGATION

Number	Title (A Side/B Side)	Yr	VG	VG+	NM
IN-1027	Pharoah	1977	3.00	6.00	12.00

MCA

Number	Title (A Side/B Side)	Yr	VG	VG+	NM
4151 [(2)]	The Best of Pharoah Sanders	1981	3.00	6.00	12.00
—Reissue of Impulse 9229					
29056	Tauhid	1981	2.00	4.00	8.00
—Reissue of Impulse 9138					
29057	Karma	1981	2.00	4.00	8.00
—Reissue of Impulse 9181					
29058	Jewels of Thought	1981	2.00	4.00	8.00
—Reissue of Impulse 9190					
29059	Thembi	1981	2.00	4.00	8.00
—Reissue of Impulse 9206					

SIGNATURE

Number	Title (A Side/B Side)	Yr	VG	VG+	NM
FA 40952	Oh Lord, Let Me Do No Wrong	1989	3.00	6.00	12.00

STRATA-EAST

Number	Title (A Side/B Side)	Yr	VG	VG+	NM
19733	Izipho Sam (My Gifts)	1973	3.75	7.50	15.00

THERESA

Number	Title (A Side/B Side)	Yr	VG	VG+	NM
108/9 [(2)]	Journey to the One	1980	3.75	7.50	15.00
112/13 [(2)]	Rejoice	1981	3.75	7.50	15.00
116	Pharoah Sanders Live	1985	2.50	5.00	10.00
118	Heart Is a Melody	1986	2.50	5.00	10.00
121	Shukuru	1986	2.50	5.00	10.00

TIMELESS

Number	Title (A Side/B Side)	Yr	VG	VG+	NM
SJP-253	Africa	1990	3.00	6.00	12.00

UPFRONT

Number	Title (A Side/B Side)	Yr	VG	VG+	NM
150	Spotlight	1973	3.00	6.00	12.00

SANDFORD, CHRIS

45s

FONTANA

Number	Title (A Side/B Side)	Yr	VG	VG+	NM
1534	(I Wish They Wouldn't Always Say) I Sound Like the Guy from USA Blues/Little Man-Nobody Cares	1965	3.00	6.00	12.00

SANDLER AND YOUNG

Also known as "Tony Sandler and Ralph Young."

45s

CAPITOL

Number	Title (A Side/B Side)	Yr	VG	VG+	NM
2083	In the Sunshine Days/Seven Lonely Days	1968	—	3.00	6.00
2157	Cotton Fields/Can I Trust You	1968	—	3.00	6.00
2333	I Sing Noel/Santa Claus Is Coming to Town	1968	—	3.00	6.00
2362	Life Is/Something Is Happening	1968	—	3.00	6.00
2423	Cuando Sali De Cuba/Viva El Amor	1969	—	3.00	6.00
2578	Heather/Pretty Things Come in Twos	1969	—	2.50	5.00
2636	Brazilian Love Song/On Days Like This	1969	—	2.50	5.00
5590	Let It Be Now/When Summer Is Gone	1966	—	3.00	6.00
5795	Chicago/Dominique	1966	—	3.00	6.00
5873	C'est Si Bon/Walk an Autumn Day with Me	1967	—	3.00	6.00
5928	More and More/Imagine Me	1967	—	3.00	6.00

P.I.P.

Number	Title (A Side/B Side)	Yr	VG	VG+	NM
6514	Medley: I Believe-Ave Maria/(B-side unknown)	1975	—	2.00	4.00

Albums

CAPITOL

Number	Title (A Side/B Side)	Yr	VG	VG+	NM
ST-159	Together	1968	3.00	6.00	12.00
ST-241	Pretty Things Come in Twos	1969	3.00	6.00	12.00
ST-449	Honey Come Back	1970	3.00	6.00	12.00
ST 2598 [S]	Side by Side	1966	3.75	7.50	15.00
T 2598 [M]	Side by Side	1966	3.00	6.00	12.00
—also known as "Tony Sandler and Ralph Young"					
ST 2686 [S]	On the Move	1967	3.75	7.50	15.00
T 2686 [M]	On the Move	1967	3.00	6.00	12.00
ST 2802 [S]	More and More	1967	3.00	6.00	12.00
T 2802 [M]	More and More	1967	3.75	7.50	15.00
ST 2967	The Christmas World of Sandler and Young	1968	3.00	6.00	12.00

HOLIDAY

Number	Title (A Side/B Side)	Yr	VG	VG+	NM
HDY 1942	Happy Holidays!	1981	2.00	4.00	8.00
—Reissue of True Value 2 (almost identical front cover, different back cover)					

RALTON

Number	Title (A Side/B Side)	Yr	VG	VG+	NM
SY 200	Re-Discover Christmas	19??	3.75	7.50	15.00
—Has same contents as "Happy Holidays, Volume 11"; is this the original?					

TRUE VALUE

Number	Title (A Side/B Side)	Yr	VG	VG+	NM
1	Happy Holidays, Album Eleven	1975	2.50	5.00	10.00
—Sold only at True Value Hardware stores					
2	Happy Holidays! Album Twelve	1976	2.50	5.00	10.00
—Sold only at True Value Hardware stores					

SANDMEN, THE (1)

45s

BLUE JAY

Number	Title (A Side/B Side)	Yr	VG	VG+	NM
5002	If You Want Me/Searching for a New Love	1965	6.25	12.50	25.00

SANDMEN, THE (2)

BROOK BENTON was in this group.

45s

OKEH

Number	Title (A Side/B Side)	Yr	VG	VG+	NM
7052	When I Grow Too Old to Dream/Somebody to Love	1955	12.50	25.00	50.00

SANDPIPERS, THE

45s

A&M

Number	Title (A Side/B Side)	Yr	VG	VG+	NM
806	Guantanamera/What Makes You Dream, Pretty Girl	1966	—	3.00	6.00
819	Louie Louie/Things We Said Today	1966	2.00	4.00	8.00
835	La Bamba/For Baby	1967	—	3.00	6.00
851	It's Over/Glass	1967	—	3.00	6.00
861	Woman/Bon Soir Dame	1967	—	3.00	6.00
880	Softly, As I Leave You/Cuando Sali De Cuba	1967	—	3.00	6.00
939	Wooden Heart/Quando M'annamoro	1968	—	3.00	6.00
968	Softly/Cancion de Amor	1968	—	3.00	6.00
997	Suzanne/Let Go!	1968	—	3.00	6.00
1085	Temptations/Wave	1969	—	3.00	6.00
1116	Kum-Ba-Ya/Yellow Days	1969	—	3.00	6.00
1134	Come Saturday Morning/Pretty Flamingo	1969	—	3.00	6.00
1185	Come Saturday Morning/To Put Up with You	1970	—	2.50	5.00
1208	Beyond the Valley of the Dolls/Santo Domingo	1970	—	2.50	5.00
1227	Free to Carry On/The Whole World in His Hands	1970	—	2.50	5.00
1249	Drifter/Sound of Love	1971	—	2.50	5.00
1280	Chotta Matte Kudasel/Free to Carry On	1971	—	2.50	5.00
1306	Never My Love/Leland Loftis	1971	—	2.50	5.00
1314	A Gift of Song/Never My Love	1971	—	2.50	5.00
1372	Old Fashioned Love Song/Never Can Say Goodbye	1972	—	2.50	5.00
1388	The World Is a Circle/(Baby I Could Be) So Good at Lovin' You	1972	—	2.50	5.00

Albums

A&M

Number	Title (A Side/B Side)	Yr	VG	VG+	NM
LP-117 [M]	Guantanamera	1966	3.00	6.00	12.00
LP-125 [M]	The Sandpipers	1967	3.75	7.50	15.00
SP-3525 [(2)]	Foursider	1973	3.00	6.00	12.00
SP-4117 [S]	Guantanamera	1966	3.75	7.50	15.00
SP-4125 [S]	The Sandpipers	1967	3.00	6.00	12.00
SP-4135	Misty Roses	1967	3.00	6.00	12.00
SP-4147	Softly	1968	3.00	6.00	12.00
SP-4159	The Spanish Album	1969	3.00	6.00	12.00
SP-4180	The Wonder of You	1969	3.00	6.00	12.00
SP-4246	Greatest Hits	1970	3.00	6.00	12.00
SP-4262	Come Saturday Morning	1970	3.00	6.00	12.00
SP-4328	A Gift of Song	1972	3.00	6.00	12.00
SP-6014 [(2)]	Foursider	198?	2.50	5.00	10.00
—Reissue of 3525					

SANDS, JODIE

45s

ABC-PARAMOUNT

Number	Title (A Side/B Side)	Yr	VG	VG+	NM
10337	We Had Words/Uno Momento	1962	3.00	6.00	12.00
10376	Hello, Heartache/This Little Fool	1962	3.00	6.00	12.00
10451	Time to Love/Charming Little Barefoot	1963	3.00	6.00	12.00

BERNLO

Number	Title (A Side/B Side)	Yr	VG	VG+	NM
1003	Love Me Always/Everybody Needs Somebody	1957	6.25	12.50	25.00

CHANCELLOR

Number	Title (A Side/B Side)	Yr	VG	VG+	NM
1003	With All My Heart/More Than Only Friends	1957	6.25	12.50	25.00
1005	If You're Not Completely Satisfied/Sayonara	1957	5.00	10.00	20.00
1009	The Way I Love You/Tantalizin' Love	1957	5.00	10.00	20.00
1015	Love Me Again/All I Ask of You	1958	5.00	10.00	20.00
1023	Someday/Always in My Heart	1958	5.00	10.00	20.00

PARIS

Number	Title (A Side/B Side)	Yr	VG	VG+	NM
543	I'd Cry No Tears/Kiss By Kiss	1960	3.75	7.50	15.00
551	Love Me Forever/Give Me a Break	1960	3.75	7.50	15.00

SIGNATURE

Number	Title (A Side/B Side)	Yr	VG	VG+	NM
12015	Turnabout Heart/Solo A Te Mio Amor	1959	3.75	7.50	15.00

TEEN

Number	Title (A Side/B Side)	Yr	VG	VG+	NM
109	Love Me Always/Everybody Needs Somebody	1955	10.00	20.00	40.00

THOR

Number	Title (A Side/B Side)	Yr	VG	VG+	NM
101	Hold Me/What Does It Mean	1959	5.00	10.00	20.00

SANDS, TOMMY

45s

ABC-PARAMOUNT

Number	Title (A Side/B Side)	Yr	VG	VG+	NM
10466	Connie/Young Man's Fancy	1963	2.50	5.00	10.00
10480	Cinderella/Only 'Cause I'm Lonely	1963	2.50	5.00	10.00
10539	Won't You Be My Girl/Ten Dollars and a Clean White Shirt	1964	2.50	5.00	10.00
10591	Something More/Kisses (Love Theme)	1964	2.50	5.00	10.00

CAPITOL

Number	Title (A Side/B Side)	Yr	VG	VG+	NM
F3639	Teen-Age Crush/Hep Dee Hootie	1957	6.25	12.50	25.00
F3690	Ring-A-Ding-A-Ding/My Love Song	1957	6.25	12.50	25.00
F3723	Goin' Steady/Ring My Phone	1957	6.25	12.50	25.00
F3743	Let Me Be Loved/Fantastically Foolish	1957	5.00	10.00	20.00
F3810	A Swingin' Romance/Man, Like Wow!	1957	5.00	10.00	20.00
F3867	Sing, Boy, Sing/Crazy 'Cause I Love You	1957	5.00	10.00	20.00
F3953	Teenage Doll/Hawaiian Rock	1958	5.00	10.00	20.00
F3985	Big Date/After the Senior Prom	1958	5.00	10.00	20.00
F4036	Blue Ribbon Baby/I Love You Because	1958	5.00	10.00	20.00
F4082	Bigger Than Texas/The Worryin' Kind	1958	5.00	10.00	20.00
F4160	Is It Ever Gonna Happen/I Ain't Gittin' Rid of You	1959	3.75	7.50	15.00
F4231	Sinner Man/Bring Me Your Love	1959	3.75	7.50	15.00
F4259	I'll Be Seeing You/That's the Way I Am	1959	3.75	7.50	15.00
F4259 [PS]	I'll Be Seeing You/That's the Way I Am	1959	7.50	15.00	30.00
4316	You Hold the Future/I Gotta Have You	1959	3.75	7.50	15.00
4366	That's Love/Crossroads	1960	3.75	7.50	15.00
4405	The Old Oaken Bucket/These Are the Things You Are	1960	3.75	7.50	15.00
4470	Doctor Heartache/On and On	1960	3.75	7.50	15.00
4580	Love in a Goldfish Bowl/I Love My Baby	1961	3.00	6.00	12.00
4611	Rainbow/Remember Me to Jennie	1961	3.00	6.00	12.00
4660	Wrong Side of Love/Jimmy's Song	1961	3.00	6.00	12.00

IMPERIAL

Number	Title (A Side/B Side)	Yr	VG	VG+	NM
66174	As Long As I'm Travelin'/It's the Only One I've Got	1966	2.00	4.00	8.00
66229	Second Star to the Left/Candy Store Prophet	1967	2.00	4.00	8.00

LIBERTY

Number	Title (A Side/B Side)	Yr	VG	VG+	NM
55807	Love's Funny/One Rose Today, One Rose Tomorrow	1965	2.00	4.00	8.00
55842	The Statue/Little Rosita	1965	2.00	4.00	8.00
55864	Waitin' in Your Welfare Line/Don't Do It Darlin'	1966	—	—	—

—Unreleased

RCA VICTOR

Number	Title (A Side/B Side)	Yr	VG	VG+	NM
47-5435	Love Pains/Transfer	1953	7.50	15.00	30.00
47-5510	Roses Speak Louder Than Words/Spanish Coquita	1953	7.50	15.00	30.00
47-5628	A Dime and a Dollar/Life Is So Lonesome	1954	7.50	15.00	30.00
47-5697	Never Let Me Go/I Know About the Bees	1954	7.50	15.00	30.00
47-5800	Don't Drop It/A Place for Girls Like You	1954	7.50	15.00	30.00
47-6007	Kissin' Ain't No Fun/Something's Bound to Go Wrong	1955	7.50	15.00	30.00
47-6868	Don't Drop It/Love Pains	1957	5.00	10.00	20.00

SUPERSCOPE

Number	Title (A Side/B Side)	Yr	VG	VG+	NM
007	Seasons in the Sun/Ain't No Big Thing	1969	—	3.00	6.00

(NO LABEL)

Number	Title (A Side/B Side)	Yr	VG	VG+	NM
T 929 [DJ]	People in Love/That's All I Want from You	1957	12.50	25.00	50.00

—"Promotion Record" with no label name; used to promote the movie "Sing Boy Sing"; T 929 is catalog number of LP and the most prominent number on label

7-Inch Extended Plays

CAPITOL

Number	Title (A Side/B Side)	Yr	VG	VG+	NM
PRO 351 [DJ]	Goin' Steady/I Don't Know Why (I Just Do)//Graduation Day/A-You're Adorable (The Alphabet Song)	1957	10.00	20.00	40.00
—Promotional sampler from "Steady Date" album					
EAP 1-848	*Goin' Steady/Teach Me Tonight/Gonna Get a Girl/Somewhere Along the Way	1957	7.50	15.00	30.00
EAP 1-848 [PS]	Steady Date with Tommy Sands, Part 1	1957	7.50	15.00	30.00
EAP 2-848	Walkin' My Baby Back Home/Too Young to Go Steady//A-You're Adorable (The Alphabet Song)/Graduation Day	1957	7.50	15.00	30.00
EAP 2-848 [PS]	Steady Date with Tommy Sands, Part 2	1957	7.50	15.00	30.00
EAP 3-848	Ring My Phone/I Don't Know Why//Too Young/I Don't Care Who Knows It	1957	7.50	15.00	30.00
EAP 3-848 [PS]	Steady Date with Tommy Sands, Part 3	1957	7.50	15.00	30.00
EAP 1-851	*Teen-Age Crush/My Love Song/Hep Dee Hootie (Cutie Wootie)/Ring-a-Ding-a-Ding	1957	7.50	15.00	30.00
EAP 1-851 [PS]	Teen-Age Crush	1957	7.50	15.00	30.00
EAP 1-929	*I'm Gonna Walk and Talk with My Lord/Who Baby/Rock of Ages/Sing Boy Sing	1958	7.50	15.00	30.00
EAP 1-929 [PS]	Sing Boy Sing, Part 1	1958	7.50	15.00	30.00
EAP 2-929	(contents unknown)	1958	7.50	15.00	30.00
EAP 2-929 [PS]	Sing Boy Sing, Part 2	1958	7.50	15.00	30.00

Albums

CAPITOL

Number	Title (A Side/B Side)	Yr	VG	VG+	NM
T 848 [M]	Steady Date with Tommy Sands	1957	15.00	30.00	60.00
T 929 [M]	Sing Boy Sing	1958	15.00	30.00	60.00
T 1081 [M]	Sands Storm	1959	12.50	25.00	50.00
ST 1123 [S]	This Thing Called Love	1959	10.00	20.00	40.00
T 1123 [M]	This Thing Called Love	1959	7.50	15.00	30.00
ST 1239 [S]	When I'm Thinking of You	1960	10.00	20.00	40.00
T 1239 [M]	When I'm Thinking of You	1960	7.50	15.00	30.00
ST 1364 [S]	Sands at the Sands	1960	10.00	20.00	40.00
T 1364 [M]	Sands at the Sands	1960	7.50	15.00	30.00
ST 1426 [S]	Dream with Me	1961	10.00	20.00	40.00
T 1426 [M]	Dream with Me	1961	7.50	15.00	30.00

GREEN LINNET

Number	Title (A Side/B Side)	Yr	VG	VG+	NM
SIF-3044	Singing of the Times	1989	3.00	6.00	12.00

SANDY, FRANK

45s

MARK

Number	Title (A Side/B Side)	Yr	VG	VG+	NM
138	Shamrock/Here She Comes	1959	10.00	20.00	40.00

MGM

Number	Title (A Side/B Side)	Yr	VG	VG+	NM
12626	Somebody Loves Me/Tarantella Rock	1958	12.50	25.00	50.00
12678	Let's Go Rock 'N' Roll/Midnight Stomp	1958	25.00	50.00	100.00

SANDY AND DICK

Also see DICK ST. JOHN.

45s

CONGRESS

Number	Title (A Side/B Side)	Yr	VG	VG+	NM
6015	Groove With What You Got/Sing Along with Groove With What You Got	1970	2.00	4.00	8.00
6021	Sweet Sweet Lovin'/Quick Like a Bunny	1970	2.00	4.00	8.00

SANETTES, THE

45s

OHN-J

Number	Title (A Side/B Side)	Yr	VG	VG+	NM
1001	Merry Christmas/Blessings From Above	1964	2.50	5.00	10.00

SANG, SAMANTHA

45s

ATCO

Number	Title (A Side/B Side)	Yr	VG	VG+	NM
6705	Don't Let It Happen Again/Love of a Woman	1969	—	3.00	6.00
6875	Nothing in the World Like Love/Mia Bamba	1972	—	2.50	5.00

PRIVATE STOCK

Number	Title (A Side/B Side)	Yr	VG	VG+	NM
45178	Emotion/When Love Is Gone	1977	—	2.00	4.00
—Originals have brown labels					
45178	Emotion/When Love Is Gone	1978	—	—	3.00
—Second pressings have skyline labels					
45188	You Keep Me Dancing/Change of Heart	1978	—	—	3.00

UNITED ARTISTS

Number	Title (A Side/B Side)	Yr	VG	VG+	NM
XW1297	I'll Never Get Enough of You/From Dance to Love	1979	—	—	3.00
1313	In the Midnight Hour/Now	1979	—	—	3.00

Albums

LIBERTY

Number	Title (A Side/B Side)	Yr	VG	VG+	NM
LN-10017	From Dance to Love	1980	2.00	4.00	8.00

—Budget-line reissue

PRIVATE STOCK

Number	Title (A Side/B Side)	Yr	VG	VG+	NM
PS-7009	Emotion	1978	2.50	5.00	10.00

UNITED ARTISTS

Number	Title (A Side/B Side)	Yr	VG	VG+	NM
UA-LA965-H	From Dance to Love	1979	2.50	5.00	10.00

SANS, PEGGY

45s

TOLLIE

Number	Title (A Side/B Side)	Yr	VG	VG+	NM
9018	Give Your Love/Snow Man	1964	2.50	5.00	10.00

SANTAMARIA, MONGO

12-Inch Singles

TAPPAN ZEE

Number	Title (A Side/B Side)	Yr	VG	VG+	NM
10912	A Mi No Me Enganan (You Better Believe It)/Watermelon Man	1979	2.00	4.00	8.00

45s

ATLANTIC

Number	Title (A Side/B Side)	Yr	VG	VG+	NM
2689	Feeling Alright/I Can't Get Next to You	1969	—	2.50	5.00
2717	Sunshine of Your Love/Heighty-Ho	1970	—	2.50	5.00
2770	Windjammer/No' Do'	1970	—	2.50	5.00
2794	Hippo Walk/Tell It	1971	—	2.50	5.00
2862	Come Cardella/I Wanna Know	1972	—	2.50	5.00

BATTLE

Number	Title (A Side/B Side)	Yr	VG	VG+	NM
45909	Watermelon Man/Don't Bother Me No More	1963	2.50	5.00	10.00
45917	Yeh-Yeh!/Get the Money	1963	2.00	4.00	8.00
45924	Creole/Fatback	1963	2.00	4.00	8.00

COLUMBIA

Number	Title (A Side/B Side)	Yr	VG	VG+	NM
43171	El Pussy Cat/Black-Eyed Peas	1964	—	3.00	6.00
43310	La Bamba/Streak O' Lean	1965	—	3.00	6.00
43613	I Got You/Walk On By	1966	—	3.00	6.00
43698	Call Me/El Bikini	1966	—	3.00	6.00
43962	Mongo's Boogaloo/Old Clothes	1967	—	3.00	6.00
44109	I Want to Know/Bossa-Negra	1967	—	3.00	6.00
44303	Funny Man/There Is a Mountain	1967	—	3.00	6.00
44397	Bloodshot/Juan Jose	1967	—	3.00	6.00
44452	Bonita/Sugar Cane Hombre	1968	—	3.00	6.00
44502	Cold Sweat/(Sittin' On) The Dock of the Bay	1968	—	3.00	6.00
44653	Hot Dog/Chili Beans	1968	—	3.00	6.00
44740	Cloud Nine/Son of a Preacher Man	1969	—	3.00	6.00
44812	Where We Are/(B-side unknown)	1969	—	3.00	6.00
44886	Twenty-Five Miles/El Tres	1969	—	3.00	6.00
44998	We Got Latin Soul/Getting It Out of My System	1969	—	3.00	6.00

FANTASY

Number	Title (A Side/B Side)	Yr	VG	VG+	NM
555	Tuli Bamba Charanga/Que Maravilloso Pachanga	196?	2.50	5.00	10.00
557	Para-Ti/Mongo's Theme	196?	2.50	5.00	10.00

RIVERSIDE

Number	Title (A Side/B Side)	Yr	VG	VG+	NM
4532	Cha Cha Blues/Tumba Le Le	196?	2.00	4.00	8.00
4574	Besito Pa Ti/Montuneando	196?	2.00	4.00	8.00
4586	Hammerhead/Tacos	196?	2.00	4.00	8.00
4587	Fatback/Sweet Tater Pie	1966	2.00	4.00	8.00

TAPPAN ZEE

Number	Title (A Side/B Side)	Yr	VG	VG+	NM
10920	A Mi No Me Enganan (You Better Believe It)/Sambita	1979	—	2.00	4.00

Albums

ATLANTIC

Number	Title (A Side/B Side)	Yr	VG	VG+	NM
SD 1567	Mongo '70	1970	3.00	6.00	12.00
SD 1581	Mongo's Way	1971	3.00	6.00	12.00
SD 1593	Mongo at Montreux	1972	3.00	6.00	12.00
SD 1621	Up from the Roots	1974	3.00	6.00	12.00
SD 8252	Feelin' Alright	1970	3.00	6.00	12.00

BATTLE

Number	Title (A Side/B Side)	Yr	VG	VG+	NM
B-6120 [M]	Watermelon Man!	1963	5.00	10.00	20.00
B-6129 [M]	Mongo at the Village Gate	1964	5.00	10.00	20.00
BS-96120 [S]	Watermelon Man!	1963	6.25	12.50	25.00
BS-96129 [S]	Mongo at the Village Gate	1964	6.25	12.50	25.00

COLUMBIA

Number	Title (A Side/B Side)	Yr	VG	VG+	NM
CS 1060	Mongo's Greatest Hits	1970	3.00	6.00	12.00
PC 1060	Mongo's Greatest Hits	198?	2.00	4.00	8.00
—Reissue with new prefix					
CL 2298 [M]	El Pussy Cat	1965	5.00	10.00	20.00
—With "Guaranteed High Fidelity" in black at bottom of red label					
CL 2298 [M]	El Pussy Cat	1965	3.00	6.00	12.00
—With "360 Sound Mono" in white at bottom of red label					
CL 2375 [M]	La Bamba	1965	3.75	7.50	15.00
CL 2375 [M]	Mr. Watermelon Man	196?	3.00	6.00	12.00
—Retitled reissue					
CL 2411 [M]	El Bravo	1966	3.00	6.00	12.00

Number	Title (A Side/B Side)	Yr	VG	VG+	NM
CL 2473 [M]	Hey! Let's Party	1966	3.00	6.00	12.00
CL 2612 [M]	Mongomania	1967	3.75	7.50	15.00
CL 2770 [M]	Mongo Santamaria Explodes at the Village Gate	1967	3.75	7.50	15.00
CS-9098 [S]	El Pussy Cat	1965	3.75	7.50	15.00
—With "360 Sound Stereo" in white at bottom of red label					
CS 9098 [S]	El Pussy Cat	1965	6.25	12.50	25.00
—With "360 Sound Stereo" in black at bottom of red label					
CS 9175 [S]	La Bamba	1965	5.00	10.00	20.00
CS 9175 [S]	Mr. Watermelon Man	196?	3.75	7.50	15.00
—Retitled reissue					
CS 9211 [S]	El Bravo	1966	3.75	7.50	15.00
CS 9273 [S]	Hey! Let's Party	1966	3.75	7.50	15.00
CS 9412 [S]	Mongomania	1967	3.00	6.00	12.00
CS 9570 [S]	Mongo Santamaria Explodes at the Village Gate	1967	3.00	6.00	12.00
CS 9653	Soul Bag	1968	3.75	7.50	15.00
CS 9780	Stone Soul	1969	3.75	7.50	15.00
CS 9937	Workin' on a Groovy Thing	1969	3.75	7.50	15.00
CS 9988	All Strung Out	1970	3.75	7.50	15.00
CONCORD JAZZ					
CJ-387	Ole Ola	1989	3.00	6.00	12.00
CONCORD PICANTE					
CJP-327	Soy Yo	1987	2.50	5.00	10.00
CJP-362	Soca Me Nice	1988	2.50	5.00	10.00
FANTASY					
OJC-276	Yambu	1987	2.50	5.00	10.00
—Reissue of 8012					
OJC-281	Sabroso	1987	2.50	5.00	10.00
—Reissue of 8058					
OJC-490	Mongo at the Village Gate	1991	3.00	6.00	12.00
—Reissue of Riverside 93529					
OJC-626	Summertime	1991	3.00	6.00	12.00
—Reissue of Pablo 2308 229					
3267 [M]	Yambu	1959	10.00	20.00	40.00
—Red vinyl					
3267 [M]	Yambu	1959	7.50	15.00	30.00
—Black vinyl					
3291 [M]	Mongo	1959	10.00	20.00	40.00
—Red vinyl					
3291 [M]	Mongo	1959	7.50	15.00	30.00
—Black vinyl					
3302 [M]	Our Man in Havana	1960	10.00	20.00	40.00
—Red vinyl					
3302 [M]	Our Man in Havana	1960	7.50	15.00	30.00
—Black vinyl					
3311 [M]	Mongo in Havana	1960	10.00	20.00	40.00
—Red vinyl					
3311 [M]	Mongo in Havana	1960	7.50	15.00	30.00
—Black vinyl					
3314 [M]	Sabroso	1960	10.00	20.00	40.00
—Red vinyl					
3314 [M]	Sabroso	1960	7.50	15.00	30.00
—Black vinyl					
3324 [M]	Arriba!	1961	10.00	20.00	40.00
—Red vinyl					
3324 [M]	Arriba!	1961	7.50	15.00	30.00
—Black vinyl					
3328 [M]	Mas Sabroso	1962	10.00	20.00	40.00
—Red vinyl					
3328 [M]	Mas Sabroso	1962	7.50	15.00	30.00
—Black vinyl					
3335 [M]	Viva Mongo!	1962	10.00	20.00	40.00
—Red vinyl					
3335 [M]	Viva Mongo!	1962	7.50	15.00	30.00
—Black vinyl					
3351 [M]	Mighty Mongo	1963	3.75	7.50	15.00
MPF-4529	Mongo Santamaria's Greatest Hits	198?	2.00	4.00	8.00
—Budget-line reissue					
8012 [S]	Yambu	1962	7.50	15.00	30.00
—Blue vinyl					
8012 [S]	Yambu	1962	5.00	10.00	20.00
—Black vinyl					
8032 [S]	Mongo	1962	7.50	15.00	30.00
—Blue vinyl					
8032 [S]	Mongo	1962	5.00	10.00	20.00
—Black vinyl					
8045 [S]	Our Man in Havana	1962	7.50	15.00	30.00
—Blue vinyl					
8045 [S]	Our Man in Havana	1962	5.00	10.00	20.00
—Black vinyl					
8055 [S]	Mongo in Havana	1962	7.50	15.00	30.00
—Blue vinyl					
8055 [S]	Mongo in Havana	1962	5.00	10.00	20.00
—Black vinyl					
8058 [S]	Sabroso	1962	7.50	15.00	30.00
—Blue vinyl					
8058 [S]	Sabroso	1962	5.00	10.00	20.00
—Black vinyl					
8067 [S]	Arriba!	1962	7.50	15.00	30.00
—Blue vinyl					
8067 [S]	Arriba!	1962	5.00	10.00	20.00
—Black vinyl					
8071 [S]	Mas Sabroso	1962	7.50	15.00	30.00
—Blue vinyl					
8071 [S]	Mas Sabroso	1962	5.00	10.00	20.00
—Black vinyl					
8087 [S]	Viva Mongo!	1962	7.50	15.00	30.00
—Blue vinyl					
8087 [S]	Viva Mongo!	1962	5.00	10.00	20.00
—Black vinyl					
8351 [S]	Mighty Mongo	1963	5.00	10.00	20.00
8373	Mongo Santamaria's Greatest Hits	1967	3.00	6.00	12.00
9431	Mongo Y La Lupe	1974	3.00	6.00	12.00
HARMONY					
H 30291	The Dock of the Bay	1971	2.50	5.00	10.00

Number	Title (A Side/B Side)	Yr	VG	VG+	NM
MILESTONE					
47012 [(2)]	Watermelon Man	1974	3.75	7.50	15.00
47038 [(2)]	Skins	1976	3.75	7.50	15.00
PABLO					
2308229	Summertime	1980	3.00	6.00	12.00
PRESTIGE					
24018 [(2)]	Afro Roots	1973	3.75	7.50	15.00
RIVERSIDE					
RLP-423 [M]	Go, Mongo!	1962	6.25	12.50	25.00
R-3008 [M]	Explosion	1967	6.25	12.50	25.00
RM-3008 [M]	Explosion	1968	6.25	12.50	25.00
RS-3008 [S]	Explosion	1968	3.75	7.50	15.00
RS-3045	Mongo Soul	1969	3.75	7.50	15.00
RM-3523 [M]	Mongo Introduces La Lupe	1963	5.00	10.00	20.00
RM-3529 [M]	Mongo at the Village Gate	1963	5.00	10.00	20.00
RM-3530 [M]	Mongo Santamaria Explodes!	1964	5.00	10.00	20.00
RS-9423 [S]	Go, Mongo!	1962	7.50	15.00	30.00
RS-93523 [S]	Mongo Introduces La Lupe	1963	6.25	12.50	25.00
RS-93529 [S]	Mongo at the Village Gate	1963	6.25	12.50	25.00
RS-93530 [S]	Mongo Santamaria Explodes!	1964	6.25	12.50	25.00
TICO					
LP-137 [10]	Chango	1955	20.00	40.00	80.00
LP-1037 [M]	Chango: Mongo Santamaria's Drums and Chants	1957	15.00	30.00	60.00
LP-1149 [M]	Mongo Santamaria's Drums and Chants	1967	5.00	10.00	20.00

SANTANA

Also see JOURNEY; CARLOS SANTANA.

Number	Title (A Side/B Side)	Yr	VG	VG+	NM
12-Inch Singles					
COLUMBIA					
AS 383 [DJ]	She's Not There (4:08) (2:58) (stereo/mono)	1977	3.75	7.50	15.00
AS 517 [DJ]	Well All Right (short) (long)	1978	3.00	6.00	12.00
AS 585 [DJ]	One Chain (Don't Make No Prison) (Long) (Short) (both on each side)	1978	2.00	4.00	8.00
AS 842 [DJ]	Love Theme from Spartacus/Song for My Brother/Swapan Tari	1980	3.00	6.00	12.00
AS 937 [DJ]	Winning/E Papa Ne	1981	2.00	4.00	8.00
AS 1266 [DJ]	Sensitive Kind/Sensitive Kind (Live)	1981	2.50	5.00	10.00
AS 1998 [DJ]	Say It Again (same on both sides)	1985	—	3.00	6.00
CAS 2068 [DJ]	I'm the One Who Loves You (same on both sides)	1985	—	3.00	6.00
CAS 2630 [DJ]	Veracruz (same on both sides)	1987	—	3.00	6.00
06762	Vera Cruz (Cool Mix)/Vera Cruz (Cool Whip Mix)	1987	—	3.00	6.00
10957	One Chain (Don't Make No Prison)/Life Is a Lady Holiday	1978	2.50	5.00	10.00
45s					
ARISTA					
13773	Maria Maria (featuring The Product G&B)/ Smooth (featuring Rob Thomas)	2000	—	2.00	4.00
COLUMBIA					
01050	Winning/The Brightest Star	1981	—	2.00	4.00
AE7 1064 [DJ]	All the Love of the Universe/Just in Time to See the Sun	1972	2.50	5.00	10.00
02178	The Sensitive Kind/American Gypsy	1981	—	2.00	4.00
02178 [PS]	The Sensitive Kind/American Gypsy	1981	—	2.50	5.00
02519	Searchin'/Tales of Kilimanjaro	1981	—	2.00	4.00
03160	Hold On/Oxun	1982	—	2.00	4.00
03268	Hold On	1982	—	3.00	6.00
—One-sided budget release					
03376	Nowhere to Run/Nueva York	1982	—	2.00	4.00
04034	Havana Moon/Lightnin'	1983	—	2.00	4.00
04758	Say It Again/Touchdown Raiders	1985	—	—	3.00
04758 [PS]	Say It Again/Touchdown Raiders	1985	—	2.00	4.00
04912	I'm the One Who Loves You/Right Now	1985	—	—	3.00
05677	They All Went to Mexico/Slow Movin' Outlaw	1985	—	—	3.00
—A-side: Willie Nelson and Carlos Santana; B-side: Willie and Lacy J. Dalton					
06654	Vera Cruz/Manuela	1987	—	2.00	4.00
07038	Vera Cruz (Remix)/Manuela	1987	—	—	3.00
07140	Praise/Love Is You	1987	—	—	3.00
10073	Mirage/Flor de Canela	1974	—	2.50	5.00
10088	Give and Take/Love Is Anew	1975	—	2.50	5.00
10336	Let It Shine/Tell Me Are You Tired	1976	—	2.50	5.00
10353	Dance Sister Dance (Baila Mi Hermana)/Let Me	1976	—	2.50	5.00
10421	Take Me with You/Europa (Earth's Cry Heaven's Smile)	1976	—	2.50	5.00
10481	Let the Children Play/Carnival	1977	—	2.50	5.00
10524	Give Me Love/Revelations	1977	—	2.50	5.00
10616	She's Not There/Zulu	1977	—	2.50	5.00
10677	Black Magic Woman/I'll Be Waiting	1978	—	2.50	5.00
10839	Well, All Right/Jericho	1978	—	2.50	5.00
10873	Stormy/Move On	1978	—	2.50	5.00
10938	One Chain (Don't Make a Prison)/Life Is a Lady-Holiday	1979	—	2.00	4.00
11144	You Know That I Love You/Aqua Marine	1979	—	2.00	4.00
11218	All I Ever Wanted/Lightning in the Sky	1980	—	2.00	4.00
45010	Jingo/Persuasion	1969	—	3.00	6.00
45010	Jin-Go-Lo-Ba/Persuasion	1969	—	3.00	6.00
—Same song, different A-side title					
45069	Evil Ways/Waiting	1970	—	3.00	6.00
45270	Black Magic Woman/Hope You're Feeling Better	1970	—	3.00	6.00
45270 [PS]	Black Magic Woman/Hope You're Feeling Better	1970	3.00	6.00	12.00
45330	Oye Como Va/Samba Pa Ti	1971	—	2.50	5.00
45330 [PS]	Oye Como Va/Samba Pa Ti	1971	2.00	4.00	8.00
45472	Everybody's Everything/Guajira	1971	—	2.50	5.00
45552	No One to Depend On/Taboo	1972	—	2.50	5.00
45552 [PS]	No One to Depend On/Taboo	1972	2.00	4.00	8.00
45753	Look Up/All the Love of the Universe	1973	—	2.50	5.00
45999	When I Look Into Your Eyes/Samba De Sausalito	1974	—	2.50	5.00
46067	Incident at Neshabur/Samba Pa Ti	1974	—	2.50	5.00
Albums					
CICADELIC					
1004	Santana '68	1988	3.00	6.00	12.00
COLUMBIA					
CS 9781	Santana	1969	3.75	7.50	15.00
—"360 Sound" on label					

Number	Title (A Side/B Side)	Yr	VG	VG+	NM
CS 9781	Santana	1970	2.50	5.00	10.00
—Orange label					
PC 9781	Santana	198?	2.00	4.00	8.00
CQ 30130 [Q]	Abraxas	1972	5.00	10.00	20.00
JC 30130	Abraxas	1977	2.00	4.00	8.00
KC 30130	Abraxas	1970	3.75	7.50	15.00
—Original copies have a poster					
KC 30130	Abraxas	197?	2.50	5.00	10.00
—With no poster					
PC 30130	Abraxas	1985	2.00	4.00	8.00
C 30595	Santana	1971	3.00	6.00	12.00
—Not the same album as CS 9781; this is often called "Santana III"					
CQ 30595 [Q]	Santana	1972	5.00	10.00	20.00
PC 30595	Santana	197?	2.00	4.00	8.00
KC 31610	Caravanserai	1972	3.00	6.00	12.00
PC 31610	Caravanserai	197?	2.00	4.00	8.00
PCQ 31610 [Q]	Caravanserai	1974	5.00	10.00	20.00
PC 32455	Welcome	1973	3.00	6.00	12.00
—No bar code on cover					
PC 32455	Welcome	1979	2.00	4.00	8.00
—With bar code on cover					
PCQ 32455 [Q]	Welcome	1974	5.00	10.00	20.00
JC 33050	Santana's Greatest Hits	1977	2.00	4.00	8.00
PC 33050	Santana's Greatest Hits	1974	3.00	6.00	12.00
—No bar code on cover					
PCQ 33050 [Q]	Santana's Greatest Hits	1974	5.00	10.00	20.00
PC 33135	Borboletta	1974	3.00	6.00	12.00
—No bar code on cover					
PC 33135	Borboletta	1979	2.00	4.00	8.00
—With bar code on cover					
PCQ 33135 [Q]	Borboletta	1974	5.00	10.00	20.00
PC 33576	Amigos	1976	3.00	6.00	12.00
—No bar code on cover					
PC 33576	Amigos	1979	2.00	4.00	8.00
—With bar code on cover					
PCQ 33576 [Q]	Amigos	1976	5.00	10.00	20.00
JC 34423	Festival	1977	3.00	6.00	12.00
JCQ 34423 [Q]	Festival	1977	5.00	10.00	20.00
PC 34423	Festival	198?	2.00	4.00	8.00
C2 34914 [(2)]	Moonflower	1977	3.75	7.50	15.00
FC 35600	Inner Secrets	1978	3.00	6.00	12.00
PC 35600	Inner Secrets	198?	2.00	4.00	8.00
—Budget-line reissue					
FC 36154	Marathon	1979	3.00	6.00	12.00
PC 36154	Marathon	198?	2.00	4.00	8.00
—Budget-line reissue					
C2 36590 [(2)]	Swing of Delight	1980	3.75	7.50	15.00
FC 37158	Zebop!	1981	3.00	6.00	12.00
PC 37158	Zebop!	198?	2.00	4.00	8.00
—Budget-line reissue					
FC 38122	Shango	1982	3.00	6.00	12.00
PC 38122	Shango	198?	2.00	4.00	8.00
—Budget-line reissue					
FC 39527	Beyond Appearances	1985	2.50	5.00	10.00
PC 39527	Beyond Appearances	198?	2.00	4.00	8.00
—Budget-line reissue					
HC 40130	Abraxas	1981	20.00	40.00	80.00
—Half-speed mastered edition					
FC 40272	Freedom	1987	2.50	5.00	10.00
C3X 44344 [(3)]	Viva Santana	1988	5.00	10.00	20.00
HC 47158	Zebop!	1981	10.00	20.00	40.00
—Half-speed mastered edition					

SANTANA, CARLOS

Also see SANTANA.

45s

COLUMBIA

Number	Title (A Side/B Side)	Yr	VG	VG+	NM
03925	Tales of Kilimanjaro/Watch Your Step	1983	—	2.00	4.00

Albums

COLUMBIA

Number	Title (A Side/B Side)	Yr	VG	VG+	NM
AS 573 [DJ]	The Solo Guitar of Devadip Carlos Santana	1979	3.75	7.50	15.00
JC 35686	Oneness/Silver Dreams-Golden Reality	1979	2.50	5.00	10.00
C2 36590 [(2)]	The Swing of Delight	1980	3.00	6.00	12.00
FC 38642	Havana Moon	1983	2.50	5.00	10.00
FC 40875	Blues for Salvador	1987	2.50	5.00	10.00

SANTANA, CARLOS, AND MAHAVISHNU JOHN MCLAUGHLIN

Also see each artist's individual listings.

Albums

COLUMBIA

Number	Title (A Side/B Side)	Yr	VG	VG+	NM
KC 32034	Love Devotion Surrender	1973	2.50	5.00	10.00
PC 32034	Love Devotion Surrender	197?	2.00	4.00	8.00
—Reissue with new prefix					

SANTANA, CARLOS, AND BUDDY MILES

Also see each artist's individual listings.

45s

COLUMBIA

Number	Title (A Side/B Side)	Yr	VG	VG+	NM
45666	Them Changes/Evil Ways	1972	—	2.50	5.00

Albums

COLUMBIA

Number	Title (A Side/B Side)	Yr	VG	VG+	NM
KC 31308	Carlos Santana and Buddy Miles! Live!	1972	3.00	6.00	12.00
PC 31308	Carlos Santana and Buddy Miles! Live!	197?	2.00	4.00	8.00
—Reissue with new prefix					

SANTO AND JOHNNY

45s

CANADIAN AMERICAN

Number	Title (A Side/B Side)	Yr	VG	VG+	NM
103	Sleep Walk/All Night Diner	1959	6.25	12.50	25.00
107	Tear Drop/The Long Walk Home	1959	3.75	7.50	15.00
111	Caravan/Summertime	1960	3.75	7.50	15.00
115	The Breeze and I/Lazy Day	1960	3.75	7.50	15.00
118	Love Lost/Annie	1960	3.75	7.50	15.00
120	Twistin' Bells/Bullseye!	1960	4.00	8.00	16.00
120 [PS]	Twistin' Bells/Bullseye!	1960	10.00	20.00	40.00
124	Hop Scotch/Sea Shells	1961	3.75	7.50	15.00
128	Theme from Come September/The Long Walk Home	1961	3.75	7.50	15.00
131	The Mouse/Birmingham	1961	3.75	7.50	15.00
132	Twistin' Bells/Christmas Day	1961	5.00	10.00	20.00
—B-side by Linda Scott					
137	Spanish Harlem/Stage to Cimarron	1962	3.00	6.00	12.00
141	Three Caballeros/Step Aside	1962	3.00	6.00	12.00
144	Misirlou/Tokyo Twilight	1962	3.00	6.00	12.00
148	Twistin' Bells/Manhattan	1962	3.00	6.00	12.00
151	On Your Mark/Manhattan	1963	3.00	6.00	12.00
155	The Wandering Sea/Manhattan Spiritual	1963	3.00	6.00	12.00
161	Love Letters in the Sand/Lido Beach	1963	3.00	6.00	12.00
164	I'll Remember (In the Still of the Night)/Song for Rosemary	1964	3.00	6.00	12.00
164 [PS]	I'll Remember (In the Still of the Night)/Song for Rosemary	1964	6.25	12.50	25.00
167	A Thousand Miles Away/Road Block	1964	3.00	6.00	12.00
167 [PS]	A Thousand Miles Away/Road Block	1964	6.25	12.50	25.00
174	Sugar Stroll/Rattler	1964	3.00	6.00	12.00
177	A Hard Day's Night/And I Love Her	1964	3.75	7.50	15.00
182	Goldfinger/Sleep Walk	1964	3.00	6.00	12.00
182 [PS]	Goldfinger/Sleep Walk	1964	6.25	12.50	25.00
189	Brazilian Summer/Off Tempo	1965	3.00	6.00	12.00
194	Watermelon Man/Return to Naples	1965	3.00	6.00	12.00
204	Come with Me/The Young World	1967	2.50	5.00	10.00

IMPERIAL

Number	Title (A Side/B Side)	Yr	VG	VG+	NM
66269	Live for Life/See You in September	1968	2.50	5.00	10.00
66292	Sleep Walk '68/It Must Be Him	1968	2.50	5.00	10.00

PAUSA

Number	Title (A Side/B Side)	Yr	VG	VG+	NM
703	Come Back Soldier/Flamingo	1976	—	2.50	5.00

UNITED ARTISTS

Number	Title (A Side/B Side)	Yr	VG	VG+	NM
970	Thunderball/Mister Kiss Kiss Bang Bang	1966	2.50	5.00	10.00

7-Inch Extended Plays

CANADIAN AMERICAN

Number	Title (A Side/B Side)	Yr	VG	VG+	NM
1001	(contents unknown)	1959	20.00	40.00	80.00
1001 [PS]	Santo and Johnny	1959	20.00	40.00	80.00

Albums

CANADIAN AMERICAN

Number	Title (A Side/B Side)	Yr	VG	VG+	NM
CALP-1001 [M]	Santo & Johnny	1959	15.00	30.00	60.00
SCALP-1001 [S]	Santo & Johnny	1959	20.00	40.00	80.00
CALP-1002 [M]	Encore	1960	10.00	20.00	40.00
SCALP-1002 [S]	Encore	1960	12.50	25.00	50.00
CALP-1004 [M]	Hawaii	1961	10.00	20.00	40.00
SCALP-1004 [S]	Hawaii	1961	12.50	25.00	50.00
CALP-1006 [M]	Come On In	1962	7.50	15.00	30.00
SCALP-1006 [S]	Come On In	1962	10.00	20.00	40.00
CALP-1008 [M]	Around the World with Santo and Johnny	1962	7.50	15.00	30.00
SCALP-1008 [S]	Around the World with Santo and Johnny	1962	10.00	20.00	40.00
CALP-1011 [M]	Off Shore	1963	7.50	15.00	30.00
SCALP-1011 [S]	Off Shore	1963	10.00	20.00	40.00
CALP-1014 [M]	In the Still of the Night	1963	7.50	15.00	30.00
SCALP-1014 [S]	In the Still of the Night	1963	10.00	20.00	40.00
CALP-1016 [M]	Wish You Love	1964	7.50	15.00	30.00
SCALP-1016 [S]	Wish You Love	1964	10.00	20.00	40.00
CALP-1017 [M]	The Beatles' Greatest Hits	1965	10.00	20.00	40.00
SCALP-1017 [S]	The Beatles' Greatest Hits	1965	12.50	25.00	50.00
CALP-1018 [M]	Mucho	1965	7.50	15.00	30.00
SCALP-1018 [S]	Mucho	1965	10.00	20.00	40.00

IMPERIAL

Number	Title (A Side/B Side)	Yr	VG	VG+	NM
LP-9363 [M]	Brilliant Guitar Sounds	1967	3.75	7.50	15.00
LP-12363 [S]	Brilliant Guitar Sounds	1967	5.00	10.00	20.00
LP-12366	Golden Guitars	1968	3.75	7.50	15.00
LP-12418	On the Road Again	1968	3.75	7.50	15.00

SANTOS, LARRY

45s

ATLANTIC

Number	Title (A Side/B Side)	Yr	VG	VG+	NM
2250	Someday (When I'm Gone)/True	1964	5.00	10.00	20.00
—With the Four Seasons on backup					

BIG TREE

Number	Title (A Side/B Side)	Yr	VG	VG+	NM
136	Life Is Beautiful/Touchin' You	1972	—	2.50	5.00

CASABLANCA

Number	Title (A Side/B Side)	Yr	VG	VG+	NM
844	Can't Get You Off My Mind/We Can't Hide It Anymore	1975	—	3.00	6.00
—With "Can't Get You Off My Mind" listed as "Side A"					
844	We Can't Hide It Anymore/Can't Get You Off My Mind	1976	—	2.00	4.00
—With "We Can't Hide It Anymore" listed as "Side A"					
869	You Are Everything I Need/Long, Long Time	1976	—	2.00	4.00
881	Magic Mountain/Don't Let the Music Stop	1977	—	2.00	4.00

EVOLUTION

Number	Title (A Side/B Side)	Yr	VG	VG+	NM
1007	Tomorrow Without Love/You Got Me Where You Want Me	1969	—	3.00	6.00
1010	Subway Man/Woman-Child	1969	—	3.00	6.00
1018	Great Divide/Paper Chase	1970	—	3.00	6.00
1024	Mornin' Sun/Wandering Man	1970	—	3.00	6.00
1029	Now That I Have Found You/Wandering Man	1970	—	3.00	6.00
1039	Let It End/Little Bit of You	1971	—	3.00	6.00
1043	I Love You More Than Everything/Let It End	1971	—	3.00	6.00

Albums

CASABLANCA

Number	Title (A Side/B Side)	Yr	VG	VG+	NM
NBLP 7030	You Are Everything I Need	1976	3.00	6.00	12.00
NBLP 7061	Don't Let the Music Stop	1977	3.00	6.00	12.00

EVOLUTION

Number	Title (A Side/B Side)	Yr	VG	VG+	NM
2002	Just a Man	1969	5.00	10.00	20.00
2015	Morning Sun	1971	3.75	7.50	15.00

SAPODILLA PUNCH

Albums

PHILIPS

Number	Title (A Side/B Side)	Yr	VG	VG+	NM
PHS 600312	Sapodilla Punch	1969	5.00	10.00	20.00

SAPPHIRES, THE (1)

Number	Title (A Side/B Side)	Yr	VG	VG+	NM
45s					
ABC-PARAMOUNT					
10559	Hearts Are Made to Be Broken/Let's Break Up for Awhile	1964	3.75	7.50	15.00
10590	Thank You for Loving Me/Our Love Is Everywhere	1964	3.75	7.50	15.00
10639	Gee I'm Sorry, Baby/Gotta Have Your Love	1965	3.75	7.50	15.00
10693	Evil One/How Could I Say Goodbye	1965	3.75	7.50	15.00
10753	You'll Never Stop Me from Loving You/Gonna Be a Big Thing	1965	3.75	7.50	15.00
10778	Our Love Is Everywhere/Slow Fizz	1966	3.75	7.50	15.00
ITZY					
8	Who Do You Love/Oh So Soon	1963	10.00	20.00	40.00
SWAN					
4143	Your True Love/Where Is Johnny Now	1963	3.75	7.50	15.00
4162	Who Do You Love/Oh So Soon	1963	3.75	7.50	15.00
4177	I Found Out Too Late/I've Got Mine, You Better Get Yours	1964	3.75	7.50	15.00
4184	Gotta Be More Than Friends/Moulin Rouge	1964	3.75	7.50	15.00
Albums					
COLLECTABLES					
COL-5007	Who Do You Love	198?	2.50	5.00	10.00
SWAN					
LP-513 [M]	Who Do You Love	1964	75.00	150.00	300.00

SAPPHIRES, THE (2)

Number	Title (A Side/B Side)	Yr	VG	VG+	NM
45s					
RCA VICTOR					
47-7357	Everyone Knows/So Glad	1958	5.00	10.00	20.00

SARATOGAS, THE

Number	Title (A Side/B Side)	Yr	VG	VG+	NM
45s					
IMPERIAL					
5738	I'll Be Loving You/Get It in a Minute	1961	7.50	15.00	30.00

SARDO, FRANKIE

Number	Title (A Side/B Side)	Yr	VG	VG+	NM
45s					
20TH FOX					
208	I Know Why and So Do You/When the Bells Stop Ringing	1960	5.00	10.00	20.00
221	Dream Lover/Bonnie, Bonnie	1960	6.25	12.50	25.00
ABC-PARAMOUNT					
9963	Class Room/Fake Out	1958	5.00	10.00	20.00
10003	No Love Like Mine/Oh Linda	1959	5.00	10.00	20.00
LIDO					
602	Kiss and Make Up/The Girl I'm Gonna Dream About	1959	5.00	10.00	20.00
MGM					
12621	May I/My Story of Love	1958	5.00	10.00	20.00
NEWTOWN					
5005	I Got You Where I Want You/Mr. Make Believe	1962	6.25	12.50	25.00
RAYNA					
5005	Ring of Love/She Taught Me How to Cry	1962	3.75	7.50	15.00
STUDIO					
9910	Just You Watch Me/I'm Sittin' at Home	1961	12.50	25.00	50.00

SARDO, JOHNNY

Number	Title (A Side/B Side)	Yr	VG	VG+	NM
45s					
CHOCK FULL-O-HITS					
104	(Hip Hop) Take a Ride with Me/Hollywood Sign	1958	25.00	50.00	100.00
WARNER BROS.					
5014	I Wanna Rock/Used Heart	1958	6.25	12.50	25.00
5044	Late, Late, Late to School/New Kid in Town	1959	6.25	12.50	25.00

SARNE, MIKE

Number	Title (A Side/B Side)	Yr	VG	VG+	NM
45s					
ASCOT					
2213	An Englishman Sings "America Swings"/Can't Wait for Spring	1966	2.50	5.00	10.00
CAMEO					
220	Come On Outside/Fountain of Love	1962	3.00	6.00	12.00
STELLAR					
1506	Come Outside/Fountain of Love	1962	3.00	6.00	12.00

SARSTEDT, PETER

Number	Title (A Side/B Side)	Yr	VG	VG+	NM
45s					
SIRE					
1028	Beirut/The Hollywood Sign	1978	—	2.00	4.00
UNITED ARTISTS					
50923	You're a Lady/What Makes One Man Feel	1972	—	2.50	5.00
WORLD PACIFIC					
77906	I Am a Cathedral/Blagged	1969	—	3.00	6.00
77911	Where Do You Go To (My Lovely)/Morning Mountain	1969	2.00	4.00	8.00
77919	Frozen Orange Juice/Aretuza Loser	1969	—	3.00	6.00
77919 [PS]	Frozen Orange Juice/Aretuza Loser	1969	2.50	5.00	10.00
77933	Step Into the Battlefield/I Thought It Was	1970	—	3.00	6.00
Albums					
UNITED ARTISTS					
UAS-5558	Every Word You Say Is Written Down	1971	2.50	5.00	10.00
WORLD PACIFIC					
WPS-21895	Where Do You Go To, My Lovely	1969	3.75	7.50	15.00
WPS-21899	As Though It Were a Movie	1969	3.75	7.50	15.00

SATAN AND THE DISCIPLES

Allegedly, this is FREDDY FENDER.

Number	Title (A Side/B Side)	Yr	VG	VG+	NM
45s					
GOLDBAND					
1188	Mummies Curse/Cat's Meow	1969	6.25	12.50	25.00
Albums					
GOLDBAND					
7750	Underground	1969	10.00	20.00	40.00

SATANS, THE

Number	Title (A Side/B Side)	Yr	VG	VG+	NM
Albums					
(NO LABEL)					
(no #) [M]	Raisin' Hell	1962	75.00	150.00	300.00

SATAN'S FOUR

Number	Title (A Side/B Side)	Yr	VG	VG+	NM
45s					
B.T. PUPPY					
515	I Can't Find the Girl on My Mind/Oh Cathy	1966	3.75	7.50	15.00
Albums					
B.T. PUPPY					
BTS-1010	Mixed Soul	1970	37.50	75.00	150.00
—With the Cinnamon Angels					

SATELLITES, THE

More than one group.

Number	Title (A Side/B Side)	Yr	VG	VG+	NM
45s					
ABC-PARAMOUNT					
10038	Linda Jean/Rockateen	1959	10.00	20.00	40.00
CLASS					
234	Heavenly Angel/You Ain't Sayin' Nothin'	1958	7.50	15.00	30.00
CUPID					
(no #)	Linda Jean/Rockateen	1959	20.00	40.00	80.00
D-M-G					
4001	Each Night/Darktown Strutters Ball	1960	7.50	15.00	30.00
MALYNN					
231	Heavenly Angel/You Ain't Sayin' Nothin'	1958	6.25	12.50	25.00
PALACE					
102	Buzz Buzz/We Like Birdland	1960	5.00	10.00	20.00
PARROT					
313	Bodacious/El San Juan	1966	6.25	12.50	25.00
UNITED ARTISTS					
141	I Found a Girl/My Piggie's Gotta Dance	1958	10.00	20.00	40.00

SATINTONES, THE

Number	Title (A Side/B Side)	Yr	VG	VG+	NM
45s					
MOTOWN					
1000	Sugar Daddy/My Beloved	1960	100.00	200.00	400.00
—Without strings. Matrix number of A-side is "MNT 12345"					
1000	Sugar Daddy/My Beloved	1960	100.00	200.00	400.00
—With strings. Matrix number of A-side is "1000 G-3"					
1006	Tomorrow and Always/A Love That Can Never Be	1961	62.50	125.00	250.00
—Without strings					
1006	Angel/A Love That Can Never Be	1961	375.00	750.00	1500.
1006	Tomorrow and Always/A Love That Can Never Be	1961	62.50	125.00	250.00
—With strings					
1010	I Know How It Feels/My Kind of Love	1961	50.00	100.00	200.00
1020	Zing Went the Strings of My Heart/Faded Letter	1962	50.00	100.00	200.00
TAMLA					
54026	Motor City/Going to the Hop	1960	200.00	400.00	800.00

SATISFACTIONS, THE (1)

Number	Title (A Side/B Side)	Yr	VG	VG+	NM
45s					
LIONEL					
3201	This Bitter Earth/Ol' Man River	1970	3.00	6.00	12.00
3205	One Light Two Lights/Turn Back the Tears	1970	3.00	6.00	12.00
3214	God I'm Losing My Baby/O-o-o La La	1971	3.75	7.50	15.00

SATISFACTIONS, THE (2)

Number	Title (A Side/B Side)	Yr	VG	VG+	NM
45s					
CHESAPEKE					
610	We Will Walk Together/Oh Why	1962	7.50	15.00	30.00

SATISFACTIONS, THE (3)

Number	Title (A Side/B Side)	Yr	VG	VG+	NM
45s					
IMPERIAL					
66170	Bring It All Down/Daddy, You Just Gotta Let Him In	1966	5.00	10.00	20.00
SMASH					
2059	Give Me Your Love/Stop Following Me	1966	3.75	7.50	15.00
2098	Take It or Leave It/You Got to Share	1967	7.50	15.00	30.00

SATISFACTIONS, THE (U)

These could be group (1) or (3).

Number	Title (A Side/B Side)	Yr	VG	VG+	NM
45s					
1-2-3					
1716	Gonna Get Right Tonight/Living on a Prayer, a Hope and a Hand-Me-Down	1969	3.00	6.00	12.00
TWIN TOWN					
714	Bad Times/Don't Tell Me	1966	6.25	12.50	25.00

SATISFIERS, THE

Number	Title (A Side/B Side)	Yr	VG	VG+	NM
45s					
CORAL					
61727	Come Away, Love/Where'll I Be Tomorrow Night	1956	3.75	7.50	15.00
61788	Over the Rainbow/Solitude	1957	3.75	7.50	15.00
61945	Will o' the Wisp/Remember That Crazy Rock and Roll	1958	3.75	7.50	15.00
JUBILEE					
5205	All or Nothing at All/Lies, Nothing But Lies	1955	5.00	10.00	20.00
VEGAS					
626	Ghost of a Chance/Fair Exchange	1960	3.00	6.00	12.00

SATURDAY, PATTY

Number	Title (A Side/B Side)	Yr	VG	VG+	NM
45s					
SWAN					
4022	Ladies Choice/Love Is a Beautiful Thing	1959	6.25	12.50	25.00

SATURDAY KNIGHTS, THE

Number	Title (A Side/B Side)	Yr	VG	VG+	NM
45s					
NOCTURNE					
1030	Sea Mist/Queen of the Nile	1963	12.50	25.00	50.00
SWAN					
4075	Ticonderoga/Tiger Lily	1961	5.00	10.00	20.00
4081	Hawaiian Tears/Texas Tommy	1961	5.00	10.00	20.00

SATURDAY'S CHILDREN

Number	Title (A Side/B Side)	Yr	VG	VG+	NM
45s					
ABC-PARAMOUNT					
10505	Raindrops/Cry Wind	1963	2.50	5.00	10.00
DUNWICH					
139	Born on Saturday/You Don't Know Better	1966	3.75	7.50	15.00
144	The Christmas Song/Deck Five	1967	3.75	7.50	15.00
156	Leave That Baby Alone/I Hardly Know Her	1967	3.75	7.50	15.00

SAUNDERS, LITTLE BUTCHIE

Number	Title (A Side/B Side)	Yr	VG	VG+	NM
45s					
HERALD					
485	Lindy Lou/Rock 'N' Roll Indian Dance	1956	12.50	25.00	50.00
491	Great Big Heart/I Wanna Holler	1956	12.50	25.00	50.00

SAUNDERS, MERL

Number	Title (A Side/B Side)	Yr	VG	VG+	NM
45s					
FANTASY					
600	High Heel Sneakers/(B-side unknown)	1964	2.50	5.00	10.00
620	Five More/Julia	1969	2.00	4.00	8.00
668	Save Mother Earth (Part 1)/Save Mother Earth (Part 2)	1971	—	3.00	6.00
678	My Problems Got Problems/Welcome to the Basement	1972	—	3.00	6.00
GALAXY					
747	I Pity the Fool/Tighten Up	1966	2.00	4.00	8.00
755	Soul Grooving/Up-Up and Away	1967	2.00	4.00	8.00
776	Iron Horse/A Little Bit of Righteousness	1970	2.00	4.00	8.00
Albums					
CRYSTAL CLEAR					
5006	Do I Move You	1980	5.00	10.00	20.00
—Direct-to-disc recording					
FANTASY					
MPF-4533	Keystone Encores, Vol. 1	1988	3.00	6.00	12.00
MPF-4534	Keystone Encores, Vol. 2	1988	3.00	6.00	12.00
MPF-4535	Live at the Keystone, Vol. 1	1988	3.00	6.00	12.00
MPF-4536	Live at the Keystone, Vol. 2	1988	3.00	6.00	12.00
8421	Heavy Turbulence	1972	3.75	7.50	15.00
9421	Fire Up	1973	5.00	10.00	20.00
—With Jerry Garcia and Tom Fogerty					
9460	Saunders	1974	3.75	7.50	15.00
9503	Leave Your Hat On	1976	3.00	6.00	12.00
79002 [(2)]	Live at the Keystone	198?	5.00	10.00	20.00
GALAXY					
8209	Soul Grooving	197?	3.75	7.50	15.00

SAVAGE, BOB

Number	Title (A Side/B Side)	Yr	VG	VG+	NM
45s					
ABC-PARAMOUNT					
9915	Rock Around the World/Butterfingers	1958	5.00	10.00	20.00

SAVAGE, DUKE, AND THE ARRIBINS

Number	Title (A Side/B Side)	Yr	VG	VG+	NM
45s					
ARGO					
5346	Your Love/Hey Baby	1959	10.00	20.00	40.00

SAVAGE GRACE

Number	Title (A Side/B Side)	Yr	VG	VG+	NM
45s					
REPRISE					
0924	Hymn to Freedom/Come On Down	1970	—	3.00	6.00
0952	Watchtower (All Alone)/Come On Down	1970	—	3.00	6.00
0988	Ivy/Save It for Me	1971	—	3.00	6.00
1022	Friends/Yonder	1971	—	3.00	6.00
Albums					
REPRISE					
RS 6399	Savage Grace	1970	3.75	7.50	15.00
RS 6484	Savage Grace 2	1971	3.75	7.50	15.00

SAVAGE RESURRECTION

Number	Title (A Side/B Side)	Yr	VG	VG+	NM
45s					
MERCURY					
72778	Thing in "E"/The Fox Is Sick	1968	3.00	6.00	12.00
Albums					
MERCURY					
SR-61156	Savage Resurrection	1968	25.00	50.00	100.00

SAVALAS, TELLY

Number	Title (A Side/B Side)	Yr	VG	VG+	NM
45s					
MCA					
40301	If/Rubber Bands and Bits of String	1974	—	2.00	4.00
40363	Help Me Make It Through the Night/You've Lost That Lovin' Feelin'	1975	—	2.00	4.00
40468	Who Loves Ya Baby/Nevertheless (I'm in Love with You)	1975	—	2.00	4.00
Albums					
AUDIO FIDELITY					
AFSD-6271	Telly Savalas	1975	3.75	7.50	15.00
MCA					
436	Telly	1974	3.75	7.50	15.00
2160	Who Loves Ya Baby	1976	3.75	7.50	15.00

SAVOY, RONNIE

Number	Title (A Side/B Side)	Yr	VG	VG+	NM
45s					
EPIC					
9619	I Hear Violins/The Marriage	1963	2.00	4.00	8.00
9708	Little Rascals/Sally Blue	1964	2.00	4.00	8.00
GONE					
5079	Ooh, What a Girl/Love Me As I Love You	1959	3.00	6.00	12.00
MGM					
12950	And the Heavens Cried/Big Chain	1960	5.00	10.00	20.00
13001	Bewitched/It's Gotta Be Love	1961	3.75	7.50	15.00
13042	Jungle Love Call/Your Cheatin' Heart	1961	3.75	7.50	15.00
PHILIPS					
40032	A Fool, A Loser, A Clown/Big Hand, Little Hand	1962	2.00	4.00	8.00
40071	Moonlight to Sunlight/21,000 Happiness Street	1962	2.00	4.00	8.00
WINGATE					
001	Memories Linger/Loving You	1965	6.25	12.50	25.00

SAVOY BROWN

Number	Title (A Side/B Side)	Yr	VG	VG+	NM
45s					
LONDON					
206	Everybody Loves a Drinkin' Man/Ride On Babe	1974	—	2.50	5.00
234	Walkin' 'n' Talkin'/Stranger Blues	1976	—	2.50	5.00
PARROT					
40034	Shake 'Em On Down/(B-side unknown)	1968	3.75	7.50	15.00
40037	Grits Ain't Groceries/She's Got a Ring in His Nose and a Ring on Her Hand	1969	2.00	4.00	8.00
40039	Train to Nowhere/Made Up My Mind	1969	2.00	4.00	8.00
40042	I'm Tired/Stay with Me Baby	1969	2.00	4.00	8.00
40046	Hard Way to Go/The Incredible Gnome Meets Jaxman	1970	—	3.00	6.00
40057	Poor Girl/Mr. Hare	1970	—	3.00	6.00
40060	Sitting and Thinking/(B-side unknown)	1971	—	3.00	6.00
40066	Tell Mama/Rock and Roll on the Radio	1971	—	3.00	6.00
40075	Coming Down Your Way/Can't Find You	1973	—	3.00	6.00
TOWN HOUSE					
1055	Run to Me/Georgie	1981	—	2.00	4.00
Albums					
GNP CRESCENDO					
GNPS-2193	Make Me Sweat	1988	2.50	5.00	10.00
GNPS-2196	Kings of Boogie	1989	2.50	5.00	10.00
LONDON					
APS 638	Boogie Brothers	1974	2.50	5.00	10.00
PS 659	Wire Fire	1975	2.50	5.00	10.00
PS 670	Skin 'n' Bone	1976	2.50	5.00	10.00
PS 718	Savage Return	1978	2.50	5.00	10.00
LC-50000	The Best of Savoy Brown	1977	2.50	5.00	10.00
PARROT					
PAS 71024	Getting to the Point	1968	6.25	12.50	25.00
PAS 71027	Blue Matter	1969	6.25	12.50	25.00
PAS 71029	A Step Further	1969	3.75	7.50	15.00
PAS 71036	Raw Sienna	1970	3.75	7.50	15.00
PAS 71042	Looking In	1970	3.75	7.50	15.00
PAS 71047	Street Corner Talking	1971	3.75	7.50	15.00
XPAS 71052	Hellbound Train	1972	3.75	7.50	15.00
XPAS 71057	Lion's Share	1972	3.75	7.50	15.00
XPAS 71059	Jack the Toad	1973	3.75	7.50	15.00
TOWN HOUSE					
ST-7002	Rock 'n' Roll Warriors	1981	3.00	6.00	12.00
SKBK-7003 [(2)]	Greatest Hits Live in Concert	1982	3.75	7.50	15.00

SAWBUCK

Number	Title (A Side/B Side)	Yr	VG	VG+	NM
Albums					
FILLMORE					
Z 31248	Sawbuck	1972	5.00	10.00	20.00

SAWYER, RAY

Also see DR. HOOK.

Number	Title (A Side/B Side)	Yr	VG	VG+	NM
45s					
CAPITOL					
4344	(One More Year of) Daddy's Little Girl/I Need That High (But I Can't Stand the Taste)	1976	—	2.00	4.00
4386	Red-Winged Blackbird/The One I'm Holding Now	1977	—	2.00	4.00
4416	Walls and Doors/I Need That HIgh (But I Can't Stand the Taste)	1977	—	2.00	4.00
4592	Dancing Fool/Rhythm Guitar	1978	—	2.00	4.00
4747	What I'm Holding/I Want Johnny's Job	1979	—	2.00	4.00
4820	Drinking Wine Alone/I Don't Feel Like Smilin'	1980	—	2.00	4.00
SANDY					
1030	Rockin' Satellite/Bells in My Heart	1961	10.00	20.00	40.00
1037	I'm Gonna Leave/You Gave Me the Right	1961	6.25	12.50	25.00
Albums					
CAPITOL					
ST-11591	Ray Sawyer	1976	2.50	5.00	10.00

SAXON, EDDIE, AND THE PARAMOUNTS

Number	Title (A Side/B Side)	Yr	VG	VG+	NM
45s					
EMPRESS					
106	Blues No More/If It's Meant to Be	1962	37.50	75.00	150.00
106 [DJ]	Blues No More	1962	50.00	100.00	200.00
—Single-sided promo					

SAXON, SKY

Later recorded with THE SEEDS. Also see RITCHIE MARSH.

45s

CONQUEST

Number	Title (A Side/B Side)	Yr	VG	VG+	NM
777	They Say/Go Ahead and Cry	1964	7.50	15.00	30.00

Albums

GNP CRESCENDO

Number	Title (A Side/B Side)	Yr	VG	VG+	NM
GNP-2040 [M]	A Full Spoon of Seedy Blues	1967	10.00	20.00	40.00
GNPS-2040 [S]	A Full Spoon of Seedy Blues	1967	7.50	15.00	30.00

SAYER, LEO

12-Inch Singles

WARNER BROS.

Number	Title (A Side/B Side)	Yr	VG	VG+	NM
PRO-A-699 [DJ]	Thunder in My Heart (Disco Version) (same on both sides)	1977	2.00	4.00	8.00

45s

WARNER BROS.

Number	Title (A Side/B Side)	Yr	VG	VG+	NM
7768	The Show Must Go On/Innocent Bystander	1974	2.00	4.00	8.00
7824	One Man Band/Drop Back	1974	—	3.00	6.00
8043	Long Tall Glasses/In My Life	1974	—	3.00	6.00
—First pressings have no A-side subtitle					
8043	Long Tall Glasses (I Can Dance)/In My Life	1975	—	2.50	5.00
—Later pressings add subtitle to A-side					
8097	One Man Band/Telepath	1975	—	2.50	5.00
8153	Moonlighting/Streets of Your Town	1975	—	2.50	5.00
8283	You Make Me Feel Like Dancing/Magdalena	1976	—	2.50	5.00
8319	How Much Love/I Hear the Laughter	1977	—	2.50	5.00
8332	When I Need You/I Think We Fell in Love Too Fast	1977	—	2.50	5.00
8465	Thunder in My Heart/Get the Girl	1977	—	2.50	5.00
8502	Easy to Love/Haunting Me	1977	—	2.50	5.00
8682	Raining in My Heart/No Looking Back	1978	—	2.00	4.00
8738	Don't Look Back/No Looking Back	1979	—	2.00	4.00
29904	Paris Dies in the Morning/We've Got Ourselves In Love	1982	—	2.00	4.00
29960	End of the Game/Heart	1982	—	2.00	4.00
49134	Oh Girl/Englishman in the U.S.A.	1979	—	2.00	4.00
49565	More Than I Can Say/Millionaire	1980	—	2.00	4.00
49657	Living in a Fantasy/Only Foolin'	1981	—	2.00	4.00
49714	Where Did We Go Wrong/She's Not Coming Back	1981	—	2.00	4.00
50060	Have You Ever Been in Love/I Don't Need Dreaming Anymore	1982	—	2.00	4.00

Albums

CHRYSALIS

Number	Title (A Side/B Side)	Yr	VG	VG+	NM
PV 41087	Another Year	1985	2.00	4.00	8.00
—Reissue of Warner Bros. 2885					
PV 41125	Endless Flight	1985	2.00	4.00	8.00
—Reissue of Warner Bros. 3101					
PV 41154	Thunder in My Heart	1985	2.00	4.00	8.00
—Reissue of Warner Bros. 3089					
PV 41198	Leo Sayer	1985	2.00	4.00	8.00
—Reissue of Warner Bros. 3200					
PV 41240	Here	1985	2.00	4.00	8.00
—Reissue of Warner Bros. 3374					

WARNER BROS.

Number	Title (A Side/B Side)	Yr	VG	VG+	NM
BS 2738	Silverbird	1973	3.00	6.00	12.00
BS 2836	Just a Boy	1974	2.50	5.00	10.00
BS 2885	Another Year	1975	2.50	5.00	10.00
BS 2962	Endless Flight	1976	2.50	5.00	10.00
BSK 3089	Thunder in My Heart	1977	2.50	5.00	10.00
BSK 3101	Endless Flight	1977	2.00	4.00	8.00
—Reissue of 2962					
BSK 3200	Leo Sayer	1978	2.50	5.00	10.00
BSK 3374	Here	1979	2.50	5.00	10.00
BSK 3483	Living in a Fantasy	1980	2.50	5.00	10.00
23560	World Radio	1982	2.50	5.00	10.00

SCAFFOLD, THE

With Mike McGear, Paul McCartney's brother.

45s

BELL

Number	Title (A Side/B Side)	Yr	VG	VG+	NM
701	Thank U Very Much/Ide B the First	1968	4.00	8.00	16.00
724	Do You Remember/Carry On Krow	1968	4.00	8.00	16.00
747	Lily the Pink/Buttons of Your Mind	1968	4.00	8.00	16.00
821	Charity Bubbles/Goose	1969	4.00	8.00	16.00
849	Jelly Covered Cloud/Liver Birds	1969	3.00	6.00	12.00

WARNER BROS.

Number	Title (A Side/B Side)	Yr	VG	VG+	NM
8001	Liverpool Lou/Ten Years After on Strawberry Jam	1974	—	3.00	6.00

Albums

BELL

Number	Title (A Side/B Side)	Yr	VG	VG+	NM
6018 [M]	Thank U Very Much	1968	12.50	25.00	50.00
—Mono copies are promo only					
6018 [S]	Thank U Very Much	1968	12.50	25.00	50.00

SCAGGS, BOZ

12-Inch Singles

COLUMBIA

Number	Title (A Side/B Side)	Yr	VG	VG+	NM
AS 380 [DJ]	Hard Times (same on both sides)	1977	2.00	4.00	8.00
11350	Look What You've Done to Me/Jojo	1980	2.50	5.00	10.00

45s

ATLANTIC

Number	Title (A Side/B Side)	Yr	VG	VG+	NM
2692	I'm Easy/I'll Be Long Gone	1969	2.50	5.00	10.00

COLUMBIA

Number	Title (A Side/B Side)	Yr	VG	VG+	NM
01023	You Can Have Me Anytime/Georgia	1981	—	2.00	4.00
02423	Jojo/Miss Sun	1981	—	—	3.00
—Reissue					
02424	Breakdown Dead Ahead/Look What You've Done to Me	1981	—	—	3.00
—Reissue					
07780	Heart of Mine/You'll Never Know	1988	—	—	3.00
07780 [PS]	Heart of Mine/You'll Never Know	1988	—	2.00	4.00
07981	Cool Running/You'll Never Know	1988	—	—	3.00
08068	What's Number 1/Claudia	1988	—	—	3.00
10027	Slow Dancer/Pain of Love	1974	—	3.00	6.00
10124	You Make It So Hard (To Say Goodbye)/There Is Something Else	1975	—	2.50	5.00
10319	It's Over/Harbor Lights	1976	—	2.50	5.00
10367	Lowdown/Harbor Lights	1976	—	2.50	5.00
10440	What Can I Say/We're All Alone	1976	—	2.50	5.00
10491	Lido Shuffle/We're All Alone	1977	—	2.50	5.00
10606	Hard Times/We're Waiting	1977	—	2.50	5.00
10606 [PS]	Hard Times/We're Waiting	1977	2.50	5.00	10.00
10679	Hollywood/A Clue	1978	—	2.50	5.00
11241	Breakdown Dead Ahead/Isn't It Time	1980	—	2.00	4.00
11281	Jojo/Do Like You Do in New York	1980	—	2.00	4.00
11349	Look What You've Done to Me/Simone	1980	—	2.00	4.00
11406	Miss Sun/Dinah Flo	1980	—	2.00	4.00
45353	We Were Always Sweethearts/Painted Bells	1971	—	3.00	6.00
45408	Near You/Downright Woman	1971	—	3.00	6.00
45540	Here to Stay/Runnin' Blue	1972	—	3.00	6.00
45670	Dinah Flo/He's a Fool for You	1972	—	3.00	6.00
46025	You Make It So Hard (To Say Goodbye)/There Is Someone Else	1974	—	3.00	6.00

FULL MOON

Number	Title (A Side/B Side)	Yr	VG	VG+	NM
49676	You Make It So Hard (To Say Goodbye)/ Something's Missing in My Life	1981	—	2.00	4.00
—B-side by Lady Sylvia					

VIRGIN

Number	Title (A Side/B Side)	Yr	VG	VG+	NM
S7-18048	I'll Be the One/Time Change	1994	—	2.00	4.00
S7-19529	It All Went Down the Drain/I've Got Your Love	1997	—	—	3.00
S7-19651	Fly Like a Bird/Sick and Tired	1997	—	—	3.00

Albums

ATLANTIC

Number	Title (A Side/B Side)	Yr	VG	VG+	NM
SD 8239	Boz Scaggs	1969	3.00	6.00	12.00
SD 19166	Boz Scaggs	1977	2.00	4.00	8.00

COLUMBIA

Number	Title (A Side/B Side)	Yr	VG	VG+	NM
A2S 71 [(2) DJ]	KSAN Live Concert	1974	12.50	25.00	50.00
—Promo-only set released in plain cardboard jacket					
AS 203 [DJ]	The Boz Scaggs Sampler	1976	5.00	10.00	20.00
KC 30454	Moments	1971	2.50	5.00	10.00
PC 30454	Moments	197?	2.00	4.00	8.00
KC 30976	Boz Scaggs & Band	1971	2.50	5.00	10.00
PC 30976	Boz Scaggs & Band	197?	2.00	4.00	8.00
KC 31384	My Time	1972	2.50	5.00	10.00
PC 31384	My Time	197?	2.00	4.00	8.00
KC 32760	Slow Dancer	1974	3.00	6.00	12.00
—Original cover has Boz Scaggs on a beach in only a bathing suit					
KC 32760	Slow Dancer	1974	2.50	5.00	10.00
—Second cover has a male dancer who is not Boz Scaggs					
PC 32760	Slow Dancer	197?	2.00	4.00	8.00
JC 33920	Silk Degrees	1976	2.50	5.00	10.00
PC 33920	Silk Degrees	1985	2.00	4.00	8.00
—Budget-line reissue					
FC 36106	Middle Man	1980	2.50	5.00	10.00
PC 36106	Middle Man	198?	2.00	4.00	8.00
—Budget-line reissue					
FC 36841	Hits!	1980	2.50	5.00	10.00
PC 36841	Hits!	198?	2.00	4.00	8.00
—Budget-line reissue					
PC 37249	Down Two Then Left	198?	2.00	4.00	8.00
—Budget-line reissue					
JC 37429	Down Two Then Left	1977	2.50	5.00	10.00
FC 40463	Other Roads	1988	2.50	5.00	10.00
HC 43920	Silk Degrees	1981	7.50	15.00	30.00
—Half-speed mastered edition					

SCARLETS, THE (1)

45s

DOT

Number	Title (A Side/B Side)	Yr	VG	VG+	NM
16004	Stampede/Park Avenue	1959	6.25	12.50	25.00

PRINCE

Number	Title (A Side/B Side)	Yr	VG	VG+	NM
1207	Stampede/Park Avenue	1959	12.50	25.00	50.00

SCARLETS, THE (2)

45s

EVENT

Number	Title (A Side/B Side)	Yr	VG	VG+	NM
4287	Dear One/I've Lost	1958	10.00	20.00	40.00

RED ROBIN

Number	Title (A Side/B Side)	Yr	VG	VG+	NM
128	Dear One/I've Lost	1954	125.00	250.00	500.00
133	Darling, I'm Yours/Love Doll	1954	125.00	250.00	500.00
135	True Love/Cry Baby	1955	125.00	250.00	500.00
138	Kiss Me/Indian Fever	1955	150.00	300.00	600.00

SCARLETS, THE (3)

45s

TOWER

Number	Title (A Side/B Side)	Yr	VG	VG+	NM
144	I've Had It/You Don't Love Me	1965	2.50	5.00	10.00

SCARLETS, THE (U)

Could be group (1).

45s

FURY

Number	Title (A Side/B Side)	Yr	VG	VG+	NM
1036	Truly Yours/East of the Sun	1960	7.50	15.00	30.00

SCAVENGERS, THE

45s

FENTON

Number	Title (A Side/B Side)	Yr	VG	VG+	NM
987	Curfew/Oasis	1964	12.50	25.00	50.00

MOBILE FIDELITY

Number	Title (A Side/B Side)	Yr	VG	VG+	NM
1005	The Angels Listened In/My Love Waits for Me	1963	7.50	15.00	30.00
1212	Devil's Reef/Little Annie	1963	7.50	15.00	30.00

STARS OF HOLLYWOOD

Number	Title (A Side/B Side)	Yr	VG	VG+	NM
1210	Shot Gun/Cream Puff	1963	12.50	25.00	50.00
1211	Shot Gun/Zip Code	1963	12.50	25.00	50.00

—"Cream Puff" and "Zip Code" are different titles for the same recording

Number	Title (A Side/B Side)	Yr	VG	VG+	NM
1212	Devil's Reef/Little Annie	1963	12.50	25.00	50.00
SUEMI					
4552	Bogus/Ghost Riders '65	1965	6.25	12.50	25.00

SCENE, THE

Number	Title (A Side/B Side)	Yr	VG	VG+	NM
45s					
B.T. PUPPY					
533	Scenes (From Another World)/You're in a Bad Way	1967	2.50	5.00	10.00

SCHAFF, MURRAY, AND THE ARISTOCRATS

Number	Title (A Side/B Side)	Yr	VG	VG+	NM
45s					
JOSIE					
788	The Unfinished Rock/Ooh How I Love Ya	1956	7.50	15.00	30.00
KING					
4977	How Many Miles/Tombstone Number 9	1956	7.50	15.00	30.00

SCHIFRIN, LALO

Listings include many of his soundtrack LPs.

Number	Title (A Side/B Side)	Yr	VG	VG+	NM
12-Inch Singles					
CTI					
OJ-2	Flamingo/Quiet Village/Jaws	1976	3.75	7.50	15.00
PABLO					
RD-11004	Unicorn/Free Ride	1977	3.00	6.00	12.00
—With Dizzy Gillespie					
TABU					
5520	No One Home/(Instrumental)	1979	3.00	6.00	12.00
45s					
20TH CENTURY					
2150	Ape Shuffle/Escape from Tomorrow	1974	—	2.50	5.00
2205	Bolero/Dona Donna	1975	—	2.50	5.00
AUDIO FIDELITY					
084	The Ugly Duckling/(B-side unknown)	196?	2.50	5.00	10.00
A&M					
1756	Theme from "The Master Gunfighter"/Theme from "The Trial of Billy Jack"	1975	—	2.50	5.00
CTI					
29	Turning Point/Flamingo	1976	—	2.00	4.00
36	Eagles in Love/Towering Toccata	1977	—	2.00	4.00
DOT					
17059	Mission Impossible/Jim on the Move	1967	2.50	5.00	10.00
MCA					
40748	Magic Carousel/Merry-Go-Round	1977	—	2.00	4.00
52175	Heliotrope Bouquet/The Entertainer	1983	—	2.00	4.00
—B-side by Marvin Hamlisch					
MGM					
13139	Broken Date/Good Life	1963	2.50	5.00	10.00
13151	Hud/Jive Orbit	1963	2.50	5.00	10.00
13163	Haunting/Theme from "Dime with a Halo"	1963	2.50	5.00	10.00
13224	Seven Faces of Dr. Lao/The Wave	1964	2.50	5.00	10.00
13251	Theme from "Rhino"/Rhino Bomp	1964	2.50	5.00	10.00
13425	The Cincinnati Kid/So Many Times	1965	2.00	4.00	8.00
13670	Venice After Dark/Our Venetian Affair	1967	2.00	4.00	8.00
14153	Burning Bridges/Kelly's Heroes	1970	—	3.00	6.00
14180	Theme from "Medical Center"/(B-side unknown)	1970	—	3.00	6.00
PABLO					
RB-11003	Unicorn/Free Ride	1977	—	2.00	4.00
—With Dizzy Gillespie					
PARAMOUNT					
0001	Self Destruct/The Getaway	1969	2.00	4.00	8.00
0002	Mannix/End Game	1969	2.00	4.00	8.00
TABU					
5509	Moonlight Gypsies/Prophecy of Love	1978	—	2.00	4.00
5519	No One Home/Middle of the Night	1979	—	2.00	4.00
TETRAGRAMMATON					
1533	Theme from "Che"/Embo Scada	1969	2.00	4.00	8.00
UNITED ARTISTS					
50649	What's New Pussycat/Pussycat, Pussycat, I Love You	1970	—	2.50	5.00
VERVE					
10290	Broken Date/Good Life	1963	2.00	4.00	8.00
10331	New Fantasy/Bachianas Brasilerias #5	1964	2.00	4.00	8.00
10365	Man from Thrush/Blues-A-Go-Go	1965	2.50	5.00	10.00
10434	The Wig/Beneath a Weeping Willow Shade	1966	2.00	4.00	8.00
10663	Theme from "Medical Center"/All for the Love of Sunshine	1971	2.00	4.00	8.00
10663	Agnus Dei/Sanctus Benedictus	1971	—	3.00	6.00
WARNER BROS.					
7173	Foxtail/That Night	1968	—	3.00	6.00
7263	Bullitt/That Night	1969	—	3.00	6.00
Albums					
AMERICAN INT'L.					
AILP 3003	The Amityville Horror	1979	2.50	5.00	10.00
AUDIO FIDELITY					
AFLP-1981 [M]	Bossa Nova — New Brazilian Jazz	1962	5.00	10.00	20.00
AFLP-2117 [M]	Eso Es Latino Jazz	1963	5.00	10.00	20.00
AFSD-5981 [S]	Bossa Nova — New Brazilian Jazz	1962	6.25	12.50	25.00
AFSD-6117 [S]	Eso Es Latino Jazz	1963	6.25	12.50	25.00
AFSD-6195	The Other Side of Lalo Schifrin	1968	3.75	7.50	15.00
COLGEMS					
COMO-5003 [M]	Murderer's Row	1967	12.50	25.00	50.00
COSO-5003 [S]	Murderer's Row	1967	25.00	50.00	100.00
CTI					
5000	Black Widow	1976	3.00	6.00	12.00
5003	Towering Toccata	1977	3.00	6.00	12.00
DOT					
DLP-3831 [M]	Music from Mission: Impossible	1967	7.50	15.00	30.00
DLP-3833 [M]	Cool Hand Luke	1968	12.50	25.00	50.00
DLP-25831 [S]	Music from Mission: Impossible	1967	10.00	20.00	40.00
DLP-25833 [S]	Cool Hand Luke	1968	12.50	25.00	50.00
DLP-25852	There's a Whole Lot of Schifrin Goin' On	1968	5.00	10.00	20.00
DRG					
SBL-12591	The Fourth Protocol	1987	3.75	7.50	15.00
ENTR'ACTE					
ERS-6508	Voyage of the Damned	1977	6.25	12.50	25.00
ERS-6510	The Eagle Has Landed/The Four Musketeers	1980	3.00	6.00	12.00
MCA					
2284	Rollercoaster	1977	3.75	7.50	15.00
2374	Nunzio	1978	3.00	6.00	12.00
5185	The Competition	1980	2.50	5.00	10.00
25012	The Cincinnati Kid	1986	2.00	4.00	8.00
25137	Liquidator	1966	2.00	4.00	8.00
MGM					
E-4110 [M]	Piano, Strings and Bossa Nova	1963	3.75	7.50	15.00
SE-4110 [S]	Piano, Strings and Bossa Nova	1963	5.00	10.00	20.00
E-4156 [M]	Between Broadway and Hollywood	1963	3.75	7.50	15.00
SE-4156 [S]	Between Broadway and Hollywood	1963	5.00	10.00	20.00
E-4313 [M]	The Cincinnati Kid	1965	5.00	10.00	20.00
SE-4313 [S]	The Cincinnati Kid	1965	6.25	12.50	25.00
E-4413 ST [M]	Liquidator	1966	5.00	10.00	20.00
SE-4413 ST [S]	Liquidator	1966	6.25	12.50	25.00
SE-4742	Medical Center and Other Great Themes	1971	5.00	10.00	20.00
NAUTILUS					
NR-51	Ins and Outs	198?	10.00	20.00	40.00
—Audiophile vinyl					
PALO ALTO					
8055	Ins and Outs	1983	3.00	6.00	12.00
PARAMOUNT					
PAS-5002	More Music from Mission: Impossible	1969	10.00	20.00	40.00
PAS-5004	Mannix	1969	7.50	15.00	30.00
ROULETTE					
SR-42013	"Lalole" — The Latin Sound	1968	3.75	7.50	15.00
R 52088 [M]	Lalo Brilliance	1962	5.00	10.00	20.00
SR 52088 [S]	Lalo Brilliance	1962	6.25	12.50	25.00
TABU					
JZ 35436	Gypsies	1978	3.00	6.00	12.00
JZ 36091	No One Home	1979	3.00	6.00	12.00
TETRAGRAMMATON					
T-5006	Che!	1969	7.50	15.00	30.00
TICO					
LP-1070 [M]	Piano Espanol	1960	6.25	12.50	25.00
LPS-1070 [S]	Piano Espanol	1960	7.50	15.00	30.00
VARESE SARABANDE					
STV-81198	The Osterman Weekend	1983	2.50	5.00	10.00
VERVE					
V-8543 [M]	Samba Paros Dos	1963	3.75	7.50	15.00
—With Bob Brookmeyer					
V6-8543 [S]	Samba Paros Dos	1963	5.00	10.00	20.00
—With Bob Brookmeyer					
V-8601 [M]	New Fantasy	1964	3.75	7.50	15.00
V6-8601 [S]	New Fantasy	1964	5.00	10.00	20.00
V-8624 [M]	Once a Thief and Other Themes	1965	3.75	7.50	15.00
V6-8624 [S]	Once a Thief and Other Themes	1965	5.00	10.00	20.00
V-8654 [M]	The Dissection and Reconstruction of Music from the Past	1966	3.75	7.50	15.00
V6-8654 [S]	The Dissection and Reconstruction of Music from the Past	1966	5.00	10.00	20.00
V6-8785	Insensatez	1968	3.75	7.50	15.00
V6-8801	Rock Requiem	1971	3.00	6.00	12.00
WARNER BROS.					
BSK 328	Boulevard Nights	1979	2.50	5.00	10.00
WS 1777	Bullitt	1968	12.50	25.00	50.00
BS 2727	Enter the Dragon	1973	12.50	25.00	50.00

SCHILLER, LAWRENCE

Number	Title (A Side/B Side)	Yr	VG	VG+	NM
Albums					
CAPITOL					
TAO 2574 [M]	LSD	1966	25.00	50.00	100.00
KAO 2630 [M]	Why Did Lenny Bruce Die?	1967	7.50	15.00	30.00
KAO 2652 [M]	Homosexuality in the American Male	1967	7.50	15.00	30.00

SCHILLING, JOHNNY, AND THE SHERWOODS

Number	Title (A Side/B Side)	Yr	VG	VG+	NM
45s					
C&A					
507	King of the World/Marcelle	1963	25.00	50.00	100.00

SCHOLARS, THE (1)

Featuring a young KENNY ROGERS.

Number	Title (A Side/B Side)	Yr	VG	VG+	NM
45s					
IMPERIAL					
5449	I Didn't Want to Do It/Beloved	1957	6.25	12.50	25.00
5459	Eternally Yours/Kan-Gu-Wa	1957	6.25	12.50	25.00

SCHOLARS, THE (U)

May or may not be group (1).

Number	Title (A Side/B Side)	Yr	VG	VG+	NM
45s					
CUE					
7927	What Did I Do Wrong/(B-side unknown)	1956	10.00	20.00	40.00
DOT					
15498	Rock Road/Spin the Wheel	1956	5.00	10.00	20.00
15519	If You Listen with Your Heart/Poor Little Doggie	1956	5.00	10.00	20.00

SCHOOLBOYS, THE

Number	Title (A Side/B Side)	Yr	VG	VG+	NM
45s					
JUANITA					
103	Angel of Love/The Slide	1958	37.50	75.00	150.00
OKEH					
7076	Shirley/Please Say You Want Me	1957	7.50	15.00	30.00
—"Shirley" was the hit, but "Please Say You Want Me" is the side that has lived on					
7085	I Am Old Enough/Mary	1957	6.25	12.50	25.00
7090	Pearl/Carol	1957	6.25	12.50	25.00

SCHORY, DICK

Albums

CONCERT DISC

Number	Title (A Side/B Side)	Yr	VG	VG+	NM
SC-21 [M]	Re-Percussion	1957	15.00	30.00	60.00

RCA VICTOR

Number	Title (A Side/B Side)	Yr	VG	VG+	NM
LPM-1866 [M]	Music for Bang, Barroom and Harp	1958	15.00	30.00	60.00
LSP-1866 [S]	Music for Bang, Barroom and Harp	1958	50.00	100.00	200.00
LPM-2125 [M]	Music to Break Any Mood	1960	7.50	15.00	30.00
LSP-2125 [S]	Music to Break Any Mood	1960	25.00	50.00	100.00
LPM-2289 [M]	Wild Percussion and Horns A-Plenty	1960	7.50	15.00	30.00
LSP-2289 [S]	Wild Percussion and Horns A-Plenty	1960	15.00	30.00	60.00
LSA-2306 [S]	Runnin' Wild	1960	10.00	20.00	40.00
LSA-2382 [S]	Stereo Action Goes Broadway	1961	10.00	20.00	40.00
LPM-2485 [M]	Holiday for Percussion	1962	7.50	15.00	30.00
LSA-2485 [S]	Holiday for Percussion	1962	10.00	20.00	40.00
LSP-2613 [S]	Supercussion	1963	10.00	20.00	40.00
LPM-2738 [M]	Politely Percussive	1963	7.50	15.00	30.00
LSP-2738 [S]	Politely Percussive	1963	10.00	20.00	40.00
LPM-2806 [M]	Dick Schory on Tour	1964	5.00	10.00	20.00
LSP-2806 [S]	Dick Schory on Tour	1964	6.25	12.50	25.00

SCHUMACHER, CHRISTINE, SINGS WITH THE SUPREMES

Also see THE SUPREMES.

45s

MOTOWN

Number	Title (A Side/B Side)	Yr	VG	VG+	NM
L-294-MO5 [DJ]	Mother You, Smother You (same on both sides)	1968	75.00	150.00	300.00

—Schumacher won a "Record a Record with the Supremes" contest on WKNR of Detroit. This is the rare result.

SCOOBY DOO

45s

ZEPHYR

Number	Title (A Side/B Side)	Yr	VG	VG+	NM
006	Moonglow/Ernie's Journey	195?	5.00	10.00	20.00

Albums

ZEPHYR

Number	Title (A Side/B Side)	Yr	VG	VG+	NM
ZMP-12002 [M]	Jerry Leiber Presents Scooby Doo	1959	12.50	25.00	50.00

SCORPION

Albums

TOWER

Number	Title (A Side/B Side)	Yr	VG	VG+	NM
ST 5171	Scorpion	1969	12.50	25.00	50.00

SCORPIONS

12-Inch Singles

MERCURY

Number	Title (A Side/B Side)	Yr	VG	VG+	NM
MK 212 [DJ]	You Give Me All I Need (same on both sides)	1982	2.00	4.00	8.00
265 [DJ]	Rock You Like a Hurricane (same on both sides)	1984	2.50	5.00	10.00
359 [DJ]	Big City Nights (Edit) (LP)/No One Like You (Live)	1985	2.00	4.00	8.00
378 [DJ]	Loving You Sunday Morning/No One Like You	1985	2.00	4.00	8.00
833 [DJ]	I'm Leaving You (Long) (Short)	1984	2.00	4.00	8.00

45s

MERCURY

Number	Title (A Side/B Side)	Yr	VG	VG+	NM
76008	Coast to Coast/Loving You Sunday Morning	1979	—	2.00	4.00
76070	Make It Real/(B-side unknown)	1980	—	2.00	4.00
76084	Lady Starlight/(B-side unknown)	1980	—	2.00	4.00
76153	No One Like You/Now	1982	—	2.00	4.00
818440-7	Rock You Like a Hurricane/Coming Home	1984	—	—	3.00
818440-7 [PS]	Rock You Like a Hurricane/Coming Home	1984	—	2.50	5.00
866236-7	Send Me an Angel/Wind of Change (Russian Version)	1991	—	2.00	4.00
868180-7	Wind of Change/Money and Fame	1991	—	2.00	4.00
870323-7	Rhythm of Love/We Let It Rock...We Let It Roll	1988	—	—	3.00
870323-7 [PS]	Rhythm of Love/We Let It Rock...We Let It Roll	1988	—	—	3.00
870559-7	Believe in Love/Love on the Run	1988	—	—	3.00
872372-7	Passion Rules the Game/Media Overkill	1988	—	—	3.00
880082-7	Still Loving You/Bad Boys Running Wild	1984	—	—	3.00
880319-7	I'm Leaving You/Same Thrill	1984	—	—	3.00

RCA VICTOR

Number	Title (A Side/B Side)	Yr	VG	VG+	NM
PB-10574	Speedy's Gone/They Need a Million	1976	—	3.00	6.00
PB-10691	In Trance/Night Lights	1976	—	3.00	6.00

Albums

BILLINGSGATE

Number	Title (A Side/B Side)	Yr	VG	VG+	NM
1004	Lonesome Crow	1974	7.50	15.00	30.00

MERCURY

Number	Title (A Side/B Side)	Yr	VG	VG+	NM
SRM-1-3795	Lovedrive	1979	2.50	5.00	10.00
SRM-1-3825	Animal Magnetism	1980	2.50	5.00	10.00
SRM-1-4039	Blackout	1982	2.50	5.00	10.00
814981-1	Love at First Sting	1984	2.50	5.00	10.00
—With man and woman on cover					
818885-1	Blackout	198?	2.00	4.00	8.00
—Reissue of 4039					
822038-1	Love at First Sting	1984	3.00	6.00	12.00
—Reissue with band on cover					
822555-1	Lovedrive	198?	2.00	4.00	8.00
—Reissue of 3795					
822556-1	Animal Magnetism	198?	2.00	4.00	8.00
—Reissue of 3825					
824344-1 [(2)]	World Wide Live	1985	3.00	6.00	12.00
832963-1	Savage Amusement	1988	2.50	5.00	10.00
842002-1	Best of Rockers 'N' Ballads	1989	2.50	5.00	10.00
846908-1	Crazy World	1990	3.75	7.50	15.00

RCA VICTOR

Number	Title (A Side/B Side)	Yr	VG	VG+	NM
AFL1-2628	Taken by Force	1978	3.00	6.00	12.00
CPL2-3039 [(2)]	Toyko Tapes	1978	3.75	7.50	15.00
AFL1-3516	Best of Scorpions	1979	2.50	5.00	10.00
AYL1-3659	Virgin Killer	1980	2.00	4.00	8.00
—"Best Buy Series" reissue					
AFL1-4025	Fly to the Rainbow	1977	2.50	5.00	10.00
—Reissue with new prefix					
PPL1-4025	Fly to the Rainbow	1975	3.00	6.00	12.00
AFL1-4128	In Trance	1977	2.50	5.00	10.00
—Reissue with new prefix					
PPL1-4128	In Trance	1976	3.00	6.00	12.00
PPL1-4225	Virgin Killer	1977	3.00	6.00	12.00
AYL1-4657	In Trance	1983	2.00	4.00	8.00
—"Best Buy Series" reissue					
AYL1-5057	Fly to the Rainbow	1984	2.00	4.00	8.00
—"Best Buy Series" reissue					
AFL1-5085	Best of Scorpions, Vol. 2	1984	2.50	5.00	10.00

SCOTT, BILLY

45s

CAMEO

Number	Title (A Side/B Side)	Yr	VG	VG+	NM
121	You're the Greatest/That's Why I Was Born	1957	6.25	12.50	25.00
143	A Million Boys/The Town of Never Worry	1958	5.00	10.00	20.00

EVEREST

Number	Title (A Side/B Side)	Yr	VG	VG+	NM
19315	Carole/Stairway to the Stars	1959	3.75	7.50	15.00

LAMON

Number	Title (A Side/B Side)	Yr	VG	VG+	NM
10114	Merry Christmas/A Night To Remember	1983	—	2.00	4.00

SCOTT, CALVIN

45s

ATCO

Number	Title (A Side/B Side)	Yr	VG	VG+	NM
6696	I'm Taking You Home to Mama/Sonny Boy (Be a Man)	1969	3.00	6.00	12.00
6729	Cry Like a Baby/More Than You'll Ever Know	1970	3.00	6.00	12.00

STAX

Number	Title (A Side/B Side)	Yr	VG	VG+	NM
0094	Shame on the Family Name/I've Made a Reservation	1971	2.50	5.00	10.00
0110	Goin' Back to Eden/The Sadness for Things	1971	2.50	5.00	10.00

Albums

STAX

Number	Title (A Side/B Side)	Yr	VG	VG+	NM
STS-2046	I'm Not Blind... I Just Can't See	1972	20.00	40.00	80.00

SCOTT, CHRISTOPHER

Albums

DECCA

Number	Title (A Side/B Side)	Yr	VG	VG+	NM
DL 75141	Switched-On Bacharach	1969	3.75	7.50	15.00
DL 75243	More Switched-On Bacharach	1970	3.75	7.50	15.00

MCA

Number	Title (A Side/B Side)	Yr	VG	VG+	NM
282	Switched-On Bacharach	1973	3.00	6.00	12.00
—Reissue of Decca 75141					

SCOTT, FREDDIE

Also see THE SYMPHONICS (2).

45s

COLPIX

Number	Title (A Side/B Side)	Yr	VG	VG+	NM
692	Hey Girl/The Slide	1963	3.00	6.00	12.00
709	I Got a Woman/Brand New World	1963	2.50	5.00	10.00
724	Where Does Love Go/Where Have All the Flowers Gone	1964	2.50	5.00	10.00
752	On Broadway/If I Had a Hammer	1964	2.50	5.00	10.00

COLUMBIA

Number	Title (A Side/B Side)	Yr	VG	VG+	NM
43112	Mr. Heartache/One Heartache Too Many	1964	2.50	5.00	10.00
43199	Lonely Man/I'll Try Again	1964	2.50	5.00	10.00
43316	Don't Let It End/Come Up Singing	1965	2.50	5.00	10.00
43623	One Iddy Biddy Needle/Forget Me If You Can	1966	2.50	5.00	10.00

JOY

Number	Title (A Side/B Side)	Yr	VG	VG+	NM
250	Baby, You're a Long Time Dead/Lost the Right	1961	3.00	6.00	12.00
255	I Gotta Stand Tall/When the Wind Changes	1961	3.00	6.00	12.00
280	I Gotta Stand Tall/When the Wind Changes	1963	2.50	5.00	10.00

PROBE

Number	Title (A Side/B Side)	Yr	VG	VG+	NM
481	I Shall Be Released/Girl I Love You	1970	—	3.00	6.00

P.I.P.

Number	Title (A Side/B Side)	Yr	VG	VG+	NM
8932	Deep Is the Night/The Great If	1972	—	2.50	5.00

SHOUT

Number	Title (A Side/B Side)	Yr	VG	VG+	NM
207	Are You Lonely for Me/Where Were You	1966	2.00	4.00	8.00
211	Cry to Me/No One Could Ever Love You	1967	2.00	4.00	8.00
212	Am I Grooving You/Never You Mind	1967	2.00	4.00	8.00
216	He Will Break Your Heart/I'll Be Gone	1967	2.00	4.00	8.00
220	He Ain't Give You None/Run Joy	1967	2.00	4.00	8.00
227	Just Like a Flower/Spanish Harlem	1968	2.00	4.00	8.00
233	(You) Got What I Need/Powerful Love	1968	2.50	5.00	10.00
238	Loving You Is Killing Me/Eileen	1968	2.00	4.00	8.00
245	Forever My Darling/(You) Got What I Need	1969	2.50	5.00	10.00

VANGUARD

Number	Title (A Side/B Side)	Yr	VG	VG+	NM
35137	I Guess God Wants It This Way/Please Listen	1971	—	2.50	5.00

Albums

COLPIX

Number	Title (A Side/B Side)	Yr	VG	VG+	NM
CP-461 [M]	Freddie Scott Sings and Sings and Sings	1964	15.00	30.00	60.00
—Gold label					
CP-461 [M]	Freddie Scott Sings and Sings and Sings	1965	10.00	20.00	40.00
—Blue label					
SCP-461 [R]	Freddie Scott Sings and Sings and Sings	1965	7.50	1.00	30.00
—Blue label					
SCP-461 [S]	Freddie Scott Sings and Sings and Sings	1964	30.00	60.00	120.00
—Gold label					

COLUMBIA

Number	Title (A Side/B Side)	Yr	VG	VG+	NM
CL 2258 [M]	Everything I Have Is Yours	1964	5.00	10.00	20.00
CL 2660 [M]	Lonely Man	1967	5.00	10.00	20.00
CS 9058 [S]	Everything I Have Is Yours	1964	6.25	12.50	25.00
CS 9460 [S]	Lonely Man	1967	6.25	12.50	25.00

PROBE

Number	Title (A Side/B Side)	Yr	VG	VG+	NM
CPLP-4517	I Shall Be Released	1970	6.25	12.50	25.00

SHOUT

Number	Title (A Side/B Side)	Yr	VG	VG+	NM
SLP-501 [M]	Are You Lonely for Me	1967	5.00	10.00	20.00
SLPS-501 [S]	Are You Lonely for Me	1967	6.25	12.50	25.00

SCOTT, FREDDIE, AND THE CHIMES

45s

ARROW

Number	Title (A Side/B Side)	Yr	VG	VG+	NM
724	Please Call/A Letter Came This Morning	1958	10.00	20.00	40.00
726	Lovin' Baby/A Faded Memory	1958	10.00	20.00	40.00

SCOTT, JACK

Number	Title (A Side/B Side)	Yr	VG	VG+	NM
45s					
ABC					
10843	Before the Bird Flies/Insane	1966	5.00	10.00	20.00
ABC-PARAMOUNT					
9818	Baby She's Gone/You Can Bet Your Bottom Dollar	1957	37.50	75.00	150.00
9860	Two Timin' Woman/I Need Your Love	1957	37.50	75.00	150.00
CAPITOL					
4554	A Little Feeling (Called Love)/Now That I	1961	6.25	12.50	25.00
4554 [PS]	A Little Feeling (Called Love)/Now That I	1961	12.50	25.00	50.00
4597	My Dream Came True/Strange Desire	1961	5.00	10.00	20.00
4597 [PS]	My Dream Came True/Strange Desire	1961	12.50	25.00	50.00
4637	Steps 1 and 2/One of These Days	1961	5.00	10.00	20.00
4637 [PS]	Steps 1 and 2/One of These Days	1961	12.50	25.00	50.00
4689	Cry, Cry, Cry/Grizzly Bear	1962	5.00	10.00	20.00
4689 [PS]	Cry, Cry, Cry/Grizzly Bear	1962	12.50	25.00	50.00
4738	The Part Where I Cry/You Only See What You Wanna See	1962	5.00	10.00	20.00
4796	Sad Story/I Can't Hold Your Letters	1962	5.00	10.00	20.00
4855	If Only/Green, Green Valley	1962	5.00	10.00	20.00
4903	Strangers/Laugh and the World Laughs With You	1963	5.00	10.00	20.00
4955	All I See Is Blue/Meo Myo	1963	5.00	10.00	20.00
CARLTON					
462	My True Love/Leroy	1958	7.50	15.00	30.00
483	With Your Love/Geraldine	1958	7.50	15.00	30.00
483 [PS]	With Your Love/Geraldine	1958	15.00	30.00	60.00
493	Goodbye Baby/Save My Soul	1959	7.50	15.00	30.00
493 [PS]	Goodbye Baby/Save My Soul	1959	15.00	30.00	60.00
504	I Never Felt Like This/Bella	1959	7.50	15.00	30.00
514	The Way I Walk/Midgie	1959	7.50	15.00	30.00
519 [M]	There Comes a Time/Baby Marie	1959	5.00	10.00	20.00
ST-519 [S]	There Comes a Time/Baby Marie	1959	10.00	20.00	40.00
DOT					
17475	May You Never Be Alone/Face to the Wall	1973	—	2.50	5.00
17504	You're Just Getting Better/Walk Through My Mind	1974	—	2.50	5.00
GROOVE					
58-0027	There's Trouble Brewin'/Jingle Bell Slide	1963	5.00	10.00	20.00
58-0031	Blue Skies (Moving In on Me)/I Knew You First	1964	3.75	7.50	15.00
58-0037	Wiggle On Out/What a Wonderful Night Out	1964	5.00	10.00	20.00
58-0042	Thou Shalt Not Steal/I Prayed for an Angel	1964	3.75	7.50	15.00
58-0049	Flakey John/Tall Tales	1964	5.00	10.00	20.00
GRT					
35	Billy Jack/Mary, Marry Me	1971	—	2.50	5.00
GUARANTEED					
209	What Am I Living For/Indiana Waltz	1960	7.50	15.00	30.00
211	No One Will Ever Know/Go Wild Little Sadie	1960	7.50	15.00	30.00
JUBILEE					
5606	My Special Angel/I Keep Changin' My Mind	1967	5.00	10.00	20.00
PONIE					
7021-10	Geraldine/Midgie	197?	—	2.00	4.00
7021-11	There's Trouble Brewin'/Jingle Bell Slide	197?	—	2.00	4.00
7021-12	Flakey John/Wiggle On Out	197?	—	2.00	4.00
5121-15	Baby She's Gone/Two Timin' Woman	197?	—	2.00	4.00
6063-20	Leroy/Go Wild Little Sadie	197?	—	2.00	4.00
6083-20	Country Witch/Blues, Stay Away from Me-Stones	197?	—	2.00	4.00
4104-30	Spirit of '76/(Instrumental)	1976	—	2.00	4.00
RCA VICTOR					
47-8505	Separation's Now Granted/I Don't Believe in Tea Leaves	1965	3.75	7.50	15.00
47-8685	Looking for Linda/I Hope I Think I Wish	1965	3.75	7.50	15.00
47-8724	Don't Hush the Laughter/Let's Learn to Live and Love Again	1965	3.75	7.50	15.00
TOP RANK					
2028 [M]	What in the World's Come Over You/Baby Baby	1959	7.50	15.00	30.00
2028 [S]	What in the World's Come Over You/Baby Baby	1959	10.00	20.00	40.00
2041 [M]	Burning Bridges/Oh Little One	1960	6.25	12.50	25.00
2041 [PS]	Burning Bridges/Oh Little One	1960	15.00	30.00	60.00
2041 [S]	Burning Bridges/Oh Little One	1960	15.00	30.00	60.00
2055	It Only Happened Yesterday/Cool Water	1960	5.00	10.00	20.00
2075	Patsy/Old Time Religion	1960	5.00	10.00	20.00
2093	Is There Something on Your Mind/Found a Woman	1960	5.00	10.00	20.00
2093 [PS]	Is There Something on Your Mind/Found a Woman	1960	15.00	30.00	60.00
7-Inch Extended Plays					
CARLTON					
EP 7/1070	Save My Soul/I Can't Help It//Geraldine/With Your Love	1959	50.00	100.00	200.00
EP 7/1070 [PS]	Presenting Jack Scott (Volume 1)	1959	50.00	100.00	200.00
EP 7/1071	Indiana Waltz,/Midgie//My True Love/Leroy	1959	50.00	100.00	200.00
EP 7/1071 [PS]	Presenting Jack Scott (Volume 2)	1959	50.00	100.00	200.00
EP 7/1072	No One Will Ever Know/Goodbye Baby//I'm Dreaming Of You/The Way I Walk	1959	50.00	100.00	200.00
EP 7/1072 [PS]	Jack Scott Sings	1959	50.00	100.00	200.00
TOP RANK					
1001	(contents unknown)	1960	50.00	100.00	200.00
1001 [PS]	What in the World's Come Over You	1960	50.00	100.00	200.00
Albums					
CAPITOL					
ST-8-2035	Burning Bridges	196?	50.00	100.00	200.00
—Capitol Record Club edition					
ST 2035 [S]	Burning Bridges	1964	37.50	75.00	150.00
T 2035 [M]	Burning Bridges	1964	20.00	40.00	80.00
CARLTON					
LP-12-107 [M]	Jack Scott	1959	37.50	75.00	150.00
STLP-12-107 [S]	Jack Scott	1959	100.00	200.00	400.00
—With "Stereo" in felt letters vertically along the left of cover					
STLP-12-107 [S]	Jack Scott	1959	75.00	150.00	300.00
—With "Stereo" in felt letters horizontally along the top of cover					
STLP-12-107 [S]	Jack Scott	1959	50.00	100.00	200.00
—With "Stereo" printed across the top					
LP-12-122 [M]	What Am I Living For	1959	30.00	60.00	120.00
STLP-12-122 [S]	What Am I Living For	1959	80.00	160.00	320.00
JADE					
J33-113	Jack Is Back	198?	3.75	7.50	15.00
J33-114	The Way I Rock	198?	3.75	7.50	15.00
PONIE					
563	Jack Scott	1974	3.75	7.50	15.00
7055	Jack Scott	1977	3.75	7.50	15.00
TOP RANK					
RM-319 [M]	I Remember Hank Williams	1960	37.50	75.00	150.00
RM-326 [M]	What in the World's Come Over You	1960	37.50	75.00	150.00
RM-348 [M]	The Spirit Moves Me	1961	37.50	75.00	150.00
SM-619 [S]	I Remember Hank Williams	1960	62.50	125.00	250.00
SM-626 [S]	What in the World's Come Over You	1960	62.50	125.00	250.00
SM-648 [S]	The Spirit Moves Me	1961	62.50	125.00	250.00

SCOTT, JOEL

Number	Title (A Side/B Side)	Yr	VG	VG+	NM
45s					
PHILLES					
101	Here I Stand/You're My Only Love	1962	6.25	12.50	25.00

SCOTT, LINDA

Number	Title (A Side/B Side)	Yr	VG	VG+	NM
45s					
CANADIAN AMERICAN					
123	I've Told Every Little Star/Three Guesses	1961	5.00	10.00	20.00
127	Don't Bet Money Honey/Starlight, Starbright	1961	5.00	10.00	20.00
129	I Don't Know Why/It's All Because	1961	5.00	10.00	20.00
132	Christmas Day/Twistin' Bells	1961	5.00	10.00	20.00
—B-side by Santo and Johnny					
133	Count Every Star/Land of Stars	1962	3.75	7.50	15.00
134	Bermuda/Lonely for You	1962	3.75	7.50	15.00
CONGRESS					
101	Yessiree/Town Crier	1962	3.75	7.50	15.00
103	Never in a Million Years/Through the Summer	1962	3.75	7.50	15.00
106	I Left My Heart in the Balcony/Lopsided Love Affair	1962	3.75	7.50	15.00
108	I'm So Afraid of Losing You/The Loneliest Girl in Town	1962	3.75	7.50	15.00
110	I'm Gonna Sit Right Down and Write Myself a Letter/Ain't That Fun	1963	3.75	7.50	15.00
200	Let's Fall in Love/I Know It, You Know It	1963	3.75	7.50	15.00
204	Who's Been Sleeping in My Bed/My Baby	1963	3.75	7.50	15.00
206	Let's Fall in Love/I Know It, You Know It	1964	3.75	7.50	15.00
209	I Envy You/Everybody Stopped Laughing at Jane	1964	3.75	7.50	15.00
KAPP					
610	That Old Feeling/This Is My Prayer	1964	2.50	5.00	10.00
641	If I Love Again/Patch It Up	1965	2.50	5.00	10.00
677	Don't Lose Your Head/I'll See You in My Dreams	1965	2.50	5.00	10.00
713	You Baby/I Can't Get Through to You	1965	2.50	5.00	10.00
762	Toys/Take a Walk Bobby	1966	2.50	5.00	10.00
RCA VICTOR					
47-9424	They Don't Know You/Three Miles High	1967	2.50	5.00	10.00
7-Inch Extended Plays					
CANADIAN AMERICAN					
CAEP 1005	Count Every Star/Catch a Falling Star//Stars Fell on Alabama/Blue Star	196?	12.50	25.00	50.00
CAEP 1005 [PS]	(title unknown)	196?	12.50	25.00	50.00
Albums					
CANADIAN AMERICAN					
CALP-1005 [M]	Starlight, Starbright	1961	25.00	50.00	100.00
SCALP-1005 [S]	Starlight, Starbright	1961	37.50	75.00	150.00
CALP-1007 [M]	Great Scott!! Her Greatest Hits	1962	25.00	50.00	100.00
SCALP-1007 [S]	Great Scott!! Her Greatest Hits	1962	37.50	75.00	150.00
CONGRESS					
CGL-3001 [M]	Linda	1962	10.00	20.00	40.00
CGS-3001 [S]	Linda	1962	12.50	25.00	50.00
KAPP					
KL-1424 [M]	Hey, Look at Me Now	1965	10.00	20.00	40.00
KS-3424 [S]	Hey, Look at Me Now	1965	12.50	25.00	50.00

SCOTT, PEGGY, AND JO JO BENSON

Number	Title (A Side/B Side)	Yr	VG	VG+	NM
45s					
SSS INTERNATIONAL					
736	Lover's Holiday/Here with Me	1968	2.00	4.00	8.00
748	Pickin' Wild Mountain Berries/Pure Love and Pleasure	1968	2.00	4.00	8.00
761	Soulshake/We Were Made for Each Other	1969	2.00	4.00	8.00
769	I Want to Love You Baby/We Got Our Bag	1969	2.00	4.00	8.00
781	Sugarmaker/Lover's Heaven	1969	2.00	4.00	8.00
805	Let's Spend a Day Out in the Country/Little Things That Count	1970	—	3.00	6.00
Albums					
SSS INTERNATIONAL					
1	Soulshake	1968	6.25	12.50	25.00
2	Lover's Heaven	1969	6.25	12.50	25.00

SCOTT, RICKY

Number	Title (A Side/B Side)	Yr	VG	VG+	NM
45s					
CUB					
9079	I Didn't Mean It/Darlin' Darlin'	1960	5.00	10.00	20.00
X-CLUSIVE					
1001	I Didn't Mean It/Darlin' Darlin'	1960	20.00	40.00	80.00

SCOTT, RODNEY

Number	Title (A Side/B Side)	Yr	VG	VG+	NM
45s					
CANON					
225	Granny Went Rockin'/Bitter Tears	1961	50.00	100.00	200.00
231	You're So Square (Baby I Don't Care)/He'll Be There	1961	50.00	100.00	200.00
MR. PEEKE					
119	You're So Square (Baby I Don't Care)/He'll Be There	1962	20.00	40.00	80.00

Number	Title (A Side/B Side)	Yr	VG	VG+	NM
126	That's the Way It Goes/Bitter Tears	1963	7.50	15.00	30.00

SCOTT, SHERREE

Number	Title (A Side/B Side)	Yr	VG	VG+	NM
45s					
ROBBINS					
105	Twinkle Toes (The Littlest Reindeer)/Our Christmas Day	1959	10.00	20.00	40.00
1036	Fascinating Baby/You and I	1957	37.50	75.00	150.00
ROCKET					
101	Whole Lotta Shakin' Goin' On/Unhappy Birthday	1958	37.50	75.00	150.00
101 [PS]	Whole Lotta Shakin' Goin' On/Unhappy Birthday	1958	50.00	100.00	200.00

SCOTT, SIMON

Number	Title (A Side/B Side)	Yr	VG	VG+	NM
45s					
IMPERIAL					
66089	My Baby's Got Soul/Midnight	1965	3.75	7.50	15.00

SCOTT, TERRY

Number	Title (A Side/B Side)	Yr	VG	VG+	NM
45s					
VALIANT					
6016	Little Angel/Love Only Me	1962	3.00	6.00	12.00

SCOTT, TOM

Number	Title (A Side/B Side)	Yr	VG	VG+	NM
12-Inch Singles					
ATLANTIC					
703 [DJ]	Got to Get Out of New York/Aerobia	1983	—	3.00	6.00
COLUMBIA					
AS 1249 [DJ]	So White and So Funky (same on both sides)	1981	—	3.00	6.00
45s					
ABC IMPULSE!					
265	The Honeysuckle Breeze/Baby I Love You	1967	2.00	4.00	8.00
ATLANTIC					
89763	Lollipoppin'/Come Back to Me	1983	—	2.00	4.00
A&M					
1345	Boss Walk/Looking Out for Number 7	1972	—	2.50	5.00
COLUMBIA					
02496	So White and So Funky/We Belong Together	1981	—	2.00	4.00
10914	Beautiful Music/Lost Inside the Love of You	1979	—	2.00	4.00
ODE					
50433	Gotcha (Theme from Starsky & Hutch)/Smoothin' On Down	1977	—	2.00	4.00
66043	Strut Your Stuff/Sneaking in the Back	1974	—	2.00	4.00
66048	Jump Back/T.C.B. in E	1974	—	2.00	4.00
66105	Tom Cat/Keep On Doin' It	1975	—	2.00	4.00
66109	Refried/Rock Island Rocket	1975	—	2.00	4.00
66118	Uptown and Country/Appolina (Foxtrata)	1976	—	2.00	4.00
66121	Time and Love/Dirty Old Man	1976	—	2.00	4.00
Albums					
ABC IMPULSE!					
A-9163 [M]	Honeysuckle Breeze	1967	10.00	20.00	40.00
AS-9163 [S]	Honeysuckle Breeze	1967	6.25	12.50	25.00
AS-9171	Rural Still Life	1968	6.25	12.50	25.00
ATLANTIC					
80106	Target	1983	2.50	5.00	10.00
A&M					
SP-4330	Great Scott!	1972	3.75	7.50	15.00
COLUMBIA					
JC 35557	Intimate Strangers	1978	2.50	5.00	10.00
PC 35557	Intimate Strangers	198?	2.00	4.00	8.00
—Budget-line reissue					
JC 36137	Street Beat	1979	2.50	5.00	10.00
JC 36352	The Best of Tom Scott	1980	2.50	5.00	10.00
FC 37419	Apple Juice	1981	2.50	5.00	10.00
ELEKTRA/MUSICIAN					
60162	Desire	1982	2.50	5.00	10.00
FLYING DUTCHMAN					
106	Hair	1969	5.00	10.00	20.00
114	Paint Your Wagon	1970	5.00	10.00	20.00
BDL1-0833	Tom Scott in L.A.	1975	2.50	5.00	10.00
AYL1-3875	Tom Scott in L.A.	1980	2.00	4.00	8.00
—"Best Buy Series" reissue					
GRP					
GR-1044	Streamlines	1987	2.50	5.00	10.00
GR-9571	Flashpoint	1988	2.50	5.00	10.00
MCA					
29060	Rural Still Life	198?	2.00	4.00	8.00
—Reissue of Impulse 9171					
ODE					
PE 34952	Tom Scott and the L.A. Express	1977	2.00	4.00	8.00
—Reissue of 77021					
PE 34956	Tom Cat	1977	2.00	4.00	8.00
—Reissue of 77029					
PE 34959	New York Connection	1977	2.00	4.00	8.00
—Reissue of 77033					
PE 34966	Blow It Out	1977	2.50	5.00	10.00
SP-77021	Tom Scott and the L.A. Express	1974	2.50	5.00	10.00
SP-77029	Tom Cat	1975	2.50	5.00	10.00
SP-77033	New York Connection	1976	2.50	5.00	10.00
SOUNDWINGS					
SW-202	Tom Scott	1986	2.50	5.00	10.00

SCOTT, WALTER

Lead singer with BOB KUBAN AND THE IN-MEN.

Number	Title (A Side/B Side)	Yr	VG	VG+	NM
45s					
MUSICLAND U.S.A.					
111	Just You Wait/Silly Girl	1967	5.00	10.00	20.00
20009	Watch Out/My Shadow Is Gone	1966	3.75	7.50	15.00
20014	It's Been a Long Time/Proud	1966	3.75	7.50	15.00
PZAZZ					
026	Soul Stew Recipe/Feeling Something New Inside	1969	2.50	5.00	10.00
WHITE WHALE					
259	Just You Wait/Silly Girl	1967	5.00	10.00	20.00
Albums					
MUSICLAND U.S.A.					
LP-3502 [M]	Great Scott	1967	5.00	10.00	20.00
SLP-3502 [S]	Great Scott	1967	6.25	12.50	25.00
WHITE WHALE					
WWS-7131	Walter Scott	1970	5.00	10.00	20.00

SCOTT-HERON, GIL

Includes records with Brian Jackson.

Number	Title (A Side/B Side)	Yr	VG	VG+	NM
12-Inch Singles					
ARISTA					
9216	Re-Ron/Re-Ron (Special Mix)	1984	2.50	5.00	10.00
45s					
ARISTA					
0117	Superman/We Beg Your Pardon America	1975	—	2.50	5.00
0152	Johannesburg/Fell Together	1975	—	2.50	5.00
0225	The Bottle Part 1/The Bottle Part 2	1976	—	2.50	5.00
0285	Hello Sunday! Hello Road!/Song of the Wind	1977	—	2.50	5.00
0317	Under the Hammer/Backtrack in France	1978	—	2.50	5.00
0366	Angel Dust/Third World Revolution	1978	—	2.00	4.00
0390	Show Bizness/Better Days Ahead	1979	—	2.00	4.00
0488	Shut 'Um Down/Baltimore	1980	—	2.00	4.00
0583	Legend in His Own Mind/(B-side unknown)	1980	—	2.00	4.00
0647	"B" Movie/(B-side unknown)	1981	—	2.00	4.00
1011	Blue Collar/Fast Lane	1982	—	2.00	4.00
9253	Re-Ron/Re-Ron (Special Mix)	1984	—	2.00	4.00
Albums					
ARISTA					
AL 4030	The First Minute of a New Day	1975	2.50	5.00	10.00
AL 4044	From South Africa to South Carolina	1975	2.50	5.00	10.00
AL 4147	Bridges	1977	2.50	5.00	10.00
AB 4189	Secrets	1978	2.50	5.00	10.00
A2L 5001 [(2)]	It's Your World	1976	3.00	6.00	12.00
AL 8248	The Best of Gil Scott-Heron	1984	2.50	5.00	10.00
AL 8301	The Mind of Gil Scott-Heron	1980	3.75	7.50	15.00
ALB6-8306	The Best of Gil Scott-Heron	1985	2.00	4.00	8.00
—Reissue of 8248					
AL 9514	1980	1980	2.50	5.00	10.00
AL 9540	Real Eyes	1980	2.50	5.00	10.00
AL 9566	Reflections	1981	2.50	5.00	10.00
AL 9606	Moving Target	1982	2.50	5.00	10.00
BLUEBIRD					
6994-1-RB	The Revolution Will Not Be Televised	1988	3.00	6.00	12.00
FLYING DUTCHMAN					
BLD1-0613	The Revolution Will Not Be Televised	1974	5.00	10.00	20.00
BXL1-0613	The Revolution Will Not Be Televised	1978	3.00	6.00	12.00
—Reissue with new prefix					
BXL1-2834	Pieces of a Man	1978	3.00	6.00	12.00
—Reissue of 10143					
AYL1-3818	The Revolution Will Not Be Televised	1980	2.00	4.00	8.00
—"Best Buy Series" reissue					
AYL1-3819	Pieces of a Man	1980	2.00	4.00	8.00
—"Best Buy Series" reissue					
FD-10143	Pieces of a Man	1971	5.00	10.00	20.00
FD-10153	Free Will	1972	5.00	10.00	20.00
STRATA-EAST					
SES-19742	Winter in America	1974	6.25	12.50	25.00

SCOTT RICHARD CASE

See SRC.

SCOTTSVILLE SQUIRREL BARKERS, THE

Chris Hillman, later of THE BYRDS, makes his first appearance on record here.

Number	Title (A Side/B Side)	Yr	VG	VG+	NM
Albums					
CROWN					
CST-346 [S]	Bluegrass Favorites	1963	15.00	30.00	60.00
CLP-5346 [M]	Bluegrass Favorites	1963	12.50	25.00	50.00

SCRAMBLERS, THE

Number	Title (A Side/B Side)	Yr	VG	VG+	NM
45s					
ARVEE					
6502	Super Surfer U.S.A./Go Getera Go	1963	6.25	12.50	25.00
DEL-FI					
4237	The Beatle Walk/The Beatle Blues	1964	6.25	12.50	25.00
Albums					
CROWN					
CST-384 [S]	Cycle Psychos	1964	6.25	12.50	25.00
CLP-5384 [M]	Cycle Psychos	1964	5.00	10.00	20.00
DIPLOMAT					
D-2316 [M]	Motorcycle Scramble	1964	5.00	10.00	20.00
DS-2316 [S]	Motorcycle Scramble	1964	6.25	12.50	25.00
WYNCOTE					
SW-9048 [S]	Little Honda	1964	6.25	12.50	25.00
W-9048 [M]	Little Honda	1964	5.00	10.00	20.00

SCREAMING GYPSY BANDITS

Number	Title (A Side/B Side)	Yr	VG	VG+	NM
Albums					
BAR-B-Q					
004	The Dancer Inside You	1974	20.00	40.00	80.00
22185	In the Eye	1973	20.00	40.00	80.00

SEA, JOHNNY

Some of these were as "Johnny Seay."

Number	Title (A Side/B Side)	Yr	VG	VG+	NM
45s					
CAPITOL					
4585	The Torch and the Flame/No Tears Tonight	1961	2.50	5.00	10.00
4646	Livin' Is Lovin'/The Wayward Wind	1961	2.50	5.00	10.00
COLUMBIA					
44423	Going Out to Tulsa/There's a Shadow Bar	1968	—	2.50	5.00

Number	Title (A Side/B Side)	Yr	VG	VG+	NM
44542	Mama When I'm Gone Don't Cry for Me/Spng Number 9 1/2 on the Album	1968	—	2.50	5.00
44634	Three Six-Packs, Two Arms and a Juke Box/ Loved Her Fine for a Time	1968	—	2.50	5.00
44717	I've Learned a Lot Today/A Poor Boy Just Trying to Get Along	1968	—	2.50	5.00
44805	Cryin' Gray Tombstone/Everybody's Friend	1969	—	2.50	5.00
NRC					
006	It Won't Be Easy to Forget/I Love You	1958	3.00	6.00	12.00
019	Frankie's Man, Johnny/Loneliness	1959	3.00	6.00	12.00
026	Stranger/Judy and Johnny	1959	3.00	6.00	12.00
049	Nobody's Darling But Mine/My Time to Cry	1959	3.00	6.00	12.00
060	Ghost Riders in the Sky/Mr. and Mrs. Sippi	1960	3.00	6.00	12.00
PHILIPS					
40164	My Baby Walks All Over Me/There's Another Man	1964	2.00	4.00	8.00
40214	All Mixed Up/Standing Room Only	1964	2.00	4.00	8.00
40267	My Old Faded Rose/It's a Shame	1965	2.00	4.00	8.00
40307	If It Wasn't for Hard Luck/Hitchin' and Hikin'	1965	2.00	4.00	8.00
VIKING					
1011	Fort Worth Girl/Willie's Drunk and Willie's Dying	1970	—	2.50	5.00
1017	Annie's Going to Sing Her Song/(B-side unknown)	1971	—	3.00	6.00
WARNER BROS.					
5820	Day for Decision/Mary Rocks Him to Sleep	1966	—	3.00	6.00
5861	Things You Gave Me/Wheels on the Highway	1966	—	3.00	6.00
5889	Nothin's Bad As Bein' Lonely/Ain't That Right	1967	—	3.00	6.00
Albums					
HILLTOP					
6018	Everybody's Favorite	196?	3.00	6.00	12.00
PHILIPS					
PHM 200139 [M]	World of a Country Boy	1964	5.00	10.00	20.00
PHM 200194 [M]	Live at the Bitter End	1965	5.00	10.00	20.00
PHS 600139 [S]	World of a Country Boy	1964	6.25	12.50	25.00
PHS 600194 [S]	Live at the Bitter End	1965	6.25	12.50	25.00
WARNER BROS.					
W 1659 [M]	Day for Decision	1966	3.75	7.50	15.00
WS 1659 [S]	Day for Decision	1966	5.00	10.00	20.00

SEA SHELLS, THE

Number	Title (A Side/B Side)	Yr	VG	VG+	NM
45s					
GOLIATH					
1357	Love Those Beach Boys/Close to Jimmy	1964	10.00	20.00	40.00
JUBILEE					
5587	Hit the Surf/Barefoot in the Sand	1967	5.00	10.00	20.00

SEALS, JIMMY

Also see THE CHAMPS; SEALS AND CROFTS.

Number	Title (A Side/B Side)	Yr	VG	VG+	NM
45s					
CARLTON					
470	Sneaky Pete/Benguela	1958	7.50	15.00	30.00
CHALLENGE					
9153	Wish for You, Want for You, Wait for You/ Runaway Heart	1962	7.50	15.00	30.00
9200	Lady Heartbreak/Grounded	1963	7.50	15.00	30.00
59270	Everybody's Doing the Jerk/Wa-Hoo	1965	5.00	10.00	20.00
59299	She's Not a Bad Girl/The Yesterday of Our Love	1965	5.00	10.00	20.00
WINSTON					
1021	Sneaky Pete/Benguela	1958	10.00	20.00	50.00
1027	Biscayne Bay/Juarez	1958	10.00	20.00	50.00

SEALS AND CROFTS

Also see THE CHAMPS; JIMMY SEALS.

Number	Title (A Side/B Side)	Yr	VG	VG+	NM
12-Inch Singles					
WARNER BROS.					
PRO-A-722 [DJ]	You're the Love (5:22) (stereo/mono)	1978	3.75	7.50	15.00
45s					
T-A					
188	In Tune/Seldom's Sister	1969	2.00	4.00	8.00
191	See My Life/(B-side unknown)	1969	2.00	4.00	8.00
206	See My Life/In Tune//Hollow Reed/Leave	1970	2.50	5.00	10.00
208	Ridin' Thumb/Leave	1970	2.00	4.00	8.00
210	Gabriel Go On Home/Robin	1971	2.00	4.00	8.00
WARNER BROS.					
7536	When I Meet Them/Irish Linen	1971	—	3.00	6.00
7565	Sudan Village/High on a Mountain	1972	—	3.00	6.00
7606	Summer Breeze/East of Ginger Trees	1972	—	2.50	5.00
7671	Hummingbird/Say	1972	—	2.50	5.00
7697	We May Never Pass This Way (Again)/Intone My Servant	1973	—	—	—
—Unreleased?					
7708	Diamond Girl/Wisdom	1973	—	2.50	5.00
7740	We May Never Pass This Way (Again)/Jessica	1973	—	2.50	5.00
7771	Unborn Child/Ledges	1974	—	2.00	4.00
7810	King of Nothing/Follow Me	1974	—	2.00	4.00
8075	I'll Play for You/Truth Is But a Woman	1975	—	2.00	4.00
8130	Castles in the Sand/Golden Rainbow	1975	—	2.00	4.00
8190	Get Closer/Don't Fail	1976	—	2.00	4.00
8190 [PS]	Get Closer/Don't Fail	1976	—	2.50	5.00
8277	Baby, I'll Give It to You/Advance Guards	1976	—	2.00	4.00
8405	My Fair Share/East of Ginger Trees	1977	—	2.00	4.00
8405 [PS]	My Fair Share/East of Ginger Trees	1977	—	3.00	6.00
8551	You're the Love/Midnight Blue	1978	—	2.00	4.00
8639	Magnolia Moon/Takin' It Easy	1978	—	2.00	4.00
49522	First Love/Kite Dreams	1980	—	2.00	4.00
7-Inch Extended Plays					
WARNER BROS.					
S 2761 [DJ]	Rachel/King of Nothing/Desert People//The Story of Her Love/Dance by the Light of the Moon	1974	2.00	4.00	8.00
—33 1/3 rpm, small hole jukebox edition					
S 2761 [PS]	Unborn Child	1974	2.50	5.00	10.00
Albums					
K-TEL					
NU 9610	Collection: 16 of Their Greatest Hits	1979	3.00	6.00	12.00
NAUTILUS					
NR-10	Summer Breeze	1979	7.50	15.00	30.00
—Audiophile vinyl					
T-A					
5001	Seals and Crofts	1969	6.25	12.50	25.00
5004	Down Home	1970	6.25	12.50	25.00
WARNER BROS.					
BS 2568	Year of Sunday	1971	3.00	6.00	12.00
—Green "WB" label					
BS 2568	Year of Sunday	1973	2.50	5.00	10.00
—"Burbank" palm-tree label					
BS 2629	Summer Breeze	1972	3.00	6.00	12.00
—Green "WB" label					
BS 2629	Summer Breeze	1973	2.50	5.00	10.00
—"Burbank" palm-tree label					
BS 2629	Summer Breeze	1979	2.00	4.00	8.00
—White or tan label					
BS4 2629 [Q]	Summer Breeze	1974	5.00	10.00	20.00
BS 2699	Diamond Girl	1973	3.00	6.00	12.00
—"Burbank" palm-tree label					
BS 2699	Diamond Girl	1979	2.00	4.00	8.00
—White or tan label					
BS4 2699 [Q]	Diamond Girl	1974	5.00	10.00	20.00
BS 2761	Unborn Child	1974	3.00	6.00	12.00
BS4 2761 [Q]	Unborn Child	1974	5.00	10.00	20.00
2WS 2809 [(2)]	Seals & Crofts I and II	1974	3.75	7.50	15.00
—Reissue of the two T-A LPs in one package					
BS 2848	I'll Play for You	1975	2.50	5.00	10.00
BS4 2848 [Q]	I'll Play for You	1975	5.00	10.00	20.00
BS 2886	Greatest Hits	1975	2.50	5.00	10.00
BS 2907	Get Closer	1976	2.50	5.00	10.00
BS 2976	Sudan Village	1976	2.50	5.00	10.00
BSK 3109	Greatest Hits	1977	2.00	4.00	8.00
—Reissue; any label variation					
BSK 3165	Takin' It Easy	1978	2.50	5.00	10.00
BSK 3365	The Longest Road	1980	2.50	5.00	10.00

SEAN AND THE BRANDYWINES

Number	Title (A Side/B Side)	Yr	VG	VG+	NM
45s					
DECCA					
31910	She Ain't No Good/Cod'ine	1966	5.00	10.00	20.00
—Produced by Gary Usher					

SEARCH PARTY

Number	Title (A Side/B Side)	Yr	VG	VG+	NM
Albums					
CENTURY					
32013	Montgomery Chapel	1969	500.00	1000.	2000.

SEARCHERS, THE

Number	Title (A Side/B Side)	Yr	VG	VG+	NM
45s					
KAPP					
KJB-22	Needles and Pins/Ain't That Just Like Me	1964	2.00	4.00	8.00
—Orange label "Winners Circle Series"					
KJB-27	Love Potion Number Nine/Hi-Heel Sneakers	1964	2.50	5.00	10.00
—Orange label "Winners Circle Series"; no black label counterpart					
KJB-29	Bumble Bee/Everything You Do	1964	2.50	5.00	10.00
—Orange label "Winners Circle Series"; no black label counterpart					
KJB-29	Bumble Bee/A Tear Fell	1965	2.50	5.00	10.00
—Orange label "Winners Circle Series"; no black label counterpart					
577	Needles and Pins/Ain't That Just Like Me	1964	3.00	6.00	12.00
577	Needles and Pins/Saturday Night Out	1964	2.50	5.00	10.00
577 [PS]	Needles and Pins/Ain't That Just Like Me	1964	7.50	15.00	30.00
577 [PS]	Needles and Pins (promo-only version)	1964	12.50	25.00	50.00
584	Ain't That Just Like Me/Ain't Gonna Kiss You	1964	2.50	5.00	10.00
584 [PS]	Ain't That Just Like Me (special promo sleeve)	1964	12.50	25.00	50.00
593	Don't Throw Your Love Away/I'll Pretend I'm with You	1964	2.50	5.00	10.00
609	Someday We're Gonna Love Again/No One Else Could Love Me	1964	2.50	5.00	10.00
609 [PS]	Someday We're Gonna Love Again/No One Else Could Love Me	1964	7.50	15.00	30.00
618	When You Walk in the Room/I'll Be Missing You	1964	2.50	5.00	10.00
644	What Have They Done to the Rain/This Feeling Inside	1965	2.50	5.00	10.00
658	Goodbye My Lover Goodbye/'Til I Met You	1965	2.50	5.00	10.00
686	He's Got No Love/So Far Away	1965	2.50	5.00	10.00
706	Don't You Know Why/You Can't Lie to a Liar	1965	2.50	5.00	10.00
729	Take Me for What I'm Worth/Too Many Miles	1966	2.50	5.00	10.00
783	Have You Ever Loved Somebody/It's Just the Way	1966	2.50	5.00	10.00
811	Lovers/Popcorn Double Feature	1966	2.50	5.00	10.00
LIBERTY					
55646	Sugar and Spice/Saints and Sinners	1963	6.25	12.50	25.00
55689	Sugar and Spice/Saints and Sinners	1964	3.75	7.50	15.00
MERCURY					
72172	Sweets for My Sweet/It's All Been a Dream	1963	6.25	12.50	25.00
72390	(Ain't That) Just Like Me/I Can Tell	1964	3.75	7.50	15.00
RCA VICTOR					
74-0484	Desdemona/The World Is Waiting for Tomorrow	1971	—	3.00	6.00
74-0652	Love Is Everywhere/And the Button	1972	—	3.00	6.00
SIRE					
49175	It's Too Late/Don't Hang On	1980	—	2.00	4.00
49665	Love's Melody/Little Bit of Heaven	1981	—	2.00	4.00
WORLD PACIFIC					
77908	Umbrella Man/Over the Weekend	1969	2.00	4.00	8.00
Albums					
KAPP					
KL-1363 [M]	Meet the Searchers	1964	10.00	20.00	40.00
—With black and blue label					

Number	Title (A Side/B Side)	Yr	VG	VG+	NM
KL-1363 [M]	Meet the Searchers	1964	6.25	12.50	25.00
—With black label					
KL-1409 [M]	This Is Us	1964	6.25	12.50	25.00
—Version 1: No sticker on front cover					
KL-1409 [M]	This Is Us	1964	6.25	12.50	25.00
—Version 2: With sticker on front cover referring to "Love Potion No. 9"					
KL-1412 [M]	The New Searchers LP	1965	6.25	12.50	25.00
KL-1449 [M]	The Searchers No. 4	1965	6.25	12.50	25.00
KL-1477 [M]	Take Me for What I'm Worth	1966	6.25	12.50	25.00
KS-3363 [S]	Meet the Searchers	1964	12.50	25.00	50.00
—With black and blue label					
KS-3363 [S]	Meet the Searchers	1964	7.50	15.00	30.00
—With black label					
KS-3409 [S]	This Is Us	1964	7.50	15.00	30.00
—Version 1: No sticker on front cover					
KS-3409 [S]	This Is Us	1964	7.50	15.00	30.00
—Version 2: With sticker on front cover referring to "Love Potion No. 9"					
KS-3412 [S]	The New Searchers LP	1965	7.50	15.00	30.00
KS-3419 [S]	The Searchers No. 4	1965	7.50	15.00	30.00
KS-3477 [S]	Take Me for What I'm Worth	1966	7.50	15.00	30.00
MERCURY					
MG-20914 [M]	Hear! Hear!	1964	12.50	25.00	50.00
—Version 1: With only the title on the front cover					
MG-20914 [M]	Hear! Hear!	1964	10.00	20.00	40.00
—Version 2: With sticker "Live from the Star Club" on cover					
MG-20914 [M]	Hear! Hear!	1964	7.50	15.00	30.00
—Version 3: With "Live from the Star Club" imprinted on cover					
MG-20914 [M-DJ]	Hear! Hear!	1964	12.50	25.00	50.00
—White label promo					
MG-20994 [M]	The Searchers Meet the Rattles	1965	18.75	37.50	75.00
SR-60914 [S]	Hear! Hear!	1964	10.00	20.00	40.00
—Version 1: With only the title on the front cover					
SR-60914 [S]	Hear! Hear!	1964	7.50	15.00	30.00
—Version 2: With sticker "Live from the Star Club" on cover					
SR-60914 [S]	Hear! Hear!	1964	6.25	12.50	25.00
—Version 3: With "Live from the Star Club" imprinted on cover					
SR-60994 [S]	The Searchers Meet the Rattles	1965	12.50	25.00	50.00
PYE					
501	The Searchers	197?	3.75	7.50	15.00
—Reissue of Kapp hits					
508	The Searchers, Vol. 2	1976	3.75	7.50	15.00
RHINO					
RNLP 162	Greatest Hits	1985	2.50	5.00	10.00
R1-70162	Greatest Hits	1988	2.00	4.00	8.00
—Reissue of RNLP 162					
SIRE					
SRK 3523	Love's Melodies	1981	2.50	5.00	10.00
SRK 6082	The Searchers	1980	2.50	5.00	10.00

SEATRAIN

45s

Number	Title (A Side/B Side)	Yr	VG	VG+	NM
A&M					
994	As I Lay Losing/Let the Duchess Know	1968	2.00	4.00	8.00
—As "Sea Train"					
994 [PS]	As I Lay Losing/Let the Duchess Know	1968	3.75	7.50	15.00
—As "Sea Train"					
CAPITOL					
3067	13 Questions/Oh My Love-Sally Goodin	1971	—	3.00	6.00
3140	Song of Job/Waiting for Elijah	1971	—	3.00	6.00
3201	Marblehead Messenger/Despair Tire	1971	—	3.00	6.00
3275	Gramercy/How Sweet Thy Song	1972	—	3.00	6.00
WARNER BROS.					
7696	Flute Thing/Freedom Is the Reason	1973	—	2.50	5.00

Albums

Number	Title (A Side/B Side)	Yr	VG	VG+	NM
A&M					
SP-4171	Sea Train	1969	3.75	7.50	15.00
CAPITOL					
SMAS-650	Seatrain	1970	3.75	7.50	15.00
SMAS-829	Marblehead Messenger	1971	3.75	7.50	15.00
SN-16102	Seatrain	1980	2.00	4.00	8.00
—Budget-line reissue					
SN-16103	Marblehead Messenger	1980	2.00	4.00	8.00
—Budget-line reissue					
WARNER BROS.					
BS 2692	Watch	1973	3.00	6.00	12.00

SEBASTIAN, JOHN

Also see THE LOVIN' SPOONFUL.

45s

Number	Title (A Side/B Side)	Yr	VG	VG+	NM
KAMA SUTRA					
254	She's a Lady/The Room Nobody Lives In	1968	2.50	5.00	10.00
254 [PS]	She's a Lady/The Room Nobody Lives In	1968	3.75	7.50	15.00
505	Younger Generation/Boredom	1970	2.00	4.00	8.00
MGM					
14122	Rainbows All Over Your Blues/You're a Big Boy Now	1970	—	3.00	6.00
REPRISE					
0902	Fa-Fana-Fa/Magical Connection	1970	—	3.00	6.00
0918	What She Thinks About/Red-Eye Express	1970	—	3.00	6.00
1026	I Don't Want Nobody Else/Sweet Muse	1971	—	3.00	6.00
1050	We'll See/Well, Well, Well	1971	—	3.00	6.00
1074	Give Us a Break/Music for People Who Don't Speak English	1972	—	3.00	6.00
1349	Welcome Back Kotter/Warm Baby	1976	2.00	4.00	8.00
—Original A-side title					
1349	Welcome Back/Warm Baby	1976	—	2.00	4.00
—Revised A-side title					
1355	Hideaway/One Step Forward, Two Steps Back	1976	—	2.00	4.00

Albums

Number	Title (A Side/B Side)	Yr	VG	VG+	NM
MGM					
SE-4654	John B. Sebastian	1969	3.75	7.50	15.00
SE-4720	John Sebastian Live	1970	3.75	7.50	15.00
REPRISE					
MS 2036	Cheapo-Cheapo Productions Presents Real Live John Sebastian	1971	3.00	6.00	12.00
MS 2041	The Four of Us	1971	3.00	6.00	12.00
MS 2187	Tarzana Kid	1974	3.00	6.00	12.00
MS 2249	Welcome Back	1976	3.00	6.00	12.00
RS 6379	John B. Sebastian	1969	5.00	10.00	20.00
—Same album as MGM 4654, but a different mix					
RHINO					
R1-70170	The Best of John Sebastian (1969-1976)	1989	3.00	6.00	12.00

SECOND TIME, THE

45s

Number	Title (A Side/B Side)	Yr	VG	VG+	NM
TOWER					
432	Listen to the Music/Psychedelic Senate	1968	2.50	5.00	10.00

Albums

Number	Title (A Side/B Side)	Yr	VG	VG+	NM
TOWER					
ST 5146	Listen to the Music	1968	5.00	10.00	20.00

SECRET OYSTER

Albums

Number	Title (A Side/B Side)	Yr	VG	VG+	NM
PETERS INT'L.					
9003	Furtive Pearl	1973	7.50	15.00	30.00
9009	Sea Son	1974	6.25	12.50	25.00

SECRETS, THE (1)

Girl group.

45s

Number	Title (A Side/B Side)	Yr	VG	VG+	NM
OMEN					
15	Here I Am/I Feel a Thrill Coming On	1966	3.00	6.00	12.00
PHILIPS					
40146	The Boy Next Door/Learnin' to Forget	1963	3.75	7.50	15.00
40173	Hey Big Boy/The Other Side of Town	1964	3.00	6.00	12.00
40173 [PS]	Hey Big Boy/The Other Side of Town	1964	5.00	10.00	20.00
40196	Here He Comes Now!/Oh Donnie	1964	3.00	6.00	12.00
40222	He's the Boy/He Doesn't Want You	1964	3.00	6.00	12.00

SECRETS, THE (2)

45s

Number	Title (A Side/B Side)	Yr	VG	VG+	NM
SWAN					
4097	Hot Toddy/Twin Exhaust	1962	6.25	12.50	25.00
4097 [PS]	Hot Toddy/Twin Exhaust	1962	12.50	25.00	50.00

SECRETS, THE (U)

Could be group (1).

45s

Number	Title (A Side/B Side)	Yr	VG	VG+	NM
RED BIRD					
10-076	Every Day/A Smile Upside Down	1966	2.50	5.00	10.00

SEDAKA, NEIL

Also see THE TOKENS.

45s

Number	Title (A Side/B Side)	Yr	VG	VG+	NM
DECCA					
30520	Laura Lee/Snowtime	1957	15.00	30.00	60.00
ELEKTRA					
45406	Amarillo/The Leaving Game	1977	—	2.00	4.00
45421	Alone at Last/Sleazy Love	1977	—	2.00	4.00
45525	Candy Kisses/All You Need Is the Music	1978	—	2.00	4.00
46017	Sad, Sad Story/Tillie the Twirler	1979	—	2.00	4.00
46615	Should've Never Let You Go/You're So Good for Me	1980	—	2.00	4.00
—With Dara Sedaka					
47017	Letting Go/It's Good to Be Alive Again	1980	—	3.00	6.00
47184	My World Keeps Slipping Away/Love Is Spreading Over the World	1981	—	2.00	4.00
GUYDEN					
2004	Ring-a-Rockin'/Fly, Don't Fly on Me	1958	12.50	25.00	50.00
KIRSHNER					
SP-45-291 [DJ]	I'm a Song (Sing Me)/Silent Movies	1971	2.00	4.00	8.00
—Promo only number (mono versions)					
SP-45-370 [DJ]	Beautiful You (Long)/Beautiful You (Short)	1972	2.00	4.00	8.00
—Promo only number					
63-5017	I'm a Song (Sing Me)/Silent Movies	1971	—	2.50	5.00
—As "Sedaka"					
63-5020	Superbird/Rosemary Blue	1972	—	2.50	5.00
63-5024	Beautiful You/Anywhere You're Gonna Be (Leba's Song)	1972	—	3.00	6.00
LEGION					
133	Ring-a-Rockin'/Fly, Don't Fly on Me	1958	25.00	50.00	100.00
MCA					
60189	Laughter in the Rain/The Immigrant	197?	—	—	3.00
—Reissue					
MCA CURB					
52307	Your Precious Love/Searchin'	1983	—	2.00	4.00
—With Dara Sedaka					
52400	New Orleans/Rhythm of the Rain	1984	—	2.00	4.00
—With Gary U.S. Bonds					
MGM					
14564	Standing on the Inside/Let Daddy Know	1973	—	2.50	5.00
14661	Alone in New York in the Rain/Suspicions	1973	—	2.50	5.00
PYRAMID					
623	Oh Delilah/Neil's Twist	1962	7.50	15.00	30.00
—B-side is an instrumental version of the A-side credited to The Marvels					
RCA VICTOR					
SP-45-96 [DJ]	RCA Victor Special DJ Spots	196?	12.50	25.00	50.00
—Promo only; Sedaka introduces six songs and promotes his current release					
37-7829	Calendar Girl/The Same Old Fool	1960	12.50	25.00	50.00
—"Compact Single 33" (small hole, plays at LP speed)					
37-7874	Little Devil/I Must Be Dreaming	1961	12.50	25.00	50.00
—"Compact Single 33" (small hole, plays at LP speed)					

Number	Title (A Side/B Side)	Yr	VG	VG+	NM
37-7922	Sweet Little You/I Found My World in You	1961	12.50	25.00	50.00
—"Compact Single 33" (small hole, plays at LP speed)					
37-7957	Happy Birthday Sweet Sixteen/Don't Lead Me On	1961	12.50	25.00	50.00
—"Compact Single 33" (small hole, plays at LP speed)					
47-7408	The Diary/No Vacancy	1958	5.00	10.00	20.00
47-7408 [DJ]	The Diary/No Vacancy	1958	10.00	20.00	40.00
—White label promo with Sedaka's photo on label					
47-7473	I Go Ape/Moon of Gold	1959	5.00	10.00	20.00
47-7530	You Gotta Learn Your Rhythm and Blues/Crying My Heart Out for You	1959	6.25	12.50	25.00
47-7595	Oh! Carol/One Way Ticket (To the Blues)	1959	5.00	10.00	20.00
47-7709	Stairway to Heaven/Forty Winks Away	1960	3.75	7.50	15.00
47-7781	You Mean Everything to Me/Run Samson Run	1960	3.75	7.50	15.00
47-7781 [PS]	You Mean Everything to Me/Run Samson Run	1960	6.25	12.50	25.00
47-7829	Calendar Girl/The Same Old Fool	1960	3.75	7.50	15.00
47-7829 [PS]	Calendar Girl/The Same Old Fool	1960	6.25	12.50	25.00
47-7874	Little Devil/I Must Be Dreaming	1961	3.75	7.50	15.00
47-7874 [PS]	Little Devil/I Must Be Dreaming	1961	6.25	12.50	25.00
47-7922	Sweet Little You/I Found My World in You	1961	3.75	7.50	15.00
47-7922 [PS]	Sweet Little You/I Found My World in You	1961	6.25	12.50	25.00
47-7957	Happy Birthday Sweet Sixteen/Don't Lead Me On	1961	3.75	7.50	15.00
47-8007	King of Clowns/Walk with Me	1962	3.75	7.50	15.00
47-8007 [PS]	King of Clowns/Walk with Me	1962	6.25	12.50	25.00
47-8046	Breaking Up Is Hard to Do/As Long As I Live	1962	3.75	7.50	15.00
47-8046 [PS]	Breaking Up Is Hard to Do/As Long As I Live	1962	6.25	12.50	25.00
47-8086	Next Door to An Angel/I Belong to You	1962	3.75	7.50	15.00
47-8086 [PS]	Next Door to An Angel/I Belong to You	1962	6.25	12.50	25.00
47-8137	Alice in Wonderland/Circulate	1963	3.00	6.00	12.00
47-8137 [PS]	Alice in Wonderland/Circulate	1963	6.25	12.50	25.00
47-8169	Let's Go Steady Again/Waiting for Never	1963	3.00	6.00	12.00
47-8169 [PS]	Let's Go Steady Again/Waiting for Never	1963	6.25	12.50	25.00
47-8209	The Dreamer/Look Inside Your Heart	1963	3.00	6.00	12.00
47-8209 [PS]	The Dreamer/Look Inside Your Heart	1963	6.25	12.50	25.00
47-8254	Bad Girl/Wait 'Til You See My Baby	1963	3.00	6.00	12.00
47-8341	The Closest Thing to Heaven/Without a Song	1964	2.50	5.00	10.00
47-8341 [PS]	The Closest Thing to Heaven/Without a Song	1964	5.00	10.00	20.00
47-8382	Sunny/She'll Never Be You	1964	2.50	5.00	10.00
47-8453	I Hope He Breaks Your Heart/Too Late	1964	2.50	5.00	10.00
47-8511	Let the People Talk/In the Chapel with You	1965	2.50	5.00	10.00
47-8511 [PS]	Let the People Talk/In the Chapel with You	1965	5.00	10.00	20.00
47-8637	The World Through a Tear/High On a Mountain	1965	2.50	5.00	10.00
47-8637 [PS]	The World Through a Tear/High On a Mountain	1965	5.00	10.00	20.00
47-8737	The Answer to My Prayer/Blue Boy	1965	2.50	5.00	10.00
47-8844	The Answer Lies Within/Grown-Up Games	1966	2.50	5.00	10.00
47-9004	We Can Make It If We Try/Too Late	1966	2.50	5.00	10.00
61-7595 [S]	Oh! Carol/One Way Ticket (To the Blues)	1959	12.50	25.00	50.00
—"Living Stereo" (large hole, plays at 45 rpm)					
61-7709 [S]	Stairway to Heaven/Forty Winks Away	1960	12.50	25.00	50.00
—"Living Stereo" (large hole, plays at 45 rpm)					
61-7781 [S]	You Mean Everything to Me/Run Samson Run	1960	12.50	25.00	50.00
—"Living Stereo" (large hole, plays at 45 rpm)					
61-7829 [S]	Calendar Girl/The Same Old Fool	1960	12.50	25.00	50.00
—"Living Stereo" (large hole, plays at 45 rpm)					
447-0575	Oh! Carol/Calendar Girl	196?	—	3.00	6.00
—Gold Standard Series; black label					
447-0575	Oh! Carol/Calendar Girl	197?	—	2.00	4.00
—Gold Standard Series; red label					
447-0597	The Diary/Happy Birthday Sweet Sixteen	196?	—	3.00	6.00
—Gold Standard Series; black label					
447-0597	The Diary/Happy Birthday Sweet Sixteen	197?	—	2.00	4.00
—Gold Standard Series; red label					
447-0701	Breaking Up Is Hard to Do/Next Door to An Angel	196?	—	3.00	6.00
—Gold Standard Series; black label					
447-0701	Breaking Up Is Hard to Do/Next Door to An Angel	197?	—	2.00	4.00
—Gold Standard Series; red label					
447-0939	Little Devil/Stairway to Heaven	196?	—	3.00	6.00
—Gold Standard Series; black label					
ROCKET					
40313	Laughter in the Rain/Endlessly	1974	—	2.00	4.00
40370	The Immigrant/Hey Mister Sunshine	1975	—	2.00	4.00
—No mention of John Lennon on label					
40370	The Immigrant/Hey Mister Sunshine	1975	2.50	5.00	10.00
—With "Dedicated to John Lennon" under title in bold					
40426	That's When the Music Takes Me/Standing on the Inside	1975	—	2.00	4.00
40460	Bad Blood/Your Favorite Entertainer	1975	—	2.00	4.00
40500	Breaking Up Is Hard to Do/Nana's Song	1975	—	2.00	4.00
40543	Love in the Shadows/Baby Don't Let It Mess Your Mind	1976	—	2.00	4.00
40582	Steppin' Out/I Let You Walk Away	1976	—	2.00	4.00
40614	You Gotta Make Your Own Sunshine/Perfect Strangers	1976	—	2.00	4.00
SGC					
005	Star-Crossed Lovers/We Had a Good Thing Going	1969	—	3.00	6.00
008	Rainy Jane/Jeannine	1970	—	3.00	6.00

7-Inch Extended Plays

Number	Title	Yr	VG	VG+	NM
RCA VICTOR					
LPC-105	Oh! Carol/Stairway to Heaven//The Diary/Run Samson Run	1961	12.50	25.00	50.00
—"Compact Double 33" with small hole					
LPC-105 [PS]	Neil's Best	1961	12.50	25.00	50.00
LPC-135	Little Devil/Circulate//Calendar Girl/We Kiss in a Shadow	1961	12.50	25.00	50.00
—"Compact Double 33" with small hole					
LPC-135 [PS]	Little Devil	1961	12.50	25.00	50.00
EPA-4334	(contents unknown)	1959	15.00	30.00	60.00
EPA-4334 [PS]	I Go Ape	1959	15.00	30.00	60.00
EPA-4353	(contents unknown)	1959	15.00	30.00	60.00
EPA-4353 [PS]	Oh! Carol	1959	15.00	30.00	60.00

Albums

Number	Title	Yr	VG	VG+	NM
ACCORD					
SN-7152	Singer, Songwriter, Melody Maker	1981	2.50	5.00	10.00
ELEKTRA					
6E-102	A Song	1977	2.50	5.00	10.00
6E-161	All You Need Is Music	1978	2.50	5.00	10.00
6E-259	In the Pocket	1980	2.50	5.00	10.00
6E-348	Neil Sedaka Now	1981	2.50	5.00	10.00
KIRSHNER					
KES-111	Emergence	1971	3.75	7.50	15.00
KES-117	Solitaire	1972	3.75	7.50	15.00
MCA					
2357	Sedaka's Back	1978	2.50	5.00	10.00
—Reissue of Rocket 463					
5466	Come See About Me	1984	2.50	5.00	10.00
PICKWICK					
ACL1-7006	Breaking Up Is Hard to Do	197?	2.00	4.00	8.00
POLYDOR					
831235-1	My Friend	1986	2.50	5.00	10.00
RCA CAMDEN					
ACL1-7006	Breaking Up Is Hard to Do	197?	2.50	5.00	10.00
RCA VICTOR					
ANL1-0879	Oh! Carol	1975	2.50	5.00	10.00
AFL1-0928	Neil Sedaka Sings His Greatest Hits	1977	2.50	5.00	10.00
—Reissue with new prefix					
APL1-0928	Neil Sedaka Sings His Greatest Hits	1975	3.00	6.00	12.00
—Reissue of LSP-2627					
ANL1-1314	Pure Gold	1976	2.50	5.00	10.00
VPL1-1540	Live in Australia	1976	3.00	6.00	12.00
APL1-1789	Emergence	1976	3.00	6.00	12.00
—Reissue of Kirshner 111					
APL1-1790	Solitaire	1976	3.00	6.00	12.00
—Reissue of Kirshner 117					
LPM-2065 [M]	Neil Sedaka	1959	15.00	30.00	60.00
LSP-2065 [S]	Neil Sedaka	1959	25.00	50.00	100.00
AFL1-2254	Sedaka — The '50s and '60s	1977	2.50	5.00	10.00
LPM-2317 [M]	Circulate	1960	12.50	25.00	50.00
LSP-2317 [S]	Circulate	1960	15.00	30.00	60.00
LPM-2421 [M]	"Little Devil" and His Other Hits	1961	12.50	25.00	50.00
LSP-2421 [S]	"Little Devil" and His Other Hits	1961	15.00	30.00	60.00
AFL1-2524	The Many Sides of Neil Sedaka	1978	2.50	5.00	10.00
LPM-2627 [M]	Neil Sedaka Sings His Greatest Hits	1962	10.00	20.00	40.00
LSP-2627 [S]	Neil Sedaka Sings His Greatest Hits	1962	12.50	25.00	50.00
ANL1-3465	Neil Sedaka Sings His Greatest Hits	1979	2.00	4.00	8.00
—Reissue of AFL1-0928					
ROCKET					
MCA-463	Sedaka's Back	1974	3.00	6.00	12.00
PIG-2157	The Hungry Years	1975	3.00	6.00	12.00
PIG-2195	Steppin' Out	1976	3.00	6.00	12.00
PIG-2297	Neil Sedaka's Greatest Hits	1977	3.00	6.00	12.00

SEDAKA, NEIL, AND THE TOKENS WITH THE COINS

Also see each artist's individual listings.

Albums

Number	Title	Yr	VG	VG+	NM
CROWN					
CST-366 [R]	Neil Sedaka and the Tokens and the Coins	1963	5.00	10.00	20.00
CLP-5366 [M]	Neil Sedaka and the Tokens and the Coins	1963	7.50	15.00	30.00

SEEDS, THE

Also see RITCHIE MARSH; SKY SAXON.

45s

Number	Title (A Side/B Side)	Yr	VG	VG+	NM
GNP CRESCENDO					
354	Can't Seem to Make You Mine/Daisy Mae	1965	3.75	7.50	15.00
354	Can't Seem to Make You Mine/I Tell Myself	1967	2.50	5.00	10.00
354 [PS]	Can't Seem to Make You Mine/I Tell Myself	1967	12.50	25.00	50.00
364	You're Pushing Too Hard/Out of the Question	1965	3.75	7.50	15.00
370	The Other Place/Try to Understand	1966	3.75	7.50	15.00
372	Pushin' Too Hard/Try to Understand	1966	3.75	7.50	15.00
—With "GNP Crescendo" standing alone at top of label (no box)					
372	Pushin' Too Hard/Try to Understand	1966	3.00	6.00	12.00
—With "GNP Crescendo" in box at top of label					
383	Mr. Farmer/No Escape	1967	2.00	4.00	8.00
383	Mr. Farmer/Up in Her Room	1967	2.00	4.00	8.00
383 [PS]	Mr. Farmer/Up in Her Room	1967	12.50	25.00	50.00
394	A Thousand Shadows/March of the Flower Children	1967	2.00	4.00	8.00
394 [PS]	A Thousand Shadows/March of the Flower Children	1967	5.00	10.00	20.00
398	The Wind Blows Your Hair/Six Dreams	1967	2.00	4.00	8.00
408	Satisfy You/900 Million People Daily	1968	2.00	4.00	8.00
422	Fallin' Off the Edge of My Mind/Wild Blood	1969	2.50	5.00	10.00
MGM					
14163	Wish Me Up/Bad Part of Town	1970	5.00	10.00	20.00
14190	Did He Die/Love in a Summer Blanket	1970	5.00	10.00	20.00
PHILCO-FORD					
HP-26	Pushin' Too Hard/Can't Seem to Make You Mine	1968	6.25	12.50	25.00
—4-inch plastic "Hip Pocket Record" with color sleeve					

Albums

Number	Title	Yr	VG	VG+	NM
GNP CRESCENDO					
GNP-2023 [M]	The Seeds	1966	15.00	30.00	60.00
GNPS-2023 [S]	The Seeds	1966	10.00	20.00	40.00
GNP-2033 [M]	A Web of Sound	1967	15.00	30.00	60.00
GNPS-2033 [S]	A Web of Sound	1967	10.00	20.00	40.00
GNP-2038 [M]	Future	1967	10.00	20.00	40.00
—Deduct 25% if two inserts are missing					
GNPS-2038 [S]	Future	1967	7.50	15.00	30.00
—Deduct 25% if two inserts are missing					
GNPS-2040	Full Spoon of Seedy Blues	1968	6.25	12.50	25.00
GNPS-2043	Raw and Alive	1968	6.25	12.50	25.00
GNPS-2107	Fallin' Off the Edge	1977	2.50	5.00	10.00
ST-91224	A Web of Sound	1968	7.50	15.00	30.00
—Capitol Record Club edition					

SEEGER, PETE

Also see THE WEAVERS.

45s

Number	Title (A Side/B Side)	Yr	VG	VG+	NM
COLUMBIA					
42940	Little Boxes/Mail Myself to You	1963	2.00	4.00	8.00

Number	Title (A Side/B Side)	Yr	VG	VG+	NM
43349	Healing River/Johnny Give Me	1965	2.00	4.00	8.00
43699	Draft Dodger Rag/Guantanamera	1966	2.00	4.00	8.00
44273	Waist Deep in the Big Muddy/Down by the Riverside	1967	2.00	4.00	8.00
FOLKWAYS					
45-201	The Battle of New Orleans/My Home's Across the Smokey Mountains	1959	3.00	6.00	12.00
Albums					
ARAVEL					
AB 1006 [M]	Live Hootenanny	1963	3.75	7.50	15.00
ARCHIVE OF FOLK AND JAZZ					
201	Pete Seeger	1966	3.00	6.00	12.00
BROADSIDE					
502 [(2)]	Pete Seeger Sings and Answers Questions	1970	3.75	7.50	15.00
BULLDOG					
BDL-2011	20 Golden Pieces of Pete Seeger	198?	2.50	5.00	10.00
CAPITOL					
DW 2172 [R]	Folk Songs	1964	3.00	6.00	12.00
W 2172 [M]	Folk Songs	1964	5.00	10.00	20.00
DT 2718 [R]	Freight Train	1967	3.00	6.00	12.00
T 2718 [M]	Freight Train	1967	5.00	10.00	20.00
COLUMBIA					
CL 1668 [M]	Pete Seeger Story Songs	1961	6.25	12.50	25.00
CL 1916 [M]	The Bitter and the Sweet	1962	6.25	12.50	25.00
CL 1947 [M]	Children's Concert at Town Hall	1963	6.25	12.50	25.00
CL 2101 [M]	We Shall Overcome	1963	3.75	7.50	15.00
CL 2257 [M]	I Can See a New Day	1965	3.75	7.50	15.00
CL 2334 [M]	Strangers and Cousins	1964	3.75	7.50	15.00
CL 2432 [M]	God Bless the Grass	1966	3.75	7.50	15.00
CL 2503 [M]	Dangerous Songs?	1966	3.75	7.50	15.00
CL 2616 [M]	Pete Seeger's Greatest Hits	1967	5.00	10.00	20.00
CL 2705 [M]	Waist Deep in the Big Muddy	1967	5.00	10.00	20.00
CS 8468 [S]	Pete Seeger Story Songs	1961	7.50	15.00	30.00
CS 8716 [S]	The Bitter and the Sweet	1962	7.50	15.00	30.00
CS 8747 [S]	Children's Concert at Town Hall	1963	7.50	15.00	30.00
CS 8901 [S]	We Shall Overcome	1963	5.00	10.00	20.00
CS 9057 [S]	I Can See a New Day	1965	5.00	10.00	20.00
CS 9134 [S]	Strangers and Cousins	1964	5.00	10.00	20.00
CS 9232 [S]	God Bless the Grass	1966	5.00	10.00	20.00
CS 9303 [S]	Dangerous Songs?	1966	5.00	10.00	20.00
CS 9416 [S]	Pete Seeger's Greatest Hits	1967	3.75	7.50	15.00
PC 9416	Pete Seeger's Greatest Hits	198?	2.00	4.00	8.00
—Reissue with new prefix					
CS 9505 [S]	Waist Deep in the Big Muddy	1967	3.75	7.50	15.00
CS 9717	Pete Seeger Now	1968	3.75	7.50	15.00
CS 9873	Young vs. Old	1969	3.75	7.50	15.00
C 30739	Rainbow Race	1971	3.00	6.00	12.00
KG 31949 [(2)]	The World of Pete Seeger	1972	3.75	7.50	15.00
DISC					
D-101 [M]	Sing with Seeger	1964	5.00	10.00	20.00
FOLKWAYS					
FP-3 [10]	Darling Corey	1950	25.00	50.00	100.00
FP-10 [10]	Lonesome Valley	195?	25.00	50.00	100.00
FP-43 [10]	A Pete Seeger Sampler	195?	25.00	50.00	100.00
FP-45 [10]	Goofing Off Suite	195?	25.00	50.00	100.00
FP-701 [10]	American Folk Songs for Children	195?	25.00	50.00	100.00
FP-710 [10]	Birds, Beasts, Bugs and Little Fishes	1954	25.00	50.00	100.00
FP-911 [10]	Folk Songs of Four Continents	195?	25.00	50.00	100.00
FA-2003 [10]	Darling Corey	1950	20.00	40.00	80.00
FA-2010 [10]	Lonesome Valley	195?	20.00	40.00	80.00
FA-2043 [10]	A Pete Seeger Sampler	1954	20.00	40.00	80.00
FA-2045 [10]	Goofing Off Suite	1954	20.00	40.00	80.00
FA-2175 [10]	Frontier Ballads, Volume 1	1954	20.00	40.00	80.00
FA-2176 [10]	Frontier Ballads, Volume 2	1954	20.00	40.00	80.00
FA-2311 [M]	Traditional Christmas Carols	1956	7.50	15.00	30.00
FA-2319 [M]	American Ballads	1957	7.50	15.00	30.00
FA-2320 [M]	American Favorite Ballads, Vol. 1	1957	7.50	15.00	30.00
FA-2321 [M]	American Favorite Ballads, Vol. 2	1958	7.50	15.00	30.00
FA-2322 [M]	American Favorite Ballads, Vol. 3	1958	7.50	15.00	30.00
FA-2323 [M]	American Favorite Ballads, Vol. 4	1961	5.00	10.00	20.00
FA-2412 [M]	Pete Seeger and Sonny Terry	1958	7.50	15.00	30.00
FA-2439 [M]	Nonesuch	196?	5.00	10.00	20.00
FA-2445 [M]	American Favorite Ballads, Vol. 5: Tunes and Songs As Sung by Pete Seeger	1962	5.00	10.00	20.00
FA-2450 [M]	Highlights of Pete Seeger at the Village Gate with Memphis Slim and Willie Dixon	1960	7.50	15.00	30.00
FA-2451 [M]	Pete Seeger at the Village Gate — Vol. 2	1960	7.50	15.00	30.00
FA-2452 [M]	With Voices Together We Sing	1956	6.25	12.50	25.00
FA-2453 [M]	Love Songs for Friends and Foes	1956	6.25	12.50	25.00
FA-2454 [M]	Rainbow Quest	1960	6.25	12.50	25.00
FA-2455 [M]	Sing Out with Pete!	1961	5.00	10.00	20.00
FA-2456 [M]	Broadsides	1964	5.00	10.00	20.00
FA-2501 [M]	Gazette, Vol. 1	1958	6.25	12.50	25.00
FA-2502 [M]	Gazette, Vol. 2	1962	5.00	10.00	20.00
FN-2511 [M]	Hootenanny Tonight!	195?	6.25	12.50	25.00
FN-2513 [M]	Sing Out! Hootenanny	1963	5.00	10.00	20.00
FS-3851 [M]	Indian Summer	1960	6.25	12.50	25.00
—With Michael Seeger					
5003 [(2)]	Frontier Ballads	1954	25.00	50.00	100.00
FH-5210 [M]	Champlain Valley Songs	1960	6.25	12.50	25.00
FH-5233 [M]	Songs of Struggle and Protest 1930-50	1959	6.25	12.50	25.00
FH-5251 [M]	American Industrial Ballads	1956	7.50	15.00	30.00
FH-5257	Fifty Sail On Newburgh Bay	1976	3.00	6.00	12.00
FH-5302 [M]	Broadside Ballads, Vol. 2	1963	5.00	10.00	20.00
FH-5436 [M]	Songs of the Spanish Civil War, Vol. 1	1961	5.00	10.00	20.00
FH-5485 [M]	Ballads of Sacco and Vanzetti	1963	5.00	10.00	20.00
FH-5595 [M]	WNEW's Story of Selma	1965	5.00	10.00	20.00
FH-5702 [(2)]	Pete Seeger Sings and Answers Questions	1968	6.25	12.50	25.00
FW-6843 [10]	German Folk Songs	1954	20.00	40.00	80.00
FW-6911 [10]	Folk Songs of Four Continents	1955	20.00	40.00	80.00
FW-6912 [10]	Bantu Choral Folk Songs	1955	20.00	40.00	80.00
FC-7020 [10]	Songs to Grow On — Vol. 2	1951	20.00	40.00	80.00
FC-7027 [10]	Songs to Grow On — Vol. 3	1951	20.00	40.00	80.00
FC-7526 [M]	Song and Play Time	195?	12.50	25.00	50.00
7527	Zhitkov's How I Hunted the Little Fellows	1980	3.00	6.00	12.00
FC-7601 [10]	American Folk Songs for Children	1953	20.00	40.00	80.00
FC-7610 [10]	Birds, Beasts, Bugs and Little Fishes	1954	20.00	40.00	80.00
FC-7611 [M]	Birds, Beasts, Bugs and Bigger Fishes	1954	12.50	25.00	50.00
FC-7674 [M]	American Game and Activity Songs for Children	1962	5.00	10.00	20.00
FI-8303 [M]	How to Play the Five String Banjo	195?	6.25	12.50	25.00
FI-8354 [M]	Folksinger's Guitar Guide Vol. 1: An Instruction Record	1955	7.50	15.00	30.00
FQ-8354 [M]	The Folksinger's Guitar Gude	1955	6.25	12.50	25.00
FI-8371 [M]	12-String Guitar As Played by Leadbelly	1962	5.00	10.00	20.00
FTS-31002 [R]	Pete Seeger Sings Woody Guthrie	1968	3.00	6.00	12.00
FTS-31017 [R]	American Favorite Ballads	1968	3.00	6.00	12.00
FTS-31018 [R]	Wimoweh and Other Songs of Freedom and Protest	1968	3.00	6.00	12.00
FTS-31022 [R]	Pete Seeger Sings Leadbelly	1968	3.00	6.00	12.00
FTS-31040 [R]	Banks of Marble and Other Songs	1974	3.00	6.00	12.00
FTS-32311 [R]	Traditional Christmas Carols	1967	3.75	7.50	15.00
FT-35001 [(2)]	The Nativity: By Sholem Asch	1963	3.75	7.50	15.00
FXM-36055 [(2)]	Sing Along	1980	3.75	7.50	15.00
37232	God Bless the Grass	1982	3.00	6.00	12.00
HARMONY					
HS 11337	John Henry and Other Folk Favorites	1969	3.00	6.00	12.00
ODYSSEY					
32160266	3 Saints, 4 Sinners and 6 Other People	1968	3.75	7.50	15.00
OLYMPIC					
7102	America's Balladeer	1973	3.00	6.00	12.00
PAIR					
PDL2-1076 [(2)]	Clearwater Classics	1986	3.00	6.00	12.00
PHILIPS					
PHM 2-300 [(2) M]	The Story of the Nativity	1963	5.00	10.00	20.00
PHM 2-300 [(2) M]	The Story of the Nativity	1963	5.00	10.00	20.00
PHS 2-300 [(2) S]	The Story of the Nativity	1963	6.25	12.50	25.00
PHS 2-300 [(2) S]	The Story of the Nativity	1963	6.25	12.50	25.00
SMITHSONIAN FOLKWAYS					
SF-40024	Traditional Christmas Carols	1989	3.00	6.00	12.00
STINSON					
SLP-52 [10]	Lincoln Brigade	1953	25.00	50.00	100.00
SLP-57 [10]	A Pete Seeger Concert	1953	25.00	50.00	100.00
SLP-90 [M]	Pete	1963	6.25	12.50	25.00
TRADITION					
2107	Folk Music of the World	1973	3.00	6.00	12.00
VANGUARD					
VSD-97/98 [(2)]	The Essential Pete Seeger	1978	3.75	7.50	15.00
VSD-73111	The Essential Pete Seeger, Vol. 1	198?	2.00	4.00	8.00
VSD-73112	The Essential Pete Seeger, Vol. 2	198?	2.00	4.00	8.00
VERVE FOLKWAYS					
FV-9008 [M]	Pete Seeger and Big Bill Broonzy in Concert	1965	5.00	10.00	20.00
FVS-9008 [S]	Pete Seeger and Big Bill Broonzy in Concert	1965	6.25	12.50	25.00
FV-9009 [M]	Pete Seeger On Campus	1965	5.00	10.00	20.00
FVS-9009 [S]	Pete Seeger On Campus	1965	6.25	12.50	25.00
FV-9013 [M]	Folk Music Live at the Village Gate	1965	5.00	10.00	20.00
FVS-9013 [S]	Folk Music Live at the Village Gate	1965	6.25	12.50	25.00
FV-9020 [M]	Little Boxes and Other Broadsides	1965	5.00	10.00	20.00
FVS-9020 [S]	Little Boxes and Other Broadsides	1965	6.25	12.50	25.00
WARNER BROS.					
BSK 3329	Circles and Seasons	1979	3.00	6.00	12.00

SEEKERS, THE

Number	Title (A Side/B Side)	Yr	VG	VG+	NM
45s					
ATMOS					
711	Myra/Wild Rover	1965	3.75	7.50	15.00
CAPITOL					
2013	When the Good Apples Fall/Myra (Shake Up the Party)	1967	2.50	5.00	10.00
2122	Love Is Kind, Love Is Wine/All I Can Remember	1968	2.50	5.00	10.00
5383	I'll Never Find Another You/Open Up Them Pearly Gates	1965	3.00	6.00	12.00
5430	A World of Our Own/Sinner Man	1965	3.00	6.00	12.00
5430 [PS]	A World of Our Own/Sinner Man	1965	5.00	10.00	20.00
5531	The Carnival Is Over/We Shall Not Be Moved	1965	2.50	5.00	10.00
5622	Some Day, One Day/Nobody Knows the Trouble I've Seen	1966	2.50	5.00	10.00
5756	Georgy Girl/When the Stars Begin to Fall	1966	3.00	6.00	12.00
5787	Morningtown Ride/Walk with Me	1967	2.50	5.00	10.00
5974	I Wish You Could Be Here/On the Other Side	1967	2.50	5.00	10.00
CAPITOL CREATIVE PRODUCTS					
50 [DJ]	Island of Dreams/Breaking My Back — Instead of Using My Mind	1966	3.75	7.50	15.00
—B-side by Lou Rawls					
50 [PS]	Island of Dreams/Breaking My Back — Instead of Using My Mind	1966	5.00	10.00	20.00
—Custom sleeve; no titles or artist, but "#50" is at right and "Capitol has specially produced this record for Frito-Lay" is under the center hole					
MARVEL					
1060	Chilly Winds/The Light from the Lighthouse	1965	3.75	7.50	15.00
Albums					
CAPITOL					
ST-135 [S]	The Seekers Live	1969	3.00	6.00	12.00
ST 2319 [S]	The New Seekers	1965	3.75	7.50	15.00
T 2319 [M]	The New Seekers	1965	3.00	6.00	12.00
DT 2369 [R]	A World of Our Own	1965	3.00	6.00	12.00
T 2369 [M]	A World of Our Own	1965	3.00	6.00	12.00
ST 2431 [S]	Georgy Girl	1966	3.75	7.50	15.00
T 2431 [M]	Georgy Girl	1966	3.00	6.00	12.00
DT 2746 [P]	The Best of the Seekers	1967	3.00	6.00	12.00
—Red and white "target" Starline label. "Morningtown Ride," Turn, Turn, Turn," and "We're Moving On" are in stereo.					
DT 2746 [P]	The Best of the Seekers	196?	2.50	5.00	10.00
—Red and white "star" Starline label					
SM-2746 [P]	The Best of the Seekers	197?	2.50	5.00	10.00
T 2746 [M]	The Best of the Seekers	1967	3.00	6.00	12.00
SKAO 2821 [S]	The Seekers Seen in Green	1968	3.75	7.50	15.00
SN-16104 [P]	The Best of the Seekers	1980	2.00	4.00	8.00

Number	Title (A Side/B Side)	Yr	VG	VG+	NM
MARVEL					
2060 [M]	The Seekers	1965	3.00	6.00	12.00
3060 [R]	The Seekers	1965	2.50	5.00	10.00

SEGAL, GEORGE

45s

Number	Title (A Side/B Side)	Yr	VG	VG+	NM
PHILIPS					
40468	The Yama-Yama Man/Yes Sir, That's My Baby	1967	2.00	4.00	8.00
SIGNATURE					
SB-10099	If You Like-a Me/What You Goin' to Do When the Rent Comes Around	1974	—	3.00	6.00

Albums

Number	Title (A Side/B Side)	Yr	VG	VG+	NM
PHILIPS					
PHM 200242 [M]	The Yama-Yama Man	1967	5.00	10.00	20.00
PHS 600242 [S]	The Yama-Yama Man	1967	5.00	10.00	20.00
SIGNATURE					
BSL1-0654	A Touch of Ragtime	1976	3.75	7.50	15.00

SEGER, BOB

Includes records with The Last Heard, The Bob Seger System and The Silver Bullet Band. Also see THE BEACH BUMS.

12-Inch Singles

Number	Title (A Side/B Side)	Yr	VG	VG+	NM
CAPITOL					
SPRO-8987 [DJ]	We've Got Tonite (single)/We've Got Tonite (LP)	1978	3.00	6.00	12.00
SPRO-9085/6 [DJ]	Old Time Rock and Roll/Sunspot Baby	1979	3.75	7.50	15.00
SPRO-9641/2 [DJ]	American Storm (Edit)/American Storm (LP)	1986	—	3.00	6.00
SPRO-9687/8 [DJ]	Tryin' to Live My Life Without You (3:00)/(3:46)	1981	2.50	5.00	10.00
SPRO-9705 [DJ]	Like a Rock (Edit)/Like a Rock (LP)	1986	2.00	4.00	8.00
SPRO-9736 [DJ]	The Aftermath (remix)/The Aftermath (LP)	1986	—	3.00	6.00
SPRO-9778 [DJ]	It's You (45 remix)/The Aftermath (remix)	1986	—	3.00	6.00
SPRO-9866/74 [DJ]	Miami (Extended)/Miami (LP)	1986	—	3.00	6.00

45s

Number	Title (A Side/B Side)	Yr	VG	VG+	NM
ABKCO					
4015	East Side Story/East Side Sound	1973	—	3.00	6.00
4016	Chain Smokin'/Persecution Smith	1973	—	3.00	6.00
4017	Heavy Music - Pt. I/Heavy Music - Pt. II	1973	—	3.00	6.00
4031	Heavy Music - Pt. I/Heavy Music - Pt. II	1973	—	2.50	5.00
CAMEO					
438	East Side Story/East Side Sound	1966	6.25	12.50	25.00
444	Sock It To Me, Santa/Florida Time	1966	7.50	15.00	30.00
465	Chain Smokin'/Persecution Smith	1967	6.25	12.50	25.00
473	Vagrant Winter/Very Few	1967	6.25	12.50	25.00
494	Heavy Music/Heavy Music (Part 2)	1967	5.00	10.00	20.00
CAPITOL					
2143	2 + 2 = ?/Death Row	1968	3.75	7.50	15.00
2297	Ramblin' Gamblin' Man/Tales of Lucy Blue	1968	3.00	6.00	12.00
2480	Ivory/The Lost Song (Love Needs to Be Loved)	1969	2.00	4.00	8.00
2576	Noah/Lennie Johnson	1969	2.00	4.00	8.00
2640	Lonely Man/Innervenus Eyes	1970	2.00	4.00	8.00
2748	Lucifer/Big River	1970	2.00	4.00	8.00
3187	Lookin' Back/Highway Child	1971	2.00	4.00	8.00
4062	Beautiful Loser/Fine Memory	1975	—	2.50	5.00
4116	Katmandu/Black Night	1975	—	2.50	5.00
4183	Nutbush City Limits/Travelin' Man	1975	—	2.50	5.00
4269	Nutbush City Limits/Lookin' Back	1976	—	2.50	5.00
4300	Beautiful Loser/Travelin' Man	1976	—	2.50	5.00
4369	Night Moves/Ship of Fools	1976	—	2.00	4.00
4422	Mainstreet/Jody Girl	1977	—	2.00	4.00
4449	Rock and Roll Never Forgets/Fire Down Below	1977	—	2.00	4.00
4581	Still the Same/Feel Like a Number	1978	—	2.00	4.00
4618	Hollywood Nights/Brave Strangers	1978	—	2.00	4.00
4653	We've Got Tonite/Ain't Got No Money	1978	—	2.00	4.00
4653 [DJ]	We've Got Tonite (mono/stereo)	1978	2.50	5.00	10.00
—Silver vinyl					
4653 [PS]	We've Got Tonite/Ain't Got No Money	1978	—	3.00	6.00
4702	Old Time Rock and Roll/Sunspot Baby	1979	—	2.00	4.00
4702 [PS]	Old Time Rock and Roll/Sunspot Baby	1979	—	3.00	6.00
4836	Fire Lake/Long Twin Silver Line	1980	—	2.00	4.00
4836 [PS]	Fire Lake/Long Twin Silver Line	1980	—	3.00	6.00
4863	Against the Wind/No Man's Land	1980	—	2.00	4.00
4863 [PS]	Against the Wind/No Man's Land	1980	—	3.00	6.00
4904	You'll Accomp'ny Me/Betty Lou's Gettin' Out Tonight	1980	—	2.50	5.00
4904 [PS]	You'll Accomp'ny Me/Betty Lou's Gettin' Out Tonight	1980	—	3.00	6.00
4951	The Horizontal Bop/Her Strut	1980	—	2.50	5.00
4951 [PS]	The Horizontal Bop/Her Strut	1980	25.00	50.00	100.00
A-5042	Tryin' to Live My Life Without You/Brave Strangers	1981	—	—	3.00
A-5042 [PS]	Tryin' to Live My Life Without You/Brave Strangers	1981	—	2.00	4.00
A-5077	Feel Like a Number/Hollywood Nights	1981	—	2.00	4.00
A-5077 [PS]	Feel Like a Number/Hollywood Nights	1981	—	2.50	5.00
B-5187	Shame on the Moon/House Behind a House	1982	—	—	3.00
B-5187 [PS]	Shame on the Moon/House Behind a House	1982	—	2.00	4.00
B-5213	Even Now/Little Victories	1983	—	—	3.00
B-5213 [PS]	Even Now/Little Victories	1983	—	2.00	4.00
B-5235	Roll Me Away/Boomtown Blues	1983	—	—	3.00
B-5235 [PS]	Roll Me Away/Boomtown Blues	1983	—	2.00	4.00
B-5276	Old Time Rock and Roll/Till It Shines	1983	—	—	3.00
B-5276 [PS]	Old Time Rock and Roll/Till It Shines	1983	—	2.50	5.00
B-5413	Understanding/East L.A.	1984	—	—	3.00
B-5413 [PS]	Understanding/East L.A.	1984	—	2.00	4.00
B-5532	American Storm/Fortunate Son	1986	—	—	3.00
B-5532 [PS]	American Storm/Fortunate Son	1986	—	—	3.00
B-5592	Like a Rock/Livin' Inside My Heart	1986	—	—	3.00
B-5592 [PS]	Like a Rock/Livin' Inside My Heart	1986	—	—	3.00
B-5623	It's You/The Aftermath (12" Remix)	1986	—	—	3.00
B-5623 [PS]	It's You/The Aftermath (12" Remix)	1986	—	—	3.00
B-5658	Miami/Somewhere Tonight	1986	—	—	3.00
B-5658 [PS]	Miami/Somewhere Tonight	1986	6.25	12.50	25.00
—May only have been released in the New York metro area, as it quotes reviewers from four different New York newspapers					
SPRO 8433 [DJ]	Travelin' Man/Beautiful Loser	1976	2.50	5.00	10.00
S7-18298	C'est La Vie/Night Moves	1995	—	2.00	4.00
NR-44761	The Real Love/Roll Me Away	1991	—	2.00	4.00
NR-44793	The Fire Inside/New Coat of Paint	1991	—	2.00	4.00
S7-56784	Like a Rock/Sunspot Baby	1992	—	2.00	4.00
S7-57732	New Coat of Paint/Blind Love	1992	—	2.00	4.00
S7-57742	Night Moves/Her Strut	1992	—	2.00	4.00
S7-57797	Old TIme Rock and Roll/Turn the Page	1992	—	2.00	4.00
HIDEOUT					
1013	East Side Story/East Side Sound	1966	12.50	25.00	50.00
1014	Chain Smokin'/Persecution Smith	1966	12.50	25.00	50.00
MCA					
53094	Shakedown/The Aftermath	1987	—	—	3.00
53094 [PS]	Shakedown/The Aftermath	1987	—	2.00	4.00
—Picture of Bob Seger on cover					
53094 [PS]	Shakedown/The Aftermath	1987	2.50	5.00	10.00
—Picture of Eddie Murphy as Axel Foley on cover					
PALLADIUM					
1079	If I Were a Carpenter/Jesse James	1972	2.50	5.00	10.00
1117	Turn On Your Love Light/Who Do You Love?	1972	2.50	5.00	10.00
1143	Rosalie/Neon Sky	1972	2.50	5.00	10.00
1171	Need Ya/Seen a Lot of Floors	1973	2.50	5.00	10.00
1205	Get Out of Denver/Long Song Comin'	1974	2.50	5.00	10.00
1316	This Ole House/U.M.C.	1974	3.75	7.50	15.00
REPRISE					
PRO 571 [DJ]	Midnight Rider (same on both sides)	1972	3.75	7.50	15.00

Albums

Number	Title (A Side/B Side)	Yr	VG	VG+	NM
CAPITOL					
(no #) [PD]	Night Moves	1977	10.00	20.00	40.00
—Promo-only picture disc					
SM-172	Ramblin' Gamblin' Man	1977	2.00	4.00	8.00
ST-172	Ramblin' Gamblin' Man	1969	7.50	15.00	30.00
—Black label with colorband					
ST-236	Noah	1969	20.00	40.00	80.00
SKAO-499	Mongrel	1970	6.25	12.50	25.00
SM-499	Mongrel	1977	2.00	4.00	8.00
ST-731	Brand New Morning	1971	25.00	50.00	100.00
SPRO-8433 [DJ]	Consensus Cuts Edited for Airplay from "Live Bullet"	1976	6.25	12.50	25.00
ST-11378	Beautiful Loser	1975	2.50	5.00	10.00
—Originals have orange labels					
ST-11378	Beautiful Loser	1978	2.00	4.00	8.00
—Purple label with large Capitol logo					
SKBB-11523 [(2)]	Live Bullet	1976	3.75	7.50	15.00
—Originals have orange labels					
SKBB-11523 [(2)]	Live Bullet	1978	3.00	6.00	12.00
—Purple label with large Capitol logo					
SKBB-11523 [(2)]	Live Bullet	1983	3.00	6.00	12.00
—Black label, print in colorband					
STBK-11523 [(2)]	Live Bullet	1988	3.00	6.00	12.00
—Purple label with smaller Capitol logo					
ST-11557	Night Moves	1976	2.50	5.00	10.00
SW-11698	Stranger in Town	1978	2.50	5.00	10.00
ST-11746	Smokin' O.P.'s	1978	2.50	5.00	10.00
ST-11748	Seven	1978	2.50	5.00	10.00
SEAX-11904 [PD]	Stranger in Town	1978	6.25	12.50	25.00
SOO-12041	Against the Wind	1980	2.50	5.00	10.00
STBX-12182 [(2)]	Nine Tonight	1981	3.75	7.50	15.00
ST-12254	The Distance	1983	2.50	5.00	10.00
PT-12398	Like a Rock	1986	2.50	5.00	10.00
SN-16105	Ramblin' Gamblin' Man	1980	2.00	4.00	8.00
SN-16106	Mongrel	1980	2.00	4.00	8.00
SN-16107	Smokin' O.P.'s	1980	2.00	4.00	8.00
SN-16108	Seven	1980	2.00	4.00	8.00
SN-16315	Beautiful Loser	1984	2.00	4.00	8.00
C1-30334	Greatest Hits	1994	3.75	7.50	15.00
C1-91134	The Fire Inside	1991	3.00	6.00	12.00
C1-99774	It's a Mystery	1995	—	—	—
—Canceled					
MOBILE FIDELITY					
1-034	Night Moves	1980	10.00	20.00	40.00
—Audiophile vinyl					
1-127	Against the Wind	1983	10.00	20.00	40.00
—Audiophile vinyl					
PALLADIUM					
P-1006	Smokin' O.P.'s	1972	6.25	12.50	25.00
REPRISE					
MS 2109	Smokin' O.P.'s	1972	3.75	7.50	15.00
MS 2126	Back in '72	1973	15.00	30.00	60.00
MS 2184	Seven	1974	5.00	10.00	20.00

SELECTIONS, THE

45s

Number	Title (A Side/B Side)	Yr	VG	VG+	NM
ANTONE					
101	Guardian Angel/Soft and Sweet	1958	62.50	125.00	250.00
MONA LEE					
129	Guardian Angel/Soft and Sweet	1959	15.00	30.00	60.00
SPECIALTY					
751	Guardian Angel/Soft and Sweet	197?	2.50	5.00	10.00

SELF, MACK

45s

Number	Title (A Side/B Side)	Yr	VG	VG+	NM
PHILLIPS INT'L.					
3548	Mad at You/Willie Brown	1959	6.25	12.50	25.00
SUN					
273	Easy to Love/Every Day	1957	7.50	15.00	30.00

SELF, RONNIE

45s

Number	Title (A Side/B Side)	Yr	VG	VG+	NM
ABC-PARAMOUNT					
9714	Pretty Bad Blues/Three Hearts Later	1956	25.00	50.00	100.00
9768	Alone/Sweet Love	1956	25.00	50.00	100.00
AMY					
11009	High on Life/The Road Keeps Winding	1968	2.50	5.00	10.00

Number	Title (A Side/B Side)	Yr	VG	VG+	NM
COLUMBIA					
40875	Big Fool/Flame of Love	1957	10.00	20.00	40.00
40989	Ain't I'm a Dog/Rocky Road Blues	1957	10.00	20.00	40.00
41101	Bop-A-Lena/I Ain't Going Nowhere	1958	7.50	15.00	30.00
41166	Big Blon' Baby/Date Bait	1958	7.50	15.00	30.00
41241	Petrified/You're So Right for Me	1958	20.00	40.00	80.00
DECCA					
30958	Big Town/This Must Be the Place	1959	6.25	12.50	25.00
31131	I've Been There/So High	1960	6.25	12.50	25.00
31351	Instant Man/Some Things You Can't Change	1962	6.25	12.50	25.00
31431	Oh Me, Oh My/Past, Present and Future	1962	6.25	12.50	25.00
KAPP					
546	Houdini/Bless My Broken Heart	1963	5.00	10.00	20.00
7-Inch Extended Plays					
COLUMBIA					
B-2149	(contents unknown)	1957	50.00	100.00	200.00
B-2149 [PS]	Ain't I'm a Dog	1957	50.00	100.00	200.00

SELLERS, PETER

Number	Title (A Side/B Side)	Yr	VG	VG+	NM
45s					
CAPITOL					
F4159	I'm So Ashamed/A Drop of the Hard Stuff	1959	3.00	6.00	12.00
5580	A Hard Day's Night/Help	1966	3.75	7.50	15.00
UNITED ARTISTS					
X1221	Thank Heaven for Little Girls/Singin' in the Rain	1978	2.50	5.00	10.00
—As "Inspector Clouseau"					
Albums					
ACAPELLA					
1	Fool Brittania	1963	6.25	12.50	25.00
—With Joan Collins and Anthony Newley					
ANGEL					
35884 [M]	The Best of Sellers	1960	7.50	15.00	30.00
S 35884 [S]	The Best of Sellers	1960	10.00	20.00	40.00
EMI AMERICA					
SN-16396	Songs for Swingin' Sellers	1986	5.00	10.00	20.00
—First American issue of 1959 U.K. LP					

SELLERS, PETER, AND SOPHIA LOREN

Number	Title (A Side/B Side)	Yr	VG	VG+	NM
45s					
CAPITOL					
4505	Bangers and Mash/Goodness Gracious Me	1961	3.00	6.00	12.00
Albums					
ANGEL					
35910 [M]	Peter Sellers and Sophia Loren	1961	7.50	15.00	30.00
S 35910 [S]	Peter Sellers and Sophia Loren	1961	10.00	20.00	40.00

SENATOR BOBBY

Number	Title (A Side/B Side)	Yr	VG	VG+	NM
45s					
PARKWAY					
127	Wild Thing/Wild Thing	1966	3.00	6.00	12.00
—B-side by "Senator McKinley"					
137	Mellow Yellow/White Christmas	1967	2.50	5.00	10.00
—A-side by "Senator Bobby & Senator McKinley"; B-side by "Bobby the Poet" (Dylan impersonation)					
150	The Congressional Record/The Hardly Worthit Melody	1967	2.50	5.00	10.00
—By The Hardly Worthit Players					
RCA VICTOR					
47-9522	Sock It To Me, Bobby/Sock It To Me, Baby	1968	2.50	5.00	10.00
—B-side by the Bobby Sockers					
Albums					
PARKWAY					
P 7057 [M]	Boston Soul with the Hardly-Worthit Players	1967	5.00	10.00	20.00
SP 7057 [S]	Boston Soul with the Hardly-Worthit Players	1967	5.00	10.00	20.00

SENATORS, THE (1)

Number	Title (A Side/B Side)	Yr	VG	VG+	NM
45s					
ABC-PARAMOUNT					
10178	There's a New Man in the White House/A Sing-Along Song	1961	3.75	7.50	15.00

SENATORS, THE (2)

Number	Title (A Side/B Side)	Yr	VG	VG+	NM
45s					
ABNER					
1031	Julie/It Doesn't Matter	1959	30.00	60.00	120.00
GOLDEN CREST					
514	Loretta/Poor Little Puppet	1958	37.50	75.00	150.00

SENATORS, THE (3)

Number	Title (A Side/B Side)	Yr	VG	VG+	NM
45s					
BRISTOL					
1916	Scheming/Tafu	1959	100.00	200.00	400.00
WINN					
1917	Wedding Bells/I Shouldn't Care	1962	62.50	125.00	250.00

SENIORS, THE (1)

Number	Title (A Side/B Side)	Yr	VG	VG+	NM
45s					
ABC-PARAMOUNT					
10736	No Surfin' 'Round Here/Cindy	1965	7.50	15.00	30.00

SENIORS, THE (2)

Number	Title (A Side/B Side)	Yr	VG	VG+	NM
45s					
DECCA					
31112	I've Lived Before/Hello Mr. Robin	1960	5.00	10.00	20.00
31244	When I Fall in Love/Baby, Say the Word	1961	5.00	10.00	20.00

SENIORS, THE (3)

Number	Title (A Side/B Side)	Yr	VG	VG+	NM
45s					
EXCELLO					
2130	Why Did You Leave Me/Sloo Foot Soo	1958	10.00	20.00	40.00
TETRA					
4446	Evening Shadows Falling (I Think of You)/I've Got Plenty of Love	1956	50.00	100.00	200.00

SENIORS, THE (U)

Number	Title (A Side/B Side)	Yr	VG	VG+	NM
45s					
ESV					
1016	Ah Sweet Mystery of Love/Rock and Rolly	1960	6.25	12.50	25.00
KENT					
342	Hully Gully Fever/Pitter Patter Heart	1960	5.00	10.00	20.00
TAMPA					
163	Who's Gonna Know/It's Been a Long Time	1959	10.00	20.00	40.00

SENORS, THE

Allegedly THE ISLEY BROTHERS in disguise.

Number	Title (A Side/B Side)	Yr	VG	VG+	NM
45s					
SUE					
756	May I Have This Dance/Searching for Olive Oil	1962	12.50	25.00	50.00

SENSATIONS, THE

Also see YVONNE BAKER.

Number	Title (A Side/B Side)	Yr	VG	VG+	NM
45s					
ARGO					
5391	Music, Music, Music/A Part of Me	1961	2.50	5.00	10.00
5405	Let Me In/Oh Yes I'll Be True	1961	3.00	6.00	12.00
—Brown label					
5405	Let Me In/Oh Yes I'll Be True	1961	5.00	10.00	20.00
—Black label					
5412	That's My Desire/Eyes	1962	2.50	5.00	10.00
—By "Yvonne Baker and the Sensations"					
5420	Party Across the Hall/No Changes	1962	2.50	5.00	10.00
—By "Yvonne Baker and the Sensations"					
5446	When My Lover Comes Home/Father Dear	1963	2.50	5.00	10.00
—By "Yvonne Baker and the Sensations"					
ATCO					
6056	Yes Sir, That's My Baby/Sympathy	1955	10.00	20.00	40.00
6067	Please Mr. Disc Jockey/Ain't He Sweet	1956	10.00	20.00	40.00
6075	Cry Baby Cry/My Heart Cries for You	1956	10.00	20.00	40.00
6083	Little Wallflower/Such a Love	1957	10.00	20.00	40.00
6090	My Debut to Love/You Made Me Love You	1957	10.00	20.00	40.00
6115	Kiddy Car Love/Romance in the Dark	1958	10.00	20.00	40.00
JUNIOR					
1002	We Were Meant to Be/It's Good Enough for Me	1963	3.00	6.00	12.00
1005	You Made a Fool of Me/That's What You've Gotta Do	1963	5.00	10.00	20.00
1010	I Can't Change/Mend the Torn Pieces	1964	3.00	6.00	12.00
1021	We Were Meant to Be/It's Good Enough for Me	1964	3.00	6.00	12.00
TOLLIE					
9009	You Made a Fool of Me/That's What You've Gotta Do	1964	2.50	5.00	10.00
Albums					
ARGO					
LP-4022 [M]	Let Me In/Music, Music, Music	1963	125.00	250.00	500.00

SENSATIONS OF LONDON, THE

Number	Title (A Side/B Side)	Yr	VG	VG+	NM
45s					
YORK					
406	Look at My Baby/What a Wonderful Feeling	1966	3.75	7.50	15.00

SENTIMENTALS, THE

Number	Title (A Side/B Side)	Yr	VG	VG+	NM
45s					
CHECKER					
875	I Want to Love You/Tommie Teenager	1957	10.00	20.00	40.00
CORAL					
62100	We Three/Understanding Love	1959	6.25	12.50	25.00
62172	Deep Down in My Heart/Two Different Worlds	1960	6.25	12.50	25.00
MINT					
801	I Want to Love You/Tommie Teenager	1957	12.50	25.00	50.00
802	Sunday Kind of Love/Wedding Bells	1957	10.00	20.00	40.00
803	I'm Your Fool, Always/Rock Me, Mama	1958	10.00	20.00	40.00
805	You're Mine/Danny Boy	1958	10.00	20.00	40.00
807	Found a New Baby/I'll Miss These Things	196?	3.00	6.00	12.00
808	This Time/I Want to Love You	196?	3.00	6.00	12.00
VANITY					
589	Love Is a Gamble/If It Isn't for You	1959	6.25	12.50	25.00

SENTINALS, THE

Number	Title (A Side/B Side)	Yr	VG	VG+	NM
45s					
ADMIRAL					
900	Roughshod/Copy Cat Walk	1961	12.50	25.00	50.00
DEL-FI					
4197	Big Surf/Sunset Beach	1963	7.50	15.00	30.00
ERA					
3082	Torchula/Latin'ia	1962	7.50	15.00	30.00
3097	Christmas Eve/Latin Soul	1962	7.50	15.00	30.00
3117	Infinity/Encinada	1963	7.50	15.00	30.00
—As "The Sentinal Six"					
POINT					
5100	The Bee/Over You	1963	12.50	25.00	50.00
5101	Blue Booze/Bony Moronie	1962	12.50	25.00	50.00
WCEB					
23	Torchula/Latin'ia	1962	12.50	25.00	50.00
WESTCO					
12	I've Been Blue/Hit the Road	1964	7.50	15.00	30.00
14	Tell Me/Hit the Road	1964	7.50	15.00	30.00
Albums					
DEL-FI					
DFLP-1232 [M]	Big Surf!	1963	25.00	50.00	100.00
DFST-1232 [S]	Big Surf!	1963	37.50	75.00	150.00
DLF 1232	Big Surf!	1997	3.00	6.00	12.00
DFLP-1241 [M]	Surfer Girl	1963	17.50	35.00	70.00

Number	Title (A Side/B Side)	Yr	VG	VG+	NM
DFST-1241 [S]	Surfer Girl	1963	25.00	50.00	100.00
DLF 1241	Surfer Girl	1997	3.00	6.00	12.00
SUTTON					
SSU-338 [S]	Vegas Go-Go	1964	12.50	25.00	50.00
SU-338 [M]	Vegas Go-Go	1964	10.00	20.00	40.00

SEQUINS, THE

More than one group.

Number	Title (A Side/B Side)	Yr	VG	VG+	NM
45s					
ASCOT					
2140	You Can't Sit Still/Mr. Leader of the Band	1963	3.75	7.50	15.00
A&M					
761	I'll Be Satisfied/Who Says You Can't Jerk to the Old Time Music	1965	3.00	6.00	12.00
CAMEO					
161	To Be Young/The Mountains	1959	5.00	10.00	20.00
GOLD STAR					
101	Hey Romeo/I've Got to Overcome	1970	—	3.00	6.00
RED ROBIN					
140	Why Can't You Treat Me Right/Don't Fall in Love	1956	100.00	200.00	400.00
TERRACE					
7511	Love Me Forever/You're Dancing Now	1962	3.75	7.50	15.00
7515	Hideaway/I Ain't Gonna Cry (No More)	1963	3.75	7.50	15.00

SERENADERS, THE (1)

Number	Title (A Side/B Side)	Yr	VG	VG+	NM
45s					
CHOCK FULL O' HITS					
101	I Wrote a Letter/Never Let Me Go	1957	75.00	150.00	300.00
102	Dance Darling, Dance/Give Me a Girl	1957	50.00	100.00	200.00
MGM					
12623	I Wrote a Letter/Never Let Me Go	1958	25.00	50.00	100.00
12666	Dance Darling, Dance/Give Me a Girl	1958	30.00	60.00	120.00
MOTOWN					
1046	If Your Heart Says Yes/I'll Cry Tomorrow	1963	1000.	1500.	2000.
RAE COX					
101	Gotta Go to School/My Girl Flip-Flop	1959	15.00	30.00	60.00
RIVERSIDE					
4549	Adios, My Love/Two Lovers Make One Fool	1963	25.00	50.00	100.00
V.I.P.					
25002	If Your Heart Says Yes/I'll Cry Tomorrow	1964	25.00	50.00	100.00

SERENADERS, THE (2)

Number	Title (A Side/B Side)	Yr	VG	VG+	NM
45s					
CORAL					
60720	It's Funny/Confession Is Good for the Soul	1952	75.00	150.00	300.00
65093	Misery/But I Forgive You	1952	75.00	150.00	300.00
DELUXE					
6022	Please, Please Forgive Me/Baby	1953	125.00	250.00	500.00
JVB					
2001	Tomorrow Night/Why Don't You Do Right	1952	100.00	200.00	400.00
RED ROBIN					
115	Will She Know?/I Want to Love You Baby	1953	375.00	750.00	1500.
SWING TIME					
347	M-A-Y-B-E-L-L/Ain't Gonna Cry No More	1954	300.00	600.00	1200.

SERENADERS, THE (3)

Number	Title (A Side/B Side)	Yr	VG	VG+	NM
45s					
HANOVER					
4507	Honolulu/Summer Job	1959	3.75	7.50	15.00
4514	Alaska/Where Did You Go	1959	3.75	7.50	15.00

SERENADERS, THE (U)

Could be group (1) or (2).

Number	Title (A Side/B Side)	Yr	VG	VG+	NM
45s					
STARFIRE					
115	Nite Owl/I'm Gonna Love You	1980	—	3.00	6.00
TEEN LIFE					
9	Love Me Now/Gates of Gold	1958	175.00	350.00	700.00

SERENADETTS, THE

Number	Title (A Side/B Side)	Yr	VG	VG+	NM
45s					
ENRICA					
1008	Boyfriend/The Big Night	1961	3.00	6.00	12.00

SERENDIPITY SINGERS, THE

Number	Title (A Side/B Side)	Yr	VG	VG+	NM
45s					
PHILIPS					
40175	Crooked Little Man/Freedom's Star	1964	3.00	6.00	12.00
40175	Don't Let the Rain Come Down (Crooked Little Man)/Freedom's Star	1964	2.50	5.00	10.00
40198	Beans in My Ears/Sailin' Away	1964	2.00	4.00	8.00
40215	The New Frankie and Johnny Song/Down Where the Winds Blow	1964	2.00	4.00	8.00
40236	Autumn Wind/Same Old Reason	1964	2.00	4.00	8.00
40246	Little Brown Jug/High North Star	1964	2.00	4.00	8.00
40273	My Heart Keeps Following You/Rider	1965	2.00	4.00	8.00
40292	Run, Run, Chicken, Run/We Belong Together	1965	2.00	4.00	8.00
40309	The Bells of Rhymney/Oh Brother	1965	2.00	4.00	8.00
40331	When Peaches Grow on Lilac Trees/Plastic	1965	2.00	4.00	8.00
40356	Phoenix Love Theme (Sinza Fina)/If You Come Back in Summer	1966	2.00	4.00	8.00
40410	Born Free/Autumn Bound	1966	2.00	4.00	8.00
UNITED ARTISTS					
50137	Hawaii/Wishing Doll	1967	—	3.00	6.00
50166	The Way West/Love to Love	1967	—	3.00	6.00
50168	Signs of Love/The Boat That I Row	1967	—	3.00	6.00
50317	Rain Doll/Love Is a State of Mind	1968	—	3.00	6.00
50457	What Will We Do with the Child/Illusions	1968	—	3.00	6.00
50532	Come Softly to Me/Cotton Mouth River	1969	—	3.00	6.00
Albums					
PHILIPS					
PHM 200115 [M]	The Serendipity Singers	1964	3.75	7.50	15.00
PHM 200134 [M]	The Many Sides of the Serendipity Singers	1964	3.75	7.50	15.00
PHM 200151 [M]	Take Your Shoes Off with the Serendipity Singers	1964	3.75	7.50	15.00
PHM 200180 [M]	We Belong Together	1965	3.75	7.50	15.00
PHM 200190 [M]	Love, Lies and Flying Festoons	1965	3.75	7.50	15.00
PHS 600115 [S]	The Serendipity Singers	1964	5.00	10.00	20.00
PHS 600134 [S]	The Many Sides of the Serendipity Singers	1964	5.00	10.00	20.00
PHS 600151 [S]	Take Your Shoes Off with the Serendipity Singers	1964	5.00	10.00	20.00
PHS 600180 [S]	We Belong Together	1965	5.00	10.00	20.00
PHS 600190 [S]	Love, Lies and Flying Festoons	1965	5.00	10.00	20.00

SERPENT POWER

Number	Title (A Side/B Side)	Yr	VG	VG+	NM
Albums					
VANGUARD					
VRS-9252 [M]	Serpent Power	1967	30.00	60.00	120.00
VSD-79252 [S]	Serpent Power	1967	15.00	30.00	60.00

SERRATT, HOWARD

Number	Title (A Side/B Side)	Yr	VG	VG+	NM
45s					
SUN					
198	I Must Be Saved/Troublesome Waters	1954	500.00	1000.	2000.

SEVEN BLENDS, THE

Number	Title (A Side/B Side)	Yr	VG	VG+	NM
Albums					
ROULETTE					
R-25172 [M]	Twistin' at the Miami Beach Peppermint Lounge	1962	5.00	10.00	20.00
SR-25172 [S]	Twistin' at the Miami Beach Peppermint Lounge	1962	6.25	12.50	25.00

SEVEN OF US

Number	Title (A Side/B Side)	Yr	VG	VG+	NM
45s					
RED BIRD					
10-069	The Way to Your Heart/How Could You	1966	7.50	15.00	30.00
10-080	Jamboree/It's Not Easy to Forget	1966	7.50	15.00	30.00

7TH AVENUE AVIATORS, THE

Number	Title (A Side/B Side)	Yr	VG	VG+	NM
45s					
CONGRESS					
255	You Should 'A Held On/The Boy Next Door	1965	30.00	60.00	120.00

SEVENTH SONS, THE

Number	Title (A Side/B Side)	Yr	VG	VG+	NM
Albums					
ESP-DISK'					
1078	The Seventh Sons	1967	7.50	15.00	30.00

SEVENTH WAVE, THE

Number	Title (A Side/B Side)	Yr	VG	VG+	NM
Albums					
JANUS					
7008	Things to Come	1974	5.00	10.00	20.00
7021	Psi-Fi	1975	5.00	10.00	20.00

SEVERINSON, DOC

Number	Title (A Side/B Side)	Yr	VG	VG+	NM
45s					
AMHERST					
110	Tonight Show Theme/Skyliner	1986	—	2.50	5.00
COMMAND					
4039	Cry Me a River/This Is All I Ask	1963	2.50	5.00	10.00
4065	It Ain't Necessarily So/Manha de Carnival	1965	2.00	4.00	8.00
4071	Phantom Trumpet/You Are My Sunshine	1965	2.00	4.00	8.00
4080	In a Little Spanish Town/Tennessee Waltz	1966	2.00	4.00	8.00
4084	If He Walked Into My Life/Mothers and Daughters	1966	2.00	4.00	8.00
4087	Sunday Morning/When the Saints Go Marching In	1967	2.00	4.00	8.00
4091	Is Paris Burning/Walk On By	1967	2.00	4.00	8.00
4098	Monday, Monday/Music to Think By	1967	2.00	4.00	8.00
4101	Canadian Sunset/One Step Above	1968	—	3.00	6.00
4117	Trumpets and Crumpets/Free Again	1968	—	3.00	6.00
4122	Lullaby from "Rosemary's Baby"/That's What Love's About	1968	—	3.00	6.00
4124	Summer's Coming Back/That's What Love's About	1969	—	3.00	6.00
4125	Barbarella/Knowing When to Leave	1969	—	3.00	6.00
4133	Come Together/Carry That Weight	1970	—	3.00	6.00
4137	Power to the People/Bottleneck	1971	—	3.00	6.00
EPIC					
9311	Do You Know a Story/Oh, Mr. Dillon	1959	3.00	6.00	12.00
50220	I Wanna Be with You/The World's Gone Home	1976	—	2.00	4.00
50318	Little Tiny Feets/Melody (Aria)	1976	—	2.00	4.00
RCA VICTOR					
74-0904	Last Tango in Paris/Alone Again	1973	—	2.00	4.00
Albums					
ABC					
S-737	16 Great Performances	1971	2.50	5.00	10.00
X-771	Trumpets, Crumpets	1973	2.50	5.00	10.00
AMHERST					
AMH-3311	The Tonight Show Band with Doc Severinson	1986	2.50	5.00	10.00
AMH-3312	The Tonight Show Band with Doc Severinson, Vol. II	1987	2.50	5.00	10.00
AMH-3319	Facets	1988	2.50	5.00	10.00
ARCHIVE OF FOLK AND JAZZ					
334	Doc Severinson and Friends	1978	2.50	5.00	10.00
COMMAND					
RS 819 SD [S]	Tempestuous Trumpet	1961	5.00	10.00	20.00
RS 33-819 [M]	Tempestuous Trumpet	1961	3.75	7.50	15.00
RS 837 SD [S]	The Big Band's Back in Town	1962	5.00	10.00	20.00
RS 33-837 [M]	The Big Band's Back in Town	1962	3.75	7.50	15.00
RS 859 SD [S]	Torch Songs for Trumpet	1963	5.00	10.00	20.00
RS 33-859 [M]	Torch Songs for Trumpet	1963	3.75	7.50	15.00
RS 883 SD [S]	High, Wide and Wonderful	1965	5.00	10.00	20.00
RS 33-883 [M]	High, Wide and Wonderful	1965	3.75	7.50	15.00
RS 893 SD [S]	Fever!	1966	3.75	7.50	15.00

Number	Title (A Side/B Side)	Yr	VG	VG+	NM
RS 33-893 [M]	Fever!	1966	3.00	6.00	12.00
RS 901 SD [S]	Live!	1966	3.75	7.50	15.00
RS 33-901 [M]	Live!	1966	3.00	6.00	12.00
RS 904 SD [S]	Command Performances	1966	3.75	7.50	15.00
RS 33-904 [M]	Command Performances	1966	3.00	6.00	12.00
RS 909 SD [S]	Swinging and Singing	1967	3.00	6.00	12.00
RS 33-909 [M]	Swinging and Singing	1967	3.75	7.50	15.00
RS 917 SD [S]	The New Sound	1967	3.00	6.00	12.00
RS 33-917 [M]	The New Sound	1967	3.75	7.50	15.00
RS 927 SD	The Great Arrival	1968	3.00	6.00	12.00
RS 937 SD	Doc Severinson with Strings	1969	3.00	6.00	12.00
RS 950 SD	The Closet	1970	3.00	6.00	12.00
RS 952 SD	The Best of Doc Severinson	1970	3.00	6.00	12.00
QD-40003 [Q]	Fever!	1972	3.75	7.50	15.00
EPIC					
PE 34078	Night Journey	1976	2.50	5.00	10.00
PE 34925	A Brand New Thing	1977	2.50	5.00	10.00
FIRSTLINE					
FDLP 5001	London Sessions	1980	3.00	6.00	12.00
JUNO					
1001	I Feel Good	1970	3.00	6.00	12.00
MCA					
4168 [(2)]	The Best of Doc Severinson	198?	2.50	5.00	10.00
PICKWICK					
SPC-3608	Torch Songs for Trumpet	1978	2.00	4.00	8.00
RCA VICTOR					
APL1-0273	Rhapsody for Now!	1973	3.00	6.00	12.00
LSP-4522	Brass Roots	1971	3.00	6.00	12.00
AFL1-4669	Doc	1977	2.50	5.00	10.00
—Reissue with new prefix					
LSP-4669	Doc	1972	3.00	6.00	12.00

SEVILLE, DAVID

Also see ROSS BAGDASARIAN; THE CHIPMUNKS.

Number	Title (A Side/B Side)	Yr	VG	VG+	NM
45s					
LIBERTY					
55041	Armen's Theme/Carousel in Rome	1956	6.25	12.50	25.00
55055	The Donkey and the Schoolboy/The Gift	1957	6.25	12.50	25.00
55079	Camel Rock/Gotta Get to Your House	1957	6.25	12.50	25.00
55079 [PS]	Camel Rock/Gotta Get to Your House	1957	12.50	25.00	50.00
55105	Pretty Dark Eyes/Cecelia	1957	6.25	12.50	25.00
55113	Bagdad Express/Starlight, Starbright	1957	6.25	12.50	25.00
55124	Bonjour Tristesse/Dance from Bonjour Tristesse	1958	6.25	12.50	25.00
55132	Witch Doctor/Don't Whistle at Me Baby	1958	7.50	15.00	30.00
55140	The Bird on My Head/Hey There Moon	1958	6.25	12.50	25.00
55153	Little Brass Band/Take Five	1958	6.25	12.50	25.00
55163	The Mountain/Mr. Grape	1958	6.25	12.50	25.00
55272	Witch Doctor/Swanee River	1960	5.00	10.00	20.00
55314	Oh Judge, Your Honor, Dear Sir, Sweetheart/ Freddy, Freddy	1961	6.25	12.50	25.00
UNITED ARTISTS					
0063	Witch Doctor/The Bird on My Head	1973	—	2.00	4.00
—"Silver Spotlight Series" reissue					
7-Inch Extended Plays					
LIBERTY					
LSX-1003	(contents unknown)	1958	10.00	20.00	40.00
LSX-1003 [PS]	Witch Doctor	1958	10.00	20.00	40.00
Albums					
LIBERTY					
LRP-3073 [M]	The Music of David Seville	1957	20.00	40.00	80.00
LRP-3092 [M]	The Witch Doctor	1958	25.00	50.00	100.00

SEVILLE, DAVID, AND THE CHIPMUNKS

See THE CHIPMUNKS.

SEWARD, ALEC

Number	Title (A Side/B Side)	Yr	VG	VG+	NM
Albums					
BLUESVILLE					
BVLP-1076 [M]	Creepin' Blues	1963	20.00	40.00	80.00
—Blue label, silver print					
BVLP-1076 [M]	Creepin' Blues	1964	6.25	12.50	25.00
—Blue label, trident logo at right					

SH-BOOMS, THE

See THE CHORDS.

SHA NA NA

Number	Title (A Side/B Side)	Yr	VG	VG+	NM
45s					
KAMA SUTRA					
503	Lovers Never Say Goodbye/Remember Then	1970	—	3.00	6.00
507	Pay Day/Rock and Roll Is Here to Stay	1970	—	3.00	6.00
522	Only One Song/Yakety Yak	1971	—	3.00	6.00
528	Top Forty of the Lord/I Wonder Why	1971	—	3.00	6.00
528 [PS]	Top Forty of the Lord/I Wonder Why	1971	2.50	5.00	10.00
555	Bounce in Your Buggy/Bless My Soul	1972	—	3.00	6.00
555 [PS]	Bounce in Your Buggy/Bless My Soul	1972	2.50	5.00	10.00
560	In the Still of the Night/Sea Cruise	1972	—	2.50	5.00
578 [DJ]	In the Still of the Night (mono/stereo)	1973	3.75	7.50	15.00
—As "Eddie and the Evergreens"; may be promo only					
592	Maybe I'm Old Fashioned/Stroll All Night	1974	—	2.50	5.00
596	Too Chubby to Boogie/(B-side unknown)	1974	—	2.50	5.00
602	Just Like Romeo and Juliet/Circles of Love	1975	—	2.50	5.00
603	You're the Only Light on My Horizon Now	1975	—	2.50	5.00
604	Shanghied/Chills in My Spine	1975	—	2.50	5.00
RSO					
909	Rock and Roll Is Here to Stay/Greased Lightnin'	1978	—	2.00	4.00
—B-side by John Travolta					
930	Blue Moon/Sandy	1979	—	2.00	4.00
—B-side by John Travolta					
Albums					
ACCORD					
SN-7115	Remember Then	1981	2.50	5.00	10.00
SN-7146	Sh-Boom	1981	2.50	5.00	10.00
BUDDAH					
BDM-5692	Rock & Roll Is Here to Stay!	1978	2.50	5.00	10.00
BDM-5703	The Best of Sha Na Na	1978	2.50	5.00	10.00
EMUS					
ES-12037	On Stage	1978	2.50	5.00	10.00
KAMA SUTRA					
KSBS-2010	Rock & Roll Is Here to Stay!	1969	3.75	7.50	15.00
KSBS-2034	Sha Na Na	1971	3.75	7.50	15.00
KSBS-2050	The Night Is Still Young	1972	3.75	7.50	15.00
KSBS-2073 [(2)]	The Golden Age of Rock 'n' Roll	1973	5.00	10.00	20.00
KSBS-2075	From the Streets of New York	1973	3.75	7.50	15.00
KSBS-2077	Rock & Roll Is Here to Stay!	1974	3.75	7.50	15.00
KSBS-2600	Hot Sox	1974	3.75	7.50	15.00
KSBS-2605	Sha Na Now	1975	3.75	7.50	15.00
KSBS-2609 [(2)]	The Best...Sha Na Na	1976	3.75	7.50	15.00
NASHVILLE					
NR-12348-122 [(2)]	Rockin' in the 80's	1980	3.00	6.00	12.00

SHA-WEES, THE

Number	Title (A Side/B Side)	Yr	VG	VG+	NM
45s					
ALADDIN					
3170	No One to Love Me/Early Sunday Morning	1953	1000.	2000.	4000.

SHADES, THE

More than one group.

Number	Title (A Side/B Side)	Yr	VG	VG+	NM
45s					
ALADDIN					
3453	Dear Lori/One Touch of Heaven	1959	75.00	150.00	300.00
AOK					
1028	Ginger Bread Man/The Hip	1967	7.50	15.00	30.00
BIG TOP					
3003	Sun Glasses/Undivided Attention	1958	25.00	50.00	100.00
—B-side by The Knott Sisters					

SHADES OF BLUE

Number	Title (A Side/B Side)	Yr	VG	VG+	NM
45s					
IMPACT					
1007	Oh, How Happy/Little Orphan Boy	1966	5.00	10.00	20.00
1014	Lonely Summer/With This Ring	1966	5.00	10.00	20.00
1015	Happiness/The Night	1966	5.00	10.00	20.00
1026	All I Want Is Love/How Do You Save a Dying Love	1967	5.00	10.00	20.00
1028	Penny Arcade/Funny Kind of Love	1967	5.00	10.00	20.00
Albums					
IMPACT					
IM-101 [M]	Happiness Is the Shades of Blue	1966	12.50	25.00	50.00
IM-1001 [S]	Happiness Is the Shades of Blue	1966	15.00	30.00	60.00

SHADES OF JOY

Number	Title (A Side/B Side)	Yr	VG	VG+	NM
45s					
FONTANA					
1659	Soul Truth/I Do Like Rock	1969	2.50	5.00	10.00
Albums					
FONTANA					
SRF-67592	Shades of Joy	1969	5.00	10.00	20.00

SHADOWS, THE (1)

Backing group for CLIFF RICHARD. Includes early records as "The Drifters" and "The Four Jets." Also see JET HARRIS AND TONY MEEHAN.

Number	Title (A Side/B Side)	Yr	VG	VG+	NM
45s					
ABC-PARAMOUNT					
10073	Saturday Dance/Lonesome Fella	1960	7.50	15.00	30.00
10138	Apache/Quartermaster's Stores	1960	7.50	15.00	30.00
ATLANTIC					
2111	FBI/The Frightened City	1961	5.00	10.00	20.00
2135	Kon-Tiki/Man of Mystery	1962	5.00	10.00	20.00
2146	Wonderful Land/Stars Fell on Stockton	1962	5.00	10.00	20.00
2166	Guitar Tango/What a Lovely Thing	1962	5.00	10.00	20.00
2177	Dance On/The Rumble	1963	5.00	10.00	20.00
2235	Theme for Young Lovers/The Rise and Fall of Flingel Bunt	1964	5.00	10.00	20.00
2257	Rhythm and Greens/The Miracle	1964	5.00	10.00	20.00
CAPITOL					
F-4220	Feelin' Fine/Don't Be a Fool	1959	10.00	20.00	40.00
—As "The Drifters"					
F-4270	Driftin'/Jet Black	1959	10.00	20.00	40.00
—As "The Four Jets"					
EPIC					
9793	Mary Anne/Chu Chi	1965	5.00	10.00	20.00
9826	Stingray/Alice in Sunderland	1965	5.00	10.00	20.00
9848	Don't Make My Baby Blue/My Grandfather's Clock	1965	5.00	10.00	20.00
10020	I Met a Girl/Last Night Set	1966	5.00	10.00	20.00
Albums					
ATLANTIC					
8084 [M]	Out of the Shadows	1962	50.00	100.00	200.00
—Canada-only release?					
8089 [M]	Surfing with the Shadows	1963	37.50	75.00	150.00
SD 8089 [S]	Surfing with the Shadows	1963	75.00	150.00	300.00
8097 [M]	The Shadows Know	1964	25.00	50.00	100.00
SD 8097 [S]	The Shadows Know	1964	50.00	100.00	200.00

SHADOWS, THE (2)

Number	Title (A Side/B Side)	Yr	VG	VG+	NM
45s					
DECCA					
28765	No Use/Stay	1953	62.50	125.00	250.00
48307	Tell Her/Don't Be Bashful	1954	75.00	150.00	300.00
48322	Big Mouth Mama/Better Than Gold	1954	75.00	150.00	300.00

SHADOWS, THE (3)

45s

DEL-FI

Number	Title (A Side/B Side)	Yr	VG	VG+	NM
4109	Under the Stars of Love/Jungle Fever	1958	15.00	30.00	60.00

SHADOWS, THE (4)

45s

DOTTIE

Number	Title (A Side/B Side)	Yr	VG	VG+	NM
1006	I Wonder Why/Tell This Lonely Heart Goodbye	1961	5.00	10.00	20.00

SHADOWS, THE (U)

Could be group (3) or an entirely different group.

45s

DELTA

Number	Title (A Side/B Side)	Yr	VG	VG+	NM
1509	Bop-A-Lena/There Stands the Glass	1958	50.00	100.00	200.00

SHADOWS OF KNIGHT, THE

45s

Number	Title (A Side/B Side)	Yr	VG	VG+	NM
ATCO					
6634	Gloria '69/A Spaniard at My Door	1968	4.00	8.00	16.00
6776	I Am the Hunter/Warwick County Affair	1970	4.00	8.00	16.00
AURAVISION					
(no #)	Potato Chip	196?	15.00	30.00	60.00
—One-sided cardboard disc, 5 inches wide with small hole					
DUNWICH					
116	Gloria/Dark Side	1966	6.25	12.50	25.00
—Gold label, no mention of Atco Records					
116	Gloria/Dark Side	1966	5.00	10.00	20.00
—Yellow label, "Distributed by Atco Record Sales Co."					
116	Gloria/Dark Side	1966	3.75	7.50	15.00
—Dark pink and yellow label; other label variations may exist					
122	Oh Yeah/Light Bulb Blues	1966	5.00	10.00	20.00
122 [PS]	Oh Yeah/Light Bulb Blues	1966	7.50	15.00	30.00
128	Bad Little Woman/Gospel Zone	1966	3.75	7.50	15.00
128 [PS]	Bad Little Woman/Gospel Zone	1966	12.50	25.00	50.00
141	I'm Gonna Make You Mine/I'll Make You Sorry	1966	6.25	12.50	25.00
151	The Behemoth/Willie Jean	1967	5.00	10.00	20.00
167	Someone Like Me/There for Love	1967	5.00	10.00	20.00
SUPER K					
108	Taurus/My Fire Department Needs a Fireman	1969	2.50	5.00	10.00
110	Run, Run, Billy Porter/My Fire Department Needs a Fireman	1969	2.50	5.00	10.00
TEAM					
520	Shake/From Way Out to Way In	1968	4.00	8.00	16.00

Albums

Number	Title (A Side/B Side)	Yr	VG	VG+	NM
DUNWICH					
666 [M]	Gloria	1966	12.50	25.00	50.00
S-666 [S]	Gloria	1966	20.00	40.00	80.00
667 [M]	Back Door Men	1966	12.50	25.00	50.00
S-667 [S]	Back Door Men	1966	20.00	40.00	80.00
SUNDAZED					
LP 5006	Raw and Live at the Cellar 1966	1992	2.50	5.00	10.00
LP 5034	Gloria	1999	3.00	6.00	12.00
—Reissue on 180-gram vinyl					
LP 5035	Back Door Men	1999	3.00	6.00	12.00
—Reissue on 180-gram vinyl					
SUPER K					
SKS-6002	The Shadows of Knight	1969	12.50	25.00	50.00

SHADRACK

Albums

IGL

Number	Title (A Side/B Side)	Yr	VG	VG+	NM
132	Chameleon	1971	75.00	150.00	300.00

SHAFTO, BOBBY

45s

RUST

Number	Title (A Side/B Side)	Yr	VG	VG+	NM
5082	She's My Girl/Wonderful You	1964	2.50	5.00	10.00
5092	I'll Never Get Over You/Who Wouldn't Love a Girl Like That	1964	2.50	5.00	10.00
5096	Baby Then/How Could You Do a Thing Like That to Me	1965	2.50	5.00	10.00
5108	Lonely Is As Lonely Does/The Same Old Room	1966	3.00	6.00	12.00
5110	See Me Cry/A Little Like You	1966	2.50	5.00	10.00

SHAG, THE

45s

CAPITOL

Number	Title (A Side/B Side)	Yr	VG	VG+	NM
5995	Stop and Listen/Melissa	1967	5.00	10.00	20.00

SHAGGS, THE (1)

45s

CAPITOL

Number	Title (A Side/B Side)	Yr	VG	VG+	NM
2511	Mean Woman Blues/She Makes Me Happy	1969	2.50	5.00	10.00

SHAGGS, THE (2)

This all-male band comprised students at the University of Notre Dame.

Albums

MCM

Number	Title (A Side/B Side)	Yr	VG	VG+	NM
1295	Wink	1967	375.00	750.00	1500.
—No number on label -- this number is found in the trail-off wax on each side					

SHAGGS, THE (3)

This band comprised three sisters from New Hampshire attempting to sing and play.

Albums

Number	Title (A Side/B Side)	Yr	VG	VG+	NM
ROUNDER					
3032	Philosophy of the World	1980	6.25	12.50	25.00
3056	Shaggs' Own Thing	1982	6.25	12.50	25.00
THIRD WORLD					
3001	Philosophy of the World	1969	500.00	1000.	2000.

SHAGGY BOYS, THE

45s

Number	Title (A Side/B Side)	Yr	VG	VG+	NM
RED BIRD					
10-074	Stop the Clock/In the Morning	1966	3.75	7.50	15.00
UNITED ARTISTS					
50100	You and Me/Joy in the Morning	1966	3.75	7.50	15.00
50135	That's the Only Way/Behind These Stained Glass Windows	1967	3.75	7.50	15.00

SHAKERS, THE

45s

Number	Title (A Side/B Side)	Yr	VG	VG+	NM
ABC					
10960	Love, Love, Love/One Wonderful Moment	1967	2.00	4.00	8.00
AUDIO FIDELITY					
119	Break It All/Ticket to Ride	1966	2.50	5.00	10.00

Albums

AUDIO FIDELITY

Number	Title (A Side/B Side)	Yr	VG	VG+	NM
AFLP-2155 [M]	The Shakers Break It All	1966	10.00	20.00	40.00
AFSD-6155 [S]	The Shakers Break It All	1966	12.50	25.00	50.00

SHAKEY JAKE

45s

BLUESVILLE

Number	Title (A Side/B Side)	Yr	VG	VG+	NM
807	My Foolish Heart/Jake's Blues	1960	5.00	10.00	20.00

Albums

Number	Title (A Side/B Side)	Yr	VG	VG+	NM
BLUESVILLE					
BVLP-1008 [M]	Good Times	1960	30.00	60.00	120.00
—Blue label, silver print					
BVLP-1008 [M]	Good Times	1964	7.50	15.00	30.00
—Blue label, trident logo at right					
BVLP-1027 [M]	Mouth Harp Blues	1961	30.00	60.00	120.00
—Blue label, silver print					
BVLP-1027 [M]	Mouth Harp Blues	1964	7.50	15.00	30.00
—Blue label, trident logo at right					
WORLD PACIFIC					
WPS-21886	Blues Makers	196?	7.50	15.00	30.00

SHAKEY VICK

Albums

JANUS

Number	Title (A Side/B Side)	Yr	VG	VG+	NM
JLS-3000	Little Woman, You're So Sweet	1970	5.00	10.00	20.00

SHAM-ETTES, THE

45s

MGM

Number	Title (A Side/B Side)	Yr	VG	VG+	NM
13618	Big Bad Wolf (Hey There)/I'd Rather Have You	1966	3.75	7.50	15.00
13798	He'll Come Back/You're Welcome Back	1967	3.00	6.00	12.00

SHANE, BOB

Also see THE KINGSTON TRIO.

45s

DECCA

Number	Title (A Side/B Side)	Yr	VG	VG+	NM
32239	Simple Gifts/Weeping Annaleah	1967	2.50	5.00	10.00
32275	Honey/I Don't Think of You Anymore	1968	2.50	5.00	10.00

SHANGRI-LAS, THE

45s

Number	Title (A Side/B Side)	Yr	VG	VG+	NM
MERCURY					
72645	I'll Never Learn/Sweet Sounds of Summer	1966	5.00	10.00	20.00
72670	Footsteps on the Roof/Take the Time	1967	5.00	10.00	20.00
RED BIRD					
10-008	Remember (Walkin' in the Sand)/It's Easier to Cry	1964	6.25	12.50	25.00
10-014	Leader of the Pack/What Is Love	1964	6.25	12.50	25.00
10-018	Give Him a Great Big Kiss/Twist and Shout	1964	6.25	12.50	25.00
10-019	Maybe/Shout	1964	5.00	10.00	20.00
10-025	Out in the Streets/The Boy	1965	5.00	10.00	20.00
10-030	Give Us Your Blessings/Heaven Only Knows	1965	5.00	10.00	20.00
10-036	Right Now and Not Later/The Train from Kansas City	1965	5.00	10.00	20.00
10-043	I Can Never Go Home Anymore/Bull Dog	1965	5.00	10.00	20.00
10-043	I Can Never Go Home Anymore/Sophisticated Boom Boom	1965	7.50	15.00	30.00
10-048	Long Live Our Love/Sophisticated Boom Boom	1966	5.00	10.00	20.00
10-048	Long Live Our Love/Bull Dog	1966	5.00	10.00	20.00
10-053	He Cried/Dressed in Black	1966	5.00	10.00	20.00
10-068	Past, Present and Future/Love You More Than Yesterday	1966	5.00	10.00	20.00
10-068	Past, Present and Future/Paradise	1966	5.00	10.00	20.00
SCEPTER					
1291	Wishing Well/Hate to Say I Told You So	1964	5.00	10.00	20.00
SMASH					
1866	Simon Says/Simon Speaks	1963	10.00	20.00	40.00
SPOKANE					
4006	Wishing Well/Hate to Say I Told You So	1964	7.50	15.00	30.00

Albums

Number	Title (A Side/B Side)	Yr	VG	VG+	NM
COLLECTABLES					
COL-5011	Remember...Their Greatest Hits	198?	2.50	5.00	10.00
MERCURY					
MG-21099 [M]	The Shangri-Las' Golden Hits	1966	10.00	20.00	40.00
SR-61099 [S]	The Shangri-Las' Golden Hits	1966	12.50	25.00	50.00
POLYDOR					
824807-1	Golden Hits of the Shangri-Las	1985	2.50	5.00	10.00
POST					
4000	The Shangri-Las Sing	196?	5.00	10.00	20.00
RED BIRD					
20101 [M]	Leader of the Pack	1965	37.50	75.00	150.00
20104 [M]	Shangri-Las '65	1965	37.50	75.00	150.00
20104 [M]	I Can Never Go Home Anymore	1966	25.00	50.00	100.00
—Retitled version with title song added and "Sophisticated Boom Boom" dropped					

SHANK, BUD

Number	Title (A Side/B Side)	Yr	VG	VG+	NM
45s					
PACIFIC JAZZ					
320	The Awakening/New Groove	1961	2.50	5.00	10.00
88131	Sidewinder/Time for Love	1966	2.00	4.00	8.00
88156	Let It Be/Something	1970	—	2.50	5.00
WORLD PACIFIC					
364	Misty/Joao	1963	2.00	4.00	8.00
370	Brassamba/Little Boat	1963	2.00	4.00	8.00
410	Don't Think Twice/Freight Train	1964	2.00	4.00	8.00
653	Steve Allen Theme/Penny Whistle Blues	195?	3.75	7.50	15.00
77814	Michelle/I Will Wait for You	1966	—	3.00	6.00
77821	You Didn't Have to Be So Nice/Sounds of Silence	1966	—	3.00	6.00
77824	California Dreamin'/Woman	1966	—	3.00	6.00
77842	Summer Samba (So Nice)/Monday, Monday	1966	—	3.00	6.00
77885	I Am the Walrus/Sounds of Silence	1968	—	3.00	6.00
77893	There's Got to Be a Better Way (Theme from Bandolero)/Tour D'Amour	1968	—	3.00	6.00
Albums					
BAINBRIDGE					
CRS-6830	Live at the Haig	1985	2.50	5.00	10.00
CONCORD CONCERTO					
CC-2002	Explorations 1980: Suite for Flute and Piano	1981	2.50	5.00	10.00
CONCORD JAZZ					
CJ-20	Sunshine Express	1976	3.00	6.00	12.00
CJ-58	Heritage	1979	3.00	6.00	12.00
CJ-126	Crystal Comments	1980	2.50	5.00	10.00
CONTEMPORARY					
C-14012	California Concert	1985	2.50	5.00	10.00
C-14019	That Old Feeling	1986	2.50	5.00	10.00
C-14027	Bud Shank at Jazz Alley	1987	2.50	5.00	10.00
C-14031	Serious Swingers	1988	2.50	5.00	10.00
—With the Bill Perkins Quartet					
C-14048	Tomorrow's Rainbow	1989	2.50	5.00	10.00
CROWN					
CST-311 [R]	Bud Shank	1963	3.00	6.00	12.00
CLP-5311 [M]	Bud Shank	1963	3.75	7.50	15.00
KIMBERLY					
2025 [M]	The Talents of Bud Shank	1963	5.00	10.00	20.00
11025 [S]	The Talents of Bud Shank	1963	6.25	12.50	25.00
MUSE					
5309	This Bud's for You	198?	2.50	5.00	10.00
NOCTURNE					
NLP-2 [10]	Compositions of Shorty Rogers	1953	50.00	100.00	200.00
PACIFIC JAZZ					
PJ-4 [M]	Bud Shank Plays Tenor	1960	6.25	12.50	25.00
ST-4 [S]	Bud Shank Plays Tenor	1960	7.50	15.00	30.00
PJLP-14 [10]	Bud Shank with Three Trombones	1954	30.00	60.00	120.00
PJLP-20 [10]	Bud Shank and Bob Brookmeyer	1954	30.00	60.00	120.00
PJ-21 [M]	New Groove	1961	6.25	12.50	25.00
ST-21 [S]	New Groove	1961	7.50	15.00	30.00
PJ-58 [M]	Bossa Nova Jazz Samba	1962	6.25	12.50	25.00
ST-58 [S]	Bossa Nova Jazz Samba	1962	7.50	15.00	30.00
PJ-64 [M]	Brassamba Bossa Nova	1963	5.00	10.00	20.00
ST-64 [S]	Brassamba Bossa Nova	1963	6.25	12.50	25.00
PJ-89 [M]	Bud Shank and His Brazilian Friends	1965	5.00	10.00	20.00
ST-89 [S]	Bud Shank and His Brazilian Friends	1965	6.25	12.50	25.00
PJM-411 [M]	The Swing's to TV	1957	15.00	30.00	60.00
PJ-1205 [M]	Bud Shank/Shorty Rogers	1955	20.00	40.00	80.00
PJ-1213 [M]	Strings and Trombones	1956	20.00	40.00	80.00
PJ-1215 [M]	The Bud Shank Quartet	1956	20.00	40.00	80.00
PJ-1219 [M]	Jazz at Cal-Tech	1956	15.00	30.00	60.00
PJ-1226 [M]	Flute 'n Oboe	1957	15.00	30.00	60.00
PJ-1230 [M]	The Bud Shank Quartet	1957	15.00	30.00	60.00
LN-10091	Bud Shank and the Sax Section	198?	2.50	5.00	10.00
PJ-10110 [M]	Bud Shank and the Sax Section	1966	3.75	7.50	15.00
ST-20110 [S]	Bud Shank and the Sax Section	1966	5.00	10.00	20.00
SUNSET					
SUM-1132 [M]	I Hear Music	1967	3.00	6.00	12.00
SUS-5132 [S]	I Hear Music	1967	3.00	6.00	12.00
WORLD PACIFIC					
PJM-411 [M]	The Swing's to TV	1958	12.50	25.00	50.00
WPM-411 [M]	The Swing's to TV	1958	10.00	20.00	40.00
ST-1002 [S]	The Swing's to TV	1959	7.50	15.00	30.00
ST-1018 [S]	Holiday in Brazil	1959	7.50	15.00	30.00
WP-1205 [M]	Bud Shank/Shorty Rogers	1958	10.00	20.00	40.00
WP-1215 [M]	The Bud Shank Quartet	1958	10.00	20.00	40.00
WP-1219 [M]	Jazz at Cal-Tech	1958	10.00	20.00	40.00
WP-1226 [M]	Flute 'n Oboe	1958	10.00	20.00	40.00
WP-1230 [M]	The Bud Shank Quartet	1958	10.00	20.00	40.00
WP-1251 [M]	I'll Take Romance	1958	10.00	20.00	40.00
WP-1259 [M]	Holiday in Brazil	1959	10.00	20.00	40.00
ST-1281 [S]	Latin Contrasts	1959	7.50	15.00	30.00
WP-1281 [M]	Latin Contrasts	1959	10.00	20.00	40.00
ST-1286 [S]	Flute 'n Alto	1960	10.00	20.00	40.00
WP-1286 [M]	Flute 'n Alto	1960	7.50	15.00	30.00
ST-1299 [S]	Koto 'n Flute	1960	10.00	20.00	40.00
WP-1299 [M]	Koto 'n Flute	1960	7.50	15.00	30.00
WP-1416 [M]	Improvisations	1961	6.25	12.50	25.00
WP-1424 [M]	Koto 'n Flute	1962	6.25	12.50	25.00
WP-1819 [M]	Folk 'n Flute	1965	3.75	7.50	15.00
WP-1827 [M]	Flute, Oboe and Strings	1965	3.75	7.50	15.00
WP-1840 [M]	Michelle	1966	3.75	7.50	15.00
WP-1845 [M]	California Dreaming	1966	3.75	7.50	15.00
WP-1853 [M]	Girl in Love	1967	5.00	10.00	20.00
WP-1855 [M]	Brazil! Brazil! Brazil!	1967	5.00	10.00	20.00
WP-1864 [M]	Bud Shank Plays Music from Today's Movies	1967	5.00	10.00	20.00
ST-20170	Let It Be	1970	3.75	7.50	15.00
ST-21819 [S]	Folk 'n Flute	1965	5.00	10.00	20.00
ST-21827 [S]	Flute, Oboe and Strings	1965	5.00	10.00	20.00
ST-21840 [S]	Michelle	1966	5.00	10.00	20.00
ST-21845 [S]	California Dreaming	1966	5.00	10.00	20.00
ST-21853 [S]	Girl in Love	1967	3.75	7.50	15.00
ST-21855 [S]	Brazil! Brazil! Brazil!	1967	3.75	7.50	15.00
ST-21864 [S]	Bud Shank Plays Music from Today's Movies	1967	3.75	7.50	15.00
ST-21868	A Spoonful of Jazz	1968	3.75	7.50	15.00
ST-21873	Magical Mystery Tour	1968	3.75	7.50	15.00

SHANK, BUD/CHET BAKER

Number	Title (A Side/B Side)	Yr	VG	VG+	NM
Albums					
KIMBERLY					
2016 [M]	Swinging Soundtrack	1963	5.00	10.00	20.00
11016 [S]	Swinging Soundtrack	1963	6.25	12.50	25.00

SHANKAR, ANANDA

Number	Title (A Side/B Side)	Yr	VG	VG+	NM
Albums					
REPRISE					
RS-6398	Ananda Shankar	1970	5.00	10.00	20.00

SHANKAR, RAVI

Also see GEORGE HARRISON AND FRIENDS.

Number	Title (A Side/B Side)	Yr	VG	VG+	NM
45s					
APPLE					
1838	Joi Bangla-Oh Bhaugowan/Raga Mishra-Jhinjhoti	1971	2.00	4.00	8.00
—By Ravi Shankar & Ali Akbar with Alla Rakah					
1838 [PS]	Joi Bangla-Oh Bhaugowan/Raga Mishra-Jhinjhoti	1971	5.00	10.00	20.00
DARK HORSE					
10001	I Am Missing You/Lost	1974	—	2.50	5.00
WORLD PACIFIC					
77871	Pather Panchali/Gat Kirawani	1967	2.00	4.00	8.00
77898	Charly Theme/Love Montage	1968	2.00	4.00	8.00
Albums					
ANGEL					
35468 [M]	Music of India	196?	6.25	12.50	25.00
S 36026 [S]	West Meets East, Vol. 2	1968	3.75	7.50	15.00
36418 [M]	West Meets East	1967	6.25	12.50	25.00
—With Yahudi Menuhin					
S 36418 [S]	West Meets East	1967	5.00	10.00	20.00
—With Yahudi Menuhin					
S 36806	Concerto for Sitar and Orchestra	1972	3.00	6.00	12.00
DS-37920	Raga Mishra Piloo	1982	2.50	5.00	10.00
DS-37935	Raga-Mala (Sitar Concert No. 2)	1983	2.50	5.00	10.00
APPLE					
SWAO-3384	Raga	1971	6.25	12.50	25.00
SVBB-3396 [(2)]	Ravi Shankar In Concert	1973	10.00	20.00	40.00
BLUESVILLE					
BVLP-1078 [M]	The Master Musician of India	1964	6.25	12.50	25.00
CAPITOL					
DT 2720 [R]	Three Ragas	1967	3.75	7.50	15.00
T 2720 [M]	Three Ragas	1967	5.00	10.00	20.00
ST 10482 [S]	Two Raga Moods	196?	6.25	12.50	25.00
T 10482 [M]	Two Raga Moods	196?	5.00	10.00	20.00
ST 10497 [S]	Exotic Sitar and Sarod	196?	6.25	12.50	25.00
T 10497 [M]	Exotic Sitar and Sarod	196?	5.00	10.00	20.00
SP-10561	Raga Parameshwari	1972	3.00	6.00	12.00
COLUMBIA					
WL 119 [M]	The Sounds of India	196?	6.25	12.50	25.00
CL 2496 [M]	Sounds of India	1966	3.75	7.50	15.00
CL 2760 [M]	The Genius of Ravi Shankar	1967	5.00	10.00	20.00
OS 3230	Chappaqua	1968	3.75	7.50	15.00
CS 9296 [S]	Sounds of India	1966	5.00	10.00	20.00
CS 9560 [S]	The Genius of Ravi Shankar	1967	3.75	7.50	15.00
DARK HORSE					
SP 22002	Shankar Family and Friends	1974	3.00	6.00	12.00
SP 22007	Music Festival from India	1975	3.00	6.00	12.00
DEUTCHE GRAMMOPHON					
2531 216	Ragas Hameer & Gara	198?	2.50	5.00	10.00
2531 280	Raga Jogeshwari	198?	2.50	5.00	10.00
2531 356	Homage to Mahatma Gandhi; Homage to Baba Allauddin	198?	2.50	5.00	10.00
2531 381	Pad Hasapa, for Koto; etc.	198?	2.50	5.00	10.00
FANTASY					
24714 [(2)]	Ragas	1973	3.75	7.50	15.00
ORIENTAL					
BGRP-108	Raga Sanjh Kalyan	198?	2.50	5.00	10.00
PRIVATE MUSIC					
2016-1-P	The Shankar Project: Tana Mana	1988	2.50	5.00	10.00
2044-1-P	Inside the Kremlin	1989	2.50	5.00	10.00
SPARK					
06	Transmigration Macabre	1973	3.00	6.00	12.00
WORLD PACIFIC					
WP-1421 [M]	Ravi Shankar In Concert	1965	3.75	7.50	15.00
WP-1422 [M]	India's Master Musician	1965	3.75	7.50	15.00
WP-1430 [M]	Ravi Shankar In London	1966	3.75	7.50	15.00
WP-1431 [M]	Ragas and Talas	1966	3.75	7.50	15.00
WP-1432 [M]	Portrait of Genius	1966	3.75	7.50	15.00
WP-1434 [M]	Sound of the Sitar	1967	3.75	7.50	15.00
WP-1438 [M]	Three Ragas	1967	3.75	7.50	15.00
WP-1441 [M]	Ravi Shankar in New York	1967	3.75	7.50	15.00
WP-1442 [M]	Ravi Shankar at the Monterey International Pop Festival	1967	5.00	10.00	20.00
ST-21421 [S]	Ravi Shankar In Concert	1965	5.00	10.00	20.00
ST-21422 [S]	India's Master Musician	1965	5.00	10.00	20.00
ST-21430 [S]	Ravi Shankar In London	1966	5.00	10.00	20.00
ST-21431 [S]	Ragas and Talas	1966	5.00	10.00	20.00
ST-21432 [S]	Portrait of Genius	1966	5.00	10.00	20.00
ST-21434 [S]	Sound of the Sitar	1967	5.00	10.00	20.00
ST-21438 [S]	Three Ragas	1967	5.00	10.00	20.00
ST-21441 [S]	Ravi Shankar in New York	1967	5.00	10.00	20.00
ST-21442 [S]	Ravi Shankar at the Monterey International Pop Festival	1967	5.00	10.00	20.00
ST-21449	Ravi Shankar in San Francisco	1968	5.00	10.00	20.00
ST-21454	Charly	1969	3.75	7.50	15.00

Number	Title (A Side/B Side)	Yr	VG	VG+	NM
ST-21464	Morning Raga/Evening Raga	1970	3.75	7.50	15.00
ST-21467	Ravi Shankar at Woodstock	1970	3.75	7.50	15.00
WPS-26201 [(2)]	His Festival from India	1968	5.00	10.00	20.00

SHANNON
See MARTY WILDE.

SHANNON, DEL

Number	Title (A Side/B Side)	Yr	VG	VG+	NM
45s					
ABC DUNHILL					
4193	Sweet Mary Lou/Comin' Back to me	1969	3.75	7.50	15.00
4224	Sister Isabelle/Colorado Rain	1970	3.75	7.50	15.00
AMY					
897	Mary Jane/Stains on My Letter	1964	6.25	12.50	25.00
905	Handy Man/Give Her Lots of Lovin'	1964	3.75	7.50	15.00
911	Do You Want to Dance/This Is All I Have to Give	1964	3.75	7.50	15.00
915	Keep Searchin' (We'll Follow the Sun)/Broken Promises	1964	4.00	8.00	16.00
919	Stranger in Town/Over You	1965	4.00	8.00	16.00
925	Why Don't You Tell Him/Break Up	1965	3.75	7.50	15.00
937	Move It On Over/She Still Remembers Tony	1965	3.75	7.50	15.00
947	I Can't Believe My Ears/I Wish I Wasn't Me Tonight	1966	10.00	20.00	40.00
—Withdrawn shortly after release; promos worth about half these values					
BERLEE					
501	Sue's Gotta Be Mine/Now She's Gone	1963	3.75	7.50	15.00
502	That's the Way Love Is/Time of the Day	1964	3.75	7.50	15.00
BIG TOP					
3067	Runaway/Jody	1961	7.50	15.00	30.00
3075	Hats Off to Larry/Don't Gild the Lily, Lily	1961	6.25	12.50	25.00
3083	So Long Baby/The Answer to Everything	1961	6.25	12.50	25.00
3091	Hey! Little Girl/I Don't Care Anymore	1961	6.25	12.50	25.00
3098	Ginny in the Mirror/I Won't Be There	1962	6.25	12.50	25.00
3112	Cry Myself to Sleep/I'm Gonna Move On	1962	6.25	12.50	25.00
3117	The Swiss Maid/You Never Talked About Me	1962	6.25	12.50	25.00
3131	Little Town Flirt/The Wamboo	1962	6.25	12.50	25.00
3143	Two Kinds of Teardrops/Kelly	1963	6.25	12.50	25.00
3152	From Me to You/Two Silhouettes	1963	15.00	30.00	60.00
—A-side is the first American version of a Beatles song					
ERIC					
189 [S]	Runaway/Hats Off to Larry	1972	—	3.00	6.00
—Both sides of this reissue are the original recordings in true stereo!					
ISLAND					
021	Tell Her No/Restless	1975	3.75	7.50	15.00
038	Cry Baby Cry/In My Arms Again	1975	3.75	7.50	15.00
LIBERTY					
55866	The Big Hurt/I Got It Bad	1966	3.00	6.00	12.00
55889	Hey Little Star/For a Little While	1966	3.00	6.00	12.00
55894	Show Me/Never Thought I Could	1966	3.00	6.00	12.00
55904	Under My Thumb/She Was Mine	1966	3.00	6.00	12.00
55939	She/What Makes You Run	1967	3.00	6.00	12.00
55961	Led Along/I Can't Be True	1967	3.00	6.00	12.00
55993	Runaway '67/He Cheated	1967	3.75	7.50	15.00
56018	Runnin' On Back/Thinkin' It Over	1968	2.50	5.00	10.00
56018 [PS]	Runnin' On Back/Thinkin' It Over	1968	7.50	15.00	30.00
56036	Magical Musical Box/Gemini	1968	2.50	5.00	10.00
56070	Raindrops/You Don't Love Me	1968	2.50	5.00	10.00
NETWORK					
47951	Sea of Love/Midnight Train	1981	—	2.50	5.00
48006	To Love Someone/Liar	1982	—	2.50	5.00
TWIRL					
4001	Runaway/Hey Little Girl	196?	—	3.00	6.00
4002	Hats Off to Larry/Little Town Flirt	196?	—	3.00	6.00
WARNER BROS.					
28853	Stranger on the Run/What You Gonna Do with That	1985	—	2.50	5.00
29098	In My Arms Again/You Can't Forgive Me	1985	—	2.50	5.00
Albums					
AMY					
8003 [M]	Handy Man	1964	12.50	25.00	50.00
S-8003 [S]	Handy Man	1964	20.00	40.00	80.00
8004 [M]	Del Shannon Sings Hank Williams	1965	12.50	25.00	50.00
S-8004 [S]	Del Shannon Sings Hank Williams	1965	20.00	40.00	80.00
8006 [M]	1,661 Seconds with Del Shannon	1965	12.50	25.00	50.00
S-8006 [S]	1,661 Seconds with Del Shannon	1965	20.00	40.00	80.00
BIG TOP					
12-1303 [M]	Runaway	1961	75.00	150.00	300.00
12-1303 [S]	Runaway	1961	400.00	800.00	1600.
12-1308 [B]	Little Town Flirt	1963	250.00	500.00	1000.
—One side is mono, one side is stereo; again, should be played to identify					
12-1308 [M]	Little Town Flirt	1963	37.50	75.00	150.00
12-1308 [S]	Little Town Flirt	1963	375.00	750.00	1500.
—Stereo copies are not identified as such on either cover or label; some, but not all, copies have an "S" in the dead wax. Playing is the best way to identify.					
DOT					
DLP 3824 [M]	The Best of Del Shannon	1967	12.50	25.00	50.00
DLP 25824 [R]	The Best of Del Shannon	1967	10.00	20.00	40.00
ELEKTRA					
5E-568	Drop Down and Get Me	1981	2.50	5.00	10.00
LIBERTY					
LRP-3453 [M]	This Is My Bag	1966	7.50	15.00	30.00
LRP-3479 [M]	Total Commitment	1966	7.50	15.00	30.00
LRP-3539 [M]	The Further Adventures of Charles Westover	1967	12.50	25.00	50.00
LST-7453 [S]	This Is My Bag	1966	10.00	20.00	40.00
LST-7479 [S]	Total Commitment	1966	10.00	20.00	40.00
LST-7539 [S]	The Further Adventures of Charles Westover	1967	20.00	40.00	80.00
PICKWICK					
SPC-3595 [R]	The Best of Del Shannon	197?	2.50	5.00	10.00
POST					
0000 [R]	Del Shannon Sings	196?	10.00	20.00	40.00
RHINO					
RNLP-71056 [M]	Runaway Hits	1986	2.50	5.00	10.00
SIRE					
SASH-3708 [(2) P]	The Vintage Years	1975	6.25	12.50	25.00
UNITED ARTISTS					
UA-LA151-E	Del Shannon Live in England	1973	6.25	12.50	25.00

SHANNON, JACKIE
See JACKIE DeSHANNON.

SHANNON, PAT

Number	Title (A Side/B Side)	Yr	VG	VG+	NM
45s					
AMOS					
152	I Ain't Got Time Anymore/(B-side unknown)	1970	—	2.50	5.00
163	Liar/Something's Coming My Way	1971	—	2.50	5.00
CAPITOL					
3802	Eleanor Jones/102 Times a Day	1973	—	2.00	4.00
DECCA					
30545	Maybelle/Knock, Knock, Who's There	1958	3.00	6.00	12.00
30666	You're So Wild/Awaiting Love	1958	7.50	15.00	30.00
30751	Summer's Over/We Found Love	1958	3.00	6.00	12.00
30905	Summertime's Comin'/The Snake and the Bookworm	1959	3.00	6.00	12.00
31072	Everything But You/So Happy Now	1960	3.00	6.00	12.00
UNI					
55191	Back to Dreamin' Again/Moody	1969	—	2.50	5.00
55229	It's So Easy/The Story of Your Life	1970	—	2.50	5.00
55229	It's So Easy/102 Times a Day	1970	—	2.50	5.00
WARNER BROS.					
7210	Candy Apple, Cotton Candy/She Sleeps Alone	1968	—	3.00	6.00
7237	Here They Come Again/Run to Home	1968	—	3.00	6.00

SHANTONS, THE

Number	Title (A Side/B Side)	Yr	VG	VG+	NM
45s					
JAY-MAR					
241	To Be in Love with You/Lucille	1959	200.00	400.00	800.00
1292	The Christmas Song/Santa Claus Is Coming To Town	1960	50.00	100.00	200.00
(# unknown)	Triangle Love/Lover's March	1959	100.00	200.00	400.00

SHANTY BOYS, THE

Number	Title (A Side/B Side)	Yr	VG	VG+	NM
Albums					
ELEKTRA					
EKL-142 [M]	Off-Beat Folk Songs	1958	7.50	15.00	30.00

SHAPIRO, HELEN

Number	Title (A Side/B Side)	Yr	VG	VG+	NM
45s					
CAPITOL					
4561	Don't Treat Me Like a Child/When I'm With You	1961	3.00	6.00	12.00
4627	You Don't Know/A Marvelous Lie	1961	3.00	6.00	12.00
4662	Walkin' Back to Happiness/Kiss 'N' Run	1961	3.00	6.00	12.00
4735	Tell Me What He Said/I Apologize	1962	3.00	6.00	12.00
EPIC					
9549	Little Miss Lonely/Keep Away from Other Girls	1962	3.00	6.00	12.00
9599	Woe Is Me/No Trespassing	1963	3.00	6.00	12.00
JANUS					
120	A Glass of Wine/Waiting on the Shores of Nowhere	1970	—	3.00	6.00
MUSICOR					
1075	It Might As Well Rain Until September/Shop Around	1965	2.50	5.00	10.00
TOWER					
346	Make Me Belong to You/The Way of the World	1967	2.00	4.00	8.00
Albums					
EPIC					
LN 24075 [M]	A Teenager in Love	1962	6.25	12.50	25.00
BN 26075 [S]	A Teenager in Love	1962	7.50	15.00	30.00

SHARKS

Number	Title (A Side/B Side)	Yr	VG	VG+	NM
45s					
MCA					
40120	Follow Me/Ole Jelly Roll	1973	—	2.50	5.00
40246	Kung Fu/Elevator Dancing	1974	—	2.50	5.00
Albums					
MCA					
351	First Water	1973	3.00	6.00	12.00
415	Jab It in Your Eye	1974	3.00	6.00	12.00

SHARMEERS, THE

Number	Title (A Side/B Side)	Yr	VG	VG+	NM
45s					
RED TOP					
109	A School Girl in Love/You're My Love	1958	37.50	75.00	150.00

SHARMETTES, THE

Number	Title (A Side/B Side)	Yr	VG	VG+	NM
45s					
KING					
5648	Answer Me/My Dream	1962	3.75	7.50	15.00
5686	I Want to Be Loved/Tell Me	1962	3.75	7.50	15.00

SHARON MARIE

Number	Title (A Side/B Side)	Yr	VG	VG+	NM
45s					
CAPITOL					
5064	Run-Around Lover/Summertime	1963	62.50	125.00	250.00
5195	The Story of My Life/Thinkin' 'Bout You Baby	1964	50.00	100.00	200.00
—Both these records were produced by Brian Wilson					

SHARP, DEE DEE

Number	Title (A Side/B Side)	Yr	VG	VG+	NM
45s					
ATCO					
6445	Bye Bye Baby/My Best Friend's Man	1966	2.50	5.00	10.00
6502	Baby I Love You/What Am I Gonna Do	1967	2.00	4.00	8.00

Number	Title (A Side/B Side)	Yr	VG	VG+	NM
6557	We Got a Thing Goin' On/What 'Cha Gonna Do About It	1968	2.00	4.00	8.00
—With Ben E. King					
6576	Woman Will Do Wrong/You're Just a Fool in Love	1968	2.00	4.00	8.00
6587	This Love Won't Run Out/Help Me Find My Glove	1968	2.00	4.00	8.00
CAMEO					
212	Mashed Potato Time/Set My Heart at Ease	1962	5.00	10.00	20.00
219	Gravy (For My Mashed Potatoes)/Baby Cakes	1962	3.75	7.50	15.00
219 [PS]	Gravy (For My Mashed Potatoes)/Baby Cakes	1962	6.25	12.50	25.00
230	Ride!/The Night	1962	3.75	7.50	15.00
230 [PS]	Ride!/The Night	1962	6.25	12.50	25.00
244	Do the Bird/Lover Boy	1963	3.75	7.50	15.00
244 [PS]	Do the Bird/Lover Boy	1963	6.25	12.50	25.00
260	Rock Me in the Cradle of Love/You'll Never Be Mine	1963	3.75	7.50	15.00
260 [PS]	Rock Me in the Cradle of Love/You'll Never Be Mine	1963	6.25	12.50	25.00
274	Wild!/Why Doncha Ask Me	1963	3.75	7.50	15.00
274 [PS]	Wild!/Why Doncha Ask Me	1963	6.25	12.50	25.00
296	Where Did I Go Wrong/Willyam, Willyam	1964	3.00	6.00	12.00
296 [PS]	Where Did I Go Wrong/Willyam, Willyam	1964	5.00	10.00	20.00
329	Never Pick a Pretty Boy/He's No Ordinary Guy	1964	3.00	6.00	12.00
335	Deep Dark Secret/Good	1964	3.00	6.00	12.00
347	To Know Him Is to Love Him/There Ain't Nothin' I Wouldn't Do for You	1965	2.50	5.00	10.00
357	Let's Twine/That's What My Mama Said	1965	2.50	5.00	10.00
375	I Really Love You/Standing in the Need of Love	1965	2.50	5.00	10.00
375 [PS]	I Really Love You/Standing in the Need of Love	1965	3.75	7.50	15.00
382	It's a Funny Situation/There Ain't Nothin' I Wouldn't Do for You	1965	2.50	5.00	10.00
FAIRMOUNT					
1004	(It's Wonderful) The Love I Feel for You/Willyam, Wilyam	1966	2.50	5.00	10.00
GAMBLE					
219	What Kind of Lady/You're Gonna Miss Me (When I'm Gone)	1968	5.00	10.00	20.00
4005	The Bottle or Me/You're Gonna Miss Me (When I'm Gone)	1969	3.75	7.50	15.00
PHILADELPHIA INT'L.					
02041	Breaking and Entering/I Love You Anyway	1981	—	2.00	4.00
3512	Conquer the World Together/We Gotta Good Thing Goin'	1971	—	3.00	6.00
—With Bunny Sigler					
3625	Flashback/Nobody Can Take Your Place	1977	—	2.50	5.00
3636	I'd Really Love to See You Tonight/What Color Is Love	1977	—	2.50	5.00
3638	I Believe in Love/Just As Long As I Know You're Mine	1978	—	2.50	5.00
3644	Tryin' to Get the Feeling Again/I Wanna Be Your Woman	1978	—	2.50	5.00
70058	I Love You Anyway/Easy Money	1981	—	2.00	4.00
—Philadelphia International records as "Dee Dee Sharp Gamble"					
TSOP					
4776	Happy 'Bout the Whole Thing/Touch My Life	1976	—	2.50	5.00
4778	I'm Not in Love/Make It Till Tomorrow	1976	—	2.50	5.00
Albums					
CAMEO					
C-1018 [M]	It's Mashed Potato Time	1962	15.00	30.00	60.00
C-1022 [M]	Songs of Faith	1962	10.00	20.00	40.00
SC-1022 [S]	Songs of Faith	1962	12.50	25.00	50.00
C-1027 [M]	All the Hits	1962	10.00	20.00	40.00
SC-1027 [S]	All the Hits	1962	12.50	25.00	50.00
C-1032 [M]	All the Hits, Vol. 2	1963	10.00	20.00	40.00
SC-1032 [S]	All the Hits, Vol. 2	1963	12.50	25.00	50.00
C-1050 [M]	Do the Bird	1963	10.00	20.00	40.00
SC-1050 [S]	Do the Bird	1963	12.50	25.00	50.00
C-1062 [M]	Biggest Hits	1963	10.00	20.00	40.00
C-1074 [M]	Down Memory Lane	1963	10.00	20.00	40.00
C-2002 [M]	18 Golden Hits	1964	10.00	20.00	40.00
SC-2002 [S]	18 Golden Hits	1964	12.50	25.00	50.00
PHILADELPHIA INT'L.					
PZ 33839	Happy 'Bout the Whole Thing	1976	2.50	5.00	10.00
PZ 34437	What Color Is Love	1977	2.50	5.00	10.00
JZ 36370	Dee Dee	1980	2.50	5.00	10.00

SHARP, DEE DEE, AND CHUBBY CHECKER

Also see each artist's individual listings.

Number	Title (A Side/B Side)	Yr	VG	VG+	NM
45s					
CAMEO					
103 [DJ]	Do You Love Me?/One More Time	1962	10.00	20.00	40.00
—Yellow label, black print, promo only					
Albums					
CAMEO					
C-1029 [M]	Down to Earth	1962	10.00	20.00	40.00
SC-1029 [S]	Down to Earth	1962	12.50	25.00	50.00

SHARPE, RAY

Number	Title (A Side/B Side)	Yr	VG	VG+	NM
45s					
ATCO					
6402	Help Me (Get the Feeling) Part 1/Help Me (Get the Feeling) Part 2	1966	2.50	5.00	10.00
6437	I Can't Take It/Mary Jane	1966	2.50	5.00	10.00
A&M					
1297	Dream On, Donna/Another Piece of the Puzzle	1971	—	2.50	5.00
DOT					
15788	Oh, My Baby's Gone/That's the Way I Feel	1958	3.75	7.50	15.00
15974	Oh, My Baby's Gone/That's the Way I Feel	1959	3.00	6.00	12.00
GREGMARK					
14	(The New) Linda Lu/The Bus Song	1963	3.00	6.00	12.00
HAMILTON					
50002	Oh, My Baby's Gone/That's the Way I Feel	1959	2.50	5.00	10.00
JAMIE					
1128	Linda Lu/Monkey's Uncle	1959	6.25	12.50	25.00
1128	Linda Lu/Red Sails in the Sunset	1959	3.75	7.50	15.00
1138	Long John/T.A. Blues	1959	3.75	7.50	15.00
1149	Bermuda/Gonna Let It Go This Time	1960	3.75	7.50	15.00
1155	For You My Love/Red Sails in the Sunset	1960	3.75	7.50	15.00
1164	Give'n Up/Kewpie Doll	1960	3.75	7.50	15.00
LHI					
1215	Linda Lu/Monkey's Uncle	1967	2.00	4.00	8.00
MONUMENT					
874	Let's Go, Let's Go, Let's Go/It's Too Cold	1965	2.50	5.00	10.00
PARK AVE.					
4904	Do the Thaxton/Baby Ora	196?	2.50	5.00	10.00
4906	Almost Grown/(B-side unknown)	196?	2.50	5.00	10.00
TREY					
3011	Justine/On the Street Where You Live	1961	3.00	6.00	12.00
Albums					
AWARD					
LMP-711 [M]	Welcome Back, Linda Lu	1964	30.00	60.00	120.00

SHARPS, THE

Possibly more than one group.

Number	Title (A Side/B Side)	Yr	VG	VG+	NM
45s					
ALADDIN					
3401	What Will I Gain/Shufflin'	1957	12.50	25.00	50.00
3401	What Will I Gain/Shufflin'	1957	100.00	200.00	400.00
—Purple vinyl					
CHESS					
1690	6 Months, 3 Weeks, 2 Days/Cha-Cho Bop	1958	7.50	15.00	30.00
—B-side by Jack McVea					
COMBO					
146	All My Love/Look What You've Done to Me	1958	12.50	25.00	50.00
DOT					
15806	All My Love/Look What You've Done to Me	1958	3.75	7.50	15.00
JAMIE					
1040	Sweet Sweetheart/Come On	1957	10.00	20.00	40.00
1108	Have Love, Will Travel/Look at Me	1958	12.50	25.00	50.00
1114	Here's My Heart/Gig-A-Lene	1958	7.50	15.00	30.00
LAMP					
2007	Our Love Is Here to Stay/Lock My Heart	1957	7.50	15.00	30.00
STAR-HI					
10406	Double Clutch/If Love Is What You Want	1960	7.50	15.00	30.00
TAG					
2200	6 Months, 3 Weeks, 2 Days/Cha-Cho Bop	1957	25.00	50.00	100.00
—B-side by Jack McVea					
VIK					
0264	Sweet Sweetheart/Come On	1957	6.25	12.50	25.00
WIN					
702	Teenage Girl/We Three	1958	12.50	25.00	50.00

SHARPTONES, THE

Number	Title (A Side/B Side)	Yr	VG	VG+	NM
45s					
POST					
2009	Since I Fell for You/Made to Love	1955	100.00	200.00	400.00

SHATNER, WILLIAM

Number	Title (A Side/B Side)	Yr	VG	VG+	NM
45s					
DECCA					
32399	How Insensitive/Transformed Man	1969	5.00	10.00	20.00
Albums					
DECCA					
DL 75043	The Transformed Man	1969	15.00	30.00	60.00
K-TEL					
NC 494 [(2)]	Captain of the Starship	1978	12.50	25.00	50.00
—Reissue of Lemli album					
LEMLI					
9400 [(2)]	William Shatner — Live!	1977	7.50	15.00	30.00

SHAW, JIMMY

Number	Title (A Side/B Side)	Yr	VG	VG+	NM
45s					
IMPERIAL					
5603	Take a Chance on Me/Big Chief Hug-Um An' Kiss-Um	1959	5.00	10.00	20.00

SHAW, JOHN, AND THE DELL-OS

Number	Title (A Side/B Side)	Yr	VG	VG+	NM
45s					
U-C					
5002	Why Did You Leave Me/Why Does It Have to Be Her	1957	2000.	3000.	4000.

SHAW, MARLENA

Number	Title (A Side/B Side)	Yr	VG	VG+	NM
12-Inch Singles					
COLUMBIA					
11025	Love Dancin'/No One Yet	1979	—	2.50	5.00
POLYDOR					
PRO 628 [DJ]	I Want to Know (same on both sides)	1988	2.00	4.00	8.00
SOUTH BAY					
1004	More Room at the Top/At Last	1982	2.50	5.00	10.00
22004	Never Give Up on You/(B-side unknown)	1983	2.00	4.00	8.00
45s					
BLUE NOTE					
XW209	Last Tango in Paris/(B-side unknown)	1973	—	2.50	5.00
XW366	Easy Evil/Just Don't Want to Be Lonely	1973	—	2.50	5.00
XW550	The Feeling's Good/But For Now	1974	—	2.50	5.00
XW649	You/Loving You Is Like a Party	1975	—	2.50	5.00
XW691	Feel Like Makin' Love/You Taught Me How to Speak in Love	1975	—	2.50	5.00
XW790	It's Better Than Walkin' Out/Be for Real	1976	—	2.50	5.00
XW844	Love Has Gone Away/This Time I'll Be Sweeter	1976	—	2.50	5.00
1981	Somewhere/You Must Believe	1972	—	3.00	6.00
CADET					
5549	Let's Wade in the Water/Show Time	1966	2.00	4.00	8.00

Number	Title (A Side/B Side)	Yr	VG	VG+	NM
5557	Mercy, Mercy, Mercy/Go Away Little Boy	1967	2.00	4.00	8.00
5571	Brother Where Are You/Waiting for Charlie to Come Home	1967	2.00	4.00	8.00
5592	Matchmaker, Matchmaker/A Couple of Losers	1968	—	3.00	6.00
5618	Looking Through the Eyes of Love/Anyone Can Move a Mountain	1968	—	3.00	6.00
5638	California Soul/The House That Jack Built	1969	—	3.00	6.00
5650	Woman of the Ghetto/I'm Satisfied	1969	—	3.00	6.00
5656	Looking Through the Eyes of Love/California Soul	1969	—	3.00	6.00
COLUMBIA					
10542	Yu-Ma/Go Away Little Boy//No Deposit, No Return	1977	—	2.50	5.00
10589	Johnny/Pictures and Memories	1977	—	2.50	5.00
10661	Don't Ask to Stay Until Tomorrow/No Deposit, No Return	1978	—	2.50	5.00
10746	Dreamin'/Places	1978	—	2.50	5.00
11034	Love Dancin'/No One Yet	1979	3.00	6.00	12.00
POLYDOR					
887776-7	I Want to Know/Love Is In Flight	1988	—	2.00	4.00

Albums

Number	Title	Yr	VG	VG+	NM
BLUE NOTE					
BN-LA143-F	From the Depths of My Soul	1974	3.75	7.50	15.00
BN-LA397-G	Who Is This Bitch, Anyway?	1975	3.75	7.50	15.00
BN-LA606-G	Just a Matter	1976	3.75	7.50	15.00
BST-84422	Marlena	1972	3.75	7.50	15.00
CADET					
LPS-803	Different Bags	1968	5.00	10.00	20.00
LPS-833	Spice of Life	1969	5.00	10.00	20.00
COLUMBIA					
PC 34458	Sweet Beginnings	1977	3.00	6.00	12.00
JC 35073	Acting Up	1978	3.00	6.00	12.00
JC 35632	Take a Bite	1979	3.00	6.00	12.00
JC 36367	The Best of Marlena Shaw	1980	2.50	5.00	10.00
VERVE					
831438-1	It Is Love	1987	2.50	5.00	10.00
837312-1	Love Is In Flight	1988	2.50	5.00	10.00

SHAW, SANDIE

45s

Number	Title (A Side/B Side)	Yr	VG	VG+	NM
MERCURY					
72315	Ya, Ya, Da, Da/As Long As You're Happy	1964	3.75	7.50	15.00
RCA VICTOR					
47-9594	Together/One More Lie	1968	2.00	4.00	8.00
74-0118	Voice in the Crowd/Monsieur Dupont	1969	2.00	4.00	8.00
74-0370	Love Is For the Two of Us/Wight Is Wight	1970	2.00	4.00	8.00
REPRISE					
0320	(There's) Always Something There to Remind Me/Don't You Know	1964	3.00	6.00	12.00
0342	Girl Don't Come/I'd Be Far Better Off Without You	1965	2.50	5.00	10.00
0365	I'll Stop at Nothing/You Can't Blame Him	1965	2.50	5.00	10.00
0375	Long Live Love/I've Heard About Him	1965	2.50	5.00	10.00
0394	Stop Feeling Sorry for Yourself/I'll Stop at Nothing	1965	2.50	5.00	10.00
0427	If Ever You Need Me/How Can You Tell	1965	2.50	5.00	10.00
0449	Tomorrow/Hurting You	1966	2.50	5.00	10.00
0488	Nothing Comes Easy/Stop Before You Start	1966	2.50	5.00	10.00
0546	Think Sometime About Me/Hide All Emotion	1967	2.50	5.00	10.00
0575	Puppet on a String/I Had a Dream Last Night	1967	2.50	5.00	10.00
20191	Me/Now	1963	3.75	7.50	15.00
—B-side by Bob Candee					

Albums

Number	Title	Yr	VG	VG+	NM
REPRISE					
PS-6166 [R]	Sandie Shaw	1965	12.50	25.00	50.00
R-6166 [M]	Sandie Shaw	1965	10.00	20.00	40.00
R-6191 [M]	Me	1966	7.50	15.00	30.00
RS-6191 [S]	Me	1966	10.00	20.00	40.00

SHAW, SERENA

Albums

Number	Title	Yr	VG	VG+	NM
RAMA					
RLP-5001 [M]	Cry My Love	1956	100.00	200.00	400.00

SHEAN AND JENKYNS

45s

Number	Title (A Side/B Side)	Yr	VG	VG+	NM
GNP CRESCENDO					
198	Goofy-Footer Ho-Dad/Do the Commercial	1963	6.25	12.50	25.00

SHEARING, GEORGE

45s

Number	Title (A Side/B Side)	Yr	VG	VG+	NM
CAPITOL					
4418	Blue Malibu/Honeysuckle Rose	1960	2.00	4.00	8.00
4922	The Stripper/Fairy Tales	1963	2.00	4.00	8.00
5850	On a Clear Day You Can See Forever/Call Me	1967	—	3.00	6.00
MGM					
10647	In a Chinese Garden/(B-side unknown)	1950	5.00	10.00	20.00
—Note: Earlier George Shearing 45s on MGM may exist					
10687	I'll Remember April/Jumping with Symphony Sid	1950	5.00	10.00	20.00
10720	I Didn't Know What Time It Was/How's Trix	1950	5.00	10.00	20.00
10763	When Your Lover Has Gone/Carnegie Horizons	1950	5.00	10.00	20.00
10859	Roses of Picardy/Pick Yourself Up	1950	5.00	10.00	20.00
10907	For You/Little White Lies	1951	3.75	7.50	15.00
10956	I'll Be Around/Quintessence	1951	3.75	7.50	15.00
10986	The Breeze and I/I Remember You	1951	3.75	7.50	15.00
11046	Don't Blame Me/Brain Waves	1951	3.75	7.50	15.00
11153	Thine Alone/Geneva's Move	1952	3.75	7.50	15.00
11199	To a Wild Rose/Swedish Pastry	1952	3.75	7.50	15.00
11282	Simplicity/5 O'Clock Whistle	1952	3.75	7.50	15.00
11354	Lullaby of Birdland/When Lights Are Low	1952	3.75	7.50	15.00
11425	There's a Lull in My Life/Midnight Belongs to You	1953	3.75	7.50	15.00
11493	Body and Soul/I Hear a Rhapsody	1953	3.75	7.50	15.00
11545	Indian Summer/Appreciation	1953	3.75	7.50	15.00
11600	Easy to Love/Wrap Your Troubles in Dreams	1953	3.75	7.50	15.00
11639	Tiempo de Concerro (Part 1)/Tiempo de Concerro (Part 2)	1953	3.75	7.50	15.00
11677	A Sinner Kissed an Angel/Mood for Milt	1954	3.00	6.00	12.00
11754	I've Never Been in Love Before/Mambo Inn	1954	3.00	6.00	12.00
11833	Lullaby of Birdland/Love Is Here to Stay	1954	3.00	6.00	12.00
11876	Adieu/Undecided	1954	3.00	6.00	12.00
11943	The Lady Is a Tramp/Cool Mambo	1955	3.00	6.00	12.00
12038	Ill Wind/Drune Negrita	1955	3.00	6.00	12.00
12079	Get Off My Back/Love Is Just Around the Corner	1955	3.00	6.00	12.00
12132	Stranger in Paradise/Point and Counterpoint	1955	3.00	6.00	12.00
12182	Hallelujah/Basso Profundo	1956	3.00	6.00	12.00
12227	Spring Is Here/Minor Trouble	1956	3.00	6.00	12.00
12309	Over the Rainbow/Lonely Moments	1956	3.00	6.00	12.00
12349	My Silent Love/As Long As There's Music	1956	3.00	6.00	12.00

Albums

Number	Title	Yr	VG	VG+	NM
ARCHIVE OF FOLK AND JAZZ					
223	Young George Shearing	1968	2.50	5.00	10.00
236	The Early Years, Vol. 2	1969	2.50	5.00	10.00
BASF					
25340	Light, Airy and Swinging	1973	3.00	6.00	12.00
25351	The Way We Are	1974	3.00	6.00	12.00
CAPITOL					
SKAO-139	The Best of George Shearing, Vol. 2	1969	3.00	6.00	12.00
ST-181	Fool on the Hill	1969	3.00	6.00	12.00
T 648 [M]	The Shearing Spell	1956	7.50	15.00	30.00
—Turquoise label					
T 648 [M]	The Shearing Spell	1959	5.00	10.00	20.00
—Black label with colorband, logo on left					
DT 720 [R]	Velvet Carpet	196?	3.00	6.00	12.00
T 720 [M]	Velvet Carpet	1956	7.50	15.00	30.00
—Turquoise label					
T 720 [M]	Velvet Carpet	1959	5.00	10.00	20.00
—Black label with colorband, logo on left					
T 720 [M]	Velvet Carpet	1962	3.75	7.50	15.00
—Black label with colorband, logo on top					
DT 737 [R]	Latin Escapade	196?	3.00	6.00	12.00
T 737 [M]	Latin Escapade	1957	7.50	15.00	30.00
—Turquoise label					
T 737 [M]	Latin Escapade	1959	5.00	10.00	20.00
—Black label with colorband, logo on left					
T 737 [M]	Latin Escapade	1962	3.75	7.50	15.00
—Black label with colorband, logo on top					
ST 858 [S]	Black Satin	1959	5.00	10.00	20.00
—Black label with colorband, logo on left					
ST 858 [S]	Black Satin	1962	3.75	7.50	15.00
—Black label with colorband, logo on top					
T 858 [M]	Black Satin	1957	7.50	15.00	30.00
—Turquoise label					
T 858 [M]	Black Satin	1959	5.00	10.00	20.00
—Black label with colorband, logo on left					
T 858 [M]	Black Satin	1962	3.75	7.50	15.00
—Black label with colorband, logo on top					
T 909 [M]	Shearing Piano	1957	7.50	15.00	30.00
—Turquoise label					
T 909 [M]	Shearing Piano	1959	5.00	10.00	20.00
—Black label with colorband, logo on left					
ST 1038 [S]	Burnished Brass	1959	6.25	12.50	25.00
—Black label with colorband, logo on left					
ST 1038 [S]	Burnished Brass	1962	5.00	10.00	20.00
—Black label with colorband, logo on top					
T 1038 [M]	Burnished Brass	1958	5.00	10.00	20.00
—Black label with colorband, logo on left					
T 1038 [M]	Burnished Brass	1962	3.75	7.50	15.00
—Black label with colorband, logo on top					
ST 1082 [S]	Latin Lace	1958	6.25	12.50	25.00
—Black label with colorband, logo on left					
ST 1082 [S]	Latin Lace	1962	5.00	10.00	20.00
—Black label with colorband, logo on top					
T 1082 [M]	Latin Lace	1958	5.00	10.00	20.00
—Black label with colorband, logo on left					
T 1082 [M]	Latin Lace	1962	3.75	7.50	15.00
—Black label with colorband, logo on top					
ST 1124 [S]	Blue Chiffon	1959	6.25	12.50	25.00
—Black label with colorband, logo on left					
ST 1124 [S]	Blue Chiffon	1962	5.00	10.00	20.00
—Black label with colorband, logo on top					
T 1124 [M]	Blue Chiffon	1959	5.00	10.00	20.00
—Black label with colorband, logo on left					
T 1124 [M]	Blue Chiffon	1962	3.75	7.50	15.00
—Black label with colorband, logo on top					
ST 1187 [S]	George Shearing On Stage	1959	6.25	12.50	25.00
—Black label with colorband, logo on left					
ST 1187 [S]	George Shearing On Stage	1962	5.00	10.00	20.00
—Black label with colorband, logo on top					
T 1187 [M]	George Shearing On Stage	1959	5.00	10.00	20.00
—Black label with colorband, logo on left					
T 1187 [M]	George Shearing On Stage	1962	3.75	7.50	15.00
—Black label with colorband, logo on top					
ST 1275 [S]	Latin Affair	1960	6.25	12.50	25.00
—Black label with colorband, logo on left					
ST 1275 [S]	Latin Affair	1962	5.00	10.00	20.00
—Black label with colorband, logo on top					
T 1275 [M]	Latin Affair	1960	5.00	10.00	20.00
—Black label with colorband, logo on left					
T 1275 [M]	Latin Affair	1962	3.75	7.50	15.00
—Black label with colorband, logo on top					
ST 1334 [S]	White Satin	1960	6.25	12.50	25.00
—Black label with colorband, logo on left					
ST 1334 [S]	White Satin	1962	5.00	10.00	20.00
—Black label with colorband, logo on top					
T 1334 [M]	White Satin	1960	5.00	10.00	20.00
—Black label with colorband, logo on left					
T 1334 [M]	White Satin	1962	3.75	7.50	15.00
—Black label with colorband, logo on top					

Number	Title (A Side/B Side)	Yr	VG	VG+	NM
ST 1416 [S]	On the Sunny Side of the Strip	1960	6.25	12.50	25.00
—Black label with colorband, logo on left					
ST 1416 [S]	On the Sunny Side of the Strip	1962	5.00	10.00	20.00
—Black label with colorband, logo on top					
T 1416 [M]	On the Sunny Side of the Strip	1960	5.00	10.00	20.00
—Black label with colorband, logo on left					
T 1416 [M]	On the Sunny Side of the Strip	1962	3.75	7.50	15.00
—Black label with colorband, logo on top					
SM-1472	The Shearing Touch	1977	2.50	5.00	10.00
—Reissue with new prefix					
ST 1472 [S]	The Shearing Touch	1961	6.25	12.50	25.00
—Black label with colorband, logo on left					
ST 1472 [S]	The Shearing Touch	1962	5.00	10.00	20.00
—Black label with colorband, logo on top					
T 1472 [M]	The Shearing Touch	1961	5.00	10.00	20.00
—Black label with colorband, logo on left					
T 1472 [M]	The Shearing Touch	1962	3.75	7.50	15.00
—Black label with colorband, logo on top					
ST 1567 [S]	Mood Latino	1961	6.25	12.50	25.00
—Black label with colorband, logo on left					
ST 1567 [S]	Mood Latino	1962	5.00	10.00	20.00
—Black label with colorband, logo on top					
T 1567 [M]	Mood Latino	1961	5.00	10.00	20.00
—Black label with colorband, logo on left					
T 1567 [M]	Mood Latino	1962	3.75	7.50	15.00
—Black label with colorband, logo on top					
ST 1628 [S]	Satin Affair	1961	6.25	12.50	25.00
—Black label with colorband, logo on left					
ST 1628 [S]	Satin Affair	1962	5.00	10.00	20.00
—Black label with colorband, logo on top					
T 1628 [M]	Satin Affair	1961	5.00	10.00	20.00
—Black label with colorband, logo on left					
T 1628 [M]	Satin Affair	1962	3.75	7.50	15.00
—Black label with colorband, logo on top					
ST 1715 [S]	San Francisco Scene	1962	5.00	10.00	20.00
T 1715 [M]	San Francisco Scene	1962	3.75	7.50	15.00
ST 1755 [S]	Concerto for My Love	1962	5.00	10.00	20.00
T 1755 [M]	Concerto for My Love	1962	3.75	7.50	15.00
ST 1827 [S]	Jazz Moments	1963	5.00	10.00	20.00
T 1827 [M]	Jazz Moments	1963	3.75	7.50	15.00
ST 1873 [S]	Bossa Nova	1963	5.00	10.00	20.00
T 1873 [M]	Bossa Nova	1963	3.75	7.50	15.00
ST 1874 [S]	Touch Me Softly	1963	5.00	10.00	20.00
T 1874 [M]	Touch Me Softly	1963	3.75	7.50	15.00
ST 1992 [S]	Jazz Concert	1963	5.00	10.00	20.00
T 1992 [M]	Jazz Concert	1963	3.75	7.50	15.00
ST 2048 [S]	Old Gold and Ivory	1964	3.75	7.50	15.00
T 2048 [M]	Old Gold and Ivory	1964	3.00	6.00	12.00
SM-2104	The Best of George Shearing	1977	2.50	5.00	10.00
—Reissue with new prefix					
ST 2104 [S]	The Best of George Shearing	1964	3.75	7.50	15.00
T 2104 [M]	The Best of George Shearing	1964	3.00	6.00	12.00
ST 2143 [S]	Deep Velvet	1964	3.75	7.50	15.00
T 2143 [M]	Deep Velvet	1964	3.00	6.00	12.00
ST 2272 [S]	Out of the Woods	1965	3.75	7.50	15.00
T 2272 [M]	Out of the Woods	1965	3.00	6.00	12.00
ST 2326 [S]	Latin Rendezvous	1965	3.75	7.50	15.00
T 2326 [M]	Latin Rendezvous	1965	3.00	6.00	12.00
ST 2372 [S]	Here and Now	1965	3.75	7.50	15.00
T 2372 [M]	Here and Now	1965	3.00	6.00	12.00
ST 2447 [S]	Rare Form	1965	3.75	7.50	15.00
T 2447 [M]	Rare Form	1965	3.00	6.00	12.00
ST 2567 [S]	That Fresh Feeling	1966	3.75	7.50	15.00
T 2567 [M]	That Fresh Feeling	1966	3.00	6.00	12.00
ST 2699 [S]	George Shearing Today	1967	3.00	6.00	12.00
T 2699 [M]	George Shearing Today	1967	3.75	7.50	15.00
SM-11454	Latin Escapade	197?	2.50	5.00	10.00
SM-11800	Black Satin	1978	2.50	5.00	10.00
CONCORD CONCERTO					
CC-2010	George Shearing and Barry Tuckwell Play the Music of Cole Porter	1986	2.50	5.00	10.00
CONCORD JAZZ					
CJ-110	Blues Alley Jazz	1980	2.50	5.00	10.00
CJ-132	On a Clear Day	1981	2.50	5.00	10.00
—With Brian Torff					
CJ-171	Alone Together	1981	2.50	5.00	10.00
CJ-177	First Edition	1982	2.50	5.00	10.00
CJ-246	Live at the Café Carlyle	1984	2.50	5.00	10.00
CJ-281	Grand Piano	1985	2.50	5.00	10.00
CJ-318	More Grand Piano	1987	2.50	5.00	10.00
CJ-335	Breakin' Out	1988	2.50	5.00	10.00
CJ-346	Dexterity	1988	2.50	5.00	10.00
CJ-357	A Perfect Match	1988	2.50	5.00	10.00
—With Ernestine Anderson					
CJ-371	The Spirit of 176	1989	3.00	6.00	12.00
—With Hank Jones					
CJ-388	George Shearing in Dixieland	1989	3.00	6.00	12.00
CJ-400	Piano	1989	3.00	6.00	12.00
DISCOVERY					
DL-3002 [10]	George Shearing Quintet	1950	15.00	30.00	60.00
FANTASY					
OJC-040	George Shearing and the Montgomery Brothers	198?	2.50	5.00	10.00
LONDON					
LL 295 [10]	Souvenirs	1951	15.00	30.00	60.00
LL 1343 [M]	By Request	1956	7.50	15.00	30.00
MGM					
E-90 [10]	A Touch of Genius	1951	12.50	25.00	50.00
GAS-143	You're Hearing George Shearing	1970	3.00	6.00	12.00
E-155 [10]	I Hear Music	1952	12.50	25.00	50.00
E-226 [10]	When Lights Are Low	1953	12.50	25.00	50.00
E-252 [10]	An Evening with George Shearing	1954	12.50	25.00	50.00
E-518 [10]	You're Hearing the George Shearing Quartet	1950	15.00	30.00	60.00
E-3122 [M]	An Evening with Shearing	1955	7.50	15.00	30.00
E-3175 [M]	Shearing Caravan	1955	7.50	15.00	30.00
E-3216 [M]	You're Hearing George Shearing	1955	7.50	15.00	30.00
E-3264 [M]	When Lights Are Low	1955	7.50	15.00	30.00
E-3265 [M]	Touch of Genius	1955	7.50	15.00	30.00
E-3266 [M]	I Hear Music	1955	7.50	15.00	30.00
E-3293 [M]	Shearing in Hi-Fi	1955	7.50	15.00	30.00
E-4041 [M]	Satin Latin	1962	3.75	7.50	15.00
SE-4041 [R]	Satin Latin	1962	3.00	6.00	12.00
E-4042 [M]	Soft and Silky	1962	3.75	7.50	15.00
SE-4042 [R]	Soft and Silky	1962	3.00	6.00	12.00
E-4043 [M]	Smooth and Swinging	1962	3.75	7.50	15.00
SE-4043 [R]	Smooth and Swinging	1962	3.00	6.00	12.00
E-4169 [M]	The Very Best of George Shearing	1963	3.75	7.50	15.00
SE-4169 [R]	The Very Best of George Shearing	1963	3.00	6.00	12.00
MOSAIC					
MQ7-157 [(7)]	The Complete Capitol Live Recordings of George Shearing	199?	30.00	60.00	120.00
PAUSA					
7035	Light, Airy and Swinging	1977	2.50	5.00	10.00
7049	The Reunion	1979	2.50	5.00	10.00
—With Stephane Grappelli					
7072	500 Miles High	1979	2.50	5.00	10.00
7088	Getting in the Swing of Things	1981	2.50	5.00	10.00
7116	On Target	198?	2.50	5.00	10.00
9030	The Shearing Touch	198?	2.50	5.00	10.00
9036	Jazz Moments	1985	2.50	5.00	10.00
9065	Latin Affair	1986	2.50	5.00	10.00
PICKWICK					
SPC-3039	Lullaby of Birdland	197?	2.50	5.00	10.00
SPC-3100	You Stepped Out of a Dream	197?	2.50	5.00	10.00
SAVOY					
MG-15003 [10]	Piano Solo	1951	15.00	30.00	60.00
SAVOY JAZZ					
SJL-1117	So Rare	198?	2.50	5.00	10.00
SHEBA					
101	Out of This World	197?	3.00	6.00	12.00
103	George Shearing Trio	197?	3.00	6.00	12.00
104	George Shearing Quartet	197?	3.00	6.00	12.00
105	As Requested	197?	3.00	6.00	12.00
106	Music to Hear	197?	3.00	6.00	12.00
107	GAS	197?	3.00	6.00	12.00
VERVE					
VSP-9 [M]	Classic Shearing	1966	3.75	7.50	15.00
VSPS-9 [R]	Classic Shearing	1966	3.00	6.00	12.00
821664-1	My Ship	198?	2.50	5.00	10.00
827977-1 [(2)]	Lullaby of Birdland	1986	3.00	6.00	12.00

SHEARING, GEORGE, AND THE MONTGOMERY BROTHERS

Albums

Number	Title (A Side/B Side)	Yr	VG	VG+	NM
JAZZLAND					
JLP-55 [M]	Love Walked In	1961	7.50	15.00	30.00
—Cover has Shearing and the brothers					
JLP-55 [M]	Love Walked In	1962	6.25	12.50	25.00
—Cover has a woman					
JLP-955 [S]	Love Walked In	1961	10.00	20.00	40.00
—Cover has Shearing and the brothers					
JLP-955 [S]	Love Walked In	1962	7.50	15.00	30.00
—Cover has a woman					
RIVERSIDE					
6087	George Shearing and the Montgomery Brothers	197?	2.50	5.00	10.00
—Reissue of Jazzland LP					

SHEARING, GEORGE, AND MEL TORME

Also see each artist's individual listings.

Albums

Number	Title (A Side/B Side)	Yr	VG	VG+	NM
CONCORD JAZZ					
CJ-190	An Evening with George Shearing and Mel Torme	1982	2.50	5.00	10.00
CJ-219	Top Drawer	1983	2.50	5.00	10.00
CJ-248	An Evening at Charlie's	1984	2.50	5.00	10.00
CJ-294	An Elegant Evening	1985	2.50	5.00	10.00
CJ-341	A Vintage Year	1988	2.50	5.00	10.00

SHEEP, THE

By the same people who gave us THE STRANGELOVES.

45s

Number	Title (A Side/B Side)	Yr	VG	VG+	NM
BOOM					
60000	Hide and Seek/Twelve Months Later	1966	5.00	10.00	20.00
60007	Dynamite/I Feel Good	1966	5.00	10.00	20.00

SHEFFIELDS, THE

45s

Number	Title (A Side/B Side)	Yr	VG	VG+	NM
DESTINATION					
613	My Loving Days Are Through/Please Come Back	1966	3.00	6.00	12.00
621	Do You Still Love Me/Nothing I Can Do	1966	3.00	6.00	12.00
DOT					
16722	Plenty of Love/Bags Groove	1965	3.75	7.50	15.00

SHEIKS, THE

More than one group. Some of these were labeled "The Shieks."

45s

Number	Title (A Side/B Side)	Yr	VG	VG+	NM
AMY					
807	Come On Back/Please Don't Take Away the Girl I Love	1960	50.00	100.00	200.00
CAT					
116	Walk That Walk/The Kissing Song (Sweetie Lover)	1955	10.00	20.00	40.00
EF-N-DE					
1000	Give Me Another Chance/Baby Don't You Cry	1955	200.00	400.00	600.00
FEDERAL					
12237	So Fine/Sentimental Heart	1955	37.50	75.00	150.00
JAMIE					
1147	Candlelight Cafe/The Song of Old Paree	1959	5.00	10.00	20.00
LEGRAND					
1013	What I'd Do for Your Love/Why Should I Dance	1961	25.00	50.00	100.00

Number	Title (A Side/B Side)	Yr	VG	VG+	NM
1016	Cocoanut Woman/Twist That Twist	1962	6.25	12.50	25.00
MGM					
12876	Baghdad Rock (Part 1)/Baghdad Rock (Part 2)	1960	5.00	10.00	20.00

SHELDON, DOUG

45s

Number	Title (A Side/B Side)	Yr	VG	VG+	NM
CONGRESS					
266	How Can I Tell Her/It's Because of You	1966	2.50	5.00	10.00
MGM					
13261	Lonely Boy/Hello There Lonely Baby	1964	3.00	6.00	12.00

SHELLS, THE

45s

Number	Title (A Side/B Side)	Yr	VG	VG+	NM
END					
1022	Pretty Little Girl/Sippin' Soda	1958	37.50	75.00	150.00
1050	Whispering Wings/Shooma Dom Dom	1959	12.50	25.00	50.00
GONE					
5103	Pretty Little Girl/Sippin' Soda	1961	6.25	12.50	25.00
JOHNSON					
099	My Cherie/Explain It to Me	1972	—	3.00	6.00
104	Baby Oh Baby/Angel Eyes	1957	10.00	20.00	40.00
104	Baby Oh Baby/What's in An Angel's Eyes	1960	3.75	7.50	15.00
—Note lengthened B-side title					
106	Don't Say Goodbye/Pleading	1958	25.00	50.00	100.00
107	Explain It to Me/An Island Unknown	1961	6.25	12.50	25.00
109	Better Forget Him/Can't Take It	1961	6.25	12.50	25.00
110	In the Dim Light of the Dark/O-Mi Yum-Mi Yum-Mi	1961	6.25	12.50	25.00
112	Sweetest One/Baby Walk On In	1961	7.50	15.00	30.00
119	Deep in My Heart/(It's a) Happy Holiday	1962	7.50	15.00	30.00
120	The Drive/A Toast to Your Birthday	1962	7.50	15.00	30.00
127	On My Honor/My Royal Love	1963	12.50	25.00	50.00
332	Explain It to Me/An Island Unknown	1961	3.75	7.50	15.00
JOSIE					
912	Deep in My Heart/Our Wedding Day	1963	5.00	10.00	20.00
ROULETTE					
4156	The Thief/She Wasn't Meant for Me	1959	7.50	15.00	30.00

Albums

Number	Title (A Side/B Side)	Yr	VG	VG+	NM
CANDELITE					
1000	Accapella	197?	3.75	7.50	15.00
COLLECTABLES					
COL-5077	Golden Classics	198?	2.50	5.00	10.00

SHELTON, GARY

45s

Number	Title (A Side/B Side)	Yr	VG	VG+	NM
ALPINE					
56	Honey Bee/Till the End of the Line	1960	7.50	15.00	30.00
MARK					
145	Goodbye Little Darlin' Goodbye/Stop the World	1960	50.00	100.00	200.00
MERCURY					
71310	Kissin' at the Drive-In/Yours Till I Die	1958	7.50	15.00	30.00

SHEP AND THE LIMELITES

Also see THE HEARTBEATS; SHANE SHEPPARD.

45s

Number	Title (A Side/B Side)	Yr	VG	VG+	NM
HULL					
740	Daddy's Home/This I Know	1961	10.00	20.00	40.00
—Pink label					
740	Daddy's Home/This I Know	1961	6.25	12.50	25.00
—Red label					
740	Daddy's Home/This I Know	1961	5.00	10.00	20.00
—Tan label. Note: Any colored vinyl version is a counterfeit.					
742	Ready for Your Love/You'll Be Sorry	1961	5.00	10.00	20.00
747	Three Steps from the Altar/Oh What a Feeling	1961	5.00	10.00	20.00
748	Our Anniversary/Who Told the Sandman	1962	5.00	10.00	20.00
751	What Did Daddy Do/Teach Me, Teach Me How to Twist	1962	5.00	10.00	20.00
753	Gee Baby, What About You/Everything Is Going to Be Alright	1962	5.00	10.00	20.00
756	Remember Baby/The Monkey	1963	5.00	10.00	20.00
757	Stick By Me (And I'll Stick By You)/It's All Over Now	1963	5.00	10.00	20.00
759	Steal Away (With Your Baby)/For All My Love	1963	5.00	10.00	20.00
761	Easy to Remember (When You Want to Forget)/Why, Why Won't You Believe Me	1964	5.00	10.00	20.00
767	I'm All Alone/Why Did You Fall for Me	1964	5.00	10.00	20.00
770	Party for Two/You Better Believe	1965	7.50	15.00	30.00
772	In Case I Forget/I'm a-Hurting Inside	1965	5.00	10.00	20.00

Albums

Number	Title (A Side/B Side)	Yr	VG	VG+	NM
HULL					
1001 [M]	Our Anniversary	1962	300.00	600.00	1200.
ROULETTE					
R-25350 [M]	Our Anniversary	1967	20.00	40.00	80.00
SR-25350 [R]	Our Anniversary	1967	12.50	25.00	50.00

SHEPARDS, THE

45s

Number	Title (A Side/B Side)	Yr	VG	VG+	NM
ABC-PARAMOUNT					
10758	Little Girl Lost/Let Yourself Go	1965	6.25	12.50	25.00

SHEPHERD, CYBILL

45s

Number	Title (A Side/B Side)	Yr	VG	VG+	NM
PARAMOUNT					
0299	My Heart Belongs to Daddy/Anything Goes	1974	2.50	5.00	10.00

Albums

Number	Title (A Side/B Side)	Yr	VG	VG+	NM
PARAMOUNT					
PAS-1018	Cybill Does It...to Cole Porter	1974	5.00	10.00	20.00
—With poster					

SHEPHERD SISTERS

Some of these spelled the name "Shepard," others "Sheppard," but they are all the same group.

45s

Number	Title (A Side/B Side)	Yr	VG	VG+	NM
20TH CENTURY FOX					
468	I've Got a Secret/Finders Keepers	1964	2.50	5.00	10.00
ATLANTIC					
2176	What Makes Little Girls Cry/Don't Mention My Name	1963	2.50	5.00	10.00
2195	Talk Is Cheap/The Greatest Lover	1963	2.50	5.00	10.00
BIG TOP					
3066	Hapsburg Serenade/Schoen-A, Schoen-A	1961	3.75	7.50	15.00
LANCE					
125	Alone (Why Must I Be Alone)/Congratulations to Someone	1957	6.25	12.50	25.00
MELBA					
100	Gone with the Wind/Rock and Roll, Cha Cha	1956	6.25	12.50	25.00
108	Remember That Crazy Rock and Roll Turf/I Walked Beside the Sea	1957	6.25	12.50	25.00
MERCURY					
71244	Gettin' Ready for Freddie/The Best Thing There Is	1957	6.25	12.50	25.00
71306	Eatin' Pizza/A Boy and a Girl	1958	5.00	10.00	20.00
71350	Dancing Baby/Is It a Crime	1958	5.00	10.00	20.00
MGM					
12766	Heart and Soul/(It's No) Sin	1959	5.00	10.00	20.00
PRIVATE STOCK					
45063	Our Town/(B-side unknown)	1975	—	3.00	6.00
UNITED ARTISTS					
350	Deeply/I'm Still Dancin'	1961	3.00	6.00	12.00
456	Lolita Ya Ya/Marvin	1962	3.00	6.00	12.00
WARWICK					
511	Here Comes Heaven Again/I Think It's Time	1959	3.75	7.50	15.00
530	Alone/Rocky	1960	3.75	7.50	15.00
548	Yea Yea Dixie/How Softly a Heart Breaks	1960	3.75	7.50	15.00
YORK					
50002	Alone (New Version)/Alone (Original Version)	1965	2.50	5.00	10.00

SHEPPARD, BUDDY, AND THE HOLIDAYS

THE BELMONTS in disguise.

45s

Number	Title (A Side/B Side)	Yr	VG	VG+	NM
SABINA					
506	My Love Is Real/Brahms' Lullaby (Time to Dream)	1962	12.50	25.00	50.00
510	Now It's All Over/That Background Sound	1963	12.50	25.00	50.00

SHEPPARD, NEIL

45s

Number	Title (A Side/B Side)	Yr	VG	VG+	NM
ALMONT					
314	You Can't Go Far Without a Guitar (Unless You're Ringo Starr)/Betty Is the Girl for You	1964	7.50	15.00	30.00

SHEPPARD, SHANE

Also see SHEP AND THE LIMELITES.

45s

Number	Title (A Side/B Side)	Yr	VG	VG+	NM
APT					
25039	Too Young to Wed/Two Loving Hearts	1960	12.50	25.00	50.00
25046	One Week from Today/I'm So Lonely (What Can I Do)	1960	10.00	20.00	40.00

SHEPPARDS, THE

More than one group?

45s

Number	Title (A Side/B Side)	Yr	VG	VG+	NM
ABNER					
7006	Elevator Operator/Loving You	1961	3.00	6.00	12.00
APEX					
7750	Loving You/Island of Love	1959	10.00	20.00	40.00
7752	Just Like You/Feel Like Lovin'	1959	6.25	12.50	25.00
7755	It's Crazy/Meant to Be	1960	6.25	12.50	25.00
7759	Just When I Need You Most/Society Gal	1960	6.25	12.50	25.00
7760	Come Home, Come Home/Just Like You	1960	6.25	12.50	25.00
7762	Tragic/Feel Like Lovin'	1961	6.25	12.50	25.00
BUNKY					
7764	Island of Love/Steal Away	1969	—	3.00	6.00
7766	I'm Not Wanted/Your Love (Has a Hole in It)	1969	—	3.00	6.00
CONSTELLATION					
123	Island of Love/Give a Hug to Me	1964	2.50	5.00	10.00
176	Island of Love/Give a Hug to Me	1966	2.00	4.00	8.00
IMPACT					
1018	Poor Man's Thing/When Johnny Comes Marching Home	1967	7.50	15.00	30.00
OKEH					
7173	Walkin'/Pretend You're Still Mine	1963	2.50	5.00	10.00
PAM					
1001	Never Let Me Go/Give a Hug to Me	1961	3.00	6.00	12.00
SHARP					
6039	What's the Name of the Game/Glitter in Your Eyes	1961	3.00	6.00	12.00
UNITED					
198	Sherry/Mozelle	1957	62.50	125.00	250.00
VEE JAY					
406	Every Now and Then/Glitter in Your Eyes	1961	3.00	6.00	12.00
441	Tragic/Come to Me	1962	5.00	10.00	20.00

Albums

Number	Title (A Side/B Side)	Yr	VG	VG+	NM
COLLECTABLES					
COL-5078	Golden Classics	198?	2.50	5.00	10.00
CONSTELLATION					
C-4 [M]	Collectors Showcase: The Sheppards	1964	20.00	40.00	80.00
CS-4 [R]	Collectors Showcase: The Sheppards	1964	10.00	20.00	40.00
SOLID SMOKE					
SS-8004	The Sheppards	1980	2.50	5.00	10.00
SS-8028	18 Dusty Diamonds	1984	2.50	5.00	10.00

SHERIDAN, BOBBY

45s

Number	Title (A Side/B Side)	Yr	VG	VG+	NM
SUN					
354	Red Man/Sad News	1961	7.50	15.00	30.00

SHERIDAN, MIKE, AND THE NIGHTRIDERS

45s

Number	Title (A Side/B Side)	Yr	VG	VG+	NM
LIVERPOOL SOUND					
902	Please Mr. Postman/In Love	1964	30.00	60.00	120.00

SHERIDAN, TONY, AND THE BEAT BROTHERS

See THE BEATLES.

SHERIFF AND THE RAVELS

45s

Number	Title (A Side/B Side)	Yr	VG	VG+	NM
VEE JAY					
306	Shombalor/Lonely One	1959	10.00	20.00	40.00

SHERLOCKS, THE

45s

Number	Title (A Side/B Side)	Yr	VG	VG+	NM
DOT					
16890	Skin of My Teeth/Turn Her Down	1966	5.00	10.00	20.00
16953	Shades of Blue/Too Good to Be True	1966	3.00	6.00	12.00

SHERMAN, ALLAN

45s

Number	Title (A Side/B Side)	Yr	VG	VG+	NM
RCA VICTOR					
47-8412	The End of a Symphony (Part 1)/The End of a Symphony (Part 2)	1964	2.50	5.00	10.00
47-9693	Fig Leaves Are Falling/Juggling	1968	—	3.00	6.00
WARNER BROS.					
5378	Hello Mudduh! Hello Fadduh! (A Letter from Camp)/Here's to the Crabgrass	1963	3.75	7.50	15.00
5378	Hello Mudduh! Hello Fadduh! (A Letter from Camp)/Rat Fink	1963	3.00	6.00	12.00
5378 [PS]	Hello Mudduh! Hello Fadduh! (A Letter from Camp)/Rat Fink	1963	5.00	10.00	20.00
5406	The Twelve Gifts of Christmas/You Went the Wrong Way, Old King Louie	1963	6.25	12.50	25.00
5419	My Son the Vampire/I Can't Dance	1964	3.00	6.00	12.00
5435	Skin (Heart)/The Drop-Outs March	1964	2.50	5.00	10.00
5449	Hello Mudduh! Hello Fadduh! New 1964 Version/ Hello Mudduh! Hello Fadduh! Original Version	1964	3.00	6.00	12.00
5449 [PS]	Hello Mudduh! Hello Fadduh! New 1964 Version/ Hello Mudduh! Hello Fadduh! Original Version	1964	5.00	10.00	20.00
5490	Pop Hates the Beatles/Grow Mrs. Goldfarb	1964	3.75	7.50	15.00
5614	Crazy Downtown/The Drop-Outs March	1965	2.50	5.00	10.00
5672	The Drinking Man's Diet/The Laarge Daark Aardvark Song	1965	2.50	5.00	10.00
5806	His Own Little Island/Odd Ball	1966	2.50	5.00	10.00
5896	Westchester Hadassah/Strange Things in My Soup	1967	2.50	5.00	10.00
7112	Hello Mudduh! Hello Fadduh! (A Letter from Camp)/Sarah Jackman	1968	—	3.00	6.00
—"Back to Back Hits" series -- originals have green "W7" labels					

Albums

Number	Title (A Side/B Side)	Yr	VG	VG+	NM
JUBLIEE					
JGM 5019 [M]	More Folk Songs by Allan Sherman	1963	5.00	10.00	20.00
—Two early Allan Sherman sides plus comedy bits by others					
RCA RED SEAL					
LM-2773 [M]	Peter and the Commissar	1964	5.00	10.00	20.00
LSC-2773 [S]	Peter and the Commissar	1964	6.25	12.50	25.00
—With Arthur Fiedler and the Boston Pops Orchestra					
RHINO					
RNLP-005	The Best of Allan Sherman	198?	2.50	5.00	10.00
RNLP 70818	A Gift of Laughter	1986	2.50	5.00	10.00
WARNER BROS.					
W 1475 [M]	My Son, the Folk Singer	1962	3.75	7.50	15.00
WS 1475 [S]	My Son, the Folk Singer	1962	5.00	10.00	20.00
—Gold label					
W 1487 [M]	My Son, the Celebrity	1963	3.75	7.50	15.00
WS 1487 [S]	My Son, the Celebrity	1963	5.00	10.00	20.00
—Gold label					
W 1501 [M]	My Son, the Nut	1963	3.75	7.50	15.00
WS 1501 [S]	My Son, the Nut	1963	5.00	10.00	20.00
—Gold label					
W 1539 [M]	Allan in Wonderland	1964	3.00	6.00	12.00
WS 1539 [S]	Allan in Wonderland	1964	3.75	7.50	15.00
—Gold label					
W 1569 [M]	For Swingin' Livers Only!	1964	3.00	6.00	12.00
WS 1569 [S]	For Swingin' Livers Only!	1964	3.75	7.50	15.00
W 1604 [M]	My Name Is Allan	1965	3.00	6.00	12.00
WS 1604 [S]	My Name Is Allan	1965	3.75	7.50	15.00
—Gold label					
W 1649 [M]	Allan Sherman — Live	1966	3.00	6.00	12.00
WS 1649 [S]	Allan Sherman — Live	1966	3.75	7.50	15.00
—Gold label					
W 1684 [M]	Togetherness	1967	3.75	7.50	15.00
WS 1684 [S]	Togetherness	1967	5.00	10.00	20.00
—Gold label					

SHERMAN, BOBBY

45s

Number	Title (A Side/B Side)	Yr	VG	VG+	NM
CAMEO					
403	Happiness Is/Can't Get Used to Loving You	1966	2.50	5.00	10.00
403 [DJ]	Happiness Is	1966	5.00	10.00	20.00
—One-sided promo					
CONDOR					
1002	I'll Never Tell You/Telegram	1969	2.50	5.00	10.00
DECCA					
31672	Man Overboard/You Make Me Happy	1964	3.75	7.50	15.00
31741	It Hurts Me/Give Me Your Word	1965	3.75	7.50	15.00
31741 [PS]	It Hurts Me/Give Me Your Word	1965	12.50	25.00	50.00
31779	Hey Little Girl/Well All Right	1965	3.75	7.50	15.00
DOT					
16566	I Want to Hear It From Her/Nobody's Sweetheart	1963	3.75	7.50	15.00
EPIC					
10181	Cold Girl/Think of Rain	1967	2.50	5.00	10.00
10181 [PS]	Cold Girl/Think of Rain	1967	5.00	10.00	20.00
JANUS					
246	Runaway/Mr. Success	1975	—	2.00	4.00
254	Our Last Song Together/Sunshine Rose	1975	—	2.00	4.00
METROMEDIA					
68-0100	Early in the Morning/Unborn Lullaby	1973	—	2.50	5.00
121	Little Woman/One Too Many Mornings	1969	—	2.50	5.00
121 [PS]	Little Woman/One Too Many Mornings	1969	—	2.50	5.00
150	La La La (If I Had You)/Time	1969	—	2.50	5.00
150 [PS]	La La La (If I Had You)/Time	1969	—	2.50	5.00
177	Easy Come, Easy Go/July Seventeen	1970	—	2.50	5.00
177	Easy Come, Easy Go/Sounds Along the Way	1970	—	2.50	5.00
177 [PS]	Easy Come, Easy Go/July Seventeen	1970	—	2.50	5.00
188	Hey, Mister Sun/Two Blind Mice	1970	—	2.50	5.00
188 [PS]	Hey, Mister Sun/Two Blind Mice	1970	—	2.50	5.00
194	Julie, Do Ya Love Me/Spend Some Time Lovin' Me	1970	—	2.50	5.00
194 [PS]	Julie, Do Ya Love Me/Spend Some Time Lovin' Me	1970	—	2.50	5.00
204	Goin' Home (Sing a Song of Christmas Cheer)/ Love's What You're Gettin' for Christmas	1970	—	3.00	6.00
204 [PS]	Goin' Home (Sing a Song of Christmas Cheer)/ Love's What You're Gettin' for Christmas	1970	2.00	4.00	8.00
206	Cried Like a Baby/Is Anybody There	1971	—	2.50	5.00
206 [PS]	Cried Like a Baby/Is Anybody There	1971	—	2.50	5.00
217	The Drum/Free Now to Roam	1971	—	2.50	5.00
217 [PS]	The Drum/Free Now to Roam	1971	—	2.50	5.00
222	Waiting at the Bus Stop/Run Away	1971	—	2.50	5.00
222 [PS]	Waiting at the Bus Stop/Run Away	1971	—	2.50	5.00
227	Jennifer/Getting Together	1971	—	2.50	5.00
227 [PS]	Jennifer/Getting Together	1971	—	2.50	5.00
240	Together Again/Picture a Little Girl	1972	—	2.50	5.00
240 [PS]	Together Again/Picture a Little Girl	1972	—	2.50	5.00
249	I Don't Believe in Magic/Just a Little While Longer	1972	—	2.50	5.00
PARKWAY					
967	Goody Galumshus/Anything Your Little Heart Desires	1966	2.50	5.00	10.00
STARCREST					
100	Judy, You'll Never Know/Telegram	1962	5.00	10.00	20.00

Albums

Number	Title (A Side/B Side)	Yr	VG	VG+	NM
METROMEDIA					
MD 1014	Bobby Sherman	1969	3.75	7.50	15.00
MD 1028	Here Comes Bobby	1970	3.75	7.50	15.00
MD 1032	With Love, Bobby	1970	3.75	7.50	15.00
MD 1038	Bobby Sherman Christmas Album	1970	3.75	7.50	15.00
MD 1040	Portrait of Bobby	1971	3.75	7.50	15.00
MD 1045	Getting Together	1971	3.75	7.50	15.00
KMD 1048	Bobby Sherman's Greatest Hits	1972	3.00	6.00	12.00
MD 1060	Just for You	1973	3.75	7.50	15.00

SHERRYS, THE

45s

Number	Title (A Side/B Side)	Yr	VG	VG+	NM
GUYDEN					
2068	Pop-Pop-Pop-Eye/Your Hand in Mine	1962	3.75	7.50	15.00
2077	Slop Time/Let's Stomp Again	1963	3.75	7.50	15.00
2084	Saturday Night/I've Got No One	1963	3.75	7.50	15.00
2094	Monk, Monk, Monkey/That Boy of Mine	1963	3.75	7.50	15.00
MERCURY					
72256	No No Baby/That Guy of Mine	1964	3.00	6.00	12.00
ROBERTS					
701	Slow Jerk/Confusion	1965	3.00	6.00	12.00

Albums

Number	Title (A Side/B Side)	Yr	VG	VG+	NM
GUYDEN					
GLP 503 [M]	At the Hop with the Sherrys	1963	62.50	125.00	250.00

SHEVELLES, THE

45s

Number	Title (A Side/B Side)	Yr	VG	VG+	NM
WORLD ARTISTS					
1023	Oo Poo Pa Doo/Like I Love You	1964	3.00	6.00	12.00
1025	How Would You Like Me to Love You/I Could Conquer the World	1964	3.00	6.00	12.00

SHEVETON, TONY

45s

Number	Title (A Side/B Side)	Yr	VG	VG+	NM
PARROT					
10616	Dance with Me/A Million Drums	1964	3.75	7.50	15.00

SHIEKS, THE

See THE SHEIKS.

SHIELDS, BILLY

Pseudonym of TONY ORLANDO.

45s

Number	Title (A Side/B Side)	Yr	VG	VG+	NM
HARBOUR					
304	I Was a Boy/Moments from Now	1969	6.25	12.50	25.00

SHIELDS, BOBBY

45s

Number	Title (A Side/B Side)	Yr	VG	VG+	NM
MELBA					
105	Land of Rock and Roll/I Wouldn't Change You for the World	1956	15.00	30.00	60.00

SHIELDS, THE

45s

Number	Title (A Side/B Side)	Yr	VG	VG+	NM
ATCO					
7071	The Way I Feel Tonight/All Right by Me	1977	—	2.50	5.00
CONTINENTAL					
4072	You Told Another Lie/Barnyard Dance	1961	100.00	200.00	400.00
DOT					
136	You Cheated/Nature Boy	196?	2.50	5.00	10.00
—Reissue; black label					
15805	You Cheated/That's the Way It's Gonna Be	1958	6.25	12.50	25.00
15856	I'm Sorry Now/Nature Boy	1958	7.50	15.00	30.00
15940	Fare Thee Well/Play the Game Fair	1959	6.25	12.50	25.00
TENDER					
513	You Cheated/That's the Way It's Gonna Be	1958	37.50	75.00	150.00
—No reference to Dot Records on label					
513	You Cheated/That's the Way It's Gonna Be	1958	10.00	20.00	40.00
—With reference to Dot Records on label					
518	I'm Sorry Now/Nature Boy	1958	15.00	30.00	60.00
521	Fare Thee Well/Play the Game Fair	1959	15.00	30.00	60.00
TRANSCONTINENTAL					
1013	The Girl Around the Corner/Fare Thee Well, My Love	1960	25.00	50.00	100.00

SHILOH

Don Henley, later of EAGLES, was in this group. The album was produced by KENNY ROGERS.

45s

Number	Title (A Side/B Side)	Yr	VG	VG+	NM
AMOS					
140	Jennifer/Tell Her to Get Out of Your Life	1970	3.00	6.00	12.00
162	Down on the Farm/Simple Little Down Home Rock & Roll Love Song for Rosie	1971	3.00	6.00	12.00

Albums

Number	Title (A Side/B Side)	Yr	VG	VG+	NM
AMOS					
AAS-7015	Shiloh	1971	20.00	40.00	80.00

SHINDIGS, THE

Also known as THE BOBBY FULLER FOUR.

45s

Number	Title (A Side/B Side)	Yr	VG	VG+	NM
MUSTANG					
3003	Thunder Reef/Wolfman	1965	10.00	20.00	40.00

SHIP, THE

Albums

Number	Title (A Side/B Side)	Yr	VG	VG+	NM
ELEKTRA					
EKS-75036	The Ship	1972	5.00	10.00	20.00

SHIRELLES, THE

45s

Number	Title (A Side/B Side)	Yr	VG	VG+	NM
BELL					
760	A Most Unusual Boy/Look What You've Done to My Heart	1969	2.50	5.00	10.00
787	Looking Glass/Playthings	1969	2.50	5.00	10.00
815	Never Give You Up/Go Away and Find Yourself	1969	2.50	5.00	10.00
BLUE ROCK					
4051	Don't Mess with Cupid/Sweet Sweet Lovin'	1968	2.50	5.00	10.00
4066	Call Me/There's a Storm Goin' Home in My Heart	1968	2.50	5.00	10.00
DECCA					
25506	I Met Him on a Sunday/My Love Is a Charm	196?	3.75	7.50	15.00
—Early reissue					
30588	I Met Him on a Sunday/I Want You to Be My Boyfriend	1958	6.25	12.50	25.00
30669	My Love Is a Charm/Slop Time	1958	10.00	20.00	40.00
30761	Stop Me/I Got the Message	1958	10.00	20.00	40.00
PHILCO-FORD					
HP-30	Soldier Boy/My Heart Belongs to You	1968	5.00	10.00	20.00
—4-inch plastic "Hip Pocket Record" with color sleeve					
RCA VICTOR					
APBO-0192	Touch the Wind (Eres Tu)/Do What You've a Mind To	1973	2.00	4.00	8.00
47-0902	Let's Give Each Other Love/Deep in the Night	1973	2.00	4.00	8.00
48-1019	No Sugar Tonight/Strange, I Still Love You	1971	2.50	5.00	10.00
48-1032	Brother, Brother/Sunday Dreaming	1972	2.50	5.00	10.00
SCEPTER					
1203	Dedicated to the One I Love/Look A Here Baby	1958	10.00	20.00	40.00
—White label					
1203	Dedicated to the One I Love/Look A Here Baby	1958	5.00	10.00	20.00
—Red label					
1205	A Teardrop and a Lollipop/Doin' the Ronde	1959	7.50	15.00	30.00
—White label					
1205	A Teardrop and a Lollipop/Doin' the Ronde	1959	5.00	10.00	20.00
—Red label					
1207	Please Be My Boyfriend/I Saw a Tear	1960	7.50	15.00	30.00
—White label					
1207	Please Be My Boyfriend/I Saw a Tear	1960	5.00	10.00	20.00
—Red label					
1208	Tonight's the Night/The Dance Is Over	1960	7.50	15.00	30.00
—White label					
1208	Tonight's the Night/The Dance Is Over	1960	5.00	10.00	20.00
—Red label					
1208	Tonight's the Night/The Dance Is Over	1960	6.25	12.50	25.00
—Pink label					
1211	Tomorrow/Boys	1960	10.00	20.00	40.00
—Original A-side title					
1211	Will You Love Me Tomorrow/Boys	1960	7.50	15.00	30.00
—Revised A-side title					
1217	Mama Said/Blue Holiday	1961	5.00	10.00	20.00
1220	A Thing of the Past/What a Sweet Thing That Was	1961	5.00	10.00	20.00
1223	Big John/Twenty-One	1961	5.00	10.00	20.00
1227	Baby It's You/Things I Want to Hear (Pretty Words)	1961	5.00	10.00	20.00
1228	Soldier Boy/Love Is a Swingin' Thing	1962	3.75	7.50	15.00
1234	Welcome Home Baby/Mama, Here Comes the Bride	1962	3.75	7.50	15.00
1237	Stop the Music/It's Love That Really Counts	1962	3.75	7.50	15.00
1243	Everybody Loves a Lover/I Don't Think So	1962	3.75	7.50	15.00
1248	Foolish Little Girl/Not for All the Money in the World	1963	3.75	7.50	15.00
1248 [PS]	Foolish Little Girl/Not for All the Money in the World	1963	10.00	20.00	40.00
1255	Don't Say Goodnight and Mean Goodbye/I Didn't Mean to Hurt You	1963	3.00	6.00	12.00
1255 [PS]	Don't Say Goodnight and Mean Goodbye/I Didn't Mean to Hurt You	1963	10.00	20.00	40.00
1259	What Does a Girl Do?/Don't Let It Happen to You	1963	3.00	6.00	12.00
1260	It's a Mad, Mad, Mad, Mad World/31 Flavors	1963	3.00	6.00	12.00
1264	Tonight You're Gonna Fall in Love with Me/20th Century Rock and Roll	1963	3.00	6.00	12.00
1267	Sha-La-La/His Lips Get In the Way	1964	3.00	6.00	12.00
1278	Thank You Baby/Doomsday	1964	3.00	6.00	12.00
1284	Maybe Tonight/Lost Love	1964	3.00	6.00	12.00
1292	Are You Still My Baby/I Saw a Tear	1964	3.00	6.00	12.00
1296	Shh, I'm Watching the Movies/A Plus B	1965	3.00	6.00	12.00
12101	March (You'll Be Sorry)/Everybody's Goin' Mad	1965	2.50	5.00	10.00
12114	My Heart Belongs to You/Love That Man	1965	2.50	5.00	10.00
12123	(Mama) My Soldier Boy Is Coming Home/Soldier Boy	1965	2.50	5.00	10.00
12132	I Met Him on a Sunday — '66/Love That Man	1966	2.50	5.00	10.00
12150	Till My Baby Comes Home/Que Sera, Sera	1966	2.50	5.00	10.00
12162	Shades of Blue/Looking Around	1966	2.50	5.00	10.00
12162	Shades of Blue/After Midnight	1966	2.50	5.00	10.00
12178	Teasin' Me/Look Away	1966	2.50	5.00	10.00
12185	Don't Go Home (My Little Baby)/Nobody Baby After You	1967	2.50	5.00	10.00
12192	Too Much of a Good Thing/Bright Shiny Colors	1967	2.50	5.00	10.00
12198	Last Minute Miracle/No Doubt About It	1967	2.50	5.00	10.00
12209	Wild and Sweet/Wait Till I Give the Signal	1968	2.50	5.00	10.00
12217	Hippie Walk (Part 1)/Hippie Walk (Part 2)	1968	2.50	5.00	10.00
TIARA					
6112	I Met Him on a Sunday/I Want You to Be My Boyfriend	1958	200.00	400.00	800.00
UNITED ARTISTS					
50648	There Goes My Baby-Be My Baby/Strange, I Still Love You	1970	2.00	4.00	8.00
50693	It's Gonna Take a Miracle/Lost	1970	2.00	4.00	8.00
50740	Take Me for a Little While/Dedicated to the One I Love	1971	2.00	4.00	8.00

Albums

Number	Title (A Side/B Side)	Yr	VG	VG+	NM
RCA VICTOR					
LSP-4581	Happy and In Love	1971	3.75	7.50	15.00
LSP-4698	The Shirelles	1972	3.75	7.50	15.00
RHINO					
RNDA-1101 [(2)]	Anthology (1959-1967)	1984	3.00	6.00	12.00
SCEPTER					
S-501 [M]	Tonight's the Night	1961	50.00	100.00	200.00
—"Scepter" in scroll at top of label					
SPM-501 [M]	Tonight's the Night	1962	15.00	30.00	60.00
—"Scepter Records" at left of label					
SPS-501 [S]	Tonight's the Night	1965	25.00	50.00	100.00
S-502 [M]	The Shirelles Sing to Trumpets and Strings	1961	50.00	100.00	200.00
—"Scepter" in scroll at top of label					
SPM-502 [M]	The Shirelles Sing to Trumpets and Strings	1962	15.00	30.00	60.00
—"Scepter Records" at left of label					
SPS-502 [S]	The Shirelles Sing to Trumpets and Strings	1965	25.00	50.00	100.00
SPM-504 [M]	Baby It's You	1962	25.00	50.00	100.00
SPS-504 [S]	Baby It's You	1965	25.00	50.00	100.00
SPM-505 [M]	A Twist Party	1962	20.00	40.00	80.00
SPS-505 [S]	A Twist Party	1965	25.00	50.00	100.00
SPM-507 [M]	The Shirelles' Greatest Hits	1962	10.00	20.00	40.00
SPS-507 [S]	The Shirelles' Greatest Hits	1965	12.50	25.00	50.00
SPM-511 [M]	Foolish Little Girl	1963	12.50	25.00	50.00
SPS-511 [S]	Foolish Little Girl	1965	20.00	40.00	80.00
SPM-514 [M]	It's a Mad, Mad, Mad, Mad World	1963	10.00	20.00	40.00
SPS-514 [S]	It's a Mad, Mad, Mad, Mad World	1963	12.50	25.00	50.00
SPM-516 [M]	The Shirelles Sing the Golden Oldies	1964	10.00	20.00	40.00
SPS-516 [S]	The Shirelles Sing the Golden Oldies	1964	12.50	25.00	50.00
SPM-560 [M]	The Shirelles' Greatest Hits, Volume 2	1967	5.00	10.00	20.00
SPS-560 [S]	The Shirelles' Greatest Hits, Volume 2	1967	6.25	12.50	25.00
SPM-562 [M]	Spontaneous Combustion	1967	10.00	20.00	40.00
SPS-562 [S]	Spontaneous Combustion	1967	12.50	25.00	50.00
SPS-569	Eternally Soul	1968	7.50	15.00	30.00
SPS-2-599 [(2)]	Remember When	1972	5.00	10.00	20.00
SPRINGBOARD					
4006	The Shirelles Sing Their Very Best	1973	2.00	4.00	8.00
UNITED ARTISTS					
UA-LA340-E	The Very Best of the Shirelles	1974	2.50	5.00	10.00

SHIRLEY (AND COMPANY)

Shirley Goodman, earlier of SHIRLEY AND LEE.

45s

Number	Title (A Side/B Side)	Yr	VG	VG+	NM
VIBRATION					
532	Shame, Shame, Shame/(Instrumental)	1974	—	2.50	5.00
—Shirley Goodman, also of Shirley and Lee					
535	Cry, Cry, Cry/(Instrumental)	1975	—	2.50	5.00
539	Disco Shirley/Keep On Rolling On	1975	—	2.50	5.00
542	I Like to Dance/Jim Doc C'ain	1976	—	2.50	5.00
579	Revelations True/(Instrumental)	1978	—	2.50	5.00

Albums

Number	Title (A Side/B Side)	Yr	VG	VG+	NM
VIBRATION					
128	Shame Shame Shame	1975	2.50	5.00	10.00

SHIRLEY AND LEE

Also see SHIRLEY (AND COMPANY).

45s

Number	Title (A Side/B Side)	Yr	VG	VG+	NM
ALADDIN					
3153	I'm Gone/Sweethearts	1952	25.00	50.00	100.00
3173	Baby/Shirley Come Back to Me	1953	30.00	60.00	120.00

Number	Title (A Side/B Side)	Yr	VG	VG+	NM
3192	Shirley's Back/So In Love	1953	15.00	30.00	60.00
3205	Two Happy People/The Proposal	1953	12.50	25.00	50.00
3222	Why Did I/Lee Goofed	1954	12.50	25.00	50.00
3244	Confessin'/Keep On	1954	12.50	25.00	50.00
3258	Comin' Over/Takes Money	1954	12.50	25.00	50.00
3289	Feel So Good/You'd Be Thinking of Me	1955	10.00	20.00	40.00
3302	Let's Dream/I'll Do It	1955	10.00	20.00	40.00
3325	Let the Good Times Roll/Do You Mean to Hurt Me So	1956	15.00	30.00	60.00
3338	I Feel Good/Now That It's Over	1956	6.25	12.50	25.00
3362	When I Saw You/That's What I Want to Do	1957	5.00	10.00	20.00
3369	I Want to Dance/Marry Me	1957	5.00	10.00	20.00
3380	Rock All Night/Don't You Know I Love You	1957	5.00	10.00	20.00
3390	Rockin' with the Clock/The Flirt	1957	5.00	10.00	20.00
3405	Love No One But You (I Love You So)/I'll Thrill You	1958	5.00	10.00	20.00
3418	Everybody's Rocking/Don't Leave Me Here to Cry	1958	5.00	10.00	20.00
3432	Come On and Have Your Fun/All I Want to Do Is Cry	1958	5.00	10.00	20.00
3455	True Love/When Day Is Done	1959	5.00	10.00	20.00
IMPERIAL					
5818	Together We Stand (Divided We Fall)/The Joker	1962	2.50	5.00	10.00
5854	My Last Letter/I'm Early Enough	1962	2.50	5.00	10.00
5868	Don't Stop Now/A Little Thing	1962	2.50	5.00	10.00
5922	The Golden Rule/Hey Little Boy	1963	2.50	5.00	10.00
5970	Dancing World/I'm Gone	1963	2.50	5.00	10.00
5979	Paper Doll/The Brink of Disaster	1963	2.50	5.00	10.00
66000	Somebody Put a Jukebox in the Study Hall/Never Let Me Go	1963	2.50	5.00	10.00
UNITED ARTISTS					
0087	Let the Good Times Roll/Feel So Good	1973	—	2.00	4.00
—"Silver Spotlight Series" reissue					
XW274	Let the Good Times Roll/That's What I Wanna Do	1973	—	2.50	5.00
WARWICK					
581	Let the Good Times Roll/Keep Loving Me	1960	3.00	6.00	12.00
609	Two Peas in a Pod/Your Love Makes the Difference	1961	3.00	6.00	12.00
664	Well-a, Well-a/Our Kids	1961	3.00	6.00	12.00
679	Let's Live It Up/Girl, You're Married Now	1962	3.00	6.00	12.00
Albums					
ALADDIN					
807 [M]	Let the Good Times Roll	1956	375.00	750.00	1500.
IMPERIAL					
LP-9179 [M]	Let the Good Times Roll	1962	75.00	150.00	300.00
—Reissue of Aladdin LP					
SCORE					
SLP-4023 [M]	Let the Good Times Roll	1957	200.00	400.00	800.00
—Reissue of Aladdin LP					
WARWICK					
W-2028 [M]	Let the Good Times Roll	1961	37.50	75.00	150.00
W-2028ST [S]	Let the Good Times Roll	1961	75.00	150.00	300.00

SHOCKING BLUE, THE

Number	Title (A Side/B Side)	Yr	VG	VG+	NM
45s					
21 RECORDS					
99517	Venus/Mighty Joe	1986	—	2.00	4.00
BUDDAH					
258	Sleepless at Midnight/Serenade	1971	—	3.00	6.00
COLOSSUS					
108	Venus/Hot Sand	1969	2.50	5.00	10.00
108 [PS]	Venus/Hot Sand	1969	3.75	7.50	15.00
111	Mighty Joe/I'm a Woman	1970	2.00	4.00	8.00
111 [PS]	Mighty Joe/I'm a Woman	1970	3.00	6.00	12.00
116	Long and Lonesome Road/Ackaragh	1970	2.00	4.00	8.00
123	Never Love a Railroad Man/Never Marry	1970	2.00	4.00	8.00
141	Boll Weevil/Long and Lonesome Road	1971	—	3.00	6.00
MGM					
14481	When I Was a Girl/Eve and the Apple	1973	—	3.00	6.00
14543	Oh Love/Inkpot	1973	—	3.00	6.00
Albums					
COLOSSUS					
CS-1000	The Shocking Blue	1970	6.25	12.50	25.00

SHONDELL, TROY

Number	Title (A Side/B Side)	Yr	VG	VG+	NM
45s					
AVM					
14	(I'm Looking for Some) New Blue Jeans/(B-side unknown)	1988	—	2.00	4.00
DECCA					
31712	You Can't Catch Me/Walkin' in a Memory	1964	2.50	5.00	10.00
EVEREST					
2015	Gone/Some People Never Learn	1963	2.50	5.00	10.00
2018	I've Got a Woman/No Fool Like an Old Fool	1963	2.50	5.00	10.00
2041	Trouble/Little Miss Tease	1964	2.50	5.00	10.00
GAYE					
2010	This Time/I Catch Myself Crying	1961	20.00	40.00	80.00
GOLDCREST					
161-A	This Time/Girl After Girl	1961	7.50	15.00	30.00
—With no "Distributed by Liberty" on label					
161-A	This Time/Girl After Girl	1961	6.25	12.50	25.00
—With "Distributed by Liberty Record Sales" on label					
ITCO					
105	And We Made Love/Imitation Woman	198?	—	2.50	5.00
LIBERTY					
55353	This Time/Girl After Girl	1961	5.00	10.00	20.00
55392	Tears from an Angel/Island in the Sky	1961	4.00	8.00	16.00
55445	Just Because/Na-No-No	1962	4.00	8.00	16.00
RIC					
174	Just a Dream/Just Like Me	1965	2.50	5.00	10.00
184	Big Windy City/I Thought That You Were Mine	1966	2.50	5.00	10.00
STAR-FOX					
77	Still Loving You/(B-side unknown)	1979	—	2.50	5.00
TELESONIC					
804	(Sittin' Here) Lovin' You/(B-side unknown)	1980	—	2.50	5.00
TRX					
5001	A Rose and a Baby Ruth/Here It Comes Again	1967	2.00	4.00	8.00
5003	Head Man/She's Got Everything She Needs	1967	2.00	4.00	8.00
5015	Let's Go All the Way/Let Me Love You	1968	2.00	4.00	8.00
5019	Something's Wrong in Indiana/A Rose and a Baby Ruth	1969	2.00	4.00	8.00
Albums					
EVEREST					
SDBR-1206 [S]	The Many Sides of Troy Shondell	1963	20.00	40.00	80.00
LPBR-5206 [M]	The Many Sides of Troy Shondell	1963	12.50	25.00	50.00
SUNSET					
SUM-1174 [M]	This Time	1967	3.75	7.50	15.00
SUS-5174 [S]	This Time	1967	3.75	7.50	15.00

SHONDELLES, THE

Number	Title (A Side/B Side)	Yr	VG	VG+	NM
45s					
KING					
5597	Don't Cry My Soldier Boy/My Love	1962	5.00	10.00	20.00
5656	Wonderful One/I Gotta Tell It	1962	5.00	10.00	20.00
5705	Muscle Bound/Special Delivery	1963	5.00	10.00	20.00
5755	Watusi, One More/Ooo, Sometimes	1963	5.00	10.00	20.00

SHONDELLS, THE

See TOMMY JAMES AND THE SHONDELLS.

SHOOTERS, THE

With OTIS REDDING.

Number	Title (A Side/B Side)	Yr	VG	VG+	NM
45s					
TRANS WORLD					
6908	Tuff Enuff/She's All Right	1960	25.00	50.00	100.00

SHORE, DINAH

Number	Title (A Side/B Side)	Yr	VG	VG+	NM
45s					
CAPITOL					
4344	So Many Things to Do Today/When the Sparrows Learn to Fly	1960	2.00	4.00	8.00
4476	I Ain't Down Yet/I Gotta Love You	1960	2.00	4.00	8.00
4618	Mississippi Mud/This Is a Changing World	1961	2.00	4.00	8.00
4774	That'll Show Him/Just a Brief Encounter	1962	2.00	4.00	8.00
COLUMBIA					
1-111	So in Love/Always True to You in My Fashion	1949	7.50	15.00	30.00
—Microgroove 33 1/3 rpm 7-inch single					
1-134	Forever and Ever/I've Been Hit	1949	7.50	15.00	30.00
—Microgroove 33 1/3 rpm 7-inch single					
1-155	Having Wonderful Time/The Story of My Life	1949	7.50	15.00	30.00
—Microgroove 33 1/3 rpm 7-inch single					
1-197	A Wonderful Guy/Younger Than Springtime	1949	7.50	15.00	30.00
—Microgroove 33 1/3 rpm 7-inch single					
1-200	Baby, It's Cold Outside/My One and Only Highland Fling	1949	7.50	15.00	30.00
—With Buddy Clark; Microgroove 33 1/3 rpm 7-inch single					
1-220 (?)	I'm Gonna Wash That Man Right Out of My Hair/Kiss Me, Sweet	1949	7.50	15.00	30.00
—Microgroove 33 1/3 rpm 7-inch single					
1-250 (?)	Till My Ship Comes In/Lovers Gold	1949	7.50	15.00	30.00
—Microgroove 33 1/3 rpm 7-inch single					
1-260 (?)	Homework/You Can Have Him	1949	7.50	15.00	30.00
—With Doris Day; Microgroove 33 1/3 rpm 7-inch single					
1-290 (?)	Through a Long and Sleepless Night/I'm Yours	1949	7.50	15.00	30.00
—Microgroove 33 1/3 rpm 7-inch single					
1-330 (?)	The Story of Annie Laurie/A Thousand Violins	1949	7.50	15.00	30.00
—Microgroove 33 1/3 rpm 7-inch single					
1-368	Dear Hearts and Gentle People/Speak a Word of Love	1949	7.50	15.00	30.00
—Microgroove 33 1/3 rpm 7-inch single					
1-369	Star of Bethlehem/Merry Christmas	1949	10.00	20.00	40.00
—Microgroove 33 1/3 rpm 7-inch single					
1-437	Bibbidi-Bobbidi-Boo (The Magic Song)/Happy Time	1950	7.50	15.00	30.00
—Microgroove 33 1/3 rpm 7-inch single					
1-440 (?)	The Shoe Is On the Other Foot Now/Wedding Dolls	1950	7.50	15.00	30.00
—With George Morgan; Microgroove 33 1/3 rpm 7-inch single					
1-445 (?)	Lucky Us/Nobody Home at My House	1950	7.50	15.00	30.00
—Microgroove 33 1/3 rpm 7-inch single					
1-450 (?)	Scarlet Ribbons (For Her Hair)/Sitting by the Window	1950	7.50	15.00	30.00
—Microgroove 33 1/3 rpm 7-inch single					
1-469	It's So Nice to Have a Man Around the House/More Than Anything Else	1950	7.50	15.00	30.00
—Microgroove 33 1/3 rpm 7-inch single					
1-580 (?)	You've Been Playing Checkers/Ask Me No Questions	1950	7.50	15.00	30.00
—With Dusty Walker; Microgroove 33 1/3 rpm 7-inch single					
1-599	Scottish Samba/Never Had a Worry	1950	7.50	15.00	30.00
—Microgroove 33 1/3 rpm 7-inch single					
1-630 (?)	A Simple Melody/I Still Get a Thrill	1950	7.50	15.00	30.00
—Microgroove 33 1/3 rpm 7-inch single					
1-660 (?)	I Didn't Know What Time It Was/I'll Always Love You	1950	7.50	15.00	30.00
—Microgroove 33 1/3 rpm 7-inch single					
1-690 (?)	Cotton Candy and a Toy Balloon/1812	1950	7.50	15.00	30.00
—Microgroove 33 1/3 rpm 7-inch single					
1-719	Tunnel of Love/With the Wind and the Rain in Your Hair	1950	7.50	15.00	30.00
—Microgroove 33 1/3 rpm 7-inch single					
1-759	Can Anyone Explain? (No! No! No!)/Dream a Little Dream of Me	1950	7.50	15.00	30.00
—Microgroove 33 1/3 rpm 7-inch single					
6-759	Can Anyone Explain? (No! No! No!)/Dream a Little Dream of Me	1950	6.25	12.50	25.00

Number	Title (A Side/B Side)	Yr	VG	VG+	NM
1-770 (?)	It's Easy to Remember/Don't Rock the Boat, Dear	1950	7.50	15.00	30.00
—Microgroove 33 1/3 rpm 7-inch single					
6-770 (?)	It's Easy to Remember/Don't Rock the Boat, Dear	1950	6.25	12.50	25.00
DECCA					
32468	Crying Time/Rocky Top	1969	—	2.50	5.00
MERCURY					
73465	Me and Ole Crazy Bill/Wait a Little Longer	1974	—	2.00	4.00
PROJECT 3					
1313	All at Once It's Love/Loneliness Is My Lover	1967	—	3.00	6.00
1328	Trains and Boats and Planes/Faces and Voices	1968	—	3.00	6.00
RCA VICTOR					
19-0001	You're Just in Love/(B-side unknown)	1951	6.25	12.50	25.00
—With Russell Nype; "Green Label Series" issue					
47-3978	My Heart Cries for You/Nobody's Chasing Me	1950	5.00	10.00	20.00
47-4015	Wait for Me/Down in Nashville, Tennessee	1951	5.00	10.00	20.00
47-4019	A Penny a Kiss/In Your Arms	1951	5.00	10.00	20.00
—With Tony Martin					
47-4045	I'm Through with Love/Makin' Whoopee	1951	3.75	7.50	15.00
47-4046	Orchids in the Moonlight/Around the Corner	1951	3.75	7.50	15.00
47-4047	My Isle of Golden Dreams/Wonder Where My Baby Is Tonight	1951	3.75	7.50	15.00
—The above three comprise a box set					
47-4060	Lonesome Gal/Too Late Now	1951	5.00	10.00	20.00
47-4107	Cause I Love You/Three Cornered Tune	1951	5.00	10.00	20.00
47-4136	I Wish, I Wish/The Kissing Song	1951	3.75	7.50	15.00
—With Tony Martin					
47-4174	Sweet Violets/If You Turn Me Down	1951	5.00	10.00	20.00
47-4175	Ten Thousand Miles/How Many Times	1951	3.75	7.50	15.00
47-4233	It's All in the Game/Stay Awhile	1951	3.75	7.50	15.00
47-4286	Getting to Know You/End of a Love Affair	1951	3.75	7.50	15.00
47-4317	The Lie-De-Lie Song/Oh How I Needed You Joe	1951	3.75	7.50	15.00
47-4345	Manhattan/If You Catch a Little Cold	1951	3.75	7.50	15.00
—With Tony Martin					
47-4421	Life Is a Beautiful Thing/Why Should I Believe in Love	1951	3.75	7.50	15.00
47-4434	Saturday Night in Punkin' Crick/Life Is a Beautiful Thing	1951	3.00	6.00	12.00
47-4436	Cheres/Pure Night	1951	3.00	6.00	12.00
—B-side by Alan Young					
47-4437	Marshmallow Moon/Why Should I Believe in Love	1951	3.00	6.00	12.00
—The above three are 75% of a box set					
47-4478	Until/Take Me Home	1952	3.00	6.00	12.00
47-4493	Marshmallow Moon/Warm Hearted Woman	1952	3.00	6.00	12.00
47-4561	Double Shuffle/Senator from Tennessee	1952	3.75	7.50	15.00
—With Tex Williams					
47-4666	I Am a Heart/To Be Loved by You	1952	3.00	6.00	12.00
47-4718	No Other Girl for Me/If Someone Had Told Me	1952	3.00	6.00	12.00
—With Tony Martin					
47-4719	Delicado/The World Has a Promise	1952	3.00	6.00	12.00
47-4768	West of the Mountains/From the Time You Say Goodbye	1952	3.00	6.00	12.00
47-4926	Blues in Advance/Bella Musica	1952	3.00	6.00	12.00
47-4992	Keep It a Secret/Hi-Lili, Hi-Lo	1952	3.00	6.00	12.00
47-5176	Let Me Know/Salomay	1953	3.00	6.00	12.00
47-5247	Sweet Thing/Why Come Crying to Me	1953	3.00	6.00	12.00
47-5335	I'm Your Girl/Marriage-Type Love	1953	3.00	6.00	12.00
47-5390	Blue Canary/Eternally	1953	3.00	6.00	12.00
47-5438	Choo Choo Train/Reflections on the Water	1953	3.00	6.00	12.00
47-5515	Changing Partners/Think	1953	3.00	6.00	12.00
47-5622	I'll Hate Myself in the Morning/Pass the Jam, Sam	1954	3.00	6.00	12.00
47-5725	Come Back to My Arms/This Must Be the Place	1954	3.00	6.00	12.00
47-5755	Three Coins in the Fountain/Pakistan	1954	3.00	6.00	12.00
47-5825	Tempting/Anyplace I Hang My Hat Is Home	1954	3.00	6.00	12.00
47-5838	If I Give My Heart to You/Tempting	1954	3.00	6.00	12.00
47-5863	I Have to Tell You/Never Underestimate	1954	3.00	6.00	12.00
47-5975	Melody of Love/You're Getting to Be a Habit with Me	1955	2.50	5.00	10.00
—With Tony Martin					
47-6010	Then I'll Be Happy/The Stow-Away	1955	2.50	5.00	10.00
47-6077	Whatever Lola Wants (Lola Gets)/Church Twice on Sundays	1955	2.50	5.00	10.00
47-6266	Love and Marriage/Compare	1955	2.50	5.00	10.00
47-6360	Stolen Love/That's All There Is to That	1955	2.50	5.00	10.00
47-6469	I Could Have Danced All Night/What a Heavenly Lover	1956	2.50	5.00	10.00
47-6683	High Heels/The Whistling Tree	1956	2.50	5.00	10.00
47-6733	A New-Fangled Tango/I'll Come Back	1956	2.50	5.00	10.00
47-6792	Chantez-Chantez (Shan-Tay, "Sing")/Honkytonk Heart	1957	2.50	5.00	10.00
47-6897	The Cattle Call/Promises, Promises	1957	2.50	5.00	10.00
47-6980	Fascination/Till	1957	2.50	5.00	10.00
47-7056	I'll Never Say "Never Again" Again/The Kiss That Rocked the Cradle	1957	2.50	5.00	10.00
47-7138	I Never Left Your Arms/Thirteen Men	1958	2.50	5.00	10.00
47-7211	The Secret of Happiness/It's the Second Time You Meet That Matters	1958	2.50	5.00	10.00
47-7349	I'm Sitting on Top of the World/Scene of the Crime	1958	2.50	5.00	10.00
7-Inch Extended Plays					
CHEVROLET					
2886/7	You Meet The Nicest People/Jingle Bells//Silent Night/The Coventry Carol	1960	2.50	5.00	10.00
—7-inch 33 1/3 rpm, small hole record from Capitol Custom Services					
2886/7 [PS]	Season's Best	1960	2.50	5.00	10.00
RCA VICTOR					
EPA-4119	Opening/You Meet the Nicest People/Have Yourself a Merry Little Christmas//Christmas Party/Happy Christmas Little Friend/Closing	1957	3.00	6.00	12.00
EPA-4119 [PS]	You Meet the Nicest People at Christmas	1957	3.00	6.00	12.00
Albums					
BAINBRIDGE					
6232	Once Upon a Summertime	198?	2.50	5.00	10.00
CAPITOL					
ST 1247 [S]	Dinah, Yes Indeed	1959	6.25	12.50	25.00
T 1247 [M]	Dinah, Yes Indeed	1959	5.00	10.00	20.00
ST 1296 [S]	Somebody Loves Me	1959	6.25	12.50	25.00
T 1296 [M]	Somebody Loves Me	1959	5.00	10.00	20.00
ST 1354 [S]	Dinah Sings Some Blues with Red	1960	7.50	15.00	30.00
T 1354 [M]	Dinah Sings Some Blues with Red	1960	6.25	12.50	25.00
ST 1422 [S]	Dinah Sings/Previn Plays	1960	6.25	12.50	25.00
T 1422 [M]	Dinah Sings/Previn Plays	1960	5.00	10.00	20.00
ST 1655 [S]	Dinah Down Home	1962	6.25	12.50	25.00
T 1655 [M]	Dinah Down Home	1962	5.00	10.00	20.00
ST 1704 [S]	The Fabulous Hits of Dinah Shore	1962	6.25	12.50	25.00
—Black label with colorband, logo at left					
ST 1704 [S]	The Fabulous Hits of Dinah Shore	1962	3.75	7.50	15.00
—Black label with colorband, logo at top					
T 1704 [M]	The Fabulous Hits of Dinah Shore	1962	5.00	10.00	20.00
—Black label with colorband, logo at left					
T 1704 [M]	The Fabulous Hits of Dinah Shore	1962	3.00	6.00	12.00
—Black label with colorband, logo at top					
COLUMBIA					
CL 6004 [10]	Dinah Shore Sings	1949	12.50	25.00	50.00
CL 6069 [10]	Reminiscing	1949	12.50	25.00	50.00
C 34395	The Best of Dinah Shore	1977	2.50	5.00	10.00
HARMONY					
HL 7010 [M]	Dinah Shore Sings Cole Porter and Richard Rodgers	195?	5.00	10.00	20.00
HL 7239 [M]	Lavender Blue	1959	3.75	7.50	15.00
PICKWICK					
SPC-3524	It's So Nice to Have a Man Around the House	197?	2.00	4.00	8.00
PROJECT 3					
PR-5018 SD	Songs for Sometime Losers	1968	3.75	7.50	15.00
RCA VICTOR					
LPM-1154 [M]	Holding Hands at Midnight	1955	7.50	15.00	30.00
ANL1-1158	The Best of Dinah Shore	1976	2.50	5.00	10.00
LPM-1214 [M]	Bouquet of Blues	1956	7.50	15.00	30.00
LPM-1719 [M]	Moments Like These	1958	6.25	12.50	25.00
LPM-3103 [10]	Dinah Shore Sings the Blues	1953	10.00	20.00	40.00
LPM-3214 [10]	The Dinah Shore TV Show	1954	10.00	20.00	40.00
REPRISE					
R-6150 [M]	The Lower East Side Revisited	1965	3.00	6.00	12.00
RS-6150 [S]	The Lower East Side Revisited	1965	3.75	7.50	15.00
SEAGULL					
LG-8203	Oh Lonesome Me	198?	2.50	5.00	10.00
STANYAN					
10071	Dinah Sings the Blues	197?	2.50	5.00	10.00
10125	Once Upon a Summertime	197?	2.50	5.00	10.00
10139	For Always	1977	2.50	5.00	10.00

SHORT, BOBBY

45s

Number	Title (A Side/B Side)	Yr	VG	VG+	NM
ATLANTIC					
1157	Down in Mexico/Sand in My Shoes	1957	3.00	6.00	12.00

Albums

Number	Title (A Side/B Side)	Yr	VG	VG+	NM
ATLANTIC					
SD 2-606 [(2)]	Bobby Short Loves Cole Porter	1972	5.00	10.00	20.00
SD 2-607 [(2)]	Mad About Noel Coward	1972	5.00	10.00	20.00
SD 2-608 [(2)]	Bobby Short Is K-RA-Z-Y for Gershwin	1973	3.75	7.50	15.00
SD 2-609 [(2)]	Live at Café Carlyle	1974	3.75	7.50	15.00
SD 2-610 [(2)]	Bobby Short Celebrates Rodgers and Hart	197?	3.75	7.50	15.00
1214 [M]	Songs by Bobby Short	1955	7.50	15.00	30.00
—Black label					
1214 [M]	Songs by Bobby Short	1961	5.00	10.00	20.00
—White "fan" logo at right of label					
1214 [M]	Songs by Bobby Short	1963	3.75	7.50	15.00
—Black "fan" logo at right of label					
1230 [M]	Bobby Short	1956	7.50	15.00	30.00
—Black label					
1230 [M]	Bobby Short	1961	5.00	10.00	20.00
—White "fan" logo at right of label					
1230 [M]	Bobby Short	1963	3.75	7.50	15.00
—Black "fan" logo at right of label					
1262 [M]	Speaking of Love	1958	7.50	15.00	30.00
—Black label					
1262 [M]	Speaking of Love	1961	5.00	10.00	20.00
—White "fan" logo at right of label					
SD 1262 [S]	Speaking of Love	1959	10.00	20.00	40.00
—Green label					
SD 1262 [S]	Speaking of Love	1961	6.25	12.50	25.00
—White "fan" logo at right of label					
1285 [M]	Sing Me a Swing Song	1958	7.50	15.00	30.00
—Black label					
1285 [M]	Sing Me a Swing Song	1961	5.00	10.00	20.00
—White "fan" logo at right of label					
1285 [M]	Sing Me a Swing Song	1963	3.75	7.50	15.00
—Black "fan" logo at right of label					
1302 [M]	The Mad Twenties	1959	7.50	15.00	30.00
—Black label					
1302 [M]	The Mad Twenties	1961	5.00	10.00	20.00
—White "fan" logo at right of label					
1302 [M]	The Mad Twenties	1963	3.75	7.50	15.00
—Black "fan" logo at right of label					
SD 1302 [S]	The Mad Twenties	1959	10.00	20.00	40.00
—Green label					
SD 1302 [S]	The Mad Twenties	1961	6.25	12.50	25.00
—White "fan" logo at right of label					
SD 1302 [S]	The Mad Twenties	1963	5.00	10.00	20.00
—Black "fan" logo at right of label					
1321 [M]	On the East Side	1960	7.50	15.00	30.00
—Black label					
1321 [M]	On the East Side	1961	5.00	10.00	20.00
—White "fan" logo at right of label					
1321 [M]	On the East Side	1963	3.75	7.50	15.00
—Black "fan" logo at right of label					
SD 1321 [S]	On the East Side	1960	10.00	20.00	40.00
—Green label					
SD 1321 [S]	On the East Side	1961	6.25	12.50	25.00
—White "fan" logo at right of label					

(Top left) In the 1965 year-end issue of Billboard magazine, "Wooly Bully" by Sam the Sham and the Pharaohs was listed as the top hit of the year — even though it never reached the top of the charts in any given week. Before it became popular, though, "Wooly Bully" was on this rare release on the XL label. (Top right) The Shadows of Knight's hit version of "Gloria" was almost as trashy as the original by Them. The group's follow-up single, "Oh Yeah," came in this scarce picture sleeve. (Bottom left) When it was first issued, the Shirelles' classic hit single was simply called "Tomorrow," as pictured above. By the time it was on its way to the top of the charts, the song was known as "Will You Love Me Tomorrow." (Bottom right) Troy Shondell was your basic one-hit wonder. His one hit, "This Time," was featured on this album that came out on the Everest label.

Number	Title (A Side/B Side)	Yr	VG	VG+	NM
SD 1321 [S]	On the East Side	1963	5.00	10.00	20.00
—Black "fan" logo at right of label					
SD 1535	Jump for Joy	1969	3.00	6.00	12.00
SD 1574	Nobody Else But Me	1971	3.00	6.00	12.00
SD 1620	The Very Best of Bobby Short	1973	3.00	6.00	12.00
SD 1664	The Mad Twenties	1974	3.00	6.00	12.00
SD 1689	Personal	1977	3.00	6.00	12.00
81715 [(4)]	50 from Bobby Short	1987	7.50	15.00	30.00
81778	Guess Who's in Town: The Lyrics of Andy Razaf	1988	2.50	5.00	10.00
ELEKTRA					
E1-60002	Moments Like This	1982	2.50	5.00	10.00

SHORT CROSS

Albums

Number	Title (A Side/B Side)	Yr	VG	VG+	NM
GRIZZLY					
S-16013	Arising	1970	62.50	125.00	250.00

SHORTER, WAYNE

Also see WEATHER REPORT.

12-Inch Singles

Number	Title (A Side/B Side)	Yr	VG	VG+	NM
COLUMBIA					
CAS 2609	Remote Control (Extended) (LP)	1985	—	3.00	6.00

45s

Number	Title (A Side/B Side)	Yr	VG	VG+	NM
VEE JAY					
363	Black Diamond/Harry's Last Stand	1960	3.00	6.00	12.00

Albums

Number	Title (A Side/B Side)	Yr	VG	VG+	NM
BLUE NOTE					
BN-LA014-G	Moto Grosso Feio	1973	3.75	7.50	15.00
LT-988	The Soothsayer	1979	3.00	6.00	12.00
LT-1056	Etcetera	1980	3.00	6.00	12.00
BLP-4173 [M]	Night Drreamer	1964	6.25	12.50	25.00
BLP-4182 [M]	Juju	1965	6.25	12.50	25.00
BLP-4194 [M]	Speak No Evil	1966	6.25	12.50	25.00
BLP-4219 [M]	The All Seeing Eye	1966	6.25	12.50	25.00
B1-29100	The All Seeing Eye	1994	3.75	7.50	15.00
B1-32096	Schizophrenia	1995	3.75	7.50	15.00
B1-33581	Etcetera	1995	3.75	7.50	15.00
B1-46509	Speak No Evil	1997	3.75	7.50	15.00
—Reissue on 180-gram vinyl					
BST-84173 [S]	Night Drreamer	1964	7.50	15.00	30.00
—With New York, USA address on label					
BST-84173 [S]	Night Drreamer	1967	3.75	7.50	15.00
—With "A Division of Liberty Records" on label					
BST-84182	Juju	198?	2.50	5.00	10.00
—"The Finest in Jazz Since 1939" reissue					
BST-84182 [S]	Juju	1965	7.50	15.00	30.00
—With New York, USA address on label					
BST-84182 [S]	Juju	1967	3.75	7.50	15.00
—With "A Division of Liberty Records" on label					
BST-84194 [S]	Speak No Evil	1966	7.50	15.00	30.00
—With New York, USA address on label					
BST-84194 [S]	Speak No Evil	1967	3.75	7.50	15.00
—With "A Division of Liberty Records" on label					
BST-84219 [S]	The All Seeing Eye	1966	7.50	15.00	30.00
—With New York, USA address on label					
BST-84219 [S]	The All Seeing Eye	1967	3.75	7.50	15.00
—With "A Division of Liberty Records" on label					
BST-84232	Adam's Apple	1967	5.00	10.00	20.00
BST-84232	Adam's Apple	1985	2.50	5.00	10.00
—"The Finest in Jazz Since 1939" reissue					
BST-84297	Schizophrenia	1969	5.00	10.00	20.00
BST-84332	Super Nova	1970	5.00	10.00	20.00
BST-84363	The Odyssey of Iska	1971	3.75	7.50	15.00
B1-91141	The Best of Wayne Shorter	1988	2.50	5.00	10.00
COLUMBIA					
PC 33418	Native Dancer	1975	3.00	6.00	12.00
—Originals have no bar code					
PC 33418	Native Dancer	198?	2.00	4.00	8.00
—Reissue with bar code					
FC 40055	Atlantis	1985	2.50	5.00	10.00
FC 40373	Phantom Navigator	1987	2.50	5.00	10.00
FC 44110	Joy Ryder	1988	2.50	5.00	10.00
GNP CRESCENDO					
GNPS-2075 [(2)]	Wayne Shorter	1973	3.75	7.50	15.00
TRIP					
5009 [(2)]	Shorter Moments	1974	3.00	6.00	12.00
VEE JAY					
LP-3006 [M]	Introducing Wayne Shorter	1960	10.00	20.00	40.00
SR-3006 [S]	Introducing Wayne Shorter	1960	12.50	25.00	50.00
VJS-3006	Introducing Wayne Shorter	1986	3.00	6.00	12.00
—1980s reissue on thinner vinyl					
LP-3029 [M]	Wayning Moments	1962	7.50	15.00	30.00
SR-3029 [S]	Wayning Moments	1962	10.00	20.00	40.00
VJS-3029	Wayning Moments	198?	3.00	6.00	12.00
—1980s reissue on thinner vinyl					
LP-3057 [M]	Second Genesis	1963	7.50	15.00	30.00
SR-3057 [S]	Second Genesis	1963	10.00	20.00	40.00
VJS-3057	Second Genesis	198?	3.00	6.00	12.00
—1980s reissue on thinner vinyl					

SHOTGUN EXPRESS

With ROD STEWART.

45s

Number	Title (A Side/B Side)	Yr	VG	VG+	NM
UPTOWN					
747	I Could Feel the Whole World Turn/Curtains	1967	7.50	15.00	30.00

SHOTGUN LTD.

45s

Number	Title (A Side/B Side)	Yr	VG	VG+	NM
PROPHESY					
55004	River of Hope/(B-side unknown)	1971	2.00	4.00	8.00

Albums

Number	Title (A Side/B Side)	Yr	VG	VG+	NM
PROPHESY					
6050	Shotgun Ltd.	1971	5.00	10.00	20.00

SHOWMEN, THE

With General Johnson, later of CHAIRMEN OF THE BOARD.

45s

Number	Title (A Side/B Side)	Yr	VG	VG+	NM
AMY					
11036	Action/What Would It Take	1968	2.00	4.00	8.00
IMPERIAL					
66033	It Will Stand/Country Fool	1964	3.00	6.00	12.00
66071	Country Fool/Somebody Help Me	1964	3.00	6.00	12.00
LIBERTY					
56166	It Will Stand/Country Fool	1970	—	3.00	6.00
MINIT					
632	It Will Stand/Country Fool	1961	7.50	15.00	30.00
—Orange label					
632	It Will Stand/Country Fool	1961	5.00	10.00	20.00
—Black label					
643	The Wrong Girl/Fate Planned It This Way	1962	12.50	25.00	50.00
647	Com'n Home/I Love You, Can't You See	1962	6.25	12.50	25.00
654	True Fine Mama/The Owl Sees You	1962	6.25	12.50	25.00
662	39-21-46/Swish Fish	1963	6.25	12.50	25.00
32007	39-21-46/Swish Fish	1966	2.50	5.00	10.00
SWAN					
4213	In Paradise/Take It Baby	1965	2.50	5.00	10.00
4219	Our Love Will Grow/You're Everything	1965	2.50	5.00	10.00
4241	Please Try and Understand/Honey House	1966	2.50	5.00	10.00
UNITED ARTISTS					
0100	It Will Stand/I'm a Happy Man	1973	—	2.50	5.00
—"Silver Spotlight Series" reissue; B-side by the Jive Five					

Albums

Number	Title (A Side/B Side)	Yr	VG	VG+	NM
COLLECTABLES					
COL-5162	Golden Classics	198?	2.50	5.00	10.00

SHUFFLES, THE

45s

Number	Title (A Side/B Side)	Yr	VG	VG+	NM
RAYCO					
508	Do You Remember My Darling/Dancin' Little Girl	1963	50.00	100.00	200.00

SHUT DOWNS, THE

45s

Number	Title (A Side/B Side)	Yr	VG	VG+	NM
DIMENSION					
1016	Four on the Floor/Beach Buggy	1963	6.25	12.50	25.00
KARSONG					
501	Four on the Floor/Straightaway	1963	12.50	25.00	50.00

SICKNICKS, THE

45s

Number	Title (A Side/B Side)	Yr	VG	VG+	NM
AMY					
824	The Presidential Press Conference (Part 1)/The Presidential Press Conference (Part 2)	1961	3.75	7.50	15.00
824 [PS]	The Presidential Press Conference (Part 1)/The Presidential Press Conference (Part 2)	1961	6.25	12.50	25.00
831	Wadja Say Mr. K (Part 1)/Wadja Say Mr. K (Part 2)	1961	3.75	7.50	15.00

Albums

Number	Title (A Side/B Side)	Yr	VG	VG+	NM
AMY					
2 [M]	Sick #2	1961	7.50	15.00	30.00

SIDEKICKS, THE

45s

Number	Title (A Side/B Side)	Yr	VG	VG+	NM
RCA VICTOR					
47-8864	Suspicions/Up on the Roof	1966	2.50	5.00	10.00
47-8969	Fifi the Flea/Not Now	1966	2.50	5.00	10.00
47-9079	He's My Friend/Miss Charlotte	1967	2.50	5.00	10.00
47-9174	Sight and Sound/You Gave Me Somebody to Love	1967	2.50	5.00	10.00

Albums

Number	Title (A Side/B Side)	Yr	VG	VG+	NM
RCA VICTOR					
LPM-3712 [M]	Fifi the Flea	1966	5.00	10.00	20.00
LSP-3712 [S]	Fifi the Flea	1966	6.25	12.50	25.00

SIDEWALK SURFERS, THE

45s

Number	Title (A Side/B Side)	Yr	VG	VG+	NM
JUBILEE					
5496	Skate Board/Fun Last Summer	1965	12.50	25.00	50.00

SIDEWINDERS, THE

45s

Number	Title (A Side/B Side)	Yr	VG	VG+	NM
RCA VICTOR					
48-1033	Rendezvous/O Miss Mary	1972	2.00	4.00	8.00

Albums

Number	Title (A Side/B Side)	Yr	VG	VG+	NM
RCA VICTOR					
LSP-4694	The Sidewinders	1972	5.00	10.00	20.00

SIERRAS, THE

45s

Number	Title (A Side/B Side)	Yr	VG	VG+	NM
DOT					
16569	Plan for Love/Then I'll Still Love You	1963	3.00	6.00	12.00
GOLDISC					
G-4	I Should Have Loved You/I'll Believe It When I See It	1963	7.50	15.00	30.00
KNOX					
102	So Many Sleepless Nights/Nearer My Heart	1962	25.00	50.00	100.00
MAIL CALL					
2333/4	Stormy Weather/Chance	1963	50.00	100.00	200.00

SIGLER, BUNNY

Number	Title (A Side/B Side)	Yr	VG	VG+	NM
12-Inch Singles					
GOLD MIND					
501	Glad to Be Your Lover (8:48)/I'm Funkin' You Tonight (5:30)	1979	3.00	6.00	12.00
45s					
CRAIG					
501	I Won't Cry/Come On Home	1961	7.50	15.00	30.00
—As Bunny "Mr. Emotions" Sigler					
DECCA					
31880	Everything's Gonna Be All Right/For Cryin' Out Loud	1965	6.25	12.50	25.00
31947	Will You Love Me Tomorrow/Comparatively Speaking	1966	3.00	6.00	12.00
32183	Will You Love Me Tomorrow/Let Them Talk	1967	2.50	5.00	10.00
GOLD MIND					
4008	Let Me Party with You (Part 1) (Party, Party, Party)/Let Me Party with You (Part 2) (Party, Party, Party)	1977	—	2.50	5.00
4010	I Got What You Need/It's Time to Twist	1978	—	2.50	5.00
4012	Only You/Good Good Feeling	1978	—	3.00	6.00
—A-side with Loleatta Holloway; B-side is Holloway solo					
4014	Don't Even Try (Give It Up)/I'm a Fool	1978	—	2.50	5.00
4018	By the Way You Dance (I Knew It Was You)/Glad to Be Your Lover	1979	—	2.50	5.00
4020	I'm Funking You Tonight with My Music/Glad to Be Your Lover	1979	—	2.50	5.00
NEPTUNE					
14	Where Do the Lonely Go/Great Big Liar	1969	2.00	4.00	8.00
15	We're Only Human/Sure Didn't Take Long	1969	2.00	4.00	8.00
—With Cindy Scott					
24	Conquer the World Together/We're Only Human	1970	2.00	4.00	8.00
—With Cindy Scott					
25	Don't Stop Doing What You're Doing/Where Do the Lonely Go	1970	2.00	4.00	8.00
PARKWAY					
123	Girl Don't Make Me Wait/Always in the Wrong Place (At the Wrong Time)	1966	2.50	5.00	10.00
153	Let the Good Times Roll & Feel So Good/There's No Love Left (In This Old Heart of Mine)	1967	3.00	6.00	12.00
6000	Lovey Dovey & You're So Fine/Sunny Sunday	1967	2.50	5.00	10.00
6001	Follow Your Heart/Can You Dig It	1967	2.50	5.00	10.00
PHILADELPHIA INT'L.					
3505	Everybody Needs Good Lovin' (Part 1)/Everybody Needs Good Lovin' (Part 2)	1971	—	3.00	6.00
3512	Conquer the World Together/We Gotta Good Thing Goin'	1971	—	3.00	6.00
—With Dee Dee Sharp					
3519	Heaven Knows I've Changed/Regina	1972	—	3.00	6.00
3523	Tossin' and Turnin'/Picture Us	1972	—	3.00	6.00
3532	Theme from "Five Fingers of Death"/Regina	1973	—	3.00	6.00
3536	That's How Long I'll Be Loving You/Heaven Knows I've Changed	1973	—	3.00	6.00
3545	Love Train (Part 1)/Love Train (Part 2)	1974	—	3.00	6.00
3554	Keep Smilin'/Somebody Free	1974	—	3.00	6.00
3560	Shake Your Booty/Your Love Is Good	1975	—	3.00	6.00
3575	Somebody Free/That's How Long I'll Be Loving You	1975	—	3.00	6.00
3582	Jingle Bells (Part 1)/Jingle Bells (Part 2)	1975	—	2.50	5.00
3597	My Music/Can't Believe That You Love Me	1976	—	3.00	6.00
3608	Somebody Loves You/Woman, Woman	1976	—	3.00	6.00
SALSOUL					
2114	How Can I Tell Her (It's Over)/Since the Day I First Saw You	1980	—	2.00	4.00
2125	Super Duper Duper Superman/Kool Aid	1980	—	2.00	4.00
V-TONE					
500	Family Dance/Hold On	196?	5.00	10.00	20.00
Albums					
GOLD MIND					
7502	Let Me Party with You	1978	3.00	6.00	12.00
9503	I've Always Wanted to Sing... Not Just Write Songs	1979	3.00	6.00	12.00
PARKWAY					
P-50000 [M]	Let the Good Times Roll	1967	10.00	20.00	40.00
PS-50000 [S]	Let the Good Times Roll	1967	10.00	20.00	40.00
PHILADELPHIA INT'L.					
KZ 32589	That's How Long I'll Be Loving You	1974	3.75	7.50	15.00
KZ 33249	Keep Smilin'	1974	3.75	7.50	15.00
PZ 34267	My Music	1976	3.75	7.50	15.00
SALSOUL					
SA-8531	Let It Snow	1980	3.00	6.00	12.00

SIGNATURES, THE

Number	Title (A Side/B Side)	Yr	VG	VG+	NM
45s					
NORMAN					
210	Julie Is Her Name/Someone in Love	1957	75.00	150.00	300.00
WHIPPET					
210	Julie Is Her Name/Someone in Love	1957	12.50	25.00	50.00
Albums					
WARNER BROS.					
W 1250 [M]	The Signatures Sing In	1958	7.50	15.00	30.00
WS 1250 [S]	The Signatures Sing In	1958	10.00	20.00	40.00
W 1353 [M]	Prepare to Flip!	1959	7.50	15.00	30.00
WS 1353 [S]	Prepare to Flip!	1959	10.00	20.00	40.00
WHIPPET					
WLP-702 [M]	The Signatures — Their Voices and Instruments	1957	15.00	30.00	60.00

SILBERMAN, BENEDICT, ORCHESTRA AND CHORUS

Number	Title (A Side/B Side)	Yr	VG	VG+	NM
45s					
PALETTE					
5037	The Chipmunk Song/Lovers of Paris	1959	2.50	5.00	10.00

SILHOUETTES, THE

Number	Title (A Side/B Side)	Yr	VG	VG+	NM
45s					
ACE					
552	I Sold My Heart to the Junkman/What Would You Do	1958	5.00	10.00	20.00
562	Evelyn/Never Will Part	1959	5.00	10.00	20.00
—As "Bill Horton and the Silhouettes"					
EMBER					
1029	Get a Job/I Am Lonely	1958	7.50	15.00	30.00
—Red label					
1029	Get a Job/I Am Lonely	1960	5.00	10.00	20.00
—Black label					
1032	Headin' for the Poorhouse/Miss Thing	1958	5.00	10.00	20.00
1037	Bing Bong/Voodoo Eyes	1958	5.00	10.00	20.00
GOODWAY					
101	Not Me Baby/Gaucho Serenade	1966	50.00	100.00	200.00
—As "The New Silhouettes"					
GRAND					
142	Wish I Could Be There/Move On Over	1956	50.00	100.00	200.00
IMPERIAL					
5899	The Push/Which Way Did She Go	1962	3.00	6.00	12.00
JUNIOR					
391	Get a Job/I Am Lonely	1957	200.00	400.00	800.00
—Brown label (first press)					
391	Get a Job/I Am Lonely	1957	150.00	300.00	600.00
—Blue label (second press)					
396	I Sold My Heart to the Junkman/What Would You Do	1958	25.00	50.00	100.00
400	Evelyn/Never Will Part	1959	50.00	100.00	200.00
993	Your Love/Rent Man	1963	7.50	15.00	30.00
UNITED ARTISTS					
147	I Sold My Heart to the Junkman/What Would You Do	1958		—	—
—Canceled					
Albums					
GOODWAY					
GLP-100	The Silhouettes 1958-1968/Get a Job	1968	75.00	150.00	300.00

SILK

Also see MICHAEL STANLEY BAND.

Number	Title (A Side/B Side)	Yr	VG	VG+	NM
45s					
DECCA					
32829	Come Over Here/Falling in Love Isn't Easy	1971	2.00	4.00	8.00
Albums					
ABC					
S-694	Smooth As Raw Silk	1969	6.25	12.50	25.00

SILKIE, THE

Number	Title (A Side/B Side)	Yr	VG	VG+	NM
45s					
FONTANA					
1525	You've Got to Hide Your Love Away/City Winds	1965	3.75	7.50	15.00
—Light blue label; A-side was produced by John Lennon and Paul McCartney, with the two and George Harrison playing along					
1525	You've Got to Hide Your Love Away/City Wind	1965	5.00	10.00	20.00
—Dark blue label					
1536	The Keys to My Soul/Leave Me to Cry	1965	2.50	5.00	10.00
1551	Born to Be With You/I'm So Sorry	1966	2.50	5.00	10.00
Albums					
FONTANA					
MGF 27548 [M]	You've Got to Hide Your Love Away	1965	12.50	25.00	50.00
—With full-color cover					
MGF 27548 [M]	You've Got to Hide Your Love Away	1965	10.00	20.00	40.00
—With purplish, black and white cover					
SRF 67548 [R]	You've Got to Hide Your Love Away	1965	10.00	20.00	40.00
—With full-color cover					
SRF 67548 [R]	You've Got to Hide Your Love Away	1965	7.50	15.00	30.00
—With purplish, black and white cover					

SILLY SURFERS, THE

Number	Title (A Side/B Side)	Yr	VG	VG+	NM
Albums					
MERCURY					
MG-20977 [M]	The Sounds of the Silly Surfers	1965	20.00	40.00	80.00
SR-60977 [S]	The Sounds of the Silly Surfers	1965	25.00	50.00	100.00

SILLY SURFERS, THE / THE WEIRD-OHS

Number	Title (A Side/B Side)	Yr	VG	VG+	NM
Albums					
HAIRY					
101 [M]	The Sounds of the Silly Surfers/The Sounds of the Weird-Ohs	1964	37.50	75.00	150.00

SILVA TONES, THE

Number	Title (A Side/B Side)	Yr	VG	VG+	NM
45s					
ARGO					
5281	Chi-Wa-Wa (That's All I Want from You)/Roses Are Blooming	1957	6.25	12.50	25.00
5281	That's All I Want from You/Roses Are Blooming	1957	7.50	15.00	30.00
MONARCH					
615	That's All I Want from You/Weepin' and a-Wailin'	1957	12.50	25.00	50.00
—Yellow label					
615	That's All I Want from You/Roses Are Blooming	1957	7.50	15.00	30.00
—Black label					

SILVER, HORACE

Number	Title (A Side/B Side)	Yr	VG	VG+	NM
45s					
BLUE NOTE					
XW325	Liberated Brother/Nothin' Can Stop Me Now	1973	—	2.50	5.00
XW905	Slow Down (Tranquilizer Suite)/Time and Effort	1976	—	2.50	5.00
XW1032	Togetherness/Out of the Night (Came You)	1977	—	2.50	5.00
1608	Safari/Thou Swell	195?	3.00	6.00	12.00
1625	Opus de Funk/Day In Day Out	195?	3.00	6.00	12.00
1630	Doodlin'/The Preacher	195?	3.00	6.00	12.00

Number	Title (A Side/B Side)	Yr	VG	VG+	NM
1631	Room 608/Creepin' In	195?	3.00	6.00	12.00
1654	Enchantment/Camouflage	195?	3.00	6.00	12.00
1655	Senor Blues/Cool Eyes	195?	3.00	6.00	12.00
1672	Home Cookin'/The Back Beat	195?	3.00	6.00	12.00
1673	Soulsville/No Smokin'	195?	3.00	6.00	12.00
1705	The Outlaw/Safari	195?	3.00	6.00	12.00
1740	Finger Poppin'/Come On Home	1959	2.50	5.00	10.00
1741	Cookin' at the Continental/Juicy Lucy	1959	2.50	5.00	10.00
1742	Mellow D/Swingin' the Samba	1959	2.50	5.00	10.00
1750	Break City/Sister Sadie	1959	2.50	5.00	10.00
1751	Blowin' the Blues Away/The Baghdad Blues	1959	2.50	5.00	10.00
1784	Strollin'/Nica's Dream	1960	2.50	5.00	10.00
1785	Where Are You?/Me and My Baby	1960	2.50	5.00	10.00
1817	Filthy McNasty (Part 1)/Filthy McNasty (Part 2)	1961	2.50	5.00	10.00
1818	Doin' the Thing (Part 1)/Doin' the Thing (Part 2)	1961	2.50	5.00	10.00
1871	Tokyo Blues (Part 1)/Tokyo Blues (Part 2)	1962	2.50	5.00	10.00
1872	Sayonara Blues (Part 1)/Sayonara Blues (Part 2)	1962	2.50	5.00	10.00
1873	Too Much Sake (Part 1)/Too Much Sake (Part 2)	1962	2.50	5.00	10.00
1902	Let's Get to the Nitty Gritty/Silver's Serenade	1963	2.50	5.00	10.00
1903	Dragon Lady/Sweet Sweetie Dee	1963	2.50	5.00	10.00
1912	Song for My Father (Part 1)/Song for My Father (Part 2)	1964	2.00	4.00	8.00
1913	Que Pasa (Part 1)/Que Pasa (Part 2)	1964	2.00	4.00	8.00
1923	The Cape Verdean Blues/Pretty Eyes	1965	2.00	4.00	8.00
1924	The African Queen (Part 1)/The African Queen (Part 2)	1965	2.00	4.00	8.00
1932	The Jody Grind (Part 1)/The Jody Grind (Part 2)	1967	2.00	4.00	8.00
1939	Serenade to a Soul Sister/Psychedelic Sally	1968	2.00	4.00	8.00
1946	Down and Out/Take a Little Love	1969	2.00	4.00	8.00
1963	The Show Has Begun/There's Much to Be Done	197?	—	3.00	6.00
1975	Acid, Pot or Pills/I've Had a Little Talk	197?	—	3.00	6.00
1978	Cause and Effect/Horn of Life	197?	—	3.00	6.00

Albums
BLUE NOTE

Number	Title (A Side/B Side)	Yr	VG	VG+	NM
BN-LA054-F	The Pursuit of the 27th Man	1973	3.75	7.50	15.00
BN-LA402-H2 [(2)]	Horace Silver	1975	5.00	10.00	20.00
BN-LA406-G	Silver 'n' Brass	1975	3.00	6.00	12.00
BN-LA581-G	Silver 'n' Wood	1976	3.00	6.00	12.00
BN-LA708-G	Silver 'n' Voices	1977	3.00	6.00	12.00
BN-LA945-H	Sterling Silver	1979	3.00	6.00	12.00
LWB-1033 [(2)]	Silver and Strings Play Music of the Spheres	1980	3.75	7.50	15.00
BLP-1518 [M]	Horace Silver and the Jazz Messengers	1956	50.00	100.00	200.00
—"Deep groove" version (deep indentation under label on both sides)					
BLP-1518 [M]	Horace Silver and the Jazz Messengers	1956	37.50	75.00	150.00
—Regular edition, Lexington Ave. address on label					
BLP-1518 [M]	Horace Silver and the Jazz Messengers	1963	6.25	12.50	25.00
—"New York, USA" address on label					
BLP-1520 [M]	Spotlight on Drums	1956	50.00	100.00	200.00
—"Deep groove" version (deep indentation under label on both sides)					
BLP-1520 [M]	Spotlight on Drums	1956	37.50	75.00	150.00
—Regular edition, Lexington Ave. address on label					
BLP-1520 [M]	Spotlight on Drums	1963	6.25	12.50	25.00
—"New York, USA" address on label					
BLP-1539 [M]	Six Pieces of Silver	1957	50.00	100.00	200.00
—"Deep groove" version (deep indentation under label on both sides)					
BLP-1539 [M]	Six Pieces of Silver	1957	37.50	75.00	150.00
—Regular edition, Lexington Ave. address on label					
BLP-1539 [M]	Six Pieces of Silver	1963	6.25	12.50	25.00
—"New York, USA" address on label					
BLP-1562 [M]	The Stylings of Silver	1957	37.50	75.00	150.00
—"Deep groove" version (deep indentation under label on both sides)					
BLP-1562 [M]	The Stylings of Silver	1957	25.00	50.00	100.00
—Regular edition, W. 63rd St. address on label					
BLP-1562 [M]	The Stylings of Silver	1963	6.25	12.50	25.00
—"New York, USA" address on label					
BST-1562 [S]	The Stylings of Silver	1959	25.00	50.00	100.00
—"Deep groove" version (deep indentation under label on both sides)					
BST-1562 [S]	The Stylings of Silver	1959	20.00	40.00	80.00
—Regular edition, W. 63rd St. address on label					
BST-1562 [S]	The Stylings of Silver	1963	5.00	10.00	20.00
—"New York, USA" address on label					
BLP-1589 [M]	Further Explorations	1958	37.50	75.00	150.00
—"Deep groove" version (deep indentation under label on both sides)					
BLP-1589 [M]	Further Explorations	1958	25.00	50.00	100.00
—Regular edition, W. 63rd St. address on label					
BLP-1589 [M]	Further Explorations	1963	6.25	12.50	25.00
—"New York, USA" address on label					
BST-1589 [S]	Further Explorations	1959	25.00	50.00	100.00
—"Deep groove" version (deep indentation under label on both sides)					
BST-1589 [S]	Further Explorations	1959	20.00	40.00	80.00
—Regular edition, W. 63rd St. address on label					
BST-1589 [S]	Further Explorations	1963	5.00	10.00	20.00
—"New York, USA" address on label					
BLP-4008 [M]	Finger Poppin'	1959	37.50	75.00	150.00
—"Deep groove" version (deep indentation under label on both sides)					
BLP-4008 [M]	Finger Poppin'	1959	25.00	50.00	100.00
—Regular edition, W. 63rd St. address on label					
BLP-4008 [M]	Finger Poppin'	1963	6.25	12.50	25.00
—"New York, USA" address on label					
BST-4008 [S]	Finger Poppin'	1959	25.00	50.00	100.00
—"Deep groove" version (deep indentation under label on both sides)					
BST-4008 [S]	Finger Poppin'	1959	20.00	40.00	80.00
—Regular edition, W. 63rd St. address on label					
BST-4008 [S]	Finger Poppin'	1963	5.00	10.00	20.00
—"New York, USA" address on label					
BLP-4017 [M]	Blowin' the Blues Away	1959	30.00	60.00	120.00
—"Deep groove" version (deep indentation under label on both sides)					
BLP-4017 [M]	Blowin' the Blues Away	1959	20.00	40.00	80.00
—Regular edition, W. 63rd St. address on label					
BLP-4017 [M]	Blowin' the Blues Away	1963	6.25	12.50	25.00
—"New York, USA" address on label					
BLP-4042 [M]	Horace-Scope	1960	30.00	60.00	120.00
—"Deep groove" version (deep indentation under label on both sides)					
BLP-4042 [M]	Horace-Scope	1960	20.00	40.00	80.00
—Regular edition, W. 63rd St. address on label					
BLP-4042 [M]	Horace-Scope	1963	6.25	12.50	25.00
—"New York, USA" address on label					
BLP-4076 [M]	Doin' the Thing at the Village Gate	1961	15.00	30.00	60.00
—61st St. address on label					
BLP-4076 [M]	Doin' the Thing at the Village Gate	1963	5.00	10.00	20.00
—"New York, USA" address on label					
BLP-4110 [M]	The Tokyo Blues	1962	7.50	15.00	30.00
BLP-4131 [M]	Silver's Serenade	1963	7.50	15.00	30.00
BLP-4185 [M]	Song for My Father (Cantiga Para Meu Pai)	1965	6.25	12.50	25.00
BLP-4220 [M]	The Cape Verdean Blues	1965	6.25	12.50	25.00
BLP-4250 [M]	The Jody Grind	1966	6.25	12.50	25.00
BLP-5018 [10]	New Faces	1953	75.00	150.00	300.00
BLP-5034 [10]	Horace Silver Trio, Vol. 2	1954	62.50	125.00	250.00
BLP-5058 [10]	Horace Silver Quintet	1955	62.50	125.00	250.00
BLP-5062 [10]	Horace Silver Quintet	1955	62.50	125.00	250.00
B1-46548	Song for My Father	1997	3.75	7.50	15.00
—Reissue on 180-gram vinyl					
BST-81518	Horace Silver and the Jazz Messengers	1985	2.50	5.00	10.00
—"The Finest in Jazz Since 1939" reissue					
BST-81518 [R]	Horace Silver and the Jazz Messengers	1967	3.00	6.00	12.00
B1-81520	The Horace Silver Trio	1989	2.50	5.00	10.00
—"The Finest in Jazz Since 1939" reissue					
BST-81520 [R]	Spotlight on Drums	1967	3.00	6.00	12.00
—With "A Division of Liberty Records" on label					
B1-81539	Six Pieces of Silver	1988	2.50	5.00	10.00
—"The Finest in Jazz Since 1939" reissue					
BST-81539 [R]	Six Pieces of Silver	1967	3.00	6.00	12.00
BST-81562 [S]	The Stylings of Silver	1967	3.75	7.50	15.00
BST-81589 [S]	Further Explorations	1967	3.75	7.50	15.00
B1-84008	Finger Poppin'	198?	2.50	5.00	10.00
—"The Finest in Jazz Since 1939" reissue					
BST-84008 [S]	Finger Poppin'	1967	3.75	7.50	15.00
BST-84017	Blowin' the Blues Away	1985	2.50	5.00	10.00
—"The Finest in Jazz Since 1939" reissue					
BST-84017 [S]	Blowin' the Blues Away	1959	15.00	30.00	60.00
—W. 63rd St. address on label					
BST-84017 [S]	Blowin' the Blues Away	1963	5.00	10.00	20.00
—"New York, USA" address on label					
BST-84017 [S]	Blowin' the Blues Away	1967	3.75	7.50	15.00
—"A Division of Liberty Records" on label					
BST-84042 [S]	Horace-Scope	1960	15.00	30.00	60.00
—W. 63rd St. address on label					
BST-84042 [S]	Horace-Scope	1963	5.00	10.00	20.00
—"New York, USA" address on label					
BST-84042 [S]	Horace-Scope	1967	3.75	7.50	15.00
—"A Division of Liberty Records" on label					
B1-84076	Doin' the Thing at the Village Gate	1989	2.50	5.00	10.00
—"The Finest in Jazz Since 1939" reissue					
BST-84076 [S]	Doin' the Thing at the Village Gate	1961	15.00	30.00	60.00
—61st St. address on label					
BST-84076 [S]	Doin' the Thing at the Village Gate	1963	5.00	10.00	20.00
—"New York, USA" address on label					
BST-84076 [S]	Doin' the Thing at the Village Gate	1967	3.75	7.50	15.00
—"A Division of Liberty Records" on label					
BST-84110 [S]	The Tokyo Blues	1962	10.00	20.00	40.00
—"New York, USA" address on label					
BST-84110 [S]	The Tokyo Blues	1967	3.75	7.50	15.00
—"A Division of Liberty Records" on label					
BST-84131 [S]	Silver's Serenade	1963	10.00	20.00	40.00
—"New York, USA" address on label					
BST-84131 [S]	Silver's Serenade	1967	3.75	7.50	15.00
—"A Division of Liberty Records" on label					
BST-84185	Song for My Father (Cantiga Para Meu Pai)	1985	2.50	5.00	10.00
—"The Finest in Jazz Since 1939" reissue					
BST-84185 [S]	Song for My Father (Cantiga Para Meu Pai)	1965	7.50	15.00	30.00
—"New York, USA" address on label					
BST-84185 [S]	Song for My Father (Cantiga Para Meu Pai)	1967	3.75	7.50	15.00
—"A Division of Liberty Records" on label					
BST-84220 [S]	The Cape Verdean Blues	1965	7.50	15.00	30.00
—"New York, USA" address on label					
BST-84220 [S]	The Cape Verdean Blues	1967	3.75	7.50	15.00
—"A Division of Liberty Records" on label					
BST-84250 [S]	The Jody Grind	1966	7.50	15.00	30.00
—"New York, USA" address on label					
BST-84250 [S]	The Jody Grind	1967	3.75	7.50	15.00
—"A Division of Liberty Records" on label					
BST-84277	Serenade to a Soul Sister	1968	3.75	7.50	15.00
BST-84309	You Gotta Take a Little Love	1969	3.75	7.50	15.00
BST-84325	The Best of Horace Silver	1970	3.75	7.50	15.00
BST-84352	That Healin' Feelin' (Phase 1)	1970	3.75	7.50	15.00
BST-84368	Total Response (Phase 2)	1971	3.75	7.50	15.00
BST-84420	Phase Three "All"	1972	3.75	7.50	15.00
B1-91143	The Best of Horace Silver	1988	2.50	5.00	10.00
B1-93206	The Best of Horace Silver, Vol. 2	1989	2.50	5.00	10.00

EPIC

Number	Title (A Side/B Side)	Yr	VG	VG+	NM
LN 3326 [M]	Silver's Blue	1956	20.00	40.00	80.00
LA 16006 [M]	Silver's Blue	1959	10.00	20.00	40.00
BA 17006 [R]	Silver's Blue	196?	5.00	10.00	20.00

SILVER APPLES

45s
KAPP

Number	Title (A Side/B Side)	Yr	VG	VG+	NM
923	Whirly Bird/Oscillations	1968	2.00	4.00	8.00

Albums
KAPP

Number	Title (A Side/B Side)	Yr	VG	VG+	NM
KS-3562	Silver Apples	1968	7.50	15.00	30.00
—Add 1/3 if poster is enclosed					
KS-3584	Contact	1969	7.50	15.00	30.00

SILVER CONVENTION

12-Inch Singles
MIDSONG INT'L.

Number	Title (A Side/B Side)	Yr	VG	VG+	NM
L33-1977 [DJ]	Spend the Night with Me (9:27)/Mission to Venus (8:45)	1978	3.75	7.50	15.00
JD-11027 [DJ]	Hollywood Music/(B-side unknown)	1976	3.75	7.50	15.00

Number	Title (A Side/B Side)	Yr	VG	VG+	NM
13906	Spend the Night with Me (9:27)/Mission to Venus (8:45)	1978	3.00	6.00	12.00

45s

MIDLAND INT'L.

Number	Title (A Side/B Side)	Yr	VG	VG+	NM
MB-10212	Save Me/Save Me Again	1975	—	2.00	4.00
MB-10339	Fly, Robin, Fly/Chains of Love	1975	—	3.00	6.00
—First pressing: "Fly, Robin, Fly" is over 4 minutes long, matrix number is 10339-A					
MB-10339	Fly, Robin, Fly/Chains of Love	1975	—	2.00	4.00
—Second pressing: "Fly, Robin, Fly" is 3:05, matrix number is 10339-Z					
MB-10571	Get Up and Boogie (That's Right)/Son of a Gun	1976	—	3.00	6.00
—First pressing: "Get Up and Boogie" is 4:05, matrix number is 10571-A					
MB-10571	Get Up and Boogie (That's Right)/Son of a Gun	1976	—	2.00	4.00
—Second pressing: "Get Up and Boogie" is under three minutes long					
MB-10571 [PS]	Get Up and Boogie (That's Right)/Son of a Gun	1976	—	3.00	6.00
MB-10723	No, No Joe/Another Girl	1976	—	2.00	4.00
MB-10849	Thank You Mr. D.J./Dancing in the Aisles (Take Me Higher)	1976	—	2.00	4.00

MIDSONG INT'L.

Number	Title (A Side/B Side)	Yr	VG	VG+	NM
GB-10939	Fly, Robin, Fly/Get Up and Boogie (That's Right)	1977	—	—	3.00
—Gold Standard Series					
MB-10972	Telegram/(B-side unknown)	1977	—	2.00	4.00
MB-11062	Save Me '77/Hotshot	1977	—	2.00	4.00
40896	Breakfast in Bed/Spend the Night with Me	1978	—	2.00	4.00

Albums

MIDLAND INT'L.

Number	Title (A Side/B Side)	Yr	VG	VG+	NM
BKL1-1129	Save Me	1975	2.50	5.00	10.00
BKL1-1369	Silver Convention	1976	2.50	5.00	10.00
BKL1-1824	Madhouse	1976	2.50	5.00	10.00

MIDSONG INT'L.

Number	Title (A Side/B Side)	Yr	VG	VG+	NM
BXL1-1129	Save Me	1978	2.00	4.00	8.00
—Reissue with new prefix					
BXL1-1369	Silver Convention	1978	2.00	4.00	8.00
—Reissue with new prefix					
BXL1-1824	Madhouse	1978	2.00	4.00	8.00
—Reissue with new prefix					
BKL1-2296	Golden Girls	1977	2.50	5.00	10.00
BXL1-2296	Golden Girls	1978	2.00	4.00	8.00
—Reissue with new prefix					

SILVER DUST

45s

SUN

Number	Title (A Side/B Side)	Yr	VG	VG+	NM
1124	Father and Son/Castle in the Sun	1971	—	2.50	5.00

SILVER FLEET

A precursor to 10CC.

45s

UNI

Number	Title (A Side/B Side)	Yr	VG	VG+	NM
55271	Look Out World/C'mon Plane	1971	6.25	12.50	25.00

SILVERSTEIN, SHEL

45s

COLUMBIA

Number	Title (A Side/B Side)	Yr	VG	VG+	NM
10053	Everybody's Makin' It Big But Me/The Man Who Got No Sign	1974	—	2.50	5.00
10153	Sahra Cynthia Sylvia Stout Would Not Take the Garbage Out/The Man Who Got No Sign	1975	—	2.50	5.00
45450	A Front Row Seat to Hear Ole Johnny Sing/26 Second Song	1971	—	3.00	6.00
45772	Sahra Cynthia Sylvia Stout Would Not Take the Garbage Out/Stacey Brown Got Two	1973	—	3.00	6.00
45885	All About You/Peace Proposal	1973	—	3.00	6.00

RCA VICTOR

Number	Title (A Side/B Side)	Yr	VG	VG+	NM
47-9844	Policeman, Woman, Taxicab/Three Legged Man	1970	2.00	4.00	8.00
74-0158	A Boy Named Sue/Somebody Stole My Rig	1969	2.00	4.00	8.00

Albums

ATLANTIC

Number	Title (A Side/B Side)	Yr	VG	VG+	NM
8072 [M]	Inside Folk Songs	1962	7.50	15.00	30.00
SD 8072 [S]	Inside Folk Songs	1962	10.00	20.00	40.00

CADET

Number	Title (A Side/B Side)	Yr	VG	VG+	NM
LP 4052 [M]	I'm So Good I Don't Have to Brag!	1965	6.25	12.50	25.00
LPS 4052 [S]	I'm So Good I Don't Have to Brag!	1965	7.50	15.00	30.00
LP 4054 [M]	Drain My Brain	1966	6.25	12.50	25.00
LPS 4054 [S]	Drain My Brain	1966	7.50	15.00	30.00

COLUMBIA

Number	Title (A Side/B Side)	Yr	VG	VG+	NM
KC 31119	Freakin' at the Freakers' Ball	1972	3.75	7.50	15.00
PC 31119	Freakin' at the Freakers' Ball	1979	2.00	4.00	8.00
—Budget-line reissue					
FC 39412	Where the Sidewalk Ends	1984	2.50	5.00	10.00
9C9 39611 [PD]	Where the Sidewalk Ends	1984	6.25	12.50	25.00
—Picture disc					
FC 40219	A Light in the Attic	1985	2.50	5.00	10.00

CRESTVIEW

Number	Title (A Side/B Side)	Yr	VG	VG+	NM
CRV 804 [M]	Stag Party	1963	6.25	12.50	25.00
CRS 7804 [S]	Stag Party	1963	7.50	15.00	30.00

ELEKTRA

Number	Title (A Side/B Side)	Yr	VG	VG+	NM
EKL-176 [M]	Hairy Jazz	1961	25.00	50.00	100.00
EKS-7176 [S]	Hairy Jazz	1961	37.50	75.00	150.00

FLYING FISH

Number	Title (A Side/B Side)	Yr	VG	VG+	NM
FF-211	Conch Train Robbery	1980	3.00	6.00	12.00

JANUS

Number	Title (A Side/B Side)	Yr	VG	VG+	NM
2JLS 3052 [(2)]	Crouching on the Outside	1973	3.75	7.50	15.00

PARACHUTE

Number	Title (A Side/B Side)	Yr	VG	VG+	NM
RRLP-9007	Songs and Stories	1978	3.00	6.00	12.00
20512 [DJ]	Selected Cuts from Songs and Stories	1978	5.00	10.00	20.00
—Promo-only EP					

RCA VICTOR

Number	Title (A Side/B Side)	Yr	VG	VG+	NM
LSP-4192	A Boy Named Sue (And His Other Country Songs)	1969	5.00	10.00	20.00

SIMMONS, "JUMPIN'" GENE

Also includes records as "Gene Simmons."

45s

AGP

Number	Title (A Side/B Side)	Yr	VG	VG+	NM
119	Back Home Again/Don't Worry About Me	1969	2.00	4.00	8.00
—Some were released as Gene Simmons					

CHECKER

Number	Title (A Side/B Side)	Yr	VG	VG+	NM
948	Bad Boy Willie/Goin' Back to Memphis	1960	3.00	6.00	12.00

EPIC

Number	Title (A Side/B Side)	Yr	VG	VG+	NM
10601	She's There When I Come Home/Magnolia Street	1970	—	3.00	6.00

HI

Number	Title (A Side/B Side)	Yr	VG	VG+	NM
2034	Teddy Bear/Your True Love	1961	2.50	5.00	10.00
2050	Caldonia/Be Her Number One	1962	2.50	5.00	10.00
2076	Haunted House/Hey, Hey Little Girl	1964	3.75	7.50	15.00
—As "Gene Simmons"					
2076	Haunted House/Hey, Hey Little Girl	1964	3.75	7.50	15.00
—As "Jumpin' Gene Simmons"					
2080	The Dodo/The Jump	1964	2.50	5.00	10.00
2086	Skinnie Minnie/I'm a Ramblin' Man	1965	2.50	5.00	10.00
2092	Mattie Rae/Folsom Prison Blues	1965	2.50	5.00	10.00
2102	The Batman/Bossy Boss	1966	3.75	7.50	15.00
2113	Go On Shoes/Keep That Meat in the Pan	1966	2.50	5.00	10.00

MALA

Number	Title (A Side/B Side)	Yr	VG	VG+	NM
12012	I'm Just a Loser/Lila	1968	2.50	5.00	10.00

SANDY

Number	Title (A Side/B Side)	Yr	VG	VG+	NM
1027	The Waiting Game/Shenandoah Waltz	1959	5.00	10.00	20.00
—As "Morris Gene Simmons"					

SUN

Number	Title (A Side/B Side)	Yr	VG	VG+	NM
299	Drinkin' Wine/I Done Told You	1958	37.50	75.00	150.00
—As "Gene Simmons"					

Albums

HI

Number	Title (A Side/B Side)	Yr	VG	VG+	NM
HL 2018 [M]	Jumpin' Gene Simmons	1964	12.50	25.00	50.00
SHL 32018 [S]	Jumpin' Gene Simmons	1964	17.50	35.00	70.00

SIMON, CARLY

Also see THE SIMON SISTERS.

12-Inch Singles

ELEKTRA

Number	Title (A Side/B Side)	Yr	VG	VG+	NM
11399 [DJ]	Tranquillo (same on both sides)	1978	2.50	5.00	10.00

EPIC

Number	Title (A Side/B Side)	Yr	VG	VG+	NM
05277	My New Boyfriend (3 versions)	1985	—	3.00	6.00

45s

ARISTA

Number	Title (A Side/B Side)	Yr	VG	VG+	NM
2083	Better Not Tell Her/Happy Birthday	1990	—	—	3.00
2164	Life Is Eternal/We Just Got Here	1990	—	—	3.00
9525	Coming Around Again/Itsy Bitsy Spider	1986	—	—	3.00
9525 [PS]	Coming Around Again/Itsy Bitsy Spider	1986	2.00	4.00	8.00
—With "Heartburn" movie scenes					
9525 [PS]	Coming Around Again/Itsy Bitsy Spider	1986	—	2.00	4.00
—Black and white photo of Carly Simon					
9525 [PS]	Coming Around Again/Itsy Bitsy Spider	1986	—	2.00	4.00
—Color photo of Carly Simon					
9587	Give Me All Night/Sleight of Hand	1987	—	—	3.00
9587 [PS]	Give Me All Night/Sleight of Hand	1987	—	—	3.00
9619	The Stuff That Dreams Are Made Of/As Time Goes By	1987	—	—	3.00
9619 [PS]	The Stuff That Dreams Are Made Of/As Time Goes By	1987	—	—	3.00
9653	All I Want Is You/On a Hot Summer Night	1987	—	—	3.00
9653 [PS]	All I Want Is You/On a Hot Summer Night	1987	—	—	3.00
9732 [DJ]	Do the Walls Come Down (same on both sides)	1988	—	2.50	5.00
—Not released as stock copy on this number					
9732 [PS]	Do the Walls Come Down (same on both sides)	1988	—	2.50	5.00
—Promo-only picture sleeve					
9754	You're So Vain/Do the Walls Come Down	1988	—	—	3.00
9754 [PS]	You're So Vain/Do the Walls Come Down	1988	—	—	3.00
9793	Let the River Run/The Turn of the Tide	1988	—	—	3.00
9793 [PS]	Let the River Run/The Turn of the Tide	1988	—	—	3.00

ELEKTRA

Number	Title (A Side/B Side)	Yr	VG	VG+	NM
45246	Attitude Dancing/Are You Ticklish	1975	—	2.50	5.00
45248	Slave/Look Me in the Eyes	1975	—	—	—
—Unreleased?					
45263	Waterfall/After the Storm	1975	—	2.50	5.00
45278	More and More/Love Out in the Street	1975	—	2.50	5.00
45325	It Keeps You Runnin'/Look Me in the Eyes	1976	—	2.00	4.00
45341	Half a Chance/Libby	1976	—	2.00	4.00
—Butterfly label					
45341	Half a Chance/Libby	1976	—	2.50	5.00
—Red label					
45413	Nobody Does It Better/After the Storm	1977	—	2.00	4.00
45477	You Belong to Me/In a Small Moment	1978	—	2.00	4.00
45477 [PS]	You Belong to Me/In a Small Moment	1978	—	3.00	6.00
45506	Devoted to You/Boys in the Trees	1978	—	2.00	4.00
—A-side with James Taylor					
45544	Tranquillo (Melt My Heart)/Back Down to Earth	1978	—	2.00	4.00
45724	That's the Way I've Always Heard It Should Be/Alone	1971	—	3.00	6.00
45748	Our First Day Together/Share the Land	1971	—	—	—
—Unreleased					
45759	Anticipation/The Garden	1971	—	3.00	6.00
45774	Legend in Your Own Time/Julie Through the Glass	1972	—	3.00	6.00
45796	The Girl You Think You Are/Share the Land	1972	—	3.00	6.00
45824	You're So Vain/His Friends Are More Than Fond of Robin	1972	—	3.00	6.00
45843	The Right Thing to Do/We Have No Secrets	1973	—	2.50	5.00
45880	Mockingbird/Grownup	1974	—	2.50	5.00
—A-side with James Taylor					
45887	Haven't Got Time for the Pain/Mind on My Man	1974	—	2.50	5.00
46051	Vengeance/Love You by Heart	1979	—	2.00	4.00
46051 [PS]	Vengeance/Love You by Heart	1979	—	2.50	5.00
46514	Spy/Pure Sin	1979	—	2.00	4.00

Number	Title (A Side/B Side)	Yr	VG	VG+	NM
69953	Hidin' Away/Fight for It	1982	—	2.00	4.00
—With Jesse Colin Young					
69953 [PS]	Hidin' Away/Fight for It	1982	—	3.00	6.00
—With Jesse Colin Young					
EPIC					
05419	Tired of Being Blonde/Black Honeymoon	1985	—	—	3.00
05419 [PS]	Tired of Being Blonde/Black Honeymoon	1985	—	2.00	4.00
05596	My New Boyfriend/The Wives Are in Connecticut	1985	—	—	3.00
MIRAGE					
4051	Why/Why	1982	—	2.00	4.00
—B-side by Chic					
99963	Why/(Instrumental)	1982	—	2.00	4.00
PLANET					
YB-13779	Someone Waits for You/(B-side unknown)	1984	—	2.00	4.00
WARNER BROS.					
29428	Hello Big Man/Dawn You Get to Me	1983	—	2.00	4.00
29484	You Know What to Do/Orpheus	1983	—	2.00	4.00
29484 [PS]	You Know What to Do/Orpheus	1983	—	2.50	5.00
49518	Jesse/Stardust	1980	—	2.00	4.00
49518 [PS]	Jesse/Stardust	1980	—	2.50	5.00
49630	Take Me As I Am/James	1980	—	2.00	4.00
49689	Come Upstairs/Them	1981	—	2.00	4.00
49880	From the Heart/Hurt	1981	—	2.00	4.00
50027	Body and Soul/Get Along Without You Very Well	1982	—	2.00	4.00
Albums					
ARISTA					
AL-8443	Coming Around Again	1987	2.00	4.00	8.00
AL-8526	Greatest Hits Live	1988	2.00	4.00	8.00
AL-8582	My Romance	1990	3.00	6.00	12.00
AL-8650	Have You Seen Me Lately?	1990	3.00	6.00	12.00
DIRECT DISK					
SD-16608	Boys in the Trees	1980	12.50	25.00	50.00
—Audiophile vinyl					
ELEKTRA					
6E-109	The Best of Carly Simon	1977	2.00	4.00	8.00
—Reissue of 7E-1048					
6E-128	Boys in the Trees	1978	2.50	5.00	10.00
5E-506	Spy	1979	2.50	5.00	10.00
7E-1002	Hotcakes	1974	2.50	5.00	10.00
EQ-1002 [Q]	Hotcakes	1974	5.00	10.00	20.00
7E-1033	Playing Possum	1975	2.50	5.00	10.00
EQ-1033 [Q]	Playing Possum	1975	5.00	10.00	20.00
7E-1048	The Best of Carly Simon	1975	2.50	5.00	10.00
EQ-1048 [Q]	The Best of Carly Simon	1975	5.00	10.00	20.00
7E-1064	Another Passenger	1976	2.50	5.00	10.00
EQ-1064 [Q]	Another Passenger	1976	5.00	10.00	20.00
EQ-4082 [Q]	Carly Simon	1974	5.00	10.00	20.00
EQ-5049 [Q]	No Secrets	1974	5.00	10.00	20.00
EKS-74082	Carly Simon	1971	3.00	6.00	12.00
EKS-75016	Anticipation	1971	3.00	6.00	12.00
EKS-75049	No Secrets	1972	3.00	6.00	12.00
—With lyrics on innersleeve					
EKS-75049	No Secrets	1973	2.50	5.00	10.00
—Without lyrics on innersleeve					
EPIC					
FE 39970	Spoiled Girl	1985	2.50	5.00	10.00
WARNER BROS.					
BSK 3443	Come Upstairs	1980	2.50	5.00	10.00
BSK 3592	Torch	1981	2.50	5.00	10.00
23886	Hello Big Man	1983	2.50	5.00	10.00

SIMON, JOE

12-Inch Singles

Number	Title (A Side/B Side)	Yr	VG	VG+	NM
SPRING					
025 [DJ]	One Step at a Time (5:33) (3:39)	1977	3.75	7.50	15.00
057 [DJ]	Love Vibration (same on both sides)	1978	3.00	6.00	12.00
45s					
COMPLEAT					
140	It Turns Me Inside Out/Morning, Noon and Night	1985	—	2.00	4.00
146	Mr. Right or Mr. Right Now/Let Me Have My Way with You	1985	—	2.00	4.00
DOT					
16570	Just Like Yesterday/Only a Dream	1964	2.00	4.00	8.00
HUSH					
103	It's a Miracle/Land of Love	1960	3.00	6.00	12.00
104	Call My Name/Everybody Needs Somebody	1961	3.00	6.00	12.00
106	Pledge of Love/It's All Over	1961	3.00	6.00	12.00
107	I See Your Face/Troubles	1961	3.00	6.00	12.00
108	Land of Love/I Keep Remembering	1962	3.00	6.00	12.00
POSSE					
5001	Baby, When Love Is In Your Heart (It's In Your Eyes)/Are We Breaking Up	1980	—	2.50	5.00
5005	Glad You Came My Way/I Don't Wanna Make Love	1980	—	2.50	5.00
5010	Are We Breaking Up/We're Together	1981	—	2.50	5.00
5014	Fallin' in Love with You/Magnolia	1981	—	2.50	5.00
5018	You Give Life to Me/(Instrumental)	1982	—	2.50	5.00
—With Clare Bathe					
5019	Go Sam/(Instrumental)	1982	—	2.50	5.00
5021	Get Down, Get Down "82"/It Be's That Way Sometime	1982	—	2.50	5.00
5038	Deeper Than Love/Step by Step	198?	—	2.50	5.00
SOUND STAGE 7					
1508	Misty Blue/That's the Way I Want Our Love	1972	—	2.50	5.00
1512	Who's Julie/The Girl's Alright with Me	1973	—	2.50	5.00
1514	Someone to Lean On/I Got a Whole Lotta Lovin'	1974	—	2.50	5.00
1521	Funny How Time Slips Away/Message from Maria	1976	—	2.50	5.00
2564	Teenager's Prayer/Long Hot Summer	1966	2.00	4.00	8.00
2569	Too Many Teardrops/What Makes a Man Feel Good	1966	2.00	4.00	8.00
2577	My Special Prayer/Travelin' Man	1966	2.00	4.00	8.00
2583	Put Your Trust in Me (Depend on Me)/Just a Dream	1967	2.00	4.00	8.00
2589	Nine Pound Steel/The Girl's Alright with Me	1967	2.00	4.00	8.00
2602	No Sad Songs/Come On and Get It	1967	2.00	4.00	8.00
2608	(You Keep Me) Hangin' On/Long Hot Summer	1968	2.00	4.00	8.00
2617	Message from Maria/I Worry About You	1968	2.00	4.00	8.00
2622	Looking Back/Standing in the Safety Zone	1968	2.00	4.00	8.00
2628	The Chokin' Kind/Come On and Get It	1969	—	3.00	6.00
2634	Baby, Don't Be Looking in My Mind/Don't Let Me Lose the Feeling	1969	—	3.00	6.00
2637	Oon-Guela (Part 1)/Oon-Guela (Part 2)	1969	2.00	4.00	8.00
2641	It's Hard to Get Along/San Francisco Is a Lonely Town	1969	—	3.00	6.00
2651	Moon Walk Part 1/Moon Walk Part 2	1969	—	3.00	6.00
2656	Farther On Down the Road/Wounded Man	1970	—	3.00	6.00
2664	Yours Love/I Got a Whole Lotta Lovin'	1970	—	3.00	6.00
2667	That's the Way I Want Our Love/When	1970	—	3.00	6.00
SPRING					
108	Your Time to Cry/I Love You More (Than Anything)	1970	—	2.50	5.00
113	Help Me Make It Through the Night/To Lay Down Beside You	1971	—	2.50	5.00
113 [PS]	Help Me Make It Through the Night/To Lay Down Beside You	1971	—	3.00	6.00
115	You're the One for Me/I Ain't Givin' Up	1971	—	2.50	5.00
118	Georgia Blues/All My Hard Times	1971	—	2.50	5.00
120	Drowning in the Sea of Love/Let Me Be the One	1971	—	2.50	5.00
124	Pool of Bad Luck/Glad to Be Your Lover	1972	—	2.50	5.00
128	Power of Love/The Mirror Don't Lie	1972	—	2.50	5.00
130	Trouble in My Home/I Found My Dad	1972	—	2.50	5.00
133	Step by Step/Talk Don't Bother Me	1973	—	2.50	5.00
138	Theme from Cleopatra Jones/Who Is That Lady	1973	—	2.50	5.00
138 [PS]	Theme from Cleopatra Jones/Who Is That Lady	1973	—	3.00	6.00
141	River/Love Never Hurt Nobody	1973	—	2.50	5.00
145	Carry Me/Do You Know What It's Like to Be Lonesome	1974	—	2.50	5.00
149	The Best Time of My Life/What We Gonna Do Now	1974	—	2.50	5.00
156	Get Down, Get Down (Get On the Floor)/In My Baby's Arms	1975	—	2.50	5.00
159	Music in My Bones/Fire Burning	1975	—	2.50	5.00
163	I Need You, You Need Me/I'll Take Care (Of You)	1975	—	2.50	5.00
166	Come Get to This/Let the Good Times Roll	1976	—	2.50	5.00
169	Easy to Love/Can't Stand the Pain	1976	—	2.50	5.00
172	You Didn't Have to Play No Games/What's Left to Do	1977	—	2.50	5.00
176	One Step at a Time/Track of Your Love	1977	—	2.50	5.00
178	For Your Love, Love, Love/I've Got a Jones on You Baby	1977	—	2.50	5.00
184	I.O.U./It Must Be Love	1978	—	2.50	5.00
190	Love Vibration/(Instrumental)	1978	—	2.50	5.00
194	Going Through These Changes/I Can't Stand a Liar	1979	—	2.50	5.00
3003	I Wanna Taste Your Love/Make Every Moment Count	1979	—	2.50	5.00
3006	Hooked on Disco Music/I Still Love You	1980	—	2.50	5.00
VEE JAY					
609	My Adorable One/Say (That My Love Is True)	1964	2.00	4.00	8.00
663	When You're Near/When I'm Gone	1965	2.00	4.00	8.00
694	Let's Do It Over/The Whoo Pee	1965	2.00	4.00	8.00
Albums					
BUDDAH					
BDS-7512	Joe Simon	1969	6.25	12.50	25.00
COMPLEAT					
671015-1	Mr. Right	1985	3.00	6.00	12.00
POSSE					
10002	Glad You Came My Way	1981	3.00	6.00	12.00
10003	By Popular Demand	1982	3.00	6.00	12.00
SOUND STAGE 7					
5000 [(2)]	The World of Joe Simon	197?	3.00	6.00	12.00
—Reissue of 32536					
SSM-5003 [M]	Pure Soul	1967	7.50	15.00	30.00
SSS-15003 [S]	Pure Soul	1967	10.00	20.00	40.00
SSS-15004	No Sad Songs	1968	10.00	20.00	40.00
SSS-15005	Simon Sings	1968	10.00	20.00	40.00
SSS-15006	The Chokin' Kind	1969	7.50	15.00	30.00
SSS-15008	Joe Simon...Better Than Ever	1969	7.50	15.00	30.00
SSS-15009	The Best of Joe Simon	1972	3.75	7.50	15.00
KZ 31916	Greatest Hits	1972	3.00	6.00	12.00
ZG 32536 [(2)]	The World of Joe Simon	1974	3.75	7.50	15.00
ZG 33879 [(2)]	The Chokin' Kind/Joe Simon...Better Than Ever	1975	3.75	7.50	15.00
SPRING					
SPR-4701	The Sounds of Simon	1971	6.25	12.50	25.00
SPR-5702	Drowning in the Sea of Love	1972	6.25	12.50	25.00
SPR-5704	The Power of Joe Simon	1973	6.25	12.50	25.00
SPR-5705	Simon Country	1973	3.75	7.50	15.00
SPR-6702	Mood, Heart and Soul	1974	3.75	7.50	15.00
SPR-6706	Get Down	1975	3.75	7.50	15.00
SPR-6710	Today	1975	3.75	7.50	15.00
SPR-6713	Easy to Love	1976	3.75	7.50	15.00
SPR-6716	Bad Case of Love	1977	3.75	7.50	15.00
SPR-6720	Love Vibrations	1979	3.75	7.50	15.00

SIMON, PAUL

Includes records under various pseudonyms, such as "Paul Kane," "Jerry Landis" and "True Taylor." Also see SIMON AND GARFUNKEL; TICO AND THE TRIUMPHS; TOM AND JERRY (1).

12-Inch Singles

Number	Title (A Side/B Side)	Yr	VG	VG+	NM
WARNER BROS.					
PRO-A-889 [DJ]	Late in the Evening/How the Heart Approaches What It Yearns	1980	2.50	5.00	10.00
PRO-A-2100 [DJ]	Allergies (LP) (7" Version)	1983	2.00	4.00	8.00
PRO-A-2610 [DJ]	Graceland (LP Version) (Edit)	1986	—	3.00	6.00
PRO-A-2652 [DJ]	The Boy in the Bubble (LP Version) (Extended)	1987	—	3.00	6.00

Number	Title (A Side/B Side)	Yr	VG	VG+	NM
PRO-A-4480 [DJ]	The Obvious Child (The Single) (same on both sides)	1990	2.00	4.00	8.00
45s					
AMY					
875	The Lone Teen Ranger/Lisa	1962	15.00	30.00	60.00
—As "Jerry Landis"					
BIG					
614	True or False/Teenage Fool	1958	25.00	50.00	100.00
—As "True Taylor"					
CANADIAN AMERICAN					
130	I'm Lonely/I Wish I Weren't in Love	1961	25.00	50.00	100.00
—As "Jerry Landis"; the rarest of his pre-Columbia solo singles					
COLUMBIA					
10197	Gone at Last/Take Me to the Mardi Gras	1975	—	2.50	5.00
—A-side with Phoebe Snow and the Jesse Dixon Singers					
10270	50 Ways to Leave Your Lover/Some Folks Lives Roll Easy	1975	—	2.50	5.00
10332	Still Crazy After All These Years/I Do It for Your Love (Live)	1976	—	2.50	5.00
10630	Slip Slidin' Away/Something So Right	1977	—	3.00	6.00
—First pressings claim the A-side came from the LP "Blatant Greatest Hits." The Oak Ridge Boys are not mentioned.					
10630	Slip Slidin' Away/Something So Right	1977	—	2.50	5.00
—Later pressings correct the LP title to "Greatest Hits, Etc." The Oak Ridge Boys are credited in the fine print.					
10711	Stranded in a Limousine/Have a Good Time	1978	—	3.00	6.00
45547	Mother and Child Reunion/Paranoia Blues	1972	—	2.50	5.00
—Orange label					
45547	Mother and Child Reunion/Paranoia Blues	1972	—	2.00	4.00
—Gray label					
45585	Me and Julio Down by the Schoolyard/ Congratulations	1972	—	2.50	5.00
—Orange label					
45585	Me and Julio Down by the Schoolyard/ Congratulations	1972	—	2.00	4.00
—Gray label					
45638	Duncan/Run That Body Down	1972	—	2.50	5.00
45859	Kodachrome/Tenderness	1973	—	3.00	6.00
—With no trademark disclaimer on label					
45859	Kodachrome/Tenderness	1973	—	3.00	6.00
—With sticker on label: "Kodachrome is a registered trademark for color film."					
45859	Kodachrome/Tenderness	1973	—	2.50	5.00
—With printing on label: "Kodachrome is a registered trademark for color film."					
45900	American Tune/One Man's Ceiling Is Another Man's Floor	1973	—	2.50	5.00
45900 [PS]	American Tune/One Man's Ceiling Is Another Man's Floor	1973	2.50	5.00	10.00
45907	Loves Me Like a Rock/Learn How to Fall	1973	—	2.50	5.00
—With the Dixie Hummingbirds					
46038	The Sound of Silence/Mother and Child Reunion	1974	2.00	4.00	8.00
MGM					
12822	Anna Belle/Loneliness	1959	12.50	25.00	50.00
—As "Jerry Landis"					
TRIBUTE					
128	Carlos Dominguez/He Was My Brother	1963	15.00	30.00	60.00
—As "Paul Kane"; authentic copies make no mention of Paul Simon on the label					
WARNER BROS.					
19464	Proof/The Coast	1991	—	—	3.00
27903	Graceland/Hearts and Bones	1988	—	2.50	5.00
28221	Under African Skies/I Know What I Know	1987	—	—	3.00
—A-side with Linda Ronstadt					
28221 [PS]	Under African Skies/I Know What I Know	1987	—	—	3.00
28389	Diamonds on the Soles of Her Shoes/All Around the World Or the Myth of Fingerprints	1987	—	—	3.00
28389 [PS]	Diamonds on the Soles of Her Shoes/All Around the World Or the Myth of Fingerprints	1987	—	—	3.00
28460	The Boy in the Bubble/Crazy Love, Part 2	1987	—	—	3.00
28460 [PS]	The Boy in the Bubble/Crazy Love, Part 2	1987	—	—	3.00
28522	Graceland/Hearts and Bones	1986	—	—	3.00
28522 [PS]	Graceland/Hearts and Bones	1986	—	—	3.00
28667	You Can Call Me Al/Gumboots	1986	—	—	3.00
28667 [PS]	You Can Call Me Al/Gumboots	1986	—	—	3.00
29333	Think Too Much/Song About the Moon	1984	—	2.00	4.00
29453	Allergies/Think Too Much (ii)	1983	—	2.00	4.00
29453 [PS]	Allergies/Think Too Much (ii)	1983	—	2.00	4.00
49511	Late in the Evening/How the Heart Approaches What It Yearns	1980	—	2.00	4.00
49511 [PS]	Late in the Evening/How the Heart Approaches What It Yearns	1980	—	2.50	5.00
49601	One-Trick Pony/Long, Long Day	1980	—	2.00	4.00
49675	Oh, Marion/God Bless the Absentee	1981	—	2.00	4.00
WARWICK					
522	Swanee/Toot, Toot, Tootsie Goodbye	1960	12.50	25.00	50.00
—As "Jerry Landis"					
552	Shy/Just a Boy	1960	12.50	25.00	50.00
—As "Jerry Landis"					
588	I'd Like to Be/Just a Boy	1960	12.50	25.00	50.00
—As "Jerry Landis"					
619	Play Me a Sad Song/It Means a Lot to Them	1961	12.50	25.00	50.00
—As "Jerry Landis"					
Albums					
COLUMBIA					
CQ 30750 [Q]	Paul Simon	1974	5.00	10.00	20.00
KC 30750	Paul Simon	1972	2.50	5.00	10.00
CQ 32280 [Q]	There Goes Rhymin' Simon	1974	5.00	10.00	20.00
KC 32280	There Goes Rhymin' Simon	1973	2.50	5.00	10.00
PC 32280	There Goes Rhymin' Simon	1980	2.00	4.00	8.00
PC 32855	Paul Simon in Concert — Live Rhymin'	1974	2.50	5.00	10.00
PC 33540	Still Crazy After All These Years	1975	2.50	5.00	10.00
—Original release has no bar code on cover					
PC 33540	Still Crazy After All These Years	1980	2.00	4.00	8.00
—With bar code on cover					
PCQ 33540 [Q]	Still Crazy After All These Years	1975	5.00	10.00	20.00
JC 35032	Greatest Hits, Etc.	1977	2.50	5.00	10.00

Number	Title (A Side/B Side)	Yr	VG	VG+	NM
C5X 37581 [(5)]	Collected Works	1981	10.00	20.00	40.00
—Contains his first four post-S&G solo albums plus the elusive "Paul Simon Songbook," otherwise unavailable in U.S.					
HC 43540	Still Crazy After All These Years	1981	10.00	20.00	40.00
—Half-speed mastered edition					
HC 45032	Greatest Hits, Etc.	1981	10.00	20.00	40.00
—Half-speed mastered edition					
DCC COMPACT CLASSICS					
LPZ-2060	Paul Simon	1998	6.25	12.50	25.00
—Audiophile vinyl					
LPZ-2062	There Goes Rhymin' Simon	1998	6.25	12.50	25.00
—Audiophile vinyl					
WARNER BROS.					
WBMS-140 [(2) DJ]	The Paul Simon Interview Show	1986	12.50	25.00	50.00
—Promo-only "Graceland"-era program in the "Warner Bros. Music Show" series					
HS 3472	One-Trick Pony	1980	2.50	5.00	10.00
23942	Hearts and Bones	1983	2.50	5.00	10.00
23942 [DJ]	Hearts and Bones	1983	5.00	10.00	20.00
—Promo only on Quiex II vinyl					
25447	Graceland	1986	2.50	5.00	10.00
25588	Paul Simon	1988	3.00	6.00	12.00
25589	There Goes Rhymin' Simon	1988	3.00	6.00	12.00
25590	Paul Simon in Concert — Live Rhymin'	1988	3.00	6.00	12.00
25591	Still Crazy After All These Years	1988	3.00	6.00	12.00
25789 [(2)]	Negotiations and Love Songs	1988	3.75	7.50	15.00
26098	The Rhythm of the Saints	1990	3.75	7.50	15.00
46814	Songs from The Capeman	1997	3.75	7.50	15.00

SIMON AND GARFUNKEL

Also see ART GARFUNKEL; PAUL SIMON; TOM AND JERRY (1).

Number	Title (A Side/B Side)	Yr	VG	VG+	NM
45s					
ABC-PARAMOUNT					
10788	That's My Story/Tia-Juana Blues	1966	5.00	10.00	20.00
—Outtakes from Tom and Jerry days					
COLUMBIA					
AS 43 [DJ]	America/Keep the Customer Satisfied	1972	3.00	6.00	12.00
10230	My Little Town//Art Garfunkel: Rag Doll/Paul Simon: You're Kind	1975	—	2.50	5.00
10230 [PS]	My Little Town//Art Garfunkel: Rag Doll/Paul Simon: You're Kind	1975	—	2.50	5.00
43396	The Sounds of Silence/We've Got a Groovey Thing Goin'	1965	2.50	5.00	10.00
43396 [DJ]	The Sounds of Silence (same on both sides)	1965	12.50	25.00	50.00
—Red vinyl promo					
43511	Homeward Bound/Leaves That Are Green	1966	2.50	5.00	10.00
43511 [DJ]	Homeward Bound (same on both sides)	1966	12.50	25.00	50.00
—Red vinyl promo					
43617	I Am a Rock/Flowers Never Bend with the Rainfall	1966	2.50	5.00	10.00
43617 [DJ]	I Am a Rock (same on both sides)	1966	12.50	25.00	50.00
—Red vinyl promo					
43728	The Dangling Conversation/The Big Bright Green Pleasure Machine	1966	2.50	5.00	10.00
43728 [DJ]	The Dangling Conversation (same on both sides)	1966	12.50	25.00	50.00
—Red vinyl promo					
43728 [PS]	The Dangling Conversation/The Big Bright Green Pleasure Machine	1966	5.00	10.00	20.00
43873	A Hazy Shade of Winter/For Emily, Wherever I May Find Her	1966	2.50	5.00	10.00
44046	At the Zoo/The 59th Street Bridge Song (Feelin' Groovy)	1967	2.50	5.00	10.00
44046 [PS]	At the Zoo/The 59th Street Bridge Song (Feelin' Groovy)	1967	10.00	20.00	40.00
44232	Fakin' It/You Don't Know Where Your Interest Lies	1967	2.50	5.00	10.00
44465	Scarborough Fair (/Canticle)/April Come She Will	1968	2.50	5.00	10.00
44511	Mrs. Robinson/Old Friends-Bookends	1968	2.50	5.00	10.00
—Label says "From the Motion Picture 'The Graduate'"					
44511	Mrs. Robinson/Old Friends-Bookends	1968	2.00	4.00	8.00
—Label says "From the Columbia Lp BOOKENDS," etc. with no reference to "The Graduate"					
44785	The Boxer/Baby Driver	1969	—	3.00	6.00
—B-side mix (mono) is different than stereo LP version, especially near the end of the song					
44785 [PS]	The Boxer/Baby Driver	1969	2.00	4.00	8.00
45079	Bridge Over Troubled Water/Keep the Customer Satisfied	1970	—	3.00	6.00
45079 [PS]	Bridge Over Troubled Water/Keep the Customer Satisfied	1970	2.00	4.00	8.00
45133	Cecilia/The Only Living Boy in New York	1970	—	3.00	6.00
—Red label, "Columbia" in black at top					
45133	Cecilia/The Only Living Boy in New York	1970	2.50	5.00	10.00
—Red label, continuous "Columbia Records" in white along outer edge					
45133 [PS]	Cecilia/The Only Living Boy in New York	1970	2.00	4.00	8.00
45237	El Condor Pasa/Why Don't You Write Me	1970	—	3.00	6.00
45663	America/For Emily, Whenever I May Find Her	1972	—	3.00	6.00
JZSP 116469 [DJ]	7 O'Clock News-Silent Night (same on both sides)	1966	6.25	12.50	25.00
—Promo-only Christmas release for radio stations					
WARNER BROS.					
50053	Wake Up Little Susie/Me and Julio Down by the Schoolyard	1982	—	2.00	4.00
Albums					
CBS					
KCS 9914	Bridge Over Troubled Water	1970	3.75	7.50	15.00
—"360 Sound Stereo" on label; pressed in U.S. for export					
COLUMBIA					
CL 2249 [M]	Wednesday Morning, 3 A.M.	1964	6.25	12.50	25.00
—"Guaranteed High Fidelity" on label					
CL 2249 [M]	Wednesday Morning, 3 A.M.	1965	3.75	7.50	15.00
—"Mono" on label					
CL 2469 [M]	Sounds of Silence	1966	7.50	15.00	30.00
—With "Simon and Garfunkel" and "Sounds of Silence" in all capital letters on front cover with no list of songs					
CL 2469 [M]	Sounds of Silence	1966	5.00	10.00	20.00
—With "Simon and Garfunkel" and "Sounds of Silence" in large upper and lowercase letters on front cover with all song titles listed; "Tiger Beat" magazine is pictured twice on back cover					

Number	Title (A Side/B Side)	Yr	VG	VG+	NM
CL 2469 [M]	Sounds of Silence	1966	3.75	7.50	15.00
—With "Simon and Garfunkel" and "Sounds of Silence" in large upper and lowercase letters on front cover with all song titles listed; "Tiger Beat" magazines on back cover are airbrushed out					
CL 2563 [M]	Parsley, Sage, Rosemary and Thyme	1966	5.00	10.00	20.00
KCL 2729 [M]	Bookends	1968	12.50	25.00	50.00
—Red label, "Mono" at bottom -- this has been proven to exist					
CS 9049 [S]	Wednesday Morning, 3 A.M.	1964	6.25	12.50	25.00
—"360 Sound Stereo" in black on label					
CS 9049 [S]	Wednesday Morning, 3 A.M.	1965	3.75	7.50	15.00
—"360 Sound Stereo" in white on label					
CS 9049 [S]	Wednesday Morning, 3 A.M.	1970	2.50	5.00	10.00
—Orange label					
PC 9049 [S]	Wednesday Morning, 3 A.M.	197?	2.00	4.00	8.00
—Budget-line reissue					
CS 9269 [S]	Sounds of Silence	1966	7.50	15.00	30.00
—With "Simon and Garfunkel" and "Sounds of Silence" in all capital letters on front cover with no list of songs					
CS 9269 [S]	Sounds of Silence	1966	5.00	10.00	20.00
—With "Simon and Garfunkel" and "Sounds of Silence" in large upper and lowercase letters on front cover with all song titles listed; "Tiger Beat" magazine is pictured twice on back cover					
CS 9269 [S]	Sounds of Silence	1966	3.00	6.00	12.00
—With "Simon and Garfunkel" and "Sounds of Silence" in large upper and lowercase letters on front cover with all song titles listed; "Tiger Beat" magazines on back cover are airbrushed out					
CS 9269 [S]	Sounds of Silence	1970	2.50	5.00	10.00
—Orange label					
JC 9269	Sounds of Silence	197?	2.00	4.00	8.00
—Reissue with new prefix					
PC 9269 [S]	Sounds of Silence	198?	2.00	4.00	8.00
—Budget-line reissue					
CS 9363 [S]	Parsley, Sage, Rosemary and Thyme	1966	3.75	7.50	15.00
—"360 Sound Stereo" on label					
CS 9363 [S]	Parsley, Sage, Rosemary and Thyme	1970	2.50	5.00	10.00
—Orange label					
PC 9363 [S]	Parsley, Sage, Rosemary and Thyme	197?	2.00	4.00	8.00
—Budget-line reissue					
KCS 9529 [M]	Bookends	1968	7.50	15.00	30.00
—White label "Special Mono Radio Station Copy"					
KCS 9529 [S]	Bookends	1968	3.00	6.00	12.00
—"360 Sound Stereo" on label; add 25% for poster					
KCS 9529 [S]	Bookends	1970	2.50	5.00	10.00
—Orange label					
PC 9529 [S]	Bookends	197?	2.00	4.00	8.00
—Budget-line reissue					
JC 9914	Bridge Over Troubled Water	197?	2.00	4.00	8.00
—Reissue with new prefix					
KCS 9914	Bridge Over Troubled Water	1970	3.00	6.00	12.00
—"360 Sound Stereo" on label					
KCS 9914	Bridge Over Troubled Water	1970	2.50	5.00	10.00
—Orange label					
KCS 9914	Bridge Over Troubled Water	2000	6.25	12.50	25.00
—Classic Records reissue on audiophile vinyl					
PC 9914	Bridge Over Troubled Water	198?	2.00	4.00	8.00
—Budget-line reissue					
CQ 30995 [Q]	Bridge Over Troubled Water	1971	6.25	12.50	25.00
JC 31350	Simon and Garfunkel's Greatest Hits	197?	2.00	4.00	8.00
—Reissue with new prefix					
KC 31350	Simon and Garfunkel's Greatest Hits	1972	3.00	6.00	12.00
—Original covers are slightly oversized					
C5X 37587 [(5)]	Collected Works	1981	10.00	20.00	40.00
HC 41350	Simon and Garfunkel's Greatest Hits	1982	7.50	15.00	30.00
—Half-speed mastered edition					
HC 49914	Bridge Over Troubled Water	1982	7.50	15.00	30.00
—Half-speed mastered edition					
MOBILE FIDELITY					
1-173	Bridge Over Troubled Water	198?	10.00	20.00	40.00
—Audiophile vinyl					
PICKWICK					
PC-3059 [M]	The Hit Sounds of Simon and Garfunkel	1966	15.00	30.00	60.00
SPC-3059 [R]	The Hit Sounds of Simon and Garfunkel	1966	7.50	15.00	30.00
SEARS					
SPS-435	Simon and Garfunkel	196?	7.50	15.00	30.00
WARNER BROS.					
2BSK 3654 [(2)]	The Concert in Central Park	1982	3.00	6.00	12.00

SIMON SISTERS, THE

CARLY SIMON and her sister Lucy.

45s

Number	Title (A Side/B Side)	Yr	VG	VG+	NM
CHILDREN'S RECORDS OF AMERICA					
100	My Love Is Like a Red, Red Rose/The Lamb	1968	5.00	10.00	20.00
COLUMBIA					
02675	Maryanne/(B-side unknown)	1982	—	2.00	4.00
—As "Carly and Lucy Simon"					
45840	Red, Red Rose/Lobster Quadrille	1973	—	3.00	6.00
—As "Carly and Lucy Simon"					
KAPP					
586	Winkin', Blinkin' and Nod/So Glad I'm Here	1964	3.75	7.50	15.00
624	Cuddlebug/No One to Talk My Troubles To	1964	3.75	7.50	15.00

Albums

Number	Title (A Side/B Side)	Yr	VG	VG+	NM
COLUMBIA					
CR 21525	The Lobster Quadrille	1969	3.75	7.50	15.00
CR 21539	The Simon Sisters Sing for Children	1972	3.75	7.50	15.00
CC 24506	The Lobster Quadrille	1969	5.00	10.00	20.00
—Special edition with booklet					
KAPP					
KL-1359 [M]	Winkin', Blinkin' and Nod	1964	7.50	15.00	30.00
KL-1397 [M]	Cuddlebug	1964	10.00	20.00	40.00
KS-3359 [S]	Winkin', Blinkin' and Nod	1964	10.00	20.00	40.00
KS-3397 [S]	Cuddlebug	1964	12.50	25.00	50.00

SIMONE, NINA

45s

Number	Title (A Side/B Side)	Yr	VG	VG+	NM
BETHLEHEM					
3031	My Baby Just Cares for Me/He Needs Me	1962	2.00	4.00	8.00
3099	I Loves You Porgy/My Baby Just Cares for Me	1970	—	2.50	5.00
11021	I Loves You, Porgy/Love Me or Leave Me	1959	3.00	6.00	12.00
11052	Little Girl Blue/He Needs Me	1960	2.50	5.00	10.00
11055	Don't Smoke in Bed/African Mailman	1960	2.50	5.00	10.00
11057	Mood Indigo/Central Park Blues	1960	2.50	5.00	10.00
11087	For All We Know/Good Bait	1960	2.50	5.00	10.00
11088	You'll Never Walk Alone/Plain Gold Ring	1960	2.50	5.00	10.00
11089	He's Got the Whole World in His Hands/Central Park Blues	1960	2.50	5.00	10.00
COLPIX					
116	Solitaire/Chilly Winds	1959	2.50	5.00	10.00
124	Children Go Where I Send Thee/Willow Weep for Me	1959	2.50	5.00	10.00
135	It Might As Well Be Spring/The Other Woman	1959	2.50	5.00	10.00
143	Summertime/Fine and Mellow	1960	2.50	5.00	10.00
151	Since My Love Has Gone/Tomorrow (We Shall Meet Once More)	1960	2.50	5.00	10.00
156	If Only for Tonight/(B-side unknown)	1960	2.50	5.00	10.00
158	Nobody Knows You When You're Down and Out/Black Is the Color of My True Love's Hair	1960	2.50	5.00	10.00
175	Trouble in Mind/Cotton-Eyed Joe	1960	2.50	5.00	10.00
197	The Work Song/Memphis in June	1961	2.50	5.00	10.00
608	You Can Have Him/Gin House Blues	1961	2.50	5.00	10.00
614	Come On Back, Jack/You've Been Gone Too Long	1961	2.50	5.00	10.00
635	In the Evening by the Moonlight/Chilly Winds Don't Blow	1962	2.00	4.00	8.00
647	I Got It Bad/I Want a Little Sugar in My Bowl	1962	2.00	4.00	8.00
703	Blackbird/Little Liza Jane	1963	2.00	4.00	8.00
CTI					
44	Baltimore/The Family	1978	—	2.50	5.00
46	Forget/Baltimore	1978	—	2.50	5.00
49	The Family/That's All I Want from You	1978	—	2.50	5.00
PHILIPS					
40194	I Loves You Porgy/Old Jim Crow	1964	2.00	4.00	8.00
40216	Mississippi Goddam/Sea Lion Woman	1964	2.00	4.00	8.00
40232	Don't Let Me Be Misunderstood/A Monster	1964	2.00	4.00	8.00
40254	I Am Blessed/How Can I	1965	2.00	4.00	8.00
40286	I Put a Spell on You/Gimme Some	1965	2.00	4.00	8.00
40337	Either Way I Lose/Break Down and Let It All Out	1965	2.00	4.00	8.00
40359	Why Keep On Breaking My Heart/I Love Your Lovin' Ways	1966	—	3.00	6.00
40376	See-Line Woman/I Love Your Lovin' Ways	1966	—	3.00	6.00
40404	What More Can I Say/Four Women	1966	—	3.00	6.00
40418	Don't Pay Them No Mind/(B-side unknown)	1966	—	3.00	6.00
RCA VICTOR					
47-9120	Do I Move You/Day and Night	1967	—	3.00	6.00
47-9286	It Be's That Way Sometime/You'll Go to Hell	1967	—	3.00	6.00
47-9375	Cherish/I Wish I Knew How It Would Feel to Be Free	1967	—	3.00	6.00
47-9447	To Love Somebody/I Can't See Nobody	1968	—	3.00	6.00
47-9532	Why (Part 1)/Why (Part 2)	1968	—	3.00	6.00
47-9602	Do What You Gotta Do/Peace of Mind	1968	—	3.00	6.00
47-9686	Ain't Got No; I Got Life/Real, Real	1968	—	3.00	6.00
47-9730	Revolution (Part 1)/Revolution (Part 2)	1969	—	3.00	6.00
47-9749	Suzanne/Turn, Turn, Turn (To Everything There Is a Season)	1969	—	3.00	6.00
74-0269	To Be Young, Gifted and Black/Save Me	1969	—	3.00	6.00
74-0311	Who Knows Where the Time Goes/The Assignment Song	1970	—	3.00	6.00
74-0467	Here Comes the Sun/New World Coming	1971	—	—	—
—Canceled					
74-0471	New World Coming/O-o-h Child	1971	—	3.00	6.00
74-0514	Here Comes the Sun/Angel of the Morning	1971	—	3.00	6.00
74-0871	My Sweet Lord-Today Is a Killer/Poppies	1973	—	3.00	6.00

Albums

Number	Title (A Side/B Side)	Yr	VG	VG+	NM
ACCORD					
SN-7108	In Concert	1981	2.50	5.00	10.00
BETHLEHEM					
BCP-6003	Nina Simone's Finest	197?	3.00	6.00	12.00
BCP-6028 [M]	Jazz As Played in an Exclusive Side Street Club	1959	20.00	40.00	80.00
BCP-6028 [M]	The Original Nina Simone	1961	7.50	15.00	30.00
—Retitled reissue					
SBCP-6028 [S]	Jazz As Played in an Exclusive Side Street Club	1959	25.00	50.00	100.00
SBCP-6028 [S]	The Original Nina Simone	1961	10.00	20.00	40.00
—Retitled reissue					
BCP-6041 [M]	Nina Simone and Her Friends	1960	10.00	20.00	40.00
SBCP-6041 [S]	Nina Simone and Her Friends	1960	12.50	25.00	50.00
—With Carmen McRae and Chris Connor					
CANYON					
7705	Gifted and Black	1971	3.75	7.50	15.00
COLPIX					
CP-407 [M]	The Amazing Nina Simone	1959	6.25	12.50	25.00
SCP-407 [S]	The Amazing Nina Simone	1959	7.50	15.00	30.00
CP-409 [M]	Nina at Town Hall	1960	6.25	12.50	25.00
SCP-409 [S]	Nina at Town Hall	1960	7.50	15.00	30.00
CP-412 [M]	Nina at Newport	1960	6.25	12.50	25.00
SCP-412 [S]	Nina at Newport	1960	7.50	15.00	30.00
CP-419 [M]	Forbidden Fruit	1961	6.25	12.50	25.00
SCP-419 [S]	Forbidden Fruit	1961	7.50	15.00	30.00
CP-421 [M]	Nina Simone at the Village Gate	1961	6.25	12.50	25.00
SCP-421 [S]	Nina Simone at the Village Gate	1961	7.50	15.00	30.00
CP-425 [M]	Nina Sings Ellington	1962	6.25	12.50	25.00
SCP-425 [S]	Nina Sings Ellington	1962	7.50	15.00	30.00
CP-443 [M]	Nina's Choice	1963	6.25	12.50	25.00
SCP-443 [S]	Nina's Choice	1963	7.50	15.00	30.00
CP-455 [M]	Nina Simone at Carnegie Hall	1963	6.25	12.50	25.00
SCP-455 [S]	Nina Simone at Carnegie Hall	1963	7.50	15.00	30.00
CP-465 [M]	Folksy Nina	1964	6.25	12.50	25.00
SCP-465 [S]	Folksy Nina	1964	7.50	15.00	30.00
CP-496 [M]	Nina with Strings	1966	6.25	12.50	25.00
SCP-496 [S]	Nina with Strings	1966	7.50	15.00	30.00
CTI					
7084	Baltimore	1078	3.00	6.00	12.00

Number	Title (A Side/B Side)	Yr	VG	VG+	NM
PHILIPS					
PHM 200135 [M]	Nina Simone In Concert	1964	3.75	7.50	15.00
PHM 200148 [M]	Broadway...Blues...Ballads	1964	3.75	7.50	15.00
PHM 200172 [M]	I Put a Spell on You	1965	3.75	7.50	15.00
PHM 200187 [M]	Pastel Blues	1965	3.75	7.50	15.00
PHM 200202 [M]	Let It All Out	1966	3.75	7.50	15.00
PHM 200207 [M]	Wild Is the Wind	1966	3.75	7.50	15.00
PHM 200219 [M]	The High Priestess of Soul	1967	3.75	7.50	15.00
PHS 600135 [S]	Nina Simone In Concert	1964	5.00	10.00	20.00
PHS 600148 [S]	Broadway...Blues...Ballads	1964	5.00	10.00	20.00
PHS 600172 [S]	I Put a Spell on You	1965	5.00	10.00	20.00
PHS 600187 [S]	Pastel Blues	1965	5.00	10.00	20.00
PHS 600202 [S]	Let It All Out	1966	5.00	10.00	20.00
PHS 600207 [S]	Wild Is the Wind	1966	5.00	10.00	20.00
PHS 600219 [S]	The High Priestess of Soul	1967	5.00	10.00	20.00
PHS 600298	The Best of Nina Simone	1969	5.00	10.00	20.00
822846-1	The Best of Nina Simone	198?	2.50	5.00	10.00
PM					
018	A Very Rare Evening	1979	3.00	6.00	12.00
QUINTESSENCE					
25421	Silk and Soul	1979	2.50	5.00	10.00
RCA VICTOR					
AFL1-0241	It Is Finished — Nina 1974	1977	2.50	5.00	10.00
—Reissue with new prefix					
APL1-0241	It Is Finished — Nina 1974	1974	3.00	6.00	12.00
AFL1-1788	Poets	1977	2.50	5.00	10.00
—Reissue with new prefix					
APL1-1788	Poets	1976	3.00	6.00	12.00
LPM-3789 [M]	Nina Simone Sings the Blues	1967	6.25	12.50	25.00
LSP-3789 [S]	Nina Simone Sings the Blues	1967	3.75	7.50	15.00
LPM-3837 [M]	Silk and Soul	1967	6.25	12.50	25.00
LSP-3837 [S]	Silk and Soul	1967	3.75	7.50	15.00
LSP-4065	'Nuff Said	1968	3.75	7.50	15.00
LSP-4102	Nina Simone and Piano	1968	3.75	7.50	15.00
LSP-4152	To Love Somebody	1969	3.75	7.50	15.00
LSP-4248	Black Gold	1970	3.75	7.50	15.00
AFL1-4374	The Best of Nina Simone	1977	2.50	5.00	10.00
—Reissue with new prefix					
LSP-4374	The Best of Nina Simone	1970	3.75	7.50	15.00
AFL1-4536	Here Comes the Sun	1977	2.50	5.00	10.00
—Reissue with new prefix					
LSP-4536	Here Comes the Sun	1971	3.75	7.50	15.00
LSP-4757	Emergency Ward!	1972	3.75	7.50	15.00
SALSOUL					
SA-8546	Little Girl Blue	1982	2.50	5.00	10.00
TRIP					
8020 [(2)]	Live in Europe	1973	3.00	6.00	12.00
8021 [(2)]	Black Is the Color	1973	3.00	6.00	12.00
9521	Portrait	197?	2.50	5.00	10.00
VERVE					
831437-1	Let It Be Me	1987	2.50	5.00	10.00

SIMPSON, VALERIE

Also see ASHFORD AND SIMPSON.

45s

Number	Title (A Side/B Side)	Yr	VG	VG+	NM
TAMLA					
54204	Back to Nowhere/Can't It Wait Until Tomorrow	1971	—	2.50	5.00
54224	Silly Wasn't I/I Believe I'm Gonna Take This Ride	1972	—	2.50	5.00
54231	Genius/One More Baby Child Born	1973	—	2.50	5.00

Albums

Number	Title (A Side/B Side)	Yr	VG	VG+	NM
TAMLA					
T 311	Valerie Simpson Exposed	1971	3.75	7.50	15.00
T 317	Valerie Simpson	1972	3.75	7.50	15.00
T6-351	Keep It Comin'	1977	3.00	6.00	12.00

SIMS, FRANKIE LEE

45s

Number	Title (A Side/B Side)	Yr	VG	VG+	NM
ACE					
524	What Will Lucy Do/Misery Blues	1957	10.00	20.00	40.00
527	Hey Little Girl/Walking with Frankie	1957	10.00	20.00	40.00
539	I Warned You Baby/My Talk Didn't Do No Good	1957	10.00	20.00	40.00
SPECIALTY					
459	Lucky Man Blues/Don't Take It Out on Me	1953	12.50	25.00	50.00
478	I'm Long, Long Gone/Yeh Baby	1953	10.00	20.00	40.00
487	I'll Get Along Somehow/Rhumba My Boogie	1954	10.00	20.00	40.00
VIN					
1006	She Likes to Boogie Low/Well Goodbye Baby	1958	7.50	15.00	30.00

SIMS TWINS, THE

45s

Number	Title (A Side/B Side)	Yr	VG	VG+	NM
KENT					
4556	Bring It On Home Where You Belong/Under the Double Eagle	1971	—	3.00	6.00
PARKWAY					
6002	Together/Baby It's Real	1968	2.50	5.00	10.00
SAR					
117	Soothe Me/I'll Never Come Running Back to You	1961	3.75	7.50	15.00
125	The Smile/Right to Love	1962	3.00	6.00	12.00
130	Double Portion of Love/You're Pickin' in the Right Cotton Patch	1962	3.00	6.00	12.00
136	I Gopher You/Good Good Lovin'	1963	3.00	6.00	12.00
138	That's Where It's At/Movin' and a Groovin'	1963	3.00	6.00	12.00
SPECIALTY					
731	Make It On Up/Something Hanging on Your Mind	197?	—	3.00	6.00

SINATRA, FRANK

Also see TOMMY DORSEY.

12-Inch Singles

Number	Title (A Side/B Side)	Yr	VG	VG+	NM
QWEST					
PRO-A-2216 [DJ]	Mack the Knife (Remix 4:50) (same on both sides)	1984	3.00	6.00	12.00
REPRISE					
PRO-A-674 [DJ]	Night and Day/Everybody Ought to Be in Love	1977	20.00	40.00	80.00
PRO-A-865 [DJ]	Theme from New York, New York (same on both sides)	1980	12.50	25.00	50.00

45s

Number	Title (A Side/B Side)	Yr	VG	VG+	NM
CAPITOL					
X1-1491 [S]	When You're Smiling/It All Depends on You	1961	5.00	10.00	20.00
—Stereo jukebox single, 33 1/3 rpm, small hole					
X2-1594 [S]	Five Minutes More/Almost Like Being in Love	1961	5.00	10.00	20.00
—Stereo jukebox single, 33 1/3 rpm, small hole					
F1699	Young at Heart/I've Got the World on a String	1955	25.00	50.00	100.00
—Early reissue					
PRO 1707/8 [DJ]	Mistletoe and Holly (with spoken intro)/Mistletoe and Holly	1960	25.00	50.00	100.00
—Christmas Seals record for 1960, with Sinatra introducing the song					
F2450	I'm Walking Behind You/Lean Baby	1953	6.25	12.50	25.00
—Add 50% for intact center					
F2505	My One and Only Love/I've Got the World on a String	1953	5.00	10.00	20.00
—Add 50% for intact center					
F2560	Anytime, Anywhere/From Here to Eternity	1953	5.00	10.00	20.00
F2638	I Love You/South of the Border	1953	5.00	10.00	20.00
F2703	Young at Heart/Take a Chance	1953	5.00	10.00	20.00
F2787	Don't Worry 'Bout Me/I Could Have Told You	1954	5.00	10.00	20.00
F2816	Three Coins in the Fountain/Rain	1954	5.00	10.00	20.00
F2864	The Girl That Got Away/Half as Lovely	1954	5.00	10.00	20.00
F2922	It Worries Me/When I Stop Loving You	1954	5.00	10.00	20.00
2954	White Christmas/The Christmas Waltz	1962	2.50	5.00	10.00
—Reissue without the "F" prefix on orange and yellow swirl label					
F2954	White Christmas/The Christmas Waltz	1954	5.00	10.00	20.00
F2993	You My Love/Someone to Watch Over Me	1954	5.00	10.00	20.00
F3018	Melody of Love/I'm Gonna Live Till I Die	1954	5.00	10.00	20.00
F3050	Why Should I Cry Over You?/Don't Change Your Mind About Me	1954	5.00	10.00	20.00
F3084	Two Hearts, Two Kisses/From the Bottom to the Top	1955	3.75	7.50	15.00
F3102	Learnin' the Blues/If I Had Three Wishes	1955	3.75	7.50	15.00
F3130	Not as a Stranger/How Could You Do a Thing Like That to Me?	1955	3.75	7.50	15.00
F3218	Same Old Saturday Night/Fairy Tale	1955	3.75	7.50	15.00
F3260	Love and Marriage/The Impatient Years	1955	5.00	10.00	20.00
F3290	(Love Is) The Tender Trap/Weep They Will	1955	3.75	7.50	15.00
F3350	Flowers Mean Forgiveness/You'll Get Yours	1956	3.75	7.50	15.00
F3423	(How Little It Maters) How Little We Know/Five Hundred Guys	1956	3.75	7.50	15.00
F3469	You're Sensational/Johnny Concho Theme (Wait for Me)	1956	3.75	7.50	15.00
F3507	Well, Did You Evah?/True Love	1956	3.75	7.50	15.00
—A-side by Bing Crosby and Frank Sinatra; B-side by Bing Crosby and Grace Kelly					
F3508	Who Wants to Be a Millionaire/Mind If I Make Love to You?	1956	3.75	7.50	15.00
F3552	Jealous Lover/You Forgot All the Words	1956	6.25	12.50	25.00
—Original pressings contain this title					
F3552	Hey! Jealous Lover/You Forgot All the Words	1956	3.75	7.50	15.00
F3608	Can I Steal a Little Love/Your Love for Me	1956	3.75	7.50	15.00
F3703	Crazy Love/So Long, My Love	1957	3.00	6.00	12.00
F3744	You're Cheatin' Yourself (If You're Cheatin' On Me)/Something Wonderful Happens in Summer	1957	3.00	6.00	12.00
F3793	All the Way/Chicago	1957	3.00	6.00	12.00
F3859	Witchcraft/Tell Her You Love Her	1957	3.00	6.00	12.00
F3900	Mistletoe and Holly/The Christmas Waltz	1957	3.75	7.50	15.00
—"The Christmas Waltz" here is a different version than that on Capitol 2954.					
F3952	How Are Ya' Fixed for Love?/Nothin' in Common	1958	3.00	6.00	12.00
—By Frank Sinatra and Keely Smith					
F4003	Same Old Song and Dance/Monique (Song from Kings Go Forth)	1958	3.00	6.00	12.00
F4070	Mr. Success/Sleep Warm	1958	3.00	6.00	12.00
F4103	To Love and Be Loved/No One Ever Tells You	1958	3.00	6.00	12.00
F4103 [PS]	To Love and Be Loved/No One Ever Tells You	1958	25.00	50.00	100.00
—Promo-only sleeve					
F4155	French Foreign Legion/Time After Time	1959	3.00	6.00	12.00
F4214	High Hopes/All My Tomorrows	1959	3.75	7.50	15.00
F4214 [PS]	High Hopes/All My Tomorrows	1959	50.00	100.00	200.00
F4284	Talk to Me/They Came to Cordura	1959	3.00	6.00	12.00
4376	River, Stay 'Way from My Door/It's Over, It's Over, It's Over	1960	3.00	6.00	12.00
4408	Nice 'N' Easy/This Was My Love	1960	3.00	6.00	12.00
4466	Ol' MacDonald/You'll Always Be the One I Love	1960	3.00	6.00	12.00
4546	My Blue Heaven/Sentimental Baby	1960	3.00	6.00	12.00
4615	American Beauty Rose/Sentimental Journey	1961	3.00	6.00	12.00
4677	The Moon Was Yellow/I've Heard That Song Before	1962	3.00	6.00	12.00
4729	Five Minutes More/I'll Remember April	1962	3.00	6.00	12.00
4815	I Love Paris/Hidden Persuasion	1962	3.00	6.00	12.00
6019	Young at Heart/Learnin' the Blues	196?	—	3.00	6.00
—Starline reissue label					
6027	All the Way/High Hopes	196?	—	3.00	6.00
—Starline reissue label					
6078	Witchcraft/Chicago	1966	—	3.00	6.00
—Starline reissue label					
6193	One for My Baby/I've Got You Under My Skin	197?	—	3.00	6.00
6195	In the Wee Small Hours of the Morning/Night and Day	197?	—	3.00	6.00
S7-17704	I've Got You Under My Skin/Come Rain or Come Shine	1994	—	—	—
—A-side with Bono, B-side with Gloria Estefan; canceled					
S7-18204	Jingle Bells/I'll Be Home for Christmas	1994	—	2.50	5.00
—Red vinyl					
58741	Mistletoe and Holly/The Christmas Waltz	1998	—	—	3.00
COLUMBIA					
1-106	Sunflower/Once in Love with Amy	1948	15.00	30.00	60.00
—All records with a "1-" prefix are Microgroove 33 1/3 rpm 7-inch singles					
1-112	Why Can't You Behave/No Orchids for My Lady	1948	15.00	30.00	60.00
B-112 [(4)]	The Voice of Frank Sinatra	1950	37.50	75.00	150.00
—Includes records 36918, 36919, 36920 and 36921 plus box					
1-130	Comme Ci, Comme Ca/While the Angelus Was Ringing	1948	15.00	30.00	60.00

Number	Title (A Side/B Side)	Yr	VG	VG+	NM
1-144	When Is Sometime/If You Stub Your Toe on the Moon	1949	15.00	30.00	60.00
1-154	Where Is the One/Bop Goes My Heart	1949	15.00	30.00	60.00
B-167 [(4)]	Christmas Songs by Sinatra	1950	37.50	75.00	150.00
—Includes records 38256, 38257, 38258 and 38259 plus box					
1-174	Bali Ha'i/Some Enchanted Evening	1949	15.00	30.00	60.00
1-191	The Right Girl for Me/Night After Night	1949	15.00	30.00	60.00
B-197 [(4)]	Dedicated to You	1950	37.50	75.00	150.00
—Includes records 38683, 38684, 38685 and 38686 plus box					
B-218 [(4)]	Sing and Dance with Frank Sinatra	1950	37.50	75.00	150.00
—Includes records 38996, 38997, 38998 and 38999 plus box					
1-222	It Happens Every Spring/The Hucklebuck	1949	15.00	30.00	60.00
1-260	Let's Take an Old-Fashioned Walk/Just One Way to Say I Love You	1949	15.00	30.00	60.00
—With Doris Day					
1-307	I Only Have Eyes for You/It All Depends on You	1949	15.00	30.00	60.00
1-315	Don't Cry Joe/The Wedding of Lili Marlene	1949	15.00	30.00	60.00
1-316	Just a Kiss Apart/Bye Bye Baby	1949	15.00	30.00	60.00
1-326	If I Ever Love Again/Every Man Should Marry	1949	15.00	30.00	60.00
1-372	Could'ja/That Lucky Old Sun	1949	15.00	30.00	60.00
1-380	On the Island of Stromboli/Mad About You	1949	15.00	30.00	60.00
1-427	The Old Master Painter/Lost in the Stars	1949	15.00	30.00	60.00
1-440	Sorry/Why Remind Me	1949	15.00	30.00	60.00
1-491	Sunshine Cake/We've Got a Sure Thing	1949	15.00	30.00	60.00
1-496	Chattanoogie Shoe Shine Boy/God's Country	1950	15.00	30.00	60.00
1-508	You'll Never Walk Alone/Begin the Beguine	1950	15.00	30.00	60.00
1-511	Among My Souvenirs/September Song	1950	15.00	30.00	60.00
1-611	Kisses and Tears/When the Sun Goes Down	1950	15.00	30.00	60.00
1-624	American Beauty Rose/Just An Old Stone House	1950	15.00	30.00	60.00
1-650	Poinciana/There's No Business Like Show Business	1950	15.00	30.00	60.00
1-669	Peachtree Street/This Is the Night	1950	15.00	30.00	60.00
1-718	Goodnight Irene/My Blue Heaven	1950	15.00	30.00	60.00
6-718	Goodnight Irene/My Blue Heaven	1950	7.50	15.00	30.00
1-780	Life Is So Peculiar/Dear Little Boy of Mine	1950	15.00	30.00	60.00
1-845	One Finger Melody/Accidents Will Happen	1950	15.00	30.00	60.00
1-888	Nevertheless/I Guess I'll Have to Dream the Rest	1950	15.00	30.00	60.00
6-888	Nevertheless/I Guess I'll Have to Dream the Rest	1950	7.50	15.00	30.00
1-924	Remember Me in Your Dreams/Let It Snow, Let It Snow, Let It Snow	1950	15.00	30.00	60.00
6-924	Remember Me in Your Dreams/Let It Snow, Let It Snow, Let It Snow	1950	7.50	15.00	30.00
1-936	I Am Loved/You Don't Remind Me	1950	15.00	30.00	60.00
6-936	I Am Loved/You Don't Remind Me	1950	7.50	15.00	30.00
13-33011	Nancy/Ol' Man River	1975	—	3.00	6.00
—Hall of Fame series; new prefix					
3-33011	Nancy/Ol' Man River	1961	12.50	25.00	50.00
—Hall of Fame series; Compact Single 33					
4-33011	Nancy/Ol' Man River	1960	2.50	5.00	10.00
33306	I've Got a Crush on You/The Birth of the Blues	1977	—	3.00	6.00
—Hall of Fame series					
33319	Among My Souvenirs/September Song	1977	—	3.00	6.00
—Hall of Fame series					
36814	If You Are But a Dream/Put Your Dreams Away	1950	5.00	10.00	20.00
—Most Columbia 45s from 36000-39000 are reissues of titles that first appeared on 78s					
36825	You'll Never Walk Alone/If I Loved You	1950	5.00	10.00	20.00
36918	You Go to My Head/I Don't Know Why	1950	5.00	10.00	20.00
36919	These Foolish Things/A Ghost of a Chance	1950	5.00	10.00	20.00
36920	Why Shouldn't I?/Try a Little Tenderness	1950	5.00	10.00	20.00
36921	Paradise/Someone to Watch Over Me	1950	5.00	10.00	20.00
—The above four comprise the box set The Voice of Frank Sinatra, B-112					
37161	Among My Souvenirs/September Song	1950	5.00	10.00	20.00
37257	That Old Black Magic/How Deep Is the Ocean?	1950	5.00	10.00	20.00
37259	She's Funny That Way/Embraceable You	1950	5.00	10.00	20.00
38151	I've Got a Crush on You/Ever Homeward	1950	5.00	10.00	20.00
38163	All of Me/I Went Down to Virginia	1950	5.00	10.00	20.00
38256	Silent Night/Adeste Fideles	1950	5.00	10.00	20.00
38257	Jingle Bells/White Christmas	1950	5.00	10.00	20.00
38258	O Little Town of Bethlehem/It Came Upon a Midnight Clear	1950	5.00	10.00	20.00
38259	Have Yourself a Merry Little Christmas/Santa Claus Is Comin' to Town	1950	5.00	10.00	20.00
—The above four comprise the box set Christmas Songs by Sinatra, B-167					
38446	Bali Ha'i/Some Enchanted Evening	1950	5.00	10.00	20.00
38683	The Moon Was Yellow/The Music Stopped	1950	5.00	10.00	20.00
38684	Strange Music/I Love You	1950	5.00	10.00	20.00
38685	Where or When/None But the Lonely Heart	1950	5.00	10.00	20.00
38686	Always/Why Was I Born?	1950	5.00	10.00	20.00
—The above four comprise the box set Dedicated to You, B-197					
38829	Poinciana/There's No Business Like Show Business	1950	5.00	10.00	20.00
38892	Goodnight Irene/My Blue Heaven	1950	3.75	7.50	15.00
—Reissue of Columbia 6-718					
38996	Lover/When You're Smiling	1950	5.00	10.00	20.00
38997	The Continental/It's Only a Paper Moon	1950	5.00	10.00	20.00
38998	Should I?/My Blue Heaven	1950	5.00	10.00	20.00
38999	It All Depends on You/You Do Something to Me	1950	5.00	10.00	20.00
—The above four comprise the box set Sing and Dance with Frank Sinatra, B-218					
39044	Nevertheless/I Guess I'll Have to Dream the Rest	1950	3.75	7.50	15.00
—Reissue of Columbia 6-888					
39069	Remember Me in Your Dreams/Let It Snow, Let It Snow, Let It Snow	1950	3.75	7.50	15.00
—Reissue of Columbia 6-924					
39079	I Am Loved/You Don't Remind Me	1950	3.75	7.50	15.00
—Reissue of Columbia 6-936					
39118	Take My Love/Come Back to Sorrento	1950	3.75	7.50	15.00
3-39118	Take My Love/Come Back to Sorrento	1950	50.00	100.00	150.00
—Microgroove 33 1/3 rpm, 7-inch single					
39141	Love Means Love/Cherry Pies Ought to Be You	1951	6.25	12.50	25.00
3-39141	Love Means Love/Cherry Pies Ought to Be You	1951	200.00	400.00	600.00
—Microgroove 33 1/3 rpm, 7-inch single					
39213	Faithful/You're the One	1951	5.00	10.00	20.00
3-39213	Faithful/You're the One	1951	50.00	100.00	150.00
—Microgroove 33 1/3 rpm, 7-inch single					
39294	Hello, Young Lovers/We Kissed in a Shadow	1951	3.75	7.50	15.00
39346	I Whistle a Happy Tune/Love Me	1951	3.75	7.50	15.00

Number	Title (A Side/B Side)	Yr	VG	VG+	NM
39425	Mama Will Bark/I'm a Fool to Want You	1951	10.00	20.00	40.00
—"Frank Sinatra & Dagmar"; the record Ol' Blue Eyes called his worst					
39493	I Fall in Love with You Everyday/It's a Long Way from Your House	1951	5.00	10.00	20.00
39498	It Never Entered My Mind/Try a Little Tenderness	1951	3.75	7.50	15.00
39527	Castle Rock/Deep Night	1951	5.00	10.00	20.00
39592	April in Paris/London by Night	1951	3.75	7.50	15.00
39652	I Hear a Rhapsody/I Could Write a Book	1952	3.75	7.50	15.00
39687	Feet of Clay/Don't Ever Be Afraid to Go Home	1952	5.00	10.00	20.00
39726	My Girl/Walkin' in the Sunshine	1952	5.00	10.00	20.00
39787	Luna Rosa/Tennessee Newsboy	1952	5.00	10.00	20.00
39819	Azure-Te/Bim Bam Baby	1952	3.75	7.50	15.00
39882	The Birth of the Blues/Why Try to Change Me Now?	1952	3.75	7.50	15.00
40229	I'm Glad There Is You/You Can Take My Word For It Baby	1954	5.00	10.00	20.00
40522	Dream/American Beauty Rose	1955	3.75	7.50	15.00
40565	Sheila/Day by Day	1955	7.50	15.00	30.00
41133	I'm a Fool to Want You/If I Forget You	1958	3.75	7.50	15.00
50003	Among My Souvenirs/September Song	1954	2.50	5.00	10.00
—Hall of Fame series					
50028	I've Got a Crush on You/The Birth of the Blues	1954	2.50	5.00	10.00
—Hall of Fame series					
50053	Nancy/The Girl That I Marry	1955	2.50	5.00	10.00
—Hall of Fame series					
50066	You'll Never Walk Alone/If I Loved You	1955	2.50	5.00	10.00
—Hall of Fame series					
50069	Saturday Night/Five Minutes More	1955	2.50	5.00	10.00
—Hall of Fame series					
50079	Silent Night/Adeste Fideles	1955	2.50	5.00	10.00
—Hall of Fame series					
JZSP 116427/8 [DJ]	White Christmas/Have Yourself A Merry Little Christmas	1966	12.50	25.00	50.00
ISLAND/CAPITOL					
858076-7	I've Got You Under My Skin/Stay (Faraway, So Close!)	1994	—	2.00	4.00
—A-side: Frank Sinatra and Bono; B-side: U2					
858076-7 [PS]	I've Got You Under My Skin/Stay (Faraway, So Close!)	1994	—	2.00	4.00
—A-side: Frank Sinatra and Bono; B-side: U2					
MCA					
55127	Fly Me to the Moon/Check Yes or No	1995	—	2.00	4.00
—A-side with George Strait; B-side is George Strait solo					
QWEST					
28844	The Best of Everything/Teach Me Tonight	1985	—	2.00	4.00
29139	Mack the Knife/It's All Right with Me	1984	—	2.50	5.00
29223	L.A. Is My Lady/Until the Real Thing Comes Along	1984	—	2.50	5.00
29223 [PS]	L.A. Is My Lady/Until the Real Thing Comes Along	1984	3.75	7.50	15.00
RCA VICTOR					
DTAO-3001	Street of Dreams/Whispering	1973	3.00	6.00	12.00
DTBO-3012	The One I Love/This Love of Mine	1973	3.00	6.00	12.00
27-0012	Night and Day/The Lamplighter's Serenade	1948	3.75	7.50	15.00
—All RCA and 45s are reissues of material first issued on 78s. Part of WPT-5					
27-0076	Stardust/(B-side unknown)	1949	3.75	7.50	15.00
—From WDT 15					
27-0077	I'll Never Smile Again/(B-side unknown)	1949	3.75	7.50	15.00
—From WDT 15					
27-0095	Somewhere A Voice Is Calling/(B-side unknown)	1949	3.75	7.50	15.00
—From WDT 20					
27-0151	Daybreak/There Are Such Things	1948	3.75	7.50	15.00
447-0116	I'll Never Smile Again/I'll Be Seeing You	1950	3.00	6.00	12.00
447-0123	Stardust/There Are Such Things	1950	3.00	6.00	12.00
447-0408	Night and Day/The Lamplighter's Serenade	1952	3.00	6.00	12.00
447-0445	Street of Dreams/East of the Sun	1952	3.00	6.00	12.00
447-0928	Night and Day/The Night We Called It a Day	1972	—	3.00	6.00
447-0929	The Song Is You/The Lamplighter's Serenade	1972	—	3.00	6.00
REPRISE					
0053	I'll Be Seeing You/Without a Song	1962	50.00	100.00	200.00
—Released in Great Britain as 20,053; pressed in the United States later					
GRE 0113	Bad, Bad Leroy Brown/Let Me Try Again	1975	5.00	10.00	20.00
—"Back to Back Hits" series					
GRE 0122	Theme from New York, New York/You and Me (We Wanted It All)	1981	—	2.00	4.00
—"Back to Back Hits" series					
S 168 [S]	Moon River/Days of Wine and Roses	1964	5.00	10.00	20.00
S 169 [S]	Three Coins in the Fountain/The Way You Look Tonight	1964	5.00	10.00	20.00
S 170 [S]	Secret Love/In the Cool, Cool, Cool of the Evening	1964	5.00	10.00	20.00
S 171 [S]	It Might As Well Be Spring/Swinging on a Star	1964	5.00	10.00	20.00
S 172 [S]	All the Way/The Continental	1964	5.00	10.00	20.00
—The above five are 33 1/3 rpm, small hole jukebox singles					
243	Have Yourself a Merry Little Christmas/How Shall I Send Thee?	1963	5.00	10.00	20.00
—B-side by Les Baxter					
0249	Stay with Me/Talk to Me Baby	1963	2.50	5.00	10.00
0279	My Kind of Town/I Like to Lead When I Dance	1964	2.50	5.00	10.00
0279 [PS]	My Kind of Town/I Like to Lead When I Dance	1964	37.50	75.00	150.00
—Sleeve issued with promo copies only					
0301	Softly, As I Leave You/Then Suddenly Love	1964	2.50	5.00	10.00
0314	I Heard the Bells on Christmas Day/The Little Drummer Boy	1964	5.00	10.00	20.00
0314 [PS]	I Heard the Bells on Christmas Day/The Little Drummer Boy	1964	12.50	25.00	50.00
0317	We Wish You the Merriest/Go Tell It on the Mountain	1964	10.00	20.00	40.00
—By Frank Sinatra/Bing Crosby/Fred Waring					
0317 [PS]	We Wish You the Merriest/Go Tell It on the Mountain	1964	15.00	30.00	60.00
—By Frank Sinatra/Bing Crosby/Fred Waring					
0332	Somewhere in Your Heart/Emily	1964	2.00	4.00	8.00
—From here through 0677, originals on dark brown & orange label					
0350	Anytime at All/Available	1964	2.00	4.00	8.00
0373	Tell Her (You Love Her Each Day)/Here's to the Losers	1965	2.00	4.00	8.00

Number	Title (A Side/B Side)	Yr	VG	VG+	NM
0380	Forget Domani/I Can't Believe I'm Losing You	1965	2.00	4.00	8.00
0398	When Somebody Loves You/When I'm Not Near the Girl I Love	1965	2.00	4.00	8.00
0410	Everybody Has the Right to Be Wrong/I'll Only Miss Her When I Think of Her	1965	2.00	4.00	8.00
0429	It Was a Very Good Year/Moment to Moment	1965	2.00	4.00	8.00
0429 [PS]	It Was a Very Good Year/Moment to Moment	1965	6.25	12.50	25.00
0470	Strangers in the Night/Oh, You Crazy Moon	1966	2.50	5.00	10.00
0493	Frank Sinatra Reads from Gunga Din	1966	125.00	250.00	500.00
—300 pressed and given away to friends; no stock copies					
0509	Summer Wind/You Make Me Feel So Young	1966	2.50	5.00	10.00
0531	That's Life/The September of My Years	1966	2.50	5.00	10.00
0531 [PS]	That's Life/The September of My Years	1966	6.25	12.50	25.00
0561	Somethin' Stupid/Give Her Love	1967	2.50	5.00	10.00
—A-side: Nancy Sinatra and Frank Sinatra					
0561	Somethin' Stupid/I Will Wait for You	1967	2.00	4.00	8.00
—A-side: Nancy Sinatra and Frank Sinatra					
0610	The World We Knew (Over and Over)/You Are There	1967	2.00	4.00	8.00
0631	This Town/This Is My Love	1967	2.00	4.00	8.00
0677	I Can't Believe I'm Losing You/How Old Am I?	1967	2.00	4.00	8.00
0702	My Kind of Town/That's Life	1968	—	2.50	5.00
—"Back to Back Hits" series					
0706	September of My Years/Softly, As I Leave You	1968	—	2.50	5.00
—"Back to Back Hits" series					
0710	Strangers in the Night/Summer Wind	1968	—	2.50	5.00
—"Back to Back Hits" series					
0713	It Was a Very Good Year/Stay with Me	1968	—	2.50	5.00
—"Back to Back Hits" series					
0727	Somethin' Stupid/The World We Knew (Over and Over)	1968	—	2.50	5.00
—"Back to Back Hits" series; A-side with Nancy Sinatra					
0734	My Way/Cycles	1970	—	2.50	5.00
—"Back to Back Hits" series					
0764	Cycles/My Way of Life	1968	—	3.00	6.00
—From here though 0865, orange/tan label with "W7/:r" logo					
0790	Whatever Happened to Christmas?/I Wouldn't Trade Christmas	1968	3.00	6.00	12.00
—B-side by The Sinatra Family					
0798	Rain in My Heart/Star	1968	—	3.00	6.00
0817	My Way/Blue Lace	1969	2.50	5.00	10.00
0852	Love's Been Good to Me/A Man Alone	1969	2.00	4.00	8.00
0865	Goin' Out of My Head/Forget to Remember	1969	2.00	4.00	8.00
0895	I Would Be in Love (Anyway)/Watertown	1970	2.00	4.00	8.00
—From here through 29903, orange (or tan) label with ":r" logo in square					
0920	The Train/What's Now Is Now	1969	2.00	4.00	8.00
0970	Lady Day/Song of the Sabia	1969	2.00	4.00	8.00
0980	Feelin' Kinda Sunday/Kids	1970	2.00	4.00	8.00
—A-side by Nancy Sinatra and Frank Sinatra; B-side by Nancy Sinatra					
0981	Something/Bein' Green	1970	2.00	4.00	8.00
PRO-S-1007	To Love a Child (mono/stereo)	1982	75.00	150.00	300.00
—Special pressing of 500 with small hole, given to Nancy Reagan for distributuion at a White House function.					
1010	Witchcraft/Young at Heart	1971	2.00	4.00	8.00
1011	Life's a Trippy Thing/I'm Not Afraid	1971	2.00	4.00	8.00
—A-side by Nancy Sinatra and Frank Sinatra					
1181	Let Me Try Again/Send In the Clowns	1973	2.00	4.00	8.00
1190	You Will Be My Music/Winners	1973	2.00	4.00	8.00
1196	Bad, Bad Leroy Brown/I'm Gonna Make It All the Way	1974	2.00	4.00	8.00
1208	You Turned My World Around/Satisfy Me One More Time	1974	2.00	4.00	8.00
1327	Anytime (I'll Be There)/The Hurt Doesn't Go Away	1975	2.00	4.00	8.00
1335	I Believe I'm Gonna Love You/The Only Couple on the Floor	1975	2.00	4.00	8.00
1335 [PS]	I Believe I'm Gonna Love You	1975	10.00	20.00	40.00
—Issued with promo copies only					
1342	A Baby Just Like You/Christmas Mem'ries	1975	2.50	5.00	10.00
1342 [PS]	A Baby Just Like You/Christmas Mem'ries	1975	10.00	20.00	40.00
—Blue printing, released with promo copies only					
1342 [PS]	A Baby Just Like You/Christmas Mem'ries	1975	5.00	10.00	20.00
—Red and black printing, released with stock copies					
1343	Empty Tables/The Saddest Thing of All	1976	2.00	4.00	8.00
1347	I Sing the Songs (I Write the Songs)/Empty Tables	1976	2.50	5.00	10.00
1364	Stargazer/The Best I Ever Had	1976	2.00	4.00	8.00
1364 [PS]	Stargazer/The Best I Ever Had	1976	3.75	7.50	15.00
—Special sleeve: "New Sinatra Single"					
1377	Dry Your Eyes/Like a Sad Song	1976	2.00	4.00	8.00
1382	I Love My Wife/Send In the Clowns	1976	2.50	5.00	10.00
1386	Night and Day/Everybody Ought to Be in Love	1977	2.00	4.00	8.00
15999	My Way/Cycles	199?	—	—	3.00
—"Back to Back Hits" series					
19355	Fly Me to the Moon/The Last Dance	1991	—	2.00	4.00
20001	The Second Time Around/Tina	1961	6.25	12.50	25.00
—Originals on light blue label					
20010	Granada/The Curse of an Aching Heart	1961	3.75	7.50	15.00
—From here through 0317, originals on peach label					
20010 [PS]	Granada/The Curse of an Aching Heart	1961	6.25	12.50	25.00
20023	I'll Be Seeing You/The One I Love	1961	3.75	7.50	15.00
20024	Imagination/It's Always You	1961	3.75	7.50	15.00
20025	I'm Getting Sentimental Over You/East of the Sun (And West of the Moon)	1961	3.75	7.50	15.00
20026	There Are Such Things/Polkadots and Moonbeams	1961	3.75	7.50	15.00
20027	Without a Song/It Started All Over Again	1961	3.75	7.50	15.00
20028	Take Me/Daybreak	1961	3.75	7.50	15.00
20040	Pocketful of Miracles/Name It and It's Yours	1961	3.75	7.50	15.00
20040 [PS]	Pocketful of Miracles/Name It and It's Yours	1961	15.00	30.00	60.00
20059	Stardust/Come Rain or Come Shine	1962	3.75	7.50	15.00
20063	Everybody's Twistin'/Nothin' But the Best	1962	3.75	7.50	15.00
20063 [PS]	Everybody's Twistin'/Nothin' But the Best	1962	7.50	15.00	30.00
20092	Goody, Goody/Love Is Just Around the Corner	1962	3.00	6.00	12.00
20107	The Look of Love/I Left My Heart in San Francisco	1962	12.50	25.00	50.00
20107	The Look of Love/Indiscreet	1962	12.50	25.00	50.00

Number	Title (A Side/B Side)	Yr	VG	VG+	NM
20128	Me and My Shadow/Sam's Song	1962	3.75	7.50	15.00
—A-side by Frank Sinatra and Sammy Davis, Jr.; B-side by Sammy Davis Jr. and Dean Martin					
20128 [PS]	Me and My Shadow/Sam's Song	1962	12.50	25.00	50.00
—A-side by Frank Sinatra and Sammy Davis, Jr.; B-side by Sammy Davis Jr. and Dean Martin					
20151	Call Me Irresponsible/Tina	1963	2.50	5.00	10.00
—B-side changed for commercial release					
20151	Call Me Irresponsible/Come Blow Your Horn	1963	125.00	250.00	500.00
—One stock copy is known to exist!					
20151 [DJ]	Call Me Irresponsible/Come Blow Your Horn	1963	25.00	50.00	100.00
20151 [PS]	Call Me Irresponsible/Come Blow Your Horn	1963	50.00	100.00	200.00
—Sleeve accompanies promo copies only					
20157 [DJ]	California/America the Beautiful	1963	62.50	125.00	250.00
—No stock copies isssued					
20157 [DJ]	California/America the Beautiful	1978	50.00	100.00	200.00
—Private pressing of 1,000 for Sinatra's personal use					
20157 [PS]	California/America the Beautiful	1963	187.50	375.00	750.00
—No stock copies isssued					
20184	I Have Dreamed/Come Blow Your Horn	1963	2.50	5.00	10.00
20209	Love Isn't Just for the Young/You Brought a New Kind of Love to Me	1963	3.00	6.00	12.00
20209 [PS]	Love Isn't Just for the Young/You Brought a New Kind of Love to Me	1963	12.50	25.00	50.00
20217	Fugue for Tinhorns/The Oldest Established (Permanent Floating Crap Game in New York)	1963	3.75	7.50	15.00
—By Frank Sinatra/Bing Crosby/Dean Martin					
20217 [PS]	Fugue for Tinhorns/The Oldest Established (Permanent Floating Crap Game in New York)	1963	18.75	37.50	75.00
—By Frank Sinatra/Bing Crosby/Dean Martin					
20235	Tangerine/A New Kind of Love	1963	—	—	—
—Unreleased					
29677	Here's to the Band/It's Sunday	1983	2.00	4.00	8.00
29903	To Love a Child/That's What God Looks Like to Me	1982	2.00	4.00	8.00
29903 [PS]	To Love a Child/That's What God Looks Like to Me	1982	3.75	7.50	15.00
49233	Theme from New York, New York/That's What God Looks Like to Me	1980	2.50	5.00	10.00
49233 [PS]	Theme from New York, New York/That's What God Looks Like to Me	1980	3.75	7.50	15.00
49517	You and Me (We Wanted It All)/I've Been There	1980	2.00	4.00	8.00
49827	Say Hello/Good Thing Going	1981	2.00	4.00	8.00
—B-side listed on label as "RE-1"					
49827	Say Hello/Good Thing Going	1981	2.00	4.00	8.00
—B-side listed on label as "RE-2"					
(NO LABEL)					
KB-2077/8	High Hopes with Jack Kennedy/Jack Kennedy All the Way	1960	75.00	150.00	300.00
—No artist or label shown, but Sinatra does sing the A-side					

7-Inch Extended Plays

CAPITOL

Number	Title (A Side/B Side)	Yr	VG	VG+	NM
EAP 488 [PS]	Songs for Young Lovers	1954	12.50	25.00	50.00
—Both of above EPs in gatefold sleeve					
EAP 1-488	My Funny Valentine/The Girl Next Door//They Can't Take That Away from Me/Violets for Your Furs	1954	5.00	10.00	20.00
EAP 1-488 [PS]	Songs for Young Lovers, Vol. 1	1954	5.00	10.00	20.00
EAP 2-488	A Foggy Day/Like Someone I Love//I Get a Kick Out of You/Little Girl Blue	1954	5.00	10.00	20.00
EAP 2-488 [PS]	Songs for Young Lovers, Vol. 2	1954	5.00	10.00	20.00
EAP 1-510	(contents unknown)	1954	6.25	12.50	25.00
EAP 1-510 [PS]	Young at Heart	1954	6.25	12.50	25.00
EAP 1-528	(contents unknown)	1954	5.00	10.00	20.00
EAP 1-528 [PS]	Swing Easy, Part I	1954	5.00	10.00	20.00
EAP 2-528	(contents unknown)	1954	5.00	10.00	20.00
EAP 2-528 [PS]	Swing Easy, Part II	1954	5.00	10.00	20.00
EBF 528 [PS]	Swing Easy	1954	12.50	25.00	50.00
—Both 1-528 and 2-528 EPs in gatefold sleeve					
EAP 1-542	Three Coins in the Fountain/My One and Only Love//Don't Worry 'Bout Me/I Love You	1954	6.25	12.50	25.00
EAP 1-542 [PS]	Three Coins in the Fountain	1954	6.25	12.50	25.00
EAP 1-571	(contents unknown)	1954	6.25	12.50	25.00
EAP 1-571 [PS]	Frank Sinatra Sings Young at Heart	1954	6.25	12.50	25.00
EAP 1-581	In the Wee Small Hours of the Morning/I See Your Face Before Me//I'll Never Be the Same/This Love of Mine	1954	5.00	10.00	20.00
EAP 1-581 [PS]	In the Wee Small Hours, Part 1	1955	5.00	10.00	20.00
EAP 2-581	I'll Be Around/I Get Along Without You Very Well //It Never Entered My Mind/Dancing on the Ceiling	1955	5.00	10.00	20.00
EAP 2-581 [PS]	In the Wee Small Hours, Part 2	1955	5.00	10.00	20.00
EAP 3-581	Deep in a Dream/Mood Indigo//Glad to Be Unhappy/Ill Wind	1955	5.00	10.00	20.00
EAP 3-581 [PS]	In the Wee Small Hours, Part 3	1955	5.00	10.00	20.00
EAP 4-581	Can't We Be Friends/When Your Lover Has Gone//What Is This Thing Called Love/Last Night When We Were Young	1955	5.00	10.00	20.00
EAP 4-581 [PS]	In the Wee Small Hours, Part 4	1955	5.00	10.00	20.00
EBF 1-581 [PS]	In the Wee Small Hours, Parts 1 and 2	1955	12.50	25.00	50.00
—Gatefold sleeve for some editions of EAP 1-581 and 2-581					
EBF 2-581 [PS]	In the Wee Small Hours, Parts 3 and 4	1955	12.50	25.00	50.00
—Gatefold sleeve for some editions of EAP 3-581 and 4-581					
EAP 1-590	(contents unknown)	1955	6.25	12.50	25.00
EAP 1-590 [PS]	Melody of Love	1955	6.25	12.50	25.00
EAP 1-629	Two Hearts, Two Kisses (Make One Love)/Don't Change Your Mind About Me//Learnin' the Blues/Why Should I Cry Over You?	1955	6.25	12.50	25.00
EAP 1-629 [PS]	Session with Sinatra	1955	6.25	12.50	25.00
EAP 1-653	You Make Me Feel So Young/It Happened in Monterey//Anything Goes/How About You	1956	5.00	10.00	20.00
EAP 1-653 [PS]	Songs for Swingin' Lovers, Part 1	1956	6.25	12.50	25.00
—With Sinatra facing away from the embracing couple					
EAP 1-653 [PS]	Songs for Swingin' Lovers, Part 1	1957	5.00	10.00	20.00
—With Sinatra facing toward the embracing couple					
EAP 2-653	You're Getting to Be a Habit with Me/You Brought a New Kind of Love to Me//Makin' Whoopee/Swingin' Down the Lane	1956	5.00	10.00	20.00

Number	Title (A Side/B Side)	Yr	VG	VG+	NM
EAP 2-653 [PS]	Songs for Swingin' Lovers, Part 2	1956	6.25	12.50	25.00
—With Sinatra facing away from the embracing couple					
EAP 2-653 [PS]	Songs for Swingin' Lovers, Part 2	1957	5.00	10.00	20.00
—With Sinatra facing toward the embracing couple					
EAP 3-653	Too Marvelous for Words/Old Devil Moon//We'll Be Together Again	1956	5.00	10.00	20.00
EAP 3-653 [PS]	Songs for Swingin' Lovers, Part 3	1956	6.25	12.50	25.00
—With Sinatra facing away from the embracing couple					
EAP 3-653 [PS]	Songs for Swingin' Lovers, Part 3	1957	5.00	10.00	20.00
—With Sinatra facing toward the embracing couple					
EAP 4-653	Pennies from Heaven/Love Is Here to Stay//I've Got You Under My Skin/I Thought About You	1956	5.00	10.00	20.00
EAP 4-653 [PS]	Songs for Swingin' Lovers, Part 4	1956	6.25	12.50	25.00
—With Sinatra facing away from the embracing couple					
EAP 4-653 [PS]	Songs for Swingin' Lovers, Part 4	1957	5.00	10.00	20.00
—With Sinatra facing toward the embracing couple					
EBF 1-653 [PS]	Songs for Swingin' Lovers, Parts 1 and 2	1956	15.00	30.00	60.00
—Gatefold sleeve for some editions of EAP 1-653 and 2-653; with Sinatra facing away from the embracing couple					
EBF 1-653 [PS]	Songs for Swingin' Lovers, Parts 1 and 2	1957	12.50	25.00	50.00
—Gatefold sleeve for some editions of EAP 1-653 and 2-653; with Sinatra facing toward the embracing couple					
EBF 2-653 [PS]	Songs for Swingin' Lovers, Parts 3 and 4	1956	15.00	30.00	60.00
—Gatefold sleeve for some editions of EAP 3-653 and 4-653; with Sinatra facing away from the embracing couple					
EBF 2-653 [PS]	Songs for Swingin' Lovers, Parts 3 and 4	1957	12.50	25.00	50.00
—Gatefold sleeve for some editions of EAP 3-653 and 4-653; with Sinatra facing toward the embracing couple					
EAP 1-673	Our Town/The Impatient Years//Love and Marriage/Look to Your Heart	1956	12.50	25.00	50.00
EAP 1-673 [PS]	Our Town	1956	12.50	25.00	50.00
EAP 1-789	Close to You/Love Locked Out//The End of a Love Affair	1956	5.00	10.00	20.00
EAP 1-789 [PS]	Close to You, Part 1	1956	5.00	10.00	20.00
EAP 2-789	P.S. I Love You//With Every Breath I Take/I Couldn't Sleep a Wink Last Night	1956	5.00	10.00	20.00
EAP 2-789 [PS]	Close to You, Part 2	1956	5.00	10.00	20.00
EAP 3-789	Everything Happens to Me/It Could Happen to You//I've Had My Moments	1956	5.00	10.00	20.00
EAP 3-789 [PS]	Close to You, Part 3	1956	5.00	10.00	20.00
EAP 4-789	Don't Like Goodbyes//It's Easy to Remember/Blame It on My Youth	1956	5.00	10.00	20.00
EAP 4-789 [PS]	Close to You, Part 4	1956	5.00	10.00	20.00
EBF 1-789 [PS]	Close to You, Parts 1 and 2	1956	12.50	25.00	50.00
—Gatefold sleeve for some editions of EAP 1-789 and 2-789					
EBF 2-789 [PS]	Close to You, Parts 3 and 4	1956	12.50	25.00	50.00
—Gatefold sleeve for some editions of EAP 3-789 and 4-789					
EAP 1-800	How Little We Know/Flowers Mean Forgiveness//You Forgot All the Words/Hey! Jealous Lover	1956	7.50	15.00	30.00
EAP 1-800 [PS]	Hey! Jealous Lover	1956	7.50	15.00	30.00
EAP 1-803	The Lonesome Road/You'd Be So Nice to Come Home To//From This Moment On/Nice Work If You Can Get It	1957	5.00	10.00	20.00
EAP 1-803 [PS]	A Swingin' Affair, Part 1	1957	5.00	10.00	20.00
EAP 2-803	I Won't Dance/At Long Last Love//I Got It Bad and That Ain't Good/I Guess I'll Have to Change My Plan	1957	5.00	10.00	20.00
EAP 2-803 [PS]	A Swingin' Affair, Part 2	1957	5.00	10.00	20.00
EAP 3-803	No One Ever Tells You/If I Had You//I Wish I Were in Love Again/I Got Plenty o' Nuttin'	1957	5.00	10.00	20.00
EAP 3-803 [PS]	A Swingin' Affair, Part 3	1957	5.00	10.00	20.00
EAP 4-803	Oh! Look at Me Now/Stars Fell on Alabama//Night and Day	1957	5.00	10.00	20.00
EAP 4-803 [PS]	A Swingin' Affair, Part 4	1957	5.00	10.00	20.00
EBF 1-803 [PS]	A Swingin' Affair, Parts 1 and 2	1957	12.50	25.00	50.00
—Gatefold sleeve for some editions of EAP 1-803 and 2-803					
EBF 2-803 [PS]	A Swingin' Affair, Parts 3 and 4	1957	12.50	25.00	50.00
—Gatefold sleeve for some editions of EAP 3-803 and 4-803					
EAP 1-855	Where Are You?/Where Is the One//Baby Won't You Please Come Home	1957	5.00	10.00	20.00
EAP 1-855 [PS]	Where Are You? Part 1	1957	5.00	10.00	20.00
EAP 2-855	I'm a Fool to Want You//I Cover the Waterfront/Laura	1957	5.00	10.00	20.00
EAP 2-855 [PS]	Where Are You? Part 2	1957	5.00	10.00	20.00
EAP 3-855	Lonelytown/The Night We Called It a Day//Autumn Leaves	1957	5.00	10.00	20.00
EAP 3-855 [PS]	Where Are You? Part 3	1957	5.00	10.00	20.00
EAP 4-855	There's No You/I Think of You//Maybe You'll Be There	1957	5.00	10.00	20.00
EAP 4-855 [PS]	Where Are You? Part 4	1957	5.00	10.00	20.00
EBF 1-855 [PS]	Where Are You? Parts 1 and 2	1957	12.50	25.00	50.00
—Gatefold sleeve for some editions of EAP 1-855 and 2-855					
EBF 2-855 [PS]	Where Are You? Parts 3 and 4	1957	12.50	25.00	50.00
—Gatefold sleeve for some editions of EAP 3-855 and 4-855					
EAP 1-894	Jingle Bells/The Christmas Song//Mistletoe and Holly/I'll Be Home for Christmas	1957	3.00	6.00	12.00
EAP 1-894 [PS]	A Jolly Christmas from Frank Sinatra, Part 1	1957	3.00	6.00	12.00
EAP 2-894	The Christmas Waltz/Have Yourself a Merry Little Christmas//The First Noel/Hark the Herald Angels Sing	1957	3.00	6.00	12.00
EAP 2-894 [PS]	A Jolly Christmas from Frank Sinatra, Part 2	1957	3.00	6.00	12.00
EAP 3-894	O Little Town of Bethlehem/Adeste Fideles//It Came Upon a Midnight Clear/Silent Night	1957	3.00	6.00	12.00
EAP 3-894 [PS]	A Jolly Christmas from Frank Sinatra, Part 3	1957	3.00	6.00	12.00
EAP 1-920	Come Fly with Me/Isle of Capri//It's Nice to Go Trav'ling	1958	3.75	7.50	15.00
EAP 1-920 [PS]	Come Fly with Me, Part 1	1958	3.75	7.50	15.00
EAP 2-920	Autumn in New York//April in Paris/Around the World	1958	3.75	7.50	15.00
EAP 2-920 [PS]	Come Fly with Me, Part 2	1958	3.75	7.50	15.00
EAP 3-920	Moonlight in Vermont//London by Night/Let's Get Away from It All	1958	3.75	7.50	15.00
EAP 3-920 [PS]	Come Fly with Me, Part 3	1958	3.75	7.50	15.00
EAP 4-920	On the Road to Mandalay//Blue Hawaii/Brazil	1958	3.75	7.50	15.00
EAP 4-920 [PS]	Come Fly with Me, Part 4	1958	3.75	7.50	15.00
EAP 1-982	Hey! Jealous Lover/Everybody Loves Somebody//I Believe/Put Your Dreams Away	1958	5.00	10.00	20.00
EAP 1-982 [PS]	This Is Sinatra, Volume Two, Part 1	1958	5.00	10.00	20.00
EAP 2-982	Something Wonderful Happens in Summer/Half As Lovely//So Long My Love/It's the Same Old Dreams	1958	5.00	10.00	20.00
EAP 2-982 [PS]	This Is Sinatra, Volume Two, Part 2	1958	5.00	10.00	20.00
EAP 3-982	You're Cheatin' Yourself/You'll Always Be the One I Love//Johnny Concho Theme (Wait for Me)/If You Are But a Dream	1958	5.00	10.00	20.00
EAP 3-982 [PS]	This Is Sinatra, Volume Two, Part 3	1958	5.00	10.00	20.00
EAP 4-982	You Forgot All the Words/How Little We Know//Time After Time/Crazy Love	1958	5.00	10.00	20.00
EAP 4-982 [PS]	This Is Sinatra, Volume 2, Part 4	1958	5.00	10.00	20.00
EAP 1-1013	The Lady Is a Tramp/Witchcraft//Come Fly with Me/Tell Her You Love Her	1958	7.50	15.00	30.00
EAP 1-1013 [PS]	Frank Sinatra!	1958	7.50	15.00	30.00
EAP 1-1053	(contents unknown)	1958	5.00	10.00	20.00
EAP 1-1053 [PS]	Frank Sinatra Sings for Only the Lonely	1958	5.00	10.00	20.00
EAP 1-1069	Come Dance with Me/Something's Gotta Give//The Song Is You/The Last Dance	1958	3.75	7.50	15.00
EAP 1-1069 [PS]	Come Dance with Me, Part 1	1958	3.75	7.50	15.00
EAP 2-1069	Just in Time/Dancing in the Dark//Cheek to Cheek/Baubles, Bangles and Beads	1958	3.75	7.50	15.00
EAP 2-1069 [PS]	Come Dance with Me, Part 2	1958	3.75	7.50	15.00
EAP 3-1069	Saturday Night/Day In — Day Out//Too Close for Comfort/I Could Have Danced All Night	1958	3.75	7.50	15.00
EAP 3-1069 [PS]	Come Dance with Me, Part 3	1958	3.75	7.50	15.00
EAP 1-1159	(contents unknown)	1958	7.50	15.00	30.00
EAP 1-1159 [PS]	Frank Sinatra Sings Angel Eyes	1958	7.50	15.00	30.00
EAP 1-1221	When No One Cares/I'll Never Smile Again//A Cottage for Sale/None But the Lonely Heart	1959	3.75	7.50	15.00
EAP 1-1221 [PS]	No One Cares, Part 1	1959	3.75	7.50	15.00
EAP 2-1221	I Don't Stand a Ghost of a Chance with You/Here's That Rainy Day//I Can't Get Started	1959	3.75	7.50	15.00
EAP 2-1221 [PS]	No One Cares, Part 2	1959	3.75	7.50	15.00
EAP 3-1221	*Stormy Weather/Where Do You Go/Why Try to Change Me Now/Just Friends	1959	3.75	7.50	15.00
EAP 3-1221 [PS]	No One Cares, Part 3	1959	3.75	7.50	15.00
EAP 1-1224	(contents unknown)	1959	7.50	15.00	30.00
EAP 1-1224 [PS]	High Hopes	1959	7.50	15.00	30.00
SEP 1-1233 [PS]	French Foreign Legion	1959	12.50	25.00	50.00
SEP 1-1233 [S]	(contents unknown)	1959	12.50	25.00	50.00
EAP 1-1348	Talk to Me/They Came to Cordura//When No One Cares/Where Do You Go?	1959	7.50	15.00	30.00
EAP 1-1348 [PS]	Talk to Me	1959	7.50	15.00	30.00
EAP 1-1417	*Nice 'n' Easy/That Old Feeling/She's Funny That Way/Dream	1960	5.00	10.00	20.00
EAP 1-1417 [PS]	Nice 'n' Easy, Part 1	1960	5.00	10.00	20.00
EAP 2-1417	How Deep Is the Ocean/Mam'selle//Try a Little Tenderness/Embraceable You	1960	5.00	10.00	20.00
EAP 2-1417 [PS]	Nice 'n' Easy, Part 2	1960	5.00	10.00	20.00
EAP 3-1417	You Go to My Head/I've Got a Crush on You//Fools Rush In/Nevertheless	1960	5.00	10.00	20.00
EAP 3-1417 [PS]	Nice 'n' Easy, Part 3	1960	5.00	10.00	20.00
EAP 1-1491	When You're Smiling (The Whole World Smiles With You)/Blue Moon//S'Posin'/It All Depends on You	1961	6.25	12.50	25.00
EAP 1-1491 [PS]	Sinatra's Swingin' Session, Part 1	1961	6.25	12.50	25.00
EAP 2-1491	Always/I Can't Believe You're in Love with Me//It's Only a Paper Moon/My Blue Heaven	1961	6.25	12.50	25.00
EAP 2-1491 [PS]	Sinatra's Swingin' Session, Part 2	1961	6.25	12.50	25.00
EAP 3-1491	Should I/September in the Rain//I Concentrate on You/You Do Something to Me	1961	6.25	12.50	25.00
EAP 3-1491 [PS]	Sinatra's Swingin' Session, Part 3	1961	6.25	12.50	25.00
EAP 1-1594	(contents unknown)	1961	6.25	12.50	25.00
EAP 1-1594 [PS]	Come Swing with Me, Part 1	1961	6.25	12.50	25.00
EAP 2-1594	(contents unknown)	1961	6.25	12.50	25.00
EAP 2-1594 [PS]	Come Swing with Me, Part 2	1961	6.25	12.50	25.00
EAP 3-1594	(contents unknown)	1961	6.25	12.50	25.00
EAP 3-1594 [PS]	Come Swing with Me, Part 3	1961	6.25	12.50	25.00
COLUMBIA					
B-167 [PS]	Christmas Songs by Sinatra	1952	12.50	25.00	50.00
—Gatefold cover for 2-EP set (1322 and 1323)					
5-1322	White Christmas/Jingle Bells//Have Yourself a Merry Little Christmas/Have Yourself a Merry Little Christmas	1952	6.25	12.50	25.00
5-1323	Silent Night, Holy Night/Adeste Fideles//O Little Town of Bethlehem/It Came Upon a Midnight Clear	1952	6.25	12.50	25.00
B-1524	(contents unknown)	1952	6.25	12.50	25.00
B-1524 [PS]	Frank Sinatra Sings Irving Berlin	1952	6.25	12.50	25.00
B-1608	(contents unknown)	1952	7.50	15.00	30.00
B-1608 [PS]	Frank Sinatra Sings Hits from South Pacific and Oklahoma	1952	7.50	15.00	30.00
B-1620	(contents unknown)	1952	7.50	15.00	30.00
B-1620 [PS]	Carousel Sung by Frank Sinatra	1952	7.50	15.00	30.00
B-1673	(contents unknown)	1953	6.25	12.50	25.00
B-1673 [PS]	Frank Sinatra Sings George Gershwin	1953	6.25	12.50	25.00
B-1702	Ol' Man River/All the Things You Are//Why Was I Born/The Song Is You	1953	6.25	12.50	25.00
B-1702 [PS]	Frank Sinatra Sings Jerome Kern	1953	6.25	12.50	25.00
B-1815	(contents unknown)	1954	6.25	12.50	25.00
B-1815 [PS]	Frank Sinatra Sings Cole Porter	1954	6.25	12.50	25.00
B-1872	(contents unknown)	1954	6.25	12.50	25.00
B-1872 [PS]	Frank Sinatra Sings Rodgers and Hart	1954	6.25	12.50	25.00
B-1984	(contents unknown)	1955	6.25	12.50	25.00
B-1984 [PS]	Frankie, Vol. 1	1955	6.25	12.50	25.00
B-1985	(contents unknown)	1955	6.25	12.50	25.00
B-1985 [PS]	Frankie, Vol. 2	1955	6.25	12.50	25.00
B-1986	(contents unknown)	1955	6.25	12.50	25.00
B-1986 [PS]	Frankie, Vol. 3	1955	6.25	12.50	25.00
B-2515	I Couldn't Sleep a Wink Last Night/A Lovely Way to Spend an Evening//People Will Say We're in Love/Oh, What a Beautiful Mornin'	1957	6.25	12.50	25.00
B-2515 [PS]	Frank Sinatra (Hall of Fame Series)	1957	6.25	12.50	25.00

Number	Title (A Side/B Side)	Yr	VG	VG+	NM
B-2516	They Say It's Wonderful/The Girl That I Marry//Nancy (With the Laughing Face)/Day by Day	1957	6.25	12.50	25.00
B-2516 [PS]	Frank Sinatra (Hall of Fame Series)	1957	6.25	12.50	25.00
B-2517	The Birth of the Blues/I've Got a Crush on You//Five Minutes More/Someone to Watch Over Me	1957	6.25	12.50	25.00
B-2517 [PS]	Frank Sinatra (Hall of Fame Series)	1957	6.25	12.50	25.00
B-2542	Castle Rock/Farewell, Farewell to Love//A Little Learnin' Is a Dangerous Thing	1957	12.50	25.00	50.00
B-2542 [PS]	Frank Sinatra with Harry James and Pearl Bailey	1957	12.50	25.00	50.00
B-2559	(contents unknown)	1958	6.25	12.50	25.00
B-2559 [PS]	Frank Sinatra (Hall of Fame Series)	1958	6.25	12.50	25.00
B-2564	Ol' Man River/You'll Never Walk Alone//Soliloquy	1958	6.25	12.50	25.00
B-2564 [PS]	Frank Sinatra (Hall of Fame Series)	1958	6.25	12.50	25.00
B-2589	September Song/Among My Souvenirs//The Things We Did Last Summer/Oh! What It Seemed to Be	1958	6.25	12.50	25.00
B-2589 [PS]	Frank Sinatra (Hall of Fame Series)	1958	6.25	12.50	25.00
B-2614	One for My Baby/If I Loved You//Put Your Dreams Away/You'll Never Know	1958	6.25	12.50	25.00
B-2614 [PS]	Frank Sinatra (Hall of Fame Series)	1958	6.25	12.50	25.00
B-2626	(contents unknown)	1958	6.25	12.50	25.00
B-2626 [PS]	Frank Sinatra (Hall of Fame Series)	1958	6.25	12.50	25.00
B-2638	(contents unknown)	1958	6.25	12.50	25.00
B-2638 [PS]	Frank Sinatra (Hall of Fame Series)	1958	6.25	12.50	25.00
B-2641	All or Nothing at All/You Go to My Head//Why Try to Change Me Now/I Concentrate on You	1958	6.25	12.50	25.00
B-2641 [PS]	Frank Sinatra (Hall of Fame Series)	1958	6.25	12.50	25.00
B-7431	I Don't Know Why (I Just Do)/Try a Little Tenderness//(I Don't Stand) A Ghost of a Chance/Paradise	1955	6.25	12.50	25.00
B-7431 [PS]	The Voice, Vol. I	1955	6.25	12.50	25.00
B-7432	(contents unknown)	1955	6.25	12.50	25.00
B-7432 [PS]	The Voice, Vol. II	1955	6.25	12.50	25.00
B-7433	Over the Rainbow/That Old Black Magic//Spring Is Here/Lover	1955	6.25	12.50	25.00
B-7433 [PS]	The Voice, Vol. III	1955	6.25	12.50	25.00
B-9021	(contents unknown)	1956	6.25	12.50	25.00
B-9021 [PS]	That Old Feeling, Vol. I	1956	6.25	12.50	25.00
B-9022	(contents unknown)	1956	6.25	12.50	25.00
B-9022 [PS]	That Old Feeling, Vol. II	1956	6.25	12.50	25.00
B-9023	A Fellow Needs a Girl/Poinciana (Song of the Tree)//For Every Man There's a Woman/Mean to Me	1956	6.25	12.50	25.00
B-9023 [PS]	That Old Feeling, Vol. III	1956	6.25	12.50	25.00
B-9531	(contents unknown)	1957	6.25	12.50	25.00
B-9531 [PS]	Adventures of the Heart, Vol. I	1957	6.25	12.50	25.00
B-9532	(contents unknown)	1957	6.25	12.50	25.00
B-9532 [PS]	Adventures of the Heart, Vol. II	1957	6.25	12.50	25.00
B-9533	Mad About You/Sorry//On the Island of Stromboli/It's Only a Paper Moon	1957	6.25	12.50	25.00
B-9533 [PS]	Adventures of the Heart, Vol. III	1957	6.25	12.50	25.00
B-10321	White Christmas/Jingle Bells//Have Yourself a Merry Little Christmas/Santa Claus Is Coming to Town	1957	7.50	15.00	30.00
B-10321 [PS]	Christmas Dreaming, Vol. 1	1957	10.00	20.00	40.00
B-10322	Silent Night, Holy Night/Adeste Fideles//O Little Town of Bethlehem/It Came Upon the Midnight Clear	1957	7.50	15.00	30.00
B-10322 [PS]	Christmas Dreaming, Vol. 2	1957	10.00	20.00	40.00
ZTEP 28595/6 [DJ]	And…I'm a Fool to Want You/Full Moon and Empty Arms//The Birth of the Blues/Nancy (With the Laughing Face)	1958	12.50	25.00	50.00
ZTEP 28595/6 [PS]	Nancy	1958	12.50	25.00	50.00
—Limited edition EP for the B.T. Babbit Soap Co.					

RCA VICTOR

Number	Title (A Side/B Side)	Yr	VG	VG+	NM
EPBT-3063 [(2)]	Fabulous Frankie	1954	25.00	50.00	100.00
—Includes two EP records in gatefold jacket. Record numbers and contents unknown.					
EPA-5014	(contents unknown)	1958	5.00	10.00	20.00
EPA-5014 [PS]	Frankie and Tommy	1958	5.00	10.00	20.00
EPA-5147	(contents unknown)	1960	6.25	12.50	25.00
EPA-5147 [PS]	Frank Sinatra	1960	6.25	12.50	25.00

REPRISE

Number	Title (A Side/B Side)	Yr	VG	VG+	NM
SR 1012 [PS]	It Might As Well Be Swing	1965	5.00	10.00	20.00
SR 1012 [S]	Fly Me to the Moon/I Wanna Be Around/More//I Can't Stop Loving You/The Good Life/I Wish You Love	1965	5.00	10.00	20.00
—33 1/3 rpm, small hole, "Promotion"					

Albums

ARTANIS

Number	Title (A Side/B Side)	Yr	VG	VG+	NM
ARZ 101 [(2)]	Sinatra '57 In Concert	2000	—	—	—
—LP was rescheduled for issue in the summer of 2000. At press time, we had no word whether it actually came out.					

BOOK-OF-THE-MONTH

Number	Title (A Side/B Side)	Yr	VG	VG+	NM
(# unknown) [(6)]	Tommy Dorsey/Frank Sinatra: The Complete Sessions	1983	25.00	50.00	100.00

CAPITOL

Number	Title (A Side/B Side)	Yr	VG	VG+	NM
DWBB-254 [(2) R]	Close-Up	1969	5.00	10.00	20.00
—Reissue in one package of "This Is Sinatra" and "This Is Sinatra, Volume Two"					
DKAO-374 [R]	Frank Sinatra's Greatest Hits	1969	3.00	6.00	12.00
H 488 [10]	Songs for Young Lovers	1954	15.00	30.00	60.00
H 528 [10]	Swing Easy	1954	15.00	30.00	60.00
STBB-529 [(2)]	What Is This Thing Called Love?/The Night We Called It a Day	1970	3.75	7.50	15.00
DW 581 [R]	In the Wee Small Hours	196?	3.00	6.00	12.00
H1-581 [10]	In the Wee Small Hours, Part 1	1955	25.00	50.00	100.00
H2-581 [10]	In the Wee Small Hours, Part 2	1955	25.00	50.00	100.00
SM-581	In the Wee Small Hours	197?	2.00	4.00	8.00
W 581 [M]	In the Wee Small Hours	1955	10.00	20.00	40.00
—Gray label original					
W 581 [M]	In the Wee Small Hours	1959	6.25	12.50	25.00
—Black label with colorband					
W 587 [M]	Swing Easy/Songs for Young Lovers	1955	10.00	20.00	40.00
—Gray label original; 12-inch version of two 10-inch LPs					
W 587 [M]	Swing Easy/Songs for Young Lovers	1959	6.25	12.50	25.00
—Black label with colorband					
DW 653 [R]	Songs for Swingin' Lovers!	196?	3.00	6.00	12.00
SM-653	Songs for Swingin' Lovers!	197?	2.00	4.00	8.00
W 653 [M]	Songs for Swingin' Lovers!	1956	12.50	25.00	50.00
—Gray label; cover has Sinatra facing away from the embracing couple					
W 653 [M]	Songs for Swingin' Lovers!	1956	10.00	20.00	40.00
—Gray label; cover has Sinatra facing toward the embracing couple					
W 653 [M]	Songs for Swingin' Lovers!	1959	6.25	12.50	25.00
—Black label with colorband					
STBB-724 [(2)]	My One and Only Love/Sentimental Journey	1971	3.75	7.50	15.00
T 735 [M]	Frank Sinatra Conducts Tone Poems of Color	1956	15.00	30.00	60.00
—Turquoise label					
T 735 [M]	Frank Sinatra Conducts Tone Poems of Color	1959	10.00	20.00	40.00
—Black label with colorband					
DT 768 [R]	This Is Sinatra!	196?	3.00	6.00	12.00
T 768 [M]	This Is Sinatra!	1956	7.50	15.00	30.00
—Turquoise label					
T 768 [M]	This Is Sinatra!	196?	5.00	10.00	20.00
—Black "Starline" label					
T 768 [M]	This Is Sinatra!	196?	3.75	7.50	15.00
—Gold "Starline" label					
DW 789 [R]	Close to You	196?	3.00	6.00	12.00
W 789 [M]	Close to You	1957	7.50	15.00	30.00
—Gray label					
W 789 [M]	Close to You	1959	5.00	10.00	20.00
—Black label with colorband					
DW 803 [R]	A Swingin' Affair!	196?	3.00	6.00	12.00
W 803 [M]	A Swingin' Affair!	1957	7.50	15.00	30.00
—Gray label					
W 803 [M]	A Swingin' Affair!	1957	5.00	10.00	20.00
—Black label with colorband					
SW 855 [S]	Where Are You?	1959	10.00	20.00	40.00
—Originals do not include "I Cover the Waterfront"					
SW 855 [S]	Where Are You?	196?	7.50	15.00	30.00
—Later releases restore "I Cover the Waterfront"					
W 855 [M]	Where Are You?	1957	7.50	15.00	30.00
—Gray label					
W 855 [M]	Where Are You?	1959	5.00	10.00	20.00
—Black label with colorband					
DT 894 [R]	The Sinatra Christmas Album	196?	2.50	5.00	10.00
—Rechanneled reissue of A Jolly Christmas with Frank Sinatra with same contents; some copies have this cover and "A Jolly Christmas" labels					
SM-894 [R]	The Sinatra Christmas Album	197?	2.00	4.00	8.00
—Reissue in rechanneled stereo; any color label					
T 894 [M]	The Sinatra Christmas Album	196?	5.00	10.00	20.00
—Reissue of A Jolly Christmas with Frank Sinatra with same contents; some copies have this cover and "A Jolly Christmas" labels					
W 894 [M]	A Jolly Christmas from Frank Sinatra	1957	10.00	20.00	40.00
—Original mono with gray label					
W 894 [M]	A Jolly Christmas from Frank Sinatra	1958	7.50	15.00	30.00
—Black colorband label, logo at left					
SM-920	Come Fly with Me	197?	2.00	4.00	8.00
SW 920 [S]	Come Fly with Me	1959	7.50	15.00	30.00
W 920 [M]	Come Fly with Me	1958	10.00	20.00	40.00
—Gray label					
W 920 [M]	Come Fly with Me	1959	5.00	10.00	20.00
—Black label with colorband					
DW 982 [R]	This Is Sinatra, Volume Two	196?	3.00	6.00	12.00
W 982 [M]	This Is Sinatra, Volume Two	1958	10.00	20.00	40.00
—Gray label					
W 982 [M]	This Is Sinatra, Volume Two	1959	5.00	10.00	20.00
—Black label with colorband					
SW 1053 [S]	Frank Sinatra Sings for Only the Lonely	1959	7.50	15.00	30.00
—Originals do not include "It's a Lonesome Old Town" and "Spring Is Here"					
SW 1053 [S]	Frank Sinatra Sings for Only the Lonely	196?	6.25	12.50	25.00
—Later releases restore "It's a Lonesome Old Town" and "Spring Is Here"					
W 1053 [M]	Frank Sinatra Sings for Only the Lonely	1958	10.00	20.00	40.00
—Gray label					
W 1053 [M]	Frank Sinatra Sings for Only the Lonely	1959	5.00	10.00	20.00
—Black label with colorband					
SW 1069 [S]	Come Dance with Me!	1959	7.50	15.00	30.00
W 1069 [M]	Come Dance with Me!	1959	5.00	10.00	20.00
DW 1164 [R]	Look to Your Heart	196?	3.00	6.00	12.00
W 1164 [M]	Look to Your Heart	1959	7.50	15.00	30.00
SM-1221	No One Cares	197?	2.00	4.00	8.00
SW 1221 [S]	No One Cares	1959	7.50	15.00	30.00
W 1221 [M]	No One Cares	1959	5.00	10.00	20.00
SW 1417 [S]	Nice 'N' Easy	1960	6.25	12.50	25.00
W 1417 [M]	Nice 'N' Easy	1960	5.00	10.00	20.00
DW 1429 [R]	Swing Easy	1960	3.00	6.00	12.00
W 1429 [M]	Swing Easy	1960	5.00	10.00	20.00
DW 1432 [R]	Songs for Young Lovers	1960	3.00	6.00	12.00
W 1432 [M]	Songs for Young Lovers	1960	5.00	10.00	20.00
SM-1491	Sinatra's Swingin' Session!!!	197?	2.00	4.00	8.00
SW 1491 [S]	Sinatra's Swingin' Session!!!	1961	6.25	12.50	25.00
W 1491 [M]	Sinatra's Swingin' Session!!!	1961	5.00	10.00	20.00
SW 1538 [S]	All the Way	1961	6.25	12.50	25.00
W 1538 [M]	All the Way	1961	5.00	10.00	20.00
SW 1594 [S]	Come Swing with Me!	1961	6.25	12.50	25.00
W 1594 [M]	Come Swing with Me!	1961	5.00	10.00	20.00
SM-1676	Point of No Return	197?	2.00	4.00	8.00
SW 1676 [S]	Point of No Return	1962	6.25	12.50	25.00
W 1676 [M]	Point of No Return	1962	5.00	10.00	20.00
SW 1729 [P]	Sinatra Sings…Of Love and Things	1962	5.00	10.00	20.00
W 1729 [M]	Sinatra Sings…Of Love and Things	1962	5.00	10.00	20.00
SWCO 1762 [(3) P]	Sinatra, The Great Years	1962	10.00	20.00	40.00
WCO 1762 [(3) M]	Sinatra, The Great Years	1962	7.50	15.00	30.00
DW 1825 [R]	Sinatra Sings Rodgers and Hart	1963	3.00	6.00	12.00
W 1825 [M]	Sinatra Sings Rodgers and Hart	1963	5.00	10.00	20.00
DT 1919 [R]	Tell Her You Love Her	1963	3.00	6.00	12.00
T 1919 [M]	Tell Her You Love Her	1963	5.00	10.00	20.00
DW 1994 [R]	Sinatra Sings the Select Johnny Mercer	1963	3.00	6.00	12.00
W 1994 [M]	Sinatra Sings the Select Johnny Mercer	1963	5.00	10.00	20.00
DT 2036 [R]	The Greatest Hits of Frank Sinatra	1964	3.00	6.00	12.00
T 2036 [M]	The Greatest Hits of Frank Sinatra	1964	5.00	10.00	20.00
PRO-2163/4/5/6 [(2) DJ]	Selections from Sinatra, The Great Years	1962	10.00	20.00	40.00
DW 2301 [R]	Sinatra Sings the Select Cole Porter	1965	3.00	6.00	12.00

Number	Title (A Side/B Side)	Yr	VG	VG+	NM
W 2301 [M]	Sinatra Sings the Select Cole Porter	1965	5.00	10.00	20.00
DT 2602 [R]	Forever Frank	1966	3.00	6.00	12.00
T 2602 [M]	Forever Frank	1966	5.00	10.00	20.00
DT 2700 [R]	The Movie Songs	1967	3.00	6.00	12.00
T 2700 [M]	The Movie Songs	1967	5.00	10.00	20.00
STFL 2814 [(6) P]	The Frank Sinatra Deluxe Set	1968	15.00	30.00	60.00
TFL 2814 [(6) M]	The Frank Sinatra Deluxe Set	1968	25.00	50.00	100.00
DKAO 2900 [R]	The Best of Frank Sinatra	1968	3.75	7.50	15.00
PRO-2974/5 [DJ]	Frank Sinatra Minute Masters	1965	10.00	20.00	40.00
—Edited version of 20 songs					
DNFR 7630 [(6) P]	The Sinatra Touch	19??	15.00	30.00	60.00
ST-11309	One More for the Road	1973	2.50	5.00	10.00
SABB-11367 [(2) P]	Round #1	1974	3.75	7.50	15.00
SM-11502	A Swingin' Affair!	1976	2.50	5.00	10.00
SM-11801	Come Swing with Me	1978	2.50	5.00	10.00
M-11883	This Is Sinatra!	1979	2.50	5.00	10.00
SN-16109	The Best of Frank Sinatra	198?	2.00	4.00	8.00
—Budget-line reissue					
DN-16110	What Is This Thing Called Love	198?	2.00	4.00	8.00
—Budget-line reissue					
SN-16111	The Night We Called It a Day	198?	2.00	4.00	8.00
—Budget-line reissue					
N-16112	My One and Only Love	198?	2.00	4.00	8.00
—Budget-line reissue					
SN-16113	Sentimental Journey	198?	2.00	4.00	8.00
—Budget-line reissue					
N-16148	Look to Your Heart	198?	2.00	4.00	8.00
—Budget-line reissue					
SN-16149	Sinatra Sings...Of Love and Things	198?	2.00	4.00	8.00
—Budget-line reissue					
SN-16202	Frank Sinatra Sings for Only the Lonely	198?	2.00	4.00	8.00
—Budget-line reissue					
SN-16203	Come Dance with Me!	198?	2.00	4.00	8.00
—Budget-line reissue					
SN-16204	Nice 'N' Easy	198?	2.00	4.00	8.00
—Budget-line reissue					
SN-16205	All the Way	198?	2.00	4.00	8.00
—Budget-line reissue					
SN-16267	Where Are You	198?	2.00	4.00	8.00
—Budget-line reissue					
DN-16268	This Is Sinatra, Volume Two	198?	2.00	4.00	8.00
—Budget-line reissue					
C1-89611	Duets	1993	5.00	10.00	20.00
DW 90986 [R]	Sentimental Journey	1966	3.75	7.50	15.00
—Capitol Record Club issue					
W 90986 [M]	Sentimental Journey	1966	6.25	12.50	25.00
—Capitol Record Club issue					
DQBO 91261 [(2) R]	Songs for the Young at Heart	196?	7.50	15.00	30.00
—Capitol Record Club issue					
C1-94777 [(5)]	The Capitol Years	1990	25.00	50.00	100.00
—With book and wraparound banner. Only 5,000 were pressed					
STBB-95191 [(2)]	Sinatra Sings the Great Ones	1973	5.00	10.00	20.00
—Longines Symphonette (formerly Capitol) Record Club issue					
CAPITOL PICKWICK SERIES					
PC-3450 [M]	The Nearness of You	196?	3.00	6.00	12.00
SPC-3450 [R]	The Nearness of You	196?	2.50	5.00	10.00
PC-3452 [M]	Try a Little Tenderness	196?	3.00	6.00	12.00
SPC-3452 [R]	Try a Little Tenderness	196?	2.50	5.00	10.00
PC-3456 [M]	Nevertheless	196?	3.00	6.00	12.00
SPC-3456 [R]	Nevertheless	196?	2.50	5.00	10.00
PC-3457 [M]	Just One of Those Things	196?	3.00	6.00	12.00
SPC-3457 [R]	Just One of Those Things	196?	2.50	5.00	10.00
PC-3458 [M]	This Love of Mine	196?	3.00	6.00	12.00
SPC-3458 [R]	This Love of Mine	196?	2.50	5.00	10.00
PC-3463 [M]	My Cole Porter	196?	3.00	6.00	12.00
SPC-3463 [R]	My Cole Porter	196?	2.50	5.00	10.00
COLUMBIA					
C2L 6 [(2) M]	The Frank Sinatra Story	1958	7.50	15.00	30.00
C3L 42 [(3) M]	The Essential Frank Sinatra	1966	25.00	50.00	100.00
C3S 42 [(3) R]	The Essential Frank Sinatra	1966	12.50	25.00	50.00
CL 606 [M]	Frankie	1955	7.50	15.00	30.00
—Cover has drawing of Frank Sinatra wearing a hat					
CL 606 [M]	Frankie	1955	6.25	12.50	25.00
—Cover has Frank with Debbie Reynolds					
CL 743 [M]	The Voice	1956	6.25	12.50	25.00
CL 743 [M]	The Voice	1999	6.25	12.50	25.00
—Classic Records reissue on audiophile vinyl					
CL 884 [M]	Frank Sinatra Conducts Music of Alec Wilder	1956	10.00	20.00	40.00
—Reissue of Columbia Masterworks ML 4271					
CL 902 [M]	That Old Feeling	1956	6.25	12.50	25.00
CL 953 [M]	Adventures of the Heart	1957	6.25	12.50	25.00
CL 1032 [M]	Christmas Dreaming	1957	20.00	40.00	80.00
CL 1136 [M]	Put Your Dreams Away	1958	6.25	12.50	25.00
CL 1241 [M]	Love Is a Kick	1958	6.25	12.50	25.00
CL 1297 [M]	The Broadway Kick	1958	6.25	12.50	25.00
CL 1359 [M]	Come Back to Sorrento	1959	6.25	12.50	25.00
CL 1448 [M]	Reflections	1959	15.00	30.00	60.00
CL 2474 [M]	Greatest Hits, The Early Years, Vol. 1	1966	3.75	7.50	15.00
CAS 2475 [DJ]	The Voice: The Columbia Years Sampler	1986	10.00	20.00	40.00
CL 2521 [10]	Get Happy	1955	15.00	30.00	60.00
—"House Party Series" release					
CL 2539 [10]	I've Got a Crush on You	1955	15.00	30.00	60.00
—"House Party Series" release; different contents from CL 6290					
CL 2542 [10]	Christmas with Sinatra	1955	15.00	30.00	60.00
—"House Party Series" release					
CL 2572 [M]	Greatest Hits, The Early Years, Vol. 2	1966	3.75	7.50	15.00
CL 2739 [M]	The Essential Frank Sinatra, Volume 1	1967	6.25	12.50	25.00
CL 2740 [M]	The Essential Frank Sinatra, Volume 2	1967	6.25	12.50	25.00
CL 2741 [M]	The Essential Frank Sinatra, Volume 3	1967	6.25	12.50	25.00
CL 2913 [M]	Frank Sinatra in Hollywood	1968	20.00	40.00	80.00
CL 6001 [10]	The Voice of Frank Sinatra	1949	17.50	35.00	70.00
—Original in pink paper cover					
CL 6001 [10]	The Voice of Frank Sinatra	1950	15.00	30.00	60.00
—Blue cardboard cover					
CL 6019 [10]	Christmas Songs by Sinatra	1948	25.00	50.00	100.00
—With "gingerbread man" cover					
CL 6019 [10]	Christmas Songs by Sinatra	1949	20.00	40.00	80.00
—With green vinylite cover					
CL 6059 [10]	Frankly Sentimental	1951	15.00	30.00	60.00
CL 6087 [10]	Songs by Sinatra, Volume 1	1952	15.00	30.00	60.00
CL 6096 [10]	Dedicated to You	1952	25.00	50.00	100.00
—Three of the tracks on this LP are alternate takes unavailable on vinyl anywhere else					
CL 6143 [10]	Sing and Dance with Frank Sinatra	1953	15.00	30.00	60.00
CL 6290 [10]	I've Got a Crush on You	1954	15.00	30.00	60.00
CS 9274 [R]	Greatest Hits, The Early Years, Vol. 1	1966	2.50	5.00	10.00
CS 9372 [R]	Greatest Hits, The Early Years, Vol. 2	1966	2.50	5.00	10.00
CS 9539 [R]	The Essential Frank Sinatra, Volume 1	1967	3.00	6.00	12.00
CS 9540 [R]	The Essential Frank Sinatra, Volume 2	1967	3.00	6.00	12.00
CS 9541 [R]	The Essential Frank Sinatra, Volume 3	1967	3.00	6.00	12.00
CS 9713 [R]	Frank Sinatra in Hollywood	1968	3.00	6.00	12.00
KG 31358 [(2)]	In the Beginning	1971	10.00	20.00	40.00
C6X 40343 [(6)]	The Voice: The Columbia Years 1943-1952	1986	20.00	40.00	80.00
PC 40707	Christmas Dreaming	1987	7.50	15.00	30.00
—Reissue of CL 1032 with an extra track					
C2X 40897 [(2)]	Hello Young Lovers	1988	7.50	15.00	30.00
PC 44238 [M]	Sinatra Rarities	1989	10.00	20.00	40.00
COLUMBIA MASTERWORKS					
ML 4271 [M]	Frank Sinatra Conducts Music of Alec Wilder	1955	25.00	50.00	100.00
COUMBIA					
PC 9274	Greatest Hits, The Early Years, Vol. 1	197?	2.00	4.00	8.00
PC 9372	Greatest Hits, The Early Years, Vol. 2	197?	2.00	4.00	8.00
PG 31358 [(2)]	In the Beginning	197?	3.00	6.00	12.00
HARMONY					
HL 7400 [M]	Have Yourself a Merry Little Christmas	1967	7.50	15.00	30.00
HL 7405 [M]	Romantic Scenes from the Early Years	1967	7.50	15.00	30.00
HS 11200 [R]	Have Yourself a Merry Little Christmas	1967	5.00	10.00	20.00
—At least two different cover designs exist					
HS 11205 [R]	Romantic Scenes from the Early Years	1967	3.00	6.00	12.00
HS 11277 [R]	Someone to Watch Over Me	1968	3.75	7.50	15.00
HS 11390 [R]	Frank Sinatra	1969	3.75	7.50	15.00
KH 30318 [R]	Greatest Hits, Early Years	1971	3.75	7.50	15.00
LONGINES SYMPHONETTE					
LS-308A [(10)]	Sinatra: The Works	1972	18.75	37.50	75.00
LS-309A [(6)]	Sinatra: The Works	1973	10.00	20.00	40.00
—Abridged version of LS-308A					
SYS-5637	Sinatra Like Never Before	1972	6.25	12.50	25.00
—Bonus LP with purchase of LS-308A					
MOBILE FIDELITY					
SC-1 [(16)]	Sinatra	1983	150.00	300.00	600.00
—Audiophile vinyl; only two of the 16 records in this box were released individually					
1-086	Nice 'N' Easy	1981	10.00	20.00	40.00
—Audiophile vinyl					
1-135 [M]	A Jolly Christmas from Frank Sinatra	1984	10.00	20.00	40.00
—Audiophile vinyl using the original title					
PAIR					
PDL2-1027 [(2)]	All-Time Classics	1986	3.00	6.00	12.00
PDL2-1028 [(2)]	Timeless	1986	3.00	6.00	12.00
PDL2-1122 [(2)]	Classic Performances	1986	3.00	6.00	12.00
QWEST					
25145	L.A. Is My Lady	1984	3.00	6.00	12.00
RCA VICTOR					
APL1-0497 [R]	What'll I Do	1974	3.00	6.00	12.00
LPV-583 [M]	This Love of Mine	1971	10.00	20.00	40.00
ANL1-1050 [R]	What'll I Do	1976	2.50	5.00	10.00
LPM-1569 [M]	Frankie and Tommy	1957	15.00	30.00	60.00
—First issue of this LP					
LPM-1569 [M]	Tommy Plays, Frankie Sings	1957	10.00	20.00	40.00
—Second issue with new title					
LPM-1632 [M]	We Three	1958	15.00	30.00	60.00
—First issue					
LPM-1632 [M]	We Three	1958	10.00	20.00	40.00
—Second issue, "RE" on cover					
LPT-3063 [10]	Fabulous Frankie	1953	15.00	30.00	60.00
CPL2-4334 [(2)]	The Sinatra/Dorsey Sessions, Vol. 1	1982	6.25	12.50	25.00
CPL2-4335 [(2)]	The Sinatra/Dorsey Sessions, Vol. 2	1982	6.25	12.50	25.00
CPL2-4336 [(2)]	The Sinatra/Dorsey Sessions, Vol. 3	1982	6.25	12.50	25.00
AFL1-4741 [R]	Radio Years (Sinatra/Dorsey/Stordahl)	1983	3.75	7.50	15.00
REPRISE					
F 1001 [M]	Ring-a-Ding-Ding!	1961	5.00	10.00	20.00
R9 1001 [S]	Ring-a-Ding-Ding!	1961	6.25	12.50	25.00
F 1002 [M]	Swing Along with Me	1961	10.00	20.00	40.00
—Original title					
F 1002 [M]	Sinatra Swings	1961	5.00	10.00	20.00
—Retitled version of "Swing Along with Me"; Capitol threatened legal action because of its "Come Swing With Me!" collection					
R9 1002 [S]	Swing Along with Me	1961	12.50	25.00	50.00
—Original title					
R9 1002 [S]	Sinatra Swings	1961	6.25	12.50	25.00
—Retitled version of "Swing Along with Me"; Capitol threatened legal action because of its "Come Swing With Me!" collection					
F 1003 [M]	I Remember Tommy	1961	5.00	10.00	20.00
R9 1003 [S]	I Remember Tommy	1961	6.25	12.50	25.00
F 1004 [M]	Sinatra & Strings	1962	3.75	7.50	15.00
R9 1004 [S]	Sinatra & Strings	1962	5.00	10.00	20.00
F 1005 [M]	Sinatra and Swingin' Brass	1962	3.75	7.50	15.00
R9 1005 [S]	Sinatra and Swingin' Brass	1962	5.00	10.00	20.00
F 1007 [M]	All Alone	1962	3.75	7.50	15.00
R9 1007 [S]	All Alone	1962	5.00	10.00	20.00
F 1008 [M]	Sinatra-Basie	1963	3.75	7.50	15.00
R9 1008 [S]	Sinatra-Basie	1963	5.00	10.00	20.00
F 1009 [M]	The Concert Sinatra	1963	3.75	7.50	15.00
R9 1009 [S]	The Concert Sinatra	1963	6.25	12.50	25.00
—Original pressings declare this was recorded in "35mm Stereo"					
R9 1009 [S]	The Concert Sinatra	196?	5.00	10.00	20.00
—Without cover reference to "35mm Stereo"					
F 1010 [M]	Sinatra's Sinatra	1963	3.75	7.50	15.00
R9 1010 [S]	Sinatra's Sinatra	1963	5.00	10.00	20.00
F 1011 [M]	Days of Wine and Roses, Moon River, and Other Academy Award Winners	1964	3.75	7.50	15.00
FS 1011 [S]	Days of Wine and Roses, Moon River, and Other Academy Award Winners	1964	5.00	10.00	20.00

Number	Title (A Side/B Side)	Yr	VG	VG+	NM
F 1012 [M]	It Might As Well Be Swing	1964	3.75	7.50	15.00
FS 1012 [S]	It Might As Well Be Swing	1964	5.00	10.00	20.00
F 1013 [M]	Softly, As I Leave You	1964	3.75	7.50	15.00
FS 1013 [S]	Softly, As I Leave You	1964	5.00	10.00	20.00
F 1014 [M]	September of My Years	1965	3.75	7.50	15.00
FS 1014 [S]	September of My Years	1965	5.00	10.00	20.00
F 1015 [M]	My Kind of Broadway	1965	3.75	7.50	15.00
FS 1015 [S]	My Kind of Broadway	1965	5.00	10.00	20.00
2F 1016 [(2) M]	A Man and His Music	1965	5.00	10.00	20.00
2FS 1016 [(2) S]	A Man and His Music	1965	6.25	12.50	25.00
2F/2FS 1016	A Man and His Music Special Box	1965	50.00	100.00	200.00
—Blue slipcase with embossed silver front, raised letters, plus 4-page booklet and a signed card (deduct 50% if card missing). Add this to LP value.					
F 1017 [M]	Strangers in the Night	1966	3.00	6.00	12.00
FS 1017 [S]	Strangers in the Night	1966	3.75	7.50	15.00
F 1018 [M]	Moonlight Sinatra	1966	3.75	7.50	15.00
FS 1018 [S]	Moonlight Sinatra	1966	5.00	10.00	20.00
2F 1019 [(2) M]	Sinatra at the Sands	1966	5.00	10.00	20.00
2FS 1019 [(2) S]	Sinatra at the Sands	1966	6.25	12.50	25.00
F 1020 [M]	That's Life	1966	3.00	6.00	12.00
FS 1020 [S]	That's Life	1966	3.75	7.50	15.00
F 1021 [M]	Francis Albert Sinatra & Antonio Carlos Jobim	1967	3.00	6.00	12.00
FS 1021 [S]	Francis Albert Sinatra & Antonio Carolos Jobim	1967	3.75	7.50	15.00
F 1022 [M]	Frank Sinatra (The World We Knew)	1967	3.75	7.50	15.00
FS 1022 [S]	Frank Sinatra (The World We Knew)	1967	3.75	7.50	15.00
FS 1023	The Sinatra Christmas Album	1967	25.00	50.00	100.00
—Album never released; value is for cover slick					
FS 1024	Francis A. and Edward K.	1968	5.00	10.00	20.00
FS 1025	Frank Sinatra's Greatest Hits	1968	3.75	7.50	15.00
FS 1027	Cycles	1969	3.75	7.50	15.00
FS 1028	SinatraJobim	1969	2000.	3000.	4000.
—Unreleased; test pressings exist (value is for one of these). 8-track tapes also exist and are 10% of this value					
FS 1029	My Way	1969	3.75	7.50	15.00
FS4 1029 [Q]	My Way	1974	6.25	12.50	25.00
FS 1030	A Man Alone & Other Songs of Rod McKuen	1969	3.75	7.50	15.00
FS 1030	A Man Alone & Other Songs of Rod McKuen	1969	100.00	200.00	400.00
—Signed copies with gatefold cover and hardbound book; 400 made					
FS 1031	Watertown	1970	6.25	12.50	25.00
—With gatefold and poster					
FS 1032	Frank Sinatra's Greatest Hits, Vol. 2	1970	—	—	—
—Canceled?					
FS 1033	Sinatra and Company	1971	3.75	7.50	15.00
FS 1034	Frank Sinatra's Greatest Hits, Vol. 2	1972	3.75	7.50	15.00
FS 2155	Ol' Blue Eyes Is Back	1973	3.00	6.00	12.00
FS4 2155 [Q]	Ol' Blue Eyes Is Back	1974	6.25	12.50	25.00
FS4 2194 [Q]	Some Nice Things I've Missed	1974	6.25	12.50	25.00
FS 2195	Some Nice Things I've Missed	1974	3.00	6.00	12.00
FS 2207	Sinatra — The Main Event Live	1974	3.00	6.00	12.00
3FS 2300 [(3)]	Trilogy: Past, Present, Future	1980	5.00	10.00	20.00
FS 2305	She Shot Me Down	1981	3.00	6.00	12.00
5004 [DJ]	A Man and His Music, Part II	1966	75.00	150.00	300.00
—Promotional album for use by Budweiser					
5230 [DJ]	Songbook, Vol. 1	1971	12.50	25.00	50.00
5267 [(2) DJ]	Songbook, Vol. 2	1972	25.00	50.00	100.00
5409 [DJ]	I Sing the Songs	1976	12.50	25.00	50.00
F 6045 [M]	Sinatra Conducts Music from Pictures and Plays	1962	7.50	15.00	30.00
R9 6045 [S]	Sinatra Conducts Music from Pictures and Plays	1962	10.00	2.00	40.00
R 6167 [M]	Sinatra '65	1965	3.75	7.50	15.00
RS 6167 [S]	Sinatra '65	1965	5.00	10.00	20.00
SMAS-92081	A Man Alone & Other Songs of Rod McKuen	1969	5.00	10.00	20.00
—Capitol Record Club edition					
TIME-LIFE					
SLGD-02 [(2)]	Legendary Singers	1982	6.25	12.50	25.00

SINATRA, FRANK; DEAN MARTIN; SAMMY DAVIS, JR.

Albums

Number	Title (A Side/B Side)	Yr	VG	VG+	NM
ARTANIS					
ARZ 102 [(2)]	The Summit	2000	—	—	—
—LP was rescheduled for issue in the summer of 2000. At press time, we had no word whether it actually came out.					

SINATRA, NANCY

Includes duets with Lee Hazlewood and Mel Tillis.

45s

Number	Title (A Side/B Side)	Yr	VG	VG+	NM
ELEKTRA					
46659	Let's Keep It That Way/One Jump Ahead of the Storm	1979	—	2.50	5.00
47157	Texas Cowboy Night/After the Lovin'	1981	—	2.00	4.00
—With Mel Tillis					
47234 [DJ]	Rudolph the Red-Nosed Reindeer/Winter Wonderland	1981	2.00	4.00	8.00
—As "Mel (Tillis) and Nancy"; B-side by Dave Rowland and Sugar					
47247	Where Would I Be/Play Me or Trade Me	1981	—	2.00	4.00
—With Mel Tillis					
PRIVATE STOCK					
45022	Annabel of Mobile/(B-side unknown)	1975	—	2.50	5.00
45075	Kinky Love/She Played the Piano and He Beat the Drum	1976	—	2.50	5.00
45108	Indian Summer/Holly and Hawkeye	1976	—	2.50	5.00
—With Lee Hazlewood					
45158	It's For My Dad/A Gentle Man Like You	1977	—	2.50	5.00
RCA VICTOR					
APBO-0029	Ain't No Sunshine/Sugar Me	1973	—	2.50	5.00
47-0864	It's the Love/Kind of a Woman	1973	2.00	4.00	8.00
74-0614	Paris Summer/Down from Dover	1971	2.00	4.00	8.00
—With Lee Hazlewood					
REPRISE					
0238	Tammy/Thanks to You	1963	5.00	10.00	20.00
0263	Where Do the Lonely Go/Just Think About the Good Times	1964	5.00	10.00	20.00
0292	This Love of Mine/There Goes the Bride	1964	5.00	10.00	20.00
0335	The Answer to Everything/True Love	1965	3.75	7.50	15.00
0407	So Long Babe/If He'd Love Me	1965	3.75	7.50	15.00
0432	These Boots Are Made for Walkin'/The City Never Sleeps at Night	1965	3.00	6.00	12.00
0461	How Does That Grab You, Darlin'?/The Last of the Secret Agents	1966	2.50	5.00	10.00
0491	Friday's Child/Hutchinson Jail	1966	2.50	5.00	10.00
0514	In Our Time/Leave My Dog Alone	1966	2.50	5.00	10.00
0527	Sugar Town/Summer Wine	1966	3.00	6.00	12.00
0559	Love Eyes/Coastin'	1967	2.50	5.00	10.00
0561	Somethin' Stupid/Give Her Love	1967	2.50	5.00	10.00
—A-side: Nancy Sinatra and Frank Sinatra; B-side: Frank Sinatra					
0561	Somethin' Stupid/I Will Wait for You	1967	2.00	4.00	8.00
—A-side: Nancy Sinatra and Frank Sinatra; B-side: Frank Sinatra					
0595	Jackson/You Only Live Twice	1967	2.50	5.00	10.00
—A-side: With Lee Hazlewood					
0620	Lightning's Girl/Until It's Time for You to Go	1967	2.50	5.00	10.00
0620 [PS]	Lightning's Girl/Until It's Time for You to Go	1967	5.00	10.00	20.00
0629	Lady Bird/Sand	1967	2.00	4.00	8.00
—With Lee Hazlewood					
0636	Tony Rome/This Town	1967	2.00	4.00	8.00
0651	Some Velvet Morning/Oh Lonesome Me	1967	2.00	4.00	8.00
—With Lee Hazlewood					
0670	100 Years/See the Little Children	1968	2.00	4.00	8.00
0701	These Boots Are Made for Walkin'/Love Eyes	1968	—	2.50	5.00
—"Back to Back Hits" series					
0721	Sugar Town/Summer Wine	1968	—	2.50	5.00
—"Back to Back Hits" series					
0726	Jackson/Summer Wine	1968	—	2.50	5.00
—With Lee Hazlewood; "Back to Back Hits" series					
0729	Lightning's Girl/One Velvet Morning	1968	—	2.50	5.00
—B-side with Lee Hazlewood; "Back to Back Hits" series					
0756	Happy/Nice 'N' Easy	1968	2.00	4.00	8.00
0789	Good Time Girl/Old Devil Moon	1968	2.00	4.00	8.00
0813	God Knows I Love You/Just Plain Old Me	1969	2.00	4.00	8.00
0821	Here We Go Again/Memories	1969	2.00	4.00	8.00
0851	Drummer Man/I Home	1969	2.00	4.00	8.00
0880	It's Such a Lonely Time of the Year/Kids	1969	2.50	5.00	10.00
0890	I Love Them All/Home	1970	2.00	4.00	8.00
0932	Hello L.A., Bye Bye Birmingham/White Tattoo	1970	2.00	4.00	8.00
0968	I'm Not a Girl Anymore/How Are Things in California	1970	2.00	4.00	8.00
0980	Feelin' Kinda Sunday/Kids	1970	2.00	4.00	8.00
—A-side by Nancy Sinatra and Frank Sinatra					
0991	Is Anybody Goin' to San Antone/Hook and Ladder	1971	2.00	4.00	8.00
0991 [PS]	Is Anybody Goin' to San Antone/Hook and Ladder	1971	3.75	7.50	15.00
1011	Life's a Trippy Thing/I'm Not Afraid	1971	2.00	4.00	8.00
—A-side by Nancy Sinatra and Frank Sinatra; B-side by Frank Sinatra solo					
1021	Did You Ever/Back on the Road	1971	2.00	4.00	8.00
—As "Nancy and Lee" (Hazlewood)					
1034	Glory Road/Is Anybody Goin' to San Antone	1971	2.00	4.00	8.00
20017	Not Just Your Friend/Cuff Links and a Tie Clip	1961	5.00	10.00	20.00
20017 [PS]	Not Just Your Friend/Cuff Links and a Tie Clip	1961	15.00	30.00	60.00
20045	To Know Him Is to Love Him/Like I Do	1962	5.00	10.00	20.00
20097	June, July and August/Think of Me	1962	5.00	10.00	20.00
20127	Tonight You Belong to Me/You Can Have Any Boy	1962	5.00	10.00	20.00
20144	Put Your Head on My Shoulder/I See the Moon	1963	5.00	10.00	20.00
20188	The Cruel War/One Way	1963	5.00	10.00	20.00

Albums

Number	Title (A Side/B Side)	Yr	VG	VG+	NM
RCA VICTOR					
LSP-4645	Nancy and Lee Again	1972	7.50	15.00	30.00
—With Lee Hazlewood					
LSP-4774	Woman	1973	6.25	12.50	25.00
VPS-6078 [(2)]	This Is Nancy Sinatra	1972	12.50	25.00	50.00
REPRISE					
R-6202 [M]	Boots	1966	6.25	12.50	25.00
RS-6202 [S]	Boots	1966	7.50	15.00	30.00
R-6207 [M]	How Does That Grab You?	1966	5.00	10.00	20.00
RS-6207 [S]	How Does That Grab You?	1966	6.25	12.50	25.00
R-6221 [M]	Nancy in London	1966	5.00	10.00	20.00
RS-6221 [S]	Nancy in London	1966	6.25	12.50	25.00
R-6239 [M]	Sugar	1967	6.25	12.50	25.00
RS-6239 [S]	Sugar	1967	5.00	10.00	20.00
R-6251 [M]	Country, My Way	1967	6.25	12.50	25.00
RS-6251 [S]	Country, My Way	1967	5.00	10.00	20.00
RS-6273	Nancy and Lee	1968	5.00	10.00	20.00
—With Lee Hazlewood					
R-6277 [M]	Movin' with Nancy	1967	6.25	12.50	25.00
RS-6277 [S]	Movin' with Nancy	1967	5.00	10.00	20.00
RS-6333	Nancy	1969	5.00	10.00	20.00
RS-6409	Nancy's Greatest Hits	1970	5.00	10.00	20.00
RHINO					
R1-70166	Fairy Tales and Fantasies: The Best of Nancy and Lee	1989	2.50	5.00	10.00
—With Lee Hazlewood					
RNLP-70227	Boots: Nancy Sinatra's All-Time Hits (1966-1970)	1987	2.50	5.00	10.00

SINATRA FAMILY, THE

See VARIOUS ARTISTS COMPILATIONS in back.

SINCERES, THE (1)

45s

Number	Title (A Side/B Side)	Yr	VG	VG+	NM
COLUMBIA					
43110	Sincerely/Snap Your Fingers	1964	3.75	7.50	15.00
EPIC					
9583	Kookie Ookie/Our Winter Love	1963	3.75	7.50	15.00
TAURUS					
377	The Magic of Love/Tell Her	1966	7.50	15.00	30.00

SINCERES, THE (2)

45s

Number	Title (A Side/B Side)	Yr	VG	VG+	NM
JORDAN					
117	You're Too Young/Forbidden Love	1960	62.50	125.00	250.00

Number	Title (A Side/B Side)	Yr	VG	VG+	NM
RICHIE					
545	Please Don't Cheat on Me/If You Should Leave Me	1961	175.00	350.00	700.00
—No mention of Roulette Records on label					
545	Please Don't Cheat on Me/If You Should Leave Me	1961	25.00	50.00	100.00
—With Roulette Records distribution mentioned on label					
SIGMA					
1003/4	Darling/Do You Remember	1960	100.00	200.00	400.00

SINFIELD, PETE

Albums

Number	Title (A Side/B Side)	Yr	VG	VG+	NM
MANTICORE					
MC 66667	Still	1973	2.50	5.00	10.00

SING A SONG WITH THE BEATLES

Albums

Number	Title (A Side/B Side)	Yr	VG	VG+	NM
TOWER					
DKAO 5000 [R]	Sing a Song with the Beatles	1965	50.00	100.00	200.00
KAO 5000 [M]	Sing a Song with the Beatles	1965	37.50	75.00	150.00
—No artist listed on label					

SINGING DOGS, THE, DON CHARLES PRESENTS

45s

Number	Title (A Side/B Side)	Yr	VG	VG+	NM
RCA					
PA-10129	Jingle Bells/Oh! Susanna	1976	—	2.00	4.00
—Black label, dog near top					
RCA VICTOR					
F2NW-7846/7 [DJ]	Pearl's Jingle Bells/Caesar's Pat-A-Cake/King's Three Blind Mice//Dolly's Oh! Susanna (Fast)/ Dolly's Oh! Susanna (Slow)	1955	10.00	20.00	40.00
—Banded version for radio use ("Jingle Bells" is 1:15)					
PA-10129	Jingle Bells/Oh! Susannah	1974	2.00	4.00	8.00
—First issue of PA-10129 has tan or brown (also possibly orange) labels					
47-6344	Oh! Susannah//Pat-a-Cake/Three Blind Mice/ Jingle Bells	1955	3.75	7.50	15.00
—"Jingle Bells" is part of a medley and lasts 1:15					
47-6344 [PS]	Oh! Susannah//Pat-a-Cake/Three Blind Mice/ Jingle Bells	1955	6.25	12.50	25.00
47-6432	Hot Dog Rock and Roll/Hot Dog Boogie	1956	3.00	6.00	12.00
48-1020	Jingle Bells/Oh! Susannah	1971	—	2.50	5.00
—First reissue; "Jingle Bells" lengthened to 1:47 on this and future issues					
48-1021	Hot Dog Rock and Roll/Hot Dog Boogie	1971	—	2.50	5.00

SINGING MCENTIRES, THE (PAKE, REBA AND SUSIE)

45s

Number	Title (A Side/B Side)	Yr	VG	VG+	NM
BOSS					
SPS-194	The Ballad of John McEntire/Interview by the Grandchildren	1969	125.00	250.00	500.00
—Supposedly only 25 copies were pressed					

SINGING NUN, THE

45s

Number	Title (A Side/B Side)	Yr	VG	VG+	NM
PHILIPS					
40152	Dominique/Entres Les Etoiles (Among the Stars)	1963	—	3.00	6.00
40152 [PS]	Dominique/Entres Les Etoiles (Among the Stars)	1963	3.00	6.00	12.00
40163	Dominique/Les Pieds de Missionaires	1963	—	3.00	6.00
40165	Tous Les Chemins/Frere "Tout Le" Monde	1964	—	2.50	5.00
40165 [PS]	Tous Les Chemins/Frere "Tout Le" Monde	1964	3.00	6.00	12.00
40195	Une Fleur (A Flower)/Avec Toi (With You)	1964	—	2.50	5.00

Albums

Number	Title (A Side/B Side)	Yr	VG	VG+	NM
PHILIPS					
PCC 203 [M]	Soeur Sourire: The Singing Nun	1963	3.75	7.50	15.00
PCC 209 [M]	Her Joy, Her Songs	1964	3.75	7.50	15.00
PCC 603 [S]	Soeur Sourire: The Singing Nun	1963	3.75	7.50	15.00
PCC 609 [S]	Her Joy, Her Songs	1964	3.75	7.50	15.00

SINGING REINDEER, THE

See DANCER, PRANCER, AND NERVOUS.

SIR DOUGLAS QUINTET

Also see THE DEVONS; DOUG SAHM.

45s

Number	Title (A Side/B Side)	Yr	VG	VG+	NM
ATLANTIC					
2965	The Nitty Gritty/I'm Just Tired of Getting Burned	1973	2.00	4.00	8.00
2985	Texas Tornado/Blue Horizon	1973	2.00	4.00	8.00
—As "Sir Douglas Band"					
CASABLANCA					
828	Roll With the Punches/I'm Not That Kat Anymore	1975	6.25	12.50	25.00
MERCURY					
73257	Michoacan/Westside Blues Again	1971	—	3.00	6.00
PACEMAKER					
280	Sugar Bee/Blue Norther	1964	5.00	10.00	20.00
PHILIPS					
40676	What About Tomorrow/A Nice Song	1970	2.00	4.00	8.00
40676 [PS]	What About Tomorrow/A Nice Song	1970	3.75	7.50	15.00
40687	Pretty Flower/Catch the Man on the Fly	1970	2.00	4.00	8.00
40708	Wasted Days, Wasted Nights/Me and My Destiny	1971	2.00	4.00	8.00
SMASH					
2169	Are Inlaws Really Outlaws/Sell a Song	1968	2.00	4.00	8.00
2191	Mendocino/I Wanna Be Your Mama Again	1968	2.00	4.00	8.00
2222	Lawd, I'm Just a Country Boy in This Great Big Freaky City/It Didn't Even Bring Me Down	1969	2.00	4.00	8.00
2233	Dynamite Woman/Too Many Dociled Minds	1969	2.00	4.00	8.00
2253	At the Crossroads/Texas Me	1969	2.00	4.00	8.00
2259	Nuevo Laredo/I Don't Wanna Go Home	1970	2.00	4.00	8.00
TRIBE					
8308	She's About a Mover/We'll Take Our Last Walk Tonight	1965	3.00	6.00	12.00
8310	The Tracker/Blue Brother	1965	2.50	5.00	10.00
8312	In Time/The Story of John Hardy	1965	2.50	5.00	10.00
8314	The Rains Came/Bacon Fat	1966	2.50	5.00	10.00
8317	She's Gotta Be Boss/Quarter to Three	1966	2.50	5.00	10.00
8318	Beginning of the End/Love Don't Treat Me Fair	1966	2.50	5.00	10.00
8321	She Digs My Love/When I Sing the Blues	1966	2.50	5.00	10.00
8323	Hang Loose/I'm Sorry	1967	2.50	5.00	10.00

Albums

Number	Title (A Side/B Side)	Yr	VG	VG+	NM
ABC DOT					
DO-2057	Texas Rock for Country Rollers	1976	3.75	7.50	15.00
—As "Sir Doug and the Texas Tornadoes"					
ATLANTIC					
SD 7287	Texas Tornado	1974	3.75	7.50	15.00
—As "Sir Douglas Band"					
BEAT ROCKET					
BR 123	The Best of the Sir Douglas Quintet	2000	3.00	6.00	12.00
—Reissue of Tribe LP on 180-gram vinyl					
BR 124	The Sir Douglas Quintet Is Back!	2000	3.00	6.00	12.00
—New compilation of Tribe material on 180-gram vinyl					
PHILIPS					
PHS 600344	1 + 1 + 1 = 4	1970	6.25	12.50	25.00
PHS 600353	The Return of Doug Saldana	1971	6.25	12.50	25.00
R&M					
UDL-2343	The Tracker	1981	5.00	10.00	20.00
SMASH					
SRS-67108	Sir Douglas Quintet + 2 = Honkey Blues	1968	7.50	15.00	30.00
SRS-67115	Mendocino	1969	6.25	12.50	25.00
SRS-67130	Together After Five	1970	6.25	12.50	25.00
TAKOMA					
TAK-7086	The Best of the Sir Douglas Quintet	1980	3.00	6.00	12.00
TAK-7088	Border Wave	1981	3.00	6.00	12.00
TAK-7095	Sir Douglas Quintet Live	1985	3.00	6.00	12.00
TRIBE					
TR 37001 [M]	The Best of the Sir Douglas Quintet	1966	17.50	35.00	70.00
TRS 47001 [R]	The Best of the Sir Douglas Quintet	1966	12.50	25.00	50.00
VARRICK					
004	Quintessence	1983	3.00	6.00	12.00

SIR LORD BALTIMORE

45s

Number	Title (A Side/B Side)	Yr	VG	VG+	NM
MERCURY					
73181	I Got a Woman/Master Headache	1970	2.00	4.00	8.00

Albums

Number	Title (A Side/B Side)	Yr	VG	VG+	NM
MERCURY					
SRM-1-613	Sir Lord Baltimore	1971	6.25	12.50	25.00
SR-61328	Kingdom Come	1970	6.25	12.50	25.00

SIR WALTER RALEIGH AND THE COUPONS

45s

Number	Title (A Side/B Side)	Yr	VG	VG+	NM
A&M					
757	White Cliffs of Dover/Something or Other	1965	2.50	5.00	10.00
764	While I Wait/Somethin'	1965	2.50	5.00	10.00
JERDEN					
760	Tomorrow's Gonna Be Another Day/Whitcomb St.	1965	3.00	6.00	12.00
TOWER					
156	Tell Her Tonight/If You Need Me	1965	2.50	5.00	10.00
220	I Don't Want to Cry/Always	1966	2.50	5.00	10.00

SISK, SHIRLEY

45s

Number	Title (A Side/B Side)	Yr	VG	VG+	NM
SUN					
365	I Forgot to Remember to Forget/The Other Side	1961	6.25	12.50	25.00

SISTER SLEDGE

12-Inch Singles

Number	Title (A Side/B Side)	Yr	VG	VG+	NM
ATLANTIC					
DSKO 97 [DJ]	As (same on both sides)	1977	3.75	7.50	15.00
850 [DJ]	Frankie (Club Mix) (Dub Mix)/Hold Out Poppy	1985	—	3.00	6.00
868 [DJ]	Dancing on the Jagged Edge/(Dub)	1985	—	3.00	6.00
979 [DJ]	Here to Stay (2 mixes)/Make a Wish	1986	—	3.00	6.00
—B-side by Joe Cruz					
86862	Dancing on the Jagged Edge/(Dub)	1985	—	3.00	6.00
COTILLION					
229 [DJ]	Reach Your Peak (5:26) (same on both sides)	1980	2.00	4.00	8.00
277 [DJ]	He's Just a Runaway (6:05) (3:57)	1981	2.00	4.00	8.00
645 [DJ]	B.Y.O.B. (Bring Your Own Body) (6:43) (3:50)	1983	—	3.00	6.00
RHINO					
76019	We Are Family (2 mixes)/Lost in Music (2 mixes)	1993	2.00	4.00	8.00

45s

Number	Title (A Side/B Side)	Yr	VG	VG+	NM
ATCO					
6924	The Weatherman/Have You Met My Friend	1973	—	3.00	6.00
6940	Mama Never Told Me/Neither One of Us	1973	—	3.00	6.00
7008	Love Don't You Go Through No Changes on Me/ Don't You Miss Him	1974	—	2.50	5.00
7020	Circle of Love (Caught in the Middle)/Cross My Heart	1975	—	2.50	5.00
7035	Love Ain't Easy/Love Has Found Me	1975	—	2.50	5.00
ATLANTIC					
89357	Here to Stay/Make a Wish	1986	—	—	3.00
—B-side by Joe Cruz					
89466	You're Fine/(B-side unknown)	1985	—	—	3.00
89520	You Need Me/Dancing on the Jagged Edge	1985	—	—	3.00
89547	Frankie/Hold Out Poppy	1985	—	—	3.00
89547 [PS]	Frankie/Hold Out Poppy	1985	—	2.00	4.00
COTILLION					
44202	Thank You for Today/Have Love Will Travel	1976	—	2.50	5.00
44208	Cream of the Crop/Love Ain't Easy	1976	—	2.50	5.00
44220	Blockbuster Boy/Moondancer	1977	—	2.50	5.00
44226	Baby, It's the Rain/Hold Onto This Feeling	1977	—	2.50	5.00
44234	Do It to the Max/I've Seen Better Days	1978	—	2.50	5.00
44245	He's the Greatest Dancer/Somebody Loves Me	1978	—	2.00	4.00
44251	We Are Family/Easier to Love	1979	—	2.00	4.00
45001	Lost in Music/Thinking of You	1979	—	2.00	4.00

Number	Title (A Side/B Side)	Yr	VG	VG+	NM
45007	Got to Love Somebody/Good Girl Now	1979	—	2.00	4.00
45013	Reach Your Peak/You Fooled Around	1980	—	2.00	4.00
45020	Let's Go on Vacation/Easy Street	1980	—	2.00	4.00
46007	All American Girls/Happy Feelings	1981	—	2.00	4.00
46012	Next Time You'll Know/If You Really Want Me	1981	—	2.00	4.00
46017	He's Just a Runaway/He's Just a Runaway (Long Version)	1981	—	2.00	4.00
47000	My Guy/Il Macquillace Lady	1982	—	2.00	4.00
47007	All the Man That I Need/Light Footin'	1982	—	2.00	4.00
99834	Gotta Get Back to Love/Lifetime Lover	1983	—	2.00	4.00
99885	B.Y.O.B. (Bring Your Own Baby)/(B-side unknown)	1983	—	2.00	4.00
Albums					
ATCO					
SD 36-105	Circle of Love	1975	5.00	10.00	20.00
ATLANTIC					
81255	When the Boys Meet the Girls	1985	2.50	5.00	10.00
COTILLION					
SD 5209	We Are Family	1979	2.50	5.00	10.00
SD 5231	The Sisters	1982	2.50	5.00	10.00
SD 9919	Together	1976	3.00	6.00	12.00
SD 16012	Love Somebody Today	1980	2.50	5.00	10.00
SD 16027	All American Girls	1981	2.50	5.00	10.00
90069	Bet Cha Say That to All the Girls	1983	2.50	5.00	10.00

SIX PENTZ, THE

Number	Title (A Side/B Side)	Yr	VG	VG+	NM
45s					
BRENT					
7062	Imitation Situation/Please Come Home	1967	5.00	10.00	20.00
7064	Don't Say You're Sorry/Tinkle Talk	1967	5.00	10.00	20.00

SIX TEENS, THE

Number	Title (A Side/B Side)	Yr	VG	VG+	NM
45s					
FLIP					
315	A Casual Look/Teenage Promise	1956	5.00	10.00	20.00
317	Send Me Flowers/Afar Into the Night	1956	3.75	7.50	15.00
320	My Special Guy/Only Jim	1956	3.75	7.50	15.00
322	Arrow of Love/Was It a Dream of Mine	1957	3.75	7.50	15.00
326	Baby You're Dynamite/My Surprise	1957	3.75	7.50	15.00
329	My Secret/Stop Playing Ping Pong	1958	3.75	7.50	15.00
333	Danny/Love's Funny That Way	1958	3.75	7.50	15.00
338	Baby-O/Oh, It's Crazy	1958	5.00	10.00	20.00
346	Why Do I Go to School/Heaven Knows I Love You	1959	6.25	12.50	25.00
350	So Happy/That Wonderful Secret of Love	1960	3.75	7.50	15.00
351	A Little Prayer/Suddenly in Love	1960	3.75	7.50	15.00

SIXPENCE, THE

Number	Title (A Side/B Side)	Yr	VG	VG+	NM
45s					
ALL AMERICAN					
313	Fortune Teller/My Flash on You	1966	10.00	20.00	40.00
333	Hey Joe/(B-side unknown)	1967	7.50	15.00	30.00
353	Fortune Teller/My Flash on You	1967	7.50	15.00	30.00
DOT					
16959	Fortune Teller/My Flash on You	1966	6.25	12.50	25.00
IMPACT					
1025	What to Do/You're the Love	1967	6.25	12.50	25.00

SKA KINGS, THE

Number	Title (A Side/B Side)	Yr	VG	VG+	NM
45s					
ATLANTIC					
2232	Jamaica Sea/Oil in My Lamp	1964	2.50	5.00	10.00
2236	Last Night Ska/Watermelon Man Ska	1964	2.50	5.00	10.00

SKARLETTONES, THE

Number	Title (A Side/B Side)	Yr	VG	VG+	NM
45s					
EMBER					
1053	Do You Remember/Will You Dream	1959	30.00	60.00	120.00

SKEE BROTHERS, THE

Number	Title (A Side/B Side)	Yr	VG	VG+	NM
45s					
EPIC					
9275	Big Deal/While I'm Away	1958	25.00	50.00	100.00
OKEH					
7108	That's All She Wrote/Four Aces	1959	12.50	25.00	50.00
ROULETTE					
4164	Romeo Joe/Lu Ann	1959	5.00	10.00	20.00

SKELLERN, PETER

Number	Title (A Side/B Side)	Yr	VG	VG+	NM
45s					
LONDON					
20075	You're a Lady/Manifesto	1972	—	2.50	5.00
PRIVATE STOCK					
45028	Hold On to Love/(B-side unknown)	1975	—	2.00	4.00
45054	Hard Times/And Then You'll Fall	1975	—	2.00	4.00

SKELTON, EDDIE

Number	Title (A Side/B Side)	Yr	VG	VG+	NM
45s					
DIXIE					
2011	Keep It Swinging/Without You	1958	500.00	1000.	1500.
STARDAY					
294	My Heart Gets Lonely/Let Me Be With You Forever	1957	37.50	75.00	150.00

SKID ROW

Number	Title (A Side/B Side)	Yr	VG	VG+	NM
Albums					
EPIC					
E 30404	Skid Row	1971	5.00	10.00	20.00
E 30913	34 Hours	1971	6.25	12.50	25.00

SKIP AND FLIP

Also see GARY PAXTON.

Number	Title (A Side/B Side)	Yr	VG	VG+	NM
45s					
BRENT					
7002	It Was I/Lunch Hour	1959	6.25	12.50	25.00
7005	Fancy Nancy/It Could Be	1959	6.25	12.50	25.00
7010	Cherry Pie/I'll Quit Cryin' Over You	1960	6.25	12.50	25.00
7013	Teenage Honeymoon/Hully Gully Cha Cha Cha	1960	5.00	10.00	20.00
7017	The Green Door/Willow Tree	1960	5.00	10.00	20.00
7028	Over the Mountain/One More Drink for Julie	1962	5.00	10.00	20.00
CALIFORNIA					
2325	Tossin' and Turnin'/Everyday I Have to Cry	1963	3.75	7.50	15.00
REV					
3523	Why Not Confess/Johnny Risk	1959	6.25	12.50	25.00
—As "Gary and Clyde"					
TIME					
1007	Why Not Confess/Johnny Risk	1959	5.00	10.00	20.00
—As "Gary and Clyde"					
1031	Betty Jean/Doubt	1961	5.00	10.00	20.00

SKIP AND THE CREATIONS

Number	Title (A Side/B Side)	Yr	VG	VG+	NM
Albums					
JUSTICE					
(# unknown)	Mobam	196?	100.00	200.00	400.00

SKY

Doug Fieger, later of The Knack, was in this group.

Number	Title (A Side/B Side)	Yr	VG	VG+	NM
45s					
RCA VICTOR					
74-0419	Goodie Two Shoes/Make It in Time	1971	—	3.00	6.00
74-0611	Let It Lie Low/Taking the Long Way Home	1971	—	3.00	6.00
Albums					
RCA VICTOR					
LSP-4457	Sky	1970	3.75	7.50	15.00
LSP-4514	Sailor's Delight	1971	3.75	7.50	15.00

SKYLARK

Number	Title (A Side/B Side)	Yr	VG	VG+	NM
45s					
CAPITOL					
3378	What Would I Do Without You/Suites for My Lady	1972	—	2.00	4.00
3511	Wildflower/The Writings on the Wall	1973	—	2.50	5.00
3661	I'll Have to Go Away/Twenty-Six Years	1973	—	2.00	4.00
3773	Virgin Green/If That's the Way You Want It	1973	—	2.00	4.00
Albums					
CAPITOL					
ST-11048	Skylark	1972	3.75	7.50	15.00
ST-11256	Skylark 2	1973	3.00	6.00	12.00

SKYLARKS, THE (1)

Number	Title (A Side/B Side)	Yr	VG	VG+	NM
45s					
ADMIRAL					
500	I'll Surf Around the World/How Many Times	1963	7.50	15.00	30.00

SKYLARKS, THE (2)

Number	Title (A Side/B Side)	Yr	VG	VG+	NM
45s					
DECCA					
48241	The Glory of Love/You and I	1951	125.00	250.00	500.00

SKYLARKS, THE (3)

Number	Title (A Side/B Side)	Yr	VG	VG+	NM
45s					
EVERLAST					
5022	Everybody's Got Somebody/Jeannie	1963	7.50	15.00	30.00

SKYLARKS, THE (4)

Number	Title (A Side/B Side)	Yr	VG	VG+	NM
45s					
RCA VICTOR					
47-5257	Home in Pasadena/I Had the Craziest Dream	1953	6.25	12.50	25.00

SKYLARKS, THE (5)

Number	Title (A Side/B Side)	Yr	VG	VG+	NM
45s					
VERVE					
10082	Ol' Man River/There's a Boat Dat's Leavin' for New York	1957	5.00	10.00	20.00

SKYLARKS, THE (U)

Number	Title (A Side/B Side)	Yr	VG	VG+	NM
45s					
THUNDERBIRD					
102	Do You Know?/Here Comes the Fool	196?	3.00	6.00	12.00

SKYLINERS, THE

Number	Title (A Side/B Side)	Yr	VG	VG+	NM
45s					
ATCO					
6270	Since I Fell for You/I'd Die	1963	10.00	20.00	40.00
CALICO					
103/4	Since I Don't Have You/One Night, One Night	1959	12.50	25.00	50.00
106	This I Swear/Tomorrow	1959	7.50	15.00	30.00
109	It Happened Today/Lonely Way	1959	7.50	15.00	30.00
114	How Much/Lorraine from Spain	1960	6.25	12.50	25.00
117	Pennies from Heaven/I'll Be Seeing You	1960	6.25	12.50	25.00
120	Believe Me/Happy Time	1960	6.25	12.50	25.00
CAMEO					
215	Three Coins in the Fountain/Everyone But You	1962	10.00	20.00	40.00
CAPITOL					
3979	Where Have They Gone/I Could Have Loved You So Well	1974	6.25	12.50	25.00
—As "Jimmy Beaumont and the Skyliners"					
CLASSIC ARTISTS					
123	You're My Christmas Present/Another Lonely New Year's Eve	1990	—	2.50	5.00

Number	Title (A Side/B Side)	Yr	VG	VG+	NM
COLPIX					
188	I'll Close My Eyes/The Door Is Still Open	1961	10.00	20.00	40.00
607	Ba'ion Rhythms/The End of a Story	196?	10.00	20.00	40.00
—As "Jimmy Beaumont and the Skyliners"					
613	Close Your Eyes/Our Love Will Last	1961	10.00	20.00	40.00
DRIVE					
6250	Our Day Is Here/The Day the Clown Cried	1976	2.00	4.00	8.00
JUBILEE					
5506	The Loser/Everything Is Fine	1965	3.75	7.50	15.00
5512	Who Do You Love/Get Yourself a Baby	1965	3.75	7.50	15.00
5520	I Run to You/Don't Hurt Me Baby	1965	3.75	7.50	15.00
MOTOWN					
1046 [DJ]	Since I Fell for You/I'd Die	1963	1000.	1500.	2000.
—Record never got beyond the test pressing stage (2 known copies)					
ORIGINAL SOUND					
35	Since I Don't Have You/One Night, One Night	1963	3.75	7.50	15.00
36	Pennies from Heaven/I'll Be Seeing You	1963	3.75	7.50	15.00
37	This I Swear/It Happened Today	1963	3.75	7.50	15.00
TORTOISE INT'L.					
PB-11243	Oh How Happy/We've Got Love on Our Side	1978	2.00	4.00	8.00
PB-11312	Smile On Me/Love Bug (Done Bit Me Again)	1978	2.00	4.00	8.00
VISCOUNT					
104	Comes Love/Tell Me	1962	5.00	10.00	20.00
Albums					
CALICO					
LP-3000 [M]	The Skyliners	1959	200.00	400.00	600.00
—Yellow and blue label					
LP-3000 [M]	The Skyliners	196?	50.00	100.00	200.00
—Blue label					
KAMA SUTRA					
KSBS-2026	Once Upon a Time	1971	6.25	12.50	25.00
ORIGINAL SOUND					
OS-5010 [M]	Since I Don't Have You	1963	12.50	25.00	50.00
OSS-8873 [S]	Since I Don't Have You	1963	17.50	35.00	70.00
OSS-8873 [S]	Since I Don't Have You	197?	3.75	7.50	15.00
—Reissue on thinner vinyl					

SLADE

Includes early releases as "Ambrose Slade." Also see THE IN-BE-TWEENS.

Number	Title (A Side/B Side)	Yr	VG	VG+	NM
45s					
CBS ASSOCIATED					
04398	Run Runaway/Don't Take a Hurricane	1984	—	2.00	4.00
04528	My Oh My/High and Dry	1984	—	2.00	4.00
04865	Little Sheila/Lock Up Your Daughters	1985	—	2.00	4.00
COTILLION					
44128	Get Down and Get With It/The Gospel According to Rasputin	1971	6.25	12.50	25.00
44139	Cos I Love You/Gotta Keep a-Rockin'	1971	6.25	12.50	25.00
44150	Look Wot You Dun/Candidate	1972	6.25	12.50	25.00
POLYDOR					
15041	Look Wot You Dun/Candidate	1972	2.50	5.00	10.00
15044	Cuz I Love You/My Life Is Natural	1972	2.50	5.00	10.00
15046	Take Me Back 'Ome/Wondering Why	1972	2.50	5.00	10.00
15053	Mama Weer All Crazee Now/Man Who Speeks Evil	1972	2.50	5.00	10.00
15060	Gudbuy T' Jane/I Won't Let It 'Appen Again	1973	2.50	5.00	10.00
15069	Cum On Feel the Noize/I'm Mee, I'm Now, An' That's Orl	1973	3.75	7.50	15.00
15080	Let the Good Times Roll/Feel So Fine-I Don' Mind	1973	2.50	5.00	10.00
REPRISE					
1182	Skweeze Me Pleeze Me/My Town	1973	2.00	4.00	8.00
WARNER BROS.					
7759	Merry Christmas Everybody/Don't Blame Me	1973	2.50	5.00	10.00
7777	Good Time Gals/We're Really Gonna Raise the Roof	1974	2.00	4.00	8.00
7808	How Can It Be/When the Lights Are Out	1974	2.00	4.00	8.00
8134	How Does It Feel/OK, Yesterday Was Yesterday	1975	2.00	4.00	8.00
8185	Nobody's Fool/When the Chips Are Down	1976	2.00	4.00	8.00
Albums					
CBS ASSOCIATED					
FZ 39336	Keep Your Hands Off My Power Supply	1984	2.50	5.00	10.00
PZ 39336	Keep Your Hands Off My Power Supply	1985	2.00	4.00	8.00
—Budget-line reissue					
FZ 39976	Rogues Gallery	1985	2.50	5.00	10.00
COTILLION					
SD 9035	Play It Loud	1970	5.00	10.00	20.00
FONTANA					
SRF-67598	Ballzy	1969	20.00	40.00	80.00
SRF-67598 [DJ]	Ballzy	1969	12.50	25.00	50.00
—White label promo					
POLYDOR					
PD-5508	Slade Alive!	1972	3.75	7.50	15.00
PD-5524	Slayed?	1973	3.75	7.50	15.00
REPRISE					
MS 2173	Sladest	1973	3.00	6.00	12.00
WARNER BROS.					
BS 2770	Stomp Your Hands, Clap Your Feet	1974	3.00	6.00	12.00
BS 2865	Slade in Flame	1975	3.00	6.00	12.00
BS 2936	Nobody's Fools	1976	3.00	6.00	12.00

SLADES, THE

Number	Title (A Side/B Side)	Yr	VG	VG+	NM
45s					
DOMINO					
500	You Cheated/The Waddle	1958	10.00	20.00	40.00
800	You Gambled/No Time	1959	10.00	20.00	40.00
901	Just You/It's Better to Love	1959	7.50	15.00	30.00
906	It's Your Turn/Take My Heart	1961	10.00	20.00	40.00
1000	Summertime/You Must Try	1961	7.50	15.00	30.00
LIBERTY					
55118	Baby/You Mean Everything to Me	1957	12.50	25.00	50.00
—As "The Spades," in error					
55118	Baby/You Mean Everything to Me	1957	6.25	12.50	25.00

SLATKIN, FELIX

Number	Title (A Side/B Side)	Yr	VG	VG+	NM
45s					
LIBERTY					
55282	Theme from The Sundowners/Gaythers Gone	1960	2.50	5.00	10.00
55299	My Own True Love/It's Not Forever	1961	2.50	5.00	10.00
55326	Streets of Laredo/(B-side unknown)	1961	2.50	5.00	10.00
55329	Theme from The Pleasure of Your Company/Street Scene	1961	2.50	5.00	10.00
55372	King of Kings/Mandolin	1961	2.50	5.00	10.00
55487	A Theme Searching for a Picture/Theme from "My Geisha"	1962	2.00	4.00	8.00
55523	Orange Blossom Special/Maiden's Prayer	1962	2.00	4.00	8.00
Albums					
LIBERTY					
LRP-3150 [M]	Fantastic Percussion	1960	3.75	7.50	15.00
LRP-3287 [M]	Our Winter Love	1963	3.00	6.00	12.00
LST-7150 [S]	Fantastic Percussion	1960	5.00	10.00	20.00
LST-7287 [S]	Our Winter Love	1963	3.75	7.50	15.00
LMM-13001 [M]	Paradise Found	1960	3.75	7.50	15.00
LMM-13008 [M]	Street Scene	1961	3.75	7.50	15.00
LMM-13011 [M]	Many Splendored Themes	1962	3.75	7.50	15.00
LMM-13019 [M]	Inspired Themes from the Inspired Films	1962	3.75	7.50	15.00
LMM-13024 [M]	Hoedown	1963	3.75	7.50	15.00
LSS-14001 [S]	Paradise Found	1960	4.50	9.00	18.00
LSS-14008 [S]	Street Scene	1961	4.50	9.00	18.00
LSS-14011 [S]	Many Splendored Themes	1962	4.50	9.00	18.00
LSS-14019 [S]	Inspired Themes from the Inspired Films	1962	4.50	9.00	18.00
LSS-14024 [S]	Hoedown	1963	4.50	9.00	18.00
SUNSET					
SUM-1106 [M]	Love Strings	196?	3.00	6.00	12.00
SUM-1141 [M]	Seasons Greetings	196?	3.00	6.00	12.00
SUM-1170 [M]	Tender Strings	196?	3.00	6.00	12.00
SUS-5106 [S]	Love Strings	196?	3.00	6.00	12.00
SUS-5141 [S]	Seasons Greetings	196?	3.00	6.00	12.00
SUS-5170 [S]	Tender Strings	196?	3.00	6.00	12.00
UNITED ARTISTS					
UAS-6818	Classic Country	1971	2.50	5.00	10.00

SLAVIN, SLICK

Number	Title (A Side/B Side)	Yr	VG	VG+	NM
45s					
IMPERIAL					
5540	Speed Crazy/She Says She's Mine	1958	7.50	15.00	30.00

SLED, BOB, AND THE TOBOGGANS

Number	Title (A Side/B Side)	Yr	VG	VG+	NM
45s					
CAMEO					
400	Here We Go (Surfer Boys Are Going Skiing)/Sea and Ski	1966	12.50	25.00	50.00

SLEDGE, PERCY

Number	Title (A Side/B Side)	Yr	VG	VG+	NM
12-Inch Singles					
CAPRICORN					
PRO 672 [DJ]	When She's Touching Me (same on both sides)	1977	3.00	6.00	12.00
45s					
ATLANTIC					
2326	When a Man Loves a Woman/Love Me Like You Mean It	1966	5.00	10.00	20.00
2342	Warm and Tender Love/Sugar Puddin'	1966	2.50	5.00	10.00
2358	It Tears Me Up/Heart of a Child	1966	2.50	5.00	10.00
2383	Baby, Help Me/You Got That Something Wonderful	1967	2.50	5.00	10.00
2396	Out of Left Field/It Can't Be Stopped	1967	2.50	5.00	10.00
2414	Love Me Tender/What Am I Living For	1967	2.50	5.00	10.00
2434	Just Out of Reach (Of My Two Empty Arms)/Hard to Believe	1967	2.50	5.00	10.00
2453	Cover Me/Behind Every Great Man There Is a Woman	1967	2.50	5.00	10.00
2490	Take Time to Know Her/It's All Wrong But It's Alright	1968	3.00	6.00	12.00
2539	Sudden Stop/Between These Arms	1968	2.50	5.00	10.00
2563	You're All Around Me/Self-Preservation	1968	2.50	5.00	10.00
2594	My Special Prayer/Bless Your Little Sweet Soul	1969	2.00	4.00	8.00
2616	Any Day Now/The Angels Listened In	1969	2.50	5.00	10.00
2646	Woman of the Night/Kind Woman	1969	2.00	4.00	8.00
2679	Faithful and True/True Love Travels on a Gravel Road	1969	2.00	4.00	8.00
2719	Too Many Rivers to Cross/Push Mr. Pride Aside	1970	2.00	4.00	8.00
2754	Help Me Make It Through the Night/Thief in the Night	1970	2.00	4.00	8.00
2826	Stop the World Tonight/That's the Way I Want to Live	1971	—	3.00	6.00
2848	Rainbow Road/Standing on the Mountain	1971	—	3.00	6.00
2886	Sunday Brother/Everything You'll Ever Need	1972	—	3.00	6.00
2963	Sunshine/Unchanging Love	1973	—	3.00	6.00
89262	When a Man Loves a Woman/Cover Me	1987	—	—	3.00
89262 [PS]	When a Man Loves a Woman/Cover Me	1987	—	2.00	4.00
CAPRICORN					
0209	I'll Be Your Everything/Blue Water	1974	—	2.50	5.00
0220	If This Is the Last Time/Behind Closed Doors	1975	—	2.50	5.00
0273	When a Boy Becomes a Man/When She Touches Me	1977	—	2.50	5.00
MONUMENT					
03612	You Had to Be There/Hard Lovin' Woman	1983	—	2.00	4.00
03878	She's Too Pretty to Cry/Home Type Thing	1983	—	2.00	4.00
PHILCO-FORD					
HP-12	When a Man Loves a Woman/Baby Help Me	1967	6.25	12.50	25.00
—4-inch plastic "Hip Pocket Record" with color sleeve					
Albums					
ATLANTIC					
8125 [M]	When a Man Loves a Woman	1966	12.50	25.00	50.00
SD 8125 [R]	When a Man Loves a Woman	1966	7.50	15.00	30.00
8132 [M]	Warm and Tender Soul	1966	12.50	25.00	50.00

Number	Title (A Side/B Side)	Yr	VG	VG+	NM
SD 8132 [R]	Warm and Tender Soul	1966	7.50	15.00	30.00
8146 [M]	The Percy Sledge Way	1967	12.50	25.00	50.00
SD 8146 [S]	The Percy Sledge Way	1967	12.50	25.00	50.00
SD 8180	Take Time to Know Her	1968	12.50	25.00	50.00
SD 8210	The Best of Percy Sledge	1969	6.25	12.50	25.00
CAPRICORN					
CP 0147	I'll Be Your Everything	1974	3.75	7.50	15.00
MONUMENT					
FW 38532	Percy	1983	3.00	6.00	12.00

SLICK, GRACE

Also see THE GREAT SOCIETY; JEFFERSON AIRPLANE; JEFFERSON STARSHIP; PAUL KANTNER AND GRACE SLICK.

12-Inch Singles

Number	Title (A Side/B Side)	Yr	VG	VG+	NM
RCA VICTOR					
JD-13708 [DJ]	All the Machines (Long)/All the Machines (Short)	1984	—	3.00	6.00

45s

Number	Title (A Side/B Side)	Yr	VG	VG+	NM
GRUNT					
BFBO-0183	Theme from "Manhole"/Come Again, Toucan	1973	—	3.00	6.00
RCA					
PB-11939	Seasons/Angel of Night	1980	—	2.00	4.00
PB-11939 [PS]	Seasons/Angel of Night	1980	—	2.50	5.00
PB-12041	Dreams/Do It the Hard Way	1980	—	2.00	4.00
PB-12171	Sea of Love/Full Moon Man	1981	—	2.00	4.00
PB-12172	Mistreater/Full Moon Man	1981	—	—	—
—Canceled					
PB-12186	Round and Round/Full Moon Man	1981	—	—	—
—Canceled					
PB-13764	Through the Window/Habits	1984	—	2.00	4.00

Albums

Number	Title (A Side/B Side)	Yr	VG	VG+	NM
GRUNT					
BFL1-0347	Manhole	1974	3.00	6.00	12.00
AYL1-3736	Manhole	1981	2.00	4.00	8.00
—"Best Buy Series" reissue					
RCA VICTOR					
AFL1-3544	Dreams	1980	2.50	5.00	10.00
AQL1-3851	Welcome to the Wrecking Ball	1981	2.50	5.00	10.00
DJL1-3922 [DJ]	Welcome to the Wrecking Ball Interview	1981	5.00	10.00	20.00
DJL1-3923 [DJ]	RCA Special Radio Series	1981	5.00	10.00	20.00

SLLEDNATS, THE

See THE STANDELLS.

SLOAN, P.F.

45s

Number	Title (A Side/B Side)	Yr	VG	VG+	NM
ALADDIN					
3461	All I Want Is Lovin'/Little Girl in the Cabin	1959	6.25	12.50	25.00
—As "Flip Sloan"					
ATCO					
6663	Star Gazin'/New Design	1969	5.00	10.00	20.00
DUNHILL					
4007	Sins of the Family/This Mornin'	1965	3.75	7.50	15.00
4016	Halloween Mary/I'd Have to Be Out of My Mind	1965	3.75	7.50	15.00
4016 [PS]	Halloween Mary/I'd Have to Be Out of My Mind	1965	6.25	12.50	25.00
—Sleeve is promo only					
4024	From a Distance/Patterns	1966	6.25	12.50	25.00
4037	City Women/Top of a Fence	1966	3.75	7.50	15.00
4054	I Found a Girl/A Melody for You	1966	3.75	7.50	15.00
4064	Sunflower, Sunflower/The Man Behind the Red Balloon	1967	6.25	12.50	25.00
4064 [PS]	Sunflower, Sunflower/The Man Behind the Red Balloon	1967	7.50	15.00	30.00
4106	Karma (Study of Divination)/I Can't Help But Wonder, Elizabeth	1967	6.25	12.50	25.00
—As "Philip Sloan"					
MART					
802	She's My Girl/If You Believe in Me	1960	20.00	40.00	80.00
MUMS					
6010	Let Me Be/Springtime	1972	5.00	10.00	20.00

Albums

Number	Title (A Side/B Side)	Yr	VG	VG+	NM
ATCO					
SD 33-268	Measure of Pleasure	1968	6.25	12.50	25.00
DUNHILL					
D-50004 [M]	Songs of Our Times	1965	6.25	12.50	25.00
DS-50004 [S]	Songs of Our Times	1965	7.50	15.00	30.00
D-50007 [M]	Twelve More Times	1966	6.25	12.50	25.00
DS-50007 [S]	Twelve More Times	1966	7.50	15.00	30.00
MUMS					
KZ 31260	Raised on Records	1972	5.00	10.00	20.00
RHINO					
RNLP-70133	Precious Times: The Best of P.F. Sloan	1986	2.50	5.00	10.00

SLY

See SLY STEWART.

SLY AND THE FAMILY STONE

Also see GRAHAM CENTRAL STATION; SLY STEWART.

45s

Number	Title (A Side/B Side)	Yr	VG	VG+	NM
EPIC					
10229	Higher/Underdog	1967	2.50	5.00	10.00
10256	Dance to the Music/Let Me Hear It from You	1967	2.50	5.00	10.00
10353	Life/M'Lady	1968	2.00	4.00	8.00
10407	Everyday People/Sing a Simple Song	1968	2.50	5.00	10.00
10407 [PS]	Everyday People/Sing a Simple Song	1968	3.00	6.00	12.00
10450	Stand!/I Want to Take You Higher	1969	2.50	5.00	10.00
10450 [PS]	Stand!/I Want to Take You Higher	1969	3.00	6.00	12.00
10497	Hot Fun in the Summertime/Fun	1969	2.50	5.00	10.00
10555	Thank You Falettinme Be Mice Elf Agin/ Everybody Is a Star	1969	—	3.00	6.00
10555 [PS]	Thank You Falettinme Be Mice Elf Agin/ Everybody Is a Star	1969	2.50	5.00	10.00
10805	Family Affair/Luv N' Haight	1971	—	3.00	6.00
10829	Runnin' Away/Brave & Strong	1972	—	3.00	6.00
10850	Smilin'/Luv N' Haight	1972	—	3.00	6.00
11017	If You Want Me to Stay/Thankful N' Thoughtful	1973	—	3.00	6.00
11017	If You Want Me to Stay/Babies Makin' Babies	1973	—	3.00	6.00
11060	Frisky/If It Were Left Up to Me	1973	—	3.00	6.00
11140	Time for Livin'/Small Talk	1974	—	3.00	6.00
50035	Loose Booty/Can't Strain My Brain	1974	—	3.00	6.00
50119	Hot Fun in the Summertime/Fun	1975	2.00	4.00	8.00
50135	I Get High on You/That's Lovin' You	1975	—	2.50	5.00
50175	Li Lo Li/Who Do You Love	1975	—	2.50	5.00
50201	Greed/Crossword Puzzle	1976	—	2.50	5.00
50331	Family Again/Nothing Less Than Happiness	1977	—	2.50	5.00
LOADSTONE					
3951	I Ain't Got Nobody/I Can't Turn You Loose	1967	5.00	10.00	20.00
WARNER BROS.					
29682	High Y'All/Ha Ha He He	1983	—	2.00	4.00
49062	Sheer Energy/Remember Who You Are	1979	—	2.00	4.00
49132	Who's to Say/Same Thing	1979	—	2.00	4.00

Albums

Number	Title (A Side/B Side)	Yr	VG	VG+	NM
EPIC					
AS 264 [DJ]	Everything You Always Wanted to Hear by Sly and the Family Stone But Were Afraid to Ask For	1976	6.25	12.50	25.00
—Promo-only compilation					
LN 24324 [M]	A Whole New Thing	1967	5.00	10.00	20.00
BN 26324 [S]	A Whole New Thing	1967	5.00	10.00	20.00
BN 26371	Dance to the Music	1968	3.75	7.50	15.00
BN 26397	Life	1968	3.75	7.50	15.00
BN 26456	Stand!	1969	3.75	7.50	15.00
PE 26456	Stand!	1986	2.00	4.00	8.00
—Budget-line reissue					
EQ 30325 [Q]	Sly and the Family Stone's Greatest Hits	1971	25.00	50.00	100.00
—Has alternate mixes of "Hot Fun in the Summertime," "Thank You" and "Everybody Is a Star," which are not rechanneled stereo as they are on other LPs					
KE 30325	Sly and the Family Stone's Greatest Hits	1970	3.00	6.00	12.00
—Yellow label, gatefold cover					
PE 30325	Sly and the Family Stone's Greatest Hits	1979	2.00	4.00	8.00
—Budget-line reissue					
E 30333	Life	1971	3.00	6.00	12.00
—Reissue of 26397					
E 30334	Dance to the Music	1971	3.00	6.00	12.00
—Reissue of 26371					
E 30335	A Whole New Thing	1971	3.00	6.00	12.00
—Reissue of 26324					
KE 30986	There's a Riot Goin' On	1971	3.00	6.00	12.00
—Yellow label, gatefold cover					
KE 32134	Fresh	1973	2.50	5.00	10.00
—Orange label					
PE 32930	Small Talk	1974	2.50	5.00	10.00
—Orange label					
PEQ 32930 [Q]	Small Talk	1974	6.25	12.50	25.00
PE 33835	High on You	1975	2.50	5.00	10.00
—Orange label					
PEQ 33835 [Q]	High on You	1975	6.25	12.50	25.00
PE 34348	Heard Ya Missed Me, Well I'm Back	1976	2.50	5.00	10.00
—Orange label					
JE 35974	Ten Years Too Soon	1979	2.50	5.00	10.00
E2 37071 [(2)]	Anthology	1981	3.75	7.50	15.00
WARNER BROS.					
BSK 3303	Back on the Right Track	1979	2.50	5.00	10.00
23700	Ain't But the Right Way	1983	2.50	5.00	10.00

SMACK, THE

Albums

Number	Title (A Side/B Side)	Yr	VG	VG+	NM
AUDIO HOUSE					
(# unknown)	The Smack	1967	500.00	1000.	2000.

SMALL, MILLIE

45s

Number	Title (A Side/B Side)	Yr	VG	VG+	NM
ATCO					
6384	Tongue Tied/Blood Shot Eyes	1965	2.50	5.00	10.00
ATLANTIC					
2266	Bring It On Home to Me/I've Fallen in Love with a Snowman	1965	2.50	5.00	10.00
BRIT					
7002	My Street/Mixed-Up, Lonely, Self-Centered, Spoiled Kind of Boy	1965	3.00	6.00	12.00
SMASH					
1893	My Boy Lollipop/Something's Gotta Be Done	1964	3.75	7.50	15.00
1920	Sweet William/What Am I Living For	1964	3.00	6.00	12.00
1940	I Love the Way You Love/Bring It On Home to Me	1964	3.00	6.00	12.00
1946	Don't You Know/Tom Hark	1964	3.00	6.00	12.00

Albums

Number	Title (A Side/B Side)	Yr	VG	VG+	NM
SMASH					
MGS-27055 [M]	My Boy Lollipop	1964	12.50	25.00	50.00
SRS-67055 [R]	My Boy Lollipop	1964	10.00	20.00	40.00

SMALL FACES

Also see FACES.

45s

Number	Title (A Side/B Side)	Yr	VG	VG+	NM
IMMEDIATE					
501	Itchykoo Park/I'm Only Dreaming	1967	3.00	6.00	12.00
1902	Here Come the Nice/Talk to You	1967	2.50	5.00	10.00
5003	Tin Soldier/I Feel Much Better	1968	2.50	5.00	10.00
5003 [PS]	Tin Soldier/I Feel Much Better	1968	6.25	12.50	25.00
5007	Lazy Sunday/Rollin' Over	1968	2.50	5.00	10.00
5009	The Universal/Donkey Rides A Penny A Glass	1968	3.75	7.50	15.00
5012	Mad John/The Journey	1969	3.75	7.50	15.00
5014	Afterglow of Your Love/Wham, Bam, Thank You Ma'am	1969	3.75	7.50	15.00
PRESS					
5007	Almost Grown/Hey Girl	1969	5.00	10.00	20.00
9794	What 'Cha Gonna Do About It/What's a Matter	1965	6.25	12.50	25.00
9826	Sha-La-La-La-Lee/Grow Your Own	1966	3.75	7.50	15.00

Number	Title (A Side/B Side)	Yr	VG	VG+	NM
PRIDE					
1006	Runaway/Shake	1972	3.00	6.00	12.00
RCA VICTOR					
47-8949	Understanding/All or Nothing	1966	5.00	10.00	20.00
47-9055	My Mind's Eye/I Can't Dance with You	1966	5.00	10.00	20.00
Albums					
ACCORD					
AN-7157	By Appointment	1982	2.50	5.00	10.00
ATLANTIC					
SD 19113	Playmates	1977	2.50	5.00	10.00
SD 19171	78 in the Shade	1978	2.50	5.00	10.00
COMPLEAT					
67-2004 [(2)]	Big Music	1985	3.00	6.00	12.00
67-5003	Ogden's Nut Gone Flake	1985	2.50	5.00	10.00
—Reissue					
IMMEDIATE					
4225	Ogden's Nut Gone Flake	1973	3.75	7.50	15.00
—Reissue has a standard square cover					
Z12 52002 [S]	There Are But Four Small Faces	1967	12.50	25.00	50.00
—Color cover (counterfeits have either black and white or black and green covers)					
Z12 52008 [S]	Ogden's Nut Gone Flake	1968	12.50	25.00	50.00
—Originals have a round cover					
MGM					
M3F-4955	Archetypes	1974	3.00	6.00	12.00
PRIDE					
PRD 0001 [R]	Early Faces	1972	3.75	7.50	15.00
PRD 0014 [P]	The History of the Small Faces	1973	3.00	6.00	12.00
SIRE					
SASH-3709 [(2)]	The Vintage Years	1976	3.75	7.50	15.00

SMART TONES, THE

Number	Title (A Side/B Side)	Yr	VG	VG+	NM
45s					
HERALD					
529	Bob-O-Link/Ginny	1958	25.00	50.00	100.00

SMILE (1)

Brian May and Roger Taylor, later of QUEEN, were in this group.

Number	Title (A Side/B Side)	Yr	VG	VG+	NM
45s					
MERCURY					
72977	Earth/Step on Me	1968	50.00	100.00	200.00

SMILE (2)

Number	Title (A Side/B Side)	Yr	VG	VG+	NM
45s					
UNI					
55313	A Year Every Night/Southbound	1972	—	3.00	6.00
55336	Tonight/One Night Stand	1972	—	3.00	6.00

SMITH

Also see GAYLE McCORMACK.

Number	Title (A Side/B Side)	Yr	VG	VG+	NM
45s					
ABC DUNHILL					
4206	Baby It's You/I Don't Believe (I Believe)	1969	2.00	4.00	8.00
4206 [PS]	Baby It's You/I Don't Believe (I Believe)	1969	3.00	6.00	12.00
4228	Take a Look Around/Mojalesky Ridge	1970	—	3.00	6.00
4238	What Am I Gonna Do/Born in Boston	1970	—	3.00	6.00
4238 [PS]	What Am I Gonna Do/Born in Boston	1970	2.50	5.00	10.00
4246	Comin' Back to Me Baby/Minus-Plus	1970	—	3.00	6.00
Albums					
ABC DUNHILL					
DS-50056	A Group Called Smith	1969	3.75	7.50	15.00
DS-50056	A Group Called Smith	1969	3.75	7.50	15.00
DS-50081	Minus-Plus	1970	3.75	7.50	15.00
DS-50081	Minus-Plus	1970	3.75	7.50	15.00

SMITH, ARLENE

Also see THE CHANTELS.

Number	Title (A Side/B Side)	Yr	VG	VG+	NM
45s					
BIG TOP					
3073	Love, Love, Love/He Knows I Love Him Too Much	1961	7.50	15.00	30.00
SPECTORIOUS					
150	Good Girls/Everything	196?	25.00	50.00	100.00

SMITH, BETTY, GROUP

Number	Title (A Side/B Side)	Yr	VG	VG+	NM
45s					
LONDON					
1763	Virginia/Double Shuffle	1958	3.00	6.00	12.00
1787	Bewitched/Hand Jive	1958	3.00	6.00	12.00
1819	My Foolsih Heart/Betty's Blues	1958	3.00	6.00	12.00

SMITH, BOB

Number	Title (A Side/B Side)	Yr	VG	VG+	NM
Albums					
KENT					
KST-551 [(2)]	The Visit	1970	25.00	50.00	100.00
—Deduct 25 percent if poster is missing					

SMITH, BOBBIE, AND THE DREAM GIRLS

See THE DREAM GIRLS.

SMITH, CAL

Number	Title (A Side/B Side)	Yr	VG	VG+	NM
45s					
DECCA					
32768	That's What It's Like to Be Lonesome/The Only Girl in the Game	1971	—	3.00	6.00
32815	Free Streets/Goin' Home to Do My Time	1971	—	3.00	6.00
32878	Woman on the Inside/To Save, My Wife	1971	—	3.00	6.00
32959	I've Found Someone of My Own/Lights of the Living	1972	—	3.00	6.00
33003	For My Baby/Handful of Stars	1972	—	3.00	6.00
33040	The Lord Knows I'm Drinking/Sweet Things I Remember About You	1972	—	3.00	6.00
KAPP					
748	I'll Just Go On Home/Silver Dew on the Blue Grass Tonight	1966	2.50	5.00	10.00
788	The Only Thing I Want/Stranger in the House	1966	2.00	4.00	8.00
834	I'll Never Be Lonesome with You/If I Had My Life to Live Over	1967	2.00	4.00	8.00
851	I'll Sail My Ship Alone/You're Not Drowning Your Heartache	1967	2.00	4.00	8.00
884	Destination Atlanta G.A./Did She Ask About Me	1968	2.00	4.00	8.00
913	Jacksonville/I Love You a Thousand Ways	1968	2.00	4.00	8.00
938	Drinking Champagne/Honky Tonk Blues	1968	2.00	4.00	8.00
960	Empty Arms/So Much to Do	1969	2.00	4.00	8.00
994	It Takes All Night Long/Daddy's Arms	1969	2.00	4.00	8.00
2037	You Can't Housebreak a Tomcat/At the Sight of You	1969	—	3.00	6.00
2059	Heaven Is Just a Touch Away/I Overlooked an Orchid	1969	—	3.00	6.00
2076	The Difference Between Going and Really Gone/My Happiness Goes Off	1970	—	3.00	6.00
MCA					
40061	I Can Feel the Leavin' Comin' On/I've Loved You All Over the World	1973	—	2.50	5.00
40136	Bleep You/An Hour and a Six-Pack	1973	—	2.50	5.00
40191	Country Bumpkin/It's Not the Miles You Traveled	1974	—	2.50	5.00
40265	Between Lust and Watching TV/Some Kind of a Woman	1974	—	2.50	5.00
40335	It's Time to Pay the Fiddler/Love Is the Foundation	1974	—	2.50	5.00
40394	She Talked a Lot About Texas/Baby's Gone	1975	—	2.50	5.00
40467	Jason's Farm/You Slip Into My Mind	1975	—	2.50	5.00
40517	Thunderstorms/19 Years and 1800 Miles	1976	—	2.00	4.00
40563	MacArthur's Hand/Sunday Morning Christian	1976	—	2.00	4.00
40618	Woman Don't Try to Sing My Song/I Play a Man	1976	—	2.00	4.00
40671	I Just Came Home to Count the Memories/Feelin' the Weight of My Chains	1976	—	2.00	4.00
40714	Come See About Me/The In Crowd	1977	—	2.00	4.00
40789	Helen/I'm Forty Now	1977	—	2.00	4.00
40839	Throwin' Memories on the Fire/Tabernacle Tom	1977	—	2.00	4.00
40864	I'm Just a Farmer/The Ghost of Jim Bob Wilson	1978	—	2.00	4.00
40911	Bits and Pieces of Life/Leona	1978	—	2.00	4.00
40982	The Rise and Fall of the Roman Empire/Oklahoma Sunshine	1978	—	2.00	4.00
41001	One Little Skinny Rib/I Fed Her Love	1979	—	2.00	4.00
41128	The Room at the Top of the Stairs/Happy Anniversary	1979	—	2.00	4.00
SOUNDWAVES					
4686	Too Many Irons in the Fire/Honky Tonk Girl	1982	—	2.00	4.00
STEP ONE					
353	Bein' Gone/I Know It's Not Over	1986	—	2.00	4.00
358	King Lear/Country Bumpkin	1986	—	2.00	4.00
Albums					
DECCA					
DL 75369	I've Found Someone of My Own	1972	3.75	7.50	15.00
KAPP					
KL-1504 [M]	All the World Is Lonely Now	1966	6.25	12.50	25.00
KL-1537 [M]	Goin' to Cal's Place	1967	6.25	12.50	25.00
KS-3504 [S]	All the World Is Lonely Now	1966	5.00	10.00	20.00
KS-3537 [S]	Goin' to Cal's Place	1967	5.00	10.00	20.00
KS-3544	Travelin' Man	1968	5.00	10.00	20.00
KS-3608	Drinking Champagne	1968	5.00	10.00	20.00
KS-3642	The Best of Cal Smith	1969	3.75	7.50	15.00
MCA					
70	The Best of Cal Smith	1973	2.50	5.00	10.00
—Reissue of Kapp 3642					
344	Cal Smith	1973	2.50	5.00	10.00
—Reissue of Decca LP					
424	Country Bumpkin	1974	2.50	5.00	10.00
467	It's Time to Pay the Fiddler	1975	2.50	5.00	10.00
485	My Kind of Country	1975	2.50	5.00	10.00
2172	Jason's Farm	1976	2.50	5.00	10.00
2266	I Just Came Home to Count the Memories	1977	2.50	5.00	10.00

SMITH, CARL

Number	Title (A Side/B Side)	Yr	VG	VG+	NM
45s					
ABC HICKORY					
54004	A Way with Words/Till I Stop Meeting You	1976	—	2.50	5.00
54009	Show Me a Brick Wall/It's Teardrop Time	1977	—	2.50	5.00
54016	This Kinda Love Ain't Meant for Sunday School/There Stands the Glass	1977	—	2.50	5.00
54022	This Lady Loving Me/Loose Talk	1978	—	2.50	5.00
54030	Remembered by Someone (Remembered by Me)/It Takes Four Feet to Make a Yard	1978	—	2.50	5.00
54037	I Can't Get the Last Memory Down/Silver Tongued Cowboy	1978	—	2.50	5.00
COLUMBIA					
4-20741	I Overlooked an Orchid/I Betcha My Heart I Love You	1950	7.50	15.00	30.00
4-20765	This Side of Heaven/I Won't Be at Home	1950	7.50	15.00	30.00
4-20796	Let's Live a Little/There's Nothing As Sweet As My Baby	1951	6.25	12.50	25.00
4-20825	Mr. Moon/If Teardrops Were Pennies	1951	6.25	12.50	25.00
4-20862	Let Old Mother Nature Have Her Way/Me and My Broken Heart	1951	6.25	12.50	25.00
4-20893	(When You Feel Like You're in Love) Don't Just Stand There/The Little Girl in My Home Town	1952	6.25	12.50	25.00
4-20922	Are You Teasing Me/It's a Lovely, Lovely World	1952	6.25	12.50	25.00
4-20942	It's a Lovely, Lovely World/(When You Feel Like You're in Love) Don't Just Stand There	1952	6.25	12.50	25.00
4-21008	Our Honeymoon/Sing Her a Love Song	1952	6.25	12.50	25.00
4-21040	The Blood That Stained the Old Rugged Cross/Gethsemane	1951	7.50	15.00	30.00
—With the Carters					
4-21051	That's the Kind of Love I'm Looking For/My Lonely Heart's Runnin' Wild	1952	5.00	10.00	20.00

Number	Title (A Side/B Side)	Yr	VG	VG+	NM
4-21087	Orchids Mean Goodbye/Just Wait 'Til I Get You Alone	1953	5.00	10.00	20.00
4-21110	Nail Scarred Hand/We Shall Meet Someday	1953	6.25	12.50	25.00
4-21119	Trademark/Do I Like It?	1953	5.00	10.00	20.00
4-21129	Hey Joe!/Darling Am I the One	1953	5.00	10.00	20.00
4-21166	Satisfaction Guaranteed/Who'll Buy My Heartaches	1953	5.00	10.00	20.00
4-21192	How About You/I'll Be Listening	1953	5.00	10.00	20.00
4-21197	Dog-Gone It, Baby, I'm in Love/What Am I Going to Do	1954	5.00	10.00	20.00
4-21226	Back Up Buddy/If You Tried As Hard to Love Me	1954	5.00	10.00	20.00
4-21266	Go, Boy, Go/If You Saw Her Through My Eyes	1954	5.00	10.00	20.00
4-21317	Loose Talk/More Than Anything Else in the World	1954	5.00	10.00	20.00
4-21340	Kisses Don't Lie/No, I Don't Believe I Will	1955	5.00	10.00	20.00
4-21368	Wait a Little Longer Please, Jesus/Works of the Lord	1955	6.25	12.50	25.00
4-21382	There She Goes/Old Lonesome Times	1955	5.00	10.00	20.00
4-21411	Baby I'm Ready/I Just Don't Care Anymore	1955	5.00	10.00	20.00
4-21429	Don't Tease Me/I Just Dropped In to Say Goodbye	1955	5.00	10.00	20.00
4-21462	You're Free to Go/I Feel Like Cryin'	1955	5.00	10.00	20.00
4-21493	I've Changed/If You Do Dear	1956	5.00	10.00	20.00
4-21507	Answers/My Dream of the Old Rugged Cross	1956	6.25	12.50	25.00
4-21522	You Are the One/Doorstep to Heaven	1956	5.00	10.00	20.00
4-21552	Before I Met You/Wicked Lies	1956	5.00	10.00	20.00
30848 [S]	(titles unknown)	1960	3.75	7.50	15.00
30849 [S]	(titles unknown)	1960	3.75	7.50	15.00
30850 [S]	(titles unknown)	1960	3.75	7.50	15.00
30851 [S]	(titles unknown)	1960	3.75	7.50	15.00
31473 [S]	(titles unknown)	1962	3.75	7.50	15.00
31474 [S]	(titles unknown)	1962	3.75	7.50	15.00
31475 [S]	(titles unknown)	1962	3.75	7.50	15.00
31476 [S]	(titles unknown)	1962	3.75	7.50	15.00
31477 [S]	(titles unknown)	1962	3.75	7.50	15.00
—The above 10 are "Stereo Seven" 7-inch 33 1/3 rpm singles with small holes					
4-40823	You Can't Hurt Me Anymore/That's the Way I Like You the Best	1957	3.75	7.50	15.00
4-40918	Mr. Lost/Try to Take It Like a Man	1957	3.75	7.50	15.00
4-40984	Why, Why/Emotions	1957	3.75	7.50	15.00
4-41092	Your Name Is Beautiful/You're So Easy to Love	1958	3.75	7.50	15.00
4-41170	Guess I've Been Around Too Long/Goodnight Mr. Sun	1958	3.75	7.50	15.00
4-41243	Walking the Slow Walk/A Love Was Born	1958	3.75	7.50	15.00
4-41290	The Best Years of Your Life/Mr. Moon	1958	3.75	7.50	15.00
4-41344	It's All My Heartache/I'll Kiss the Past Goodbye	1959	3.00	6.00	12.00
4-41417	Ten Thousand Drums/The Tall, Tall Gentleman	1959	3.00	6.00	12.00
4-41417 [PS]	Ten Thousand Drums/The Tall, Tall Gentleman	1959	6.25	12.50	25.00
4-41489	Tomorrow Night/I'll Walk with You	1959	3.00	6.00	12.00
4-41557	Make the Waterwheel Roll/Past	1960	3.00	6.00	12.00
4-41610	A Pain a Pill Can't Locate/If I Had You (I'd Live for You Only)	1962	3.00	6.00	12.00
4-41642	Cut Across Shorty/Why Did You Come My Way	1960	3.00	6.00	12.00
4-41729	If the World Don't End Tomorrow/Lonely Old Room	1960	3.00	6.00	12.00
4-41819	You Make Me Live Again/I Don't Know How	1960	3.00	6.00	12.00
4-41948	Are You True to Me/More Habit Than Desire	1961	3.00	6.00	12.00
4-42042	Kisses Never Lie/Why Can't You Be Satisfied with Me	1961	3.00	6.00	12.00
4-42222	Air Mail to Heaven/Things That Mean the Most	1961	3.00	6.00	12.00
4-42349	The Best Dressed Beggar (In Town)/I Used to Be	1962	3.00	6.00	12.00
4-42490	Gettin' Even/I Volunteer	1962	3.00	6.00	12.00
4-42610	A Pain a Pill Can't Locate/If I Had You (I'd Live for You Only)	1962	3.00	6.00	12.00
4-42686	Live for Tomorrow/Let's Talk This Thing Over	1963	3.00	6.00	12.00
4-42768	In the Back Room Tonight/Take My Love with You	1963	3.00	6.00	12.00
4-42858	Triangle/I Almost Forgot Her Today	1963	3.00	6.00	12.00
4-42949	The Pillow That Whispers/Sweet Little Country Girl	1964	3.00	6.00	12.00
4-43033	Take My Ring Off Your Finger/The Ballad of Hershel Lawson	1964	3.00	6.00	12.00
4-43124	Lonely Girl/When It's Over	1964	3.00	6.00	12.00
4-43200	She Called Me Baby/My Friends Are Gonna Be Strangers	1965	2.50	5.00	10.00
4-43266	Be Good to Her/Keep Me Fooled	1965	2.50	5.00	10.00
4-43361	Let's Walk Away Strangers/Ain't Love a Hurting Thing	1965	2.50	5.00	10.00
4-43485	Why Do I Keep Doing This to Us/Why Can't You Feel Sorry for Me	1966	2.50	5.00	10.00
4-43599	Sweet Temptation/(Is My) Ring on Your Finger	1966	2.50	5.00	10.00
4-43753	Man with a Plan/You Mean Ol' Moon	1966	2.50	5.00	10.00
4-43866	You Better Be Better to Me/It's Only a Matter of Time	1966	2.50	5.00	10.00
4-44034	I Should Get Away for Awhile (From You)/Mighty Day	1967	2.00	4.00	8.00
4-44233	Deep Water/I Really Don't Want to Know	1967	2.00	4.00	8.00
4-44396	Foggy River/When Will the Rainbow Follow the Rain	1967	2.00	4.00	8.00
4-44486	You Ought to Hear Me Cry/I Used Up My Last Chance Last Night	1968	2.00	4.00	8.00
4-44620	There's No More Love/Remember Me (I'm the One Who Loves You)	1968	2.00	4.00	8.00
4-44702	Faded Love and Winter Roses/Until I Looked at You	1968	2.00	4.00	8.00
4-44816	Good Deal, Lucille/Never Gonna Cry No More	1969	2.00	4.00	8.00
4-44939	I Love You Because/Mister, Come and Get Your Wife	1969	2.00	4.00	8.00
4-45031	Heartbreak Avenue/It's Nice to See You Once Again	1969	2.00	4.00	8.00
4-45086	Pull My String and Wind Me Up/It's All Right	1970	2.00	4.00	8.00
4-45177	Pick Me Up on Your Way Down/Bonaparte's Retreat	1970	2.00	4.00	8.00
4-45225	How I Love Them Old Songs/Little Crop of Cotton Tops	1970	2.00	4.00	8.00
4-45262	Big Murph/My Mother's Eyes	1970	2.00	4.00	8.00
4-45293	Don't Worry 'Bout the Mule (Just Load the Wagon)/Darling Days	1970	2.00	4.00	8.00
4-45382	Lost It on the Road/I'm Wound Up Tight	1971	2.00	4.00	8.00
4-45436	Red Door/You Walked in My Sleep Last Night	1971	2.00	4.00	8.00
4-45497	Don't Say You're Mine/Country Soul Man	1971	2.00	4.00	8.00
4-45558	Mama Bear/Before My Time	1972	2.00	4.00	8.00
4-45648	If This Is Goodbye/If You Saw Her	1972	2.00	4.00	8.00
4-45832	What a Difference Your Love Would Make/When You're Gone (There Will Be Nothing Left)	1973	2.00	4.00	8.00
4-45923	I Need Help/Yesterday Is Gone	1973	2.00	4.00	8.00
HICKORY/MGM					
329	Dreaming Again/I Ain't Getting Nowhere with You	1974	—	3.00	6.00
337	The Way I Lose My Mind/Happy Birthday My Darlin'	1975	—	2.50	5.00
347	Everything I Touch Turns to Sugar/Lost Highway	1975	—	2.50	5.00
352	The Girl I Love/Me and My Broken Heart	1975	—	2.50	5.00
357	Roly Poly/Remembered by Someone (Remembered by Me)	1975	—	2.50	5.00
363	She Is/I Can't Go On Like This	1976	—	2.50	5.00
371	If You Don't, Somebody Else Will/It's Gonna Be One of Those Days	1976	—	2.50	5.00

7-Inch Extended Plays

Number	Title (A Side/B Side)	Yr	VG	VG+	NM
COLUMBIA					
B-10221	San Antonio Rose/Time Changes Everything//Lovin' Is Livin'/Oh, No!	1957	5.00	10.00	20.00
B-10221 [PS]	Smith's the Name, Vol. I	1957	5.00	10.00	20.00
B-10222	If I Could Hold Back the Dawn/That's What You Think//Live and Let Live/If You Want It, I've Got It	1957	5.00	10.00	20.00
B-10222 [PS]	Smith's the Name, Vol. II	1957	5.00	10.00	20.00
B-10223	Please Come Back Home/Look What Thoughts Done to Me//The House That Love Built/Come Back to Me	1957	5.00	10.00	20.00
B-10223 [PS]	Smith's the Name, Vol. III	1957	5.00	10.00	20.00

Albums

Number	Title	Yr	VG	VG+	NM
ABC HICKORY					
HB 44005	This Lady Loves Me	1977	3.00	6.00	12.00
HB-44015	The Silver-Tongued Cowboy	1978	3.00	6.00	12.00
COLUMBIA					
GP 31 [(2)]	The Carl Smith Anniversary Album/20 Years of Hits	1970	6.25	12.50	25.00
CL 959 [M]	Sunday Down South	1957	12.50	25.00	50.00
CL 1022 [M]	Smith's the Name	1957	12.50	25.00	50.00
CL 1172 [M]	Let's Live a Little	1958	12.50	25.00	50.00
CL 1532 [M]	The Carl Smith Touch	1960	6.25	12.50	25.00
CL 1740 [M]	Easy to Please	1961	6.25	12.50	25.00
CL 1937 [M]	Carl Smith's Greatest Hits	1962	5.00	10.00	20.00
CL 2091 [M]	The Tall, Tall Gentleman	1963	5.00	10.00	20.00
CL 2173 [M]	There Stands the Glass	1964	5.00	10.00	20.00
CL 2293 [M]	I Want to Live and Love	1965	5.00	10.00	20.00
CL 2358 [M]	Kisses Don't Lie	1965	5.00	10.00	20.00
CL 2501 [M]	Man with a Plan	1966	5.00	10.00	20.00
CL 2579 [10]	Carl Smith	1955	25.00	50.00	100.00
CL 2610 [M]	The Country Gentleman	1967	5.00	10.00	20.00
CL 2687 [M]	The Country Gentleman Sings His Favorites	1967	6.25	12.50	25.00
CL 2822 [M]	Deep Water	1968	7.50	15.00	30.00
CS 8352 [S]	The Carl Smith Touch	1960	7.50	15.00	30.00
CS 8540 [S]	Easy to Please	1961	7.50	15.00	30.00
CS 8737 [S]	Carl Smith's Greatest Hits	1962	6.25	12.50	25.00
CS 8891 [S]	The Tall, Tall Gentleman	1963	6.25	12.50	25.00
CS 8973 [S]	There Stands the Glass	1964	6.25	12.50	25.00
CL 9023 [10]	Sentimental Songs	195?	25.00	50.00	100.00
CL 9026 [10]	Softly and Tenderly	195?	20.00	40.00	80.00
CS 9093 [S]	I Want to Live and Love	1965	6.25	12.50	25.00
CS 9158 [S]	Kisses Don't Lie	1965	6.25	12.50	25.00
CS 9301 [S]	Man with a Plan	1966	6.25	12.50	25.00
CS 9410 [S]	The Country Gentleman	1967	6.25	12.50	25.00
CS 9487 [S]	The Country Gentleman Sings His Favorites	1967	5.00	10.00	20.00
CS 9622 [S]	Deep Water	1968	5.00	10.00	20.00
CS 9688	Country on My Mind	1968	5.00	10.00	20.00
CS 9786	Faded Love and Winter Roses	1969	5.00	10.00	20.00
CS 9807	Carl Smith's Greatest Hits, Vol. 2	1969	5.00	10.00	20.00
CS 9870	Carl Smith Sings a Tribute to Roy Acuff	1969	5.00	10.00	20.00
CS 9898	I Love You Because	1970	5.00	10.00	20.00
C 30215	Carl Smith with the Tunesmiths	1970	5.00	10.00	20.00
C 30548	Bluegrass	1971	5.00	10.00	20.00
C 31277	Don't Say You're Mine	1972	5.00	10.00	20.00
KC 31606	If This Is Goodbye	1972	5.00	10.00	20.00
FC 38906	Carl Smith	198?	2.50	5.00	10.00
HICKORY/MGM					
H3G 4518	The Way I Lose My Mind	1975	3.00	6.00	12.00
H3G 4522	The Girl I Love	1975	3.00	6.00	12.00
ROUNDER					
SS-25	Old Lonesome Times	1988	2.50	5.00	10.00

SMITH, CARL; LEFTY FRIZZELL; MARTY ROBBINS

Albums

Number	Title	Yr	VG	VG+	NM
COLUMBIA					
CL 2544 [10]	Carl, Lefty and Marty	1955	100.00	200.00	400.00

SMITH, CONNIE

45s

Number	Title (A Side/B Side)	Yr	VG	VG+	NM
COLUMBIA					
10051	I've Got My Baby on My Mind/Why Don't You Love Me	1974	—	2.00	4.00
10086	I Got a Lot of Hurtin' Done Today/Back in the Country	1975	—	2.00	4.00
10135	Why Don't You Love Me/Loving You (Has Changed My Whole Life)	1975	—	2.00	4.00
10210	The Song We Fell in Love To/One Little Reason	1975	—	2.00	4.00
10277	('Til) I Kissed You/Ridin' on a Rainbow	1975	—	2.00	4.00
10345	So Sad (To Watch Good Love Go Bad)/Constantly	1976	—	2.00	4.00
10393	I Don't Wanna Talk It Over Anymore/You Crossed My Mind a Thousand Times	1976	—	2.00	4.00
10501	The Latest Shade of Blue/I'm All Wrapped Up in You	1977	—	2.00	4.00

Number	Title (A Side/B Side)	Yr	VG	VG+	NM
45816	You've Got Me (Right Where You Want Me)/A Picture of Me	1973	—	2.50	5.00
45954	Ain't Love a Good Thing/I Still Feel the Same About You	1973	—	2.50	5.00
46008	Dallas/That's the Way Love Goes	1974	—	2.50	5.00
46058	I Never Knew (What That Song Meant Before)/ Did We Have to Come This Far	1974	—	2.50	5.00
EPIC					
05414	A Far Cry from You/Don't Touch (The Pain's Not Dry)	1986	—	—	3.00
MONUMENT					
03857	Rough at the Edges/Don't Make Me Dream	1983	—	2.00	4.00
45219	Coming Around/You and Love and I	1977	—	2.00	4.00
45231	I Just Want to Be Your Everything/Scrapbook	1977	—	2.00	4.00
45241	Lovin' You Baby/All of a Sudden	1978	—	2.00	4.00
45252	There'll Never Be Another for Me/The Wayward Wind	1978	—	2.00	4.00
45266	Smooth Sailin'/Loving You Has Sure Been Good to Me	1978	—	2.00	4.00
45281	Lovin' You, Lovin' Me/Ten Thousand and One	1979	—	2.00	4.00
45284	Don't Say Love/I Don't Want to Be Free	1979	—	2.00	4.00
RCA VICTOR					
APBO-0156	Everybody Loves Somebody/I Don't Want Your Memories	1973	—	2.50	5.00
PB-10051	Someone to Give My Love To/I'm Sorry If My Love Got In Your Way	1974	—	2.50	5.00
47-8416	Once a Day/The Threshold	1964	2.50	5.00	10.00
47-8489	Then and Only Then/Tiny Blue Transistor Radio	1964	2.00	4.00	8.00
47-8551	I Can't Remember/Senses	1965	2.00	4.00	8.00
47-8663	If I Talk to Him/I Don't Have Anyplace to Go	1965	2.00	4.00	8.00
47-8746	Nobody But a Fool (Would Love Him)/I'll Never Get Over Loving You	1965	2.00	4.00	8.00
47-8842	Ain't Had No Lovin'/Five Fingers to Spare	1966	2.00	4.00	8.00
47-8964	The Hurtin's All Over/Invisible Tears	1966	2.00	4.00	8.00
47-9108	I'll Come Runnin'/It's Now or Never	1967	2.00	4.00	8.00
47-9214	Cincinnati, Ohio/Don't Feel Sorry for Me	1967	2.00	4.00	8.00
47-9335	Burning a Hole in My Mind/Only for Me	1967	2.00	4.00	8.00
47-9413	Baby's Back Again/It Only Hurts for a Little While	1967	2.00	4.00	8.00
47-9513	Run Away Little Tears/Let Me Halp You Work It Out	1968	2.00	4.00	8.00
47-9624	Cry, Cry, Cry/The Hurt Goes On	1968	2.00	4.00	8.00
47-9805	If God Is Dead (Who's That Living in My Soul)/ His Love Takes Care of Me	1970	2.00	4.00	8.00
—With Nat Stuckey					
47-9832	I Never Once Stopped Loving You/The Sun Shines Down on Me	1970	—	3.00	6.00
47-9887	Louisiana Man/Alone with You	1970	—	3.00	6.00
47-9938	Where Is My Castle/Clinging to a Saving Hand	1970	—	3.00	6.00
47-9981	Just One Time/Don't Walk Away	1971	—	3.00	6.00
74-0101	Ribbon of Darkness/A Lonely Woman	1969	2.00	4.00	8.00
74-0181	Young Love/Something Pretty	1969	2.00	4.00	8.00
—With Nat Stuckey					
74-0258	You and Your Sweet Love/I Can't Get Used to Being Lonely	1969	2.00	4.00	8.00
74-0535	I'm Sorry If My Love Got In Your Way/Plenty of Time	1971	—	3.00	6.00
74-0655	Just for What I Am/I'd Still Want to Serve Him Today	1972	—	3.00	6.00
74-0752	If It Ain't Love (Let's Leave It Alone)/Living Without You	1972	—	3.00	6.00
74-0860	Love Is the Look You're Looking For/My Ecstasy	1972	—	3.00	6.00
74-0971	Dream Painter/Once a Day	1973	—	3.00	6.00

Albums

Number	Title (A Side/B Side)	Yr	VG	VG+	NM
COLUMBIA					
KC 32185	A Lady Named Smith	1973	3.00	6.00	12.00
KC 32492	God Is Abundant	1973	3.00	6.00	12.00
KC 32581	That's the Way Love Goes	1974	3.00	6.00	12.00
KC 33055	I Never Knew (What That Song Meant Before)	1974	3.00	6.00	12.00
KC 33375	Got My Baby on My Mind	1975	3.00	6.00	12.00
KC 33414	Connie Smith Sings Hank Williams Gospel	1975	3.00	6.00	12.00
KC 33918	The Song We Fell in Love To	1976	3.00	6.00	12.00
KC 34270	I Don't Want to Talk It Over Anymore	1976	3.00	6.00	12.00
KC 34877	The Best of Connie Smith	1977	3.00	6.00	12.00
MONUMENT					
7609	Pure Connie Smith	1977	3.00	6.00	12.00
7624	New Horizons	1978	3.00	6.00	12.00
RCA CAMDEN					
ACL1-0250	Even the Bad Times Are Good	1973	2.50	5.00	10.00
—With Nat Stuckey					
CAL-2120 [M]	Connie in the Country	1967	3.75	7.50	15.00
CAS-2120 [S]	Connie in the Country	1967	3.00	6.00	12.00
CAS-2495	My Heart Has a Mind of Its Own	1971	2.50	5.00	10.00
CAS-2550	City Lights — Country Favorites	1972	2.50	5.00	10.00
RCA VICTOR					
APL1-0188	Dream Painter	1973	3.00	6.00	12.00
APL1-0275	Connie Smith's Greatest Hits, Volume 1	1973	3.00	6.00	12.00
APL1-0607	Now	1974	3.00	6.00	12.00
LPM-3341 [M]	Connie Smith	1965	5.00	10.00	20.00
LSP-3341 [S]	Connie Smith	1965	6.25	12.50	25.00
LPM-3444 [M]	Cute 'n' Country	1965	5.00	10.00	20.00
LSP-3444 [S]	Cute 'n' Country	1965	6.25	12.50	25.00
LPM-3520 [M]	Miss Smith Goes to Nashville	1966	5.00	10.00	20.00
LSP-3520 [S]	Miss Smith Goes to Nashville	1966	6.25	12.50	25.00
LPM-3589 [M]	Connie Smith Sings Great Sacred Songs	1966	5.00	10.00	20.00
LSP-3589 [S]	Connie Smith Sings Great Sacred Songs	1966	6.25	12.50	25.00
LPM-3628 [M]	Born to Sing	1966	5.00	10.00	20.00
LSP-3628 [S]	Born to Sing	1966	6.25	12.50	25.00
LPM-3725 [M]	Downtown Country	1967	6.25	12.50	25.00
LSP-3725 [S]	Downtown Country	1967	5.00	10.00	20.00
LPM-3768 [M]	Connie Smith Sings Bill Anderson	1967	6.25	12.50	25.00
LSP-3768 [S]	Connie Smith Sings Bill Anderson	1967	5.00	10.00	20.00
LPM-3848 [M]	The Best of Connie Smith	1967	6.25	12.50	25.00
LSP-3848 [S]	The Best of Connie Smith	1967	5.00	10.00	20.00
LPM-3889 [M]	Soul of Country Music	1968	12.50	25.00	50.00
LSP-3889 [S]	Soul of Country Music	1968	5.00	10.00	20.00
LSP-4002	I Love Charley Brown	1968	5.00	10.00	20.00
LSP-4077	Sunshine and Rain	1968	5.00	10.00	20.00
LSP-4132	Connie's Country	1969	5.00	10.00	20.00
LSP-4190	Young Love	1969	5.00	10.00	20.00
—With Nat Stuckey					
LSP-4229	Back in Baby's Arms	1969	5.00	10.00	20.00
LSP-4324	The Best of Connie Smith Volume II	1970	5.00	10.00	20.00
LSP-4394	I Never Once Stopped Loving You	1970	5.00	10.00	20.00
LSP-4474	Where's My Castle	1971	3.75	7.50	15.00
LSP-4537	Just One Time	1971	3.75	7.50	15.00
LSP-4598	Come Along and Walk with Me	1971	5.00	10.00	20.00
LSP-4694	Ain't We Having a Good Time	1972	3.75	7.50	15.00
LSP-4748	"If It Ain't Love" And Other Great Dallas Frazier Songs	1972	3.75	7.50	15.00
LSP-4840	Love Is the Look You're Looking For	1973	3.75	7.50	15.00

SMITH, HUEY "PIANO"

45s

Number	Title (A Side/B Side)	Yr	VG	VG+	NM
ACE					
521	Everybody's Wailin'/Little Liza Jane	1956	6.25	12.50	25.00
530	Rockin' Pneumonia and the Boogie Woogie Flu (Part 1/Part 2)	1957	7.50	15.00	30.00
538	Free, Single and Disengaged/Just a Lonely Clown	1957	6.25	12.50	25.00
545	Don't You Just Know It/High Blood Pressure	1958	6.25	12.50	25.00
548	Havin' a Good Time/We Like Birdland	1958	6.25	12.50	25.00
553	Don't You Know Yockomo/Well, I'll Be John Brown	1958	6.25	12.50	25.00
562	Would You Believe It (I Have a Cold)/Genevieve	1959	5.00	10.00	20.00
571	Tu-Ber-Cu-Lucas and the Sinus Blues/Dearest Darling	1959	5.00	10.00	20.00
584	Beatnik Blues/For Cryin' Out Loud	1960	3.75	7.50	15.00
638	She Got Low Down/Mean, Mean, Mean	1961	3.75	7.50	15.00
639	She Got Low Down/Mean, Mean, Mean//Little Liza Jane/Rockin' Pnuemonia	1961	6.25	12.50	25.00
649	Pop-Eye/Scald Dog	1962	3.75	7.50	15.00
672	Every Once in a While/Somebody Told It	1962	3.00	6.00	12.00
8002	Talk to Me Baby/If It Ain't One Thing, It's Another	1962	3.00	6.00	12.00
8008	Let's Bring 'Em Back Again/Quiet as It's Kept	1963	3.75	7.50	15.00
CONSTELLATION					
102	He's Back Again/Quiet As It's Kept	1963	2.50	5.00	10.00
COTILLION					
44142	Rockin' Pneumonia and the Boogie Woogie Flu (Part 1/Part 2)	1971	—	3.00	6.00
IMPERIAL					
5721	The Little Moron/Someone to Love	1961	3.00	6.00	12.00
5747	Behind the Wheel — Part 1/Behind the Wheel — Part 2	1961	3.00	6.00	12.00
5772	More Girls/Sassy Sara	1961	3.00	6.00	12.00
5789	Don't Knock It/Shag-a-Tooth	1961	3.00	6.00	12.00
INSTANT					
3287	I'll Never Forget/Bury Me Dead	1967	2.00	4.00	8.00
3297	Two Way Pockaway (Part 1)/Two Way Pockaway (Part 2)	1969	2.00	4.00	8.00
3301	Epitaph of Uncle Tom/Eight Bars of Amen	1969	2.00	4.00	8.00
3303	You Got Too (Part 1)/You Got Too (Part 2)	1969	2.00	4.00	8.00
3305	Ballad of a Black Man/The Whatcha Call 'Em	1970	2.00	4.00	8.00
SAVOY					
1113	You Made Me Cry/You're Down with Me	1953	25.00	50.00	100.00
VIN					
1024	I Didn't Do It/They Kept On	1960	3.75	7.50	15.00

Albums

Number	Title (A Side/B Side)	Yr	VG	VG+	NM
ACE					
LP-1004 [M]	Having a Good Time	1959	100.00	200.00	400.00
LP-1015 [M]	For Dancing	1961	62.50	125.00	250.00
LP-1027 [M]	'Twas the Night Before Christmas	1962	62.50	125.00	250.00
LP-1027 [M]	'Twas the Night Before Christmas	198?	3.75	7.50	15.00
—Reissue with "Dr. John Band" credited on front cover and label					
LP-2021	Rock 'n' Roll Revival	197?	7.50	15.00	30.00
2038	Good Old Rock & Roll	198?	3.75	7.50	15.00
GRAND PRIX					
K-418 [M]	Huey "Piano" Smith	196?	5.00	10.00	20.00
KS-418 [R]	Huey "Piano" Smith	196?	3.00	6.00	12.00
RHINO					
RNLP-70222	Serious Clownin': The History of Huey "Piano" Smith and the Clowns	1986	3.00	6.00	12.00

SMITH, HURRICANE

45s

Number	Title (A Side/B Side)	Yr	VG	VG+	NM
CAPITOL					
3148	Don't Let It Die/The Writer Sings His Song	1971	—	2.50	5.00
3383	Oh Babe, What Would You Say?/Getting to Know You	1972	—	3.00	6.00
—Red and orange "target" label					
3383	Oh Babe, What Would You Say?/Getting to Know You	1972	—	2.00	4.00
—Orange label with "Capitol" at bottom					
3455	Who Was It?/Take Suki Home	1972	—	2.00	4.00
EMI					
3809	Beautiful Day-Beautiful Night/Sam	1973	—	2.00	4.00

Albums

Number	Title (A Side/B Side)	Yr	VG	VG+	NM
CAPITOL					
ST-11139	Hurricane Smith	1972	2.50	5.00	10.00

SMITH, JIMMY

45s

Number	Title (A Side/B Side)	Yr	VG	VG+	NM
BLUE NOTE					
1635	High and Mighty/You Get Cha	195?	3.00	6.00	12.00
1636	The Preacher/Midnight Sun	195?	3.00	6.00	12.00
1637	Tenderly/Joy	195?	3.00	6.00	12.00
1641	The Champ (Part 1)/The Champ (Part 2)	195?	3.00	6.00	12.00
1642	Bubbis/Bayou	195?	3.00	6.00	12.00
1643	Judo Mambo/Autumn Leaves	195?	3.00	6.00	12.00

Number	Title (A Side/B Side)	Yr	VG	VG+	NM
1644	Willow Weep for Me/Fiddlin' the Minors	195?	3.00	6.00	12.00
1652	I Cover the Waterfront/I Can't Give You Anything	195?	3.00	6.00	12.00
1660	New Preacher (Part 1)/New Preacher (Part 2)	195?	3.00	6.00	12.00
1665	Where or When (Part 1)/Where or When (Part 2)	195?	3.00	6.00	12.00
1666	Love Is a Many-Splendored Thing (Part 1)/Love Is a Many-Splendored Thing (Part 2)	195?	3.00	6.00	12.00
1667	How High the Moon/Summertime	195?	3.00	6.00	12.00
1668	Plum Nellie/I'm Getting Sentimental	195?	3.00	6.00	12.00
1676	All Day Long (Part 1)/All Day Long (Part 2)	195?	3.00	6.00	12.00
1677	Funk's Oasis (Part 1)/Funk's Oasis (Part 2)	195?	3.00	6.00	12.00
1682	I Can't Get Started/Penthouse Serenade	195?	3.00	6.00	12.00
1683	East of the Sun/The Very Thought of You	195?	3.00	6.00	12.00
1685	Blue Moon (Part 1)/Blue Moon (Part 2)	195?	3.00	6.00	12.00
1686	There'll Never Be Another You/Jitterbug Waltz	195?	3.00	6.00	12.00
1703	After Hours (Part 1)/After Hours (Part 2)	195?	3.00	6.00	12.00
1704	Just Friends/Lover Man	195?	3.00	6.00	12.00
1711	The Swingin' Shepherd Blues/Cha Cha J.	195?	3.00	6.00	12.00
1727	Ain't No Use/Angel Eyes	195?	3.00	6.00	12.00
—With Bill Henderson					
1728	Ain't That Love/Willow Weep for Me	195?	3.00	6.00	12.00
—With Bill Henderson					
1765	Makin' Whoopee/What's New	196?	2.50	5.00	10.00
1766	Mack the Knife/When Johnny Comes Marching Home	196?	2.50	5.00	10.00
1767	Alfredo/I Got a Woman	196?	2.50	5.00	10.00
1768	Come On Baby/See See Rider	196?	2.50	5.00	10.00
1769	Since I Fell for You/Motorin' Along	196?	2.50	5.00	10.00
—With Kenny Burrell					
1819	Midnight Special (Part 1)/Midnight Special (Part 2)	1962	2.50	5.00	10.00
1820	Jumpin' the Blues/One O'Clock Blues	1962	2.50	5.00	10.00
1851	Ain't She Sweet/Everybody Loves My Baby	1962	2.50	5.00	10.00
1852	Honeysuckle Rose/Lulu's Back in Town	1962	2.50	5.00	10.00
1877	Back at the Chicken Shack (Part 1)/Back at the Chicken Shack (Part 2)	1963	2.50	5.00	10.00
1878	Minor Chant (Part 1)/Minor Chant (Part 2)	1963	2.50	5.00	10.00
1879	Sermon (Part 1)/Sermon (Part 2)	1963	2.50	5.00	10.00
1904	When My Dreamboat Comes Home (Part 1)/When My Dreamboat Comes Home (Part 2)	1964	2.50	5.00	10.00
1905	Matilda, Matilda/Can Heat	1964	2.50	5.00	10.00
1906	Pork Chop (Part 1)/Pork Chop (Part 2)	1964	2.50	5.00	10.00
1909	Prayer Meetin' (Part 1)/Prayer Meetin' (Part 2)	1964	2.50	5.00	10.00
1910	Red Top (Part 1)/Red Top (Part 2)	1964	2.50	5.00	10.00
1925	I Cover the Waterfront/I Can't Give You Anything But Love	1966	2.00	4.00	8.00
1927	Bucket!/Sassy Mae	1966	2.00	4.00	8.00

MERCURY

Number	Title (A Side/B Side)	Yr	VG	VG+	NM
73895	Can't Hide Love/No Place in Space	1977	—	2.00	4.00
73972	I've Got Love on My Mind/Side Mouthin'	1977	—	2.00	4.00

PRIDE

Number	Title (A Side/B Side)	Yr	VG	VG+	NM
7602	Groovin'/Why Can't We Live Together	1974	—	2.50	5.00

VERVE

Number	Title (A Side/B Side)	Yr	VG	VG+	NM
CS6-5 [(5)]	Celebrity Scene: Jimmy Smith	1967	15.00	30.00	60.00
—Box set of five singles (10502-10506). Price includes box, all 5 singles, jukebox title strips, bio. Records are sometimes found by themselves, so they are also listed separately.					
10255	Walk on the Wild Side (Part 1)/Walk on the Wild Side (Part 2)	1962	2.00	4.00	8.00
10262	Ol' Man River/Bashin'	1962	2.00	4.00	8.00
10278	Step Right Up (Part 1)/Step Right Up (Part 2)	1963	2.00	4.00	8.00
10283	Hobo Flats (Part 1)/Hobo Flats (Part 2)	1963	2.00	4.00	8.00
10298	Blueberry Hill/Walk Right In	1963	2.00	4.00	8.00
10299	Theme from "Any Number Can Win"/What'd I Say	1963	2.00	4.00	8.00
10314	Who's Afraid of Virginia Woolf?/Who's Afraid of Virginia Woolf? (Part 2)	1964	2.00	4.00	8.00
10330	The Cat/Basin Street Blues	1964	2.00	4.00	8.00
10346	Goldfinger (Part 1)/Goldfinger (Part 2)	1965	2.00	4.00	8.00
10363	The Organ Grinder's Swing/I'll Close My Eyes	1965	2.00	4.00	8.00
—With Kenny Burrell and Grady Tate					
10382	Theme from "Where the Spies Are"/Slow Theme from "Where the Spies Are"	1966	2.00	4.00	8.00
10393	Got My Mojo Working (Part 1)/Got My Mojo Working (Part 2)	1966	2.00	4.00	8.00
10424	Who Do You Love (Part 1)/Who Do You Love (Part 2)	1966	2.00	4.00	8.00
10467	Cat in a Tree (Part 1)/Cat in a Tree (Part 2)	1966	2.00	4.00	8.00
10502 [DJ]	Walk on the Wild Side (Part 1)/Walk on the Wild Side (Part 2)	1967	2.50	5.00	10.00
10503 [DJ]	The Cat/Basin Street Blues	1967	2.50	5.00	10.00
10504 [DJ]	Got My Mojo Working (Part 1)/Got My Mojo Working (Part 2)	1967	2.50	5.00	10.00
10505 [DJ]	I'm Your Hoochie Coochie Man (Part 1)/I'm Your Hoochie Coochie Man (Part 2)	1967	2.50	5.00	10.00
10506 [DJ]	Cat in a Tree (Part 1)/Cat in a Tree (Part 2)	1967	2.50	5.00	10.00
10536	Respect/Funky Broadway	1967	2.00	4.00	8.00
10583	Chain of Fools (Part 1)/Chain of Fools (Part 2)	1968	2.00	4.00	8.00
10623	Mission: Impossible/Gentle Rain	1968	2.00	4.00	8.00
10652	Groove Drops/By the Time I Get to Phoenix	1970	—	3.00	6.00
10660	One Bad Apple/Theme from "The Night Visitor"	1971	—	3.00	6.00
10668	Jimmy Smith Is a Midnight Cowboy/Recession or Depression	1971	—	3.00	6.00
10672	For Everyone Under the Sun/Sag' Shootin' His Arrow	1972	—	3.00	6.00
10695	Lolita/Straight Ahead	1972	—	3.00	6.00
10724	And I Love You So/Ritual (Funky 5/4)	1973	—	3.00	6.00

Albums

BLUE NOTE

Number	Title	Yr	VG	VG+	NM
BN-LA400-H2 [(2)]	Jimmy Smith	1975	3.75	7.50	15.00
LT-992	Confirmation	1979	2.50	5.00	10.00
LT-1054	Cool Blues	1980	2.50	5.00	10.00
LT-1092	On the Sunny Side	1981	2.50	5.00	10.00
BLP-1512 [M]	Jimmy Smith at the Organ, Vol. 1	1956	37.50	75.00	150.00
—"Deep groove" version (deep indentation under label on both sides)					
BLP-1512 [M]	Jimmy Smith at the Organ, Vol. 1	1956	25.00	50.00	100.00
—Regular edition, Lexington Ave. address on label					
BLP-1512 [M]	Jimmy Smith at the Organ, Vol. 1	1963	6.25	12.50	25.00
—With New York, USA address on label					
BLP-1514 [M]	Jimmy Smith at the Organ, Vol. 2	1956	37.50	75.00	150.00
—"Deep groove" version (deep indentation under label on both sides)					
BLP-1514 [M]	Jimmy Smith at the Organ, Vol. 2	1956	25.00	50.00	100.00
—Regular edition, Lexington Ave. address on label					
BLP-1514 [M]	Jimmy Smith at the Organ, Vol. 2	1963	6.25	12.50	25.00
—With New York, USA address on label					
BLP-1525 [M]	The Incredible Jimmy Smith at the Organ, Vol. 3	1956	37.50	75.00	150.00
—"Deep groove" version (deep indentation under label on both sides)					
BLP-1525 [M]	The Incredible Jimmy Smith at the Organ, Vol. 3	1956	25.00	50.00	100.00
—Regular edition, Lexington Ave. address on label					
BLP-1525 [M]	The Incredible Jimmy Smith at the Organ, Vol. 3	1963	6.25	12.50	25.00
—With New York, USA address on label					
BLP-1528 [M]	The Incredible Jimmy Smith at Club Baby Grand, Wilmington, Delaware, Vol. 1	1956	37.50	75.00	150.00
—"Deep groove" version (deep indentation under label on both sides)					
BLP-1528 [M]	The Incredible Jimmy Smith at Club Baby Grand, Wilmington, Delaware, Vol. 1	1956	25.00	50.00	100.00
—Regular edition, Lexington Ave. address on label					
BLP-1528 [M]	The Incredible Jimmy Smith at Club Baby Grand, Wilmington, Delaware, Vol. 1	1963	6.25	12.50	25.00
—With New York, USA address on label					
BLP-1529 [M]	The Incredible Jimmy Smith at Club Baby Grand, Wilmington, Delaware, Vol. 2	1956	37.50	75.00	150.00
—"Deep groove" version (deep indentation under label on both sides)					
BLP-1529 [M]	The Incredible Jimmy Smith at Club Baby Grand, Wilmington, Delaware, Vol. 2	1956	25.00	50.00	100.00
—Regular edition, Lexington Ave. address on label					
BLP-1529 [M]	The Incredible Jimmy Smith at Club Baby Grand, Wilmington, Delaware, Vol. 2	1963	6.25	12.50	25.00
—With New York, USA address on label					
BLP-1547 [M]	A Date with Jimmy Smith, Vol. 1	1957	30.00	60.00	120.00
—"Deep groove" version (deep indentation under label on both sides)					
BLP-1547 [M]	A Date with Jimmy Smith, Vol. 1	1957	20.00	40.00	80.00
—Regular edition, W. 63rd St. address on label					
BLP-1547 [M]	A Date with Jimmy Smith, Vol. 1	1963	6.25	12.50	25.00
—With New York, USA address on label					
BLP-1548 [M]	A Date with Jimmy Smith, Vol. 2	1957	30.00	60.00	120.00
—"Deep groove" version (deep indentation under label on both sides)					
BLP-1548 [M]	A Date with Jimmy Smith, Vol. 2	1957	20.00	40.00	80.00
—Regular edition, W. 63rd St. address on label					
BLP-1548 [M]	A Date with Jimmy Smith, Vol. 2	1963	6.25	12.50	25.00
—With New York, USA address on label					
BLP-1551 [M]	Jimmy Smith at the Organ, Vol. 1	1957	30.00	60.00	120.00
—"Deep groove" version (deep indentation under label on both sides)					
BLP-1551 [M]	Jimmy Smith at the Organ, Vol. 1	1957	20.00	40.00	80.00
—Regular edition, W. 63rd St. address on label					
BLP-1551 [M]	Jimmy Smith at the Organ, Vol. 1	1963	6.25	12.50	25.00
—With New York, USA address on label					
BLP-1552 [M]	Jimmy Smith at the Organ, Vol. 2	1957	30.00	60.00	120.00
—"Deep groove" version (deep indentation under label on both sides)					
BLP-1552 [M]	Jimmy Smith at the Organ, Vol. 2	1957	20.00	40.00	80.00
—Regular edition, W. 63rd St. address on label					
BLP-1552 [M]	Jimmy Smith at the Organ, Vol. 2	1963	6.25	12.50	25.00
—With New York, USA address on label					
BLP-1556 [M]	The Sounds of Jimmy Smith	1957	30.00	60.00	120.00
—"Deep groove" version (deep indentation under label on both sides)					
BLP-1556 [M]	The Sounds of Jimmy Smith	1957	20.00	40.00	80.00
—Regular edition, W. 63rd St. address on label					
BLP-1556 [M]	The Sounds of Jimmy Smith	1963	6.25	12.50	25.00
—With New York, USA address on label					
BLP-1563 [M]	Jimmy Smith Plays Pretty Just for You	1957	30.00	60.00	120.00
—"Deep groove" version (deep indentation under label on both sides)					
BLP-1563 [M]	Jimmy Smith Plays Pretty Just for You	1957	20.00	40.00	80.00
—Regular edition, W. 63rd St. address on label					
BLP-1563 [M]	Jimmy Smith Plays Pretty Just for You	1963	6.25	12.50	25.00
—With New York, USA address on label					
BST-1563 [S]	Jimmy Smith Plays Pretty Just for You	1959	20.00	40.00	80.00
—"Deep groove" version (deep indentation under label on both sides)					
BST-1563 [S]	Jimmy Smith Plays Pretty Just for You	1959	12.50	25.00	50.00
—Regular edition, W. 63rd St. address on label					
BST-1563 [S]	Jimmy Smith Plays Pretty Just for You	1963	5.00	10.00	20.00
—With New York, USA address on label					
BLP-1585 [M]	Groovin' at Small's Paradise, Vol. 1	1958	30.00	60.00	120.00
—"Deep groove" version (deep indentation under label on both sides)					
BLP-1585 [M]	Groovin' at Small's Paradise, Vol. 1	1958	20.00	40.00	80.00
—Regular edition, W. 63rd St. address on label					
BLP-1585 [M]	Groovin' at Small's Paradise, Vol. 1	1963	6.25	12.50	25.00
—With New York, USA address on label					
BST-1585 [S]	Groovin' at Small's Paradise, Vol. 1	1959	20.00	40.00	80.00
—"Deep groove" version (deep indentation under label on both sides)					
BST-1585 [S]	Groovin' at Small's Paradise, Vol. 1	1959	12.50	25.00	50.00
—Regular edition, W. 63rd St. address on label					
BST-1585 [S]	Groovin' at Small's Paradise, Vol. 1	1963	5.00	10.00	20.00
—With New York, USA address on label					
BLP-1586 [M]	Groovin' at Small's Paradise, Vol. 2	1958	30.00	60.00	120.00
—"Deep groove" version (deep indentation under label on both sides)					
BLP-1586 [M]	Groovin' at Small's Paradise, Vol. 2	1958	20.00	40.00	80.00
—Regular edition, W. 63rd St. address on label					
BLP-1586 [M]	Groovin' at Small's Paradise, Vol. 2	1963	6.25	12.50	25.00
—With New York, USA address on label					
BST-1586 [S]	Groovin' at Small's Paradise, Vol. 2	1959	20.00	40.00	80.00
—"Deep groove" version (deep indentation under label on both sides)					
BST-1586 [S]	Groovin' at Small's Paradise, Vol. 2	1959	12.50	25.00	50.00
—Regular edition, W. 63rd St. address on label					
BST-1586 [S]	Groovin' at Small's Paradise, Vol. 2	1963	5.00	10.00	20.00
—With New York, USA address on label					
BLP-4002 [M]	House Party	1959	30.00	60.00	120.00
—"Deep groove" version (deep indentation under label on both sides)					
BLP-4002 [M]	House Party	1959	20.00	40.00	80.00
—Regular edition, W. 63rd St. address on label					
BLP-4002 [M]	House Party	1963	6.25	12.50	25.00
—With New York, USA address on label					
BST-4002 [S]	House Party	1959	20.00	40.00	80.00
—"Deep groove" version (deep indentation under label on both sides)					

Number	Title (A Side/B Side)	Yr	VG	VG+	NM
BST-4002 [S]	House Party	1959	12.50	25.00	50.00
—Regular edition, W. 63rd St. address on label					
BST-4002 [S]	House Party	1963	5.00	10.00	20.00
—With New York, USA address on label					
BLP-4011 [M]	The Sermon	1959	30.00	60.00	120.00
—"Deep groove" version (deep indentation under label on both sides)					
BLP-4011 [M]	The Sermon	1959	20.00	40.00	80.00
—Regular edition, W. 63rd St. address on label					
BLP-4011 [M]	The Sermon	1963	6.25	12.50	25.00
—With New York, USA address on label					
BST-4011 [S]	The Sermon	1959	20.00	40.00	80.00
—"Deep groove" version (deep indentation under label on both sides)					
BST-4011 [S]	The Sermon	1959	12.50	25.00	50.00
—Regular edition, W. 63rd St. address on label					
BST-4011 [S]	The Sermon	1963	5.00	10.00	20.00
—With New York, USA address on label					
BLP-4030 [M]	Crazy Baby	1960	30.00	60.00	120.00
—"Deep groove" version (deep indentation under label on both sides)					
BLP-4030 [M]	Crazy Baby	1960	20.00	40.00	80.00
—Regular edition, W. 63rd St. address on label					
BLP-4030 [M]	Crazy Baby	1963	6.25	12.50	25.00
—With New York, USA address on label					
BLP-4050 [M]	Home Cookin'	1961	12.50	25.00	50.00
—With W. 63rd St. address on label					
BLP-4050 [M]	Home Cookin'	1963	5.00	10.00	20.00
—With New York, USA address on label					
BLP-4078 [M]	Midnight Special	1961	12.50	25.00	50.00
—With 61st St. address on label					
BLP-4078 [M]	Midnight Special	1963	5.00	10.00	20.00
—With New York, USA address on label					
BLP-4100 [M]	Jimmy Smith Plays Fats Waller	1962	12.50	25.00	50.00
—With 61st St. address on label					
BLP-4100 [M]	Jimmy Smith Plays Fats Waller	1963	5.00	10.00	20.00
—With New York, USA address on label					
BLP-4117 [M]	Back at the Chicken Shack	1963	6.25	12.50	25.00
BLP-4141 [M]	Rockin' the Boat	1963	6.25	12.50	25.00
BLP-4164 [M]	Prayer Meetin'	1964	6.25	12.50	25.00
BLP-4200 [M]	Softly as a Summer Breeze	1965	6.25	12.50	25.00
BLP-4235 [M]	Bucket!	1966	6.25	12.50	25.00
BLP-4255 [M]	I'm Movin' On	1967	7.50	15.00	30.00
BST-81512 [R]	Jimmy Smith at the Organ, Vol. 1	1967	3.00	6.00	12.00
BST-81514 [R]	Jimmy Smith at the Organ, Vol. 2	1967	3.00	6.00	12.00
BST-81525 [R]	The Incredible Jimmy Smith at the Organ, Vol. 3	1967	3.00	6.00	12.00
BST-81528 [R]	The Incredible Jimmy Smith at Club Baby Grand, Wilmington, Delaware, Vol. 1	1967	3.00	6.00	12.00
BST-81529 [R]	The Incredible Jimmy Smith at Club Baby Grand, Wilmington, Delaware, Vol. 2	1967	3.00	6.00	12.00
BST-81547 [R]	A Date with Jimmy Smith, Vol. 1	1967	3.00	6.00	12.00
BST-81548 [R]	A Date with Jimmy Smith, Vol. 2	1967	3.00	6.00	12.00
BST-81551 [R]	Jimmy Smith at the Organ, Vol. 1	1967	3.00	6.00	12.00
BST-81552 [R]	Jimmy Smith at the Organ, Vol. 2	1967	3.00	6.00	12.00
BST-81556 [R]	The Sounds of Jimmy Smith	1967	3.00	6.00	12.00
BST-81563 [S]	Jimmy Smith Plays Pretty Just for You	1967	3.75	7.50	15.00
BST-81585 [S]	Groovin' at Small's Paradise, Vol. 1	1967	3.75	7.50	15.00
BST-81586 [S]	Groovin' at Small's Paradise, Vol. 1	1967	3.75	7.50	15.00
BST-84002	House Party	1985	2.50	5.00	10.00
—"The Finest in Jazz Since 1939" reissue					
BST-84002 [S]	House Party	1967	3.75	7.50	15.00
BST-84011 [S]	The Sermon	1967	3.75	7.50	15.00
B1-84030	Crazy Baby	1988	2.50	5.00	10.00
—"The Finest in Jazz Since 1939" reissue					
BST-84030 [S]	Crazy Baby	1960	12.50	25.00	50.00
—With W. 63rd St. address on label					
BST-84030 [S]	Crazy Baby	1963	5.00	10.00	20.00
—With New York, USA address on label					
BST-84030 [S]	Crazy Baby	1967	3.75	7.50	15.00
—With "A Division of Liberty Records" on label					
BST-84050 [S]	Home Cookin'	1961	12.50	25.00	50.00
—With W. 63rd St. address on label					
BST-84050 [S]	Home Cookin'	1963	5.00	10.00	20.00
—With New York, USA address on label					
BST-84050 [S]	Home Cookin'	1967	3.75	7.50	15.00
—With "A Division of Liberty Records" on label					
B1-84078	Midnight Special	1989	2.50	5.00	10.00
—"The Finest in Jazz Since 1939" reissue					
BST-84078 [S]	Midnight Special	1961	12.50	25.00	50.00
—With 61st St. address on label					
BST-84078 [S]	Midnight Special	1963	5.00	10.00	20.00
—With New York, USA address on label					
BST-84078 [S]	Midnight Special	1967	3.75	7.50	15.00
—With "A Division of Liberty Records" on label					
BST-84100 [S]	Jimmy Smith Plays Fats Waller	1962	12.50	25.00	50.00
—With 61st St. address on label					
BST-84100 [S]	Jimmy Smith Plays Fats Waller	1963	5.00	10.00	20.00
—With New York, USA address on label					
BST-84100 [S]	Jimmy Smith Plays Fats Waller	1967	3.75	7.50	15.00
—With "A Division of Liberty Records" on label					
BST-84117	Back at the Chicken Shack	1985	2.50	5.00	10.00
—"The Finest in Jazz Since 1939" reissue					
BST-84117 [S]	Back at the Chicken Shack	1963	7.50	15.00	30.00
—With New York, USA address on label					
BST-84117 [S]	Back at the Chicken Shack	1967	3.75	7.50	15.00
—With "A Division of Liberty Records" on label					
BST-84141 [S]	Rockin' the Boat	1963	7.50	15.00	30.00
—With New York, USA address on label					
BST-84141 [S]	Rockin' the Boat	1967	3.75	7.50	15.00
—With "A Division of Liberty Records" on label					
B1-84164	Prayer Meetin'	1988	2.50	5.00	10.00
—"The Finest in Jazz Since 1939" reissue					
BST-84164 [S]	Prayer Meetin'	1964	7.50	15.00	30.00
—With New York, USA address on label					
BST-84164 [S]	Prayer Meetin'	1967	3.75	7.50	15.00
—With "A Division of Liberty Records" on label					
BST-84200 [S]	Softly as a Summer Breeze	1965	7.50	15.00	30.00
—With New York, USA address on label					
BST-84200 [S]	Softly as a Summer Breeze	1967	3.75	7.50	15.00
—With "A Division of Liberty Records" on label					
BST-84225 [S]	Bucket!	1967	3.75	7.50	15.00
—With "A Division of Liberty Records" on label					
BST-84235 [S]	Bucket!	1966	7.50	15.00	30.00
—With New York, USA address on label					
BST-84255 [S]	I'm Movin' On	1967	5.00	10.00	20.00
BST-84269	Open House	1968	5.00	10.00	20.00
BST-84296	Plain Talk	1969	5.00	10.00	20.00
B1-85125	Go For Whatcha Know	198?	2.50	5.00	10.00
BST-89901 [(2)]	Jimmy Smith's Greatest Hits!	1969	6.25	12.50	25.00
B1-91140	The Best of Jimmy Smith	1988	2.50	5.00	10.00
ELEKTRA MUSICIAN					
60175	Off the Top	1983	2.50	5.00	10.00
60301	Keep On Comin'	1984	2.50	5.00	10.00
GUEST STAR					
1344 [M]	Jimmy Smith	196?	3.00	6.00	12.00
G 1914 [M]	Jimmy Smith	196?	3.00	6.00	12.00
INNER CITY					
1121	The Cat Strikes Again	1981	2.50	5.00	10.00
MERCURY					
SRM-1-1127	Sit On It!	1976	2.50	5.00	10.00
SRM-1-1189	It's Necessary	1977	2.50	5.00	10.00
SRM-1-3716	Unfinished Business	1978	2.50	5.00	10.00
METRO					
M-521 [M]	Jimmy Smith at the Village Gate	1965	3.00	6.00	12.00
MS-521 [S]	Jimmy Smith at the Village Gate	1965	3.00	6.00	12.00
MGM					
GAS-107	Jimmy Smith (Golden Archive Series)	1970	3.75	7.50	15.00
SE-4709	The Other Side	1970	3.00	6.00	12.00
SE-4751	I'm Gon' Git Myself Together	1971	3.00	6.00	12.00
MILESTONE					
M-9176	Prime Time	198?	2.50	5.00	10.00
MOSAIC					
MQ5-154 [(5)]	The Complete February 1957 Jimmy Smith Blue Note Sessions	199?	20.00	40.00	80.00
PICKWICK					
SPC-3023	Stranger in Paradise	196?	2.50	5.00	10.00
PRIDE					
6011	Black Smith	1974	3.00	6.00	12.00
SUNSET					
SUM-1175 [M]	Jimmy Smith Plays the Standards	1967	3.75	7.50	15.00
SUS-5175 [S]	Jimmy Smith Plays the Standards	1967	3.00	6.00	12.00
SUS-5316	Just Friends	1971	3.00	6.00	12.00
VERVE					
V6-652-2 [(2)]	24 Karat Hits	196?	3.75	7.50	15.00
UMV-2073	Organ Grinder Swing	198?	2.50	5.00	10.00
—Reissue of 8628					
V-8474 [M]	Bashin'	1962	5.00	10.00	20.00
V6-8474 [S]	Bashin'	1962	6.25	12.50	25.00
V-8544 [M]	Hobo Flats	1963	5.00	10.00	20.00
V6-8544 [S]	Hobo Flats	1963	6.25	12.50	25.00
V-8552 [M]	Any Number Can Win	1963	5.00	10.00	20.00
V6-8552 [S]	Any Number Can Win	1963	6.25	12.50	25.00
V-8583 [M]	Who's Afraid of Virginia Woolf?	1964	5.00	10.00	20.00
V6-8583 [S]	Who's Afraid of Virginia Woolf?	1964	6.25	12.50	25.00
V-8587 [M]	The Cat	1964	5.00	10.00	20.00
V6-8587 [S]	The Cat	1964	6.25	12.50	25.00
V-8604 [M]	Christmas '64	1964	5.00	10.00	20.00
V6-8604 [S]	Christmas '64	1964	6.25	12.50	25.00
V-8618 [M]	The Monster	1965	3.75	7.50	15.00
V6-8618 [S]	The Monster	1965	5.00	10.00	20.00
V-8628 [M]	Organ Grinder Swing	1965	3.75	7.50	15.00
V6-8628 [S]	Organ Grinder Swing	1965	5.00	10.00	20.00
V-8641 [M]	Got My Mojo Workin'	1966	3.75	7.50	15.00
V6-8641 [S]	Got My Mojo Workin'	1966	5.00	10.00	20.00
V-8652 [M]	Peter and the Wolf	1966	5.00	10.00	20.00
V6-8652 [S]	Peter and the Wolf	1966	6.25	12.50	25.00
V-8666 [M]	Christmas Cookin'	1966	5.00	10.00	20.00
V6-8666 [S]	Christmas Cookin'	1966	6.25	12.50	25.00
V-8667 [M]	Hoochie Coochie Man	1966	3.75	7.50	15.00
V6-8667 [S]	Hoochie Coochie Man	1966	5.00	10.00	20.00
V-8705 [M]	Respect	1967	5.00	10.00	20.00
V6-8705 [S]	Respect	1967	3.75	7.50	15.00
V-8721 [M]	The Best of Jimmy Smith	1967	5.00	10.00	20.00
V6-8721 [S]	The Best of Jimmy Smith	1967	3.75	7.50	15.00
V6-8745 [S]	Stay Loose	1968	3.75	7.50	15.00
V6-8750	Livin' It Up!	1968	3.75	7.50	15.00
V6-8770	The Boss	1969	3.75	7.50	15.00
V6-8794	Groove Drops	1970	3.75	7.50	15.00
V6-8800	Plain Brown Wrapper	1971	3.00	6.00	12.00
V6-8806	Root Down	1972	3.00	6.00	12.00
V6-8809	Bluesmith	1973	3.00	6.00	12.00
V6-8814 [(2)]	History of Jimmy Smith	1973	3.75	7.50	15.00
V6-8832	Portuguese Soul	1974	3.00	6.00	12.00
SMAS-90643 [S]	The Monster	1965	6.25	12.50	25.00
—Capitol Record Club edition					
823308-1	Bashin'	1986	2.50	5.00	10.00
—Reissue of 8474					

SMITH, JIMMY, AND WES MONTGOMERY

Also see each artist's individual listings.

Albums

Number	Title (A Side/B Side)	Yr	VG	VG+	NM
VERVE					
UMV-2069	Jimmy and Wes, The Dynamic Duo	198?	2.50	5.00	10.00
—Reissue of 8678					
V-8678 [M]	Jimmy and Wes, The Dynamic Duo	1967	5.00	10.00	20.00
V6-8678 [S]	Jimmy and Wes, The Dynamic Duo	1967	3.75	7.50	15.00
V6-8766	The Further Adventures of Jimmy Smith and Wes Montgomery	1969	3.75	7.50	15.00

Number	Title (A Side/B Side)	Yr	VG	VG+	NM

SMITH, JOHNNY "HAMMOND"
See JOHNNY HAMMOND.

SMITH, KEELY
Also see LOUIS PRIMA AND KEELY SMITH.

45s

Number	Title (A Side/B Side)	Yr	VG	VG+	NM
ATLANTIC					
2429	One Less Bell to Answer/Begin the Beguine	1967	—	3.00	6.00
2457	Open Your Heart/All Fall Down	1967	—	3.00	6.00
CAPITOL					
F3445	I Wish You Love/Shy	1956	3.75	7.50	15.00
F3545	High School Affair/Hurt Me	1956	3.00	6.00	12.00
F3663	Sentimental Journey/Baby, Won't You Please Come Home	1957	3.00	6.00	12.00
F3698	Young and In Love/You Better Go Now	1957	3.00	6.00	12.00
F3740	You'll Never Know/Good Behavior	1957	3.00	6.00	12.00
F3820	Autumn Leaves/I Keep Forgetting	1957	3.00	6.00	12.00
F3952	How Are Ya' Fixed for Love?/Nothin' in Common	1958	3.00	6.00	12.00
—By Frank Sinatra and Keely Smith					
F3975	The Whippoorwill/Sometimes	1958	3.00	6.00	12.00
DOT					
15989	Don't Let the Stars Get In Your Eyes/I'd Climb the Highest Mountain	1959	3.00	6.00	12.00
16089	Close/Tea Leaves	1960	3.00	6.00	12.00
16146	Here in My Heart/Clearance Sale	1960	3.00	6.00	12.00
16147	Christmas Island/Silent Night	1960	3.75	7.50	15.00
16182	La-Bou-Lay-A/Young in Years	1961	2.50	5.00	10.00
16228	I Keep Coming Back for More/Little Lover Boy	1961	2.50	5.00	10.00
16257	Prisoner of Love/The Loveliest Night of the Year	1961	2.50	5.00	10.00
16298	Can't Help Falling in Love/You'll Never Walk Alone	1961	2.50	5.00	10.00
16338	Confidential/How Deep Is the Ocean	1962	2.50	5.00	10.00
16386	What Kind of Fool Am I/If I Should Lose You	1962	2.50	5.00	10.00
RCA VICTOR					
74-0543	Your Love/Loving Gift	1971	—	2.50	5.00
REPRISE					
0294	Let Me Call You Sweetheart/Sunday Mornin'	1964	2.00	4.00	8.00
0303	I'll Always Love You/I Can't Get You Out of My Heart	1964	2.00	4.00	8.00
0346	You're Breaking My Heart/Crazy	1965	—	3.00	6.00
0374	Have You Ever Been Lonely/Something Wonderful Happened	1965	—	3.00	6.00
0396	Someday (You'll Want Me to Love You)/Standing in the Ruins	1965	—	3.00	6.00
0402	That Old Black Magic/Standing in the Ruins	1965	—	3.00	6.00
0428	It's All in the Way You Look at Life/I'll Bring You Water	1965	—	3.00	6.00
0452	Good-Bye My Love/Where Are You	1966	—	3.00	6.00
0482	The Wonder of You/Who's Afraid	1966	—	3.00	6.00
20148	Going Through the Motions/When You Cry	1963	—	—	—
—Foreign release					
20149	Going Through the Motions/When You Cry	1963	2.00	4.00	8.00
20211	Love Again/No One Ever Tells You	1963	2.00	4.00	8.00

Albums

Number	Title (A Side/B Side)	Yr	VG	VG+	NM
CAPITOL					
SW 914 [S]	I Wish You Love	1959	7.50	15.00	30.00
—Black label with colorband, Capitol logo at left					
SW 914 [S]	I Wish You Love	1962	3.75	7.50	15.00
—Black label with colorband, Capitol logo at top					
W 914 [M]	I Wish You Love	1957	12.50	25.00	50.00
—Turquoise label					
W 914 [M]	I Wish You Love	1959	7.50	15.00	30.00
—Black label with colorband, Capitol logo at left					
W 914 [M]	I Wish You Love	1962	3.75	7.50	15.00
—Black label with colorband, Capitol logo at top					
ST 1073 [S]	Politely!	1959	12.50	25.00	50.00
—Black label with colorband, Capitol logo at left					
ST 1073 [S]	Politely!	1962	5.00	10.00	20.00
—Black label with colorband, Capitol logo at top					
T 1073 [M]	Politely!	1958	10.00	20.00	40.00
—Black label with colorband, Capitol logo at left					
T 1073 [M]	Politely!	1962	3.75	7.50	15.00
—Black label with colorband, Capitol logo at top					
ST 1145 [S]	Swingin' Pretty	1959	12.50	25.00	50.00
—Black label with colorband, Capitol logo at left					
ST 1145 [S]	Swingin' Pretty	1962	5.00	10.00	20.00
—Black label with colorband, Capitol logo at top					
T 1145 [M]	Swingin' Pretty	1959	10.00	20.00	40.00
—Black label with colorband, Capitol logo at left					
T 1145 [M]	Swingin' Pretty	1962	3.75	7.50	15.00
—Black label with colorband, Capitol logo at top					
DOT					
DLP-3241 [M]	Be My Love	1959	6.25	12.50	25.00
DLP-3265 [M]	Swing, You Lovers	1960	6.25	12.50	25.00
DLP-3287 [M]	Dearly Beloved	1961	6.25	12.50	25.00
DLP-3345 [M]	A Keely Christmas	1961	6.25	12.50	25.00
DLP-3415 [M]	Because You're Mine	1962	6.25	12.50	25.00
DLP-3423 [M]	Twist with Keely Smith	1962	6.25	12.50	25.00
DLP-3460 [M]	Cherokeely Swings	1962	6.25	12.50	25.00
DLP-3461 [M]	What Kind of Fool Am I	1962	6.25	12.50	25.00
DLP-25241 [S]	Be My Love	1959	7.50	15.00	30.00
DLP-25265 [S]	Swing, You Lovers	1960	7.50	15.00	30.00
DLP-25287 [S]	Dearly Beloved	1961	7.50	15.00	30.00
DLP-25345 [S]	A Keely Christmas	1961	7.50	15.00	30.00
DLP-25415 [S]	Because You're Mine	1962	7.50	15.00	30.00
DLP-25423 [S]	Twist with Keely Smith	1962	7.50	15.00	30.00
DLP-25460 [S]	Cherokeely Swings	1962	7.50	15.00	30.00
DLP-25461 [S]	What Kind of Fool Am I	1962	7.50	15.00	30.00
HARMONY					
HS 11333	That Old Black Magic	1968	3.00	6.00	12.00
REPRISE					
R-6086 [M]	Little Girl Blue, Little Girl New	1963	5.00	10.00	20.00
R9-6086 [S]	Little Girl Blue, Little Girl New	1963	6.25	12.50	25.00
R-6132 [M]	The Intimate Keely Smith	1964	5.00	10.00	20.00
RS-6132 [S]	The Intimate Keely Smith	1964	6.25	12.50	25.00
R-6142 [M]	Keely Smith Sings the John Lennon/Paul McCartney Songbook	1964	6.25	12.50	25.00
RS-6142 [S]	Keely Smith Sings the John Lennon/Paul McCartney Songbook	1964	7.50	15.00	30.00
R-6175 [M]	That Old Black Magic	1965	5.00	10.00	20.00
RS-6175 [S]	That Old Black Magic	1965	6.25	12.50	25.00

SMITH, LENDON, AND THE JESTERS

45s

Number	Title (A Side/B Side)	Yr	VG	VG+	NM
METEOR					
5030	Women/Lost Love	1956	37.50	75.00	150.00

SMITH, LEON

45s

Number	Title (A Side/B Side)	Yr	VG	VG+	NM
EPIC					
9326	Little 40 Ford/Cry All the Time	1959	10.00	20.00	40.00
LAVENDER					
1851	Basic Surf/Jailer, Bring Me Water	196?	7.50	15.00	30.00
WILLIAMETTE					
101	Little 40 Ford/Once I Had a Heart	1959	30.00	60.00	120.00
105	Honey Honey/That's the Way	1959	7.50	15.00	30.00
109	Flip, Flop and Fly/Sweet Love	1960	7.50	15.00	30.00

SMITH, LONNIE

12-Inch Singles

Number	Title (A Side/B Side)	Yr	VG	VG+	NM
T.K. DISCO					
78	For the Love of It (7:03)/Funk Reaction (5:50)	1978	3.00	6.00	12.00

45s

Number	Title (A Side/B Side)	Yr	VG	VG+	NM
BLUE NOTE					
1945	Think/Son of Ice Bag	1969	—	3.00	6.00
1955	Soul Talk (Part 1)/Soul Talk (Part 2)	1969	—	3.00	6.00
GROOVE MERCHANT					
1034	Afro-Desia (Part 1)/Afro-Desia (Part 2)	1975	—	2.00	4.00
1037	Keep On Lovin'/Lean Meat	1976	—	2.00	4.00

Albums

Number	Title (A Side/B Side)	Yr	VG	VG+	NM
BLUE NOTE					
B1-28266	Drives	1994	3.75	7.50	15.00
B1-31249	Move Your Hand	1996	3.75	7.50	15.00
B1-31880	Live at Club Mozambique	1995	3.75	7.50	15.00
BST-84290	Think!	1968	5.00	10.00	20.00
BST-84313	Turning Point	1969	5.00	10.00	20.00
BST-84326	Move Your Hand	1970	3.75	7.50	15.00
BST-84351	Drives	1971	3.75	7.50	15.00
CHIAROSCURO					
2019	When the Night Is Right	1979	3.00	6.00	12.00
COLUMBIA					
CL 2696 [M]	Finger-Lickin' Good Soul Organ	1967	6.25	12.50	25.00
CS 9496 [S]	Finger-Lickin' Good Soul Organ	1967	5.00	10.00	20.00
GROOVE MERCHANT					
3308	Afro-Desia	1975	3.00	6.00	12.00
3312	Keep On Lovin'	1976	3.00	6.00	12.00
KUDU					
02	Mama Wailer	1972	3.00	6.00	12.00

SMITH, LONNIE LISTON

12-Inch Singles

Number	Title (A Side/B Side)	Yr	VG	VG+	NM
COLUMBIA					
01882	Space Princess (7:01)/Quiet Moments	1979	2.50	5.00	10.00
DOCTOR JAZZ					
04624	If You Take Care of Me (2 versions)/Silhouettes	1984	—	3.00	6.00
STARTRAK					
P-044	Obsession (# of versions unknown)	1990	—	3.00	6.00
—With Phyllis Hyman					
P-050	Dance Floor (3 versions)	199?	—	3.00	6.00
P-056	Star Flower (3 versions)	199?	—	3.00	6.00

45s

Number	Title (A Side/B Side)	Yr	VG	VG+	NM
COLUMBIA					
10747	Journey Into Love/Sunburst	1978	—	2.00	4.00
10810	Bright Moments/We Can Dream	1978	—	2.00	4.00
10903	Space Princess/Quiet Moments	1979	—	2.00	4.00
11057	A Song for the Children/A Gift of Love	1979	—	2.00	4.00
11217	Give Peace a Chance (Make Love Not War)/Free and Easy	1980	—	2.00	4.00
11269	Love Is the Answer/Bridge Through Time	1980	—	2.00	4.00
DOCTOR JAZZ					
03836	Never Too Late/Divine Light	1983	—	—	3.00
03996	Mystic Woman/A Lonely Way to Be	1983	—	—	3.00
04623	If You Take Care of Me/Silhouettes	1984	—	—	3.00
FLYING DUTCHMAN					
DB-10214	Expansions — Part 1/Expansions — Part 2	1975	—	2.50	5.00
DB-10392	A Chance for Peace/Sunset	1975	—	2.50	5.00
DB-10616	Goddess of Love/Get Down Everybody (It's Time for World Peace)	1976	—	2.50	5.00
DB-10702	Peace and Love/Quiet Down	1976	—	2.50	5.00
RCA					
PB-10920	Renaissance/Space Lady	1977	—	2.50	5.00

Albums

Number	Title (A Side/B Side)	Yr	VG	VG+	NM
COLUMBIA					
JC 35332	Loveland	1978	2.50	5.00	10.00
JC 35654	Exotic Mysteries	1979	2.50	5.00	10.00
JC 36141	Song for the Children	1979	2.50	5.00	10.00
JC 36366	The Best of Lonnie Liston Smith	1980	2.50	5.00	10.00
JC 36373	Love Is the Answer	1980	2.50	5.00	10.00
DOCTOR JAZZ					
FW 38447	Dreams of Tomorrow	1983	2.50	5.00	10.00
FW 39420	Silhouettes	1984	2.50	5.00	10.00
FW 40063	Rejuvenation	1985	2.50	5.00	10.00
FLYING DUTCHMAN					
BDL1-0591	Cosmic Funk	1974	3.00	6.00	12.00

Number	Title (A Side/B Side)	Yr	VG	VG+	NM
BXL1-0591	Cosmic Funk	1978	2.00	4.00	8.00
—Reissue with new prefix					
BDL1-0934	Expressions	1975	3.00	6.00	12.00
BXL1-0934	Expressions	1978	2.00	4.00	8.00
—Reissue with new prefix					
BDL1-1196	Visions of a New World	1975	3.00	6.00	12.00
BXL1-1196	Visions of a New World	1978	2.00	4.00	8.00
—Reissue with new prefix					
BDL1-1460	Reflections of a Golden Dream	1976	3.00	6.00	12.00
BXL1-1460	Reflections of a Golden Dream	1978	2.00	4.00	8.00
—Reissue with new prefix					
10163	Astral Travelling	1973	3.00	6.00	12.00
RCA VICTOR					
AFL1-1822	Renaissance	1978	2.00	4.00	8.00
—Reissue with new prefix					
APL1-1822	Renaissance	1976	2.50	5.00	10.00
AFL1-2433	Live!	1978	2.00	4.00	8.00
—Reissue with new prefix					
APL1-2433	Live!	1977	2.50	5.00	10.00
AFL1-2897	The Best of Lonnie Liston Smith	1978	2.50	5.00	10.00
STARTRAK					
STA-4021	Love Goddess	198?	2.50	5.00	10.00

SMITH, O.C.

Number	Title (A Side/B Side)	Yr	VG	VG+	NM
45s					
BIG TOP					
3039	You Are My Sunshine/Well I'm Dancin'	1960	3.00	6.00	12.00
—As "Ocie Smith"					
CADENCE					
1304	Slow Walk/Forbidden Fruit	1956	3.75	7.50	15.00
—As "Ocie Smith"					
1312	If You Don't Love Me/Bad Man of Missouri	1957	3.75	7.50	15.00
—As "Ocie Smith"					
1329	Lighthouse/Too Many	1957	3.75	7.50	15.00
—As "Ocie Smith"					
CARIBOU					
9017	Together/Just Couldn't Help Myself	1976	—	2.50	5.00
9021	Simple Wife/Come with Me	1977	—	2.50	5.00
COLUMBIA					
10031	La La Peace Song/When Morning Comes	1974	—	2.50	5.00
43525	That's Life/I'm Your Man	1966	2.00	4.00	8.00
43809	Beyond the Next Hill/On Easy Street	1966	2.00	4.00	8.00
44151	Double Life/The Season	1967	2.00	4.00	8.00
44425	The Son of Hickory Holler's Tramp/The Best Man	1968	2.00	4.00	8.00
44555	Main Street Mission/Gas Food Lodging	1968	2.00	4.00	8.00
44616	Little Green Apples/Long Black Limousine	1968	2.00	4.00	8.00
44705	Isn't It Lonely Together/I Ain't the Worryin' Kind	1968	—	3.00	6.00
44751	Honey (I Miss You)/Keep On Keepin' On	1969	—	3.00	6.00
44859	Friend, Lover, Woman, Wife/I Taught Her Everything She Knows	1969	—	3.00	6.00
44948	Daddy's Little Man/If I Leave You Now	1969	—	3.00	6.00
44948 [PS]	Daddy's Little Man/If I Leave You Now	1969	2.00	4.00	8.00
45038	Me and You/Can't Take My Eyes Off You	1969	—	3.00	6.00
45098	Isn't Life Beautiful/Moody	1970	—	3.00	6.00
45160	Primrose Lane/Melodee	1970	—	3.00	6.00
45206	Baby I Need Your Loving/San Francisco Is a Lonely Town	1970	—	3.00	6.00
45301	Downtown U.S.A./That's What Life Is All About	1971	—	3.00	6.00
45343	Clean Up Your Own Back Yard/I've Been There	1971	—	3.00	6.00
45435	Help Me Make It Through the Night/Diamond in the Rough	1971	—	3.00	6.00
45655	Don't Misunderstand/If You Touch Me	1972	—	3.00	6.00
45863	La La Peace Song/When Morning Comes	1973	—	3.00	6.00
FAMILY					
5000	Dreams Come True/(B-side unknown)	1980	—	2.50	5.00
MGM					
12321	Just Kiss Me/At Last My Baby's Coming Home	1956	3.75	7.50	15.00
—As "Ocie Smith"					
MOTOWN					
1623	Love Changes/Got to Know	1982	—	2.50	5.00
1636	I Betcha/That's One for Love	1982	—	2.50	5.00
RENDEZVOUS					
101	What'cha Gonna Do/(B-side unknown)	1986	—	2.00	4.00
102	You're the First, the Last, My Everything/(B-side unknown)	1986	—	2.00	4.00
103	Brenda/(B-side unknown)	1986	—	2.00	4.00
SHADY BROOK					
1045	Love to Burn/Give Me Time	1978	—	2.50	5.00
1049	Living Without Your Love/Can't Be the One to Say It's Over	1978	—	2.50	5.00
45012	Love Is Forever/(B-side unknown)	197?	—	2.50	5.00
SOUTH BAY					
1003	Love Changes/Got to Know	1982	—	3.00	6.00
Albums					
CARIBOU					
PZ 34471	Together	1977	2.50	5.00	10.00
COLUMBIA					
CL 2714 [M]	The Dynamic O.C. Smith	1967	5.00	10.00	20.00
CS 9514 [S]	The Dynamic O.C. Smith	1967	3.75	7.50	15.00
CS 9680	Hickory Holler Revisited	1968	3.00	6.00	12.00
CS 9756	For Once in My Life	1969	3.00	6.00	12.00
CS 9908	O.C. Smith at Home	1969	3.00	6.00	12.00
C 30227	O.C. Smith's Greatest Hits	1970	3.00	6.00	12.00
C 30664	Help Me Make It Through the Night	1971	3.00	6.00	12.00
KC 33247	La La Peace Song	1974	2.50	5.00	10.00
HARMONY					
KH 30317	O.C. Smith	1971	2.50	5.00	10.00
MOTOWN					
6019 ML	Love Changes	1982	2.50	5.00	10.00
SHADYBROOK					
012	Love	1978	2.50	5.00	10.00

SMITH, OCIE

See O.C. SMITH.

SMITH, PATTI, GROUP

Number	Title (A Side/B Side)	Yr	VG	VG+	NM
12-Inch Singles					
ARISTA					
SP-62 [DJ]	Frederick (Studio)/Frederick (Live)	1977	3.75	7.50	15.00
9688	People Have the Power/Where Duty Calls/Wild Leaves	1988	—	3.00	6.00
45s					
ARISTA					
SP-2 [DJ]	Pissing in the River (mono/stereo)	1976	6.25	12.50	25.00
SP-4 [DJ]	Ask the Angels (mono/stereo)	1977	6.25	12.50	25.00
—With lyric insert (deduct 20% if missing)					
0171	Gloria/My Generation	1976	2.50	5.00	10.00
0171 [PS]	Gloria/My Generation	1976	2.50	5.00	10.00
0318	Because the Night/God Speed	1978	—	2.00	4.00
—A-side co-written by Bruce Springsteen					
0318 [PS]	Because the Night/God Speed	1978	2.00	4.00	8.00
0427	Frederick/Frederick (Live)	1979	—	2.00	4.00
0427 [PS]	Frederick/Frederick (Live)	1979	2.00	4.00	8.00
0453	So You Want to Be a Rock and Roll Star//5-4-3-2-1/A Fire of Unknown Origin	1979	—	2.00	4.00
0453 [PS]	So You Want to Be a Rock and Roll Star//5-4-3-2-1/A Fire of Unknown Origin	1979	5.00	10.00	20.00
9173	Because the Night/So You Want to Be a Rock 'n' Roll Star	198?	—	—	3.00
—"Flashback" reissue					
9689	People Have the Power/Wild Leaves	1988	—	—	3.00
9689 [PS]	People Have the Power/Wild Leaves	1988	—	—	3.00
9762	I Was (Looking for You)/Up There Down There	1988	—	—	3.00
MER					
601	Hey Joe/Piss Factory	1974	20.00	40.00	80.00
SIRE					
1009	Hey Joe/Piss Factory	1977	2.00	4.00	8.00
1009	Hey Joe/Piss Factory	1977	2.00	4.00	8.00
Albums					
ARISTA					
AL 4066	Horses	1975	3.00	6.00	12.00
—With the word "Horses" in white letters on the front cover					
AL 4066	Horses	1975	3.75	7.50	15.00
—With the word "Horses" in black letters on the front cover					
AL 4097	Radio Ethiopia	1977	3.00	6.00	12.00
AB 4171	Easter	1978	3.00	6.00	12.00
AB 4221	Wave	1979	2.50	5.00	10.00
ALB6-8349	Easter	198?	2.00	4.00	8.00
—Reissue					
ALB6-8362	Horses	198?	2.00	4.00	8.00
—Reissue					
ALB6-8379	Radio Ethiopia	198?	2.00	4.00	8.00
—Reissue					
AL 8453	Dreams of Life	1988	2.50	5.00	10.00
AL 8546	Wave	1990	2.00	4.00	8.00
—Reissue					
R 100469	Dreams of Life	1988	3.00	6.00	12.00
—BMG Music Service edition					

SMITH, RAY

Number	Title (A Side/B Side)	Yr	VG	VG+	NM
45s					
CELEBRITY CIRCLE					
6901	I Walk the Line/Fool #1	1964	3.75	7.50	15.00
CINNAMON					
755	Tiilted Cup of Love/I'd Traded Better for Worse	1973	—	2.50	5.00
760	It Wasn't Easy/It's Just Not the Same	1973	—	2.50	5.00
773	The First Lonely Weekend/A Handful of Friends	1973	—	2.50	5.00
795	Ten Steps Out in Front/Because of Losing You	1974	—	2.50	5.00
COLUMBIA					
20604	An Old Christmas Card/Jolly Old St. Nicholas	1949	—	—	—
—Unconfirmed on 45 rpm					
DIAMOND					
193	Everybody's Goin' Somewhere/Au-Go-Go-Go	1965	3.75	7.50	15.00
ERA BACK TO BACK HITS					
048	Rockin' Little Angel/Robbin' the Cradle	197?	—	2.50	5.00
—B-side by Tony Bellus					
HEART					
250	Gone, Baby, Gone/(B-side unknown)	195?	1000.	1500.	2000.
INFINITY					
003	After This Night Is Through/Turn On the Moonlight	1961	3.75	7.50	15.00
007	Let Yourself Go/Johnny the Hummer	1961	3.75	7.50	15.00
JUDD					
1016	Rockin' Little Angel/That's All Right	1959	7.50	15.00	30.00
1017	Maria Elena/Put Your Arms Around Me Honey	1960	7.50	15.00	30.00
1019	One Wonderful Love/Makes Me Feel Good	1960	7.50	15.00	30.00
1021	Blonde Hair, Blue Eyes/You Don't Want Me	1960	7.50	15.00	30.00
NU-TONE					
1182	Deep in My Heart/She's Mine	1964	3.75	7.50	15.00
SHI-RAY					
101	Sleepy Eyed Woman/Pretty Juke Box	197?	—	3.00	6.00
SMASH					
1787	Room 503/These Four Precious Years	1962	3.75	7.50	15.00
SUN					
298	So Right/Right Behind You Baby	1958	7.50	15.00	30.00
308	Why, Why, Why/You Made a Hit	1958	7.50	15.00	30.00
319	Rockin' Bandit/Sail Away	1959	7.50	15.00	30.00
372	Travelin' Salesman/I Won't Miss You ('Til You're Gone)	1961	7.50	15.00	30.00
375	Hey Boss Man/Candy Doll	1962	7.50	15.00	30.00
TOLLIE					
9029	There Comes My Baby Back Again/Did We Have a Party	1964	5.00	10.00	20.00
TOPPA					
1071	Almost Alone/A Place Within My Heart	1962	5.00	10.00	20.00

Number	Title (A Side/B Side)	Yr	VG	VG+	NM
VEE JAY					
579	Rockin' Robin/Robbin' the Cradle	1964	3.75	7.50	15.00
WARNER BROS.					
5371	I'm Snowed/Turn Over a New Leaf	1963	3.75	7.50	15.00
ZIRKON					
1055	After This Night Is Through/Turn On the Moonlight	1961	5.00	10.00	20.00
Albums					
COLUMBIA					
CL 1937 [M]	Ray Smith's Greatest Hits	1963	6.25	12.50	25.00
CS 8737 [S]	Ray Smith's Greatest Hits	1963	7.50	15.00	30.00
JUDD					
JLPA-701 [M]	Travelin' with Ray	1960	175.00	350.00	700.00
STOMP OFF					
SOS-1012	Jungle Blues	198?	3.00	6.00	12.00
WIX					
1000	I'm Gonna Rock Some More	197?	3.75	7.50	15.00
"T"					
56062 [M]	The Best of Ray Smith	196?	25.00	50.00	100.00

SMITH, ROBERT CURTIS

Number	Title (A Side/B Side)	Yr	VG	VG+	NM
45s					
ARHOOLIE					
502	Love Each Other/Please Don't Drive Me Away	1961	5.00	10.00	20.00
Albums					
BLUESVILLE					
BVLP-1064 [M]	Clarksdale Blues	1963	20.00	40.00	80.00
—Blue label, silver print					
BVLP-1064 [M]	Clarksdale Blues	1964	6.25	12.50	25.00
—Blue label, trident logo at right					

SMITH, RONNIE

Number	Title (A Side/B Side)	Yr	VG	VG+	NM
45s					
BRUNSWICK					
55137	Lookie, Lookie, Lookie/Tiny Kisses	1959	10.00	20.00	40.00
HAMILTON					
50003	My Babe/I've Got a Love	1959	6.25	12.50	25.00
IMPERIAL					
5667	It Hurts Me So/Long Time No Love	1960	7.50	15.00	30.00
5679	I Hear You Knocking/I Started Out Walkin'	1960	7.50	15.00	30.00

SMITH, SAMMI

Number	Title (A Side/B Side)	Yr	VG	VG+	NM
45s					
COLUMBIA					
44370	So Long, Charlie Brown, Don't Look for Me Around/Turn Around	1967	2.00	4.00	8.00
44523	Why Do You Do Me Like You Do/22 Road Markers to a Mile	1968	2.00	4.00	8.00
44663	It's Not Time Now/Sand Covered Angels	1968	2.00	4.00	8.00
44905	Brownsville Lumberyard/Shadows of Your Mind	1969	2.00	4.00	8.00
CYCLONE					
100	What a Lie/It's Not My Way	1979	—	2.00	4.00
104	The Letter/It's a Day for Sad Songs	1979	—	2.00	4.00
ELEKTRA					
45292	Huckleberry Pie/I Won't Sing No Love Songs Anymore	1975	—	2.00	4.00
—With Even Stevens					
45300	As Long As There's a Sunday/Children	1976	—	2.00	4.00
45334	Sunday School to Broadway/Goodmornin', Sunshine, Goodbye	1976	—	2.00	4.00
45374	Loving Arms/I Just Wanted to Sing	1977	—	2.00	4.00
45398	I Can't Stop Loving You/De Grazia's Song	1977	—	2.00	4.00
45429	Days That End in "Y"/Hallelujah for Beer	1977	—	2.00	4.00
45476	It Just Won't Feel Like Cheating (With You)/I Ain't Got Time to Rock No Babies	1978	—	2.00	4.00
45504	Norma Jean/Lookin' for Lovin'	1978	—	2.00	4.00
MEGA					
0001	He's Everywhere/This Room for Rent	1970	—	2.50	5.00
0015	Help Me Make It Through the Night/When Michael Calls	1970	—	3.00	6.00
0026	Then You Walk In/Willie	1971	—	2.50	5.00
0039	For the Ride/Saunder's Ferry Lane	1971	—	2.50	5.00
0056	Kentucky/The Marionette	1971	—	2.50	5.00
0068	Girl in New Orleans/Isn't It Sad	1972	—	2.50	5.00
0079	I've Got to Have You/Jimmy's in Georgia	1972	—	2.50	5.00
0097	The Toast of '45/Tony	1972	—	2.50	5.00
0109	I Miss You Most When You're Here/Billy Jacks	1973	—	2.50	5.00
0118	City of New Orleans/Don't Blow No Smoke on Me	1973	—	2.50	5.00
204	The Rainbow in Daddy's Eyes/Birmingham Mistake	1974	—	2.50	5.00
210	Never Been to Spain/It's Not Easy	1974	—	2.50	5.00
212	Help Me Make It Through the Night/When Michael Calls	1974	—	2.00	4.00
—Reissue of 0015					
1214	Long Black Veil/Paste Me On Some Feathers`	1974	—	2.50	5.00
1222	Cover Me/He Makes It Hard to Say Goodbye	1975	—	2.50	5.00
1233	She's in Love with a Rodeo Man/Fool for Something Years	1975	—	2.50	5.00
1236	Today I Started Loving You Again/Fine As Wine	1975	—	2.50	5.00
1246	My Window Faces the South/Before the Next Teardrop Falls	1976	—	2.50	5.00
SOUND FACTORY					
425	I Just Want to Be with You/(B-side unknown)	1980	—	2.00	4.00
427	Cheatin's a Two-Way Street/(B-side unknown)	1981	—	2.00	4.00
446	Sometimes I Cry When I'm Alone/(B-side unknown)	1981	—	2.00	4.00
453	Gypsy and Joe/(B-side unknown)	1982	—	2.00	4.00
STEP ONE					
342	You Just Hurt My Last Feeling/Lying in My Arms	1985	—	2.00	4.00
347	An Offer I Couldn't Refuse/One Away from One Too Many	1985	—	2.00	4.00
351	Love Me All Over/Don't Let It Happen Again	1986	—	2.00	4.00
ZODIAC					
1000	Help Me Make It Through the Night/Saunder's Ferry Drive	1976	—	2.00	4.00
1005	Just You 'n' Me/Walking in the Sunshine	1976	—	2.00	4.00
1013	Rings for Sale/You Don't Want My Love	1976	—	2.00	4.00
Albums					
ELEKTRA					
7E-1058	As Long As There's a Sunday	1976	2.50	5.00	10.00
7E-1108	Mixed Emotions	1977	2.50	5.00	10.00
HARMONY					
H 30616	The World of Sammi Smith	1971	2.50	5.00	10.00
MEGA					
601	Rainbow in Daddy's Eyes	1974	3.00	6.00	12.00
612	Today I Started Loving You Again	1975	3.00	6.00	12.00
31-1000	Help Me Make It Through the Night	1971	3.00	6.00	12.00
31-1007	Lonesome	1971	3.00	6.00	12.00
31-1011	Something Old, Something New, Something Blue	1972	3.00	6.00	12.00
31-1019	The Best of Sammi Smith	1973	3.00	6.00	12.00
31-1021	The Toast of '45	1973	3.00	6.00	12.00
PICKWICK					
6167	Help Me Make It Through the Night	197?	2.50	5.00	10.00
ZODIAC					
5004	Her Way	1976	2.50	5.00	10.00

SMITH, SHELBY

Number	Title (A Side/B Side)	Yr	VG	VG+	NM
45s					
REBEL					
728	Rockin' Mama/Since My Baby Said Goodbye	1962	100.00	200.00	400.00

SMITH, SOMETHIN', AND THE REDHEADS

Number	Title (A Side/B Side)	Yr	VG	VG+	NM
45s					
EPIC					
5-9025	Gee/Just in Case You Change Your Mind	1954	3.00	6.00	12.00
—As "Somethin' Smith and the Skylarks"					
5-9048	If I Could Be with You/Oh Jane	1954	2.50	5.00	10.00
5-9093	It's a Sin to Tell a Lie/My Baby Just Cares for Me	1955	2.50	5.00	10.00
5-9106	The Ace in the Hole/Charley, My Boy	1955	2.50	5.00	10.00
5-9119	When All the Streets Are Dark/Pretty Baby	1955	2.50	5.00	10.00
5-9140	Red Head/Pinch Me (I Must Be Dreamin')	1956	2.50	5.00	10.00
5-9168	In a Shanty in Old Shanty Town/Coal Dust on the Fiddle	1956	2.50	5.00	10.00
5-9179	Heartaches/Cecelia	1956	2.50	5.00	10.00
5-9188	When I Grow Too Old to Dream/We'll Build a Bungalow	1956	2.50	5.00	10.00
5-9197	Sweet Stuff/I Hope You Know What You're Doin'	1957	2.50	5.00	10.00
5-9208	Ma (She's Makin' Eyes at Me)/Mambo, Tango, Samba, Chalypso Rhumba Blues	1957	2.50	5.00	10.00
5-9221	You Always Hurt the One You Love/My Melancholy Baby	1957	2.50	5.00	10.00
5-9247	Ev'ry Night at 9 O'Clock/I'm Gonna Wrap Up All My Heartaches	1957	2.50	5.00	10.00
5-9264	School Bus Rock/I Thank You, Mr. Moon	1958	3.00	6.00	12.00
5-9269	My Secret Inspiration/The Brush Off	1958	2.50	5.00	10.00
5-9280	I Don't Want to Set the World on Fire/You Made Me Love You	1958	2.50	5.00	10.00
5-9313	Mr. D.J. (Please Play a Song for Me)/That's Togetherness	1959	2.50	5.00	10.00
5-9340	Poor Butterfly/Ten Chaperones	1959	2.50	5.00	10.00
5-9389	Ballin' the Jack/It's a Sin to Tell a Lie	1960	2.00	4.00	8.00
MGM					
13023	Ain't We Got Fun/We'll Meet Again	1961	2.00	4.00	8.00
Albums					
EPIC					
LN 3138 [M]	Somethin' Smith and the Redheads	1959	7.50	15.00	30.00
LN 3373 [M]	Put the Blame on Mame	196?	6.25	12.50	25.00
MGM					
E-3941 [M]	Ain't We Got Fun Kinda Songs	1961	5.00	10.00	20.00
SE-3941 [S]	Ain't We Got Fun Kinda Songs	1961	6.25	12.50	25.00

SMITH, WARREN

Number	Title (A Side/B Side)	Yr	VG	VG+	NM
45s					
LIBERTY					
55248	I Don't Believe I'll Fall in Love Today/Cave-In	1960	5.00	10.00	20.00
55302	Odds and Ends (Bits and Pieces)/A Whole Lot of Nothin'	1961	5.00	10.00	20.00
55336	Call of the Wild/Old Lonesome Feeling	1961	5.00	10.00	20.00
55361	Why Baby Why/Why I'm Walking	1961	5.00	10.00	20.00
—With Shirley Collie					
55409	Bad News Gets Around/Five Minutes of the Latest Blues	1962	5.00	10.00	20.00
55475	Book of Broken Hearts/160 Pounds of Hurt	1962	5.00	10.00	20.00
55615	Big City Ways/That's Why I Sing in a Honky Tonk	1963	3.75	7.50	15.00
55699	Blue Smoke/Judge and Jury	1964	3.75	7.50	15.00
MERCURY					
72825	Lie to Me/When the Heartaches Get to Me	1968	2.50	5.00	10.00
SUN					
239	Rock and Roll Ruby/I'd Rather Be Safe Than Sorry	1956	20.00	40.00	80.00
250	Ubangi Stomp/Black Jack David	1956	15.00	30.00	60.00
268	Miss Froggie/So Long, I'm Gone	1957	10.00	20.00	40.00
286	I Fell in Love/I've Got Love If You Want It	1958	7.50	15.00	30.00
314	Goodbye Mr. Love/Sweet Sweet Girl	1959	10.00	20.00	40.00
WARNER BROS.					
5125	Dear Santa/The Meaning of Christmas	1959	6.25	12.50	25.00
Albums					
LIBERTY					
LRP-3199 [M]	The First Country Collection of Warren Smith	1961	12.50	25.00	50.00
LST-7199 [S]	The First Country Collection of Warren Smith	1961	17.50	35.00	70.00

Number	Title (A Side/B Side)	Yr	VG	VG+	NM
SMITH, WHISTLING JACK					
45s					
DERAM					
85005	I Was Kaiser Bill's Batman/The British Grin 'N' Bear	1967	2.00	4.00	8.00
85041	Only When I Laff/Early One Morning	1969	—	3.00	6.00
SMOKE, THE					
45s					
UNI					
55154	Choose It (Part 1)/Choose It (Part 2)	1969	2.50	5.00	10.00
Albums					
SIDEWALK					
ST 5912	The Smoke	1968	10.00	20.00	40.00
UNI					
73052	The Smoke	1969	6.25	12.50	25.00
73065	The Smoke at George's Coffee Shop	1970	6.25	12.50	25.00
SMOKE RINGS, THE					
45s					
DOT					
16975	Love's the Thing/She Gives Me Love	1966	5.00	10.00	20.00
PROSPECT					
101	Love's the Thing/She Gives Me Love	1966	10.00	20.00	40.00
SMOKE RISE, THE					
45s					
PARAMOUNT					
0113	I'm Here (Love Me)/Survival	1971	2.00	4.00	8.00
Albums					
PARAMOUNT					
PAS-9000 [(2)] *—With booklet*	The Survival of St. Joan	1971	5.00	10.00	20.00
SMOKESTACK LIGHTNIN'					
45s					
BELL					
755	Light in My Window/Long Stemmed Eyes	1968	—	3.00	6.00
777	I Idolize You/Something's Got a Hold on You	1969	—	3.00	6.00
836	Baby Don't Get Crazy/The Blue Albino Shuffle	1969	—	3.00	6.00
861	Hello L.A., Bye-Bye Birmingham/Well Tuesday	1970	—	3.00	6.00
WHITE WHALE					
243	Nadine/Crossroadds Blues	1967	2.00	4.00	8.00
256	Look What You've Done/Got a Good Love	1967	2.00	4.00	8.00
Albums					
BELL					
6026	Off the Wall	1969	5.00	10.00	20.00
SMOKEY JOE					
45s					
FLIP					
228	The Signifying Monkey/Listen to Me Baby	1955	125.00	250.00	500.00
SUN					
228	The Signifying Monkey/Listen to Me Baby	1956	75.00	150.00	300.00
393	The Signifying Monkey/Listen to Me Baby	1964	50.00	100.00	200.00
SMOKIE					
45s					
MCA					
40429 *—As "Smokey"*	If You Think You Know How to Love Me/'Tis Me	1975	—	2.50	5.00
40471 *—As "Smokey"*	Don't Play Your Rock 'N' Roll to Me/Talking Her 'Round	1975	—	2.50	5.00
RSO					
860	Living Next Door to Alice/When My Back Was Against the Wall	1976	—	2.50	5.00
874	If You Think You Know How to Love Me/Make Ya Boogie	1977	—	2.00	4.00
881	Needles and Pins/No One Could Ever Love You More	1977	—	2.00	4.00
900	For a Few Dollars More/I Can't Stay Here Tonight	1978	—	2.00	4.00
934	No More Letters/Oh Carol	1979	—	2.00	4.00
Albums					
MCA					
2152 *—As "Smokey"*	Smokey	1975	3.00	6.00	12.00
RSO					
RS-1-3005	Midnight Café	1976	2.50	5.00	10.00
RS-1-3029	Bright Lights and Back Alleys	1978	2.50	5.00	10.00
SMOOTHIES, THE					
With JOHN PHILLIPS and SCOTT McKENZIE.					
45s					
DECCA					
31105	Softly/Joanie	1960	5.00	10.00	20.00
31159	Ride, Ride, Ride/Lonely Boy and Pretty Girl	1960	5.00	10.00	20.00
SMOTHERS, DICK					
Also see THE SMOTHERS BROTHERS.					
45s					
MERCURY					
72717	Saturday Night at the World/They Are Gone	1967	5.00	10.00	20.00
72717 [PS]	Saturday Night at the World/They Are Gone	1967	6.25	12.50	25.00
SMOTHERS BROTHERS, THE					
Also see DICK SMOTHERS.					
45s					
MERCURY					
72027	Fly Ezekiel/They Call the Wind Maria	1962	2.50	5.00	10.00
72182	Jenny Brown/You Go This-a-Way	1963	2.50	5.00	10.00
72323	Coo Coo/Slithery Dee	1964	2.50	5.00	10.00
72483	The Three Song/The World I Used to Know	1965	2.00	4.00	8.00
72483 [PS]	The Three Song/The World I Used to Know	1965	3.75	7.50	15.00
72519	The Toy Song/Little Sacha Sugar	1966	2.00	4.00	8.00
72519 [PS]	The Toy Song/Little Sacha Sugar	1966	3.75	7.50	15.00
72573	Writer of Songs/Lark Day	1966	2.00	4.00	8.00
SMOTHERS INC.					
79151	The Christmas Bunny Part 1/The Christmas Bunny Part 2	1969	6.25	12.50	25.00
79151 [PS]	The Christmas Bunny Part 1/The Christmas Bunny Part 2	1969	12.50	25.00	50.00
Albums					
MERCURY					
MGDJ-20 [DJ]	Best of the Smothers Brothers	1964	10.00	20.00	40.00
MGDJ-25 [DJ]	It's Brothers Smothers Month	1964	10.00	20.00	40.00
MG-20611 [M]	The Songs and Comedy of the Smothers Brothers!	1962	3.75	7.50	15.00
MG-20675 [M]	The Two Sides of the Smothers Brothers	1962	3.75	7.50	15.00
MG-20777 [M]	(Think Ethnic!)	1963	3.75	7.50	15.00
MG-20862 [M]	Curb Your Tongue, Knave!	1963	3.75	7.50	15.00
MG-20904 [M]	It Must Have Been Something I Said!	1964	3.75	7.50	15.00
MG-20948 [M]	Tour De Farce American History and Other Unrelated Subjects	1964	3.75	7.50	15.00
MG-20989 [M]	Aesop's Fables the Smothers Brothers Way	1965	3.75	7.50	15.00
MG-21051 [M]	Mom Always Liked You Best!	1965	3.75	7.50	15.00
MG-21064 [M]	The Smothers Brothers Play It Straight	1966	3.75	7.50	15.00
MG-21089 [M]	Golden Hits of the Smothers Brothers, Vol. 2	1966	3.75	7.50	15.00
SR-60611 [S]	The Songs and Comedy of the Smothers Brothers!	1962	5.00	10.00	20.00
SR-60675 [S]	The Two Sides of the Smothers Brothers	1962	5.00	10.00	20.00
SR-60777 [S]	(Think Ethnic!)	1963	5.00	10.00	20.00
SR-60862 [S]	Curb Your Tongue, Knave!	1963	5.00	10.00	20.00
SR-60904 [S]	It Must Have Been Something I Said!	1964	5.00	10.00	20.00
SR-60948 [S]	Tour De Farce American History and Other Unrelated Subjects	1964	5.00	10.00	20.00
SR-60989 [S]	Aesop's Fables the Smothers Brothers Way	1965	5.00	10.00	20.00
SR-61051 [S]	Mom Always Liked You Best!	1965	5.00	10.00	20.00
SR-61064 [S]	The Smothers Brothers Play It Straight	1966	5.00	10.00	20.00
SR-61089 [S]	Golden Hits of the Smothers Brothers, Vol. 2	1966	5.00	10.00	20.00
SR-61193	Smothers Comedy Brothers Hour	1968	5.00	10.00	20.00
RHINO					
R1-70188	Sibling Revelry: The Best of the Smothers Brothers	1988	2.50	5.00	10.00
SNOW, EDDIE					
45s					
SUN					
226	Ain't That Right/Bring Your Love Back Home	1955	50.00	100.00	200.00
SNOW, PHOEBE					
12-Inch Singles					
ELEKTRA					
ED 5370 [DJ]	If I Can Just Get Through the Night (same on both sides)	1989	—	3.00	6.00
ED 5383 [DJ]	Something Real (same on both sides)	1989	—	3.00	6.00
45s					
COLUMBIA					
10315	Two Fisted Love/Inspired Insanity	1976	—	2.50	5.00
10351	All Over/No Regrets	1976	—	2.50	5.00
10463	Shakey Ground/Don't Sleep with Your Eyes Closed	1976	—	2.50	5.00
10504	Teach Me Tonight/Autobiography (Shine, Shine, Shine)	1977	—	2.50	5.00
10626	Never Letting Go/The Middle of the Night	1977	—	2.50	5.00
10654	Love Makes a Woman/Electra	1977	—	2.50	5.00
10856	Every Night/Random Time	1978	—	2.50	5.00
ELEKTRA					
69290	Something Real/Best of My Love	1989	—	—	3.00
69305	If I Can Just Get Through the Night/Soothin'	1989	—	—	3.00
MIRAGE					
3800	Games/Down in the Basement	1981	—	2.00	4.00
3818	Mercy, Mercy, Mercy/Something Good	1981	—	2.00	4.00
3843	Rock Away/Baby Please	1981	—	2.00	4.00
SHELTER					
40278	Harpo's Blues/Let the Good Times Roll	1974	—	2.50	5.00
40353	Poetry Man/Either or Both	1974	—	3.00	6.00
40400	Easy Street/Harpo's Blues	1975	—	2.50	5.00
Albums					
COLUMBIA					
PC 33952 *—Original with no bar code*	Second Childhood	1976	2.50	5.00	10.00
PC 33952 *—Budget-line reissue with bar code*	Second Childhood	198?	2.00	4.00	8.00
PCQ 33952 [Q]	Second Childhood	1976	3.75	7.50	15.00
PC 34387 *—Original with no bar code*	It Looks Like Snow	1976	2.50	5.00	10.00
PC 34387 *—Budget-line reissue with bar code*	It Looks Like Snow	198?	2.00	4.00	8.00
JC 34875	Never Letting Go	1977	2.50	5.00	10.00
JC 35456	Against the Grain	1978	2.50	5.00	10.00
JC 37091	The Best of Phoebe Snow	1981	2.50	5.00	10.00
PC 37091 *—Budget-line reissue*	The Best of Phoebe Snow	1981	2.00	4.00	8.00
DCC COMPACT CLASSICS					
LPZ-2027 *—Audiophile vinyl*	Phoebe Snow	1996	6.25	12.50	25.00

Number	Title (A Side/B Side)	Yr	VG	VG+	NM
ELEKTRA					
60852	Something Real	1989	2.50	5.00	10.00
MCA					
37119	Phoebe Snow	198?	2.00	4.00	8.00
—Budget-line reissue of Shelter LP					
MIRAGE					
SD 19297	Rock Away	1981	2.50	5.00	10.00
SHELTER					
2109	Phoebe Snow	1974	2.50	5.00	10.00
52017	Phoebe Snow	1977	2.00	4.00	8.00
—Reissue with ABC distribution					

SNOW MEN, THE

Early version of THE SUNRAYS.

45s

Number	Title (A Side/B Side)	Yr	VG	VG+	NM
CHALLENGE					
59227	Ski Storm (Part 1)/Ski Storm (Part 2)	1964	7.50	15.00	30.00

SNYDER, TERRY, AND THE ALL-STARS

See ENOCH LIGHT.

SOCIALITES, THE

45s

Number	Title (A Side/B Side)	Yr	VG	VG+	NM
ARRAWAK					
1004	Jimmy/The Click	1962	5.00	10.00	20.00
WARNER BROS.					
5476	You're Losing Your Touch/Jive Jimmy	1964	3.00	6.00	12.00

SOCIETY'S CHILDREN

45s

Number	Title (A Side/B Side)	Yr	VG	VG+	NM
ATCO					
6538	White Christmas/I'll Let You Know	1967	3.00	6.00	12.00
6553	Count the Ways/Golden Child	1968	2.50	5.00	10.00
6597	Live for Today/I'll Let You Know	1968	2.50	5.00	10.00
6618	A Tribute to the Four Seasons/Golden Child	1968	5.00	10.00	20.00

SOF-TONES, THE

45s

Number	Title (A Side/B Side)	Yr	VG	VG+	NM
CEE BEE					
1062	Oh Why/(B-side unknown)	195?	4000.	6000.	8000.

SOFT MACHINE, THE

45s

Number	Title (A Side/B Side)	Yr	VG	VG+	NM
PROBE					
452	Joy of a Toy/Why Are We Sleeping	1969	2.50	5.00	10.00

Albums

Number	Title (A Side/B Side)	Yr	VG	VG+	NM
ACCORD					
SN-7178	Memories	1981	2.50	5.00	10.00
COLUMBIA					
G 30339 [(2)]	Third	1970	3.75	7.50	15.00
C 30754	Fourth	1971	3.00	6.00	12.00
KC 31604	5	1972	3.00	6.00	12.00
KG 32260 [(2)]	Six	1973	3.75	7.50	15.00
KC 32716	Seven	1974	3.00	6.00	12.00
COMMAND					
964 SD [(2)]	Soft Machine	1973	3.75	7.50	15.00
—Reissue of Probe LPs in one package					
PROBE					
CPLP-4500	The Soft Machine	1968	10.00	20.00	40.00
—Cover with moving parts					
CPLP-4500	The Soft Machine	1969	5.00	10.00	20.00
—Regular cover					
CPLP-4505	The Soft Machine, Vol. 2	1969	6.25	12.50	25.00

SOLDIER BOYS, THE

Also see DON COVAY.

45s

Number	Title (A Side/B Side)	Yr	VG	VG+	NM
SCEPTER					
1230	I'm Your Soldier Boy/You Picked Me	1962	15.00	30.00	60.00

SOLITAIRES, THE

45s

Number	Title (A Side/B Side)	Yr	VG	VG+	NM
ARGO					
5316	Walking Along/Please Kiss This Letter	1958	7.50	15.00	30.00
MGM					
13221	Fool That I Am/Fair Weather Lover	1964	7.50	15.00	30.00
OLD TOWN					
1000	Blue Valentine/Wonder Boy	1954	100.00	200.00	400.00
—Black vinyl					
1000	Blue Valentine/Wonder Boy	1954	375.00	750.00	1500.
—Red vinyl					
1003	Chapel of St. Clair/If I Loved You	1954	—	—	—
—Unreleased?					
1006/7	Please Remember My Heart/South of the Border	1954	175.00	350.00	700.00
—Black vinyl					
1006/7	Please Remember My Heart/South of the Border	1954	1000.	2000.	3000.
—Red vinyl					
1006/8	Please Remember My Heart/Chances I've Taken	1954	37.50	75.00	150.00
1008	Chances I've Taken/Lonely	1954	175.00	350.00	700.00
1008	Please Remember My Heart/Chances I've Taken	196?	6.25	12.50	25.00
—Blue label					
1010	I Don't Stand a Ghost of a Chance/Girl of Mine	1955	125.00	250.00	500.00
1012	My Dear/What Did She Say	1955	100.00	200.00	400.00
—Logo in Old English style					
1012	My Dear/What Did She Say	1956	18.75	37.50	75.00
—Logo in block letters					
1014	The Wedding/Don't Fall in Love	1955	25.00	50.00	100.00
1015	Magic Rose/Later for You Baby	1955	25.00	50.00	100.00
1019	The Honeymoon/Fine Little Girl	1956	25.00	50.00	100.00
1026	You've Sinned/The Angels Sang	1956	25.00	50.00	100.00
1026	You've Sinned/You're Back with Me	1956	75.00	150.00	300.00
1032	Give Me One More Chance/Nothing Like a Little Love	1956	50.00	100.00	200.00
1034	Walking Along/Please Kiss This Letter	1957	18.75	37.50	75.00
—Yellow label					
1034	Walking Along/Please Kiss This Letter	196?	6.25	12.50	25.00
—Blue label					
1044	I Really Love You So/Thrill of Love	1957	100.00	200.00	400.00
1049	Walkin' and Talkin'/No More Sorrows	1958	25.00	50.00	100.00
1059	Please Remember My Heart/Big Mary's House	1958	10.00	20.00	40.00
1066	Embraceable You/Round Goes My Heart	1959	10.00	20.00	40.00
1071	Light a Candle in the Chapel/Helpless	1959	10.00	20.00	40.00
1096	Lonesome Lover/Pretty Thing	1961	10.00	20.00	40.00
1139	The Time Is Here/Honey Babe	1963	7.50	15.00	30.00

SOMETHING WILD

45s

Number	Title (A Side/B Side)	Yr	VG	VG+	NM
PSYCHEDELIC					
1691	Trippin' Out/She's Kinda Weird	1966	12.50	25.00	50.00

SOMETHING YOUNG

45s

Number	Title (A Side/B Side)	Yr	VG	VG+	NM
FONTANA					
1556	Oh, Don't Come Crying/The Words I'm Seeking	1966	6.25	12.50	25.00

SOMMERS, JOANIE

45s

Number	Title (A Side/B Side)	Yr	VG	VG+	NM
ABC					
12323	Peppermint Choo Choo/Peppermint Engineer	1978	—	2.50	5.00
CAPITOL					
5936	Trains and Boats and Planes/Yesterday's Morning	1967	2.00	4.00	8.00
COLUMBIA					
43567	You've Got Possibilities/Never Throw Your Dreams	1966	2.00	4.00	8.00
43731	Alfie/You Take What Comes Along	1966	2.00	4.00	8.00
43950	It Doesn't Matter Anymore/Take a Broken Heart	1966	2.00	4.00	8.00
HAPPY TIGER					
522	Step Inside Love/Little Girl from Greenwood, Ga.	1970	—	3.00	6.00
537	Sunshine After the Rain/Tell Him	1970	—	3.00	6.00
WARNER BROS.					
5157	One Boy/I'll Never Be Free	1960	3.75	7.50	15.00
5177	Be My Love/Why Don't You Do Right	1960	3.75	7.50	15.00
5183	Ruby Duby Du/Bob White	1960	3.75	7.50	15.00
5201	I Don't Want to Walk Without You/Seems Like Long, Long Ago	1961	3.75	7.50	15.00
5226	Piano Boy/Serenade of the Bells	1961	3.75	7.50	15.00
5241	Makin' Whoopee/What's Wrong with Me	1961	3.75	7.50	15.00
5275	Johnny Get Angry/Theme from "A Summer Place"	1962	5.00	10.00	20.00
5308	When the Boys Get Together/Passing Strangers	1962	3.00	6.00	12.00
5324	Goodbye Joey/Bobby's Hobbies	1962	3.00	6.00	12.00
5339	Memories, Memories/Since Randy Moved Away	1963	3.00	6.00	12.00
5350	Little Bit of Everything/Henny Penny	1963	3.00	6.00	12.00
5361	One Boy/June Is Bustin' Out All Over	1963	3.00	6.00	12.00
5374	Little Girl Bad/Wishing Well	1963	3.00	6.00	12.00
5390	Goodbye Summer/Big Man	1963	3.00	6.00	12.00
5437	I'd Be So Good for You/I'm Gonna Know He's Mine	1964	2.50	5.00	10.00
5454	If You Love Him/I Think I'm Gonna Cry Now	1964	2.50	5.00	10.00
5507	Makin' Whoopee/What's Wrong with Me + 2	1961	6.25	12.50	25.00
—Part of Warner Bros. "+2" series, with two new songs and excerpts of two prior hits					
5507 [PS]	Makin' Whoopee/What's Wrong with Me + 2	1961	7.50	15.00	30.00
5629	Don't Pity Me/My Block	1965	2.50	5.00	10.00
7129	Johnny Get Angry/One Boy	1968	—	3.00	6.00
—"Back to Back Hits" series -- originals have green labels with "W7" logo					
7251	Great Divide/Talk Until Midnight	1968	2.00	4.00	8.00

Albums

Number	Title (A Side/B Side)	Yr	VG	VG+	NM
COLUMBIA					
CL 2495 [M]	Come Alive	1966	5.00	10.00	20.00
CS 9295 [S]	Come Alive	1966	6.25	12.50	25.00
DISCOVERY					
DS-883	Dream	1983	3.00	6.00	12.00
—With Bob Florence					
WARNER BROS.					
W 1346 [M]	Positively the Most	1960	7.50	15.00	30.00
WS 1346 [S]	Positively the Most	1960	10.00	20.00	40.00
B 1348 [M]	Behind Closed Doors at a Recording Session	1960	37.50	75.00	150.00
—Record comes in a box with a booklet included					
W 1412 [M]	Joanie Sommers	1961	7.50	15.00	30.00
WS 1412 [S]	Joanie Sommers	1961	10.00	20.00	40.00
W 1436 [M]	For Those Who Think Young	1962	7.50	15.00	30.00
WS 1436 [S]	For Those Who Think Young	1962	10.00	20.00	40.00
W 1470 [M]	Johnny Get Angry	1962	10.00	20.00	40.00
WS 1470 [S]	Johnny Get Angry	1962	12.50	25.00	50.00
W 1474 [M]	Let's Talk About Love	1962	7.50	15.00	30.00
WS 1474 [S]	Let's Talk About Love	1962	10.00	20.00	40.00
W 1504 [M]	Sommers' Seasons	1963	6.25	12.50	25.00
WS 1504 [S]	Sommers' Seasons	1963	7.50	15.00	30.00
W 1575 [M]	Softly, The Brazilian Sound	1964	6.25	12.50	25.00
WS 1575 [S]	Softly, The Brazilian Sound	1964	7.50	15.00	30.00

SOMMERS, RONNY

See SONNY.

SONICS, THE (1)

Male vocal group.

45s

Number	Title (A Side/B Side)	Yr	VG	VG+	NM
AMCO					
001	It's You/Preacher Man	1962	50.00	100.00	200.00
CHECKER					
922	This Broken Heart/You Made Me Cry	1959	6.25	12.50	25.00
HARVARD					
801	This Broken Heart/You Made Me Cry	1959	100.00	200.00	400.00

Number	Title (A Side/B Side)	Yr	VG	VG+	NM
922	This Broken Heart/You Made Me Cry	1959	12.50	25.00	50.00
JAMIE					
1235	Sugaree/Beautiful Brown Eyes	1962	5.00	10.00	20.00
X-TRA					
107	Once in a Lifetime/It Ain't True	1958	500.00	1000.	2000.

SONICS, THE (2)

Rock band from the Pacific Northwest.

45s

Number	Title (A Side/B Side)	Yr	VG	VG+	NM
BURDETTE					
106	Dirty Old Man/Bama Lama Bama Loo	1975	2.00	4.00	8.00
ETIQUETTE					
11	Keep a-Knockin'/The Witch	1965	7.50	15.00	30.00
16	The Hustler/Boss Hoss	1965	7.50	15.00	30.00
18	Don't Be Afraid of the Dark/Shot Down	1965	7.50	15.00	30.00
22	Don't Believe in Christmas/Christmas Spirit	1965	7.50	15.00	30.00
—B-side by the Wailers					
23	Louie Louie/Cinderella	1966	7.50	15.00	30.00
GREAT NORTHWEST					
702	The Witch/Bama Lama Bama Loo	1979	—	2.50	5.00
JERDEN					
809	Love Lights/You Got Your Head On Backwards	1966	3.75	7.50	15.00
810	The Witch/Like No Other	1966	3.75	7.50	15.00
811	Psycho/Maintaining My Cool	1966	3.75	7.50	15.00
NORTON					
45-066	Don't Believe in Christmas/Santa Claus	1997	—	—	2.00
—A-side is reissue of Etiquette 22					
45-066 [PS]	Don't Believe in Christmas/Santa Claus	1997	—	—	2.00
PICCADILLY					
244	Anyway the Wind Blows/Lost Love	1967	5.00	10.00	20.00
—A-side written by Frank Zappa					
UNI					
55039	Anyway the Wind Blows/Lost Love	1967	3.75	7.50	15.00
—A-side written by Frank Zappa					

Albums

Number	Title	Yr	VG	VG+	NM
BOMP!					
4011	Sinderella	1980	3.75	7.50	15.00
BUCKSHOT					
001	Explosives	1973	50.00	100.00	200.00
ETIQUETTE					
ETALB-024 [M]	Here Are the Sonics!!!	1965	62.50	125.00	250.00
—Red label					
ETALB-024 [M]	Here Are the Sonics!!!	1965	50.00	100.00	200.00
—Purple label					
ETLPS-024	Here Are the Sonics!!!	1984	2.50	5.00	10.00
—Purple label, flimsier vinyl, with date on back cover					
ETLPS-024 [S]	Here Are the Sonics!!!	1965	100.00	200.00	400.00
—Red label					
ETLPS-024 [S]	Here Are the Sonics!!!	1965	75.00	150.00	300.00
—Purple label					
ETALB-027 [M]	The Sonics Boom	1966	75.00	150.00	300.00
ETLPS-027	The Sonics Boom	1984	2.50	5.00	10.00
—Flimsier vinyl, with date on back cover					
ETLPS-027 [R]	The Sonics Boom	1966	50.00	100.00	200.00
FIRST AMERICAN					
FA-7715	Original Northwest Punk	1978	5.00	10.00	20.00
FA-7719	Unreleased	1980	5.00	10.00	20.00
FA-7779	Fire and Ice	1983	5.00	10.00	20.00
JERDEN					
JRL-7007 [M]	Introducing the Sonics	1967	50.00	100.00	200.00
JRS-7007 [R]	Introducing the Sonics	1967	37.50	75.00	150.00

SONICS, THE (2); THE WAILERS; THE GALAXIES

Albums

Number	Title	Yr	VG	VG+	NM
ETIQUETTE					
ETALB-025	Merry Christmas	1984	2.50	5.00	10.00
—Flimsier vinyl, with date on back cover					
ETALB-025 [M]	Merry Christmas	1965	125.00	250.00	500.00

SONICS, THE (U)

Some of these could be group (1); none of these are group (2).

45s

Number	Title (A Side/B Side)	Yr	VG	VG+	NM
ARMONIA					
102	Funny/I Get That Feeling	1962	37.50	75.00	150.00
GAITY					
114	Marlene/(B-side unknown)	1959	1000.	1500.	2000.
GROOVE					
0112	Bumble Bee/As I Live On	1955	50.00	100.00	200.00
NOCTURNE					
110	Triangle Love/Evil Eye	1959	20.00	40.00	80.00
RKO UNIQUE					
411	Triangle Love/Evil Eye	1957	15.00	30.00	60.00

SONNETS, THE

45s

Number	Title (A Side/B Side)	Yr	VG	VG+	NM
GUYDEN					
2112	I Can't Get Sentimental/Forever for You	1964	3.75	7.50	15.00
HERALD					
477	Please Won't You Call Me/Why Should We Break Up	1956	15.00	30.00	60.00

SONNY

Contains many records he made under aliases. Also see .

45s

Number	Title (A Side/B Side)	Yr	VG	VG+	NM
ATCO					
6369	Laugh at Me/Gip Pony	1965	3.00	6.00	12.00
6386	The Revolution Kind/Georgia and John Quetzal	1965	3.00	6.00	12.00
6505	Misty Roses/I Told My Girl to Go Away	1967	2.50	5.00	10.00
6531	Pammie's on a Bummer/My Best Friend's Girl Is Out of Sight	1967	2.50	5.00	10.00
FIDELITY					
3020	Wearing Black/Don't Have to Tell Me	1960	6.25	12.50	25.00
—As "Don Christy"					
GO					
1001	As Long As You Love Me/I'll Always Be Grateful	1960	6.25	12.50	25.00
—As "Don Christy"					
HIGHLAND					
1160	I'll Change/Try It Out on Me	1963	7.50	15.00	30.00
—As "Sonny Bono"					
MCA					
40139	Laugh at Me/Rub Your Nose	1973	—	2.00	4.00
—As "Sonny Bono"					
40271	Classified 1A/Our Last Show	1974	—	2.00	4.00
—As "Sonny Bono"					
NAME					
3	As Long As You Love Me/I'll Always Be Grateful	1960	6.25	12.50	25.00
—As "Don Christy"					
SPECIALTY					
672	Wearing Black/One Little Answer	1959	6.25	12.50	25.00
—As "Don Christy"					
733	One Little Answer/Comin' Down the Chimney	1974	—	3.00	6.00
—As "Sonny Bono and Little Tootsie"					
SWAMI					
1001	Don't Shake My Tree/(Mama) Come Get Your Baby Boy	1961	6.25	12.50	25.00
—As "Ronny Sommers"					
VEE JAY					
710	Midnight Surf/Ride the Wild Quetzal	1966	6.25	12.50	25.00
—As "Sonny Bono"					

Albums

Number	Title	Yr	VG	VG+	NM
ATCO					
33-229 [M]	Inner Views	1967	5.00	10.00	20.00
SD 33-229 [S]	Inner Views	1967	5.00	10.00	20.00

SONNY AND CHER

Includes early records as "Caesar and Cleo." Also see CHER; SONNY.

45s

Number	Title (A Side/B Side)	Yr	VG	VG+	NM
ATCO					
6345	Just You/Sing C'est La Vie	1965	2.50	5.00	10.00
6359	I Got You Babe/It's Gonna Rain	1965	3.00	6.00	12.00
6381	But You're Mine/Hello	1965	3.00	6.00	12.00
6395	What Now My Love/I Look for You	1965	3.00	6.00	12.00
6420	Have I Stayed Too Long/Leave Me Be	1966	2.50	5.00	10.00
6440	Little Man/Monday	1966	2.50	5.00	10.00
6449	Living for You/Love Don't Come	1966	2.50	5.00	10.00
6461	The Beat Goes On/Love Don't Come	1967	3.00	6.00	12.00
6480	A Beautiful Story/Podunk	1967	2.50	5.00	10.00
6486	Plastic Man/It's the Little Things	1967	2.50	5.00	10.00
6507	It's the Little Things/Don't Talk to Strangers	1967	2.50	5.00	10.00
6541	Good Combination/You and Me	1968	2.50	5.00	10.00
6555	Circus/I Would Marry You Today	1968	2.50	5.00	10.00
6605	You Gotta Have a Thing of Your Own/I Got You Babe	1968	2.50	5.00	10.00
6684	You're a Friend of Mine/I Would Marry You Today	1969	2.50	5.00	10.00
6758	Get It Together/Hold Me Tighter	1970	2.00	4.00	8.00
KAPP					
2141	Real People/Somebody	1971	—	2.00	4.00
2151	All I Ever Need Is You/I Got You Babe	1971	—	2.50	5.00
2163	A Cowboy's Work Is Never Done/Somebody	1972	—	2.50	5.00
2176	When You Say Love/Crystal Clear and Muddy Waters	1972	—	2.00	4.00
MCA					
40026	Mama Was a Rock and Roll Singer, Papa Used to Write All Her Songs (Parts 1 & 2)	1973	—	2.00	4.00
40083	The Greatest Show on Earth/You Know Darn Well	1973	—	2.00	4.00
PHILCO-FORD					
HP-8	I Got You Babe/The Beat Goes On	1967	6.25	12.50	25.00
—4-inch plastic "Hip Pocket Record" with color sleeve					
REPRISE					
0308	Love Is Strange/Do You Want to Dance	1964	5.00	10.00	20.00
—As "Caesar and Cleo"					
0309	Baby Don't Go/Walkin' the Quetzal	1964	5.00	10.00	20.00
0392	Baby Don't Go/Walkin' the Quetzal	1965	3.75	7.50	15.00
0419	Love Is Strange/Let the Good Times Roll	1965	5.00	10.00	20.00
—As "Caesar and Cleo"					
0419 [PS]	Love Is Strange/Let the Good Times Roll	1965	10.00	20.00	40.00
—As "Caesar and Cleo"					
0723	Baby Don't Go/Love Is Strange	1968	—	2.50	5.00
—"Back to Back Hits" series -- originals have both "r:" and "W7" logos					
VAULT					
909	The Letter/Spring Fever	1964	7.50	15.00	30.00
—As "Caesar and Cleo"					
916	The Letter/Spring Fever	1965	3.00	6.00	12.00
916 [PS]	The Letter/Spring Fever	1965	12.50	25.00	50.00
WARNER BROS.					
8341	You're Not Right for Me/Wrong Number	1977	—	2.50	5.00

7-Inch Extended Plays

Number	Title	Yr	VG	VG+	NM
ATCO					
LSD 33-177 [DJ]	It's Gonna Rain/You've Really Got a Hold on Me //I Got You Babe/The Letter/Why Don't They Let Us Fall in Love	1965	6.25	12.50	25.00
—Jukebox mini-LP					
LSD 33-177 [PS]	Look at Us	1965	6.25	12.50	25.00

Albums

Number	Title	Yr	VG	VG+	NM
ATCO					
33-177 [M]	Look At Us	1965	5.00	10.00	20.00
SD 33-177 [S]	Look At Us	1965	6.25	12.50	25.00
33-183 [M]	The Wondrous World of Sonny and Cher	1966	3.75	7.50	15.00
SD 33-183 [S]	The Wondrous World of Sonny and Cher	1966	5.00	10.00	20.00
33-203 [M]	In Case You're in Love	1967	3.75	7.50	15.00
SD 33-203 [S]	In Case You're in Love	1967	5.00	10.00	20.00
33-214 [M]	Good Times	1967	3.75	7.50	15.00
SD 33-214 [S]	Good Times	1967	5.00	10.00	20.00

Number	Title (A Side/B Side)	Yr	VG	VG+	NM
33-219 [M]	The Best of Sonny and Cher	1967	3.75	7.50	15.00
SD 33-219 [S]	The Best of Sonny and Cher	1967	5.00	10.00	20.00
SD 2-804 [(2)]	The Two of Us	1972	5.00	10.00	20.00
—Combines "Look at Us" and "In Case You're in Love"					
A2M 5177 [(2) M]	Sonny & Cher's Greatest Hits	1967	7.50	15.00	30.00
—Columbia Record Club exclusive					
A2S 5178 [(2) S]	Sonny & Cher's Greatest Hits	1967	7.50	15.00	30.00
—Columbia Record Club exclusive					
KAPP					
KS-3654	Sonny & Cher Live	1971	3.75	7.50	15.00
KS-3660	All I Ever Need Is You	1972	3.75	7.50	15.00
MCA					
2009	Sonny & Cher Live	1973	3.00	6.00	12.00
—Reissue of Kapp 3654					
2021	All I Ever Need Is You	1973	3.00	6.00	12.00
—Reissue of Kapp 3660					
2101	Mama Was a Rock & Roll Singer Papa Used to Write All Her Songs	1973	3.00	6.00	12.00
2117	Greatest Hits	1974	3.00	6.00	12.00
2-8004 [(2)]	Sonny & Cher Live in Las Vegas, Vol. 2	1973	3.75	7.50	15.00
PAIR					
PDL2-1140 [(2)]	Sonny & Cher At Their Best	1986	3.00	6.00	12.00
REPRISE					
R 6177 [M]	Baby Don't Go	1965	7.50	15.00	30.00
RS 6177 [P]	Baby Don't Go	1965	7.50	15.00	30.00
—By "Sonny & Cher & Friends" (also includes The Lettermen, Bill Medley and The Blendells)					

SONNY AND THE DEMONS

Albums

Number	Title (A Side/B Side)	Yr	VG	VG+	NM
UNITED ARTISTS					
UAL-3316 [M]	Drag Kings	1964	12.50	25.00	50.00
UAS-6316 [S]	Drag Kings	1964	15.00	30.00	60.00

SONS OF CHAMPLIN, THE

With Bill Champlin, later of CHICAGO.

45s

Number	Title (A Side/B Side)	Yr	VG	VG+	NM
ARIOLA AMERICA					
7606	Look Out/Queen of the Rain	1975	—	2.00	4.00
7627	Hold On/Still in Love with You	1976	—	2.00	4.00
7633	You/Imagination's Sake	1976	—	2.00	4.00
7653	Follow Your Heart/Here Is Where Your Love Belongs	1976	—	2.00	4.00
7664	Saved by the Grace of Your Love/West End	1977	—	2.00	4.00
CAPITOL					
2437	1982-A/Black and Blue Rainbow	1969	2.00	4.00	8.00
2534	Freedom/Hello Sunlight	1969	2.00	4.00	8.00
2663	It's Time/Why Do People Run	1969	2.00	4.00	8.00
2786	You Can Fly/Terry's Tune	1970	—	3.00	6.00
COLUMBIA					
45872	Welcome to the Dance/Swim	1973	—	2.50	5.00
GOLDMINE					
101	Look Out/Queen of the Rain	1975	—	2.50	5.00
VERVE					
10500	Sing Me a Lullaby/Fat City	1967	2.50	5.00	10.00

Albums

Number	Title (A Side/B Side)	Yr	VG	VG+	NM
ARIOLA AMERICA					
SW-50002	The Sons of Champlin	1975	2.50	5.00	10.00
SW-50007	A Circle Filled with Love	1976	2.50	5.00	10.00
SW-50017	Loving Is Why	1977	2.50	5.00	10.00
CAPITOL					
SWBB-200 [(2)]	Loosen Up Naturally	1969	12.50	25.00	50.00
—With the F-word clearly visible as part of the cover artwork					
SWBB-200 [(2)]	Loosen Up Naturally	1969	6.25	12.50	25.00
—With the F-word scratched off the cover artwork					
SWBB-200 [(2)]	Loosen Up Naturally	1969	5.00	10.00	20.00
—With the F-word airbrushed off the cover artwork					
SKAO-322	The Sons	1969	6.25	12.50	25.00
ST-675	Follow Your Heart	1971	5.00	10.00	20.00
COLUMBIA					
KC 32341	Welcome to the Dance	1973	3.75	7.50	15.00
GOLDMINE					
GM 94930	The Sons of Champlin	1975	5.00	10.00	20.00
SONS OF CHAMPLIN					
(no #)	Minus Seeds and Stems	1969	125.00	250.00	500.00

SOOTZ, MANNY

45s

Number	Title (A Side/B Side)	Yr	VG	VG+	NM
PIRATE					
841	Cape Canaveral (Part 1)/Cape Canaveral (Part 2)	1957	6.25	12.50	25.00

SOPHISTICATES, THE

45s

Number	Title (A Side/B Side)	Yr	VG	VG+	NM
VIVA					
61	When Elvis Comes Marching Home/Woody's Place	1960	12.50	25.00	50.00

SOPHOMORES, THE (1)

45s

Number	Title (A Side/B Side)	Yr	VG	VG+	NM
CHORD					
1302	Charades/What Can I Do	1957	10.00	20.00	40.00
DAWN					
216	Cool, Cool Baby/Every Night About This Time	1956	6.25	12.50	25.00
218	Linda/I Get a Thrill	1956	6.25	12.50	25.00
223	Ocean Blue/I Left My Sugar	1956	6.25	12.50	25.00
225	Is There Someone for Me/Everybody Loves Me	1957	6.25	12.50	25.00
228	I Just Can't Keep the Tears from Tumblin' Down/If I Should Lose Your Love	1957	6.25	12.50	25.00
237	Checkers/Each Time I Hold You	1958	6.25	12.50	25.00
EPIC					
9259	Charades/What Can I Do	1957	5.00	10.00	20.00

SOPHOMORES, THE (2)

45s

Number	Title (A Side/B Side)	Yr	VG	VG+	NM
SOUND STAGE 7					
2533	Summer of '64/I Know I Should (Every Night)	1964	2.50	5.00	10.00

SOPWITH "CAMEL", THE

45s

Number	Title (A Side/B Side)	Yr	VG	VG+	NM
KAMA SUTRA					
217	Hello Hello/Treadin'	1966	3.00	6.00	12.00
224	Postcard from Jamaica/Little Orphan Annie	1967	3.00	6.00	12.00
224 [PS]	Postcard from Jamaica/Little Orphan Annie	1967	5.00	10.00	20.00
236	Great Morpheum/Saga of the Lowdown Letdown	1967	3.00	6.00	12.00
REPRISE					
1179	Sleazy Love/Fazon	1973	2.00	4.00	8.00

Albums

Number	Title (A Side/B Side)	Yr	VG	VG+	NM
KAMA SUTRA					
KSBS-2063	Hello Hello	1973	5.00	10.00	20.00
KLP-8060 [M]	The Sopwith Camel	1967	7.50	15.00	30.00
KLPS-8060 [S]	The Sopwith Camel	1967	7.50	15.00	30.00
REPRISE					
MS 2108	The Miraculous Hump Returns	1973	6.25	12.50	25.00

SORENSON BROTHERS, THE

45s

Number	Title (A Side/B Side)	Yr	VG	VG+	NM
MARLINDA					
7507/8	They've Landed/Stowaway	196?	12.50	25.00	50.00

SORROWS, THE

45s

Number	Title (A Side/B Side)	Yr	VG	VG+	NM
WARNER BROS.					
5662	Take a Heart/We Should Get Along Fine	1965	3.00	6.00	12.00

SOUL, DAVID

45s

Number	Title (A Side/B Side)	Yr	VG	VG+	NM
MGM					
13510	The Covered Man/I Will Warm Your Heart	1966	2.50	5.00	10.00
13589	Was I Ever So Wrong/Before	1966	2.50	5.00	10.00
13842	No One's Gonna Cry/Quiet Kind of Hate	1967	2.50	5.00	10.00
PRIVATE STOCK					
45129	Don't Give Up on Us/Black Bean Soup	1976	—	2.00	4.00
45150	Going In with My Eyes Open/Topanga	1977	—	2.00	4.00
45163	Silver Lady/The Rider	1977	—	2.00	4.00

Albums

Number	Title (A Side/B Side)	Yr	VG	VG+	NM
PRIVATE STOCK					
PS-2019	David Soul	1977	2.50	5.00	10.00
PS-7001	Playing to an Audience of One	1977	2.50	5.00	10.00

SOUL, JIMMY

45s

Number	Title (A Side/B Side)	Yr	VG	VG+	NM
20TH FOX					
413	Respectable/I Wish I Could Dance	1963	2.50	5.00	10.00
SPQR					
3221	My Little Room/Ella Is Yella	1964	2.50	5.00	10.00
3300	Twistin' Matilda/I Can't Hold Out Any Longer	1962	3.00	6.00	12.00
3302	When Matilda Comes Back/Some Kinda Nut	1962	3.00	6.00	12.00
3304	Guess Things Happen That Way/My Baby Loves to Bowl	1963	3.00	6.00	12.00
3305	If You Wanna Be Happy/Don't Release Me	1963	3.75	7.50	15.00
3305 [PS]	If You Wanna Be Happy/Don't Release Me	1963	7.50	15.00	30.00
3310	Treat 'Em Tough/Church Street in the Summertime	1963	3.00	6.00	12.00
3312	Go 'Way Christina/Everybody's Gone Ape	1963	3.00	6.00	12.00
3314	Change Partners/I Hate You Baby	1963	3.00	6.00	12.00
3315	My Girl-She Sure Can Cook/A Woman Is Smarter in Every Kinda Way	1964	2.50	5.00	10.00
3318	You Can't Have Your Cake/Take Me to Los Angeles	1964	2.50	5.00	10.00
3319	Twistin' Matilda/Treat 'Em Tough	1964	2.50	5.00	10.00

Albums

Number	Title (A Side/B Side)	Yr	VG	VG+	NM
SPQR					
E 16001	If You Wanna Be Happy	1963	37.50	75.00	150.00

SOUL AGENTS, THE

45s

Number	Title (A Side/B Side)	Yr	VG	VG+	NM
CAMEO					
350	Let's Make It Pretty Baby/The Seventh Son	1965	5.00	10.00	20.00
INTERPHON					
7702	I Just Want to Make Love to You/Mean Woman Blues	1964	5.00	10.00	20.00

SOUL BROTHERS SIX

45s

Number	Title (A Side/B Side)	Yr	VG	VG+	NM
ATLANTIC					
2406	Some Kind of Wonderful/I'll Be Loving You	1967	3.75	7.50	15.00
2456	You Better Check Yourself/What Can You Do When You Ain't Got Nobody	1967	3.00	6.00	12.00
2535	Your Love Is Such a Wonderful Love/I Can't Live Without You	1968	3.00	6.00	12.00
2592	Somebody Else Is Loving My Baby/Thank You Baby for Loving Me	1969	3.00	6.00	12.00
2645	What You Got (Is So Good for Me)/Drive	1969	3.00	6.00	12.00
PHIL-L.A. OF SOUL					
355	Funky Funky Way of Making Love/Let Me Be the One	1972	—	3.00	6.00
360	You're My World/You Gotta Come a Little Closer	1973	—	3.00	6.00
365	Let Me Do What We Ain't Doin'/Lost the Will to Live	1974	—	3.00	6.00

SOUL CHILDREN, THE

Number	Title (A Side/B Side)	Yr	VG	VG+	NM
45s					
EPIC					
50178	Finders Keepers/Midnight Sunshine	1976	—	2.50	5.00
50236	If You Move I'll Fall/Little Understanding	1976	—	2.50	5.00
50345	Where Is Your Woman Tonight?/Merry-Go-Round	1977	—	2.50	5.00
50405	There Always/You Don't Need a Ring	1977	—	2.50	5.00
STAX					
0008	Give 'Em Love/Move Over	1968	2.00	4.00	8.00
0018	I'll Understand/Doin' Our Thing	1969	2.00	4.00	8.00
0030	Tighten Up My Thang/Take Up the Slack	1969	2.00	4.00	8.00
0050	The Sweeter He Is — Part 1/The Sweeter He Is — Part 2	1969	2.00	4.00	8.00
0062	Hold On, I'm Coming/Make It Good	1970	—	3.50	7.00
0075	Give Me One Good Reason Why/Finish Me Off	1970	—	3.50	7.00
0086	Let's Make a Sweet Thing Sweeter/Finish Me Off	1971	—	3.50	7.00
0119	Hearsay/Don't Take My Sunshine	1972	—	3.50	7.00
0132	Don't Take My Kindness for Weakness/Just the One	1972	—	3.50	7.00
0152	It Ain't Always What You Do (It's Who You Let See You Do It)/All That Shines Ain't Gold	1973	—	3.50	7.00
0170	Love Is a Hurtin' Thing/Poem on the School House Door	1973	—	3.50	7.00
0182	I'll Be the Other Woman/Come Back Kind of Love	1973	—	3.00	6.00
0218	Love Makes It Right/Love Makes It Right — Part 2	1974	—	3.00	6.00
0230	What's Happening Baby/What's Happening Baby — Part 2	1974	—	3.00	6.00
3206	Can't Give Up a Good Thing/Signed, Sealed and Delivered	1978	—	2.50	5.00
3211	Summer in the Shade/Hard Living with a Woman	1978	—	2.50	5.00
3214	Who You Used to Be/Believing	1978	—	2.50	5.00
Albums					
EPIC					
PE 33902	Finders Keepers	1976	3.75	7.50	15.00
PE 34455	Where Is Your Woman Tonight	1977	3.75	7.50	15.00
STAX					
STS-2018	Soul Children	1969	7.50	15.00	30.00
STS-2043	The Best of Two Worlds	1971	7.50	15.00	30.00
STS-3003	Genesis	1972	7.50	15.00	30.00
STX-4105	Open Door Policy	1978	3.75	7.50	15.00
STX-4120	Chronicle	1979	3.00	6.00	12.00
STS-5507	Friction	1974	7.50	15.00	30.00

SOUL CLAN, THE

SOLOMON BURKE, ARTHUR CONLEY, DON COVAY, BEN E. KING and JOE TEX.

Number	Title (A Side/B Side)	Yr	VG	VG+	NM
45s					
ATLANTIC					
2530	Soul Meeting/That's How It Feels	1968	2.50	5.00	10.00
2530 [PS]	Soul Meeting/That's How It Feels	1968	3.75	7.50	15.00

SOUL COMFORTERS, THE

Number	Title (A Side/B Side)	Yr	VG	VG+	NM
45s					
HOLLYWOOD					
1042	White Christmas/Silent Night	1955	7.50	15.00	30.00

SOUL FINDERS, THE

Number	Title (A Side/B Side)	Yr	VG	VG+	NM
Albums					
RCA CAMDEN					
CAL-2170 [M]	Sweet Soul Music	1967	7.50	15.00	30.00
CAS-2170 [S]	Sweet Soul Music	1967	7.50	15.00	30.00
CAL-2239 [M]	An Explosive Album of Soul	1968	7.50	15.00	30.00
CAS-2239 [S]	An Explosive Album of Soul	1968	7.50	15.00	30.00

SOUL SURFERS, THE

Number	Title (A Side/B Side)	Yr	VG	VG+	NM
45s					
CHALLENGE					
9209	Cannonball/Home from Camp	1963	10.00	20.00	40.00
59249	Cannonball/In the Misty Moonlight	1964	3.75	7.50	15.00
—B-side by Jerry Wallace					

SOUL SURVIVORS

Number	Title (A Side/B Side)	Yr	VG	VG+	NM
45s					
ATCO					
6627	Turn Out the Fire/Go Out Walking	1968	2.00	4.00	8.00
6650	Tell Daddy/Mama Soul	1969	2.00	4.00	8.00
6735	Still Got My Head/Tempting 'Bout to Get Me	1970	2.00	4.00	8.00
CRIMSON					
1010	Expressway to Your Heart/Hey Gyp	1967	3.00	6.00	12.00
1012	Explosion (In Your Soul)/Dathon's Theme	1967	2.50	5.00	10.00
1016	Poor Man's Dream/Impossible Mission	1968	2.50	5.00	10.00
DECCA					
32080	Devil with a Blue Dress On/Shakin' with Linda	1967	3.75	7.50	15.00
DOT					
16793	Look at Me/Can't Stand to Be in Love with You	1965	5.00	10.00	20.00
16830	Hung Up on Losin'/Snow Man	1966	3.00	6.00	12.00
PHILADELPHIA INT'L.					
3595	Happy Birthday America (Part 1)/Happy Birthday America (Part 2)	1976	—	2.50	5.00
3595 [PS]	Happy Birthday America (Part 1)/Happy Birthday America (Part 2)	1976	2.00	4.00	8.00
TSOP					
4756	City of Brotherly Love/The Best Time Was the Last Time	1974	—	3.00	6.00
4760	What It Takes/Virgin Girl	1974	—	3.00	6.00
4768	Your Love/Lover to Me	1975	—	3.00	6.00
Albums					
ATCO					
SD 33-277	Take Another Look	1969	6.25	12.50	25.00
CRIMSON					
CR-502 [M]	When the Whistle Blows Anything Goes	1967	12.50	25.00	50.00
CR-502 S [S]	When the Whistle Blows Anything Goes	1967	7.50	15.00	30.00
TSOP					
KZ 33186	The Soul Survivors	1975	3.00	6.00	12.00

SOULFUL STRINGS, THE

Number	Title (A Side/B Side)	Yr	VG	VG+	NM
45s					
CADET					
5559	Paint It Black/Love Is a Hurtin' Thing	1967	—	3.00	6.00
5576	Burning Spear/Within You Without You	1968	—	3.00	6.00
5607	(Sittin' On) The Dock of the Bay/The Stripper	1968	—	3.00	6.00
5617	The Who Who Song/Jericho	1968	—	3.00	6.00
5633	I Wish It Would Rain/Listen Here	1969	—	3.00	6.00
5654	A Love Song/Zabezi	1969	—	3.00	6.00
Albums					
CADET					
LP-776 [M]	Paint It Black	1967	3.75	7.50	15.00
LPS-776 [S]	Paint It Black	1967	3.00	6.00	12.00
LPS-796	Groovin' with the Soulful Strings	1967	3.00	6.00	12.00
LPS-805	Another Exposure	1968	3.00	6.00	12.00
LPS-814	The Magic of Christmas	1968	3.00	6.00	12.00
LPS-820	In Concert/Back by Demand	1969	3.00	6.00	12.00
LPS-834	String Fever	1969	3.00	6.00	12.00
LPS-846	Gamble-Huff	1971	2.50	5.00	10.00
50022 [(2)]	Best of the Soulful Strings	1973	3.00	6.00	12.00

SOUND SYMPOSIUM, THE

Number	Title (A Side/B Side)	Yr	VG	VG+	NM
45s					
DOT					
17296	The Mighty Quinn/I'll Be Your Baby Tonight	1969	2.50	5.00	10.00
Albums					
DOT					
DLP-25952	Bob Dylan Interpreted	1969	5.00	10.00	20.00

SOUNDS, INC.

Number	Title (A Side/B Side)	Yr	VG	VG+	NM
45s					
LIBERTY					
55709	The Spartans/Detroit	1964	2.00	4.00	8.00
55729	Rinky Dink/Spanish Harlem	1964	2.00	4.00	8.00
55789	In the Hall of the Mountain King/Time for You	1965	2.00	4.00	8.00
55844	On the Brink/I Am Comin' Thru	1965	2.00	4.00	8.00

SOUNDS LIKE US

Number	Title (A Side/B Side)	Yr	VG	VG+	NM
45s					
FONTANA					
1570	Outside Chance/Clock on the Wall	1967	6.25	12.50	25.00
JILL ANN					
101	Outside Chance/Clock on the Wall	1966	12.50	25.00	50.00
SOMA					
8108	It Was a Very Good Year/The Other Side of the Record	1967	5.00	10.00	20.00

SOUNDS OF SUNSHINE

Number	Title (A Side/B Side)	Yr	VG	VG+	NM
45s					
P.I.P.					
6527	Nadia's Theme (Vocal)/Nadia's Theme (Instrumental)	1976	—	2.00	4.00
RANWOOD					
896	Love Means (You Never Have to Say You're Sorry)/Linda, the Untouchable	1971	—	2.50	5.00
912	It's Hard to Say Goodbye Forever/I Do All My Crying in the Rain	1971	—	2.00	4.00
913	Yesterday Keeps Getting in the Way/Anything Can Happen	1971	—	2.00	4.00
921	Make It Happy/Nature Boy	1972	—	2.00	4.00
925	Today Is the First Day (Of the Rest of Your Life)/Make Believe Saturday Night	1972	—	2.00	4.00
932	The End of the World/Over and Over	1972	—	2.00	4.00
940	Sea Gull/She Takes Care of Me	1973	—	2.00	4.00
Albums					
P.I.P.					
6823	Nadia's Theme	1976	2.50	5.00	10.00
RANWOOD					
8089	Love Means You Never Have to Say You're Sorry	1971	2.50	5.00	10.00
8095	Today Is the First Day (Of the Rest of Your Life)	1972	2.50	5.00	10.00

SOUNDS ORCHESTRAL

Number	Title (A Side/B Side)	Yr	VG	VG+	NM
45s					
JANUS					
124	Love in the Shadows/Louie, Louie	1970	—	3.00	6.00
PARKWAY					
120	Pretty Flamingo/Sounds Like Jacques	1966	2.00	4.00	8.00
155	A Man and a Woman/West of Carnaby	1967	2.00	4.00	8.00
942	Cast Your Fate to the Wind/To Wendy With Love	1965	2.50	5.00	10.00
958	Canadian Sunset/Have Faith in Your Love	1965	2.00	4.00	8.00
968	A Boy and a Girl/Go Home Girl	1966	2.00	4.00	8.00
973	Thunderball/Mr. Kiss Kiss Bang Bang	1966	2.00	4.00	8.00
Albums					
JANUS					
JLS-3014	One More Time	197?	3.75	7.50	15.00
PARKWAY					
P 7046 [M]	Cast Your Fate to the Wind	1965	3.75	7.50	15.00
SP 7046 [S]	Cast Your Fate to the Wind	1965	5.00	10.00	20.00
P 7050 [M]	Impressions of James Bond	1966	5.00	10.00	20.00
SP 7050 [S]	Impressions of James Bond	1966	7.50	15.00	30.00

SOUNDS UNLIMITED

Number	Title (A Side/B Side)	Yr	VG	VG+	NM
45s					
ABC					
10803	Nobody But Me/Why Doesn't She Believe Me	1966	5.00	10.00	20.00

Number	Title (A Side/B Side)	Yr	VG	VG+	NM
DUNWICH					
157	A Girl As Sweet As You/Little Brother	1967	6.25	12.50	25.00

SOUP

Albums

Number	Title (A Side/B Side)	Yr	VG	VG+	NM
ARF ARM					
1	Soup	1970	30.00	60.00	120.00
BIG TREE					
BTS 2007	The Album Soup	1971	6.25	12.50	25.00

SOUTH, JOE

45s

Number	Title (A Side/B Side)	Yr	VG	VG+	NM
ALLWOOD					
402	Just Remember You're Mine/Silly Me	1962	3.00	6.00	12.00
APT					
25084	Deep Inside Me/I Want to Be Somebody	1965	2.50	5.00	10.00
CAPITOL					
2060	Birds of a Feather/It Got Away	1967	2.00	4.00	8.00
2169	How Can I Unlove You/She's Almost You	1968	2.00	4.00	8.00
2248	Games People Play/Mirror of Your Mind	1968	2.00	4.00	8.00
2284	Redneck/Don't Throw Your Love to the Wind	1968	2.00	4.00	8.00
2491	Leanin' On You/Don't You Be Ashamed	1969	—	3.00	6.00
2532	Birds of a Feather/These Are Not My People	1969	—	3.00	6.00
2592	Don't It Make You Want to Go Home/Heart's Desire	1969	—	3.00	6.00
2704	Walk a Mile in My Shoes/Sheltered	1969	—	3.00	6.00
2755	Children/The Clock Up On the Wall	1970	—	2.50	5.00
2916	Why Does a Man Do What He Has to Do/Be a Believer	1970	—	2.50	5.00
3008	Rose Garden/Mirror of Your Mind	1971	—	3.00	6.00
3053	United We Stand/So the Seeds Are Growing	1971	—	2.50	5.00
3204	Fool Me/Devil May Care	1971	—	2.50	5.00
3450	One Man Band/Coming Down All Alone	1972	—	2.50	5.00
3487	I'm a Star/Misunderstanding	1972	—	2.50	5.00
3554	Real Thing/Save Your Best	1973	—	2.50	5.00
3717	Riverdog/It Hurts Me Too	1973	—	2.50	5.00
COLUMBIA					
43983	Backfield in Motion/I'll Come Back to You	1967	3.00	6.00	12.00
44218	A Fool in Love/Great Day	1967	3.00	6.00	12.00
FAIRLANE					
21006	You're the Reason/Jukebox	1961	3.00	6.00	12.00
21010	Masquerade/I'm Sorry for You	1961	3.00	6.00	12.00
21015	Slippin' Around/Just to Be with You Again	1962	3.00	6.00	12.00
ISLAND					
034	To Have, to Hold and Let Go/Midnight Rainbows	1975	—	2.00	4.00
MGM					
13145	Same Old Song/Standing Invitation	1963	2.50	5.00	10.00
13196	Concrete Jungle/The Last One to Know	1963	2.50	5.00	10.00
13276	Naughty Claudie/Little Queenie	1964	2.50	5.00	10.00
NRC					
002	I'm Snowed/It's Only You	1958	10.00	20.00	40.00
022	Chills/What a Night	1959	3.75	7.50	15.00
041	Little Bluebird/Play It Cool	1959	3.75	7.50	15.00
053	Tell the Truth/If You Only Knew Her	1960	3.75	7.50	15.00
065	Let's Talk It Over/Formality	1961	3.75	7.50	15.00
5000	The Purple People Eater Meets the Witch Doctor/My Fondest Memories	1958	3.75	7.50	15.00
5001	One Fool to Another/Texas Ain't the Biggest Anymore	1958	3.75	7.50	15.00

Albums

Number	Title (A Side/B Side)	Yr	VG	VG+	NM
ACCORD					
SN-7119	Party People	1981	2.50	5.00	10.00
CAPITOL					
ST-108	Introspect	1968	5.00	10.00	20.00
ST-235	Games People Play	1969	3.75	7.50	15.00
ST-392	Don't It Make You Want to Go Home	1969	3.75	7.50	15.00
SM-450	Joe South's Greatest Hits	1977	2.00	4.00	8.00
—Reissue with new prefix					
ST-450	Joe South's Greatest Hits	1970	3.75	7.50	15.00
ST-637	So the Seeds Are Growing	1971	3.00	6.00	12.00
ST-845	Joe South	1972	3.00	6.00	12.00
ST-11074	A Look Inside	1972	3.00	6.00	12.00
ISLAND					
ILPS-9328	Midnight Rainbows	1975	2.50	5.00	10.00
MINE					
1100	Walkin' South	1971	3.00	6.00	12.00
NASHVILLE					
2092	You're the Reason	1970	3.00	6.00	12.00
PICKWICK					
SPC-3314	Games People Play	197?	2.50	5.00	10.00

SOUTH 40

45s

Number	Title (A Side/B Side)	Yr	VG	VG+	NM
METROBEAT					
4450	The Penny Song/Good Lovin'	1967	3.00	6.00	12.00
4457	I Want Sunshine/Goin' Someplace Else	1968	3.00	6.00	12.00

Albums

Number	Title (A Side/B Side)	Yr	VG	VG+	NM
METROBEAT					
MBS-1000	Live at the Someplace Else	1968	6.25	12.50	25.00

SOUTHER, J.D.

Includes records as "John David Souther." Also see THE SOUTHER, HILLMAN, FURAY BAND.

12-Inch Singles

Number	Title (A Side/B Side)	Yr	VG	VG+	NM
WARNER BROS.					
PRO-A-2140 [DJ]	Bad News/Homeby Down/Go Ahead	1984	—	3.00	6.00

45s

Number	Title (A Side/B Side)	Yr	VG	VG+	NM
ASYLUM					
11009	How Long/The Fast One	1972	—	2.50	5.00
45364	Faithless Love/Midnight Prowl	1976	—	2.00	4.00
—As "John David Souther"					
COLUMBIA					
02422	You're Only Lonely/If You Don't Want My Love	1981	—	—	3.00
—Reissue					
11079	You're Only Lonely/Songs of Love	1979	—	2.00	4.00
11196	White Rhythm and Blues/The Last in Love	1980	—	2.00	4.00
11302	'Til the Bar Burns Down/If You Don't Want My Love	1980	—	2.00	4.00
—With Johnny Duncan					
FULL MOON					
49612	You're Only Lonely/Once in a Lifetime	1980	—	2.00	4.00
—B-side by Bonnie Raitt					
WARNER BROS.					
29289	Go Ahead and Rain/All I Want	1984	—	—	3.00

Albums

Number	Title (A Side/B Side)	Yr	VG	VG+	NM
ASYLUM					
7E-1059	Black Rose	1976	2.50	5.00	10.00
SD 5055	John David Souther	1972	3.00	6.00	12.00
COLUMBIA					
JC 36093	You're Only Lonely	1979	2.50	5.00	10.00
PC 36093	You're Only Lonely	198?	2.00	4.00	8.00
—Budget-line reissue					
WARNER BROS.					
25081	Home By Dawn	1985	2.50	5.00	10.00

SOUTHER, HILLMAN, FURAY BAND, THE

Also see J.D. SOUTHER.

45s

Number	Title (A Side/B Side)	Yr	VG	VG+	NM
ASYLUM					
45201	Fallin' in Love/Heavenly Fire	1974	—	2.00	4.00
45217	Border Town/Safe at Home	1974	—	2.00	4.00
45251	Mexico/Move Me Real Slow	1975	—	2.00	4.00
45267	Trouble in Paradise/On the Line	1975	—	2.00	4.00
45280	For Someone I Love/Move Me Real Slow	1975		2.00	4.00

Albums

Number	Title (A Side/B Side)	Yr	VG	VG+	NM
ASYLUM					
7E-1006	The Souther, Hillman, Furay Band	1974	2.50	5.00	10.00
7E-1036	Trouble in Paradise	1975	2.50	5.00	10.00
EQ-1036 [Q]	Trouble in Paradise	1975	4.50	9.00	18.00

SOUTHWEST F.O.B.

ENGLAND DAN AND JOHN FORD COLEY were in this group.

45s

Number	Title (A Side/B Side)	Yr	VG	VG+	NM
GPC					
1945	Smell of Incense/Green Skies	1968	3.75	7.50	15.00
HIP					
8002	Smell of Incense/Green Skies	1968	2.00	4.00	8.00
8009	Nadine/All One Big Game	1969	2.00	4.00	8.00
8015	Independent Me/As I Look at You	1969	2.00	4.00	8.00
8022	Feelin' Groovy/Beggar Man	1969	2.00	4.00	8.00

Albums

Number	Title (A Side/B Side)	Yr	VG	VG+	NM
HIP					
7001	Smell of Incense	1969	7.50	15.00	30.00

SOUVENIRS, THE

May be three different groups.

45s

Number	Title (A Side/B Side)	Yr	VG	VG+	NM
DOOTO					
412	So Long Daddy/Arlene, Sweet Little Texas Queen	1957	12.50	25.00	50.00
INFERNO					
2001	I Could Have Danced All Night/It's Too Bad	1967	12.50	25.00	50.00
REPRISE					
20065	The Worm/The Bump	1962	3.75	7.50	15.00
20066	The Real McCoy/The Watusi	1962	3.75	7.50	15.00

SOVINE, RED

Also see JOHNNY BOND.

45s

Number	Title (A Side/B Side)	Yr	VG	VG+	NM
CHART					
5142	Old Pine Tree/Two Hearts on a Post Card	1971	—	2.50	5.00
5152	Six Broken Hearts/The Greatest Grand Ol' Opry	1972	—	2.50	5.00
5161	Down Through the Years/Petunia	1972	—	2.50	5.00
5176	The Guilty One/The Day the Preacher Came	1973	—	2.50	5.00
5207	Midnight Rider/Why the Grass Is Green	1974	—	2.50	5.00
5216	From Champagne to Beer/Mama's Birthday	1974	—	2.50	5.00
5220	It'll Come Back/Down Through the Years	1974	—	2.50	5.00
5230	Can I Keep Him Daddy/Red's So Fine	1974	—	2.50	5.00
5231	Santa Claus Is a Texas Cowboy/The Legend of the Christmas Rose	1974	—	2.50	5.00
7507	Daddy's Girl/(B-side unknown)	1975	—	2.50	5.00
DECCA					
29068	My New Love Affair/How Do You Think I Feel	1954	3.75	7.50	15.00
29211	Don't Drop It/Don't Be the One	1954	3.75	7.50	15.00
29335	Outlaw/Which One Should I Choose	1954	3.75	7.50	15.00
29411	Are You Mine/Ko Ko Mo	1955	3.75	7.50	15.00
—With Goldie Hill					
29529	I Hope You Don't Care/I'm Glad You Found a Place for Me	1955	3.75	7.50	15.00
29739	Why Baby Why/Sixteen Tons	1955	3.75	7.50	15.00
—A-side with Webb Pierce					
29755	Why Baby Why/Missing You	1955	3.75	7.50	15.00
—A-side with Webb Pierce					
29825	If Jesus Came to Your House/I Got Religion	1956	3.75	7.50	15.00
29876	Little Rosa/Hold Everything (Till I Get Home)	1956	3.75	7.50	15.00
—A-side with Webb Pierce					
30018	The Best Years of Your Life/My Little Rat	1956	3.00	6.00	12.00
30162	A Poor Man's Riches/Down on the Corner of Love	1956	3.00	6.00	12.00
30239	Juke Joint Johnny/No Thanks, Bartender	1957	7.50	15.00	30.00
30458	Wrong/Who Knows Better Than You and I	1957	3.00	6.00	12.00
30595	Once More/For Arms	1958	3.00	6.00	12.00
30715	Courtin' Time in Tennessee/Where Will Mommie Go	1958	3.00	6.00	12.00

Number	Title (A Side/B Side)	Yr	VG	VG+	NM
30814	You Used to Be My Baby/Leave Me Alone	1959	2.50	5.00	10.00
30920	Cold Hands of Fate/One Sided Love Affair	1959	2.50	5.00	10.00
31028	A Lot Like You/Ooooh How I Love You	1959	2.50	5.00	10.00
31903	You Used to Be My Baby/Leave Me Alone	1966	2.00	4.00	8.00
GUSTO					
169	Woman Behind the Man Behind the Wheel/ Jealous Heart	1977	—	2.00	4.00
175	Lay Down Sally/The Farmers and the Miners	1978	—	2.00	4.00
180	Lay Down Sally/The King's Last Concert	1978	—	3.00	6.00
188	The Days of Me and You/I'd Love to Make Love	1978	—	2.00	4.00
9005	A Place for Mama's Roses/Does Steppin' Out Mean Daddy Took a Walk	1978	—	2.00	4.00
9015	Christmas Is For Kids/What Does Christmas Look Like	1978	—	2.00	4.00
9016	The Waylon and Willie Machine/Colorado Cool-Aid	1979	—	2.50	5.00
9017	Mr. F.C.C./Flesh and Blood	1979	—	2.00	4.00
9019	The Prettiest Dress/Flesh and Blood	1979	—	2.00	4.00
9021	The Hero/Flesh and Blood	1979	—	2.00	4.00
9026	The First Time I Saw Her/18 Wheels a-Hummin' Home Sweet Home	1980	—	2.00	4.00
9028	The Little Family Soldier/She Was Loving Me Goodbye	1980	—	2.00	4.00
9030	It'll Come Back/Love Is	1980	—	2.00	4.00
MGM					
10717	When I Get Rich/You're Barking Up the Wrong Tree	1950	6.25	12.50	25.00
10782	Christmas Alone/Dear Mister Santa Claus	1950	6.25	12.50	25.00
10887	Billy Goat Boogie/Big Dipper	1951	5.00	10.00	20.00
10981	Four Flusher/Farewell, So Long	1951	5.00	10.00	20.00
11090	Don't Worry/Sundown Sue	1951	5.00	10.00	20.00
11214	It'd Surprise You/Loveless Marriage	1952	5.00	10.00	20.00
11323	Okey Dokey/Till Today	1952	5.00	10.00	20.00
11402	A Quarter's Worth of Heartaches/I'm Gonna Lock My Heart	1953	5.00	10.00	20.00
11567	You Taught Me How/If You'll Be a Baby	1953	5.00	10.00	20.00
RCA VICTOR					
47-7981	The Cajun Queen/Big Dreams	1962	3.00	6.00	12.00
RIC					
131	Big Ol' Ugly Fool/Hiding Out	1964	2.00	4.00	8.00
154	Losing My Grip/Star of the Show	1965	2.00	4.00	8.00
168	I Wish I Had Seen Sunshine/Salt on My Eggs	1965	2.00	4.00	8.00
STARDAY					
101	Phantom 309/(B-side unknown)	1975	—	2.00	4.00
137	Giddyup Go/Tonight My Lady Learns to Love	1976	—	2.00	4.00
142	Teddy Bear/Daddy	1976	—	2.50	5.00
144	Little Joe/Cold Love to Go	1976	—	2.00	4.00
147	Last Goodbye/Lonely Arms of Mine	1976	—	2.00	4.00
148	Just Gettin' By/I'm Gonna Move	1977	—	2.00	4.00
152	I'm Only Seventeen/No One's Too Big to Cry	1977	—	2.00	4.00
158	Daddy's Girl/Love Is All She Ever Wants from Me	1977	—	2.00	4.00
510	Burn the School/One Is a Lonely Number	1960	2.50	5.00	10.00
521	No Money in This Deal/If I Could Come Back	1960	2.50	5.00	10.00
540	Why Baby Why/Little Rosa	1961	2.50	5.00	10.00
553	Heart of a Man/Brand New Low	1961	2.50	5.00	10.00
567	Color of the Blues/Hold Everything	1961	2.50	5.00	10.00
598	Rose of Love/She Can't Read My Writing	1962	2.50	5.00	10.00
616	Sittin' and Thinkin'/A Million to One	1962	2.50	5.00	10.00
632	Waltzing with Sin/I Forgot to Keep Her with Me	1963	2.50	5.00	10.00
650	Dream House for Sale/King of the Open Road	1963	2.50	5.00	10.00
672	Old Pipeliner/Peace of Mind	1964	2.50	5.00	10.00
737	Giddyup Go/A Kiss and the Keys	1965	2.00	4.00	8.00
757	Long Night/Too Much	1966	2.00	4.00	8.00
766	I'm the Man/I Think I Can Sleep Tonight	1966	2.00	4.00	8.00
774	Alabam/Nobody's Business	1966	2.00	4.00	8.00
—With Minnie Pearl					
779	Class of '49/I Hope My Wife Don't Find Out	1966	2.00	4.00	8.00
794	I Didn't Jump the Fence/Don't Let My Glass Run Dry	1967	2.00	4.00	8.00
811	Phantom 309/In Your Heart	1967	2.50	5.00	10.00
823	Tell Maude I Slipped/Not Like It Was with You	1967	2.00	4.00	8.00
831	Twenty-One/Sparkling Wine	1968	2.00	4.00	8.00
842	Loser Making Good/Good Enough for Nothing	1968	2.00	4.00	8.00
852	Normally, Norma Loves Me/Live and Let Live and Be Happy	1968	2.00	4.00	8.00
857	Between Closing Time and Dawn/The Father of Judy Ann	1968	2.00	4.00	8.00
864	Blues Stay Away from Me/Whiskey Flavored Kisses	1969	—	3.00	6.00
872	Who Am I/Three Hearts in a Tangle	1969	—	3.00	6.00
882	Truck Drivers Prayer/Chairman of the Board	1969	2.00	4.00	8.00
885	Castle of Shame/Why Don't You Haul Off and Love Me	1969	—	3.00	6.00
—With Lois Williams					
889	I Know You're Married But I Love You Still/Money, Marbles and Chalk	1970	—	3.00	6.00
896	Freightliner Fever/Mr. Sunday Sun	1970	—	3.00	6.00
915	Enough to Take the Me Out of Men/I'm Waiting Just for You	1970	—	3.00	6.00
918	Unfinished Letter/The Thought of Losing You	1970	—	3.00	6.00
926	Get in Touch/Violets Blue	1971	—	3.00	6.00
933	Happy Birthday, My Darlin'/I'll Sail My Ship Alone	1971	—	3.00	6.00
934	I Am a Pilgrim/Beautiful Life	1971	—	3.00	6.00
960	Go Hide John/Tear Stained Guitar	1973	—	2.50	5.00
977	Take Time to Remember/(B-side unknown)	1973	—	2.50	5.00
7004	Why Baby Why/Little Rosa	197?	—	2.00	4.00
—Reissue of 540					
7022	Six Days on the Road/Truck Drivin' Man	197?	—	2.00	4.00
7037	He'll Have to Go/I'll Step Aside	197?	—	2.00	4.00
8000	Giddyup Go/Phantom 309	197?	—	2.00	4.00
8023	Little Rosa/Ruby, Don't Take Your Love to Town	197?	—	2.00	4.00
8033	Truck Driving Son-of-a-Gun/Radar Blues	197?	—	2.00	4.00
—B-side by Coleman Wilson					

Number	Title (A Side/B Side)	Yr	VG	VG+	NM
Albums					
CHART					
1052	The Greatest Grand Ol' Opry	1972	3.75	7.50	15.00
2056	It'll Come Back	1974	3.75	7.50	15.00
DECCA					
DL 4445 [M]	Red Sovine	1963	7.50	15.00	30.00
DL 4736 [M]	Country Music Time	1966	7.50	15.00	30.00
DL 74445 [R]	Red Sovine	1963	5.00	10.00	20.00
DL 74736 [R]	Country Music Time	1966	5.00	10.00	20.00
GUSTO					
3010	16 All-Time Favorites	1978	3.00	6.00	12.00
MGM					
E-3465 [M]	Red Sovine	1957	15.00	30.00	60.00
NASHVILLE					
2033	Giddy-Up Go	196?	3.00	6.00	12.00
2044	A Dear John Letter	196?	3.00	6.00	12.00
2056	Anytime	196?	3.00	6.00	12.00
2083	Don't Take Your Love to Town	1969	3.00	6.00	12.00
POWER PAK					
270	Phantom 309	197?	2.50	5.00	10.00
STARDAY					
SLP-132 [M]	The One and Only Red Sovine	1961	10.00	20.00	40.00
SLP-197 [M]	Golden Country Ballads of the 1960s	1962	10.00	20.00	40.00
SLP-341 [M]	Little Rosa	1965	6.25	12.50	25.00
SLP-357	That's Truckdrivin'	196?	5.00	10.00	20.00
SLP-363 [M]	Giddy-Up Go	1966	5.00	10.00	20.00
SLP-383 [M]	Town and Country Action	1966	5.00	10.00	20.00
SLP-396 [M]	The Nashville Sound of Red Sovine	1967	5.00	10.00	20.00
SLP-405 [M]	I Didn't Jump the Fence	1967	5.00	10.00	20.00
SLP-414 [M]	Phantom 309	1967	5.00	10.00	20.00
SLP-420	Tell Maude I Slipped	1968	5.00	10.00	20.00
SLP-427	Sunday with Sovine	1968	5.00	10.00	20.00
SLP-436	Classic Narrations	1968	5.00	10.00	20.00
SLP-441	Closing Time 'Til Dawn	1969	5.00	10.00	20.00
SLP-445	Who Am I	1969	5.00	10.00	20.00
SLP-459	I Know You're Married But I Love You Still	1970	5.00	10.00	20.00
952	The Best of Red Sovine	197?	3.75	7.50	15.00
968	Teddy Bear	1976	3.75	7.50	15.00
970	Woodrow Wilson Sovine	1977	3.75	7.50	15.00
991	Red Sovine's 16 Greatest Hits	1977	3.75	7.50	15.00
VOCALION					
VL 3829 [M]	The Country Way	196?	3.75	7.50	15.00
VL 73829 [R]	The Country Way	196?	3.00	6.00	12.00

SPADES, THE (1)

For records on Liberty, see THE SLADES.

SPADES, THE (2)

Number	Title (A Side/B Side)	Yr	VG	VG+	NM
45s					
MAJOR					
1007	Close to You/I'm on Fire	1959	15.00	30.00	60.00

SPADES, THE (3)

Evolved into THE THIRTEENTH FLOOR ELEVATORS. Zero 10001 was recorded before Roky Erickson joined the group.

Number	Title (A Side/B Side)	Yr	VG	VG+	NM
45s					
ZERO					
10001	I Need a Girl/Do You Want to Dance	1965	15.00	30.00	60.00
10002	You're Gonna Miss Me/We Sell Soul	1966	100.00	200.00	400.00

SPANIELS, THE

Number	Title (A Side/B Side)	Yr	VG	VG+	NM
45s					
BUDDAH					
153	Goodnight Sweetheart/Maybe	1969	2.00	4.00	8.00
CALLA					
172	Fairy Tales/Jealous Heart	1970	—	3.00	6.00
CANTERBURY					
101	Peace of Mind/She Sang to Me/Danny Boy	1974	—	2.50	5.00
CHANCE					
1141	Baby It's You/Bounce	1953	125.00	250.00	500.00
1141	Baby It's You/Bounce	1953	375.00	750.00	1500.
—Red vinyl					
LOST-NITE					
262	Baby It's You/Bounce	197?	—	2.00	4.00
265	The Bells Ring Out/House Cleaning	197?	—	2.00	4.00
268	Goodnite, Sweetheart, Goodnite/You Don't Move Me	197?	—	2.00	4.00
271	Do-Wah/Don'cha Go	197?	—	2.00	4.00
274	Play It Cool/Let's Make Up	197?	—	2.00	4.00
277	False Love/Do You Really	197?	—	2.00	4.00
280	You Painted Pictures/Hey, SIster Lizzie	197?	—	2.00	4.00
283	Dear Heart/Why Won't You Dance	197?	—	2.00	4.00
286	Everyone's Laughing/I.O.U.	197?	—	2.00	4.00
289	I Lost You/Crazy Baby	197?	—	2.00	4.00
292	You Gave Me Peace of Mind/Please Don't Tease	197?	—	2.00	4.00
295	You're Gonna Cry/I Like It Like That	197?	—	2.00	4.00
298	Stormy Weather/Here Is Why I Love You	197?	—	2.00	4.00
301	Tina/Great Googley Moo	197?	—	2.00	4.00
304	Since I Fell for You/Baby Come Along with Me	197?	—	2.00	4.00
307	This Is a Lovely Way to Spend an Evening/Red Sails in the Sunset	197?	—	2.00	4.00
446	I Know/Bus Fare Home	197?	—	2.00	4.00
NEPTUNE					
124	I Love You For Sentimental Reasons/Meek Man	1961	5.00	10.00	20.00
—As "Pookie Hudson and the Spaniels"					
NORTH AMERICAN					
001	Fairy Tales/Jealous Heart	1970	—	2.50	5.00
002	Stand in Line/Lonely Man	1970	—	2.50	5.00
1114	Come Back to These Arms/Money Blues	1970	—	2.50	5.00
OWL					
328	Little Goe/The Posse	1973	—	2.50	5.00

Number	Title (A Side/B Side)	Yr	VG	VG+	NM
VEE JAY					
101	Baby It's You/Bounce	1953	1125.	2250.	4500.
—Red vinyl					
101	Baby It's You/Bounce	1953	200.00	400.00	800.00
—Black vinyl, maroon label					
101	Baby It's You/Bounce	1961	10.00	20.00	40.00
—Black vinyl, black label					
103	The Bells Ring Out/House Cleaning	1953	150.00	300.00	600.00
—Red vinyl					
103	The Bells Ring Out/House Cleaning	1953	75.00	150.00	300.00
107	Goodnite, Sweetheart, Goodnite/You Don't Move Me	1953	200.00	400.00	800.00
—Red vinyl; no "Trade Mark Reg" on label					
107	Goodnite, Sweetheart, Goodnite/You Don't Move Me	1953	75.00	150.00	300.00
—Black vinyl; as "Spanials"					
107	Goodnite, Sweetheart, Goodnite/You Don't Move Me	1953	50.00	100.00	200.00
—Black vinyl, correct spelling					
107	Goodnite, Sweetheart, Goodnite/You Don't Move Me	1993	2.00	4.00	8.00
—Red vinyl; "Trade Mark Reg" on label; included in Vee-Jay CD box set					
116	Play It Cool/Let's Make Up	1954	125.00	250.00	500.00
—Red vinyl					
116	Play It Cool/Let's Make Up	1954	25.00	50.00	100.00
131	Do-Wah/Don'cha Go	1955	125.00	250.00	500.00
—Red vinyl					
131	Do-Wah/Don'cha Go	1955	20.00	40.00	80.00
154	You Painted Pictures/Hey, Sister Lizzie	1955	15.00	30.00	60.00
154	You Painted Pictures/Hey, Sister Lizzie	1955	12.50	25.00	50.00
—As "Spanials"					
178	False Love/Do You Really	1956	37.50	75.00	150.00
189	Dear Heart/Why Won't You Dance	1956	37.50	75.00	150.00
202	Since I Fell for You/Baby Come Along with Me	1956	37.50	75.00	150.00
229	Please Don't Tease/You Gave Me Peace of Mind	1956	15.00	30.00	60.00
246	Everyone's Laughing/I.O.U.	1957	15.00	30.00	60.00
257	You're Gonna Cry/I Need Your Kisses	1957	15.00	30.00	60.00
264	I Love You/Crazee Babee	1958	15.00	30.00	60.00
278	Tina/Great Googly Moo	1958	15.00	30.00	60.00
290	Stormy Weather/Here Is Why I Love You	1958	15.00	30.00	60.00
301	Baby It's You/Heart and Soul	1958	15.00	30.00	60.00
310	Trees/I Like It Like That	1959	15.00	30.00	60.00
328	These Three Words/100 Years from Today	1959	15.00	30.00	60.00
342	People Will Say We're in Love/The Bells Ring Out	1960	25.00	50.00	100.00
350	I Know/Bus Fare Home	1960	10.00	20.00	40.00
Albums					
LOST-NITE					
LLP-19 [10]	The Spaniels	1981	3.00	6.00	12.00
—Red vinyl					
VEE JAY					
LP-1002 [M]	Goodnite, It's Time to Go	1958	150.00	300.00	600.00
—Maroon label; group pictured on cover					
LP-1002 [M]	Goodnite, It's Time to Go	1961	50.00	100.00	200.00
—Black label; dogs on cover					
VJLP-1002 [M]	Goodnite, It's Time to Go	198?	3.00	6.00	12.00
—Legitimate reissue on flimsier vinyl than originals					
LP-1024 [M]	The Spaniels	1960	75.00	150.00	300.00

SPANKY AND OUR GANG

Number	Title (A Side/B Side)	Yr	VG	VG+	NM
45s					
EPIC					
50170	When I Wanna/I Won't Brand You	1975	—	2.50	5.00
50206	L.A. Freeway/Standing Room Only	1976	—	2.50	5.00
MERCURY					
DJ-101 [DJ]	Give a Damn (mono/stereo)	1968	3.00	6.00	12.00
—Special promo for the New York Urban Coalition					
DJ-101 [PS]	Give a Damn (mono/stereo)	1968	5.00	10.00	20.00
—Fold-open sleeve with insert letter					
72598	And Your Bird Can Sing/Sealed with a Kiss	1966	5.00	10.00	20.00
72679	Sunday Will Never Be the Same/Distance	1967	2.00	4.00	8.00
72714	Making Every Minute Count/If You Could Only Be Me	1967	2.00	4.00	8.00
72714 [PS]	Making Every Minute Count/If You Could Only Be Me	1967	2.50	5.00	10.00
72732	Lazy Day/(It Ain't Necessarily) Byrd Avenue	1967	2.00	4.00	8.00
72732 [PS]	Lazy Day/(It Ain't Necessarily) Byrd Avenue	1967	2.50	5.00	10.00
72765	Sunday Morning/Echoes	1968	2.00	4.00	8.00
72765 [PS]	Sunday Morning/Echoes	1968	2.50	5.00	10.00
72795	Like to Get to Know You/Three Ways from Tomorrow	1968	2.00	4.00	8.00
—Orange and tan swirl label					
72795	Like to Get to Know You/Three Ways from Tomorrow	1968	2.50	5.00	10.00
—Red label with white "Mercury" in all caps across top of label					
72795 [PS]	Like to Get to Know You/Three Ways from Tomorrow	1968	2.50	5.00	10.00
72831	Give a Damn/Swinging Gate	1968	2.00	4.00	8.00
72871	Yesterday's Rain/Without Rhyme or Reason	1968	2.00	4.00	8.00
72890	Anything You Choose/Mecca Flat Blues	1969	2.00	4.00	8.00
72926	And She's Mine/Leopard Skinned Phones	1969	2.00	4.00	8.00
72982	Everybody's Talkin'/(B-side unknown)	1969	2.00	4.00	8.00
PHILCO-FORD					
HP-19	Making Every Minute Count/Byrd Avenue	1968	3.75	7.50	15.00
—4-inch plastic "Hip Pocket Record" with color sleeve					
Albums					
EPIC					
PE 33580	Change	1975	3.00	6.00	12.00
MERCURY					
MG-21124 [M]	Spanky and Our Gang	1967	7.50	15.00	30.00
SR-61124 [S]	Spanky and Our Gang	1967	5.00	10.00	20.00
SR-61161	Like to Get to Know You	1968	5.00	10.00	20.00
SR-61183	Anything You Choose/Without Rhyme or Reason	1969	5.00	10.00	20.00
SR-61227	Spanky's Greatest Hit(s)	1969	5.00	10.00	20.00
SR-61326	Live	1971	3.75	7.50	15.00
RHINO					
RNLP-70131	The Best of Spanky and Our Gang (1967-1969)	1986	3.00	6.00	12.00

SPARKLETONES, THE

Also see JOE BENNETT AND THE SPARKLETONES.

Number	Title (A Side/B Side)	Yr	VG	VG+	NM
45s					
ABC-PARAMOUNT					
10659	Run Rabbit Run/Well Dressed Man	1965	3.75	7.50	15.00

SPARKS

Includes records as "Halfnelson." This group did not use the article "The" before its name.

Number	Title (A Side/B Side)	Yr	VG	VG+	NM
Albums					
ANTILLES					
ANT-7044	Kimono My House	198?	2.50	5.00	10.00
—Reissue of Island 9272					
ATLANTIC					
SD 19347	Angst in My Pants	1982	2.50	5.00	10.00
80055	Sparks in Outer Space	1983	2.50	5.00	10.00
80160	Pulling Rabbits Out of a Hat	1984	2.50	5.00	10.00
BEARSVILLE					
BV 2048	Halfnelson	1971	6.25	12.50	25.00
—Original issue of "Sparks" as "Halfnelson"					
BV 2048	Sparks	1972	3.00	6.00	12.00
—Reissue under the group's new name					
BR 2110	A Woofer in Tweeter's Clothing	1973	3.00	6.00	12.00
COLUMBIA					
PC 34359	Big Beat	1976	2.50	5.00	10.00
—Originals have no bar code					
PC 34901	Introducing Sparks	1977	2.50	5.00	10.00
—Originals have no bar code					
ELEKTRA					
6E-186	No. 1 in Heaven	1979	2.50	5.00	10.00
ISLAND					
ILPS-9272	Kimono My House	1974	3.00	6.00	12.00
—Originals have multicolor island-scene label					
ILPS-9312	Propaganda	1975	3.00	6.00	12.00
—Originals have multicolor island-scene label					
ILPS-9345	Indiscreet	1975	3.00	6.00	12.00
—Originals have black label and no Warner Bros. distribution					
MCA CURB					
5780	Music That You Can Dance To	1986	2.50	5.00	10.00
RCA VICTOR					
AFL1-4091	Whomp That Sucker	1981	2.50	5.00	10.00
RHINO					
R1-70841	Interior Design	1988	2.50	5.00	10.00

SPARKS, THE

Possibly more than one group.

Number	Title (A Side/B Side)	Yr	VG	VG+	NM
45s					
ARWIN					
114	Something's Happened/Robin Redbreast	1958	5.00	10.00	20.00
CARLTON					
522	The Genie/Gee, That's Bad	1959	5.00	10.00	20.00
CUB					
9151	Woe, Woe/Cool It	1967	2.50	5.00	10.00
DECCA					
30378	Ol' Man River/Merry, Merry Lou	1957	3.00	6.00	12.00
30509	Roamin' Candle/A Cuddle and a Kiss	1957	3.00	6.00	12.00
30974	Why Did You Leave/La Macerena	1959	2.50	5.00	10.00
HULL					
723	Danny Boy/Run Run Run	1957	100.00	200.00	400.00
724	Adreann/Finger	1957	37.50	75.00	150.00

SPARKS OF RHYTHM, THE

Number	Title (A Side/B Side)	Yr	VG	VG+	NM
45s					
APOLLO					
479	Women, Women, Women/Don't Love You Anymore	1955	75.00	150.00	300.00
481	Hurry Home/Stars Are in the Sky	1955	75.00	150.00	300.00
541	Handy Man/Everybody Rock and Roll	1959	12.50	25.00	50.00

SPARROW, THE

Evolved into STEPPENWOLF. Also see MARS BONFIRE.

Number	Title (A Side/B Side)	Yr	VG	VG+	NM
45s					
COLUMBIA					
10234	Eli's Coming/Oh Doctor	1975	2.50	5.00	10.00
43755	Tomorrow's Ship/Isn't It Strange	1966	6.25	12.50	25.00
—As "The Sparrows"					
43755 [PS]	Tomorrow's Ship/Isn't It Strange	1966	25.00	50.00	100.00
—As "The Sparrows"					
43960	Green Bottle Lover/Down Goes Your Love Life	1967	6.25	12.50	25.00
—As "The Sparrows"					
Albums					
COLUMBIA					
CS 9758	John Kay and Sparrow	1969	10.00	20.00	40.00
—Red "360 Sound" label					

SPARROWS, THE

Probably three different groups.

Number	Title (A Side/B Side)	Yr	VG	VG+	NM
45s					
DAVIS					
456	Love Me Tender/Come Back to Me	1957	75.00	150.00	300.00
JAY DEE					
783	Tell Me Baby/Why Did You Leave Me	1953	125.00	250.00	500.00
790	I'll Be Loving You/Hey!	1954	125.00	250.00	500.00
Albums					
ELKAY					
3009 [M]	That Mersey Sound	1964	10.00	20.00	40.00

SPATS, THE

45s

Number	Title (A Side/B Side)	Yr	VG	VG+	NM
ABC-PARAMOUNT					
10585	Gator Tails and Monkey Ribs/The Roach	1964	2.50	5.00	10.00
10600	She Kissed Me Last Night/There's a Party in the Pad Down Below	1964	2.50	5.00	10.00
10640	Billy, the Blue Grasshoper/Gotta Tell Ya All About It, Baby	1965	2.50	5.00	10.00
10711	Go Go Yamaha/Have You Ever Seen Me Crying	1965	2.50	5.00	10.00
10790	Scoobee Doo/She Done Moved	1966	2.50	5.00	10.00
ENITH					
1268	Gator Tails and Monkey Ribs/The Roach	1964	6.25	12.50	25.00

Albums

Number	Title (A Side/B Side)	Yr	VG	VG+	NM
ABC-PARAMOUNT					
502 [M]	Cookin' with the Spats	1965	5.00	10.00	20.00
S-502 [S]	Cookin' with the Spats	1965	7.50	15.00	30.00

SPECTOR, PHIL

Also see THE TEDDY BEARS; THE RIGHTEOUS BROTHERS.

45s

Number	Title (A Side/B Side)	Yr	VG	VG+	NM
PAVILLION					
AE7 1354 [DJ]	Phil Spector's Christmas Medley (same on both sides)	1981	3.75	7.50	15.00
—Promo-only sampler from the Pavillion reissue of Phil Spector's Christmas Album					
PHILLES					
(no #) [DJ]	Thanks for Giving Me the Right Time! (same on both sides)	1965	250.00	500.00	1000.
—Has Phil's picture on label; actually plays "Ebb Tide" by the Righteous Brothers					

SPECTOR, RONNIE

Also see THE RONETTES; VERONICA.

12-Inch Singles

Number	Title (A Side/B Side)	Yr	VG	VG+	NM
COLUMBIA					
CAS 2701 [DJ]	Who Can Sleep (same on both sides)	1987	2.00	4.00	8.00
EPIC					
ASF 350 [DJ]	Say Goodbye to Hollywood/Baby Please Don't Go	1977	10.00	20.00	40.00
TOM CAT					
JD-10380 [DJ]	You'd Be Good for Me (same on both sides)	197?	7.50	15.00	30.00
—Promo only on red vinyl					

45s

Number	Title (A Side/B Side)	Yr	VG	VG+	NM
ALSTON					
3738	It's a Heartache/I Wanna Come Over	1978	2.00	4.00	8.00
APPLE					
1832	Try Some, Buy Some/Tandoori Chicken	1971	—	3.50	7.00
1832	Try Some, Buy Some/Tandoori Chicken	1971	2.00	4.00	8.00
—With star on A-side label					
1832 [PS]	Try Some, Buy Some/Tandoori Chicken	1971	2.50	5.00	10.00
COLUMBIA					
07082	Who Can Sleep/When We Danced	1987	—	2.00	4.00
07082 [PS]	Who Can Sleep/When We Danced	1987	—	2.00	4.00
07300	Love on a Rooftop/Good Love Is Hard to Find	1987	—	2.00	4.00
EPIC					
50374	Say Goodbye to Hollywood/Baby Please Don't Go	1977	2.50	5.00	10.00
50374 [PS]	Say Goodbye to Hollywood/Baby Please Don't Go	1977	6.25	12.50	25.00
POLISH					
202	Darlin'/Tonight	1980	—	2.50	5.00
TOM CAT					
JB-10380 [DJ]	You'd Be Good for Me/Something Tells Me	1975	2.50	5.00	10.00
—Promo only on blue vinyl					
PB-10380	You'd Be Good for Me/Something Tells Me	1975	—	2.50	5.00
WARNER/SPECTOR					
0409	Paradise/When I Saw You	1976	2.50	5.00	10.00

Albums

Number	Title (A Side/B Side)	Yr	VG	VG+	NM
COLUMBIA					
C 40620	Unfinished Business	1987	2.50	5.00	10.00
POLISH					
PRG-808	Siren	1980	3.00	6.00	12.00

SPECTORS THREE, THE

45s

Number	Title (A Side/B Side)	Yr	VG	VG+	NM
TREY					
3001	I Really Do/I Know Why	1959	6.25	12.50	25.00
3005	My Heart Stood Still/Mr. Robin	1960	6.25	12.50	25.00

SPEEDO AND THE IMPALAS

See THE IMPALAS.

SPEEDY AND THE REVERBS

45s

Number	Title (A Side/B Side)	Yr	VG	VG+	NM
REVERB					
51	100 Proof/Gas Chamber	196?	12.50	25.00	50.00

SPELLMAN, BENNY

45s

Number	Title (A Side/B Side)	Yr	VG	VG+	NM
ACE					
630	That's All I Ask of You/Roll On Big Wheel	1961	5.00	10.00	20.00
ALON					
9018	Tain't the Truth/No Don't Stop	1965	2.50	5.00	10.00
9024	The Word Game/I Feel Good	1965	5.00	10.00	20.00
9027	It Must Be Love/Spirit of Loneliness	1965	2.50	5.00	10.00
9031	It's for You/This Is My Love	1966	2.50	5.00	10.00
ATLANTIC					
2291	The Word Game/I Feel Good	1965	2.50	5.00	10.00
MINIT					
606	Life Is Too Short/Ammerette	1960	3.75	7.50	15.00
613	Darling No Matter Where/I Didn't Know	1960	3.75	7.50	15.00
644	Lipstick Traces (On a Cigarette)/Fortune Teller	1962	3.00	6.00	12.00
652	Every Now and Then/I'm in Love	1962	3.00	6.00	12.00
659	Stickin' Whicha' Baby/You Got to Get It	1963	3.00	6.00	12.00
664	Ammerette/Talk About Love	1963	3.00	6.00	12.00
SANSU					
462	But If You Love Her/Sinner Girl	1967	2.00	4.00	8.00
WATCH					
6336	Slow Down Baby (You Drive Too Fast)/Someday They'll Understand	1964	2.50	5.00	10.00

SPELLMAN, JIMMY

45s

Number	Title (A Side/B Side)	Yr	VG	VG+	NM
DOT					
15564	Here I Am/Make Up Your Mind	1957	7.50	15.00	30.00
15607	Doggonit/I'll Never Smile Again	1957	7.50	15.00	30.00

SPENCE, ALEXANDER "SKIP"

Also see MOBY GRAPE.

Albums

Number	Title (A Side/B Side)	Yr	VG	VG+	NM
COLUMBIA					
CS 9831	Oar	1969	15.00	30.00	60.00
SUNDAZED					
LP 5030	Oar	2000	3.00	6.00	12.00
—Reissue on 180-gram vinyl					

SPENCER, JEREMY

Also see FLEETWOOD MAC.

45s

Number	Title (A Side/B Side)	Yr	VG	VG+	NM
ATLANTIC					
3588	Cool Breeze/You Got the Right	1979	—	2.50	5.00
3601	Cool Breeze/You Got the Right	1979	—	2.50	5.00
3624 [DJ]	Travelin' (same on both sides)	1979	—	2.50	5.00
—May be promo-only					
COLUMBIA					
45854	Can You Hear the Song/The World in Her Heart	1973	—	2.50	5.00

Albums

Number	Title (A Side/B Side)	Yr	VG	VG+	NM
ATLANTIC					
SD 19236	Flee	1979	2.50	5.00	10.00
COLUMBIA					
KC 31990	Jeremy Spencer and the Children of God	1972	3.75	7.50	15.00

SPENCER AND SPENCER

DICKIE GOODMAN and Mickey Shorr.

45s

Number	Title (A Side/B Side)	Yr	VG	VG+	NM
ARGO					
5331	Russian Bandstand/Brass Wail	1959	6.25	12.50	25.00
GONE					
5053	Stagger Lawrence/Strogonoff Cha Cha	1959	6.25	12.50	25.00

SPHEERIS, JIMMY

45s

Number	Title (A Side/B Side)	Yr	VG	VG+	NM
COLUMBIA					
45646	I Am the Mercury/The Nest	1972	—	2.50	5.00
45875	The Original Tap Dancing Kid/Beautiful News	1973	—	2.50	5.00
EPIC					
50159	Tequila Moonlight/Sunken Skies	1975	—	2.00	4.00
50286	It's All in the Game/The Captain Comes Cold	1976	—	2.00	4.00

Albums

Number	Title (A Side/B Side)	Yr	VG	VG+	NM
COLUMBIA					
C 30988	The Isle of View	1972	3.75	7.50	15.00
KC 32157	The Original Tap Dancing Kid	1973	3.75	7.50	15.00
EPIC					
PE 33565	The Dragon Is Dancing	1975	3.00	6.00	12.00
PE 34276	Ports of the Heart	1976	3.00	6.00	12.00

SPICES, THE

45s

Number	Title (A Side/B Side)	Yr	VG	VG+	NM
CARLTON					
480	Tell Me Little Girl/Money, Fortune and Fame	1958	75.00	150.00	300.00

SPIDELLS, THE

45s

Number	Title (A Side/B Side)	Yr	VG	VG+	NM
CORAL					
62508	Pushed Out of the Picture/With You in Mind	1966	12.50	25.00	50.00
62531	Don't You Forget That You're My Baby/If It Ain't One Thing (It's Another)	1967	5.00	10.00	20.00

SPIDERS, THE (1)

45s

Number	Title (A Side/B Side)	Yr	VG	VG+	NM
IMPERIAL					
5265	I Didn't Want to Do It/You're the One	1954	25.00	50.00	100.00
5280	Tears Begin to Flow/I'll Stop Cryin'	1954	25.00	50.00	100.00
5291	I'm Searching/I'm Slippin' In	1954	62.50	125.00	250.00
5305	The Real Thing/Mm Mm Baby	1954	25.00	50.00	100.00
5318	She Keeps Me Wondering/(3 x 7) = "21"	1954	25.00	50.00	100.00
5331	That's Enough/Lost and Bewildered	1955	18.75	37.50	75.00
5344	Am I the One/Sukey, Sukey, Sukey	1955	18.75	37.50	75.00
5354	Bells in My Heart/For a Thrill	1955	25.00	50.00	100.00
—Red label					
5354	Bells in My Heart/For a Thrill	1957	7.50	15.00	30.00
—Black label					
5366	Is It True/Witchcraft	1955	25.00	50.00	100.00
—Blue label					
5366	Is It True/Witchcraft	1955	10.00	20.00	40.00
—Red label					
5376	Don't Pity Me/How I Feel	1956	10.00	20.00	40.00
—Featuring Chuck Carbo					
5393	A-1 in My Heart/Dear Mary	1956	7.50	15.00	30.00
—As "The Spiders with Chuck Carbo"					
5618	I Didn't Want to Do It/You're the One	1959	7.50	15.00	30.00
5714	You're the One/Tennessee Slim	1960	7.50	15.00	30.00
5739	Witchcraft/(True) You Don't Love Me	1961	7.50	15.00	30.00

Albums

IMPERIAL

Number	Title (A Side/B Side)	Yr	VG	VG+	NM
LP-9142 [M]	I Didn't Wanna Do It	1961	150.00	300.00	600.00

SPIDERS, THE (2)

Early ALICE COOPER.

45s

Number	Title (A Side/B Side)	Yr	VG	VG+	NM
MASCOT					
112	Why Don't You Love Me/Hitch Hike	1965	375.00	750.00	1500.
SANTA CRUZ					
003	Don't Blow Your Mind/No Price Tag	1966	250.00	500.00	1000.

SPIDERS, THE (U)

Definitely not group (2); could be group (1).

45s

Number	Title (A Side/B Side)	Yr	VG	VG+	NM
LAWN					
234	Run Boy Run/Baby Doll	1964	3.00	6.00	12.00
PHILIPS					
40363	No No Boy/How Could I Fall in Love	1966	2.00	4.00	8.00

SPIKE DRIVERS, THE

45s

Number	Title (A Side/B Side)	Yr	VG	VG+	NM
OM 1000					
1676	High Time/Baby Won't You Let Me Tell You How I Lost My Mind	1966	7.50	15.00	30.00
REPRISE					
0535	High Time/Baby Won't You Let Me Tell You How I Lost My Mind	1966	5.00	10.00	20.00
0558	Strange Mysterious Sounds/Break Out the Wine	1967	5.00	10.00	20.00

SPINDLES, THE

45s

Number	Title (A Side/B Side)	Yr	VG	VG+	NM
ABC					
10802	To Make You Mine/And the Band Played On	1966	5.00	10.00	20.00
10850	No One Loves You (The Way I Do)/Ten Shades of Blue	1966	6.25	12.50	25.00

SPINDRIFTS, THE

45s

Number	Title (A Side/B Side)	Yr	VG	VG+	NM
ABC-PARAMOUNT					
9904	Belinda/Cha Cha Doo	1958	6.25	12.50	25.00

SPINNERS

Many, though not all, of these did not use the article "The" before the name. These are all by the group known as "The Detroit Spinners" in the U.K.

45s

Number	Title (A Side/B Side)	Yr	VG	VG+	NM
ATLANTIC					
2904	I'll Be Around/How Could I Let You Get Away	1972	—	2.50	5.00
2927	Could It Be I'm Falling in Love/Just You and Me Baby	1972	—	2.50	5.00
2962	One of a Kind (Love Affair)/Don't Let the Green Grass Fool You	1973	—	2.50	5.00
2973	Ghetto Child/We Belong Together	1973	—	2.50	5.00
3006	Mighty Love — Pt. 1/Mighty Love — Pt. 2	1974	—	2.50	5.00
3027	I'm Coming Home/He'll Never Love You Like I Do	1974	—	2.50	5.00
3029	Then Came You/Just As Long As We Have Love	1974	—	3.00	6.00
—With Dionne Warwicke					
3202	Then Came You/Just As Long As We Have Love	1974	—	2.50	5.00
—With Dionne Warwicke					
3206	Love Don't Love Nobody (Part 1)/Love Don't Love Nobody (Part 2)	1974	—	2.50	5.00
3252	Living a Little, Loving a Little/Smile, We Have Each Other	1975	—	2.50	5.00
3268	Sadie/Lazy Susan	1975	—	2.50	5.00
3284	Games People Play/I Don't Want to Lose You	1975	2.50	5.00	10.00
3284	They Just Can't Stop it the (Games People Play)/ I Don't Want to Lose You	1975	—	2.50	5.00
—Same A-side, altered title					
3309	Love Or Leave/You Made a Promise to Me	1975	—	2.50	5.00
3341	Wake Up Susan/If You Can't Be in Love	1976	—	2.50	5.00
3355	The Rubberband Man/Now That We're Together	1976	—	2.50	5.00
3382	You're Throwing a Good Love Away/You're All I Need in Life	1977	—	2.50	5.00
3400	Me and My Music/I'm Riding Your Shadow	1977	—	2.50	5.00
3425	Heaven on Earth (So Fine)/I'm Tired of Giving	1977	—	2.50	5.00
3462	Easy Come, Easy Go/Love Is One Step Away	1978	—	2.50	5.00
3483	If You Wanna Do a Dance/One in a Life Proposal	1978	—	2.50	5.00
3546	Are You Ready for Love/Once You Fall in Love	1978	—	2.50	5.00
3590	Don't Let the Man Get You/I Love the Music	1979	—	2.50	5.00
3619	Body Language/With My Eyes	1979	—	2.50	5.00
3637	Working My Way Back to You/Disco Ride	1979	2.00	4.00	8.00
—Original pressings mention only one song on the A-side					
3637	Working My Way Back to You-Forgive Me, Girl/ Disco Ride	1979	—	2.00	4.00
3664	Cupid-I've Loved You for a Long Time/ Pipedreams	1980	—	2.00	4.00
3757	Love Trippin'/Now That You're Mine Again	1980	—	2.00	4.00
3765	I Just Want to Fall in Love/Heavy on the Sunshine	1980	—	2.00	4.00
3798	Yesterday Once More-Nothing Remains the Same/Be My Love	1981	—	2.00	4.00
3814	Long Live Soul Music/Give Your Lady What She Wants	1981	—	2.00	4.00
3827	Winter of Our Love/The Deacon	1981	—	2.00	4.00
3848	What You Feel Is Real/Street Talk	1981	—	2.00	4.00
—With Gino Soccio					
3865	You Go Your Way (I'll Go Mine)/Got to Be Love	1981	—	2.00	4.00
3882 [DJ]	Love Connection (same on both sides)	1981	—	2.50	5.00
—May be promo only					
4007	Never Thought I'd Fall in Love/Send a Little Love	1982	—	2.00	4.00
89226	Spaceballs/Spaceballs (Dub Version)	1987	—	—	3.00
89648	(We Have Come Into) Our Time for All/All Your Love	1984	—	2.00	4.00
89689	Right or Wrong/Love Is In Season	1984	—	2.00	4.00
89862	City Full of Memories/No Other Love	1983	—	2.00	4.00
89922	Funny How Time Slips Away/I'm Calling You Now	1982	—	2.00	4.00
89962	Magic in the Moonlight/So Far Away	1982	—	2.00	4.00
MIRAGE					
99580	She Does/(B-side unknown)	1986	—	—	3.00
99604	Put Us Together Again/Show Us Your Magic	1985	—	—	3.00
MOTOWN					
1067	Sweet Thing/How Can I	1964	3.75	7.50	15.00
1078	I'll Always Love You/Tomorrow May Never Come	1965	3.75	7.50	15.00
1093	Truly Yours/Where Is That Girl	1966	3.75	7.50	15.00
1109	For All We Know/Cross My Heart	1967	3.75	7.50	15.00
1136	I Just Can't Help But Feel the Pain/Bad, Bad Weather	1968	3.75	7.50	15.00
1155	In My Diary/(She's Gonna Love Me) At Sundown	1969	375.00	750.00	1500.
1235	Together We Can Make Such Sweet Music/Bad, Bad Weather	1973	2.00	4.00	8.00
TRI-PHI					
1001	That's What Girls Are Made For/Heebie-Jeebies	1961	6.25	12.50	25.00
1004	Love (I'm So Glad I Found You)/Sudbuster	1961	6.25	12.50	25.00
1007	What Did She Use/Itching for My Baby, I Know Where to Scratch	1962	6.25	12.50	25.00
1010	She Loves Me So/Whistling About You	1962	6.25	12.50	25.00
1013	I've Been Hurt/I Got Your Water Boiling Baby (I'm Gonna Cook Your Goose)	1962	6.25	12.50	25.00
1018	She Don't Love Me/Too Young, Too Much, Too Soon	1962	7.50	15.00	30.00
V.I.P.					
25050	In My Diary/(She's Gonna Love Me) At Sundown	1969	6.25	12.50	25.00
25054	Message from a Black Man/(She's Gonna Love Me) At Sundown	1970	3.00	6.00	12.00
25057	It's a Shame/Together We Can Make Such Sweet Music	1970	3.00	6.00	12.00
25060	We'll Have It Made/My Whole World Ended (The Moment You Left Me)	1971	3.00	6.00	12.00

Albums

Number	Title (A Side/B Side)	Yr	VG	VG+	NM
ATLANTIC					
SD 2-910 [(2)]	Spinners Live!	1975	3.75	7.50	15.00
QD 7256 [Q]	Spinners	1974	5.00	10.00	20.00
SD 7256	Spinners	1973	3.00	6.00	12.00
SD 7296	Mighty Love	1974	3.00	6.00	12.00
SD 16032	Labor of Love	1981	2.50	5.00	10.00
QD 18118 [Q]	New and Improved	1974	5.00	10.00	20.00
SD 18118	New and Improved	1974	3.00	6.00	12.00
SD 18141	Pick of the Litter	1975	3.00	6.00	12.00
SD 18181	Happiness is Being with the Spinners	1976	3.00	6.00	12.00
SD 19100	Yesterday, Today & Tomorrow	1977	3.00	6.00	12.00
SD 19146	Spinners/8	1977	3.00	6.00	12.00
SD 19179	The Best of the Spinners	1978	3.00	6.00	12.00
SD 19219	From Here to Eternally	1979	3.00	6.00	12.00
SD 19256	Dancin' and Lovin'	1980	2.50	5.00	10.00
SD 19270	Love Trippin'	1980	2.50	5.00	10.00
SD 19318	Can't Shake This Feelin'	1981	2.50	5.00	10.00
80020	Grand Slam	1982	2.50	5.00	10.00
MIRAGE					
90456	Lovin' Feelings	1985	2.50	5.00	10.00
MOTOWN					
M5-109V1	Motown Superstar Series, Vol. 9	1982	2.00	4.00	8.00
M5-132V1	The Original Spinners	1981	3.00	6.00	12.00
—Reissue of Motown 639					
M5-199V1	The Best of the Spinners	1981	3.00	6.00	12.00
—Reissue of Motown 769					
M 639 [M]	The Original Spinners	1967	6.25	12.50	25.00
MS 639 [P]	The Original Spinners	1967	7.50	15.00	30.00
MS 769	The Best of the Spinners	1973	3.75	7.50	15.00
VOLT					
V-3403	Down to Business	1989	3.00	6.00	12.00
V.I.P.					
405	2nd Time Around	1970	10.00	20.00	40.00

SPINNERS, THE

None of these are the popular soul group.

45s

Number	Title (A Side/B Side)	Yr	VG	VG+	NM
CAPITOL					
F3955	Love's Prayer/Goofin'	1958	10.00	20.00	40.00
CRYSTALETTE					
736	Boomerang/Slave Chain	1960	12.50	25.00	50.00
—Reissued under different titles and on different labels credited to the Crestriders and Duke Mitchell					
END					
1045	Bird Watcher/Richard Pry, Private Eye	1959	25.00	50.00	100.00
—Gray label					
1045	Bird Watcher/Richard Pry, Private Eye	1959	10.00	20.00	40.00
—Multicolor label					
LAWSON					
324	Surfing Monkey/Beatle Mania	1964	7.50	15.00	30.00
LIBERTY					
55339	Till the End of Time/Dream	1961	2.50	5.00	10.00
RCA VICTOR					
47-8427	All I Want/It Must Be Love	1964	2.50	5.00	10.00
RHYTHM					
125	Marvella/My Love and Your Love	1958	100.00	200.00	400.00
SMASH					
1845	Happy Hootenanny/Nothin'	1963	2.50	5.00	10.00
WARNER BROS.					
5084	Little Otis/Rag Mop	1959	3.00	6.00	12.00

Albums

Number	Title (A Side/B Side)	Yr	VG	VG+	NM
TIME					
S-2092 [S]	Party — My Pad After Surfin'	1963	7.50	15.00	30.00
52092 [M]	Party — My Pad After Surfin'	1963	6.25	12.50	25.00

Number	Title (A Side/B Side)	Yr	VG	VG+	NM
SPIRAL STARECASE					
45s					
COLUMBIA					
44442	Makin' My Mind Up/Baby What I Mean	1968	—	3.00	6.00
44566	Inside, Outside, Upside Down/I'll Run	1968	—	3.00	6.00
44741	More Today Than Yesterday/Broken Hearted Man	1969	2.00	4.00	8.00
44924	Sweet Little Thing/No One for Me to Turn To	1969	—	2.50	5.00
45048	She's Ready/Judas to the Love We Know	1969	—	2.50	5.00
Albums					
COLUMBIA					
CS 9852	More Today Than Yesterday	1969	6.25	12.50	25.00
—"360 Sound" label					
SPIRALS, THE					
45s					
CAPITOL					
F4084	Rockin' Cow/Everybody Knows	1958	12.50	25.00	50.00
SMASH					
1719	Please Be My Love/Forever and a Day	1961	25.00	50.00	100.00
SPIRES, BIG BOY					
45s					
CHANCE					
1137	About to Lose My Mind/Which One Do I Love	1953	625.00	1250.	2500.
SPIRIT					
Also see RANDY CALIFORNIA.					
12-Inch Singles					
MERCURY					
301 [DJ]	I Got a Line on You (Edit)/Black Satin Nights	1984	—	3.00	6.00
45s					
EPIC					
10648	Animal Zoo/Red Light Roll On	1970	—	3.00	6.00
10685	Soldier/Mr. Skin	1970	—	3.00	6.00
10701	Mr. Skin/Nature's Way	1971	—	2.50	5.00
10849	Darkness/Cadillac Cowboys	1972	—	2.50	5.00
11020	Mr. Skin/Nature's Way	1973	—	2.00	4.00
MERCURY					
73697	America the Beautiful-The Times They Are a-Changin'/Lady of the Lakes	1975	—	2.50	5.00
73722	Holy Man/Looking Into Darkness	1975	—	2.50	5.00
73837	Atomic Boogie/Farther Along	1976	—	2.00	4.00
ODE					
108	Mechanical World/Uncle Jack	1967	2.50	5.00	10.00
115	I Got a Line on You/She Smiles	1968	2.50	5.00	10.00
122	Dark Eyed Woman/New Dope in Town	1969	2.00	4.00	8.00
128	1984/Sweet Stella Baby	1969	2.00	4.00	8.00
POTATO					
1722	Nature's Way/Rock and Roll Planet	1978	—	2.50	5.00
1722 [PS]	Nature's Way/Rock and Roll Planet	1978	—	2.50	5.00
RHINO					
008	Turn to the Right/Potato Land Theme Song	1980	—	2.50	5.00
Albums					
EPIC					
E 30267	Twelve Dreams of Dr. Sardonicus	1970	5.00	10.00	20.00
—Yellow label					
KE 30267	Twelve Dreams of Dr. Sardonicus	1973	2.50	5.00	10.00
—Orange label					
PE 30267	Twelve Dreams of Dr. Sardonicus	197?	2.00	4.00	8.00
—Orange or dark blue label, with or without bar code					
KE 31175	Feedback	1972	5.00	10.00	20.00
—Yellow label					
KE 31175	Feedback	1973	2.50	5.00	10.00
—Orange label					
KEG 31457 [(2)]	Spirit	1972	3.75	7.50	15.00
—Reissue of Ode 44004 and 44016 in one package; yellow labels					
PEG 31457 [(2)]	Spirit	197?	3.00	6.00	12.00
—Reissue with new prefix and orange labels					
KE 31461	The Family That Plays Together	1972	3.00	6.00	12.00
—Reissue of Ode 44014 with slightly different cover; yellow label					
KE 31461	The Family That Plays Together	1973	2.50	5.00	10.00
—Orange label					
KE 32271	The Best of Spirit	1973	3.00	6.00	12.00
PE 32271	The Best of Spirit	1979	2.00	4.00	8.00
—Dark blue label; bar code on cover					
BG 33761 [(2)]	The Family That Plays Together/Feedback	1976	3.00	6.00	12.00
I.R.S.					
82007	Rapture in the Chambers	1989	3.00	6.00	12.00
MERCURY					
SRM-2-804 [(2)]	Spirit of '76	1975	3.75	7.50	15.00
SRM-1-1053	Son of Spirit	1975	3.00	6.00	12.00
SRM-1-1094	Farther Along	1976	3.00	6.00	12.00
SRM-1-1122	Future Games	1977	3.00	6.00	12.00
818514-1	Spirit of '84	1984	2.50	5.00	10.00
ODE					
Z12 44004	Spirit	1968	6.25	12.50	25.00
Z12 44014	The Family That Plays Together	1968	6.25	12.50	25.00
Z12 44016	Clear Spirit	1969	6.25	12.50	25.00
POTATO					
2001	Live	1978	2.50	5.00	10.00
RHINO					
RNSP-303	Potatoland	1981	2.50	5.00	10.00
SPIRITS AND WORM					
45s					
A&M					
1104	Fanny Firecracker/You and I Together	1969	10.00	20.00	40.00
Albums					
A&M					
SP-4229	Spirits and Worm	1969	200.00	400.00	800.00

Number	Title (A Side/B Side)	Yr	VG	VG+	NM
SPLINTER					
Also see BILL ELLIOTT AND THE ELASTIC OZ BAND.					
45s					
DARK HORSE					
8439	Round and Round/I'll Bend for You	1977	—	2.00	4.00
8523	I Need Your Love/Motions of Love	1978	—	2.00	4.00
10002	Costafine Town/Elly-Mae	1974	—	3.00	6.00
10002 [PS]	Costafine Town/Elly-Mae	1974	2.00	4.00	8.00
10003	China Light/Haven't Got Time	1975	—	3.00	6.00
10007	Which Way Will I Get Home/What Is It (If You Never Tried It Yourself)	1975	—	3.00	6.00
10010	After Five Years/Halfway There	1976	—	2.50	5.00
Albums					
DARK HORSE					
DH 3073	Two Man Band	1977	2.50	5.00	10.00
SP-22001	The Place I Love	1974	2.50	5.00	10.00
SP-22006	Harder to Live	1975	2.50	5.00	10.00
SPOKESMEN, THE					
45s					
DECCA					
31844	The Dawn of Correction/For You Babe	1965	3.00	6.00	12.00
31874	It Ain't Fair/Have Courage, Be Careful	1965	2.50	5.00	10.00
31895	Michelle/Better Days Are Yet to Come	1966	2.50	5.00	10.00
31949	Today's the Day/Enchante	1966	2.50	5.00	10.00
32049	I Love How You Love Me/Beautiful Girl	1966	2.50	5.00	10.00
WINCHESTER					
1001	Mary Jane/Flashback	1967	3.00	6.00	12.00
Albums					
DECCA					
DL 4712 [M]	The Dawn of Correction	1965	6.25	12.50	25.00
DL 74712 [S]	The Dawn of Correction	1965	7.50	15.00	30.00
SPOOKY TOOTH					
Also see PATTO; GARY WRIGHT.					
45s					
A&M					
1144	That Was Only Yesterday/Waitin' for the Wind	1969	2.00	4.00	8.00
ISLAND					
004	The Mirror/Hell or High Water	1974	—	2.50	5.00
1219	All Sewn Up/Things Change	1973	—	3.00	6.00
MALA					
12013	Love Really Changed Me/Spooky Blow	1968	2.50	5.00	10.00
12022	The Weight/Do Right People	1968	2.50	5.00	10.00
Albums					
ACCORD					
SN-7168	Hell or High Water	1982	2.50	5.00	10.00
A&M					
SP-3124	Spooky Two	198?	2.00	4.00	8.00
—Budget-line reissue					
SP-4194	Spooky Two	1969	3.75	7.50	15.00
SP-4225	Ceremony	1970	3.75	7.50	15.00
SP-4266	The Last Puff	1970	3.75	7.50	15.00
SP-4300	Tobacco Road	1971	3.75	7.50	15.00
—Reissue of Bell LP					
SP-4385	You Broke My Heart So I Busted Your Jaw	1973	3.75	7.50	15.00
BELL					
6019	Spooky Tooth	1968	6.25	12.50	25.00
ISLAND					
SW-9255	Witness	1973	3.00	6.00	12.00
SW-9292	The Mirror	1974	3.00	6.00	12.00
ILPS-9337	Witness	1974	2.50	5.00	10.00
SPORTONES, THE					
45s					
MUNICH					
101	In My Dreams/So Sincere	1959	125.00	250.00	500.00
SPOTLIGHTERS, THE					
Two different groups?					
45s					
ALADDIN					
3436	Please Be My Girlfriend/Whisper	1958	25.00	50.00	100.00
3441	This Is My Story/Preaching	1959	25.00	50.00	100.00
IMPERIAL					
5342	It's Cold/Bam Jingle Jingle	1955	31.25	62.50	125.00
5342	It's Cold/Bam Jingle Jingle	1955	62.50	125.00	250.00
—Red vinyl					
SPOTNICKS, THE					
45s					
ATCO					
6261	Orange Blossom Special/Hava Nagila	1963	3.00	6.00	12.00
FELSTED					
8649	Spotnick/Old Spinning Wheel	1962	3.00	6.00	12.00
LAURIE					
3241	I'm Goin' Home/Orange Blossom Special	1964	2.50	5.00	10.00
3260	Summer in Sweden/Endless Sleep	1964	2.50	5.00	10.00
3297	Just Listen to My Heart/Pony Express	1965	2.50	5.00	10.00
3333	Drum Didley/Orange Blossom Special	1966	2.50	5.00	10.00
SPOTSWOOD, KENDRA					
45s					
TUFF					
407	Stickin' with My Baby/Jive Guy	1965	2.50	5.00	10.00

SPRING

Also see AMERICAN SPRING.

45s

Number	Title (A Side/B Side)	Yr	VG	VG+	NM
UNITED ARTISTS					
50848	Now Everything's Been Said/Awake	1971	7.50	15.00	30.00
50907	Good Times/Sweet Mountain	1972	20.00	40.00	80.00

Albums

Number	Title (A Side/B Side)	Yr	VG	VG+	NM
UNITED ARTISTS					
UAS-5571	Spring	1972	6.25	12.50	25.00
UAS-5571 [DJ]	Spring	1972	25.00	50.00	100.00
—Special promo package in 12x12 folder; includes LP, press kit and a packet of seeds					

SPRINGFIELD, DUSTY

Also see THE SPRINGFIELDS.

12-Inch Singles

Number	Title (A Side/B Side)	Yr	VG	VG+	NM
CASABLANCA					
20245 [DJ]	Donnez-Moi/I Am Curious + 1	1982	3.75	7.50	15.00
UNITED ARTISTS					
SP-178 [DJ]	That's the Kind of Love I've Got for You (7:06) (same on both sides)	1978	5.00	10.00	20.00

45s

Number	Title (A Side/B Side)	Yr	VG	VG+	NM
20TH CENTURY					
2457	It Goes Like It Goes/I Wish That Love Would Last	1980	—	2.50	5.00
ABC DUNHILL					
4341	Who Gets Your Love/Of All the Things	1973	—	3.00	6.00
4344	Mama's Little Girl/Learn to Say Goodbye	1973	—	3.00	6.00
4357	Mama's Little Girl/Learn to Say Goodbye	1973	2.00	4.00	8.00
ATLANTIC					
2580	Son-of-a-Preacher-Man/Just a Little Lovin'	1968	2.50	5.00	10.00
2580 [PS]	Son-of-a-Preacher-Man/Just a Little Lovin'	1968	3.75	7.50	15.00
2606	Breakfast in Bed/Don't Forget About Me	1969	2.00	4.00	8.00
2623	The Windmills of Your Mind/I Don't Want to Hear It Anymore	1969	2.00	4.00	8.00
2647	Willie & Laura May Jones/That Old Sweet Roll	1969	—	3.00	6.00
2673	In the Land of Make Believe/So Much Love	1969	—	3.00	6.00
2685	A Brand New Me/Bad Case of the Blues	1969	—	3.00	6.00
2705	Silly, Silly, Fool/Joe	1970	—	3.00	6.00
2729	I Wanna Be a Free Girl/Let Me In Your Way	1970	—	3.00	6.00
2739	Never Love Again/Lost	1970	—	3.00	6.00
2771	What Good Is I Love You/What Do You Do When Love Dies	1970	—	3.00	6.00
2825	Nothing Is Forever/Haunted	1971	—	3.00	6.00
2841	I Believe in You/Someone Who Cared	1971	—	3.00	6.00
CASABLANCA					
2356	I Am Curious/Donnez-Moi	1981	—	2.00	4.00
ENIGMA					
75042	Nothing Has Been Proved/(Instrumental)	1989	—	2.50	5.00
PHILIPS					
40162	I Only Want to Be with You/Once Upon a Time	1963	3.00	6.00	12.00
40180	Stay Awhile/Something Special	1964	2.50	5.00	10.00
40180 [PS]	Stay Awhile/Something Special	1964	5.00	10.00	20.00
40207	Wishin' and Hopin'/Do Re Mi (Forget About the Do and Think About Me)	1964	3.00	6.00	12.00
40229	All Cried Out/I Wish I'd Never Loved You	1964	2.50	5.00	10.00
40229 [PS]	All Cried Out/I Wish I'd Never Loved You	1964	5.00	10.00	20.00
40245	Guess Who/Live It Up	1964	2.50	5.00	10.00
40245 [PS]	Guess Who/Live It Up	1964	5.00	10.00	20.00
40270	Losing You/Here She Comes	1965	2.50	5.00	10.00
40270 [PS]	Losing You/Here She Comes	1965	5.00	10.00	20.00
40303	In the Middle of Nowhere/Baby, Don't You Know	1965	2.50	5.00	10.00
40303 [PS]	In the Middle of Nowhere/Baby, Don't You Know	1965	5.00	10.00	20.00
40319	I Just Don't Know What to Do with Myself/Some of Your Lovin'	1965	2.50	5.00	10.00
40319 [PS]	I Just Don't Know What to Do with Myself/Some of Your Lovin'	1965	5.00	10.00	20.00
40371	You Don't Have to Say You Love Me/Little by Little	1966	2.50	5.00	10.00
40371 [PS]	You Don't Have to Say You Love Me/Little by Little	1966	5.00	10.00	20.00
40396	All I See Is You/I'm Gonna Leave You	1966	2.50	5.00	10.00
40396 [PS]	All I See Is You/I'm Gonna Leave You	1966	5.00	10.00	20.00
40439	I'll Try Anything/The Corrupt Ones	1967	2.50	5.00	10.00
40439 [PS]	I'll Try Anything/The Corrupt Ones	1967	5.00	10.00	20.00
40465	The Look of Love/Give Me Time	1967	2.50	5.00	10.00
40498	What's It Gonna Be/Small Town Girl	1967	2.50	5.00	10.00
40498 [PS]	What's It Gonna Be/Small Town Girl	1967	4.00	8.00	16.00
40547	Sweet Ride/No Stranger Am I	1968	2.50	5.00	10.00
40553	La Bamba/I Close My Eyes and Count to Ten	1968	2.50	5.00	10.00
UNITED ARTISTS					
XW1006	Let Me Love You Once Before You Go/I'm Your Child	1977	—	2.50	5.00
XW1205	Checkmate/Sandra	1978	—	2.50	5.00
XW1225	Give Me the Night/Checkmate	1978	—	2.50	5.00
XW1255	Living Without Your Love/Get Yourself to Love	1978	—	2.50	5.00

Albums

Number	Title (A Side/B Side)	Yr	VG	VG+	NM
ABC DUNHILL					
DSX-50128	Cameo	1973	3.75	7.50	15.00
DSX-50186	Longings	1974	—	—	—
—Unreleased					
ATLANTIC					
SD 8214	Dusty in Memphis	1969	7.50	15.00	30.00
—Originals have purple and brown labels					
SD 8214	Dusty in Memphis	1969	3.75	7.50	15.00
—Second pressings have green and red labels					
SD 8249	A Brand New Me	1970	3.75	7.50	15.00
CASABLANCA					
NBLP-7271	White Heat	1982	3.00	6.00	12.00
LIBERTY					
LN-10024	It Begins Again	1980	2.00	4.00	8.00
—Budget-line reissue of United Artists LP of same name					
LN-10026	Living Without Your Love	1980	2.00	4.00	8.00
—Budget-line reissue of United Artists LP of same name					
PHILIPS					
PHM-200133 [M]	Stay Awhile	1964	7.50	15.00	30.00
PHM-200156 [M]	Dusty	1964	7.50	15.00	30.00
PHS-200156 [P]	Dusty	1964	10.00	20.00	40.00
PHM-200174 [M]	Oooooo Weeeee!	1965	10.00	20.00	40.00
PHM-200210 [M]	You Don't Have to Say You Love Me	1966	7.50	15.00	30.00
PHM-200220 [M]	Dusty Springfield's Golden Hits	1966	6.25	12.50	25.00
—With "Goin' Back"					
PHM-200220 [M]	Dusty Springfield's Golden Hits	1967	5.00	10.00	20.00
—Without "Goin' Back"					
PHM-200256 [M]	The Look of Love	1967	6.25	12.50	25.00
PHM-200303 [M]	Everything's Coming Up Dusty	1967	6.25	12.50	25.00
PHS-600133 [P]	Stay Awhile	1964	10.00	20.00	40.00
PHS-600174 [S]	Oooooo Weeeee!	1965	12.50	25.00	50.00
PHS-600210 [S]	You Don't Have to Say You Love Me	1966	10.00	20.00	40.00
PHS-600220 [P]	Dusty Springfield's Golden Hits	1966	8.75	17.50	35.00
—With "Goin' Back"					
PHS-600220 [P]	Dusty Springfield's Golden Hits	1967	6.25	12.50	25.00
—Without "Goin' Back"					
PHS-600256 [S]	The Look of Love	1967	7.50	15.00	30.00
PHS-600303 [S]	Everything's Coming Up Dusty	1967	7.50	15.00	30.00
POLYDOR					
824467-1	Dusty Springfield's Golden Hits	1985	2.50	5.00	10.00
UNITED ARTISTS					
UA-LA791	It Begins Again	1978	3.75	7.50	15.00
UA-LA936	Living Without Your Love	1979	3.75	7.50	15.00
WING					
PKW-2-120 [(2)]	Something Special	196?	5.00	10.00	20.00
SRW-16380	Just Dusty	196?	3.00	6.00	12.00

SPRINGFIELD, RICK

12-Inch Singles

Number	Title (A Side/B Side)	Yr	VG	VG+	NM
RCA					
8393-1-R	Honeymoon in Beirut/Tear It All Down	1988	—	3.00	6.00
PD-12273	I've Done Everything for You/Love Is Alright Tonite	1981	2.00	4.00	8.00
PD-13009	Love Is Alright Tonite/Everybody's Girl	1981	2.00	4.00	8.00
PD-13075	Don't Talk to Strangers/Calling All Girls	1982	2.00	4.00	8.00
JD-13509 [DJ]	Affair of the Heart (Long) (Short)	1983	2.00	4.00	8.00
JR-13577 [DJ]	Human Touch (same on both sides)	1983	2.00	4.00	8.00
PD-13617	Human Touch (Vocal)/(Instrumental)	1983	2.50	5.00	10.00
PD-13651	Souls/Souls (Live)	1983	2.00	4.00	8.00
JR-13747 [DJ]	Love Somebody (same on both sides)	1984	2.00	4.00	8.00
JD-13815 [DJ]	Don't Walk Away (3:38) (4:00)	1984	2.00	4.00	8.00
PD-13868	Bop 'Til You Drop/Taxi Dancing	1984	2.00	4.00	8.00
JR-13882 [DJ]	Bop 'Til You Drop (same on both sides)	1984	2.00	4.00	8.00
JR-14051 [DJ]	Celebrate Youth (same on both sides)	1985	—	3.00	6.00
PD-14052	Celebrate Youth (Long) (Short)	1985	—	3.00	6.00
JR-14119 [DJ]	State of the Heart (Special Rock Radio Edited Version) (same on both sides)	1985	2.00	4.00	8.00

45s

Number	Title (A Side/B Side)	Yr	VG	VG+	NM
CAPITOL					
3340	Speak to the Sky/Why	1972	2.00	4.00	8.00
3340 [PS]	Speak to the Sky/Why	1972	3.75	7.50	15.00
3466	What Would the Children Think/Come On Everybody	1972	2.00	4.00	8.00
3466 [PS]	What Would the Children Think/Come On Everybody	1972	3.75	7.50	15.00
3637	I'm Your Superman/Why Are You Waiting	1973	2.00	4.00	8.00
3713	Believe in Me/The Liar	1973	3.00	6.00	12.00
CHELSEA					
3051	Take a Hand/Archangel	1976	—	2.50	5.00
3055	Million Dollar Face/(B-side unknown)	1976	—	2.50	5.00
3056	Jessica/(B-side unknown)	1976	—	2.50	5.00
COLUMBIA					
45935	Believe in Me/The Liar	1973	—	3.00	6.00
46032	Streakin' Across the U.S.A./Music to Streak By	1974	—	3.00	6.00
46057	American Girls/Weep No More	1974	—	2.50	5.00
MERCURY					
880405-7	Bruce/Guenevere	1984	—	2.00	4.00
880405-7 [PS]	Bruce/Guenevere	1984	—	2.50	5.00
RCA					
6853-7-R	Rock of Life/The Language of Love	1988	—	—	3.00
6853-7-R [PS]	Rock of Life/The Language of Love	1988	—	—	3.00
8391-7-R	Honeymoon in Beirut/My Father's Chair	1988	—	—	3.00
8391-7-R [PS]	Honeymoon in Beirut/My Father's Chair	1988	—	—	3.00
PB-12166	I've Done Everything for You/Red Hot and Blue Love	1981	—	2.00	4.00
PB-12166 [PS]	I've Done Everything for You/Red Hot and Blue Love	1981	—	2.00	4.00
PB-12201	Jessie's Girl/Carry Me Away	1981	—	2.00	4.00
PB-12201 [PS]	Jessie's Girl/Carry Me Away	1981	—	2.50	5.00
PB-13008	Love Is Alright Tonite/Everybody's Girl	1981	—	2.00	4.00
PB-13008 [PS]	Love Is Alright Tonite/Everybody's Girl	1981	—	2.00	4.00
PB-13070	Don't Talk to Strangers/Tonight	1982	—	2.00	4.00
PB-13070 [PS]	Don't Talk to Strangers/Tonight	1982	—	2.00	4.00
PB-13245	What Kind of Fool Am I/How Do You Talk to Girls	1982	—	2.00	4.00
PB-13303	I Get Excited/Kristina	1982	—	2.00	4.00
PB-13303 [PS]	I Get Excited/Kristina	1982	—	2.00	4.00
GB-13482	Jessie's Girl/I've Done Everything for You	1983	—	—	3.00
—Gold Standard Series					
GB-13483	Don't Talk to Strangers/What Kind of Fool Am I	1983	—	—	3.00
—Gold Standard Series					
PB-13497	Affair of the Heart/Like Father, Like Son	1983	—	—	3.00
PB-13497 [PS]	Affair of the Heart/Like Father, Like Son	1983	—	2.00	4.00
PB-13576	Human Touch/Alyson	1983	—	—	3.00
PB-13650	Souls/Souls (Live)	1983	—	—	3.00
PB-13650 [PS]	Souls/Souls (Live)	1983	—	2.00	4.00
PB-13738	Love Somebody/The Great Lost Art of Conversation	1984	—	—	3.00
PB-13738 [PS]	Love Somebody/The Great Lost Art of Conversation	1984	—	—	3.00
GB-13794	Affair of the Heart/Human Touch	1984	—	—	3.00
—Gold Standard Series					
PB-13813	Don't Walk Away/S.F.O.	1984	—	—	3.00
PB-13813 [PS]	Don't Walk Away/S.F.O.	1984	—	—	3.00

Number	Title (A Side/B Side)	Yr	VG	VG+	NM
PB-13861	Bop 'Til You Drop/Taxi Dancing	1984	—	—	3.00
—B-side: With Randy Crawford					
PB-13861 [PS]	Bop 'Til You Drop/Taxi Dancing	1984	—	—	3.00
PB-14047	Celebrate Youth/Stranger in the House	1985	—	—	3.00
PB-14047 [PS]	Celebrate Youth/Stranger in the House	1985	—	—	3.00
PB-14120	State of the Heart/The Power of Love (The Tao of Love)	1985	—	—	3.00
PB-14120 [PS]	State of the Heart/The Power of Love (The Tao of Love)	1985	—	—	3.00

Albums

CAPITOL

Number	Title (A Side/B Side)	Yr	VG	VG+	NM
SMAS-11047	Beginnings	1972	5.00	10.00	20.00
SMAS-11206	Comic Book Heroes	1973	10.00	20.00	40.00
—Withdrawn and reissued on Columbia					
SN-16251	Beginnings	1981	2.00	4.00	8.00
—Budget-line reissue					

CHELSEA

Number	Title (A Side/B Side)	Yr	VG	VG+	NM
515	Wait for Night	1976	3.75	7.50	15.00

COLUMBIA

Number	Title (A Side/B Side)	Yr	VG	VG+	NM
KC 32704	Comic Book Heroes	1973	3.75	7.50	15.00
PC 32704	Comic Book Heroes	1981	2.00	4.00	8.00
—Budget-line reissue					

MERCURY

Number	Title (A Side/B Side)	Yr	VG	VG+	NM
824107-1	Beautiful Feelings	1984	2.50	5.00	10.00

RCA

Number	Title (A Side/B Side)	Yr	VG	VG+	NM
6620-1-R	Rock of Life	1988	2.00	4.00	8.00
9817-1-R	Rick Springfield's Greatest Hits	1989	3.00	6.00	12.00

RCA VICTOR

Number	Title (A Side/B Side)	Yr	VG	VG+	NM
ARL1-3697	Working Class Dog	1981	2.50	5.00	10.00
AFL1-4125	Success Hasn't Spoiled Me Yet	1982	2.50	5.00	10.00
AFL1-4235	Wait for Night	1982	2.50	5.00	10.00
—Reissue of Chelsea LP					
AFL1-4660	Living in Oz	1983	2.50	5.00	10.00
AYL1-4766	Working Class Dog	1983	2.00	4.00	8.00
—"Best Buy Series" reissue					
AYL1-4767	Success Hasn't Spoiled Me Yet	1983	2.00	4.00	8.00
—"Best Buy Series" reissue					
ABL1-4935	Hard to Hold	1984	2.50	5.00	10.00
AJL1-5370	Tao	1985	2.50	5.00	10.00

SPRINGFIELD RIFLE, THE

45s

ABC

Number	Title (A Side/B Side)	Yr	VG	VG+	NM
10878	The Bears/There Is Life on Mars	1966	2.50	5.00	10.00

JERDEN

Number	Title (A Side/B Side)	Yr	VG	VG+	NM
812	Stop and Take a Look Around/100 or Two	1967	3.00	6.00	12.00
815	All She Said/It Ain't Happened	1967	3.00	6.00	12.00
901	I'll Be Standing There/Will You Love Me Tomorrow	196?	3.00	6.00	12.00
902	Left of Nowhere/I Must Go for a Walk	196?	3.00	6.00	12.00
905	I Love You/That's All I Really Need	196?	3.00	6.00	12.00

TOWER

Number	Title (A Side/B Side)	Yr	VG	VG+	NM
455	I Love Her/That's All I Really Need	1968	2.50	5.00	10.00

Albums

BURDETTE

Number	Title (A Side/B Side)	Yr	VG	VG+	NM
ST-5159	The Springfield Rifle	1969	6.25	12.50	25.00

SPRINGFIELDS, THE

Also see DUSTY SPRINGFIELD.

45s

PHILIPS

Number	Title (A Side/B Side)	Yr	VG	VG+	NM
40038	Silver Threads and Golden Needles/Aunt Rhody	1962	3.75	7.50	15.00
40072	Dear Hearts and Gentle People/Gotta Travel On	1962	3.00	6.00	12.00
40092	Little By Little/Waf-Woof	1963	3.00	6.00	12.00
40099	Foggy Mountain Top/Island of Dreams	1963	3.00	6.00	12.00
40121	Say I Won't Be There/Little Boat	1963	3.00	6.00	12.00

Albums

PHILIPS

Number	Title (A Side/B Side)	Yr	VG	VG+	NM
PHM 200052 [M]	Silver Threads and Golden Needles	1962	7.50	15.00	30.00
PHM 200076 [M]	Folksongs from the Hills	1963	7.50	15.00	30.00
PHS 600052 [S]	Silver Threads and Golden Needles	1962	10.00	20.00	40.00
PHS 600076 [S]	Folksongs from the Hills	1963	10.00	20.00	40.00

SPRINGSTEEN, BRUCE

12-Inch Singles

ASYLUM

Number	Title (A Side/B Side)	Yr	VG	VG+	NM
11442 [DJ]	Devil with a Blue Dress Medley/Before the Deluge	1979	10.00	20.00	40.00
—B-side by Jackson Browne					

COLUMBIA

Number	Title (A Side/B Side)	Yr	VG	VG+	NM
AS 928 [DJ]	Fade Away/Be True/Held Up Without a Gun	1981	12.50	25.00	50.00
AS 1329 [DJ]	Santa Claus Is Comin' to Town (same on both sides)	1981	10.00	20.00	40.00
—White label promo					
AS 1862 [DJ]	Dancing in the Dark (same on both sides)	1984	5.00	10.00	20.00
—Red label, black and white cover					
AS 1959 [DJ]	Born in the U.S.A. (same on both sides)	1984	5.00	10.00	20.00
—Red label, black and white cover					
AS 2007 [DJ]	I'm on Fire (same on both sides)	1985	5.00	10.00	20.00
—Red label, black and white cover					
AS 2082 [DJ]	Glory Days (same on both sides)	1985	5.00	10.00	20.00
—Red label, black and white cover					
CAS 2147 [DJ]	I'm Goin' Down (same on both sides)	1985	5.00	10.00	20.00
—Red label, black and white cover					
CAS 2223 [DJ]	My Hometown (same on both sides)	1985	5.00	10.00	20.00
—Red label, black and white cover					
CAS 2636 [DJ]	Fire/Because the Night/Seeds	1986	6.25	12.50	25.00
CAS 2806 [DJ]	Brilliant Disguise (same on both sides)	1987	3.75	7.50	15.00
05028	Dancing in the Dark (Blaster Mix)/(Radio) (Dub)	1984	3.00	6.00	12.00
05087	Cover Me (Undercover Mix) (Dub 1)/(Dub 2) (Radio)	1984	3.00	6.00	12.00
05147	Born in the U.S.A. (Freedom Mix)/(Dub) (Radio)	1984	3.00	6.00	12.00
74416	57 Channels (And Nothin' On) (Little Steven Remix 1 & 2)//There's a Riot Goin' On/Part Man Part Monkey	1992	3.75	7.50	15.00

45s

COLUMBIA

Number	Title (A Side/B Side)	Yr	VG	VG+	NM
AE7 1088 [DJ]	Rosalita (Come Out Tonight)//Spirit in the Night/ Growin' Up	1974	75.00	150.00	300.00
—Small hole, plays at 33 1/3 RPM					
AE7 1332 [DJ]	Santa Claus Is Coming to Town (same on both sides)	1981	5.00	10.00	20.00
AE7 1332 [PS]	Santa Claus Is Coming to Town (same on both sides)	1981	6.25	12.50	25.00
03243	Hungry Heart/Fade Away	1983	—	2.00	4.00
—"Columbia Hall of Fame" series; red label					
03243	Hungry Heart/Fade Away	198?	—	—	3.00
—"Columbia Hall of Fame" series; gray label					
04463	Dancing in the Dark/Pink Cadillac	1984	—	2.00	4.00
04463 [PS]	Dancing in the Dark/Pink Cadillac	1984	—	2.50	5.00
04561	Cover Me/Jersey Girl	1984	2.50	5.00	10.00
—First pressings have a spoken intro to "Jersey Girl." Dead wax has matrix number followed by "-1" and a letter.					
04561	Cover Me/Jersey Girl	1984	—	2.00	4.00
—Spoken intro to "Jersey Girl" is deleted. Dead wax has matrix number followed by "-2" and a letter.					
04561 [PS]	Cover Me/Jersey Girl	1984	—	2.50	5.00
04680	Born in the U.S.A./Shut Out the Light	1984	—	2.00	4.00
04680 [PS]	Born in the U.S.A./Shut Out the Light	1984	—	2.50	5.00
04772	I'm on Fire/Johnny Bye Bye	1985	—	2.00	4.00
04772 [PS]	I'm on Fire/Johnny Bye Bye	1985	—	2.50	5.00
04924	Glory Days/Stand On It	1985	—	2.00	4.00
04924 [PS]	Glory Days/Stand On It	1985	—	2.50	5.00
05603	I'm Goin' Down/Janey, Don't You Lose Heart	1985	—	2.00	4.00
05603 [PS]	I'm Goin' Down/Janey, Don't You Lose Heart	1985	—	2.50	5.00
05728	My Hometown/Santa Claus Is Coming to Town	1985	—	2.00	4.00
05728 [PS]	My Hometown/Santa Claus Is Coming to Town	1985	—	2.00	4.00
06432	War/Merry Christmas Baby	1986	—	2.00	4.00
06432 [PS]	War/Merry Christmas Baby	1986	—	2.00	4.00
06657	Fire/Incident on 57th Street	1987	—	2.50	5.00
06657 [PS]	Fire/Incident on 57th Street	1987	—	2.50	5.00
07595	Brilliant Disguise/Lucky Man	1987	—	2.00	4.00
07595 [PS]	Brilliant Disguise/Lucky Man	1987	—	2.00	4.00
07663	Tunnel of Love/Two for the Road	1987	—	2.00	4.00
07663 [PS]	Tunnel of Love/Two for the Road	1987	—	2.00	4.00
07726	One Step Up/Roulette	1988	—	2.00	4.00
07726 [PS]	One Step Up/Roulette	1988	—	2.00	4.00
08408	Dancing in the Dark/Pink Cadillac	1984	—	—	3.00
—Gray label reissue					
08409	Cover Me/Jersey Girl	1984	—	—	3.00
—Gray label reissue					
08410	Born in the U.S.A./Shut Out the Light	1984	—	—	3.00
—Gray label reissue					
08411	I'm on Fire/Johnny Bye Bye	1985	—	—	3.00
—Gray label reissue					
08412	Glory Days/Stand On It	1985	—	—	3.00
—Gray label reissue					
08413	I'm Goin' Down/Janey, Don't You Lose Heart	1985	—	—	3.00
—Gray label reissue					
08414	My Hometown/Santa Claus Is Coming to Town	1985	—	—	3.00
—Gray label reissue; many copies of this were issued with Columbia 05728 picture sleeves					
10209	Born to Run/Meeting Across the River	1975	5.00	10.00	20.00
10274	Tenth Avenue Freeze-Out/She's the One	1976	3.75	7.50	15.00
10763	Prove It All Night/Factory	1978	3.00	6.00	12.00
10801	Badlands/Streets of Fire	1978	3.00	6.00	12.00
11391	Hungry Heart/Held Up Without a Gun	1980	—	2.00	4.00
11391 [PS]	Hungry Heart/Held Up Without a Gun	1980	—	3.00	6.00
11431	Fade Away/To Be True	1981	6.25	12.50	25.00
—Erroneous first pressing					
11431	Fade Away/Be True	1981	—	2.00	4.00
—Corrected second pressing					
11431 [PS]	Fade Away/Be True	1981	—	3.00	6.00
33323	Born to Run/Spirit in the Night	1976	—	2.00	4.00
—"Columbia Hall of Fame" series; red label					
33323	Born to Run/Spirit in the Night	198?	—	—	3.00
—"Columbia Hall of Fame" series; gray label					
45805	Blinded by the Light/The Angel	1972	125.00	250.00	500.00
45805 [DJ]	Blinded by the Light (mono/stereo)	1972	12.50	25.00	50.00
45805 [PS]	Blinded by the Light/The Angel	1972	100.00	200.00	400.00
45864	Spirit in the Night/For You	1973	375.00	750.00	1500.
45864 [DJ]	Spirit in the Night (mono/stereo)	1973	12.50	25.00	50.00
73796	Tunnel of Love/Two for the Road	1991	—	—	3.00
—Reissue					
73943	One Step Up/Roulette	1991	—	—	3.00
—Reissue					
74273	Human Touch/Better Days	1992	—	2.00	4.00
74354	57 Channels (And Nothin' On)/Part Man Part Monkey	1992	—	2.00	4.00
77384	Streets of Philadelphia/If I Should Fall Behind	1994	—	2.00	4.00
77847	Secret Garden/Thunder Road (Live)	1995	—	—	3.00
77847 [PS]	Secret Garden/Thunder Road (Live)	1995	—	—	3.00

Albums

COLUMBIA

Number	Title (A Side/B Side)	Yr	VG	VG+	NM
AS 978 [DJ]	As Requested Around the World	1981	12.50	25.00	50.00
AS 1957 [DJ]	Bruce Springsteen	1985	7.50	15.00	30.00
—Five-song mini-LP with five B-sides of singles from Born in the U.S.A.					
AS 1957 [DJ]	Bruce Springsteen	1987	5.00	10.00	20.00
—Five-song mini-LP with five B-sides of singles from Born in the U.S.A.; second pressings say so on the label					
AS 2543 [DJ]	Bruce Springsteen and the E Street Band: Live 1975-1985	1986	7.50	15.00	30.00
—Sampler from 5-LP live set					
JC 31903	Greetings from Asbury Park, N.J.	1977	2.00	4.00	8.00
—Reissue of the first PC-prefix version					
KC 31903	Greetings from Asbury Park, N.J.	1973	5.00	10.00	20.00
KC 31903 [DJ]	Greetings from Asbury Park, N.J.	1973	50.00	100.00	200.00
—Promotional copy with timing strip and "Bruce Springsteen Fact Sheet" attached to back cover. Authentic fact sheets are on glossy stock					

Number	Title (A Side/B Side)	Yr	VG	VG+	NM
PC 31903	Greetings from Asbury Park, N.J.	1975	2.50	5.00	10.00
—Without bar code on cover					
PC 31903	Greetings from Asbury Park, N.J.	1979	2.00	4.00	8.00
—With bar code on cover					
JC 32432	The Wild, the Innocent & the E Street Shuffle	1977	2.00	4.00	8.00
—Reissue of the first PC-prefix version					
KC 32432	The Wild, the Innocent & the E Street Shuffle	1973	5.00	10.00	20.00
PC 32432	The Wild, the Innocent & the E Street Shuffle	1975	2.50	5.00	10.00
—Without bar code on cover					
PC 32432	The Wild, the Innocent & the E Street Shuffle	1979	2.00	4.00	8.00
—With bar code on cover					
HC 33795	Born to Run	1981	12.50	25.00	50.00
—Half-speed mastered edition (original)					
JC 33795	Born to Run	1977	2.00	4.00	8.00
PC 33795	Born to Run	1975	6.25	12.50	25.00
—Jon Landau's name is misspelled "John" on the back cover					
PC 33795	Born to Run	1975	3.75	7.50	15.00
—Sticker with the correct spelling of Jon Landau is on the back cover					
PC 33795	Born to Run	1975	2.50	5.00	10.00
—Jon Landau's name is correct on the back cover					
PC 33795	Born to Run	1999	10.00	20.00	40.00
—Classic Records reissue, identified as such on back cover; "error" first pressing with no gatefold					
PC 33795	Born to Run	1999	6.25	12.50	25.00
—Classic Records reissue, identified as such on back cover; corrected pressing with gatefold					
PC 33795 [DJ]	Born to Run	1975	400.00	800.00	1200.
—Test pressing with "Bruce Springsteen -- Born to Run" in script print. Also includes mailing envelope, letter from CBS and orange patch					
PC 33795 [DJ]	Born to Run	1975	25.00	50.00	100.00
—White label promo					
JC 35318	Darkness on the Edge of Town	1978	2.50	5.00	10.00
—Original pressings have thick paper innersleeves and small titles on back cover					
JC 35318	Darkness on the Edge of Town	198?	2.00	4.00	8.00
—Later pressings have thin paper innersleeves and larger titles on back cover					
JC 35318 [DJ]	Darkness on the Edge of Town	1978	25.00	50.00	100.00
—White label promo					
PC2 36854 [(2)]	The River	1980	3.00	6.00	12.00
PC2 36854 [(2) DJ]	The River	1980	18.75	37.50	75.00
—White label promo, with photocopied letter from CBS					
PC2 36854 [(2) DJ]	The River	1980	10.00	20.00	40.00
—White label promo, without letter					
QC 38358	Nebraska	1982	2.50	5.00	10.00
QC 38653	Born in the U.S.A.	1984	2.50	5.00	10.00
C5X 40558 [(5)]	Bruce Springsteen and the E Street Band: Live 1975-1985	1986	10.00	20.00	40.00
OC 40999	Tunnel of Love	1987	2.50	5.00	10.00
HC 43795	Born to Run	1982	10.00	20.00	40.00
—Half-speed mastered edition (reissue)					
3C 44445 [EP]	Chimes of Freedom	1988	2.50	5.00	10.00
HC 45318	Darkness on the Edge of Town	1981	10.00	20.00	40.00
—Half-speed mastered edition					
C 53000	Human Touch	1992	3.00	6.00	12.00
C 53001	Lucky Town	1992	3.00	6.00	12.00
C2 67060 [(2)]	Greatest Hits	1995	3.75	7.50	15.00
C 67484	The Ghost of Tom Joad	1995	3.00	6.00	12.00
C2 69746 [(2)]	18 Tracks	1999	3.75	7.50	15.00
(# unknown) [PD]	Darkness on the Edge of Town	1978	37.50	75.00	150.00
—Promo-only picture disc					

SPUR

Albums

CINEMA

Number	Title (A Side/B Side)	Yr	VG	VG+	NM
CSLP-1500	Spur of the Moment	196?	20.00	40.00	80.00

SPUTNIKS, THE

45s

Number	Title (A Side/B Side)	Yr	VG	VG+	NM
CLASS					
217	My Love Is Gone/Hey Maryann	1958	12.50	25.00	50.00
222	Wait a Little While/Johnny's Little Lamb	1958	10.00	20.00	40.00
PAM MAR					
601	My Love Is Gone/Hey Maryann	1957	62.50	125.00	250.00

SQUIRES, THE (1)

45s

Number	Title (A Side/B Side)	Yr	VG	VG+	NM
ALADDIN					
3360	Dreamy Eyes/Danglin' with My Heart	1957	25.00	50.00	100.00
KICKS					
1	Dream Come True/Lucy Lou	1954	200.00	400.00	800.00
MAMBO					
105	Sindy/Do-Be-Do-Be-Wop-Wop	1955	37.50	75.00	150.00
VITA					
105	Sindy/Do-Be-Do-Be-Wop-Wop	1960	25.00	50.00	100.00
113	Sweet Girl/Me and My Deal	1955	25.00	50.00	100.00
116	Heavenly Angel/Sweet Girl	1955	25.00	50.00	100.00

SQUIRES, THE (2)

45s

Number	Title (A Side/B Side)	Yr	VG	VG+	NM
ATCO					
6442	Go Ahead/Going All the Way	1966	10.00	20.00	40.00

SQUIRES, THE (3)

45s

Number	Title (A Side/B Side)	Yr	VG	VG+	NM
CHAN					
102	Movin' Out/Our Theme	1961	7.50	15.00	30.00
105	Mean Misery/Chattanooga Choo Choo	1962	7.50	15.00	30.00
MGM					
13044	Movin' Out/Our Theme	1961	3.75	7.50	15.00

SQUIRES, THE (4)

45s

Number	Title (A Side/B Side)	Yr	VG	VG+	NM
COMBO					
35	Let's Give Love a Try/Whop	1952	125.00	250.00	500.00
42	Oh Darling/My Little Girl	1953	150.00	300.00	600.00

SQUIRES, THE (U)

We can't conclusively place any of these with the above groups. Of course, they may not be any of the above groups.

45s

Number	Title (A Side/B Side)	Yr	VG	VG+	NM
CONGRESS					
223	Joyce/Can't Believe That You've Grown Up	1964	15.00	30.00	60.00
FLAIR					
1030	Sayonara/Mia Bella Donna	1954	7.50	15.00	30.00
GEE					
1082	Don't Accuse Me/So Many Tears Ago	1962	12.50	25.00	50.00
HERALD					
580	Why Should I Suffer/Walkin'	1963	7.50	15.00	30.00
STARLITE					
1/2	Movin'/Night Road	1964	12.50	25.00	50.00
V					
109	The Sultan/Aurora	1961	250.00	500.00	1000.
—Canadian release only; with a very early Neil Young					

SQUIRRELS, THE

45s

Number	Title (A Side/B Side)	Yr	VG	VG+	NM
CAMEO					
284	Grandma's House/The Girl That I'll Adore	1963	2.50	5.00	10.00
—B-side by the Philadelphia Minstrels					

SRC

45s

Number	Title (A Side/B Side)	Yr	VG	VG+	NM
A-SQUARE					
301	I'm So Glad/Who Is That Girl	1967	6.25	12.50	25.00
—As "Scott Richard Case"					
402	Get the Picture/I Need You	1967	6.25	12.50	25.00
—B-side by the Rationals					
CAPITOL					
2327	Black Sheep/Morning Hood	1968	2.50	5.00	10.00
2457	Turn Into Love/Up All Night	1969	2.50	5.00	10.00
2726	My Fortune's Coming True/Never Before Now	1970	2.50	5.00	10.00

Albums

Number	Title (A Side/B Side)	Yr	VG	VG+	NM
CAPITOL					
ST-134	Milestones	1969	10.00	20.00	40.00
SKAO-273	Travellers Tale	1970	10.00	20.00	40.00
ST 2991	SRC	1968	15.00	30.00	60.00

STACKRIDGE

45s

Number	Title (A Side/B Side)	Yr	VG	VG+	NM
DECCA					
32923	Dora the Female Explorer/(B-side unknown)	1972	2.50	5.00	10.00
SIRE					
717	The Last Plimsoul/Spin Around the Room	1974	—	2.50	5.00

Albums

Number	Title (A Side/B Side)	Yr	VG	VG+	NM
DECCA					
DL 75317	Stackridge	1971	6.25	12.50	25.00
MCA					
308	Friendliness	1973	2.50	5.00	10.00
SIRE					
SASD-7503	Pinafore Days	1974	2.50	5.00	10.00
SASD-7509	Extravaganza	1975	2.50	5.00	10.00

STAFFORD, JIM

45s

Number	Title (A Side/B Side)	Yr	VG	VG+	NM
COLUMBIA					
04339	Little Bits and Pieces/Banjo Billy	1984	—	—	3.00
ELEKTRA					
47013	Don't Fool Around (When There's a Fool Around)/I Took Your Love Lightly	1980	—	2.00	4.00
47226	Isabel and Samantha/Yeller Dog Blues	1981	—	2.00	4.00
MGM					
14496	Swamp Witch/Nifty Fifties Blues	1973	—	2.00	4.00
14648	Spiders and Snakes/Undecided	1973	—	2.00	4.00
14718	My Girl Bill/L.A. Mama	1974	—	2.00	4.00
14737	Wildwood Weed/The Last Chant	1974	—	2.00	4.00
14775	Your Bulldog Drinks Champagne/Real Good Time	1974	—	2.00	4.00
14819	I Got Stoned and I Missed It/I Ain't Workin'	1975	—	2.00	4.00
POLYDOR					
14309	Jasper/I Can't Find Nobody Home	1976	—	2.00	4.00
TOWN HOUSE					
1062	What Mama Don't Know/(B-side unknown)	1982	—	2.00	4.00
WARNER BROS.					
8299	Turn Loose of My Leg/The Fight	1976	—	2.00	4.00
8538	You Can Call Me Clyde/One Step Ahead of the Law	1978	—	2.00	4.00
49611	Cow Patti/Texas Guitar Song	1980	—	2.00	4.00

Albums

Number	Title (A Side/B Side)	Yr	VG	VG+	NM
MGM					
M3G-4947	Jim Stafford	1974	2.50	5.00	10.00
M3G-4984	Not Just Another Pretty Foot	1975	2.50	5.00	10.00
POLYDOR					
PD-1-6072	Jim Stafford	1976	2.00	4.00	8.00
—Reissue of MGM 4947					

STAFFORD, JO

Also see JONATHAN AND DARLENE EDWARDS.

45s

Number	Title (A Side/B Side)	Yr	VG	VG+	NM
CAPITOL					
54-785	Scarlet Ribbons (For Her Hair)/Happy Times	1949	6.25	12.50	25.00
F808	Fools Rush In/Just One of Those Things	1950	5.00	10.00	20.00
F824	Diamonds Are a Girl's Best Friend/Open Door, Open Arms	1950	5.00	10.00	20.00
F868	Near Me/Beyond the Sunset	1950	5.00	10.00	20.00
F914	Day by Day/When April Comes Again	1950	5.00	10.00	20.00
F927	Tumbling Tumbleweeds/Someone to Love	1950	5.00	10.00	20.00

Number	Title (A Side/B Side)	Yr	VG	VG+	NM
F946	Ask Me No Questions/On the Outgoing Tide	1950	5.00	10.00	20.00
F989	Begin the Beguine/In the Still of the Night	1950	3.75	7.50	15.00
F990	September Song/Yesterdays	1950	3.75	7.50	15.00
F991	The Best Things in Life Are Free/The Gentleman Is a Dope	1950	3.75	7.50	15.00
F992	Here I'll Stay/Almost Like Being in Love	1950	3.75	7.50	15.00
F993	Sometimes I'm Happy/Why Can't You Believe Me	1950	3.75	7.50	15.00
F994	Barbara Allen/He's Gone Away	1950	3.75	7.50	15.00
F995	Walkin' My Baby Back Home/Over the Rainbow	1950	3.75	7.50	15.00
F996	On the Alamo/Roses of Picardy	1950	3.75	7.50	15.00
F997	Baby Won't You Please Come Home/I'll Be With You in Apple Blossom Time	1950	3.75	7.50	15.00
F998	Ave Maria/Shinin' Through	1950	3.75	7.50	15.00
F999	Where Are You Gonna Be/Driftin' Down the Dreamy Old Ohio	1950	3.75	7.50	15.00
—Whether the above 11 (F989-F999) were released individually, as a box set, or as several box sets, we don't know.					
F1039	Play a Simple Melody/Pagan Love Song	1950	5.00	10.00	20.00
F1053	No Other Love/Sometime	1950	5.00	10.00	20.00
F1061	The Rosary/Perfect Day	1950	5.00	10.00	20.00
F1142	Goodnight Irene/Our Very Own	1950	5.00	10.00	20.00
F1153	La Vie En Rose/La Vie En Rose	1950	5.00	10.00	20.00
—B-side by Paul Weston					
F1195	In the Middle of a Riddle/Tea for Two	1950	5.00	10.00	20.00
F1248	Autumn Leaves/Autumn in New York	1950	5.00	10.00	20.00
F1262	White Christmas/Silent Night	1950	3.75	7.50	15.00
F1312	Love Is a Masquerade/It Was So Beautiful	1950	5.00	10.00	20.00
F1651	Tumbling Tumbleweeds/On the Sunny Side of the Street	1951	3.75	7.50	15.00
—Reissue					
F1685	Sometime/No Other Love	1951	3.75	7.50	15.00
—Reissue					
PRO 2756 [DJ]	Christmas Is The Season/Merry Christmas	1964	2.50	5.00	10.00
54-90042	Silent Night/White Christmas	1949	3.75	7.50	15.00
COLPIX					
623	Misty/Adios My Love	1962	2.50	5.00	10.00
633	My Heart Had a Window/Symphony	1962	2.50	5.00	10.00
COLUMBIA					
1-900 (?)	Where or When/Use Your Imagination	1950	7.50	15.00	30.00
—Microgroove 33 1/3 rpm 7-inch single					
6-900 (?)	Where or When/Use Your Imagination	1950	6.25	12.50	25.00
—First edition of 45					
1-905 (?)	Stardust/You Don't Remind Me	1950	7.50	15.00	30.00
—Microgroove 33 1/3 rpm 7-inch single					
6-905 (?)	Stardust/You Don't Remind Me	1950	6.25	12.50	25.00
—First edition of 45					
1-910 (?)	Tennessee Waltz/If You've Got the Money, I've Got the Time	1950	7.50	15.00	30.00
—Microgroove 33 1/3 rpm 7-inch single					
6-910 (?)	Tennessee Waltz/If You've Got the Money, I've Got the Time	1950	6.25	12.50	25.00
—First edition of 45					
39049	Where or When/Use Your Imagination	1950	5.00	10.00	20.00
—Second edition of this 45					
39056	Stardust/You Don't Remind Me	1950	5.00	10.00	20.00
—Second edition of this 45					
39065	Tennessee Waltz/If You've Got the Money, I've Got the Time	1950	5.00	10.00	20.00
—Second edition of this 45					
39082	If/It Is No Secret (What God Can Do)	1950	5.00	10.00	20.00
3-39082	If/It Is No Secret (What God Can Do)	1950	7.50	15.00	30.00
—Microgroove 33 1/3 rpm 7-inch single					
39129	Tennessee Waltz/Goodnight Pillow	1950	5.00	10.00	20.00
39130	If You've Got the Money, I've Got the Time/Handsome Stranger	1950	5.00	10.00	20.00
39206	San Antonio Rose/Lovely Is the Evening	1951	5.00	10.00	20.00
39301	Make Man Love Me/Along the Colorado Trail	1951	5.00	10.00	20.00
39389	Somebody/Allentown Jail	1951	5.00	10.00	20.00
39448	Star of Hope/He Bought My Soul	1951	5.00	10.00	20.00
39529	Kissin' Bug Boogie/Hawaiian War Chant	1951	5.00	10.00	20.00
39581	Shrimp Boats/Love Mystery	1951	5.00	10.00	20.00
39653	Ay-Round the Corner (Bee-Hind the Bush)/Heaven Drops the Curtain	1952	3.75	7.50	15.00
39720	Don't Worry 'Bout Me/As You Desire Me	1952	3.00	6.00	12.00
39721	Something to Remember You By/Spring Is Here	1952	3.00	6.00	12.00
39722	September in the Rain/Easy Come, Easy Go	1952	3.00	6.00	12.00
39723	Blue Moon/I'm In the Mood for Love	1952	3.00	6.00	12.00
—The above four comprise a box set					
39725	Raminay/With You in My Arms	1952	3.75	7.50	15.00
39811	You Belong to Me/Pretty Boy	1952	3.75	7.50	15.00
39838	Jambalaya/Early Autumn	1952	3.75	7.50	15.00
39891	Keep It a Secret/Once to Every Heart	1952	3.75	7.50	15.00
39893	Christmas Roses/Chow, Willy	1952	3.75	7.50	15.00
—With Frankie Laine					
39930	(Now and Then, There's) A Fool Such As I/Just Because You're You	1953	3.75	7.50	15.00
39951	Smoking My Sad Cigarette/Without My Lover	1953	3.75	7.50	15.00
40000	My Dearest, My Darling/Just Another Polka	1953	3.75	7.50	15.00
40021	Someone's Been Readin' My Mail/I'm Your Girl	1953	3.75	7.50	15.00
40034	Till We Meet Again/With These Hands	1953	3.75	7.50	15.00
—With Nelson Eddy					
40059	Living for Only You/Cups of Joy	1953	3.75	7.50	15.00
40103	The Christmas Blues/What Good Am I Without You	1953	3.75	7.50	15.00
40143	Make Love to Me!/Adi-Adios, Amigo	1953	3.00	6.00	12.00
40170	April and You/Indiscretion	1954	3.00	6.00	12.00
—With Liberace					
40190	It Is No Secret (What God Can Do)/Beautiful Garden of Prayer	1954	2.50	5.00	10.00
40191	Star of Hope/Peace in the Valley (For Me)	1954	2.50	5.00	10.00
40192	You Bought My Soul at Calvary/Invisible Hands	1954	2.50	5.00	10.00
40193	I Found a Friend/Beautiful Isle of Somewhere	1954	2.50	5.00	10.00
—The above four comprise a box set					
40230	The Temple of an Understanding Heart/Don't Get Around Much Anymore	1954	—	—	—
—Canceled					

Number	Title (A Side/B Side)	Yr	VG	VG+	NM
40250	Thank You for Calling/Where Are You	1954	3.00	6.00	12.00
40291	Nearer My Love to Me/The Temple of an Understanding Heart	1954	3.00	6.00	12.00
40351	Teach Me Tonight/Suddenly	1954	3.00	6.00	12.00
40406	Don't Get Around Much Anymore/Darling! Darling! Darling!	1955	3.00	6.00	12.00
40451	Please Don't Go So Soon/I Got a Sweetie	1955	3.00	6.00	12.00
40495	Be Sure, Beloved/Young and Foolish	1955	3.00	6.00	12.00
40538	Ain'tcha Comin' Out T-Tonight/St. Louis Blues	1955	3.00	6.00	12.00
40559	Suddenly There's a Valley/The Night Watch	1955	3.00	6.00	12.00
40595	It's Almost Tomorrow/If You Want to Love Me, You Have to Cry	1955	3.00	6.00	12.00
40640	All Night Long/As I Love You	1956	2.50	5.00	10.00
40697	Warm All Over/Big D	1956	2.50	5.00	10.00
40718	With a Little Bit of Luck/One Little Kiss	1956	2.50	5.00	10.00
40745	Love Me Good/A Perfect Love	1956	2.50	5.00	10.00
40782	On London Bridge/Bells Are Ringing	1956	2.50	5.00	10.00
40832	Wind in the Willow/King of Paris	1957	2.50	5.00	10.00
40926	I'll Be There (When We Get Lonely)/Underneath the Overpass	1957	2.50	5.00	10.00
41006	Star of Love/What's Botherin' You Baby	1957	2.50	5.00	10.00
41007	Echoes in the Night/Beyond the Stars	1957	2.50	5.00	10.00
41078	Sweet Little Darlin'/I'll Buy It	1957	2.50	5.00	10.00
41129	Sweet Little Darlin'/It's Never Quite the Same	1958	2.50	5.00	10.00
41160	I May Never Pass This Way Again/It Won't Be Easy	1958	2.50	5.00	10.00
41281	Lazy Moon/Hibiscus	1958	2.50	5.00	10.00
41321	How Can We Say Goodbye/My Heart Is From Missouri	1959	2.50	5.00	10.00
41413	All Yours/Pine Top's Boogie	1959	2.50	5.00	10.00
41517	It's Been So Long/Just Tell 'Em You Love Me	1959	2.50	5.00	10.00
41535	You're Starting to Get to Me/Every Night When the Sun Goes In	1959	2.50	5.00	10.00
41640	Happy Is the Word/What a Feeling	1960	2.50	5.00	10.00
41690	Candy/Indoor Sport	1960	2.50	5.00	10.00
DECCA					
25734	You Belong to Me/St. Louis Blues	1968	—	3.00	6.00
25740	Make Love to Me/I'll Be Seeing You	1968	—	3.00	6.00
DOT					
16791	Do I Hear a Waltz/Down in the Valley	1965	2.00	4.00	8.00
16904	Falling in Love Again/Cry, Cry Darling	1966	2.00	4.00	8.00
REPRISE					
20205	Country Bumpkin/Writing on the Wall	1963	2.00	4.00	8.00
7-Inch Extended Plays					
COLUMBIA					
B-2526	*You Belong to Me/Shrimp Boats/Keep It a Secret/Jambalaya	1957	3.75	7.50	15.00
B-2526 [PS]	Jo Stafford (Hall of Fame Series)	1957	3.75	7.50	15.00
B-2527	*Make Love to Me!/Early Autumn/Stardust/Teach Me Tonight	1957	3.75	7.50	15.00
B-2527 [PS]	Jo Stafford (Hall of Fame Series)	1957	3.75	7.50	15.00
B-9101	(contents unknown)	1956	3.00	6.00	12.00
B-9101 [PS]	Ski Trails, Vol. 1	1956	3.00	6.00	12.00
B-9102	(contents unknown)	1956	3.00	6.00	12.00
B-9102 [PS]	Ski Trails, Vol. 2	1956	3.00	6.00	12.00
B-9103	(contents unknown)	1956	3.00	6.00	12.00
B-9103 [PS]	Ski Trails, Vol. 3	1956	3.00	6.00	12.00
Albums					
BAINBRIDGE					
6234	Look at Me Now	1982	2.50	5.00	10.00
CAPITOL					
H 75 [10]	American Folk Songs	1950	15.00	30.00	60.00
H 197 [10]	Autumn in New York	195?	15.00	30.00	60.00
T 197 [M]	Autumn in New York	1955	12.50	25.00	50.00
—Turquoise or gray label					
T 197 [M]	Autumn in New York	1959	7.50	15.00	30.00
—Black colorband label, Capitol logo at left					
H 247 [10]	Songs for Sunday Evening	195?	15.00	30.00	60.00
T 423 [M]	Memory Songs	1955	12.50	25.00	50.00
—Turquoise or gray label					
T 423 [M]	Memory Songs	1959	7.50	15.00	30.00
—Black colorband label, Capitol logo at left					
H 435 [10]	Starring Jo Stafford	1953	15.00	30.00	60.00
T 435 [M]	Starring Jo Stafford	1955	12.50	25.00	50.00
—Turquoise or gray label					
T 435 [M]	Starring Jo Stafford	1959	7.50	15.00	30.00
—Black colorband label, Capitol logo at left					
ST 1653 [S]	American Folk Songs	1962	6.25	12.50	25.00
T 1653 [M]	American Folk Songs	1962	5.00	10.00	20.00
SM-1696	Whispering Hope	1977	2.50	5.00	10.00
—Reissue with new prefix					
ST 1921 [S]	The Hits of Jo Stafford	1963	6.25	12.50	25.00
T 1921 [M]	The Hits of Jo Stafford	1963	5.00	10.00	20.00
ST 2069 [S]	Sweet Hour of Prayer	1964	6.25	12.50	25.00
T 2069 [M]	Sweet Hour of Prayer	1964	5.00	10.00	20.00
ST 2166 [S]	The Joyful Season	1964	6.25	12.50	25.00
T 2166 [M]	The Joyful Season	1964	5.00	10.00	20.00
H 9014 [10]	Songs of Faith	1950	15.00	30.00	60.00
SM-11889	The Hits of Jo Stafford	1979	2.50	5.00	10.00
COLUMBIA					
CL 578 [M]	New Orleans	1954	10.00	20.00	40.00
—Maroon label, gold print					
CL 578 [M]	New Orleans	1955	7.50	15.00	30.00
—Red and black label with six "eye" logos					
CL 584 [M]	Jo Stafford Sings Broadway's Best	1954	10.00	20.00	40.00
—Maroon label, gold print					
CL 584 [M]	Jo Stafford Sings Broadway's Best	1955	7.50	15.00	30.00
—Red and black label with six "eye" logos					
CL 691 [M]	Happy Holiday	1955	15.00	30.00	60.00
CL 910 [M]	Ski Trails	1956	10.00	20.00	40.00
CL 968 [M]	Once Over Lightly	1957	10.00	20.00	40.00
CL 1043 [M]	Songs of Scotland	1957	10.00	20.00	40.00
CL 1124 [M]	Swingin' Down Broadway	1958	10.00	20.00	40.00

Number	Title (A Side/B Side)	Yr	VG	VG+	NM
CL 1228 [M]	Jo Stafford's Greatest Hits	1958	10.00	20.00	40.00
—Red and black label with six "eye" logos					
CL 1228 [M]	Jo Stafford's Greatest Hits	1963	5.00	10.00	20.00
—Red label with "Guaranteed High Fidelity" in black					
CL 1228 [M]	Jo Stafford's Greatest Hits	1965	3.75	7.50	15.00
—Red label with "360 Sound Mono" in white					
CL 1262 [M]	I'll Be Seeing You	1959	7.50	15.00	30.00
CL 1339 [M]	Ballad of the Blues	1959	7.50	15.00	30.00
CL 1561 [M]	Jo + Jazz	1960	10.00	20.00	40.00
CL 2501 [10]	Soft and Sentimental	1955	10.00	20.00	40.00
CL 2591 [10]	A Gal Named Jo	1955	10.00	20.00	40.00
CL 6210 [10]	As You Desire Me	1952	12.50	25.00	50.00
CL 6238 [10]	Jo Stafford Sings Broadway's Best	1953	12.50	25.00	50.00
CL 6268 [10]	New Orleans	1954	12.50	25.00	50.00
CL 6274 [10]	My Heart's in the Highland	1954	12.50	25.00	50.00
CL 6286 [10]	Garden of Prayer	1954	12.50	25.00	50.00
CS 8080 [S]	I'll Be Seeing You	1959	10.00	20.00	40.00
CS 8139 [S]	Ballad of the Blues	1959	10.00	20.00	40.00
CS 8361 [S]	Jo + Jazz	1960	15.00	30.00	60.00
CORINTHIAN					
COR-105	G.I. Jo	1977	2.50	5.00	10.00
COR-106	Greatest Hits	1977	2.50	5.00	10.00
COR-108	Jo + Jazz	197?	2.50	5.00	10.00
COR-110	Jo Stafford Sings American Folk Songs	197?	2.50	5.00	10.00
COR-111	Songs of Faith, Hope and Love	197?	2.50	5.00	10.00
COR-112	Jo + Broadway	197?	2.50	5.00	10.00
COR-113	Ski Trails	197?	2.50	5.00	10.00
COR-114	Jo + Blues	197?	2.50	5.00	10.00
COR-115	International Hits	197?	2.50	5.00	10.00
COR-118	Broadway Revisited	198?	2.50	5.00	10.00
COR-119	By Request	198?	2.50	5.00	10.00
COR-123	Music of My Life	1986	2.50	5.00	10.00
DECCA					
DL 74973	Jo Stafford's Greatest Hits	1968	3.75	7.50	15.00
DOT					
DLP-3673 [M]	Do I Hear a Waltz?	1966	3.75	7.50	15.00
DLP-3745 [M]	This Is Jo Stafford	1967	3.75	7.50	15.00
DLP-25673 [S]	Do I Hear a Waltz?	1966	5.00	10.00	20.00
DLP-25745 [S]	This Is Jo Stafford	1967	5.00	10.00	20.00
REPRISE					
R-6090 [M]	Getting Sentimental Over Tommy Dorsey	1963	5.00	10.00	20.00
R9-6090 [S]	Getting Sentimental Over Tommy Dorsey	1963	6.25	12.50	25.00
STANYAN					
10073	Look at Me Now	197?	3.00	6.00	12.00
VOCALION					
VL 73856 [R]	Happy Holidays	1968	3.00	6.00	12.00
VL 73892	In the Mood for Love	1970	3.00	6.00	12.00

STAFFORD, JO, AND VIC DAMONE

Also see each artist's individual listings.

45s

Number	Title (A Side/B Side)	Yr	VG	VG+	NM
COLUMBIA					
40968	Silence Is Golden/Good Nite	1957	2.50	5.00	10.00

STAFFORD, JO, AND GORDON MACRAE

45s

Number	Title (A Side/B Side)	Yr	VG	VG+	NM
CAPITOL					
54-782	Bibbidi-Bobbidi-Boo (The Magic Song)/Echoes	1949	6.25	12.50	25.00
F858	Dearie/Monday, Tuesday, Wednesday	1950	5.00	10.00	20.00
F969	Down the Lane/You Are My Love	1950	5.00	10.00	20.00
F1235	Yesterday/I'll See You After Church	1950	5.00	10.00	20.00
F1307	To Think You've Chosen Me/Hold Me, Hold Me	1950	5.00	10.00	20.00
F1642	Whispering Hope/I'll String Along with You	1951	3.75	7.50	15.00
—Reissue of 1949 hit					
F1659	Wunderbar/Beyond the Sunset	1951	3.75	7.50	15.00
—Reissue					

7-Inch Extended Plays

Number	Title (A Side/B Side)	Yr	VG	VG+	NM
CAPITOL					
EAP 1-9021	Songs Of Christmas Part 1/Songs Of Christmas Part 2	195?	2.50	5.00	10.00
EAP 1-9021 [PS]	Songs Of Christmas	195?	2.50	5.00	10.00

Albums

Number	Title (A Side/B Side)	Yr	VG	VG+	NM
CAPITOL					
T 423 [M]	Memory Songs	1955	12.50	25.00	50.00
ST 1696 [S]	Whispering Hope	1962	6.25	12.50	25.00
T 1696 [M]	Whispering Hope	1962	5.00	10.00	20.00
ST 1916 [S]	Peace in the Valley	1963	6.25	12.50	25.00
T 1916 [M]	Peace in the Valley	1963	5.00	10.00	20.00

STAFFORD, TERRY

45s

Number	Title (A Side/B Side)	Yr	VG	VG+	NM
ATLANTIC					
4006	Amarillo by Morning/Say, Has Anybody Seen My Sweet Gypsy Rose	1973	2.00	4.00	8.00
4015	Captured/It Sure Is Bad to Love Her	1974	—	3.00	6.00
4026	Stop If You Love Me/We've Grown Close	1974	—	3.00	6.00
A&M					
707	Heartaches on the Way/You Left Me Here to Cry	1963	3.00	6.00	12.00
CASINO					
113	It Sure Is Bad to Love Her/(B-side unknown)	1977	—	3.00	6.00
CRUSADER					
101	Suspicion/Judy	1964	3.75	7.50	15.00
105	I'll Touch a Star/Playing with Fire	1964	3.00	6.00	12.00
109	Follow the Rainbow/Are You a Fool Like Me	1964	3.00	6.00	12.00
110	A Little Bit Better/Hoping	1964	3.00	6.00	12.00
EASTLAND					
101	Back Together/Life's Railway to Heaven	198?	—	2.50	5.00
MELODYLAND					
6009	Darling, Think It Over/I Can't Find It	1975	—	2.50	5.00
MERCURY					
72538	Out of the Picture/Forbidden	1966	2.50	5.00	10.00
MGM					
14232	Mean Woman Blues-Candy Man/Chilly Chicago	1971	—	3.00	6.00
14271	California Dancer/The Walk	1971	—	3.00	6.00
PLAYER					
134	Lonestar Lonesome/(B-side unknown)	1989	—	3.00	6.00
SIDEWALK					
902	Soldier Boy/When Sin Stops, Love Begins	1966	2.50	5.00	10.00
914	A Step or Two Behind You/The Joke's on Me	1967	2.50	5.00	10.00
WARNER BROS.					
7286	Big in Dallas/Will a Man Ever Learn	1969	—	3.00	6.00

Albums

Number	Title (A Side/B Side)	Yr	VG	VG+	NM
ATLANTIC					
SD 7282	Say, Has Anybody Seen My Sweet Gypsy Rose	1974	3.00	6.00	12.00
CRUSADER					
CLP-1001S [S]	Suspicion!	1964	15.00	30.00	60.00
CLP-1001 [M]	Suspicion!	1964	10.00	20.00	40.00

STAIRSTEPS, THE

See THE FIVE STAIRSTEPS.

STALK-FORREST GROUP, THE

Early version of BLUE OYSTER CULT.

45s

Number	Title (A Side/B Side)	Yr	VG	VG+	NM
ELEKTRA					
45693	What Is Quicksand/Arthur Comics	1970	12.50	25.00	50.00

STAMPEDERS

45s

Number	Title (A Side/B Side)	Yr	VG	VG+	NM
BELL					
45120	Sweet City Woman/Gator Road	1971	—	3.00	6.00
45154	Devil You/Giant in the Streets	1971	—	2.50	5.00
45188	Monday Morning Choo-Choo/Then Came the White Man	1972	—	3.00	6.00
45226	Wild Eyes/Carryin' On	1972	—	3.00	6.00
45331	Oh My Lady/No Destination	1973	—	3.00	6.00
CAPITOL					
3868	Goodbye Goodbye/Me and My Stone	1974	—	2.00	4.00
3964	Running Out of Time/Ramona	1974	—	2.00	4.00
MGM					
13970	Be a Woman/I Don't Believe	1968	3.00	6.00	12.00
POLYDOR					
14060	Carry Me/I Didn't Need You Anyhow	1970	2.50	5.00	10.00
QUALITY					
501	Hard Lovin' Woman/Hit the Road Jack	1976	—	2.00	4.00
505	Sweet Love Bandit/Let It Begin	1976	—	2.00	4.00

Albums

Number	Title (A Side/B Side)	Yr	VG	VG+	NM
BELL					
6068	Sweet City Woman	1971	3.75	7.50	15.00
CAPITOL					
ST-11288	From the Fire	1973	3.00	6.00	12.00
ST-11328	New Day	1974	3.00	6.00	12.00
QUALITY					
1001	Hit the Road	1976	3.00	6.00	12.00

STANDARDS, THE

The record on Amos may be by a different group than the others.

45s

Number	Title (A Side/B Side)	Yr	VG	VG+	NM
AMOS					
134	When You Wish Upon a Star/(Instrumental)	1969	2.50	5.00	10.00
CHESS					
1869	My Heart Belongs to You/Hello Love	1963	10.00	20.00	40.00
DEBRO					
3178	Tears Bring Heartaches/No, No, No	1963	50.00	100.00	200.00
GLENDEN					
1315	It Isn't Fair/Everybody Knows	1964	5.00	10.00	20.00
MAGNA					
1314	My Heart Belongs to You/Hello Love	1963	20.00	40.00	80.00
1315	It Isn't Fair/Everybody Knows	1963	12.50	25.00	50.00
ROULETTE					
4487	Tears Bring Heartaches/No, No, No	1963	7.50	15.00	30.00

STANDELLS, THE

Also see DICK DODD.

45s

Number	Title (A Side/B Side)	Yr	VG	VG+	NM
LIBERTY					
55680	The Peppermint Beatle/The Shake	1964	6.25	12.50	25.00
55722	Help Yourself/I'll Go Crazy	1964	5.00	10.00	20.00
55743	So Fine/Linda Lou	1964	5.00	10.00	20.00
MGM					
13350	Someday You'll Cry/Zebra in the Kitchen	1965	7.50	15.00	30.00
SUNSET					
61000	Ooh Poo Pah Doo/Help Yourself	1966	5.00	10.00	20.00
TOWER					
185	Dirty Water/Rari	1966	5.00	10.00	20.00
257	Sometimes Good Guys Don't Wear White/Why Did You Hurt Me	1966	3.75	7.50	15.00
282	Why Pick on Me/Mr. Nobody	1966	3.75	7.50	15.00
310	Try It/Poor Shell of a Man	1967	3.75	7.50	15.00
310 [PS]	Try It/Poor Shell of a Man	1967	12.50	25.00	50.00
312	Don't Tell Me What to Do/When I Was a Cowboy	1967	5.00	10.00	20.00
—By "The Sllednats" (Standells backwards)					
314	Riot on Sunset Strip/Black Hearted Woman	1967	3.75	7.50	15.00
314 [PS]	Riot on Sunset Strip/Black Hearted Woman	1967	20.00	40.00	80.00
348	Can't Help But Love You/Ninety-Nine and One Half	1967	3.75	7.50	15.00
398	Animal Girl/Soul Drippin'	1968	3.75	7.50	15.00
VEE JAY					
643	The Boy Next Door/B.J. Quetzal	1965	5.00	10.00	20.00
643 [PS]	The Boy Next Door/B.J. Quetzal	1965	50.00	100.00	200.00
679	Big Boss Man/Don't Say Goodbye	1965	5.00	10.00	20.00

Number	Title (A Side/B Side)	Yr	VG	VG+	NM
Albums					
LIBERTY					
LRP-3384 [M]	The Standells In Person at P.J.'s	1964	20.00	40.00	80.00
LST-7384 [S]	The Standells In Person at P.J.'s	1964	25.00	50.00	100.00
RHINO					
RNLP-107	The Best of the Standells	1983	2.50	5.00	10.00
RNLP-115	Rarities	1983	2.50	5.00	10.00
RNLP-70176	The Best of the Standells (Golden Archive Series)	1987	2.50	5.00	10.00
SUNSET					
SUM-1136 [M]	Live and Out of Sight	1966	6.25	12.50	25.00
SUS-5136 [S]	Live and Out of Sight	1966	7.50	15.00	30.00
TOWER					
ST 5027 [R]	Dirty Water	1966	12.50	25.00	50.00
T 5027 [M]	Dirty Water	1966	15.00	30.00	60.00
ST 5044 [S]	Why Pick on Me	1966	15.00	30.00	60.00
T 5044 [M]	Why Pick on Me	1966	12.50	25.00	50.00
ST 5049 [S]	The Hot Ones	1966	15.00	30.00	60.00
T 5049 [M]	The Hot Ones	1966	12.50	25.00	50.00
ST 5098 [S]	Try It	1967	15.00	30.00	60.00
T 5098 [M]	Try It	1967	12.50	25.00	50.00

STANLEY, MICHAEL, BAND

Number	Title (A Side/B Side)	Yr	VG	VG+	NM
45s					
ARISTA					
0348	Why Should Love Be This Way/Late Show	1978	—	2.00	4.00
0368	Baby If You Wanna Dance/Fool's Parade	1978	—	2.00	4.00
0436	Last Night/Down to the Wire	1979	—	2.00	4.00
EMI AMERICA					
8063	He Can't Love You/Carolyn	1980	—	—	3.00
8064	Lover/Save a Little Piece for Me	1981	—	—	3.00
8090	Falling in Love Again/Does It Hurt	1981	—	—	3.00
8097	Victim of Circumstance/When Your Heart Says It's Right	1981	—	—	3.00
8130	When I'm Holding You Tight/In Between the Lines	1982	—	—	3.00
8146	Take the Time/Just a Little Bit Longer	1982	—	—	3.00
8178	My Town/Just How Good	1983	—	—	3.00
8189	Someone Like You/Highlife	1983	—	—	3.00
EPIC					
50116	I'm Gonna Love You/Step the Way	1975	—	2.00	4.00
50151	Face the Music/Song for My Children	1975	—	2.00	4.00
50242	Ladies' Choice/Sweet Refrain	1976	—	2.00	4.00
50416	Love Hasn't Been Here/Nothing's Gonna Change My Mind	1977	—	2.00	4.00
MCA					
40177	Roll On/Yours for a Song	1974	—	2.50	5.00
Albums					
ARISTA					
AL 4182	Cabin Fever	1978	2.50	5.00	10.00
AL 4236	Greatest Hints	1979	2.50	5.00	10.00
EMI AMERICA					
SN-16352	Heartland	1985	2.00	4.00	8.00
—Budget-line reissue					
SN-16353	You Can't Fight Fashion	1985	2.00	4.00	8.00
—Budget-line reissue					
SN-16392	MSB	1986	2.00	4.00	8.00
—Budget-line reissue					
SW-17040	Heartland	1980	2.50	5.00	10.00
SW-17056	North Coast	1981	2.50	5.00	10.00
ST-17071	MSB	1982	2.50	5.00	10.00
ST-17100	You Can't Fight Fashion	1983	2.50	5.00	10.00
EPIC					
PE 33492	You Break It...You Bought It!	1975	3.00	6.00	12.00
—Original with orange label and no bar code					
PE 33492	You Break It...You Bought It!	198?	2.00	4.00	8.00
—Reissue with dark blue label and bar code					
PE 33917	Ladies' Choice	1976	3.00	6.00	12.00
—Original with orange label and no bar code					
PE 33917	Ladies' Choice	198?	2.00	4.00	8.00
—Reissue with dark blue label and bar code					
PEG 34661 [(2)]	Stagepass	1977	3.75	7.50	15.00
MCA					
372	Friends and Legends	1973	3.00	6.00	12.00
TUMBLEWEED					
TWS 106	Michael Stanley	1972	5.00	10.00	20.00
—Blue textured cover					

STAPLE SINGERS, THE

Also see MAVIS STAPLES.

Number	Title (A Side/B Side)	Yr	VG	VG+	NM
12-Inch Singles					
PRIVATE I					
05078	Slippery People (5:30)/(Instrumental)	1984	—	2.50	5.00
05266	Are You Ready? (Extended) (Dub)	1985	—	2.50	5.00
45s					
20TH CENTURY					
2508	Hold On to Your Dreams/Cold and Windy Night	1981	—	2.00	4.00
CURTOM					
0109	Let's Do It Again/After Sex	1975	—	2.00	4.00
0113	New Orleans/A Whole Lot of Love	1976	—	2.00	4.00
EPIC					
9748	Be Careful of Stones That You Throw/More Than a Hammer and Nail	1964	2.50	5.00	10.00
9776	Do Something for Yourself/Samson and Delilah	1965	2.50	5.00	10.00
9825	Freedom Highway/The Funeral	1965	2.50	5.00	10.00
9880	Why/What Are They Doing	1965	2.50	5.00	10.00
10054	King of Kings/Step Aside	1966	2.50	5.00	10.00
10104	Pray On/It's Been a Change	1966	2.50	5.00	10.00
10158	Why (Am I Treated So Bad)/What Are They Doing (In Heaven Today)	1967	2.00	4.00	8.00
10220	For What It's Worth/Are You Sure	1967	2.00	4.00	8.00
10264	Deliver Me/He	1967	2.00	4.00	8.00
10294	Let's Get Together/Power of Love	1968	2.00	4.00	8.00
10339	Crying in the Chapel/Nothing Lasts Forever	1968	2.00	4.00	8.00
10742	For What It's Worth/Why	1971	—	3.00	6.00
PRIVATE I					
04384	H-A-T-E (Don't Live Here Anymore)/Can You Hang	1984	—	2.00	4.00
04583	Slippery People/On My Own Again	1984	—	2.00	4.00
04711	This Is Our Night/Turning Point	1984	—	2.00	4.00
05565	Are You Ready/Love Wowks in Strange Ways	1985	—	2.00	4.00
05565 [PS]	Are You Ready/Love Wowks in Strange Ways	1985	—	3.00	6.00
05727	Nobody Can Make It on Their Own/Reasons to Love	1985	—	2.00	4.00
RIVERSIDE					
4518	Gloryland/Hammer and Nails	1962	3.00	6.00	12.00
4531	Gambling Man/Use What You Got	1962	3.00	6.00	12.00
4540	There Was a Star/The Virgin Mary Had One Son	1962	3.00	6.00	12.00
4553	I Can't Help from Cryin'/Let That Liar Again	1963	3.00	6.00	12.00
4563	Cotton Fields/This Land	1963	3.00	6.00	12.00
4568	Blowing in the Wind/Wish I Had Answered	1963	3.00	6.00	12.00
SHARP					
603	This May Be the Last Time/This Same Jesus	1960	3.75	7.50	15.00
STAX					
0007	Long Walk to D.C./Stay with Us	1968	—	3.00	6.00
0019	The Ghetto/Got to Be Some Changes Made	1968	—	3.00	6.00
0031	(Sittin' On) The Dock of the Bay/Top of the Mountain	1969	—	3.00	6.00
0039	The Gardener/The Challenge	1969	—	3.00	6.00
0052	When Will We Be Paid/Tend to Your Own Business	1969	—	3.00	6.00
0066	Give a Damn/God Bless the Children	1970	—	3.00	6.00
0074	Brand New Day/God Bless the Children	1970	—	3.00	6.00
0083	Heavy Makes You Happy (Sha-Na-Boom-Boom)/Love Is Plentiful	1970	—	3.00	6.00
0084	Who Took the Merry Out of Christmas/(Instrumental)	1970	2.00	4.00	8.00
0093	You've Got to Earn It/I'm a Lover	1971	—	2.50	5.00
0104	Respect Yourself/You're Gonna Make Me Cry	1971	—	2.50	5.00
0125	I'll Take You There/I'm Just Another Soldier	1972	—	2.50	5.00
0137	This World/Are You Sure	1972	—	2.50	5.00
0156	Oh La De Da/We the People	1973	—	2.50	5.00
0164	Be What You Are/I Like the Things About Me	1973	—	2.50	5.00
—B-side by Cal Starr					
0179	If You're Ready (Come Go with Me)/Love Comes in All Colors	1973	—	2.50	5.00
0196	Touch a Hand, Make a Friend/Tellin' Lies	1974	—	2.50	5.00
0213	What's Your Thing/Whicha Way Did It Go	1974	—	2.50	5.00
—B-side by Pops Staples					
0215	City in the Sky/That's What Friends Are For	1974	—	2.50	5.00
0227	My Main Man/Who Made the Man	1974	—	2.50	5.00
0248	Back Road Into Town/My Main Man	1975	—	2.50	5.00
UNITED					
165	It Rained Children/Won't You Sit Down	1955	100.00	200.00	400.00
VEE JAY					
169	God's Wonderful Love/If I Could Hear My Mother	1956	5.00	10.00	20.00
224	Uncloudy Day/I Know I Got Religion	1956	5.00	10.00	20.00
846	Let Me Ride/I'm Coming Home	1957	5.00	10.00	20.00
856	I Had a Dream/Help Me Jesus	1958	3.75	7.50	15.00
866	Love Is the Way/On My Way to Heaven	1959	3.75	7.50	15.00
870	I'm Leaving/Going Away	1959	3.75	7.50	15.00
881	Downward Road/So Soon	1959	3.75	7.50	15.00
893	Pray On/Too Close	1960	3.00	6.00	12.00
902	I've Been Scorned/Don't Knock	1961	3.00	6.00	12.00
912	Sit Down Servant/Swing Low	1962	3.00	6.00	12.00
930	Swing Low Sweet Chariot/I'm So Glad	1963	3.00	6.00	12.00
WARNER BROS.					
8279	Love Me, Love Me, Love Me/Pass It On	1976	—	2.00	4.00
8317	Sweeter Than the Sweet/Making Love	1977	—	2.00	4.00
8460	See a Little Further (Than My Bed)/Let's Go to the Disco	1977	—	2.00	4.00
8510	I Honestly Love You/Family Tree	1978	—	2.00	4.00
8669	Unlock Your Mind/Mystery Train	1978	—	2.00	4.00
8748	Chica Boom/Handwriting on the Wall	1979	—	2.00	4.00
49598	God Can/Unlock Your Mind	1980	—	2.00	4.00
—Warner Bros. titles as "The Staples"					
Albums					
20TH CENTURY					
T-636	Hold On to Your Dream	1981	2.50	5.00	10.00
ARCHIVE OF GOSPEL MUSIC					
62	The Staple Singers	1968	3.00	6.00	12.00
72	The Staple Singers, Vol. 2	1969	3.00	6.00	12.00
BUDDAH					
BDS-2009	The Best of the Staple Singers	1969	5.00	10.00	20.00
BDS-7508	Will the Circle Be Unbroken	1969	5.00	10.00	20.00
CURTOM					
CU 5005	Let's Do It Again	1975	3.00	6.00	12.00
EPIC					
LN 24132 [M]	Amen	1965	5.00	10.00	20.00
LN 24163 [M]	Freedom Highway	1965	5.00	10.00	20.00
LN 24196 [M]	Why	1966	5.00	10.00	20.00
LN 24237 [M]	Pray On	1967	6.25	12.50	25.00
LN 24332 [M]	For What It's Worth	1967	6.25	12.50	25.00
BN 26132 [S]	Amen	1965	6.25	12.50	25.00
BN 26163 [S]	Freedom Highway	1965	6.25	12.50	25.00
BN 26196 [S]	Why	1966	6.25	12.50	25.00
BN 26237 [S]	Pray On	1967	5.00	10.00	20.00
BN 26332 [S]	For What It's Worth	1967	5.00	10.00	20.00
BN 26373	What the World Needs Now Is Love	1968	5.00	10.00	20.00
EG 30635 [(2)]	The Staple Singers Make You Happy	1971	5.00	10.00	20.00
FANTASY					
9423	Use What You Got	1973	3.75	7.50	15.00
9442	The 25th Day of December	1973	3.75	7.50	15.00
HARMONY					
KH 31775	Tell It Like It Is	1972	3.00	6.00	12.00
MILESTONE					
47028 [(2)]	A Great Day	197?	3.75	7.50	15.00

Number	Title (A Side/B Side)	Yr	VG	VG+	NM
PICKWICK					
7001	The Staple Singers	197?	2.50	5.00	10.00
PRIVATE I					
FZ 39460	The Turning Point	1984	2.50	5.00	10.00
BFZ 40109	The Staple Singers	1985	2.50	5.00	10.00
STAX					
STS-2004	Soul Folk in Action	1968	6.25	12.50	25.00
STS-2016	We'll Get Over	1969	5.00	10.00	20.00
STS-2034	The Staple Swingers	1971	5.00	10.00	20.00
STS-3002	Be Altitude: Respect Yourself	1972	3.75	7.50	15.00
STS-3015	Be What You Are	1973	3.75	7.50	15.00
STX-4116	Be Altitude: Respect Yourself	198?	2.50	5.00	10.00
—Reissue of 3002					
STX-4119	Chronicle	198?	2.50	5.00	10.00
STS-5515	City in the Sky	1974	3.75	7.50	15.00
STS-5523	The Best of the Staple Singers	1975	3.75	7.50	15.00
MPS-8511	This Time Around	198?	2.50	5.00	10.00
MPS-8532	We'll Get Over	198?	2.50	5.00	10.00
—Reissue of 2016					
MPS-8553	Be What You Are	1990	3.00	6.00	12.00
—Reissue of 3015					
TRIP					
7000	Uncloudy Day	197?	2.50	5.00	10.00
7014	Swing Low	197?	2.50	5.00	10.00
7019	The Best of the Staple Singers	197?	2.50	5.00	10.00
8014	The Other Side of the Staple Singers	1972	2.50	5.00	10.00
VEE JAY					
LP-5000 [M]	Uncloudy Day	1959	7.50	15.00	30.00
LP-5008 [M]	Will the Circle Be Unbroken	1960	7.50	15.00	30.00
LP-5014 [M]	Swing Low	1961	7.50	15.00	30.00
LP-5019 [M]	Best of the Staple Singers	1962	7.50	15.00	30.00
LP-5030 [M]	Swing Low Sweet Chariot	1963	7.50	15.00	30.00
VEE JAY/CHAMELEON					
D1-74782 [(2)]	The Best of the Staple Singers	1988	3.75	7.50	15.00
WARNER BROS.					
BS 2945	Pass It On	1976	3.00	6.00	12.00
—As "The Staples"					
BS 3084	Family Tree	1977	3.00	6.00	12.00
—As "The Staples"					
BSK 3192	Unlock Your Mind	1978	3.00	6.00	12.00
—As "The Staples"					

STAPLES, GORDON, AND THE MOTOWN STRINGS

45s

Number	Title (A Side/B Side)	Yr	VG	VG+	NM
MOTOWN					
1180	Strung Out/Sounds of the Zodiac	1971	7.50	15.00	30.00
1180 [DJ]	Strung Out (same on both sides)	1971	7.50	15.00	30.00
—Red vinyl promo					

STAPLES, MAVIS

Also see THE STAPLE SINGERS.

12-Inch Singles

Number	Title (A Side/B Side)	Yr	VG	VG+	NM
PAISLEY PARK					
PRO-A-4397 [DJ]	Melody Cool (Edit) (LP)	1990	2.00	4.00	8.00
PRO-A-5991 [DJ]	The Voice (same on both sides)	1993	2.50	5.00	10.00
21287	Jaguar (4 versions)	1989	2.00	4.00	8.00
21748	Melody Cool (4 versions)/Time Waits for No One (Edit)	1990	2.00	4.00	8.00
WARNER BROS.					
PRO-A-2444 [DJ]	Show Me How It Works (same on both sides)	1986	—	3.00	6.00
8837	Tonight I Feel Like Dancing/If I Can't Have You	1979	3.00	6.00	12.00

45s

Number	Title (A Side/B Side)	Yr	VG	VG+	NM
CURTOM					
0132	A Piece of the Action/Till Blossoms Bloom	1977	—	2.00	4.00
PAISLEY PARK					
22968	20th Century Express/All the Discomforts of Home	1989	—	—	3.00
PHONO					
1051	Love Gone Bad/(B-side unknown)	1984	—	2.50	5.00
VOLT					
4044	I Have Learned to Do Without You/Since I Fell for You	1970	—	2.50	5.00
4086	Endlessly/Don't Change Me Now	1972	—	2.50	5.00
WARNER BROS.					
PRO-S-3878 [DJ]	Christmas Vacation (same on both sides)	1989	—	2.50	5.00
8838	Tonight I Feel Like Dancing/If I Can't Have You	1979	—	2.00	4.00
28765	Show Me How It Works/Half Time	1986	—	—	3.00
49054	Oh What a Feeling/If I Can't Have You	1979	—	2.00	4.00

Albums

Number	Title (A Side/B Side)	Yr	VG	VG+	NM
CURTOM					
CU 5019	A Piece of the Action	1977	3.00	6.00	12.00
PAISLEY PARK					
25798	Time Waits for No One	1989	3.00	6.00	12.00
STAX					
STX-4118	Mavis Staples	198?	2.50	5.00	10.00
—Reissue of Volt 6007					
MPS-8539	Only for the Lonely	1987	2.50	5.00	10.00
—Reissue of Volt 6010					
VOLT					
VOS-6007	Mavis Staples	1969	5.00	10.00	20.00
VOS-6010	Only for the Lonely	1970	5.00	10.00	20.00
WARNER BROS.					
BSK 3319	Oh What a Feeling	1979	3.00	6.00	12.00

STAR FIRES, THE

45s

Number	Title (A Side/B Side)	Yr	VG	VG+	NM
HARAL					
777	Each Night at Nine/What Good Is Money	1962	25.00	50.00	100.00
LAURIE					
3332	You Done Me Wrong/Like Socks and Shoes	1966	5.00	10.00	20.00

STARFIRES, THE (1)

45s

Number	Title (A Side/B Side)	Yr	VG	VG+	NM
APT					
25030	Fender Bender/Camel Walk	1959	5.00	10.00	20.00
PACE					
101	Fender Bender/Camel Walk	1959	10.00	20.00	40.00

STARFIRES, THE (2)

45s

Number	Title (A Side/B Side)	Yr	VG	VG+	NM
BARGAIN					
5001	You're the One/So Much	1961	15.00	30.00	60.00
5003	Love Will Break Your Heart/The Dances	1961	15.00	30.00	60.00
D&H					
200	These Foolish Things/Let's Do the Pony	1961	30.00	60.00	120.00

STARFIRES, THE (3)

45s

Number	Title (A Side/B Side)	Yr	VG	VG+	NM
BERNICE					
201	Yearning for You/Do-Ko-Icki-No	1958	37.50	75.00	150.00
DECCA					
30730	Three Roses/I Have Someone	1958	10.00	20.00	40.00
30916	Love Is Here to Stay/Tomorrow	1959	12.50	25.00	50.00

STARFIRES, THE (4)

45s

Number	Title (A Side/B Side)	Yr	VG	VG+	NM
DUEL					
518	Fools Fall in Love/Under the Stars	1962	12.50	25.00	50.00
TRIUMPH					
61	Fink/Work Out Fine	1965	5.00	10.00	20.00

Albums

Number	Title (A Side/B Side)	Yr	VG	VG+	NM
OHIO RECORDING SERVICE					
31 [M]	The Starfires Play	1964	12.50	25.00	50.00

STARFIRES, THE (5)

45s

Number	Title (A Side/B Side)	Yr	VG	VG+	NM
G.I.					
4001	I Never Loved Her/Linda	1965	625.00	1250.	2500.
4002	Rockin' Dixie/(B-side unknown)	1965	25.00	50.00	100.00
4004	Cry for Freedom/(B-side unknown)	1965	25.00	50.00	100.00

Albums

Number	Title (A Side/B Side)	Yr	VG	VG+	NM
LABREA					
LS-8018 [M]	Teenbeat A-Go-Go	1965	12.50	25.00	50.00

STARFIRES, THE (6)

Early version of THE OUTSIDERS.

45s

Number	Title (A Side/B Side)	Yr	VG	VG+	NM
PAMA					
115	Ring of Love/Cheating Game	196?	10.00	20.00	40.00
117	Chartreuse Caboose/Billy's Blues	196?	10.00	20.00	40.00

STARFIRES, THE (7)

45s

Number	Title (A Side/B Side)	Yr	VG	VG+	NM
ROUND					
1016	Space Needle/The Jordan Stomp	1962	10.00	20.00	40.00
1016 [PS]	Space Needle/The Jordan Stomp	1962	15.00	30.00	60.00

STARFIRES, THE (8)

45s

Number	Title (A Side/B Side)	Yr	VG	VG+	NM
SONIC					
7163	Re-Entry/Hand Full of Blood	1963	7.50	15.00	30.00

STARLETS, THE (1)

Later recorded as THE ANGELS (1).

45s

Number	Title (A Side/B Side)	Yr	VG	VG+	NM
ASTRO					
202/3	P.S. I Love You/Where Is My Love Tonight	1960	7.50	15.00	30.00
204	Romeo and Juliet/Listen for a Lonely Tambourine	1960	6.25	12.50	25.00

STARLETS, THE (2)

45s

Number	Title (A Side/B Side)	Yr	VG	VG+	NM
CHESS					
1997	My Baby's Real/Loving You Is Something New	1967	6.25	12.50	25.00
2038	I Wanna Be Good to You/Watered Down	1968	5.00	10.00	20.00

STARLETS, THE (3)

This is the same group that, as THE BLUE-BELLES, recorded "I Sold My Heart to the Junkman."

45s

Number	Title (A Side/B Side)	Yr	VG	VG+	NM
LUTE					
5909	I'm So Young/He's Got It	1960	6.25	12.50	25.00
PAM					
1003	Better Tell Him No/You Are the One	1961	5.00	10.00	20.00
1004	My Last Cry/Money Hungry	1961	5.00	10.00	20.00

STARLETTES, THE

45s

Number	Title (A Side/B Side)	Yr	VG	VG+	NM
CHECKER					
895	Please Ring My Phone/Jungle Love	1958	37.50	75.00	150.00

STARLIGHTERS, THE

45s

Number	Title (A Side/B Side)	Yr	VG	VG+	NM
CAPITOL					
F844	Rag Mop/It's Not Bad	1950	7.50	15.00	30.00
CRYSTALETTE					
661	Sweetheart of Sigma Chi/Don't Call Me Coach, Call Me George	1952	6.25	12.50	25.00
END					
1031	It's Twelve O'Clock/The Birdland	1958	125.00	250.00	500.00
1049	I Cried/You're the One to Blame	1959	20.00	40.00	80.00

Number	Title (A Side/B Side)	Yr	VG	VG+	NM
1072	A Story of Love/Let's Take a Stroll	1960	30.00	60.00	120.00
IRMA					
101	Love Cry/Last Night	1956	100.00	200.00	400.00
LAMP					
2014	Slipping Out/Rocking Too Much	1958	12.50	25.00	50.00
SUN COAST					
1001	Until You Return/Whomp, Whomp	1956	62.50	125.00	250.00
WHEEL					
1004	Hot Licks/Creepin'	1960	3.75	7.50	15.00

STARLINGS, THE (1)

45s

Number	Title (A Side/B Side)	Yr	VG	VG+	NM
DAWN					
212	I'm Just a Crying Fool/Hokey-Smokey Mama	1955	150.00	300.00	600.00
213	A-Loo, A-Loo/I Gotta Go Now	1955	100.00	200.00	400.00
JOSIE					
760	My Plea for Love/Music, Maestro, Please	1954	125.00	250.00	500.00

STARLINGS, THE (2)

45s

Number	Title (A Side/B Side)	Yr	VG	VG+	NM
WORLD PACIFIC					
809	All I Want/That's Me	1959	10.00	20.00	40.00

STARR, ANDY

45s

Number	Title (A Side/B Side)	Yr	VG	VG+	NM
KAPP					
190	Do It Right Now/I Waited for You to Remember	1957	6.25	12.50	25.00
MGM					
12263	Rockin' Rollin' Stone/I Wanna Go South	1956	37.50	75.00	150.00
12315	She's a-Going, Jessie/Old Deacon Jones	1956	37.50	75.00	150.00
12364	Round and Round/Give Me a Woman	1957	37.50	75.00	150.00
12421	No Room for Your Kind/One More Time	1957	37.50	75.00	150.00

STARR, EDWIN

12-Inch Singles

Number	Title (A Side/B Side)	Yr	VG	VG+	NM
20TH CENTURY					
TCD-62	I Just Wanna Do My Thing/Mr. Davenport and Mr. James	1977	3.75	7.50	15.00
TCD-107 [DJ]	Tell a Star (same on both sides)	1980	2.50	5.00	10.00
TCD-128 [DJ]	Real Live #10 (stereo/mono)	1981	2.50	5.00	10.00
A.S.K.					
S-29116	Hit Me with Your Love/Over and Over	198?	2.00	4.00	8.00

45s

Number	Title (A Side/B Side)	Yr	VG	VG+	NM
20TH CENTURY					
2338	I Just Wanna Do My Thing/Mr. Davenport and Mr. James	1977	—	2.00	4.00
2389	I'm So Into You/Don't Waste Your Time	1978	—	2.00	4.00
2396	Contact/Don't Waste Your Time	1978	—	2.00	4.00
2408	H.A.P.P.Y. Radio/My Friend	1979	—	2.00	4.00
2420	It's Called the Rock/Patiently	1979	—	2.00	4.00
2423	It's Called the Rock/H.A.P.P.Y. Radio	1979	—	2.00	4.00
2441	It's Called the Rock/H.A.P.P.Y. Radio	1980	—	2.00	4.00
2445	Stronger Than You Think I Am/(Instrumental)	1980	—	2.00	4.00
2450	Tell-A-Star/Boop Boop Song	1980	—	2.00	4.00
2455	Get Up-Whirlpool/Better and Better	1980	—	2.00	4.00
2477	Twenty-Five Miles/Never Turn My Back on You	1980	—	2.00	4.00
2496	Real Live #10/Sweat	1981	—	2.00	4.00
GORDY					
7066	Gonna Keep On Tryin' Til I Win Your Love/I Want My Baby Back	1967	—	3.00	6.00
7071	I Am the Man for You Baby/My Weakness Is You	1968	—	3.00	6.00
7078	Way Over There/If My Heart Could Tell the Story	1968	—	3.00	6.00
7083	Twenty-Five Miles/Love Is the Destination	1969	—	3.00	6.00
7087	I'm Still a Struggling Man/Pretty Little Angel	1969	—	3.00	6.00
7090	Oh How Happy/Ooh Baby Baby	1969	—	3.00	6.00
—With Blinky					
7097	Time/Running Back and Forth	1970	—	3.00	6.00
7101	War/He Who Picks a Rose	1970	—	3.00	6.00
7104	Stop the War Now/Gonna Keep On Tryin' Til I Win Your Love	1970	—	3.00	6.00
7107	Funky Music Sho Nuff Turns Me On/Cloud Nine	1971	—	3.00	6.00
GRANITE					
522	Pain/I'll Never Forget You	1975	—	2.50	5.00
528	Stay with Me/Party	1975	—	2.50	5.00
532	Abyssinia Jones/Beginning	1975	—	2.50	5.00
MONTAGE					
1216	Tired of It/(B-side unknown)	1982	—	2.00	4.00
MOTOWN					
1276	You've Got My Soul on Fire/Love (The Lonely People's Prayer)	1973	—	2.50	5.00
1284	Ain't It Hell Up in Harlem/Don't It Feel Good to Be Free	1973	—	2.50	5.00
1300	Big Papa/Like We Used to Do	1974	—	2.50	5.00
1326	Who's Right or Wrong/Lonely Rainy Days in San Diego	1974	—	2.50	5.00
RIC-TIC					
103	Agent Double-O-Soul/(Instrumental)	1965	3.75	7.50	15.00
107	Back Street/(Instrumental)	1965	3.75	7.50	15.00
109X [DJ]	Scott's On Swingers (S.O.S.)/I Have Faith in You	1966	12.50	25.00	50.00
109	Stop Her on Sight (S.O.S.)/I Have Faith in You	1966	3.75	7.50	15.00
114	Headline News/Harlem	1966	3.75	7.50	15.00
118	It's My Turn Now/Girls Are Getting Prettier	1967	3.75	7.50	15.00
120	You're My Mellow/My Kind of Woman	1967	15.00	30.00	60.00
SOUL					
35096	Take Me Clear from Here/Ball of Confusion	1972	—	3.00	6.00
35100	Who Is the Leader of the People/Don't Tell Me I'm Crazy	1972	—	3.00	6.00
35103	There You Go/(Instrumental)	1973	—	3.00	6.00

Albums

Number	Title (A Side/B Side)	Yr	VG	VG+	NM
20TH CENTURY					
T-538	Edwin Starr	1977	2.50	5.00	10.00
T-559	Clean	1978	2.50	5.00	10.00
T-591	Happy Radio	1979	2.50	5.00	10.00
T-615	Stronger Than You	1980	2.50	5.00	10.00
T-634	The Best of Edwin Starr	1981	2.50	5.00	10.00
GORDY					
GS-931	Soul Master	1968	6.25	12.50	25.00
GS-940	25 Miles	1969	6.25	12.50	25.00
GS-945	Just We Two	1969	5.00	10.00	20.00
—With Blinky					
GS-948	War & Peace	1970	5.00	10.00	20.00
GS-956	Involved	1971	5.00	10.00	20.00
GRANITE					
1005	Free to Be Myself	1975	3.00	6.00	12.00
MOTOWN					
M5-103V1	Superstar Series, Vol. 3	1981	2.50	5.00	10.00
M5-170V1	War & Peace	1981	2.50	5.00	10.00
PICKWICK					
SPC-3387	25 Miles	197?	2.50	5.00	10.00

STARR, KAY

45s

Number	Title (A Side/B Side)	Yr	VG	VG+	NM
ABC					
11013	When the Lights Go On Again (All Over the World)/Only When You're Lonely	1967	—	2.50	5.00
11049	My Melancholy Baby/Some Sweet Tomorrow	1968	—	2.50	5.00
CAPITOL					
F936	Bonaparte's Retreat/Someday Sweetheart	1950	5.00	10.00	20.00
F980	Hoop-Dee-Doo/A Woman Likes to Be Told	1950	5.00	10.00	20.00
F1072	Mississippi/He's a Good Man to Have Around	1950	5.00	10.00	20.00
F1124	I'll Never Be Free/Ain't Nobody's Business But My Own	1950	3.75	7.50	15.00
—With Tennessee Ernie Ford					
F1152	When You're a Long Way from Home/Is There Anything Wrong with Texas (The Texas Song)	1950	3.75	7.50	15.00
F1194	Nobody's Sweetheart/The Honeymoon	1950	3.75	7.50	15.00
F1205	Mama Goes Everywhere Papa Goes/Please Love Me	1950	3.75	7.50	15.00
—With Tennessee Ernie Ford					
F1256	Christopher Robin/The Man with the Bag	1950	3.75	7.50	15.00
F1278	Oh Babe/Everybody's Somebody's Fool	1950	3.75	7.50	15.00
F1357	Lovesick Blues/Evenin'	1951	3.75	7.50	15.00
F1492	Come Back Darling/Then You've Never Been Blue	1951	3.75	7.50	15.00
F1567	Oceans of Tears/You're My Sugar	1951	3.75	7.50	15.00
—With Tennessee Ernie Ford					
F1615	You Were Only Fooling (While I Was Falling in Love)/If I Could Be with You	1951	3.00	6.00	12.00
—Reissue of 78 from 1948					
F1649	I'm the Lonesomest Gal in Town/You've Got to See Mama Every Night	1951	3.00	6.00	12.00
—Reissue					
F1652	Bonaparte's Retreat/The Honeymoon	1951	3.00	6.00	12.00
—Reissue					
F1677	Wheel of Fortune/Angry	195?	2.50	5.00	10.00
—Reissue					
F1688	Side by Side/Breeze	1954	2.50	5.00	10.00
—Reissue					
F1710	Come On-a My House/Hold Me, Hold Me	1951	3.75	7.50	15.00
F1796	Don't Tell Him What's Happened to Me/Angry	1951	3.75	7.50	15.00
F1856	Two Brothers/On Honky Tonk Hardwood Floor	1951	3.75	7.50	15.00
F1902	So Help Me/Hold Me, Hold Me	1951	3.75	7.50	15.00
F1964	Wheel of Fortune/I Wanna Love You	1952	3.75	7.50	15.00
F2062	I Waited a Little Too Long/Me Too	1952	3.00	6.00	12.00
F2151	Fool, Fool, Fool/Kay's Lament	1952	3.00	6.00	12.00
F2213	Comes A-Long A-Love/Three Letters	1952	3.00	6.00	12.00
F2334	Side by Side/Noah	1953	3.00	6.00	12.00
F2464	Half a Photograph/Allez-Vous-En	1953	3.00	6.00	12.00
F2595	When My Dreamboat Comes Home/Swamp Fire	1953	3.75	7.50	15.00
F2657	Changing Partners/I'll Always Be in Love with You	1953	3.00	6.00	12.00
F2769	If You Love Me (Really Love Me)/The Man Upstairs	1954	3.00	6.00	12.00
F2887	Fortune in Dreams/Am I a Toy or Treasure	1954	3.00	6.00	12.00
F4295	Riders in the Sky/Night Train	1959	2.00	4.00	8.00
4419	Out in the Cold Again/Just for a Thrill	1960	2.00	4.00	8.00
4542	Foolin' Around/Kay's Lament	1961	2.00	4.00	8.00
4583	I'll Never Be Free/Nobody	1961	2.00	4.00	8.00
4620	Well I Ask Ya/Rough Riders	1961	2.00	4.00	8.00
4835	Four Walls/Oh Lonesome Me	1962	2.00	4.00	8.00
4835 [PS]	Four Walls/Oh Lonesome Me	1962	3.00	6.00	12.00
4894	Bossa Nova Casanova/Swingin' at the Hungry-O	1962	2.00	4.00	8.00
4983	No Regrets/Cherche La Rose	1963	2.00	4.00	8.00
5046	To Each His Own/Make a Circle	1963	2.00	4.00	8.00
5194	It's Happening All Over Again/Dancing on My Tears	1964	—	3.00	6.00
5259	Together Again/Friends	1964	—	3.00	6.00
5328	Look on the Brighter Side/Lorna's Here	1965	—	3.00	6.00
5386	Happy/I Forgot to Forget	1965	—	3.00	6.00
5492	I Never Dreamed I Could Love You/I Know That You Know That We...	1965	—	3.00	6.00
5601	Old Records/Tears and Photographs	1966	—	3.00	6.00
DOT					
17183	Something Happened to Me/12th Street Marching Band	1968	—	2.50	5.00
GNP CRESCENDO					
468	The Ranger's Waltz/Saturday Night	1973	—	2.00	4.00
476	The New Frankie and Johnny/(B-side unknown)	1974	—	2.00	4.00
488	Tie a Yellow Ribbon Round the Ole Oak Tree/Something's Missing	1974	—	2.00	4.00
493	What Can I Say After I Say I'm Sorry/What Is This Thing Called Love	1975	—	2.00	4.00
HAPPY TIGER					
553	Knock, Knock (Who's There)/Sweet Blindness	1970	—	2.50	5.00
RCA VICTOR					
AMBO-0131	Rock and Roll Waltz/Down by the Riverside	1973	—	2.00	4.00
—"Gold Standard Series" reissue					

Number	Title (A Side/B Side)	Yr	VG	VG+	NM
47-5999	Turn Right/If Anyone Finds This, I Love You	1955	2.50	5.00	10.00
47-6079	For Better or Worse/Foolishly Yours	1955	2.50	5.00	10.00
47-6146	Good and Lonesome/Where, What or When	1955	2.50	5.00	10.00
47-6247	Home Sweet Home on the Range/Without a Song	1955	2.50	5.00	10.00
47-6359	Rock and Roll Waltz/I've Changed My Mind a Thousand Times	1955	2.50	5.00	10.00
47-6541	Second Fiddle/Love Ain't Right	1956	2.50	5.00	10.00
47-6617	The Good Book/The Things I Never Had	1956	2.50	5.00	10.00
47-6748	The Brass Ring/Touch and Go	1956	2.50	5.00	10.00
47-6864	Jamie Boy/A Little Loneliness	1957	2.50	5.00	10.00
47-6981	My Heart Reminds Me/Flim Flam Floo	1957	2.50	5.00	10.00
47-7114	The Last Song and Dance/Help Me	1957	2.50	5.00	10.00
47-7218	Stroll Me/Rockin' Chair	1958	2.50	5.00	10.00
47-7338	Voodoo Man/Bridge of Sighs	1958	2.50	5.00	10.00
47-7414	He Cha-Cha'd Me/Oh How I Miss You Tonight	1958	2.50	5.00	10.00
47-7521	I Couldn't Care Less/Only Love Me	1959	2.50	5.00	10.00

Albums

ABC

Number	Title (A Side/B Side)	Yr	VG	VG+	NM
S-631	When the Lights Go On Again	1968	3.00	6.00	12.00

CAPITOL

Number	Title (A Side/B Side)	Yr	VG	VG+	NM
H 211 [10]	Songs by Starr	1950	17.50	35.00	70.00
T 211 [M]	Songs by Starr	1955	12.50	25.00	50.00
H 363 [10]	Kay Starr Style	1953	17.50	35.00	70.00
T 363 [M]	Kay Starr Style	1955	12.50	25.00	50.00
DT 415 [R]	The Hits of Kay Starr	196?	3.00	6.00	12.00
H 415 [10]	The Hits of Kay Starr	1953	17.50	35.00	70.00
T 415 [M]	The Hits of Kay Starr	1955	12.50	25.00	50.00
—Turquoise or gray label					
T 415 [M]	The Hits of Kay Starr	1958	7.50	15.00	30.00
—Black label with colorband, Capitol logo at left					
T 415 [M]	The Hits of Kay Starr	1962	5.00	10.00	20.00
—Black label with colorband, Capitol logo at top					
T 580 [M]	In a Blue Mood	1955	12.50	25.00	50.00
ST 1254 [S]	Movin'	1959	7.50	15.00	30.00
T 1254 [M]	Movin'	1959	6.25	12.50	25.00
ST 1303 [S]	Losers Weepers	1960	7.50	15.00	30.00
T 1303 [M]	Losers Weepers	1960	6.25	12.50	25.00
ST 1358 [S]	One More Time	1960	7.50	15.00	30.00
T 1358 [M]	One More Time	1960	6.25	12.50	25.00
ST 1374 [S]	Movin' on Broadway	1960	7.50	15.00	30.00
T 1374 [M]	Movin' on Broadway	1960	6.25	12.50	25.00
ST 1438 [S]	Kay Starr, Jazz Singer	1960	10.00	20.00	40.00
T 1438 [M]	Kay Starr, Jazz Singer	1960	7.50	15.00	30.00
ST 1468 [S]	All Starr Hits	1961	7.50	15.00	30.00
T 1468 [M]	All Starr Hits	1961	6.25	12.50	25.00
ST 1681 [S]	I Cry by Night	1962	6.25	12.50	25.00
T 1681 [M]	I Cry by Night	1962	5.00	10.00	20.00
ST-8-1795 [S]	Just Plain Country	196?	7.50	15.00	30.00
—Capitol Record Club edition					
ST 1795 [S]	Just Plain Country	1962	6.25	12.50	25.00
T 1795 [M]	Just Plain Country	1962	5.00	10.00	20.00
ST 2106 [S]	The Fabulous Favorites	1964	3.75	7.50	15.00
T 2106 [M]	The Fabulous Favorites	1964	3.00	6.00	12.00
ST 2550 [S]	Tears and Heartaches/Old Records	1966	3.75	7.50	15.00
T 2550 [M]	Tears and Heartaches/Old Records	1966	3.00	6.00	12.00
SM-11323	Kay Starrs Again	1977	2.00	4.00	8.00
—Reissue with new prefix					
ST-11323	Kay Starrs Again	1974	2.50	5.00	10.00
SM-11880	Movin'	1979	2.50	5.00	10.00

CORONET

Number	Title (A Side/B Side)	Yr	VG	VG+	NM
CX-106 [M]	Kay Starr Sings	196?	3.00	6.00	12.00

GNP CRESCENDO

Number	Title (A Side/B Side)	Yr	VG	VG+	NM
GNPS-2083	Country	1974	2.50	5.00	10.00
GNPS-2090	Back to the Roots	1975	2.50	5.00	10.00

HINDSIGHT

Number	Title (A Side/B Side)	Yr	VG	VG+	NM
HSR-214	Kay Starr 1947	1985	2.50	5.00	10.00

LIBERTY

Number	Title (A Side/B Side)	Yr	VG	VG+	NM
LRP-3280 [M]	Swingin' with the Starr	1963	6.25	12.50	25.00
—Reissue of 9001					
LRP-9001 [M]	Swingin' with the Starr	1956	12.50	25.00	50.00

PARAMOUNT

Number	Title (A Side/B Side)	Yr	VG	VG+	NM
PAS-5001	How About This	1969	3.00	6.00	12.00

RCA CAMDEN

Number	Title (A Side/B Side)	Yr	VG	VG+	NM
CAL-567 [M]	Kay Starr	196?	3.00	6.00	12.00

RCA VICTOR

Number	Title (A Side/B Side)	Yr	VG	VG+	NM
LPM-1149 [M]	The One and Only Kay Starr	1955	7.50	15.00	30.00
ANL1-1311	Pure Gold	1976	2.00	4.00	8.00
LPM-1549 [M]	Blue Starr	1957	7.50	15.00	30.00
LPM-1720 [M]	Rockin' with Kay	1958	12.50	25.00	50.00
LPM-2055 [M]	I Hear the Word	1959	6.25	12.50	25.00
LSP-2055 [S]	I Hear the Word	1959	7.50	15.00	30.00

RONDO-LETTE

Number	Title (A Side/B Side)	Yr	VG	VG+	NM
A-3 [M]	Them There Eyes	1958	6.25	12.50	25.00

SUNSET

Number	Title (A Side/B Side)	Yr	VG	VG+	NM
SUM-1126 [M]	Portrait of a Starr	196?	3.75	7.50	15.00
SUS-5126 [R]	Portrait of a Starr	196?	2.50	5.00	10.00

STARR, KAY/ERROLL GARNER

Also see each artist's individual listings.

Albums

CROWN

Number	Title (A Side/B Side)	Yr	VG	VG+	NM
CLP-5003 [M]	Singin' Kay Starr, Swingin' Erroll Garner	1957	7.50	15.00	30.00

MODERN

Number	Title (A Side/B Side)	Yr	VG	VG+	NM
LMP-1203 [M]	Singin' Kay Starr, Swingin' Erroll Garner	1956	20.00	40.00	80.00

STARR, RAY

45s

KING

Number	Title (A Side/B Side)	Yr	VG	VG+	NM
5652	I Have to Laugh to Keep from Crying/In the Middle of Two Hearts	1962	2.50	5.00	10.00

STARR, RINGO

Also see THE BEATLES; GEORGE HARRISON AND FRIENDS.

12-Inch Singles

ATLANTIC

Number	Title (A Side/B Side)	Yr	VG	VG+	NM
DSKO 93 [DJ]	Drowning in the Sea of Love (5:08) (same on both sides)	1977	7.50	15.00	30.00

45s

APPLE

Number	Title (A Side/B Side)	Yr	VG	VG+	NM
1826 [PS]	Beaucoups of Blues/Coochy-Coochy	1970	10.00	20.00	40.00
—Sleeve with wrong catalog number (actually 2969)					
1831	It Don't Come Easy/Early 1970	1971	2.00	4.00	8.00
1831	It Don't Come Easy/Early 1970	1971	3.00	6.00	12.00
—With star on A-side label					
1831	It Don't Come Easy/Early 1970	1975	7.50	15.00	30.00
—With "All rights reserved" on label					
1831 [PS]	It Don't Come Easy/Early 1970	1971	7.50	15.00	30.00
1849	Back Off Boogaloo/Blindman	1972	2.00	4.00	8.00
—Green-background label					
1849	Back Off Boogaloo/Blindman	1972	18.75	37.50	75.00
—Blue-background label					
1849 [DJ]	Back Off Boogaloo/Blindman	1972	37.50	75.00	150.00
—White label					
1849 [PS]	Back Off Boogaloo/Blindman	1972	3.75	7.50	15.00
—Black paper with flat finish					
1849 [PS]	Back Off Boogaloo/Blindman	1972	10.00	20.00	40.00
—Glossy black paper on both sides					
1849 [PS]	Back Off Boogaloo/Blindman	1972	10.00	20.00	40.00
—Glossy black on one side, gray on the other					
1865	Photograph/Down and Out	1973	—	3.00	6.00
—Custom star label					
1865 [PS]	Photograph/Down and Out	1973	5.00	10.00	20.00
P-1865 [DJ]	Photograph (mono/stereo)	1973	12.50	25.00	50.00
1870	You're Sixteen/Devil Woman	1973	—	3.00	6.00
—Custom star label					
1870	You're Sixteen/Devil Woman	1973	6.25	12.50	25.00
—Regular Apple label					
1870 [PS]	You're Sixteen/Devil Woman	1973	6.25	12.50	25.00
P-1870 [DJ]	You're Sixteen (mono/stereo)	1973	12.50	25.00	50.00
1872	Oh My My/Step Lightly	1974	—	3.00	6.00
—Custom star label					
1872	Oh My My/Step Lightly	1974	2.00	4.00	8.00
—Regular Apple label					
P-1872 [DJ]	Oh My My (Edited Mono)/Oh My My (Long Stereo)	1974	12.50	25.00	50.00
1876	Only You/Call Me	1974	—	3.00	6.00
—Custom nebula label					
1876	Only You/Call Me	1974	2.00	4.00	8.00
—Regular Apple label					
1876 [PS]	Only You/Call Me	1974	5.00	10.00	20.00
P-1876 [DJ]	Only You (mono/stereo)	1974	10.00	20.00	40.00
1880	No No Song/Snookeroo	1975	—	3.00	6.00
—Custom nebula label					
P-1880 [DJ]	No No Song/Snookeroo (both mono)	1975	10.00	20.00	40.00
P-1880 [DJ]	No No Song/Snookeroo (both stereo)	1975	10.00	20.00	40.00
1882	It's All Down to Goodnight Vienna/Oo-Wee	1975	—	3.00	6.00
—Custom star label					
1882 [PS]	It's All Down to Goodnight Vienna/Oo-Wee	1975	5.00	10.00	20.00
P-1882 [DJ]	It's All Down to Goodnight Vienna (mono/stereo)	1975	10.00	20.00	40.00
P-1882 [DJ]	Oo-Wee/Oo-Wee	1975	17.50	35.00	70.00
2969	Beaucoups of Blues/Coochy-Coochy	1970	6.25	12.50	25.00
—With small Capitol logo on bottom of B-side label and star on A-side label					
2969	Beaucoups of Blues/Coochy-Coochy	1970	10.00	20.00	40.00
—With "Mfd. by Apple" on label and star on A-side label					
2969	Beaucoups of Blues/Coochy-Coochy	1970	2.00	4.00	8.00
—With "Mfd. by Apple" on label and no star on A-side label					
2969 [PS]	Beaucoups of Blues/Coochy-Coochy	1970	12.50	25.00	50.00
—Sleeve with correct catalog number					

ATLANTIC

Number	Title (A Side/B Side)	Yr	VG	VG+	NM
3361	A Dose of Rock 'N' Roll/Cryin'	1976	2.50	5.00	10.00
3371	Hey Baby/Lady Gaye	1976	7.50	15.00	30.00
3412	Drowning in the Sea of Love/Just a Dream	1977	30.00	60.00	120.00
3429	Wings/Just a Dream	1977	7.50	15.00	30.00

BOARDWALK

Number	Title (A Side/B Side)	Yr	VG	VG+	NM
NB7-11-130	Wrack My Brain/Drumming Is My Madness	1981	—	2.50	5.00
NB7-11-130 [PS]	Wrack My Brain/Drumming Is My Madness	1981	—	2.50	5.00
NB7-11-134	Private Property/Stop and Take the Time to Smell the Roses	1982	3.00	6.00	12.00

CAPITOL

Number	Title (A Side/B Side)	Yr	VG	VG+	NM
1831	It Don't Come Easy/Early 1970	1976	6.25	12.50	25.00
—Orange label					
1831	It Don't Come Easy/Early 1970	1978	—	3.00	6.00
—Purple late-1970s label					
1831	It Don't Come Easy/Early 1970	1983	—	3.00	6.00
—Black colorband label					
1831	It Don't Come Easy/Early 1970	1988	—	2.50	5.00
—Purple late-1980s label (wider)					
1849	Back Off Boogaloo/Blindman	1976	7.50	15.00	30.00
—Orange label					
1849	Back Off Boogaloo/Blindman	1978	2.00	4.00	8.00
—Purple late-1970s label					
1865	Photograph/Down and Out	1978	2.00	4.00	8.00
—Purple late-1970s label					
1865	Photograph/Down and Out	1983	2.00	4.00	8.00
—Black colorband label					
1865	Photograph/Down and Out	1988	—	3.00	6.00
—Purple late-1980s label (wider)					
1870	You're Sixteen/Devil Woman	1976	15.00	30.00	60.00
—Orange label					
1870	You're Sixteen/Devil Woman	1978	2.00	4.00	8.00
—Purple late-1970s label					
1870	You're Sixteen/Devil Woman	1983	2.00	4.00	8.00
—Black colorband label					
1870	You're Sixteen/Devil Woman	1988	—	2.50	5.00
—Purple late-1980s label (wider)					

Number	Title (A Side/B Side)	Yr	VG	VG+	NM
1876	Only You/Call Me	1978	2.00	4.00	8.00
—Purple late-1970s label					
1876	Only You/Call Me	1983	25.00	50.00	100.00
—Black colorband label					
1880	No No Song/Snookeroo	1978	2.00	4.00	8.00
—Purple late-1970s label					
1880	No No Song/Snookeroo	1983	2.00	4.00	8.00
—Black colorband label					
1880	No No Song/Snookeroo	1988	7.50	15.00	30.00
—Purple late-1980s label (wider)					
1882	It's All Down to Goodnight Vienna/Oo-Wee	1978	2.00	4.00	8.00
—Purple late-1970s label					
2969	Beaucoups of Blues/Coochy-Coochy	1976	10.00	20.00	40.00
—Orange label					
B-44409	Act Naturally/Key's in the Mailbox	1989	3.75	7.50	15.00
—A-side with Buck Owens; B-side is Owens solo					
MERCURY					
MELP-195 [DJ]	La De Da/Everyday	1998	3.75	7.50	15.00
—Number only in the dead wax					
MELP-195 [PS]	La De Da/Everyday	1998	3.75	7.50	15.00
—The above record and sleeve were a giveaway from Beatlefest and J&R's Music World with advance purchase of the CD "Vertical Man" and later from Beatlefest with any Ringo Starr Mercury CD.					
PORTRAIT					
70015	Lipstick Traces (On a Cigarette)/Old Time Relovin'	1978	3.75	7.50	15.00
70018	Heart on My Sleeve/Who Needs a Heart	1978	3.75	7.50	15.00
THE RIGHT STUFF					
S7-18178	In My Car/She's About a Mover	1994	2.00	4.00	8.00
—Gold/orange vinyl					
S7-18179	Wrack My Brain/Private Property	1994	2.00	4.00	8.00
—Red vinyl					

Albums

Number	Title (A Side/B Side)	Yr	VG	VG+	NM
APPLE					
SW-3365	Sentimental Journey	1970	5.00	10.00	20.00
SMAS-3368	Beaucoups of Blues	1970	5.00	10.00	20.00
SWAL-3413	Ringo	1973	5.00	10.00	20.00
—Standard issue with booklet; Side 1, Song 2 identified on cover as "Hold On"					
SWAL-3413	Ringo	1973	100.00	200.00	400.00
—With a 5:26 version of "Six O'Clock." On later copies, the song is shortened to 4:05 though the label still says 5:26. All known copies have a promo punch-hole in top corner of jacket; on Side 2 record, "Six O'Clock" will be the widest track.					
SWAL-3413	Ringo	1974	6.25	12.50	25.00
—Later issue with booklet; Side 1, Song 2 identified on cover as "Have You Seen My Baby"					
SW-3417	Goodnight Vienna	1974	3.00	6.00	12.00
SW-3422	Blast from Your Past	1975	3.75	7.50	15.00
ATLANTIC					
SD 18193	Ringo's Rotogravure	1976	3.75	7.50	15.00
—Deduct 2/3 for cut-outs					
SD 18193 [DJ]	Ringo's Rotogravure	1976	7.50	15.00	30.00
—With "DJ Only" scrawled into trail-off area					
SD 19108	Ringo the 4th	1977	3.75	7.50	15.00
—Deduct 1/2 for cut-outs					
SD 19108 [DJ]	Ringo the 4th	1977	7.50	15.00	30.00
—With "DJ Only" scrawled into trail-off area					
BOARDWALK					
NB1-33246	Stop and Smell the Roses	1981	2.50	5.00	10.00
—Deduct 1/2 for cut-outs					
CAPITOL					
SW-3365	Sentimental Journey	197?	10.00	20.00	40.00
—Purple label, large Capitol logo					
SN-16114	Ringo	198?	3.75	7.50	15.00
—Green label budget-line reissue with all errors corrected					
SN-16218	Sentimental Journey	198?	6.25	12.50	25.00
—Green label budget-line reissue					
SN-16218	Goodnight Vienna	198?	6.25	12.50	25.00
—Green label budget-line reissue					
SN-16235	Beaucoups of Blues	198?	5.00	10.00	20.00
—Green label budget-line reissue					
SN-16236	Blast from Your Past	198?	3.75	7.50	15.00
—Green label budget-line reissue					
PORTRAIT					
JR 35378	Bad Boy	1978	3.75	7.50	15.00
—Deduct 1/3 for cut-outs					
JR 35378 [DJ]	Bad Boy	1978	25.00	50.00	100.00
—White label promo with "Advance Promotion" on label; in plain white cover					
JR 35378 [DJ]	Bad Boy	1978	7.50	15.00	30.00
—Regular white-label promo in standard jacket					
RHINO					
R1 70199	Starr Struck: Ringo's Best 1976-1983	1989	6.25	12.50	25.00
RYKODISC					
RALP 0190	Ringo Starr and His All-Starr Band	1990	7.50	15.00	30.00
—With limited, numbered obi (deduct $5 if missing)					

STARR, SALLY

Philadelphia TV star backed by members of BILL HALEY AND HIS COMETS.

45s

Number	Title (A Side/B Side)	Yr	VG	VG+	NM
ARCADE					
157	Rocky the Rockin' Rabbit/Sing a Song of Happiness	1960	7.50	15.00	30.00
CLYMAX					
301	Rockin' in the Nursery/Little Pedro	1959	10.00	20.00	40.00

7-Inch Extended Plays

Number	Title (A Side/B Side)	Yr	VG	VG+	NM
CLYMAX					
EP-1001/2/3 [PS]	Our Gal Sal	1959	10.00	20.00	40.00
—Triple gatefold cover for all three EP-1001 records (despite what the cover says, the records are each numbered 1001)					
EP-1001	Toy Shop in the Town/Happy Birthday//Candy Red/Blue Ranger	1959	7.50	15.00	30.00
—First record of 3-EP set; master numbers are JB-140/JB-141					
EP-1001	Cuckoo in the Clock/Sing a Song of Happiness//TV Pal/A.B.C. Rock	1959	7.50	15.00	30.00
—Second record of 3-EP set; master numbers are JB 142/JB 143					
EP-1001	Rockin' in the Nursery/Little Pedro//Rockin' Horse Cowgirl/Good Night Dear Lord	1959	7.50	15.00	30.00
—Third record of 3-EP set; master numbers are JB-144/JB-145					

Albums

Number	Title (A Side/B Side)	Yr	VG	VG+	NM
ARCADE					
1001 [M]	Our Gal Sal	1960	20.00	40.00	80.00
CLYMAX					
1001 [M]	Our Gal Sal	1959	50.00	100.00	200.00

STARSHIP

No relation to the 1980s Starship, this features MICKEY DOLENZ.

45s

Number	Title (A Side/B Side)	Yr	VG	VG+	NM
LION					
132	Johnny B. Goode/It's Amazing to Me	1973	6.25	12.50	25.00

STATENS, THE

45s

Number	Title (A Side/B Side)	Yr	VG	VG+	NM
MARK-X					
8011	Summertime Is the Time for Love/That Certain Kind	1961	20.00	40.00	80.00

STATLER BROTHERS, THE

45s

Number	Title (A Side/B Side)	Yr	VG	VG+	NM
COLUMBIA					
43069	The Wreck of the Old 97/Hammer and Nails	1964	3.00	6.00	12.00
43146	I Still Miss Someone/You're a Foolish Game	1964	3.00	6.00	12.00
43315	Flowers on the Wall/Billy Christian	1965	2.50	5.00	10.00
43315 [DJ]	Flowers on the Wall (same on both sides)	1965	5.00	10.00	20.00
—Promo only on red vinyl					
43526	The Doodlin' Song/My Darling Hildegarde	1966	2.00	4.00	8.00
43624	The Right One/Is That What You'd Have Me Do	1966	2.00	4.00	8.00
43868	That'll Be the Day/Makin' Rounds	1966	2.00	4.00	8.00
44070	Ruthless/Do You Love Me Tonight	1967	2.00	4.00	8.00
44245	You Can't Have Your Kate and Edith, Too/Walking in the Sunshine	1967	2.00	4.00	8.00
44480	Jump for Joy/Take a Bow, Rufus Humfry	1968	2.00	4.00	8.00
44608	Sissy/I Am the Boy	1968	2.00	4.00	8.00
44899	Oh Happy Day/How Great Thou Art	1969	2.00	4.00	8.00
MERCURY					
55000	Silver Medals and Sweet Memories/The Regular Saturday Night Setback Card Game	1977	—	2.00	4.00
55013	Some I Wrote/Carried Away	1977	—	2.00	4.00
55022	Do You Know You Are My Sunshine/You're the First	1978	—	2.00	4.00
55037	Who Am I to Say/I Dreamed About You	1978	—	2.00	4.00
55046	I Believe in Santa's Cause/Who Do You Think	1978	—	2.00	4.00
55048	The Official Historian on Shirley Jean Berrell/The Best That I Can Do	1978	—	2.00	4.00
55057	How to Be a Country Star/A Little Farther Down the Road	1979	—	2.00	4.00
55066	Here We Are Again/Mr. Autry	1979	—	2.00	4.00
57007	Nothing As Original As You/Counting My Memories	1979	—	2.00	4.00
57012	(I'll Even Love You) Better Than I Did Then/Almost in Love	1980	—	2.00	4.00
57031	Charlotte's Web/One Less Day to Go	1980	—	2.00	4.00
57037	Don't Forget Yourself/We Got Paid by Cash	1980	—	2.00	4.00
57048	In the Garden/How Are Things in Clay, Kentucky	1981	—	2.00	4.00
57051	Don't Wait on Me/Chet Atkins' Band	1981	—	2.00	4.00
57059	Years Ago/Dad	1981	—	2.00	4.00
73141	Bed of Rose's/The Last Goodbye	1970	—	2.50	5.00
73194	New York City/This Part of the World	1971	—	2.50	5.00
73229	Pictures/Making Memories	1971	—	2.50	5.00
73253	You Can't Go Home/Second Thoughts	1971	—	2.50	5.00
73275	Do You Remember These/Since Then	1972	—	2.50	5.00
73315	The Class of '57/Every Time I Trust a Gal	1972	—	2.50	5.00
73360	Monday Morning Secretary/Special Song for Wanda	1973	—	2.50	5.00
73392	Woman Without a Home/I'll Be Your Baby Tonight	1973	—	2.50	5.00
73415	Carry Me Back/I Wish I Could Be	1973	—	2.50	5.00
73448	Whatever Happened to Randolph Scott/The Strand	1974	—	2.50	5.00
73485	Thank You World/The Blackwood Brothers by the Statler Brothers	1974	—	2.50	5.00
73625	Susan When She Tried/She's Too Good	1974	—	2.50	5.00
73665	All American Girl/A Few Old Memories	1975	—	2.50	5.00
73687	I'll Go to My Grave Loving You/You've Been Like a Mother to Me	1975	—	2.50	5.00
73732	How Great Thou Art/Noah Found Grace in the Eyes of the Lord	1975	—	2.50	5.00
73785	Your Picture in the Paper/All the Times	1976	—	2.50	5.00
73846	Thank God I've Got You/Hat and Boots	1976	—	2.50	5.00
73877	The Movies/You Could Be Coming to Me	1976	—	2.50	5.00
73906	I Was There/Somebody New Will Be Coming Along	1977	—	2.50	5.00
76130	I Never Spend A Christmas That I Don't Think Of You/Who Do You Think?	1981	—	2.00	4.00
76142	You'll Be Back (Every Night in My Dreams)/We Ain't Even Started Yet	1982	—	—	3.00
76162	Whatever/Do You Know You Are My Sunshine	1982	—	—	3.00
76184	A Child of the Fifties/I'll Love You All Over Again	1982	—	—	3.00
811488-7	Oh Baby Mine (I Get So Lonely)/I'm Dyin' a Little Each Day	1983	—	—	3.00
812988-7	Guilty/I Never Want to Kiss You Goodbye	1983	—	—	3.00
814881-7	Elizabeth/Class of '57	1983	—	—	3.00
818700-7	Atlanta Blue/If It Makes Any Difference	1984	—	—	3.00
818700-7 [PS]	Atlanta Blue/If It Makes Any Difference	1984	—	2.00	4.00
866302-7	Atlanta Blue/Put It on the Card	1991	—	2.00	4.00
868140-7	Remember Me/My Music, My Memories and You	1991	—	—	3.00
868484-7	You've Been Like a Mother to Me/Jesus Is the Answer	1991	—	2.00	4.00
868892-7	There's Still Times/Elizabeth	1991	—	—	3.00
870164-7	The Best I Know How/I Lost My Heart to You	1988	—	—	3.00
870442-7	Am I Crazy?/Beyond Romance	1988	—	—	3.00

Number	Title (A Side/B Side)	Yr	VG	VG+	NM
870681-7	Let's Get Started If We're Gonna Break My Heart/Guilty	1988	—	—	3.00
872604-7	Moon Pretty Moon/I'll Be the One	1989	—	—	3.00
874196-7	More Than a Name on the Wall/Atlanta Blue	1989	—	—	3.00
875498-7	Small Small World/My Music, My Memories and You	1990	—	—	3.00
876112-7	Don't Wait on Me/A Hurt I Can't Handle	1989	—	—	3.00
876876-7	Walkin' Heartache in Disguise/The Official Historian on Shirley Jean Berrell	1990	—	—	3.00
878386-7	He Is There/Nobody Else	1991	—	2.00	4.00
880130-7	One Takes the Blame/Give It Your Best	1984	—	—	3.00
880411-7	My Only Love/Let's Just Take One Night at a Time	1984	—	—	3.00
880685-7	Hello Mary Lou/Remembering You	1985	—	—	3.00
884016-7	Too Much on My Heart/Her Heart or Mine	1985	—	—	3.00
884317-7	Sweeter and Sweeter/Amazing Grace	1985	—	—	3.00
884320-7	Christmas Eve (Kodia's Theme)/Mary's Sweet Smile	1985	—	—	3.00
884721-7	Count On Me/Will You Be There?	1986	—	—	3.00
888042-7	Only You/We Got the Mem'ries	1986	—	—	3.00
888219-7	Forever/More Like Daddy Than Me	1986	—	—	3.00
888650-7	I'll Be the One/Deja Vu	1987	—	—	3.00
888920-7	Maple Street Mem'ries/Jesus Showed Me So	1987	—	—	3.00
7-Inch Extended Plays					
MERCURY					
DJ 577 [DJ]	I Never Spend a Christmas That I Don't Think of You/Jingle Bells//Away in a Manger/The Carols Those Kids Used to Sing	1978	—	3.00	6.00
DJ 577 [PS]	A Very Merry Christmas from the Statler Brothers	1978	2.00	4.00	8.00
Albums					
COLUMBIA					
CL 2449 [M]	Flowers on the Wall	1966	6.25	12.50	25.00
CL 2719 [M]	The Big Hits	1967	7.50	15.00	30.00
CS 9249 [S]	Flowers on the Wall	1966	7.50	15.00	30.00
PC 9249	Flowers on the Wall	198?	2.00	4.00	8.00
—Reissue with new prefix					
CS 9519 [S]	The Big Hits	1967	6.25	12.50	25.00
PC 9519	The Big Hits	198?	2.00	4.00	8.00
—Reissue with new prefix					
CS 9878	Oh Happy Day	1969	6.25	12.50	25.00
PC 9878	Oh Happy Day	198?	2.00	4.00	8.00
—Reissue with new prefix					
CG 31557 [(2)]	The World of the Statler Brothers	198?	3.00	6.00	12.00
—Reissue with new prefix					
KG 31557 [(2)]	The World of the Statler Brothers	1972	5.00	10.00	20.00
C 31560	How Great Thou Art	197?	2.50	5.00	10.00
—Reissue of Harmony 31560					
HARMONY					
H 30610	Big Country Hits	1971	3.00	6.00	12.00
KH 31560	How Great Thou Art	1972	3.00	6.00	12.00
KH 32256	Do You Love Me Tonight	1973	3.00	6.00	12.00
MERCURY					
SRM-2-101 [(2)]	Holy Bible/The Old and New Testaments	1978	5.00	10.00	20.00
—Reissue of 1051 and 1052 in one package					
SRM-1-676	Carry Me Back	1973	3.75	7.50	15.00
SRM-1-707	Thank You World	1974	3.75	7.50	15.00
SRM-1-1019	Sons of the Motherland	1975	3.75	7.50	15.00
SRM-1-1037	The Best of the Statler Brothers	1975	3.00	6.00	12.00
SRM-1-1051	Holy Bible: Old Testament	1975	3.75	7.50	15.00
SRM-1-1052	Holy Bible: New Testament	1975	3.75	7.50	15.00
SRM-1-1077	Harold, Lew, Phil & Don	1976	3.75	7.50	15.00
SRM-1-1125	The Country America Loves	1977	3.75	7.50	15.00
SRM-1-4048	The Legend Goes On	1982	3.00	6.00	12.00
SRM-1-5001	Short Stories	1977	3.00	6.00	12.00
SRM-1-5007	Entertainers...On and Off the Record	1978	3.00	6.00	12.00
SRM-1-5012	Christmas Card	1978	2.50	5.00	10.00
SRM-1-5016	The Originals	1979	3.00	6.00	12.00
SRM-1-5024	The Best of the Statler Brothers Rides Again, Volume II	1980	3.00	6.00	12.00
SRM-1-5027	10th Anniversary	1980	3.00	6.00	12.00
SRM-1-6002	Years Ago	1981	3.00	6.00	12.00
SR-61317	Bed of Rose's	1970	3.75	7.50	15.00
SR-61349	Pictures of Moments to Remember	1971	3.75	7.50	15.00
SR-61358	Innerview	1972	3.75	7.50	15.00
SR-61367	Country Music "Then and Now"	1972	3.75	7.50	15.00
SR-61374	The Statler Brothers Sing Country Symphonies in E Major	1973	3.75	7.50	15.00
812184-1	Today	1983	2.50	5.00	10.00
812282-1	10th Anniversary	1983	2.00	4.00	8.00
812283-1	Entertainers...On and Off the Record	1983	2.00	4.00	8.00
812284-1	Carry Me Back	1983	2.00	4.00	8.00
818652-1	Atlanta Blue	1984	2.50	5.00	10.00
822524-1	The Best of the Statler Brothers	1984	2.00	4.00	8.00
822525-1	The Best of the Statler Brothers Rides Again, Volume II	1984	2.00	4.00	8.00
822743-1	Christmas Card	1985	2.00	4.00	8.00
824420-1	Pardners in Rhyme	1985	2.50	5.00	10.00
824785-1	Christmas Present	1985	2.50	5.00	10.00
826247-1	Bed of Rose's	1986	2.00	4.00	8.00
826259-1	Innerview	1986	2.00	4.00	8.00
826260-1	Country Music "Then and Now"	1986	2.00	4.00	8.00
826264-1 [(2)]	Holy Bible/The Old and New Testaments	1986	2.50	5.00	10.00
826267-1	Holy Bible: Old Testament	1986	2.00	4.00	8.00
826268-1	Holy Bible: New Testament	1986	2.00	4.00	8.00
826269-1	Harold, Lew, Phil & Don	1986	2.00	4.00	8.00
826275-1	The Country America Loves	1986	2.00	4.00	8.00
826278-1	The Legend Goes On	1986	2.00	4.00	8.00
826280-1	Short Stories	1986	2.00	4.00	8.00
826281-1	The Originals	1986	2.00	4.00	8.00
826710-1	Radio Gospel Favorites	1986	2.50	5.00	10.00
826782-1	Four for the Show	1986	2.50	5.00	10.00
832404-1	Maple Street Memories	1987	2.50	5.00	10.00
834626-1	The Statlers Greatest Hits	1988	2.50	5.00	10.00
838231-1	Statler Brothers Live — Sold Out	1989	3.75	7.50	15.00
PRIORITY					
PU 37709	Country Gospel	1982	2.50	5.00	10.00

STATLERS, THE

Number	Title (A Side/B Side)	Yr	VG	VG+	NM
45s					
LITTLE STAR					
108	Vicky/Gone	1962	37.50	75.00	150.00

STATON, CANDI

Number	Title (A Side/B Side)	Yr	VG	VG+	NM
12-Inch Singles					
LA					
8012	Without You I Cry (4:47)/(B-side unknown)	1981	2.50	5.00	10.00
SUGAR HILL					
568	Count On Me/(Instrumental)	1981	2.50	5.00	10.00
571	Suspicious Minds/Love and Be Free	1982	2.50	5.00	10.00
WARNER BROS.					
PRO-A-772 [DJ]	Honest I Do Love You (6:31) (same on both sides)	1978	3.00	6.00	12.00
PRO-A-827 [DJ]	Chance (5:34)/Rock (7:16)	1979	3.00	6.00	12.00
PRO-A-867 [DJ]	Looking for Love (same on both sides)	1980	3.00	6.00	12.00
8820	When You Wake Up Tomorrow/Rough Times	1979	3.00	6.00	12.00
45s					
FAME					
XW256	Something's Burning/It's Not Love	1973	—	2.50	5.00
XW328	Love Chain/I'm Gonna Hold On	1973	—	2.50	5.00
1456	I'd Rather Be an Old Man's Sweetheart (Than a Young Man's Fool)/For You	1969	—	3.00	6.00
1459	Never in Public/You Don't Love Me No More	1969	—	3.00	6.00
1460	I'm Just a Prisoner (Of Your Good Lovin')/Heart on a String	1969	—	3.00	6.00
1466	Sweet Feeling/Evidence	1970	—	3.00	6.00
1472	Stand By Your Man/How Can I Put Out the Flame (When You Keep the Fire Burning)	1970	—	3.00	6.00
1476	He Called Me Baby/What Would Become of Me	1970	—	3.00	6.00
1478	Mr. and Mrs. Untrue/Too Hurt to Cry	1971	—	3.00	6.00
91000	In the Ghetto/Sure As Sin	1972	—	2.50	5.00
91005	Lovin' You, Lovin' Me/You Don't Love Me No More	1972	—	2.50	5.00
91009	Do It in the Name of Love/The Thanks I Get for Loving You	1972	—	2.50	5.00
LA					
0080	Without You I Cry/(B-side unknown)	1981	—	2.50	5.00
SUGAR HILL					
770	Count on Me/(B-side unknown)	1981	—	2.50	5.00
776	Suspicious Minds/(B-side unknown)	1982	—	2.50	5.00
784	Hurry Sundown/Count on Me	1982	—	2.50	5.00
UNITY					
711	Now That You Have the Upper Hand/(B-side unknown)	196?	37.50	75.00	150.00
WARNER BROS.					
8038	As Long As He Takes Care of Business/Little Taste of Love	1974	—	2.00	4.00
8078	Here I Am Again/Your Opening Night	1975	—	2.00	4.00
8112	Six Nights and a Day/We Can Work It Out	1975	—	2.00	4.00
8181	Young Hearts Run Free/I Know	1976	—	2.00	4.00
8249	Run to Me/What a Feeling	1976	—	2.00	4.00
8320	A Dreamer of a Dream/When You Want Love	1977	—	2.00	4.00
8387	Nights on Broadway/You Are	1977	—	2.00	4.00
8461	Music Speaks Louder Than Words/Cotton Candi	1977	—	2.00	4.00
8477	Listen to the Music/Music Speaks Louder Than Words	1977	—	2.00	4.00
8582	Victim/So Blue	1978	—	2.00	4.00
8691	Honest I Do Love You/I'm Gonna Make Me Love You	1978	—	2.00	4.00
8821	When You Wake Up Tomorrow/Rough Times	1979	—	2.00	4.00
49061	Chance/I Live	1979	—	2.00	4.00
49240	Looking for Love/It's Real	1980	—	2.00	4.00
49240 [PS]	Looking for Love/It's Real	1980	—	3.00	6.00
49536	The Hunter Gets Captured by the Game/If You Feel the Need	1980	—	2.00	4.00
Albums					
FAME					
1800	Candi Staton	1972	5.00	10.00	20.00
ST-4201	I'm a Prisoner	1970	5.00	10.00	20.00
ST-4202	Stand By Your Man	1971	5.00	10.00	20.00
WARNER BROS.					
BS 2830	Candi	1974	3.00	6.00	12.00
BS 2948	Young Hearts Run Free	1976	3.00	6.00	12.00
BS 3040	Music Speaks Louder Than Words	1977	3.00	6.00	12.00
BSK 3207	House of Love	1978	3.00	6.00	12.00
BSK 3333	Chance	1979	3.00	6.00	12.00
BSK 3428	Candi Staton	1980	3.00	6.00	12.00

STATON, DAKOTA

Number	Title (A Side/B Side)	Yr	VG	VG+	NM
45s					
CAPITOL					
F3010	My Heart's Delight/What Do You Know About Love	1955	3.00	6.00	12.00
F3059	For the Rest of My Life/No Mama, No Papa	1955	3.00	6.00	12.00
F3128	Don't Leave Me Now/Little You	1955	3.00	6.00	12.00
F3181	Abracadabra/I Never Dreamt	1955	3.00	6.00	12.00
F3293	It Feels So Nice/Dangerous Age	1955	3.00	6.00	12.00
F3361	How High the Moon/Weak for the Man	1956	3.00	6.00	12.00
F3489	My Friend/Don't Mean Maybe	1956	3.00	6.00	12.00
F3546	You Know I Do/I Told You So	1956	3.00	6.00	12.00
F3876	The Late Late Show/Trust in Me	1958	2.50	5.00	10.00
F3958	Invitation/The Party's Over	1958	2.50	5.00	10.00
F4012	Confessin' the Blues/Blues in My Heart	1958	2.50	5.00	10.00
F4299	Where Did You Go?/Avalon	1959	2.50	5.00	10.00
4372	My Babe/Romance in the Dark	1960	2.50	5.00	10.00
4465	First Things First/I Don't Worry	1960	2.50	5.00	10.00
4512	All in My Mind/Hey Lawdy Mama	1961	2.50	5.00	10.00
4673	When I Grow Too Old to Dream/Mean and Evil Blues	1961	2.50	5.00	10.00
4790	Porgy/On Chapel Hill	1962	2.50	5.00	10.00
4910	Once There Lived a Fool/You'd Better Go Now	1963	2.50	5.00	10.00
GROOVE MERCHANT					
1011	Let It Be Me/Losing Battle	1972	—	2.50	5.00

Number	Title (A Side/B Side)	Yr	VG	VG+	NM
1017	(I Want a) Country Man/I Love You More Than You'll Ever Know	1973	—	2.50	5.00
1019	How Did He Look/Girl Talk	1973	—	2.50	5.00
UNITED ARTISTS					
611	When It's Sleepy Time Down South/ Massachusetts	1963	2.00	4.00	8.00
7-Inch Extended Plays					
CAPITOL					
EAP 1-876	*Broadway/Trust in Me/Moonray/Ain't No Use	1958	3.75	7.50	15.00
EAP 1-876 [PS]	The Late, Late Show, Part 1	1958	3.75	7.50	15.00
EAP 2-876	(contents unknown)	1958	3.75	7.50	15.00
EAP 2-876 [PS]	The Late, Late Show, Part 2	1958	3.75	7.50	15.00
EAP 1-1170	*Crazy He Calls Me/Idaho/How Does It Feel?/ How High the Moon	1959	3.75	7.50	15.00
EAP 1-1170 [PS]	Crazy He Calls Me, Part 1	1959	3.75	7.50	15.00
EAP 2-1170	(contents unknown)	1959	3.75	7.50	15.00
EAP 2-1170 [PS]	Crazy He Calls Me, Part 2	1959	3.75	7.50	15.00
Albums					
CAPITOL					
DT 876 [R]	The Late, Late Show	196?	3.00	6.00	12.00
SM-876	The Late, Late Show	1977	2.50	5.00	10.00
—Reissue with new prefix					
T 876 [M]	The Late, Late Show	1957	12.50	25.00	50.00
—Turquoise or gray label					
T 876 [M]	The Late, Late Show	1959	7.50	15.00	30.00
—Black label with colorband, Capitol logo at left					
T 876 [M]	The Late, Late Show	1962	3.75	7.50	15.00
—Black label with colorband, Capitol logo at top					
M-1003	In the Night	1976	2.50	5.00	10.00
—Reissue with new prefix					
T 1003 [M]	In the Night	1958	12.50	25.00	50.00
—Turquoise or gray label					
T 1003 [M]	In the Night	1959	7.50	15.00	30.00
—Black label with colorband, Capitol logo at left					
ST 1054 [S]	Dynamic!	1959	10.00	20.00	40.00
—Black label with colorband, Capitol logo at left					
ST 1054 [S]	Dynamic!	1962	5.00	10.00	20.00
—Black label with colorband, Capitol logo at top					
T 1054 [M]	Dynamic!	1958	7.50	15.00	30.00
—Black label with colorband, Capitol logo at left					
T 1054 [M]	Dynamic!	1962	3.75	7.50	15.00
—Black label with colorband, Capitol logo at top					
ST 1170 [S]	Crazy He Calls Me	1959	10.00	20.00	40.00
—Black label with colorband, Capitol logo at left					
ST 1170 [S]	Crazy He Calls Me	1962	5.00	10.00	20.00
—Black label with colorband, Capitol logo at top					
T 1170 [M]	Crazy He Calls Me	1959	7.50	15.00	30.00
—Black label with colorband, Capitol logo at left					
T 1170 [M]	Crazy He Calls Me	1962	3.75	7.50	15.00
—Black label with colorband, Capitol logo at top					
ST 1241 [S]	Time to Swing	1959	10.00	20.00	40.00
—Black label with colorband, Capitol logo at left					
ST 1241 [S]	Time to Swing	1962	5.00	10.00	20.00
—Black label with colorband, Capitol logo at top					
T 1241 [M]	Time to Swing	1959	7.50	15.00	30.00
—Black label with colorband, Capitol logo at left					
T 1241 [M]	Time to Swing	1962	3.75	7.50	15.00
—Black label with colorband, Capitol logo at top					
ST 1325 [S]	More Than the Most	1960	10.00	20.00	40.00
—Black label with colorband, Capitol logo at left					
ST 1325 [S]	More Than the Most	1962	5.00	10.00	20.00
—Black label with colorband, Capitol logo at top					
T 1325 [M]	More Than the Most	1960	7.50	15.00	30.00
—Black label with colorband, Capitol logo at left					
T 1325 [M]	More Than the Most	1962	3.75	7.50	15.00
—Black label with colorband, Capitol logo at top					
ST 1387 [S]	Ballads and the Blues	1960	10.00	20.00	40.00
—Black label with colorband, Capitol logo at left					
ST 1387 [S]	Ballads and the Blues	1962	5.00	10.00	20.00
—Black label with colorband, Capitol logo at top					
T 1387 [M]	Ballads and the Blues	1960	7.50	15.00	30.00
—Black label with colorband, Capitol logo at left					
T 1387 [M]	Ballads and the Blues	1962	3.75	7.50	15.00
—Black label with colorband, Capitol logo at top					
ST 1427 [S]	Softly	1961	10.00	20.00	40.00
—Black label with colorband, Capitol logo at left					
ST 1427 [S]	Softly	1962	5.00	10.00	20.00
—Black label with colorband, Capitol logo at top					
T 1427 [M]	Softly	1961	7.50	15.00	30.00
—Black label with colorband, Capitol logo at left					
T 1427 [M]	Softly	1962	3.75	7.50	15.00
—Black label with colorband, Capitol logo at top					
ST 1490 [S]	Dakota	1961	10.00	20.00	40.00
—Black label with colorband, Capitol logo at left					
ST 1490 [S]	Dakota	1962	5.00	10.00	20.00
—Black label with colorband, Capitol logo at top					
T 1490 [M]	Dakota	1961	7.50	15.00	30.00
—Black label with colorband, Capitol logo at left					
T 1490 [M]	Dakota	1962	3.75	7.50	15.00
—Black label with colorband, Capitol logo at top					
ST 1597 [S]	'Round Midnight	1961	10.00	20.00	40.00
—Black label with colorband, Capitol logo at left					
ST 1597 [S]	'Round Midnight	1962	5.00	10.00	20.00
—Black label with colorband, Capitol logo at top					
T 1597 [M]	'Round Midnight	1961	7.50	15.00	30.00
—Black label with colorband, Capitol logo at left					
T 1597 [M]	'Round Midnight	1962	3.75	7.50	15.00
—Black label with colorband, Capitol logo at top					
ST 1649 [S]	Dakota at Storyville	1962	6.25	12.50	25.00
T 1649 [M]	Dakota at Storyville	1962	5.00	10.00	20.00
GROOVE MERCHANT					
510	Madame Foo-Foo	1972	3.00	6.00	12.00
521	I Want a Country Man	1973	3.00	6.00	12.00
532	Ms. Soul	1974	3.00	6.00	12.00
4410 [(2)]	Confessin'	197?	3.75	7.50	15.00

Number	Title (A Side/B Side)	Yr	VG	VG+	NM
LONDON					
PS 495 [S]	Dakota '67	1967	3.75	7.50	15.00
LL 3495 [M]	Dakota '67	1967	5.00	10.00	20.00
MUSE					
MR-5401	Dakota Staton	1991	3.75	7.50	15.00
UNITED ARTISTS					
UAL-3292 [M]	From Dakota with Love	1963	5.00	10.00	20.00
UAL-3312 [M]	Live and Swinging	1963	5.00	10.00	20.00
UAL-3355 [M]	Dakota Staton with Strings	1964	5.00	10.00	20.00
UAS-6292 [S]	From Dakota with Love	1963	6.25	12.50	25.00
UAS-6316 [S]	Live and Swinging	1963	6.25	12.50	25.00
UAS-6355 [S]	Dakota Staton with Strings	1964	6.25	12.50	25.00
VERVE					
V6-8799	I've Been There	1971	3.75	7.50	15.00
STATUES, THE					
45s					
HOLIDAY					
1026 [DJ]	White Christmas/Get Off My Roof	197?	3.00	6.00	12.00
—B-side by Jerry and the Landsliders					
LIBERTY					
55245	Blue Velvet/Keep the Hall Light Burning	1959	5.00	10.00	20.00
55292	White Christmas/Jeannie with the Light Brown Hair	1960	6.25	12.50	25.00
55363	Ten Commandments of Love/Love at First Sight	1961	5.00	10.00	20.00
STATUS QUO					
45s					
A&M					
1425	Don't Waste My TIme/All the Reasons	1973	—	2.50	5.00
1445	Paper Plane/All the Reasons	1973	—	2.50	5.00
1510	Carolina/Softer Ride	1974	—	2.50	5.00
BELL					
45417	Gerdundula/(B-side unknown)	1973	—	2.50	5.00
CADET CONCEPT					
7001	Pictures of Matchstick Men/Gentleman Joe's Sidewalk Café	1968	2.50	5.00	10.00
7006	Ice in the Sun/When My Mind Is Not Live	1968	2.00	4.00	8.00
7010	Technicolor Dreams/Spicks and Specks	1969	2.00	4.00	8.00
7015	Black Veils of Melancholy/To Be Free	1969	2.00	4.00	8.00
7017	The Price of Love/Little Miss Nothing	1969	2.00	4.00	8.00
CAPITOL					
4039	Nightride/Down Down	1975	—	2.00	4.00
4125	Bye Bye Johnny/Down Down	1975	—	2.00	4.00
4407	Wild Side of Life/All Through the Night	1977	—	2.00	4.00
JANUS					
127	Down the Dustpipe/Face Without a Soul	1970	—	3.00	6.00
141	Gerdundula/In My Chair	1970	—	3.00	6.00
PYE					
65000	Good Thinking/Tuned to the Music	1971	—	3.00	6.00
65017	Mean Girl/Everything	1971	—	3.00	6.00
RIVA					
206	Living on an Island/(B-side unknown)	1980	—	2.50	5.00
Albums					
A&M					
SP-3615	Hello!	1974	3.00	6.00	12.00
SP-3649	Quo	1974	3.00	6.00	12.00
SP-4381	Piledriver	1973	3.00	6.00	12.00
CADET CONCEPT					
LPS-315	Messages from the Status Quo	1968	12.50	25.00	50.00
CAPITOL					
ST-11381	On the Level	1975	2.50	5.00	10.00
ST-11509	Status Quo	1976	2.50	5.00	10.00
SKBB-11623 [(2)]	Status Quo Live	1977	3.00	6.00	12.00
ST-11779	Rockin' All Over the World	1978	2.50	5.00	10.00
JANUS					
JLS-3018	Ma Kelly's Greasy Spoon	1970	3.75	7.50	15.00
MERCURY					
836651-1	Status Quo	1989	3.00	6.00	12.00
PYE					
3301	Dog of Two Heads	1971	3.75	7.50	15.00
RIVA					
7402	Now Here This	1980	2.50	5.00	10.00
STEALERS WHEEL					
Also see GERRY RAFFERTY.					
45s					
A&M					
1416	Stuck in the Middle with You/Jose	1973	—	2.50	5.00
1450	Everyone's Agreed That Everything Will Turn Out Fine/Next to Me	1973	—	2.00	4.00
1483	Star/What More Could You Want	1973	—	2.00	4.00
1483 [PS]	Star/What More Could You Want	1973	—	3.00	6.00
1529	You Put Something Better Inside of Me/Wheelin'	1974	—	2.00	4.00
1675	This Morning/Found My Way to You	1975	—	2.00	4.00
2075	(Everyone's Agreed That) Everything Will Turn Out Fine/Who Cares	1978	—	2.50	5.00
Albums					
A&M					
SP-4377	Stealers Wheel	1973	3.00	6.00	12.00
SP-4419	Ferguslie Park	1974	3.00	6.00	12.00
SP-4517	Right or Wrong	1974	3.00	6.00	12.00
SP-4708	Stuck in the Middle with You — The Best of Stealers Wheel	1978	2.50	5.00	10.00
STEAM					
45s					
FONTANA					
1667	Na Na Hey Hey Kiss Him Goodbye/It's the Magic in You Girl	1969	2.00	4.00	8.00

Number	Title (A Side/B Side)	Yr	VG	VG+	NM
MERCURY					
30160	Na Na Hey Hey Kiss Him Goodbye/Don't Stop Lovin' Me	1976	—	2.00	4.00
—Reissue					
30160 [PS]	Na Na Hey Hey Kiss Him Goodbye/Don't Stop Lovin' Me	1976	5.00	10.00	20.00
—Special Chicago White Sox sleeve, available only in that area					
73020	I've Gotta Make You Love Me/One Good Woman	1970	—	3.00	6.00
73053	What I'm Saying Is True/I'm the One Who Loves You	1970	—	3.00	6.00
73117	Don't Stop Lovin' Me/Do Unto Others	1970	—	3.00	6.00
Albums					
MERCURY					
SR 61254	Steam	1969	5.00	10.00	20.00

STEAMHAMMER

Number	Title (A Side/B Side)	Yr	VG	VG+	NM
Albums					
EPIC					
BN 26490	Reflection	1969	7.50	15.00	30.00
BN 26552	Steamhammer	1970	7.50	15.00	30.00

STEEL

Number	Title (A Side/B Side)	Yr	VG	VG+	NM
45s					
EPIC					
5-10753	Never on a Monday/Rosie Lee	1971	2.00	4.00	8.00
Albums					
EPIC					
E 30875	Steel	1971	5.00	10.00	20.00

STEELE, TOMMY

Number	Title (A Side/B Side)	Yr	VG	VG+	NM
45s					
BUENA VISTA					
457	Fortuosity/I'm a Brass Band Today	1067	2.00	4.00	8.00
LONDON					
1706	Doomsday Rock/Elevator Rock	1957	3.75	7.50	15.00
1735	Butterfingers/Teenage Party	1957	3.75	7.50	15.00
1760	Water, Water/A Handful of Songs	1958	3.75	7.50	15.00
1795	Nairobi/Neon Sign	1958	3.75	7.50	15.00
1824	Swaller Tail Coat/The Only Man Across the Way	1959	3.75	7.50	15.00
1838	Hey You/Number 22 Across the Way	1959	3.75	7.50	15.00
1878	The Trail/Give, Give, Give	1959	3.75	7.50	15.00
1950	She's My Baby/Happy-Go-Lucky Blues	1960	3.75	7.50	15.00
RCA VICTOR					
47-8602	Half a Sixpence/If the Rain's Got to Fall	1965	2.50	5.00	10.00
47-9458	Half a Sixpence/If the Rain's Got to Fall	1968	2.00	4.00	8.00
Albums					
LIBERTY					
LRP-3426 [M]	Everything's Coming Up Broadway	1965	5.00	10.00	20.00
LST-7426 [S]	Everything's Coming Up Broadway	1965	6.25	12.50	25.00
LST-7566 [S]	Sixpenny Millionaire	1968	3.75	7.50	15.00
LONDON					
LL 1770 [M]	Rock Around the World	195?	12.50	25.00	50.00

STEELEYE SPAN

Number	Title (A Side/B Side)	Yr	VG	VG+	NM
45s					
CHRYSALIS					
2008	Gaudete/Royal Forester	1972	—	3.00	6.00
2102	Gaudete/Royal Forester	1974	—	2.50	5.00
2262	Rag Doll/Hunting the Wren	1978	—	2.00	4.00
Albums					
BIG TREE					
BTS-2004	Please to See the King	1971	7.50	15.00	30.00
CHRYSALIS					
CHR 1008	Below the Salt	1972	3.75	7.50	15.00
—Green label, "3300 Warner Blvd." address					
CHR 1008	Below the Salt	1977	3.00	6.00	12.00
—Blue label, New York address					
CHR 1046	Parcel of Rogues	1973	3.75	7.50	15.00
—Green label, "3300 Warner Blvd." address					
CHR 1046	Parcel of Rogues	1977	3.00	6.00	12.00
—Blue label, New York address					
CHR 1053	Now We Are Six	1974	3.75	7.50	15.00
—Green label, "3300 Warner Blvd." address					
CHR 1053	Now We Are Six	1977	3.00	6.00	12.00
—Blue label, New York address					
CHR 1071	Commoners Crown	1975	3.75	7.50	15.00
—Green label, "3300 Warner Blvd." address					
CHR 1071	Commoners Crown	1977	3.00	6.00	12.00
—Blue label, New York address					
CHR 1091	All Around My Hat	1975	3.75	7.50	15.00
—Green label, "3300 Warner Blvd." address					
CHR 1091	All Around My Hat	1977	3.00	6.00	12.00
—Blue label, New York address					
CHR 1119	Please to See the King	1976	3.75	7.50	15.00
—Reissue of Big Tree LP; green label, "3300 Warner Blvd." address					
CHR 1119	Please to See the King	1977	3.00	6.00	12.00
—Blue label, New York address					
CHR 1120	Hark the Village Wait	1976	3.75	7.50	15.00
—First US issue of debut LP; green label, "3300 Warner Blvd." address					
CHR 1120	Hark the Village Wait	1977	3.00	6.00	12.00
—Blue label, New York address					
CHR 1121	Ten Man Mop	1976	3.75	7.50	15.00
—First US issue of third UK LP; green label, "3300 Warner Blvd." address					
CHR 1121	Ten Man Mop	1977	3.00	6.00	12.00
—Blue label, New York address					
CHR 1123	Rocket Cottage	1976	3.75	7.50	15.00
—Green label, "3300 Warner Blvd." address					
CHR 1123	Rocket Cottage	1977	3.00	6.00	12.00
—Blue label, New York address					
CHR2 1136 [(2)]	The Steeleye Span Story: Original Masters	1977	3.75	7.50	15.00
CHR 1151	Storm Force Ten	1978	3.00	6.00	12.00
CHR 1199	Live at Last	1978	3.00	6.00	12.00
V2X 41136 [(2)]	The Steeleye Span Story: Original Masters	1984	3.00	6.00	12.00
—Reissue of 1136					
MOBILE FIDELITY					
1-027	All Around My Hat	1980	6.25	12.50	25.00
—Audiophile vinyl					
SHANACHIE					
64020	Tempted and Tried	1989	3.00	6.00	12.00
79039	Below the Salt	1989	3.00	6.00	12.00
79045	Parcel of Rogues	1989	3.00	6.00	12.00
79049	Ten Man Mop	1989	3.00	6.00	12.00
79052	Hark the Village Wait	1989	3.00	6.00	12.00
79059	All Around My Hat	1989	3.00	6.00	12.00
79060	Now We Are Six	1989	3.00	6.00	12.00
79063	Back in Line	1989	3.00	6.00	12.00
79071/2 [(2)]	Portfolio	1990	5.00	10.00	20.00
TAKOMA					
TAK-7097	Sails of Silver	1981	2.50	5.00	10.00

STEELY DAN

Number	Title (A Side/B Side)	Yr	VG	VG+	NM
12-Inch Singles					
ABC					
SPDJ-26 [DJ]	Aja (same on both sides)	1977	5.00	10.00	20.00
SPDJ-32 [DJ]	Deacon Blues (same on both sides)	1978	5.00	10.00	20.00
SPDJ-36 [DJ]	Josie (same on both sides)	1978	5.00	10.00	20.00
SPDJ-47 [DJ]	Here at the Western World (same on both sides)	1978	3.75	7.50	15.00
45s					
ABC					
11323	Dallas/Sail the Waterway	1972	7.50	15.00	30.00
—Neither of these songs has appeared on a U.S. Steely Dan album -- not even the "complete" CD box set!					
11338	Do It Again/Fire in the Hole	1972	—	2.00	4.00
11352	Reeling In the Years/Only a Fool Would Say That	1973	—	2.00	4.00
11382	Show Biz Kids/Razor Boy	1973	—	2.00	4.00
11396	My Old School/Pearl of the Quarter	1973	—	2.00	4.00
11439	Rikki Don't Lose That Number/Any Major Dude Will Tell You	1974	—	2.00	4.00
12014	Rikki Don't Lose That Number/Any Major Dude Will Tell You	1974	—	3.00	6.00
12033	Pretzel Logic/Through with Buzz	1974	—	2.00	4.00
12101	Black Friday/Throw Back the Little Ones	1975	—	2.00	4.00
12128	Chain Lightning/Bad Sneakers	1975	—	2.00	4.00
12195	Kid Charlemagne/Green Earrings	1976	—	2.00	4.00
12222	The Fez/Sign In Stranger	1976	—	2.00	4.00
12320	Peg/I Got the News	1977	—	2.00	4.00
12355	Deacon Blues/Home at Last	1978	—	2.00	4.00
12404	Josie/Black Cow	1978	—	2.00	4.00
MCA					
40894	FM (No Static at All)/(Instrumental)	1978	—	2.00	4.00
51036	Hey Nineteen/Bodhisattva	1980	—	2.00	4.00
51082	Time Out of Mind/Bodhisattva	1981	—	2.00	4.00
Albums					
ABC					
758	Can't Buy a Thrill	1972	3.00	6.00	12.00
—Black label					
758	Can't Buy a Thrill	1974	2.50	5.00	10.00
—Multicolor label					
779	Countdown to Ecstasy	1973	3.00	6.00	12.00
—Black label					
779	Countdown to Ecstasy	1974	2.50	5.00	10.00
—Multicolor label					
806	Pretzel Logic	1974	3.00	6.00	12.00
—Black label					
806	Pretzel Logic	1974	2.50	5.00	10.00
—Multicolor label					
846	Katy Lied	1975	3.00	6.00	12.00
931	The Royal Scam	1976	3.00	6.00	12.00
AA-1006	Aja	1977	3.00	6.00	12.00
AK-1107 [(2)]	Greatest Hits	1978	3.75	7.50	15.00
ABC DUNHILL					
SMAS-94976	Can't Buy a Thrill	1973	6.25	12.50	25.00
—Capitol Record Club edition pressed on the wrong label					
COMMAND					
QD-40009 [Q]	Can't Buy a Thrill	1974	5.00	10.00	20.00
QD-40010 [Q]	Countdown to Ecstasy	1974	5.00	10.00	20.00
QD-40015 [Q]	Pretzel Logic	1974	5.00	10.00	20.00
MCA					
AA-1006	Aja	1980	2.50	5.00	10.00
1591	Can't Buy a Thrill	1987	—	3.00	6.00
1592	Countdown to Ecstasy	1987	—	3.00	6.00
1593	Pretzel Logic	1987	—	3.00	6.00
1594	Katy Lied	1987	—	3.00	6.00
1595	The Royal Scam	1987	—	3.00	6.00
1688	Aja	1987	—	3.00	6.00
—Many in the 1500 and 1600 series have a gold stamp with the new number on the cover					
1693	Gaucho	1987	—	3.00	6.00
5324	Gold	1982	2.50	5.00	10.00
2-6008 [(2)]	Greatest Hits	1980	3.00	6.00	12.00
6102	Gaucho	1980	2.50	5.00	10.00
16009	Gaucho	1981	12.50	25.00	50.00
—Audiophile pressing					
16016	Gold	1982	12.50	25.00	50.00
—Audiophile pressing					
37040	Can't Buy a Thrill	1980	2.00	4.00	8.00
37041	Countdown to Ecstasy	1980	2.00	4.00	8.00
37042	Pretzel Logic	1980	2.00	4.00	8.00
37043	Katy Lied	1980	2.00	4.00	8.00
37044	The Royal Scam	1980	2.00	4.00	8.00
37243	Gold	1984	2.00	4.00	8.00
MOBILE FIDELITY					
1-007	Katy Lied	1979	20.00	40.00	80.00
—Audiophile vinyl					
1-033	Aja	1980	12.50	25.00	50.00
—Audiophile vinyl					

STEIN, FRANK N., AND THE TOMBSTONES

Number	Title (A Side/B Side)	Yr	VG	VG+	NM
45s					
MARCO					
003	Mess Around/Graveyard Giggle	1962	10.00	20.00	40.00

STEIN, FRANKIE, AND THE GHOULS

Number	Title (A Side/B Side)	Yr	VG	VG+	NM
45s					
KING					
6414	Franken Boogie/All She Wants to Do Is Boogie	1972	2.50	5.00	10.00
POWER					
338	Goon River/Weerdo the Wolf	1964	6.25	12.50	25.00
338 [PS]	Goon River/Weerdo the Wolf	1964	7.50	15.00	30.00

STEINBERG, DAVID

Number	Title (A Side/B Side)	Yr	VG	VG+	NM
45s					
COLUMBIA					
46075	The Nixon Tapes/The Exam	1974	—	2.50	5.00
Albums					
COLUMBIA					
KC 32563	Booga Booga	1974	2.50	5.00	10.00
PC 33390	Goodbye to the Seventies	1975	2.50	5.00	10.00
ELEKTRA					
EKS-74063	Disguised as a Normal Person	1970	3.00	6.00	12.00
UNI					
73013	The Incredible Shrinking God	1968	3.75	7.50	15.00

STEPHENS, LEIGH

Number	Title (A Side/B Side)	Yr	VG	VG+	NM
45s					
PHILIPS					
40628	Red Weather/Saki Swadoo	1969	3.00	6.00	12.00
Albums					
PHILIPS					
PHS 600294	Red Weather	1969	20.00	40.00	80.00

STEPPENWOLF

Also see SPARROW.

Number	Title (A Side/B Side)	Yr	VG	VG+	NM
45s					
ABC					
1436	The Pusher/Born to Be Wild	1970	—	2.00	4.00
—"Goldies 45" series					
1436 [PS]	The Pusher/Born to Be Wild	1970	—	3.00	6.00
ABC DUNHILL					
4138	Born to Be Wild/Everybody's Next One	1968	2.00	4.00	8.00
4161	Magic Carpet Ride/Sookie Sookie	1968	2.00	4.00	8.00
4182	Rock Me/Jupiter Child	1969	2.00	4.00	8.00
4192	It's Never Too Late/Happy Birthday	1969	—	3.00	6.00
4205	Move Over/Power Play	1969	—	3.00	6.00
4221	Monster/Berry Rides Again	1969	—	3.00	6.00
4234	Hey Lawdy Mama/Twisted	1970	—	3.00	6.00
4248	Screaming Night Hog/Spiritual Fantasy	1970	—	3.00	6.00
4261	Who Needs Ya/Earschplittenloudenboomer	1970	—	3.00	6.00
4269	Snow Blind Friend/Hippo Stomp	1971	—	2.50	5.00
4283	Ride with Me/Black Pit	1971	—	2.50	5.00
4283	Ride with Me/For Madmen Only	1971	—	2.50	5.00
4283 [PS]	Ride with Me/For Madmen Only	1971	—	3.00	6.00
4292	For Ladies Only/Sparkle Eyes	1971	—	2.50	5.00
ALLEGIANCE					
3909	Hot Night in a Cold Town/Every Man for Himself	1983	—	2.00	4.00
—As "John Kay and Steppenwolf"					
DUNHILL					
4109	The Ostrich/A Girl I Know	1967	2.50	5.00	10.00
4123	Sookie Sookie/Take What You Need	1968	2.50	5.00	10.00
MUMS					
6031	Straight Shootin' Woman/Justice, Don't Be Slow	1974	—	2.00	4.00
6031 [PS]	Straight Shootin' Woman/Justice, Don't Be Slow	1974	—	3.00	6.00
6034	Get Into the Wind/Morning Blue	1974	—	2.00	4.00
6036	Fool's Fantasy/Smokey Factory Blues	1975	—	2.00	4.00
6040	Caroline (Are You Ready for the Outlaw)/Angel Drawers	1975	—	2.00	4.00
Albums					
ABC					
AC-30008	The ABC Collection	1976	3.75	7.50	15.00
ABC DUNHILL					
DS-50029 [S]	Steppenwolf	1968	5.00	10.00	20.00
DS-50037	The Second	1968	6.25	12.50	25.00
—With chrome border on cover					
DS-50037	The Second	1968	7.50	15.00	30.00
—With white border on cover					
DSX-50053	At Your Birthday Party	1969	5.00	10.00	20.00
DSX-50060	Early Steppenwolf	1969	5.00	10.00	20.00
—Actually a 1967 concert by Sparrow (pre-Steppenwolf)					
DSX-50066	Monster	1969	5.00	10.00	20.00
DSD-50075 [(2)]	Steppenwolf 'Live'	1970	6.25	12.50	25.00
DSX-50090	Steppenwolf 7	1970	5.00	10.00	20.00
DSX-50099	Steppenwolf Gold/Their Great Hits	1971	5.00	10.00	20.00
DSX-50101	For Ladies Only	1971	5.00	10.00	20.00
DSX-50124	Rest in Peace	1972	5.00	10.00	20.00
DSX-50135	16 Greatest Hits	1973	5.00	10.00	20.00
DUNHILL					
D-50029 [M]	Steppenwolf	1968	37.50	75.00	150.00
DS-50029 [S]	Steppenwolf	1968	10.00	20.00	40.00
EPIC					
PE 33583	Hour of the Wolf	1975	3.00	6.00	12.00
PE 34120	Skullduggery	1976	3.00	6.00	12.00
JE 34382	Reborn to Be Wild	1977	3.00	6.00	12.00
MCA					
2-6013 [(2)]	Steppenwolf 'Live'	198?	2.50	5.00	10.00
37045	Steppenwolf	1979	2.00	4.00	8.00
37046	The Second	1979	2.00	4.00	8.00
37047	Steppenwolf 7	1979	2.00	4.00	8.00
37049	16 Greatest Hits	1979	2.00	4.00	8.00
DSX-50099	Steppenwolf Gold/Their Great Hits	1980	3.00	6.00	12.00
—Columbia House edition on blue rainbow label, but retaining the original ABC Dunhill catalog number					
MUMS					
KZ 33093	Slow Flux	1974	3.75	7.50	15.00
NAUTILUS					
NR-53	Wolftracks	198?	12.50	25.00	50.00
—As "John Kay and Steppenwolf"; audiophile vinyl					

STEVE & EYDIE

See STEVE LAWRENCE AND EYDIE GORME.

STEVENS, APRIL

Also see NINO TEMPO AND APRIL STEVENS.

Number	Title (A Side/B Side)	Yr	VG	VG+	NM
45s					
ATCO					
6346	Teach Me Tiger 1965/Morning Till Midnight	1965	2.00	4.00	8.00
6380	Lovin' Valentine/No Hair Say	1965	2.00	4.00	8.00
A&M					
1636	Marry Me Again/Gotta Leave You Baby	1974	—	2.00	4.00
CONTRACT					
429	You and Only You/Love Kitten	1961	3.75	7.50	15.00
IMPERIAL					
5626	Teach Me, Tiger/That Warm Afternoon	1959	5.00	10.00	20.00
5666	In Other Words/Jonny	1960	3.75	7.50	15.00
5761	You and Only You/Love Kitten	1961	3.75	7.50	15.00
5907	Fly Me to the Moon/That's My Name	1963	3.75	7.50	15.00
KING					
5826	Soft Warm Lips/How Could Red Riding Hood	1963	2.50	5.00	10.00
RCA VICTOR					
47-4148	I'm in Love Again/Roller Coaster	1951	5.00	10.00	20.00
—With Henri Rene					
47-4208	Gimme a Little Kiss, Will Ya, Huh?/Dreamy Melody	1951	5.00	10.00	20.00
—With Henri Rene					
47-4283	And So to Sleep Again/Aw, C'mon	1951	5.00	10.00	20.00
47-4381	Put Me in Your Pocket/The Tricks of the Trade	1951	5.00	10.00	20.00
47-4567	I Love the Way You're Breaking My Heart/Meant to Tell You	1952	5.00	10.00	20.00
47-4876	I Like to Talk to Myself/That Naughty Waltz	1952	5.00	10.00	20.00
Albums					
AUDIO LAB					
AL-1534 [M]	Torrid Tunes	1959	50.00	100.00	200.00
IMPERIAL					
LP-9118 [M]	Teach Me Tiger	1960	15.00	30.00	60.00
LP-12055 [S]	Teach Me Tiger	1960	25.00	50.00	100.00

STEVENS, CAT

Number	Title (A Side/B Side)	Yr	VG	VG+	NM
12-Inch Singles					
A&M					
8440 [DJ]	Was Dog a Doughnut (Remix) (same on both sides)	1977	3.75	7.50	15.00
45s					
A&M					
1211	Lady D'Arbanville/Time — Fill My Eyes	1970	—	2.50	5.00
1231	Wild World/Miles from Nowhere	1970	—	2.50	5.00
1265	Moon Shadow/I Think I See the Light	1971	—	2.00	4.00
1265 [PS]	Moon Shadow/I Think I See the Light	1971	—	3.00	6.00
1291	Peace Train/Where Do the Children Play	1971	—	2.00	4.00
1291 [PS]	Peace Train/Where Do the Children Play	1971	—	3.00	6.00
1335	Morning Has Broken/I Want to Live in a Wigwam	1972	—	2.00	4.00
1335 [PS]	Morning Has Broken/I Want to Live in a Wigwam	1972	—	3.00	6.00
1396	Sitting/Crab Dance	1972	—	2.00	4.00
1396 [PS]	Sitting/Crab Dance	1972	—	3.00	6.00
1418	The Hurt/Silent Sunlight	1973	—	2.00	4.00
1418 [PS]	The Hurt/Silent Sunlight	1973	—	3.00	6.00
1503	Oh Very Young/100 I Dream	1974	—	2.00	4.00
1503 [PS]	Oh Very Young/100 I Dream	1974	—	3.00	6.00
1549	Another Saturday Night/Home in the Sky	1974	—	—	—
—Unreleased?					
1602	Another Saturday Night/Home in the Sky	1974	—	2.00	4.00
1602 [PS]	Another Saturday Night/Home in the Sky	1974	—	3.00	6.00
1645	Ready/I Think I See the Light	1974	—	2.00	4.00
1700	Two Fine People/Bad Penny	1975	—	2.00	4.00
1785	Banapple Gas/Ghost Town	1976	—	2.00	4.00
1785 [PS]	Banapple Gas/Ghost Town	1976	—	3.00	6.00
1924	(I Never Wanted) To Be a Star/Land O' Freelove and Goodbye	1977	—	2.00	4.00
1948	(Remember the Days of the) Old School Yard/ Land O' Freelove and Goodbye	1977	—	2.00	4.00
1948 [PS]	(Remember the Days of the) Old School Yard/ Land O' Freelove and Goodbye	1977	—	3.00	6.00
1971	Was Dog a Doughnut/Sweet Jamaica	1977	—	2.00	4.00
2109	Bad Brakes/Nascimento	1979	—	2.00	4.00
2126	Randy/Nascimento	1979	—	2.00	4.00
2683	If You Want to Sing Out, Sing Out/I Want to Live in a Wigwam	1984	—	2.00	4.00
2711 [DJ]	Father and Son (same on both sides)	1985	2.50	5.00	10.00
—No stock copies issued					
DERAM					
7501	I Love My Dog/Portobello Road	1966	2.50	5.00	10.00
7505	Matthew and Son/Granny	1967	2.50	5.00	10.00
7518	Kitty/The Blackness of the Night	1968	2.00	4.00	8.00
85006	I'm Gonna Get Me a Gun/School Is Out	1967	2.50	5.00	10.00
85015	Laughing Apple/Bad Night	1967	2.50	5.00	10.00
85079	Kitty/Where Are You	1972	—	3.00	6.00
Albums					
A&M					
SP-3160	Mona Bone Jakon	198?	2.00	4.00	8.00
—Reissue of 4260					
SP-3285	Footsteps in the Dark — Greatest Hits, Volume Two	1986	2.00	4.00	8.00
—Reissue of 3736					

Number	Title (A Side/B Side)	Yr	VG	VG+	NM
SP-3623	Buddha and the Chocolate Box	1974	3.00	6.00	12.00
SP-3736	Footsteps in the Dark — Greatest Hits, Volume Two	1984	2.50	5.00	10.00
SP-4260	Mona Bone Jakon	1970	3.00	6.00	12.00
—Brown label					
SP-4260	Mona Bone Jakon	1974	2.50	5.00	10.00
—Mostly silver label with gradually fading "A&M"					
SP-4280	Tea for the Tillerman	1971	3.00	6.00	12.00
—Brown label					
SP-4280	Tea for the Tillerman	1974	2.50	5.00	10.00
—Mostly silver label with gradually fading "A&M"					
SP-4313	Teaser and the Firecat	1971	3.00	6.00	12.00
—Brown label					
SP-4313	Teaser and the Firecat	1974	2.50	5.00	10.00
—Mostly silver label with gradually fading "A&M"					
SP-4365	Catch Bull at Four	1972	3.00	6.00	12.00
SP-4391	Foreigner	1973	3.00	6.00	12.00
SP-4519	Greatest Hits	1975	3.00	6.00	12.00
SP-4555	Numbers	1975	3.00	6.00	12.00
SP-4702	Izitso	1977	3.00	6.00	12.00
SP-4735	Back to Earth	1978	3.00	6.00	12.00
QU-53623 [Q]	Buddha and the Chocolate Box	1974	5.00	10.00	20.00
QU-54280 [Q]	Tea for the Tillerman	1974	5.00	10.00	20.00
QU-54313 [Q]	Teaser and the Firecat	1974	5.00	10.00	20.00
QU-54365 [Q]	Catch Bull at Four	1974	5.00	10.00	20.00
QU-54391 [Q]	Foreigner	1974	5.00	10.00	20.00
QU-54519 [Q]	Greatest Hits	1975	5.00	10.00	20.00
DERAM					
DE 16005 [M]	Matthew and Son	1967	5.00	10.00	20.00
DES 18005 [P]	Matthew and Son	1967	3.75	7.50	15.00
DES 18005/10 [(2) P]	Matthew and Son/New Masters	1971	3.75	7.50	15.00
DES 18010 [S]	New Masters	1968	3.75	7.50	15.00
DES 18061 [P]	Very Young and Early Songs	1972	3.00	6.00	12.00
LONDON					
LC 50010	Cat's Cradle	1977	3.00	6.00	12.00
820321-1	Cat's Cradle	1985	2.00	4.00	8.00
MOBILE FIDELITY					
1-035	Tea for the Tillerman	1979	10.00	20.00	40.00
—Audiophile vinyl					
MFQR-035	Tea for the Tillerman	1984	30.00	60.00	120.00
—Ultra High Quality Recording in a box					
1-244	Teaser and the Firecat	1996	10.00	20.00	40.00
—Audiophile vinyl					
1-254	Izitso	1996	6.25	12.50	25.00
—Audiophile vinyl					

STEVENS, CONNIE

Also see EDD BYRNES.

45s

Number	Title (A Side/B Side)	Yr	VG	VG+	NM
BELL					
866	She'll Never Understand Him/5:30 Plane	1970	—	2.50	5.00
922	Keep Growing Strong/Tick-Tock	1970	—	2.50	5.00
992	Keep Growing Strong/(B-side unknown)	1971	—	2.50	5.00
45234	Simple Girl/(B-side unknown)	1972	—	2.50	5.00
MGM					
13906	Cinderella Could Have Saved Us All/Wouldn't It Be Nice (To Have Wings and Fly)	1968	—	3.00	6.00
WARNER BROS.					
5092	Apollo/Why Do I Cry for Joey	1959	5.00	10.00	20.00
5137	Sixteen Reasons/Little Sister	1960	3.75	7.50	15.00
—First pressing has pink labels					
5137	Sixteen Reasons/Little Sister	1960	3.00	6.00	12.00
—Second pressing has red label with arrows					
5159	Too Young to Go Steady/A Little Kiss Is a Kiss Is a Kiss	1960	3.00	6.00	12.00
5159 [PS]	Too Young to Go Steady/A Little Kiss Is a Kiss Is a Kiss	1960	7.50	15.00	30.00
5217	Make Believe Lover/And This Is Mine	1961	3.00	6.00	12.00
5232	If You Don't, Somebody Else Will/Greenwood Tree	1961	3.00	6.00	12.00
5265	Why'd You Wanna Make Me Cry/Just One Kiss	1962	3.00	6.00	12.00
5289	Mr. Songwriter/I Couldn't Say No	1962	3.00	6.00	12.00
5318	Hey, Good Lookin'/Nobody's Lonesome for Me	1962	3.00	6.00	12.00
5380	Little Miss Understood/There Goes Your Guy	1963	2.50	5.00	10.00
5425	A Girl Never Knows/They're Jealous of Me	1964	2.50	5.00	10.00
5610	Now That You've Gone/Lost in Wonderland	1965	3.00	6.00	12.00
5656	In the Deep of Night/Something Beautiful	1965	2.50	5.00	10.00
5691	Don't You Want to Love Me/In My Room (El Amor)	1966	2.50	5.00	10.00
5804	All of My Life/That's All I Want from You	1966	2.50	5.00	10.00
5834	How Bitter the Taste of Love/Most of All	1966	2.50	5.00	10.00
5872	It'll Never Happen Again/What Will I Tell Him	1966	2.50	5.00	10.00
7128	Sixteen Reasons/Make Believe Lover	1968	—	2.50	5.00
—"Back to Back Hits" series -- originals have green labels with "W7" logo					

Albums

Number	Title (A Side/B Side)	Yr	VG	VG+	NM
HARMONY					
HS 11312	The Hank Williams Songbook	1969	3.75	7.50	15.00
WARNER BROS.					
W 1208 [M]	Conchetta	1958	12.50	25.00	50.00
WS 1208 [S]	Conchetta	1958	15.00	30.00	60.00
W 1382 [M]	Connie Stevens from "Hawaiian Eye"	1960	7.50	15.00	30.00
WS 1382 [S]	Connie Stevens from "Hawaiian Eye"	1960	10.00	20.00	40.00
W 1431 [M]	From Me to You	1962	7.50	15.00	30.00
WS 1431 [S]	From Me to You	1962	10.00	20.00	40.00
W 1432 [M]	Connie	1962	7.50	15.00	30.00
WS 1432 [S]	Connie	1962	10.00	20.00	40.00
W 1460 [M]	The Hank Williams Songbook	1962	7.50	15.00	30.00
WS 1460 [S]	The Hank Williams Songbook	1962	10.00	20.00	40.00

STEVENS, DEBBIE

45s

Number	Title (A Side/B Side)	Yr	VG	VG+	NM
ABC-PARAMOUNT					
10034	Billy Boy's Theme/I Sit and Cry	1959	3.75	7.50	15.00
APT					
25027	If You Can't Rock Me/What Will I Tell My Heart	1959	6.25	12.50	25.00

STEVENS, DODIE

45s

Number	Title (A Side/B Side)	Yr	VG	VG+	NM
CRYSTALETTE					
724	Pink Shoe Laces/Coming of Age	1959	5.00	10.00	20.00
724 [PS]	Pink Shoe Laces/Coming of Age	1959	—	—	—
—Rumored to exist, but without conclusive evidence, we will delete this from future editions					
728	Yes-Sir-Ee/The Five Pennies	1959	5.00	10.00	20.00
DOLTON					
83	You Don't Have to Prove a Thing to Me/I Wore Out Our Record	1963	3.00	6.00	12.00
88	Sailor Boy/Does Goodnight Mean Goodbye	1964	3.00	6.00	12.00
DOT					
15975	Miss Lonely Heart/Poor Butterfly	1959	5.00	10.00	20.00
16002	Steady Date/Mairzy Doats	1959	5.00	10.00	20.00
16067	Candy Store Blues/Gringo's Guitar	1960	3.75	7.50	15.00
16103	No/A Tisket, A Tasket	1960	3.75	7.50	15.00
16139	Am I Too Young/So Let's Dance	1960	3.75	7.50	15.00
16166	Merry Christmas Baby/Jingle Bells	1960	5.00	10.00	20.00
16167	Yes, I'm Lonesome Tonight/Too Young	1960	5.00	10.00	20.00
16200	I Fall to Pieces/Turn Around	1961	3.75	7.50	15.00
16259	Let Me Tell You About Johnny/You Are the Only One	1961	3.75	7.50	15.00
16279	The In-Between Years/Trade Winds	1961	3.75	7.50	15.00
16339	I Cried/Dancing on My Ceiling	1962	3.75	7.50	15.00
16389	Pink Shoelaces/Yes-Sir-Ee	1962	3.75	7.50	15.00
IMPERIAL					
5908	Don't Send Me No Roses/Daddy Could Get Me One of These	1963	3.75	7.50	15.00
5930	Hello Stranger/For a Little While	1963	3.75	7.50	15.00

Albums

Number	Title (A Side/B Side)	Yr	VG	VG+	NM
DOT					
DLP-3212 [M]	Dodie Stevens	1960	7.50	15.00	30.00
DLP-3323 [M]	Over the Rainbow	1900	7.50	15.00	30.00
DLP-3371 [M]	Pink Shoelaces	1961	7.50	15.00	30.00
DLP-25212 [S]	Dodie Stevens	1960	10.00	20.00	40.00
DLP-25323 [S]	Over the Rainbow	1960	10.00	20.00	40.00
DLP-25371 [S]	Pink Shoelaces	1961	10.00	20.00	40.00

STEVENS, JOHNNY

45s

Number	Title (A Side/B Side)	Yr	VG	VG+	NM
FORD					
123	Oh Yeah/Last Chicken in the Shack	1963	7.50	15.00	30.00
PARKWAY					
805	Apple Taffy/Mm, Baby, Mm	1959	6.25	12.50	25.00

STEVENS, MARK, AND THE CHARMERS

45s

Number	Title (A Side/B Side)	Yr	VG	VG+	NM
ALLISON					
921	Magic Rose/Come Back to My Heart	1962	15.00	30.00	60.00

STEVENS, NEIL

45s

Number	Title (A Side/B Side)	Yr	VG	VG+	NM
BRUNSWICK					
55095	More and More/What Could Be Better	1958	7.50	15.00	30.00
—With the Dee-Vines					
GOLDISC					
3019	Ballad of Love/Tonight My Heart She Is Crying	1961	5.00	10.00	20.00
—With the Temptations					
GONE					
5067	Ballad of Love/Gambler's Game	1959	12.50	25.00	50.00

STEVENS, RAY

45s

Number	Title (A Side/B Side)	Yr	VG	VG+	NM
BARNABY					
514	Gitarzan/Unwind	197?	—	2.00	4.00
515	Everything Is Beautiful/Turn Your Radio On	197?	—	2.00	4.00
516	Mr. Businessman/Sunday Morning Comin' Down	197?	—	2.00	4.00
517	Ahab the Arab/Along Came Jones	197?	—	2.00	4.00
518	Freddie Feelgood (And His Funky Little Five Piece Band)/Isn't It Lonely Together	197?	—	2.00	4.00
519	Have a Little Talk with Myself/Bridget the Midget (The Queen of the Blues)	197?	—	2.00	4.00
—Barnaby releases in the 500 series are reissues; some may be re-recordings					
600	The Streak/You've Got the Music Inside	1974	—	2.50	5.00
—White label (not a promo)					
600	The Streak/You've Got the Music Inside	1974	—	2.00	4.00
—Multicolor label					
605	Moonlight Special/Just So Proud to Be Here	1974	—	2.00	4.00
610	Everybody Needs a Rainbow/Inside	1974	—	2.00	4.00
614	Misty/Sunshine	1975	—	2.00	4.00
616	Indian Love Call/Piece of Paradise	1975	—	2.00	4.00
618	Young Love/Deep Purple	1975	—	2.00	4.00
619	Lady of Spain/Mockingbird Hill	1976	—	2.00	4.00
2011	Everything Is Beautiful/A Brighter Day	1970	—	3.00	6.00
2016	America, Communicate with Me/Monkey See, Monkey Do	1970	—	2.50	5.00
2021	Sunset Strip/Islands	1970	—	2.50	5.00
2024	Bridget the Midget (The Queen of the Blues)/Night People	1970	—	2.50	5.00
2024 [PS]	Bridget the Midget (The Queen of the Blues)/Night People	1970	2.50	5.00	10.00
2029	A Mama and a Papa/Melt	1971	—	2.50	5.00
2039	All My Trials/Have a Little Talk with Myself	1971	—	2.50	5.00
2048	Turn Your Radio On/Loving You on Paper	1971	—	2.50	5.00
2058	Love Lifted Me/Glory Special	1972	—	2.50	5.00
2058	Love Lifted Me/Monkey See, Monkey Do	1972	—	2.50	5.00
2065	Losing Streak/Inside	1972	—	2.50	5.00
5020	Golden Age/Nashville	1973	—	2.00	4.00
5028	Love Me Longer/Float	1973	—	2.00	4.00
CAPITOL					
F3967	Chickie Chickie Wah Wah/Crying Goodbye	1958	6.25	12.50	25.00
F4030	Cat Pants/Love Goes On Forever	1958	7.50	15.00	30.00

Number	Title (A Side/B Side)	Yr	VG	VG+	NM
F4101	The School/The Clown	1958	6.25	12.50	25.00
7PRO-79430 [DJ]	Help Me Make It Through the Night (same on both sides)	1991	—	2.50	5.00
—Vinyl is promo only					
MCA					
52451	Joggin'/I'm Kissin' You Goodbye	1984	—	2.00	4.00
52492	Mississippi Squirrel Revival/Ned Nostril	1984	—	2.00	4.00
52548	It's Me Again, Margaret/Joggin'	1985	—	—	3.00
52657	The Haircut Song/Punk Country Love	1985	—	—	3.00
52738	Santa Claus Is Watching You/Armchair Quarterback	1985	—	2.00	4.00
52738 [PS]	Santa Claus Is Watching You/Armchair Quarterback	1985	—	2.00	4.00
52771	Vacation Bible School/The Ballad of the Blue Cyclone	1986	—	—	3.00
52906	The Camping Trip/Southern Air	1986	—	—	3.00
52924	People's Court/Dudley Doright (Of the Highway Patrol)	1986	—	—	3.00
53007	Can He Love You Half As Much As I Do/Dudley Doright (Of the Highway Patrol)	1987	—	—	3.00
53007 [DJ]	Can He Love You Half As Much As I Do (same on both sides)	1987	2.50	5.00	10.00
—Blue vinyl promo					
53101	Would Jesus Wear a Rolex?/Cool Down Willard	1987	—	2.00	4.00
53178	Three-Legged Man/Doctor, Doctor (Have Mercy on Me)	1987	—	—	3.00
53232	Sex Symbols/The Ballad of Cactus Pete and Lefty	1987	—	—	3.00
53372	Surfin' U.S.S.R./Language, Nudity, Violence & Sex	1988	—	—	3.00
53423	The Day I Tried to Teach Charlene MacKenzie How to Drive/I Don't Need None of That	1988	—	—	3.00
53661	I Saw Elvis in a U.F.O./I Used to Be Crazy	1989	2.50	5.00	10.00
MERCURY					
71843	Jeremiah Peabody's Poly Unsaturated Quick Dissolving Fast Acting Pleasant Tasting Green and Purple Pills/Teen Years	1961	3.75	7.50	15.00
71843 [PS]	Jeremiah Peabody's Poly Unsaturated Quick Dissolving Fast Acting Pleasant Tasting Green and Purple Pills/Teen Years	1961	6.25	12.50	25.00
71888	Scratch My Back/When You Wish Upon a Star	1961	3.75	7.50	15.00
71966	Ahab, the Arab/It's Been So Long	1962	3.75	7.50	15.00
71966 [PS]	Ahab, the Arab/It's Been So Long	1962	7.50	15.00	30.00
72039	Further More/Saturday Night at the Movies	1962	3.75	7.50	15.00
72058	Santa Claus Is Watching You/Loved and Lost	1962	3.75	7.50	15.00
72058 [PS]	Santa Claus Is Watching You/Loved and Lost	1962	6.25	12.50	25.00
72098	Funny Man/Just One of Life's Little Tragedies	1963	3.75	7.50	15.00
72125	Harry the Hairy Ape/Little Stone Statue	1963	3.75	7.50	15.00
72125 [PS]	Harry the Hairy Ape/Little Stone Statue	1963	6.25	12.50	25.00
72189	Speed Ball/It's Party Time	1963	3.75	7.50	15.00
72255	Butch Barbarian (Sure Footed Mountain Climber World Famous Yodeling Champion)/Don't Say Anything	1963	3.75	7.50	15.00
72307	Bubble Gum the Bubble Dancer/Laughing Over My Grave	1964	3.75	7.50	15.00
72382	Rockin' Teenage Mummies/It Only Hurts When I Love	1965	5.00	10.00	20.00
72430	Mr. Baker the Undertaker/Old English Surfer	1965	5.00	10.00	20.00
72816	Funny Man/Just One of Life's Little Tragedies	1968	3.00	6.00	12.00
812496-7	Pice of Paradise Called Tennessee/Mary Lou Nights	1983	—	2.00	4.00
812906-7	My Dad/Game Show Love	1983	—	2.50	5.00
814196-7	Love Will Beat Your Brains Out/Game Show Love	1983	—	2.00	4.00
818057-7	My Dad/Me	1984	—	2.00	4.00
MONUMENT					
911	A-B-C/Party People	1966	2.50	5.00	10.00
927	Devil-May-Care/Make a Few Memories	1966	2.50	5.00	10.00
946	Freddy Feelgood (And His Funky Little Five Piece Band)/There's One in Every Crowd	1966	2.50	5.00	10.00
1001	Mary, My Secretary/Answer Me, My Love	1967	2.00	4.00	8.00
1048	Unwind/For He's a Jolly Good Fellow	1968	2.00	4.00	8.00
1083	Mr. Businessman/Face the Music	1968	2.00	4.00	8.00
1099	Isn't It Lonely Together/The Great Escape	1968	2.00	4.00	8.00
1131	Gitarzan/Bagpipes-That's My Bag	1969	2.00	4.00	8.00
1150	Along Came Jones/Yakety Yak	1969	2.00	4.00	8.00
1163	Sunday Mornin' Comin' Down/The Minority	1969	—	3.00	6.00
1171	Have a Little Talk with Myself/Little Woman	1969	—	3.00	6.00
1187	I'll Be Your Baby Tonight/Fool on the Hill	1970	—	3.00	6.00
NRC					
031	High School Yearbook (Deck of Cards)/Truly True	1959	6.25	12.50	25.00
042	What Would I Do Without You/My Heart Cries for You	1959	6.25	12.50	25.00
057	Sergeant Preston of the Yukon/Who Do You Love	1960	6.25	12.50	25.00
063	Happy Blue Year/White Christmas	1960	6.25	12.50	25.00
PREP					
108	Rang Tang Ding Dong (I'm the Japanese Sandman)/Silver Bracelet	1957	6.25	12.50	25.00
122	Five More Steps/Tingle	1957	6.25	12.50	25.00
RCA					
PB-11911	Shriner's Convention/You're Never Goin' to Tampa With Me	1980	—	2.00	4.00
PB-12069	Night Games/Let's Do It Right This Time	1980	—	2.00	4.00
PB-12170	One More Last Chance/I Believe You Love Me	1981	—	2.00	4.00
PB-12185	The Streak/Misty	1981	—	2.00	4.00
GB-12368	Everything Is Beautiful/Gitarzan	1981	—	—	3.00
—Gold Standard Series					
GB-12370	Shriner's Convention/You're Never Goin' to Tampa with Me	1981	—	—	3.00
—Gold Standard Series					
PB-13038	Written Down in My Heart/Country Boy, Country Club Girl	1981	—	2.00	4.00
PB-13207	Where the Sun Don't Shine/Why Don't We Go Somewhere and Love	1982	—	2.00	4.00
WARNER BROS.					
8198	You Are So Beautiful/One Man Band	1976	—	2.00	4.00
8237	Honky Tonk Waltz/Om	1976	—	2.00	4.00
8301	In the Mood/Classical Cluck	1976	—	3.00	6.00
—As "Henhouse Five Plus Too"					
8318	Get Crazy with Me/Dixie Hummingbird	1977	—	2.00	4.00
8393	Dixie Hummingbird/Feel the Music	1977	—	2.00	4.00
8603	Be Your Own Best Friend/With a Smile	1978	—	2.00	4.00
8785	I Need Your Help Barry Manilow/Daydream Romance	1979	—	2.00	4.00
8785 [PS]	I Need Your Help Barry Manilow/Daydream Romance	1979	—	3.00	6.00
8849	The Feeling's Not Right Again/Get Crazy with Me	1979	—	2.00	4.00

Albums

Number	Title	Yr	VG	VG+	NM
BARNABY					
5004	Ray Stevens' Greatest Hits	1974	2.50	5.00	10.00
—Reissue of 30770					
5005	Nashville	1974	2.50	5.00	10.00
—Reissue of 15007					
6003	Boogity Boogity	1974	3.00	6.00	12.00
6012	Misty	1975	3.00	6.00	12.00
6018	The Very Best of Ray Stevens	1975	3.00	6.00	12.00
15007	Nashville	1973	3.00	6.00	12.00
Z 30092	Ray Stevens...Unreal!!!	1970	3.00	6.00	12.00
Z 30770	Ray Stevens' Greatest Hits	1971	3.00	6.00	12.00
Z 30809	Turn Your Radio On	1972	3.00	6.00	12.00
KZ 32139	Losin' Streak	1972	3.00	6.00	12.00
Z12 35005	Everything Is Beautiful	1970	3.75	7.50	15.00
MCA					
5517	He Thinks He's Ray Stevens	1984	2.50	5.00	10.00
5635	I Have Returned	1985	2.50	5.00	10.00
5795	Surely You Joust	1986	2.50	5.00	10.00
5918	Greatest Hits	1987	2.50	5.00	10.00
42020	Crackin' Up!	1987	2.50	5.00	10.00
42062	Greatest Hits, Volume 2	1987	2.50	5.00	10.00
42172	I Never Made a Record I Didn't Like	1988	2.50	5.00	10.00
42303	Beside Myself	1989	2.50	5.00	10.00
MERCURY					
MG-20732 [M]	1,837 Seconds of Humor	1962	10.00	20.00	40.00
MG-20828 [M]	This Is Ray Stevens	1963	6.25	12.50	25.00
SR-60732 [S]	1,837 Seconds of Humor	1962	12.50	25.00	50.00
SR-60828 [S]	This Is Ray Stevens	1963	7.50	15.00	30.00
SR-61272	The Best of Ray Stevens	1968	3.75	7.50	15.00
812780-1	Me	1984	2.50	5.00	10.00
MONUMENT					
SLP-18102	Even Stevens	1968	3.75	7.50	15.00
SLP-18115	Gitarzan	1969	3.75	7.50	15.00
SLP-18134	Have a Little Talk with Myself	1970	3.75	7.50	15.00
PICKWICK					
SPC-3266	Rock and Roll Show	1971	2.50	5.00	10.00
PRIORITY					
PU 38075	Turn Your Radio On	1982	2.50	5.00	10.00
—Reissue of Barnaby 30809					
RCA VICTOR					
AHL1-3574	Shriner's Convention	1980	2.50	5.00	10.00
AHL1-3841	One More Last Chance	1981	2.50	5.00	10.00
AYL1-4253	Shriner's Convention	1982	2.00	4.00	8.00
—"Best Buy Series" reissue					
AHL1-4288	Don't Laugh Now	1982	2.50	5.00	10.00
AHL1-4727	Greatest Hits	1983	2.50	5.00	10.00
AYL1-5153	Greatest Hits	1985	2.00	4.00	8.00
—"Best Buy Series" reissue					
CPL1-7161	Collector's Series	1986	2.50	5.00	10.00
WARNER BROS.					
BS 2914	Just for the Record	1976	2.50	5.00	10.00
BS 2997	Feel the Music	1977	2.50	5.00	10.00
BS 3098	There Is Something...	1977	2.50	5.00	10.00
BS 3195	Be Your Own Best Friend	1978	2.50	5.00	10.00
BSK 3332	The Feeling's Not Right Again	1979	2.50	5.00	10.00

STEVENS, TERRI

45s

Number	Title (A Side/B Side)	Yr	VG	VG+	NM
RCA VICTOR					
47-6165	Why Am I to Blame/What Am I Trying to Forget	1955	5.00	10.00	20.00
47-6300	All I Want Is You/I've Always Loved You	1955	5.00	10.00	20.00
47-6393	Dood-ly Dood-ly/I'll Come When You Call	1956	5.00	10.00	20.00
47-6633	Sweet World/That's How I Cried Over You	1956	5.00	10.00	20.00
47-7014	Pick-Up Girl/Untouched Heart	1957	5.00	10.00	20.00

STEVENSON, B.W.

45s

Number	Title (A Side/B Side)	Yr	VG	VG+	NM
MCA					
41151	A Special Wish/Holding a Special Place for You	1979	—	2.00	4.00
41166	Headin' Home/Holding a Special Place for You	1980	—	2.00	4.00
PRIVATE STOCK					
45208	Holdin' On for Dear Love/I'm a Better Man for Lovin' You	1979	—	2.00	4.00
RCA VICTOR					
APBO-0030	My Maria/August Evening Lady	1973	—	3.00	6.00
APBO-0171	River of Love/Lucky Touch	1973	—	2.50	5.00
APBO-0242	Song for Katy/Look for the Light	1974	—	2.00	4.00
APBO-0279	Remember Me/Roll On	1974	—	2.00	4.00
PB-10012	Here We Go Again/Little Bit of Understanding	1974	—	2.00	4.00
GB-10158	My Maria/Shambala	1975	—	—	3.00
—Gold Standard Series					
47-0728	Say What I Feel/Lonesome Song	1972	—	2.50	5.00
47-0778	On My Own/Highway One	1972	—	2.50	5.00
47-0840	Minuet for My Lady/Don't Go to Mexico	1972	—	2.50	5.00
47-0952	Shambala/My Feet Are So Weary	1973	—	3.00	6.00
WARNER BROS.					
8184	Jerrry's Bar and Grill/Way Down by the Ocean	1976	—	2.00	4.00
8247	Dream Baby/Wastin' Time	1976	—	2.00	4.00
8343	Down to the Station/May You Find Yourself in Heaven	1977	—	2.00	4.00

Number	Title (A Side/B Side)	Yr	VG	VG+	NM
Albums					
MCA					
3215	Lifeline	1980	2.50	5.00	10.00
RCA VICTOR					
APL1-0088	My Maria	1973	3.00	6.00	12.00
APL1-0410	Calabasas	1974	3.00	6.00	12.00
APL1-2394	The Best of B.W. Stevenson	1977	2.50	5.00	10.00
LSP-4685	B.W. Stevenson	1972	3.75	7.50	15.00
LSP-4794	Lead Free	1972	3.75	7.50	15.00
WARNER BROS.					
BS 2901	We Be Sailin'	1976	2.50	5.00	10.00
BS 3012	Lost	1977	2.50	5.00	10.00

STEWART, AL

Number	Title (A Side/B Side)	Yr	VG	VG+	NM
45s					
ARISTA					
0362	Time Passages/Almost Lucy	1978	—	2.00	4.00
0389	Song on the Radio/A Man for All Seasons	1979	—	2.00	4.00
0552	Midnight Rocks/Constantinople	1980	—	2.00	4.00
0576	Paint by Numbers/Optical Illusion	1980	—	2.00	4.00
0585	Running Man/Merlin's Theme	1981	—	2.00	4.00
0639	Indian Summer/Soko (Needless to Say)	1981	—	2.00	4.00
JANUS					
243	Nostradamus/Terminal Eyes	1974	—	2.50	5.00
250	Carol/Sirens of Titan	1975	—	2.50	5.00
266	Year of the Cat/Broadway Hotel	1976	—	2.50	5.00
267	On the Border/Flying Sorcery	1977	—	2.50	5.00
Albums					
ARISTA					
AL 4190	Time Passages	1978	2.50	5.00	10.00
AL6-8326	Year of the Cat	198?	2.00	4.00	8.00
—Reissue of Arista 9503					
AL6-8342	Time Passages	198?	2.00	4.00	8.00
—Reissue of 4190					
AL6-8359	Past, Present and Future	198?	2.00	4.00	8.00
—Reissue of Arista 9524					
A2L 8607 [(2)]	Live/Indian Summer	1981	3.00	6.00	12.00
AL 9503	Year of the Cat	1979	2.50	5.00	10.00
—Reissue of Janus 7022					
AL 9520	24 Carrots	1980	2.50	5.00	10.00
AL 9524	Past, Present and Future	1980	2.50	5.00	10.00
—Reissue of Janus 3063					
AL 9525	Modern Times	1980	2.50	5.00	10.00
—Reissue of Janus 7012					
ENIGMA					
D1-73316	Last Days of the Century	1988	3.00	6.00	12.00
EPIC					
BN 26564	Love Chronicles	1970	5.00	10.00	20.00
JANUS					
3063	Past, Present and Future	1974	3.75	7.50	15.00
7012	Modern Times	1975	3.00	6.00	12.00
7022	Year of the Cat	1976	3.00	6.00	12.00
7026 [DJ]	The Early Years	1977	7.50	15.00	30.00
—Promo-only condensation of 2-LP set with rubber-stamp cover					
7026 [(2)]	The Early Years	1977	3.75	7.50	15.00
MOBILE FIDELITY					
1-009	Year of the Cat	1979	10.00	20.00	40.00
—Audiophile vinyl					
1-082	Time Passages	1981	7.50	15.00	30.00
—Audiophile vinyl					
NAUTILUS					
NR-34	24 Carrots	198?	7.50	15.00	30.00
—Audiophile vinyl					
PASSPORT					
PB-6042	Russians and Americans	1986	3.00	6.00	12.00

STEWART, ANDY

Number	Title (A Side/B Side)	Yr	VG	VG+	NM
45s					
CAPITOL					
4809	The Road and the Miles to Dundee/Take Me Back	1962	2.50	5.00	10.00
WARWICK					
627	The Scottish Soldier/The Muckin' O' Georgie's Brye	1961	3.00	6.00	12.00
665	Donald Where's Your Troosers?/The Battle's Over	1961	3.00	6.00	12.00
676	The Road and the Miles to Dundee/Take Me Back	1962	3.00	6.00	12.00
Albums					
CAPITOL					
ST 10320 [S]	Andy Stewart's Scotland	196?	5.00	10.00	20.00
T 10320 [M]	Andy Stewart's Scotland	196?	3.75	7.50	15.00
EPIC					
LF 18027 [M]	A Scottish Soldier	196?	3.00	6.00	12.00
LF 18031 [M]	Tunes of Glory	196?	3.00	6.00	12.00
LF 18048 [M]	I'm Off to Bonnie Scotland	196?	3.00	6.00	12.00
BF 19027 [S]	A Scottish Soldier	196?	3.75	7.50	15.00
BF 19031 [S]	Tunes of Glory	196?	3.75	7.50	15.00
BF 19048 [S]	I'm Off to Bonnie Scotland	196?	3.75	7.50	15.00
WARWICK					
W 3043 [M]	A Scottish Soldier	1961	5.00	10.00	20.00
WST 3043 [S]	A Scottish Soldier	1961	7.50	15.00	30.00

STEWART, BILLY

Number	Title (A Side/B Side)	Yr	VG	VG+	NM
45s					
ARGO					
5256	Billy's Blues (Part 1)/Billy's Blues (Part 2)	1956	10.00	20.00	40.00
CHESS					
1625	Billy's Blues (Part 1)/Billy's Blues (Part 2)	1956	15.00	30.00	60.00
1820	Reap What You Sow/Fat Boy	1962	3.00	6.00	12.00
1835	True Fine Lovin'/Wedding Bells	1962	3.00	6.00	12.00
1852	Scramble/Oh What Can the Matter Be	1963	3.00	6.00	12.00
1868	Strange Feeling/Sugar and Spice	1963	3.00	6.00	12.00
1888	Count Me Out/A Fat Boy Can Cry	1964	2.50	5.00	10.00
1905	Tell It Like It Is/My Sweet Senorita	1964	2.50	5.00	10.00
1922	I Do Love You/Keep Loving	1965	2.50	5.00	10.00
1932	Sitting in the Park/Once Again	1965	2.50	5.00	10.00
1941	How Nice It Is/No Girl	1965	2.50	5.00	10.00
1948	Because I Love You/Mountain of Love	1965	2.50	5.00	10.00
1960	Love Me/Why Am I Lonely	1966	2.50	5.00	10.00
1966	Summertime/To Love, To Love	1966	3.75	7.50	15.00
—Black label					
1966	Summertime/To Love, To Love	1966	3.00	6.00	12.00
—Blueish label					
1978	Secret Love/Look Back and Smile	1966	2.50	5.00	10.00
1991	Every Day I Have the Blues/Ol' Man River	1967	2.50	5.00	10.00
2002	Cross My Heart/Why (Do I Love You So)	1967	2.50	5.00	10.00
2053	Tell Me the Truth/What Have I Done	1968	2.50	5.00	10.00
2063	I'm in Love (Oh Yes I Am)/Crazy 'Bout You Baby	1969	2.50	5.00	10.00
2080	By the Time I Get to Phoenix/We'll Always Be Together	1969	2.50	5.00	10.00
OKEH					
7095	Baby, You're My Only Love/Billy's Heartache	1957	75.00	150.00	300.00
UNITED ARTISTS					
340	This Is a Fine Time/Young in Years	1961	3.75	7.50	15.00
Albums					
CHESS					
LP-1496 [M]	I Do Love You	1965	20.00	40.00	80.00
—Red cover, black "wheel"					
LP-1496 [M]	I Do Love You	196?	7.50	15.00	30.00
—Green "woman" cover					
LPS-1496 [S]	I Do Love You	1965	25.00	50.00	100.00
—Red cover, black "wheel"					
LPS-1496 [S]	I Do Love You	196?	10.00	20.00	40.00
—Green "woman" cover					
LP-1499 [M]	Unbelievable	1966	7.50	15.00	30.00
LPS-1499 [S]	Unbelievable	1966	10.00	20.00	40.00
LP-1513 [M]	Billy Stewart Teaches Old Standards New Tricks	1967	7.50	15.00	30.00
LPS-1513 [S]	Billy Stewart Teaches Old Standards New Tricks	1967	10.00	20.00	40.00
LPS-1547	Billy Stewart Remembered	1970	6.25	12.50	25.00
CH-9104	The Greatest Sides	198?	2.50	5.00	10.00
CH-50059	Cross My Heart	1974	3.75	7.50	15.00

STEWART, DANNY

See SLY STEWART.

STEWART, JOHN

Also see THE KINGSTON TRIO.

Number	Title (A Side/B Side)	Yr	VG	VG+	NM
45s					
ALLEGIANCE					
3900	The Queen of Hollywood High/Judy in G Major	198?	—	2.00	4.00
CAPITOL					
2469	Mother Country/Shackles and Chains	1969	—	3.00	6.00
2538	July, You're a Woman/She Believes in Me	1969	—	3.00	6.00
2605	Armstrong/Anna on a Memory	1969	—	3.00	6.00
2711	Earth Rider/The Lady and the Outlaw	1969	—	3.00	6.00
2712	World of No Return/Wild Is Love	1969	2.00	4.00	8.00
—B-side by Patti Drew					
2842	Clack Clack/Marshall Wind	1970	—	3.00	6.00
RCA VICTOR					
APBO-0109	Anna on a Memory/Wheatfield	1973	—	2.50	5.00
PB-10003	July, You're a Woman/Runaway Fool of Love	1974	—	2.50	5.00
PB-10227	Survivors/Josie	1975	—	2.50	5.00
PB-10268	Survivors/Josie	1975	—	2.50	5.00
74-0970	Chilly Winds/Durango	1973	—	2.50	5.00
RSO					
894	Promise the Wind/Morning Thunder	1978	—	2.00	4.00
931	Gold/Comin' Out of Nowhere	1979	—	2.00	4.00
1000	Midnight Wind/Somewhere Down the Line	1979	—	2.00	4.00
1016	Lost Her in the Sun/Heart of the Dream	1979	—	2.00	4.00
1031	(Odin) Spirit of the Water/Love Has Tied My Wings	1980	—	2.00	4.00
VITA					
169	Rockin' Anna/Lorraine	1958	62.50	125.00	250.00
—As "Johnny Stewart"					
WARNER BROS.					
7525	Daydream Believer/Sweet Lizard	1971	—	2.50	5.00
7552	Light Come Shine/A Little Road and a Stone to Roll	1972	—	2.50	5.00
7592	An Accent of Halley's Comet/Arkansas Breakout	1972	—	2.50	5.00
Albums					
AFFORDABLE DREAMS					
AD-01	Trancas	1984	2.50	5.00	10.00
ALLEGIANCE					
AV-431	Blondes	198?	2.50	5.00	10.00
CAPITOL					
ST-203	California Bloodlines	1969	3.75	7.50	15.00
ST-540	Willard	1970	3.75	7.50	15.00
SM-2975	Signals Through the Glass	1977	2.50	5.00	10.00
—Reissue with new prefix					
ST 2975	Signals Through the Glass	1968	5.00	10.00	20.00
SN-16150	California Bloodlines	198?	2.00	4.00	8.00
—Budget-line reissue					
SN-16151	Willard	198?	2.00	4.00	8.00
—Budget-line reissue					
CYPRESS					
661117-1	Punch the Big Guy	1987	2.50	5.00	10.00
HOMECOMING					
HC-0200	Centennial	1984	2.50	5.00	10.00
HC-0300	The Last Campaign	1985	2.50	5.00	10.00
HC-0500	The Trio Years	1986	2.50	5.00	10.00
RCA VICTOR					
CPL2-0265 [(2)]	The Phoenix Concerts — Live	1974	3.75	7.50	15.00
APL1-0816	Wingless Angels	1975	3.00	6.00	12.00
AFL1-3513	John Stewart in Concert	1980	2.50	5.00	10.00
AYL1-3731	Cannons in the Rain	1981	2.00	4.00	8.00
—"Best Buy Series" reissue					

Number	Title (A Side/B Side)	Yr	VG	VG+	NM
LSP-4827	Cannons in the Rain	1973	3.00	6.00	12.00
RSO					
RS-1-3027	Fire in the Wind	1977	2.50	5.00	10.00
RS-1-3051	Bombs Away Dream Babies	1979	2.50	5.00	10.00
RS-1-3074	Dream Babies Go Hollywood	1980	2.50	5.00	10.00
WARNER BROS.					
WS 1948	The Lonesome Picker Rides Again	1971	3.00	6.00	12.00
BS 2611	Sunstorm	1972	3.00	6.00	12.00

STEWART, ROD

Also see JEFF BECK; FACES; PYTHON LEE JACKSON; SHOTGUN EXPRESS.

12-Inch Singles

Number	Title (A Side/B Side)	Yr	VG	VG+	NM
GEFFEN					
PRO-A-2787 [DJ]	Twistin' the Night Away (same on both sides)	1987	—	3.00	6.00
WARNER BROS.					
PRO-A-680 [DJ]	The Killing of Georgie (6:31) (same on both sides)	1977	3.75	7.50	15.00
PRO-A-921 [DJ]	Passion (7:30) (5:35)	1980	2.50	5.00	10.00
PRO-A-989 [DJ]	Young Turks (Edit) (LP Version)	1981	2.00	4.00	8.00
PRO-A-1078 [DJ]	Guess I'll Always Love You (same on both sides)	1982	2.50	5.00	10.00
PRO-A-2063 [DJ]	Dancin' Alone/Ghetto Blaster/What Am I Gonna Do	1983	—	3.00	6.00
PRO-A-2184 [DJ]	Some Guys Have All the Luck (Edit)/Bad for You	1984	—	3.00	6.00
PRO-A-2505 [DJ]	Love Touch (same on both sides)	1986	—	3.00	6.00
PRO-A-2538 [DJ]	A Night Like This (same on both sides)	1986	—	2.50	5.00
PRO-A-2559 [DJ]	Another Heartache (LP Version) (Edit)	1986	—	3.00	6.00
PRO-A-2618 [DJ]	Every Beat of My Heart (UK Edit) (LP Version)	1986	—	3.00	6.00
8727	Da Ya Think I'm Sexy?/Scarred and Scared	1978	2.50	5.00	10.00
21268	Crazy About Her (4 versions)/Dynamite	1989	—	2.50	5.00

45s

Number	Title (A Side/B Side)	Yr	VG	VG+	NM
GEFFEN					
28303	Twistin' the Night Away/Let's Get Small	1987	—	2.00	4.00
—B-side by Steve Martin					
28303 [PS]	Twistin' the Night Away/Let's Get Small	1987	—	2.00	4.00
MERCURY					
73009	Handbags and Gladrags/An Old Raincoat Won't Ever Let You Down	1970	2.50	5.00	10.00
73031	Handbags and Gladrags/Man of Constant Sorrow	1970	2.00	4.00	8.00
73095	It's All Over Now/Joe's Lament	1970	2.50	5.00	10.00
73115	Only a Hero/Gasoline Alley	1970	2.50	5.00	10.00
73156	Cut Across Shorty/Gasoline Alley	1970	2.50	5.00	10.00
73175	My Way of Giving/Lady Day	1971	—	3.00	6.00
73196	Country Comfort/Gasoline Alley	1971	—	3.00	6.00
73224	Maggie May/Reason to Believe	1971	—	3.00	6.00
73244	(I Know) I'm Losing You/Mandolin Wind	1971	—	2.50	5.00
73330	You Wear It Well/True Blue	1972	—	2.50	5.00
73330 [PS]	You Wear It Well/True Blue	1972	3.75	7.50	15.00
73344	Angel/Lost Paraguayos	1972	—	2.50	5.00
73412	Twistin' the Night Away//True Blue-Lady Day	1973	—	2.50	5.00
73412 [PS]	Twistin' the Night Away//True Blue-Lady Day	1973	—	3.00	6.00
73426	Oh No Not My Baby/Jodie	1973	—	2.50	5.00
73426 [PS]	Oh No Not My Baby/Jodie	1973	—	3.00	6.00
73636	Mine for Me/Farewell	1974	—	2.50	5.00
73660	Let Me Be Your Car/Sailor	1974	—	3.00	6.00
73802	Every Picture Tells a Story/What's Made Milwaukee Famous (Has Made a Loser Out of Me)	1976	—	2.50	5.00
PRESS					
9722	Good Morning Little Schoolgirl/I'm Gonna Move to the Outskirts of Town	1965	10.00	20.00	40.00
PRIVATE STOCK					
45130	Shake/Bright Lights, Big City	1976	—	3.00	6.00
WARNER BROS.					
8066	As Long As You Tell Him/You Can Make Me Dance, Sing or Anything	1975	—	2.50	5.00
—As "Rod Stewart and Faces"					
8102	As Long As You Tell Him/You Can Make Me Dance, Sing or Anything	1975	—	2.00	4.00
—As "Rod Stewart and Faces"					
8146	Sailing/All in the Name of Rock and Roll	1975	—	2.00	4.00
8170	This Old Heart of Mine/Still Love Again	1975	—	2.50	5.00
8262	Tonight's the Night (Gonna Be Alright)/Fool for You	1976	—	2.00	4.00
8321	The First Cut Is the Deepest/Ball Trap	1977	—	2.00	4.00
8396	The Killing of Georgie (Part 1 and 2)/Rosie	1977	—	2.00	4.00
8475	You're In My Heart (The Final Acclaim)/You Got a Nerve	1977	—	2.00	4.00
8535	Hot Legs/You're Insane	1978	—	2.00	4.00
8535 [PS]	Hot Legs/You're Insane	1978	—	2.50	5.00
8568	I Was Only Joking/Born Loose	1978	—	2.00	4.00
8568 [PS]	I Was Only Joking/Born Loose	1978	—	2.50	5.00
8724	Da Ya Think I'm Sexy?/Scarred and Scared	1978	—	2.00	4.00
8724 [PS]	Da Ya Think I'm Sexy?/Scarred and Scared	1978	—	2.50	5.00
8810	Ain't Love a Bitch/Last Summer	1979	—	2.00	4.00
8810 [PS]	Ain't Love a Bitch/Last Summer	1979	—	2.50	5.00
15995	Broken Arrow/Downtown Train	1993	—	—	3.00
—"Back to Back Hits" series; only 45 release of A-side					
17195	Ooh La La/A Night Like This	1998	—	—	3.00
17459	If We Fall in Love Tonight/Tom Traubert's Blues (Waltzing Matilda)	1996	—	—	3.00
17847	Leave Virginia Alone/Shock to the System	1995	—	—	3.00
17854	This/The Groom's Still Waiting at the Altar	1995	—	—	3.00
18424	Having a Party/Sweet Little Rock and Roller	1993	—	—	3.00
18427	Reason to Believe/It's All Over Now	1993	—	—	3.00
18511	Have I Told You Lately/Gasoline Alley	1993	—	2.00	4.00
—Note: Warner Bros. 19274 does not exist on 45					
19322	The Motown Song/Sweet Soul Marie	1991	—	—	3.00
19366	Rhythm of My Heart/Moment of Glory	1991	—	—	3.00
19983	This Old Heart of Mine/You're In My Heart	1990	—	—	3.00
22685	Downtown Train/The Killing of Georgie (Part 1 and 2)	1989	—	—	3.00
22685 [PS]	Downtown Train/The Killing of Georgie (Part 1 and 2)	1989	—	3.00	6.00
27657	Crazy About Her/Dynamite	1989	—	—	3.00
27729	My Heart Can't Tell You No/The Wild Horse	1988	—	—	3.00
27729 [PS]	My Heart Can't Tell You No/The Wild Horse	1988	—	—	3.00
27796	Forever Young/Days of Rage	1988	—	—	3.00
27796 [PS]	Forever Young/Days of Rage	1988	—	—	3.00
27927	Lost in You/Almost Illegal	1988	—	—	3.00
27927 [PS]	Lost in You/Almost Illegal	1988	—	—	3.00
28625	Every Beat of My Heart/Trouble	1986	—	—	3.00
28625 [PS]	Every Beat of My Heart/Trouble	1986	—	—	3.00
28631	Another Heartache/You're In My Heart (The Final Acclaim)	1986	—	—	3.00
28631 [PS]	Another Heartache/You're In My Heart (The Final Acclaim)	1986	—	—	3.00
28668	Love Touch (Love Theme from Legal Eagles)/Heart Is on the Line	1986	—	—	3.00
28668 [PS]	Love Touch (Love Theme from Legal Eagles)/Heart Is on the Line	1986	—	—	3.00
29122	All Right Now/Dancin' Alone	1984	—	2.00	4.00
29215	Some Guys Have All the Luck/I Was Only Joking	1984	—	2.00	4.00
29215 [PS]	Some Guys Have All the Luck/I Was Only Joking	1984	—	2.00	4.00
29256	Infatuation/She Won't Dance with Me	1984	—	2.00	4.00
29256 [PS]	Infatuation/She Won't Dance with Me	1984	—	2.00	4.00
29564	What Am I Gonna Do (I'm So in Love with You)/Dancin' Alone	1983	—	2.00	4.00
29564 [PS]	What Am I Gonna Do (I'm So in Love with You)/Dancin' Alone	1983	—	2.00	4.00
29608	Baby Jane/Ready Now	1983	—	2.00	4.00
29874	Guess I'll Always Love You/Rock My Plimsoul	1982	—	2.00	4.00
29874 [PS]	Guess I'll Always Love You/Rock My Plimsoul	1982	—	2.50	5.00
49138	I Don't Want to Talk About It/Best Days of My Life	1979	—	2.00	4.00
49138 [PS]	I Don't Want to Talk About It/Best Days of My Life	1979	—	2.50	5.00
49617	Passion/Better Off Dead	1980	—	2.00	4.00
49617 [PS]	Passion/Better Off Dead	1980	—	2.50	5.00
49686	Somebody Special/She Won't Dance with Me	1981	—	2.00	4.00
49843	Young Turks/Sonny	1981	—	2.00	4.00
49843 [PS]	Young Turks/Sonny	1981	—	2.50	5.00
49886	Tonight I'm Yours (Don't Hurt Me)/Tora, Tora, Tora	1981	—	2.00	4.00
49886 [PS]	Tonight I'm Yours (Don't Hurt Me)/Tora, Tora, Tora	1981	—	2.50	5.00
50051	How Long/Jealous	1982	—	2.00	4.00
50051 [PS]	How Long/Jealous	1982	—	2.50	5.00

7-Inch Extended Plays

Number	Title (A Side/B Side)	Yr	VG	VG+	NM
MERCURY					
MEPL-28 [DJ]	I'd Rather Go Blind/What's Made Milwaukee Famous//Italian Girls/Twistin' the Night Away	1972	2.50	5.00	10.00
MEPL-28 [PS]	(title unknown)	1972	2.50	5.00	10.00

Albums

Number	Title (A Side/B Side)	Yr	VG	VG+	NM
ACCORD					
SN-7142	Rod the Mod	1981	3.00	6.00	12.00
DCC COMPACT CLASSICS					
LPZ-2010	Never a Dull Moment	1995	5.00	10.00	20.00
—Audiophile vinyl					
MERCURY					
SRM-1-609	Every Picture Tells a Story	1971	3.75	7.50	15.00
—Original cover has an attached, perforated poster					
SRM-1-609	Every Picture Tells a Story	1971	2.50	5.00	10.00
—With poster missing; red label					
SRM-1-646	Never a Dull Moment	1972	3.00	6.00	12.00
—Red label					
SRM-1-680	Sing It Again Rod	1973	3.00	6.00	12.00
—Red label					
SRM-1-697	Rod Stewart/Faces Live: Coast to Coast Overtures and Beginners	1973	3.75	7.50	15.00
—By "Rod Stewart/Faces"					
SRM-1-1017	Smiler	1974	3.00	6.00	12.00
—Chicago skyline label					
SRM-2-7507 [(2)]	The Best of Rod Stewart	1976	3.75	7.50	15.00
SRM-2-7509 [(2)]	The Best of Rod Stewart, Volume 2	1977	3.75	7.50	15.00
SR-61237	The Rod Stewart Album	1969	6.25	12.50	25.00
—Cover is yellow with no black border					
SR-61237	The Rod Stewart Album	1971	3.75	7.50	15.00
—Cover is yellow with black border; red label					
SR-61264	Gasoline Alley	1970	5.00	10.00	20.00
—Cover is textured, most noticeably on the pebbles					
SR-61264	Gasoline Alley	1971	3.75	7.50	15.00
—Cover is not textured; red label					
822385-1	Every Picture Tells a Story	1984	2.00	4.00	8.00
822791-1 [(2)]	The Best of Rod Stewart, Volume 2	1985	3.00	6.00	12.00
824881-1	Gasoline Alley	1985	2.00	4.00	8.00
824882-1	Sing It Again Rod	1985	2.00	4.00	8.00
826287-1 [(2)]	The Best of Rod Stewart	1985	3.00	6.00	12.00
MOBILE FIDELITY					
1-054	Blondes Have More Fun	1980	6.25	12.50	25.00
—Audiophile vinyl					
PRIVATE STOCK					
PS-2021	A Shot of Rhythm and Blues	1976	3.75	7.50	15.00
SPRINGBOARD					
SPB-4030	Rod Stewart and The Faces	197?	3.00	6.00	12.00
TRIP					
TOP-16-31	Looking Back/16 Early Hits	1974	3.00	6.00	12.00
UNITED DISTRIBUTORS					
UDL-2391	The Day Will Come	1981	5.00	10.00	20.00
WARNER BROS.					
BS 2875	Atlantic Crossing	1975	2.50	5.00	10.00
BS 2938	A Night on the Town	1976	2.50	5.00	10.00
BSK 3092	Foot Loose and Fancy Free	1977	2.50	5.00	10.00
BSK 3108	Atlantic Crossing	1977	2.00	4.00	8.00
—Reissue of 2875					
BSK 3116	A Night on the Town	1977	2.00	4.00	8.00
—Reissue of 2938					
BSK 3261	Blondes Have More Fun	1978	2.50	5.00	10.00
BSP 3276 [PD]	Blondes Have More Fun	1978	5.00	10.00	20.00
HS 3373	Rod Stewart Greatest Hits	1979	2.50	5.00	10.00
HS 3485	Foolish Behaviour	1980	2.50	5.00	10.00
BSK 3602	Tonight I'm Yours	1981	2.50	5.00	10.00

Number	Title (A Side/B Side)	Yr	VG	VG+	NM
23743 [(2)]	Absolutely Live	1982	3.00	6.00	12.00
23743 [(2) DJ]	Absolutely Live	1982	6.25	12.50	25.00
—Promo only on Quiex II vinyl					
23877	Body Wishes	1983	2.00	4.00	8.00
23877 [DJ]	Body Wishes	1983	3.75	7.50	15.00
—Promo only on Quiex II vinyl					
25095	Camouflage	1984	2.00	4.00	8.00
—Issued with 16 different back covers, all of equal value, that, when assembled, form a giant poster					
25446	Rod Stewart	1986	2.00	4.00	8.00
25884	Out of Order	1988	2.00	4.00	8.00
26158	Downtown Train: Selections from the Storyteller Anthology	1990	3.00	6.00	12.00

STEWART, SANDY

45s

Number	Title (A Side/B Side)	Yr	VG	VG+	NM
20TH CENTURY					
5007	The Game of Love/Do Ya Do Ya	1954	3.00	6.00	12.00
5014	I'm Goin' Home/Saturday Night	1954	3.00	6.00	12.00
ATCO					
6137	Playmates/Heavenly Father	1959	2.50	5.00	10.00
COLPIX					
669	My Coloring Book/I Heard You Cried Last Night	1962	2.00	4.00	8.00
669 [PS]	My Coloring Book/I Heard You Cried Last Night	1962	3.75	7.50	15.00
681	My Favorite Song/Promise of Love	1963	2.00	4.00	8.00
704	I Know He Needs Her/Please Don't Fall in Love with Me Again	1963	2.00	4.00	8.00
DCP					
1004	Draw Me a Circle/Little Child (Mommy Dear)	1964	2.00	4.00	8.00
EASTWEST					
122	To My Love/Music, Music, Music	1958	2.50	5.00	10.00
EPIC					
9070	No One Came to My Party/Mama, Mama	1954	3.00	6.00	12.00
OKEH					
6941	Since You Went Away from Me/Before	1953	3.00	6.00	12.00
6967	If My Heart Had a Window/Punch Brother Punch	1953	3.00	6.00	12.00
6991	Loved and Lost/Please Come Home	1953	3.00	6.00	12.00
UNITED ARTISTS					
232	Indoor Sports/Time Waits for No One	1960	2.50	5.00	10.00
287	Past the Age of Innocence/Richest Girl in the World	1961	2.50	5.00	10.00
332	Nice Guy/Lord and Master	1961	2.50	5.00	10.00
"X"					
0126	Johnny Darling/No More Love	1955	3.00	6.00	12.00
0156	Puddin' 'n' Pie/In Nuevo Laredo	1955	3.00	6.00	12.00
0176	Could It Be?/I'll Take Care of You	1955	3.00	6.00	12.00

Albums

Number	Title (A Side/B Side)	Yr	VG	VG+	NM
AUDIOPHILE					
AP-205	Sandy Stewart Sings Songs of Jerome Kern	1985	2.50	5.00	10.00
—Accompanied by Dick Hyman on piano					
COLPIX					
CP-441 [M]	My Coloring Book	1963	6.25	12.50	25.00
SCP-441 [S]	My Coloring Book	1963	7.50	15.00	30.00

STEWART, SLY

Sylvester Stewart, later "Sly" of SLY AND THE FAMILY STONE.

12-Inch Singles

Number	Title (A Side/B Side)	Yr	VG	VG+	NM
EPIC					
50794	Dance to the Music/Sing a Simple Song	1979	3.75	7.50	15.00
—As "Sly Stone"					

45s

Number	Title (A Side/B Side)	Yr	VG	VG+	NM
AUTUMN					
3	I Just Learned How to Swim/Scat Swim	1964	5.00	10.00	20.00
—Sylvester Stewart, later "Sly" of The Family Stone					
14	Buttermilk — Part 1/Buttermilk — Part 2	1965	5.00	10.00	20.00
—As "Sly"					
26	Temptation Walk/Temptation Walk — Part 2	1966	5.00	10.00	20.00
A&M					
2890	Eek-Ah-Bo-Static Automatic/Black Girls	1986	—	—	3.00
—B-side by Rae Dawn Chong					
2896	Love and Affection/Black Girls	1986	—	—	3.00
—A-side as "Sly Stone and Martha Davis"; B-side by Rae Dawn Chong					
EPIC					
50795	Dance to the Music/Sing a Simple Song	1979	—	2.50	5.00
—As "Sly Stone"					
G&P					
901	Help Me With My Heart/A Long Time Away	1962	62.50	125.00	250.00
—As "Sylvester Stewart"					
LUKE					
1008	A Long Time Alone/I'm Just a Fool	1961	62.50	125.00	250.00
—As "Danny Stewart"					

STEWART, WYNN

45s

Number	Title (A Side/B Side)	Yr	VG	VG+	NM
ATLANTIC					
4025	When/Why Don't You Come to Me	1974	—	2.50	5.00
CAPITOL					
2012	Love's Gonna Happen to Me/Waltz of the Angels	1967	2.00	4.00	8.00
2012 [PS]	Love's Gonna Happen to Me/Waltz of the Angels	1967	3.00	6.00	12.00
2137	Something Pretty/Built in Love	1968	—	3.50	7.00
2137 [PS]	Something Pretty/Built in Love	1968	3.00	6.00	12.00
2240	In Love/My Own Little World	1968	—	3.50	7.00
2240 [PS]	In Love/My Own Little World	1968	3.00	6.00	12.00
2341	Strings/Happy Blues	1968	—	3.50	7.00
2421	Let the Whole World Sing It with Me/Who Are You	1969	—	3.50	7.00
2549	World-Wide Travelin' Man/Cry Baby	1969	—	3.50	7.00
2657	Yours Forever/Goin' Steady	1969	—	3.50	7.00
2751	You Don't Care What Happens to Me/Young As Spring	1970	—	3.00	6.00
2888	It's a Beautiful Day/Prisoner on the Run	1970	—	3.00	6.00
3000	Heavenly/You're No Secret of Mine	1970	—	3.00	6.00
3080	Baby, It's Yours/I Was the First One to Know	1971	—	3.00	6.00
3157	Hello Little Rock/You Can't Take It With You	1971	—	3.00	6.00
F-3408	The Waltz of the Angels/Why Do I Love You So	1956	5.00	10.00	20.00
F-3515	The Keeper of the Keys/Slowly But Surely	1956	5.00	10.00	20.00
F-3594	That Just Kills Me/You Took Her Off My Hands	1956	5.00	10.00	20.00
F-3651	Hold Back Tomorrow/New Love	1957	5.00	10.00	20.00
F-3803	A Night to Remember/I Wish I Could Say the Same	1957	5.00	10.00	20.00
5271	Half of This, Half of That	1964	2.00	4.00	8.00
5271 [PS]	Half of This, Half of That	1964	3.75	7.50	15.00
5397	Sha Marie/Does He Love You Like I Do	1965	2.00	4.00	8.00
5485	I Keep Forgettin' That I Forgot About You/My Rosalie	1965	2.00	4.00	8.00
5593	Angels Don't Lie/The Tourist	1966	2.00	4.00	8.00
5831	It's Such a Pretty World Today/Ol' What's Her Name	1967	2.00	4.00	8.00
5937	'Cause I Love You/That's the Only Way to Cry	1967	2.00	4.00	8.00
5937 [PS]	'Cause I Love You/That's the Only Way to Cry	1967	3.00	6.00	12.00
CHALLENGE					
9121	Big Big Love/One More Memory	1961	3.75	7.50	15.00
9142	I Done Done It/I Don't Feel at Home	1962	—	—	—
9155	Don't Look Back/Loversville	1962	3.75	7.50	15.00
9164	Another Day, Another Dollar/Donna on My Mind	1962	3.75	7.50	15.00
9192	Slightly Used/I'm Not the Man I Used to Be	1963	3.75	7.50	15.00
59061	Wishful Thinking/Uncle Tom Got Caught	1958	15.00	30.00	60.00
—The B-side is sought after by rockabilly collectors					
59084	Heartaches for a Dime/Playboy	1960	3.75	7.50	15.00
59095	If You See My Baby/I'd Rather Have America	1960	3.75	7.50	15.00
59216	Big City/One Way to Go	1963	3.75	7.50	15.00
59379	Girl in White/Fallin' for You	1967	2.00	4.00	8.00
FOUR STAR					
8001	Inflation Blues/Heartbreak Mountain	1980	—	3.00	6.00
JACKPOT					
48005	Come On/School Bus Love Affair	1959	75.00	150.00	300.00
48019	Open Up My Heart/Above and Beyond	1960	5.00	10.00	20.00
PLAYBOY					
6035	Lonely Rain/Just Now Thought of You	1975	—	2.50	5.00
6060	I'm Gonna Kill You/Seasons of My Heart	1976	—	3.00	6.00
6080	After the Storm/Don't Monkey with My Widow	1976	—	2.50	5.00
6091	Sing a Sad Song/It's Such a Pretty World Today	1976	—	2.50	5.00
PRETTY WORLD					
001	Wait Till I Get My Hands on You/Would You Want the World to End	1985	2.00	4.00	8.00
RCA VICTOR					
APBO-0004	Love Ain't Worth a Dime Unless It's Free/Me and My Jesus Would Know	1973	—	2.50	5.00
APBO-0114	It's Raining in Seattle/If I Were You	1973	—	2.50	5.00
74-0819	Paint Me a Rainbow/I Know They'll Make Room for You	1972	—	2.50	5.00
74-0891	Everything Needs a Little Woman's Touch/Search Through the Ashes	1973	—	2.50	5.00
WIN					
126	Eyes Big as Dallas/Such a Perfect Day for Making Love	1978	—	3.00	6.00
127	Could I Talk You Into Loving Me Again/I Was Raised Down on the Farm	1979	—	3.00	6.00

STEWART, WYNN, AND JAN HOWARD

45s

Number	Title (A Side/B Side)	Yr	VG	VG+	NM
CHALLENGE					
59071	Wrong Company/We'll Never Love Again	1960	3.75	7.50	15.00
59264	How the Other Half Lives/We'll Never Love Again	1964	3.00	6.00	12.00
JACKPOT					
48014	How the Other Half Lives/Yankee Go Home	1960	5.00	10.00	20.00

STEWART BROTHERS, THE

With Sylvester "SLY" STEWART, later of SLY AND THE FAMILY STONE.

45s

Number	Title (A Side/B Side)	Yr	VG	VG+	NM
ENSIGN					
4032	The Rat/Ra Ra Roo	1959	25.00	50.00	100.00
KEEN					
2113	Sleep on the Porch/Yum Yum	1960	25.00	50.00	100.00

STILLROVEN, THE

45s

Number	Title (A Side/B Side)	Yr	VG	VG+	NM
AUGUST					
101	Little Picture Playhouse/Cast Thy Burden Upon the Stone	1968	6.25	12.50	25.00
102	Necessary Person/Come in the Morning	1968	25.00	50.00	100.00
102	Necessary Person/Have You Ever Seen Me	1968	6.25	12.50	25.00
FALCON					
69	Hey Joe/Sunny Day	1967	12.50	25.00	50.00
7296	She's Your Woman/I'm Not Your Steppin' Stone	1966	50.00	100.00	200.00
ROULETTE					
4748	Hey Joe/Sunny Day	1967	3.75	7.50	15.00

STILLS, STEPHEN

Also see BUFFALO SPRINGFIELD; CROSBY, STILLS AND NASH; CROSBY, STILLS, NASH AND YOUNG; THE STILLS-YOUNG BAND.

12-Inch Singles

Number	Title (A Side/B Side)	Yr	VG	VG+	NM
ATLANTIC					
PR 623 [DJ]	Stranger (same on both sides)	1984	—	3.00	6.00
PR 650 [DJ]	Can't Let Go (same on both sides)	1984	—	3.00	6.00

45s

Number	Title (A Side/B Side)	Yr	VG	VG+	NM
ATLANTIC					
2778	Love the One You're With/To a Flame	1970	—	3.00	6.00
2790	Sit Yourself Down/We Are Not Helpless	1971	—	2.50	5.00
2806	Change Partners/Relaxing Town	1971	—	2.50	5.00
2806 [PS]	Change Partners/Relaxing Town	1971	—	3.00	6.00
2820	Marianne/Nothin' to Do But Today	1971	—	2.50	5.00
2876	It Doesn't Matter/Rock & Roll's Crazy Medley	1972	—	2.50	5.00
2888	Rock and Roll Crazies/Colorado	1972	—	2.50	5.00
—With Manassas					

Number	Title (A Side/B Side)	Yr	VG	VG+	NM
2917	Down the Road/Guaguanco De Vero	1972	—	2.50	5.00
—With Manassas					
2959	So Many Times/Isn't It About Time	1973	—	2.50	5.00
89597	Only Love Can Break Your Heart/Love Again	1984	—	2.00	4.00
89611	Can't Let Go/Grey to Green	1984	—	2.00	4.00
—With Walter Finnegan					
89633	Stranger/No Hiding Place	1984	—	2.00	4.00
89633 [PS]	Stranger/No Hiding Place	1984	—	2.00	4.00
COLUMBIA					
10179	Turn Back the Pages/Shuffle Just as Bad	1975	—	2.50	5.00
10369	Buyin' Time/Soldier	1976	—	2.50	5.00
10804	Lowdown/Can't Get No Booty	1978	—	2.50	5.00
10872	Thoroughfare Gap/Lowdown	1978	—	2.50	5.00
Albums					
ATLANTIC					
SD 2-903 [(2)]	Manassas	1972	3.75	7.50	15.00
SD 7202	Stephen Stills	1970	3.00	6.00	12.00
SD 7206	Stephen Stills 2	1971	3.00	6.00	12.00
SD 7250	Down the Road	1973	3.00	6.00	12.00
SD 18156	Stephen Stills Live	1975	3.00	6.00	12.00
SD 18201	Still Stills — The Best of Stephen Stills	1976	2.50	5.00	10.00
80177	Right By You	1984	2.00	4.00	8.00
COLUMBIA					
PC 33575	Stills	1975	2.50	5.00	10.00
—No bar code on cover					
PC 33575	Stills	198?	2.00	4.00	8.00
—Bar code on cover					
PCQ 33575 [Q]	Stills	1975	5.00	10.00	20.00
PC 34348	Illegal Stills	1976	2.50	5.00	10.00
JC 35380	Thoroughfare Gap	1978	2.50	5.00	10.00

STILLS-YOUNG BAND, THE

STEPHEN STILLS and NEIL YOUNG.

Number	Title (A Side/B Side)	Yr	VG	VG+	NM
45s					
REPRISE					
1365	Long May You Run//12/8 Blues (All the Same)	1976	—	3.00	6.00
1378	Midnight on the Bay/Black Coral	1976	—	2.50	5.00
Albums					
REPRISE					
MS 2253	Long May You Run	1976	2.50	5.00	10.00

STINGERS, THE

Number	Title (A Side/B Side)	Yr	VG	VG+	NM
Albums					
CROWN					
CST-476 [S]	Guitars A Go Go	196?	10.00	20.00	40.00
CLP-5476 [M]	Guitars A Go Go	196?	7.50	15.00	30.00

STINIT, DANE

Number	Title (A Side/B Side)	Yr	VG	VG+	NM
45s					
SUN					
402	Always on the Go/Don't Knock What You Don't Understand	1966	3.75	7.50	15.00
405	Sweet Country Girl/That Muddy Ole River	1967	3.75	7.50	15.00

STITES, GARY

Number	Title (A Side/B Side)	Yr	VG	VG+	NM
45s					
CARLTON					
508	Lonely for You/Shine That Ring	1959	5.00	10.00	20.00
516	A Girl Like You/Hey Little Girl	1959	5.00	10.00	20.00
521	Starry Eyed/Without Your Love	1959	5.00	10.00	20.00
525	Lawdy Miss Clawdy/Don't Wanna Say Goodbye	1960	5.00	10.00	20.00
529	Gloria Lee/Hey, Hey	1960	5.00	10.00	20.00
EPIC					
10064	Hurting/Thinking of You	1966	3.00	6.00	12.00
MADISON					
138	Young Love/Little Tear	1960	3.75	7.50	15.00
155	Honey Girl/Little Lonely One	1961	3.75	7.50	15.00
MR. PEEKE					
122	You Doubted Me/Only a Fool Would Say	1962	3.75	7.50	15.00
Albums					
CARLTON					
LP-120 [M]	Lonely for You	1960	20.00	40.00	80.00
STLP-120 [S]	Lonely for You	1960	30.00	60.00	120.00

STITT, SONNY

Number	Title (A Side/B Side)	Yr	VG	VG+	NM
45s					
ARGO					
5403	It All Depends on You (Part 1)/It All Depends on You (Part 2)	1961	2.50	5.00	10.00
5433	Rearin' Back (Part 1)/Rearin' Back (Part 2)	1963	2.00	4.00	8.00
5493	Flame and Frost/My Main Man	1965	2.00	4.00	8.00
—With Bennie Green					
CADET					
5701	Mr. Bojangles/Blue Monsoon	1974	—	2.00	4.00
5705	Will You Love Me Tomorrow/Satan	1974	—	2.00	4.00
5708	Theme from The Godfather Part II/Ocho Nos	1974	—	2.50	5.00
ENTERPRISE					
9001	Private Number/Heads or Tails	1969	—	3.00	6.00
IMPULSE!					
230	Salt and Pepper (Part 1)/Salt and Pepper (Part 2)	1964	2.00	4.00	8.00
—With Paul Gonsalves					
PRESTIGE					
239	'Nuther Fu'ther (Part 1)/'Nuther Fu'ther (Part 2)	1963	2.50	5.00	10.00
263	Ringin' In/Pam Ain't Blue	1963	2.50	5.00	10.00
282	Thirty-Three Ninety-Six (Part 1)/Thirty-Three Ninety-Six (Part 2)	1963	2.50	5.00	10.00
304	Shangri-La/Soul Shack	1964	2.50	5.00	10.00
392	Night Crawler/Answering Service	1965	2.00	4.00	8.00
404	Star Eyes/Who Can I Turn To	196?	2.00	4.00	8.00
438	Blue Lights/Up and Over	196?	2.00	4.00	8.00
710	Candy/Lover Man	1969	—	3.00	6.00
ROULETTE					
4701	What's New/Morgan's Song	1966	2.00	4.00	8.00
4713	Stardust (Part 1)/Stardust (Part 2)	1966	2.00	4.00	8.00
WINGATE					
006	The Double-O-Soul of Sonny Stitt (Part 1 and 2)	1965	2.00	4.00	8.00
010	Just Dust/Concerto for Jazz Lovers	1966	2.00	4.00	8.00
011	Stitt's Groove/Marr's Groove	1966	2.00	4.00	8.00
—With Hank Marr					
WORLD PACIFIC					
398	My Mother's Eyes/Summer Special	1963	2.50	5.00	10.00
Albums					
ABC IMPULSE!					
AS-43 [S]	Sonny Stitt Now!	1968	3.00	6.00	12.00
AS-52 [S]	Salt and Pepper	1968	3.00	6.00	12.00
—With Paul Gonsalves					
ARGO					
LP-629 [M]	Sonny Stitt	1958	10.00	20.00	40.00
LP-661 [M]	Burnin'	1960	6.25	12.50	25.00
LPS-661 [S]	Burnin'	1960	7.50	15.00	30.00
LP-683 [M]	Sonny Stitt at the D.J. Lounge	1961	6.25	12.50	25.00
LPS-683 [S]	Sonny Stitt at the D.J. Lounge	1961	7.50	15.00	30.00
LP-709 [M]	Rearin' Back	1962	6.25	12.50	25.00
LPS-709 [S]	Rearin' Back	1962	7.50	15.00	30.00
LP-730 [M]	Move On Over	1964	6.25	12.50	25.00
LPS-730 [S]	Move On Over	1964	7.50	15.00	30.00
LP-744 [M]	My Main Man	1965	6.25	12.50	25.00
LPS-744 [S]	My Main Man	1965	7.50	15.00	30.00
ATLANTIC					
1395 [M]	Sonny Stitt and the Top Brass	1962	6.25	12.50	25.00
SD 1395 [S]	Sonny Stitt and the Top Brass	1962	7.50	15.00	30.00
1418 [M]	Stitt Plays Bird	1964	7.50	15.00	30.00
SD 1418 [S]	Stitt Plays Bird	1964	10.00	20.00	40.00
SD 3008	Deuces Wild	1970	3.75	7.50	15.00
90139	Sonny Stitt and Top Brass	198?	2.50	5.00	10.00
BLACK LION					
307	Night Work	197?	2.50	5.00	10.00
CADET					
LP-629 [M]	Sonny Stitt	1966	3.75	7.50	15.00
LP-661 [M]	Burnin'	1966	3.00	6.00	12.00
LPS-661 [S]	Burnin'	1966	3.75	7.50	15.00
LP-683 [M]	Sonny Stitt at the D.J. Lounge	1966	3.00	6.00	12.00
LPS-683 [S]	Sonny Stitt at the D.J. Lounge	1966	3.75	7.50	15.00
LP-709 [M]	Rearin' Back	1966	3.00	6.00	12.00
LPS-709 [S]	Rearin' Back	1966	3.75	7.50	15.00
LP-730 [M]	Move On Over	1966	3.00	6.00	12.00
LPS-730 [S]	Move On Over	1966	3.75	7.50	15.00
LP-744 [M]	My Main Man	1966	3.00	6.00	12.00
LPS-744 [S]	My Main Man	1966	3.75	7.50	15.00
LP-760 [M]	Inter-Action	1966	3.75	7.50	15.00
LPS-760 [S]	Inter-Action	1966	5.00	10.00	20.00
LP-770 [M]	Soul in the Night	1966	3.75	7.50	15.00
LPS-770 [S]	Soul in the Night	1966	5.00	10.00	20.00
50026	Mr. Bojangles	1973	3.00	6.00	12.00
50039 [(2)]	I Cover the Waterfront	1974	3.75	7.50	15.00
50060	Satan	1974	3.00	6.00	12.00
60040	Never Can Say Goodbye	197?	3.00	6.00	12.00
CATALYST					
7608	Forecast	1976	3.00	6.00	12.00
—With Red Holloway					
7616	I Remember Bird	1976	3.00	6.00	12.00
7620	Tribute to Duke Ellington	1977	3.00	6.00	12.00
CHESS					
405 [(2)]	Interaction	197?	3.75	7.50	15.00
—With Zoot Sims					
CH-9317	Sonny Stitt	1990	2.50	5.00	10.00
CH-91523	Sonny Stitt at the D.J. Lounge	198?	2.50	5.00	10.00
COBBLESTONE					
9013	Tune-Up	1972	3.00	6.00	12.00
9021	Constellation	1973	3.00	6.00	12.00
COLPIX					
CP-499 [M]	Broadway Soul	1964	7.50	15.00	30.00
SCP-499 [S]	Broadway Soul	1964	7.50	15.00	30.00
DELMARK					
426	Made for Each Other	197?	3.00	6.00	12.00
FANTASY					
OJC-009	Sonny Stitt/Bud Powell/J.J. Johnson	198?	2.50	5.00	10.00
OJC-060	Kaleidoscope	198?	2.50	5.00	10.00
FLYING DUTCHMAN					
BDL1-1538	Stomp Off Let's Go	1976	2.50	5.00	10.00
GALAXY					
8204	In the Beginning	197?	3.00	6.00	12.00
GRP/IMPULSE!					
IMP-210	Salt and Pepper	199?	3.75	7.50	15.00
—Reissue on audiophile vinyl					
IMPULSE!					
A-43 [M]	Sonny Stitt Now!	1963	6.25	12.50	25.00
AS-43 [S]	Sonny Stitt Now!	1963	7.50	15.00	30.00
A-52 [M]	Salt and Pepper	1964	6.25	12.50	25.00
AS-52 [S]	Salt and Pepper	1964	7.50	15.00	30.00
—With Paul Gonsalves					
JAZZ MAN					
5040	Night Work	198?	2.50	5.00	10.00
JAZZLAND					
JLP-71 [M]	Low Flame	1962	6.25	12.50	25.00
JLP-971 [S]	Low Flame	1962	7.50	15.00	30.00
JAZZTONE					
J-1231 [M]	Early Modern	1956	12.50	25.00	50.00
J-1263 [M]	Early Modern	1957	10.00	20.00	40.00
MUSE					
MR-5006	12!	1973	3.00	6.00	12.00
MR-5023	The Champ	1974	3.00	6.00	12.00
MR-5067	Mellow	1975	3.00	6.00	12.00
MR-5091	My Buddy: Plays for Ammons	1976	3.00	6.00	12.00

Number	Title (A Side/B Side)	Yr	VG	VG+	NM
MR-5129	Blues for Duke	197?	3.00	6.00	12.00
MR-5204	Sonny's Back	1981	2.50	5.00	10.00
MR-5228	In Style	1982	2.50	5.00	10.00
MR-5269	The Last Stitt Sessions, Vol. 1	1983	2.50	5.00	10.00
MR-5280	The Last Stitt Sessions, Vol. 2	1984	2.50	5.00	10.00
MR-5323	Constellation	1986	2.50	5.00	10.00
MR-5334	Tune-Up	1987	2.50	5.00	10.00
NEW JAZZ					
NJLP-103 [10]	Sonny Stitt and Bud Powell	1950	75.00	150.00	300.00
PACIFIC JAZZ					
PJ-71 [M]	My Mother's Eyes	1963	5.00	10.00	20.00
ST-71 [S]	My Mother's Eyes	1963	6.25	12.50	25.00
PAULA					
4004	Soul Girl	1974	3.00	6.00	12.00
PHOENIX					
15	Superstitt	197?	2.50	5.00	10.00
19	Battles	197?	2.50	5.00	10.00
PRESTIGE					
PRLP-103 [10]	Sonny Stitt Plays	1951	50.00	100.00	200.00
PRLP-111 [10]	Mr. Saxophone	1951	50.00	100.00	200.00
PRLP-126 [10]	Favorites, Volume 1	1952	50.00	100.00	200.00
PRLP-148 [10]	Favorites, Volume 2	1953	50.00	100.00	200.00
PRLP-7024 [M]	Sonny Stitt with Bud Powell and J.J. Johnson	1956	25.00	50.00	100.00
PRLP-7077 [M]	Kaleidoscope	1957	25.00	50.00	100.00
PRLP-7133 [M]	Stitt's Bits	1958	25.00	50.00	100.00
PRLP-7244 [M]	Stitt Meets Brother Jack	1962	12.50	25.00	50.00
—Yellow label					
PRLP-7244 [M]	Stitt Meets Brother Jack	1964	6.25	12.50	25.00
—Blue label with trident logo					
PRST-7244 [S]	Stitt Meets Brother Jack	1962	12.50	25.00	50.00
PRLP-7248 [M]	All God's Chillun Got Rhythm	1962	12.50	25.00	50.00
—Yellow label					
PRLP-7248 [M]	All God's Chillun Got Rhythm	1964	6.25	12.50	25.00
—Blue label with trident logo					
PRST-7248 [R]	All God's Chillun Got Rhythm	1962	7.50	15.00	30.00
PRLP-7297 [M]	Soul Shack	1964	12.50	25.00	50.00
—Yellow label					
PRLP-7297 [M]	Soul Shack	1965	6.25	12.50	25.00
—Blue label with trident logo					
PRST-7297 [S]	Soul Shack	1964	12.50	25.00	50.00
—Silver label					
PRST-7297 [S]	Soul Shack	1965	6.25	12.50	25.00
—Blue label with trident logo					
PRLP-7302 [M]	Primitive Soul!	1964	10.00	20.00	40.00
—Yellow label					
PRLP-7302 [M]	Primitive Soul!	1965	6.25	12.50	25.00
—Blue label with trident logo					
PRST-7302 [S]	Primitive Soul!	1964	10.00	20.00	40.00
—Silver label					
PRST-7302 [S]	Primitive Soul!	1965	6.25	12.50	25.00
—Blue label with trident logo					
PRLP-7332 [M]	Shangri-La	1964	5.00	10.00	20.00
PRST-7332 [S]	Shangri-La	1964	6.25	12.50	25.00
PRLP-7372 [M]	Soul People	1965	5.00	10.00	20.00
PRST-7372 [S]	Soul People	1965	6.25	12.50	25.00
PRLP-7436 [M]	Night Crawler	1966	5.00	10.00	20.00
PRST-7436 [S]	Night Crawler	1966	6.25	12.50	25.00
PRLP-7452 [M]	'Nuther Fu'ther	1966	5.00	10.00	20.00
PRST-7452 [S]	'Nuther Fu'ther	1966	6.25	12.50	25.00
PRLP-7459 [M]	Pow!	1967	6.25	12.50	25.00
PRST-7459 [S]	Pow!	1967	5.00	10.00	20.00
PRST-7585	Stitt's Bits, Volume 1	1968	3.75	7.50	15.00
PRST-7606	We'll Be Together Again	1969	3.75	7.50	15.00
PRST-7612	Stitt's Bits, Volume 2	1969	3.75	7.50	15.00
PRST-7635	Soul Electricity	1969	3.75	7.50	15.00
PRST-7701	The Best of Sonny Stitt with Brother Jack McDuff	1969	3.75	7.50	15.00
PRST-7759	Night Letter	1970	3.75	7.50	15.00
PRST-7769	Best for Lovers	1970	3.75	7.50	15.00
PRST-7839	Bud's Blues	1974	3.00	6.00	12.00
10012	Turn It On	1971	3.00	6.00	12.00
10032	Black Vibrations	1972	3.00	6.00	12.00
10048	Goin' Down Slow	1973	3.00	6.00	12.00
10074	So Doggone Good	1974	3.00	6.00	12.00
24044 [(2)]	Genesis	1974	3.75	7.50	15.00
PROGRESSIVE					
7034	Sonny Stitt Meets Sadik Hakim	1978	2.50	5.00	10.00
ROOST					
LP-415 [10]	Sonny Stitt Plays Arrangements from the Pen of Johnny Richards	1952	75.00	150.00	300.00
LP-418 [10]	Jazz at the Hi-Hat	1954	75.00	150.00	300.00
LP-1203 [M]	Battle of Birdland	1955	20.00	40.00	80.00
LP-1208 [M]	Sonny Stitt	1956	20.00	40.00	80.00
LP-2204 [M]	Sonny Stitt Plays Arrangements of Quincy Jones	1957	12.50	25.00	50.00
LP-2208 [M]	Sonny Stitt	1957	12.50	25.00	50.00
LP-2219 [M]	37 Minutes and 48 Seconds of Sonny Stitt	1957	12.50	25.00	50.00
LP-2226 [M]	Sonny Stitt with the New Yorkers	1958	12.50	25.00	50.00
LP-2230 [M]	The Saxophone of Sonny Stitt	1959	10.00	20.00	40.00
SLP-2230 [S]	The Saxophone of Sonny Stitt	1959	7.50	15.00	30.00
LP-2235 [M]	A Little Bit of Stitt	1959	10.00	20.00	40.00
SLP-2235 [S]	A Little Bit of Stitt	1959	7.50	15.00	30.00
LP-2240 [M]	The Sonny Side of Stitt	1960	10.00	20.00	40.00
SLP-2240 [S]	The Sonny Side of Stitt	1960	7.50	15.00	30.00
LP-2244 [M]	Stittsville	1960	10.00	20.00	40.00
SLP-2244 [S]	Stittsville	1960	7.50	15.00	30.00
LP-2245 [M]	Sonny Side Up	196?	6.25	12.50	25.00
SLP-2245 [S]	Sonny Side Up	196?	6.25	12.50	25.00
LP-2247 [M]	Feelin's	1962	6.25	12.50	25.00
SLP-2247 [S]	Feelin's	1962	6.25	12.50	25.00
LP-2252 [M]	Sonny Stitt in Orbit	1963	6.25	12.50	25.00
SLP-2252 [S]	Sonny Stitt in Orbit	1963	6.25	12.50	25.00
LP-2253 [M]	Sonny Stitt Goes Latin	1963	6.25	12.50	25.00
SLP-2253 [S]	Sonny Stitt Goes Latin	1963	6.25	12.50	25.00
ROULETTE					
R-25339 [M]	The Matadors Meet the Bull	1965	5.00	10.00	20.00
SR-25339 [S]	The Matadors Meet the Bull	1965	6.25	12.50	25.00

Number	Title (A Side/B Side)	Yr	VG	VG+	NM
R-25343 [M]	What's New?	1966	5.00	10.00	20.00
SR-25343 [S]	What's New?	1966	6.25	12.50	25.00
R-25348 [M]	I Keep Comin' Back	1967	6.25	12.50	25.00
SR-25348 [S]	I Keep Comin' Back	1967	5.00	10.00	20.00
SR-25354	Parallel-O-Stitt	1968	3.75	7.50	15.00
SR-42035	Make Someone Happy	1969	3.00	6.00	12.00
SR-42048	Stardust	1970	3.00	6.00	12.00
SAVOY					
MG-9006 [10]	All Star Series: Sonny Stitt	1953	50.00	100.00	200.00
MG-9012 [10]	New Sounds in Modern Music	1953	50.00	100.00	200.00
MG-9014 [10]	New Trends of Jazz	1953	50.00	100.00	200.00
SAVOY JAZZ					
SJL-1165	Symphony Hall Swing	1986	2.50	5.00	10.00
SOLID STATE					
SS-18047	Little Green Apples	1968	3.75	7.50	15.00
SS-18057	Come Hither	1969	3.75	7.50	15.00
TRIP					
5008 [(2)]	Two Sides of Sonny Stitt	1974	3.00	6.00	12.00
UPFRONT					
UPF-196	Sonny's Blues	197?	2.50	5.00	10.00
VERVE					
UMV-2558	New York Jazz	198?	2.50	5.00	10.00
UMV-2634	Only the Blues	198?	2.50	5.00	10.00
MGVS-6038 [S]	The Hard Swing	1960	10.00	20.00	40.00
MGVS-6041 [S]	Sonny Stitt Plays Jimmy Giuffre Arrangements	1960	10.00	20.00	40.00
MGVS-6108 [S]	Sonny Stitt Sits In with the Oscar Peterson Trio	1960	10.00	20.00	40.00
MGVS-6149-45 [(4)]	Sonny Stitt Blows the Blues	1999	10.00	20.00	40.00
—Audiophile reissue by Classic Records; plays at 45 rpm					
MGVS-6149	Sonny Stitt Blows the Blues	1996	10.00	20.00	40.00
—Audiophile reissue by Classic Records					
MGVS-6149 [S]	Sonny Stitt Blows the Blues	1960	10.00	20.00	40.00
MGVS-6154 [S]	Saxophone Supremacy	1960	—	—	—
—Canceled					
MGVS-6162 [S]	Sonny Stitt Swings the Most	1960	—	—	—
—Canceled					
MGV-8219 [M]	New York Jazz	1957	12.50	25.00	50.00
V-8219 [M]	New York Jazz	1961	6.25	12.50	25.00
MGV-8250 [M]	Only the Blues	1958	12.50	25.00	50.00
V-8250 [M]	Only the Blues	1961	6.25	12.50	25.00
MGV-8262 [M]	Sonny Side Up	1958	15.00	30.00	60.00
V-8262 [M]	Sonny Side Up	1961	7.50	15.00	30.00
MGV-8306 [M]	The Hard Swing	1959	12.50	25.00	50.00
V-8306 [M]	The Hard Swing	1961	6.25	12.50	25.00
V6-8306 [S]	The Hard Swing	1961	5.00	10.00	20.00
MGV-8309 [M]	Sonny Stitt Plays Jimmy Giuffre Arrangements	1959	12.50	25.00	50.00
V-8309 [M]	Sonny Stitt Plays Jimmy Giuffre Arrangements	1961	6.25	12.50	25.00
V6-8309 [S]	Sonny Stitt Plays Jimmy Giuffre Arrangements	1961	5.00	10.00	20.00
MGV-8324 [M]	Personal Appearance	1959	12.50	25.00	50.00
V-8324 [M]	Personal Appearance	1961	6.25	12.50	25.00
MGV-8344 [M]	Sonny Stitt Sits In with the Oscar Peterson Trio	1959	12.50	25.00	50.00
V-8344 [M]	Sonny Stitt Sits In with the Oscar Peterson Trio	1961	6.25	12.50	25.00
V6-8344 [S]	Sonny Stitt Sits In with the Oscar Peterson Trio	1961	5.00	10.00	20.00
MGV-8374 [M]	Sonny Stitt Blows the Blues	1960	12.50	25.00	50.00
V-8374 [M]	Sonny Stitt Blows the Blues	1961	6.25	12.50	25.00
V6-8374 [S]	Sonny Stitt Blows the Blues	1961	5.00	10.00	20.00
MGV-8377 [M]	Saxophone Supremacy	1960	12.50	25.00	50.00
V-8377 [M]	Saxophone Supremacy	1961	6.25	12.50	25.00
MGV-8380 [M]	Sonny Stitt Swings the Most	1960	12.50	25.00	50.00
V-8380 [M]	Sommy Stitt Swings the Most	1961	6.25	12.50	25.00
MGV-8403 [M]	Sonny Stitt	1960	—	—	—
—Canceled					
V-8451 [M]	The Sensual Sound of Sonny Stitt	1962	5.00	10.00	20.00
V6-8451 [S]	The Sensual Sound of Sonny Stitt	1962	6.25	12.50	25.00
V6-8837	Previously Unreleased Recordings	1974	3.00	6.00	12.00
WHO'S WHO IN JAZZ					
21022	Sonny, Sweets and Jaws	1981	2.50	5.00	10.00
21025	The Bubba's Sessions	1982	2.50	5.00	10.00

STITT, SONNY, AND GENE AMMONS

Also see each artist's individual listings.

Albums

Number	Title (A Side/B Side)	Yr	VG	VG+	NM
CADET					
LP-785 [M]	Jug and Sonny	1967	6.25	12.50	25.00
LPS-785 [S]	Jug and Sonny	1967	3.75	7.50	15.00
CHESS					
CH-91549	Jug and Sonny	198?	2.50	5.00	10.00
PRESTIGE					
PRLP-107 [10]	Battle of the Saxes: Ammons vs. Stitt	1951	62.50	125.00	250.00
PRLP-7234 [M]	Soul Summit	1962	10.00	20.00	40.00
—Yellow label					
PRST-7234 [S]	Soul Summit	1962	12.50	25.00	50.00
—Yellow label					
PRLP-7454 [M]	Soul Summit	1966	5.00	10.00	20.00
—Blue label, trident logo at right					
PRST-7454 [S]	Soul Summit	1966	6.25	12.50	25.00
—Blue label, trident logo at right					
PRST-7606	We'll Be Together Again	1969	5.00	10.00	20.00
VERVE					
V-8426 [M]	Boss Tenors	1962	5.00	10.00	20.00
V6-8426 [S]	Boss Tenors	1962	6.25	12.50	25.00
V-8468 [M]	Boss Tenors in Orbit	1962	5.00	10.00	20.00
V6-8468 [S]	Boss Tenors in Orbit	1962	6.25	12.50	25.00

STOECKLEIN, VAL

45s

Number	Title (A Side/B Side)	Yr	VG	VG+	NM
DOT					
17200	Sounds of Yesterday/Say It's Not Over	1969	3.75	7.50	15.00
17234	All the Way Home/I Wonder Who I'll Be Tomorrow	1969	3.75	7.50	15.00

Albums

Number	Title (A Side/B Side)	Yr	VG	VG+	NM
DOT					
DLP-25904	Grey Life	1968	10.00	20.00	40.00

STOMPERS, THE

45s

Number	Title (A Side/B Side)	Yr	VG	VG+	NM
GONE					
5120	Stompin' Round the Christmas Tree/Forgive Me	1961	37.50	75.00	150.00
LANDA					
684	Foolish One/Quarter to Four Stomp	1962	6.25	12.50	25.00
684	Foolish One/Surf Stompin'	1962	6.25	12.50	25.00
MERCURY					
72111	Frump/Blacksmith Blues	1963	3.75	7.50	15.00
—As "The Ski Stompers"					
SOUVENIR					
1003	I Miss You So/Blue Moon of Kentucky	1960	25.00	50.00	100.00

STONE, JIMMY

45s

Number	Title (A Side/B Side)	Yr	VG	VG+	NM
CROSS COUNTRY					
523	Found/Mine	1956	75.00	150.00	300.00
GONE					
5001	Found/Mine	1957	50.00	100.00	200.00

STONE, SLY

See SLY STEWART.

STONE CIRCUS, THE

45s

Number	Title (A Side/B Side)	Yr	VG	VG+	NM
MAINSTREAM					
694	Mister Grey/(B-side unknown)	1969	5.00	10.00	20.00

Albums

Number	Title (A Side/B Side)	Yr	VG	VG+	NM
MAINSTREAM					
S-6119	The Stone Circus	1969	20.00	40.00	80.00

STONE COUNTRY

45s

Number	Title (A Side/B Side)	Yr	VG	VG+	NM
RCA VICTOR					
47-9534	Wheels on Fire/Million Dollar Bash	1968	2.00	4.00	8.00

Albums

Number	Title (A Side/B Side)	Yr	VG	VG+	NM
RCA VICTOR					
LSP-3958	Stone Country	1968	5.00	10.00	20.00

STONE PONEYS

Also see LINDA RONSTADT.

45s

Number	Title (A Side/B Side)	Yr	VG	VG+	NM
CAPITOL					
2004	Different Drum/I've Got to Know	1967	3.75	7.50	15.00
2110	Up to My Neck in High Muddy Water/Carnival Bear	1968	2.50	5.00	10.00
2110 [PS]	Up to My Neck in High Muddy Water/Carnival Bear	1968	10.00	20.00	40.00
—By "Linda Ronstadt and the Stone Poneys"					
2195	Hobo (Mornin' Glory)/Some of Shelly's Blues	1968	2.50	5.00	10.00
5838	All the Beautiful Things/Sweet Summer Blue and Gold	1967	2.50	5.00	10.00
5910	One for One/Evergreen	1967	2.50	5.00	10.00
SIDEWALK					
937	So Fine/Everyone Has Their Own Ideas	1968	50.00	100.00	200.00

Albums

Number	Title (A Side/B Side)	Yr	VG	VG+	NM
CAPITOL					
ST 2666 [S]	The Stone Poneys	1967	7.50	15.00	30.00
T 2666 [M]	The Stone Poneys	1967	6.25	12.50	25.00
ST 2763 [S]	Evergreen, Vol. 2	1967	7.50	15.00	30.00
T 2763 [M]	Evergreen, Vol. 2	1967	10.00	20.00	40.00
ST 2863	Linda Ronstadt/Stone Poneys and Friends Vol. III	1968	12.50	25.00	50.00
ST-11383	The Stone Poneys Featuring Linda Ronstadt	1974	2.50	5.00	10.00
PICKWICK					
SPC-3298	Stoney End	197?	2.00	4.00	8.00

STONE THE CROWS

45s

Number	Title (A Side/B Side)	Yr	VG	VG+	NM
POLYDOR					
14033	Fool on the Hill/Raining in My Heart	1969	—	—	—
—Canceled					

Albums

Number	Title (A Side/B Side)	Yr	VG	VG+	NM
POLYDOR					
24-4019	Stone the Crows	1970	5.00	10.00	20.00
PD-5020	Teenage Licks	1972	5.00	10.00	20.00
PD-5037	Continuous Performance	1972	5.00	10.00	20.00

STONES, THE

45s

Number	Title (A Side/B Side)	Yr	VG	VG+	NM
SOLLY					
928	She Said Yeah/Watch Me	1966	6.25	12.50	25.00
—Reissued with group renamed "The Tracers"					

STONEY AND MEATLOAF

Also see MEAT LOAF.

45s

Number	Title (A Side/B Side)	Yr	VG	VG+	NM
RARE EARTH					
5027	What You See Is What You Get/Lady Be Mine	1971	—	3.00	6.00
5033	The Way You Do the Things You Do/It Takes All Kinds of People	1971	—	3.00	6.00

Albums

Number	Title (A Side/B Side)	Yr	VG	VG+	NM
PRODIGAL					
10	Stoney and Meatloaf	1978	3.00	6.00	12.00
RARE EARTH					
R 528	Stoney and Meatloaf	1971	5.00	10.00	20.00

STOOGES, THE

See IGGY AND THE STOOGES.

STOOKEY, PAUL

Also see PETER, PAUL AND MARY.

45s

Number	Title (A Side/B Side)	Yr	VG	VG+	NM
BENSON					
5616 [DJ]	For Christmas (same on both sides)	198?	—	2.00	4.00
—As "Noel Paul Stookey and the Bodyworks Band"					
5616 [PS]	For Christmas (same on both sides)	198?	—	2.00	4.00
WARNER BROS.					
7511	Wedding Song (There Is Love)/Give a Damn	1971	—	3.00	6.00
—Of Peter, Paul and Mary					
7602	Hey, Sad Sack/Sebastian	1972	—	2.50	5.00
7683	Funky Monkey (Part 1)/Blessed	1973	—	2.50	5.00
—As "Noel Paul Stookey"					

Albums

Number	Title (A Side/B Side)	Yr	VG	VG+	NM
WARNER BROS.					
WS 1912	Paul and...	1971	2.50	5.00	10.00
BS 2674	One Night Stand	1973	2.50	5.00	10.00
—As "Noel Paul Stookey"					

STORIES

45s

Number	Title (A Side/B Side)	Yr	VG	VG+	NM
KAMA SUTRA					
545	I'm Coming Home/You Told Me	1972	—	2.00	4.00
558	Top of the City/Stepback	1972	—	2.00	4.00
566	Darling/Take Cover	1972	—	2.00	4.00
574	Love in Motion/Changes Have Begun	1973	—	2.00	4.00
577	Brother Louie/Changes Have Begun	1973	—	3.00	6.00
577	Brother Louie/What Comes After	1973	—	2.50	5.00
584	Mammy Blue/Travelling Underground	1973	—	2.00	4.00
588	Circles/If It Feels Good	1974	—	2.00	4.00
594	Another Love/Love Is In Motion	1974	—	2.00	4.00

Albums

Number	Title (A Side/B Side)	Yr	VG	VG+	NM
KAMA SUTRA					
KSBS-2051	Stories	1972	3.00	6.00	12.00
KSBS-2068	About Us	1973	7.50	15.00	30.00
—Gatefold; does NOT contain "Brother Louie"					
KSBS-2068	About Us	1973	3.00	6.00	12.00
—Regular cover; with "Brother Louie"					
KSBS-2078	Traveling Underground	1974	3.00	6.00	12.00

STORM, BILLY

45s

Number	Title (A Side/B Side)	Yr	VG	VG+	NM
ATLANTIC					
2076	In the Chapel in the Moonlight/Sure As You're Born	1960	3.00	6.00	12.00
2098	When You Dance/Dear One	1961	3.00	6.00	12.00
2112	Honey Love/A Kiss from Your Lips	1961	3.00	6.00	12.00
BUENA VISTA					
403	Puppy Love Is Here to Stay/Push Over	1962	3.75	7.50	15.00
413	Love Theme from El Cid/Cee Cee Rider	1962	3.75	7.50	15.00
415	Double Date/Good Girl	1963	3.75	7.50	15.00
418	'Deed I Do/Lonely People Do Foolish Things	1963	3.75	7.50	15.00
424	He Knows How Much We Can Bear/Motherless Child	1963	5.00	10.00	20.00
429	Since I Fell for You/Body and Soul	1964	5.00	10.00	20.00
COLUMBIA					
41431	Easy Chair/You Just Can't Plan These Things	1959	3.75	7.50	15.00
41494	I Can't Stop Crying for You/Emotion	1959	3.75	7.50	15.00
41545	Enchanted/When the Whole World Smiles Again	1959	3.75	7.50	15.00
GREGMARK					
9	3000 Tears/Who'll Keep an Eye on Jane	1961	3.00	6.00	12.00
HANNA-BARBERA					
474	Please Don't Mention Her Name/The Warmest Love	1966	5.00	10.00	20.00
474 [PS]	Please Don't Mention Her Name/The Warmest Love	1966	6.25	12.50	25.00
INFINITY					
013	Love Theme from El Cid/Don't Let Go	1962	3.00	6.00	12.00
018	Since I Fell for You/A Million Miles from Nowhere	1963	3.00	6.00	12.00
023	I Can't Help It/Educated Fool	1963	3.00	6.00	12.00
LOMA					
2001	Baby, Don't Look Down/I Never Want to Dream Again	1964	2.50	5.00	10.00
2009	Goldfinger Theme/Debbie and Mitch	1965	2.50	5.00	10.00
ODE					
120	Coal Mine/Tonight I'll Be Staying Here with You	1968	2.00	4.00	8.00

Albums

Number	Title (A Side/B Side)	Yr	VG	VG+	NM
BUENA VISTA					
BV-3315 [M]	Billy Storm	1963	25.00	50.00	100.00
STER-3315 [S]	Billy Storm	1963	30.00	60.00	120.00
FAMOUS					
F-504	This Is the Night	1969	25.00	50.00	100.00

STORM, GALE

45s

Number	Title (A Side/B Side)	Yr	VG	VG+	NM
DOT					
15412	I Hear You Knocking/Never Leave Me	1955	5.00	10.00	20.00
15436	Teen-Age Prayer/Memories Are Made of This	1955	3.75	7.50	15.00
15448	Why Do Fools Fall in Love/I Walk Alone	1956	3.75	7.50	15.00
15458	Ivory Tower/I Ain't Gonna Worry	1956	3.75	7.50	15.00
15474	Tell Me Why/Don't Be That Way	1956	3.75	7.50	15.00
15492	Now Is the Hour/A Heart Without a Sweetheart	1956	3.75	7.50	15.00
—Originals have maroon labels					
15492	Now Is the Hour/A Heart Without a Sweetheart	1956	2.50	5.00	10.00
—Second pressings have black labels					
15515	My Heart Belongs to You/Orange Blossoms	1956	2.50	5.00	10.00
15528	I Need You So/On Treasure Island	1957	2.50	5.00	10.00
15539	On Treasure Island/Lucky Lips	1957	2.50	5.00	10.00
15558	Dark Moon/A Little Too Late	1957	2.50	5.00	10.00

Number	Title (A Side/B Side)	Yr	VG	VG+	NM
15606	On My Mind Again/Love by the Jukebox Light	1957	2.50	5.00	10.00
15666	Go 'Way from My Window/Winter Warm	1957	2.50	5.00	10.00
15691	A Farewell to Arms/I Get That Feeling	1958	2.50	5.00	10.00
15734	Angry/You	1958	2.50	5.00	10.00
15783	South of the Border/Soon I'll Wed My Love	1958	2.50	5.00	10.00
15861	Oh, Lonely Crowd/Happiness Left Yesterday	1958	2.50	5.00	10.00
16031	I Hear You Knocking/Ivory Tower	1960	2.00	4.00	8.00
16032	Dark Moon/Memories Are Made of This	1960	2.00	4.00	8.00
16057	On Treasure Island/I Need You So	1960	2.00	4.00	8.00
16111	Please Help Me, I'm Falling/He's There	1960	2.00	4.00	8.00
Albums					
DOT					
DLP-3011 [M]	Gale Storm	1956	12.50	25.00	50.00
DLP-3017 [M]	Sentimental Me	1956	12.50	25.00	50.00
DLP-3098 [M]	Gale Storm Hits	1958	10.00	20.00	40.00
DLP-3197 [M]	Softly and Tenderly	1959	7.50	15.00	30.00
DLP-3209 [M]	Gale Storm Sings	1959	7.50	15.00	30.00
DLP-25197 [S]	Softly and Tenderly	1959	10.00	20.00	40.00
DLP-25209 [S]	Gale Storm Sings	1959	10.00	20.00	40.00
HAMILTON					
HLP-171 [M]	I Don't Want to Walk	1966	3.00	6.00	12.00
HLP-12171 [S]	I Don't Want to Walk	1966	3.75	7.50	15.00
MCA					
1504	Gale Storm	198?	2.50	5.00	10.00

STORM, RORY, AND THE HURRICANES

The group that Ringo Starr drummed for before joining the Beatles. He is not on this record.

Number	Title (A Side/B Side)	Yr	VG	VG+	NM
45s					
COLUMBIA					
43018	I Can Tell/Let's Stomp	1964	6.25	12.50	25.00
—B-side by Faron's Flamingos					

STORM, TOM, AND THE PEPS

Number	Title (A Side/B Side)	Yr	VG	VG+	NM
45s					
GE GE					
501	I Love You/That's the Way Love Is	1965	7.50	15.00	30.00

STORME, ROBB

Number	Title (A Side/B Side)	Yr	VG	VG+	NM
45s					
AURORA					
162	Here Today/Don't Cry	1966	3.00	6.00	12.00
CAPITOL					
5452	Love Is Strange/Shy Guy	1965	2.50	5.00	10.00

STORMS, THE

Also see JODY REYNOLDS.

Number	Title (A Side/B Side)	Yr	VG	VG+	NM
45s					
SUNDOWN					
114	Thunder/Tarantula	1959	12.50	25.00	50.00
—This was re-recorded on Indigo 127					

STORYTELLERS, THE

Number	Title (A Side/B Side)	Yr	VG	VG+	NM
45s					
CAPITOL					
5042	I Don't Want an Angel/Down in the Valley	1964	6.25	12.50	25.00
CLASSIC ARTISTS					
137	Christmas Time Is Coming/White Christmas	1990	—	2.50	5.00
—B-side by The Storytellers and Vicky Tafoya					
DIMENSION					
1014	When Two People/Time Will Tell	1963	5.00	10.00	20.00
RAMARCA					
501	When Two People/Time Will Tell	1963	7.50	15.00	30.00
STACK					
500	Hey Baby/You Played Me for a Fool	1959	50.00	100.00	200.00

STOWAWAYS, THE

Number	Title (A Side/B Side)	Yr	VG	VG+	NM
Albums					
JUSTICE					
JLP-148	The Stowaways	1968	125.00	250.00	500.00

STRANGE, BILLY

Number	Title (A Side/B Side)	Yr	VG	VG+	NM
45s					
BUENA VISTA					
406	I'll Remember April/The Mooncussors	1962	2.50	5.00	10.00
417	Johnny Shiloh/Day by Day	1963	2.50	5.00	10.00
COLISEUM					
605	A Lotta Limbo (Part 1)/A Lotta Limbo (Part 2)	1963	3.00	6.00	12.00
GNP CRESCENDO					
308	Wildwood Flower/Wabash Cannonball	1964	2.00	4.00	8.00
309	Charade/Where's Baby Gone	1964	2.00	4.00	8.00
320	The James Bond Theme/007 Theme	1964	2.00	4.00	8.00
334	Goldfinger/(Theme from) The Munsters	1965	2.00	4.00	8.00
341	The Man with the Golden Arm/Raunchy	1965	2.00	4.00	8.00
360	Remember Me (I'm the One Who Loves You)/ Trains and Boats and Planes	1965	2.00	4.00	8.00
367	Our Man Flint/Run, Spy, Run	1966	2.00	4.00	8.00
374	Caliente/Have Tequila	1966	2.00	4.00	8.00
390	Go Ahead and Cry/Yours Is a World I Can't Live In	1967	—	3.00	6.00
395	You Only Live Twice/For a Few Dollars More	1967	—	3.00	6.00
413	Hang 'Em High/Five Card Stud	1968	—	3.00	6.00
417	The High Chaparral/Gunsmoke	1968	—	3.00	6.00
477	Chattanooga Choo Choo/Track Walkin'	1974	—	2.00	4.00
800	Star Trek/Theme from "Jaws"	1975	—	2.50	5.00
LIBERTY					
55362	Long Steel Road/Soft Chains of Love	1961	2.50	5.00	10.00
55414	A Life of Pretend/I'm Still Crying	1962	2.50	5.00	10.00
TOWER					
515	De Sade/Nocturne Permission	1969	2.00	4.00	8.00
Albums					
CHESS					
CH2-6027 [(2)]	One More Time	1988	3.00	6.00	12.00
COLISEUM					
CM-1001 [M]	Limbo Rock	1962	10.00	20.00	40.00
GNP CRESCENDO					
GNP-94 [M]	Twelve String Guitar	1963	3.00	6.00	12.00
GNPS-94 [S]	Twelve String Guitar	1963	3.75	7.50	15.00
GNP-97 [M]	Mr. Guitar	1963	3.00	6.00	12.00
GNPS-97 [S]	Mr. Guitar	1963	3.75	7.50	15.00
GNP-98 [M]	Five String Banjo	1964	3.00	6.00	12.00
GNPS-98 [S]	Five String Banjo	1964	3.75	7.50	15.00
GNP-2004 [M]	The James Bond Theme	1964	3.00	6.00	12.00
GNPS-2004 [S]	The James Bond Theme	1964	3.75	7.50	15.00
GNP-2006 [M]	Goldfinger	1965	3.00	6.00	12.00
GNPS-2006 [S]	Goldfinger	1965	3.75	7.50	15.00
GNP-2009 [M]	English Hits of '65	1965	3.00	6.00	12.00
GNPS-2009 [S]	English Hits of '65	1965	3.75	7.50	15.00
GNP-2012 [M]	Billy Strange Plays the Hits	1965	3.00	6.00	12.00
GNPS-2012 [S]	Billy Strange Plays the Hits	1965	3.75	7.50	15.00
GNP-2016 [M]	Folk Rock Hits	1965	3.00	6.00	12.00
GNPS-2016 [S]	Folk Rock Hits	1965	3.75	7.50	15.00
GNP-2019 [M]	Secret Agent File	1966	3.00	6.00	12.00
GNPS-2019 [S]	Secret Agent File	1966	3.75	7.50	15.00
GNP-2022 [M]	In the Mexican Bag	1966	3.00	6.00	12.00
GNPS-2022 [S]	In the Mexican Bag	1966	3.75	7.50	15.00
GNP-2024 [M]	Billy Strange Plays Roger Miller Hits	1966	3.00	6.00	12.00
GNPS-2024 [S]	Billy Strange Plays Roger Miller Hits	1966	3.75	7.50	15.00
GNP-2030 [M]	Billy Strange with the Challengers	1966	3.75	7.50	15.00
GNPS-2030 [S]	Billy Strange with the Challengers	1966	5.00	10.00	20.00
GNP-2037 [M]	The Best of Billy Strange	1967	3.00	6.00	12.00
GNPS-2037 [S]	The Best of Billy Strange	1967	3.00	6.00	12.00
GNPS-2039	A James Bond Double Feature	1967	3.00	6.00	12.00
GNPS-2041	Railroad Man	1968	3.00	6.00	12.00
GNPS-2046	Great Western Themes	1969	3.00	6.00	12.00
GNPS-2094	Dyn-o-mite Guitar	197?	2.50	5.00	10.00
SUNSET					
SUS-5209	Mr. Guitar	1968	2.50	5.00	10.00
SURREY					
SS-1002	The Best of Billy Strange	1965	3.75	7.50	15.00
TRADITION					
2080	Strange Country	1969	2.50	5.00	10.00

STRANGE, TOMMY

Number	Title (A Side/B Side)	Yr	VG	VG+	NM
45s					
ERA					
3157	Don't Bug Me Baby/Two Steps Forward	1965	2.00	4.00	8.00
RAMCO					
1986	Piano Man from Louisiana/My Mind Just Don't Fit My Head	1967	2.00	4.00	8.00
1995	She Was Never Mine to Lose/One More Time	1967	2.00	4.00	8.00
ROCKO					
504	Nervous and Shakin' All Over/What Am I to Do	1958	50.00	100.00	200.00

STRANGEBREW

Number	Title (A Side/B Side)	Yr	VG	VG+	NM
45s					
ABC					
11217	Union Man/I Can Hardly Wait to Live	1969	3.00	6.00	12.00
Albums					
ABC					
ABCS-672	Very Strangebrew	1969	5.00	10.00	20.00

STRANGELOVES, THE

Also see THE SHEEP.

Number	Title (A Side/B Side)	Yr	VG	VG+	NM
45s					
BANG					
501	I Want Candy/It's About My Baby	1965	3.75	7.50	15.00
508	Cara-Lin/(Roll On) Mississippi	1965	3.00	6.00	12.00
514	Night Time/Rhythm of Love	1965	3.00	6.00	12.00
524	Hand Jive/I Gotta Dance	1966	3.00	6.00	12.00
544	Just the Way You Are/Quarter to Three	1967	3.00	6.00	12.00
SIRE					
4102	I Wanna Do It/Honey Do	1968	2.50	5.00	10.00
SWAN					
4192	Love Love (That's All I Want from You)/I'm on Fire	1964	5.00	10.00	20.00
Albums					
BANG					
BLP-211 [M]	I Want Candy	1965	20.00	40.00	80.00
BLPS-211 [S]	I Want Candy	1965	25.00	50.00	100.00

STRANGERS, THE (1)

Instrumental group; the only Strangers that made the charts.

Number	Title (A Side/B Side)	Yr	VG	VG+	NM
45s					
TITAN					
1701	The Caterpillar Crawl/Rockin' Rebel	1959	7.50	15.00	30.00
1702	Hill Stomp/A Lost Soul	1959	6.25	12.50	25.00
1704	Boogie Man/Young Maggie	1960	6.25	12.50	25.00
1711	Navajo/Dance of the Ants	1960	6.25	12.50	25.00

STRANGERS, THE (2)

Number	Title (A Side/B Side)	Yr	VG	VG+	NM
45s					
CHATTAHOOCHIE					
710	Like a Stranger/Can't Get the Water from My Eye	1966	3.00	6.00	12.00
JUBILEE					
5514	Plan On Someone New/What's the Matter Baby	1965	3.00	6.00	12.00

STRANGERS, THE (3)

Number	Title (A Side/B Side)	Yr	VG	VG+	NM
45s					
CHECKER					
1010	Darlin'/Pa and Billie	1962	3.75	7.50	15.00

STRANGERS, THE (4)

45s

CHOICE

Number	Title (A Side/B Side)	Yr	VG	VG+	NM
5	"Bart" Maverick/"Bret" Maverick	1960	5.00	10.00	20.00

STRANGERS, THE (5)

45s

CHRISTY

Number	Title (A Side/B Side)	Yr	VG	VG+	NM
107	We're in Love, We're in Love, We're in Love/Crab Louie	1959	7.50	15.00	30.00
108	J-U-D-Y/The Lord Will Welcome You	1959	6.25	12.50	25.00

STRANGERS, THE (6)

Group that backed BOBBY VEE on some of his later records, most notably "Come Back When You Grow Up."

45s

CUCA

Number	Title (A Side/B Side)	Yr	VG	VG+	NM
1172	Runaway/John Henry	1960	50.00	100.00	200.00

LIBERTY

Number	Title (A Side/B Side)	Yr	VG	VG+	NM
55481	Toy Soldier/Loco	1962	5.00	10.00	20.00
55550	Card Shark/Mindreader	1963	5.00	10.00	20.00

STRANGERS, THE (7)

45s

KING

Number	Title (A Side/B Side)	Yr	VG	VG+	NM
4697	My Friends/I've Got Eyes	1954	100.00	200.00	400.00
4709	Blue Flowers/Beg and Steal	1954	125.00	250.00	500.00
4728	Hoping You'll Understand/Just Don't Care	1954	100.00	200.00	400.00
4745	Drop Down to My Place/Get It One More Time	1954	75.00	150.00	300.00
4766	How Long Must I Wait/Dreams Came True	1955	62.50	125.00	250.00
4821	Without a Friend/Think Again	1955	15.00	30.00	60.00
—With "High Fidelity" on label					
4821	Without a Friend/Think Again	1955	62.50	125.00	250.00
—Without "High Fidelity" on label (original)					

STRANGERS, THE (8)

45s

LINDA

Number	Title (A Side/B Side)	Yr	VG	VG+	NM
118	Easy Livin'/Tell Me	1965	7.50	15.00	30.00

WARNER BROS.

Number	Title (A Side/B Side)	Yr	VG	VG+	NM
5438	Night Winds/These Are the Things I Love	1964	5.00	10.00	20.00

STRANGERS, THE (9)

45s

MGM

Number	Title (A Side/B Side)	Yr	VG	VG+	NM
11980	Strange Lady in Town/North Dakota	1955	10.00	20.00	40.00

STRASSMAN, MARCIA

45s

UNI

Number	Title (A Side/B Side)	Yr	VG	VG+	NM
55006	The Flower Children/Out of the Picture	1967	2.50	5.00	10.00
55023	The Groovy World of Jack and Jill/The Flower Shop	1967	2.50	5.00	10.00
55023 [PS]	The Groovy World of Jack and Jill/The Flower Shop	1967	3.75	7.50	15.00
55056	Star Gazer/Self-Analysis	1968	2.50	5.00	10.00

STRAWBERRY ALARM CLOCK

45s

ALL AMERICAN

Number	Title (A Side/B Side)	Yr	VG	VG+	NM
373	Incense and Peppermints/The Birdman of Alcatrash	1967	50.00	100.00	200.00

UNI

Number	Title (A Side/B Side)	Yr	VG	VG+	NM
55018	Incense and Peppermints/The Birdman of Alcatrash	1967	3.00	6.00	12.00
55046	Tomorrow/Birds in My Tree	1967	2.50	5.00	10.00
55055	Pretty Song from Psych-Out/Sit with the Guru	1968	2.50	5.00	10.00
55076	Barefoot in Baltimore/Angry Young Man	1968	2.50	5.00	10.00
55093	Paxton's Back Street Carnival/Sea Shell	1968	2.50	5.00	10.00
55113	Stand By/Miss Attraction	1969	2.00	4.00	8.00
55125	Good Morning Starshine/Me and the Township	1969	2.00	4.00	8.00
55158	Desiree/Changes	1969	2.00	4.00	8.00
55185	Small Package/Starting Out the Day	1969	2.00	4.00	8.00
55190	I Climbed the Mountain/Three	1969	2.00	4.00	8.00
55218	California Day/Three	1970	5.00	10.00	20.00
55241	Girl from the City/Three	1970	5.00	10.00	20.00

Albums

UNI

Number	Title (A Side/B Side)	Yr	VG	VG+	NM
3014 [M]	Incense and Peppermints	1967	12.50	25.00	50.00
73014 [S]	Incense and Peppermints	1967	10.00	20.00	40.00
73025	Wake Up It's Tomorrow	1968	10.00	20.00	40.00
73035	The World in a Sea Shell	1968	10.00	20.00	40.00
73054	Good Morning Starshine	1969	10.00	20.00	40.00
73074	The Best of the Strawberry Alarm Clock	1970	10.00	20.00	40.00

VOCALION

Number	Title (A Side/B Side)	Yr	VG	VG+	NM
VL 73915	Changes	1971	12.50	25.00	50.00

STRAWBS, THE

45s

ARISTA

Number	Title (A Side/B Side)	Yr	VG	VG+	NM
0327	I Don't Want to Talk About It/Words of Wisdom	1978	—	2.00	4.00

A&M

Number	Title (A Side/B Side)	Yr	VG	VG+	NM
944	Oh How She Changed/Or Am I Dreaming	1968	—	2.50	5.00
998	Poor Jimmy Wilson/The Man Who Called Himself Jesus	1968	—	2.50	5.00
1242 [DJ]	Where Is This Dream of Your Youth (mono/stereo)	1971	—	3.00	6.00
—No stock copies known					
1364	Heavy Disguise/Benedictus	1972	—	2.50	5.00
1419	Part of the Union/Tomorrow	1973	—	2.50	5.00
1451	Lay Down/The Winter and the Summer	1973	—	2.50	5.00
1476	Shine On Silver Sun/And Wherefore	1973	—	2.50	5.00
1519	Round and Round/The Heroine's Theme	1974	—	2.50	5.00
1687	Where Do You Go/Lemon Pie	1975	—	2.00	4.00
1747	Little Sleepy/Golden Salamander	1975	—	2.00	4.00

OYSTER

Number	Title (A Side/B Side)	Yr	VG	VG+	NM
702	I Only Want My Love to Grow on You/(Wasting My Time) Thinking of You	1976	—	2.00	4.00
704	So Close and Yet So Far Away/(B-side unknown)	1977	—	2.00	4.00
705	Burning for Me/Heartbreaker	1977	—	2.00	4.00

Albums

ARISTA

Number	Title (A Side/B Side)	Yr	VG	VG+	NM
AB 4172	Deadlines	1978	2.50	5.00	10.00

A&M

Number	Title (A Side/B Side)	Yr	VG	VG+	NM
SP-3607	Hero and Heroine	1974	3.75	7.50	15.00
SP-4288	Just a Collection of Antiques and Curios	1971	3.75	7.50	15.00
SP-4304	From the Witchwood	1971	3.75	7.50	15.00
SP-4344	Grave New World	1972	3.75	7.50	15.00
SP-4383	Bursting at the Seams	1973	3.75	7.50	15.00
SP-4506	Ghosts	1975	3.75	7.50	15.00
SP-4544	Nomadness	1975	3.75	7.50	15.00
SP-6005 [(2)]	Best of the Strawbs	1978	3.00	6.00	12.00

OYSTER

Number	Title (A Side/B Side)	Yr	VG	VG+	NM
OY-1603	Deep Cuts	1976	3.00	6.00	12.00
OY-1604	Burning for You	1977	3.00	6.00	12.00

STREAMERS, THE

45s

DOT

Number	Title (A Side/B Side)	Yr	VG	VG+	NM
16648	Slip-Stream/Blue Mountain	1964	7.50	15.00	30.00

STREET CLEANERS, THE

Yet another incarnation of P.F. SLOAN and STEVE BARRI.

45s

AMY

Number	Title (A Side/B Side)	Yr	VG	VG+	NM
914	Garbage City/That's Cool, That's Trash	1964	7.50	15.00	30.00

STREET NOISE

45s

EVOLUTION

Number	Title (A Side/B Side)	Yr	VG	VG+	NM
1014	Run or Die/Six Days on the Road	1969	2.00	4.00	8.00

Albums

EVOLUTION

Number	Title (A Side/B Side)	Yr	VG	VG+	NM
2010	Street Noise	1970	5.00	10.00	20.00

STREISAND, BARBRA

Also see BARBRA AND NEIL.

12-Inch Singles

CASABLANCA

Number	Title (A Side/B Side)	Yr	VG	VG+	NM
NBD 20199	No More Tears (Enough Is Enough) (11:40)	1979	2.50	5.00	10.00
—With Donna Summer; B-side is blank					

COLUMBIA

Number	Title (A Side/B Side)	Yr	VG	VG+	NM
05167	Emotion (6:34) (4:44)	1985	2.50	5.00	10.00

45s

ARISTA

Number	Title (A Side/B Side)	Yr	VG	VG+	NM
0123	How Lucky Can You Get/More Than You Know	1975	—	3.00	6.00
—Also see "Barbra and Neil"					

COLUMBIA

Number	Title (A Side/B Side)	Yr	VG	VG+	NM
02065	Promises/Make It Like a Memory	1981	—	2.00	4.00
02621	Comin' In and Out of Your Life/Lost Inside of You	1981	—	2.00	4.00
02717	Memory/Love Theme from "A Star Is Born"	1982	—	2.00	4.00
04177	The Way He Makes Me Feel (Studio)/The Way He Makes Me Feel (Film Version)	1983	—	—	3.00
04177 [PS]	The Way He Makes Me Feel (Studio)/The Way He Makes Me Feel (Film Version)	1983	—	2.00	4.00
04357	Papa Can You Hear Me?/Will Someone Ever Look at Me That Way	1984	—	—	3.00
04357 [PS]	Papa Can You Hear Me?/Will Someone Ever Look at Me That Way	1984	—	2.00	4.00
04605	Left in the Dark/Here We Are at Last	1984	—	—	3.00
04605 [PS]	Left in the Dark/Here We Are at Last	1984	—	2.00	4.00
04695	Make No Mistake, He's Mine/Clear Sailing	1984	—	—	3.00
—A-side with Kim Carnes					
04695 [PS]	Make No Mistake, He's Mine/Clear Sailing	1984	—	2.00	4.00
04707	Emotion/Here We Are at Last	1984	—	—	3.00
04707 [PS]	Emotion/Here We Are at Last	1984	—	2.00	4.00
05680	Somewhere/Not While I'm Around	1985	—	—	3.00
05680 [PS]	Somewhere/Not While I'm Around	1985	—	2.00	4.00
05837	Send In the Clowns/Being Alive	1986	—	—	3.00
05837 [PS]	Send In the Clowns/Being Alive	1986	2.00	4.00	8.00
08026	All I Ask of You/On My Way to You	1988	—	2.00	4.00
08026 [PS]	All I Ask of You/On My Way to You	1988	—	2.00	4.00
08062	Till I Loved You/Two People	1988	—	—	3.00
—A-side with Don Johnson					
08062 [PS]	Till I Loved You/Two People	1988	—	2.00	4.00
10075	Love in the Afternoon/Guava Jelly	1974	—	2.50	5.00
10130	Let the Good Times Roll/Jubilation	1975	—	2.50	5.00
10198	My Father's Song/By the Way	1975	—	2.50	5.00
10272	Shake Me, Wake Me, When It's Over/Widescreen	1975	—	2.50	5.00
10450	Love Theme from "A Star Is Born" (Evergreen)/I Believe in Love	1976	—	2.50	5.00
10450 [PS]	Love Theme from "A Star Is Born" (Evergreen)/I Believe in Love	1976	—	3.00	6.00
10555	My Heart Belongs to Me/Answer Me	1977	—	2.50	5.00
10756	Songbird/Honey Can I Put On Your Clothes	1978	—	2.00	4.00
10777	Love Theme from "Eyes of Laura Mars" (Prisoner)/Laura and Nevil	1978	—	2.00	4.00
10931	Superman/A Man I Loved	1979	—	2.00	4.00
11008	The Main Event/Fight/(Instrumental)	1979	—	2.00	4.00
11125	No More Tears (Enough Is Enough)/Wet	1979	—	2.00	4.00
—A-side with Donna Summer					
11125 [PS]	No More Tears (Enough Is Enough)/Wet	1979	—	2.50	5.00
11179	Kiss Me in the Rain/I Ain't Gonna Cry Tonight	1980	—	2.00	4.00

Number	Title (A Side/B Side)	Yr	VG	VG+	NM
11364	Woman in Love/Run Wild	1980	—	2.00	4.00
11390	Guilty/Life Story	1980	—	2.00	4.00
—A-side with Barry Gibb					
11430	What Kind of Fool/The Lovin' Side	1981	—	2.00	4.00
—A-side with Barry Gibb					
42631	Happy Days Are Here Again/When the Sun Comes Out	1962	5.00	10.00	20.00
42648	My Coloring Book/Lover Come Back to Me	1962	3.75	7.50	15.00
42937	Gotta Move/Make Believe	1964	3.75	7.50	15.00
42965	People/I Am Woman	1964	2.50	5.00	10.00
43127	Funny Girl/Absent Minded Me	1964	2.50	5.00	10.00
43248	Why Did I Choose You/My Love	1965	2.00	4.00	8.00
43323	My Man/Where Is the Wonder	1965	2.00	4.00	8.00
43403	He Touched Me/I Like Him	1965	2.00	4.00	8.00
43469	Second Hand Rose/The Kind of Man a Woman Needs	1965	2.00	4.00	8.00
43518	Where Am I Going?/You Wanna Bet	1966	—	3.00	6.00
43612	Sam, You Made the Pants Too Long/The Minute Waltz	1966	—	3.00	6.00
43739	La Mer/C'est Rien	1966	2.00	4.00	8.00
43808	Free Again/I've Been Here	1966	—	3.00	6.00
43896	Sleep in Heavenly Peace (Silent Night)/Gounod's Ave Maria	1966	2.50	5.00	10.00
43896 [PS]	Sleep in Heavenly Peace (Silent Night)/Gounod's Ave Maria	1966	5.00	10.00	20.00
44225	Stout-Hearted Men/Look	1967	—	3.00	6.00
44331	Lover Man (Oh, Where Can You Be)/My Funny Valentine	1967	—	3.00	6.00
44350	Jingle Bells?/White Christmas	1967	7.50	15.00	30.00
44350 [PS]	Jingle Bells?/White Christmas	1967	10.00	20.00	40.00
44351	Have Yourself a Merry Little Christmas/The Best Gift	1967	2.50	5.00	10.00
44351 [PS]	Have Yourself a Merry Little Christmas/The Best Gift	1967	5.00	10.00	20.00
44352	My Favorite Things/The Christmas Song	1967	7.50	15.00	30.00
44352 [PS]	My Favorite Things/The Christmas Song	1967	10.00	20.00	40.00
44354	I Wonder As I Wander/The Lord's Prayer	1967	7.50	15.00	30.00
44476	Our Corner of the Night/He Could Show Me	1968	—	2.50	5.00
44532	Morning After/Where Is the Wonder	1968	—	2.50	5.00
44622	Funny Girl/I'd Rather Be Blue Over You	1968	—	2.50	5.00
44704	Don't Rain on My Parade/My Man	1968	—	3.00	6.00
44775	Punky's Dilemma/Frank Mills	1969	—	2.50	5.00
44921	Honey Pie/Little Tin Soldier	1969	—	2.50	5.00
45040	What About Today/What Are You Doing the Rest of Your Life	1969	—	2.50	5.00
45072	Love Is Only Love/Before the Parade Passes By	1970	—	2.50	5.00
45147	The Best Thing You've Ever Done/Summer Me, Winter Me	1970	—	2.50	5.00
45236	Stoney End/I'll Be Home	1970	—	2.50	5.00
45341	Time and Love/No Easy Way Down	1971	—	2.50	5.00
45384	Flim Flam Man/Maybe	1971	—	2.50	5.00
45414	Where You Lead/Since I Fell for You	1971	—	2.50	5.00
45471	Mother/The Summer Knows	1971	—	2.50	5.00
45511	One Less Bell to Answer-A House Is Not a Home/Space Captain	1971	—	2.50	5.00
45626	Sweet Inspiration-Where You Lead/Didn't We	1972	—	2.50	5.00
45686	Sing a Song-Make Your Own Kind of Music/Starting Here-Starting Now	1972	—	2.50	5.00
45739	Didn't We/On a Clear Day	1972	—	2.50	5.00
45780	If I Close My Eyes/(Instrumental)	1973	—	2.50	5.00
45944	The Way We Were/What Are You Doing the Rest of Your Life	1973	—	2.50	5.00
—A-side contains a different vocal than most of the album versions					
46024	All in Love Is Fair/My Buddy-How About Me	1974	—	2.50	5.00
68691	What Were We Thinking Of/Why Let It Go	1989	—	—	3.00
73016	We're Not Makin' Love Anymore/Here We Are at Last	1989	—	—	3.00
73794	Till I Loved You/Two People	1991	—	—	3.00
—Reissue					
73944	All I Ask of You/On My Way to You	1991	—	—	3.00
—Reissue					
77533	Ordinary Miracles/Ordinary Miracles (Live)	1994	—	2.00	4.00
JZSP 79183/4 [DJ]	I'm All Smiles/Autumn	1964	7.50	15.00	30.00
—White label promo only					

Albums

COLUMBIA

Number	Title (A Side/B Side)	Yr	VG	VG+	NM
AS 1779 [DJ]	The Legend of Barbra Streisand	1983	10.00	20.00	40.00
—Promo-only interview LP for "Yentl"					
CL 2007 [M]	The Barbra Streisand Album	1963	5.00	10.00	20.00
—"Guaranteed High Fidelity" on label					
CL 2007 [M]	The Barbra Streisand Album	1966	3.00	6.00	12.00
—"360 Sound Mono" on label					
CL 2054 [M]	The Second Barbra Streisand Album	1963	5.00	10.00	20.00
—"Guaranteed High Fidelity" on label					
CL 2054 [M]	The Second Barbra Streisand Album	1966	3.00	6.00	12.00
—"360 Sound Mono" on label					
CL 2054 [M-DJ]	The Second Barbra Streisand Album	1963	50.00	100.00	200.00
—Promo only on blue vinyl (white label)					
CL 2154 [M]	The Third Album	1964	5.00	10.00	20.00
—"Guaranteed High Fidelity" on label					
CL 2154 [M]	The Third Album	1966	3.00	6.00	12.00
—"360 Sound Mono" on label					
CL 2215 [M]	People	1964	5.00	10.00	20.00
—"Guaranteed High Fidelity" on label					
CL 2215 [M]	People	1966	3.00	6.00	12.00
—"360 Sound Mono" on label					
CL 2336 [M]	My Name Is Barbra	1965	5.00	10.00	20.00
—"Guaranteed High Fidelity" on label					
CL 2336 [M]	My Name Is Barbra	1966	3.00	6.00	12.00
—"360 Sound Mono" on label					
CL 2409 [M]	My Name Is Barbra, Two	1965	3.75	7.50	15.00
CL 2478 [M]	Color Me Barbra	1966	3.75	7.50	15.00
CL 2478 [M-DJ]	Color Me Barbra	1966	50.00	100.00	200.00
—Promo only on red vinyl (white label)					
CL 2547 [M]	Je M'Appelle Barbra	1966	3.75	7.50	15.00
CL 2682 [M]	Simply Streisand	1967	7.50	15.00	30.00
CL 2757 [M]	A Christmas Album	1967	6.25	12.50	25.00
CS 8807 [S]	The Barbra Streisand Album	1963	6.25	12.50	25.00
—"360 Sound Stereo" in black on label					
CS 8807 [S]	The Barbra Streisand Album	1966	3.75	7.50	15.00
—"360 Sound Stereo" in white on label					
CS 8807 [S]	The Barbra Streisand Album	1970	2.50	5.00	10.00
—Orange label					
PC 8807	The Barbra Streisand Album	197?	2.00	4.00	8.00
—Reissue with new prefix					
CS 8854 [S]	The Second Barbra Streisand Album	1963	6.25	12.50	25.00
—"360 Sound Stereo" in black on label					
CS 8854 [S]	The Second Barbra Streisand Album	1966	3.75	7.50	15.00
—"360 Sound Stereo" in white on label					
CS 8854 [S]	The Second Barbra Streisand Album	1970	2.50	5.00	10.00
—Orange label					
CS 8854 [S-DJ]	The Second Barbra Streisand Album	1963	50.00	100.00	200.00
—Promo only on blue vinyl (white label)					
PC 8854	The Second Barbra Streisand Album	197?	2.00	4.00	8.00
—Reissue with new prefix					
CS 8954 [S]	The Third Album	1964	6.25	12.50	25.00
—"360 Sound Stereo" in black on label					
CS 8954 [S]	The Third Album	1966	3.75	7.50	15.00
—"360 Sound Stereo" in white on label					
CS 8954 [S]	The Third Album	1970	2.50	5.00	10.00
—Orange label					
PC 8954	The Third Album	197?	2.00	4.00	8.00
—Reissue with new prefix					
CS 9015 [S]	People	1964	6.25	12.50	25.00
—"360 Sound Stereo" in black on label					
CS 9015 [S]	People	1966	3.75	7.50	15.00
—"360 Sound Stereo" in white on label					
CS 9015 [S]	People	1970	2.50	5.00	10.00
—Orange label					
PC 9015	People	197?	2.00	4.00	8.00
—Reissue with new prefix					
CS 9136 [S]	My Name Is Barbra	1965	6.25	12.50	25.00
—"360 Sound Stereo" in black on label					
CS 9136 [S]	My Name Is Barbra	1966	3.75	7.50	15.00
—"360 Sound Stereo" in white on label					
CS 9136 [S]	My Name Is Barbra	1970	2.50	5.00	10.00
—Orange label					
PC 9136	My Name Is Barbra	197?	2.00	4.00	8.00
—Reissue with new prefix					
CS 9209 [S]	My Name Is Barbra, Two	1965	5.00	10.00	20.00
—Red "360 Sound Stereo" label					
CS 9209 [S]	My Name Is Barbra, Two	1970	2.50	5.00	10.00
—Orange label					
PC 9209	My Name Is Barbra, Two	197?	2.00	4.00	8.00
—Reissue with new prefix					
CS 9278 [S]	Color Me Barbra	1966	5.00	10.00	20.00
—Red "360 Sound Stereo" label					
CS 9278 [S]	Color Me Barbra	1970	2.50	5.00	10.00
—Orange label					
CS 9278 [S-DJ]	Color Me Barbra	1966	50.00	100.00	200.00
—Promo only on red vinyl (white label)					
PC 9278	Color Me Barbra	197?	2.00	4.00	8.00
—Reissue with new prefix					
CS 9347 [S]	Je M'Appelle Barbra	1966	5.00	10.00	20.00
—Red "360 Sound Stereo" label					
CS 9347 [S]	Je M'Appelle Barbra	1970	2.50	5.00	10.00
—Orange label					
PC 9347	Je M'Appelle Barbra	197?	2.00	4.00	8.00
—Reissue with new prefix					
CS 9482 [S]	Simply Streisand	1967	5.00	10.00	20.00
—Red "360 Sound Stereo" label					
CS 9482 [S]	Simply Streisand	1970	2.50	5.00	10.00
—Orange label					
PC 9482	Simply Streisand	197?	2.00	4.00	8.00
—Reissue with new prefix					
CS 9557 [S]	A Christmas Album	1967	5.00	10.00	20.00
—Red "360 Sound Stereo" label					
CS 9557 [S]	A Christmas Album	1970	2.00	4.00	8.00
—Orange label					
PC 9557	A Christmas Album	198?	—	3.00	6.00
—Reissue with new prefix and bar code					
CS 9710	A Happening in Central Park	1968	3.75	7.50	15.00
—Red "360 Sound Stereo" label					
CS 9710	A Happening in Central Park	1970	2.50	5.00	10.00
—Orange label					
PC 9710	A Happening in Central Park	197?	2.00	4.00	8.00
—Reissue with new prefix					
CS 9816	What About Today?	1969	3.75	7.50	15.00
—Red "360 Sound Stereo" label					
CS 9816	What About Today?	1970	2.50	5.00	10.00
—Orange label					
PC 9816	What About Today?	197?	2.00	4.00	8.00
—Reissue with new prefix					
JC 9968	Barbra Streisand's Greatest Hits	197?	—	3.00	6.00
—Another reissue with a new prefix (postdates PC)					
KCS 9968	Barbra Streisand's Greatest Hits	1970	3.75	7.50	15.00
—Red "360 Sound Stereo" label					
KCS 9968	Barbra Streisand's Greatest Hits	1970	2.50	5.00	10.00
—Orange label					
PC 9968	Barbra Streisand's Greatest Hits	197?	2.00	4.00	8.00
—Reissue with new prefix					
CQ 30378 [Q]	Stoney End	1972	6.25	12.50	25.00
KC 30378	Stoney End	1971	3.75	7.50	15.00
PC 30378	Stoney End	197?	2.00	4.00	8.00
—Reissue with new prefix					
CQ 30792 [Q]	Barbra Joan Streisand	1972	6.25	12.50	25.00
KC 30792	Barbra Joan Streisand	1971	3.75	7.50	15.00
PC 30792	Barbra Joan Streisand	197?	2.00	4.00	8.00
—Reissue with new prefix					
CQ 31760 [Q]	Live Concert at the Forum	1972	6.25	12.50	25.00
KC 31760	Live Concert at the Forum	1972	3.75	7.50	15.00

Number	Title (A Side/B Side)	Yr	VG	VG+	NM
PC 31760	Live Concert at the Forum	197?	2.00	4.00	8.00
—Reissue with new prefix					
KC 32655	Barbra Streisand...And Other Musical Instruments	1973	3.00	6.00	12.00
PC 32655	Barbra Streisand...And Other Musical Instruments	197?	2.00	4.00	8.00
—Reissue with new prefix					
JC 32801	The Way We Were	197?	2.00	4.00	8.00
—Reissue with new prefix					
PC 32801	Barbra Streisand Featuring The Way We Were and All In Love Is Fair	1974	5.00	10.00	20.00
—Original version with this title on spine and label, and no title on front cover					
PC 32801	The Way We Were	1974	3.00	6.00	12.00
—Revised version; has this title on spine, label and front cover					
PCQ 32801 [Q]	The Way We Were	1974	6.25	12.50	25.00
PC 33095	Butterfly	1974	3.00	6.00	12.00
—Original with no bar code					
PC 33095	Butterfly	198?	2.00	4.00	8.00
—Reissue with bar code					
PC 33815	Lazy Afternoon	1975	3.00	6.00	12.00
—Original with no bar code					
PC 33815	Lazy Afternoon	198?	2.00	4.00	8.00
—Reissue with bar code					
PCQ 33815 [Q]	Lazy Afternoon	1975	6.25	12.50	25.00
JS 34403	A Star Is Born	1976	3.00	6.00	12.00
—With Kris Kristofferson					
JC 34830	Streisand Superman	1977	3.00	6.00	12.00
PC 34830	Streisand Superman	198?	2.00	4.00	8.00
—Budget-line reissue					
PC 35275	Songbird	198?	2.00	4.00	8.00
—Budget-line reissue					
JC 35375	Songbird	1978	3.00	6.00	12.00
FC 35679	Barbra Streisand's Greatest Hits, Volume 2	1978	3.00	6.00	12.00
FC 36258	Wet	1979	2.50	5.00	10.00
FC 36750	Guilty	1980	2.50	5.00	10.00
TC 37678	Memories	1981	2.50	5.00	10.00
JS 39152	Yentl	1983	2.50	5.00	10.00
QC 39480	Emotion	1984	2.50	5.00	10.00
OC 40092	The Broadway Album	1985	2.50	5.00	10.00
OC 40880	Till I Loved You	1988	2.50	5.00	10.00
HC 42801	The Way We Were	1982	7.50	5.00	30.00
—Half-speed mastered edition					
OC 45369	A Collection: Greatest Hits.. And More	1989	3.75	7.50	15.00
HC 45679	Barbra Streisand's Greatest Hits, Volume 2	1980	7.50	15.00	30.00
—Half-speed mastered edition					
HC 46750	Guilty	1982	7.50	15.00	30.00
—Half-speed mastered edition					
HC 47678	Memories	1982	7.50	15.00	30.00
—Half-speed mastered edition					
COLUMBIA MASTERWORKS					
M 33452	Classical Barbra	1976	3.00	6.00	12.00

STRENGTH, BILL

Number	Title (A Side/B Side)	Yr	VG	VG+	NM
45s					
SUN					
346	Guess I'd Better Go/Senorita	1960	6.25	12.50	25.00

STRIDER

Number	Title (A Side/B Side)	Yr	VG	VG+	NM
Albums					
WARNER BROS.					
BS 2722	Exposed	1973	5.00	10.00	20.00

STRIDERS, THE (1)

Number	Title (A Side/B Side)	Yr	VG	VG+	NM
45s					
APOLLO					
480	I Wonder/Hesitating Fool	1955	75.00	150.00	300.00
DERBY					
857	Come Back to Me Tomorrow/Rollin'	1954	50.00	100.00	200.00

STRIDERS, THE (2)

Number	Title (A Side/B Side)	Yr	VG	VG+	NM
45s					
COLUMBIA					
43738	Sorrow/Say You Love Me	1966	5.00	10.00	20.00
43948	Am I On Your Mind/There's a Storm Comin'	1966	5.00	10.00	20.00
44143	When You Walk In the Room/Do It Now	1967	3.75	7.50	15.00

STRIKES, THE

Number	Title (A Side/B Side)	Yr	VG	VG+	NM
45s					
IMPERIAL					
5433	Baby I'm Sorry/If You Can't Rock Me	1957	12.50	25.00	50.00
5446	Rockin'/I Don't Want to Cry Over You	1957	12.50	25.00	50.00
LIN					
5006	Baby I'm Sorry/If You Can't Rock Me	1957	18.75	37.50	75.00

STRING-A-LONGS, THE

Number	Title (A Side/B Side)	Yr	VG	VG+	NM
45s					
7 ARTS					
700	Tell the World/For My Angel	1961	3.75	7.50	15.00
—As "Mickey Boyd and the Plain Viewers"					
ATCO					
6694	Popi/Places I Remember	1969	2.00	4.00	8.00
DOT					
16331	Twistwatch/Sunday	1962	2.50	5.00	10.00
16379	Spinnin' My Wheels/My Blue Heaven	1962	2.50	5.00	10.00
16393	Matilda/Replica	1962	2.50	5.00	10.00
16448	Heartaches/Happy Melody	1963	2.50	5.00	10.00
16575	Myna Bird/My Babe	1964	2.50	5.00	10.00
16592	Beatles, You Bug Me/Bloomin' Bird	1964	4.00	8.00	16.00
—As "The Bug Men"					
16708	Caravan/Mathilda	1965	2.50	5.00	10.00
WARWICK					
603	Wheels/Am I Asking Too Much	1960	3.75	7.50	15.00
603	Wheels/Tell the World	1960	5.00	10.00	20.00
—Red label					
603	Wheels/Tell the World	1960	6.25	12.50	25.00
—White label (not marked as a promo)					
606	Tell the World/For an Angel	1960	3.75	7.50	15.00
625	Brass Buttons/Panic Button	1961	3.75	7.50	15.00
654	Take a Minute/Should I	1961	3.75	7.50	15.00
668	Myna Bird/Scottie	1961	3.75	7.50	15.00
675	Theme for Twisters/Nearly Sunrise	1962	3.75	7.50	15.00
Albums					
ATCO					
SD 33-241	Wide World Hits	1969	6.25	12.50	25.00
DOT					
DLP-3463 [M]	Matilda	1962	6.25	12.50	25.00
DLP-3723 [M]	Great Instrumental Hits	1966	5.00	10.00	20.00
DLP-25463 [S]	Matilda	1962	7.50	15.00	30.00
DLP-25723 [S]	Great Instrumental Hits	1966	6.25	12.50	25.00
WARWICK					
W-2036ST [S]	Pick-A-Hit Featuring "Wheels"	1961	20.00	40.00	80.00
W-2036 [M]	Pick-A-Hit Featuring "Wheels"	1961	12.50	25.00	50.00

STRING CHEESE

Number	Title (A Side/B Side)	Yr	VG	VG+	NM
Albums					
WOODEN NICKEL					
WNS-1001	String Cheese	1971	5.00	10.00	20.00

STRONG, BARRETT

Number	Title (A Side/B Side)	Yr	VG	VG+	NM
45s					
ANNA					
1111	Money (That's What I Want)/Oh I Apologize	1960	7.50	15.00	30.00
1116	You Know What to Do/Yes, No, Maybe So	1960	6.25	12.50	25.00
ATCO					
6225	Seven Sins/What Went Wrong	1962	10.00	20.00	40.00
CAPITOL					
4052	Is It True/Anywhere	1975	—	2.50	5.00
4120	Surrender/There's Something About You	1975	—	2.50	5.00
4223	Gonna Make It Right/The Man Up in the Sky	1976	—	2.50	5.00
EPIC					
11011	Stand Up and Cheer for the Preacher (Part 1)/ Stand Up and Cheer for the Preacher (Part 2)	1973	—	2.50	5.00
PHASE II					
02048	Rock It Easy/Love Will Make It Right	1981	—	2.00	4.00
TAMLA					
54022	Let's Rock/(B-side unknown)	1960	1000.	1500.	2000.
54027	Money (That's What I Want)/Oh I Apologize	1960	30.00	60.00	120.00
—Horizontal lines label					
54027	Money (That's What I Want)/Oh I Apologize	1960	12.50	25.00	50.00
—Globe label					
54029	You Know What to Do/Yes, No, Maybe So	1960	12.50	25.00	50.00
54033	I'm Gonna Cry/Whirl Wind	1960	12.50	25.00	50.00
54035	You Got What It Takes/Money and Me	1961	12.50	25.00	50.00
54043	Two Wrongs Don't Make a Right/Misery	1961	12.50	25.00	50.00
TOLLIE					
9023	Make Up Your Mind/I Better Run	1964	7.50	15.00	30.00
Albums					
CAPITOL					
ST-11376	Stronghold	1975	3.00	6.00	12.00

STRONG, NOLAN, AND THE DIABLOS

Some of these refer only to "The Diablos," others only to "Nolan Strong."

Number	Title (A Side/B Side)	Yr	VG	VG+	NM
45s					
FORTUNE					
509/10	Adios, My Desert Love/(I Want) An Old Fashioned Girl	1954	25.00	50.00	100.00
511	The Wind/Baby, Be Mine	1954	25.00	50.00	100.00
511	The Wind/Baby, Be Mine	196?	5.00	10.00	20.00
—Later pressing adds reference to LP on which it appears					
514	Hold Me Until Eternity/Route 16	1955	25.00	50.00	100.00
516	Daddy Rockin' Strong/Do You Remember What You Did Last Night	1955	25.00	50.00	100.00
518	The Way You Dog Me Around/Jump, Shake and Move	1955	25.00	50.00	100.00
519	You're the Only Girl, Dolores/You Are	1956	20.00	40.00	80.00
522	Teardrop from Heaven/Try Me One More Time	1956	20.00	40.00	80.00
525	Can't We Talk This Over/The Mambo of Love	1957	20.00	40.00	80.00
529	For Old Times' Sake/My Heart Will Always Belong to You	1959	10.00	20.00	40.00
531	I Am With You/Goodbye Matilda	1959	10.00	20.00	40.00
532	If I Could Be with You Tonite/I Wanna Know	1959	10.00	20.00	40.00
536	Since You're Gone/What You Gonna Do	1960	7.50	15.00	30.00
544	Blue Moon/I Don't Care	1962	5.00	10.00	20.00
546	Mind Over Matter (I'm Gonna Make You Mine)/ Beside You	1962	5.00	10.00	20.00
553	I Really Love You/You're My Love	1963	5.00	10.00	20.00
556	(Yeah, Baby) It's Because of You/You're Every Beat of My Heart	1963	5.00	10.00	20.00
564	Are You Making a Fool Out of Me/You're My Happiness	1964	3.75	7.50	15.00
569	(What Did That Genie Mean When He Said) Ali-Coochie/(You're Not Good Looking But) You're Presentable	1964	3.75	7.50	15.00
574	The Way You Dog Me Around/Jump with Me	1980	3.75	7.50	15.00
PYRAMID					
159	White Christmas/Danny Boy	19??	3.75	7.50	15.00
Albums					
FORTUNE					
LP-8010 [M]	Fortune of Hits	1961	55.00	110.00	220.00
—Purple label, thick vinyl					
LP-8010 [M]	Fortune of Hits	196?	12.50	25.00	50.00
—Yellow label					
LP-8010 [M]	Fortune of Hits	197?	3.75	7.50	15.00
—Purple label, thinner, more flexible vinyl					

Number	Title (A Side/B Side)	Yr	VG	VG+	NM
LP-8012 [M]	Fortune of Hits, Vol. 2	1962	55.00	110.00	220.00
—Purple label, thick vinyl					
LP-8012 [M]	Fortune of Hits, Vol. 2	196?	12.50	25.00	50.00
—Yellow label					
LP-8012 [M]	Fortune of Hits, Vol. 2	197?	3.75	7.50	15.00
—Purple label, thinner, more flexible vinyl					
LP-8015 [M]	Mind Over Matter	1963	62.50	125.00	250.00
—Purple label, thick vinyl					
LP-8015 [M]	Mind Over Matter	196?	15.00	30.00	60.00
—Yellow label					
LP-8015 [M]	Mind Over Matter	197?	5.00	10.00	20.00
—Purple label, thinner, more flexible vinyl					

STRUNK, JUD

45s

Number	Title (A Side/B Side)	Yr	VG	VG+	NM
AD-MEDIA					
6416	The Santa Song/A Special Christmas Tree	1969	2.50	5.00	10.00
6416 [PS]	The Santa Song/A Special Christmas Tree	1969	3.75	7.50	15.00
CAPITOL					
3960	My Country/The Will	1974	—	3.00	6.00
COLUMBIA					
4-45189	Self-Eating Watermelon/Children at Play	1970	2.00	4.00	8.00
MCA					
40872	Tell Me Where I Am Tonight/Fool on My Shoulder	1978	—	2.00	4.00
MELODYLAND					
6015	The Biggest Parakeets in Town/I Wasn't Wrong About You	1975	—	2.50	5.00
6027	Pamela Brown/They're Tearing Down a Town	1975	—	2.50	5.00
MGM					
14388	Jacob Brown/Long Ride Home	1972	—	3.00	6.00
14463	Daisy a Day/The Searchers	1972	—	3.50	7.00
14572	Next Door Neighbor's Kid/I'd Prefer to Do It All Again	1973	—	3.00	6.00

Albums

Number	Title (A Side/B Side)	Yr	VG	VG+	NM
COLUMBIA					
CS 9990	Downeast Viewpoint	1970	3.75	7.50	15.00
HARMONY					
KH 32344	Mr. Bojangles and Other Favorites	1973	2.50	5.00	10.00
MCA					
2309	A Semi-Reformed Tequila Crazed Gypsy	1977	2.50	5.00	10.00
MGM					
SE-4790	Jones General Store	1972	3.00	6.00	12.00
SE-4898	Daisy a Day	1973	3.00	6.00	12.00

STUART, CHAD

Also see CHAD AND JEREMY.

45s

Number	Title (A Side/B Side)	Yr	VG	VG+	NM
SIDEWALK					
944	Good Morning Sunrise/Paxton's Song	1968	2.00	4.00	8.00
944 [PS]	Good Morning Sunrise/Paxton's Song	1968	3.75	7.50	15.00

STUART, CHAD AND JILL

Also see CHAD STUART.

45s

Number	Title (A Side/B Side)	Yr	VG	VG+	NM
COLUMBIA					
43467	The Cruel War/I Can't Talk to You	1965	2.00	4.00	8.00
43467 [PS]	The Cruel War/I Can't Talk to You	1965	3.75	7.50	15.00

STUART, CHAD, AND JEREMY CLYDE

See CHAD AND JEREMY.

STUBBS, JOE

45s

Number	Title (A Side/B Side)	Yr	VG	VG+	NM
LU-PINE					
120	Keep On Loving Me/What's My Destiny	1964	50.00	100.00	200.00

STUDENT NURSES, THE

45s

Number	Title (A Side/B Side)	Yr	VG	VG+	NM
RCA VICTOR					
47-8482	Kiss Me Goodnight/Simply	1964	6.25	12.50	25.00

STUDENTS, THE

45s

Number	Title (A Side/B Side)	Yr	VG	VG+	NM
ARGO					
5386	I'm So Young/Every Day of the Week	1961	5.00	10.00	20.00
CHECKER					
902	I'm So Young/Every Day of the Week	1958	10.00	20.00	40.00
1004	My Vow to You/That's How I Feel	1962	3.75	7.50	15.00
NOTE					
10012	I'm So Young/Every Day of the Week	1958	125.00	250.00	500.00
10019	My Vow to You/That's How I Feel	1959	100.00	200.00	400.00
RED TOP					
100	My Heart Is an Open Door/Mommy and Daddy	1958	50.00	100.00	200.00
—Blue label					
100	My Heart Is an Open Door/Mommy and Daddy	1958	10.00	20.00	40.00
—Red label					

STUFFY AND HIS FROZEN PARACHUTE BAND

Albums

Number	Title (A Side/B Side)	Yr	VG	VG+	NM
PARAMOUNT					
PAS-6070	Stuffy and His Frozen Parachute Band	1974	6.25	12.50	25.00

STYLERS, THE (1)

45s

Number	Title (A Side/B Side)	Yr	VG	VG+	NM
GOLDEN CREST					
117	You Tell Me/Blues in the Night	1957	10.00	20.00	40.00
117 [PS]	You Tell Me/Blues in the Night	1957	25.00	50.00	100.00
129	Kiss and Run Lover/Girlie, Girlie, Girlie	1957	10.00	20.00	40.00
JUBILEE					
5168	Believe It or Not/The World Is Yours	1954	10.00	20.00	40.00
5188	Shoo Shoo Sha La La/I Love Ya Like Crazy	1955	10.00	20.00	40.00
5246	Lost John/Huffin' and Puffin'	1956	10.00	20.00	40.00
5253	Confession of a Sinner/Gonna Tell 'Em	1956	10.00	20.00	40.00
5279	Breaker of Hearts/Miracle in Milan	1957	7.50	15.00	30.00

STYLERS, THE (U)

These could both be by group (1), or they may be different groups.

45s

Number	Title (A Side/B Side)	Yr	VG	VG+	NM
GORDY					
7018	Going Steady Anniversary/Pushing Up Daisies	1963	15.00	30.00	60.00
KICKS					
2	Gentle as a Teardrop/There Were Others	1954	125.00	250.00	500.00

STYLES, THE (1)

45s

Number	Title (A Side/B Side)	Yr	VG	VG+	NM
JOSIE					
920	I Love You for Sentimental Reasons/School Bells to Chapel Bells	1964	15.00	30.00	60.00
SERENE					
1501	Scarlet Angel/Gotta Go, Go, Go	1961	37.50	75.00	150.00

STYLES, THE (2)

45s

Number	Title (A Side/B Side)	Yr	VG	VG+	NM
MODERN					
1048	I Know You Know That I Know/Baby You're Alive	1967	3.00	6.00	12.00
SWAN					
4258	I Do Love You/Hush Little Girl	1966	3.00	6.00	12.00

STYLISTICS, THE

12-Inch Singles

Number	Title (A Side/B Side)	Yr	VG	VG+	NM
H&L					
2008	The Lion Sleeps Tonight (5:29)/Fly! (6:09)	1977	3.75	7.50	15.00
STREETWISE					
2236	Give a Little Love/Give a Little Love (Sing Along Version)	1984	2.00	4.00	8.00
2237	Some Things Never Change/Row Your Love	1985	2.00	4.00	8.00
2238	Special/(B-side unknown)	1985	2.00	4.00	8.00
2241	Let's Go Rockin' (Tonight)/(B-side unknown)	1986	2.00	4.00	8.00

45s

Number	Title (A Side/B Side)	Yr	VG	VG+	NM
AMHERST					
301	Because I Love You Girl/My Love, Come Live With Me	1985	—	2.00	4.00
AVCO					
4581	You Are Everything/Country Living	1971	—	2.50	5.00
4591	Betcha by Golly, Wow/Ebony Eyes	1972	—	2.50	5.00
4595	People Make the World Go Round/Point of No Return	1972	—	2.50	5.00
4603	I'm Stone in Love with You/Make It Last	1972	—	2.50	5.00
4611	Break Up to Make Up/You and Me	1973	—	2.50	5.00
4618	You'll Never Get to Heaven (If You Break My Heart)/If You Don't Watch Out	1973	—	2.50	5.00
4625	Rockin' Roll Baby/Pieces	1973	—	2.50	5.00
4634	You Make Me Feel Brand New/Only for the Children	1974	—	2.50	5.00
4640	Let's Put It All Together/I Take It Out on You	1974	—	2.50	5.00
4647	Heavy Fallin' Out/Go Now	1974	—	2.50	5.00
4649	Star on a TV Show/Hey Girl, Come and Get It	1975	—	2.50	5.00
4652	Thank You Baby/Sing, Baby, Sing	1975	—	2.50	5.00
4656	Can't Give You Anything (But My Love)/I'd Rather Be Hurt by You	1975	—	2.50	5.00
4661	Funky Weekend/If You Are There	1975	—	2.50	5.00
4664	You Are Beautiful/Michael and Me	1976	—	2.50	5.00
4664 [PS]	You Are Beautiful/Michael and Me	1976	2.50	5.00	10.00
AVCO EMBASSY					
4555	You're a Big Girl Now/Let the Junkie Beat the Pusher	1970	—	3.00	6.00
4572	Stop, Look, Listen (To Your Heart)/If I Love You	1971	—	3.00	6.00
H&L					
4669	Can't Help Falling in Love/Jenny	1976	—	2.00	4.00
4674	Because I Love You, Girl/You Are	1976	—	2.00	4.00
4676	Only You/What Goes Around Comes Around	1976	—	2.00	4.00
4678	I Got a Letter/Satin Doll	1977	—	2.00	4.00
4681	Shame and Scandal in the Family/That Don't Shake Me	1977	—	2.00	4.00
4686	I'm Coming Home/I Run to You	1977	—	2.00	4.00
4695	Fool of the Year/Good Thing Goin'	1978	—	2.00	4.00
MERCURY					
74005	First Impressions/Your Love's Too Good to Be Forgotten	1978	—	2.00	4.00
74022	I Can't Stop Livin'/You're the Best Thing in My Life	1978	—	2.00	4.00
74042	Love at First Sight/Broken Wing	1979	—	2.00	4.00
74057	Don't Know Where I'm Going/You Make Me Feel So Doggone Good	1979	—	2.00	4.00
PHILADELPHIA INT'L.					
02901	Callin' You/Don't Come Telling Me Lies	1982	—	2.00	4.00
03085	Lighten Up/We Should Be Lovers	1982	—	2.00	4.00
SEBRING					
8370	You're a Big Girl Now/Let the Junkie Beat the Pusher	1970	7.50	15.00	30.00
STREETWISE					
1136	Give a Little Love/Give a Little Love (Sing Along Version)	1984	—	2.00	4.00
1137	Some Things Never Change/Row Your Love	1985	—	2.00	4.00
1138	Special/(B-side unknown)	1985	—	2.00	4.00
TSOP					
02195	What's Your Name/Almost There	1981	—	2.00	4.00
02588	Mine All Mine/Closer Than Close	1981	—	2.00	4.00
02702	Habit/I've Got This Feeling	1982	—	2.00	4.00
4789	Hurry Up This Way Again/It Started Out	1980	—	2.00	4.00
4798	And I'll See You No More/Driving Me Wild	1980	—	2.00	4.00

Albums

Number	Title (A Side/B Side)	Yr	VG	VG+	NM
AMHERST					
AMH-743	The Best of the Stylistics	1986	2.50	5.00	10.00
AMH-744	All-Time Classics	1986	2.50	5.00	10.00
AMH-745	The Best of the Stylistics, Vol. 2	1986	2.50	5.00	10.00
AMH-746	Greatest Love Hits	1986	2.50	5.00	10.00
AVCO					
11006	Round 2: The Stylistics	1972	5.00	10.00	20.00
11010	Rockin' Roll Baby	1973	5.00	10.00	20.00
33023	The Stylistics	1971	5.00	10.00	20.00
69001	Let's Put It All Together	1974	3.75	7.50	15.00
69004	Heavy	1974	3.75	7.50	15.00
69005	The Best of the Stylistics	1975	3.75	7.50	15.00
69008	Thank You Baby	1975	3.75	7.50	15.00
69010	You Are Beautiful	1975	3.75	7.50	15.00
H&L					
69013	Fabulous	1976	3.00	6.00	12.00
69032	Wonder Woman	1978	3.00	6.00	12.00
MERCURY					
SRM-1-3727	In Fashion	1978	3.00	6.00	12.00
SRM-1-3753	Love Spell	1979	3.00	6.00	12.00
PHILADELPHIA INT'L.					
FZ 37955	1982	1982	2.50	5.00	10.00
TSOP					
JZ 36470	Hurry Up This Way Again	1980	2.50	5.00	10.00
FZ 37458	Closer Than Close	1981	2.50	5.00	10.00

STYLISTS, THE

45s

Number	Title (A Side/B Side)	Yr	VG	VG+	NM
V.I.P.					
25066	What Is Love/Where Did the Children Go	1970	6.25	12.50	25.00

STYX

12-Inch Singles

Number	Title (A Side/B Side)	Yr	VG	VG+	NM
A&M					
SP-17021 [DJ]	The Grand Illusion (same on both sides)	1977	3.75	7.50	15.00

45s

Number	Title (A Side/B Side)	Yr	VG	VG+	NM
A&M					
1786	Lorelei/Midnight Ride	1976	—	2.00	4.00
1818	Born for Adventure/Light Up	1976	—	2.50	5.00
1877	Mademoiselle/Light Up	1976	—	2.50	5.00
1900	Jennifer/Shooz	1976	—	2.50	5.00
1931	Crystal Ball/Put Me On	1977	—	2.50	5.00
1977	Come Sail Away/Put Me On	1977	—	2.00	4.00
1977 [PS]	Come Sail Away/Put Me On	1977	—	3.00	6.00
2007	Fooling Yourself (The Angry Young Man)/The Grand Finale	1978	—	2.00	4.00
2007 [PS]	Fooling Yourself (The Angry Young Man)/The Grand Finale	1978	—	3.00	6.00
2087	Blue Collar Man (Long Nights)/Superstars	1978	—	2.00	4.00
2087 [PS]	Blue Collar Man (Long Nights)/Superstars	1978	—	3.00	6.00
2110	Sing for the Day/Queen of Spades	1979	—	2.50	5.00
2110	Renegade/Sing for the Day	1979	—	2.00	4.00
2110 [PS]	Renegade/Sing for the Day	1979	—	2.50	5.00
2188	Babe/I'm O.K.	1979	—	2.00	4.00
2206	Why Me/Lights	1979	—	2.00	4.00
2228	Borrowed Time/Eddie	1980	—	2.00	4.00
2294	The Best of Times/Lights	1980	—	—	—
—Unreleased?					
2300	The Best of Times/Lights	1981	—	2.00	4.00
2300 [PS]	The Best of Times/Lights	1981	—	2.00	4.00
2323	Too Much Time on My Hands/Queen of Spades	1981	—	2.00	4.00
2348	Nothing Ever Goes As Planned/Never Say Never	1981	—	2.00	4.00
2525	Mr. Roboto/Snowblind	1983	—	—	3.00
2525 [PS]	Mr. Roboto/Snowblind	1983	—	—	3.00
2543	Don't Let It End/Rockin' the Paradise	1983	—	—	3.00
2543 [PS]	Don't Let It End/Rockin' the Paradise	1983	—	—	3.00
2560	Double Life/Haven't We Been Here Before	1983	—	—	3.00
2568	High Time/Double Life	1983	—	—	3.00
2625	Music Time/Heavy Metal Poisoning	1984	—	—	3.00
2625 [PS]	Music Time/Heavy Metal Poisoning	1984	—	—	3.00
8696	Show Me the Way/Love at First Sight	1993	—	2.00	4.00
—Reissue series; both songs were unreleased on 45 until this record					
WOODEN NICKEL					
BWBO-0065	You Need Love/Winner Take All	1973	—	2.50	5.00
65-0106	Best Thing/What Has Come Between	1972	—	2.50	5.00
65-0111	I'm Gonna Make You Feel It/Quick Is the Beat of My Heart	1972	—	2.50	5.00
65-0116	Lady/You Better Ask	1973	2.50	5.00	10.00
BWBO-0252	Young Man/Unfinished Song	1974	—	2.50	5.00
WB-10027	Lies/22 Years	1974	—	2.50	5.00
WB-10102	Lady/Children of the Land	1974	—	2.50	5.00
WB-10272	You Need Love/You Better Ask	1975	—	2.50	5.00
WB-10329	Best Thing/Havin' a Ball	1975	—	2.50	5.00
GB-10492	Lady/Children of the Land	1975	—	2.00	4.00
—Gold Standard Series					
WB-11205	Winner Take All/Best Thing	1978	—	2.50	5.00

Albums

Number	Title (A Side/B Side)	Yr	VG	VG+	NM
A&M					
SP-3217	Equinox	1984	2.00	4.00	8.00
SP-3218	Crystal Ball	1984	2.00	4.00	8.00
SP-3223	The Grand Illusion	1984	2.00	4.00	8.00
SP-3224	Pieces of Eight	1984	2.00	4.00	8.00
SP-3239	Cornerstone	1984	2.00	4.00	8.00
SP-3240	Paradise Theater	1984	2.00	4.00	8.00
—3200 series LPs are reissues					
SP-3711	Cornerstone	1979	7.50	15.00	30.00
—Silver vinyl pressing, reportedly for fan club members					
SP-3711	Cornerstone	1979	2.50	5.00	10.00
SP-3719	Paradise Theater	1981	2.50	5.00	10.00
SP-3734	Kilroy Was Here	1983	2.50	5.00	10.00
SP-4559	Equinox	1975	2.50	5.00	10.00
SP-4604	Crystal Ball	1976	2.50	5.00	10.00
SP-4637	The Grand Illusion	1977	2.50	5.00	10.00
PR-4724 [PD]	Pieces of Eight	1978	6.25	12.50	25.00
SP-4724	Pieces of Eight	1978	2.50	5.00	10.00
75021 5327 1	Edge of the Century	1990	3.75	7.50	15.00
SP-6514 [(2)]	Caught in the Act	1984	3.00	6.00	12.00
SP-8431 [(2) DJ]	The Styx Radio Special	1977	6.25	12.50	25.00
—Promo only; green cover					
SP-17053 [(3) DJ]	Styx Radio Special	1978	10.00	20.00	40.00
—Promo-only box set					
SP-17222 [(2) DJ]	Radio Sampler and Interview Album	1983	6.25	12.50	25.00
—Promo only; with "Kilroy Was Here" album graphic on cover					
MOBILE FIDELITY					
1-026	The Grand Illusion	1979	7.50	15.00	30.00
—Audiophile vinyl					
NAUTILUS					
NR-15	Pieces of Eight	1981	6.25	12.50	25.00
—Audiophile vinyl					
NR-27	Cornerstone	1982	5.00	10.00	20.00
—Audiophile vinyl					
NR-45	Paradise Theater	198?	7.50	15.00	30.00
—Audiophile vinyl					
RCA VICTOR					
AFL1-3593	Styx	1979	2.50	5.00	10.00
AFL1-3594	Lady	1979	2.50	5.00	10.00
—Retitled version of "Styx II"					
AFL1-3595	Serpent	1979	2.50	5.00	10.00
—Retitled version of "The Serpent Is Rising"					
AFL1-3596	Miracles	1979	2.50	5.00	10.00
—Retitled version of "Man of Miracles"					
AFL1-3597	Best of Styx	1979	2.50	5.00	10.00
AYL1-3888	Styx	1980	2.00	4.00	8.00
AYL1-4233	Lady	1981	2.00	4.00	8.00
—Retitled version of "Styx II"					
AYL1-4756	Best of Styx	1982	2.00	4.00	8.00
WOODEN NICKEL					
BWL1-0287	The Serpent Is Rising	1974	5.00	10.00	20.00
BWL1-0638	Man of Miracles	1974	7.50	15.00	30.00
—Original version contains "Lies"					
BWL1-0638	Man of Miracles	1974	5.00	10.00	20.00
—Second version contains "Best Thing"					
BWL1-1008	Styx	1975	3.75	7.50	15.00
WNS-1008	Styx	1972	5.00	10.00	20.00
BWL1-1012	Styx II	1975	3.75	7.50	15.00
WNS-1012	Styx II	1973	5.00	10.00	20.00
—With die-cut cover					
BWL1-2250	Best of Styx	1977	3.00	6.00	12.00

STYX (2)

45s

Number	Title (A Side/B Side)	Yr	VG	VG+	NM
ABC					
10848	Don't Bring Me Down/MacDougal Street	1966	3.00	6.00	12.00

STYX (U)

Definitely not the more famous Styx; could be group (2), though.

45s

Number	Title (A Side/B Side)	Yr	VG	VG+	NM
ONYX					
2200	Puppetmaster/Hey, I'm Lost	1966	6.25	12.50	25.00
PARAMOUNT					
0104	Promised Land/Soul Flow	1971	—	3.00	6.00

SUDDENS, THE

Also recorded as THE SAFARIS.

45s

Number	Title (A Side/B Side)	Yr	VG	VG+	NM
SUDDEN					
103	Garden of Love/Childish Ways	1961	25.00	50.00	100.00

SUGAR BEARS, THE

KIM CARNES was in this group.

45s

Number	Title (A Side/B Side)	Yr	VG	VG+	NM
BIG TREE					
122	Someone Like You/You Are the One	1971	—	3.00	6.00
143	Right On/Happiness Train	1972	—	3.00	6.00
151	Some Kind of a Summer/Put Some Love Into It	1972	—	3.00	6.00

Albums

Number	Title (A Side/B Side)	Yr	VG	VG+	NM
BIG TREE					
BTS-2009	Introducing the Sugar Bears	1972	5.00	10.00	20.00

SUGAR CANES, THE

45s

Number	Title (A Side/B Side)	Yr	VG	VG+	NM
KING					
5157	Poor Boy/Sioux Rock	1958	6.25	12.50	25.00

SUGAR CREEK

Albums

Number	Title (A Side/B Side)	Yr	VG	VG+	NM
METROMEDIA					
MD 1020	Please Tell a Friend	1969	15.00	30.00	60.00

SUGARLOAF

45s

Number	Title (A Side/B Side)	Yr	VG	VG+	NM
BRUT					
805	Round and Round/Colorado Jones	1973	—	2.50	5.00
815	I Got a Song/Myra, Myra	1973	—	2.50	5.00
815 [PS]	I Got a Song/Myra, Myra	1973	—	3.00	6.00
CLARIDGE					
402	Don't Call Us, We'll Call You/Texas Two-Lane	1974	—	2.50	5.00
405	Stars in My Eyes/Myra, Myra	1975	—	2.50	5.00
408	Boogie Man/I Got a Song	1975	—	2.50	5.00
415	Have a Good Time/You Set My Dreams to Music	1976	—	2.50	5.00
422	Last Dance, Take a Chance/Satisfaction Guaranteed	1976	—	2.50	5.00
LIBERTY					
56183	Green-Eyed Lady/West of Tomorrow	1970	—	3.00	6.00

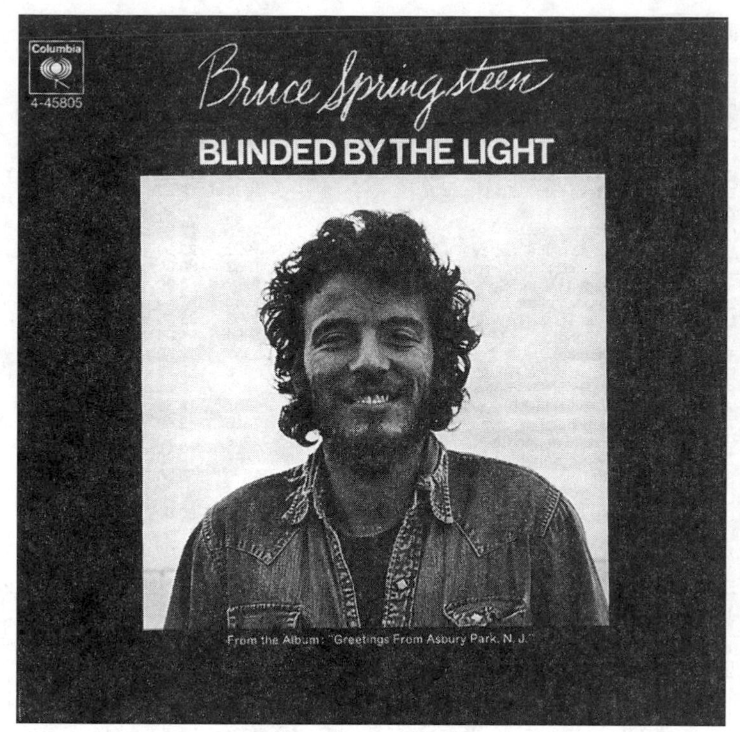

(Top left) Only one of Bruce Springsteen's American picture sleeves is rare — but what a rarity it is! An uncomfirmed rumor says that most, if not all, of the few existing copies of the "Blinded by the Light" picture sleeve were fished out of a trash bin in 1973. Today, it's every bit that difficult to find. (Top right) Agreeable people may disagree on whether Dusty Springfield was truly worthy of her 1999 Rock and Roll Hall of Fame induction, but few can disagree that she put out at least one great album, *Dusty In Memphis*. Here's the picture sleeve for its hit single, "Son-of-a Preacher Man." (Bottom left) Few of Rod Stewart's classic singles on Mercury were issued with picture sleeves. One of them was "You Wear It Well," from 1972. (Bottom right) Here's proof that you can't always trust the dates you see on records. This is the hit version of Styx's "Lady" 45 on Wooden Nickel. The label has both 1971 and 1973 dates on it, yet this single was not issued until early 1975 with the catalog number WB-10102. And of course, the year 1975 is nowhere on the label.

Number	Title (A Side/B Side)	Yr	VG	VG+	NM
56218	Tongue in Cheek/Woman	1970	—	2.50	5.00
56218 [PS]	Tongue in Cheek/Woman	1970	2.50	5.00	10.00
UNITED ARTISTS					
0062	Green-Eyed Lady/Tongue in Cheek	1973	—	2.00	4.00
—"Silver Spotlight Series" reissue					
50757	Woman/Tongue in Cheek	1971	—	—	—
—Unreleased					
50784	Chest Fever/Mother Nature's Wine	1971	—	2.50	5.00
Albums					
BRUT					
6006	I Got a Song	1973	3.75	7.50	15.00
CLARIDGE					
1000	Don't Call Us, We'll Call You	1975	3.00	6.00	12.00
LIBERTY					
LST-7640	Sugarloaf	1970	5.00	10.00	20.00
LST-11010	Spaceship Earth	1971	5.00	10.00	20.00

SUGGS, BRAD

Number	Title (A Side/B Side)	Yr	VG	VG+	NM
45s					
METEOR					
5034	Charcoal Suit/Bop Baby Bop	1956	100.00	200.00	400.00
PHILLIPS INT'L.					
3545	Low Outside/706 Union	1959	6.25	12.50	25.00
3549	I Walk the Line/Ooh-Wee	1959	6.25	12.50	25.00
3554	Cloudy/Partly Cloudy	1960	6.25	12.50	25.00
3563	My Gypsy/Sam's Tune	1960	6.25	12.50	25.00
3571	Elephant Walk/Catching Up	1961	6.25	12.50	25.00

SULLIVAN, JIM

Number	Title (A Side/B Side)	Yr	VG	VG+	NM
45s					
LONDON					
9585	Back and Forth/Toad Stool	1963	3.00	6.00	12.00

SULLIVAN, NIKI

Also see THE CRICKETS.

Number	Title (A Side/B Side)	Yr	VG	VG+	NM
45s					
DOT					
15751	Three Steps to Heaven/It's All Over	1958	25.00	50.00	100.00
JOLI					
073	Do the Dive/My Lost Dream	196?	15.00	30.00	60.00
075	It Really Doesn't Matter/You Better Get a Move On	196?	18.75	37.50	75.00

SULTANS, THE (1)

Number	Title (A Side/B Side)	Yr	VG	VG+	NM
45s					
ASCOT					
2228	I Wanna Know/Gloria	1967	5.00	10.00	20.00

SULTANS, THE (2)

Number	Title (A Side/B Side)	Yr	VG	VG+	NM
45s					
DUKE					
125	Good Thing Baby/How Deep Is the Ocean	1954	25.00	50.00	100.00
133	I Cried My Heart Out/Baby Don't Put Me Down	1954	25.00	50.00	100.00
135	Boppin' with the Mambo/What Makes Me Feel This Way	1954	25.00	50.00	100.00
178	My Love Is So High/If I Could Tell	1957	12.50	25.00	50.00

SULTANS, THE (3)

Number	Title (A Side/B Side)	Yr	VG	VG+	NM
45s					
GUYDEN					
2079	Someone You Can Trust/Christina	1963	3.75	7.50	15.00
JAM					
103	Toss in My Sleep/I Feel Your Love Growing Cold	1962	7.50	15.00	30.00
107	Mary, Mary/How Far Does a Friendship Go	1963	7.50	15.00	30.00
113	Poor Boy/Don't Tie Me Down	1964	7.50	15.00	30.00
TILT					
782	It'll Be Easy/You Got Me Goin'	1961	25.00	50.00	100.00
—Yellow label					
782	It'll Be Easy/You Got Me Goin'	1961	10.00	20.00	40.00
—Black label					

SULTANS, THE (4)

Number	Title (A Side/B Side)	Yr	VG	VG+	NM
45s					
JUBILEE					
5054	Lemon Squeezing Daddy/You Captured My Heart	1951	62.50	125.00	250.00
5077	Blues at Dawn/Don't Be Angry	1952	200.00	400.00	800.00

SUMAC, YMA

Number	Title (A Side/B Side)	Yr	VG	VG+	NM
45s					
CAPITOL					
F1717	Virgin of the Sun God/Lure of the Unknown Love	1951	5.00	10.00	20.00
F1819	Birds/Najalas Lament	1951	5.00	10.00	20.00
F1819 [PS]	Birds/Najalas Lament	1951	10.00	20.00	40.00
F2079	Babalu/Wimoweh	1952	5.00	10.00	20.00
CORAL					
60741	The Sun Maidens/Beautiful Eyes	1952	5.00	10.00	20.00
60742	Cholitas Punenas/The Hummingbird	1952	5.00	10.00	20.00
60743	One Love/Indian Love	1952	5.00	10.00	20.00
60744	La Benita/I Love Only You	1952	5.00	10.00	20.00
—The above four comprise a box set					
7-Inch Extended Plays					
CAPITOL					
EAP 1-299	(contents unknown)	1955	6.25	12.50	25.00
EAP 1-299 [PS]	Legend of the Sun Virgin, Part 1	1955	6.25	12.50	25.00
EAP 2-299	(contents unknown)	1955	6.25	12.50	25.00
EAP 2-299 [PS]	Legend of the Sun Virgin, Part 2	1955	6.25	12.50	25.00
EAP 1-564	(contents unknown)	1955	6.25	12.50	25.00
EAP 1-564 [PS]	Mambo!	1955	6.25	12.50	25.00
EAP 2-564	(contents unknown)	1955	6.25	12.50	25.00
EAP 2-564 [PS]	Mambo!	1955	6.25	12.50	25.00
EAP 1-770	(contents unknown)	1956	5.00	10.00	20.00
EAP 1-770 [PS]	Legend of the Jivaro, Part 1	1956	5.00	10.00	20.00
EAP 2-770	(contents unknown)	1956	5.00	10.00	20.00
EAP 2-770 [PS]	Legend of the Jivaro, Part 2	1956	5.00	10.00	20.00
EAP 3-770	(contents unknown)	1956	5.00	10.00	20.00
EAP 3-770 [PS]	Legend of the Jivaro, Part 3	1956	5.00	10.00	20.00
CORAL					
EC 81050	(contents unknown)	1954	12.50	25.00	50.00
EC 81050 [PS]	Presenting Yma Sumac	1954	12.50	25.00	50.00
EC 81051	(contents unknown)	1954	12.50	25.00	50.00
EC 81051 [PS]	Presenting Yma Sumac	1954	12.50	25.00	50.00
Albums					
CAPITOL					
H 244 [10]	Voice of the Xtabay	1952	25.00	50.00	100.00
L 299 [10]	Legend of the Sun Virgin	1952	30.00	60.00	120.00
SM-299	Legend of the Sun Virgin	197?	3.00	6.00	12.00
T 299 [M]	Legend of the Sun Virgin	1955	12.50	25.00	50.00
L 423 [10]	Inca Taqui	1953	25.00	50.00	100.00
H 564 [10]	Mambo!	1954	25.00	50.00	100.00
T 564 [M]	Mambo!	1955	12.50	25.00	50.00
DW 684 [R]	Voice of the Xtabay and Inca Taqui	1963	3.75	7.50	15.00
SM-684	Voice of the Xtabay and Inca Taqui	197?	3.00	6.00	12.00
W 684 [M]	Voice of the Xtabay and Inca Taqui	1955	12.50	25.00	50.00
T 770 [M]	Legend of the Jivaro	1956	12.50	25.00	50.00
ST 1169 [S]	Fuego del Andes	1959	12.50	25.00	50.00
T 1169 [M]	Fuego del Andes	1959	10.00	20.00	40.00
SM-11892	Mambo!	1979	3.00	6.00	12.00
CORAL					
CRL 56058 [10]	Presenting Yma Sumac	1952	30.00	60.00	120.00
LONDON					
XPS 608	Miracles	1972	5.00	10.00	20.00

SUMMER, DONNA

Number	Title (A Side/B Side)	Yr	VG	VG+	NM
12-Inch Singles					
ATLANTIC					
1382 [DJ]	Love's About to Change My Heart (5 versions)	1989	2.00	4.00	8.00
DMD 1431 [DJ]	Breakaway (Extended Mix) (Power Radio Mix)/I Don't Wanna Get Hurt (12" Mix)	1989	—	3.50	7.00
1709 [DJ]	When Love Cries (4 versions)	1991	—	3.00	6.00
1758 [DJ]	Work That Magic (4:34) (6:20) (5:00)/Let There Be Peace	1991	—	3.50	7.00
86255	Breakaway (Extended Mix) (Power Radio Mix)/I Don't Wanna Get Hurt (12" Mix)	1989	2.00	4.00	8.00
86309	Love's About to Change My Heart (5 versions)	1989	2.50	5.00	10.00
86415	This Time I Know It's for Real (Extended) (Instrumental) (LP Version)	1989	2.50	5.00	10.00
CASABLANCA					
NBD 100	Winter Melody/Spring Affair	1977	3.75	7.50	15.00
PRO 1148 [DJ]	Love to Love You Baby (16:49)/Flash Light (10:43)	1994	5.00	10.00	20.00
—B-side by Parliament; promo-only reissue					
NBLP 7041	Love to Love You Baby (16:50)/Try Me, I Know We Can Make It (17:55)	1976	3.75	7.50	15.00
—One song on each side, yet it has an LP catalog number					
NBD 20112 [DJ]	Rumour Has It/I Love You	1978	3.00	6.00	12.00
—B-side is blank (both tracks are on Side 1)					
NBD 20159 [DJ]	Hot Stuff (Long)	1979	3.00	6.00	12.00
—B-side is blank					
NBD 20167	Hot Stuff/Bad Girls	1979	3.75	7.50	15.00
—B-side is blank (both tracks are on Side 1)					
NBD 20199	No More Tears (Enough Is Enough) (11:40)	1979	2.50	5.00	10.00
—With Barbra Streisand; B-side is blank					
NBD 20226 [DJ]	Walk Away (7:15)	1979	2.50	5.00	10.00
—B-side is blank					
856357-1	Melody of Love (4 versions)	1994	—	3.00	6.00
GEFFEN					
PRO-A-910 [DJ]	The Wanderer (stereo/mono)	1980	3.00	6.00	12.00
PRO-A-925 [DJ]	Cold Love/Looking Up/Who Do You Think You're Foolin'	1980	2.00	4.00	8.00
PRO-A-1041 [DJ]	Love Is In Control (Edit) (LP)	1982	3.00	6.00	12.00
—Promo only on Quiex II vinyl					
PRO-A-2180 [DJ]	There Goes My Baby (same on both sides)	1984	—	3.00	6.00
PRO-A-2802 [DJ]	Dinner with Gershwin (7:43) (same on both sides)	1987	2.50	5.00	10.00
PRO-A-3036 [DJ]	All Systems Go (Dance Mix)/Fascination	1987	2.00	4.00	8.00
20273	Supernatural Love (Extended)/Face the Music	1984	2.00	4.00	8.00
20635	Dinner with Gershwin (Extended) (Instrumental)	1987	2.00	4.00	8.00
29938	Love Is In Control (7:03)/(Instrumental)	1982	2.00	4.00	8.00
MERCURY					
PRO 226-1 [DJ]	Unconditional Love (Club Mix)/(Instrumental)	1983	—	3.00	6.00
814592-1	Unconditional Love (Remix)/She Works Hard for the Money (Remix)	1983	2.00	4.00	8.00
45s					
ATLANTIC					
88792	Breakaway/Thinkin' Bout My Baby	1989	—	—	3.00
88840	Love's About to Change My Heart/Love's About to Change My Heart	1989	—	—	3.00
88899	This Time I Know It's for Real/If It Makes You Feel Good	1989	—	—	3.00
88899 [PS]	This Time I Know It's for Real/If It Makes You Feel Good	1989	—	2.00	4.00
CASABLANCA					
872	Spring Affair/The Landing	1976	—	2.50	5.00
874	Winter Melody/Spring Affair	1977	—	2.50	5.00
884	Can't We Just Sit Down (And Talk It Over)/I Feel Love	1977	—	3.00	6.00
—Original copies have "I Feel Love" listed as "Side B"					
884	I Feel Love/Can't We Just Sit Down (And Talk It Over)	1977	—	2.50	5.00
—Second pressings have "I Feel Love" listed as "Side A"					
907	I Love You/Once Upon a Time	1977	—	2.50	5.00
916	Rumour Has It/Once Upon a Time	1978	—	2.50	5.00
926	Last Dance/With Your Love	1978	—	2.00	4.00
939	Mac Arthur Park/Once Upon a Time	1978	—	2.00	4.00

Number	Title (A Side/B Side)	Yr	VG	VG+	NM
959	Heaven Knows/Only One Love	1979	—	2.00	4.00
—A-side with Brooklyn Dreams					
978	Hot Stuff/Journey to the Center of Your Heart	1979	—	2.00	4.00
988	Bad Girls/On My Honor	1979	—	2.00	4.00
2201	Dim All the Lights/There Will Always Be a You	1979	—	2.00	4.00
2236	On the Radio/There Will Always Be a You	1980	—	2.00	4.00
2273	Our Love/Sunset People	1980	—	2.50	5.00
2300	Walk Away/Could It Be Magic	1980	—	2.00	4.00
858366-7	Melody of Love/The Christmas Song	1994	—	—	3.00
858366-7 [PS]	Melody of Love/The Christmas Song	1994	—	—	3.00
EPIC					
79201	I Will Go with You (Con Te Partiro)/Love On & On	1999	—	—	3.00
GEFFEN					
27939	Fascination/All Systems Go	1988	—	2.00	4.00
28165	Only the Fool Survives/Love Shock	1987	—	2.00	4.00
—A-side with Mickey Thomas					
28165 [PS]	Only the Fool Survives/Love Shock	1987	—	2.00	4.00
—A-side with Mickey Thomas					
28418	Dinner with Gershwin/(Instrumental)	1987	—	2.00	4.00
28418 [PS]	Dinner with Gershwin/(Instrumental)	1987	—	2.00	4.00
29142	Supernatural Love/Face the Music	1984	—	2.00	4.00
29142 [PS]	Supernatural Love/Face the Music	1984	—	2.00	4.00
29291	There Goes My Baby/Maybe It's Over	1984	—	2.00	4.00
29291 [PS]	There Goes My Baby/Maybe It's Over	1984	—	2.00	4.00
29805	The Woman in Me/Livin' in America	1982	—	2.00	4.00
29805 [PS]	The Woman in Me/Livin' in America	1982	—	2.00	4.00
29895	State of Independence/Love Is Just a Breath Away	1982	—	2.00	4.00
29895 [PS]	State of Independence/Love Is Just a Breath Away	1982	—	2.00	4.00
29982	Love Is In Control (Finger on the Trigger)/ Sometimes Like Butterflies	1982	—	2.00	4.00
29982 [PS]	Love Is In Control (Finger on the Trigger)/ Sometimes Like Butterflies	1982	—	2.50	5.00
49563	The Wanderer/Stop Me	1980	—	2.00	4.00
—Second pressings have WB logo replaced by Geffen logo					
49563 [PS]	The Wanderer/Stop Me	1980	—	2.50	5.00
49634	Cold Love/Grand Illusion	1980	—	2.00	4.00
49634 [PS]	Cold Love/Grand Illusion	1980	—	2.50	5.00
49664	Who Do You Think You're Foolin'/Runnin' for Cover	1981	—	2.00	4.00
MERCURY					
812370-7	She Works Hard for the Money/I Do Believe (I'll Fall in Love)	1983	—	2.00	4.00
812370-7 [PS]	She Works Hard for the Money/I Do Believe (I'll Fall in Love)	1983	—	2.50	5.00
814088-7	Unconditional Love/People, People	1983	—	2.00	4.00
814088-7 [PS]	Unconditional Love/People, People	1983	—	2.50	5.00
814922-7	Love Has a Mind of Its Own/Stop, Look and Listen	1983	—	2.00	4.00
OASIS					
401 A /B	Love to Love You Baby/Need-A-Man Blues	1975	3.00	6.00	12.00
—"Love to Love You Baby" has a radically different mix on the above first pressing					
401 AA/BB	Love to Love You Baby (4:55)/Love to Love You Baby (3:24)	1975	—	3.00	6.00
405	Could It Be Magic/Whispering Waves	1976	—	3.00	6.00
406	Try Me, I Know We Can Make It/Wasted	1976	—	3.00	6.00
406 [PS]	Try Me, I Know We Can Make It/Wasted	1976	2.00	4.00	8.00
WARNER BROS./GEFFEN					
49563	The Wanderer/Stop Me	1980	—	3.00	6.00
—Original pressings have a WB logo on the left side and "Geffen Records" in a box at the top of the label					
Albums					
ATLANTIC					
81987	Another Place and Time	1989	3.00	6.00	12.00
CASABLANCA					
NBLP 7038	Four Seasons of Love	1976	2.50	5.00	10.00
NBLP 7056	I Remember Yesterday	1977	2.50	5.00	10.00
NBLP 7078 [(2)]	Once Upon a Time...	1977	3.00	6.00	12.00
NBLP 7119 [(2)]	Live and More	1978	3.00	6.00	12.00
NBPIX 7119 [PD]	The Best of Live and More	1979	5.00	10.00	20.00
NBLP 7150 [(2)]	Bad Girls	1979	3.00	6.00	12.00
NBLP 7191 [(2)]	On the Radio — Greatest Hits Vols. 1 and 2	1979	3.00	6.00	12.00
NBLP 7201	Greatest Hits, Vol. 1	1979	2.00	4.00	8.00
NBLP 7202	Greatest Hits, Vol. 2	1979	2.00	4.00	8.00
NBLP 7244	Walk Away — Collector's Edition (The Best of 1977-1980)	1980	2.50	5.00	10.00
811123-1 [(2)]	Live and More	1985	2.50	5.00	10.00
822557-1 [(2)]	Bad Girls	1984	2.50	5.00	10.00
822558-1 [(2)]	On the Radio — Greatest Hits Vols. 1 and 2	1984	2.50	5.00	10.00
822559-1	Greatest Hits, Vol. 2	1984	2.00	4.00	8.00
822560-1	Walk Away	1984	2.00	4.00	8.00
EPIC					
E2 69910 [(2)]	Live and More Encore	1999	3.75	7.50	15.00
GEFFEN					
GHS 2000	The Wanderer	1980	2.50	5.00	10.00
GHS 2005	Donna Summer	1982	2.50	5.00	10.00
GHS 24040	Cats Without Claws	1984	2.50	5.00	10.00
GHS 24040 [DJ]	Cats Without Claws	1984	3.75	7.50	15.00
—Promo only on Quiex II vinyl					
GHS 24102	All Systems Go	1987	2.50	5.00	10.00
MERCURY					
812265-1	She Works Hard for the Money	1983	2.50	5.00	10.00
826144-1	The Summer Collection	1985	2.50	5.00	10.00
OASIS					
OCLP 5003	Love to Love You Baby	1975	3.00	6.00	12.00
—Add 50% if poster is included					
OCLP 5004	A Love Trilogy	1976	3.00	6.00	12.00
822792-1	Love to Love You Baby	1985	2.00	4.00	8.00

SUMMER SOUNDS, THE

Number	Title (A Side/B Side)	Yr	VG	VG+	NM
Albums					
LAUREL					
90973	Up Down	196?	250.00	500.00	1000.

SUMMERHILL

Number	Title (A Side/B Side)	Yr	VG	VG+	NM
45s					
TETRAGRAMMATON					
1528	Soft Voice/The Last Day	1969	2.50	5.00	10.00
Albums					
TETRAGRAMMATON					
T-114	Summerhill	1969	7.50	15.00	30.00

SUMMERS, DAVEY, AND THE SINGING ANTS

Number	Title (A Side/B Side)	Yr	VG	VG+	NM
45s					
DORE					
684	Gonna Climb That Big Ole Hill/Doin' the Davey Drag	1963	10.00	20.00	40.00

SUMMERS, GENE

Number	Title (A Side/B Side)	Yr	VG	VG+	NM
45s					
CAPRI					
502	Blue Diamond/You Said You Loved Me	196?	5.00	10.00	20.00
507	Alabama Shake/Just Because	1964	15.00	30.00	60.00
JAMIE					
1273	Blue Diamond/You Said You Loved Me	1964	3.75	7.50	15.00
JAN					
100	School of Rock 'N' Roll/Straight Skirt	1958	15.00	30.00	60.00
102	Nervous/Gotta Love That	1959	15.00	30.00	60.00
106	Twixteen/I'll Never Be Lonely	1959	15.00	30.00	60.00
MERCURY					
72606	Green-Eyed Monster/The Clown	1966	3.75	7.50	15.00
TEARDROP					
3405	Goodbye Priscilla (Bye Bye Baby Blue)/Down on the Farm	1977	2.00	4.00	8.00
3405 [DJ]	Goodbye Priscilla (Bye Bye Blue Baby)	1977	3.00	6.00	12.00
—Single-sided promo copies have erroneous subtitle					

SUN-RAYS, THE

Number	Title (A Side/B Side)	Yr	VG	VG+	NM
45s					
SUN					
293	Love Is a Stranger/The Lonely Hours	1958	10.00	20.00	40.00

SUNBEAMS, THE (1)

Number	Title (A Side/B Side)	Yr	VG	VG+	NM
45s					
ACME					
109	Please Say You'll Be Mine/You've Got to Rock and Roll	1957	750.00	1500.	3000.
HERALD					
451	Tell Me Why/Come Back Baby	1955	75.00	150.00	300.00

SUNBEAMS, THE (2)

Number	Title (A Side/B Side)	Yr	VG	VG+	NM
45s					
DOT					
1271	I'm Gonna Go Home to Mama/Blue Mountain Waltz	1955	7.50	15.00	30.00
1280	How About It/Wrap It Up and Save It	1956	7.50	15.00	30.00

SUNBEAMS, THE (3)

Number	Title (A Side/B Side)	Yr	VG	VG+	NM
45s					
TOLLIE					
9022	Sing a Song/Good Old Days	1964	3.00	6.00	12.00

SUNDAY FUNNIES, THE

Number	Title (A Side/B Side)	Yr	VG	VG+	NM
45s					
CAPITOL					
5614	Another Time, Another Place/Headlines	1966	3.00	6.00	12.00
HIDEOUT					
1070	Heavy Music/Path of Freedom	196?	7.50	15.00	30.00
MERCURY					
72571	Wonder Woman/She's Not at All Like You	1966	3.00	6.00	12.00
RARE EARTH					
5035	Walk Down the Path of Freedom/It's Just a Dream	1971	2.00	4.00	8.00
UNI					
55157	Baby, I Could Be So Good at Loving You/See Things My Way	1969	2.50	5.00	10.00
Albums					
RARE EARTH					
RS-526	The Sunday Funnies	1971	3.00	6.00	12.00
RS-538	Benediction	1972	3.00	6.00	12.00

SUNDIALS, THE

Number	Title (A Side/B Side)	Yr	VG	VG+	NM
45s					
GUYDEN					
2065	Chapel of Love/Whether to Resist	1962	50.00	100.00	200.00

SUNDOWN PLAYBOYS, THE

Number	Title (A Side/B Side)	Yr	VG	VG+	NM
45s					
APPLE					
1852	Saturday Night Special/Valse De Soleil Coucher	1972	3.75	7.50	15.00

SUNDOWNERS, THE

Number	Title (A Side/B Side)	Yr	VG	VG+	NM
45s					
JAMIE					
1271	A Shot of Rhythm 'N' Blues/Come On In	1964	3.00	6.00	12.00
Albums					
LIBERTY					
LRP-3269 [M]	Folk Songs for the Rich	1962	5.00	10.00	20.00
LST-7269 [S]	Folk Songs for the Rich	1962	6.25	12.50	25.00

SUNGLOWS, THE
See SUNNY AND THE SUNLINERS.

SUNLINERS, THE
45s

Number	Title (A Side/B Side)	Yr	VG	VG+	NM
GOLDEN WORLD					
31	The Swingin' Kind/All Alone	1965	7.50	15.00	30.00
MGM					
13809	Land of Nod/Well One	1967	6.25	12.50	25.00

SUNNY AND THE HORIZONS
45s

Number	Title (A Side/B Side)	Yr	VG	VG+	NM
LUXOR					
1013	Nature's Creation/Because They Tell Me	1962	50.00	100.00	200.00
—Yellow label					
1013	Nature's Creation/Because They Tell Me	1962	18.75	37.50	75.00
—Red label					

SUNNY AND THE SUNGLOWS
See SUNNY AND THE SUNLINERS.

SUNNY AND THE SUNLINERS
45s

Number	Title (A Side/B Side)	Yr	VG	VG+	NM
DISCO GRANDE					
1021	Peanuts (La Cacahuata)/The Happy Hippo	1965	5.00	10.00	20.00
KEY-LOC					
1010	I Want To Come Home For Christmas/(B-side unknown)	1966	2.00	4.00	8.00
OKEH					
7143	Golly Gee/Touring	1962	3.00	6.00	12.00
—As "Sunny and the Sunglows"					
SUNGLOW					
102	Sylvia/(B-side unknown)	1961	3.75	7.50	15.00
103	A Dream/The Lasso	1961	3.75	7.50	15.00
104	Golly Gee/Touring	1961	3.75	7.50	15.00
105	Once in a While/Ho Ho Ha Ha	1962	3.75	7.50	15.00
106	Won't You Tell Me/(B-side unknown)	1962	3.75	7.50	15.00
107	Peanuts (La Cacahuata)/The Happy Hippo	1962	3.75	7.50	15.00
107	Peanuts (La Cacahuata)/Falasette Corazon	1962	3.75	7.50	15.00
109	Close Your Eyes/Ooo Poo Pa Doo	1963	3.75	7.50	15.00
110	Talk to Me/Pony Time	1963	5.00	10.00	20.00
111	Rags to Riches/It Won't Be Me	1963	4.50	9.00	18.00
112	The Dog/You Can Make It If You Try	1963	3.75	7.50	15.00
115	Till the End of Time/La Bamba	1964	3.75	7.50	15.00
116	Guess Who/Just as I Thought	1964	3.75	7.50	15.00
117	Love Me/Honey Child	1964	3.75	7.50	15.00
118	Popcorn/The Circus	1964	3.75	7.50	15.00
118	Popcorn/All Night Worker	1965	3.75	7.50	15.00
119	Baby I Apologize/Cut Across Shorty	1965	3.75	7.50	15.00
120	Oh Heart/Latin Trumpet	1965	3.75	7.50	15.00
122	Fly Me to the Moon/La Macarena	1966	3.75	7.50	15.00
123	If You Don't Love Me/(B-side unknown)	1966	3.75	7.50	15.00
124	Just a Game/Maria Elena	1966	3.75	7.50	15.00
125	Again/Roly Poly	1967	3.75	7.50	15.00
127	It's Okay/99 + 1	1968	3.75	7.50	15.00
—All Sunglow releases as "The Sunglows"					
TEAR DROP					
3014	Talk to Me/Every Week, Every Month, Every Year	1963	2.50	5.00	10.00
—As "Sunny and the Sunglows"					
3016	Carino Nuevo/(B-side unknown)	1963	3.00	6.00	12.00
3022	Rags to Riches/Not Even Judgment Day	1963	2.50	5.00	10.00
3025	Cuando El Destino/(B-side unknown)	1963	3.00	6.00	12.00
3027	Out of Sight, Out of Mind/No One Else Will Do	1964	2.50	5.00	10.00
3031	Pa Que Sientas, Lo Que Sientex Que Tal Te Sientes/De Mi Nada Mas, Usted	1964	3.00	6.00	12.00
—As "Sunny Ozuna"					
3035	It's Too Late/You Gave Me a True Love	1964	2.50	5.00	10.00
3037	Tu Nueva Viva/Dime Como Le Haces	1964	3.00	6.00	12.00
3040	You Send Me/His Greatest Creation	1964	2.50	5.00	10.00
3045	Something's Got a Hold on Me/Teenage Promise-I'm Not a Fool Anymore	1964	2.50	5.00	10.00
3056	Token of Love/Little Dancing Girl	1965	2.50	5.00	10.00
—As "Sunny Ozuna"					
3066	El Ta Conazo/La Diudades	1965	3.00	6.00	12.00
3067	Hitch Hike/That Night in San Antonio	1965	2.50	5.00	10.00
3071	Too Young/The Very Thought of You	1965	2.50	5.00	10.00
3079	Trick Bag/Cheatin' Traces	1965	2.50	5.00	10.00
3094	Fly Me to the Moon/Short Short Shorty	1966	2.00	4.00	8.00
3096	Tristie Y Lastimado/(B-side unknown)	1966	3.00	6.00	12.00
3123	No One Else Will Do/Cheatin' Traces	1966	2.00	4.00	8.00
3183	Wonderful Girl/Talk That Trash	1966	2.00	4.00	8.00
WHITE WHALE					
324	It's Okay/99 + 1	1969	2.00	4.00	8.00
—As "The Sunglows"					

Albums

Number	Title	Yr	VG	VG+	NM
KEY-LOC					
3001 [M]	Smile Now, Cry Later	196?	6.25	12.50	25.00
3002 [M]	No Te Chifles	196?	6.25	12.50	25.00
3003 [M]	Sunny and the Sunliners Live in Hollywood	196?	6.25	12.50	25.00
3004 [M]	Canta Sunny	196?	6.25	12.50	25.00
3005 [M]	A Little Brown-Eyed Soul	196?	6.25	12.50	25.00
3006 [M]	This Is My Band	196?	6.25	12.50	25.00
3007 [M]	Versatile	196?	6.25	12.50	25.00
3008 [M]	Adelante	196?	6.25	12.50	25.00
3009 [M]	Sky High	196?	6.25	12.50	25.00
3010 [M]	The Missing Link	196?	6.25	12.50	25.00
SUNGLOW					
SLP-101 [M]	Sunny Ozuna and the Sunglows	1963	25.00	50.00	100.00
—As "The Sunglows"					
SLP-102 [M]	The Fabulous Sunglows	1964	25.00	50.00	100.00
—As "The Sunglows"					
SLP-103S [S]	The Original Peanuts	1965	25.00	50.00	100.00
—As "The Sunglows"					
SLP-103 [M]	The Original Peanuts	1965	20.00	40.00	80.00
—As "The Sunglows"					
TEAR DROP					
LPM-2000 [M]	Talk to Me	1963	25.00	50.00	100.00
LPM-2001 [M]	Las Vegas Welcomes Sunny and the Sunliners	1964	10.00	20.00	40.00
LPM-2008 [M]	Teardrop Presents Sunny and the Sunliners	196?	10.00	20.00	40.00

SUNRAYS, THE
Also see THE SNOW MEN.

45s

Number	Title (A Side/B Side)	Yr	VG	VG+	NM
TOWER					
101	Outta Gas/Car Party	1964	5.00	10.00	20.00
148	I Live for the Sun/Bye Baby Bye	1965	3.00	6.00	12.00
191	Andrea/You Don't Phase Me	1966	3.00	6.00	12.00
224	Still/When You're Not There	1966	3.00	6.00	12.00
256	Don't Take Yourself Too Seriously/I Look Baby, I Can't See	1966	3.00	6.00	12.00
256 [PS]	Don't Take Yourself Too Seriously/I Look Baby, I Can't See	1966	6.25	12.50	25.00
290	Hi, How Are You/Just 'Round the River Bend	1966	3.75	7.50	15.00
340	Loaded with Love/Time (A Special Thing)	1967	3.75	7.50	15.00
WARNER BROS.					
5253	Talk to Him/Gideon	1962	3.75	7.50	15.00

Albums

Number	Title	Yr	VG	VG+	NM
TOWER					
ST 5017 [S]	Andrea	1966	15.00	30.00	60.00
T 5017 [M]	Andrea	1966	12.50	25.00	50.00

SUNSET DRAGSTERS, THE
Albums

Number	Title	Yr	VG	VG+	NM
PALACE					
M-775 [M]	Hot Rod Rally	196?	15.00	30.00	60.00
PST-775 [S]	Hot Rod Rally	196?	20.00	40.00	80.00

SUNSETS, THE (1)
45s

Number	Title (A Side/B Side)	Yr	VG	VG+	NM
CHALLENGE					
9186	C.C. Rider/The Chug-a-Lug	1963	10.00	20.00	40.00
9198	Lonely Surfer Boy/Playmate of the Year	1963	10.00	20.00	40.00
9208	My Little Beach Bunny/My Little Surfin' Woody	1963	12.50	25.00	50.00
PETAL					
1040	Lydia/Only You, Only Me	1963	12.50	25.00	50.00

Albums

Number	Title	Yr	VG	VG+	NM
PALACE					
M-752 [M]	Surfing with the Sunsets	1963	10.00	20.00	40.00
PST-752 [S]	Surfing with the Sunsets	1963	12.50	25.00	50.00

SUNSETS, THE (2)
45s

Number	Title (A Side/B Side)	Yr	VG	VG+	NM
RAE COX					
102	How Will I Remember/Sittin' and Cryin'	1959	10.00	20.00	40.00

SUNSHINE COMPANY, THE
45s

Number	Title (A Side/B Side)	Yr	VG	VG+	NM
IMPERIAL					
66241	Up Up and Away/Blue May	1967	—	—	—
—Unreleased					
66247	Happy/Blue May	1967	2.50	5.00	10.00
66260	Back on the Street Again/I Just Want to Be Your Friend	1967	2.50	5.00	10.00
66278	Reflections on an Angel/It's Sunday	1968	—	—	—
—Unreleased					
66280	Look, Here Comes the Sun/It's Sunday	1968	2.50	5.00	10.00
66298	Let's Get Together/Sunday Brought the Rain	1968	2.50	5.00	10.00
66308	On a Beautiful Day/Darcy Farrow	1968	2.50	5.00	10.00
66324	Love Poem/Willie Jean	1968	2.50	5.00	10.00
66399	The Only Thing That Matters/Bolaro	1969	2.50	5.00	10.00
UNITED ARTISTS					
0132	Happy/Back on the Street Again	1973	—	2.00	4.00
—"Silver Spotlight Series" reissue					

Albums

Number	Title	Yr	VG	VG+	NM
IMPERIAL					
LP-9359 [M]	Happy Is the Sunshine Company	1967	5.00	10.00	20.00
LP-9368 [M]	The Sunshine Company	1968	6.25	12.50	25.00
—Mono copies are promo only					
LP-12359 [S]	Happy Is the Sunshine Company	1967	5.00	10.00	20.00
LP-12368 [S]	The Sunshine Company	1968	5.00	10.00	20.00
LP-12399	Sunshine and Shadows	1969	5.00	10.00	20.00

SUPER K GENERATION, THE
45s

Number	Title (A Side/B Side)	Yr	VG	VG+	NM
LAURIE					
3413	Heartful O'Soul (Part 1)/Heartful O'Soul (Part 2)	1967	2.50	5.00	10.00

SUPER STOCKS, THE
45s

Number	Title (A Side/B Side)	Yr	VG	VG+	NM
CAPITOL					
5153	Thunder Road/Wheel Stands	1964	6.25	12.50	25.00

Albums

Number	Title	Yr	VG	VG+	NM
CAPITOL					
ST 1997 [S]	Hot Rod Rally	1963	17.50	35.00	70.00
T 1997 [M]	Hot Rod Rally	1963	12.50	25.00	50.00
ST 2060 [S]	Thunder Road	1964	31.25	62.50	125.00
T 2060 [M]	Thunder Road	1964	25.00	50.00	100.00
(S)T 2060	Thunder Road Bonus Poster	1964	12.50	25.00	50.00
ST 2113 [S]	Surf Route 101	1964	37.50	75.00	150.00
—With bonus single, "Doin' the Surfink"/"Finksville, U.S.A." by Mr. Gasser and the Weirdos, in special pocket on front cover					
ST 2113 [S]	Surf Route 101	1964	31.25	62.50	125.00
—Without bonus single					

Number	Title (A Side/B Side)	Yr	VG	VG+	NM
T 2113 [M]	Surf Route 101	1964	31.25	62.50	125.00
—With bonus single, "Doin' the Surfink"/"Finksville, U.S.A." by Mr. Gasser and the Weirdos, in special pocket on front cover					
T 2113 [M]	Surf Route 101	1964	25.00	50.00	100.00
—Without bonus single					
ST 2190 [S]	School Is a Drag	1964	30.00	60.00	120.00
T 2190 [M]	School Is a Drag	1964	25.00	50.00	100.00

SUPERFINE DANDELION, THE

Number	Title (A Side/B Side)	Yr	VG	VG+	NM
45s					
MAINSTREAM					
672	People in the Street/(B-side unknown)	1967	3.00	6.00	12.00
673	Crazy Town/Janie's Tomb	1967	3.00	6.00	12.00
Albums					
MAINSTREAM					
S-6102 [S]	The Superfine Dandelion	1967	10.00	20.00	40.00
56102 [M]	The Superfine Dandelion	1967	10.00	20.00	40.00

SUPERIORS, THE (1)

Number	Title (A Side/B Side)	Yr	VG	VG+	NM
45s					
ATCO					
6106	Lost Love/Don't Say Goodbye	1957	17.50	35.00	70.00
MAIN LINE					
104	Lost Love/Don't Say Goodbye	1958	150.00	300.00	600.00
—With Fairmount Ave., Philadelphia street address on label					
104	Lost Love/Don't Say Goodbye	1962	10.00	20.00	40.00
—No address on label or only "Philadelphia, Pennsylvania" address on label					

SUPERIORS, THE (2)

Number	Title (A Side/B Side)	Yr	VG	VG+	NM
45s					
FAL					
301	What Is Love/Flee the Scene	1961	20.00	40.00	80.00
FEDERAL					
12436	I'm Sorry Baby (I Didn't Mean to Do You Wrong)/ Dance of Love	1961	7.50	15.00	30.00

SUPERIORS, THE (3)

Number	Title (A Side/B Side)	Yr	VG	VG+	NM
45s					
MGM					
13503	Can't Make It Without You/Let Me Make You Happy	1966	3.00	6.00	12.00
SUE					
12	Heavenly Angel/I'd Rather Die	1969	2.00	4.00	8.00
VERVE					
10370	Tell Me to Go/What Would I Do	1965	5.00	10.00	20.00

SUPERSAX

Number	Title (A Side/B Side)	Yr	VG	VG+	NM
Albums					
CAPITOL					
ST-11177	Supersax Plays Bird	1973	2.50	5.00	10.00
ST-11271	Supersax Plays Bird, Volume 2/Salt Peanuts	1974	2.50	5.00	10.00
ST-11371	Supersax Plays Bird with Strings	1975	2.50	5.00	10.00
COLUMBIA					
FC 39140	Supersax and L.A. Voices	1984	2.50	5.00	10.00
FC 39925	Supersax and L.A. Voices, Vol. 2	1985	2.50	5.00	10.00
FC 44436	Stone Bird	1989	3.00	6.00	12.00
MOBILE FIDELITY					
1-511	Supersax Plays Bird	1981	10.00	20.00	40.00
—Audiophile vinyl					
PAUSA					
7038	Chasin' the Bird	1977	2.50	5.00	10.00
7082	Dynamite!	1979	2.50	5.00	10.00
9028	Supersax Plays Bird, Volume 2/Salt Peanuts	198?	2.00	4.00	8.00

SUPERSISTER

Number	Title (A Side/B Side)	Yr	VG	VG+	NM
Albums					
DWARF					
PDLP-2001	Supersister	197?	7.50	15.00	30.00

SUPERTRAMP

Number	Title (A Side/B Side)	Yr	VG	VG+	NM
12-Inch Singles					
A&M					
SP-12254	I'm Beggin' You (3 remixes)	1987	2.00	4.00	8.00
SP-17320 [DJ]	Cannonball (Edit) (Single Version) (Direct-to-Disc Version)	1985	2.50	5.00	10.00
45s					
A&M					
1305	Forever/Your Poppa Don't Mind	1971	—	3.00	6.00
1660	Bloody Well Right/Dreamer	1975	—	2.50	5.00
1766	Lady/You Started Laughing When I Held You in My Arms	1975	—	—	—
—Unreleased?					
1793	Lady/You Started Laughing When I Held You in My Arms	1976	—	2.50	5.00
1814	Sister Moonshine/Ain't Nobody But Me	1976	—	2.50	5.00
1938	Give a Little Bit/Downstream	1977	—	2.00	4.00
1938 [PS]	Give a Little Bit/Downstream	1977	—	3.00	6.00
1981	Dreamer/From Now On	1977	—	2.50	5.00
1981 [PS]	Dreamer/From Now On	1977	—	3.00	6.00
2128	The Logical Song/Just Another Nervous Wreck	1979	—	2.00	4.00
2128 [PS]	The Logical Song/Just Another Nervous Wreck	1979	—	2.50	5.00
2162	Goodbye Stranger/Even in the Quietest Moments	1979	—	2.00	4.00
2162 [PS]	Goodbye Stranger/Even in the Quietest Moments	1979	—	2.50	5.00
2193	Take the Long Way Home/Ruby	1979	—	2.00	4.00
2193 [PS]	Take the Long Way Home/Ruby	1979	—	2.00	4.00
—With yellow maze					
2193 [PS]	Take the Long Way Home/Ruby	1979	—	2.50	5.00
—With green maze					
2193 [PS]	Take the Long Way Home/Ruby	1979	—	2.50	5.00
—With red maze. Other colors may exist as well.					
2269	Dreamer/From Now On	1980	—	2.00	4.00
2269 [PS]	Dreamer/From Now On	1980	—	2.50	5.00
2292	Breakfast in America/You Started Laughing	1980	—	2.00	4.00
2502	It's Raining Again/Monnie	1982	—	2.00	4.00
2502 [PS]	It's Raining Again/Monnie	1982	—	2.00	4.00
2517	My Kind of Lady/Know Who You Are	1983	—	2.00	4.00
2517 [PS]	My Kind of Lady/Know Who You Are	1983	—	2.00	4.00
2720 [DJ]	Still in Love with You (same on both sides)	1985	—	—	—
—Unreleased?					
2731	Cannonball/Every Open Door	1985	—	—	3.00
2731 [PS]	Cannonball/Every Open Door	1985	—	—	3.00
2760	Better Days/No In-Between	1985	—	—	3.00
2985	I'm Beggin' You/No Inbetween	1987	—	—	3.00
2985 [PS]	I'm Beggin' You/No Inbetween	1987	—	—	3.00
2996	Free as a Bird/Thing for You	1987	—	—	3.00
Albums					
A&M					
SP-3129	Indelibly Stamped	198?	2.00	4.00	8.00
—Budget-line reissue					
SP-3149	Supertramp	198?	2.00	4.00	8.00
—Budget-line reissue					
SP-3214	Crisis? What Crisis?	1982	2.00	4.00	8.00
—Budget-line reissue					
SP-3215	Even in the Quietest Moments	1982	2.00	4.00	8.00
—Budget-line reissue					
SP-3284	...Famous Last Words...	1986	2.00	4.00	8.00
—Budget-line reissue					
SP-3647	Crime of the Century	1974	3.00	6.00	12.00
SP-3707	Breakfast in America	1979	2.50	5.00	10.00
SP-3730 [PD]	Breakfast in America	1979	125.00	250.00	500.00
—In-house picture discs featuring A&M staff members posing with the cover model					
SP-3732	...Famous Last Words...	1982	2.50	5.00	10.00
SP-4274	Supertramp	1970	5.00	10.00	20.00
—First edition with brown label					
SP-4274	Supertramp	197?	2.50	5.00	10.00
—Second edition with silverish label					
SP-4311	Indelibly Stamped	1971	5.00	10.00	20.00
—First edition with brown label					
SP-4311	Indelibly Stamped	197?	2.50	5.00	10.00
—Second edition with silverish label					
SP-4560	Crisis? What Crisis?	1975	3.00	6.00	12.00
SP-4634	Even in the Quietest Moments...	1977	3.00	6.00	12.00
SP-4665	Supertramp	1978	3.00	6.00	12.00
—Reissue of 4274					
SP-5013	Brother Where You Bound	1985	2.50	5.00	10.00
SP-5181	Free as a Bird	1987	2.50	5.00	10.00
SP-6702 [(2)]	Paris	1980	3.00	6.00	12.00
MOBILE FIDELITY					
1-005	Crime of the Century	1979	10.00	20.00	40.00
—Audiophile vinyl					
MFQR-005	Crime of the Century	1983	30.00	60.00	120.00
—Ultra High Quality Recording; in box					
1-045	Breakfast in America	1980	12.50	25.00	50.00
—Audiophile vinyl					
SWEET THUNDER					
5	Even in the Quietest Moments...	198?	10.00	20.00	40.00
—Audiophile vinyl					

SUPREMES, THE

Motown girl group. Also see FLORENCE BALLARD; THE PRIMETTES; DIANA ROSS.

Number	Title (A Side/B Side)	Yr	VG	VG+	NM
45s					
EEOC					
SL4M-3114 [DJ]	Things Are Changing (same on both sides)	1965	37.50	75.00	150.00
SL4M-3114 [PS]	Things Are Changing (same on both sides)	1965	37.50	75.00	150.00
—Promotional item for the Equal Employment Opportunity Commission (number not on sleeve)					
GEORGE ALEXANDER INC.					
1079 [DJ]	The Only Time I'm Happy/Supremes Interview	1965	15.00	30.00	60.00
MOTOWN					
1008	I Want a Guy/Never Again	1961	75.00	150.00	300.00
1027	Your Heart Belongs to Me/(He's) Seventeen	1962	6.25	12.50	25.00
1027 [PS]	Your Heart Belongs to Me/(He's) Seventeen	1962	100.00	200.00	400.00
1034	Let Me Go the Right Way/Time Changes Things	1962	12.50	25.00	50.00
1040	My Heart Can't Take It No More/You Bring Back Memories	1963	10.00	20.00	40.00
1044	A Breath Taking, First Sight Soul Shaking, One Night Love Making, Next Day Heart Breaking Guy/Rock and Roll Banjo Band	1963	25.00	50.00	100.00
—Original pressing with long title. This does exist on stock copies as well as on promos.					
1044	A Breath Taking Guy/Rock and Roll Banjo Band	1963	6.25	12.50	25.00
1051	When the Lovelight Starts Shining Through His Eyes/Standing at the Crossroads of Love	1963	5.00	10.00	20.00
1054	Run, Run, Run/I'm Giving You Your Freedom	1964	6.25	12.50	25.00
1060	Where Did Our Love Go/He Means the World to Me	1964	5.00	10.00	20.00
1060 [PS]	Where Did Our Love Go/He Means the World to Me	1964	7.50	15.00	30.00
1066	Baby Love/Ask Any Girl	1964	5.00	10.00	20.00
1066 [PS]	Baby Love/Ask Any Girl	1964	7.50	15.00	30.00
1068	Come See About Me/Always in My Heart	1964	5.00	10.00	20.00
1074	Stop! In the Name of Love/I'm in Love Again	1965	3.75	7.50	15.00
1074 [PS]	Stop! In the Name of Love/I'm in Love Again	1965	7.50	15.00	30.00
1075	Back in My Arms Again/Whisper You Love Me Boy	1965	3.75	7.50	15.00
1075 [PS]	Back in My Arms Again/Whisper You Love Me Boy	1965	7.50	15.00	30.00
1080	Nothing But Heartaches/He Holds His Own	1965	3.75	7.50	15.00
1080 [PS]	Nothing But Heartaches/He Holds His Own	1965	7.50	15.00	30.00
1083	I Hear a Symphony/Who Could Ever Doubt My Love	1965	3.75	7.50	15.00
1085	Children's Christmas Song/Twinkle, Twinkle Little Me	1965	5.00	10.00	20.00
1085 [DJ]	Children's Christmas Song/Twinkle, Twinkle Little Me	1965	6.25	12.50	25.00
—Promo only on red vinyl					
1085 [PS]	Children's Christmas Song/Twinkle, Twinkle Little Me	1965	8.75	17.50	35.00

Number	Title (A Side/B Side)	Yr	VG	VG+	NM
1089	My World Is Empty Without You/Everything Is Good About You	1966	3.75	7.50	15.00
1094	Love Is Like an Itching in My Heart/He's All I Got	1966	3.75	7.50	15.00
1097	You Can't Hurry Love/Put Yourself in My Place	1966	3.75	7.50	15.00
1097 [PS]	You Can't Hurry Love/Put Yourself in My Place	1966	7.50	15.00	30.00
1101	You Keep Me Hangin' On/Remove This Doubt	1966	3.75	7.50	15.00
1101 [PS]	You Keep Me Hangin' On/Remove This Doubt	1966	7.50	15.00	30.00
1103	Love Is Here and Now You're Gone/There's No Stopping Us Now	1967	3.00	6.00	12.00
1107	The Happening/All I Know About You	1967	3.00	6.00	12.00
1111	Reflections/Going Down for the Third Time	1967	2.00	4.00	8.00
—Starting here, through 1156, as "Diana Ross and the Supremes"					
1116	In and Out of Love/I Guess I'll Always Love You	1967	2.00	4.00	8.00
1122	Forever Came Today/Time Changes Things	1968	2.00	4.00	8.00
1125	What the World Needs Now/Your Kiss of Fire	1968	—	—	—
—Unreleased					
1126	Some Things You Never Get Used To/You've Been So Wonderful to Me	1968	2.00	4.00	8.00
1135	Love Child/Will This Be the Day	1968	2.00	4.00	8.00
1139	I'm Livin' in Shame/I'm So Glad I Got Somebody	1969	2.00	4.00	8.00
1146	The Composer/The Beginning of the End	1969	2.00	4.00	8.00
1148	No Matter What Sign You Are/The Young Folks	1969	2.00	4.00	8.00
1156	Someday We'll Be Together/He's My Sunny Boy	1969	2.00	4.00	8.00
1162	Up the Ladder to the Roof/Bill, When Are You Coming Home	1970	—	3.00	6.00
—Starting here, name reverts to "The Supremes" (unless noted)					
1167	Everybody's Got the Right to Love/But I Love You More	1970	—	3.00	6.00
1172	Stoned Love/Shine on Me	1970	—	3.00	6.00
1182	Nathan Jones/Happy (Is a Bumpy Road)	1971	—	3.00	6.00
1190	Touch/It's So Hard for Me to Say Goodbye	1971	—	3.00	6.00
1195	Floy Joy/This Is the Story	1972	—	2.50	5.00
1200	Automatically Sunshine/Precious Little Things	1972	—	2.50	5.00
1206	Your Wonderful, Sweet Sweet Love/The Wisdom of Time	1972	—	2.50	5.00
1213	I Guess I'll Miss the Man/Over and Over	1972	—	2.50	5.00
1225	Bad Weather/Oh Be My Love	1973	—	2.50	5.00
1350	It's All Been Said Before/(B-side unassigned)	1975	—	—	—
—Unreleased					
1357	He's My Man/Give Out But Don't Give Up	1975	—	2.50	5.00
1374	Where Do I Go from Here/Give Out But Don't Give Up	1975	—	2.50	5.00
1391	I'm Gonna Let My Heart Do the Walking/Early Morning Love	1976	—	2.50	5.00
1407	You're My Driving Wheel/You're What's Missing in My Life	1976	—	2.50	5.00
1415	Let Yourself Go/You Are the Heart of Me	1977	—	2.50	5.00
1488	Medley of Hits/Where Did We Go Wrong	1980	—	2.00	4.00
—As "Diana Ross and the Supremes"					
1523	Medley of Hits/Where Did We Go Wrong	1981	—	2.00	4.00
—As "Diana Ross and the Supremes"					

TAMLA

Number	Title (A Side/B Side)	Yr	VG	VG+	NM
54038	I Want a Guy/Never Again	1961	31.25	62.50	125.00
—Lines label					
54038	I Want a Guy/Never Again	1961	15.00	30.00	60.00
—Globes label					
54045	Buttered Popcorn/Who's Lovin' You	1961	31.25	62.50	125.00
—Lines label					
54045	Buttered Popcorn/Who's Lovin' You	1961	15.00	30.00	60.00
—Globes label					

TOPPS/MOTOWN

Number	Title (A Side/B Side)	Yr	VG	VG+	NM
1	Baby Love	1967	18.75	37.50	75.00
—Cardboard record					
2	Stop in the Name of Love	1967	18.75	37.50	75.00
—Cardboard record					
3	Where Did Our Love Go	1967	18.75	37.50	75.00
—Cardboard record					
15	Come See About Me	1967	18.75	37.50	75.00
—Cardboard record					
16	My World Is Empty Without You	1967	18.75	37.50	75.00
—Cardboard record					

7-Inch Extended Plays

MOTOWN

Number	Title (A Side/B Side)	Yr	VG	VG+	NM
S 621 [PS]	Where Did Our Love Go	1965	6.25	12.50	25.00
S 621 [S]	He Means the World to Me/Baby Love/Ask Any Girl//Where Did Our Love Go/Come See About Me/Run, Run, Run	1965	6.25	12.50	25.00
—33 1/3 rpm, small hole					

Albums

DORAL

Number	Title (A Side/B Side)	Yr	VG	VG+	NM
(# unknown)	Doral Presents Diana Ross and the Supremes	1971	12.50	25.00	50.00
—Available through Doral cigarettes					

MOTOWN

Number	Title (A Side/B Side)	Yr	VG	VG+	NM
M5-101	Superstar Series, Vol. 1	1981	3.00	6.00	12.00
—By "Diana Ross and the Supremes"					
PR-102 [DJ]	Touch Interview	1971	6.25	12.50	25.00
M5-138V1	The Supremes A' Go-Go	1981	3.00	6.00	12.00
—Reissue of Motown 649					
M5-147V1	I Hear a Symphony	1981	3.00	6.00	12.00
—Reissue of Motown 643					
M5-162V1	The Supremes at the Copa	1981	3.00	6.00	12.00
—Reissue of Motown 636					
M5-182V1	The Supremes Sing Holland-Dozier-Holland	1981	3.00	6.00	12.00
—Reissue of Motown 650					
M5-203V1	Diana Ross and the Supremes Greatest Hits, Volume 3	1981	3.00	6.00	12.00
—Reissue of Motown 702					
M 606 [M]	Meet the Supremes	1963	225.00	450.00	900.00
—With group sitting on stools					
M 606 [M]	Meet the Supremes	1963	7.50	15.00	30.00
—With close-up of group's faces					
MS 606 [S]	Meet the Supremes	1964	10.00	20.00	40.00
—With close-up of group's faces					
MT/MS 610	The Supremes Sing Ballads and Blues	1963	—	—	—
—Unreleased					
M 621 [M]	Where Did Our Love Go	1964	7.50	15.00	30.00
MS 621 [S]	Where Did Our Love Go	1964	10.00	20.00	40.00
M 623 [M]	A Bit of Liverpool	1964	10.00	20.00	40.00
MS 623 [S]	A Bit of Liverpool	1964	12.50	25.00	50.00
M 625 [M]	The Supremes Sing Country Western & Pop	1965	6.25	12.50	25.00
MS 625 [S]	The Supremes Sing Country Western & Pop	1965	7.50	15.00	30.00
MT/MS 626	The Supremes Live! Live! Live!	1965	—	—	—
—Unreleased					
M 627 [M]	More Hits by the Supremes	1965	6.25	12.50	25.00
MS 627 [S]	More Hits by the Supremes	1965	7.50	15.00	30.00
MT/MS 628	There's a Place for Us	1965	—	—	—
—Unreleased					
M 629 [M]	We Remember Sam Cooke	1965	6.25	12.50	25.00
MS 629 [S]	We Remember Sam Cooke	1965	7.50	15.00	30.00
—The above LP came out before Motown 627					
M 636 [M]	The Supremes at the Copa	1965	6.25	12.50	25.00
MS 636 [S]	The Supremes at the Copa	1965	7.50	15.00	30.00
MT/MS 637	A Tribute to the Girls	1965	—	—	—
—Unreleased					
MS 638 [S]	Merry Christmas	1965	10.00	20.00	40.00
—Same as above, but in stereo					
MT 638 [M]	Merry Christmas	1965	7.50	15.00	30.00
M 643 [M]	I Hear a Symphony	1966	6.25	12.50	25.00
MS 643 [S]	I Hear a Symphony	1966	7.50	15.00	30.00
MTMS 648	Pure Gold	1966	—	—	—
—Unreleased					
M 649 [M]	The Supremes A' Go-Go	1966	6.25	12.50	25.00
MS 649 [S]	The Supremes A' Go-Go	1966	7.50	15.00	30.00
M 650 [M]	The Supremes Sing Holland-Dozier-Holland	1967	6.25	12.50	25.00
MS 650 [S]	The Supremes Sing Holland-Dozier-Holland	1967	7.50	15.00	30.00
M 659 [M]	The Supremes Sing Rodgers & Hart	1967	6.25	12.50	25.00
MS 659 [S]	The Supremes Sing Rodgers & Hart	1967	7.50	15.00	30.00
M 663 [(2) M]	Diana Ross and the Supremes Greatest Hits	1967	7.50	15.00	30.00
MS 663 [(2) S]	Diana Ross and the Supremes Greatest Hits	1967	10.00	20.00	40.00
MT/MS 663	Diana Ross and the Supremes Greatest Hits Poster	1967	2.50	5.00	10.00
M 665 [M]	Reflections	1968	7.50	15.00	30.00
MS 665 [S]	Reflections	1968	5.00	10.00	20.00
MS 670	Love Child	1968	5.00	10.00	20.00
M 672 [M]	Funny Girl	1968	7.50	15.00	30.00
—Mono appears to be promo only					
MS 672 [S]	Funny Girl	1968	5.00	10.00	20.00
—The above LP came out before Motown 670					
M 676 [M]	Live at London's Talk of the Town	1968	7.50	51.00	30.00
—Mono is promo only					
MS 676 [S]	Live at London's Talk of the Town	1968	5.00	10.00	20.00
—The above LP came out before Motown 670 and 672					
MS 689	Let the Sunshine In	1969	5.00	10.00	20.00
MS 694	Cream of the Crop	1969	5.00	10.00	20.00
MS 702	Diana Ross and the Supremes Greatest Hits, Volume 3	1970	5.00	10.00	20.00
MS 705	Right On	1970	3.75	7.50	15.00
—By "The Supremes"; the first LP after Diana Ross left					
MS 708 [(2)]	Farewell	1970	6.25	12.50	25.00
—By "Diana Ross and the Supremes"					
MS 720	New Ways But Love Stays	1970	3.75	7.50	15.00
MS 737	Touch	1971	3.75	7.50	15.00
MS 746	Promises Kept	1972	—	—	—
—Unreleased					
M 751L	Floy Joy	1972	3.75	7.50	15.00
M 756L	The Supremes	1972	3.75	7.50	15.00
M9-794L3 [(3)]	Anthology (1962-1969)	1974	6.25	12.50	25.00
—By "Diana Ross and the Supremes"					
M6-828	The Supremes	1975	3.75	7.50	15.00
M6-863	High Energy	1976	3.75	7.50	15.00
M6-873	Mary, Scherrie and Susaye	1976	3.75	7.50	15.00
M7-904	The Supremes at Their Best	1978	3.75	7.50	15.00
5252 ML	Merry Christmas	1982	2.50	5.00	10.00
—Reissue of MS 638 with same contents					
5381 ML [(3)]	25th Anniversary	1986	5.00	10.00	20.00
—By "Diana Ross and the Supremes"					

NATURAL RESOURCES

Number	Title (A Side/B Side)	Yr	VG	VG+	NM
NR 4006T1	Where Did Our Love Go	1978	3.00	6.00	12.00
—Reissue of Motown 621					

SUPREMES, THE (2)

45s

ACE

Number	Title (A Side/B Side)	Yr	VG	VG+	NM
534	Just for You and I/Don't Leave Me Here to Cry	1957	20.00	40.00	80.00

SUPREMES, THE (3)

45s

APT

Number	Title (A Side/B Side)	Yr	VG	VG+	NM
25055	Another Chance to Love/Fidgety	1961	10.00	20.00	40.00

SUPREMES, THE (4)

45s

KITTEN

Number	Title (A Side/B Side)	Yr	VG	VG+	NM
6969	Could This Be You/Margie	1956	125.00	250.00	500.00

SUPREMES, THE (5)

45s

MARK

Number	Title (A Side/B Side)	Yr	VG	VG+	NM
129	Nobody Can Love You/Snap, Crackle and Pop	1958	200.00	400.00	800.00

SUPREMES, THE (6)

45s

MASCOT

Number	Title (A Side/B Side)	Yr	VG	VG+	NM
126	Little Sally Walker/Just Yell	1960	25.00	50.00	100.00

SUPREMES, THE (7)

45s

OLD TOWN

Number	Title (A Side/B Side)	Yr	VG	VG+	NM
1024	Tonight/My Babe	1956	25.00	50.00	100.00
1024	Tonight/She Don't Want Me No More	1956	37.50	75.00	150.00

SUPREMES, THE, AND THE FOUR TOPS

Also see each artist's individual listings.

45s

MOTOWN

Number	Title (A Side/B Side)	Yr	VG	VG+	NM
1173	River Deep-Mountain High/Together We Can Make Such Sweet Music	1970	—	3.00	6.00
1181	You Gotta Have Love in Your Heart/I'm Glad About It	1971	—	3.00	6.00

Albums

MOTOWN

Number	Title (A Side/B Side)	Yr	VG	VG+	NM
M5-123V1A	The Magnificent Seven	1981	3.00	6.00	12.00
—Reissue of Motown 717					
MS 717	The Magnificent Seven	1970	3.75	7.50	15.00
MS 736	The Return of the Magnificent Seven	1971	3.75	7.50	15.00
MS 745	Dynamite	1971	3.75	7.50	15.00

SUPREMES, THE, DIANA ROSS AND, AND THE TEMPTATIONS

Also see each artist's individual listings.

45s

MOTOWN

Number	Title (A Side/B Side)	Yr	VG	VG+	NM
1137	I'm Gonna Make You Love Me/A Place in the Sun	1968	—	3.50	7.00
1137 [PS]	I'm Gonna Make You Love Me/A Place in the Sun	1968	5.00	10.00	20.00
1142	I'll Try Something New/The Way You Do the Things You Do	1969	—	3.50	7.00
1150	Stubborn Kind of Fellow/Try It Baby	1969	—	3.50	7.00
1153	The Weight/For Better or Worse	1969	—	3.50	7.00

Albums

MOTOWN

Number	Title (A Side/B Side)	Yr	VG	VG+	NM
M5-139V1	Diana Ross and the Supremes Join the Temptations	1981	3.00	6.00	12.00
—Reissue of Motown 679					
M5-171V1	TCB	1981	3.00	6.00	12.00
—Reissue of Motown 682					
M 679 [M]	Diana Ross and the Supremes Join the Temptations	1968	7.50	15.00	30.00
MS 679 [S]	Diana Ross and the Supremes Join the Temptations	1968	5.00	10.00	20.00
MS 682	TCB	1968	5.00	10.00	20.00
MS 692	Together	1969	5.00	10.00	20.00
MS 699	On Broadway	1969	5.00	10.00	20.00

SUPREMES FOUR, THE

45s

SARA

Number	Title (A Side/B Side)	Yr	VG	VG+	NM
1032	I Lost My Job/I Love You Patricia	1958	500.00	1000.	2000.

SURF BOYS, THE

45s

KARATE

Number	Title (A Side/B Side)	Yr	VG	VG+	NM
526	Da Doo Ron Ron/Hurt	1966	6.25	12.50	25.00

SCEPTER

Number	Title (A Side/B Side)	Yr	VG	VG+	NM
12180	Stuck in the Chimney/I Told Santa Claus I Want You	1966	6.25	12.50	25.00

SURF BREAKERS, THE

45s

MERCURY

Number	Title (A Side/B Side)	Yr	VG	VG+	NM
72174	Hang Ten/Ridin' In #9	1963	12.50	25.00	50.00

SURF BUNNIES, THE

45s

DOT

Number	Title (A Side/B Side)	Yr	VG	VG+	NM
16523	Our Surfer Boys/Surf Bunny Beach	1963	7.50	15.00	30.00

GOLIATH

Number	Title (A Side/B Side)	Yr	VG	VG+	NM
1352	Our Surfer Boys/Surf Bunny Beach	1963	12.50	25.00	50.00
1353	Surf City High/Met the Boy I Adore	1963	12.50	25.00	50.00

SURF RIDERS, THE

45s

DECCA

Number	Title (A Side/B Side)	Yr	VG	VG+	NM
31477	The Birds/Blues for the Birds	1963	7.50	15.00	30.00

NASCO

Number	Title (A Side/B Side)	Yr	VG	VG+	NM
6008	I'm Out/Rocko Socko	1958	15.00	30.00	60.00

SURF STOMPERS, THE

Also see BRUCE JOHNSTON.

Albums

DEL-FI

Number	Title (A Side/B Side)	Yr	VG	VG+	NM
DFLP-1236 [M]	The Original Surfer Stomp	1963	15.00	30.00	60.00
DFST-1236 [S]	The Original Surfer Stomp	1963	20.00	40.00	80.00
DLF-1236	The Original Surfer Stomp	1997	3.00	6.00	12.00

SURF TEENS, THE

Albums

SUTTON

Number	Title (A Side/B Side)	Yr	VG	VG+	NM
SSU-339 [S]	Surf Mania	1963	15.00	30.00	60.00
SU-339 [M]	Surf Mania	1963	12.50	25.00	50.00

SURFARIS, THE (1)

45s

DECCA

Number	Title (A Side/B Side)	Yr	VG	VG+	NM
31538	Point Panic/Waikiki Run	1963	3.75	7.50	15.00
31561	A Surfer's Christmas List/Santa's Speed Shop	1963	7.50	15.00	30.00
31581	I Wanna Take a trip to the Islands/Scatter Shield	1964	5.00	10.00	20.00
31605	Murphy the Surfie/Go Go Go For Louie's Place	1964	3.75	7.50	15.00
31641	Bossa Barracuda/Dune Buggy	1964	3.75	7.50	15.00
31682	Hot Rod High/Karen	1964	3.75	7.50	15.00
31731	Beat '65/Black Denim	1965	5.00	10.00	20.00
31784	Theme of the Battle Maiden/Somethin' Else	1965	5.00	10.00	20.00
31835	Catch a Little Ride with Me/Don't Hurt My Little Sister	1965	5.00	10.00	20.00
31954	Hey Joe Where Are You Going/So Get Out	1966	5.00	10.00	20.00
32003	Wipe Out/I'm a Hog for You	1966	2.50	5.00	10.00

DFS

Number	Title (A Side/B Side)	Yr	VG	VG+	NM
11/12	Wipe Out/Surfer Joe	1963	1500.	2250.	3000.

DOT

Number	Title (A Side/B Side)	Yr	VG	VG+	NM
144	Wipe Out/Surfer Joe	1966	2.50	5.00	10.00
—Black label, script "Dot" in multicolor letters					
144	Wipe Out/Surfer Joe	1969	—	3.00	6.00
—Muilticolor label, "DOT" in all capital letters in box at top					
144 [DJ]	Wipe Out (same on both sides)	1966	25.00	50.00	100.00
—Red vinyl					
144 [DJ]	Wipe Out (same on both sides)	1966	37.50	75.00	150.00
—Red vinyl; error pressing with "Surfer Joe" on both sides					
16479	Wipe Out/Surfer Joe	1963	3.75	7.50	15.00
16757	Surfer Joe/Can't Sit Down	1965	7.50	15.00	30.00
—B-side by the Challengers, but credited to the Surfaris					
16757	Surfer Joe/Can't Sit Down	1965	12.50	25.00	50.00
—B-side by the Challengers, and credited correctly					
16966	Show Biz/Chicago Green	1966	2.50	5.00	10.00
17008	Shake/The Search	1967	2.50	5.00	10.00

PRINCESS

Number	Title (A Side/B Side)	Yr	VG	VG+	NM
50	Wipe Out/Surfer Joe	1963	100.00	200.00	400.00
—With long versions of both songs. No "RE-1" is in the trail-off area.					
50	Wipe Out/Surfer Joe	1963	37.50	75.00	150.00
—With short versions of both songs. "RE-1" is in the trail-off area.					

Albums

DECCA

Number	Title (A Side/B Side)	Yr	VG	VG+	NM
DL 4470 [M]	The Surfaris Play Wipe Out	1963	6.25	12.50	25.00
DL 4487 [M]	Hit City '64	1964	10.00	20.00	40.00
DL 4560 [M]	Fun City, U.S.A.	1964	10.00	20.00	40.00
DL 4614 [M]	Hit City '65	1965	10.00	20.00	40.00
DL 4663 [M]	It Ain't Me, Babe	1965	10.00	20.00	40.00
DL 74470 [S]	The Surfaris Play Wipe Out	1963	7.50	15.00	30.00
DL 74487 [S]	Hit City '64	1964	12.50	25.00	50.00
DL 74560 [S]	Fun City, U.S.A.	1964	12.50	25.00	50.00
DL 74614 [S]	Hit City '65	1965	12.50	25.00	50.00
DL 74663 [S]	It Ain't Me, Babe	1965	12.50	25.00	50.00

DOT

Number	Title (A Side/B Side)	Yr	VG	VG+	NM
DLP-3535 [M]	Wipe Out	1963	12.50	25.00	50.00
—With back cover photo featuring five Surfaris					
DLP-3535 [M]	Wipe Out	1963	10.00	20.00	40.00
—With back cover photo featuring four Surfaris					
DLP-3535 [M]	Wipe Out	1963	7.50	15.00	30.00
—With no back cover photo of the Surfaris					
DLP-25535 [S]	Wipe Out	1963	20.00	40.00	80.00
—With back cover photo featuring five Surfaris					
DLP-25535 [S]	Wipe Out	1963	12.50	25.00	50.00
—With back cover photo featuring four Surfaris					
DLP-25535 [S]	Wipe Out	1963	10.00	20.00	40.00
—With no back cover photo of the Surfaris					

SURFARIS, THE (2)

This group was forced to change its name to "The Original Surfaris."

45s

CHANCELLOR

Number	Title (A Side/B Side)	Yr	VG	VG+	NM
1142	The Midnight Surf/Psyche-Out	1963	12.50	25.00	50.00

DEL-FI

Number	Title (A Side/B Side)	Yr	VG	VG+	NM
4219	Surfari/Bombora	1963	25.00	50.00	100.00

FELSTED

Number	Title (A Side/B Side)	Yr	VG	VG+	NM
8688	Tor-Chula/Psyche-Out	1964	12.50	25.00	50.00

NORTHRIDGE

Number	Title (A Side/B Side)	Yr	VG	VG+	NM
1001	Moment of Truth/Church Key	1963	15.00	30.00	60.00
—B-side by the Biscaynes					

REGANO

Number	Title (A Side/B Side)	Yr	VG	VG+	NM
1062	Surfin' '63/Boss Beat	1963	12.50	25.00	50.00
—As "The Original Surfaris"					

REPRISE

Number	Title (A Side/B Side)	Yr	VG	VG+	NM
20180	Moment of Truth/Church Key	1963	7.50	15.00	30.00
—B-side by the Biscaynes					

SURFARI

Number	Title (A Side/B Side)	Yr	VG	VG+	NM
301	Gum Dipped Slicks/High Time	1964	25.00	50.00	100.00
—As "The Original Surfaris"					

Albums

DIPLOMAT

Number	Title (A Side/B Side)	Yr	VG	VG+	NM
D-2309 [M]	Wheels-Shorts-Hot Rods	1963	6.25	12.50	25.00
—As "The Original Surfaris"					
DS-2309 [S]	Wheels-Shorts-Hot Rods	1963	7.50	15.00	30.00
—As "The Original Surfaris"					

SURFRIDERS, THE

Albums

VAULT

Number	Title (A Side/B Side)	Yr	VG	VG+	NM
LP-105 [M]	Surfbeat, Volume 2	1963	7.50	15.00	30.00
VS-105 [S]	Surfbeat, Volume 2	1963	10.00	20.00	40.00

SURFSIDERS, THE

Albums

DESIGN

Number	Title (A Side/B Side)	Yr	VG	VG+	NM
DLP-208 [M]	The Beach Boys Songbook	1965	3.75	7.50	15.00
DLPS-208 [S]	The Beach Boys Songbook	1965	5.00	10.00	20.00

SURVIVORS, THE
Dave Nowlen, Bob Norberg and friends with help from BRIAN WILSON. This record is NOT by the Beach Boys.

Number	Title (A Side/B Side)	Yr	VG	VG+	NM
45s					
CAPITOL					
5102	Pamela Jean/After the Game	1963	250.00	500.00	1000.

SUSIE AND THE FOUR TRUMPETS

Number	Title (A Side/B Side)	Yr	VG	VG+	NM
45s					
UNITED ARTISTS					
471	Starry Eyes/Blue Little Girl	1962	15.00	30.00	60.00

SUTCH, SCREAMING LORD

Number	Title (A Side/B Side)	Yr	VG	VG+	NM
45s					
CAMEO					
341	She's Fallen in Love with the Monster Man/Bye Bye Baby	1964	3.75	7.50	15.00
COTILLION					
44149	Gotta Keep a-Rocking/Country Club	1972	2.50	5.00	10.00
—As "Lord Sutch"					
Albums					
COTILLION					
SD 9015	Lord Sutch and Heavy Friends	1970	7.50	15.00	30.00
—With Jimmy Page, John Bonham and Jeff Beck					
SD 9049	Hands of Jack the Ripper	1972	7.50	15.00	30.00

SUTHERLAND BROTHERS
Also see SUTHERLAND BROTHERS AND QUIVER.

Number	Title (A Side/B Side)	Yr	VG	VG+	NM
45s					
COLUMBIA					
10758	One More Night with You/When I Say I Love You (The Pie)	1978	—	2.00	4.00
11003	On the Rocks/As Long As I've Got You	1979	—	2.00	4.00
ISLAND					
1203	Long Long Day/The Pie	1972	—	2.50	5.00
1209	Sailing/Hallelujah	1972	—	2.50	5.00
Albums					
COLUMBIA					
JC 35293	Down to Earth	1978	2.50	5.00	10.00
JC 35703	When the Night Comes Down	1979	2.50	5.00	10.00
ISLAND					
SW-9315	The Sutherland Brothers Band	1972	3.00	6.00	12.00

SUTHERLAND BROTHERS AND QUIVER
Also see each artist's individual listings.

Number	Title (A Side/B Side)	Yr	VG	VG+	NM
45s					
COLUMBIA					
10284	Arms of Mary/Love on the Moon	1976	—	2.50	5.00
10362	When the Train Comes/Mad Trail	1976	—	2.50	5.00
10460	Secrets/Something's Burning	1976	—	2.50	5.00
ISLAND					
1217	(I Don't Want to Love You But) You Got Me Anyway/Rock and Roll Show	1973	—	2.00	4.00
1220	Dream Kid/Silver Sister	1974	—	2.00	4.00
Albums					
COLUMBIA					
PC 33982	Reach for the Sky	1976	2.50	5.00	10.00
PC 34376	Slipstream	1977	2.50	5.00	10.00
ISLAND					
SW-9326	Lifeboat	1973	2.50	5.00	10.00
SW-9341	Dream Kid	1974	2.50	5.00	10.00

SUZY AND THE RED STRIPES
Actually Linda McCartney with Wings. Also see PAUL McCARTNEY.

Number	Title (A Side/B Side)	Yr	VG	VG+	NM
12-Inch Singles					
CAPITOL					
V-15244	Seaside Woman/B-Side to Seaside	1986	10.00	20.00	40.00
EPIC					
ASF 361 [DJ]	Seaside Woman (same on both sides)	1977	7.50	15.00	30.00
45s					
CAPITOL					
B-5608	Seaside Woman/B-Side to Seaside	1986	7.50	15.00	30.00
EPIC					
50403	Seaside Woman/B-Side to Seaside	1977	2.50	5.00	10.00
—Linda McCartney and Wings					
50403 [DJ]	Seaside Woman (mono/stereo)	1977	25.00	50.00	100.00
—"Advance Promotion" label, black vinyl					
50403 [DJ]	Seaside Woman (mono/stereo)	1977	6.25	12.50	25.00
—Red vinyl, orange label on one side, white on the other					
50403 [DJ]	Seaside Woman (mono/stereo)	1977	25.00	50.00	100.00
—Black vinyl, orange label on one side, white on the other					

SWALLOWS, THE

Number	Title (A Side/B Side)	Yr	VG	VG+	NM
45s					
AFTER HOURS					
104	My Baby/Good Time Girls	1954	800.00	1600.	2400.
FEDERAL					
12319	Oh Lonesome Me/Angel Baby	1958	10.00	20.00	40.00
12328	We Want to Rock/Rock-a-Bye-Baby Rock	1958	10.00	20.00	40.00
12329	Beside You/Laughing Boy	1958	10.00	20.00	40.00
12333	Itchy Twitchy Feeling/Who Knows, Do You?	1958	10.00	20.00	40.00
KING					
4458	Will You Be Mine/Dearest	1951	500.00	1000.	1500.
4466	Since You've Been Away/Wishing for You	1951	—	—	—
—Unconfirmed on 45 rpm					
4501	Eternally/It Ain't the Meat	1952	200.00	400.00	800.00
—Black vinyl					
4501	Eternally/It Ain't the Meat	1952	625.00	1250.	2500.
—Blue vinyl					
4501	Eternally/It Ain't the Meat	1952	625.00	1250.	2500.
—Green vinyl					
4515	Tell Me Why/Roll, Roll, Pretty Baby	1952	1000.	1500.	2000.
4525	Beside You/You Left Me	1952	100.00	200.00	400.00
4533	You Walked In/I Only Have Eyes for You	1952	200.00	400.00	800.00
4579	Where Do I Go from Here/Please, Baby, Please	1952	200.00	400.00	800.00
4612	Laugh (Though You Want to Cry)/Our Love Is Dying	1953	125.00	250.00	500.00
4632	Nobody's Lovin' Me/Bicycle Tillie	1953	125.00	250.00	500.00
4656	Trust Me/Pleading Blues	1953	100.00	200.00	400.00
4676	I'll Be Waiting/It Feels So Good	1953	100.00	200.00	400.00

SWALLOWS, THE (2)

Number	Title (A Side/B Side)	Yr	VG	VG+	NM
45s					
GUYDEN					
2023	How Long Must a Fool Go On/You Must Try	1959	12.50	25.00	50.00
—Reissued credited to "The Guides"					

SWAMP RATS, THE

Number	Title (A Side/B Side)	Yr	VG	VG+	NM
45s					
CO & CE					
245	In the Midnight Hour/It's Not Easy	1967	5.00	10.00	20.00
ST. CLAIR					
69	Louie Louie/Hey Joe	1966	12.50	25.00	50.00
2222	Psycho/Here, There and Everywhere	1966	50.00	100.00	200.00
3333	Two Tymes Two/(B-side unknown)	1966	12.50	25.00	50.00
711711	It's Not Easy/No Friend of Mine	1966	12.50	25.00	50.00

SWAN, BILLY

Number	Title (A Side/B Side)	Yr	VG	VG+	NM
45s					
A&M					
2046	Hello! Remember Me/Never Go Lookin' Again	1978	—	2.00	4.00
2103	No Way Around It (It's Love)/Forever in Your Love	1978	—	2.00	4.00
COLUMBIA					
10443	Shake, Rattle and Roll/I Got It for You	1976	—	2.00	4.00
10486	Swept Away/California Song (For Malibu)	1977	—	2.00	4.00
EPIC					
02196	I'm Into Lovin' You/Not Far from Forty	1981	—	—	3.00
02601	Stuck Right in the Middle of Your Love/Soft Touch	1981	—	—	3.00
02841	With Their Kind of Money and Our Kind of Love/Lay Down and Love Me Tonight	1982	—	—	3.00
03226	Your Picture Still Loves Me (And I Still Love You)/Give Your Lovin' to Me	1982	—	—	3.00
03505	Rainbows and Butterflies/Only Be You	1982	—	—	3.00
03917	Yes/I Can't Stop Writing Love Songs	1983	—	—	3.00
51000	Do I Have to Draw a Picture/I Want to Change Your Life	1981	—	—	3.00
MERCURY					
884668-7	You Must Be Lookin' for Me/Three Chord Rock & Roll	1986	—	—	3.00
888320-7	I'm Gonna Get You/Three Chord Rock & Roll	1987	—	—	3.00
MGM					
14008	El Paso/The Sweet Sound of Your Name	1968	2.50	5.00	10.00
MONUMENT					
8597	Wedding Bells/P.M.S.	1974	—	2.50	5.00
8621	I Can Help/The Ways of a Woman in Love	1974	—	2.50	5.00
8641	I'm Her Fool/I'd Like to Work for You	1975	—	2.00	4.00
8651	Come By/Woman Handled My Mind	1975	—	2.00	4.00
8661	Everything's the Same (Ain't Nothing Changed)/Overnite Thing (Usually)	1975	—	2.00	4.00
8682	Just Want to Taste Your Wine/Love You Baby to the Bone	1976	—	2.00	4.00
8697	Vanessa/Number 1	1976	—	2.00	4.00
8706	You're the One/Mr. Misery	1976	—	2.00	4.00
45275	Don't Be Cruel/Vanessa	1979	—	2.00	4.00
RISING SONS					
702	Friendship/You Got Me Laughing	1967	2.50	5.00	10.00
Albums					
A&M					
SP-4686	You're OK, I'm OK	1978	2.50	5.00	10.00
COLUMBIA					
PZ 33279	I Can Help	1977	2.00	4.00	8.00
—Reissue of Monument 33279					
PZ 33805	Rock 'n' Roll Moon	1977	2.00	4.00	8.00
—Reissue of Monument 33805					
PZ 34183	Billy Swan	1977	2.00	4.00	8.00
—Reissue of Monument 34183					
PC 34473	Four	1977	2.50	5.00	10.00
EPIC					
FE 37079	I'm Into Lovin' You	1981	2.50	5.00	10.00
MONUMENT					
7629	Billy Swan At His Best	1978	2.50	5.00	10.00
KZ 33279	I Can Help	1974	2.50	5.00	10.00
PZ 33805	Rock 'n' Roll Moon	1975	2.50	5.00	10.00
PZ 34183	Billy Swan	1976	2.50	5.00	10.00

SWANS, THE (1)

Number	Title (A Side/B Side)	Yr	VG	VG+	NM
45s					
BALLAD					
1003/6	It's a Must/Night Train	1954	150.00	300.00	600.00
1007	Happy/The Santa Claus Boogie	1955	150.00	300.00	600.00
FORTUNE					
822	I'll Forever Love You/Mister Cool Breeze	1955	200.00	400.00	800.00
RAINBOW					
233	No More/My True Love	1954	375.00	750.00	1500.
—Red vinyl					
STEAMBOAT					
101	Believe in Me/In the Morning	1956	625.00	1250.	2500.

SWANS, THE (2)

45s

Number	Title (A Side/B Side)	Yr	VG	VG+	NM
CAMEO					
302	The Boy with the Beatle Hair/Please Hurry Home	1964	10.00	20.00	40.00
PARKWAY					
881	Daydreamin' of You/The Promise	1963	7.50	15.00	30.00
SWAN					
4151	He's Mine/You Better Be a Good Girl Now	1963	7.50	15.00	30.00

SWANS, THE (3)

45s

Number	Title (A Side/B Side)	Yr	VG	VG+	NM
ROULETTE					
4213	He Wasn't On the Air Again Today/If I Could Stop Every Clock	1959	6.25	12.50	25.00

SWANSON, BOBBY

45s

Number	Title (A Side/B Side)	Yr	VG	VG+	NM
DONNA					
1326	Tom and Susie/China Doll	1960	6.25	12.50	25.00
1336	Janie's Face/Peggy's Last Birthday	1961	6.25	12.50	25.00
1356	Twisting at the Top/Hello There Lover Doll	1962	6.25	12.50	25.00
IGLOO					
1003	Rockin' Little Eskimo/Ballad of an Angel	1959	100.00	200.00	400.00

SWATLEY, HANK

45s

Number	Title (A Side/B Side)	Yr	VG	VG+	NM
AARON					
101	Oakie Boogie/I Can't Help It	1957	125.00	250.00	500.00

SWEATHOG

45s

Number	Title (A Side/B Side)	Yr	VG	VG+	NM
COLUMBIA					
45416	Things Yet to Come/Hunneth Over	1971	—	2.50	5.00
45492	Hallelujah/Still on the Road	1971	—	2.50	5.00
45575	Things Yet to Come/Rejoice, Rejoice, Rejoice	1972	—	2.50	5.00
45609	Rock and Roll Revival/Ride Louise Ride	1972	—	2.50	5.00

Albums

Number	Title (A Side/B Side)	Yr	VG	VG+	NM
COLUMBIA					
C 30601	Sweathog	1971	3.00	6.00	12.00
KC 31144	Hallelujah	1972	3.00	6.00	12.00

SWEET, THE (1)

British pop-rock band.

45s

Number	Title (A Side/B Side)	Yr	VG	VG+	NM
20TH CENTURY					
2033	It's Lonely Out There/I'm On My Way	1973	2.50	5.00	10.00
—U.S. issue of 1968 material that was on Fontana in the U.K.					
BELL					
45106	Funny, Funny/You're Not Wrong for Loving Me	1971	2.00	4.00	8.00
45126	Co-Co/You're Not Wrong for Loving Me	1971	—	3.00	6.00
45184	Poppa Joe/Jeanie	1972	—	3.00	6.00
45251	Little Willy/Man from Mecca	1972	—	3.00	6.00
45361	Blockbuster/Need a Lot of Lovin'	1973	—	2.50	5.00
45408	Wig-Wam Bam/New York Connection	1973	—	2.50	5.00
CAPITOL					
4055	Ballroom Blitz/Restless	1975	—	2.50	5.00
4157	Fox on the Run/Burn On the Flame	1975	—	2.50	5.00
4220	Action/Medussa	1976	—	2.50	5.00
4429	Fever of Love/Heartbreak Today	1977	—	2.50	5.00
4454	Funk It Up (David's Song)/Stairway to the Stars	1977	—	2.50	5.00
4549	Love Is Like Oxygen/Cover Girl	1978	—	2.50	5.00
4610	California Nights/Dream On	1978	—	2.50	5.00
4730	Mother Earth/Why Don't You	1979	—	2.00	4.00
4908	Sixties Man/Water's Edge	1980	—	2.00	4.00
PARAMOUNT					
0044	All You'll Ever Get from Me/The Juicer	1970	5.00	10.00	20.00

Albums

Number	Title (A Side/B Side)	Yr	VG	VG+	NM
BELL					
1125	The Sweet	1973	6.25	12.50	25.00
CAPITOL					
SPRO-8371/2 [DJ]	For A.O.R. Radio Only	1976	6.25	12.50	25.00
SPRO-8849 [DJ]	Short and Sweet	1978	7.50	15.00	30.00
ST-11395	Desolation Boulevard	1975	3.00	6.00	12.00
ST-11496	Give Us a Wink	1976	3.00	6.00	12.00
STAO-11636	Off the Record	1977	3.00	6.00	12.00
SKAO-11744	Level Headed	1978	3.00	6.00	12.00
PRO-11929 [DJ]	Cut Above the Rest	1979	12.50	25.00	50.00
—Special promo box contains record, cassette, 8-track, photo, bio					
ST-11929	Cut Above the Rest	1979	3.00	6.00	12.00
ST-12106	Sweet VI	1980	3.00	6.00	12.00
SN-16115	Give Us a Wink	1980	2.00	4.00	8.00
—Budget-line reissue					
SN-16116	Off the Record	1980	2.00	4.00	8.00
—Budget-line reissue					
SN-16117	Level Headed	1980	2.00	4.00	8.00
—Budget-line reissue					
SN-16118	Cut Above the Rest	1980	2.00	4.00	8.00
—Budget-line reissue					
SN-16287	Desolation Boulevard	1981	2.00	4.00	8.00
—Budget-line reissue					
KORY					
3009	The Sweet	1977	2.50	5.00	10.00
—Reissue of Bell LP					

SWEET, THE (2)

45s

Number	Title (A Side/B Side)	Yr	VG	VG+	NM
SMASH					
2116	Got to Have More Love/You Can't Win at Love	1967	3.75	7.50	15.00
2136	Broken Heart Attack/Don't Do It	1967	3.75	7.50	15.00

SWEET INSPIRATIONS, THE

Also see CISSY HOUSTON.

12-Inch Singles

Number	Title (A Side/B Side)	Yr	VG	VG+	NM
CARIBOU					
ASD 333 [DJ]	Black Sunday Parts 1 and 2 (same on both sides)	1977	3.75	7.50	15.00
RSO					
304 [DJ]	Love Is On the Way (6:10)/(Instrumental)	1979	3.00	6.00	12.00

45s

Number	Title (A Side/B Side)	Yr	VG	VG+	NM
ATLANTIC					
2410	Why (Am I Treated So Bad)/I Don't Want to Go On Without You	1967	2.00	4.00	8.00
2418	Let It Be Me/When Something Is Wrong with My Baby	1967	2.00	4.00	8.00
2436	I've Been Loving You Too Long (To Stop Now)/That's How Strong My Love Is	1967	2.00	4.00	8.00
2449	O' What a Fool I've Been/Don't Fight It	1967	2.00	4.00	8.00
2465	Reach Out for Me/Do Right Woman — Do Right Man	1967	2.00	4.00	8.00
2476	Sweet Inspiration/I'm Blue	1968	2.00	4.00	8.00
2529	To Love Somebody/Where Did It Go	1968	2.00	4.00	8.00
2551	Unchained Melody/Am I Ever Gonna See My Baby Again	1968	2.00	4.00	8.00
2571	What the World Needs Now Is Love/You Really Didn't Mean It	1968	2.00	4.00	8.00
2620	Crying in the Rain/Everyday WIll Be Like a Holiday	1969	2.00	4.00	8.00
2638	Sweets for My Sweet/Get a Little Order	1969	2.00	4.00	8.00
2653	Don't Go/Chained	1969	2.00	4.00	8.00
2686	(Gotta Find) A Brand New Lover — Part I/(Gotta Find) A Brand New Lover — Part II	1969	2.00	4.00	8.00
2720	At Last I Found a Love/That's the Way My Baby Is	1970	—	3.00	6.00
2732	Them Boys/Flash in the Pan	1970	—	3.00	6.00
2750	This World/A Light Sings	1970	—	3.00	6.00
2779	Evidence/Change Me Not	1970	—	3.00	6.00
CARIBOU					
9022	Black Sunday/(Instrumental)	1977	—	2.00	4.00
RSO					
932	Love Is On the Way/(Instrumental)	1979	—	2.50	5.00
1013	Love Is On the Way/(Instrumental)	1979	—	2.00	4.00
STAX					
0178	Emercury/Slipped and Tripped	1973	—	2.50	5.00
0203	Try a Little Tenderness/Dirty Tricks	1974	—	2.50	5.00

Albums

Number	Title (A Side/B Side)	Yr	VG	VG+	NM
ATLANTIC					
SD 8155	The Sweet Inspirations	1968	5.00	10.00	20.00
SD 8182	Songs of Faith and Inspiration	1968	5.00	10.00	20.00
SD 8201	What the World Needs Now Is Love	1969	5.00	10.00	20.00
SD 8225	Sweets for My Sweet	1969	5.00	10.00	20.00
SD 8253	Sweet, Sweet Soul	1970	5.00	10.00	20.00
RSO					
RS-1-3058	Hot Butterfly	1979	2.50	5.00	10.00
STAX					
STS-3017	Estelle, Myrna and Sylvia	1973	5.00	10.00	20.00

SWEET MARQUEES, THE

45s

Number	Title (A Side/B Side)	Yr	VG	VG+	NM
APACHE					
1516	You Lied/I Love My Baby	1961	75.00	150.00	300.00

SWEET PANTS

Albums

Number	Title (A Side/B Side)	Yr	VG	VG+	NM
BARKLEY					
1141	Fat Peter Presents Sweet Pants	1969	50.00	100.00	200.00

SWEET SENSATION

45s

Number	Title (A Side/B Side)	Yr	VG	VG+	NM
PYE					
71002	Sad Sweet Dreamer/Surething, Yes I Do	1974	—	2.00	4.00
71026	Ride Away from the Sun/(B-side unknown)	1975	—	2.00	4.00
71049	Mr. Cool/(B-side unknown)	1975	—	2.00	4.00

Albums

Number	Title (A Side/B Side)	Yr	VG	VG+	NM
PYE					
12110	Sweet Sensation	1975	2.50	5.00	10.00

SWEET SICK TEENS, THE

45s

Number	Title (A Side/B Side)	Yr	VG	VG+	NM
RCA VICTOR					
37-7940	The Pretzel/Agnes, the Teenage Russian Spy	1961	20.00	40.00	80.00
—"Compact Single 33" (small hole, plays at LP speed)					
47-7940	The Pretzel/Agnes, the Teenage Russian Spy	1961	10.00	20.00	40.00

SWEET TEENS, THE

45s

Number	Title (A Side/B Side)	Yr	VG	VG+	NM
FLIP					
311	Forever More/Don't Worry About a Thing	1955	15.00	30.00	60.00
GEE					
1030	My Valentine/With This Ring	1957	15.00	30.00	60.00

SWEET TOOTHE

Albums

Number	Title (A Side/B Side)	Yr	VG	VG+	NM
DOMINION					
NR-7360	Testing	1974	75.00	150.00	300.00

SWEETIES, THE

45s

Number	Title (A Side/B Side)	Yr	VG	VG+	NM
END					
1110	After You/Paul's Love	1962	5.00	10.00	20.00

Number	Title (A Side/B Side)	Yr	VG	VG+	NM

SWEETWATER

45s

REPRISE

Number	Title (A Side/B Side)	Yr	VG	VG+	NM
0787	My Crystal Spiker/What's Wrong	1968	2.00	4.00	8.00
0816	Motherless Child/Why Oh Why	1969	2.00	4.00	8.00
0835	For Pete's Sake/Bondeau	1969	2.00	4.00	8.00
0987	Just for You/Look Out	1971	—	3.00	6.00
1002	Day Song/Without Me	1971	—	3.00	6.00
1076	Join the Band (Part 1)/Join the Band (Part 2)	1972	—	3.00	6.00

Albums

REPRISE

Number	Title (A Side/B Side)	Yr	VG	VG+	NM
RS 6313	Sweetwater	1968	3.75	7.50	15.00
RS 6417	Just for You	1970	3.75	7.50	15.00
RS 6473	Melon	1971	3.75	7.50	15.00

SWENSONS, THE

45s

X-TRA

Number	Title (A Side/B Side)	Yr	VG	VG+	NM
100	Remember Me to My Darling/Golly Boo	1957	50.00	100.00	200.00

SWIFT, BASIL, AND THE SEEGRAMS

Also see DANNY HUTTON.

45s

MERCURY

Number	Title (A Side/B Side)	Yr	VG	VG+	NM
72386	Farmer's Daughter/Shambles	1965	50.00	100.00	200.00

SWIFT RAIN

Albums

HI

Number	Title (A Side/B Side)	Yr	VG	VG+	NM
SHL-32064	Coming Down	1971	6.25	12.50	25.00

SWINGIN' MEDALLIONS

45s

1-2-3

Number	Title (A Side/B Side)	Yr	VG	VG+	NM
1723	We're Gonna Hate Ourselves in the Morning/It's Alright	1970	2.00	4.00	8.00
1732	Rollin' Rovin' River/Don't Let Your Feet Touch the Ground	1971	2.00	4.00	8.00

4 SALE

Number	Title (A Side/B Side)	Yr	VG	VG+	NM
002	Double Shot (Of My Baby's Love)/Here It Comes Again	1966	25.00	50.00	100.00

CAPITOL

Number	Title (A Side/B Side)	Yr	VG	VG+	NM
2338	Sun, Sand and Sea/Hey, Hey Baby	1968	2.00	4.00	8.00

DOT

Number	Title (A Side/B Side)	Yr	VG	VG+	NM
16721	Bye Bye, Silly Girl/I Want to Be Your Guy	1965	3.00	6.00	12.00

SMASH

Number	Title (A Side/B Side)	Yr	VG	VG+	NM
2033	Double Shot (Of My Baby's Love)/Here It Comes Again	1966	3.75	7.50	15.00
2050	She Drives Me Out of My Mind/You Gotta Have Faith	1966	3.00	6.00	12.00
2075	I Don't Want to Lose It for You Baby/Night Owl	1966	3.00	6.00	12.00
2084	Don't Cry No More/I Found a Rainbow	1967	2.50	5.00	10.00
2107	Turn On the Music/Summer's Not the Same This Year	1967	2.50	5.00	10.00
2129	Bow and Arrow/Where Can I Go to Get Soul	1967	2.50	5.00	10.00

Albums

SMASH

Number	Title (A Side/B Side)	Yr	VG	VG+	NM
MGS-27083 [M]	Double Shot (Of My Baby's Love)	1966	10.00	20.00	40.00
—First pressing contains the original 45 version of the title song					
MGS-27083 [M]	Double Shot (Of My Baby's Love)	1966	7.50	15.00	30.00
—Later pressings contain a "censored" version of the title song					
SRS-67083 [S]	Double Shot (Of My Baby's Love)	1966	12.50	25.00	50.00
—First pressing contains the original 45 version of the title song					
SRS-67083 [S]	Double Shot (Of My Baby's Love)	1966	10.00	20.00	40.00
—Later pressings contain a "censored" version of the title song					

SWINGING BLUE JEANS, THE

Also see TERRY SYLVESTER.

45s

IMPERIAL

Number	Title (A Side/B Side)	Yr	VG	VG+	NM
66021	Hippy Hippy Shake/Now I Must Go	1964	3.75	7.50	15.00
66030	Good Golly Miss Molly/Shaking Feeling	1964	3.00	6.00	12.00
66049	Shake, Rattle and Roll/You're No Good	1964	3.00	6.00	12.00
66059	Tutti Frutti/Promise You'll Tell Her	1964	3.00	6.00	12.00
66090	It Isn't There/One of These Days	1965	3.00	6.00	12.00
66154	Don't Make Me Over/What Can I Do Today	1966	3.00	6.00	12.00
66225	Now the Summer's Gone/Rumors, Gossip, Words Untrue	1967	2.50	5.00	10.00
66255	Something's Coming Along/Tremblin'	1967	2.50	5.00	10.00

Albums

IMPERIAL

Number	Title (A Side/B Side)	Yr	VG	VG+	NM
LP-9261 [M]	Hippy Hippy Shake	1964	20.00	40.00	80.00
LP-12261 [R]	Hippy Hippy Shake	1964	20.00	40.00	80.00

SWINGING TIGERS

45s

TAMLA

Number	Title (A Side/B Side)	Yr	VG	VG+	NM
54024	Snake Walk (Part 1)/Snake Walk (Part 2)	1960	75.00	150.00	300.00

SWINGLE SINGERS, THE

45s

PHILIPS

Number	Title (A Side/B Side)	Yr	VG	VG+	NM
40157	Fugue in D Minor/Prelude in F Minor	1963	—	3.00	6.00

Albums

COLUMBIA

Number	Title (A Side/B Side)	Yr	VG	VG+	NM
PC 34194	Rags and All That Jazz	1976	2.50	5.00	10.00

COLUMBIA MASTERWORKS

Number	Title (A Side/B Side)	Yr	VG	VG+	NM
M 33013	Love Songs for Madrigals and Madriguys	1976	2.50	5.00	10.00

MMG

Number	Title (A Side/B Side)	Yr	VG	VG+	NM
1115	Swingle Skyliner	198?	2.00	4.00	8.00
1125	Folio	198?	2.00	4.00	8.00

PHILIPS

Number	Title (A Side/B Side)	Yr	VG	VG+	NM
PHS 2-5400 [(2)]	Bachanalia	1972	3.00	6.00	12.00
—Reissue of 600-197 and 600-126 in same package					
PHM 200097 [M]	Bach's Greatest Hits	1963	2.50	5.00	10.00
PHM 200126 [M]	Going Baroque	1964	2.50	5.00	10.00
PHM 200149 [M]	Anyone for Mozart?	1965	2.50	5.00	10.00
PHM 200191 [M]	Getting Romantic	1965	2.50	5.00	10.00
PHM 200214 [M]	Rococo A-Go-Go	1966	2.50	5.00	10.00
PHM 200225 [M]	Encounter	1966	3.00	6.00	12.00
—With the Modern Jazz Quartet					
PHM 200261 [M]	Spanish Masters	1967	2.50	5.00	10.00
PHS 600097 [S]	Bach's Greatest Hits	1963	3.00	6.00	12.00
PHS 600126 [S]	Going Baroque	1964	3.00	6.00	12.00
PHS 600149 [S]	Anyone for Mozart?	1965	3.00	6.00	12.00
PHS 600191 [S]	Getting Romantic	1965	3.00	6.00	12.00
PHS 600214 [S]	Rococo A-Go-Go	1966	3.00	6.00	12.00
PHS 600225 [S]	Encounter	1966	3.75	7.50	15.00
—With the Modern Jazz Quartet					
PHS 600261 [S]	Spanish Masters	1967	3.00	6.00	12.00
PHS 600288	Back to Bach	1968	2.50	5.00	10.00
PHS 700004	The Joy of Singing	1973	2.50	5.00	10.00
824544-1	Jazz Sebastian Bach	1985	2.00	4.00	8.00
824545-1	Place Vendome	1985	2.00	4.00	8.00
—With the Modern Jazz Quartet; reissue of 600-225					

SWISHER, DEBRA

45s

BOOM

Number	Title (A Side/B Side)	Yr	VG	VG+	NM
60001	You're So Good to Me/Thank You and Goodnight	1966	3.00	6.00	12.00

SYCAMORES, THE

45s

GROOVE

Number	Title (A Side/B Side)	Yr	VG	VG+	NM
0121	I'll Be Waiting/Darling, Is It True	1955	50.00	100.00	200.00

SYDELLS, THE

45s

BELTONE

Number	Title (A Side/B Side)	Yr	VG	VG+	NM
2032	In the Night/The Hokey Pokey	1963	3.75	7.50	15.00

SYLVERS, FOSTER

Also see THE SYLVERS.

45s

CAPITOL

Number	Title (A Side/B Side)	Yr	VG	VG+	NM
4553	Don't Let Me Go for Someone Else/Super Scoop	1978	—	2.00	4.00

MGM

Number	Title (A Side/B Side)	Yr	VG	VG+	NM
14580	Misdemeanor/So Close	1973	—	2.50	5.00
14630	Hey Little Girl/I'll Get You in the End	1973	—	2.50	5.00

PRIDE

Number	Title (A Side/B Side)	Yr	VG	VG+	NM
1031	Misdemeanor/So Close	1973	2.50	5.00	10.00

Albums

PRIDE

Number	Title (A Side/B Side)	Yr	VG	VG+	NM
0027	Foster Sylvers	1973	3.00	6.00	12.00

SYLVERS, THE

Also see FOSTER SYLVERS.

12-Inch Singles

GEFFEN

Number	Title (A Side/B Side)	Yr	VG	VG+	NM
20258	In One Love and Out the Other (Extended)/(Instrumental)	1984	—	3.00	6.00

45s

CAPITOL

Number	Title (A Side/B Side)	Yr	VG	VG+	NM
4179	Boogie Fever/Free Style	1975	—	2.00	4.00
4255	Cotton Candy/I Can Be for Real	1976	—	2.00	4.00
4336	Hot Line/That's What Love Is Made Of	1976	—	2.00	4.00
4405	High School Dance/Lovin' You Is Like Lovin' the Wind	1977	—	2.00	4.00
4493	Any Way You Want Me/Lovin' Me Back	1977	—	2.00	4.00
4532	New Horizon/Charisma	1978	—	2.00	4.00

CASABLANCA

Number	Title (A Side/B Side)	Yr	VG	VG+	NM
938	Don't Stop, Get Off/Love Won't Let Me Go	1978	—	2.00	4.00
953	Forever Yours/Diamonds Are Rare	1978	—	2.00	4.00
992	I Feel So Good Tonight/Hoochie Coochie Dancin'	1979	—	2.00	4.00
2207	I Feels So Good Tonight/Mahogany	1979	—	2.00	4.00

GEFFEN

Number	Title (A Side/B Side)	Yr	VG	VG+	NM
29061	Falling for Your Love/(Instrumental)	1985	—	—	3.00
29293	In One Love and Out the Other/Falling for Your Love	1984	—	—	3.00
29293 [PS]	In One Love and Out the Other/Falling for Your Love	1984	—	—	3.00

MGM

Number	Title (A Side/B Side)	Yr	VG	VG+	NM
14352	You Got What It Takes/Time to Ride	1972	—	3.00	6.00
14579	Stay Away from Me/I'll Never Be Ashamed	1973	—	3.00	6.00
14678	Through the Love in My Heart/Cry of a Dreamer	1973	—	2.00	4.00
14698	Hang On Sloopy/Na Na Hey Hey Kiss Him Goodbye	1974	—	2.00	4.00
—As "Foster, Pat & Angie Sylivers"					
14721	I Aim to Please/Wish You Were Here	1974	—	2.00	4.00

PRIDE

Number	Title (A Side/B Side)	Yr	VG	VG+	NM
1001	Fool's Paradise/I'm Truly Happy	1972	—	2.50	5.00
1019	Wish That I Could Talk to You/How Love Hurts	1972	—	2.50	5.00
1029	Stay Away from Me/I'll Never Be Ashamed	1973	—	2.50	5.00
1029 [PS]	Stay Away from Me/I'll Never Be Ashamed	1973	—	3.00	6.00

SOLAR

Number	Title (A Side/B Side)	Yr	VG	VG+	NM
47949	Come Back, Lover, Come Back/There's a Place	1981	—	2.00	4.00
48002	Take It to the Top/I'm Getting Over	1982	—	2.00	4.00

VERVE

Number	Title (A Side/B Side)	Yr	VG	VG+	NM
10664	Come On Give Me a Chance/I'm Just a Lonely Soul	1071	2.50	5.00	10.00

Number	Title (A Side/B Side)	Yr	VG	VG+	NM
Albums					
CAPITOL					
ST-11465	Showcase	1976	2.50	5.00	10.00
ST-11580	Something Special	1976	2.50	5.00	10.00
ST-11705	New Horizons	1977	2.50	5.00	10.00
ST-11868	Best of the Sylvers	1978	2.50	5.00	10.00
CASABLANCA					
NBLP 7103	Forever Yours	1978	2.50	5.00	10.00
NBLP 7151	Disco Fever	1979	2.50	5.00	10.00
GEFFEN					
GHS 24039	Bizarre	1984	2.50	5.00	10.00
MGM					
SE-4930	The Sylvers III	1974	2.50	5.00	10.00
PRIDE					
0007	The Sylvers	1972	3.00	6.00	12.00
0026	The Sylvers II	1973	3.00	6.00	12.00
SOLAR					
22	Concept	1981	2.50	5.00	10.00

SYLVESTER, TERRY

Also see THE HOLLIES; THE SWINGING BLUE JEANS.

Number	Title (A Side/B Side)	Yr	VG	VG+	NM
45s					
EPIC					
20002	It's Better Off This Way/For the Peace of All Mankind	1974	—	2.00	4.00
20002 [PS]	It's Better Off This Way/For the Peace of All Mankind	1974	—	2.50	5.00
50017	It's Better Off This Way/For the Peace of All Mankind	1974	—	2.00	4.00
50532	Silver and Gold/Realistic Situation	1978	—	2.00	4.00
Albums					
EPIC					
KE 33076	Terry Sylvester	1974	3.00	6.00	12.00

SYLVESTER, TONY, AND THE NEW INGREDIENT

See THE MAIN INGREDIENT.

SYLVIA, MARGO

See TUNE WEAVERS.

SYLVIA (1)

R&B singer and record company mogul (All Platinum/Stang/Vibration, Sugar Hill). Also see MICKEY AND SYLVIA.

Number	Title (A Side/B Side)	Yr	VG	VG+	NM
45s					
ALL PLATINUM					
2303	I Can't Help It/It's a Good Life	1969	2.00	4.00	8.00
2350	Sho Nuff Boogie (Part 1)/Sho Nuff Boogie (Part 2)	1974	—	2.50	5.00
—With the Moments					
JUBILEE					
5093	Drive, Daddy, Drive/I Found Somebody to Love	1952	12.50	25.00	50.00
—As "Little Sylvia"					
STANG					
5015	Have You Had Any Lately/Anytime	1970	—	3.00	6.00
SUGAR HILL					
781	It's Good to Be the Queen/(B-side unknown)	1982	—	2.00	4.00
VIBRATION					
512	Next Time I See You/Gimme a Little Action	1972	—	3.00	6.00
521	Pillow Talk/My Thing	1973	—	3.00	6.00
524	Didn't I/Had Any Lately	1973	—	2.50	5.00
525	Soul Je T'Aime/Sunday	1973	—	2.50	5.00
—With Ralfi Pagan					
527	Alfredo/Lay It On Me	1973	—	2.50	5.00
528	Private Performance/If You Get the Notion	1974	—	2.50	5.00
529	Sweet Stuff/Had Any Lately	1974	—	2.50	5.00
530	Easy Evil/Give It Up in Vain	1974	—	2.50	5.00
536	Pussy Cat (Part 1)/Pussy Cat (Part 2)	1975	—	2.50	5.00
567	L.A. Sunshine/Taxi	1976	—	2.50	5.00
570	Lay It On Me (Vocal)/(Instrumental)	1977	—	2.50	5.00
572	Lollipop Man/Lay It On Me	1977	—	2.50	5.00
576	Automatic Lover/Stop Boy	1978	—	2.50	5.00
Albums					
STANG					
1010	Sylvia	197?	5.00	10.00	20.00
SUGAR HILL					
258	Sylvia I	1981	2.50	5.00	10.00
VIBRATION					
126	Pillow Talk	1973	3.75	7.50	15.00
131	Lay It On Me	1977	3.00	6.00	12.00
143	Brand New Funk	197?	3.00	6.00	12.00

SYMBOLS, THE (1)

Number	Title (A Side/B Side)	Yr	VG	VG+	NM
45s					
DORE					
666	Last Year About This Time/Better Get Your Own One Buddy	1963	3.75	7.50	15.00

SYMBOLS, THE (2)

Number	Title (A Side/B Side)	Yr	VG	VG+	NM
45s					
IMPERIAL					
66382	I Will Still Be There/The Wrong Girl	1969	2.00	4.00	8.00

SYMBOLS, THE (3)

Number	Title (A Side/B Side)	Yr	VG	VG+	NM
45s					
MGM					
13348	One Fine Girl/Don't Go	1965	2.50	5.00	10.00
13463	Don't Go/Oo Wee Baby	1966	2.50	5.00	10.00

SYMBOLS, THE (4)

Number	Title (A Side/B Side)	Yr	VG	VG+	NM
45s					
VINTAGE					
1007	Bye Bye/I Love You	1973	—	2.50	5.00

SYMBOLS, THE (U)

Number	Title (A Side/B Side)	Yr	VG	VG+	NM
45s					
LAURIE					
3401	Bye Bye Baby/The Things You Do to Me	1967	2.50	5.00	10.00
3435	The Best Part of Breaking Up/Again	1968	2.50	5.00	10.00
PRESIDENT					
102	Canadian Sunset/The Gentle Art of Loving	1966	2.50	5.00	10.00

SYMPHONICS, THE (1)

Number	Title (A Side/B Side)	Yr	VG	VG+	NM
45s					
ABC					
11068	Boy (Please Help Me)/It's Gonna Be Real Hard	1968	2.00	4.00	8.00
BRUNSWICK					
55303	Don't Fail Me Now/Silent Kind of Guy	1966	2.50	5.00	10.00
55313	No More/(She's Just a) Sad Girl	1967	2.50	5.00	10.00

SYMPHONICS, THE (2)

This Symphonics features FREDDIE SCOTT.

Number	Title (A Side/B Side)	Yr	VG	VG+	NM
45s					
ENRICA					
1002	Come On Honey/A Blessing to You	1959	5.00	10.00	20.00

SYNDICATE, THE

Number	Title (A Side/B Side)	Yr	VG	VG+	NM
45s					
DORE					
743	My Baby Is Barefoot/Love Will Take Away	1965	10.00	20.00	40.00
DOT					
16807	Egyptian Thing/She Haunts You	1965	10.00	20.00	40.00

SYNDICATE OF SOUND

Number	Title (A Side/B Side)	Yr	VG	VG+	NM
45s					
BELL					
640	Little Girl/You	1966	5.00	10.00	20.00
646	Rumors/Upper Hand	1966	3.75	7.50	15.00
655	Goodtime Music/Keep It Up	1966	3.75	7.50	15.00
666	Mary/That Kind of Man	1967	3.75	7.50	15.00
BUDDAH					
156	Brown Paper Bag/Reverb Beat	1970	2.50	5.00	10.00
183	Mexico/First to Love You	1970	2.50	5.00	10.00
CAPITOL					
2426	You're Looking Fine/Change the World	1969	2.50	5.00	10.00
DEL-FI					
4304	Prepare for Love/Tell the World	1965	5.00	10.00	20.00
HUSH					
228	Little Girl/You	1966	12.50	25.00	50.00
PHILCO-FORD					
HP-29	Little Girl/Rumors	1968	5.00	10.00	20.00
—4-inch plastic "Hip Pocket Record" with color sleeve					
SCARLET					
503	Prepare for Love/Tell the World	1965	7.50	15.00	30.00
Albums					
BELL					
6001 [M]	Little Girl	1966	12.50	25.00	50.00
S-6001 [S]	Little Girl	1966	20.00	40.00	80.00

SYNERGY

Number	Title (A Side/B Side)	Yr	VG	VG+	NM
12-Inch Singles					
AUDION					
12204 [DJ]	Redstone/Metropolitan Theme	1987	3.00	6.00	12.00
PASSPORT					
SP-30 [DJ]	Phobos and Deimos Go to Mars (Edit) (LP)	1978	3.75	7.50	15.00
45s					
PASSPORT					
7907	Classical Gas/Cybersports	1976	2.00	4.00	8.00
Albums					
AUDION					
SYN 204	Metropolitan Suite	1987	2.50	5.00	10.00
PASSPORT					
PG-1	Computer Experiments Volume One	1981	3.75	7.50	15.00
PB 6000	Cords	1978	3.75	7.50	15.00
—First pressing on clear vinyl					
PB 6000	Cords	1978	2.50	5.00	10.00
—Later pressings on black vinyl					
PB 6001	Electronic Realizations for Rock Orchestra	1979	2.50	5.00	10.00
—Reissue of 98009					
PB 6002	Sequencer	1979	2.50	5.00	10.00
—Reissue of 98014					
PB 6003	Games	1979	2.50	5.00	10.00
PB 6005	Audion	1981	2.50	5.00	10.00
P2B 11002 [(2)]	Semi-Conductor	1984	3.00	6.00	12.00
PPSD-98009	Electronic Realizations for Rock Orchestra	1975	3.00	6.00	12.00
PPSD-98014	Sequencer	1976	3.00	6.00	12.00

SYREETA

Also see BILLY PRESTON AND SYREETA.

Number	Title (A Side/B Side)	Yr	VG	VG+	NM
12-Inch Singles					
MOTOWN					
PR 90 [DJ]	Quick Slick/Out of the Box	1981	2.50	5.00	10.00
45s					
MOTOWN					
1297	Come and Get This Stuff/Black Maybe	1974	—	2.50	5.00
1317	I'm Goin' Left/Heavy day	1974	—	2.50	5.00
1328	Your Kiss Is Sweeter/Spinnin' and Spinnin'	1975	—	2.50	5.00
1353	Harmour Love/Cause We've Ended As Lovers	1975	—	2.50	5.00

Number	Title (A Side/B Side)	Yr	VG	VG+	NM
1353 [DJ]	Harmour Love (same on both sides?)	1975	2.50	5.00	10.00
—Promo only on red vinyl					
MOWEST					
5016	I Love Every Little Thing About You/Black Maybe	1972	—	3.00	6.00
5021	Happiness/To Know You Is to Love You	1972	—	3.00	6.00
TAMLA					
1610	I Must Be in Love/Wish Upon a Star	1982	—	2.00	4.00
1675	Forever Is Not Enough/She's Leaving Home	1983	—	2.00	4.00
54333	Quick Slick/I Don't Know	1981	—	2.00	4.00
Albums					
MOTOWN					
M6-808	Stevie Wonder Presents Syreeta	1974	2.50	5.00	10.00
M6-891	Rich Love, Poor Love	1977	2.50	5.00	10.00
—With G.C. Cameron					
MOWEST					
113	Syreeta	1972	3.00	6.00	12.00
TAMLA					
T6-349	One	1977	2.50	5.00	10.00
T7-372	Syreeta	1980	2.50	5.00	10.00
T8-376	Set My Love in Motion	1981	2.50	5.00	10.00
6039 TF	The Spell	1983	2.50	5.00	10.00

SZABO, GABOR

Number	Title (A Side/B Side)	Yr	VG	VG+	NM
45s					
BLUE THUMB					
200	Breezin'/Azure Blue	1971	—	2.50	5.00
—With Bobby Womack					
7118	Close to You/Love Theme from "Spartacus"	1971	—	2.50	5.00
BUDDAH					
215	That's What Happens/Rocky Raccoon	1971	—	3.00	6.00
—With Lena Horne					
CTI					
14	It's Going to Take Some Time/(B-side unknown)	1973	—	2.50	5.00
IMPULSE!					
244	Yesterday/Walk On By	1966	2.00	4.00	8.00
248	Gypsy Queen/Bang Bang	1966	2.00	4.00	8.00
254	Spellbinder/Witchcraft	1966	2.00	4.00	8.00
257	Paint It Black/Sophisticated Wheels	1967	2.00	4.00	8.00
263	The Beat Goes On/Space	1967	2.00	4.00	8.00
268	Twelve Thirty (Young Girls Are Coming to the Canyon)/Saigon Bride	1968	2.00	4.00	8.00
MERCURY					
73840	Keep Smilin'/Baby Rattle Shake	1976	—	2.00	4.00
73957	Alicia/The Biz	1977	—	2.00	4.00
SKYE					
451	Theme from "Valley of the Dolls"/Sunshine Superman	1968	—	3.00	6.00
454	Bacchanal/The Look of Love	1968	—	3.00	6.00
459	Fire Dance/Ferris Wheel	1969	—	3.00	6.00
4515	Dear Prudence/Stormy	1969	—	3.00	6.00
Albums					
ABC IMPULSE!					
AS-9105	Gypsy 66	1968	3.00	6.00	12.00
AS-9123	Spellbinder	1968	3.00	6.00	12.00
AS-9128	Jazz Raga	1968	3.00	6.00	12.00
AS-9146	The Sorcerer	1968	3.00	6.00	12.00
AS-9151	Wind, Sky and Diamonds	1968	3.75	7.50	15.00
AS-9159	Light My Fire	1968	3.75	7.50	15.00
AS-9167	More Sorcery	1968	3.75	7.50	15.00
AS-9173	The Best of Gabor Szabo	1968	3.75	7.50	15.00
AS-9204 [(2)]	His Great Hits	1971	3.75	7.50	15.00
BLUE THUMB					
BTS-28	High Contrast	1972	3.00	6.00	12.00
—With Bobby Womack					
6014	Live	1974	3.00	6.00	12.00
BTS-8823	Magical Connection	1971	3.00	6.00	12.00
BUDDAH					
18-SK	Watch What Happens	1970	3.00	6.00	12.00
20-SK	Blowin' Some Old Smoke	1971	3.00	6.00	12.00
CTI					
6026	Mizrab	1973	3.00	6.00	12.00
6035	Rambler	1974	3.00	6.00	12.00
GRP/IMPULSE!					
IMP-211	The Sorcerer	199?	3.75	7.50	15.00
—Reissue on audiophile vinyl					
IMPULSE!					
A-9105 [M]	Gypsy 66	1966	5.00	10.00	20.00
AS-9105 [S]	Gypsy 66	1966	6.25	12.50	25.00
A-9123 [M]	Spellbinder	1966	5.00	10.00	20.00
AS-9123 [S]	Spellbinder	1966	6.25	12.50	25.00
A-9128 [M]	Jazz Raga	1967	6.25	12.50	25.00
AS-9128 [S]	Jazz Raga	1967	5.00	10.00	20.00
A-9146 [M]	The Sorcerer	1967	6.25	12.50	25.00
AS-9146 [S]	The Sorcerer	1967	5.00	10.00	20.00
AS-9151	Wind, Sky and Diamonds	1968	6.25	12.50	25.00
—This exists on the pre-ABC Impulse! label, though theoretically it shouldn't. Other titles may exist on that label also.					
MCA					
4155 [(2)]	His Great Hits	198?	3.00	6.00	12.00
MERCURY					
SRM-1-1091	Nightflight	1976	2.50	5.00	10.00
SRM-1-1141	Faces	1976	2.50	5.00	10.00
PEPITA					
707	Femme Fatalo	198?	2.50	5.00	10.00
SALVATION					
704	Macho	1975	3.00	6.00	12.00
SKYE					
SK-3	Bacchanal	1968	3.75	7.50	15.00
SK-7	Dreams	1969	3.75	7.50	15.00
SK-9	Gabor Szabo 1969	1969	3.75	7.50	15.00
SK-15	Lena & Gabor	1970	3.75	7.50	15.00
—With Lena Horne					

SZIGETI, SANDY

Number	Title (A Side/B Side)	Yr	VG	VG+	NM
45s					
DECCA					
32862	America's Sweetheart/My Steady Diet	1971	2.50	5.00	10.00
—Produced by Rick Nelson					

T

T-BIRDS, THE

45s

Number	Title (A Side/B Side)	Yr	VG	VG+	NM
CHESS					
1778	Green Stamps/Come On Dance with Me	1961	6.25	12.50	25.00
1792	Hog Wild/Taco Harry	1961	6.25	12.50	25.00
GONE					
5141	Wild Stomp/Soft Smoke	1962	5.00	10.00	20.00
T-BIRD					
101	Green Stamps/Come On Dance with Me	1961	10.00	20.00	40.00
VEGAS					
720	Nobody But You/Have You Ever Been in Love Before	1968	15.00	30.00	60.00

T-BONES, THE

Members of this group later formed HAMILTON, JOE FRANK AND REYNOLDS.

45s

Number	Title (A Side/B Side)	Yr	VG	VG+	NM
LIBERTY					
55677	Draggin'/Rail-Vette	1964	5.00	10.00	20.00
55814	That's Where It's At/Pearlin'	1965	3.75	7.50	15.00
55836	No Matter What Shape (Your Stomach's In)/ Feelin' Fine	1965	3.00	6.00	12.00
55867	Sippin' & Chippin'/Moment of Softness	1966	2.50	5.00	10.00
55885	Underwater/Wherever You Look, Wherever You Go	1966	2.50	5.00	10.00
55906	Let's Go Get Stoned/Farre Thee Well	1966	2.50	5.00	10.00
55925	Balboa Blues/Walkin' My Cat Named Dog	1966	2.50	5.00	10.00
55951	Tee Hee Hee (My Life Seems Different Now)/ Proper Thing to Do	1967	2.50	5.00	10.00
UNITED ARTISTS					
0060	No Matter What Shape (Your Stomach's In)/ Sippin' N Chippin'	1973	—	2.50	5.00
—"Silver Spotlight Series" reissue					

Albums

Number	Title (A Side/B Side)	Yr	VG	VG+	NM
LIBERTY					
LRP-3346 [M]	Boss Drag	1963	15.00	30.00	60.00
LRP-3363 [M]	Boss Drag at the Beach	1964	15.00	30.00	60.00
LRP-3404 [M]	Doin' the Jerk	1965	10.00	20.00	40.00
LRP-3439 [M]	No Matter What Shape (Your Stomach's In)	1966	5.00	10.00	20.00
LRP-3446 [M]	Sippin' and Chippin'	1966	5.00	10.00	20.00
LRP-3471 [M]	Everyone's Gone to the Moon	1966	5.00	10.00	20.00
LST-7346 [S]	Boss Drag	1963	25.00	50.00	100.00
LST-7363 [S]	Boss Drag at the Beach	1964	25.00	50.00	100.00
LST-7404 [S]	Doin' the Jerk	1965	15.00	30.00	60.00
LST-7439 [S]	No Matter What Shape (Your Stomach's In)	1966	6.25	12.50	25.00
LST-7446 [S]	Sippin' and Chippin'	1966	6.25	12.50	25.00
LST-7471 [S]	Everyone's Gone to the Moon	1966	6.25	12.50	25.00
SUNSET					
SUM-1119 [M]	Shapin' Things Up	196?	3.00	6.00	12.00
SUS-5119 [S]	Shapin' Things Up	196?	3.75	7.50	15.00

T.C. ATLANTIC

45s

Number	Title (A Side/B Side)	Yr	VG	VG+	NM
AESOP'S LABEL					
6044	Once Upon a Melody/I Love You So, Little Girl	1965	10.00	20.00	40.00
B. SHARP					
272	Mona/My Babe	1966	7.50	15.00	30.00
CANDY FLOSS					
101	I'm So Glad/Twenty Years Ago	1968	10.00	20.00	40.00
PARAMOUNT					
0098	Judgment Train/Shine the Light	1971	3.75	7.50	15.00
PARROT					
330	I'm So Glad/Twenty Years Ago	1968	5.00	10.00	20.00
338	Love Is Just/Faces	1969	5.00	10.00	20.00
TURTLE					
1103	Faces/Baby, Please Don't Go	1966	25.00	50.00	100.00
1105	Shake/Spanish Harlem	1967	10.00	20.00	40.00

Albums

Number	Title (A Side/B Side)	Yr	VG	VG+	NM
DOVE					
LP-4459	T.C. Atlantic	1966	25.00	50.00	100.00

T.I.M.E.

45s

Number	Title (A Side/B Side)	Yr	VG	VG+	NM
LIBERTY					
56020	Take Me Along/Make It Right	1968	2.50	5.00	10.00
56020 [PS]	Take Me Along/Make It Right	1968	3.75	7.50	15.00
56060	Tripping Into Sunshine/What Would Life Be Without You	1968	2.50	5.00	10.00

Albums

Number	Title (A Side/B Side)	Yr	VG	VG+	NM
LIBERTY					
LST-7558	T.I.M.E.	1968	6.25	12.50	25.00
LST-7605	Smooth Ball	1969	6.25	12.50	25.00

T. REX

45s

Number	Title (A Side/B Side)	Yr	VG	VG+	NM
A&M					
955	Child Star/Debora	1968	3.00	6.00	12.00
—As "Tyrannosaurus Rex"					
BLUE THUMB					
212	By the Light of the Magical Moon/Fina a Little Wood	1971	—	3.00	6.00
SP-6115/6 [DJ]	Ride a White Swan/Is It Love	1970	3.00	6.00	12.00
—As "Tyrannosaurus Rex"					
7121	Ride a White Swan/Summertime Blues	1970	2.00	4.00	8.00
—As "Tyrannosaurus Rex"					
CASABLANCA					
810	Precious Star/(B-side unknown)	1974	—	3.00	6.00
REPRISE					
1006	Hot Love//One Inch Rock/Seagull Woman	1971	—	3.00	6.00
1032	Bang a Gong (Get It On)/Raw Ramp	1971	2.00	4.00	8.00
1056	Jeepster/Rip Off	1971	—	3.00	6.00
1078	Telegram Sam/Cadillac	1972	—	3.00	6.00
1095	Metal Guru/Lady	1972	—	3.00	6.00
1122	The Slider/Rock On	1972	—	3.00	6.00
1150	Bang a Gong (Get It On)/Telegram Sam	1972	—	2.00	4.00
—"Back to Back Hits" series					
1151	Jeepster/Metal Guru	1972	—	2.00	4.00
—"Back to Back Hits" series					
1161	Born to Boogie/The Groover	1973	—	2.50	5.00
1161 [PS]	Born to Boogie/The Groover	1973	6.25	12.50	25.00
1170	Hot Love/Rip Off	1973	—	2.50	5.00

Albums

Number	Title (A Side/B Side)	Yr	VG	VG+	NM
A&M					
SP-3514 [(2)]	Tyrannosaurus Rex (A Beginning)	1972	3.75	7.50	15.00
—Compilation of early LPs Prophets, Seers & Sages and My People Were Fair and Had Sky in Their Hair But Now They're Content to Wear Stars on Their Brows					
BLUE THUMB					
BTS 7	Unicorn	1969	5.00	10.00	20.00
BTS 18	A Beard of Stars	1970	5.00	10.00	20.00
—Add $5 for bonus single SP-6115/6, "Ride a White Swan"/"Is It Love." For reasons unknown, the single seems to be much more readily available than the LP					
CASABLANCA					
NBLP 7005	Light of Love	1974	3.00	6.00	12.00
MARC ON WAX/RELATIVITY					
8249	Bolan's Zip Gun	198?	2.50	5.00	10.00
8250	Zinc Alloy & The Hidden Riders of Tomorrow	198?	2.50	5.00	10.00
8251	Dandy in the Underworld	198?	2.50	5.00	10.00
8252	Futuristic Dragon	198?	2.50	5.00	10.00
8253	The Slider	198?	2.50	5.00	10.00
8254	Tanx	198?	2.50	5.00	10.00
REPRISE					
PRO 511 [DJ]	An Interview with Marc Bolan	1971	25.00	50.00	100.00
MS 2095	The Slider	1972	3.00	6.00	12.00
MS 2132	Tanx	1973	3.00	6.00	12.00
RS 6440	T. Rex	1971	3.00	6.00	12.00
RS 6466	Electric Warrior	1971	3.00	6.00	12.00
WARNER BROS.					
25333	T. Rextasy: The Best of T. Rex, 1970-1973	1985	2.50	5.00	10.00

T.S.U. TORONADOES, THE

45s

Number	Title (A Side/B Side)	Yr	VG	VG+	NM
ATLANTIC					
2579	Getting the Corners/What Good Am I!	1968	2.00	4.00	8.00
2614	Got to Get Through to You/The Goose	1969	2.00	4.00	8.00
VOLT					
4030	My Thing Is a Moving Thing/Still Love You	1969	—	3.00	6.00
4038	One Flight Too Many/Play the Music Toronadoes	1970	—	3.00	6.00

T2

Albums

Number	Title (A Side/B Side)	Yr	VG	VG+	NM
LONDON					
PS 583	It'll All Work Out in Boomland	1971	20.00	40.00	80.00

T.V. AND THE TRIBESMEN

Albums

Number	Title (A Side/B Side)	Yr	VG	VG+	NM
HANNA-BARBERA					
HLP-9507 [S]	Barefootin'	1966	6.25	12.50	25.00

TABBYS, THE

45s

Number	Title (A Side/B Side)	Yr	VG	VG+	NM
TIME					
1008	Yes I Do/My Darling	1959	12.50	25.00	50.00
—Blue label					
1008	Yes I Do/My Darling	1959	6.25	12.50	25.00
—Red label					

TABS, THE

45s

Number	Title (A Side/B Side)	Yr	VG	VG+	NM
DOT					
15887	Avenue of Tears/The First Star	1959	7.50	15.00	30.00
GARDENA					
110	Never Forget/Rock and Roll Holiday	1960	12.50	25.00	50.00
NASCO					
6016	Will We Meet Again/Still Love You Baby	1958	7.50	15.00	30.00
NOBLE					
719	Never Forget/Rock and Roll Holiday	1959	37.50	75.00	150.00
720	Oops/My Girl Is Gone	1959	100.00	200.00	400.00
VEE JAY					
418	Dance All By Myself/Dance Party	1961	5.00	10.00	20.00
446	Mash Dem Taters/But You're My Baby	1962	5.00	10.00	20.00
WAND					
130	Two Stupid Feet/Footsteps	1962	3.75	7.50	15.00
139	I'm with You/Take My Love Along with You	1963	3.75	7.50	15.00

TADS, THE

45s

Number	Title (A Side/B Side)	Yr	VG	VG+	NM
DOT					
15518	Your Reason/The Pink Panther	1956	6.25	12.50	25.00
LIBERTY BELL					
9010	Your Reason/The Pink Panther	1956	12.50	25.00	50.00
REV					
3513	Wolf Call/She Is My Dream	1958	12.50	25.00	50.00

TAFFYS, THE

45s

Number	Title (A Side/B Side)	Yr	VG	VG+	NM
AMY					
933	Bongo Man/The Game Called Love	1965	2.50	5.00	10.00

Number	Title (A Side/B Side)	Yr	VG	VG+	NM
FAIRMOUNT					
610	Everybody South Street/Key to My Heart	1963	2.50	5.00	10.00
PAGEANT					
608	Can't We Just Be Friends/Peter Cottontail	1963	2.50	5.00	10.00

TAGES, THE

With PETER FRAMPTON.

45s

Number	Title (A Side/B Side)	Yr	VG	VG+	NM
VERVE					
10626	Halcyon Days/I Read You Like an Open Book	1968	5.00	10.00	20.00

TAKERS, THE

45s

Number	Title (A Side/B Side)	Yr	VG	VG+	NM
INTERPHON					
7709	Think/If You Don't Come Back	1964	2.50	5.00	10.00

TALLEY, JOHNNY T.

45s

Number	Title (A Side/B Side)	Yr	VG	VG+	NM
MERCURY					
70902	Lonesome Train/(I've Changed My) Wild Mind	1956	75.00	150.00	300.00

TALLYSMEN, THE

45s

Number	Title (A Side/B Side)	Yr	VG	VG+	NM
TALLY					
200688	Little By Little/You Don't Care About Me	1966	15.00	30.00	60.00

TAMANEERS, THE

45s

Number	Title (A Side/B Side)	Yr	VG	VG+	NM
BRAMLEY					
102	Searching/Be Anything (But Be Mine)	1960	100.00	200.00	400.00

TAMBLYN, LARRY

45s

Number	Title (A Side/B Side)	Yr	VG	VG+	NM
FARO					
601	Patty Ann/Dearest	1960	5.00	10.00	20.00
603	The Lie/My Bride-to-Be	1960	5.00	10.00	20.00
612	This Is the Night/Destiny	1961	6.25	12.50	25.00
LINDA					
112	You'll Be Mine Someday/The Girl in My Heart	1963	5.00	10.00	20.00
—With the Standells					

TAMMI AND THE BACHELORS

45s

Number	Title (A Side/B Side)	Yr	VG	VG+	NM
BANGAR					
00610	My Summer Love/My Love	1964	6.25	12.50	25.00

TAMMYS, THE

45s

Number	Title (A Side/B Side)	Yr	VG	VG+	NM
UNITED ARTISTS					
632	Take Back Your Ring/Part of Growing Up	1963	3.00	6.00	12.00
678	Egyptian Shamba/What's So Sweet About Sweet Sixteen	1963	3.00	6.00	12.00
VEEP					
1210	Gypsy/Hold Back the Light of Dawn	1965	3.00	6.00	12.00
1220	His Actions Speak Louder Than Words/Blues Sixteen	1965	3.00	6.00	12.00

TAMPA RED

45s

Number	Title (A Side/B Side)	Yr	VG	VG+	NM
RCA VICTOR					
47-4275	Boogie Woogie Women/I Won't Let Her Do It	1951	12.50	25.00	50.00
47-4399	She's a Cool Operator/Green and Lucky Blues	1951	12.50	25.00	50.00
47-4722	But I Forgive You/I'm Gonna Put You Down	1952	12.50	25.00	50.00
47-4898	True Love/Look-a There, Look-a There	1952	12.50	25.00	50.00
47-5134	All Mixed Up Over You/Too Late Too Long	1953	10.00	20.00	40.00
47-5273	I'll Never Let You Go/Got a Mind to Leave This Town	1953	10.00	20.00	40.00
47-5523	So Craazy About You Baby/So Much Trouble	1953	10.00	20.00	40.00
47-5594	If She Don't Come Back/Big Stars Falling	1954	10.00	20.00	40.00
50-0002	If You Ever Change Your Ways/Chicago Breakdown	1949	30.00	60.00	120.00
—Gray label, orange vinyl; With Big Maceo					
50-0019	Come On If You're Coming/When Things Go Wrong with You	1950	30.00	60.00	120.00
—Gray label, orange vinyl					
50-0027	It's a Brand New Boogie/Put Your Money Where Your Mouth Is	1950	30.00	60.00	120.00
—Gray label, orange vinyl					
50-0041	I'll Find My Way/That's Her Own Business	1950	30.00	60.00	120.00
—Gray label, orange vinyl					
50-0071	It's Too Late Now/Please Try to See It My Way	1950	25.00	50.00	100.00
—Gray label, orange vinyl					
50-0084	1950 Blues/Love Her with a Feelin'	1950	25.00	50.00	100.00
—Gray label, orange vinyl					
50-0094	It's Good Like That/New Deal Blues	1950	25.00	50.00	100.00
—Gray label, orange vinyl					
50-0107	Sweet Little Angel/Don't Blame Shorty for That	1951	20.00	40.00	80.00
50-0112	Midnight Boogie/I Miss My Lovin' Blues	1951	20.00	40.00	80.00
50-0123	She's Dynamite/Early in the Morning	1951	20.00	40.00	80.00
50-0136	Pretty Baby Blues/Since My Baby's Been Gone	1951	20.00	40.00	80.00

Albums

Number	Title (A Side/B Side)	Yr	VG	VG+	NM
BLUEBIRD					
AXM2-5501 [(2)]	Guitar Wizard	1975	3.75	7.50	15.00
BLUES CLASSICS					
25	Guitar Wizard (1935-53)	197?	3.00	6.00	12.00
BLUESVILLE					
BVLP-1030 [M]	Don't Tampa with the Blues	1961	30.00	60.00	120.00
—Blue label, silver print					
BVLP-1030 [M]	Don't Tampa with the Blues	1963	7.50	15.00	30.00
—Blue label, trident logo at right					
BVLP-1043 [M]	Don't Jive Me	1962	30.00	60.00	120.00
—Blue label, silver print					
BVLP-1043 [M]	Don't Jive Me	1963	7.50	15.00	30.00
—Blue label, trident logo at right					
FANTASY					
OBC-516	Don't Tampa with the Blues	198?	2.50	5.00	10.00
YAZOO					
1039	Bottleneck Guitar	197?	3.00	6.00	12.00

TAMS, THE

45s

Number	Title (A Side/B Side)	Yr	VG	VG+	NM
1-2-3					
1726	How Long Love/Too Much Foolin' Around	1970	—	3.00	6.00
ABC					
10825	Holding On/Is It Better to Have Loved a Little	1966	2.00	4.00	8.00
10885	Shelter/Get Away (Leave Me Alone)	1966	2.00	4.00	8.00
10929	Breaking Up/How 'Bout It	1967	2.00	4.00	8.00
10956	Everything Else Is Gone/Mary, Mary, Row Your Boat	1967	2.00	4.00	8.00
11019	All My Heard Times/A Little More Soul	1967	2.00	4.00	8.00
11066	Be Young, Be Foolish, Be Happy/That Same Old Song	1968	2.00	4.00	8.00
11128	Laugh at the World/Trouble Maker	1968	2.00	4.00	8.00
11183	Sunshine, Rainbow, Blue Sky, Brown Eyed Girl/There's a Great Big Change in Me	1969	2.00	4.00	8.00
11228	Be Young, Be Foolish, Be Happy/Love, Love, Love	1969	2.00	4.00	8.00
11358	Don't You Just Know It/Making Music	1973	—	2.50	5.00
ABC-PARAMOUNT					
10502	What Kind of Fool (Do You Think I Am)/Laugh It Off	1963	3.75	7.50	15.00
10533	It's All Right (You're Just in Love)/You Lied to Your Daddy	1964	3.00	6.00	12.00
10573	Hey Girl Don't Bother Me/Take Away	1964	3.00	6.00	12.00
10601	Silly Little Girl/Weep Little Girl	1964	3.00	6.00	12.00
10614	The Truth Hurts/Why Did My Little Girl Cry	1965	2.50	5.00	10.00
10635	What Do You Do/Unlove You	1965	2.50	5.00	10.00
10702	Concrete Jungle/Till the End of Time	1965	2.50	5.00	10.00
10741	Carryin' On/I've Been Hurt	1965	2.50	5.00	10.00
10779	Got to Get Used to a Broken Heart/Riding for a Fall	1966	2.50	5.00	10.00
ABC DUNHILL					
4290	Hey Girl Don't Bother Me/Weep Little Girl	1971	—	3.00	6.00
4290 [PS]	Hey Girl Don't Bother Me/Weep Little Girl	1971	2.50	5.00	10.00
—Title sleeve with "#1 in England"					
APT					
26010	Long Distance Operator/Numbers	1970	—	3.00	6.00
ARLEN					
711	Untie Me/Disillusioned	1962	3.00	6.00	12.00
717	Deep Inside Me/If You're So Smart (Why Do You Have a Broken Heart)	1962	3.00	6.00	12.00
720	You'll Never Know/Blue Shadows	1963	3.00	6.00	12.00
729	Don't Ever Go/Find Another Love	1963	3.00	6.00	12.00
CAPITOL					
3050	The Tams Medley/Wire Help	1971	—	3.00	6.00
COMPLEAT					
109	My Baby Sure Can Shag/Making True Love	1983	—	2.00	4.00
GENERAL AMERICAN					
714	My Baby Loves Me/Find Another Love	1962	3.75	7.50	15.00
HERITAGE					
101	Vacation Time/If Love Were Like Rivers	1961	75.00	150.00	300.00
KING					
6012	Untie Me/Find Another Love	1965	2.50	5.00	10.00
SWAN					
4055	Sorry/Valley of Love	1960	3.75	7.50	15.00

Albums

Number	Title (A Side/B Side)	Yr	VG	VG+	NM
1-2-3					
567	The Best of the Tams	1970	5.00	10.00	20.00
ABC					
596 [M]	Time for the Tams	1967	7.50	15.00	30.00
S-596 [S]	Time for the Tams	1967	7.50	15.00	30.00
S-627	A Little More Soul	1968	6.25	12.50	25.00
S-673	A Portrait of the Tams	1969	6.25	12.50	25.00
ABC-PARAMOUNT					
481 [M]	Presenting the Tams	1964	12.50	25.00	50.00
S-481 [R]	Presenting the Tams	1964	7.50	15.00	30.00
499 [M]	Hey Girl, Don't Bother Me	1964	7.50	15.00	30.00
S-499 [S]	Hey Girl, Don't Bother Me	1964	10.00	20.00	40.00
CAPITOL					
SM-11839	The Best of the Tams	1979	3.00	6.00	12.00
COMPLEAT					
CMLP-5001 [EP]	Beach Music from the Tams	198?	2.00	4.00	8.00
SOUNDS SOUTH					
SO-16010	The Mighty, Mighty Tams	1977	3.75	7.50	15.00

TAMS, THE (2)

45s

Number	Title (A Side/B Side)	Yr	VG	VG+	NM
MINK					
22	Memory Lane/Teenage Kids	1959	10.00	20.00	40.00
—Originally issued as "The Stereos"					
PARKWAY					
863	Memory Lane/A Lovely Piano	1963	5.00	10.00	20.00
—The same record was reissued as "The Hippies"					

TANEGA, NORMA

45s

Number	Title (A Side/B Side)	Yr	VG	VG+	NM
NEW VOICE					
807	Walkin' My Cat Named Dog/I'm the Sky	1966	3.00	6.00	12.00
810	A Street That Rhymes at 6 A.M./Treat Me Right	1966	2.50	5.00	10.00
815	Bread/Waves	1966	2.50	5.00	10.00
821	No Stranger Am I/Run on the Run	1967	2.50	5.00	10.00

Number	Title (A Side/B Side)	Yr	VG	VG+	NM
Albums					
NEW VOICE					
NV-2001 [M]	Walkin' My Cat Named Dog	1966	10.00	20.00	40.00
NVS-2001 [S]	Walkin' My Cat Named Dog	1966	20.00	40.00	80.00

TANGEERS, THE

Number	Title (A Side/B Side)	Yr	VG	VG+	NM
45s					
OKEH					
7319	Let My Heart and Soul Be Free/What's the Use of Me Trying	1968	10.00	20.00	40.00

TANGERINE DREAM

Number	Title (A Side/B Side)	Yr	VG	VG+	NM
12-Inch Singles					
RELATIVITY					
EMC 8044	Streethawk (2 versions)/Tiergarten	1985	5.00	10.00	20.00
45s					
MCA					
40740	Betrayal (Sorcerer's Theme)/Grind	1977	2.50	5.00	10.00
VIRGIN					
9516	Moonlight (Part 2)/Coldwater Canyon (Part 2)	1977	2.50	5.00	10.00
9516 [DJ]	Moonlight/Desert Dream	1977	2.50	5.00	10.00
9516 [DJ]	Moonlight/Cherokee Lane	1977	2.50	5.00	10.00
9516 [DJ]	Moonlight (Part 2) (mono/stereo)	1977	2.50	5.00	10.00
Albums					
CAROLINE					
CAROL 1349	Livemiles	1988	3.00	6.00	12.00
ELEKTRA					
5E-521	Thief	1981	2.50	5.00	10.00
5E-557	Exit	1981	2.50	5.00	10.00
EMI AMERICA					
ST-17141	Flashpoint	1984	2.50	5.00	10.00
MCA					
2277	Sorcerer	1977	3.00	6.00	12.00
6165	Legend	1986	2.00	4.00	8.00
PRIVATE MUSIC					
2042-1-P	Optical Race	1988	3.75	7.50	15.00
2047-1-P	Miracle Mile	1989	3.75	7.50	15.00
2057-1-P	Lily on the Beach	1989	3.75	7.50	15.00
RELATIVITY					
EMC 8043	Le Parc	198?	3.00	6.00	12.00
EMC 8045 [(2)]	Poland	198?	3.75	7.50	15.00
86561 8068	Electronic Meditation	1986	3.00	6.00	12.00
86561 8069	Alpha Centauri	1986	3.00	6.00	12.00
86561 8070 [(2)]	Zeit	1986	3.75	7.50	15.00
86561 8071	Atam	1986	3.00	6.00	12.00
86561 8072	Green Desert	1986	3.00	6.00	12.00
86561 8113	Underwater Sunlight	1986	3.00	6.00	12.00
VIRGIN					
VR 13-108	Phaedra	1974	3.75	7.50	15.00
VR 13-116	Rubycon	1975	3.75	7.50	15.00
PZ 34427	Stratosfear	1976	3.75	7.50	15.00
PZG 35014 [(2)]	Encore	1977	5.00	10.00	20.00
VIRGIN INTERNATIONAL					
VI 2010 *—Reissue*	Phaedra	1979	2.50	5.00	10.00
VI 2025 *—Reissue*	Rubycon	1979	2.50	5.00	10.00
VI 2044	Ricochet	1975	3.75	7.50	15.00
VI 2068 *—Reissue of 34427*	Stratosfear	1979	3.00	6.00	12.00
VI 2097 *—Reissue*	Cyclone	1979	2.50	5.00	10.00
VI 2111	Force Majeure	1979	3.00	6.00	12.00

TANGERINE ZOO, THE

Number	Title (A Side/B Side)	Yr	VG	VG+	NM
45s					
MAINSTREAM					
682	A Trip to the Zoo/One More Heartache	1968	5.00	10.00	20.00
690	Like People/(B-side unknown)	1968	5.00	10.00	20.00
Albums					
MAINSTREAM					
S-6107	Tangerine Zoo	1968	12.50	25.00	50.00
S-6118	Outside Looking In	1969	17.50	35.00	70.00

TANGIERS, THE

Possibly more than one group. Also see THE HOLLYWOOD FLAMES.

Number	Title (A Side/B Side)	Yr	VG	VG+	NM
45s					
A-J					
905	The Plea/The Waddle	1962	6.25	12.50	25.00
CLASS					
224	School Days Will Be Over/Don't Try	1958	7.50	15.00	30.00
DECCA					
29603	I Won't Be Around/Tabarin	1955	37.50	75.00	150.00
29971	Remember Me/Oh, Baby!	1956	37.50	75.00	150.00
STRAND					
25039	Ping Pong/Don't Stop the Music	1961	7.50	15.00	30.00

TANTONES, THE

Number	Title (A Side/B Side)	Yr	VG	VG+	NM
45s					
LAMP					
2002	No Matter/I Love You, Really I Do	1957	37.50	75.00	150.00
2008	So Afraid/Tell Me	1957	37.50	75.00	150.00

TARANTULA

Number	Title (A Side/B Side)	Yr	VG	VG+	NM
45s					
A&M					
1156	Billy the Birdman/Love Is for Peace	1969	2.00	4.00	8.00
Albums					
A&M					
SP-4202	Tarantula	1969	5.00	10.00	20.00

TARANTULAS, THE

Number	Title (A Side/B Side)	Yr	VG	VG+	NM
45s					
ATLANTIC					
2102	Tarantula/Black Widow	1961	6.25	12.50	25.00
STOP					
102	Herky Jerky/Vera Brown	1964	2.50	5.00	10.00

TARGETS, THE

Number	Title (A Side/B Side)	Yr	VG	VG+	NM
45s					
KING					
5538	It Doesn't Matter/Girls, Girls, Girls	1961	10.00	20.00	40.00

TARRIERS, THE

Also see VINCE MARTIN.

Number	Title (A Side/B Side)	Yr	VG	VG+	NM
45s					
DECCA					
31387	Last Night I Had the Strangest Dream/Lonesome Traveler	1962	2.50	5.00	10.00
31470	Casey Jones/Mary Ann	1963	2.50	5.00	10.00
31524	Lonesome Traveller/Seven Daffodils	1963	2.50	5.00	10.00
31631	San Francisco Bay Blues/Guantanamera	1964	2.50	5.00	10.00
GLORY					
246	Wishing Well Song/East Virginia	1956	3.75	7.50	15.00
249	The Banana Boat Song/No Hidin' Place	1956	5.00	10.00	20.00
254	Those Brown Eyes/Chaucon	1957	3.75	7.50	15.00
255	I Know Where I'm Going/Pretty Boy	1957	3.75	7.50	15.00
264	Dunya/Quinto	1957	3.75	7.50	15.00
271	Lonesome Traveler/East Virginia	1958	3.75	7.50	15.00
286	Tom Dooley/Everybody Loves Saturday Night	1958	3.75	7.50	15.00
UNITED ARTISTS					
168	Hard Travelin'/Times Are Getting Hard	1959	3.00	6.00	12.00
Albums					
ATLANTIC					
8042 [M]	Tell the World	1960	7.50	15.00	30.00
SD 8042 [S]	Tell the World	1960	10.00	20.00	40.00
DECCA					
DL 4342 [M]	The Tarriers	1962	6.25	12.50	25.00
DL 4538 [M]	Gather 'Round	1964	6.25	12.50	25.00
DL 74342 [S]	The Tarriers	1962	7.50	15.00	30.00
DL 74538 [S]	Gather 'Round	1964	7.50	15.00	30.00
GLORY					
PG-1200 [M]	The Tarriers	1958	15.00	30.00	60.00
KAPP					
KL 1349 [M]	The Original Tarriers	1963	6.25	12.50	25.00
KS 3349 [S]	The Original Tarriers	1963	7.50	15.00	30.00
UNITED ARTISTS					
UAL-4033 [M]	Hard Travelin'	1959	7.50	15.00	30.00
UAS-5033 [S]	Hard Travelin'	1959	10.00	20.00	40.00

TARRYTONS, THE

Number	Title (A Side/B Side)	Yr	VG	VG+	NM
45s					
DOT					
16537	Rough Surfin'/Mansion on the Hill	1963	6.25	12.50	25.00
EXCLUSIVE					
2270	Rough Surfin'/Mansion on the Hill	1963	10.00	20.00	40.00

TASSELS, THE

Number	Title (A Side/B Side)	Yr	VG	VG+	NM
45s					
AMY					
946	To a Soldier Boy/The Boy for Me	1966	2.50	5.00	10.00
MADISON					
117	To a Soldier Boy/The Boy for Me	1959	6.25	12.50	25.00
121	To a Young Lover/My Guy and I	1959	5.00	10.00	20.00

TASTE

RORY GALLAGHER was in this group.

Number	Title (A Side/B Side)	Yr	VG	VG+	NM
Albums					
ATCO					
SD 33-296	Taste	1969	6.25	12.50	25.00
SD 33-322	On the Boards	1970	6.25	12.50	25.00

TATE, BILLY

Number	Title (A Side/B Side)	Yr	VG	VG+	NM
45s					
IMPERIAL					
5337 *—Script logo*	Single Life/You Told Me	1955	50.00	100.00	200.00
PEACOCK					
1671	Don't Call My Name/Right from Wrong	1957	7.50	15.00	30.00

TATE, HOWARD

Number	Title (A Side/B Side)	Yr	VG	VG+	NM
45s					
ATLANTIC					
2836	Keep Cool (Don't Be a Fool)/Strugglin'	1971	—	3.00	6.00
2860	She's a Burglar/You Don't Know Nothing About Love	1972	—	3.00	6.00
2894	Eight Days on the Road/Girl of the North Country	1972	—	3.00	6.00
EPIC					
11118	Can You Top This/Ain't Got Nobody to Give It To	1974	—	2.50	5.00
TURNTABLE					
505	These Are the Things That Make Me Know You're Gone/That's What Happens	1969	2.00	4.00	8.00
1018	My Soul's Got a Hole In It/It's Too Late	1970	2.00	4.00	8.00
UTOPIA					
510	Half a Man/(B-side unknown)	1966	6.25	12.50	25.00
VERVE					
10420	Ain't Nobody Home/How Come My Bull Dog Don't Bark	1966	2.00	4.00	8.00
10464	Look at Granny Run, Run/Half a Man	1966	2.00	4.00	8.00
10496	Get It While You Can/Glad I Knew Better	1967	2.00	4.00	8.00
10525	Baby I Love You/How Blue Can You Get	1967	2.00	4.00	8.00

Number	Title (A Side/B Side)	Yr	VG	VG+	NM
10547	I Learned It All the Hard Way/Part-Time Love	1967	2.00	4.00	8.00
10573	Stop/Shoot 'Em All Down	1967	2.00	4.00	8.00
10604	Night Owl/Everyday I Have the Blues	1968	2.00	4.00	8.00
10625	I'm Your Servant/Sweet Love Child	1968	2.00	4.00	8.00
Albums					
ATLANTIC					
SD 8303	Howard Tate	1971	5.00	10.00	20.00
TURNTABLE					
5002	Reaction	1969	5.00	10.00	20.00
VERVE					
V-5022 [M]	Get It While You Can	1967	5.00	10.00	20.00
V6-5022 [S]	Get It While You Can	1967	6.25	12.50	25.00

TATE, LAURIE

45s

Number	Title (A Side/B Side)	Yr	VG	VG+	NM
ATLANTIC					
965	Rock Me Daddy/You Can't Stop My Crying	1952	25.00	50.00	100.00

TATE, TOMMY

45s

Number	Title (A Side/B Side)	Yr	VG	VG+	NM
ABC-PARAMOUNT					
10626	What's the Matter/Ordinarily	1965	6.25	12.50	25.00
KOKO					
722	Hardtimes S.O.S./Always	1976	—	3.00	6.00
723	If You Ain't Man Enough/Revelations	1976	—	3.00	6.00
727	I'm So Satisfied/If You Ain't Man Enough	1977	—	3.00	6.00
2109	I Remember/Help Me Love	1971	—	3.00	6.00
2112	School of Life/I Remember	1972	—	3.00	6.00
2114	I Ain't Gonna Worry/More Power To You	1972	—	3.00	6.00
OKEH					
7242	Are You From Heaven/I'm Taking On Pain	1966	5.00	10.00	20.00
7253	Big Blue Diamonds/Lover's Reward	1967	5.00	10.00	20.00

TAUPIN, BERNIE

ELTON JOHN's songwriting partner.

45s

Number	Title (A Side/B Side)	Yr	VG	VG+	NM
RCA					
5162-7-R	Friend of the Flag/Backbone	1987	—	—	3.00
5162-7-R [PS]	Friend of the Flag/Backbone	1987	—	—	3.00
5216-7-R	Citizen Jane/White Boys in Chains	1987	—	—	3.00
5216-7-R [PS]	Citizen Jane/White Boys in Chains	1987	—	—	3.00
Albums					
ASYLUM					
6E-263	He Who Rides the Tiger	1980	3.00	6.00	12.00
ELEKTRA					
EKS-75020	Bernie Taupin	1972	3.75	7.50	15.00
RCA					
5922-1-R	Tribe	1987	2.50	5.00	10.00
6420-1-RAB [(2) DJ]	Interview Album	1987	5.00	10.00	20.00

TAVARES

Also see CHUBBY AND THE TURNPIKES.

12-Inch Singles

Number	Title (A Side/B Side)	Yr	VG	VG+	NM
CAPITOL					
SPRO-9087 [DJ]	Straight from the Heart (7:23) (same on both sides)	1979	3.00	6.00	12.00
JDC					
002	C'est La Vie/Good 'n' Plenty/On My Mind Tonight	198?	—	3.00	6.00
003	She Freaks Out on the Floor (4 versions)	198?	—	3.00	6.00
RCA					
PD-13434	Got to Find My Way Back to You/I Hope You Will Be Very Unhappy Without Me	1983	2.00	4.00	8.00
PD-13612	Deeper in Love/I Really Miss You Baby	1983	2.00	4.00	8.00
45s					
CAPITOL					
3674	Check It Out/The Judgment Day	1973	—	2.50	5.00
3794	That's the Sound That Lonely Makes/Little Girl	1973	—	2.50	5.00
3882	Too Late/Leave It Up to the Lady	1974	—	2.50	5.00
3957	She's Gone/To Love You	1974	—	2.50	5.00
4010	Remember What I Told You to Forget/My Ship	1974	—	2.50	5.00
4111	It Only Takes a Minute/I Hope She Chooses Me	1975	—	2.50	5.00
4184	Free Ride/In the Eyes of Love	1975	—	2.50	5.00
4221	The Love I Never Had/In the City	1976	—	2.50	5.00
4270	Heaven Must Be Missing An Angel (Part 1)/Heaven Must Be Missing An Angel (Part 2)	1976	—	2.50	5.00
4348	Don't Take Away the Music/Guiding Star	1976	—	2.50	5.00
4398	Whodunit/Fool of the Year	1977	—	2.50	5.00
4453	Goodnight My Love/Watchin' the Woman's Movement	1977	—	2.50	5.00
4500	More Than a Woman/Keep in Touch	1977	—	2.00	4.00
4544	The Ghost of Love (Part 1)/The Ghost of Love (Part 2)	1978	—	2.00	4.00
4583	Timber/Feel So Good	1978	—	2.00	4.00
4658	Never Had a Love Like This Before/Positive Forces	1978	—	2.00	4.00
4703	Straight from the Heart/I'm Back for Me	1979	—	2.00	4.00
4738	One Telephone Call Away/Let Me Heal the Bruises	1979	—	2.00	4.00
4781	Hard Core Poetry/Stabilize	1979	—	2.00	4.00
4811	Bad Times/Got to Have Your Love	1979	—	2.00	4.00
4846	I Can't Go On Living Without You/Why Can't We Fall in Love	1980	—	2.00	4.00
4880	I Don't Want You Anymore/Paradise	1980	—	2.00	4.00
4933	Love Uprising/Not Love	1980	—	2.00	4.00
4969	Loneliness/Break Down for Love	1981	—	2.00	4.00
A-5019	Turn Out the Nightlight/House of Music	1981	—	2.00	4.00
A-5043	Loveline/Right On Time	1981	—	2.00	4.00
RCA					
PB-13292	A Penny for Your Thoughts/The Skin You're In	1982	—	2.00	4.00
PB-13433	Got to Find My Way Back to You/I Hope You Will Be Very Unhappy Without Me	1983	—	2.00	4.00
PB-13530	Abra-Ca-Dabra Love You Too/Mystery Lady	1983	—	2.00	4.00
PB-13611	Deeper in Love/I Really Miss You Baby	1983	—	2.00	4.00
PB-13684	Words and Music/I'll Send Love (We Go Together)	1983	—	2.00	4.00
GB-13799	A Penny for Your Thoughts/Got to Find My Way Back to You	1984	—	—	3.00
—Gold Standard Series					
Albums					
CAPITOL					
ST-11258	Check It Out	1973	2.50	5.00	10.00
ST-11316	Hard Core Poetry	1974	2.50	5.00	10.00
ST-11396	In the City	1975	2.50	5.00	10.00
ST-11533	Sky-High!	1976	2.50	5.00	10.00
ST-11628	Love Storm	1977	2.50	5.00	10.00
ST-11701	The Best of Tavares	1977	2.50	5.00	10.00
SW-11719	Future Bound	1978	2.50	5.00	10.00
SW-11874	Madam Butterfly	1979	2.50	5.00	10.00
ST-12026	Supercharged	1980	2.50	5.00	10.00
ST-12117	Love Uprising	1981	2.50	5.00	10.00
ST-12167	Loveline	1982	2.50	5.00	10.00
SN-16206	Love Storm	1981	2.00	4.00	8.00
—Budget-line reissue					
SN-16207	Future Bound	1981	2.00	4.00	8.00
—Budget-line reissue					
RCA VICTOR					
AFL1-4357	New Directions	1982	2.50	5.00	10.00
AFL1-4700	Words and Music	1983	2.50	5.00	10.00

TAVARES, ERNIE, TRIO

45s

Number	Title (A Side/B Side)	Yr	VG	VG+	NM
DOOTONE					
325	I'm Alone Tonight/It's Christmas	1953	37.50	75.00	150.00
—B-side by the Bonairs					

TAVENER, JOHN

Albums

Number	Title (A Side/B Side)	Yr	VG	VG+	NM
APPLE					
SMAS-3369	The Whale	1972	5.00	10.00	20.00

TAX FREE

Albums

Number	Title (A Side/B Side)	Yr	VG	VG+	NM
POLYDOR					
24-4053	Tax Free	1971	5.00	10.00	20.00

TAYLOR, ALEX

45s

Number	Title (A Side/B Side)	Yr	VG	VG+	NM
BANG					
739	Don't Look at Me That Way/Sunny Day to Rain	1978	—	2.00	4.00
CAPRICORN					
0004	Comin' Back to You/Who Will the Next Fool Be	1972	—	2.50	5.00
0018	Lizzie and the Rainman/Change Your Sexy Ways	1973	—	2.50	5.00
8013	Highway Song/C Song	1971	—	2.50	5.00
8016	Baby Ruth/All in Line	1971	—	2.50	5.00
8019	Night Owl/Southern Kids	1971	—	2.50	5.00
Albums					
CAPRICORN					
CP 101	Dinnertime	1972	2.50	5.00	10.00
860	With Friends and Neighbors	1971	2.50	5.00	10.00

TAYLOR, ANDREW

45s

Number	Title (A Side/B Side)	Yr	VG	VG+	NM
GONE					
5109	That's How I Feel About You/Never Bite Off More Than You Could Chew	1961	50.00	100.00	200.00

TAYLOR, BILL, AND SMOKEY JO

45s

Number	Title (A Side/B Side)	Yr	VG	VG+	NM
FLIP					
502	Split Personality/Lonely Sweetheart	1955	375.00	750.00	1500.

TAYLOR, BILLY

45s

Number	Title (A Side/B Side)	Yr	VG	VG+	NM
CITATION					
5002	Income Taxes and You/Lullaby to Carolyn	1962	3.75	7.50	15.00
FAME					
502	Little Jewel/Study Hall Romance	196?	75.00	150.00	300.00
FELCO					
101	Wombie Zombie/I'm Young	1959	5.00	10.00	20.00
FELSTED					
8564	Bandstand Baby/Cat with No Future	1959	5.00	10.00	20.00
TOWER					
421	Sunny/I Wish I Knew How I Would Feel to Be Free	1968	2.00	4.00	8.00
Albums					
ABC-PARAMOUNT					
ABC-112 [M]	Evergreens	1956	12.50	25.00	50.00
ABC-134 [M]	Billy Taylor At the London House	1956	12.50	25.00	50.00
ABC-162 [M]	Billy Taylor Introduces Ira Sullivan	1957	12.50	25.00	50.00
ABC-177 [M]	My Fair Lady Loves Jazz	1957	12.50	25.00	50.00
ABC-226 [M]	The New Trio	1958	12.50	25.00	50.00
ABCS-226 [S]	The New Trio	1958	10.00	20.00	40.00
ABC IMPULSE!					
AS-71 [S]	My Fair Lady Loves Jazz	1968	3.75	7.50	15.00
ARGO					
LP-650 [M]	Taylor Made Flute	1959	12.50	25.00	50.00
LPS-650 [S]	Taylor Made Flute	1959	10.00	20.00	40.00
ATLANTIC					
ALR-113 [10]	Piano Panorama	1951	37.50	75.00	150.00
1277 [M]	The Billy Taylor Touch	1958	12.50	25.00	50.00
—Black label					
1277 [M]	The Billy Taylor Touch	1961	6.25	12.50	25.00
—Multicolor label, white "fan" logo at right					

Number	Title (A Side/B Side)	Yr	VG	VG+	NM
1329 [M]	One for Fun	1960	12.50	25.00	50.00
—Black label					
SD 1329 [S]	One for Fun	1960	12.50	25.00	50.00
—Green label					
BELL					
S-6049	OK Billy!	1970	3.75	7.50	15.00
CAPITOL					
ST 2039 [S]	Right Here, Right Now	1963	6.25	12.50	25.00
T 2039 [M]	Right Here, Right Now	1963	5.00	10.00	20.00
ST 2302 [S]	Midnight Piano	1965	6.25	12.50	25.00
T 2302 [M]	Midnight Piano	1965	5.00	10.00	20.00
CONCORD JAZZ					
CJ-145	Where've You Been	1981	2.50	5.00	10.00
FANTASY					
OJC-015	The Billy Taylor Trio with Candido	1982	2.50	5.00	10.00
OJC-1730	Cross Section	198?	2.50	5.00	10.00
IMPULSE!					
A-71 [M]	My Fair Lady Loves Jazz	1965	5.00	10.00	20.00
AS-71 [S]	My Fair Lady Loves Jazz	1965	6.25	12.50	25.00
MERCURY					
MG-20722 [M]	Impromptu	1962	5.00	10.00	20.00
SR-60722 [S]	Impromptu	1962	6.25	12.50	25.00
MONMOUTH-EVERGREEN					
7089	Jazz Alive	1978	3.00	6.00	12.00
MOODSVILLE					
MVLP-16 [M]	Interlude	1961	12.50	25.00	50.00
—Green label					
MVLP-16 [M]	Interlude	1965	6.25	12.50	25.00
—Blue label, trident logo at right					
NEW JAZZ					
NJLP-8313 [M]	Live! At Town Hall	1963	—	—	—
—Canceled; reassigned to Status					
PAUSA					
7096	Sleeping Bee	198?	2.50	5.00	10.00
PRESTIGE					
PRLP-139 [10]	Billy Taylor Trio, Volume 1	1953	55.00	110.00	220.00
PRLP-165 [10]	Billy Taylor Trio, Volume 2	1953	55.00	110.00	220.00
PRLP-168 [10]	Billy Taylor Trio, Volume 3	1953	55.00	110.00	220.00
PRLP-184 [10]	Billy Taylor Trio	1954	50.00	100.00	200.00
PRLP-188 [10]	Billy Taylor Trio	1954	50.00	100.00	200.00
PRLP-194 [10]	Billy Taylor Trio In Concert at Town Hall, December 17, 1954	1955	50.00	100.00	200.00
PRLP-7001 [M]	A Touch of Taylor	1955	20.00	40.00	80.00
PRLP-7015 [M]	Billy Taylor Trio, Volume 1	1956	20.00	40.00	80.00
PRLP-7016 [M]	Billy Taylor Trio, Volume 2	1956	20.00	40.00	80.00
PRLP-7051 [M]	The Billy Taylor Trio with Candido	1956	20.00	40.00	80.00
PRLP-7071 [M]	Cross Section	1956	20.00	40.00	80.00
PRLP-7093 [M]	Billy Taylor Trio at Town Hall	1957	20.00	40.00	80.00
PRST-7664 [R]	A Touch of Taylor	1969	3.75	7.50	15.00
PRST-7762	Today!	1970	3.75	7.50	15.00
RIVERSIDE					
RLP 12-306 [M]	Billy Taylor with Four Flutes	1959	12.50	25.00	50.00
RLP 12-319 [M]	Billy Taylor Trio Uptown	1960	12.50	25.00	50.00
RLP 12-339 [M]	Warming Up	1960	12.50	25.00	50.00
RLP-1151 [S]	Billy Taylor with Four Flutes	1959	10.00	20.00	40.00
RLP-1168 [S]	Billy Taylor Trio Uptown	1960	10.00	20.00	40.00
RLP-1195 [S]	Warming Up	1960	10.00	20.00	40.00
ROOST					
R-406 [10]	Jazz at Storyville	1952	30.00	60.00	120.00
R-409 [10]	Taylor Made Jazz	1952	30.00	60.00	120.00
SAVOY					
MG-9035 [10]	Billy Taylor Piano	1953	30.00	60.00	120.00
SESAC					
N-3001 [M]	Custom Taylored	1959	15.00	30.00	60.00
SN-3001 [S]	Custom Taylored	1959	12.50	25.00	50.00
STATUS					
ST-8313 [M]	Live! At Town Hall	1965	10.00	20.00	40.00
SURREY					
S-1033 [M]	Easy Life	1966	6.25	12.50	25.00
SS-1033 [S]	Easy Life	1966	7.50	15.00	30.00
TOWER					
ST-5111 [S]	I Wish I Knew	1968	6.25	12.50	25.00
WEST 54					
8008	Live at Storyville	198?	3.00	6.00	12.00

TAYLOR, BOBBY, AND THE VANCOUVERS

45s

Number	Title (A Side/B Side)	Yr	VG	VG+	NM
GORDY					
7069	Does Your Mama Know About Me/Fading Away	1968	5.00	10.00	20.00
7073	I Am Your Man/If You Love Her	1968	5.00	10.00	20.00
7079	Malinda/It's Growing	1968	5.00	10.00	20.00
7088	Oh I've Been Blessed/It Should Have Been Me Loving Her	1969	150.00	300.00	600.00
7092	My Girl Is Gone/It Should Have Been Me Loving Her	1969	5.00	10.00	20.00
INTEGRA					
103	This Is My Woman/(B-side unknown)	1968	25.00	50.00	100.00
MOWEST					
5006	Hey Lordy/Just a Little Bit Closer	1971	3.75	7.50	15.00
PLAYBOY					
6046	Why Play Games/Don't Wonder Why	1975	—	2.50	5.00
SUNFLOWER					
126	There Are Roses Somewhere in the World/It Was a Good Time	1972	6.25	12.50	25.00
V.I.P.					
25053	Oh I've Been Blessed/Blackmail	1969	6.25	12.50	25.00

Albums

Number	Title (A Side/B Side)	Yr	VG	VG+	NM
GORDY					
G-930 [M]	Bobby Taylor and the Vancouvers	1968	20.00	40.00	80.00
—Mono is promo only					
GS-930 [S]	Bobby Taylor and the Vancouvers	1968	15.00	30.00	60.00
GS-942	Taylor Made Soul	1969	15.00	30.00	60.00

TAYLOR, CARMEN

45s

Number	Title (A Side/B Side)	Yr	VG	VG+	NM
APOLLO					
489	Oh Please/Teen Age Ball	1956	15.00	30.00	60.00
ATLANTIC					
1002	Lovin' Daddy/Ding Dong	1953	12.50	25.00	50.00
1015	Big Mamou Daddy/Mamma Me and Johnny Free	1953	12.50	25.00	50.00
1041	Freddie/Ooh I	1954	30.00	60.00	120.00
GUYDEN					
100	Let Me Go Lover/No More, No Less	1954	10.00	20.00	40.00
KAMA SUTRA					
206	My Son/You're Puttin' Me On	1966	3.00	6.00	12.00
KING					
5085	So What/Why Did You Leave Me Alone	1957	12.50	25.00	50.00

TAYLOR, CHIP

45s

Number	Title (A Side/B Side)	Yr	VG	VG+	NM
BUDDAH					
325	Angel of the Morning/(B-side unknown)	1972	—	3.00	6.00
344	Londonderry Company/(B-side unknown)	1973	—	3.00	6.00
CAPITOL					
4692	Saint Sebastian/One Night Out with the Boys	1979	—	2.00	4.00
COLUMBIA					
10446	Hello Atlanta/Farmer's Daughter	1976	—	2.00	4.00
10520	Three Younger Bandits/Nothing Like You Girl	1977	—	2.00	4.00
44736	It's Such a Lonely Time of the Year/(B-side unknown)	1968	3.00	6.00	12.00
EPIC					
10567	It's Such a Lonely Time of Year/(Instrumental)	1969	2.50	5.00	10.00
MALA					
476	On My World/Joanie's Blues	1964	3.00	6.00	12.00
489	Suzannah (Comin' Home to Louisiana)/(B-side unknown)	1964	3.00	6.00	12.00
507	Young Love/Betty Ann	1965	2.50	5.00	10.00
MGM					
12993	Foolin' Around/Innocent Eyes	1961	5.00	10.00	20.00
13040	If You Don't Want Me Now/Sad Songs	1961	5.00	10.00	20.00
WARNER BROS.					
5314	Here I Am/I Love You But I Know	1962	3.75	7.50	15.00
5333	Lucky Star/A Guy Don't Need a Lot of Time	1963	3.75	7.50	15.00
8050	Me As I Am/Comin' From Behind	1974	—	2.00	4.00
8090	Early Sunday Morning/Shickshinny	1975	—	2.00	4.00
8128	Big River/John Tucker's On the Wagon Again	1975	—	2.00	4.00
8159	Circle of Tears/You're Alright, Charlie	1975	—	2.00	4.00

Albums

Number	Title (A Side/B Side)	Yr	VG	VG+	NM
BUDDAH					
BDS-5118	Gasoline	1972	3.00	6.00	12.00
CAPITOL					
ST-11909	Saint Sebastian	1979	2.50	5.00	10.00
COLUMBIA					
KC 34345	Somebody Shoot	1977	2.50	5.00	10.00
WARNER BROS.					
BS 2718	Last Chance	1973	3.00	6.00	12.00
BS 2824	Some of Us	1974	3.00	6.00	12.00

TAYLOR, EDDIE

45s

Number	Title (A Side/B Side)	Yr	VG	VG+	NM
VEE JAY					
149	Bad Boy/E.T. Blues	1955	30.00	60.00	120.00
185	Big Town Playboy/Ride 'Em On Down	1956	20.00	40.00	80.00
206	You'll Always Have a Home/Don't Knock at My Door	1956	15.00	30.00	60.00
267	I'm Gonna Love You/Looking for Trouble	1958	10.00	20.00	40.00
VIVID					
104	I'm Sitting Here/Do You Want Me to Cry	1964	5.00	10.00	20.00

TAYLOR, FAITH, AND THE SWEET TEENS

45s

Number	Title (A Side/B Side)	Yr	VG	VG+	NM
BEA & BABY					
104	I Need Him to Love Me/I Love You Darling	1959	12.50	25.00	50.00
FEDERAL					
12334	Your Candy Kisses/Won't Someone Tell Me Why?	1958	12.50	25.00	50.00

TAYLOR, JAMES

12-Inch Singles

Number	Title (A Side/B Side)	Yr	VG	VG+	NM
COLUMBIA					
ASF 358 [DJ]	Handy Man (mono/stereo)	1977	3.75	7.50	15.00
AS 1240 [DJ]	Summer's Here/Hard Times	1981	2.00	4.00	8.00

45s

Number	Title (A Side/B Side)	Yr	VG	VG+	NM
APPLE					
1805	Carolina in My Mind/Taking It In	1969	75.00	150.00	300.00
1805	Carolina in My Mind/Something's Wrong	1970	2.50	5.00	10.00
—With star on A-side label					
1805	Carolina in My Mind/Something's Wrong	1970	2.00	4.00	8.00
—Without star on A-side label					
1805 [DJ]	Carolina on My Mind/Something's Wrong	1970	7.50	15.00	30.00
—Promo with error in title on A-side					
COLUMBIA					
02093	Hard Times/Summer's Here	1981	—	—	3.00
02093 [PS]	Hard Times/Summer's Here	1981	—	2.00	4.00
05681	Everyday/Limousine Driver	1985	—	—	3.00
05681 [PS]	Everyday/Limousine Driver	1985	—	2.00	4.00
05785	Only One/Mona	1986	—	—	3.00
05785 [PS]	Only One/Mona	1986	—	—	3.00
05884	That's Why I'm Here/Going Around One More Time	1986	—	—	3.00
06278	Only a Dream in Rio/Turn Away	1986	—	—	3.00
07616	Never Die Young/Valentine's Day	1987	—	—	3.00
07616 [PS]	Never Die Young/Valentine's Day	1987	—	2.00	4.00
07948	Baby Boom Baby/Letter in the Mail	1988	—	—	3.00

Number	Title (A Side/B Side)	Yr	VG	VG+	NM
08493	Sweet Potato Pie/First of May	1988	—	—	3.00
10557	Handy Man/Bartender's Blues	1977	—	2.00	4.00
10602	Your Smiling Face/If I Keep My Heart Out of Sight	1977	—	2.00	4.00
10676	(What a) Wonderful World/Wooden Planes	1978	—	3.00	6.00
—By Art Garfunkel with Paul Simon and James Taylor; B-side is Garfunkel solo					
10689	Honey Don't Leave L.A./Another Grey Morning	1978	—	2.00	4.00
11005	Up on the Roof/Chanson Francaise	1979	—	2.00	4.00
60514	Her Town Too/Believe It or Not	1981	—	2.00	4.00
—A-side: James Taylor and J.D. Souther					
WARNER BROS.					
7387	Sweet Baby James/Suite for 20G	1970	2.00	4.00	8.00
7423	Fire and Rain/Anywhere Like Heaven	1970	2.00	4.00	8.00
7460	Country Road/Sunny Skies	1970	—	3.00	6.00
7498	You've Got a Friend/You Can Close Your Eyes	1971	—	3.00	6.00
7521	Long Ago and Far Away/Let Me Ride	1971	—	2.50	5.00
7655	Don't Let Me Be Lonely Tonight/Wow, Don't You Know	1972	—	2.50	5.00
7682	One Man Parade/Nobody But You	1973	—	2.50	5.00
7695	Hymn/Fanfare	1973	—	2.50	5.00
8015	Let It All Fall Down/Daddy's Baby	1974	—	2.50	5.00
8028	Walking Man/Daddy's Baby	1974	—	2.50	5.00
8109	How Sweet It Is (To Be Loved By You)/Sarah Maria	1975	—	2.50	5.00
8137	Mexico/Gorilla	1975	—	2.50	5.00
8222	Shower the People/I Can Dream of You	1976	—	2.50	5.00
8278	Woman's Gotta Have It/You Make It Easy	1976	—	2.50	5.00

Albums

Number	Title	Yr	VG	VG+	NM
APPLE					
SKAO 3352	James Taylor	1969	6.25	12.50	25.00
—With title in black print					
SKAO 3352	James Taylor	1970	5.00	10.00	20.00
—With title in orange print					
COLUMBIA					
JC 34811	JT	1977	2.50	5.00	10.00
PC 34811	JT	198?	2.00	4.00	8.00
FC 36058	Flag	1979	2.50	5.00	10.00
PC 36058	Flag	198?	2.00	4.00	8.00
PC 37009	Dad Loves His Work	198?	2.00	4.00	8.00
TC 37009	Dad Loves His Work	1981	2.50	5.00	10.00
FC 40052	That's Why I'm Here	1985	2.50	5.00	10.00
FC 40851	Never Die Young	1988	2.50	5.00	10.00
HC 47009	Dad Loves His Work	1983	10.00	20.00	40.00
—Half-speed mastered edition					
EUPHORIA					
EST-2	James Taylor and the Original Flying Machine 1967	1971	3.00	6.00	12.00
NAUTILUS					
NR-29	Gorilla	1981	10.00	20.00	40.00
—Audiophile pressing					
TRIP					
TLP-9513	Rainy Day Man	197?	2.50	5.00	10.00
—Reissue of Euphoria album					
WARNER BROS.					
WS 1843	Sweet Baby James	1970	6.25	12.50	25.00
—Very early pressings have green label with "W7" logo					
WS 1843	Sweet Baby James	1970	3.75	7.50	15.00
—Green "WB" label with no reference to other songs on front cover					
WS 1843	Sweet Baby James	1970	2.50	5.00	10.00
—Green "WB" label with "Contains Fire and Rain and Country Road" added to front cover					
WS 1843	Sweet Baby James	1973	2.00	4.00	8.00
—"Burbank" label or cream label					
BS 2561	Mud Slide Slim and the Blue Horizon	1971	2.50	5.00	10.00
—Green "WB" label					
BS 2561	Mud Slide Slim and the Blue Horizon	1973	2.00	4.00	8.00
—"Burbank" label or cream label					
BS 2660	One Man Dog	1972	2.50	5.00	10.00
—Green "WB" label					
BS 2660	One Man Dog	1973	2.00	4.00	8.00
—"Burbank" label or cream label					
BS4 2660 [Q]	One Man Dog	1975	3.75	7.50	15.00
BS 2794	Walking Man	1973	2.50	5.00	10.00
—"Burbank" label					
BS 2794	Walking Man	1979	2.00	4.00	8.00
—Cream label					
BS 2866	Gorilla	1975	2.50	5.00	10.00
—"Burbank" label					
BS 2866	Gorilla	1979	2.00	4.00	8.00
—Cream label					
BS4 2866 [Q]	Gorilla	1975	3.75	7.50	15.00
BS 2912	In the Pocket	1976	2.50	5.00	10.00
—"Burbank" label					
BS 2912	In the Pocket	1979	2.00	4.00	8.00
—Cream label					
BS 2979	Greatest Hits	1976	3.00	6.00	12.00
—This and other variations of this title have re-recorded versions of "Carolina in My Mind" and "Something in the Way She Moves."					
BSK 3113	Greatest Hits	1977	2.50	5.00	10.00
—"Burbank" label					
BSK 3113	Greatest Hits	1979	2.00	4.00	8.00
—Cream label					
ST-93138	Sweet Baby James	1970	5.00	10.00	20.00
—Capitol Record Club edition					

TAYLOR, JOHNNIE

12-Inch Singles

Number	Title (A Side/B Side)	Yr	VG	VG+	NM
BEVERLY GLEN					
BG 2002	What About My Love/Reaganomics	1982	2.50	5.00	10.00

45s

Number	Title (A Side/B Side)	Yr	VG	VG+	NM
BEVERLY GLEN					
2003	What About My Love/Reaganomics	1982	—	2.00	4.00
2004	I'm So Proud/I Need a Freak	1982	—	2.00	4.00
2007	Just Ain't Good Enough/Don't Wait	1983	—	2.00	4.00
2016	Seconds of Your Love/Shoot for the Stars	1983	—	2.00	4.00
COLUMBIA					
AE7 1153 [DJ]	God Is Standing By/God Is Amazing	1977	2.00	4.00	8.00
—B-side by Deniece Williams; promo with "Suggested Christmas Programming" on label					
10281	Disco Lady/You're the Best in the World	1976	—	2.50	5.00
10334	Somebody's Gettin' It/Please Don't Stop (That Song from Playing)	1976	—	2.50	5.00
10478	Love Is Better in the A.M. (Part 1)/Love Is Better in the A.M. (Part 2)	1977	—	2.50	5.00
10541	Your Love Is Rated X/Here I Go (Through These Chains Again)	1977	—	2.50	5.00
10610	Disco 9000/Right Now	1977	—	2.00	4.00
10709	Keep On Dancing/I Love to Make Love When It's Raining	1978	—	2.00	4.00
10776	Give Me My Baby/Ever Ready	1978	—	2.00	4.00
11084	(Ooh-Wee) She's Killing Me/Play Something Pretty	1979	—	2.00	4.00
11315	I Got This Thing for Your Love/Signing Off with Love	1980	—	2.00	4.00
11373	I Wanna Get Into You/Baby Don't Hesitate	1980	—	2.00	4.00
DERBY					
101	Shine, Shine, Shine/Dance What You Wanna	1963	3.75	7.50	15.00
1006	Baby, We've Got Love/In Love with You	1963	3.75	7.50	15.00
1010	I Need Lots of Love/Getting Married Soon	1964	3.75	7.50	15.00
MALACO					
2107	Lady, My Whole World Is You/L-O-V-E	1984	—	—	3.00
2111	Good with My Hips/This Is Your Night	1985	—	—	3.00
2118	Still Called the Blues/She's Cheatin' on Me	1985	—	—	3.00
2125	Wall to Wall/(B-side unknown)	1986	—	—	3.00
2128	Can I Love You/There's Nothing I Wouldn't Do	1986	—	—	3.00
2132	Just Because/When She Stops Asking	1987	—	—	3.00
2135	Don't Make Me Late/Happy Time	1987	—	—	3.00
2140	If I Lose Your Love/Something Is Going Wrong	1987	—	—	3.00
2143	Everything's Out in the Open/Got to Leave This Woman	1988	—	—	3.00
2153	In Control/I Found a Love	1989	—	—	3.00
2159	Still Crazy for You/(B-side unknown)	1989	—	—	3.00
RCA					
PB-11137	I Want You Back Again/Heaven Bless This Home	1977	—	2.50	5.00
SAR					
114	A Whole Lotta Woman/Why Oh Why	1961	5.00	10.00	20.00
131	Never Never/Rome (Wasn't Built in a Day)	1962	10.00	20.00	40.00
156	Oh, How I Love You/Run, But You Can't Hide	1964	3.75	7.50	15.00
STAX					
0009	Who's Making Love/I'm Trying	1968	2.00	4.00	8.00
0023	Take Care of Your Homework/Hold On This Time	1969	2.00	4.00	8.00
0033	Testify (I Wanna)/I Had a Fight with Love	1969	2.00	4.00	8.00
0042	Just Keep On Loving Me/My Life	1969	2.00	4.00	8.00
—With Carla Thomas					
0046	I Could Never Be President/It's Amazing	1969	2.00	4.00	8.00
0055	Love Bones/Mr. Nobody Is Somebody	1969	2.00	4.00	8.00
0068	Steal Away/Friday Night	1970	—	3.00	6.00
0078	I Am Somebody (Part 1)/I Am Somebody (Part 2)	1970	—	3.00	6.00
0085	Jody's Got Your Girl and Gone/A Fool Like Me	1970	—	3.00	6.00
0089	I Don't Wanna Lose You/Party Life	1971	—	3.00	6.00
0096	Hijackin' Love/Love in the Streets	1971	—	3.00	6.00
0114	Standing In for Jody/Shackin' Up	1972	—	3.00	6.00
0122	Doing My Own Thing (Part 1)/Doing My Own Thing (Part 2)	1972	—	3.00	6.00
0142	Stop Doggin' Me/Stop Teasin' Me	1972	—	3.00	6.00
0155	Don't You Fool with My Soul (Part 1)/Don't You Fool with My Soul (Part 2)	1973	—	3.00	6.00
0161	I Believe in You (You Believe in Me)/Love Depression	1973	—	3.00	6.00
—With A-side time listed at 4:37					
0161	I Believe in You (You Believe in Me)/Love Depression	1973	—	3.00	6.00
—With A-side time listed at 3:58					
0176	Cheaper to Keep Her/I Can Read Between the Lines	1973	—	3.00	6.00
186	I Had a Dream/Changes	1966	2.50	5.00	10.00
193	I Got to Love Somebody's Baby/Just the One I've Been Looking For	1966	2.50	5.00	10.00
0193	We're Getting Careless with Our Love/Poor Make Believer	1974	—	3.00	6.00
202	Little Bluebird/Toe Hold	1967	2.50	5.00	10.00
0208	I've Been Born Again/At Night Time	1974	—	3.00	6.00
209	Ain't That Loving You/Outside Love	1967	2.50	5.00	10.00
226	If I Had It to Do Over/You Can't Get Away from It	1967	2.50	5.00	10.00
0226	It's September/Just One Moment	1974	—	3.00	6.00
235	Somebody's Sleeping in My Bed/Strange Thing	1967	2.50	5.00	10.00
0241	Try Me Tonight/Free	1975	—	3.00	6.00
247	Next Time/Sundown	1968	2.50	5.00	10.00
253	I Ain't Particular/Where There's Smoke There's Fire	1968	2.50	5.00	10.00
3201	It Don't Pay to Get Up in the Mornin'/Just Keep On Loving Me	1977	—	2.50	5.00

Albums

Number	Title	Yr	VG	VG+	NM
BEVERLY GLEN					
10001	Just Ain't Good Enough	1982	3.00	6.00	12.00
COLUMBIA					
PC 33951	Eargasm	1976	3.00	6.00	12.00
—Originals have no bar code					
PC 33951	Eargasm	1986	2.00	4.00	8.00
—Budget-line reissue with bar code					
PCQ 33951 [Q]	Eargasm	1976	5.00	10.00	20.00
PC 34401	Rated Extraordinaire	1977	3.00	6.00	12.00
PCQ 34401 [Q]	Rated Extraordinaire	1977	5.00	10.00	20.00
JC 35340	Ever Ready	1978	3.00	6.00	12.00
JC 36061	She's Killing Me	1979	3.00	6.00	12.00
JC 36548	A New Day	1980	3.00	6.00	12.00
JC 37127	The Best of Johnnie Taylor	1981	3.00	6.00	12.00
ICHIBAN					
ICH-1022	Stuck in the Mud	198?	2.50	5.00	10.00
ICH-1042	Ugly Man	198?	2.50	5.00	10.00

Number	Title (A Side/B Side)	Yr	VG	VG+	NM
MALACO					
MAL-7421	This Is Your Night	198?	2.50	5.00	10.00
MAL-7431	Wall to Wall	198?	2.50	5.00	10.00
MAL-7440	Lover Boy	198?	2.50	5.00	10.00
MAL-7446	In Control	198?	2.50	5.00	10.00
MAL-7452	Crazy 'Bout You	1989	2.50	5.00	10.00
MAL-7460	Just Can't Do Right	1991	2.50	5.00	10.00
MAL-7463	The Best of Johnnie Taylor on Malaco, Vol. 1	1992	2.50	5.00	10.00
STAX					
ST-715 [M]	Wanted: One Soul Singer	1967	12.50	25.00	50.00
STS-715 [S]	Wanted: One Soul Singer	1967	15.00	30.00	60.00
STS-2005	Who's Making Love	1968	10.00	20.00	40.00
STS-2008	Raw Blues	1969	6.25	12.50	25.00
STS-2012	Rare Stamps	1969	6.25	12.50	25.00
STS-2023	The Johnnie Taylor Philosophy Continues	1969	6.25	12.50	25.00
STS-2030	One Step Beyond	1971	6.25	12.50	25.00
STS-2032	Johnnie Taylor's Greatest Hits	1970	6.25	12.50	25.00
STS-3014	Taylored in Silk	1973	5.00	10.00	20.00
STX-4115	Who's Making Love	198?	2.50	5.00	10.00
—Reissue of 2005					
STS-5509	Super Taylor	1974	5.00	10.00	20.00
STS-5521	The Best of Johnnie Taylor	1975	5.00	10.00	20.00
MPS-8508	Raw Blues	1982	2.50	5.00	10.00
MPS-8520	Super Hits	1983	2.50	5.00	10.00
MPS-8537	Taylored in Silk	1987	2.50	5.00	10.00
—Reissue of 3014					
MPS-8558	Little Bluebird	1988	2.50	5.00	10.00
88001 [(2)]	Chronicle	1977	5.00	10.00	20.00

TAYLOR, KATE

Number	Title (A Side/B Side)	Yr	VG	VG+	NM
45s					
COLUMBIA					
10596	It's In His Kiss (The Shoop Shoop Song)/Jason and Ida	1977	—	2.00	4.00
10787	It's Growin'/Slow and Steady	1978	—	2.00	4.00
11017	It's the Same Old Song/Champagne and Wine	1979	—	2.00	4.00
COTILLION					
44112	Handbags and Gladrags/You Can Close Your Eyes	1971	—	2.50	5.00
44124	Lo and Behold-Jesus Is Just Alright/Home Again	1971	—	2.50	5.00
Albums					
COLUMBIA					
JC 35089	Kate Taylor	1978	2.50	5.00	10.00
JC 36034	It's In There and It's Got to Come Out	1979	2.50	5.00	10.00
COTILLION					
SD 9045	Sister Kate	1971	2.50	5.00	10.00

TAYLOR, KINGSIZE, AND THE DOMINOES

Number	Title (A Side/B Side)	Yr	VG	VG+	NM
Albums					
MIDNIGHT					
HLP-2101 [M]	Real Gonk Man	1965	12.50	25.00	50.00
HST-2101 [S]	Real Gonk Man	1965	25.00	50.00	100.00

TAYLOR, LITTLE JOHNNY

Number	Title (A Side/B Side)	Yr	VG	VG+	NM
45s					
GALAXY					
718	You'll Need Another Favor/What You Need Is a Ball	1963	3.00	6.00	12.00
722	Part Time Love/Somewhere Down the Line	1963	5.00	10.00	20.00
725	Since I Found a New Love/My Heart Is Filled with Pain	1963	3.00	6.00	12.00
729	First Class Love/If You Love Me	1964	2.50	5.00	10.00
731	You Win, I Lose/Nightingale Melody	1964	2.50	5.00	10.00
733	True Love/I Smell Trouble	1964	2.50	5.00	10.00
735	For Your Precious Love/I've Never Had a Woman Like You Before	1965	2.00	4.00	8.00
736	Help Yourself/Somebody's Got to Pay	1965	2.00	4.00	8.00
739	One More Chance/Looking at the Future	1965	2.00	4.00	8.00
743	Please Come Home For Christmas/Miracle Maker	1965	2.00	4.00	8.00
745	My Love Is Real/All I Want Is You	1966	2.00	4.00	8.00
748	Zig Zag Lightning/The Things I Used to Do	1966	2.00	4.00	8.00
752	I Know You Hear Me Calling/Big Blue Diamonds	1967	2.00	4.00	8.00
756	Driving Wheel/Darling Believe in Me	1967	2.00	4.00	8.00
764	Double or Nothing/Sometimey Woman	1968	2.00	4.00	8.00
ICHIBAN					
169	Christmas Is Here Again/Ugly Man	1988	—	3.00	6.00
174	Christmas Is Here Again/I Enjoy You	1989	—	3.00	6.00
RONN					
43	Make Love to Me Baby/Sweet Soul Woman	1970	—	3.00	6.00
48	How Can a Broke Man Survive/Make Love to Me Baby	1970	—	3.00	6.00
51	How Are You Fixed for Love/Keep On Keepin' On	1971	—	3.00	6.00
55	Everybody Knows About My Good Thing Pt. 1/Pt. 2	1971	—	3.00	6.00
59	It's My Fault Darling/There Is Something On Your Mind	1972	—	3.00	6.00
64	Open House at My House (Part 1)/Open House at My House (Part 2)	1972	—	3.00	6.00
66	As Long As I Don't See You/Strange Bed with a Bad Head	1972	—	3.00	6.00
69	I'll Make It Worth Your While/You're Not the Only One	1973	—	3.00	6.00
73	My Special Rose/A Thousand Miles Away	1973	—	3.00	6.00
78	You're Savin' Your Best Lovin' for Me/What Would I Do Without You	1974	—	3.00	6.00
83	I Don't Want It All/I Can't See Myself As a One-Woman Man	1974	—	3.00	6.00
85	Found a New Love/Oh, How I Love My Baby	1975	—	3.00	6.00
87	True Love/When Are You Coming Home	1975	—	3.00	6.00
88	A Hard Head Makes a Sore Behind/The Future	1976	—	3.00	6.00
92	L.J.T./I Should Have Known	197?	—	3.00	6.00
98	Just One More Chance/New Song	197?	—	3.00	6.00
Albums					
FANTASY					
MPF-4510	Little Johnny Taylor's Greatest Hits	1982	2.50	5.00	10.00
GALAXY					
203 [M]	Little Johnny Taylor	1963	25.00	50.00	100.00
207 [M]	Little Johnny Taylor's Greatest Hits	1964	25.00	50.00	100.00
8203 [S]	Little Johnny Taylor	1963	37.50	75.00	150.00
8207 [S]	Little Johnny Taylor's Greatest Hits	1964	37.50	75.00	150.00
RONN					
LPS-7530	Everybody Knows About My Good Thing	1972	6.25	12.50	25.00
LSP-7532	Open House at My House	1973	6.25	12.50	25.00
LSP-7535	L.J.T.	1975	5.00	10.00	20.00

TAYLOR, LITTLE JOHNNY, AND TED TAYLOR

Number	Title (A Side/B Side)	Yr	VG	VG+	NM
45s					
RONN					
75	Walking the Floor/Cry It Out Baby	1973	—	3.00	6.00
89	Pretending Love/Funky Ghetto	1976	—	3.00	6.00
Albums					
RONN					
LSP-7533	The Super Taylors	1973	5.00	10.00	20.00

TAYLOR, LIVINGSTON

Number	Title (A Side/B Side)	Yr	VG	VG+	NM
45s					
CAPRICORN					
0032	Somewhere Over the Rainbow/Lady Tomorrow	1973	—	2.00	4.00
0045	I Can Dream of You/Loving Be My New Horizon	1974	—	2.00	4.00
8012	Carolina Day/Sit On Back	1971	—	2.50	5.00
8025	Get Out of Bed/Mom, Dad	1971	—	2.50	5.00
CRITIQUE					
99255	City Lights/Louie	1989	—	—	3.00
EPIC					
50604	I Will Be in Love with You/How Much Your Sweet Love Means to Me	1978	—	2.00	4.00
50667	I'll Come Running/No Thank You Skycap	1979	—	2.00	4.00
50894	First Time Love/Pajamas	1980	—	2.00	4.00
Albums					
ATCO					
SD 33-334	Livingston Taylor	1970	3.00	6.00	12.00
CAPRICORN					
CP 0114	Over the Rainbow	1973	2.50	5.00	10.00
863	Liv	1971	2.50	5.00	10.00
EPIC					
JE 36153	Man's Best Friend	1979	2.50	5.00	10.00

TAYLOR, MAD MAN

Number	Title (A Side/B Side)	Yr	VG	VG+	NM
45s					
EASTWEST					
117	Rumble Tumble/Rock and Roll Espanola	1958	18.75	37.50	75.00

TAYLOR, R. DEAN

Number	Title (A Side/B Side)	Yr	VG	VG+	NM
45s					
20TH CENTURY					
2510	Let's Talk It Over/Add Up the Score	1981	—	2.00	4.00
AUDIO MASTER					
1	At the High School Dance/How Wrong Can You Be?	1960	50.00	100.00	200.00
FARR					
001	We'll Show Them All/Magdalena	1976	—	2.50	5.00
MALA					
444	I'll Remember/It's a Long Way to St. Louis	1962	25.00	50.00	100.00
RARE EARTH					
5013	Indiana Wants Me/Love's Your Name	1970	—	3.00	6.00
5023	Ain't It a Sad Thing/Back Street	1970	—	2.50	5.00
5023 [PS]	Ain't It a Sad Thing/Back Street	1970	2.50	5.00	10.00
5026	Gotta See Jane/Back Street	1971	—	2.50	5.00
5030	Candy Apple Red/Woman Alive	1971	—	2.50	5.00
5041	Taos New Mexico/Shadow	1972	—	2.50	5.00
STRUMMER					
3748	Let's Talk It Over/(B-side unknown)	1982	—	2.00	4.00
V.I.P.					
25042	Don't Fool Around/There's a Ghost in My House	1966	6.25	12.50	25.00
25045	Gotta See Jane/Don't Fool Around	1967	6.25	12.50	25.00
Albums					
RARE EARTH					
RS-522	I Think, Therefore I Am	1971	3.75	7.50	15.00

TAYLOR, RENEE

Number	Title (A Side/B Side)	Yr	VG	VG+	NM
45s					
FELSTED					
8620	His Pigs/I'm in Love with Jack	1961	3.00	6.00	12.00

TAYLOR, SHEILA

Number	Title (A Side/B Side)	Yr	VG	VG+	NM
45s					
MELODYLAND					
6013	How Important Can It Be/She Satisfies	1975	—	2.50	5.00

TAYLOR, SHERRI

Number	Title (A Side/B Side)	Yr	VG	VG+	NM
45s					
GLORECO					
1002	I've Got a Crush/(B-side unknown)	196?	15.00	30.00	60.00
MOTOWN					
1004	Lover/That's Why I Love You So Much	1960	10.00	20.00	40.00
—With Singin' Sammy Ward					

Number	Title (A Side/B Side)	Yr	VG	VG+	NM

TAYLOR, TRUE
See PAUL SIMON.

TAYLOR, VERNON
45s
DOT

15632	I've Got the Blues/The Losing Game	1957	25.00	50.00	100.00
15697	Satisfaction Guaranteed/Why Must You Leave Me	1958	12.50	25.00	50.00
SUN					
310	Breeze/Today Is a Blue Day	1958	6.25	12.50	25.00
325	Sweet and Easy to Love/Mystery Train	1959	8.75	17.50	35.00

TAYLOR, VINCE
45s
PALETTE

5065	I'll Be Your Hero/Jet Black Machine	1960	3.00	6.00	12.00
5084	Move Over Tiger/What Cha Gonna Do	1961	3.00	6.00	12.00

TAYLOR, ZOLA
45s
RPM

405	Make Love to Me/Oh My Dear	1954	75.00	150.00	300.00

TAZMEN, THE
45s
ABC-PARAMOUNT

9812	Easy Pickin'/The Chicken	1957	3.75	7.50	15.00

TEA COMPANY, THE
45s
SMASH

2176	Come and Have Some Tea with Me/Flowers	1968	3.75	7.50	15.00

Albums
SMASH

SRS-67105	Come and Have Some Tea	1968	12.50	25.00	50.00

TEAM MATES, THE
45s
ABC-PARAMOUNT

10760	If Only I Had Known/You Must Pay	1965	3.00	6.00	12.00
LE CAM					
701	I Just Might/Sooner or Later	196?	6.25	12.50	25.00
706	If Only I Had Known/You Must Pay	196?	6.25	12.50	25.00
707	Once There Was a Time/Come On Baby	1962	6.25	12.50	25.00
PAULA					
220	Most of All/Please Believe Me	1965	7.50	15.00	30.00
PHILIPS					
40029	Once There Was a Time/Never Believed in Love	1962	3.00	6.00	12.00

TEARDROPS, THE (1)
45s
DORE

679	Little Orphan Boy/(Instrumental)	1963	3.00	6.00	12.00

TEARDROPS, THE (2)
45s
DOT

15669	Bridge of Love/Jellyfish	1957	6.25	12.50	25.00
RENDEZVOUS					
102	Catch Me, I'm Falling Again/Sugar Baby	1958	7.50	15.00	30.00

TEARDROPS, THE (3)
45s
JOSIE

766	The Stars Are Out Tonight/Oh Stop It	1954	75.00	150.00	300.00
771	My Heart/Ooh Baby	1954	125.00	250.00	500.00
PORT					
70019	The Stars Are Out Tonight/Oh Stop It	1960	6.25	12.50	25.00

TEARDROPS, THE (4)
Even though on the same label as group (3), this is a different group.
45s
JOSIE

856	We Won't Tell/Al Chiar Di Luna (Porto Fortuna)	1959	6.25	12.50	25.00
862	Cry No More/You're My Hollywood Star	1959	6.25	12.50	25.00
873	Daddy's Little Girl/Always You	1960	6.25	12.50	25.00

TEARDROPS, THE (5)
45s
KING

5004	My Inspiration/I Prayed for Love	1956	6.25	12.50	25.00
5037	After School/Don't Be Afraid to Love	1957	6.25	12.50	25.00

TEARDROPS, THE (6)
Girl group.
45s
MUSICOR

1139	Tears Come Tumbling/You Won't Be There	1965	3.75	7.50	15.00
1218	I Will Love You Dear Forever/Bubblegummers	1966	3.75	7.50	15.00
SAXONY					
1007	Tonight I'm Gonna Fall in Love Again/That's Why I'll Get By	1964	20.00	40.00	80.00
1008	I'm Gonna Steal Your Boyfriend/Call Me and I'll Be Happy	1965	6.25	12.50	25.00
1009	Tears Come Tumbling/You Won't Be There	1965	5.00	10.00	20.00

TEARDROPS, THE (7)
45s
SAMPSON

634	Come Back to Me/Sweet Lovin' Daddy-O	1952	100.00	200.00	400.00

TEARDROPS, THE (U)
Albums
20TH CENTURY FOX

FXG-5011 [M]	The Teardrops at Trinchi's	1963	6.25	12.50	25.00

TEASERS, THE
45s
CHECKER

800	I Was a Fool to Love You/How Could You Hurt One So	1954	150.00	300.00	600.00
800	I Was a Fool to Love You/How Could You Hurt One So	1954	300.00	600.00	1200.
—Red vinyl					

TECHNICS, THE
45s
CHEX

1010	Has He Told You/Workout With a Pretty Girl	1963	7.50	15.00	30.00
—As "Tony and the Technics"					
1012	Because I Really Love You/A Man's Confusion	1963	7.50	15.00	30.00
1013	Hey Girl Don't Leave Me/I Met Her on the First of September	1963	10.00	20.00	40.00

TECHNIQUES, THE
45s
ROULETTE

4030	Hey! Little Girl/In a Round-About Way	1957	6.25	12.50	25.00
4048	(Why Did I Ever) Let Her Go/Marindy	1958	6.25	12.50	25.00
4097	The Wisest Man You Know/Moon Tan	1958	6.25	12.50	25.00
STARS					
551	Hey Little Girl/In a Round-About Way	1957	10.00	20.00	40.00

TEDDY AND HIS PATCHES
45s
CHANCE

100	Suzy Creamcheese/From Day to Day	1967	25.00	50.00	100.00
668	Suzy Creamcheese/It Ain't Nothin'	1967	25.00	50.00	100.00
669	Haight Ashbury/It Ain't Nothin'	1967	25.00	50.00	100.00

TEDDY AND THE CONTINENTALS
45s
PIK

235	Tick Tick Tock/Everybody Pony	1961	6.25	12.50	25.00
RAGO					
201	Tick Tick Tock/Wild Christening Party	1962	6.25	12.50	25.00
—B-side by the Teen Kings					
RICHIE					
445	Do You/Tighten Up	1961	25.00	50.00	100.00
—With no mention of Roulette distribution on label					
445	Do You/Tighten Up	1961	10.00	20.00	40.00
—With Roulette Records distribution mentioned on label					
453	Crying Over You/Crossfire With Me Baby	1963	12.50	25.00	50.00
1001	Tick Tick Tock/Everybody Pony	1961	15.00	30.00	60.00

TEDDY BEARS, THE
With PHIL SPECTOR and Annette Kleinbard (a.k.a. Carol Connors).
45s
DORE

503	To Know Him, Is to Love Him/Don't You Worry My Little Pet	1958	7.50	15.00	30.00
520	Wonderful Loveable You/Till You'll Be Mine	1959	5.00	10.00	20.00
IMPERIAL					
5562	Oh Why/I Don't Need You Anymore	1959	7.50	15.00	30.00
5581	You Said Goodbye/If You Only Knew	1959	7.50	15.00	30.00
5594	Seven Lonely Days/Don't Go Away	1959	7.50	15.00	30.00

Albums
IMPERIAL

LP-9067 [M]	The Teddy Bears Sing!	1959	75.00	150.00	300.00
LP-12010 [S]	The Teddy Bears Sing!	1959	300.00	600.00	1200.

TEDDY BOYS, THE
45s
CAMEO

433	Where Have All the Good Times Gone/La La	1966	5.00	10.00	20.00
448	Mona/Good Morning Blues	1966	5.00	10.00	20.00
MGM					
13515	Jezebel/It's You	1966	5.00	10.00	20.00

TEE, WILLIE
45s
ATLANTIC

2273	Teasin' You/Walkin' Up a One-Way Street	1965	2.50	5.00	10.00
2287	Thank You John/Dedicated to You	1965	2.50	5.00	10.00
2302	I Want Somebody/You Better Say Yes	1965	2.50	5.00	10.00
A.F.O.					
307	All for One/Always Accused	1962	3.75	7.50	15.00
311	Why Lie/I Found Out You Are My Cousin	1963	3.75	7.50	15.00
CAPITOL					
2369	Walk Tall (Baby, That's What I Need)/I'm Only a Man	1968	2.00	4.00	8.00
2892	Reach Out for Me/The Love of a Married Man	1970	2.00	4.00	8.00
CINDERELLA					
1202	Foolish Girl/(B-side unknown)	196?	10.00	20.00	40.00
GATOR					
701	She Really Did Surprise Me/(B-side unknown)	196?	7.50	15.00	30.00

Number	Title (A Side/B Side)	Yr	VG	VG+	NM
HOT LINE					
910	Close Your Eyes/I Heard Everything You Said	196?	2.00	4.00	8.00
NOLA					
708	Teasin' You/Walkin' Up a One-Way Street	1964	62.50	125.00	250.00
UNITED ARTISTS					
XW910	I'd Give It to You/Look Out World	1976	—	2.50	5.00
Albums					
CAPITOL					
ST-199	I'm Only a Man	1969	3.75	7.50	15.00
UNITED ARTISTS					
UA-LA655-G	Anticipation	1976	3.00	6.00	12.00

TEE SET, THE

Number	Title (A Side/B Side)	Yr	VG	VG+	NM
45s					
COLOSSUS					
107	Ma Belle Amie/Angels Coming in the Holy Night	1969	—	2.50	5.00
107 [PS]	Ma Belle Amie/Angels Coming in the Holy Night	1969	—	3.00	6.00
114	If You Do Believe in Love/Charmaine	1970	—	2.00	4.00
139	She Likes Weeds/(B-side unknown)	1971	—	2.00	4.00
Albums					
COLOSSUS					
CCS-1001	Ma Belle Amie	1970	3.75	7.50	15.00

TEEGARDEN AND VAN WINKLE

Number	Title (A Side/B Side)	Yr	VG	VG+	NM
45s					
PLUMM					
68102	God, Love, and Rock & Roll (We Believe)/Work Me Tomorrow	1970	3.75	7.50	15.00
WESTBOUND					
170	God, Love and Rock & Roll/Work Me Tomorrow	1970	—	2.50	5.00
170 [PS]	God, Love and Rock & Roll/Work Me Tomorrow	1970	—	3.00	6.00
171	Everything Is Going to Be All Right/You Do	1970	—	2.50	5.00
187	Stoned on the Love for Jesus/I Need You	1971	—	2.50	5.00
200	Passing Gas/Ride Away with Me	1971	—	2.50	5.00
210	Carry On/Ride Away with Me	1972	—	2.50	5.00
Albums					
ATCO					
SD 33-272	An Evening at Home	1968	3.75	7.50	15.00
WESTBOUND					
2003	But Anyhow	1969	3.75	7.50	15.00
2010	On Our Way	1971	3.75	7.50	15.00

TEEMATES, THE

Number	Title (A Side/B Side)	Yr	VG	VG+	NM
45s					
AUDIO FIDELITY					
104	Dream On Little Girl/Moving Out	1964	3.75	7.50	15.00
105	Night Fall/No More Tomorrows	1964	3.75	7.50	15.00
Albums					
AUDIO FIDELITY					
AFLP-3042 [M]	Jet Set Dance Discotheque	1964	10.00	20.00	40.00
AFSD-7042 [S]	Jet Set Dance Discotheque	1964	12.50	25.00	50.00

TEEN ANGELS, THE

Number	Title (A Side/B Side)	Yr	VG	VG+	NM
45s					
SUN					
388	Ain't Gonna Let You (Break My Heart)/Tell Me My Love	1964	7.50	15.00	30.00

TEEN CLEFS, THE

Number	Title (A Side/B Side)	Yr	VG	VG+	NM
45s					
DICE					
98/99	Sputnik/Hiding My Tears with a Smile	1959	37.50	75.00	150.00

TEEN KINGS, THE

See ROY ORBISON.

TEEN-KINGS, THE

Number	Title (A Side/B Side)	Yr	VG	VG+	NM
45s					
BEE					
1114/5	That's a Teen-Age Love/Tell Me If You Know	1959	500.00	1000.	1500.
—Legitimate original copies are on black vinyl					
WILLETT					
118	Don't Just Stand There/My Greatest Wish	1959	62.50	125.00	250.00

TEEN QUEENS, THE

Number	Title (A Side/B Side)	Yr	VG	VG+	NM
45s					
ANTLER					
4014	There's Nothing on My Mind (Part 1)/There's Nothing on My Mind (Part 2)	1959	3.75	7.50	15.00
4015	Politician/I'm a Fool	1959	3.75	7.50	15.00
4016	Donny (Part 1)/Donny (Part 2)	1960	3.75	7.50	15.00
4017	I Hear Violins/Magoo Can See	1960	3.75	7.50	15.00
KENT					
359	Eddie My Love/Just Goofed	1961	3.00	6.00	12.00
RCA VICTOR					
47-7206	Dear Tommy/You Good Boy-You Get Cookie	1958	4.00	8.00	16.00
47-7396	Movie Star/First Crush	1958	4.00	8.00	16.00
RPM					
453	Eddie My Love/Just Goofed	1956	7.50	15.00	30.00
—Black label					
453	Eddie My Love/Just Goofed	1956	30.00	60.00	120.00
—Red label					
460	So All Alone/Baby Mine	1956	6.25	12.50	25.00
464	Billy Boy/Until the Day I Die	1956	6.25	12.50	25.00
470	Red Top/Love Sweet Love	1956	6.25	12.50	25.00
480	My First Love/(B-side unknown)	1956	6.25	12.50	25.00
484	Rock Everybody/My Heart's Desire	1957	5.00	10.00	20.00
500	I Miss You/Two Loves and Two Lives	1957	5.00	10.00	20.00
Albums					
CROWN					
CST-373 [R]	The Teen Queens	1963	7.50	15.00	30.00
CLP-5022 [M]	Eddie My Love	1956	62.50	125.00	250.00
CLP-5373 [M]	The Teen Queens	1963	12.50	25.00	50.00
RPM					
LRP-3007 [M]	Eddie My Love	1956	—	—	—
—Canceled					

TEEN TONES, THE

More than one group. Some may be listed as "Teen-Tones."

Number	Title (A Side/B Side)	Yr	VG	VG+	NM
45s					
DANDY DAN					
2	Darling I Love You/My Sweet	1958	20.00	40.00	80.00
DECCA					
30895	Don't Call Me Baby, I'll Call You/Yes You May	1959	7.50	15.00	30.00
GONE					
5061	The Rockin' Rumble/Latino Part 2	1959	7.50	15.00	30.00
SWAN					
4040	My Little Baby/Head Strong Baby	1959	7.50	15.00	30.00
TRI-DISC					
102	I'm So Happy/Shoutin' Twist	1961	3.75	7.50	15.00
WYNNE					
107	Faded Love/Gypsy Boogie	1958	6.25	12.50	25.00

TEENAGE MOONLIGHTERS

Number	Title (A Side/B Side)	Yr	VG	VG+	NM
45s					
MARK					
134	Sorry Sorry/I Want to Cry	1960	1000.	1500.	2000.

TEENAGERS, THE

These are records by the original group without FRANKIE LYMON. Also see FRANKIE LYMON AND THE TEENAGERS.

Number	Title (A Side/B Side)	Yr	VG	VG+	NM
45s					
END					
1071	Crying/Tonight's the Night	1960	15.00	30.00	60.00
1076	Can You Tell Me/A Little Wiser Now	1960	10.00	20.00	40.00
GEE					
1046	Flip Flop/Everything to Me	1957	7.50	15.00	30.00
ROULETTE					
4086	My Broken Heart/Momma Wanna Rock	1958	20.00	40.00	80.00

TEENBEATS, THE

Number	Title (A Side/B Side)	Yr	VG	VG+	NM
45s					
TEENBEAT					
(No #)	Surfbound/Mr. Moto	1963	20.00	40.00	80.00

TEENETTES, THE

Number	Title (A Side/B Side)	Yr	VG	VG+	NM
45s					
BRUNSWICK					
55125	I Want a Boy with a Hi-Fi Supersonic Stereophonic Bloop Bleep/From the Word Go	1959	6.25	12.50	25.00
JOSIE					
830	My Lucky Star/Too Young to Fall in Love	1958	15.00	30.00	60.00

TELSTARS, THE

Number	Title (A Side/B Side)	Yr	VG	VG+	NM
45s					
COLUMBIA					
44141	Keep On Running/Hold Tight	1967	5.00	10.00	20.00
IMPERIAL					
5903	Continental Mash/Stomp Happy	1962	6.25	12.50	25.00
TEEN					
510	Continental Mash/Stomp Happy	1962	10.00	20.00	40.00
513	Pow Wow/Lovina	1963	8.75	17.50	35.00
516	Topless/Spaghetti Strap	1964	8.75	17.50	35.00
517	Tough George/'Cause I Really Do	1964	8.75	17.50	35.00

TEMPEST

Number	Title (A Side/B Side)	Yr	VG	VG+	NM
Albums					
WARNER BROS.					
BS 2682	Tempest	1973	6.25	12.50	25.00

TEMPLE, BOB

Number	Title (A Side/B Side)	Yr	VG	VG+	NM
45s					
KING					
4958	Come Back, Come Back/Vam Vam Vamoose	1956	7.50	15.00	30.00

TEMPO, NINO

Also see NINO TEMPO AND APRIL STEVENS.

Number	Title (A Side/B Side)	Yr	VG	VG+	NM
45s					
A&M					
1461	Sister James/Clair De Lune (In Jazz)	1973	—	2.00	4.00
1499	Roll It/Hawkeye	1974	—	2.00	4.00
1532	High on the Music/Come See Me 'Round Midnight	1974	—	2.00	4.00
1625	Gettin' Off/Don't Stop Now	1974	—	2.00	4.00
2131	Hooked on Young Stuff/Ronan's Road	1979	—	2.00	4.00
RCA VICTOR					
47-7424	15 Girl Friends/Loonie 'Bout Junie	1958	3.00	6.00	12.00
47-7647	Ding-a-Ling/When You Were Sweet Sixteen	1959	3.00	6.00	12.00
47-7694	Jack the Ripper/Main Theme from "Jack the Ripper"	1960	2.50	5.00	10.00
—B-side by Pete Rugolo					
TOWER					
369	Boys Town/Boys Town (Sing Along)	1967	—	3.00	6.00
UNITED ARTISTS					
256	What Is Love to a Teenager/Lipstick on Your Lips	1960	2.50	5.00	10.00
Albums					
A&M					
SP-3629	Come See Me 'Round Midnight	1974	2.50	5.00	10.00

Number	Title (A Side/B Side)	Yr	VG	VG+	NM
LIBERTY					
LRP-3023 [M]	Rock 'n' Roll Beach Party	1958	30.00	60.00	120.00

TEMPO, NINO, AND APRIL STEVENS

Also see each artist's individual listings.

45s

Number	Title (A Side/B Side)	Yr	VG	VG+	NM
ATCO					
6224	Sweet and Lovely/True Love	1962	2.50	5.00	10.00
6248	Indian Love Call/Paradise	1962	2.50	5.00	10.00
6263	Together We'll Always Be/Baby Weemus	1963	2.50	5.00	10.00
6273	Deep Purple/I've Been Carrying a Torch for You So Long That I Burned a Great Big Hole in My Heart	1963	3.00	6.00	12.00
6281	Whispering/Tweedledee	1963	2.50	5.00	10.00
6286	Stardust/I-45	1964	2.00	4.00	8.00
6294	Tea for Two/I'm Confessin' (That I Love You)	1964	2.00	4.00	8.00
6306	I Surrender Dear/Who	1964	2.00	4.00	8.00
6314	Melancholy Baby/Ooh La La	1964	2.00	4.00	8.00
6325	Our Love/Honeywell Rose	1964	2.00	4.00	8.00
6337	These Arms of Mine/The Coldest Night of the Year	1965	2.00	4.00	8.00
6350	Swing Me/Tomorrow Is Soon a Memory	1965	2.00	4.00	8.00
6360	Think of You/I'm Sweet on You	1965	2.00	4.00	8.00
6368	That's My Desire/King Kong	1965	2.00	4.00	8.00
6375	I Love How You Love Me/Tears of Sorrow	1965	2.00	4.00	8.00
6391	Hey Baby/The Poison of Your Kisses	1965	2.00	4.00	8.00
6410	Bye Bye Blues/King Kong	1966	2.00	4.00	8.00
6897	She's My Baby/Tomorrow Is Soon a Memory	1972	—	3.00	6.00
A&M					
1394	Love Story/Hoochy Coochy — Wing Dang Doo	1972	—	2.00	4.00
1443	Put It Where You Want It/I Can't Get Over You Baby	1973	—	2.00	4.00
1674	Never Had a Lover/You Turn Me On	1975	—	2.00	4.00
BELL					
769	Did I or Didn't I/Yesterday I Heard the Rain	1969	2.00	4.00	8.00
823	Seas of Love-Dock of the Bay/Twilight	1969	2.00	4.00	8.00
CHELSEA					
3052	What Kind of Fool Am I/(B-side unknown)	1976	—	2.00	4.00
MGM					
13825	Falling in Love Again/Wanting You	1967	2.00	4.00	8.00
14266	How About Me/Makin' Love to Rainbow Colors	1971	—	3.00	6.00
UNITED ARTISTS					
272	Ooeah (That's What You Do to Me)/High School Sweetheart	1960	2.50	5.00	10.00
WHITE WHALE					
236	All Strung Out/I Can't Go On Living (Baby Without You)	1966	2.00	4.00	8.00
241	You'll Be Needing Me Baby/Habit of Lovin' You Baby	1966	2.00	4.00	8.00
246	Wings of Love/My Old Flame	1967	2.00	4.00	8.00
252	I Can't Go On Living Baby Without You/Little Child	1967	2.00	4.00	8.00
268	Let It Be Me/Words of Love	1968	2.00	4.00	8.00
271	Ooh Poo Pa Doo/Let It Be Me	1968	2.00	4.00	8.00

Albums

Number	Title (A Side/B Side)	Yr	VG	VG+	NM
ATCO					
33-156 [M]	Deep Purple	1963	10.00	20.00	40.00
SD 33-156 [S]	Deep Purple	1963	12.50	25.00	50.00
33-162 [M]	Nino Tempo and April Stevens Sing the Great Songs	1964	7.50	15.00	30.00
SD 33-162 [S]	Nino Tempo and April Stevens Sing the Great Songs	1964	10.00	20.00	40.00
33-180 [M]	Hey Baby	1966	7.50	15.00	30.00
SD 33-180 [S]	Hey Baby	1966	10.00	20.00	40.00
WHITE WHALE					
WW-113 [M]	All Strung Out	1967	5.00	10.00	20.00
WWS-7113 [S]	All Strung Out	1967	6.25	12.50	25.00

TEMPO-TONES, THE

45s

Number	Title (A Side/B Side)	Yr	VG	VG+	NM
ACME					
713	Get Yourself Another Fool/Ride Along	1957	37.50	75.00	150.00
715	In My Dreams/My Boy Sleep Pete	1957	125.00	250.00	500.00
718	Come Into My Heart/Somewhere There Is Sunshine	1957	125.00	250.00	500.00
722	The Day I Met You/Wishing All the Time	1957	100.00	200.00	400.00

TEMPOS, THE

Probably more than one group.

45s

Number	Title (A Side/B Side)	Yr	VG	VG+	NM
ASCOT					
2167	When You Loved Me/My Barbara Ann	1965	6.25	12.50	25.00
2173	I Wish It Were Summer/My Barbara Ann	1965	6.25	12.50	25.00
CANTERBURY					
504	Here I Come (Countdown) Part 1/Here I Come (Countdown) Part 2	1967	3.75	7.50	15.00
CLIMAX					
102	See You in September/Bless You My Love	1959	5.00	10.00	20.00
105	The Crossroads of Love/Whatever Happens	1959	5.00	10.00	20.00
FAIRMOUNT					
611	Oh Play That Thing/Monkey Doo	1963	3.00	6.00	12.00
HI-Q					
100	It's Tough/Sham-Rock	1959	10.00	20.00	40.00
KAPP					
178	Kingdom of Love/That's What You Do to Me	1957	6.25	12.50	25.00
199	Prettiest Girl in School/Never You Mind	1957	6.25	12.50	25.00
213	I Got a Job/Strollin' with My Baby	1958	6.25	12.50	25.00
MONTEL					
955	I Gotta Make a Move/It Was You	1966	3.75	7.50	15.00
PARIS					
550	Look Homeward, Angel/Under Ten Flags	1960	5.00	10.00	20.00
RHYTHM					
121	Promise Me/Never Let Me Go	1958	125.00	250.00	500.00
RILEY'S					
8781	Don't Leave Me/I Need You	1966	7.50	15.00	30.00
U.S.A.					
810	Why Don't You Write Me/A Thief in the Night	1965	6.25	12.50	25.00

Albums

Number	Title (A Side/B Side)	Yr	VG	VG+	NM
JUSTICE					
JLP-104	Speaking of the Tempos	1966	125.00	250.00	500.00

TEMPREES

45s

Number	Title (A Side/B Side)	Yr	VG	VG+	NM
EPIC					
50192	I Found Love on a Disco Floor/There Ain't a Dream Been Dreamed	1976	—	2.50	5.00
WE PRODUCE					
1801	I'm for You, You for Me/Rules and Regulations	1971	2.00	4.00	8.00
1803	(Girl) I Love You/I Love You, You Love Me	1971	2.00	4.00	8.00
1805	My Baby Love/If I Could Say What's On My Mind	1972	2.00	4.00	8.00
1807	Explain It to Her Mama/Love Can Be So Wonderful	1972	2.00	4.00	8.00
1808	Dedicated to the One I Love/I Love You, You Love Me	1972	2.00	4.00	8.00
1810	A Thousand Miles Away/Chalk It Up to Experience	1973	2.00	4.00	8.00
1811	Love's Maze/Wrap Me in Love	1973	2.00	4.00	8.00
1812	At Last/Love Can Be So Wonderful	1974	—	3.50	7.00
1813	You Make Me Love You/You Make the Sunshine	1974	—	3.50	7.00
1814	Mr. Cool That Ain't Cool/Lovin' You Is So Easy	1974	—	3.50	7.00
1815	I Love, I Love/Your Love	1975	—	3.50	7.00
1816	Come and Get Your Love/I'll Live Her Life	1975	—	3.50	7.00

Albums

Number	Title (A Side/B Side)	Yr	VG	VG+	NM
WE PRODUCE					
1901	Love Men	1972	15.00	30.00	60.00
1903	Love Maze	1973	15.00	30.00	60.00
1905	Temprees 3	1974	15.00	30.00	60.00

TEMPTATIONS, THE

The famous Detroit/Motown male vocal group. Also see EDDIE KENDRICKS; DAVID RUFFIN; THE SUPREMES AND THE TEMPTATIONS.

12-Inch Singles

Number	Title (A Side/B Side)	Yr	VG	VG+	NM
MOTOWN					
180 [DJ]	A Fine Mess (same on both sides)	1986	—	3.00	6.00
37463 1025 1 [DJ]	Hoops on Fire (3 versions)	1992	2.00	4.00	8.00
1132 [DJ]	Get Ready 1990 (4 versions)	1990	2.00	4.00	8.00
1604 [DJ]	The Jones (4 versions)	1991	2.00	4.00	8.00
4550	Do You Really Love Your Baby (3 versions)/I'll Keep My Light in Your Window	1985	—	3.00	6.00
4598	Look What You Started (4 versions)/More Love, Your Love	1987	—	3.00	6.00
4649	All I Want from You/(Instrumental)	1989	—	3.00	6.00
L33-17880 [DJ]	All I Want from You (Club Mix)/(Debbie Favorite Mix)	1989	2.00	4.00	8.00
L33-18149 [DJ]	Soul to Soul (3 versions)	1990	2.00	4.00	8.00
L33-18206 [DJ]	One Step at a Time (3 versions)	1990	2.00	4.00	8.00
53954	Get Ready 1990 (4 versions)	1990	2.00	4.00	8.00

45s

Number	Title (A Side/B Side)	Yr	VG	VG+	NM
ATLANTIC					
3436	In a Lifetime/I Could Never Stop Loving You	1977	—	2.00	4.00
3461	Think for Yourself/Let's Live in Place	1978	—	2.00	4.00
3517	Bare Back/I See My Child	1978	—	2.00	4.00
3538	Ever Ready Love/Touch Me Again	1978	—	2.00	4.00
3567	Mystic Woman/I Just Don't Know How to Let You Go	1979	—	2.00	4.00
GORDY					
1616	Standing on the Top-Part 1/Standing on the Top-Part 2	1982	—	2.00	4.00
—With Rick James					
1631	More on the Inside/Money's Hard to Get	1982	—	2.00	4.00
1654	Silent Night/Everything for Christmas	1982	—	3.00	6.00
1666	Love on My Mind Tonight/Bring Your Body Here	1983	—	2.00	4.00
1683	Made in America/Surface Thrills	1983	—	2.00	4.00
1707	Miss Busy Body (Get Your Body Busy)/(Instrumental)	1983	—	2.00	4.00
1713	Silent Night/Everything for Christmas	1983	—	2.50	5.00
1720	Sail Away/Isn't the Night Fantastic	1984	—	2.00	4.00
1765	Treat Her Like a Lady/Isn't the Night Fantastic	1984	—	2.00	4.00
1781	My Love Is True (Truly for You)/Set Your Love Right	1985	—	2.00	4.00
1789	How Can You Say That It's Over/I'll Keep My Light in My Window	1985	—	2.00	4.00
1818	Do You Really Love Your Baby/I'll Keep My Light in My Window	1985	—	2.00	4.00
1834	Touch Me/Set Your Love Right	1986	—	2.00	4.00
1856	Lady Soul/Put Us Together Again	1986	—	2.00	4.00
1871	To Be Continued/You're the One	1986	—	2.00	4.00
1871 [PS]	To Be Continued/You're the One	1986	—	3.00	6.00
1881	Someone/Love Me Right	1987	—	2.00	4.00
7001	Dream Come True/Isn't She Pretty	1962	10.00	20.00	40.00
7010	Paradise/Slow Down Heart	1962	7.50	15.00	30.00
7015	I Want a Love I Can See/The Further You Look, The Less You See	1963	6.25	12.50	25.00
7020	May I Have This Dance?/Farewell, My Love	1963	6.25	12.50	25.00
7028	The Way You Do the Things You Do/Just Let Me Know	1964	3.75	7.50	15.00
7032	I'll Be in Trouble/The Girl's Alright with Me	1964	3.75	7.50	15.00
7035	Girl (Why You Wanna Make Me Blue)/Baby, Baby I Need You	1964	3.75	7.50	15.00
7038	My Girl/Nobody But My Baby	1965	3.75	7.50	15.00
7038 [PS]	My Girl/Nobody But My Baby	1965	30.00	60.00	120.00
7040	It's Growing/What Love Has Joined Together	1965	3.75	7.50	15.00
7043	Since I Lost My Baby/You've Got to Earn It	1965	3.75	7.50	15.00
7047	My Baby/Don't Look Back	1965	3.75	7.50	15.00
7049	Get Ready/Fading Away	1966	3.75	7.50	15.00

Number	Title (A Side/B Side)	Yr	VG	VG+	NM
7054	Ain't Too Proud to Beg/You'll Lose a Precious Love	1966	3.75	7.50	15.00
7055	Beauty Is Only Skin Deep/You're Not an Ordinary Girl	1966	3.75	7.50	15.00
7055 [PS]	Beauty Is Only Skin Deep/You're Not an Ordinary Girl	1966	10.00	20.00	40.00
7057	(I Know) I'm Losing You/I Couldn't Cry If I Wanted To	1966	3.75	7.50	15.00
7061	All I Need/Sorry Is a Sorry Word	1967	2.50	5.00	10.00
7063	You're My Everything/I've Been Good to You	1967	2.50	5.00	10.00
—"Gordy" on left					
7063	You're My Everything/I've Been Good to You	1967	3.75	7.50	15.00
—"Gordy" on top					
7065	(Loneliness Made Me Realize) It's You That I Need/Don't Send Me Away	1967	2.50	5.00	10.00
7068	I Wish It Would Rain/I Truly, Truly Believe	1967	2.50	5.00	10.00
7072	I Could Never Love Another (After Loving You)/ Gonna Give Her All the Love I've Got	1968	2.50	5.00	10.00
7074	Please Return Your Love to Me/How Can I Forget	1968	2.50	5.00	10.00
7081	Cloud Nine/Why Did She Have to Leave Me	1968	2.00	4.00	8.00
7082	Silent Night/Rudolph, the Red-Nosed Reindeer	1968	3.00	6.00	12.00
7084	Run Away Child, Running Wild/I Need Your Love	1969	2.00	4.00	8.00
7086	Don't Let the Joneses Get You Down/Since I've Lost You	1969	2.00	4.00	8.00
7093	I Can't Get Next to You/Running Away (Ain't Gonna Help You)	1969	2.00	4.00	8.00
7096	Psychedelic Shack/That's the Way Love Is	1970	—	3.00	6.00
7099	Ball of Confusion (That's What the World Is Today)/It's Summer	1970	—	3.00	6.00
7099 [PS]	Ball of Confusion (That's What the World Is Today)/It's Summer	1970	5.00	10.00	20.00
7102	Ungena Za Ulimwengu (Unite the World)/Hum Along and Dance	1970	—	3.00	6.00
7105	Just My Imagination (Running Away with Me)/ You Make Your Own Heaven and Hell Right Here on Earth	1971	—	3.00	6.00
7109	It's Summer/I'm the Exception to the Rule	1971	—	3.00	6.00
7111	Superstar (Remember How You Got Where You Are)/Gonna Keep On Tryin' Till I Win Your Love	1971	—	3.00	6.00
7115	Take a Look Around/Smooth Sailing (From Now On)	1972	—	3.00	6.00
7119	Mother Nature/Funky Music Sho Nuff Turns Me On	1972	—	3.00	6.00
7121	Papa Was a Rollin' Stone/(Instrumental)	1972	—	3.00	6.00
7126	Masterpiece/(Instrumental)	1973	—	3.00	6.00
7129	Plastic Man/Hurry Tomorrow	1973	—	3.00	6.00
7131	Hey Girl (I Like Your Style)/Ma	1973	—	3.00	6.00
7133	Let Your Hair Down/Ain't No Justice	1973	—	3.00	6.00
7135	Heavenly/Zoom	1974	—	3.00	6.00
7136	You've Got My Soul on Fire/I Need You	1974	—	3.00	6.00
7138	Happy People/(Instrumental)	1974	—	3.00	6.00
7142	Shakey Ground/I'm a Bachelor	1975	—	3.00	6.00
7144	Glasshouse/The Prophet	1975	—	3.00	6.00
7146	Keep Holding On/What You Need Most (I Do Best of All)	1975	—	3.00	6.00
7150	Up the Creek (Without a Paddle)/Darling Stand By Me (Song for a Woman)	1976	—	3.00	6.00
7151	Who Are You (And What Are You Doing the Rest of Your Life)/Darling Stand By Me (Song for a Woman)	1976	—	—	—
—Unreleased					
7152	Let Me Count the Ways (I Love You)/Who Are You (And What Are You Doing the Rest of Your Life)	1976	—	3.00	6.00
7183	Power/Power (Part 2)	1980	—	2.00	4.00
7183 [DJ]	Power (same on both sides)	1980	2.50	5.00	10.00
—Promo only on red vinyl					
7188	Struck by Lightning Twice/I'm Coming Home	1980	—	2.00	4.00
7208	Aiming at Your Heart/Life of a Cowboy	1981	—	2.00	4.00
7213	Oh What a Night/Isn't the Night Fantastic	1981	—	2.00	4.00
MIRACLE					
5	Oh, Mother of Mine/Romance Without Finance	1961	25.00	50.00	100.00
12	Check Yourself/Your Wonderful Love	1961	25.00	50.00	100.00
MOTOWN					
903	One Step at a Time/(Instrumental)	1990	—	—	3.00
1501	Take Me Away/There's More Where That Came From	1980	—	2.00	4.00
1837	A Fine Mess/Wishful Thinking	1986	—	2.00	4.00
1837 [PS]	A Fine Mess/Wishful Thinking	1986	—	3.00	6.00
1908	I Wonder Who She's Seeing Now/Girls (They Like It)	1987	—	—	3.00
1908 [PS]	I Wonder Who She's Seeing Now/Girls (They Like It)	1987	—	2.00	4.00
1920	Look What You Started/More Love, Your Love	1987	—	—	3.00
1933	Do You Wanna Go with Me/Put Your Foot Down	1988	—	—	3.00
1974	All I Want from You/(Instrumental)	1989	—	—	3.00
860862-7	Stay/My Girl	1998	—	—	3.00
MOTOWN YESTERYEAR					
690	Silent Night/Everything For Christmas	198?	—	2.00	4.00
TOPPS/MOTOWN					
4	My Girl	1967	18.75	37.50	75.00
—Cardboard record					
13	The Way You Do the Things You Do	1967	18.75	37.50	75.00
—Cardboard record					
Albums					
ATLANTIC					
SD 19143	Hear to Tempt You	1977	3.00	6.00	12.00
SD 19188	Bare Back	1978	3.00	6.00	12.00
GORDY					
G 911 [M]	Meet the Temptations	1964	7.50	15.00	30.00
GS 911 [S]	Meet the Temptations	1964	10.00	20.00	40.00
—Script "Gordy" at top of label					
GS 911 [S]	Meet the Temptations	1967	5.00	10.00	20.00
—Block "GORDY" inside "G" on left of label					
G 912 [M]	The Temptations Sing Smokey	1965	7.50	15.00	30.00
GS 912 [S]	The Temptations Sing Smokey	1965	10.00	20.00	40.00
—Script "Gordy" at top of label					
GS 912 [S]	The Temptations Sing Smokey	1967	5.00	10.00	20.00
—Block "GORDY" inside "G" on left of label					
G 914 [M]	Temptin' Temptations	1965	6.25	12.50	25.00
GS 914 [S]	Temptin' Temptations	1965	7.50	15.00	30.00
—Script "Gordy" at top of label					
GS 914 [S]	Temptin' Temptations	1967	5.00	10.00	20.00
—Block "GORDY" inside "G" on left of label					
G 918 [M]	Gettin' Ready	1966	6.25	12.50	25.00
GS 918 [S]	Gettin' Ready	1966	7.50	15.00	30.00
—Script "Gordy" at top of label					
GS 918 [S]	Gettin' Ready	1967	5.00	10.00	20.00
—Block "GORDY" inside "G" on left of label					
G 919 [M]	The Temptations' Greatest Hits	1966	6.25	12.50	25.00
GS 919 [S]	The Temptations' Greatest Hits	1966	7.50	15.00	30.00
—Script "Gordy" at top of label					
GS 919 [S]	The Temptations' Greatest Hits	1967	5.00	10.00	20.00
—Block "GORDY" inside "G" on left of label					
G 921 [M]	Temptations Live!	1967	6.25	12.50	25.00
GS 921 [S]	Temptations Live!	1967	7.50	15.00	30.00
—Script "Gordy" at top of label					
GS 921 [S]	Temptations Live!	1967	5.00	10.00	20.00
—Block "GORDY" inside "G" on left of label					
G 922 [M]	With a Lot o' Soul	1967	6.25	12.50	25.00
GS 922 [S]	With a Lot o' Soul	1967	6.25	12.50	25.00
—Script "Gordy" at top of label					
GS 922 [S]	With a Lot o' Soul	1967	5.00	10.00	20.00
—Block "GORDY" inside "G" on left of label					
G 924 [M]	The Temptations in a Mellow Mood	1967	6.25	12.50	25.00
GS 924 [S]	The Temptations in a Mellow Mood	1967	6.25	12.50	25.00
G 927 [M]	The Temptations Wish It Would Rain	1968	10.00	20.00	40.00
—Mono is white-label promo only					
GS 927 [S]	The Temptations Wish It Would Rain	1068	5.00	10.00	20.00
GS 933	The Temptations Show	1969	5.00	10.00	20.00
GS 938	Live at the Copa	1968	5.00	10.00	20.00
GS 939	Cloud Nine	1969	5.00	10.00	20.00
GS 947	Psychedelic Shack	1970	5.00	10.00	20.00
GS 949	Puzzle People	1969	5.00	10.00	20.00
GS 951	The Temptations' Christmas Card	1969	6.25	12.50	25.00
GS 953	Live at London's Talk of the Town	1970	5.00	10.00	20.00
GS 954	Temptations Greatest Hits II	1970	5.00	10.00	20.00
GS 957	Sky's the Limit	1971	5.00	10.00	20.00
GS 961	Solid Rock	1972	5.00	10.00	20.00
G 962L	All Directions	1972	5.00	10.00	20.00
G 965L	Masterpiece	1973	5.00	10.00	20.00
G 966L	1990	1973	3.75	7.50	15.00
G7-969	A Song for You	1975	3.75	7.50	15.00
G7-971	Wings of Love	1976	3.75	7.50	15.00
G7-973	House Party	1975	3.75	7.50	15.00
G7-975	The Temptations Do the Temptations	1976	3.75	7.50	15.00
994	Power	1980	3.00	6.00	12.00
G8-998M1	Give Love at Christmas	1980	3.75	7.50	15.00
G8-1006	The Temptations	1981	3.00	6.00	12.00
6008 GL	Reunion	1982	3.00	6.00	12.00
6032 GL	Surface Thrills	1983	3.00	6.00	12.00
6085 GL	Back to Basics	1984	3.00	6.00	12.00
6119 GL	Truly for You	1984	3.00	6.00	12.00
6164 GL	Touch Me	1986	3.00	6.00	12.00
6207 GL	To Be Continued	1986	3.00	6.00	12.00
MOTOWN					
M5-140V1	Meet the Temptations	1981	3.00	6.00	12.00
—Reissue of Gordy 911					
M5-144V1	Masterpiece	1981	3.00	6.00	12.00
—Reissue of Gordy 965					
M5-159V1	Cloud Nine	1981	3.00	6.00	12.00
—Reissue of Gordy 939					
M5-164V1	Psychedelic Shack	1981	3.00	6.00	12.00
—Reissue of Gordy 947					
M5-172V1	Puzzle People	1981	3.00	6.00	12.00
—Reissue of Gordy 949					
M5-205V1	The Temptations Sing Smokey	1981	3.00	6.00	12.00
—Reissue of Gordy 912					
M5-212V1	All the Million Sellers	1982	3.00	6.00	12.00
M 782 [(3)]	Anthology	1973	6.25	12.50	25.00
5251 ML	The Temptations Christmas Card	1982	2.50	5.00	10.00
—Reissue of Gordy 951					
5279 ML	Give Love at Christmas	1983	2.50	5.00	10.00
—Reissue of Gordy 998					
5389 ML [(2)]	25th Anniversary	1986	3.75	7.50	15.00
6246 ML	Together Again	1987	3.00	6.00	12.00
MOT-6275	Special	1989	3.00	6.00	12.00
NATURAL RESOURCES					
NR 4005T1	The Temptations in a Mellow Mood	1978	3.00	6.00	12.00
—Reissue of Gordy 924					

TEMPTATIONS, THE (2)

White doo-wop group.

45s

Number	Title (A Side/B Side)	Yr	VG	VG+	NM
GOLDISC					
3001	Barbara/Someday	1960	7.50	15.00	30.00
—All-black label					
3001	Barbara/Someday	1960	5.00	10.00	20.00
—Multicolor (black, red, gold) label					
3007	Letter of Devotion/Fickle Little Girl	1960	6.25	12.50	25.00

TEMPTATIONS, THE (3)

45s

Number	Title (A Side/B Side)	Yr	VG	VG+	NM
KING					
5118	Standing Alone/Roaches Rock	1958	75.00	150.00	300.00

TEMPTATIONS, THE (4)

45s

Number	Title (A Side/B Side)	Yr	VG	VG+	NM
PARKWAY					
803	Temptations/Birds N' Bees	1959	7.50	15.00	30.00

TEMPTATIONS, THE (5)

45s

Number	Title (A Side/B Side)	Yr	VG	VG+	NM
P&L					
1001	Blue Surf/Egyptian Surf	1963	15.00	30.00	60.00

TEMPTATIONS, THE (6)

45s

Number	Title (A Side/B Side)	Yr	VG	VG+	NM
SAVOY					
1532	Mister Juke Box/Mad at Love	1958	5.00	10.00	20.00
1550	I Love You/Don't You Know	1958	5.00	10.00	20.00

TEMPTONES, THE

DARYL HALL was in this group.

45s

Number	Title (A Side/B Side)	Yr	VG	VG+	NM
ARCTIC					
130	Girl, I Love You/Good-Bye	1967	10.00	20.00	40.00
136	Say These Words of Love/This Could Be the Start of Something Good	1967	10.00	20.00	40.00

TEN BROKEN HEARTS

Allegedly, NEIL DIAMOND appears on this record.

45s

Number	Title (A Side/B Side)	Yr	VG	VG+	NM
DIAMOND					
123	Ten Lonely Guys/Shining Star	1962	10.00	20.00	40.00

10CC

Also see GRAHAM GOULDMAN; HOTLEGS.

45s

Number	Title (A Side/B Side)	Yr	VG	VG+	NM
MERCURY					
73678	I'm Not in Love/Channel Swimmer	1975	—	2.50	5.00
73725	Art for Art's Sake/Get It While You Can	1975	—	2.50	5.00
73725 [PS]	Art for Art's Sake/Get It While You Can	1975	2.00	4.00	8.00
73779	I'm Mandy Fly Me/How Dare You	1976	—	2.50	5.00
73875	The Things We Do for Love/Hot to Trot	1976	—	2.50	5.00
73917	People in Love/Don't Squeeze Me Like Toothpaste	1977	—	2.50	5.00
73943	Good Morning Judge/I'm So Laid Back I'm Laid Out	1977	—	2.50	5.00
73980	You've Got a Cold/The Wall Street Shuffle	1977	—	2.50	5.00
POLYDOR					
14511	Dreadlock Holiday/Nothing Can Move Me	1978	—	2.50	5.00
14528	For You and I/Take These Chains	1978	—	2.50	5.00
UK					
49005	Donna/Hot Sun Rock	1972	—	3.00	6.00
49015	Ruber Bullets/Waterfall	1973	—	3.00	6.00
49019	Headline Hustler/Speed Kills	1973	—	3.00	6.00
49023	The Wall Street Shuffle/Gismo My Way	1974	—	3.00	6.00
WARNER BROS.					
29973	Power of Love/Action Man in Motown Suit	1982	—	2.50	5.00
49266	It Doesn't Matter Anymore/Strange Lover	1980	—	2.50	5.00

Albums

Number	Title (A Side/B Side)	Yr	VG	VG+	NM
MERCURY					
SRM-1-1029	The Original Soundtrack	1975	3.00	6.00	12.00
SRM-1-1061	How Dare You!	1976	3.00	6.00	12.00
SRM-1-3702	Deceptive Bends	1977	3.00	6.00	12.00
SRM-2-8600 [(2)]	Live and Let Live	1977	3.75	7.50	15.00
POLYDOR					
PD-1-6161	Bloody Tourists	1978	2.50	5.00	10.00
PD-1-6244	Greatest Hits 1972-1978	1979	2.50	5.00	10.00
U.K.					
53105	10cc	1973	3.75	7.50	15.00
53107	Sheet Music	1974	3.75	7.50	15.00
53110	100cc	1975	3.75	7.50	15.00
WARNER BROS.					
BSK 3442	Look Hear?	1980	2.50	5.00	10.00
BSK 3575	Ten Out of Ten	1981	2.50	5.00	10.00

TEN WHEEL DRIVE

45s

Number	Title (A Side/B Side)	Yr	VG	VG+	NM
CAPITOL					
3700	Monsoon Rain/Close Up the Cheese	1973	—	2.50	5.00
POLYDOR					
14015	Tightrope/Lapidary	1969	—	2.50	5.00
14024	Eye of the Needle/I Am a Want Ad	1970	—	2.50	5.00
14037	Morning Much Better/Stay with Me	1970	—	2.50	5.00
14052	Don't Blame Me/20 Miles from Home	1971	—	2.50	5.00

Albums

Number	Title (A Side/B Side)	Yr	VG	VG+	NM
CAPITOL					
ST-11199	Ten Wheel Drive	1973	2.50	5.00	10.00
POLYDOR					
24-4008	Construction #1	1969	3.00	6.00	12.00
24-4024	Brief Replies	1970	3.00	6.00	12.00
24-4062	Peculiar Friends	1971	3.00	6.00	12.00

TEN YEARS AFTER

45s

Number	Title (A Side/B Side)	Yr	VG	VG+	NM
COLUMBIA					
45457	I'd Love to Change the World/Let the Sky Fall	1971	—	2.50	5.00
45530	Baby Won't You Let Me Rock 'N' Roll You/Once There Was a Time	1972	—	2.50	5.00
45736	You Can't Win Them All/Choo Choo Mama	1972	—	2.50	5.00
45787	Tomorrow, I'll Be Out of Town/Convention Prevention	1973	—	2.50	5.00
45915	I'm Going Home/You Give Me Loving	1973	—	2.50	5.00
46061	It's Getting Harder/I Wanted to Boogie	1974	—	2.50	5.00
DERAM					
7529	If You Should Love Me/Love Like a Man	1970	2.00	4.00	8.00
85027	Portable People/The Sounds	1968	2.00	4.00	8.00
85035	Hear Me Calling/I'm Going Home	1968	2.00	4.00	8.00

Albums

Number	Title (A Side/B Side)	Yr	VG	VG+	NM
CHRYSALIS					
CHS 1083	Ssssh	1975	2.50	5.00	10.00
CHS 1084	Cricklewood Green	1975	2.50	5.00	10.00
CHS 1085	Watt	1975	2.50	5.00	10.00
F1-21001	A Space in Time	1989	2.00	4.00	8.00
F1-21009	Rock and Roll Music to the World	1989	2.00	4.00	8.00
F1-21083	Ssssh	1989	2.00	4.00	8.00
F1-21084	Cricklewood Green	1989	2.00	4.00	8.00
F1-21085	Watt	1989	2.00	4.00	8.00
F1-21573	Positive Vibrations	1989	2.00	4.00	8.00
F1-21580	Universal	1989	2.00	4.00	8.00
F1-21722	About Time	1989	3.00	6.00	12.00
PV 41001	A Space in Time	1987	2.00	4.00	8.00
PV 41009	Rock and Roll Music to the World	1987	2.00	4.00	8.00
FV 41049 [(2)]	Recorded Live	1987	2.50	5.00	10.00
PV 41083	Ssssh	1983	2.00	4.00	8.00
PV 41084	Cricklewood Green	1983	2.00	4.00	8.00
PV 41085	Watt	1983	2.00	4.00	8.00
PV 41573	Positive Vibrations	1987	2.00	4.00	8.00
FV 41580	Universal	1988	2.50	5.00	10.00
COLUMBIA					
CQ 30801 [Q]	A Space in Time	1973	4.00	8.00	16.00
KC 30801	A Space in Time	1971	3.00	6.00	12.00
PC 30801	A Space in Time	1979	2.00	4.00	8.00
C 31779	Rock and Roll Music to the World	197?	2.50	5.00	10.00
—Reissue with new prefix					
KC 31779	Rock and Roll Music to the World	1972	3.00	6.00	12.00
C2X 32288 [(2)]	Recorded Live	1973	3.75	7.50	15.00
PC 32851	Positive Vibrations	1974	2.50	5.00	10.00
PC 34366	Classic Performances of Ten Years After	1976	2.50	5.00	10.00
DERAM					
DE 16009 [M]	Ten Years After	1968	12.50	25.00	50.00
DES 18009 [S]	Ten Years After	1968	5.00	10.00	20.00
DES 18016	Undead	1968	3.75	7.50	15.00
DES 18021	Stonedhenge	1969	3.75	7.50	15.00
DES 18029	Ssssh	1969	3.75	7.50	15.00
DES 18038	Cricklewood Green	1970	3.75	7.50	15.00
DES 18050	Watt	1970	3.75	7.50	15.00
DES 18064	Alvin Lee and Company	1972	3.00	6.00	12.00
DES 18072	Goin' Home! Their Greatest Hits	1975	3.00	6.00	12.00
LONDON					
LC 50008	Greatest Hits	1977	2.50	5.00	10.00
820324-1	Greatest Hits	1986	2.00	4.00	8.00

TENDER TONES, THE

45s

Number	Title (A Side/B Side)	Yr	VG	VG+	NM
DUCKY					
713	I Love You So/Just for a Little While	1959	200.00	400.00	800.00

TENDERFOOTS, THE

45s

Number	Title (A Side/B Side)	Yr	VG	VG+	NM
FEDERAL					
12214	Kissing Bug/Watussi Wussi Wo	1955	15.00	30.00	60.00
12219	My Confession/Save Me Some Kisses	1955	15.00	30.00	60.00
12225	Those Golden Bells/I'm Yours Anyhow	1955	20.00	40.00	80.00
12228	Sindy/Sugar Ways	1955	30.00	60.00	120.00

TENNESSEE DRIFTERS, THE

45s

Number	Title (A Side/B Side)	Yr	VG	VG+	NM
DOT					
1166	Boogie Woogie Baby/Drive Those Blues Away	1953	7.50	15.00	30.00
1187	Corrine, Corrina/Somebody Loves You	1954	7.50	15.00	30.00

TENNESSEE ERNIE

See TENNESSEE ERNIE FORD.

TENNESSEE GUITARS, THE

45s

Number	Title (A Side/B Side)	Yr	VG	VG+	NM
SUN					
1102	Tennessee Toddy/Trophy Run	1969	—	3.00	6.00

TERMITES, THE

45s

Number	Title (A Side/B Side)	Yr	VG	VG+	NM
BEE					
1825	Give Me Your Heart/Carrie Lou	1964	12.50	25.00	50.00

TERRACETONES, THE

45s

Number	Title (A Side/B Side)	Yr	VG	VG+	NM
APT					
25016	Words of Wisdom/Ride of Paul Revere	1958	25.00	50.00	100.00

TERRELL, ERNIE

45s

Number	Title (A Side/B Side)	Yr	VG	VG+	NM
ARGO					
5511	Dear Abbie/I Can't Wait	1965	3.00	6.00	12.00

TERRELL, TAMMI

Also see MARVIN GAYE AND TAMMI TERRELL; TAMMY MONTGOMERY.

45s

Number	Title (A Side/B Side)	Yr	VG	VG+	NM
MOTOWN					
1086	I Can't Believe You Love Me/Hold Me Oh My Darling	1965	2.50	5.00	10.00
1095	Come On and See Me/Baby Don'tcha Worry	1966	2.50	5.00	10.00
1115	What a Good Man He Is/There Are Things	1967	2.50	5.00	10.00
1138	This Old Heart of Mine (Is Weak for You)/Just Too Much to Hope For	1968	2.50	5.00	10.00

Number	Title (A Side/B Side)	Yr	VG	VG+	NM
Albums					
MOTOWN					
M5-231V1	Irresistible Tammi	1982	2.50	5.00	10.00
MS-652	Irresistible Tammi	1969	12.50	25.00	50.00

TERRI AND THE KITTENS

Number	Title (A Side/B Side)	Yr	VG	VG+	NM
45s					
IMPERIAL					
5728	Wedding Bells/You Cheated	1961	5.00	10.00	20.00

TERRI AND THE VELVETEENS

Number	Title (A Side/B Side)	Yr	VG	VG+	NM
45s					
KERWOOD					
711	Bells of Love/You've Broken My Heart	1962	10.00	20.00	40.00

TERRI-TONES, THE

Number	Title (A Side/B Side)	Yr	VG	VG+	NM
45s					
CORTLAND					
105	Go/The Sinner	1962	12.50	25.00	50.00
REGENCY					
929	Go/The Sinner	1962	7.50	15.00	30.00

TERRY, DON

Number	Title (A Side/B Side)	Yr	VG	VG+	NM
45s					
LIN					
5018	Knees Shakin'/She Giggles	1959	37.50	75.00	150.00

TERRY, DOSSIE

Number	Title (A Side/B Side)	Yr	VG	VG+	NM
45s					
KING					
5072	Thunderbird/I Got a Watch Dog	1957	12.50	25.00	50.00
5890	Thunderbird/Be-Bop Wino	1964	3.75	7.50	15.00
—B side by the Lamplighters					
RCA VICTOR					
47-4474	Didn't Satisfy You/24 Years	1952	15.00	30.00	60.00
47-4648	When I Hit the Number/My Love Is Gone	1952	15.00	30.00	60.00
47-4864	Lost My Head/Sad, Sad Affair	1952	15.00	30.00	60.00

TERRY, GENE

Number	Title (A Side/B Side)	Yr	VG	VG+	NM
45s					
GOLDBAND					
1066	Cindy Lou/Teardrops in My Eyes	1958	30.00	60.00	120.00
1081	Never Let Her Go/No Mail Today	1958	10.00	20.00	40.00
1088	Cinderella, Cinderella/Guy with a Million Dreams	1959	7.50	15.00	30.00
SAVOY					
1559	This Should Go On Forever/Fine, Fine, Fine	1959	5.00	10.00	20.00

TERRY, LARRY

Number	Title (A Side/B Side)	Yr	VG	VG+	NM
45s					
TESTA					
006	Hep Cat/Why Did She Go	1960	300.00	600.00	1200.

TERRY, NAT

Number	Title (A Side/B Side)	Yr	VG	VG+	NM
45s					
IMPERIAL					
5150	Take It Easy/I Don't Know Why	1951	25.00	50.00	100.00

TERRY, SONNY

Number	Title (A Side/B Side)	Yr	VG	VG+	NM
45s					
CAPITOL					
F931	Telephone Blues/Dirty Mistreater Don't You Know	1950	30.00	60.00	120.00
CHESS					
1860	Dangerous Woman/Hootenanny Blues	1963	5.00	10.00	20.00
CHOICE					
15	Hootin'/Dupre	1961	5.00	10.00	20.00
GOTHAM					
517	Baby Let's Have Some Fun/Four O'Clock Blues	1951	10.00	20.00	40.00
518	Harmonica Rhumba/Lonesome Room	1951	10.00	20.00	40.00
GRAMERCY					
1004	Hootin' Blues/(B-side unknown)	1952	12.50	25.00	50.00
—Black vinyl					
1004	Hootin' Blues/(B-side unknown)	1952	25.00	50.00	100.00
—Colored vinyl					
GROOVE					
0015	Lost Jawbone/Louise	1954	7.50	15.00	30.00
0135	Ride and Roll/Hootin' Blues #2	1956	7.50	15.00	30.00
HARLEM					
2327	Dangerous Woman/I Love You Baby	1954	75.00	150.00	300.00
JAX					
305	I Don't Worry (Sittin' on Top of the World)/Man Ain't Nothin' But a Fool	195?	100.00	200.00	400.00
—Colored vinyl					
OLD TOWN					
1023	Uncle Bud/Climbing on Top of the Hill	1956	6.25	12.50	25.00
RCA VICTOR					
47-5492	Hootin' and Jumpin'/Hooray, Hooray	1953	25.00	50.00	100.00
47-5577	Sonny Is Drinking/I'm Gonna Rock My Wig	1954	25.00	50.00	100.00
RED ROBIN					
110	Harmonica Hop/Doggin' My Heart Around	1952	75.00	150.00	300.00
Albums					
ALLIGATOR					
AL-4734	Whoopin'	198?	3.00	6.00	12.00
—With Johnny Winter, Willie Dixon and others					
BLUE LABOR					
101	Robbin' the Grave	197?	3.00	6.00	12.00
BLUESVILLE					
BVLP-1025 [M]	Sonny's Story	1961	20.00	40.00	80.00
—Bright blue label, no trident logo					
BVLP-1025 [M]	Sonny's Story	1964	6.25	12.50	25.00
—Blue label with trident logo on right					
BVLP-1069 [M]	Sonny Is King	1963	20.00	40.00	80.00
—Bright blue label, no trident logo					
BVLP-1069 [M]	Sonny Is King	1964	6.25	12.50	25.00
—Blue label with trident logo on right					
COLLECTABLES					
COL-5195	Chain Gang Blues	198?	2.50	5.00	10.00
COL-5307	Sonny Terry	198?	2.50	5.00	10.00
ELEKTRA					
EKL-14 [10]	Folk Blues	1954	37.50	75.00	150.00
EKL-15 [10]	City Blues	1954	37.50	75.00	150.00
—With Alec Stewart					
FANTASY					
OBC-521	Sonny Is King	198?	2.50	5.00	10.00
FOLKWAYS					
FP-35 [10]	Harmonica and Vocal Solos	1952	37.50	75.00	150.00
FA-2006 [10]	Sonny Terry's Washboard Band	195?	25.00	50.00	100.00
—Black and white cover (reissue)					
FP-2006 [10]	Sonny Terry's Washboard Band	1950	37.50	75.00	150.00
—Blue and white cover					
FA-2035 [10]	Harmonica and Vocal Solos	1952	25.00	50.00	100.00
FS-2369	On the Road	196?	3.75	7.50	15.00
3821	A New Sound	198?	3.00	6.00	12.00
PRESTIGE					
PRST-7802	Sonny Is King	1970	3.75	7.50	15.00
RIVERSIDE					
RLP-644 [M]	Sonny Terry and His Mouth Harp	195?	20.00	40.00	80.00
STINSON					
55	Sonny Terry and His Mouth Harp	197?	3.00	6.00	12.00
—Reissue of 10-inch LP					
SLP-55 [10]	Sonny Terry and His Mouth Harp	1950	37.50	75.00	150.00

TERRY, SONNY, AND BROWNIE MCGHEE

Also see each artist's individual listings.

Number	Title (A Side/B Side)	Yr	VG	VG+	NM
45s					
BLUESVILLE					
802	Let Me Be Your Big Dig/Stranger Here	196?	5.00	10.00	20.00
809	Pawnshop/Too Nicey Mama	196?	5.00	10.00	20.00
818	Freight Train/Beggin' and Tryin'	196?	5.00	10.00	20.00
CHOICE					
1	John Henry/Oh Lawdy Pick a Bale of Cotton	196?	5.00	10.00	20.00
—As "Brownie & Sonny"					
7	Study War No More/I'm Gonna Tell God	196?	5.00	10.00	20.00
—As "Brownie & Sonny"					
Albums					
ARCHIVE OF FOLK MUSIC					
242	Brownie & Sonny	198?	3.00	6.00	12.00
A&M					
SP-4379	Sonny & Brownie	1973	3.00	6.00	12.00
BLUESVILLE					
BVLP-1002 [M]	Down Home Blues	1960	20.00	40.00	80.00
—Bright blue label, no trident logo					
BVLP-1002 [M]	Down Home Blues	1964	6.25	12.50	25.00
—Blue label with trident logo on right					
BVLP-1005 [M]	Blues and Folk	1960	20.00	40.00	80.00
—Bright blue label, no trident logo					
BVLP-1005 [M]	Blues and Folk	1964	6.25	12.50	25.00
—Blue label with trident logo on right					
BVLP-1020 [M]	Blues All Around My Head	1961	20.00	40.00	80.00
—Bright blue label, no trident logo					
BVLP-1020 [M]	Blues All Around My Head	1964	6.25	12.50	25.00
—Blue label with trident logo on right					
BVLP-1033 [M]	Blues in My Soul	1961	20.00	40.00	80.00
—Bright blue label, no trident logo					
BVLP-1033 [M]	Blues in My Soul	1964	6.25	12.50	25.00
—Blue label with trident logo on right					
BVLP-1058 [M]	Live at the Second Fret	1962	20.00	40.00	80.00
—Bright blue label, no trident logo					
BVLP-1058 [M]	Live at the Second Fret	1964	6.25	12.50	25.00
—Blue label with trident logo on right					
BLUESWAY					
BLS-6028	Long Way from Home	1969	3.75	7.50	15.00
BLS-6059	Couldn't Believe My Eyes	1970	3.75	7.50	15.00
COLLECTABLES					
COL-5198	Golden Classics: Blowin' the Fuses	198?	2.50	5.00	10.00
EVEREST					
206	Sonny Terry	1968	6.25	12.50	25.00
242	Brownie McGhee and Sonny Terry	1969	6.25	12.50	25.00
FANTASY					
OBC-503	Sonny's Story	1984	2.50	5.00	10.00
OBC-505	Brownie's Blues	1984	2.50	5.00	10.00
F-3254 [M]	Sonny Terry & Brownie McGhee	1961	37.50	75.00	150.00
—Red vinyl					
F-3254 [M]	Sonny Terry & Brownie McGhee	1961	10.00	20.00	40.00
—Black vinyl					
F-3296 [M]	Just a Closer Walk with Thee	1962	37.50	75.00	150.00
—Red vinyl					
F-3296 [M]	Just a Closer Walk with Thee	1962	10.00	20.00	40.00
—Black vinyl					
F-3317 [M]	Blues and Shouts	1962	37.50	75.00	150.00
—Red vinyl					
F-3317 [M]	Blues and Shouts	1962	10.00	20.00	40.00
—Black vinyl					
F-3340 [M]	Sonny and Brownie at Sugar Hill	1962	37.50	75.00	150.00
—Red vinyl					
F-3340 [M]	Sonny and Brownie at Sugar Hill	1962	10.00	20.00	40.00
—Black vinyl					
FS-8091 [S]	Sonny and Brownie at Sugar Hill	1962	37.50	75.00	150.00
—Blue vinyl					
FS-8091 [S]	Sonny and Brownie at Sugar Hill	1962	10.00	20.00	40.00
—Black vinyl					
24708 [(2)]	Back to New Orleans	1972	3.75	7.50	15.00

Number	Title (A Side/B Side)	Yr	VG	VG+	NM
24721 [(2)]	Midnight Special	1977	3.75	7.50	15.00
24723 [(2)]	California Blues	1981	3.75	7.50	15.00
FOLKLORE					
FRLP-14013 [M]	Down Home Blues	1964	10.00	20.00	40.00
FRST-14013 [S]	Down Home Blues	1964	12.50	25.00	50.00
FOLKWAYS					
FA-2327 [M]	Blues and Folk Songs	1960	7.50	15.00	30.00
F-2421 [M]	Traditional Blues, Volume 1	1961	7.50	15.00	30.00
FS-2421 [S]	Traditional Blues, Volume 1	1961	10.00	20.00	40.00
F-2422 [M]	Traditional Blues, Volume 2	1961	7.50	15.00	30.00
FS-2422 [S]	Traditional Blues, Volume 2	1961	10.00	20.00	40.00
FONTANA					
SGF-67599	Where the Blues Begin	1969	6.25	12.50	25.00
KIMBERLEY					
2017 [M]	Southern Meetin'	1963	5.00	10.00	20.00
11017 [S]	Southern Meetin'	1963	6.25	12.50	25.00
MAINSTREAM					
M-6049 [M]	Hometown Blues	1966	5.00	10.00	20.00
MS-6049 [S]	Hometown Blues	1966	6.25	12.50	25.00
MOBILE FIDELITY					
1-233	Sonny and Brownie	1996	5.00	10.00	20.00
—Audiophile vinyl					
MUSE					
5117	Hootin'	198?	3.00	6.00	12.00
5131	You Hear Me Talkin'	198?	3.00	6.00	12.00
OLYMPIC					
7108	Hootin' & Hollerin'	1972	3.00	6.00	12.00
PRESTIGE					
PRLP-7715	Best of Sonny Terry and Brownie McGhee	1969	3.75	7.50	15.00
PRLP-7803	Live at the Second Fret	1970	3.75	7.50	15.00
ROULETTE					
R-25074 [M]	The Folk Songs of Sonny & Brownie	1959	12.50	25.00	50.00
RS-25074 [S]	The Folk Songs of Sonny & Brownie	1959	20.00	40.00	80.00
SAVOY					
SJL-1137	Climbin' Up	1984	2.50	5.00	10.00
12218	Down Home Blues	1973	3.00	6.00	12.00
SHARP					
2003 [M]	Down Home Blues	195?	37.50	75.00	150.00
SMASH					
MGS-27067 [M]	Brownie McGhee at the Bunkhouse	1965	7.50	15.00	30.00
SRS-67067 [S]	Brownie McGhee at the Bunkhouse	1965	10.00	20.00	40.00
SMITHSONIAN/FOLKWAYS					
SF-40011	Sing	198?	2.50	5.00	10.00
STORYVILLE					
4007	Brownie & Sonny	1972	3.00	6.00	12.00
TOPIC					
T-29 [M]	Songs	1958	12.50	25.00	50.00
VEE JAY					
VJLP-1138	Coffee House Blues	198?	2.50	5.00	10.00
—With Lightnin' Hopkins					
VERVE					
MGV 3008 [M]	Blues Is My Companion	1961	20.00	40.00	80.00
VERVE FOLKWAYS					
FV 9010 [M]	Get Together	1965	6.25	12.50	25.00
FVS 9010 [S]	Get Together	1965	7.50	15.00	30.00
FV 9019 [M]	Guitar Highway	1965	6.25	12.50	25.00
FVS 9019 [S]	Guitar Highway	1965	7.50	15.00	30.00
WASHINGTON					
W-702 [M]	Talkin' 'Bout the Blues	1961	12.50	25.00	50.00
WORLD PACIFIC					
ST-1294 [S]	Blues Is a Story	1960	20.00	40.00	80.00
WP-1294 [M]	Blues Is a Story	1960	12.50	25.00	50.00
ST-1296 [S]	Down South Summit Meetin'	1960	20.00	40.00	80.00
WP-1296 [M]	Down South Summit Meetin'	1960	12.50	25.00	50.00

TERRY AND THE MACS

45s

Number	Title (A Side/B Side)	Yr	VG	VG+	NM
ABC-PARAMOUNT					
9668	Baby-O-Mine/Love Is a Beautiful Thing	1956	5.00	10.00	20.00
9721	You Don't Have to Explain/Spinning, Spinning, Spinning	1956	5.00	10.00	20.00
9753	Please Don't Tease/The Mystery of Love	1956	5.00	10.00	20.00

TERRY AND THE PIRATES

45s

Number	Title (A Side/B Side)	Yr	VG	VG+	NM
CHESS					
1696	Talk About the Girl/What Did He Say	1958	10.00	20.00	40.00

TERRY AND THE TAGS

45s

Number	Title (A Side/B Side)	Yr	VG	VG+	NM
SYLVESTER					
100	Rampage/The Twomp	1962	12.50	25.00	50.00

TEX, JOE

12-Inch Singles

Number	Title (A Side/B Side)	Yr	VG	VG+	NM
EPIC					
50352	Ain't Gonna Bump No More (With No Big Fat Woman)/Be Cool (Willie Is Dancing with a Sissy)	1977	5.00	10.00	20.00

45s

Number	Title (A Side/B Side)	Yr	VG	VG+	NM
ACE					
544	Cut It Out/Just for You and Me	1958	15.00	30.00	60.00
550	Mother's Advice/You Little Baby Face Thing	1958	20.00	40.00	80.00
559	Charlie Brown Got Expelled/Blessed Are These Tears	1959	15.00	30.00	60.00
572	Don't Hold It Against Me/Yum, Yum, Yum	1959	15.00	30.00	60.00
591	Boys Will Be Boys/Grannie Stole the Show	1960	10.00	20.00	40.00
674	Boys Will Be Boys/Baby You're Right	1963	3.75	7.50	15.00
ANNA					
1119	All I Could Do Was Cry (Part 1)/All I Could Do Was Cry (Part 2)	1960	10.00	20.00	40.00
1124	I'll Never Break Your Heart (Part 1)/I'll Never Break Your Heart (Part 2)	1960	10.00	20.00	40.00
1128	Baby, You're Right/Ain't It a Mess	1961	10.00	20.00	40.00
ATLANTIC					
2874	I'll Never Fall in Love Again (Part 1)/I'll Never Fall in Love Again (Part 2)	1972	—	3.00	6.00
CHECKER					
1104	Baby, You're Right/All I Could Do Was Cry (Part 2)	1965	3.00	6.00	12.00
DIAL					
1001	Bad Feet/I Know Him	1971	—	3.00	6.00
1003	Papa's Dream/I'm Comin' Home	1971	—	3.00	6.00
1006 [DJ]	King Thaddeus (mono/stereo)	1971	—	3.50	7.00
—May be promo only					
1008	Give the Baby Anything the Baby Wants/Takin' a Chance	1971	—	3.00	6.00
1010	I Gotcha/A Mother's Prayer	1972	—	3.00	6.00
1012	You Said a Bad Word/It Ain't Gonna Work Baby	1972	—	3.00	6.00
1018	Rain Go Away/King Thaddeus	1973	—	3.00	6.00
1020	Woman Stealer/Cat's Got Her Tongue	1973	—	3.00	6.00
1020 [PS]	Woman Stealer/Cat's Got Her Tongue	1973	2.00	4.00	8.00
1021	All the Heaven a Man Really Needs/Let's Go Somewhere and Talk	1973	—	3.00	6.00
1024	Trying to Win Your Love/I've Seen Enough	1973	—	3.00	6.00
1154	Sassy Sexy Wiggle/Under Your Powerful Love	1975	—	3.00	6.00
1155	I'm Goin' Back Again/My Body Wants You	1975	—	3.00	6.00
1156	Baby, It's Rainin'/Have You Ever	1975	—	3.00	6.00
1157	Mama Red/Love Shortage	1975	—	3.00	6.00
2800	Loose Caboose/Music Ain't Got No Color	1979	—	2.50	5.00
2801	Who Gave Birth to the Funk/If You Don't Want the Man	1979	—	2.50	5.00
2802	Discomania/Fat People	1979	—	2.50	5.00
3000	What Should I Do/The Only Girl I've Ever Loved	1961	3.00	6.00	12.00
3002	One Giant Step/The Rib	1961	3.00	6.00	12.00
3003	Popeye Johnny/Hand Shakin', Love Makin', Girl Talkin', Son-of-a-Gun From Next Door	1962	3.00	6.00	12.00
3007	Meet Me in Church/Be Your Own Judge	1962	3.00	6.00	12.00
3009	I Let Her Get Away/The Peck	1963	3.00	6.00	12.00
3013	Someone to Take Your Place/I Should Have Kissed You More	1963	3.00	6.00	12.00
3016	I Wanna Be Free/Blood's Thicker Than Water	1963	3.00	6.00	12.00
3019	Looking for My Pig/Say Thank You	1964	3.00	6.00	12.00
3020	I'd Rather Have You/Old Time Lover	1964	3.00	6.00	12.00
3023	I Had a Good Thing But I Left (Part 1)/I Had a Good Thing But I Left (Part 2)	1964	3.00	6.00	12.00
4001	Hold What You've Got/Fresh Out of Tears	1964	3.75	7.50	15.00
4003	You Better Get It/You Got What It Takes	1965	2.50	5.00	10.00
4006	A Woman Can Change a Man/Don't Let Your Left Hand Know	1965	2.50	5.00	10.00
4011	One Monkey Don't Stop No Show/Build Your Love on a Solid Foundation	1965	2.50	5.00	10.00
4016	I Want To (Do Everything For You)/Funny Bone	1965	2.50	5.00	10.00
4022	A Sweet Woman Like You/Close the Door	1965	2.50	5.00	10.00
4026	The Love You Save (May Be Your Own)/If Sugar Was As Sweet As You	1966	2.50	5.00	10.00
4028	S.Y.S.L.J.F.M. (Letter Song)/I'm a Man	1966	2.50	5.00	10.00
4033	I Believe I'm Gonna Make It/Better Believe It, Baby	1966	2.50	5.00	10.00
4045	I've Got to Do a Little Bit Better/What in the World	1966	2.50	5.00	10.00
4051	Papa Was Too/Truest Woman in the World	1966	2.50	5.00	10.00
4055	Show Me/A Woman Sees a Hard Time (When Her Man Is Gone)	1967	2.00	4.00	8.00
4059	Woman Like That, Yeah/I'm Going and Get It	1967	2.00	4.00	8.00
4061	A Woman's Hands/See See Rider	1967	2.00	4.00	8.00
4063	Skinny Legs and All/Watch the One	1967	2.50	5.00	10.00
4068	I'll Make Everyday Christmas (For My Woman)/Don't Give Up	1967	3.00	6.00	12.00
4069	Men Are Gettin' Scarce/You're Gonna Thank Me, Woman	1968	2.00	4.00	8.00
4076	I'll Never Do You Wrong/Wooden Spoon	1968	2.00	4.00	8.00
4079	Chocolate Cherry/Betwixt and Between	1968	2.00	4.00	8.00
4083	Keep the One You Got/Go Home and Do It	1968	2.00	4.00	8.00
4086	You Need Me, Baby/Baby, Be Good	1968	2.00	4.00	8.00
4089	That's Your Baby/Sweet, Sweet Woman	1968	2.00	4.00	8.00
4090	Buying a Book/Chicken Crazy	1969	2.00	4.00	8.00
4093	That's the Way/Anything You Wanna Know	1969	2.00	4.00	8.00
4094	We Can't Sit Down Now/It Ain't Sanitary	1969	2.00	4.00	8.00
4095	I Can't See You No More (When Johnny Comes Marching Home Again)/Sure Is Good	1969	2.00	4.00	8.00
4096	Everything Happens on Time/You're Right, Ray Charles	1970	2.00	4.00	8.00
4098	I'll Never Fall in Love Again/The Only Way I Know to Love You	1970	2.00	4.00	8.00
EPIC					
50313	Ain't Gonna Bump No More (With No Big Fat Woman)/I Mess Up Everything I Get My Hands On	1976	—	2.50	5.00
50426	Hungry for Your Love/I Almost Got to Heaven Once	1977	—	2.50	5.00
50494	Rub Down/Be Kind to Old People	1977	—	2.50	5.00
50530	Get Back, Leroy/You Can Be My Star	1978	—	2.50	5.00
HANDSHAKE					
02565	Don't Do Da Do/Here Comes No. 34 (Do the Earl Campbell)	1981	—	2.00	4.00
KING					
4840	Come In This House/Baby, You Upset My Home	1955	15.00	30.00	60.00
4884	My Biggest Mistake/Right Back to My Arms	1956	12.50	25.00	50.00
4911	She's Mine/I Had to Come Back to You	1956	12.50	25.00	50.00
4980	Get Way Back/Pneumonia	1956	12.50	25.00	50.00
5064	I Want to Have a Talk with You/Ain't Nobody's Business	1957	12.50	25.00	50.00
5981	Come In This House/I Want to Have a Talk with You	1965	2.50	5.00	10.00

Albums

Number	Title (A Side/B Side)	Yr	VG	VG+	NM
ACCORD					
SN-7174	J.T.'s Funk	1982	2.50	5.00	10.00

Number	Title (A Side/B Side)	Yr	VG	VG+	NM
ATLANTIC					
8106 [M]	Hold What You've Got	1965	10.00	20.00	40.00
SD 8106 [P]	Hold What You've Got	1965	12.50	25.00	50.00
8115 [M]	The New Boss	1965	10.00	20.00	40.00
SD 8115 [S]	The New Boss	1965	12.50	25.00	50.00
8124 [M]	The Love You Save	1966	10.00	20.00	40.00
SD 8124 [S]	The Love You Save	1966	12.50	25.00	50.00
8133 [M]	I've Got to Do a Little Better	1966	10.00	20.00	40.00
SD 8133 [S]	I've Got to Do a Little Better	1966	12.50	25.00	50.00
8144 [M]	The Best of Joe Tex	1967	5.00	10.00	20.00
SD 8144 [P]	The Best of Joe Tex	1967	6.25	12.50	25.00
SD 8156	Live and Lively	1968	5.00	10.00	20.00
SD 8187	Soul Country	1968	5.00	10.00	20.00
SD 8211	Happy Soul	1969	5.00	10.00	20.00
SD 8231	Buying a Book	1969	5.00	10.00	20.00
SD 8254	Joe Tex Sings with Strings and Things	1970	3.75	7.50	15.00
SD 8292	From the Roots Came the Rapper	1972	3.75	7.50	15.00
81278	The Best of Joe Tex	1985	2.50	5.00	10.00
CHECKER					
LP-2993 [M]	Hold On	1965	37.50	75.00	150.00
DIAL					
DL 6002	I Gotcha	1972	3.75	7.50	15.00
DL 6004	Joe Tex Spills the Beans	1973	3.75	7.50	15.00
DL 6100	He Who Is Without Funk Cast the First Stone	1979	2.50	5.00	10.00
EPIC					
PE 34666	Bumps and Bruises	1977	3.00	6.00	12.00
KING					
935 [M]	The Best of Joe Tex	1965	25.00	50.00	100.00
KS-935 [R]	The Best of Joe Tex	1965	18.75	37.50	75.00
LONDON					
LC-50017	Super Soul	1977	2.50	5.00	10.00
PARROT					
PA 61002 [M]	The Best of Joe Tex	1965	12.50	25.00	50.00
PAS 71002 [R]	The Best of Joe Tex	1965	7.50	15.00	30.00
PRIDE					
PRD-20	The History of Joe Tex	1973	2.50	5.00	10.00
RHINO					
RNLP-70191	I Believe I'm Gonna Make It: The Best of Joe Tex 1964-1972	1988	2.50	5.00	10.00

TEX AND THE CHEX

45s

Number	Title (A Side/B Side)	Yr	VG	VG+	NM
20TH FOX					
411	Beach Party/Now (Love Me)	1963	7.50	15.00	30.00
ATLANTIC					
2116	I Do Love You/My Love	1961	15.00	30.00	60.00
NEWTOWN					
5010	Watching Willie Wobble/Be on the Lookout for My Girl	1963	5.00	10.00	20.00

TEXANS, THE

Also see JOHNNY AND DORSEY BURNETTE.

45s

Number	Title (A Side/B Side)	Yr	VG	VG+	NM
GOTHIC					
001	Old Reb/Rockin' Johnny Home	1961	7.50	15.00	30.00
INFINITY					
001	Green Grass of Texas/Bloody River	1961	7.50	15.00	30.00
JOX					
001	Old Reb/Rockin' Johnny Home	1965	7.50	15.00	30.00
VEE JAY					
658	Green Grass of Texas/Bloody River	1965	5.00	10.00	20.00

THARP, CHUCK, AND THE FIREBALLS

See THE FIREBALLS.

THEE MIDNITERS

45s

Number	Title (A Side/B Side)	Yr	VG	VG+	NM
CHATTAHOOCHIE					
666-2	Land of a Thousand Dances (Part 1)/Ball O' Twine	1965	3.75	7.50	15.00
666	Land of a Thousand Dances (Part 1)/Land of a Thousand Dances (Part 2)	1965	3.75	7.50	15.00
674	Sad Girl/Heat Wave	1965	4.00	8.00	16.00
675	Sad Girl/Heat Wave	1965	3.75	7.50	15.00
684	Whittier Blvd./Evil Love	1965	3.75	7.50	15.00
693	I Need Someone/Empty Heart	1965	5.00	10.00	20.00
695	Brother, Where Are You/Heat Wave	1966	3.75	7.50	15.00
706	Are You Angry/I Found a Peanut	1966	3.75	7.50	15.00
UNI					
55170	She Only Wants What She Can't Get/I've Come Alive	1969	2.50	5.00	10.00
WHITTIER					
201	That's All/To Be with You	196?	3.00	6.00	12.00
500	Love, Special Delivery/Don't Go Away	1966	5.00	10.00	20.00
501	The Midnite Feeling/It'll Never Be Over for Me	1966	5.00	10.00	20.00
503	Dragon Fly/The Big Ranch	1966	5.00	10.00	20.00
504	Never Knew I Had It So Bad/The Walking Song	1967	5.00	10.00	20.00
504	Never Knew I Had It So Bad/Everybody Needs Somebody	1967	7.50	15.00	30.00
507	Jump Five and Harmonize/Looking Out a Window	1967	5.00	10.00	20.00
508	Chile Con Soul/Tu Despedida	1967	5.00	10.00	20.00
509	Breakfast on the Grass/Dreaming Casually	1967	5.00	10.00	20.00
511	You're Gonna Make Me Cry/Make Ends Meet	1968	50.00	100.00	200.00
512	The Ballad of Cesar Chavez/The Ballad of Cesar Chavez (Spanish)	1968	5.00	10.00	20.00
513	Chicano Power/Never Goin' to Give You Up	1968	5.00	10.00	20.00
674	Sad Girl/Heat Wave	1968	3.00	6.00	12.00
694	It's Not Unusual/It's Not Unusual	1969	3.00	6.00	12.00

Albums

Number	Title (A Side/B Side)	Yr	VG	VG+	NM
CHATTAHOOCHIE					
C-1001 [M]	Thee Midniters	1965	15.00	30.00	60.00
CS-1001 [S]	Thee Midniters	1965	20.00	40.00	80.00
WHITTIER					
W-5000 [M]	Bring You Love Special Delivery	1966	10.00	20.00	40.00
WS-5000 [S]	Bring You Love Special Delivery	1966	12.50	25.00	50.00
W-5001 [M]	Unlimited	1966	10.00	20.00	40.00
WS-5001 [S]	Unlimited	1966	12.50	25.00	50.00
W-5002 [M]	Giants	1967	10.00	20.00	40.00
WS-5002 [S]	Giants	1967	12.50	25.00	50.00
ZYANYA/RHINO					
RNLP-63	The Best of Thee Midniters	1983	3.00	6.00	12.00

THEE MUFFINS

Albums

Number	Title (A Side/B Side)	Yr	VG	VG+	NM
(NO LABEL)					
(no #)	Thee Muffins Pop Up!	1967	50.00	100.00	200.00

THEE PROPHETS

45s

Number	Title (A Side/B Side)	Yr	VG	VG+	NM
KAPP					
962	Playgirl/Patricia Ann	1969	2.50	5.00	10.00
997	Some Kind of Wonderful/They Call Her Sorrow	1969	2.50	5.00	10.00
2038	Rag Doll Boy/It Isn't So Easy	1969	2.50	5.00	10.00
2087	Little Bit of Love/Come to Me Girl	1970	2.50	5.00	10.00

Albums

Number	Title (A Side/B Side)	Yr	VG	VG+	NM
KAPP					
KS-3596	Playgirl	1969	5.00	10.00	20.00

THEM

Also see BELFAST GYPSIES; VAN MORRISON.

45s

Number	Title (A Side/B Side)	Yr	VG	VG+	NM
A&M					
1201	Baby Please Don't Go/Danger Heartbreak Dead Ahead	1988	—	2.00	4.00
—B-side by the Marvelettes					
1201 [PS]	Danger Heartbreak Dead Ahead/Baby Please Don't Go	1988	—	2.00	4.00
—"Good Morning Vietnam" sleeve					
HAPPY TIGER					
525	Lonely Weekends/I Am Waiting	1969	3.75	7.50	15.00
534	Memphis Lady/Nobody Cares	1970	3.00	6.00	12.00
PARROT					
365	Gloria/Bring 'Em On In	1971	2.50	5.00	10.00
3003	Richard Cory/Don't You Know	1966	3.75	7.50	15.00
3006	Don't Start Crying Now/I Can Only Give You Everything	1966	3.75	7.50	15.00
9702	Don't Start Crying Now/One, Two Brown Eyes	1964	5.00	10.00	20.00
9727	Gloria/Baby, Please Don't Go	1965	4.00	8.00	16.00
9749	Here Comes the Night/All By Myself	1965	3.75	7.50	15.00
9784	Gonna Dress in Black/Half As Much	1965	3.75	7.50	15.00
9796	Mystic Eyes/If You and I Could Be As Two	1965	3.75	7.50	15.00
9819	Call My Name/Bring 'Em On In	1966	3.75	7.50	15.00
RUFF					
1088	Walking in the Queen's Garden/I Happen to Love You	1967	6.25	12.50	25.00
TOWER					
384	Walking in the Queen's Garden/I Happen to Love You	1967	3.00	6.00	12.00
384 [PS]	Walking in the Queen's Garden/I Happen to Love You	1967	7.50	15.00	30.00
407	But It's Alright/Square Room	1968	3.00	6.00	12.00
461	Waltz of the Flies/We All Agreed to Help	1969	3.00	6.00	12.00
493	Corina/Dark Are the Shadows	1969	3.00	6.00	12.00

Albums

Number	Title (A Side/B Side)	Yr	VG	VG+	NM
HAPPY TIGER					
HT-1004	Them	1969	12.50	25.00	50.00
HT-1012	Them In Reality	1971	30.00	60.00	120.00
LONDON					
PS 639 [P]	Backtrackin'	1974	2.50	5.00	10.00
LC-50001 [R]	The Story of Them	1977	2.50	5.00	10.00
820326-1	Them Featuring Van Morrison	1985	2.50	5.00	10.00
PARROT					
PA 61005 [M]	Them Featuring "Here Comes the Night"	1965	20.00	40.00	80.00
PA 61005 [M]	Them Featuring "Gloria"	1966	12.50	25.00	50.00
—Same album as above, but with slightly different title					
PA 61008 [M]	Them Again	1966	20.00	40.00	80.00
PAS 71005 [R]	Them Featuring "Here Comes the Night"	1965	17.50	35.00	70.00
PAS 71005 [R]	Them Featuring "Gloria"	1966	10.00	20.00	40.00
—Same album as above, but with slightly different title					
PAS 71008 [R]	Them Again	1966	12.50	25.00	50.00
BP 71053 [(2) P]	Them Featuring Van Morrison	1972	3.00	6.00	12.00
—"Gloria," "Here Comes the Night," "If You and I Could Be as Two," "One More Time" and "One Two Brown Eyes" are true stereo.					
TOWER					
ST 5104 [S]	Now and Them	1967	20.00	40.00	80.00
T 5104 [M]	Now and Them	1967	12.50	25.00	50.00
ST 5116 [S]	Time Out! Time In for Them	1968	25.00	50.00	100.00

THEM (2)

45s

Number	Title (A Side/B Side)	Yr	VG	VG+	NM
KING					
5967	Don't Look Now/A Girl Like You	1964	3.75	7.50	15.00

THEMES, INC.

Yet another creation of STEVE BARRI and P.F. SLOAN.

45s

Number	Title (A Side/B Side)	Yr	VG	VG+	NM
VEE JAY					
635	Theme from Petyon Place/Paula's Percussion	1964	3.75	7.50	15.00

THERRIEN, JOE, JR.

45s

Number	Title (A Side/B Side)	Yr	VG	VG+	NM
BRUNSWICK					
9-55005	Hey Babe, Let's Go Downtown/Come Back to Me Darling	1957	10.00	20.00	40.00
9-55017	Wheels/You're Long Gone	1957	20.00	40.00	80.00
JAT					
101	I Ain't Gonna Be Around/Play Me a Blue Song	1958	20.00	40.00	80.00
LIDO					
505	Hey Babe, Let's Go Downtown/Come Back to Me Darling	1957	30.00	60.00	120.00

THESE TRAILS

Albums

Number	Title (A Side/B Side)	Yr	VG	VG+	NM
SINERGIA					
(# unknown)	These Trails	1973	30.00	60.00	120.00

THIN LIZZY

12-Inch Singles

Number	Title (A Side/B Side)	Yr	VG	VG+	NM
WARNER BROS.					
PRO-A-754 [DJ]	Cowboy Song/The Boys Are Back in Town/Rosalie	1978	5.00	10.00	20.00

45s

Number	Title (A Side/B Side)	Yr	VG	VG+	NM
LONDON					
20076	Whiskey in the Jar/Black Boys on the Corner	1972	2.00	4.00	8.00
20078	Broken Dreams/Randolph's Tango	1973	2.00	4.00	8.00
20082	Little Darling/The Rocket	1973	2.00	4.00	8.00
MERCURY					
73786	The Boys Are Back in Town/Jailbreak	1976	—	2.50	5.00
73841	Cowboy Song/Angel from the Coast	1976	—	2.50	5.00
73867	Rocky/Half-Caste	1976	—	2.50	5.00
73882	Old Flame/Johnny the Fox Meets Jimmy the Weed	1977	—	2.50	5.00
73892	Don't Believe a Word/Boogie Woogie Dance	1977	—	2.50	5.00
73945	Bad Reputation/Dancing in the Moonlight (It's Caught Me in the Spotlight)	1977	—	2.50	5.00
VERTIGO					
202	Night Life/Showdown	1974	—	3.00	6.00
205	Wild One/Freedom Song	1975	—	3.00	6.00
WARNER BROS.					
8648	Cowboy Song/Johnny the Fox Meets Jimmy the Weed	1978	—	2.50	5.00
49019	S & M/Do Anything You Want To	1979	—	2.50	5.00
49078	Got to Give It Up/With Love	1979	—	2.50	5.00
49643	Killer on the Loose/Sugar Blues	1980	—	2.00	4.00
49679	We Will Be Strong/Sweetheart	1981	—	2.00	4.00
50056	Hollywood/Pressure Will Blow	1982	—	2.00	4.00

Albums

Number	Title (A Side/B Side)	Yr	VG	VG+	NM
LONDON					
PS 594	Thin Lizzy	1971	10.00	20.00	40.00
PS 636	Vagabonds of the Western World	1973	7.50	15.00	30.00
LC-50004	The Rocker (1971-1974)	1977	3.00	6.00	12.00
MERCURY					
SRM-1-1081	Jailbreak	1976	3.00	6.00	12.00
SRM-1-1107	Night Life	1976	3.00	6.00	12.00
—Reissue of Vertigo 2002					
SRM-1-1108	Fighting	1976	3.00	6.00	12.00
—Reissue of Vertigo 2005					
SRM-1-1119	Johnny the Fox	1976	3.00	6.00	12.00
SRM-1-1186	Bad Reputation	1977	3.00	6.00	12.00
VERTIGO					
VEL-2002	Night Life	1974	3.75	7.50	15.00
VEL-2005	Fighting	1975	3.75	7.50	15.00
WARNER BROS.					
BS2 3213 [(2)]	Live and Dangerous	1978	3.00	6.00	12.00
BSK 3338	Black Rose/A Rock Legend	1979	2.50	5.00	10.00
BSK 3496	Chinatown	1980	2.50	5.00	10.00
BSK 3622	Renegade	1982	2.50	5.00	10.00
23831	Thunder and Lightning	1983	2.50	5.00	10.00
23986 [(2)]	"Life" — Live	1984	3.00	6.00	12.00

THINGS TO COME

45s

Number	Title (A Side/B Side)	Yr	VG	VG+	NM
DUNWICH					
124	I'm Not Talkin'/'Til the End	1966	12.50	25.00	50.00
STARFIRE					
103	Sweet Gina/(B-side unknown)	1966	10.00	20.00	40.00
WARNER BROS.					
7164	Come Alive/Dancer	1968	3.75	7.50	15.00
7228	Cool Day/Hello	1968	3.75	7.50	15.00

THINK

45s

Number	Title (A Side/B Side)	Yr	VG	VG+	NM
BIG TREE					
15000	Once You Understand/Gather	1974	—	2.00	4.00
COLUMBIA					
44627	Faster Faster/Stop Runnin' Away	1968	—	3.00	6.00
44848	California (Is Getting So Heavy)/It's a Good Thing	1969	—	3.00	6.00
LAURIE					
3583	Once You Understand/Gather	1972	—	2.50	5.00
3594	It's Not the World — It's the People/Who Are You to Tell Me What to Do?	1972	—	2.50	5.00

Albums

Number	Title (A Side/B Side)	Yr	VG	VG+	NM
LAURIE					
SLLP-2052	Encounter	1972	3.00	6.00	12.00

THIRD POWER

Albums

Number	Title (A Side/B Side)	Yr	VG	VG+	NM
VANGUARD					
VSD-6554	Believe	1970	7.50	15.00	30.00

THIRD RAIL, THE

45s

Number	Title (A Side/B Side)	Yr	VG	VG+	NM
CAMEO					
445	The Subway Train That Came to Life/Train Rush Hour Stomp	1966	3.75	7.50	15.00
EPIC					
10191	Run, Run, Run/No Return	1967	2.50	5.00	10.00
10240	Boppa Do Down Down/Invisible Man	1967	2.00	4.00	8.00
10285	Overdose of Love/It's Time to Say Goodbye	1968	2.00	4.00	8.00
10323	Shape of Things to Come/She Ain't No Choir Girl	1968	2.00	4.00	8.00
10457	The Ballad of General Humpty/Beggin' Me to Stay	1969	2.00	4.00	8.00

Albums

Number	Title (A Side/B Side)	Yr	VG	VG+	NM
EPIC					
LN 24327 [M]	Id Music	1967	7.50	15.00	30.00
BN 26327 [S]	Id Music	1967	10.00	20.00	40.00

THIRTEENTH FLOOR ELEVATORS, THE

45s

Number	Title (A Side/B Side)	Yr	VG	VG+	NM
CONTACT					
5269	You're Gonna Miss Me/Tried to Hide	1966	25.00	50.00	100.00
HANNA-BARBERA					
492	You're Gonna Miss Me/Tried to Hide	1966	50.00	100.00	200.00
INTERNATIONAL ARTISTS					
107	You're Gonna Miss Me/Tried to Hide	1967	7.50	15.00	30.00
—Blue label					
107	You're Gonna Miss Me/Tried to Hide	1967	5.00	10.00	20.00
—Yellow label					
111	Reverberation (Doubt)/Fire Engine	1967	5.00	10.00	20.00
113	Before You Accuse Me/Levitation	1968	5.00	10.00	20.00
121	Baby Blue/She Lives	1968	5.00	10.00	20.00
122	Slip Inside This House/Splash 1	1968	5.00	10.00	20.00
126	May the Circle Remain Unbroken/I'm Gonna Love You Too	1968	5.00	10.00	20.00
130	Livin' On/Scarlet and Gold	1969	10.00	20.00	40.00

Albums

Number	Title (A Side/B Side)	Yr	VG	VG+	NM
INTERNATIONAL ARTISTS					
1 [M]	Psychedelic Sounds	1967	62.50	125.00	250.00
—Green and yellow label					
1 [M]	Psychedelic Sounds	1968	37.50	75.00	150.00
—All-yellow label					
1 [S]	Psychedelic Sounds	1968	37.50	75.00	150.00
—All-yellow label					
1 [S]	Psychedelic Sounds	1968	50.00	100.00	200.00
—Aqua-blue label					
1 [S]	Psychedelic Sounds	1979	7.50	15.00	30.00
—Repressing with "Masterfonics" in dead wax					
5 [M]	Easter Everywhere	1968	100.00	200.00	400.00
—Mono is promo only					
5 [S]	Easter Everywhere	1968	37.50	75.00	150.00
—With custom inner sleeve					
5 [S]	Easter Everywhere	1968	37.50	75.00	150.00
—Without custom inner sleeve					
5 [S]	Easter Everywhere	1979	7.50	15.00	30.00
—Repressing with "Masterfonics" in dead wax					
8	13th Floor Elevators Live	1968	25.00	50.00	100.00
8	13th Floor Elevators Live	1979	6.25	12.50	25.00
—Repressing with "Masterfonics" in dead wax					
9	Bull of the Woods	1968	20.00	40.00	80.00
9	Bull of the Woods	1979	6.25	12.50	25.00
—Repressing with "Masterfonics" in dead wax					

31ST OF FEBRUARY, THE

45s

Number	Title (A Side/B Side)	Yr	VG	VG+	NM
VANGUARD					
35066	Sandcastles/Pick a Gripe	1968	2.50	5.00	10.00
35087	In the Morning When I'm Real/Porcelain Mirrors	1969	2.50	5.00	10.00

Albums

Number	Title (A Side/B Side)	Yr	VG	VG+	NM
VANGUARD					
VSD-6503	The 31st of February	1969	10.00	20.00	40.00

31 FLAVORS, THE

Albums

Number	Title (A Side/B Side)	Yr	VG	VG+	NM
CROWN					
CST-592	Hair	1968	12.50	25.00	50.00

THOMAS, B.J.

45s

Number	Title (A Side/B Side)	Yr	VG	VG+	NM
ABC					
12054	(Hey, Won't You Play) Another Somebody Done Somebody Wrong Song/City Blues	1974	—	2.00	4.00
12121	We Are Happy Together/Help Me Make It (To My Rockin' Chair)	1975	—	2.00	4.00
BRAGG					
103	Billy and Sue/Never Tell	1964	5.00	10.00	20.00
CLEVELAND INT'L.					
03492	Whatever Happened to Old Fashioned Love/I Just Sing	1983	—	2.00	4.00
04608	From This Moment On/The Girl Most Likely To	1984	—	2.00	4.00
COLUMBIA					
03985	New Looks from an Old Lover/You Keep the Man in Me Happy	1983	—	2.00	4.00
04237	Two Car Garage/Beautiful World	1983	—	2.00	4.00
04431	The Whole World's in Love When You're Lonely/We're Here to Love	1984	—	—	3.00
04531	Rock and Roll Shoes/Then I'll Be Over You	1984	—	—	3.00
—Ray Charles and B.J. Thomas					
05647	A Part of Me That Needs You Most/Northern Lights	1985	—	—	3.00
05771	America Is/Broken Toys	1986	—	—	3.00
05771 [PS]	America Is/Broken Toys	1986	—	2.00	4.00
06314	Night Life/Make the World Go Away	1986	—	—	3.00

Number	Title (A Side/B Side)	Yr	VG	VG+	NM
HICKORY					
1395	Billy and Sue/Never Tell	1966	2.50	5.00	10.00
LORI					
9547	I've Got a Feeling/Hey Judy	1963	6.25	12.50	25.00
9561	For Your Precious Love/Here I Am Again	1964	6.25	12.50	25.00
MCA					
40735	Don't Worry Baby/My Love	1977	—	2.00	4.00
40812	Still the Lovin' Is Fun/Play Me a Little Traveling Music	1977	—	2.00	4.00
40854	Everybody Loves a Rain Song/Dusty Roads	1978	—	2.00	4.00
40914	Sweet Young America/Aloha	1978	—	2.00	4.00
40986	We Could Have Been the Closest of Friends/In My Heart	1979	—	2.00	4.00
41134	God Bless the Children/On This Christmas Night	1979	—	2.00	4.00
41134 [PS]	God Bless the Children/On This Christmas Night	1979	—	2.50	5.00
41207	Nothin' Could Be Better/Walkin' on a Cloud	1980	—	2.00	4.00
41281	Everything Always Works Out for the Best/No Limit	1980	—	2.00	4.00
51087	Some Love Songs Never Die/There Ain't No Love	1981	—	2.00	4.00
51151	The Lovin' Kind/I Recall a Gypsy Woman	1981	—	2.00	4.00
52053	I Really Got the Feeling/But Love Me	1982	—	2.00	4.00
MYRRH					
166	Home Where I Belong/Hallelujah	1977	—	2.50	5.00
176	Without a Doubt/(B-side unknown)	1977	—	2.50	5.00
234	Uncloudy Day/(B-side unknown)	1981	—	2.50	5.00
PACEMAKER					
227	I'm So Lonesome I Could Cry/Candy Baby	1964	5.00	10.00	20.00
231	Mama/Wendy	1965	3.75	7.50	15.00
234	Bring Back the Time/I Don't Have a Mind of My Own	1965	3.75	7.50	15.00
239	Tomorrow Never Comes/Your Tears Leave Me Cold	1965	3.75	7.50	15.00
247	Plain Jane/My Home Town	1965	3.75	7.50	15.00
253	I'm Not a Fool Anymore/Baby Cried	1965	3.75	7.50	15.00
256	I Can't Help It (If I'm Still in Love with You)/Baby Cried	1965	3.75	7.50	15.00
259	Pretty Country Girl/Houston Town	1965	3.75	7.50	15.00
PARAMOUNT					
0218	Songs/Goodbye's a Long, Long Time	1973	—	2.50	5.00
0218 [PS]	Songs/Goodbye's a Long, Long Time	1973	—	3.00	6.00
0239	Sunday Sunrise/Talkin' Confidentially	1973	—	2.50	5.00
0239	Sunday Sunrise/Early Morning Rush	1973	—	2.50	5.00
0277	Play Something Sweet (Brickyard Blues)/Talkin' Confidentially	1974	—	2.50	5.00
REPRISE					
22837	Don't Leave Love (Out There All Alone)/One Woman	1989	—	—	3.00
SCEPTER					
12129	I'm So Lonesome I Could Cry/Candy Baby	1966	2.50	5.00	10.00
12139	Mama/Wendy	1966	2.00	4.00	8.00
12154	Bring Back the Time/I Don't Have a Mind of My Own	1966	2.00	4.00	8.00
12165	Tomorrow Never Comes/Your Tears Leave Me Cold	1966	2.00	4.00	8.00
12179	Plain Jane/My Home Town	1966	2.00	4.00	8.00
12194	I Can't Help It (If I'm Still in Love with You)/Baby Cried	1967	2.00	4.00	8.00
12200	Just the Wisdom of a Fool/Treasure of Love	1967	2.00	4.00	8.00
12201	Wisdom of a Fool/Human	1967	2.00	4.00	8.00
12205	The Girl Can't Help It/Walkin' Back	1967	2.00	4.00	8.00
12219	The Eyes of a New York Woman/I May Never Get to Heaven	1968	2.00	4.00	8.00
12230	Hooked on a Feeling/I've Been Down This Road Before	1968	2.00	4.00	8.00
12244	It's Only Love/You Don't Love Me Anymore	1969	—	3.00	6.00
12255	Pass the Apple Eve/Fairy Tale of Time	1969	—	3.00	6.00
12259	You Don't Love Me Anymore/Skip a Rope	1969	—	3.00	6.00
12265	Raindrops Keep Fallin' on My Head/Never Had It So Good	1969	—	3.50	7.00
12277	Everybody's Out of Town/Living Again	1970	—	3.00	6.00
12283	I Just Can't Help Believing/Send My Picture to Scranton, Pa.	1970	—	3.00	6.00
12299	Most of All/The Mask	1970	—	2.50	5.00
12307	No Love at All/Have a Heart	1971	—	2.50	5.00
12320	Mighty Clouds of Joy/Life	1971	—	2.50	5.00
12335	Long Ago Tomorrow/Burnin' a Hole in My Mind	1971	—	2.50	5.00
12344	Rock and Roll Lullaby/Are We Losing Touch	1972	—	3.00	6.00
12354	That's What Friends Are For/I Get Enthused	1972	—	2.50	5.00
12364	Happier Than the Morning Sun/We Have Got to Get Out Ship Together	1972	—	2.50	5.00
12379	Sweet Cherry Wine/Roads	1973	—	2.50	5.00
VALERIE					
226	I've Got a Feeling/Hey Judy	1963	5.00	10.00	20.00
WARNER BROS.					
5491	Billy and Sue/Never Tell	1964	5.00	10.00	20.00

Albums

Number	Title	Yr	VG	VG+	NM
ABC					
ABCD-858	Reunion	1975	2.50	5.00	10.00
ABCD-912	Help Me Make It to My Rockin' Chair	1976	2.50	5.00	10.00
ACCORD					
SN-7106	Lovin' You	198?	2.50	5.00	10.00
BUCKBOARD					
1023	B.J. Thomas Sings Hank Williams and Other Favorites	198?	2.50	5.00	10.00
CLEVELAND INT'L.					
FC 38561	New Looks	1983	2.50	5.00	10.00
PC 38561	New Looks	1984	2.00	4.00	8.00
—Budget-line reissue					
FC 39111	The Great American Dream	1983	2.50	5.00	10.00
PC 39111	The Great American Dream	1984	2.00	4.00	8.00
—Budget-line reissue					
FC 39337	Shining	1984	2.50	5.00	10.00
FC 40157	Throwing Rocks at the Moon	1985	2.50	5.00	10.00
COLUMBIA					
PC 38400	Love Shines	1984	2.00	4.00	8.00
—Reissue of Priority 38400					
PC 40148	All Is Calm, All Is Bright...	1985	2.50	5.00	10.00
FC 40496	Night Life	1986	2.50	5.00	10.00
DORAL					
(# unknown)	Doral Presents B.J. Thomas	1971	5.00	10.00	20.00
—Mail-order promotion from Doral cigarettes					
EVEREST					
4104	Golden Greats	1981	2.50	5.00	10.00
HICKORY					
LPM-133 [M]	The Very Best of B.J. Thomas	1966	5.00	10.00	20.00
LPS-133 [S]	The Very Best of B.J. Thomas	1966	6.25	12.50	25.00
ST 90956 [S]	The Very Best of B.J. Thomas	1966	7.50	15.00	30.00
—Capitol Record Club edition					
T 90956 [M]	The Very Best of B.J. Thomas	1966	6.25	12.50	25.00
—Capitol Record Club edition					
MCA					
746	Everybody Loves a Rain Song	1980	2.00	4.00	8.00
—Budget-line reissue					
2286	B.J. Thomas	1977	2.50	5.00	10.00
3035	Everybody Loves a Rain Song	1978	2.50	5.00	10.00
3231	For the Best	1979	2.50	5.00	10.00
5155	In Concert	1980	2.50	5.00	10.00
5195	Some Love Songs Never Die	1980	2.50	5.00	10.00
5296	As We Know Him	1982	2.50	5.00	10.00
27032	In Concert	198?	2.00	4.00	8.00
—Reissue of MCA 5155					
MYRRH					
MSB-6574	Home Where I Belong	1978	2.50	5.00	10.00
MSB-6593	A Happy Man	1979	2.50	5.00	10.00
MSB-6633	You Gave Me Love	1979	2.50	5.00	10.00
MSB-6653	The Best of B.J. Thomas	1980	2.50	5.00	10.00
MSB 6675	Amazing Grace	1981	2.50	5.00	10.00
MSB-6705	Miracle	1983	2.50	5.00	10.00
MSB-6710	Peace in the Valley	1983	2.50	5.00	10.00
MSB-6725	The Best of B.J. Thomas, Volume 2	1984	2.50	5.00	10.00
WR-8153	Peace in the Valley	1985	2.50	5.00	10.00
—Reissue of 6710					
WR-8200	Amazing Grace	1985	2.00	4.00	8.00
—Reissue of 6675					
PACEMAKER					
PLP-3001 [M]	B.J. Thomas and the Triumphs	1965	50.00	100.00	200.00
PAIR					
PDL2-1099 [(2)]	Greatest Hits	1986	3.00	6.00	12.00
PARAMOUNT					
PAS 1020	Longhorns & Londonbridges	1974	3.00	6.00	12.00
PAS-6052	B.J. Thomas Songs	1973	3.00	6.00	12.00
PICKWICK					
SPC-3623	The Best of B.J. Thomas	197?	2.50	5.00	10.00
PRIORITY					
JU 38400	Love Shines	1982	2.50	5.00	10.00
REPRISE					
25898	Midnight Minute	1989	3.00	6.00	12.00
SCEPTER					
SPS-535 [S]	I'm So Lonesome I Could Cry	1966	6.25	12.50	25.00
SRM-535 [M]	I'm So Lonesome I Could Cry	1966	5.00	10.00	20.00
SPS-556 [S]	Tomorrow Never Comes	1966	5.00	10.00	20.00
SRM-556 [M]	Tomorrow Never Comes	1966	3.75	7.50	15.00
SPS-561 [S]	For Lovers and Losers	1967	3.75	7.50	15.00
SRM-561 [M]	For Lovers and Losers	1967	5.00	10.00	20.00
SPS-570	On My Way	1968	3.75	7.50	15.00
SPS-576	Young and In Love	1969	3.75	7.50	15.00
SPS-578	Greatest Hits, Volume 1	1969	3.00	6.00	12.00
SPS-580	Raindrops Keep Fallin' on My Head	1970	3.75	7.50	15.00
—Original "muddy mix"; trail-off wax number on Side 1 is "SPS-580-A-1B" and on Side 2 is "SPS-580-B-1A"					
SPS-580	Raindrops Keep Fallin' on My Head	1970	3.00	6.00	12.00
—Remixed version; trail-off wax number on Side 1 is "SPS-580-A-1C" and on Side 2 is "SPS-580-B-1C"					
SPS-582	Everybody's Out of Town	1970	3.00	6.00	12.00
SPS-586	Most of All	1970	3.00	6.00	12.00
SPS-597	Greatest Hits, Volume Two	1971	3.00	6.00	12.00
5101	Billy Joe Thomas	1972	3.00	6.00	12.00
5108	B.J. Thomas Country	1972	3.00	6.00	12.00
5112 [(2)]	Greatest All-Time Hits	1973	3.75	7.50	15.00
STARDAY					
992	The Best of B.J. Thomas	197?	2.50	5.00	10.00
UNITED ARTISTS					
UA-LA389-E	The Very Best of B.J. Thomas	1974	3.00	6.00	12.00

THOMAS, BUELL

45s

Number	Title (A Side/B Side)	Yr	VG	VG+	NM
DALTON					
102	Shepherds & Kings/My Christmas Star	19??	—	2.00	4.00
—B-side by Jean Doran					
DOOTONE					
316	Santa Claus Walks Just Like Daddy/You're My Christmas	1953	7.50	15.00	30.00
—B-side by Gerri Goodley					
318	Green Christmas/For My Bride At Christmas Time	1953	7.50	15.00	30.00

THOMAS, CARLA

Also see OTIS AND CARLA; RUFUS AND CARLA.

45s

Number	Title (A Side/B Side)	Yr	VG	VG+	NM
ATLANTIC					
2086	Gee Whiz (Look at His Eyes)/For You	1960	3.75	7.50	15.00
2101	A Love of My Own/Promises	1961	3.00	6.00	12.00
2113	Wish Me Good Luck/In Your Spare Time	1961	3.00	6.00	12.00
2132	The Masquerade Is Over/I Kinda Think He Does	1962	3.00	6.00	12.00
2163	I'll Bring It On Home to You/I Can't Take It	1962	3.00	6.00	12.00
2189	What a Fool I've Been/The Life I Live	1963	3.00	6.00	12.00

Number	Title (A Side/B Side)	Yr	VG	VG+	NM
2212	Gee Whiz, It's Christmas/All I Want for Christmas Is You	1963	3.75	7.50	15.00
2238	I've Got No Time to Lose/A Boy Named Tom	1964	3.00	6.00	12.00
2258	A Woman's Love/Don't Let the Love Light Leave	1964	3.00	6.00	12.00
2272	How Do You Quit (Someone You Love)/The Puppet	1965	3.00	6.00	12.00
GUSTO					
816	All I Want For Christmas Is You/Gee Whiz, It's Christmas	1979	2.50	5.00	10.00
—A Canadian import ($5) from 1986 exists on King					
SATELLITE					
104	Gee Whiz (Look at His Eyes)/For You	1960	125.00	250.00	500.00
STAX					
0011	I've Fallen in Love/Where Do I Go	1968	2.00	4.00	8.00
0024	I Like What You're Doing (To Me)/Strung Out	1969	2.00	4.00	8.00
0042	Just Keep On Loving Me/My Love	1969	2.00	4.00	8.00
—With Johnnie Taylor					
0044	I Can't Stop/I Need You Woman	1969	—	2.50	5.00
—With William Bell					
0056	Guide Me Well/Some Other Man (Is Beating Your Time)	1970	2.00	4.00	8.00
0061	The Time for Love Is Anytime/Living in the City	1970	—	3.00	6.00
0067	All I Have to Do Is Dream/Leave the Girl Alone	1970	—	2.50	5.00
—With William Bell					
0080	Hi De Ho (That Old Sweet Roll)/I Loved You Like I Love My Very Life	1970	—	3.00	6.00
0113	You've Got a Cushion to Fall On/Love Means (You Never Have to Say You're Sorry)	1972	—	3.00	6.00
0133	Sugar/You've Got a Cushion to Fall On	1972	—	3.00	6.00
0149	I May Not Be All You Want/Sugar	1972	—	3.00	6.00
172	Stop! Look What You're Doing/Every Ounce of Strength	1965	3.00	6.00	12.00
0173	I Have a God Who Loves/Love Among People	1973	—	3.00	6.00
183	Comfort Me/I'm for You	1966	3.00	6.00	12.00
188	Let Me Be Good to You/Another Night Without My Man	1966	3.00	6.00	12.00
195	B-A-B-Y/What Have You Got to Offer Me	1966	3.75	7.50	15.00
206	All I Want for Christmas Is You/Winter Snow	1966	3.00	6.00	12.00
207	Something Good (Is Going to Happen to You)/It's Starting to Grow	1967	2.50	5.00	10.00
214	Unchanging Love/When Tomorrow Comes	1967	2.50	5.00	10.00
222	I'll Always Have Faith in You/Stop Thief	1967	2.50	5.00	10.00
239	Pick Up the Pieces/Separation	1967	2.50	5.00	10.00
251	A Dime a Dozen/I Want You Back	1968	2.50	5.00	10.00
Albums					
ATLANTIC					
8057 [M]	Gee Whiz	1961	25.00	50.00	100.00
—With white "fan" logo					
8057 [M]	Gee Whiz	1963	10.00	20.00	40.00
—With black "fan" logo					
SD 8057 [S]	Gee Whiz	1961	37.50	75.00	150.00
—With white "fan" logo					
SD 8057 [S]	Gee Whiz	1963	12.50	25.00	50.00
—With black "fan" logo					
SD 8232	The Best of Carla Thomas	1969	6.25	12.50	25.00
STAX					
ST-706 [M]	Comfort Me	1966	8.75	17.50	35.00
STS-706 [P]	Comfort Me	1966	12.50	25.00	50.00
ST-709 [M]	Carla	1966	8.75	17.50	35.00
STS-709 [S]	Carla	1966	12.50	25.00	50.00
ST-718 [M]	The Queen Alone	1967	8.75	17.50	35.00
STS-718 [S]	The Queen Alone	1967	12.50	25.00	50.00
STS-2019	Memphis Queen	1969	8.75	17.50	35.00
STS-2044	Love Means Carla Thomas	1971	8.75	17.50	35.00
MPS-8538	Memphis Queen	1987	2.50	5.00	10.00
—Budget-line reissue					

THOMAS, CARLA, AND RUFUS THOMAS

See RUFUS AND CARLA.

THOMAS, GENE

Also see GENE AND DEBBE.

Number	Title (A Side/B Side)	Yr	VG	VG+	NM
45s					
HICKORY					
1608	Lay It Down/Remembered by Someone	1971	—	3.50	7.00
1631	Touch Something Good/Watching It Go	1972	—	3.50	7.00
VENUS					
1439	Sometime/Every Night	1961	7.50	15.00	30.00
1441	Lamp of Love/Two Lips	1961	5.00	10.00	20.00
1444	Down the Road/(B-side unknown)	1962	20.00	40.00	80.00

THOMAS, IRMA

Number	Title (A Side/B Side)	Yr	VG	VG+	NM
45s					
CANYON					
21	Save a Little Bit for Me/That's How I Feel About You	1970	—	3.00	6.00
31	I'll Do It All Over You/We Won't Be In Your Way Anymore	1970	—	3.00	6.00
CHESS					
2010	Cheater Man/Somewhere Crying	1967	2.00	4.00	8.00
2017	A Woman Will Do Wrong/I Gave You Everything	1967	2.00	4.00	8.00
2036	Good to Me/We Got Something Good	1968	2.00	4.00	8.00
COTILLION					
44144	Full Time Woman/She's Taken My Part	1972	—	3.00	6.00
IMPERIAL					
66013	Wish Someone Would Care/Break-A-Way	1964	3.00	6.00	12.00
66041	Time Is On My Side/Anyone Who Knows What Love Is (Will Understand)	1964	3.00	6.00	12.00
66069	Times Have Changed/Moments to Remember	1964	2.50	5.00	10.00
66080	He's My Guy/(I Want a) True, True Love	1964	2.50	5.00	10.00
66095	Some Things You Better Get Used To/You Don't Miss a Good Thing	1965	2.50	5.00	10.00
66106	Nobody Wants to Hear Nobody's Troubles/I'm Gonna Cry Till My Tears Run Dry	1965	2.50	5.00	10.00
66120	Hurts All Over/It's Starting to Get Me Now	1965	2.50	5.00	10.00
66137	Take a Look/What Are You Trying to Do	1965	2.50	5.00	10.00
66178	It's a Man-Woman's World (Part 1)/It's a Man-Woman's World (Part 2)	1966	2.50	5.00	10.00
MINIT					
625	Cry On/Girl Needs Boy	1961	3.00	6.00	12.00
633	It's Too Soon to Know/That's All I Ask	1961	3.00	6.00	12.00
642	Gone/Done Got Over It	1962	3.00	6.00	12.00
653	It's Raining/I Did My Part	1962	3.00	6.00	12.00
660	Somebody Told Me/Two Winters Long	1963	3.00	6.00	12.00
666	Ruler of My Heart/Hitting on Nothing	1963	3.00	6.00	12.00
RON					
328	Don't Mess with My Man/Set Me Free	1960	3.75	7.50	15.00
330	Good Man/I May Be Wrong	1960	3.75	7.50	15.00
UNITED ARTISTS					
0088	Wish Someone Would Care/Take a Look	1973	—	2.00	4.00
—"Silver Spotlight Series" reissue					
Albums					
BANDY					
70003	Irma Thomas Sings	197?	7.50	15.00	30.00
FUNGUS					
FB-25150	In Between Tears	1973	10.00	20.00	40.00
IMPERIAL					
LP-9266 [M]	Wish Someone Would Care	1964	12.50	25.00	50.00
LP-9302 [M]	Take a Look	1966	12.50	25.00	50.00
LP-12266 [S]	Wish Someone Would Care	1964	15.00	30.00	60.00
LP-12302 [S]	Take a Look	1966	15.00	30.00	60.00
RCS					
1004	Safe with Me	1980	7.50	15.00	30.00

THOMAS, JON

Number	Title (A Side/B Side)	Yr	VG	VG+	NM
45s					
ABC-PARAMOUNT					
10122	Heartbreak (It's Hurtin' Me)/Tearin'	1960	3.75	7.50	15.00
10140	Hey Hey Baby/Buffalo Blues	1960	3.75	7.50	15.00
10190	The Snake/Story Telling	1961	3.00	6.00	12.00
10238	Boss Hoss/Flip, Flop, Fly	1961	3.00	6.00	12.00
10274	The Thomas Twist/So Good	1961	3.00	6.00	12.00
CHECKER					
809	Rib Tips/Hi-Fi	1955	7.50	15.00	30.00
MERCURY					
71078	Hard Head (Part 1)/Hard Head (Part 2)	1957	7.50	15.00	30.00
71151	St. Louis Blues/Fat Back	1957	6.25	12.50	25.00
NOTE					
10001	Rib Tips/Hi-Fi	1954	10.00	20.00	40.00
Albums					
ABC-PARAMOUNT					
351 [M]	Heartbreak	1960	7.50	15.00	30.00
S-351 [S]	Heartbreak	1960	10.00	20.00	40.00
WING					
MGW-12258 [M]	The Big Beat on the Organ	1963	5.00	10.00	20.00
SRW-16258 [R]	The Big Beat on the Organ	1963	3.00	6.00	12.00

THOMAS, RAY

Also see THE MOODY BLUES.

Number	Title (A Side/B Side)	Yr	VG	VG+	NM
45s					
THRESHOLD					
67020	High Above My Head/Love Is the Key	1975	—	2.50	5.00
67023	One Night Stand/Carousel	1975	—	2.50	5.00
Albums					
THRESHOLD					
THS 16	From Mighty Oaks	1975	3.75	7.50	15.00
THS 17	Hopes Wishes & Dreams	1976	3.75	7.50	15.00
THSX-102 [DJ]	Ray Thomas Discusses The Recording of His First Solo Album From Mighty Oaks	1975	12.50	25.00	50.00

THOMAS, RUFUS

Also see RUFUS AND CARLA.

Number	Title (A Side/B Side)	Yr	VG	VG+	NM
12-Inch Singles					
ICHIBAN					
12-103	Rappin' Rufus (3 versions)	1985	2.00	4.00	8.00
45s					
ARTISTS OF AMERICA					
126	If There Were No Music/Blues in the Basement	1976	—	2.50	5.00
AVI					
149	Who's Makin' Love to Your Old Lady/Hot Grits	1977	—	2.00	4.00
178	I Ain't Gettin' Older, I'm Gettin' Better (Part 1)/I Ain't Gettin' Older, I'm Gettin' Better (Part 2)	1977	—	2.00	4.00
HI					
78520	Fried Chicken/I Ain't Got Time	1978	—	2.00	4.00
HIGH STACKS					
9801	Hey Rufus!/Body Fine	1999	—	—	3.00
—B-side by the Barkays					
ICHIBAN					
85-103	Rappin' Rufus/(Instrumental)	1985	—	2.00	4.00
METEOR					
5039	I'm Steady Holdin' On/The Easy Livin' Plan	1956	37.50	75.00	150.00
STAX					
0010	Funky Mississippi/So Hard to Get Along With	1968	—	3.00	6.00
0022	Funky Way/I Want to Hold You	1969	—	3.00	6.00
0059	Do the Funky Chicken/Turn Your Damper Down	1969	—	3.00	6.00
0071	Sixty Minute Man/The Preacher and the Bear	1970	—	3.00	6.00
0079	(Do the) Push and Pull Part I/(Do the) Push and Pull Part II	1970	—	3.00	6.00
0090	The World Is Round/(I Love You) For Sentimental Reasons	1971	—	3.00	6.00
0098	The Breakdown (Part 1)/The Breakdown (Part 2)	1971	—	3.00	6.00
0112	Do the Funky Penguin (Part 1)/Do the Funky Penguin (Part 2)	1971	—	3.00	6.00

Number	Title (A Side/B Side)	Yr	VG	VG+	NM
126	It's Aw-Rite/Can't Ever Let You Go	1962	3.75	7.50	15.00
0129	Love Trap/6-3-8	1972	—	3.00	6.00
130	The Dog/Did You Ever Love a Woman	1963	3.75	7.50	15.00
140	Walking the Dog/You Said	1963	3.00	6.00	12.00
140	Walking the Dog/Fine and Mellow	1963	7.50	15.00	30.00
0140	Itch and Scratch (Part 1)/Itch and Scratch (Part 2)	1972	—	3.00	6.00
144	Can Your Monkey Do the Dog/I Want to Get Married	1964	3.00	6.00	12.00
149	Somebody Stole My Dog/I Want to Be Loved	1964	3.00	6.00	12.00
0153	Funky Robot (Part 1)/Funky Robot (Part 2)	1973	—	3.00	6.00
157	Jump Back/All Night Worker	1964	3.00	6.00	12.00
167	Baby Walk/Little Sally Walker	1965	2.00	4.00	8.00
173	Willy Nilly/Sho' Gonna Mess Him Up	1965	2.00	4.00	8.00
0177	I Know You Don't Want Me No More/I'm Still in Love with You	1973	—	3.00	6.00
178	Chicken Scratch/The World Is Round	1965	2.00	4.00	8.00
0187	That Makes Christmas Day/I'll Be Your Santa Baby	1973	—	3.00	6.00
0192	The Funky Bird/Steal a Little	1974	—	3.00	6.00
200	Talkin' 'Bout True Love/Sister's Got a Boyfriend	1967	2.00	4.00	8.00
0219	Boogie Ain't Nothin' (But Gettin' Down) (Part 1)/ Boogie Ain't Nothin' (But Gettin' Down) (Part 2)	1974	—	3.00	6.00
221	Sophisticated Sissy/Grasy Spoon	1967	2.00	4.00	8.00
0236	Do the Double Bump/Do the Double Bump	1975	—	3.00	6.00
240	Down Ta My House/Steady Holding On	1968	2.00	4.00	8.00
250	The Memphis Train/I Think I Made a Boo-Boo	1968	2.00	4.00	8.00
0254	Jump Back '75 (Part 1)/Jump Back '75 (Part 2)	1975	—	3.00	6.00
1073	I'll Be Your Santa Claus/Christmas Comes Once A Year	197?	—	2.50	5.00
—B-side by Albert King; reissue					
SUN					
181	Bear Cat (The Answer to Hound Dog)/Walking in the Rain	1953	87.50	175.00	350.00
—With subtitle on A-side					
181	Bear Cat/Walking in the Rain	1953	50.00	100.00	200.00
—No subtitle on A-side					
188	Tiger Man (King of the Jungle)/Save Your Money	1953	125.00	250.00	500.00
Albums					
ALLIGATOR					
AV-4769	That Woman Is Poison	1988	2.50	5.00	10.00
A.V.I.					
6015	If There Were No Music	1977	3.75	7.50	15.00
6046	I Ain't Gettin' Older, I'm Gettin' Better	1978	3.75	7.50	15.00
GUSTO					
64	Rufus Thomas	1980	2.50	5.00	10.00
STAX					
ST-704 [M]	Walking the Dog	1963	37.50	75.00	150.00
STS-2028	Do the Funky Chicken	1970	6.25	12.50	25.00
STS-2039	Rufus Thomas Live/Doing the Push and Pull at P.J.'s	1971	6.25	12.50	25.00
STS-3004	Did You Hear Me	1972	6.25	12.50	25.00
STS-3008	Crown Prince of Dance	1973	6.25	12.50	25.00

THOMAS, TIMMY

Number	Title (A Side/B Side)	Yr	VG	VG+	NM
12-Inch Singles					
GOLD MOUNTAIN					
81203	Gotta Give a Little Love/Gotta Give a Little Love (Dub)	1984	—	3.00	6.00
81203 [DJ]	Gotta Give a Little Love (5:26) (4:35)	1984	2.00	4.00	8.00
45s					
GLADES					
1703	Why Can't We Live Together/Funky Me	1972	—	3.00	6.00
1709	People Are Changin'/Rainbow Power	1973	—	3.00	6.00
1712	Let Me Be Your Eyes/Cold Cold People	1973	—	3.00	6.00
1717	What Can I Tell Her/Opportunity	1973	—	3.00	6.00
1719	One Brief Moment/Rio Girl	1974	—	3.00	6.00
1721	Deep in You/Spread Us Around	1974	—	2.50	5.00
1723	I've Got to See You Tonight/You're the Song (I've Always Wanted to Sing)	1974	—	2.50	5.00
1727	Sexy Woman/Sweet Brown Sugar	1975	—	2.50	5.00
1730	Ebony Affair/It's What They Can't See	1975	—	2.50	5.00
1735	Love Shine/Running Out of Time	1976	—	2.50	5.00
1740	Stone to the Bone/Watch It! Watch It!	1977	—	2.50	5.00
1748	Touch to Touch/When a House Got Music	1978	—	2.50	5.00
1749	Freak In, Freak Out/Say Love, Can You Chase	1978	—	2.50	5.00
1758	Drown in My Own Tears (Part 1)/Drown in My Own Tears (Part 2)	1980	—	2.50	5.00
GOLD MOUNTAIN					
82004	Gotta Give a Little Love (Ten Years After)/Same Old Song	1984	—	2.00	4.00
82008	Love Is Never Too Late/Let It Flow	1984	—	2.00	4.00
GOLDWAX					
320	Have Some Boogaloo/Liquid Mood	1967	3.75	7.50	15.00
327	It's My Life/Whole Lotta Shakin' Goin' On	1967	3.75	7.50	15.00
MARLIN					
3348	Are You Crazy??? (Pt. 1)/Are You Crazy??? (Pt. 2)	1981	—	2.00	4.00
Albums					
GLADES					
33-6501	Why Can't We Live Together	1973	3.75	7.50	15.00
GOLD MOUNTAIN					
GM-80006	Gotta Give a Little Love	1984	2.50	5.00	10.00

THOMAS, VIC

Number	Title (A Side/B Side)	Yr	VG	VG+	NM
45s					
PHILIPS					
40183	Napoleon Bonaparte/Marianne	1964	18.75	37.50	75.00
40228	Village of Love/There Stands An Empty Man	1964	18.75	37.50	75.00

THOMPSON, BILLY

Number	Title (A Side/B Side)	Yr	VG	VG+	NM
45s					
COLUMBUS					
1043	Black Eyed Girl/Kiss Tomorrow Goodbye	1965	50.00	100.00	200.00
WAND					
1108	Black Eyed Girl/Kiss Tomorrow Goodbye	1966	15.00	30.00	60.00

THOMPSON, JUNIOR

Number	Title (A Side/B Side)	Yr	VG	VG+	NM
45s					
ATCO					
6500	You're the One/Jungle Girl	1967	3.00	6.00	12.00
METEOR					
5029	Mama's Little Baby/Raw Deal	1956	100.00	200.00	400.00

THOMPSON, LORETTA

Number	Title (A Side/B Side)	Yr	VG	VG+	NM
45s					
SKOOP					
1050	Buddy-Big Bopper-Ritchie/Square from Nowhere	1959	12.50	25.00	50.00
UNITED					
214	He Do Ho Rock 'N' Roll/Let's Change the Alphabet	1958	10.00	20.00	40.00

THOMPSON, RICHARD

Also see FAIRPORT CONVENTION; RICHARD AND LINDA THOMPSON.

Number	Title (A Side/B Side)	Yr	VG	VG+	NM
45s					
CAPITOL					
S7-18043	I Can't Wake Up to Save My Life/Easy There	1994	—	2.50	5.00
58810	Crawl Back (Under My Stone)/Bathsheba Smiles	1999	—	—	3.00
Albums					
BONG LOAD					
BL 44 [(2)]	Mock Tudor	1999	3.75	7.50	15.00
CAPITOL					
C1-48845	Amnesia	1988	2.00	4.00	8.00
C1-95713	Rumor & Sigh	1991	3.00	6.00	12.00
CARTHAGE					
CGLP-4405	Henry the Human Fly	1983	2.00	4.00	8.00
—Reissue of Reprise LP					
CGLP-4409	Strict Tempo	1983	2.00	4.00	8.00
CGLP-4413 [(2)]	Richard Thompson (Guitar/Vocal)	1983	2.50	5.00	10.00
—Reissue of Island 9421 with original UK title					
HANNIBAL					
HNLP-1313	Heart of Kindness	1983	2.50	5.00	10.00
HNLP-1316	Small Town Romance	1984	2.50	5.00	10.00
POLYDOR					
825421-1	Across a Crowded Room	1985	2.00	4.00	8.00
829728-1	Daring Adventures	1986	2.00	4.00	8.00
REPRISE					
MS 2112	Henry the Human Fly	1972	5.00	10.00	20.00

THOMPSON, RICHARD AND LINDA

Number	Title (A Side/B Side)	Yr	VG	VG+	NM
Albums					
CARTHAGE					
CGLP-4403	Sunnyvista	1983	2.50	5.00	10.00
—First U.S. issue of this LP					
CGLP-4404	Pour Down Like Silver	1983	2.00	4.00	8.00
—Reissue of Island 9348					
CGLP-4407	I Want to See the Bright Lights Tonight	1983	2.50	5.00	10.00
—Reissue of Island 9266 (UK)					
CGLP-4408	Hokey Pokey	1983	2.00	4.00	8.00
—Reissue of Island 9305					
CGLP-4412	First Light	1983	2.00	4.00	8.00
—Reissue of Chrysalis 1177					
CHRYSALIS					
CHR 1177	First Light	1978	3.75	7.50	15.00
CHR 1247	Sunnyvista	1979	—	—	—
—Unreleased in U.S.					
HANNIBAL					
HNBL 1303	Shoot Out the Lights	1982	2.50	5.00	10.00
ISLAND					
ILPS 9266	I Want to See the Bright Lights Tonight	1974	—	—	—
—Unreleased in U.S. on this number					
ILPS 9305	Hokey Pokey	1974	3.75	7.50	15.00
ILPS 9348	Pour Down Like Silver	1975	3.75	7.50	15.00
ISLA 9421 [(2)]	Bright Lights and Live! More or Less	1977	5.00	10.00	20.00
—First U.S. issue of "I Want to See the Bright Lights Tonight" plus an LP of unreleased material					

THOMPSON, SUE

Also see DON GIBSON AND SUE THOMPSON.

Number	Title (A Side/B Side)	Yr	VG	VG+	NM
45s					
DECCA					
29314	Walkin' in the Snow/Come a Little Bit Closer	1954	6.25	12.50	25.00
—With Hank Penny					
29545	Day Dreaming/Your Mommie and Your Daddy	1955	6.25	12.50	25.00
30435	Walkin' to Missouri/Red Hot Honey Brown	1957	6.25	12.50	25.00
HICKORY					
308	Just Plain Country/Oh Johnny, Oh Johnny, Oh	1973	—	2.50	5.00
313	Find Out/Stay Another Day	1974	—	2.50	5.00
320	Making Love to You Is Just Like Eating Peanuts/ Sweet Memories	1974	—	2.50	5.00
330	Trains/And Love Me	1974	—	2.50	5.00
339	The Thought of Losing You/Tennessee Waltz	1975	—	2.00	4.00
346	I Can't Stop Loving You/Any Other Morning	1975	—	2.00	4.00
354	Big Mabel Murphy/Big Daddy	1975	—	2.00	4.00
364	Never Naughty Rosie/He Cheats on Me	1976	—	2.00	4.00
370	Baby's Not Home/I Want It All	1976	—	2.00	4.00
1144	Throwin' Kisses/Angel, Angel	1961	5.00	10.00	20.00
1153	Sad Movies (Make Me Cry)/Nine Little Teardrops	1961	5.00	10.00	20.00
1159	Norman/Never Love Again	1961	5.00	10.00	20.00
1166	Two of a Kind/It Has to Be	1962	3.75	7.50	15.00
1174	Have a Good Time/If the Boy Only Knew	1962	3.75	7.50	15.00
1183	James (Hold the Ladder Steady)/My Hero	1962	3.75	7.50	15.00

Number	Title (A Side/B Side)	Yr	VG	VG+	NM
1196	Willie Can/Too Much in Love	1962	3.75	7.50	15.00
1204	What's Wrong Bill/I Need a Harbor	1963	3.75	7.50	15.00
1204 [PS]	What's Wrong Bill/I Need a Harbor	1963	5.00	10.00	20.00
1217	True Confession/Suzie	1963	3.75	7.50	15.00
1217 [PS]	True Confession/Suzie	1963	5.00	10.00	20.00
1221	Too Hot to Dance/I Like Your Kind of Love	1963	3.00	6.00	12.00
—With Bob Luman					
1234	'Cause I Ask You To/It's 12:35	1963	3.00	6.00	12.00
1240	Big Daddy/I'd Like to Know You Better	1964	3.00	6.00	12.00
1255	Bad Boy/Toys	1964	3.00	6.00	12.00
1270	Big Hearted Me/Looking for a Good Boy	1964	3.00	6.00	12.00
1284	Paper Tiger/Mama, Don't Cry at My Wedding	1964	3.75	7.50	15.00
1308	Stop Th' Music/What I'm Needin' Is You	1965	3.00	6.00	12.00
1328	Afraid/It's Break-Up Time	1965	3.00	6.00	12.00
1340	Just Kiss Me/Sweet Hunk of Misery	1965	3.00	6.00	12.00
1359	Walkin' My Baby/I'm Lookin' (For a World)	1965	3.00	6.00	12.00
1381	What Should I Do/After the Heartache	1966	2.50	5.00	10.00
1403	I Can't Help It/Put It Back	1966	2.50	5.00	10.00
1423	Someone/From My Balcony	1966	2.50	5.00	10.00
1431	Language of Love/Let Me Down Hard	1967	2.50	5.00	10.00
1457	Don't Forget to Cry/Ferris Wheel	1967	2.50	5.00	10.00
1469	That's Just Too Much/Straight to Helen	1967	2.50	5.00	10.00
1488	Dear Boy/Love Has Come My Way	1967	2.50	5.00	10.00
1493	How Do You Start Over/Why Not	1968	2.00	4.00	8.00
1512	You Deserve Each Other/Doin' Nothing	1968	2.00	4.00	8.00
1524	Don't Try to Change Me/The Real Me	1968	2.00	4.00	8.00
1534	Tennessee Waltz/Who's Gonna Mow Your Grass	1969	2.00	4.00	8.00
1547	Pair of Broken Hearts/You Two-Timed Me One Time Too Often	1969	2.00	4.00	8.00
1558	Talk Back Trembling Lips/Till I Can't Take It Anymore	1970	—	3.00	6.00
—With Roy Acuff, Jr.					
1560	I Just Keep Hangin' On/Lost Highway	1970	—	3.00	6.00
1573	Don't Let the Stars Get In Your Eyes/Why You Been Gone	1970	—	3.00	6.00
—With Roy Acuff, Jr.					
1577	Whole Lot of Walkin'/Guess Who's Coming to Dinner Tonight	1970	—	3.00	6.00
1587	Because You Love Me/Take a Little Time	1971	—	3.00	6.00
1596	Here's To Forever/What You See Is What You Get	1971	—	3.00	6.00
1612	Swiss Cottage Place/Thanks to Rumors	1971	—	3.00	6.00
1622	Let Your Thoughts Be Sweet/What a Woman in Love Won't Do	1972	—	3.00	6.00
1641	Sweet Memories/Take Me As I Am	1972	—	3.00	6.00
1652	Candy and Roses/Full Time Job	1972	—	3.00	6.00
1669	How I Love Them Old Songs/Just Two Young People	1973	—	2.50	5.00
MERCURY					
6325	You're Getting a Good Girl (When You Get Me)/What've You Got (That Makes Me Love You So)	1951	10.00	20.00	40.00
6377	Just Walking Out the Door/I'll Hate Myself in the Morning	1952	7.50	15.00	30.00
6390	Junior's a Big Boy Now/Tadpole	1952	7.50	15.00	30.00
6407	You Belong to Me/You're an Angel on the Outside	1952	7.50	15.00	30.00
6416	Red Hot Henrietta Brown/Last Night I Heard Somebody Cry	1952	7.50	15.00	30.00
70066	How Many Tears/If You Should Change	1953	6.25	12.50	25.00
70084	Take Care My Love/Things I Might Have Been	1953	6.25	12.50	25.00
70089	You and Me/Say It with Your Heart	1953	6.25	12.50	25.00
70152	I'm Not That Kind of Girl/I Long to Tell You	1953	6.25	12.50	25.00
70309	Donna Wanna/Gee But I Hate to Go Home Alone	1954	6.25	12.50	25.00
Albums					
HICKORY					
LPM-104 [M]	Meet Sue Thompson	1962	12.50	25.00	50.00
LPS-104 [S]	Meet Sue Thompson	1962	20.00	40.00	80.00
LPM-107 [M]	Two of a Kind	1962	7.50	15.00	30.00
LPS-107 [S]	Two of a Kind	1962	10.00	20.00	40.00
LPM-111 [M]	Sue Thompson's Golden Hits	1963	7.50	15.00	30.00
LPS-111 [S]	Sue Thompson's Golden Hits	1963	10.00	20.00	40.00
LPM-121 [M]	Paper Tiger	1965	7.50	15.00	30.00
LPS-121 [S]	Paper Tiger	1965	10.00	20.00	40.00
LPM-130 [M]	Sue Thompson with Strings Attached	1966	7.50	15.00	30.00
LPS-130 [S]	Sue Thompson with Strings Attached	1966	10.00	20.00	40.00
LPS-148	This Is Sue Thompson Country	1969	5.00	10.00	20.00
H3F-4511	Sweet Memories	1974	3.75	7.50	15.00
H3G-4515	...And Love Me	1974	3.75	7.50	15.00
WING					
MGW-12317 [M]	The Country Side of Sue Thompson	1965	5.00	10.00	20.00
SRW-16317 [R]	The Country Side of Sue Thompson	1965	3.75	7.50	15.00

THOR-ABLES, THE

Number	Title (A Side/B Side)	Yr	VG	VG+	NM
45s					
TITANIC					
1001	Our Love Song/Get That Bread	1962	75.00	150.00	300.00
1002	My Reckless Heart/Batman and Robin	1962	75.00	150.00	300.00

THORINSHIELD

Number	Title (A Side/B Side)	Yr	VG	VG+	NM
45s					
PHILIPS					
40492	The Best of All/Life Is a Dream	1967	2.00	4.00	8.00
40521	Family of Man/Lonely Mountain Again	1968	2.00	4.00	8.00
Albums					
PHILIPS					
PHS 600251	Thorinshield	1968	5.00	10.00	20.00

THORNTON, BIG MAMA

Number	Title (A Side/B Side)	Yr	VG	VG+	NM
45s					
ARHOOLIE					
512	Swing It On Home/My Heavy Load	1968	2.00	4.00	8.00
520	Ball and Chain/Wade in the Water	1968	2.00	4.00	8.00
BAYTONE					
107	You Did Me Wrong/Big Mama's Blues	1961	3.75	7.50	15.00
GALAXY					
749	Life Goes On/Because It's Love	1966	2.50	5.00	10.00
KENT					
424	Before Day/Me and My Chauffeur	1965	2.50	5.00	10.00
MERCURY					
72981	Hound Dog/Let's Go Get Started	1969	2.00	4.00	8.00
PEACOCK					
1603	Everytime I Think of You/Mischievous Boogie	1952	25.00	50.00	100.00
1612	Hound Dog/Rock-a-Bye Baby	1953	50.00	100.00	200.00
1612	Hound Dog/Nightmare	1953	45.00	90.00	180.00
1621	They Call Me Big Mama/Cotton Pickin' Blues	1953	25.00	50.00	100.00
1626	Big Change/I Ain't No Fool Either	1953	25.00	50.00	100.00
1632	I've Searched the Whole World/I Smell a Rat	1954	15.00	30.00	60.00
1642	Stop Hoppin' on Me/Story of My Blues	1954	15.00	30.00	60.00
1647	Walking Blues/Rock-a-Bye Baby	1955	15.00	30.00	60.00
1650	The Fish/Laugh, Laugh, Laugh	1955	15.00	30.00	60.00
1681	Just Like a Dog/My Man Called Me	1957	10.00	20.00	40.00
Albums					
ARHOOLIE					
F-1028 [M]	Big Mama Thornton in Europe	1966	7.50	15.00	30.00
F-1032 [M]	Chicago Blues: The Queen at Monterey	1967	7.50	15.00	30.00
F-1039 [M]	Ball and Chain	1968	7.50	15.00	30.00
BACK BEAT					
BLP-68	She's Back	1970	6.25	12.50	25.00
MERCURY					
SR-61225	Stronger Than Dirt	1969	6.25	12.50	25.00
SR-61249	The Way It Is	1970	6.25	12.50	25.00
PENTAGRAM					
PE-10005	Saved	1971	5.00	10.00	20.00
VANGUARD					
VSD-79351	Jail	1974	3.75	7.50	15.00
VSD-79354	Sassy Mama	1975	3.75	7.50	15.00

THORNTON, FRADKIN AND UNGER

Number	Title (A Side/B Side)	Yr	VG	VG+	NM
45s					
ESP-DISK					
63019	God Bless California/Sometimes	1972	3.75	7.50	15.00
—Paul McCartney appears on this record					

THREE BELLS, THE

Number	Title (A Side/B Side)	Yr	VG	VG+	NM
45s					
LAWN					
251	He Doesn't Love Me/Softly in the Night	1965	3.00	6.00	12.00

THREE BLONDE MICE

Number	Title (A Side/B Side)	Yr	VG	VG+	NM
45s					
ATCO					
6324	Ringo Bells/The 12 Days of Christmas	1964	7.50	15.00	30.00
6353	Alley Cat/What Did I Say	1965	2.50	5.00	10.00

THREE CHUCKLES, THE

Also see TEDDY RANDAZZO.

Number	Title (A Side/B Side)	Yr	VG	VG+	NM
45s					
BOULEVARD					
100	Runaround/At Last You Understand	1954	20.00	40.00	80.00
VIK					
0186	Anyway/The Funny Little Things We Used to Do	1956	5.00	10.00	20.00
0194	Tell Me/And the Angels Sing	1956	5.00	10.00	20.00
0216	Gypsy in My Soul/We're Still Holding Hands	1956	5.00	10.00	20.00
0232	Fallen Out of Love/Midnight 'Til Dawn	1956	5.00	10.00	20.00
0244	Won't You Give Me a Chance/We're Gonna Rock Tonight	1956	5.00	10.00	20.00
"X"					
0066	Runaround/At Last You Understand	1954	6.25	12.50	25.00
0095	Foolishly/If I Should Love Again	1955	6.25	12.50	25.00
0134	So Long/You Should Have Told Me	1955	6.25	12.50	25.00
0150	Blue Lover/Realize	1955	6.25	12.50	25.00
0162	Times Two, I Love You/Still Thinking of You	1955	6.25	12.50	25.00
0186	Anyway/The Funny Little Things We Used to Do	1956	6.25	12.50	25.00
0194	Tell Me/And the Angels Sing	1956	6.25	12.50	25.00
0216	Gypsy in My Soul/We're Still Holding Hands	1956	6.25	12.50	25.00
7-Inch Extended Plays					
"X"					
EXA-192	(contents unknown)	1955	10.00	20.00	40.00
EXA-192 [PS]	The Three Chuckles (Vol. 1)	1955	10.00	20.00	40.00
EXA-193	(contents unknown)	1955	10.00	20.00	40.00
EXA-193 [PS]	The Three Chuckles (Vol. 2)	1955	10.00	20.00	40.00
EXA-194	(contents unknown)	1955	10.00	20.00	40.00
EXA-194 [PS]	The Three Chuckles (Vol. 3)	1955	10.00	20.00	40.00
Albums					
VIK					
LX-1067 [M]	The Three Chuckles	1956	62.50	125.00	250.00

THREE D'S, THE (1)

Number	Title (A Side/B Side)	Yr	VG	VG+	NM
45s					
BRUNSWICK					
55152	Nothing to Wear/The Happiest Boy and Girl	1959	6.25	12.50	25.00
PARIS					
503	Little Billy Boy/Let Me Know	1957	5.00	10.00	20.00
508	Never Let You Go/Birth of An Angel	1957	5.00	10.00	20.00
511	Baby Doll/Crazy Little Woman	1958	5.00	10.00	20.00
514	Jumpin' Jack/I Never Saw My Pretty Little Baby Alone	1958	5.00	10.00	20.00
PILGRIM					
719	Broken Dreams/Tell Me That You Love Me	1956	6.25	12.50	25.00
SQUARE					
502	Squeeze/Graveyard Cha-Cha	1959	20.00	40.00	80.00

THREE D'S, THE (2)

Number	Title (A Side/B Side)	Yr	VG	VG+	NM
45s					
CAPITOL					
5188	Sinner Man/Give, Said the Little Stream	1964	2.50	5.00	10.00
5249	Chim Chim Cheree/Crayon Box	1964	2.50	5.00	10.00
Albums					
CAPITOL					
ST 2171 [S]	New Dimensions in Folk Songs	1964	6.25	12.50	25.00
T 2171 [M]	New Dimensions in Folk Songs	1964	5.00	10.00	20.00
ST 2314 [S]	I Won't Be Worried Long	1965	6.25	12.50	25.00
T 2314 [M]	I Won't Be Worried Long	1965	5.00	10.00	20.00

THREE D'S, THE (U)

Number	Title (A Side/B Side)	Yr	VG	VG+	NM
45s					
DEAN					
521	Broken Hearted/I Love You So	1961	5.00	10.00	20.00

THREE DEGREES, THE

Number	Title (A Side/B Side)	Yr	VG	VG+	NM
45s					
ARIOLA AMERICA					
801	My Simple Heart/Hot Summer Night	1980	—	2.00	4.00
7721	Giving Up, Giving In/Woman in Love	1978	—	2.00	4.00
7742	Woman in Love/Out of Love Again	1979	—	2.00	4.00
7746	The Runner/Out of Love Again	1979	—	2.00	4.00
EPIC					
50283	What I Did for Love/Macaronie Man	1976	—	2.00	4.00
50330	In Love We Grow/Standing Up for Love	1977	—	2.00	4.00
ICHIBAN					
89-167	Tie U Up/(B-side unknown)	1989	—	2.50	5.00
METROMEDIA					
109	Down in the Boondocks/Warm Weather Music	1969	2.00	4.00	8.00
128	Feeling of Love/Warm Weather Music	1969	2.00	4.00	8.00
NEPTUNE					
23	Reflections of Yesterday/What I See	1970	—	3.00	6.00
PHILADELPHIA INT'L.					
3534	Dirty Ol Man/Can't You See What You're Doing to Me	1973	—	3.00	6.00
3539	Year of Decision/A Woman Needs a Good Man	1974	—	2.50	5.00
3550	When Will I See You Again/Year of Decision	1974	—	2.50	5.00
3561	I Didn't Know/Dirty Ol Man	1975	—	2.50	5.00
3568	Take Good Care of Yourself/Here I Am	1975	—	2.50	5.00
3585	Free Ride/Loving Cup	1976	—	2.50	5.00
ROULETTE					
7072	Melting Pot/The Grass Will Sing for You	1970	—	3.00	6.00
7079	Maybe/Collage	1970	—	3.00	6.00
7088	I Do Take You/You're the Fool	1970	—	3.00	6.00
7097	You're the One/Stardust	1971	—	3.00	6.00
7102	There's So Much Love All Around/Yours	1971	—	3.00	6.00
7105	Ebb Tide/Low Down	1971	—	3.00	6.00
7117	Trade Winds/I Turn to You	1972	—	3.00	6.00
7125	Find My Way/I Wanna Be Your Baby	1972	—	3.00	6.00
7137	I Won't Let You Go/Through Misty Eyes	1972	—	3.00	6.00
SWAN					
4197	Gee Baby (I'm Sorry)/Do What You're Supposed to Do	1965	3.00	6.00	12.00
4214	I'm Gonna Need You/Just Right for Love	1965	3.00	6.00	12.00
4224	Close Your Eyes/Gotta Draw the Line	1965	3.00	6.00	12.00
4235	Look in My Eyes/Drivin' Me Mad	1965	3.00	6.00	12.00
4245	Maybe/Yours	1966	3.00	6.00	12.00
4253	I Wanna Be Your Baby/Tales Are True	1966	3.00	6.00	12.00
4267	Love of My Life/Are You Satisfied	1967	3.00	6.00	12.00
WARNER BROS.					
7198	Contact/Oh No Not Again	1968	2.50	5.00	10.00
Albums					
ARIOLA AMERICA					
OL 1501	Three D	1980	2.50	5.00	10.00
SW-50044	New Dimensions	1978	2.50	5.00	10.00
EPIC					
PE 34385	Standing Up for Love	1977	3.00	6.00	12.00
ICHIBAN					
ICH-1041	Three Degrees...And Holding	198?	2.50	5.00	10.00
PHILADELPHIA INT'L.					
KZ 32406	The Three Degrees	1974	3.00	6.00	12.00
KZ 33162	International	1975	3.00	6.00	12.00
PZ 33840	The Three Degrees Live	1975	3.00	6.00	12.00
ROULETTE					
3015	So Much Love	1975	2.50	5.00	10.00
SR-42050	Maybe	1970	10.00	20.00	40.00

THREE DOG NIGHT

Also see DANNY HUTTON; CORY WELLS AND THE ENEMYS.

Number	Title (A Side/B Side)	Yr	VG	VG+	NM
45s					
ABC					
12114	'Til the World Ends/Yo Te Quiero Hablo (Take You Down)	1975	—	2.00	4.00
12192	Everybody Is a Masterpiece/Drive On, Ride On	1976	—	2.00	4.00
ABC DUNHILL					
4168	Nobody/It's for You	1968	3.00	6.00	12.00
4168 [PS]	Nobody/It's for You	1968	7.50	15.00	30.00
—Sleeve is promo only					
4177	Try a Little Tenderness/That No One Ever Hurt So Bad	1969	2.00	4.00	8.00
4191	One/Chest Fever	1969	2.00	4.00	8.00
4203	Easy to Be Hard/Dreaming Isn't Good for You	1969	2.00	4.00	8.00
4215	Eli's Coming/Circle for a Landing	1969	2.00	4.00	8.00
4229	Celebrate/Feeling Alright	1970	—	3.00	6.00
4239	Mama Told Me (Not to Come)/Rock and Roll Widow	1970	—	3.00	6.00
4239 [PS]	Mama Told Me (Not to Come)/Rock and Roll Widow	1970	3.00	6.00	12.00
4250	Out in the Country/Good Time Living	1970	—	3.00	6.00
4262	One Man Band/It Ain't Easy	1970	—	3.00	6.00
4272	Joy to the World/I Can Hear You Calling	1971	—	2.50	5.00
4282	Liar/Can't Get Enough of It	1971	—	2.50	5.00
4294	An Old Fashioned Love Song/Jam	1971	—	2.50	5.00
4299	Never Been to Spain/Peace of Mind	1972	—	2.50	5.00
4306	The Family of Man/Going in Circles	1972	—	2.50	5.00
4317	Black and White/Freedom for the Stallion	1972	—	2.50	5.00
4331	Pieces of April/The Writings on the Wall	1972	—	2.50	5.00
4352	Shambala/Our "B" Side	1973	—	2.50	5.00
—First pressings have "Dunhill" spelled out in children's blocks					
4352	Shambala/Our "B" Side	1973	—	2.50	5.00
—Transitional pressings have "Dunhill" in children's blocks on one label and "Dunhill" in a box on the other label					
4352	Shambala/Our "B" Side	1973	—	2.00	4.00
—Later pressings have "Dunhill" in a box on both labels (1968-72 style)					
4370	Let Me Serenade You/Storybook Feeling	1973	—	2.00	4.00
4382	The Show Must Go On/On the Way Back Home	1974	—	2.00	4.00
15001	Sure As I'm Sittin' Here/Anytime Babe	1974	—	2.00	4.00
15010	The Show Must Go On/On the Way Back Home	1974	2.00	4.00	8.00
15013	Play Something Sweet (Brickyard Blues)/I'd Be So Happy	1974	—	2.00	4.00
PASSPORT					
7921	It's a Jungle Out There/Somebody's Gonna Get Hurt	1983	—	2.50	5.00
Albums					
ABC					
888	Coming Down Your Way	1975	2.50	5.00	10.00
928	American Pastime	1976	2.50	5.00	10.00
ABC DUNHILL					
DS-50048	Three Dog Night	1968	3.75	7.50	15.00
DS-50048	Three Dog Night "One"	1969	3.00	6.00	12.00
—Same album as above, but with revised title on cover					
DS-50058	Suitable for Framing	1969	3.00	6.00	12.00
DS-50068	Three Dog Night Was Captured Live at the Forum	1969	3.00	6.00	12.00
DS-50078	It Ain't Easy	1970	25.00	50.00	100.00
—Original cover with band members in the nude					
DS-50078	It Ain't Easy	1970	3.00	6.00	12.00
—Regular front cover with gatefold					
DSX-50088	Naturally	1970	3.00	6.00	12.00
—With detachable cardboard poster intact					
DSX-50098	Golden Bisquits	1971	3.00	6.00	12.00
—With detachable cardboard poster intact					
DSX-50108	Harmony	1971	3.00	6.00	12.00
DSD-50118	Seven Separate Fools	1972	3.00	6.00	12.00
—With seven oversize playing cards included					
DSY-50138 [(2)]	Around the World with Three Dog Night	1973	3.75	7.50	15.00
DSX-50158	Cyan	1973	3.00	6.00	12.00
DSD-50168	Hard Labor	1974	7.50	15.00	30.00
—With uncensored "childbirth" front cover					
DSD-50168	Hard Labor	1974	3.75	7.50	15.00
—With huge Band-Aid attached to jacket, covering the "childbirth"					
DSD-50168	Hard Labor	1974	2.50	5.00	10.00
—With huge Band-Aid as part of the LP artwork					
DSD-50178	Joy to the World: Their Greatest Hits	1974	3.00	6.00	12.00
—With gatefold cover					
DSD-50178	Joy to the World: Their Greatest Hits	1975	2.50	5.00	10.00
—With standard cover					
AT EASE					
MD 11109	Three Dog Night: Their Greatest Recordings	1978	5.00	10.00	20.00
—"This Album Compiled Exclusively for Military Personnel" by ABC					
COMMAND					
QD-40014 [Q]	Hard Labor	1974	5.00	10.00	20.00
QD-40018 [Q]	Coming Down Your Way	1975	5.00	10.00	20.00
MCA					
6018 [(2)]	The Best of Three Dog Night	1982	3.00	6.00	12.00
37120	Joy to the World: Their Greatest Hits	1980	2.00	4.00	8.00
PASSPORT					
PB 5001 [RP]	It's a Jungle	1983	2.00	4.00	8.00

THREE DOTS AND A DASH

With JESSE BELVIN.

Number	Title (A Side/B Side)	Yr	VG	VG+	NM
45s					
IMPERIAL					
5164	I'll Never Love Again/Let's Do It	1951	125.00	250.00	500.00

THREE FRIENDS, THE (1)

Number	Title (A Side/B Side)	Yr	VG	VG+	NM
45s					
CAL-GOLD					
169	Walkin' Shoes/Blue Ribbon Baby	1961	50.00	100.00	200.00
IMPERIAL					
5763	Dedicated (To the Songs I Love)/Happy as a Man Can Be	1961	7.50	15.00	30.00
5773	You're a Square/Go On to School	1961	5.00	10.00	20.00

THREE FRIENDS, THE (2)

Number	Title (A Side/B Side)	Yr	VG	VG+	NM
45s					
BRUNSWICK					
55032	Jinx/Chinese Tearoom	1957	7.50	15.00	30.00
LIDO					
500	Baby I'll Cry/Blanche	1956	15.00	30.00	60.00
—Gray label					
500	Baby I'll Cry/Blanche	1956	10.00	20.00	40.00
—Blue label					
502	I'm Only a Boy/Jinx	1957	12.50	25.00	50.00
504	Now That You've Gone/Chinese Tea Room	1957	12.50	25.00	50.00

THREE MAN ARMY, THE

Number	Title (A Side/B Side)	Yr	VG	VG+	NM
Albums					
KAMA SUTRA					
KSBS-2044	A Third of a Lifetime	1971	7.50	15.00	30.00
—Pink label, gatefold cover					
REPRISE					
MS 2150	Three Man Army	1973	5.00	10.00	20.00

Number	Title (A Side/B Side)	Yr	VG	VG+	NM
MS 2182	Three Man Army Two	1974	5.00	10.00	20.00

THREE PENNIES, THE

45s

B.T. PUPPY

Number	Title (A Side/B Side)	Yr	VG	VG+	NM
501	A Penny for Your Thoughts/Why Am I So Shy	1964	3.00	6.00	12.00

THREE SOULS, THE

45s

ARGO

Number	Title (A Side/B Side)	Yr	VG	VG+	NM
5369	The Horse/Madisonville	1960	5.00	10.00	20.00
5472	Hi-Heel Sneakers/Dangerous Dan Express	1964	3.75	7.50	15.00
5514	You're No Good/Chitterlins Con Carne	1965	3.00	6.00	12.00

NOTE

Number	Title (A Side/B Side)	Yr	VG	VG+	NM
10015	Night Time/Smorgasbord	1959	5.00	10.00	20.00

Albums

ARGO

Number	Title (A Side/B Side)	Yr	VG	VG+	NM
LP-4005 [M]	Almost Like Being In Love	1960	—	—	—
—Canceled					
LPS-4005 [S]	Almost Like Being In Love	1960	—	—	—
—Canceled					
LP-4036 [M]	Dangerous Dan Express	1964	5.00	10.00	20.00
LPS-4036 [S]	Dangerous Dan Express	1964	6.25	12.50	25.00
LP-4044 [M]	Soul Sounds	1965	5.00	10.00	20.00
LPS-4044 [S]	Soul Sounds	1965	6.25	12.50	25.00

THREE SUNS, THE

45s

RCA VICTOR

Number	Title (A Side/B Side)	Yr	VG	VG+	NM
WP 250 [(3)]	Your Christmas Favorites	1949	10.00	20.00	40.00
—Three records (47-3057, 47-3058, 47-3059) plus box					
47-2756	Dancing Tambourine/Stumbling	1949	2.50	5.00	10.00
47-2757	Dizzy Fingers/Eccentric	1949	2.50	5.00	10.00
47-2758	Nola/The Doll Dance	1949	2.50	5.00	10.00
47-2759	Canadian Capers/The Wedding of the Painted Doll	1949	2.50	5.00	10.00
—The above four comprise a box set					
47-2839	Twilight Time/Hindustan	1949	2.50	5.00	10.00
47-2840	Deep Purple/Dardanella	1949	2.50	5.00	10.00
47-2841	Sunrise Serenade/When Day Is Done	1949	2.50	5.00	10.00
47-2842	I'll Never Wish for More Than This/The Breeze and I	1949	2.50	5.00	10.00
—The above four comprise a box set					
47-2898	Hurry! Hurry! Hurry!/Ballin' the Jack	1949	3.00	6.00	12.00
47-2924	Ting-a-Ling/Everybody Kiss the Bride	1949	3.00	6.00	12.00
47-2964	Lover's Gold/In a Shady Nook by a Babbling Brook	1949	3.00	6.00	12.00
47-2996	Hop Scotch Polka/The Windmill's Turning	1949	3.00	6.00	12.00
47-3025	Soft Lips/Give Me Some Sugar, Sugar Baby	1949	3.00	6.00	12.00
47-3057	Adeste Fideles/Santa Claus Is Coming to Town	1949	2.50	5.00	10.00
47-3058	Winter Wonderland/White Christmas	1949	2.50	5.00	10.00
47-3059	Jingle Bells/Silent Night	1949	2.50	5.00	10.00
—The above three comprise box set WP 250, "The Three Suns Present Your Christmas Favorites"					
47-3079	Close Your Eyes and Dream/Merry Maiden Polka	1949	3.00	6.00	12.00
47-3094	The Donkey Serenade/Serenade	1949	2.50	5.00	10.00
47-3095	Penthouse Serenade/Frasquita Serenade	1949	2.50	5.00	10.00
47-3096	Serenade from the Student Prince/Serenade in the Night	1949	2.50	5.00	10.00
—The above three comprise a box set					
47-3105	Beyond the Sunset/Game of Broken Hearts	1949	3.00	6.00	12.00
47-3202	Sugar Blues/The French Can-Can Song	1949	3.00	6.00	12.00
47-3230	Goofus/Ragging the Scale	1949	2.50	5.00	10.00
47-3231	Josephine/Parade of the Wooden Soldiers	1949	2.50	5.00	10.00
47-3232	The Darktown Strutters' Ball/The Glow-Worm	1949	2.50	5.00	10.00
—The above three comprise a box set					
47-3272	Cruising Down the River/Allah's Holiday	1949	3.00	6.00	12.00
47-3722	Blue Prelude/I May Hate Myself in the Morning	1950	3.00	6.00	12.00
47-3768	The Flying Red Horse Polka/Leicester Square Rag	1950	3.00	6.00	12.00
47-3786	Abide with Me/Ave Maria	1950	2.50	5.00	10.00
47-3787	Lead Kindly Light/Whispering Hope	1950	2.50	5.00	10.00
47-3788	Beautiful Isle of Somewhere/In the Garden	1950	2.50	5.00	10.00
—The above three comprise a box set					
47-3817	Miaianne/When the Saints Go Marching In	1950	3.00	6.00	12.00
47-3824	Gone Fishin'/So Tall a Tree	1950	3.00	6.00	12.00
47-3843	Jalousie (Jealousy)/Fiddle Faddle	1950	3.00	6.00	12.00
47-3844	Ritual Fire Dance/Malaguena	1950	3.00	6.00	12.00
47-3924	Sleigh Ride/I'll Find You	1949	3.75	7.50	15.00
47-3976	It Is No Secret (What God Can Do)/To Think You've Chosen Me	1950	3.00	6.00	12.00
47-4010	After You've Gone/Remember Me in Your Dreams	1950	3.00	6.00	12.00
47-4090	The Syncopated Clock/March of Cards	1951	3.00	6.00	12.00
47-4122	What Will I Tell My Heart/I Whistle a Happy Tune	1951	3.00	6.00	12.00
47-4150	Tom's Tune/These Things I Offer You	1951	3.00	6.00	12.00
47-4199	Come On-a My House/Hula Blues	1951	2.50	5.00	10.00
47-4200	Auf Wiedersehn/Hands Across the Table	1951	2.50	5.00	10.00
47-4201	Autumn Leaves/La Vie En Rose	1951	2.50	5.00	10.00
47-4202	You and the Night and the Music/Yours Is My Heart Alone	1951	2.50	5.00	10.00
—The above four comprise a box set					
47-4221	The Bird of Happiness/At the End of Day	1951	3.00	6.00	12.00
47-4258	Kol Nidre/Eili Eili	1951	3.00	6.00	12.00
47-4287	Little Jumping Jack/Painting Clouds with Sunshine	1951	3.00	6.00	12.00
47-4323	Sleigh Ride/Uncle Mistletoe	1951	3.75	7.50	15.00
47-4385	Sunshower/Sleepy Serenade	1951	3.00	6.00	12.00
47-4463	Laura/My Reverie	1952	2.50	5.00	10.00
47-4464	April in Paris/Moonglow	1952	2.50	5.00	10.00
47-4465	Intermezzo/Moonlight Sonata	1952	2.50	5.00	10.00
47-4466	My Silent Love/Smoke Rings	1952	2.50	5.00	10.00
—The above four comprise a box set					
47-4510	Cool, Cool Kisses/Stolen Love	1952	3.00	6.00	12.00
47-4562	You're Not Worth My Tears/Two Wrongs Never Make a Right	1952	3.00	6.00	12.00
47-4677	Delicado/Plink, Plank, Plunk	1952	3.00	6.00	12.00
47-4790	Birds 'n' Bees/Sky-High	1952	3.00	6.00	12.00
47-5082	Twilight Boogie/Junga-Junga	1952	3.00	6.00	12.00
47-5185	Waggashoe/Ecstacy Tango	1953	3.00	6.00	12.00
47-5246	Anna/Little Red Monkey	1953	3.00	6.00	12.00
47-5347	Under Paris Skies/Don't Take Love from Me	1953	3.00	6.00	12.00
47-5417	Invisible Hands/One Step	1953	3.00	6.00	12.00
47-5463	Peg o' My Heart/Jealous	1953	3.00	6.00	12.00
47-5553	The Creep/Just One More Chance	1953	3.00	6.00	12.00
47-5711	Under a Blanket of Blue/Gimme a Little Kiss	1954	3.00	6.00	12.00
47-5768	Moonlight and Roses (Bring Mem'ries of You)/ Crazy Legs	1954	3.00	6.00	12.00
47-5874	Touch/Southern Star	1954	3.00	6.00	12.00
47-5961	For You/Perdido	1954	3.00	6.00	12.00
47-6084	I Wonder, I Wonder, I Wonder/Dancing with Tears in My Eyes	1955	2.50	5.00	10.00
47-6202	Satan Takes a Holiday/You and You Alone	1955	2.50	5.00	10.00
47-6273	Arrividerci Roma/Cha Cha Joe	1955	2.50	5.00	10.00
47-6461	The Beautiful Girls of Vienna/Petite Papillon	1956	2.50	5.00	10.00
47-6574	Theme from The Proud Ones/Haunted Guitar	1956	2.50	5.00	10.00
47-6713	Postmark: Vienna/Wind River Valley	1956	2.50	5.00	10.00
47-6881	The Lovers/Wailin' Guitar	1957	2.50	5.00	10.00
47-7072	Tumbling Tumbleweeds/Sentimental Journey	1957	2.50	5.00	10.00
47-7187	Rainbow/Tweety	1958	2.50	5.00	10.00
47-7416	Volcano/Cha Cha Charleston	1958	2.50	5.00	10.00
47-7970	Honey Bee/Fun in the Sun	1961	2.00	4.00	8.00
47-8373	My Man/Happy Wedding Song	1964	2.00	4.00	8.00

7-Inch Extended Plays

RCA VICTOR

Number	Title (A Side/B Side)	Yr	VG	VG+	NM
547-0032	Sunrise Serenade/I'll Never Wish for More Than This//Deep Purple/Hindustan	1952	3.00	6.00	12.00
—Part of 2-EP set EPB 3034					
547-0208	Sweet & Low/Out of Nowhere//Someone to Watch Over Me/My Prayer		3.00	6.00	12.00
—One record of 2-EP set EPB 3075					
547-0209	Because/Yesterdays//Lullaby of the Leaves/ Deep Night		3.00	6.00	12.00
—One record of 2-EP set EPB 3075					
EPA 250	White Christmas/Winter Wonderland//Silent Night/Jingle Bells	195?	3.00	6.00	12.00
EPA 250 [PS]	The Three Suns Present Your Christmas Favorites	195?	3.00	6.00	12.00
EPA 655	White Christmas	1955	3.00	6.00	12.00
EPA 655	White Christmas/Santa Claus Is Coming to Town/ Der Tannenbaum//It Came Upon a Midnight Clear/Greensleeves/God Rest Ye Merry Gentlemen	1955	3.00	6.00	12.00
EPA 736	My Reverie/Intermezzo//Tenderly/Laura	1956	2.50	5.00	10.00
EPA 736 [PS]	(title unknown)	1956	2.50	5.00	10.00
547-1040	There Is No Greater Love/A Sinner Kissed an Angel//Autumn Nocturne/Blue Orchids	1954	2.50	5.00	10.00
—One record of 2-EP set EPB 1041					
547-1041	Stars Fell on Alabama/The Touch of Your Lips// Moonlight in Vermont/Flamingo	1954	2.50	5.00	10.00
—One record of 2-EP set EPB 1041					
EPB 1041 [PS]	Soft and Sweet	1954	2.50	5.00	10.00
EPB 3034 [PS]	The Three Suns Present	1952	3.00	6.00	12.00
—Two-pocket jacket for two-EP set					
EPB 3075 [PS]	Slumber Time		3.00	6.00	12.00

Albums

PICKWICK

Number	Title (A Side/B Side)	Yr	VG	VG+	NM
SPC-3037	Twilight Time	197?	2.50	5.00	10.00

RCA CAMDEN

Number	Title (A Side/B Side)	Yr	VG	VG+	NM
CAL-633 [M]	The Sound of Christmas	1964	3.00	6.00	12.00
CAS-633(e) [R]	The Sound of Christmas	1964	3.00	6.00	12.00

RCA VICTOR

Number	Title (A Side/B Side)	Yr	VG	VG+	NM
LPM-3 [10]	Three-Quarter Time	1951	12.50	25.00	50.00
LPM-28 [10]	Hands Across the Table	1951	12.50	25.00	50.00
LPM-52 [10]	Christmas Favorites	1951	12.50	25.00	50.00
LPM-1041 [M]	Soft and Sweet	1955	7.50	15.00	30.00
LPM-1132 [M]	Sounds of Christmas	1955	7.50	15.00	30.00
LPM-1171 [M]	Twilight Time	1956	7.50	15.00	30.00
LPM-1173 [M]	My Reverie	1956	7.50	15.00	30.00
LPM-1219 [M]	Slumber Time	1956	7.50	15.00	30.00
LPM-1220 [M]	Malaguena	1956	7.50	15.00	30.00
LPM-1249 [M]	High Fi and Wide	1956	7.50	15.00	30.00
LPM-1316 [M]	Easy Listening	1956	7.50	15.00	30.00
LPM-1333 [M]	Midnight for Two	1957	7.50	15.00	30.00
LPM-1543 [M]	The Things in Love in Hi-Fi	1958	5.00	10.00	20.00
LSP-1543 [S]	The Things in Love in Hi-Fi	1958	7.50	15.00	30.00
LPM-1578 [M]	Let's Dance with the Three Suns	1958	5.00	10.00	20.00
LSP-1578 [S]	Let's Dance with the Three Suns	1958	7.50	15.00	30.00
LPM-1669 [M]	Love in the Afternoon	1959	5.00	10.00	20.00
LSP-1669 [S]	Love in the Afternoon	1959	7.50	15.00	30.00
LPM-1734 [M]	Having a Ball with the Three Suns	1959	5.00	10.00	20.00
LSP-1734 [S]	Having a Ball with the Three Suns	1959	7.50	15.00	30.00
ANL1-1779(e)	Pure Gold	1974	2.50	5.00	10.00
LPM-1964 [M]	Swingin' on a Star	1959	5.00	10.00	20.00
LSP-1964 [S]	Swingin' on a Star	1959	7.50	15.00	30.00
LPM-2054 [M]	A Ding Dong Dandy Christmas!	1959	5.00	10.00	20.00
LSP-2054 [S]	A Ding Dong Dandy Christmas!	1959	7.50	15.00	30.00
LPM-2120 [M]	Twilight Memories	1960	5.00	10.00	20.00
LSP-2120 [S]	Twilight Memories	1960	6.25	12.50	25.00
LPM-2235 [M]	On a Magic Carpet	1960	5.00	10.00	20.00
LSP-2235 [S]	On a Magic Carpet	1960	6.25	12.50	25.00
LPM-2307 [M]	Dancing on a Cloud	1961	5.00	10.00	20.00
LSP-2307 [S]	Dancing on a Cloud	1961	6.25	12.50	25.00
LPM-2310 [M]	Fever and Smoke	1961	5.00	10.00	20.00
LSP-2310 [S]	Fever and Smoke	1961	6.25	12.50	25.00
LPM-2437 [M]	Fun in the Sun	1961	5.00	10.00	20.00
LSP-2437 [S]	Fun in the Sun	1961	6.25	12.50	25.00
LPM-2532 [M]	Movin' 'N' Groovin'	1962	5.00	10.00	20.00
LSP-2532 [S]	Movin' 'N' Groovin'	1962	6.25	12.50	25.00

Number	Title (A Side/B Side)	Yr	VG	VG+	NM
LPM-2617 [M]	Warm and Tender	1962	5.00	10.00	20.00
LSP-2617 [S]	Warm and Tender	1962	6.25	12.50	25.00
LPM-2717 [M]	Everything Under the Sun	1963	3.75	7.50	15.00
LSP-2717 [S]	Everything Under the Sun	1963	5.00	10.00	20.00
LPM-2904 [M]	One Enchanted Evening	1964	3.75	7.50	15.00
LSP-2904 [S]	One Enchanted Evening	1964	5.00	10.00	20.00
LPM-2963 [M]	A Swingin' Thing	1964	3.75	7.50	15.00
LSP-2963 [S]	A Swingin' Thing	1964	5.00	10.00	20.00
LPM-3012 [10]	Twilight Moods	1952	12.50	25.00	50.00
LPM-3034 [10]	The Three Suns Present	1952	12.50	25.00	50.00
LPM-3040 [10]	Busy Fingers	1952	12.50	25.00	50.00
LPM-3056 [10]	Christmas Party	1952	12.50	25.00	50.00
LPM-3075 [10]	Slumbertime	1953	12.50	25.00	50.00
LPM-3113 [10]	Pops Concert Favorites	1953	12.50	25.00	50.00
LPM-3125 [10]	Mods	1953	12.50	25.00	50.00
LPM-3130 [10]	Top Pops	1953	12.50	25.00	50.00
LPM-3146 [10]	Polka Time	1954	12.50	25.00	50.00
LPM-3174 [10]	Sacred Hymns	1954	12.50	25.00	50.00
LPM-3354 [M]	Country Music Shindig	1965	3.75	7.50	15.00
LSP-3354 [S]	Country Music Shindig	1965	5.00	10.00	20.00
LPM-3447 [M]	The Best of the Three Suns	1965	3.75	7.50	15.00
LSP-3447 [S]	The Best of the Three Suns	1965	5.00	10.00	20.00
VPS-6075 [(2)]	This Is the Three Suns	1972	3.75	7.50	15.00
ROYALE					
1 [10]	Twilight Time	1951	12.50	25.00	50.00
29 [10]	Midnight Time	1951	12.50	25.00	50.00
SEARS					
SPS-437	Twilight Time	1969	3.00	6.00	12.00
VARSITY					
VLP-6001 [10]	Twilight Time	1950	12.50	25.00	50.00
VLP-6048 [10]	Midnight Time	1950	12.50	25.00	50.00

THREE VALES, THE

Number	Title (A Side/B Side)	Yr	VG	VG+	NM
45s					
CINDY					
3007	Blue Lights/Ay, Ay, Ay	1957	30.00	60.00	120.00

THREETEENS, THE

Number	Title (A Side/B Side)	Yr	VG	VG+	NM
45s					
REV					
3516	Dear 53310761/Doowaddie	1958	10.00	20.00	40.00
3522	X + Y = Z/For the Love of Mike	1959	6.25	12.50	25.00
TODD					
1021	X + Y = Z/For the Love of Mike	1959	5.00	10.00	20.00

THRILLERS, THE (1)

Number	Title (A Side/B Side)	Yr	VG	VG+	NM
45s					
BIG TOWN					
109	The Drunkard/Mattie, Leave Me Alone	1953	100.00	200.00	400.00
HERALD					
432	Lizabeth/Please Talk to Me	1954	100.00	200.00	400.00
THRILLER					
3530	Lessie Mae/I'm Going to Live My Life Alone	1953	250.00	500.00	1000.

THRILLERS, THE (2)

Number	Title (A Side/B Side)	Yr	VG	VG+	NM
45s					
UPTOWN					
715	Come What May/This I Know Little Girl	1965	3.00	6.00	12.00

THRILLINGTON, PERCY "THRILLS"

See PAUL McCARTNEY.

THRILLS, THE

Number	Title (A Side/B Side)	Yr	VG	VG+	NM
45s					
CAPITOL					
5631	What Can Go Wrong/No One	1966	5.00	10.00	20.00
5719	Here's a Heart/Bring It On Home to Me	1966	5.00	10.00	20.00
5871	Show the World Where It's At/Underneath My Make-Up	1967	5.00	10.00	20.00

THUNDER, JOHNNY

Number	Title (A Side/B Side)	Yr	VG	VG+	NM
45s					
CALLA					
161	I'm Alive/Verbal Expressions of T.V.	1969	—	3.00	6.00
DIAMOND					
129	Loop De Loop/Don't Be Ashamed	1962	3.75	7.50	15.00
132	Rock-a-Bye My Darling/The Rosy Dance	1963	2.50	5.00	10.00
132 [PS]	Rock-a-Bye My Darling/The Rosy Dance	1963	5.00	10.00	20.00
137	The Outlaw/Jailer, Bring Me Water	1963	2.50	5.00	10.00
148	Hey Child/Darling Je Vous Aime Beaucoup	1963	2.50	5.00	10.00
152	Constitution of Love/Good Morning Sadness	1964	2.00	4.00	8.00
155	Everybody Likes to Dance with Johnny/Zoo-Lee-Oh	1964	2.00	4.00	8.00
169	More, More More Love, Love, Love/Shout It to the World	1964	2.00	4.00	8.00
175	Send Her to Me/Shout It to the World	1964	2.00	4.00	8.00
185	Suzie-Q/Dear John, I'm Going to Leave You	1965	2.00	4.00	8.00
192	Everybody Do the Sloopy/Beautiful	1965	2.00	4.00	8.00
196	My Prayer/A Broken Heart	1966	2.00	4.00	8.00
206	Bewildered/Just Me and You	1966	2.00	4.00	8.00
218	Make Love to Me/Teach Me Tonight	1967	2.00	4.00	8.00
—With Ruby Winters					
222	Am I Right or Am I Wrong/You Send Me	1967	2.00	4.00	8.00
238	We Only Have One Life (Let's Live It Together)/ Teach Me Tonight	1968	2.00	4.00	8.00
—With Ruby Winters					
246	Put It in Motion/Groovy Two Shoes	1968	2.00	4.00	8.00
EPIC					
9329	Ever Your Man/Horror Show	1959	3.75	7.50	15.00
UNITED ARTISTS					
50736	Power to the People/Love Trip	1971	—	3.00	6.00
Albums					
DIAMOND					
D-5001 [M]	Loop De Loop	1963	25.00	50.00	100.00
DS-5001 [S]	Loop De Loop	1963	37.50	75.00	150.00
REAL					
RR-1	So Alone	196?	3.75	7.50	15.00

THUNDER AND ROSES

Number	Title (A Side/B Side)	Yr	VG	VG+	NM
45s					
UNITED ARTISTS					
50536	Country Life/I Love a Woman	1969	3.00	6.00	12.00
Albums					
UNITED ARTISTS					
UAS-6709	King of the Black Sunrise	1969	7.50	15.00	30.00

THUNDER BOLTS, THE

Number	Title (A Side/B Side)	Yr	VG	VG+	NM
45s					
RONDACK					
7546	Thunder Head/Blending	196?	12.50	25.00	50.00

THUNDER HEADS, THE

Number	Title (A Side/B Side)	Yr	VG	VG+	NM
45s					
CARTWHEEL					
100	Thunder Head/Unemployment	1966	7.50	15.00	30.00

THUNDERBOLTS, THE

Number	Title (A Side/B Side)	Yr	VG	VG+	NM
45s					
DOT					
16496	Lost Planets/March of the Spacemen	1963	5.00	10.00	20.00

THUNDERCLAP NEWMAN

Jimmy McCulloch, later of WINGS, was in this group.

Number	Title (A Side/B Side)	Yr	VG	VG+	NM
45s					
TRACK					
2656	Something in the Air/Wilhelmina	1969	2.50	5.00	10.00
2769	Something in the Air/Wilhelmina	1970	—	3.00	6.00
Albums					
MCA					
354	Hollywood Dream	1974	2.50	5.00	10.00
—Reissue of Track 354					
TRACK					
354	Hollywood Dream	1973	3.00	6.00	12.00
—Reissue of Track 8264					
SD 8264	Hollywood Dream	1970	6.25	12.50	25.00

THUNDERGRIN

Number	Title (A Side/B Side)	Yr	VG	VG+	NM
45s					
EPIC					
10215	Women in the Street/Mr. Simms	1967	2.50	5.00	10.00

THUNDERPUSSY

Number	Title (A Side/B Side)	Yr	VG	VG+	NM
Albums					
M.R.T.					
31748	Documents of Captivity	1973	37.50	75.00	150.00

THUNDERTONES, THE

Number	Title (A Side/B Side)	Yr	VG	VG+	NM
45s					
DONNA					
1343	Thunder Rhythm/Pay Day	1961	7.50	15.00	30.00
DOT					
16137	Jungle Fever/Hot Ice	1960	7.50	15.00	30.00
16177	The Street Beat/Happy Little Jug	1961	7.50	15.00	30.00
—As "Lenny and the Thundertones"					

THUNDERTREE

Number	Title (A Side/B Side)	Yr	VG	VG+	NM
Albums					
ROULETTE					
SR-42038	Thundertree	1970	7.50	15.00	30.00

THURSDAY'S CHILDREN

Number	Title (A Side/B Side)	Yr	VG	VG+	NM
45s					
INTERNATIONAL ARTISTS					
110	Air Conditioned Man/Sominoes	1967	37.50	75.00	150.00
115	Help, Murder, Police/You Can't Forget About That	1967	37.50	75.00	150.00
N-JOY					
1019	Running Around on Me/I Don't Need Your Love	1967	3.75	7.50	15.00

THYME

Number	Title (A Side/B Side)	Yr	VG	VG+	NM
45s					
A-SQUARE					
201	Somehow/Shame, Shame	1969	10.00	20.00	40.00
202	Time of the Season/I Found a Love	1969	10.00	20.00	40.00
BANG					
546	Love to Love/Very Last Day	1967	5.00	10.00	20.00

TIATT, LYNN, AND THE COMETS

Number	Title (A Side/B Side)	Yr	VG	VG+	NM
45s					
PUSSYCAT					
1	Dad Is Home/Vilma's Jump-Up	195?	75.00	150.00	300.00

TICO AND THE TRIUMPHS

PAUL SIMON was a member.

Number	Title (A Side/B Side)	Yr	VG	VG+	NM
45s					
AMY					
835	Motorcycle/I Don't Believe Them	1961	25.00	50.00	100.00
845	Wildflower/Express Train	1962	25.00	50.00	100.00
860	Cry, Lil' Boy, Cry/Get Up and Do the Wobble	1962	25.00	50.00	100.00
876	Cards of Love/Noise	1963	50.00	100.00	200.00

Number	Title (A Side/B Side)	Yr	VG	VG+	NM
MADISON					
169	Motorcycle/I Don't Believe Them	1961	50.00	100.00	200.00

TIEKEN, FREDDIE, AND THE ROCKERS

Albums

Number	Title (A Side/B Side)	Yr	VG	VG+	NM
I.T.					
2301 [M]	By Popular Demand	1957	12.50	25.00	50.00
2304 [M]	Freddie Tieken and the Rockers	1958	12.50	25.00	50.00

TIFFANY SHADE, THE

45s

Number	Title (A Side/B Side)	Yr	VG	VG+	NM
MAINSTREAM					
677	One Good Reason/Would You Take My Mind Out for a Walk	1968	3.75	7.50	15.00
680	An Older Man/Sam	1968	3.75	7.50	15.00

Albums

Number	Title (A Side/B Side)	Yr	VG	VG+	NM
MAINSTREAM					
S-6105	The Tiffany Shade	1968	25.00	50.00	100.00

TIFFANYS, THE

Probably not all the same group.

45s

Number	Title (A Side/B Side)	Yr	VG	VG+	NM
ARCTIC					
101	Love Me/Happiest Girl in the World	1964	5.00	10.00	20.00
ATLANTIC					
2240	Please Tell Me/Gossip	1964	5.00	10.00	20.00
JOSIE					
942	I Feel the Same Way Too/I Just Wanna Be a Girl	1965	3.00	6.00	12.00
952	Heaven on Earth/Take Another Look at Me	1966	3.00	6.00	12.00
KR					
120	He's Good for Me/It's Got to Be a Great Song	1967	5.00	10.00	20.00
—As "The Tiffanies"					
MRS					
777	Please Tell Me/Gossip	1964	20.00	40.00	80.00
RKO					
120	He's Good for Me/It's Got to Be a Great Song	1967	2.50	5.00	10.00
—Are the KR and RKO releases one and the same? We don't know					
ROCKIN' ROBIN					
1	I've Got a Girl/I Don't Dig Western Movies	1963	75.00	150.00	300.00
SWAN					
4104	Atlanta/The Pleasure of Love	1962	5.00	10.00	20.00

TIGERS, THE

45s

Number	Title (A Side/B Side)	Yr	VG	VG+	NM
COLPIX					
773	GeeTO Tiger/The Prowl	1965	12.50	25.00	50.00
SPEC-773	GeeTO Tiger/The Big Sounds of the GeeTO Tiger	1965	20.00	40.00	80.00
—Special promotional issue					
SPEC-773 [PS]	GeeTO Tiger/The Big Sounds of the GeeTO Tiger	1965	50.00	100.00	200.00
—Sleeve appears to have been available only with the promotional B-side					

TIKIS, THE

45s

Number	Title (A Side/B Side)	Yr	VG	VG+	NM
ASCOT					
2186	Stop-Look-Listen/Cream in My Coffee	1965	2.50	5.00	10.00
2204	High School Dropout Blues/Whole Lotta Soul	1966	2.50	5.00	10.00
AUTUMN					
18	If I've Been Dreaming/Pay Attention to Me	1965	2.50	5.00	10.00
—As "The Other Tikis"					
28	Bye Bye Bye/Lost My Love Today	1966	2.50	5.00	10.00
—As "The Other Tikis"					
DIAL					
4048	Somebody's Sun/Little Miss Lovelight	1966	2.50	5.00	10.00
MINARET					
115	Big Feet/One More Chance	196?	3.00	6.00	12.00
116	Popsicle/All That Talk	196?	3.00	6.00	12.00
118	Traveling Shoes/Valley of Tears	196?	3.00	6.00	12.00
WARNER BROS.					
5818	Bye Bye Bye/Lost My Love Today	1966	2.50	5.00	10.00

Albums

Number	Title (A Side/B Side)	Yr	VG	VG+	NM
MINARET					
TLP-7001 [M]	The Tikis	196?	25.00	50.00	100.00
PHILIPS					
PHM 200043 [M]	The Tikis	1962	6.25	12.50	25.00
PHS 600043 [S]	The Tikis	1962	7.50	15.00	30.00

TIKIS, THE, AND THE FABULONS

45s

Number	Title (A Side/B Side)	Yr	VG	VG+	NM
PANORAMA					
13	Take a Look/For Your Love	1965	5.00	10.00	20.00
TOWER					
181	Take a Look/Cherry Pie	1965	3.00	6.00	12.00

TIL, SONNY

Also see THE ORIOLES.

45s

Number	Title (A Side/B Side)	Yr	VG	VG+	NM
JUBILEE					
5060	I Never Knew (I Could Love Anybody)/My Prayer	1951	75.00	150.00	300.00
5066	Fool's World/For All We Know	1951	75.00	150.00	300.00
—Black vinyl					
5066	Fool's World/For All We Know	1951	200.00	400.00	800.00
—Red vinyl					
5090	Once in Awhile/I Only Have Eyes for You	1952	12.50	25.00	50.00
—With Edna McGriff					
5099	Good/Picadilly	1952	20.00	40.00	80.00
—With Edna McGriff					
5112	Have You Heard/Lonely Wine	1953	50.00	100.00	200.00
5118	(Danger) Soft Shoulders/Congratulations to Someone	1953	50.00	100.00	200.00
5394	Night and Day/Shimmy Time	1960	5.00	10.00	20.00
RCA VICTOR					
47-9733	You're All I Need/After You	1969	2.00	4.00	8.00
47-9759	Tears and Misery/I Better Leave Love Alone	1969	2.00	4.00	8.00
74-0390	Don't Feel No Pain/One Big Happy Family	1970	2.00	4.00	8.00
74-0432	Colours/Love Is What It's All About	1971	2.00	4.00	8.00
74-0529	'Til Then/Love or Desire	1971	2.00	4.00	8.00
74-0606	Crying in the Chapel/What Are You Doing New Year's Eve	1971	2.00	4.00	8.00
ROULETTE					
4079	Shy/First Blush	1958	5.00	10.00	20.00

Albums

Number	Title (A Side/B Side)	Yr	VG	VG+	NM
DOBRE					
1026	Back to the Chapel	1978	3.00	6.00	12.00
RCA VICTOR					
LSP-4451	Sonny Til Returns	1970	5.00	10.00	20.00
LSP-4538	Old Gold/New Gold	1971	3.75	7.50	15.00

TILLOTSON, JOHNNY

45s

Number	Title (A Side/B Side)	Yr	VG	VG+	NM
AMOS					
117	Tears on My Pillow/Remember When	1969	—	3.00	6.00
125	What Am I Living For/Joy to the World	1969	—	3.00	6.00
128	Raining in My Heart/Today I Started Loving You Again	1969	—	3.00	6.00
136	Susan/Love Waits for Me	1970	—	3.00	6.00
146	I Don't Believe In It Anymore/Kansas City, Kansas	1970	—	3.00	6.00
ATLANTIC					
87978	Bim Bam Boom/(B-side unknown)	1990	—	2.00	4.00
BUDDAH					
232	Star Spangled Bus/Apple Bend	1971	—	2.50	5.00
256	Welfare Hero/The Flower Kissed the Shoes That Jesus Wore	1971	—	2.50	5.00
279	Make Me Believe/The Flower Kissed the Shoes That Jesus Wore	1972	—	2.50	5.00
311	Your Love's Been a Long Time Comin'/Apple Bend	1972	—	2.50	5.00
CADENCE					
1353	Dreamy Eyes/Well, I'm Your Man	1958	5.00	10.00	20.00
1354	I'm Never Gonna Kiss You/Cherie, Cherie	1958	6.25	12.50	25.00
—With Genevieve					
1365	True True Happiness/Love Is Blind	1959	5.00	10.00	20.00
1372	Why Do I Love You So/Never Let Me Go	1959	5.00	10.00	20.00
1377	Earth Angel/Pledging My Love	1960	5.00	10.00	20.00
1377 [PS]	Earth Angel/Pledging My Love	1960	7.50	15.00	30.00
1384	Poetry in Motion/Princess, Princess	1960	5.00	10.00	20.00
1391	Jimmy's Girl/His True Love Said Godbye	1960	3.75	7.50	15.00
1391 [PS]	Jimmy's Girl/His True Love Said Godbye	1960	7.50	15.00	30.00
1404	Without You/Cutie Pie	1961	3.75	7.50	15.00
1409	Dreamy Eyes/Well, I'm Your Man	1961	3.75	7.50	15.00
1418	It Keeps Right On a-Hurtin'/She Gave Sweet Love to Me	1962	3.75	7.50	15.00
1424	Send Me the Pillow You Dream On/What'll I Do	1962	3.75	7.50	15.00
1432	I Can't Help It (If I'm Still in Love with You)/I'm So Lonesome I Could Cry	1962	3.75	7.50	15.00
1434	Out of My Mind/Empty Feelin'	1963	3.75	7.50	15.00
1437	You Can Never Stop Me Loving You/Judy, Judy, Judy	1963	3.75	7.50	15.00
1441	Funny How Time Slips Away/A Very Good Year for Girls	1963	3.75	7.50	15.00
COLUMBIA					
10125	Big Ole Jean/Mississippi Lady	1975	—	2.50	5.00
10199	Right Here in Your Arms/Willow County Request Live	1975	—	2.50	5.00
45842	Sunshine of My Life/If You Wouldn't Be My Lady	1973	—	2.50	5.00
45984	So Much of My Life/I Love How She Needs Me	1973	—	2.50	5.00
46065	Till I Can't Take It Anymore/Sunday Kind of Woman	1974	—	2.50	5.00
MGM					
13181	Talk Back Trembling Lips/Another You	1963	3.00	6.00	12.00
13181 [PS]	Talk Back Trembling Lips/Another You	1963	5.00	10.00	20.00
13193	Worried Guy/Please Don't Go Away	1963	2.50	5.00	10.00
13193 [PS]	Worried Guy/Please Don't Go Away	1963	5.00	10.00	20.00
13232	I Rise, I Fall/I'm Watching My Watch	1964	2.50	5.00	10.00
13232 [PS]	I Rise, I Fall/I'm Watching My Watch	1964	5.00	10.00	20.00
13255	Worry/Sufferin' from a Heartache	1964	2.50	5.00	10.00
13255 [PS]	Worry/Sufferin' from a Heartache	1964	5.00	10.00	20.00
13284	She Understands Me/Tomorrow	1964	2.50	5.00	10.00
13284 [PS]	She Understands Me/Tomorrow	1964	5.00	10.00	20.00
13316	Angel/Little Boy	1965	2.50	5.00	10.00
13316 [PS]	Angel/Little Boy	1965	5.00	10.00	20.00
13344	Then I'll Count Again/One's Yours, One's Mine	1965	2.50	5.00	10.00
13344 [PS]	Then I'll Count Again/One's Yours, One's Mine	1965	5.00	10.00	20.00
13376	Heartaches by the Number/Your Mem'ry Comes Along	1965	2.50	5.00	10.00
13376 [PS]	Heartaches by the Number/Your Mem'ry Comes Along	1965	5.00	10.00	20.00
13408	Our World/(Wait 'Till You See) My Gidget	1965	2.50	5.00	10.00
13445	Hello Enemy/I Never Loved You Anyway	1966	2.50	5.00	10.00
13499	Me, Myself and I/Country Boy, Country Boy	1966	2.50	5.00	10.00
13519	No Love at All/What Am I Gonna Do	1966	2.50	5.00	10.00
13598	More Than Before/Baby's Gone	1966	2.50	5.00	10.00
13598	More Than Before/Open Up Your Heart	1966	2.50	5.00	10.00
13633	Christmas Country Style/Christmas Is the Best of All	1966	2.50	5.00	10.00
13684	Strange Things Happen/Tommy Jones	1967	2.50	5.00	10.00
13738	Don't Tell Me It's Raining/Takin' It Easy	1967	2.50	5.00	10.00
13829	You're the Reason/Countin' My Teardrops	1967	2.50	5.00	10.00
13888	I Can Spot a Cheater/It Keeps Right On a-Hurtin'	1968	2.00	4.00	8.00
13924	I Haven't Begun to Love You Yet/Why So Lonely	1968	2.00	4.00	8.00
13977	Letter to Emily/Your Mem'ry Comes Along	1968	2.00	4.00	8.00
REWARD					
03327	Baby You Do It for Me (And I'll Do It for You)/She's Not As Married As She Used to Be	1982	—	2.00	4.00
03901	Crying/You're a Beautiful Place to Be	1983	—	2.00	4.00

Number	Title (A Side/B Side)	Yr	VG	VG+	NM
04123	Burnin'/What's Another Year	1983	—	2.00	4.00
04346	Lay Back (In the Arms of Somebody)/What's Another Year	1984	—	2.00	4.00
SCEPTER					
12389	Song for Hank Williams (mono/stereo)	1973	2.00	4.00	8.00
—With John Edward Beland; may be promo-only					
UNITED ARTISTS					
XW860	It Could've Been Nashville/Summertime Lovin'	1976	—	2.50	5.00
XW986	Toy Hearts/Just An Ordinary Man	1977	—	2.50	5.00
7-Inch Extended Plays					
CADENCE					
CEP-114	True True Happiness/Love Is Blind//Dreamy Eyes/Well I'm Your Man	1960	6.25	12.50	25.00
CEP-114 [PS]	Johnny Tillotson	1960	6.25	12.50	25.00
Albums					
ACCORD					
SN-7194	Scrapbook	1982	2.50	5.00	10.00
AMOS					
7006	Tears on My Pillow	1969	5.00	10.00	20.00
BARNABY					
BR-4007	Johnny Tillotson's Greatest	1977	3.00	6.00	12.00
BUDDAH					
BDS-5112	Johnny Tillotson	1972	3.75	7.50	15.00
CADENCE					
CLP-3052 [M]	Johnny Tillotson's Best	1961	10.00	20.00	40.00
—Maroon and silver label					
CLP-3052 [M]	Johnny Tillotson's Best	1962	6.25	12.50	25.00
—Red and black label					
CLP-3058 [M]	It Keeps Right On a-Hurtin'	1962	7.50	15.00	30.00
CLP-3067 [M]	You Can Never Stop Me Loving You	1963	7.50	15.00	30.00
CLP-25052 [P]	Johnny Tillotson's Best	1961	12.50	25.00	50.00
—Maroon and silver label					
CLP-25052 [P]	Johnny Tillotson's Best	1962	7.50	15.00	30.00
—Red and black label					
CLP-25058 [S]	It Keeps Right On a-Hurtin'	1962	10.00	20.00	40.00
CLP-25067 [P]	You Can Never Stop Me Loving You	1963	10.00	20.00	40.00
EVEREST					
4113	Johnny Tillotson's Greatest Hits	1982	2.50	5.00	10.00
METRO					
M-561 [M]	Johnny Tillotson Sings Tillotson	1967	3.75	7.50	15.00
MS-561 [S]	Johnny Tillotson Sings Tillotson	1967	5.00	10.00	20.00
MGM					
E-4188 [M]	Talk Back Trembling Lips	1964	5.00	10.00	20.00
SE-4188 [S]	Talk Back Trembling Lips	1964	6.25	12.50	25.00
E-4224 [M]	The Tillotson Touch	1964	5.00	10.00	20.00
SE-4224 [S]	The Tillotson Touch	1964	6.25	12.50	25.00
E-4270 [M]	She Understands Me	1965	5.00	10.00	20.00
SE-4270 [S]	She Understands Me	1965	6.25	12.50	25.00
E-4302 [M]	That's My Style	1965	5.00	10.00	20.00
SE-4302 [S]	That's My Style	1965	6.25	12.50	25.00
E-4328 [M]	Our World	1965	5.00	10.00	20.00
SE-4328 [S]	Our World	1965	6.25	12.50	25.00
E-4395 [M]	No Love at All	1966	5.00	10.00	20.00
SE-4395 [S]	No Love at All	1966	6.25	12.50	25.00
E-4402 [M]	The Christmas Touch	1966	5.00	10.00	20.00
SE-4402 [S]	The Christmas Touch	1966	6.25	12.50	25.00
E-4452 [M]	Here I Am	1967	5.00	10.00	20.00
SE-4452 [S]	Here I Am	1967	6.25	12.50	25.00
E-4532 [M]	The Best of Johnny Tillotson	1968	7.50	15.00	30.00
—May be promo only (yellow label)					
SE-4532 [S]	The Best of Johnny Tillotson	1968	5.00	10.00	20.00
SE-4814	The Very Best of Johnny Tillotson	1971	3.00	6.00	12.00
ST 90410 [S]	The Tillotson Touch	1965	7.50	15.00	30.00
—Capitol Record Club edition					
T 90410 [M]	The Tillotson Touch	1965	7.50	15.00	30.00
—Capitol Record Club edition					
UNITED ARTISTS					
UA-LA759-G	Johnny Tillotson	1977	2.50	5.00	10.00

TIM TAM AND THE TURN-ONS

Number	Title (A Side/B Side)	Yr	VG	VG+	NM
45s					
PALMER					
5002	Wait a Minute/Ophelia	1965	6.25	12.50	25.00
5003	Cheryl Ann/Sealed with a Kiss	1966	7.50	15.00	30.00
5006	Kimberly/I Leave You in Tears	1966	10.00	20.00	40.00
5014	Don't Say Hi/(Instrumental)	1967	6.25	12.50	25.00

TIMBER CREEK

Number	Title (A Side/B Side)	Yr	VG	VG+	NM
Albums					
RENEGADE					
95014	Hellbound Highway	1975	37.50	75.00	150.00

TIMERS, THE

With GARY USHER and BRIAN WILSON.

Number	Title (A Side/B Side)	Yr	VG	VG+	NM
45s					
REPRISE					
20231	No-Go Showboat/Competition Coupe	1963	25.00	50.00	100.00

TIMMOTHY

Number	Title (A Side/B Side)	Yr	VG	VG+	NM
Albums					
PEAR					
(# unknown)	Strange But True	1972	50.00	100.00	200.00

TIN HOUSE

Number	Title (A Side/B Side)	Yr	VG	VG+	NM
45s					
EPIC					
10739	I Want Your Baby/Be Good and Be Kind	1971	2.00	4.00	8.00
Albums					
EPIC					
E 30511	Tin House	1971	5.00	10.00	20.00

Number Title (A Side/B Side) Yr VG VG+ NM

TIN TIN

Number	Title (A Side/B Side)	Yr	VG	VG+	NM
45s					
ATCO					
6794	Toast and Marmalade for Tea/Manhattan Woman	1971	2.00	4.00	8.00
6821	Is That the Way/Swans on the Canal	1971	—	3.00	6.00
6853	Set Sail for England/The Cavalry Is Coming	1971	—	3.00	6.00
POLYDOR					
15055	Talking Turkey/The Cavalry Is Coming	1972	—	3.00	6.00
SIRE					
29750	Kiss Me/Kiss Me	1983	—	2.50	5.00
Albums					
ATCO					
SD 33-350	Tin Tin	1970	3.75	7.50	15.00
SD 33-370	Astral Taxi	1971	3.75	7.50	15.00

TINA WITH DADDY AND MOMMY

"Mommy and Daddy" are TAMMY WYNETTE and GEORGE JONES; Tina is their stepdaughter.

Number	Title (A Side/B Side)	Yr	VG	VG+	NM
45s					
EPIC					
11099	Telephone Call/No Charge	1974	—	2.50	5.00

TINDLEY, GEORGE

Number	Title (A Side/B Side)	Yr	VG	VG+	NM
45s					
EMBER					
1058	The Gypsy/I Wish	1960	3.75	7.50	15.00
1060	Wedding Bells/No Lonely Nights	1960	3.75	7.50	15.00
HERALD					
558	Close Your Eyes/Heart of Gold	1961	3.00	6.00	12.00
PARKWAY					
834	Fairy Tales/Just For You	1962	3.00	6.00	12.00
WAND					
11205	Ain't That Peculiar/It's All Over But the Shouting	1969	2.00	4.00	8.00
11208	Honky Tonk Women/So Help Me Woman	1969	2.00	4.00	8.00
11215	Wan-Tu-Wah-Zuree/Pity the Poor Man	1970	2.00	4.00	8.00

TINGLING MOTHER'S CIRCUS

Number	Title (A Side/B Side)	Yr	VG	VG+	NM
45s					
MUSICOR					
1335	Positively Negative/Sunday Kind of Feeling	1968	2.50	5.00	10.00
1359	I Found a New Love/Happy Bubble	1969	2.50	5.00	10.00
ROULETTE					
4758	Face in My Mind/Isn't It Strange	1967	3.75	7.50	15.00
Albums					
MUSICOR					
MS-3167	Circus of the Mind	1968	6.25	12.50	25.00

TINY TIM

Number	Title (A Side/B Side)	Yr	VG	VG+	NM
45s					
BLUE CAT					
127	April Showers/Little Girl	1966	3.00	6.00	12.00
CLOUDS					
17	Tip Toe to the Gas Pumps/Hickey on Your Neck	1979	2.50	5.00	10.00
REPRISE					
0679	Tip-Toe Thru' the Tulips with Me/Fill Your Heart	1968	2.00	4.00	8.00
0740	Tip-Toe Thru' the Tulips with Me/Don't Bite the Hand That's Feeding You	1971	—	2.00	4.00
—"Back to Back Hits" series					
0760	Bring Back Those Rock-A-Bye Baby Days/Hello, Hello	1968	—	3.00	6.00
0760	Bring Back Those Rock-A-Bye Baby Days/This Is All I Ask	1968	—	3.00	6.00
0769	Be My Love/This Is All I Ask	1968	—	3.00	6.00
0802	Great Balls of Fire/As Time Goes By	1969	—	3.00	6.00
0837	On the Good Ship Lollipop/America I Love You	1969	—	3.00	6.00
0855	Mickey the Monkey/Neighborhood Children	1969	—	3.00	6.00
0867	I'm a Lonesome Little Raindrop/What the World Needs Now Is Love	1969	—	3.00	6.00
0939	Don't Bite the Hand That's Feeding You/What Kind of American Are You	1970	—	3.00	6.00
0985	Why/Spaceship Song	1971	—	3.00	6.00
—With Miss Vicky					
20174	Bring Back Rockabye Baby Days/Just Say I Love Her	1963	3.00	6.00	12.00
—B-side by Johnny Prophet					
SCEPTER					
12351	Am I Just Another Pretty Face/The Movies	1972	—	3.00	6.00
VICTIM					
1001	Rudolph The Red-Nosed Reindeer/White Christmas	198?	3.00	6.00	12.00
Albums					
BOUQUET					
SLP-711	Love and Kisses from Tiny Tim	1968	3.00	6.00	12.00
REPRISE					
RS 6292	God Bless Tiny Tim	1968	3.75	7.50	15.00
RS 6323	Tiny Tim's Second Album	1969	3.75	7.50	15.00
RS 6351	For All My Little Friends	1969	3.75	7.50	15.00

TINY TIM AND THE HITS

Number	Title (A Side/B Side)	Yr	VG	VG+	NM
45s					
ROULETTE					
4123	Wedding Bells/Doll Baby	1958	12.50	25.00	50.00

TITANS, THE

More than one group.

Number	Title (A Side/B Side)	Yr	VG	VG+	NM
45s					
BANGAR					
00611	Surfer's Lullaby/Motivation	1964	6.25	12.50	25.00
CLASS					
244	No Time/The Tootin' Tutor	1959	6.25	12.50	25.00

Number	Title (A Side/B Side)	Yr	VG	VG+	NM
DUFF'S					
111	Little Girl/Pretty Young Thing	1969	3.00	6.00	12.00
112	Ode to Billy Martin/Please Don't Be Angry	1970	3.00	6.00	12.00
FIDELITY					
3016	What Have I Done/Everybody Happy?	1960	7.50	15.00	30.00
METROBEAT					
4452	To Covet the Turf/Mountain of Love	196?	5.00	10.00	20.00
MGM					
13207	Yojimbo/Midnight in Tokyo	1964	3.00	6.00	12.00
—B-side by the Tokyo Boys					
NOLTA					
351	A-Rab/Marquette	1961	6.25	12.50	25.00
SOMA					
1402	A Summer Place/Tchaikovsky Rides Again	1963	5.00	10.00	20.00
1411	The No Place Special/Reveille Rock	1964	5.00	10.00	20.00
SOUND OF MUSIC					
12186	Need You/Fun Seekers	196?	3.00	6.00	12.00
12186 [PS]	Need You/Fun Seekers	196?	12.50	25.00	50.00
SPECIALTY					
614	Sweet Peach/Free and Easy	1957	6.25	12.50	25.00
625	Don't You Just Know It/Can It Be	1958	6.25	12.50	25.00
632	Arlene/Love Is a Wonderful Thing	1958	6.25	12.50	25.00
STUDIO CITY					
1008	The No Place Special/Reveille Rock	1964	10.00	20.00	40.00
VITA					
148	Rhythm and Blues/So Hard to Laugh, So Easy to Cry	1957	18.75	37.50	75.00
158	G'Wan Home Calypso/Look What You're Doing Baby	1957	15.00	30.00	60.00
Albums					
MGM					
E-3992 [M]	Today's Teen Beat	1961	7.50	15.00	30.00
SE-3992 [S]	Today's Teen Beat	1961	10.00	20.00	40.00
TITONES, THE					
45s					
SCEPTER					
1206	Symbol of Love/The Movies	1960	12.50	25.00	50.00
—White label					
1206	Symbol of Love/The Movies	1960	6.25	12.50	25.00
—Red label					
WAND					
105	Symbol of Love/My Movie Queen	1960	5.00	10.00	20.00
TITUS GROAN					
Albums					
JANUS					
JLS-3024	Titus Groan	1971	7.50	15.00	30.00
TITUS OATES					
Albums					
LIPS					
(no #)	Jungle Lady	1974	50.00	100.00	200.00
TJADER, CAL					
45s					
FANTASY					
531	Yesterdays/Bei Mir Bist Du Schoen	195?	3.75	7.50	15.00
—Red vinyl					
532	Fascinatin' Rhythm/I Concentrate on You	195?	3.75	7.50	15.00
—Red vinyl					
533	Wachi Wara/For Heaven's Sake	195?	3.75	7.50	15.00
—Red vinyl					
534	It Ain't Necessarily So/Mambo Macumba	195?	3.75	7.50	15.00
—Red vinyl; the above four comprise a box set					
536	Lucero/Chloe	195?	3.75	7.50	15.00
538	Sonny Boy/Mamblues	195?	3.75	7.50	15.00
540	As I Love You/I've Waited So Long	195?	3.75	7.50	15.00
544	Black Orchid/Afro Blue	195?	3.75	7.50	15.00
547	Doxie (Part 1)/Doxie (Part 2)	195?	3.75	7.50	15.00
552	Cool/Maria	1960	2.50	5.00	10.00
562	The Continental/(B-side unknown)	196?	2.50	5.00	10.00
605	Dixie/Mamblues	196?	2.50	5.00	10.00
659	Evil Ways/First There Is a Mountain	1971	—	3.00	6.00
SAVOY					
1117	Love Me or Leave Me/Tangerine	1953	5.00	10.00	20.00
1120	I Want to Be Happy/Minority	1954	5.00	10.00	20.00
SKYE					
452	Ode to Billie Joe/Solar Heat	1968	2.00	4.00	8.00
4510	My Little Red Book/Moneypenny	1968	2.00	4.00	8.00
VERVE					
10275	Weeping Bossa Nova/Silenciosa	1962	2.50	5.00	10.00
10300	The Fakir/China Nights	1963	2.50	5.00	10.00
10315	Sake and Greens/Shoji	1964	2.50	5.00	10.00
10325	People/Poor Butterfly	1964	2.50	5.00	10.00
10345	Soul Sauce (Guacha Guaro)/Somewhere in the Night	1965	2.00	4.00	8.00
10364	Soul Bird/The Whiffenpoof Song	1965	2.00	4.00	8.00
10397	Soul Burst/Cuchy Frito Man	1966	2.00	4.00	8.00
10431	Guajira en Azul/Modesty	1966	2.00	4.00	8.00
10552	Trick or Treat/Quando Quando Que Sera	1967	2.00	4.00	8.00
Albums					
CONCORD JAZZ					
CJ-159	Shining Sea	1981	2.50	5.00	10.00
CONCORD PICANTE					
CJP-113	La Onda Va Bien	1979	3.00	6.00	12.00
CJP-133	Gozame! Pero Ya...	1980	3.00	6.00	12.00
CJP-176	A Fuego Vivo	1981	2.50	5.00	10.00
CJP-247	Good Vibes	1983	2.50	5.00	10.00

Number	Title (A Side/B Side)	Yr	VG	VG+	NM
CRYSTAL CLEAR					
8003	Huracan	1978	6.25	12.50	25.00
—Direct-to-disc recording					
FANTASY					
3-9 [10]	The Cal Tjader Trio	1953	37.50	75.00	150.00
—Any of various non-black vinyl pressings					
3-9 [10]	The Cal Tjader Trio	1953	25.00	50.00	100.00
—Black vinyl					
3-17 [10]	Ritmo Caliente	1954	37.50	75.00	150.00
—Any of various non-black vinyl pressings					
3-17 [10]	Ritmo Caliente	1954	25.00	50.00	100.00
—Black vinyl					
OJC-271	Mambo with Tjader	1987	2.50	5.00	10.00
—Reissue of 3202					
OJC-274	Tjader Plays Mambo	1987	2.50	5.00	10.00
—Reissue of 3221					
OJC-277	San Francisco Moods	1987	2.50	5.00	10.00
—Reissue of 8017					
OJC-278	A Night at the Blackhawk	1987	2.50	5.00	10.00
—Reissue of 8026					
OJC-279	Concert on the Campus	1987	2.50	5.00	10.00
—Reissue of 8044					
OJC-285	Cal Tjader Plays the Harold Arlen Songbook	1987	2.50	5.00	10.00
—Reissue of 8072					
OJC-436	Jazz at the Blackhawk	1990	2.50	5.00	10.00
—Reissue of 8096					
OJC-642	Latin Kick	1991	3.00	6.00	12.00
—Reissue of 8033					
OJC-643	Cal Tjader's Latin Concert	1991	3.00	6.00	12.00
—Reissue of 8014					
3202 [M]	Mambo with Tjader	1955	25.00	50.00	100.00
—Red vinyl					
3202 [M]	Mambo with Tjader	1956	12.50	25.00	50.00
—Black vinyl, red label, non-flexible vinyl					
3202 [M]	Mambo with Tjader	196?	6.25	12.50	25.00
—Black vinyl, red label, flexible vinyl					
3211 [M]	Tjader Plays Tjazz	1956	25.00	50.00	100.00
—Red vinyl					
3211 [M]	Tjader Plays Tjazz	1956	12.50	25.00	50.00
—Black vinyl, red label, non-flexible vinyl					
3216 [M]	Ritmo Caliente	1956	25.00	50.00	100.00
—Red vinyl					
3216 [M]	Ritmo Caliente	1956	12.50	25.00	50.00
—Black vinyl, red label, non-flexible vinyl					
3216 [M]	Ritmo Caliente	196?	6.25	12.50	25.00
—Black vinyl, red label, flexible vinyl					
3221 [M]	Tjader Plays Mambo	1956	25.00	50.00	100.00
—Red vinyl					
3221 [M]	Tjader Plays Mambo	1956	12.50	25.00	50.00
—Black vinyl, red label, non-flexible vinyl					
3221 [M]	Tjader Plays Mambo	196?	6.25	12.50	25.00
—Black vinyl, red label, flexible vinyl					
3227 [M]	Cal Tjader Quartet	1956	25.00	50.00	100.00
—Red vinyl					
3232 [M]	The Cal Tjader Quintet	1956	25.00	50.00	100.00
—Red vinyl					
3232 [M]	The Cal Tjader Quintet	1956	12.50	25.00	50.00
—Black vinyl, red label, non-flexible vinyl					
3232 [M]	The Cal Tjader Quintet	196?	6.25	12.50	25.00
—Black vinyl, red label, flexible vinyl					
3241 [M]	Jazz at the Blackhawk	1957	12.50	25.00	50.00
—Red vinyl					
3241 [M]	Jazz at the Blackhawk	1957	7.50	15.00	30.00
—Black vinyl, red label, non-flexible vinyl					
3241 [M]	Jazz at the Blackhawk	196?	3.75	7.50	15.00
—Black vinyl, red label, flexible vinyl					
3250 [M]	Latin Kick	1957	12.50	25.00	50.00
—Red vinyl					
3250 [M]	Latin Kick	1957	7.50	15.00	30.00
—Black vinyl, red label, non-flexible vinyl					
3250 [M]	Latin Kick	196?	3.75	7.50	15.00
—Black vinyl, red label, flexible vinyl					
3253 [M]	Cal Tjader	1958	15.00	30.00	60.00
—Red vinyl					
3253 [M]	Cal Tjader	1958	10.00	20.00	40.00
—Black vinyl, non-flexible vinyl					
3262 [M]	Mas Ritmo Caliente	1958	12.50	25.00	50.00
—Red vinyl					
3262 [M]	Mas Ritmo Caliente	1958	7.50	15.00	30.00
—Black vinyl, red label, non-flexible vinyl					
3262 [M]	Mas Ritmo Caliente	196?	3.75	7.50	15.00
—Black vinyl, red label, flexible vinyl					
3271 [M]	San Francisco Moods	1958	12.50	25.00	50.00
—Red vinyl					
3271 [M]	San Francisco Moods	1958	7.50	15.00	30.00
—Black vinyl, red label, non-flexible vinyl					
3271 [M]	San Francisco Moods	196?	3.75	7.50	15.00
—Black vinyl, red label, flexible vinyl					
3275 [M]	Cal Tjader's Latin Concert	1958	12.50	25.00	50.00
—Red vinyl					
3275 [M]	Cal Tjader's Latin Concert	1958	7.50	15.00	30.00
—Black vinyl, red label, non-flexible vinyl					
3275 [M]	Cal Tjader's Latin Concert	196?	3.75	7.50	15.00
—Black vinyl, red label, flexible vinyl					
3278 [M]	Tjader Plays Tjazz	1958	12.50	25.00	50.00
—Red vinyl; reissue of 3211					
3278 [M]	Tjader Plays Tjazz	1958	7.50	15.00	30.00
—Black vinyl, red label, non-flexible vinyl					
3278 [M]	Tjader Plays Tjazz	196?	3.75	7.50	15.00
—Black vinyl, red label, flexible vinyl					
3279 [M]	Latin for Lovers	1958	12.50	25.00	50.00
—Red vinyl					
3279 [M]	Latin for Lovers	1958	7.50	15.00	30.00
—Black vinyl, red label, non-flexible vinyl					
3279 [M]	Latin for Lovers	196?	3.75	7.50	15.00
—Black vinyl, red label, flexible vinyl					

Number	Title (A Side/B Side)	Yr	VG	VG+	NM
3283 [M]	A Night at the Blackhawk	1959	12.50	25.00	50.00
—Red vinyl					
3283 [M]	A Night at the Blackhawk	1959	7.50	15.00	30.00
—Black vinyl, red label, non-flexible vinyl					
3283 [M]	A Night at the Blackhawk	196?	3.75	7.50	15.00
—Black vinyl, red label, flexible vinyl					
3289 [M]	Tjader Goes Latin	1959	12.50	25.00	50.00
—Red vinyl					
3289 [M]	Tjader Goes Latin	1959	7.50	15.00	30.00
—Black vinyl, red label, non-flexible vinyl					
3289 [M]	Tjader Goes Latin	196?	3.75	7.50	15.00
—Black vinyl, red label, flexible vinyl					
3295 [M]	Concert by the Sea	1959	12.50	25.00	50.00
—Red vinyl					
3295 [M]	Concert by the Sea	1959	7.50	15.00	30.00
—Black vinyl, red label, non-flexible vinyl					
3295 [M]	Concert by the Sea	196?	3.75	7.50	15.00
—Black vinyl, red label, flexible vinyl					
3299 [M]	Concert on the Campus	1960	10.00	20.00	40.00
—Red vinyl					
3299 [M]	Concert on the Campus	1960	6.25	12.50	25.00
—Black vinyl, red label, non-flexible vinyl					
3299 [M]	Concert on the Campus	196?	3.75	7.50	15.00
—Black vinyl, red label, flexible vinyl					
3307 [M]	Cal Tjader Quartet	1960	10.00	20.00	40.00
—Red vinyl					
3307 [M]	Cal Tjader Quartet	1960	6.25	12.50	25.00
—Black vinyl, red label, non-flexible vinyl					
3307 [M]	Cal Tjader Quartet	196?	3.75	7.50	15.00
—Black vinyl, red label, flexible vinyl					
3309 [M]	Demasiado Caliente	1960	10.00	20.00	40.00
—Red vinyl					
3309 [M]	Demasiado Caliente	1960	6.25	12.50	25.00
—Black vinyl, red label, non-flexible vinyl					
3309 [M]	Demasiado Caliente	196?	3.75	7.50	15.00
—Black vinyl, red label, flexible vinyl					
3310 [M]	West Side Story	1960	10.00	20.00	40.00
—Red vinyl					
3310 [M]	West Side Story	1960	6.25	12.50	25.00
—Black vinyl, red label, non-flexible vinyl					
3310 [M]	West Side Story	196?	3.75	7.50	15.00
—Black vinyl, red label, flexible vinyl					
3313 [M]	Cal Tjader Quintet	1961	10.00	20.00	40.00
—Red vinyl; evidently a different album than 3232					
3313 [M]	Cal Tjader Quintet	1961	6.25	12.50	25.00
—Black vinyl, red label, non-flexible vinyl					
3313 [M]	Cal Tjader Quintet	196?	3.75	7.50	15.00
—Black vinyl, red label, flexible vinyl					
3315 [M]	Cal Tjader Live and Direct	1961	10.00	20.00	40.00
—Red vinyl					
3315 [M]	Cal Tjader Live and Direct	1961	6.25	12.50	25.00
—Black vinyl, red label, non-flexible vinyl					
3315 [M]	Cal Tjader Live and Direct	196?	3.75	7.50	15.00
—Black vinyl, red label, flexible vinyl					
3326 [M]	Mambo	1961	10.00	20.00	40.00
—Red vinyl					
3326 [M]	Mambo	1961	6.25	12.50	25.00
—Black vinyl, red label, non-flexible vinyl					
3326 [M]	Mambo	196?	3.75	7.50	15.00
—Black vinyl, red label, flexible vinyl					
3330 [M]	Cal Tjader Plays the Harold Arlen Songbook	1961	10.00	20.00	40.00
—Red vinyl					
3330 [M]	Cal Tjader Plays the Harold Arlen Songbook	1961	6.25	12.50	25.00
—Black vinyl, red label, non-flexible vinyl					
3330 [M]	Cal Tjader Plays the Harold Arlen Songbook	196?	3.75	7.50	15.00
—Black vinyl, red label, flexible vinyl					
3339 [M]	Latino	1962	10.00	20.00	40.00
—Red vinyl					
3339 [M]	Latino	1962	6.25	12.50	25.00
—Black vinyl, red label, non-flexible vinyl					
3339 [M]	Latino	196?	3.75	7.50	15.00
—Black vinyl, red label, flexible vinyl					
3341 [M]	Concert by the Sea, Volume 2	1962	10.00	20.00	40.00
—Red vinyl					
3341 [M]	Concert by the Sea, Volume 2	1962	6.25	12.50	25.00
—Black vinyl, red label, non-flexible vinyl					
3341 [M]	Concert by the Sea, Volume 2	196?	3.75	7.50	15.00
—Black vinyl, red label, flexible vinyl					
3366 [M]	Cal Tjader's Greatest Hits	1965	3.75	7.50	15.00
3374 [M]	Cal Tjader's Greatest Hits, Violume 2	1966	3.75	7.50	15.00
MPF-4527	Cal Tjader's Greatest Hits	1987	2.50	5.00	10.00
—Reissue of 8366					
MPF-4530	Cal Tjader's Greatest Hits, Volume 2	1987	2.50	5.00	10.00
—Reissue of 8374					
8003 [S]	Mas Ritmo Caliente	196?	7.50	15.00	30.00
—Blue vinyl					
8003 [S]	Mas Ritmo Caliente	196?	5.00	10.00	20.00
—Black vinyl, blue label, non-flexible vinyl					
8003 [S]	Mas Ritmo Caliente	196?	3.00	6.00	12.00
—Black vinyl, blue label, flexible vinyl					
8014 [S]	Cal Tjader's Latin Concert	196?	7.50	15.00	30.00
—Blue vinyl					
8014 [S]	Cal Tjader's Latin Concert	196?	5.00	10.00	20.00
—Black vinyl, blue label, non-flexible vinyl					
8014 [S]	Cal Tjader's Latin Concert	196?	3.00	6.00	12.00
—Black vinyl, blue label, flexible vinyl					
8016 [S]	Latin for Lovers	196?	7.50	15.00	30.00
—Blue vinyl					
8016 [S]	Latin for Lovers	196?	5.00	10.00	20.00
—Black vinyl, blue label, non-flexible vinyl					
8016 [S]	Latin for Lovers	196?	3.00	6.00	12.00
—Black vinyl, blue label, flexible vinyl					
8017 [S]	San Francisco Moods	196?	7.50	15.00	30.00
—Blue vinyl					
8017 [S]	San Francisco Moods	196?	5.00	10.00	20.00
—Black vinyl, blue label, non-flexible vinyl					
8017 [S]	San Francisco Moods	196?	3.00	6.00	12.00
—Black vinyl, blue label, flexible vinyl					
8019 [S]	Latin for Dancers	196?	25.00	50.00	100.00
—Blue vinyl; the existence of this has been confirmed. Black vinyl copies of 8019 are unknown.					
8026 [S]	A Night at the Blackhawk	196?	7.50	15.00	30.00
—Blue vinyl					
8026 [S]	A Night at the Blackhawk	196?	5.00	10.00	20.00
—Black vinyl, blue label, non-flexible vinyl					
8026 [S]	A Night at the Blackhawk	196?	3.00	6.00	12.00
—Black vinyl, blue label, flexible vinyl					
8030 [S]	Tjader Goes Latin	196?	7.50	15.00	30.00
—Blue vinyl					
8030 [S]	Tjader Goes Latin	196?	5.00	10.00	20.00
—Black vinyl, blue label, non-flexible vinyl					
8030 [S]	Tjader Goes Latin	196?	3.00	6.00	12.00
—Black vinyl, blue label, flexible vinyl					
8033 [S]	Latin Kick	196?	7.50	15.00	30.00
—Blue vinyl					
8033 [S]	Latin Kick	196?	5.00	10.00	20.00
—Black vinyl, blue label, non-flexible vinyl					
8033 [S]	Latin Kick	196?	3.00	6.00	12.00
—Black vinyl, blue label, flexible vinyl					
8038 [S]	Concert by the Sea	196?	7.50	15.00	30.00
—Blue vinyl					
8038 [S]	Concert by the Sea	196?	5.00	10.00	20.00
—Black vinyl, blue label, non-flexible vinyl					
8038 [S]	Concert by the Sea	196?	3.00	6.00	12.00
—Black vinyl, blue label, flexible vinyl					
8044 [S]	Concert on the Campus	196?	7.50	15.00	30.00
—Blue vinyl					
8044 [S]	Concert on the Campus	196?	5.00	10.00	20.00
—Black vinyl, blue label, non-flexible vinyl					
8044 [S]	Concert on the Campus	196?	3.00	6.00	12.00
—Black vinyl, blue label, flexible vinyl					
8053 [S]	Demasiado Caliente	196?	7.50	15.00	30.00
—Blue vinyl					
8053 [S]	Demasiado Caliente	196?	5.00	10.00	20.00
—Black vinyl, blue label, non-flexible vinyl					
8053 [S]	Demasiado Caliente	196?	3.00	6.00	12.00
—Black vinyl, blue label, flexible vinyl					
8054 [S]	West Side Story	196?	7.50	15.00	30.00
—Blue vinyl					
8054 [S]	West Side Story	196?	5.00	10.00	20.00
—Black vinyl, blue label, non-flexible vinyl					
8054 [S]	West Side Story	196?	3.00	6.00	12.00
—Black vinyl, blue label, flexible vinyl					
8057 [S]	Mambo	1962	7.50	15.00	30.00
—Blue vinyl					
8057 [S]	Mambo	1962	5.00	10.00	20.00
—Black vinyl, blue label, non-flexible vinyl					
8057 [S]	Mambo	196?	3.00	6.00	12.00
—Black vinyl, blue label, flexible vinyl					
8059 [S]	Cal Tjader Live and Direct	1962	7.50	15.00	30.00
—Blue vinyl					
8059 [S]	Cal Tjader Live and Direct	1962	5.00	10.00	20.00
—Black vinyl, blue label, non-flexible vinyl					
8059 [S]	Cal Tjader Live and Direct	196?	3.00	6.00	12.00
—Black vinyl, blue label, flexible vinyl					
8072 [S]	Cal Tjader Plays the Harold Arlen Songbook	1962	7.50	15.00	30.00
—Blue vinyl					
8072 [S]	Cal Tjader Plays the Harold Arlen Songbook	1962	5.00	10.00	20.00
—Black vinyl, blue label, non-flexible vinyl					
8072 [S]	Cal Tjader Plays the Harold Arlen Songbook	196?	3.00	6.00	12.00
—Black vinyl, blue label, flexible vinyl					
8077 [R]	Ritmo Caliente	1962	7.50	15.00	30.00
—Blue vinyl					
8077 [R]	Ritmo Caliente	1962	5.00	10.00	20.00
—Black vinyl, blue label, non-flexible vinyl					
8077 [R]	Ritmo Caliente	196?	3.00	6.00	12.00
—Black vinyl, blue label, flexible vinyl					
8079 [S]	Latino	1962	7.50	15.00	30.00
—Blue vinyl					
8079 [S]	Latino	1962	5.00	10.00	20.00
—Black vinyl, blue label, non-flexible vinyl					
8079 [S]	Latino	196?	3.00	6.00	12.00
—Black vinyl, blue label, flexible vinyl					
8083 [R]	Cal Tjader Quartet	1962	7.50	15.00	30.00
—Blue vinyl					
8083 [R]	Cal Tjader Quartet	1962	5.00	10.00	20.00
—Black vinyl, blue label, non-flexible vinyl					
8083 [R]	Cal Tjader Quartet	1962	3.00	6.00	12.00
—Black vinyl, blue label, flexible vinyl					
8084 [S]	Cal Tjader Quintet	1962	7.50	15.00	30.00
—Blue vinyl; stereo version of 3313					
8084 [S]	Cal Tjader Quintet	1962	5.00	10.00	20.00
—Black vinyl, blue label, non-flexible vinyl					
8084 [S]	Cal Tjader Quintet	1962	3.00	6.00	12.00
—Black vinyl, blue label, flexible vinyl					
8085 [R]	The Cal Tjader Quintet	196?	7.50	15.00	30.00
—Blue vinyl; stereo version of 3232					
8085 [R]	The Cal Tjader Quintet	196?	5.00	10.00	20.00
—Black vinyl, blue label, non-flexible vinyl					
8085 [R]	The Cal Tjader Quintet	196?	3.00	6.00	12.00
—Black vinyl, blue label, flexible vinyl					
8096 [R]	Jazz at the Blackhawk	1962	7.50	15.00	30.00
—Blue vinyl					
8096 [R]	Jazz at the Blackhawk	1962	5.00	10.00	20.00
—Black vinyl, blue label, non-flexible vinyl					
8096 [R]	Jazz at the Blackhawk	196?	3.00	6.00	12.00
—Black vinyl, blue label, flexible vinyl					
8097 [R]	Tjader Plays Tjazz	1962	7.50	15.00	30.00
—Blue vinyl					
8097 [R]	Tjader Plays Tjazz	1962	5.00	10.00	20.00
—Black vinyl, blue label, non-flexible vinyl					
8097 [R]	Tjader Plays Tjazz	196?	3.00	6.00	12.00
—Black vinyl, blue label, flexible vinyl					

Number	Title (A Side/B Side)	Yr	VG	VG+	NM
8098 [S]	Concert by the Sea, Volume 2	1962	7.50	15.00	30.00
—Blue vinyl					
8098 [S]	Concert by the Sea, Volume 2	1962	5.00	10.00	20.00
—Black vinyl, blue label, non-flexible vinyl					
8098 [S]	Concert by the Sea, Volume 2	196?	3.00	6.00	12.00
—Black vinyl, blue label, flexible vinyl					
8366 [S]	Cal Tjader's Greatest Hits	1965	3.00	6.00	12.00
8374 [S]	Cal Tjader's Greatest Hits, Volume 2	1966	3.00	6.00	12.00
8379	West Side Story	1967	3.00	6.00	12.00
—Reissue of 8054					
8406	Tjader	1970	3.00	6.00	12.00
8416	Agua Dulce	1971	3.00	6.00	12.00
9409	Live at the Funky Quarters	1970	3.00	6.00	12.00
9422	Primo	1972	3.00	6.00	12.00
9424	Mambo with Tjader	1973	3.00	6.00	12.00
9446	Last Bolero in Berkeley	1974	3.00	6.00	12.00
9463	Puttin' It Together	1974	3.00	6.00	12.00
9482	Last Night When We Were Young	1975	3.00	6.00	12.00
9502	Amazonas	1975	3.00	6.00	12.00
9521	At Grace Cathedral	1977	3.00	6.00	12.00
9533	Guarabe	1977	3.00	6.00	12.00
24712 [(2)]	Los Ritmos Caliente	197?	3.75	7.50	15.00
GALAXY					
5107	Breathe Easy	1977	3.00	6.00	12.00
5121	Here	1978	3.00	6.00	12.00
MGM					
10008	Sonido Nuevo	197?	3.75	7.50	15.00
PRESTIGE					
24026 [(2)]	The Monterey Concerts	1973	3.75	7.50	15.00
SAVOY					
MG-9036 [10]	Cal Tjader — Vibist	1954	25.00	50.00	100.00
SKYE					
SK-1	Solar Heat	1968	5.00	10.00	20.00
SK-10	Cal Tjader Plugs In	1969	5.00	10.00	20.00
SK-19	Tjader-Ade	1970	3.75	7.50	15.00
VERVE					
V-8419 [M]	In a Latin Bag	1961	5.00	10.00	20.00
V6-8419 [S]	In a Latin Bag	1961	6.25	12.50	25.00
V-8459 [M]	Saturday Night...Sunday Night at the Blackhawk	1962	5.00	10.00	20.00
V6-8459 [S]	Saturday Night...Sunday Night at the Blackhawk	1962	6.25	12.50	25.00
V-8470 [M]	The Contemporary Music of Mexico and Brazil	1962	5.00	10.00	20.00
V6-8470 [S]	The Contemporary Music of Mexico and Brazil	1962	6.25	12.50	25.00
V-8507 [M]	Several Shades of Jade	1963	5.00	10.00	20.00
V6-8507 [S]	Several Shades of Jade	1963	6.25	12.50	25.00
V-8531 [M]	Sona Libre	1963	5.00	10.00	20.00
V6-8531 [S]	Sona Libre	1963	6.25	12.50	25.00
V-8575 [M]	Breeze from the East	1964	5.00	10.00	20.00
V6-8575 [S]	Breeze from the East	1964	6.25	12.50	25.00
V-8585 [M]	Warm Wave	1964	5.00	10.00	20.00
V6-8585 [S]	Warm Wave	1964	6.25	12.50	25.00
V-8614 [M]	Soul Sauce	1965	5.00	10.00	20.00
V6-8614 [S]	Soul Sauce	1965	6.25	12.50	25.00
V-8626 [M]	Soul Bird: Whippenpoof	1965	5.00	10.00	20.00
V6-8626 [S]	Soul Bird: Whippenpoof	1965	6.25	12.50	25.00
V-8637 [M]	Soul Burst	1965	5.00	10.00	20.00
V6-8637 [S]	Soul Burst	1965	6.25	12.50	25.00
V-8651 [M]	El Soni Do Nuevo — The New Soul Sound	1966	3.75	7.50	15.00
V6-8651 [S]	El Soni Do Nuevo — The New Soul Sound	1966	5.00	10.00	20.00
V-8671 [M]	Along Comes Cal	1966	3.75	7.50	15.00
V6-8671 [S]	Along Comes Cal	1966	5.00	10.00	20.00
V-8725 [M]	The Best of Cal Tjader	1967	3.75	7.50	15.00
V6-8725 [S]	The Best of Cal Tjader	1967	5.00	10.00	20.00
V-8730 [M]	Hip Vibrations	1967	5.00	10.00	20.00
V6-8730 [S]	Hip Vibrations	1967	3.75	7.50	15.00
V6-8769	The Prophet	1969	3.75	7.50	15.00
827756-1	Soul Sauce	1986	2.50	5.00	10.00
—Reissue of 8614					

TJADER, CAL, AND CHARLIE BYRD

Also see each artist's individual listings.

Number	Title (A Side/B Side)	Yr	VG	VG+	NM
Albums					
FANTASY					
9453	Tambu	1974	3.00	6.00	12.00

TJADER, CAL/DON ELLIOTT

Number	Title (A Side/B Side)	Yr	VG	VG+	NM
Albums					
SAVOY					
MG-12054 [M]	Vib-Rations	1956	10.00	20.00	40.00
—Reissue of 9036 and 9033					

TJADER, CAL, AND STAN GETZ

Also see each artist's individual listings.

Number	Title (A Side/B Side)	Yr	VG	VG+	NM
45s					
FANTASY					
566	For All We Know/Ginza Samba	196?	2.50	5.00	10.00
Albums					
FANTASY					
3266 [M]	Cal Tjader-Stan Getz Sextet	1958	12.50	25.00	50.00
—Red vinyl					
3266 [M]	Cal Tjader-Stan Getz Sextet	1958	7.50	15.00	30.00
—Black vinyl, red label, non-flexible vinyl					
3266 [M]	Cal Tjader-Stan Getz Sextet	196?	3.75	7.50	15.00
—Black vinyl, red label, flexible vinyl					
3348 [M]	Cal Tjader-Stan Getz Sextet	1963	3.75	7.50	15.00
—Reissue of 3266					
8005 [S]	Cal Tjader-Stan Getz Sextet	196?	7.50	15.00	30.00
—Blue vinyl					
8005 [S]	Cal Tjader-Stan Getz Sextet	196?	5.00	10.00	20.00
—Black vinyl, blue label, non-flexible vinyl					
8005 [S]	Cal Tjader-Stan Getz Sextet	196?	3.00	6.00	12.00
—Black vinyl, blue label, flexible vinyl					
8348 [S]	Cal Tjader-Stan Getz Quartet	1963	3.00	6.00	12.00
—Reissue of 8005					

TJADER, CAL, AND CARMEN MCRAE

Number	Title (A Side/B Side)	Yr	VG	VG+	NM
Albums					
CONCORD JAZZ					
CJ-189	Heat Wave	1982	2.50	5.00	10.00

TOAD HALL

Number	Title (A Side/B Side)	Yr	VG	VG+	NM
Albums					
LIBERTY					
LST-7580	Toad Hall	1968	6.25	12.50	25.00

TODAY AND TOMORROW

Number	Title (A Side/B Side)	Yr	VG	VG+	NM
45s					
NOOSE					
812	Dooley Swings (Part 1)/Dooley Swings (Part 2)	1959	10.00	20.00	40.00

TODD, ART AND DOTTY

Number	Title (A Side/B Side)	Yr	VG	VG+	NM
45s					
ABBOTT					
3006	Busy Signal/Oh Honey Why Don't Cha	1955	5.00	10.00	20.00
CAPITOL					
4778	Sweet Someone/Ring-a-Ding	1962	2.00	4.00	8.00
DART					
404	Wait for Me/Joie de Vivre	1956	3.00	6.00	12.00
405	Chop Chop/Say You	1956	3.00	6.00	12.00
51986	Blueberry Hill/Wonderful, Loveable You	1959	2.50	5.00	10.00
DECCA					
31227	Ca C'est La Vie/Drifting and Dreaming	1961	2.50	5.00	10.00
31329	Your Cheatin' Heart/Sweet Cha Cha Chariot	1961	2.50	5.00	10.00
DOT					
16939	I'll Take Care of Your Cares/Bodie Tree	1966	—	3.00	6.00
ERA					
1064	Chanson D'Amour (Song of Love)/Along the Trail with You	1957	3.00	6.00	12.00
1076	Au Revoir Amour/Der Glockenspiel	1958	2.50	5.00	10.00
1087	Pray/Don't You Worry My Little Pet	1958	2.50	5.00	10.00
1088	Straight as an Arrow/Stand There Mountain	1959	2.50	5.00	10.00
3001	Paradise/Ayuh Ayuh	1959	2.50	5.00	10.00
RCA VICTOR					
47-5029	Heavenly-Heavenly/Broken Wings	1952	3.75	7.50	15.00
SIGNET					
2020	Bernadette Soubirous/Bodie Tree	1965	2.00	4.00	8.00
Albums					
DART					
D-444 [M]	Black Velvet Eyes	1959	10.00	20.00	40.00
DOT					
DLP-3742 [M]	Chanson d'Amour (Song of Love)	1966	6.25	12.50	25.00
DLP-25742 [S]	Chanson d'Amour (Song of Love)	1966	7.50	15.00	30.00

TODD, DYLAN

Number	Title (A Side/B Side)	Yr	VG	VG+	NM
45s					
RCA VICTOR					
47-6463	The Ballad of James Dean/More Precious Than Gold	1956	7.50	15.00	30.00
47-6463 [PS]	The Ballad of James Dean/More Precious Than Gold	1956	12.50	25.00	50.00
47-6711	Timber/Golden Spurs and a Silver Saddle	1956	5.00	10.00	20.00

TODD, FULLER

Number	Title (A Side/B Side)	Yr	VG	VG+	NM
45s					
KING					
5048	Old Fashioned/Proud Lady Heart Stealer	1957	6.25	12.50	25.00
5075	Real True Love/Young Hearts Are True	1957	6.25	12.50	25.00
5111	Top Ten Rock/Jeannie Marie	1958	6.25	12.50	25.00

TODD, JOHNNY

Number	Title (A Side/B Side)	Yr	VG	VG+	NM
45s					
MODERN					
1003	Pink Cadillac/What's Up	1956	30.00	60.00	120.00

TODD, NICK

Number	Title (A Side/B Side)	Yr	VG	VG+	NM
45s					
DOT					
15643	Plaything/The Honey Song	1957	5.00	10.00	20.00
15675	At the Hop/I Do	1957	5.00	10.00	20.00
15688	Teen-Age Cutie/Ever Since I Met Lucy	1958	5.00	10.00	20.00
15772	Forever and a Day/Too Much Rosita	1958	5.00	10.00	20.00
15860	My Little Girl/Does Your Heart Beat for Me?	1958	5.00	10.00	20.00
15893	Red Roses for a Blue Lady/Little Rosey Red	1959	3.75	7.50	15.00
15951	Tiger/Twice As Nice	1959	3.75	7.50	15.00
15981	Invisible Man/Sayin' Something	1959	3.75	7.50	15.00
16109	Each Moment/Your Love's Gotta Grip on Me	1960	3.75	7.50	15.00

TOE FAT

Number	Title (A Side/B Side)	Yr	VG	VG+	NM
45s					
RARE EARTH					
5019	Bad Side of the Moon/Just Like Me	1970	—	3.00	6.00
Albums					
RARE EARTH					
RS-511	Toe Fat	1970	6.25	12.50	25.00
RS-525	Toe Fat Two	1971	6.25	12.50	25.00

TOGGERY FIVE, THE

Also see FREDDIE AND THE DREAMERS.

Number	Title (A Side/B Side)	Yr	VG	VG+	NM
45s					
TOWER					
119	I'm Gonna Jump/Bye Bye Bird	1965	3.75	7.50	15.00

TOKAYS, THE

45s

Number	Title (A Side/B Side)	Yr	VG	VG+	NM
BONNIE					
102	Lost and Found/Fatty-Boom Bi Laddy	1962	25.00	50.00	100.00
BRUTE					
001	Hey Senorita/Baby Baby Baby	1967	30.00	60.00	120.00
SCORPIO					
403	Now/Ask Me No Questions	1966	5.00	10.00	20.00

TOKENS, THE

NEIL SEDAKA was (very) briefly a member. Also see THE COEDS; CROSS COUNTRY; THE FOUR WINDS (1); JOHNNY AND THE TOKENS; UNITED STATES DOUBLE QUARTET.

45s

Number	Title (A Side/B Side)	Yr	VG	VG+	NM
ATCO					
7009	The Lord Can't Sing a Solo/Penny Whistle Band	1974	—	3.00	6.00
BELL					
45190	You and Me/I Like to Throw My Head Back and Sing	1972	—	3.00	6.00
BUDDAH					
151	She Lets Her Hair Down (Early in the Morning)/Oh to Get Away	1970	—	3.00	6.00
159	Don't Worry Baby/If the Shoe Fits Ya Baby	1970	—	2.50	5.00
159	Don't Worry Baby/Some People Sleep	1970	—	2.50	5.00
174	Both Sides Now/I Could See Me (Dancin' with You)	1970	—	2.50	5.00
187	Listen to the Words (Listen to the Music)/Groovin' On the Sunshine	1970	—	2.50	5.00
B.T. PUPPY					
500	A Girl Named Arlene/Swing	1964	3.00	6.00	12.00
502	He's in Town/Oh Cathy	1964	3.00	6.00	12.00
504	You're My Girl/Havin' Fun	1964	3.00	6.00	12.00
505	Nobody But You/Mr. Cupid	1965	2.50	5.00	10.00
507	A Message to the World/Sylvie Sleepin'	1965	2.50	5.00	10.00
512	Only My Friend/Cattle Call	1965	2.50	5.00	10.00
513	The Bells of St. Mary/Just One Smile	1966	2.50	5.00	10.00
515	The Three Bells/Message to the World	1966	2.50	5.00	10.00
518	I Hear Trumpets Blow/Don't Cry, Sing Along with the Music	1966	2.50	5.00	10.00
519	Breezy/Greatest Moments of a Girl's Life	1966	2.50	5.00	10.00
519 [PS]	Breezy/Greatest Moments of a Girl's Life	1966	6.25	12.50	25.00
525	Green Plant/Saloogy	1967	2.50	5.00	10.00
552	Please Say You Want Me/Get a Job	1969	2.50	5.00	10.00
DATE					
2737	Oh What a Night/(Hey Hey) Juanita	1961	12.50	25.00	50.00
GARY					
1006	Doom-Lang/Come Dance with Me	1961	25.00	50.00	100.00
LAURIE					
3180	I'll Always Love You/Please Write	1963	5.00	10.00	20.00
MELBA					
104	While I Dream/I Love My Baby	1956	12.50	25.00	50.00
RCA					
8749-7-R	Re-Doo-Wopp/I'm Through with You	1988	—	2.00	4.00
8836-7-R	Re-Doo-Wopp (Edit)/I'm Through with You	1988	—	2.00	4.00
RCA VICTOR					
37-7896	When I Go to Sleep at Night/Dry Your Eyes	1961	10.00	20.00	40.00
—"Compact Single 33" (small hole, plays at LP speed)					
37-7925	Sincerely/When the Summer Is Through	1961	10.00	20.00	40.00
—"Compact Single 33" (small hole, plays at LP speed)					
37-7954	The Lion Sleeps Tonight/Tina	1961	12.50	25.00	50.00
—"Compact Single 33" (small hole, plays at LP speed)					
37-7991	B'wa Nina/Weeping River	1962	10.00	20.00	40.00
—"Compact Single 33" (small hole, plays at LP speed)					
37-8018	The Riddle/Big Boat	1962	10.00	20.00	40.00
—"Compact Single 33" (small hole, plays at LP speed)					
47-7896	When I Go to Sleep at Night/Dry Your Eyes	1961	5.00	10.00	20.00
47-7896 [PS]	When I Go to Sleep at Night/Dry Your Eyes	1961	10.00	20.00	40.00
47-7925	Sincerely/When the Summer Is Through	1961	5.00	10.00	20.00
47-7954	The Lion Sleeps Tonight/Tina	1961	6.25	12.50	25.00
47-7991	B'wa Nina/Weeping River	1962	5.00	10.00	20.00
47-7991 [PS]	B'wa Nina/Weeping River	1962	12.50	25.00	50.00
—No mention of "The Lion Sleeps Tonight" LP on sleeve					
47-7991 [PS]	B'wa Nina/Weeping River	1962	7.50	15.00	30.00
—"The Lion Sleeps Tonight" LP mentioned on sleeve					
47-8018	The Riddle/Big Boat	1962	5.00	10.00	20.00
47-8018 [PS]	The Riddle/Big Boat	1962	10.00	20.00	40.00
47-8052	La Bomba/A Token of Love	1962	5.00	10.00	20.00
47-8052 [PS]	La Bomba/A Token of Love	1962	10.00	20.00	40.00
47-8089	I'll Do My Crying Tomorrow/Dream Angel Goodnight	1962	5.00	10.00	20.00
47-8089 [PS]	I'll Do My Crying Tomorrow/Dream Angel Goodnight	1962	10.00	20.00	40.00
47-8114	A Bird Flies Out of Sight/Wishing	1962	5.00	10.00	20.00
47-8114 [PS]	A Bird Flies Out of Sight/Wishing	1962	10.00	20.00	40.00
47-8148	Tonight I Met An Angel/Hindi Lullabye	1963	3.75	7.50	15.00
47-8148 [PS]	Tonight I Met An Angel/Hindi Lullabye	1963	7.50	15.00	30.00
47-8210	Hear the Bells/ABC 1-2-3	1963	3.75	7.50	15.00
47-8210 [PS]	Hear the Bells/ABC 1-2-3	1963	7.50	15.00	30.00
47-8309	Two Cars/Let's Go to the Drag Strip	1963	3.75	7.50	15.00
47-8309 [PS]	Two Cars/Let's Go to the Drag Strip	1963	20.00	40.00	80.00
ROULETTE					
4174	Roses Are Red/Pictures in My Wallet	1959	7.50	15.00	30.00
—As "Darrell and the Oxfords"					
4230	Can't You Tell/Your Mother Said So	1960	7.50	15.00	30.00
—As "Darrell and the Oxfords"					
RUST					
5094	Arlene/Rumble in the Park	1965	2.50	5.00	10.00
WARNER BROS.					
5900	Portrait of My Love/She Comes and Goes	1967	2.00	4.00	8.00
5900 [PS]	Portrait of My Love/She Comes and Goes	1967	5.00	10.00	20.00
7056	It's a Happening World/How Nice	1967	—	3.00	6.00
7099	Ain't That Peculiar/Bye, Bye, Bye	1967	—	3.00	6.00
7118	Portrait of My Love/It's a Happening World	1968	—	2.50	5.00
—"Back to Back Hits" series -- originals have green labels with "W7" logo					
7169	Till/Poor Man	1968	—	3.00	6.00
7183	Mister Swail/Needles of Evergreen	1968	2.50	5.00	10.00
—As "Margo, Margo, Medress and Siegel"					
7202	Animal/Bathroom Wall	1968	—	3.00	6.00
7233	Grandfather/The Banana Boat Song	1968	—	3.00	6.00
7255	The World Is Full of Wonderful Things/Some People Sleep	1968	—	3.00	6.00
7280	Go Away Little Girl-Young Girl/I Want to Make Love to You	1969	—	3.00	6.00
7323	I Could Be/End of the World	1969	—	3.00	6.00
WARWICK					
615	Tonight I Fell in Love/I'll Always Love You	1961	7.50	15.00	30.00

Albums

Number	Title (A Side/B Side)	Yr	VG	VG+	NM
BUDDAH					
BDS-5059	Both Sides Now	1971	3.75	7.50	15.00
B.T. PUPPY					
BTP-1000 [M]	I Hear Trumpets Blow	1966	5.00	10.00	20.00
BTPS-1000 [S]	I Hear Trumpets Blow	1966	6.25	12.50	25.00
BTPS-1006	Tokens of Gold	1969	6.25	12.50	25.00
BTPS-1012	Greatest Moments	1970	6.25	12.50	25.00
BTPS-1014	December 5th	1971	50.00	100.00	200.00
BTPS-1027	Intercourse	1971	150.00	300.00	600.00
DIPLOMAT					
D-2308 [M]	Kings of the Hot Rods	196?	6.25	12.50	25.00
DS-2308 [S]	Kings of the Hot Rods	196?	7.50	15.00	30.00
RCA					
8534-1-R	Re-Doo-Wopp	1988	2.50	5.00	10.00
RCA VICTOR					
LPM-2514 [M]	The Lion Sleeps Tonight	1961	20.00	40.00	80.00
LSP-2514 [S]	The Lion Sleeps Tonight	1961	37.50	75.00	150.00
LPM-2631 [M]	We, The Tokens, Sing Folk	1962	10.00	20.00	40.00
LSP-2631 [S]	We, The Tokens, Sing Folk	1962	12.50	25.00	50.00
LPM-2886 [M]	Wheels	1964	20.00	40.00	80.00
LSP-2886 [S]	Wheels	1964	25.00	50.00	100.00
LPM-3685 [M]	The Tokens Again	1966	10.00	20.00	40.00
LSP-3685 [S]	The Tokens Again	1966	12.50	25.00	50.00
WARNER BROS.					
W 1685 [M]	It's a Happening World	1967	6.25	12.50	25.00
WS 1685 [S]	It's a Happening World	1967	5.00	10.00	20.00

TOKENS, THE AND THE HAPPENINGS

Also see each artist's individual listings.

Albums

Number	Title (A Side/B Side)	Yr	VG	VG+	NM
B.T. PUPPY					
BTP-1002 [M]	Back to Back	1967	6.00	10.00	20.00
—Half this LP is by the Tokens, the other half by the Happenings					
BTPS-1002 [S]	Back to Back	1967	6.25	12.50	25.00

TOLLIVER, MICKEY, AND THE CAPITOLS

45s

Number	Title (A Side/B Side)	Yr	VG	VG+	NM
CINDY					
3002	Rose Marie/Millie	1957	50.00	100.00	200.00

TOM AND JERRIO

45s

Number	Title (A Side/B Side)	Yr	VG	VG+	NM
ABC-PARAMOUNT					
10638	Boo-Ga-Loo/Boomerang	1965	3.00	6.00	12.00
10704	Great Goo-Ga Moo-Ga/Come On and Love Me	1965	3.00	6.00	12.00
10787	Oolya-Coo/Bacardi	1966	3.00	6.00	12.00

TOM AND JERRY (1)

"Tommy Graph" and "Jerry Landis," i.e., ART GARFUNKEL and PAUL SIMON. Also see SIMON AND GARFUNKEL.

45s

Number	Title (A Side/B Side)	Yr	VG	VG+	NM
ABC-PARAMOUNT					
10363	Surrender, Please Surrender/Fightin' Mad	1962	10.00	20.00	40.00
10788	That's My Story/Tia-Juana Blues	1966	5.00	10.00	20.00
—As "Simon and Garfunkel" (may have been reissued as "Tom and Jerry", but we don't know)					
BELL					
120	Baby Talk/I'm Gonna Get Married	1959	12.50	25.00	50.00
—B-side by Ronnie Lawrence					
120 [PS]	Baby Talk/I'm Gonna Get Married	1959	25.00	50.00	100.00
BIG					
613	Hey, Schoolgirl/Dancin' Wild	1957	12.50	25.00	50.00
—With songwriting credits as "Tommy Graph-Jerry Landis"					
613	Hey, Schoolgirl/Dancin' Wild	1957	12.50	25.00	50.00
—With songwriting credits as "Paul Simon-Art Garfunkel"					
616	Our Song/Two Teen Agers	1958	12.50	25.00	50.00
618	That's My Story/Don't Say Goodbye	1958	12.50	25.00	50.00
621	Baby Talk/Two Teen Agers	1959	—	—	—
—Unreleased?					
EMBER					
1094	I'm Lonesome/Looking at You	1959	12.50	25.00	50.00
HUNT					
319	That's My Story/Don't Say Goodbye	1959	12.50	25.00	50.00
KING					
5167	Hey, Schoolgirl/Dancin' Wild	1958	20.00	40.00	80.00

TOM AND JERRY (2)

Tommy Tomlinson and Jerry Kennedy, a country instrumental duo.

45s

Number	Title (A Side/B Side)	Yr	VG	VG+	NM
MERCURY					
71753	Golden Wildwood Flower/South	1961	5.00	10.00	20.00
71827	Swing Low/Sungarfoot Rag	1961	5.00	10.00	20.00
71930	I'll Drown in My Tears/French Twist	1961	5.00	10.00	20.00

Albums

Number	Title (A Side/B Side)	Yr	VG	VG+	NM
MERCURY					
MG-20626 [M]	Guitar's Greatest Hits	1961	7.50	15.00	30.00
MG-20671 [M]	Guitars Play the Sound of Ray Charles	1962	7.50	15.00	30.00
MG-20756 [M]	Guitar's Greatest Hits, Vol. 2	1962	7.50	15.00	30.00
MG-20842 [M]	Surfin' Hootenanny	1963	10.00	20.00	40.00

Number	Title (A Side/B Side)	Yr	VG	VG+	NM
SR-60626 [S]	Guitar's Greatest Hits	1961	10.00	20.00	40.00
SR-60671 [S]	Guitars Play the Sound of Ray Charles	1962	10.00	20.00	40.00
SR-60756 [S]	Guitar's Greatest Hits, Vol. 2	1962	10.00	20.00	40.00
SR-60842 [S]	Surfin' Hootenanny	1963	12.50	25.00	50.00

TOMBSTONES, THE

45s

Number	Title (A Side/B Side)	Yr	VG	VG+	NM
CAPITOL					
5997	Times Will Be Hard/Mary Jane	1967	2.50	5.00	10.00

TOMITA

45s

Number	Title (A Side/B Side)	Yr	VG	VG+	NM
RCA					
PB-10819	Planet Mars/Planet Venus	1976	—	2.00	4.00
RCA VICTOR					
APBO-0308	Golliwog's Cakewalk/Clair de Lune	1974	—	2.50	5.00
APBO-0308 [PS]	Golliwog's Cakewalk/Clair de Lune	1974	2.00	4.00	8.00
PB-10296	The Great Gate of Kiev/Baba Yaya	1975	—	2.50	5.00
PB-10683	Firebird Suite: Infernal Dance/Firebird Suite: Finale	1976	—	2.50	5.00

Albums

Number	Title (A Side/B Side)	Yr	VG	VG+	NM
RCA RED SEAL					
ARL1-0488	Snowflakes Are Dancing	1974	2.50	5.00	10.00
ARL1-0838	Moussorgsky: Pictures at an Exhibition	1975	2.50	5.00	10.00
ARD1-1312 [Q]	Firebird	1976	3.75	7.50	15.00
ARL1-1312	Firebird	1976	2.50	5.00	10.00
ARL1-1919	Holst: The Planets	1976	2.50	5.00	10.00
ARL1-2616	Kosmos	1978	2.50	5.00	10.00
ARL1-2885	The Bermuda Triangle	1979	2.50	5.00	10.00
ARL1-3412	Ravel: Bolero	1980	2.50	5.00	10.00
ARL1-3439	Greatest Hits	1980	2.50	5.00	10.00
ARL1-4019	A Voyage Through His Greatest Hits, Vol. 2	1981	2.50	5.00	10.00
ARL1-4317	Grand Canyon Suite	1982	2.50	5.00	10.00
ATL1-4332	Snowflakes Are Dancing	1982	3.00	6.00	12.00
—Reissue with die-cut cover and custom innersleeve					
ARL1-5037	Spacewalk — Impressions of an Astronaut	1984	2.50	5.00	10.00
ARL1-5184	Canon of the 3 Stars	1984	2.50	5.00	10.00
ARL1-5461	Live at Linz, 1984 — The Mind of the Universe	1985	2.50	5.00	10.00

TOMLIN, LILY

45s

Number	Title (A Side/B Side)	Yr	VG	VG+	NM
POLYDOR					
14180	20th Century Blues/Blues	1973	—	2.50	5.00
14283	Edith Ann/Detroit City	1975	—	2.50	5.00

Albums

Number	Title (A Side/B Side)	Yr	VG	VG+	NM
ARISTA					
AB 4142	Lily Tomlin On Stage	1977	3.00	6.00	12.00
POLYDOR					
24-4055	This Is a Recording	1971	2.50	5.00	10.00
PD 5023	And That's the Truth	1972	2.50	5.00	10.00
PD 6051	Modern Scream	1976	3.00	6.00	12.00

TOMMY AND THE HUSTLERS

45s

Number	Title (A Side/B Side)	Yr	VG	VG+	NM
FANTASY					
573	Diggin' Out/The Right Size	1963	10.00	20.00	40.00
—Green vinyl					
573	Diggin' Out/The Right Size	1963	6.25	12.50	25.00

TOMMY AND THE TWISTERS

45s

Number	Title (A Side/B Side)	Yr	VG	VG+	NM
REGENT					
205	Mr. Twist/Hucklebuck Twist	1962	3.00	6.00	12.00

Albums

Number	Title (A Side/B Side)	Yr	VG	VG+	NM
REGENT					
MG-6104 [M]	Let's All Do the Twist	1961	10.00	20.00	40.00

TOMS, GARY, EMPIRE

45s

Number	Title (A Side/B Side)	Yr	VG	VG+	NM
MCA					
40770	Turn It Out (Tear This Building Down)/Hurricane	1977	—	2.00	4.00
MERCURY					
74012	1-2-3-4/Feelin' Good Again	1978	—	2.00	4.00
74023	Welcome to Harlem/(B-side unknown)	1978	—	2.00	4.00
P.I.P.					
6504	7-6-5-4-3-2-1 (Blow Your Whistle)/7-6-5-4-3-2-1 (Blow Your Whistle) (Long Version)	1975	—	2.50	5.00
6509	Drive My Car/The New Empire	1975	—	2.50	5.00
6517	Love Me Right (Short Version)/Love Me Right (Long Version)	1976	—	2.50	5.00
6524	Stand Up and Shout/Party Hardy	1976	—	2.50	5.00

Albums

Number	Title (A Side/B Side)	Yr	VG	VG+	NM
MCA					
2289	Turn It Out	1977	2.50	5.00	10.00
MERCURY					
SRM-1-3731	Do It Again	1978	2.50	5.00	10.00
P.I.P.					
6814	7-6-5-4-3-2-1 Blow Your Whistle	1975	2.50	5.00	10.00

TONETTES, THE

Two different groups?

45s

Number	Title (A Side/B Side)	Yr	VG	VG+	NM
ABC-PARAMOUNT					
9905	Oh What a Baby/Howie	1958	5.00	10.00	20.00
DOE					
101	Oh What a Baby/Howie	1958	20.00	40.00	80.00
103	Uh Oh/He Loves Me, He Loves Me Not	1958	15.00	30.00	60.00
MODERN					
997	Tonight You Belong to Me/Don't Fall in Love Too Soon	1956	6.25	12.50	25.00
VOLT					
101	Please Don't Go/No Tears	1962	5.00	10.00	20.00
104	Stolen Angel/Teardrop Sea	1963	5.00	10.00	20.00

TONEY, OSCAR, JR.

45s

Number	Title (A Side/B Side)	Yr	VG	VG+	NM
BELL					
672	For Your Precious Love/Ain't That True Love	1967	2.50	5.00	10.00
681	Turn On Your Love Light/Any Day Now	1967	2.50	5.00	10.00
688	Unlucky Guy/You Can Lead Your Woman to the Altar	1967	2.50	5.00	10.00
699	Without Love (There Is Nothing)/Love That Never Grows Old	1968	2.50	5.00	10.00
714	Never Get Enough of Your Love/Love That Never Grows Old	1968	2.50	5.00	10.00
CAPRICORN					
0005	I Do What You Wish/Thank You, Honey Chile	1972	—	3.00	6.00
8005	Down on My Knees/Seven Days Tomorrow	1970	2.00	4.00	8.00
8010	I Wouldn't Be a Poor Boy/Person to Person	1970	2.00	4.00	8.00
8018	Workin' Together/Baby Is Mine	1971	2.00	4.00	8.00
KING					
5906	Can It All Be Love/You Are Going to Need Me	1964	5.00	10.00	20.00
6108	Keep On Loving Me/I've Found a True Love	1967	3.00	6.00	12.00

Albums

Number	Title (A Side/B Side)	Yr	VG	VG+	NM
BELL					
6006 [M]	For Your Precious Love	1967	6.25	12.50	25.00
S-6006 [S]	For Your Precious Love	1967	7.50	15.00	30.00

TONGUE AND GROOVE

45s

Number	Title (A Side/B Side)	Yr	VG	VG+	NM
FONTANA					
1640	Cherry Ball/Devil	1969	2.00	4.00	8.00
1653	Come On in My Kitchen/Mailman's Sack	1969	2.00	4.00	8.00

Albums

Number	Title (A Side/B Side)	Yr	VG	VG+	NM
FONTANA					
SRF-67593	Tongue and Groove	1968	5.00	10.00	20.00

TONTO'S EXPANDING HEAD BAND

Albums

Number	Title (A Side/B Side)	Yr	VG	VG+	NM
EMBRYO					
SD 732	Zero Time	1971	5.00	10.00	20.00

TONY AND THE DAYDREAMS

45s

Number	Title (A Side/B Side)	Yr	VG	VG+	NM
PLANET					
1008	Why Don't You Be Nice/I'll Never Tell	1958	25.00	50.00	100.00
1054	Christmas Lullaby/Handin' Hand	1961	50.00	100.00	200.00

TONY AND THE HOLIDAYS

45s

Number	Title (A Side/B Side)	Yr	VG	VG+	NM
ABC-PARAMOUNT					
10295	There Goes My Heart Again/My Love Is Real	1962	50.00	100.00	200.00

TONY AND THE MASQUINS

45s

Number	Title (A Side/B Side)	Yr	VG	VG+	NM
RUTHIE					
1000	My Angel Eyes/Fugi Womma	1961	25.00	50.00	100.00

TONY AND THE RAINDROPS

45s

Number	Title (A Side/B Side)	Yr	VG	VG+	NM
CHESAPEKE					
609	While Walking/Our Love Is Over	1961	15.00	30.00	60.00
CROSLEY					
340	Tina/My Heart Cried	1962	50.00	100.00	200.00

TONY AND THE TECHNICS

See THE TECHNICS.

TONY AND THE TWILIGHTERS

Early version of ANTHONY AND THE SOPHOMORES.

45s

Number	Title (A Side/B Side)	Yr	VG	VG+	NM
JALYNNE					
106	Be My Girl/Did You Make Up Your Mind	1960	20.00	40.00	80.00
RED TOP					
127	Key to My Heart/Yes or No	1960	50.00	100.00	200.00

TONY AND TYRONE

45s

Number	Title (A Side/B Side)	Yr	VG	VG+	NM
ATLANTIC					
2458	Please Operator/Apple of My Eye	1967	7.50	15.00	30.00
COLUMBIA					
43432	Turn It On/Talkin' About the People	1965	3.75	7.50	15.00

TOOMORROW

OLIVIA NEWTON-JOHN was in this group.

45s

Number	Title (A Side/B Side)	Yr	VG	VG+	NM
KIRSHNER					
63-5005	Goin' Back/You're My Baby Now	1970	15.00	30.00	60.00

TOONE, GENE

45s

Number	Title (A Side/B Side)	Yr	VG	VG+	NM
ANNETTE					
1001	You're My Baby/Jose	1964	50.00	100.00	200.00
—Produced by Phil Spector					
WAND					
11293	Baby Boy (Part 1)/Baby Boy (Part 2)	1975	—	3.00	6.00

Number	Title (A Side/B Side)	Yr	VG	VG+	NM

TOOTIE AND THE BOUQUETS

45s

PARKWAY

Number	Title (A Side/B Side)	Yr	VG	VG+	NM
887	The Conqueror/You Done Me Wrong	1963	6.25	12.50	25.00

TOOTS AND THE MAYTALS

Albums

Number	Title (A Side/B Side)	Yr	VG	VG+	NM
ISLAND					
ILPS 9330	Funky Kingston	1975	3.00	6.00	12.00
MANGO					
MLPS 9330	Funky Kingston	197?	2.50	5.00	10.00
—Reissue of Island 9330					
MLPS 9374	Reggae Got Soul	1976	3.00	6.00	12.00
MLPS 9534	Pass the Pipe	198?	2.50	5.00	10.00
MLPS 9590	Just Like That	1980	2.50	5.00	10.00
MLPS 9647	Live	1980	3.00	6.00	12.00
MLPS 9670	Knock Out	1982	2.50	5.00	10.00
9781	Reggae Greats	198?	2.50	5.00	10.00

TOP DRAWER

Albums

WISH BONE

Number	Title (A Side/B Side)	Yr	VG	VG+	NM
721207	Solid Oak	1969	100.00	200.00	400.00

TOP HITS, THE

45s

NORMAN

Number	Title (A Side/B Side)	Yr	VG	VG+	NM
504	Love No One/Thum-A-Lum-A	1961	50.00	100.00	200.00

TOP NOTES, THE

45s

Number	Title (A Side/B Side)	Yr	VG	VG+	NM
ABC-PARAMOUNT					
10399	I Love You So Much/It's Alright	1963	2.50	5.00	10.00
ATLANTIC					
2066	A Wonderful Time/Walkin' with Love	1960	3.75	7.50	15.00
2080	Say Man/Warm Your Heart	1960	3.75	7.50	15.00
2097	Hearts of Stone/The Basic Things	1961	3.75	7.50	15.00
2115	Twist and Shout/Always Late (Why Lead Me On)	1961	6.25	12.50	25.00

TOPICS, THE

Also see THE FOUR SEASONS.

45s

PERRI

Number	Title (A Side/B Side)	Yr	VG	VG+	NM
1007	The Girl in My Dreams	1961	37.50	75.00	150.00
—One-sided record					

TOPPERS, THE

More than one group.

45s

Number	Title (A Side/B Side)	Yr	VG	VG+	NM
ABC-PARAMOUNT					
9667	George Washington/Honey, Honey	1956	5.00	10.00	20.00
9699	God Bless Kids and Little Animals/Tornado	1956	5.00	10.00	20.00
9759	Three Roads/Lonely	1956	5.00	10.00	20.00
AVALON					
63707	I Love You, I Love You/Bow-Legged Boy	1954	10.00	20.00	40.00
DECCA					
30209	The Purple Hills/Stashu Pandowski	1957	3.75	7.50	15.00
30297	Pots and Pans/It Was Twice As Big As I Thought It Was	1957	3.75	7.50	15.00
JUBILEE					
5136	Let Me Bang Your Box/You're Laughing 'Cause I'm Crying	1954	37.50	75.00	150.00
STACY					
927	Tell Me Why/All Around	1962	3.00	6.00	12.00

TOPPS, THE

45s

RED ROBIN

Number	Title (A Side/B Side)	Yr	VG	VG+	NM
126	What Do You Do (To Make Me Love You So)/ Tippin'	1954	75.00	150.00	300.00
131	I've Got a Feeling/Won't You Come Home Baby	1954	75.00	150.00	300.00

TOPS, THE

45s

SINGULAR

Number	Title (A Side/B Side)	Yr	VG	VG+	NM
712	An Innocent Kiss/Walkin' with My Baby	1957	30.00	60.00	120.00

TOPSIDERS, THE

45s

JOSIE

Number	Title (A Side/B Side)	Yr	VG	VG+	NM
907	Heartbreak Hotel/Let the Good Times Roll	1963	3.00	6.00	12.00

Albums

JOSIE

Number	Title (A Side/B Side)	Yr	VG	VG+	NM
JOZ-4000 [M]	Rock Goes Folk	1963	6.25	12.50	25.00

TORME, MEL

45s

Number	Title (A Side/B Side)	Yr	VG	VG+	NM
ATLANTIC					
2165	Comin' Home Baby/Right Now	1962	2.50	5.00	10.00
2183	Cast Your Fate to the Wind/The Gift	1963	2.50	5.00	10.00
2187	Gravy Waltz/My Gal's Back in Town	1963	2.50	5.00	10.00
2202	You Belong to Me/You Can't Love 'Em All	1963	2.50	5.00	10.00
2219	42nd Street/Sunday in New York	1964	2.50	5.00	10.00
BETHLEHEM					
11008	Lulu's Back in Town/Keeping Myself for You	1958	3.00	6.00	12.00
CAPITOL					
F1000	Bewitched/Piccolino	1950	5.00	10.00	20.00
F1177	Recipe for Romance/Do Do Do	1950	5.00	10.00	20.00
F1237	I Owe a Kiss/Say No More	1950	5.00	10.00	20.00
F1291	Skylark/Lullaby of the Leaves	1950	5.00	10.00	20.00
F1383	Around the World/Sidewalk Shufflers	1951	5.00	10.00	20.00
F1402	You're Getting to Be a Habit with Me/Sailin' Away on Henry Clay	1951	5.00	10.00	20.00
F1524	The World Is Yours/Bundle of Love	1951	5.00	10.00	20.00
F1598	You Locked My Heart/Qho Sends You Orchids	1951	5.00	10.00	20.00
F1662	Bewitched/Blue Moon	1951	3.75	7.50	15.00
—Reissue					
F1712	One for Me/Love Is Such a Cheat	1951	5.00	10.00	20.00
F1761	My Buddy/Take My Heart	1951	5.00	10.00	20.00
F1864	Foolish Rumors/You're a Heavenly Thing	1951	5.00	10.00	20.00
F2131	Don't Leave Me/Black Moonlight	1952	5.00	10.00	20.00
F2263	Casually/Anywhere I Wander	1952	5.00	10.00	20.00
2613	Games People Play/Willie and Laura Mae Jones	1969	—	3.00	6.00
2743	Requiem: 820 Latham/Spinning Wheel	1970	—	3.00	6.00
COLUMBIA					
43022	I Know Your Heart/You Better Love Me	1964	2.00	4.00	8.00
43087	Once in a Lifetime/I See It Now	1964	2.00	4.00	8.00
43167	Every Day's a Holiday/One Little Snowflake	1964	3.00	6.00	12.00
43167 [DJ]	Every Day's a Holiday/One Little Snowflake	1964	3.75	7.50	15.00
—Promo only on green vinyl					
43230	Do I Love You Because You're Beautiful/That's All	1965	2.00	4.00	8.00
43383	Ho-Ba-La-Ba/My Romance	1965	2.00	4.00	8.00
43550	The Power of Love/Dominique's Discotheque	1966	2.00	4.00	8.00
43677	All That Jazz/Hang On to Me	1966	2.00	4.00	8.00
44180	Lover's Roulette/I Remember Suzanne	1967	2.00	4.00	8.00
44399	Wait Until Dark/Lima Lady	1967	2.00	4.00	8.00
45283	The Christmas Song/(B-side unknown)	1970	—	3.00	6.00
CORAL					
61136	Anything Can Happen Mambo/Just One More Chance	1954	3.75	7.50	15.00
61295	All of You/Spellbound	1954	3.75	7.50	15.00
61452	It Don't Mean a Thing/Rose O'Day	1955	3.75	7.50	15.00
61507	Goody Goody/Jeepers Creepers	1955	3.75	7.50	15.00
LIBERTY					
56022	A Day in the Life of Bonnie and Clyde/Brother Can You Spare a Dime	1968	2.50	5.00	10.00
56066	Didn't We/Five-Four	1968	2.00	4.00	8.00
VERVE					
10174	The Crossroads/Frenesi	1959	3.00	6.00	12.00
10211	Wayfaring Stranger/Walk Like a Dragon	1960	3.00	6.00	12.00
10232	Her Face/Yes Indeed	1961	3.00	6.00	12.00

Albums

Number	Title (A Side/B Side)	Yr	VG	VG+	NM
ALLEGRO ELITE					
4117 [10]	Mel Torme Sings	195?	7.50	15.00	30.00
ARCHIVE OF FOLK AND JAZZ					
324	The Velvet Fog	198?	2.50	5.00	10.00
ATLANTIC					
8066 [M]	Mel Torme at the Red Hill Inn	1962	7.50	15.00	30.00
SD 8066 [S]	Mel Torme at the Red Hill Inn	1962	10.00	20.00	40.00
8069 [M]	Comin' Home Baby	1962	7.50	15.00	30.00
SD 8069 [S]	Comin' Home Baby	1962	10.00	20.00	40.00
8091 [M]	Sunday in New York	1963	7.50	15.00	30.00
SD 8091 [S]	Sunday in New York	1963	10.00	20.00	40.00
SD 18129	Live at the Maisonette	1975	3.00	6.00	12.00
80078	Songs of New York	1982	2.50	5.00	10.00
AUDIOPHILE					
67	Mel Torme Sings About Love	198?	5.00	10.00	20.00
BETHLEHEM					
BCP-34 [M]	It's a Blue World	1956	12.50	25.00	50.00
BCP-52 [M]	Mel Torme and the Marty Paich Dektette	1956	12.50	25.00	50.00
BCP 6013 [M]	Mel Torme Sings Fred Astaire	1957	12.50	25.00	50.00
BCP 6016 [M]	California Suite	1957	12.50	25.00	50.00
BCP 6020 [M]	Mel Torme Live at the Crescendo	1958	12.50	25.00	50.00
BCP 6031 [M]	Songs for Any Taste	1959	12.50	25.00	50.00
CAPITOL					
P 200 [10]	California Suite	1950	25.00	50.00	100.00
ST-313	A Time for Us	1969	3.00	6.00	12.00
COLUMBIA					
CL 2318 [M]	That's All — A Lush Romantic Album	1965	3.75	7.50	15.00
CL 2535 [M]	Mel Torme Right Now	1966	3.00	6.00	12.00
CS 9118 [S]	That's All — A Lush Romantic Album	1965	5.00	10.00	20.00
CS 9335 [S]	Mel Torme Right Now	1966	3.75	7.50	15.00
COLUMBIA SPECIAL PRODUCTS					
P 13090	That's All	1976	3.00	6.00	12.00
CONCORD JAZZ					
CJ-306	Mel Torme with Rob McConnell and the Boss Brass	1986	2.50	5.00	10.00
CJ-360	Reunion	1988	2.50	5.00	10.00
CJ-382	In Concert Tokyo	1989	2.50	5.00	10.00
—Above two with the Marty Paich Dek-Tette					
CORAL					
CRL 57012 [M]	Gene Norman Presents Mel Torme "Live" at the Crescendo	1955	12.50	25.00	50.00
CRL 57044 [M]	Musical Sounds Are the Best Songs	1956	12.50	25.00	50.00
DISCOVERY					
910	Sings His California Suite	1986	2.50	5.00	10.00
—Reissue of Capitol 200					
FINESSE					
W2X 37484 [(2)]	Mel Torme & Friends Recorded at Marty's, New York City	1981	3.00	6.00	12.00
GLENDALE					
6007	Mel Torme	1978	2.50	5.00	10.00
6018	Easy to Remember	1979	2.50	5.00	10.00
GRYPHON					
796	A New Album	1979	2.50	5.00	10.00
LIBERTY					
LST-7560	A Day in the Life of Bonnie and Clyde	1968	5.00	10.00	20.00
METRO					
M-523 [M]	I Wished on the Moon	1965	3.00	6.00	12.00
MS-523 [S]	I Wished on the Moon	1965	3.75	7.50	15.00
MGM					
E 552 [10]	Songs by Mel Torme	1952	25.00	50.00	100.00

Number	Title (A Side/B Side)	Yr	VG	VG+	NM
MUSICRAFT					
508	Mel Torme, Volume 1	1983	2.50	5.00	10.00
510	It Happened in Monterey	1983	2.50	5.00	10.00
2005	Gone with the Wind	1986	2.50	5.00	10.00
STASH					
ST-252	'Round Midnight	1985	2.50	5.00	10.00
STRAND					
SL-1076 [M]	Mel Torme Sings	1960	5.00	10.00	20.00
SLS-1076 [S]	Mel Torme Sings	1960	6.25	12.50	25.00
TOPS					
L-1615 [M]	Prelude to a Kiss	1958	6.25	12.50	25.00
VERVE					
MGV 2105 [M]	Torme	1958	12.50	25.00	50.00
V-2105 [M]	Torme	1961	5.00	10.00	20.00
—Reissue					
V6-2105 [S]	Torme	1961	6.25	12.50	25.00
—Reissue					
MGV 2117 [M]	Ole Torme! Mel Torme Goes South of the Border with Billy May	1959	12.50	25.00	50.00
V-2117 [M]	Ole Torme! Mel Torme Goes South of the Border with Billy May	1961	5.00	10.00	20.00
—Reissue					
V6-2117 [S]	Ole Torme! Mel Torme Goes South of the Border with Billy May	1961	6.25	12.50	25.00
—Reissue					
MGV 2120 [M]	Back in Town	1959	12.50	25.00	50.00
V-2120 [M]	Back in Town	1961	5.00	10.00	20.00
—Reissue					
V6-2120 [S]	Back in Town	1961	6.25	12.50	25.00
—Reissue					
MGV 2132 [M]	Mel Torme Swings Schubert Alley	1960	12.50	25.00	50.00
V-2132 [M]	Mel Torme Swings Schubert Alley	1961	5.00	10.00	20.00
—Reissue					
V6-2132 [S]	Mel Torme Swings Schubert Alley	1961	6.25	12.50	25.00
—Reissue					
MGV 2144 [M]	Swingin' on the Moon	1960	12.50	25.00	50.00
V-2144 [M]	Swingin' on the Moon	1961	5.00	10.00	20.00
—Reissue					
V6-2144 [S]	Swingin' on the Moon	1961	6.25	12.50	25.00
MGV 2146 [M]	Broadway, Right Now	1961	12.50	25.00	50.00
V-2146 [M]	Broadway, Right Now	1961	5.00	10.00	20.00
—Reissue					
V6-2146 [S]	Broadway, Right Now	1961	6.25	12.50	25.00
MGV 2153 [M]	I Dig the Duke! I Dig the Count!	1961	—	—	—
—Canceled; moved to 8491					
UMV-2521	Mel Torme Swings Shubert Alley	1981	2.50	5.00	10.00
UMV-2675	Back in Town	1982	2.50	5.00	10.00
MGVS 6015 [S]	Torme	1960	12.50	25.00	50.00
MGVS 6058 [S]	Ole Torme! Mel Torme Goes South of the Border with Billy May	1960	12.50	25.00	50.00
MGVS 6063 [S]	Back in Town	1960	12.50	25.00	50.00
MGVS 6146 [S]	Mel Torme Swings Schubert Alley	1960	12.50	25.00	50.00
V-8440 [M]	My Kind of Music	1962	6.25	12.50	25.00
V6-8440 [S]	My Kind of Music	1962	7.50	15.00	30.00
V-8491 [M]	I Dig the Duke! I Dig the Count!	1962	6.25	12.50	25.00
V6-8491 [S]	I Dig the Duke! I Dig the Count!	1962	7.50	15.00	30.00
V-8593 [M]	Verve's Choice — The Best of Mel Torme	1964	3.00	6.00	12.00
V6-8593 [S]	Verve's Choice — The Best of Mel Torme	1964	3.75	7.50	15.00
823248-1	The Duke Ellington and Count Basie Songbooks	1984	2.50	5.00	10.00
—Reissue of Verve 8491					
VOCALION					
VL 73905	The Velvet Fog	197?	2.50	5.00	10.00

TORME, MEL, AND BUDDY RICH

Albums

Number	Title (A Side/B Side)	Yr	VG	VG+	NM
CENTURY					
1100	Together Again — For the First Time	1978	6.25	12.50	25.00
—Direct-to-disc recording					
GRYPHON					
784	Together Again — For the First Time	1978	2.50	5.00	10.00

TORNADOES, THE (1)

British band.

45s

Number	Title (A Side/B Side)	Yr	VG	VG+	NM
DATE					
1519	Hey Baby!/Next Stop Kansas City	1966	3.00	6.00	12.00
LONDON					
9561	Telstar/Jungle Fever	1962	6.25	12.50	25.00
9579	Globetrottin'/Like Locomotion	1963	5.00	10.00	20.00
9581	Ridin' the Wind/The Breeze and I	1963	5.00	10.00	20.00
9599	Life on Venus (Telstar II)/Robot	1963	5.00	10.00	20.00
9614	Theme from "The Scales of Justice"/The Ice Cream Man	1963	5.00	10.00	20.00
11003	Telestar/Jungle Fever	1964	5.00	10.00	20.00
—Gold label "Demand Performance" with misspelled A-side					
TOWER					
152	Stompin' Through the Rye/Early Bird	1965	3.75	7.50	15.00
171	Stingray/Aqua Marina	1965	3.75	7.50	15.00

Albums

Number	Title (A Side/B Side)	Yr	VG	VG+	NM
LONDON					
LL 3279 [M]	Telstar	1963	50.00	100.00	200.00
LL 3293 [M]	The Sounds of the Tornadoes	1963	50.00	100.00	200.00

—Basically the same album as above, but with a new cover, one different track and the song order shuffled.

TORNADOES, THE (2)

California surf band, also called "Hollywood Tornadoes."

45s

Number	Title (A Side/B Side)	Yr	VG	VG+	NM
AERTAUN					
100	Bustin' Surfboards/Beyond the Surf	1962	10.00	20.00	40.00
101	The Gremmie (Part 1)/The Gremmie (Part 2)	1963	6.25	12.50	25.00
—As "The Hollywood Tornadoes"					
102	Inebriated Surfer/Moon Dawg	1963	7.50	15.00	30.00
—As "The Hollywood Tornadoes"					
103	Phantom Surfer/Shootin' Beavers	1963	7.50	15.00	30.00
103	Phantom Surfer/Lightnin'	1964	6.25	12.50	25.00
—B-side is same recording as "Shootin' Beavers" but retitled					

Albums

Number	Title (A Side/B Side)	Yr	VG	VG+	NM
JOSIE					
J-4005 [M]	Bustin' Surfboards	1963	50.00	100.00	200.00
JS-4005 [S]	Bustin' Surfboards	1963	75.00	150.00	300.00

TORNADOES, THE (3)

45s

Number	Title (A Side/B Side)	Yr	VG	VG+	NM
ABC-PARAMOUNT					
10174	Cora/Like a Frog	1960	5.00	10.00	20.00

TORNADOES, THE (4)

45s

Number	Title (A Side/B Side)	Yr	VG	VG+	NM
CUCA					
1092	Scalping Party/7-0-7	1962	10.00	20.00	40.00
1099	Loneliest Guy in the World/It Always Makes Me Cry	1962	7.50	15.00	30.00
1104	Hey There/Standing Watch	1963	7.50	15.00	30.00

TOROK, MITCHELL

45s

Number	Title (A Side/B Side)	Yr	VG	VG+	NM
ABBOTT					
136	Little Hoo-Wee/Judalina	1953	6.25	12.50	25.00
140	Caribbean/Weep Away	1953	7.50	15.00	30.00
150	Hootchy Kootchy Henry (From Hawaii)/Gigolo	1953	6.25	12.50	25.00
156	Edgar the Eager Easter Bunny/Living on Love	1954	6.25	12.50	25.00
162	Dancerette/Haunting Waterfall	1954	6.25	12.50	25.00
CAPITOL					
4846	Rio Grande/Fools Disguise	1962	2.00	4.00	8.00
4946	Mighty Mighty Man/For Someone Who's Supposed to Be Hurtin'	1963	2.00	4.00	8.00
DECCA					
29326	Roulette/Havana Huddle	1954	5.00	10.00	20.00
29408	Peasant's Guitar/The World Keeps Turning Around	1955	3.75	7.50	15.00
29576	Too Late Now/Smooth Talk	1955	3.75	7.50	15.00
29661	Marching My Blues Away/Country and Western	1955	3.75	7.50	15.00
29863	No Money Down/Red Light, Green Light	1956	3.75	7.50	15.00
29986	I Wish I Was a Little Bit Younger/When Mexico Gave Up Rhumba	1956	3.75	7.50	15.00
30134	Take This Heart/Drink Up and Go Home	1956	3.75	7.50	15.00
30230	Pledge of Love/What's Behind That Strange Door	1957	3.75	7.50	15.00
30424	Two Words/You're Tempting Me	1957	3.75	7.50	15.00
30599	Be Kind to Me/How Much Do I Love You	1958	3.00	6.00	12.00
30661	Sweet Revenge/Love Me Like You Mean It	1958	3.00	6.00	12.00
30742	Date with a Teardrop/These Things I Hold Dear	1958	3.00	6.00	12.00
30859	Go Ahead and Be a Fool/Memories of You Haunting Me Night and Day	1959	3.00	6.00	12.00
30901	PTA Rock and Roll/Teenie Weenie Bikini	1959	5.00	10.00	20.00
GUYDEN					
2018	Caribbean/Hootchy Kootchy Henry (From Hawaii)	1959	3.00	6.00	12.00
2028	You Are the One/Mexican Joe	1959	2.50	5.00	10.00
2032	Guardian Angel/I Want to Know Everything	1960	2.50	5.00	10.00
2034	Pink Chiffon/What You Don't Know	1960	2.50	5.00	10.00
2034 [PS]	Pink Chiffon/What You Don't Know	1960	5.00	10.00	20.00
2040	Happy Street/Little Boy in Love	1960	2.50	5.00	10.00
MERCURY					
71826	El Tigre/Eating My Heart Out	1961	2.50	5.00	10.00
RCA VICTOR					
47-8646	I Needed All the Help I Can Get/Man with a Golden Hand	1965	2.00	4.00	8.00
47-8703	Caribbean/Witch Woman	1965	2.00	4.00	8.00
REPRISE					
0541	Instant Love/Put Me in the Driver's Seat	1966	—	3.00	6.00
0568	Falling in Love Again/Baby, Baby, Baby	1967	—	3.00	6.00

Albums

Number	Title (A Side/B Side)	Yr	VG	VG+	NM
GUYDEN					
GLP-502 [M]	Caribbean	1960	10.00	20.00	40.00
ST-502 [S]	Caribbean	1960	12.50	25.00	50.00
REPRISE					
R 6223 [M]	Guitar Course	1966	5.00	10.00	20.00
RS 6223 [S]	Guitar Course	1966	6.25	12.50	25.00

TORQUAYS, THE

45s

Number	Title (A Side/B Side)	Yr	VG	VG+	NM
AERTAUN					
1020	Turmoil/Crying in the Chapel	1964	7.50	15.00	30.00
COLPIX					
782	Image of a Girl/Stolen Moments	1965	5.00	10.00	20.00
GEE CEE					
8163	Escondido/Surfer's City	1963	12.50	25.00	50.00
GYPSY					
265	Busting Point/The Other Side	1965	12.50	25.00	50.00
ORIGINAL SOUND					
66	Harmonica Man/Our Teenage Love	1967	5.00	10.00	20.00
PUNCH					
1007	Shake a Tail Feather/Temptation	196?	5.00	10.00	20.00
ROCK-IT					
1004	Image of a Girl/Stolen Moments	1965	7.50	15.00	30.00
1005	Hooked on Her/Harmonica Man	1965	7.50	15.00	30.00

TORQUES, THE

45s

Number	Title (A Side/B Side)	Yr	VG	VG+	NM
DIAL					
4060	Merry Maker/You Make Me Feel So Good	1967	5.00	10.00	20.00

Number	Title (A Side/B Side)	Yr	VG	VG+	NM
LEMCO					
880	Tidal Wave/Harlem Nocturne	1965	7.50	15.00	30.00
890	Mercy Mercy/Bumpin'	1966	7.50	15.00	30.00
1001	Linden Walk/Deep Blue, At Dusk	196?	7.50	15.00	30.00
1007	I've Been Hurt/Bumpin'	1966	6.25	12.50	25.00

Albums

Number	Title (A Side/B Side)	Yr	VG	VG+	NM
LEMCO					
604	The Torques Live	1966	50.00	100.00	200.00
WIGGINS					
64010	Zoom!	1967	50.00	100.00	200.00

TORQUETTS, THE

45s

Number	Title (A Side/B Side)	Yr	VG	VG+	NM
SANTA CRUZ					
10002	Any More/(Who's Got The) Tortillas	196?	12.50	25.00	50.00
TORQUETT					
005/6	Feedback/Bacardi	196?	12.50	25.00	50.00
007/8	Side Swiped/Blue Corral	196?	6.25	12.50	25.00

TORRANCE, RICHARD

45s

Number	Title (A Side/B Side)	Yr	VG	VG+	NM
CAPITOL					
4417	Leave My Love Behind/Rio De Janeiro Blue	1977	—	2.00	4.00
4554	Long Lonely Nights/I Can't Ask for Anymore Than You	1978	—	2.00	4.00
4644	Be Bop 'n Holla/Let's Call It a Night	1978	—	2.00	4.00
SHELTER					
40374	Don't Let Me Down Again/Hard Heavy Road	1975	—	2.00	4.00
40419	Lady/Southern Belles	1975	—	2.00	4.00

Albums

Number	Title (A Side/B Side)	Yr	VG	VG+	NM
CAPITOL					
SW-11610	Bareback	1977	2.50	5.00	10.00
SW-11660	Anything's Possible	1978	2.50	5.00	10.00
SW-11699	Double Take	1978	2.50	5.00	10.00
SHELTER					
2112	Eureka	1974	3.00	6.00	12.00
2134	Belle of the Ball	1975	2.50	5.00	10.00

TORRENCE, JOHNNY

45s

Number	Title (A Side/B Side)	Yr	VG	VG+	NM
IMPERIAL					
5230	Sad Day/Bad Habit	1953	30.00	60.00	120.00
5897	Rat Race/Your Lover Man	1962	3.75	7.50	15.00
R&B					
1306	Rosalie/Living from Day to Day	1954	50.00	100.00	200.00
—With the Jewels					

TOUCH

Albums

Number	Title (A Side/B Side)	Yr	VG	VG+	NM
MAINLINE					
PS-70-116-7	Street Suite	1969	1000.	1500.	2000.

TOUCHSTONE

Albums

Number	Title (A Side/B Side)	Yr	VG	VG+	NM
UNITED ARTISTS					
UAS-5563	Tarot	1972	7.50	15.00	30.00

TOUSAN, AL

See ALLEN TOUSSAINT.

TOUSSAINT, ALLEN

45s

Number	Title (A Side/B Side)	Yr	VG	VG+	NM
ALON					
9021	Go Back Home/Poor Boy, Got to Move	1965	2.50	5.00	10.00
BELL					
732	Get Out of My Life, Woman/Gotta Travel On	1968	2.00	4.00	8.00
748	Hans Christian Anderson/I've Got That Feeling Now	1968	2.00	4.00	8.00
782	Tequila/We the People	1969	2.00	4.00	8.00
RCA VICTOR					
47-7192	Whirlaway/Happy Times	1958	6.25	12.50	25.00
—As "Al Tousan"					
REPRISE					
1109	Soul Sister/She Once Belonged to Me	1972	—	2.50	5.00
1132	Am I Expecting Too Much/Out of the City	1972	—	2.50	5.00
1334	Country John/When the Party's Over	1975	—	2.00	4.00
SCEPTER					
12317	From a Whisper to a Scream/Secret Touch of Love	1971	—	3.00	6.00
12334	Working in a Coal Mine/What Is Success	1971	—	3.00	6.00
SEVILLE					
103	Chico/Sweetie-Pie	1960	3.75	7.50	15.00
—All Seville releases as "Al Tousan"					
110	Back Home in Indiana/Naomi	1960	3.75	7.50	15.00
113	A Blue Mood/Moo Moo	1961	3.75	7.50	15.00
124	Twenty Years Later/Real Churchy	1962	3.75	7.50	15.00
WARNER BROS.					
8561	Night People/Optimism Blues	1978	—	2.00	4.00
8609	Happiness/Lover of Love	1978	—	2.00	4.00

Albums

Number	Title (A Side/B Side)	Yr	VG	VG+	NM
RCA VICTOR					
LPM-1767 [M]	The Wild Sounds of New Orleans	1958	75.00	150.00	300.00
—As "Al Tousan"					
REPRISE					
MS 2062	Life, Love and Faith	1972	6.25	12.50	25.00
SCEPTER					
24003	Toussaint	1971	6.25	12.50	25.00
WARNER BROS.					
BSK 3142	Motion	1978	3.00	6.00	12.00

TOWER OF POWER

12-Inch Singles

Number	Title (A Side/B Side)	Yr	VG	VG+	NM
COLUMBIA					
10738	Lovin' You Is Gonna See Me Through/Yin-Yang Thang	1978	2.50	5.00	10.00

45s

Number	Title (A Side/B Side)	Yr	VG	VG+	NM
COLUMBIA					
10409	You Ought to Be Havin' Fun/While We Went to the Moon	1976	—	2.50	5.00
10461	Ain't Nothin' Stoppin' Us Now/Because I Think the World of You	1976	—	2.50	5.00
10718	Lovin' You Is Gonna See Me Through/I Am a Fool	1978	—	2.00	4.00
10780	Love Bug/We Came to Play	1978	—	2.00	4.00
11012	Rock Baby/Heaven Must Have Made You	1979	—	2.00	4.00
11157	In Due Time/And You Know It	1979	—	2.00	4.00
WARNER BROS.					
7612	You're Still a Young Man/Skating on Thin Ice	1972	—	3.00	6.00
7635	Down to the Nightclub/What Happened to the World That Day	1972	—	3.00	6.00
7687	So Very Hard to Go/Clean Slate	1973	—	3.00	6.00
7733	This Time It's Real/Soul Vaccination	1973	—	3.00	6.00
7748	What is Hip?/Clever Girl	1973	—	3.00	6.00
7796	Time Will Tell/Oakland Stroke	1974	—	3.00	6.00
7828	Don't Change Horses (In the Middle of a Stream)/I Got the Chop	1974	—	3.00	6.00
8055	Only So Much Oil in the Ground/Give Me the Proof	1974	—	3.00	6.00
8083	Willing to Learn/Walkin' Up Hip Street	1975	—	2.50	5.00
8121	You're So Wonderful, So Marvelous/Stroke '75	1975	—	2.50	5.00
8151	Soul of a Child/Treat Me Like Your Man	1975	—	2.50	5.00

Albums

Number	Title (A Side/B Side)	Yr	VG	VG+	NM
COLUMBIA					
PC 34302	Ain't Nothin' Stoppin' Us Now	1976	2.50	5.00	10.00
—No bar code on cover					
PC 34302	Ain't Nothin' Stoppin' Us Now	198?	2.00	4.00	8.00
—Budget-line reissue with bar code					
JC 34906	We Came to Play!	1978	2.50	5.00	10.00
JC 35784	Back on the Streets	1979	2.50	5.00	10.00
DIRECT DISC					
SD 16601	Back to Oakland	1980	6.25	12.50	25.00
—Audiophile vinyl					
SAN FRANCISCO					
SD 204	East Bay Grease	1971	12.50	25.00	50.00
SHEFFIELD LABS					
17	Direct	1982	6.25	12.50	25.00
—Direct-to-disc recording					
WARNER BROS.					
BS 2616	Bump City	1972	3.75	7.50	15.00
—Green "WB" label					
BS 2681	Tower of Power	1973	3.75	7.50	15.00
—Green "WB" label					
BS 2681	Tower of Power	1973	3.00	6.00	12.00
—"Burbank" palm trees label					
BS 2681	Tower of Power	1979	2.00	4.00	8.00
—White or tan label					
BS 2749	Back to Oakland	1974	3.75	7.50	15.00
—"Burbank" palm trees label					
BS 2749	Back to Oakland	1979	2.00	4.00	8.00
—White or tan label					
BS 2834	Urban Renewal	1975	3.75	7.50	15.00
—"Burbank" palm trees label					
BS 2880	In the Slot	1975	3.75	7.50	15.00
—"Burbank" palm trees label					
BS 2924	Live and In Living Color	1976	3.75	7.50	15.00
—"Burbank" palm trees label					
BS 2924	Live and In Living Color	1979	2.00	4.00	8.00
—White or tan label					

TOWNSEND, BOB

45s

Number	Title (A Side/B Side)	Yr	VG	VG+	NM
MINARET					
106	Christmas Message From Space/The Night Before New Year's	1962	2.50	5.00	10.00

TOWNSEND, ED

45s

Number	Title (A Side/B Side)	Yr	VG	VG+	NM
ALADDIN					
3373	Every Night/Love Never Dies	1957	6.25	12.50	25.00
CAPITOL					
F3926	For Your Love/Over and Over Again	1958	3.75	7.50	15.00
F3994	What Shall I Do/Please Never Change	1958	3.00	6.00	12.00
F4048	When I Grow Too Old to Dream/You Are My Everything	1958	3.00	6.00	12.00
F4104	Richer Than I/Getting By Without You	1958	3.00	6.00	12.00
F4171	Don't Ever Leave Me/Lover Come Back to Me	1959	3.00	6.00	12.00
F4240	This Little Love of Mine/Hold On	1959	3.00	6.00	12.00
4314	Be My Love/With No One to Love	1959	3.00	6.00	12.00
CHALLENGE					
9118	Ed Townsend's Boogie Woogie (Part 1)/Ed Townsend's Boogie Woogie (Part 2)	1961	3.00	6.00	12.00
9129	And Then Came Love/Little Bitty Dave	1961	3.00	6.00	12.00
9144	You Walked In/I Love to Hear That Best	1962	3.00	6.00	12.00
DOT					
15596	Tall Grows the Sycamore/My Need for You	1957	5.00	10.00	20.00
LIBERTY					
55516	Tell Her/Down Home	1962	3.00	6.00	12.00
55516	Tell Her/Hard Way to Go	1962	3.00	6.00	12.00
55542	That's What I Get for Loving You/There's No End	1963	3.00	6.00	12.00
MAXX					
325	I Love You/I Might Like It	1964	2.50	5.00	10.00
MGM					
13784	Mommy's Never Comin' Back Again/Who Would Deny Me	1967	2.50	5.00	10.00

Number	Title (A Side/B Side)	Yr	VG	VG+	NM
POLYDOR					
14021	No/Color Me Human	1970	—	3.00	6.00
WARNER BROS.					
5174	Stay with Me/I Love Everything About You	1960	3.00	6.00	12.00
5200	Cherrigale/Dream World	1961	3.00	6.00	12.00
Albums					
CAPITOL					
ST 1140 [S]	New in Town	1959	7.50	15.00	30.00
T 1140 [M]	New in Town	1959	6.25	12.50	25.00
ST 1214 [S]	Glad to Be Here	1959	7.50	15.00	30.00
T 1214 [M]	Glad to Be Here	1959	6.25	12.50	25.00
CURTOM					
5006	Ed Townsend Now	1976	3.00	6.00	12.00

TOWNSEND, HENRY

Number	Title (A Side/B Side)	Yr	VG	VG+	NM
Albums					
BLUESVILLE					
BVLP-1041 [M]	Tired Bein' Mistreated	1962	30.00	60.00	120.00
—Blue label, silver print					
BVLP-1041 [M]	Tired Bein' Mistreated	1964	7.50	15.00	30.00
—Blue label, trident logo at side					

TOWNSEND, SHERRELL

Number	Title (A Side/B Side)	Yr	VG	VG+	NM
45s					
GONE					
5135	He Thinks I Still Care/Glass of Tears	1962	5.00	10.00	20.00
LITTLE STAR					
115	I Love You Alone/Summer Days Are Here	1962	10.00	20.00	40.00
LUTE					
6015	I Love You Alone/Summer Days Are Here	1961	7.50	15.00	30.00

TOWNSHEND, PETE

Also see THE WHO.

Number	Title (A Side/B Side)	Yr	VG	VG+	NM
12-Inch Singles					
ATCO					
PR 804 [DJ]	Face the Face (long and short)/Hiding Out	1985	3.75	7.50	15.00
PR 863 [DJ]	Secondhand Love (same on both sides)	1985	2.00	4.00	8.00
96833	Face the Face (6:08)/Won't Get Fooled Again (Live)	1985	—	3.50	7.00
45s					
ATCO					
7217	Let My Love Open the Door/And I Moved	1980	—	2.00	4.00
7312	A Little Is Enough/Cat's in a Cupboard	1980	—	2.00	4.00
7318	Rough Boys/Jools and Jim	1980	—	2.00	4.00
99499	Barefootin'/Behind Blue Eyes	1986	—	—	3.00
99499 [PS]	Barefootin'/Behind Blue Eyes	1986	—	2.00	4.00
99553	Secondhand Love/White City Fighting	1986	—	—	3.00
99577	Give Blood/Magic Bus	1986	—	—	3.00
99577 [PS]	Give Blood/Magic Bus	1986	—	—	3.00
99590	Face the Face/Hiding Out	1985	—	—	3.00
99590 [PS]	Face the Face/Hiding Out	1985	—	—	3.00
99884	Bargain/Dirty Water	1983	—	2.00	4.00
99884 [PS]	Bargain/Dirty Water	1983	—	2.00	4.00
99973	Slit Skirts/Uniforms	1982	—	2.00	4.00
99989	Face Dances Part Two/Man Watching	1982	—	2.00	4.00
99989 [PS]	Face Dances Part Two/Man Watching	1982	—	2.00	4.00
ATLANTIC					
88875	A Friend Is a Friend/Man Machines	1989	—	—	3.00
88875 [PS]	A Friend Is a Friend/Man Machines	1989	—	—	3.00
Albums					
ATCO					
SD 32-100	Empty Glass	1980	2.50	5.00	10.00
SD 38-149	All the Best Cowboys Have Chinese Eyes	1982	2.50	5.00	10.00
PR 940 [RP]	Deep End Sampler	1986	5.00	10.00	20.00
—Promo-only sampler from Deep End Live					
90063 [(2)]	Scoop	1983	3.00	6.00	12.00
90473	White City — A Novel	1985	2.50	5.00	10.00
90539 [(2)]	Another Scoop	1987	3.00	6.00	12.00
90553	Pete Townshend's Deep End Live!	1986	2.50	5.00	10.00
ATLANTIC					
81996	The Iron Man: The Musical by Pete Townshend	1989	2.50	5.00	10.00
—Also includes tracks by John Lee Hooker, Simon Townshend, Nina Simone, The Who					
DECCA					
79189	Who Came First	1972	5.00	10.00	20.00
—With poster (deduct 50% if missing). Evidently a near-simultaneous release with Track 79189					
MCA					
2026	Who Came First	1973	3.00	6.00	12.00
—Reissue of 79189					
TRACK					
PR-A-160 [DJ]	Pete Townshend Talks To and About Thunderclap Newman	1970	25.00	50.00	100.00
—One-sided promo-only interview record					
79189	Who Came First	1972	5.00	10.00	20.00
—With poster (deduct 50% if missing)					

TOWNSHEND, PETE, AND RONNIE LANE

Also see each artist's individual listings.

Number	Title (A Side/B Side)	Yr	VG	VG+	NM
45s					
MCA					
40818	My Baby Gives It Away/April Fool	1977	—	2.00	4.00
40878	Nowhere to Run/Keep Me Turning	1978	—	2.00	4.00
Albums					
ATCO					
90097	Rough Mix	1983	2.00	4.00	8.00
—Reissue of MCA LP					
MCA					
2295	Rough Mix	1977	2.50	5.00	10.00

TOWNSMEN, THE

Number	Title (A Side/B Side)	Yr	VG	VG+	NM
45s					
CARDINAL					
1022	Pretty Patricia/(B-side unknown)	195?	3.75	7.50	15.00
COLUMBIA					
43207	Please Don't Say Goodbye/Gotta Get Moving	1965	2.50	5.00	10.00
HERALD					
585	Is It All Over/Just a Little Bit	1963	3.75	7.50	15.00
JOEY					
6202	Moonlight Was Made for Lovers/I'm in the Mood for Love	1963	6.25	12.50	25.00
PJ					
1341	That's All I'll Ever Need/I Can't Let Go	1963	50.00	100.00	200.00
VANITY					
579/80	It's Time/Little Jeanie	1960	5.00	10.00	20.00
WARNER BROS.					
5190	You're Having the Last Dance with Me/Gloria's Theme from "Butterfield-8"	1960	3.00	6.00	12.00

TOYS, THE

Number	Title (A Side/B Side)	Yr	VG	VG+	NM
45s					
DYNO VOICE					
209	A Lover's Concerto/This Night	1965	3.00	6.00	12.00
214	Attack/See How They Run	1965	2.50	5.00	10.00
218	My My Heart Be Cast Into Stone/On Backstreet	1966	2.50	5.00	10.00
219	Can't Get Enough of You Baby/Silver Spoon	1966	2.50	5.00	10.00
222	Baby Toys/Happy Birthday Broken Heart	1966	2.50	5.00	10.00
MUSICOR					
1300	You Got It Baby/You've Got to Give Her Love	1968	2.00	4.00	8.00
1319	Sealed with a Kiss/I Got My Heart Set on You	1968	2.00	4.00	8.00
PHILIPS					
40432	Ciao Baby/I Got Carried Away	1967	2.50	5.00	10.00
40456	My Love Sonata/I Close My Eyes	1967	2.50	5.00	10.00
Albums					
DYNOVOICE					
9002 [M]	The Toys Sing "A Lover's Concerto" and "Attack!"	1966	10.00	20.00	40.00
S-9002 [P]	The Toys Sing "A Lover's Concerto" and "Attack!"	1966	12.50	25.00	50.00

TRACERS, THE

Number	Title (A Side/B Side)	Yr	VG	VG+	NM
45s					
SULLY					
928	She Said Yeah/Watch Me	1966	6.25	12.50	25.00
—Originally released under the name "The Stones"					

TRACEY, WREG

Number	Title (A Side/B Side)	Yr	VG	VG+	NM
45s					
ANNA					
1105	All I Want Is You/Take Me Back	1959	10.00	20.00	40.00
1126	All I Want for Christmas (Is Your Love)/Take Me Back	1960	10.00	20.00	40.00

TRACEY TWINS, THE

Number	Title (A Side/B Side)	Yr	VG	VG+	NM
45s					
EASTWEST					
108	Heartbreak Hill/Don't Mean Maybe Baby	1958	5.00	10.00	20.00
EPIC					
9230	Kissin' Diploma/Because We Are Young	1957	5.00	10.00	20.00
RESERVE					
110	Tonight You Belong to Me/(B-side unknown)	1956	6.25	12.50	25.00
114	Do You Ever Think of Me/(B-side unknown)	195?	6.25	12.50	25.00

TRACY, BILL

Number	Title (A Side/B Side)	Yr	VG	VG+	NM
45s					
DEL-FI					
4124	You're My Girl/Tops to Summer	1959	5.00	10.00	20.00
4132	I'm So Happy/January Love	1959	5.00	10.00	20.00
DOT					
15797	One Chance/Hold Me, Thrill Me, Kiss Me	1958	15.00	30.00	60.00
15868	Flame Out/Disappointed	1958	10.00	20.00	40.00
RADIANT					
1504	High School Hero/Lost Love	1961	3.75	7.50	15.00
RPM					
489	Kiss at Daybreak/No One But You	1957	10.00	20.00	40.00

TRADE WINDS, THE

Number	Title (A Side/B Side)	Yr	VG	VG+	NM
45s					
KAMA SUTRA					
212	Mind Excursion/Little Susan's Dreamin'	1966	3.00	6.00	12.00
218	I Believe in Her/Catch Me in the Meadow	1966	3.00	6.00	12.00
234	Mind Excursion/Only When I'm Dreamin'	1967	3.00	6.00	12.00
RED BIRD					
10-020	New York's a Lonely Town/Club Seventeen	1965	5.00	10.00	20.00
10-028	Girl from Greenwich Village/There's a Rock and Roll Show in Town	1965	5.00	10.00	20.00
10-033	Summertime Girl/The Party Starts at Nine	1965	10.00	20.00	40.00
Albums					
KAMA SUTRA					
KLP-8057 [M]	Excursions	1967	6.25	12.50	25.00
KSLP-8057 [S]	Excursions	1967	7.50	15.00	30.00

TRADER HORNE

Number	Title (A Side/B Side)	Yr	VG	VG+	NM
Albums					
JANUS					
JLS-3012	Morning Way	1970	7.50	15.00	30.00

TRADEWINDS, THE

Number	Title (A Side/B Side)	Yr	VG	VG+	NM
45s					
DAWN CORY					
1005	Surfin' Thunder/Gotcha	196?	20.00	40.00	80.00

Number	Title (A Side/B Side)	Yr	VG	VG+	NM
RCA VICTOR					
47-7511	Toni/Twins	1959	5.00	10.00	20.00
47-7553	Crossroads/Furry Murry	1959	5.00	10.00	20.00

TRAFFIC

Also see JIM CAPALDI; DAVE MASON; STEVE WINWOOD.

45s

Number	Title (A Side/B Side)	Yr	VG	VG+	NM
ASYLUM					
45207	Walking in the Wind/(Instrumental)	1974	—	2.50	5.00
—Also see "Capaldi, Jim"; "Mason, Dave"; "Winwood, Steve"					
ISLAND					
1201	Rock and Roll Stew (Part 1)/Rock and Roll Stew (Part 2)	1972	—	2.50	5.00
UNITED ARTISTS					
0129	Paper Sun/Empty Pages	1973	—	2.00	4.00
—"Silver Spotlight Series" reissue					
1694	Feelin' Alright?/You Can All Join In	197?	—	2.50	5.00
—"Silver Spotlight Series" reissue					
50195	Paper Sun/Giving to You	1967	2.50	5.00	10.00
50218	Hole in My Shoe/Smiling Phases	1967	2.50	5.00	10.00
50232	Here We Go 'Round the Mulberry Bush/Coloured Rain	1967	2.50	5.00	10.00
50261	Heaven Is In Your Mind/No Face, No Name and No Number	1968	2.00	4.00	8.00
50460	Feelin' Alright?/Withering Tree	1968	2.00	4.00	8.00
50500	Medicated Goo/Pearly Queen	1969	—	3.00	6.00
50692	Empty Pages/Stranger to Himself	1970	—	3.00	6.00
50841	Gimme Some Lovin' (Part 1)/Gimme Some Lovin' (Part 2)	1971	—	3.00	6.00
—By "Traffic, Etc."					
50883	Glad (Part 1)/Glad (Part 2)	1972	—	3.00	6.00
VIRGIN					
S7-17971	Here Comes a Man (Rock Mix)/Glad (Live)	1994	—	2.00	4.00
S7-18134	Some Kinda Woman/Forty Thousand Headmen (Live)	1994	—	2.00	4.00

Albums

Number	Title (A Side/B Side)	Yr	VG	VG+	NM
ASYLUM					
7E-1020	When the Eagle Flies	1974	3.00	6.00	12.00
ISLAND					
ILSD 2 [(2)]	Traffic — On the Road	197?	3.75	7.50	15.00
—Reissue					
ILPS 9180	The Low Spark of High Heeled Boys	197?	3.00	6.00	12.00
—Reissue					
ILPS 9224	Shoot Out at the Fantasy Factory	197?	3.00	6.00	12.00
—Reissue					
SW-9306	The Low Spark of High Heeled Boys	1971	3.75	7.50	15.00
SW-9323	Shoot Out at the Fantasy Factory	1973	3.75	7.50	15.00
SMAS-9336 [(2)]	Traffic — On the Road	1973	5.00	10.00	20.00
90026	The Low Spark of High Heeled Boys	1983	2.00	4.00	8.00
—Reissue					
90027	Shoot Out at the Fantasy Factory	1983	2.00	4.00	8.00
—Reissue					
90028 [(2)]	Traffic — On the Road	1983	3.00	6.00	12.00
—Reissue					
90058	John Barleycorn Must Die	1983	2.00	4.00	8.00
—Reissue					
90059	Traffic	1983	2.00	4.00	8.00
—Reissue					
90060	Mr. Fantasy	1983	2.00	4.00	8.00
—Reissue					
MOBILE FIDELITY					
1-209	The Low Spark of High Heeled Boys	1994	6.25	12.50	25.00
—Audiophile vinyl					
UNITED ARTISTS					
UA-LA421-G	Heavy Traffic	1975	3.75	7.50	15.00
UA-LA526-G	More Heavy Traffic	1975	3.75	7.50	15.00
UAL-3651 [M]	Heaven Is In Your Mind	1967	15.00	30.00	60.00
UAS-5500	Best of Traffic	1969	5.00	10.00	20.00
—Originals have pink and orange labels					
UAS-5504	John Barleycorn Must Die	1970	5.00	10.00	20.00
—Originals have black and orange labels					
UAS-5550	Welcome to the Canteen	1971	3.75	7.50	15.00
UAS-6651 [S]	Heaven Is In Your Mind	1967	12.50	25.00	50.00
UAS-6651 [S]	Mr. Fantasy	1968	8.75	17.50	35.00
—Retitled version of "Heaven Is In Your Mind" with old title still on back cover					
UAS-6651 [S]	Mr. Fantasy	1968	6.25	12.50	25.00
—Retitled version of "Heaven Is In Your Mind" with green strip across top of back with song titles					
UAS-6676	Traffic	1968	5.00	10.00	20.00
—Originals have purple and orange labels					
UAS-6702	Last Exit	1969	5.00	10.00	20.00
—Originals have purple and orange labels					

TRAILER, REX, AND THE PLAYBOYS

Albums

Number	Title (A Side/B Side)	Yr	VG	VG+	NM
CROWN					
CLP-5158 [M]	Country & Western	1958	6.25	12.50	25.00

TRAITS, THE

Also see ROY HEAD.

45s

Number	Title (A Side/B Side)	Yr	VG	VG+	NM
ASCOT					
2108	Linda Lou/Little Mama	1962	7.50	15.00	30.00
PACEMAKER					
254	Too Good to Be True/Gotta Keep Cool	1967	5.00	10.00	20.00
RENNER					
221	Linda Lou/Little Mama	1962	10.00	20.00	40.00
229	Got My Mojo Working/Woe Woe	1962	6.25	12.50	25.00
—Black vinyl					
229 [DJ]	Got My Mojo Working/Woe Woe	1962	10.00	20.00	40.00
—Promo only on colored vinyl					
SCEPTER					
12169	Harlem Shuffle/Strange Lips Start Old Memories	1966	2.00	4.00	8.00
TNT					
164	One More Time/Don't Be Blue	1959	5.00	10.00	20.00
—Later reissued on TNT 194 credited to "Roy Head"					
175	Live It Up/Yes I Do	1960	5.00	10.00	20.00
177	My Baby's Fine/Here I Am in Love Again	1960	5.00	10.00	20.00
181	Summer Time Love/Your Turn to Cry	1960	5.00	10.00	20.00
185	Night Time Blues/Walking All Day	1961	5.00	10.00	20.00
UNIVERSAL					
30494	Harlem Shuffle/Strange Lips Start Old Memories	1966	7.50	15.00	30.00

TRAMLINE

Albums

Number	Title (A Side/B Side)	Yr	VG	VG+	NM
A&M					
SP-4208	Somewhere Down the Line	1969	5.00	10.00	20.00

TRAMMELL, BOBBY LEE

45s

Number	Title (A Side/B Side)	Yr	VG	VG+	NM
ABC-PARAMOUNT					
9890	Shirley Lee/I Sure Do Love You Baby	1958	20.00	40.00	80.00
ALLEY					
1001	It's All Your Fault/Arkansas Twist	1962	6.25	12.50	25.00
1004	Come On Baby/I Tried Not to Cry	1963	6.25	12.50	25.00
ATLANTIC					
2332	Shimmy Loo/You Make Me Feel So Fine	1966	3.00	6.00	12.00
CAPITOL					
3718	Love Don't Let Me Down/I Couldn't Believe My Eyes	1973	2.00	4.00	8.00
3801	You Mostest Girl/You Stand a Chance of Losing What You've Got	1973	2.00	4.00	8.00
FABOR					
127	You Mostest Girl/Uh Oh	1964	3.00	6.00	12.00
4038	Shirley Lee/I Sure Do Love You Baby	1957	37.50	75.00	150.00
RADIO					
102	You Mostest Girl/Uh Oh	1958	12.50	25.00	50.00
114	My Susie Jane/Should I Make Amends	1958	10.00	20.00	40.00
SANTO					
9052	Hi-O Silver/Don't You Know I Love You	196?	5.00	10.00	20.00
SIMS					
183	Good Lovin'/New Dance in France	1964	3.00	6.00	12.00
195	Come On and Love Me/If You Don't Wanna, You Don't Have To	1964	3.00	6.00	12.00
225	Twenty-Four Hours/Just Let Me Move You One More Time	1965	3.00	6.00	12.00
SKYLA					
1307	You Mostest Girl/Uh Oh	1961	3.75	7.50	15.00
SOUNCOT					
1100	I Dare America to Be Great/A Gift from God	1970	—	3.00	6.00
1104	24 Hours a Day/I Lost the Girl I Love Tonight	1970	—	3.00	6.00
1113	You Mostest Girl/Whole Lotta Shakin' Goin' On	1971	—	3.00	6.00
1119	My Shoes Keep Walkin' Back to You/Let's Wash the World and Make It Clean	1971	—	3.00	6.00
1128	Don't Let the Stars Get In Your Eyes/Sheila	1971	—	3.00	6.00
1130	You Were Worth the Wait/Wadin' in the Water	1972	—	3.00	6.00
1135	Love Isn't Love (Till You Give It Away)/Tell Me That You Want Me	1972	—	3.00	6.00
1143	I Believe in You/My Love Keeps Growing	1972	—	3.00	6.00
1145	You Put Love Back in My Heart/I Lost the Girl I Love Tonight	1972	—	3.00	6.00
SUN					
1135	Jenny Lee/It's All Your Fault	1977	—	3.00	6.00

Albums

Number	Title (A Side/B Side)	Yr	VG	VG+	NM
ATLANTA					
1503 [M]	Arkansas Twist	1962	250.00	500.00	1000.
SOUNCOT					
SC-1102	I Dare America to Be Great	1971	5.00	10.00	20.00
SC-1141	Love Isn't Love Till You Give It Away	1972	3.75	7.50	15.00

TRAMMPS, THE

Also see THE VOLCANOS.

12-Inch Singles

Number	Title (A Side/B Side)	Yr	VG	VG+	NM
ATLANTIC					
PR 102 [DJ]	The Night the Lights Went Out (same on both sides)	1977	3.00	6.00	12.00
PR 139 [DJ]	Soul Bones/Love Magnet	1978	3.00	6.00	12.00
PR 170 [DJ]	Teaser/Life Insurance Policy	1979	3.00	6.00	12.00
DSKO 173	The Night the Lights Went Out (7:06)/Hooked for Life (4:40)	1977	3.75	7.50	15.00
PR 224 [DJ]	Hard Rock and Disco (same on both sides)	1980	3.00	6.00	12.00
PR 251 [DJ]	Looking for You/Mellow Out	1980	3.00	6.00	12.00
VENTURE					
5024	Up on the Hill (Mt. U)	1983	—	3.50	7.00

45s

Number	Title (A Side/B Side)	Yr	VG	VG+	NM
ATLANTIC					
3286	Hooked for Life/I'm Alright	1975	—	2.50	5.00
3306	That's Where the Happy People Go (Short)/That's Where the Happy People Go (Long)	1975	—	2.50	5.00
3345	Soul Searchin' Time/Love Is a Funky Thing	1976	—	2.50	5.00
3365	Ninety-Nine and a Half (Won't Do)/Can We Come Together	1976	—	2.50	5.00
3389	Disco Inferno/You Touch My Hot Line	1977	—	3.00	6.00
3389	Disco Inferno/That's Where the Happy People Go	1978	—	2.50	5.00
—Reissue in conjunction with the success of "Saturday Night Fever"					
3389 [PS]	Disco Inferno/You Touch My Hot Line	1977	2.00	4.00	8.00
3403	I Feel Like I've Been Livin' (On the Dark Side of the Moon)/Don't Burn Bridges	1977	—	2.50	5.00
3442	The Night the Lights Went Out/I'm So Glad You Came Along	1977	—	2.50	5.00
3460	Seasons for Girls/Love Ain't Been Easy	1978	—	2.50	5.00
3460	Seasons for Girls/Body Contact Contract	1978	—	2.50	5.00
3537	Soul Bones/Love Magnet	1978	—	2.50	5.00
3573	More Good Times to Remember/Teaser	1979	—	2.50	5.00
3654	Dance Contest/Hard Rock and Disco	1980	—	2.00	4.00

Number	Title (A Side/B Side)	Yr	VG	VG+	NM
3669	Music Freek/V.I.P.	1980	—	2.00	4.00
3777	Mellow Out/Looking for You	1980	—	2.00	4.00
3797	I Don't Want to Ever Lose Your Love/Breathtaking View	1981	—	2.00	4.00
BUDDAH					
306	Zing Went the Strings of My Heart/Penguin at the Big Apple	1972	2.50	5.00	10.00
—As "Tramps"					
306	Zing Went the Strings of My Heart/Penguin at the Big Apple	1972	—	3.00	6.00
—As "Trammps"					
321	Sixty Minute Man/Scrub Board	1972	—	3.00	6.00
339	Rubber Band/Pray All You Sinners	1973	—	3.00	6.00
507	Hold Back the Night/Tom's Song	1975	—	2.50	5.00
GOLDEN FLEECE					
3251	Love Epidemic/I Know That Feeling	1973	—	3.00	6.00
3253	Where Do We Go from Here/Shout	1974	—	3.00	6.00
3255	Trusting Heart/Down These Dark Streets	1974	—	3.00	6.00
Albums					
ATLANTIC					
SD 18172	Where the Happy People Go	1976	2.50	5.00	10.00
SD 18211	Disco Inferno	1977	2.50	5.00	10.00
SD 19148	The Trammps III	1977	2.50	5.00	10.00
SD 19194	The Best of the Trammps	1978	2.50	5.00	10.00
SD 19210	The Whole World's Dancing	1979	2.50	5.00	10.00
SD 19267	Mixin' It Up	1980	2.50	5.00	10.00
SD 19290	Slipping Out	1981	2.50	5.00	10.00
BUDDAH					
BDS-5641	The Legendary Zing Album Featuring the Fabulous Trammps	1975	3.00	6.00	12.00
GOLDEN FLEECE					
KZ 33163	Trammps	1975	2.50	5.00	10.00
PHILADELPHIA INT'L.					
PZ 33163	Disco Champs	1977	2.00	4.00	8.00
—Reissue of Golden Fleece LP					

TRANQUILS, THE

45s

Number	Title (A Side/B Side)	Yr	VG	VG+	NM
HAMILTON					
50005	You're Such a Much/One Billion, Seven Million and Thirty-Three	1959	7.50	15.00	30.00

TRANSIENTS, THE

Albums

Number	Title (A Side/B Side)	Yr	VG	VG+	NM
HORIZON					
WP-1633 [M]	The Funky 12 String Guitar	1963	5.00	10.00	20.00
WPS-1633 [S]	The Funky 12 String Guitar	1963	6.25	12.50	25.00

TRAPEZE

45s

Number	Title (A Side/B Side)	Yr	VG	VG+	NM
THRESHOLD					
67001	Send Me No More Letters/Another Day	1970	2.00	4.00	8.00
67005 [DJ]	Black Cloud (mono/stereo)	1971	2.50	5.00	10.00
67011	Coast to Coast/Your Love Is Alright	1972	2.00	4.00	8.00
Albums					
PAID					
2003	Hold On	1981	2.50	5.00	10.00
THRESHOLD					
THS 2	Trapeze	1970	10.00	20.00	40.00
THS 4	Medusa	1971	20.00	40.00	80.00
THS 8	You Are the Music, We're Just the Band	1972	10.00	20.00	40.00
THS 11	The Final Swing	1974	10.00	20.00	40.00
WARNER BROS.					
BS 2828	Hot Wire	1974	3.00	6.00	12.00
BS 2887	Trapeze	1975	3.00	6.00	12.00

TRASH

45s

Number	Title (A Side/B Side)	Yr	VG	VG+	NM
APPLE					
1804	Road to Nowhere/Illusions	1969	25.00	50.00	100.00
—With star on A-side label					
1804	Road to Nowhere/Illusions	1969	12.50	25.00	50.00
—Without star on A-side label					
1811	Golden Slumbers-Carry That Weight/Trash Can	1969	3.75	7.50	15.00
—A-side listed as "Golden Slumbers/Carry That Weight"					
1811	Golden Slumbers-Carry That Weight/Trash Can	1969	5.00	10.00	20.00
—A-side listed as "Golden Slumbers and Carry That Weight"					
1811	Golden Slumbers-Carry That Weight/Trash Can	1969	5.00	10.00	20.00
—A-side listed as "Golden Slumbers Carry That Weight"					
PRO-4671/2	Road to Nowhere (Edit)/Road to Nowhere	1969	20.00	40.00	80.00

TRASHMEN, THE

45s

Number	Title (A Side/B Side)	Yr	VG	VG+	NM
ARGO					
5516	Bird '65/Ubangi Stomp	1965	12.50	25.00	50.00
BEAR					
1966	Keep Your Hands Off My Baby/Lost Angel	1965	5.00	10.00	20.00
ERA BACK TO BACK HITS					
016	Liar, Liar/Surfin' Bird	197?	—	2.50	5.00
—B-side by the Castaways					
ERIC					
247	Surfin' Bird/Liar, Liar	197?	—	2.50	5.00
—B-side by the Castaways; reissue					
GARRETT					
4002	Surfin' Bird/King of the Surf	1963	7.50	15.00	30.00
4003	Bird Dance Beat/A-Bone	1964	5.00	10.00	20.00
4005	Bad News/On the Move	1964	5.00	10.00	20.00
4010	Peppermint Man/New Generation	1964	5.00	10.00	20.00
4012	Whoa Dad/Walkin' My Baby	1964	5.00	10.00	20.00
4012 [PS]	Whoa Dad/Walkin' My Baby	1964	62.50	125.00	250.00
4013	Dancing with Santa/Real Live Doll	1964	6.25	12.50	25.00
4013 [PS]	Dancing with Santa/Real Live Doll	1964	62.50	125.00	250.00
GET HIP					
2	Well All Right/That's What They Say	1994	—	2.00	4.00
METROBEAT					
7927	Green, Green Backs of Home/Address Enclosed	1968	3.75	7.50	15.00
OLDIES 45					
301	Surfin' Bird/King of the Surf	1965	3.00	6.00	12.00
—Early reissue					
SOMA					
1469	Surfin' Bird/Liar, Liar	1966	3.00	6.00	12.00
—B-side by the Castaways					
SUNDAZED					
102	Henrietta/Rumble	1995	—	—	2.00
102 [PS]	Henrietta/Rumble	1995	—	—	2.00
103	Lucille/Green Onions	1995	—	—	2.00
103 [PS]	Lucille/Green Onions	1995	—	—	2.00
104	Roll Over Beethoven/Betty Jean	1995	—	—	2.00
104 [PS]	Roll Over Beethoven/Betty Jean	1995	—	—	2.00
112	Dancing with Santa/Real Live Doll	1996	—	—	2.00
—Red vinyl					
112 [PS]	Dancing with Santa/Real Live Doll	1996	—	—	2.00
TERRIFIC					
5003	Surfin' Bird/Bird Dance Beat	196?	2.50	5.00	10.00
—Early reissue					
TRIBE					
8315	Hanging On Me/Some Lies	1966	6.25	12.50	25.00
Albums					
BEAT ROCKET					
BR 107	Surfin' Bird	1999	3.00	6.00	12.00
—Reissue on 180-gram vinyl					
GARRETT					
GA-200 [M]	Surfin' Bird	1964	55.00	110.00	220.00
GAS-200 [R]	Surfin' Bird	1964	87.50	175.00	350.00
SUNDAZED					
LP 5002	Live Bird '65-'67	1991	2.50	5.00	10.00
LP 5003	Great Lost Album	1991	2.50	5.00	10.00

TRAVELERS, THE

Probably more than one group.

45s

Number	Title (A Side/B Side)	Yr	VG	VG+	NM
ABC-PARAMOUNT					
10119	June, July, August and September/What a Weekend	1960	5.00	10.00	20.00
ANDEX					
2011	I'll Be Home for Christmas/Katie the Kangaroo	1958	7.50	15.00	30.00
4033	I Go for You/I'll Always Be in Love with You	1959	7.50	15.00	30.00
34006	Why/Teenage Machine Age	1957	7.50	15.00	30.00
34012	He's Got the Whole World in His Hands/Green Town Girl	1957	7.50	15.00	30.00
DECCA					
31215	Ivy on the Old School Wall/Cadwallader 0002	1961	10.00	20.00	40.00
31282	White Rose/Oh My Love (Love Me)	1961	10.00	20.00	40.00
DON RAY					
5965	Traveler/Seven Minutes Till Four	1963	12.50	25.00	50.00
MAGIC LAMP					
516	Big House/Goin' Home	1964	3.00	6.00	12.00
VAULT					
911	Spanish Moon/She's Got the Blues	1964	3.75	7.50	15.00
YELLOW SAND					
2	Windy and Warm/Last Date	1963	12.50	25.00	50.00
451	Groovy/(B-side unknown)	1965	7.50	15.00	30.00
452	Malibu Sunset/Hang On	1965	7.50	15.00	30.00

TRAVELING SALESMEN

45s

Number	Title (A Side/B Side)	Yr	VG	VG+	NM
RCA VICTOR					
47-9167	I'm Alive/Days of My Years	1967	5.00	10.00	20.00

TRAVELLERS, THE

45s

Number	Title (A Side/B Side)	Yr	VG	VG+	NM
GASS					
1000	Tie Me Surfer Board Down, Sport/In the Pines	1963	10.00	20.00	40.00

TRAVERS, MARY

Also see PETER, PAUL AND MARY.

45s

Number	Title (A Side/B Side)	Yr	VG	VG+	NM
CHRYSALIS					
2202	The Air That I Breathe/You Turn Me Around	1977	—	2.50	5.00
2367	Freedom/(B-side unknown)	1979	—	2.00	4.00
WARNER BROS.					
7481	Follow Me/I Guess He'd Rather Be in Colorado	1971	—	2.50	5.00
7517	The Song Is Love/Ericka with the Windy Yellow Hair	1971	—	2.50	5.00
7588	Morning Glory/That's Enough for Me	1972	—	2.50	5.00
7675	Too Many Mondays/That Year There Was No Winter	1972	—	2.50	5.00
7731	Five Hundred Miles/Oh, What a Feeling	1973	—	2.50	5.00
7790	Circles/I'll Have to Say I Love You in a Song	1974	—	2.50	5.00
Albums					
CHRYSALIS					
CHR 1168	It's In Everyone of Us	1978	2.50	5.00	10.00
WARNER BROS.					
WS 1907	Mary	1971	3.00	6.00	12.00
—Green "WB" label					
BS 2609	Morning Glory	1972	3.00	6.00	12.00
—Green "WB" label					
BS 2677	All My Choices	1973	3.00	6.00	12.00
—Green "WB" label					
BS 2795	Circles	1974	3.00	6.00	12.00
—"Burbank" palm-trees label					

TRAVIS AND BOB

Number	Title (A Side/B Side)	Yr	VG	VG+	NM
45s					
BIG TOP					
3054	Pocahontas/Day Dreams	1960	3.75	7.50	15.00
MERCURY					
71797	Give Your Love to Me/Stay Close to Me	1961	3.75	7.50	15.00
71866	The Spider and the Fly/What a Change	1961	3.75	7.50	15.00
SANDY					
1017	Tell Him No/We're Too Young	1959	6.25	12.50	25.00
—With no mention of Dot Records on label					
1017	Tell Him No/We're Too Young	1959	5.00	10.00	20.00
—With Dot Records distribution mentioned on label					
1019	Teenage Vision/Little Bitty Johnny	1959	5.00	10.00	20.00
1024	Lover's Rendezvous/Oh Yeah	1959	5.00	10.00	20.00
1029	That's How Long/Wake Up and Cry	1960	5.00	10.00	20.00

TRAYNOR, JAY

Also see JAY AND THE AMERICANS.

Number	Title (A Side/B Side)	Yr	VG	VG+	NM
45s					
ABC					
10809	Come On/The Merry-Go-Round Is Slowing You Down	1966	3.75	7.50	15.00
10845	Up and Over/Don't Let the End Begin	1966	7.50	15.00	30.00
CORAL					
62396	How Sweet It Is/I Rise, I Fall	1964	3.00	6.00	12.00
62420	I've Known You All My Life/Little Sister	1964	3.00	6.00	12.00

TREADWELL, IRENE

Number	Title (A Side/B Side)	Yr	VG	VG+	NM
45s					
JAY DEE					
782	Church Bells Are Ringing on Christmas Morning/Dear Santa Bring Back My Daddy to Me	1953	5.00	10.00	20.00

TREASURERS, THE

Number	Title (A Side/B Side)	Yr	VG	VG+	NM
45s					
CROWN					
005	Story of Love/I Walk with An Angel	1961	75.00	150.00	300.00

TREASURES, THE

Number	Title (A Side/B Side)	Yr	VG	VG+	NM
45s					
SHIRLEY					
500	Hold Me Tight/Pete Meets Vinnie	1964	7.50	15.00	30.00
VALOR					
(# unknown)	Minor Chaos/Valley of the Broken Hearts	1964	100.00	200.00	400.00
—Marbled vinyl					
(# unknown)	Minor Chaos/Valley of the Broken Hearts	1964	50.00	100.00	200.00
—Green vinyl					
(# unknown)	Minor Chaos/Valley of the Broken Hearts	1964	25.00	50.00	100.00
—Sources differ as to what the number of this record is, and we've never seen a copy, so we haven't listed one.					

TREBELAIRES, THE

Number	Title (A Side/B Side)	Yr	VG	VG+	NM
45s					
NESTOR					
16	There Goes That Train/I Gotta	1954	25.00	50.00	100.00

TREBLE CHORDS, THE

Number	Title (A Side/B Side)	Yr	VG	VG+	NM
45s					
DECCA					
31015	Teresa/My Little Girl	1959	25.00	50.00	100.00

TREE

Number	Title (A Side/B Side)	Yr	VG	VG+	NM
Albums					
GOAT FARM					
580	Tree	1970	17.50	35.00	70.00

TREMAINES, THE

Number	Title (A Side/B Side)	Yr	VG	VG+	NM
45s					
CASH					
100/1	Jingle, Jingle/Moon Shining Bright	1958	100.00	200.00	400.00
KANE					
008	Heavenly/Wonderful, Marvelous	1959	12.50	25.00	50.00
OLD TOWN					
1051	Jingle, Jingle/Moon Shining Bright	1958	12.50	25.00	50.00
V-TONE					
507	Heavenly/Wonderful, Marvelous	1959	6.25	12.50	25.00
VAL					
100/1	Jingle, Jingle/Moon Shining Bright	1958	62.50	125.00	250.00

TREMELOES, THE

Also see BRIAN POOLE AND THE TREMELOES.

Number	Title (A Side/B Side)	Yr	VG	VG+	NM
45s					
DJM					
1008	Hard Woman/My Friend Delaney	1976	—	2.50	5.00
1016	September, November, December/(B-side unknown)	1976	—	2.50	5.00
EPIC					
10075	Good Day Sunshine/What a State I'm In	1966	3.00	6.00	12.00
10139	Here Comes My Baby/Gentlemen of Pleasure	1967	2.50	5.00	10.00
10184	Silence Is Golden/Let Your Hair Hang Down	1967	2.50	5.00	10.00
10184 [PS]	Silence Is Golden/Let Your Hair Hang Down	1967	3.75	7.50	15.00
10233	Even the Bad Times Are Good/Jenny's All Right	1967	2.00	4.00	8.00
10233 [PS]	Even the Bad Times Are Good/Jenny's All Right	1967	3.75	7.50	15.00
10293	Suddenly You Love Me/Suddenly Winter	1968	2.00	4.00	8.00
10328	Girl from Nowhere/Helule, Helule	1968	2.00	4.00	8.00
10376	My Little Lady/All the World to Me	1968	2.00	4.00	8.00
10437	I Shall Be Released/I Miss My Baby	1969	2.00	4.00	8.00
10467	Up, Down, All Around/Hello World	1969	2.00	4.00	8.00
10548	(Call Me) Number One/Instant Whip	1969	2.00	4.00	8.00
10621	Breakheart Motel/By the Way	1970	2.50	5.00	10.00
10682	Try Me/Me and My Life	1970	2.00	4.00	8.00
10807	My Woman/Hello Buddy	1971	—	3.00	6.00
10996	Yodelay/Blue Suede Tie	1973	—	3.00	6.00
Albums					
DJM					
2	Shiner	1974	3.00	6.00	12.00
EPIC					
LN 24310 [M]	Here Comes My Baby	1967	7.50	15.00	30.00
LN 24326 [M]	Even the Bad Times Are Good	1967	6.25	12.50	25.00
LN 24363 [M]	Suddenly You Love Me	1968	7.50	15.00	30.00
BN 26310 [R]	Here Comes My Baby	1967	5.00	10.00	20.00
BN 26326 [P]	Even the Bad Times Are Good	1967	7.50	15.00	30.00
BN 26363 [R]	Suddenly You Love Me	1968	5.00	10.00	20.00
BN 26388 [S]	World Explosion '58/'68	1968	7.50	15.00	30.00

TREMELOS, THE

Number	Title (A Side/B Side)	Yr	VG	VG+	NM
45s					
ROCKLAND					
102	Jaguar/Fly	196?	12.50	25.00	50.00

TREMONTS, THE

Number	Title (A Side/B Side)	Yr	VG	VG+	NM
45s					
BRUNSWICK					
55217	Believe My Heart/Legend of Love	1961	7.50	15.00	30.00
PAT RICCIO					
101	Believe My Heart/Legend of Love	1961	25.00	50.00	100.00

TREN-DELLS, THE

Number	Title (A Side/B Side)	Yr	VG	VG+	NM
45s					
CAPITOL					
4852	Nite Owl/Hully Gully Jones	1962	3.00	6.00	12.00
JAM					
101	Nite Owl/Hully Gully Jones	1962	6.25	12.50	25.00
111	Hey Da-Da Dow/Tough Little Buggy	1962	6.25	12.50	25.00
SOUND STAGE 7					
2508	Mr. Doughnut Man/Ain't That Funny	1963	3.00	6.00	12.00
TILT					
779	I'm So Young/Don't You Hear Me Calling Baby	1961	7.50	15.00	30.00
—As "The Trend-Els"					
788	Moments Like This/I Miss You So	1962	7.50	15.00	30.00

TREN-TEENS, THE

Number	Title (A Side/B Side)	Yr	VG	VG+	NM
45s					
CARNIVAL					
501	My Baby's Gone/Your Yah Yah Is Gone	1964	25.00	50.00	100.00

TRENDS, THE (1)

Number	Title (A Side/B Side)	Yr	VG	VG+	NM
45s					
ABC					
10817	A Night for Love/Gonna Have to Show You	1966	6.25	12.50	25.00
10881	No One There/That's How I Like It	1966	6.25	12.50	25.00
10944	Check My Tears/Don't Drop Out of School	1967	5.00	10.00	20.00
10993	Thanks for a Little Lovin'/I Never Knew How Good I Had It	1967	5.00	10.00	20.00
11091	Soul Clap/Big Parade	1968	5.00	10.00	20.00
11150	Not Another Day/You Sure Know How to Hurt a Guy	1968	10.00	20.00	40.00
ABC-PARAMOUNT					
10731	Not Too Old to Cry/If You Don't Dig the Blues	1965	10.00	20.00	40.00
SMASH					
1914	Dance with My Baby/To Be Happy Enough	1964	6.25	12.50	25.00
1933	Get Something Going/That's the Way the Story Goes	1964	6.25	12.50	25.00

TRENDS, THE (2)

Number	Title (A Side/B Side)	Yr	VG	VG+	NM
45s					
ARGO					
5341	I'll Be True/Class Ring	1959	7.50	15.00	30.00
SCOPE					
102	Gone Again/Silly Grin	1959	20.00	40.00	80.00

TRENDS, THE (U)

Definitely not group (1), but it may not be group (2), either.

Number	Title (A Side/B Side)	Yr	VG	VG+	NM
45s					
RCA VICTOR					
47-7733	The Beard/Chug-a-Lug	1960	3.75	7.50	15.00

TRENIERS, THE

Number	Title (A Side/B Side)	Yr	VG	VG+	NM
45s					
BRUNSWICK					
55014	Holy Mackerel Andy/Rock Calypso Joe	1957	5.00	10.00	20.00
55033	Pennies from Heaven/Ooh-La-La	1957	5.00	10.00	20.00
55047	Goodnight Irene/Rubbing Noses in the Midnight Sun	1958	5.00	10.00	20.00
DOM					
410	Gotta Travel On/Let It All Hang Out	1968	2.00	4.00	8.00
DOT					
15882	Never Never/When Your Hair Has Turned to Silver	1958	5.00	10.00	20.00
EPIC					
9127	Go! Go! Go!/Doin' 'Em Up	1955	6.25	12.50	25.00
9144	Rock'n Roll Call/Day-Old Bread and Canned Beans	1956	6.25	12.50	25.00
9162	Boodie Green/Good Rockin' Tonight	1956	6.25	12.50	25.00
OKEH					
6804	Go! Go! Go!/Plenty of Money	1951	12.50	25.00	50.00
6826	Hey, Little Girl/Old Woman Blues	1951	10.00	20.00	40.00
6853	It Rocks, It Rolls, It Swings/Taxi Blues	1952	10.00	20.00	40.00
6876	Hadacol, That's All/Long Distance Blues	1952	10.00	20.00	40.00
6904	Rockin' on Sunday Night/Cheatin' On Me	1952	10.00	20.00	40.00

Number	Title (A Side/B Side)	Yr	VG	VG+	NM
6932	Hi-Yo Silver/Poon-Tang!	1953	10.00	20.00	40.00
6937	The Moondog/Poon-Tang!	1953	12.50	25.00	50.00
6960	Rockin' Is Our Bizness/Sugar Doo	1953	10.00	20.00	40.00
6984	I'd Do Nothin' But Grieve/This Is It	1953	10.00	20.00	40.00
7012	You Know, Yeah! Tiger/Bug Dance	1953	10.00	20.00	40.00
7023	Rock-a-Beatin' Boogie/Trapped	1954	10.00	20.00	40.00
7035	Bald Head/Come On Let's Face It	1954	10.00	20.00	40.00
7050	Who Put the "Ungh" in the Mambo/Get Out of the Car	1955	7.50	15.00	30.00
7057	Devil's Mambo/Do, Do, Do (Do-Be-Oo-Be-Oo)	1955	7.50	15.00	30.00
VIK					
0214	Lover Come Back to Me/Sorrento	1956	6.25	12.50	25.00
0227	Rock and Roll President/Cool It Baby	1956	6.25	12.50	25.00

7-Inch Extended Plays

Number	Title (A Side/B Side)	Yr	VG	VG+	NM
EPIC					
EG-7014	(contents unknown)	1955	12.50	25.00	50.00
EG-7014 [PS]	Go! Go! Go!	1955	12.50	25.00	50.00
EG-7114	(contents unknown)	195?	12.50	25.00	50.00
EG-7114 [PS]	Those Crazy Treniers	195?	12.50	25.00	50.00

Albums

Number	Title (A Side/B Side)	Yr	VG	VG+	NM
DOT					
DLP-3257 [M]	Souvenir Album	1960	25.00	50.00	100.00
EPIC					
LG 3125 [M]	The Treniers on TV	1955	50.00	100.00	200.00

TRENT, JACKIE

The record on Nasco may be by a different singer than the others.

45s

Number	Title (A Side/B Side)	Yr	VG	VG+	NM
A&M					
1022	Hollywood/Don't Send Me Away	1969	—	3.00	6.00
KAPP					
583	Only One Such As You/If You Love Me, Really Love Me	1964	3.00	6.00	12.00
630	Somewhere in the World/I Heard Someone Say	1964	3.00	6.00	12.00
NASCO					
6012	Little Andy/What's He Got	1958	6.25	12.50	25.00
—Is this the same Jackie Trent as the others? We don't know.					
PARKWAY					
941	Don't Stand in My Way/How Soon	1965	3.00	6.00	12.00
955	Where Are You Now My Love/On the Other Side of the Tracks	1965	3.00	6.00	12.00
963	To Show I Love Him/When Summertime Is Over	1965	3.00	6.00	12.00
WARNER BROS.					
5683	It's All in the Way You Look at Life/Time After Time	1965	2.50	5.00	10.00
5865	If You Ever Leave Me/Take Me Away	1966	2.50	5.00	10.00
7022	Hummingbird/I'll Be with You	1967	2.00	4.00	8.00
7070	It's Not Easy Loving You/Your Love Is Everywhere	1967	2.00	4.00	8.00
7178	7:10 to Suburbia/Stop Me and Buy One	1968	2.00	4.00	8.00
7189	I'll Be With You/Two of Us	1968	2.00	4.00	8.00

TRENTONS, THE

45s

Number	Title (A Side/B Side)	Yr	VG	VG+	NM
SHEPHERD					
2204	All Alone/Star Bright	1962	20.00	40.00	80.00

TREVOR, VAN

45s

Number	Title (A Side/B Side)	Yr	VG	VG+	NM
ATLANTIC					
2175	Tuesday Girl/I Want to Cry	1963	2.50	5.00	10.00
BAND BOX					
367	Born to Be in Love with You/It's So Good to Be Loved	1966	2.00	4.00	8.00
371	Our Side/When You've Lost Your Baby	1966	2.00	4.00	8.00
373 [DJ]	Christmas In The Country/PSA Announcements	1966	2.50	5.00	10.00
374	He's Losing His Mind/A Fool Called Me	1967	2.00	4.00	8.00
CANADIAN AMERICAN					
181	Louisiana Hot Sauce/Satisfaction Is Guaranteed	1964	5.00	10.00	20.00
188	The Girl from the Main Street Diner/For This Girl	1965	3.75	7.50	15.00
CLARIDGE					
305	Christmas in Washington Square/Melting Snow	1965	3.75	7.50	15.00
DATE					
1565	You've Been So Good to Me/Sunday Morning	1967	2.00	4.00	8.00
1594	Take Me Along with You/Guitar	1968	2.00	4.00	8.00
ROYAL AMERICAN					
3	Mercy Hospital/Something Missing in Me	1970	—	2.50	5.00
9	Luziana River/Sweet Diana	1970	—	2.50	5.00
23	Wish I Was Home Instead/Did I Have a Good Time	1970	—	2.50	5.00
31	Lonely Looking Woman/Johnnie and Annie	1971	—	2.50	5.00
280	The Things That Matter/Band of Gold	1969	—	3.00	6.00
283	A Man Away from Home/I've Got Today to Live For	1969	—	3.00	6.00
289	Funny Familiar Forgotten Feelings/Daddy's Little Man	1969	—	3.00	6.00
VIVID					
1004	C'mon Now Baby/Fling of the Past	1963	7.50	15.00	30.00
—Backing group is The Four Seasons					

Albums

Number	Title (A Side/B Side)	Yr	VG	VG+	NM
BAND BOX					
(# unknown)	Come On Over to Our Side	1967	5.00	10.00	20.00
DATE					
DES-4008	You've Been So Good to Me	1967	3.75	7.50	15.00
ROYAL AMERICAN					
2800	Funny Familiar Forgotten Feelings	1969	3.75	7.50	15.00

TREXLER, GARY

45s

Number	Title (A Side/B Side)	Yr	VG	VG+	NM
RCA VICTOR					
47-7258	I Flipped/Turn About	1958	3.75	7.50	15.00
47-7420	The Look/You Made Up for Everything	1958	3.75	7.50	15.00
REV					
3507	Teen Baby/Cloud Full of Tears	1957	5.00	10.00	20.00

TRIANGLE, THE

45s

Number	Title (A Side/B Side)	Yr	VG	VG+	NM
AMARET					
108	Music, Music, Music/Magic Touch	1969	2.50	5.00	10.00
113	Ninety Nine and a Half/Lucille	1969	2.50	5.00	10.00

Albums

Number	Title (A Side/B Side)	Yr	VG	VG+	NM
AMARET					
5000	How Now Brown Cow	1969	6.25	12.50	25.00

TRIANGLES, THE

45s

Number	Title (A Side/B Side)	Yr	VG	VG+	NM
FARGO					
1023	Dance the Magoo/Step-Up-and-Go	1962	3.75	7.50	15.00
FIFO					
107	My Oh My/Really I Do	1964	50.00	100.00	200.00
HERALD					
549	Savin' My Love/'Tis a Pity	1960	10.00	20.00	40.00

TRIBULATIONS, THE

45s

Number	Title (A Side/B Side)	Yr	VG	VG+	NM
IMPERIAL					
66416	Mama's Love/You Gave Me Up for Promises	1969	7.50	15.00	30.00

TRICKELS, THE

45s

Number	Title (A Side/B Side)	Yr	VG	VG+	NM
GONE					
5078	With Each Step a Tear/Outside the Chapel Door	1959	25.00	50.00	100.00
POWER					
250	With Each Step a Tear/When I Fall in Love	1958	50.00	100.00	200.00

TRICYCLE

Albums

Number	Title (A Side/B Side)	Yr	VG	VG+	NM
ABC					
S-674	Tricycle	1969	5.00	10.00	20.00

TRIDELS, THE

45s

Number	Title (A Side/B Side)	Yr	VG	VG+	NM
SAN-DEE					
1009	Land of Love/Image of My Love	1963	12.50	25.00	50.00

TRINA, MARGUERITE

45s

Number	Title (A Side/B Side)	Yr	VG	VG+	NM
BELLA					
19	The Rocking Tree/The Brat	1959	3.00	6.00	12.00

TRINIDADS, THE

45s

Number	Title (A Side/B Side)	Yr	VG	VG+	NM
FORMAL					
1005	Don't Say Goodbye/On My Happy Way	1959	50.00	100.00	200.00
1006	One Lonely Night/When We're Together	1959	50.00	100.00	200.00

TRIOLO, FRANK

45s

Number	Title (A Side/B Side)	Yr	VG	VG+	NM
FLAGSHIP					
106	Ice Cream Baby/Pretty Little Woman	1958	100.00	200.00	400.00

TRIPP, PAUL

45s

Number	Title (A Side/B Side)	Yr	VG	VG+	NM
MUSICOR					
1125	An Old-Fashioned Christmas/I've Got a Date with Santa	1965	3.00	6.00	12.00

TRIPSICHORD MUSIC BOX, THE

Albums

Number	Title (A Side/B Side)	Yr	VG	VG+	NM
JANUS					
JLS-3016	The Tripsichord Music Box	1971	50.00	100.00	200.00

TRIUMVIRAT

45s

Number	Title (A Side/B Side)	Yr	VG	VG+	NM
CAPITOL					
4700	Waterfall/Jo Ann Walker	1979	—	2.50	5.00

Albums

Number	Title (A Side/B Side)	Yr	VG	VG+	NM
CAPITOL					
ST-11392	Spartacus	1975	3.00	6.00	12.00
ST-11551	Old Loves Die Hard	1976	3.00	6.00	12.00
ST-11697	Pompeii	1977	3.00	6.00	12.00
ST-11862	A La Carte	1978	3.00	6.00	12.00
SN-16119	Illusions on a Double Dimple	1980	2.00	4.00	8.00
—Budget-line reissue					
SN-16120	Pompeii	1980	2.00	4.00	8.00
—Budget-line reissue					
SN-16121	Spartacus	1980	2.00	4.00	8.00
—Budget-line reissue					
SN-16122	Old Loves Die Hard	1980	2.00	4.00	8.00
—Budget-line reissue					
SN-16123	A La Carte	1980	2.00	4.00	8.00
—Budget-line reissue					
HARVEST					
ST-11311	Illusions on a Double Dimple	1974	3.75	7.50	15.00

TROGGS, THE

45s

Number	Title (A Side/B Side)	Yr	VG	VG+	NM
ATCO					
6415	Wild Thing/With a Girl Like You	1966	6.25	12.50	25.00
—"Wild Thing" writer is incorrectly credited as "Presley."					

Number	Title (A Side/B Side)	Yr	VG	VG+	NM
6415	Wild Thing/With a Girl Like You	1966	5.00	10.00	20.00
—"Wild Thing" writer is correctly credited as "Taylor."					
6415	Wild Thing/I Want You	1966	5.00	10.00	20.00
6444	I Can't Control Myself/Gonna Make You	1966	3.75	7.50	15.00
BELL					
45405	Listen to the Man/Queen of Sorrow	1973	2.00	4.00	8.00
45426	Strange Movies/I'm on Fire	1973	2.00	4.00	8.00
FONTANA					
1548	Wild Thing/From Home	1966	2.50	5.00	10.00
1552	With a Girl Like You/I Want You	1966	2.50	5.00	10.00
1557	I Can't Control Myself/Gonna Make You	1966	2.50	5.00	10.00
1576	You're Lying/Give It To Me	1967	2.00	4.00	8.00
1585	6-5-4-3-2-1/Anyway That You Want Me	1967	2.00	4.00	8.00
1593	Night of the Long Grass/Girl in Black	1967	2.00	4.00	8.00
1607	Love Is All Around/When Will the Rain Come	1967	2.50	5.00	10.00
1622	You Can Cry If You Want To/There's Something About You	1968	2.00	4.00	8.00
1630	Surprise, Surprise/Cousin Jane	1968	2.00	4.00	8.00
1634	Hip Hip Hooray/Say Darlin'	1968	2.00	4.00	8.00
PAGE ONE					
21026	Evil Woman/Heads Or Tails	1969	—	3.00	6.00
21030	Easy Lovin'/Give Me Something	1970	—	3.00	6.00
21032	Come Now/Lover	1970	—	3.00	6.00
21035	The Raver/You	1970	—	3.00	6.00
PRIVATE STOCK					
45102	Rolling Stone/(B-side unknown)	1976	—	2.50	5.00
PYE					
65011	Feels Like a Woman/Everything's Funny	1972	2.00	4.00	8.00
71015	Good Vibrations/Push It Up to Me	1975	—	2.50	5.00
71035	Summertime/Jerry Come Down	1975	—	2.50	5.00
71054	Satisfaction/(B-side unknown)	1975	—	2.50	5.00
Albums					
ATCO					
33-193 [M]	Wild Thing	1966	12.50	25.00	50.00
SD 33-193 [R]	Wild Thing	1966	10.00	20.00	40.00
FONTANA					
MGF 27556 [M]	Wild Thing/With a Girl Like You	1966	10.00	20.00	40.00
—Contents identical to the Atco LP; two slightly different cover variations are known					
SRF 67556 [R]	Wild Thing/With a Girl Like You	1966	7.50	15.00	30.00
—Contents identical to the Atco LP; two slightly different cover variations are known					
SRF 67576 [R]	Love Is All Around	1968	7.50	15.00	30.00
MKC					
214	Live at Max's Kansas City	1980	3.00	6.00	12.00
PRIVATE STOCK					
PS-2008	The Troggs Tapes	1976	3.00	6.00	12.00
PYE					
12112	The Troggs	1975	3.00	6.00	12.00
RHINO					
RNLP-118	The Best of the Troggs	1985	2.50	5.00	10.00
R1 70118	The Best of the Troggs	1988	2.00	4.00	8.00
SIRE					
SASH-3714 [(2)]	The Vintage Years	1976	3.75	7.50	15.00

TROLL, THE

Number	Title (A Side/B Side)	Yr	VG	VG+	NM
45s					
SMASH					
2208	Satin City News/Professor Potts' Pornographic Projector	1969	3.00	6.00	12.00
Albums					
SMASH					
SRS-67114	Animated Music	1969	12.50	25.00	50.00

TROLLS, THE

Number	Title (A Side/B Side)	Yr	VG	VG+	NM
45s					
ABC					
10823	Every Day and Every Night/Are You the One	1966	3.00	6.00	12.00
10884	Laughing All the Way/Someone Here Inside	1966	2.50	5.00	10.00
10916	They Don't Know/There Was a Time	1967	2.50	5.00	10.00
10952	Baby. What You Ain't Got (I Ain't in Need)/Who Was That Boy	1967	2.50	5.00	10.00
RUFF					
1010	Into My Arms/That's the Way My Love Is	1966	10.00	20.00	40.00
U.S.A.					
905	I Got to Have You/Don't Come Around	1968	6.25	12.50	25.00
WARRIOR					
173	Stupid Girl/I Don't Recall	1967	3.00	6.00	12.00
173 [PS]	Stupid Girl/I Don't Recall	1967	5.00	10.00	20.00

TROMBONES UNLIMITED

Number	Title (A Side/B Side)	Yr	VG	VG+	NM
45s					
LIBERTY					
55874	The Phoenix Love Theme/Daydream	1966	2.00	4.00	8.00
55908	You're Gonna Hear from Me/Modesty	1966	2.00	4.00	8.00
55980	Holiday for Trombones/A Night in Israel	1967	2.00	4.00	8.00
Albums					
LIBERTY					
LRP-3449 [M]	These Bones are Made for Walking	1966	3.75	7.50	15.00
LRP-3472 [M]	You're Gonna Hear from Me	1966	3.75	7.50	15.00
LRP-3494 [M]	Big Boss Bones	1967	5.00	10.00	20.00
LRP-3527 [M]	Holiday for Trombones	1967	5.00	10.00	20.00
LRP-3549 [M]	One of Those Songs	1968	6.25	12.50	25.00
LST-7449 [S]	These Bones are Made for Walking	1966	5.00	10.00	20.00
LST-7472 [S]	You're Gonna Hear from Me	1966	5.00	10.00	20.00
LST-7494 [S]	Big Boss Bones	1967	3.75	7.50	15.00
LST-7527 [S]	Holiday for Trombones	1967	3.75	7.50	15.00
LST-7549 [S]	One of Those Songs	1968	3.75	7.50	15.00
LST-7592	Grazing in the Grass	1968	3.75	7.50	15.00

TROPHIES, THE

More than one group?

Number	Title (A Side/B Side)	Yr	VG	VG+	NM
45s					
CHALLENGE					
9133	Desire/Doggone It	1962	15.00	30.00	60.00
9149	Peg O' My Heart/I Laughed So Hard I Cried	1962	3.75	7.50	15.00
9170	That's All I Want from You/Felicia	1962	3.75	7.50	15.00
KAPP					
714	Everywhere I Go/Baby Don't Live Here Anymore	1965	3.75	7.50	15.00
750	Leave My Girl Alone/You're the Queen	1966	3.75	7.50	15.00
NORK					
79907	Walkin' the Dog/Somethin' Blue	196?	5.00	10.00	20.00

TROUBADOURS DE ROI BAUDOUIN

Number	Title (A Side/B Side)	Yr	VG	VG+	NM
Albums					
PHILIPS					
PCC 206 [M]	Missa Luba	1963	3.75	7.50	15.00
PCC 606 [S]	Missa Luba	1963	3.75	7.50	15.00
—Released in '63, this didn't chart until 1969					

TROWER, ROBIN

Also see JACK BRUCE/ROBIN TROWER; PROCOL HARUM.

Number	Title (A Side/B Side)	Yr	VG	VG+	NM
12-Inch Singles					
ATLANTIC					
PR 2251 [DJ]	Shattered (LP version)/Shattered (Live Version)	1988	2.00	4.00	8.00
PR 2374 [DJ]	Love Won't Wait Forever (same on both sides)	1988	—	3.00	6.00
GNP CRESCENDO					
PRO-1 [DJ]	Secret Doors (same on both sides)	1986	2.00	4.00	8.00
PRO-2 [DJ]	No Time (same on both sides)	1987	2.00	4.00	8.00
PRO-3 [DJ]	Caroline (same on both sides)	1987	2.00	4.00	8.00
45s					
CHRYSALIS					
2009	Man of the World/Take a Fast Train	1973	—	3.00	6.00
2113	Too Rolling Stoned (Part 1)/Too Rolling Stoned (Part 2)	1976	—	3.00	6.00
2122	Caledonia/Messin' the Blues	1976	—	3.00	6.00
2172	Sweet Wine of Love/In City Dreams	1977	—	2.50	5.00
2206	Somebody Calling/Bluebird	1978	—	2.50	5.00
2238	My Love (Burning Love)/(B-side unknown)	1978	—	2.50	5.00
2272	It's for You/Birthday Boy	1979	—	2.50	5.00
Albums					
ATLANTIC					
81838	Take What You Need	1988	2.50	5.00	10.00
82080	In the Line of Fire	1990	3.00	6.00	12.00
CHRYSALIS					
CHR 1039	Twice Removed from Yesterday	1973	3.00	6.00	12.00
—Green label, "3300 Warner Blvd." address					
CHR 1039	Twice Removed from Yesterday	1977	2.50	5.00	10.00
—Blue label, New York address					
CHR 1057	Bridge of Sighs	1974	3.00	6.00	12.00
—Green label, "3300 Warner Blvd." address					
CHR 1057	Bridge of Sighs	1977	2.50	5.00	10.00
—Blue label, New York address					
CHR 1073	For Earth Below	1975	3.00	6.00	12.00
—Green label, "3300 Warner Blvd." address					
CHR 1073	For Earth Below	1977	2.50	5.00	10.00
—Blue label, New York address					
CHR 1089	Robin Trower Live!	1976	3.00	6.00	12.00
—Green label, "3300 Warner Blvd." address					
CHR 1089	Robin Trower Live!	1977	2.50	5.00	10.00
—Blue label, New York address					
CHR 1107	Long Misty Days	1976	3.00	6.00	12.00
—Green label, "3300 Warner Blvd." address					
CHR 1107	Long Misty Days	1977	2.50	5.00	10.00
—Blue label, New York address					
CHR 1148	In City Dreams	1977	3.00	6.00	12.00
CHR 1189	Caravan to Midnight	1978	3.00	6.00	12.00
CHR 1215	Victims of the Fury	1980	3.00	6.00	12.00
CHR 1324	B.L.T.	1981	2.50	5.00	10.00
PV 41039	Twice Removed from Yesterday	1983	2.00	4.00	8.00
—Reissue					
FV 41057	Bridge of Sighs	1984	2.00	4.00	8.00
—Reissue					
PV 41057	Bridge of Sighs	1986	2.00	4.00	8.00
—Reissue					
PV 41073	For Earth Below	1984	2.00	4.00	8.00
—Reissue					
PV 41089	Robin Trower Live!	1983	2.00	4.00	8.00
—Reissue					
PV 41107	Long Misty Days	1983	2.00	4.00	8.00
—Reissue					
PV 41148	In City Dreams	1984	2.00	4.00	8.00
—Reissue					
PV 41189	Caravan to Midnight	1984	2.00	4.00	8.00
—Reissue					
PV 41215	Victims of the Fury	1983	2.00	4.00	8.00
—Reissue					
PV 41324	B.L.T.	1984	2.00	4.00	8.00
—Reissue					
FV 41420	Back It Up	1983	2.50	5.00	10.00
PV 41420	Back it Up	1986	2.00	4.00	8.00
—Reissue					
GNP CRESCENDO					
2187	Passion	1986	2.50	5.00	10.00
PASSPORT					
PB-6049	Beyond the Mist	1985	2.50	5.00	10.00

TROY, DORIS

Number	Title (A Side/B Side)	Yr	VG	VG+	NM
45s					
APPLE					
1820	Ain't That Cute/Vaya Con Dios	1970	2.00	4.00	8.00
1824	Jacob's Ladder/Get Back	1970	2.00	4.00	8.00

Number	Title (A Side/B Side)	Yr	VG	VG+	NM
ATLANTIC					
2188	Just One Look/Bossa Nova Blues	1963	5.00	10.00	20.00
2206	Tomorrow Is Another Day/What'cha Gonna Do About It	1963	3.00	6.00	12.00
2222	One More Chance/Please Little Angel	1964	3.00	6.00	12.00
2269	Hurry/He Don't Belong to Me	1965	3.00	6.00	12.00
CALLA					
114	Heartaches/I'll Do Anything	1966	5.00	10.00	20.00
CAPITOL					
2043	Face Up to the Truth/He's Qualified	1967	2.00	4.00	8.00
MIDLAND INT'L.					
MB-10806	Lyin' Eyes/Give God Glory	1976	—	2.50	5.00
MB-11082	Can't Hold On/Another Look	1977	—	2.50	5.00
Albums					
APPLE					
ST-3371	Doris Troy	1970	6.25	12.50	25.00
ATLANTIC					
8088 [M]	Just One Look	1964	7.50	15.00	30.00
SD 8088 [S]	Just One Look	1964	12.50	25.00	50.00

TROYKA

Number	Title (A Side/B Side)	Yr	VG	VG+	NM
Albums					
COTILLION					
SD 9020	Troyka	1970	7.50	15.00	30.00

TRU-TONES, THE

Number	Title (A Side/B Side)	Yr	VG	VG+	NM
45s					
CHART					
634	Tears in My Eyes/Magic	1957	200.00	400.00	800.00
DEN RIC					
4527	I'm the Guy/(B-side unknown)	196?	10.00	20.00	40.00
KEB					
6037	Soldier's Last Letter/(B-side unknown)	196?	10.00	20.00	40.00

TRUELEERS, THE

Number	Title (A Side/B Side)	Yr	VG	VG+	NM
45s					
CHECKER					
1026	Forget About Him/Waiting for You	1962	3.00	6.00	12.00

TRUMPETEERS, THE

Number	Title (A Side/B Side)	Yr	VG	VG+	NM
45s					
IMPERIAL					
5972	Milky White Way/Leave That Lie Alone	1963	3.75	7.50	15.00
5994	Seven Angels/Just a Little Walk with Jesus	1963	3.75	7.50	15.00
SPLASH					
800	A String of Trumpets/(B-side unknown)	1959	3.00	6.00	12.00

TRYTHALL, GIL

Number	Title (A Side/B Side)	Yr	VG	VG+	NM
45s					
ATHENA					
5013	Yakety Moog/Foggy Mountain Breakdown	1970	—	3.00	6.00
Albums					
ATHENA					
6003	Switched On Nashville/Country Moog	1970	2.50	5.00	10.00
6004	Nashville Gold	1970	2.50	5.00	10.00

TUBB, ERNEST, AND LORETTA LYNN

Also see LORETTA LYNN.

Number	Title (A Side/B Side)	Yr	VG	VG+	NM
45s					
DECCA					
31643	Mr. and Mrs. Used to Be/Love Was Right Here All the Time	1964	2.50	5.00	10.00
31793	Our Hearts Are Holding Hands/We're Not Kids Anymore	1965	2.50	5.00	10.00
32091	Sweet Thang/Beautiful, Unhappy Home	1967	2.50	5.00	10.00
32496	Who's Gonna Take the Garbage Out/Somewhere Between	1969	2.00	4.00	8.00
32570	I Chased You Till You Caught Me/If We Put Our Heads Together	1969	2.00	4.00	8.00
Albums					
DECCA					
DL 4639 [M]	Mr. and Mrs. Used to Be	1965	7.50	15.00	30.00
DL 4872 [M]	Singin' Again	1967	7.50	15.00	30.00
DL 74639 [S]	Mr. and Mrs. Used to Be	1965	10.00	20.00	40.00
DL 74872 [S]	Singin' Again	1967	6.25	12.50	25.00
DL 75115	If We Put Our Heads Together	1969	6.25	12.50	25.00
MCA					
4000	The Ernest Tubb/Loretta Lynn Story	1973	3.75	7.50	15.00

TUBES, THE

Number	Title (A Side/B Side)	Yr	VG	VG+	NM
12-Inch Singles					
A&M					
17068 [DJ]	Prime Time/No Way Out	1979	2.00	4.00	8.00
CAPITOL					
SPRO 9332 [DJ]	Piece by Piece (same on both sides)	198?	—	3.00	6.00
SPRO 9728 [DJ]	Gonna Get It Next Time (same on both sides)	1982	—	3.00	6.00
45s					
A&M					
1733	White Punks on Dope (Part 1)/White Punks on Dope (Part 2)	1975	—	2.50	5.00
1733 [PS]	White Punks on Dope (Part 1)/White Punks on Dope (Part 2)	1975	2.00	4.00	8.00
1755	What Do You Want from Life/Space Baby	1975	—	2.50	5.00
1826	Don't Touch Me There/Proud to Be an American	1976	—	2.50	5.00
1956	This Town/I'm Just a Mess	1977	—	2.50	5.00
2037	Show Me a Reason/I Saw Her Standing There	1978	—	2.50	5.00
2120	Prime Time/No Way Out	1979	—	2.50	5.00
2149	Love's a Mystery (I Don't Understand)/Telecide	1979	—	2.50	5.00
8591	White Punks on Dope/What Do You Want from Life?	198?	—	—	3.00
—Reissue					
CAPIROL					
SPRO-9740 [DJ]	Sports Fans (same on both sides)	1982	—	2.50	5.00
CAPITOL					
5007	Don't Want to Wait Anymore/Think About Me	1981	—	—	3.00
5007 [PS]	Don't Want to Wait Anymore/Think About Me	1981	—	—	3.00
5016	Talk To Ya Later/Power Tools	1981	—	2.00	4.00
5091	Gonna Get It Next Time/Sports Fans	1982	—	2.00	4.00
B-5217	She's a Beauty/When You're Ready to Come	1983	—	2.00	4.00
—First pressing: Purple label					
B-5217	She's a Beauty/When You're Ready to Come	1983	—	—	3.00
—Second pressing: Black label with multi-colored ring					
B-5217 [PS]	She's a Beauty/When You're Ready to Come	1983	—	2.00	4.00
—Sleeve only came with first pressing, and then not with all of them					
B-5254	The Monkey Time/Sports Fans	1983	—	—	3.00
B-5254 [PS]	The Monkey Time/Sports Fans	1983	—	—	3.00
B-5258	Tip of My Tongue/Keyboard Kids	1983	—	—	3.00
B-5443	Piece by Piece/Night People	1985	—	—	3.00
B-5443 [PS]	Piece by Piece/Night People	1985	—	2.00	4.00
TUBES					
12682XS	Tubular Holiday	1982	12.50	25.00	50.00
—Fan club flexidisc					
833502XS	Happy Holidaze	1983	12.50	25.00	50.00
—Fan club flexidisc					
Albums					
A&M					
SP-3161	The Tubes	198?	2.00	4.00	8.00
—Reissue					
SP-3222	Young and Rich	198?	2.00	4.00	8.00
—Reissue					
SP-3242	Remote Control	198?	2.00	4.00	8.00
—Reissue					
SP-3243	Now	198?	2.00	4.00	8.00
—Reissue					
SP-3244	T.R.A.S.H. (Tubes Rarities And Smash Hits)	198?	2.00	4.00	8.00
—Reissue					
SP-4535	The Tubes	1975	3.75	7.50	15.00
SP-4580	Young and Rich	1976	3.75	7.50	15.00
SP-4632	Now	1977	3.75	7.50	15.00
SP-4751	Remote Control	1979	3.75	7.50	15.00
SP-4870	T.R.A.S.H. (Tubes Rarities And Smash Hits)	1981	3.00	6.00	12.00
SP-6003 [(2)]	What Do You Want From Live!	1978	3.75	7.50	15.00
SP-17012 [DJ]	Tubes Live/Edited for Trouble-Free Airplay	1978	6.25	12.50	25.00
—Generic cover with sticker; promo only					
CAPITOL					
SOO-12151	The Completion Backward Principle	1981	3.00	6.00	12.00
ST-12260	Outside/Inside	1983	2.50	5.00	10.00
ST-12381	Love Bomb	1985	2.50	5.00	10.00
SN-16360	Outside/Inside	1985	2.00	4.00	8.00
—Reissue					
SN-16378	The Completion Backward Principle	1986	2.00	4.00	8.00
—Reissue					
SN-16446	Love Bomb	1987	2.00	4.00	8.00
—Reissue					

TUCKER, BILLY JOE

Number	Title (A Side/B Side)	Yr	VG	VG+	NM
45s					
DOT					
16240	Boogie Woogie Bill/Mail Train	1961	25.00	50.00	100.00
MAHA					
103	Boogie Woogie Bill/Mail Train	1961	75.00	150.00	300.00

TUCKER, RICK

Number	Title (A Side/B Side)	Yr	VG	VG+	NM
45s					
COLUMBIA					
4-41041	Patty Baby/Don't Do Me This Way	1957	25.00	50.00	100.00
HITSVILLE					
6035	I Heard a Song/Plans That We Made	1976	—	3.00	6.00
OAK					
1066	Honey I'm Just Walking Out the Door/(B-side unknown)	1989	—	2.50	5.00

TUCKER, TANYA

Number	Title (A Side/B Side)	Yr	VG	VG+	NM
45s					
ARISTA					
0677	Feel Right/Cry	1982	—	2.00	4.00
1053	Changes/Too Long	1983	—	2.00	4.00
9006	Changes/Too Long	1983	—	—	3.00
9046	Baby I'm Yours/I Don't Want You to Go	1983	—	—	3.00
CAPITOL					
4986	Why Don't We Just Sleep on It Tonight/It's Your World	1981	—	2.00	4.00
—With Glen Campbell					
B-5533	One Love at a Time/(B-side unknown)	1985	—	—	3.00
B-5533 [PS]	One Love at a Time/(B-side unknown)	1985	—	—	3.00
B-5604	Just Another Love/You Could Change My Mind	1986	—	—	3.00
B-5604 [PS]	Just Another Love/You Could Change My Mind	1986	—	—	3.00
B-5652	I'll Come Back As Another Woman/Somebody to Care	1986	—	—	3.00
B-5694	It's Only for You/Girls Like Me	1987	—	2.50	5.00
—First pressing had erroneous A-side title					
B-5694	It's Only Over for You/Girls Like Me	1987	—	—	3.00
B-44036	Love Me Like You Used To/If I Didn't Love You	1987	—	—	3.00
B-44036 [PS]	Love Me Like You Used To/If I Didn't Love You	1987	—	—	3.00
B-44100	I Won't Take Less Than Your Love/Heartbreaker	1987	—	—	3.00
—With Paul Davis and Paul Overstreet					
B-44142	If It Don't Come Easy/I'll Tennessee You in My Dreams	1988	—	—	3.00
B-44188	Strong Enough to Bend/Back on My Feet	1988	—	—	3.00
B-44271	Highway Robbery/Lonesome Town	1989	—	—	3.00
B-44348	Call on Me/Daddy and Home	1989	—	—	3.00

Number	Title (A Side/B Side)	Yr	VG	VG+	NM
B-44401	Daddy and Home/Playing for Keeps	1989	—	—	3.00
B-44469	My Arms Stay Open All Night/Love Me Like You Used To	1989	—	—	3.00
NR-44520	Walking Shoes/This Heart of Mine	1990	—	2.00	4.00
NR-44586	Don't Go Out/(B-side unknown)	1990	—	2.50	5.00
—With T. Graham Brown; may only have been released on cassette single					
CAPITOL NASHVILLE					
S7-19515	Little Things/You Don't Do It	1997	—	—	3.00
S7-19628	Ridin' Out the Heartache/I Don't Believe That's How You Feel	1997	—	—	3.00
NR-44774	(Without You) What Do I Do with Me/Oh What It Did to Me	1991	—	2.50	5.00
7PRO-79338 [DJ]	It Won't Be Me (same on both sides)	1990	—	2.50	5.00
—Vinyl is promo only					
7PRO-79535 [DJ]	Oh What It Did to Me (same on both sides)	1991	—	2.50	5.00
—Vinyl is promo only					
7PRO-79711 [DJ]	Down to My Last Teardrop (same on both sides)	1991	—	2.50	5.00
—Vinyl is promo only					
COLUMBIA					
10069	I Believe the South Is Gonna Rise Again/Old Dan Tucker's Daughter	1974	—	2.50	5.00
10127	Spring/Bed of Roses	1975	—	2.50	5.00
10236	Greener Than the Grass (We Laid On)/Guess I'll Have to Love Him More	1975	—	2.50	5.00
10577	You Are So Beautiful/Almost Persuaded	1977	—	2.00	4.00
45588	Delta Dawn/I Love the Way He Loves Me	1972	—	2.50	5.00
45588 [PS]	Delta Dawn/I Love the Way He Loves Me	1972	2.50	5.00	10.00
45721	Love's the Answer/The Jamestown Ferry	1972	—	2.50	5.00
45799	What's Your Mama's Name/Rainy Girl	1973	—	2.50	5.00
45892	Blood Red and Goin' Down/Missing Piece of Puzzle	1973	—	2.50	5.00
45991	Would You Lay with Me (In a Field of Stone)/No Man's Land	1974	—	2.50	5.00
46047	The Man That Turned My Mama On/Satisfied with Missing You	1974	—	2.50	5.00
LIBERTY					
S7-17594	Soon/Sneaky Moon	1993	—	2.00	4.00
S7-17803	We Don't Have to Do This/Silence Is King	1994	—	2.00	4.00
S7-17908	Hangin' In/Let the Good Times Roll	1994	—	2.00	4.00
S7-18135	You Just Watch Me/I Love You Anyway	1994	—	2.00	4.00
S7-18485	Between the Two of Them/Love Will	1995	—	2.00	4.00
S7-18583	Something/All My Loving	1995	—	2.00	4.00
—B-side by Suzy Bogguss and Chet Atkins					
S7-56825	Two Sparrows in a Hurricane/Danger Ahead	1992	—	2.00	4.00
S7-56953	It's a Little Too Late/Rainbow Rider	1993	—	2.00	4.00
S7-56985	Tell Me About It/What Do They Know	1993	—	2.00	4.00
—A-side with Delbert McClinton					
S7-57703	Some Kind of Trouble/Oh What It Did to Me	1992	—	2.50	5.00
S7-57768	If Your Heart Ain't Busy Tonight/Down to My Last Teardrop	1992	—	2.50	5.00
S7-57895	Winter Wonderland/What Child Is This	1992	—	2.00	4.00
MCA					
40402	Lizzie and the Rainman/Traveling Salesman	1975	—	2.00	4.00
40444	San Antonio Stroll/The Serenade That We Played	1975	—	2.00	4.00
40497	Don't Believe My Heart Can Stand Another You/Depend on You	1975	—	2.00	4.00
40540	You've Got Me to Hold On To/Ain't That a Shame	1976	—	2.00	4.00
40598	Here's Some Love/The Pride of Franklin County	1976	—	2.00	4.00
40650	Ridin' Rainbows/Short Cut	1976	—	2.00	4.00
40708	It's a Cowboy Lovin' Night/Morning Comes	1977	—	2.00	4.00
40755	Dancing the Night Away/Let's Keep It That Way	1977	—	2.00	4.00
40902	Save Me/Slippin' Away	1978	—	2.00	4.00
40902 [PS]	Save Me/Slippin' Away	1978	—	3.00	6.00
40976	Texas (When I Die)/Not Fade Away	1978	—	2.00	4.00
40976 [PS]	Texas (When I Die)/Not Fade Away	1978	—	3.00	6.00
41005	I'm the Singer, You're the Song/Lover Goodbye	1979	—	2.00	4.00
41144	Lay Back in the Arms of Someone/By Day By Day	1979	—	2.00	4.00
41194	Tear Me Apart/Better Late Than Never	1980	—	2.00	4.00
41305	Pecos Promenade/King of Country Music	1980	—	2.00	4.00
41323	Dream Lover/Bronco	1980	—	2.00	4.00
—A-side with Glen Campbell					
51037	Can I See You Tonight/Let Me Count the Ways	1980	—	2.00	4.00
51096	Love Knows We Tried/Somebody (Trying to Tell You Something)	1981	—	2.00	4.00
51131	Should I Do It/Lucky Enough for Two	1981	—	2.00	4.00
51184	Rodeo Girls/Halfway to Heaven	1981	—	2.00	4.00
52017	Somebody Buy This Cowgirl a Beer/Delta Dawn	1982	—	2.00	4.00
Albums					
ARISTA					
AL 8381	Changes	1984	2.00	4.00	8.00
—Reissue of 9596					
AL 9596	Changes	1982	2.50	5.00	10.00
CAPITOL					
ST-12474	Girls Like Me	1986	2.50	5.00	10.00
CLT-46870	Love Me Like You Used To	1987	2.50	5.00	10.00
C1-48865	Strong Enough to Bend	1988	2.50	5.00	10.00
C1-91814	Greatest Hits	1989	3.00	6.00	12.00
CAPITOL NASHVILLE					
1P 8140	What Do I Do with Me	1991	5.00	10.00	20.00
—Only available on vinyl through Columbia House					
COLUMBIA					
KC 31742	Delta Dawn	1972	3.75	7.50	15.00
PC 31742	Delta Dawn	198?	2.00	4.00	8.00
KC 32272	What's Your Mama's Name	1973	3.75	7.50	15.00
KC 32744	Would You Lay with Me (In a Field of Stone)	1974	3.00	6.00	12.00
PC 32744	Would You Lay with Me (In a Field of Stone)	197?	2.00	4.00	8.00
PC 33355	Greatest Hits	1975	3.00	6.00	12.00
—No bar code on cover					
PC 33355	Greatest Hits	197?	2.00	4.00	8.00
—With bar code on cover					
PC 34733	You Are So Beautiful	1977	3.00	6.00	12.00
—No bar code on cover					
PC 34733	You Are So Beautiful	197?	2.00	4.00	8.00
—With bar code on cover					

Number	Title (A Side/B Side)	Yr	VG	VG+	NM
MCA					
654	Tanya Tucker	1980	2.00	4.00	8.00
—Reissue of 2141					
655	Lovin' and Learnin'	1980	2.00	4.00	8.00
—Reissue of 21??					
656	Here's Some Love	1980	2.00	4.00	8.00
—Reissue of 22??					
657	Ridin' Rainbows	1980	2.00	4.00	8.00
—Reissue of 2253					
2141	Tanya Tucker	1975	3.00	6.00	12.00
2167	Lovin' and Learnin'	1976	3.00	6.00	12.00
2213	Here's Some Love	1976	3.00	6.00	12.00
2253	Ridin' Rainbows	1977	3.00	6.00	12.00
3032	Tanya Tucker's Greatest Hits	1978	3.00	6.00	12.00
3066	TNT	1978	3.00	6.00	12.00
—Original gatefold cover					
5106	Tear Me Apart	1979	2.50	5.00	10.00
5140	Dreamlovers	1980	2.50	5.00	10.00
5228	Should I Do It	1981	2.50	5.00	10.00
5299	Tanya Tucker Live	1982	2.50	5.00	10.00
5357	The Best of Tanya Tucker	1983	2.50	5.00	10.00
27030	Dreamlovers	198?	2.00	4.00	8.00
—Reissue of 5140					
37075	TNT	1981	2.00	4.00	8.00
—Reissue of 3066; gatefold removed					
37158	Tear Me Apart	1981	2.00	4.00	8.00
—Reissue of 5106					
37225	Greatest Hits	1984	2.00	4.00	8.00
—Reissue of 3032					
37242	Tanya Tucker Live	1984	2.00	4.00	8.00
—Reissue of 5299					

TUCKER, TOMMY

May be two different performers.

Number	Title (A Side/B Side)	Yr	VG	VG+	NM
45s					
CHECKER					
1067	Hi-Heel Sneakers/I Don't Want 'Cha	1964	6.25	12.50	25.00
1075	Long Tall Shorty/Mo' Shorty	1964	3.75	7.50	15.00
1112	Alimony/All About Melanie	1965	3.75	7.50	15.00
1133	Chewing Gun/I've Been a Fool	1966	2.50	5.00	10.00
1178	I'm Shorty/Sitting Home Alone	1967	2.00	4.00	8.00
1186	A Whole Lot of Fun Before the Weekend Is Done/Real True Love	1967	2.00	4.00	8.00
HI					
2014	Loving Lil/A Man in Love	1959	7.50	15.00	30.00
2020	Miller's Cave/The Strangers	1960	6.25	12.50	25.00
MGM					
10854	Christmas In Killarney/Jing-A-Ling	1950	3.75	7.50	15.00
RCA VICTOR					
37-7838	The Return of the Teenage Queen/Since You Have Gone	1961	6.25	12.50	25.00
—"Compact Single 33" (small hole, plays at LP speed)					
47-7838	The Return of the Teenage Queen/Since You Have Gone	1961	3.75	7.50	15.00
68-7838	The Return of the Teenage Queen/Since You Have Gone	1961	7.50	15.00	30.00
—"Compact Single 33" in "Living Stereo"					
SUNBEAM					
128	My Blue Heaven/That Man Comes Around	1959	3.75	7.50	15.00
Albums					
CHECKER					
LP-2990 [M]	Hi-Heel Sneakers	1964	62.50	125.00	250.00
—Black label					
LP-2990 [M]	Hi-Heel Sneakers	1965	30.00	60.00	120.00
—Blue label with checkers					

TUCKY BUZZARD

Number	Title (A Side/B Side)	Yr	VG	VG+	NM
45s					
CAPITOL					
3171	Pisces Apple Lady/Time Will Be Your Doctor	1971	—	3.00	6.00
PASSPORT					
7901	Gold Medallions/Fast Bluesy Woman	1974	—	2.50	5.00
Albums					
CAPITOL					
ST-787	Tucky Buzzard	1971	3.75	7.50	15.00
ST-864	Warm Slash	1972	3.75	7.50	15.00
PASSPORT					
97001	Alright in the Night	1973	3.75	7.50	15.00
98002	Tucky Buzzard	1974	3.75	7.50	15.00

TUDOR MINSTRELS, THE

Number	Title (A Side/B Side)	Yr	VG	VG+	NM
45s					
LONDON					
1012	Love in the Open Air/A Theme from "The Family Way"	1966	12.50	25.00	50.00

TUFFS, THE

Number	Title (A Side/B Side)	Yr	VG	VG+	NM
45s					
DORE					
757	I Only Cry Once a Day Now/The Moon Out There	1966	6.25	12.50	25.00
DOT					
16304	Surfer Stomp (Part 1)/Surfer Stomp (Part 2)	1962	6.25	12.50	25.00

TULLY, LEE, AND MILT MOSS

Number	Title (A Side/B Side)	Yr	VG	VG+	NM
45s					
FLAIR-X					
3007	Around the World with Elwood Pretzel (Part 1)/Around the World with Elwood Pretzel (Part 2)	1956	12.50	25.00	50.00

Number	Title (A Side/B Side)	Yr	VG	VG+	NM
TUNE ROCKERS, THE					
45s					
UNITED ARTISTS					
139	The Green Mosquito/Warm Up	1958	5.00	10.00	20.00
0145	The Green Mosquito/Bust Out	1973	—	2.00	4.00
—"Silver Spotlight Series" reissue; B-side by the Busters					
TUNE WEAVERS, THE					
45s					
CASA GRANDE					
101	Little Boy/Look Down That Lonesome Road	1959	10.00	20.00	40.00
3038	My Congratulations Baby/This Can't Be Love	1960	7.50	15.00	30.00
4037	Happy, Happy Birthday Baby/Ol' Man River	1957	37.50	75.00	150.00
4038	I Remember Dear/Pamela Jean	1957	7.50	15.00	30.00
4040	There Stands My Love/I'm Cold	1958	10.00	20.00	40.00
CHECKER					
872	Happy, Happy Birthday Baby/Ol' Man River	1957	6.25	12.50	25.00
872	Happy, Happy Birthday Baby/Yo Yo Walk	1957	6.25	12.50	25.00
—B-side by Paul Gayten					
880	Ol' Man River/Tough Enough	1957	6.25	12.50	25.00
—B-side by Paul Gayten					
1007	Congratulations on Your Wedding/Your Skies of Blue	1962	6.25	12.50	25.00
CLASSIC ARTISTS					
104	Come Back to Me/I've Tried	1988	—	2.00	4.00
—As "Margo Sylvia and Tune Weavers"					
107	Merry, Merry Christmas Baby/What Are You Doing New Year's Eve	1988	—	2.00	4.00
—As "Margo Sylvia and Tune Weavers"					
TUNEDROPS, THE					
45s					
GONE					
5003	Rosie Lee/Speak for Yourself	1957	10.00	20.00	40.00
5072	Smoothie/Jumpin' Jellybeans	1959	6.25	12.50	25.00
METRO					
20028	Smoothie/Jumpin' Jelly Beans	1959	10.00	20.00	40.00
TUNEMASTERS, THE					
45s					
MARK					
7002	Sending This Letter/It's All Over	1957	75.00	150.00	300.00
TURBANS, THE					
Also see THE TURKS/THE TURBANS.					
45s					
HERALD					
458	When You Dance/Let Me Show You (Around My Heart)	1955	12.50	25.00	50.00
—Yellow label, script print inside flag					
458	When You Dance/Let Me Show You (Around My Heart)	195?	5.00	10.00	20.00
—Yellow label, block print inside flag					
469	Sister Sookey/I'll Always Watch Over You	1956	7.50	15.00	30.00
478	B-I-N-G-O (Bingo)/I'm Nobody's	1956	7.50	15.00	30.00
486	It Was a Nite Like This/All of My Love	1956	7.50	15.00	30.00
495	Valley of Love/Bye and Bye	1957	7.50	15.00	30.00
510	Congratulations/The Wadda-Do	1957	6.25	12.50	25.00
IMPERIAL					
5807	Six Questions/The Lament of Silver Gulch	1962	10.00	20.00	40.00
5828	This Is My Story/Clicky Clicky Clack	1962	6.25	12.50	25.00
5847	I Wonder (I Wanna Know)/The Damage Is Done	1962	5.00	10.00	20.00
MONEY					
209	Tick Tock Awoo/No No Cherry	1955	50.00	100.00	200.00
209	Tick Tock Awoo/Nest Is Warm	1955	50.00	100.00	200.00
PARKWAY					
820	When You Dance/Golden Rings	1961	6.25	12.50	25.00
RED TOP					
115	I Promise You Love/Curfew Time	1959	12.50	25.00	50.00
ROULETTE					
4281	Diamonds and Pearls/Bad Man	1960	5.00	10.00	20.00
4326	Three Friends (Two Lovers)/I'm Not Your Fool Anymore	1961	5.00	10.00	20.00
Albums					
HERALD					
5009	Presenting the Turbans	197?	5.00	10.00	20.00
—No such album was released in the 1950s; this is a bootleg that has some collector value.					
LOST-NITE					
LLP-25 [10]	The Turbans	1981	2.50	5.00	10.00
—Red vinyl					
RELIC					
5009	The Turbans' Greatest Hits	198?	3.00	6.00	12.00
TURKS, THE					
More than one group.					
45s					
BALLY					
1017	This Heart of Mine/Why Did You	1956	7.50	15.00	30.00
CASH					
1042	It Can't Be True/Wagon Wheels	1956	7.50	15.00	30.00
—As "The Original Turks"					
CLASS					
256	Hully Gully/Rockville U.S.A.	1959	5.00	10.00	20.00
IMPERIAL					
5783	I'm a Fool/It Can't Be True	1961	3.00	6.00	12.00
KEEN					
3-4016	Father Time/Okay	1958	5.00	10.00	20.00
KNIGHT					
2005	I'm a Fool/It Can't Be True	1958	5.00	10.00	20.00
MONEY					
215	I'm a Fool/I've Been Accused	1956	10.00	20.00	40.00

Number	Title (A Side/B Side)	Yr	VG	VG+	NM
P.B.D.					
112	Baja/Dianne	196?	7.50	15.00	30.00
113	Wipeout/Hideaway	196?	7.50	15.00	30.00
TURKS, THE / THE TURBANS					
Also see each artist's individual listings.					
45s					
MONEY					
211	Emily/When I Return	1955	15.00	30.00	60.00
TURLEY, RICHARD					
45s					
DOT					
16231	I Wanna Dance/Since I Met You	1961	10.00	20.00	40.00
FRATERNITY					
845	Makin' Love with My Baby/All About Ann	1959	10.00	20.00	40.00
TURNER, IKE					
Also see IKE AND TINA TURNER.					
45s					
ARTISTIC					
1504	(I Know) You Don't Love Me/Down and Out	1958	7.50	15.00	30.00
COBRA					
5033	Box Top/Walking Down the Aisle	1959	7.50	15.00	30.00
FEDERAL					
12297	Do You Mean It/She Made My Blood Run Cold	1957	25.00	50.00	100.00
12304	Rock a Bucket/The Big Question	1957	12.50	25.00	50.00
12307	You've Changed My Love/Trail Blazer	1957	10.00	20.00	40.00
FLAIR					
1040	Cubano Jump/Loosely	1954	15.00	30.00	60.00
1059	Cuban Getaway/Go To It	1955	15.00	30.00	60.00
KING					
5553	The Big Question/She Made My Blood Run Cold	1961	3.75	7.50	15.00
LIBERTY					
56194	Takin' Back My Name/Love Is a Game	1970	—	2.50	5.00
RPM					
356	You're Driving Me Insane/Trouble and Heartaches	1952	100.00	200.00	400.00
362	My Heart Belongs to You/Lookin' for My Baby	1952	15.00	30.00	60.00
—As "Bonnie and Ike Turner"					
446	As Long As I Have You/I Wanna Make Love to You	1955	10.00	20.00	40.00
SUE					
722	My Love/That's All I Need	1959	5.00	10.00	20.00
UNITED ARTISTS					
XW460	Take My Hand, Precious Lord/Father Alone	1974	—	2.50	5.00
50865	River Deep Mountain High/Na Na	1971	—	2.50	5.00
50900	Right On/Tacks in My Shoes	1972	—	2.50	5.00
50930	Lawdy Miss Clawdy/Tacks in My Shoes	1972	—	2.50	5.00
51102	Dust My Broom/You Won't Let Me Go	1973	—	2.50	5.00
Albums					
CROWN					
CST-367 [R]	Ike Turner Rocks the Blues	1963	25.00	50.00	100.00
CLP-5367 [M]	Ike Turner Rocks the Blues	1963	50.00	100.00	200.00
FANTASY					
F-9597	The Edge	1980	2.50	5.00	10.00
POMPEII					
SD 6003	A Black Man's Soul	1969	3.75	7.50	15.00
UNITED ARTISTS					
UA-LA087-F	Bad Dreams	1973	3.75	7.50	15.00
UAS-5576	Blues Roots	1972	3.75	7.50	15.00
TURNER, IKE AND TINA					
Also see IKE TURNER; TINA TURNER.					
12-Inch Singles					
STRIPED HORSE					
1201	Living for the City (5:02)/Bootsy Whitelaw (4:01)	1985	3.75	7.50	15.00
45s					
A&M					
1118	River Deep, Mountain High/I'll Keep You Happy	1969	2.50	5.00	10.00
1170	A Love Like Yours/Save the Last Dance for Me	1970	2.50	5.00	10.00
BLUE THUMB					
101	I've Been Loving You Too Long/Grumbling	1969	—	3.00	6.00
102	The Hunter/Crazy 'Bout You Baby	1969	—	3.00	6.00
104	Bold Soul Sister/I Know	1969	—	3.00	6.00
202	I've Been Loving You Too Long/Crazy 'Bout You Baby	1971	—	2.50	5.00
CENCO					
112	Get It-Get It/You Weren't Ready (For My Love)	1967	3.75	7.50	15.00
INNIS					
6666	Betcha Can't Kiss Me/Don't Lie to Me	1968	2.50	5.00	10.00
6667	So Fine/So Blue Over You	1968	2.50	5.00	10.00
KENT					
402	I Can't Believe What You Say (For Seeing What You Do)/My Baby Now	1964	2.50	5.00	10.00
409	Am I a Fool in Love/Please, Please, Please	1964	2.50	5.00	10.00
418	Chicken Shack/He's the One	1965	2.50	5.00	10.00
4514	Plaese, Please, Please (Part 1)/Please, Please, Please (Part 2)	1970	—	3.00	6.00
LIBERTY					
56177	I Want to Take You Higher/Contact High	1970	—	3.00	6.00
56207	Workin' Together/The Way You Love Me	1970	—	3.00	6.00
56216	Proud Mary/Funkier Than a Mosquito's Tweeter	1970	—	3.00	6.00
LOMA					
2011	I'm Thru with Love/Tell Her I'm Not Home	1965	2.50	5.00	10.00
2015	Somebody Needs You/Just to Be with You	1965	2.50	5.00	10.00
MINIT					
32000	I'm Gonna Do All I Can (To Do Right By My Man)/You've Got Too Many Ties That Bind	1969	—	3.00	6.00

Number	Title (A Side/B Side)	Yr	VG	VG+	NM
32068	I Wish It Would Rain/With a Little Help from My Friends	1969	—	3.00	6.00
32077	I Wanna Jump/Treating Us Funky	1969	—	3.00	6.00
32087	Come Together/Honky Tonk Women	1970	—	3.00	6.00
MODERN					
1007	Good Bye, So Long/Hurt Is All You Gave Me	1965	2.50	5.00	10.00
1012	I Don't Need/Gonna Have Fun	1965	2.50	5.00	10.00
PHILLES					
131	River Deep — Mountain High/I'll Keep You Happy	1966	5.00	10.00	20.00
134	Two to Tango/A Man Is a Man Is a Man	1966	3.75	7.50	15.00
135	I'll Never Need More Love Than This/The Cash Box Blues Or (Oops We Printed the Wrong Story Again)	1967	3.75	7.50	15.00
136	I Idolize You/A Love Like Yours	1967	3.75	7.50	15.00
POMPEII					
7003	Betcha Can't Kiss Me/Cussin', Cryin', and Carryin' On	1969	2.00	4.00	8.00
66675	It Sho' Ain't Me/We Need An Understanding	1968	2.00	4.00	8.00
66700	Shake a Tail Feather/Cussin', Cryin', and Carryin' On	1969	2.00	4.00	8.00
SONJA					
2005	You Can't Miss Nothing That You Never Had/(B-side unknown)	1968	3.00	6.00	12.00
SUE					
135	Two Is a Couple/Tin Top House	1965	3.75	7.50	15.00
138	The New Breed (Part 1)/The New Breed (Part 2)	1965	3.75	7.50	15.00
139	Stagger Lee and Billy/Can't Chance a Breakup	1965	3.75	7.50	15.00
146	Dear John/I Made a Promise Up Above	1966	3.00	6.00	12.00
730	A Fool in Love/The Way You Love Me	1960	7.50	15.00	30.00
734	You're My Baby/A Fool Too Long	1960	6.25	12.50	25.00
735	I Idolize You/Letter from Tina	1960	6.25	12.50	25.00
740	I'm Jealous/You're My Baby	1961	6.25	12.50	25.00
749	It's Gonna Work Out Fine/Won't You Forgive Me	1961	7.50	15.00	30.00
753	Poor Fool/You Can't Blame Me	1961	5.00	10.00	20.00
757	Tra La La La La/Puppy Love	1962	3.75	7.50	15.00
760	Prancing/It's Gonna Work Out Fine	1962	3.75	7.50	15.00
765	You Shoulda Treated Me Right/Sleepless	1962	3.75	7.50	15.00
768	Tina's Dilemma/I Idolize You	1962	3.75	7.50	15.00
772	The Argument/Mind in a Whirl	1962	3.75	7.50	15.00
774	Please Don't Hurt Me/Worried and Hurtin' Inside	1962	3.75	7.50	15.00
784	Don't Play Me Cheap/Wake Up	1963	3.75	7.50	15.00
TANGERINE					
963	Beauty Is Only Skin Deep/Anything You Wasn't Born With	1966	2.50	5.00	10.00
967	Dust My Broom/I'm Hooked	1966	2.50	5.00	10.00
UNITED ARTISTS					
SP-48 [DJ]	I Want to Take You Higher/Ooh Poo Pah Doo	1971	2.50	5.00	10.00
0119	A Fool in Love/I Idolize You	1973	—	2.00	4.00
0120	It's Gonna Work Out Fine/Poor Fool	1973	—	2.00	4.00
0121	I Want to Take You Higher/Come Together	1973	—	2.00	4.00
0122	Proud Mary/Tra La La La La	1973	—	2.00	4.00
—0119 through 0122 are "Silver Spotlight Series" reissues					
XW174	With a Little Help from My Friends/Early One Morning	1973	—	2.50	5.00
XW257	Work On Me/Born Free	1973	—	2.50	5.00
XW298	Nutbosh City Limits/Help Him	1973	—	3.00	6.00
XW409	Get it Out of Your Mind/Sweet Rhode Island Red	1974	—	2.50	5.00
XW524	Nutbush City Limits/Ooh Poo Pah Doo	1974	—	2.00	4.00
—Reissue					
XW528	Sexy Ida (Part 1)/Sexy Ida (Part 2)	1974	—	2.50	5.00
XW598X	Baby, Get It On/Baby, Get It On (Disco Version)	1975	—	2.50	5.00
50782	Ooh Poo Pah Doo/I Wanna Jump	1971	—	2.50	5.00
50837	I'm Yours/Doin' It	1971	—	2.50	5.00
50881	Do Wah Ditty (Got to Get Ya)/Up in Heah	1972	—	2.50	5.00
50913	Outrageous/Feel Good	1972	—	2.50	5.00
50939	Games People Play/Pick Me Up	1972	—	2.50	5.00
50955	Let Me Touch Your Mind/Chopper	1972	—	2.50	5.00
WARNER BROS.					
5433	A Fool for a Fool/No Tears to Cry	1964	3.00	6.00	12.00
5433 [PS]	A Fool for a Fool/No Tears to Cry	1964	10.00	20.00	40.00
5461	It's All Over/Finger Poppin'	1964	3.00	6.00	12.00
5493	Ooh Poop A Doo/Merry Christmas Baby	1964	3.00	6.00	12.00
Albums					
ABC					
4014	16 Great Performances	1975	3.00	6.00	12.00
ACCORD					
SN-7147	Hot and Sassy	1981	2.50	5.00	10.00
A&M					
SP-3179	River Deep — Mountain High	1982	2.50	5.00	10.00
—Budget-line reissue					
SP-4178	River Deep — Mountain High	1969	6.25	12.50	25.00
—Official release of Philles 4011					
BLUE THUMB					
BTS 5	Outta Season	1968	3.75	7.50	15.00
BTS 11	The Hunter	1969	3.75	7.50	15.00
BTS 49	The Best of Ike & Tina Turner	1973	3.00	6.00	12.00
BTS-8805	Outta Season	1971	3.00	6.00	12.00
—Early reissue of Blue Thumb 5					
CAPITOL					
ST-571	Her Man, His Woman	1971	3.75	7.50	15.00
COLLECTABLES					
COL-5107	Golden Classics	198?	2.50	5.00	10.00
COL-5137	It's Gonna Work Out Fine	198?	2.50	5.00	10.00
EMI AMERICA					
ST-17212	It's Gonna Work Out Fine	1986	2.50	5.00	10.00
SQ-17216	Workin' Together	1986	2.50	5.00	10.00
HARMONY					
HS 11360	Ooh Poo Pah Doo	1969	3.75	7.50	15.00
H 30567	Something's Got a Hold on Me	1971	3.75	7.50	15.00
KENT					
KST-514 [S]	The Ike and Tina Turner Revue Live	1964	10.00	20.00	40.00
KST-519 [S]	The Soul of Ike and Tina	1966	10.00	20.00	40.00
KST-538	Festival of Live Performances	1969	7.50	15.00	30.00
KST-550	Please Please Please	1971	7.50	15.00	30.00
K-5014 [M]	The Ike and Tina Turner Revue Live	1964	7.50	15.00	30.00
K-5019 [M]	The Soul of Ike and Tina	1966	7.50	15.00	30.00
LIBERTY					
LT-917	Airwaves	1981	2.00	4.00	8.00
LST-7637	Come Together	1970	3.75	7.50	15.00
LST-7650	Workin' Together	1970	3.75	7.50	15.00
LO-51156	Get Back!	1985	2.50	5.00	10.00
LOMA					
5904 [M]	Live! The Ike & Tina Turner Show	1966	6.25	12.50	25.00
5904 [S]	Live! The Ike & Tina Turner Show	1966	7.50	15.00	30.00
—Reissue of Warner Bros. 1579?					
MINIT					
24018	In Person	1969	5.00	10.00	20.00
PHILLES					
PHLP 4011 [M]	River Deep — Mountain High	1966	2000.	4000.	8000.
—Value is for record alone; covers were not printed					
PICKWICK					
SPC-3284	Too Hot to Hold	197?	2.50	5.00	10.00
POMPEII					
SD 6000	So Fine	1968	6.25	12.50	25.00
SD 6004	Cussin', Cryin' and Carryin' On	1969	6.25	12.50	25.00
SD 6006	Get It Together	1969	6.25	12.50	25.00
STRIPED HORSE					
SHL-2001	Golden Empire	1986	2.50	5.00	10.00
SUE					
LP 1038 [M]	Ike and Tina Turner's Greatest Hits	1965	75.00	150.00	300.00
LP 2001 [M]	The Soul of Ike and Tina Turner	1961	100.00	200.00	400.00
LP 2003 [M]	Ike and Tina Turner's Kings of Rhythm Dance	1962	100.00	200.00	400.00
LP 2004 [M]	Dynamite	1963	100.00	200.00	400.00
LP 2005 [M]	Don't Play Me Cheap	1963	100.00	200.00	400.00
LP 2007 [M]	It's Gonna Work Out Fine	1963	100.00	200.00	400.00
SUNSET					
SUS-5265	The Fantastic Ike & Tina Turner	1969	3.75	7.50	15.00
SUS-5286	Ike & Tima Turner's Greatest Hits	1969	3.75	7.50	15.00
UNART					
S 21021	Greatest Hits	197?	2.50	5.00	10.00
UNITED ARTISTS					
UA-LA064-G [(2)]	The World of Ike & Tina Live	1973	3.75	7.50	15.00
UA-LA180-F	Nutbush City Limits	1973	3.00	6.00	12.00
UA-LA203-G	The Gospel According to Ike & Tina Turner	1974	3.00	6.00	12.00
UA-LA312-G	Sweet Rhode Island Red	1974	3.00	6.00	12.00
UA-LA592-G	Greatest Hits	1976	3.00	6.00	12.00
UA-LA707-G	Delilah's Power	1977	3.00	6.00	12.00
UA-LA917-H	Airwaves	1978	3.00	6.00	12.00
UAS-5530	'Nuff Said	1971	3.00	6.00	12.00
UAS-5598	Feel Good	1972	3.00	6.00	12.00
UAS-5660	Let Me Touch Your Mind	1972	3.00	6.00	12.00
UAS-5667	Ike & Tina Turner's Greatest Hits	1972	3.00	6.00	12.00
UAS-9953 [(2)]	Live at Carnegie Hall/What You Hear Is What You Get	1971	3.75	7.50	15.00
WARNER BROS.					
W 1579 [M]	Live! The Ike & Tina Turner Show	1965	7.50	15.00	30.00
WS 1579 [S]	Live! The Ike & Tina Turner Show	1965	10.00	20.00	40.00
WS 1810	Ike & Tina Turner's Greatest Hits	1969	6.25	12.50	25.00

TURNER, JESSE LEE

45s

Number	Title (A Side/B Side)	Yr	VG	VG+	NM
CARLTON					
496	The Little Space Girl/Shake, Baby, Shake	1959	5.00	10.00	20.00
509	Baby Please Don't Tease/Thinkin'	1959	5.00	10.00	20.00
509 [PS]	Baby Please Don't Tease/Thinkin'	1959	10.00	20.00	40.00
FRATERNITY					
855	Teen-Age Misery/That's My Girl	1959	5.00	10.00	20.00
855 [PS]	Teen-Age Misery/That's My Girl	1959	10.00	20.00	40.00
GNP CRESCENDO					
184	All You Gotta Do (Is Ask Me To)/Voice Changing Song	1962	3.00	6.00	12.00
188	Shotgun Boogie/Ballad of Billy Sol Estes	1962	15.00	30.00	60.00
IMPERIAL					
5635	Slippin' Around/Early in the Morning	1960	—	—	—
5649	I'm the Little Space Girl's Father/Valley of Lost Soldiers	1960	—	—	—
TOP RANK					
2064	Do I Worry/All Right, Be That Way	1960	5.00	10.00	20.00

TURNER, JOE

45s

Number	Title (A Side/B Side)	Yr	VG	VG+	NM
ATLANTIC					
939	Chains of Love/After My Laughter Came Tears	1951	125.00	250.00	500.00
949	The Chill Is On/Bump Miss Suzie	1951	200.00	400.00	800.00
960	Sweet Sixteen/I'll Never Stop Loving You	1952	30.00	60.00	120.00
970	Don't You Cry/Poor Lover's Blues	1952	25.00	50.00	100.00
982	Still in Love/Baby I Still Want You	1953	25.00	50.00	100.00
1001	Honey Hush/Crawdad Hole	1953	50.00	100.00	200.00
1016	TV Mama/Oke-She-Moke-She-Pop	1954	30.00	60.00	120.00
1026	Shake, Rattle, and Roll/You Know I Love You	1954	20.00	40.00	80.00
1040	Well All Right/Married Woman	1954	17.50	35.00	70.00
1053	Flip, Flop, and Fly/Ti-Ri-Lee	1955	12.50	25.00	50.00
1069	Hide and Seek/Midnight Cannonball	1955	12.50	25.00	50.00
1080	Morning, Noon and Night/The Chicken and the Hawk	1956	12.50	25.00	50.00
1088	Corinne, Corinna/Boogie Woogie Country Girl	1956	7.50	15.00	30.00
1100	Rock a While/Lipstick, Powder, and Paint	1956	7.50	15.00	30.00
1122	Midnight Special Train/Feeling Happy	1957	7.50	15.00	30.00
1131	Red Sails in the Sunset/After a While	1957	7.50	15.00	30.00
1146	Love Roller Coaster/A World of Trouble	1957	7.50	15.00	30.00
1155	I Need a Girl/Trouble in Mind	1957	7.50	15.00	30.00
1167	Teen-Age Letter/Wee Baby Blues	1957	7.50	15.00	30.00
1184	Blues in the Night/Jump for Joy	1958	7.50	15.00	30.00
2034	Got You On My Mind/Love, Oh Careless Love	1959	5.00	10.00	20.00
2044	Tomorrow Night/Honey Hush	1959	5.00	10.00	20.00
2054	Chains of Love/My Little Honey Dripper	1960	5.00	10.00	20.00

Number	Title (A Side/B Side)	Yr	VG	VG+	NM
2072	My Reason for Living/Sweet Sue	1960	5.00	10.00	20.00
BAYOU					
015	The Blues Jumped the Rabbit/The Sun Is Shining	1951	75.00	150.00	300.00
BLUESTIME					
45001	Two Loves Have I/Shake, Rattle and Roll	195?	10.00	20.00	40.00
BLUESWAY					
61009	Big Wheel/Bluer Than Blue	1967	2.00	4.00	8.00
CORAL					
62408	I Walk a Lonely Mile/I'm Packin' Up	1964	3.75	7.50	15.00
62429	Shake, Rattle and Roll/There'll Be Some Tears Falling	1964	3.75	7.50	15.00
DECCA					
29711	Piney Brown Blues/I Got a Gal for Every Day of the Week	1955	10.00	20.00	40.00
29924	Corrine, Corrina/It's the Same Old Story	1956	10.00	20.00	40.00
KENT					
512	Love Ain't Nothin'/10-20-25-30	1969	—	3.00	6.00
4561	Chains of Love/Battle Hymn of the Republic	1971	—	3.00	6.00
4569	One Hour in Your Garden/You've Been Squeezin' My Lemons	1972	—	3.00	6.00
MGM					
10719	Moody Baby/Feeling So Sad	1951	75.00	150.00	300.00
OKEH					
6829	Cherry Red/Joe Turner Blues	1951	50.00	100.00	200.00
RONN					
28	Up on the Mountain/I Love You Baby	1969	—	3.00	6.00
35	Morning Glory/Night-Time Is the Right Time	1969	—	3.00	6.00
RPM					
345	Riding Blues/Playful Baby	1952	50.00	100.00	200.00
—With Pete Johnson					
7-Inch Extended Plays					
ATLANTIC					
536	(contents unknown)	1955	37.50	75.00	150.00
536 [PS]	Joe Turner Sings	1955	37.50	75.00	150.00
565	(contents unknown)	1956	37.50	75.00	150.00
565 [PS]	Joe Turner	1956	37.50	75.00	150.00
586	*Corrine Corrina/The Chicken and the Hawk/Feeling Happy/Hide and Seek	195?	37.50	75.00	150.00
586 [PS]	Joe Turner	195?	37.50	75.00	150.00
EMARCY					
EP-1-6132	(contents unknown)	195?	25.00	50.00	100.00
EP-1-6132 [PS]	Joe Turner	195?	25.00	50.00	100.00
Albums					
ARHOOLIE					
2004 [M]	Jumpin' the Blues	1962	5.00	10.00	20.00
ATCO					
SD 33-376	Joe Turner — His Greatest Recordings	1971	3.75	7.50	15.00
ATLANTIC					
1234 [M]	The Boss of the Blues	1956	30.00	60.00	120.00
—Black label					
1234 [M]	The Boss of the Blues	1960	25.00	50.00	100.00
—White "bullseye" label					
1234 [M]	The Boss of the Blues	1961	10.00	20.00	40.00
—White "fan" logo on label					
1234 [M]	The Boss of the Blues	1963	3.75	7.50	15.00
—Black "fan" logo on label					
SD 1234 [S]	The Boss of the Blues	1959	45.00	90.00	180.00
—Green label					
SD 1234 [S]	The Boss of the Blues	1960	37.50	75.00	150.00
—White "bullseye" label					
SD 1234 [S]	The Boss of the Blues	1961	12.50	25.00	50.00
—White "fan" logo on label					
SD 1234 [S]	The Boss of the Blues	1963	5.00	10.00	20.00
—Black "fan" logo on label					
1332 [M]	Big Joe Rides Again	1959	37.50	75.00	150.00
—Black label					
1332 [M]	Big Joe Rides Again	1960	10.00	20.00	40.00
—White "fan" logo on label					
1332 [M]	Big Joe Rides Again	1963	3.75	7.50	15.00
—Black "fan" logo on label					
SD 1332 [S]	Big Joe Rides Again	1959	50.00	100.00	200.00
—Green label					
SD 1332 [S]	Big Joe Rides Again	1960	12.50	25.00	50.00
—White "fan" logo on label					
SD 1332 [S]	Big Joe Rides Again	1963	5.00	10.00	20.00
—Black "fan" logo on label					
8005 [M]	Joe Turner	1957	37.50	75.00	150.00
—Black label					
8005 [M]	Joe Turner	1961	10.00	20.00	40.00
—White "fan" logo on label					
8005 [M]	Joe Turner	1963	3.75	7.50	15.00
—Black "fan" logo on label					
8023 [M]	Rockin' the Blues	1958	30.00	60.00	120.00
—Black label					
8023 [M]	Rockin' the Blues	1960	10.00	20.00	40.00
—White "fan" logo on label					
8023 [M]	Rockin' the Blues	1963	3.75	7.50	15.00
—Black "fan" logo on label					
8033 [M]	Big Joe Is Here	1959	30.00	60.00	120.00
—Black label					
8033 [M]	Big Joe Is Here	1960	25.00	50.00	100.00
—White "bullseye" label					
8033 [M]	Big Joe Is Here	1960	10.00	20.00	40.00
—White "fan" logo on label					
8033 [M]	Big Joe Is Here	1963	3.75	7.50	15.00
—Black "fan" logo on label					
8081 [M]	The Best of Joe Turner	1963	12.50	25.00	50.00
SD 8812	Boss of the Blues	1981	2.50	5.00	10.00
—Reissue of 1234					
81752	Greatest Hits	1987	2.50	5.00	10.00
BLUES SPECTRUM					
BS-104	Great Rhythm and Blues Oldies Vol. 4	197?	3.75	7.50	15.00
BLUESTIME					
9002 [M]	The Real Boss of the Blues	196?	10.00	20.00	40.00
29002 [S]	The Real Boss of the Blues	196?	7.50	15.00	30.00
BLUESWAY					
BL 6006 [M]	Singing the Blues	1967	5.00	10.00	20.00
BLS-6006 [S]	Singing the Blues	1967	6.25	12.50	25.00
S-6060	Roll 'Em	1973	3.75	7.50	15.00
CHIAROSCURO					
147	King of Stride	1976	3.75	7.50	15.00
CLASSIC JAZZ					
138	Effervescent	1976	3.75	7.50	15.00
DECCA					
DL 8044 [M]	Joe Turner Sings Kansas City Jazz	1953	62.50	125.00	250.00
FANTASY					
OJC-497	Trumpet Kings Meet Joe Turner	1991	3.00	6.00	12.00
INTERMEDIA					
QS-5008	Rock This Joint	198?	2.50	5.00	10.00
QS-5026	The Very Best of Joe Turner — Live	198?	2.50	5.00	10.00
QS-5030	The Blues Boss — Live	198?	2.50	5.00	10.00
QS-5036	Everyday I Have the Blues	198?	2.50	5.00	10.00
QS-5043	Roll Me Baby	198?	2.50	5.00	10.00
KENT					
KST-542	Joe Turner Turns On the Blues	1973	3.75	7.50	15.00
MCA					
1325	Early Big Joe	198?	2.50	5.00	10.00
MUSE					
MR-5293	Blues Train	198?	2.50	5.00	10.00
—With Roomful of Blues and Dr. John					
PABLO					
2310717	Trumpet Kings Meet Joe Turner	197?	3.00	6.00	12.00
2310760	Nobody in Mind	197?	3.00	6.00	12.00
2310763	Another Epoch Stride Piano	197?	3.00	6.00	12.00
2310776	In the Evening	197?	3.00	6.00	12.00
2310800	Things That I Used to Do	197?	3.00	6.00	12.00
2310818	Every Day I Have the Blues	198?	3.00	6.00	12.00
2310848	The Best of Joe Turner	1980	3.00	6.00	12.00
2310863	Have No Fear, Joe Turner Is Here	1983	3.00	6.00	12.00
2310883	Singing the Same, Sad, Happy, Forever Blues	1983	3.00	6.00	12.00
2310913	Patcha, Patcha, All Night Long	198?	3.00	6.00	12.00
2310937	Flip, Flop and Fly	1989	3.00	6.00	12.00
2405404	The Best of "Big" Joe Turner	198?	3.00	6.00	12.00
SAVOY					
MG-14012 [M]	Blues'll Make You Happy	1958	37.50	75.00	150.00
MG-14106 [M]	Careless Love	1963	20.00	40.00	80.00
SAVOY JAZZ					
SJC-406	Blues'll Make You Happy	1985	2.50	5.00	10.00
—Reissue of Savoy 14012					
SJL-2223 [(2)]	Have No Fear	197?	3.75	7.50	15.00

TURNER, JOE, AND PETE JOHNSON

Number	Title (A Side/B Side)	Yr	VG	VG+	NM
Albums					
EMARCY					
MG-36014 [M]	Joe Turner and Pete Johnson	1955	50.00	100.00	200.00

TURNER, ODELLE

Number	Title (A Side/B Side)	Yr	VG	VG+	NM
45s					
ATLANTIC					
964	Alarm Clock Boogie/Draggin' Hours	1952	37.50	75.00	150.00

TURNER, SAMMY

Number	Title (A Side/B Side)	Yr	VG	VG+	NM
45s					
20TH FOX					
6610	For Your Love I'll Die/The House I Live In	1965	2.50	5.00	10.00
BIG TOP					
3007	Thunderbolt/Sweet Annie Laurie	1959	6.25	12.50	25.00
3016 [M]	Lavender-Blue/Wrapped Up in a Dream	1959	5.00	10.00	20.00
3016 [S]	Lavender-Blue/Wrapped Up in a Dream	1959	15.00	30.00	60.00
3029 [M]	Always/Symphony	1959	5.00	10.00	20.00
3029 [S]	Always/Symphony	1959	12.50	25.00	50.00
3032	Paradise/I'd Be a Fool Again	1960	5.00	10.00	20.00
3038	Goodnight Irene/I Want to Be Loved	1960	5.00	10.00	20.00
3049	Fools Fall in Love/Stay My Love	1960	5.00	10.00	20.00
3061	Falling/The Things I Do	1961	3.75	7.50	15.00
3065	Little Sir Echo/Love Keeps Calling	1961	3.75	7.50	15.00
3070	Starlight, Starbright/Let's Donkey On Down	1961	3.75	7.50	15.00
3082	Pour It On/The Fool of the Year	1961	3.75	7.50	15.00
3089	Falling/Raincoat in the River	1961	6.25	12.50	25.00
—B-side produced by Phil Spector					
MILLENNIUM					
616	Do You Know (What Life Is All About)/Nothing Can Separate Me (From Your Love)	1978	—	2.50	5.00
MOTOWN					
1055	Only You/Right Now	1964	7.50	15.00	30.00
PACIFIC					
3016	Lavender-Blue/Wrapped Up in a Dream	1959	10.00	20.00	40.00
—Despite label name, Pacific Records was in North Carolina!					
VERVE					
10465	A Child Was Born/Come to Me Comf'tably	1966	7.50	15.00	30.00
Albums					
BIG TOP					
12-1301 [M]	Lavender Blue Moods	1959	75.00	150.00	300.00
—May not exist in stereo					

TURNER, SPYDER

Number	Title (A Side/B Side)	Yr	VG	VG+	NM
45s					
KWANZA					
7688	Since I Don't Have You/Happy Days	1973	—	3.00	6.00
MGM					
13617	Stand By Me/You're Good Enough for Me	1966	2.50	5.00	10.00
13692	Don't Hold Back/I Can't Take It Anymore	1967	2.00	4.00	8.00

Number	Title (A Side/B Side)	Yr	VG	VG+	NM
13739	For Your Precious Love/I Can't Wait to See My Baby's Face	1967	2.00	4.00	8.00
14263	I Can't Make It Anymore/I'm Alive with a Lovin' Feeling	1971	—	3.00	6.00
WHITFIELD					
8526	I've Been Waiting/Tomorrow's Only Yesterday	1978	—	2.00	4.00
8596	Get Down/Is It Love You're After	1978	—	2.00	4.00
49190	You're So Fine/Only Love	1980	—	2.00	4.00
Albums					
MGM					
E-4450 [M]	Stand By Me	1967	6.25	12.50	25.00
SE-4450 [S]	Stand By Me	1967	7.50	15.00	30.00
WHITFIELD					
BSK 3124	Music Web	1978	2.50	5.00	10.00
BSK 3397	Only Love	1979	2.50	5.00	10.00

TURNER, TINA

Also see IKE AND TINA TURNER.

Number	Title (A Side/B Side)	Yr	VG	VG+	NM
12-Inch Singles					
CAPITOL					
8579	Let's Stay Together/I Wrote a Letter	1983	2.00	4.00	8.00
8597	What's Love Got to Do with It/Rock 'n' Roll Widow	1984	2.00	4.00	8.00
8609	Better Be Good to Me (7:40)/When I Was Young	1984	2.00	4.00	8.00
8635	Show Some Respect/Let's Pretend We're Married	1985	2.00	4.00	8.00
8655	We Don't Need Another Hero/(Instrumental)	1985	2.00	4.00	8.00
SPRO-9196 [DJ]	What's Love Got to Do with It (Extended) (same on both sides)	1984	3.00	6.00	12.00
SPRO-9264 [DJ]	Better Be Good to Me (Live) (same on both sides)	1984	2.50	5.00	10.00
SPRO-9425/6 [DJ]	We Don't Need Another Hero/(Instrumental)	1985	—	3.00	6.00
SPRO-9493/4 [DJ]	One of the Living (Club Version)/One of the Living (Single Version)	1985	2.50	5.00	10.00
SPRO-9826 [DJ]	Back Where You Started (same on both sides)	198?	—	3.00	6.00
SPRO-9867 [DJ]	Overnight Sensation (same on both sides)	1987	—	3.00	6.00
V-15205	One of the Living (3 versions)	1985	2.00	4.00	8.00
V-15249	Typical Male (3 versions)/Don't Turn Around	1986	2.00	4.00	8.00
V-15261	Two People (3 versions)/Havin' a Party	1986	2.00	4.00	8.00
V-15543	Steamy Windows (4 versions)	1989	—	3.00	6.00
SPRO-79168/92 [DJ]	Afterglow (4 versions)	1987	—	3.00	6.00
FANTASY					
D-161	Party Vibes (8:11)/Shame, Shame, Shame (5:06)	1980	3.00	6.00	12.00
45s					
CAPITOL					
B-5322	Let's Stay Together/I Wrote a Letter	1984	—	—	3.00
B-5322 [PS]	Let's Stay Together/I Wrote a Letter	1984	—	2.50	5.00
B-5354	What's Love Got to Do with It/Rock 'N' Roll Widow	1984	—	—	3.00
B-5354 [PS]	What's Love Got to Do with It/Rock 'N' Roll Widow	1984	—	2.00	4.00
B-5387	Better Be Good to Me/When I Was Young	1984	—	—	3.00
B-5387 [PS]	Better Be Good to Me/When I Was Young	1984	—	2.00	4.00
B-5433	Private Dancer/Nutbush City Limits	1984	—	—	3.00
B-5433 [PS]	Private Dancer/Nutbush City Limits	1984	—	2.00	4.00
B-5461	Show Some Respect/Let's Pretend We're Married	1985	—	—	3.00
B-5461 [PS]	Show Some Respect/Let's Pretend We're Married	1985	—	2.00	4.00
B-5491	We Don't Need Another Hero (Thunderdome)/(Instrumental)	1985	—	—	3.00
B-5491 [PS]	We Don't Need Another Hero (Thunderdome)/(Instrumental)	1985	—	2.00	4.00
B-5518	One of the Living/One of the Living (Dub)	1985	—	—	3.00
B-5518 [PS]	One of the Living/One of the Living (Dub)	1985	—	2.00	4.00
B-5615	Typical Male/Don't Turn Around	1986	—	—	3.00
B-5615 [PS]	Typical Male/Don't Turn Around	1986	—	—	3.00
B-5644	Two People/Havin' a Party	1986	—	—	3.00
B-5644 [PS]	Two People/Havin' a Party	1986	—	—	3.00
B-5668	What You Get Is What You See/What You Get Is What You See (Live)	1987	—	—	3.00
B-5668 [PS]	What You Get Is What You See/What You Get Is What You See (Live)	1987	—	—	3.00
B-44003	Break Every Rule/Take Me to the River	1987	—	—	3.00
B-44003 [PS]	Break Every Rule/Take Me to the River	1987	—	—	3.00
B-44111	Afterglow/Afterglow	1987	—	—	3.00
B-44442	The Best/Undercover Agent for the Blues	1989	—	—	3.00
B-44442 [PS]	The Best/Undercover Agent for the Blues	1989	—	—	3.00
B-44473	Steamy Windows/The Best	1989	—	—	3.00
B-44473 [PS]	Steamy Windows/The Best	1989	—	—	3.00
NR-44510	Look Me in the Heart/Stronger Than the Wind	1990	—	—	3.00
S7-57702	Way of the World/You Know Who	1992	—	—	3.00
FANTASY					
948	Lean On Me/Shame, Shame, Shame	1984	—	2.00	4.00
POLYDOR					
PRO-002 [DJ]	Acid Queen/Pinball Wizard	1975	10.00	20.00	40.00
—B-side by Elton John; promo-only					
POMPEII					
66682	Too Hot to Hold/You Got What You Wanted	1968	2.50	5.00	10.00
UNITED ARTISTS					
XW 724	Whole Lotta Love/Rockin' 'N' Rollin'	1975	—	3.00	6.00
XW 730	Delilah's Power/That's My Power	1975	—	3.00	6.00
XW 920	Come Together/I Want to Take You Higher	1977	—	3.00	6.00
XW 1265	Fire Down Below/Viva La Money	1979	—	2.50	5.00
VIRGIN					
S7-17401	I Don't Wanna Fight/Tina's Wish	1993	—	—	3.00
S7-17498	Why Must We Wait Until Tomorrow/Shake a Tail Feather	1993	—	—	3.00
S7-18047	Proud Mary (Edit Live Version)/The Best (Live)	1994	—	—	3.00
—Red vinyl					
S7-19217	Missing You/Do Something	1996	—	—	3.00
38691	When the Heartache Is Over/On Silent Wings	2000	—	—	3.00
Albums					
CAPITOL					
1P 8192 [(2)]	Simply the Best	1991	5.00	10.00	20.00
—Columbia House edition (only US vinyl version)					
ST-12330	Private Dancer	1984	2.00	4.00	8.00
SJ-12530	Break Every Rule	1986	2.00	4.00	8.00
C1-90126 [(2)]	Tina Live in Europe	1988	3.00	6.00	12.00
C1-91873	Foreign Affair	1989	2.00	4.00	8.00
FANTASY					
MFP-4520 [EP]	Mini	1984	2.00	4.00	8.00
SPRINGBOARD					
SPB-4033	The Queen	1972	2.50	5.00	10.00
UNITED ARTISTS					
UA-LA200-F	Tina Turns the Country On	1973	3.75	7.50	15.00
UA-LA495-G	Acid Queen	1975	3.00	6.00	12.00
UA-LA919-G	Rough	1978	3.00	6.00	12.00
WAGNER					
14108	Good Hearted Woman	1979	3.00	6.00	12.00

TURNER, TITUS

Number	Title (A Side/B Side)	Yr	VG	VG+	NM
45s					
ATCO					
6310	Baby Girl (Part 1)/Baby Girl (Part 2)	1964	2.00	4.00	8.00
ATLANTIC					
1127	A-Knockin' at My Baby's Door/Hungry Man	1957	5.00	10.00	20.00
COLUMBIA					
42873	Young Wings Can Fly/Goodbye Rose	1963	2.50	5.00	10.00
42947	Make Someone Love You/I'm a Fool About My Mama	1964	2.50	5.00	10.00
ENJOY					
1005	People Sure Act Funny/My Darkest Hour	1962	2.50	5.00	10.00
1015	Soulville/My Darkest Hour	1963	2.50	5.00	10.00
2010	Bow Wow/I Love You Baby	1963	2.50	5.00	10.00
GLOVER					
201	We Told You Not to Marry/Taking Care of Business	1959	6.25	12.50	25.00
202	When the Sergeant Comes Marching Home/(B-side unknown)	1960	6.25	12.50	25.00
JAMIE					
1177	Pony Train/Bla, Bla, Cha Cha Cha	1961	3.00	6.00	12.00
1184	Hey Doll Baby/I Want a Steady Girl	1961	3.00	6.00	12.00
1189	Horsin' Around/Chances Go Around	1961	3.00	6.00	12.00
1202	Shake the Hand of a Fool/Beautiful Stranger	1961	3.00	6.00	12.00
1213	Walk on the Wild Twist/Twistin' Train	1962	2.50	5.00	10.00
JOSIE					
990	I Just Can't Keep It to Myself/People Sure Are Funny	1968	—	3.00	6.00
1012	His Funeral, My Trial/Do You Dig It	1969	—	3.00	6.00
KING					
5067	Have Mercy Baby/You Turned Lamps Too	1957	3.00	6.00	12.00
5095	Hold Your Loving/Stop the Rain	1957	3.00	6.00	12.00
5129	Follow Me/Way Down Yonder	1958	3.00	6.00	12.00
5140	Coralee/Tears of Joy Fill My Eyes	1958	3.00	6.00	12.00
5186	The Return of Staggolee/Answer Me	1959	3.00	6.00	12.00
5213 [M]	Tarzan/Fall Guy	1959	3.00	6.00	12.00
S-5213 [S]	Tarzan/Fall Guy	1959	7.50	15.00	30.00
5243	Bonnie Baby/Miss Rubberneck Jones	1959	3.00	6.00	12.00
5465	Way Down Yonder/Miss Rubberneck Jones	1961	2.50	5.00	10.00
MURBO					
1001	Huckle Buckle Beanstalk/Hoop Hoop Hoop a Hoopa Doo	1965	2.00	4.00	8.00
OKEH					
6844	Same Old Feeling/Don't Take Everybody to Be Your Friend	1951	7.50	15.00	30.00
6883	What'cha Gonna Do for Me/Got So Much Trouble	1952	6.25	12.50	25.00
6907	Jambalaya/Please Baby	1952	6.25	12.50	25.00
6929	Christmas Morning/Be Sure You Know	1952	7.50	15.00	30.00
6938	My Plea/It's Too Late Now	1953	6.25	12.50	25.00
6961	Big Mary's/Living in Misery	1953	6.25	12.50	25.00
7027	Over the Rainbow/My Lonely Room	1954	6.25	12.50	25.00
7038	Hello Stranger/Devilish Woman	1954	6.25	12.50	25.00
7244	Eye to Eye/What Kinda Deal Is This	1966	2.00	4.00	8.00
PHILIPS					
40445	(I'm Afraid the) Masquerade Is Over/Mary Mack	1967	2.00	4.00	8.00
WING					
90006	All Around the World/Do You Know	1955	5.00	10.00	20.00
90033	Sweet and Low/Big John	1955	5.00	10.00	20.00
90058	Get on the Right Track, Baby/I'll Wait Forever	1956	5.00	10.00	20.00
Albums					
JAMIE					
JLP-3018 [M]	Sound Off	1961	5.00	10.00	20.00
JLPS-3018 [S]	Sound Off	1961	7.50	15.00	30.00

TURNER, VELVERT, GROUP

Number	Title (A Side/B Side)	Yr	VG	VG+	NM
Albums					
FAMILY PRODUCTIONS					
FPS-2704	Velvert Turner Group	1972	12.50	25.00	50.00

TURNER, ZEB

Number	Title (A Side/B Side)	Yr	VG	VG+	NM
Albums					
AUDIO LAB					
AL-1537 [M]	Country Music in the Turner Style	1959	37.50	75.00	150.00

TURNPIKES, THE

Number	Title (A Side/B Side)	Yr	VG	VG+	NM
45s					
CAPITOL					
2234	Cast a Spell/Nothing But Promises	1968	6.25	12.50	25.00

TURNQUIST REMEDY

Number	Title (A Side/B Side)	Yr	VG	VG+	NM
Albums					
PENTAGRAM					
PE-10004	Turnquist Remedy	1970	6.25	12.50	25.00

TURRENTINE, STANLEY

12-Inch Singles

Number	Title (A Side/B Side)	Yr	VG	VG+	NM
BLUE NOTE					
SPRO-79031 [DJ]	Boogie On Reggae Woman (2 versions)/Creepin'	1987	—	3.00	6.00
ELEKTRA					
11472 [DJ]	Deja Vu (mono/stereo)	1980	2.50	5.00	10.00
FANTASY					
D-108	Disco Dancing (7:58)//Heritage/Feed the Fire	1978	2.50	5.00	10.00

45s

Number	Title (A Side/B Side)	Yr	VG	VG+	NM
BLUE NOTE					
1780	Look Out/Journey Into Melody	196?	2.50	5.00	10.00
1781	Little Cheri/Minor Chant	196?	2.50	5.00	10.00
1845	Smile, Stacy (Part 1)/Smile, Stacy (Part 2)	196?	2.00	4.00	8.00
1846	Soft Pedal Blues (Part 1)/Soft Pedal Blues (Part 2)	196?	2.00	4.00	8.00
1847	Pia/Dorene, Don't Cry	196?	2.00	4.00	8.00
1848	We'll See You After Awhile, Ya Hear? (Part 1/Part 2)	196?	2.00	4.00	8.00
1893	Trouble #2 (Part 1)/Trouble #2 (Part 2)	196?	2.00	4.00	8.00
1894	Never Let Me Go/Major's Minor	196?	2.00	4.00	8.00
1917	River's Invitation (Part 1)/River's Invitation (Part 2)	196?	2.00	4.00	8.00
1929	Walk On By/And Satisfy	196?	2.00	4.00	8.00
1933	Feeling Good/What Could I Do Without You	196?	2.00	4.00	8.00
1936	Love Is Blue/Spooky	1969	—	3.00	6.00
1940	The Look of Love/This Guy's in Love with You	1969	—	3.00	6.00
1948	Always Something There (To Remind Me)/When I Look Into Your Eyes	1970	—	3.00	6.00
CTI					
1	Sugar (Part 1)/Sugar (Part 2)	1971	—	2.50	5.00
10	I Told Jesus/(B-side unknown)	1972	—	2.50	5.00
ELEKTRA					
46509	Take Me Home/Long Time Gone	1979	—	2.00	4.00
46533	Concentrate on You/Together Again	1979	—	2.00	4.00
46576	Betcha/Hamlet (So Peaceful)	1980	—	2.00	4.00
47008	Is It You/Inflation	1980	—	2.00	4.00
47074	Deja Vu/Don't Misunderstand	1981	—	2.00	4.00
47156	Having Fun with Mr. T/World Chimes	1981	—	2.00	4.00
47245	After the Love Is Gone/I'll Give You My Love	1981	—	2.00	4.00
FANTASY					
745	Spaced/Naked as the Day I Was Born	1975	—	2.50	5.00
772	All By Myself/There Is a Place	1976	—	2.50	5.00
778	Hope That We Can Be Together Soon/There Is a Place	1976	—	2.50	5.00
782	You'll Never Find Another Love Like Mine/The Man with the Sad Face	1976	—	2.50	5.00
790	Evil Ways/Love Hangover	1977	—	2.50	5.00
804	Papa "T" (Part 1)/Papa "T" (Part 2)	1977	—	2.50	5.00
816	Walkin'/Ann, Wonderful One	1977	—	2.50	5.00
834	Disco Dancing/Heritage	1978	—	2.50	5.00
IMPULSE!					
256	Let It Go/Good Looking Out	1967	2.00	4.00	8.00

Albums

Number	Title (A Side/B Side)	Yr	VG	VG+	NM
BAINBRIDGE					
1038	Stan The Man	1981	2.50	5.00	10.00
BLUE NOTE					
BN-LA883-J2 [(2)]	Jubilee Shout!!	1977	3.75	7.50	15.00
LT-933	New Time Shuffle	1978	2.50	5.00	10.00
LT-1037	In Memory Of...	1980	2.50	5.00	10.00
LT-1075	Mr. Natural	1980	2.50	5.00	10.00
LT-1095	Ain't No Way	1981	2.50	5.00	10.00
BLP-4039 [M]	Look Out!	1960	30.00	60.00	120.00
—"Deep groove" version (deep indentation under label on both sides)					
BLP-4039 [M]	Look Out!	1960	20.00	40.00	80.00
—Regular version with W. 63rd St. address on label					
BLP-4039 [M]	Look Out!	1963	6.25	12.50	25.00
—With New York, USA address on label					
BLP-4057 [M]	Blue Hour	1961	20.00	40.00	80.00
—With W. 63rd St. addresss on label					
BLP-4057 [M]	Blue Hour	1963	6.25	12.50	25.00
—With New York, USA address on label					
BLP-4065 [M]	Comin' Your Way	1961	—	—	—
—Canceled					
BLP-4069 [M]	Up at Minton's, Volume 1	1961	20.00	40.00	80.00
—With W. 63rd St. addresss on label					
BLP-4069 [M]	Up at Minton's, Volume 1	1963	6.25	12.50	25.00
—With New York, USA address on label					
BLP-4070 [M]	Up at Minton's, Volume 2	1961	20.00	40.00	80.00
—With W. 63rd St. addresss on label					
BLP-4070 [M]	Up at Minton's, Volume 2	1963	6.25	12.50	25.00
—With New York, USA address on label					
BLP-4081 [M]	Dearly Beloved	1961	18.75	37.50	75.00
—With 61st St. address on label					
BLP-4081 [M]	Dearly Beloved	1963	6.25	12.50	25.00
—With New York, USA address on label					
BLP-4096 [M]	That's Where It's At	1962	15.00	30.00	60.00
—With 61st St. address on label					
BLP-4096 [M]	That's Where It's At	1963	6.25	12.50	25.00
—With New York, USA address on label					
BLP-4122 [M]	Jubilee Shout!!!	1963	—	—	—
—Canceled					
BLP-4129 [M]	Never Let Me Go	1963	7.50	15.00	30.00
BLP-4150 [M]	A Chip Off the Old Block	1963	7.50	15.00	30.00
BLP-4162 [M]	Hustlin'	1964	7.50	15.00	30.00
BLP-4201 [M]	Joyride	1965	6.25	12.50	25.00
BLP-4234 [M]	Stanley Turrentine	1965	—	—	—
—Canceled					
BLP-4240 [M]	Rough 'n Tumble	1966	6.25	12.50	25.00
BLP-4256 [M]	The Spoiler	1967	6.25	12.50	25.00
BLP-4268 [M]	Easy Walker	1967	6.25	12.50	25.00
BST-84039 [S]	Look Out!	1960	15.00	30.00	60.00
—With W. 63rd St. addresss on label					
BST-84039 [S]	Look Out!	1963	5.00	10.00	20.00
—With New York, USA address on label					
BST-84039 [S]	Look Out!	1967	3.75	7.50	15.00
—With "A Division of Liberty Records" on label					
BST-84057	Blue Hour	1986	2.50	5.00	10.00
—"The Finest in Jazz Since 1939" label reissue					
BST-84057 [S]	Blue Hour	1961	15.00	30.00	60.00
—With W. 63rd St. addresss on label					
BST-84057 [S]	Blue Hour	1963	5.00	10.00	20.00
—With New York, USA address on label					
BST-84057 [S]	Blue Hour	1967	3.75	7.50	15.00
—With "A Division of Liberty Records" on label					
BST-84057 [S]	Blue Hour	1970	2.50	5.00	10.00
—With United Artists distribution					
B1-84065	Comin' Your Way	1988	2.50	5.00	10.00
—"The Finest in Jazz Since 1939" label; first issue of LP					
BST-84065 [S]	Comin' Your Way	1961	—	—	—
—Canceled					
BST-84069 [S]	Up at Minton's, Volume 1	1961	15.00	30.00	60.00
—With W. 63rd St. addresss on label					
BST-84069 [S]	Up at Minton's, Volume 1	1963	5.00	10.00	20.00
—With New York, USA address on label					
BST-84069 [S]	Up at Minton's, Volume 1	1967	3.75	7.50	15.00
—With "A Division of Liberty Records" on label					
BST-84070 [S]	Up at Minton's, Volume 2	1961	15.00	30.00	60.00
—With W. 63rd St. addresss on label					
BST-84070 [S]	Up at Minton's, Volume 2	1963	5.00	10.00	20.00
—With New York, USA address on label					
BST-84070 [S]	Up at Minton's, Volume 2	1967	3.75	7.50	15.00
—With "A Division of Liberty Records" on label					
BST-84081 [S]	Dearly Beloved	1961	15.00	30.00	60.00
—With 61st St. address on label					
BST-84081 [S]	Dearly Beloved	1963	5.00	10.00	20.00
—With New York, USA address on label					
BST-84081 [S]	Dearly Beloved	1967	3.75	7.50	15.00
—With "A Division of Liberty Records" on label					
BST-84096	That's Where It's At	1986	2.50	5.00	10.00
—"The Finest in Jazz Since 1939" reissue					
BST-84096 [S]	That's Where It's At	1962	15.00	30.00	60.00
—With 61st St. address on label					
BST-84096 [S]	That's Where It's At	1963	5.00	10.00	20.00
—With New York, USA address on label					
BST-84096 [S]	That's Where It's At	1967	3.75	7.50	15.00
—With "A Division of Liberty Records" on label					
BST-84122	Jubilee Shout!!	1986	3.00	6.00	12.00
—"The Finest in Jazz Since 1939" label; first issue of LP					
BST-84129 [S]	Never Let Me Go	1963	7.50	15.00	30.00
—With New York, USA address on label					
BST-84129 [S]	Never Let Me Go	1967	3.75	7.50	15.00
—With "A Division of Liberty Records" on label					
BST-84150 [S]	A Chip Off the Old Block	1963	7.50	15.00	30.00
—With New York, USA address on label					
BST-84150 [S]	A Chip Off the Old Block	1967	3.75	7.50	15.00
—With "A Division of Liberty Records" on label					
BST-84162 [S]	Hustlin'	1964	7.50	15.00	30.00
—With New York, USA address on label					
BST-84162 [S]	Hustlin'	1967	3.75	7.50	15.00
—With "A Division of Liberty Records" on label					
BST-84162 [S]	Hustlin'	1970	2.50	5.00	10.00
—With United Artists distribution					
BST-84201	Joyride	1984	2.50	5.00	10.00
—"The Finest in Jazz Since 1939" label reissue					
BST-84201 [S]	Joyride	1964	6.25	12.50	25.00
—With New York, USA address on label					
BST-84201 [S]	Joyride	1967	3.75	7.50	15.00
—With "A Division of Liberty Records" on label					
BST-84234 [S]	Stanley Turrentine	1965	—	—	—
—Canceled					
BST-84240 [S]	Rough 'n Tumble	1966	5.00	10.00	20.00
—With New York, USA address on label					
BST-84240 [S]	Rough 'n Tumble	1967	3.75	7.50	15.00
—With "A Division of Liberty Records" on label					
BST-84256 [S]	The Spoiler	1967	5.00	10.00	20.00
BST-84268 [S]	Easy Walker	1967	5.00	10.00	20.00
BST-84286	The Look of Love	1968	5.00	10.00	20.00
—With "A Division of Liberty Records" on label					
BST-84286	The Look of Love	1970	3.75	7.50	15.00
—With United Artists distribution					
BST-84298	Always Something There	1968	5.00	10.00	20.00
BST-84315	Common Touch!	1969	5.00	10.00	20.00
BST-84336	Another Story	1969	5.00	10.00	20.00
BST-84424	Z.T.'s Blues	1985	2.50	5.00	10.00
BST-85105	Straight Ahead	1984	2.50	5.00	10.00
BST-85140	Wonderland	1987	2.50	5.00	10.00
B1-90261	La Place	1987	2.50	5.00	10.00
B1-93201	The Best of Stanley Turrentine	1989	3.00	6.00	12.00
CTI					
6005	Sugar	1971	3.00	6.00	12.00
6010	Salt Song	1971	3.00	6.00	12.00
6017	Cherry	1972	3.00	6.00	12.00
6030	Don't Mess with Mister T.	1973	3.00	6.00	12.00
6048	The Baddest Turrentine	1974	3.00	6.00	12.00
6052	The Sugar Man	1975	3.00	6.00	12.00
8006	Sugar	1981	2.50	5.00	10.00
—Reissue					
8008	Salt Song	1981	2.50	5.00	10.00
—Reissue					
8010	Cherry	1981	2.50	5.00	10.00
—Reissue					
8011	Don't Mess with Mister T.	1981	2.50	5.00	10.00
—Reissue					
ELEKTRA					
6E-217	Betcha	1979	2.50	5.00	10.00
6E-269	Inflation	1980	2.50	5.00	10.00
5E-534	Tender Togetherness	1981	2.50	5.00	10.00
60201	Home Again	1982	2.50	5.00	10.00
FANTASY					
FPM-4002 [Q]	Pieces of Dreams	1974	5.00	10.00	20.00

(Top left) The closest thing the Thirteenth Floor Elevators had to a hit song was "You're Gonna Miss Me." It finally saw some action when issued on the International Artists label, but before that it was on two other labels, including the Texas label Contact. (Top right) Three Dog Night was one of the most popular bands of the early 1970s, yet the only stock-copy picture sleeve was for the Number One hit "Mama Told Me (Not to Come)." (Bottom left) Thanks to a licensing dispute, the early records by the Troggs were issued on two different to find. Here is the only Atco Troggs LP. (Bottom right) Records don't get much rarer than this one. Here's the Philles-label edition of Ike and Tina Turner's *River Deep — Mountain High* LP, which was never officially released. Only when issued on A&M in 1969 did this record have a jacket — none were ever made for the Phillies version.

Number	Title (A Side/B Side)	Yr	VG	VG+	NM
9465	Pieces of Dreams	1974	2.50	5.00	10.00
9478	In the Pocket	1975	2.50	5.00	10.00
9493	Have You Ever Seen the Rain	1975	2.50	5.00	10.00
9508	Everybody Come On Out	1976	2.50	5.00	10.00
9519	The Man with the Sad Face	1976	2.50	5.00	10.00
9534	Nightwings	1977	2.50	5.00	10.00
9548	West Side Highway	1978	2.50	5.00	10.00
9563	What About You!	1978	2.50	5.00	10.00
9604	Use the Stairs	1980	2.50	5.00	10.00
IMPULSE!					
AS-9115	Let It Go	1967	6.25	12.50	25.00
MAINSTREAM					
S-6041 [S]	Tiger Tail	1965	6.25	12.50	25.00
56041 [M]	Tiger Tail	1965	5.00	10.00	20.00
SUNSET					
SUS-5255	The Soul of Stanley Turrentine	196?	3.00	6.00	12.00
TIME					
S-2086 [S]	Stan the Man	1962	10.00	20.00	40.00
52086 [M]	Stan the Man	1962	10.00	20.00	40.00

TURTLES, THE

Also see FLO AND EDDIE.

45s

Number	Title (A Side/B Side)	Yr	VG	VG+	NM
WHITE WHALE					
222	It Ain't Me, Babe/Almost There	1965	3.00	6.00	12.00
224	Let Me Be/Your Maw Said You Cried	1965	2.50	5.00	10.00
227	You Baby/Wanderin' Kind	1966	2.50	5.00	10.00
231	Grim Reaper of Love/Come Back	1966	5.00	10.00	20.00
234	We'll Meet Again/Outside Chance	1966	3.75	7.50	15.00
237	Outside Chance/Making My Mind Up	1966	2.50	5.00	10.00
238	Can I Get to Know You Better?/Like the Seasons	1966	2.50	5.00	10.00
244	Happy Together/Like the Seasons	1967	2.00	4.00	8.00
244 [PS]	Happy Together/Like the Seasons	1967	5.00	10.00	20.00
249	She'd Rather Be with Me/The Walking Song	1967	2.00	4.00	8.00
249 [PS]	She'd Rather Be with Me/The Walking Song	1967	6.25	12.50	25.00
251	Guide for the Married Man/Think I'll Run Away	1967	10.00	20.00	40.00
—Withdrawn shortly after release					
254	You Know What I Mean/Rugs of Woods and Flowers	1967	2.00	4.00	8.00
254 [PS]	You Know What I Mean/Rugs of Woods and Flowers	1967	3.75	7.50	15.00
260	She's My Girl/Chicken Little Was Right	1967	2.50	5.00	10.00
—All-blue label					
260	She's My Girl/Chicken Little Was Right	1967	2.00	4.00	8.00
—White concentric circles on mostly blue label					
260 [PS]	She's My Girl/Chicken Little Was Right	1967	5.00	10.00	20.00
264	Sound Asleep/Umbassa the Dragon	1968	2.00	4.00	8.00
264 [PS]	Sound Asleep/Umbassa the Dragon	1968	3.75	7.50	15.00
273	The Story of Rock and Roll/Can't You Hear the Cows	1968	2.00	4.00	8.00
273 [PS]	The Story of Rock and Roll/Can't You Hear the Cows	1968	7.50	15.00	30.00
276	Elenore/Surfer Dan	1968	2.00	4.00	8.00
276 [PS]	Elenore/Surfer Dan	1968	3.00	6.00	12.00
292	You Showed Me/Buzz Saw	1969	2.00	4.00	8.00
292 [PS]	You Showed Me/Buzz Saw	1969	3.00	6.00	12.00
306	House on the Hill/Come Over	1969	5.00	10.00	20.00
308	You Don't Have to Walk in the Rain/Come Over	1969	2.00	4.00	8.00
308 [PS]	You Don't Have to Walk in the Rain/Come Over	1969	2.50	5.00	10.00
326	Love in the City/Bachelor Mother	1969	2.00	4.00	8.00
326 [PS]	Love in the City/Bachelor Mother	1969	2.50	5.00	10.00
334	Lady-O/Somewhere Friday Nite	1969	2.00	4.00	8.00
341	Who Would Ever Think That I Would Marry Margaret?/We Ain't Gonna Party No More	1970	3.75	7.50	15.00
350	Is It Any Wonder?/Wanderin' Kind	1970	2.00	4.00	8.00
355	Eve of Destruction/Wanderin' Kind	1970	2.00	4.00	8.00
364	Me About You/Think I'll Run Away	1970	2.00	4.00	8.00

Albums

Number	Title (A Side/B Side)	Yr	VG	VG+	NM
RHINO					
RNLP 151	It Ain't Me Babe	1983	2.50	5.00	10.00
RNLP 152	Happy Together	1983	2.50	5.00	10.00
RNLP 153	You Baby	1983	2.50	5.00	10.00
RNLP 154	Wooden Head	1983	2.50	5.00	10.00
RNLP 160	Greatest Hits	1983	2.50	5.00	10.00
RNDF 280 [RP]	Turtle-Sized	1984	3.00	6.00	12.00
—Green vinyl turtle-shaped EP					
RNPD 900	1968	1984	2.00	4.00	8.00
RNPD 901 [PD]	1968	1984	3.00	6.00	12.00
RNLP 70155	Chalon Road	1986	2.50	5.00	10.00
RNLP 70156	The Turtles Present the Battle of the Bands	1986	2.50	5.00	10.00
RNLP 70157	Turtle Soup	1986	2.50	5.00	10.00
RNLP 70158	Shell Shock	1986	2.50	5.00	10.00
RNLP 70159	Turtle Wax: The Best of the Turtles, Vol. 2	1988	2.50	5.00	10.00
RNLP 70177	The Best of the Turtles (Golden Archives Series)	1987	2.50	5.00	10.00
SIRE					
SASH-3703 [(2)]	The Turtles' Greatest Hits/Happy Together Again	1974	5.00	10.00	20.00
WHITE WHALE					
WW 111 [M]	It Ain't Me Babe	1965	7.50	15.00	30.00
WW 112 [M]	You Baby	1966	7.50	15.00	30.00
WW 114 [M]	Happy Together	1967	5.00	10.00	20.00
WW 115 [M]	The Turtles! Golden Hits	1967	6.25	12.50	25.00
WWS 7111 [S]	It Ain't Me Babe	1965	10.00	20.00	40.00
WWS 7112 [S]	You Baby	1966	10.00	20.00	40.00
WWS 7114 [S]	Happy Together	1967	6.25	12.50	25.00
WWS 7115 [S]	The Turtles! Golden Hits	1967	5.00	10.00	20.00
WWS 7118	The Turtles Present the Battle of the Bands	1968	6.25	12.50	25.00
WWS 7124	Turtle Soup	1969	6.25	12.50	25.00
WWS 7127	The Turtles! More Golden Hits	1970	5.00	10.00	20.00
WWS 7133	Wooden Head	1970	5.00	10.00	20.00

TURTLES, THE (2)

45s

Number	Title (A Side/B Side)	Yr	VG	VG+	NM
RCA VICTOR					
47-6356	Mystery Train/Say You Care	1955	6.25	12.50	25.00

TWEETERS, THE

45s

Number	Title (A Side/B Side)	Yr	VG	VG+	NM
DECCA					
30725	Mascara Mama/The Campus Rock	1958	7.50	15.00	30.00

TWENTIETH CENTURY ZOO, THE

45s

Number	Title (A Side/B Side)	Yr	VG	VG+	NM
CAZ					
103	You Don't Remember/Love in Your Face	1967	6.25	12.50	25.00
VAULT					
948	Rainbow/Bullfrog	1969	3.00	6.00	12.00

7-Inch Extended Plays

Number	Title (A Side/B Side)	Yr	VG	VG+	NM
SUNDAZED					
SEP 145	You Don't Remember//Love in Your Face/Tossin' and Turnin'	1999	—	—	2.00
SEP 145 [PS]	You Don't Remember	1999	—	—	2.00

Albums

Number	Title (A Side/B Side)	Yr	VG	VG+	NM
VAULT					
LPS-122	Thunder on a Clear Day	1968	15.00	30.00	60.00

23 SKIDOO

45s

Number	Title (A Side/B Side)	Yr	VG	VG+	NM
MERCURY					
72874	The New Year's Song/Courtesy	1968	2.50	5.00	10.00

TWICE AS MUCH

45s

Number	Title (A Side/B Side)	Yr	VG	VG+	NM
MGM					
13530	Sittin' on a Fence/Baby I Want You	1966	3.75	7.50	15.00
—A-side is a Mick Jagger-Keith Richards song that only later was released by the Rolling Stones.					
13530 [PS]	Sittin' on a Fence/Baby I Want You	1966	7.50	15.00	30.00
13600	Step Out of Line/Simplified	1966	2.50	5.00	10.00

TWIGGY

45s

Number	Title (A Side/B Side)	Yr	VG	VG+	NM
CAPITOL					
5903	Over and Over/When I Think of You	1967	2.50	5.00	10.00
MERCURY					
73863	Rain on the Roof/Vanilla Olay	1976	—	3.00	6.00
73923	I Lie Awake and Dream of You/Woman in Love	1977	—	3.00	6.00

Albums

Number	Title (A Side/B Side)	Yr	VG	VG+	NM
MERCURY					
SRM-1-1093	Twiggy	1976	3.00	6.00	12.00
SRM-1-1138	Please Get My Name Right	1977	3.00	6.00	12.00

TWILIGHTERS, THE (1)

45s

Number	Title (A Side/B Side)	Yr	VG	VG+	NM
BELL					
624	Be Faithful/Thumper	1965	5.00	10.00	20.00

TWILIGHTERS, THE (2)

45s

Number	Title (A Side/B Side)	Yr	VG	VG+	NM
BUBBLE					
1334	My Silent Prayer/Little Bitty Bed Bug	1962	10.00	20.00	40.00
CHESS					
1803	Scratchin'/Tears	1961	6.25	12.50	25.00
CHOLLY					
712	Let There Be Love/Eternally	1957	250.00	500.00	1000.
DOT					
15526	Eternally/I Believe	1957	10.00	20.00	40.00
EBB					
117	Pride and Joy/Live Like a King	1957	10.00	20.00	40.00
ELDO					
115	Nothin'/Do You Believe	1961	6.25	12.50	25.00
IMPERIAL					
66201	Shake a Tail Feather/Road to Fortune	1966	3.00	6.00	12.00
66238	I Still Love You/Meat Ball	1967	3.00	6.00	12.00
JVB					
83	How Many Times/Water-Water	1957	200.00	400.00	800.00
MGM					
55011	Little Did I Dream/Gotta Get On the Train	1955	75.00	150.00	300.00
55014	Lovely Lady/Half Angel	1955	100.00	200.00	400.00
PICO					
2801	Eternally/I Believe	1957	20.00	40.00	80.00

TWILIGHTERS, THE (3)

45s

Number	Title (A Side/B Side)	Yr	VG	VG+	NM
CADDY					
103	Eternally/I Believe	1955	62.50	125.00	250.00

TWILIGHTERS, THE (4)

45s

Number	Title (A Side/B Side)	Yr	VG	VG+	NM
FRATERNITY					
889	To Love in Vain/The Beginning of Love	1961	6.25	12.50	25.00
—As "The Twi-Lighters"					

TWILIGHTERS, THE (5)

45s

Number	Title (A Side/B Side)	Yr	VG	VG+	NM
MARSHALL					
702	Please Tell Me You're Mine/Wondering	1953	50.00	100.00	200.00
—Black vinyl					
702	Please Tell Me You're Mine/Wondering	1953	250.00	500.00	1000.
—Red vinyl					

TWILIGHTERS, THE (6)

45s

Number	Title (A Side/B Side)	Yr	VG	VG+	NM
SPECIALTY					
548	It's True/Wha-Bop-Sh-Wah	1955	15.00	30.00	60.00

TWILIGHTERS, THE (7)

45s

Number	Title (A Side/B Side)	Yr	VG	VG+	NM
SPIN					
0001	Yes You Are/A Possibility	1960	50.00	100.00	200.00

TWILIGHTERS, THE (U)

45s

Number	Title (A Side/B Side)	Yr	VG	VG+	NM
GROOVE					
0154	Sittin' in a Corner/It's a Cold, Cold, Rainy Day	1956	15.00	30.00	60.00
—As "The Twi-Lighters"					
RICKI					
907	Help Me/Rockin' Mule	1961	10.00	20.00	40.00
SARA					
1048	Restless Love/Can't You Stay a Little Longer	1961	15.00	30.00	60.00
VANCO					
204	Out of My Mind/I Need Your Lovin'	1968	2.50	5.00	10.00

TWILLEY, DWIGHT

12-Inch Singles

Number	Title (A Side/B Side)	Yr	VG	VG+	NM
ARISTA					
SP-79 [DJ]	Somebody to Love/Money	1979	3.00	6.00	12.00
CBS ASSOCIATED					
ZAS 2360 [DJ]	Sexual (same on both sides)	1986	2.50	5.00	10.00
EMI AMERICA					
SPRO-9104 [DJ]	Little Bit of Love (Edit)/Little Bit of Love (LP)	1984	2.00	4.00	8.00

45s

Number	Title (A Side/B Side)	Yr	VG	VG+	NM
ARISTA					
0278	Rock and Roll 47/Twilley Don't Mind	1977	—	2.50	5.00
0299	Trying to Find My Baby/Here She Comes	1977	—	2.50	5.00
0311	Looking for the Magic/Invasion	1978	—	2.50	5.00
0415	Out of My Hands/Nothing's Ever Gonna Change So Fast	1979	—	2.00	4.00
0433	Runaway/Burnin' Sand	1979	—	2.00	4.00
0478	Somebody to Love/Money (That's What I Want)	1979	—	2.00	4.00
CBS ASSOCIATED					
06050	Sexual/Wild Dogs	1986	—	—	3.00
EMI AMERICA					
8109	Later That Night/Somebody to Love	1982	—	2.00	4.00
8115	I Found the Magic/I'm Back Again	1982	—	2.00	4.00
8196	Girls/To Get to You	1984	—	—	3.00
8196 [PS]	Girls/To Get to You	1984	—	2.00	4.00
8206	Little Bit of Love/Mad Dog	1984	—	—	3.00
8206 [PS]	Little Bit of Love/Mad Dog	1984	—	2.00	4.00
8235	Why You Wanna Break My Heart/Chilly D's Theme	1984	—	—	3.00
8235 [PS]	Why You Wanna Break My Heart/Chilly D's Theme	1984	—	—	3.00
PRIVATE I					
04820	Keep On Working/(Instrumental)	1985	—	—	3.00
SHELTER					
40380	I'm on Fire/Did You See What Happened	1975	—	2.50	5.00
40380 [PS]	I'm on Fire/Did You See What Happened	1975	2.50	5.00	10.00
40450	Sincerely/You Were So Warm	1975	—	2.50	5.00
62003	Could Be Love/Feeling in the Dark	1976	—	2.50	5.00
62003 [PS]	Could Be Love/Feeling in the Dark	1976	2.00	4.00	8.00
THE RIGHT STUFF					
S7-19563	I'm on Fire/Looking for the Magic	1997	—	—	3.00

Albums

Number	Title (A Side/B Side)	Yr	VG	VG+	NM
ARISTA					
AL 4140	Twilley Don't Mind	1977	2.50	5.00	10.00
AB 4214	Twilley	1979	2.50	5.00	10.00
AB 4251	Blueprint	1980	—	—	—
—Unreleased					
CBS ASSOCIATED					
BFZ 40266	Wild Dogs	1986	2.00	4.00	8.00
EMI AMERICA					
ST-17064	Scuba Divers	1982	2.50	5.00	10.00
ST-17107	Jungle	1984	2.50	5.00	10.00
MCA					
688	Sincerely	1981	2.00	4.00	8.00
—Reissue of Shelter LP					
SHELTER					
SA-52001	Sincerely	1976	2.50	5.00	10.00

TWIN-TONES, THE

See THE TWINS.

TWINK

Albums

Number	Title (A Side/B Side)	Yr	VG	VG+	NM
SIRE					
SES-97022	Think Pink	1970	25.00	50.00	100.00

TWINKLE

45s

Number	Title (A Side/B Side)	Yr	VG	VG+	NM
AURORA					
163	The End of the World/What Am I Doing Here with You	1966	2.50	5.00	10.00
TOLLIE					
9040	The Boy of My Dreams/Terry	1965	3.00	6.00	12.00
9047	Ain't Nobody Home But Me/Golden Lights	1965	3.00	6.00	12.00

TWINS, THE

45s

Number	Title (A Side/B Side)	Yr	VG	VG+	NM
LANCER					
106	Heart of Gold/Buttercup	1959	3.75	7.50	15.00
RCA VICTOR					
47-7148	My Dear/The Flip Skip	1958	5.00	10.00	20.00
—As "The Twin-Tones"					
47-7235	Jo-Ann's Sister/Who Knows the Secret	1958	5.00	10.00	20.00
47-7382	Classroom Rock/Gee Whiz	1958	5.00	10.00	20.00

7-Inch Extended Plays

Number	Title (A Side/B Side)	Yr	VG	VG+	NM
RCA VICTOR					
EPA-4107	Jo-Ann/Before You Go//My Dancing Lady/One Mail a Day	1957	5.00	10.00	20.00
—As "The Twin-Tones"					
EPA-4107 [PS]	Jim and John The Twin-Tones	1957	5.00	10.00	20.00
EPA-4237	My Dear/The Flip Skip//I Want a Girl/Together Forever	1958	5.00	10.00	20.00
EPA-4237 [PS]	Teenagers Love the Twins	1958	5.00	10.00	20.00

Albums

Number	Title (A Side/B Side)	Yr	VG	VG+	NM
RCA VICTOR					
LPM-1708 [M]	Teenagers Love the Twins	1958	12.50	25.00	50.00

TWISTERS, THE

45s

Number	Title (A Side/B Side)	Yr	VG	VG+	NM
APT					
25045	Come Go with Me/Pretty Little Girl Next Door	1960	5.00	10.00	20.00
CAMPUS					
125	Elvis Leaves Sorrento/Street Dance	1961	7.50	15.00	30.00
CAPITOL					
4451	Turn the Page/Dancing Little Clown	1960	5.00	10.00	20.00
DUAL					
502	Silly Chilli/Peppermint Twist Time	1962	3.00	6.00	12.00
FELCO					
103	Count Down 1-2-3/Speed Limit	1959	6.25	12.50	25.00
SUN-SET					
501	Please Come Back/This Is the End	1961	150.00	300.00	600.00

Albums

Number	Title (A Side/B Side)	Yr	VG	VG+	NM
TREASURE					
TLP-890 [M]	Doin' the Twist	1962	7.50	15.00	30.00

TWISTIN' KINGS

45s

Number	Title (A Side/B Side)	Yr	VG	VG+	NM
MOTOWN					
1022	Xmas Twist/White House Twist	1961	10.00	20.00	40.00
1023	Congo (Part 1)/Congo (Part 2)	1962	10.00	20.00	40.00

Albums

Number	Title (A Side/B Side)	Yr	VG	VG+	NM
MOTOWN					
M-601 [M]	Twistin' the World Around	1961	75.00	150.00	300.00

TWITTY, CONWAY

Also see CONWAY TWITTY AND LORETTA LYNN.

45s

Number	Title (A Side/B Side)	Yr	VG	VG+	NM
ABC-PARAMOUNT					
10507	Go On and Cry/She Loves Me	1963	3.75	7.50	15.00
10550	Such a Night/My Baby Left Me	1964	6.25	12.50	25.00
DECCA					
31833	Together Forever/That Kind of Girl	1965	2.50	5.00	10.00
31897	Guess My Eyes Were Bigger Than Her Heart/Honky Tonk Man	1966	2.00	4.00	8.00
31983	Look Into My Teardrops/If You Were Mine to Lose	1966	2.00	4.00	8.00
32081	I Don't Want to Be with Me/Before I'll Set Her Free	1967	2.00	4.00	8.00
32147	Don't Put Your Hurt in My Heart/Walk Me to the Door	1967	2.00	4.00	8.00
32208	Funny (But I'm Not Laughing)/Working Girl	1967	2.00	4.00	8.00
32272	The Image of Me/Dim Lights, Truck Smoke (And Loud, Loud Music)	1968	2.00	4.00	8.00
32361	Next in Line/I'm Checking Out	1968	2.00	4.00	8.00
32424	Darling, You Know I Wouldn't Lie/Table in the Corner	1968	2.00	4.00	8.00
32481	I Love You More Today/Bad Girl	1969	2.00	4.00	8.00
32546	To See My Angel Cry/I Did the Best I Could	1969	2.00	4.00	8.00
32599	That's When She Started to Stop Loving You/I'll Get Over Losing You	1969	2.00	4.00	8.00
32661	Hello Darlin'/Girl at the Bar	1970	—	3.50	7.00
32742	Fifteen Years Ago/Up Comes the Bottle	1970	—	3.50	7.00
32801	How Much More Can She Stand/Just Like a Stranger	1971	—	3.50	7.00
32842	I Wonder What She'll Think About Me Leaving/A Heartache Just Walked In	1971	—	3.50	7.00
32895	I Can't See Me Without You/I Didn't Lose Her	1971	—	3.50	7.00
32945	(Lost Her Love) On Our Last Date/I'll Never Make It Home Tonight	1972	—	3.50	7.00
32988	I Can't Stop Loving You/She Needs Someone to Hold Her (When She Cries)	1972	—	3.50	7.00
32988	I Can't Stop Loving You/Since She's Not with the One She Loves	1972	—	3.50	7.00
33033	She Needs Someone to Hold Her (When She Cries)/This Road That I Walk	1972	—	3.50	7.00
ELEKTRA					
47302	The Clown/The Boy Next Door	1982	—	2.00	4.00
47302 [PS]	The Clown/The Boy Next Door	1982	—	2.50	5.00
47443	Slow Hand/When Love Was Something Else	1982	—	2.00	4.00
69854	The Rose/It's Only Make Believe	1982	—	2.00	4.00
69854 [PS]	The Rose/It's Only Make Believe	1982	—	2.50	5.00
69964	We Did But Now You Don't/(B-side unknown)	1982	—	2.00	4.00
MCA					
40027	Baby's Gone/Dim Lovely Places	1973	—	2.50	5.00
40094	You've Never Been This Far Before/You Make It Hard	1973	—	2.50	5.00
40173	There's a Honky Tonk Angel (Who'll Take Me Back In)/Don't Let It Go to Your Heart	1973	—	2.50	5.00
40224	I'm Not Through Loving You Yet/Before Your Time	1974	—	2.50	5.00
40282	I See the Want To in Your Eyes/Girl from Tupelo	1974	—	2.50	5.00
40339	Linda on My Mind/She's Just Not Over You Yet	1974	—	2.50	5.00
40407	Touch the Hand/Don't Cry Joni	1975	—	2.50	5.00
40492	This Time I've Hurt Her More Than She Loves Me/She Did, It Did, I Didn't	1975	—	2.50	5.00
40534	After All the Good Is Gone/I Got a Good Thing Going	1976	—	2.50	5.00

Number	Title (A Side/B Side)	Yr	VG	VG+	NM
40601	The Games That Daddies Play/There's More Love in the Arms You're Leaving	1976	—	2.50	5.00
40649	I Can't Believe She Gives It All to Me/I Can't Help It If She Can't Stop Loving Me	1976	—	2.50	5.00
40682	Play, Guitar, Play/One in a Million	1977	—	2.50	5.00
40754	I've Already Loved You in My Mind/I Changed My Mind	1977	—	2.50	5.00
40805	Talkin' 'Bout You/Georgia Keeps Pulling on My Ring	1977	—	2.50	5.00
40857	I'm Used to Losing You/The Grandest Lady of Them All	1978	—	2.50	5.00
40929	That's All She Wrote/Boogie Grass Band	1978	—	2.50	5.00
40963	Your Love Had Taken Me That High/My Woman Knows	1978	—	2.50	5.00
41002	Don't Take It Away/Draggin' Chains	1979	—	2.00	4.00
41059	I May Never Get to Heaven/Grand Ole Blues	1979	—	2.00	4.00
41135	Happy Birthday Darlin'/Heavy Tears	1979	—	2.00	4.00
41174	I'd Just Love to Lay You Down/She Thinks I Still Care	1980	—	2.00	4.00
41174	I'd Love to Lay You Down/She Thinks I Still Care	1980	—	2.50	5.00
—Note slightly different A-side title					
41271	I've Never Seen the Likes of You/Soulful Woman	1980	—	2.00	4.00
51011	A Bridge That Just Won't Burn/You'll Be Back	1980	—	2.00	4.00
51059	Rest Your Love on Me/I Am the Dreamer (You Are the Dream)	1981	—	2.00	4.00
51137	Tight Fittin' Jeans/I Made You a Woman	1981	—	2.00	4.00
51199	Red Neckin' Love Makin' Night/Hearts	1981	—	2.00	4.00
52032	Over Thirty (Not Over the Hill)/Love Salvation	1982	—	2.00	4.00
52154	We Had It All/Cheatin' Fire	1983	—	2.00	4.00
53034	Julia/Everybody Needs a Hero	1987	—	2.00	4.00
53134	I Want to Know You Before We Make Love/Snake Boots	1987	—	2.00	4.00
53200	That's My Job/Lonely Town	1987	—	2.00	4.00
53276	Goodbye Time/Your Loving Side	1988	—	2.00	4.00
53373	Saturday Night Special/If You Were Mine to Lose	1988	—	2.00	4.00
53456	I Wish I Was Still in Your Dreams/If You Were Mine to Lose	1988	—	2.00	4.00
53633	She's Got a Single Thing in Mind/Too White to Sing the Blues	1989	—	2.00	4.00
53688	The House on Old Lonesome Road/Nobody Can Fill Your Shoes	1989	—	2.00	4.00
53759	Who's Gonna Know/Private Part of My Heart	1989	—	2.00	4.00
53983	I Couldn't See You Leavin'/Just the Thought of Losing You	1991	—	2.00	4.00
54077	One Bridge I Didn't Burn/I'm Tired of Being Something	1991	—	2.00	4.00
54186	She's Got a Man on Her Mind/You Put It There	1991	—	2.00	4.00
54281	Who Did They Think He Was/Let the Pretty Lady Dance	1991	—	2.00	4.00
54717	I'm the Only Thing (I'll Hold Against You)/Final Touches	1993	—	2.00	4.00
54766	Don't It Make You Lonely/I Don't Love You	1993	—	2.00	4.00
79000	Fit to Be Tied Down/When You're Cool (The Sun Shines All the Time)	1990	—	2.00	4.00
79067	Crazy in Love/Hearts Breakin' All Over Town	1990	—	2.00	4.00
MERCURY					
71086	I Need Your Lovin'/Born to Sing the Blues	1957	10.00	20.00	40.00
71148	Maybe Baby/Shake It Up	1957	10.00	20.00	40.00
71384	Why Can't I Get Through to You/Double Talk Baby	1958	10.00	20.00	40.00
MGM					
12677 [M]	It's Only Make Believe/I'll Try	1958	6.25	12.50	25.00
12748	The Story of My Love/Make Me Know You're Mine	1959	6.25	12.50	25.00
12785	Hey Little Lucy! (Don'tcha Put No Lipstick On)/ When I'm Not with You	1959	6.25	12.50	25.00
12804	Mona Lisa/Heavenly	1959	6.25	12.50	25.00
12826 [M]	Danny Boy/Halfway to Heaven	1959	6.25	12.50	25.00
—First pressings on yellow labels					
12826 [M]	Danny Boy/Halfway to Heaven	1959	5.00	10.00	20.00
—Second pressings on black labels					
12857	Lonely Blue Boy/Star Spangled Heaven	1959	5.00	10.00	20.00
12886	What Am I Living For/The Hurt in My Heart	1960	5.00	10.00	20.00
12886 [PS]	What Am I Living For/The Hurt in My Heart	1960	12.50	25.00	50.00
12911	Is a Blue Bird Blue/She's Mine	1960	5.00	10.00	20.00
12911 [PS]	Is a Blue Bird Blue/She's Mine	1960	12.50	25.00	50.00
12918	What a Dream/Tell Me One More Time	1960	3.75	7.50	15.00
12943	Teasin'/I Need You So	1960	3.75	7.50	15.00
12962	Whole Lot of Shakin' Going On/The Flame	1960	3.75	7.50	15.00
12969	C'est Si Bon (It's So Good)/Don't You Dare Let Me Down	1960	3.75	7.50	15.00
12969 [PS]	C'est Si Bon (It's So Good)/Don't You Dare Let Me Down	1960	12.50	25.00	50.00
12998	The Next Kiss (Is the Last Goodbye)/A Man Alone	1961	3.75	7.50	15.00
12998 [PS]	The Next Kiss (Is the Last Goodbye)/A Man Alone	1961	12.50	25.00	50.00
13011	I'm in a Blue, Blue Mood/A Million Teardrops	1961	3.75	7.50	15.00
13034	It's Drivin' Me Wild/Sweet Sorrow	1961	3.75	7.50	15.00
13034 [PS]	It's Drivin' Me Wild/Sweet Sorrow	1961	10.00	20.00	40.00
13050	Portrait of a Fool/Tower of Tears	1961	3.75	7.50	15.00
13072	Little Piece of My Heart/Comfy N' Cozy	1962	3.75	7.50	15.00
13089	There's Something on Your Mind/Unchained Melody	1962	3.75	7.50	15.00
13112	I Hope, I Think, I Wish/The Pickup	1962	3.75	7.50	15.00
13149	I Got My Mojo Working/She Ain't No Angel	1963	3.75	7.50	15.00
14172	It's Only Make Believe/Lonely Blue Boy	1970	—	2.50	5.00
14205	What Am I Living For/I'll Try	1970	—	2.50	5.00
14274	What a Dream/Long Black Train	1971	—	2.50	5.00
14355	It's Too Late/I Hope, I Think, I Wish	1972	—	2.50	5.00
14408	Walk On By/Hey Miss Ruby	1972	—	2.50	5.00
14447	Boss Man/Fever	1972	—	2.50	5.00
14582	Danny Boy/The Pickup	1973	—	2.50	5.00
SK-50107 [S]	It's Only Make Believe/I'll Try	1958	25.00	50.00	100.00
SK-50130 [S]	Danny Boy/Halfway to Heaven	1959	25.00	50.00	100.00
WARNER BROS.					
28577	Fallin' for You for Years/I'll Try	1986	—	2.00	4.00
28692	Desperado Love/I Can't See Me Without You	1986	—	2.00	4.00
28772	You'll Never Know How Much I Needed You Today/Fifteen Years Ago	1986	—	2.00	4.00
28866	The Legend and the Man/(I Can't Believe) She Gives It All to Me	1985	—	2.00	4.00
28966	Between Blue Eyes and Jeans/Baby's Gone	1985	—	2.00	4.00
29057	Don't Call Him a Cowboy/After All the Good Is Gone	1985	—	2.00	4.00
29129	White Christmas/Happy the Christmas Clown	1984	—	2.50	5.00
29129 [PS]	White Christmas/Happy The Christmas Clown	1984	—	2.50	5.00
29137	Ain't She Somethin' Else/The Games That Daddies Play	1984	—	2.00	4.00
29227	I Don't Know a Thing About Love (The Moon Song)/Don't Cry Joni	1984	—	2.00	4.00
29308	Somebody's Needin' Somebody/(Lying Here with) Linda on My Mind	1984	—	2.00	4.00
29395	Three Times a Lady/I Think I'm in Love	1983	—	2.00	4.00
29505	Heartache Tonight/Hello Darlin'	1983	—	2.00	4.00
29636	Lost in the Feeling/You've Never Been This Far Before	1983	—	2.00	4.00
7-Inch Extended Plays					
MGM					
X-1623	(contents unknown)	1958	37.50	75.00	150.00
X-1623 [PS]	It's Only Make Believe	1958	37.50	75.00	150.00
X-1640	It's Only Make Believe/Hallelujah, I Love Her So //First Romance/Make Me Know You're Mine	1959	25.00	50.00	100.00
X-1640 [PS]	Conway Twitty Sings, Volume 1	1959	25.00	50.00	100.00
X-1641	(contents unknown)	1959	25.00	50.00	100.00
X-1641 [PS]	Conway Twitty Sings, Volume 2	1959	25.00	50.00	100.00
X-1642	(contents unknown)	1959	25.00	50.00	100.00
X-1642 [PS]	Conway Twitty Sings, Volume 3	1959	25.00	50.00	100.00
X-1678	Danny Boy/Heavenly//She's Mine/Blueberry Hill	1959	25.00	50.00	100.00
X-1678 [PS]	Saturday Night with Conway Twitty, Volume 1	1959	25.00	50.00	100.00
X-1679	(contents unknown)	1959	25.00	50.00	100.00
X-1679 [PS]	Saturday Night with Conway Twitty, Volume 2	1959	25.00	50.00	100.00
X-1680	(contents unknown)	1959	25.00	50.00	100.00
X-1680 [PS]	Saturday Night with Conway Twitty, Volume 3	1959	25.00	50.00	100.00
X-1701	(contents unknown)	1960	25.00	50.00	100.00
X-1701 [PS]	Lonely Blue Boy	1960	25.00	50.00	100.00
Albums					
ACCORD					
SN-7169	Early Favorites	1982	3.00	6.00	12.00
ALLEGIANCE					
AV-5012	You Made Me What I Am	1983	3.75	7.50	15.00
DECCA					
DL 4724 [M]	Conway Twitty Sings	1965	6.25	12.50	25.00
DL 4828 [M]	Look Into My Teardrops	1966	6.25	12.50	25.00
DL 4913 [M]	Conway Twitty Country	1967	7.50	15.00	30.00
DL 4990 [M]	Here's Conway Twitty	1968	12.50	25.00	50.00
DL 74724 [S]	Conway Twitty Sings	1965	7.50	15.00	30.00
DL 74828 [S]	Look Into My Teardrops	1966	7.50	15.00	30.00
DL 74913 [S]	Conway Twitty Country	1967	7.50	15.00	30.00
DL 74990 [S]	Here's Conway Twitty	1968	7.50	15.00	30.00
DL 75062	Next in Line	1968	6.25	12.50	25.00
DL 75105	Darling, You Know I Wouldn't Lie	1968	5.00	10.00	20.00
DL 75131	I Love You More Today	1969	5.00	10.00	20.00
DL 75172	To See My Angel Cry	1970	5.00	10.00	20.00
DL 75209	Hello Darlin'	1970	5.00	10.00	20.00
DL 75248	Fifteen Years Ago	1970	5.00	10.00	20.00
DL 75276	How Much More Can She Stand	1971	5.00	10.00	20.00
DL 75292	I Wonder What She'll Think About Me Leaving	1971	5.00	10.00	20.00
DL 75335	I Can't See Me Without You	1972	5.00	10.00	20.00
DL 75352	Conway Twitty's Greatest Hits	1972	5.00	10.00	20.00
DL 75361	I Can't Stop Loving You/Last Date	1972	5.00	10.00	20.00
ELEKTRA					
60005	Southern Confort	1982	2.50	5.00	10.00
60115	#1 Classics, Volume 1	1982	2.50	5.00	10.00
60182	Dream Maker	1982	2.50	5.00	10.00
60209	#1 Classics, Volume 2	1982	2.50	5.00	10.00
HEARTLAND					
HL-1088/9 [(2)]	The Very Best of Conway Twitty	1989	5.00	10.00	20.00
MCA					
19	Hello Darlin'	1973	3.00	6.00	12.00
—Reissue of Decca 75209					
53	I Can't Stop Loving You/Last Date	1973	3.00	6.00	12.00
—Reissue of Decca 75361					
303	She Needs Someone to Hold Her (When She Cries)	1973	3.75	7.50	15.00
359	You've Never Been This Far Before/Baby's Gone	1973	3.75	7.50	15.00
376	Clinging to a Saving Hand	1973	15.00	30.00	60.00
406	Honky Tonk Angel	1974	3.75	7.50	15.00
441	I'm Not Through Loving You Yet/I See the Want To in Your Eyes	1974	3.75	7.50	15.00
469	Linda on My Mind	1975	3.75	7.50	15.00
625	High Priest of Country	197?	2.50	5.00	10.00
—Reissue of MCA 2144					
702	Conway	197?	2.50	5.00	10.00
—Reissue of MCA 3063					
2144	High Priest of Country Music	1975	3.75	7.50	15.00
2176	Twitty (This Time I've Hurt Her More Than She Loves Me)	1975	3.75	7.50	15.00
2206	Now and Then	1976	3.75	7.50	15.00
2235	Conway Twitty's Greatest Hits, Vol. 2	1976	3.75	7.50	15.00
2262	Play Guitar Play	1977	3.00	6.00	12.00
2293	I've Already Loved You in My Mind	1977	3.00	6.00	12.00
2328	Georgia Keeps Pullin' on My Ring	1978	3.00	6.00	12.00
2345	Conway Twitty's Greatest Hits, Vol. 1	1978	3.00	6.00	12.00
—Reissue of Decca 75352					
3042	The Very Best of Conway Twitty	1978	3.00	6.00	12.00
3063	Conway	1978	3.00	6.00	12.00
3086	Cross Winds	1979	3.00	6.00	12.00
3210	Heart and Soul	1980	3.00	6.00	12.00
5138	Rest Your Love on Me	1980	3.00	6.00	12.00
5204	Mr. T.	1981	3.00	6.00	12.00
5318	Number Ones	1982	3.00	6.00	12.00

Number	Title (A Side/B Side)	Yr	VG	VG+	NM
5424	Classic Conway	1983	2.50	5.00	10.00
5700	Songwriter	1986	2.00	4.00	8.00
5817	A Night with Conway Twitty	1986	2.00	4.00	8.00
5969	Borderline	1987	2.00	4.00	8.00
37081	Georgia Keeps Pullin' on My Ring	198?	2.00	4.00	8.00
—Budget-line reissue					
37163	Cross Winds	198?	2.00	4.00	8.00
—Budget-line reissue					
37227	Heart and Soul	1983	2.00	4.00	8.00
—Budget-line reissue					
37228	Rest Your Love on Me	1983	2.00	4.00	8.00
—Budget-line reissue					
37229	Conway Twitty's Greatest Hits, Vol. 1	1983	2.00	4.00	8.00
—Budget-line reissue					
42115	Still in Your Dreams	1988	2.00	4.00	8.00
42297	House on Old Lonesome Road	1989	3.00	6.00	12.00

MCA CORAL

Number	Title (A Side/B Side)	Yr	VG	VG+	NM
CB-20000	I'm So Used to Loving You	1973	3.00	6.00	12.00

METRO

Number	Title (A Side/B Side)	Yr	VG	VG+	NM
M-512 [M]	It's Only Make Believe	1966	3.75	7.50	15.00
MS-512 [S]	It's Only Make Believe	1966	5.00	10.00	20.00

MGM

Number	Title (A Side/B Side)	Yr	VG	VG+	NM
GAS-110	Conway Twitty (Golden Archive Series)	1970	5.00	10.00	20.00
E-3744 [M]	Conway Twitty Sings	1959	25.00	50.00	100.00
—Yellow label					
E-3744 [M]	Conway Twitty Sings	1960	10.00	20.00	40.00
—Black label					
E-3744 [M]	Conway Twitty Sings	196?	75.00	150.00	300.00
—Reissue with orange cover and a clean-cut photo of Conway					
SE-3744 [S]	Conway Twitty Sings	1959	37.50	75.00	150.00
—Yellow label					
SE-3744 [S]	Conway Twitty Sings	1960	12.50	25.00	50.00
—Black label					
SE-3744 [S]	Conway Twitty Sings	196?	75.00	150.00	300.00
—Reissue with orange cover and a clean-cut photo of Conway					
E-3786 [M]	Saturday Night with Conway Twitty	1960	17.50	35.00	70.00
SE-3786 [S]	Saturday Night with Conway Twitty	1960	25.00	50.00	100.00
E-3818 [M]	Lonely Blue Boy	1960	17.50	35.00	70.00
SE-3818 [S]	Lonely Blue Boy	1960	25.00	50.00	100.00
E-3849 [M]	Conway Twitty's Greatest Hits	1960	17.50	35.00	70.00
—With poster					
E-3849 [M]	Conway Twitty's Greatest Hits	1960	10.00	20.00	40.00
—Without poster					
SE-3849 [P]	Conway Twitty's Greatest Hits	1960	20.00	40.00	80.00
—With poster					
SE-3849 [P]	Conway Twitty's Greatest Hits	1960	12.50	25.00	50.00
—Without poster					
E-3907 [M]	The Rock and Roll Story	1961	12.50	25.00	50.00
SE-3907 [S]	The Rock and Roll Story	1961	20.00	40.00	80.00
E-3943 [M]	The Conway Twitty Touch	1961	12.50	25.00	50.00
SE-3943 [S]	The Conway Twitty Touch	1961	20.00	40.00	80.00
E-4019 [M]	Portrait of a Fool and Others	1962	10.00	20.00	40.00
SE-4019 [S]	Portrait of a Fool and Others	1962	12.50	25.00	50.00
E-4089 [M]	R & B '63	1963	10.00	20.00	40.00
SE-4089 [S]	R & B '63	1963	12.50	25.00	50.00
E-4217 [M]	Hit the Road	1964	6.25	12.50	25.00
SE-4217 [S]	Hit the Road	1964	7.50	15.00	30.00
SE-4650	You Can't Take the Country Out of Conway	1969	3.75	7.50	15.00
SE-4799	Conway Twitty Hits	1971	3.75	7.50	15.00
SE-4837	Conway Twitty Sings the Blues	1972	3.75	7.50	15.00
SES-4844 [(2)]	20 Great Hits by Conway Twitty	1973	4.50	9.00	18.00

PICKWICK

Number	Title (A Side/B Side)	Yr	VG	VG+	NM
SPC-3360	Shake It Up	1973	3.00	6.00	12.00

TEE VEE

Number	Title (A Side/B Side)	Yr	VG	VG+	NM
1009	20 Certified #1 Hits	1978	3.75	7.50	15.00

WARNER BROS.

Number	Title (A Side/B Side)	Yr	VG	VG+	NM
23869	Lost in the Feeling	1983	2.50	5.00	10.00
23971	Merry Twismas	1983	5.00	10.00	20.00
25078	By Heart	1984	2.50	5.00	10.00
25170	Conway's Latest Greatest Hits	1984	2.50	5.00	10.00
25207	Don't Call Him a Cowboy	1985	2.50	5.00	10.00
25294	Chasin' Rainbows	1985	2.50	5.00	10.00
25406	Fallin' for You for Years	1986	2.50	5.00	10.00
25777	#1's — The Warner Bros. Years	1988	2.00	4.00	8.00
60115	#1 Classics, Volume 1	1983	2.00	4.00	8.00
—Reissue of Elektra LP					
60182	Dream Maker	1983	2.00	4.00	8.00
—Reissue of Elektra LP					
60209	#1 Classics, Volume 2	1983	2.00	4.00	8.00
—Reissue of Elektra LP					

TWITTY, CONWAY, AND LORETTA LYNN

Also see each artist's individual listings.

45s

DECCA

Number	Title (A Side/B Side)	Yr	VG	VG+	NM
32776	After the Fire Is Gone/The One I Can't Live Without	1971	—	3.50	7.00
32873	Lead Me On/Four Glass Walls	1971	—	3.50	7.00

MCA

Number	Title (A Side/B Side)	Yr	VG	VG+	NM
40079	Louisiana Woman, Mississippi Man/Living Together Alone	1973	—	2.50	5.00
40251	As Soon As I Hang Up the Phone/A Lifetime Before	1974	—	2.50	5.00
40283	Trouble in Paradise/We've Already Tasted Love	1974	—	2.50	5.00
40420	Feelin's/You Done Lost Your Baby	1975	—	2.50	5.00
40572	The Letter/God Bless America Again	1976	—	2.50	5.00
40728	The Bed I'm Dreaming On/I Can't Love You Enough	1977	—	2.50	5.00
40920	You're the Reason Our Kids Are Ugly/From Seven Until Ten	1978	—	2.50	5.00
41141	The Sadness of It All/You Know Just What I'd Do	1979	—	2.50	5.00
41232	Hit the Road Jack/It's True Love	1980	—	2.00	4.00
51050	Lovin' What Your Lovin' Does to Me/Silent Partners	1981	—	2.00	4.00
51114	I Still Believe in Waltzes/Oh Honey	1981	—	2.00	4.00
53417	Making Believe/As Soon As I Hang Up the Phone (The Telephone Song)	1988	—	2.00	4.00

Albums

DECCA

Number	Title (A Side/B Side)	Yr	VG	VG+	NM
DL 75251	We Only Make Believe	1971	5.00	10.00	20.00
DL 75326	Lead Me On	1972	5.00	10.00	20.00

HEARTLAND

Number	Title (A Side/B Side)	Yr	VG	VG+	NM
HL-1059/60 [(2)]	The Best of Conway and Loretta	1987	5.00	10.00	20.00

MCA

Number	Title (A Side/B Side)	Yr	VG	VG+	NM
8	We Only Make Believe	1973	3.00	6.00	12.00
—Reissue of Decca 75251					
9	Lead Me On	1973	3.00	6.00	12.00
—Reissue of Decca 75326					
335	Louisiana Woman, Mississippi Man	1973	3.75	7.50	15.00
427	Country Partners	1974	3.75	7.50	15.00
629	United Talent	198?	2.50	5.00	10.00
—Reissue of MCA 2209					
722	Honky Tonk Heroes	198?	2.50	5.00	10.00
—Reissue of MCA 2372					
723	Diamond Duet	198?	2.50	5.00	10.00
—Reissue of MCA 3190					
2143	Feelins'	1975	3.75	7.50	15.00
2209	United Talent	1976	3.75	7.50	15.00
2278	Dynamic Duo	1977	3.00	6.00	12.00
2354	Country Partners	1978	2.50	5.00	10.00
—Reissue of MCA 427					
2372	Honky Tonk Heroes	1978	3.00	6.00	12.00
3164	The Very Best of Loretta and Conway	1979	3.00	6.00	12.00
3190	Diamond Duet	1979	3.00	6.00	12.00
5178	Two's a Party	1981	3.00	6.00	12.00
37237	The Very Best of Loretta and Conway	1983	2.00	4.00	8.00
—Budget-line reissue					
42216	Making Believe	1988	2.00	4.00	8.00

MCA CORAL

Number	Title (A Side/B Side)	Yr	VG	VG+	NM
CDL-8006	Never Ending Song of Love	1973	3.00	6.00	12.00

TWO CHAPS, THE

With JAY BLACK, later of JAY AND THE AMERICANS.

45s

ATLANTIC

Number	Title (A Side/B Side)	Yr	VG	VG+	NM
1195	Forgive Me/No More	1958	7.50	15.00	30.00

TYLER, FRANKIE

See FRANKIE VALLI.

TYLER, KIP

45s

CHALLENGE

Number	Title (A Side/B Side)	Yr	VG	VG+	NM
1014	She Got Eyes/Shadow Street	1957	7.50	15.00	30.00
59008	Jungle Hop/Ooh Yeah Baby	1958	10.00	20.00	40.00

EBB

Number	Title (A Side/B Side)	Yr	VG	VG+	NM
154	She's My Witch/Rumble Rock	1959	12.50	25.00	50.00
156	Oh Linda/Kali Lou	1959	12.50	25.00	50.00

GYRO DISC

Number	Title (A Side/B Side)	Yr	VG	VG+	NM
711	Surfer's Lament (Eternity)/Toledo	1963	12.50	25.00	50.00
711 [PS]	Surfer's Lament (Eternity)/Toledo	1963	25.00	50.00	100.00

IMPERIAL

Number	Title (A Side/B Side)	Yr	VG	VG+	NM
5641	Rocket 'Round the Universe/The Goblin Trot	1960	7.50	15.00	30.00

TYLER, WILLIE, AND LESTER

Albums

TAMLA

Number	Title (A Side/B Side)	Yr	VG	VG+	NM
TM-265 [M]	Hello Dummy	1965	50.00	100.00	200.00

TYMES, THE

12-Inch Singles

RCA

Number	Title (A Side/B Side)	Yr	VG	VG+	NM
PD-11068	How Am I to Know/I'll Take You There	1977	3.00	6.00	12.00

45s

CAPITOL

Number	Title (A Side/B Side)	Yr	VG	VG+	NM
3440	When I Look Around Me/Smile a Tender Smile	1972	—	3.00	6.00

COLUMBIA

Number	Title (A Side/B Side)	Yr	VG	VG+	NM
44630	People/For Love of Ivy	1968	2.00	4.00	8.00
44799	God Bless the Child/The Love That You're Looking For	1969	—	3.00	6.00
44917	Find My Way/If You Love Me Baby	1969	—	3.00	6.00
45078	Love Child/Most Beautiful Married Lady	1970	—	3.00	6.00
45336	She's Gone/Someone to Watch Over Me	1971	—	3.00	6.00

MGM

Number	Title (A Side/B Side)	Yr	VG	VG+	NM
13536	Pretend/Street Talk	1966	5.00	10.00	20.00
13631	(Touch of) Baby/What Would I Do	1966	5.00	10.00	20.00

PARKWAY

Number	Title (A Side/B Side)	Yr	VG	VG+	NM
871	So in Love/Roscoe James McClain	1963	6.25	12.50	25.00
—Original title of A-side					
871	So Much in Love/Roscoe James McClain	1963	3.75	7.50	15.00
871 [PS]	So Much in Love/Roscoe James McClain	1963	7.50	15.00	30.00
884	Wonderful! Wonderful!/Come with Me to the Sea	1963	3.75	7.50	15.00
884 [PS]	Wonderful! Wonderful!/Come with Me to the Sea	1963	6.25	12.50	25.00
891	Somewhere/View from My Window	1963	3.75	7.50	15.00
891 [PS]	Somewhere/View from My Window	1963	6.25	12.50	25.00
908	To Each His Own/Wonderland By Night	1964	3.75	7.50	15.00
908 [PS]	To Each His Own/Wonderland By Night	1964	6.25	12.50	25.00
919	The Magic of Our Summer Love/With All My Heart	1964	3.75	7.50	15.00
919 [PS]	The Magic of Our Summer Love/With All My Heart	1964	6.25	12.50	25.00
924	Here She Comes/Malibu	1964	3.75	7.50	15.00
924 [PS]	Here She Comes/Malibu	1964	6.25	12.50	25.00
933	The Twelfth of Never/Here She Comes	1964	3.75	7.50	15.00
7039	Isle of Love/I'm Always Chasing Rainbows	1964	3.75	7.50	15.00
—Included as a bonus with album 7039					

RCA

Number	Title (A Side/B Side)	Yr	VG	VG+	NM
PB-10862	Love's Illusion/Savannah Sunny Sunday	1976	—	2.00	4.00

Number	Title (A Side/B Side)	Yr	VG	VG+	NM
PB-11136	I'll Take You There/How Am I to Know (The Things a Girl in Love Should Know)	1977	—	2.00	4.00
GB-12082	You Little Trustmaker/Ms. Grace	1980	—	—	—
—Unreleased?					
RCA VICTOR					
PB-10022	You Little Trustmaker/The North Hills	1974	—	2.50	5.00
PB-10128	Ms. Grace/The Crutch	1974	—	2.00	4.00
PB-10244	Interloop/Someday, Somehow I'm Keeping You	1975	—	2.00	4.00
PB-10422	God's Gonna Punish You/If I Can't Make You Smile	1975	—	2.00	4.00
GB-10493	You Little Trustmaker/The North Hills	1975	—	2.00	4.00
—Gold Standard Series					
PB-10561	Good Morning Dear Lord/It's Cool	1976	—	2.00	4.00
PB-10713	Goin' Through the Motions/Only Your Love	1976	—	2.00	4.00
WINCHESTER					
1002	These Foolish Things (Remind Me of You)/This Time It's Love	1967	2.50	5.00	10.00
Albums					
ABKCO					
4228	The Best of Tymes	1973	3.00	6.00	12.00
COLUMBIA					
CS 9778	People	1969	3.75	7.50	15.00
PARKWAY					
P 7032 [M]	So Much in Love	1963	10.00	20.00	40.00
—With group standing in front-cover photo					
P 7032 [M]	So Much in Love	1963	50.00	100.00	200.00
—With head-and-shoulders group photo on front cover					
P 7038 [M]	The Sound of the Wonderful Tymes	1963	10.00	20.00	40.00
SP 7038 [S]	The Sound of the Wonderful Tymes	1963	12.50	25.00	50.00
P 7039 [M]	Somewhere	1964	12.50	25.00	50.00
—Includes bonus single 7039 (deduct 20 percent if missing)					
P 7049 [M]	18 Greatest Hits	1964	10.00	20.00	40.00
RCA VICTOR					
APL1-0727	Trustmaker	1974	3.00	6.00	12.00
APL1-1835	Turning Point	1976	3.00	6.00	12.00
APL1-2406	Diggin' Their Roots	1977	3.00	6.00	12.00

TYNER, MCCOY

Number	Title (A Side/B Side)	Yr	VG	VG+	NM
45s					
COLUMBIA					
03151	Island Birdie/Love Surrounds Us Everywhere	1982	—	2.00	4.00
IMPULSE!					
240	Duke's Place/Searchin'	1965	2.00	4.00	8.00
MILESTONE					
304	Rotunda/For Tomorrow	197?	—	2.50	5.00
Albums					
ABC IMPULSE!					
AS-18	Inception	1968	3.00	6.00	12.00
AS-33	Reaching Fourth	1968	3.00	6.00	12.00
AS-39	Nights of Ballads and Blues	1968	3.00	6.00	12.00
AS-48	McCoy Tyner Live at Newport	1968	3.00	6.00	12.00
AS-63	Today and Tomorrow	1968	3.00	6.00	12.00
AS-79	McCoy Tyner Plays Duke Ellington	1968	3.00	6.00	12.00
IA-9235 [(2)]	Reevaluation: The Impulse! Years	197?	3.75	7.50	15.00
IA-9338 [(2)]	Early Trios	1978	3.75	7.50	15.00
BLUE NOTE					
BN-LA022-F	Extensions	1973	3.75	7.50	15.00
BN-LA223-G	Asante	1974	3.75	7.50	15.00
BLP-4264 [M]	The Real McCoy	1967	6.25	12.50	25.00
BLP-84264	The Real McCoy	1987	2.50	5.00	10.00
—"The Finest in Jazz Since 1939" label					
BST-84264	The Real McCoy	1970	3.00	6.00	12.00
—With United Artists distribution					
BST-84264 [S]	The Real McCoy	1967	5.00	10.00	20.00
—With "A Division of Liberty Records" on label					
BST-84275	Tender Moments	1968	5.00	10.00	20.00
—With "A Division of Liberty Records" on label					
BST-84275	Tender Moments	1970	3.00	6.00	12.00
—With United Artists distribution					
BST-84275	Tender Moments	1985	2.50	5.00	10.00
—"The Finest in Jazz Since 1939" label					
BLP-84307	Time for Tyner	1987	2.50	5.00	10.00
—"The Finest in Jazz Since 1939" label					
BST-84307	Time for Tyner	1969	5.00	10.00	20.00
—With "A Division of Liberty Records" on label					
BST-84338	Expansions	1969	5.00	10.00	20.00
—With "A Division of Liberty Records" on label					
BST-84338	Expansions	1970	3.00	6.00	12.00
—With United Artists distribution					
BST-84338	Expansions	1984	2.50	5.00	10.00
—"The Finest in Jazz Since 1939" label					
B1-91651	Revelations	1989	3.00	6.00	12.00
COLUMBIA					
FC 37375	La Leyenda de la Hora (The Legend of the Hour)	1981	2.50	5.00	10.00

Number	Title (A Side/B Side)	Yr	VG	VG+	NM
FC 38053	Looking Out	1982	2.50	5.00	10.00
ELEKTRA/MUSICIAN					
60350	Dimensions	1984	2.50	5.00	10.00
FANTASY					
OJC-311	Sahara	1988	2.50	5.00	10.00
—Reissue of Milestone 9039					
OJC-313	Song for My Lady	1988	2.50	5.00	10.00
—Reissue of Milestone 9044					
OJC-618	Song of the New World	1991	2.50	5.00	10.00
—Reissue of Milestone 9049					
OJC-650	Echoes of a Friend	1991	2.50	5.00	10.00
—Reissue of Milestone 9055					
GRP/IMPULSE!					
216	McCoy Tyner Plays Duke Ellington	1997	5.00	10.00	20.00
—Reissue on audiophile vinyl					
220	Inception	1997	5.00	10.00	20.00
—Reissue on audiophile vinyl					
221	Nights of Ballads and Blues	1997	5.00	10.00	20.00
—Reissue on audiophile vinyl					
IMPULSE!					
A-18 [M]	Inception	1962	6.25	12.50	25.00
AS-18 [S]	Inception	1962	6.25	12.50	25.00
A-33 [M]	Reaching Fourth	1963	6.25	12.50	25.00
AS-33 [S]	Reaching Fourth	1963	6.25	12.50	25.00
A-39 [M]	Nights of Ballads and Blues	1963	6.25	12.50	25.00
AS-39 [S]	Nights of Ballads and Blues	1963	6.25	12.50	25.00
A-48 [M]	McCoy Tyner Live at Newport	1963	6.25	12.50	25.00
AS-48 [S]	McCoy Tyner Live at Newport	1963	6.25	12.50	25.00
A-63 [M]	Today and Tomorrow	1964	6.25	12.50	25.00
AS-63 [S]	Today and Tomorrow	1964	6.25	12.50	25.00
A-79 [M]	McCoy Tyner Plays Duke Ellington	1965	6.25	12.50	25.00
AS-79 [S]	McCoy Tyner Plays Duke Ellington	1965	6.25	12.50	25.00
MCA					
4126 [(2)]	Great Moments with McCoy Tyner	1981	3.00	6.00	12.00
4156 [(2)]	Reevaluation: The Impulse Years	1981	3.00	6.00	12.00
—Reissue of Impulse! 9235					
4157 [(2)]	Early Trios	1981	3.00	6.00	12.00
—Reissue of Impulse! 9338					
MILESTONE					
FPM-4006 [Q]	Song of the New World	197?	5.00	10.00	20.00
9039	Sahara	197?	2.50	5.00	10.00
9044	Song for My Lady	197?	2.50	5.00	10.00
9049	Song of the New World	197?	2.50	5.00	10.00
9055	Echoes of a Friend	1974	2.50	5.00	10.00
9056	Sama Layuca	1974	2.50	5.00	10.00
9063	Trident	1975	2.50	5.00	10.00
9067	Fly with the Wind	1976	2.50	5.00	10.00
9072	Focal Point	1977	2.50	5.00	10.00
9079	Inner Voices	1978	2.50	5.00	10.00
9085	The Greeting	1978	2.50	5.00	10.00
9087	Together	1979	2.50	5.00	10.00
9091	Passion Dance	1979	2.50	5.00	10.00
9094	Horizon	1980	2.50	5.00	10.00
9102	13th House	1981	2.50	5.00	10.00
9167	Uptown/Downtown	1988	2.50	5.00	10.00
47062	Reflections	198?	2.50	5.00	10.00
55001 [(2)]	Enlightenment	197?	3.00	6.00	12.00
55002 [(2)]	Atlantis	1975	3.00	6.00	12.00
55003 [(2)]	Supertrios	1977	3.00	6.00	12.00
55007 [(2)]	4 x 4	1980	3.00	6.00	12.00
PALO ALTO					
PA-8083	Just Feelin'	1985	2.50	5.00	10.00
PAUSA					
9007	Time for Tyner	198?	2.00	4.00	8.00
—Reissue of Blue Note 84307					
QUICKSILVER					
QS-4010	Just Feelin'	1990	2.50	5.00	10.00
—Reissue of Palo Alto LP					
TIMELESS					
SJP-260	Bon Voyage	1990	2.50	5.00	10.00

TYRANNOSAURUS REX

See T. REX.

TYRELL, DANNY, AND THE CLEESHAYS

Number	Title (A Side/B Side)	Yr	VG	VG+	NM
45s					
EASTMAN					
784	You're Only Seventeen/Let's Walk, Let's Talk	1958	10.00	20.00	40.00

TYSON, ROY

Number	Title (A Side/B Side)	Yr	VG	VG+	NM
45s					
DOUBLE L					
723	Oh What a Night for Love/Not Too Young	1963	20.00	40.00	80.00
733	The Girl I Love/I Want to Be Your Boyfriend	1964	25.00	50.00	100.00

U

U.K.'S, THE

45s

Number	Title (A Side/B Side)	Yr	VG	VG+	NM
CAMEO					
342	Ever Faithful Ever True/Your Love Is All I Want	1965	2.50	5.00	10.00

UBANS, THE

45s

Number	Title (A Side/B Side)	Yr	VG	VG+	NM
RADIANT					
102	Gloria/On the Bridge	1964	50.00	100.00	200.00

UFO

12-Inch Singles

Number	Title (A Side/B Side)	Yr	VG	VG+	NM
CHRYSALIS					
28 [DJ]	Lonely Heart (same on both sides)	1981	2.00	4.00	8.00
VAS 2363 [DJ]	Night Run/Blue	1986	3.00	6.00	12.00

45s

Number	Title (A Side/B Side)	Yr	VG	VG+	NM
CHRYSALIS					
2040	Doctor Doctor/Lipstick Traces	1974	—	2.50	5.00
2157	Too Hot to Handle/Electric Phase	1977	—	2.50	5.00
2178	Try Me/Gettin' Ready	1977	—	2.50	5.00
2239	Cherry/You Don't Fool Me	1978	—	2.50	5.00
2263	Only You Can Rock Me/Ain't No Baby	1978	—	2.50	5.00
2308	Lights Out/Doctor Doctor	1979	—	2.50	5.00
2590	Back in My Life/(B-side unknown)	1981	—	2.00	4.00

Albums

Number	Title (A Side/B Side)	Yr	VG	VG+	NM
CHRYSALIS					
CHR 1059	Phenomenon	1974	3.00	6.00	12.00
CHR 1074	Force It	1975	3.00	6.00	12.00
CHR 1103	No Heavy Petting	1976	3.00	6.00	12.00
CHR 1127	Lights Out	1977	3.00	6.00	12.00
CHR 1182	Obsession	1978	3.00	6.00	12.00
CHR 1209 [(2)]	Strangers in the Night	1979	3.75	7.50	15.00
CHR 1239	No Place to Run	1980	3.00	6.00	12.00
CHR 1307	The Wild, the Willing and the Innocent	1981	3.00	6.00	12.00
CHR 1360	Mechanix	1982	3.00	6.00	12.00
PV 41059	Phenomenon	1983	2.00	4.00	8.00
PV 41074	Force It	1983	2.00	4.00	8.00
PV 41103	No Heavy Petting	1983	2.00	4.00	8.00
FV 41127	Lights Out	1983	2.00	4.00	8.00
PV 41127	Lights Out	1986	2.00	4.00	8.00
—Reissue of FV 41127					
PV 41182	Obsession	1983	2.00	4.00	8.00
V2X 41209 [(2)]	Strangers in the Night	1983	2.50	5.00	10.00
PV 41239	No Place to Run	1983	2.00	4.00	8.00
PV 41307	The Wild, the Willing and the Innocent	1983	2.00	4.00	8.00
PV 41360	Mechanix	1983	2.00	4.00	8.00
FV 41402	Making Contact	1983	2.50	5.00	10.00
PV 41402	Making Contact	1986	2.00	4.00	8.00
—Reissue of FV 41402					
BFV 41518	Misdemeanor	1986	2.50	5.00	10.00
FV 41644	The Best of the Rest	1988	2.50	5.00	10.00
ENIGMA/METAL BLADE					
D1-73404	Ain't Misbehavin'	1989	3.00	6.00	12.00
RARE EARTH					
RS 624	UFO 1	1971	6.25	12.50	25.00

UGGAMS, LESLIE

45s

Number	Title (A Side/B Side)	Yr	VG	VG+	NM
ATLANTIC					
2313	Don't You Care/Who Killed Teddy Bear	1965	3.75	7.50	15.00
2371	If My Friends Could See Me Now/We Can Work It Out	1967	2.50	5.00	10.00
2397	Hallelujah Baby/My Own Morning	1967	2.50	5.00	10.00
2469	I (Who Have Nothing)/The House Built on Sand	1967	2.50	5.00	10.00
2524	River Deep, Mountain High/Land of Make Believe	1968	2.50	5.00	10.00
2675	Just to Satisfy You/That Old Sweet Roll (Hi-De-Ho)	1969	2.00	4.00	8.00
2698	Home/Save the Country	1969	2.00	4.00	8.00
2727	He Can Do It/Walk Him Up the Stairs	1970	2.00	4.00	8.00
COLUMBIA					
41451	One More Sunrise (Morgen)/The Eyes of God	1959	3.00	6.00	12.00
41531	My Favorite Things/Sixteen Going on Seventeen	1959	3.00	6.00	12.00
41564	Carefree Years/Lullaby of the Leaves	1960	2.50	5.00	10.00
41654	I Grew Up Last Night/I'm Just a Little Sparrow	1960	2.50	5.00	10.00
41798	Inherit the Wind/Love Is Like a Violin	1960	2.50	5.00	10.00
42055	He Doesn't Know/I Love Him	1961	2.50	5.00	10.00
42255	Get Happy/Birth of the Blues	1961	2.50	5.00	10.00
42611	Each and Ev'ry Day/Is He the Only Man in the World	1962	2.50	5.00	10.00
43012	A Legend in My Time/My Wish	1964	2.50	5.00	10.00
43064	Little Bird/This Is My Prayer	1964	2.50	5.00	10.00
GORDY					
7149	I Want to Make It Easy on You/Two Shoes	1976	—	3.00	6.00
MGM					
11437	Easter Sunny Day/Percy the Pale Faced Bear	1953	5.00	10.00	20.00
—As "Lesley 'Uggams' Crayne"					
11626	My Stocking Is Empty/This Is Santa Claus	1953	5.00	10.00	20.00
—As "Leslie 'Uggams' Crayne"					
11676	My Candy Apple/Kickin' Up a Storm	1954	5.00	10.00	20.00
—As "Lesley 'Uggams' Crayne"					
11755	Ev'ry Little Piggy's Curley Tail/Palsy Walsy Land	1954	5.00	10.00	20.00
11868	Uncle Santa/The Fat, Fat Man	1954	5.00	10.00	20.00
11965	Meet My Friend, Mr. Sun/Did You Ever Dream	1955	3.75	7.50	15.00

Albums

Number	Title (A Side/B Side)	Yr	VG	VG+	NM
ATLANTIC					
8128 [M]	Time to Love	1967	3.75	7.50	15.00
SD 8128 [S]	Time to Love	1967	5.00	10.00	20.00
SD 8196	What's an Uggams	1968	3.75	7.50	15.00
SD 8241	Just to Satisfy You	1969	3.75	7.50	15.00
COLUMBIA					
CL 1706 [M]	Leslie Uggams on TV	1962	3.75	7.50	15.00
CL 1865 [M]	More Leslie Uggams on TV	1963	3.75	7.50	15.00
CL 2071 [M]	So in Love	1963	3.75	7.50	15.00
CS 8506 [S]	Leslie Uggams on TV	1962	5.00	10.00	20.00
CS 8665 [S]	More Leslie Uggams on TV	1963	5.00	10.00	20.00
CS 8871 [S]	So in Love	1963	5.00	10.00	20.00
CS 9936	Leslie	1970	3.00	6.00	12.00
MOTOWN					
M6-846	Leslie Uggams	1975	3.00	6.00	12.00
SONDAY					
8000	Try to See It My Way	1972	3.00	6.00	12.00

UGLYS, THE

45s

Number	Title (A Side/B Side)	Yr	VG	VG+	NM
ABC-PARAMOUNT					
10707	Wake Up My Mind/Ugly Blues	1965	3.00	6.00	12.00
10748	It's Alright/A Friend	1965	3.00	6.00	12.00
10773	Quiet Explosion/A Good Idea	1966	3.00	6.00	12.00

ULANO, SAM

45s

Number	Title (A Side/B Side)	Yr	VG	VG+	NM
MGM					
SK-37	Santa & The Doodle-Li-Boop/The Story Of Santa Claus	1954	2.50	5.00	10.00
SK-37 [PS]	Santa & The Doodle-Li-Boop/The Story Of Santa Claus	1954	5.00	10.00	20.00

ULTIMATE SPINACH

45s

Number	Title (A Side/B Side)	Yr	VG	VG+	NM
MGM					
14023	(Just Like) Romeo and Juliet/Some Days You Just Can't Win	1969	3.00	6.00	12.00

Albums

Number	Title (A Side/B Side)	Yr	VG	VG+	NM
MGM					
E-4518 [M]	Ultimate Spinach	1968	7.50	15.00	30.00
SE-4518 [S]	Ultimate Spinach	1968	6.25	12.50	25.00
E-4570 [M]	Behold & See	1968	12.50	25.00	50.00
—Mono is promo only (yellow label)					
SE-4570 [S]	Behold & See	1968	6.25	12.50	25.00
SE-4600	Ultimate Spinach	1969	6.25	12.50	25.00

ULTRA VIOLET

45s

Number	Title (A Side/B Side)	Yr	VG	VG+	NM
CAPITOL					
3743	Shanghai Bill/La Vie En Rose	1973	—	3.00	6.00

Albums

Number	Title (A Side/B Side)	Yr	VG	VG+	NM
CAPITOL					
ST-11244	Ultra Violet	1973	6.25	12.50	25.00

UNBEATABLES, THE

45s

Number	Title (A Side/B Side)	Yr	VG	VG+	NM
DAWN					
552	I Love Paris/What I Say	1964	10.00	20.00	40.00

Albums

Number	Title (A Side/B Side)	Yr	VG	VG+	NM
DAWN					
5050 [M]	Live at Palisades Park	1964	37.50	75.00	150.00

UNCHAINED MYNDS, THE

45s

Number	Title (A Side/B Side)	Yr	VG	VG+	NM
BUDDAH					
111	We Can't Go On This Way/Going Back to Miami	1969	3.75	7.50	15.00
119	Every Day/(B-side unknown)	1969	3.75	7.50	15.00
140	You, Me, and My Yo-Yo/Every Day	1970	3.75	7.50	15.00
TEEN TOWN					
106	We Can't Go On This Way/Going Back to Miami	1969	10.00	20.00	40.00

UNDERBEATS, THE

45s

Number	Title (A Side/B Side)	Yr	VG	VG+	NM
BANGAR					
00632	Annie Do the Dog/Sweet Words of Love	1964	15.00	30.00	60.00
00657	Broken Arrow/Little Romance	1964	15.00	30.00	60.00
GARRETT					
4004	Foot Stompin'/Route 66	1964	6.25	12.50	25.00
METROBEAT					
4449	Sweetest Girl in the World/It's Gonna Rain Today	1967	6.25	12.50	25.00
SOMA					
1449	Book of Love/Darling Lorraine	1966	6.25	12.50	25.00
1458	I Can't Stand It/Shake It for Me	1966	5.00	10.00	20.00
TWIN-TOWN					
706	Jo Jo Gunne/Our Love	1965	7.50	15.00	30.00

UNDERDOGS, THE

45s

Number	Title (A Side/B Side)	Yr	VG	VG+	NM
HIDEOUT					
1001	The Man in the Glass/Friday at the Hideout (Judy Be Mine)	1965	7.50	15.00	30.00
1004	Little Girl/Don't Pretend	1965	7.50	15.00	30.00
1011	Surprise Surprise/Get Down on Your Knees	1966	10.00	20.00	40.00
REPRISE					
0422	The Man in the Glass/Friday at the Hideout (Judy Be Mine)	1965	3.75	7.50	15.00
0446	Little Girl/Don't Pretend	1966	3.75	7.50	15.00
V.I.P.					
25040	Love's Gone Bad/Mo Jo Hanna	1966	6.25	12.50	25.00

UNDERGROUND, THE

45s

MAINSTREAM

Number	Title (A Side/B Side)	Yr	VG	VG+	NM
660	Easy/Satisfy'n Sunday	1967	6.25	12.50	25.00
667	Get Him Out of Your Mind/Take Me Back	1967	6.25	12.50	25.00

UNDERGROUND SUNSHINE

Also see THE CHALLENGERS (4).

45s

INTREPID

Number	Title (A Side/B Side)	Yr	VG	VG+	NM
ITDJ-3 [DJ]	Don't Shut Me Out (mono/stereo)	1969	3.00	6.00	12.00
—Promo issue of 75012					
75002	Birthday/All I Want Is You	1969	3.00	6.00	12.00
75012	Don't Shut Me Out/Take Me, Break Me	1969	2.50	5.00	10.00
75019	Nine to Five (Ain't My Bag)/Rotten Woman Blues	1969	2.50	5.00	10.00
75029	Jesus Is Just Alright/Six O'Clock	1970	2.50	5.00	10.00

Albums

INTREPID

Number	Title (A Side/B Side)	Yr	VG	VG+	NM
IT-74003	Let There Be Light	1969	7.50	15.00	30.00

UNDERTAKERS, THE

45s

PARKWAY

Number	Title (A Side/B Side)	Yr	VG	VG+	NM
909	Just a Little Bit/Stupidity	1964	3.00	6.00	12.00

UNDISPUTED TRUTH, THE

12-Inch Singles

WHITFIELD

Number	Title (A Side/B Side)	Yr	VG	VG+	NM
8306	Let's Go Down to the Disco (9:10)/You + Me = Love	1976	5.00	10.00	20.00
8783	Show Time (8:59)/Misunderstood	1979	3.75	7.50	15.00

45s

GORDY

Number	Title (A Side/B Side)	Yr	VG	VG+	NM
7106	Save My Love for a Rainy Day/Since I've Lost You	1971	2.00	4.00	8.00
7108	Smiling Faces Sometimes/You Got the Love I Need	1971	—	3.00	6.00
7112	You Make Your Own Heaven and Hell Right Here on Earth/Ball of Confusion (That's What the World Is Today)	1971	—	3.00	6.00
7114	What It Is/California Soul	1972	—	3.00	6.00
7117	Papa Was a Rollin' Stone/Friendship Train	1972	—	3.00	6.00
7122	With a Little Help from My Friends/Girl You're Alright	1972	—	3.00	6.00
7124	Mama I Got a Brand New Thing (Don't Say No)/Gonna Keep On Tryin' Till I Win Your Love	1973	—	3.00	6.00
7130	Law of the Land/Just My Imagination (Running Away with Me)	1973	—	3.00	6.00
7134	Help Yourself/What's Going On	1974	—	3.00	6.00
7139	I'm a Fool for You/Girl's Alright with Me	1974	—	3.00	6.00
7140	Big John Is My Name/L'il Red Ridin' Hood	1974	—	3.00	6.00
7141	Earthquake Shake/Spaced Out	1975	—	—	—
—Unreleased					
7143	UFO's/Got to Get My Hands on Some Lovin'	1975	—	3.00	6.00
7145	Higher Than High/Spaced Out	1975	—	3.00	6.00
7147	Boogie Bump Boogie/I Saw Her When You Met Her	1975	—	3.00	6.00

WHITFIELD

Number	Title (A Side/B Side)	Yr	VG	VG+	NM
8231	You + Me = Love/You + Me = Love (Disco Version)	1976	—	2.50	5.00
8295	Let's Get Down to the Disco/Loose	1977	—	2.50	5.00
8362	Hole in the Wall/Sunshine	1977	—	2.50	5.00
8781	Show Time (Part 1)/Show Time (Part 2)	1979	—	2.00	4.00
8873	I Can't Get Enough of Your Love/Misunderstood	1979	—	2.00	4.00

Albums

GORDY

Number	Title (A Side/B Side)	Yr	VG	VG+	NM
G 955L	The Undisputed Truth	1971	6.25	12.50	25.00
G5-959	Face to Face with the Truth	1972	5.00	10.00	20.00
G5-963	Law of the Land	1973	5.00	10.00	20.00
G6-968	Down to Earth	1974	5.00	10.00	20.00
G6-970	Cosmic Truth	1975	5.00	10.00	20.00
G6-972	Higher Than High	1975	5.00	10.00	20.00

WHITFIELD

Number	Title (A Side/B Side)	Yr	VG	VG+	NM
BS 2967	Method to the Madness	1977	3.00	6.00	12.00
BSK 3202	Smokin'	1979	3.00	6.00	12.00

UNFOLDING

Albums

AUDIO FIDELITY

Number	Title (A Side/B Side)	Yr	VG	VG+	NM
AFLP-2184 [M]	How to Blow Your Mind and Have a Freak-Out Party	1967	17.50	35.00	70.00
AFSD-6184 [S]	How to Blow Your Mind and Have a Freak-Out Party	1967	25.00	50.00	100.00

UNFORGETTABLES, THE

45s

COLPIX

Number	Title (A Side/B Side)	Yr	VG	VG+	NM
192	It Hurts/Was It All Right	1961	7.50	15.00	30.00

PAMELA

Number	Title (A Side/B Side)	Yr	VG	VG+	NM
204	Oh Wishing Well/Daddy Must Be a Man	1961	125.00	250.00	500.00
—Blue vinyl					
204	Oh Wishing Well/Daddy Must Be a Man	1961	75.00	150.00	300.00

TITANIC

Number	Title (A Side/B Side)	Yr	VG	VG+	NM
5012	He'll Be Sorry/Oh There He Goes	1963	10.00	20.00	40.00

UNICORN

45s

CAPITOL

Number	Title (A Side/B Side)	Yr	VG	VG+	NM
3954	Bog Trotter/Ooh, Mother	1974	—	2.50	5.00
3993	Blue Pine Trees/Electric Night	1974	—	2.50	5.00

Albums

CAPITOL

Number	Title (A Side/B Side)	Yr	VG	VG+	NM
ST-11334	Blue Pine Trees	1974	2.50	5.00	10.00
—Produced by David Gilmour (Pink Floyd)					
ST-11453	Unicorn 2	1976	2.50	5.00	10.00
ST-11692	One More Tomorrow	1977	2.50	5.00	10.00

UNIFICS, THE

45s

KAPP

Number	Title (A Side/B Side)	Yr	VG	VG+	NM
935	Court of Love/Which One Should I Choose	1968	3.00	6.00	12.00
957	The Beginning of My End/Sentimental Man	1968	3.00	6.00	12.00
957 [PS]	The Beginning of My End/Sentimental Man	1968	3.75	7.50	15.00
985	It's a Groovy World!/Memories	1969	3.00	6.00	12.00
985 [PS]	It's a Groovy World!/Memories	1969	3.75	7.50	15.00
2026	Toshisumasu/It's All Over	1969	3.00	6.00	12.00
2058	Got to Get You/Memories	1969	3.00	6.00	12.00

Albums

KAPP

Number	Title (A Side/B Side)	Yr	VG	VG+	NM
KS-3582	Sittin' In at the Court of Love	1968	6.25	12.50	25.00

UNION GAP, THE

See GARY PUCKETT AND THE UNION GAP.

UNIQUE ECHOES, THE

45s

SOUTHERN SOUND

Number	Title (A Side/B Side)	Yr	VG	VG+	NM
108	Zoom/Italian Twist	1962	12.50	25.00	50.00

UNIQUE TEENS, THE

45s

DYNAMIC

Number	Title (A Side/B Side)	Yr	VG	VG+	NM
110	Whatcha Know Now/Run Fast	1959	7.50	15.00	30.00

HANOVER

Number	Title (A Side/B Side)	Yr	VG	VG+	NM
4510	Jeannie/At the Ball	1959	10.00	20.00	40.00

IVY

Number	Title (A Side/B Side)	Yr	VG	VG+	NM
112	Jeannie/At the Ball	1958	10.00	20.00	40.00

UNIQUES, THE (1)

Country singer Joe Stampley was a member of this group.

45s

PARAMOUNT

Number	Title (A Side/B Side)	Yr	VG	VG+	NM
0017	Eunice/No One But You	1970	—	2.50	5.00
0058	Shadow of Love/Lazy Afternoon	1970	—	2.50	5.00
0116	Lucille/One Night with You	1971	—	2.50	5.00
0172	Will You Love Me Tomorrow/I Am a Gemini	1972	—	2.50	5.00

PAULA

Number	Title (A Side/B Side)	Yr	VG	VG+	NM
219	Not Too Long Ago/Fast Way of Living	1965	2.50	5.00	10.00
222	Too Good to Be True/Never Been in Love	1965	2.00	4.00	8.00
227	Lady's Man/Bolivar	1965	2.00	4.00	8.00
231	Strange/You Ain't Tuff	1966	2.00	4.00	8.00
238	All These Things/Tell Me What to Do	1966	2.00	4.00	8.00
245	Goodbye, So Long/Run and Hide	1966	2.00	4.00	8.00
255	Please Come Home for Christmas/(Instrumental)	1966	3.00	6.00	12.00
264	Groovin' Out/Areba	1967	2.00	4.00	8.00
275	Every Now and Then (I Cry)/Love Is a Precious Thing	1967	2.00	4.00	8.00
289	Go On and Leave/I'll Do Anything	1967	2.00	4.00	8.00
—B-side by University of Utah Chamber Choir					
299	It's All Over Now/All I Took Was Love	1968	—	3.00	6.00
307	It Hurts Me to Remember/I Sure Feel More (Like I Do Then I Did When I Got Here)	1968	—	3.00	6.00
313	How Lucky Can One Man Be/You Don't Miss Your Water	1968	—	3.00	6.00
320	Sha-La Love/You Know (That I Love You)	1970	—	2.50	5.00
324	My Babe/Toys Are Made for Children	1970	—	2.50	5.00
332	All These Things/You Know That I Love You	1970	—	2.50	5.00

Albums

PAULA

Number	Title (A Side/B Side)	Yr	VG	VG+	NM
LP-2190 [M]	Uniquely Yours	1966	6.25	12.50	25.00
LPS-2190 [S]	Uniquely Yours	1966	7.50	15.00	30.00
LP-2194 [M]	Happening Now	1967	6.25	12.50	25.00
LPS-2194 [S]	Happening Now	1967	7.50	15.00	30.00
LP-2199 [M]	Playtime	1968	6.25	12.50	25.00
LPS-2199 [S]	Playtime	1968	6.25	12.50	25.00
LPS-2204	The Uniques	1969	6.25	12.50	25.00
LPS-2208	Golden Hits	1970	6.25	12.50	25.00

UNIQUES, THE (2)

45s

AMBER

Number	Title (A Side/B Side)	Yr	VG	VG+	NM
2004	Taboo/Ghost Riders in the Sky	1961	12.50	25.00	50.00

UNITED SOUTHERN

Number	Title (A Side/B Side)	Yr	VG	VG+	NM
104	Renegade/Malaguena	1961	75.00	15.00	30.00

UNIQUES, THE (3)

45s

BANGAR

Number	Title (A Side/B Side)	Yr	VG	VG+	NM
00609	Baby Don't Cry/Little Angel	1967	5.00	10.00	20.00

UNIQUES, THE (4)

45s

BLISS

Number	Title (A Side/B Side)	Yr	VG	VG+	NM
1004	I'm So Unhappy/I'm Confessin'	1961	125.00	250.00	500.00

END

Number	Title (A Side/B Side)	Yr	VG	VG+	NM
1012	Tell the Angels/Hey, Little Cupid	1958	62.50	125.00	250.00

FLIPPIN'

Number	Title (A Side/B Side)	Yr	VG	VG+	NM
202	Come Marry Me/Do You Remember	1959	12.50	25.00	50.00

GONE

Number	Title (A Side/B Side)	Yr	VG	VG+	NM
5113	I'm So Unhappy/I'm Confessin'	1961	50.00	100.00	200.00
5113	I'm So Unhappy/It's Got to Come	1961	17.50	35.00	70.00

Number	Title (A Side/B Side)	Yr	VG	VG+	NM
MR. CEE					
100	Look at Me/Bossa Nova Cha Cha	1960	75.00	150.00	300.00
PRIDE					
1018	I'm So Unhappy/It's Got to Come	1960	62.50	125.00	250.00
TEE KAY					
112	One Million Miles Away/All at Once	1962	12.50	25.00	50.00

UNIQUES, THE (5)

Number	Title (A Side/B Side)	Yr	VG	VG+	NM
45s					
CAPITOL					
4949	Loving You/Blue Skies	1963	3.00	6.00	12.00
ROULETTE					
4528	Send Him to Me/This Little Boy of Mine	1963	5.00	10.00	20.00

UNIQUES, THE (6)

Number	Title (A Side/B Side)	Yr	VG	VG+	NM
45s					
DEMAND					
1994	Merry Christmas, Darling/I Wanna Chance	198?	2.00	4.00	8.00
—B-side by the Vows; green vinyl "collector's issue"					
2490	Times Change/Alright, OK, You Win	1964	12.50	25.00	50.00
2936	Merry Christmas Darling/Rockin' Rudolph	1963	20.00	40.00	80.00
3950	Merry Christmas Darling (And A Happy New Year Too)/Times Change	1963	12.50	25.00	50.00
DOT					
16533	Merry Christmas Darling/Times Change	1963	10.00	20.00	40.00

UNIQUES, THE (7)

Number	Title (A Side/B Side)	Yr	VG	VG+	NM
45s					
PEACOCK					
1677	Right Now/Somewhere	1957	7.50	15.00	30.00
1695	Mysterious/Picture of My Baby	1960	6.25	12.50	25.00

UNIQUES, THE (U)

Number	Title (A Side/B Side)	Yr	VG	VG+	NM
45s					
CLIFTON					
62	After New Year's Eve/Kiss, Kiss, Kiss	19??	2.00	4.00	8.00
LUCKY FOUR					
1024	Silvery Moon/Chocolate Bar	1962	50.00	100.00	200.00

UNIT FOUR PLUS TWO

Number	Title (A Side/B Side)	Yr	VG	VG+	NM
45s					
LONDON					
1009	I Was Only Playing Games/I Won't Let You Down	1966	3.00	6.00	12.00
9732	Sorrow and Pain/Woman from Liberia	1965	3.00	6.00	12.00
9751	Concrete and Clay/When I Fall in Love	1965	3.00	6.00	12.00
9751	Concrete and Clay/Wild Is the Wind	1965	4.00	8.00	16.00
9761	You've Never Been in Love Like This Before/Tell Somebody You Know	1965	3.00	6.00	12.00
9790	Stop Wasting Your Time/Hark	1965	3.00	6.00	12.00
Albums					
LONDON					
PS 427 [P]	Unit Four Plus Two #1	1965	12.50	25.00	50.00
LL 3427 [M]	Unit Four Plus Two #1	1965	10.00	20.00	40.00

UNITED FRUIT CO.

Number	Title (A Side/B Side)	Yr	VG	VG+	NM
45s					
LAURIE					
3408	On the Good Ship Lollipop/Sunshine Street	1967	2.50	5.00	10.00

UNITED STATES DOUBLE QUARTET

THE TOKENS and The Kirby Stone Four.

Number	Title (A Side/B Side)	Yr	VG	VG+	NM
45s					
B.T. PUPPY					
524	Life Is Groovy/Split	1966	2.50	5.00	10.00
547	Walking Along-Happy Wanderer/When I Lock My Door	1968	2.50	5.00	10.00
551	Do Re Mi/When I Lock My Door	1969	2.50	5.00	10.00
Albums					
B.T. PUPPY					
BTS-1005	Life Is Groovy	1969	12.50	25.00	50.00

UNITED STATES OF AMERICA, THE

Number	Title (A Side/B Side)	Yr	VG	VG+	NM
Albums					
COLUMBIA					
CL 2814 [M]	The United States of America	1968	25.00	50.00	100.00
—Mono is promo only					
CS 9614 [S]	The United States of America	1968	20.00	40.00	80.00
—With outer bag					
CS 9614 [S]	The United States of America	1968	10.00	20.00	40.00
—Without outer bag					

UNIVERSALS, THE

Probably more than one group.

Number	Title (A Side/B Side)	Yr	VG	VG+	NM
45s					
ASCOT					
2124	Dear Ruth/Gotta Little Girl	1963	15.00	30.00	60.00
CORA-LEE					
501	The Picture/He's So Right	1958	10.00	20.00	40.00
FESTIVAL					
1601	Dreaming/Love Bound	1961	15.00	30.00	60.00
—No subtitle on A-side					
25001	(I'll Just Have to Go On) Dreaming/Love Bound	1961	6.25	12.50	25.00
MARK-X					
7004	Teenage Love/Again	1957	50.00	100.00	200.00
MODERN					
1057	New Lease on Life/Without Friends	1968	2.50	5.00	10.00
SHEPHERD					
2200	A Love Only You Can Give/I'm in Love	1962	12.50	25.00	50.00
SOUTHERN					
102	Dear Ruth/Prayer of Love	1963	12.50	25.00	50.00

Number	Title (A Side/B Side)	Yr	VG	VG+	NM
Albums					
RELIC					
5006	Acapella Showcase	197?	2.50	5.00	10.00

UNKNOWN, THE

Number	Title (A Side/B Side)	Yr	VG	VG+	NM
45s					
AUTOGRAPH					
206	I Have Returned/Keep Talking, Baby	1960	10.00	20.00	40.00

UNKNOWNS, THE (1)

Also see STEVE ALAIMO; MARK LINDSAY.

Number	Title (A Side/B Side)	Yr	VG	VG+	NM
45s					
PARROT					
307	Melody for an Unknown Girl/Keith's Song	1966	6.25	12.50	25.00

UNKNOWNS, THE (2)

Number	Title (A Side/B Side)	Yr	VG	VG+	NM
45s					
SHIELD					
7101	One More Chance/You and Me	196?	50.00	100.00	200.00
X-TRA					
102	One More Chance/You and Me	1957	250.00	500.00	1000.

UNKNOWNS, THE (U)

Number	Title (A Side/B Side)	Yr	VG	VG+	NM
45s					
MARLIN					
16008	Tighter/Young Enough to Cry	1966	6.25	12.50	25.00

UNRELATED SEGMENTS, THE

Number	Title (A Side/B Side)	Yr	VG	VG+	NM
45s					
HANNA-BARBERA					
514	It's Unfair/Story of My Life	1967	5.00	10.00	20.00
LIBERTY					
55992	It's Gonna Rain/Where You Gonna Go	1967	6.25	12.50	25.00
56052	Cry, Cry, Cry/It's Not Fair	1968	10.00	20.00	40.00

UNTAMED, THE

Number	Title (A Side/B Side)	Yr	VG	VG+	NM
45s					
PLANET					
117	It's Not True/Gimme Gimme Some Shade	1966	3.00	6.00	12.00
—Also reported to be Planet 103; do both exist as U.S. editions?					

UNTOUCHABLES, THE

At least two different groups.

Number	Title (A Side/B Side)	Yr	VG	VG+	NM
45s					
ALAN K					
6901	Little Mary/Funny What a Little Kiss Can Do	1962	50.00	100.00	200.00
DOT					
16306	Blues in the Night/Bondaru	1962	3.75	7.50	15.00
LIBERTY					
55335	You're on Top/Lovely Dee	1961	5.00	10.00	20.00
55423	Papa/Medicine Man	1962	5.00	10.00	20.00
MADISON					
128	Poor Boy Need a Preacher/New Fad	1960	6.25	12.50	25.00
134	Goodnight Sweetheart Goodnight/Vickie Lee	1960	6.25	12.50	25.00
139	Sixty Minute Man/Everybody's Laughin'	1960	6.25	12.50	25.00
147	Do Your Best/Raisin' Cain	1961	6.25	12.50	25.00
MCA/STIFF					
52725	I Spy (For the F.B.I.)/Freak in the Streets	1985	—	—	3.00
52725 [PS]	I Spy (For the F.B.I.)/Freak in the Streets	1985	—	2.00	4.00
NAU VOO					
809	Blue Chip Bounce (Part 1)/Blue Chip Bounce (Part 2)	1960	3.75	7.50	15.00
WASP					
105	Don't Go, I'm Beggin'/Baby, Let's Wait	1967	6.25	12.50	25.00

UNUSUAL WE

Number	Title (A Side/B Side)	Yr	VG	VG+	NM
Albums					
PULSAR					
10608	Unusual We	1969	7.50	15.00	30.00

UPCHURCH, PHIL

Number	Title (A Side/B Side)	Yr	VG	VG+	NM
45s					
BOYD					
3398	You Can't Sit Down Part 2/You Can't Sit Down Part 1	1961	3.00	6.00	12.00
CADET					
5661	You Don't Know the Reason/I Don't Know	1970	—	3.00	6.00
KUDU					
926	You Got Style/Ave Maria	1975	—	2.50	5.00
—With Tennyson Stephens					
MARLIN					
3325	Strawberry Letter 23/(B-side unknown)	1978	—	2.00	4.00
UNITED ARTISTS					
329	You Can't Sit Down Part 2/You Can't Sit Down Part 1	1961	2.50	5.00	10.00
355	Pink Lollipop/Straw Hat	1961	2.50	5.00	10.00
385	The Hog/That's Where It Is	1961	2.50	5.00	10.00
417	Organ Grinder's Swing/The Persian	1962	2.50	5.00	10.00
488	The Stonewall/Flap Jack	1962	2.50	5.00	10.00
Albums					
BLUE THUMB					
BTS-59	Lovin' Feelin'	1973	3.00	6.00	12.00
BTS-6005 [(2)]	Darkness, Darkness	1971	5.00	10.00	20.00
BOYD					
B-398 [M]	You Can't Sit Down	1961	20.00	40.00	80.00
BS-398 [S]	You Can't Sit Down	1961	25.00	50.00	100.00
CADET					
LPS-826	Upchurch	1969	3.75	7.50	15.00
LPS-840	The Way I Feel	1970	3.75	7.50	15.00

Number	Title (A Side/B Side)	Yr	VG	VG+	NM
JAM					
007	Free and Easy	198?	3.00	6.00	12.00
KUDU					
22	Phil Upchurch and Tennyson Stevens	1975	3.00	6.00	12.00
MILESTONE					
MSP-9010	Feeling Blue	1968	3.75	7.50	15.00
UNITED ARTISTS					
UAL-3162 [M]	You Can't Sit Down, Part 2	1961	7.50	15.00	30.00
UAL-3175 [M]	Big Hit Dances	1962	6.25	12.50	25.00
UAS-6162 [S]	You Can't Sit Down, Part 2	1961	10.00	20.00	40.00
UAS-6175 [S]	Big Hit Dances	1962	7.50	15.00	30.00

UPFRONTS, THE

45s

Number	Title (A Side/B Side)	Yr	VG	VG+	NM
LUMMTONE					
103	It Took Time/Betty Lou and the Lions	1960	12.50	25.00	50.00
104	Too Far to Turn Around/Married Jive	1960	10.00	20.00	40.00
106	Why You Kiss Me/Little Girl	1961	12.50	25.00	50.00
107	Send Me Someone to Love Who Will Love Me/Baby For Your Love	1961	12.50	25.00	50.00
—White label					
107	Send Me Someone to Love Who Will Love Me/Baby For Your Love	1961	7.50	15.00	30.00
—Black label					
108	It Took Time/Baby For Your Love	1962	6.25	12.50	25.00
114	Do the Beetle/Most of the Pretty Girls	1964	15.00	30.00	60.00

UPSETTERS, THE

45s

Number	Title (A Side/B Side)	Yr	VG	VG+	NM
ABC					
11081	Tossin' and Turnin'/Always in the Wrong Place at the Wrong Time	1968	2.50	5.00	10.00
11120	Don't Be Cruel/Down Home	1968	2.50	5.00	10.00
AUTUMN					
4	Autumn's Here/Draggin' the Main	1964	6.25	12.50	25.00
FALCON					
1010	The Upsetter/The Strip	1958	5.00	10.00	20.00
FIRE					
1029	Jaywalking/Steppin' Out	1960	5.00	10.00	20.00
GEE					
1055	The Blues/Rollin' On	1960	5.00	10.00	20.00
LITTLE STAR					
123	Yes, It's Me/Every Night About This Time	1962	12.50	25.00	50.00
—With Little Richard					

UPTONES, THE

45s

Number	Title (A Side/B Side)	Yr	VG	VG+	NM
LUTE					
6225	No More/I'll Be There	1962	7.50	15.00	30.00
—Black label					
6225	No More/I'll Be There	1962	5.00	10.00	20.00
—Multicolor label					
6229	Be Mine/Dreamin'	1962	10.00	20.00	40.00
MAGNUM					
714	Dreaming/Wear My Ring	1963	5.00	10.00	20.00
WATTS					
1080	Dreaming/Wear My Ring	1963	7.50	15.00	30.00

URIAH HEEP

45s

Number	Title (A Side/B Side)	Yr	VG	VG+	NM
CHRYSALIS					
2274	Come Back to Me/Love or Nothing	1978	—	2.00	4.00
MERCURY					
73103	Gypsy/Real Turned On	1970	2.00	4.00	8.00
73145	Come Away Melinda/Wake Up	1970	2.00	4.00	8.00
73154	I Wanna Be Free/What Should Be Done	1971	2.00	4.00	8.00
73174	High Priestess/(B-side unknown)	1970	2.50	5.00	10.00
73243	Look at Yourself/Love Machine	1971	2.00	4.00	8.00
73271	Why/The Wizard	1971	2.00	4.00	8.00
73307	Easy Livin'/All My Life	1972	2.00	4.00	8.00
73349	Sweet Lorraine/Blind Eye	1972	—	3.00	6.00
73406	Tears in My Eyes/July Morning	1973	—	3.00	6.00
76177	That's the Way It Is/Son of a Bitch	1982	—	2.00	4.00
76177 [PS]	That's the Way It Is/Son of a Bitch	1982	—	2.50	5.00
WARNER BROS.					
7738	Stealin'/Sunshine	1973	—	2.50	5.00
7836	Something or Nothing/What Can I Do	1974	—	—	—
—Unreleased?					
8013	Something or Nothing/What Can I Do	1974	—	2.50	5.00
8132	Prima Dance/Stealin'	1975	—	2.50	5.00
8581	Masquerade/Free Me	1978	—	2.50	5.00

Albums

Number	Title (A Side/B Side)	Yr	VG	VG+	NM
CHRYSALIS					
CHR 1204	Fallen Angel	1978	2.50	5.00	10.00
COLUMBIA					
BFC 40132	Equator	1985	2.00	4.00	8.00
MERCURY					
SRM-1-614	Look at Yourself	1971	2.50	5.00	10.00
SRM-1-630	Demons and Wizards	1972	2.50	5.00	10.00
SRM-1-652	The Magician's Birthday	1972	2.50	5.00	10.00
SRM-1-1070	The Best of Uriah Heep	1976	2.50	5.00	10.00
SRM-1-4057	Abominog	1982	2.00	4.00	8.00
SRM-2-7503 [(2)]	Uriah Heep Live	1973	3.00	6.00	12.00
SR-61294	Uriah Heep	1970	3.00	6.00	12.00
SR-61319	Salisbury	1970	3.00	6.00	12.00
812313-1	Head First	1983	2.00	4.00	8.00
822476-1	The Best of Uriah Heep	1986	2.00	4.00	8.00
—Reissue of Mercury 1070					
WARNER BROS.					
BS 2724	Sweet Freedom	1973	2.50	5.00	10.00
BS 2800	Wonderworld	1974	2.50	5.00	10.00
BS 2869	Return to Fantasy	1975	2.50	5.00	10.00
BS 2949	High and Mighty	1976	2.50	5.00	10.00
BS 3013	Firefly	1977	2.50	5.00	10.00
BSK 3145	Innocent Victim	1978	2.50	5.00	10.00

USHER, GARY

Also see THE TIMERS.

45s

Number	Title (A Side/B Side)	Yr	VG	VG+	NM
CAPITOL					
5128	The Beetle/Jody	1964	12.50	25.00	50.00
5193	Sacramento/That's the Way I Feel	1964	20.00	40.00	80.00
—Produced by Brian Wilson					
5403	It's a Lie/Jody	1965	12.50	25.00	50.00
DOT					
16518	Three Surfer Boys/Milky Way	1963	100.00	200.00	400.00
LAN-CET					
144	Tomorrow/Lies	1961	15.00	30.00	60.00
TITAN					
1716	Driven Insane/You're the Girl	1961	37.50	75.00	150.00

UTMOSTS, THE

45s

Number	Title (A Side/B Side)	Yr	VG	VG+	NM
PAN-OR					
1123	I Need You/Big Man	1962	30.00	60.00	120.00

UTOPIA

Also see TODD RUNDGREN.

45s

Number	Title (A Side/B Side)	Yr	VG	VG+	NM
BEARSVILLE					
0317	Sunburst Finish/Communion with the Sun	1977	—	2.00	4.00
0321	Love Is the Answer/Marriage of Heaven and Hell	1977	—	2.00	4.00
29947	Junk Rock/Lysistrata	1982	—	2.50	5.00
49180	Set Me Free/Umbrella Man	1980	—	2.50	5.00
49247	Love Alone/Very Last Time	1980	—	2.00	4.00
49545	Second Nature/You Make Me Crazy	1980	—	2.00	4.00
49579	Always Late/I Just Want to Touch You	1980	—	2.00	4.00
50062	One World/Special Interest	1982	—	2.50	5.00
NETWORK					
69830	Hammer in My Heart/I'm Looking at You But I'm Talking to Myself	1983	—	2.00	4.00
69859	Feet Don't Fail Me Now/There Goes My Inspiration	1982	—	2.00	4.00
PASSPORT					
7923	Cry Baby/Winston Smith Takes It on the Jaw	1984	—	2.00	4.00
7923 [PS]	Cry Baby/Winston Smith Takes It on the Jaw	1984	—	2.50	5.00
7927	Stand for Something/Mated	1985	—	2.00	4.00

Albums

Number	Title (A Side/B Side)	Yr	VG	VG+	NM
BEARSVILLE					
BRK 3487	Deface the Music	1980	3.00	6.00	12.00
BRK 3666	Swing to the Right	1982	3.00	6.00	12.00
BR 6954	Todd Rundgren's Utopia	1974	3.00	6.00	12.00
BR 6961	Todd Rundgren's Utopia/Another Live	1975	3.00	6.00	12.00
BR 6965	RA	1977	3.00	6.00	12.00
BRK 6970	Oops! Wrong Planet	1977	3.00	6.00	12.00
BRK 6991	Adventures in Utopia	1979	3.00	6.00	12.00
NETWORK					
60183 [(2)]	Utopia	1982	3.75	7.50	15.00
PASSPORT					
PB 6029	Oblivion	1984	2.50	5.00	10.00
PB 6044	POV	1985	2.50	5.00	10.00
RHINO					
RNLP 70865	Todd Rundgren's Utopia	1987	2.00	4.00	8.00
RNLP 70867	Todd Rundgren's Utopia/Another Live	1987	2.00	4.00	8.00
RNLP 70869	RA	1987	2.00	4.00	8.00
RNLP 70870	Oops! Wrong Planet	1987	2.00	4.00	8.00
RNLP 70872	Adventures in Utopia	1987	2.00	4.00	8.00
RNLP 70873	Deface the Music	1987	2.00	4.00	8.00
RNLP 70875	Swing to the Right	1987	2.00	4.00	8.00
R1-70892	Anthology (1974-1985)	1989	2.50	5.00	10.00

UTOPIANS, THE

45s

Number	Title (A Side/B Side)	Yr	VG	VG+	NM
IMPERIAL					
5861	Dutch Treat/Ain't No Such Thing	1962	7.50	15.00	30.00
5876	Along My Lonely Way/Hurry to Your Date	1962	100.00	200.00	400.00
5921	Let Love Come Later/Opera vs. the Blues	1963	6.25	12.50	25.00

V

V-EIGHTS, THE

45s

Number	Title (A Side/B Side)	Yr	VG	VG+	NM
ABC-PARAMOUNT					
10201	Papa's Yellow Tie/My Heart	1961	5.00	10.00	20.00
MOST					
711/3	Pretty Girl/Please Come Back	1959	25.00	50.00	100.00
VIBRO					
4005	Papa's Yellow Tie/My Heart	1960	7.50	15.00	30.00
4007	Let's Take a Chance/Hot Water	1961	7.50	15.00	30.00

V.I.P.'S

45s

Number	Title (A Side/B Side)	Yr	VG	VG+	NM
BIG TOP					
100	Don't Pass Me By/You Ain't Good for Nothing	1965	3.00	6.00	12.00
518	You Pulled a Fast One/Flashback	1964	3.00	6.00	12.00
521	I'm On to You Baby/If He Wants Me	1964	3.00	6.00	12.00
CONGRESS					
211	My Girl Cried/Strange Little Girl	1964	3.75	7.50	15.00

VACELS, THE

Also see RICKY AND THE VACELS.

45s

Number	Title (A Side/B Side)	Yr	VG	VG+	NM
KAMA SUTRA					
200	You're My Baby (And Don't You Forget It)/Hey Girl, Stop Leading Me On	1965	2.50	5.00	10.00
204	Can You Please Crawl Out Your Window/I'm Just a Poor Boy	1965	2.50	5.00	10.00

VAGRANTS, THE

45s

Number	Title (A Side/B Side)	Yr	VG	VG+	NM
ATCO					
6473	Respect/I Love You Yes I Do	1967	2.50	5.00	10.00
6513	Beside the Sea/Sunny Summer Rain	1967	2.50	5.00	10.00
6552	And When It's Over/I Don't Need Your Lovin'	1968	2.50	5.00	10.00
SOUTHERN SOUND					
204	Oh, Those Eyes/You're Too Young	1966	6.25	12.50	25.00
VANGUARD					
35038	I Can't Make a Friend/Young Blues	1966	3.75	7.50	15.00
35042	Final Hour/Your Hasty Heart	1966	5.00	10.00	20.00

Albums

Number	Title (A Side/B Side)	Yr	VG	VG+	NM
ARISTA					
AL-8459	The Great Lost Vagrants Album	1987	5.00	10.00	20.00

VAL-AIRES, THE

Forerunner to THE VOGUES.

45s

Number	Title (A Side/B Side)	Yr	VG	VG+	NM
CORAL					
62177	Laurie My Love/Which One Will It Be	1960	20.00	40.00	80.00
WILLETTE					
114	Laurie My Love/Which One Will It Be	1959	100.00	200.00	400.00

VAL-CHORDS, THE

45s

Number	Title (A Side/B Side)	Yr	VG	VG+	NM
GAME TIME					
104	Candy Store Love/You're Laughing at Me	1957	75.00	150.00	300.00
—With no sword logo					
104	Candy Store Love/You're Laughing at Me	1957	25.00	50.00	100.00
—With sword logo					

VAL-TONES, THE

45s

Number	Title (A Side/B Side)	Yr	VG	VG+	NM
DELUXE					
6084	Tender Darling/Siam Sam	1955	37.50	75.00	150.00

VALADIERS, THE

45s

Number	Title (A Side/B Side)	Yr	VG	VG+	NM
GORDY					
7003	While I'm Away/Because I Love Her	1962	15.00	30.00	60.00
7013	I Found a Girl/You'll Be Sorry Someday	1963	15.00	30.00	60.00
MIRACLE					
6	Greetings/Take a Chance	1961	20.00	40.00	80.00
—With no subtitle on A-side and 2:23 version of B-side					
6	Greeting (This Is Uncle Sam)/Take a Chance	1961	12.50	25.00	50.00
—With subtitle on A-side and 2:15 version of B-side					

VALAQUONS, THE

45s

Number	Title (A Side/B Side)	Yr	VG	VG+	NM
LAGUNA					
102	Teardrops/Madeleine	1964	50.00	100.00	200.00
RAYCO					
516	Jolly Green Giant/Diddy Bop	1965	7.50	15.00	30.00
TANGERINE					
951	I Wanna Woman/Window Shopping on Girl's Avenue	1965	6.25	12.50	25.00

VALE, JERRY

45s

Number	Title (A Side/B Side)	Yr	VG	VG+	NM
BUDDAH					
591	Toot Toot Tootsie (Goodbye)/Now Is Forever	1978	—	2.00	4.00
COLUMBIA					
10042	If I Could Write a Song/Woman of the World	1974	—	2.00	4.00
31163 [S]	(titles unknown)	1961	2.50	5.00	10.00
31164 [S]	(titles unknown)	1961	2.50	5.00	10.00
31165 [S]	(titles unknown)	1961	2.50	5.00	10.00
31166 [S]	(titles unknown)	1961	2.50	5.00	10.00
31167 [S]	(titles unknown)	1961	2.50	5.00	10.00
31468 [S]	(titles unknown)	1962	2.50	5.00	10.00
31469 [S]	(titles unknown)	1962	2.50	5.00	10.00
31470 [S]	(titles unknown)	1962	2.50	5.00	10.00
31471 [S]	(titles unknown)	1962	2.50	5.00	10.00
31472 [S]	(titles unknown)	1962	2.50	5.00	10.00
—Anyone who can fill in these gaps -- the above 10 all are Columbia "Stereo 7" singles -- please let us know.					
39929	And No One Knows/You Can Never Give Me Back Your Heart	1953	5.00	10.00	20.00
39990	For Me/Tired of Waiting	1953	5.00	10.00	20.00
40058	Ask Me/A Tear, a Kiss, a Smile	1953	5.00	10.00	20.00
40131	Two Purple Shadows/And This Is My Beloved	1953	3.75	7.50	15.00
40201	The Ghost in the Vine/I Live Each Day	1954	3.75	7.50	15.00
40260	I'll Follow You/Go	1954	3.75	7.50	15.00
40322	Love Is a Circus/For You, My Love	1954	3.75	7.50	15.00
40404	A Million Moons Ago/Lolly Linger Longer	1955	3.75	7.50	15.00
40429	Hey Punchinello/I Live for Only You	1955	3.75	7.50	15.00
40463	When I Let You Go/And No One Knows	1955	3.75	7.50	15.00
40499	Only Beautiful/How Do I Love You	1955	3.75	7.50	15.00
40541	Magic Night/Heaven Came Down to Earth	1955	3.75	7.50	15.00
40584	Miracle in the Rain/Adelaide	1955	3.75	7.50	15.00
40634	Innamorata (Sweetheart)/Second Ending	1956	3.00	6.00	12.00
40710	You Don't Know Me/Enchanted	1956	3.00	6.00	12.00
40825	All Dressed Up with a Brand New Broken Heart/It Looks Like Love	1957	3.00	6.00	12.00
40880	Don't You Know Me Anymore/For You My Love	1957	3.00	6.00	12.00
40941	Love in the Afternoon/I'm Not Ashamed	1957	3.00	6.00	12.00
41010	Pretend You Don't See Her/The Spreading Chestnut	1957	3.00	6.00	12.00
41120	I Always Say/She	1958	2.50	5.00	10.00
41182	With You/Blue Tears	1958	2.50	5.00	10.00
41238	Go Chase a Moonbeam/Around the Clock	1958	2.50	5.00	10.00
41314	Me and My Shadow/A Warm Spot	1959	2.50	5.00	10.00
41373	Bella, Bella Sue/The Heart Has Won the Game	1959	2.50	5.00	10.00
41423	The Flame/The Moon Is My Pillow	1959	2.50	5.00	10.00
41503	Prima Donna/What Do I Care	1959	2.50	5.00	10.00
41594	Solitaire/Please Believe Me	1960	2.50	5.00	10.00
41681	If/The Dawn of Love	1960	2.50	5.00	10.00
41732	No Moon at All/Making Believe You're Here	1960	2.50	5.00	10.00
41823	Just Friends/To Belong	1960	2.50	5.00	10.00
41942	Camelot/Thirteen Girls Too Much	1961	2.50	5.00	10.00
42027	Al Di La/Thinking of Your Happiness	1961	2.50	5.00	10.00
42201	Another Time, Another Place/If He Leaves You	1961	2.00	4.00	8.00
42304	If Ever I Would Leave You/Who Knows	1962	2.00	4.00	8.00
42439	Ah, Camminare/One Paradise for Sale	1962	2.00	4.00	8.00
42508	My Geisha/It's My Way	1962	2.00	4.00	8.00
42637	From the Bottom of My Heart/Here's to Us	1962	2.00	4.00	8.00
42783	One More Blessing/Doin' What I Said I'd Never Do	1963	2.00	4.00	8.00
42826	Old Cape Cod/Theme for Young Lovers (Where Is My Someone)	1963	2.00	4.00	8.00
42872	Maria Elena/Mala Femina	1963	2.00	4.00	8.00
42951	The Peking Theme (So Little Time)/On and On	1964	2.00	4.00	8.00
42994	The Lights of Rome/As Sure As Night Must Fall	1964	2.00	4.00	8.00
43105	Love Goddess/Where Love Has Gone	1964	2.00	4.00	8.00
43181	Have You Looked Into Your Heart/Andiamo	1964	—	3.00	6.00
43232	For Mama/Ti Adora	1965	—	3.00	6.00
43252	Tears Keep On Falling/Now	1965	—	3.00	6.00
43337	Where Were You When I Needed You/I Don't Wanna Go Home	1965	—	3.00	6.00
43413	Deep in Your Heart/If It Isn't in Your Heart	1965	—	3.00	6.00
43473	Big Wide World/Ashamed	1965	—	3.00	6.00
43605	Less Than Tomorrow/This Day of Days	1966	—	3.00	6.00
43656	My Melancholy Baby/It's Magic	1966	—	3.00	6.00
43696	It'll Take a Little Time/Palermo	1966	—	3.00	6.00
43774	Dommage, Dommage (Too Bad, Too Bad)/Promises	1966	—	3.00	6.00
43895	Somewhere/I've Lost My Heart Again	1966	—	3.00	6.00
44027	Have You Seen the One I Love Go By/Signs	1967	—	2.50	5.00
44087	So Near, Yet So Far/Time Alone Will Tell	1967	—	2.50	5.00
44185	I Love New England/In the Back of My Heart	1967	—	2.50	5.00
44274	In Time/Blame It on Me	1967	—	2.50	5.00
44280	Santa Mouse/Silent Night, Holy Night	1967	—	3.00	6.00
44347	What a Wonderful World/Love Me the Way I Love You	1967	—	2.50	5.00
44432	Don't Tell My Heart to Stop Loving You/When I'm With You	1968	—	2.50	5.00
44512	My Love, Forgive Me/I Never Let a Day Go By	1968	—	2.50	5.00
44572	The Look of Love/With Pen in Hand	1968	—	2.50	5.00
44615	Till Now/That Girl Would Be So Happy	1968	—	2.50	5.00
44687	There's a Baby/Where Are They Now	1968	—	2.50	5.00
44753	Life/Congratulations, I Guess	1969	—	2.50	5.00
44823	Close to Cathy/Fa Fa Fa (Live for Today)	1969	—	2.50	5.00
44914	He Who Loves/Close to You	1969	—	2.50	5.00
44969	This Is My Life/What's Wrong with My World	1969	—	2.50	5.00
45043	Stay Awhile/It's All in the Game	1969	—	2.50	5.00
45118	Hello and Goodbye/Look Homeward Angel	1970	—	2.00	4.00
45188	I'l Never Fall in Love Again/Lovin' Time	1970	—	2.00	4.00
45216	I Climbed the Mountain/Love Never Goes Away	1970	—	2.00	4.00
45308	Point Me in the Direction of Albuquerque/Perfect Love	1971	—	2.50	5.00
45361	My Little Girl/Is It Asking Too Much	1971	—	2.00	4.00
45407	Which Way You Goin' Girl/Moonlight	1971	—	2.00	4.00
45463	Two Purple Shadows/I Found You	1971	—	2.00	4.00
45545	Pretend/Too Young	1972	—	2.00	4.00
45597	Smile/All I Ever Wanted	1972	—	2.00	4.00
45677	Mister Good Times/Till We Two Are One	1972	—	2.00	4.00
45797	He/If I Give My Heart to You	1973	—	2.00	4.00
45896	Mon Amour/The Circle Ends	1973	—	2.00	4.00
45992	Free As the Wind/Reason to Believe	1974	—	2.00	4.00
JZSP 79175/6 [DJ]	Silent Night, Holy Night/Oh Holy Night	1963	2.50	5.00	10.00
JZSP 111776 [DJ]	Blue Christmas (same on both sides)	1965	2.50	5.00	10.00

7-Inch Extended Plays

Number	Title (A Side/B Side)	Yr	VG	VG+	NM
COLUMBIA					
B-2568	*Innamorata/Two Purple Shadows/Pretend You Don't See Her/And This Is My Beloved	1958	2.50	5.00	10.00
B-2568 [PS]	Jerry Vale (Hall of Fame Series)	1958	2.50	5.00	10.00

Number	Title (A Side/B Side)	Yr	VG	VG+	NM
7-9073 [PS]	Standing Ovation!	1964	2.50	5.00	10.00
7-9073 [S]	Hey, Look Me Over/Lulu's Back in Town/With a Song in My Heart//If I Had You/I'm Always Chasing Rainbows/Lonesome Road	1964	2.50	5.00	10.00
—33 1/3 rpm, small hole, "Special Coin Operator Release"					
7-9187 [PS]	There Goes My Heart	1965	2.50	5.00	10.00
7-9187 [S]	There Goes My Heart/Sogni D'Oro (Dreams of Gold/Can't You See I'm Sorry//Without Saying a Word/No One Will Ever Know/Somebody Else Is Taking My Place	1965	2.50	5.00	10.00
—33 1/3 rpm, small hole, "Special Coin Operator Release"					

Albums

COLUMBIA

Number	Title (A Side/B Side)	Yr	VG	VG+	NM
GP 16 [(2)]	With Love, Jerry Vale	1969	3.75	7.50	15.00
CS 1021	Let It Be	1970	3.00	6.00	12.00
CL 1114 [M]	I Remember Buddy	1958	3.75	7.50	15.00
CL 1164 [M]	I Remember Russ	1958	3.75	7.50	15.00
CL 1380 [M]	The Same Old Moon	1959	3.75	7.50	15.00
CL 1529 [M]	Jerry Vale's Greatest Hits	1961	3.75	7.50	15.00
CL 1797 [M]	I Have But One Heart	1962	3.00	6.00	12.00
CL 1955 [M]	Arrividerci, Roma	1963	3.00	6.00	12.00
CL 2043 [M]	The Language of Love	1963	3.00	6.00	12.00
CL 2116 [M]	Till the End of Time	1964	3.00	6.00	12.00
CL 2181 [M]	Be My Love	1964	3.00	6.00	12.00
CL 2225 [M]	Christmas Greetings from Jerry Vale	1964	3.00	6.00	12.00
CL 2273 [M]	Standing Ovation!	1965	3.00	6.00	12.00
CL 2313 [M]	Have You Looked Into Your Heart	1965	3.00	6.00	12.00
CL 2371 [M]	Moonlight Becomes You	1965	3.00	6.00	12.00
CL 2387 [M]	There Goes My Heart	1965	3.00	6.00	12.00
CL 2444 [M]	It's Magic	1966	3.00	6.00	12.00
CL 2489 [M]	Great Moments on Broadway	1966	3.00	6.00	12.00
CL 2530 [M]	Everybody Loves Somebody	1966	3.00	6.00	12.00
CL 2583 [M]	The Impossible Dream	1967	3.00	6.00	12.00
CL 2659 [M]	More Jerry Vale's Greatest Hits	1967	3.75	7.50	15.00
CL 2684 [M]	Time Alone Will Tell	1967	3.00	6.00	12.00
CL 2774 [M]	You Don't Have to Say You Love Me	1968	3.75	7.50	15.00
CS 8016 [S]	I Remember Russ	1958	5.00	10.00	20.00
—Originals have red and black "6 eye" labels					
CS 8069 [S]	I Remember Buddy	1959	5.00	10.00	20.00
—Originals have red and black "6 eye" labels					
CS 8175 [S]	The Same Old Moon	1960	3.75	7.50	15.00
CS 8597 [S]	I Have But One Heart	1962	3.75	7.50	15.00
CS 8755 [S]	Arrividerci, Roma	1963	3.75	7.50	15.00
CS 8778 [R]	Jerry Vale's Greatest Hits	1963	3.00	6.00	12.00
CS 8843 [S]	The Language of Love	1963	3.75	7.50	15.00
CS 8916 [S]	Till the End of Time	1964	3.75	7.50	15.00
CS 8981 [S]	Be My Love	1964	3.75	7.50	15.00
CS 9025 [S]	Christmas Greetings from Jerry Vale	1964	3.75	7.50	15.00
CS 9073 [S]	Standing Ovation!	1965	3.75	7.50	15.00
CS 9113 [S]	Have You Looked Into Your Heart	1965	3.75	7.50	15.00
CS 9171 [S]	Moonlight Becomes You	1965	3.75	7.50	15.00
CS 9187 [S]	There Goes My Heart	1965	3.75	7.50	15.00
CS 9244 [S]	It's Magic	1966	3.75	7.50	15.00
CS 9289 [S]	Great Moments on Broadway	1966	3.75	7.50	15.00
CS 9383 [S]	The Impossible Dream	1967	3.75	7.50	15.00
CS 9459 [S]	More Jerry Vale's Greatest Hits	1967	3.00	6.00	12.00
CS 9484 [S]	Time Alone Will Tell	1967	3.75	7.50	15.00
CS 9574 [S]	You Don't Have to Say You Love Me	1968	3.75	7.50	15.00
CS 9634	I Hear a Rhapsody	1968	3.75	7.50	15.00
CS 9694	This Guy's in Love with You	1968	3.75	7.50	15.00
CS 9757	Till	1969	3.75	7.50	15.00
CS 9838	Where's the Playground Susie?	1969	3.75	7.50	15.00
CS 9982	Jerry Vale Sings 16 Greatest Hits of the 60's	1970	3.00	6.00	12.00
LE 10058	Till	197?	2.50	5.00	10.00
—Reissue of 9757					
LE 10164 [S]	Christmas Greetings from Jerry Vale	197?	2.50	5.00	10.00
—Reissue					
C 30104	We've Only Just Begun	1971	2.50	5.00	10.00
C 30389	The Italian Album	1970	2.50	5.00	10.00
C 30799	I Don't Know How to Love Her	1971	2.50	5.00	10.00
C 31147	Jerry Vale Sings the Great Hits of Nat King Cole	1972	3.00	6.00	12.00
KG 31543 [(2)]	All-Time Greatest Hits	1972	3.00	6.00	12.00
KC 31716	Alone Again (Naturally)	1972	2.50	5.00	10.00
KG 31938 [(2)]	Great Italian Hits	1973	3.00	6.00	12.00
KG 32083 [(2)]	Jerry Vale Sings the Great Love Songs	1973	3.00	6.00	12.00
C 32238	Love Is a Many-Splendored Thing	1973	2.50	5.00	10.00
KC 32454	Jerry Vale's World	1973	2.50	5.00	10.00
KC 32829	Free as the Wind	1974	2.50	5.00	10.00
CG 33615 [(2)]	The Italian Album/Arrividerci, Roma	1974	3.00	6.00	12.00

HARMONY

Number	Title (A Side/B Side)	Yr	VG	VG+	NM
HS 11298	As Long As She Needs Me	1969	2.50	5.00	10.00
HS 11376	Hey Look Me Over	1970	2.50	5.00	10.00
KH 30345	Born Free	1971	2.50	5.00	10.00
KH 30759	More	1971	2.50	5.00	10.00
KH 32478	What a Wonderful World	1973	2.50	5.00	10.00

VALE, RICKY, AND THE SURFERS

Albums

STRAND

Number	Title (A Side/B Side)	Yr	VG	VG+	NM
SL-1104 [M]	Everybody's Surfin'	1963	10.00	20.00	40.00
SLS-1104 [S]	Everybody's Surfin'	1963	12.50	25.00	50.00

VALENS, RITCHIE

45s

DEL-FI

Number	Title (A Side/B Side)	Yr	VG	VG+	NM
1287	La Bamba '87/La Bamba	1987	—	2.50	5.00
4106	Come On, Let's Go/Framed	1958	20.00	40.00	80.00
4110	Donna/La Bamba	1958	17.50	35.00	70.00
—Blue/green/black label with circles					
4110	Donna/La Bamba	1958	10.00	20.00	40.00
—Green label					
4110	Donna/La Bamba	1958	7.50	15.00	30.00
—Light blue label					
4110	Donna/La Bamba	196?	3.75	7.50	15.00
—Black label with light blue sawtooth border					
4110	Donna/La Bamba	196?	6.25	12.50	25.00
—Light blue label with black sawtooth border					
4111	Fast Freight/Big Baby Blues	1959	12.50	25.00	50.00
—As "Arvee Allens"					
4111	Fast Freight/Big Baby Blues	1959	10.00	20.00	40.00
—As "Ritchie Valens"					
4114	That's My Little Susie/In a Turkish Town	1959	10.00	20.00	40.00
4114 [PS]	That's My Little Susie/In a Turkish Town	1959	—	—	—
—Rumored to exist, but without conclusive evidence, we will delete this from future editions					
4117	Little Girl/We Belong Together	1959	7.50	15.00	30.00
4117 [PS]	Little Girl/We Belong Together	1959	25.00	50.00	100.00
4128	Stay Beside Me/Big Baby Blues	1959	6.25	12.50	25.00
4133	The Paddiwack Song/Cry, Cry, Cry	1960	6.25	12.50	25.00
51341 [DJ]	Come On Let's Go/La Bamba	1998	—	2.50	5.00
51341 [PS]	Come On Let's Go/La Bamba	1998	—	2.50	5.00
—Promotional issue in advance of box set; number is not on sleeve, but is on record					

7-Inch Extended Plays

DEL-FI

Number	Title (A Side/B Side)	Yr	VG	VG+	NM
PR-1 [DJ]	La Bamba/We Belong Together//Donna/Framed	1960	37.50	75.00	150.00
PR-1 [PS]	Ritchie Valens (Limited Valens Memorial Series)	1960	50.00	100.00	200.00
—Sleeve accompanying promo-only EP states "February Is Ritchie Valens Memorial Month"					
DFEP-101	(contents unknown)	1959	37.50	75.00	150.00
DFEP-101 [PS]	Ritchie Valens	1959	37.50	75.00	150.00
—Cardboard sleeve					
DFEP-101 [PS]	Ritchie Valens	1959	37.50	75.00	150.00
—Paper sleeve					
DFEP-111	(contents unknown)	1960	37.50	75.00	150.00
DFEP-111 [PS]	Ritchie Valens	1960	37.50	75.00	150.00

Albums

DEL-FI

Number	Title (A Side/B Side)	Yr	VG	VG+	NM
DFLP 1201 [M]	Ritchie Valens	1959	62.50	125.00	250.00
—Blue label with black border					
DFLP 1201 [M]	Ritchie Valens	1959	37.50	75.00	150.00
—Black label with "diamonds" border					
DFLP 1206 [M]	Ritchie	1959	37.50	75.00	150.00
DFLP 1214 [M]	In Concert at Pacoima Jr. High	1960	62.50	125.00	250.00
DFLP 1225 [M]	His Greatest Hits	1963	87.50	175.00	350.00
—Black cover					
DFLP 1225 [M]	His Greatest Hits	1963	37.50	75.00	150.00
—White cover					
DFLP 1247 [M]	His Greatest Hits, Volume 2	1965	37.50	75.00	150.00

GUEST STAR

Number	Title (A Side/B Side)	Yr	VG	VG+	NM
GS-1469 [M]	The Original Ritchie Valens	1963	7.50	15.00	30.00
GSS-1469 [R]	The Original Ritchie Valens	1963	5.00	10.00	20.00
GS-1484 [M]	The Original La Bamba	1963	7.50	15.00	30.00
GSS-1484 [R]	The Original La Bamba	1963	5.00	10.00	20.00

MGM

Number	Title (A Side/B Side)	Yr	VG	VG+	NM
GAS-117	Ritchie Valens (Golden Archive Series)	1970	7.50	15.00	30.00

RHINO

Number	Title (A Side/B Side)	Yr	VG	VG+	NM
RNDF-200	The Best of Ritchie Valens	1981	3.00	6.00	12.00
RNBC-2798 [(3)]	The History of Ritchie Valens	198?	6.25	12.50	25.00
RNLP-70178	The Best of Ritchie Valens (Golden Archive Series)	1987	2.50	5.00	10.00
RNLP-70231	Ritchie Valens	1987	2.50	5.00	10.00
RNLP-70232	Ritchie	1987	2.50	5.00	10.00
RNLP-70233	In Concert at Pacoima Jr. High	1987	2.50	5.00	10.00

VALENS, RITCHIE / JERRY KOLE

Albums

CROWN

Number	Title (A Side/B Side)	Yr	VG	VG+	NM
CLP-5336 [M]	Ritchie Valens and Jerry Kole	1963	7.50	15.00	30.00

VALENTI, DINO

Also see QUICKSILVER MESSENGER SERVICE.

45s

ELEKTRA

Number	Title (A Side/B Side)	Yr	VG	VG+	NM
45012	Birdses/Don't Let It Down	1964	3.75	7.50	15.00

Albums

EPIC

Number	Title (A Side/B Side)	Yr	VG	VG+	NM
LN 24335 [M]	Dino Valenti	1967	5.00	10.00	20.00
BN 26335 [S]	Dino Valenti	1967	5.00	10.00	20.00

VALENTINE, HILTON

Former member of THE ANIMALS.

Albums

CAPITOL

Number	Title (A Side/B Side)	Yr	VG	VG+	NM
ST-330	All in Your Head	1969	7.50	15.00	30.00

VALENTINE, PENNY

45s

LIBERTY

Number	Title (A Side/B Side)	Yr	VG	VG+	NM
55774	I Want to Kiss Ringo Goodbye/Show Me the Way to Love You	1964	7.50	15.00	30.00

VALENTINES, THE (1)

45s

BETHLEHEM

Number	Title (A Side/B Side)	Yr	VG	VG+	NM
3055	I'll Forget You/Yes, You Made It That Way	1962	6.25	12.50	25.00

KING

Number	Title (A Side/B Side)	Yr	VG	VG+	NM
5338	Please Don't Leave, Please Don't Go/That's It Man	1960	6.25	12.50	25.00
5433	That's How I Feel/Hey Ruby	1960	6.25	12.50	25.00
5830	I Have Two Loves/Camping Out	1963	5.00	10.00	20.00

UNITED ARTISTS

Number	Title (A Side/B Side)	Yr	VG	VG+	NM
764	Alone in the Night/Mink Coats and Sneakers	1964	3.75	7.50	15.00

VALENTINES, THE (2)

45s

OLD TOWN

Number	Title (A Side/B Side)	Yr	VG	VG+	NM
1009	Tonight Kathleen/Summer Love	1954	200.00	400.00	800.00

Number	Title (A Side/B Side)	Yr	VG	VG+	NM
RAMA					
171	Lily Maebelle/Falling for You	1955	50.00	100.00	200.00
—Blue label					
171	Lily Maebelle/Falling for You	1955	12.50	25.00	50.00
—Red label					
181	I Love You Darling/Hand Me Down Love	1955	37.50	75.00	150.00
186	Christmas Prayer/K-I-S-S Me	1955	125.00	250.00	500.00
—Blue label					
186	Christmas Prayer/K-I-S-S Me	1955	12.50	25.00	50.00
—Red label					
196	Why/The Woo Woo Train	1956	25.00	50.00	100.00
—Blue label					
196	Why/The Woo Woo Train	1956	12.50	25.00	50.00
—Red label					
201	Twenty Minutes (Before the Hour)/I'll Never Let You Go	1956	25.00	50.00	100.00
208	Nature's Creation/My Story of Love	1956	25.00	50.00	100.00
228	Don't Say Goodnight/I Cried Oh, Oh	1957	50.00	100.00	200.00
ROULETTE					
58	Christmas Prayer/Nature's Creation	196?	2.50	5.00	10.00
—"Golden Goodies Series"					

VALENTINES, THE (3)

45s

Number	Title (A Side/B Side)	Yr	VG	VG+	NM
SOUND STAGE 7					
2646	I'm Alright Now/Gotta Get Yourself Together	1969	3.75	7.50	15.00
2663	If You Love Me/Breakaway	1970	3.00	6.00	12.00

VALENTINES, THE (U)

45s

Number	Title (A Side/B Side)	Yr	VG	VG+	NM
IONA					
1003	The Sock/Sixteen Senoritas	196?	3.75	7.50	15.00
LUDIX					
102	Johnny One Heart/Mama I Have Come Home	1962	5.00	10.00	20.00

VALENTINO, MARK

45s

Number	Title (A Side/B Side)	Yr	VG	VG+	NM
SWAN					
4121	The Push and Kick/Walking Alone	1962	3.75	7.50	15.00
4135	Hey You're Lookin' Good/Do It	1963	3.00	6.00	12.00
4142	Jivin' at the Drive-In/Part Time Job	1963	3.00	6.00	12.00

Albums

Number	Title (A Side/B Side)	Yr	VG	VG+	NM
SWAN					
SLP-508 [M]	Mark Valentino	1963	12.50	25.00	50.00

VALENTINO, SAL

Of THE BEAU BRUMMELS.

45s

Number	Title (A Side/B Side)	Yr	VG	VG+	NM
FALCO					
306	Lisa Marie/I Wanna Twist	1962	10.00	20.00	40.00
WARNER BROS.					
7268	An Added Attraction (Come and See Me)/Alligator Man	1969	2.50	5.00	10.00
7289	Friends and Lovers/Alligator Man	1969	2.50	5.00	10.00
7368	Silkie/Going for Rochelle	1970	2.50	5.00	10.00

VALENTINO AND THE LOVERS

45s

Number	Title (A Side/B Side)	Yr	VG	VG+	NM
DONNA					
1345	One Teardrop Too Late/I'm Gonna Love	1961	10.00	20.00	40.00

VALENTYNE, RUDY

45s

Number	Title (A Side/B Side)	Yr	VG	VG+	NM
ROULETTE					
4610	Don't Ever Leave Me/I Won't Cry Anymore	1965	2.50	5.00	10.00
4618	When I Fall in Love/When I Was a Child	1965	2.00	4.00	8.00
4619	And Now/Ev'rything Beautiful	1965	2.00	4.00	8.00
4620	Who Can I Turn To/More Than This I Cannot Give	1965	2.00	4.00	8.00

Albums

Number	Title (A Side/B Side)	Yr	VG	VG+	NM
ROULETTE					
R-25299 [M]	And Now... Rudy Valentyne	1965	5.00	10.00	20.00
SR-25299 [S]	And Now... Rudy Valentyne	1965	6.25	12.50	25.00

VALERY, DANA

45s

Number	Title (A Side/B Side)	Yr	VG	VG+	NM
ABC					
11138	The Lamplighter's Psalm/Didn't I	1968	3.00	6.00	12.00
11161	A Girl Without Love/Happy Birthday to Me	1968	3.00	6.00	12.00
11214	Surround Yourself with Sorrow/Breakfast in Bed	1969	3.00	6.00	12.00
COLUMBIA					
44004	Having You Around/You Don't Know Where Your Interest Lies	1967	6.25	12.50	25.00
—With Paul Simon					
44301	Imagine/You	1967	3.00	6.00	12.00
44389	Zabadak/Having You Around	1967	3.00	6.00	12.00
LIBERTY					
56156	Clinging Vine/Get In Line Girl	1970	2.00	4.00	8.00
56209	Point of No Return/Put Your Hand in the Hand	1970	2.00	4.00	8.00
PHANTOM					
HB-10566	Will You Love Me Tomorrow/I Never Had It So Good	1975	—	2.50	5.00
SCOTTI BROS.					
509	I Don't Want to Be Lonely/Rainbow Connection	1979	—	2.00	4.00
612	I Gave You My Love/Roses and Rainbows	1980	—	2.00	4.00

VALETS, THE

45s

Number	Title (A Side/B Side)	Yr	VG	VG+	NM
JON					
4025	I Need Someone/When I Met You	1958	25.00	50.00	100.00
4219	Sherry/You and You Alone	1959	7.50	15.00	30.00
VULCAN					
135	Sherry/You and You Alone	1959	50.00	100.00	200.00

VALHALLA

Albums

Number	Title (A Side/B Side)	Yr	VG	VG+	NM
UNITED ARTISTS					
UAS-6730	Valhalla	1969	6.25	12.50	25.00

VALIANTS, THE (1)

45s

Number	Title (A Side/B Side)	Yr	VG	VG+	NM
ANDEX					
4026	Please Wait My Love/Freida, Freida	1958	30.00	60.00	120.00
—Some copies were pressed with this label in error (Keen 4026 is the "correct" issue)					
KEEN					
4008	Temptation of My Heart/Freida, Freida	1958	12.50	25.00	50.00
4026	Please Wait My Love/Freida, Freida	1958	15.00	30.00	60.00
34004	This Is the Nite/Good Golly Miss Molly	1957	10.00	20.00	40.00
34007	Lover Lover/Walkin' Girl	1958	10.00	20.00	40.00
82120	This Is the Nite/Walkin' Girl	1960	5.00	10.00	20.00
SHAR-DEE					
703	Dear Cindy/Surprise	1959	30.00	60.00	120.00
—No mention of London distribution on label					
703	Dear Cindy/Surprise	1959	10.00	20.00	40.00
—With London distribution credit on label					

VALIANTS, THE (2)

45s

Number	Title (A Side/B Side)	Yr	VG	VG+	NM
ALLSTAR					
3677	Jack the Ripper/(B-side unknown)	196?	5.00	10.00	20.00

VALIANTS, THE (3)

45s

Number	Title (A Side/B Side)	Yr	VG	VG+	NM
DOT					
16884	I'll Return to You/Don't Make the Same Mistake	1966	3.00	6.00	12.00

VALIANTS, THE (4)

45s

Number	Title (A Side/B Side)	Yr	VG	VG+	NM
FAIRLANE					
21007	Blue Jeans and a Pony Tail/See Saw	1961	5.00	10.00	20.00
IMPERIAL					
5843	Love Comes in Many Ways/You Are Sweeter Than Wine	1962	3.75	7.50	15.00
5915	Living in Paradise/I'm in a World of My Own	1963	3.75	7.50	15.00
KC					
108	Frankie's Angel/Are You Ready	1962	3.75	7.50	15.00

VALIANTS, THE (5)

45s

Number	Title (A Side/B Side)	Yr	VG	VG+	NM
SPECK					
1001	Wedding Bells/Velma	1958	625.00	1250.	2500.

VALIANTS, THE (U)

45s

Number	Title (A Side/B Side)	Yr	VG	VG+	NM
JOY					
235	Let Me Go Lover/Let Me Ride	1960	5.00	10.00	20.00
ROULETTE					
4510	Johnny Lonely/Eternal Triangle	1963	5.00	10.00	20.00

VALINO, JOE

45s

Number	Title (A Side/B Side)	Yr	VG	VG+	NM
BAND BOX					
261	Turn Back the Dawn/Now	1961	2.50	5.00	10.00
CROSLEY					
216	Back to Your Eyes/Hidden Persuasion	1958	3.00	6.00	12.00
219	Game of Fools/Vesta La Giubba	1959	3.00	6.00	12.00
DEBUT					
143	Christmas Is Here/In Old Judea	1967	2.00	4.00	8.00
144	Vicki/Most Charming	1968	2.00	4.00	8.00
RCA VICTOR					
AMAO-0132	Garden of Eden/Caravan	1973	—	2.50	5.00
—Gold Standard Series reissue					
47-7535	Out of Darkness/Everything I Touched Turned to Gold	1959	2.50	5.00	10.00
47-7723	Garden of Eden/Caravan	1960	2.50	5.00	10.00
UNITED ARTISTS					
101	Legend of the Lost/Declaration of Love	1957	3.00	6.00	12.00
101 [PS]	Legend of the Lost/Declaration of Love	1957	5.00	10.00	20.00
119	God's Little Acre/I'm Happy with What I've Got	1958	3.00	6.00	12.00
VIK					
0204	Buckets of Love (Zoop Zoop Do U Ba)/Four Seasons	1956	3.00	6.00	12.00
0226	Garden of Eden/Caravan	1956	3.75	7.50	15.00
0257	The Wind in the Riggin'/In the Arms of My Love	1957	3.00	6.00	12.00
0275	I'll Be Good/Tears (That I Cry Over You)	1957	3.00	6.00	12.00

7-Inch Extended Plays

Number	Title (A Side/B Side)	Yr	VG	VG+	NM
VIK					
EXA-223	(contents unknown)	1956	5.00	10.00	20.00
EXA-223 [PS]	Garden of Eden	1956	5.00	10.00	20.00

VALJEAN

45s

Number	Title (A Side/B Side)	Yr	VG	VG+	NM
CARLTON					
573	Theme from Ben Casey/Theme from Dr. Kildare	1962	2.50	5.00	10.00
573 [PS]	Theme from Ben Casey/Theme from Dr. Kildare	1962	5.00	10.00	20.00
576	Till There Was You/18th Variation	1962	2.50	5.00	10.00
576 [PS]	Till There Was You/18th Variation	1962	3.75	7.50	15.00
582	Mr. Mozart's Mash/Newsette	1962	2.50	5.00	10.00
586	For the Birds/Hungarian Hash	1963	2.00	4.00	8.00

Number	Title (A Side/B Side)	Yr	VG	VG+	NM
Albums					
CARLTON					
LP-142 [M]	The Theme from Ben Casey	1962	5.00	10.00	20.00
STLP-142 [S]	The Theme from Ben Casey	1962	6.25	12.50	25.00
LP-146 [M]	Mashin' the Classics	1963	5.00	10.00	20.00
STLP-146 [S]	Mashin' the Classics	1963	6.25	12.50	25.00

VALLEY, JIM

Of PAUL REVERE AND THE RAIDERS.

Number	Title (A Side/B Side)	Yr	VG	VG+	NM
45s					
DUNHILL					
4096	Try, Try, Try/Invitations	1967	3.00	6.00	12.00
4103	Go-Go Round/Maintain	1967	3.00	6.00	12.00
JERDEN					
814	I'm Real/There Is Love	196?	2.50	5.00	10.00

VALLI

Number	Title (A Side/B Side)	Yr	VG	VG+	NM
45s					
SCEPTER					
1233	Hurry Home to Me (Soldier Boy)/Jimmy's in a Hurry	1962	3.75	7.50	15.00
—With the Shirelles backing up					

VALLI, FRANKIE

Includes records under numerous pseudonyms. Also see THE FOUR LOVERS; THE FOUR SEASONS.

Number	Title (A Side/B Side)	Yr	VG	VG+	NM
45s					
ATLANTIC					
89720	American Pop/Why	1983	—	2.00	4.00
—With Manhattan Transfer					
CAPITOL					
B-5115	Can't Say No to You/You Make It Beautiful	1982	—	2.00	4.00
—With Cheryl Ladd					
B-5115 [PS]	Can't Say No to You/You Make It Beautiful	1982	—	2.50	5.00
CINDY					
3012	Come Si Bella/Real (This Is Real)	1958	50.00	100.00	200.00
—As "Franke Valli and the Romans"					
CORONA					
1234	My Mother's Eyes/The Laugh's on Me	1953	500.00	1000.	1500.
—As "Frank Valley"					
DECCA					
30994	It May Be Wrong/Please Take a Chance	1959	50.00	100.00	200.00
—As "Frankie Vally"					
MCA					
41253	Doctor Dance/Where Did We Go Wrong	1980	—	2.50	5.00
—With Chris Forde					
MERCURY					
70381	Forgive and Forget/Somebody Else Took Her Home	1954	75.00	150.00	300.00
—As "Frankie Valley"; maroon label					
70381	Forgive and Forget/Somebody Else Took Her Home	1954	50.00	100.00	200.00
—As "Frankie Valley"; black label					
MOTOWN					
1251	You've Got Your Troubles/Listen to Yesterday	1973	3.00	6.00	12.00
1279	The Scalawag Song (And I Will Love You)/Listen to Yesterday	1973	3.00	6.00	12.00
MOWEST					
5011	Love Isn't Here/Poor Fool	1972	3.00	6.00	12.00
5025	The Night (mono/stereo)	1972	2.50	5.00	10.00
—Evidently, stock copies do not exist					
OKEH					
7103	I Go Ape/If You Care	1958	75.00	150.00	300.00
—As "Frankie Tyler"					
PHILIPS					
DJP-16 [DJ]	My Mother's Eyes (mono/stereo)	1967	12.50	25.00	50.00
—Only issued as a promo; alternate number is 40460, but actual issue of 40460 is "C'mon Marianne" by the Four Seasons					
40407	The Proud One/Ivy	1966	2.50	5.00	10.00
40407 [PS]	The Proud One/Ivy	1966	3.75	7.50	15.00
40446	Can't Take My Eyes Off You/The Trouble with Me	1967	2.50	5.00	10.00
40446 [PS]	Can't Take My Eyes Off You/The Trouble with Me	1967	3.75	7.50	15.00
40484	I Make a Fool of Myself/September Rain (Here Comes the Rain)	1967	2.50	5.00	10.00
40484 [PS]	I Make a Fool of Myself/September Rain (Here Comes the Rain)	1967	3.75	7.50	15.00
40510	To Give (The Reason I Live)/Watch Where You Walk	1967	2.50	5.00	10.00
40510 [PS]	To Give (The Reason I Live)/Watch Where You Walk	1967	3.75	7.50	15.00
40622	The Girl I'll Never Know (Angels Never Fly This Low)/A Face Without a Name	1969	2.50	5.00	10.00
40622 [PS]	The Girl I'll Never Know (Angels Never Fly This Low)/A Face Without a Name	1969	3.75	7.50	15.00
40661	You've Got Your Troubles/A Dream of Kings	1970	3.00	6.00	12.00
40680	Circles in the Sand/My Mother's Eyes	1970	2.50	5.00	10.00
PRIVATE STOCK					
45003	My Eyes Adored You/Watch Where You Walk	1974	—	2.50	5.00
45021	Swearin' to God/Why	1975	—	2.50	5.00
45043	Our Day Will Come/You Can Bet	1975	—	2.50	5.00
45074	Fallen Angel/Carrie (I Would Marry You)	1976	—	2.50	5.00
45098	We're All Alone/You to Me Are Everything	1976	—	2.50	5.00
45109	Boomerang/Look at the World, It's Changing	1976	—	2.50	5.00
45140	Easily/What Good Am I Without You	1977	—	2.50	5.00
45154	Second Thoughts/So She Says	1977	—	2.50	5.00
45169	I Need You/I'm Gonna Love You	1977	—	2.50	5.00
45180	I Could Have Loved You/Rainstorm	1978	—	2.50	5.00
RSO					
897	Grease/Grease (Instrumental)	1978	—	3.00	6.00
SMASH					
1995	The Sun Ain't Gonna Shine (Anymore)/This Is Goodbye	1965	2.50	5.00	10.00
2015	(You're Gonna) Hurt Yourself/Night Hawk	1965	3.75	7.50	15.00
—B-side by the Valli Boys					
2037	You're Ready Now/Cry for Me	1966	2.50	5.00	10.00
WARNER BROS.					
8670	No Love at All/Save Me, Save Me	1978	—	2.50	5.00
8734	Fancy Dancer/Needing You	1979	—	2.50	5.00
Albums					
MCA					
743	Heaven Above Me	1982	2.00	4.00	8.00
—Reissue of 5134					
756	The Very Best of Frankie Valli	1982	2.00	4.00	8.00
—Reissue of 3198					
3198	The Very Best of Frankie Valli	1980	2.50	5.00	10.00
5134	Heaven Above Me	1979	2.50	5.00	10.00
MOTOWN					
M5-104V1	Motown Superstar Series, Vol. 4	1981	2.50	5.00	10.00
M6-852	Inside You	1975	3.75	7.50	15.00
PHILIPS					
PHM 200247 [M]	Frankie Valli — Solo	1967	10.00	20.00	40.00
PHS 600247 [S]	Frankie Valli — Solo	1967	7.50	15.00	30.00
PHS 600274	Timeless	1968	6.25	12.50	25.00
PRIVATE STOCK					
PS-2000	Closeup	1975	3.00	6.00	12.00
PS-2001	Frankie Valli Gold	1975	3.00	6.00	12.00
PS-2006	Our Day Will Come	1975	3.00	6.00	12.00
PS-2017	Valli	1976	3.00	6.00	12.00
PS-7002	Lady Put the Light Out	1977	3.00	6.00	12.00
PS-7012	Hits	1978	3.00	6.00	12.00
WARNER BROS.					
BSK 3233	Frankie Valli...Is the Word	1978	2.50	5.00	10.00

VALLI, FRANKIE, AND THE FOUR SEASONS

See THE FOUR SEASONS.

VALOR, TONY

Number	Title (A Side/B Side)	Yr	VG	VG+	NM
45s					
MUSICTONE					
1119	There's a Story in My Heart/So Tenderly	1963	37.50	75.00	150.00

VALQUINS, THE

Number	Title (A Side/B Side)	Yr	VG	VG+	NM
45s					
GAITY					
161/2	My Dear/Falling Star	1959	200.00	400.00	800.00
161/2	My Dear/Falling Star	1959	500.00	1000.	1500.
—Red vinyl					

VALRAYS, THE

Number	Title (A Side/B Side)	Yr	VG	VG+	NM
45s					
PARKWAY					
880	Get A Board/Pee Wee	1963	7.50	15.00	30.00
904	Yo Me Pregunto/Tonky	1964	5.00	10.00	20.00

VALS, THE

Number	Title (A Side/B Side)	Yr	VG	VG+	NM
45s					
ASCOT					
2163	Too Late/I'm Stepping Out with My Memories	1964	7.50	15.00	30.00
UNIQUE LABORATORIES					
(no #)	The Song of a Lover/Compensation Blues	1962	250.00	500.00	1000.

VALTONES, THE

Number	Title (A Side/B Side)	Yr	VG	VG+	NM
45s					
GEE					
1004	You Belong to My Heart/Have You Ever Met an Angel	1956	75.00	150.00	300.00

VALUMES, THE

See THE VOLUMES.

VAMPIRES, THE

Number	Title (A Side/B Side)	Yr	VG	VG+	NM
45s					
CARROLL					
104	Why Didn't I Listen to Mother/Did Anybody Lose a Tear	1962	37.50	75.00	150.00
Albums					
UNITED ARTISTS					
UAL-3378 [M]	The Vampires at the Monster Ball	1964	6.25	12.50	25.00
UAS-6378 [S]	The Vampires at the Monster Ball	1964	7.50	15.00	30.00

VAN DER GRAAF GENERATOR

Number	Title (A Side/B Side)	Yr	VG	VG+	NM
45s					
MERCURY					
72979	Necromancer/Afterwards	1969	5.00	10.00	20.00
Albums					
ABC DUNHILL					
DS 50097	H to He Who Am the Only One	1971	3.75	7.50	15.00
CHARISMA					
CAS-1051	Pawn Hearts	1971	3.75	7.50	15.00
MERCURY					
SRM-1-1069	Godbluff	1975	3.00	6.00	12.00
SRM-1-1096	Still Life	1976	3.00	6.00	12.00
SRM-1-1116	World Record	1976	3.00	6.00	12.00
SR-61238	The Aerosol Grey Machine	1969	25.00	50.00	100.00
PROBE					
CLP-4515	The Least We Can Do Is Wave	1970	7.50	5.00	30.00
PVC					
9901 [(2)]	Vital	1979	3.75	7.50	15.00

Number	Title (A Side/B Side)	Yr	VG	VG+	NM
VAN DERBUR, MARILYN					
Albums					
DECCA					
DL 8770 [M]	Miss America	1958	10.00	20.00	40.00
VAN DYKE, CONNIE					
45s					
MOTOWN					
1041	Oh Freddie/It Hurt Me Too	1963	12.50	25.00	50.00
WHEELSVILLE					
112	Don't Do Nothin' I Wouldn't Do/The Words Won't Come	196?	37.50	75.00	150.00
VAN DYKE, EARL, AND THE SOUL BROTHERS					
45s					
RENAISSANCE					
5000	September Song/(B-side unknown)	196?	18.75	37.50	75.00
SOUL					
35006	Soul Stomp/Hot 'N' Tot	1964	5.00	10.00	20.00
35009	All for You/Too Many Fish in the Sea	1965	200.00	400.00	800.00
35014	I Can't Help Myself/How Sweet It Is To Be Loved By You	1965	5.00	10.00	20.00
35018	The Flick (Part 1)/The Flick (Part 2)	1966	5.00	10.00	20.00
35028	6 x 6/There Is No Greater Love	1967	5.00	10.00	20.00
—By Earl Van Dyke and the Motown Brass					
35059	Runaway Child, Running Wild/Gonna Give Her All the Love I've Got	1969	5.00	10.00	20.00
Albums					
MOTOWN					
M-631 [M]	The Motown Sound	1965	10.00	20.00	40.00
MS-631 [S]	The Motown Sound	1965	12.50	25.00	50.00
SOUL					
SS-715	The Earl of Funk	1970	10.00	20.00	40.00
VAN DYKE, LEROY					
45s					
ABC					
12070	Unfaithful Fools/What Will You Do Now, Mrs. Jones	1975	—	2.00	4.00
ABC/DOT					
17567	You Sure Look Good on My Pillow/Busted	1975	—	2.00	4.00
17597	Who's Gonna Run the Truck Stop in Tuba City When I'm Gone?/There Ain't No Roses in My Bed	1975	—	2.00	4.00
17691	Texas Tea/Las Vegas Girl	1977	—	2.00	4.00
DECCA					
32756	Mister Professor/People Gonna Turn You Off	1970	—	3.00	6.00
32825	Birmingham/What Am I Gonna Tell Them Now	1971	—	3.00	6.00
32866	I Get Lonely When It Rains/Party Girl	1971	—	3.00	6.00
32933	I'd Rather Be Wantin' Love/My Mind Is On You	1972	—	3.00	6.00
32999	I'll Be Around/Yesterday Will Come Again Tonight	1972	—	3.00	6.00
33055	Untie Me/Sittin' In for Me	1973	—	3.00	6.00
DOT					
15503	Auctioneer/I Fell in Love with a Pony Tail	1956	5.00	10.00	20.00
—Originals have maroon labels					
15503	Auctioneer/I Fell in Love with a Pony Tail	1956	3.75	7.50	15.00
—Second pressings have black labels					
15561	The Pocket Book Song/Honky Tonk Song	1957	3.75	7.50	15.00
15652	One Heart/Everytime I Ask My Heart	1957	3.75	7.50	15.00
15698	Leather Jacket/My Good Mind Went Bad	1958	25.00	50.00	100.00
16299	Auctioneer/I Fell in Love with a Pony	1961	2.50	5.00	10.00
KAPP					
908	Lonely Thing/One More Minute of Lonely	1968	—	3.00	6.00
931	You May Be Too Much for Memphis, Baby/Road of Love	1968	—	3.00	6.00
951	Lonesome Is/The Long Drive Home	1968	—	3.00	6.00
983	Goin' Back to Boston/The Straw	1969	—	3.00	6.00
2021	Steal Away/This Beginning of a Man	1969	—	3.00	6.00
2054	Crack in the World/Try a Little Bit Harder	1969	—	3.00	6.00
2091	Belle-O/An Old Love Affair Now Showing	1970	—	3.00	6.00
MCA					
40114	I'm O.K., You're O.K./Everytime Seems Like the First Time	1973	—	2.50	5.00
MERCURY					
71779	Faded Love/Big Man in a Big House	1961	3.00	6.00	12.00
71834	Walk On By/My World Is Caving In	1961	3.75	7.50	15.00
71926	If a Woman Answers (Hang Up the Phone)/A Broken Promise	1962	3.00	6.00	12.00
71988	The Life You Offered Me/Dim, Dark Corner	1962	3.00	6.00	12.00
72018	How Long Must You Keep Me a Secret/I Sat Back and Let It Happen	1962	3.00	6.00	12.00
72057	Black Cloud/Five Steps	1962	3.00	6.00	12.00
72097	Be a Good Girl/The Other Boys Are Talking	1963	3.00	6.00	12.00
72155	Wrong Side of the Tracks/What Are the Lips of Janet	1963	3.00	6.00	12.00
72198	Happy to Be Unhappy/Now I Lay Me Down	1963	3.00	6.00	12.00
72232	Night People/Baby (Where Can You Be)	1964	2.50	5.00	10.00
72277	Afraid of a Heartbreak/Your Money	1964	2.50	5.00	10.00
72360	Anne of a Thousand Days/Poor Guy	1964	2.50	5.00	10.00
PLANTATION					
170	Runaround Sue/House of the Rising Sun	1978	—	2.00	4.00
192	Don't Bite the Hand That Feeds You/A Gay Ranchero	1978	—	2.00	4.00
SUN					
1146	Save Me a Seat by the Fire/Rev. Edmond Giles	1979	—	2.00	4.00
WARNER BROS.					
5650	It's All Over Now, Baby Blue/Just a State of Mind	1965	2.50	5.00	10.00
5692	Big Wide Wonderful World of Country/Ol' Man Moses	1966	2.50	5.00	10.00
5807	(Now and Then There's) A Fool Such As I/You Couldn't Get My Love Back (If You Tried)	1966	2.50	5.00	10.00
5841	Roses from a Stranger/Before I Change My Mind	1966	2.00	4.00	8.00
7001	I've Never Been Loved/Less of Me	1967	2.00	4.00	8.00
7064	I'll Make It Up to You/What Am I Bid	1967	2.00	4.00	8.00
7155	Louisville/There's Always Tomorrow	1967	2.00	4.00	8.00
Albums					
DOT					
DLP 3693 [M]	Auctioneer	1966	5.00	10.00	20.00
HARMONY					
HS 11308	I've Never Been Loved	196?	3.00	6.00	12.00
KAPP					
KS-3571	Lonesome Is	1968	3.75	7.50	15.00
KS-3605	Greatest Hits	1969	3.75	7.50	15.00
KS-3607	Just a Closer Walk with Thee	1969	3.75	7.50	15.00
MCA					
145	Greatest Hits	1973	3.00	6.00	12.00
MERCURY					
MG-20682 [M]	Walk On By	1962	5.00	10.00	20.00
MG-20716 [M]	Movin' Van Dyke	1963	5.00	10.00	20.00
MG-20802 [M]	Leroy Van Dyke's Greatest Hits	1963	5.00	10.00	20.00
MG-20922 [M]	Songs for Mom and Dad	1964	5.00	10.00	20.00
MG-20950 [M]	Leroy Van Dyke at the Tradewinds	1964	5.00	10.00	10.00
SR-60682 [S]	Walk On By	1962	6.25	12.50	25.00
SR-60716 [S]	Movin' Van Dyke	1963	6.25	12.50	25.00
SR-60802 [S]	Leroy Van Dyke's Greatest Hits	1963	6.25	12.50	25.00
SR-60922 [S]	Songs for Mom and Dad	1964	6.25	12.50	25.00
SR-60950 [S]	Leroy Van Dyke at the Tradewinds	1964	6.25	12.50	25.00
PLANTATION					
516	Gospel Greats	1977	3.00	6.00	12.00
SUN					
131	Golden Hits	1974	3.00	6.00	12.00
WARNER BROS.					
W 1618 [M]	The Leroy Van Dyke Show	1965	3.75	7.50	15.00
WS 1618 [S]	The Leroy Van Dyke Show	1965	5.00	10.00	20.00
W 1652 [M]	Country Hits	1966	3.75	7.50	15.00
WS 1652 [S]	Country Hits	1966	5.00	10.00	20.00
WING					
MGW-12302 [M]	Out of Love	196?	3.00	6.00	12.00
MGW-12322 [M]	Movin'	196?	3.00	6.00	12.00
SRW-16302 [S]	Out of Love	196?	3.75	7.50	15.00
SRW-16322 [S]	Movin'	196?	3.75	7.50	15.00
VAN DYKES, THE (1)					
45s					
DELUXE					
6193	The Bells Are Ringing/The Meaning of Love	1960	6.25	12.50	25.00
DONNA					
1333	Gift of Love/Guardian Angel	1961	10.00	20.00	40.00
FELSTED					
8565	Once Upon a Dream/Dame Tu Corazon	1959	6.25	12.50	25.00
KING					
5158	The Bells Are Ringing/The Meaning of Love	1958	17.50	35.00	70.00
SPRING					
1113	Gift of Love/Guardian Angel	1961	30.00	60.00	120.00
VAN DYKES, THE (2)					
45s					
HUE					
6501	No Man Is an Island/I Won't Hold It Against You	1965	7.50	15.00	30.00
MALA					
520	No Man Is an Island/I Won't Hold It Against You	1965	3.75	7.50	15.00
530	I've Got to Go On Without You/What Will I Do If I Lose You	1966	3.00	6.00	12.00
539	Never Let Me Go/I've Got to Find a Love	1966	3.00	6.00	12.00
549	You Need Confidence/You're Shakin' Me Up	1966	3.00	6.00	12.00
566	A Sunday Kind of Love/I'm So Happy	1967	5.00	10.00	20.00
584	Tears of Joy/Save My Love for a Rainy Day	1967	10.00	20.00	40.00
Albums					
BELL					
6004 [M]	Tellin' It Like It Is	1967	12.50	25.00	50.00
S-6004 [S]	Tellin' It Like It Is	1967	15.00	30.00	60.00
VAN DYKES, THE (3)					
45s					
CO-OP					
515	Rich Girl/Miracle After Miracle	1967	5.00	10.00	20.00
516	Rock-a-Bye Girl/I'll Be By	1967	5.00	10.00	20.00
GREEN SEA					
101	Rich Girl/Again and Again	1965	10.00	20.00	40.00
105	Rock-a-Bye Girl/I'll Be By	1966	12.50	25.00	50.00
108	Miracle After Miracle/How Can I Forget Her	1966	10.00	20.00	40.00
VAN DYKES, THE (4)					
45s					
DECCA					
30654	The Fixer/Run Betty, Run	1958	10.00	20.00	40.00
30762	Come On Baby/Lambie Baby	1958	10.00	20.00	40.00
31036	Better Come Back to Me/I Don't Know What to Do	1959	15.00	30.00	60.00
VAN DYKES, THE (U)					
45s					
ATLANTIC					
2161	King of Fools/Stupidity	1962	3.75	7.50	15.00
VAN EATEN, LON AND DERREK					
45s					
APPLE					
1845	Sweet Music/Song of Songs	1972	2.00	4.00	8.00
1845 [PS]	Sweet Music/Song of Songs	1972	2.50	5.00	10.00
A&M					
1643	Wildfire/Music Lover	1974	—	2.50	5.00
—All A&M records as "Lon and Derrek"					

Number	Title (A Side/B Side)	Yr	VG	VG+	NM
1662	Who Do You Outdo/All You're Hungry For Is Love	1975	—	2.50	5.00
1696	The Harder You Pull... The Tighter It Gets/ Dancing in the Dark	1975	—	2.50	5.00
1845	Loving You/Baby It's You	1976	—	2.00	4.00
Albums					
APPLE					
SMAS-3360	Brother	1972	3.75	7.50	15.00
A&M					
SP-4507	Who Do You Outdo	1975	2.50	5.00	10.00

VAN ZANDT, TOWNES

Number	Title (A Side/B Side)	Yr	VG	VG+	NM
45s					
POPPY					
XW170	Fraulein/Don't Let the Sunshine Fool You	1973	—	3.00	6.00
XW238	Pancho and Lefty/(B-side unknown)	1973	2.50	5.00	10.00
506	Talking Karate Blues/Waiting Around to Die	1968	2.00	4.00	8.00
510	Second Lovers/(B-side unknown)	1968	2.00	4.00	8.00
90104	Come Tomorrow/Delta Momma Blues	1970	2.00	4.00	8.00
90108	Greensboro Woman/Stand-In	1971	2.00	4.00	8.00
90113	If I Needed You/Sunshine Boy	1971	2.00	4.00	8.00
90116	Honky Tonkin'/Snow Don't Fall	1972	2.00	4.00	8.00
TOMATO					
10003	Who Do You Love/(B-side unknown)	1977	—	2.50	5.00
10005	When She Don't Need Me/No Place to Fall	1978	—	2.50	5.00
Albums					
POPPY					
PP-LA004-F	The Late Great Townes Van Zandt	1973	3.75	7.50	15.00
PYS-5700	High, Low and In Between	1972	3.75	7.50	15.00
PYS-40001	For the Sake of a Song	1968	6.25	12.50	25.00
PYS-40004	Our Mother, The Mountain	1969	3.75	7.50	15.00
PYS-40007	Townes Van Zandt	1969	3.75	7.50	15.00
PYS-40012	Delta Momma Blues	1970	3.75	7.50	15.00
SUGAR HILL					
SH-1020	At My Window	1987	2.50	5.00	10.00
SH-1026	Live and Obscure	1989	2.50	5.00	10.00
TOMATO					
7001 [(2)]	Live at the Old Quarter, Houston, Texas	1977	3.75	7.50	15.00
7011	The Late Great Townes Van Zandt	1978	3.00	6.00	12.00
—Reissue of Poppy 004					
7012	High, Low and In Between	1978	3.00	6.00	12.00
—Reissue of Poppy 5700					
7013	Delta Momma Blues	1978	3.00	6.00	12.00
—Reissue of Poppy 40012					
7014	Townes Van Zandt	1978	3.00	6.00	12.00
—Reissue of Poppy 40007					
7015	Our Mother, The Mountain	1978	3.00	6.00	12.00
—Reissue of Poppy 40004					
7017	Flyin' Shoes	1978	3.00	6.00	12.00

VANGUARDS, THE (1)

Number	Title (A Side/B Side)	Yr	VG	VG+	NM
45s					
LAMP					
652	It's To Late for Love/The Thought of Losing Your Love	1970	3.00	6.00	12.00
—Yes, the label misspelled the A-side					
653	Girl Go Away/Man Without Knowledge	1970	3.00	6.00	12.00
WHIZ					
612	Somebody Please/(B-side unknown)	1969	2.50	5.00	10.00

VANGUARDS, THE (2)

Number	Title (A Side/B Side)	Yr	VG	VG+	NM
45s					
DERBY					
854	Don't Let It Happen Again/So Live	1954	100.00	200.00	400.00

VANGUARDS, THE (3)

Number	Title (A Side/B Side)	Yr	VG	VG+	NM
45s					
IVY					
103	Moonlight/I'm Movin'	1958	30.00	60.00	120.00
—With mention of "Billy Butler's Orchestra"					
103	Moonlight/I'm Movin'	1958	10.00	20.00	40.00
—No mention of "Billy Butler's Orchestra"					

VANGUARDS, THE (4)

Number	Title (A Side/B Side)	Yr	VG	VG+	NM
45s					
WARNER BROS.					
5800	Girl/A Stranger in Your Town	1966	3.00	6.00	12.00

VANGUARDS, THE (U)

Number	Title (A Side/B Side)	Yr	VG	VG+	NM
45s					
DOT					
15791	Baby Doll/My Friend Mary Ann	1958	6.25	12.50	25.00

VANILLA FUDGE

Number	Title (A Side/B Side)	Yr	VG	VG+	NM
45s					
ATCO					
6495	You Keep Me Hangin' On/Take Me for a Little While	1967	3.00	6.00	12.00
6554	The Look of Love/Where Is My Mind	1968	2.00	4.00	8.00
6590	You Keep Me Hangin' On/Come by Day, Come by Night	1968	2.50	5.00	10.00
6616	Take Me for a Little While/Thoughts	1968	2.00	4.00	8.00
6632	Season of the Witch (Part 1)/Season of the Witch (Part 2)	1968	2.00	4.00	8.00
6655	Good Good Lovin'/Shot Gun	1969	2.00	4.00	8.00
6679	People/Some Velvet Morning	1969	2.00	4.00	8.00
6703	Need Love/I Can't Make It Alone	1969	2.00	4.00	8.00
6728	Windmills of Your Mind/Lord in the Country	1970	—	3.00	6.00
99729	Mystery/The Stranger	1984	—	2.00	4.00
7-Inch Extended Plays					
ATCO					
SP-4516 [DJ]	Eleanor Rigby-Part 1/You Keep Me Hanging On/ /Eleanor Rigby-Part 2/Ticket to Ride	1968	5.00	10.00	20.00
—Promo only, white label					
SP-4516 [PS]	(title unknown)	1968	5.00	10.00	20.00
—Paper sleeve with above EP					
Albums					
ATCO					
33-224 [M]	Vanilla Fudge	1967	6.25	12.50	25.00
SD 33-224	Vanilla Fudge	197?	2.00	4.00	8.00
—Any later label					
SD 33-224 [S]	Vanilla Fudge	1967	5.00	10.00	20.00
—Purple and brown label					
SD 33-224 [S]	Vanilla Fudge	1969	3.00	6.00	12.00
—Yellow label					
33-237 [M]	The Beat Goes On	1968	10.00	20.00	40.00
SD 33-237	The Beat Goes On	1968	5.00	10.00	20.00
—Purple and brown label					
SD 33-237	The Beat Goes On	1969	3.00	6.00	12.00
—Yellow label					
SD 33-244	Renaissance	1968	5.00	10.00	20.00
—Purple and brown label					
SD 33-244	Renaissance	1969	3.00	6.00	12.00
—Yellow label					
SD 33-278	Near the Beginning	1969	3.75	7.50	15.00
SD 33-303	Rock 'n' Roll	1969	3.75	7.50	15.00
90006	The Best of Vanilla Fudge	1982	2.50	5.00	10.00

VANITY FARE

Number	Title (A Side/B Side)	Yr	VG	VG+	NM
45s					
20TH CENTURY					
2012	Rock and Roll Is Back/Making for the Sun	1973	—	2.50	5.00
2036	Down Home/Take It, Shake It, Break My Heart	1973	—	2.50	5.00
BRENT					
7067	Peter Who (Peter Pan)/Salt Water Babies	1967	2.00	4.00	8.00
DJM					
70024	Where Did All the Good Times Go/Stand	1971	—	2.50	5.00
70029	Big Parade/Nowhere to Go	1971	—	2.50	5.00
PAGE ONE					
21007	I Live for the Sun/On the Other Side of Life	1969	—	3.00	6.00
21020	Highway of Dreams/Waiting for the Nightfall	1969	—	3.00	6.00
21027	Early in the Morning/You Made Me Love You	1969	2.00	4.00	8.00
21029	Hitchin' a Ride/Man Child	1970	2.00	4.00	8.00
21033	(I Remember) Summer Morning/Megowd (Something Tells Me)	1970	—	3.00	6.00
21036	Where Did All the Good Times Go/Stand	1970	—	3.50	7.00
SOMA					
5000	Hitchin' a Ride/Early in the Morning	197?	—	2.50	5.00
—Reissue					
Albums					
PAGE ONE					
2502	Early in the Morning	1970	5.00	10.00	20.00

VANNELLI, GINO

Number	Title (A Side/B Side)	Yr	VG	VG+	NM
12-Inch Singles					
CBS ASSOCIATED					
ZAS 2663 [DJ]	Wild Horses (same on both sides)	1987	2.00	4.00	8.00
06728	In the Name of Money (3 versions)	1987	—	3.00	6.00
HME					
ZAS 2059 [DJ]	Black Cars (Dance Mix) (LP Version)	1985	2.00	4.00	8.00
05205	Black Cars (Dance Mix) (Instrumental) (LP Version)	1985	2.00	4.00	8.00
45s					
ARISTA					
0588	Living Inside Myself/Stay with Me	1981	—	—	3.00
0588 [PS]	Living Inside Myself/Stay with Me	1981	—	2.00	4.00
0613	Nightwalker/Sally She Says the Sweetest Things	1981	—	—	3.00
0613 [PS]	Nightwalker/Sally She Says the Sweetest Things	1981	—	2.00	4.00
0664	The Longer You Wait/Bandito	1982	—	—	3.00
0664 [PS]	The Longer You Wait/Bandito	1982	—	2.00	4.00
A&M					
1449	Granny Goodbye/Hollywood Holiday	1973	—	2.50	5.00
1467	Crazy Life/There's No Time	1973	—	2.50	5.00
1614	People Gotta Move/Son of a New York Gun	1974	—	2.00	4.00
1652	Powerful People/Lady	1974	—	2.00	4.00
1732	Father and Son/Love Me Now	1975	—	2.00	4.00
1760	Gettin' High/Mama Coco	1975	—	2.00	4.00
1790	Keep On Walking/Love Is a Night	1976	—	2.00	4.00
1861	Love of My Life/Omens of Love	1976	—	2.00	4.00
1861 [PS]	Love of My Life/Omens of Love	1976	—	2.50	5.00
1879	Summers of My Life/Omens of Love	1976	—	2.00	4.00
1911	Fly Into This Night/Ugly Man	1977	—	2.00	4.00
2002	Feel the Fire (Valleys of Valhalla)/Black and Blue	1977	—	2.00	4.00
2025	One Night with You/Black and Blue	1978	—	2.00	4.00
2072	I Just Wanna Stop/The Surest Things Can Change	1978	—	2.00	4.00
2072 [PS]	I Just Wanna Stop/The Surest Things Can Change	1978	—	2.50	5.00
2114	Wheels of Life/Mardi Gras	1979	—	2.00	4.00
2114 [PS]	Wheels of Life/Mardi Gras	1979	—	2.50	5.00
2133	The River Must Flow/Mardi Gras	1979	—	2.00	4.00
CBS ASSOCIATED					
05586	Hurts to Be in Love/Here She Comes	1985	—	—	3.00
05586 [PS]	Hurts to Be in Love/Here She Comes	1985	—	—	3.00
06663	In the Name of Money/Shape Me Like a Man	1987	—	—	3.00
06699	Wild Horses/Shape Me Like a Man	1987	—	—	3.00
06699 [PS]	Wild Horses/Shape Me Like a Man	1987	—	—	3.00
HME					
04889	Black Cars/Imagination	1985	—	—	3.00
04889 [PS]	Black Cars/Imagination	1985	—	—	3.00

Number	Title (A Side/B Side)	Yr	VG	VG+	NM
Albums					
ARISTA					
AB 9539	Nightwalker	1981	2.50	5.00	10.00
A&M					
SP-3112	The Gist of the Gemini	1981	2.00	4.00	8.00
—Reissue of 4596					
SP-3120	Powerful People	1981	2.00	4.00	8.00
—Reissue of 3630					
SP-3139	Crazy Life	1981	2.00	4.00	8.00
—Reissue of 4395					
SP-3170	Brother to Brother	1981	2.00	4.00	8.00
—Reissue of 4722					
SP-3260	The Best of Gino Vannelli	1982	2.00	4.00	8.00
—Reissue of 3729					
SP-3630	Powerful People	1974	2.50	5.00	10.00
SP-3729	The Best of Gino Vannelli	1981	2.50	5.00	10.00
SP-4395	Crazy Life	1973	3.00	6.00	12.00
SP-4533	Storm at Sunup	1975	2.50	5.00	10.00
SP-4596	The Gist of the Gemini	1976	2.50	5.00	10.00
SP-4664	A Pauper in Paradise	1977	2.50	5.00	10.00
SP-4722	Brother to Brother	1978	2.50	5.00	10.00
CBS ASSOCIATED					
BFZ 40337	Big Dreamers Never Sleep	1987	2.50	5.00	10.00
HME					
FZ 40077	Black Cars	1985	2.50	5.00	10.00
MOBILE FIDELITY					
1-041	Powerful People	1980	5.00	10.00	20.00
—Audiophile vinyl					
NAUTILUS					
NR-35	Brother to Brother	198?	6.25	12.50	25.00
—Audiophile vinyl					

VAQUEROS, THE

Number	Title (A Side/B Side)	Yr	VG	VG+	NM
45s					
AUDITION					
6102	Desert Wind/Echo	1964	12.50	25.00	50.00
BANGAR					
00647	Birds and Bees/80-Foot Wave	1964	10.00	20.00	40.00

VARE, RONNIE, AND THE INSPIRATIONS

Number	Title (A Side/B Side)	Yr	VG	VG+	NM
45s					
DELL					
5203	Let's Rock, Little Girl/Love Is Just for Two	1959	12.50	25.00	50.00

VAREEATIONS, THE

Number	Title (A Side/B Side)	Yr	VG	VG+	NM
45s					
DIONN					
506	The Time/Ssab-Bbrom	1968	3.75	7.50	15.00
510	Foolish One/It's the Loving Season	1969	3.75	7.50	15.00

VARNER, DON

Number	Title (A Side/B Side)	Yr	VG	VG+	NM
45s					
QUINCY					
8002	Tear Stained Face/Meet Me in the Church	1969	62.50	125.00	250.00
VEEP					
1296	Tear Stained Face/Meet Me in the Church	1969	50.00	100.00	200.00

VAUGHAN, FRANKIE

Number	Title (A Side/B Side)	Yr	VG	VG+	NM
45s					
COLUMBIA					
41279	One Thing Led to Another/So Happy in Love	1958	3.75	7.50	15.00
41406	Honey Bunny Baby/Big Deal	1959	3.75	7.50	15.00
41480	Ain't Gonna Lead This Life No More/Heart of a Man	1959	3.75	7.50	15.00
41537	The Very Very Young/If You Ever Fall in Love	1959	3.75	7.50	15.00
41638	Hey You with the Crazy Eyes/The Key	1960	3.75	7.50	15.00
41859	Do You Still Love Me/Milord	1960	3.75	7.50	15.00
EPIC					
9238	Pebble on the Beach/Isn't This a Lovely Evening	1957	3.75	7.50	15.00
9265	We're Not Alone/Can't Get Along Without You	1958	3.75	7.50	15.00
9273	Judy/Am I Wasting My Time with You	1958	4.00	8.00	16.00
MALA					
588	If I Didn't Care/So Tired	1968	—	3.00	6.00
12004	Nevertheless/Girl Talk	1968	—	3.00	6.00
PHILIPS					
40070	Hercules/I'm Gonna Clip Your Wings	1962	3.00	6.00	12.00
40349	Forgotten Man/Wait	1965	2.00	4.00	8.00
Albums					
PHILIPS					
PHM 200006 [M]	Singin' Happy	1962	5.00	10.00	20.00
PHS 600006 [S]	Singin' Happy	1962	6.25	12.50	25.00

VAUGHAN, SARAH

Number	Title (A Side/B Side)	Yr	VG	VG+	NM
45s					
ATLANTIC					
1012	It Might As Well Be Spring/You Go to My Head	1953	25.00	50.00	100.00
3835	Fool on the Hill/Get Back	1981	—	2.50	5.00
COLUMBIA					
1-199	Black Coffee/As You Desire Me	1949	10.00	20.00	40.00
—Microgroove 33 1/3 rpm single					
1-250 (?)	Tonight I Shall Sleep (With a Smile on My Face)/While You're Gone	1949	10.00	20.00	40.00
—Microgroove 33 1/3 rpm single					
1-321	That Lucky Old Sun (Just Rolls Around Heaven All Day)/Make Believe (You Are Glad When You're Sorry)	1949	10.00	20.00	40.00
—Microgroove 33 1/3 rpm single					
1-380 (?)	Fool's Paradise/Lonely Girl	1949	10.00	20.00	40.00
—Microgroove 33 1/3 rpm single					
1-390 (?)	I Cried for You/You Say You Care	1950	10.00	20.00	40.00
—Microgroove 33 1/3 rpm single					
1-485	I'm Crazy to Love You/Summertime	1950	10.00	20.00	40.00
—Microgroove 33 1/3 rpm single					
1-620 (?)	Just Friends/You Taught Me to Love Again	1950	10.00	20.00	40.00
—Microgroove 33 1/3 rpm single					
1-679	Our Very Own/Don't Be Afraid	1950	10.00	20.00	40.00
—Microgroove 33 1/3 rpm single					
1-750 (?)	(I Love the Girl) I Love the Guy/Thinking of You	1950	10.00	20.00	40.00
—Microgroove 33 1/3 rpm single					
6-750 (?)	(I Love the Girl) I Love the Guy/Thinking of You	1950	7.50	15.00	30.00
1-830 (?)	Perdido/Whippa Whippa Woo	1950	10.00	20.00	40.00
—Microgroove 33 1/3 rpm single					
6-830 (?)	Perdido/Whippa Whippa Woo	1950	7.50	15.00	30.00
1-926	The Nearness of You/You're Mine You	1950	10.00	20.00	40.00
—Microgroove 33 1/3 rpm single					
6-926	The Nearness of You/You're Mine You	1950	7.50	15.00	30.00
38925	(I Love the Girl) I Love the Guy/Thinking of You	1950	6.25	12.50	25.00
39001	Perdido/Whippa Whippa Woo	1950	6.25	12.50	25.00
39071	The Nearness of You/You're Mine You	1950	6.25	12.50	25.00
39124	I'll Know/Gas Pipe Leaking	1950	6.25	12.50	25.00
39207	Ave Maria/A City Called Heaven	1951	6.25	12.50	25.00
39370	These Things I Offer You (For a Lifetime)/Deep Purple	1951	6.25	12.50	25.00
39446	Vanity/My Reverie	1951	6.25	12.50	25.00
39494	After Hours/Out of Breath	1951	6.25	12.50	25.00
39576	I Ran All the Way Home/Just a Moment More	1951	6.25	12.50	25.00
39634	Pinky/A Miracle Happened	1952	5.00	10.00	20.00
39719	If Someone Had Told Me/Corner to Corner	1952	5.00	10.00	20.00
39789	Time to Go/Street of Dreams	1952	5.00	10.00	20.00
39839	Say You'll Wait for Me/My Tormented Heart	1952	5.00	10.00	20.00
39873	Sinner or Saint/Mighty Lonesome Feeling	1952	5.00	10.00	20.00
39932	Lovers' Quarrel/I Confess	1953	5.00	10.00	20.00
39963	Spring Will Be a Little Late This Year/A Blues Serenade	1953	5.00	10.00	20.00
40041	Time/Linger Awhile	1953	5.00	10.00	20.00
MAINSTREAM					
5517	Imagine/Sweet Gingerbread Man	1971	—	2.50	5.00
5521	Pieces of Dreams/Once You've Been in Love	1972	—	2.50	5.00
5522	What Are You Doing the Rest of Your Life/The Summer Knows	1972	—	2.50	5.00
5523	Summer Me, Winter Me/The Story of a Frasier	1972	—	2.50	5.00
5527	And the Feeling's Good/Deep in the Night	1972	—	2.50	5.00
5533	Rainy Days and Mondays/Just a Little Lovin'	1973	—	2.50	5.00
5541	Send In the Clowns/(B-side unknown)	1973	—	2.50	5.00
5544	Alone Again (Naturally)/Run to Me	1973	—	2.50	5.00
5553	Do Away with April/I Need You More	1974	—	2.50	5.00
MERCURY					
70423	Ol' Devil Moon/Saturday	1954	3.75	7.50	15.00
70469	Make Yourself Comfortable/Idle Gossip	1954	3.75	7.50	15.00
70534	How Important Can It Be/Waltzing Down the Aisle	1955	3.75	7.50	15.00
70595	Whatever Lola Wants/Oh Yeah	1955	3.75	7.50	15.00
70646	Experience Unnecessary/Slowly, With Feeling	1955	3.75	7.50	15.00
70693	Johnny, Be Smart/Hey Naughty Papa	1955	3.75	7.50	15.00
70727	C'est La Vie/Never	1955	3.75	7.50	15.00
70777	Mr. Wonderful/You Ought to Have a Wife	1956	3.00	6.00	12.00
70846	Hot and Cold Running Tears/That's Not the Kind of Love I Want	1956	3.00	6.00	12.00
70885	Fabulous Character/The Other Woman	1956	3.00	6.00	12.00
70947	It Happened Again/I Wanna Play House	1956	3.00	6.00	12.00
71020	The Banana Boat Song/I've Got a New Heartache	1956	3.00	6.00	12.00
71030	Leave It to Love/The Bashful Matador	1957	3.00	6.00	12.00
71085	Poor Butterfly/April Give Me One More Day	1957	3.00	6.00	12.00
71157	Band of Angels/Please Mr. Brown	1957	3.00	6.00	12.00
71235	Gone Train/Next Time Around	1957	3.00	6.00	12.00
71303	Padre/Spin the Bottle	1958	3.00	6.00	12.00
71326	What's So Bad About It/Too Much Too Soon	1958	3.00	6.00	12.00
71380	I Ain't Hurtin'/Everything I Do	1958	3.00	6.00	12.00
71407	Are You Certain/Cool Baby	1959	3.00	6.00	12.00
71433	Separate Ways/Careless	1959	3.00	6.00	12.00
71477	Broken-Hearted Melody/Misty	1959	3.00	6.00	12.00
71519	Smooth Operator/Maybe It's Because (I Love You Too Much)	1959	3.00	6.00	12.00
71562	Eternally/You're My Baby	1960	3.00	6.00	12.00
71610	Some Other Spring/Our Waltz	1960	3.00	6.00	12.00
71642	Maybe You'll Be There/Doodlin'	1960	3.00	6.00	12.00
71669	For All We Know/The Rough Years	1960	3.00	6.00	12.00
71702	Close to You/Out of This World	1960	3.00	6.00	12.00
71742	If You Are But a Dream/Mary Contrary	1960	3.00	6.00	12.00
72510	Darling/I'll Never Be Lonely Again	1965	2.00	4.00	8.00
72543	A Lover's Concerto/First Thing Every Morning	1966	2.00	4.00	8.00
72588	Everybody Loves Somebody/1-2-3	1966	2.00	4.00	8.00
MGM					
10705	Tenderly/I'll Wait and Pray	1950	7.50	15.00	30.00
10762	What a Difference A Day Made/I Can't Get Started	1950	7.50	15.00	30.00
10819	I Cover the Waterfront/Don't Worry 'Bout Me	1950	7.50	15.00	30.00
10890	Sit Right Down/I'm Through with Love	1951	6.25	12.50	25.00
11068	Don't Blame Me/If You Could See Me Now	1951	6.25	12.50	25.00
ROULETTE					
4285	Serenata/Let's	1960	2.50	5.00	10.00
4325	True Believer/What's the Use	1961	2.50	5.00	10.00
4359	April/Oh Lover	1961	2.50	5.00	10.00
4378	Untouchable/The Hills of Assisi	1961	2.50	5.00	10.00
4397	If Love Is Good to Me/A Great Day	1961	2.50	5.00	10.00
4413	One Mint Julep/Mama (He Treats Your Daughter Mean)	1962	2.50	5.00	10.00
4482	Call Me Irresponsible/There'll Be Other Times	1963	2.00	4.00	8.00
4497	Once Upon a Summertime/Snowbound	1963	2.00	4.00	8.00
4516	What'll I Do/I Believe in You	1963	2.00	4.00	8.00
4547	The Wallflower Waltz/Only	1964	2.00	4.00	8.00
4604	A Taste of Honey/The Good Life	1965	2.00	4.00	8.00
WARNER BROS.					
49890	Theme from "Sharkey's Machine"/Sharkey's Theme	1981	—	2.00	4.00
—B-side by Eddie Harris					

Number	Title (A Side/B Side)	Yr	VG	VG+	NM
7-Inch Extended Plays					
COLUMBIA					
B-2588	*Perdido/Linger Awhile/Time/Corner to Corner	1959	5.00	10.00	20.00
B-2588 [PS]	Sarah Vaughan (Hall of Fame Series)	1959	5.00	10.00	20.00
B-7452	Come Rain or Come Shine/Mean to Me//It Might As Well Be Spring/Can't Get Out of This Mood	195?	6.25	12.50	25.00
B-7452 [PS]	Sarah Vaughan in Hi-Fi	195?	6.25	12.50	25.00
Albums					
ACCORD					
SN-7195	Simply Divine	1981	2.50	5.00	10.00
ALLEGRO					
1592 [M]	Sarah Vaughan	1955	12.50	25.00	50.00
1608 [M]	Sarah Vaughan	1955	12.50	25.00	50.00
3080 [10]	Early Sarah	195?	20.00	40.00	80.00
ALLEGRO ELITE					
4106 [10]	Sarah Vaughan Sings	195?	7.50	15.00	30.00
ARCHIVE OF FOLK AND JAZZ					
250	Sarah Vaughan	197?	2.50	5.00	10.00
271	Sarah Vaughan, Volume 2	197?	2.50	5.00	10.00
325	Sarah Vaughan, Volume 3	197?	2.50	5.00	10.00
ATLANTIC					
SD 16037	Songs of the Beatles	1981	3.00	6.00	12.00
CBS MASTERWORKS					
FM 37277	Gershwin Live!	1982	2.50	5.00	10.00
—With the Los Angeles Philharmonic Orchestra					
FM 42519	Brazilian Romance	1987	2.50	5.00	10.00
COLUMBIA					
CL 660 [M]	After Hours with Sarah Vaughan	1955	12.50	25.00	50.00
CL 745 [M]	Sarah Vaughan in Hi-Fi	1956	12.50	25.00	50.00
CL 914 [M]	Linger Awhile	1956	12.50	25.00	50.00
CL 6133 [10]	Sarah Vaughan	1950	30.00	60.00	120.00
COLUMBIA SPECIAL PRODUCTS					
P 13084	Sarah Vaughan in Hi-Fi	1976	2.50	5.00	10.00
—Reissue of Columbia 745					
P 14364	Linger Awhile	1978	2.50	5.00	10.00
—Reissue of Columbia 914					
CONCORD					
3018 [M]	Sarah Vaughan Concert	1957	7.50	15.00	30.00
CORONET					
277	Sarah Vaughan Belts the Hits	196?	3.75	7.50	15.00
EMARCY					
EMS-2-412 [(2)]	Sarah Vaughan Live	197?	3.00	6.00	12.00
MG-26005 [10]	Images	1954	20.00	40.00	80.00
MG-36004 [M]	Sarah Vaughan	1955	20.00	40.00	80.00
MG-36058 [M]	In the Land of Hi-Fi	1956	20.00	40.00	80.00
MG-36089 [M]	Sassy	1956	12.50	25.00	50.00
MG-36109 [M]	Swingin' Easy	1957	12.50	25.00	50.00
814187-1 [(2)]	The George Gershwin Songbook	1983	3.00	6.00	12.00
824864-1	The Rodgers & Hart Songbook	1985	2.50	5.00	10.00
826454-1	In the Land of Hi-Fi	1986	2.50	5.00	10.00
—Reissue of 36058					
FORUM					
F-9034 [M]	Dreamy	196?	3.00	6.00	12.00
SF-9034 [S]	Dreamy	196?	3.75	7.50	15.00
HARMONY					
HL 7158 [M]	The Great Sarah Vaughan	196?	3.00	6.00	12.00
LION					
L 70052 [M]	Tenderly	1958	6.25	12.50	25.00
MAINSTREAM					
MRL 340	Time in My Life	1972	3.75	7.50	15.00
MRL 361	Sarah Vaughan/Michel Legrand	1972	3.75	7.50	15.00
MRL 379	Feelin' Good	1973	3.75	7.50	15.00
MRL 404	Sarah Vaughan and the Jimmy Rowles Quintet	1974	3.75	7.50	15.00
MRL 419	More Sarah Vaughan from Japan	1974	3.75	7.50	15.00
MASTERSEAL					
MS-55 [M]	Sarah Vaughan Sings	195?	6.25	12.50	25.00
MERCURY					
MGP-2-100 [(2) M]	Great Songs from Hit Shows	1957	15.00	30.00	60.00
MGP-2-101 [(2) M]	Sarah Vaughan Sings George Gershwin	1957	15.00	30.00	60.00
MG-20094 [M]	Sarah Vaughan at the Blue Note	1956	10.00	20.00	40.00
MG-20219 [M]	Wonderful Sarah	1957	10.00	20.00	40.00
MG-20223 [M]	In a Romantic Mood	1957	10.00	20.00	40.00
MG-20244 [M]	Great Songs from Hit Shows, Vol. 1	1958	7.50	15.00	30.00
MG-20245 [M]	Great Songs from Hit Shows, Vol. 2	1958	7.50	15.00	30.00
MG-20310 [M]	Sarah Vaughan Sings George Gershwin, Vol. 1	1958	7.50	15.00	30.00
MG-20311 [M]	Sarah Vaughan Sings George Gershwin, Vol. 2	1958	7.50	15.00	30.00
MG-20326 [M]	Sarah Vaughan and Her Trio at Mr. Kelly's	1958	10.00	20.00	40.00
MG-20370 [M]	Vaughan and Violins	1958	10.00	20.00	40.00
MG-20383 [M]	After Hours at the London House	1958	10.00	20.00	40.00
MG-20438 [M]	The Magic of Sarah Vaughan	1959	7.50	15.00	30.00
MG-20441 [M]	No 'Count Sarah	1959	7.50	15.00	30.00
MG-20540 [M]	The Divine Sarah Vaughan	1960	6.25	12.50	25.00
MG-20580 [M]	Close to You	1960	6.25	12.50	25.00
MG-20617 [M]	My Heart Sings	1961	6.25	12.50	25.00
MG-20645 [M]	Sarah Vaughan's Golden Hits	1961	5.00	10.00	20.00
MG-20831 [M]	Sassy Swings the Tivoli	1962	5.00	10.00	20.00
MG-20882 [M]	Vaughan with Voices	1963	5.00	10.00	20.00
MG-20941 [M]	Viva Vaughan	1964	3.75	7.50	15.00
MG-21009 [M]	Sarah Vaughan Sings the Mancini Songbook	1965	3.75	7.50	15.00
MG-21069 [M]	The Pop Artistry of Sarah Vaughan	1966	3.75	7.50	15.00
MG-21079 [M]	The New Scene	1966	3.75	7.50	15.00
MG-21116 [M]	Sassy Swings Again	1967	3.75	7.50	15.00
MG-21122 [M]	It's a Man's World	1967	3.75	7.50	15.00
MG-25188 [10]	Divine Sarah	1955	25.00	50.00	100.00
SR-60020 [S]	After Hours at the London House	1959	10.00	20.00	40.00
SR-60038 [S]	Vaughan and Violins	1959	10.00	20.00	40.00
SR-60041 [S]	Great Songs from Hit Shows, Vol. 1	1959	10.00	20.00	40.00
SR-60045 [S]	Sarah Vaughan Sings George Gershwin, Vol. 1	1959	10.00	20.00	40.00
SR-60046 [S]	Sarah Vaughan Sings George Gershwin, Vol. 2	1959	10.00	20.00	40.00
SR 60078 [S]	Great Songs from Hit Shows, Vol. 2	1959	10.00	20.00	40.00
SR-60110 [S]	The Magic of Sarah Vaughan	1959	10.00	20.00	40.00
SR-60116 [S]	No 'Count Sarah	1959	10.00	20.00	40.00
SR-60240 [S]	Close to You	1960	7.50	15.00	30.00
SR-60255 [S]	The Divine Sarah Vaughan	1960	7.50	15.00	30.00
SR-60617 [S]	My Heart Sings	1961	7.50	15.00	30.00
SR-60645 [S]	Sarah Vaughan's Golden Hits	1961	6.25	12.50	25.00
—Original black label version					
SR-60831 [S]	Sassy Swings the Tivoli	1962	6.25	12.50	25.00
SR-60882 [S]	Vaughan with Voices	1963	6.25	12.50	25.00
SR-60941 [S]	Viva Vaughan	1964	5.00	10.00	20.00
SR-61009 [S]	Sarah Vaughan Sings the Mancini Songbook	1965	5.00	10.00	20.00
SR-61069 [S]	The Pop Artistry of Sarah Vaughan	1966	5.00	10.00	20.00
SR-61079 [S]	The New Scene	1966	5.00	10.00	20.00
SR-61116 [S]	Sassy Swings Again	1967	5.00	10.00	20.00
SR-61122 [S]	It's a Man's World	1967	5.00	10.00	20.00
826320-1 [(6)]	The Complete Sarah Vaughan on Mercury Vol. 1: Great Jazz years (1954-56)	1986	10.00	20.00	40.00
826327-1 [(5)]	The Complete Sarah Vaughan on Mercury Vol. 2: Great American Songs (1956-57)	1986	10.00	20.00	40.00
826333-1 [(6)]	The Complete Sarah Vaughan on Mercury Vol. 3: Great Show on Stage (1954-56)	1986	10.00	20.00	40.00
830721-1 [(4)]	The Complete Sarah Vaughan on Mercury Vol. 4 Part 1: Live in Europe (1963-64)	1987	10.00	20.00	40.00
830726-1 [(5)]	The Complete Sarah Vaughan on Mercury Vol. 4 Part 2: Sassy Swings Again	1987	10.00	20.00	40.00
METRO					
M-539 [M]	Tenderly	1965	3.00	6.00	12.00
MS-539 [S]	Tenderly	1965	3.75	7.50	15.00
MGM					
E-165 [10]	Tenderly	1950	30.00	60.00	120.00
E-544 [10]	Sarah Vaughan Sings	1951	30.00	60.00	120.00
E-3274 [M]	My Kinda Love	1955	12.50	25.00	50.00
—Combination of two 10-inch LPs on one 12-inch LP					
MUSICRAFT					
504	Divine Sarah	197?	2.50	5.00	10.00
MVS-2002	The Man I Love	1986	2.50	5.00	10.00
MVS-2006	Lover Man	1986	2.50	5.00	10.00
PABLO					
2310821	How Long	1978	2.50	5.00	10.00
2310885	The Best of Sarah Vaughan	1983	2.50	5.00	10.00
2312101	I Love Brazil	1978	2.50	5.00	10.00
2312111	The Duke Ellington Songbook One	1979	2.50	5.00	10.00
2312116	The Duke Ellington Songbook Two	1980	2.50	5.00	10.00
2312125	Copacabana	1981	2.50	5.00	10.00
2312137	Crazy and Mixed Up	1981	2.50	5.00	10.00
2405416	The Best of Sarah Vaughan	1990	2.50	5.00	10.00
PALACE					
5191 [M]	Sarah Vaughan Sings	195?	6.25	12.50	25.00
PICKWICK					
PCS-3035	Fabulous Sarah Vaughan	197?	2.50	5.00	10.00
REMINGTON					
RLP-1024 [10]	Hot Jazz	1953	50.00	100.00	200.00
RIVERSIDE					
RLP 2511 [10]	Sarah Vaughan Sings with John Kirby	1955	25.00	50.00	100.00
RONDO-LETTE					
A-35 [M]	Songs of Broadway	1958	6.25	12.50	25.00
A-53 [M]	Sarah Vaughan Sings	1959	6.25	12.50	25.00
ROULETTE					
103 [(2)]	Echoes of An Era	197?	3.00	6.00	12.00
R 52046 [M]	Dreamy	1960	7.50	15.00	30.00
SR 52046 [S]	Dreamy	1960	10.00	20.00	40.00
R 52060 [M]	Divine One	1960	6.25	12.50	25.00
SR 52060 [S]	Divine One	1960	7.50	15.00	30.00
R 52070 [M]	After Hours	1961	6.25	12.50	25.00
SR 52070 [S]	After Hours	1961	7.50	15.00	30.00
R 52082 [M]	You're Mine	1962	6.25	12.50	25.00
SR 52082 [S]	You're Mine	1962	7.50	15.00	30.00
—Black vinyl					
SR 52082 [S]	You're Mine	1962	15.00	30.00	60.00
—Red vinyl					
R 52091 [M]	Snowbound	1962	5.00	10.00	20.00
SR 52091 [S]	Snowbound	1962	6.25	12.50	25.00
R 52092 [M]	The Explosive Side of Sarah	1962	5.00	10.00	20.00
SR 52092 [S]	The Explosive Side of Sarah	1962	6.25	12.50	25.00
R 52100 [M]	Star Eyes	1963	3.75	7.50	15.00
SR 52100 [S]	Star Eyes	1963	5.00	10.00	20.00
R 52104 [M]	Lonely Hours	1963	3.75	7.50	15.00
SR 52104 [S]	Lonely Hours	1963	5.00	10.00	20.00
R 52109 [M]	The World of Sarah Vaughan	1964	3.75	7.50	15.00
SR 52109 [S]	The World of Sarah Vaughan	1964	5.00	10.00	20.00
R 52112 [M]	Sweet 'N Sassy	1964	3.75	7.50	15.00
SR 52112 [S]	Sweet 'N Sassy	1964	5.00	10.00	20.00
R 52116 [M]	Sarah Sings Soulfully	1965	3.75	7.50	15.00
SR 52116 [S]	Sarah Sings Soulfully	1965	5.00	10.00	20.00
R 52118 [M]	Sarah Plus Two	1965	3.75	7.50	15.00
SR 52118 [S]	Sarah Plus Two	1965	5.00	10.00	20.00
SCEPTER					
CTN-18029	The Best of Sarah Vaughan	1972	3.00	6.00	12.00
SPIN-O-RAMA					
73 [M]	Sweet, Sultry and Swinging	196?	10.00	20.00	40.00
S-73 [S]	Sweet, Sultry and Swinging	196?	12.50	25.00	50.00
114 [M]	The Divine Sarah Vaughan	196?	10.00	20.00	40.00
S-114 [S]	The Divine Sarah Vaughan	196?	12.50	25.00	50.00
TRIP					
5501	Sarah Vaughan	197?	2.50	5.00	10.00
5517	Sassy	197?	2.50	5.00	10.00
5523	In the Land of Hi-Fi	197?	2.50	5.00	10.00
5551	Swingin' Easy	197?	2.50	5.00	10.00
WING					
MGW-12123 [M]	All Time Favorites	1963	3.00	6.00	12.00
MGW-12280 [M]	The Magic of Sarah Vaughan	1964	3.00	6.00	12.00
SRW-16123 [S]	All Time Favorites	1963	3.75	7.50	15.00
SRW-16123 [S]	The Magic of Sarah Vaughan	1964	3.75	7.50	15.00

VAUGHAN, SARAH, AND COUNT BASIE
Also see each artist's individual listings.

Albums

Number	Title (A Side/B Side)	Yr	VG	VG+	NM
PABLO					
2312130	Send In the Clowns	1980	2.50	5.00	10.00
ROULETTE					
SR 42018	Count Basie and Sarah Vaughan	1968	3.75	7.50	15.00
R 52061 [M]	Count Basie and Sarah Vaughan	1960	6.25	12.50	25.00
SR 52061 [S]	Count Basie and Sarah Vaughan	1960	7.50	15.00	30.00

VAUGHAN, SARAH, AND BILLY ECKSTINE
Also see each artist's individual listings.

45s

Number	Title (A Side/B Side)	Yr	VG	VG+	NM
MERCURY					
71122	Passing Strangers/The Door Is Open	1957	3.00	6.00	12.00
71393	Alexander's Ragtime Band/No Limit	1959	3.00	6.00	12.00

Albums

Number	Title (A Side/B Side)	Yr	VG	VG+	NM
EMARCY					
822526-1	The Irving Berlin Songbook	1984	2.50	5.00	10.00
LION					
L-70088 [M]	Billy and Sarah	195?	6.25	12.50	25.00
MERCURY					
MG-20316 [M]	Sarah Vaughan and Billy Eckstine Sing the Best of Irving Berlin	1959	7.50	15.00	30.00
SR-60002 [S]	Sarah Vaughan and Billy Eckstine Sing the Best of Irving Berlin	1959	10.00	20.00	40.00

VAUGHAN, SARAH; DINAH WASHINGTON; JOE WILLIAMS

Albums

Number	Title (A Side/B Side)	Yr	VG	VG+	NM
ROULETTE					
R 52108 [M]	We Three	1964	3.75	7.50	15.00
SR 52108 [S]	We Three	1964	5.00	10.00	20.00

VAUGHN, BILLY

45s

Number	Title (A Side/B Side)	Yr	VG	VG+	NM
DOT					
225 [S]	Look for a Star/He'll Have to Go	1960	3.00	6.00	12.00
15247	Melody of Love/Joy Ride	1954	3.00	6.00	12.00
15347	Silver Moon/Baby o' Mine	1955	3.00	6.00	12.00
15374	The Waltz You Saved for Me/Billy Vaughn's Boogie	1955	3.00	6.00	12.00
15409	The Shifting, Whispering Sands (Part 1)/The Shifting, Whispering Sands (Part 2)	1955	3.00	6.00	12.00
15430	I'd Give a Million Tomorrows/Calico Cathy	1955	3.00	6.00	12.00
15444	A Theme from (The Three Penny Opera) "Moritat"/Little Boy Blue	1956	2.50	5.00	10.00
15454	Till I Waltz Again with You/Sleep	1956	2.50	5.00	10.00
15466	Angel, Angel/Autumn Concerto	1956	2.50	5.00	10.00
15479	Sweetheart Polka/The Left Bank	1956	2.50	5.00	10.00
15491	When the White Lilacs Bloom Again/Spanish Diary	1956	2.50	5.00	10.00
15506	Petticoats of Portugal/La La Colette	1956	2.50	5.00	10.00
15514	Sweet Leilani/Cradle Love Call	1956	2.50	5.00	10.00
15530	Sugar Blues/Pennsylvania Waltz	1957	2.50	5.00	10.00
15546	The Ship That Never Sailed/Song of the Nairobi Trio	1957	2.50	5.00	10.00
15575	Tell My Love/Ve'Borriquito	1957	2.50	5.00	10.00
15598	Johnny Tremain/Naughty Annette	1957	3.00	6.00	12.00
15661	Sail Along Silvery Moon/Raunchy	1957	2.00	4.00	8.00
15710	Tumbling Tumbleweeds/Trying	1958	2.00	4.00	8.00
15771	Singing Hills/Chimes of Arcady	1958	2.00	4.00	8.00
15795	La Paloma/Here Is My Love	1958	2.00	4.00	8.00
15836	Cimarron (Roll On)/You're My Baby Doll	1958	2.00	4.00	8.00
15836 [PS]	Cimarron (Roll On)/You're My Baby Doll	1958	3.00	6.00	12.00
15879	Blue Hawaii/Tico Tico	1958	2.00	4.00	8.00
15900	Hawaiian War Chant/Trade Winds	1959	2.00	4.00	8.00
15900 [PS]	Hawaiian War Chant/Trade Winds	1959	3.00	6.00	12.00
15936	Your Cheatin' Heart/Lights Out	1959	2.00	4.00	8.00
15976	Wabash Blues/Carnival in Paris	1959	2.00	4.00	8.00
15993	It's No Sin/After Hours	1959	2.00	4.00	8.00
16021	You're the Only Star (In My Blue Heaven)/Chop Stick	1959	2.00	4.00	8.00
16026 *—Reissue*	Melody of Love/Sail Along Silvery Moon	1960	—	3.00	6.00
16030 *—Reissue*	The Shifting, Whispering Sands (Part 1)/The Shifting, Whispering Sands (Part 2)	1960	—	3.00	6.00
16064	Skaters' Waltz/Beg Your Pardon	1960	2.00	4.00	8.00
16064 [PS]	Skaters' Waltz/Beg Your Pardon	1960	2.50	5.00	10.00
16106	Look for a Star/He'll Have to Go	1960	2.00	4.00	8.00
16121	Theme from The Apartment/(B-side unknown)	1960	2.00	4.00	8.00
16133	The Sundowners/Old Cape Cod	1960	2.00	4.00	8.00
16174	Wheels/Orange Blossom Special	1961	2.00	4.00	8.00
16220	Blue Tomorrow/Red Wing	1961	2.00	4.00	8.00
16245	Down Yonder/Born to Be with You	1961	2.00	4.00	8.00
16262	Berlin Melody/Come September	1961	2.00	4.00	8.00
16295	Everybody's Twisting Down in Mexico/Melody in the Night	1961	2.00	4.00	8.00
16329	Chapel by the Sea/One Love, One Heartache	1962	—	3.00	6.00
16359	Continental Melody/Born to Be with You	1962	—	3.00	6.00
16374	A Swingin' Safari/Indian Love Call	1962	2.00	4.00	8.00
16397	Blue Flame/Someone	1962	—	3.00	6.00
16417	Down Yonder/I'm Waitin'	1963	—	3.00	6.00
16436	Meditation (Meditacao)/Release Me	1963	—	3.00	6.00
16477	Happy Cowboy/Broken Date	1963	—	3.00	6.00
16484	Sukiyaki/Theme from A Summer Place	1963	—	3.00	6.00
16522	Rag Mop/I'm Sorry	1963	—	3.00	6.00
16549	Cumberland County Feud/Chow Chow Amore	1963	—	3.00	6.00
16580	Boss/Blue Tango	1964	—	3.00	6.00
16604	One Rose/Lucky Duck	1964	—	3.00	6.00
16622	Guitar Song/Chianti Song	1964	—	3.00	6.00
16647	People/The World I Used to Know	1964	—	3.00	6.00
16664	Maybe/Pearly Shells	1964	—	3.00	6.00
16670	Song of Peace/Billy's Theme	1964	—	3.00	6.00
16686	There's a Star Spangled Banner Waving Somewhere/In the Ocean of Time	1965	—	3.00	6.00
16706	Mexican Pearls/Woodpecker	1965	—	3.00	6.00
16739	Making Other Plans/Our Dream of Love	1965	—	3.00	6.00
16762	Moon Over Naples/Tonight	1965	—	3.00	6.00
16774	Anniversary Song/Please	1965	—	3.00	6.00
16809	Michelle/Elaine	1965	—	3.00	6.00
16835	Mexican Shuffle/Organ Grinder's Swing	1966	—	2.50	5.00
16841	Things Go Better/James (Steady Does It)	1966	—	2.50	5.00
16883	Did You Ever Have to Make Up Your Mind/It's Over	1966	—	2.50	5.00
16900	Because They're Young/Buckaroo	1966	—	2.50	5.00
16924	Alfie/Lara's Theme	1966	—	2.50	5.00
16957	Tiny Bubbles/Too Many Hot Tacos	1966	—	2.50	5.00
16985	There Goes My Everything/Sweet Maria	1966	—	2.50	5.00
17000	That's Life/Pineapple Market	1967	—	2.50	5.00
17021	I Love You/Yellow Roses Mean Goodbye	1967	—	2.50	5.00
17054	Last Hearts of Kyoto/The Last Safari	1967	—	2.50	5.00
17074	Lolly/Moonlight Makes Memories	1968	—	2.50	5.00
17111	St. James Infirmary/Soulitude	1968	—	2.50	5.00
17214	You Win Again/No One Will Ever Know	1969	—	2.50	5.00
17215	A Mansion on the Hill/I've Got You on My Mind Again	1969	—	2.50	5.00
17229	The Windmills of Your Mind/The Way That I Live	1969	—	2.50	5.00
17295	True Grit/Odds and Ends	1969	—	2.50	5.00
17314	Color It Cool/On Days Like This	1969	—	2.50	5.00
17337	Coco/Always Mademoiselle	1970	—	2.00	4.00
17346	Come Saturday Morning/True Grit	1970	—	2.00	4.00
PARAMOUNT					
0036	Boulevard Saint/Michelle	1970	—	2.00	4.00
0073	Look What They've Done to My Song, Ma/Rooftops of Tokyo	1971	—	2.00	4.00
0156	Butterfly/To the End of This Day	1972	—	2.00	4.00

7-Inch Extended Plays

Number	Title (A Side/B Side)	Yr	VG	VG+	NM
DOT					
DEP-1071	Canadian Sunset/Moonglow and Picnic//Fascination/Around the World	195?	2.50	5.00	10.00
DEP-1071 [PS]	Billy Vaughn Plays Million Sellers	195?	2.50	5.00	10.00

Albums

Number	Title (A Side/B Side)	Yr	VG	VG+	NM
ABC					
4005	16 Great Performances	1974	2.50	5.00	10.00
DOT					
DLP 3001 [M] *—Maroon label*	Sweet Music and Memories	1955	6.25	12.50	25.00
DLP 3001 [M] *—Black label*	Sweet Music and Memories	1957	3.75	7.50	15.00
DLP 3016 [M] *—Maroon label*	The Golden Instrumentals	1956	6.25	12.50	25.00
DLP 3016 [M] *—Black label*	The Golden Instrumentals	1957	3.75	7.50	15.00
DLP 3045 [M]	Instrumental Souvenirs	1957	3.75	7.50	15.00
DLP 3064 [M]	Melodies in Gold	1957	3.75	7.50	15.00
DLP 3086 [M]	Music for the Golden Hours	1958	3.75	7.50	15.00
DLP 3100 [M]	Sail Along Silv'ry Moon	1958	3.75	7.50	15.00
DLP 3119 [M]	Billy Vaughn Plays the Million Sellers	1958	3.75	7.50	15.00
DLP 3140 [M]	La Paloma	1959	3.75	7.50	15.00
DLP 3148 [M]	Christmas Carols	1958	3.75	7.50	15.00
DLP 3156 [M]	Billy Vaughn Plays	1959	3.75	7.50	15.00
DLP 3165 [M]	Blue Hawaii	1959	3.75	7.50	15.00
DLP 3201 [M]	Golden Hits	1959	3.75	7.50	15.00
DLP 3205 [M]	Golden Saxophones	1959	3.75	7.50	15.00
DLP 3260 [M]	Billy Vaughn Plays Stephen Foster	1960	3.75	7.50	15.00
DLP 3275 [M]	Linger Awhile	1960	3.75	7.50	15.00
DLP 3276 [M]	Theme from A Summer Place	1960	3.75	7.50	15.00
DLP 3280 [M]	Golden Waltzes	1961	3.75	7.50	15.00
DLP 3288 [M]	Great Golden Hits	1960	3.75	7.50	15.00
DLP 3322 [M]	Look for a Star	1960	3.75	7.50	15.00
DLP 3349 [M]	Theme from The Sundowners	1960	3.75	7.50	15.00
DLP 3366 [M]	Orange Blossom Special and Wheels	1961	3.75	7.50	15.00
DLP 3396 [M]	Berlin Melody	1961	3.75	7.50	15.00
DLP 3409 [M]	Greatest String Band Hits	1962	3.75	7.50	15.00
DLP 3424 [M]	Chapel by the Sea	1962	3.75	7.50	15.00
DLP 3442 [M]	The Shifting, Whispering Sands	1962	3.75	7.50	15.00
DLP 3458 [M]	A Swingin' Safari	1962	3.75	7.50	15.00
DLP 3497 [M]	1962's Greatest Hits	1963	3.00	6.00	12.00
DLP 3523 [M]	Sukiyaki and 11 Hawaiian Hits	1963	3.00	6.00	12.00
DLP 3540 [M]	Number One Hits, Vol. #1	1963	3.00	6.00	12.00
DLP 3558 [M]	Greatest Boogie Woogie Hits	1963	3.00	6.00	12.00
DLP 3559 [M]	Blue Velvet & 1963's Great Hits	1964	3.00	6.00	12.00
DLP 3578 [M]	Forever	1964	3.00	6.00	12.00
DLP 3593 [M]	Another Hit Album!	1964	3.00	6.00	12.00
DLP 3605 [M]	Pearly Shells	1965	3.00	6.00	12.00
DLP 3625 [M]	12 Golden Hits from Latin America	1965	3.00	6.00	12.00
DLP 3628 [M]	Mexican Pearls	1965	3.00	6.00	12.00
DLP 3654 [M]	Moon Over Naples	1965	3.00	6.00	12.00
DLP 3679 [M]	Michelle	1966	3.00	6.00	12.00
DLP 3698 [M]	Great Country Hits	1966	3.00	6.00	12.00
DLP 3751 [M]	Alfie	1966	3.00	6.00	12.00
DLP 3782 [M]	Sweet Maria	1967	3.00	6.00	12.00
DLP 3788 [M]	That's Life & Pineapple Market	1967	3.00	6.00	12.00
DLP 3796 [M]	Josephine	1967	3.00	6.00	12.00
DLP 3800 [M]	Billy Vaughn Presents Friends from Rio Playing "Something Stupid"	1967	3.00	6.00	12.00
DLP 3811 [M]	Golden Hits/The Best of Billy Vaughn	1967	3.00	6.00	12.00
DLP 3813 [M]	I Love You	1967	3.00	6.00	12.00
DLP 3828 [M]	Ode to Billy Joe	1967	3.00	6.00	12.00
DLP 5857	Quietly Wild	1968	2.50	5.00	10.00
DLP 25001 [R]	Sweet Music and Memories	196?	2.50	5.00	10.00
DLP 25016 [R]	The Golden Instrumentals	196?	2.50	5.00	10.00
DLP 25064 [R]	Melodies in Gold	196?	2.50	5.00	10.00
DLP 25086 [R]	Music for the Golden Hours	196?	2.50	5.00	10.00
DLP 25100 [S]	Sail Along Silv'ry Moon	1959	5.00	10.00	20.00
DLP 25119 [S]	Billy Vaughn Plays the Million Sellers	1959	5.00	10.00	20.00
DLP 25140 [S]	La Paloma	1959	5.00	10.00	20.00

Number	Title (A Side/B Side)	Yr	VG	VG+	NM
DLP 25156 [S]	Billy Vaughn Plays	1959	5.00	10.00	20.00
DLP 25165 [S]	Blue Hawaii	1959	5.00	10.00	20.00
DLP 25201 [S]	Golden Hits	1959	5.00	10.00	20.00
DLP 25205 [S]	Golden Saxophones	1959	5.00	10.00	20.00
DLP 25260 [S]	Billy Vaughn Plays Stephen Foster	1960	5.00	10.00	20.00
DLP 25275 [S]	Linger Awhile	1960	5.00	10.00	20.00
DLP 25276 [S]	Theme from A Summer Place	1960	5.00	10.00	20.00
DLP 25280 [S]	Golden Waltzes	1961	5.00	10.00	20.00
DLP 25288 [S]	Great Golden Hits	1960	5.00	10.00	20.00
DLP 25322 [S]	Look for a Star	1960	5.00	10.00	20.00
DLP 25349 [S]	Theme from The Sundowners	1960	5.00	10.00	20.00
DLP 25366 [S]	Orange Blossom Special and Wheels	1961	5.00	10.00	20.00
DLP 25396 [S]	Berlin Melody	1961	5.00	10.00	20.00
DLP 25409 [S]	Greatest String Band Hits	1962	5.00	10.00	20.00
DLP 25424 [S]	Chapel by the Sea	1962	5.00	10.00	20.00
DLP 25442 [S]	The Shifting, Whispering Sands	1962	5.00	10.00	20.00
DLP 25458 [S]	A Swingin' Safari	1962	5.00	10.00	20.00
DLP 25497 [S]	1962's Greatest Hits	1963	3.75	7.50	15.00
DLP 25523 [S]	Sukiyaki and 11 Hawaiian Hits	1963	3.75	7.50	15.00
DLP 25540 [S]	Number One Hits, Vol. #1	1963	3.75	7.50	15.00
DLP 25558 [S]	Greatest Boogie Woogie Hits	1963	3.75	7.50	15.00
DLP 25559 [S]	Blue Velvet & 1963's Great Hits	1964	3.75	7.50	15.00
DLP 25578 [S]	Forever	1964	3.75	7.50	15.00
DLP 25593 [S]	Another Hit Album!	1964	3.75	7.50	15.00
DLP 25605 [S]	Pearly Shells	1965	3.75	7.50	15.00
DLP 25625 [S]	12 Golden Hits from Latin America	1965	3.75	7.50	15.00
DLP 25628 [S]	Mexican Pearls	1965	3.75	7.50	15.00
DLP 25654 [S]	Moon Over Naples	1965	3.75	7.50	15.00
DLP 25679 [S]	Michelle	1966	3.75	7.50	15.00
DLP 25698 [S]	Great Country Hits	1966	3.75	7.50	15.00
DLP 25751 [S]	Alfie	1966	3.75	7.50	15.00
DLP 25782 [S]	Sweet Maria	1967	2.50	5.00	10.00
DLP 25788 [S]	That's Life & Pineapple Market	1967	2.50	5.00	10.00
DLP 25796 [S]	Josephine	1967	2.50	5.00	10.00
DLP 25800 [S]	Billy Vaughn Presents Friends from Rio Playing "Something Stupid"	1967	2.50	5.00	10.00
DLP 25811 [S]	Golden Hits/The Best of Billy Vaughn	1967	2.50	5.00	10.00
DLP 25813 [S]	I Love You	1967	2.50	5.00	10.00
DLP 25828 [S]	Ode to Billy Joe	1967	2.50	5.00	10.00
DLP 25837	Pretty Country	1968	2.50	5.00	10.00
DLP 25841	As Requested	1968	2.50	5.00	10.00
DLP 25882	A Current Set of Standards	1968	2.50	5.00	10.00
DLP-25897	Alone with Today	1968	2.50	5.00	10.00
DLP 25899	Have Yourself a Merry Merry Christmas	1968	3.00	6.00	12.00
DLP 25911	Nashville Saxophones	1969	2.50	5.00	10.00
DLP 25937	The Windmills of Your Mind	1969	2.50	5.00	10.00
DLP 25969	True Grit	1969	2.50	5.00	10.00
DLP 25975	Winter World of Love	1970	2.50	5.00	10.00
DLP 25985	Everything Is Beautiful	1970	2.50	5.00	10.00
HAMILTON					
HLP 113 [M]	Golden Gems	196?	3.00	6.00	12.00
HLP 147 [M]	Strauss Waltz Concert	196?	3.00	6.00	12.00
HLP 162 [M]	Songs I Wrote	196?	3.00	6.00	12.00
HLP 12113 [S]	Golden Gems	196?	3.00	6.00	12.00
HLP 12147 [S]	Strauss Waltz Concert	196?	3.00	6.00	12.00
HLP 12162 [S]	Songs I Wrote	196?	3.00	6.00	12.00
MCA					
801	La Paloma	198?	2.00	4.00	8.00
—Budget-line reissue					
4164 [(2)]	The Best of Billy Vaughn	198?	3.00	6.00	12.00
27018	Blue Hawaii	198?	2.00	4.00	8.00
—Budget-line reissue					
PARAMOUNT					
PAS-1031 [(2)]	Billy Vaughn Plays His Greatest Hits	1974	3.00	6.00	12.00
PAS-1033	Electrified	1974	2.50	5.00	10.00
PAS-5032	Theme from Love Story	1971	2.50	5.00	10.00
PAS-5037	I Don't Know How to Love Him	1971	2.50	5.00	10.00
PAS-6025	An Old Fashioned Love Song	1972	2.50	5.00	10.00
PAS-6035	Soundstage!	1972	2.50	5.00	10.00
PAS-6044	Country's Greatest Hits	1973	2.50	5.00	10.00
PICKWICK					
SPC-3093	Embraceable You	197?	2.50	5.00	10.00
SPC-3146	Up, Up and Away	197?	2.50	5.00	10.00
SPC-3213	Moon River	197?	2.50	5.00	10.00
RANWOOD					
7025 [(2)]	Billy Vaughn and His Orchestra Play 22 Greatest Hits	1982	3.00	6.00	12.00

VAUGHN, YVONNE

Later recorded as DONNA FARGO.

45s

Number	Title (A Side/B Side)	Yr	VG	VG+	NM
DOT					
16751	Lonely Little Girl/When You Gonna Tell Her About Me	1965	37.50	75.00	150.00

VEE, BOBBY

45s

Number	Title (A Side/B Side)	Yr	VG	VG+	NM
COGNITO					
010	Tremble On/Always Be Each Other's Best Friend	1981	—	2.50	5.00
LIBERTY					
55208	Suzie Baby/Flyin' High	1959	6.25	12.50	25.00
55234	What Do You Want/My Love Loves Me	1959	5.00	10.00	20.00
55251	Laurie/One Last Kiss	1960	3.75	7.50	15.00
55270	Devil or Angel/Since I Met You Baby	1960	5.00	10.00	20.00
55270 [PS]	Devil or Angel/Since I Met You Baby	1960	7.50	15.00	30.00
55287	Rubber Ball/Everyday	1960	5.00	10.00	20.00
55287 [PS]	Rubber Ball/Everyday	1960	7.50	15.00	30.00
55296	More Than I Can Say/Stayin' In	1961	3.75	7.50	15.00
55296 [PS]	More Than I Can Say/Stayin' In	1961	7.50	15.00	30.00
55325	How Many Tears/Baby Face	1961	3.75	7.50	15.00
55331 [PS]	How Many Tears/Baby Face	1961	7.50	15.00	30.00
55354	Take Good Care of My Baby/Bashful Bob	1961	3.75	7.50	15.00
55388	Run to Him/Walkin' with My Angel	1961	5.00	10.00	20.00
55419	Please Don't Ask About Barbara/I Can't Say Goodbye	1962	3.75	7.50	15.00
55419 [PS]	Please Don't Ask About Barbara/I Can't Say Goodbye	1962	6.25	12.50	25.00
55451	Sharing You/In My Baby's Eyes	1962	3.75	7.50	15.00
55479	Punish Her/Someday (When I'm Gone from You)	1962	5.00	10.00	20.00
55479 [PS]	Punish Her/Someday (When I'm Gone from You)	1962	7.50	15.00	30.00
—With the Crickets					
55517	A Not-So-Merry Christmas/Christmas Vacation	1962	7.50	15.00	30.00
—This record's existence has been questioned					
55521	The Night Has a Thousand Eyes/Anonymous Phone Call	1962	3.00	6.00	12.00
55530	Charms/Bobby Tomorrow	1963	3.00	6.00	12.00
55530 [PS]	Charms/Bobby Tomorrow	1963	5.00	10.00	20.00
55581	Be True to Yourself/A Letter from Betty	1963	2.50	5.00	10.00
55581 [PS]	Be True to Yourself/A Letter from Betty	1963	5.00	10.00	20.00
55636	Yesterday and You (Armen's Theme)/Never Love a Robin	1963	2.50	5.00	10.00
55654	Stranger in Your Arms/1963	1963	2.50	5.00	10.00
55654 [PS]	Stranger in Your Arms/1963	1963	5.00	10.00	20.00
55670	I'll Make You Mine/She's Sorry	1964	2.50	5.00	10.00
55700	Hickory, Dick and Doc/I Wish You Were Mine Again	1964	2.50	5.00	10.00
55726	Where Is She/How to Make a Farewell	1964	2.50	5.00	10.00
55751	(There'll Come a Day When) Ev'ry Little Bit Hurts/Pretend You Don't See Her	1964	2.50	5.00	10.00
55761	Cross My Heart/This Is the End	1965	2.00	4.00	8.00
55790	Keep On Trying/You Won't Forget Me	1965	2.00	4.00	8.00
55828	Run Like the Devil/Take a Look Around Us	1965	2.00	4.00	8.00
55843	The Story of My Life/High Coin	1965	2.00	4.00	8.00
55854	A Girl I Used to Know/Gone	1965	2.00	4.00	8.00
55877	Butterfly/Save a Love	1966	2.00	4.00	8.00
55877	Butterfly/Look at Me Girl	1966	2.00	4.00	8.00
55921	Before You Go/Here Today	1966	2.00	4.00	8.00
55964	Come Back When You Grow Up/Swahili Serenade	1967	2.00	4.00	8.00
55964	Come Back When You Grow Up/That's All There Is to That	1967	2.00	4.00	8.00
56009	Beautiful People/I May Be Gone	1967	2.00	4.00	8.00
56014	Maybe Just Today/You're a Big Girl Now	1968	—	3.00	6.00
56014 [PS]	Maybe Just Today/You're a Big Girl Now	1968	3.00	6.00	12.00
56033	Medley: My Girl-Hey Girl/Just Keep It Up	1968	—	3.00	6.00
56057	Do What You Gotta Do/Thank You	1968	—	3.00	6.00
56080	I'm Into Lookin' for Someone to Love Me/Thank You	1968	—	3.00	6.00
56096	Jenny Come to Me/Santa Cruz	1969	—	3.00	6.00
56124	Let's Call It a Day Girl/I'm Gonna Make It Up to You	1969	—	3.00	6.00
56149	Electric Trains and You/In and Out of Love	1969	—	3.00	6.00
56178	The Woman in My Life/No Obligations	1970	—	3.00	6.00
56208	Sweet Sweetheart/Rock and Roll Music and You	1970	—	3.00	6.00
SHADYBROOK					
45013	Saying Goodbye/(I'm) Lovin' You	1975	—	2.50	5.00
45026	You're Never Gonna Find Someone Like Me (Long Version)/You're Never Gonna Find Someone Like Me (Short Version)	1976	—	2.50	5.00
45030	It's Good to Be Here/If I Needed You	1976	—	2.50	5.00
SOMA					
1110	Suzie Baby/Flyin' High	1959	15.00	30.00	60.00
UNITED ARTISTS					
0020	Devil or Angel/Stayin' In	1973	—	2.00	4.00
—0020 through 0025 are "Silver Spotlight Series" reissues					
0021	Rubber Ball/Punish Her	1973	—	2.00	4.00
0022	Take Good Care of My Baby/Please Don't Ask About Barbara	1973	—	2.00	4.00
0023	Run to Him/Sharing You	1973	—	2.00	4.00
0024	The Night Has a Thousand Eyes/Charms	1973	—	2.00	4.00
0025	Come Back When You Grow Up/Beautiful People	1973	—	2.00	4.00
XW199	Take Good Care of My Baby/Every Opportunity	1973	—	2.50	5.00
—As "Robert Thomas Velline"					
XW1142	Well All Right/Something Has Come Between Us	1978	—	2.50	5.00
50755	Signs/Something to Say	1971	—	2.50	5.00
50875	Sweet Sweetheart/Electric Trains and You	1972	—	2.50	5.00

7-Inch Extended Plays

Number	Title (A Side/B Side)	Yr	VG	VG+	NM
LIBERTY					
LSX-1006	(contents unknown)	1960	12.50	25.00	50.00
LSX-1006 [PS]	Devil or Angel	1960	12.50	25.00	50.00
LSX-1010	(contents unknown)	1960	12.50	25.00	50.00
LSX-1010 [PS]	Bobby Vee's Hits	1960	12.50	25.00	50.00
LSX-1013	(contents unknown)	1961	12.50	25.00	50.00
LSX-1013 [PS]	Bobby Vee	1961	12.50	25.00	50.00

Albums

Number	Title (A Side/B Side)	Yr	VG	VG+	NM
LIBERTY					
LRP-3165 [M]	Bobby Vee Sings Your Favorites	1960	12.50	25.00	50.00
LRP-3181 [M]	Bobby Vee	1961	10.00	20.00	40.00
LRP-3186 [M]	Bobby Vee With Strings and Things	1961	10.00	20.00	40.00
LRP-3205 [M]	Bobby Vee Sings Hits of the Rockin' 50's	1961	10.00	20.00	40.00
LRP-3211 [M]	Take Good Care of My Baby	1962	7.50	15.00	30.00
LRP-3228 [M]	Bobby Vee Meets the Crickets	1962	10.00	20.00	40.00
LRP-3232 [M]	A Bobby Vee Recording Session	1962	7.50	15.00	30.00
LRP-3245 [M]	Bobby Vee's Golden Greats	1962	7.50	15.00	30.00
LRP-3267 [M]	Merry Christmas from Bobby Vee	1962	7.50	15.00	30.00
LRP-3285 [M]	The Night Has a Thousand Eyes	1963	7.50	15.00	30.00
LRP-3289 [M]	Bobby Vee Meets the Ventures	1963	10.00	20.00	40.00
LRP-3336 [M]	I Remember Buddy Holly	1963	10.00	20.00	40.00
LRP-3352 [M]	Bobby Vee Sings the New Sound from England!	1964	6.25	12.50	25.00
LRP-3385 [M]	30 Big Hits From the 60's	1964	6.25	12.50	25.00
LRP-3393 [M]	Bobby Vee Live on Tour	1965	6.25	12.50	25.00
LRP-3448 [M]	30 Big Hits From the 60's, Volume 2	1966	6.25	12.50	25.00
LRP-3464 [M]	Bobby Vee's Golden Greats, Volume 2	1966	5.00	10.00	20.00
LRP-3480 [M]	Look at Me Girl	1966	5.00	10.00	20.00
LRP-3534 [M]	Come Back When You Grow Up	1967	5.00	10.00	20.00
LST-7165 [S]	Bobby Vee Sings Your Favorites	1960	20.00	40.00	80.00
LST-7181 [S]	Bobby Vee	1961	12.50	25.00	50.00
LST-7186 [S]	Bobby Vee With Strings and Things	1961	12.50	25.00	50.00

Number	Title (A Side/B Side)	Yr	VG	VG+	NM
LST-7205 [S]	Bobby Vee Sings Hits of the Rockin' 50's	1961	12.50	25.00	50.00
LST-7211 [S]	Take Good Care of My Baby	1962	10.00	20.00	40.00
LST-7228 [S]	Bobby Vee Meets the Crickets	1962	12.50	25.00	50.00
LST-7232 [S]	A Bobby Vee Recording Session	1962	10.00	20.00	40.00
LST-7245 [S]	Bobby Vee's Golden Greats	1962	10.00	20.00	40.00
LST-7267 [S]	Merry Christmas from Bobby Vee	1962	10.00	20.00	40.00
LST-7285 [S]	The Night Has a Thousand Eyes	1963	10.00	20.00	40.00
LST-7289 [S]	Bobby Vee Meets the Ventures	1963	12.50	25.00	50.00
LST-7336 [S]	I Remember Buddy Holly	1963	12.50	25.00	50.00
LST-7352 [S]	Bobby Vee Sings the New Sound from England!	1964	7.50	15.00	30.00
LST-7385 [S]	30 Big Hits From the 60's	1964	7.50	15.00	30.00
LST-7393 [S]	Bobby Vee Live on Tour	1965	7.50	15.00	30.00
LST-7448 [S]	30 Big Hits From the 60's, Volume 2	1966	7.50	15.00	30.00
LST-7464 [S]	Bobby Vee's Golden Greats, Volume 2	1966	6.25	12.50	25.00
LST-7480 [S]	Look at Me Girl	1966	6.25	12.50	25.00
LST-7534 [S]	Come Back When You Grow Up	1967	6.25	12.50	25.00
LST-7554	Just Today	1968	6.25	12.50	25.00
LST-7592	Do What You Gotta Do	1968	7.50	15.00	30.00
LST-7612	Gates, Grills and Railings	1969	7.50	15.00	30.00
LN-10223	I Remember Buddy Holly	198?	2.00	4.00	8.00
LM-51008	Bobby Vee's Golden Greats	198?	2.00	4.00	8.00
SUNSET					
SUM-1111 [M]	Bobby Vee	1966	2.50	5.00	10.00
SUM-1162 [M]	A Forever Kind of Love	1967	2.50	5.00	10.00
SUM-1186 [M]	The Christmas Album	1967	3.00	6.00	12.00
—Reissue of Liberty album with two fewer tracks					
SUS-5111 [S]	Bobby Vee	1966	3.00	6.00	12.00
SUS-5162 [S]	A Forever Kind of Love	1967	3.00	6.00	12.00
SUS-5186 [S]	The Christmas Album	1967	3.00	6.00	12.00
UNITED ARTISTS					
UA-LA025-G2 [(2)]	Legendary Masters Series	1973	75.00	150.00	300.00
—Withdrawn before release, but a few copies survived					
UA-LA085-G	Robert Thomas Velline	1973	5.00	10.00	20.00
UA-LA332-E	The Very Best of Bobby Vee	1975	3.00	6.00	12.00
LT 1008	Bobby Vee's Golden Greats	1980	2.50	5.00	10.00
UAS-5656	Nothin' Like a Sunny Day	1972	3.00	6.00	12.00

VEERS, RUSS

Number	Title (A Side/B Side)	Yr	VG	VG+	NM
45s					
TREND					
30010	Warm As Toast/The Answer	1958	125.00	250.00	500.00

VEGAS, PAT AND LOLLY

Also see REDBONE.

Number	Title (A Side/B Side)	Yr	VG	VG+	NM
45s					
APOGEE					
101	Don't You Remember/The Robot Walk	1964	3.75	7.50	15.00
MERCURY					
72509	Walk On (Right Out of My Life)/Let's Get It On	1965	3.00	6.00	12.00
REPRISE					
20199	Boom Boom/Two Figures (On the Wedding Cake)	1963	5.00	10.00	20.00
Albums					
MERCURY					
MG-21059 [M]	At the Haunted House	1966	7.50	15.00	30.00
SR-61059 [S]	At the Haunted House	1966	10.00	20.00	40.00

VEJTABLES, THE

Number	Title (A Side/B Side)	Yr	VG	VG+	NM
45s					
AUTUMN					
15	Anything/I Still Love You	1965	3.00	6.00	12.00
23	The Last Thing on My Mind/Mansion of Texas	1965	3.00	6.00	12.00
UPTOWN					
741	Feel the Music/Shadows	1967	2.50	5.00	10.00

VEL-TONES, THE

More than one group.

Number	Title (A Side/B Side)	Yr	VG	VG+	NM
45s					
COY					
101	Cal's Tune/Playboy	1959	1000.	1500.	2000.
GOLDWAX					
301	Darling/I Do	1966	3.75	7.50	15.00
JIN					
107	Lover Blues/Take a Ride	1959	10.00	20.00	40.00
115	Jailbird/I'm Yours Now	1959	10.00	20.00	40.00
KAPP					
268	Cal's Tune/Playboy	1959	25.00	50.00	100.00
LOST-NITE					
103	Now/I Need You So	1961	25.00	50.00	100.00
MERCURY					
71526	Fool in Love/Someday	1959	7.50	15.00	30.00
SATELLITE					
100	Fool in Love/Someday	1959	25.00	50.00	100.00
VEL					
9178	Broken Heart/Please Say You'll Be True	1960	375.00	750.00	1500.
WEDGE					
1013	My Dear/I Want to Know	1964	50.00	100.00	200.00
ZARA					
901	Now/I Need You So	1960	20.00	40.00	80.00

VELEZ, MARTHA

Number	Title (A Side/B Side)	Yr	VG	VG+	NM
45s					
MCA					
41244	What Becomes of the Brokenhearted/Wild Night in Paradise	1980	—	2.00	4.00
POLYDOR					
14158	Magic in His Hands/Black Rose	1973	—	3.00	6.00
SIRE					
722	Mockingbird/Aggravation	1975	—	2.50	5.00
—With Pete Wingfield					
727	Disco Night/Come On In	1976	—	2.50	5.00
735	Money Man/There You Are	1976	—	2.50	5.00
1010	When You Were Beautiful/Up to You	1977	—	2.50	5.00
4111	Tell Mama/Swamp Man	1969	2.50	5.00	10.00
Albums					
POLYDOR					
PD 5034	Hypnotized	1972	3.75	7.50	15.00
SIRE					
SR 6040	American Heartbeat	1977	2.50	5.00	10.00
SES-7409	Matinee Weepers	1973	3.75	7.50	15.00
SASD-7515	Escape from Babylon	1976	2.50	5.00	10.00
—Produced by Bob Marley					
SES-97008	Fiends and Angels	1969	7.50	15.00	30.00

VELLS, THE

Later recorded as MARTHA AND THE VANDELLAS.

Number	Title (A Side/B Side)	Yr	VG	VG+	NM
45s					
MEL-O-DY					
103	There He Is At My Door/You'll Never Cherish a Love So True	1962	25.00	50.00	100.00

VELONS, THE

Number	Title (A Side/B Side)	Yr	VG	VG+	NM
45s					
BJM					
6568	Summer Love/Why Don't You Write	1965	5.00	10.00	20.00
6569	That's What Love Can Do/That's All Right	1965	5.00	10.00	20.00
BLAST					
216	Shelly/From the Chapel	1964	25.00	50.00	100.00

VELOURS, THE

Number	Title (A Side/B Side)	Yr	VG	VG+	NM
45s					
CLIFTON					
1987	Old Fashion Christmas/I Wish You Love	19??	—	3.00	6.00
CUB					
9014	Crazy Love/I'll Never Smile Again	1958	6.25	12.50	25.00
9029	Blue Velvet/Tired of Your Rock and Rollin'	1959	6.25	12.50	25.00
END					
1090	Lover Come Back/The Lonely One	1961	5.00	10.00	20.00
GOLDISC					
3012	Daddy Warbucks/Sweet Sixteen	1960	6.25	12.50	25.00
GONE					
5092	Can I Come Over Tonight/Where There's a Way	1960	5.00	10.00	20.00
MGM					
13780	Don't Pity Me/I'm Gonna Change	1967	7.50	15.00	30.00
ONYX					
501	My Love Come Back/Honey Drop	1956	50.00	100.00	200.00
508	What You Do to Me/Romeo	1957	200.00	400.00	800.00
512	Can I Come Over Tonight/Where There's a Will (There's a Way)	1957	50.00	100.00	200.00
515	This Could Be the Night/Hands Across the Table	1957	30.00	60.00	120.00
520	Remember/Can I Walk You Home	1958	15.00	30.00	60.00
ORBIT					
9001	Remember/Can I Walk You Home	1958	12.50	25.00	50.00
RONA					
010	Woman for Me/(B-side unknown)	1966	6.25	12.50	25.00
STUDO					
9902	I Promise/Little Sweetheart	1959	12.50	25.00	50.00

VELVATONES, THE

Number	Title (A Side/B Side)	Yr	VG	VG+	NM
45s					
METEOR					
5042	Real Gone Baby/Feeling Kinda Lonely	1957	50.00	100.00	200.00
NU KAT					
110	Impossible/I'm Leaving Home	1959	12.50	25.00	50.00

VELVELETTES, THE

Number	Title (A Side/B Side)	Yr	VG	VG+	NM
45s					
I.P.G.					
1002	There He Goes/That's the Reason Why	1963	25.00	50.00	100.00
SOUL					
35025	These Things Will Keep Me Loving You/Since You've Been Loving Me	1966	5.00	10.00	20.00
V.I.P.					
25007	Needle in a Haystack/Should I Tell Them	1964	6.25	12.50	25.00
25013	He Was Realy Sayin' Somethin'/Throw a Farewell Kiss	1965	6.25	12.50	25.00
25017	I'm the Exception to the Rule/Lonely, Lonely Girl Am I	1965	5.00	10.00	20.00
25021	A Bird in the Hand (Is Worth Two in the Bush)/(B-side unknown)	1965	200.00	400.00	800.00
25030	A Bird in the Hand (Is Worth Two in the Bush)/Since You've Been Loving Me	1965	5.00	10.00	20.00
25034	These Things Will Keep Me Loving You/Since You've Been Loving Me	1966	7.50	15.00	30.00

VELVET, JIMMY

Two different singers, both of whom also recorded as "Jimmy Velvit"! If someone can help us tell who's who, we'd really appreciate it.

Number	Title (A Side/B Side)	Yr	VG	VG+	NM
45s					
ABC-PARAMOUNT					
10488	We Belong Together/History of Love	1963	5.00	10.00	20.00
10528	To the Aisle/Lonely, Lonely Night	1964	5.00	10.00	20.00
BELL					
692	Let Me Keep Your Love/Woman in Bloom	1967	2.00	4.00	8.00
CAMEO					
464	Take Me Tonight/Young Hearts	1967	6.25	12.50	25.00
CORREC-TONE					
102	When I Needed You/Bouquet of Flowers	1962	25.00	50.00	100.00
—As "James Velvet"; the Supremes sing backup					
CUB					
9100	Sometimes at Night/Look at Me	1961	3.75	7.50	15.00

Number	Title (A Side/B Side)	Yr	VG	VG+	NM
9111	When I Needed You/Bouquet of Flowers	1962	3.75	7.50	15.00
DIVISION					
102	Sometimes at Night/Look at Me	1961	5.00	10.00	20.00
PHILIPS					
40285	It's Almost Tomorrow/Blue Eyes (Don't Run Away)	1965	5.00	10.00	20.00
40314	I Won't Be Back This Year/Young Hearts	1965	5.00	10.00	20.00
ROYAL AMERICAN					
286	It's You/A Woman	1968	2.00	4.00	8.00
291	Blue Velvet/Missing You	1969	2.00	4.00	8.00
STARTIME					
103	Wisdom of a Fool/Want to Be Loved	196?	3.00	6.00	12.00
TEAR DROP					
3353	Don't Go Near a Woman/Hey Nashville	196?	3.00	6.00	12.00
3395	Oh Lonesome Me-Detroit City/Crazy Arms	196?	3.00	6.00	12.00
—As "James Velvit"					
TOLLIE					
9037	Teen Angel/Mission Bell	1964	3.75	7.50	15.00
UNITED ARTISTS					
50272	Good Good Lovin'/Heart Breakin' Misery	1968	5.00	10.00	20.00
VELVET					
201	We Belong Together/You're Mine	1963	25.00	50.00	100.00
—As "Jimmy Velvit"					
VELVET TONE					
102	It's Almost Tomorrow/Young Hearts	1965	7.50	15.00	30.00
Albums					
UNITED ARTISTS					
UAS-6653	A Touch of Velvet	1968	6.25	12.50	25.00
VELVET TONE					
501	A Touch of Velvet	1968	15.00	30.00	60.00

VELVET KEYS, THE

45s

Number	Title (A Side/B Side)	Yr	VG	VG+	NM
KING					
5090	My Baby's Gone/Let's Stay After School	1957	20.00	40.00	80.00
5109	Don't Take My Picture, Take Me/The Truth About Youth	1958	20.00	40.00	80.00

VELVET NIGHT

45s

Number	Title (A Side/B Side)	Yr	VG	VG+	NM
METROMEDIA					
110	Velvet Night/I'm Sure He'll Come Most Anytime	1969	2.00	4.00	8.00
Albums					
METROMEDIA					
MD-1028	Velvet Night	1970	7.50	15.00	30.00

VELVET SOUNDS, THE

45s

Number	Title (A Side/B Side)	Yr	VG	VG+	NM
COSMOPOLITAN					
100/101	Silver Star/The Devil and the Stocker	1953	150.00	300.00	600.00
105/106	Pretty Darling/Who'll Take My Place	1953	100.00	200.00	400.00
530/531	Hanging Up Christmas Stockings/Sing A Song Of Christmas Cheer	1953	125.00	250.00	500.00

VELVET UNDERGROUND, THE

Includes releases with NICO. Also see JOHN CALE; LOU REED.

12-Inch Singles

Number	Title (A Side/B Side)	Yr	VG	VG+	NM
POLYDOR					
PRO 349 [DJ]	Foggy Notion (same on both sides)	1985	3.75	7.50	15.00
45s					
COTILLION					
44107	Who Loves the Sun/Oh, Sweet Nothin'	1971	75.00	150.00	300.00
44107 [DJ]	Who Loves the Sun (mono/stereo)	1971	25.00	50.00	100.00
MGM					
14057	What Goes On/Jesus	1969	75.00	150.00	300.00
—Existence of a stock copy of this record has been questioned.					
14057 [DJ]	What Goes On/Jesus	1969	50.00	100.00	200.00
VERVE					
10427	All Tomorrow's Parties/I'll Be Your Mirror	1966	150.00	300.00	600.00
10427 [DJ]	All Tomorrow's Parties/I'll Be Your Mirror	1966	75.00	150.00	300.00
10427 [PS]	All Tomorrow's Parties/I'll Be Your Mirror	1966	2000.	4000.	8000.
10466	Femme Fatale/Sunday Morning	1966	100.00	200.00	400.00
10466 [DJ]	Femme Fatale/Sunday Morning	1966	75.00	150.00	300.00
10560	White Light/White Heat//Here She Comes Now	1967	75.00	150.00	300.00
10560 [DJ]	White Light/White Heat//I Heard Her Call My Name	1967	50.00	100.00	200.00
Albums					
COTILLION					
SD 9034	Loaded	1970	5.00	10.00	20.00
—Original pressing has a light blue label					
SD 9034	Loaded	197?	3.75	7.50	15.00
—Reissue with purplish label					
SD 9034	Loaded	198?	3.00	6.00	12.00
—Reissue with purplish label and bar code on back cover					
SD 9034 [DJ]	Loaded	1970	18.75	37.50	75.00
—White label promo					
SD 9500	Live at Max's Kansas City	1972	5.00	10.00	20.00
—Original pressing has a light blue label					
SD 9500	Live at Max's Kansas City	197?	3.75	7.50	15.00
—Reissue with purplish label					
SD 9500	Live at Max's Kansas City	198?	3.00	6.00	12.00
—Reissue with purplish label and bar code on back cover					
SD 9500 [DJ]	Live at Max's Kansas City	1972	18.75	37.50	75.00
—White label promo					
MERCURY					
SRM-2-7504 [(2)]	1969 (Live)	1974	3.75	7.50	15.00
—Reissues with Chicago skyline or black labels					
SRM-2-7504 [(2)]	1969 (Live)	1974	12.50	25.00	50.00
—Originals with red labels					
MGM					
GAS-131	The Velvet Underground (Golden Archive Series)	1970	10.00	20.00	40.00
SE-4617	The Velvet Underground	1969	12.50	25.00	50.00
SE-4617 [DJ]	The Velvet Underground	1969	75.00	125.00	250.00
—Yellow label promo					
M3G 4950	Archetypes	1974	5.00	10.00	20.00
PRIDE					
0022	Lou Reed and the Velvet Underground	1973	3.75	7.50	15.00
VERVE					
V-5008 [M]	The Velvet Underground and Nico	1967	75.00	150.00	300.00
—Version 1: With peel-off banana peel, photo of band framed by a male torso (deduct 50% if banana sticker is gone)					
V-5008 [M]	The Velvet Underground and Nico	1967	75.00	150.00	300.00
—Version 2: With peel-off banana peel, photo of torso obscured by a sticker (deduct 50% if stickers removed)					
V-5008 [M]	The Velvet Underground and Nico	1967	50.00	100.00	200.00
—Version 3: With peel-off banana peel, torso is airbrushed off the cover (deduct 50% if banana sticker removed)					
V6-5008 [S]	The Velvet Underground and Nico	1967	50.00	100.00	200.00
—Version 1: With peel-off banana peel, photo of band framed by a male torso (deduct 50% if banana sticker is gone)					
V6-5008 [S]	The Velvet Underground and Nico	1967	50.00	100.00	200.00
—Version 2: With peel-off banana peel, photo of torso obscured by a sticker (deduct 50% if stickers removed)					
V6-5008 [S]	The Velvet Underground and Nico	1967	37.50	75.00	150.00
—Version 3: With peel-off banana peel, torso is airbrushed off the cover (deduct 50% if banana sticker removed)					
V6-5008 [S]	The Velvet Underground and Nico	1968	25.00	50.00	100.00
—Version 4: With unpeelable banana					
V-5046 [M]	White Light/White Heat	1967	37.50	75.00	150.00
—Version 1: "Skeleton" cover -- a black-on-black skeleton is visible when cover is viewed at an angle					
V-5046 [M]	White Light/White Heat	1967	15.00	30.00	60.00
—Version 2: No "skeleton" on cover					
V-5046 [M/DJ]	White Light/White Heat	1967	75.00	150.00	300.00
—White label promo					
V6-5046 [S]	White Light/White Heat	1967	20.00	40.00	80.00
—Version 1: "Skeleton" cover -- a black-on-black skeleton is visible when cover is viewed at an angle					
V6-5046 [S]	White Light/White Heat	1967	10.00	20.00	40.00
—Version 2: No "skeleton" on cover					
V6-5046 [S/DJ]	White Light/White Heat	1967	62.50	125.00	250.00
—Yellow label promo					
815454-1	The Velvet Underground	1985	3.00	6.00	12.00
—Reissue of MGM SE-4617					
823290-1	The Velvet Underground and Nico	1985	3.00	6.00	12.00
—Reissue of Verve V6-5008					
823721-1	VU	1985	3.00	6.00	12.00
825119-1	White Light/White Heat	1985	3.00	6.00	12.00
—Reissue of Verve V6-5046					
826284-1 [(2)]	1969 (Live)	1985	3.00	6.00	12.00
—Reissue of Mercury SRM-2-7504					
829405-1	Another View	1986	3.00	6.00	12.00

VELVETEENS, THE

45s

Number	Title (A Side/B Side)	Yr	VG	VG+	NM
GOLDEN ARTISTS					
614	I Feel Sorry for You Baby/Ching Bam Bah	1965	2.50	5.00	10.00
LAURIE					
3126	I Thank You/Meant to Be	1962	3.75	7.50	15.00
STARK					
101	Please Holy Father/Baby Baby	1961	12.50	25.00	50.00
—Original title of A-side					
101	The Teen Prayer/Baby Baby	1961	7.50	15.00	30.00
—New A-side title					
101	Teen Prayer/Baby Baby	1961	5.00	10.00	20.00
—Slightly altered A-side title					
105	I Thank You/Meant to Be	1962	6.25	12.50	25.00

VELVETEERS, THE

45s

Number	Title (A Side/B Side)	Yr	VG	VG+	NM
SPITFIRE					
15	Tell Me You're Mine/Boo Wacka Boo	1956	2000.	3000.	4000.

VELVETIERS, THE

45s

Number	Title (A Side/B Side)	Yr	VG	VG+	NM
RIC					
958	Oh Baby/Feelin' Right Saturday Night	1958	75.00	150.00	300.00

VELVETONES, THE (1)

45s

Number	Title (A Side/B Side)	Yr	VG	VG+	NM
ALADDIN					
3372	Glory of Love/I Love Her So	1957	50.00	100.00	200.00
3391	I Found My Love/Melody of Love	1957	50.00	100.00	200.00
3463	My Every Thought/Little Girl I Love You So	1960	75.00	150.00	300.00
D					
1049	Come Back/Penalty of Love	1959	37.50	75.00	150.00
1072	Worried Over You/Space Man	1959	25.00	50.00	100.00
DEB					
1008	Stars of Wonder/Who Took My Girl	1959	37.50	75.00	150.00
IMPERIAL					
5878	The Glory of Love/I Love Her So	1962	7.50	15.00	30.00
66020	The Glory of Love/I Found My Love	1964	3.75	7.50	15.00

VELVETONES, THE (2)

Girl group.

45s

Number	Title (A Side/B Side)	Yr	VG	VG+	NM
ASCOT					
2117	I Want Him So Bad/Yes I Will	1962	3.75	7.50	15.00
2126	Starry Eyed/I'm Ashamed	1963	3.75	7.50	15.00

VELVETONES, THE (3)

45s

Number	Title (A Side/B Side)	Yr	VG	VG+	NM
GARP					
102	Mister X/(B-side unknown)	1965	15.00	30.00	60.00
—Black vinyl					

Number	Title (A Side/B Side)	Yr	VG	VG+	NM
102	Mister X/(B-side unknown)	1965	30.00	60.00	120.00

—Red vinyl

VELVETONES, THE (4)

45s

VERVE

Number	Title (A Side/B Side)	Yr	VG	VG+	NM
10514	What Can the Matter Be/Hairy Lumpty Bump	1967	3.00	6.00	12.00

VELVETONES, THE (U)

Could be group (3); could be someone completely different.

45s

Number	Title (A Side/B Side)	Yr	VG	VG+	NM
GLENN					
309	Doheny Run/Static	1965	7.50	15.00	30.00
VELVET					
101	Doheny Run/Static	1965	17.50	35.00	70.00

VELVETS, THE (1)

45s

MONUMENT

Number	Title (A Side/B Side)	Yr	VG	VG+	NM
435	That Lucky Old Sun/Time and Again	1961	7.50	15.00	30.00
441	Tonight (Could Be the Night)/Spring Fever	1961	7.50	15.00	30.00
448	Lana/Laugh	1961	7.50	15.00	30.00
458	The Love Express/Don't Let Him Take My Baby	1962	6.25	12.50	25.00
464	Let the Good Times Roll/The Lights Go On, The Lights Go Off	1962	6.25	12.50	25.00
810	Crying in the Chapel/Dawn	1963	5.00	10.00	20.00
836	Nightmare/Here Comes That Song Again	1964	5.00	10.00	20.00
861	If/Let the Fool Kiss You	1964	5.00	10.00	20.00
961	Baby the Magic Is Gone/Let the Fool Kiss You	1966	3.75	7.50	15.00
8917	Tonight (Could Be the Night)/That Lucky Old Sun (Just Rolls Around Heaven)	197?	—	2.50	5.00

—"Golden Series" reissue

VELVETS, THE (2)

45s

Number	Title (A Side/B Side)	Yr	VG	VG+	NM
EVENT					
4285	I/At Last	197?	2.00	4.00	8.00
FURY					
1012	I-I-I (Love You So-So-So)/Dance Honey Dance	1958	12.50	25.00	50.00
PILGRIM					
706	I/At Last	1956	12.50	25.00	50.00
710	Tell Her/I Cried	1956	12.50	25.00	50.00
RED ROBIN					
120	They Tried/She's Gotta Grin	1953	50.00	100.00	200.00
122	I/At Last	1953	37.50	75.00	150.00
127	Tell Her/I Cried	1954	37.50	75.00	150.00

VELVETS, THE (U)

These could be by group (1).

45s

Number	Title (A Side/B Side)	Yr	VG	VG+	NM
20TH FOX					
165	Happy Days Are Here Again/If I Could Be with You	1959	6.25	12.50	25.00
PLAID					
101	Everybody Knows/Hand Jivin' Baby	1959	20.00	40.00	80.00

VENEERS, THE

45s

Number	Title (A Side/B Side)	Yr	VG	VG+	NM
PRINCETON					
102	Believe Me (My Angel)/I	1960	10.00	20.00	40.00
TREYCO					
402	With All My Love/Recipe of Love	1963	3.75	7.50	15.00

VENET, NICK

45s

Number	Title (A Side/B Side)	Yr	VG	VG+	NM
DECCA					
31939	Theme from "Out of Sight"/Camp Side	1966	2.50	5.00	10.00
IMPERIAL					
5522	Love In Be-Bop Time/Honey Baby	1958	5.00	10.00	20.00

VENTRILLS, THE

45s

PARKWAY

Number	Title (A Side/B Side)	Yr	VG	VG+	NM
141	Alone in the Night/Confusion	1967	3.00	6.00	12.00

VENTURES, THE

12-Inch Singles

TRIDEX

Number	Title (A Side/B Side)	Yr	VG	VG+	NM
1245	Surfin' and Spyin'/Showdown at Newport	1981	5.00	10.00	20.00

45s

BLUE HORIZON

Number	Title (A Side/B Side)	Yr	VG	VG+	NM
100	The Real McCoy/Cookies and Coke	1960	150.00	300.00	600.00
101	Walk-Don't Run/Home	1960	625.00	1250.	2500.
102	Hold Me, Thrill Me, Kiss Me/No Next Time	1960	50.00	100.00	200.00

—As "Scott Douglas and the Venture Quintet"

DOLTON

Number	Title (A Side/B Side)	Yr	VG	VG+	NM
25X	Walk — Don't Run/The McCoy	1960	5.00	10.00	20.00
25	Walk — Don't Run/Home	1960	6.25	12.50	25.00
28	Perfidia/No Trespassing	1960	5.00	10.00	20.00
28 [PS]	Perfidia/No Trespassing	1960	12.50	25.00	50.00
32	Ram-Bunk-Shush/Lonely Heart	1961	5.00	10.00	20.00
41	Lullaby of the Leaves/Ginchy	1961	5.00	10.00	20.00
44	(Theme from) Silver City/Bluer Than Blue	1961	5.00	10.00	20.00
47	Blue Moon/Lady of Spain	1961	5.00	10.00	20.00
50	Yellow Jacket/Genesis	1962	5.00	10.00	20.00
55	Instant Mashed/My Bonnie	1962	5.00	10.00	20.00
60	Lolita Ya-Ya/Lucille	1962	5.00	10.00	20.00
67	The 2,000 Pound Bee (Part 1)/The 2,000 Pound Bee (Part 2)	1962	5.00	10.00	20.00
68	El Cumbanchero/Skip To M'Limbo	1963	3.75	7.50	15.00
78	The Ninth Wave/Damaged Goods	1963	3.75	7.50	15.00
85	The Savage/The Chase	1963	3.75	7.50	15.00
91	Journey to the Stars/Walkin' with Pluto	1964	3.75	7.50	15.00
94	Fugitive/Scratchin'	1964	3.75	7.50	15.00
96	Walk... Don't Run '64/The Cruel Sea	1964	3.75	7.50	15.00
96 [PS]	Walk... Don't Run '64/The Cruel Sea	1964	7.50	15.00	30.00
300	Slaughter on Tenth Avenue/Rap City	1964	3.00	6.00	12.00
300 [PS]	Slaughter on Tenth Avenue/Rap City	1964	6.25	12.50	25.00
303	Diamond Head/Lonely Girl	1965	3.00	6.00	12.00
306	Pedal Pusher/The Swingin' Creeper	1965	3.00	6.00	12.00
308	Ten Seconds to Heaven/Bird Rockers	1965	3.00	6.00	12.00
311	La Bomba/Gemini	1965	3.00	6.00	12.00
312	Sleigh Ride/Snow Flakes	1965	3.75	7.50	15.00
316	Secret Agent Man/00-711	1966	3.00	6.00	12.00
320	Blue Star/Comin' Home Baby	1966	3.00	6.00	12.00
320 [PS]	Blue Star/Comin' Home Baby	1966	6.25	12.50	25.00
321	Arabesque/Ginza Lights	1966	3.00	6.00	12.00
323	Green Hornet Theme/Fuzzy and Wild	1966	3.00	6.00	12.00
323 [PS]	Green Hornet Theme/Fuzzy and Wild	1966	7.50	15.00	30.00
325	Penetration/Wild Thing	1966	3.00	6.00	12.00
325 [PS]	Penetration/Wild Thing	1966	6.25	12.50	25.00
327	Theme from "The Wild Angels"/Kickstand	1967	3.00	6.00	12.00
S7-19770	Rudolph the Red-Nosed Reindeer/Frosty (The Snow Man)	1997	—	—	3.00

—B-side by Jan and Dean on Liberty

EMI

Number	Title (A Side/B Side)	Yr	VG	VG+	NM
S7-18212	Jingle Bell Rock/Jingle Bells	1994	—	2.50	5.00

—Red vinyl

Number	Title (A Side/B Side)	Yr	VG	VG+	NM
SPRO 19949 [DJ]	Rudolf The Red-Nosed Reindeer/Depression	1994	—	2.50	5.00

—B-side by Johnny and the Dwellers

Number	Title (A Side/B Side)	Yr	VG	VG+	NM
SPRO 19949 [PS]	Rudolf The Red-Nosed Reindeer/Depression	1994	—	2.50	5.00
LIBERTY					
55967	Strawberry Fields Forever/Endless Dream	1967	2.00	4.00	8.00
55977	Theme from "Endless Summer"/Strawberry Fields Forever	1967	2.00	4.00	8.00
56007	On the Road/Mirrors and Shadows	1967	2.00	4.00	8.00
56019	Flights of Fantasy/Vibrations	1968	—	3.00	6.00
56044	Walk Don't Run-Land of 1000 Dances/Too Young to Know My Mind	1968	—	3.00	6.00
56068	Hawaii Five-O/Soul Breeze	1968	2.00	4.00	8.00
56115	Theme from A Summer Place/A Summer Love	1969	—	3.00	6.00
56153	Expo '70/Swan Lake	1970	—	3.00	6.00
56169	The Wanderer/The Mercenary	1970	—	3.00	6.00
56189	Storefront Lawyers (Theme)/Kern County Line	1970	—	3.00	6.00
TRIDEX					
501	Surfin' and Spyin'/Rumble at Newport	1981	—	2.50	5.00

—A-side with Charlotte Caffey and Jane Wiedlin of the Go-Go's, who did their own version on an early single

Number	Title (A Side/B Side)	Yr	VG	VG+	NM
501 [PS]	Surfin' and Spyin'/Rumble at Newport	1981	—	2.50	5.00
UNITED ARTISTS					
0050	Walk—Don't Run/Ram-Bunk-Shush	1973	—	2.00	4.00

—0050, 0051 and 0052 are "Silver Spotlight Series" reissues

Number	Title (A Side/B Side)	Yr	VG	VG+	NM
0051	Perfidia/Telstar	1973	—	2.00	4.00
0052	Hawaii Five-O/Walk—Don't Run '64	1973	—	2.00	4.00
XW207	Last Tango in Paris/Prima Vera	1973	—	3.00	6.00
XW277	Skylab/The Little People	1973	—	3.00	6.00
XW333	Also Sprach Zarathustra (2001)/The Cisco Kid	1973	—	3.00	6.00
XW369	Main Theme from The Young and the Restless/Eloise	1973	—	3.00	6.00
XW392	Main Theme from The Young and the Restless/Eloise	1974	—	3.00	6.00
XW392 [PS]	Main Theme from The Young and the Restless/Eloise	1974	2.00	4.00	8.00
XW578	Theme from "Airport 1975"/The Man with the Golden Gun	1974	—	3.00	6.00
XW687	Superstar Revue (Part 1)/Superstar Revue (Part 2)	1975	—	3.00	6.00
XW784	Moonlight Serenade (Part 1)/Moonlight Serenade (Part 2)	1976	2.00	4.00	8.00

—As "The New Ventures"

Number	Title (A Side/B Side)	Yr	VG	VG+	NM
XW942	Theme from "Charlie's Angels"/Theme from "Starsky and Hutch"	1977	2.00	4.00	8.00
XW1100	Walk Don't Run '77/Amanda's Theme	1977	—	3.00	6.00
XW1161	Wipe Out/Nadia's Theme	1978	—	2.00	4.00

—Reissue

Number	Title (A Side/B Side)	Yr	VG	VG+	NM
50800	Indian Sun/Squaw Man	1971	—	3.00	6.00
50800 [PS]	Indian Sun/Squaw Man	1971	2.00	4.00	8.00
50851	Theme from "Shaft"/Tight Fit	1971	—	3.00	6.00
50872	Joy/Cherries Jubilee	1972	—	3.00	6.00
50903	Beethoven's Sonata in G Minor/Peter and the Wolf	1972	—	3.00	6.00
50925	Honky Tonk (Part 1)/Honky Tonk (Part 2)	1972	—	3.00	6.00
50989	Last Night/Ram-Bunk-Shush	1972	—	3.00	6.00

7-Inch Extended Plays

DOLTON

Number	Title (A Side/B Side)	Yr	VG	VG+	NM
BEP-503	Walk — Don't Run/The McCoy//Honky Tonk/Raunchy	1960	20.00	40.00	80.00
BEP-503 [PS]	Walk — Don't Run	1960	20.00	40.00	80.00
4-8031 [DJ]	House of the Rising Sun/Night Train/Rap City//Walk Don't Run '64/One Mint Julep/The Creeper	1964	3.75	7.50	15.00

—Jukebox single, small hole, plays at 33 1/3 rpm

Number	Title (A Side/B Side)	Yr	VG	VG+	NM
4-8031 [PS]	Walk Don't Run '64	1964	3.75	7.50	15.00

Albums

Number	Title (A Side/B Side)	Yr	VG	VG+	NM
COMPLEAT					
672013-1	The Best of the Ventures	1986	2.50	5.00	10.00
DOLTON					
BLP 2003 [M]	Walk Don't Run	1960	12.50	25.00	50.00

—Pale blue label with dolphins on top

Number	Title (A Side/B Side)	Yr	VG	VG+	NM
BLP 2003 [M]	Walk Don't Run	1963	5.00	10.00	20.00

—Dark label, logo on left

Number	Title (A Side/B Side)	Yr	VG	VG+	NM
BLP 2004 [M]	The Ventures	1961	12.50	25.00	50.00

—Pale blue label with dolphins on top

Number	Title (A Side/B Side)	Yr	VG	VG+	NM
BLP 2004 [M]	The Ventures	1963	5.00	10.00	20.00

—Dark label, logo on left

Number	Title (A Side/B Side)	Yr	VG	VG+	NM
BLP 2006 [M]	Another Smash!!!	1961	12.50	25.00	50.00

—Pale blue label with dolphins on top

Number	Title (A Side/B Side)	Yr	VG	VG+	NM
BLP 2006 [M]	Another Smash!!!	1963	5.00	10.00	20.00
—Dark label, logo on left					
BLP 2008 [M]	The Colorful Ventures	1961	12.50	25.00	50.00
—Pale blue label with dolphins on top					
BLP 2008 [M]	The Colorful Ventures	1963	5.00	10.00	20.00
—Dark label, logo on left					
BLP 2010 [M]	Twist with the Ventures	1962	12.50	25.00	50.00
—Pale blue label with dolphins on top					
BLP 2010 [M]	Dance!	1963	5.00	10.00	20.00
—Dark label, logo on left; retitled version of "Twist with the Ventures"					
BLP 2014 [M]	The Ventures' Twist Party, Vol. 2	1962	12.50	25.00	50.00
—Pale blue label with dolphins on top					
BLP 2014 [M]	Dance with the Ventures	1963	5.00	10.00	20.00
—Dark label, logo on left' retitled version of "The Ventures' Twist Party, Vol. 2"					
BLP 2016 [M]	Mashed Potatoes and Gravy	1962	7.50	15.00	30.00
BLP 2016 [M]	Beach Party	1963	5.00	10.00	20.00
—Retitled version of "Mashed Potatoes and Gravy"					
BLP 2017 [M]	Going to the Ventures Dance Party!	1962	7.50	15.00	30.00
BLP 2019 [M]	The Ventures Play Telstar, The Lonely Bull	1962	7.50	15.00	30.00
BLP 2022 [M]	Surfing	1963	6.25	12.50	25.00
BLP 2023 [M]	The Ventures Play the Country Classics	1963	6.25	12.50	25.00
BLP 2024 [M]	Let's Go!	1963	6.25	12.50	25.00
BLP 2027 [M]	(The) Ventures in Space	1964	10.00	20.00	40.00
BLP 2029 [M]	The Fabulous Ventures	1964	6.25	12.50	25.00
BLP 2031 [M]	Walk, Don't Run, Vol. 2	1964	6.25	12.50	25.00
BLP 2033 [M]	The Ventures Knock Me Out!	1965	6.25	12.50	25.00
BLP 2035 [M]	The Ventures on Stage	1965	6.25	12.50	25.00
BLP 2037 [M]	The Ventures A-Go-Go	1965	6.25	12.50	25.00
BLP-2038 [M]	The Ventures' Christmas Album	1965	7.50	15.00	30.00
BLP 2040 [M]	Where the Action Is	1966	5.00	10.00	20.00
BLP 2042 [M]	The Ventures/Batman Theme	1966	7.50	15.00	30.00
BLP 2045 [M]	Go with the Ventures!	1966	5.00	10.00	20.00
BLP 2047 [M]	Wild Things!	1966	5.00	10.00	20.00
BLP 2050 [M]	Guitar Freakout	1967	5.00	10.00	20.00
BST 8003 [S]	Walk Don't Run	1960	15.00	30.00	60.00
—Pale blue label with dolphins on top					
BST 8003 [S]	Walk Don't Run	1963	6.25	12.50	25.00
—Dark label, logo on left					
BST 8004 [S]	The Ventures	1961	15.00	30.00	60.00
—Pale blue label with dolphins on top					
BST 8004 [S]	The Ventures	1963	6.25	12.50	25.00
—Dark label, logo on left					
BST 8006 [S]	Another Smash!!!	1961	15.00	30.00	60.00
—Pale blue label with dolphins on top					
BST 8006 [S]	Another Smash!!!	1963	6.25	12.50	25.00
—Dark label, logo on left					
BST 8008 [S]	The Colorful Ventures	1961	15.00	30.00	60.00
—Pale blue label with dolphins on top					
BST 8008 [S]	The Colorful Ventures	1963	6.25	12.50	25.00
—Dark label, logo on left					
BST 8010 [S]	Twist with the Ventures	1962	15.00	30.00	60.00
—Pale blue label with dolphins on top					
BST 8010 [S]	Dance!	1963	6.25	12.50	25.00
—Dark label, logo on left; retitled version of "Twist with the Ventures"					
BST 8014 [S]	The Ventures' Twist Party, Vol. 2	1962	15.00	30.00	60.00
—Pale blue label with dolphins on top					
BST 8014 [S]	Dance with the Ventures	1963	6.25	12.50	25.00
—Dark label, logo on left' retitled version of "The Ventures' Twist Party, Vol. 2"					
BST 8016 [S]	Mashed Potatoes and Gravy	1962	10.00	20.00	40.00
BST 8016 [S]	Beach Party	1963	6.25	12.50	25.00
—Retitled version of "Mashed Potatoes and Gravy"					
BST 8017 [S]	Going to the Ventures Dance Party!	1962	10.00	20.00	40.00
BST 8019 [S]	The Ventures Play Telstar, The Lonely Bull	1962	10.00	20.00	40.00
BST 8022 [S]	Surfing	1963	7.50	15.00	30.00
BST 8023 [S]	The Ventures Play the Country Classics	1963	7.50	15.00	30.00
BST 8024 [S]	Let's Go!	1963	7.50	15.00	30.00
BST 8027 [S]	(The) Ventures in Space	1964	12.50	25.00	50.00
BST 8029 [S]	The Fabulous Ventures	1964	7.50	15.00	30.00
BST 8031 [S]	Walk, Don't Run, Vol. 2	1964	7.50	15.00	30.00
BST 8033 [S]	The Ventures Knock Me Out!	1965	7.50	15.00	30.00
BST 8035 [S]	The Ventures on Stage	1965	7.50	15.00	30.00
BST 8037 [S]	The Ventures A-Go-Go	1965	7.50	15.00	30.00
BST-8038 [S]	The Ventures' Christmas Album	1965	5.00	10.00	20.00
BST 8040 [S]	Where the Action Is	1966	6.25	2.50	25.00
BST 8042 [S]	The Ventures/Batman Theme	1966	10.00	20.00	40.00
BST 8045 [S]	Go with the Ventures!	1966	6.25	12.50	25.00
BST 8047 [S]	Wild Things!	1966	6.25	12.50	25.00
BST 8050 [S]	Guitar Freakout	1967	6.25	12.50	25.00
BLP 16501 [M]	Play Guitar with the Ventures	1965	6.25	12.50	25.00
BLP 16502 [M]	Play Guitar with the Ventures, Vol. 2	196?	6.25	12.50	25.00
BLP 16503 [M]	Play Guitar with the Ventures, Vol. 3	196?	6.25	12.50	25.00
BLP 16504 [M]	Play Guitar with the Ventures, Vol. 4	196?	6.25	12.50	25.00
BST 16504 [S]	Play Guitar with the Ventures, Vol. 4	196?	7.50	15.00	30.00
BST 17501 [S]	Play Guitar with the Ventures	1965	7.50	15.00	30.00
BST 17502 [S]	Play Guitar with the Ventures, Vol. 2	196?	7.50	15.00	30.00
BST 17503 [S]	Play Guitar with the Ventures, Vol. 3	196?	7.50	15.00	30.00

LIBERTY

Number	Title (A Side/B Side)	Yr	VG	VG+	NM
LRP-2052 [M]	Super Psychedelics	1967	5.00	10.00	20.00
LRP-2053 [M]	Golden Greats by the Ventures	1967	5.00	10.00	20.00
LRP-2054 [M]	$1,000,000.00 Weekend	1967	5.00	10.00	20.00
LRP-2055 [M]	Flights of Fancy	1968	7.50	15.00	30.00
LST-8003	Walk Don't Run	1970	3.75	7.50	15.00
—Reissue of Dolton 8003 with new front cover, original back cover					
LST-8003	Walk Don't Run	1970	5.00	10.00	20.00
—Reissue of Dolton 8003 with new front and back covers					
LT-8003	Walk Don't Run	1981	2.00	4.00	8.00
LST-8023	I Walk the Line and Other Giant Hits	1970	5.00	10.00	20.00
—Reissue of "The Ventures Play the Country Classics"					
LST-8031	Walk, Don't Run, Vol. 2	1970	6.25	12.50	25.00
—Reissue of Dolton 8031 with new cover					
LST-8050	Revolving Sounds	1970	7.50	15.00	30.00
—Reissue of "Guitar Freakout"					
LST-8052 [S]	Super Psychedelics	1967	6.25	12.50	25.00
LST-8052 [S]	Changing Times	1970	10.00	20.00	40.00
—Reissue of "Super Psychedelics"					
LST-8053 [S]	Golden Greats by the Ventures	1967	5.00	10.00	20.00
LTAO-8053	Golden Greats by the Ventures	1981	2.00	4.00	8.00
LST-8054 [S]	$1,000,000.00 Weekend	1967	5.00	10.00	20.00
LST-8055 [S]	Flights of Fancy	1968	5.00	10.00	20.00
LST-8057	The Horse	1968	5.00	10.00	20.00
LST-8057	On the Scene	1970	3.75	7.50	15.00
—Reissue of "The Horse"					
LST-8059	Underground Fire	1969	5.00	10.00	20.00
LST-8060	More Golden Greats	1970	3.75	7.50	15.00
LST-8061	Hawaii Five-O	1969	3.75	7.50	15.00
LST-8062	Swamp Rock	1969	3.75	7.50	15.00
LN-10122	The Very Best of the Ventures	1981	2.00	4.00	8.00
LN-10155	The Ventures Play Telstar, The Lonely Bull	1981	2.00	4.00	8.00
LN-10156	The Ventures Play the Country Classics	1981	2.00	4.00	8.00
LN-10188	Walk, Don't Run, Vol. 2	1984	2.00	4.00	8.00
LN-10190	(The) Ventures in Space	1984	2.00	4.00	8.00
LN-10203	The Ventures	1984	2.00	4.00	8.00
LN-10224	TV Themes	1984	2.00	4.00	8.00
LST-35000 [(2)]	The Ventures 10th Anniversary Album	1970	5.00	10.00	20.00

SUNSET

Number	Title (A Side/B Side)	Yr	VG	VG+	NM
SUM-1160 [M]	The Guitar Genius of the Ventures	1967	3.00	6.00	12.00
SUS-5160 [S]	The Guitar Genius of the Ventures	1967	3.75	7.50	15.00
SUS-5270	Super Group	1969	3.00	6.00	12.00

UNITED ARTISTS

Number	Title (A Side/B Side)	Yr	VG	VG+	NM
UXS-80 [(2)]	The Ventures	1971	3.75	7.50	15.00
UA-LA147-G [(2)]	Only Hits	1973	3.75	7.50	15.00
UA-LA217-E	The Jim Croce Songbook	1973	3.00	6.00	12.00
UA-LA331-E	The Very Best of the Ventures	1974	3.00	6.00	12.00
UA-LA586-F	Rocky Road	1976	3.00	6.00	12.00
UA-LA717-F	TV Themes	1977	6.25	12.50	25.00
UAS-5547	Theme from Shaft	1971	3.00	6.00	12.00
UAS-5575	Joy/The Ventures Play the Classics	1972	3.00	6.00	12.00
UAS-5649	Rock and Roll Forever	1972	3.00	6.00	12.00
UAS-6796	New Testament	1971	3.00	6.00	12.00

VENUS, VIC

45s

BUDDAH

Number	Title (A Side/B Side)	Yr	VG	VG+	NM
118	Moonflight/Everybody's On Strike	1969	2.50	5.00	10.00
138	Moon Jack/Moon Welcome	1969	2.00	4.00	8.00

VERA, BILLY

Includes records as "Billy and the Beaters."

45s

ALFA

Number	Title (A Side/B Side)	Yr	VG	VG+	NM
7002	I Can Take Care of Myself/Corner of the Night	1981	—	2.00	4.00
—As "Billy and the Beaters"					
7005	At This Moment/Someone Will School You, Someone Will Cool You	1981	—	2.50	5.00
7005 [PS]	At This Moment/Someone Will School You, Someone Will Cool You	1981	—	2.50	5.00
—As "Billy and the Beaters"					
7012	Millie, Make Me Some Chili/Someone Will School You, Someone Will Cool You	1981	—	2.00	4.00
—As "Billy and the Beaters"					
7020	We Got It All/You Own It	1982	—	2.00	4.00

ATLANTIC

Number	Title (A Side/B Side)	Yr	VG	VG+	NM
2526	With Pen in Hand/Good Morning Blues	1968	2.00	4.00	8.00
2555	I've Been Loving You Too Long/Are You Coming to My Party	1968	2.00	4.00	8.00
2586	Julie/Time Doesn't Matter Anymore	1968	2.00	4.00	8.00
2628	Bible Salesman/Are You Coming to My Party	1969	—	3.00	6.00
2700	I've Never Been Loved Like This Before/J.W.'s Dream	1970	—	3.00	6.00

CAPITOL

Number	Title (A Side/B Side)	Yr	VG	VG+	NM
B-44149	Between Like and Love/Heart Be Still	1988	—	—	3.00
B-44149 [PS]	Between Like and Love/Heart Be Still	1988	—	—	3.00
B-44200	Ronnie's Song/Between Like and Love	1988	—	—	3.00

MIDLAND INT'L.

Number	Title (A Side/B Side)	Yr	VG	VG+	NM
MB-10639	Back Door Man/Run and Tell the People	1976	—	2.50	5.00
MB-10909	Private Clown/Billy, Meet Your Son	1977	—	2.50	5.00
MB-11042	I've Had Enough/Something Like Nothing Before	1977	—	2.50	5.00

RHINO

Number	Title (A Side/B Side)	Yr	VG	VG+	NM
74403	At This Moment/I Can Take Care of Myself	1986	—	2.50	5.00
74403	At This Moment/Peanut Butter	1986	—	—	3.00
74404	I Can Take Care of Myself/(B-side unknown)	1987	—	—	3.00
74407	Hopeless Romantic/(B-side unknown)	1987	—	—	3.00

RUST

Number	Title (A Side/B Side)	Yr	VG	VG+	NM
5051	My Heart Cries/All My Love	1962	5.00	10.00	20.00

Albums

ALFA

Number	Title (A Side/B Side)	Yr	VG	VG+	NM
10001	Billy and the Beaters	1981	3.75	7.50	15.00
10012	Billy Vera	1982	3.00	6.00	12.00

ATLANTIC

Number	Title (A Side/B Side)	Yr	VG	VG+	NM
8197 [M]	With Pen in Hand	1968	10.00	20.00	40.00
SD 8197 [S]	With Pen in Hand	1968	6.25	12.50	25.00

CAPITOL

Number	Title (A Side/B Side)	Yr	VG	VG+	NM
C1-46948	Retro Nuevo	1988	2.50	5.00	10.00

MACOLA

Number	Title (A Side/B Side)	Yr	VG	VG+	NM
961	The Billy Vera Album	1987	2.50	5.00	10.00
—Reissue of Midsong Int'l. LP					

MIDSONG INT'L.

Number	Title (A Side/B Side)	Yr	VG	VG+	NM
BKL1-2219	Out of the Darkness	1977	3.00	6.00	12.00

RHINO

Number	Title (A Side/B Side)	Yr	VG	VG+	NM
RNLP 70185	The Atlantic Years	1987	2.50	5.00	10.00
RNLP 70858	By Request — The Best of Billy Vera and the Beaters	1986	3.00	6.00	12.00

THUNDER

Number	Title (A Side/B Side)	Yr	VG	VG+	NM
TVLP 0018	The Hollywood Sessions	1987	2.50	5.00	10.00

VERA, BILLY, AND JUDY CLAY

45s

ATLANTIC

Number	Title (A Side/B Side)	Yr	VG	VG+	NM
2445	Storybook Children/Really Together	1967	2.00	4.00	8.00
2480	Country Girl — City Man/So Good	1968	2.00	4.00	8.00
2515	Ever Since/When Do We Go	1968	2.00	4.00	8.00
2654	Tell It Like It Is/Reaching for the Moon	1969	—	3.00	6.00

Albums

ATLANTIC

Number	Title (A Side/B Side)	Yr	VG	VG+	NM
8174 [M]	Storybook Children	1967	6.25	12.50	25.00
SD 8174 [S]	Storybook Children	1967	7.50	15.00	30.00

VERA, RICKY, AND STEVE ALLEN

45s

CORAL

Number	Title (A Side/B Side)	Yr	VG	VG+	NM
61098	How Can Santa Come to Puerto Rico/Can I Wait Up for Santa Claus	1953	7.50	15.00	30.00

VERITY, JOHN, BAND

Albums

ABC DUNHILL

Number	Title (A Side/B Side)	Yr	VG	VG+	NM
DSX-50170	The John Verity Band	1974	5.00	10.00	20.00

VERNE, LARRY

45s

ERA

Number	Title (A Side/B Side)	Yr	VG	VG+	NM
3024	Mr. Custer/Okefenokee Two-Step	1960	3.75	7.50	15.00
3034	Mister Livingston/Roller Coaster	1960	3.00	6.00	12.00
3034 [PS]	Mister Livingston/Roller Coaster	1960	6.25	12.50	25.00
3044	Abdul's Party/Tubby Tilly	1961	3.00	6.00	12.00
3051	Charlie at the Bat/Pow, Right in the Kisser	1961	3.00	6.00	12.00
3065	Beatnik/Speck	1961	3.00	6.00	12.00
3091	The Coward Who Won the West/The Porcupine Patrol	1962	3.00	6.00	12.00
3139	Return of Mr. Custer/Running Through the Forest	1964	3.00	6.00	12.00

Albums

ERA

Number	Title (A Side/B Side)	Yr	VG	VG+	NM
104 [M]	Mister Larry Verne	1961	15.00	30.00	60.00

VERNON, MARIE

45s

ALLIED

Number	Title (A Side/B Side)	Yr	VG	VG+	NM
5012	I Want You For Christmas/Christmas Tree Waltz	195?	3.75	7.50	15.00

VERNON GIRLS, THE

45s

CHALLENGE

Number	Title (A Side/B Side)	Yr	VG	VG+	NM
59234	We Love the Beatles/Hey Lover Boy	1964	7.50	15.00	30.00
59261	Only You Can Do It/Stupid Little Girl	1964	2.50	5.00	10.00

VERONICA

Also see RONNIE SPECTOR.

45s

PHIL SPECTOR

Number	Title (A Side/B Side)	Yr	VG	VG+	NM
1	So Young/Larry L	1964	50.00	100.00	200.00
2	Why Can't They Let Us Fall in Love/Chubby Danny D	1964	150.00	300.00	600.00
—Note slightly different A-side title					
2	Why Don't They Let Us Fall in Love/Chubby Danny D	1964	50.00	100.00	200.00

VERSATILES, THE

More than one group.

45s

Number	Title (A Side/B Side)	Yr	VG	VG+	NM
ATLANTIC					
2004	Passing By/Crying	1958	10.00	20.00	40.00
PEACOCK					
1910	White Cliffs of Dover/Just Words	1963	7.50	15.00	30.00
RAMCO					
3717	Blue Feeling/Just Pretending	1962	50.00	100.00	200.00
RO-CAL					
1002	I'll Whisper in Your ear/Lundee Dundee	1960	25.00	50.00	100.00
SEA CREST					
6001	Lonely Boy/Moon Dawg	1964	6.25	12.50	25.00

VERSATONES, THE

Probably more than one group.

45s

Number	Title (A Side/B Side)	Yr	VG	VG+	NM
ALL STAR					
501	Tight Skirt and Sweater/Bila	1958	10.00	20.00	40.00
ATLANTIC					
2211	Tight Skirt and Sweater/Bila	1963	5.00	10.00	20.00
FENWAY					
7001	Tight Skirt and Sweater/Bila	1960	6.25	12.50	25.00
RCA VICTOR					
47-6917	Wait for Me/De Obeah Man	1957	3.75	7.50	15.00
47-6976	Lovely Teenage Girl/Bikini Baby	1957	3.75	7.50	15.00

Albums

RCA VICTOR

Number	Title (A Side/B Side)	Yr	VG	VG+	NM
LPM-1538 [M]	The Versatones	1957	25.00	50.00	100.00

VERTUES FOUR, THE

45s

SEA SEVEN

Number	Title (A Side/B Side)	Yr	VG	VG+	NM
22	Angel Baby/Uphill, Downhill	1963	10.00	20.00	40.00

VESPERS, THE

45s

SWAN

Number	Title (A Side/B Side)	Yr	VG	VG+	NM
4156	Cupid/When I Walk with My Angel	1963	10.00	20.00	40.00

VESTELLES, THE

45s

DECCA

Number	Title (A Side/B Side)	Yr	VG	VG+	NM
9-30733	Come Home/Ditta Wa Do	1958	7.50	15.00	30.00

VETTES, THE

With BRUCE JOHNSTON.

45s

MGM

Number	Title (A Side/B Side)	Yr	VG	VG+	NM
13186	Little Ford Ragtop/Happy Hodaddy (With Ragtop Caddy)	1963	12.50	25.00	50.00

Albums

MGM

Number	Title (A Side/B Side)	Yr	VG	VG+	NM
E-4193 [M]	Rev-Up	1963	25.00	50.00	100.00
SE-4193 [S]	Rev-Up	1963	30.00	60.00	120.00

VIBES, THE (1)

45s

ABC-PARAMOUNT

Number	Title (A Side/B Side)	Yr	VG	VG+	NM
9810	Darling/Come Back Baby	1957	12.50	25.00	50.00

VIBES, THE (2)

Probably the same group as THE VIBRANAIRES.

45s

Number	Title (A Side/B Side)	Yr	VG	VG+	NM
AFTER HOURS					
105	Stop Torturing Me/Stop Jibing, Baby	1954	500.00	1000.	2000.
CHARIOT					
105	Stop Torturing Me/Stop Jibing, Baby	1954	375.00	750.00	1500.

VIBES, THE (3)

45s

ALLIED

Number	Title (A Side/B Side)	Yr	VG	VG+	NM
10006	What's Her Name/You Are	1958	15.00	30.00	60.00
10007	Misunderstood/Let the Old Folks Talk	1959	10.00	20.00	40.00

VIBES, THE (4)

45s

PERSPECTIVE

Number	Title (A Side/B Side)	Yr	VG	VG+	NM
5858	Pretty Baby (I Saw You Last Night)/Crying for You	1960	25.00	50.00	100.00

VIBES, THE (5)

45s

RAYNA

Number	Title (A Side/B Side)	Yr	VG	VG+	NM
103	You Got Me Crying/A Killer Came to Town	196?	10.00	20.00	40.00

VIBRA-SONICS, THE

45s

IDEAL

Number	Title (A Side/B Side)	Yr	VG	VG+	NM
94874	Thunder Storm/Drag Race	1964	12.50	25.00	50.00

VIBRANAIRES, THE

Probably the same group as THE VIBES (2).

45s

Number	Title (A Side/B Side)	Yr	VG	VG+	NM
AFTER HOURS					
103	Doll Face/Ooh,I Feel So Good	1954	625.00	1250.	2500.
CHARIOT					
103	Doll Face/Ooh,I Feel So Good	1954	500.00	1000.	2000.

VIBRATIONS, THE

Also see THE JAYHAWKS; THE MARATHONS (1).

45s

Number	Title (A Side/B Side)	Yr	VG	VG+	NM
ATLANTIC					
2204	Between Hello and Goodbye/Lonesome Little Lonely Girl	1963	3.00	6.00	12.00
2221	My Girl Sloopy/Daddy Woo-Woo	1964	3.00	6.00	12.00
BET					
1	So BLue/Love Me Like You Should	1960	25.00	50.00	100.00
CHECKER					
954	So BLue/Love Me Like You Should	1960	7.50	15.00	30.00
961	Feel So Bad/Cave Man	1960	5.00	10.00	20.00
967	Doing the Slop/So Little Time	1961	5.00	10.00	20.00
969	The Watusi/Wallflower	1961	5.00	10.00	20.00
974	The Continental/The Junkeroo	1961	5.00	10.00	20.00
982	Don't Say Goodbye/Stranded in the Jungle	1961	5.00	10.00	20.00
987	All My Love Belongs to You/Stop Right Now	1961	10.00	20.00	40.00
990	Let's Pony Again/What Made You Change Your Mind	1961	5.00	10.00	20.00
1002	Over the Rainbow/Oh, Cindy	1962	3.75	7.50	15.00
1011	The New Hully Gully/Anytime	1962	3.75	7.50	15.00
1022	Hamburgers on a Bun/If He Don't	1962	3.75	7.50	15.00
1038	Since I Fell for You/May the Best Man Win	1963	3.75	7.50	15.00
1061	Dancing Danny/(Instrumental)	1963	3.75	7.50	15.00
CHESS					
2151	Shake It Up/Make It Last	1974	—	3.00	6.00
EPIC					
10418	I Took an Overdose/Because You're Mine	1968	5.00	10.00	20.00
MANDALA					
2511	Ain't No Greens in Harlem/Wind-Up Toy	1972	—	3.00	6.00
2514	Man Overboard/(B-side unknown)	1972	—	3.00	6.00
NEPTUNE					
19	Expressway to Your Heart/Who's Gonna Help Me Now	1969	2.00	4.00	8.00
21	Smoke Signals/Who's Gonna Help Me Now	1970	2.00	4.00	8.00

Number	Title (A Side/B Side)	Yr	VG	VG+	NM
28	Right On Brothers, Right On/Surprise Party for Baby	1970	2.00	4.00	8.00
OKEH					
7205	Sloop Dance/Watusi Time	1964	3.00	6.00	12.00
7212	Hello Happiness/Keep On Keeping On	1965	3.00	6.00	12.00
7220	End Up Crying/Ain't Love That Way	1965	3.00	6.00	12.00
7228	Talkin' 'Bout Love/If You Only Knew	1965	3.00	6.00	12.00
7230	Misty/Finding Out the Hard Way	1965	3.00	6.00	12.00
7238	Gina/The Story of a Starry Night	1966	—	—	—
—Unreleased					
7241	Canadian Sunset/The Story of a Starry Night	1966	2.50	5.00	10.00
7249	Forgive and Forget/Gonna Get Along Without You Now	1966	2.50	5.00	10.00
7257	And I Love Her/Soul a-Go-Go	1966	2.50	5.00	10.00
7276	Pick Me/You Better Beware	1967	2.50	5.00	10.00
7297	Together/Come To Yourself	1967	2.50	5.00	10.00
7311	Love in Them There Hills/Remember the Rain	1968	2.50	5.00	10.00
Albums					
CHECKER					
LP-2978 [M]	The Watusi	1961	50.00	100.00	200.00
MANDALA					
3006	Taking a New Step	1972	5.00	10.00	20.00
OKEH					
OKM-12111 [M]	Shout	1965	7.50	15.00	30.00
OKM-12112 [M]	Misty	1966	7.50	15.00	30.00
OKM-12114 [M]	New Vibrations	1967	7.50	15.00	30.00
OKS-12114 [S]	New Vibrations	1967	10.00	20.00	40.00
OKS-12129	The Vibrations' Greatest Hits	1969	7.50	15.00	30.00
OKS-14111 [S]	Shout	1965	10.00	20.00	40.00
OKS-14112 [S]	Misty	1966	10.00	20.00	40.00

VIC, PAUL AND BRUCE

See THE CANADIAN BEADLES.

VICEROYS, THE (1)

Number	Title (A Side/B Side)	Yr	VG	VG+	NM
45s					
ALADDIN					
3273	Please, Baby, Please/I'm Yours As Long As I Live	1955	100.00	200.00	400.00

VICEROYS, THE (2)

Number	Title (A Side/B Side)	Yr	VG	VG+	NM
45s					
BETHLEHEM					
3045	Seagrams/Moasin'	1962	6.25	12.50	25.00
—Original A-side title					
3045	Sea Green/Moasin'	1962	5.00	10.00	20.00
3070	The Fox/Buzz Bomb	1963	6.25	12.50	25.00
—Original A-side title					
3070	Joshin'/Buzz Bomb	1963	5.00	10.00	20.00
3088	Not Too Much Twist/Tears on My Pillow	1965	5.00	10.00	20.00

VICEROYS, THE (3)

Number	Title (A Side/B Side)	Yr	VG	VG+	NM
45s					
BOLO					
736	Granny's Pad/Blues Bouquet	1962	3.00	6.00	12.00
739	Goin' Back to Granny's/Get Set	1963	3.00	6.00	12.00
743	Granny's Medley/Dartell Stomp	1964	2.50	5.00	10.00
749	Tiger Shark/Please, Please, Please	1964	2.50	5.00	10.00
750	Bacon Fat/Until	1965	2.50	5.00	10.00
754	That Sound/Tired of Waiting for You	1965	2.50	5.00	10.00
DOT					
16456	Granny's Pad/Blues Bouquet	1963	2.00	4.00	8.00
Albums					
BOLO					
BLP-8000 [M]	The Viceroys at Granny's Pad	1963	10.00	20.00	40.00

VICEROYS, THE (4)

Number	Title (A Side/B Side)	Yr	VG	VG+	NM
45s					
LITTLE STAR					
107	I'm So Sorry (It's Ending with You)/Uncle Sam Needs You	1961	37.50	75.00	150.00
ORIGINAL SOUND					
15	Dreamy Eyes/Ball 'N' Chain	1961	10.00	20.00	40.00
RAMCO					
3715	My Heart/I Need Your Love So Bad	1962	2000.	3000.	4000.
SMASH					
1716	I'm So Sorry (It's Ending with You)/Uncle Sam Needs You	1961	5.00	10.00	20.00

VICEROYS, THE (U)

Number	Title (A Side/B Side)	Yr	VG	VG+	NM
45s					
E'DEN					
9001	Don't Let Go/Down Beat Blues	1962	3.00	6.00	12.00
IMPERIAL					
66058	Death of an Angel/Earth Angel	1964	3.00	6.00	12.00

VICTORIALS, THE

Number	Title (A Side/B Side)	Yr	VG	VG+	NM
45s					
IMPERIAL					
5398	I Get That Feeling/The Prettiest Girl in the World	1956	12.50	25.00	50.00

VICTORIANS, THE

More than one group.

Number	Title (A Side/B Side)	Yr	VG	VG+	NM
45s					
ARNOLD					
571	Move In a Little Closer/Lovin'	1963	5.00	10.00	20.00
BANG					
550	Merry-Go-Round/Wasn't the Summer Short	1967	3.75	7.50	15.00
LIBERTY					
55574	Climb Every Mountain/What Makes Little Girls Cry	1963	5.00	10.00	20.00
55656	The Monkey Stroll/You're Invited to a Party	1964	3.75	7.50	15.00
55693	Happy Birthday Blues/Oh What a Night for Love	1964	3.75	7.50	15.00
55728	If I Loved You/The Monkey Stroll	1964	3.75	7.50	15.00
REPRISE					
0434	I Saw My Girl/Baby Toys	1965	3.75	7.50	15.00
SAXONY					
103	Heartbreaking Moon/I'm Rollin'	1956	125.00	250.00	500.00
SELMA					
1002	Wedding Bells/Please Say You Do	1956	75.00	150.00	300.00

VICTORY FIVE, THE

Number	Title (A Side/B Side)	Yr	VG	VG+	NM
45s					
TERP					
101	I Never Knew/Swing Low	1958	150.00	300.00	600.00
—All copies on colored vinyl					

VIDALTONES, THE

Number	Title (A Side/B Side)	Yr	VG	VG+	NM
45s					
JOSIE					
900	Forever/Someone to Love	1962	10.00	20.00	40.00

VIDELS, THE

Number	Title (A Side/B Side)	Yr	VG	VG+	NM
45s					
EARLY					
702	I Wish/Blow, Winds, Blow	1960	100.00	200.00	400.00
JDS					
5004	Mr. Lonely/I'll Forget You	1960	7.50	15.00	30.00
—Gray label					
5004	Mr. Lonely/I'll Forget You	1960	5.00	10.00	20.00
—Multicolor label					
5005	She's Not Coming Home/Now That Summer Is Here	1960	7.50	15.00	30.00
—Gray label					
5005	She's Not Coming Home/Now That Summer Is Here	1960	5.00	10.00	20.00
—Multicolor label					
KAPP					
361	Streets of Love/I'll Keep On Waiting	1960	5.00	10.00	20.00
405	A Letter from Ann/This Year's Mister New	1961	10.00	20.00	40.00
MEDIEVAL					
203	Be My Girl/A Place in Your Heart	1961	3.75	7.50	15.00
MUSICNOTE					
117	We Belong Together/It's All Over	1963	12.50	25.00	50.00
RHODY					
2000	Be My Girl/A Place in Your Heart	1959	12.50	25.00	50.00
TIC TAC TOE					
5005	She's Not Coming Home/Now That Summer Is Here	1962	12.50	25.00	50.00

VIDEOS, THE

Number	Title (A Side/B Side)	Yr	VG	VG+	NM
45s					
CASINO					
102	Trickle, Trickle/Moonglow You Know	1958	12.50	25.00	50.00
—No playing cards; no mention of distribution by Gone					
102	Trickle, Trickle/Moonglow You Know	1958	5.00	10.00	20.00
—With playing cards on label					
102	Trickle, Trickle/Moonglow You Know	1961	6.25	12.50	25.00
—No playing cards; with distribution by Gone					
105	Love or Infatuation/Shoo-Be-Doo-Be Cha Cha Cha	1959	75.00	150.00	300.00

VIGRASS AND OSBORNE

With Gary Osborne, later a collaborator with Elton John.

Number	Title (A Side/B Side)	Yr	VG	VG+	NM
45s					
EPIC					
50044	Gypsy Woman/Haystacks	1974	—	2.50	5.00
UNI					
55330	Forever Autumn/Men of Learning	1972	—	3.00	6.00
55344	Virginia/Ballerina	1972	—	2.50	5.00
55355	Remember Pearl Harbor/Mister Deadline	1972	—	2.50	5.00
Albums					
EPIC					
KE 33077	Steppin' Out	1975	3.00	6.00	12.00
UNI					
73129	Queues	1971	3.75	7.50	15.00

VILLAGE STOMPERS, THE

Number	Title (A Side/B Side)	Yr	VG	VG+	NM
45s					
EPIC					
9617	Washington Square/Turkish Delight	1963	2.00	4.00	8.00
9617 [PS]	Washington Square/Turkish Delight	1963	2.50	5.00	10.00
9655	Blue Grass/The La-Dee-La Song	1964	—	3.00	6.00
9655 [PS]	Blue Grass/The La-Dee-La Song	1964	2.00	4.00	8.00
9674	From Russia with Love/The Bridges of Budapest	1964	—	3.00	6.00
9702	Haunted House/Mozambique	1964	—	3.00	6.00
9718	Oh, Marie/Lonesome Blues	1964	—	3.00	6.00
9740	Fiddler on the Roof/Moonlight on the Ganges	1964	—	3.00	6.00
9785	Brother, Can You Spare a Dime/Magic Horn	1965	—	3.00	6.00
9785 [PS]	Brother, Can You Spare a Dime/Magic Horn	1965	2.00	4.00	8.00
9824	Those Magnificant Men in Their Flying Machines/Sweetwater Bay	1965	—	3.00	6.00
9868	The Bride of Bleecker Street/Call Me	1965	—	3.00	6.00
10017	Second Hand Rose/The Poet and the Prophet	1966	—	3.00	6.00
10106	Chopsticks/Wilkommen	1966	—	3.00	6.00
10142	Rose of Washington Square/When I Tell You That I Love You	1967	—	3.00	6.00
Albums					
EPIC					
LN 24078 [M]	Washington Square	1963	3.75	7.50	15.00
LN 24090 [M]	More Sounds of Washington Square	1964	3.75	7.50	15.00
LN 24109 [M]	Around the World with the Village Stompers	1964	3.00	6.00	12.00

Number	Title (A Side/B Side)	Yr	VG	VG+	NM
LN 24161 [M]	Some Folk, a Bit of Country and a Whole Lot of Dixie	1965	3.00	6.00	12.00
LN 24180 [M]	A Taste of Honey	1965	3.00	6.00	12.00
LN 24235 [M]	One More Time	1966	3.00	6.00	12.00
LN 24318 [M]	The Village Stompers' Greatest Hits	1967	3.00	6.00	12.00
BN 26078 [S]	Washington Square	1963	5.00	10.00	20.00
BN 26090 [S]	More Sounds of Washington Square	1964	5.00	10.00	20.00
BN 26109 [S]	Around the World with the Village Stompers	1964	3.75	7.50	15.00
BN 26161 [S]	Some Folk, a Bit of Country and a Whole Lot of Dixie	1965	3.75	7.50	15.00
BN 26180 [S]	A Taste of Honey	1965	3.75	7.50	15.00
BN 26235 [S]	One More Time	1966	3.75	7.50	15.00
BN 26318 [S]	The Village Stompers' Greatest Hits	1967	3.75	7.50	15.00

VILLAGE VOICES, THE

See THE FOUR SEASONS.

VINCE AND THE WAIKIKI RUMBLERS

45s

Number	Title (A Side/B Side)	Yr	VG	VG+	NM
BIG BEN					
1003	Waikiki Rumble/Pacifica	1965	12.50	25.00	50.00
ZODIAC					
1004	Waikiki Rumble/Pacifica	1965	20.00	40.00	80.00

VINCENT, GENE

45s

Number	Title (A Side/B Side)	Yr	VG	VG+	NM
CAPITOL					
F3450	Be-Bop-a-Lula/Woman Love	1956	17.50	35.00	70.00
—With large Capitol logo					
F3450	Be-Bop-a-Lula/Woman Love	1956	12.50	25.00	50.00
—With small Capitol logo					
F3530	Race with the Devil/Gonna Back Up, Baby	1956	10.00	20.00	40.00
F3558	Bluejean Bop/Who Slapped John	1956	10.00	20.00	40.00
F3617	Crazy Legs/Important Words	1956	12.50	25.00	50.00
F3678	B-I-Bickey-Bi-Bo-Bo-Go/Five Days, Five Days	1957	12.50	25.00	50.00
F3763	Lotta Lovin'/Wear My Ring	1957	12.50	25.00	50.00
F3839	Dance to the Bop/I Got It	1957	7.50	15.00	30.00
3871	Be-Bop-a-Lula/Lotta Lovin'	1974	3.75	7.50	15.00
F3874	Walkin' Home from School/I Gotta Baby	1958	10.00	20.00	40.00
F3959	Baby Blue/True to You	1958	12.50	25.00	50.00
F4010	Yes I Love You Baby/Rocky Road Blues	1958	10.00	20.00	40.00
F4051	Little Lover/Git It	1958	10.00	20.00	40.00
F4105	Say Mama/Be-Bop Boogie Boy	1958	12.50	25.00	50.00
F4153	Over the Rainbow/Who's Pushin' Your Swing	1959	12.50	25.00	50.00
F4237	The Night Is So Lonely/Right Now	1959	12.50	25.00	50.00
F4237 [PS]	The Night Is So Lonely/Right Now	1959	500.00	1000.	2000.
4313	Wild Cat/Right Here on Earth	1959	12.50	25.00	50.00
4442	Pistol Packin' Mama/Anna Annabella	1960	10.00	20.00	40.00
4525	Mister Loneliness/If You Want My Lovin'	1961	6.25	12.50	25.00
4665	Lucy Star/Baby Don't Believe Him	1961	6.25	12.50	25.00
CHALLENGE					
59337	Bird Doggin'/Ain't That Too Much	1966	5.00	10.00	20.00
59347	Lonely Street/I've Got My Eyes on You	1966	5.00	10.00	20.00
59365	Born to Be a Rolling Stone/Pickin' Poppies	1967	5.00	10.00	20.00
FOREVER					
6001	Story of the Rockers/Pickin' Poppies	1969	12.50	25.00	50.00
KAMA SUTRA					
514	Sunshine/Geese	1970	3.00	6.00	12.00
518	High On Life/The Day the World Turned Blue	1971	3.00	6.00	12.00
PLAYGROUND					
100	Story of the Rockers/Pickin' Poppies	1968	50.00	100.00	200.00

7-Inch Extended Plays

Number	Title (A Side/B Side)	Yr	VG	VG+	NM
CAPITOL					
EAP 1-764	Bluejean Bop/Jezebel//Jumps, Giggles and Shouts/Ain't She Sweet	1957	37.50	75.00	150.00
EAP 1-764 [PS]	Bluejean Bop! Part 1	1957	37.50	75.00	150.00
EAP 2-764	*Who Slapped John/Wedding Bells/Up a Lazy River/Bop Street	1957	37.50	75.00	150.00
EAP 2-764 [PS]	Bluejean Bop! Part 2	1957	37.50	75.00	150.00
EAP 3-764	*Jump Back, Honey, Jump Back/Waltz of the Wind/I Flipped/Peg o' My Heart	1957	37.50	75.00	150.00
EAP 3-764 [PS]	Bluejean Bop! Part 3	1957	37.50	75.00	150.00
EAP 1-811	*Red Bluejeans and a Ponytail/You Told a Fib/Hold Me, Hug Me, Rock Me/Unchained Melody	1957	37.50	75.00	150.00
EAP 1-811 [PS]	Gene Vincent and the Blue Caps, Part 1	1957	37.50	75.00	150.00
EAP 2-811	*Cruisin'/You Better Believe/Double Talkin' Baby/Blues Stay Away from Me	1957	37.50	75.00	150.00
EAP 2-811 [PS]	Gene Vincent and the Blue Caps, Part 2	1957	37.50	75.00	150.00
EAP 3-811	*Pink Thunderbird/Pretty, Pretty Baby/Cat Man/I Sure Miss You	1957	37.50	75.00	150.00
EAP 3-811 [PS]	Gene Vincent and the Blue Caps, Part 3	1957	37.50	75.00	150.00
EAP 1-970	*Frankie and Johnnie/In My Dreams/You'll Never Walk Alone/Brand New Beat	1958	37.50	75.00	150.00
EAP 1-970 [PS]	Gene Vincent Rocks! And the Blue Caps Roll, Part 1	1958	37.50	75.00	150.00
EAP 2-970	*By the Light of the Silvery Moon/Flea Brain/Rollin' Danny/Your Cheatin' Heart	1958	37.50	75.00	150.00
EAP 2-970 [PS]	Gene Vincent Rocks! And the Blue Caps Roll, Part 2	1958	37.50	75.00	150.00
EAP 3-970	*You Belong to Me/Time Will Bring You Everything/Should I Ever Love Again/It's No Lie	1958	37.50	75.00	150.00
EAP 3-970 [PS]	Gene Vincent Rocks! And the Blue Caps Roll, Part 3	1958	37.50	75.00	150.00
EAP 1-985	Lovely Loretta/Dance to the Bop//Dance in the Street/Baby Blue	1958	50.00	100.00	200.00
EAP 1-985 [PS]	Hot Rod Gang	1958	50.00	100.00	200.00
EAP 1-1059	*Five Feet of Lovin'/The Wayward Wind/Somebody Help Me/Keep It a Secret	1958	37.50	75.00	150.00
EAP 1-1059 [PS]	A Gene Vincent Record Date, Part 1	1958	37.50	75.00	150.00
EAP 2-1059	Git It/Teenage Partner//Hey, Good Lookin'/I Can't Help It	1958	37.50	75.00	150.00
EAP 2-1059 [PS]	A Gene Vincent Record Date, Part 2	1958	37.50	75.00	150.00
EAP 3-1059	*Look What You Gone and Done to Me/Peace of Mind/Summertime/I Love You	1958	37.50	75.00	150.00
EAP 3-1059 [PS]	A Gene Vincent Record Date, Part 3	1958	37.50	75.00	150.00
NORTON					
EP-076	My Love (In Love Again)/Lonesome Boy//The Night Is So Lonely/In My Dreams	1999	—	—	2.00
EP-076 [PS]	Blue Gene	1999	—	—	2.00

Albums

Number	Title (A Side/B Side)	Yr	VG	VG+	NM
CAPITOL					
DKAO-380 [R]	Gene Vincent's Greatest	1969	12.50	25.00	50.00
SM-380 [R]	Gene Vincent's Greatest	197?	3.75	7.50	15.00
—Abridged reissue of DKAO-380					
T 764 [M]	Bluejean Bop!	1957	250.00	500.00	1000.
—Yellow label promo					
T 764 [M]	Bluejean Bop!	1957	250.00	500.00	1000.
—Black label promo					
T 764 [M]	Bluejean Bop!	1957	100.00	200.00	400.00
—Turquoise label stock copy					
T 811 [M]	Gene Vincent and the Blue Caps	1957	250.00	500.00	1000.
—Yellow label promo					
T 811 [M]	Gene Vincent and the Blue Caps	1957	250.00	500.00	1000.
—Black label promo					
T 811 [M]	Gene Vincent and the Blue Caps	1957	100.00	200.00	400.00
—Turquoise label stock copy					
T 970 [M]	Gene Vincent Rocks! And the Blue Caps Roll	1958	250.00	500.00	1000.
—Yellow label promo					
T 970 [M]	Gene Vincent Rocks! And the Blue Caps Roll	1958	250.00	500.00	1000.
—Black label promo					
T 970 [M]	Gene Vincent Rocks! And the Blue Caps Roll	1958	100.00	200.00	400.00
—Turquoise label stock copy					
T 1059 [M]	A Gene Vincent Record Date	1958	250.00	500.00	1000.
—Yellow label promo					
T 1059 [M]	A Gene Vincent Record Date	1958	250.00	500.00	1000.
—Black label promo					
T 1059 [M]	A Gene Vincent Record Date	1958	100.00	200.00	400.00
—Turquoise label stock copy					
T 1207 [M]	Sounds Like Gene Vincent	1959	75.00	150.00	300.00
—Black label with colorband, Capitol logo at left					
ST 1342 [S]	Crazy Times	1960	125.00	250.00	500.00
—Black label with colorband, Capitol logo at left					
T 1342 [M]	Crazy Times	1960	75.00	150.00	300.00
—Black label with colorband, Capitol logo at left					
SM-11287	The Bop That Just Won't Stop	1974	3.75	7.50	15.00
N-16208	Gene Vincent's Greatest	198?	3.00	6.00	12.00
—Budget-line reissue					
N-16209	The Bop That Just Won't Stop	198?	3.00	6.00	12.00
—Budget-line reissue					
DANDELION					
9-102	I'm Back and I'm Proud	1970	12.50	25.00	50.00
INTERMEDIA					
QS-5074	Rockabilly Fever	198?	3.00	6.00	12.00
KAMA SUTRA					
KSBS 2019	Gene Vincent	1970	12.50	25.00	50.00
KSBS 2027	The Day the World Turned Blue	1971	12.50	25.00	50.00
ROLLIN' ROCK					
022	Forever	1981	3.75	7.50	15.00

VINCENT & PESCI

The "Pesci" is future movie star Joe Pesci.

45s

Number	Title (A Side/B Side)	Yr	VG	VG+	NM
MAINSTREAM					
5531	Can You Fix The Way I Talk For Christmas?/Little People Blues	1972	2.50	5.00	10.00

VINSON, EDDIE "CLEANHEAD"

45s

Number	Title (A Side/B Side)	Yr	VG	VG+	NM
BETHLEHEM					
11097	Cherry Red/Kidney Stew	1961	5.00	10.00	20.00
BLUESWAY					
61005	Cadillac Blues/Old Maid Got Married	1967	3.00	6.00	12.00
KING					
4563	Good Bread Alley/I Need You Tonight	1952	15.00	30.00	60.00
4582	Lonesome Train/Person to Person	1952	15.00	30.00	60.00
6305	Person to Person/Cherry Red Blues	1970	—	3.00	6.00
MERCURY					
70334	Old Man Boogie/You Can't Have My Love No More	1954	50.00	100.00	200.00
70525	Anxious Heart/Suffer Fool	1954	30.00	60.00	120.00
70621	Tomorrow May Never Come/Big Chief Rain in the Face	1955	25.00	50.00	100.00
RIVERSIDE					
4512	Back Door Blues/Hold It	1962	5.00	10.00	20.00

Albums

Number	Title (A Side/B Side)	Yr	VG	VG+	NM
AAMCO					
312 [M]	Cleanhead's Back in Town	196?	10.00	20.00	40.00
BETHLEHEM					
BCP-5005 [M]	Eddie "Cleanhead" Vinson Sings	1957	25.00	50.00	100.00
6036	Back in Town	1978	3.75	7.50	15.00
BLUESWAY					
BL-6007 [M]	Cherry Red	1967	6.25	12.50	25.00
BLS-6007 [S]	Cherry Red	1967	6.25	12.50	25.00
CIRCLE					
CLP-57	Kidney Stew	1983	3.00	6.00	12.00
DELMARK					
631	Old Kidney Stew Is Fine	1980	3.00	6.00	12.00
FLYING DUTCHMAN					
31-1012	You Can't Make Love Alone	197?	3.75	7.50	15.00
KING					
KS-1087	Cherry Red	1969	6.25	12.50	25.00
MUSE					
MR-5116	The Clean Machine	1978	3.75	7.50	15.00
MR-5208	Eddie "Cleanhead" Vinson and the Muse All-Stars: Live at Sandy's	1979	3.00	6.00	12.00

Number	Title (A Side/B Side)	Yr	VG	VG+	NM
MR-5243	Eddie "Cleanhead" Vinson and the Muse All-Stars: Hold It Right There	198?	3.00	6.00	12.00
MR-5282	Cleanhead and Roomful of Blues	1982	3.00	6.00	12.00
MR-5310	Eddie "Cleanhead" Vinson Sings the Blues	198?	3.00	6.00	12.00
PABLO					
2310866	I Want a Little Girl	198?	3.00	6.00	12.00
REGGIES					
1000	Rollin' Over the Devil	1981	3.00	6.00	12.00
RIVERSIDE					
RLP-502 [M]	Back Door Blues	1965	10.00	20.00	40.00
RLS-9502 [S]	Back Door Blues	1965	10.00	20.00	40.00

VINSON, EDDIE "CLEANHEAD"/JIMMY WITHERSPOON

Also see each artist's individual listings.

Albums

Number	Title (A Side/B Side)	Yr	VG	VG+	NM
KING					
634 [M]	Battle of the Blues, Volume 3	1960	375.00	750.00	1500.

VINTON, BOBBY

45s

Number	Title (A Side/B Side)	Yr	VG	VG+	NM
ABC					
12022	My Melody of Love/I'll Be Loving You	1974	—	2.50	5.00
—Black label					
12022	My Melody of Love/I'll Be Loving You	1974	—	2.00	4.00
—Multi-colored label					
12056	Beer Barrel Polka/Dick and Jane	1974	—	2.00	4.00
12100	Wooden Heart/Polka Pose	1975	—	2.00	4.00
12131	My Gypsy Love/Midnight Show	1975	—	2.00	4.00
12178	Moonight Serenade/Why Can't I Get Over You	1976	—	2.00	4.00
12186	Save Your Kisses for Me/Love Shine	1976	—	2.00	4.00
12229	Love Is the Reason/Nobody But Me	1976	—	2.00	4.00
12265	Only Love Can Break a Heart/Once More with Feeling	1977	—	2.00	4.00
12293	Hold Me, Thrill Me, Kiss Me/Her Name Is Love	1977	—	2.00	4.00
12308	All My Todays/Strike Up the Band for Love	1977	—	2.00	4.00
ALPINE					
50	First Impression/You'll Never Forget	1959	7.50	15.00	30.00
59	The Sheik/A Freshman and a Sophomore	1960	6.25	12.50	25.00
BOBBY VINTON					
100	Santa Must Be Polish/Santa Claus Is Coming to Town	1987	—	—	3.00
100 [PS]	Santa Must Be Polish/Santa Claus Is Coming to Town	1987	—	—	3.00
CURB					
10512	The Last Rose/Sealed with a Kiss	1988	—	—	3.00
10541	Please Tell Her That I Said Hello/Getting Used to Being Loved Again	1989	—	—	3.00
10560	It's Been One of Those Days/(Now and Then There's) A Fool Such As I	1989	—	—	3.00
DIAMOND					
121	I Love You the Way You Are/You're My Girl	1962	5.00	10.00	20.00
—B-side by Chuck and Johnny					
ELEKTRA					
45503	My First, My Only Love/Summerlove Sensation	1978	—	2.00	4.00
EPIC					
06537	Blue Velvet/Blue on Blue	1986	—	2.50	5.00
9417	Posin'/Tornado	1960	3.75	7.50	15.00
9440	Corrina, Corrina/Little Lonely One	1961	3.75	7.50	15.00
9469	Hip-Swinging, High-Stepping, Drum Majorette/Will I Ask Ya	1961	3.75	7.50	15.00
9509	Roses Are Red (My Love)/You and I	1962	3.00	6.00	12.00
9509 [PS]	Roses Are Red (My Love)/You and I	1962	3.75	7.50	15.00
—Bobby Vinton looks straight ahead, chin in hand					
9509 [PS]	Roses Are Red (My Love)/You and I	1962	3.75	7.50	15.00
—Bobby Vinton looks toward the lower right corner					
9532	Rain, Rain Go Away/Over and Over	1962	3.00	6.00	12.00
9532 [PS]	Rain, Rain Go Away/Over and Over	1962	3.75	7.50	15.00
9550	Excerpts from "Roses Are Red"	1962	3.00	6.00	12.00
9551	Excerpts from "Roses Are Red"	1962	3.00	6.00	12.00
9552	Excerpts from "Roses Are Red"	1962	3.00	6.00	12.00
9553	Excerpts from "Roses Are Red"	1962	3.00	6.00	12.00
9554	Excerpts from "Roses Are Red"	1962	3.00	6.00	12.00
9561	Trouble Is My Middle Name/Let's Kiss and Make Up	1962	2.50	5.00	10.00
9561 [PS]	Trouble Is My Middle Name/Let's Kiss and Make Up	1962	3.75	7.50	15.00
9577	Over the Mountain (Across the Sea)/Faded Pictures	1963	2.50	5.00	10.00
9577 [PS]	Over the Mountain (Across the Sea)/Faded Pictures	1963	3.75	7.50	15.00
9593	Blue on Blue/Those Little Things	1963	3.00	6.00	12.00
9593 [PS]	Blue on Blue/Those Little Things	1963	3.75	7.50	15.00
9614	Blue Velvet/Is There a Place (Where I Can Go)	1963	3.00	6.00	12.00
9614 [PS]	Blue Velvet/Is There a Place (Where I Can Go)	1963	3.75	7.50	15.00
9638	There! I've Said It Again/The Girl with the Bow in Her Hair	1963	3.00	6.00	12.00
9638 [PS]	There! I've Said It Again/The Girl with the Bow in Her Hair	1963	3.75	7.50	15.00
9662	My Heart Belongs to Only You/Warm and Tender	1964	2.50	5.00	10.00
9662 [PS]	My Heart Belongs to Only You/Warm and Tender	1964	3.75	7.50	15.00
9687	Tell Me Why/Remembering	1964	2.00	4.00	8.00
9687 [PS]	Tell Me Why/Remembering	1964	3.75	7.50	15.00
9705	Clinging Vine/Imagination Is a Magic Dream	1964	2.00	4.00	8.00
9705 [PS]	Clinging Vine/Imagination Is a Magic Dream	1964	3.00	6.00	12.00
9730	Mr. Lonely/It's Better to Have Loved	1964	2.50	5.00	10.00
9730 [PS]	Mr. Lonely/It's Better to Have Loved	1964	3.00	6.00	12.00
9741	The Bell That Couldn't Jingle/Dearest Santa	1964	2.50	5.00	10.00
9768	Long Lonely Nights/Satin	1965	2.00	4.00	8.00
9768 [PS]	Long Lonely Nights/Satin	1965	3.00	6.00	12.00
9791	L-O-N-E-L-Y/Graduation Tears	1965	2.00	4.00	8.00
9791 [PS]	L-O-N-E-L-Y/Graduation Tears	1965	3.00	6.00	12.00
9814	Theme from "Harlow" (Lonely Girl)/If I Should Lose Your Love	1965	2.00	4.00	8.00
9814 [PS]	Theme from "Harlow" (Lonely Girl)/If I Should Lose Your Love	1965	3.00	6.00	12.00
9846	What Color (Is a Man)/Love or Infatuation	1965	2.00	4.00	8.00
9869	Satin Pillows/Careless	1965	2.00	4.00	8.00
9869 [PS]	Satin Pillows/Careless	1965	3.00	6.00	12.00
9894	Tears/Go Away Pain	1966	—	3.00	6.00
10014	Dum-De-Da/Blue Clarinet	1966	—	3.00	6.00
10014 [PS]	Dum-De-Da/Blue Clarinet	1966	2.50	5.00	10.00
10048	Petticoat White (Summer Sky Blue)/All the King's Horses	1966	—	3.00	6.00
10048 [PS]	Petticoat White (Summer Sky Blue)/All the King's Horses	1966	2.50	5.00	10.00
10090	Coming Home Soldier/Don't Let My Mary Go Around	1966	—	3.00	6.00
10090 [PS]	Coming Home Soldier/Don't Let My Mary Go Around	1966	2.50	5.00	10.00
10136	For He's a Jolly Good Fellow/Sweet Maria	1967	—	3.00	6.00
10136 [PS]	For He's a Jolly Good Fellow/Sweet Maria	1967	2.50	5.00	10.00
10168	Red Roses for Mom/College Town	1967	—	3.00	6.00
10228	Please Love Me Forever/Miss America	1967	2.00	4.00	8.00
10228 [PS]	Please Love Me Forever/Miss America	1967	2.50	5.00	10.00
10266	Just As Much As Ever/Another Memory	1967	—	3.00	6.00
10266 [PS]	Just As Much As Ever/Another Memory	1967	2.50	5.00	10.00
10305	Take Good Care of My Baby/Strange Sensations	1968	—	3.00	6.00
10305 [PS]	Take Good Care of My Baby/Strange Sensations	1968	2.50	5.00	10.00
10350	Halfway to Paradise/(My Little) Christie	1968	—	3.00	6.00
10350	Halfway to Paradise/(My Little) Kristie	1968	2.50	5.00	10.00
—Note variation in B-side spelling					
10350 [PS]	Halfway to Paradise/(My Little) Christie	1968	2.50	5.00	10.00
10397	I Love How You Love Me/Little Barefoot Boy	1968	—	3.00	6.00
10397 [PS]	I Love How You Love Me/Little Barefoot Boy	1968	2.50	5.00	10.00
10461	To Know You Is to Love You/The Beat of My Heart	1969	—	2.50	5.00
10461 [PS]	To Know You Is to Love You/The Beat of My Heart	1969	2.50	5.00	10.00
10485	The Days of Sand and Shovels/So Many Lonely Girls	1969	—	2.50	5.00
10485 [PS]	The Days of Sand and Shovels/So Many Lonely Girls	1969	2.50	5.00	10.00
10554	Where Is Love/For All We Know	1969	—	2.50	5.00
10576	My Elusive Dreams/Over and Over	1970	—	2.50	5.00
10576 [PS]	My Elusive Dreams/Over and Over	1970	2.50	5.00	10.00
10629	No Arms Can Ever Hold You/I've Got That Lovin' Feelin'	1970	—	2.50	5.00
10629 [PS]	No Arms Can Ever Hold You/I've Got That Lovin' Feelin'	1970	2.00	4.00	8.00
10651	Why Don't They Understand/Where Is Love	1970	—	2.50	5.00
10651 [PS]	Why Don't They Understand/Where Is Love	1970	2.00	4.00	8.00
10689	Christmas Eve in My Home Town/The Christmas Angel	1970	—	3.00	6.00
10711	She Loves Me/I'll Make You My Baby	1971	—	2.50	5.00
10736	And I Love You So/She Loves Me	1971	—	2.50	5.00
10790	A Little Bit of You/God Bless America	1971	—	2.50	5.00
10822	Every Day of My Life/You Can Do It to Me Anytime	1972	—	2.50	5.00
10822 [PS]	Every Day of My Life/You Can Do It to Me Anytime	1972	2.00	4.00	8.00
10861	Sealed with a Kiss/All My Life	1972	—	2.50	5.00
10861 [PS]	Sealed with a Kiss/All My Life	1972	2.00	4.00	8.00
10936	But I Do/When You Love	1972	—	2.50	5.00
10936 [PS]	But I Do/When You Love	1972	2.00	4.00	8.00
10980	I Love You the Way You Are/Hurt	1973	—	2.50	5.00
11038	Where Are the Children/I Can't Believe That It's All Over	1973	—	2.50	5.00
50080	Clinging Vine/I Can't Believe That It's All Over	1975	—	2.50	5.00
50169	Christmas Eve in My Home Town/The Christmas Angel	1975	—	2.50	5.00
LARC					
81019	You Are Love/Ghost of Another Man	1983	—	2.00	4.00
MELODY					
5001/2	Always in My Heart/Harlem Nocturne	1960	6.25	12.50	25.00
TAPESTRY					
001	Disco Polka (Pennsylvania Polka)/I Could Have Danced All Night	1979	—	2.00	4.00
002	Make Believe It's Your First Time/I Remember Loving You	1979	—	2.00	4.00
003	He/My First and Only Love	1980	—	2.00	4.00
005	It Was Nice to Know You John/Ain't That Lovin' You	1981	—	2.50	5.00
006	Let Me Love You, Goodbye/You Are Love	1981	—	2.00	4.00
007	Forever and Ever/(B-side unknown)	1982	—	2.00	4.00
008	She WIll Survive (Poland)/Love Is the Reason	1982	—	2.00	4.00
008 [PS]	She WIll Survive (Poland)/Love Is the Reason	1982	—	2.50	5.00
010	It Hurts to Be in Love/Love Makes Everything Better	1985	—	2.00	4.00
013	What Did You Do with Your Old 45s/(B-side unknown)	1986	—	2.00	4.00
1986	Sweet Lady of Liberty (same on both sides)	1986	—	2.00	4.00
4009	Bed of Roses/I Know a Goodbye	1984	—	2.00	4.00

7-Inch Extended Plays

Number	Title (A Side/B Side)	Yr	VG	VG+	NM
ABC					
LLP-271 [DJ]	The Most Beautiful Girl/My Melody of Love/Never Ending Song of Love//You'll Never Know/Am I Losing You/Here in My Heart	1974	2.50	5.00	10.00
—33 1/3 rpm, small hole jukebox issue					
LLP-271 [PS]	Melodies of Love	1974	2.50	5.00	10.00
EPIC					
EG 7215	Silver Bells/White Christmas//O Holy Night/The Christmas Song	1963	2.50	5.00	10.00
EG 7215 [PS]	Songs of Christmas	1963	2.50	5.00	10.00
7-26437 [DJ]	Why Don't You Believe Me/Together/Save the Last Dance for Me//If I Didn't Care/Shangri-La/It's No Sin	1968	2.50	5.00	10.00
—33 1/3 rpm, small hole jukebox issue					
7-26437 [PS]	I Love How You Love Me	1968	2.50	5.00	10.00
7-31642 [DJ]	Our Day Will Come/Song Sung Blue/Come Softly to Me//Some Kind of Wonderful/Somebody's Breaking My Heart/I'm Leaving It Up to You	1972	2.50	5.00	10.00
—33 1/3 rpm, small hole jukebox issue					

Number	Title (A Side/B Side)	Yr	VG	VG+	NM
7-31642 [PS]	Sealed with a Kiss	1972	2.50	5.00	10.00
Albums					
ABC					
X-851	Melodies of Love	1974	2.50	5.00	10.00
D-891	Heart of Hearts	1975	2.50	5.00	10.00
D-924	The Bobby Vinton Show	1975	2.50	5.00	10.00
D-957	Serenades of Love	1976	2.50	5.00	10.00
AB-981	The Name Is Love	1977	2.50	5.00	10.00
COLUMBIA LIMITED EDITION					
LE 10140	Blue Velvet	197?	2.50	5.00	10.00
—Reissue of Epic 26068					
EPIC					
BN 579 [S]	Dancing at the Hop	1961	12.50	25.00	50.00
BN 597 [S]	Young Man with a Big Band	1961	12.50	25.00	50.00
LN 3727 [M]	Dancing at the Hop	1961	7.50	15.00	30.00
LN 3780 [M]	Young Man with a Big Band	1961	7.50	15.00	30.00
LN 24020 [M]	Roses Are Red	1962	3.75	7.50	15.00
LN 24035 [M]	Bobby Vinton Sings the Big Ones	1962	3.75	7.50	15.00
LN 24049 [M]	The Greatest Hits of the Greatest Groups	1963	3.75	7.50	15.00
LN 24068 [M]	Blue On Blue	1963	37.50	75.00	150.00
—Promo only on blue vinyl					
LN 24068 [M]	Blue On Blue	1963	6.25	12.50	25.00
—Stock copy on black vinyl					
LN 24068 [M]	Blue Velvet	1963	3.75	7.50	15.00
—Retitled version of "Blue On Blue"					
LN 24081 [M]	There! I've Said It Again	1964	3.75	7.50	15.00
LN 24098 [M]	Bobby Vinton's Greatest Hits	1964	3.00	6.00	12.00
—Despite lower number, this came out after "Tell Me Why"					
LN 24113 [M]	Tell Me Why	1964	3.00	6.00	12.00
LN 24122 [M]	A Very Merry Christmas	1964	3.00	6.00	12.00
LN 24136 [M]	Mr. Lonely	1965	3.00	6.00	12.00
LN 24154 [M]	Bobby Vinton Sings for Lonely Nights	1965	3.00	6.00	12.00
LN 24170 [M]	Drive-In Movie Time	1965	3.00	6.00	12.00
LN 24182 [M]	Satin Pillows and Careless	1966	3.00	6.00	12.00
LN 24187 [M]	More of Bobby Vinton's Greatest Hits	1966	3.00	6.00	12.00
LN 24188 [M]	Country Boy	1966	3.00	6.00	12.00
LN 24203 [M]	Live at the Copa	1967	3.00	6.00	12.00
LN 24245 [M]	Bobby Vinton's Newest Hits	1967	3.00	6.00	12.00
LN 24341 [M]	Please Love Me Forever	1967	3.75	7.50	15.00
BN 26020 [S]	Roses Are Red	1962	5.00	10.00	20.00
BN 26035 [S]	Bobby Vinton Sings the Big Ones	1962	5.00	10.00	20.00
BN 26049 [S]	The Greatest Hits of the Greatest Groups	1963	5.00	10.00	20.00
BN 26068 [S]	Blue On Blue	1963	7.50	15.00	30.00
BN 26068 [S]	Blue Velvet	1963	5.00	10.00	20.00
—Retitled version of "Blue On Blue"					
BN 26081 [S]	There! I've Said It Again	1964	5.00	10.00	20.00
BN 26098 [S]	Bobby Vinton's Greatest Hits	1964	3.75	7.50	15.00
—Despite lower number, this came out after "Tell Me Why"					
PE 26098	Bobby Vinton's Greatest Hits	198?	2.00	4.00	8.00
—Budget-line reissue					
BN 26113 [S]	Tell Me Why	1964	3.75	7.50	15.00
BN 26122 [S]	A Very Merry Christmas	1964	3.75	7.50	15.00
—Same as above, but in stereo					
BN 26136 [S]	Mr. Lonely	1965	3.75	7.50	15.00
BN 26154 [S]	Bobby Vinton Sings for Lonely Nights	1965	3.75	7.50	15.00
BN 26170 [S]	Drive-In Movie Time	1965	3.75	7.50	15.00
BN 26182 [S]	Satin Pillows and Careless	1966	3.75	7.50	15.00
BN 26187 [S]	More of Bobby Vinton's Greatest Hits	1966	3.75	7.50	15.00
BN 26188 [S]	Country Boy	1966	3.75	7.50	15.00
BN 26203 [S]	Live at the Copa	1967	3.75	7.50	15.00
BN 26245 [S]	Bobby Vinton's Newest Hits	1967	3.75	7.50	15.00
BN 26341 [S]	Please Love Me Forever	1967	3.75	7.50	15.00
BN 26382	Take Good Care of My Baby	1968	3.75	7.50	15.00
BN 26437	I Love How You Love Me	1968	3.75	7.50	15.00
BN 26471	Vinton	1969	3.75	7.50	15.00
BN 26510	Bobby Vinton's Greatest Hits of Love	1970	3.75	7.50	15.00
BN 26540	My Elusive Dreams	1970	3.75	7.50	15.00
KE 31286	Ev'ry Day of My Life	1972	3.00	6.00	12.00
KEG 31487 [(2)]	Bobby Vinton's All-Time Greatest Hits	1972	3.75	7.50	15.00
PEG 31487 [(2)]	Bobby Vinton's All-Time Greatest Hits	197?	3.00	6.00	12.00
—Reissue					
KE 31642	Sealed with a Kiss	1972	3.00	6.00	12.00
PE 32921	With Love	1974	2.50	5.00	10.00
KEG 33468 [(2)]	Bobby Vinton Sings the Golden Decade of Love	1975	3.00	6.00	12.00
KEG 33767 [(2)]	Greatest Hits/Greatest Hits of Love	1976	3.00	6.00	12.00
JE 35605	Autumn Memories	1979	2.50	5.00	10.00
JE 35998	Spring Sensations	1979	2.50	5.00	10.00
JE 35999	Summer Serenade	1979	2.50	5.00	10.00
HARMONY					
KH 11402	Vinton Sings Vinton	197?	2.50	5.00	10.00
PICKWICK					
SPC-3353	Melodies of Love	197?	2.00	4.00	8.00
TAPESTRY					
TRS-1001 [EP]	Santa Must Be Polish	1987	2.50	5.00	10.00

VIPERS SKIFFLE GROUP, THE

Number	Title (A Side/B Side)	Yr	VG	VG+	NM
45s					
CAPITOL					
F3673	Don't You Rock Me Daddy-O/10,000 Years Ago	1957	5.00	10.00	20.00
F3711	Cumberland Gap/Maggie Mae	1957	3.75	7.50	15.00

VIRGIN INSANITY

Number	Title (A Side/B Side)	Yr	VG	VG+	NM
Albums					
FUNKY					
71411	Illusions of the Maintenance Man	1970	50.00	100.00	200.00

VIRTUES, THE

Includes records by "Frank Virtue" and "Frank Virtuoso."

Number	Title (A Side/B Side)	Yr	VG	VG+	NM
45s					
ABC-PARAMOUNT					
10071	Blues in the Cellar/Vaya Con Dios	1959	3.75	7.50	15.00
ARCADE					
135	Ooh You Gotta/I Make a Mistake	1955	7.50	15.00	30.00
—As "Frank Virtue"					
FAYETTE					
1626	Guitar Boogie Shuffle '65/Moon Maid	1965	3.75	7.50	15.00
HIGHLAND					
2505X	Bye Bye Blues/Strollin' Again	1960	6.25	12.50	25.00
2505	Bye Bye Blues/Happy Guitar	1960	6.25	12.50	25.00
HUNT					
324 [M]	Guitar Boogie Shuffle/Guitar in Orbit	1959	6.25	12.50	25.00
S-324 [S]	Guitar Boogie Shuffle/Guitar in Orbit	1959	12.50	25.00	50.00
327	Flippin' In/Shufflin' Along	1959	5.00	10.00	20.00
328	Pickin' the Stroll/Virtue's Boogie Woogie	1959	5.00	10.00	20.00
329	Pony Walk/Virtue's Boogie Woogie	1959	5.00	10.00	20.00
331	Blues in the Cellar/Vaya Con Dios	1960	5.00	10.00	20.00
LIBERTY					
55706	Dream World/Move On	1964	3.00	6.00	12.00
—As "Frank Virtuoso"					
SURE					
501	Guitar Boogie Shuffle/Guitar in Orbit	1959	20.00	40.00	80.00
1733	Guitar Boogie Shuffle Twist/Guitar Boogie Stomp	1962	3.75	7.50	15.00
1779	Tel-Star Guitar/Jersey Bounce	1962	3.75	7.50	15.00
VIRNON					
603	Guitar Boogie Twist/Guitar Shimmy	1960	3.75	7.50	15.00
VIRTUE					
190	Cotton Candy/Love You	1966	2.50	5.00	10.00
2503	Guitar on the Wild Side/Meditation of the Soul	1970	—	3.00	6.00
WYNNE					
123	Highland Guitar/Pickin' Plankin' Boogie	1960	3.75	7.50	15.00
Albums					
FAYETTE					
1816 [M]	Frank Virtue and the Virtues	1964	15.00	30.00	60.00
—Blue cover					
1816 [M]	Frank Virtue and the Virtues	1964	10.00	20.00	40.00
—White cover					
STRAND					
L-1061 [M]	Guitar Boogie Shuffle	1960	7.50	15.00	30.00
SL-1061 [S]	Guitar Boogie Shuffle	1960	10.00	20.00	40.00
WYNNE					
WLP-111 [M]	Guitar Boogie Shuffle	1960	30.00	60.00	120.00
WLP-711 [S]	Guitar Boogie Shuffle	1960	45.00	90.00	180.00

VISCAYNES, THE

Sylvester Stewart [Sly Stone] was a member.

Number	Title (A Side/B Side)	Yr	VG	VG+	NM
45s					
TROPO					
101	I Guess I'll Be/Stop What You're Doing	1958	37.50	75.00	150.00
VPM					
1006	Yellow Moon/Heavenly Angel	1961	10.00	20.00	40.00

VISCOUNTS, THE (1)

Number	Title (A Side/B Side)	Yr	VG	VG+	NM
45s					
AMY					
940	Harlem Nocturne/Dig	1965	3.00	6.00	12.00
949	Night Train/When the Saints Go Marching In	1966	3.00	6.00	12.00
CORAL					
62490	Come, Come On Back/Off Shore	1966	2.50	5.00	10.00
62520	Moonlight in Vermont/Sweet Georgia Brown	1967	2.50	5.00	10.00
MADISON					
123	Harlem Nocturne/Dig	1959	6.25	12.50	25.00
129	The Touch/Chug-a-Lug	1960	3.75	7.50	15.00
133	Night Train/Summertime	1960	3.75	7.50	15.00
140	Wabash Blues/So Slow	1960	3.75	7.50	15.00
152	Shadrack/This Place	1961	3.75	7.50	15.00
159	Little Brown Jug/Opus One	1961	3.75	7.50	15.00
165	Drag Race/Sophisticated Lady	1961	3.75	7.50	15.00
MR. PEACOCK					
101	When Johnny Comes Marching Home/Mark's Mood	1961	3.00	6.00	12.00
107	The Continental Walk/Hully Gully	1962	3.00	6.00	12.00
112	Night Flight/A Girl Like You	1962	3.00	6.00	12.00
MR. PEEKE					
125	Night for Love/Ballin' the Jack	1963	3.00	6.00	12.00
Albums					
AMY					
8008 [M]	Harlem Nocturne	1965	10.00	20.00	40.00
S-8008 [S]	Harlem Nocturne	1965	12.50	25.00	50.00
MADISON					
1001 [M]	The Viscounts	1960	50.00	100.00	200.00

VISCOUNTS, THE (2)

Number	Title (A Side/B Side)	Yr	VG	VG+	NM
45s					
MERCURY					
71073	My Girl/Raindrop	1957	10.00	20.00	40.00

VISION OF SUNSHINE

Number	Title (A Side/B Side)	Yr	VG	VG+	NM
Albums					
AVCO EMBASSY					
33007	Vision of Sunshine	1970	7.50	15.00	30.00

VISIONS, THE

Several different groups.

Number	Title (A Side/B Side)	Yr	VG	VG+	NM
45s					
BIG TOP					
3092	Tell Me You're Mine/All Through the Night	1961	5.00	10.00	20.00
3119	Secret Worlds of Tears/Swingin' Wedding	1962	5.00	10.00	20.00
BRUNSWICK					
55206	So Close/There'll Be No Next Time	1961	6.25	12.50	25.00
COED					
598	Down in My Heart/Tell Her Now	1964	3.00	6.00	12.00

Number	Title (A Side/B Side)	Yr	VG	VG+	NM
ELGEY					
1003	Teenager's Life/Little Moon	1960	10.00	20.00	40.00
LOST-NITE					
102	Teenager's Life/Little Moon	1961	6.25	12.50	25.00
MERCURY					
72188	Oh Boy What a Girl/Tommy's Girl	1963	3.75	7.50	15.00
ORIGINAL SOUND					
32	Look at Me Now/Cigarette	1963	3.75	7.50	15.00
UNI					
55031	How Can I Be Down/Threshold of Love	1967	3.00	6.00	12.00
55042	Keepin' Your Eyes on the Sun/Small Town Commotion	1967	3.00	6.00	12.00
WARNER BROS.					
5898	Black and White Rainbow/Bulldog Cadillac	1967	2.50	5.00	10.00

VISITORS, THE (1)

45s

Number	Title (A Side/B Side)	Yr	VG	VG+	NM
DAKAR					
603	I'm in Danger/Until You Came Along	1969	2.00	4.00	8.00
613	I'm Gonna Stay/Lonely One, Only Son	1969	2.00	4.00	8.00
TANGERINE					
1003	My Love Is Ready and Waiting/What About Me	1970	2.00	4.00	8.00
1010	Anytime Is the Right Time/Nevertheless	1970	2.00	4.00	8.00

VISITORS, THE (2)

45s

Number	Title (A Side/B Side)	Yr	VG	VG+	NM
TOWER					
268	Theme from The Wild Angels/Is It Them or Me	1966	3.75	7.50	15.00

VISTAS, THE

45s

Number	Title (A Side/B Side)	Yr	VG	VG+	NM
REBEL					
77755	Ghost Wave/Surfer's Minuet	1963	12.50	25.00	50.00
VENPRO					
1000	Ghost Wave/Surfer's Minuet	1963	20.00	40.00	80.00

VISUALS, THE

45s

Number	Title (A Side/B Side)	Yr	VG	VG+	NM
POPLAR					
115	The Submarine Race/Maybe You	1962	10.00	20.00	40.00
117	My Juanita/A Boy, a Girl, and a Dream	1963	12.50	25.00	50.00
121	Please Don't Be Mad at Me/Blue Enough to Cry	1963	75.00	150.00	300.00

VITALE, JOE

45s

Number	Title (A Side/B Side)	Yr	VG	VG+	NM
ASYLUM					
47169	Never Gonna Leave You Alone/Theme from Cabin Weirdos	1981	—	2.00	4.00
47210	The Lady on the Rock (It's America)/Plantation Harbor	1981	—	2.00	4.00
47251	Man Gonna Love You/I'm Flyin'	1981	—	2.00	4.00
ATLANTIC					
3204	Roller Coaster Weekend/Take a Chance on Love	1974	—	2.00	4.00
3260	Two of Us/Shot 'Em Up	1975	—	2.00	4.00

Albums

Number	Title (A Side/B Side)	Yr	VG	VG+	NM
ASYLUM					
5E-529	Plantation Harbor	1981	2.50	5.00	10.00
ATLANTIC					
SD 18114	Rollercoaster Weekend	1975	2.50	5.00	10.00

VITELLS, THE

45s

Number	Title (A Side/B Side)	Yr	VG	VG+	NM
DECCA					
31362	Shirley/The Dip	1962	7.50	15.00	30.00

VITO, SONNY

45s

Number	Title (A Side/B Side)	Yr	VG	VG+	NM
ABC-PARAMOUNT					
9958	Cameo Ring/Teen-Age Blues	1958	3.00	6.00	12.00
STRAND					
25045	An Angel Cries/Mister Groovy	1961	3.00	6.00	12.00

VITO AND THE SALUTATIONS

45s

Number	Title (A Side/B Side)	Yr	VG	VG+	NM
APT					
25079	High Noon/Walkin'	1965	12.50	25.00	50.00
BOOM					
60020	Bring Back Yesterday/I Want You to Be My Baby	1966	5.00	10.00	20.00
CRYSTAL BALL					
105	Unchained Melody/So Much	1978	—	2.50	5.00
HERALD					
583	Unchained Melody/Hey Hey Baby	1963	7.50	15.00	30.00
586	Eenie Meenie/Extraordinary Girl	1964	6.25	12.50	25.00
KRAM					
5002	Your Way/Hey, Hey Baby	1962	12.50	25.00	50.00
RAYNA					
5009	Gloria/Let's Untwist the Twist	1962	12.50	25.00	50.00
RED BOY					
1001	So Wonderful (My Love)/I'd Best Be Going	1966	6.25	12.50	25.00
5009	Gloria/Let's Untwist the Twist	1962	7.50	15.00	30.00
REGINA					
1320	Get a Job/Girls I Know	1964	7.50	15.00	30.00
RUST					
5106	Can I Depend on You/Hello Dolly	1966	5.00	10.00	20.00
SANDBAG					
103	So Wonderful (My Love)/I'd Best Be Going	1966	5.00	10.00	20.00
WELLS					
1008	Can I Depend on You/Liverpool Bound	1964	12.50	25.00	50.00
—Yellow vinyl					
1008	Can I Depend on You/Liverpool Bound	1964	6.25	12.50	25.00
1010	The Banana Boat Song (Day-O)/Don't Count on Me	1964	6.25	12.50	25.00

VOCALEERS, THE

Possibly more than one group.

45s

Number	Title (A Side/B Side)	Yr	VG	VG+	NM
OLD TOWN					
1089	This Is the Night/Love and Devotion	1960	6.25	12.50	25.00
PARADISE					
113	I Need Your Love So Bad/Have You Ever Loved Someone	1959	10.00	20.00	40.00
RED ROBIN					
113	Be True/Oh! Where	1953	150.00	300.00	600.00
114	Is It a Dream/Hurry Home	1953	75.00	150.00	300.00
119	I Walk Alone/How Soon	1953	100.00	200.00	400.00
125	Will You Be True/Love You	1954	75.00	150.00	300.00
132	Angel Face/Lovin' Baby	1954	75.00	150.00	300.00
TWISTIME					
11	Cootie Snap/A Golden Tear	1962	7.50	15.00	30.00
VEST					
832	Hear My Plea/The Night Is Quiet	1960	20.00	40.00	80.00

VOGUES, THE

Also see THE VAL-AIRES.

45s

Number	Title (A Side/B Side)	Yr	VG	VG+	NM
20TH CENTURY					
2041	My Prayer/I've Got to Learn to Live Without You	1973	—	2.50	5.00
2060	Wonderful Summer/Guess Who	1973	—	2.50	5.00
2085	As Time Goes By/Prisoner of Love	1974	—	2.50	5.00
ABC-PARAMOUNT					
10672	Big Man/Golden Locket	1965	5.00	10.00	20.00
ASTRA					
1029	You're the One/Goodnight My Love	1973	—	2.50	5.00
1030	Five O'Clock World/Land of Milk and Honey	1973	—	2.50	5.00
BELL					
991	Love Song/We're On Our Way	1971	—	2.50	5.00
45127	Take Time to Tell Her/I'll Be with You	1971	—	2.50	5.00
45158	An American Family/Gotta Have You Back	1971	—	2.50	5.00
BLUE STAR					
229	You're the One/Some Words	1965	6.25	12.50	25.00
CO & CE					
229	You're the One/Some Words	1965	3.00	6.00	12.00
232	Five O'Clock World/Nothing to Offer You	1965	3.00	6.00	12.00
234	Magic Town/Humpty Dumpty	1966	2.50	5.00	10.00
238	The Land of Milk and Honey/True Lovers	1966	2.50	5.00	10.00
240	Please Mr. Sun/Don't Blame the Rain	1966	2.50	5.00	10.00
242	That's the Tune/Midnight Dreams	1966	2.50	5.00	10.00
244	Take a Chance on My Heart/Summer Afternoon	1967	2.50	5.00	10.00
246	Brighter Days/Lovers of the World Unite	1967	2.50	5.00	10.00
MAINSTREAM					
5524	Need You/(B-side unknown)	1972	—	2.50	5.00
MGM					
13813	Brighter Days/Lovers of the World Unite	1967	2.00	4.00	8.00
REPRISE					
0663	I've Got You on My Mind/Just What I've Been Looking For	1968	2.50	5.00	10.00
0686	Turn Around, Look at Me/Then	1968	2.00	4.00	8.00
0731	Turn Around, Look at Me/My Special Angel	1969	—	2.50	5.00
—"Back to Back Hits" series					
0736	No, Not Much/Earth Angel (Will You Be Mine)	1970	—	2.50	5.00
—"Back to Back Hits" series					
0741	Five O'Clock World/Magic Town	1970	—	3.00	6.00
—"Back to Back Hits" series; "Five O'Clock World" has overdubbed strings					
0766	My Special Angel/I Keep It Hid	1968	2.00	4.00	8.00
0788	Till/I Will	1968	2.00	4.00	8.00
0803	Woman Helping Man/I'll Know My Love	1969	2.00	4.00	8.00
0803	Woman Helping Man/No, Not Much	1969	—	3.00	6.00
0820	Earth Angel (Will You Be Mine)/P.S. I Love You	1969	—	3.00	6.00
0831	Moments to Remember/Once in a While	1969	—	3.00	6.00
0844	Green Fields/Easy to Say	1969	—	3.00	6.00
0856	See That Girl/If We Only Have Love	1969	—	3.00	6.00
0887	God Only Knows/Moody	1970	—	3.00	6.00
0909	Over the Rainbow/Hey, That's No Way to Say Goodbye	1970	—	3.00	6.00
0931	50's Medley/Come Into My Arms	1970	—	3.00	6.00
0969	Since I Don't Have You/I Know You as a Woman	1970	—	3.00	6.00

Albums

Number	Title (A Side/B Side)	Yr	VG	VG+	NM
CO & CE					
LP-1229 [M]	Meet the Vogues	1965	12.50	25.00	50.00
LP-1230 [M]	Five O'Clock World	1966	12.50	25.00	50.00
—Stereo pressings of these two albums are not known to exist!					
PICKWICK					
SPC-3188	Five O'Clock World	1971	2.50	5.00	10.00
SPC-3214	A Lover's Concerto	1971	2.50	5.00	10.00
REPRISE					
RS 6314	Turn Around, Look at Me	1968	3.75	7.50	15.00
—With "W7" and "r:" logos on two-tone orange label					
RS 6326	Till	1969	3.75	7.50	15.00
—With "W7" and "r:" logos on two-tone orange label					
RS 6347	Memories	1969	3.75	7.50	15.00
—With "W7" and "r:" logos on two-tone orange label					
RS 6371	The Vogues' Greatest Hits	1969	3.75	7.50	15.00
—With "W7" and "r:" logos on two-tone orange label					
RS 6395	The Vogues Sing the Good Old Songs	1970	3.00	6.00	12.00
ST-91559	Turn Around, Look at Me	1968	5.00	10.00	20.00
—Capitol Record Club edition					
SW-93040	The Vogues' Greatest Hits	1970	5.00	10.00	20.00
—Capitol Record Club edition					
SSS INTERNATIONAL					
34	The Vogues' Greatest Hits	1977	2.50	5.00	10.00

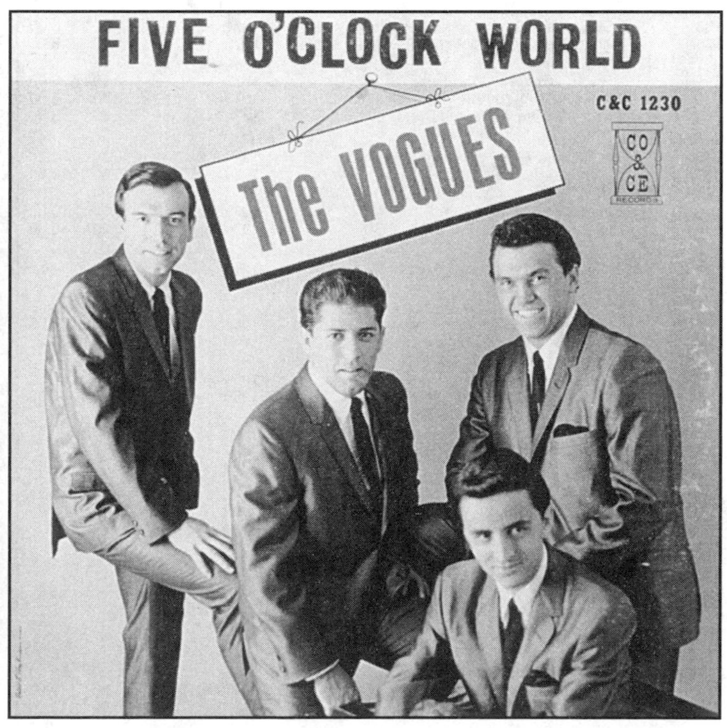

(Top left) One of the more obscure British Invasion acts who actually had an LP released in America was Unit 4+ 2. Their only Top 40 hit was "Concrete and Clay," which served as the basis for this album. (Top right) The only Velvet Underground album to remain in print from the day it was issued through the present was *Loaded*. It also features two of their best-known songs, "Sweet Jane" and "Rock and Roll." (Bottom left) All of Gene Vincent's original albums are scarce and highly collectible. No exception to the rule is this one, *Gene Vincent Rocks! And the Blue Caps Roll.* (Bottom right) The second album by The Vogues was named after their second hit, "Five O'Clock World." Despite prior reports to the contrary, neither this nor its predecessor LP on the Co&Ce label was ever released in stereo.

VOGUES, THE (2)

No relation to the more famous group above.

45s

Number	Title (A Side/B Side)	Yr	VG	VG+	NM
DOT					
15798	Love Is a Funny Little Game/Which Witch Doctor	1958	6.25	12.50	25.00
15859	Try, Baby. Try/Falling Star	1958	6.25	12.50	25.00

VOGUES, THE (U)

Definitely not group (1); could be group (2).

45s

Number	Title (A Side/B Side)	Yr	VG	VG+	NM
CASCADE					
5908	Ev'ry Day, Ev'ry Night/Now I Lay Me Down to Cry	1959	5.00	10.00	20.00

VOICE MASTERS, THE

LAMONT DOZIER and DAVID RUFFIN were originally in this group, though they did not appear on the later sides.

45s

Number	Title (A Side/B Side)	Yr	VG	VG+	NM
ANNA					
101	Hope and Pray/Oop's I'm Sorry	1959	50.00	100.00	200.00
102	Needed/Needed (For Lovers Only)	1959	50.00	100.00	200.00
BAMBOO					
103	You've Hurt Me Baby/If a Woman Catches a Fool	1968	6.25	12.50	25.00
105	Never Gonna Leave You/If a Woman Catches a Fool	1969	3.75	7.50	15.00
113	Dance Right Into My Heart/If a Woman Catches a Fool	1970	3.75	7.50	15.00
FRISCO					
15235	In Love in Vain/Two Lovers	196?	25.00	50.00	100.00

VOICES, THE

45s

Number	Title (A Side/B Side)	Yr	VG	VG+	NM
CASH					
1011	Why/Two Things I Love	1955	15.00	30.00	60.00
1014	Hey Now/My Love Grows Stronger	1955	15.00	30.00	60.00
1015	I Want to Be Ready/Takes Two to Make a Home	1955	15.00	30.00	60.00
1016	Santa Claus Boogie/Santa Claus Baby	1955	20.00	40.00	80.00
1016	Santa Claus Boogie/Santa Claus Baby	197?	—	2.50	5.00
—Reproduction					
SPECIALTY					
754	Santa Claus Boogie/Santa Claus Baby	197?	3.75	7.50	15.00
—Red vinyl					

VOICES OF EAST HARLEM, THE

45s

Number	Title (A Side/B Side)	Yr	VG	VG+	NM
ELEKTRA					
45753	Sit Yourself Down/Oxford Town	1971	—	3.00	6.00
45775	Angry/New York Lightning	1972	—	3.00	6.00
JUST SUNSHINE					
504	Giving Love/New Vibrations	1973	—	2.50	5.00
510	I Like Having You Around/Cashing In	1973	—	2.50	5.00
517	Can You Feel It/Wanted Dead or Alive	1974	—	2.50	5.00

Albums

Number	Title (A Side/B Side)	Yr	VG	VG+	NM
ELEKTRA					
EKS-74080	Right On Be Free	1970	2.50	5.00	10.00
JUST SUNSHINE					
7	Voices of East Harlem	1973	2.50	5.00	10.00
3504	Can You Feel It?	1974	2.50	5.00	10.00

VOIGHT, WES

45s

Number	Title (A Side/B Side)	Yr	VG	VG+	NM
DELUXE					
6176	Midnight Blues/Another Guy's Line	1958	25.00	50.00	100.00
6180	I Want a Lover/Little Joan	1958	10.00	20.00	40.00
KING					
5211 [M]	I'm Loving It/Everything's the Same	1959	15.00	30.00	60.00
S-5211 [S]	I'm Loving It/Everything's the Same	1959	50.00	100.00	200.00
5231 [M]	I'm Ready to Go Steady/The Wind and the Cold Black Night	1959	10.00	20.00	40.00
S-5231 [S]	I'm Ready to Go Steady/The Wind and the Cold Black Night	1959	25.00	50.00	100.00

VOLCANOES, THE

45s

Number	Title (A Side/B Side)	Yr	VG	VG+	NM
EPIC					
9490	Shotgun/Stardust	1962	3.00	6.00	12.00

VOLCANOS, THE

Early version of THE TRAMMPS.

45s

Number	Title (A Side/B Side)	Yr	VG	VG+	NM
ARCTIC					
103	Make Your Move/Baby	1965	3.00	6.00	12.00
106	Storm Warning/Baby	1965	3.00	6.00	12.00
111	Help Wanted/Make Your Move	1965	3.00	6.00	12.00
115	(It's Against the) Laws of Love/(Instrumental)	1965	3.00	6.00	12.00
125	Lady's Man/Help Wanted	1966	2.50	5.00	10.00
128	You're Number 1/Make Your Move	1967	2.50	5.00	10.00

VOLK, VAL, AND THE MATCHED ACES

45s

Number	Title (A Side/B Side)	Yr	VG	VG+	NM
ROCKET					
1050	A Rockin' Party Tonight/Spring Time Rock	195?	50.00	100.00	200.00

VOLUMES, THE

45s

Number	Title (A Side/B Side)	Yr	VG	VG+	NM
AMERICAN ARTS					
6	Gotta Give Her Love/I Can't Live Without You	1964	7.50	15.00	30.00
18	I Just Can't Help Myself/One Way Lover	1965	7.50	15.00	30.00
CHEX					
1002	I Love You/Dreams	1962	75.00	150.00	300.00
—With typographical error crediting "The Valumes"					
1002	I Love You/Dreams	1962	10.00	20.00	40.00
—With no reference to Jay-Gee Records on label					
1002	I Love You/Dreams	1962	6.25	12.50	25.00
—With "Nationally Dist. by Jay-Gee Rec. Co. Inc." on label					
1005	Come Back Into My Heart/The Bell	1962	10.00	20.00	40.00
IMPACT					
1017	That Same Old Feeling/The Trouble I've Seen	1966	12.50	25.00	50.00
INFERNO					
2001	A Way to Love You/You Got It Baby	1967	5.00	10.00	20.00
2004	My Road Is the Right Road/My Kind of Girl	1967	5.00	10.00	20.00
5001	Ain't That Lovin' You/I Love You Baby	1968	5.00	10.00	20.00
JUBILEE					
5446	Sandra/Teenage Paradise	1963	5.00	10.00	20.00
5454	Our Song/Oh My Mother-in-Law	1963	5.00	10.00	20.00
KAREN					
1551	Am I Losing You/Ain't Gonna Give You Up	1970	2.00	4.00	8.00
OLD TOWN					
1154	Why/Monkey Hop	1964	6.25	12.50	25.00

VONNS, THE

45s

Number	Title (A Side/B Side)	Yr	VG	VG+	NM
KING					
5793	Leave Us Alone/So Many Days	1963	5.00	10.00	20.00

VOWS, THE

45s

Number	Title (A Side/B Side)	Yr	VG	VG+	NM
MARKAY					
103	I Wanna Chance/Have You Heard	1962	10.00	20.00	40.00
—Black label					
103	I Wanna Chance/Have You Heard	1962	100.00	200.00	400.00
—Orange label					
RAN-DEE					
112	Girl in Red/Born with the Rhythm	196?	15.00	30.00	60.00
STA-SET					
402	Say You'll Be Mine/When a Boy Loves a Girl	1963	15.00	30.00	60.00
TAMARA					
506	The Things You Do to Me/Dottie	1963	10.00	20.00	40.00
760	Say You'll Be Mine/When a Boy Loves a Girl	1964	6.25	12.50	25.00
V.I.P.					
25016	Buttered Popcorn/Tell Me	1965	10.00	20.00	40.00

VOXPOPPERS, THE

45s

Number	Title (A Side/B Side)	Yr	VG	VG+	NM
AMP 3					
1004	Wishing for Your Love/The Last Drag	1958	10.00	20.00	40.00
MERCURY					
71282	Wishing for Your Love/The Last Drag	1958	5.00	10.00	20.00
71315	Pony Tail/Ping Pong Baby	1958	5.00	10.00	20.00
POPLAR					
107	Come Back Little Girl/A Love to Last a Lifetime	1959	5.00	10.00	20.00
VERSAILLES					
200	Can't Understand It/A Blessing After All	1959	7.50	15.00	30.00
WARWICK					
589	Lonely for You/Helen Isn't Tellin'	1960	3.00	6.00	12.00
—As "Freddie and the Voxpoppers"					

7-Inch Extended Plays

Number	Title (A Side/B Side)	Yr	VG	VG+	NM
MERCURY					
EP 1-3391	Wishing for Your Love/The Last Drag//Stroll Roll/Guitar Stroll	1958	25.00	50.00	100.00
EP 1-3391 [PS]	The Voxpoppers	1958	25.00	50.00	100.00

VY-DELLS, THE

45s

Number	Title (A Side/B Side)	Yr	VG	VG+	NM
GARNET					
101	What I'm Gonna Do/Unknown	196?	25.00	50.00	100.00

W

WADE, ADAM

45s

COED

Number	Title (A Side/B Side)	Yr	VG	VG+	NM
520	Tell Her for Me/Don't Cry, My Love	1959	3.00	6.00	12.00
526	Ruby/Too Far	1960	3.00	6.00	12.00
530	I Can't Help It/I Had the Craziest Dream	1960	3.00	6.00	12.00
536	Speaking of Her/Black Out the Moon	1960	3.00	6.00	12.00
539	For the Want of Your Love/In Pursuit of Happiness	1960	3.00	6.00	12.00
541	Gloria's Theme/Dreamy	1960	3.00	6.00	12.00
541 [PS]	Gloria's Theme/Dreamy	1960	3.75	7.50	15.00
546	Take Good Care of Her/Sleepy Time Gal	1961	2.50	5.00	10.00
550	The Writing on the Wall/Point of No Return	1961	2.50	5.00	10.00
550 [PS]	The Writing on the Wall/Point of No Return	1961	3.75	7.50	15.00
553	As If I Didn't Know/Playin' Around	1961	2.50	5.00	10.00
553 [PS]	As If I Didn't Know/Playin' Around	1961	3.75	7.50	15.00
556	Tonight I Won't Be There/Linda	1961	2.50	5.00	10.00
556 [PS]	Tonight I Won't Be There/Linda	1961	3.75	7.50	15.00
560	Cold Cold Winter/Preview of Paradise	1961	2.50	5.00	10.00
565	How Are Things in Lover's Lane/It's Good to Have You Back with Me	1962	2.50	5.00	10.00
567	Little Miss Lovely/For the First Time in My Life	1962	2.50	5.00	10.00

EPIC

Number	Title (A Side/B Side)	Yr	VG	VG+	NM
9521	I'm Climbin' (The Wall)/They Didn't Believe Me	1962	2.00	4.00	8.00
9557	There'll Be No Teardrops Tonight/Here Comes the Pain	1962	2.00	4.00	8.00
9566	Don't Let Me Cross Over/Rain from the Skies	1963	2.00	4.00	8.00
9590	Teenage Mona Lisa/Why Do We Have to Wait So Long	1963	2.00	4.00	8.00
9609	Let's Make the Most of a Beautiful Thing/Theme from "Irma La Douce" (Look Again)	1963	2.00	4.00	8.00
9639	Charade/Does Goodnight Mean Goodbye	1963	2.00	4.00	8.00
9659	Seven Loves for Seven Days/Whisper Away	1964	2.00	4.00	8.00
9686	Love Song from "Flight to Ashiya"/Pencil and Paper	1964	2.00	4.00	8.00
9752	Crying in the Chapel/Broken Hearted Stranger	1964	2.00	4.00	8.00
9771	It's Been a Long Time Comin'/A Lover's Question	1965	2.00	4.00	8.00
9808	Garden in the Rain/Play Some Music for Broken Hearts	1965	2.00	4.00	8.00
9840	Garden of Eden/Time for Dreams	1965	2.00	4.00	8.00
10024	How Can I Leave You/Solitude	1966	—	3.00	6.00
10112	A Man Alone/Wheels on the Highway	1966	—	3.00	6.00

KIRSHNER

Number	Title (A Side/B Side)	Yr	VG	VG+	NM
4272	Russell Never Had a Chance/Keeping Up with the Joneses	1977	—	2.00	4.00

REMEMBER

Number	Title (A Side/B Side)	Yr	VG	VG+	NM
7791	Half the World/My Time for Love	1969	—	3.00	6.00

WARNER BROS.

Number	Title (A Side/B Side)	Yr	VG	VG+	NM
7068	Julie on My Mind/With an Exception	1967	—	3.00	6.00
7179	Everybody Is Looking for That Someone/Maybe	1968	—	3.00	6.00
7225	Old Devil Woman/Rome	1968	—	3.00	6.00

Albums

COED

Number	Title (A Side/B Side)	Yr	VG	VG+	NM
LPC-902 [M]	And Then Came Adam	1960	12.50	25.00	50.00
LPCS-902 [S]	And Then Came Adam	1960	15.00	30.00	60.00
LPC-903 [M]	Adam and Evening	1961	12.50	25.00	50.00
LPCS-903 [S]	Adam and Evening	1961	15.00	30.00	60.00

EPIC

Number	Title (A Side/B Side)	Yr	VG	VG+	NM
LN 24019 [M]	Adam Wade's Greatest Hits	1962	6.25	12.50	25.00
LN 24026 [M]	One Is a Lonely Number	1962	6.25	12.50	25.00
LN 24044 [M]	What Kind of Fool Am I?	1963	6.25	12.50	25.00
LN 24056 [M]	A Very Good Year for Girls	1963	6.25	12.50	25.00
BN 26019 [S]	Adam Wade's Greatest Hits	1962	7.50	15.00	30.00
BN 26026 [S]	One Is a Lonely Number	1962	7.50	15.00	30.00
BN 26044 [S]	What Kind of Fool Am I?	1963	7.50	15.00	30.00
BN 26056 [S]	A Very Good Year for Girls	1963	7.50	15.00	30.00

KIRSHNER

Number	Title (A Side/B Side)	Yr	VG	VG+	NM
PZ 34919	Adam Wade	1977	3.00	6.00	12.00

WADE, BILLY, AND THE 3 DEGREES

45s

ABC

Number	Title (A Side/B Side)	Yr	VG	VG+	NM
45-10991	Tear It Up (Part 1)/Tear It Up (Part 2)	1967	2.50	5.00	10.00

WADE, DON

45s

SAN

Number	Title (A Side/B Side)	Yr	VG	VG+	NM
206	Gone, Gone, Gone/(B-side unknown)	1958	75.00	150.00	300.00
207	Forever Yours/Oh Love	1958	7.50	15.00	30.00

WADE, RONNY

45s

KING

Number	Title (A Side/B Side)	Yr	VG	VG+	NM
5061	Gotta Make Her Mine/Let Me Cry	1957	20.00	40.00	80.00
5078	I Know But I'll Never Tell/I Never Fall in Love Again	1957	12.50	25.00	50.00
5099	Annie Don't Work/I'll Sail My Ship Alone	1958	12.50	25.00	50.00
5112	All I Want/A King and a Vow	1958	12.50	25.00	50.00

WADE AND DICK

45s

SUN

Number	Title (A Side/B Side)	Yr	VG	VG+	NM
269	Bop Bop Baby/Don't Need Your Lovin' Baby	1957	7.50	15.00	30.00

WADSWORTH MANSION

45s

SUSSEX

Number	Title (A Side/B Side)	Yr	VG	VG+	NM
209	Sweet Mary/What's On Tonight	1970	2.00	4.00	8.00

—First pressings have a much longer version of A-side

Number	Title (A Side/B Side)	Yr	VG	VG+	NM
209	Sweet Mary/What's On Tonight	1970	—	3.00	6.00

—Later pressings have a short version of A-side

Number	Title (A Side/B Side)	Yr	VG	VG+	NM
215	Havin' Such a Good Time/Michigan Harry Slaughter	1971	—	2.50	5.00
221	Nine on the Line/Queenie Dew	1971	—	2.50	5.00

Albums

SUSSEX

Number	Title (A Side/B Side)	Yr	VG	VG+	NM
SXBS-7008	Wadsworth Mansion	1971	5.00	10.00	20.00
SXBS-7008	Wadsworth Manison	1971	6.25	12.50	25.00

—Some copies of this LP have the above typographical error

WAGNER, DANNY, AND KINDRED SOUL

45s

IMPERIAL

Number	Title (A Side/B Side)	Yr	VG	VG+	NM
66305	I Lost a True Love/My Buddy	1968	7.50	15.00	30.00
66327	Harlem Shuffle/When Johnny Comes Marching Home	1968	5.00	10.00	20.00

Albums

IMPERIAL

Number	Title (A Side/B Side)	Yr	VG	VG+	NM
LP-12405	The Kindred Soul of Danny Wagner	1968	7.50	15.00	30.00

WAGNER, DAVID

See CROW.

WAGNER, DICK, AND THE FROSTS

See THE FROST.

WAGONER, PORTER

Also see PORTER WAGONER AND DOLLY PARTON.

45s

RCA

Number	Title (A Side/B Side)	Yr	VG	VG+	NM
PB-10803	When Lea Jane Sang/Storm of Love	1976	—	2.00	4.00
PB-10974	I Haven't Learned a Thing/Hand Me Down My Walking Cane	1977	—	2.00	4.00
PB-11186	Mountain Music/Natural Wonder	1977	—	2.00	4.00
PB-11411	Ole Slew Foot/I'm Gonna Feed 'Em Now	1978	—	2.00	4.00
PB-11491	I Want to Walk You Home/Old Love Letter	1979	—	2.00	4.00
PB-11671	Everything I've Always Wanted/No Bed of Roses	1979	—	2.00	4.00
PB-11771	Hold On Tight/Someone Just Like You	1979	—	2.00	4.00
PB-11998	Is It Only 'Cause You're Lonely/When She Was Mine	1980	—	2.00	4.00

RCA VICTOR

Number	Title (A Side/B Side)	Yr	VG	VG+	NM
APBO-0013	Wake Up, Jacob/Stella, Dear Sweet Stella	1973	—	2.50	5.00
APBO-0187	George Leory Chickashea/Cassie	1973	—	2.50	5.00
APBO-0233	Tore Down/Nothing Between	1974	—	2.50	5.00
APBO-0328	Highway Headin' South/Freda	1974	—	2.50	5.00
PB-10124	Carolina Moonshiner/Not a Cloud in the Sky	1974	—	2.50	5.00
PB-10281	It's My Time (To Say I Love You)/Just for the Lonely Ones	1975	—	3.00	6.00
PB-10411	Indian Creek/Thank You for the Happiness	1975	—	2.50	5.00
47-5086	Takin' Chances/I Can't Live with You	1952	7.50	15.00	30.00
47-5215	That's It/Don't Play That Song	1953	6.25	12.50	25.00
47-5330	Trademark/A Beggar for Your Love	1953	6.25	12.50	25.00
47-5430	Bringing Home the Bacon/An Angel Made for Love	1953	6.25	12.50	25.00
47-5527	Flame of Love/Dig That Crazy Moon	1953	6.25	12.50	25.00
47-5631	Trinidad/Bad News Travels Fast	1954	6.25	12.50	25.00
47-5754	Be Glad You Ain't Me/Love at First Sight	1954	6.25	12.50	25.00
47-5848	Company's Comin'/Tricks of the Trade	1954	6.25	12.50	25.00
47-6105	A Satisfied Mind/Itchin' for My Baby	1955	5.00	10.00	20.00
47-6289	Eat, Drink and Be Merry (Tomorrow You'll Cry)/Let's Squiggle	1955	5.00	10.00	20.00
47-6421	What Would You Do? (If Jesus Came to Your House)/How Can You Refuse Him Now	1956	5.00	10.00	20.00
47-6494	Uncle Pen/How I've Tried	1956	5.00	10.00	20.00
47-6598	Tryin' to Forget the Blues/I've Known You from Somewhere	1956	5.00	10.00	20.00
47-6803	I'm Day Dreamin' Tonight/I Should Be with You	1957	5.00	10.00	20.00
47-6844	Good Mornin', Neighbor/Who Will He Be	1957	5.00	10.00	20.00
47-6964	I Thought I Heard You Call My Name/Pay Day	1957	5.00	10.00	20.00
47-7073	Doll Face/Your Love	1957	5.00	10.00	20.00
47-7279	Haven't You Heard/Tell Her Lies and Feed Her Candy	1958	3.75	7.50	15.00
47-7374	Just Before Dawn/Dear Lonesome	1958	3.75	7.50	15.00
47-7457	Me and Fred and Joe and Bill/Out of Sight, Out of Mind	1959	3.75	7.50	15.00
47-7532	I'm Gonna Sing/I Thought of God	1959	3.75	7.50	15.00
47-7568	The Battle of Little Big Horn/Our Song of Love	1959	3.75	7.50	15.00
47-7638	The Girl Who Didn't Need Love/Your Kind of People	1959	3.75	7.50	15.00
47-7708	Legend of the Big Steeple/Wakin' Up the Crowd	1960	3.75	7.50	15.00
47-7770	Falling Again/An Old Log Cabin for Sale	1960	3.75	7.50	15.00
47-7837	Your Old Love Letters/Heartbreak Affair	1961	3.00	6.00	12.00
47-7901	Everything She Touches Gets the Blues/Sugar Foot Rag	1961	3.00	6.00	12.00
47-7967	Misery Loves Company/I Cried Again	1961	3.00	6.00	12.00
47-8026	Cold Dark Waters/Ain't It Awful	1962	3.00	6.00	12.00
47-8105	I've Enjoyed As Much of This As I Can Stand/One Way Ticket to the Blues	1962	3.00	6.00	12.00
47-8178	My Baby's Not Here (In Town Tonight)/In the Shadows of the Wine	1963	3.00	6.00	12.00
47-8257	Howdy Neighbor Howdy/Find Out	1963	3.00	6.00	12.00
47-8338	Sorrow on the Rocks/The Life of the Party	1964	3.00	6.00	12.00
47-8432	I'll Go Down Swinging/Country Music Has Gone to Town	1964	3.00	6.00	12.00
47-8524	I'm Gonna Feed You Now/The Bride's Bouquet	1965	2.50	5.00	10.00
47-8622	Green, Green Grass of Home/Dooley	1965	2.50	5.00	10.00
47-8723	Skid Row Joe/Love Your Neighbor	1965	2.50	5.00	10.00
47-8800	I Just Came to Smell the Flowers/I'm a Long Way from Home	1966	2.50	5.00	10.00
47-8882	I Dreamed I Saw America on Her Knees/When I Reach That City	1966	2.50	5.00	10.00
47-8977	Old Slew-Foot/Let Me In	1966	2.50	5.00	10.00

Number	Title (A Side/B Side)	Yr	VG	VG+	NM
47-9067	The Cold Hard Facts of Life/You Can't Make a Heel Toe the Mark	1967	2.50	5.00	10.00
47-9243	Julie/Try Being Lonely	1967	2.50	5.00	10.00
47-9379	Woman Hungry/Out of the Silence (Came a Song)	1967	2.50	5.00	10.00
47-9530	Be Proud of Your Man/Wino	1968	2.00	4.00	8.00
47-9651	The Carroll County Accident/Sorrow Overtakes the Wine	1968	2.00	4.00	8.00
47-9802	You Got-Ta Have a License/Fairchild	1970	—	3.00	6.00
47-9811	Little Boy's Prayer/Roses Out of Season	1970	—	3.00	6.00
47-9895	Jim Johnson/One More Dime	1970	—	3.00	6.00
47-9939	The Last One to Touch Me/The Alley	1970	—	3.00	6.00
47-9979	Charley's Picture/As Simple As I Am	1971	—	3.00	6.00
48-1007	Be a Little Quieter/Watching	1971	—	3.00	6.00
74-0168	Big Wind/Tennessee Stud	1969	2.00	4.00	8.00
74-0267	When You're Hot You're Hot/The Answer Is Love	1969	2.00	4.00	8.00
74-0648	What Ain't to Be, Just Might Happen/Little Bird	1972	—	3.00	6.00
74-0753	A World Without Music/Denise Mayree	1972	—	3.00	6.00
74-0820	Katy Did/Darlin' Debra Jean	1972	—	3.00	6.00
74-0923	Lightening the Load/Tomorrow Is Forever	1973	—	3.00	6.00
WARNER BROS.					
29772	This Cowboy's Hat/She Don't Have a License to Drive Me Up the Wall	1983	—	—	3.00
29875	Turn the Pencil Over/Texas Moonbeam Waltz	1982	—	—	3.00
—B-side by Johnny Gimble/Texas Swing Band					

7-Inch Extended Plays

Number	Title (A Side/B Side)	Yr	VG	VG+	NM
RCA VICTOR					
EPA-937	A Satisfied Mind/I Like Girls//Living in the Past/ Midnight	1956	6.25	12.50	25.00
EPA-937 [PS]	Satisfied Mind	1956	6.25	12.50	25.00

Albums

Number	Title (A Side/B Side)	Yr	VG	VG+	NM
ACCORD					
SN-7179	Down Home Country	1982	3.00	6.00	12.00
DOT/MCA					
39053	Porter Wagoner	1986	2.50	5.00	10.00
RCA CAMDEN					
CAL-769 [M]	A Satisfied Mind	1963	3.00	6.00	12.00
CAS-769(e) [R]	A Satisfied Mind	1963	2.50	5.00	10.00
CAL-861 [M]	An Old Log Cabin for Sale	1965	3.00	6.00	12.00
CAS-861 [S]	An Old Log Cabin for Sale	1965	3.00	6.00	12.00
CAL-942 [M]	"Your Old Love Letters" And Other Country Hits	1966	3.00	6.00	12.00
CAS-942 [S]	"Your Old Love Letters" And Other Country Hits	1966	3.00	6.00	12.00
CAL-2116 [M]	I'm Day Dreamin' Tonight	1967	3.00	6.00	12.00
CAS-2116 [S]	I'm Day Dreamin' Tonight	1967	3.00	6.00	12.00
CAL-2191 [M]	Green, Green Grass of Home	1967	3.00	6.00	12.00
CAS-2191 [S]	Green, Green Grass of Home	1967	3.00	6.00	12.00
CAS-2321	Country Feeling	1968	3.00	6.00	12.00
CAS-2409	Howdy Neighbor	1970	3.00	6.00	12.00
CAS-2478	Porter Wagoner Country	1971	3.00	6.00	12.00
CAS-2588	The Silent Kind	1972	3.00	6.00	12.00
CXS-9010 [(2)]	Blue Moon of Kentucky	1971	3.75	7.50	15.00
RCA VICTOR					
APL1-0142	I'll Keep on Lovin' You	1973	3.75	7.50	15.00
APL1-0346	The Farmer	1974	3.75	7.50	15.00
APL1-0496	Tore Down	1974	3.75	7.50	15.00
APL1-0713	Highway Headin' South	1974	3.75	7.50	15.00
APL1-1056	Sing Love	1975	3.75	7.50	15.00
ANL1-1213	The Best of Porter Wagoner	1975	3.00	6.00	12.00
LPM-1358 [M]	A Satisfied Mind	1956	50.00	100.00	200.00
AHL1-2432	Porter	1977	3.00	6.00	12.00
LPM-2447 [M]	A Slice of Life — Songs Happy 'N' Sad	1962	6.25	12.50	25.00
LSP-2447 [S]	A Slice of Life — Songs Happy 'N' Sad	1962	7.50	15.00	30.00
LPM-2650 [M]	The Porter Wagoner Show	1963	6.25	12.50	25.00
LSP-2650 [S]	The Porter Wagoner Show	1963	7.50	15.00	30.00
LPM-2706 [M]	Y'All Come	1963	6.25	12.50	25.00
LSP-2706 [S]	Y'All Come	1963	7.50	15.00	30.00
LPM-2840 [M]	In Person	1964	6.25	12.50	25.00
LSP-2840 [S]	In Person	1964	7.50	15.00	30.00
LPM-2960 [M]	The Bluegrass Story	1964	5.00	10.00	20.00
LSP-2960 [S]	The Bluegrass Story	1964	6.25	12.50	25.00
LPM-3389 [M]	The Thin Man from West Plains	1965	5.00	10.00	20.00
LSP-3389 [S]	The Thin Man from West Plains	1965	6.25	12.50	25.00
LPM-3488 [M]	Grand Old Gospel	1966	5.00	10.00	20.00
LSP-3488 [S]	Grand Old Gospel	1966	6.25	12.50	25.00
LPM-3509 [M]	On the Road	1966	5.00	10.00	20.00
LSP-3509 [S]	On the Road	1966	6.25	12.50	25.00
LPM-3560 [M]	The Best of Porter Wagoner	1966	5.00	10.00	20.00
LSP-3560 [S]	The Best of Porter Wagoner	1966	6.25	12.50	25.00
LPM-3593 [M]	Confessions of a Broken Man	1966	5.00	10.00	20.00
LSP-3593 [S]	Confessions of a Broken Man	1966	6.25	12.50	25.00
LPM-3683 [M]	Soul of a Convict	1967	6.25	12.50	25.00
LSP-3683 [S]	Soul of a Convict	1967	5.00	10.00	20.00
LPM-3797 [M]	The Cold Hard Facts of Life	1967	6.25	12.50	25.00
LSP-3797 [S]	The Cold Hard Facts of Life	1967	5.00	10.00	20.00
LPM-3855 [M]	More Grand Old Gospel	1967	6.25	12.50	25.00
LSP-3855 [S]	More Grand Old Gospel	1967	5.00	10.00	20.00
LPM-3968 [M]	The Bottom of the Bottle	1968	25.00	50.00	100.00
LSP-3968 [S]	The Bottom of the Bottle	1968	5.00	10.00	20.00
LSP-4034	Gospel Country	1968	5.00	10.00	20.00
LSP-4116	The Carroll County Accident	1969	5.00	10.00	20.00
LSP-4181	Me and My Boys	1969	5.00	10.00	20.00
LSP-4286	You Got-ta Have a License	1970	5.00	10.00	20.00
LSP-4321	The Best of Porter Wagoner, Volume 2	1970	5.00	10.00	20.00
LSP-4386	Down in the Alley	1970	5.00	10.00	20.00
LSP-4508	Simple As I Am	1971	5.00	10.00	20.00
LSP-4586	Porter Wagoner Sings His Own	1971	3.75	7.50	15.00
LSP-4661	What Ain't to Be	1972	3.75	7.50	15.00
LSP-4734	Ballads of Love	1972	3.75	7.50	15.00
LSP-4810	The Porter Wagoner Experience	1973	3.75	7.50	15.00
AHL1-7000	Collector's Series	1985	2.50	5.00	10.00
WARNER BROS.					
23783	Viva Porter Wagoner!	1983	2.50	5.00	10.00

WAGONER, PORTER, AND SKEETER DAVIS

Also see each artist's individual listings.

Albums

Number	Title (A Side/B Side)	Yr	VG	VG+	NM
RCA VICTOR					
LPM-2529 [M]	Porter Wagoner and Skeeter Davis Sing Duets	1962	6.25	12.50	25.00
LSP-2529 [S]	Porter Wagoner and Skeeter Davis Sing Duets	1962	7.50	15.00	30.00

WAGONER, PORTER, AND DOLLY PARTON

Also see each artist's individual listings.

45s

Number	Title (A Side/B Side)	Yr	VG	VG+	NM
RCA					
PB-11983	Making Plans/Beneath the Sweet Magnolia Trees	1980	—	2.00	4.00
PB-12119	If You Go, I'll Follow You/Hide Me Away	1980	—	2.00	4.00
RCA VICTOR					
PB-10010	Please Don't Stop Loving Me/Sounds of Nature	1974	—	2.00	4.00
PB-10328	Say Forever You'll Be Mine/How Can I Help You Forgive Me	1975	—	2.00	4.00
GB-10506	Please Don't Stop Loving Me/Sounds of Nature	1975	—	2.00	4.00
—Gold Standard Series					
PB-10652	Is Forever Longer Than Always/If You Say I Can	1976	—	2.00	4.00
GB-10675	Say Forever You'll Be Mine/How Can I Help You Forgive Me	1976	—	2.00	4.00
—Gold Standard Series					
47-9369	The Last Thing on My Mind/Love Is Worth Living	1967	2.00	4.00	8.00
47-9490	Holding On to Nothing/Just Between You and Me	1968	2.00	4.00	8.00
47-9577	We'll Get Ahead Someday/Jeannie's Afraid of the Dark	1968	2.00	4.00	8.00
47-9799	Tomorrow Is Forever/Mandy Never Sleeps	1969	—	3.00	6.00
47-9875	Daddy Was An Old Time Preacher Man/Good Understanding	1970	—	3.00	6.00
47-9958	Better Move It On Home/Two of a Kind	1971	—	3.00	6.00
47-9994	The Right Combination/The Part of Loving You	1971	—	3.00	6.00
74-0104	Malena/Yours, Love	1969	—	3.00	6.00
74-0172	Always, Always/No Need to Hurry Home	1969	—	3.00	6.00
74-0247	Just Someone I Used to Know/My Hands Are Tied	1969	—	3.00	6.00
74-0565	Burning the Midnight Oil/More Than Words Can Tell	1971	—	3.00	6.00
74-0675	Lost Forever in Your Kiss/The Fog Has Lifted	1972	—	2.50	5.00
74-0773	Together Always/Love's All Over	1972	—	2.50	5.00
74-0893	We Found It/Lord Have Mercy on Us	1973	—	2.50	5.00
74-0981	If Teardrops Were Pennies/Come to Me	1973	—	2.50	5.00

Albums

Number	Title (A Side/B Side)	Yr	VG	VG+	NM
PAIR					
PDL1-1013 [(2)]	Sweet Harmony	1986	3.00	6.00	12.00
RCA VICTOR					
APL1-0248	Love and Music	1973	3.75	7.50	15.00
APL1-0646	Porter 'N' Dolly	1974	3.75	7.50	15.00
APL1-1116	Say Forever	1975	3.75	7.50	15.00
AHL1-3700	Porter Wagoner and Dolly Parton	1980	3.00	6.00	12.00
LPM-3926 [M]	Just Between You and Me	1968	25.00	50.00	100.00
LSP-3926 [S]	Just Between You and Me	1968	5.00	10.00	20.00
LSP-4039	Just the Two of Us	1968	5.00	10.00	20.00
LSP-4186	Always, Always	1969	5.00	10.00	20.00
AYL1-4251	Porter Wagoner and Dolly Parton	1982	2.00	4.00	8.00
—"Best Buy Series" reissue					
LSP-4305	Porter Wayne and Dolly Rebecca	1970	5.00	10.00	20.00
LSP-4388	Once More	1970	5.00	10.00	20.00
LSP-4490	Two of a Kind	1971	5.00	10.00	20.00
AHL1-4556	The Best of Porter Wagoner and Dolly Parton	1983	2.50	5.00	10.00
LSP-4556	The Best of Porter Wagoner and Dolly Parton	1971	5.00	10.00	20.00
LSP-4628	The Right Combination/Burning the Midnight Oil	1972	3.75	7.50	15.00
LSP-4761	Together Always	1972	3.75	7.50	15.00
LSP-4841	We Found It	1973	3.75	7.50	15.00

WAIKIKIS, THE

45s

Number	Title (A Side/B Side)	Yr	VG	VG+	NM
KAPP					
KJB-30	Hawaii Tattoo/Tahiti Tamoure	1964	2.00	4.00	8.00
KJB-52	Hawaii Honeymoon/Remember Boa-Boa	1965	2.00	4.00	8.00
891	Pearly Shells/Tiny Bubbles	1968	—	2.50	5.00
PALETTE					
5091	Hawaii Tattoo/Aloha Parade	1962	3.00	6.00	12.00
5109	Tikitiki Puki/Tanita Tamoure	1963	2.50	5.00	10.00

Albums

Number	Title (A Side/B Side)	Yr	VG	VG+	NM
KAPP					
KL-1366 [M]	Hawaii Tattoo	1964	3.75	7.50	15.00
KL-1432 [M]	Hawaii Honeymoon	1965	3.75	7.50	15.00
KL-1437 [M]	Beach Party	1965	3.75	7.50	15.00
KL-1473 [M]	Lollipops and Roses	1966	3.75	7.50	15.00
KL-1484 [M]	A Taste of Hawaii	1966	3.75	7.50	15.00
KS-3366 [S]	Hawaii Tattoo	1964	5.00	10.00	20.00
KS-3432 [S]	Hawaii Honeymoon	1965	5.00	10.00	20.00
KS-3437 [S]	Beach Party	1965	5.00	10.00	20.00
KS-3473 [S]	Lollipops and Roses	1966	5.00	10.00	20.00
KS-3484 [S]	A Taste of Hawaii	1966	5.00	10.00	20.00
KS-3555	Pearly Shells from Hawaii	1968	3.75	7.50	15.00
KS-3575	Midnight Luau	1969	3.75	7.50	15.00
KS-3593	Moonlight on Diamond Head	1969	3.75	7.50	15.00
KS-3612	Greatest Hits	1970	3.00	6.00	12.00
MCA					
544	Pearly Shells from Hawaii	197?	2.50	5.00	10.00
547	Greatest Hits	197?	2.50	5.00	10.00

WAILERS, THE

45s

Number	Title (A Side/B Side)	Yr	VG	VG+	NM
BELL					
694	Thinking Out Loud/You Can't Fly	1967	2.50	5.00	10.00
ETIQUETTE					
2	Mashi/Velva	1962	3.75	7.50	15.00
4	Stompin' Willie/Doin' the Seaside	1963	3.75	7.50	15.00
6	We're Goin' Surfin'/Shakedown	1963	3.75	7.50	15.00
7	Seattle/Party Time U.S.A.	1963	3.75	7.50	15.00

Number	Title (A Side/B Side)	Yr	VG	VG+	NM
9	Tall Cool One/Frenzy	1964	3.75	7.50	15.00
12	You Better Believe It/Don't Take It So Hard	1965	3.75	7.50	15.00
15	You Weren't Using Your Head/Back to You	1965	3.75	7.50	15.00
19	Hang Up/Dirty Robber	1965	3.75	7.50	15.00
21	Out of Our Tree/I Got Me	1966	3.75	7.50	15.00
22	Christmas Spirit/Don't Believe in Christmas	1965	7.50	15.00	30.00
—B-side by the Sonics					
24	It's You Alone/Tears	1966	6.25	12.50	25.00
GOLDEN CREST					
375	Beat Guitar/Driftwood	19??	2.50	5.00	10.00
518	Tall Cool One/Roadrunner	1959	7.50	15.00	30.00
—Photo of group on label					
518	Tall Cool One/Roadrunner	1964	3.75	7.50	15.00
—No photo on label					
526	Mau-Mau/Dirty Robber	1959	6.25	12.50	25.00
—Photo of group on label					
526	Mau-Mau/Dirty Robber	1964	3.00	6.00	12.00
—No photo on label					
532	Wailin'/Shanghai'd	1960	6.25	12.50	25.00
—Photo of group on label					
532	Wailin'/Shanghai'd	1964	3.00	6.00	12.00
—No photo on label					
545	Lucille/Scratchin'	1960	6.25	12.50	25.00
—Photo of group on label					
545	Lucille/Scratchin'	1964	3.00	6.00	12.00
—No photo of group					
591	Mau-Mau/Beat Guitar	1964	2.50	5.00	10.00
IMPERIAL					
66028	Tall Cool One/Frenzy	1964	—	—	—
—Unreleased					
66045	Mashi/On the Rocks	1964	3.75	7.50	15.00
UNITED ARTISTS					
50026	Tears/It's You Alone	1966	2.50	5.00	10.00
50065	End of the Summer/Think Kindly Baby	1966	2.50	5.00	10.00
50110	Tears (Don't Have to Fall)/You Won't Lead Me On	1967	2.50	5.00	10.00
VIVA					
614	I'm Determined/I Don't Want to Follow You	1967	2.50	5.00	10.00
7-Inch Extended Plays					
NORTON					
EP-085	Scotch on the Rocks/Snake Pit//Dirty Robber/High Wall	1999	—	—	2.00
EP-085 [PS]	Scotch on the Rocks/Snake Pit//Dirty Robber/High Wall	1999	—	—	2.00
—Custom yellow sleeve with center hole					
Albums					
BELL					
6016	Walk Thru the People	1969	7.50	15.00	30.00
ETIQUETTE					
ALB-01 [M]	The Fabulous Wailers at the Castle	196?	25.00	50.00	100.00
ALB-022 [M]	The Wailers and Company	196?	20.00	40.00	80.00
ALB-023 [M]	Wailers, Wailers, Everywhere	196?	25.00	50.00	100.00
ALB-026 [M]	Out of Our Tree	1966	25.00	50.00	100.00
22296/7 [(2)]	The Wailers and Their Greatest Hits	1979	6.25	12.50	25.00
GOLDEN CREST					
CR-3075 [M]	Fabulous Wailers	1959	62.50	125.00	250.00
—Full-color photo on cover					
CR-3075 [M]	Fabulous Wailers	1962	25.00	50.00	100.00
—Black and white photo on cover					
CR-3075 [M]	Fabulous Wailers	196?	12.50	25.00	50.00
—Title, no photo, on cover					
IMPERIAL					
LP-9262 [M]	Tall Cool One	1964	12.50	25.00	50.00
LP-12262 [S]	Tall Cool One	1964	20.00	40.00	80.00
UNITED ARTISTS					
UAL-3557 [M]	Outburst!	1966	12.50	25.00	50.00
UAS-6557 [S]	Outburst!	1966	20.00	40.00	80.00

WAILERS, THE (2)

Number	Title (A Side/B Side)	Yr	VG	VG+	NM
45s					
COLUMBIA					
40288	Hot Love/Stop the Clock	1954	30.00	60.00	120.00

WAINWRIGHT, LOUDON, III

Number	Title (A Side/B Side)	Yr	VG	VG+	NM
45s					
ARISTA					
0174	Bicentennial/Talking Big Apple '75	1976	—	2.50	5.00
0340	Final Exam/(B-side unknown)	1978	—	2.50	5.00
COLUMBIA					
45726	Dead Skunk/Needless to Say	1972	2.00	4.00	8.00
—Gray label					
45726	Dead Skunk/Needless to Say	1973	—	3.00	6.00
—Orange label					
45849	New Paint/Say That You Love Me	1973	—	2.50	5.00
45949	Down Drinking at the Bar/I Am the Way	1973	—	2.50	5.00
46064	Swimming Song/Bell Bottom Pants	1974	—	2.50	5.00
Albums					
ARISTA					
AL 4063	T Shirt	1976	3.00	6.00	12.00
AB 4173	Final Exam	1978	3.00	6.00	12.00
ATLANTIC					
SD 8260	Loudon Wainwright III	1970	5.00	10.00	20.00
SD 8291	Album II	1971	5.00	10.00	20.00
COLUMBIA					
KC 31462	Album III	1972	3.75	7.50	15.00
PC 31462	Album III	198?	2.00	4.00	8.00
—Budget-line reissue					
KC 32710	Attempted Mustache	1973	3.75	7.50	15.00
PC 32710	Attempted Mustache	198?	2.00	4.00	8.00
—Budget-line reissue					
PC 33369	Unrequited	1975	3.00	6.00	12.00
—No bar code on cover					
PC 33369	Unrequited	198?	2.00	4.00	8.00
—Budget-line reissue with bar code					
ROUNDER					
3050	A Live One	1979	3.00	6.00	12.00
3076	Fame and Wealth	1983	3.00	6.00	12.00
3096	I'm Alright	1986	2.50	5.00	10.00
3106	More Love Songs	1987	2.50	5.00	10.00
SILVERTONE					
1203-1-J	Therapy	1989	3.00	6.00	12.00

WAITE, GENEVIEVE

Number	Title (A Side/B Side)	Yr	VG	VG+	NM
Albums					
PARAMOUR					
5088	Romance Is on the Rise	1974	6.25	12.50	25.00

WAITS, TOM

Number	Title (A Side/B Side)	Yr	VG	VG+	NM
12-Inch Singles					
ISLAND					
96750	Hang On St. Christopher (Extended Remix)/(Instrumental)	1987	3.75	7.50	15.00
45s					
ASYLUM					
11014	Ol' 55/(B-side unknown)	1973	—	3.00	6.00
45213	San Diego Serenade/Diamonds on My Windshield	1974	—	2.50	5.00
45233	New Coat of Paint/Blue Skies	1975	—	2.50	5.00
45371	Step Right Up/The Piano Has Been Drinking	1976	—	2.50	5.00
45539	Red Shoes by the Drugstore/Somewhere	1978	—	2.50	5.00
47077	Jersey Girl/Heartattack and Vine	1980	2.00	4.00	8.00
Albums					
ASYLUM					
6E-162	Blue Valentine	1978	2.50	5.00	10.00
6E-295	Heartattack and Vine	1980	2.50	5.00	10.00
7E-1015	The Heart of Saturday	1974	3.00	6.00	12.00
7E-1078	Small Change	1976	2.50	5.00	10.00
7E-1117	Foreign Affairs	1977	2.50	5.00	10.00
7E-2008 [(2)]	Nighthawks at the Diner	1975	3.00	6.00	12.00
SD 5061	Closing Time	1973	3.00	6.00	12.00
ELEKTRA					
60416	Anthology of Tom Waits	1985	2.50	5.00	10.00
EPITAPH					
86547	Mule Variations	1999	3.00	6.00	12.00
ISLAND					
90095	Swordfishtrombone	1983	2.50	5.00	10.00
90299	Rain Dogs	1985	2.50	5.00	10.00
90572	Franks Wild Years	1987	2.50	5.00	10.00
90987	Big Time	1988	2.50	5.00	10.00

WAKEFIELD SUN

Number	Title (A Side/B Side)	Yr	VG	VG+	NM
45s					
MGM					
14028	When I See You/Get Out	1969	5.00	10.00	20.00
14072	Tryst on Love/Sing a Simple Song	1969	7.50	15.00	30.00
Albums					
MGM					
SE-4626	Wakefield Sun	1969	6.25	12.50	25.00

WAKEMAN, RICK

Also see YES.

Number	Title (A Side/B Side)	Yr	VG	VG+	NM
45s					
A&M					
1430	Catherine/Anne	1973	—	2.50	5.00
1627	The Journey/The Return	1974	—	2.50	5.00
1635	The Battle/And Now a Word from Our Sponsor	1974	—	2.50	5.00
1708	Merlin the Magician/Sir Galahad	1975	—	2.50	5.00
1937	White Rock/After the Ball	1977	—	2.50	5.00
2010	The Birdman of Alcatraz/And Now a Word from Our Sponsor	1978	—	2.50	5.00
Albums					
A&M					
SP-3156	Journey to the Centre of the Earth	198?	2.00	4.00	8.00
—Budget-line reissue of 3621					
SP-3229	The Six Wives of Henry VIII	1984	2.00	4.00	8.00
—Budget-line reissue of 4361					
SP-3230	The Myths and Legends of King Arthur and the Knights of the Round Table	1984	2.00	4.00	8.00
—Budget-line reissue of 4515					
SP-3621	Journey to the Centre of the Earth	1974	3.00	6.00	12.00
SP-4361	The Six Wives of Henry VIII	1973	3.00	6.00	12.00
—Originals have brown labels					
SP-4361	The Six Wives of Henry VIII	1974	2.50	5.00	10.00
—Silver label with "fading" A&M logo					
SP-4515	The Myths and Legends of King Arthur and the Knights of the Round Table	1975	3.00	6.00	12.00
SP-4583	No Earthly Connection	1976	3.00	6.00	12.00
SP-4614	White Rock	1977	3.00	6.00	12.00
SP-4660	Rick Wakeman's Criminal Record	1977	3.00	6.00	12.00
SP-6501 [(2)]	Rhapsodies	1979	3.75	7.50	15.00
QU-53621 [Q]	Journey to the Centre of the Earth	1974	6.25	12.50	25.00
QU-54361 [Q]	The Six Wives of Henry VIII	1974	6.25	12.50	25.00
QU-54515 [Q]	The Myths and Legends of King Arthur and the Knights of the Round Table	1975	6.25	12.50	25.00
MOBILE FIDELITY					
1-230	Journey to the Centre of the Earth	1995	5.00	10.00	20.00
—Audiophile vinyl					
SWEET THUNDER					
1	Journey to the Centre of the Earth	1981	12.50	25.00	50.00
—Audiophile vinyl					

WALCOS, THE

45s

DRUM

Number	Title (A Side/B Side)	Yr	VG	VG+	NM
011	Tell Me Why/Moonlight Rock	1959	25.00	50.00	100.00

WALES, HOWARD, AND JERRY GARCIA

Also see JERRY GARCIA.

45s

DOUGLAS

Number	Title (A Side/B Side)	Yr	VG	VG+	NM
76501	South Side Strut/Uncle Martin's	1971	3.75	7.50	15.00

Albums

DOUGLAS

Number	Title (A Side/B Side)	Yr	VG	VG+	NM
Z 30589	Hooteroll	1971	10.00	20.00	40.00

WALKER, DAVID T.

45s

ODE

Number	Title (A Side/B Side)	Yr	VG	VG+	NM
66025	Hot Fun in the Summertime/I Want to Talk to You	1972	—	2.50	5.00
66037	Press On/Brother, Brother	1973	—	2.50	5.00
66042	I Got Work to Do/The Real T.	1974	—	2.50	5.00
66045	Loving You Is Sweeter Than Ever/Didn't I Blow Your Mind This Time	1974	—	2.50	5.00
66125	I Wish You Love/Oh Love	1976	—	2.50	5.00

REVUE

Number	Title (A Side/B Side)	Yr	VG	VG+	NM
11060	My Baby Loves Me/Can I Change My Mind	1969	—	3.00	6.00
11070	Watch Out Dynamite/Baby I Need Your Loving	1970	—	3.00	6.00

ZEA

Number	Title (A Side/B Side)	Yr	VG	VG+	NM
50005	Love Vibrations/(B-side unknown)	1970	—	2.50	5.00

Albums

ODE

Number	Title (A Side/B Side)	Yr	VG	VG+	NM
SP-77011	David T. Walker	1971	2.50	5.00	10.00
SP-77020	Press On	1974	2.50	5.00	10.00
SP-77035	On Love	1976	2.50	5.00	10.00

ZEA

Number	Title (A Side/B Side)	Yr	VG	VG+	NM
1000	Plum Happy	1970	3.75	7.50	15.00

WALKER, JERRY JEFF

45s

ATCO

Number	Title (A Side/B Side)	Yr	VG	VG+	NM
6594	Mr. Bojangles/Round and Round	1968	2.50	5.00	10.00
6767	I'm Gonna Tell on You/But For the Time	1970	—	3.00	6.00

ELEKTRA

Number	Title (A Side/B Side)	Yr	VG	VG+	NM
46016	Comfort and Crazy/Eastern Ave. River Railway Blues	1979	—	2.00	4.00

MCA

Number	Title (A Side/B Side)	Yr	VG	VG+	NM
40054	L.A. Freeway/Charlie Dunn	1973	—	2.00	4.00
40167	Desperadoes Waitin' for a Train/Gettin' By	1973	—	2.00	4.00
40250	Sangria Wine/Hill Country Rain	1974	—	2.00	4.00
40389	Goodbye Easy Street/Salvation Army Band	1975	—	2.00	4.00
40487	Jaded Lover/I Love You	1975	—	2.00	4.00
40570	Dear John Letter Lounge/It's a Good Night for Singing	1976	—	2.00	4.00
40622	(Looking for the) Heart of Saturday Night/Stoney	1976	—	2.00	4.00
40760	Mr. Bojangles/Don't It Make You Wanna Dance	1977	—	2.00	4.00
40822	Ro-Deo-Deo Cowboy/Leavin' Texas	1977	—	2.00	4.00

SOUTH COAST

Number	Title (A Side/B Side)	Yr	VG	VG+	NM
51146	Got Lucky Last Night/Maybe Mexico	1981	—	2.00	4.00
51215	Take It As It Comes/She Knows Her Daddy Sings	1981	—	2.00	4.00
52122	Don't Think Twice, It's Alright/Laying My Life on the Line	1982	—	2.00	4.00

TRIED & TRUE

Number	Title (A Side/B Side)	Yr	VG	VG+	NM
1690	I Feel Like Hank Williams Tonight/(B-side unknown)	1989	—	2.00	4.00
1695	The Pickup Truck Song/(B-side unknown)	1989	—	2.00	4.00
1698	Trashy Women/(B-side unknown)	1989	—	2.00	4.00

Albums

ATCO

Number	Title (A Side/B Side)	Yr	VG	VG+	NM
SD 33-259	Mr. Bojangles	1968	6.25	12.50	25.00
SD 33-297	Five Years Gone	1969	7.50	15.00	30.00
SD 33-336	Bein' Free	1970	5.00	10.00	20.00

BAINBRIDGE

Number	Title (A Side/B Side)	Yr	VG	VG+	NM
6222	Mr. Bojangles	198?	2.50	5.00	10.00

DECCA

Number	Title (A Side/B Side)	Yr	VG	VG+	NM
DL 75384	Jerry Jeff Walker	1972	3.75	7.50	15.00

ELEKTRA

Number	Title (A Side/B Side)	Yr	VG	VG+	NM
6E-163	Jerry Jeff	1978	2.50	5.00	10.00
6E-239	Too Old to Change	1980	2.50	5.00	10.00

MCA

Number	Title (A Side/B Side)	Yr	VG	VG+	NM
382	Viva Terlingua!	1973	2.50	5.00	10.00
450	Walker's Collectibles	1974	2.50	5.00	10.00
510	Jerry Jeff Walker	1975	2.50	5.00	10.00
—Reissue of Decca LP					
2156	Ridin' High	1975	2.50	5.00	10.00
2202	It's a Good Night for Singin'	1976	2.50	5.00	10.00
2350	Viva Terlingua!	1977	2.00	4.00	8.00
—Reissue of MCA 382					
2355	Walker's Collectibles	1977	2.00	4.00	8.00
—Reissue of MCA 450					
2358	Jerry Jeff Walker	1977	2.00	4.00	8.00
—Reissue of MCA 510					
3041	Contrary to Ordinary	1978	2.50	5.00	10.00
5128	The Best of Jerry Jeff Walker	1980	2.50	5.00	10.00
5355	Cowjazz	1983	2.50	5.00	10.00
6003 [(2)]	A Man Must Carry On	198?	2.50	5.00	10.00
—Budget-line reissue					
8013 [(2)]	A Man Must Carry On	1977	3.00	6.00	12.00
27026	It's a Good Night for Singin'	198?	2.00	4.00	8.00
—Budget-line reissue					
27027	Walker's Collectibles	198?	—	3.00	6.00
—Budget-line reissue					
37004	Jerry Jeff Walker	198?	—	3.00	6.00
—Budget-line reissue					
37005	Viva Terlingua!	198?	—	3.00	6.00
—Budget-line reissue					
37006	Ridin' High	198?	2.00	4.00	8.00
—Budget-line reissue					
37162	Contrary to Ordinary	198?	2.00	4.00	8.00
—Budget-line reissue					

SOUTHCOAST

Number	Title (A Side/B Side)	Yr	VG	VG+	NM
5199	Reunion	1981	2.50	5.00	10.00

VANGUARD

Number	Title (A Side/B Side)	Yr	VG	VG+	NM
VSD-6521	Driftin' Way of Life	1969	5.00	10.00	20.00
VMS-73124	Driftin' Way of Life	1985	2.00	4.00	8.00
—Reissue of 6521					

WALKER, JIMMIE

Albums

BUDDAH

Number	Title (A Side/B Side)	Yr	VG	VG+	NM
BDS 5635	Dyn-O-Mite	1975	2.50	5.00	10.00

WALKER, JR., AND THE ALL STARS

45s

HARVEY

Number	Title (A Side/B Side)	Yr	VG	VG+	NM
113	Willie's Blues/Twist Lackawanna	1962	6.25	12.50	25.00
117	Cleo's Mood/Brain Washer	1963	5.00	10.00	20.00
119	Good Rockin'/Brain Washer	1963	5.00	10.00	20.00

MOTOWN

Number	Title (A Side/B Side)	Yr	VG	VG+	NM
1352	Country Boy/What Does It Take (To Win Your Love)	1975	—	2.50	5.00
1380	I'm So Glad/Hot Shot	1976	—	—	—
—Unreleased					
1689	Blow the House Down/Ball Baby	1983	—	2.00	4.00

SOUL

Number	Title (A Side/B Side)	Yr	VG	VG+	NM
35003	Monkey Jump/Satan's Blues	1964	3.75	7.50	15.00
35008	Shotgun/Hot Cha	1965	3.75	7.50	15.00
35008 [PS]	Shotgun/Hot Cha	1965	6.25	12.50	25.00
35012	Do the Boomerang/Tune Up	1965	2.50	5.00	10.00
35013	Shake and Fingerpop/Cleo's Back	1965	2.50	5.00	10.00
35015	(I'm a) Road Runner/Shoot Your Shot	1965	2.50	5.00	10.00
35017	Cleo's Mood/Baby You Know It Ain't Right	1966	2.00	4.00	8.00
35024	How Sweet It Is (To Be Loved By You)/Nothing But Soul	1966	2.00	4.00	8.00
35024 [PS]	How Sweet It Is (To Be Loved By You)/Nothing But Soul	1966	5.00	10.00	20.00
35026	Money (That's What I Want) Part I/Money (That's What I Want) Part II	1966	2.00	4.00	8.00
35030	Pucker Up Buttercup/Anyway You Wanna	1967	2.00	4.00	8.00
35036	Shoot Your Shot/Ain't That the Truth	1967	2.00	4.00	8.00
35041	Come See About Me/Sweet Soul	1967	2.00	4.00	8.00
35048	Hip City — Part 1/Hip City — Part 2	1968	2.00	4.00	8.00
35055	Home Cookin'/Mutiny	1969	2.00	4.00	8.00
35062	What Does It Take (To Win Your Love)/Brainwasher — Part 1	1969	2.00	4.00	8.00
35067	These Eyes/Got to Find a Way to Win Maria Back	1969	—	3.00	6.00
35070	Gotta Hold On to This Feeling/Clinging to the Theory That She's Coming Back	1970	—	3.00	6.00
35073	Do You See My Love (For You Growing)/Groove and More	1970	—	3.00	6.00
35081	Holly Holy/Carry Your Own Load	1970	—	3.00	6.00
35084	Take Me Girl, I'm Ready/Right On Brothers and Sisters	1971	—	3.00	6.00
35090	Way Back Home/(Instrumental)	1971	—	3.00	6.00
35095	Walk in the Night/I Don't Want to Do Wrong	1972	—	3.00	6.00
35097	Groove Thang/Me and My Family	1972	—	3.00	6.00
35104	Gimme That Beat (Part 1)/Gimme That Beat (Part 2)	1973	—	3.00	6.00
35106	I Don't Need No Reason/Country Boy	1973	—	3.00	6.00
35108	Peace and Understanding (Is Hard to Find)/Soul Clappin'	1973	—	3.00	6.00
35110	Dancing Like They Do on Soul Train/I Ain't That Easy to Love	1973	—	3.00	6.00
35114 [DJ]	You Are the Sunshine of My Life/Until You Come Back to Me	1974	—	—	—
—Unreleased					
35116	I'm So Glad/Soul Clappin'	1975	—	2.50	5.00
35118	Hot Shot/You're No Ordinary Woman	1976	—	2.50	5.00
35122	Whopper Bopper Show Stopper/Hard Love	1977	—	2.50	5.00

WHITFIELD

Number	Title (A Side/B Side)	Yr	VG	VG+	NM
8861	Back Street Boogie/Don't Let Me Go Away	1979	—	2.00	4.00
49052	Wishing on a Star/Hole in the Wall	1979	—	2.00	4.00

Albums

MOTOWN

Number	Title (A Side/B Side)	Yr	VG	VG+	NM
M5-105V1	Motown Superstar Series, Vol. 5	1981	2.50	5.00	10.00
M5-141V1	Shotgun	1981	2.50	5.00	10.00
—Reissue of Soul 701					
M5-208V1	Greatest Hits	1981	2.50	5.00	10.00
—Reissue of Soul 718					
M7-786 [(2)]	Anthology	1974	5.00	10.00	20.00
5297 ML	All the Great Hits of Jr. Walker and the All Stars	1984	2.50	5.00	10.00
6053 ML	Blow the House Down	1983	2.50	5.00	10.00

PICKWICK

Number	Title (A Side/B Side)	Yr	VG	VG+	NM
SPC-3391	Shotgun	197?	3.00	6.00	12.00

SOUL

Number	Title (A Side/B Side)	Yr	VG	VG+	NM
701 [M]	Shotgun	1965	15.00	30.00	60.00
—Mostly white label with vertical "Soul" at left					
701 [M]	Shotgun	1965	5.00	10.00	20.00
—Purple swirl label with "Soul" at top					
SS-701 [S]	Shotgun	1965	7.50	15.00	30.00
702 [M]	Soul Session	1966	15.00	30.00	60.00
—Mostly white label with vertical "Soul" at left					
702 [M]	Soul Session	1966	5.00	10.00	20.00
—Purple swirl label with "Soul" at top					
SS-702 [S]	Soul Session	1966	7.50	15.00	30.00
703 [M]	Road Runner	1966	5.00	10.00	20.00

Number	Title (A Side/B Side)	Yr	VG	VG+	NM
SS-703 [S]	Road Runner	1966	7.50	15.00	30.00
705 [M]	"Live"	1967	5.00	10.00	20.00
SS-705 [S]	"Live"	1967	7.50	15.00	30.00
SS-710	Home Cookin'	1969	5.00	10.00	20.00
SS-718	Greatest Hits	1969	5.00	10.00	20.00
SS-721	Gotta Hold on to This Feeling	1969	6.25	12.50	25.00
SS-721	What Does It Take to Win Your Love	1970	5.00	10.00	20.00
—Retitled version of above					
SS-726	A Gasssss	1970	3.75	7.50	15.00
SS-732	Rainbow Funk	1971	3.75	7.50	15.00
SS-733	Moody Jr.	1971	3.75	7.50	15.00
SS-738	Peace and Understanding Is Hard to Find	1973	3.75	7.50	15.00
S6-742	Jr. Walker and the All Stars	1973	—	—	—
—Canceled					
S6-745	Hot Shot	1976	3.75	7.50	15.00
S6-747	Sax Appeal	1976	3.75	7.50	15.00
S6-748	Whopper Bopper Show Stopper	1977	3.75	7.50	15.00
S7-750	Smooth	1978	3.75	7.50	15.00
WHITFIELD					
WHK 3331	Back Street Boogie	1980	3.00	6.00	12.00

WALKER, T-BONE

45s

Number	Title (A Side/B Side)	Yr	VG	VG+	NM
ATLANTIC					
1045	Papa Ain't Salty/T-Bone Shuffle	1955	12.50	25.00	50.00
1074	Why Not/Play On Little Girl	1955	10.00	20.00	40.00
BLUESWAY					
61008	Confusion Blues/Every Night I Have to Cry	1967	2.00	4.00	8.00
CAPITOL					
F799	Go Back to the One You Love/On Your Way Blues	1950	37.50	75.00	150.00
F944	Too Much Trouble Blues/She's My Old Time Used to Be	1950	37.50	75.00	150.00
IMPERIAL					
5202	Street Walkin' Woman/The Blues Is a Woman	1952	100.00	200.00	400.00
—Note: T-Bone Walker records on Imperial before 5202 are unconfirmed on 45 rpm.					
5216	Blue Mood/Got No Use for You	1953	50.00	100.00	200.00
5228	Railroad Station Blues/Long Distance Blues	1953	50.00	100.00	200.00
5239	Party Girl/You're Here in the Dark	1953	75.00	150.00	300.00
5247	Everytime/Tell Me What's the Reason	1953	37.50	75.00	150.00
5261	I'm About to Lose My Mind/I Miss You Baby	1954	25.00	50.00	100.00
5264	Pony Tail/When the Sun Goes Down	1954	20.00	40.00	80.00
5274	Vida Lee/My Baby Is Now on My Mind	1954	20.00	40.00	80.00
5284	Bye Bye Baby/Wanderin' Heart	1954	20.00	40.00	80.00
5299	Teenage Baby/Strugglin' Blues	1954	20.00	40.00	80.00
5311	Love Is Just a Gamble/High Society	1954	20.00	40.00	80.00
5330	I'll Understand/The Hard Way	1955	12.50	25.00	50.00
5384	You Don't Understand/Say! Pretty Baby	1956	12.50	25.00	50.00
5695	Travelin' Blues/Strollin' with Bones	1960	3.75	7.50	15.00
5832	Evil Hearted Woman/Life Is Too Short	1962	3.75	7.50	15.00
5962	Doin' Time/Cold, Cold Water	1963	3.00	6.00	12.00
JETSTREAM					
726	Reconsider Baby/I'm Not Your Fool Anymore	1966	2.50	5.00	10.00
730	T-Bone's Back/She's a Hit	1967	2.50	5.00	10.00
MODERN					
1004	Should I Let Her Go/Hey Hey Baby	1965	2.50	5.00	10.00
POST					
2002	I Get So Weary/Tell Me What's the Reason	1955	15.00	30.00	60.00

7-Inch Extended Plays

Number	Title (A Side/B Side)	Yr	VG	VG+	NM
CAPITOL					
EAP 370	(contents unknown)	1953	50.00	100.00	200.00
EAP 370 [PS]	Classics in Jazz	1953	50.00	100.00	200.00

Albums

Number	Title (A Side/B Side)	Yr	VG	VG+	NM
ATLANTIC					
8020 [M]	T-Bone Blues	1959	55.00	110.00	220.00
—Black label					
8020 [M]	T-Bone Blues	1960	17.50	35.00	70.00
—Red and purple label					
SD 8256	T-Bone Blues	1970	5.00	10.00	20.00
BLUE NOTE					
BN-LA533-H2 [(2)]	Classics	1975	5.00	10.00	20.00
BLUESTIME					
29004	Everyday I Have the Blues	1968	7.50	15.00	30.00
29010	Blue Rocks	1969	7.50	15.00	30.00
BLUESWAY					
BLS-6008	Stormy Monday Blues	1968	7.50	15.00	30.00
—Reissue of Wet Soul LP?					
BLS-6014	Funky Town	1968	7.50	15.00	30.00
BLS-6058	Dirty Mistreater	1973	3.75	7.50	15.00
BRUNSWICK					
BL 754126	The Truth	1968	7.50	15.00	30.00
CAPITOL					
H 370 [10]	Classics in Jazz	1953	250.00	500.00	1000.
T 370 [M]	Classics in Jazz	1953	75.00	150.00	300.00
T 1958 [M]	Great Blues Vocal and Guitar	1963	37.50	75.00	150.00
—Black "The Star Line" label (existence of black colorband label not confirmed)					
DELMARK					
D-633 [M]	I Want a Little Girl	1967	10.00	20.00	40.00
DS-633 [S]	I Want a Little Girl	1967	12.50	25.00	50.00
IMPERIAL					
LP-9098 [M]	T-Bone Walker Sings the Blues	1959	75.00	150.00	300.00
LP-9116 [M]	Singing the Blues	1960	62.50	125.00	250.00
LP-9146 [M]	I Get So Weary	1961	75.00	150.00	300.00
MOSAIC					
M9-130 [(9)]	The Complete Recordings of T-Bone Walker 1940-1954	199?	50.00	100.00	200.00
POLYDOR					
24-4502	Good Feelin'	1972	3.75	7.50	15.00
PD-5521	Fly Walker Airlines	1973	3.75	7.50	15.00
REPRISE					
2RS 6483 [(2)]	Very Rare	1973	5.00	10.00	20.00
WET SOUL					
1002	Stormy Monday Blues	1967	12.50	25.00	50.00

WALKER, WAYNE

45s

Number	Title (A Side/B Side)	Yr	VG	VG+	NM
ABC-PARAMOUNT					
9735	It's My Way/All I Can Do Is Cry	1956	15.00	30.00	60.00
BRUNSWICK					
55133	Little Ole You/What Kind of God Do You Think You Are	1959	10.00	20.00	40.00
COLUMBIA					
40905	A Teenage Love Affair/Whatever You Desire	1957	6.25	12.50	25.00
40979	Just a-Walkin' Around/Sands of Gold	1957	6.25	12.50	25.00
41042	Bo-Bo Sha Diddle Diddle/Come Away from His Arms	1957	6.25	12.50	25.00
41130	I'm Finally Free/It's Written in Your Arms	1958	6.25	12.50	25.00
CORAL					
62328	Battle of the Bulge/Reaching for the Impossible	1962	3.75	7.50	15.00
EVEREST					
19380	Love, Love, Love/Sweet Chains of Love	1960	3.75	7.50	15.00

WALKER BROTHERS, THE

Also see SCOTT ENGEL.

45s

Number	Title (A Side/B Side)	Yr	VG	VG+	NM
KAY-Y					
66785	Beautiful Brown Eyes/Ninety-Seven	1960	12.50	25.00	50.00
SMASH					
1952	Doin' the Jerk/Pretty Girls Everywhere	1964	3.00	6.00	12.00
1976	Love Her/Seventh Dawn	1965	3.00	6.00	12.00
2000	Make It Easy on Yourself/But I Do	1965	3.75	7.50	15.00
2009	Make It Easy on Yourself/Doin' the Jerk	1965	3.00	6.00	12.00
2009 [PS]	Make It Easy on Yourself/Doin' the Jerk	1965	5.00	10.00	20.00
2016	My Ship Is Comin' In/You're All Around Me	1966	3.00	6.00	12.00
2016 [PS]	My Ship Is Comin' In/You're All Around Me	1966	5.00	10.00	20.00
2032	The Sun Ain't Gonna Shine (Anymore)/After the Lights Go Out	1966	3.00	6.00	12.00
2048	(Baby) You Don't Have to Tell Me/Young Man Cried	1966	3.00	6.00	12.00
2063	Another Tear Falls/Saddest Night in the World	1966	3.00	6.00	12.00
TOWER					
218	I Only Came to Dance with You/Greens	1966	3.00	6.00	12.00

Albums

Number	Title (A Side/B Side)	Yr	VG	VG+	NM
SMASH					
MGS-27076 [M]	Introducing the Walker Brothers	1965	12.50	25.00	50.00
MGS-27082 [M]	The Sun Ain't Gonna Shine (Anymore)	1966	10.00	20.00	40.00
SRS-67076 [R]	Introducing the Walker Brothers	1965	10.00	20.00	40.00
SRS-67082 [P]	The Sun Ain't Gonna Shine (Anymore)	1966	12.50	25.00	50.00
—"The Sun Ain't Gonna Shine (Anymore)" and "When the Lights Go Out" are rechanneled.					
TOWER					
ST 5026 [S]	I Only Came to Dance with You	1966	5.00	10.00	20.00
—As "Scott Engel and John Stewart"					
T 5026 [M]	I Only Came to Dance with You	1966	3.75	7.50	15.00
—As "Scott Engel and John Stewart"					

WALLACE, BILLY

45s

Number	Title (A Side/B Side)	Yr	VG	VG+	NM
DEB					
883	Wolf Call/(B-side unknown)	1957	37.50	75.00	150.00
1003	Don't Flirt with My Baby/You'll Never Cheat Me Anymore	1958	37.50	75.00	150.00
MERCURY					
70876	What'll I Do/That's My Reward	1956	50.00	100.00	200.00
70957	Mean Mistrteating Baby/Burning the Wind	1956	75.00	150.00	300.00

WALLACE, JERRY

45s

Number	Title (A Side/B Side)	Yr	VG	VG+	NM
4-STAR					
1035	I Wanna Go to Heaven/After You	1978	—	2.00	4.00
1036	Yours Love/(B-side unknown)	1979	—	2.00	4.00
ALLIED					
5015	Little Miss One/Petrillo	1954	12.50	25.00	50.00
—B-side by Eddie Oliver and the Oliver Twisters					
5019	That's What a Woman Can Do/I Hate to Go Home Alone	1954	10.00	20.00	40.00
5023	Runnin' After Love/Dixie Anna	1954	10.00	20.00	40.00
BMA					
7-002	I Miss You Already/At the End of a Rainbow	1977	—	2.00	4.00
7-005	I'll Promise You Tomorrow/Youre on the Run	1977	—	2.00	4.00
8-006	At the End of a Rainbow/Looking for a Memory	1978	—	2.00	4.00
8-008	My Last Sad Song/Wickenburg Way	1978	—	2.00	4.00
CHALLENGE					
1003	Blue Jean Baby/Fool's Hall of Fame	1957	5.00	10.00	20.00
9107	Life's a Holiday/I Can See an Angel Walking	1961	3.00	6.00	12.00
9117	Eyes (Don't Give My Secrets Away)/Lonesome	1961	3.00	6.00	12.00
9130	Rollin' River/I Hang My Head and Cry	1961	3.00	6.00	12.00
9139	Little Miss Tease/Mr. Lonely	1962	3.00	6.00	12.00
9152	Here I Go/You'll Never Know	1962	3.00	6.00	12.00
9171	Shutters and Boards/Am I That Easy to Forget	1962	3.00	6.00	12.00
9185	Move Over/On a Merry-Go-Round	1963	3.00	6.00	12.00
9195	Just Walking in the Rain/San Francisco Mama	1963	3.00	6.00	12.00
9205	Empty Arms Again/Bambola (My Darling One)	1963	3.00	6.00	12.00
59000	The Other Me/Good and Bad	1958	5.00	10.00	20.00
59013	How the Time Flies/With This Ring	1958	5.00	10.00	20.00
59027	Diamond Ring/All My Love Belongs to You	1958	5.00	10.00	20.00
59040	A Touch of Pink/Off Stage	1959	3.75	7.50	15.00
59047	Primrose Lane/By Your Side	1959	4.50	9.00	18.00
59060	Little Coco Palm/Mission Bell Blues	1959	3.75	7.50	15.00
59060 [PS]	Little Coco Palm/Mission Bell Blues	1959	10.00	20.00	40.00
59072	King of the Mountain/You're Singing Our Love Song to Somebody Else	1960	3.75	7.50	15.00
59082	Swingin' Down the Lane/Teardrops in the Rain	1960	3.75	7.50	15.00
59098	There She Goes/Angel on My Shoulder	1960	3.75	7.50	15.00
59223	Auf Wiedesehn/If I Make It Through Today	1963	2.50	5.00	10.00
59246	In the Misty Moonlight/Even the Bad Times Are Good	1964	2.50	5.00	10.00

Number	Title (A Side/B Side)	Yr	VG	VG+	NM
59249	In the Misty Moonlight/Cannon Ball	1964	3.75	7.50	15.00
—B-side by the Soul Surfers					
59265	Even the Bad Times Are Good/Spanish Guitars	1964	2.50	5.00	10.00
59278	You're Driving You Out of My Mind/Helpless	1965	2.50	5.00	10.00
CLASS					
502	Taj Mahal/Autumn Has Come and Gone	1955	6.25	12.50	25.00
DECCA					
32777	After You/She'll Remember	1971	—	3.50	7.00
32859	The Morning After/I Can't Take It Anymore	1971	—	3.50	7.00
32914	To Get to You/Time	1972	—	3.50	7.00
32989	If You Leave Me Tonight I'll Cry/What's He Doin' in My World	1972	—	3.50	7.00
33036	Do You Know What It's Like to Be Lonesome/ Where Did He Come From	1972	—	3.50	7.00
DOOR KNOB					
116	You've Still Got Me/Now That Sandy's Gone	1979	—	2.00	4.00
127	Cling to Me/Paper Madonna	1980	—	2.00	4.00
134	If I Could Set My Love to Music/Cling to Me	1980	—	2.00	4.00
GLENOLDEN					
159	Are You Ready/That's the Fool in Me	1968	—	3.00	6.00
LIBERTY					
55957	Runaway Bay/Dispossessed	1967	2.00	4.00	8.00
56001	This One's on the House/A New Sun Risin'	1967	2.00	4.00	8.00
56027	The Closest I Ever Came/That's What Fools Are For	1968	—	—	—
—Unreleased					
56028	Another Time, Another Place, Another World/ That's What Fools Are For	1968	—	3.00	6.00
56059	Sweet Child of Sunshine/Our House on Paper	1968	—	3.00	6.00
56095	Temptation/Son	1969	—	3.00	6.00
56105	Venus/Soon We'll Be There	1969	—	3.00	6.00
56130	Swiss Cottage Place/With Aging	1969	—	3.00	6.00
56147	Honey Eyed Girl/Glory of My Girl	1969	—	3.00	6.00
56155	Even the Bad Times Are Good/For All We Know	1970	—	3.00	6.00
MCA					
40037	A Song Nobody Sings/Sound of Goodbye	1973	—	2.50	5.00
40111	Don't Give Up on Me/You Look Like Forever	1973	—	2.50	5.00
40183	Guess Who/All I Ever Want from You	1974	—	2.50	5.00
40248	My Wife's House/A Better Way to Say I Love You	1974	—	2.50	5.00
40321	Make Hay While the Sun Shines/I Wonder Whose Baby	1974	—	2.50	5.00
MERCURY					
70684	Taj Mahal/Autumn Has Come and Gone	1955	5.00	10.00	20.00
70758	The Greatest Magic of All/Walking in the Rain	1955	5.00	10.00	20.00
70812	One Night When Flowers Were Dancing/Gloria	1956	5.00	10.00	20.00
72246	In the Misty Moonlight/Even the Bad Times Are Good	1964	3.00	6.00	12.00
72258	Butterfly/Let the Tears Begin	1964	2.50	5.00	10.00
72292	It's a Cotton Candy World/Keep a Lamp Burning	1964	2.50	5.00	10.00
72356	Careless Hands/San Francisco d'Assisi	1964	2.50	5.00	10.00
72406	Rainbow/Time	1965	2.50	5.00	10.00
72461	Life's Gone and Slipped Away/Twelve Little Roses	1965	2.50	5.00	10.00
72529	Diamonds and Horseshoes/Will the Pain Fade Away	1966	2.50	5.00	10.00
72589	Wallpaper Roses/Son of a Green Beret	1966	2.50	5.00	10.00
72619	Not That I Care/Release Me	1966	2.50	5.00	10.00
MGM					
14788	Comin' Home to You/The River St. Marie	1975	—	2.50	5.00
14809	Wanted Man/Your Love	1975	—	2.50	5.00
14832	Georgia Rain/In the Garden	1975	—	2.50	5.00
POLYDOR					
14322	The Fool I've Been Today/Jenny Angel	1976	—	2.00	4.00
TOPS					
369	P.S. I Love You/Vaya Con Dios (May God Be With You)	1953	10.00	20.00	40.00
—B-side by Betty Ford					
UNITED ARTISTS					
XW239	Take Me As I Am/Touch Me	1973	—	2.50	5.00
XW618	With Pen in Hand/All I Want Is You	1975	—	2.50	5.00
50971	Funny How Time Slips Away/Thanks to You for Loving Me	1972	—	2.50	5.00
WING					
90065	Eyes of Fire, Lips of Wine/Monkey See, Monkey Do	1956	5.00	10.00	20.00
Albums					
CHALLENGE					
CHL 606 [M]	Just Jerry	1959	15.00	30.00	60.00
CHL 612 [M]	There She Goes	1961	7.50	15.00	30.00
CHS 612 [S]	There She Goes	1961	10.00	20.00	40.00
CHL 616 [M]	Shutters and Boards	1962	7.50	15.00	30.00
CHS 616 [S]	Shutters and Boards	1962	10.00	20.00	40.00
CHL 619 [M]	In the Misty Moonlight	1964	5.00	10.00	20.00
CHS 619 [S]	In the Misty Moonlight	1964	6.25	12.50	25.00
2002	Greatest Hits	1969	3.75	7.50	15.00
DECCA					
DL 75294	This Is Jerry Wallace	1971	3.75	7.50	15.00
DL 75349	To Get to You	1972	3.75	7.50	15.00
LIBERTY					
LST-7545	This One's on the House	1967	5.00	10.00	20.00
LST-7564	Another Time, Another World	1968	5.00	10.00	20.00
LST-7597	Sweet Child of Sunshine	1968	5.00	10.00	20.00
MCA					
301	Do You Know What It's Like to Be Lonesome?	1973	3.00	6.00	12.00
366	Primrose Lane/Don't Give Up on Me	1973	3.00	6.00	12.00
408	For Wives and Lovers	1974	3.00	6.00	12.00
462	I Wonder Whose Baby (You Are Now)/Make Hay While the Sun Shines	1975	3.00	6.00	12.00
MERCURY					
MG 21072 [M]	The Best of Jerry Wallace	1966	3.75	7.50	15.00
SR-61072 [S]	The Best of Jerry Wallace	1966	5.00	10.00	20.00
MGM					
M3G-4990	Greatest Hits	1975	2.50	5.00	10.00

Number	Title (A Side/B Side)	Yr	VG	VG+	NM
M3G-4995	Comin' Home to You	1976	3.00	6.00	12.00
M3G-5007	Jerry Wallace	1976	2.50	5.00	10.00
SUNSET					
SUS-5294	Primrose Lane	1969	3.00	6.00	12.00
UNITED ARTISTS					
UXS-95 [(2)]	Jerry Wallace Superpak	1972	5.00	10.00	20.00

WALLACE, SONNY

45s

Number	Title (A Side/B Side)	Yr	VG	VG+	NM
YUCCA					
127	Black Cadillac/If a Man Could See	1961	25.00	50.00	100.00

WALLER, GORDON

Also see PETER AND GORDON.

45s

Number	Title (A Side/B Side)	Yr	VG	VG+	NM
BELL					
794	The Lady in the Window/I Was a Boy When You Needed a Man	1969	2.00	4.00	8.00
882	Sunshine/You Gonna Hurt Yourself	1970	—	3.00	6.00
CAPITOL					
2346	Everyday/Because of a Woman	1968	2.00	4.00	8.00
5886	Speak for Me/Little Nonie	1967	2.00	4.00	8.00
Albums					
ABC					
X-749	And Gordon	1972	3.75	7.50	15.00

WALLIS, RUTH

Albums

Number	Title (A Side/B Side)	Yr	VG	VG+	NM
KING					
265-6 [10]	Rhumba Party	1952	30.00	60.00	120.00
265-9 [10]	House Party	1952	30.00	60.00	120.00
395-507 [M]	House Party	1956	25.00	50.00	100.00
904 [M]	Saucy Hit Parade	1964	7.50	15.00	30.00
986 [M]	Here's Looking Up Your Hatch	1966	7.50	15.00	30.00
987 [M]	Davy's Little Dinghy	1966	7.50	15.00	30.00
988 [M]	Marry Go Round	1966	7.50	15.00	30.00
989 [M]	Red Lights	1966	7.50	15.00	30.00
990 [M]	Ubangi Me	1966	7.50	15.00	30.00
991 [M]	Oil Man from Texas	1966	7.50	15.00	30.00
992 [M]	He Wants a Little...Pizza	1966	7.50	15.00	30.00
993 [M]	Bahama Mama	1966	7.50	15.00	30.00
WALLIS ORIGINAL					
2 [M]	Ruth Wallis	1957	10.00	20.00	40.00

WALLS, VAN

45s

Number	Title (A Side/B Side)	Yr	VG	VG+	NM
ATLANTIC					
980	After Midnight/Blue Sender	1952	25.00	50.00	100.00

WALSH, JOE

Also see EAGLES; THE JAMES GANG (1).

12-Inch Singles

Number	Title (A Side/B Side)	Yr	VG	VG+	NM
ABC					
SPDJ-46 [DJ]	Turn to Stone (same on both sides)	1978	5.00	10.00	20.00
WARNER BROS.					
PRO-A-2038 [DJ]	Space Age Whiz Kids (same on both sides)	1983	—	3.00	6.00
PRO-A-2340 [DJ]	Good Man Down (same on both sides)	1985	—	2.50	5.00
PRO-A-2756 [DJ]	Radio Song (same on both sides)	1985	—	2.50	5.00
PRO-A-2833 [DJ]	Malibu (same on both sides)	1985	—	2.50	5.00
45s					
ABC					
12115	Time Out/Help Me Through the Night	1975	—	2.50	5.00
12187	Walk Away/Help Me Through the Night	1976	—	2.50	5.00
12426	Rocky Mountain Way/Turn to Stone	1978	—	2.00	4.00
ABC DUNHILL					
4327	I'll Tell the World About You/Mother Says	1972	—	2.50	5.00
4361	Rocky Mountain Way/Prayer	1973	—	2.50	5.00
4373	Meadows/Bookends	1973	—	2.50	5.00
15026	Turn to Stone/All Night Laundromat Blues	1974	—	2.50	5.00
ASYLUM					
45493	Life's Been Good/Theme from Boat Weirdos	1978	—	2.00	4.00
45536	At the Station/Over and Over	1978	—	2.00	4.00
47144	A Life of Illusion/Rockets	1981	—	2.00	4.00
47197	Made Your Mind Up/Things	1981	—	2.00	4.00
EPIC					
73843	Ordinary Average Guy/Alphabetical Order	1991	—	—	3.00
FULL MOON					
69951	Waffle Stomp/Things	1982	—	2.00	4.00
69951 [PS]	Waffle Stomp/Things	1982	—	2.00	4.00
FULL MOON/ASYLUM					
46639	All Night Long/Orange Blossom Special	1980	—	2.00	4.00
—B-side by Gilley's Urban Cowboy Band					
46639 [PS]	All Night Long/Orange Blossom Special	1980	—	2.50	5.00
WARNER BROS.					
28225	In My Car/How Ya Doin'?	1987	—	—	3.00
28304	The Radio Song/How Ya Doin'?	1987	—	—	3.00
28304 [PS]	The Radio Song/How Ya Doin'?	1987	—	—	3.00
28910	Good Man Down/I Broke My Leg	1985	—	2.00	4.00
29454	I.L.B.T.'s/Love Letters	1983	—	2.00	4.00
29519	Here We Are Now/I Can Play That Rock and Roll	1983	—	2.00	4.00
29611	Space Age Whiz Kids/Theme from Island Weirdos	1983	—	2.00	4.00
29611 [PS]	Space Age Whiz Kids/Theme from Island Weirdos	1983	—	2.50	5.00
Albums					
ABC					
ABCD-932	You Can't Argue with a Sick Mind	1976	2.50	5.00	10.00
AA-1083	The Best of Joe Walsh	1978	2.50	5.00	10.00
—Also contains two James Gang tracks					
ABC COMMAND					
QD-40016 [Q]	The Smoker You Drink, the Player You Get	1974	5.00	10.00	20.00

Number	Title (A Side/B Side)	Yr	VG	VG+	NM
QD-40017 [Q]	So What	1975	5.00	10.00	20.00
ABC DUNHILL					
DS-50130	Barnstorm	1972	2.50	5.00	10.00
—Of the James Gang and the Eagles					
DS-50140	The Smoker You Drink, the Player You Get	1973	2.50	5.00	10.00
DS-51071	So What	1974	2.50	5.00	10.00
ASYLUM					
6E-141	But Seriously, Folks...	1978	2.50	5.00	10.00
5E-523	There Goes the Neighborhood	1981	2.00	4.00	8.00
MCA					
37051	You Can't Argue with a Sick Mind	1979	2.00	4.00	8.00
—Reissue of ABC 932					
37052	The Best of Joe Walsh	1979	2.00	4.00	8.00
—Reissue of ABC 1083					
37053	Barnstorm	1979	2.00	4.00	8.00
—Reissue of ABC Dunhill 50130					
37054	The Smoker You Drink, the Player You Get	1979	2.00	4.00	8.00
—Reissue of ABC Dunhill 50140					
37055	So What	1979	2.00	4.00	8.00
—Reissue of ABC Dunhill 50171					
WARNER BROS.					
23884	You Bought It — You Name It	1983	2.00	4.00	8.00
25281	The Confessor	1985	2.00	4.00	8.00
25281 [DJ]	The Confessor	1985	3.75	7.50	15.00
—Promo only on Quiex II vinyl					
25606	Got Any Gum?	1987	2.00	4.00	8.00

WALSTON, RAY

Number	Title (A Side/B Side)	Yr	VG	VG+	NM
Albums					
VEE JAY					
LP-1110 [M]	My Favorite Songs from "Mary Poppins" and Other Songs to Delight	1965	6.25	12.50	25.00
SR-1110 [S]	My Favorite Songs from "Mary Poppins" and Other Songs to Delight	1965	7.50	15.00	30.00

WANDERERS, THE (1)

Number	Title (A Side/B Side)	Yr	VG	VG+	NM
45s					
CUB					
9003	A Teenage Quarrel/My Shining Hour	1958	7.50	15.00	30.00
9019	Collecting Hearts/Two Hearts on a Window Pane	1958	10.00	20.00	40.00
9023	Please/Shadrack, Meshack, and Abednego	1959	7.50	15.00	30.00
9035	Only When You're Lonely/I'm Not Ashamed	1959	7.50	15.00	30.00
9054	I Walked Through a Forest/I'm Waiting for Green Pastures	1959	7.50	15.00	30.00
9075	I Need You More/I Could Make You Mine	1960	7.50	15.00	30.00
9089	For Your Love/Sally Goodheart	1961	7.50	15.00	30.00
9094	I'll Never Smile Again/A Little Too Long	1961	7.50	15.00	30.00
9099	She Wears My Ring/Somebody Else's Sweetheart	1961	12.50	25.00	50.00
9109	There Is No Greater Love/As Time Goes By	1962	7.50	15.00	30.00
MGM					
13082	There Is No Greater Love/As Time Goes By	1962	5.00	10.00	20.00
ONYX					
518	Thinking of You/Great Jumpin' Catfish	1957	15.00	30.00	60.00
ORBIT					
9003	A Teenage Quarrel/My Shining Hour	1958	15.00	30.00	60.00
SAVOY					
1109	We Could Find Happiness/Holy Mae Ethel	1953	125.00	250.00	500.00
UNITED ARTISTS					
570	After He Breaks Your Heart/Run, Run Senorita	1963	3.75	7.50	15.00
648	I'll Know/You Can't Run Away from Me	1963	7.50	15.00	30.00

WANDERERS, THE (2)

Number	Title (A Side/B Side)	Yr	VG	VG+	NM
45s					
PANAMA					
3900	Quiet Night/One Look	1960	3.75	7.50	15.00

WANDERERS, THE (U)

May be by group (1).

Number	Title (A Side/B Side)	Yr	VG	VG+	NM
45s					
GONE					
5005	Mask Off/My Lady Chocaonine	1957	7.50	15.00	30.00

WANDERLEY, WALTER

Number	Title (A Side/B Side)	Yr	VG	VG+	NM
45s					
A&M					
1023	Surfboard/When It Was Done	1969	—	3.00	6.00
GNP CRESCENDO					
824	Perpetual Motion Love/Monica	197?	—	2.00	4.00
TOWER					
296	You and I/What Do You Know About Me	1966	2.00	4.00	8.00
334	Brazilian Samba/Murmurio	1967	2.00	4.00	8.00
VERVE					
10421	Summer Samba (So Nice)/Call Me	1966	2.00	4.00	8.00
10456	Chaganca/Amanha	1966	2.00	4.00	8.00
10539	On the South Side of Chicago/Minha Saudade	1967	2.00	4.00	8.00
10579	Sensuous/Kee-Ka-Roo	1968	2.00	4.00	8.00
WORLD PACIFIC					
77861	Jet Samba (Samba Do Aviao)/Sad Samba (Samba Triste)	1966	2.00	4.00	8.00
Albums					
A&M					
SP-3018	When It Was Done	1969	3.00	6.00	12.00
SP-3022	Moondreams	1969	3.00	6.00	12.00
CANYON					
7711	Return of the Original Sound	196?	3.00	6.00	12.00
GNP CRESCENDO					
GNPS-2137	Brazil's Greatest Hits	197?	2.50	5.00	10.00
GNPS-2142	Perpetual Motion Love	197?	2.50	5.00	10.00
PHILIPS					
PHM 200227 [M]	Brazilian Blend	1967	3.00	6.00	12.00
PHM 200233 [M]	Organ-ized	1967	3.00	6.00	12.00
PHS 600227 [S]	Brazilian Blend	1967	3.75	7.50	15.00
PHS 600233 [S]	Organ-ized	1967	3.75	7.50	15.00
TOWER					
ST 5047 [S]	From Rio with Love	1966	3.75	7.50	15.00
T 5047 [M]	From Rio with Love	1966	3.75	7.50	15.00
ST 5058 [S]	Murmurio	1967	3.75	7.50	15.00
T 5058 [M]	Murmurio	1967	3.75	7.50	15.00
VERVE					
V-8658 [M]	Rain Forest	1966	3.75	7.50	15.00
V6-8658 [S]	Rain Forest	1966	5.00	10.00	20.00
V-8676 [M]	Cheganca	1966	3.75	7.50	15.00
V6-8676 [S]	Cheganca	1966	5.00	10.00	20.00
V-8706 [M]	Batucada	1967	5.00	10.00	20.00
V6-8706 [S]	Batucada	1967	3.75	7.50	15.00
V-8739 [M]	Kee-Ka-Roo	1967	5.00	10.00	20.00
V6-8739 [S]	Kee-Ka-Roo	1967	3.75	7.50	15.00
WORLD PACIFIC					
WP-1856 [M]	Samba So!	1967	5.00	10.00	20.00
WP-1866 [M]	Quarteto Bossamba	1967	6.25	12.50	25.00
ST-21856 [S]	Samba So!	1967	3.75	7.50	15.00
ST-21866 [S]	Quarteto Bossamba	1967	3.75	7.50	15.00

WAR

Also see ERIC BURDON AND WAR.

Number	Title (A Side/B Side)	Yr	VG	VG+	NM
12-Inch Singles					
AVENUE					
76028	Da Roof (3 versions)	1994	2.00	4.00	8.00
LAX					
02122	Cinco de Mayo (7:29) (3:59)	1981	2.50	5.00	10.00
PRIORITY					
VL-9364	Low Rider '87 (Extended Version 7:45) (Radio Edit) (Instrumental)	1987	3.75	7.50	15.00
VL-9502	Livin' In the Red (versions unknown)	1987	3.00	6.00	12.00
RCA					
PD-13062	You Got the Power/Cinco de Mayo	1982	2.50	5.00	10.00
PD-13239	Outlaw/I'm About Somebody	1982	2.50	5.00	10.00
JD-13323 [DJ]	Just Because (same on both sides)	1982	2.00	4.00	8.00
PD-13323	Just Because (Long Version)/The Jungle (Medley)	1982	2.50	5.00	10.00
SISAPA					
76707	Truth Be Known (4 versions)	1991	2.00	4.00	8.00
UNITED ARTISTS					
SP-184 [DJ]	Youngblood (Livin' in the Streets) (9:07)/Keep On Doin'	1978	3.75	7.50	15.00
45s					
BLUE NOTE					
1009	L.A. Sunshine/Slowly We Walk Together	1977	—	2.50	5.00
COCO PLUM					
2002	Groovin'/(B-side unknown)	1985	—	2.00	4.00
LAX					
02120	Cinco de Mayo/Don't Let No One Get You Down	1981	—	2.50	5.00
MCA					
40820	Galaxy (Part 1)/Galaxy (Part 2)	1977	—	2.50	5.00
40820 [PS]	Galaxy (Part 1)/Galaxy (Part 2)	1977	—	3.00	6.00
40883	Hey Senorita/Sweet Fighting Lady	1978	—	2.50	5.00
40995	Good, Good Feelin'/Baby Face (She Said Do Do Do Do)	1979	—	2.50	5.00
41061	I'm the One Who Understands/Corns & Callouses	1979	—	2.50	5.00
41158	Don't Take It Away/The Music Band 2 (We Are the Music Band)	1979	—	2.50	5.00
41209	I'll Be Around/The Music Band 2 (We Are the Music Band)	1980	—	2.50	5.00
RCA					
PB-13061	You Got the Power/Cinco de Mayo	1982	—	2.00	4.00
PB-13239	Outlaw/I'm About Somebody	1982	—	2.00	4.00
PB-13322	Just Because/The Jungle (Medley)	1982	—	2.00	4.00
JH-13426 [DJ]	Baby, It's Cold Outside (same on both sides)	1982	—	2.50	5.00
PB-13544	Life (Is So Strange)/W.W. III	1983	—	2.00	4.00
UNITED ARTISTS					
XW163	The Cisco Kid/Beetles in the Bog	1973	—	2.50	5.00
XW281	Gypsy Man/Deliver the Word	1973	—	2.50	5.00
XW350	Me and Baby Brother/In Your Eyes	1973	—	2.50	5.00
XW432	Ballero/Slippin' Into Darkness	1974	—	2.50	5.00
XW629	Why Can't We Be Friends?/In Mazatlin	1975	—	2.50	5.00
XW629 [PS]	Why Can't We Be Friends?/In Mazatlin	1975	—	3.00	6.00
XW706	Low Rider/So	1975	—	2.50	5.00
XW706 [PS]	Low Rider/So	1975	—	3.00	6.00
XW834	Summer/All Day Music	1976	—	2.50	5.00
XW1213	Youngblood/(Instrumental)	1978	—	2.50	5.00
XW1247	Sing a Happy Song/This Funky Music Makes You Feel Good	1978	—	2.50	5.00
50746	Lonely Feelin'/Sun Oh Sun	1971	2.00	4.00	8.00
50746 [PS]	Lonely Feelin'/Sun Oh Sun	1971	3.00	6.00	12.00
50815	All Day Music/Get Down	1971	2.00	4.00	8.00
50867	Slippin' Into Darkness/Happy Head	1971	—	3.00	6.00
50975	The World Is a Ghetto/Four Cornered Room	1972	—	3.00	6.00
Albums					
AVENUE					
R1 71706	Peace Sign	1994	3.75	7.50	15.00
BLUE NOTE					
BN-LA690-G [(2)]	Platinum Jazz	1977	3.00	6.00	12.00
LAX					
PW 37111	All Day Music	1981	2.50	5.00	10.00
—Reissue of United Artists 5546					
PW 37112	The World Is a Ghetto	1981	2.50	5.00	10.00
—Reissue of United Artists 5652					
PW 37113	Why Can't We Be Friends?	1981	2.50	5.00	10.00
—Reissue of United Artists 441					
MCA					
745	Galaxy	1983	2.00	4.00	8.00
—Reissue of MCA 3030					

Number	Title (A Side/B Side)	Yr	VG	VG+	NM
747	The Music Band	1983	2.00	4.00	8.00
—Reissue of MCA 3085					
751	The Music Band 2	1983	2.00	4.00	8.00
—Reissue of MCA 3193					
3030	Galaxy	1977	2.50	5.00	10.00
3085	The Music Band	1979	2.50	5.00	10.00
3193	The Music Band 2	1979	2.50	5.00	10.00
5156	The Music Band Live	1980	2.50	5.00	10.00
5362	Best of the Music Band	1982	2.50	5.00	10.00
5411	Music Band Jazz	1983	2.50	5.00	10.00
PRIORITY					
SL 9467	The Best of War...And More	1987	2.50	5.00	10.00
RCA VICTOR					
AFL1-4208	Outlaw	1982	2.50	5.00	10.00
AFL1-4598	Life (Is So Strange)	1983	2.50	5.00	10.00
UNITED ARTISTS					
SP-103 [DJ]	Radio Free War	1974	6.25	12.50	25.00
—Promo only on blue vinyl					
UA-LA128-F	Deliver the Word	1973	3.00	6.00	12.00
UA-LA193-J [(2)]	War Live!	1974	3.75	7.50	15.00
UA-LA441-G	Why Can't We Be Friends?	1975	2.50	5.00	10.00
UA-LA648-G	Greatest Hits	1976	2.50	5.00	10.00
UAS-5508	War	1971	3.75	7.50	15.00
—Also see "Burdon, Eric, and War"					
UAS-5546	All Day Music	1971	3.75	7.50	15.00
UAS-5652	The World Is a Ghetto	1972	3.00	6.00	12.00

WAR BABIES, THE

45s

Number	Title (A Side/B Side)	Yr	VG	VG+	NM
UNI					
55164	War Baby/Together Forever	1969	2.00	4.00	8.00

WARD, BILLY, AND THE DOMINOES

Also includes "The Dominoes."

45s

Number	Title (A Side/B Side)	Yr	VG	VG+	NM
ABC-PARAMOUNT					
10128	You're Mine/The World Is Waiting for the Sunrise	1960	5.00	10.00	20.00
10156	You/Gypsy	1960	5.00	10.00	20.00
DECCA					
29933	St. Therese of the Roses/Home Is Where You Hang Your Hat	1956	7.50	15.00	30.00
30043	Come On, Shake, Let's Crawl/Will You Remember	1956	7.50	15.00	30.00
30149	Half a Love (Is Better Than None)/Evermore	1956	7.50	15.00	30.00
30199	Rock, Plymouth Rock/Till Kingdom Come	1957	7.50	15.00	30.00
30420	To Each His Own/I Don't Stand a Ghost of a Chance	1957	7.50	15.00	30.00
30514	September Song/When the Saints Go Marching In	1957	7.50	15.00	30.00
FEDERAL					
12001	Do Something For Me/Chicken Blues	1951	200.00	400.00	800.00
—Note: Federal 12010 and 12016 were issued only on 78s					
12022AA	Sixty Minute Man/I Can't Escape from You	1951	125.00	250.00	500.00
12036	Heart to Heart/Looking for a Man to Satisfy My Soul	1951	125.00	250.00	500.00
—With Little Esther					
12039	I Am with You/Weeping Willow Blues	1951	100.00	200.00	400.00
12059	That's What You're Doing to Me/When the Swallows Come Back to Capistrano	1952	100.00	200.00	400.00
12068AA	Have Mercy Baby/Deep Sea Blues	1952	62.50	125.00	250.00
12072	Love, Love, Love/That's What You're Doing to Me	1952	50.00	100.00	200.00
12105	I'd Be Satisfied/No Room	1952	45.00	90.00	180.00
12106	I'm Lonely/Yours Forever	1952	45.00	90.00	180.00
12114	The Bells/Pedal Pushin' Papa	1952	50.00	100.00	200.00
12129	These Foolish Things Remind Me of You/Don't Leave Me This Way	1953	75.00	150.00	300.00
—Green label, gold top					
12129	These Foolish Things Remind Me of You/Don't Leave Me This Way	1954	25.00	50.00	100.00
—Green label, silver top					
12129	These Foolish Things Remind Me of You/Don't Leave Me This Way	1955	7.50	15.00	30.00
—All-green label					
12139	You Can't Keep a Good Man Down/Where Now Little Heart	1953	25.00	50.00	100.00
12162	Until the Real Thing Comes Along/My Baby's 3 D	1954	25.00	50.00	100.00
12178	Tootsie Roll/Move to the Outskirts of Town	1954	25.00	50.00	100.00
12184	Handwriting on the Wall/One Moment with You	1954	50.00	100.00	200.00
12193	Above Jacob's Ladder/Little Black Train	1954	12.50	25.00	50.00
12209	Can't Do Sixty No More/If I Never Get to Heaven	1955	25.00	50.00	100.00
12218	Love Me Now or Let Me Go/Cave Man	1955	12.50	25.00	50.00
12263	Bobby Sox Baby/How Long, How Long Blues	1956	12.50	25.00	50.00
12301	St. Louis Blues/One Moment with You	1957	12.50	25.00	50.00
12308	Have Mercy Baby/Love, Love, Love	1957	10.00	20.00	40.00
JUBLIEE					
5163	Gimme, Gimme, Gimme/Come to Me, Baby	1954	7.50	15.00	30.00
5213	Sweethearts on Parade/Take Me Back to Heaven	1955	7.50	15.00	30.00
KING					
1280	Rags to Riches/Don't Ask Me	1953	12.50	25.00	50.00
1281	Christmas in Heaven/Ringing In a Brand New Year	1953	25.00	50.00	100.00
1342	Tenderly/Little Lie	1954	12.50	25.00	50.00
1364	Three Coins in the Fountain/Lonesome Road	1954	12.50	25.00	50.00
1368	Little Things Mean a Lot/I Really Don't Want to Know	1954	10.00	20.00	40.00
1492	Learnin' the Blues/May I Never Love	1955	10.00	20.00	40.00
1502	Over the Rainbow/Give Me You	1955	10.00	20.00	40.00
5322	Sixty Minute Man/Have Mercy Baby	1960	5.00	10.00	20.00
5463	Lay It on the Line/That's How You Know You're Growing Old	1961	5.00	10.00	20.00
6002	I'm Walking Behind You/This Love of Mine	1965	5.00	10.00	20.00
6016	O Holy Night/What Are You Doin' New Year's Eve	1965	5.00	10.00	20.00
6106	O Holy Night/What Are You Doin' New Year's Eve	1967	3.75	7.50	15.00
LIBERTY					
55071	Star Dust/Lucinda	1957	6.25	12.50	25.00
55099	Deep Purple/Do It Again	1957	6.25	12.50	25.00
55111	My Proudest Possession/Someone Greater Than I	1957	6.25	12.50	25.00
55126	Solitude/You Grow Sweeter As the Years Go By	1958	6.25	12.50	25.00
55136	Jennie Lee/Music, Maestro, Please	1958	6.25	12.50	25.00
55181	Please Don't Say No/Behave, Hula Girl	1959	6.25	12.50	25.00
RO-ZAN					
10001	Man in the Stain Glass Window/My Fair Weather Friend	1961	5.00	10.00	20.00
UNITED ARTISTS					
0017	Stardust/These Foolish Things	1973	—	2.50	5.00
—"Silver Spotlight Series" reissue					

7-Inch Extended Plays

Number	Title (A Side/B Side)	Yr	VG	VG+	NM
DECCA					
ED 2549	(contents unknown)	1958	50.00	100.00	200.00
ED 2549 [PS]	Billy Ward and His Dominoes	1958	50.00	100.00	200.00
FEDERAL					
212	(contents unknown)	1956	100.00	200.00	400.00
—Green label, silver top					
212	(contents unknown)	1956	25.00	50.00	100.00
—All-green label					
212 [PS]	Billy Ward and His Dominoes, Vol. 1	1956	25.00	50.00	100.00
262	(contents unknown)	1957	100.00	200.00	400.00
—Green label, silver top					
262	(contents unknown)	1957	25.00	50.00	100.00
—All-green label					
262 [PS]	Billy Ward and His Dominoes, Vol. 2	1957	25.00	50.00	100.00
269	(contents unknown)	1957	100.00	200.00	400.00
—Green label, silver top					
269	(contents unknown)	1957	25.00	50.00	100.00
—All-green label					
269 [PS]	Billy Ward and His Dominoes, Vol. 3	1957	25.00	50.00	100.00
LIBERTY					
LEP-1-3056	(contents unknown)	1959	25.00	50.00	100.00
LEP-1-3056 [PS]	Sea of Glass (Part One)	1959	25.00	50.00	100.00
LEP-2-3056	Deep River/By and By//The House of the Lord/The Lullaby Divine	1959	25.00	50.00	100.00
LEP-2-3056 [PS]	Sea of Glass (Part 2)	1959	25.00	50.00	100.00
LEP-3-3056	(contents unknown)	1959	25.00	50.00	100.00
LEP-3-3056 [PS]	Sea of Glass (Part 3)	1959	25.00	50.00	100.00
LEP-1-3083	Stardust/Eatin' and Sleepin'//Music, Maestro, Please/I'll Never Ask for More Than This	1959	25.00	50.00	100.00
LEP-1-3083 [PS]	Yours Forever (Part One)	1959	25.00	50.00	100.00
LEP-2-3083	(contents unknown)	1959	25.00	50.00	100.00
LEP-2-3083 [PS]	Yours Forever (Part 2)	1959	25.00	50.00	100.00
LEP-3-3083	Smoke Gets in Your Eyes/Do It Again//If You Please/Yours Forever	1959	25.00	50.00	100.00
LEP-3-3083 [PS]	Yours Forever (Part 3)	1959	25.00	50.00	100.00

Albums

Number	Title (A Side/B Side)	Yr	VG	VG+	NM
DECCA					
DL 8621 [M]	Billy Ward and the Dominoes	1958	50.00	100.00	200.00
FEDERAL					
295-94 [10]	Billy Ward and His Dominoes	1955	6000.	9500.	13000.
548 [M]	Billy Ward and His Dominoes	1958	375.00	750.00	1500.
559 [M]	Clyde McPhatter with Billy Ward and His Dominoes	1958	300.00	600.00	1200.
KING					
548 [M]	Billy Ward and His Dominoes	1958	—	—	—
—Unknown					
559 [M]	Clyde McPhatter with Billy Ward and His Dominoes	1958	150.00	300.00	600.00
—Yellow cover					
559 [M]	Clyde McPhatter with Billy Ward and His Dominoes	196?	75.00	150.00	300.00
—Pink cover					
733 [M]	Billy Ward and His Dominoes Featuring Clyde McPhatter and Jackie Wilson	1961	150.00	300.00	600.00
952 [M]	24 Songs	1966	12.50	25.00	50.00
5005	14 Hits	197?	3.00	6.00	12.00
5008	21 Hits	197?	3.00	6.00	12.00
LIBERTY					
LRP-3056 [M]	Sea of Glass	1957	15.00	30.00	60.00
LRP-3083 [M]	Yours Forever	1958	15.00	30.00	60.00
LRP-3113 [M]	Pagan Love Song	1959	15.00	30.00	60.00
LST-7113 [S]	Pagan Love Song	1959	25.00	50.00	100.00

WARD, BURT

45s

Number	Title (A Side/B Side)	Yr	VG	VG+	NM
MGM					
13632	Boy Wonder I Love You/Orange Colored Sky	1966	50.00	100.00	200.00
—Written and produced by Frank Zappa					

WARD, HERB

45s

Number	Title (A Side/B Side)	Yr	VG	VG+	NM
ARGO					
5510	Strange Change/Why Do You Want to Leave	1965	20.00	40.00	80.00
RCA VICTOR					
47-9688	Honest to Goodness/If You Got to Leave Me	1968	15.00	30.00	60.00

WARD, JOE

45s

Number	Title (A Side/B Side)	Yr	VG	VG+	NM
GUSTO					
814	Nuttin' For Christmas/Christmas Time's A Coming	1979	—	2.00	4.00
—B-side by Mac Wiseman					
KING					
4854	Nuttin' for Xmas/Christmas Questions	1955	3.00	6.00	12.00
4897	Upsy Down Town/Mama Darling	1956	5.00	10.00	20.00
4931	Rock and Roll Merry-Go-Round/Freckle Face	1956	5.00	10.00	20.00

WARD, ROBIN

45s

DOT

Number	Title (A Side/B Side)	Yr	VG	VG+	NM
16530	Wonderful Summer/Dream Boy	1963	3.00	6.00	12.00
16578	Winter's Here/Bobby	1963	2.50	5.00	10.00
16599	Johnny Come and Get Me/Where the Blue of the Night Meets the Gold of the Day	1964	5.00	10.00	20.00
16624	In His Car/Wishing	1964	6.25	12.50	25.00

Albums

DOT

Number	Title (A Side/B Side)	Yr	VG	VG+	NM
DLP 3555 [M]	Wonderful Summer	1963	50.00	100.00	200.00
DLP 25555 [S]	Wonderful Summer	1963	75.00	150.00	300.00

WARD, SINGIN' SAMMY

45s

MOTOWN

Number	Title (A Side/B Side)	Yr	VG	VG+	NM
1004	Lover/That's Why I Love You So Much	1960	10.00	20.00	40.00

—With Sherri Taylor

SOUL

Number	Title (A Side/B Side)	Yr	VG	VG+	NM
35004	Bread Winner/You've Got to Change	1964	12.50	25.00	50.00

TAMLA

Number	Title (A Side/B Side)	Yr	VG	VG+	NM
54030	What Makes You Love Him/The Child Is Really Wild	1960	50.00	100.00	200.00
—With lines label					
54030	What Makes You Love Him/The Child Is Really Wild	1960	18.75	37.50	75.00
—With globe label					
54049	What Makes You Love Him/Don't Take It Away	1961	12.50	25.00	50.00
54057	Everybody Knew It/Big Joe Moe	1962	12.50	25.00	50.00
54071	Part Time Love/Someday Pretty Baby	1962	12.50	25.00	50.00

WARD, WALTER, AND THE CHALLENGERS

Later recorded as THE OLYMPICS.

45s

MELATONE

Number	Title (A Side/B Side)	Yr	VG	VG+	NM
1002	I Can Tell/The Mambo Beat	1957	100.00	200.00	400.00

WARDELL AND THE SULTANS

45s

IMPERIAL

Number	Title (A Side/B Side)	Yr	VG	VG+	NM
5812	The Original Popeye/Dance Time	1962	5.00	10.00	20.00
5886	I Need Your Love/I'm Broke	1962	3.75	7.50	15.00

WARE, CURTIS, AND THE FOUR DO-MATICS

45s

KAYBEE

Number	Title (A Side/B Side)	Yr	VG	VG+	NM
101	Flame in My Heart/Am I in Love	1961	125.00	250.00	500.00

WARE, EDDIE

45s

STATES

Number	Title (A Side/B Side)	Yr	VG	VG+	NM
130	That's the Stuff I Like/Lonely Broken Heart	1954	30.00	60.00	120.00

WARING, FRED, AND THE PENNSYLVANIANS

45s

CAPITOL

Number	Title (A Side/B Side)	Yr	VG	VG+	NM
F3901	Christmas Was Meant for Children/I Heard the Bells on Christmas Day	1958	3.00	6.00	12.00
4289	Inch Worm/The Donkey Song	1959	2.00	4.00	8.00

DECCA

Number	Title (A Side/B Side)	Yr	VG	VG+	NM
9-67 [(4)]	'Twas the Night Before Christmas	1950	12.50	25.00	50.00
—Contains 4 records (23642, 23643, 23644, 23645) and box					
9-74 [(3)]	The Song of Christmas	1950	10.00	20.00	40.00
—Includes records and box					
9-97 [(4)]	(title unknown)	195?	12.50	25.00	50.00
—Contains 4 records (27283, 27284, 27285, 27286) and box					
23642	Twas the Night Before Christmas (Part 1)/Twas the Night Before Christmas (Part 2)	1950	3.00	6.00	12.00
—Sides 1 and 2 of "Album No. 9-67"					
23643	Silent Night/Oh Gathering Clouds	1950	3.00	6.00	12.00
—Sides 3 and 4 of "Album No. 9-67"					
23644	Adeste Fideles/Cantique De Noel	1950	3.00	6.00	12.00
—Sides 5 and 6 of "Album No. 9-67"					
23645	The First Noel/O Little Town of Bethlehem//Carol of the Bells/Beautiful Saviour	1950	3.00	6.00	12.00
—Sides 7 and 8 of "Album No. 9-67"					
24500	White Christmas/Twelve Days Of Christmas	195?	3.00	6.00	12.00
—78 originally released in 1948					
24500	White Christmas/Twelve Days Of Christmas	1960	2.00	4.00	8.00
—Also known to exist on color bars label					
25698	Lollytoodum/On Top of Old Smoky	1966	—	2.50	5.00
27146	Ave Maria/The Rosary	1950	3.00	6.00	12.00
27147	The Bells of St. Mary's/In a Monastery Garden	1950	3.00	6.00	12.00
27148	The Lord's Prayer/Were You There When They Crucified My Lord	1950	3.00	6.00	12.00
27149	Faith of Our Fathers/Blest Be the Tie That Binds	1950	3.00	6.00	12.00
—The above four comprise a box set					
27150	A Cigarette, Sweet Music and You/So Beats My Heart for You	1950	3.00	6.00	12.00
27151	Remember/Day In-Day Out	1950	3.00	6.00	12.00
27152	Besame Mucho/Marcheta	1950	3.00	6.00	12.00
27153	Beyond the Blue Horizon/My Ideal	1950	3.00	6.00	12.00
—The above four comprise a box set					
27283	When Angels Sang Of Peace/The Christmas Song (Merry Christmas To You)	1950	3.00	6.00	12.00
—Sides 1 and 2 of "Album No. 9-97"					
27284	A Musical Christmas Card/O Christmas Tree//Kentucky Wassailsong/Parade Of The Wooden Soldiers	1950	3.00	6.00	12.00
—Sides 3 and 4 of "Album No. 9-97"					
27285	Heigh Ho the Holly/See Amid the Winter's Snow//Behold That Star/Carol of the Bells	1950	3.00	6.00	12.00
—Sides 5 and 6 of "Album No. 9-97"					
27286	Jingle Bells (Part 1)/Jingle Bells (Part 2)	1950	3.00	6.00	12.00
—Sides 7 and 8 of "Album No. 9-97"					
27291	Oklahoma!/The Surrey with the Fringe on Top	1950	3.00	6.00	12.00
27292	This Was A Real Nice Christmas/You'll Never Walk Alone	1950	3.00	6.00	12.00
27292	You'll Never Walk Alone/This Was a Real Nice Christmas	1950	3.00	6.00	12.00
27293	If I Loved You/What's the Use of Wond'rin'	1950	3.00	6.00	12.00
27294	Bali Ha'i/Some Enchanted Evening	1950	3.00	6.00	12.00
27295	A Wonderful Guy/People Will Say We're in Love	1950	3.00	6.00	12.00
27297	It Might As Well Be Spring/A Fellow Needs a Girl	1950	3.00	6.00	12.00
27454	No Man Is an Island/Worship	1951	3.00	6.00	12.00
27465	Palms/Before the Crucifix	1951	3.00	6.00	12.00
27480	The Place Where I Worship/A Home That's Filled with Love	1951	3.00	6.00	12.00
27496	Faithful/My Lost Melody	1951	3.00	6.00	12.00
27507	The Loveliest Night of the Year/Tulips and Heather	1951	3.00	6.00	12.00
27581	Something Wonderful/Hello, Young Lovers	1951	3.00	6.00	12.00
27600	I Whistle a Happy Tune/We Kiss in the Shadows	1951	3.00	6.00	12.00
27855	Monastery Bells/A Little Foolish Pride	1951	3.00	6.00	12.00
27935	Remember Your Promise (Say the Bells of St. Thomas)/Two Sleepy People	1952	3.00	6.00	12.00
27964	You'll Never Walk Alone/Tulips and Heather	1952	3.00	6.00	12.00
27988	Heigh-Ho/Whistle While You Work	1952	3.00	6.00	12.00
28020	The Caissons Go Rolling Along/Army Air Corps	1952	3.00	6.00	12.00
28235	It Happened in Monterey/You	1952	3.00	6.00	12.00
28298	Peace in the Valley/Just a Closer Walk with Thee	1952	3.00	6.00	12.00
28305	My Gal Sal/I Do, I Do, I Do	1952	3.00	6.00	12.00
28400	Bibbidi-Bobbidi-Boo/Zip-a-Dee-Doo-Dah	1952	3.00	6.00	12.00
28401	When You Wish Upon a Star/One Song	1952	3.00	6.00	12.00
28402	Lavender Blue/Tico Tico	1952	3.00	6.00	12.00
28449	High Noon (Do Not Forsake Me)/Outside of Heaven	1952	3.00	6.00	12.00
28512	God Bless America/Where in the World	1952	3.00	6.00	12.00
28527	Somebody Loves You/True, Be True, My Love	1953	2.50	5.00	10.00
28559	Mamie/Ike, Mr. President	1953	5.00	10.00	20.00
28600	One to Remember/Just a Dream of You Dear	1953	2.50	5.00	10.00
28970	Winter Wonderland/Snow, Snow	1953	3.00	6.00	12.00
29063	Easter Parade/Say It with Music	1954	2.50	5.00	10.00
29192	My Friend/He Was There	1954	2.50	5.00	10.00
29304	Fanny/Restless Heart	1954	2.50	5.00	10.00
29305	Be Kind to Your Parents/I Have to Tell You	1954	2.50	5.00	10.00
29331	Without Love/Silk Stockings	1954	2.50	5.00	10.00
29351	Rudolph the Red-Nosed Reindeer/Santa Claus Is Comin' to Town	1954	3.00	6.00	12.00
29451	We'll Go a Long Way Together/He Was the Happiest	1955	2.50	5.00	10.00
29619	(I'll Be With You) In Apple Blossom Time/Drug Store Cowboy	1955	2.50	5.00	10.00
30197	The Navy Hymn/Anchors Aweigh	1957	2.00	4.00	8.00
32323	Big Man/Kites Are Fun	1968	—	2.50	5.00
88023	A Visit From St. Nicholas Part 1/A Visit From St. Nicholas Part 2	195?	3.00	6.00	12.00
88023 [PS]	A Visit From St. Nicholas Part 1/A Visit From St. Nicholas Part 2	195?	5.00	10.00	20.00

REPRISE

Number	Title (A Side/B Side)	Yr	VG	VG+	NM
0315	It's Christmas Time Again/Christmas Candles	1964	3.00	6.00	12.00
—With Bing Crosby					
0316	The 12 Days of Christmas/Do You Hear What I Hear	1964	2.50	5.00	10.00

7-Inch Extended Plays

CAPITOL

Number	Title (A Side/B Side)	Yr	VG	VG+	NM
EAP 1-896	*Now Is the Caroling Season/We Three Kings/Winter Wonderland/It Was a Night of Wonder/White Christmas	1957	3.00	6.00	12.00
EAP 1-896 [PS]	Now Is the Caroling Season, Part 1	1957	3.00	6.00	12.00
EAP 2-896	O Christmas Tree/Silver Bells/Angels We Have Heard on High/In Sweetest Jubilee//I Heard the Bells on Christmas Day/The Christmas Song	1957	3.00	6.00	12.00
EAP 2-896 [PS]	Now Is the Caroling Season, Part 2	1957	3.00	6.00	12.00
EAP 3-896	(contents unknown)	1957	3.00	6.00	12.00
EAP 3-896 [PS]	Now Is the Caroling Season, Part 3	1957	3.00	6.00	12.00

DECCA

Number	Title (A Side/B Side)	Yr	VG	VG+	NM
ED 678 [PS]	Christmas Time	195?	2.50	5.00	10.00
—Cover for 2-EP set					
ED 2007	Holiday for Strings/Prelude of the Bells//Cornish Rhapsody/Pearls on Velvet	195?	3.00	6.00	12.00
ED 2007 [PS]	Fred Waring and the Pennsylvanians, Vol. 1	195?	3.00	6.00	12.00
ED 2039	(contents unknown)	195?	3.00	6.00	12.00
ED 2039 [PS]	Fred Waring and the Pennsylvanians	195?	3.00	6.00	12.00
ED 2198	(contents unknown)	195?	3.00	6.00	12.00
ED 2198 [PS]	The Holy City	195?	3.00	6.00	12.00
ED 2199	(contents unknown)	195?	3.00	6.00	12.00
ED 2199 [PS]	Songs of Easter	195?	3.00	6.00	12.00
ED 2546	(contents unknown)	195?	3.00	6.00	12.00
ED 2546 [PS]	Christmastime	195?	3.00	6.00	12.00
ED 2656	(contents unknown)	195?	3.00	6.00	12.00
ED 2656 [PS]	Christmas Songs	195?	3.00	6.00	12.00
91329	When Angels Sang Of Peace/The Christmas Song//Medley: A Musical Christmas Card-O Christmas Tree-The Sleigh/Medley: Kentucky Wassail Song-Parade of the Wooden Soldiers	195?	2.50	5.00	10.00
—Part of 2-EP set ED 678					
91330	Medley: Heigh Ho The Holly-See Amid The Winter's Snow/Medley: Behold That Star-Carol Of The Bells//Jingle Bells	195?	2.50	5.00	10.00
—Part of 2-EP set ED 678					

Albums

CAPITOL

Number	Title (A Side/B Side)	Yr	VG	VG+	NM
STBB-347 [(2)]	Christmas Magic	1969	3.75	7.50	15.00

—Collects ST 1260 and ST 1610 in one package (abridged); green label original

Number	Title (A Side/B Side)	Yr	VG	VG+	NM
STBB-347 [(2)]	Christmas Magic	1972	3.00	6.00	12.00
—Orange label reissue					
ST 896 [S]	Now Is the Caroling Season	1959	3.75	7.50	15.00
—Black colorband label, logo at left					
ST 896 [S]	Now Is the Caroling Season	1962	3.00	6.00	12.00
—Black colorband label, logo at top					
T 896 [M]	Now Is the Caroling Season	1957	5.00	10.00	20.00
—Originals have turquoise labels					
T 896 [M]	Now Is the Caroling Season	1959	3.75	7.50	15.00
—Black colorband label, logo at left					
T 896 [M]	Now Is the Caroling Season	1962	3.00	6.00	12.00
—Black colorband label, logo at top					
ST 936 [S]	All Through the Night	1958	5.00	10.00	20.00
T 936 [M]	All Through the Night	1958	5.00	10.00	20.00
—Black colorband label, logo at left					
ST 1260 [S]	The Sounds of Christmas	1959	5.00	10.00	20.00
—Originals have black label with colorband and "Capitol" logo at 9 o'clock					
T 1260 [M]	The Sounds of Christmas	1959	3.75	7.50	15.00
—Black colorband label, logo at left					
SM-1610	The Meaning of Christmas	197?	2.00	4.00	8.00
—Reissue of ST 1610 with same contents					
ST 1610 [S]	The Meaning of Christmas	1961	5.00	10.00	20.00
T 1610 [M]	The Meaning of Christmas	1961	3.75	7.50	15.00
ST 2054 [S]	This I Believe	1964	3.75	7.50	15.00
T 2054 [M]	This I Believe	1964	3.00	6.00	12.00
ST 2625 [S]	The Best of Fred Waring and the Pennsylvanians	1967	3.75	7.50	15.00
T 2625 [M]	The Best of Fred Waring and the Pennsylvanians	1967	3.00	6.00	12.00
CAPITOL CREATIVE PRODUCTS					
L-6550 [M]	Fred Waring and the Pennsylvanians Sing of Faith, Home and Christmas	1967	3.75	7.50	15.00
—Compiled for the E.F. MacDonald Company, Dayton, Ohio					
CAPITOL PICKWICK SERIES					
PC-3451 [M]	The Romantic Sound	196?	2.50	5.00	10.00
SPC-3451 [S]	The Romantic Sound	196?	3.00	6.00	12.00
PC-3454 [M]	Some Enchanted Evening	196?	2.50	5.00	10.00
SPC-3454 [S]	Some Enchanted Evening	196?	3.00	6.00	12.00
DECCA					
DBX 186 [(2) M]	The Best of Fred Waring	1965	3.75	7.50	15.00
DL 4158 [M]	This Is My Country	1961	3.00	6.00	12.00
DL 4234 [M]	Songs of Faith	1962	3.00	6.00	12.00
DL 4345 [M]	God's Trombones	1962	3.00	6.00	12.00
DL 4511 [M]	Song of Easter	1965	2.50	5.00	10.00
DL 4753 [M]	Fred Waring Showcase	1966	2.50	5.00	10.00
DL 4759 [M]	Magic Music	1966	2.50	5.00	10.00
DL 4809 [M]	A-Caroling We Go	1966	3.00	6.00	12.00
DL 4875 [M]	Barbershop Sing	1967	3.00	6.00	12.00
DLP 5004 [10]	Jerome Kern Songs	1950	12.50	25.00	50.00
DLP 5005 [10]	Cole Porter Songs	1950	12.50	25.00	50.00
DLP 5009 [10]	Selections from Miss Liberty	1950	12.50	25.00	50.00
DLP 5021 [10]	'Twas the Night Before Christmas	1950	12.50	25.00	50.00
DLP 5036 [10]	Pleasure Time	1951	10.00	20.00	40.00
DL 5061 [10]	Songs of Devotion, Vol. 1	1950	10.00	20.00	40.00
DL 5062 [10]	Songs of Devotion, Vol. 2	1950	10.00	20.00	40.00
DL 5141 [10]	This Is My Country	1950	10.00	20.00	40.00
DL 5202 [10]	Columbia, the Gem of the Ocean (Patriotic and Service Songs)	1950	10.00	20.00	40.00
DL 5292 [10]	Richard Rodgers and Oscar Hammerstein II Songs, Vol. 1	1950	10.00	20.00	40.00
DL 5293 [10]	Richard Rodgers and Oscar Hammerstein II Songs, Vol. 2	1950	10.00	20.00	40.00
DL 5295 [10]	Christmas Time	1950	10.00	20.00	40.00
DXSB 7186 [(2) S]	The Best of Fred Waring	1965	3.75	7.50	15.00
DL 8005 [M]	Listening Time	1950	10.00	20.00	40.00
DL 8026 [M]	Program Time	1950	7.50	15.00	30.00
DL 8033 [M]	Song of America	195?	10.00	20.00	40.00
DL 8039 [M]	Songs of Faith, Vols. 1 and 2	195?	7.50	15.00	30.00
DL 8047 [M]	God's Trombones and Other Spirituals	195?	7.50	15.00	30.00
DL 8082 [M]	For Listening Only	1954	6.25	12.50	25.00
DL 8084 [M]	Song of Christmas	1954	6.25	12.50	25.00
DL 8110 [M]	Lullaby Time	1955	5.00	10.00	20.00
DL 8111 [M]	Songs in Reverence	1955	5.00	10.00	20.00
DL 8171 [M]	'Twas the Night Before Christmas	1955	5.00	10.00	20.00
DL 8172 [M]	Christmas Time	1955	5.00	10.00	20.00
DL 8222 [M]	College Memories	1956	3.75	7.50	15.00
DL 8335 [M]	Harmonizin' the Old Songs	1956	3.75	7.50	15.00
DL 8670 [M]	Songs of Devotion	1958	3.75	7.50	15.00
DL 8708 [M]	Excerpts from Carousel and Oklahoma	1958	3.75	7.50	15.00
DL 8709 [M]	Songs of Inspiration	1958	3.75	7.50	15.00
DL 8710 [M]	Stars and Stripes Forever	1958	3.75	7.50	15.00
DL 8829	Memorable Moments from Broadway Musicals	1959	3.75	7.50	15.00
DL 9031 [M]	Hear, Hear	195?	3.75	7.50	15.00
DL 74158 [S]	This Is My Country	1961	3.75	7.50	15.00
DL 74234 [S]	Songs of Faith	1962	3.75	7.50	15.00
DL 74345 [S]	God's Trombones	1962	3.75	7.50	15.00
DL 74511 [S]	Song of Easter	1965	3.00	6.00	12.00
DL 74753 [S]	Fred Waring Showcase	1966	3.00	6.00	12.00
DL 74759 [S]	Magic Music	1966	3.00	6.00	12.00
DL 74809 [S]	A-Caroling We Go	1966	3.75	7.50	15.00
DL 74875 [S]	Barbershop Sing	1967	3.00	6.00	12.00
DL 75007	Two Sides of Fred Waring and the Pennsylvanians	1968	3.00	6.00	12.00
DL 78171 [R]	'Twas the Night Before Christmas	196?	3.00	6.00	12.00
DL 78172 [R]	Christmas Time	196?	3.00	6.00	12.00
HARMONY					
HS 11363	In Concert	1970	2.50	5.00	10.00
MCA					
193	This Is My Country	1973	2.00	4.00	8.00
—Reissue of Decca 74158					
207	God's Trombones	1973	2.00	4.00	8.00
—Reissue of Decca 74345					
4008 [(2)]	The Best of Fred Waring and the Pennsylvanians	197?	3.00	6.00	12.00
—Reissue of Decca 7186					
15009	A-Caroling We Go	1973	2.50	5.00	10.00
—Reissue of DL 74809; black label with rainbow					
15009	A-Caroling We Go	1980	2.00	4.00	8.00
—Blue label with rainbow					
15011	Christmas Time	1973	2.50	5.00	10.00
—Reissue of DL 78172; black label with rainbow					
15011	Christmas Time	1980	2.00	4.00	8.00
—Blue label with rainbow					
15016	'Twas the Night Before Christmas	1973	2.50	5.00	10.00
—Reissue of DL 78171; black label with rainbow					
15016	'Twas the Night Before Christmas	1980	2.00	4.00	8.00
—Blue label with rainbow					
MEGA					
31-1005	Nashville	1971	2.50	5.00	10.00
REPRISE					
R 6137 [M]	To You...Forever	1964	3.00	6.00	12.00
RS 6137 [S]	To You...Forever	1964	3.75	7.50	15.00
R 6148 [M]	Fred Waring and the Pennsylvanians in Concert	1964	3.00	6.00	12.00
RS 6148 [S]	Fred Waring and the Pennsylvanians in Concert	1964	3.75	7.50	15.00
STASH					
126	Memorial Album	1985	2.50	5.00	10.00

WARLOCKS, THE (1)

Members of this group later joined ZZ TOP.

Number	Title (A Side/B Side)	Yr	VG	VG+	NM
45s					
ARA					
1017	If You Really Want Me to Stay/Good Time Trippin'	1968	37.50	75.00	150.00

WARLOCKS, THE (2)

Number	Title (A Side/B Side)	Yr	VG	VG+	NM
45s					
DECCA					
31806	I'll Go Crazy/Temper Tantrum	1965	5.00	10.00	20.00
WASHINGTON SQUARE					
2023	Hey Joe/Girl	1966	5.00	10.00	20.00

WARMEST SPRING, THE

Number	Title (A Side/B Side)	Yr	VG	VG+	NM
45s					
PARKWAY					
985	Younger Girl/It Doesn't Matter Now	1966	2.50	5.00	10.00
985 [DJ]	Younger Girl	1966	5.00	10.00	20.00
—One-sided white label promo					
990	Suddenly (You Find Love)/Hard, Hard Girl	1966	2.50	5.00	10.00

WARREN, BEVERLY

Number	Title (A Side/B Side)	Yr	VG	VG+	NM
45s					
B.T. PUPPY					
521	Would You Believe/So Glad You're My Baby	1966	2.50	5.00	10.00
526	He's So Fine/March	1967	2.50	5.00	10.00
RUST					
5098	Baby Hullabaloo/Let Me Get Close to You	1964	3.00	6.00	12.00
UNITED ARTISTS					
543	It Was Me Yesterday/Like a Million Years	1963	3.75	7.50	15.00

WARREN, BOBBY, FIVE

Number	Title (A Side/B Side)	Yr	VG	VG+	NM
45s					
JORDAN					
119	Nite-Beat/Medicine Man	1960	10.00	20.00	40.00

WARREN, DOUG

Number	Title (A Side/B Side)	Yr	VG	VG+	NM
45s					
IMAGE					
1011	Around Midnight/If the World Don't End Tomorrow	1960	10.00	20.00	40.00
1013	Ain't Gonna Wait No Longer/Ain't That Love	1960	7.50	15.00	30.00

WARREN, RUSTY

Number	Title (A Side/B Side)	Yr	VG	VG+	NM
45s					
JUBILEE					
5473	Lil' Lizzy Beth/Life Is Really Worth Living	1964	3.00	6.00	12.00
Albums					
GNP CRESCENDO					
2079 [(2)]	Knockers Up!/Songs for Sinners	1975	3.75	7.50	15.00
2080 [(2)]	Rusty Warren Bounces Back/Sin-Sational	1975	3.75	7.50	15.00
2081	Rusty Warren Lays It on the Line	1975	3.00	6.00	12.00
2088	Knockers Up! '76	1976	3.00	6.00	12.00
2103	Bottoms Up!	1976	3.00	6.00	12.00
2114	Sexplosion	1977	3.00	6.00	12.00
JUBILEE					
JLP 2024 [M]	Songs for Sinners	1960	6.25	12.50	25.00
JLP 2029 [M]	Knockers Up!	1960	6.25	12.50	25.00
JLP 2034 [M]	Sin-Sational	1961	6.25	12.50	25.00
JGM 2039 [M]	Rusty Warren Bounces Back	1961	6.25	12.50	25.00
JGM 2044 [M]	Rusty Warren in Orbit	1962	6.25	12.50	25.00
JLP 2049 [M]	Banned in Boston?	1963	6.25	12.50	25.00
JLP 2054 [M]	Sex-X-Ponent	1964	6.25	12.50	25.00
JLP 2059 [M]	More Knockers Up!	1965	6.25	12.50	25.00
JGM 2069 [M]	Bottoms Up!	1967	5.00	10.00	20.00
JGM 2074	Look What I've Got for You	1967	5.00	10.00	20.00
JLP 5025 [M]	Portrait of Life	196?	5.00	10.00	20.00
JLPS 5025 [S]	Portrait of Life	196?	5.00	10.00	20.00

WARWICK, DEE DEE

Number	Title (A Side/B Side)	Yr	VG	VG+	NM
45s					
ATCO					
6754	Make Love to Me/She Didn't Know (She Kept On Talkin')	1970	—	3.00	6.00
6769	I'm Only Human/If This Was the Last Song	1970	—	3.00	6.00
6796	Cold Night in Georgia/Searchin'	1971	—	3.00	6.00
6810	Suspicious Minds/I'm Glad I'm a Woman	1971	—	3.00	6.00
6840	Everybody's Got to Believe in Somebody/Signed, Dee Dee	1971	—	3.00	6.00
BLUE ROCK					
4008	Do It with All Your Heart/Happiness	1965	2.50	5.00	10.00

Number	Title (A Side/B Side)	Yr	VG	VG+	NM
4027	We're Doing Fine/I Want to Be with You	1965	2.50	5.00	10.00
4032	Baby I'm Yours/Gotta Get a Hold of Myself	1965	2.50	5.00	10.00
JUBILEE					
5459	You're No Good/Don't Call Me	1963	3.00	6.00	12.00
MERCURY					
72584	I Want to Be with You/Lover's Chant	1966	2.00	4.00	8.00
72638	I'm Gonna Make You Love Me/Yours Until Tomorrow	1966	2.00	4.00	8.00
72667	When Love Slips Away/House of Gold	1967	2.00	4.00	8.00
72710	Locked in Your Love/Alfie	1967	2.00	4.00	8.00
72738	Don't You Ever Give Up on Me/We've Got Everything Going for Us	1967	2.00	4.00	8.00
72788	Girls Need Love/It's Not Fair	1968	2.00	4.00	8.00
72834	I'll Be Better Off (Without You)/Monday, Monday	1968	2.00	4.00	8.00
72880	Foolish Fool/Thank You Girl	1969	2.00	4.00	8.00
72927	That's Not Love/It's Not Fair	1969	2.00	4.00	8.00
72940	Next Time (You Fall in Love)/Ring of Bright Water	1969	2.00	4.00	8.00
72966	I (Who Have Nothing)/Where Is That Rainbow	1969	2.00	4.00	8.00
PRIVATE STOCK					
45011	Get Out of My Life/Funny How We Change Places	1975	—	2.50	5.00
45033	This Time May Be My Last/Funny How We Change Places	1975	—	2.50	5.00
SUTRA					
134	Move with the World/The Way We Used to Be	1984	—	2.00	4.00
134 [PS]	Move with the World/The Way We Used to Be	1984	—	2.00	4.00
Albums					
ATCO					
SD 33-337	Turnin' Around	1970	6.25	12.50	25.00
MERCURY					
MG-21100 [M]	I Want to Be with You	1967	6.25	12.50	25.00
SR-61100 [S]	I Want to Be with You	1967	6.25	12.50	25.00
SR-61221	Foolish Fool	1968	6.25	12.50	25.00

WARWICK, DIONNE

Number	Title (A Side/B Side)	Yr	VG	VG+	NM
12-Inch Singles					
ARISTA					
ADP 9145 [DJ]	Got a Date (7:04) (4:07)	1983	2.00	4.00	8.00
45s					
ARISTA					
0419	I'll Never Love This Way Again/In Your Eyes	1979	—	2.00	4.00
0459	Deja Vu/All the Time	1979	—	2.00	4.00
0498	After You/Out of My Hands	1980	—	2.00	4.00
0527	No Night So Long/Reaching for the Sky	1980	—	2.00	4.00
0572	Easy Love/You Never Said Goodbye	1980	—	2.00	4.00
0602	Some Changes Are For Good/This Time Is Ours	1981	—	2.00	4.00
0630	There's a Long Road Ahead of Me/Medley of Hits	1981	—	2.00	4.00
0673	Friends in Love/What Is This	1982	—	2.00	4.00
—A-side with Johnny Mathis					
0701	For You/What Is This	1982	—	2.00	4.00
1015	Heartbreaker/I Can't See Anything But You	1982	—	2.00	4.00
1040	Take the Short Way Home/Just One More Night	1983	—	2.00	4.00
1067	All the Love in the World/You Are My Love	1983	—	—	—
—Unreleased?					
9032	All the Love in the World/You Are My Love	1983	—	2.00	4.00
9073	How Many Times Can We Say Goodbye/What Can a Miracle Do	1983	—	2.00	4.00
—With Luther Vandross					
9145	Got a Date/Two Ships Passing in the Night	1984	—	2.00	4.00
9281	Finder of Lost Loves/It's Love	1984	—	2.00	4.00
—A-side with Glen Jones					
9341	Run to Me/No Love in Sight	1985	—	—	3.00
—A-side with Barry Manilow					
9460	Whisper in the Dark/Extravagant Gestures	1986	—	—	3.00
9460 [PS]	Whisper in the Dark/Extravagant Gestures	1986	—	—	3.00
9567	Love Power/In a World Such As This	1987	—	—	3.00
—A-side with Jeffrey Osborne					
9567 [PS]	Love Power/In a World Such As This	1987	—	—	3.00
9638	Reservations for Two/For Everything You Are	1987	—	—	3.00
—A-side with Kashif					
9638 [PS]	Reservations for Two/For Everything You Are	1987	—	—	3.00
9652	Another Chance for Love/Cry on Me	1987	—	—	3.00
—A-side with Howard Hewett					
9652 [PS]	Another Chance for Love/Cry on Me	1987	—	—	3.00
9901	Take Good Care of You and Me/Heartbreak of Love	1989	—	—	3.00
—A-side with Jeffrey Osborne; B-side with June Pointer					
9940	I Don't Need Another Love/Hertbreaker	1990	—	—	3.00
—A-side with the Spinners					
9940 [PS]	I Don't Need Another Love/Hertbreaker	1990	—	—	3.00
ATLANTIC					
3029	Then Came You/Just As Long As We Have Love	1974	—	3.00	6.00
—With the Spinners					
3202	Then Came You/Just As Long As We Have Love	1974	—	2.50	5.00
—With the Spinners					
MUSICOR					
6303	If I Ruled the World/Only Love Can Break a Heart	1977	—	2.50	5.00
SCEPTER					
1239	Don't Make Me Over/I Smiled Yesterday	1962	3.00	6.00	12.00
1247	This Empty Place/Wishin' and Hopin'	1963	3.00	6.00	12.00
1247 [PS]	This Empty Place/Wishin' and Hopin'	1963	5.00	10.00	20.00
1253	Make the Music Play/Please Make Him Love Me	1963	3.00	6.00	12.00
1262	Anyone Who Had a Heart/The Love of a Boy	1963	3.00	6.00	12.00
1274	Walk On By/Any Old Time of Day	1964	3.00	6.00	12.00
1282	You'll Never Get to Heaven (If You Break My Heart)/A House Is Not a Home	1964	2.50	5.00	10.00
1285	Reach Out for Me/How Many Days of Sadness	1964	2.50	5.00	10.00
1294	You Can Have Him/Is There Another Way to Love Him	1965	2.50	5.00	10.00
1298	Who Can I Turn To/Don't Say I Didn't Tell You Something	1965	2.50	5.00	10.00
12104	Here I Am/They Long to Be Close to You	1965	2.50	5.00	10.00
12111	Looking with My Eyes/Only the Strong, Only the Brave	1965	2.50	5.00	10.00

Number	Title (A Side/B Side)	Yr	VG	VG+	NM
12122	Are You There (With Another Girl)/If I Ever Make You Cry	1965	2.50	5.00	10.00
12133	Message to Michael/Here Where There Is Love	1966	2.00	4.00	8.00
12153	Trains and Boats and Planes/Don't Go Breaking My Heart	1966	2.00	4.00	8.00
12167	I Just Don't Know What to Do with Myself/In Between the Heartaches	1966	2.00	4.00	8.00
12181	Another Night/Go with Love	1966	2.00	4.00	8.00
12187	Alfie/The Beginning of Loneliness	1967	2.00	4.00	8.00
12196	The Windows of the World/Walk Little Dolly	1967	2.00	4.00	8.00
12203	I Say a Little Prayer/(Theme from) Valley of the Dolls	1967	2.00	4.00	8.00
12216	Do You Know the Way to San Jose?/Let Me Be Lonely	1968	2.00	4.00	8.00
12226	Who Is Gonna Love Me?/(There's) Always Something There to Remind Me	1968	2.00	4.00	8.00
12231	Promises, Promises/Whoever You Are, I Love You	1968	—	3.50	7.00
12241	This Girl's In Love with You/Dream Sweet Dreamer	1969	—	3.50	7.00
12249	The April Fools/Slaves	1969	—	3.50	7.00
12256	Odds and Ends/As Long As There's an Apple Tree	1969	—	3.50	7.00
12262	You've Lost That Lovin' Feeling/Window Wishing	1969	—	3.50	7.00
12273	I'll Never Fall in Love Again/What the World Needs Now Is Love	1970	—	3.50	7.00
12276	Let Me Go to Him/Loneliness Remembers What Happiness Forgets	1970	—	3.00	6.00
12285	Paper Mache/The Wine Is Young	1970	—	3.00	6.00
12294	Make It Easy on Yourself/Knowing When to Leave	1970	—	3.00	6.00
12300	The Green Grass Starts to Grow/They Don't Give Medals to Yesterday's Heroes	1970	—	3.00	6.00
12309	Who Gets the Guy/Walk the Way You Talk	1971	—	3.00	6.00
12326	Amanda/He's Moving On	1971	—	3.00	6.00
12336	The Love of My Man/Hurts So Bad	1971	—	3.00	6.00
12346	Raindrops Keep Falling on My Head/Is There Another Way to Love You	1972	—	3.00	6.00
12352	I'm Your Puppet/Don't Make Me Over	1972	—	3.00	6.00
12383	Medley: Reach Out and Touch (Somebody's Hand)-All Kinds of People/The Good Life	1973	—	3.00	6.00
WARNER BROS.					
7560	If We Only Have Love/Close to You	1972	—	2.50	5.00
7669	Don't Let My Teardrops Bother TYou/I Think You Need Love	1973	—	2.50	5.00
7693	(I'm) Just Being Myself/You're Gonna Need Me	1973	—	2.50	5.00
8026	Sure Thing/Who Knows	1974	—	2.50	5.00
8088	Take it from Me/It's Magic	1975	—	2.50	5.00
8154	Once You Hit the Road/World of My Dreams	1975	—	2.50	5.00
8183	His House and Me/Ronnie Lee	1976	—	2.50	5.00
8280	I Didn't Mean to Love You/He's Not for You	1976	—	2.50	5.00
8419	Do You Believe in Love at First Sight/Do I Have to Cry	1977	—	2.50	5.00
8501	Keepin' My Head Above Water/Livin' It Up Is Startin' to Get Me Down	1977	—	2.50	5.00
8530	Don't Ever Take Your Love Away/Do I Have to Cry	1978	—	2.00	4.00
Albums					
ARISTA					
AB 4230	Dionne	1979	2.50	5.00	10.00
AL 8104	How Many Times Can We Say Goodbye	1983	2.50	5.00	10.00
A2L 8111 [(2)]	Hot! Live and Otherwise	1983	2.50	5.00	10.00
—Budget-line reissue					
AL 8262	Finder of Lost Loves	1985	2.50	5.00	10.00
AL 8295	Dionne	1985	2.00	4.00	8.00
—Budget-line reissue					
AL 8338	Heartbreaker	1985	2.00	4.00	8.00
—Budget-line reissue					
AL 8358	Friends in Love	1985	2.00	4.00	8.00
—Budget-line reissue					
AL 8398	Friends	1985	2.50	5.00	10.00
AL 8446	Reservations for Two	1987	2.50	5.00	10.00
AL 8540	Greatest Hits 1979-1990	1989	3.00	6.00	12.00
AL 8573	Dionne Warwick Sings Cole Porter	1990	3.00	6.00	12.00
A2L 8605 [(2)]	Hot! Live and Otherwise	1981	3.00	6.00	12.00
AL 9526	No Night So Long	1980	2.50	5.00	10.00
AL 9585	Friends in Love	1982	2.50	5.00	10.00
AL 9609	Heartbreaker	1982	2.50	5.00	10.00
EVEREST					
4103	Dionne Warwick	1981	2.50	5.00	10.00
MOBILE FIDELITY					
2-098 [(2)]	Hot! Live and Otherwise	1982	7.50	15.00	30.00
—Audiophile vinyl					
MUSICOR					
2501	Only Love Can Break a Heart	1977	3.00	6.00	12.00
PAIR					
PDL2-1043 [(2)]	The Dynamic Dionne Warwick	1986	3.00	6.00	12.00
PDL2-1098 [(2)]	Masterpieces	1986	3.00	6.00	12.00
PICKWICK					
PTP-2056 [(2)]	Alfie	1973	3.00	6.00	12.00
—As "Dionne Warwicke"					
RHINO					
RNDA-1100 [(2)]	Anthology 1962-1971	1985	3.75	7.50	15.00
SCEPTER					
S-508 [M]	Presenting Dionne Warwick	1963	3.75	7.50	15.00
SS-508 [S]	Presenting Dionne Warwick	1963	5.00	10.00	20.00
S-517 [M]	Anyone Who Had a Heart	1964	3.75	7.50	15.00
SS-517 [S]	Anyone Who Had a Heart	1964	5.00	10.00	20.00
SPS-523 [S]	Make Way for Dionne Warwick	1964	5.00	10.00	20.00
SRM-523 [M]	Make Way for Dionne Warwick	1964	3.75	7.50	15.00
SPS-528 [S]	The Sensitive Sound of Dionne Warwick	1965	5.00	10.00	20.00
SRM-528 [M]	The Sensitive Sound of Dionne Warwick	1965	3.75	7.50	15.00
SPS-531 [S]	Here I Am	1965	5.00	10.00	20.00
SRM-531 [M]	Here I Am	1965	3.75	7.50	15.00
SPS-534 [S]	Dionne Warwick in Paris	1966	3.75	7.50	15.00
SRM-534 [M]	Dionne Warwick in Paris	1966	3.00	6.00	12.00

Number	Title (A Side/B Side)	Yr	VG	VG+	NM
SPS-555 [S]	Here Where There Is Love	1966	3.75	7.50	15.00
SRM-555 [M]	Here Where There Is Love	1966	3.00	6.00	12.00
SPS-559 [S]	On Stage and in the Movies	1967	3.75	7.50	15.00
SRM-559 [M]	On Stage and in the Movies	1967	3.00	6.00	12.00
SPS-563 [S]	The Windows of the World	1967	3.75	7.50	15.00
SRM-563 [M]	The Windows of the World	1967	3.00	6.00	12.00
SPS-565 [S]	Dionne Warwick's Golden Hits, Part One	1967	3.75	7.50	15.00
SRM-565 [M]	Dionne Warwick's Golden Hits, Part One	1967	5.00	10.00	20.00
SPS-567 [S]	The Magic of Believing	1968	5.00	10.00	20.00
SRM-567 [M]	The Magic of Believing	1968	7.50	15.00	30.00
SPS-568	Valley of the Dolls	1968	3.75	7.50	15.00
SPS-571	Promises, Promises	1968	3.75	7.50	15.00
SPS-573	Soulful	1969	3.75	7.50	15.00
SPS-575	Dionne Warwick's Greatest Motion Picture Hits	1969	3.75	7.50	15.00
SPS-577	Dionne Warwick's Golden Hits, Part 2	1969	3.75	7.50	15.00
SPS-581	I'll Never Fall in Love Again	1970	3.75	7.50	15.00
SPS-587	Very Dionne	1970	3.75	7.50	15.00
SPS-596 [(2)]	The Dionne Warwicke Story	1971	5.00	10.00	20.00
—As "Dionne Warwicke"					
SPS-598 [(2)]	From Within	1972	5.00	10.00	20.00
—As "Dionne Warwicke"					
SPRINGBOARD					
SPS-4001	The Golden Voice of Dionne Warwicke	1972	2.50	5.00	10.00
—As "Dionne Warwicke"					
SPS-4002	Dionne Warwicke Sings Her Very Best	1972	2.50	5.00	10.00
—As "Dionne Warwicke"					
SPS-4003	One Hit After Another	1972	2.50	5.00	10.00
—As "Dionne Warwicke"					
SPS-4032	Greatest Hits, Vol. 2	197?	2.50	5.00	10.00
UNITED ARTISTS					
UA-LA337-G	The Very Best of Dionne Warwicke	1974	3.00	6.00	12.00
—As "Dionne Warwicke"					
WARNER BROS.					
BS 2585	Dionne	1971	3.00	6.00	12.00
—As "Dionne Warwicke"					
BS 2658	Just Being Myself	1973	3.00	6.00	12.00
—As "Dionne Warwicke"					
BS 2846	Then Came You	1975	3.00	6.00	12.00
—As "Dionne Warwicke"					
BS4 2846 [Q]	Then Came You	1975	5.00	10.00	20.00
—As "Dionne Warwicke"					
BS 2893	Track of the Cat	1975	3.00	6.00	12.00
BS 3119	Love at First Sight	1976	3.00	6.00	12.00

WASHINGTON, BABY

Also includes records as "Justine Washington."

45s

Number	Title (A Side/B Side)	Yr	VG	VG+	NM
ABC-PARAMOUNT					
10223	My Time to Cry/Let Love Go By	1961	3.75	7.50	15.00
—As Jeanette "Baby" Washington					
10245	There You Go Again/Don't Cry, Foolish Heart	1961	3.75	7.50	15.00
AVI					
253	I Wanna Dance/I Can't Get Over Losing You	1978	—	2.50	5.00
—As Jeanette "Baby" Washington					
CHECKER					
918	I Hate to See You Go/Knock Yourself Out	1959	6.25	12.50	25.00
CHESS					
2099	Happy Birthday/Is It Worth It	1970	—	3.00	6.00
COTILLION					
44047	I Don't Know/I Can't Afford to Lose Him	1969	—	3.00	6.00
44065	Let Them Talk/I Love You Brother	1970	—	3.00	6.00
44086	Don't Let Me Lose This Dream/I'm Good Enough for You	1970	—	3.00	6.00
J&S					
1604	There Must Be a Reason/Congratulations Honey	1957	12.50	25.00	50.00
1632	I Hate to See You Go/Knock Yourself Out	1958	7.50	15.00	30.00
1656	Every Day/Smitty's Rock	1961	15.00	30.00	60.00
LIBERTY					
1393	Silent Night/Merry Christmas Baby	1980	—	2.50	5.00
—B-side by Charles Brown					
MASTER 5					
3500	Can't Get Over Losing You/(B-side unknown)	1974	—	3.00	6.00
9103	Forever/(B-side unknown)	1973	—	3.00	6.00
—With Don Gardner					
9104	Just Can't Get You Out of My Mind/(B-side unknown)	1973	—	3.00	6.00
9107	I've Got to Break Away/(B-side unknown)	1973	—	3.00	6.00
NEPTUNE					
101	The Time/(B-side unknown)	1959	5.00	10.00	20.00
104	The Bells (On Our Wedding Day)/(B-side unknown)	1959	5.00	10.00	20.00
122	Nobody Cares (About Me)/(B-side unknown)	1961	3.75	7.50	15.00
—As Jeanette (Baby) Washington					
SUE					
104	The Clock/Standing on the Pier	1964	2.00	4.00	8.00
114	It'll Never Be Over for Me/Move On Drifter	1964	2.00	4.00	8.00
119	Your Fool/Run My Heart	1965	2.00	4.00	8.00
124	I Can't Wait Until I See My Baby/Who's Going to Take Care of Me	1965	2.00	4.00	8.00
—As Justine Washington					
129	Only Those in Love/The Ballad of Bobby Dawn	1965	2.00	4.00	8.00
149	Silent Night/White Christmas	1967	5.00	10.00	20.00
150	Either You're With Me (Or Either You're Not)/You Are What You Are	1967	3.75	7.50	15.00
764	Hey Lonely One/No Tears	1962	3.00	6.00	12.00
767	Handful of Memories/Careless Hands	1962	2.50	5.00	10.00
769	Hush Heart/I've Got a Feeling	1962	2.50	5.00	10.00
783	That's How Heartaches Are Made/There He Is	1963	2.50	5.00	10.00
790	Leave Me Alone/You and the Night and the Music	1963	2.50	5.00	10.00
794	Hey Lonely One/Doodlin'	1963	2.50	5.00	10.00
797	I Can't Wait Until I See My Baby/Who's Going to Take Care of Me	1964	2.50	5.00	10.00
—As Justine Washington					
UNITED ARTISTS					
0143	That's How Heartaches Are Made/Leave Me Alone	1973	—	2.50	5.00
—"Silver Spotlight Series" reissue					
VEEP					
1274	Silent Night/White Christmas	1967	5.00	10.00	20.00
1297	Think About the Good Times/Hold Back the Dawn	1969	2.00	4.00	8.00

Albums

Number	Title (A Side/B Side)	Yr	VG	VG+	NM
AVI					
6038	I Wanna Dance	1978	2.50	5.00	10.00
COLLECTABLES					
COL-5040	The Best of Baby Washington	198?	2.50	5.00	10.00
COL-5108	Only Those in Love	198?	2.50	5.00	10.00
COL-5124	That's How Heartaches Are Made	198?	2.50	5.00	10.00
SUE					
LP-1014 [M]	That's How Heartaches Are Made	1963	37.50	75.00	150.00
LP-1042 [M]	Only Those in Love	1965	37.50	75.00	150.00
LPS-1042 [S]	Only Those in Love	1965	75.00	150.00	300.00
TRIP					
8009	The One and Only Baby Washington	1971	3.75	7.50	15.00
VEEP					
VPS-16528	With You in Mind	1968	6.25	12.50	25.00

WASHINGTON, DINAH

45s

Number	Title (A Side/B Side)	Yr	VG	VG+	NM
MERCURY					
5488	Harbor Lights/I Cross My Fingers	1950	6.25	12.50	25.00
5503	Time Out for Tears/Only a Moment Ago	1950	6.25	12.50	25.00
5510	How Deep Is the Ocean/Harbor Lights	1950	6.25	12.50	25.00
5665	I'm a Fool/If You Don't Believe I'm Leaving	1951	6.25	12.50	25.00
5728	Cold, Cold Heart/Mixed Emotions	1951	6.25	12.50	25.00
5736	Just One More Chance/Baby Did You Hear	1951	6.25	12.50	25.00
5804	No Time for Blues/(B-side unknown)	1952	6.25	12.50	25.00
5842	I Can't Face the Music/Mad About the Boy	1952	6.25	12.50	25.00
5906	Stormy Weather/Make Believe Dreams	1952	6.25	12.50	25.00
8181	I Wanna Be Loved/Love with Misery	1950	10.00	20.00	40.00
—Note: Earlier Dinah Washington 45s in the Mercury 8000 series may exist.					
8187	I'll Never Be Free/Big Deal	1950	6.25	12.50	25.00
8192	How Deep Is the Ocean/Why Don't You Think Things Over	1950	6.25	12.50	25.00
8194	My Kind of Man/I Wanna Be Loved by You	1950	6.25	12.50	25.00
8195	It Isn't Fair/I'll Never Be Free	1950	6.25	12.50	25.00
8206	If I Loved You/My Kind of Man	1950	6.25	12.50	25.00
8207	Fast Movin' Mama/Juice Head Man of Mine	1950	6.25	12.50	25.00
8209	My Heart Cries for You/I Apologize	1951	6.25	12.50	25.00
8211	I Won't Cry Anymore/Don't Say You're Sorry Again	1951	6.25	12.50	25.00
8231	Ain't Nobody's Bizness If I Do/Please Send Me Someone to Love	1951	6.25	12.50	25.00
8232	I'm So Lonely I Could Cry/Fine Fine Daddy	1951	6.25	12.50	25.00
8249	Saturday Night/Be Fair to Me	1951	6.25	12.50	25.00
8257	Hey Good Lookin'/Out in the Cold Again	1951	20.00	40.00	80.00
—With The Ravens					
8267	Wheel of Fortune/Tell Me Why	1952	6.25	12.50	25.00
8269	Trouble in Mind/New Blowtop Blues	1952	6.25	12.50	25.00
8292	Pillow Blues/Double Dealin' Daddy	1952	6.25	12.50	25.00
8294	My Song/Half As Much	1952	6.25	12.50	25.00
10008 [S]	What a Diff'rence a Day Makes/Come Home	1959	6.25	12.50	25.00
70046	I Cried for You/Gambler's Blues	1953	6.25	12.50	25.00
70125	Ain't Nothing Good/You Let My Love Grow Old	1953	6.25	12.50	25.00
70175	My Lean Baby/Never Never	1953	6.25	12.50	25.00
70214	TV Is the Thing (This Year)/Fat Daddy	1953	6.25	12.50	25.00
70263	Silent Night/The Lord's Prayer	1953	6.25	12.50	25.00
70284	Since My Man Has Gone and Went/My Man's an Undertaker	1953	6.25	12.50	25.00
70329	Short John/Feel Like I Wanna Cry	1954	5.00	10.00	20.00
70336	Such a Night/Until Sunrise	1954	5.00	10.00	20.00
70392	(No, No, No) You Can't Love Two/Big Long Slidin' Thing	1954	10.00	20.00	40.00
70439	I Don't Hurt Anymore/Dream	1954	5.00	10.00	20.00
70497	Teach Me Tonight/Wishing Well	1954	5.00	10.00	20.00
70537	That's All I Want from You/You Stay on My Mind	1955	5.00	10.00	20.00
70600	If It's the Last Thing I Do/I Diddie	1955	5.00	10.00	20.00
70653	I Hear Those Bells/The Cheat	1955	5.00	10.00	20.00
70694	I Concentrate on You/Not Without You	1955	5.00	10.00	20.00
70728	I'm Lost Without You Tonight/You Might Have Told Me	1955	5.00	10.00	20.00
70776	The Show Must Go On/I Just Couldn't Stand It No More	1956	3.75	7.50	15.00
70833	Let's Get Busy Too/Let's Go Around Together	1956	3.75	7.50	15.00
70868	Cat on a Hot Tin Roof/The First Time	1956	3.75	7.50	15.00
70906	Soft Winds/Tears to Burn	1956	3.75	7.50	15.00
70968	Relax, Max/The Kissing Way Home	1956	3.75	7.50	15.00
71018	All Because of You/To Love and Be Loved	1956	3.75	7.50	15.00
71043	You Let My Love Grow Old/I Know	1957	3.75	7.50	15.00
71087	Ain't Nobody Home/I'm Gonna Keep My Eyes on You	1957	3.75	7.50	15.00
71220	Everybody Loves My Baby/Blues Down Home	1957	3.75	7.50	15.00
71317	Ring-a My Phone/Never Again	1958	3.75	7.50	15.00
71377	Make Me a Present of You/All of Me	1958	3.75	7.50	15.00
71435	What a Diff'rence a Day Makes/Come Home	1959	3.75	7.50	15.00
71508	Unforgettable/Nothing in the World	1959	2.50	5.00	10.00
71557	Ol' Santa/The Light	1959	3.00	6.00	12.00
71560	It Could Happen to You/Age of Miracles	1960	2.50	5.00	10.00
71635	This Bitter Earth/I Understand	1960	2.50	5.00	10.00
71696	Love Walked In/I'm in Heaven Tonight	1960	2.50	5.00	10.00
71744	We Have Love/Looking Back	1960	2.50	5.00	10.00
71744 [PS]	We Have Love/Looking Back	1960	3.75	7.50	15.00
71778	Early Every Morning (Early Every Evening Too)/Do You Want It That Way	1961	2.50	5.00	10.00
71778 [PS]	Early Every Morning (Early Every Evening Too)/Do You Want It That Way	1961	3.75	7.50	15.00
71812	Our Love Is Here to Stay/Congratulations to Someone	1961	2.50	5.00	10.00

Number	Title (A Side/B Side)	Yr	VG	VG+	NM
71812 [PS]	Our Love Is Here to Stay/Congratulations to Someone	1961	3.75	7.50	15.00
71876	September in the Rain/Wake the Town and Tell the People	1961	2.50	5.00	10.00
71876 [PS]	September in the Rain/Wake the Town and Tell the People	1961	3.75	7.50	15.00
71922	Tears and Laughter/If I Should Lose You	1962	2.50	5.00	10.00
71922 [PS]	Tears and Laughter/If I Should Lose You	1962	3.75	7.50	15.00
71958	Dream/Such a Night	1962	2.50	5.00	10.00
71958 [PS]	Dream/Such a Night	1962	3.75	7.50	15.00
72015	I Want to Be Loved/Am I Blue	1962	2.00	4.00	8.00
72040	Cold, Cold Heart/I Don't Hurt Anymore	1962	2.00	4.00	8.00
72040 [PS]	Cold, Cold Heart/I Don't Hurt Anymore	1962	3.75	7.50	15.00
ROULETTE					
4424	Where Are You/You're Nobody 'Til Somebody Loves You	1962	2.00	4.00	8.00
4444	For All We Know/I Wouldn't Know (What to Do)	1962	2.00	4.00	8.00
4455	You're a Sweetheart/It's a Mean Old Man's World	1962	2.00	4.00	8.00
4476	Romance in the Dark/No Hard Feelings	1963	2.00	4.00	8.00
4490	Soulsville/Let Me Be the First to Know	1963	2.00	4.00	8.00
4520	The Show Must Go On/I'll Drown in My Own Tears	1963	2.00	4.00	8.00
4534	That Sunday (That Summer)/A Stranger on Earth	1963	2.00	4.00	8.00
4538	Call Me Irresponsible/Funny Thing	1963	2.00	4.00	8.00
7-Inch Extended Plays					
EMARCY					
EP 1-6054	(contents unknown)	195?	6.25	12.50	25.00
EP 1-6054 [PS]	After Hours with Miss "D"	195?	6.25	12.50	25.00
MERCURY					
EP 1-3395	(contents unknown)	195?	5.00	10.00	20.00
EP 1-3395 [PS]	Dinah Washington	195?	5.00	10.00	20.00
EP 1-4035	(contents unknown)	195?	5.00	10.00	20.00
EP 1-4035 [PS]	Dinah Washington	195?	5.00	10.00	20.00
EP 1-4041	(contents unknown)	195?	5.00	10.00	20.00
EP 1-4041 [PS]	For Lonely Lovers	195?	5.00	10.00	20.00
Albums					
ACCORD					
SN-7207	Retrospective	1982	2.50	5.00	10.00
ARCHIVE OF FOLK AND JAZZ					
297	Dinah Washington	197?	3.00	6.00	12.00
COLLECTABLES					
COL-5200	Golden Classics	1989	2.50	5.00	10.00
DELMARK					
DL-451	Mellow Mama	1992	5.00	10.00	20.00
EMARCY					
EMS-2-401 [(2)]	Jazz Sides	197?	3.75	7.50	15.00
MG-26032 [10]	After Hours with Miss D	1954	30.00	60.00	120.00
MG-36000 [M]	Dinah Jams	1955	12.50	25.00	50.00
MG-36011 [M]	For Those in Love	1955	12.50	25.00	50.00
MG-36028 [M]	After Hours with Miss D	1955	12.50	25.00	50.00
—Reissue of 26032					
MG-36065 [M]	Dinah	1956	12.50	25.00	50.00
MG-36073 [M]	In the Land of Hi-Fi	1956	12.50	25.00	50.00
MG-36104 [M]	The Swingin' Miss "D"	1956	12.50	25.00	50.00
MG-36119 [M]	Dinah Washington Sings Fats Waller	1957	12.50	25.00	50.00
MG-36130 [M]	Dinah Washington Sings Bessie Smith	1957	12.50	25.00	50.00
MG-36141 [M]	Newport '58	1958	10.00	20.00	40.00
814184-1 [(2)]	Slick Chick (On the Mellow Side)	1983	3.00	6.00	12.00
824883-1 [(2)]	Jazz Sides	198?	3.00	6.00	12.00
—Reissue of 401					
826453-1	In the Land of Hi-Fi	1986	2.50	5.00	10.00
GRAND AWARD					
GA 33-318 [M]	Dinah Washington Sings the Blues	1955	12.50	25.00	50.00
—Add 50% if removable wrap-around cover is still there					
HARLEM HIT PARADE					
8002	Finer Dinah	197?	2.50	5.00	10.00
MERCURY					
MGP-2-103 [(2) M]	This Is My Story	1963	6.25	12.50	25.00
—Combines 20788 and 20789 in one package					
MGP-2-603 [(2) S]	This Is My Story	1963	7.50	15.00	30.00
—Combines 60788 and 60789 in one package					
MG-20119 [M]	Music for a First Love	1957	12.50	25.00	50.00
MG-20120 [M]	Music for Late Hours	1957	12.50	25.00	50.00
MG-20247 [M]	The Best in Blues	1958	12.50	25.00	50.00
MG-20439 [M]	The Queen	1959	7.50	15.00	30.00
MG-20479 [M]	What a Diff'rence a Day Makes!	1960	7.50	15.00	30.00
MG-20523 [M]	Newport '58	1960	7.50	15.00	30.00
—Reissue of EmArcy 36141					
MG-20525 [M]	Dinah Washington Sings Fats Waller	1960	7.50	15.00	30.00
—Reissue of EmArcy 36119					
MG-20572 [M]	Unforgettable	1961	6.25	12.50	25.00
MG-20604 [M]	I Concentrate on You	1961	6.25	12.50	25.00
MG-20614 [M]	For Lonely Lovers	1961	6.25	12.50	25.00
MG-20638 [M]	September in the Rain	1961	6.25	12.50	25.00
MG-20661 [M]	Tears and Laughter	1962	6.25	12.50	25.00
MG-20729 [M]	I Wanna Be Loved	1962	6.25	12.50	25.00
MG-20788 [M]	This Is My Story — Dinah Washington's Golden Hits, Volume 1	1963	3.75	7.50	15.00
MG-20789 [M]	This Is My Story — Dinah Washington's Golden Hits, Volume 2	1963	3.75	7.50	15.00
MG-20829 [M]	The Good Old Days	1963	3.75	7.50	15.00
MG-20928 [M]	The Queen and Quincy	1965	3.75	7.50	15.00
MG-21119 [M]	Dinah Discovered	1967	5.00	10.00	20.00
MG-25060 [10]	Dinah Washington	1950	30.00	60.00	120.00
MG-25138 [10]	Dynamic Dinah	1952	30.00	60.00	120.00
MG-25140 [10]	Blazing Ballads	1952	30.00	60.00	120.00
SR-60111 [S]	The Queen	1959	10.00	20.00	40.00
SR-60158 [S]	What a Diff'rence a Day Makes!	1960	10.00	20.00	40.00
SR-60200 [S]	Newport '58	1960	10.00	20.00	40.00
SR-60202 [S]	Dinah Washington Sings Fats Waller	1960	10.00	20.00	40.00
SR-60232 [S]	Unforgettable	1961	7.50	15.00	30.00
SR-60604 [S]	I Concentrate on You	1961	7.50	15.00	30.00
SR-60614 [S]	For Lonely Lovers	1961	7.50	15.00	30.00
SR-60638 [S]	September in the Rain	1961	7.50	15.00	30.00
SR-60661 [S]	Tears and Laughter	1962	7.50	15.00	30.00
SR-60729 [S]	I Wanna Be Loved	1962	7.50	15.00	30.00
SR-60788 [S]	This Is My Story — Dinah Washington's Golden Hits, Volume 1	1963	5.00	10.00	20.00
SR-60789 [S]	This Is My Story — Dinah Washington's Golden Hits, Volume 2	1963	5.00	10.00	20.00
SR-60829 [S]	The Good Old Days	1963	5.00	10.00	20.00
SR-60928 [S]	The Queen and Quincy	1965	5.00	10.00	20.00
SR-61119 [S]	Dinah Discovered	1967	3.75	7.50	15.00
818815-1	What a Diff'rence a Day Makes!	198?	2.00	4.00	8.00
—Reissue					
822867-1	This Is My Story — Dinah Washington's Golden Hits, Volume 1	1985	2.00	4.00	8.00
—Reissue					
PICKWICK					
SPC-3043	Dinah Washington	196?	2.50	5.00	10.00
SPC-3230	I Don't Hurt Anymore	197?	2.50	5.00	10.00
SPC-3536	Greatest Hits	197?	2.50	5.00	10.00
ROULETTE					
RE 104 [(2)]	Echoes of An Era	196?	3.75	7.50	15.00
RE 117 [(2)]	Queen of the Blues	1971	3.75	7.50	15.00
RE 125 [(2)]	The Immortal Dinah Washington	1973	3.75	7.50	15.00
R 25170 [M]	Dinah '62	1962	3.75	7.50	15.00
SR 25170 [S]	Dinah '62	1962	5.00	10.00	20.00
R 25180 [M]	In Love	1962	3.75	7.50	15.00
SR 25180 [S]	In Love	1962	5.00	10.00	20.00
R 25183 [M]	Drinking Again	1962	3.75	7.50	15.00
SR 25183 [S]	Drinking Again	1962	5.00	10.00	20.00
R 25189 [M]	Back to the Blues	1963	3.75	7.50	15.00
SR 25189 [S]	Back to the Blues	1963	5.00	10.00	20.00
R 25220 [M]	Dinah '63	1963	3.75	7.50	15.00
SR 25220 [S]	Dinah '63	1963	5.00	10.00	20.00
R 25244 [M]	In Tribute	1963	3.75	7.50	15.00
SR 25244 [S]	In Tribute	1963	5.00	10.00	20.00
R 25253 [M]	A Stranger on Earth	1964	3.75	7.50	15.00
SR 25253 [S]	A Stranger on Earth	1964	5.00	10.00	20.00
R 25269 [M]	Dinah Washington	1964	3.75	7.50	15.00
SR 25269 [S]	Dinah Washington	1964	5.00	10.00	20.00
R 25289 [M]	The Best of Dinah Washington	1965	3.75	7.50	15.00
SR 25289 [S]	The Best of Dinah Washington	1965	5.00	10.00	20.00
42014	The Best of Dinah Washington	1968	3.00	6.00	12.00
—Reissue of 25289					
TRIP					
5500	Dinah Jams	1973	2.50	5.00	10.00
5516	After Hours	1973	2.50	5.00	10.00
5524	Tears and Laughter	1974	2.50	5.00	10.00
5556	Dinah Washington Sings Bessie Smith	197?	2.50	5.00	10.00
5565	The Swingin' Miss D	197?	2.50	5.00	10.00
TLX 9505 [(2)]	Sad Songs — Blue Songs	197?	3.00	6.00	12.00
VERVE					
818930-1	The Fats Waller Songbook	1984	2.50	5.00	10.00
WING					
PKW-2-121 [(2)]	The Original Queen of Soul	1969	5.00	10.00	20.00
MGW-12140 [M]	The Late Late Show	1963	3.00	6.00	12.00
MGW-12271 [M]	Dinah Washington Sings Fats Waller	1964	3.00	6.00	12.00
SRW-16140 [S]	The Late Late Show	1963	3.00	6.00	12.00
SRW-16271 [S]	Dinah Washington Sings Fats Waller	1964	3.00	6.00	12.00
SRW-16386	The Original Soul Sister	196?	3.00	6.00	12.00

WASHINGTON, DINAH, AND BROOK BENTON

Also see each artist's individual listings.

Number	Title (A Side/B Side)	Yr	VG	VG+	NM
45s					
MERCURY					
71565	Baby (You Got What It Takes)/I Do	1960	3.75	7.50	15.00
71629	A Rockin' Good Way (To Mess Arounf and Fall in Love)/I Believe	1960	3.75	7.50	15.00
71629 [PS]	A Rockin' Good Way (To Mess Arounf and Fall in Love)/I Believe	1960	6.25	12.50	25.00
Albums					
MERCURY					
MG-20588 [M]	The Two of Us	1960	6.25	12.50	25.00
SR-60588 [S]	The Two of Us	1960	7.50	15.00	30.00
824823-1	The Two of Us	1985	2.00	4.00	8.00
—Reissue					

WASHINGTON, GINO

Number	Title (A Side/B Side)	Yr	VG	VG+	NM
45s					
ATAC					
101	Doin' the Popcorn/(B-side unknown)	1969	7.50	15.00	30.00
102	I'll Be Around/(B-side unknown)	1969	10.00	20.00	40.00
2830	Rat Race/(B-side unknown)	1969	7.50	15.00	30.00
7823	Like My Baby/(B-side unknown)	1969	10.00	20.00	40.00
CONGRESS					
269	Understanding/Water	1966	3.00	6.00	12.00
273	Beach Bash/Hi Hi Hazel	1966	3.00	6.00	12.00
CORREC-TONE					
503	Gino Is a Coward/Puppet on a String	1962	15.00	30.00	60.00
DJM					
1011	You Lovely Witch/Love Me, Love Me	1976	—	3.00	6.00
KAPP					
796	All I Need/Whatever Will Be, Will Be	1966	2.50	5.00	10.00
MALA					
12029	Like My Baby/I'll Be Around When You Want Me	1968	10.00	20.00	40.00
RIC-TIC					
100	Gino Is a Coward/Puppet on a String	1964	5.00	10.00	20.00
SIDRA					
9005	Romeo/Now You're Lonely	196?	6.25	12.50	25.00
SONBERT					
3770	Gino Is a Coward/Puppet on a String	1963	6.25	12.50	25.00
WAND					
147	Out of This World/Come Monday with Me	1964	5.00	10.00	20.00

Albums

Number	Title (A Side/B Side)	Yr	VG	VG+	NM
ATAC					
2730	Gino Washington's Golden Hits	1969	7.50	15.00	30.00
KAPP					
KL-1415 [M]	Gino Washington's Ram Jam Band	1967	5.00	10.00	20.00
KS-3415 [S]	Gino Washington's Ram Jam Band	1967	6.25	12.50	25.00

WASHINGTON, GROVER, JR.

45s

Number	Title (A Side/B Side)	Yr	VG	VG+	NM
COLUMBIA					
07240	Summer Nights/Strawberry Moon	1987	—	—	3.00
07621	The Look of Love/Shwaree Ride	1987	—	—	3.00
73040	Jamaica/Split Second (Act II, The Bar Scene)	1989	—	2.00	4.00
ELEKTRA					
46060	Tell Me About It Now/Feel It Comin'	1979	—	2.00	4.00
47071	Let It Flow (For Dr. J.)/Winelight	1980	—	2.00	4.00
47103	Just the Two of Us/Make Me a Memory (Sad Samba)	1981	—	2.00	4.00
—Bill Withers sings on A-side, but is not credited on the record					
47103 [PS]	Just the Two of Us/Make Me a Memory (Sad Samba)	1981	—	2.50	5.00
47140	Let It Flow (For Dr. J.)/Winelight	1981	—	2.00	4.00
47246	Be Mine (Tonight)/Reaching Out	1981	—	2.00	4.00
47246 [PS]	Be Mine (Tonight)/Reaching Out	1981	—	2.50	5.00
47425	Jamming/East River Drive	1982	—	2.00	4.00
69680	When I Look at You/Secret Sounds	1984	—	2.00	4.00
69708	Inside Moves/Sassy Stew	1984	—	2.00	4.00
69834	I'll Be with You/Brazilian Memories	1983	—	2.00	4.00
69887	The Best Is Yet to Come/Bye Bye Love	1982	—	2.00	4.00
—With Patti LaBelle					
KUDU					
902	Inner City Blues/Ain't No Sunshine	1972	—	3.00	6.00
903	Mercy Mercy Me (Part 1)/Mercy Mercy Me (Part 2)	1972	—	3.00	6.00
909	No Tears in the End/Body and Soul	1972	—	3.00	6.00
912	Where Is the Love (Part 1)/Where Is the Love (Part 2)	1973	—	3.00	6.00
916	Masterpiece (Part 1)/Masterpiece (Part 2)	1973	—	3.00	6.00
924	Mister Magic/Black Frost	1975	—	2.50	5.00
930	Knuckle Head (Part 1)/Knuckle Head (Part 2)	1976	—	2.50	5.00
937	A Secret Place (Part 1)/A Secret Place (Part 2)	1977	—	2.50	5.00
942	Summer Song/Juffere	1978	—	2.50	5.00
MOTOWN					
1454	Do Dat/Reed Seed (This Tune)	1978	—	2.00	4.00
1486	Snake Eyes/Love	1979	—	2.00	4.00

Albums

Number	Title (A Side/B Side)	Yr	VG	VG+	NM
COLUMBIA					
FC 40510	Strawberry Moon	1987	2.50	5.00	10.00
OC 44256	Then and Now	1988	2.50	5.00	10.00
OC 45253	Time Out of Mind	1989	2.50	5.00	10.00
C 48530	Next Exit	1992	5.00	10.00	20.00
ELEKTRA					
6E-182	Paradise	1979	2.50	5.00	10.00
6E-305	Winelight	1980	2.50	5.00	10.00
5E-562	Come Morning	1981	2.50	5.00	10.00
60215	The Best Is Yet to Come	1982	2.50	5.00	10.00
60318	Inside Moves	1984	2.50	5.00	10.00
60415	Anthology of Grover Washington, Jr.	1985	2.50	5.00	10.00
KUDU					
KS-03	Inner City Blues	1971	3.00	6.00	12.00
KS-07	All the King's Horses	1972	3.00	6.00	12.00
KS-20	Mister Magic	1975	3.00	6.00	12.00
KS-24	Feels So Good	1975	3.00	6.00	12.00
KS-32	A Secret Place	1976	3.00	6.00	12.00
KSQX-1213 [(2) Q]	Soul Box	1973	6.25	12.50	25.00
KSX-1213 [(2)]	Soul Box	1973	3.75	7.50	15.00
KSX-3637 [(2)]	Live at the Bijou	1977	3.75	7.50	15.00
MOTOWN					
M5-165V1	A Secret Place	1981	2.00	4.00	8.00
—Reissue of Kudu 32					
M5-175V1	Mister Magic	1981	2.00	4.00	8.00
—Reissue of Kudu 20					
M5-177V1	Feels So Good	1981	2.00	4.00	8.00
—Reissue of Kudu 24					
M5-184V1	Soul Box Vol. 1	1981	2.00	4.00	8.00
—Reissue of half of Kudu 1213					
M5-186V1	All the King's Horses	1981	2.00	4.00	8.00
—Reissue of Kudu 07					
M5-187V1	Soul Box Vol. 2	1981	2.00	4.00	8.00
—Reissue of half of Kudu 1213					
M5-189V1	Inner City Blues	1981	2.00	4.00	8.00
—Reissue of Kudu 03					
M7-910	Reed Seed	1978	2.50	5.00	10.00
M7-933	Skylarkin'	1980	2.50	5.00	10.00
M9-940 [(2)]	Baddest	1980	3.00	6.00	12.00
M9-961 [(2)]	Anthology	1981	3.00	6.00	12.00
5232 ML	Skylarkin'	1982	2.00	4.00	8.00
—Reissue of 933					
5236 ML	Reed Seed	1982	2.00	4.00	8.00
—Reissue of 910					
5307 ML	Greatest Performances	198?	2.50	5.00	10.00
6126 ML	Grover Washington Jr. at His Best	198?	2.50	5.00	10.00
8239 ML2 [(2)]	Live at the Bijou	198?	3.00	6.00	12.00
NAUTILUS					
NR-39	Winelight	1981	12.50	25.00	50.00
—Audiophile vinyl					

WATERS, MUDDY

45s

Number	Title (A Side/B Side)	Yr	VG	VG+	NM
CHESS					
1509	All Night Long/Country Boy	1952	625.00	1250.	2500.
—Note: Muddy Waters records on Chess before 1509 are unconfirmed on 45 rpm					
1514	Please Have Mercy/Looking for My Baby	1952	200.00	400.00	800.00
1526	Standing Around Crying/Gone to Main St.	1952	175.00	350.00	700.00
1537	She's All Right/Sad, Sad Day	1953	100.00	200.00	400.00
1542	Who's Gonna Be Your Sweet Man/Turn the Lamp Down Low	1953	75.00	150.00	300.00
1550	Mad Love/Blow, Wind, Blow	1953	30.00	60.00	120.00
1560	I'm Your Hoochie Coochie Man/You're So Pretty	1954	25.00	50.00	100.00
1571	Just Make Love to Me/Oh Yeh!	1954	15.00	30.00	60.00
1579	I'm Ready/I Don't Know Why	1954	15.00	30.00	60.00
1585	Lovin' Man/I'm a Natural Born Lover	1955	12.50	25.00	50.00
1596	I Want to Be Loved/My Eyes Keep Me in Trouble	1955	12.50	25.00	50.00
1602	Manish Boy/Young Fashion Ways	1955	17.50	35.00	70.00
1612	Trouble, No More/Sugar Sweet	1955	20.00	40.00	80.00
1620	Forty Days and Forty Nights/All Aboard	1956	10.00	20.00	40.00
1630	Don't Go No Farther/Diamonds at Your Feet	1956	12.50	25.00	50.00
1644	I Got to Find My Baby/Just to Be with You	1956	10.00	20.00	40.00
1652	Got My Mojo Working/Rock Me	1957	12.50	25.00	50.00
1667	Good News/Come Home Baby	1957	7.50	15.00	30.00
1680	I Live the Life I Love/Evil	1958	7.50	15.00	30.00
1692	I Won't Go/She's Got It	1958	7.50	15.00	30.00
1704	Close to You/She's Nineteen Years Old	1958	7.50	15.00	30.00
1718	Mean Mistreater/Walking Thru the Park	1959	6.25	12.50	25.00
1724	Ooh Wee/Clouds in My Heart	1959	6.25	12.50	25.00
1733	Take the Bitter with the Sweet/She's Into Somethin'	1959	6.25	12.50	25.00
1739	Recipe for Love/Tell Me Baby	1959	6.25	12.50	25.00
1748	I Feel So Good/When I Get to Thinking	1960	6.25	12.50	25.00
1752	I'm Your Doctor/Ready Way Back	1960	6.25	12.50	25.00
1758	Love Affair/Look What You've Done	1960	6.25	12.50	25.00
1765	Tiger in Your Tank/Meanest Woman	1960	6.25	12.50	25.00
1774	Got My Mojo Working/Woman Wanted	1960	6.25	12.50	25.00
1796	Messin' with the Man/Lonesome Room Blues	1961	5.00	10.00	20.00
1819	Going Home/Tough Times	1962	5.00	10.00	20.00
1827	Muddy Waters Twist/You Shook Me	1962	6.25	12.50	25.00
1839	You Need Love/Little Brown Bird	1962	6.25	12.50	25.00
1862	Five Long Years/Twenty-Four Hours	1963	3.75	7.50	15.00
1895	The Same Thing/You Can't Lose What You Never Had	1964	3.75	7.50	15.00
1914	Short Dress Woman/My John the Conqueror	1964	3.75	7.50	15.00
1921	Put Me in Your Lay-A-Way/Still a Fool	1965	3.00	6.00	12.00
1937	My Dog Can't Bark/I Got a Rich Man's Woman	1965	3.00	6.00	12.00
1973	I'm Your Hoochie Coochie Man/Corrina, Corrina	1966	3.00	6.00	12.00
2018	When the Eagle Flies/Birdnest on the Ground	1967	2.50	5.00	10.00
2085	Going Home/I Feel So Good	1970	2.00	4.00	8.00
2107	Making Friends/Two Steps Forward	1971	2.00	4.00	8.00
2143	Garbage Man/Can't Get No Grindin'	1973	—	3.00	6.00

Albums

Number	Title (A Side/B Side)	Yr	VG	VG+	NM
BLUE SKY					
PZ 34449	Hard Again	1977	3.00	6.00	12.00
—No bar code on cover					
PZ 34449	Hard Again	198?	2.00	4.00	8.00
—Budget-line reissue with bar code					
JZ 34928	I'm Ready	1978	3.00	6.00	12.00
PZ 34928	I'm Ready	198?	2.00	4.00	8.00
—Budget-line reissue					
JZ 35712	Muddy "Missisiippi" Waters Live	1980	3.00	6.00	12.00
PZ 35712	Muddy "Missisiippi" Waters Live	198?	2.00	4.00	8.00
—Budget-line reissue					
JZ 37064	King Bee	1981	3.00	6.00	12.00
PZ 37064	King Bee	198?	2.00	4.00	8.00
—Budget-line reissue					
CADET CONCEPT					
CS-314	Electric Mud	1968	6.25	12.50	25.00
CS-320	After the Rain	1969	6.25	12.50	25.00
CHESS					
127 [(2)]	Fathers and Sons	1969	6.25	12.50	25.00
LP-1427 [DJ]	The Best of Muddy Waters	1957	500.00	1000.	1500.
—White label promo					
LP-1427 [M]	The Best of Muddy Waters	1957	125.00	250.00	500.00
—Black label					
LPS-1427 [R]	The Best of Muddy Waters	196?	3.00	6.00	12.00
—Black label					
LP-1444 [DJ]	Muddy Waters Sings Big Bill	1960	250.00	500.00	1000.
—White label promo					
LP-1444 [M]	Muddy Waters Sings Big Bill	1960	75.00	150.00	300.00
LP-1449 [M]	Muddy Waters at Newport	1962	30.00	60.00	120.00
LP-1483 [M]	Folk Singer	1964	30.00	60.00	120.00
LP-1501 [M]	The Real Folk Blues of Muddy Waters	1965	15.00	30.00	60.00
LP-1507 [M]	Muddy, Brass and Blues	1966	10.00	20.00	40.00
LPS-1507 [S]	Muddy, Brass and Blues	1966	12.50	25.00	50.00
LP-1511 [M]	More Real Folk Blues	1967	12.50	25.00	50.00
LPS-1511 [S]	More Real Folk Blues	1967	10.00	20.00	40.00
LP-1533 [M]	Blues from Big Bill's Copacabana	1968	12.50	25.00	50.00
LPS-1539	Sail On	1969	6.25	12.50	25.00
LPS-1553	They Call Me Muddy Waters	1971	5.00	10.00	20.00
CH-9101	Rolling Stone	1985	3.00	6.00	12.00
CH-9180	Rare and Unissued	1986	3.00	6.00	12.00
CH-9197	Muddy Waters Sings Big Bill	1986	2.50	5.00	10.00
—Reissue of 1444					
CH-9198	Muddy Waters at Newport	1986	2.50	5.00	10.00
—Reissue of 1449					
CH-9255	The Best of Muddy Waters	1987	2.50	5.00	10.00
—Reissue of 1427					
CH-9261	Folk Singer	1987	2.50	5.00	10.00
—Reissue of 1483					
CH-9274	The Real Folk Blues of Muddy Waters	1988	2.50	5.00	10.00
—Reissue of 1501					
CH-9278	More Real Folk Blues	1988	2.50	5.00	10.00
—Reissue of 1511					
CH-9286	Muddy, Brass and the Blues	1989	2.50	5.00	10.00
—Reissue of 1507					
CH-9291	Trouble No More: Singles 1955-1959	1989	3.00	6.00	12.00
CH-9298	The London Muddy Waters Sessions	1989	2.50	5.00	10.00
—Reissue of 60013					
CH-9299	They Call Me Muddy Waters	1989	2.50	5.00	10.00
—Reissue of 1553					

Number	Title (A Side/B Side)	Yr	VG	VG+	NM
CH-9319	Can't Get No Grindin'	1990	2.50	5.00	10.00
—Reissue of 50023					
CH-50012	Muddy Waters Live	1972	5.00	10.00	20.00
CH-50023	Can't Get No Grindin'	1973	5.00	10.00	20.00
2CH-50033 [(2)]	Fathers and Sons	1974	5.00	10.00	20.00
—Reissue of 127					
CH-50035	The Muddy Waters Woodstock Album	1976	3.75	7.50	15.00
2CH-60006 [(2)]	McKinley Morganfield, A.K.A. Muddy Waters	1971	6.25	12.50	25.00
CH-60013	The London Muddy Waters Sessions	1972	5.00	10.00	20.00
CH-60026	London Revisited	1974	3.75	7.50	15.00
CH-60031	"Unk" in Funk	1975	3.75	7.50	15.00
Ch6-80002 [(6)]	The Chess Box	1990	12.50	25.00	50.00
INTERMEDIA					
QS-5071	Sweet Home Chicago	198?	2.50	5.00	10.00
MOBILE FIDELITY					
1-201	Folk Singer	1994	6.25	12.50	25.00
—Audiophile vinyl					
MUSE					
MR-5008	Mud in Your Ear	198?	3.00	6.00	12.00
TESTAMENT					
2210	Stovall's Plantation	197?	3.00	6.00	12.00

WATERS, MUDDY, AND HOWLIN' WOLF

Also see each artist's individual listings.

Albums

Number	Title (A Side/B Side)	Yr	VG	VG+	NM
CHESS					
CH-9100	Muddy and The Wolf	1985	3.00	6.00	12.00

WATKINS, LOVELACE

45s

Number	Title (A Side/B Side)	Yr	VG	VG+	NM
GROOVE					
58-0016	Tender Love/Ma Cherie Au Revoir	1963	7.50	15.00	30.00
58-0023	I Won't Believe It/He'[s Lookin' Out for the World	1963	7.50	15.00	30.00
MGM					
12875	Hello Young Lovers/When I Fall in Love	1960	3.75	7.50	15.00
SUE					
10-003	Who Am I/Dreams	1968	3.00	6.00	12.00
UNI					
55211	Fool on the Hill/Je Vous Aime Beaucoup	1970	3.00	6.00	12.00

Albums

Number	Title (A Side/B Side)	Yr	VG	VG+	NM
MGM					
E-3831 [M]	The Voice of Lovelace Watkins	1960	6.25	12.50	25.00
SE-3831 [S]	The Voice of Lovelace Watkins	1960	10.00	20.00	40.00

WATSON, CLAYTON

45s

Number	Title (A Side/B Side)	Yr	VG	VG+	NM
LAVENDER					
2454	Everybody's Boppin'/Tall Skinny Annie	1958	100.00	200.00	400.00

WATSON, DOC

45s

Number	Title (A Side/B Side)	Yr	VG	VG+	NM
POPPY					
XW169	If I Needed You/Bonaparte's Retreat	1973	—	2.00	4.00
—With Merle Watson					
XW276	Bottle of Wine/Corinna, Corinna	1973	—	2.00	4.00
—With Merle Watson					
XW370	New Born King/Peace in the Valley	1973	—	2.00	4.00
XW414	Poor Boy Blues/Doc's Rag	1974	—	2.00	4.00
—With Merle Watson					
90110	Freight Train Boogie/Going Down the Road Feeling Bad	1971	—	2.50	5.00
90114	Summertime/I Couldn't Believe It Was True	1972	—	2.50	5.00
—With Merle Watson					
90119	New Born King/Peace in the Valley	1972	—	2.50	5.00
UNITED ARTISTS					
XW713	Make Me a Pallet/Shady Grove	1975	—	2.00	4.00
XW824	I Can't Help But Wonder (Where I'm Bound)/ Southbound Passenger Train	1976	—	2.00	4.00
XW894	Little Maggie/Cypress Grove Blues	1976	—	2.00	4.00
XW1020	My Creole Belle/Minglewood Blues	1977	—	2.00	4.00
—With Merle Watson					
1231	Don't Think Twice, It's All Right/Under the Double Eagle	1978	—	2.00	4.00
—With Merle Watson					
1275	All I Have to Do Is Dream/'Rangement Blues	1979	—	2.00	4.00
—With Merle Watson					
VANGUARD					
35079	Peach Picking Time in Georgia/Memphis Blues	1968	—	3.00	6.00

Albums

Number	Title (A Side/B Side)	Yr	VG	VG+	NM
FLYING FISH					
FF-252	Red Rocking Chair	1981	3.00	6.00	12.00
FF-301	Guitar Album	1983	3.00	6.00	12.00
FF-352	Pickin' the Blues	1985	2.50	5.00	10.00
FOLKWAYS					
FA-2366 [M]	Doc Watson and Family	1963	6.25	12.50	25.00
FA-31021 [S]	Doc Watson and Family	196?	3.75	7.50	15.00
INTERMEDIA					
QS-5031	Out in the Country	198?	2.50	5.00	10.00
LIBERTY					
LWB-423	Memories	1981	3.00	6.00	12.00
—Reissue of United Artists 423					
LW-601	Doc and the Boys	1981	2.50	5.00	10.00
—Reissue of United Artists 601					
LT-887	Look Away!	1981	2.50	5.00	10.00
—Reissue of United Artists 887					
LT-943	Live and Pickin'	1981	2.50	5.00	10.00
—Reissue of United Artists 943					
LN-10027	Lonesome Road	1981	2.00	4.00	8.00
—Budget-line reissue					
POPPY					
PP-LA022-F	Then and Now	1973	3.75	7.50	15.00
PP-LA210-G	Two Days in November	1974	3.75	7.50	15.00
PYS-5703	The Elementary Doc Watson	1972	3.75	7.50	15.00
SMITHSONIAN/FOLKWAYS					
SF-40012	The Doc Watson Family	1990	3.00	6.00	12.00
—Reissue of Folkways LP					
SUGAR HILL					
SH-3742	Down South	1985	2.50	5.00	10.00
SH-3752	Riding the Midnight Train	1986	2.50	5.00	10.00
SH-3759	Portrait	1987	2.50	5.00	10.00
UNITED ARTISTS					
UA-LA423-G [(2)]	Memories	1975	3.75	7.50	15.00
UA-LA601-G	Doc and the Boys	1976	3.00	6.00	12.00
UA-LA725-G	Lonesome Road	1977	3.00	6.00	12.00
UA-LA887-H	Look Away!	1978	3.00	6.00	12.00
UA-LA943-H	Live and Pickin'	1979	3.00	6.00	12.00
VANGUARD					
VSD-9/10 [(2)]	Doc Watson on Stage	1970	5.00	10.00	20.00
VSD 45/46 [(2)]	The Essential Doc Watson	1973	5.00	10.00	20.00
VSD 107/8 [(2)]	Old Timey Concert	1977	5.00	10.00	20.00
VSD-6576	Ballads from Deep Gap	1971	3.75	7.50	15.00
VRS-9152 [M]	Doc Watson	1964	5.00	10.00	20.00
VRS-9170 [M]	Doc Watson and Son	1965	5.00	10.00	20.00
VRS-9213 [M]	Southbound	1966	3.75	7.50	15.00
VRS-9239 [M]	Home Again	1967	3.75	7.50	15.00
VMS-73108	The Essential Doc Watson, Vol. 1	1985	2.50	5.00	10.00
VMS-73121	The Essential Doc Watson, Vol. 2	1985	2.50	5.00	10.00
VSD-79152 [S]	Doc Watson	1964	6.25	12.50	25.00
VSD-79170 [S]	Doc Watson and Son	1965	6.25	12.50	25.00
VSD-79213 [S]	Southbound	1966	5.00	10.00	20.00
VSD-79239 [S]	Home Again	1967	5.00	10.00	20.00
VSD-79276	Good Deal	1968	3.75	7.50	15.00

WATSON, JOHNNY "GUITAR"

45s

Number	Title (A Side/B Side)	Yr	VG	VG+	NM
ARVEE					
5016	Untouchable/Johnny Guitar	1960	6.25	12.50	25.00
—As "Johnny Watson"					
A&M					
2383	Planet Funk/First Timothy Six	1981	—	2.00	4.00
2398	That's What Time It Is/First Timothy Six	1982	—	2.00	4.00
CACTUS					
118	Let's Rock/(B-side unknown)	1959	37.50	75.00	150.00
CLASS					
246	The Bear/One More Kiss	1959	7.50	15.00	30.00
—As "Johnny Watson"					
DJM					
1013	I Need It/Since I Met You Baby	1976	—	2.50	5.00
1019	Superman Lover/We're No Exception	1976	—	2.50	5.00
1020	Ain't That a Bitch/Won't You Forgive Me Baby	1977	—	3.00	6.00
1024	A Real Mother For Ya/Nothing Left to Be Desired	1977	—	2.50	5.00
1029	Lover Jones/Tarzan	1977	—	2.50	5.00
1034	Love That Will Not Die/A Damn Shame	1978	—	2.50	5.00
1100	Virginia's Pretty Funky/The Institute	1978	—	2.50	5.00
—As "Watsonian Institute"					
1101	Gangster of Love/Guitar Disco	1978	—	2.50	5.00
1106	What the Hell Is This?/Can You Handle It	1979	—	2.50	5.00
1304	Love Jones/(B-side unknown)	1980	—	2.50	5.00
1305	Telephone Bill/(B-side unknown)	1980	—	2.50	5.00
FANTASY					
721	Like I'm Not Your Man/You Bring Love	1974	—	3.00	6.00
739	I Don't Want to Be a Lone Ranger/You Can Stay But the Noise Must Go	1975	—	3.00	6.00
752	It's Too Late/Tripping	1975	—	3.00	6.00
FEDERAL					
12120	Highway 60/No I Can't	1953	37.50	75.00	150.00
12131	Motor Head Baby/Sad Fool	1953	37.50	75.00	150.00
12143	I Got Eyes/Walkin' to My Baby	1953	37.50	75.00	150.00
12157	What's Going On/Thinking	1953	37.50	75.00	150.00
12175	Half Pint of Whiskey/Space Guitar	1954	62.50	125.00	250.00
12183	Gettin' Drunk/You Can't Take It With You	1954	50.00	100.00	200.00
—All Federal 45s as "Young John Watson"					
KEEN					
3-4005	Gangster of Love/One Room Country Shack	1957	7.50	15.00	30.00
3-4023	Deana Baby/Honey	1957	7.50	15.00	30.00
KENT					
328	Those Lonely, Lonely Nights/(B-side unknown)	1959	5.00	10.00	20.00
KING					
5536	Posin'/Embraceable You	1961	5.00	10.00	20.00
5579	Broke and Lonely/Cuttin' In	1961	6.25	12.50	25.00
5607	The Nearness of You/I Just Want Me Some Love	1962	3.75	7.50	15.00
5666	What You Do to Me/Sweet Lovin' Mama	1962	3.75	7.50	15.00
5716	Cold, Cold Heart/That's the Chance You've Got to Take	1963	3.75	7.50	15.00
5774	Gangster of Love/In the Evening	1963	3.75	7.50	15.00
5833	I Say, I Love You/You Better Love Me	1964	3.75	7.50	15.00
OKEH					
7263	Keep On Lovin' You/South Like West	1966	3.00	6.00	12.00
7270	Hold On, I'm Comin'/Wolfman	1967	3.00	6.00	12.00
RPM					
423	Hot Little Mama/I Love to Love You	1955	12.50	25.00	50.00
431	Too Tired/Don't Touch Me	1955	12.50	25.00	50.00
436	Those Lonely, Lonely Nights/Someone Cares for Me	1955	10.00	20.00	40.00
447	Oh Baby/Give a Little	1955	10.00	20.00	40.00
455	Three Hours Past Midnight/Ruben	1956	10.00	20.00	40.00
471	She Moves Me/Love Me Baby	1956	10.00	20.00	40.00
VALLEY VUE					
769	Strike On Computers/(B-side unknown)	1984	—	2.50	5.00

Albums

Number	Title (A Side/B Side)	Yr	VG	VG+	NM
A&M					
SP-4880	That's What Time It Is	1981	2.50	5.00	10.00
CADET					
LP-4056 [M]	I Cried for You	1967	6.25	12.50	25.00
LPS-4056 [S]	I Cried for You	1967	7.50	15.00	30.00

Number	Title (A Side/B Side)	Yr	VG	VG+	NM
CHESS					
LP-1490 [M]	Blues Soul	1965	17.50	35.00	70.00
LPS-1490 [S]	Blues Soul	1965	20.00	40.00	80.00
DJM					
3	Ain't That a Bitch	1976	2.50	5.00	10.00
7	A Real Mother for Ya	1977	2.50	5.00	10.00
13	Master Funk	1978	2.50	5.00	10.00
—As "Watsonian Institute"					
19	Giant	1978	2.50	5.00	10.00
24	What the Hell Is This?	1979	2.50	5.00	10.00
27	E.D.P. Extra Disco Perception	1979	2.50	5.00	10.00
—As "Watsonian Institute"					
31	Love Jones	1980	2.50	5.00	10.00
501	Johnny "Guitar" Watson and the Family Clone	1981	2.50	5.00	10.00
714	Funk Beyond the Call of Duty	1977	2.50	5.00	10.00
FANTASY					
MPF-4503	Greatest Hits	1981	2.50	5.00	10.00
9437	Listen	1973	3.00	6.00	12.00
9484	I Don't Want to Be Alone Stranger	1975	3.00	6.00	12.00
KING					
857 [M]	Johnny Guitar Watson	1963	100.00	200.00	400.00
MCA					
5273	The Very Best of Johnny "Guitar" Watson	1981	2.50	5.00	10.00
OKEH					
OKM 12118 [M]	Bad	1967	7.50	15.00	30.00
OKM 12124 [M]	In the Fats Bag	1967	7.50	15.00	30.00
OKS 14118 [S]	Bad	1967	10.00	20.00	40.00
OKS 14124 [S]	In the Fats Bag	1967	10.00	20.00	40.00
POWER PAK					
306	Gangster of Love	1978	2.50	5.00	10.00

WATSON, JOHNNY "GUITAR", AND LARRY WILLIAMS

Also see each artist's individual listings.

Number	Title (A Side/B Side)	Yr	VG	VG+	NM
45s					
OKEH					
7274	Mercy, Mercy, Mercy/A Quitter Never Wins	1967	2.50	5.00	10.00
7281	Too Late/Two for the Price of One	1967	2.50	5.00	10.00
7300	Find Yourself Someone to Love/Nobody	1967	6.25	12.50	25.00
—Backed by Kaleidoscope					
Albums					
OKEH					
OKM 12122 [M]	Two for the Price of One	1967	10.00	20.00	40.00
OKS 14122 [S]	Two for the Price of One	1967	15.00	30.00	60.00

WATSONIAN INSTITUTE

See JOHNNY "GUITAR" WATSON.

WATTS, ALAN

Number	Title (A Side/B Side)	Yr	VG	VG+	NM
Albums					
ASCENSION					
(# unknown)	Dhyana: of the Art of Meditation, Vol. 1	1970	7.50	15.00	30.00
(# unknown)	Dhyana: of the Art of Meditation, Vol. 2	1970	7.50	15.00	30.00
MEA					
LP-1001 [M]	Haiku Poems	1962	12.50	25.00	50.00
LP-1002 [M]	Zen and Senryu	1962	12.50	25.00	50.00
LP-1007 [M]	This Is It	1962	15.00	30.00	60.00
TOGETHER					
1025	Why Not Now	1970	6.25	12.50	25.00
WARNER BROS.					
W 1923	The Sounds of Hinduism	1968	6.25	12.50	25.00

WATTS, NOBLE

Number	Title (A Side/B Side)	Yr	VG	VG+	NM
45s					
BATON					
246	Easy Going (Part 1)/Easy Going (Part 2)	1957	6.25	12.50	25.00
249	The Slop/Midnite Flight	1957	6.25	12.50	25.00
249	Hard Times (The Slop)/Midnite Flight	1957	3.75	7.50	15.00
251	Rickey Tick/Blast Off	1958	3.75	7.50	15.00
254	The Slide/Shakin'	1958	3.75	7.50	15.00
257	Great Times/The Creep	1958	3.75	7.50	15.00
266	Flap Jack/Hot Tamales	1959	3.75	7.50	15.00
BRUNSWICK					
55382	Thingamajig/F.L.A.	1968	2.00	4.00	8.00
CUB					
9078	The Beaver/Frog Hop	1960	3.00	6.00	12.00
DELUXE					
6066	Mashing Potatoes/Pig Ears and Rice	1954	7.50	15.00	30.00
ENJOY					
1008	Jookin'/What Ya Gonna Do	1963	3.00	6.00	12.00
SIR					
273	Boogie Woogie/Mashed Potatoes	1959	3.75	7.50	15.00

WATTS 103RD STREET RHYTHM BAND, THE

See CHARLES WRIGHT AND THE WATTS 103RD STREET RHYTHM BAND.

WAYLON AND JESSI

Also see JESSI COLTER; WAYLON JENNINGS.

Number	Title (A Side/B Side)	Yr	VG	VG+	NM
45s					
RCA					
PB-12176	Storms Never Last/I Ain't the One	1982	—	2.00	4.00
PB-12245	Wild Side of Life/It Wasn't God Who Made Honky Tonk Angels	1982	—	2.00	4.00
RCA VICTOR					
PB-10653	Suspicious Minds/I Ain't the One	1976	—	2.50	5.00
47-9920	Suspicious Minds/I Ain't the One	1970	—	3.00	6.00
47-9992	Under Your Spell Again/Bridge Over Troubled Water	1971	—	3.00	6.00
Albums					
RCA VICTOR					
AHL1-3931	Leather and Lace	1981	2.50	5.00	10.00

WAYLON AND WILLIE

Also see WAYLON JENNINGS; WILLIE NELSON.

Number	Title (A Side/B Side)	Yr	VG	VG+	NM
45s					
COLUMBIA					
04131	Take It to the Limit/Till I Gain Control Again	1983	—	2.00	4.00
04131 [PS]	Take It to the Limit/Till I Gain Control Again	1983	—	2.50	5.00
EPIC					
73832	If I Can Find a Clean Shirt/Put Me on a Train Back to Texas	1991	—	—	3.00
74024	Tryin' to Outrun the Wind/The Makin's of a Song	1991	—	—	3.00
RCA					
PB-11198	Mammas Don't Let Your Babies Grow Up to Be Cowboys/I Can Get Off on You	1978	—	2.00	4.00
GB-11499	Mammas Don't Let Your Babies Grow Up to Be Cowboys/Luckenbach, Texas (Back to the Basics of Love)	1979	—	2.00	4.00
—Gold Standard Series					
GB-11996	Mammas Don't Let Your Babies Grow Up to Be Cowboys/I Can Get Off on You	1980	—	—	3.00
—Gold Standard Series					
PB-13073	Just to Satisfy You/Get Naked With You	1982	—	2.00	4.00
PB-13319	(Sittin' On) The Dock of the Bay/Luckenbach, Texas	1982	—	2.00	4.00
RCA VICTOR					
PB-10529	Good Hearted Woman/Heaven or Hell	1975	—	2.50	5.00
Albums					
COLUMBIA					
FC 38562	Take It to the Limit	1983	2.50	5.00	10.00
RCA VICTOR					
AAL1-2686	Waylon and Willie	198?	2.00	4.00	8.00
—Reissue with new prefix					
AFL1-2686	Waylon and Willie	1978	2.50	5.00	10.00
AFL1-2686 [DJ]	Waylon and Willie	1978	6.25	12.50	25.00
—Promo only on gold vinyl					
AHL1-4455	WW II	1982	2.50	5.00	10.00
AYL1-5134	Waylon and Willie	198?	2.00	4.00	8.00
—"Best Buy Series" reissue					
AYL1-5138	WW II	198?	2.00	4.00	8.00
—"Best Buy Series" reissue					

WAYLON AND WILLIE/WAYLON AND JESSI

Number	Title (A Side/B Side)	Yr	VG	VG+	NM
45s					
RCA					
GB-10928	Good Hearted Woman/Suspicious Minds	1977	—	—	3.00
—Gold Standard Series					

WAYNE, ALVIS

Number	Title (A Side/B Side)	Yr	VG	VG+	NM
45s					
WESTPORT					
132	Swing Bop Boogie/Sleep, Rock-a-Roll Rock-a-Baby	1956	50.00	100.00	200.00
138	Don't Mean Maybe Baby/I'd Rather Be with You	1957	37.50	75.00	150.00
—As "Tony Wayne"					
138	Don't Mean Maybe Baby/I'd Rather Be with You	1958	25.00	50.00	100.00
—As "Alvis Wayne"					

WAYNE, BERNIE

Number	Title (A Side/B Side)	Yr	VG	VG+	NM
45s					
20TH CENTURY FOX					
559	Christmas Is Over/Christmas Is Over	1964	2.00	4.00	8.00
—B-side by the Hushtones					
ABC-PARAMOUNT					
9664	Vanessa/Piff, Paff, Puff	1956	5.00	10.00	20.00
9679	You're Kinda Cute/The Night Was Made for Dreamers	1956	5.00	10.00	20.00
9727	Shalimar/South of Saigon	1956	5.00	10.00	20.00
9752	Flirtango/Maracaibo	1956	5.00	10.00	20.00
9815	Leaky Faucet/Theme from "Abner the Baseball"	1957	5.00	10.00	20.00
9967	The Telegraph Operator and the Chorus Girl/Cool Caballero	1958	5.00	10.00	20.00
HANOVER					
4528	Now/Chickie	1960	5.00	10.00	20.00
IMPERIAL					
5575	Soft Shoe Rock/Whistling Pixie	1959	3.75	7.50	15.00
RUST					
5063	38-24-38/Martinique	1963	3.00	6.00	12.00

WAYNE, BILLY

Number	Title (A Side/B Side)	Yr	VG	VG+	NM
45s					
FEDORA					
1008	Telegram/Heartbreak and Blues	1962	6.25	12.50	25.00
HILLCREST					
778	I Love My Baby/Walkin' n' Strollin'	1960	200.00	400.00	800.00

WAYNE, CARL, AND THE VIKINGS

Number	Title (A Side/B Side)	Yr	VG	VG+	NM
45s					
ABC-PARAMOUNT					
10752	Shimmy Shammy Jingle/My Girl	1965	3.00	6.00	12.00

WAYNE, JOHN

Number	Title (A Side/B Side)	Yr	VG	VG+	NM
45s					
CASABLANCA					
1002	I Have Faith/The Prayer	1979	—	3.00	6.00
Albums					
RCA VICTOR					
AFL1-3484	America, Why I Love Her	1979	2.50	5.00	10.00
—Reissue of 4828					
AYL1-3959	America, Why I Love Her	1981	2.00	4.00	8.00
—"Best Buy Series" reissue					
LSP-4828	America, Why I Love Her	1973	6.25	12.50	25.00

WAYNE, THOMAS

45s

Number	Title (A Side/B Side)	Yr	VG	VG+	NM
CAPEHART					
5009	Tragedy/No More, No More	1961	7.50	15.00	30.00
CHALET					
1054	No One/You're Tearin' Down My Mind	1969	—	3.00	6.00
FERNWOOD					
106	You're the One That Done It/This Time	1958	75.00	150.00	300.00
109	Tragedy/Saturday Date	1959	7.50	15.00	30.00
111	Eternally/Scandalizing My Name	1959	7.50	15.00	30.00
113	Gonna Be Waitin'/Just Beyond	1959	7.50	15.00	30.00
120	Guilty of Love/Pancho Villa	1960	7.50	15.00	30.00
122	Girl Next Door/Because of You	1960	7.50	15.00	30.00
128	Tragedy/No More, No More	1961	7.50	15.00	30.00
MERCURY					
71287	You're the One That Done It/This Time	1958	20.00	40.00	80.00
71454	You're the One That Done It/This Time	1959	10.00	20.00	40.00
PHILLIPS INT'L.					
3577	I've Got It Made/The Quiet Look	1962	6.25	12.50	25.00
SANTO					
9053	Stop the River/Eighth Wonder of the World	1962	6.25	12.50	25.00
9057	Tragedy/Gonna Be Waiting	1962	6.25	12.50	25.00

WE FIVE

45s

Number	Title (A Side/B Side)	Yr	VG	VG+	NM
A&M					
XMAS 1 [DJ]	My Favorite Things/The 12 Days Of Christmas	1968	3.00	6.00	12.00
—B-side by the Baja Marimba Band					
XMAS 1 [PS]	My Favorite Things/The 12 Days Of Christmas	1968	3.75	7.50	15.00
—B-side by the Baja Marimba Band					
770	You Were On My Mind/Small World	1965	3.00	6.00	12.00
784	Let's Get Together/Cast Your Fate to the Wind	1965	2.00	4.00	8.00
793	You Let a Love Burn Out/Somewhere Beyond the Sea	1966	2.00	4.00	8.00
800	Somewhere/There Stands the Door	1966	2.00	4.00	8.00
820	What's Goin' On/The First Time	1966	2.00	4.00	8.00
894	High Flying Bird/What Do I Do	1967	—	3.00	6.00
1072	Walk On By/It Really Doesn't Matter	1969	—	3.00	6.00
MGM					
14618	Seven Day Change/Natural Way	1973	—	2.50	5.00
VAULT					
964	Never Goin' Back/Here Comes the Sun	1970	—	3.00	6.00
969	Catch the Wind/Oh, Lonesome Me	1970	—	3.00	6.00
VERVE					
10716	Bandstand Dancer/Rejoice	1973	—	2.50	5.00

Albums

Number	Title	Yr	VG	VG+	NM
A&M					
SP-111 [M]	You Were on My Mind	1965	3.75	7.50	15.00
SP-138 [M]	Make Someone Happy	1967	5.00	10.00	20.00
SP-4111 [S]	You Were on My Mind	1965	5.00	10.00	20.00
SP-4138 [S]	Make Someone Happy	1967	3.75	7.50	15.00
SP-4168	The Return of We Five	1969	3.75	7.50	15.00
VAULT					
136	Catch the Wind	1970	3.75	7.50	15.00

WE TWO

45s

Number	Title (A Side/B Side)	Yr	VG	VG+	NM
ABC					
10930	Magic Moments/Way Down Deep Inside	1967	6.25	12.50	25.00

WEASELS, THE

Albums

Number	Title	Yr	VG	VG+	NM
WING					
MGW-12282 [M]	The Liverpool Beat	1964	6.25	12.50	25.00
SRW-16282 [S]	The Liverpool Beat	1964	7.50	15.00	30.00

WEATHER REPORT

Also see WAYNE SHORTER.

45s

Number	Title (A Side/B Side)	Yr	VG	VG+	NM
ARC					
10861	River People/Pursuit of the Woman with the Feathered Hat	1978	—	2.00	4.00
11166	Birdland/Brown Street	1979	—	2.00	4.00
11422	Rockin' in Rhythm/(B-side unknown)	1981	—	2.00	4.00
COLUMBIA					
10004	American Tango/(B-side unknown)	1974	—	2.50	5.00
10215	Between the Thighs/Lusitano	1975	—	2.50	5.00
10532	Birdland/Palladium	1977	—	2.50	5.00
45883	Adios/Boogie Woogie Waltz	1973	—	2.50	5.00
45964	125th Street Congress/Will	1973	—	2.50	5.00

Albums

Number	Title	Yr	VG	VG+	NM
ARC					
JC 35358	Mr. Gone	1978	2.50	5.00	10.00
PC2 36030 [(2)]	8:30	1979	3.00	6.00	12.00
PC 36358	Mr. Gone	1980	2.00	4.00	8.00
—Budget-line reissue					
JC 36793	Night Passage	1980	2.50	5.00	10.00
PC 36793	Night Passage	198?	2.00	4.00	8.00
—Budget-line reissue					
FC 37616	Weather Report	1982	2.50	5.00	10.00
PC 37616	Weather Report	198?	2.00	4.00	8.00
—Budget-line reissue					
HC 47616	Weather Report	1982	10.00	20.00	40.00
—Half-speed mastered edition					
COLUMBIA					
C 30661	Weather Report	1971	3.00	6.00	12.00
KC 30661	Weather Report	1974	2.50	5.00	10.00
—Reissue of C 30661					
PC 30661	Weather Report	1977	2.00	4.00	8.00
—Reissue					
KC 31352	I Sing the Body Electric	1972	3.00	6.00	12.00
PC 31352	I Sing the Body Electric	1977	2.00	4.00	8.00
—Reissue					
KC 32210	Sweetnighter	1973	3.00	6.00	12.00
CQ 32494 [Q]	Mysterious Traveller	1974	5.00	10.00	20.00
KC 32494	Mysterious Traveller	1974	3.00	6.00	12.00
PC 32494	Mysterious Traveller	1977	2.00	4.00	8.00
—Reissue					
PC 33417	Tale Spinnin'	1975	3.00	6.00	12.00
—No bar code on cover					
PC 33417	Tale Spinnin'	1977	2.00	4.00	8.00
—Budget-line reissue with bar code					
PCQ 33417 [Q]	Tale Spinnin'	1975	5.00	10.00	20.00
PC 34099	Black Market	1976	3.00	6.00	12.00
—No bar code on cover					
PC 34418	Heavy Weather	1977	3.00	6.00	12.00
—No bar code on cover					
PC 34418	Heavy Weather	198?	2.00	4.00	8.00
—Budget-line reissue					
FC 38427	Procession	1983	2.50	5.00	10.00
FC 39147	Domino Theory	1984	2.50	5.00	10.00
FC 39908	Sportin' Life	1985	2.50	5.00	10.00
FC 40280	This Is This	1986	2.50	5.00	10.00
HC 44418	Heavy Weather	198?	10.00	20.00	40.00
—Half-speed mastered edition					

WEATHERLY, JIM

45s

Number	Title (A Side/B Side)	Yr	VG	VG+	NM
20TH CENTURY FOX					
565	I'm Gonna Make It/Wise Men Never Speak	1965	3.00	6.00	12.00
ABC					
12193	(Apples Won't Grow In) Colorado Snow/To a Gentler Time	1976	—	2.00	4.00
12252	Storms of Troubled Times/(B-side unknown)	1977	—	2.00	4.00
12288	All That Keeps Me Going/I Hope It Never Rains Like That Again	1977	—	2.00	4.00
BUDDAH					
420	The Need to Be/Like Old Times Again	1974	—	2.00	4.00
420 [PS]	The Need to Be/Like Old Times Again	1974	—	2.50	5.00
444	I'll Still Love You/My First Day Without Her	1974	—	2.00	4.00
467	It Must Have Been the Rain/Mississippi	1975	—	2.00	4.00
505	What's One More Time/How'd We Ever Get This Way	1975	—	2.00	4.00
ELEKTRA					
46547	Smooth Sailin'/Let Me Love It Away	1979	—	—	3.00
46592	Gift from Missouri/All I Need to Know	1980	—	—	3.00
47027	Safe in the Arms of Your Love (Cold in the Streets)/All I Need to Know	1980	—	—	3.00
RCA VICTOR					
APBO-0020	Leavin' Dallas/It Must Be Love This Time	1973	—	2.00	4.00
APBO-0153	Rebel Keeps On Rollin'/Same Old Song and Dance	1973	—	2.00	4.00
PB-10134	High on Love/Like a First Time Thing	1974	—	2.00	4.00
74-0828	Loving You Is Just an Old Habit/Between His Goodbye and My Hello	1972	—	2.00	4.00
74-0897	Old Kentucky Moon/Until Your Ship Comes In	1973	—	2.00	4.00
74-0949	Where Peaceful Waters Flow/Like a First Time Thing	1973	—	2.00	4.00

Albums

Number	Title	Yr	VG	VG+	NM
ABC					
D-937	People Choose to Love	1976	2.50	5.00	10.00
D-982	Pictures and Rhymes	1977	2.50	5.00	10.00
BUDDAH					
BDS-5608	The Songs of Jim Weatherly	1974	2.50	5.00	10.00
RCA VICTOR					
APL1-0090	A Simpler Time	1973	3.00	6.00	12.00
APL1-0267	Jim Weatherly	1974	3.00	6.00	12.00
LSP-4747	Weatherly	1972	3.00	6.00	12.00

WEAVER, DENNIS

45s

Number	Title (A Side/B Side)	Yr	VG	VG+	NM
CASCADE					
5906	Girls (Wuz Made to Be Loved)/Michael Finnigan	1959	5.00	10.00	20.00
CENTURY CITY					
701	Days Like These/Cobwebs of Your Mind	1969	2.00	4.00	8.00
EVA					
103	The Apes/Chicken Mash	1963	3.00	6.00	12.00
IM'PRESS					
716	20th Century Man/No Name	1973	—	3.00	6.00
OVATION					
1056	Hubbardville Store/Prairie Dog Blues	1975	—	2.00	4.00
1056 [PS]	Hubbardville Store/Prairie Dog Blues	1975	—	2.50	5.00
WARNER BROS.					
5352	The Sinking of the Reuben James/Genesis Through Exodus	1963	3.75	7.50	15.00

Albums

Number	Title	Yr	VG	VG+	NM
ABC					
DP-847	People Songs	1974	3.00	6.00	12.00
IM'PRESS					
1614	Dennis Weaver	1972	3.75	7.50	15.00
OVATION					
OVOD-1440	One More Road	1975	3.00	6.00	12.00

WEAVERS, THE

Also see PETE SEEGER.

45s

Number	Title (A Side/B Side)	Yr	VG	VG+	NM
DECCA					
9-284 [(4)]	We Wish You a Merry Christmas	1951	18.75	37.50	75.00
—Four records (27783, 27817, 27818, 27819) plus box					
27053	Tzena, Tzena, Tzena/Around the World	1950	5.00	10.00	20.00
27077	Goodnight Irene/Tzena, Tzena, Tzena	1950	3.75	7.50	15.00
27332	The Roving Kind/(The Wreck of the) John B	1950	3.75	7.50	15.00

Number	Title (A Side/B Side)	Yr	VG	VG+	NM
27376	So Long (It's Been Good to Know Yuh)/Lonesome Traveller	1951	3.75	7.50	15.00
27515	On Top of Old Smoky/Across the Wide Missouri	1951	3.75	7.50	15.00
—With Terry Gilkyson					
27670	Kisses Sweeter Than Wine/When the Saints Go Marching In	1951	3.75	7.50	15.00
27726	The Frozen Logger/Darling Corey	1951	3.75	7.50	15.00
27727	I Know Where I'm Going-Hush Little Baby/ Suliram	1951	3.75	7.50	15.00
27728	Drinking Gourd/Easy Rider Blues	1951	3.75	7.50	15.00
27783	We Wish You a Merry Christmas/One for the Little Bitty Baby	1951	3.75	7.50	15.00
—Sides 1 and 2 of "Album No. 9-284"					
27817	The Seven Blessings of Mary/The Twelve Days of Christmas	1951	3.75	7.50	15.00
—Sides 3 and 4 of "Album No. 9-284"					
27818	Go Tell It on the Mountain/Poor Little Jesus	1951	3.75	7.50	15.00
—Sides 5 and 6 of "Album No. 9-284"					
27819	Lulloo Lullay-It's Almost Day/Burgundian Carol-God Rest Ye Merry Gentlemen	1951	3.75	7.50	15.00
—Sides 7 and 8 of "Album No. 9-284"					
27928	Wimoweh/Old Paint	1952	3.75	7.50	15.00
28054	Around the Corner (Beneath the Berry Tree)/The Gandy Dancer's Ball	1952	3.75	7.50	15.00
28228	Run Home to Ma-Ma/Hard Ain't It Hard	1952	3.75	7.50	15.00
28434	Clementine/True Love	1952	3.75	7.50	15.00
28542	Down in the Valley/The Bay of Mexico	1953	3.75	7.50	15.00
28637	Taking It Easy/Benoni	1953	3.75	7.50	15.00
28919	Rock Island Shuffle/Sylvia	1953	3.75	7.50	15.00
VANGUARD					
35001	Done Laid Around/Take This Letter	196?	3.00	6.00	12.00
35005	Aunt Rhodie/Bury Me Beneath the Willows	196?	3.00	6.00	12.00
35009	This Land Is Your Land/Aweigh, Santy Ano	196?	3.00	6.00	12.00
35010	On My Journey/The Sinking of the Reuben James	196?	3.00	6.00	12.00
35014	The Keeper/Twelve Gates to the City	196?	3.00	6.00	12.00
35015	Fight On/Rally Round the Flag	196?	3.00	6.00	12.00

7-Inch Extended Plays

Number	Title (A Side/B Side)	Yr	VG	VG+	NM
DECCA					
ED 2015	*Goodnight Irene/Tzena, Tzena, Tzena/On Top of Old Smoky/So Long (It's Been Good to Know Yuh)	195?	12.50	25.00	50.00
ED 2015 [PS]	The Weavers, Vol. 1	195?	12.50	25.00	50.00

Albums

Number	Title (A Side/B Side)	Yr	VG	VG+	NM
ANALOGUE PRODUCTIONS					
005	Reunion at Carnegie Hall, 1963	199?	7.50	15.00	30.00
—Audiophile vinyl					
DECCA					
DXB 173 [(2) M]	The Best of the Weavers	1965	6.25	12.50	25.00
DL 4277 [M]	Weavers' Gold	1962	5.00	10.00	20.00
DL 5285 [10]	Folk Songs of America and Other Lands	1951	25.00	50.00	100.00
DL-5373 [10]	We Wish You a Merry Christmas	1952	25.00	50.00	100.00
DXSB 7173 [(2) R]	The Best of the Weavers	1965	5.00	10.00	20.00
DL 8893 [M]	The Best of the Weavers	1959	10.00	20.00	40.00
—Black label, silver print					
DL 8893 [M]	Folk Songs Made Famous by the Weavers	196?	5.00	10.00	20.00
DL 8909 [M]	Folk Songs Around the World	1959	10.00	20.00	40.00
DL 74277 [R]	Weavers' Gold	1962	3.75	7.50	15.00
DL 75169 [R]	The Weavers' Greatest Hits	1971	3.00	6.00	12.00
DL 78893 [R]	Folk Songs Made Famous by the Weavers	196?	3.75	7.50	15.00
MCA					
4052 [(2)]	The Best of the Weavers	197?	3.75	7.50	15.00
—Reissue of Decca 7173					
VANGUARD					
VSD-15/16 [(2)]	The Weavers' Greatest Hits	1971	3.75	7.50	15.00
VSD 2022 [S]	Travelling on with the Weavers	1959	10.00	20.00	40.00
VSD 2030 [S]	The Weavers at Home	1959	10.00	20.00	40.00
VSD 2069 [S]	The Weavers at Carnegie Hall, Vol. 2	1960	10.00	20.00	40.00
VSD 2101 [S]	Almanac	1961	10.00	20.00	40.00
VSD 2150 [S]	Reunion at Carnegie Hall, 1963	1963	7.50	15.00	30.00
SRV-3001 [(2) M]	The Weavers Song Bag	1967	5.00	10.00	20.00
VRS-6533 [R]	The Weavers at Carnegie Hall	1970	3.00	6.00	12.00
VRS-6537 [R]	The Weavers on Tour	1970	3.00	6.00	12.00
VRS 9010 [M]	The Weavers at Carnegie Hall	1957	10.00	20.00	40.00
VRS 9013 [M]	The Weavers on Tour	1957	10.00	20.00	40.00
VRS 9024 [M]	The Weavers at Home	1959	7.50	15.00	30.00
VRS 9043 [M]	Travelling on with the Weavers	1959	7.50	15.00	30.00
VRS 9075 [M]	The Weavers at Carnegie Hall, Vol. 2	1960	7.50	15.00	30.00
VRS 9100 [M]	Almanac	1961	7.50	15.00	30.00
VRS 9130 [M]	Reunion at Carnegie Hall, 1963	1963	5.00	10.00	20.00
VRS 9161 [M]	Reunion at Carnegie Hall, Part 2	1965	5.00	10.00	20.00
SRV-73001 [(2) S]	The Weavers Song Bag	1967	6.25	12.50	25.00
VMS-73101	The Weavers at Carnegie Hall	1984	2.00	4.00	8.00
—Reissue of 6533					
VMS-73116	The Weavers on Tour	1985	2.00	4.00	8.00
—Reissue of 6537					
VMS-73122	Classics	1985	2.50	5.00	10.00
VSD 79161 [S]	Reunion at Carnegie Hall, Part 2	1965	7.50	15.00	30.00

WEB, THE

Albums

Number	Title (A Side/B Side)	Yr	VG	VG+	NM
DERAM					
DES 18018	Fully Interlocking	1968	6.25	12.50	25.00

WEBB, BOOGIE BILL

45s

Number	Title (A Side/B Side)	Yr	VG	VG+	NM
IMPERIAL					
5257	Bad Dog/I Ain't For It	1953	62.50	125.00	250.00

WEBB, JACK

45s

Number	Title (A Side/B Side)	Yr	VG	VG+	NM
WARNER BROS.					
5003	Try a Little Tenderness/You'd Never Know the Old Place Now	1958	5.00	10.00	20.00

7-Inch Extended Plays

Number	Title (A Side/B Side)	Yr	VG	VG+	NM
RCA VICTOR					
547-0342	The Christmas Story (Part 1)/The Christmas Story (Part 4)	1953	7.50	15.00	30.00
547-0343	The Christmas Story (Part 2)/The Christmas Story (Part 3)	1953	7.50	15.00	30.00
EPB 3199 [PS]	The Christmas Story	1953	10.00	20.00	40.00
—Cover for 2-EP set					

Albums

Number	Title (A Side/B Side)	Yr	VG	VG+	NM
RCA VICTOR					
LPM-1126 [M]	Pete Kelly's Blues	1955	12.50	25.00	50.00
—Webb narrates; jazz combo plays					
LPM-2053 [M]	Pete Kelly's Blues	1959	7.50	15.00	30.00
—Reissue of 1126					
LSP-2053(e) [R]	Pete Kelly's Blues	1959	5.00	10.00	20.00
LPM-3199 [10]	Dragnet — The Christmas Story	1954	37.50	75.00	150.00
WARNER BROS.					
W 1207 [M]	You're My Girl	1958	7.50	15.00	30.00
W 1207 [M]	You're My Girl	1958	7.50	15.00	30.00
WS 1207 [S]	You're My Girl	1958	10.00	20.00	40.00
WS 1207 [S]	You're My Girl	1958	10.00	20.00	40.00

WEBS, THE (1)

R&B group.

45s

Number	Title (A Side/B Side)	Yr	VG	VG+	NM
ATLANTIC					
2415	Let's Party/Keep Your Love Strong	1967	3.00	6.00	12.00
MGM					
13602	People Sure Act Funny/You Pretty Fool	1966	3.00	6.00	12.00
POPSIDE					
4593	This Thing Called Love/Tomorrow	1967	2.50	5.00	10.00
4595	Give In/It's So Hard to Break a Habit	1968	2.50	5.00	10.00
VERVE					
10610	We Belong Together/I Want You Back	1968	2.50	5.00	10.00

WEBS, THE (2)

BOBBY GOLDSBORO was in this group.

45s

Number	Title (A Side/B Side)	Yr	VG	VG+	NM
HEART					
333	Blue Skies/Lost (Cricket in My Ear)	1962	10.00	20.00	40.00
LITE					
9004	Blue Skies/Lost (Cricket in My Ear)	1962	5.00	10.00	20.00

WEBTONES, THE

45s

Number	Title (A Side/B Side)	Yr	VG	VG+	NM
MGM					
12724	My Lost Love/Walk, Talk and Kiss	1958	6.25	12.50	25.00

WECHTER, JULIUS

See BAJA MARIMBA BAND.

WEDGES, THE

Albums

Number	Title (A Side/B Side)	Yr	VG	VG+	NM
TIME					
S-2090 [S]	Hang Ten (For Surfers Only)	1963	17.50	35.00	70.00
52090 [M]	Hang Ten (For Surfers Only)	1963	12.50	25.00	50.00

WEIR, BOB

Also see THE GRATEFUL DEAD.

45s

Number	Title (A Side/B Side)	Yr	VG	VG+	NM
ARISTA					
0315	Bombs Away/Easy to Slip	1978	—	3.00	6.00
0336	I'll Be Doggone/Shade of Grey	1978	3.00	6.00	12.00
—May be promo only					
WARNER BROS.					
7611	One More Saturday Night/Cassidy	1972	3.00	6.00	12.00

Albums

Number	Title (A Side/B Side)	Yr	VG	VG+	NM
ARISTA					
AL 4155	Heaven Help the Fool	1978	2.50	5.00	10.00
AL 8366	Heaven Help the Fool	1985	2.00	4.00	8.00
—Budget-line reissue					
AL 8367	Bobby and the Midnites	1985	2.00	4.00	8.00
—Budget-line reissue					
AL 9568	Bobby and the Midnites	1981	2.50	5.00	10.00
WARNER BROS.					
BS 2627	Ace	1972	10.00	20.00	40.00
—Color photo on back cover					
BS 2627	Ace	1972	7.50	15.00	30.00
—Black and white photo on back cover					

WEIRD-OHS, THE

Albums

Number	Title (A Side/B Side)	Yr	VG	VG+	NM
MERCURY					
MG-20976 [M]	The Sounds of the Weird-Ohs	1964	37.50	75.00	150.00
SR-60976 [S]	The Sounds of the Weird-Ohs	1964	50.00	100.00	200.00

WEISBERG, TIM

Also see DAN FOGELBERG.

45s

Number	Title (A Side/B Side)	Yr	VG	VG+	NM
A&M					
1318	Long Ago and Far Away/Hard Way to Go	1971	—	2.50	5.00
1330	Fog and Spice/For Those Who Never Dream	1972	—	2.50	5.00
1397	Our Thing/Tyme Cube	1972	—	2.50	5.00
1427	Killing Me Softly with His Song/Tibetan Silver	1973	—	2.50	5.00
1493	Do Dah/A Night for Crying	1973	—	2.50	5.00
1520	Streak-Out/A Night for Crying	1974	—	2.50	5.00
1680	Dion Blue/The Visit	1975	—	2.00	4.00
MCA					
41036	Midsummer's Dream/Moonchild	1979	—	2.00	4.00
41307	I'm the Lucky One/Magic Lady	1980	—	2.00	4.00
51042	What's Going On/Page One	1981	—	2.00	4.00

Number	Title (A Side/B Side)	Yr	VG	VG+	NM
51163	Sleep Walk/Paula	1981	—	2.00	4.00
UNITED ARTISTS					
XW933	Gonna Fly Now (Theme from "Rocky")/Just for Fun	1976	—	2.00	4.00
XW1083	Cascade/Gene, Jean	1977	—	2.00	4.00
1227	Every Time I See Your Smile/So Good to Me	1978	—	2.00	4.00
Albums					
A&M					
SP-3039	Tim Weisberg	1971	3.00	6.00	12.00
SP-3045	Dreamspeaker	1973	2.50	5.00	10.00
SP-3121	Tim Weisberg 4	198?	2.00	4.00	8.00
—Budget-line reissue					
SP-3261	Smile/The Best of Tim Weisberg	198?	2.00	4.00	8.00
—Budget-line reissue					
SP-3658	Tim Weisberg 4	1974	2.50	5.00	10.00
SP-4352	Hurtwood Edge	1972	3.00	6.00	12.00
SP-4545	Listen to the City	1975	2.50	5.00	10.00
SP-4600	Live at Last!	1976	2.50	5.00	10.00
SP-4749	Smile/The Best of Tim Weisberg	1979	2.50	5.00	10.00
CYPRESS					
YL-0123	Outrageous Temptations	1989	3.00	6.00	12.00
661112-1	High Risk	1986	2.50	5.00	10.00
DESERT ROCK					
DR-001	High Risk	1985	3.75	7.50	15.00
LIBERTY					
LN-10029	Rotations	198?	2.00	4.00	8.00
—Budget-line reissue					
LN-10031	The Tim Weisberg Band	198?	2.00	4.00	8.00
—Budget-line reissue					
MCA					
3084	Night-Rider!	1979	2.50	5.00	10.00
5125	Party of One	1980	2.50	5.00	10.00
5245	Travelin' Light	1981	2.50	5.00	10.00
NAUTILUS					
NR-7	Tip of the Weisberg	1980	7.50	15.00	30.00
—Audiophile vinyl					
UNITED ARTISTS					
UA-LA773-G	The Tim Weisberg Band	1977	2.50	5.00	10.00
UA-LA857-H	Rotations	1978	2.50	5.00	10.00

WEISSBERG, ERIC, AND MARSHALL BRICKMAN

Number	Title (A Side/B Side)	Yr	VG	VG+	NM
Albums					
ELEKTRA					
EKL-238 [M]	New Dimensions in Banjo and Bluegrass	1963	5.00	10.00	20.00
EKS-7238 [S]	New Dimensions in Banjo and Bluegrass	1963	6.25	12.50	25.00
—Mandolin-player label					
EKS-7238 [S]	New Dimensions in Banjo and Bluegrass	1967	5.00	10.00	20.00
—Tan label with large stylized "E" at top					
EKS-7238 [S]	New Dimensions in Banjo and Bluegrass	1969	3.75	7.50	15.00
—Red label with large stylized "E" at top					
EKS-7238 [S]	New Dimensions in Banjo and Bluegrass	1971	3.00	6.00	12.00
—Butterfly label					
EKS-7238 [S]	New Dimensions in Banjo and Bluegrass	1980	2.50	5.00	10.00
—Red label with Warner Communications logo in lower right					

WEISSBERG, ERIC, AND DELIVERANCE

Number	Title (A Side/B Side)	Yr	VG	VG+	NM
45s					
EPIC					
50072	Yakety Yak/Meadow Muffins	1975	—	2.00	4.00
WARNER BROS.					
7718	Reuben's Train/Scalded Cat	1973	—	2.00	4.00
7756	Opening Day/Concrete Canyon Boogie	1973	—	2.00	4.00
Albums					
WARNER BROS.					
BS 2720	Rural Free Delivery	1973	2.50	5.00	10.00

WEISSBERG, ERIC, AND STEVE MANDELL

Number	Title (A Side/B Side)	Yr	VG	VG+	NM
45s					
WARNER BROS.					
7659	Dueling Banjos/End of a Dream	1972	—	3.00	6.00
—First pressings mark the A-side as "from the Warner Bros. motion picture Deliverance" and no artist is mentioned on the B-side					
7659	Dueling Banjos/End of a Dream	1973	—	2.00	4.00
—Later pressings credit the musicians					
Albums					
WARNER BROS.					
BS 2683	Dueling Banjos from Deliverance	1973	2.50	5.00	10.00
—Except for the title song and "End of a Dream," this is actually a reissue of Elektra 7238; green label					
BS 2683	Dueling Banjos from Deliverance	1973	2.00	4.00	8.00
—"Burbank" palm trees label					
BS 2683	Dueling Banjos from Deliverance	1979	—	3.00	6.00
—Tan or white label					

WELCH, LENNY

Number	Title (A Side/B Side)	Yr	VG	VG+	NM
45s					
ATCO					
6894	A Sunday Kind of Love/I Wish You Could Know Me	1972	—	2.50	5.00
6915	Goodnight My Love/Fancy Meeting You Here Baby	1973	—	2.50	5.00
BIG TREE					
16107	Six Million Dollar Woman/(B-side unknown)	1977	—	2.50	5.00
CADENCE					
1373	You Don't Know Me/I Need Someone	1959	2.50	5.00	10.00
1386	Darlin'/Three Handed Woman	1960	2.50	5.00	10.00
1394	I'd Like to Know/Darlin'	1960	2.50	5.00	10.00
1399	Changa Rock/Boogie Cha Cha	1961	2.50	5.00	10.00
1416	It's Just Not That Easy/Mama Don't You Hit That Boy	1962	2.50	5.00	10.00
1422	Ebb Tide/Congratulations Baby	1962	5.00	10.00	20.00
—The A-side was the hit, but this is sought after for its group sound on the B-side					
1428	A Taste of Honey/The Old Cathedral	1962	2.50	5.00	10.00
1439	Since I Fell for You/Are You Sincere	1963	3.00	6.00	12.00
1446	If You See My Love/Father Sebastian	1964	2.50	5.00	10.00
COLUMBIA					
44007	Since I Fell for You/A Taste of Honey	1967	2.00	4.00	8.00
COMMONWEALTH UNITED					
3004	Breaking Up Is Hard to Do/Get Mommy to Come Back Home	1969	—	3.00	6.00
3011	To Be Loved and Glory of Love/My Heart Won't Let Me	1970	—	3.00	6.00
DECCA					
30637	Rocket to the Moon/My One Sincere	1958	3.00	6.00	12.00
30829	Blessing of Love/Last Star of the Evening	1959	3.00	6.00	12.00
KAPP					
648	I'm Dreaming Again/My Fool of a Heart	1965	2.00	4.00	8.00
662	Darling Take Me Back/Time After Time	1965	2.00	4.00	8.00
689	Two Different Worlds/I'll Be There	1965	2.00	4.00	8.00
712	Run to My Lovin' Arms/Coronet Blue	1965	2.00	4.00	8.00
740	Rags to Riches/I Want to Worry (About Me)	1966	2.00	4.00	8.00
751	What Now My Love/Gonna Hear from Me	1966	2.00	4.00	8.00
761	Please Help Me I'm Falling/Just One Smile	1966	2.00	4.00	8.00
778	If You Love Me, Really Love Me/Once Before I Die	1966	2.00	4.00	8.00
808	Until the Real Thing Comes Along/A Right to Cry	1967	2.00	4.00	8.00
827	Let's Start All Over Again/Love Don't Live Here Anymore	1967	2.00	4.00	8.00
854	I'm Over You/Coronet Blue	1967	2.00	4.00	8.00
MAINSTREAM					
5545	Since I Don't Have You/Right in the Next Room	1973	—	2.50	5.00
5554	Eyewitness News/I Need You More	1973	—	2.50	5.00
5560	A Hundred Pounds of Pain/The Iguana	1974	—	2.50	5.00
5561	When There's No Such Thing As Love/Minx	1974	—	2.50	5.00
MERCURY					
72777	Darling Stay with Me/Wait a While Longer	1968	2.00	4.00	8.00
72811	Tennessee Waltz/He Who Loves	1968	2.00	4.00	8.00
72866	Halfway to Your Arms/You Can't Run Away	1968	2.00	4.00	8.00
Albums					
CADENCE					
CLP 3068 [M]	Since I Fell for You	1963	7.50	15.00	30.00
CLP 25068 [S]	Since I Fell for You	1963	12.50	25.00	50.00
COLUMBIA					
CL 2430 [M]	Since I Fell for You	1965	5.00	10.00	20.00
—Reissue of Cadence 3068					
CS 9230 [S]	Since I Fell for You	1965	7.50	15.00	30.00
—Reissue of Cadence 25068					
KAPP					
KL-1457 [M]	Two Different Worlds	1965	3.75	7.50	15.00
KL-1481 [M]	Rags to Riches	1966	3.75	7.50	15.00
KL-1517 [M]	Lenny	1967	3.75	7.50	15.00
KS-3457 [S]	Two Different Worlds	1965	5.00	10.00	20.00
KS-3481 [S]	Rags to Riches	1966	5.00	10.00	20.00
KS-3517 [S]	Lenny	1967	5.00	10.00	20.00

WELK, LAWRENCE

Also see THE LENNON SISTERS.

Number	Title (A Side/B Side)	Yr	VG	VG+	NM
45s					
CORAL					
60405	Shenandoah Waltz/Metro Polka	1951	3.00	6.00	12.00
—Note: Earlier Lawrence Welk 45s on Coral may exist					
60444	Moonlight Bay/Boomp! Pa-Deedle Doodle	1951	3.00	6.00	12.00
60514	Sad and Lonely/Irving	1951	3.00	6.00	12.00
60516	Slow Drive/Moonlight Bay	1951	3.00	6.00	12.00
60517	Tell Me/Cuddle Up a Little Closer, Lovey Mine	1951	3.00	6.00	12.00
60518	Yoo Hoo/I'm Forever Blowing Bubbles	1951	3.00	6.00	12.00
60519	Every Little Moment/Till We Meet Again	1951	3.00	6.00	12.00
60575	Sweetheart Waltz/I Wanna Say Hello	1951	3.00	6.00	12.00
60618	My Extraordinary Gal/Irene	1952	2.50	5.00	10.00
60619	Dolores/Emaline	1952	2.50	5.00	10.00
60620	Mary Lou/Annabelle	1952	2.50	5.00	10.00
60621	Louise/Sweet Eloise	1952	2.50	5.00	10.00
60630	Swingin' Down the Lane/You're Somebody	1952	2.50	5.00	10.00
60677	The Gandy Dancer's Ball/Ivory Rag	1952	2.50	5.00	10.00
60689	Bubbles in the Wine/Josephine	1952	3.75	7.50	15.00
60752	Dream House/Small Talk	1952	2.50	5.00	10.00
60784	Watermelon Weather/Busybody	1952	2.50	5.00	10.00
60806	Padam Padam (How It Echoes the Beat of My Heart)/Your Eyes So Lovely	1952	2.50	5.00	10.00
60813	Rustic Dance/Cocoanut Grove	1952	2.50	5.00	10.00
60828	Meet Mister Callaghan/Flirtation Waltz	1952	2.50	5.00	10.00
60893	Oh Happy Day/Your Mother and Mine	1952	2.50	5.00	10.00
60905	She Looked Down from Her Window/I'm Gonna Ring the Bell Tonight	1953	2.50	5.00	10.00
—Vocalist: Jack Smith					
60947	Minnie the Mermaid/Say It Isn't So	1953	2.50	5.00	10.00
60973	Ohio/It's Love	1953	2.50	5.00	10.00
60974	Canadian Capers/Did I Remember	1953	2.50	5.00	10.00
60975	Good Morning, Mr. Zip Zip Zip/Just Once Again	1953	2.50	5.00	10.00
60976	I'll See You in My Dreams/Peggy O'Neill	1953	2.50	5.00	10.00
60998	Bubbling Over/The La-De-Da Song	1953	2.50	5.00	10.00
61003	High Life Polka/Town and Country Polka	1953	2.50	5.00	10.00
61017	Hallejulah Brother/"O"	1953	2.50	5.00	10.00
61075	Ebb Tide/Beautiful Ohio	1953	2.50	5.00	10.00
61081	Angel on the Christmas Tree/Are My Ears On Straight	1953	3.75	7.50	15.00
—With Sara Berner					
61095	Christmas Carols (Part 1)/Christmas Carols (Part 2)	1953	3.00	6.00	12.00
61100	Joey's Theme/Coney Island	1953	2.50	5.00	10.00
61135	The Darktown Strutter's Ball/In the Mood	1954	2.50	5.00	10.00
61174	The Man with the Banjo/Until Sunrise	1954	2.50	5.00	10.00
61207	Nimble Fingers/Doll Dance	1954	2.50	5.00	10.00
—With Sara Berner					
61240	The Greatest Feeling in the World/Luxembourg Polka	1954	2.50	5.00	10.00
61318	At the Junior Prom/Home Again Blues	1954	2.50	5.00	10.00
61372	Elephant's Tango/Lazy Gondolier	1955	2.00	4.00	8.00

Number	Title (A Side/B Side)	Yr	VG	VG+	NM
61387	I See God/Pray for Me	1955	2.00	4.00	8.00
61408	Hey, Mr. Banjo/Love Me or Leave Me	1955	2.00	4.00	8.00
61442	Ball of Fire/Go 'Way, Go 'Way	1955	2.00	4.00	8.00
61477	Wake the Town and Tell the People/I Hear Those Bells	1955	2.00	4.00	8.00
61508	Champagne Waltz/Musette	1955	2.00	4.00	8.00
61515	Bonnie Blue Gal/Sam the Old Accordian Man	1955	2.00	4.00	8.00
61524	It's Almost Tomorrow/Rice	1955	2.00	4.00	8.00
61574	Moritat (A Theme from the Threepenny Opera)/ Stompin' at the Savoy	1956	2.00	4.00	8.00
61592	The Poor People of Paris/Nobody Knows But the Lord	1956	2.00	4.00	8.00
61595	Lisbon Antigua/Chain Gang	1956	2.00	4.00	8.00
61597	Mickey Mouse Mambo/Hi! to You	1956	3.00	6.00	12.00
61621	Practice, Practice What You Preach/What a Heavenly Night for Love	1956	2.00	4.00	8.00
61629	Helena Polka/Hot Pretzels	1956	2.00	4.00	8.00
61630	Jenny Lind/The Jolly Coppersmith	1956	2.00	4.00	8.00
61644	On the Street Where You Live/I Could Have Danced All Night	1956	2.00	4.00	8.00
61645	With a Little Bit of Luck/I've Grown Accustomed to Her Face	1956	2.00	4.00	8.00
61670	Weary Blues/In the Alps	1956	2.50	5.00	10.00
—With the McGuire Sisters					
61701	Tonight You Belong to Me/When the White Lilacs Bloom Again	1956	2.50	5.00	10.00
—With the Lennon Sisters					
61741	Around the World/Champagne Time	1956	2.00	4.00	8.00
61745	Ring Those Christmas Bells/Let's Have an Old-Fashioned Christmas	1956	2.50	5.00	10.00
61746	Christmas Waltz/Santa from Santa Fe	1956	3.00	6.00	12.00
—With the Lennon Sisters					
61765	Cinco Robles/Whispering Heart	1956	2.00	4.00	8.00
61783	McNamara's Band/Wild Colonial Boy	1957	2.00	4.00	8.00
61784	Dance Around a Stack of Barley/When Irish Eyes Are Smiling	1957	2.00	4.00	8.00
61786	Falling Star/It Was That Kiss	1957	2.00	4.00	8.00
61806	Ten Little Trees/The Bridge of Saint Lo	1957	2.00	4.00	8.00
61849	By the Bend of the River/Keyboard Serenade	1957	2.00	4.00	8.00
61870	Ricky-Dicky-Doo/To Be with You	1957	2.00	4.00	8.00
61893	Moon Love/We'll Be There	1957	2.00	4.00	8.00
61894	My Reverie/Fool Moon and Empty Arms	1957	2.00	4.00	8.00
61900	Lichtenstein Polka/You Know Too Much	1957	2.00	4.00	8.00
61914	Merry Christmas from Our House to Your House/ Santa Claus Is Here Again	1957	3.00	6.00	12.00
—With the Lennon Sisters					
61937	One Note Polka/The Lovers on the Park Bench	1958	2.00	4.00	8.00
61958	I Want a Girl/When My Baby Smiles at Me	1958	2.00	4.00	8.00
62018	Walk with Me/Be Thankful	1958	2.00	4.00	8.00
62031	Mary Ann/Indiana Holiday	1958	2.00	4.00	8.00
62053	Outer Space Santa/All Around The Merry Christmas Tree	1958	3.00	6.00	12.00
—As "Lawrence Welk's Little Band"					
62056	Cha Cha Polka/I Never Should Have Let You Go	1958	2.00	4.00	8.00
62091	Gunsmoke/The Ballad of Paladin	1959	3.00	6.00	12.00
65511	Bubbles in the Wine/Josephine	196?	—	3.00	6.00
65517	Cocoanut Grove/Rustic Dance	196?	—	3.00	6.00
65523	Ave Maria/He'll Be There	196?	—	3.00	6.00
65541	Gold and Silver/Lichtenstein Polka	196?	—	3.00	6.00
65574	Pony Tail/The Wreck of the Old '88	196?	—	3.00	6.00
65604	I'll See You in My Dreams/Till We Meet Again	1966	—	2.50	5.00
98054 [DJ]	Christmas Carols (Part 1)/Christmas Carols (Part 2)	19??	2.00	4.00	8.00
—"Mery Christmas from Lawrence Welk" custom label					
DECCA					
23855	Beer Barrel Polka/Pennsylvania Polka	1950	2.50	5.00	10.00
—Reissue of 78; part of "Album No. 9-24"					
23857	Clarinet Polka/Pound Your Table Polka	1950	2.50	5.00	10.00
—Reissue of 78; part of "Album No. 9-24"					
23858	Barbara Polka/Friendly Tavern Polka	1950	2.50	5.00	10.00
—Reissue of 78; part of "Album No. 9-24"					
24442	Bubbles in the Wine/Kentucky Waltz	1950	5.00	10.00	20.00
—78 originally released in 1948; original 45 has black label with "rays" on either side of the word "Decca"					
24442	Bubbles in the Wine/Kentucky Waltz	1955	3.00	6.00	12.00
—Second 45 has star under "Decca"					
24442	Bubbles in the Wine/Kentucky Waltz	1960	2.00	4.00	8.00
—Third 45 has color bars on label					
DOT					
15924	The Swingin' Burglar/Bell Boogie	1959	2.00	4.00	8.00
—By "Lawrence Welk's Little Band"					
15967	Goodnight Sweetheart/This Night Is Young and You're So Beautiful	1959	2.00	4.00	8.00
—By "The Lawrence Welk Glee Club"					
15995	Every Night When You Say a Prayer/Thank the Lord for This Thanksgiving	1959	2.50	5.00	10.00
—With the Lennon Sisters					
16017	Christmas Moon/Peppy the Peppermint Bear	1959	3.00	6.00	12.00
—With the Lennon Sisters					
16062	Just Because/Tick-Tock Polka	1960	2.00	4.00	8.00
—With Myron Floren					
16063	Hour of Parting/Summer Set	1960	2.00	4.00	8.00
16114	It Started in Naples/I Get So Lonely (Oh Baby Mine)	1960	2.00	4.00	8.00
16145	Last Date/Remember Lolita	1960	—	3.00	6.00
16153	The Cradle to the Cross/Laura-Jean	1960	—	3.00	6.00
16161	Calcutta/My Grandfather's Clock	1960	2.00	4.00	8.00
16198	Theme from My Three Sons/Out of a Clear Blue Sky	1961	2.50	5.00	10.00
16222	Yellow Bird/Cruising Down the River	1961	—	3.00	6.00
16237	Riders in the Sky/My Love for You	1961	—	3.00	6.00
16285	You Gave Me Wings/A-One, a-Two, a-Cha Cha Cha	1961	—	3.00	6.00
16336	Runaway/Happy Love	1962	—	3.00	6.00
16364	Baby Elephant Walk/Theme from the Brothers Grimm	1962	2.00	4.00	8.00
16420	Zero-Zero/Night Theme	1962	—	3.00	6.00
16488	Scarlett O'Hara/Breakwater	1963	—	3.00	6.00
16582	Stockholm/Girl from Barbados	1964	—	3.00	6.00
16603	Hello, Dolly/Clair de Lune	1964	—	3.00	6.00
16620	Poodle Walk/Do I Need You	1964	—	3.00	6.00
16680	Sixteen Reasons/Little Things Mean a Lot	1964	—	3.00	6.00
16697	Apples and Bananas/Theme from "The Addams Family"	1965	2.00	4.00	8.00
16741	There's No One Like You/Schatzie	1965	—	3.00	6.00
16764	Down, Down, Down, Down/Jenny Dear	1965	—	3.00	6.00
16778	Summer Nights/La Bamba	1965	—	3.00	6.00
16794	Moonlight and Roses/Send Me the Pillow You Dream On	1965	—	3.00	6.00
16810	Currier and Ives/Tia-Juana	1965	—	3.00	6.00
16885	Wabash Cannonball/Tennessee Waltz	1966	—	2.50	5.00
16943	Family Affair/Tarzan (Tarzan's March)	1966	2.00	4.00	8.00
16981	Born Free/Winchester Cathedral	1966	—	2.50	5.00
17001	The Beat Goes On/Then You Can Tell Me Goodbye	1967	—	2.50	5.00
MERCURY					
5411	Doo-Wacka-Doo/Pizzacata	1950	3.75	7.50	15.00
—Note: Earlier Lawrence Welk 45s on Mercury may exist					
5419	Hoop-De-Dee/If You Can Get a Drum with a Boom, Boom, Boom	1950	3.75	7.50	15.00
5434	Dakota Polka/Windy River	1950	3.75	7.50	15.00
5440	Deep Freezer Dinah/Fancy Free	1950	3.75	7.50	15.00
5469	Mama's Samba/Skaters Waltz in Springtime	1950	3.75	7.50	15.00
—Vocalist: Roberta Linn					
5487	Petite Waltz/The Middle of a Riddle	1950	3.75	7.50	15.00
5518	Emilia Polka/Tinker Polka	1950	3.75	7.50	15.00
5519	Julida Polka/Laughing Polka	1950	3.75	7.50	15.00
5529	Tiger Rag/Military Polka	1950	3.75	7.50	15.00
5666	Bubbles in the Wine/Back Home in Illinois	1951	5.00	10.00	20.00
5735	Merry Christmas Polka/Julida Polka	1951	3.75	7.50	15.00
70065	Julinda Polka/Swiss Lullaby	1953	3.00	6.00	12.00
70149	Fiddle-Dee-Dee/Dancing Doll	1953	3.00	6.00	12.00
70734	Hoop-De-Dee/Bar Room Polka	1955	2.50	5.00	10.00
70735	Amilia Polka/Tinker Polka	1955	2.50	5.00	10.00
70736	Julida Polka/Military Polka	1955	2.50	5.00	10.00
70737	Dakota Polka/Kit Kat Polka	1955	2.50	5.00	10.00
70738	Merry Christmas Polka/Laughing Polka	1955	3.00	6.00	12.00
70739	Tiger Rag/Chopsticks Polka	1955	2.50	5.00	10.00
RANWOOD					
801	Green Tambourine/Watch What Happens	1968	—	2.00	4.00
814	Let's Make America What It Used to Be/To America with Love	1968	—	2.00	4.00
842	Galveston/Gentle on My Mind	1969	—	2.00	4.00
845	Land of Dreams/Chee Chee Kookaroo	1969	—	2.00	4.00
860	Jean/Spinning Wheel	1970	—	2.00	4.00
865	Hello Dolly/Southtown U.S.A.	1970	—	2.00	4.00
874	Applause/Smiles	1970	—	2.00	4.00
888	Candida/Endlessly	1971	—	2.00	4.00
905	No, No, Nanette/Too Many Rings Around Rosie	1971	—	2.00	4.00
915	Theme from Summer of '42/Adios, Au Revoir, Auf Wiedersehn	1971	—	2.00	4.00
920	Melody of Love (Parody)/Melody of Love	1972	2.00	4.00	8.00
—With Bob Hudson (of Hudson and Landry) on A-side					
1039	Fantastic, That's You/Oh Harry	1975	—	—	3.00
—With Henry Questa					
1068	Nadia's Theme (The Young and the Restless)/ Johnny's Theme	1976	—	—	3.00
1073	Keep Your Eyes on the Sparrow/Paloma Blanca	1977	—	—	3.00
1091	Christmas In Los Angeles/Carol Of The Bells	1980	—	2.00	4.00
—By "The Lawrence Welk Christmas Chorale"					
(NO LABEL)					
(no #)	Season's Greetings From Your Dodge Dealer	196?	2.00	4.00	8.00
—Cardboard record					

7-Inch Extended Plays

Number	Title (A Side/B Side)	Yr	VG	VG+	NM
CORAL					
EC 81133	(contents unknown)	1956	2.50	5.00	10.00
EC 81133 [PS]	My Fair Lady	1956	2.50	5.00	10.00
EC 81134	(contents unknown)	195?	2.50	5.00	10.00
EC 81134	(contents unknown)	195?	2.50	5.00	10.00
EC 81134 [PS]	Champagne Medley Time	195?	2.50	5.00	10.00
EC 81134 [PS]	Say It with Music	195?	2.50	5.00	10.00
EC 81146	(contents unknown)	195?	2.50	5.00	10.00
EC 81146 [PS]	Pick-a-Polka	195?	2.50	5.00	10.00
EC 81148	(contents unknown)	195?	2.50	5.00	10.00
EC 81148 [PS]	Moments to Remember	195?	2.50	5.00	10.00
EC 81154	(contents unknown)	195?	2.50	5.00	10.00
EC 81154 [PS]	The Stars Visit Lawrence Welk	195?	2.50	5.00	10.00
EC 81157	(contents unknown)	195?	2.50	5.00	10.00
EC 81157 [PS]	Waltz with Lawrence Welk	195?	2.50	5.00	10.00
EC 81160	(contents unknown)	195?	2.50	5.00	10.00
EC 81160 [PS]	Champagne and Roses	195?	2.50	5.00	10.00
EC 81171	(contents unknown)	195?	2.50	5.00	10.00
EC 81171 [PS]	Champagne Dancing Party, Vol. I	195?	2.50	5.00	10.00
EC 81172	(contents unknown)	195?	2.50	5.00	10.00
EC 81172 [PS]	Champagne Dancing Party, Vol. II	195?	2.50	5.00	10.00
EC 81180	All Around the Merry Christmas Tree/Merry Christmas from Our House to Your House//Outer Space Santa/Santa from Santa Fe	195?	2.50	5.00	10.00
EC 81180 [PS]	Merry Christmas	195?	2.50	5.00	10.00
EC 81502	Bubbles in the Wine/Cocoanut Grove//Metro Polka/Oh Happy Day	195?	2.50	5.00	10.00
EC 81502 [PS]	Lawrence Welk	195?	2.50	5.00	10.00
EC 82032 [PS]	Jingle Bells	1956	3.00	6.00	12.00
—Cover for 2-EP set					
83068	(contents unknown)	1956	2.50	5.00	10.00
—Part of 2-EP set EC 82032					
83069	Santa Claus Is Comin' To Town/Winter Wonderland//Christmas Dreaming (A Little Early This Year)/The Twelve Gifts Of Christmas	1956	2.50	5.00	10.00
—Part of 2-EP set EC 82032					

Number	Title (A Side/B Side)	Yr	VG	VG+	NM
DECCA					
ED 2023	Bubbles in the Wine/Josephine//Kentucky Waltz/ Canadian Capers	195?	3.00	6.00	12.00
ED 2023 [PS]	Lawrence Welk, Vol. 1	195?	3.00	6.00	12.00
ED 2568	(contents unknown)	195?	3.00	6.00	12.00
ED 2568 [PS]	Polkas and Champagne	195?	3.00	6.00	12.00
Albums					
CORAL					
7CXSB 5 [(2) S]	The Best of Lawrence Welk	196?	3.75	7.50	15.00
CXB 5 [(2) M]	The Best of Lawrence Welk	196?	5.00	10.00	20.00
CRL 56120 [10]	Viennese Waltzes for Dancing	1954	7.50	15.00	30.00
CRL 57011 [M]	Lawrence Welk and His Sparkling Strings	1955	5.00	10.00	20.00
CRL 57025 [M]	TV Favorites	1955	5.00	10.00	20.00
CRL 57036 [M]	Shamrocks and Champagne	1955	5.00	10.00	20.00
CRL 57038 [M]	Bubbles in the Wine	1956	5.00	10.00	20.00
CRL 57041 [M]	Say It With Music	1956	5.00	10.00	20.00
CRL 57066 [M]	Lawrence Welk at Madison Square Garden	1956	5.00	10.00	20.00
CRL 57067 [M]	Pick-A-Polka!	1956	5.00	10.00	20.00
CRL 57068 [M]	Moments to Remember	1956	5.00	10.00	20.00
CRL 57078 [M]	Champagne Pops Parade	1956	5.00	10.00	20.00
CRL 57093 [M]	Merry Christmas from Lawrence Welk	1956	5.00	10.00	20.00
CRL 57111 [M]	Show Time	1957	5.00	10.00	20.00
CRL 57113 [M]	The World's Finest Music	1957	5.00	10.00	20.00
CRL 57119 [M]	Waltz with Lawrence Welk	1957	5.00	10.00	20.00
CRL 57146 [M]	Lawrence Welk Plays Dixieland	1957	5.00	10.00	20.00
CRL 57178 [M]	Nimble Fingers	1957	5.00	10.00	20.00
CRL 57186 [M]	Jingle Bells	1957	5.00	10.00	20.00
CRL 57191 [M]	Songs of Faith	1958	3.75	7.50	15.00
CRL 57214 [M]	Lawrence Welk Presents Keyboard Kapers	1958	3.75	7.50	15.00
CRL 57226 [M]	Champagne Dancing Party	1958	3.75	7.50	15.00
CRL 57260 [M]	Lawrence Welk Featuring the Lennon Sisters	1959	3.75	7.50	15.00
CRL 57262 [M]	Lawrence Welk Featuring Larry Hooper	1959	3.75	7.50	15.00
CRL 57267 [M]	TV Western Theme Songs	1959	3.75	7.50	15.00
CRL 57353 [M]	My Golden Favorites	1961	3.00	6.00	12.00
CRL 57383 [M]	Lawrence Welk Showcase	1962	3.00	6.00	12.00
CRL 57439 [M]	Songs Everybody Knows	1964	3.00	6.00	12.00
CRL 757036 [R]	Shamrocks and Champagne	196?	3.00	6.00	12.00
CRL 757041 [R]	Say It With Music	196?	3.00	6.00	12.00
CRL 757067 [R]	Pick-A-Polka!	1959	3.00	6.00	12.00
CRL 757093 [R]	Merry Christmas from Lawrence Welk	196?	3.00	6.00	12.00
CRL 757113 [R]	The World's Finest Music	196?	3.00	6.00	12.00
CRL 757186 [R]	Jingle Bells	196?	3.00	6.00	12.00
CRL 757226 [S]	Champagne Dancing Party	1958	5.00	10.00	20.00
CRL 757267 [S]	TV Western Theme Songs	1959	5.00	10.00	20.00
CRL 757353 [S]	My Golden Favorites	1961	3.00	6.00	12.00
CRL 757383 [S]	Lawrence Welk Showcase	1962	3.00	6.00	12.00
CRL 757439 [S]	Songs Everybody Knows	1964	3.00	6.00	12.00
CORONET					
275	Lawrence Welk and His Orchestra	196?	2.50	5.00	10.00
DECCA					
DL 8213 [M]	Lawrence Welk's Polka Party	1956	3.75	7.50	15.00
DL 8323 [M]	Around We Go	1956	3.75	7.50	15.00
DL 8324 [M]	Welktime	1956	3.75	7.50	15.00
DESIGN					
200	Champagne Time	196?	2.50	5.00	10.00
912	Three of a Kind	196?	2.50	5.00	10.00
DOT					
DLP 3164 [M]	Mr. Music Maker	1959	3.00	6.00	12.00
DLP 3200 [M]	The Voices and Strings of Lawrence Welk	1959	3.00	6.00	12.00
DLP 3218 [M]	The Lawrence Welk Glee Club	1959	3.00	6.00	12.00
DLP 3224 [M]	Dance with Lawrence Welk	1959	3.00	6.00	12.00
DLP 3238 [M]	Lawrence Welk Presents Great American Composers	1960	2.50	5.00	10.00
DLP 3247 [M]	Lawrence Welk Presents Great Overtures in Dance Time	1960	2.50	5.00	10.00
DLP 3248 [M]	I'm Forever Blowing Bubbles	1960	2.50	5.00	10.00
DLP 3251 [M]	Songs of the Islands	1960	2.50	5.00	10.00
DLP 3274 [M]	Strictly for Dancing	1960	2.50	5.00	10.00
DLP 3284 [M]	To Mother	1960	2.50	5.00	10.00
DLP 3296 [M]	Sweet and Lovely	1960	2.50	5.00	10.00
DLP 3302 [M]	Polkas	1960	2.50	5.00	10.00
DLP 3317 [M]	Lawrence in Dixieland	1960	2.50	5.00	10.00
DLP 3318 [M]	Double Shuffle	1960	2.50	5.00	10.00
DLP 3342 [M]	The Champagne Music of Lawrence Welk	1960	2.50	5.00	10.00
DLP 3350 [M]	Last Date	1960	2.50	5.00	10.00
DLP 3359 [M]	Calcutta!	1961	2.50	5.00	10.00
DLP 3389 [M]	Yellow Bird	1961	2.50	5.00	10.00
DLP 3395 [M]	Diamond Jubilee	1961	2.50	5.00	10.00
DLP 3397 [M]	Silent Night and 13 Other Best-Loved Christmas Songs	1961	3.00	6.00	12.00
DLP 3412 [M]	Moon River	1961	2.50	5.00	10.00
DLP 3428 [M]	Young World	1962	2.50	5.00	10.00
DLP 3432 [M]	Sing-a-Long Party	1962	2.50	5.00	10.00
DLP 3457 [M]	Baby Elephant Walk and Theme from The Brothers Grimm	1962	2.50	5.00	10.00
DLP 3489 [M]	Bubbles in the Wine	1962	2.50	5.00	10.00
DLP 3499 [M]	Waltz Time	1963	2.50	5.00	10.00
DLP 3510 [M]	1963's Early Hits	1963	2.50	5.00	10.00
DLP 3528 [M]	Scarlett O'Hara	1963	2.50	5.00	10.00
DLP 3544 [M]	A Tribute to the All-Time Greats	1963	2.50	5.00	10.00
DLP 3552 [M]	Wonderful! Wonderful!	1963	2.50	5.00	10.00
DLP 3572 [M]	Early Hits of 1964	1964	2.50	5.00	10.00
DLP 3591 [M]	The Lawrence Welk Television Show 10th Anniversary	1964	2.50	5.00	10.00
DLP 3611 [M]	The Golden Millions	1964	2.50	5.00	10.00
DLP 3616 [M]	My First of 1965	1965	2.50	5.00	10.00
DLP 3629 [M]	Apples and Bananas	1965	2.50	5.00	10.00
DLP 3653 [M]	The Happy Wanderer	1966	2.50	5.00	10.00
DLP 3663 [M]	Today's Great Hits	1966	2.50	5.00	10.00
DLP 3688 [M]	Champagne on Broadway	1966	2.50	5.00	10.00
DLP 3774 [M]	Winchester Cathedral	1966	2.50	5.00	10.00
DLP 3779 [M]	Hymns We Love	1967	2.50	5.00	10.00
DLP 3790 [M]	Lawrence Welk's "Hits of Our Time"	1967	2.50	5.00	10.00
DLP 3812 [M]	Golden Hits/The Best of Lawrence Welk	1967	3.00	6.00	12.00
DLP 25164 [S]	Mr. Music Maker	1959	3.75	7.50	15.00
DLP 25200 [S]	Voices and Strings	1959	3.75	7.50	15.00
DLP 25218 [S]	The Lawrence Welk Glee Club	1959	3.75	7.50	15.00
DLP 25224 [S]	Dance with Lawrence Welk	1959	3.75	7.50	15.00
DLP 25238 [S]	Lawrence Welk Presents Great American Composers	1960	3.00	6.00	12.00
DLP 25247 [S]	Lawrence Welk Presents Great Overtures in Dance Time	1960	3.00	6.00	12.00
DLP 25248 [S]	I'm Forever Blowing Bubbles	1960	3.00	6.00	12.00
DLP 25251 [S]	Songs of the Islands	1960	3.00	6.00	12.00
DLP 25274 [S]	Strictly for Dancing	1960	3.00	6.00	12.00
DLP 25284 [S]	To Mother	1960	3.00	6.00	12.00
DLP 25296 [S]	Sweet and Lovely	1960	3.00	6.00	12.00
DLP 25302 [S]	Polkas	1960	3.00	6.00	12.00
DLP 25317 [S]	Lawrence in Dixieland	1960	3.00	6.00	12.00
DLP 25318 [S]	Double Shuffle	1960	3.00	6.00	12.00
DLP 25342 [S]	The Champagne Music of Lawrence Welk	1960	3.00	6.00	12.00
DLP 25350 [S]	Last Date	1960	3.00	6.00	12.00
DLP 25359 [S]	Calcutta!	1961	3.00	6.00	12.00
DLP 25389 [S]	Yellow Bird	1961	3.00	6.00	12.00
DLP 25395 [S]	Diamond Jubilee	1961	3.00	6.00	12.00
DLP 25397 [S]	Silent Night and 13 Other Best-Loved Christmas Songs	1961	3.75	7.50	15.00
DLP 25412 [S]	Moon River	1961	3.00	6.00	12.00
DLP 25428 [S]	Young World	1962	3.00	6.00	12.00
DLP 25432 [S]	Sing-a-Long Party	1962	3.00	6.00	12.00
DLP 25457 [S]	Baby Elephant Walk and Theme from The Brothers Grimm	1962	3.00	6.00	12.00
DLP 25489 [S]	Bubbles in the Wine	1962	3.00	6.00	12.00
DLP 25499 [S]	Waltz Time	1963	3.00	6.00	12.00
DLP 25510 [S]	1963's Early Hits	1963	3.00	6.00	12.00
DLP 25528 [S]	Scarlett O'Hara	1963	3.00	6.00	12.00
DLP 25544 [S]	A Tribute to the All-Time Greats	1963	3.00	6.00	12.00
DLP 25552 [S]	Wonderful! Wonderful!	1963	3.00	6.00	12.00
DLP 25572 [S]	Early Hits of 1964	1964	3.00	6.00	12.00
DLP 25591 [S]	The Lawrence Welk Television Show 10th Anniversary	1964	3.00	6.00	12.00
DLP 25611 [S]	The Golden Millions	1964	3.00	6.00	12.00
DLP 25616 [S]	My First of 1965	1965	3.00	6.00	12.00
DLP 25629 [S]	Apples and Bananas	1965	3.00	6.00	12.00
DLP 25653 [S]	The Happy Wanderer	1966	3.00	6.00	12.00
DLP 25663 [S]	Today's Great Hits	1966	3.00	6.00	12.00
DLP 25688 [S]	Champagne on Broadway	1966	3.00	6.00	12.00
DLP 25774 [S]	Winchester Cathedral	1966	3.00	6.00	12.00
DLP 25779 [S]	Hymns We Love	1967	3.00	6.00	12.00
DLP 25790 [S]	Lawrence Welk's "Hits of Our Time"	1967	3.00	6.00	12.00
DLP 25812 [S]	Golden Hits/The Best of Lawrence Welk	1967	2.50	5.00	10.00
HAMILTON					
HLP 152 [M]	Mary Poppins	1965	2.50	5.00	10.00
HLP 12152 [S]	Mary Poppins	1965	3.00	6.00	12.00
HARMONY					
HL 7394 [M]	Vintage Champagne	1966	3.00	6.00	12.00
HS 11194 [S]	Vintage Champagne	1966	3.00	6.00	12.00
HS 11301	Champagne Dance Party	1969	2.50	5.00	10.00
HEARTLAND					
1006	Musical Family Reunion	198?	2.50	5.00	10.00
MCA					
733	Polka and Waltz Time	197?	2.00	4.00	8.00
—Reissue of Vocalion 73670					
4026 [(2)]	The Best of Lawrence Welk, Volume 2	197?	3.00	6.00	12.00
4044 [(2)]	The Best of Lawrence Welk	197?	3.00	6.00	12.00
4104 [(2)]	The Best Polkas	197?	3.00	6.00	12.00
MCA CORAL					
20100	Champagne Music	197?	2.00	4.00	8.00
MERCURY					
MG-20092 [M]	Dance Party	1956	3.75	7.50	15.00
MISTLETOE					
MLP-1215	Christmas with Lawrence Welk	197?	2.50	5.00	10.00
PICKWICK					
SPC-1019	The Christmas Song	197?	2.50	5.00	10.00
—Reissue of Coral LP "Jingle Bells" with shuffled running order					
SPC-3070	Save the Last Dance for Me	196?	2.50	5.00	10.00
SPC-3092	I'll See You Again	196?	2.50	5.00	10.00
SPC-3116	You'll Never Walk Alone	196?	2.50	5.00	10.00
SPC-3143	If You Were the Only One	196?	2.50	5.00	10.00
SPC-3157	As Time Goes By	196?	2.50	5.00	10.00
SPC-3196	Love Is a Many-Splendored Thing	197?	2.50	5.00	10.00
SPC-3212	Blue Hawaii	197?	2.50	5.00	10.00
SPC-3252	Polkas!	197?	2.50	5.00	10.00
PREMIER					
9043	Lawrence Welk	196?	2.50	5.00	10.00
RANWOOD					
2000	Merry Christmas	197?	2.50	5.00	10.00
2004	Polkas	197?	2.00	4.00	8.00
—With Myron Floren					
2005	Moon River	197?	—	3.00	6.00
—Reissue of Ranwood 8016					
2006	Yellow Bird	197?	—	3.00	6.00
—Reissue of Ranwood 8021					
2007	Songs of the Islands	197?	—	3.00	6.00
—Reissue of Ranwood 8022					
2008	Waltz Time	197?	—	3.00	6.00
—Reissue of Ranwood 8025					
2009	Hymns We Love	197?	—	3.00	6.00
—Reissue of Ranwood 8042					
2010	Memories	197?	—	3.00	6.00
—Reissue of Ranwood 8044					
4100	On Tour, Volume 1	198?	2.00	4.00	8.00
4101	On Tour, Volume 2	198?	2.00	4.00	8.00
5001 [(2)]	Reminiscing	1972	3.00	6.00	12.00
5005 [(2)]	24 of the World's Greatest Polkas	197?	3.00	6.00	12.00
—With Myron Floren					
6001 [(2)]	Lawrence Welk and His Musical Family in Concert	1973	3.00	6.00	12.00

Number	Title (A Side/B Side)	Yr	VG	VG+	NM
6002	Lawrence Welk and His Musical Family Celebrate 50 Years in Music	1974	2.50	5.00	10.00
7002 [(2)]	200 Years of American Music	1976	3.00	6.00	12.00
7004 [(2)]	22 Great Waltzes	1977	3.00	6.00	12.00
7009 [(2)]	22 Great Songs for Dancing	1978	3.00	6.00	12.00
7016 [(2)]	22 Great Songs for Easy Listening	198?	3.00	6.00	12.00
7023 [(2)]	22 All-Time Big Band Favorites	1983	3.00	6.00	12.00
7028 [(2)]	22 All-Time Favorite Waltzes	198?	3.00	6.00	12.00
7029 [(2)]	22 Merry Christmas Favorites	198?	3.00	6.00	12.00
8003	Love Is Blue	1968	2.50	5.00	10.00
8016	Moon River	1968	2.00	4.00	8.00
—Reissue of Dot 25412					
8017	Winchester Cathedral	1968	2.00	4.00	8.00
—Reissue of Dot 25774					
8020	Silent Night and 13 Other Best-Loved Christmas Songs	1968	2.00	4.00	8.00
—Reissue of Dot 25397					
8021	Yellow Bird	1968	2.00	4.00	8.00
—Reissue of Dot 25389					
8022	Songs of the Islands	1968	2.00	4.00	8.00
—Reissue of Dot 25251					
8023	The Champagne Music of Lawrence Welk	1968	2.00	4.00	8.00
—Reissue of Dot 25342					
8024	Calcutta!	1968	2.00	4.00	8.00
—Reissue of Dot 25359					
8025	Waltz Time	1968	2.00	4.00	8.00
—Reissue of Dot 25499					
8026	The Lawrence Welk Television Show	1968	2.00	4.00	8.00
—Reissue of Dot 25591					
8027	Country Music's Great Hits	1968	2.50	5.00	10.00
8028	Golden Hits/The Best of Lawrence Welk	1968	2.00	4.00	8.00
—Reissue of Dot 25812					
8030	To America with Love	1968	2.50	5.00	10.00
8034	The Lawrence Welk Singers and Orchestra	1968	2.50	5.00	10.00
8042	Hymns We Love	1968	2.00	4.00	8.00
—Reissue of Dot 25779					
8044	Memories	1969	2.50	5.00	10.00
8049	Galveston	1969	2.50	5.00	10.00
8053	Lawrence Welk Plays I Love You Truly and Other Songs of Love	1969	2.50	5.00	10.00
8060	Jean	1969	2.50	5.00	10.00
8068	The Golden 60's	1970	2.50	5.00	10.00
8077	The Big Band Sound	1970	2.50	5.00	10.00
8079	Champagne Strings	1970	2.50	5.00	10.00
8083	Candida	1970	2.50	5.00	10.00
8087	No, No, Nanette	1971	2.50	5.00	10.00
8091	Go Away Little Girl	1971	2.50	5.00	10.00
8109	(More of) The Big Band Sound	1972	2.50	5.00	10.00
8114	The Good Life	1973	2.50	5.00	10.00
8130	Lawrence Welk Plays From That's Entertainment	1974	2.50	5.00	10.00
8140	Most Requested TV Favorites	1974	2.50	5.00	10.00
8145	25 Years on Television	1975	2.50	5.00	10.00
8162	The Best of Lawrence Welk: 20 Great Hits	1976	2.50	5.00	10.00
8165	Nadia's Theme	1976	2.50	5.00	10.00
8183	My Personal Favorites	1978	2.50	5.00	10.00
8184	Hallelujah!	1978	2.50	5.00	10.00
8191	Remembering the Sweet and Swing Band Era, Vol. 1	1979	2.50	5.00	10.00
8192	Remembering the Sweet and Swing Band Era, Vol. 2	1979	2.50	5.00	10.00
8194	Lawrence Welk Plays Dixieland	1980	2.50	5.00	10.00
8195 [(2)]	Reminiscing, Vol. 2	1980	3.00	6.00	12.00
8201	Lawrence Welk Presents Anacani	1982	2.50	5.00	10.00
8210	Musical Memories with Lawrence Welk	1984	2.00	4.00	8.00
8211	Come Waltz with Me	1984	2.00	4.00	8.00
10001 [(2)]	Live at Lake Tahoe	1978	3.00	6.00	12.00
10002 [(2)]	The Sweet and Swing Band Era	1979	3.00	6.00	12.00
READER'S DIGEST					
RDA-07-A [(4)]	Merry Christmas from Lawrence Welk and His Champagne Music Makers	1970	6.25	12.50	25.00
RDA 95 [(6)]	Champagne Music Varieties	196?	6.25	12.50	25.00
RDA 156	Champagne Dance Time with Lawrence Welk	196?	2.50	5.00	10.00
SUNNYVALE					
SVL-1015	Silent Night and 13 Other Best-Loved Christmas Songs	1978	2.00	4.00	8.00
—Same contents as Dot 25397					
THOMAS					
20052	The Magic of Color-Glo	196?	3.00	6.00	12.00
VOCALION					
VL 3670 [M]	Polka and Waltz Time	196?	2.50	5.00	10.00
VL 3671 [M]	Lawrence Welk and His Champagne Music	196?	2.50	5.00	10.00
VL 3783 [M]	Lawrence Welk and His Champagne Music Makers Play for You	1967	3.00	6.00	12.00
VL 73670 [R]	Polka and Waltz Time	196?	2.50	5.00	10.00
VL 73671 [R]	Lawrence Welk and His Champagne Music	196?	2.50	5.00	10.00
VL 73783 [R]	Lawrence Welk and His Champagne Music Makers Play for You	1967	2.50	5.00	10.00
VL 73865	Champagne Polkas	1969	2.50	5.00	10.00
VL 73888	Til the End of Time	1969	2.50	5.00	10.00
VL 73921	Wonderful Music	1970	2.50	5.00	10.00
WING					
PKW-2-114 [(2)]	With a-One and a-Two	1969	3.75	7.50	15.00
MGW-12119 [M]	Dance Party	196?	3.00	6.00	12.00
MGW-12210 [M]	Music for Polka Lovers	196?	3.00	6.00	12.00
MGW-12214 [M]	Aragon Trianon Memories	196?	3.00	6.00	12.00
SRW-16210 [S]	Music for Polka Lovers	196?	2.50	5.00	10.00
SRW-16214 [R]	Aragon Trianon Memories	196?	2.50	5.00	10.00
SRW-16379	The Best of Welk	196?	2.50	5.00	10.00

WELLER, FREDDY

Also see PAUL REVERE AND THE RAIDERS.

45s

Number	Title (A Side/B Side)	Yr	VG	VG+	NM
APT					
25096	Walk Away Slowly/You Better Go Join the Campfire	1966	2.50	5.00	10.00
COLUMBIA					
10016	You're Not Getting Older (You're Getting Better)/Are We Makin' Love	1974	—	2.00	4.00
10300	Ask Any Old Cheater Who Knows/A Legend in My Home	1976	—	2.00	4.00
10352	Liquor, Love and Life/Celia Brown	1976	—	2.00	4.00
10411	Room 269/I Drank Myself Sober	1976	—	2.00	4.00
10482	Strawberry Curls/When You Were Mine	1977	—	2.00	4.00
10539	Merry-Go-Round/One Man Show	1977	—	2.00	4.00
10598	Nobody Cares But You/Love Doctor	1977	—	2.00	4.00
10682	Let Me Fall Back in Your Arms/Snuff Queens	1978	—	2.00	4.00
10769	Bar Wars/One of the Mysteries of Love	1978	—	2.00	4.00
10837	Love Got in the Way/You Win Again	1978	—	2.00	4.00
10890	Fantasy Island/Take a Little Bit	1979	—	2.00	4.00
10973	Nadine/Too Many Memories	1979	—	2.00	4.00
11044	That Run-Away Woman of Mine/Atlanta	1979	—	2.00	4.00
11149	Go for the Night/Two Makes One Wonderful	1979	—	2.00	4.00
11221	A Million Old Goodbyes/Sleep with Me	1980	—	2.00	4.00
11266	Lost in Austin/Explosion!	1980	—	2.00	4.00
11394	Still Your Fool/Tonight I'm Drinkin'	1980	—	2.00	4.00
44800	Games People Play/Home	1969	—	2.50	5.00
44916	These Are Not My People/Never Knew Julie	1969	—	2.50	5.00
45026	Down in the Boondocks/Amarillo, Texas	1969	—	2.50	5.00
45087	I Shook the Hand/We Gotta All Get Together	1970	—	2.50	5.00
45138	Listen to the Young Folks/That Little Boy	1970	—	3.00	6.00
45276	The Promised Land/Goodnight Sandy	1970	—	2.50	5.00
45388	Indian Lake/Over You	1971	—	2.50	5.00
45451	Another Night of Love/Always Something Special	1971	—	2.50	5.00
45542	Ballad of a Hillbilly Singer/Good Old-Fashioned Music	1972	—	2.50	5.00
45624	The Roadmaster/Who Do You Love	1972	—	2.50	5.00
45723	She Loves Me (Right Out of My Mind)/Angel on My Shoulder	1972	—	2.50	5.00
45827	Too Much Monkey Business/It Sure Feels Good	1973	—	2.50	5.00
45902	The Perfect Stranger/Betty Ann and Shirley Cole	1973	—	2.50	5.00
45968	I've Just Got to Know (How Loving You Would Be)/Georgia Girl	1973	—	2.50	5.00
46040	Sexy Lady/Bobby Crabtree's Grave	1974	—	2.50	5.00
DORE					
595	No One to Love/Mary, I'm Glad to See You	1961	3.75	7.50	15.00

Albums

Number	Title (A Side/B Side)	Yr	VG	VG+	NM
ABC/DOT					
DO-2026	Love You Back to Georgia	1975	3.00	6.00	12.00
COLUMBIA					
CS 1036	Listen to the Young Folks	1970	3.75	7.50	15.00
CS 9904	Games People Play/These Are Not My People	1969	3.75	7.50	15.00
C 30638	Promised Land	1971	3.00	6.00	12.00
KC 31769	Roadmaster	1972	3.00	6.00	12.00
KC 32218	Too Much Monkey Business	1973	3.00	6.00	12.00
KC 32958	Sexy Lady	1974	3.00	6.00	12.00
KC 33883	Greatest Hits	1975	3.00	6.00	12.00
KC 34244	Liquor, Love and Life	1976	2.50	5.00	10.00
PC 34709	One Man Show	1977	2.50	5.00	10.00
KC 35658	Love Got in the Way	1979	2.50	5.00	10.00
HARMONY					
KH 31784	Country Collection	1972	2.50	5.00	10.00

WELLES, ORSON

12-Inch Singles

Number	Title (A Side/B Side)	Yr	VG	VG+	NM
GNP CRESCENDO					
1206	I Know What It Is to Be Young/Love Is a Lovely Word	1984	3.75	7.50	15.00

45s

Number	Title (A Side/B Side)	Yr	VG	VG+	NM
GNP CRESCENDO					
8345	I Know What It Is to Be Young/Love Is a Lovely Word	1984	2.00	4.00	8.00

Albums

Number	Title (A Side/B Side)	Yr	VG	VG+	NM
MEDIARTS					
41-2	The Begatting of the President	1970	3.75	7.50	15.00
UNITED ARTISTS					
UAS-5521	The Begatting of the President	1971	3.00	6.00	12.00
—Reissue of Mediarts LP					

WELLINGTON, MARY SUE

45s

Number	Title (A Side/B Side)	Yr	VG	VG+	NM
TUFF					
400	Spoiled/Save a Little Monkey	1964	2.00	4.00	8.00

WELLINGTON, RUSTY

45s

Number	Title (A Side/B Side)	Yr	VG	VG+	NM
ARCADE					
116	Dog-Gone It Baby, I'm in Love/Every Precious Memory	1953	10.00	20.00	40.00
124	I Want a Little Lovin'/Slowly But Surely	1954	10.00	20.00	40.00
140	Blues from Tennessee/Jump Jump Honey	1955	10.00	20.00	40.00
144	The Convict and the Rose/I Ain't A-Movin' On No More	1957	10.00	20.00	40.00
184	The Allegash/I've Been Away from You So Long	1965	3.75	7.50	15.00
185	Soft Shoulders/The Old Man	1966	3.75	7.50	15.00
191	Lonely Lips/Isle of Wild Roses	1967	3.75	7.50	15.00
MGM					
12581	Rocking Chair on the Moon/I Lost My Someone	1957	75.00	150.00	300.00

WELLS, BILLY, AND THE CRESCENTS

45s

Number	Title (A Side/B Side)	Yr	VG	VG+	NM
RESERVE					
105	I Love Only You/Julie	1956	150.00	300.00	600.00

WELLS, DONNIE

45s

Number	Title (A Side/B Side)	Yr	VG	VG+	NM
SCEPTER					
12119	Real Love/You've Got My Love	1965	6.25	12.50	25.00

WELLS, MARY

Also see MARVIN GAYE AND MARY WELLS.

45s

Number	Title (A Side/B Side)	Yr	VG	VG+	NM
20TH CENTURY FOX					
544	Ain't It the Truth/Stop Takin' Me for Granted	1964	3.75	7.50	15.00
555	Use Your Head/Everlovin' Boy	1965	3.75	7.50	15.00
570	Never, Never Leave Me?Why Don't You Let Yourself Go	1965	3.75	7.50	15.00
590	He's a Lover/I'm Learnin'	1965	3.75	7.50	15.00
590 [PS]	He's a Lover/I'm Learnin'	1965	7.50	15.00	30.00
6606	Me Without You/I'm Sorry	1965	3.75	7.50	15.00
6619	I Should Have Known Better/Please Please Me	1965	5.00	10.00	20.00
ATCO					
6392	Dear Lover/Can't You See	1965	3.00	6.00	12.00
6423	Keep Me in Suspense/Such a Sweet Thing	1966	3.00	6.00	12.00
6436	Fancy Free/Me and My Baby	1966	3.00	6.00	12.00
6469	Coming Home/Hey You Set My Soul on Fire	1967	3.00	6.00	12.00
EPIC					
02664	Gigolo/I'm Changing My Ways	1982	—	2.00	4.00
02855	These Arms/Spend the Night With Me	1982	—	2.00	4.00
JUBILEE					
5621	The Doctor/Two Lovers' History	1968	3.75	7.50	15.00
5629	Can't Get Away From Your Love/A Woman in Love	1968	3.75	7.50	15.00
5639	Don't Look Back/500 Miles	1968	3.75	7.50	15.00
5676	Mind Reader/Never Give a Man the World	1969	3.00	6.00	12.00
5684	Dig the Way I Feel/Love Shooting Bandit	1969	3.00	6.00	12.00
5695	Sweet Love/It Must Be	1970	3.00	6.00	12.00
5718	Mr. Tough/Never Give a Man the World	1971	3.00	6.00	12.00
MOTOWN					
1003	Bye Bye Baby/Please Forgive Me	1960	12.50	25.00	50.00
1011	I Don't Want to Take a Chance/I'm Sorry	1961	7.50	15.00	30.00
—Pink "lines" label					
1011	I Don't Want to Take a Chance/I'm Sorry	1961	5.00	10.00	20.00
—Blue "map" label					
1011 [PS]	I Don't Want to Take a Chance/I'm Sorry	1961	20.00	40.00	80.00
1016	Strange Love/Come to Me	1961	5.00	10.00	20.00
1016 [PS]	Strange Love/Come to Me	1961	20.00	40.00	80.00
1024	The One Who Really Loves You/I'm Gonna Stay	1962	5.00	10.00	20.00
1024 [PS]	The One Who Really Loves You/I'm Gonna Stay	1962	20.00	40.00	80.00
1032	You Beat Me to the Punch/Old Love (Let's Try It Again)	1962	5.00	10.00	20.00
1032 [PS]	You Beat Me to the Punch/Old Love (Let's Try It Again)	1962	30.00	60.00	120.00
1035	Two Lovers/Operator	1962	5.00	10.00	20.00
1039	Laughing Boy/Two Wrongs Don't Make a Right	1963	5.00	10.00	20.00
1042	Your Old Stand By/What Love Has Joined Together	1963	5.00	10.00	20.00
1048	You Lost the Sweetest Boy/What's Easy for Two Is So Hard for One	1963	5.00	10.00	20.00
1056	My Guy/Oh Little Boy (What Did You Do to Me)	1964	5.00	10.00	20.00
1061	When I'm Gone/Guarantee for a Lifetime	1964	150.00	300.00	600.00
1065	Whisper You Love Me/I'll Be Available	1964	—	—	—
—Unreleased?					
REPRISE					
1031	I Found What I Wanted/I See a Future in You	1971	2.50	5.00	10.00
1308	If You Can't Give Her Love (Give Her Up)/Cancel My Subscription	1974	2.50	5.00	10.00

Albums

Number	Title (A Side/B Side)	Yr	VG	VG+	NM
20TH FOX					
TFM 3171 [M]	Mary Wells	1965	10.00	20.00	40.00
TFM 3178 [M]	Love Songs to the Beatles	1965	20.00	40.00	80.00
TFS 4171 [S]	Mary Wells	1965	15.00	30.00	60.00
TFS 4178 [S]	Love Songs to the Beatles	1965	25.00	50.00	100.00
ALLEGIANCE					
AV-444	The Old, the New, and the Best of Mary Wells	1984	2.50	5.00	10.00
ATCO					
33-199 [M]	Two Sides of Mary Wells	1966	6.25	12.50	25.00
SD 33-199 [S]	Two Sides of Mary Wells	1966	7.50	15.00	30.00
EPIC					
ARE 37540	In and Out of Love	1981	3.75	7.50	15.00
JUBILEE					
JGS-8018	Servin' Up Some Soul	1968	6.25	12.50	25.00
MOTOWN					
M5-161V1	Bye Bye Baby/I Don't Want to Take a Chance	1981	2.50	5.00	10.00
M5-167V1	Mary Wells Sings My Guy	1981	2.50	5.00	10.00
M5-221V1	Two Lovers	1981	2.50	5.00	10.00
M 600 [M]	Bye Bye Baby/I Don't Want to Take a Chance	1961	75.00	150.00	300.00
—White label stock copy					
M 600 [M]	Bye Bye Baby/I Don't Want to Take a Chance	1962	62.50	125.00	250.00
—With map; label address above the center hole					
M 605 [M]	The One Who Really Loves You	1962	40.00	80.00	160.00
—With map; label address above the center hole					
M 605 [M]	The One Who Really Loves You	1964	10.00	20.00	40.00
—With map; label address around lower part of label					
M 607 [M]	Two Lovers and Other Great Hits	1963	30.00	60.00	120.00
—With map; label address above the center hole					
M 607 [M]	Two Lovers and Other Great Hits	1964	10.00	20.00	40.00
—With map; label address around lower part of label					
M 611 [M]	Recorded Live on Stage	1963	30.00	60.00	120.00
—With map; label address above the center hole					
M 611 [M]	Recorded Live on Stage	1964	10.00	20.00	40.00
—With map; label address around lower part of label					
M 612	Second Time Around	1963	—	—	—
—Canceled					
M 616 [M]	Greatest Hits	1964	10.00	20.00	40.00
MS 616 [S]	Greatest Hits	1964	10.00	20.00	40.00
M 617 [M]	Mary Wells Sings My Guy	1964	12.50	25.00	50.00
M 653 [M]	Vintage Stock	1967	12.50	25.00	50.00
MS 653 [S]	Vintage Stock	1967	12.50	25.00	50.00
5233 ML	Greatest Hits	1982	2.50	5.00	10.00
MOVIETONE					
71010 [M]	Ooh	1966	6.25	12.50	25.00
72010 [S]	Ooh	1966	7.50	15.00	30.00

WENDIGO

45s

Number	Title (A Side/B Side)	Yr	VG	VG+	NM
SCEPTER					
12211	Gimmie Some Lovin' (Part 1)/Gimmie Some Lovin' (Part 2)	1968	3.00	6.00	12.00

WESLEY, FRED

Also includes the J.B.'s.

45s

Number	Title (A Side/B Side)	Yr	VG	VG+	NM
ATLANTIC					
3408	Up for the Down Stroke/When In Doubt	1977	—	2.50	5.00
KING					
6317	The Grunt (Part 1)/The Grunt (Part 2)	1970	2.50	5.00	10.00
—As "The J.B.'s"					
6333	These Are the J.B.'s (Part 1)/These Are the J.B.'s (Part 2)	1970	2.50	5.00	10.00
—As "The J.B.'s"					
PEOPLE					
602	Gimme Some More/The Rabbit Got the Gun	1972	—	3.00	6.00
—As "The J.B.'s"					
607	Pass the Peas/Hot Pants Road	1972	—	3.00	6.00
—As "The J.B.'s"					
610	Givin' Up Food for Funk (Part 1)/Givin' Up Food for Funk (Part 2)	1972	—	3.00	6.00
—As "The J.B.'s"					
614	Backstabbers/J.B. Shout	1972	—	3.00	6.00
616	If You Don't Get It the First Time/You Can Have Her Boogie	1973	—	3.00	6.00
617	Alone Again (Naturally)/Watermelon Man	1973	—	3.00	6.00
619	Sportin' Life/Dirty Harri	1973	—	3.00	6.00
621	Doing It to Death/Everybody Got Soul	1973	—	3.00	6.00
627	If You Don't Get It the First Time, Back Up and Try It Again, Party/You Can Have Watergate, Just Give Me Some Bucks and I'll Be Straight	1973	—	3.00	6.00
632	Same Beat - Part 1/Same Beat - Part 2	1974	—	3.00	6.00
638	Damn Right I Am Somebody-Part 1/Damn Right I Am Somebody-Part 2	1974	—	3.00	6.00
643	Rockin' Funky Watergate (Part 1)/Rockin' Funky Watergate (Part 2)	1974	—	3.00	6.00
646	Little Boy Black/Rockin' Funky Watergate (Part 2)	1974	—	3.00	6.00
648	Breakin' Bread/Funky Music Is My Style	1974	—	2.50	5.00
651	Makin' Love/Rice and Ribs	1975	—	2.50	5.00
654	Thank You for Lettin' Me Be Myself and Be Yours (Part 1)/Thank You for Lettin' Me Be Myself and Be Yours (Part 2)	1975	—	2.50	5.00
655	(It's Not the Express) It's the J.B.'s Monaurail, Part 1/(It's Not the Express) It's the J.B.'s Monaurail, Part 2	1975	—	2.50	5.00
660	Thank You for Lettin' Me Be Myself (Part 1)/Thank You for Lettin' Me Be Myself (Part 2)	1975	—	2.50	5.00
663	All Aboard the Funky Soul Train/Thank You for Lettin' Me Be Myself and You Be Yourself	1976	—	2.50	5.00
2502	My Brother (Part 1)/My Brother (Part 2)	1971	—	3.00	6.00
—As "The J.B.'s"					
RSO/CURTOM					
1037	House Party/I Make Music	1980	—	2.00	4.00

Albums

Number	Title (A Side/B Side)	Yr	VG	VG+	NM
ATLANTIC					
SD 18214	A Blow for Me, A Toot to You	1977	3.00	6.00	12.00
SD 19254	Say Blow by Blow Backwards	1979	3.00	6.00	12.00
PEOPLE					
PE-5601	Food for Thought	1972	20.00	40.00	80.00
PE-5603	Doing It to Death	1973	20.00	40.00	80.00
PE-6602	Damn Right I Am Somebody	1974	5.00	10.00	20.00
PE-6604	Breakin' Bread	1974	5.00	10.00	20.00

WESLEY, GATE

45s

Number	Title (A Side/B Side)	Yr	VG	VG+	NM
ATLANTIC					
2319	Do the Batman/Do the Thing	1966	6.25	12.50	25.00

WEST

45s

Number	Title (A Side/B Side)	Yr	VG	VG+	NM
EPIC					
5-10335	Just Like Tom Thumb's Blues/Baby You Been On My Mind	1968	2.50	5.00	10.00
5-10378	Step by Step/Summer Flower	1968	2.00	4.00	8.00
5-10449	Peaceful Times/You Only Think You've Come Home	1969	2.00	4.00	8.00

Albums

Number	Title (A Side/B Side)	Yr	VG	VG+	NM
EPIC					
BN 26380	West	1968	5.00	10.00	20.00
BN 26433	Bridges	1969	5.00	10.00	20.00

WEST, DOTTIE

Also see KENNY ROGERS AND DOTTIE WEST.

45s

Number	Title (A Side/B Side)	Yr	VG	VG+	NM
ATLANTIC					
2155	You Said I'd Never Love Again/I'll Pick Up My Heart (And Go Home)	1962	3.75	7.50	15.00
LIBERTY					
1392	Are You Happy Baby/Right or Wrong	1980	—	—	3.00
1404	What Are We Doin' in Love/Choosin' Means Losin'	1981	—	—	3.00
—Duet with Kenny Rogers, who is not credited on the label					
1419	(I'm Gonna) Put You Back on the Rack/Sorry Seems to Be the Hardest Word	1981	—	—	3.00
1436	It's High Time/Don't Be Kind	1981	—	—	3.00
1451	You're Not Easy to Forget/Something's Missing	1982	—	—	3.00
1479	She Can't Get My Love Off the Bed/Hurt	1982	—	—	3.00

Number	Title (A Side/B Side)	Yr	VG	VG+	NM
1490	If It Takes All Night/Try to Win a Friend	1982	—	—	3.00
1500	Tulsa Ballroom/A Woman in Love with You	1983	—	—	3.00
1506	The Night Love Let You Down/He's All I Need	1983	—	—	3.00

PERMIAN

Number	Title (A Side/B Side)	Yr	VG	VG+	NM
82006	What's Good for the Goose (Is Good for the Gander)/Tell Me Again	1984	—	2.00	4.00
82007	Let Love Come Lookin' for You/Blue Fiddle Waltz	1984	—	2.00	4.00
82010	We Know Better Now/Let Love Come Lookin' for You	1985	—	2.00	4.00

RCA

Number	Title (A Side/B Side)	Yr	VG	VG+	NM
PB-12284	Once You Were Mine/Dream Baby (How Long Must I Dream)	1981	—	2.00	4.00

RCA VICTOR

Number	Title (A Side/B Side)	Yr	VG	VG+	NM
APBO-0072	Country Sunshine/Wish I Didn't Love You Any More	1973	2.00	4.00	8.00
APBO-0231	Last Time I Saw Him/Everybody Bring a Song	1974	—	2.50	5.00
APBO-0321	House of Love/Love As Long As We Can	1974	—	2.50	5.00
PB-10125	Lay Back Lover/Good Lovin' You	1974	—	2.50	5.00
PB-10269	Rollin' in Your Sweet Sunshine/Carolina Cousins	1975	—	2.50	5.00
PB-10553	Here Come the Flowers/He's Not for You	1976	—	2.50	5.00
PB-10699	If I'm a Fool for Loving You/Home Made Love	1976	—	2.50	5.00
47-8166	Touch Me/More Than I Meant To	1963	3.00	6.00	12.00
47-8225	Let Me Off at the Corner/I Wish You Wouldn't Do That	1963	2.50	5.00	10.00
47-8324	Love Is No Excuse/Look Who's Talking	1964	2.50	5.00	10.00
—With Jim Reeves					
47-8374	Here Comes My Baby/(How Can I Face) These Heartaches Alone	1964	2.50	5.00	10.00
47-8467	Didn't I/In Its Own Little Way	1964	2.50	5.00	10.00
47-8525	Gettin' Married Has Made Us Strangers/It Just Takes Practice	1965	2.50	5.00	10.00
47-8615	No Sign of Living/Night Life	1965	2.50	5.00	10.00
47-8702	Before the Ring on Your Finger Turns Green/Wear Away	1965	2.50	5.00	10.00
47-8770	Would You Hold It Against Me/You're Just the Only World I Know	1965	2.00	4.00	8.00
47-8900	Mommy, Can I Still Call Him Daddy/Suffertime	1966	2.00	4.00	8.00
47-9011	What's Come Over My Baby/How Many Lifetimes Will It Take	1966	2.00	4.00	8.00
47-9118	Paper Mansions/Someone's Gotta Cry	1967	2.00	4.00	8.00
47-9267	Like a Fool/Everything's a Wreck	1967	2.00	4.00	8.00
47-9377	Childhood Places/No One	1967	2.00	4.00	8.00
47-9497	Country Girl/That's Where Our Love Must Be	1968	2.00	4.00	8.00
47-9604	Reno/My Heart Has Changed Its Mind	1968	2.00	4.00	8.00
47-9792	I Heard Our Song/Makin' Memories	1969	—	3.00	6.00
47-9834	Jack Daniels, Old Grand-Dad, Johnnie Walker and You/Long Black Limousine	1970	—	3.00	6.00
47-9872	It's Dawned on Me You're Gone/Love's Farewell	1970	—	3.00	6.00
47-9911	Forever Yours/Cold Hand of Fate	1970	—	3.00	6.00
47-9947	Slowly/Sweet Thang	1971	—	3.00	6.00
—With Jimmy Dean					
47-9957	Careless Hands/Only One Thing Left to Do	1971	—	3.00	6.00
47-9982	Lonely Is/Cancel Tomorrow	1971	—	3.00	6.00
48-1012	Six Weeks Every Summer (Christmas Every Day)/Wish I Didn't Love You Anymore	1971	—	2.50	5.00
74-0239	Clinging to My Baby's Hand/Don't Say a Word	1969	—	3.00	6.00
74-0711	I'm Only a Woman/Baby, I Tried	1972	—	2.50	5.00
74-0828	If It's All Right with You/Special Memory	1972	—	2.50	5.00
74-0930	Just What I've Been Looking For/Everything's a Wreck	1973	—	2.50	5.00

STARDAY

Number	Title (A Side/B Side)	Yr	VG	VG+	NM
517	Angel on Paper/No Time Will I Ever	1960	5.00	10.00	20.00
547	I Lost, You Win, I'm Leavin'/I Should Start Runnin'	1961	5.00	10.00	20.00
574	My Big John/Men with Evil Hearts	1961	5.00	10.00	20.00
724	I'd Be Lying/Walking in the Dark	1965	2.50	5.00	10.00

UNITED ARTISTS

Number	Title (A Side/B Side)	Yr	VG	VG+	NM
XW898	When It's Just You and Me/We Love Each Other	1976	—	2.00	4.00
XW946	Every Word I Write/We Love Each Other	1977	—	2.00	4.00
XW1010	Tonight You Belong to Me/Tiny Fingers	1977	—	2.00	4.00
XW1084	That's All I Wanted to Know/Who's Gonna Love Me Now	1977	—	2.00	4.00
XW1209	Come See Me and Come Lonely/Decorate Your Conscience	1978	—	2.00	4.00
XW1257	Reaching Out to Hold You/My Two Empty Arms	1978	—	2.00	4.00
1324	You Pick Me Up (And Put Me Down)/We Got Tonight	1979	—	2.00	4.00
1339	A Lesson in Leavin'/Love's So Easy for Two	1980	—	2.00	4.00
1352	Leavin's for Unbelievers/Blue As I Want To	1980	—	2.00	4.00

Albums

LIBERTY

Number	Title (A Side/B Side)	Yr	VG	VG+	NM
LT-740	When It's Just You and Me	1981	2.00	4.00	8.00
—Reissue of United Artists 740					
LT-860	Dottie	1981	2.00	4.00	8.00
—Reissue of United Artists 860					
LT-1000	Special Delivery	1981	2.00	4.00	8.00
—Reissue of United Artists 1000					
LT-1062	Wild West	1981	2.50	5.00	10.00
LT-51114	High Times	1982	2.50	5.00	10.00
LT-51129	Full Circle	1982	2.50	5.00	10.00
LT-51145	New Horizons	1983	2.50	5.00	10.00
LT-51155	Greatest Hits	1984	2.50	5.00	10.00

POWER PAK

Number	Title (A Side/B Side)	Yr	VG	VG+	NM
274	Country Girl Singing Sensation	197?	2.50	5.00	10.00

RCA CAMDEN

Number	Title (A Side/B Side)	Yr	VG	VG+	NM
ACL1-0125	Would You Hold It Against Me	1973	2.50	5.00	10.00
ACL1-0482	Loving You	1974	2.50	5.00	10.00
CAL-2155 [M]	The Sound of Country Music	1967	3.75	7.50	15.00
CAS-2155 [S]	The Sound of Country Music	1967	3.00	6.00	12.00
CAS-2454	A Legend in My Time	1971	3.00	6.00	12.00

RCA VICTOR

Number	Title (A Side/B Side)	Yr	VG	VG+	NM
APD1-0151 [Q]	If It's All Right with You	1973	5.00	10.00	20.00
APL1-0151	If It's All Right with You	1973	3.00	6.00	12.00
APL1-0344	Country Sunshine	1973	3.00	6.00	12.00
APL1-0543	House of Love	1974	3.00	6.00	12.00
APL1-1041	Carolina Cousins	1975	3.00	6.00	12.00
ANL1-2327	Country Sunshine	1977	2.50	5.00	10.00
—Reissue of APL1-0344					
LPM-3368 [M]	Here Comes My Baby	1965	6.25	12.50	25.00
LSP-3368 [S]	Here Comes My Baby	1965	7.50	15.00	30.00
LPM-3490 [M]	Dottie West Sings	1966	6.25	12.50	25.00
LSP-3490 [S]	Dottie West Sings	1966	7.50	15.00	30.00
LPM-3587 [M]	Suffer Time	1966	6.25	12.50	25.00
LSP-3587 [S]	Suffer Time	1966	7.50	15.00	30.00
LPM-3693 [M]	With All My Heart and Soul	1967	7.50	15.00	30.00
LSP-3693 [S]	With All My Heart and Soul	1967	6.25	12.50	25.00
LPM-3784 [M]	Dottie West Sings Sacred Ballads	1967	7.50	15.00	30.00
LSP-3784 [S]	Dottie West Sings Sacred Ballads	1967	6.25	12.50	25.00
LPM-3830 [M]	I'll Help You Forget Her	1967	7.50	15.00	30.00
LSP-3830 [S]	I'll Help You Forget Her	1967	6.25	12.50	25.00
LPM-3932 [M]	What I'm Cut Out to Be	1968	12.50	25.00	50.00
LSP-3932 [S]	What I'm Cut Out to Be	1968	6.25	12.50	25.00
LSP-4004	Country Girl	1968	6.25	12.50	25.00
LSP-4095	Feminine Fancy	1969	5.00	10.00	20.00
AHL1-4117	Once You Were Mine	1981	2.50	5.00	10.00
LSP-4154	Dottie Sings Eddy	1969	5.00	10.00	20.00
LSP-4276	Makin' Memories	1970	5.00	10.00	20.00
AYL1-4302	Once You Were Mine	1982	2.00	4.00	8.00
LSP-4332	Country and West	1970	5.00	10.00	20.00
LSP-4433	Forever Yours	1970	5.00	10.00	20.00
LSP-4482	Careless Hands	1971	3.75	7.50	15.00
LSP-4606	Have You Heard	1971	3.75	7.50	15.00
LSP-4704	I'm Only a Woman	1972	3.75	7.50	15.00
LSP-4811	The Best of Dottie West	1973	3.75	7.50	15.00
CPL1-7047	Collector's Series	1985	2.50	5.00	10.00

STARDAY

Number	Title (A Side/B Side)	Yr	VG	VG+	NM
SLP-302 [M]	Country Girl Singing Sensation	1964	10.00	20.00	40.00

UNITED ARTISTS

Number	Title (A Side/B Side)	Yr	VG	VG+	NM
UA-LA740-G	When It's Just You and Me	1977	2.50	5.00	10.00
UA-LA860-G	Dottie	1978	2.50	5.00	10.00
LT-1000	Special Delivery	1980	2.50	5.00	10.00

WEST, DOTTIE, AND DON GIBSON

Also see each artist's individual listings.

45s

RCA VICTOR

Number	Title (A Side/B Side)	Yr	VG	VG+	NM
47-9715	Rings of Gold/Final Examination	1969	—	3.00	6.00
47-9867	Till I Can't Take It Anymore/I Love You Because	1970	—	3.00	6.00
74-0178	Sweet Memories/How's the World Treating You	1969	—	3.00	6.00
74-0291	There's a Story (Goin' 'Round)/Lock, Stock and Teardrops	1969	—	3.00	6.00

Albums

RCA VICTOR

Number	Title (A Side/B Side)	Yr	VG	VG+	NM
LSP-4131	Dottie and Don	1969	5.00	10.00	20.00

WEST, LESLIE

Also see MOUNTAIN; WEST, BRUCE & LAING.

45s

PHANTOM

Number	Title (A Side/B Side)	Yr	VG	VG+	NM
?B-10301	E.S.P./Don't Burn Me	1975	—	2.00	4.00

WINDFALL

Number	Title (A Side/B Side)	Yr	VG	VG+	NM
530	This Wheel's On Fire/Dreams of Milk and Honey	1969	—	2.50	5.00
531	Blood of the Sun/Long Red	1969	—	2.50	5.00

7-Inch Extended Plays

PHANTOM

Number	Title (A Side/B Side)	Yr	VG	VG+	NM
JF-10424 [DJ]	Honey/Dear Prudence//Get It Up/The Setting Sun	1975	2.50	5.00	10.00

Albums

PHANTOM

Number	Title (A Side/B Side)	Yr	VG	VG+	NM
BPL1-0954	The Great Fatsby	1975	3.00	6.00	12.00
BPL1-1258	The Leslie West Band	1976	3.00	6.00	12.00

WINDFALL

Number	Title (A Side/B Side)	Yr	VG	VG+	NM
4500	Mountain	1969	3.75	7.50	15.00

WEST, MAE

45s

20TH CENTURY FOX

Number	Title (A Side/B Side)	Yr	VG	VG+	NM
6718	Hard to Handle/You Gotta Taste All the Fruit	1968	2.50	5.00	10.00
6718 [PS]	Hard to Handle/You Gotta Taste All the Fruit	1968	6.25	12.50	25.00

DAGONET

Number	Title (A Side/B Side)	Yr	VG	VG+	NM
6	Put the Loot in the Boot, Santa/With Love from Me to You	1966	3.75	7.50	15.00

DECCA

Number	Title (A Side/B Side)	Yr	VG	VG+	NM
29452	Love Is the Greatest Thing/All of Me	1955	3.75	7.50	15.00
32738	The Sayings of Mae West/More Sayings of Mae West	1970	2.50	5.00	10.00

MGM

Number	Title (A Side/B Side)	Yr	VG	VG+	NM
14491	Great Balls of Fire/Naked Ape	1973	2.00	4.00	8.00

TOWER

Number	Title (A Side/B Side)	Yr	VG	VG+	NM
260	Day Tripper/Treat Him Right	1966	2.50	5.00	10.00
260 [PS]	Day Tripper/Treat Him Right	1966	5.00	10.00	20.00
261	Shakin' All Over/If You Gotta Go	1966	2.50	5.00	10.00
261 [PS]	Shakin' All Over/If You Gotta Go	1966	5.00	10.00	20.00

Albums

DAGONET

Number	Title (A Side/B Side)	Yr	VG	VG+	NM
DG-4 [M]	Wild Christmas	1966	7.50	15.00	30.00
DGS-4 [S]	Wild Christmas	1966	10.00	20.00	40.00

DECCA

Number	Title (A Side/B Side)	Yr	VG	VG+	NM
DL 9016 [M]	The Fabulous Mae West	1955	15.00	30.00	60.00
—All-black label with silver print					
DL 9016 [M]	The Fabulous Mae West	1960	7.50	15.00	30.00
—Black label with colorband					
DL 79016 [R]	The Fabulous Mae West	1960	3.75	7.50	15.00
DL 79176	The Original Voice Tracks	196?	3.75	7.50	15.00

MCA

Number	Title (A Side/B Side)	Yr	VG	VG+	NM
2053	The Fabulous Mae West	1974	3.00	6.00	12.00
—Reissue of Decca LP					

Number	Title (A Side/B Side)	Yr	VG	VG+	NM
MEZZOTONE					
1 [10]	Mae West Songs, Vol. 1	1952	25.00	50.00	100.00
2 [10]	Mae West Songs, Vol. 2	1952	25.00	50.00	100.00
MGM					
SE-4869	Great Balls of Fire	1972	5.00	10.00	20.00
ROUND					
RS-100	Under the Mistletoe with Mae West	1977	5.00	10.00	20.00
TOWER					
ST 5028 [S]	Way Out West	1966	10.00	20.00	40.00
T 5028 [M]	Way Out West	1966	7.50	15.00	30.00

WEST, RED

45s

Number	Title (A Side/B Side)	Yr	VG	VG+	NM
DOT					
16268	Midnight Ride/Unforgiven	1961	5.00	10.00	20.00
JARO					
77031	FBI Story/What Must I Do	1960	12.50	25.00	50.00
SANTO					
9006	Bossa Nova Mamza/My Babe	1963	3.75	7.50	15.00

WEST, SONNY

45s

Number	Title (A Side/B Side)	Yr	VG	VG+	NM
ATLANTIC					
1174	Rave On!/Call On Cupid	1958	10.00	20.00	40.00
NOR VA JAK					
1956	Rock-Ola Ruby/Sweet Rockin' Baby	1959	25.00	50.00	100.00
—As "Sonee West"					

WEST, BRUCE & LAING

Also see JACK BRUCE; LESLIE WEST.

45s

Number	Title (A Side/B Side)	Yr	VG	VG+	NM
COLUMBIA					
45751	Shake Ma Thing (Rollin' Jack)/The Doctor	1973	—	2.50	5.00
45829	Why Don'tcha/Mississippi Queen	1973	—	2.50	5.00

Albums

Number	Title (A Side/B Side)	Yr	VG	VG+	NM
WINDFALL					
CQ 31929 [Q]	Why Dontcha	1972	5.00	10.00	20.00
KC 31929	Why Dontcha	1972	3.00	6.00	12.00
CQ 32216 [Q]	Whatever Turns You On	1973	5.00	10.00	20.00
KC 32216	Whatever Turns You On	1973	3.00	6.00	12.00
KC 32899	Live 'N' Kickin'	1974	3.00	6.00	12.00

WEST COAST POP ART EXPERIMENTAL BAND, THE

45s

Number	Title (A Side/B Side)	Yr	VG	VG+	NM
AMOS					
119	Free As a Bird/Where's My Daddy	1969	3.75	7.50	15.00
REPRISE					
0552	Shifting Sands/1906	1967	6.25	12.50	25.00
0582	Help, I'm a Rock/Transparent Day	1967	6.25	12.50	25.00
0776	Smell of Incense/Unfree Child	1968	6.25	12.50	25.00

Albums

Number	Title (A Side/B Side)	Yr	VG	VG+	NM
AMOS					
AAS-7004	Where's My Daddy	1969	12.50	25.00	50.00
FIFO					
M 101	West Coast Pop Art Experimental Band	1966	1000.	1500.	2000.
—With regular cover					
M 101	West Coast Pop Art Experimental Band	1966	125.00	250.00	500.00
—With plain cardboard cover					
RAZZBERRY SAWFLY					
800	West Coast Pop Art Experimental Band	1980	25.00	50.00	100.00
—Reissue of Fifo LP					
REPRISE					
R 6247 [M]	The West Coast Pop Art Experimental Band, Part One	1967	20.00	40.00	80.00
RS 6247 [S]	The West Coast Pop Art Experimental Band, Part One	1967	25.00	50.00	100.00
R 6270 [M]	The West Coast Pop Art Experimental Band, Part Two	1967	20.00	40.00	80.00
RS 6298	A Child's Guide to Good and Evil	1968	25.00	50.00	100.00
RS 6370 [S]	The West Coast Pop Art Experimental Band, Part Two	1967	25.00	50.00	100.00

WESTON, KIM

Also see MARVIN GAYE AND KIM WESTON.

45s

Number	Title (A Side/B Side)	Yr	VG	VG+	NM
ENTERPRISE					
9101	Beautiful People/Goodness Gracious	1974	—	2.50	5.00
GORDY					
7041	I'll Never See My Love Again/A Thrill a Moment	1965	5.00	10.00	20.00
7046	Take Me in Your Arms (Rock Me A Little While)/ Don't Compare Me to Her	1965	5.00	10.00	20.00
7050	Helpless/A Love Like Yours (Don't Come Knocking Every Day)	1966	5.00	10.00	20.00
MGM					
13720	I Got What You Need/Someone Like You	1967	5.00	10.00	20.00
13804	That's Groovy/Land of Tomorrow	1967	5.00	10.00	20.00
13881	Nobody/You're Just the Kind of Guy	1967	5.00	10.00	20.00
13927	Lift Every Voice and Sing/This Is America	1968	5.00	10.00	20.00
13928	The Impossible Dream/When Johnny Comes Marching Home	1968	3.75	7.50	15.00
13992	I Will Understand/Thankful	1968	3.75	7.50	15.00
PEOPLE					
1001	Danger, Heartbreak Ahead/I'll Be Thinkin'	1970	2.50	5.00	10.00
PRIDE					
1	Lift Every Voice and Sing/This Is America	1970	2.50	5.00	10.00
TAMLA					
54076	It Should Have Been Me/Love Me All the Way	1963	12.50	25.00	50.00
54085	Just Loving You/Another Train Coming	1963	12.50	25.00	50.00
54100	Looking for the Right Guy/Feel Alright Tonight	1964	12.50	25.00	50.00
54106	A Little More Love/Go Ahead and Laugh	1964	25.00	50.00	100.00
54110	I'm Still Loving You/Go Ahead and Laugh	1964	15.00	30.00	60.00
VOLT					
1502	If I Had My Way/Gonna Be Alright	1971	3.75	7.50	15.00
1503	Little By Little, Bit By Bit/(B-side unknown)	1971	3.75	7.50	15.00

Albums

Number	Title (A Side/B Side)	Yr	VG	VG+	NM
MGM					
E-4477 [M]	For the First Time	1967	7.50	15.00	30.00
SE-4477 [S]	For the First Time	1967	10.00	20.00	40.00
SE-4561	This Is America	1968	10.00	20.00	40.00
VOLT					
VOS-6014	Kim, Kim, Kim	1971	6.25	12.50	25.00

WESTON, PAUL

Also see JONATHAN AND DARLENE EDWARDS.

45s

Number	Title (A Side/B Side)	Yr	VG	VG+	NM
CAPITOL					
F826	Fairy Tales/Am I Wasting My Time	1950	3.75	7.50	15.00
—Note: Earlier Paul Weston 45s on Capitol may exist					
F833	Big Movie Show in the Sky/Little Gray House	1950	3.75	7.50	15.00
F890	La Vie En Rose/Les Fevilles Mortes	1950	3.75	7.50	15.00
F918	Orchids in the Moonlight/I'll Be Seeing You	1950	3.75	7.50	15.00
F949	Panama/Original Dixieland One-Step	1950	3.75	7.50	15.00
F1022	I'll Get By/Blue Prelude	1950	3.75	7.50	15.00
F1251	Autumn Leaves/No Other Love	1950	3.75	7.50	15.00
F1640	Deep Purple/Etude	1951	3.75	7.50	15.00
—Reissue of 78 rpm from 1948					
F1670	Laura/Intermezzo	1951	3.75	7.50	15.00
—Reissue					
4350	The Thrill Is Gone/I Love You	1960	2.00	4.00	8.00
COLUMBIA					
39000	So Long Sally/These Foolish Things	1950	3.75	7.50	15.00
39114	When You Return/In Your Arms	1950	3.75	7.50	15.00
39160	So Long/Across the Wide Missouri	1951	3.00	6.00	12.00
39210	Lonesome Gal/Never Let the Sun Set on a Quarrel	1951	3.00	6.00	12.00
39424	Morningside/What Will I Tell	1951	3.00	6.00	12.00
39465	Bonne Nuit/Maybe It's Because	1951	3.00	6.00	12.00
39508	Stardust/When Your Lover Has Gone	1951	2.50	5.00	10.00
39509	Moon Song/Among My Souvenirs	1951	2.50	5.00	10.00
39510	Then I'll Be Tired of You/My Silent Love	1951	2.50	5.00	10.00
39511	Yesterdays/Under a Blanket of Blue	1951	2.50	5.00	10.00
—The above four comprise a box set					
39569	Story of Love/And So to Sleep	1951	3.00	6.00	12.00
39608	What'll I Do/One Night of Love	1951	2.50	5.00	10.00
39609	Wonderful One/Sweethearts	1951	2.50	5.00	10.00
39610	I'll Follow My Secret Heart/All Alone	1951	2.50	5.00	10.00
39611	Together/I'll See You Again	1951	2.50	5.00	10.00
—The above four comprise a box set					
39616	Charmaine/At Dawning	1951	3.00	6.00	12.00
39644	You Were Meant for Me/S'Posin'	1952	2.50	5.00	10.00
39645	This Can't Be Love/Why Shouldn't I?	1952	2.50	5.00	10.00
39646	Embraceable You/Pennies from Heaven	1952	2.50	5.00	10.00
39647	How High the Moon/Over the Rainbow	1952	2.50	5.00	10.00
—The above four comprise a box set					
39662	Charmaine/Jealousy (Jalousie)	1952	3.00	6.00	12.00
—B-side by Frankie Laine; part of a box set					
39666	Low in Lehigh Valley/Flapperette	1952	3.00	6.00	12.00
39736	So Help Me/Beautiful Ohio	1952	3.00	6.00	12.00
39864	Forgetting You/Wonderful Copenhagen	1952	3.00	6.00	12.00
39968	Anna/Dutch Treat	1953	3.00	6.00	12.00
40014	Shane/Gigi	1953	3.00	6.00	12.00
40086	You're the Right One/Planters Punch	1953	3.00	6.00	12.00
40152	Autumn in Rome/Indiscretion	1954	2.50	5.00	10.00
40237	The Bells of Notre Dame/I Went Out of My Way	1954	2.50	5.00	10.00
40292	Bimbo/Champagne Wine	1954	2.50	5.00	10.00
40359	The Song from Desiree/Maria, Maria, Maria	1954	3.00	6.00	12.00
40385	Tara's Theme/Love Letters	1954	3.00	6.00	12.00
40484	A Streetcar Named Desire/For Whom the Bell Tolls	1955	3.00	6.00	12.00
40527	The Kentuckian Song/You and You Alone	1955	3.00	6.00	12.00
40561	Nice Work If You Can Get It/A Chance at Love	1955	2.50	5.00	10.00
40605	Memories of You/Naked Sea	1956	2.50	5.00	10.00
40675	Theme from My Foolish Heart/Infatuation	1956	2.50	5.00	10.00
40737	The Kentuckian Song/Love Theme from "La Strada"	1956	2.50	5.00	10.00
40861	Ten Minutes Ago/Where Is Cinderella	1957	2.50	5.00	10.00
40876	Mardi Gras/Storyville	1957	2.50	5.00	10.00
40901	High Society/Riverfront Blues	1957	2.50	5.00	10.00

Albums

Number	Title (A Side/B Side)	Yr	VG	VG+	NM
CAPITOL					
H 222 [10]	Music for Dreaming	195?	10.00	20.00	40.00
ST 1154 [S]	Music for Dreaming	1959	3.75	7.50	15.00
T 1154 [M]	Music for Dreaming	1959	3.00	6.00	12.00
ST 1192 [S]	Music for the Fireside	1959	3.75	7.50	15.00
T 1192 [M]	Music for the Fireside	1959	3.00	6.00	12.00
ST 1222 [S]	Music for Memories	1959	3.75	7.50	15.00
T 1222 [M]	Music for Memories	1959	3.00	6.00	12.00
ST 1563 [S]	Music for My Love	1961	3.75	7.50	15.00
T 1563 [M]	Music for My Love	1961	3.00	6.00	12.00
ST-91212	Romantic Reflections	196?	3.75	7.50	15.00
—Capitol Record Club exclusive					
COLUMBIA					
CL 572 [M]	Caribbean Cruise	1955	3.75	7.50	15.00
CL 693 [M]	Mood for 12	1955	3.75	7.50	15.00
CL 794 [M]	Love Music	1956	3.75	7.50	15.00
CL 879 [M]	Solo Mood	1956	3.75	7.50	15.00
CL 909 [M]	Moonlight Becomes You	1956	3.75	7.50	15.00
CL 977 [M]	Crescent City	1956	3.75	7.50	15.00
CL 1112 [M]	Hollywood	1958	3.75	7.50	15.00
CL 6232 [10]	Whispers in the Dark	195?	10.00	20.00	40.00
CORINTHIAN					
107	Cinema Cameos	198?	2.00	4.00	8.00
109	Easy Jazz	198?	2.00	4.00	8.00
116	Crescent City	198?	2.00	4.00	8.00

Number	Title (A Side/B Side)	Yr	VG	VG+	NM
HARMONY					
KH 31578	Paul Weston Plays Jerome Kern	1972	2.50	5.00	10.00
KH 31603	Paul Weston Plays Jerome Kern, Vol. 2	1972	2.50	5.00	10.00

WET WILLIE

45s

Number	Title (A Side/B Side)	Yr	VG	VG+	NM
CAPRICORN					
0008	Shout Bamalama/Airport	1972	—	3.00	6.00
0022	Shout Bamalama/Airport	1973	—	3.00	6.00
0031	Country Side of Life/In Our Hearts	1973	—	3.00	6.00
0043	Keep On Smilin'/Soul Jones	1974	—	3.00	6.00
0052	Keep On Smilin'/Country Side of Life	1975	—	2.00	4.00
—"Back to Back Hits" reissue					
0206	Keep On Smilin'/Soul Jones	1974	—	2.00	4.00
0212	Country Side of Life/Don't Wait Too Long	1974	—	2.00	4.00
0224	Leona/Ain't He a Mess	1975	—	2.00	4.00
0231	Dixie Rock/She's My Lady	1975	—	2.00	4.00
0254	Everything That 'Cha Do (Will Come Back to You)/ Walkin' By Myself	1976	—	2.00	4.00
0260	Comic Book Hero/Baby Fat	1976	—	2.00	4.00
8020	Rock and Roll Band/Dirty Leg	1971	2.00	4.00	8.00
EPIC					
50478	Street Corner Serenade/We Got Lovin'	1977	—	2.00	4.00
50528	Let It Shine/Make You Feel Love Again	1978	—	2.00	4.00
50714	Weekend/Mr. Streamline	1979	—	2.00	4.00
50760	The Hard Way/Ramona	1979	—	2.00	4.00

Albums

Number	Title (A Side/B Side)	Yr	VG	VG+	NM
CAPRICORN					
CP 0109	Wet Willie II	1972	3.00	6.00	12.00
CP 0113	Drippin' Wet/Live	1973	3.00	6.00	12.00
CP 0128	Keep on Smilin'	1974	2.50	5.00	10.00
CP 0138	Wet Willie	1974	2.50	5.00	10.00
—Reissue of 861					
CP 0149	Dixie Rock	1975	2.50	5.00	10.00
CP 0166	The Wetter the Better	1976	2.50	5.00	10.00
CP 0182	Left Coast Live	1977	2.50	5.00	10.00
CP 0200	Greatest Hits	1978	2.50	5.00	10.00
SD 861	Wet Willie	1971	3.75	7.50	15.00
EPIC					
JE 34983	Manorisms	1977	2.50	5.00	10.00
JE 35794	Which One's Willie?	1979	2.50	5.00	10.00

WHALEFEATHERS, THE

Albums

Number	Title (A Side/B Side)	Yr	VG	VG+	NM
NASCO					
9003	The Whalefeathers Declare	1969	25.00	50.00	100.00
9005	The Whalefeathers	1970	25.00	50.00	100.00

WHAT FOUR, THE

45s

Number	Title (A Side/B Side)	Yr	VG	VG+	NM
CAPITOL					
5449	Anything for a Laugh/Baby Can't You Hear Me Call Your Name	1965	3.00	6.00	12.00
COLUMBIA					
43711	Baby, I Dig Love/It's Hard to Live on Promises	1966	3.00	6.00	12.00
DESTINATION					
633	We Could Be Happy/Where Love Can Go	1967	3.00	6.00	12.00
—As "What For"					
ESP-DISK'					
109	Our Love Should Last Forever/(B-side unknown)	1966	7.50	15.00	30.00
MERCURY					
72716	Dandelion Wine/You're Wishin' I Was Someone Else	1967	6.25	12.50	25.00
—As "Whatt Four"					
REPRISE					
0387	Gemini 4/Night Surf	1965	6.25	12.50	25.00
TOWER					
404	Asparagus/Stop in the Name of Love	1968	3.00	6.00	12.00

WHAT-KNOTS, THE

45s

Number	Title (A Side/B Side)	Yr	VG	VG+	NM
DIAL					
4067	I Ain't Dead Yet/Talkin' 'Bout Our Breakup	1967	6.25	12.50	25.00

WHEEL MEN, THE

GARY USHER was in this group.

45s

Number	Title (A Side/B Side)	Yr	VG	VG+	NM
WARNER BROS.					
5480	Hon-Da Beach/School Is a Gas	1964	12.50	25.00	50.00

WHEELER, BILLY EDD

45s

Number	Title (A Side/B Side)	Yr	VG	VG+	NM
CAPITOL					
4149	Humperdink (The Coon Huntin' Monkey)/Baby Martin	1975	—	2.00	4.00
4231	The Hole (In Uncle Vincent's Wooden Leg)/Dust Marks	1976	—	2.00	4.00
KAPP					
595	On the Outside (Lookin' In)/The Right Foot in His World	1964	2.50	5.00	10.00
606	The Bachelor/Anne	1964	2.50	5.00	10.00
617	Ode to the Little Shack Out Back/Goin' Down to Town	1964	2.50	5.00	10.00
655	Burning Bridges/Tonight I'm Singing Just for You	1965	2.00	4.00	8.00
670	Jackson/The Politician's Dog	1965	2.00	4.00	8.00
687	Hillbilly Bossa Nova/The Waltz of Miss Sarah Green	1965	2.00	4.00	8.00
739	The Coming of the Roads/The Doves of San Morey	1966	2.00	4.00	8.00
845	Half a Man/She	1967	2.00	4.00	8.00
873	High Flying Bird/They Can't Put It Back	1967	2.00	4.00	8.00
928	I Ain't the Worryin' Kind/It's More Than Home	1968	—	3.00	6.00
NSD					
47	Mama's Going Down in the Mine/Time to Make Love	1980	—	2.00	4.00
84	Bald Headed Men/The Spinster and the Cowboy	1981	—	2.00	4.00
94	Daddy/Long Arm of the Law	1981	—	2.00	4.00
—With Rashell Richmond					
108	In Your Spanish Eyes/The Memory	1981	—	2.00	4.00
124	Pepsi/Chain Gang of Love	1982	—	2.00	4.00
RADIO CINEMA					
001	Duel Under the Snow/(B-side unknown)	1979	—	2.00	4.00
RCA VICTOR					
47-9898	The Day After Tomorrow/Soon As Buddy Gets Home	1970	—	2.50	5.00
47-9943	Woman's Talkin' Liberation Blues/Little Lucy	1971	—	2.50	5.00
48-1001	Ode to a Critter/Sally	1971	—	2.50	5.00
74-0610	Plutebobelle/Gifts	1971	—	2.50	5.00
74-0656	Betty Bow Legs/Does Mel Tillis Really Stutter	1972	—	2.50	5.00
74-0739	200 Lbs. o' Slingin' Hound/The Hoedown	1972	—	2.50	5.00
74-0832	The Girl Who Loved the Man Who Robbed the Bank at Santa Fe/Gabriel's Horn	1972	—	2.50	5.00
74-0881	Gentle Big Man/Peter Gonzales	1973	—	2.50	5.00
UNITED ARTISTS					
50507	West Virginia Woman/One Stop	1969	—	3.00	6.00
50579	Fried Chicken and a Country Tune/One Excuse	1969	—	3.00	6.00
50583	Bow of Love/Young Billy Young	1969	—	3.00	6.00
50597	Coon Hunters/Fried Chicken and a Country Tune	1969	—	3.00	6.00

Albums

Number	Title (A Side/B Side)	Yr	VG	VG+	NM
FLYING FISH					
FF-085	Wild Mountain Flowers	1979	3.00	6.00	12.00
FOLKWAYS					
31014	When Kentucky Had No Union Men	196?	5.00	10.00	20.00
KAPP					
KL-1351 [M]	A New Bag of Songs Written and Sung by Billy Edd Wheeler	1964	3.75	7.50	15.00
KL-1425 [M]	Memories of America/Ode to the Little Brown Shack Out Back	1965	3.75	7.50	15.00
KL-1443 [M]	Wheeler Man	1965	3.75	7.50	15.00
KL-1479 [M]	Goin' Town and Country	1966	3.75	7.50	15.00
KL-1533 [M]	Paper Birds	1967	5.00	10.00	20.00
KS-3351 [S]	A New Bag of Songs Written and Sung by Billy Edd Wheeler	1964	5.00	10.00	20.00
KS-3425 [S]	Memories of America/Ode to the Little Brown Shack Out Back	1965	5.00	10.00	20.00
KS-3443 [S]	Wheeler Man	1965	5.00	10.00	20.00
KS-3479 [S]	Goin' Town and Country	1966	5.00	10.00	20.00
KS-3533 [S]	Paper Birds	1967	3.75	7.50	15.00
KS-3567	I Ain't the Worryin' Kind	1968	3.75	7.50	15.00
MONITOR					
MF-354 [M]	Billy Edd U.S.A.	1961	7.50	15.00	30.00
MF-367 [M]	Billy Edd and Bluegrass	1962	7.50	15.00	30.00
RCA VICTOR					
LSP-4491	Love	1971	3.75	7.50	15.00
UNITED ARTISTS					
UAS-6711	Nashville Zodiac	1969	3.75	7.50	15.00

WHEELER, MARY, AND THE KNIGHTS

45s

Number	Title (A Side/B Side)	Yr	VG	VG+	NM
ATOM					
701	A Falling Tear/I Feel in My Heart	196?	10.00	20.00	40.00

WHEELER, ONIE

45s

Number	Title (A Side/B Side)	Yr	VG	VG+	NM
COLUMBIA					
4-21371	Little Mama/She Wiggled and Giggled	1955	5.00	10.00	20.00
4-21418	My Home Is Not a Home at All/That's What I Like	1955	5.00	10.00	20.00
4-21454	Cut It Out/I'm Satisfied with My Dreams	1955	5.00	10.00	20.00
4-21500	No I Don't Guess I Will/I Tried and I Tried	1956	5.00	10.00	20.00
4-21523	Onie's Bop/I Wanna Hold My Baby	1956	15.00	30.00	60.00
40787	A Beggar for Your Love/A Booger Gonna Getcha	1956	12.50	25.00	50.00
40911	Steppin' Out/Going Back to the City	1957	3.75	7.50	15.00
EPIC					
9540	What About Tomorrow/Sunnyland Farmer	1962	2.50	5.00	10.00
OKEH					
18022	When We All Get There/Run 'Em Off	1952	7.50	15.00	30.00
18026	Mother Prayed Loud in Her Sleep/A Million Years in Glory	195?	6.25	12.50	25.00
18037	Closing Time/I'll Swear You Don't Love Me	195?	6.25	12.50	25.00
18049	Love Me Like You Used to Do/Little Mama	195?	7.50	15.00	30.00
18058	Would You Like to Wear a Crown/I Saw Mother with God Last Night	1954	6.25	12.50	25.00
ROYAL AMERICAN					
76	John's Been Shucking My Corn/Make 'Em All Go Home	1973	—	2.50	5.00
85	Shuckin' My Way to the Hall of Fame/I Can't Pass an Orchard	1973	—	2.50	5.00
SUN					
315	Jump Right Out of This Jukebox/Tell 'Em Off	1959	7.50	15.00	30.00

WHEELERS, THE

45s

Number	Title (A Side/B Side)	Yr	VG	VG+	NM
CENCO					
107	Once I Had a Girl/Shine 'Em On	196?	15.00	30.00	60.00

WHEELS, BURT, AND THE SPEEDSTERS

Albums

Number	Title (A Side/B Side)	Yr	VG	VG+	NM
CORONET					
CX-216 [M]	Sounds of the Big Racers	196?	6.25	12.50	25.00
CXS-216 [S]	Sounds of the Big Racers	196?	7.50	15.00	30.00

WHEELS, THE (1)
British group.

45s

AURORA

Number	Title (A Side/B Side)	Yr	VG	VG+	NM
157	Bad Little Woman/Don't You Know	1966	6.25	12.50	25.00

WHEELS, THE (2)
45s

FOLLY

Number	Title (A Side/B Side)	Yr	VG	VG+	NM
800	Clap Your Hands (Part 1)/Clap Your Hands (Part 2)	1959	3.75	7.50	15.00

WHEELS, THE (3)
45s

IMPACT

Number	Title (A Side/B Side)	Yr	VG	VG+	NM
1029	Dancing in the Streets/A Taste of Money	1967	6.25	12.50	25.00

WHEELS, THE (4)
45s

PREMIUM

Number	Title (A Side/B Side)	Yr	VG	VG+	NM
405	My Heart's Desire/Let's Have a Ball	1956	15.00	30.00	60.00
408	Teasin' Heart/Loco	1956	20.00	40.00	80.00
410	I Can't Forget/How Could I Ever Leave Me	1956	37.50	75.00	150.00

WHEELS, THE (5)
45s

ROULETTE

Number	Title (A Side/B Side)	Yr	VG	VG+	NM
4271	No One But You/I've Waited for a Lifetime	1960	5.00	10.00	20.00

WHEELS, THE (U)
45s

TIME

Number	Title (A Side/B Side)	Yr	VG	VG+	NM
1003	Where Were You/So Young and So In Love	1958	20.00	40.00	80.00

WHIPPOORWILLS, THE
45s

Number	Title (A Side/B Side)	Yr	VG	VG+	NM
JOSIE					
892	Deep Within/Going to a Party	1961	15.00	30.00	60.00
VITA					
1005	Blue Raindrops/I Must Have Holes in My Head	195?	25.00	50.00	100.00

WHIPS, THE
More than one group.

45s

Number	Title (A Side/B Side)	Yr	VG	VG+	NM
DORE					
502	Yes, Master/Rosie's Blues	1958	5.00	10.00	20.00
FLAIR					
1025	Pleadin' Heart/She Done Me Wrong	1954	200.00	400.00	800.00
MGM					
13401	Whip It on Me, Baby/First Dance Fear	1965	3.00	6.00	12.00

WHIRLERS, THE
45s

Number	Title (A Side/B Side)	Yr	VG	VG+	NM
PORT					
70025	Tonight and Forever/Magic Mirror	1961	5.00	10.00	20.00
WHIRLIN' DISC					
108	Tonight and Forever/Magic Mirror	1956	20.00	40.00	80.00

WHIRLWINDS, THE
45s

Number	Title (A Side/B Side)	Yr	VG	VG+	NM
GUYDEN					
2052	Angel Love/The Mountain	1961	7.50	15.00	30.00
PHILIPS					
40139	Heartbeat/At the Party	1963	31.25	62.50	125.00

WHISPERS, THE
Well-known male R&B vocal group.

12-Inch Singles

Number	Title (A Side/B Side)	Yr	VG	VG+	NM
CAPITOL					
V-15598	Innocent (5 versions)	1990	—	3.00	6.00
V-15637	Is It Good to You (5 versions)	1990	—	3.00	6.00
SOLAR					
ED 5017 [DJ]	Contagious (LP Version) (Edit Version)/Keep Your Love Around	1984	2.00	4.00	8.00
ED 5036 [DJ]	Some Kinda Lover (same on both sides)	1984	2.00	4.00	8.00
11895	And the Beat Goes On (7:30)/Can You Do the Boogie (6:07)	1979	3.75	7.50	15.00
12052	Out the Box/Welcome Into My Dream	1980	3.00	6.00	12.00
12233	I Can Make It Better/Say You (Would Love Me Too)	1980	3.00	6.00	12.00
V-71163	No Pain No Gain (7 versions)	1988	2.00	4.00	8.00

45s

Number	Title (A Side/B Side)	Yr	VG	VG+	NM
CANADIAN AMERICAN					
179	It's Rainin', It's Pourin'/Tomorrow's On Your Side	1964	7.50	15.00	30.00
CAPITOL					
S7-18394	Make Sweet Love to Me/My Funny Valentine	1995	—	—	3.00
S7-18727	Come On Home/Better Watch Your Heart	1995	—	—	3.00
7PRO-79170/215 [DJ]	Innocent (7" Edit)/Innocent (Club Edit)	1990	2.00	4.00	8.00
—Vinyl is promo only					
DORE					
724	It Only Hurts for a Little While/The Happy One	1964	6.25	12.50	25.00
729	Slow Jerk/Never Again	1965	5.00	10.00	20.00
735	The Dip/Weirdo	1965	5.00	10.00	20.00
740	As I Sit Here/Shake It, Shake It	1965	5.00	10.00	20.00
751	Doctor Love/Lonely Avenue	1966	5.00	10.00	20.00
758	Walkin' the Fat Man/I Was Born When You Kissed Me	1966	5.00	10.00	20.00
768	Take a Lesson from the Teacher/Claire De Looney	1966	5.00	10.00	20.00
792	You Got a Man on Your Hands/You Can't Fight What's Right	1967	3.75	7.50	15.00
794	Needle in a Haystack/Waltz for You	1967	3.75	7.50	15.00
833	Never Again/I Was Born When You Kissed Me	1969	3.00	6.00	12.00
842	The Dip/It Only Hurts for a Little While	1970	2.50	5.00	10.00
FONTANA					
1564	My Long and Sleepless Night/Knowin'	1966	5.00	10.00	20.00
JANUS					
140	There's a Love for Everyone/It Sure Ain't Pretty	1970	—	3.00	6.00
150	Your Love Is So Doggone Good/Cracker Jack	1971	—	3.00	6.00
174	Can't Help But Love You/A Hopeless Situation	1971	—	3.00	6.00
184	I Only Meant to Wet My Feet/You Fill My Life with Music	1972	—	3.00	6.00
200	Somebody Loves You/Can We Love Forever	1972	—	3.00	6.00
212	POW-MIA/Does She Care	1973	—	3.00	6.00
222	Feel Like Comin' Home/I Love the Way You Make Me Feel	1973	—	3.00	6.00
231	A Mother for My Children/What More Can a Girl Ask For	1973	—	3.00	6.00
238	Bingo/Once More with Feeling	1974	—	3.00	6.00
244	What More Can a Girl Ask For/Broken Home	1974	—	3.00	6.00
247	All I Ever Do (Is Dream of You)/Here Comes Tomorrow	1975	—	3.00	6.00
253	You're What's Been Missing in My Life/Given a Little Love	1975	—	3.00	6.00
SOLAR					
YB-11246	(Let's Go) All the Way/Chocolate Girl	1978	—	2.00	4.00
GB-11328	Living Together (In Sin)/One for the Money	1978	—	—	3.00
—Gold Standard Series					
YB-11353	(Olivia) Lost and Turned Out/Try and Make It Better	1978	—	2.00	4.00
YB-11449	Happy Holidays to You/Try and Make It Better	1978	—	3.00	6.00
YB-11590	Can't Do Without Love/Headlights	1979	—	2.00	4.00
YB-11685	Homemade Lovin'/You'll Never Get Away	1979	—	2.00	4.00
YB-11739	A Song for Donny/(Instrumental)	1979	—	2.00	4.00
YB-11739 [PS]	A Song for Donny/(Instrumental)	1979	—	3.00	6.00
YB-11894	And the Beat Goes On/Can You Do the Boogie	1980	—	2.00	4.00
YB-11928	Lady/I Love You	1980	—	2.00	4.00
GB-11977	(Let's Go) All the Way/Lost and Turned Out	1980	—	—	3.00
—Gold Standard Series					
YB-12050	Welcome Into My Dream/Out the Box	1980	—	2.00	4.00
YB-12154	It's a Love Thing/Girl I Need You	1981	—	2.00	4.00
GB-12230	And the Beat Goes On/Lady	1981	—	—	3.00
—Gold Standard Series					
YB-12232	I Can Make It Better/Say You (Would Love for Me Too)	1981	—	2.00	4.00
YB-12295	This Kind of Lovin'/What Will I Do	1981	—	2.00	4.00
YB-13005	I'm the One for You/I'm Gonna Love You More	1981	—	2.00	4.00
GB-13486	It's a Love Thing/Make That Move	1983	—	—	3.00
—Gold Standard Series; B-side by Shalamar					
47961	In the Raw/Small Talkin'	1982	—	2.00	4.00
48008	Emergency/Only You	1982	—	2.00	4.00
48008 [PS]	Emergency/Only You	1982	—	3.00	6.00
69639	Don't Keep Me Waiting/Suddenly	1985	—	2.00	4.00
69658	Some Kinda Lover/Never Too Late	1985	—	2.00	4.00
69683	Contagious/(B-side unknown)	1984	—	2.00	4.00
69809	This Time/Love for Real	1983	—	2.00	4.00
69827	Keep On Lovin' Me/Try It Again	1983	—	2.00	4.00
69842	Tonight/Small Talkin'	1983	—	2.00	4.00
69965	Love Is Where You Find It/Say Yes	1982	—	2.00	4.00
70006	Rock Steady/Are You Going My Way	1987	—	—	3.00
70012	Just Gets Better with Time/Say Yes	1987	—	—	3.00
70017	In the Mood/(Instrumental)	1987	—	—	3.00
70020	No Pain, No Gain/(Instrumental)	1988	—	—	3.00
SOUL CLOCK					
104	Great Day/I Can't See Myself Leaving	1969	2.50	5.00	10.00
107	The Time Will Come/Flying High	1969	2.50	5.00	10.00
109	What Will I Do/Remember	1969	2.50	5.00	10.00
1001	I Can Remember/Planets of Life	1970	2.00	4.00	8.00
1004	Seems Like I Gotta Do Wrong/Needle in a Haystack	1970	2.00	4.00	8.00
1005	I'm the One/You Must Be Doing All Right	1970	2.00	4.00	8.00
SOUL TRAIN					
SB-10430	In Love Forever/Fairytale	1975	—	2.50	5.00
SB-10628	(You're a) Special Part of My Life/Grove Street	1976	—	2.50	5.00
SB-10700	One for the Money (Part 1)/One for the Money (Part 2)	1976	—	2.50	5.00
SB-10773	Living Together (In Sin)/I've Got a Feeling	1976	—	2.50	5.00
SB-10878	You're Only As Good As You Think You Are/Sounds Like a Love Song	1977	—	2.50	5.00
SB-10996	Make It With You/You Are Number One	1977	—	2.50	5.00
SB-11139	I'm Gonna Make You My Wife/You Never Miss Your Water	1977	—	2.50	5.00

Albums

Number	Title (A Side/B Side)	Yr	VG	VG+	NM
ACCORD					
SN-7100	I Can Remember	1981	2.50	5.00	10.00
ALLEGIANCE					
AV-5004	Excellence	1985	2.50	5.00	10.00
CAPITOL					
C1-92957	More of the Night	1990	3.00	6.00	12.00
DORE					
338	Shhh	197?	3.00	6.00	12.00
INTERMEDIA					
QS-5075	Doctor Love	198?	2.50	5.00	10.00
JANUS					
JLS-3041	The Whispers' Love Story	1972	12.50	25.00	50.00
JLS-3046	Life and Breath	1973	10.00	20.00	40.00
7006	Bingo	1974	10.00	20.00	40.00
7013	Greatest Hits	1975	7.50	15.00	30.00
SOLAR					
S-27	Love Is Where You Find It	1982	2.50	5.00	10.00
BXL1-2270	Open Up Your Love	1978	3.00	6.00	12.00
—Reissue of Soul Train 2270					
BXL1-2774	Headlights	1978	3.00	6.00	12.00

Number	Title (A Side/B Side)	Yr	VG	VG+	NM
BXL1-3105	Whisper in Your Ear	1979	3.00	6.00	12.00
BXL1-3521	The Whspers	1979	3.00	6.00	12.00
BXL1-3578	Imagination	1980	3.00	6.00	12.00
AYL1-3839	Open Up Your Love	1981	2.00	4.00	8.00
—"Best Buy Series" reissue					
BXL1-3976	This Kind of Lovin'	1981	3.00	6.00	12.00
BXL1-4242	The Best of the Whispers	1982	3.00	6.00	12.00
60216	Love for Love	1983	2.50	5.00	10.00
60356	So Good	1984	2.50	5.00	10.00
60451	Happy Holidays to You	1985	3.00	6.00	12.00
ST-72554	Just Gets Better with Time	1987	2.50	5.00	10.00
PZ 75306	Vintage Whispers	1989	3.00	6.00	12.00
SOUL CLOCK					
22001	Planets of Life	1969	25.00	50.00	100.00
SOUL TRAIN					
BVL1-1450	One for the Money	1976	3.75	7.50	15.00
BVL1-2270	Open Up Your Love	1977	3.75	7.50	15.00

WHISPERS, THE (2)

45s

Number	Title (A Side/B Side)	Yr	VG	VG+	NM
GOTHAM					
309	Fool Heart/Don't Fool with Lizzie	1953	62.50	125.00	250.00
312	Are You Sorry/We're Getting Married	1953	375.00	750.00	1500.

WHISPERS, THE (3)

45s

Number	Title (A Side/B Side)	Yr	VG	VG+	NM
LAURIE					
3344	Here Comes Summer/If You Don't Care	1966	5.00	10.00	20.00

WHITCOMB, IAN

45s

Number	Title (A Side/B Side)	Yr	VG	VG+	NM
JERDEN					
735	Soho/Bony Moronie	1964	3.75	7.50	15.00
747	This Sporting Life/Soho	1964	3.75	7.50	15.00
TOWER					
120	This Sporting Life/Fizz	1965	2.50	5.00	10.00
134	You Turn Me On (Turn On Song)/Poor But Honest	1965	3.75	7.50	15.00
155	N-N-Nervous/The End	1965	2.50	5.00	10.00
170	18 Whitcomb St./Fizz	1965	2.50	5.00	10.00
189	No Tears for Johnny/Be My Baby	1966	2.50	5.00	10.00
192	High Blood Pressure/Good Hard Rock	1966	2.50	5.00	10.00
212	Lover's Prayer/Your Baby Has Gone Down the Plug Hole	1966	2.50	5.00	10.00
251	You Won't See Me/Please Don't Put Me on the Shelf	1966	2.50	5.00	10.00
274	Where Did Robinson Crusoe Go (With Friday on Saturday Night)/Poor Little Bird	1966	3.00	6.00	12.00
336	You Really Bent Me Out of Shape/Rolling Home Georgeanne	1967	2.50	5.00	10.00
355	You Really Bent Me Out of Shape/Rolling Home Georgeanne	1967	2.50	5.00	10.00
385	Groovy Day/Sally Sails the Sky	1967	2.50	5.00	10.00
UNITED ARTISTS					
XW162	They Go Wild, Simply Wild Over Me/Yaaka Hula Hickey Dula	1973	—	3.00	6.00

Albums

Number	Title (A Side/B Side)	Yr	VG	VG+	NM
AUDIOPHILE					
AP-115	Treasures of Tin Pan Alley	197?	3.00	6.00	12.00
AP-147	At the Ragtime Ball	1983	3.00	6.00	12.00
FIRST AMERICAN					
7704	Crooner Tunes	1979	2.50	5.00	10.00
7725	Red Hot "Blue Heaven"	1980	2.50	5.00	10.00
7729	The Rock and Roll Years	1981	2.50	5.00	10.00
7751	Instrumentals	1981	2.50	5.00	10.00
7789	In Hollywood	1982	2.50	5.00	10.00
RHINO					
RNLP-127	The Best of Ian Whitcomb (1964-1968)	1986	2.00	4.00	8.00
SIERRA					
8708	Pianomelt	1980	2.50	5.00	10.00
TOWER					
DT 5004 [R]	You Turn Me On	1965	5.00	10.00	20.00
T 5004 [M]	You Turn Me On	1965	6.25	12.50	25.00
ST 5042 [S]	Mod, Mod Music Hall	1966	5.00	10.00	20.00
T 5042 [M]	Mod, Mod Music Hall	1966	3.75	7.50	15.00
ST 5071 [S]	Yellow Underground	1967	5.00	10.00	20.00
T 5071 [M]	Yellow Underground	1967	3.75	7.50	15.00
ST 5100	Sock Me Some Rock	1968	5.00	10.00	20.00
UNITED ARTISTS					
UA-LA021-F	Under the Ragtime Moon	1972	2.50	5.00	10.00

WHITCOMB, IAN, AND DICK ZIMMERMAN

Albums

Number	Title (A Side/B Side)	Yr	VG	VG+	NM
AUDIOPHILE					
AP-225	Steppin' Out	1987	2.50	5.00	10.00
STOMP OFF					
SOS-1017	Don't Say Goodbye Miss Ragtime	198?	3.00	6.00	12.00
SOS-1049	My Wife Is Dancing Mad	198?	3.00	6.00	12.00

WHITE, BARRY

12-Inch Singles

Number	Title (A Side/B Side)	Yr	VG	VG+	NM
20TH CENTURY					
TCD-88	I Love to Sing the Songs I Sing/(B-side unknown)	1979	3.00	6.00	12.00
TCD-102	How Did You Know It Was Me?/(B-side unknown)	1979	3.00	6.00	12.00
A&M					
31458 1027 1	Come On (6 versions)	1995	2.00	4.00	8.00
31458 8375 1 [DJ]	Practice What You Preach (7 versions)	1994	2.00	4.00	8.00
SP-12237	Sho You Right (Remix) (Instrumental)	1987	—	3.00	6.00
—Black vinyl					
SP-12237 [DJ]	Sho You Right (Remix) (Instrumental)	1987	3.00	6.00	12.00
—White vinyl					
SP-12317	Super Lover (3 versions)	1989	—	3.00	6.00
SP-12327	I Wanna Do It Good to Ya (3 versions)	1989	2.00	4.00	8.00
18026 [DJ]	I Wanna Do It Good to Ya (5 versions)	1989	—	3.00	6.00
UNLIMITED GOLD					
AS 864 [DJ]	I Believe in Love (3:26) (8:01)	1980	2.50	5.00	10.00
1403	It Ain't Love, Baby (Until You Give It)/Hung Up in Your Love	1979	3.00	6.00	12.00
AS 1509 [DJ]	Change (4:22) (7:04)	1982	2.50	5.00	10.00
02429	Louie Louie/Ghetto Letto	1981	2.50	5.00	10.00
03051	Change/I Like You, You Like Me	1982	2.50	5.00	10.00
03381	Passion (Long)/Passion (Short)	1982	2.50	5.00	10.00
03958	America/Life	1983	2.50	5.00	10.00
04099	Don't Let 'Em Blow Your Mind/Dreams	1983	2.50	5.00	10.00
70075	Mi Nueva Cancion (Love Makin' Music)/Ella Es Todo Para Mi (She's Everything to Me)	1981	5.00	10.00	20.00

45s

Number	Title (A Side/B Side)	Yr	VG	VG+	NM
20TH CENTURY					
(no #) [PS]	"With Love from Barry White"	1975	5.00	10.00	20.00
—Pink and white sleeve issued with some stock copies of "What Am I Gonna Do with You"					
2018	I'm Gonna Love You Just a Little More Baby/Just a Little More Baby	1973	—	2.50	5.00
2042	I've Got So Much to Give/I've Got So Much to Give	1973	—	2.50	5.00
2058	Never Never Gonna Give Ya Up/No, I'm Never Gonna Give Ya Up	1973	—	2.50	5.00
2077	Honey Please Can't You See/Honey Please Can't You See	1974	—	2.50	5.00
2120	Can't Get Enough of Your Love, Babe/Just Not Enough	1974	—	2.50	5.00
2133	You're the First, the Last, My Everything/More Than Anything, You're My Everything	1974	—	2.50	5.00
2177	What Am I Gonna Do with You/What Am I Gonna Do with You, Baby	1975	—	2.50	5.00
2208	I'll Do for You Anything You Want Me To/Anything You Want Me To	1975	—	2.50	5.00
2265	Let the Music Play/(Instrumental)	1975	—	2.50	5.00
2277	You See the Trouble with Me/I'm So Blue When You Are Too	1976	—	2.50	5.00
2298	Baby, We Better Try to Get It Together/If You Know, Won't You Tell Me	1976	—	2.50	5.00
2309	Don't Make Me Wait Too Long/Can't You See It's Only You I Want	1976	—	2.50	5.00
2328	I'm Qualified to Satisfy You/(Instrumental)	1977	—	2.50	5.00
2350	It's Ecstasy When You Lay Down Next to Me/I Never Thought I'd Fall in Love with You	1977	—	2.50	5.00
2361	Playing Your Game, Baby/Of All the Guys in the World	1977	—	2.50	5.00
2365	Oh What a Night for Dancing/You're So Good You're Bad	1978	—	2.50	5.00
2380	Your Sweetness Is My Weakness/It's Only Love Doing Its Thing	1978	—	2.50	5.00
2395	Just the Way You Are/Now I'm Gonna Make Love to You	1979	—	2.50	5.00
2416	I Love to Sing the Songs I Sing/Oh Me Oh My	1979	—	2.50	5.00
2433	How Did You Know It Was Me?/Oh Me Oh My	1979	—	2.50	5.00
A&M					
31458 0924 7	Practice What You Preach/Come On	1995	—	—	3.00
—Second pressing indeed contains these two songs					
31458 0924 7	Practice What You Preach/Come On	1995	—	2.50	5.00
—First pressing actually contains Lo-Key?'s "I Got a Thang 4 Ya!"/"Sweet On U," which are otherwise unavailable on 45. Can be identified without playing by checking the trail-off vinyl for a different number than that on the record.					
1203	Right Night/There's a Place (Where Love Never Ends)	1988	—	—	3.00
1459	Super Lover/I Wanna Do It Good to Ya	1989	—	—	3.00
75021 1511 7	When Will I See You Again/Goodnight My Love	1990	—	—	3.00
2943	Sho' You Right/You're What's On My Mind	1987	—	—	3.00
2943 [PS]	Sho' You Right/You're What's On My Mind	1987	—	—	3.00
3000	For Your Love (I'd Do Most Anything)/I'm Ready for Love	1987	—	—	3.00
3000 [PS]	For Your Love (I'd Do Most Anything)/I'm Ready for Love	1987	—	—	3.00
UNLIMITED GOLD					
1401	Any Fool Could See (You Were Meant for Me)/You're the One I Need	1979	—	2.00	4.00
1404	It Ain't Love, Babe (Until You Give It)/Hung Up in Your Love	1979	—	2.00	4.00
1411	Love Ain't Easy/I Found Love	1980	—	2.00	4.00
1415	Sheet Music/(Instrumental)	1980	—	2.00	4.00
1418	Love Makin' Music/Ella Es Todo Mi (She's Everything to Me)	1980	—	2.00	4.00
1420	I Believe in Love/You're the One I Need	1980	—	2.00	4.00
02425	Louie Louie/Ghetto Letto	1981	—	2.00	4.00
02580	Beware/Tell Me Who Do You Love	1981	—	2.00	4.00
02956	Change/I Like You, You Like Me	1982	—	2.00	4.00
03379	Passion/It's All About Love	1982	—	2.00	4.00
03957	America/Life	1983	—	2.00	4.00
04098	Don't Let 'Em Blow Your Mind/Dreams	1983	—	2.00	4.00

Albums

Number	Title (A Side/B Side)	Yr	VG	VG+	NM
20TH CENTURY					
T-407	I've Got So Much to Give	1973	2.50	5.00	10.00
T-423	Stone Gon'	1973	2.50	5.00	10.00
T-444	Can't Get Enough	1974	2.50	5.00	10.00
T-466	Just Another Way to Say I Love You	1975	2.50	5.00	10.00
T-493	Barry White's Greatest Hits	1975	2.50	5.00	10.00
T-502	Let the Music Play	1976	2.50	5.00	10.00
T-516	Is This Whatcha Want?	1976	2.50	5.00	10.00
T-543	Barry White Sings for Someone You Love	1977	2.50	5.00	10.00
T-571	Barry White The Man	1978	2.50	5.00	10.00
T-590	I Love to Sing the Songs I Sing	1979	2.50	5.00	10.00
T-599	Barry White's Greatest Hits, Volume 2	1981	2.50	5.00	10.00
A&M					
SP-5154	The Right Night and Barry White	1987	2.50	5.00	10.00
SP-5256	The Man Is Back!	1990	2.50	5.00	10.00
75021 5377 1	Put Me in Your Mix	1991	3.00	6.00	12.00
CASABLANCA					
822782-1	Barry White's Greatest Hits	1984	2.00	4.00	8.00
822783-1	Barry White's Greatest Hits, Volume 2	1984	2.00	4.00	8.00

Number	Title (A Side/B Side)	Yr	VG	VG+	NM
UNLIMITED GOLD					
JZ 35763	The Message Is Love	1979	2.50	5.00	10.00
FZ 36208	Barry White's Sheet Music	1980	2.50	5.00	10.00
Z2X 36957 [(2)]	The Best of Our Love	1981	3.00	6.00	12.00
FZ 37176	Beware	1982	2.50	5.00	10.00
FZ 38048	Change	1982	2.50	5.00	10.00
FZ 38711	Dedicated	1983	2.50	5.00	10.00
WHITE, BARRY AND GLODEAN					
45s					
UNLIMITED GOLD					
02087	I Want You/Our Theme (Part 1)	1981	—	2.00	4.00
02419	You're the Only One for Me/This Love	1981	—	2.00	4.00
70064	Didn't We Make It Happen, Baby/Our Theme (Part 2)	1981	—	2.00	4.00
Albums					
UNLIMITED GOLD					
FZ 37054	Barry and Glodean White	1981	2.50	5.00	10.00
WHITE, BEN, AND THE DARCHAES					
45s					
ALJON					
1247/8	Jocko Sent Me/Nationwide Stamps	1962	100.00	200.00	400.00
WHITE, LENNY					
45s					
NEMPEROR					
003	Chicken Fried Steak/(B-side unknown)	1975	—	2.00	4.00
012	Sweet Dreamer/(B-side unknown)	1976	—	2.00	4.00
Albums					
ELEKTRA					
6E-121	Adventures of Astral Pirates	1978	2.50	5.00	10.00
6E-164	Streamline	1978	2.50	5.00	10.00
6E-223	Best of Friends	1979	2.50	5.00	10.00
6E-304	Twennynine with Lenny White	1980	2.50	5.00	10.00
5E-551	Just Like Dreamin'	1981	2.50	5.00	10.00
NEMPEROR					
SD 435	Venusian Summer	1975	3.00	6.00	12.00
SD 441	Big City	1977	3.00	6.00	12.00
WHITE, TONY JOE					
12-Inch Singles					
CASABLANCA					
NBD 20218	I Get Off On It	1980	2.00	4.00	8.00
—B-side is blank					
45s					
20TH CENTURY					
2276	It Must Be Love/Susie-Q	1976	—	2.00	4.00
2322	Texas Woman/Hold On to Your Hiney	1976	—	2.00	4.00
ARISTA					
0376	We'll Live on Love/You and Me Baby	1978	—	2.00	4.00
0395	It Must Be Love/We'll Live on Love	1979	—	2.00	4.00
CASABLANCA					
2279	I Get Off on It/Feelin' Loose	1980	—	2.00	4.00
2304	Mamas Don't Let Your Cowboys Grow Up to Be Babies/Disco Blues	1980	—	2.00	4.00
COLUMBIA					
03967	Swamp Rap/Living in the River City	1983	—	2.00	4.00
04134	The Lady in My Life/We Belong Together	1983	—	2.00	4.00
04356	We Belong Together/Naughty Lady	1984	—	2.00	4.00
04476	You Just Get Better All the Time/Do You Have a Garter Belt	1984	—	2.00	4.00
04683	Nobody's Baby Tonight/Down by the Border	1984	—	2.00	4.00
MONUMENT					
1003	Georgia Pines/Ten More Miles to Louisiana	1967	2.00	4.00	8.00
1053	Watching the Trains Go By/Old Man Willie	1968	2.00	4.00	8.00
1070	I Protest/Man Can Only Stand So Much Pain	1968	2.00	4.00	8.00
1086	Soul Francisco/Whompt Out on You	1968	2.00	4.00	8.00
1104	Polk Salad Annie/Aspen Colorado	1968	2.50	5.00	10.00
1169	Roosevelt and Ira Lee (Night of the Moccasin)/The Migrant	1969	—	3.00	6.00
1193	High Sheriff/Groupy Girl	1970	—	3.00	6.00
1206	Save Your Sugar for Me/My Friend	1970	—	3.00	6.00
1227	Old Man Willie/Scratch My Back	1970	—	3.00	6.00
WARNER BROS.					
7468	The Daddy/Voodoo Village	1971	—	2.50	5.00
7477	My Kind of Woman/I Just Walked Away	1971	—	2.50	5.00
7505	Lustful Earl and the Married Woman/I Just Walked Away	1971	—	2.50	5.00
7523	Delta Love/That On the Road Look	1971	—	2.50	5.00
7591	Even Trolls Love Rock and Roll/If I Ever Saw a Good Thing	1972	—	2.50	5.00
7607	I've Got a Thing About You, Baby/Gospel Singer	1972	—	2.50	5.00
7712	Backwoods Preacher Man/Saturday Night in Oak Grove, La.	1973	—	2.50	5.00
7780	Love 'Tween You and Me/Sign of the Lion	1974	—	2.50	5.00
8042	Wishful Thinking/Don't Let the Door	1974	—	2.50	5.00
Albums					
20TH CENTURY					
T-523	Eyes	1977	3.00	6.00	12.00
CASABLANCA					
NBLP 7233	Real Thang	1980	2.50	5.00	10.00
COLUMBIA					
FC 38817	Dangerous	1983	2.50	5.00	10.00
MONUMENT					
SLP-18114	Black and White	1969	3.75	7.50	15.00
SLP-18133	...Continued	1969	3.75	7.50	15.00
SLP-18142	Tony Joe	1970	3.75	7.50	15.00
WARNER BROS.					
WS 1900	Tony Joe White	1971	3.00	6.00	12.00
BS 2580	The Train I'm On	1972	3.00	6.00	12.00
BS 2708	Homemade Ice Cream	1973	3.00	6.00	12.00
WHITE LIGHT					
Albums					
CENTURY					
39955	White Light	1968	75.00	150.00	300.00
WHITE PLAINS					
45s					
DERAM					
85058	My Baby Loves Lovin'/Show Me Your Hand	1970	2.00	4.00	8.00
85066	Lovin' You Baby/Noises (In My Head)	1970	—	3.00	6.00
85072	Carolina's Coming Home/Every Little Move She Makes	1971	—	3.00	6.00
85076	When You Are a King/The World Gets Better with Love	1971	—	3.00	6.00
85080	I Can't Stop/Julie Anne	1972	—	3.00	6.00
85086	Step Into a Dream/Look to See	1973	—	3.00	6.00
85089	Does Anybody Know Where My Baby Is/Just for a Change	1973	—	3.00	6.00
Albums					
DERAM					
DES 18045	My Baby Loves Lovin'	1970	3.75	7.50	15.00
WHITE WITCH					
45s					
CAPRICORN					
0012	And I'm Leaving/Parabrahm Greeting-Dweller of the Threshold	1972	—	3.00	6.00
0016	Don't Close Your Mind/You're the One	1973	—	3.00	6.00
0023	Home Grown Girl/It's So Nice to Be Stoned	1973	—	3.00	6.00
0025	Home Grown Girl/Help Me Lord	1973	—	3.00	6.00
0080	Showdown/Walk On	1974	—	3.00	6.00
Albums					
CAPRICORN					
CP 0107	White Witch	1973	6.25	12.50	25.00
CP 0129	A Spiritual Greeting	1974	6.25	12.50	25.00
WHITEMAN, PAUL					
45s					
CAPITOL					
F1668	Travelin' Light/The General Jumped at Dawn	1951	5.00	10.00	20.00
—Reissue of 78 rpm hit from 1942					
CORAL					
61228	Whispering/You're Driving Me Crazy	1954	2.50	5.00	10.00
61254	I Love You/Japanese Sandman	1954	2.50	5.00	10.00
61273	Saw Your Eyes/There's a Small Hotel	1954	2.50	5.00	10.00
61336	Mississippi Mud/Then and Now	1955	2.50	5.00	10.00
61403	Three O'Clock in the Morning/Jukin'	1955	2.50	5.00	10.00
61516	Charleston/Black Bottom	1955	2.50	5.00	10.00
Albums					
CAPITOL					
T 622 [M]	Classics in Jazz	1955	12.50	25.00	50.00
DT 1678 [R]	Paul Whiteman Conducts George Gershwin	1962	3.00	6.00	12.00
T 1678 [M]	Paul Whiteman Conducts George Gershwin	1962	3.75	7.50	15.00
COLUMBIA					
CL 2830 [M]	Paul Whiteman Featuring Bing Crosby	1968	3.75	7.50	15.00
CORAL					
CRL 57021 [M]	The Great Gershwin	1955	5.00	10.00	20.00
GRAND AWARD					
GA-208 SD [S]	Hawaiian Magic	1958	7.50	15.00	30.00
GA-241 SD [S]	The Night I Played at 666 Fifth Ave.	1960	7.50	15.00	30.00
GA-244 SD [S]	Cavalcade of Music	1960	7.50	15.00	30.00
GA-33-351 [M]	Fiddle on Fire	195?	7.50	15.00	30.00
GA-33-356 [M]	Hawaiian Magic	1958	5.00	10.00	20.00
GA-33-409 [M]	The Night I Played at 666 Fifth Ave.	1960	5.00	10.00	20.00
GA-33-412 [M]	Cavalcade of Music	1960	5.00	10.00	20.00
GA-33-502 [M]	Great Whiteman Hits	195?	7.50	15.00	30.00
GA-33-503 [M]	The Greatest Stars of My Life	195?	12.50	25.00	50.00
—In red velvet jacket					
GA-33-901 [(2) M]	Paul Whiteman/50th Anniversary	1956	12.50	25.00	50.00
MARK 56					
761 [M]	Tribute to Gershwin 1936	197?	3.00	6.00	12.00
RCA VICTOR					
LPV-555 [M]	Paul Whiteman, Volume 1	195?	3.75	7.50	15.00
SUNBEAM					
18 [M]	In Concert 1927-32	197?	3.00	6.00	12.00
"X"					
LVA-3040 [10]	Paul Whiteman's Orchestra Featuring Bix Beiderbecke	1955	20.00	40.00	80.00
WHITING, MARGARET					
45s					
CAPITOL					
F809	You're An Old Smoothie/He's Funny That Way	1950	5.00	10.00	20.00
—Note: Earlier Margaret Whiting 45s on Capitol may exist					
F841	I Said My Pajamas (And Put On My Pray'rs)/Be Mine	1950	5.00	10.00	20.00
F851	Solid As a Rock/Sure Thing	1950	5.00	10.00	20.00
F874	It Might As Well Be Spring/How Deep Is the Ocean	1950	5.00	10.00	20.00
F879	Come Rain or Come Shine/Dream Peddler's Serenade	1950	5.00	10.00	20.00
F934	My Foolish Heart/Stay with the Happy People	1950	5.00	10.00	20.00
F1027	Razza-Ma-Tazz/I Gotta Get Out of the Habit	1950	5.00	10.00	20.00
F1041	Shawl of Galway Gray/If You Were Only Mine	1950	5.00	10.00	20.00
F1042	Blind Date/Home Cookin'	1950	7.50	15.00	30.00
—With Bob Hope					
F1103	I Didn't Know What Time It Was/This Can't Be Love	1950	5.00	10.00	20.00
F1123	You're Mine You/I've Forgotten You	1950	5.00	10.00	20.00
F1132	Let's Do It Again/Friendly Star	1950	5.00	10.00	20.00

Number	Title (A Side/B Side)	Yr	VG	VG+	NM
F1160	Don't Rock the Boat/I'm in Love with You	1950	3.75	7.50	15.00
—With Dean Martin					
F1213	I've Never Been in Love Before/The Best Things for You	1950	3.75	7.50	15.00
F1309	Once You Find Your Guy/Man Ain't Nothin' But a Nothin'	1950	3.75	7.50	15.00
F1343	Over and Over and Over/The Moon Was Yellow	1950	3.75	7.50	15.00
F1391	Faithful/Lonesome Gal	1951	3.75	7.50	15.00
F1417	You Are One/Sing You Sinners	1951	3.75	7.50	15.00
F1469	We Kiss in a Shadow/Make Man Love Me	1951	3.75	7.50	15.00
F1491	Something Wonderful/Hello Young Lovers	1951	3.75	7.50	15.00
F1566	Happy, Topper and Me/This Little Pig	1951	3.75	7.50	15.00
F1645	It Might As Well Be Spring/How Deep Is the Ocean	1951	3.75	7.50	15.00
—Reissue of 78 rpm hit of 1945					
F1671	Moonlight in Vermont/My Ideal	1951	3.75	7.50	15.00
—Reissue					
F1702	Good Morning, Mr. Echo/River Road Two-Step	1951	3.75	7.50	15.00
F1784	And So to Sleep/Beer Barrel Polka	1951	3.75	7.50	15.00
F1801	Bill/More More More	1951	3.75	7.50	15.00
F1845	That's For Sure/If I Can Love You	1951	3.75	7.50	15.00
F1939	Round and Round/Oops	1952	3.75	7.50	15.00
F1984	Foggy River/Try Me One More Time	1952	3.75	7.50	15.00
F2000	I'll Walk Alone/I Could Write a Book	1952	3.75	7.50	15.00
F2177	Till We Meet Again/The Gods Were Angry with Me	1952	3.75	7.50	15.00
F2217	Alone Together/Outside of Heaven	1952	3.75	7.50	15.00
F2292	Why Don't You Believe Me/Come Back to Me Johnny	1952	3.75	7.50	15.00
F2331	Singing Bells/Take Care My Love	1953	3.75	7.50	15.00
F2489	Something Wonderful Happens/Where Did He Go	1953	3.75	7.50	15.00
F2550	Waltz to the Blues/C.O.D.	1953	3.75	7.50	15.00
F2599	I Just Love You/The Night Holds No Fear	1953	3.75	7.50	15.00
F2681	Kiss or Get Off the Spot/In the Still of the Night	1953	3.75	7.50	15.00
F2717	I Speak to the Stars/It's Nice to Have You Home	1954	3.75	7.50	15.00
F2853	Joey/Ask Me	1954	3.75	7.50	15.00
F2869	How Long Has It Been/Affair of the Heart	1954	3.75	7.50	15.00
F2913	All I Want Is All There Is And Then Some/Can This Be Mine	1954	3.75	7.50	15.00
F2996	My Son, My Son/My Own True Love	1954	3.75	7.50	15.00
F3067	Stowaway/Allah Be Praised	1955	3.00	6.00	12.00
F3189	Mama's Pearls/Man	1955	3.00	6.00	12.00
F3232	Lover Lover/I Kiss You a Million Times	1955	3.00	6.00	12.00
F3314	I Love a Mystery/Bidin' My Time	1956	3.00	6.00	12.00
F3412	Second Time in Love/Old Enough	1956	3.00	6.00	12.00
F3473	True Love/Haunting Love	1956	3.00	6.00	12.00
F3509	Hello Young Lovers/We Kiss in a Shadow	1956	3.00	6.00	12.00
F3586	The Money Tree/Maybe I Love Him	1956	3.00	6.00	12.00
F3666	Tippy Toe/Spring in Maine	1957	3.00	6.00	12.00
4638	On Second Thought/Who Can You Can	1961	2.50	5.00	10.00
DOT					
15583	Kill Me with Kisses/Speak for Yourself, John	1957	2.50	5.00	10.00
15680	I Can't Help It (If I'm Still in Love with You)/That's Why I Was Born	1957	2.50	5.00	10.00
15742	I'm So Lonely I Could Cry/Hot Spell	1958	2.50	5.00	10.00
15804	Just a Dream/Pretty-Eyed Baby	1958	2.50	5.00	10.00
15826	I Love You Because/The Waiting Game	1958	2.50	5.00	10.00
15931	I'm Alone Because I Love You/Top of the Moon	1959	2.50	5.00	10.00
15973	Half As Much/My Ideal	1959	2.50	5.00	10.00
LONDON					
101	The Wheel of Hurt/Nothing Lasts Forever	1966	—	3.00	6.00
106	Just Like a Man/World Inside Your Arms	1967	—	3.00	6.00
108	Only Love Can Break a Heart/Where Do I Stand	1967	—	3.00	6.00
115	I Almost Called Your Name/Let's Pretend	1968	—	3.00	6.00
122	Faithfully/Am I Losing You	1968	—	3.00	6.00
124	Maybe Just One More/Can't Get You Out of My Mind	1968	—	3.00	6.00
126	Love's the Only Answer/Where Was I	1969	—	3.00	6.00
128	Love Has a Way/At the End of the Ocean	1969	—	3.00	6.00
132	Theme from Z/Life Goes On	1970	—	2.50	5.00
137	Until It's Time for You to Go/I'll Tell Him Today	1970	—	2.50	5.00
VERVE					
10212	Why Was I Born/You Couldn't Be Cuter	1960	2.50	5.00	10.00
10230	Hey, Look Me Over/What's New at the Zoo	1960	2.50	5.00	10.00
—With Mel Torme					

Albums

Number	Title (A Side/B Side)	Yr	VG	VG+	NM
AUDIOPHILE					
AP-152	Too Marvelous for Words	198?	2.50	5.00	10.00
AP-173	Come a Little Closer	198?	2.50	5.00	10.00
AP-207	This Lady's in Love with You	1986	2.50	5.00	10.00
CAPITOL					
H 163 [10]	South Pacific	1950	12.50	25.00	50.00
H 209 [10]	Margaret Whiting Sings Rodgers and Hart	1950	12.50	25.00	50.00
H 234 [10]	Songs	1950	12.50	25.00	50.00
T 410 [M]	Love Songs	1954	10.00	20.00	40.00
T 685 [M]	For the Starry-Eyed	1955	10.00	20.00	40.00
DOT					
DLP 3072 [M]	Goin' Places	1957	6.25	12.50	25.00
DLP 3113 [M]	Margaret	1958	3.75	7.50	15.00
DLP 3176 [M]	Margaret Whiting's Great Hits	1959	3.75	7.50	15.00
DLP 3235 [M]	Ten Top Hits	1960	3.75	7.50	15.00
DLP 3337 [M]	Just a Dream	1960	3.75	7.50	15.00
DLP 25113 [S]	Margaret	1958	5.00	10.00	20.00
DLP 25176 [S]	Margaret Whiting's Great Hits	1959	5.00	10.00	20.00
DLP 25235 [S]	Ten Top Hits	1960	5.00	10.00	20.00
DLP 25337 [S]	Just a Dream	1960	5.00	10.00	20.00
HAMILTON					
HLP 143 [M]	My Ideal	196?	3.00	6.00	12.00
HLP 12143 [S]	My Ideal	196?	3.75	7.50	15.00
LONDON					
PS 497 [S]	The Wheel of Hurt	1967	3.75	7.50	15.00
PS 510 [S]	Maggie Isn't Margaret Anymore	1967	3.75	7.50	15.00
PS 527	Pop Country	1968	3.75	7.50	15.00
LL 3497 [M]	The Wheel of Hurt	1967	5.00	10.00	20.00
LL 3510 [M]	Maggie Isn't Margaret Anymore	1967	5.00	10.00	20.00
MGM					
E-4006 [M]	Past Midnight	1961	3.75	7.50	15.00
SE-4006 [S]	Past Midnight	1961	5.00	10.00	20.00
VERVE					
V-4038 [M]	The Jerome Kern Song Book	1960	3.75	7.50	15.00
V6-4038 [S]	The Jerome Kern Song Book	1960	5.00	10.00	20.00

WHITING, MARGARET, AND JIMMY WAKELY

45s

Number	Title (A Side/B Side)	Yr	VG	VG+	NM
CAPITOL					
F-800	Broken Down Merry-Go-Round/The Gods Were Angry with Me	1950	5.00	10.00	20.00
—Note: Earlier Capitol 45s by this duo may exist					
F960	Let's Go to Church (Next Sunday Morning)/Why Do You Say Those Things	1950	5.00	10.00	20.00
F1065	Close Your Pretty Eyes/Fools' Paradise	1950	5.00	10.00	20.00
F1234	A Bushel and a Peck/Beyond the Reef	1950	3.75	7.50	15.00
F1255	Silver Bells/Christmas Candy	1950	5.00	10.00	20.00
F1500	When You and I Were Young Maggie Blues/Till We Meet Again	1951	3.75	7.50	15.00
F1555	Star of Hope/Why Am I Losing You	1951	3.75	7.50	15.00
F1634	Slipping Around/Wedding Bells	1951	3.75	7.50	15.00
—Reissue of 78 rpm hits from 1948					
F1816	Let's Live a Little/I Don't Want to Be Free	1951	3.75	7.50	15.00
F1965	Give Me More, More, More/Let Old Mother Nature Have Her	1952	3.75	7.50	15.00
F2402	Gomen Nasai/I Learned to Love You Too Late	1953	3.75	7.50	15.00
F2528	My Heart Knows/When Love Goes Wrong	1953	3.75	7.50	15.00
F2689	Tennessee Church Bells/There's a Silver Moon on Golden Gate	1953	3.75	7.50	15.00
F3905	Silver Bells/Christmas Candy	1958	3.00	6.00	12.00

7-Inch Extended Plays

Number	Title (A Side/B Side)	Yr	VG	VG+	NM
CAPITOL					
EAP 1-403	Slipping Around/Wedding Bells//I'll Never Slip Around Again/Six Times a Week and Twice on Sundays	195?	5.00	10.00	20.00
EAP 1-403 [PS]	Margaret Whiting and Jimmy Wakely Sing	195?	5.00	10.00	20.00

WHITLOCK, BOBBY

45s

Number	Title (A Side/B Side)	Yr	VG	VG+	NM
ABC DUNHILL					
4312	Song for Paula/Where There's a Will, There's a Way	1972	—	2.50	5.00
4318	Ease Your Pain/Satisfied	1972	—	2.50	5.00
4326	Hello L.A., Bye Bye Birmingham/Start All Over	1972	—	2.50	5.00
4332	Tell the Truth/You Came Along	1972	—	2.50	5.00

Albums

Number	Title (A Side/B Side)	Yr	VG	VG+	NM
ABC DUNHILL					
DS-50121	Bobby Whitlock	1972	3.00	6.00	12.00
DSX-50131	Raw Velvet	1972	3.00	6.00	12.00
CAPRICORN					
CP 0160	One of a Kind	1975	2.50	5.00	10.00
CP 0168	Rock Your Sox Off	1976	2.50	5.00	10.00

WHITMAN, SLIM

45s

Number	Title (A Side/B Side)	Yr	VG	VG+	NM
CLEVELAND INT'L.					
02402	Can't Help Falling in Love with You/Oh My Darlin' (I Love You)	1981	—	2.00	4.00
02544	If I Had My Life to Live Over/Flowers	1981	—	2.00	4.00
02779	My Melody of Love/Open Up Your Heart	1982	—	2.00	4.00
03370	Where Is the Christ in Christmas/Sleep My Child (All Through the Night)	1982	—	2.00	4.00
50912	When/Since You Went Away	1980	—	2.00	4.00
50946	That Silver-Haired Daddy of Mine/If I Could Only Dream	1980	—	2.00	4.00
50957	Where Is the Christ in Christmas/Sleep My Child (All Through the Night)	1980	—	2.00	4.00
50971	I Remember You/Where Do I Go from Here	1981	—	2.00	4.00
EPIC					
04358	Blue Memories/Cry Baby Heart	1983	—	2.00	4.00
04549	Four Walls/Tryin' to Outrun the Wind	1984	—	2.00	4.00
IMPERIAL					
5731	Remember Me/Just Call Me Lonesome	1961	2.50	5.00	10.00
5746	The Bells That Broke My Heart/I'd Climb the Highest Mountain	1961	2.50	5.00	10.00
5766	Once in a Lifetime/When I Call on You	1961	2.50	5.00	10.00
5778	The Old Spinning Wheel/In a Hundred Years	1961	2.50	5.00	10.00
5791	Yesterday's Love/It Sure Looks Lonesome Outside	1961	2.50	5.00	10.00
5821	Valley of Tears/Annie Laurie	1962	2.50	5.00	10.00
5859	I Forgot More Than You'll Ever Know (About Her)/Backward, Turn Backward	1962	2.50	5.00	10.00
5871	Blues Stay Away from Me/You Have My Heart	1962	2.50	5.00	10.00
5900	The Wayward Wind/Straight from Heaven	1962	2.50	5.00	10.00
5919	Love Letters in the Sand/You're the Only One	1963	2.50	5.00	10.00
5938	What'll I Do/So Long Mary	1963	2.50	5.00	10.00
5966	Broken Down Merry-Go-Round/Never	1963	2.50	5.00	10.00
5990	My Wild Irish Rose/Chime Bells	1963	2.50	5.00	10.00
8134	Love Song of the Waterfall/My Love's Growing Stale	1951	6.25	12.50	25.00
8144	Bandera Waltz/(B-side unknown)	1952	6.25	12.50	25.00
8147	Cold Empty Arms/In a Hundred Years or More	1952	6.25	12.50	25.00
8156	Indian Love Call/China Doll	1952	6.25	12.50	25.00
—Black vinyl					
8156	Indian Love Call/China Doll	1952	12.50	25.00	50.00
—Opaque red vinyl					
8163	By the Waters of the Winnetonka/An Amateur in Love	1952	6.25	12.50	25.00
8169	Keep It a Secret/My Heart Is Broken in Threes	1952	6.25	12.50	25.00
8180	How Can I Tell/All That I'm Asking Is Sympathy	1953	6.25	12.50	25.00
8189	Restless Heart/Song of the Old Water Wheel	1953	6.25	12.50	25.00

Number	Title (A Side/B Side)	Yr	VG	VG+	NM
8194	Once Before/Have Mercy on Me	1953	6.25	12.50	25.00
8201	Danny Boy/There's a Rainbow in Every Teardrop	1953	6.25	12.50	25.00
8208	North Wind/Darlin' Don't Cry	1953	6.25	12.50	25.00
8223	Secret Love/Why	1954	5.00	10.00	20.00
8236	Rose-Marie/We Stood at the Altar	1954	5.00	10.00	20.00
8257	Beautiful Dreamer/Ride Away	1954	5.00	10.00	20.00
8267	Singing Hills/I Hate to See You Cry	1954	5.00	10.00	20.00
8281	Cattle Call/When I Grow Too Old to Dream	1954	5.00	10.00	20.00
8290	Roll On Silvery Moon/Haunted Hungry Heart	1955	5.00	10.00	20.00
8298	I'll Never Stop Loving You/I'll Never Take You Back Again	1955	5.00	10.00	20.00
8299	Song of the Wild/You Have My Heart	1955	5.00	10.00	20.00
8304	Tumbling Tumbleweeds/Tell Me	1955	5.00	10.00	20.00
8305	I'm a Fool/Serenade	1956	5.00	10.00	20.00
8307	The Whiffenpoof Song/Dear Mary	1956	5.00	10.00	20.00
8308	Smoke Signals/Curtain of Tears	1956	5.00	10.00	20.00
8309	Careless Love/I Must Have Been Blind	1957	3.75	7.50	15.00
8310	I'll Take You Home Again Kathleen/Lovesick Blues	1957	3.75	7.50	15.00
8312	Unchain My Heart/Hush-a-Bye	1957	3.75	7.50	15.00
8316	A Very Precious Love/Careless	1958	3.75	7.50	15.00
8317	Candy Kisses/Tormented	1958	3.75	7.50	15.00
8318	When It's Springtime in the Rockies/Put Your Trust in Me	1958	3.75	7.50	15.00
8319	At the End of Nowhere/Wherever You Are	1958	3.75	7.50	15.00
8320	The Letter Edged in Black/I Never See Maggie	1959	3.75	7.50	15.00
8321	A Tree in the Meadow/What Kind of God	1959	3.75	7.50	15.00
8322	A Fool Such As I/The Prisoner's Song	1959	3.75	7.50	15.00
8323	Indian Love Call/Haunted Hungry Heart	1960	3.00	6.00	12.00
8326	Roll, River, Roll/Twilla Lee	1960	3.00	6.00	12.00
8327	Sunrise/I'll Walk with God	1960	3.00	6.00	12.00
8328	A Lonesome Heart/The Wind	1960	3.00	6.00	12.00
8329	Vaya Con Dios/Ramona	1960	3.00	6.00	12.00
66002	Maria Elena/Gortamona	1963	2.50	5.00	10.00
66012	Tell Me Pretty Words/Only You And You Alone	1964	2.00	4.00	8.00
66040	I'll Hold You in My Heart (Till I Can Hold You in My Arms)/No Other Arms, No Other Lips	1964	2.00	4.00	8.00
66077	Love Song of the Waterfall/Virginia	1964	2.00	4.00	8.00
66103	Mansion on the Hill/Reminiscing	1965	2.00	4.00	8.00
66130	More Than Yesterday/La Golondrina	1965	2.00	4.00	8.00
66153	The Twelfth of Never/Straight from Heaven	1966	2.00	4.00	8.00
66181	I Remember You/Travelin' Man	1966	2.50	5.00	10.00
66212	One Dream/Jerry	1966	2.00	4.00	8.00
66226	What's This World a-Comin' To/You Bring Out the Best in Me	1967	2.00	4.00	8.00
66248	I'm a Fool/North Wind	1967	2.00	4.00	8.00
66262	The Keeper of the Key/Broken Wings	1967	2.00	4.00	8.00
66283	Rainbows Are Back in Style/How Could I Not Love You	1968	—	3.00	6.00
66311	Happy Street/My Heart Is In the Roses	1968	—	3.00	6.00
66337	Livin' On Lovin' (And Lovin' Livin' with You)/ Heaven Says Hello	1968	—	3.00	6.00
66358	My Happiness/Promises	1969	—	3.00	6.00
66384	Irresistible/Flower of Love	1969	—	3.00	6.00
66411	When You Were 16/Love Song of the Waterfall	1969	—	3.00	6.00
66441	Tomorrow Never Comes/Come Take My Hand	1970	—	3.00	6.00
RCA VICTOR					
47-5431	There's a Rainbow in Every Teardrop/I'm Casting My Lasso	1953	6.25	12.50	25.00
47-5557	Birmingham Jail/Wabash Waltz	1953	6.25	12.50	25.00
47-5724	I'll Never Pass This Way Again/Please Paint a Rose on the Garden Wall	1954	6.25	12.50	25.00
48-0069	Please Paint a Rose on the Garden Wall/Tears Can Never Drown the Flame	1949	15.00	30.00	60.00
—Green vinyl					
48-0145	I'll Never Pass This Way Again/Birmingham Jail	1949	15.00	30.00	60.00
—Green vinyl					
48-0358	I'm Crying for You/Wabash Waltz	1950	15.00	30.00	60.00
—Green vinyl					
UNITED ARTISTS					
0138	Indian Love Call/China Doll	1973	—	2.00	4.00
—"Silver Spotlight Series" reissue					
0139	Rose Marie/Secret Love	1973	—	2.00	4.00
—"Silver Spotlight Series" reissue					
XW178	Hold Me/So Close to Home	1973	—	2.50	5.00
XW269	Where the Lilacs Grow/Something Beautiful	1973	—	2.50	5.00
XW402	It's All in the Game/Make Believe	1974	—	2.50	5.00
XW530	Happy Anniversary/What I Had with You	1974	—	2.00	4.00
XW619	The Most Beautiful Girl/Foolish Question	1975	—	2.00	4.00
XW690	Everything Leads Back to You/I'm Beginning to Love You	1975	—	2.00	4.00
XW731	Mexicali Rose/As You Take a Walk Through My Mind	1975	—	2.00	4.00
XW1022	Red River Valley/Somewhere My Love	1977	—	2.00	4.00
50697	Shutters and Boards/I Pretend	1970	—	2.50	5.00
50731	Guess Who/From Heaven to Heartache	1970	—	2.50	5.00
50775	Something Beautiful (To Remember)/Jerry	1971	—	2.50	5.00
50806	It's a Sin to Tell a Lie/That's Enough for Me	1971	—	2.50	5.00
50852	Loveliest Night of the Year/Near You	1971	—	2.50	5.00
50899	Little Drops of Silver/Tammy	1972	—	2.50	5.00
50952	(It's No) Sin/(B-side unknown)	1972	—	2.50	5.00

7-Inch Extended Plays

Number	Title (A Side/B Side)	Yr	VG	VG+	NM
IMPERIAL					
IMP 104	(contents unknown)	1954	12.50	25.00	50.00
IMP 104 [PS]	America's Favorite Folk Artist	1954	12.50	25.00	50.00
IMP-130	(contents unknown)	1956	10.00	20.00	40.00
IMP-130 [PS]	Slim Whitman Singing…	1956	10.00	20.00	40.00
IMP-131	(contents unknown)	1956	10.00	20.00	40.00
IMP-131 [PS]	Songs by Slim Whitman	1956	10.00	20.00	40.00
IMP-132	(contents unknown)	1956	10.00	20.00	40.00
IMP-132 [PS]	Songs by Slim Whitman	1956	10.00	20.00	40.00
IMP-133	(contents unknown)	1956	10.00	20.00	40.00
IMP-133 [PS]	Songs by Slim Whitman	1956	10.00	20.00	40.00
IMP-134	(contents unknown)	1956	10.00	20.00	40.00
IMP-134 [PS]	Songs by Slim Whitman	1956	10.00	20.00	40.00
IMP-135	(contents unknown)	1956	10.00	20.00	40.00
IMP-135 [PS]	Slim Whitman	1956	10.00	20.00	40.00
IMP-136	(contents unknown)	1956	10.00	20.00	40.00
IMP-136 [PS]	Songs by Slim Whitman	1956	10.00	20.00	40.00
IMP-137	(contents unknown)	1956	10.00	20.00	40.00
IMP-137 [PS]	Slim Whitman	1956	10.00	20.00	40.00

Albums

Number	Title (A Side/B Side)	Yr	VG	VG+	NM
CLEVELAND INT'L.					
AS99-875 [DJ]	Songs I Love to Sing	1980	7.50	15.00	30.00
—Promo-only picture disc					
JE 36768	Songs I Love to Sing	1980	2.50	5.00	10.00
JE 36847	Christmas with Slim Whitman	1980	3.00	6.00	12.00
FE 37403	Mr. Songman	1982	2.50	5.00	10.00
COLUMBIA SPECIAL PRODUCTS					
P 16323	Christmas with Slim Whitman	1981	2.50	5.00	10.00
EPIC					
PE 36768	Songs I Love to Sing	198?	2.00	4.00	8.00
—Reissue of Cleveland Int'l. JE 36768					
PE 36847	Christmas with Slim Whitman	1981	2.00	4.00	8.00
—Reissue of Cleveland Int'l. JE 36847					
IMPERIAL					
LP-3004 [10]	America's Favorite Folk Artist	1954	150.00	300.00	600.00
LP-9003 [M]	Favorites	1956	12.50	25.00	50.00
—Maroon label					
LP-9003 [M]	Favorites	1958	7.50	15.00	30.00
—Black label with stars on top					
LP-9003 [M]	Favorites	1964	5.00	10.00	20.00
—Black and pink label					
LP-9003 [M]	Favorites	1966	3.75	7.50	15.00
—Black and green label					
LP-9026 [M]	Slim Whitman Sings	1957	12.50	25.00	50.00
—Maroon label					
LP-9026 [M]	Slim Whitman Sings	1958	7.50	15.00	30.00
—Black label with stars on top					
LP-9026 [M]	Slim Whitman Sings	1964	5.00	10.00	20.00
—Black and pink label					
LP-9026 [M]	Slim Whitman Sings	1966	3.75	7.50	15.00
—Black and green label					
LP-9056 [M]	Slim Whitman Sings	1958	12.50	25.00	50.00
—Maroon label					
LP-9056 [M]	Slim Whitman Sings	1958	7.50	15.00	30.00
—Black label with stars on top					
LP-9056 [M]	Slim Whitman Sings	1964	5.00	10.00	20.00
—Black and pink label					
LP-9056 [M]	Slim Whitman Sings	1966	3.75	7.50	15.00
—Black and green label					
LP-9064 [M]	Slim Whitman Sings	1959	7.50	15.00	30.00
—Black label with stars on top					
LP-9064 [M]	Slim Whitman Sings	1964	5.00	10.00	20.00
—Black and pink label					
LP-9064 [M]	Slim Whitman Sings	1966	3.75	7.50	15.00
—Black and green label					
LP-9088 [M]	I'll Walk with God	1960	7.50	15.00	30.00
—Black label with stars on top					
LP-9088 [M]	I'll Walk with God	1964	5.00	10.00	20.00
—Black and pink label					
LP-9088 [M]	I'll Walk with God	1966	3.75	7.50	15.00
—Black and green label					
LP-9102 [M]	Million Record Hits	1960	7.50	15.00	30.00
—Black label with stars on top					
LP-9102 [M]	Million Record Hits	1964	5.00	10.00	20.00
—Black and pink label					
LP-9102 [M]	Million Record Hits	1966	3.75	7.50	15.00
—Black and green label					
LP-9135 [M]	Slim Whitman's First Visit to Britain	1960	6.25	12.50	25.00
—Black label with stars on top					
LP-9135 [M]	Slim Whitman's First Visit to Britain	1964	3.75	7.50	15.00
—Black and pink label					
LP-9135 [M]	Slim Whitman's First Visit to Britain	1966	3.00	6.00	12.00
—Black and green label					
LP-9137 [M]	Just Call Me Lonesome	1961	6.25	12.50	25.00
—Black label with stars on top					
LP-9137 [M]	Just Call Me Lonesome	1964	3.75	7.50	15.00
—Black and pink label					
LP-9137 [M]	Just Call Me Lonesome	1966	3.00	6.00	12.00
—Black and green label					
LP-9156 [M]	Once in a Lifetime	1961	6.25	12.50	25.00
—Black label with stars on top					
LP-9156 [M]	Once in a Lifetime	1964	3.75	7.50	15.00
—Black and pink label					
LP-9156 [M]	Once in a Lifetime	1966	3.00	6.00	12.00
—Black and green label					
LP-9163 [M]	Slim Whitman Sings Annie Laurie	1961	6.25	12.50	25.00
—Black label with stars on top					
LP-9163 [M]	Slim Whitman Sings Annie Laurie	1964	3.75	7.50	15.00
—Black and pink label					
LP-9163 [M]	Slim Whitman Sings Annie Laurie	1966	3.00	6.00	12.00
—Black and green label					
LP-9171 [M]	Forever	1961	6.25	12.50	25.00
—Black label with stars on top					
LP-9171 [M]	Forever	1964	3.75	7.50	15.00
—Black and pink label					
LP-9171 [M]	Forever	1966	3.00	6.00	12.00
—Black and green label					
LP-9194 [M]	Slim Whitman Sings	1962	6.25	12.50	25.00
—Black label with stars on top					
LP-9194 [M]	Slim Whitman Sings	1964	3.75	7.50	15.00
—Black and pink label					
LP-9194 [M]	Slim Whitman Sings	1966	3.00	6.00	12.00
—Black and green label					
LP-9209 [M]	Heart Songs and Love Songs	1962	6.25	12.50	25.00
—Black label with stars on top					
LP-9209 [M]	Heart Songs and Love Songs	1964	3.75	7.50	15.00
—Black and pink label					

Number	Title (A Side/B Side)	Yr	VG	VG+	NM
LP-9209 [M]	Heart Songs and Love Songs	1966	3.00	6.00	12.00
—Black and green label					
LP-9226 [M]	I'm a Lonely Wanderer	1963	6.25	12.50	25.00
—Black label with stars on top					
LP-9226 [M]	I'm a Lonely Wanderer	1964	3.75	7.50	15.00
—Black and pink label					
LP-9226 [M]	I'm a Lonely Wanderer	1966	3.00	6.00	12.00
—Black and green label					
LP-9235 [M]	Yodeling	1963	6.25	12.50	25.00
—Black label with stars on top					
LP-9235 [M]	Yodeling	1964	3.75	7.50	15.00
—Black and pink label					
LP-9235 [M]	Yodeling	1966	3.00	6.00	12.00
—Black and green label					
LP-9245 [M]	Irish Songs The Whitman Way	1963	6.25	12.50	25.00
—Black label with stars on top					
LP-9245 [M]	Irish Songs The Whitman Way	1964	3.75	7.50	15.00
—Black and pink label					
LP-9245 [M]	Irish Songs The Whitman Way	1966	3.00	6.00	12.00
—Black and green label					
LP-9252 [M]	All-Time Favorites	1964	7.50	15.00	30.00
—Black label with stars on top					
LP-9252 [M]	All-Time Favorites	1964	3.75	7.50	15.00
—Black and pink label					
LP-9252 [M]	All-Time Favorites	1966	3.00	6.00	12.00
—Black and green label					
LP-9268 [M]	Country Songs/City Hits	1964	3.75	7.50	15.00
—Black and pink label					
LP-9268 [M]	Country Songs/City Hits	1966	3.00	6.00	12.00
—Black and green label					
LP-9277 [M]	Love Song of the Waterfall	1964	3.75	7.50	15.00
—Black and pink label					
LP-9277 [M]	Love Song of the Waterfall	1966	3.00	6.00	12.00
—Black and green label					
LP-9288 [M]	Reminiscing	1965	3.75	7.50	15.00
—Black and pink label					
LP-9288 [M]	Reminiscing	1966	3.00	6.00	12.00
—Black and green label					
LP-9303 [M]	More Than Yesterday	1965	3.75	7.50	15.00
—Black and pink label					
LP-9303 [M]	More Than Yesterday	1966	3.00	6.00	12.00
—Black and green label					
LP-9308 [M]	God's Hand in Mine	1966	3.00	6.00	12.00
LP-9313 [M]	A Travelin' Man	1966	3.00	6.00	12.00
LP-9333 [M]	A Time for Love	1966	3.00	6.00	12.00
LP-9342 [M]	15th Anniversary	1967	3.75	7.50	15.00
LP-9356 [M]	Country Memories	1967	3.75	7.50	15.00
LP-12032 [S]	I'll Walk with God	1959	10.00	20.00	40.00
—Black label with silver top					
LP-12032 [S]	I'll Walk with God	1964	6.25	12.50	25.00
—Black and pink label					
LP-12032 [S]	I'll Walk with God	1966	5.00	10.00	20.00
—Black and green label					
LP-12077 [S]	Slim Whitman Sings Annie Laurie	1961	7.50	15.00	30.00
—Black label with silver top					
LP-12077 [S]	Slim Whitman Sings Annie Laurie	1964	5.00	10.00	20.00
—Black and pink label					
LP-12077 [S]	Slim Whitman Sings Annie Laurie	1966	3.75	7.50	15.00
—Black and green label					
LP-12100 [R]	Slim Whitman	1964	3.75	7.50	15.00
—Black and pink label					
LP-12100 [R]	Slim Whitman	1966	3.00	6.00	12.00
—Black and green label					
LP-12102 [R]	Song of the Old Waterwheel	1964	3.75	7.50	15.00
—Black and pink label					
LP-12102 [R]	Song of the Old Waterwheel	1966	3.00	6.00	12.00
—Black and green label					
LP-12194 [S]	Slim Whitman Sings	1962	7.50	15.00	30.00
—Black label with silver top					
LP-12194 [S]	Slim Whitman Sings	1964	5.00	10.00	20.00
—Black and pink label					
LP-12194 [S]	Slim Whitman Sings	1966	3.75	7.50	15.00
—Black and green label					
LP-12268 [S]	Country Songs/City Hits	1964	5.00	10.00	20.00
—Black and pink label					
LP-12268 [S]	Country Songs/City Hits	1966	3.75	7.50	15.00
—Black and green label					
LP-12277 [S]	Love Song of the Waterfall	1964	5.00	10.00	20.00
—Black and pink label					
LP-12277 [S]	Love Song of the Waterfall	1966	3.75	7.50	15.00
—Black and green label					
LP-12288 [S]	Reminiscing	1965	5.00	10.00	20.00
—Black and pink label					
LP-12288 [S]	Reminiscing	1966	3.75	7.50	15.00
—Black and green label					
LP-12303 [S]	More Than Yesterday	1965	5.00	10.00	20.00
—Black and pink label					
LP-12303 [S]	More Than Yesterday	1966	3.75	7.50	15.00
—Black and green label					
LP-12313 [S]	A Travelin' Man	1966	3.75	7.50	15.00
LP-12333 [S]	A Time for Love	1966	3.75	7.50	15.00
LP-12342 [S]	15th Anniversary	1967	3.00	6.00	12.00
LP-12356 [S]	Country Memories	1967	3.00	6.00	12.00
LP-12375	In Love, The Whitman Way	1968	3.00	6.00	12.00
LP-12411	Happy Street	1969	3.00	6.00	12.00
LP-12436	Slim	1969	3.00	6.00	12.00
LP-12448	The Slim Whitman Christmas Album	1969	3.75	7.50	15.00

LIBERTY

Number	Title (A Side/B Side)	Yr	VG	VG+	NM
LM-1005	The Very Best of Slim Whitman	1981	2.00	4.00	8.00
—Reissue of United Artists 1005					
LM-1067	The Slim Whitman Christmas Album	1980	2.00	4.00	8.00
—Abridged reissue of Imperial 12448					
SL-8128	All My Best	1981	3.00	6.00	12.00
—Mail-order album					
LN-10033	Red River Valley	1981	2.00	4.00	8.00
—Budget-line reissue					
LN-10123	Till We Meet Again	1981	2.00	4.00	8.00
—Budget-line reissue					
LN-10124	Ghost Riders in the Sky	1981	2.00	4.00	8.00
—Budget-line reissue					
LN-10125	The Best of Slim Whitman, Vol. 2	1981	2.00	4.00	8.00
—Budget-line reissue					
LN-10152	God's Hand in Mine	1981	2.00	4.00	8.00
—Budget-line reissue					
LN-10153	Country Songs/City Hits	1981	2.00	4.00	8.00
—Budget-line reissue					

PAIR

Number	Title (A Side/B Side)	Yr	VG	VG+	NM
PDL2-1085 [(2)]	One of a Kind	1986	3.00	6.00	12.00

PICKWICK

Number	Title (A Side/B Side)	Yr	VG	VG+	NM
SPC-3590	Happy Anniversary	1978	2.50	5.00	10.00

RCA CAMDEN

Number	Title (A Side/B Side)	Yr	VG	VG+	NM
CAL-954 [M]	Birmingham Jail	1966	5.00	10.00	20.00
CAS-954(e) [R]	Birmingham Jail	1966	3.00	6.00	12.00

RCA VICTOR

Number	Title (A Side/B Side)	Yr	VG	VG+	NM
LPM-3217 [10]	Slim Whitman Sings and Yodels	1954	75.00	150.00	300.00
AYL1-3774	Birmingham Jail	1980	2.00	4.00	8.00
—"Best Buy Series" reissue					

SUNSET

Number	Title (A Side/B Side)	Yr	VG	VG+	NM
SUM-1112 [M]	Unchain Your Heart	1966	3.00	6.00	12.00
SUM-1167 [M]	Lonesome Heart	1967	3.00	6.00	12.00
SUS-5112 [R]	Unchain Your Heart	1966	3.00	6.00	12.00
SUS-5167 [R]	Lonesome Heart	1967	3.00	6.00	12.00
SUS-5267	Slim Whitman	1969	3.00	6.00	12.00
SUS-5320	Ramblin' Rose	1970	2.50	5.00	10.00

UNITED ARTISTS

Number	Title (A Side/B Side)	Yr	VG	VG+	NM
UA-LA046-F	I'll See You When I Get There	1973	2.50	5.00	10.00
UA-LA245-G	The Very Best of Slim Whitman	1974	2.50	5.00	10.00
UA-LA319-G	Happy Anniversary	1974	2.50	5.00	10.00
UA-LA386-E	The Very Best of Slim Whitman	1974	2.50	5.00	10.00
UA-LA513-G	Everything Leads Back to You	1975	2.50	5.00	10.00
UA-LA752-G	Red River Valley	1977	2.50	5.00	10.00
UA-LA787-G	Home on the Range	1978	2.50	5.00	10.00
LM-1005	The Very Best of Slim Whitman	1980	2.50	5.00	10.00
UAS-6763	Tomorrow Never Comes	1970	3.00	6.00	12.00
UAS-6783	Guess Who	1970	3.00	6.00	12.00
UAS-6819	It's a Sin to Tell a Lie	1971	3.00	6.00	12.00
UAS-6832	The Best of Slim Whitman	1972	3.00	6.00	12.00

WHITNEY SUNDAY

Albums

DECCA

Number	Title (A Side/B Side)	Yr	VG	VG+	NM
DL 75239	Whitney Sunday	1970	5.00	10.00	20.00

WHITTAKER, ROGER

45s

MAIN STREET

Number	Title (A Side/B Side)	Yr	VG	VG+	NM
93016	I Love You Because/Eternally	1983	—	2.50	5.00

RCA

Number	Title (A Side/B Side)	Yr	VG	VG+	NM
PB-10874	Here We Stand/Before She Breaks My Heart	1976	—	2.00	4.00
PB-11218	Last Song/Sea Gull	1978	—	2.00	4.00
PB-11300	Love Last Forever/If I Knew Just What to Say	1978	—	2.00	4.00
PB-11760	You Are My Miracle/Blow Gentle Breeze	1979	—	2.00	4.00
PB-11941	You Are My Miracle/Blow Gentle Breeze	1980	—	—	3.00
PB-11966	Wishes/I Was Born	1980	—	—	3.00
PB-12096	River Lady/Lighthouse	1980	—	—	—
—Unreleased					
PB-12110	A Man Without Love/I Am But a Small Voice	1980	—	—	3.00
PB-12165	Tall Dark Stranger/Goodbye	1981	—	—	3.00
PB-12330	How Does It Feel/Moonshine	1981	—	—	3.00
PB-13030	River Lady/Smooth Sailing	1981	—	—	3.00
JB-13379 [DJ]	Too Beautiful to Cry/Together	1982	—	2.50	5.00
PB-14043	Take a Little-Give a Little/Dover to Calais	1985	—	—	3.00
PB-14147	My Silver Eagle/Chicago Girl	1985	—	—	3.00
PB-14333	The Genius of Love/Everybody's Got a Lonely Heart	1986	—	—	3.00

RCA VICTOR

Number	Title (A Side/B Side)	Yr	VG	VG+	NM
PB-10356	I Don't Believe In It Anymore/New World in the Morning	1975	—	2.00	4.00
PB-10447	Durham Town (The Leaving)/Mexican Whistler	1975	—	2.00	4.00
GB-10494	The Last Farewell/Paradise	1975	—	—	3.00
—Gold Standard Series					
PB-10732	Summer Days/The First Hello, The Last Goodbye	1976	—	2.00	4.00
PB-50030	The Last Farewell/Paradise	1975	—	2.00	4.00
—Canadian number, but pressed and released in the U.S. as well					
74-0320	New World in the Morning/Durham Town	1970	2.00	4.00	8.00
74-0355	I Don't Believe in It Anymore/I Should Have Taken My Time	1970	—	3.00	6.00
74-0442	Why/Moonshine	1971	—	3.00	6.00
74-0501	The Mexican Whistler/What Love Is	1971	—	3.00	6.00

UNIVERSAL

Number	Title (A Side/B Side)	Yr	VG	VG+	NM
UVL-66010	Have I Told You Lately That I Love You/Just Across the Rio Grande	1989	—	2.00	4.00
UVL-66030	There Goes My Everything/Love Still Means You to Me	1989	—	2.00	4.00

Albums

CAPITOL NASHVILLE

Number	Title (A Side/B Side)	Yr	VG	VG+	NM
C1 594058	World's Most Beautiful Christmas Songs	1990	3.75	7.50	15.00
—Available on vinyl through Columbia House only					

PAIR

Number	Title (A Side/B Side)	Yr	VG	VG+	NM
PDL2-1039 [(2)]	Golden Tones	1986	3.00	6.00	12.00
PDL2-1111 [(2)]	Fire and Rain	1986	3.00	6.00	12.00

RCA VICTOR

Number	Title (A Side/B Side)	Yr	VG	VG+	NM
AFL1-0078	Traveling with Roger Whittaker	1978	2.50	5.00	10.00
—Reissue of APL1-0078					
APL1-0078	Traveling with Roger Whittaker	1973	3.75	7.50	15.00
AFL1-0855	"The Last Farewell" and Other Hits	1978	2.50	5.00	10.00
—Reissue of APL1-0855					
APL1-0855	"The Last Farewell" and Other Hits	1975	3.00	6.00	12.00

Number	Title (A Side/B Side)	Yr	VG	VG+	NM
AQL1-0855	"The Last Farewell" and Other Hits	198?	2.00	4.00	8.00
—Reissue of AFL1-0855					
AFL1-1313	The Magical World of Roger Whittaker	1978	2.50	5.00	10.00
—Reissue of APL1-1313					
APL1-1313	The Magical World of Roger Whittaker	1976	3.00	6.00	12.00
ANL1-1405	Roger Whittaker	1976	3.00	6.00	12.00
AFL1-1853	Reflections of Love	1978	2.50	5.00	10.00
—Reissue of APL1-1853					
APL1-1853	Reflections of Love	1976	3.00	6.00	12.00
AFL1-2255	The Best of Roger Whittaker	1978	2.50	5.00	10.00
—Reissue of APL1-2255					
APL1-2255	The Best of Roger Whittaker	1977	3.00	6.00	12.00
AQL1-2255	The Best of Roger Whittaker	198?	2.00	4.00	8.00
—Reissue of AFL1-2255					
AFL1-2525	Folk Songs	1978	3.00	6.00	12.00
AQL1-2525	Folk Songs	198?	2.50	5.00	10.00
—Reissue of AFL1-2525					
ANL1-2933	The Roger Whittaker Christmas Album	1978	3.00	6.00	12.00
AFL1-3077	Imagine	1978	3.00	6.00	12.00
AQL1-3077	Imagine	198?	2.00	4.00	8.00
—Reissue of AFL1-3077					
AFL1-3355	When I Need You	1979	2.50	5.00	10.00
AFL1-3501	Mirrors of My Mind	1979	2.50	5.00	10.00
AQL1-3501	Mirrors of My Mind	198?	2.00	4.00	8.00
—Reissue of AFL1-3501					
AFL1-3518	Voyager	1980	2.50	5.00	10.00
AQL1-3518	Voyager	198?	2.00	4.00	8.00
—Reissue of AFL1-3518					
AYL1-3670	The Magical World of Roger Whittaker	1980	2.00	4.00	8.00
—"Best Buy Series" reissue					
AFL1-3778	With Love	1980	2.50	5.00	10.00
AYL1-3911	When I Need You	1981	2.00	4.00	8.00
—"Best Buy Series" reissue					
AYL1-3946	A Special Kind of Man	1981	2.00	4.00	8.00
—"Best Buy Series" reissue					
CPL2-4057 [(2)]	Live in Concert	1981	3.00	6.00	12.00
AFL1-4129	Changes	1982	2.50	5.00	10.00
AYL1-4177	I Don't Believe in It Any More	1982	2.00	4.00	8.00
—"Best Buy Series" reissue					
AYL1-4178	New World in the Morning	1982	2.00	4.00	8.00
—"Best Buy Series" reissue					
AFL1-4321	The Wind Beneath My Wings	1983	2.50	5.00	10.00
AFL1-4340	New World in the Morning	1978	2.50	5.00	10.00
—Reissue of LSP-4340					
LPM-4340	New World in the Morning	1970	3.75	7.50	15.00
AFL1-4405	I Don't Believe in It Any More	1978	2.50	5.00	10.00
—Reissue of LSP-4405					
LPM-4405	I Don't Believe in It Any More	1970	3.75	7.50	15.00
AFL1-4505	A Special Kind of Man	1978	2.50	5.00	10.00
—Reissue of LSP-4505					
LPM-4505	A Special Kind of Man	1971	3.75	7.50	15.00
LPM-4652	Loose and Fiery	1972	3.75	7.50	15.00
AYL1-5166	The Best of Roger Whittaker	1985	—	3.00	6.00
—"Best Buy Series" reissue					
AFL1-5803	The Genius of Love	1986	2.50	5.00	10.00
NFL1-8047	Take a Little — Give a Little	1985	2.50	5.00	10.00

WHO, THE

Also see ROGER DALTREY; JOHN ENTWISTLE; KEITH MOON; PETE TOWNSHEND.

12-Inch Singles

Number	Title (A Side/B Side)	Yr	VG	VG+	NM
MCA					
L33-1257 [DJ]	Twist and Shout/I Can't Explain/My Generation	1984	2.50	5.00	10.00
WARNER BROS.					
PRO-A-938 [DJ]	You Better You Bet (LP Version) (Edited Version)	1981	2.50	5.00	10.00
PRO-A-1065 [DJ]	Athena (same on both sides)	1982	2.00	4.00	8.00
PRO-A-1087 [DJ]	Eminence Front (LP Version) (Edited Version)	1982	2.50	5.00	10.00

45s

Number	Title (A Side/B Side)	Yr	VG	VG+	NM
ATCO					
6409	Substitute/Waltz for a Pig	1966	12.50	25.00	50.00
6509	Substitute/Waltz for a Pig	1967	5.00	10.00	20.00
DECCA					
31725	I Can't Explain/Bald Headed Woman	1965	7.50	15.00	30.00
31801	Anyway, Anyhow, Anywhere/Anytime You Want Me	1965	12.50	25.00	50.00
31877	My Generation/Out in the Street (You're Going to Know Me)	1965	7.50	15.00	30.00
31988	The Kids Are Alright/A Legal Matter	1966	7.50	15.00	30.00
32058	I'm a Boy/In the City	1966	7.50	15.00	30.00
32114	Happy Jack/Whiskey Man	1967	7.50	15.00	30.00
32114 [PS]	Happy Jack/Whiskey Man	1967	12.50	25.00	50.00
32156	Pictures of Lily/Doctor, Doctor	1967	5.00	10.00	20.00
32206	I Can See for Miles/Mary-Anne with the Shaky Hands	1967	5.00	10.00	20.00
32288	Call Me Lightning/Dr. Jeckyll & Mr. Hyde	1968	6.25	12.50	25.00
32362	Magic Bus/Someone's Coming	1968	3.75	7.50	15.00
32465	Pinball Wizard/Dogs Part Two	1969	2.50	5.00	10.00
32465 [PS]	Pinball Wizard/Dogs Part Two	1969	5.00	10.00	20.00
32519	I'm Free/We're Not Gonna Take It	1969	2.50	5.00	10.00
32670	The Seeker/Here for More	1970	3.00	6.00	12.00
32708	Summertime Blues/Heaven and Hell	1970	3.00	6.00	12.00
32729	See Me, Feel Me/Overture from Tommy	1970	3.00	6.00	12.00
—With custom gold label					
32729 [PS]	See Me, Feel Me/Overture from Tommy	1970	5.00	10.00	20.00
32737	Young Man (Blues)/Substitute	1970	62.50	125.00	250.00
—Stock copies do exist					
32737 [DJ]	Young Man (Blues)/Substitute	1970	37.50	75.00	150.00
32737 [PS]	Young Man (Blues)/Substitute	1970	125.00	250.00	500.00
32846	Won't Get Fooled Again/I Don't Even Know Myself	1971	2.50	5.00	10.00
32888	Behind Blue Eyes/My Wife	1971	2.50	5.00	10.00
32983	Join Together/Baby, Don't You Do It	1972	2.50	5.00	10.00
34444 [DJ]	Happy Jack (same on both sides)	1967	10.00	20.00	40.00
—Promo-only number, pink label					
34470 [DJ]	Pictures of Lily (same on both sides)	1967	10.00	20.00	40.00
—Promo-only number, pink label					
7-34610/3 [DJ]	Excerpts from Tommy	1970	50.00	100.00	200.00
—Promo-only four-record box set with box and 4-page insert. As the records are sometimes found separately, they are also priced individually below.					
7-34610 [DJ]	Amazing Journey/The Acid Queen	1970	6.25	12.50	25.00
7-34611 [DJ]	Go to the Mirror Boy/Tommy Can You Hear Me	1970	6.25	12.50	25.00
7-34612 [DJ]	Smash the Mirror/Sensation	1970	6.25	12.50	25.00
7-34613 [DJ]	Sally Simpson/I'm Free	1970	6.25	12.50	25.00
MCA					
L45-1809 [DJ]	Had Enough (same on both sides)	1978	2.50	5.00	10.00
40475	Squeeze Box/Success Story	1975	—	2.50	5.00
40475 [PS]	Squeeze Box/Success Story	1975	7.50	15.00	30.00
—Sleeve is promo only					
40603	Slip Kid/Dreaming from the Waist	1976	—	2.50	5.00
40948	Who Are You/Had Enough	1978	—	2.50	5.00
40978	Trick of the Light/9:05	1978	—	2.50	5.00
41053	Long Live Rock/My Wife	1979	—	2.50	5.00
MERCURY					
DJ-570 [DJ]	I'm the Face/Zoot Suit	1980	—	2.50	5.00
DJ-570 [PS]	I'm the Face/Zoot Suit	1980	—	2.50	5.00
—As "The High Numbers"					
POLYDOR					
2022	5:15/I'm One	1979	—	2.00	4.00
2022 [PS]	5:15/I'm One	1979	—	2.50	5.00
TRACK					
32983	Join Together/Baby, Don't You Do It	1972	5.00	10.00	20.00
—Later pressing than Decca 32983, but much scarcer					
33041	The Relay/Waspman	1972	2.50	5.00	10.00
40152	Love, Reign O'er Me/Water	1973	2.00	4.00	8.00
40182	The Real Me/I'm One	1974	2.00	4.00	8.00
40330	Postcard/Put the Money Down	1974	10.00	20.00	40.00
WARNER BROS.					
29731	It's Hard/Dangerous	1983	—	2.50	5.00
29814	Eminence Front/One at a Time	1983	—	2.50	5.00
29905	Athena/It's Your Turn	1982	—	2.00	4.00
29905 [PS]	Athena/It's Your Turn	1982	—	2.50	5.00
49698	You Better You Bet/Quiet One	1981	—	2.00	4.00
49698 [PS]	You Better You Bet/Quiet One	1981	—	2.50	5.00
49743	Don't Let Go the Coat/You	1981	—	2.00	4.00

Albums

Number	Title (A Side/B Side)	Yr	VG	VG+	NM
DECCA					
DL 4664 [M]	The Who Sing My Generation	1966	25.00	50.00	100.00
DL 4664 [M-DJ]	The Who Sing My Generation	1966	50.00	100.00	200.00
—White label promo					
DL 4892 [M]	Happy Jack	1967	12.50	25.00	50.00
DL 4892 [M-DJ]	Happy Jack	1967	37.50	75.00	150.00
—White label promo					
DL 4950 [M]	The Who Sell Out	1967	25.00	50.00	100.00
DL 4950 [M-DJ]	The Who Sell Out	1967	50.00	100.00	200.00
—White label promo with songs in the same order as the stock copy					
DL 4950 [M-DJ]	The Who Sell Out	1967	75.00	150.00	300.00
—White label promo with side 1 banded for airplay and all the commercials on one side					
DL 5064 [M-DJ]	Magic Bus — The Who on Tour	1968	50.00	100.00	200.00
—White label promo; no stock copies were released in mono					
DXSW 7205 [(2)]	Tommy	1969	10.00	20.00	40.00
—With booklet					
DXSW 7205 [(2) DJ]	Tommy	1969	50.00	100.00	200.00
—White label promo					
DL 74664 [R]	The Who Sing My Generation	1966	15.00	30.00	60.00
DL 74664 [R-DJ]	The Who Sing My Generation	1966	50.00	100.00	200.00
—White label promo					
DL 74892 [P]	Happy Jack	1967	12.50	25.00	50.00
—All stereo except that "Happy Jack" and "Don't Look Away" are rechanneled					
DL 74892 [P-DJ]	Happy Jack	1967	37.50	75.00	150.00
—White label promo					
DL 74950 [S]	The Who Sell Out	1967	12.50	25.00	50.00
DL 74950 [S-DJ]	The Who Sell Out	1967	62.50	125.00	250.00
—White label promo with songs in the same order as the stock copy					
DL 74950 [S-DJ]	The Who Sell Out	1967	100.00	200.00	400.00
—White label promo with side 1 banded for airplay and all the commercials on one side					
DL 75064 [P]	Magic Bus — The Who on Tour	1968	12.50	25.00	50.00
—All rechanneled except "Magic Bus" and "I Can't Reach You," which are true stereo.					
DL 75064 [P-DJ]	Magic Bus — The Who on Tour	1968	37.50	75.00	150.00
DL 79175	Live at Leeds	1970	10.00	20.00	40.00
—With gatefold cover and numerous inserts					
DL 79182	Who's Next	1971	6.25	12.50	25.00
DL 79184	Meaty Beaty Big and Bouncy	1971	7.50	15.00	30.00
—With poster (deduct 1/3 if missing)					
DL 734586	The Who/The Strawberry Alarm Clock	1969	25.00	50.00	100.00
—Special Products release for Philco. One side has Who songs, the other, Strawberry Alarm Clock songs					
DIRECT DISC					
SD 16610	Who Are You	1980	7.50	15.00	30.00
—Audiophile vinyl					
LIFE					
DL 74664 [R]	The Who Sing My Generation	1967	37.50	75.00	150.00
MCA					
1496	Who's Greatest Hits	1987	2.00	4.00	8.00
1577	Live at Leeds	1988	2.00	4.00	8.00
1578	Meaty Beaty Big and Bouncy	1988	2.00	4.00	8.00
1579	The Who By Numbers	1988	2.00	4.00	8.00
1580	Who Are You	1988	2.00	4.00	8.00
L33-1987 [DJ]	Who Are You	1978	6.25	12.50	25.00
—White label promo with sticker "Who Are You Edited for Broadcast" on cover -- the line "Who the fuck are you?" is deleted twice.					
2022	Live at Leeds	1973	3.00	6.00	12.00
2023	Who's Next	1973	3.00	6.00	12.00
2025	Meaty Beaty Big and Bouncy	1973	3.00	6.00	12.00
2044 [R]	The Who Sing My Generation	1974	12.50	25.00	50.00
2045 [P]	Happy Jack	1974	12.50	25.00	50.00
2161	The Who By Numbers	1975	3.00	6.00	12.00
3023	Live at Leeds	1977	2.50	5.00	10.00
3024	Who's Next	1977	2.50	5.00	10.00
3025	Meaty Beaty Big and Bouncy	1977	2.50	5.00	10.00
3026	The Who By Numbers	1977	2.50	5.00	10.00
3050	Who Are You	1978	2.50	5.00	10.00

Number	Title (A Side/B Side)	Yr	VG	VG+	NM
4067 [(2) P]	A Quick One/The Who Sell Out	1976	5.00	10.00	20.00
—Black labels with rainbow					
4067 [(2) P]	A Quick One/The Who Sell Out	1978	3.75	7.50	15.00
—Tan labels					
4067 [(2) P]	A Quick One/The Who Sell Out	1980	3.00	6.00	12.00
—Blue labels with rainbow					
4068 [(2) P]	Magic Bus/The Who Sing My Generation	1976	5.00	10.00	20.00
—Black labels with rainbow					
4068 [(2) P]	Magic Bus/The Who Sing My Generation	1978	3.75	7.50	15.00
—Tan labels					
4068 [(2) P]	Magic Bus/The Who Sing My Generation	1980	3.00	6.00	12.00
—Blue labels with rainbow					
5220	Who's Next	1979	2.00	4.00	8.00
5408	Who's Greatest Hits	1983	2.00	4.00	8.00
5641	Who's Missing	1986	2.50	5.00	10.00
5712	Two's Missing	1987	2.50	5.00	10.00
6895 [(2)]	Quadrophenia	1980	2.50	5.00	10.00
6899 [(2)]	The Kids Are Alright	1980	2.50	5.00	10.00
—Early versions have number stamped in gold on cover with 11005 records. No difference in value.					
8018 [(2)]	Who's Last	1984	2.50	5.00	10.00
8031 [(2)]	Who's Better, Who's Best	1989	3.75	7.50	15.00
10004 [(2)]	Quadrophenia	1973	3.75	7.50	15.00
—Black labels with rainbow					
10004 [(2)]	Quadrophenia	1978	3.00	6.00	12.00
—Tan labels					
10005 [(2)]	Tommy	1973	3.75	7.50	15.00
—Black labels with rainbow					
10005 [(2)]	Tommy	1978	3.00	6.00	12.00
—Tan labels					
10005 [(2)]	Tommy	1980	2.50	5.00	10.00
—Blue labels with rainbow					
11005 [(2)]	The Kids Are Alright	1979	3.00	6.00	12.00
11164	Who's Next	1995	6.25	12.50	25.00
—"Heavy Vinyl" reissue on 180-gram vinyl with gatefold cover					
12001 [(2)]	Hooligans	1981	2.50	5.00	10.00
14950 [PD]	Who Are You	1978	3.75	7.50	15.00
—Picture disc					
19501 [(3)]	Join Together	1990	5.00	10.00	20.00
—Box set with booklet					
25986	It's Hard	1989	2.00	4.00	8.00
25987	Face Dances	1989	2.00	4.00	8.00
37000	Live at Leeds	1979	2.00	4.00	8.00
37001	Meaty Beaty Big and Bouncy	1979	2.00	4.00	8.00
37002	The Who By Numbers	1979	2.00	4.00	8.00
37003	Who Are You	1979	2.00	4.00	8.00
37169	Odds and Sods	1980	2.00	4.00	8.00
MOBILE FIDELITY					
1-115	Face Dances	1984	6.25	12.50	25.00
—Audiophile vinyl					
TRACK					
2126	Odds and Sods	1974	6.25	12.50	25.00
2-4067 [(2) P]	A Quick One/The Who Sell Out	1974	6.25	12.50	25.00
2-4068 [(2) P]	Magic Bus/The Who Sing My Generation	1974	6.25	12.50	25.00
10004 [(2)]	Quadrophenia	1973	5.00	10.00	20.00
WARNER BROS.					
WBMS-116 [DJ]	Filling in the Gaps	1981	20.00	40.00	80.00
—With drawing on cover					
WBMS-116 [DJ]	Filling in the Gaps	1981	12.50	25.00	50.00
—With generic "Warner Bros. Music Show" cover					
HS 3516	Face Dances	1981	2.00	4.00	8.00
23731	It's Hard	1982	2.00	4.00	8.00
23731 [DJ]	It's Hard	1982	7.50	15.00	30.00
—Promo version on Quiex II vinyl					

WHOLE OATS

See DARYL HALL AND JOHN OATES.

WHYTE BOOTS, THE

45s

Number	Title (A Side/B Side)	Yr	VG	VG+	NM
PHILIPS					
40422	Nightmare/Let No One Come Between Us	1967	20.00	40.00	80.00

WICHITA TRAIN WHISTLE, THE

Produced by MICHAEL NESMITH.

45s

Number	Title (A Side/B Side)	Yr	VG	VG+	NM
DOT					
17152	Tapioca Tundra/Don't Cry Now	1968	3.75	7.50	15.00

Albums

Number	Title (A Side/B Side)	Yr	VG	VG+	NM
DOT					
DLP-25861	Mike Nesmith Presents/The Wichita Train Whistle Sings	1968	7.50	15.00	30.00

WIER, RUSTY

45s

Number	Title (A Side/B Side)	Yr	VG	VG+	NM
20TH CENTURY					
2219	Don't It Make You Wanna Dance/I Believe in the Way That You Love Me	1975	—	2.50	5.00
2273	I Don't Want to Lay This Guitar Down/Long and Lonesome Highway Blues	1976	—	2.50	5.00
ABC					
12019	Stoned, Slow and Rugged/Jeremiah Black	1974	—	3.00	6.00
BLACK HAT					
102	Close Your Eyes/Kum-Back Bar and Grill	1987	—	3.00	6.00
103	(Lover of the) Other Side of the Hill/I Kept Thinkin' About You	1987	—	3.00	6.00
COLUMBIA					
3-10445	I Think It's Time (I Learned How to Let Her Go)/Me and Daisy on the Run	1976	—	2.00	4.00
COMPLEAT					
107	Don't It Make You Wanna Dance/You Gave Me a Reason	1983	—	2.50	5.00
121	Lone Star Lady/I Still Believe in You	1984	—	2.50	5.00
LONGHORN					
101	(Lover of the) Other Side of the Hill/(B-side unknown)	1965	3.75	7.50	15.00

Albums

Number	Title (A Side/B Side)	Yr	VG	VG+	NM
20TH CENTURY					
T-469	Don't It Make You Wanna Dance?	1975	2.50	5.00	10.00
T-495	Rusty Wier	1975	2.50	5.00	10.00
ABC					
D-820	Stoned, Slow and Rugged	1974	3.00	6.00	12.00
COLUMBIA					
KC 34319	Black Hat Saloon	1976	2.50	5.00	10.00
PC 34775	Stacked Deck	1977	2.50	5.00	10.00
MCA					
820	Stoned, Slow and Rugged	1980	2.00	4.00	8.00
—Reissue of ABC 820					

WIGGINS, JAY

45s

Number	Title (A Side/B Side)	Yr	VG	VG+	NM
AMY					
955	Sad Girl/No, Not Me	1966	2.50	5.00	10.00
I.P.G.					
1008	Sad Girl/No, Not Me	196?	3.75	7.50	15.00
1015	Forgive Then Forget/My Lonely Girl	196?	3.00	6.00	12.00

WIGGINS, WALLY

45s

Number	Title (A Side/B Side)	Yr	VG	VG+	NM
MERCURY					
71645	I Need You/Maybe Someday	1960	20.00	40.00	80.00
71713	Maybellene/Sweeter Than Sweet	1960	5.00	10.00	20.00
71953	The Habit of Loving You/Little Old Lady Who Lives in a Shoe	1962	7.50	15.00	30.00

WIGWAM

45s

Number	Title (A Side/B Side)	Yr	VG	VG+	NM
VERVE FORECAST					
5114	Call Me on Your Telephone/Wishful Thinker	1970	2.00	4.00	8.00

Albums

Number	Title (A Side/B Side)	Yr	VG	VG+	NM
VERVE FORECAST					
FTS-3089	Tombstone Valentine	1970	5.00	10.00	20.00

WILBURN BROTHERS, THE

45s

Number	Title (A Side/B Side)	Yr	VG	VG+	NM
DECCA					
29459	I Wanna Wanna Wanna/My Heart or My Mind	1955	5.00	10.00	20.00
29614	Temptation Go Away/Mixed-Up Medley	1955	5.00	10.00	20.00
29747	You're Not Play Love/Look Around, Take a Look at Me	1955	5.00	10.00	20.00
29887	I'm So in Love with You/Deep Elem Blues	1956	5.00	10.00	20.00
30087	Go Away with Me/Great Big Love	1956	5.00	10.00	20.00
30228	Nothing at All/I'm Setting You Free	1957	3.75	7.50	15.00
30428	I Close My Eyes/I Got Over the Blues	1957	3.75	7.50	15.00
30591	Oo Bop Sha Boom/My Baby Ain't My Baby No More	1958	7.50	15.00	30.00
30686	Cry Baby Cry/Till I'm the Only One	1958	3.75	7.50	15.00
30787	Which One Is to Blame/The Knoxville Girl	1958	3.75	7.50	15.00
30871	Somebody's Back in Town/I Love Everybody	1959	3.75	7.50	15.00
30968	A Woman's Intuition/A Town That Never Sleeps	1959	3.75	7.50	15.00
31062	Sentenced to Die/You Can't Take It With You	1960	3.00	6.00	12.00
31114	When Will You Know It/Big Heartbreak	1960	3.00	6.00	12.00
31152	The Best of All My Heartaches/Someone Else's Love	1960	3.00	6.00	12.00
31214	The Flame's Still Burning/The Legend of the Big River Train	1961	3.00	6.00	12.00
31276	Blue Blue Day/No Legal Right	1961	3.00	6.00	12.00
31333	Tag Along/Gift of the Blues	1961	3.00	6.00	12.00
31363	Trouble's Back in Town/Young But True Love	1962	3.00	6.00	12.00
31425	The Sound of Your Footsteps/Day After Day	1962	3.00	6.00	12.00
31464	Roll Muddy River/Not That I Care	1963	3.00	6.00	12.00
31520	Tell Her So/Here Comes a Million Memories	1963	3.00	6.00	12.00
31578	Hangin' Around/Never Alone	1964	2.50	5.00	10.00
31625	Impossible/I'll Take What's Left of Me	1964	2.50	5.00	10.00
31674	I'm Gonna Tie One On Tonight/Making Plans	1964	2.50	5.00	10.00
31764	I Had One Too Many/Left Out	1965	2.50	5.00	10.00
31819	It's Another World/My Day Won't Be Complete	1965	2.50	5.00	10.00
31894	Someone Before Me/Something About You	1966	2.50	5.00	10.00
31974	I Can't Keep Away from You/I'm Gonna Dress Up	1966	2.50	5.00	10.00
32038	Hurt Her Once for Me/Just to Be Where You Are	1966	2.50	5.00	10.00
32117	Roarin' Again/Go Mena Si (I'm Sorry)	1967	2.00	4.00	8.00
32169	Goody, Goody Gumdrop/You're Standing in the Way	1967	2.00	4.00	8.00
32225	I'm Leavin'/Wastin' My Time	1967	2.00	4.00	8.00
32292	Shakiest Gun in the West/She'll Walk All Over You	1968	2.00	4.00	8.00
32386	We Need a Lot More Happiness/If You're with Me	1968	2.00	4.00	8.00
32449	It Looks Like the Sun's Gonna Shine/Make My Heart Die Away	1969	2.00	4.00	8.00
32531	Signs Are Everywhere/Who Could Ask for More	1969	2.00	4.00	8.00
32597	Gift of the Blues/Tag Along	1969	2.00	4.00	8.00
32608	Little Johnny from Down the Street/Which Side's the Wrong Side	1970	2.00	4.00	8.00
32683	Lilacs in Winter/Country Boy (Sing Your Heart Out)	1970	2.00	4.00	8.00
32771	Little Eyes That Look at Me/I've Gotta Hang My Hat Up on the Wind	1971	2.00	4.00	8.00
32835	That She's Leaving Feeling/Everything I Am	1971	2.00	4.00	8.00
32909	The War Keeps Draggin' On/Bloomin' Fools	1971	2.00	4.00	8.00
32921	Arkansas/Santa Fe Rolls Royce	1972	2.00	4.00	8.00
32978	Opryland/Hard Times Have Been There	1972	2.00	4.00	8.00
33027	The City's Goin' Country/Minds of Lonely Men	1972	2.00	4.00	8.00
MCA					
40042	Simon Crutchfield's Grave/Treat the Dog Like a Dog	1973	—	2.50	5.00

Number	Title (A Side/B Side)	Yr	VG	VG+	NM
40264	There Must Be More to Love Than This/You've Still Got a Place in My Heart	1974	—	2.50	5.00
40473	Country Honey/Milwaukee, You're in Trouble	1975	—	2.50	5.00
40577	Country Kind of Feeling/Goin' and Comin'	1975	—	2.50	5.00
SCORPION					
0558	Mama's Shoe Box/What a Way to Go	1978	—	2.00	4.00
Albums					
DECCA					
DL 4058 [M]	The Big Heartbreak	1960	7.50	15.00	30.00
DL 4142 [M]	The Wilburn Brothers Sing	1961	7.50	15.00	30.00
DL 4211 [M]	City Limits	1961	7.50	15.00	30.00
DL 4225 [M]	Folk Songs	1962	5.00	10.00	20.00
DL 4391 [M]	Trouble's Back in Town	1963	5.00	10.00	20.00
DL 4464 [M]	Take Up Thy Cross	1964	5.00	10.00	20.00
DL 4544 [M]	Never Alone	1964	5.00	10.00	20.00
DL 4615 [M]	Country Gold	1965	5.00	10.00	20.00
DL 4645 [M]	I'm Gonna Tie One on Tonight	1965	5.00	10.00	20.00
DL 4721 [M]	The Wilburn Brothers Show	1966	15.00	30.00	60.00
—With guests Loretta Lynn, Ernest Tubb, Harold Morrison					
DL 4764 [M]	Let's Go Country	1966	5.00	10.00	20.00
DL 4824 [M]	Two for the Show	1967	6.25	12.50	25.00
DL 4871 [M]	Cool	1967	7.50	15.00	30.00
DL 4954 [M]	It's Another World	1968	10.00	20.00	40.00
DL 8576 [M]	The Wilburn Brothers	1957	10.00	20.00	40.00
DL 8774 [M]	Side by Side	1958	10.00	20.00	40.00
DL 8959 [M]	Livin' in God's Country	1959	10.00	20.00	40.00
DL 74058 [S]	The Big Heartbreak	1960	10.00	20.00	40.00
DL 74142 [S]	The Wilburn Brothers Sing	1961	10.00	20.00	40.00
DL 74211 [S]	City Limits	1961	10.00	20.00	40.00
DL 74225 [S]	Folk Songs	1962	7.50	15.00	30.00
DL 74391 [S]	Trouble's Back in Town	1963	7.50	15.00	30.00
DL 74464 [S]	Take Up Thy Cross	1964	6.25	12.50	25.00
DL 74544 [S]	Never Alone	1964	6.25	12.50	25.00
DL 74615 [S]	Country Gold	1965	6.25	12.50	25.00
DL 74645 [S]	I'm Gonna Tie One on Tonight	1965	6.25	12.50	25.00
DL 74721 [S]	The Wilburn Brothers Show	1966	20.00	40.00	80.00
—With guests Loretta Lynn, Ernest Tubb, Harold Morrison					
DL 74764 [S]	Let's Go Country	1966	6.25	12.50	25.00
DL 74824 [S]	Two for the Show	1967	5.00	10.00	20.00
DL 74871 [S]	Cool	1967	5.00	10.00	20.00
DL 74954 [S]	It's Another World	1968	5.00	10.00	20.00
DL 75173	Little Johnny from Down the Street	1970	5.00	10.00	20.00
DL 75214	Sing Your Heart Out Country Boy	1971	5.00	10.00	20.00
DL 75291	That She's Leaving Feeling	1972	5.00	10.00	20.00
DL 88774 [S]	Side by Side	1959	15.00	30.00	60.00
DL 88959 [S]	Livin' in God's Country	1959	15.00	30.00	60.00
KING					
746 [M]	The Wonderful Wilburn Brothers	1961	25.00	50.00	100.00
MCA					
4011 [(2)]	Portrait	197?	3.75	7.50	15.00
MCA CORAL					
20058	That Country Feeling	1973	2.50	5.00	10.00
VOCALION					
VL 3691 [M]	Carefree Moments	1962	3.75	7.50	15.00
VL 73691 [S]	Carefree Moments	1962	3.75	7.50	15.00
VL 73876	That Country Feeling	197?	3.00	6.00	12.00
VL 73889	I Walk the Line	197?	3.00	6.00	12.00

WILCOX THREE, THE

Number	Title (A Side/B Side)	Yr	VG	VG+	NM
Albums					
RCA CAMDEN					
CAL-669 [M]	The Greatest Folk Songs Ever Sung	1961	5.00	10.00	20.00

WILD, JACK

Number	Title (A Side/B Side)	Yr	VG	VG+	NM
45s					
BUDDAH					
241	(Holy Moses) Everything's Coming Up Roses/Bring Yourself Back to Me	1971	2.00	4.00	8.00
CAPITOL					
2742	Some Beautiful/A Picture of You	1970	—	3.00	6.00
2742 [PS]	Some Beautiful/A Picture of You	1970	3.00	6.00	12.00
2868	Wait for Summer/Melody	1970	—	3.00	6.00
Albums					
BUDDAH					
BDS-5083	Everything's Coming Up Roses	1971	6.25	12.50	25.00
BDS-5110	A Beautiful World	1972	6.25	12.50	25.00
CAPITOL					
SKAO-545	The Jack Wild Album	1970	6.25	12.50	25.00

WILD BEES, THE

Number	Title (A Side/B Side)	Yr	VG	VG+	NM
45s					
RCA VICTOR					
47-7275	Doctor Rock/Bamboozled	1958	7.50	15.00	30.00

WILD BUTTER

Number	Title (A Side/B Side)	Yr	VG	VG+	NM
45s					
UNITED ARTISTS					
50688	Roxanna/Terribly Blind	1970	—	3.00	6.00
Albums					
UNITED ARTISTS					
UAS-6766	Wild Butter	1970	6.25	12.50	25.00

WILD-CATS, THE

Number	Title (A Side/B Side)	Yr	VG	VG+	NM
45s					
UNITED ARTISTS					
154	Gazachstahagen/Billy's Cha Cha	1958	6.25	12.50	25.00
169	Dancing Elephants/King Size Guitar	1959	6.25	12.50	25.00
Albums					
UNITED ARTISTS					
UAL-3031 [M]	Bandstand Record Hop	1958	12.50	25.00	50.00

WILD CHERRY

Number	Title (A Side/B Side)	Yr	VG	VG+	NM
45s					
A&M					
1656	Voodoo Doll/Because Your Love Is Mine	1974	—	2.50	5.00
EPIC					
50225	Play That Funky Music/The Lady Wants Your Money	1976	—	2.50	5.00
50306	Get It Up/Baby Don't You Know	1976	—	2.00	4.00
50362	Hot to Trot/Put Yourself in My Shoes	1977	—	2.00	4.00
50401	Are You Boogieing Around on Your Daddy/Hold On (With Strings)	1977	—	2.00	4.00
50500	Don't Stop, Get Off/I Love My Music	1978	—	2.00	4.00
50551	1-2-3 Kind of Love/Fools Fall in Love	1978	—	2.00	4.00
50619	This Old Heart of Mine (Is Weak for You)/Lana	1978	—	2.00	4.00
50702	Try a Piece of My Love/Take Me Back	1979	—	2.00	4.00
UNITED ARTISTS					
XW217 [DJ]	Get Down (mono/stereo)	1973	—	2.50	5.00
—Stock copy not known to exist					
Albums					
EPIC					
PE 34195	Wild Cherry	1976	3.00	6.00	12.00
PE 34462	Electrified Funk	1977	2.50	5.00	10.00
JE 35011	I Love My Music	1978	2.50	5.00	10.00
JE 35760	Only the Wild	1979	2.50	5.00	10.00

WILD COUNTRY

See ALABAMA.

WILD MAN STEVE

Number	Title (A Side/B Side)	Yr	VG	VG+	NM
Albums					
DEALER'S CHOICE					
777	Is It Good Baby	198?	3.75	7.50	15.00
780	Did He Really Say That	198?	3.75	7.50	15.00
DICK-ER					
D 70	Do Not Disturb	1972	5.00	10.00	20.00
LAFF					
181	Eatin' Ain't Cheatin'	1973	3.00	6.00	12.00
191	When You're Hot You're Hot	1976	3.00	6.00	12.00
RAW					
7000	My Man! Wild Man!	1969	3.75	7.50	15.00
7001	Wild! Wild! Wild! Wild!	1970	3.75	7.50	15.00
7002	King of Them All	1971	3.75	7.50	15.00

WILD ONES, THE (1)

Number	Title (A Side/B Side)	Yr	VG	VG+	NM
45s					
MAINLINE					
500	Caught in the Cookie Jar/Super Fox	1965	2.50	5.00	10.00
MALA					
564	High-Ho/Valerie	1967	2.00	4.00	8.00
UNITED ARTISTS					
947	Wild Thing/Just Can't Cry Anymore	1965	3.00	6.00	12.00
971	My Love/Lord Love a Duck	1966	2.50	5.00	10.00
971 [PS]	My Love/Lord Love a Duck	1966	3.75	7.50	15.00
50043	For Your Love (I Would Do Almost Anything)/Never Givin' Up (On Your Love)	1966	2.50	5.00	10.00
Albums					
UNITED ARTISTS					
UAL-3450 [M]	The Arthur Sound	1965	6.25	12.50	25.00
UAS-6450 [S]	The Arthur Sound	1965	7.50	15.00	30.00

WILD ONES, THE (2)

Number	Title (A Side/B Side)	Yr	VG	VG+	NM
45s					
SEARS					
2180	Come On Back/(Instrumental)	1966	2.50	5.00	10.00
2180 [PS]	Come On Back/(Instrumental)	1966	7.50	15.00	30.00

WILD ONES, THE (3)

Number	Title (A Side/B Side)	Yr	VG	VG+	NM
45s					
S.P.Q.R.					
3316	A Little Bit o' Soul/I've Been Crying	1964	6.25	12.50	25.00

WILD TURKEY

Number	Title (A Side/B Side)	Yr	VG	VG+	NM
Albums					
CHRYSALIS					
CHR 1010	Turkey	1973	2.50	5.00	10.00
REPRISE					
MS 2070	Battle Hymn	1972	3.00	6.00	12.00

WILDCATS, THE (1)

Number	Title (A Side/B Side)	Yr	VG	VG+	NM
45s					
RCA VICTOR					
47-6386	Keep Talkin'/Beatin' on a Rug	1956	10.00	20.00	40.00

WILDCATS, THE (2)

Actually THE BLOSSOMS.

Number	Title (A Side/B Side)	Yr	VG	VG+	NM
45s					
REPRISE					
0253	3625 Groovy Street/What Are We Gonna Do in '64	1964	5.00	10.00	20.00

WILDE, MARTY

Number	Title (A Side/B Side)	Yr	VG	VG+	NM
45s					
BELL					
45603	All Night Girl/(B-side unknown)	1974	—	2.50	5.00
EPIC					
9291	My Lucky Love/Misery's Child	1958	3.75	7.50	15.00
9356	Bad Boy/Teenage Years	1960	3.00	6.00	12.00
9392	Little Girl/Your Seventeenth Spring	1960	3.00	6.00	12.00
9400	Angry/My Baby Is Gone (Stop This World)	1960	3.00	6.00	12.00

Number	Title (A Side/B Side)	Yr	VG	VG+	NM
9424	The Part of a Fool/Forgotten Dreams	1960	—	—	—
—Unreleased?					
HERITAGE					
814	Abergavenny/Alice in Blue	1969	—	3.00	6.00
—As "Shannon"					
814 [PS]	Abergavenny/Alice in Blue	1969	2.50	5.00	10.00
—As "Shannon"					
819	Jesamine/Lullaby	1969	—	3.00	6.00
—As "Shannon"					
JAMIE					
1282	Kiss Me/My, What a Woman	1964	2.50	5.00	10.00
Albums					
EPIC					
BN 575 [S]	Wilde About Marty	1960	25.00	50.00	100.00
LN 3686 [M]	Bad Boy	1960	20.00	40.00	80.00
LN 3711 [M]	Wilde About Marty	1960	20.00	40.00	80.00

WILDERNESS ROAD

Number	Title (A Side/B Side)	Yr	VG	VG+	NM
45s					
COLUMBIA					
4-45565	Bounty Man/Dr. Morpho's Revenge	1972	2.00	4.00	8.00
Albums					
COLUMBIA					
C 31118	Wilderness Road	1972	5.00	10.00	20.00
REPRISE					
MS 2125	Sold for the Prevention of Disease Only	1973	5.00	10.00	20.00

WILDING, BOBBY

Number	Title (A Side/B Side)	Yr	VG	VG+	NM
45s					
ABC-PARAMOUNT					
10275	Mama/You Give Me No Choice	1961	3.00	6.00	12.00
DCP					
1009	I Want to Be a Beatle/Since I've Been Wearing My Hair Like a Beatle	1964	5.00	10.00	20.00
1106	I Want You/Too Young to Fall in Love	1964	3.00	6.00	12.00
MAY					
125	Slide (Part 1)/Slide (Part 2)	1962	3.00	6.00	12.00

WILDWOODS, THE

Actually THE FIVE SATINS.

Number	Title (A Side/B Side)	Yr	VG	VG+	NM
45s					
CAPRICE					
101	When the Swallows Come Back to Capistrano/Heart of Mine	1961	37.50	75.00	150.00
MAY					
106	Golden Sunset/Here Comes Big Ed	1961	7.50	15.00	30.00

WILEY, CHUCK

Number	Title (A Side/B Side)	Yr	VG	VG+	NM
45s					
JAX					
1004	I Love You So Much/I Begin to Miss You	1959	25.00	50.00	100.00
UNITED ARTISTS					
113	Tear It Up/Shake Up the Dance	1958	18.75	37.50	75.00
120	By My Side/Door to Door	1958	—	—	—
—Unreleased					

WILKENS, ARTIE, AND THE PALMS

Number	Title (A Side/B Side)	Yr	VG	VG+	NM
45s					
STATES					
157	Darling Patricia/Please Come Back	1956	150.00	300.00	600.00

WILKINSON TRI-CYCLE

Number	Title (A Side/B Side)	Yr	VG	VG+	NM
Albums					
DATE					
TES 4016	Wilkinson Tri-Cycle	1969	10.00	20.00	40.00

WILLIAMS, ANDRE

Number	Title (A Side/B Side)	Yr	VG	VG+	NM
45s					
AVIN					
103	Rib Tips (Part 1)/Rib Tips (Part 2)	1965	3.00	6.00	12.00
CHECKER					
1187	The Stroke/Humpin' Bumpin' and Trumpin'	1967	3.00	6.00	12.00
1205	Cadillac Jack/Mrs. Mother USA	1968	3.00	6.00	12.00
1214	Do the Popcorn/It's Gonna Be Fine in '69	1969	3.00	6.00	12.00
1219	Girdle Up/(Instrumental)	1969	3.00	6.00	12.00
EPIC					
9196	Bacon Fat/Just Because of a Kiss	1956	6.25	12.50	25.00
FORTUNE					
824	Pulling Time/Going Down to Tia-Juana	1955	20.00	40.00	80.00
827	Mozelle/Just Want a Little Lovin'	1956	10.00	20.00	40.00
828	Bobby Jean/It's All Over	1956	10.00	20.00	40.00
831	Bacon Fat/Just Because of a Kiss	1956	7.50	15.00	30.00
834	Mean Jean/You Are My Sunshine	1957	7.50	15.00	30.00
837	Jail Bait/My Tears	1957	20.00	40.00	80.00
839	Come On Baby/The Greasy Chicken	1957	7.50	15.00	30.00
—With Gino Park					
839	Don't Touch/Please Pass the Biscuits	1957	20.00	40.00	80.00
—With Gino Park					
839	The Greasy Chicken/Please Pass the Biscuits	1957	15.00	30.00	60.00
—With Gino Park					
842	My Last Dance with You/Hey! Country Girl	1958	7.50	15.00	30.00
847	Put a Chain on It/I'm All For You	1959	7.50	15.00	30.00
851	(Georgia May Is) Movin'/(Mmmm — Andre Williams Is) Movin'	1960	15.00	30.00	60.00
—With Gino Park					
856	Jail House Blues/I Still Love You	1960	7.50	15.00	30.00
MIRACLE					
4	Rosa Loo/Shoo Shoo	1960	300.00	600.00	1200.
NORTON					
45-069	Poor Mr. Santa (N-N-Naughty!)/Poor Mr. Santa (N-n-nice!)	1997	—	—	2.00
45-069 [PS]	Poor Mr. Santa (N-N-Naughty!)/Poor Mr. Santa (N-n-nice!)	1997	—	—	2.00
RIC-TIC					
124	You Got It And I Want It/I Can't Stop Crying	1967	6.25	12.50	25.00
RONALD					
1001	Please Give Me a Chance/(B-side unknown)	196?	6.25	12.50	25.00
SPORT					
105	Pearl Time/Soul Groove	1967	6.25	12.50	25.00
WINGATE					
014	Loose Juice/Sweet Little Pussycat	1966	3.75	7.50	15.00
021	Do It! (Part 1)/Do It! (Part 2)	1966	5.00	10.00	20.00
Albums					
SDEG					
4020	Directly from the Streets	198?	2.50	5.00	10.00

WILLIAMS, ANDY

Number	Title (A Side/B Side)	Yr	VG	VG+	NM
12-Inch Singles					
COLUMBIA					
10953	Love Theme from "Oliver's Story"/Love Story (Where Do I Begin)	1979	3.75	7.50	15.00
45s					
CADENCE					
1282	Christmas Is a Feeling in Your Heart/The Wind, The Sand and The Stars	1955	3.75	7.50	15.00
1288	Walk Hand in Hand/Not Anymore	1956	3.00	6.00	12.00
1297	Canadian Sunset/High Upon a Mountain	1956	3.00	6.00	12.00
1303	Baby Doll/Since I've Found My Baby	1956	3.00	6.00	12.00
1308	Butterfly/It Doesn't Take Very Long	1957	3.00	6.00	12.00
1323	I Like Your Kind of Love/Stop Teasin' Me	1957	3.00	6.00	12.00
1336	Lips of Wine/Straight from the Heart	1957	3.00	6.00	12.00
1340	Are You Sincere/Be Mine Tonight	1957	3.00	6.00	12.00
1351	Promise Me, Love/Your Hand, Your Heart, Your Love	1958	2.50	5.00	10.00
1358	The Hawaiian Wedding Song/House of Bamboo	1958	2.50	5.00	10.00
1370	Lonely Street/Summer Love	1959	2.50	5.00	10.00
1374	The Village of St. Bernadette/I'm So Lonesome I Could Cry	1959	2.50	5.00	10.00
1374 [PS]	The Village of St. Bernadette/I'm So Lonesome I Could Cry	1959	3.75	7.50	15.00
1378	Wake Me When It's Over/We Have a Date	1960	2.50	5.00	10.00
1381	Do You Mind?/Dreamsville	1960	2.50	5.00	10.00
1389	In the Summertime (You Don't Want My Love)/Don't Go to Strangers	1960	2.50	5.00	10.00
1389	You Don't Want My Love/Don't Go to Strangers	1960	3.00	6.00	12.00
1398	The Bilbao Song/How Wonderful to Know	1961	2.50	5.00	10.00
1433	Twilight Time/So Rare	1962	2.50	5.00	10.00
1447	Let It Be Me/Under Paris Skies	1964	2.50	5.00	10.00
2501 [S]	Unchained Melody/I'm So Alone	1960	3.75	7.50	15.00
2502 [S]	You Don't Know What Love Is/Say It Isn't So	1960	3.75	7.50	15.00
COLUMBIA					
AE7 1108 [DJ]	It's the Most Wonderful Time of the Year/Kay Thompson's Jingle Bells	1976	2.50	5.00	10.00
—Special radio promo for Christmas Seals. Also contains public service announcements for Christmas Seals by Williams on each side.					
AE7 1108 [PS]	It's the Most Wonderful Time of the Year/Kay Thompson's Jingle Bells	1976	2.50	5.00	10.00
10029	A Mi Esposa Con Amor (To My Wife with Love)/Another Lonely Song	1974	—	2.00	4.00
10054	Christmas Present/The Lord's Prayer	1974	—	2.00	4.00
10054 [PS]	Christmas Present/The Lord's Prayer	1974	—	2.50	5.00
10078	Love Said Goodbye/One More Time	1974	—	2.00	4.00
10113	Cry Softly/You Lay So Easy on My Mind	1975	—	2.00	4.00
10144	Feelings/Quits	1975	—	2.00	4.00
10208	Sad Eyes/Quits	1975	—	2.00	4.00
10263	Tell It Like It Is/Goin' Through the Motions	1975	—	2.00	4.00
10471	Are You In There?/Are You In There? (Disco)	1977	—	2.00	4.00
10878	Love Theme from "Oliver's Story"/Everytime I See Laureen	1979	—	2.00	4.00
10952	Love Theme from "Oliver's Story"/Love Story (Where Do I Begin)	1979	—	2.00	4.00
11152	Jason/I'll Never Love Anyone Anymore	1979	—	2.00	4.00
31458 [S]	(titles unknown)	1962	3.00	6.00	12.00
31459 [S]	(titles unknown)	1962	3.00	6.00	12.00
31460 [S]	(titles unknown)	1962	3.00	6.00	12.00
31461 [S]	(titles unknown)	1962	3.00	6.00	12.00
31462 [S]	(titles unknown)	1962	3.00	6.00	12.00
31495 [S]	(titles unknown)	1962	3.00	6.00	12.00
31496 [S]	(titles unknown)	1962	3.00	6.00	12.00
31497 [S]	(titles unknown)	1962	3.00	6.00	12.00
—Anyone who can fill in these gaps -- the above 8 all are Columbia "Stereo 7" singles -- please let us know.					
31498 [S]	Tonight/The Second Time Around	1962	3.00	6.00	12.00
31499 [S]	It Might As Well Be Spring/Three Coins in the Fountain	1962	3.00	6.00	12.00
42199	Danny Boy/Fly by Night	1961	2.00	4.00	8.00
42199 [PS]	Danny Boy/Fly by Night	1961	3.00	6.00	12.00
42265	The Wonderful World of the Young/Help Me	1962	2.00	4.00	8.00
42265 [PS]	The Wonderful World of the Young/Help Me	1962	2.50	5.00	10.00
42451	Stranger on the Shore/I Want to Be Wanted	1962	2.00	4.00	8.00
42451 [PS]	Stranger on the Shore/I Want to Be Wanted	1962	2.50	5.00	10.00
42523	Don't You Believe It/Summertime	1962	2.00	4.00	8.00
42523 [PS]	Don't You Believe It/Summertime	1962	2.50	5.00	10.00
42674	Can't Get Used to Losing You/Days of Wine and Roses	1963	2.00	4.00	8.00
42674 [PS]	Can't Get Used to Losing You/Days of Wine and Roses	1963	2.50	5.00	10.00
42784	Hopeless/The Peking Theme (So Little Time)	1963	2.00	4.00	8.00
42894	The Christmas Song (Chestnuts Roasting On An Open Fire)/White Christmas	1963	2.00	4.00	8.00
—Stock copy or black vinyl promo					
42894 [DJ]	The Christmas Song (Chestnuts Roasting On An Open Fire)/White Christmas	1963	3.00	6.00	12.00
—Promo only on green vinyl					
42950	A Fool Never Learns/Charade	1963	2.00	4.00	8.00

Number	Title (A Side/B Side)	Yr	VG	VG+	NM
43015	Wrong for Each Other/Madrigal	1964	—	3.00	6.00
43128	On the Street Where You Live/Almost There	1964	—	3.00	6.00
43180	Dear Heart/Emily	1964	—	3.00	6.00
43257	...And Roses and Roses/My Carousel	1965	—	3.00	6.00
43257 [PS]	...And Roses and Roses/My Carousel	1965	2.00	4.00	8.00
43358	Ain't It True/Loved One	1965	—	3.00	6.00
43458	Do You Hear What I Hear/Some Children See Him	1965	2.00	4.00	8.00
43519	Bye Bye Blues/You're Gonna Hear from Me!	1966	—	3.00	6.00
43650	The Summer of Our Love/How Can I Tell Her It's Over	1966	—	3.00	6.00
43737	In the Arms of Love/The Many Faces of Love	1966	—	3.00	6.00
44065	Music to Watch Girls By/The Face I Love	1967	—	2.50	5.00
44202	More and More/I Want to Be Free	1967	—	2.50	5.00
44325	When I Look in Your Eyes/Holly	1967	—	2.50	5.00
44527	Sweet Memories/You Are Where Everything Is	1968	—	2.50	5.00
44650	Battle Hymn of the Republic/Ave Maria	1968	—	2.50	5.00
44650 [PS]	Battle Hymn of the Republic/Ave Maria	1968	—	3.00	6.00
44709	The Christmas Song (Chestnuts Roasting On An Open Fire)/It's The Most Wonderful Time Of The Year	1968	—	3.00	6.00
44818	Happy Heart/Our Last Goodbye	1969	—	2.50	5.00
44929	Live and Learn/You Are	1969	—	2.50	5.00
45003	What Am I Living For/A Woman's Way	1969	—	2.50	5.00
45094	Can't Help Falling in Love/Sweet Memories	1970	—	2.50	5.00
45175	One Day of Your Life/Long Time Blues	1970	—	2.50	5.00
45246	Whistling Away the Dark/Home Lovin' Man	1970	—	2.50	5.00
45317	(Where Do I Begin) Love Story/Something	1971	—	2.00	4.00
45434	You've Got a Friend/A Song for You	1971	—	2.00	4.00
45494	Help Me Make It Through the Night/Love Is All	1971	—	2.00	4.00
45531	The Last Time I Saw Her/Music from Across the Way	1972	—	2.00	4.00
45533	Love Story (Spanish Version)/Music from Across the Way (Spanish Version)	1972	—	3.00	6.00
45579	Love Theme from "The Godfather" (Speak Softly Love)/Home for Thee	1972	—	2.00	4.00
45647	MacArthur Park/Amazing Grace	1972	—	2.00	4.00
45716	Who Was It/Home Lovin' Man	1972	—	2.00	4.00
45757	Marmalade, Molenaisse and Honey/Who Was It	1973	—	2.00	4.00
45814	Last Tango in Paris/I'll Never Be the Same	1973	—	2.00	4.00
45936	Solitaire/My Love	1973	—	2.00	4.00
45985	Walk Right Back/Remember	1974	—	2.00	4.00
—With Noelle					
46049	Love's Theme/You're the Best Thing That's Ever Happened to Me	1974	—	2.00	4.00
JZSP 76322/3 [DJ]	Away In A Manger/O Holy Night	1963	2.50	5.00	10.00
JZSP 111911/2 [DJ]	Have Yourself A Merry Little Christmas/The Bells Of St. Mary's	1966	2.00	4.00	8.00
—Yellow label					
JZSP 111911/2 [DJ]	Have Yourself A Merry Little Christmas/The Bells Of St. Mary's	1966	2.00	4.00	8.00
—White label					

MGM

Number	Title (A Side/B Side)	Yr	VG	VG+	NM
11076	Gentle Hands/From the Manger to the Cross	1951	6.25	12.50	25.00

"X"

Number	Title (A Side/B Side)	Yr	VG	VG+	NM
0036	Why Should I Cry Over You/You Can't Buy Happiness	1954	5.00	10.00	20.00
0091	Now I Know/Here Comes That Dream Again	1955	5.00	10.00	20.00

7-Inch Extended Plays

CADENCE

Number	Title (A Side/B Side)	Yr	VG	VG+	NM
CEP-112	The Hawaiian Wedding Song/Sail Along Silv'ry Moon//Blue Hawaii/Sweet Leilani	1959	3.00	6.00	12.00
CEP-112 [PS]	Andy Williams	1959	3.00	6.00	12.00
CEP-116	It's All in the Game/My Happiness//Twilight Time/Love Letters in the Sand	1959	3.00	6.00	12.00
CEP-116 [PS]	Two Time Winners	1959	3.00	6.00	12.00
CEP-119	To You Sweetheart, Aloha/The Moon of Manakoora//I'll Weave a Lot of Stars for You/Beyond the Reef	1959	3.00	6.00	12.00
CEP-119 [PS]	To You Sweetheart, Aloha	1959	3.00	6.00	12.00
CEP-120	Aloha Oe/A Song of Old Hawaii//Song of the Islands/Love Song of Kalua	1959	3.00	6.00	12.00
CEP-120 [PS]	Song of the Islands	1959	3.00	6.00	12.00

COLUMBIA

Number	Title (A Side/B Side)	Yr	VG	VG+	NM
7-9138 [PS]	Dear Heart	1965	2.50	5.00	10.00
7-9138 [S]	Dear Heart/Red Roses for a Blue Lady/Who Can I Turn To//You're Nobody 'Til Somebody Loves You/Everybody Loves Somebody/I Can't Stop Loving You	1965	2.50	5.00	10.00
—33 1/3 rpm, small hole, "Special Coin Operator Release"					
7-9299 [PS]	The Shadow of Your Smile	1966	2.50	5.00	10.00
7-9299 [S]	The Shadow of Your Smile/Try to Remember/Yesterday//Michelle/A Taste of Honey/Somewhere	1966	2.50	5.00	10.00
—33 1/3 rpm, small hole, "Special Coin Operator Release"					

Albums

ATCO

Number	Title (A Side/B Side)	Yr	VG	VG+	NM
90561	Close Enough for Love	1987	2.50	5.00	10.00

CADENCE

Number	Title (A Side/B Side)	Yr	VG	VG+	NM
CLP 1018 [M]	Andy Williams	1957	12.50	25.00	50.00
CLP 3002 [M]	Andy Williams	1958	12.50	25.00	50.00
—Cover depicts Andy standing					
CLP 3002 [M]	Andy Williams	1960	5.00	10.00	20.00
—Cover depicts Andy reclining					
CLP 3005 [M]	Andy Williams Sings Rodgers and Hammerstein	1958	10.00	20.00	40.00
—Cover depicts a café scene					
CLP 3005 [M]	Andy Williams Sings Rodgers and Hammerstein	1960	5.00	10.00	20.00
—Cover depicts a close-up of Andy's face					
CLP 3026 [M]	Two Time Winners	1959	5.00	10.00	20.00
CLP 3027 [M]	Andy Williams Sings...Steve Allen	1959	5.00	10.00	20.00
CLP 3029 [M]	To You Sweetheart, Aloha	1959	5.00	10.00	20.00
CLP 3030 [M]	Lonely Street	1960	5.00	10.00	20.00
CLP 3038 [M]	The Village of St. Bernadette	1960	5.00	10.00	20.00
CLP 3047 [M]	Under Paris Skies	1961	5.00	10.00	20.00
CLP 3054 [M]	Andy Williams' Best	1962	5.00	10.00	20.00
CLP 3061 [M]	Million Seller Songs	1962	5.00	10.00	20.00
CLP 25026 [S]	Two Time Winners	1959	7.50	15.00	30.00
—Black vinyl					
CLP 25026 [S]	Two Time Winners	1959	20.00	40.00	80.00
—Red vinyl					
CLP 25027 [R]	Andy Williams Sings...Steve Allen	1959	3.75	7.50	15.00
CLP 25029 [S]	To You Sweetheart, Aloha	1959	7.50	15.00	30.00
CLP 25030 [S]	Lonely Street	1960	7.50	15.00	30.00
CLP 25038 [S]	The Village of St. Bernadette	1960	7.50	15.00	30.00
CLP 25047 [S]	Under Paris Skies	1961	7.50	15.00	30.00
CLP 25054 [S]	Andy Williams' Best	1962	6.25	12.50	25.00
CLP 25061 [S]	Million Seller Songs	1962	6.25	12.50	25.00

CAPITOL

Number	Title (A Side/B Side)	Yr	VG	VG+	NM
ST-12387	Greatest Love Classics	1984	2.50	5.00	10.00

COLUMBIA

Number	Title (A Side/B Side)	Yr	VG	VG+	NM
GP 5 [(2)]	The Andy Williams Sound of Music	1969	5.00	10.00	20.00
CL 1751 [M]	Danny Boy And Other Songs I Love to Sing	1962	3.75	7.50	15.00
CL 1809 [M]	Moon River and Other Great Movie Themes	1962	3.00	6.00	12.00
CL 1879 [M]	Warm and Willing	1962	3.00	6.00	12.00
CL 2015 [M]	Days of Wine and Roses	1963	3.00	6.00	12.00
CL 2087 [M]	The Andy Williams Christmas Album	1963	3.00	6.00	12.00
CL 2137 [M]	The Wonderful World of Andy Williams	1964	3.00	6.00	12.00
CL 2171 [M]	The Academy Award Winning "Call Me Irresponsible" and Other Hits Songs from the Movies	1964	3.00	6.00	12.00
CL 2205 [M]	The Great Songs from "My Fair Lady" and Other Broadway Hits	1964	3.00	6.00	12.00
CL 2323 [M]	Hawaiian Wedding Song	1965	3.00	6.00	12.00
—Reissue of Cadence 3029					
CL 2324 [M]	Canadian Sunset	1965	3.00	6.00	12.00
—Reissue of Cadence 3054					
CL 2338 [M]	Dear Heart	1965	3.00	6.00	12.00
CL 2383 [M]	Andy Williams' Newest Hits	1966	3.00	6.00	12.00
CL 2420 [M]	Merry Christmas	1965	3.00	6.00	12.00
CL 2499 [M]	The Shadow of Your Smile	1966	3.00	6.00	12.00
CL 2533 [M]	In the Arms of Love	1967	3.00	6.00	12.00
CL 2680 [M]	Born Free	1967	3.00	6.00	12.00
CL 2766 [M]	Love, Andy	1967	3.75	7.50	15.00
CS 8551 [S]	Danny Boy And Other Songs I Love to Sing	1962	5.00	10.00	20.00
CS 8609 [S]	Moon River and Other Great Movie Themes	1962	3.75	7.50	15.00
CS 8679 [S]	Warm and Willing	1962	3.75	7.50	15.00
CS 8815 [S]	Days of Wine and Roses	1963	3.75	7.50	15.00
CS 8887 [S]	The Andy Williams Christmas Album	1963	3.00	6.00	12.00
CS 8937 [S]	The Wonderful World of Andy Williams	1964	3.75	7.50	15.00
CS 8971 [S]	The Academy Award Winning "Call Me Irresponsible" and Other Hits Songs from the Movies	1964	3.75	7.50	15.00
CS 9005 [S]	The Great Songs from "My Fair Lady" and Other Broadway Hits	1964	3.75	7.50	15.00
CS 9123 [S]	Hawaiian Wedding Song	1965	3.75	7.50	15.00
—Reissue of Cadence 25029					
CS 9124 [S]	Canadian Sunset	1965	3.75	7.50	15.00
—Reissue of Cadence 25054					
CS 9138 [S]	Dear Heart	1965	3.75	7.50	15.00
CS 9183 [S]	Andy Williams' Newest Hits	1966	3.75	7.50	15.00
CS 9220 [S]	Merry Christmas	1965	3.00	6.00	12.00
CS 9299 [S]	The Shadow of Your Smile	1966	3.75	7.50	15.00
CS 9333 [S]	In the Arms of Love	1967	3.75	7.50	15.00
CS 9480 [S]	Born Free	1967	3.75	7.50	15.00
CS 9566 [S]	Love, Andy	1967	3.00	6.00	12.00
CS 9662	Honey	1968	3.00	6.00	12.00
CS 9844	Happy Heart	1969	3.00	6.00	12.00
CS 9896	Raindrops Keep Fallin' on My Head	1970	3.00	6.00	12.00
CS 9922	Get Together with Andy Williams	1969	3.75	7.50	15.00
—The Osmonds appear on three tracks					
KCS 9979	Andy Williams' Greatest Hits	1970	3.00	6.00	12.00
KC 30105	The Andy Williams Show	1970	2.50	5.00	10.00
CQ 30497 [Q]	Love Story	1972	3.75	7.50	15.00
KC 30497	Love Story	1971	2.50	5.00	10.00
CQ 30797 [Q]	You've Got a Friend	1971	3.75	7.50	15.00
KC 30797	You've Got a Friend	1971	2.50	5.00	10.00
CG 31064 [(2)]	The Impossible Dream	1971	3.75	7.50	15.00
CQ 31303 [Q]	Love Theme from "The Godfather"	1972	3.75	7.50	15.00
KC 31303	Love Theme from "The Godfather"	1972	2.50	5.00	10.00
CQ 31625 [Q]	Alone Again (Naturally)	1972	3.75	7.50	15.00
KC 31625	Alone Again (Naturally)	1972	2.50	5.00	10.00
KC 32383	Solitaire	1973	2.50	5.00	10.00
KC 32384	Andy Williams' Greatest Hits, Vol. 2	1973	2.50	5.00	10.00
KC 32949	The Way We Were	1974	2.50	5.00	10.00
C 33191	Christmas Present	1974	2.50	5.00	10.00
KC 33234	You Lay So Easy on My Mind	1974	2.50	5.00	10.00
PC 33563	The Other Side of Me	1975	2.50	5.00	10.00
CG 33597 [(2)]	Love Story/Born Free	1975	3.00	6.00	12.00
CG 33600 [(2)]	Moon River/Days of Wine and Roses	1975	3.00	6.00	12.00
PC 34299	Andy	1976	2.50	5.00	10.00
PCQ 34299 [Q]	Andy	1976	3.75	7.50	15.00

HARMONY

Number	Title (A Side/B Side)	Yr	VG	VG+	NM
KH 30133	Andy Williams	1970	2.50	5.00	10.00

PAIR

Number	Title (A Side/B Side)	Yr	VG	VG+	NM
PDL2-1103 [(2)]	The Best of Andy Williams	1986	3.00	6.00	12.00

WILLIAMS, BARRY

Greg Brady of THE BRADY BUNCH.

45s

PARAMOUNT

Number	Title (A Side/B Side)	Yr	VG	VG+	NM
0122	Sweet Sweetheart/Sunny	1971	3.75	7.50	15.00
0122 [PS]	Sweet Sweetheart/Sunny	1971	5.00	10.00	20.00

WILLIAMS, BERNIE

45s

BELL

Number	Title (A Side/B Side)	Yr	VG	VG+	NM
768	Ever Again/Next to You	1969	50.00	100.00	200.00

WILLIAMS, BIG JOE

Albums

Number	Title (A Side/B Side)	Yr	VG	VG+	NM
BLUESVILLE					
BVLP-1056 [M]	Blues for 9 Strings	1962	25.00	50.00	100.00
—Blue label, silver print					
BVLP-1056 [M]	Blues for 9 Strings	1964	6.25	12.50	25.00
—Blue label with trident logo					
BVLP-1067 [M]	Big Joe Williams at Folk City	1963	25.00	50.00	100.00
—Blue label, silver print					
BVLP-1067 [M]	Big Joe Williams at Folk City	1964	6.25	12.50	25.00
—Blue label with trident logo					
BVLP-1083 [M]	Studio Blues	1964	25.00	50.00	100.00
—Blue label, silver print					
BVLP-1083 [M]	Studio Blues	1964	6.25	12.50	25.00
—Blue label with trident logo					
DELMARK					
DL-604 [M]	Blues on Highway 49	1962	15.00	30.00	60.00
DL-609 [M]	Starvin' Chain Blues	1966	6.25	12.50	25.00
FOLKWAYS					
FA-3820 [M]	Mississippi's Big Joe Williams	1962	7.50	15.00	30.00
FAS-3820 [R]	Mississippi's Big Joe Williams	1962	5.00	10.00	20.00
MILESTONE					
3001 [M]	Classic Delta Blues	1966	6.25	12.50	25.00

WILLIAMS, BILLY

Also see THE CHARIOTEERS.

45s

Number	Title (A Side/B Side)	Yr	VG	VG+	NM
CORAL					
61212	Sh-Boom (Life Could Be a Dream)/Whenever Wherever	1954	3.00	6.00	12.00
61264	Love Me/The Honeydripper	1954	3.00	6.00	12.00
61346	Fools Rush In/He Follows She	1955	3.00	6.00	12.00
61462	Glory of Love/Wonderful, Wonderful One	1955	3.00	6.00	12.00
61498	Just a Little Bit More/Learning to Love	1955	3.00	6.00	12.00
61576	Cry Baby/A Crazy Little Place	1956	2.50	5.00	10.00
61639	Pray/You'll Reach Your Star	1956	2.50	5.00	10.00
61684	This Planet Earth/I Guess I'll Be On My Way	1956	2.50	5.00	10.00
61730	Shame, Shame, Shame/Don't Cry on My Shoulder	1956	2.50	5.00	10.00
61751	Stormy/Follow Me	1956	2.50	5.00	10.00
61795	Butterfly/The Pied Piper	1957	2.50	5.00	10.00
61830	I'm Gonna Sit Right Down and Write Myself a Letter/Date with the Blues	1957	3.00	6.00	12.00
61886	Got a Date with an Angel/The Lord Will Understand	1957	2.50	5.00	10.00
61932	Don't Let Go/Baby, Baby	1958	2.50	5.00	10.00
61961	There! I've Said It Again/Steppin' Out Tonight	1958	2.50	5.00	10.00
61999	I'll Get By/It's Prayin' Time	1958	2.50	5.00	10.00
62029	It Hurts So Much/So Long	1958	2.50	5.00	10.00
62069	Nola/Tied to the Strings of Your Heart	1959	2.50	5.00	10.00
62101	Goodnight Irene/Red Hot Love	1959	2.50	5.00	10.00
62131	Go to Sleep, Go to Sleep, Go to Sleep/Telephone Conversation	1959	2.00	4.00	8.00
—With Barbara McNair					
62140	Smack Dab in the Middle/I Wonder	1959	2.00	4.00	8.00
62218	I Cried for You/The Lover of All Lovers	1960	2.00	4.00	8.00
62230	Begin the Beguine/For You	1960	2.00	4.00	8.00
62438	Why Do I Love You So/Raise Your Hand	1964	—	3.00	6.00
62438	Why Do I Love You So/The Honeydripper	1964	—	3.00	6.00
MERCURY					
5866	Stay/Azure-Te (Paris Blues)	1952	3.75	7.50	15.00
5884	Who Knows/It's Best We Say Goodbye	1952	3.75	7.50	15.00
5902	That's What I'm Here For/Some Folks Do, Some Folks Don't	1952	3.75	7.50	15.00
70012	I Don't Know Why/Mad About 'Cha	1952	3.75	7.50	15.00
70094	Pour Me a Glass of Teardrops/It's a Miracle	1953	3.75	7.50	15.00
70180	This Side of Heaven/You're the One for Me	1953	3.75	7.50	15.00
70210	Why Do You Have to Go?/Cattle Call	1953	3.75	7.50	15.00
70271	If I Ever Get to Heaven/Ask Me No Questions	1953	3.75	7.50	15.00
70324	Invitation to Dance/I'll Close My Eyes	1954	3.75	7.50	15.00
70376	Go Home, Joe/You're the Only One I Adore	1954	3.75	7.50	15.00
MGM					
10764	Longing/I Didn't Slip	1950	5.00	10.00	20.00
10857	The Room I'm Sleeping In/Music by Angels	1950	5.00	10.00	20.00
10928	Gaucho Serenade/I Won't Cry Anymore	1951	3.75	7.50	15.00
10967	Pretty Eyed Baby/You Made Me Love You	1951	3.75	7.50	15.00
10998	Shang-Hai/A Wondrous Word	1951	3.75	7.50	15.00
11066	Sin/It's Over	1951	3.75	7.50	15.00
11117	I'll Never Find You/Busy Line	1951	3.75	7.50	15.00
11145	No Other Love/Callaway Went That-A-Way	1952	3.75	7.50	15.00
11172	Wheel of Fortune/What Can I Say	1952	3.75	7.50	15.00
11184	Confetti/Don't Grieve	1952	3.75	7.50	15.00
12537	Shang-Hai/Gaucho Serenade	1957	2.50	5.00	10.00

Albums

Number	Title (A Side/B Side)	Yr	VG	VG+	NM
CORAL					
CRL 57184 [M]	Billy Williams	1957	15.00	30.00	60.00
CRL 57251 [M]	Half Sweet, Half Beat	1959	12.50	25.00	50.00
CRL 57343 [M]	The Billy Williams Revue	1960	12.50	25.00	50.00
CRL 757251 [S]	Half Sweet, Half Beat	1959	20.00	40.00	80.00
CRL 757343 [S]	The Billy Williams Revue	1960	15.00	30.00	60.00
MERCURY					
MG 20317 [M]	Oh Yeah!	1958	15.00	30.00	60.00
MGM					
E-3400 [M]	The Billy Williams Quartet	1957	15.00	30.00	60.00
WING					
MGW-12131 [M]	Vote for Billy Williams	1959	10.00	20.00	40.00

WILLIAMS, BILLY DEE

Albums

Number	Title (A Side/B Side)	Yr	VG	VG+	NM
PRESTIGE LIVELY ARTS					
30001 [M]	Let's Misbehave	1962	10.00	20.00	40.00

WILLIAMS, CORA/SHIRLEY HAVEN AND THE FOUR JACKS

45s

Number	Title (A Side/B Side)	Yr	VG	VG+	NM
FEDERAL					
12079	I Ain't Coming Back Anymore/Sure Cure for the Blues	1952	150.00	300.00	600.00

WILLIAMS, DANNY

45s

Number	Title (A Side/B Side)	Yr	VG	VG+	NM
UNITED ARTISTS					
348	Lonely/We Will Never Be As Young As This Again	1961	3.00	6.00	12.00
411	Jeannie/Weaver of Dreams	1962	3.00	6.00	12.00
480	Something's Gotta Give/Miracle of You	1962	3.00	6.00	12.00
493	Tears/Miracle of You	1962	3.00	6.00	12.00
601	More (Theme from Mondo Cane)/Rhapsody	1963	3.00	6.00	12.00
685	White on White/The Comedy Is Ended	1964	3.75	7.50	15.00
729	The Truth Hurts/Little Toy Balloon	1964	2.50	5.00	10.00
762	I Watched a Flower Grow/Forget Her, Forget Her	1964	2.50	5.00	10.00
825	How Soon/The Seventh Dawn	1965	2.50	5.00	10.00
860	All's Fair in Love and War/Masquerade	1965	2.50	5.00	10.00
959	The Stranger/I Can't Believe I'm Losing You	1965	2.50	5.00	10.00
50020	Blue on White/It's Not for Me to Say	1966	2.00	4.00	8.00

Albums

Number	Title (A Side/B Side)	Yr	VG	VG+	NM
UNITED ARTISTS					
UAL-3297 [M]	The Exciting Danny Williams	1963	3.75	7.50	15.00
UAL-3359 [M]	White on White	1964	3.75	7.50	15.00
UAL-3380 [M]	With You in Mind	1964	3.75	7.50	15.00
UAL-3493 [M]	Magic Town	1966	3.75	7.50	15.00
UAS-6297 [S]	The Exciting Danny Williams	1963	5.00	10.00	20.00
UAS-6359 [S]	White on White	1964	5.00	10.00	20.00
UAS-6380 [S]	With You in Mind	1964	5.00	10.00	20.00
UAS-6493 [S]	Magic Town	1966	5.00	10.00	20.00

WILLIAMS, DENIECE

12-Inch Singles

Number	Title (A Side/B Side)	Yr	VG	VG+	NM
ARC					
10991	I've Got the Next Dance/When Love Comes Calling	1979	3.00	6.00	12.00
11141	I Found Love/Are You Thinking?	1979	3.00	6.00	12.00
60504	What Two Can Do/Suspicious	1981	—	2.00	4.00
COLUMBIA					
AS 1838 [DJ]	Let's Hear It for the Boy (6:00) (3:34)	1984	3.75	7.50	15.00
CAS 2688 [DJ]	Never Say Never (3 versions)	1987	—	3.00	6.00
04988	Let's Hear It for the Boy (6:00) (4:13)	1984	2.00	4.00	8.00
05043	Next Love (7:07)/(Instrumental)	1984	2.00	4.00	8.00
05918	Wiser and Weaker (6:15) (5:50 Instrumental)	1986	2.00	4.00	8.00
06929	I Confess (3 versions)	1987	—	3.00	6.00
10513	Free/It's Important to Me	1977	3.75	7.50	15.00

45s

Number	Title (A Side/B Side)	Yr	VG	VG+	NM
ARC					
02108	It's Your Conscience/Sweet Surrender	1981	—	2.00	4.00
02406	Silly/My Melody	1981	—	2.00	4.00
02812	It's Gonna Take a Miracle/Part of Love	1982	—	2.00	4.00
03015	Waiting by the Hotline/Love Notes	1982	—	2.00	4.00
03242	It's Gonna Take a Miracle/Silly	1982	—	—	3.00
—Reissue					
03261	Waiting/How Does It Feel	1982	—	2.00	4.00
10971	I've Got the Next Dance/When Love Comes Calling	1979	—	2.00	4.00
11063	I Found Love/Are You Thinking?	1979	—	2.00	4.00
COLUMBIA					
AE7 1153 [DJ]	God Is Amazing/God Is Standing By	1977	2.00	4.00	8.00
—B-side by Johnnie Taylor; promo with "Suggested Christmas Programming" on label					
03807	Do What You Feel/Love, Peace and Unity	1983	—	2.00	4.00
03807 [PS]	Do What You Feel/Love, Peace and Unity	1983	—	2.00	4.00
04037	I'm So Proud/It's Okay	1983	—	2.00	4.00
04218	Heaven in Your Eyes/Love, Peace and Unity	1983	—	2.00	4.00
04417	Let's Hear It for the Boy/(Instrumental)	1984	—	—	3.00
04417 [PS]	Let's Hear It for the Boy/(Instrumental)	1984	—	2.00	4.00
04537	Next Love/Picking Up the Pieces	1984	—	—	3.00
04537 [PS]	Next Love/Picking Up the Pieces	1984	—	2.00	4.00
04641	Black Butterfly/Blind Dating	1984	—	—	3.00
06157	Wiser and Weaker/(Instrumental)	1986	—	—	3.00
06157 [PS]	Wiser and Weaker/(Instrumental)	1986	—	—	3.00
06318	Healing/I Feel the Night	1986	—	—	3.00
07021	Never Say Never/Love Finds You	1987	—	—	3.00
07021 [PS]	Never Say Never/Love Finds You	1987	—	—	3.00
07357	I Confess/(Instrumental)	1987	—	—	3.00
07633	Water Under the Bridge/Love Finds You	1987	—	—	3.00
07704	I Believe in You/(Instrumental)	1988	—	—	3.00
08014	I Can't Wait/(Instrumental)	1988	—	—	3.00
08014 [PS]	I Can't Wait/(Instrumental)	1988	—	—	3.00
08425	Let's Hear It for the Boy/(Instrumental)	1988	—	—	3.00
—Reissue					
08507	This Is As Good As It Gets/Don't Stop the Love	1988	—	—	3.00
10429	Free/Cause You Love Me Baby	1976	—	2.50	5.00
10556	That's What Friends Are For/It's Important to Me	1977	—	2.50	5.00
10648	Baby, Baby My Love's All for You/Be Good to Me	1977	—	2.50	5.00
MCA					
53707	Every Moment/Do You Hear What I Hear?	1989	—	—	3.00
SPARROW					
S7-18215	Do You Hear What I Hear/Silent Night	1994	—	2.50	5.00
—B-side by Bebe and Cece Winans; green vinyl					
TODDLIN' TOWN					
107	Love Is Tears/I'm Walkin' Away	1968	2.50	5.00	10.00
—As "Deniece Chandler"					
113	Hey Baby/Glorious Feeling	1968	2.50	5.00	10.00
—As "Deniece Chandler"; with Lee Sain					
118	I Don't Wanna Cry/Goodbye Cruel World	1969	2.50	5.00	10.00
—As "Deniece Chandler"					
127	Shy Boy/(B-side unknown)	1969	2.50	5.00	10.00
—As "Deniece Chandler"					

Number	Title (A Side/B Side)	Yr	VG	VG+	NM
Albums					
ARC					
AS 1432 [DJ]	Niecy	1982	6.25	12.50	25.00
—Promo-only picture disc					
JC 35568	When Love Comes Calling	1979	2.50	5.00	10.00
FC 37048	My Melody	1981	2.50	5.00	10.00
PC 37048	My Melody	198?	2.00	4.00	8.00
—Budget-line reissue					
FC 37952	Niecy	1982	2.50	5.00	10.00
PC 37952	Niecy	198?	2.00	4.00	8.00
—Budget-line reissue					
HC 47952	Niecy	1983	12.50	25.00	50.00
—Half-speed mastered edition					
COLUMBIA					
PC 34242	This Is Niecy	1976	2.50	5.00	10.00
—No bar code on cover					
PC 34242	This Is Niecy	198?	2.00	4.00	8.00
—Reissue with bar code on cover					
JC 34911	Song Bird	1977	2.50	5.00	10.00
PC 34911	Song Bird	198?	2.00	4.00	8.00
—Budget-line reissue					
FC 38622	I'm So Proud	1983	2.50	5.00	10.00
PC 38622	I'm So Proud	198?	2.00	4.00	8.00
—Budget-line reissue					
FC 39366	Let's Hear It for the Boy	1984	2.50	5.00	10.00
FC 40084	Hot on the Trail	1986	2.50	5.00	10.00
FC 44322	As Good As It Gets	1989	2.50	5.00	10.00
MCA					
6338	Special Love	1989	2.50	5.00	10.00
SPARROW					
SPR-1256	From the Beginning	1990	3.00	6.00	12.00
ST-41039	So Glad I Know	1986	3.00	6.00	12.00

WILLIAMS, DON

Also see THE POZO-SECO SINGERS.

Number	Title (A Side/B Side)	Yr	VG	VG+	NM
45s					
ABC					
12332	I've Got a Winner in You/Overlookin' and Underthinkin'	1978	—	2.00	4.00
12373	Rake and Ramblin' Man/Too Many Tears	1978	—	2.00	4.00
12425	Tulsa Time/When I'm With You	1978	—	2.50	5.00
12458	Lay Down Beside Me/I Would Like to See You Again	1979	—	2.50	5.00
ABC DOT					
17531	The Ties That Bind/Goodbye Isn't Really Good at All	1974	—	2.00	4.00
17550	You're My Best Friend/Where Are You	1975	—	2.00	4.00
17568	(Turn Out the Light And) Love Me Tonight/Reason to Be	1975	—	2.00	4.00
17604	Till the Rivers All Run Dry/Don't You Think It's Time	1976	—	2.00	4.00
17631	Say It Again/I Don't Want the Money	1976	—	2.00	4.00
17658	She Never Knew Me/Ramblin'	1976	—	2.00	4.00
17683	Some Broken Hearts Never Mend/I'll Forgive But I'll Never Forget	1977	—	2.00	4.00
17717	I'm Just a Country Boy/It's Gotta Be Magic	1977	—	2.00	4.00
CAPITOL					
B-5526	We've Got a Good Fire Goin'/Shot Full of Love	1985	—	—	3.00
B-5588	Heartbeat in the Darkness/Light in Your Eyes	1986	—	—	3.00
B-5638	Then It's Love/It's About Time	1986	—	—	3.00
B-5683	Senorita/Send Her Roses	1987	—	—	3.00
B-44019	I'll Never Be in Love Again/Send Her Roses	1987	—	—	3.00
B-44066	I Wouldn't Be a Man/Light in Your Eyes	1987	—	—	3.00
B-44131	Another Place, Another Time/Running Out of Reasons to Run	1988	—	—	3.00
B-44216	Desperately/You Loved Me Through It All	1988	—	—	3.00
B-44274	Old Coyote Town/You Loved Me Through It All	1988	—	—	3.00
DOT					
17516	I Wouldn't Want to Live If You Didn't Love Me/Fly Away	1974	—	2.50	5.00
GIANT					
17126	Pretty Little Baby Child/'Twas the Night Before Christmas	1998	—	—	3.00
JMI					
7	Don't You Believe/You Have a Star	1972	—	3.00	6.00
12	The Shelter of Your Eyes/Playin' Around	1972	—	3.00	6.00
24	Come Early Morning/Amanda	1973	—	3.00	6.00
32	Atta Way to Go/I Recall a Gypsy Woman	1973	—	3.00	6.00
36	We Should Be Together/Miller's Cave	1974	—	3.00	6.00
42	Down the Road I Go/She's in Love with a Rodeo Man	1974	—	3.00	6.00
MCA					
S45-1763 [DJ]	A Special Message from Don Williams For Your Radio Station and Audience	1982	3.00	6.00	12.00
12458	Lay Down Beside Me/I Would Like to See You Again	1979	—	—	3.00
—Reissue of ABC 12458					
41069	It Must Be Love/Not a Chance	1979	—	—	3.00
41155	Love Me Over Again/Circle Driveway	1979	—	—	3.00
41205	Good Ole Boys Like Me/We're All the Way	1980	—	—	3.00
41304	I Believe in You/It Only Rains on Me	1980	—	2.00	4.00
51065	Falling Again/I Keep Putting Off Getting Over You	1981	—	—	3.00
51134	Miracles/I Don't Want to Love You	1981	—	—	3.00
51207	Lord, I Hope This Day Is Good/Smooth Talking Baby	1981	—	—	3.00
52037	Listen to the Radio/Only Love	1982	—	—	3.00
52097	Mistakes/Fool, Fool Heart	1982	—	—	3.00
52152	If Hollywood Don't Need You/Help Yourselves to Each Other	1982	—	—	3.00
52205	Love Is on a Roll/I'll Take Your Love Anytime	1983	—	—	3.00
52245	Nobody But You/If Love Gets There Before I Do	1983	—	—	3.00
52310	Stay Young/Pressure Makes Diamonds	1983	—	—	3.00
52389	That's the Thing About Love/I'm Still Looking for You	1984	—	—	3.00
52448	Maggie's Dream/Leavin'	1984	—	—	3.00
52514	Walkin' a Broken Heart/True Blue Hearts	1984	—	—	3.00
52692	It's Time for Love/I'll Never Need Another You	1985	—	—	3.00
RCA					
2507-7-R	Maybe That's All It Takes/We're All the Way	1990	—	2.00	4.00
2677-7-R	Back in My Younger Days/Diamonds to Dust	1990	—	2.00	4.00
2745-7-R	True Love/Learn to Let It Go	1990	—	2.00	4.00
2820-7-R	Lord Have Mercy on a Country Boy/Jamaica Farewell	1991	—	2.00	4.00
8867-7-R	One Good Well/Flowers Won't Grow (In a Field of Stone)	1989	—	2.00	4.00
9017-7-R	I've Been Loved by the Best/If You Love, Won't You Love Me	1989	—	2.00	4.00
9119-7-R	Just As Long As I Have You/Why Get Up	1989	—	2.00	4.00
62055	Donald and June/Come a Little Closer	1991	—	2.00	4.00
62180	Too Much Love/Back on the Street Again	1992	—	2.00	4.00
62240	It's Who You Love/The Old Trail	1992	—	2.00	4.00
62317	Catfish Bates/That Song About the River	1992	—	2.00	4.00
Albums					
ABC					
AA-1069	Expressions	1978	3.00	6.00	12.00
ABC/DOT					
DO-2004	Don Williams, Vol. III	1974	3.00	6.00	12.00
DO-2014	Don Williams, Vol. 1	1974	3.00	6.00	12.00
—Reissue of JMI 4004					
DO-2018	Don Williams, Vol. 2	1974	3.00	6.00	12.00
—Reissue of JMI 4006					
DO-2021	You're My Best Friend	1975	3.00	6.00	12.00
DO-2035	Greatest Hits	1975	3.00	6.00	12.00
DO-2049	Harmony	1976	3.00	6.00	12.00
DO-2064	Visions	1976	3.00	6.00	12.00
DO-2088	I'm Just a Country Boy	1977	3.00	6.00	12.00
CAPITOL					
ST 12440	New Moves	1987	2.00	4.00	8.00
CLT-48034	Traces	1988	2.00	4.00	8.00
C1-91444	Prime Cuts	1989	2.00	4.00	8.00
JMI					
4004	Don Williams	1973	6.25	12.50	25.00
4006	Don Williams, Vol. 2	1974	5.00	10.00	20.00
MCA					
1442	The Best of Don Williams, Vol. 3	1985	2.00	4.00	8.00
—Budget-line reissue					
3096	The Best of Don Williams, Vol. 2	1979	2.50	5.00	10.00
3192	Portrait	1980	2.50	5.00	10.00
3279	Expressions	1980	2.00	4.00	8.00
—Reissue of ABC 1069					
5133	I Believe in You	1980	2.50	5.00	10.00
5210	Especially for You	1981	2.50	5.00	10.00
5306	Listen to the Radio	1982	2.50	5.00	10.00
5407	Yellow Moon	1983	2.50	5.00	10.00
5465	The Best of Don Williams, Vol. 3	1984	2.50	5.00	10.00
5493	Café Carolina	1984	2.50	5.00	10.00
5671	The Best of Don Williams, Vol. 4	1985	2.50	5.00	10.00
5697	Don Williams Sings Bob McDill	1986	2.50	5.00	10.00
5803	Lovers and Best Friends	1986	2.50	5.00	10.00
37135	Greatest Hits	198?	2.00	4.00	8.00
—Budget-line reissue					
37155	The Best of Don Williams, Vol. 2	198?	2.00	4.00	8.00
—Budget-line reissue					
37230	Visions	198?	2.00	4.00	8.00
—Budget-line reissue					
37231	Portrait	198?	2.00	4.00	8.00
—Budget-line reissue					
37232	I'm Just a Country Boy	198?	2.00	4.00	8.00
—Budget-line reissue					
37233	Especially for You	198?	2.00	4.00	8.00
—Budget-line reissue					
37234	I Believe in You	198?	2.00	4.00	8.00
—Budget-line reissue					
RCA					
9656-1-R	One Good Well	1989	2.50	5.00	10.00
R 124814	True Love	1990	3.75	7.50	15.00
—BMG Music Service pressing; only US vinyl edition					

WILLIAMS, HANK

Number	Title (A Side/B Side)	Yr	VG	VG+	NM
45s					
MGM					
8010	Lovesick Blues/Never Again	1949	15.00	30.00	60.00
10352	Lovesick Blues/Never Again	1950	10.00	20.00	40.00
—Reissue has original 45 rpm number in parentheses under this number					
10401	Wedding Bells/I've Just Told Mama Goodbye	1949	12.50	25.00	50.00
10434	Dear Brother/Lost on the River	1949	12.50	25.00	50.00
10461	Mind Your Own Business/There'll Be No Teardrops Tonight	1949	12.50	25.00	50.00
10506	You're Gonna Change (Or I'm Gonna Leave)/Lost Highway	1949	12.50	25.00	50.00
10560	My Bucket's Got a Hole In It/I'm So Lonesome I Could Cry	1949	12.50	25.00	50.00
10609	I Just Don't Like This Kind of Lovin'/May You Never Be Alone	1950	10.00	20.00	40.00
10630	Beyond the Sunset/The Funeral	1950	15.00	30.00	60.00
—As "Luke the Drifter"					
10645	Long Gone Lonesome Blues/My Son Calls Another Man Daddy	1950	10.00	20.00	40.00
10696	Why Don't You Love Me/A House Without Love	1950	10.00	20.00	40.00
10718	Everything's OK/Too Many Parties	1950	15.00	30.00	60.00
—As "Luke the Drifter"					
10760	They'll Never Take Her Love from Me/Why Should We Try Anymore	1950	10.00	20.00	40.00
10806	No, No, Joe/Help Me Understand	1950	15.00	30.00	60.00
—As "Luke the Drifter"					
10813	I Heard My Mother Praying for Me/Jesus Remembered Me	1950	12.50	25.00	50.00
10832	Moanin' the Blues/Nobody's Lonesome for Me	1950	10.00	20.00	40.00

Number	Title (A Side/B Side)	Yr	VG	VG+	NM
10904	Cold, Cold Heart/Dear John	1951	7.50	15.00	30.00
10932	Just Waitin'/Men with Broken Hearts	1951	12.50	25.00	50.00
—As "Luke the Drifter"					
10961	I Can't Help It (If I'm Still in Love with You)/Howlin' at the Moon	1951	7.50	15.00	30.00
11000	Hey, Good Lookin'/My Heart Would Know	1951	7.50	15.00	30.00
11017	I Dreamed About Mama Last Night/I've Been Down That Road Before	1951	12.50	25.00	50.00
—As "Luke the Drifter"					
11054	Crazy Heart/Lonesome Whistle	1951	7.50	15.00	30.00
11083	Leave Us Women Alone/If You See My Baby	1951	10.00	20.00	40.00
11100	Baby, We're Really in Love/I'd Still Want You	1951	7.50	15.00	30.00
11120	Ramblin' Man/A Picture from Life's Other Side	1952	10.00	20.00	40.00
—As "Luke the Drifter"					
11160	Honky Tonk Blues/I'm Sorry for You My Friend	1952	7.50	15.00	30.00
11202	Half As Much/Let's Turn Back the Years	1952	7.50	15.00	30.00
11283	Jambalaya (On the Bayou)/Window Shopping	1952	7.50	15.00	30.00
11309	Be Careful of Stones That You Throw/Why Don't You Make Up Your Mind	1952	10.00	20.00	40.00
—As "Luke the Drifter"					
11318	Settin' the Woods On Fire/You Win Again	1952	7.50	15.00	30.00
11366	I'll Never Get Out of This World Alive/I Could Never Be Ashamed	1952	7.50	15.00	30.00
11416	Kaw-Liga/Your Cheatin' Heart	1953	7.50	15.00	30.00
11479	Take These Chains from My Heart/Ramblin' Man	1953	6.25	12.50	25.00
11533	I Won't Be Home No More/My Love for You	1953	6.25	12.50	25.00
11574	Weary Blues from Waitin'/I Can't Escape from You	1953	6.25	12.50	25.00
11628	Calling You/When God Comes and Gathers His Jewels	1953	6.25	12.50	25.00
11675	You Better Keep It on Your Mind/Low Down Blues	1954	6.25	12.50	25.00
11707	How Can You Refuse Him Now/A House of Gold	1954	6.25	12.50	25.00
11768	I Ain't Got Nothin' But Time/I'm Satisfied with You	1954	6.25	12.50	25.00
11861	Angel of Death/(I'm Gonna) Sing, Sing, Sing	1954	6.25	12.50	25.00
11928	Please Don't Let Me Love You/Faded Love and Winter's Roses	1955	6.25	12.50	25.00
11975	Message to My Mother/Mother Is Gone	1955	6.25	12.50	25.00
12029	A Teardrop on a Rose/Alone and Forsaken	1955	6.25	12.50	25.00
12077	Someday You'll Call My Name/The First Fall of Snow	1955	6.25	12.50	25.00
12127	The Battle of Armageddon/Thank God	1955	6.25	12.50	25.00
12185	California Zephyr/Thy Burdens Are Greater Than Mine	1956	6.25	12.50	25.00
12244	I Wish I Had a Nickel/There's No Room in My Heart	1956	6.25	12.50	25.00
12332	Blue Love (In My Heart)/Singing Waterfall	1956	6.25	12.50	25.00
12394	The Pale Horse and His Rider/A Home in Heaven	1956	5.00	10.00	20.00
—As "Hank and Audrey Williams"					
12431	Alimony Blues/Because You've Been Away	1957	5.00	10.00	20.00
12438	Ready to Go Home/We're Getting Closer	1957	5.00	10.00	20.00
12484	Leave Me Alone with the Blues/With Tears in My Eyes	1957	5.00	10.00	20.00
12535	No One Will Ever Know/The Waltz of the Wind	1957	5.00	10.00	20.00
12611	Why Don't You Love Me/I Can't Help It (If I'm Still in Love with You)	1958	5.00	10.00	20.00
12635	We Live in Two Different Worlds/My Bucket's Got a Hole In It	1958	5.00	10.00	20.00
12727	Just Waitin'/Roly-Poly	1958	5.00	10.00	20.00
13305	Your Cheatin' Heart/Lovesick Blues	1964	3.00	6.00	12.00
13305 [PS]	Your Cheatin' Heart/Lovesick Blues	1964	5.00	10.00	20.00
13489	I'm So Lonesome I Could Cry/You Win Again	1966	3.00	6.00	12.00
13542	Kaw-Liga/Let's Turn Back the Years	1966	3.00	6.00	12.00
13630	There'll Be No Teardrops Tonight/They'll Never Take Her Love from Me	1966	3.00	6.00	12.00
13717	Long Gone Lonesome Blues/Hang On the Bell, Nellie	1967	3.00	6.00	12.00
14849	Why Don't You Love Me/Ramblin' Man	1976	—	3.00	6.00

7-Inch Extended Plays

MGM

Number	Title (A Side/B Side)	Yr	VG	VG+	NM
X-168 [PS]	Moanin' the Blues	1953	10.00	20.00	40.00
—Cover with X-4041 and X-4042					
X-202 [PS]	(title unknown)	1953	10.00	20.00	40.00
—Cover with X-4102 and X-4103					
X-1014	Crazy Heart/Baby We're Really in Love//My Heart Would Know/I Can't Help It (If I'm Still in Love with You)	1953	20.00	40.00	80.00
—Yellow label					
X-1014	Crazy Heart/Baby We're Really in Love//My Heart Would Know/I Can't Help It (If I'm Still in Love with You)	1960	5.00	10.00	20.00
—Black label					
X-1014 [PS]	Crazy Heart	1953	5.00	10.00	20.00
X-1047	Pictures from Life's Other Side/Men with Broken Hearts//Help Me Understand/Too Many Parties (And Too Many Pals)	1955	15.00	30.00	60.00
—Yellow label					
X-1047	Pictures from Life's Other Side/Men with Broken Hearts//Help Me Understand/Too Many Parties (And Too Many Pals)	1960	5.00	10.00	20.00
—Black label					
X-1047 [PS]	Hank Williams As Luke the Drifter	1955	5.00	10.00	20.00
X-1076	Move It On Over/Fly Trouble//Window Shopping/Pan American	1955	15.00	30.00	60.00
—Yellow label					
X-1076	Move It On Over/Fly Trouble//Window Shopping/Pan American	1960	5.00	10.00	20.00
—Black label					
X-1076 [PS]	Move It On Over	1955	5.00	10.00	20.00
X-1082	(contents unknown)	1955	15.00	30.00	60.00
—Yellow label					
X-1082	(contents unknown)	1960	5.00	10.00	20.00
—Black label					
X-1082 [PS]	There'll Be No Teardrops Tonight	1955	5.00	10.00	20.00
X-1101	I Saw the Light/Mansion on the Hill//Six More Miles/Wedding Bells	1955	15.00	30.00	60.00
—Yellow label					

Number	Title (A Side/B Side)	Yr	VG	VG+	NM
X-1101	I Saw the Light/Mansion on the Hill//Six More Miles/Wedding Bells	1960	5.00	10.00	20.00
—Black label					
X-1101 [PS]	Hank Williams Sings	1955	5.00	10.00	20.00
X-1102	Lost Highway/I've Just Told Mama Goodbye//Wealth Won't Save Your Soul/A House Without Love	1955	15.00	30.00	60.00
—Yellow label					
X-1102	Lost Highway/I've Just Told Mama Goodbye//Wealth Won't Save Your Soul/A House Without Love	1960	5.00	10.00	20.00
—Black label					
X-1102 [PS]	Hank Williams Sings Vol. 2	1955	5.00	10.00	20.00
X-1135	Ramblin' Man/My Son Calls Another Man Daddy//I Can't Escape from You/Nobody's Lonesome for Me	1955	10.00	20.00	40.00
—Yellow label					
X-1135	Ramblin' Man/My Son Calls Another Man Daddy//I Can't Escape from You/Nobody's Lonesome for Me	1960	3.75	7.50	15.00
—Black label					
X-1135 [PS]	Ramblin' Man Vol. 1	1955	3.75	7.50	15.00
X-1136	Lonesome Whistle/I Jus' Don't Like This Kind of Livin'//Take These Chains from My Heart/Why Don't You Love Me?	1955	10.00	20.00	40.00
—Yellow label					
X-1136	Lonesome Whistle/I Jus' Don't Like This Kind of Livin'//Take These Chains from My Heart/Why Don't You Love Me?	1960	3.75	7.50	15.00
—Black label					
X-1136 [PS]	Ramblin' Man Vol. 2	1955	3.75	7.50	15.00
X-1165	Why Don't You Make Up Your Mind/I've Been Down That Road Before//Just Waitin'/Everything's Okay	1955	10.00	20.00	40.00
—Yellow label					
X-1165	Why Don't You Make Up Your Mind/I've Been Down That Road Before//Just Waitin'/Everything's Okay	1960	3.75	7.50	15.00
—Black label					
X-1165 [PS]	Luke the Drifter	1955	3.75	7.50	15.00
X-1215	(contents unknown)	1956	10.00	20.00	40.00
—Yellow label					
X-1215	(contents unknown)	1960	3.75	7.50	15.00
—Black label					
X-1215 [PS]	Moanin' the Blues Vol. 1	1956	3.75	7.50	15.00
X-1216	Moanin' the Blues/I'm So Lonesome I Could Cry//My Sweet Love Ain't Around/Honky Tonk Blues	1956	10.00	20.00	40.00
—Yellow label					
X-1216	Moanin' the Blues/I'm So Lonesome I Could Cry//My Sweet Love Ain't Around/Honky Tonk Blues	1960	3.75	7.50	15.00
—Black label					
X-1216 [PS]	Moanin' the Blues Vol. 2	1956	3.75	7.50	15.00
X-1217	Lovesick Blues/The Blues Come Around//I'm a Long Gone Daddy/Long Gone Lonesome Blues	1956	10.00	20.00	40.00
—Yellow label					
X-1217	Lovesick Blues/The Blues Come Around//I'm a Long Gone Daddy/Long Gone Lonesome Blues	1960	3.75	7.50	15.00
—Black label					
X-1217 [PS]	Moanin' the Blues Vol. 3	1956	3.75	7.50	15.00
X-1218	I'm Gonna Sing/Message to My Mother//Thank God/The Angel of Death	1956	10.00	20.00	40.00
—Yellow label					
X-1218	I'm Gonna Sing/Message to My Mother//Thank God/The Angel of Death	1960	3.75	7.50	15.00
—Black label					
X-1218 [PS]	I Saw the Light	1956	3.75	7.50	15.00
X-1235	*Honky Tonkin'/Mind Your Own Business/Rootie Tootie/I Ain't Got Nothing But Time	1956	10.00	20.00	40.00
—Yellow label					
X-1235	*Honky Tonkin'/Mind Your Own Business/Rootie Tootie/I Ain't Got Nothing But Time	1960	3.75	7.50	15.00
—Black label					
X-1235 [PS]	Honky Tonkin'	1956	3.75	7.50	15.00
X-1317	Jambalaya (On the Bayou)/I Won't Be Home No More//Honky Tonk Blues/I'll Never Get Out of This World Alive	1957	10.00	20.00	40.00
—Yellow label					
X-1317	Jambalaya (On the Bayou)/I Won't Be Home No More//Honky Tonk Blues/I'll Never Get Out of This World Alive	1960	3.75	7.50	15.00
—Black label					
X-1317 [PS]	Honky Tonkin' Vol. 1	1957	3.75	7.50	15.00
X-1318	Honky Tonkin'/Howlin' at the Moon//My Bucket's Got a Hole in It/Baby, We're Really in Love	1957	10.00	20.00	40.00
—Yellow label					
X-1318	Honky Tonkin'/Howlin' at the Moon//My Bucket's Got a Hole in It/Baby, We're Really in Love	1960	3.75	7.50	15.00
—Black label					
X-1318 [PS]	Honky Tonkin' Vol. 2	1957	3.75	7.50	15.00
X-1319	Mind Your Own Business/Rootie Tootie//I Ain't Got Nothin' But Time/You Better Keep It on Your Mind	1957	10.00	20.00	40.00
—Yellow label					
X-1319	Mind Your Own Business/Rootie Tootie//I Ain't Got Nothin' But Time/You Better Keep It on Your Mind	1960	3.75	7.50	15.00
—Black label					
X-1319 [PS]	Honky Tonkin' Vol. 3	1957	3.75	7.50	15.00
X-1491	Wedding Bells/May You Never Be Alone//Lost Highway/Why Should We Try Anymore	1958	7.50	5.00	30.00
—Yellow label					
X-1491	Wedding Bells/May You Never Be Alone//Lost Highway/Why Should We Try Anymore	1960	3.75	7.50	15.00
—Black label					
X-1491 [PS]	Sing Me a Blue Song Vol. 1	1958	3.75	7.50	15.00

Number	Title (A Side/B Side)	Yr	VG	VG+	NM
X-1492	I Heard You Crying in Your Sleep/Blue Love//Mansion on the Hill/They'll Never Take Her Love from Me	1958	7.50	15.00	30.00
—Yellow label					
X-1492	I Heard You Crying in Your Sleep/Blue Love//Mansion on the Hill/They'll Never Take Her Love from Me	1960	3.75	7.50	15.00
—Black label					
X-1492 [PS]	Sing Me a Blue Song Vol. 2	1958	3.75	7.50	15.00
X-1493	I've Just Told Mama Goodbye/House Without Love//Six More Miles/Singing Waterfall	1958	7.50	15.00	30.00
—Yellow label					
X-1493	I've Just Told Mama Goodbye/House Without Love//Six More Miles/Singing Waterfall	1960	3.75	7.50	15.00
—Black label					
X-1493 [PS]	Sing Me a Blue Song Vol. 3	1958	3.75	7.50	15.00
X-1554	There's No Room in My Heart/Waltz of the Wind//Pan American/With Tears in My Eyes	1958	7.50	15.00	30.00
—Yellow label					
X-1554	There's No Room in My Heart/Waltz of the Wind//Pan American/With Tears in My Eyes	1960	3.75	7.50	15.00
—Black label					
X-1554 [PS]	The Immortal Hank Williams Vol. 1	1958	3.75	7.50	15.00
X-1555	I Wish I Had a Nickel/Fly Trouble//Please Don't Let Me Love You/I'm Satisfied with You	1958	7.50	15.00	30.00
—Yellow label					
X-1555	I Wish I Had a Nickel/Fly Trouble//Please Don't Let Me Love You/I'm Satisfied with You	1960	3.75	7.50	15.00
—Black label					
X-1555 [PS]	The Immortal Hank Williams Vol. 2	1958	3.75	7.50	15.00
X-1556	No One Will Ever Know/Faded Love and Winter Roses//First Fall of Snow/California Zephyr	1958	7.50	15.00	30.00
—Yellow label					
X-1556	No One Will Ever Know/Faded Love and Winter Roses//First Fall of Snow/California Zephyr	1960	3.75	7.50	15.00
—Black label					
X-1556 [PS]	The Immortal Hank Williams Vol. 3	1958	3.75	7.50	15.00
X-1612	Your Cheatin' Heart/Settin' the Woods on Fire//You Win Again/Hey, Good Lookin'	1959	7.50	15.00	30.00
—Yellow label					
X-1612	Your Cheatin' Heart/Settin' the Woods on Fire//You Win Again/Hey, Good Lookin'	1960	3.75	7.50	15.00
—Black label					
X-1612 [PS]	Hank Williams Memorial Album Vol. 1	1959	3.75	7.50	15.00
X-1613	Cold, Cold Heart/Kaw-Liga//I Could Never Be Ashamed of You/Half As Much	1959	7.50	15.00	30.00
—Yellow label					
X-1613	Cold, Cold Heart/Kaw-Liga//I Could Never Be Ashamed of You/Half As Much	1960	3.75	7.50	15.00
—Black label					
X-1613 [PS]	Hank Williams Memorial Album Vol. 2	1959	3.75	7.50	15.00
X-1614	Crazy Heart/Move It On Over//My Heart Would Know/I'm Sorry for You My Friend	1959	7.50	15.00	30.00
—Yellow label					
X-1614	Crazy Heart/Move It On Over//My Heart Would Know/I'm Sorry for You My Friend	1960	3.75	7.50	15.00
—Black label					
X-1614 [PS]	Hank Williams Memorial Album Vol. 3	1959	3.75	7.50	15.00
X-1637	*I Can't Get You Off My Mind/I Don't Care (If Tomorrow Never Comes)/Dear John/My Love for You (Has Turned to Hate)	1959	7.50	15.00	30.00
—Yellow label					
X-1637	*I Can't Get You Off My Mind/I Don't Care (If Tomorrow Never Comes)/Dear John/My Love for You (Has Turned to Hate)	1959	3.75	7.50	15.00
—Black label					
X-1637 [PS]	The Unforgettable Hank Williams, Vol. 1	1959	3.75	7.50	15.00
X-1643	Pictures from Life's Other Side/Men with Broken Hearts//Help Me Understand/Too Many Parties and Too Many Pals	1959	7.50	15.00	30.00
—Yellow label					
X-1643	Pictures from Life's Other Side/Men with Broken Hearts//Help Me Understand/Too Many Parties and Too Many Pals	1960	3.75	7.50	15.00
—Black label					
X-1643 [PS]	Hank Williams As Luke The Drifter	1959	3.75	7.50	15.00
X-1644	Be Careful of Stones That You Throw/I Dreamed About Mama Last Night//Funeral/Beyond the Sunset	1959	7.50	15.00	30.00
—Yellow label					
X-1644	Be Careful of Stones That You Throw/I Dreamed About Mama Last Night//Funeral/Beyond the Sunset	1960	3.75	7.50	15.00
—Black label					
X-1644 [PS]	Hank Williams As Luke The Drifter	1959	3.75	7.50	15.00
X-1698	(contents unknown)	1960	3.75	7.50	15.00
X-1698 [PS]	The Lonesome Sound of Hank Williams Vol. 1	1960	3.75	7.50	15.00
X-1699	(contents unknown)	1960	3.75	7.50	15.00
X-1699 [PS]	The Lonesome Sound of Hank Williams Vol. 2	1960	3.75	7.50	15.00
X-1700	(contents unknown)	1960	3.75	7.50	15.00
X-1700 [PS]	The Lonesome Sound of Hank Williams Vol. 3	1960	3.75	7.50	15.00
X-4041	Moanin' the Blues/I'm So Lonesome I Could Cry//My Sweet Love Ain't Around/Honky Tonk Blues	1953	10.00	20.00	40.00
—One record of "X168"					
X-4042	Lovesick Blues/The Blues Come Around//I'm a Long Gone Daddy/Long Gone Lonesome Blues	1953	10.00	20.00	40.00
—One record of "X168"					
X-4102	Your Cheatin' Heart/Settin' the Woods on Fire//You Win Again/Hey, Good Lookin'	1953	10.00	20.00	40.00
—One record of "X202"					
X-4103	Cold, Cold Heart/Kaw-Liga//I Could Never Be Ashamed of You/Half as Much	1953	10.00	20.00	40.00
—One record of "X202"					
Albums					
COUNTRY MUSIC FOUNDATION					
CMF-006	Just Me and My Guitar	198?	2.50	5.00	10.00
CMF-007	The First Recordings	198?	2.50	5.00	10.00
METRO					
M-509 [M]	Hank Williams	1966	5.00	10.00	20.00
MS-509 [R]	Hank Williams	1966	3.00	6.00	12.00
M-547 [M]	Mr. and Mrs. Hank Williams	1966	5.00	10.00	20.00
MS-547 [R]	Mr. and Mrs. Hank Williams	1966	3.00	6.00	12.00
M-602 [M]	The Immortal Hank Williams	1967	5.00	10.00	20.00
MS-602 [R]	The Immortal Hank Williams	1967	3.00	6.00	12.00
MGM					
3E-2 [(3) M]	36 of Hank Williams' Greatest Hits	1957	50.00	100.00	200.00
—Yellow labels					
3E-2 [(3) M]	36 of Hank Williams' Greatest Hits	1960	25.00	50.00	100.00
—Black labels					
3E-4 [(3) M]	36 More of Hank Williams' Greatest Hits	1958	50.00	100.00	200.00
—Yellow labels					
3E-4 [(3) M]	36 More of Hank Williams' Greatest Hits	1960	25.00	50.00	100.00
—Black labels					
E-107 [10]	Hank Williams Sings	1952	100.00	200.00	400.00
E-168 [10]	Moanin' the Blues	1952	100.00	200.00	400.00
E-202 [10]	Memorial Album	1953	100.00	200.00	400.00
E-203 [10]	Hank Williams as Luke the Drifter	1953	100.00	200.00	400.00
E-242 [10]	Honky Tonkin'	1954	100.00	200.00	400.00
E-243 [10]	I Saw the Light	1954	100.00	200.00	400.00
E-291 [10]	Ramblin' Man	1954	100.00	200.00	400.00
PRO-912 [(3) DJ]	Reflections of Those Who Loved Him	1975	62.50	125.00	250.00
—Promo-only box set					
E-3219 [M]	Ramblin' Man	1955	25.00	50.00	100.00
—Yellow label					
E-3219 [M]	Ramblin' Man	1960	10.00	20.00	40.00
—Black label					
E-3267 [M]	Hank Williams as Luke the Drifter	1955	25.00	50.00	100.00
—Yellow label					
E-3267 [M]	Hank Williams as Luke the Drifter	1960	10.00	20.00	40.00
—Black label					
E-3272 [M]	Memorial Album	1955	25.00	50.00	100.00
—Yellow label					
E-3272 [M]	Memorial Album	1960	10.00	20.00	40.00
—Black label					
E-3330 [M]	Moanin' the Blues	1956	25.00	50.00	100.00
—Yellow label					
E-3330 [M]	Moanin' the Blues	1960	10.00	20.00	40.00
—Black label					
E-3331 [M]	I Saw the Light	1956	50.00	100.00	200.00
—Yellow label; green cover					
E-3331 [M]	I Saw the Light	1959	25.00	50.00	100.00
—Yellow label; church on cover					
E-3331 [M]	I Saw the Light	1960	10.00	20.00	40.00
—Black label					
SE-3331 [R]	I Saw the Light	1968	3.00	6.00	12.00
—Blue and gold label					
E-3412 [M]	Honky Tonkin'	1957	25.00	50.00	100.00
—Yellow label					
E-3412 [M]	Honky Tonkin'	1960	10.00	20.00	40.00
—Black label					
E-3560 [M]	Sing Me a Blue Song	1957	25.00	50.00	100.00
—Yellow label					
E-3560 [M]	Sing Me a Blue Song	1960	10.00	20.00	40.00
—Black label					
E-3605 [M]	The Immortal Hank Williams	1958	25.00	50.00	100.00
—Yellow label					
E-3605 [M]	The Immortal Hank Williams	1960	10.00	20.00	40.00
—Black label					
E-3733 [M]	The Unforgettable Hank Williams	1959	25.00	50.00	100.00
—Yellow label					
E-3733 [M]	The Unforgettable Hank Williams	1960	10.00	20.00	40.00
—Black label					
SE-3733 [R]	The Unforgettable Hank Williams	1968	3.00	6.00	12.00
—Blue and gold label					
E-3803 [M]	The Lonesome Sound of Hank Williams	1960	10.00	20.00	40.00
E-3850 [M]	Wait for the Light to Shine	1960	10.00	20.00	40.00
SE-3850 [R]	Wait for the Light to Shine	1968	3.00	6.00	12.00
—Blue and gold label					
E-3918 [M]	Hank Williams' Greatest Hits	1961	10.00	20.00	40.00
SE-3918 [R]	Hank Williams' Greatest Hits	1963	5.00	10.00	20.00
—Black label					
SE-3918 [R]	Hank Williams' Greatest Hits	1968	3.00	6.00	12.00
—Blue and gold label					
E-3923 [M]	Hank Williams Lives Again	1961	10.00	20.00	40.00
E-3924 [M]	Sing Me a Blue Song	1961	10.00	20.00	40.00
E-3925 [M]	Wanderin' Around	1961	10.00	20.00	40.00
E-3926 [M]	I'm Blue Inside	1961	10.00	20.00	40.00
E-3927 [M]	Luke the Drifter	1961	10.00	20.00	40.00
E-3928 [M]	First, Last and Always	1961	10.00	20.00	40.00
SE-3928 [R]	First, Last and Always	1968	3.00	6.00	12.00
—Blue and gold label					
E-3955 [M]	The Spirit of Hank Williams	1961	10.00	20.00	40.00
SE-3955 [R]	The Spirit of Hank Williams	1968	3.00	6.00	12.00
—Blue and gold label					
E-3999 [M]	On Stage! Hank Williams Recorded Live	1962	15.00	30.00	60.00
E-3999 [M]	Hank Williams on Stage Recorded Live	1962	10.00	20.00	40.00
—Note revised title					
SE-3999 [R]	Hank Williams on Stage Recorded Live	1968	3.00	6.00	12.00
—Blue and gold label					
E-4040 [M]	Hank Williams' Greatest Hits, Volume 2	1962	10.00	20.00	40.00
SE-4040 [R]	Hank Williams' Greatest Hits, Volume 2	1963	3.75	7.50	15.00
—Black label					
SE-4040 [R]	Hank Williams' Greatest Hits, Volume 2	1968	3.00	6.00	12.00
—Blue and gold label					
E-4109 [M]	Hank Williams on Stage, Volume 2	1963	10.00	20.00	40.00
SE-4109 [R]	Hank Williams on Stage, Volume 2	1963	5.00	10.00	20.00
—Black label					
SE-4109 [R]	Hank Williams on Stage, Volume 2	1968	3.00	6.00	12.00
—Blue and gold label					
E-4138 [M]	Beyond the Sunset	1963	7.50	15.00	30.00
SE-4138 [R]	Beyond the Sunset	1963	3.75	7.50	15.00
—Black label					

Number	Title (A Side/B Side)	Yr	VG	VG+	NM
E-4140 [M]	14 More of Hank Williams' Greatest Hits (Volume 3)	1963	7.50	15.00	30.00
SE-4140 [R]	14 More of Hank Williams' Greatest Hits (Volume 3)	1963	3.75	7.50	15.00
—Black label					
SE-4140 [R]	14 More of Hank Williams' Greatest Hits (Volume 3)	1968	3.00	6.00	12.00
—Blue and gold label					
E-4168 [M]	The Very Best of Hank Williams	1963	7.50	15.00	30.00
SE-4168 [R]	The Very Best of Hank Williams	1963	3.75	7.50	15.00
—Black label					
SE-4168 [R]	The Very Best of Hank Williams	1968	3.00	6.00	12.00
—Blue and gold label					
E-4227 [M]	The Very Best of Hank Williams, Volume 2	1964	7.50	15.00	30.00
SE-4227 [R]	The Very Best of Hank Williams, Volume 2	1964	3.75	7.50	15.00
—Black label					
SE-4227 [R]	The Very Best of Hank Williams, Volume 2	1968	3.00	6.00	12.00
—Blue and gold label					
E-4254 [M]	Lost Highway (and Other Folk Ballads)	1964	10.00	20.00	40.00
SE-4254 [R]	Lost Highway (and Other Folk Ballads)	1964	5.00	10.00	20.00
—Black label					
SE-4254 [R]	Lost Highway (and Other Folk Ballads)	1968	3.00	6.00	12.00
—Blue and gold label					
E-4267-4 [(4) M]	The Hank Williams Story	1965	15.00	30.00	60.00
E-4300 [M]	Kaw-Liga and Other Humorous Songs	1965	7.50	15.00	30.00
SE-4300 [R]	Kaw-Liga and Other Humorous Songs	1965	3.75	7.50	15.00
—Black label					
SE-4300 [R]	Kaw-Liga and Other Humorous Songs	1968	3.00	6.00	12.00
—Blue and gold label					
E-4377 [M]	The Legend Lives Anew — Hank Williams with Strings	1966	5.00	10.00	20.00
SE-4377 [S]	The Legend Lives Anew — Hank Williams with Strings	1966	6.25	12.50	25.00
—Black label					
SE-4377 [S]	The Legend Lives Anew — Hank Williams with Strings	1968	3.75	7.50	15.00
—Blue and gold label					
E-4380 [M]	Movin' on — Luke the Drifter	1966	7.50	15.00	30.00
SE-4380 [R]	Movin' on — Luke the Drifter	1968	3.00	6.00	12.00
—Blue and gold label					
E-4429 [M]	More Hank Williams and Strings	1966	5.00	10.00	20.00
SE-4429 [S]	More Hank Williams and Strings	1966	6.25	12.50	25.00
—Black label					
SE-4429 [S]	More Hank Williams and Strings	1968	3.75	7.50	15.00
—Blue and gold label					
E-4481 [M]	I Won't Be Home No More	1967	7.50	15.00	30.00
SE-4481 [S]	I Won't Be Home No More	1967	5.00	10.00	20.00
—Black label					
SE-4481 [S]	I Won't Be Home No More	1968	3.75	7.50	15.00
—Blue and gold label					
E-4529 [M]	Hank Williams and Strings, Volume 3	1968	10.00	20.00	40.00
SE-4529 [S]	Hank Williams and Strings, Volume 3	1968	5.00	10.00	20.00
E-4576 [M]	Hank Williams in the Beginning	1968	10.00	20.00	40.00
SE-4576 [R]	Hank Williams in the Beginning	1968	3.75	7.50	15.00
SE-4651	Essential Hank Williams	1969	3.00	6.00	12.00
SE-4680	Life to Legend	1970	3.00	6.00	12.00
SE-4755-2 [(2)]	24 Greatest Hits	1971	3.75	7.50	15.00
M3G-4954	Archetypes	1974	3.00	6.00	12.00
MG-1-5019	Hank Williams, Sr., Live at the Grand Old Opry	1976	3.00	6.00	12.00
MG-2-5401 [(2)]	24 Greatest Hits, Volume 2	197?	3.75	7.50	15.00
ST-90511 [R]	The Very Best of Hank Williams	1965	5.00	10.00	20.00
—Capitol Record Club edition					
T-90511 [M]	The Very Best of Hank Williams	1965	10.00	20.00	40.00
—Capitol Record Club edition					
ST-90884 [R]	Movin' on — Luke the Drifter	1968	3.75	7.50	15.00
—Capitol Record Club edition; blue and gold label					
ST-91115 [S]	The Legend Lives Anew — Hank Williams with Strings	1968	5.00	10.00	20.00
—Capitol Record Club edition; blue and gold label					
POLYDOR					
821233-1 [(2)]	40 Greatest Hits	1984	3.75	7.50	15.00
823291-1	Hank Williams' Greatest Hits	1984	2.00	4.00	8.00
823292-1	The Very Best of Hank Williams	1984	2.00	4.00	8.00
823293-1 [(2)]	24 Greatest Hits	1984	3.00	6.00	12.00
823294-1 [(2)]	24 Greatest Hits, Volume 2	1984	3.00	6.00	12.00
823695-1	Rare Takes and Radio Cuts	1984	2.50	5.00	10.00
825531-1	On the Air	1985	2.50	5.00	10.00
825548-1	I Ain't Got Nothin' But Time	1985	2.50	5.00	10.00
825551-1	Lovesick Blues	1985	2.50	5.00	10.00
825554-1	Lost Highway	1986	2.50	5.00	10.00
825557-1	I'm So Lonesome I Could Cry	1986	2.50	5.00	10.00
831574-1	Beyond the Sunset	1987	2.50	5.00	10.00
831633-1	Long Gone Lonesome Blues	1987	2.50	5.00	10.00
831634-1	Hey, Good Lookin'	1987	2.50	5.00	10.00
833749-1	Let's Turn Back the Years	1988	2.50	5.00	10.00
833752-1	I Won't Be Home No More	1988	2.50	5.00	10.00
TIME-LIFE					
3003 [(3)]	Country and Western Classics	1981	7.50	15.00	30.00

WILLIAMS, HANK /ROY ACUFF

Albums

Number	Title (A Side/B Side)	Yr	VG	VG+	NM
LAMB AND LION					
LL-706 [(3)]	Hank Williams, Sr./Roy Acuff "Collector's Item!"	197?	10.00	20.00	40.00
—Sides 1-4 are reissues of Hank Williams; side 5-6 are Roy Acuff					

WILLIAMS, HANK, AND HANK WILLIAMS, JR.

Also see each artist's individual listings.

45s

Number	Title (A Side/B Side)	Yr	VG	VG+	NM
WARNER BROS.					
27584	There's a Tear in My Beer/You Brought Me Down to Earth	1989	—	2.00	4.00
—B-side by Hank Jr. solo					

Albums

Number	Title (A Side/B Side)	Yr	VG	VG+	NM
MGM					
E-4276 [M]	Father and Son	1965	5.00	10.00	20.00
SE-4276 [S]	Father and Son	1965	6.25	12.50	25.00
E-4378 [M]	Again	1966	5.00	10.00	20.00
SE-4378 [S]	Again	1966	6.25	12.50	25.00
2SES-4865 [(2)]	Hank Williams: The Legend in Story and Song	1973	3.75	7.50	15.00
M3HB 4975 [(2)]	Insights Into Hank Williams in Song and Story	1974	3.75	7.50	15.00

WILLIAMS, HANK, JR.

12-Inch Singles

Number	Title (A Side/B Side)	Yr	VG	VG+	NM
WARNER BROS.					
PRO-A-2088 [DJ]	Woman on the Run (same on both sides)	1983	2.00	4.00	8.00
PRO-A-2662 [DJ]	My Name Is Bocephus (same on both sides)	1987	2.00	4.00	8.00

45s

Number	Title (A Side/B Side)	Yr	VG	VG+	NM
CAPRICORN					
18486	Diamond Mine/Dirty Mind	1993	—	—	3.00
18614	Everything Comes Down to Money and Love/S.O.B. I'm Tired	1993	—	—	3.00
18800	Lyin' Jukebox/Fax Me a Beer	1992	—	—	3.00
18923	Come On Over to the Country/Wild Weekend	1992	—	—	3.00
19023	Hotel Whiskey/The Count Song	1992	—	—	3.00
ELEKTRA					
46018	To Love Somebody/We Can Work It All Out	1979	—	2.50	5.00
46046	Family Tradition/Paying On Time	1979	—	2.50	5.00
46535	Whiskey Bent and Hell Bound/O.D.'d in Denver	1979	—	2.50	5.00
46593	Women I've Never Had/Tired of Being Johnny B. Goode	1980	—	2.50	5.00
46636	Kaw-Liga/The American Way	1980	—	2.50	5.00
47012	If You Don't Like Hank Williams/Outlaw Women	1980	—	3.00	6.00
47016	Old Habits/Won't It Be Nice	1980	—	2.50	5.00
47102	Texas Women/You Can't Find Many Kisses	1981	—	2.50	5.00
47137	Dixie on My Mind/Ramblin' Man	1981	—	2.50	5.00
47191	All My Rowdy Friends (Have Settled Down)/Everytime I Hear That Song	1981	—	2.50	5.00
47231 [DJ]	Little Drummer Boy/The Christmas Song	1981	2.00	4.00	8.00
—B-side by Sonny Curtis					
47257	A Country Boy Can Survive/Weatherman	1982	—	2.50	5.00
47462	Honky Tonkin'/High and Pressurized	1982	—	2.50	5.00
69846	Gonna Go Huntin' Tonight/Twodot, Montana	1983	—	2.00	4.00
69960	The American Dream/If Heaven Ain't a Lot Like Dixie	1982	—	2.00	4.00
MCG CURB					
76932	I Ain't Goin' Peacefully/Greeted in Enid	1995	—	2.00	4.00
76948	Hog Wild/Wild Thing	1995	—	2.00	4.00
MGM					
13208	Long Gone Lonesome Blues/Doesn't Anybody Know My Name	1964	3.00	6.00	12.00
13253	Guess What, That's Right, She's Gone/Goin' Steady with the Blues	1964	3.00	6.00	12.00
13278	Endless Sleep/My Bucket's Got a Hole In It	1964	3.00	6.00	12.00
13318	I'm So Lonesome I Could Cry/Is It That Much Fun to Hurt Someone	1965	3.00	6.00	12.00
13353	I Went to All That Trouble for Nothin'/Mule Skinner Blues	1965	3.00	6.00	12.00
13392	Pecos Jail/You're Ruinin' My Life	1965	3.00	6.00	12.00
13443	Rainmaker/The River	1966	3.00	6.00	12.00
13504	Standing in the Shadows/It's Written All Over Your Face	1966	3.00	6.00	12.00
13640	I Can't Take It No Longer/You Can Hear a Tear Drop	1966	3.00	6.00	12.00
13730	I'm In No Condition/I'm Gonna Break Your Heart	1967	3.00	6.00	12.00
13782	Nobody's Child/The Next Best Thing to Nothing	1967	3.00	6.00	12.00
13857	I Wouldn't Change a Thing About You (But Your Name)/No Meaning and No End	1967	3.00	6.00	12.00
13922	The Old Ryman/I Wonder Where You Are Tonight	1968	2.50	5.00	10.00
13968	It's All Over But the Crying/Rock in My Shoes	1968	2.50	5.00	10.00
14002	I Was With Red Foley (The Night He Passed Away)/On Trial	1968	3.00	6.00	12.00
—As "Luke the Drifter, Jr."					
14020	Custody/My Home Town Circle "R"	1968	3.00	6.00	12.00
—As "Luke the Drifter, Jr."					
14024	A Baby Again/Swim Across a Tear	1969	2.50	5.00	10.00
14047	Cajun Baby/My Heart Won't Let Me Go	1969	2.50	5.00	10.00
14062	Be Careful of Stones That You Throw/Book of Memories	1969	2.50	5.00	10.00
—As "Luke the Drifter, Jr."					
14077	I'd Rather Be Gone/Try, Try Again	1969	2.50	5.00	10.00
14095	Something to Think About/(There Must Be) A Better Way to Love	1969	2.50	5.00	10.00
—As "Luke the Drifter, Jr."					
14107	I Walked Out on Heaven/Your Love's One Thing	1970	2.00	4.00	8.00
14120	It Don't Take But One Mistake/Goin' Home	1970	2.00	4.00	8.00
—As "Luke the Drifter, Jr."					
14136	Removing the Shadow/Party People	1970	2.00	4.00	8.00
—With Lois Johnson					
14152	All for the Love of Sunshine/Ballad of the Moonshine	1970	2.00	4.00	8.00
14164	So Sad (To Watch Good Love Go Bad)/Let's Talk It Over Again	1970	2.00	4.00	8.00
—With Lois Johnson					
14194	Rainin' in My Heart/A-Eee	1970	2.00	4.00	8.00
14240	I've Got a Right to Cry/Jesus Loved the Devil Out of Me	1971	2.00	4.00	8.00
14277	After All They All Used to Belong to Me/Happy Kind of Sadness	1971	2.00	4.00	8.00
14317	Ain't That a Shame/End of a Bad Day	1971	2.00	4.00	8.00
14356	Send Me Some Lovin'/What We Used to Hang On To	1972	2.00	4.00	8.00
—With Lois Johnson					
14371	Eleven Roses/Richmond Valley Breeze	1972	2.00	4.00	8.00
14421	Pride's Not Hard to Swallow/Hamburger Steak, Holiday Inn	1972	2.00	4.00	8.00
14443	Whole Lotta Loving/Why Should We Try Anymore	1972	2.00	4.00	8.00
—With Lois Johnson					
14486	After You/Knoxville Courthouse Blues	1973	—	3.00	6.00
14550	Hank/Hank (Part 2)	1973	—	3.00	6.00
14656	The Last Love Song/Those Tear Jerking Songs	1973	—	3.00	6.00

Number	Title (A Side/B Side)	Yr	VG	VG+	NM
14700	Rainy Night in Georgia/Country Music in My Soul	1974	—	3.00	6.00
14731	I'll Think of Something/Country Music Lover	1974	—	3.00	6.00
14755	Angels Are Hard to Find/Getting Over You	1974	—	3.00	6.00
14794	Where He's Going, I've Already Gone/The Kind of Woman I've Got	1975	—	3.00	6.00
14813	The Same Old Story/Country Love	1975	—	3.00	6.00
14833	Stoned at the Jukebox/The Devil in the Bottle	1975	—	3.00	6.00
14845	Living Proof/Brothers of the Road	1976	—	3.00	6.00
VERVE					
10540	Meter Reader Maid/Just a Dream	1967	12.50	25.00	50.00
—As "Bocephus"					
10572	Mental Revenge/Splish Splash	1967	10.00	20.00	40.00
—As "Bocephus"					
WARNER BROS.					
PRO-S-3838 [DJ]	All My Rowdy Friends (Are Here on Monday Night) (same on both sides)	1989	3.75	7.50	15.00
PRO-S-4492 [DJ]	Don't Give Us a Reason (same on both sides)	1990	2.00	4.00	8.00
8361	Mobile Boogie/She's the Star (On the Stage of My Mind)	1977	—	2.50	5.00
8410	I'm Not Responsible/(Honey, Won't You) Call Me	1977	—	2.50	5.00
8451	One Night Stands/I'm Not Responsible	1977	—	2.50	5.00
8507	Feelin' Better/Once and For All	1977	—	2.50	5.00
8549	The New South/Storms Never Last	1978	—	3.00	6.00
8564	You Love the Thunder/I Just Ain't Been Able	1978	—	2.50	5.00
8641	I Fought the Law/It's Different with You	1978	—	2.50	5.00
8715	Old Flame, New Fire/Payin' On Time	1978	—	2.50	5.00
19193	Angels Are Hard to Find/Hollywood Honeys	1991	—	—	3.00
19352	If It Will It Will/Won't It Be Nice	1991	—	—	3.00
19463	I Mean I Love You/Stoned at the Jukebox	1990	—	—	3.00
19542	Don't Give Us a Reason/U.S.A. Today	1990	—	—	3.00
19818	Man to Man/Whiskey Bent and Hell Bound	1990	—	—	3.00
19872	Good Friends, Good Whiskey, Good Lovin'/Family Tradition	1990	—	—	3.00
19957	Ain't Nobody's Business/Big Mamou	1990	—	—	3.00
22945	Finders Are Keepers/What You Don't Know (Won't Hurt You)	1989	—	—	3.00
27722	Early in the Morning and Late at Night/I'm Just a Man	1988	—	—	3.00
27862	If the South Woulda Won/Wild Steak	1988	—	—	3.00
28120	Young Country/Buck Naked	1988	—	—	3.00
28227	Heaven Can't Be Found/Doctor's Song	1987	—	—	3.00
28369	Born to Boogie/What It Boils Down To	1987	—	—	3.00
28452	When Something Is Good (Why Does It Change)/Loving Instructor	1987	—	—	3.00
28581	Mind Your Own Business/My Name Is Bocephus	1986	—	2.00	4.00
28691	Country State of Mind/Fat Friends	1986	—	2.00	4.00
28794	Ain't Misbehavin'/I've Been Around	1986	—	2.00	4.00
28912	This Ain't Dallas/I Really Like Girls	1985	—	2.00	4.00
29022	I'm for Love/Lawyers, Guns and Money	1985	—	2.00	4.00
29095	Major Moves/Mr. Lincoln	1985	—	2.00	4.00
29184	All My Rowdy Friends Are Coming Over Tonight/Video Blues	1984	—	2.00	4.00
29253	Attitude Adjustment/Knoxville Courthouse Blues	1984	—	2.00	4.00
29382	Man of Steel/Now I Know How George Feels	1984	—	2.00	4.00
29500	Queen of My Heart/She Had Me	1983	—	2.00	4.00
29633	Leave Them Boys Alone/The Girl in the Front Row at Fort Worth	1983	—	2.00	4.00
Albums					
CAPRICORN					
W1-26806	Maverick	1992	5.00	10.00	20.00
—Columbia House edition (only U.S. vinyl release)					
ELEKTRA					
6E-194	Family Tradition	1979	3.00	6.00	12.00
6E-237	Whiskey Bent and Hell Bound	1979	2.50	5.00	10.00
6E-278	Habits Old and New	1980	2.50	5.00	10.00
6E-330	Rowdy	1981	2.50	5.00	10.00
5E-535	The Pressure Is On	1981	2.50	5.00	10.00
5E-538	One Night Stands	1982	2.50	5.00	10.00
—Reissue					
5E-539	The New South	1982	2.50	5.00	10.00
—Reissue					
60100	High Notes	1982	2.50	5.00	10.00
60193	Hank Williams, Jr.'s, Greatest Hits	1982	2.50	5.00	10.00
60223	Strong Stuff	1983	3.75	7.50	15.00
MGM					
GAS-119	Hank Williams, Jr. (Golden Archive Series)	1970	3.75	7.50	15.00
E-4213 [M]	Sings the Songs of Hank Williams	1964	5.00	10.00	20.00
SE-4213 [S]	Sings the Songs of Hank Williams	1964	6.25	12.50	25.00
E-4260 [M]	Your Cheatin' Heart	1964	5.00	10.00	20.00
SE-4260 [S]	Your Cheatin' Heart	1964	6.25	12.50	25.00
E-4316 [M]	Ballads of the Hills and Plains	1965	5.00	10.00	20.00
SE-4316 [S]	Ballads of the Hills and Plains	1965	6.25	12.50	25.00
E-4344 [M]	Blues My Name	1966	5.00	10.00	20.00
SE-4344 [S]	Blues My Name	1966	6.25	12.50	25.00
E-4391 [M]	Country Shadows	1966	5.00	10.00	20.00
SE-4391 [S]	Country Shadows	1966	6.25	12.50	25.00
E-4428 [M]	In My Own Way	1967	5.00	10.00	20.00
SE-4428 [S]	In My Own Way	1967	6.25	12.50	25.00
E-4513 [M]	The Best of Hank Williams, Jr.	1967	5.00	10.00	20.00
SE-4513 [S]	The Best of Hank Williams, Jr.	1967	6.25	12.50	25.00
E-4527 [M]	My Songs	1968	—	—	—
—Unreleased?					
SE-4527 [S]	My Songs	1968	6.25	12.50	25.00
SE-4540	A Time to Sing	1968	6.25	12.50	25.00
SE-4559	Luke the Drifter, Jr.	1969	5.00	10.00	20.00
SE-4621	Songs My Father Left Me	1969	5.00	10.00	20.00
SE-4632	Luke the Drifter, Jr. (Vol. 2)	1969	5.00	10.00	20.00
SE-4644	Live at Cobo Hall, Detroit	1969	5.00	10.00	20.00
SE-4656	Hank Williams, Jr.'s Greatest Hits	1970	3.75	7.50	15.00
SE-4657	Sunday Morning	1970	3.75	7.50	15.00
SE-4673	Luke the Drifter, Jr. (Vol. 3)	1970	3.75	7.50	15.00
SE-4675	Hank Williams, Jr., Singing My Songs (Johnny Cash)	1970	3.75	7.50	15.00
SE-4721	Removing the Shadows	1971	3.75	7.50	15.00
SE-4774	I've Got a Right to Cry/They All Used to Belong to Me	1971	3.75	7.50	15.00
SE-4798	Sweet Dreams	1972	3.00	6.00	12.00
—With the Mike Curb Congregation					
SE-4822	Hank Williams, Jr.'s Greatest Hits, Volume 2	1972	3.00	6.00	12.00
SE-4843	Eleven Roses	1972	3.00	6.00	12.00
SE-4862	After You/Pride's Not Hard to Swallow	1973	3.00	6.00	12.00
M3G-4906	Just Pickin' — No Singin'	1973	3.00	6.00	12.00
M3G-4936	The Last Love Song	1973	3.00	6.00	12.00
M3G-4971	Living Proof	1974	3.00	6.00	12.00
M3G-4988	Bocephus	1974	3.00	6.00	12.00
MG-1-5009	Hank Williams, Jr., and Friends	1975	10.00	20.00	40.00
MG-1-5020	14 Greatest Hits	1976	3.00	6.00	12.00
ST-90695 [S]	Blues My Name	1966	7.50	15.00	30.00
—Capitol Record Club edition					
T-90695 [M]	Blues My Name	1966	6.25	12.50	25.00
—Capitol Record Club edition					
PAIR					
PDL2-1164 [(2)]	I'm Walkin'	1987	3.00	6.00	12.00
POLYDOR					
811902-1	Live at Cobo Hall, Detroit	1983	2.00	4.00	8.00
—Reissue					
811903-1	Hank Williams, Jr.'s Greatest Hits	1983	2.00	4.00	8.00
811906-1	Hank Williams, Jr.'s Greatest Hits, Volume 2	1983	2.00	4.00	8.00
825091-1	14 Greatest Hits	1985	2.00	4.00	8.00
831575-1	Hank Williams, Jr., and Friends	1987	3.00	6.00	12.00
833069-1	Blues My Name	1987	2.00	4.00	8.00
833070-1	Eleven Roses	1987	2.00	4.00	8.00
835132-1	Standing in the Shadows	1988	2.00	4.00	8.00
WARNER BROS.					
6E-194	Family Tradition	1983	2.00	4.00	8.00
6E-237	Whiskey Bent and Hell Bound	1983	2.00	4.00	8.00
6E-278	Habits Old and New	1983	2.00	4.00	8.00
6E-330	Rowdy	1983	2.00	4.00	8.00
5E-535	The Pressure Is On	1983	2.00	4.00	8.00
5E-538	One Night Stands	1983	2.00	4.00	8.00
5E-539	The New South	1983	2.00	4.00	8.00
PRO-A-2092 [DJ]	The Hank Williams, Jr., Interview	1983	6.25	12.50	25.00
BS 2988	One Night Stands	1977	3.00	6.00	12.00
BS 3127	The New South	1977	3.00	6.00	12.00
23924	Man of Steel	1983	2.50	5.00	10.00
25088	Major Moves	1984	2.50	5.00	10.00
25267	Five-O	1985	2.50	5.00	10.00
25328	Greatest Hits — Volume 2	1985	2.00	4.00	8.00
25412	Montana Café	1986	2.00	4.00	8.00
25538	Hank "Live"	1987	2.00	4.00	8.00
25593	Born to Boogie	1987	2.00	4.00	8.00
25725	Wild Streak	1988	2.00	4.00	8.00
25834	Greatest Hits III	1989	2.00	4.00	8.00
26090	Lone Wolf	1990	3.00	6.00	12.00
60100	High Notes	1983	2.00	4.00	8.00
60193	Hank Williams, Jr.'s, Greatest Hits	1983	2.00	4.00	8.00
60223	Strong Stuff	1983	2.50	5.00	10.00
R 120612	America (The Way I See It)	1990	5.00	10.00	20.00
—BMG Music Service edition (no regular vinyl release)					
R 160351	Pure Hank	1991	5.00	10.00	20.00
—BMG Music Service edition (no regular vinyl release)					

WILLIAMS, HANK, JR., AND LOIS JOHNSON

Albums

MGM

Number	Title (A Side/B Side)	Yr	VG	VG+	NM
SE-4750	All for the Love of Sunshine	1971	5.00	10.00	20.00
SE-4857	Send Me Some Lovin'/Whole Lotta Lovin'	1972	5.00	10.00	20.00

WILLIAMS, JIM

45s

SUN

Number	Title (A Side/B Side)	Yr	VG	VG+	NM
270	Please Don't Cry Over Me/That Depends on You	1957	7.50	15.00	30.00

WILLIAMS, JIMMY

45s

Number	Title (A Side/B Side)	Yr	VG	VG+	NM
ABC-PARAMOUNT					
10471	I Gave My Love a Cherry/Half Man	1963	3.00	6.00	12.00
10523	Green Pastures (23rd Psalm)/I'm Strung Out Over You, Baby	1964	3.00	6.00	12.00
ATLANTIC					
2296	Walking on Air/I'm So Lost	1965	2.50	5.00	10.00
CUB					
9031	My Pledge and My Promise/Keep Me with You	1959	3.75	7.50	15.00
9039	C'mon Baby (What's Your Name)/Don't Put It Off (Do It Now)	1959	3.75	7.50	15.00
DUB					
2842	You're Always Late/I Belong to You	1958	25.00	50.00	100.00
DYNO VOICE					
931	Mushroom City/Standing There	1969	2.00	4.00	8.00
HULL					
765	I Can't Help Falling in Love/Smile	1964	2.50	5.00	10.00
LIMELIGHT					
3038	Mrs. Cherry/Keoto'To	1964	2.50	5.00	10.00
MGM					
11938	No One Knows/These Blues Are Over You	1955	5.00	10.00	20.00
12262	Alpha and Omega/Where Will I Shelter My Sheep	1956	5.00	10.00	20.00
12362	Throwing My Life Away/We're Drifting Further Apart	1956	5.00	10.00	20.00
12596	You're the One/I'll Only Give My Love	1957	6.25	12.50	25.00
ORBIT					
9002	You're the One/I'll Only Give My Love	1958	3.75	7.50	15.00
ROULETTE					
4303	There Is No Doubt/What a Change	1960	3.75	7.50	15.00

WILLIAMS, LARRY

Also see JOHNNY "GUITAR" WATSON AND LARRY WILLIAMS.

Number	Title (A Side/B Side)	Yr	VG	VG+	NM
45s					
BELL					
813	I Could Love You Baby/Can't Find No Substitute for Love	1969	2.50	5.00	10.00
—With Johnny Watson					
CHESS					
1736	My Baby's Got Soul/Every Day I Wonder	1959	5.00	10.00	20.00
1745	Get Ready/Baby, Baby	1959	5.00	10.00	20.00
1761	I Wanna Know/Like a Gentle Man	1960	5.00	10.00	20.00
1764	Oh Baby/I Hear My Baby	1960	5.00	10.00	20.00
1805	Lawdy Mama/Fresh Out of Tears	1961	5.00	10.00	20.00
EL BAM					
69	Call on Me/Boss Lovin'	1965	3.00	6.00	12.00
FANTASY					
806	Doing the Best I Can (With What I Got)/Gimme Some	1977	—	2.50	5.00
810	One Thing or the Other (Part 1)/One Thing or the Other (Part 2)	1977	—	2.50	5.00
841	The Resurrection of Funk/(B-side unknown)	1978	—	2.50	5.00
MERCURY					
72147	Woman/Can't Help Myself	1963	3.75	7.50	15.00
OKEH					
7259	This Old Heart (Is So Lonely)/I'd Rather Fight Than Switch	1966	2.50	5.00	10.00
7280	I Am the One/You Ask for One Good Reason	1967	2.50	5.00	10.00
7294	Just Because/Boss Lovin'	1967	2.50	5.00	10.00
SMASH					
2035	Call on Me/Boss Lovin'	1966	3.00	6.00	12.00
SPECIALTY					
597	Just Because/Let Me Tell You Baby	1957	7.50	15.00	30.00
608	Short Fat Fannie/High School Dance	1957	10.00	20.00	40.00
608	Short Fat Fannie/High School Dance	1984	—	2.00	4.00
—Gold vinyl					
615	Bony Moronie/You Bug Me, Baby	1957	10.00	20.00	40.00
615	Bony Moronie/You Bug Me, Baby	1984	—	2.00	4.00
—Red vinyl					
626	Dizzy, Miss Lizzy/Slow Down	1958	10.00	20.00	40.00
626	Dizzy, Miss Lizzy/Slow Down	1984	—	2.00	4.00
—Blue vinyl					
626 [PS]	Dizzy, Miss Lizzy/Slow Down	1958	20.00	40.00	80.00
634	Hootchy-Koo/The Dummy	1958	6.25	12.50	25.00
634	Hootchy-Koo/The Dummy	1984	—	2.00	4.00
—Green vinyl					
647	I Was a Fool/Peaches and Cream	1958	6.25	12.50	25.00
658	Bad Boy/She Said "Yeah"	1959	7.50	15.00	30.00
658	Bad Boy/She Said "Yeah"	1984	—	2.00	4.00
—Orange vinyl					
665	Steal a Little Kiss/I Can't Stop Loving You	1959	6.25	12.50	25.00
677	Give Me Your Love/Teardrops	1959	6.25	12.50	25.00
682	Ting-a-Ling/Little Schoolgirl	1960	6.25	12.50	25.00
682	Ting-a-Ling/Little Schoolgirl	1984	—	2.00	4.00
—Gold vinyl					
VENTURE					
622	Shake Your Body Girl/Love I Can't Seem to Find It	1968	2.50	5.00	10.00
627	Wake Up (Nothing Comes to a Sleeper But a Dream)/Love I Can't Seem to Find It	1968	2.50	5.00	10.00
Albums					
CHESS					
LP-1457 [M]	Larry Williams	1961	50.00	100.00	200.00
OKEH					
OKM-12123 [M]	Larry Williams' Greatest Hits	1967	7.50	15.00	30.00
OKS-14123 [S]	Larry Williams' Greatest Hits	1967	10.00	20.00	40.00
SPECIALTY					
SP-2109 [M]	Here's Larry Williams	1959	50.00	100.00	200.00
—Original pressing on thick vinyl with no copyright information on back cover					
SP-2109 [M]	Here's Larry Williams	198?	2.50	5.00	10.00
—Reissue with thinner vinyl and copyright information on back					
SP-7002 [(2)]	Bad Boy	1990	5.00	10.00	20.00

WILLIAMS, LENNY

Number	Title (A Side/B Side)	Yr	VG	VG+	NM
Albums					
ABC					
AB-1023	Choosing You	1977	2.50	5.00	10.00
AA-1073	Spark of Love	1978	2.50	5.00	10.00
MCA					
3155	Love Current	1979	2.50	5.00	10.00
5147	Let's Do It Today	1980	2.50	5.00	10.00
5253	Taking Chances	1982	2.50	5.00	10.00
MOTOWN					
M6-843	Rise Sleeping Beauty	1975	3.00	6.00	12.00

WILLIAMS, LESTER

Number	Title (A Side/B Side)	Yr	VG	VG+	NM
45s					
DUKE					
123	Let's Do It/Good Lovin' Baby	1954	12.50	25.00	50.00
131	Crazy 'Bout You Baby/Don't Take Your Love from Me	1954	10.00	20.00	40.00
IMPERIAL					
5402	McDonald's Daughter/Daddy Loves You	1956	12.50	25.00	50.00
SPECIALTY					
422	I Can't Lose with the Stuff I Use/My Home Ain't Here	1952	25.00	50.00	100.00
431	Let Me Tell You a Thing or Two/Tryin' to Forget	1952	37.50	75.00	150.00
437	Sweet Lovin' Daddy/Lost Gal	1952	37.50	75.00	150.00
450	Brand New Baby/If I Knew How Much I Loved You	1953	25.00	50.00	100.00

WILLIAMS, LEW

Number	Title (A Side/B Side)	Yr	VG	VG+	NM
45s					
IMPERIAL					
5394	Cat Talk/Gone Ape Man	1956	30.00	60.00	120.00
5411	Bop Bop Ba Doo Bop/Something I Said	1956	30.00	60.00	120.00
5429	Centipede/Abra Cadabra	1957	30.00	60.00	120.00
8306	Don't Mention My Name/I'll Play Your Game	1956	—	—	—

WILLIAMS, MASON

Number	Title (A Side/B Side)	Yr	VG	VG+	NM
45s					
WARNER BROS.					
7190	Classical Gas/Long Time Blues	1968	—	3.00	6.00
7235	Baroque-a-Nova/Wanderlove	1968	—	2.50	5.00
7245	Cinderella Rockafella/Generatah-Oscillath	1968	—	2.50	5.00
7248	Saturday Night at the World/One Minute Commercial	1968	—	2.50	5.00
7272	Greensleeves/13 Dollar Stella	1969	—	2.50	5.00
7301	Gift of Song/Major Thang	1969	—	2.50	5.00
7402	Find a Reason to Believe/Jose's Piece	1970	—	2.50	5.00
7513	Here I Am Again/Train Ride in G	1971	—	2.50	5.00
Albums					
AMERICAN GRAMAPHONE					
AG-800	Classical Gas	1987	2.50	5.00	10.00
—With Mannheim Steamroller					
EVEREST					
3265	Listening Matter	1969	3.00	6.00	12.00
FLYING FISH					
FF-059	Fresh Fish	1978	2.50	5.00	10.00
VEE JAY					
VJ-1103 [M]	Them Poems and Things	1964	5.00	10.00	20.00
VJS-1103 [S]	Them Poems and Things	1964	6.25	12.50	25.00
WARNER BROS.					
WS 1729	The Mason Williams Phonograph Record	1968	3.00	6.00	12.00
—Green label with "W7" logo					
WS 1729	The Mason Williams Phonograph Record	1970	2.50	5.00	10.00
—Green label with "WB" logo					
WS 1729	The Mason Williams Phonograph Record	1973	2.00	4.00	8.00
—"Burbank" palm trees label					
WS 1729	The Mason Williams Phonograph Record	1979	—	3.00	6.00
—White or tan label					
WS 1776	The Mason Williams Ear Show	1968	3.00	6.00	12.00
WS 1788	Music by Mason Williams	1969	3.00	6.00	12.00
WS 1838	Hand Made	1970	3.00	6.00	12.00
WS 1941	Sharepickers	1971	3.00	6.00	12.00

WILLIAMS, MAURICE, AND THE ZODIACS

Also see THE GLADIOLAS.

Number	Title (A Side/B Side)	Yr	VG	VG+	NM
45s					
ATLANTIC					
2199	Funny/Loneliness	1963	3.75	7.50	15.00
—As "The Zodiacs"					
2741	Sweetness/Whirlpool	1970	—	2.50	5.00
COLE					
100	Golly Gee/"I" Town	1959	12.50	25.00	50.00
101	Lover (Where Are You)/She's Mine	1959	10.00	20.00	40.00
DEESU					
302	Baby Baby/Being Without You	1967	5.00	10.00	20.00
304	May I/This Feeling	1967	5.00	10.00	20.00
307	Ooh Poo Pa Doo (Part 1)/Ooh Poo Pa Doo (Part 2)	1967	5.00	10.00	20.00
309	Don't Ever Leave Me/Surely	1967	5.00	10.00	20.00
311	Don't Be Half Safe/How to Pick a Winner	1967	5.00	10.00	20.00
318	Stay '68 (Live Version)/Dance, Dance, Dance	1968	3.75	7.50	15.00
HERALD					
552	Stay/Do You Believe	1960	5.00	10.00	20.00
556	Always/I Remember	1961	3.75	7.50	15.00
559	Do I/Come Along	1961	3.75	7.50	15.00
563	Someday/Come and Get It	1961	3.75	7.50	15.00
565	Please/High Blood Pressure	1961	3.75	7.50	15.00
572	It's Alright/Here I Stand	1962	3.75	7.50	15.00
RCA					
5363-7-R	Stay/She's Like the Wind	1987	—	—	3.00
—B-side by Patrick Swayze					
SCEPTER					
12113	Nobody Knows/I Know	1965	3.75	7.50	15.00
SEA HORN					
503	My Baby's Gone/Return	1964	3.75	7.50	15.00
SELWYN					
5121	Say Yeah/College Girl	1959	12.50	25.00	50.00
SPHERE SOUND					
707	So Fine/The Winds	1965	3.00	6.00	12.00
VEE JAY					
678	May I/Lollipop	1965	5.00	10.00	20.00
VEEP					
1294	My Reason for Living/The Four Corners	1969	2.00	4.00	8.00
Albums					
COLLECTABLES					
COL-5021	The Best of Maurice Williams and the Zodiacs	198?	2.50	5.00	10.00
HERALD					
HLP-1014 [M]	Stay	1961	125.00	250.00	500.00
RELIC					
5017	Greatest Hits	197?	3.75	7.50	15.00
SNYDER					
5586 [M]	At the Beach	196?	25.00	50.00	100.00
SPHERE SOUND					
SR-7007 [M]	Stay	1965	30.00	60.00	120.00
SSR-7007 [R]	Stay	1965	20.00	40.00	80.00

WILLIAMS, OTIS, AND HIS CHARMS

Also see THE CHARMS.

Number	Title (A Side/B Side)	Yr	VG	VG+	NM
45s					
DELUXE					
6088	Miss the Love/Tell Me Now	1955	7.50	15.00	30.00
—As "Otis Williams and His New Group"					

Number	Title (A Side/B Side)	Yr	VG	VG+	NM
6090	Gum Drop/Save Me, Save Me	1955	7.50	15.00	30.00
—As "Otis Williams and His New Group"					
6091	That's Your Mistake/Too Late I Learned	1955	7.50	15.00	30.00
6092	Rolling Home/Do Be You	1956	7.50	15.00	30.00
6093	Ivory Tower/In Paradise	1956	7.50	15.00	30.00
6095	One Night Only/It's All Over	1956	7.50	15.00	30.00
6097	I'd Like to Thank You Mr. D.J./Whirlwind	1956	7.50	15.00	30.00
6098	Gypsy Lady/I'll Remember You	1956	7.50	15.00	30.00
6105	Blues Stay Away from Me/Pardon Me	1957	6.25	12.50	25.00
6115	Walkin' After Midnight/I'm Waiting Just for You	1957	6.25	12.50	25.00
6130	Nowhere on Earth/No Got De Woman	1957	6.25	12.50	25.00
6137	Talking to Myself/One Kind Word from You	1957	6.25	12.50	25.00
6138	United/Don't Deny Me	1957	6.25	12.50	25.00
6149	Dynamite Darling/Well Oh Well	1957	6.25	12.50	25.00
6158	Could This Be Magic/Oh Julie	1958	6.25	12.50	25.00
6160	Let Some Love in Your Heart/Baby-O	1958	6.25	12.50	25.00
6165	Burnin' Lips/Red Hot Love (Do This Love)	1958	6.25	12.50	25.00
6174	Don't Wake Up the Kids/You'll Remain Forever	1958	6.25	12.50	25.00
6178	My Friends/The Secret	1958	6.25	12.50	25.00
6181	Pretty Little Things Called Girls/Welcome Home	1959	6.25	12.50	25.00
6183	My Prayer Tonight/Watch Dog	1959	6.25	12.50	25.00
6185	I Knew It All the Time/Tears of Happiness	1959	6.25	12.50	25.00
6186	In Paradise/Who Knows	1959	6.25	12.50	25.00
6187	Blues Stay Away from Me/Funny What True Love Can Do	1959	6.25	12.50	25.00
KING					
5323	Chief Um (Take It Easy)/It's a Treat	1960	5.00	10.00	20.00
5332	Silver Star/Rickety Rickshaw Man	1960	5.00	10.00	20.00
5372	Image of a Girl/Wait a Minute Baby	1960	12.50	25.00	50.00
5389	The First Sign of Love/So Be It	1960	5.00	10.00	20.00
5421	Wait/And Take My Love	1960	5.00	10.00	20.00
5455	Little Turtle Dove/So Can I	1961	5.00	10.00	20.00
5497	Just Forget About Me/You Know How Much I Care	1961	5.00	10.00	20.00
5527	Pardon Me/Panic	1961	5.00	10.00	20.00
5558	Two Hearts/The Secret	1961	5.00	10.00	20.00
5682	When We Get Together/Only Young Once	1962	3.75	7.50	15.00
5816	It Just Ain't Right/It'll Never Happen Again	1963	3.75	7.50	15.00
5880	Unchain My Heart/Friends Call Me a Fool	1964	3.75	7.50	15.00
6034	Bye Bye Baby/Please Believe in Me	1966	3.75	7.50	15.00
OKEH					
7225	Baby, You Turn Me On/Love Don't Grow on Trees	1965	3.75	7.50	15.00
7235	I Fall to Pieces/Gotta Get Myself Together	1965	3.75	7.50	15.00
7248	I Got Loving/Welcome Home	1966	3.75	7.50	15.00
7261	Ain't Gonna Walk Your Dog No More/Your Sweet Love (Rained Over Me)	1966	3.75	7.50	15.00
SCEPTER					
12376	Here Lie the Bones of Nellie Jones/When You Turn On the Love	1973	2.00	4.00	8.00
STOP					
301	Begging to You/(B-side unknown)	1968	2.50	5.00	10.00
306	Begging to You/Everybody's Got a Song But Me	1968	2.50	5.00	10.00
346	Jesus Is a Soul Man/Make a Woman Feel Like a Woman	1969	2.50	5.00	10.00
360	Ling, Ting, Tong/For the Love	1970	2.50	5.00	10.00
388	I Wanna Go Country/Rocky Top	1971	2.00	4.00	8.00
—As "Otis Williams and the Midnight Cowboys"					
7-Inch Extended Plays					
DELUXE					
385	(contents unknown)	1956	75.00	150.00	300.00
385	Otis Williams and His Charms	1956	75.00	150.00	300.00
Albums					
DELUXE					
570 [M]	Their All Time Hits	1957	250.00	500.00	1000.
KING					
570 [M]	Their All Time Hits	1957	150.00	300.00	600.00
614 [M]	This Is Otis Williams and His Charms	1959	100.00	200.00	400.00
STOP					
STLP-1022	Otis Williams and the Midnight Cowboys	1971	6.25	12.50	25.00

WILLIAMS, PAUL

Number	Title (A Side/B Side)	Yr	VG	VG+	NM
45s					
A&M					
1325	We've Only Just Begun/Waking Up Alone	1972	—	2.00	4.00
1356	My Love and I/I Never Had It So Good	1972	—	2.00	4.00
1409	I Won't Last a Day Without You/Little Girl	1973	—	2.00	4.00
1429	Lady in Waiting/Look What I Found	1973	—	2.00	4.00
1479	What Would They Say/Inspiration	1973	—	2.00	4.00
1525	That's What Friends Are For/Dream Away	1974	—	2.00	4.00
1659	A Little Bit of Love/Nice to Be Around	1975	—	2.00	4.00
1686	One More Angel/This Is Supposed to Be a Party	1975	—	2.00	4.00
1797	Don't Call It Love/Time and Tide	1976	—	2.00	4.00
1853	Even Better Than I Know Myself/Time and Tide	1976	—	2.00	4.00
1868	Bugsy Malone/Ordinary Fool	1976	—	2.00	4.00
1961	Love Theme from "A Star Is Born"/Waking Up Alone	1977	—	2.00	4.00
PAID					
146	Making Believe/Oh, How I Miss You Tonight	1981	—	2.00	4.00
PORTRAIT					
70029	The Gift/A Little on the Windy Side	1979	—	2.00	4.00
REPRISE					
0903	Someday/Mornin' I'll Be Movin' On	1970	—	3.00	6.00
Albums					
A&M					
SP-3131	Just an Old Fashioned Love Song	198?	2.00	4.00	8.00
—Budget-line reissue					
SP-3606	Here Comes Inspiration	1974	2.50	5.00	10.00
SP-3655	A Little Bit of Love	1974	2.50	5.00	10.00
SP-4327	Just an Old Fashioned Love Song	1971	2.50	5.00	10.00
SP-4367	Life Goes On	1972	2.50	5.00	10.00
SP-4550	Ordinary Fool	1975	2.50	5.00	10.00
SP-4701	Classics	1977	2.50	5.00	10.00
PORTRAIT					
JR 35610	Windy Side	1979	2.50	5.00	10.00
REPRISE					
RS 6401	Someday Man	1970	3.00	6.00	12.00

WILLIAMS, ROGER

Number	Title (A Side/B Side)	Yr	VG	VG+	NM
45s					
KAPP					
KJB-48	Try to Remember/(B-side unknown)	1965	—	3.00	6.00
KJB-87	White Christmas/Winter Wonderland	196?	2.00	4.00	8.00
101	You'll Never Walk Alone/The Boy Next Door	1955	2.50	5.00	10.00
116	Autumn Leaves/Take Care	1955	2.50	5.00	10.00
116 [PS]	Autumn Leaves/Take Care	1955	5.00	10.00	20.00
127	Wanting You/Night Wind	1955	2.50	5.00	10.00
138	La Mer (Beyond the Sea)/Song of Devotion	1956	2.50	5.00	10.00
144	Hi-Lili, Hi-Lo/My Dream Sonata	1956	2.50	5.00	10.00
156	Tumbling Tumbleweeds/I'll Always Walk with You	1956	2.50	5.00	10.00
161	Two Different Worlds/Nights in Verona	1956	2.50	5.00	10.00
—With Jane Morgan					
169	Anastasia/A Serenade for Joy	1956	2.50	5.00	10.00
175	Almost Paradise/For the First Time	1957	2.00	4.00	8.00
186	Moonlight Love/Every Little Movement	1957	2.00	4.00	8.00
197	Till/Big Town	1957	2.00	4.00	8.00
210	Arrivederci Roma/Sentimental Touch	1958	2.00	4.00	8.00
224	Indiscreet/Young and Warm and Wonderful	1958	2.00	4.00	8.00
233	Near You/Merry Widow Waltz	1958	2.00	4.00	8.00
246	The World Outside/Tchaikovsky Piano Concerto	1958	2.00	4.00	8.00
257	Dearer Than Dear/The Key to the Kingdom	1959	2.00	4.00	8.00
265	Mockin' Bird Hill/Memories Are Made of This	1959	2.00	4.00	8.00
299	Adeste Fideles/Hark the Herald Angels Sing	1959	2.50	5.00	10.00
300	Mary's Little Boy Child/Winter Wonderland	1959	2.50	5.00	10.00
301	Sunrise Serenade/Cool Water	1959	2.00	4.00	8.00
331	La Montana (If She Should Come to You)/What Lies Over the Hill	1960	—	3.50	7.00
345	Little Rock Get Away/Riviera Concerto	1960	—	3.50	7.00
347	Temptation/Homesick for New England	1960	—	3.50	7.00
364	Maria Maria/I Get a Kick Out of You	1961	—	3.50	7.00
386	A Lover's Symphony/Song of the Rain	1961	—	3.50	7.00
408	Yellow Bird/Roger's Bumble Bee	1961	—	3.50	7.00
437	Maria/Even Tide	1961	—	3.50	7.00
437 [PS]	Maria/Even Tide	1961	3.00	6.00	12.00
440	Santa Claus, Santa Claus (We Love You)/Jingle Bells	1961	2.50	5.00	10.00
447	Amor/Maria	1962	—	3.50	7.00
454	Intermezzo/Skaters' Waltz	1962	—	3.50	7.00
470	Hatari/On Top of Old Smoky	1962	—	3.50	7.00
479	Lorelei/Niagara Theme	1962	—	3.50	7.00
492	Theme from Mutiny on the Bounty/It's Now or Never	1962	—	3.50	7.00
505	Cold, Cold Heart/San Antonio Rose	1963	—	3.00	6.00
522	Walking Alone/On the Trail	1963	—	3.00	6.00
533	Theme from "11th Hour"/Janie Is Her Name	1963	—	3.00	6.00
545	Danke Schoen/Look Again	1963	—	3.00	6.00
560	Cardinal/Walking Alone	1963	—	3.00	6.00
574	Felicia/Takewood Nocturne	1964	—	3.00	6.00
587	This Is My Prayer/Roger's Bumble Bee	1964	—	3.00	6.00
607	Lollipops and Roses/Whistlin'	1964	—	3.00	6.00
707	Autumn Leaves 1965/Autumn Leaves 1955	1965	—	3.00	6.00
738	Lara's Theme from "Dr. Zhivago"/Dulcinea	1966	—	3.00	6.00
767	Born Free/Jimmie's Train	1966	—	3.00	6.00
801	Sunrise, Sunset/Edelweiss	1966	—	2.50	5.00
821	Love Me Forever/Sweet Pea	1967	—	2.50	5.00
843	Tiny Bubbles/More Than a Miracle	1967	—	2.50	5.00
890	Spinning Song/Glory of Love	1968	—	2.50	5.00
907	The Impossible Dream/If You Go	1968	—	2.50	5.00
929	Who Killed Ezra Brymay/Marlena	1968	—	2.50	5.00
949	Elvira Madigan Theme/Only for Lovers	1968	—	2.50	5.00
975	Love Theme from La Strada/Gentle on My Mind	1969	—	2.50	5.00
995	Love Theme from Romeo and Juliet/As Long As He Needs Me	1969	—	2.50	5.00
2007	Galveston/Mini Minuet	1969	—	2.00	4.00
2043	The Windmills of Your Mind/Fill the World with Love	1969	—	2.00	4.00
2064	Let It Be Me/Fill the World with Love	1969	—	2.00	4.00
2078	The Lonely Ones/I'm a Believer	1970	—	2.00	4.00
2084	Suicide Is Painless/The Time for Love Is Anytime	1970	—	2.00	4.00
2106	Junk/Butterflies	1970	—	2.00	4.00
2110	America the Beautiful/Ain't No Mountain High Enough	1970	—	2.00	4.00
2123	Theme from Love Story/For All We Know	1971	—	2.00	4.00
2135	Wandering Star/Your Song	1971	—	2.00	4.00
2140	Summer Knows/Your Song	1971	—	2.00	4.00
2148	How Can You Mend a Broken Heart/Bach Talk	1971	—	2.00	4.00
2165	Love Theme from The Godfather/Life Is What You Name It	1972	—	2.00	4.00
2177	The Way of Love/Tchaikovsky '73	1972	—	2.00	4.00
2189	Lady Sings the Blues/Play Me	1972	—	2.00	4.00
MCA					
40044	Theme from "Baxter"/Rain Song	1973	—	—	3.00
40098	Tie a Yellow Ribbon Round the Ole Oak Tree/Rain Song	1973	—	—	3.00
40155	Theme from "Exodus"/Hungarian Dance No. 5	1973	—	—	3.00
40185	Dark Lady/Solace	1974	—	—	3.00
40341	Theme from "Murder on the Orient Express"/Half-Breed	1974	—	—	3.00
40373	Theme from "The Young and the Restless"/Melody to Dawn	1975	—	2.00	4.00
40451	Theme from "Rollerball"/Bolero	1975	—	—	3.00
40529	Country Comfort/Roger's Bumble Bee (Latter Day)	1976	—	—	3.00
40571	God Bless America/Grieg's You Know What By Roger You Know Who	1976	—	—	3.00
40625	Jesu Joy of Man's Desiring/Cast Your Fate to the Wind	1976	—	—	3.00
40669	Main Title from "King Kong"/Love Song	1976	—	—	3.00

Number	Title (A Side/B Side)	Yr	VG	VG+	NM
40725	Love Theme from "A Star Is Born"/Theme from "Airport '77"	1977	—	—	3.00
40741	Theme from "New York, New York"/Me	1977	—	—	3.00
40845	You Light Up My Life/Candle on the Water	1977	—	—	3.00
40873	Verde (Green)/How Can You Mend a Broken Heart	1978	—	—	3.00

WARNER BROS.

Number	Title (A Side/B Side)	Yr	VG	VG+	NM
49584	Somewhere in Time/Bee Side	1980	—	—	3.00

7-Inch Extended Plays

KAPP

Number	Title (A Side/B Side)	Yr	VG	VG+	NM
KE-708	*Autumn Leaves/Take Care/Summertime/'Til Roses Cry	1956	2.00	4.00	8.00
KE-708 [PS]	Roger Williams Plays…	1956	2.00	4.00	8.00
KE-714	*True Love/Because of You/Young at Heart/Three Coins in the Fountain	195?	2.00	4.00	8.00
KE-714 [PS]	Songs of the Fabulous Fifties 1	195?	2.00	4.00	8.00
KE-715	(contents unknown)	195?	2.00	4.00	8.00
KE-715 [PS]	Songs of the Fabulous Fifties 2	195?	2.00	4.00	8.00
KE-716	(contents unknown)	195?	2.00	4.00	8.00
KE-716 [PS]	Songs of the Fabulous Fifties 3	195?	2.00	4.00	8.00
KE-717	*Tennessee Waltz/High Noon/Blue Tango/Hey There	195?	2.00	4.00	8.00
KE-717 [PS]	Songs of the Fabulous Fifties 4	195?	2.00	4.00	8.00
KE-737	*Holiday for Strings/The Last Time I Saw Paris/Anniversary Song/Some Enchanted Evening	195?	2.00	4.00	8.00
KE-737 [PS]	Songs of the Fabulous Forties Vol. 1	195?	2.00	4.00	8.00
KE-751	*Till/Marcheta/Always/The Merry Widow Waltz	1958	2.00	4.00	8.00
KE-751 [PS]	Roger Williams	1958	2.00	4.00	8.00

Albums

BAINBRIDGE

Number	Title (A Side/B Side)	Yr	VG	VG+	NM
6265	Somewhere in Time	1986	2.50	5.00	10.00
8002 [(2)]	Ivory Impact	1982	3.00	6.00	12.00

HOLIDAY

Number	Title (A Side/B Side)	Yr	VG	VG+	NM
HDY 1927	Golden Christmas	1981	2.00	4.00	8.00

KAPP

Number	Title (A Side/B Side)	Yr	VG	VG+	NM
KLE-1 [(3) M]	10th Anniversary/Limited Edition	1964	5.00	10.00	20.00
—Reissue of Kapp 1088, 1130 and 1172 in one package					
SKLE-1 [(3) S]	10th Anniversary/Limited Edition	1964	6.25	12.50	25.00
KW-900 [M]	Roger Williams Showcase	196?	3.00	6.00	12.00
SKW-900 [S]	Roger Williams Showcase	196?	3.75	7.50	15.00
KL-1003 [M]	The Boy Next Door	1955	6.25	12.50	25.00
—Maroon and silver (or blue and silver) labels					
KL-1003 [M]	The Boy Next Door	1962	3.00	6.00	12.00
—Any later label variation					
KL-1008 [M]	It's a Big, Wide, Wonderful World	1955	6.25	12.50	25.00
—Maroon and silver (or blue and silver) labels					
KL-1008 [M]	It's a Big, Wide, Wonderful World	1962	3.00	6.00	12.00
—Any later label variation					
KL-1012 [M]	Roger Williams	1956	6.25	12.50	25.00
KL-1012 [M]	Autumn Leaves	1956	5.00	10.00	20.00
—Retitled version of above; maroon and silver (or blue and silver) label					
KL-1012 [M]	Autumn Leaves	1962	3.00	6.00	12.00
—Any later label variation					
KL-1031 [M]	Daydreams	1956	3.75	7.50	15.00
—Maroon and silver (or blue and silver) label					
KL-1031 [M]	Daydreams	1962	3.00	6.00	12.00
—Any later label variation					
KL-1040 [M]	Roger Williams Plays the Wonderful Music of the Masters	1956	3.75	7.50	15.00
—Maroon and silver (or blue and silver) label					
KL-1040 [M]	Roger Williams Plays the Wonderful Music of the Masters	1962	3.00	6.00	12.00
—Any later label variation					
KL-1042 [M]	Roger Williams Plays Christmas Songs	1956	3.75	7.50	15.00
—Maroon and silver label; unbanded					
KL-1062 [M]	Roger Williams Plays Beautiful Waltzes	1957	3.75	7.50	15.00
—Maroon and silver (or blue and silver) label					
KL-1062 [M]	Roger Williams Plays Beautiful Waltzes	1962	3.00	6.00	12.00
—Any later label variation					
KL-1063 [M]	Almost Paradise	1957	3.75	7.50	15.00
—Maroon and silver (or blue and silver) label					
KL-1063 [M]	Almost Paradise	1962	3.00	6.00	12.00
—Any later label variation					
K-1081-S [S]	Till	1959	5.00	10.00	20.00
—Maroon and silver (or blue and silver) labels					
KL-1081 [M]	Till	1958	3.75	7.50	15.00
—Maroon and silver (or blue and silver) label					
KL-1081 [M]	Till	1962	3.00	6.00	12.00
—Any later label variation					
KS-1081 [S]	Till	1962	3.75	7.50	15.00
—Any later label variation					
KL-1088 [M]	Roger Williams Plays Gershwin	1958	3.75	7.50	15.00
—Maroon and silver (or blue and silver) labels					
KL-1088 [M]	Roger Williams Plays Gershwin	1962	3.00	6.00	12.00
—Any later label variation					
KL-1112 [M]	Near You	1959	3.75	7.50	15.00
—Maroon and silver (or blue and silver) labels					
KL-1112 [M]	Near You	1962	3.00	6.00	12.00
—Any later label variation					
KS-1112 [S]	Near You	1959	5.00	10.00	20.00
—Maroon and silver (or blue and silver) labels					
KS-1112 [S]	Near You	1962	3.75	7.50	15.00
—Any later label variation					
KL-1130 [M]	More Songs of the Fabulous Fifties	1959	3.75	7.50	15.00
—Maroon and silver (or blue and silver) labels					
KL-1130 [M]	More Songs of the Fabulous Fifties	1962	3.00	6.00	12.00
—Any later label variation					
KL-1147 [M]	With These Hands	1959	3.75	7.50	15.00
—Maroon and silver (or blue and silver) labels					
KL-1147 [M]	With These Hands	1962	3.00	6.00	12.00
—Any later label variation					
KL-1164 [M]	Christmas Time	1959	3.75	7.50	15.00
—"Merry Christmas" silver, red and green label					
KL-1164 [M]	Christmas Time	1962	3.00	6.00	12.00
—Any later label variation					
KL-1172 [M]	Always	1960	3.75	7.50	15.00
—Maroon and silver (or blue and silver) labels					
KL-1172 [M]	Always	1962	3.00	6.00	12.00
—Any later label variation					
KL-1207 [M]	Songs of the Fabulous Forties, Volume 1	1960	3.00	6.00	12.00
KL-1208 [M]	Songs of the Fabulous Forties, Volume 2	1960	3.00	6.00	12.00
KL-1209 [M]	Songs of the Fabulous Fifties, Volume 1	1960	3.00	6.00	12.00
KL-1210 [M]	Songs of the Fabulous Fifties, Volume 2	1960	3.00	6.00	12.00
KL-1211 [M]	Songs of the Fabulous Century, Volume 1	1960	3.00	6.00	12.00
KL-1212 [M]	Songs of the Fabulous Century, Volume 2	1960	3.00	6.00	12.00
KL-1217 [M]	Temptation	1960	3.75	7.50	15.00
—Maroon and silver (or blue and silver) labels					
KL-1217 [M]	Temptation	1962	3.00	6.00	12.00
—Any later label variation					
KL-1222 [M]	Roger Williams Invites You to Dance	1961	3.75	7.50	15.00
KL-1244 [M]	Yellow Bird	1961	3.75	7.50	15.00
KL-1251 [M]	Songs of the Soaring '60s	1961	3.75	7.50	15.00
KL-1260 [M]	Greatest Hits	1962	3.00	6.00	12.00
KL-1266 [M]	Maria	1962	3.00	6.00	12.00
KL-1290 [M]	Mr. Piano	1962	3.00	6.00	12.00
KL-1305 [M]	Country Style	1963	3.00	6.00	12.00
KL-1336 [M]	For You	1963	3.00	6.00	12.00
KL-1354 [M]	The Solid Gold Steinway	1964	3.00	6.00	12.00
KL-1395 [M]	Family Album of Hymns	1964	2.50	5.00	10.00
KL-1406 [M]	Academy Award Winners	1964	2.50	5.00	10.00
KL-1414 [M]	Roger Williams Plays the Hits	1965	2.50	5.00	10.00
KL-1434 [M]	Summer Wind	1965	2.50	5.00	10.00
KL-1452 [M]	Autumn Leaves — 1965	1965	2.50	5.00	10.00
KL-1470 [M]	I'll Remember You	1966	2.50	5.00	10.00
KL-1483 [M]	Academy Award Winners, Vol. 2	1966	2.50	5.00	10.00
KL-1501 [M]	Born Free	1966	2.50	5.00	10.00
KL-1512 [M]	Roger!	1967	2.50	5.00	10.00
KL-1530 [M]	Roger Williams/Golden Hits	1967	3.00	6.00	12.00
KS-3000 [S]	Waltzes in Stereo	1959	5.00	10.00	20.00
—Maroon and silver (or blue and silver) labels					
KS-3000 [S]	Waltzes in Stereo	1962	3.75	7.50	15.00
—Any later label variation					
KS-3013 [S]	More Songs of the Fabulous Fifties	1959	5.00	10.00	20.00
—Maroon and silver (or blue and silver) labels					
KS-3013 [S]	More Songs of the Fabulous Fifties	1962	3.75	7.50	15.00
—Any later label variation					
KS-3030 [S]	With These Hands	1959	5.00	10.00	20.00
—Maroon and silver (or blue and silver) labels					
KS-3030 [S]	With These Hands	1962	3.75	7.50	15.00
—Any later label variation					
KS-3048 [S]	Christmas Time	1959	5.00	10.00	20.00
KS-3056 [S]	Always	1960	5.00	10.00	20.00
—Maroon and silver (or blue and silver) labels					
KS-3056 [S]	Always	1962	3.75	7.50	15.00
—Any later label variation					
KS-3164 [S]	Christmas Time	196?	3.00	6.00	12.00
—Reissue of KS-3048 (new cover, no gatefold)					
KS-3207 [S]	Songs of the Fabulous Forties, Volume 1	1960	3.75	7.50	15.00
KS-3208 [S]	Songs of the Fabulous Forties, Volume 2	1960	3.75	7.50	15.00
KS-3209 [S]	Songs of the Fabulous Fifties, Volume 1	1960	3.75	7.50	15.00
KS-3210 [S]	Songs of the Fabulous Fifties, Volume 2	1960	3.75	7.50	15.00
KS-3211 [S]	Songs of the Fabulous Century, Volume 1	1960	3.75	7.50	15.00
KS-3212 [S]	Songs of the Fabulous Century, Volume 2	1960	3.75	7.50	15.00
KS-3217 [S]	Temptation	1960	5.00	10.00	20.00
KS-3222 [S]	Roger Williams Invites You to Dance	1961	5.00	10.00	20.00
KS-3244 [S]	Yellow Bird	1961	5.00	10.00	20.00
KS-3251 [S]	Songs of the Soaring '60s	1961	5.00	10.00	20.00
KS-3260 [S]	Greatest Hits	1962	3.75	7.50	15.00
KS-3266 [S]	Maria	1962	3.75	7.50	15.00
KS-3290 [S]	Mr. Piano	1962	3.75	7.50	15.00
KS-3305 [S]	Country Style	1963	3.75	7.50	15.00
KS-3336 [S]	For You	1963	3.75	7.50	15.00
KS-3354 [S]	The Solid Gold Steinway	1964	3.75	7.50	15.00
KS-3395 [S]	Family Album of Hymns	1964	3.00	6.00	12.00
KS-3406 [S]	Academy Award Winners	1964	3.00	6.00	12.00
KS-3414 [S]	Roger Williams Plays the Hits	1965	3.00	6.00	12.00
KS-3434 [S]	Summer Wind	1965	3.00	6.00	12.00
KS-3452 [S]	Autumn Leaves — 1965	1965	3.00	6.00	12.00
KS-3470 [S]	I'll Remember You	1966	3.00	6.00	12.00
KS-3483 [S]	Academy Award Winners, Vol. 2	1966	3.00	6.00	12.00
KS-3501 [S]	Born Free	1966	3.00	6.00	12.00
KS-3512 [S]	Roger!	1967	3.00	6.00	12.00
KS-3530 [S]	Roger Williams/Golden Hits	1967	3.00	6.00	12.00
KS-3549	Amore	1968	3.00	6.00	12.00
KS-3550	More Than a Miracle	1968	3.00	6.00	12.00
KS-3565	Only for Lovers	1969	3.00	6.00	12.00
KS-3595	Happy Heart	1969	3.00	6.00	12.00
KS-3610	Love Theme from "Romeo and Juliet"	1969	3.00	6.00	12.00
KS-3629	Themes from Great Movies	1970	3.00	6.00	12.00
KS-3638	Roger Williams/Golden Hits, Volume 2	1970	3.00	6.00	12.00
KS-3645	Love Story	1971	2.50	5.00	10.00
KS-3650	Summer of '42	1971	2.50	5.00	10.00
KS-3665	Love Theme from "The Godfather"	1972	2.50	5.00	10.00
KS-3671	Play Me	1972	2.50	5.00	10.00
KXL-5000 [(2) M]	Songs of the Fabulous Fifties	1957	5.00	10.00	20.00
—Maroon and silver (or blue and silver) labels					
KXL-5000 [(2) M]	Songs of the Fabulous Fifties	1962	3.75	7.50	15.00
—Any later label variation					
KXS-5000 [(2) S]	Songs of the Fabulous Fifties	1959	6.25	12.50	25.00
—Maroon and silver (or blue and silver) labels					
KXS-5000 [(2) S]	Songs of the Fabulous Fifties	1962	5.00	10.00	20.00
—Any later label variation					
KXL-5003 [(2) M]	Songs of the Fabulous Forties	1957	5.00	10.00	20.00
—Maroon and silver (or blue and silver) labels					
KXL-5003 [(2) M]	Songs of the Fabulous Forties	1962	3.75	7.50	15.00
—Any later label variation					
KXS-5003 [(2) S]	Songs of the Fabulous Forties	1959	6.25	12.50	25.00
—Maroon and silver (or blue and silver) labels					
KXS-5003 [(2) S]	Songs of the Fabulous Forties	1962	5.00	10.00	20.00
—Any later label variation					

Number	Title (A Side/B Side)	Yr	VG	VG+	NM
KXL-5005 [(2) M]	Songs of the Fabulous Century	195?	5.00	10.00	20.00
—Maroon and silver (or blue and silver) labels					
KXL-5005 [(2) M]	Songs of the Fabulous Century	1962	3.75	7.50	15.00
—Any later label variation					
KXS-5005 [(2) S]	Songs of the Fabulous Century	1959	6.25	12.50	25.00
—Maroon and silver (or blue and silver) labels					
KXS-5005 [(2) S]	Songs of the Fabulous Century	1962	5.00	10.00	20.00
—Any later label variation					
KXL-5008 [(2) M]	Tonight! Roger Williams at Town Hall	196?	5.00	10.00	20.00
KXS-5008 [(2) S]	Tonight! Roger Williams at Town Hall	196?	6.25	12.50	25.00
MCA					
63	Greatest Hits	1973	2.00	4.00	8.00
—Reissue of Kapp 3260					
64	Roger Williams/Golden Hits	1973	2.00	4.00	8.00
—Reissue of Kapp 3530					
68	Roger Williams/Golden Hits, Volume 2	1973	2.00	4.00	8.00
—Reissue of Kapp 3638					
71	Somewhere My Love	1973	2.00	4.00	8.00
—Retitled reissue of unknown Kapp LP					
76	Play Me	1973	2.00	4.00	8.00
—Reissue of Kapp 3671					
324	Last Tango in Paris	1973	2.50	5.00	10.00
378	Live	1973	2.50	5.00	10.00
403	The Way We Were	1974	2.50	5.00	10.00
438	I Honestly Love You	1974	2.50	5.00	10.00
539	Family Album of Hymns	1975	2.00	4.00	8.00
—Reissue of Kapp 3395					
542	Somewhere My Love	1975	—	3.00	6.00
—Reissue of MCA 71					
2175	Virtuoso	1975	2.50	5.00	10.00
2237	Nadia's Theme	1976	2.50	5.00	10.00
2279	Evergreen	1977	2.50	5.00	10.00
4106 [(2)]	The Best of Roger Williams	197?	3.00	6.00	12.00
5574	To Amadeus With Love	1985	2.50	5.00	10.00
15005	Christmas Time	197?	2.00	4.00	8.00
—Reissue of Kapp material					
20202	Autumn Leaves	198?	2.00	4.00	8.00
—Reissue of Kapp material					
PICKWICK					
PTP-2086 [(2)]	Roger Williams at the Piano	197?	3.00	6.00	12.00
SPC-3367	Spanish Eyes	197?	2.00	4.00	8.00
SPC-3511	Sunrise, Sunset	197?	2.00	4.00	8.00
VOCALION					
VL 73918	Moments to Remember	1970	2.50	5.00	10.00

WILLIAMS, TIMMY

45s

Number	Title (A Side/B Side)	Yr	VG	VG+	NM
MALA					
515	Competition/Wipe Away Your Tears	1965	75.00	150.00	300.00

WILLIAMS, TONY

Also see THE PLATTERS.

45s

Number	Title (A Side/B Side)	Yr	VG	VG+	NM
DOT					
16806	Endless Street/Smoke, Drink, Play 21	1965	2.00	4.00	8.00
MERCURY					
71158	Let's Start All Over Again/When You Return	1957	5.00	10.00	20.00
71532	Charmaine/Peg o' My Heart	1959	5.00	10.00	20.00
PHILIPS					
40069	Chloe/Second Best	1962	2.50	5.00	10.00
40123	Twenty-Four Lonely Hours/Save Me	1963	2.50	5.00	10.00
40141	How Come/When I Had You	1963	2.50	5.00	10.00
REPRISE					
20019	Sleepless Nights/Movin' In	1961	3.75	7.50	15.00
20030	Miracle/My Prayer	1961	3.75	7.50	15.00
20067	Come Along Now/That's More Like It	1962	3.75	7.50	15.00

Albums

Number	Title (A Side/B Side)	Yr	VG	VG+	NM
MERCURY					
MG-20454 [M]	A Girl Is a Girl Is a Girl	1959	10.00	20.00	40.00
SR-60138 [S]	A Girl Is a Girl Is a Girl	1959	12.50	25.00	50.00
PHILIPS					
PHM 200051 [M]	The Magic Touch of Tony	1962	6.25	12.50	25.00
PHS 600051 [S]	The Magic Touch of Tony	1962	7.50	15.00	30.00
REPRISE					
R-6006 [M]	His Greatest Hits	1961	6.25	12.50	25.00
R9-6006 [S]	His Greatest Hits	1961	7.50	15.00	30.00

WILLIAMSON, SONNY BOY (1)

The "original," born John Lee Williamson and murdered in 1948.

45s

Number	Title (A Side/B Side)	Yr	VG	VG+	NM
RCA VICTOR					
50-0005	Little Girl/Bring Another Half a Pint	1949	75.00	150.00	300.00
—Orange vinyl					
50-0030	Southern Dream/I Love You For Myself	1949	75.00	150.00	300.00
—Orange vinyl					

Albums

Number	Title (A Side/B Side)	Yr	VG	VG+	NM
BLUES CLASSICS					
3	Blues Classics by Sonny Boy Williamson	196?	6.25	12.50	25.00
20	Blues Classics by Sonny Boy Williamson, Vol. 2	196?	6.25	12.50	25.00

WILLIAMSON, SONNY BOY (2)

Really Aleck Ford, also known as Alex "Rice" Miller, before taking the name of his predecessor.

45s

Number	Title (A Side/B Side)	Yr	VG	VG+	NM
ACE					
511	Boppin' with Sonny/No Nights By Myself	1955	30.00	60.00	120.00
CHECKER					
824	Don't Start Me Talkin'/All My Love In Vain	1955	25.00	50.00	100.00
834	Let Me Explain/Your Imagination	1956	15.00	30.00	60.00
847	Keep It To Yourself/The Key to Your Door	1956	12.50	25.00	50.00
864	I Don't Know/Fattening Frogs for Snakes	1957	12.50	25.00	50.00
883	Born Blind/Ninety-Nine	1958	10.00	20.00	40.00
894	Your Funeral & My Trial/Wake Up, Baby	1958	10.00	20.00	40.00
910	Cross My Heart/Dissatisfied	1958	10.00	20.00	40.00
927	Let Your Conscience Be Your Guide/Unseeing Eye	1959	10.00	20.00	40.00
943	The Goat/It's Sad to Be Alone	1960	7.50	15.00	30.00
956	Temperature 110/Lonesome Cabin	1960	7.50	15.00	30.00
963	Trust Me Baby/Too Close Together	1960	7.50	15.00	30.00
975	The Hurt/Stop Right Now	1961	7.50	15.00	30.00
1003	One Way Out/Nine Below Zero	1962	7.50	15.00	30.00
1036	Bye Bye Bird/Help Me	1963	7.50	15.00	30.00
1065	Trying to Get Back on My Feet/Decoration Day	1963	7.50	15.00	30.00
1080	My Younger Days/I Want You Close to Me	1964	7.50	15.00	30.00
1134	Bring It On Home/Down Child	1966	6.25	12.50	25.00
TRUMPET					
144	West Memphis Blues/I Cross My Heart	1951	25.00	50.00	100.00
145	Sonny Boy's Christmas Blues/Pontiac Blues	195?	30.00	60.00	120.00
166	Nine Below Zero/Mighty Long Time	1952	25.00	50.00	100.00
167	Too Close Together/She Brought Life Back to the Dead	1952	—	—	—
—Unreleased					
168	Stop Now Baby/Mr. Downchild	1952	25.00	50.00	100.00
212	Cat Hop/Too Close Together	1952	20.00	40.00	80.00
215	Gettin' Out of Time/She Brought Life Back to the Dead	1952	20.00	40.00	80.00
216	Red Hot Kisses/Going in Your Direction	1952	20.00	40.00	80.00
228	From the Bottom/Empty Bedroom	1953	17.50	35.00	70.00

Albums

Number	Title (A Side/B Side)	Yr	VG	VG+	NM
ALLIGATOR					
AL-4787	Keep It To Ourselves	1990	3.00	6.00	12.00
ARHOOLIE					
2020	King Biscuit Time	197?	3.00	6.00	12.00
CHECKER					
LP-1437 [M]	Down and Out Blues	1959	80.00	160.00	320.00
CHESS					
2ACMB-206 [(2)]	Sonny Boy Williamson	1976	5.00	10.00	20.00
—Reissue of 50027					
CHV-417	One Way Out	1975	3.75	7.50	15.00
LP-1503 [M]	The Real Folk Blues	1966	20.00	40.00	80.00
LP-1509 [M]	More Real Folk Blues	1966	20.00	40.00	80.00
LPS-1536	Bummer Road	1969	6.25	12.50	25.00
CH-9116	One Way Out	198?	2.50	5.00	10.00
CH-9257	Down and Out Blues	1988	2.50	5.00	10.00
CH-9272	The Real Folk Blues	1988	2.50	5.00	10.00
CH-9277	More Real Folk Blues	1988	2.50	5.00	10.00
2CH-50027 [(2)]	This Is My Story	1972	6.25	12.50	25.00
GNP CRESCENDO					
GNPS-10003	Sonny Boy Williamson in Chicago	198?	2.50	5.00	10.00
STORYVILLE					
4016	A Portrait in Blues	197?	3.00	6.00	12.00
4062	The Blues of Sonny Boy Williamson	197?	3.00	6.00	12.00

WILLIAMSON, SONNY BOY (2), AND THE YARDBIRDS

Albums

Number	Title (A Side/B Side)	Yr	VG	VG+	NM
MERCURY					
MG-21071 [M]	Sonny Boy Williamson and the Yardbirds	1965	20.00	40.00	80.00
SR-61071 [R]	Sonny Boy Williamson and the Yardbirds	1965	12.50	25.00	50.00
—First cover with a picture of the bluesman and the band					
SR-61071 [R]	Sonny Boy Williamson and the Yardbirds	196?	6.25	12.50	25.00
—Later cover with cartoon artwork on the cover					

WILLIE AND THE WHEELS

Still another creation of STEVE BARRI and P.F. SLOAN.

45s

Number	Title (A Side/B Side)	Yr	VG	VG+	NM
DUNHILL					
4002	Skateboard Craze/Do What You Do	1965	10.00	20.00	40.00

WILLIS, CHUCK

Also see THE ROYALS (2).

45s

Number	Title (A Side/B Side)	Yr	VG	VG+	NM
ATLANTIC					
1098	It's Too Late/Kansas City Woman	1956	6.25	12.50	25.00
1112	Juanita/Whatcha' Gonna Do When Your Baby Leaves You	1956	6.25	12.50	25.00
1130	C.C. Rider/Ease the Pain	1957	6.25	12.50	25.00
1148	Love Me, Cherry/That Train Has Gone	1957	6.25	12.50	25.00
1168	Betty and Dupree/My Crying Eyes	1958	6.25	12.50	25.00
1179	What Am I Living For/Hang Up My Rock And Roll Shoes	1958	7.50	15.00	30.00
1192	Thunder and Lightning/My Life	1958	5.00	10.00	20.00
2005	You'll Be My Love/Keep a-Driving	1958	5.00	10.00	20.00
2029	My Baby/Just One Kiss	1959	5.00	10.00	20.00
OKEH					
6810	I Tried/I Rule My House	1951	25.00	50.00	100.00
6841	Let's Jump Tonight/It's Too Late Baby	1951	20.00	40.00	80.00
6873	Lud Mouth Lucy/Here I Come	1952	20.00	40.00	80.00
6905	My Story/Caldonia	1952	12.50	25.00	50.00
6930	Salty Tears/Wrong Lake to Catch a Fish	1953	12.50	25.00	50.00
6952	Going to the River/Baby Has Left Me Again	1953	12.50	25.00	50.00
6985	Don't Deceive Me/I've Been Treated Wrong Too Long	1953	12.50	25.00	50.00
7004	My Baby's Coming Home/When My Day Is Over	1953	12.50	25.00	50.00
7015	You're Still My Baby/What's Your Name	1954	12.50	25.00	50.00
7029	I Feel So Bad/Need One More Chance	1954	15.00	30.00	60.00
7041	Change My Mind/My Heart's Been Broke Again	1954	10.00	20.00	40.00
7048	Give and Take/I've Been Away Too Long	1954	10.00	20.00	40.00
7051	Lawdy Miss Mary/Love-Struck	1955	10.00	20.00	40.00
7055	I Can Tell/One More Break	1955	10.00	20.00	40.00
7062	Search My Heart/Ring-Ding-Doo	1955	10.00	20.00	40.00
7067	Come On Home/It Were You	1956	10.00	20.00	40.00
7070	Two Spoons of Tears/Charged with Cheating	1956	10.00	20.00	40.00

7-Inch Extended Plays

Number	Title (A Side/B Side)	Yr	VG	VG+	NM
ATLANTIC					
561	(contents unknown)	1957	50.00	100.00	200.00
561 [PS]	Chuck Willis	1957	50.00	100.00	200.00

Number	Title (A Side/B Side)	Yr	VG	VG+	NM
609	(contents unknown)	1958	30.00	60.00	120.00
609 [PS]	Rock with Chuck Willis	1958	30.00	60.00	120.00
612	(contents unknown)	1958	37.50	75.00	150.00
612 [PS]	What Am I Living For	1958	50.00	100.00	200.00
EPIC					
7070	(contents unknown)	1956	50.00	100.00	200.00
7070 [PS]	Chuck Willis Sings the Blues	1956	50.00	100.00	200.00
Albums					
ATLANTIC					
8018 [M]	The King of the Stroll	1958	75.00	150.00	300.00
—Black label					
8018 [M]	The King of the Stroll	1960	37.50	75.00	150.00
—Purple and orange label					
8079 [M]	I Remember Chuck Willis	1963	37.50	75.00	150.00
SD 8079 [P]	I Remember Chuck Willis	1963	50.00	100.00	200.00
EPIC					
LN 3425 [M]	Chuck Willis Wails the Blues	1958	125.00	250.00	500.00
LN 3728 [M]	A Tribute to Chuck Willis	1960	75.00	150.00	300.00

WILLIS, HAL

Number	Title (A Side/B Side)	Yr	VG	VG+	NM
45s					
ATHENS					
704	Crazy Little Mama/Walkin' Dream	1958	37.50	75.00	150.00
ATLANTIC					
1114	Bop-A-Dee, Bop-A-Doo/My Pink Cadillac	1956	50.00	100.00	200.00
DECCA					
30949	Poor Little Jimmy/That's the Way It Goes	1959	3.00	6.00	12.00
MERCURY					
71933	Bayou Pierre/I Love You (Around the World)	1962	3.00	6.00	12.00
SIMS					
288	The Battle of Viet Nam/Doggin' in the U.S. Mail	1966	2.50	5.00	10.00
307	Parson from Paint Rock/Private Dick	1966	2.50	5.00	10.00

WILLOWS, THE (1)

Number	Title (A Side/B Side)	Yr	VG	VG+	NM
45s					
MELBA					
102	Church Bells Are Ringing/Beby Tell Me	1956	75.00	150.00	300.00
—Original A-side title					
102	Church Bells May Ring/Baby Tell Me	1956	25.00	50.00	100.00
106	Do You Love Me/My Angel	1956	15.00	30.00	60.00
115	Little Darlin'/My Angel	1957	20.00	40.00	80.00

WILLOWS, THE (2)

Number	Title (A Side/B Side)	Yr	VG	VG+	NM
45s					
4-STAR					
1753	There's a Dance Goin' On/Now That I Have You	1961	75.00	150.00	300.00

WILLOWS, THE (3)

Number	Title (A Side/B Side)	Yr	VG	VG+	NM
45s					
HEIDI					
103	It's Such a Shame/Tears in Your Eyes	1964	3.75	7.50	15.00
107	Sit by the Fire/Such a Night	1965	3.75	7.50	15.00

WILLOWS, THE (4)

Number	Title (A Side/B Side)	Yr	VG	VG+	NM
45s					
MGM					
13484	Hurtin' All Over/My Kinda Guy	1966	3.00	6.00	12.00
13714	Snow Song/Outside the City	1967	3.00	6.00	12.00

WILMER AND THE DUKES

Number	Title (A Side/B Side)	Yr	VG	VG+	NM
45s					
APHRODISIAC					
260	Give Me One More Chance/Git It	1968	2.00	4.00	8.00
262	Living in the U.S.A./(B-side unknown)	1969	2.00	4.00	8.00
Albums					
APHRODISIAC					
6001	Wilmer and the Dukes	1969	5.00	10.00	20.00

WILSON, AL

Number	Title (A Side/B Side)	Yr	VG	VG+	NM
45s					
BELL					
867	Mississippi Woman/Sometimes a Man Must Cry	1970	—	3.50	7.00
909	You Do the Right Thing/Bachelor Man	1970	—	3.50	7.00
CAROUSEL					
30051	I Hear You Knocking/Sugar Cane Girl	1971	—	3.00	6.00
30052	Falling/Bachelor Man	1971	—	3.00	6.00
PLAYBOY					
6062	I've Got a Feeling (We'll Be Seeing Each Other Again)/Be Concerned	1976	—	2.50	5.00
6076	Baby I Want Your Body/Stay with Me	1976	—	2.50	5.00
6076 [PS]	Baby I Want Your Body/Stay with Me	1976	—	3.00	6.00
6085	You Did It for Me/Differently	1976	—	2.50	5.00
ROADSHOW					
PB-11583	Count the Days/Is This the End	1979	—	2.00	4.00
PB-11714	Earthquake/You Got It	1979	—	2.00	4.00
ROCKY ROAD					
30060	Heavy Church/(B-side unknown)	1972	—	3.00	6.00
30067	Born on the Bayou/(B-side unknown)	1972	—	3.00	6.00
30073	Show and Tell/Listen to Me	1973	—	3.00	6.00
30076	Touch and Go/Settle Me Down	1974	—	3.00	6.00
30200	La La Peace Song/Keep On Loving You	1974	—	3.00	6.00
30202	I Won't Last a Day Without You-Let Me Be the One/Willoughbry Brook Road	1974	—	3.00	6.00
SOUL CITY					
759	When You Love, You're Loved Too/Who Could Be Lovin' You	1967	2.50	5.00	10.00
761	Do What You Gotta Do/Now I Know What Love Is	1968	2.00	4.00	8.00
767	The Snake/Getting Ready for Tomorrow	1968	2.00	4.00	8.00
771	Poor Side of Town/The Dolphins	1969	2.00	4.00	8.00
773	I Stand Accused/Shake Me, Wake Me	1969	2.00	4.00	8.00
775	Lodi/By the Time I Get to Phoenix	1969	2.00	4.00	8.00
WAND					
1135	Help Me/(Instrumental)	1966	7.50	15.00	30.00
Albums					
PLAYBOY					
PB 410	I've Got a Feeling	1976	3.00	6.00	12.00
JZ 34744	I've Got a Feeling	1977	2.50	5.00	10.00
—Reissue of 410					
ROCKY ROAD					
3600	Weighing In	1973	3.75	7.50	15.00
3601	Show and Tell	1973	3.75	7.50	15.00
3700	La La Peace Song	1974	3.75	7.50	15.00
SOUL CITY					
SCS-92006	Searching for the Dolphins	1969	6.25	12.50	25.00

WILSON, ANN, AND THE DAYBREAKS

Ann Wilson was later with Heart.

Number	Title (A Side/B Side)	Yr	VG	VG+	NM
45s					
TOPAZ					
1311	Standin' Watchin' You/Wonder How I Managed	1967	30.00	60.00	120.00
1312	Through Eyes and Glass/I'm Gonna Drink My Hurt Away	1967	30.00	60.00	120.00

WILSON, BRIAN

Also see THE BEACH BOYS.

Number	Title (A Side/B Side)	Yr	VG	VG+	NM
45s					
CAPITOL					
5610	Caroline, No/Summer Means New Love	1966	6.25	12.50	25.00
—Actually a Beach Boys recording released as a solo Brian record					
GIANT					
17216	Your Imagination/Your Imagination (A Cappella)	1998	—	—	3.00
SIRE					
27694	Melt Away/Being with the One You Love	1988	5.00	10.00	20.00
27787 [DJ]	Night Time (same on both sides)	1988	7.50	15.00	30.00
—Stock copies not known to exist					
27787 [PS]	Night Time	1988	15.00	30.00	60.00
27814	Love and Mercy/He Couldn't Get His Poor Old Body to Move	1988	2.50	5.00	10.00
—Promo copies go for 50% of this price					
27814 [PS]	Love and Mercy/He Couldn't Get His Poor Old Body to Move	1988	—	2.50	5.00
—Accompanied both stock and promo copies					
28350	Let's Go to Heaven in My Car/Too Much Sugar	1987	2.50	5.00	10.00
—Promo copies go for 50% of this price					
28350 [PS]	Let's Go to Heaven in My Car/Too Much Sugar	1987	—	2.50	5.00
—Accompanied both stock and promo copies					
Albums					
SIRE					
PRO-A-3248 [DJ]	Words and Music	1988	6.25	12.50	25.00
—Promo-only music and interview					
25669	Brian Wilson	1988	2.50	5.00	10.00

WILSON, BRIAN, AND MIKE LOVE

Also see THE BEACH BOYS; BRIAN WILSON.

Number	Title (A Side/B Side)	Yr	VG	VG+	NM
45s					
BROTHER					
1002	Gettin' Hungry/Devoted to You	1967	7.50	15.00	30.00
—Beach Boys recordings released under these two names					

WILSON, FLIP

Number	Title (A Side/B Side)	Yr	VG	VG+	NM
45s					
LITTLE DAVID					
721	Don't Fight the Feeling/Geraldine-Killer	1972	—	2.50	5.00
730	There Oughta Be a Law/Berries in Salinas	1975	—	2.50	5.00
8113	There Oughta Be a Law/Berries in Salinas	1975	—	2.00	4.00
Albums					
ATLANTIC					
8149 [M]	Cowboys and Colored People	1967	6.25	12.50	25.00
SD 8149 [S]	Cowboys and Colored People	1967	3.75	7.50	15.00
—Green and blue label					
SD 8149 [S]	Cowboys and Colored People	1969	3.00	6.00	12.00
—Red and green label					
SD 8179	You Devil You	1968	3.75	7.50	15.00
—Green and blue label					
SD 8179	You Devil You	1969	3.00	6.00	12.00
—Red and green label					
IMPERIAL					
LP-9155 [M]	Flippin'	1961	6.25	12.50	25.00
LITTLE DAVID					
LD 1000	The Devil Made Me Buy This Dress	1970	3.00	6.00	12.00
LD 1001	Geraldine/Don't Fight the Feeling	1972	3.00	6.00	12.00
LD 2000	The Flip Wilson Show	1970	3.00	6.00	12.00
MINIT					
24012	Flippin'	1968	3.75	7.50	15.00
—Reissue of Imperial LP					
SCEPTER					
S-520	Flip Wilson's Pot Luck	1964	5.00	10.00	20.00
SPRINGBOARD					
SPB-4004	Funny and Live at the Village Gate	1972	3.00	6.00	12.00
—Reissue of Scepter LP					
SUNSET					
SUS-5297	Flipped Out	1970	3.00	6.00	12.00
—Reissue of Minit LP					

WILSON, FRANK

Number	Title (A Side/B Side)	Yr	VG	VG+	NM
45s					
SOUL					
35019	Do I Love You (Indeed I Do)/Sweeter As the Days Go By	1966	10000.	15000.	20000.

WILSON, HANK
See LEON RUSSELL.

WILSON, J. FRANK, AND THE CAVALIERS

Number	Title (A Side/B Side)	Yr	VG	VG+	NM
45s					
CHARAY					
13	Last Kiss '69/Black Car	1969	—	3.00	6.00
JOSIE					
923	Last Kiss/That's How Much I Love You	1964	3.00	6.00	12.00
924	Tears of Happiness/Summertime	1964	2.50	5.00	10.00
—As "The Cavaliers"					
926	Hey Little One/Speak to Me	1964	2.50	5.00	10.00
929	Say It Now/Six Boys	1965	2.50	5.00	10.00
931	Dreams of a Fool/Open Your Eyes	1965	2.50	5.00	10.00
938	Forget Me Not/A White Sport Coat (And a Pink Carnation)	1965	2.50	5.00	10.00
LE CAM					
722	Last Kiss/Carla	1964	7.50	15.00	30.00
SOLLY					
927	Me and My Teardrops/Unmarked and Uncovered with Sand	1966	2.50	5.00	10.00
TAMARA					
761	Last Kiss/That's How Much I Love You	1964	6.25	12.50	25.00
VIRGO					
506	Last Kiss/(B-side unknown)	1973	—	3.50	7.00
Albums					
JOSIE					
JM-4006 [M]	Last Kiss	1964	18.75	37.50	75.00
JS-4006 [S]	Last Kiss	1964	25.00	50.00	100.00

WILSON, JACKIE
Also see THE DOMINOES.

Number	Title (A Side/B Side)	Yr	VG	VG+	NM
45s					
BRUNSWICK					
55024	Reet Petite (The Finest Girl You Ever Want to Meet)/By the Light of the Silvery Moon	1957	7.50	15.00	30.00
55052	To Be Loved/Come Back to Me	1958	6.25	12.50	25.00
55070	As Long As I Live/I'm Wanderin'	1958	6.25	12.50	25.00
55086	We Have Love/Singing a Song	1958	6.25	12.50	25.00
55105	Lonely Teardrops/In the Blue of the Evening	1958	7.50	15.00	30.00
55121	That's Why (I Love You So)/Love Is All	1959	6.25	12.50	25.00
55121 [PS]	That's Why (I Love You So)/Love Is All	1959	15.00	30.00	60.00
55136	I'll Be Satisfied/Ask	1959	6.25	12.50	25.00
55149	You Better Know It/Never Go Away	1959	5.00	10.00	20.00
55165	Talk That Talk/Only You and Only Me	1959	5.00	10.00	20.00
55165 [PS]	Talk That Talk/Only You and Only Me	1959	15.00	30.00	60.00
55166	Night/Doggin' Around	1960	10.00	20.00	40.00
—Maroon label (scarce original)					
55166	Night/Doggin' Around	1960	3.75	7.50	15.00
—Orange label					
55166 [PS]	Night/Doggin' Around	1960	12.50	25.00	50.00
55167	(You Were Made for) All My Love/A Woman, A Lover, A Friend	1960	5.00	10.00	20.00
55170	Alone at Last/Am I the Man	1960	5.00	10.00	20.00
55170 [PS]	Alone at Last/Am I the Man	1960	12.50	25.00	50.00
55201	My Empty Arms/The Tear of the Year	1961	3.75	7.50	15.00
55201 [PS]	My Empty Arms/The Tear of the Year	1961	10.00	20.00	40.00
55208	Please Tell Me Why/Your One and Only Love	1961	3.75	7.50	15.00
55216	I'm Comin' On Back to You/Lonely Life	1961	3.75	7.50	15.00
55219	Years from Now/You Don't Know What It Means	1961	3.75	7.50	15.00
55220	The Way I Am/My Heart Belongs to Only You	1961	3.75	7.50	15.00
55220 [PS]	The Way I Am/My Heart Belongs to Only You	1961	10.00	20.00	40.00
55221	The Greatest Hurt/There'll Be No Next Time	1962	3.75	7.50	15.00
55221 [PS]	The Greatest Hurt/There'll Be No Next Time	1962	10.00	20.00	40.00
55224	I Found Love/There's Nothing Like Love	1962	3.00	6.00	12.00
—With Linda Hopkins					
55225	Hearts/Sing (And Tell the Blues So Long)	1962	3.75	7.50	15.00
55229	I Just Can't Help It/My Tale of Woe	1962	3.75	7.50	15.00
55233	Forever and a Day/Baby That's All	1962	3.75	7.50	15.00
55236	What Good Am I Without You/A Girl Named Tamiko	1962	3.75	7.50	15.00
55236 [PS]	What Good Am I Without You/A Girl Named Tamiko	1962	7.50	15.00	30.00
55239	Baby Workout/I'm Going Crazy	1963	5.00	10.00	20.00
55243	Shake a Hand/Say I Do	1963	3.00	6.00	12.00
—With Linda Hopkins					
55246	Shake! Shake! Shake!/He's a Fool	1963	3.00	6.00	12.00
55250	Baby Get It (And Don't Quit It)/The New Breed	1963	3.00	6.00	12.00
55254	Silent Night/Oh Holy Night	1963	3.75	7.50	15.00
55260	Haunted House/I'm Travelin' On	1964	2.50	5.00	10.00
55263	Call Her Up/The Kickapoo	1964	2.50	5.00	10.00
55266	Big Boss Line/Be My Girl	1964	2.50	5.00	10.00
55269	Squeeze Her-Tease Her (But Love Her)/Give Me Back My Heart	1964	2.50	5.00	10.00
55273	Watch Out/She's All Right	1964	2.50	5.00	10.00
55277	Danny Boy/Soul Time	1965	2.00	4.00	8.00
55278	Yes Indeed/When the Saints Go Marching In	1965	2.00	4.00	8.00
—With Linda Hopkins					
55280	No Pity (In the Naked City)/I'm So Lonely	1965	2.00	4.00	8.00
55283	I Believe I'll Love On/Lonely Teardrops	1965	2.00	4.00	8.00
55287	Think Twice/Please Don't Hurt Me	1965	2.00	4.00	8.00
—With LaVern Baker					
55289	I've Got to Get Back/3 Days, 1 Hour, 30 Minutes	1966	2.00	4.00	8.00
55290	Soul Galore/Brand New Things	1966	2.00	4.00	8.00
55294	I Believe/Be My Love	1966	2.00	4.00	8.00
55300	Whispers (Gettin' Louder)/The Fairest of Them All	1966	2.00	4.00	8.00
55309	I Don't Want to Lose You/Just Be Sincere	1967	2.00	4.00	8.00
55321	I've Lost You/Those Heartaches	1967	2.00	4.00	8.00
55336	(Your Love Keeps Lifting Me) Higher and Higher/I'm the One to Do It	1967	2.50	5.00	10.00
55354	Since You Showed Me How to Be Happy/The Who Who Song	1967	2.00	4.00	8.00
55365	For Your Precious Love/Uptight	1968	2.00	4.00	8.00
55373	Chain Gang/Funky Broadway	1968	2.00	4.00	8.00
55381	I Get the Sweetest Feeling/Nothing But Heartaches	1968	2.00	4.00	8.00
55392	For Once in My Life/You Brought About a Change in Me	1968	2.00	4.00	8.00
55402	I Still Love You/Hum De Dum De Do	1969	2.00	4.00	8.00
55418	Helpless/Do It the Right Way	1969	2.00	4.00	8.00
55423	With These Hands/Why Don't You (Do Your Thing)	1969	2.00	4.00	8.00
55435	Let This Be a Letter (To My Baby)/Didn't I	1970	—	3.00	6.00
55435 [PS]	Let This Be a Letter (To My Baby)/Didn't I	1970	3.00	6.00	12.00
55443	(I Can Feel Those Vibrations) This Love Is Real/Love Uprising	1970	—	3.00	6.00
55449	This Guy's in Love with You/Say You Will	1971	—	3.00	6.00
55454	Say You Will/(B-side unknown)	1971	—	3.00	6.00
55461	Love Is Funny That Way/Try It Again	1971	—	3.00	6.00
55467	You Got Me Walking/The Mountain	1972	—	3.00	6.00
55475	The Girl Turned Me On/Forever and a Day	1972	—	3.00	6.00
55480	What a Lovely Way/You Left the Fire Burning	1972	—	3.00	6.00
55490	Beautiful Day/What 'Cha Gonna Do About Love	1973	—	3.00	6.00
55495	Because of You/Go Away	1973	—	3.00	6.00
55499	Sing a Little Song/No More Goodbyes	1973	—	3.00	6.00
55504	It's All Over/Shake a Leg	1973	—	3.00	6.00
55522	Don't Burn No Bridges/(Instrumental)	1975	—	3.00	6.00
—With the Chi-Lites					
55536	Nobody But You/I've Learned About Life	1977	—	3.00	6.00
COLUMBIA					
07329	Reet Petite/You Better Know It	1987	—	2.50	5.00
07329 [PS]	Reet Petite/You Better Know It	1987	—	2.50	5.00
7-Inch Extended Plays					
BRUNSWICK					
EB 71040	To Be Loved/Reet Petite//Danny Boy/As Long As I Live	1959	15.00	30.00	60.00
EB 71040 [PS]	The Versatile Jackie Wilson	1959	15.00	30.00	60.00
EB 71042	Lonely Teardrops/It's Too Bad We Had to Say Goodbye//Someone to Need Me/Joke	1960	15.00	30.00	60.00
EB 71042 [PS]	Jumpin' Jack	1960	15.00	30.00	60.00
EB 71045 [M]	That's Why/Love Is All//You Better Know It/Each Time	1960	15.00	30.00	60.00
EB 71045 [PS]	Jackie Wilson	1960	15.00	30.00	60.00
EB 71046	Talk That Talk/Ask//I'll Be Satisfied/Wishing Well	1960	15.00	30.00	60.00
EB 71046 [PS]	Talk That Talk	1960	15.00	30.00	60.00
EB 71047	(contents unknown)	1960	15.00	30.00	60.00
EB 71047 [PS]	Mr. Excitement	1960	15.00	30.00	60.00
EB 71048	So Much/Only You, Only Me//Happiness/Magic of Love	1960	15.00	30.00	60.00
EB 71048 [PS]	Jackie Wilson	1960	15.00	30.00	60.00
EB 71049	Night/Doggin' Around//All My Love/A Woman, a Lover, a Friend	1960	15.00	30.00	60.00
EB 71049 [PS]	Jackie Wilson	1960	15.00	30.00	60.00
EB 71101	The Greatest Hurt/I Don't Know You Anymore//Tear of the Year/There'll Be No Next Time	1962	15.00	30.00	60.00
EB 71101 [PS]	Jackie Wilson	1962	15.00	30.00	60.00
EB 71102	I Just Can't Help It/My Tale of Woe//Bad News Travels Fast/You Ought to Be Ashamed	1962	15.00	30.00	60.00
EB 71102 [PS]	Jackie Wilson	1962	15.00	30.00	60.00
EB 71103	Baby Workout/Say You Will//Kickapoo/Yeah Yeah Yeah	1963	15.00	30.00	60.00
EB 71103 [PS]	Baby Workout	1963	15.00	30.00	60.00
EB 71104	(contents unknown)	1963	15.00	30.00	60.00
EB 71104 [PS]	Shake a Hand	1963	15.00	30.00	60.00
EB 771045 [PS]	Jackie Wilson	1960	20.00	40.00	80.00
EB 771045 [S]	That's Why/Love Is All//You Better Know It/Each Time	1960	20.00	40.00	80.00
Albums					
BRUNSWICK					
BL 54042 [M]	He's So Fine	1959	30.00	60.00	120.00
—All-black label					
BL 54042 [M]	He's So Fine	1964	6.25	12.50	25.00
—Black label with color bars					
BL 54045 [M]	Lonely Teardrops	1959	37.50	75.00	150.00
—All-black label					
BL 54045 [M]	Lonely Teardrops	1964	6.25	12.50	25.00
—Black label with color bars					
BL 54050 [M]	So Much	1960	25.00	50.00	100.00
—All-black label					
BL 54050 [M]	So Much	1964	5.00	10.00	20.00
—Black label with color bars					
BL 54055 [M]	Jackie Sings the Blues	1960	37.50	75.00	150.00
—All-black label					
BL 54055 [M]	Jackie Sings the Blues	1964	5.00	10.00	20.00
—Black label with color bars					
BL 54058 [M]	My Golden Favorites	1960	15.00	30.00	60.00
—All-black label					
BL 54058 [M]	My Golden Favorites	1964	6.25	12.50	25.00
—Black label with color bars					
BL 54059 [M]	A Woman, a Lover, a Friend	1961	12.50	25.00	50.00
—All-black label					
BL 54059 [M]	A Woman, a Lover, a Friend	1964	5.00	10.00	20.00
—Black label with color bars					
BL 54100 [M]	You Ain't Heard Nothin' Yet	1961	12.50	25.00	50.00
—All-black label					
BL 54100 [M]	You Ain't Heard Nothin' Yet	1964	5.00	10.00	20.00
—Black label with color bars					
BL 54101 [M]	By Special Request	1961	12.50	25.00	50.00
—All-black label					
BL 54101 [M]	By Special Request	1964	5.00	10.00	20.00
—Black label with color bars					
BL 54105 [M]	Body and Soul	1962	12.50	25.00	50.00
—All-black label					
BL 54105 [M]	Body and Soul	1964	5.00	10.00	20.00
—Black label with color bars					
BL 54106 [M]	The World's Greatest Melodies	1962	12.50	25.00	50.00
—All-black label					
BL 54106 [M]	The World's Greatest Melodies	1964	5.00	10.00	20.00
—Black label with color bars					

Number	Title (A Side/B Side)	Yr	VG	VG+	NM
BL 54108 [M]	Jackie Wilson at the Copa	1962	12.50	25.00	50.00
—All-black label					
BL 54108 [M]	Jackie Wilson at the Copa	1964	5.00	10.00	20.00
—Black label with color bars					
BL 54110 [M]	Baby Workout	1963	12.50	25.00	50.00
—All-black label					
BL 54110 [M]	Baby Workout	1963	5.00	10.00	20.00
—Black label with color bars					
BL 54112 [M]	Merry Christmas from Jackie Wilson	1963	7.50	15.00	30.00
BL 54113 [M]	Shake a Hand	1964	6.25	12.50	25.00
BL 54115 [M]	My Golden Favorites, Volume 2	1964	6.25	12.50	25.00
BL 54117 [M]	Somethin' Else	1964	6.25	12.50	25.00
BL 54118 [M]	Soul Time	1965	6.25	12.50	25.00
BL 54119 [M]	Spotlight on Jackie	1965	6.25	12.50	25.00
BL 54120 [M]	Soul Galore	1966	6.25	12.50	25.00
BL 54122 [M]	Whispers	1966	6.25	12.50	25.00
BL 54130 [M]	Higher and Higher	1967	6.25	12.50	25.00
BL 54134 [M]	Manufacturers of Soul	1968	12.50	25.00	50.00
—With Count Basie					
BL 754050 [S]	So Much	1960	37.50	75.00	150.00
—All-black label					
BL 754050 [S]	So Much	1964	6.25	12.50	25.00
—Black label with color bars					
BL 754055 [S]	Jackie Sings the Blues	1960	50.00	100.00	200.00
—All-black label					
BL 754055 [S]	Jackie Sings the Blues	1964	6.25	12.50	25.00
—Black label with color bars					
BL 754059 [S]	A Woman, a Lover, a Friend	1961	20.00	40.00	80.00
—All-black label					
BL 754059 [S]	A Woman, a Lover, a Friend	1964	6.25	12.50	25.00
—Black label with color bars					
BL 754100 [S]	You Ain't Heard Nothin' Yet	1961	20.00	40.00	80.00
—All-black label					
BL 754100 [S]	You Ain't Heard Nothin' Yet	1964	6.25	12.50	25.00
—Black label with color bars					
BL 754101 [S]	By Special Request	1961	20.00	40.00	80.00
—All-black label					
BL 754101 [S]	By Special Request	1964	6.25	12.50	25.00
—Black label with color bars					
BL 754105 [S]	Body and Soul	1962	20.00	40.00	80.00
—All-black label					
BL 754105 [S]	Body and Soul	1964	6.25	12.50	25.00
—Black label with color bars					
BL 754106 [S]	The World's Greatest Melodies	1962	20.00	40.00	80.00
—All-black label					
BL 754106 [S]	The World's Greatest Melodies	1964	6.25	12.50	25.00
—Black label with color bars					
BL 754108 [S]	Jackie Wilson at the Copa	1962	20.00	40.00	80.00
—All-black label					
BL 754108 [S]	Jackie Wilson at the Copa	1964	6.25	12.50	25.00
—Black label with color bars					
BL 754110 [S]	Baby Workout	1963	20.00	40.00	80.00
—All-black label					
BL 754110 [S]	Baby Workout	1963	6.25	12.50	25.00
—Black label with color bars					
BL 754112 [S]	Merry Christmas from Jackie Wilson	1963	10.00	20.00	40.00
BL 754113 [S]	Shake a Hand	1964	7.50	15.00	30.00
BL 754115 [S]	My Golden Favorites, Volume 2	1964	7.50	15.00	30.00
BL 754117 [S]	Somethin' Else	1964	7.50	15.00	30.00
BL 754118 [S]	Soul Time	1965	7.50	15.00	30.00
BL 754119 [S]	Spotlight on Jackie	1965	7.50	15.00	30.00
BL 754120 [S]	Soul Galore	1966	7.50	15.00	30.00
BL 754122 [S]	Whispers	1966	7.50	15.00	30.00
BL 754130 [S]	Higher and Higher	1967	7.50	15.00	30.00
BL 754134 [S]	Manufacturers of Soul	1968	5.00	10.00	20.00
—With Count Basie					
BL 754138	I Get the Sweetest Feeling	1968	5.00	10.00	20.00
BL 754140	Jackie Wilson's Greatest Hits	1969	5.00	10.00	20.00
BL 754154	Do Your Thing	1969	5.00	10.00	20.00
BL 754158	It's All a Part of Love	1970	5.00	10.00	20.00
BL 754167	This Love Is Real	1971	5.00	10.00	20.00
BL 754172	You Got Me Walking	1971	5.00	10.00	20.00
BL 754185	Beautiful Day	1972	3.75	7.50	15.00
BL 754199	Nowstalgia	1974	3.75	7.50	15.00
BL 754212	Nobody But You	1977	3.75	7.50	15.00
COLUMBIA					
FC 40866	Reet Petite: The Best of Jackie Wilson	1987	3.00	6.00	12.00
EPIC					
EG 38623 [(2)]	The Jackie Wilson Story	1983	5.00	10.00	20.00
FE 39408	The Jackie Wilson Story, Vol. 2	1985	3.00	6.00	12.00
PE 39408	The Jackie Wilson Story, Vol. 2	198?	2.00	4.00	8.00
—Budget-line reissue					
RHINO					
RNLP-70230	Through the Years: A Collection of Rare Album Tracks and Single Sides	1987	3.00	6.00	12.00

WILSON, MARTY

45s

Number	Title (A Side/B Side)	Yr	VG	VG+	NM
DECCA					
30544	Super Sonic/I'm All Woke Up	1958	7.50	15.00	30.00
30644	Po-Go/Hey Eula	1958	7.50	15.00	30.00
TEL					
1008	Stroll Me/Hot Foot	1959	6.25	12.50	25.00

WILSON, MURRY

Father of Brian, Carl and Dennis Wilson of the Beach Boys.

45s

Number	Title (A Side/B Side)	Yr	VG	VG+	NM
CAPITOL					
2063	Leaves/Plumber's Tune	1967	3.00	6.00	12.00

Albums

Number	Title (A Side/B Side)	Yr	VG	VG+	NM
CAPITOL					
ST 2819 [S]	The Many Moods of Murry Wilson	1967	12.50	25.00	50.00
T 2819 [M]	The Many Moods of Murry Wilson	1967	15.00	30.00	60.00

WILSON, NANCY

45s

Number	Title (A Side/B Side)	Yr	VG	VG+	NM
CAPITOL					
2061	Ode to Billie Joe/I'm Always Drunk in San Francisco	1967	—	3.00	6.00
2136	Face It Girl, It's Over/The End of Our Love	1968	—	3.00	6.00
2283	Peace of Mind/This Bitter Earth	1968	—	3.00	6.00
2422	You'd Better Go/I'm Your Special Fool	1969	—	3.00	6.00
2555	Got It Together/One Soft Night	1969	—	3.00	6.00
2644	Can't Take My Eyes Off You/Do You Know Why	1969	—	3.00	6.00
2749	Waitin' for Charlie to Come Home/Words and Music	1970	—	3.00	6.00
2831	This Girl Is a Woman Now/Trip with Me	1970	—	3.00	6.00
2934	Now I'm a Woman/The Real Me	1970	—	3.00	6.00
3212	The Greatest Performance of My Life/Everybody Knows	1971	—	3.00	6.00
3956	Streetrunner/Ocean of Love	1974	—	2.50	5.00
3973	You're As Right As Rain/There'll Always Be Forever	1974	—	2.50	5.00
4117	He Called Me Baby/Like a Circle Never Stops	1975	—	2.50	5.00
4189	Don't Let Me Be Lonely Tonight/Happy Tears	1975	—	2.50	5.00
4284	Now/This Mother's Daughter	1976	—	2.00	4.00
4359	In My Loneliness (When We Were One)/He Never Had It So Good	1976	—	2.00	4.00
4476	I've Never Been to Me/Here It Comes	1977	—	2.00	4.00
4558	Next Time You See Him/Give Him Love	1961	2.50	5.00	10.00
4578	I'm Gonna Let Ya/Light	1978	—	2.00	4.00
4741	Life, Love and Harmony/Open Up Your Heart and Take Me In	1979	—	2.00	4.00
4801	Sunshine/This Is Our Song	1979	—	2.00	4.00
4816	Put On a Happy Face/You Don't Know What Love Is	1962	2.00	4.00	8.00
4839	Welcome Home/Let's Hold On to Love	1980	—	2.00	4.00
4926	You Can Have Him/A Lot of Livin' to Do	1963	2.00	4.00	8.00
4991	Tell Me the Truth/My Sweet Thing	1963	2.00	4.00	8.00
5084	That's What I Want for Christmas/What Are You Doing New Year's Eve	1963	2.50	5.00	10.00
5133	Don't Rain on My Parade/The Grass Is Greener	1964	2.00	4.00	8.00
5198	(You Don't Know) How Glad I Am/Never Less Than Yesterday	1964	—	3.50	7.00
5254	I Wanna Be with You/It's Time for Me	1964	—	3.50	7.00
5319	And Satisfy/Take What I Have	1964	—	3.50	7.00
5340	Don't Come Running Back to Me/Love Has Many Faces	1965	—	3.50	7.00
5340 [PS]	Don't Come Running Back to Me/Love Has Many Faces	1965	3.00	6.00	12.00
5408	The Best Is Yet to Come/Welcome, Welcome	1965	—	3.50	7.00
5455	Where Does That Leave Me/Gentle Is My Love	1965	—	3.50	7.00
5515	I'll Only Miss Him When I Think of Him/Afterthoughts	1965	—	3.50	7.00
5564	No One Else But You/Have a Heart	1966	—	3.50	7.00
5639	The Power of Love/Rain Sometime	1966	—	3.50	7.00
5673	Uptight (Everything's Alright)/You've Got Your Troubles	1966	—	3.50	7.00
5720	Go Away/That Special Way	1966	—	3.50	7.00
5771	Love Can Do Anything/I'll Make a Man of the Man	1966	—	3.50	7.00
5841	In the Dark/Ten Years of Tears	1967	—	3.50	7.00
5935	Don't Look Over Your Shoulder/But Only Sometimes	1967	—	3.50	7.00
6275	That's What I Want for Christmas/What Are You Doing New Year's Eve	197?	—	2.50	5.00
—Starline reissue					
S7-19763	That's What I Want for Christmas/What Are You Doing New Year's Eve	1997	—	—	3.00
COLUMBIA					
07037	Forbidden Lover/A Song for You	1987	—	—	3.00
08058	Quiet Fire/The Power, The Glory	1988	—	—	3.00

7-Inch Extended Plays

Number	Title (A Side/B Side)	Yr	VG	VG+	NM
CAPITOL					
SXA-2351 [PS]	Gentle Is My Love	1965	2.50	5.00	10.00
SXA-2351 [S]	Who Can I Turn To/Gentle Is My Love/There Will Never Be Another You//Funnier Than Funny/More/If Ever I Would Leave You	1965	2.50	5.00	10.00
—33 1/3 rpm, small hole					
SU-2555 [PS]	Tender Loving Care	1966	2.50	5.00	10.00
SU-2555 [S]	Don't Go to Strangers/Like Someone in Love/Tender Loving Care//Gee Baby, Ain't I Good to You/Close Your Eyes/As You Desire Me	1966	2.50	5.00	10.00
—33 1/3 rpm, small hole					

Albums

Number	Title (A Side/B Side)	Yr	VG	VG+	NM
CAPITOL					
ST-148	Nancy	1969	3.75	7.50	15.00
ST-234	Son of a Preacher Man	1969	3.75	7.50	15.00
SWBB-256 [(2)]	Close-Up	1969	5.00	10.00	20.00
—Combines 1828 and 1934 into one package					
ST-353	Hurt So Bad	1969	3.75	7.50	15.00
ST-429	Can't Take My Eyes Off You	1970	3.75	7.50	15.00
ST-541	Now I'm a Woman	1970	3.75	7.50	15.00
STBB-727 [(2)]	For Once in My Life/Who Can I Turn To	1971	5.00	10.00	20.00
ST-763	The Right to Love	1971	3.75	7.50	15.00
—Retitled reissue of 2757					
SM-798	But Beautiful	197?	2.50	5.00	10.00
—Reissue					
ST-798	But Beautiful	1971	3.75	7.50	15.00
ST-842	Kaleidoscope	1971	3.75	7.50	15.00
ST 1319 [S]	Like in Love	1960	7.50	15.00	30.00
—Black label with colorband, Capitol logo on left					
ST 1319 [S]	Like in Love	1960	5.00	10.00	20.00
—Black label with colorband, Capitol logo on top					
T 1319 [M]	Like in Love	1960	6.25	12.50	25.00
—Black label with colorband, Capitol logo on left					
T 1319 [M]	Like in Love	1960	3.75	7.50	15.00
—Black label with colorband, Capitol logo on top					
ST 1440 [S]	Something Wonderful	1960	7.50	15.00	30.00
—Black label with colorband, Capitol logo on left					

Number	Title (A Side/B Side)	Yr	VG	VG+	NM
ST 1440 [S]	Something Wonderful	1960	5.00	10.00	20.00
—Black label with colorband, Capitol logo on top					
T 1440 [M]	Something Wonderful	1960	6.25	12.50	25.00
—Black label with colorband, Capitol logo on left					
T 1440 [M]	Something Wonderful	1960	3.75	7.50	15.00
—Black label with colorband, Capitol logo on top					
ST 1524 [S]	The Swingin's Mutual	1961	7.50	15.00	30.00
—Black label with colorband, Capitol logo on left					
ST 1524 [S]	The Swingin's Mutual	1961	5.00	10.00	20.00
—Black label with colorband, Capitol logo on top					
T 1524 [M]	The Swingin's Mutual	1961	6.25	12.50	25.00
—Black label with colorband, Capitol logo on left					
T 1524 [M]	The Swingin's Mutual	1961	3.75	7.50	15.00
—Black label with colorband, Capitol logo on top					
ST 1767 [S]	Hello Young Lovers	1962	6.25	12.50	25.00
T 1767 [M]	Hello Young Lovers	1962	5.00	10.00	20.00
SM-1828	Broadway My Way	197?	2.50	5.00	10.00
—Reissue					
ST 1828 [S]	Broadway My Way	1963	5.00	10.00	20.00
T 1828 [M]	Broadway My Way	1963	3.75	7.50	15.00
SM-1934	Hollywood My Way	197?	2.50	5.00	10.00
—Reissue					
ST 1934 [S]	Hollywood My Way	1963	5.00	10.00	20.00
T 1934 [M]	Hollywood My Way	1963	3.75	7.50	15.00
ST 2012 [S]	Yesterday's Love Songs/Today's Blues	1964	5.00	10.00	20.00
T 2012 [M]	Yesterday's Love Songs/Today's Blues	1964	3.75	7.50	15.00
ST 2082 [S]	Today, Tomorrow, Forever	1964	5.00	10.00	20.00
T 2082 [M]	Today, Tomorrow, Forever	1964	3.75	7.50	15.00
KAO 2136 [M]	The Nancy Wilson Show!	1965	3.75	7.50	15.00
SKAO 2136 [S]	The Nancy Wilson Show!	1965	5.00	10.00	20.00
ST 2155 [S]	How Glad I Am	1964	5.00	10.00	20.00
T 2155 [M]	How Glad I Am	1964	3.75	7.50	15.00
ST 2321 [S]	Today — My Way	1965	5.00	10.00	20.00
T 2321 [M]	Today — My Way	1965	3.75	7.50	15.00
ST 2351 [S]	Gentle Is My Love	1965	5.00	10.00	20.00
T 2351 [M]	Gentle Is My Love	1965	3.75	7.50	15.00
ST 2433 [S]	From Broadway with Love	1966	5.00	10.00	20.00
T 2433 [M]	From Broadway with Love	1966	3.75	7.50	15.00
SM-2495	A Touch of Today	197?	2.50	5.00	10.00
—Reissue					
ST 2495 [S]	A Touch of Today	1966	5.00	10.00	20.00
T 2495 [M]	A Touch of Today	1966	3.75	7.50	15.00
ST 2555 [S]	Tender Loving Care	1966	5.00	10.00	20.00
T 2555 [M]	Tender Loving Care	1966	3.75	7.50	15.00
ST 2634 [S]	Nancy — Naturally	1967	5.00	10.00	20.00
T 2634 [M]	Nancy — Naturally	1967	3.75	7.50	15.00
ST 2712 [S]	Just for Now	1967	5.00	10.00	20.00
T 2712 [M]	Just for Now	1967	3.75	7.50	15.00
ST 2757 [S]	Lush Life	1967	3.75	7.50	15.00
T 2757 [M]	Lush Life	1967	5.00	10.00	20.00
ST 2844 [S]	Welcome to My Love	1968	3.75	7.50	15.00
T 2844 [M]	Welcome to My Love	1968	6.25	12.50	25.00
ST 2909	Easy	1968	3.75	7.50	15.00
SKAO 2947	The Best of Nancy Wilson	1968	3.75	7.50	15.00
ST 2970	The Sound of Nancy Wilson	1968	3.75	7.50	15.00
SY-4575	Broadway My Way	197?	2.50	5.00	10.00
—Odd reissue					
ST-11131	I Know I Love Him	1972	3.00	6.00	12.00
ST-11317	All in Love Is Fair	1974	3.00	6.00	12.00
ST-11386	Come Get to This	1975	3.00	6.00	12.00
ST-11518	This Mother's Daughter	1976	3.00	6.00	12.00
ST-11659	I've Never Been to Me	1977	3.00	6.00	12.00
SM-11767	How Glad I Am	1978	2.50	5.00	10.00
—Reissue of 2155					
SMAS-11786	Music on My Mind	1978	3.00	6.00	12.00
SM-11802	Easy	1978	2.50	5.00	10.00
—Reissue of 2909					
SM-11819	Come Get to This	1978	2.50	5.00	10.00
—Reissue of 11386					
SM-11884	Nancy — Naturally	1979	2.50	5.00	10.00
—Reissue of 2634					
ST-11943	Life, Love and Happiness	1979	3.00	6.00	12.00
SM-12031	Can't Take My Eyes Off You	1980	2.50	5.00	10.00
—Reissue of 429					
ST-12055	Take My Love	1980	3.00	6.00	12.00
SN-16198	The Best of Nancy Wilson	198?	2.00	4.00	8.00
—Budget-line reissue					
COLUMBIA					
FC 40330	Keep You Satisfied	1986	2.50	5.00	10.00
FC 40787	Forbidden Lover	1987	2.50	5.00	10.00
FC 44464	Nancy Now!	1989	2.50	5.00	10.00
PAUSA					
PR-9041	Nancy — Naturally	1985	2.50	5.00	10.00
PICKWICK					
SPC-3273	Goin' Out of My Head	197?	2.50	5.00	10.00
SPC-3348	The Good Life	197?	2.50	5.00	10.00

WILSON, NANCY, AND CANNONBALL ADDERLEY

Also see each artist's individual listings.

Number	Title (A Side/B Side)	Yr	VG	VG+	NM
45s					
CAPITOL					
4693	Save Your Love for Me/Never Will I Marry	1962	2.00	4.00	8.00
Albums					
CAPITOL					
SM-1657	Nancy Wilson/Cannonball Adderley	197?	2.50	5.00	10.00
—Reissue					
ST 1657 [S]	Nancy Wilson/Cannonball Adderley	1962	7.50	15.00	30.00
—Black label with colorband, Capitol logo on left					
ST 1657 [S]	Nancy Wilson/Cannonball Adderley	1962	5.00	10.00	20.00
—Black label with colorband, Capitol logo on top					
T 1657 [M]	Nancy Wilson/Cannonball Adderley	1962	6.25	12.50	25.00
—Black label with colorband, Capitol logo on left					
T 1657 [M]	Nancy Wilson/Cannonball Adderley	1962	3.75	7.50	15.00
—Black label with colorband, Capitol logo on top					

WILSON, PEANUTS

Number	Title (A Side/B Side)	Yr	VG	VG+	NM
45s					
BRUNSWICK					
55039	Cast Iron Arm/You've Got Love	1957	37.50	75.00	150.00

WILSON, SONNY

Number	Title (A Side/B Side)	Yr	VG	VG+	NM
45s					
CANDIX					
327	I Ain't Givin' Up Nothin'/Troubled Time	1962	5.00	10.00	20.00
SUN					
341	The Great Pretender/I'm Gonna Take a Walk	1960	5.00	10.00	20.00

WILSON, WALLY

Number	Title (A Side/B Side)	Yr	VG	VG+	NM
45s					
SABRE					
106	If You Don't Love Me/The Hunt	1954	150.00	300.00	600.00

WIMBERLEY, MAGGIE SUE

Number	Title (A Side/B Side)	Yr	VG	VG+	NM
45s					
SUN					
229	Daydreams Come True/How Long	1956	15.00	30.00	60.00

WINCHELL, DANNY

Number	Title (A Side/B Side)	Yr	VG	VG+	NM
45s					
MGM					
11335	Carolina in the Morning/There Goes My Heart	1952	7.50	15.00	30.00
RECORTE					
406	Jeannie/Beware You've Fallen in Love	1959	10.00	20.00	40.00
410	We're Gonna Have a Rockin' Party/Don't Say You're Sorry	1959	12.50	25.00	50.00
415	Come Back Baby/I've Chosen You	1959	10.00	20.00	40.00

WINCHESTER, JESSE

Number	Title (A Side/B Side)	Yr	VG	VG+	NM
45s					
AMPEX					
11004	Yankee Lady/That's the Touch I Like	1970	—	3.00	6.00
11018	Quiet About It/Biloxi	1970	—	3.00	6.00
BEARSVILLE					
0311	The Brand New Tennessee Waltz/Let the Rough Side Drag	1976	—	2.00	4.00
0314	Everybody Knows But Me/Damned If You Do	1976	—	2.00	4.00
0318	Nothing But a Breeze/Twigs and Seeds	1977	—	2.00	4.00
0320	Rhumba Man/Twigs and Seeds	1977	—	2.00	4.00
0332	Sassy/Wintry Feeling	1978	—	2.00	4.00
49711	Say What/If Only	1981	—	2.00	4.00
49781	Baby Blue/Sure Enough	1981	—	2.00	4.00
Albums					
AMPEX					
A 10104	Jesse Winchester	1970	5.00	10.00	20.00
BEARSVILLE					
PRO 560 [DJ]	The Jesse Winchester Radio Show	1976	10.00	20.00	40.00
PRO-A-693 [(2) DJ]	Live at the Bijou Café Plus a Live Interview at Media College in Montreal	1977	10.00	20.00	40.00
BR 2045	Jesse Winchester	1971	3.75	7.50	15.00
—Reissue of Ampex LP					
BR 2102	Third Down, 110 to Go	1972	3.75	7.50	15.00
BR 6953	Learn to Love It	1974	3.00	6.00	12.00
BR 6964	Let the Rough Side Drag	1976	3.00	6.00	12.00
BR 6968	Nothing But a Breeze	1977	2.50	5.00	10.00
BRK 6984	A Touch on the Rainy Side	1978	2.50	5.00	10.00
BRK 6989	Talk Memphis	1981	2.50	5.00	10.00
RHINO					
R1-70085	The Best of Jesse Winchester	1989	2.50	5.00	10.00
RNLP-70885	Jesse Winchester	1988	2.50	5.00	10.00
RNLP-70886	Third Down, 110 to Go	1988	2.50	5.00	10.00
SUGAR HILL					
SH-1023	Humour Me	1988	3.00	6.00	12.00

WIND

TONY ORLANDO was in this group.

Number	Title (A Side/B Side)	Yr	VG	VG+	NM
45s					
FORWARD					
152	Groovin' with Mr. Bloe/Are You Nuts?	1970	—	2.50	5.00
—As "Cool Heat"					
LIFE					
200	Make Believe/Groovin' with Mr. Bloe	1969	—	2.50	5.00
202	Teeny Bopper/I'll Hold Out My Hand	1969	—	2.50	5.00
203	Groovin' with Mr. Bloe/Are You Nuts?	1970	—	3.00	6.00
—As "Cool Heat"					
Albums					
LIFE					
LLPS-2000	Make Believe	1969	5.00	10.00	20.00

WIND HARP, THE

Number	Title (A Side/B Side)	Yr	VG	VG+	NM
Albums					
UNITED ARTISTS					
UAS-9963 [(2)]	Song from the Hill	1972	5.00	10.00	20.00

WIND IN THE WILLOWS, THE

With Debbie Harry, later of Blondie.

Number	Title (A Side/B Side)	Yr	VG	VG+	NM
45s					
CAPITOL					
2274	Uptown Girl/Moments Spent	1968	5.00	10.00	20.00
Albums					
CAPITOL					
SKAO 2956	The Wind in the Willows	1968	12.50	25.00	50.00

WINDING, KAI

45s

Number	Title (A Side/B Side)	Yr	VG	VG+	NM
A&M					
1035	Wichita Lineman/Betwixt and Between	1969	—	3.00	6.00
COLUMBIA					
41330	Manhattan/Cha Cha Chicago	1959	2.50	5.00	10.00
IMPULSE!					
201	Theme from Picnic/Side by Side	1961	2.50	5.00	10.00
—With J.J. Johnson					
VERVE					
10258	Baby Elephant Walk/Experiment in Terror	1963	2.00	4.00	8.00
10295	More/Comin' Home Baby	1963	2.50	5.00	10.00
10301	Ice Cream Man/The Lonely One	1963	2.00	4.00	8.00
10307	Time Is On My Side/Baby Don't Come On with Me	1963	2.00	4.00	8.00
10313	Portrait of My Love/Mondo Cane	1964	2.00	4.00	8.00
10328	Don't Blow Your Cool (In the Merry Old Summertime)/New Song of India	1964	2.00	4.00	8.00
10334	Theme from The Luck of Ginger Coffey/Do Anything You Wanna	1964	2.00	4.00	8.00
10335	Dear Heart/Wolverton Mountain	1964	2.00	4.00	8.00
10343	I Will Wait for You/Baker Street Mystery	1965	—	3.00	6.00
10348	Marriage, Italian Style/My Hands Reach Out to You	1965	—	3.00	6.00
10355	Singin' in the Rain/Half a Crown	1965	—	3.00	6.00
10372	A Sign of the Times/You've Lost That Lovin' Feelin'	1965	—	3.00	6.00
10407	Dirty Dog/Sunrise	1966	—	3.00	6.00
10433	The Sidewinder/Something You Got	1966	—	3.00	6.00
10455	All/More	1966	—	3.00	6.00
10488	Penny Lane/Time	1967	—	3.00	6.00

Albums

Number	Title	Yr	VG	VG+	NM
ABC IMPULSE!					
AS 3 [S]	The Incredible Kai Winding Trombones	1968	3.00	6.00	12.00
—Black and red label					
A&M					
SP-3008	Israel	1969	3.00	6.00	12.00
COLUMBIA					
CL 936 [M]	Trombone Sound	1956	12.50	25.00	50.00
CL 999 [M]	Trombone Panorama	1957	12.50	25.00	50.00
CL 1264 [M]	Swingin' State	1958	12.50	25.00	50.00
CL 1329 [M]	Dance to the City Beat	1959	10.00	20.00	40.00
CS 8062 [S]	Swingin' State	1958	10.00	20.00	40.00
CS 8136 [S]	Dance to the City Beat	1959	7.50	15.00	30.00
GATEWAY					
7022	Jazz Showcase	1979	2.50	5.00	10.00
GLENDALE					
6003	Danish Blue	1976	2.50	5.00	10.00
6004	Caravan	1977	2.50	5.00	10.00
HARMONY					
HL 7341 [M]	The Great Kai Winding Sound	1962	3.75	7.50	15.00
IMPULSE!					
A 3 [M]	The Incredible Kai Winding Trombones	1960	7.50	15.00	30.00
AS 3 [S]	The Incredible Kai Winding Trombones	1960	6.25	12.50	25.00
—Orange and black label					
MCA					
29062	Incredible Kai Winding Trombones	198?	2.50	5.00	10.00
—Reissue of Impulse! 3					
PICKWICK					
SPC-3004	Trombones	196?	3.00	6.00	12.00
RED RECORD					
VPA-143	Duo Bones	198?	3.00	6.00	12.00
ROOST					
LP 408 [10]	Kai Winding All Stars	1952	30.00	60.00	120.00
SAVOY					
MG-9017 [10]	New Trends of Jazz	1952	30.00	60.00	120.00
MG-12119 [M]	In the Beginning	196?	3.75	7.50	15.00
VERVE					
V-8427 [M]	Kai Ole	1962	6.25	12.50	25.00
V6-8427 [S]	Kai Ole	1962	6.25	12.50	25.00
V-8493 [M]	Suspense Themes in Jazz	1962	6.25	12.50	25.00
V6-8493 [S]	Suspense Themes in Jazz	1962	6.25	12.50	25.00
V-8525 [M]	Kai Winding Solo	1963	6.25	12.50	25.00
V6-8525 [S]	Kai Winding Solo	1963	6.25	12.50	25.00
V-8551 [M]	More!!!	1963	6.25	12.50	25.00
V6-8551 [S]	More!!!	1963	6.25	12.50	25.00
V-8556 [M]	The Lonely One	1963	6.25	12.50	25.00
V6-8556 [S]	The Lonely One	1963	6.25	12.50	25.00
V-8573 [M]	Mondo Cane #2	1964	6.25	12.50	25.00
V6-8573 [S]	Mondo Cane #2	1964	7.50	15.00	30.00
V-8602 [M]	Modern Country	1964	3.75	7.50	15.00
V6-8602 [S]	Modern Country	1964	5.00	10.00	20.00
V-8620 [M]	Rainy Day	1965	3.75	7.50	15.00
V6-8620 [S]	Rainy Day	1965	5.00	10.00	20.00
V-8639 [M]	The "In" Instrumentals	1965	3.75	7.50	15.00
V6-8639 [S]	The "In" Instrumentals	1965	5.00	10.00	20.00
V-8657 [M]	More Brass	1966	3.00	6.00	12.00
V6-8657 [S]	More Brass	1966	3.75	7.50	15.00
V-8661 [M]	Dirty Dog	1966	3.00	6.00	12.00
V6-8661 [S]	Dirty Dog	1966	3.75	7.50	15.00
V-8691 [M]	Penny Lane and Time	1967	3.75	7.50	15.00
V6-8691 [S]	Penny Lane and Time	1967	3.00	6.00	12.00
WHO'S WHO IN JAZZ					
21001	Lionel Hampton Presents Kai Winding	1978	2.50	5.00	10.00

WINDING, KAI, AND SONNY STITT

Also see each artist's individual listings.

Albums

Number	Title	Yr	VG	VG+	NM
HALL OF FAME					
612	Early Modern	197?	2.50	5.00	10.00

WINDSORS, THE (1)

45s

Number	Title (A Side/B Side)	Yr	VG	VG+	NM
ABC-PARAMOUNT					
10563	Keep Away/Fingers and Thumbs	1964	3.75	7.50	15.00

WINDSORS, THE (2)

45s

Number	Title (A Side/B Side)	Yr	VG	VG+	NM
BACK BEAT					
506	My Gloria/Cool Seabreeze	1958	4000.	6000.	8000.

WINDSORS, THE (U)

45s

Number	Title (A Side/B Side)	Yr	VG	VG+	NM
UNITED ARTISTS					
128	Saki Rock/Caramba	1958	5.00	10.00	20.00
WIG WAG					
203	Carol Ann/Keep Me from Crying	1959	50.00	100.00	200.00

WINE, TONI

45s

Number	Title (A Side/B Side)	Yr	VG	VG+	NM
ATCO					
6736	Sisters in Sorrow/Take a Little Time Out for Love	1970	—	3.00	6.00
COLPIX					
715	My Boyfriend's Coming Home for Christmas/What a Pity	1963	3.75	7.50	15.00
732	I Love That Boy/The Thirteenth Hour	1964	3.00	6.00	12.00
742	A Boy Like You/Funny Little Heart	1964	3.00	6.00	12.00
756	Only Fools/A Girl Is Not a Girl	1964	3.00	6.00	12.00
SENATE					
2104	River Deep, Mountain High/Toni's Tune	1967	2.50	5.00	10.00

WINGFIELD, PETE

Also see OLYMPIC RUNNERS.

45s

Number	Title (A Side/B Side)	Yr	VG	VG+	NM
ISLAND					
026	Eighteen with a Bullet/Shadow of a Doubt	1975	2.00	4.00	8.00
—First pressing: Mostly yellow label with island scene					
026	Eighteen with a Bullet/Shadow of a Doubt	1975	—	2.50	5.00
—Second pressing: Mostly black label with Island logo at bottom					
051	Lovin' As You Wanna Be/Please	1975	—	2.00	4.00
065	Scratchy 45's/A Whole Pot of Jelly (For a Little Slice of Toast)	1976	—	2.00	4.00

Albums

Number	Title	Yr	VG	VG+	NM
ISLAND					
ILPS 9333	Breakfast Special	1975	3.00	6.00	12.00

WINGS

See PAUL McCARTNEY.

WINKLEY AND NUTLEY

45s

Number	Title (A Side/B Side)	Yr	VG	VG+	NM
MK					
101	Report to the Nation (Part 1)/Report to the Nation (Part 2)	1960	5.00	10.00	20.00

WINSTON, GEORGE

45s

Number	Title (A Side/B Side)	Yr	VG	VG+	NM
WINDHAM HILL					
WS-0005	Variations on the Kanon by Johann Pachelbel/Carol of the Bells	1984	—	2.50	5.00
WS-0005 [PS]	Variations on the Kanon by Johann Pachelbel/Carol of the Bells	1984	—	2.50	5.00

Albums

Number	Title	Yr	VG	VG+	NM
LOST LAKE ARTS					
LL-0081	Ballads and Blues	197?	3.00	6.00	12.00
TAKOMA					
9016	Piano Solos	197?	3.00	6.00	12.00
WINDHAM HILL					
WH-1012	Autumn	1980	2.50	5.00	10.00
WH-1019	Winter Into Spring	1982	2.50	5.00	10.00
C-1025	December	1982	3.75	7.50	15.00
—NOT distributed by A&M Records; "December" in black letters					
WD 1025	December	1982	3.00	6.00	12.00
—Distributed by A&M Records; "December" in raised white letters					

WINSTONS, THE

45s

Number	Title (A Side/B Side)	Yr	VG	VG+	NM
METROMEDIA					
117	Color Him Father/Amen, Brother	1969	2.00	4.00	8.00
142	Love of the Common People/Wheel of Fortune	1969	—	3.00	6.00
151	Birds of a Feather/The Greatest Love	1969	—	3.00	6.00

Albums

Number	Title	Yr	VG	VG+	NM
METROMEDIA					
MD-1010	Color Him Father	1969	12.50	25.00	50.00

WINTER, EDGAR

45s

Number	Title (A Side/B Side)	Yr	VG	VG+	NM
BLUE SKY					
2758	One Day Tomorrow/Jasmine Nightdream	1975	—	2.00	4.00
2761	Outa Control/I Always Wanted You	1975	—	2.00	4.00
2762	Cool Dance/People Music	1975	—	2.00	4.00
2763	Diamond Eyes/Infinite Peace in Rhythm	1976	—	2.00	4.00
2769	Stickin' It Out/Puttin' It Back	1977	—	2.00	4.00
2780	Forever in Love/It's Your Life to Live	1979	—	2.00	4.00
2786	Above and Beyond/(Instrumental)	1980	—	2.00	4.00
70068	Love Is Everywhere/Everyday Man	1981	—	2.00	4.00
EPIC					
10618	Tobacco Road/Now Is the Time	1970	2.00	4.00	8.00
10740	Good Morning Music/Where Would I Be	1971	2.00	4.00	8.00
10750	Where Would I Be/Feeling Like a Woman	1971	—	3.00	6.00
—B-side by Patsy Sledd					

Number	Title (A Side/B Side)	Yr	VG	VG+	NM
10762	Give It Everything You've Got/You Were My Light	1971	—	3.00	6.00
10788	Keep Playin' That Rock 'N' Roll/Dying to Live	1971	—	3.00	6.00
10855	I Can't Turn You Loose/Cool Fool	1972	—	3.00	6.00
10903	Free Ride/Catchin' Up	1972	2.00	4.00	8.00
10922	Round and Round/Catchin' Up	1972	2.00	4.00	8.00
10945	Frankenstein/Hangin' Around	1973	2.00	4.00	8.00
10967	Frankenstein/Undercover Man	1973	—	3.00	6.00
—Yellow label					
10967	Frankenstein/Undercover Man	1973	—	2.00	4.00
—Orange label					
11024	Free Ride/When It Comes	1973	—	2.00	4.00
11069	Hangin' Around/We All Had a Real Good Time	1973	—	2.00	4.00
11143	River's Risin'/Animal	1974	—	2.00	4.00
50034	Easy Street/Do Like Me	1974	—	2.00	4.00
50060	Miracle of Love/Someone Take My Heart Away	1975	—	2.00	4.00
Albums					
BLUE SKY					
PZ 33483	Jasmine Nightdreams	1975	3.00	6.00	12.00
PZQ 33483 [Q]	Jasmine Nightdreams	1975	5.00	10.00	20.00
PZ 33798	The Edgar Winter Group with Rick Derringer	1975	3.00	6.00	12.00
PZQ 33798 [Q]	The Edgar Winter Group with Rick Derringer	1975	5.00	10.00	20.00
PZ 34858	Re-Cycled	1977	3.00	6.00	12.00
JZ 35989	The Edger Winter Album	1979	3.00	6.00	12.00
JZ 36494	Standing on Rock	1981	3.00	6.00	12.00
EPIC					
BN 26503	Entrance	1970	3.75	7.50	15.00
—Yellow label					
BN 26503	Entrance	1973	3.00	6.00	12.00
—Orange label					
E 30512	Edgar Winter's White Trash	1971	3.75	7.50	15.00
—Yellow label					
KE 30512	Edgar Winter's White Trash	1973	3.00	6.00	12.00
—Orange label					
PE 30512	Edger Winter's White Trash	1985	2.00	4.00	8.00
—Budget-line reissue; dark blue label					
EG 31249 [(2)]	Roadwork	1987	2.50	5.00	10.00
—Budget-line reissue; dark blue labels					
KEG 31249 [(2)]	Roadwork	1972	5.00	10.00	20.00
—Yellow labels					
KEG 31249 [(2)]	Roadwork	1973	3.75	7.50	15.00
—Orange labels					
EQ 31584 [Q]	They Only Come Out at Night	1973	6.25	12.50	25.00
KE 31584	They Only Come Out at Night	1972	3.75	7.50	15.00
—Yellow label					
KE 31584	They Only Come Out at Night	1973	3.00	6.00	12.00
—Orange label					
PE 31584	They Only Come Out at Night	1979	2.00	4.00	8.00
—Budget-line reissue; dark blue label					
PE 31584	They Only Come Out at Night	197?	2.50	5.00	10.00
—Reissue with new prefix; orange label					
PE 32461	Shock Treatment	1974	3.75	7.50	15.00
—Orange label					
PE 32461	Shock Treatment	1985	2.00	4.00	8.00
—Budget-line reissue; dark blue label					
PEQ 32461 [Q]	Shock Treatment	1974	6.25	12.50	25.00
BG 33770 [(2)]	Entrance/White Trash	1975	3.75	7.50	15.00
—Combines 26503 and 30512 into one package					
RHINO					
R1-70709	Mission Earth	1989	3.00	6.00	12.00
R1-70895	The Edger Winter Collection	1989	2.50	5.00	10.00

WINTER, JOHNNY

Also see JOHNNY AND THE JAMMERS.

Number	Title (A Side/B Side)	Yr	VG	VG+	NM
45s					
ATLANTIC					
2248	Gangster of Love/Eternally	1964	2.50	5.00	10.00
BLUE SKY					
2754	Raised on Rock/Pick Up on My Mojo	1974	—	2.00	4.00
2756	Golden Olden Days of Rock 'N' Roll/Stranger	1975	—	2.00	4.00
BUDDAH					
168	Out of Sight/Bad News	1970	2.50	5.00	10.00
COLUMBIA					
44900	I'll Drown in My Tears/I'm Yours and I'm Here	1969	—	2.50	5.00
45058	Johnny B. Goode/I'm Not Sure	1969	—	2.50	5.00
45260	Rock and Roll Hoochie Koo/21st Century Man	1970	—	2.50	5.00
45368	Jumpin' Jack Flash/Good Morning, Little Schoolgirl	1971	—	2.50	5.00
45860	Silver Train/Rock and Roll	1973	—	2.50	5.00
45899	Can't You Feel It/Rock and Roll	1973	—	2.50	5.00
46006	Bad Luck Situation/Stone County	1974	—	2.50	5.00
46036	Boney Moroney/Hurtin' So Bad	1974	—	2.50	5.00
FROLIC					
501	That's What Love Does/Shed So Many Tears	1962	12.50	25.00	50.00
503	Voo Doo Twist/Ease My Pain	1962	25.00	50.00	100.00
509	Gangster of Love/Eternally	1963	12.50	25.00	50.00
512	Gone for Bad/I Won't Believe It	1963	15.00	30.00	60.00
GRT					
9	Gangster of Love/Roadrunner	1969	2.00	4.00	8.00
IMPERIAL					
66376	Forty-Four/Rollin' & Tumblin'	1969	2.00	4.00	8.00
MGM					
13380	Gone for Bad/I Won't Believe It	1965	2.00	4.00	8.00
PACEMAKER					
243	Leavin' Blues/Birds Can't Row Boats	1966	5.00	10.00	20.00
TODD					
1084	Road Runner/The Guy You Left Behind	1963	5.00	10.00	20.00
Albums					
ACCORD					
SN-7135	Ready for Winter	1981	2.50	5.00	10.00
ALLIGATOR					
4735	Guitar Slinger	1984	2.50	5.00	10.00
4742	Serious Business	1985	2.50	5.00	10.00
4748	Third Degree	1986	2.50	5.00	10.00
BLUE SKY					
PZ 33292	John Dawson Winter III	1974	3.00	6.00	12.00
PZQ 33292 [Q]	John Dawson Winter III	1974	5.00	10.00	20.00
PZ 33944	Captured Live!	1976	3.00	6.00	12.00
—No bar code on cover					
PZ 33944	Captured Live	198?	2.00	4.00	8.00
—Budget-line reissue with bar code on cover					
PZ 34813	Nothin' But the Blues	1977	3.00	6.00	12.00
—No bar code on cover					
PZ 34813	Nothin' But the Blues	198?	2.00	4.00	8.00
—Budget-line reissue with bar code on cover					
JZ 35475	White, Hot and Blue	1978	3.00	6.00	12.00
JZ 36343	Raisin' Cain	1980	3.00	6.00	12.00
BUDDAH					
BDS-7513	First Winter	1969	5.00	10.00	20.00
COLUMBIA					
CS 9826	Johnny Winter	1969	5.00	10.00	20.00
—"360 Sound" label					
CS 9826	Johnny Winter	1970	3.00	6.00	12.00
—Orange label					
PC 9826	Johnny Winter	198?	2.00	4.00	8.00
—Budget-line reissue					
KCS 9947 [(2)]	Second Winter	1969	6.25	12.50	25.00
—"360 Sound" labels; record 2 has music on only one side (other side is blank)					
KCS 9947 [(2)]	Second Winter	1970	3.75	7.50	15.00
—Orange labels					
PC 9947 [(2)]	Second Winter	198?	2.50	5.00	10.00
—Budget-line reissue					
C 30221	Johnny Winter And	1970	5.00	10.00	20.00
—"360 Sound" label					
C 30221	Johnny Winter And	1970	3.00	6.00	12.00
—Orange labels					
PC 30221	Johnny Winter And	198?	2.00	4.00	8.00
—Budget-line reissue					
C 30475	Live/Johnny Winter And	1971	3.75	7.50	15.00
PC 30475	Live/Johnny Winter And	198?	2.00	4.00	8.00
—Budget-line reissue					
CQ 32188 [Q]	Still Alive and Well	1973	6.25	12.50	25.00
KC 32188	Still Alive and Well	1973	3.75	7.50	15.00
PC 32188	Still Alive and Well	198?	2.00	4.00	8.00
—Budget-line reissue					
CQ 32715 [Q]	Saints and Sinners	1974	6.25	12.50	25.00
KC 32715	Saints and Sinners	1974	3.75	7.50	15.00
PC 32715	Saints and Sinners	197?	2.00	4.00	8.00
—Budget-line reissue					
CG 33651 [(2)]	Johnny Winter And//Live/Johnny Winter And	1975	3.75	7.50	15.00
GRT					
10010	The Johnny Winter Story	1969	5.00	10.00	20.00
IMPERIAL					
LP-12431	The Progressive Blues Experiment	1969	12.50	25.00	50.00
JANUS					
3008	About Blues	1970	5.00	10.00	20.00
3023	Early Times	1970	6.25	12.50	25.00
3056 [(2)]	Before the Storm	197?	5.00	10.00	20.00
LIBERTY					
LN-10294	The Progressive Blues Experiment	1986	2.50	5.00	10.00
—Reissue of Imperial LP					
MCA/VOYAGER					
42241	The Winter of '88	1988	2.50	5.00	10.00
SONOBEAT					
RS-1002	The Progressive Blues Experiment	1968	75.00	150.00	300.00
—Released in plain white cardboard jacket					
UNITED ARTISTS					
UA-LA139-F	Austin, Tex.	1974	3.75	7.50	15.00

WINTER, JOHNNY AND EDGAR

Also see each artist's individual listings.

Number	Title (A Side/B Side)	Yr	VG	VG+	NM
45s					
BLUE SKY					
2764	Soul Man/Let the Good Times Roll	1976	—	2.00	4.00
Albums					
BLUE SKY					
ASZ 242 [DJ]	Johnny and Edgar Winter Discuss Together	1976	6.25	12.50	25.00
—Promo-only interview album					
PZ 34033	Together	1976	3.00	6.00	12.00

WINTER, PAUL

Number	Title (A Side/B Side)	Yr	VG	VG+	NM
45s					
A&M					
1058	Both Sides Now/Little Train of the Caipira	1969	—	3.00	6.00
—As "The Winter Consort"					
1182	Mr. Bojangles/Jenny	1970	—	2.50	5.00
1986	Icarus/Jenny	1977	—	2.00	4.00
COLUMBIA					
42627	Maria Nobody/Journey to Recife	1962	2.00	4.00	8.00
EPIC					
10928	Icarus/Minuet	1972	—	2.00	4.00
Albums					
A&M					
SP-4170	The Winter Consort	1968	3.75	7.50	15.00
SP-4207	Something in the Wind	1969	3.75	7.50	15.00
SP-4279	The Road	1970	3.75	7.50	15.00
SP-4653	Earthdance	1977	3.00	6.00	12.00
SP-4698	Common Ground	1978	3.00	6.00	12.00
COLUMBIA					
CL 1925 [M]	Jazz Meets the Bossa Nova	1962	3.75	7.50	15.00
CL 1997 [M]	Jazz Premiere: Washington	1963	3.75	7.50	15.00
CL 2064 [M]	New Jazz on Campus	1963	3.75	7.50	15.00
CL 2155 [M]	Jazz Meets the Folk Song	1964	3.75	7.50	15.00
CL 2272 [M]	The Sound of Ipanema	1965	3.75	7.50	15.00
CL 2315 [M]	Rio	1965	3.75	7.50	15.00
CS 8725 [S]	Jazz Meets the Bossa Nova	1962	5.00	10.00	20.00
CS 8797 [S]	Jazz Premiere: Washington	1963	5.00	10.00	20.00

Number	Title (A Side/B Side)	Yr	VG	VG+	NM
CS 8864 [S]	New Jazz on Campus	1963	5.00	10.00	20.00
CS 8955 [S]	Jazz Meets the Folk Song	1964	5.00	10.00	20.00
CS 9072 [S]	The Sound of Ipanema	1965	5.00	10.00	20.00
CS 9115 [S]	Rio	1965	5.00	10.00	20.00
EPIC					
KE 31643	Icarus	1972	3.00	6.00	12.00
PE 31643	Icarus	197?	2.50	5.00	10.00
—Reissue					
LIVING MUSIC					
LM-0001 [(2)]	Callings	198?	3.75	7.50	15.00
—Reissue of LMR-1					
LMR-1 [(2)]	Callings	1981	5.00	10.00	20.00
—With 20-page booklet					
LMR-2 [(2)]	Missa Gaia/Earth Mass	1983	5.00	10.00	20.00
LM-0003	Sun Singer	198?	2.50	5.00	10.00
—Reissue of LMR-3					
LMR-3	Sun Singer	1984	3.00	6.00	12.00
LM-0004	Icarus	198?	2.50	5.00	10.00
—Reissue of LMR-4					
LMR-4	Icarus	1985	3.00	6.00	12.00
—Reissue of Epic LP					
LMR-5	Concert for the Earth Live at the United Nations	1985	3.00	6.00	12.00
LMR-6	Canyon	1986	3.00	6.00	12.00
LM-0012	Wintersong	1986	2.50	5.00	10.00
LM-0015	Earthbeat	1987	2.50	5.00	10.00

WINTERS, JONATHAN

Number	Title (A Side/B Side)	Yr	VG	VG+	NM
Albums					
COLUMBIA					
CL 2811 [M]	Jonathan Winters Wings It!	1968	6.25	12.50	25.00
CS 9611 [S]	Jonathan Winters Wings It!	1968	3.75	7.50	15.00
CS 9799	Stuff 'N' Nonsense	1969	3.75	7.50	15.00
KG 31985 [(2)]	Jonathan Winters Laughs Live	1972	5.00	10.00	20.00
—Reissue of 9611 and 9799 in one package					
PG 31985 [(2)]	Jonathan Winters Laughs Live	197?	3.00	6.00	12.00
—Reissue with new prefix					
VERVE					
MGVS-6099 [S]	The Wonderful World of Jonathan Winters	1960	6.25	12.50	25.00
MGVS-6155 [S]	Down to Earth	1960	6.25	12.50	25.00
MGV-15009 [M]	The Wonderful World of Jonathan Winters	1960	6.25	12.50	25.00
V-15009 [M]	The Wonderful World of Jonathan Winters	1961	5.00	10.00	20.00
V6-15009 [S]	The Wonderful World of Jonathan Winters	1961	5.00	10.00	20.00
—Reissue of 6099					
MGV-15011 [M]	Down to Earth	1960	6.25	12.50	25.00
V-15011 [M]	Down to Earth	1961	5.00	10.00	20.00
V6-15011 [S]	Down to Earth	1961	5.00	10.00	20.00
—Reissue of 6155					
V-15025 [M]	Here's Jonathan	1961	6.25	12.50	25.00
V6-15025 [S]	Here's Jonathan	1961	6.25	12.50	25.00
V-15032 [M]	Another Day, Another World	1962	6.25	12.50	25.00
V6-15032 [R]	Another Day, Another World	196?	3.00	6.00	12.00
V-15035 [M]	Humor As Seen Through the Eyes of Jonathan Winters	1963	6.25	12.50	25.00
V6-15035 [S]	Humor As Seen Through the Eyes of Jonathan Winters	1963	6.25	12.50	25.00
V-15037 [M]	Whistle Stopping with Jonathan Winters	1964	5.00	10.00	20.00
V6-15037 [R]	Whistle Stopping with Jonathan Winters	196?	3.00	6.00	12.00
V-15041 [M]	Jonathan Winters' Mad, Mad, Mad, Mad World	1964	5.00	10.00	20.00
V6-15041 [R]	Jonathan Winters' Mad, Mad, Mad, Mad World	196?	3.00	6.00	12.00
V-15047 [M]	Great Moments in Comedy	1965	5.00	10.00	20.00
V6-15047 [R]	Great Moments in Comedy	196?	3.00	6.00	12.00
V-15052 [M]	The Best of Frickert and Suggins	1966	5.00	10.00	20.00
V6-15052 [R]	The Best of Frickert and Suggins	196?	3.00	6.00	12.00
V-15057 [M]	Movies Are Better Than Ever	1967	5.00	10.00	20.00
V6-15057 [R]	Movies Are Better Than Ever	196?	3.00	6.00	12.00

WINWOOD, STEVE

Also see BLIND FAITH; THE SPENCER DAVIS GROUP; TRAFFIC.

Number	Title (A Side/B Side)	Yr	VG	VG+	NM
12-Inch Singles					
ISLAND					
PRO-A-1054 [DJ]	Still in the Game (same on both sides)	1982	2.00	4.00	8.00
PRO-A-2562 [DJ]	Freedom Overspill (Edit) (LP Version)	1986	—	3.00	6.00
PRO-A-2908 [DJ]	Talking Back to the Night (same on both sides)	1987	—	3.00	6.00
20537	Freedom Overspill (2 versions)/Higher Love/ + 1	1986	2.00	4.00	8.00
VIRGIN					
2637 [DJ]	Hearts on Fire (Remix) (LP Version)	1988	—	3.00	6.00
96620	Don't You Know What the Night Can Do? (Extended)/(Instrumental)	1988	2.00	4.00	8.00
45s					
ISLAND					
091	Time Is Running Out/Hold On	1977	—	2.50	5.00
28122	Talking Back to the Night/There's a River	1988	—	2.00	4.00
28122 [PS]	Talking Back to the Night/There's a River	1988	—	2.00	4.00
28231	Valerie/Talking Back to the Night (Instrumental)	1987	—	—	3.00
28231 [PS]	Valerie/Talking Back to the Night (Instrumental)	1987	—	—	3.00
28472	Back in the High Life Again/Night Train	1987	—	—	3.00
28472 [PS]	Back in the High Life Again/Night Train	1987	—	—	3.00
28498	The Finer Things/Night Train	1987	—	—	3.00
28498 [PS]	The Finer Things/Night Train	1987	—	—	3.00
28595	Freedom Overspill/Help Me Angel	1986	—	—	3.00
28595 [PS]	Freedom Overspill/Help Me Angel	1986	—	—	3.00
28710	Higher Love/And I Go	1986	—	—	3.00
28710 [PS]	Higher Love/And I Go	1986	—	—	3.00
29879	Valerie/Slowdown	1982	—	2.50	5.00
29940	Still in the Game/Dust	1982	—	2.00	4.00
49656	While You See a Chance/Vacant Chair	1981	—	2.00	4.00
49656 [PS]	While You See a Chance/Vacant Chair	1981	—	2.50	5.00
49726	Arc of a Diver/Dust	1981	—	2.00	4.00
49726 [PS]	Arc of a Diver/Dust	1981	—	2.50	5.00
49773	Night Train (Part 1)/Night Train (Part 2)	1981	—	2.00	4.00
VIRGIN					
98892	One and Only Man/(instrumental)	1990	—	—	3.00
99234	Hearts On Fire (7" Remix)/(Instrumental)	1989	—	—	3.00
99234 [PS]	Hearts On Fire (7" Remix)/(Instrumental)	1989	—	—	3.00
99261	Holding On/(Instrumental)	1988	—	—	3.00
99261 [PS]	Holding On/(Instrumental)	1988	—	—	3.00
99290	Don't You Know What the Night Can Do/ (Instrumental)	1988	—	—	3.00
99290 [PS]	Don't You Know What the Night Can Do/ (Instrumental)	1988	—	—	3.00
99326	Roll With It/The Morning Side	1988	—	—	3.00
99326 [PS]	Roll With It/The Morning Side	1988	—	—	3.00
Albums					
ISLAND					
ILPS 9387	Go	1976	3.00	6.00	12.00
—With Stomo Yamahita and Michael Shrieve					
ILPS 9494	Steve Winwood	1977	2.50	5.00	10.00
ILPS 9576	Arc of a Diver	1981	2.50	5.00	10.00
ILPS 9777	Talking Back to the Night	1982	2.50	5.00	10.00
25448	Back in the High Life	1986	2.00	4.00	8.00
25660	Chronicles	1987	2.00	4.00	8.00
UNITED ARTISTS					
UAS-9950 [(2)]	Winwood	1971	6.25	12.50	25.00
—Collection of tracks Winwood recorded with the Spencer Davis Group, Traffic and Blind Faith; with booklet					
UAS-9950 [(2)]	Winwood	1971	3.75	7.50	15.00
—Without booklet					
VIRGIN					
90946	Roll With It	1988	2.00	4.00	8.00
91405	Refugees of the Heart	1990	3.75	7.50	15.00

WISDOMS, THE

Number	Title (A Side/B Side)	Yr	VG	VG+	NM
45s					
GAITY					
169	Two Hearts Make One Love/Lost in Dreams	1959	150.00	300.00	600.00

WISHBONE ASH

Number	Title (A Side/B Side)	Yr	VG	VG+	NM
45s					
ATLANTIC					
3381	Lorelei/(B-side unknown)	1977	—	2.50	5.00
DECCA					
32826	Blind Eye/Queen of Torture	1971	2.00	4.00	8.00
32902	Jail Bait/Vas Dis	1971	2.00	4.00	8.00
33004	Blowin' Free/No Easy Road	1972	2.00	4.00	8.00
MCA					
40041	Rock and Roll Widow/No Easy Road	1973	—	3.00	6.00
40362	Persephone/Silver Shoes	1975	—	3.00	6.00
40829	Front Page News/Goodbye Baby, Hello Friends	1977	—	2.00	4.00
Albums					
ATLANTIC					
SD 18164	Locked In	1976	2.50	5.00	10.00
SD 18200	New England	1976	2.50	5.00	10.00
DECCA					
DL 75249	Wishbone Ash	1971	3.75	7.50	15.00
DL 75295	Pilgrimage	1971	3.75	7.50	15.00
DL 75437	Argus	1972	3.75	7.50	15.00
FANTASY					
9629	Twin Barrels Burning	1983	2.50	5.00	10.00
I.R.S.					
42101	Nouveau Calls	1988	3.00	6.00	12.00
82006	Here to Hear	1989	3.00	6.00	12.00
MCA					
36	Pilgrimage	1973	3.00	6.00	12.00
—Reissue of Decca 75295					
49	Argus	1973	3.00	6.00	12.00
—Reissue of Decca 75437					
327	Wishbone Four	1973	3.00	6.00	12.00
464	There's the Rub	1974	3.00	6.00	12.00
769	No Smoke Without Fire	198?	2.00	4.00	8.00
—Reissue					
770	Just Testing	198?	2.00	4.00	8.00
—Reissue					
786	Wishbone Four	198?	2.00	4.00	8.00
—Reissue					
787	Argus	198?	2.00	4.00	8.00
—Reissue					
2311	Front Page News	1977	2.50	5.00	10.00
2343	Wishbone Ash	1978	2.50	5.00	10.00
—Reissue of Decca 75249					
2344	Argus	1978	2.50	5.00	10.00
—Reissue of MCA 49					
2348	Wishbone Four	1978	2.50	5.00	10.00
—Reissue of MCA 327					
3060	No Smoke Without Fire	1978	2.50	5.00	10.00
3221	Just Testing	1980	2.50	5.00	10.00
5283	Hot Ash	1981	2.50	5.00	10.00
8006 [(2)]	Live Dates	1973	3.75	7.50	15.00

WITHERS, BILL

Number	Title (A Side/B Side)	Yr	VG	VG+	NM
12-Inch Singles					
COLUMBIA					
CAS 2112 [DJ]	Something That Turns You On (same on both sides)	1985	2.00	4.00	8.00
45s					
COLUMBIA					
02071	I Want to Spend the Night/Memories Are That Way	1981	—	2.00	4.00
02651	USA/Paint Your Pretty Picture	1981	—	2.00	4.00
02651 [PS]	USA/Paint Your Pretty Picture	1981	—	2.50	5.00
04841	Oh Yeah!/Just Like the First Time	1985	—	2.00	4.00
05424	Something That Turns You On/You Tried to Find a Love	1985	—	2.00	4.00
05424 [PS]	Something That Turns You On/You Tried to Find a Love	1985	—	2.00	4.00
05675	We Could Be Sweet Lovers/You Just Can't Smile It Away	1985	—	2.00	4.00

Number	Title (A Side/B Side)	Yr	VG	VG+	NM
10255	Make Love to Your Mind/I Love You Dawn	1975	—	2.50	5.00
10308	I Wish You Well/She's Lonely	1976	—	2.50	5.00
10357	Family Table/Hello Like Before	1976	—	2.50	5.00
10420	If I Didn't Mean You Well/My Imagination	1976	—	2.50	5.00
10459	Close to Me/I'll Be with You	1976	—	2.50	5.00
10627	Lovely Day/It Ain't Because of Me Baby	1977	—	2.50	5.00
10702	Lovely Night for Dancing/I Want to Spend the Night	1978	—	2.50	5.00
10892	Don't It Make It Better/Love Is	1979	—	2.00	4.00
10958	You Got the Stuff/Look to Each Other for Love	1979	—	2.00	4.00
SUSSEX					
219	Ain't No Sunshine/Harlem	1971	—	3.00	6.00
227	Grandma's Hands/Sweet Wanomi	1971	—	2.50	5.00
235	Lean On Me/Better Off Dead	1972	—	3.00	6.00
241	Use Me/Let Me In Your Life	1972	—	2.50	5.00
247	Let Us Love/The Gift of Giving	1972	—	2.50	5.00
247 [PS]	Let Us Love/The Gift of Giving	1972	2.00	4.00	8.00
250	Kissing My Love/I Don't Know	1973	—	2.50	5.00
257	Friend of Mine/Lonely Town, Lonely Street	1973	—	2.50	5.00
513	The Same Love That Made Me Laugh/Make a Smile for Me	1974	—	2.50	5.00
518	You/Stories	1974	—	2.50	5.00
629	Heartbreak Road/Ruby Lee	1974	—	2.50	5.00
638	Who Is He (And What Is He to You)/Harlem	1975	—	2.50	5.00
Albums					
COLUMBIA					
PC 33704	Making Music	1975	2.50	5.00	10.00
PC 34327	Naked and Warm	1976	2.50	5.00	10.00
JC 34903	Menagerie	1977	2.50	5.00	10.00
JC 35596	'Bout Love	1979	2.50	5.00	10.00
JC 36877	The Best of Bill Withers	1981	—	—	—
—Canceled?					
FC 37199	Bill Withers' Greatest Hits	1981	2.50	5.00	10.00
—Re-release of 36877 with "Just the Two of Us" added					
FC 39887	Watching You Watching Me	1985	2.50	5.00	10.00
PC 40177	Still Bill	1985	2.00	4.00	8.00
—Reissue of Sussex 7014					
PC 40178	Just As I Am	1985	2.00	4.00	8.00
—Reissue of Sussex 7006					
SUSSEX					
SUX-7006	Just As I Am	1971	5.00	10.00	20.00
SUX-7014	Still Bill	1972	5.00	10.00	20.00
SUX-7025 [(2)]	Bill Withers Live at Carnegie Hall	1973	5.00	10.00	20.00
SUX-8032	+'Justments	1974	3.75	7.50	15.00
SUX-8037	The Best of Bill Withers	1975	3.75	7.50	15.00

WITHERSPOON, JIMMY

Number	Title (A Side/B Side)	Yr	VG	VG+	NM
45s					
ABC					
11288	Handbags and Gladrags/Stay with Me Baby	1971	—	3.00	6.00
BLUE NOTE					
XW716	Pearly Whites/Sign on the Building	1975	—	2.50	5.00
BLUESWAY					
61028	Just a Dream/I Don't Know	1969	—	3.00	6.00
CAPITOL					
3998	Love Is a Five Letter Word/Other Side of Love	1974	—	2.50	5.00
CHECKER					
798	Big Daddy/When the Lights Go Out	1954	7.50	15.00	30.00
810	Time Brings About a Change/Waiting for Your Return	1955	7.50	15.00	30.00
826	It Ain't No Secret/Why Do I Love You Like I Do	1955	7.50	15.00	30.00
FEDERAL					
12095	Foolish Prayer/Two Little Girls	1952	7.50	15.00	30.00
12099	Lucille/Blues in Trouble	1952	7.50	15.00	30.00
12107	Don't Tell Me Now/Corn Whiskey	1952	7.50	15.00	30.00
12118	Jay's Blues (Part 1)/Jay's Blues (Part 2)	1953	7.50	15.00	30.00
12128	One Fine Gal/Back Home	1953	7.50	15.00	30.00
12138	Back Door Blues/Last Mile	1953	7.50	15.00	30.00
12155	Fast Women and Sloe Gin/Miss Mistreater	1953	7.50	15.00	30.00
12156	Sad Life/Move Me Baby	1953	12.50	25.00	50.00
—With the Lamplighters					
12173	24 Sad Hours/Just for You	1954	7.50	15.00	30.00
12180	It/Highway to Happiness	1954	7.50	15.00	30.00
12189	Oh Boy/I Done Told You	1954	7.50	15.00	30.00
GNP CRESCENDO					
156	Ain't Nobody's Business/No Rollin' Blues	1959	3.00	6.00	12.00
HIFI					
594	Everytime I Feel the Spirit/Oh Mary Don't You Weep	1960	3.00	6.00	12.00
KENT					
4551	Ain't Nobody's Business (Part 1)/Ain't Nobody's Business (Part 2)	1971	—	3.00	6.00
KING					
5997	Foolish Prayer/Two Little Girls	1965	2.50	5.00	10.00
MODERN					
857	The Wind Is Blowin'/My Baby Make a Change	1952	10.00	20.00	40.00
—Note: Earlier Jimmy Witherspoon 45s on Modern are not known to exist					
877	Love My Baby/Daddy Pinocchio	1952	10.00	20.00	40.00
895	Baby Baby/Slow Your Speed	1953	10.00	20.00	40.00
903	Each Step of the Way/Let Jesus Fix It for You	1953	10.00	20.00	40.00
909	Oh Mother, Dear Mother/I'll Be Right On Down	1953	10.00	20.00	40.00
PACIFIC JAZZ					
327	Ain't Nobody's Business/Times Have Changed	1961	2.50	5.00	10.00
PRESTIGE					
266	One Scotch, One Bourbon, One Beer/Baby, Baby, Baby	196?	2.50	5.00	10.00
274	Mean Ole Frisco/Sail On Little Girl	196?	2.50	5.00	10.00
291	Goin' to Chicago Blues/You Made Me Love You	196?	2.50	5.00	10.00
298	I Had a Dream/S.K. Blues	1963	2.50	5.00	10.00
307	Money's Gettin' Cheaper/Ever In	1963	2.50	5.00	10.00
340	I Never Will Marry/Happy Blues	1964	2.50	5.00	10.00
341	Some of My Best Friends Are the Blues/You're Next	1964	2.50	5.00	10.00
358	Come On and Walk with Me/Two Hearts Are Better Than One	196?	2.00	4.00	8.00
378	Love Me Right/Make This Heart of Mine Smile Again	196?	2.00	4.00	8.00
402	I Never Thought I'd See the Day/If There Wasn't Any You	196?	2.00	4.00	8.00
RCA VICTOR					
47-6977	Ain't Nobody's Business/Who Baby Who	1957	5.00	10.00	20.00
47-7377	Confessin' the Blues/Ooo Wee, Then the Lights Go Out	1958	5.00	10.00	20.00
REPRISE					
0275	Key to the Highway/I'd Rather Drink Muddy Water	1964	2.00	4.00	8.00
20013	The Masquerade Is Over/I Don't Know	1961	2.50	5.00	10.00
20029	Warm Your Heart/Hey Mrs. Jones	1961	2.50	5.00	10.00
VEE JAY					
322	Everything But You/I Know, I Know	1959	3.00	6.00	12.00
VERVE					
10439	It's All Over But the Crying/My Blue Tears	1966	2.00	4.00	8.00
10495	Fast Forty Blues/My Baby Quit Me	1967	2.00	4.00	8.00
WORLD PACIFIC					
814	Ain't Nobody's Business/There's Good Rockin' Tonight	1960	3.00	6.00	12.00
Albums					
ABC					
717	Handbags and Gladrags	1970	6.25	12.50	25.00
ANALOGUE PRODUCTIONS					
APR 3008	Evenin' Blues	199?	3.75	7.50	15.00
BLUE NOTE					
BN-LA534-G	Spoonful	1976	3.00	6.00	12.00
BLUESWAY					
BLS-6026	Blues Singer	1969	6.25	12.50	25.00
BLS-6040	Hunh	1970	6.25	12.50	25.00
BLS-6051	The Best of Jimmy Witherspoon	1970	6.25	12.50	25.00
CAPITOL					
ST-11360	Love Is a Five Letter Word	1975	3.00	6.00	12.00
CHESS					
CH-93003	Spoon So Easy: The Chess Years	1990	3.00	6.00	12.00
CONSTELLATION					
CM 1422 [M]	Take This Hammer	1964	12.50	25.00	50.00
CMS 1422 [R]	Take This Hammer	1964	7.50	15.00	30.00
CROWN					
CST-215 [S]	Jimmy Witherspoon Sings the Blues	1961	37.50	75.00	150.00
—Red vinyl; contrary to prior reports, this album -- at least the red vinyl version -- is in true stereo!					
CST-215 [S]	Jimmy Witherspoon Sings the Blues	1961	25.00	50.00	100.00
—Black vinyl; this value assumes that this is in true stereo, as the red vinyl version is, but this has not been confirmed					
CLP-5156 [M]	Jimmy Witherspoon	1959	20.00	40.00	80.00
—Black label, silver print					
CLP-5156 [M]	Jimmy Witherspoon	1961	6.25	12.50	25.00
—Gray label, black print					
CLP-5192 [M]	Jimmy Witherspoon Sings the Blues	1959	20.00	40.00	80.00
—Black label, silver print					
CLP-5192 [M]	Jimmy Witherspoon Sings the Blues	1961	6.25	12.50	25.00
—Gray label, black print					
FANTASY					
OBC-511	Evenin' Blues	1988	3.00	6.00	12.00
—Reissue of Prestige 7300					
OBC-527	Baby, Baby, Baby	1990	3.00	6.00	12.00
—Reissue of Prestige 7290					
9660	Rockin' L.A.	1989	3.00	6.00	12.00
24701 [(2)]	The 'Spoon Concerts	1972	5.00	10.00	20.00
HIFI					
R-421 [M]	At the Monterey Jazz Festival	1959	25.00	50.00	100.00
SR-421 [S]	At the Monterey Jazz Festival	1959	15.00	30.00	60.00
R-422 [M]	Feelin' the Spirit	1959	25.00	50.00	100.00
SR-422 [S]	Feelin' the Spirit	1959	15.00	30.00	60.00
R-426 [M]	Jimmy Witherspoon at the Renaissance	1959	25.00	50.00	100.00
SR-426 [S]	Jimmy Witherspoon at the Renaissance	1959	15.00	30.00	60.00
JAZZ MAN					
5013	Jimmy Witherspoon Sings the Blues	1980	3.00	6.00	12.00
LAX					
PW 37115	Love Is a Five Letter Word	1981	2.50	5.00	10.00
—Reissue of Capitol LP					
MUSE					
MR-5288	Jimmy Witherspoon Sings the Blues	1983	2.50	5.00	10.00
MR-5327	Midnight Lady Called the Blues	1986	2.50	5.00	10.00
PRESTIGE					
PRLP-7290 [M]	Baby, Baby, Baby	1963	10.00	20.00	40.00
PRST-7290 [S]	Baby, Baby, Baby	1963	10.00	20.00	40.00
PRLP-7300 [M]	Evenin' Blues	1964	10.00	20.00	40.00
PRST-7300 [S]	Evenin' Blues	1964	10.00	20.00	40.00
PRLP-7314 [M]	Blues Around the Clock	1964	10.00	20.00	40.00
PRST-7314 [S]	Blues Around the Clock	1964	10.00	20.00	40.00
PRLP-7327 [M]	Blue Spoon	1964	10.00	20.00	40.00
PRST-7327 [S]	Blue Spoon	1964	10.00	20.00	40.00
PRLP-7356 [M]	Some of My Best Friends Are the Blues	1965	6.25	12.50	25.00
PRST-7356 [S]	Some of My Best Friends Are the Blues	1965	6.25	12.50	25.00
PRLP-7418 [M]	Spoon in London	1966	6.25	12.50	25.00
PRST-7418 [S]	Spoon in London	1966	6.25	12.50	25.00
PRLP-7475 [M]	Blues for Easy Livers	1967	6.25	12.50	25.00
PRST-7475 [S]	Blues for Easy Livers	1967	5.00	10.00	20.00
PRST-7713	The Best of Jimmy Witherspoon	1969	5.00	10.00	20.00
7855	Mean Old Frisco	1974	3.75	7.50	15.00
RCA VICTOR					
ANL1-1048	Goin' to Kansas City Blues	1976	2.50	5.00	10.00
—Reissue					
LPM-1639 [M]	Goin' to Kansas City Blues	1957	25.00	50.00	100.00
REPRISE					
R-2008 [M]	Spoon	1961	10.00	20.00	40.00
R9-2008 [S]	Spoon	1961	15.00	30.00	60.00
R-6012 [M]	Hey, Mrs. Jones	1961	10.00	20.00	40.00
R9-6012 [S]	Hey, Mrs. Jones	1961	15.00	30.00	60.00
R-6059 [M]	Roots	1962	10.00	20.00	40.00

Number	Title (A Side/B Side)	Yr	VG	VG+	NM
R9-6059 [S]	Roots	1962	15.00	30.00	60.00
UNITED					
7715	A Spoonful of Blues	197?	3.00	6.00	12.00
VERVE					
V-5007 [M]	Blue Point of View	1966	5.00	10.00	20.00
V6-5007 [S]	Blue Point of View	1966	6.25	12.50	25.00
V-5030 [M]	Blues Is Now	1967	6.25	12.50	25.00
V6-5030 [S]	Blues Is Now	1967	5.00	10.00	20.00
V-5050 [M]	A Spoonful of Soul	1968	7.50	15.00	30.00
V6-5050 [S]	A Spoonful of Soul	1968	5.00	10.00	20.00
WORLD PACIFIC					
WP-1267 [M]	Singin' the Blues	1959	25.00	50.00	100.00
WP-1402 [M]	There's Good Rockin' Tonight	1961	15.00	30.00	60.00
—Reissue of 1267					

WITHERSPOON, JIMMY, AND RICHARD "GROOVE" HOLMES

Albums

Number	Title (A Side/B Side)	Yr	VG	VG+	NM
OLYMPIC GOLD MEDAL					
7107	Groovin' and Spoonin'	1974	3.00	6.00	12.00
SURREY					
S-1106 [M]	Blues for Spoon and Groove	1965	6.25	12.50	25.00
SS-1106 [S]	Blues for Spoon and Groove	1965	7.50	15.00	30.00

WITHERSPOON, JIMMY, AND GERRY MULLIGAN

Albums

Number	Title (A Side/B Side)	Yr	VG	VG+	NM
ARCHIVE OF FOLK AND JAZZ					
264	Jimmy Witherspoon and Gerry Mulligan	197?	3.00	6.00	12.00

WITHERSPOON, JIMMY, AND BEN WEBSTER

Albums

Number	Title (A Side/B Side)	Yr	VG	VG+	NM
VERVE					
V6-8835	Previously Unreleased Recordings	197?	3.75	7.50	15.00

WIZARDS FROM KANSAS, THE

Albums

Number	Title (A Side/B Side)	Yr	VG	VG+	NM
MERCURY					
SR-61309	The Wizards from Kansas	1970	37.50	75.00	150.00

WOLFE, DANNY

45s

Number	Title (A Side/B Side)	Yr	VG	VG+	NM
DOT					
15591	Pretty Blue Jean Baby/Once with You	1957	10.00	20.00	40.00
15667	Let's Flat Get It/I'm Glad I Waited	1957	15.00	30.00	60.00
15715	I'd Rather Be Lucky/Pucker Paint	1958	10.00	20.00	40.00

WOMACK, BOBBY

12-Inch Singles

Number	Title (A Side/B Side)	Yr	VG	VG+	NM
MCA					
L33-17104 [DJ]	Gypsy Woman/Whatever Happened to the Times? (2 versions)	1986	2.00	4.00	8.00
23688	(I Wanna) Make Love to You/Whatever Happened to the Times?	1986	2.00	4.00	8.00
23795	Living in a Box (3 versions)	1987	—	3.00	6.00
23827	Outside Myself (3 versions)	1988	—	3.00	6.00
SOLAR					
ZAS 1923 [DJ]	Save the Children (3 versions)	1989	2.00	4.00	8.00

45s

Number	Title (A Side/B Side)	Yr	VG	VG+	NM
ARISTA					
0421	How Could You Break My Heart/I Honestly Love You	1979	—	2.00	4.00
0446	The Roads of Life/Give It Up	1979	—	2.00	4.00
ATLANTIC					
2388	Night Train/It's Karate Time	1967	2.50	5.00	10.00
BEVERLY GLEN					
2000	If You Think You're Lonely Now/Secrets	1981	—	2.00	4.00
2001	Where Do We Go from Here/Just My Imagination	1982	—	2.00	4.00
2012	Love Has Finally Come at Last/American Dream	1984	—	2.00	4.00
—With Patti LaBelle					
2014	Tell Me Why/Through the Eyes of a Child	1984	—	2.00	4.00
—B-side with Patti LaBelle					
2018	It Takes a Lot of Strength to Say Goodbye/Who's Foolin' Who	1984	—	2.00	4.00
—A-side with Patti LaBelle					
2021	Someday We'll All Be Free/I Wish I Had Someone to Go Home To	1985	—	2.00	4.00
2023	I'm So Proud/Searching for My Love	1985	—	2.00	4.00
CHECKER					
1122	Lonesome Man/I Found a True Love	1965	3.75	7.50	15.00
COLUMBIA					
10437	Home Is Where the Heart Is/We've Only Just Begun	1976	—	2.50	5.00
10493	Standing in the Safety Zone/A Change Is Gonna Come	1977	—	2.50	5.00
10672	Trust Your Heart/When Love Begins, Friendship Ends	1978	—	2.50	5.00
10732	Wind It Up/Stop Before We Start	1978	—	2.50	5.00
LIBERTY					
56186	I'm Gonna Forget About You/Don't Look Back	1970	2.00	4.00	8.00
56206	Something/Everybody's Talkin'	1970	2.00	4.00	8.00
MCA					
52624	I Wish He Didn't Trust Me So Much/Got to Be with You Tonight	1985	—	2.00	4.00
52624 [PS]	I Wish He Didn't Trust Me So Much/Got to Be with You Tonight	1985	—	2.00	4.00
52709	Let Me Kiss It Where It Hurts/Check It Out	1985	—	2.00	4.00
52793	Gypsy Woman/What Evert Happened to the Times	1986	—	—	3.00
52955	(I Wanna) Make Love to You/The Launch	1986	—	—	3.00
52955 [PS]	(I Wanna) Make Love to You/The Launch	1986	—	—	3.00
53190	Living in a Box/I Can't Stay Mad	1987	—	—	3.00
53263	Outside Myself/A Woman Likes to Hear Than	1988	—	—	3.00
MINIT					
32024	Baby, I Can't Stand It/Trust Me	1967	2.50	5.00	10.00
32030	Somebody Special/Broadway Walk	1967	2.50	5.00	10.00
32037	What Is This/What You Gonna Do (When Your Love Is Gone)	1968	2.50	5.00	10.00
32048	Fly Me to the Moon/Take Me	1968	2.50	5.00	10.00
32055	California Dreamin'/Baby, You Oughta Think It Over	1968	2.50	5.00	10.00
32059	I Left My Heart in San Francisco/Love, The Time Is Now	1969	2.00	4.00	8.00
32071	It's Gonna Rain/Thank You	1969	2.00	4.00	8.00
32081	How I Miss You Baby/Tried and Convicted	1969	2.00	4.00	8.00
32093	More Than I Can Stand/Arkansas State Prison	1970	2.00	4.00	8.00
SOLAR					
74006	Save the Children/(Instrumental)	1989	—	—	3.00
THE RIGHT STUFF					
58815	Dear Santa Claus/Dear Santa Claus (Kids Version)	1999	—	—	3.00
UNITED ARTISTS					
0123	That's the Way I Feel About Cha/Woman's Gotta Have It	1973	—	2.00	4.00
—"Silver Spotlight Series" reissue					
XW196	Across 110th Street/Hang On In There	1973	—	2.50	5.00
XW255	Nobody Wants You When You're Down and Out/I'm Thru Trying to Prove My Love	1973	—	2.50	5.00
XW375	Lookin' for a Love/Let It Hang Out	1973	—	2.50	5.00
XW439	You're Welcome, Stop On By/I Don't Want to Be Hurt	1974	—	2.50	5.00
XW525	Lookin' for a Love/Nobody Wants You When You're Down and Out	1974	—	2.00	4.00
—Reissue					
XW526	Harry Hippie/Sweet Caroline	1974	—	2.00	4.00
—Reissue					
XW527	California Dreamin'/Fly Me to the Moon	1974	—	2.50	5.00
XW561	I Don't Know/Yes, Jesus Loves Me	1974	—	2.50	5.00
XW621	Check It Out/Interlude No. 2	1975	—	2.50	5.00
XW674	It's All Over Now/Git It	1975	—	2.50	5.00
XW735	Where There's a Will, There's a Way/Everything's Gonna Be Alright	1975	—	2.50	5.00
XW763	Daylight/Trust Me	1976	—	2.50	5.00
XW804	I Feel a Groove Comin' On/Trust Me	1976	—	2.50	5.00
50773	The Preacher/More Than I Can Stand	1971	—	3.00	6.00
50816	Communication/Fire and Rain	1971	—	3.00	6.00
50847	That's the Way I Feel About 'Cha/Come L'Amore	1971	—	3.00	6.00
50902	Woman's Gotta Have It/Give It Back	1972	—	3.00	6.00
50946	Harry Hippie/Sweet Caroline (Good Times Never Seemed So Good)	1972	—	3.00	6.00
50988 [DJ]	Harry Hippie (mono/stereo)	1972	2.00	4.00	8.00
—Apparently, no stock copy exists					

Albums

Number	Title (A Side/B Side)	Yr	VG	VG+	NM
ARISTA					
AB 4222	Roads of Life	1979	2.50	5.00	10.00
BEVERLY GLEN					
10000	The Poet	1981	2.50	5.00	10.00
10003	The Poet II	1984	2.50	5.00	10.00
COLUMBIA					
PC 34384	Home Is Where the Heart Is	1977	2.50	5.00	10.00
JC 35083	Pieces	1978	2.50	5.00	10.00
LIBERTY					
LST-7645	The Womack "Live"	1971	3.00	6.00	12.00
LN-10171	Bobby Womack's Greatest Hits	198?	2.00	4.00	8.00
—Budget-line reissue of United Artists 346					
MCA					
5617	So Many Rivers	1985	2.00	4.00	8.00
MINIT					
24014	Fly Me to the Moon	1968	7.50	15.00	30.00
24027	My Prescription	1969	7.50	15.00	30.00
UNITED ARTISTS					
UA-LA043-F	Facts of Life	1973	3.00	6.00	12.00
UA-LA199-G	Lookin' for a Love Again	1974	3.00	6.00	12.00
UA-LA346-G	Bobby Womack's Greatest Hits	1974	3.00	6.00	12.00
UA-LA353-G	I Don't Know What the World Is Coming To	1975	3.00	6.00	12.00
UA-LA544-G	Safety Zone	1975	3.00	6.00	12.00
UA-LA638-G	B.W. Goes C and W	1976	3.00	6.00	12.00
LM-1002	Understanding	1980	2.00	4.00	8.00
—Reissue of 5577					
UAS-5225	Across 110th Street	1972	3.00	6.00	12.00
UAS-5539	Communication	1971	3.00	6.00	12.00
UAS-5577	Understanding	1972	3.00	6.00	12.00

WOMB

45s

Number	Title (A Side/B Side)	Yr	VG	VG+	NM
DOT					
17250	Hang On/My Baby Thinks About the Good Things	1969	3.00	6.00	12.00

Albums

Number	Title (A Side/B Side)	Yr	VG	VG+	NM
DOT					
DLP-25933	Womb	1969	5.00	10.00	20.00
DLP-25959	Overdub	1969	5.00	10.00	20.00

WOMBLES, THE

45s

Number	Title (A Side/B Side)	Yr	VG	VG+	NM
COLUMBIA					
10013	Wombling Summer Party/Wimbledon Sunset	1974	—	2.00	4.00
10033	Remember You're a Womble/The Wellington Womble	1974	—	2.00	4.00
EPIC					
11119	Wombling Song/Wombles Everywhere	1974	—	2.50	5.00

Albums

Number	Title (A Side/B Side)	Yr	VG	VG+	NM
COLUMBIA					
KC 33140	Remember You're a Womble	1974	3.00	6.00	12.00

WOMENFOLK, THE

45s

RCA VICTOR

Number	Title (A Side/B Side)	Yr	VG	VG+	NM
47-8301	Little Boxes/Love Came a-Tricklin' Down	1964	2.00	4.00	8.00
47-8562	My Heart Tells Me to Believe/The Way I Feel	1965	2.00	4.00	8.00
47-8782	The Last Thing on My Mind/Meditation	1966	2.00	4.00	8.00

Albums

RCA VICTOR

Number	Title (A Side/B Side)	Yr	VG	VG+	NM
LPM-2832 [M]	The Womenfolk	1964	3.00	6.00	12.00
LSP-2832 [S]	The Womenfolk	1964	3.75	7.50	15.00
LPM-2919 [M]	Never Underestimate the Power of the Womenfolk	1964	3.00	6.00	12.00
LSP-2919 [S]	Never Underestimate the Power of the Womenfolk	1964	3.75	7.50	15.00
LPM-2991 [M]	The Womenfolk at the Hungry I	1965	3.00	6.00	12.00
LSP-2991 [S]	The Womenfolk at the Hungry I	1965	3.75	7.50	15.00
LPM-3527 [M]	Man Oh Man	1966	3.00	6.00	12.00
LSP-3527 [S]	Man Oh Man	1966	3.75	7.50	15.00

WONDER, STEVIE

Also see PAUL McCARTNEY AND STEVIE WONDER.

12-Inch Singles

MOTOWN

Number	Title (A Side/B Side)	Yr	VG	VG+	NM
PR 161 [DJ]	Love Light in Flight (Remix) (Instrumental)	1984	—	3.00	6.00
1065 [DJ]	Keep Our Love Alive/(Instrumental)	1990	—	3.50	7.00
1093 [DJ]	Gotta Have You (3 versions)	1991	2.00	4.00	8.00
37463 1261 [DJ]	For Your Love (4 versions)	1995	2.00	4.00	8.00
1602 [DJ]	Fun Day (Edit) (LP) (Instrumental)	1991	2.00	4.00	8.00
1690 [DJ]	Fun Day (8 versions)	1991	2.00	4.00	8.00
4527	Don't Drive Drunk (12" Version) (Instrumental)/Did I Hear You Say You Love Me	1984	—	3.00	6.00
4593	Skeletons (6:43)/(Instrumental)	1987	—	3.00	6.00
4616	My Eyes Don't Cry (3 versions)	1988	—	3.00	6.00
4665	Keep Our Love Alive/(Instrumental)	1990	2.00	4.00	8.00
4759	Gotta Have You (4 versions)	1991	—	3.50	7.00
4826	With Each Beat of My Heart (LP) (Edit) (Instrumental)	1988	—	3.00	6.00
L33-17755 [DJ]	With Each Beat of My Heart (LP) (Edit) (Instrumental)	1987	—	3.00	6.00

TAMLA

Number	Title (A Side/B Side)	Yr	VG	VG+	NM
PR 61 [DJ]	A Seed's a Star-Tree (Medley)/Power Flower/Black Orchid/Outside My Window	1979	3.75	7.50	15.00
98/99 [(2) DJ]	Do I Do (LP)/Instrumental//Front Line (LP) (Instrumental)	1982	3.75	7.50	15.00
—Two-record promo set					
PR 186 [DJ]	Land of La La (8:40)/(Instrumental)	1986	—	3.00	6.00
4553	Go Home (3 versions)	1985	—	3.00	6.00

45s

GORDY

Number	Title (A Side/B Side)	Yr	VG	VG+	NM
7076	Alfie/More Than a Dream	1968	6.25	12.50	25.00
—As "Eivets Rednow" (read it backwards)					

MOTOWN

Number	Title (A Side/B Side)	Yr	VG	VG+	NM
1650	Used to Be/I Want to Come Back As A Song	1982	—	—	3.00
—A-side with Charlene; B-side is Charlene solo					
1650 [PS]	Used to Be/I Want to Come Back As A Song	1982	—	—	3.00
1745	I Just Called to Say I Love You/(Instrumental)	1984	—	—	3.00
1745 [PS]	I Just Called to Say I Love You/(Instrumental)	1984	12.50	25.00	50.00
1769	Love Light in Flight/It's More Than You	1984	—	—	3.00
1769 [PS]	Love Light in Flight/It's More Than You	1984	—	2.00	4.00
1907	Skeletons/(Instrumental)	1987	—	—	3.00
1907 [PS]	Skeletons/(Instrumental)	1987	—	2.00	4.00
1919	You Will Know/(Instrumental)	1988	—	—	3.00
1919 [PS]	You Will Know/(Instrumental)	1988	—	2.00	4.00
1946	My Eyes Don't Cry/(Instrumental)	1988	—	—	3.00
1946 [PS]	My Eyes Don't Cry/(Instrumental)	1988	—	—	3.00
1953	With Each Beat of My Heart/(Instrumental)	1989	—	—	3.00
1990	Keep Our Love Alive/(Instrumental)	1990	—	2.50	5.00
2081	Gotta Have You/Feeding Off the Love of the Land	1991	—	2.00	4.00
2127	Fun Day/(Instrumental)	1991	—	2.00	4.00
2143	These Three Words (same on both sides)	1991	—	2.00	4.00
860310-7	For Your Love/(Instrumental)	1995	—	—	3.00
860418-7	Tomorrow Robins Will Sing/For Your Love	1995	—	—	3.00

TAMLA

Number	Title (A Side/B Side)	Yr	VG	VG+	NM
1602	That Girl/All I Do	1982	—	2.00	4.00
1612	Do I Do/Rocket Love	1982	—	2.00	4.00
1639	Ribbon in the Sky/Black Orchid	1982	—	2.00	4.00
1639 [PS]	Ribbon in the Sky/Black Orchid	1982	—	2.00	4.00
1808	Part-Time Lover/(Instrumental)	1985	—	—	3.00
1808 [PS]	Part-Time Lover/(Instrumental)	1985	—	2.00	4.00
1817	Go Home/(Instrumental)	1985	—	—	3.00
1817 [PS]	Go Home/(Instrumental)	1985	—	2.00	4.00
1832	Overjoyed/(Instrumental)	1986	—	—	3.00
1832 [PS]	Overjoyed/(Instrumental)	1986	—	2.00	4.00
1846	Land of La La/(Instrumental)	1986	—	—	3.00
1846 [PS]	Land of La La/(Instrumental)	1986	—	2.00	4.00
54061	I Call It Pretty Music But The Old People Call It the Blues (Part 1)/I Call It Pretty Music But The Old People Call It the Blues (Part 2)	1962	7.50	15.00	30.00
54061 [PS]	I Call It Pretty Music But The Old People Call It the Blues (Part 1)/I Call It Pretty Music But The Old People Call It the Blues (Part 2)	1962	20.00	40.00	80.00
54070	Little Water Boy/La La La La La	1962	6.25	12.50	25.00
54074	Contract on Love/Sunset	1963	6.25	12.50	25.00
54080	Fingertips — Pt. 2/Fingertips — Pt. 1	1963	5.00	10.00	20.00
54080 [PS]	Fingertips — Pt. 2/Fingertips — Pt. 1	1963	12.50	25.00	50.00
54086	Workout Stevie, Workout/Monkey Talk	1963	3.75	7.50	15.00
54090	Castles in the Sand/Thank You (For Loving Me All the Way)	1964	3.75	7.50	15.00
—Up to and including this, as "Little Stevie Wonder"					
54096	Hey Harmonica Man/This Little Girl	1964	3.75	7.50	15.00
54096 [PS]	Hey Harmonica Man/This Little Girl	1964	10.00	20.00	40.00
54103	Sad Boy/Happy Street	1964	5.00	10.00	20.00
54108	Pretty Little Angel/Tears in Vain	1964	—	—	—
—Unreleased					
54114	Kiss Me Baby/Tears in Vain	1965	3.00	6.00	12.00
54119	High Heel Sneakers/Music Talk	1965	3.00	6.00	12.00
54119	High Heel Sneakers/Funny How Time Slips Away	1965	5.00	10.00	20.00
54124	Uptight (Everything's Alright)/Purple Rain Drops	1965	3.75	7.50	15.00
54130	Nothing's Too Good for My Baby/With a Child's Heart	1966	3.00	6.00	12.00
54136	Blowin' in the Wind/Ain't That Asking for Trouble	1966	3.00	6.00	12.00
54136 [PS]	Blowin' in the Wind/Ain't That Asking for Trouble	1966	6.25	12.50	25.00
54139	A Place in the Sun/Sylvia	1966	3.00	6.00	12.00
54139 [PS]	A Place in the Sun/Sylvia	1966	6.25	12.50	25.00
54142	Some Day at Christmas/The Miracles of Christmas	1966	3.75	7.50	15.00
54147	Travlin' Man/Hey Love	1967	2.50	5.00	10.00
54151	I Was Made to Love Her/Hold Me	1967	2.50	5.00	10.00
54157	I'm Wondering/Every Time I See You I Go Wild	1967	2.50	5.00	10.00
54165	Shoo-Be-Doo-Be-Doo-Da-Day/Why Don't You Lead Me to Love	1968	2.00	4.00	8.00
54168	You Met Your Match/My Girl	1968	2.00	4.00	8.00
54174	For Once in My Life/Angie Girl	1968	2.00	4.00	8.00
54180	I Don't Know Why/My Cherie Amour	1969	2.50	5.00	10.00
54180	My Cherie Amour/Don't Know Why I Love You	1969	2.00	4.00	8.00
—Re-release with A and B side switched and new title on B-side					
54188	Yester-Me, Yester-You, Yesterday/I'd Be a Fool Right Now	1969	2.00	4.00	8.00
54191	Never Had a Dream Come True/Somebody Knows, Somebody Cares	1970	—	3.00	6.00
54196	Signed, Sealed, Delivered, I'm Yours/I'm More Than Happy	1970	—	3.00	6.00
54200	Heaven Help Us All/I Gotta Have a Song	1970	—	3.00	6.00
54202	We Can Work It Out/Never Dreamed You'd Leave in Summer	1971	—	3.00	6.00
54208	If You Really Love Me/Think of Me As Your Soldier	1971	—	3.00	6.00
54214	What Christmas Means to Me/Bedtime for Toys	1971	—	3.00	6.00
54216	Superwoman (Where Were You When I Needed You)/I Love Every Little Thing About You	1972	—	3.00	6.00
54223	Keep On Running/Evil	1972	—	3.00	6.00
54226	Superstition/You've Got It Bad Girl	1972	—	2.50	5.00
54232	You Are the Sunshine of My Life/Tuesday Heartbreak	1973	—	2.50	5.00
54235	Higher Ground/Too High	1973	—	2.50	5.00
54242	Living for the City/Visions	1973	—	2.50	5.00
54245	Don't You Worry 'Bout a Thing/Blame It on the Sun	1974	—	2.50	5.00
54252	You Haven't Done Nothin'/Big Brother	1974	—	2.50	5.00
54254	Boogie On Reggae Woman/Seems So Long	1974	—	2.50	5.00
54274	I Wish/You and I	1976	—	2.50	5.00
54281	Sir Duke/He's Misstra Know-It-All	1977	—	2.50	5.00
54281 [PS]	Sir Duke/He's Misstra Know-It-All	1977	2.50	5.00	10.00
54286	Another Star/Creepin'	1977	—	2.50	5.00
54291	As/Contusion	1977	—	2.50	5.00
54303	Send One Your Love/(Instrumental)	1979	—	2.00	4.00
54303 [PS]	Send One Your Love/(Instrumental)	1979	—	3.00	6.00
54308	Outside My Window/Same Old Story	1980	—	2.00	4.00
54308 [PS]	Outside My Window/Same Old Story	1980	—	3.00	6.00
54317	Master Blaster (Jammin')/(Instrumental)	1980	—	2.00	4.00
54317 [PS]	Master Blaster (Jammin')/(Instrumental)	1980	—	3.00	6.00
54320	I Ain't Gonna Stand For It/Knocks Me Off My Feet	1980	—	2.00	4.00
54323	Lately/If It's Magic	1981	—	2.00	4.00
54328	Did I Hear You Say You Love Me/As If You Read My Mind	1981	—	2.00	4.00
54331	Happy Birthday/(Instrumental)	1981	—	—	—
—Unreleased					

TOPPS/MOTOWN

Number	Title (A Side/B Side)	Yr	VG	VG+	NM
8	Fingertips Part 2	1967	18.75	37.50	75.00
—Cardboard record					
10	Uptight (Everything's Alright)	1967	18.75	37.50	75.00
—Cardboard record					

Albums

GORDY

Number	Title (A Side/B Side)	Yr	VG	VG+	NM
GS 932	Eivets Rednow	1968	7.50	15.00	30.00
—As "Eivets Rednow"					

JOBETE

Number	Title (A Side/B Side)	Yr	VG	VG+	NM
JSA-6253 [DJ]	The Wonder of Stevie	1988	5.00	10.00	20.00
—Publisher's demo with excerpts of 105 (!) Stevie Wonder songs					

MOTOWN

Number	Title (A Side/B Side)	Yr	VG	VG+	NM
M5-131V1	Recorded Live/Little Stevie Wonder/The 12 Year Old Genius	1981	3.00	6.00	12.00
—Reissue of Tamla 240					
M5-150V1	With a Song in My Heart	1981	3.00	6.00	12.00
—Reissue of Tamla 250					
M5-166V1	Down to Earth	1981	3.00	6.00	12.00
—Reissue of Tamla 272					
M5-173V1	Tribute to Uncle Ray	1981	3.00	6.00	12.00
—Reissue of Tamla 232					
M5-176V1	Signed, Sealed and Delivered	1981	3.00	6.00	12.00
—Reissue of Tamla 304					
M5-179V1	My Cherie Amour	1981	3.00	6.00	12.00
—Reissue of Tamla 296					
M5-183V1	Up-Tight Everything's Alright	1981	3.00	6.00	12.00
—Reissue of Tamla 268					
M5-219V1	The Jazz Soul of Little Stevie	1981	3.00	6.00	12.00
—Reissue of Tamla 233					
31453 0238-1 [(2) DJ]	Conversation Peace	1995	6.25	12.50	25.00
—Vinyl is promo only; white cover with custom sticker					
M-804LP3 [(3)]	Looking Back	1977	6.25	12.50	25.00
—Withdrawn after Stevie Wonder objected to its release					
5255 ML	Someday at Christmas	1982	2.50	5.00	10.00
—Reissue of Tamla 281					
6108 ML	The Woman in Red	1984	3.00	6.00	12.00
—With no sticker proclaiming "New Stevie Wonder Album"					
6108 ML	The Woman in Red	1984	2.50	5.00	10.00
—With sticker at top proclaiming "New Stevie Wonder Album"					
6248 ML	Characters	1987	2.50	5.00	10.00
6291 ML	Music from the Movie Jungle Fever	1991	5.00	10.00	20.00

Number	Title (A Side/B Side)	Yr	VG	VG+	NM
TAMLA					
T 232 [M]	Tribute to Uncle Ray	1962	37.50	75.00	150.00
T 233 [M]	The Jazz Soul of Little Stevie	1962	37.50	75.00	150.00
T 240 [M]	Recorded Live/Little Stevie Wonder/The 12 Year Old Genius	1963	30.00	60.00	120.00
—The above three LPs as "Little Stevie Wonder"					
T 248 [M]	Workout Stevie, Workout	1963	250.00	500.00	1000.
—Canceled; test pressings or acetates may exist					
T 250 [M]	With a Song in My Heart	1964	20.00	40.00	80.00
T 255 [M]	Stevie at the Beach	1964	20.00	40.00	80.00
T 268 [M]	Up-Tight Everything's Alright	1966	6.25	12.50	25.00
TS 268 [S]	Up-Tight Everything's Alright	1966	7.50	15.00	30.00
T 272 [M]	Down to Earth	1966	5.00	10.00	20.00
TS 272 [S]	Down to Earth	1966	6.25	12.50	25.00
T 279 [M]	I Was Made to Love Her	1967	5.00	10.00	20.00
TS 279 [S]	I Was Made to Love Her	1967	6.25	12.50	25.00
T 281 [M]	Someday at Christmas	1967	7.50	15.00	30.00
TS 281 [S]	Someday at Christmas	1967	10.00	20.00	40.00
T 282 [M]	Greatest Hits	1968	7.50	15.00	30.00
TS 282 [S]	Greatest Hits	1968	5.00	10.00	20.00
TS 291	For Once in My Life	1968	5.00	10.00	20.00
TS 296	My Cherie Amour	1969	5.00	10.00	20.00
TS 298	Stevie Wonder Live	1970	5.00	10.00	20.00
TS 304	Signed Sealed and Delivered	1970	5.00	10.00	20.00
TS 308	Where I'm Coming From	1971	5.00	10.00	20.00
TS 313	Stevie Wonder's Greatest Hits, Vol. 2	1971	5.00	10.00	20.00
T 314L	Music of My Mind	1972	5.00	10.00	20.00
T 319L	Talking Book	1972	3.75	7.50	15.00
—Original pressings have a braille note on cover					
T 319L	Talking Book	1973	2.50	5.00	10.00
—No braille note on cover					
T 326L	Innervisions	1973	3.75	7.50	15.00
T6-332S1	Fulfillingness' First Finale	1974	3.75	7.50	15.00
T13-340C2 [(2)]	Songs in the Key of Life	1976	5.00	10.00	20.00
—With booklet and bonus 7-inch EP (deduct 25% if missing)					
T7-362R1	Someday at Christmas	1978	5.00	10.00	20.00
—Unusual reissue of 281					
T13-371C2 [(2)]	Journey Through the Secret Life of Plants	1979	3.75	7.50	15.00
T8-373S1	Hotter Than July	1980	3.00	6.00	12.00
6002 TL2 [(2)]	Stevie Wonder's Original Musiquarium I	1982	3.75	7.50	15.00
6134 TL	In Square Circle	1985	2.50	5.00	10.00

WONDER, STEVIE, AND MICHAEL JACKSON

Also see each artist's individual listings.

Number	Title (A Side/B Side)	Yr	VG	VG+	NM
45s					
MOTOWN					
1930	Get It/(Instrumental)	1988	—	—	3.00
1930 [PS]	Get It/(Instrumental)	1988	—	—	3.00

WONDER WHO?, THE

See THE FOUR SEASONS.

WONDERETTES, THE

Number	Title (A Side/B Side)	Yr	VG	VG+	NM
45s					
ENTERPRISE					
5025	Love's Got a Hold on Me/Work Out Fine	1964	6.25	12.50	25.00
RUBY					
5065	I Feel Strange/Wait Until Tonight	1965	10.00	20.00	40.00
UNITED ARTISTS					
944	I Feel Strange/Wait Until Tonight	1965	6.25	12.50	25.00
997	Mend My Broken Heart/And If I Had My Way	1966	5.00	10.00	20.00
—By "Rose St. John and the Wonderettes"					
VEEP					
1231	Fool Don't Laugh/I Know the Meeting	1966	6.25	12.50	25.00
—As "Rose St. John and the Wonderettes"					

WOOD, ANITA

Number	Title (A Side/B Side)	Yr	VG	VG+	NM
45s					
SUN					
361	I'll Wait Forever/I Can't Show How I Feel	1961	7.50	15.00	30.00

WOOD, BOBBY

Number	Title (A Side/B Side)	Yr	VG	VG+	NM
45s					
CHALLENGE					
9160	The Day After Forever/Everybody's Searchin'	1962	2.50	5.00	10.00
CINNAMON					
790	I'm a Fool for Loving You/Secret Love Affair	1974	—	2.00	4.00
JOY					
277	I Still Hurt/Just the Same	1963	2.50	5.00	10.00
279	Do Darlin' (Do Remember Me)/That's All I Need	1963	2.50	5.00	10.00
285	If I'm a Fool for Loving You/My Heart Went Boing! Boing! Boing!	1964	2.50	5.00	10.00
288	That's All I Need to Know/This Time	1964	2.50	5.00	10.00
291	So Cruel/I'd Do It Again	1964	2.50	5.00	10.00
295	Bed of Roses/Show Me	1965	2.00	4.00	8.00
298	Human Emotions/When a Lonely Boy Meets a Lonely Girl	1965	2.00	4.00	8.00
301	Fool's Paradise/What Am I Gonna Tell Myself	1965	2.00	4.00	8.00
LUCKY ELEVEN					
361	One Day Behind/Sound of Sadness	1973	—	2.50	5.00
MALA					
526	My Special Angel/I'd Rather Forgive You	1966	2.00	4.00	8.00
MGM					
13729	My Last Date (With You)/Everybody's Baby	1967	—	3.00	6.00
13797	Break My Mind/This Thing Called Love	1967	—	3.00	6.00
13912	Is That All There Is To It/Say It's Not You	1968	—	3.00	6.00
13952	Mary/Big Buildup	1968	—	3.00	6.00
14051	(Margie's at the) Lincoln Park Inn/I'm the Name of Her Game	1969	—	3.00	6.00
SUN					
369 [DJ]	Everybody's Searchin'/Human Emotions	1961	200.00	400.00	600.00
—No stock copies known; should one be discovered, it would be worth much more					
Albums					
JOY					
1001 [M]	Bobby Wood	1964	10.00	20.00	40.00

WOOD, BRENTON

Number	Title (A Side/B Side)	Yr	VG	VG+	NM
45s					
BRENT					
7052	Good Lovin'/I Want to Love	1966	3.75	7.50	15.00
7057	Cross the Bridge/Sweet Molly Malone	1966	6.25	12.50	25.00
7068	I Want Love/Sweet Molly Malone	1967	2.50	5.00	10.00
CREAM					
7602	All That Jazz/Bless Your Little Heart	1976	—	2.00	4.00
7716	Come Softly to Me/You're Everything I Need	1977	—	2.00	4.00
7720	Number One/(B-side unknown)	1977	—	2.00	4.00
7833	Let's Get Crazy Together/Love Is Free	1978	—	2.00	4.00
DOUBLE SHOT					
111	The Oogum Boogum Song/I Like the Way You Love Me	1967	2.50	5.00	10.00
116	Gimme Little Sign/I Think You've Got Your Fools Mixed Up	1967	2.50	5.00	10.00
121	Baby You Got It/Catch You on the Rebound	1967	2.00	4.00	8.00
126	Lovey Dovey Kinda Lovin'/Two-Time Loser	1968	2.00	4.00	8.00
130	Some Got It, Some Don't/Me and You	1968	2.00	4.00	8.00
135	Trouble/It's Just a Game, Love	1968	2.00	4.00	8.00
137	Where Are You/A Change Is Gonna Come	1969	2.00	4.00	8.00
142	Whoop It On Me/Take a Chance	1969	2.00	4.00	8.00
147	Can You Dig It/Great Big Bubble of Love	1970	—	3.00	6.00
150	Bogaloosa, Lousiana/I Need Your Love So Bad	1970	—	3.00	6.00
156	Sad Little Song/Who But a Fool	1971	—	3.00	6.00
MIDGET					
101	Rainin' Love/All That Jazz	197?	—	2.50	5.00
PHILCO-FORD					
HP-38	Gimme Little Sign/Oogum Boogum	1969	5.00	10.00	20.00
—4-inch plastic "Hip Pocket Record" with color sleeve					
PROPHESY					
3002	Sticky Boom Boom Too Cold (Part 1)/Sticky Boom Boom Too Cold (Part 2)	1973	—	2.50	5.00
3003	Another Saturday Night/(B-side unknown)	1973	—	2.50	5.00
WAND					
145	Mr. Schemer/Hide-A-Way	1963	10.00	20.00	40.00
WARNER BROS.					
8079	All That Jazz/Rainin' Love	1975	—	2.50	5.00
8144	Better Believe It/It Only Makes Me Want It More	1975	—	2.50	5.00
Albums					
BRENT					
S-100 [S]	Introducing Brenton Wood! Boogaloo	1967	15.00	30.00	60.00
—Four tracks by Brenton Wood, six by other artists					
5100 [M]	Introducing Brenton Wood! Boogaloo	1967	10.00	20.00	40.00
CREAM					
1006	Come Softly	1977	3.75	7.50	15.00
DOUBLE SHOT					
1002 [M]	Oogum Boogum	1967	6.25	12.50	25.00
1003 [M]	Baby You Got It	1967	6.25	12.50	25.00
5002 [S]	Oogum Boogum	1967	7.50	15.00	30.00
5003 [S]	Baby You Got It	1967	7.50	15.00	30.00
—Black vinyl					
5003 [S]	Baby You Got It	1967	50.00	100.00	200.00
—Multi-color vinyl					
RHINO					
RNLP-70223	The Best of Brenton Wood	1986	2.50	5.00	10.00

WOOD, RONNIE

Also see FACES; THE ROLLING STONES.

Number	Title (A Side/B Side)	Yr	VG	VG+	NM
45s					
COLUMBIA					
11014	Seven Days/Breakin' My Heart	1979	—	3.00	6.00
WARNER BROS.					
8036	Breathe on Me/I Can Feel the Fire	1974	—	3.00	6.00
8131	I Got a Feeling/If You Don't Want My Love	1975	—	3.00	6.00
Albums					
COLUMBIA					
JC 35702	Gimme Some Neck	1979	3.75	7.50	15.00
PC 35702	Gimme Some Neck	198?	2.00	4.00	8.00
—Budget-line reissue					
FC 37473	1234	1981	3.75	7.50	15.00
WARNER BROS.					
BS 2819	I've Got My Own Album to Do	1974	5.00	10.00	20.00
BS 2872	Now Look	1975	3.75	7.50	15.00

WOOD, ROY

Also see ELECTRIC LIGHT ORCHESTRA; THE MOVE.

Number	Title (A Side/B Side)	Yr	VG	VG+	NM
45s					
UNITED ARTISTS					
XW160	Ball Park Incident/Carlsberg Special	1973	—	2.50	5.00
—As "Wizzard/Roy Wood"					
XW272	See My Baby Jive/Bend Over Beethoven	1973	—	2.50	5.00
XW320	Dear Elaine/Song of Praise	1973	—	2.50	5.00
XW394	Forever/Woodbe	1974	—	2.50	5.00
XW792	Any Old Time Will Do/Why Does Such a Pretty Girl Sing Those Sad Songs	1976	—	2.00	4.00
Albums					
TOWNHOUSE					
SN-7127	One Man Band	1981	3.00	6.00	12.00
UNITED ARTISTS					
UA-LA042-F	Wizzard's Brew	1973	2.50	5.00	10.00
UA-LA168-F	Boulders	1973	2.50	5.00	10.00
UA-LA219-G	Introducing Eddy and the Falcons	1974	2.50	5.00	10.00
UA-LA575-G	Mustard	1976	2.50	5.00	10.00
(# unknown) [DJ]	Boulders Folder	1973	10.00	20.00	40.00
—Promo version of 168 in 13x13 folder with press kit and postcards					

Number	Title (A Side/B Side)	Yr	VG	VG+	NM
WARNER BROS.					
BS 3065	Super Active Wizzo	1977	2.50	5.00	10.00
BSK 3247	On the Road Again	1979	2.50	5.00	10.00

WOODBURY, WOODY

Albums

Number	Title (A Side/B Side)	Yr	VG	VG+	NM
STEREODDITIES					
MW 1	Woody Woodbury Looks at Love and Life	1960	6.25	12.50	25.00
MW 2	Woody Woodbury's Laughing Room	1960	6.25	12.50	25.00
MW 3	Woody Woodbury's Concert in Comedy	1961	6.25	12.50	25.00
MW 4	Woody Woodbury's Saloonatics	1961	6.25	12.50	25.00
MW 5	The Spice Is Right	1962	6.25	12.50	25.00
MW 6	The Best of Woody Woodbury	1963	5.00	10.00	20.00
MW 7	Through the Keyhole	1964	5.00	10.00	20.00
BITOA	Booze Is the Only Answer	1961	10.00	20.00	40.00
—With record, paperback book and smaller booklets					

WOODS, BENNIE

45s

Number	Title (A Side/B Side)	Yr	VG	VG+	NM
ATLAS					
1040	I Cross My Fingers/Wheel Baby Wheel	1955	200.00	400.00	800.00
—As "Bennie Woods and the Five Dukes"					
1040	I Cross My Fingers/Wheel Baby Wheel	1955	125.00	250.00	500.00
—As "Bennie Woods and Rockin' Townies"					

WOODS, KENNI

45s

Number	Title (A Side/B Side)	Yr	VG	VG+	NM
PHILIPS					
40112	Can't He Take a Hint/That Guy Is Mine	1963	2.50	5.00	10.00
40156	Back with My Baby/Do You Really Love Me	1963	2.50	5.00	10.00

WOODS, MICKEY

45s

Number	Title (A Side/B Side)	Yr	VG	VG+	NM
TAMLA					
54039	They Rode Through the Valley/Poor Sam Jones	1961	12.50	25.00	50.00
54052	Please Mr. Kennedy/(They Call Me) Cupid	1962	10.00	20.00	40.00

WOODY, DON

45s

Number	Title (A Side/B Side)	Yr	VG	VG+	NM
DECCA					
30277	You're Barking Up the Wrong Tree/Bird-Dog	1957	25.00	50.00	100.00

WOOFERS, THE

Albums

Number	Title (A Side/B Side)	Yr	VG	VG+	NM
WYNCOTE					
SW 9011 [S]	Dragsville	1964	12.50	25.00	50.00
W 9011 [M]	Dragsville	1964	10.00	20.00	40.00

WOOLERY, CHUCK

Also see THE AVANT-GARDE.

45s

Number	Title (A Side/B Side)	Yr	VG	VG+	NM
COLUMBIA					
45017	I've Been Wrong/Soft Velvet Love	1969	—	3.00	6.00
45135	Heaven Here on Earth/Pleasure of Her Company	1970	—	3.00	6.00
45224	Your Name Is Woman/Soft Velvet Love	1970	—	3.00	6.00
45274	Hey, Baby/Soft Velvet Love	1970	—	3.00	6.00
EPIC					
50897	The Greatest Love Affair/Heroes and Lovers	1980	—	2.00	4.00
RCA VICTOR					
74-0554	Deja Vu/Forgive My Heart	1971	—	2.50	5.00
74-0703	Kiss Me Three Times/If Only	1972	—	2.50	5.00
74-0771	Time and Time Again/Pen of a Poet	1972	—	2.50	5.00
74-0865	Forgive My Heart/Love Me, Love Me	1973	—	2.50	5.00
WARNER BROS.					
8381	Painted Lady/Growing Up in a Country Way	1977	—	2.50	5.00

WOOLEY, SHEB

Includes records by his comedic alter ego, "Ben Colder."

45s

Number	Title (A Side/B Side)	Yr	VG	VG+	NM
BLUE BONNET					
124	Wooley's Polka/Lazy Mary	1954	17.50	35.00	70.00
125	Peeping Thru the Keyhole/Time Won't Heal an Achin' Heart	1954	17.50	35.00	70.00
130	Too Long with the Wrong Mama/Your Papa Ain't Steppin' Anymore	1954	15.00	30.00	60.00
MGM					
10697	Mule Boogie/Changing Your Name	1950	7.50	15.00	30.00
10960	Hoot Owl Boogie/Country Kisses	1951	7.50	15.00	30.00
11059	Over the Barrel/Air Castles	1951	7.50	15.00	30.00
11180	Backroom Boogie/Down in the Toolies	1952	7.50	15.00	30.00
11272	You're the Cat's Meow/Wha' Happened to Me Baby	1952	7.50	15.00	30.00
11308	A Cowboy Had Ought to Be Single/You Never Can Tell	1952	7.50	15.00	30.00
11403	Heart Bound in Chains/Freight Train Cinders	1953	6.25	12.50	25.00
11580	Love Is a Merry-Go-Round/Texas Tango	1953	6.25	12.50	25.00
11640	Goodbye Texas, Hello Tennessee/I'll Rerturn the Letters	1953	6.25	12.50	25.00
11665	Don't Stop Kissing Me Goodnight/Knew I Had Lost	1954	5.00	10.00	20.00
11717	Blue Guitar/Panama Pete	1954	5.00	10.00	20.00
11792	White Lightnin'/Fool About You	1954	5.00	10.00	20.00
11836	Hillbilly Mambo/I Go Outta My Mind	1954	5.00	10.00	20.00
11910	38-24-35/I Flipped	1955	3.75	7.50	15.00
11976	Speak of the Devil/Love at First Sight	1955	3.75	7.50	15.00
12048	Listening to Your Footsteps/Love Is a Prayer	1955	3.75	7.50	15.00
12060	It Takes a Heap of Livin'/Listen for Your Footsteps	1955	3.75	7.50	15.00
12114	Are You Satisfied/Humdinger	1955	3.75	7.50	15.00
12202	The Birth of the Rock 'N' Roll/A King or a Clown	1956	3.75	7.50	15.00
12260	You Can Do It/Do I Remember?	1956	3.75	7.50	15.00
12328	First Day of School/The Lonely Man	1956	3.75	7.50	15.00
12382	Honey I'm Lonesome/Let the Big Winds Blow	1956	3.75	7.50	15.00
12467	Plenty of Love/I Won't Come Back	1957	3.00	6.00	12.00
12541	Recipe for Love/I'm Too Young	1957	3.00	6.00	12.00
12584	So Close to Heaven/I Found Me An Angel	1957	3.00	6.00	12.00
12651	The Purple People Eater/I Can't Believe You're Mine	1958	4.50	9.00	18.00
12704	The Chase/Monkey Jive	1958	3.00	6.00	12.00
12733	Santa and the Purple People Eater/Star of Love	1958	5.00	10.00	20.00
12733 [PS]	Santa and the Purple People Eater/Star of Love	1958	10.00	20.00	40.00
12743	Cherry Street/Star of Love	1958	3.00	6.00	12.00
12778	More/Deep Goes the Love	1959	2.50	5.00	10.00
12781	Sweet Chile/More	1959	2.50	5.00	10.00
12817	Careless Hands/Pigmy Love	1959	2.50	5.00	10.00
12851	Love Like Mine/Josie	1959	2.50	5.00	10.00
12853	It's Almost Time/Roughneck	1959	2.50	5.00	10.00
12882	Luke the Spook/My Only Treasure	1960	2.50	5.00	10.00
12931	Taste of Ashes/Reach for the Moon	1960	2.50	5.00	10.00
13013	Skin Tight, Pin Striped, Pink Pedal Pushers/Till the End of the World	1961	2.50	5.00	10.00
13046	That's My Pa/Meet Mr. Lonely	1961	2.50	5.00	10.00
13065	Laughin' the Blues/Somebody Please	1962	2.50	5.00	10.00
13079	That's My Ma/Land of No Love	1962	2.50	5.00	10.00
13094	The Leged of Echo Mountain/Give That Ball to Willie B	1962	2.50	5.00	10.00
13104	Don't Go Near the Eskimos/Louisiana Trapper	1962	2.50	5.00	10.00
—As "Ben Colder"					
13122	Hello Wall No. 2/Shudders and Screams	1963	2.50	5.00	10.00
—As "Ben Colder"					
13125	Little Bitty Bilbo Abernathy Nathan Allen Quincy Jones/Daddy Kiss and Make It Well	1963	2.50	5.00	10.00
13147	Still No. 2/Goin' Surfin'	1963	3.75	7.50	15.00
—As "Ben Colder"					
13152	Buildin' a Railroad/Cowboy Hero	1963	2.50	5.00	10.00
13166	Hootenanny Hoot/Old Rag Doll	1963	2.50	5.00	10.00
13167	Detroit City No. 2/Ring of Smoke	1963	2.50	5.00	10.00
—As "Ben Colder"					
13195	Papa's Ole Fiddle/She Called Me Baby	1963	2.50	5.00	10.00
13197	I Walk the Line No. 2/Talk Back Blubberin' Lips	1963	2.50	5.00	10.00
—As "Ben Colder"					
13241	Blue Guitar/Natchez Landing	1964	2.00	4.00	8.00
13262	TV Westerns/Dobro's Catchin' On Again (And I'm Gonna Be a Star)	1964	2.00	4.00	8.00
—As "Ben Colder"					
13294	Wild and Wooley, Big Unruly Me/Sittin' and Thinkin'	1964	2.00	4.00	8.00
13351	Silver (The Wonder Horse)/Blistered	1965	2.00	4.00	8.00
13395	Big Land/Sally's Arms	1965	2.00	4.00	8.00
13444	Make the World Go Away No. 2/May the Bird of Paradise Fly Up Your Snoot	1966	2.00	4.00	8.00
—As "Ben Colder"					
13477	Buba Hoo Boba Dee/I'll Leave the Singin' to the Bluebirds	1966	2.00	4.00	8.00
13556	Tonight's the Night My Angel's Halo Fell/Anchors Aweigh	1966	2.00	4.00	8.00
13590	Almost Persuaded No. 2/A Packet of Pencils	1966	2.00	4.00	8.00
—As "Ben Colder"					
13668	There Goes My Everything No. 2/Great Men Repeat Themselves	1967	2.00	4.00	8.00
—As "Ben Colder"					
13705	Letter to Daddy/Draggin' the River	1967	2.00	4.00	8.00
13771	The Purple People Eater No. 2/Undertaker's Love Lament	1967	2.00	4.00	8.00
—As "Ben Colder"					
13806	Number One on the Survey/Big Ole, Good Ole Girl	1967	2.00	4.00	8.00
13827	The Love-In/Wildwood Flower on the Autoharp	1967	2.00	4.00	8.00
13897	Ain't It Funny How Wine Sips Away/The Doo-Hickey Song	1968	2.00	4.00	8.00
—As "Ben Colder"					
13914	By the Time I Get to Phoenix No. 2/Skip a Rope No. 2	1968	2.00	4.00	8.00
—As "Ben Colder"					
13938	Make 'Em Laugh/Tie a Tiger Down	1968	—	3.00	6.00
13997	Harper Valley P.T.A. (Later That Same Day)/Folsom Prison Blues No. 1 1/2	1968	2.50	5.00	10.00
—As "Ben Colder"					
14005	That Girl/I Remember Loving You	1968	—	3.00	6.00
14015	Little Green Apples No. 2/It's Such a Pretty World Tonight	1968	2.00	4.00	8.00
—As "Ben Colder"					
14044	Ode to the Little Shack Out Back/You're a Real Good Friend	1969	—	3.00	6.00
—As "Ben Colder"					
14065	The Carroll County Accident No. 2/His Lincoln's Parked at Margie's Again	1969	—	3.00	6.00
—As "Ben Colder"					
14070	The Recipient/Big Ole, Good Ole Girl	1969	—	3.00	6.00
14076	Ruby Please Bring Your Love to Town/Yet	1969	—	3.00	6.00
—As "Ben Colder"					
14085	One Man Band/You Still Turn Me On	1969	—	3.00	6.00
14111	Big Sweet John/Games People Play	1970	—	3.00	6.00
—As "Ben Colder"					
14123	Daddy's Home/The Will	1970	—	3.00	6.00
14133	Tennessee Bird Talk/What Is Youth	1970	—	3.00	6.00
—As "Ben Colder"					
14165	One of Them Roarin' Songs/I Don't Belong in Her Arms	1970	—	3.00	6.00
14209	Fifteen Beers Ago/Sunday Mornin' Fallin' Down	1970	—	3.00	6.00
—As "Ben Colder"					
14247	Help Me Fake It Through the Night/Rose Garden	1971	—	3.00	6.00
—As "Ben Colder"					
14287	Goodbye Wabash Cannonball/Joy	1971	—	3.00	6.00
14327	Easy Loving No. 2/Sing a Drinkin' Song	1971	—	3.00	6.00
—As "Ben Colder"					
14384	Life Is a Fountain/Somebody Gonna Come Along	1972	—	3.00	6.00

Number	Title (A Side/B Side)	Yr	VG	VG+	NM
14420	The Unhappiest Squirrel in the Whole U.S.A./ Runnin' Bare	1972	—	2.50	5.00
—As "Ben Colder"					
14444	A Kick in the Head/Personality	1972	—	3.00	6.00
14471	Glossy 8 x 10/Moontan	1972	—	2.50	5.00
—As "Ben Colder"					
14610	Early in the Morning/Getting High on Love	1973	—	3.00	6.00
14639	Behind Cloe's Door/Satin Sheets	1973	—	2.50	5.00
—As "Ben Colder"					
14647	The Purple People Eater/I Can't Believe You're Mine	1973	2.50	5.00	10.00
SCORPION					
0556	Lucille No. 2/Senior Citizen's Lament	1978	—	2.00	4.00
—As "Ben Colder"					
SUNBIRD					
104	The Rambler/Amazania	1979	—	2.00	4.00
—As "Ben Colder"					
109	Flower of the County (Censored Version)/Flower of the County (Uncensored Version)	1980	—	2.00	4.00
—As "Ben Colder"					
7566	Jack Hammer Man/Belly Button	1981	—	2.00	4.00
Albums					
MGM					
GAS-139	Ben Colder (Golden Archive Series)	1970	3.75	7.50	15.00
—As "Ben Colder"					
E-3299 [M]	Sheb Wooley	1956	37.50	75.00	150.00
E-3904 [M]	Songs from the Days of Rawhide	1961	10.00	20.00	40.00
SE-3904 [S]	Songs from the Days of Rawhide	1961	12.50	25.00	50.00
E-4026 [M]	That's My Ma and That's My Pa	1962	7.50	15.00	30.00
SE-4026 [S]	That's My Ma and That's My Pa	1962	10.00	20.00	40.00
E-4117 [M]	Spoofing the Big Ones	1961	10.00	20.00	40.00
SE-4117 [S]	Spoofing the Big Ones	1961	12.50	25.00	50.00
—MGM 4117 as "Ben Colder"					
E-4136 [M]	Tales of How the West Was Won	1963	7.50	15.00	30.00
SE-4136 [S]	Tales of How the West Was Won	1963	10.00	20.00	40.00
E-4173 [M]	Ben Colder	1963	7.50	15.00	30.00
SE-4173 [S]	Ben Colder	1963	10.00	20.00	40.00
—MGM 4173 as "Ben Colder"					
E-4275 [M]	The Very Best of Sheb Wooley	1965	5.00	10.00	20.00
SE-4275 [S]	The Very Best of Sheb Wooley	1965	6.25	12.50	25.00
E-4325 [M]	It's a Big Land	1965	5.00	10.00	20.00
SE-4325 [S]	It's a Big Land	1965	6.25	12.50	25.00
E-4421 [M]	Big Ben Strikes Again	1967	5.00	10.00	20.00
SE-4421 [S]	Big Ben Strikes Again	1967	5.00	10.00	20.00
—MGM 4421 as "Ben Colder"					
E-4482 [M]	Wine, Women and Song	1967	5.00	10.00	20.00
SE-4482 [S]	Wine, Women and Song	1967	5.00	10.00	20.00
—MGM 4482 as "Ben Colder"					
SE-4530	The Best of Ben Colder	1968	5.00	10.00	20.00
—As "Ben Colder"					
SE-4614	Harper Valley P.T.A.	1968	5.00	10.00	20.00
—As "Ben Colder"					
SE-4615	Warm and Wooley	1969	5.00	10.00	20.00
SE-4629	Have One On	1969	3.75	7.50	15.00
—As "Ben Colder"					
SE-4674	Wild Again	1970	3.75	7.50	15.00
—As "Ben Colder"					
SE-4758	Live and Loaded	1971	3.75	7.50	15.00
—As "Ben Colder"					
SE-4807	Warming Up to Colder	1972	3.75	7.50	15.00
—As "Ben Colder"					
SE-4876	The Wacky World of Ben Colder	1973	3.75	7.50	15.00
—As "Ben Colder"					

WORLD OF OZ, THE

Number	Title (A Side/B Side)	Yr	VG	VG+	NM
45s					
DERAM					
85029	The Muffin Man/Peter's Birthday	1968	2.50	5.00	10.00
85034	King Croesus/Jack	1968	2.50	5.00	10.00
85043	Mandy-Ann/Beside the Fire	1969	2.50	5.00	10.00
Albums					
DERAM					
DES 18022	The World of Oz	1969	12.50	25.00	50.00

WOULD

Number	Title (A Side/B Side)	Yr	VG	VG+	NM
Albums					
PERCEPTION					
24	Would	1972	7.50	15.00	30.00

WRAY, LINK

Number	Title (A Side/B Side)	Yr	VG	VG+	NM
45s					
CADENCE					
1347	Rumble/The Swag	1958	10.00	20.00	40.00
EPIC					
9300	Raw-Hide/Dixie-Doodle	1958	6.25	12.50	25.00
9321	Comanche/Lillian	1959	6.25	12.50	25.00
9343	Rendezvous/Slinky	1959	6.25	12.50	25.00
9343 [PS]	Rendezvous/Slinky	1959	62.50	125.00	250.00
9361	Trail of the Lonesome Pine/Golden Strings	1960	6.25	12.50	25.00
9419	Mary Ann/Ain't That Lovin' You Baby	1960	6.25	12.50	25.00
9454	El Toro/Tijuana	1961	6.25	12.50	25.00
HEAVY					
101	Rumble '68/Blow Your Mind	1968	3.75	7.50	15.00
KAY					
3690	I Sez Baby/(B-side unknown)	1958	25.00	50.00	100.00
MALA					
458	There's a Hole in the Middle of the Moon/Dancing Party	1963	5.00	10.00	20.00
MR. G.					
820	Rumble '69/Mind Blower	1969	2.50	5.00	10.00
NORTON					
801	Jack the Ripper/Bo Diddley	199?	—	—	3.00
802	Ace of Spades/Fat Back	199?	—	—	3.00
803	Hidden Charms/Five and Ten	199?	—	—	3.00
804	The Black Widow/Mustang	199?	—	—	3.00
805	Run Chicken Run/Scatter	199?	—	—	3.00
806	Branded/Law of the Jungle	199?	—	—	3.00
807	Deuces Wild/The Sweeper	199?	—	—	3.00
808	The Shadow Knows/Hang On	199?	—	—	3.00
809	Good Rockin' Tonight/Soul Train	199?	—	—	3.00
810	Batman Theme/Zip Code	199?	—	—	3.00
(no #) [PS]	Link Wray and the Wraymen	199?	—	—	2.00
—Custom sleeve with large hole to reveal the record label. The same generic sleeve was issued with each of 801-810.					
OKEH					
7166	Rumble Mambo/Ham Bone	1963	5.00	10.00	20.00
—B-side by Red Saunders					
7282	Rumble Mambo/Ham Bone	1967	3.75	7.50	15.00
—B-side by Red Saunders					
POLYDOR					
14084	Fire and Brimstone/June Box Mama	1970	2.00	4.00	8.00
14096	Fallin' Rain/Juke Box Mama	1971	2.00	4.00	8.00
14188	Shine the Light/Lawdy Miss Clawdy	1973	—	3.00	6.00
14256	I Got to Ramble/She's That Kind of Woman	1974	—	3.00	6.00
RUMBLE					
1000	Jack the Ripper/The Stranger	1961	10.00	20.00	40.00
SWAN					
4137	Jack the Ripper/The Black Widow	1963	5.00	10.00	20.00
4154	Weekend/Turnpike U.S.A.	1963	5.00	10.00	20.00
4163	Run Chicken Run/The Sweeper	1963	5.00	10.00	20.00
4171	The Shadow Knows/My Alberta	1964	5.00	10.00	20.00
4187	Deuces Wild/Summer Dream	1964	5.00	10.00	20.00
4201	Good Rockin' Tonight/I'll Do Anything for You	1965	6.25	12.50	25.00
4211	Branded/Hang On	1965	5.00	10.00	20.00
4232	Girl from the North Country/You Hurt Me So	1965	5.00	10.00	20.00
4239	The Fuzz/Ace of Spades	1966	5.00	10.00	20.00
4244	Batman Theme/Alone	1966	6.25	12.50	25.00
4261	Ace of Spades/Hidden Charms	1966	6.25	12.50	25.00
4284	Jack the Ripper/I'll Do Anything for You	1967	3.75	7.50	15.00
TRANS ATLAS					
687	Big City Stomp/Poppin' Popeye	1962	5.00	10.00	20.00
Albums					
EPIC					
LN 3661 [M]	Link Wray and the Wraymen	1960	62.50	125.00	250.00
NORTON					
210	Hillbilly Wolf (Missing Links Vol. 1)	199?	2.50	5.00	10.00
211	Big City After Dark (Missing Links Vol. 2)	199?	2.50	5.00	10.00
212	Some Kinda Nut (Missing Links Vol. 3)	199?	2.50	5.00	10.00
253	Streets of Chicago (Missing Links Vol. 4)	1995	2.50	5.00	10.00
POLYDOR					
24-4064	Link Wray	1971	5.00	10.00	20.00
PD-5047	Be What You Want To	1972	5.00	10.00	20.00
PD-6025	The Link Wray Rumble	1974	5.00	10.00	20.00
RECORD FACTORY					
1929	Yesterday and Today	1969	20.00	40.00	80.00
SWAN					
SLP-510 [M]	Jack the Ripper	1963	37.50	75.00	150.00
VERMILLION					
1924 [M]	Great Guitar Hits	196?	20.00	40.00	80.00
1925 [M]	Link Wray Sings and Plays Guitar	196?	20.00	40.00	80.00
VISA					
7009	Bullshot	1979	3.00	6.00	12.00
7010	Live at the Paradiso	1980	3.00	6.00	12.00

WRENS, THE

Number	Title (A Side/B Side)	Yr	VG	VG+	NM
45s					
RAMA					
53	Love's Something That's Made for Two/Beggin' for Love	1955	375.00	750.00	1500.
65	Come Back My Love/Beggin' for Love	1955	37.50	75.00	150.00
65	Come Back My Love/Eleven Roses	1955	100.00	200.00	400.00
110	Love's Something That's Made for Two/Eleven Roses	1955	75.00	150.00	300.00
174	Hey Girl/Serenade of the Bells	1955	100.00	200.00	400.00
184	I Won't Come to Your Wedding/What Makes You Do the Things That You Do	1956	100.00	200.00	400.00
194	C'est La Vie/C'est La Vie	1956	100.00	200.00	400.00
—B-side by Jimmy Wright and His Orchestra					

WRIGHT, BETTY

Number	Title (A Side/B Side)	Yr	VG	VG+	NM
12-Inch Singles					
FIRST STRING					
268	I Can (2 versions)/Music Street	1986	2.50	5.00	10.00
JAMAICA					
9002	One Step Up, Two Steps Back (9:52) (7:57 Dub)	1984	2.00	4.00	8.00
9004	Sinderella (6:30) (5:28)	1985	2.00	4.00	8.00
MS. B.					
1217	From Pain to Joy (Project Mix)/From Pain to Joy (Project Mix with Rap)	1989	2.00	4.00	8.00
1230	We Down (5 versions)	1989	2.00	4.00	8.00
T.K. DISCO					
125	Lovin' Is Really My Game (2 versions)	1979	3.00	6.00	12.00
VISION					
7005	After the Pain (6:56)/After the Pain (Project Mix)	1988	2.00	4.00	8.00
45s					
ALSTON					
3711	Shoorah! Shoorah!/Tonight Is the Night	1974	—	2.50	5.00
3713	Where Is the Love/My Baby Ain't My Baby Anymore	1975	—	2.50	5.00
3715	Ooola La/To Love and Be Loved	1975	—	2.50	5.00
3718	Slip and Do It/I Think I Better Think About It	1975	—	2.50	5.00
3719	Everybody Was Rockin'/Show Your Girl	1976	—	2.50	5.00
3722	If I Ever Do Wrong/Rock On Baby, Rock On	1976	—	2.50	5.00
3725	Life/If I Was a Kid	1976	—	2.50	5.00

Number	Title (A Side/B Side)	Yr	VG	VG+	NM
3734	You Can't See for Lookin'/Sometime Kind of Thing	1977	—	2.50	5.00
3736	Man of Mine/Sweet	1978	—	2.50	5.00
3740	Tonight Is the Night (Part 1)/Tonight Is the Night (Part 2)	1978	—	2.50	5.00
3745	Lovin' Is Really My Game/A Song for You	1979	—	2.50	5.00
3747	My Love Is/I Believe It's Love	1979	—	2.50	5.00
3749	Thank You for the Many Things You've Done/Child of the Man	1979	—	2.50	5.00
4569	Girls Can't Do What the Guys Do/Sweet Lovin' Daddy	1968	2.00	4.00	8.00
4571	He's Bad Bad Bad/Watch Out, Love	1968	2.00	4.00	8.00
4573	The Best Girls Don't Always Win/Circle of Heartbreaks	1969	2.00	4.00	8.00
4575	The Wrong Girl/The Joy of Becoming a Woman	1969	2.00	4.00	8.00
4580	I'm Not Free Hearted/A Woman Was Made for One Man	1969	2.00	4.00	8.00
4581	Soldier Boy/A Woman Was Made for One Man	1969	2.00	4.00	8.00
4587	Pure Love/If You Ain't Got It	1970	—	3.50	7.00
4589	I Found That Guy/If You Love Like I Love You	1970	—	3.50	7.00
4594	I Love the Way You Love/When We Get Together Again	1971	—	3.50	7.00
4601	Clean Up Woman/I'll Love You Forever	1971	—	3.00	6.00
4609	If You Love Me Like You Say You Love Me/I'm Gettin' Tired Baby	1972	—	3.00	6.00
4611	Is It You Girl/Crying in My Sleep	1972	—	3.00	6.00
4614	Baby Sitter/Outside Woman	1972	—	3.00	6.00
4617	It's Hard to Stop (Doing Something When It's Good to You)/Who'll Be the Fool	1973	—	3.00	6.00
4619	Let Me Be Your Lovemaker/Jealous Man	1973	—	3.00	6.00
4620	It's Bad for Me to See You/One Thing Leads to Another	1974	—	3.00	6.00
4622	Secretary/Value Your Love	1974	—	3.00	6.00
EPIC					
02143	I Like Your Loving/Body Slang	1981	—	2.00	4.00
02521	Goodbye Him Hello You/Make Me Love the Rain	1981	—	2.00	4.00
03523	He's Older Now/Special Love	1983	—	2.00	4.00
03954	Burning Desire/Show Me	1983	—	2.00	4.00
51009	What Are We Gonna Do About It/I Believe in You	1981	—	2.00	4.00
FIRST STRING					
965	Pain/(B-side unknown)	1985	—	2.00	4.00
968	The Sun Don't Shine/Music Street	1986	—	2.00	4.00
JAMAICA					
3	One Step Up, Two Steps Back/(B-side unknown)	1984	—	2.00	4.00
MS. B.					
4501	No Pain, No Gain/(Instrumental)	1988	—	2.00	4.00
4503	After the Pain/Love Days	1988	—	2.00	4.00
4504	A Christmas To Remember/2nd Chapter Of The Book Of Mathew	1988	—	—	3.00
4505	From Pain to Joy/From Pain to Joy (The Project Mix)	1989	—	2.00	4.00
4508	Quiet Storm/We Down	1989	—	2.00	4.00
Albums					
ALSTON					
SD 33-388	I Love the Way You Love	1972	3.75	7.50	15.00
4400	Danger High Voltage	1974	3.00	6.00	12.00
4406	This Time for Real	1977	3.00	6.00	12.00
4408	Betty Wright Live	1978	3.00	6.00	12.00
4410	Betty Travelin' in the Wright Circle	1979	3.00	6.00	12.00
SD 7026	Hard to Stop	1973	3.75	7.50	15.00
ATCO					
SD 33-260	My First Time Around	1968	6.25	12.50	25.00
COLLECTABLES					
COL-5118	Golden Classics	198?	2.50	5.00	10.00
EPIC					
JE 36879	Betty Wright	1981	2.50	5.00	10.00
FE 38558	Wright Back at You	1983	2.50	5.00	10.00
FANTASY					
9644	Sevens	1986	2.50	5.00	10.00
MS. B.					
3301	Mother Wit	1988	2.50	5.00	10.00
3318	Passion and Compassion	198?	3.75	7.50	15.00

WRIGHT, CHARLES, AND THE WATTS 103RD STREET RHYTHM BAND

45s

Number	Title (A Side/B Side)	Yr	VG	VG+	NM
ABC					
12127	Is It Real/One Lie	1975	—	2.00	4.00
—Charles Wright solo					
ABC DUNHILL					
4363	Liberated Lady/You Threw It All Away	1973	—	2.00	4.00
4364	(Well I'm) Doing What Cums Naturally Part 1/Part 2	1973	—	2.00	4.00
4381	The Weight of Hate/You Threw It All Away	1974	—	2.00	4.00
15027	Don't Rush Tomorrow/Is It Real	1974	—	2.00	4.00
KEYMEN					
108	Spreadin' Honey/(B-side unknown)	1967	2.50	5.00	10.00
—As "The Watts 103rd Street Rhythm Band"					
WARNER BROS.					
7175	Brown Sugar/Caesar's Palace	1968	2.50	5.00	10.00
—Through 7298, as "The Watts 103rd Street Rhythm Band"					
7222	Bottomless/65 Bars and a Taste of Soul	1968	2.50	5.00	10.00
7250	Do Your Thing/A Dance, a Kiss, and a Song	1969	2.00	4.00	8.00
7298	Till You Get Enough/Light My Fire	1969	2.00	4.00	8.00
7338	Must Be Your Thing/Comment	1969	—	3.00	6.00
7365	Love Land/Sorry Charlie	1970	—	3.00	6.00
7417	Express Yourself/Living on Borrowed Time	1970	—	3.00	6.00
7475	Your Love (Means Everything to Me)/What Can You Bring Me	1971	—	2.50	5.00
7504	Nobody/Wine	1971	—	2.50	5.00
7577	I've Got Love/Let's Make Love — Not War	1972	—	2.50	5.00
7600	Soul Train/Run Judy Run	1972	—	2.50	5.00
7630	Here Comes the Sun/You Gotta Know Whatcha Doin'	1972	—	2.50	5.00
Albums					
ABC					
D-887	Lil' Encouragement	1975	3.00	6.00	12.00
ABC DUNHILL					
DS-50162 [(2)]	Doin' What Comes Naturally	1973	3.75	7.50	15.00
DS-50187	Ninety Day Cycle People	1974	3.00	6.00	12.00
WARNER BROS.					
WS 1741	The Watts 103rd Street Rhythm Band	1968	5.00	10.00	20.00
—Green label with "W7" logo					
WS 1761	Together	1969	5.00	10.00	20.00
—Green label with "W7" logo					
WS 1761	Together	1970	3.75	7.50	15.00
—Green label with "WB" logo					
WS 1801	In the Jungle, Babe	1969	5.00	10.00	20.00
—Green label with "W7" logo					
WS 1801	In the Jungle, Babe	1970	3.75	7.50	15.00
—Green label with "WB" logo					
WS 1864	Express Yourself	1970	3.75	7.50	15.00
WS 1904	You're So Beautiful	1971	3.75	7.50	15.00
BS 2620	Rhythm and Poetry	1972	3.75	7.50	15.00
—Green label with "WB" logo					
BS 2620	Rhythm and Poetry	1973	3.00	6.00	12.00
—"Burbank" palm-trees logo					

WRIGHT, GARY

Also see SPOOKY TOOTH.

45s

Number	Title (A Side/B Side)	Yr	VG	VG+	NM
A&M					
1228	Over You Now/Get On the Right Road	1970	—	2.50	5.00
1267	Stand for Our Rights/I Can't See the Reason	1971	—	2.50	5.00
1319	Love to Survive/Fascinating Things	1972	—	2.50	5.00
1344	Two-Faced Man/I Know	1972	—	2.50	5.00
WARNER BROS.					
8143	Love Is Alive/Much Higher	1975	—	2.00	4.00
—Reissued in 1976 with the same number					
8167	Dream Weaver/Let It Out	1975	—	2.00	4.00
8250	Made to Love You/Power of Love	1976	—	2.00	4.00
8331	Phantom Writer/Child of Light	1977	—	2.00	4.00
8383	Empty Inside/Water Sign	1977	—	2.00	4.00
8426	Light of Smiles/Silent Fury	1977	—	2.00	4.00
8548	Something Very Special/Starry Eyed	1978	—	2.00	4.00
8598	Can't Get Above Losing You/Starry Eyed	1978	—	2.00	4.00
8809	Follow Next to You/I'm the One Who'll Be At Your Side	1979	—	2.00	4.00
49769	Really Wanna Know You/More Than a Heartache	1981	—	2.00	4.00
49836	Comin' Apart/Heartbeat	1981	—	2.00	4.00
49879	Got the Feelin'/Close to You	1981	—	2.00	4.00
Albums					
A&M					
SP-3528 [(2)]	That Was Only Yesterday	1976	3.75	7.50	15.00
—By "Gary Wright/Spooky Tooth"					
SP-4277	Extraction	1970	3.75	7.50	15.00
SP-4296	Footprint	1971	3.75	7.50	15.00
CYPRESS					
0111	Who I Am	1988	3.00	6.00	12.00
WARNER BROS.					
BS 2868	The Dream Weaver	1975	2.50	5.00	10.00
BS 2951	The Light of Smiles	1976	2.50	5.00	10.00
BSK 3137	Touch and Gone	1977	2.50	5.00	10.00
BSK 3244	Headin' Home	1979	2.50	5.00	10.00
BSK 3511	The Right Place	1981	2.50	5.00	10.00

WRIGHT, O.V.

45s

Number	Title (A Side/B Side)	Yr	VG	VG+	NM
ABC					
12119	What More Can I Do (To Prove My Love to You)/Henpecked Man	1975	—	3.00	6.00
12154	Nobody But You/Slow and Easy	1976	—	3.00	6.00
BACK BEAT					
544	Don't Want to Sit Down/Can't Find True Love	1965	2.50	5.00	10.00
548	You're Gonna Make Me Cry/Monkey Dog	1965	2.50	5.00	10.00
551	I'm In Your Corner/Poor Boy	1965	2.50	5.00	10.00
558	Gone for Good/How Long Baby	1966	2.50	5.00	10.00
580	Eight Men, Four Women/Fed Up with the Blues	1967	2.00	4.00	8.00
583	Heartaches-Heartaches/Treasured Moments	1967	2.00	4.00	8.00
586	What About You/What Did You Tell This Girl of Mine	1967	2.00	4.00	8.00
591	Oh Baby Mine/Working Your Game	1968	2.00	4.00	8.00
597	I Want Everyone to Know/I'm Gonna Forget About You	1968	2.00	4.00	8.00
604	Missing You/This Must Be Real	1969	2.00	4.00	8.00
607	I'll Take Care of You/Why Not Give Me a Chance	1969	2.00	4.00	8.00
611	Love the Way You Love/Blowin' in the Wind	1970	2.00	4.00	8.00
615	Ace of Spade/Afflicted	1970	2.00	4.00	8.00
620	When You Took Your Love from Me/I Was Born All Over	1971	—	3.00	6.00
622	A Nickel and a Nail/Pledging My Love	1971	—	3.00	6.00
625	He Made Woman for Man/Don't Let My Baby Ride	1972	—	3.00	6.00
626	Drowning on Dry Land/I'm Gonna Forget About You	1973	—	3.00	6.00
628	I'd Rather Be (Blind, Cripple and Crazy)/Please Forgive Me	1973	—	3.00	6.00
631	I've Been Searching/I'm Going Home	1974	—	3.00	6.00
5103	I'm In Your Corner/Poor Boy	1974	—	3.00	6.00
GOLDWAX					
106	That's How Strong My Love Is/There Goes My Used to Be	1964	3.00	6.00	12.00
HI					
2315	Rhymes/Without You	1976	—	3.00	6.00
77501	Into Something (Can't Shake Loose)/The Time We Have	1977	—	3.00	6.00

Number	Title (A Side/B Side)	Yr	VG	VG+	NM
77506	Precious, Precious/You Gotta Have Love	1977	—	3.00	6.00
78514	I Don't Do Windows/I Feel Love Growin'	1978	—	3.00	6.00
78521	No Easy Way to Say Goodbye/Bottom Line	1978	—	3.00	6.00
79531	We're Still Together/I Don't Know Why	1979	—	3.00	6.00
Albums					
BACK BEAT					
61 [M]	If It's Only for Tonight	1965	25.00	50.00	100.00
S-61 [S]	If It's Only for Tonight	1965	37.50	75.00	150.00
66	Eight Men, Four Women	1968	15.00	30.00	60.00
67	Nucleus of Soul	1969	15.00	30.00	60.00
70	A Nickel and a Nail and Ace of Spade	1971	15.00	30.00	60.00
72	Memphis Unlimited	1973	12.50	25.00	50.00
HI					
6001	Into Something	1977	6.25	12.50	25.00
6008	Bottom Line	1978	6.25	12.50	25.00
6011	We're Still Together	1979	6.25	12.50	25.00

WRIGHT, RANDY

Number	Title (A Side/B Side)	Yr	VG	VG+	NM
45s					
ATLANTIC					
1115	What My Heart Didn't Know/Snake in the Grass	1956	5.00	10.00	20.00

WRIGHT, RITA

Later recorded as SYREETA.

Number	Title (A Side/B Side)	Yr	VG	VG+	NM
45s					
GORDY					
7064	I Can't Give Back the Love I Feel for You/ Something on My Mind	1967	2.50	5.00	10.00

WRIGHT, RUBY

Number	Title (A Side/B Side)	Yr	VG	VG+	NM
45s					
CANDEE					
502	This Is Christmas/(B-side unknown)	196?	5.00	10.00	20.00
FRATERNITY					
787	Let's Light the Christmas Tree/Merry Merry Christmas	1957	3.75	7.50	15.00
KING					
1288	Santa's Little Sleigh Bells/Toodle Oo To You	1953	5.00	10.00	20.00
4850	Do You Believe/I Fall in Love with You Every Day	1955	3.75	7.50	15.00
4870	Rummy Dumb Bunny/Don't Take Me for Granted	1956	3.75	7.50	15.00
5192	Three Stars/I Only Have One Lifetime	1959	3.00	6.00	12.00
5208	Goodbye, Jimmy, Goodbye/Don't Take Me for Granted	1959	2.50	5.00	10.00
5225	Don't Take Me for Granted/I Only Have One Lifetime	1959	2.50	5.00	10.00
5261	Sweet Night of Love/You're Just a Flower from an Old Bouquet	1959	2.50	5.00	10.00
5297	Free-Hearted/When You're Away	1959	2.50	5.00	10.00
7-Inch Extended Plays					
CANDEE					
EP-50-50	Christmas Is A Birthday Time//Have A Merry Merry Merry Merry Christmas/The Happy Time	196?	2.00	4.00	8.00
—B-side by Ruth Lyons					

WRITIS, ARTHUR, AND THE NAGGING PAINS

Number	Title (A Side/B Side)	Yr	VG	VG+	NM
45s					
REPRISE					
0589	Say What/Welcome to San Francisco	1967	2.50	5.00	10.00

WYATT, GENE

Number	Title (A Side/B Side)	Yr	VG	VG+	NM
45s					
EBB					
123	Love Fever/Lover Boy	1957	25.00	50.00	100.00
MERCURY					
72752	I Stole the Flowers/I'm a One Woman Man	1967	2.50	5.00	10.00
PAULA					
308	I Just Ain't Got (As Much As He's Got Going for Me)/Chains Around My Heart	1968	2.50	5.00	10.00
1206	Little Liza Jane/Country Music Peyton Place	1968	2.50	5.00	10.00
1211	My Story of Love/Evangeline	1969	2.50	5.00	10.00
1216	Milk and Honey Memories/Failure of T Crop	1969	2.50	5.00	10.00
1223	Twelve Men/Back Door of My Mind	1970	2.00	4.00	8.00
1224	Go Together/As Long As I Live	1970	2.00	4.00	8.00

WYMAN, BILL

Also see THE ROLLING STONES.

Number	Title (A Side/B Side)	Yr	VG	VG+	NM
45s					
A&M					
2367	(Si Si) Je Suis Un Rock Star/Rio De Janeiro	1981	—	2.50	5.00
2367 [PS]	(Si Si) Je Suis Un Rock Star/Rio De Janeiro	1981	2.50	5.00	10.00
ROLLING STONES					
19111	White Lightning/I Wanna Get Me a Gun	1974	—	2.50	5.00
19119	A Quarter to Three/Soul Satisfying	1975	—	2.50	5.00
19303	Apache Woman/Soul Satisfying	1975	—	2.50	5.00
Albums					
ROLLING STONES					
COC 59102	Monkey Grip	1974	3.75	7.50	15.00
COC 79100	Monkey Grip	1974	3.00	6.00	12.00
—Reissue of 59102					
QD 79100 [Q]	Monkey Grip	1974	5.00	10.00	20.00
COC 79103	Stone Alone	1976	3.00	6.00	12.00
QD 79103 [Q]	Stone Alone	1976	5.00	10.00	20.00

WYNDER K. FROG

Number	Title (A Side/B Side)	Yr	VG	VG+	NM
45s					
UNITED ARTISTS					
50156	The Green Door/Dancing Frog	1967	—	3.00	6.00
50320	I'm a Man/Oh Mary	1968	—	3.00	6.00
50453	Jumpin' Jack Flash/I Feel So Bad	1968	—	3.00	6.00
Albums					
UNITED ARTISTS					
UAS-5740	Into the Fire	1971	3.00	6.00	12.00
UAS-6695	Out of the Frying Pan	1970	3.00	6.00	12.00

WYNETTE, TAMMY

Also see DAVID HOUSTON AND TAMMY WYNETTE; GEORGE JONES AND TAMMY WYNETTE.

Number	Title (A Side/B Side)	Yr	VG	VG+	NM
45s					
COLUMBIA					
04782	Sometimes When We Touch/You're Gonna Be the Last One	1985	—	—	3.00
—A-side with Mark Gray; B-side is Gray solo					
77294	Silver Threads and Golden Needles/Let Her Fly	1993	—	—	3.00
—Dolly Parton/Tammy Wynette/Loretta Lynn					
EPIC					
AS 60 [DJ]	White Christmas/One Happy Christmas	1973	2.00	4.00	8.00
—1973 Christmas Seals promotional record					
AS 60 [PS]	White Christmas/One Happy Christmas	1973	2.50	5.00	10.00
02439	Crying in the Rain/Bring Back My Baby to Me	1981	—	2.00	4.00
02770	Another Chance/What's It Like to Be a Woman	1982	—	2.00	4.00
03064	You Still Get To Me in My Dreams/If I Didn't Have a Heart	1982	—	2.00	4.00
03384	A Good Night's Love/I'm Going On with Everything Gone	1982	—	2.00	4.00
03811	I Just Heard a Heart Break (And I'm So Afraid It's Mine)/Back to the Wall	1983	—	2.00	4.00
03971	Unwed Fathers/I'm So Afraid That I'd Live Through It	1983	—	2.00	4.00
04101	Still in the Ring/Midnight Love	1983	—	2.00	4.00
04467	Lonely Heart/(I'm Not) A Candle in the Wind	1984	—	—	3.00
05399	You Can Lead a Heart to Love (But You Can't Make It Fall)/He Talks to Me	1985	—	—	3.00
06263	Alive and Well/I'll Be Thinking of You	1986	—	—	3.00
07226	Your Love/I Wasn't Meant to Live My Life Alone	1987	—	—	3.00
07635	Talkin' to Myself Again/A Slow Burning Fire	1987	—	—	3.00
07788	Beneath a Painted Sky/Some Things Will Never Change	1988	—	—	3.00
10095	Apartment No. 9/I'm Not Mine to Give	1966	2.50	5.00	10.00
10134	Your Good Girl's Gonna Go Bad/Send Me No Roses	1967	2.00	4.00	8.00
10211	I Don't Wanna Play House/Soakin' Wet	1967	2.00	4.00	8.00
10269	Take Me to Your World/Good	1967	2.00	4.00	8.00
10315	D-I-V-O-R-C-E/Don't Make It Now	1968	2.00	4.00	8.00
10398	Stand By Your Man/I Stayed Long Enough	1968	2.50	5.00	10.00
10462	Singing My Song/Too Far Gone	1969	—	3.00	6.00
10462 [PS]	Singing My Song/Too Far Gone	1969	2.50	5.00	10.00
10512	The Ways to Love a Man/Still Around	1969	—	3.00	6.00
10571	I'll See Him Through/Enough of a Woman	1970	—	3.00	6.00
10612	He Loves Me All the Way/One Last Night Together	1970	—	3.00	6.00
10653	Run, Woman, Run/My Daddy Doll	1970	—	3.00	6.00
10687	The Wonders You Perform/Gentle Shepherd	1970	—	3.00	6.00
10690	One Happy Christmas/(Merry Christmas) We Must Be Having One	1970	2.00	4.00	8.00
10707	We Sure Can Love Each Other/Fun	1971	—	3.00	6.00
10759	Good Lovin' (Makes It Right)/I Love You, Mr. Jones	1971	—	3.00	6.00
10818	Bedtime Story/Reach Out Your Hand	1971	—	3.00	6.00
10856	Reach Out Your Hand/Love's the Answer	1972	—	3.00	6.00
10909	My Man/Things I Love to Do	1972	—	3.00	6.00
10969	Kids Say the Darnedest Things/I Wish I Had a Mommy Like You	1973	—	3.00	6.00
11044	One Final Stand/Crying Steel Guitar	1973	—	—	—
—Canceled?					
11079	Another Lonely Song/The Only Time I'm Really Me	1973	—	3.00	6.00
50008	Woman to Woman/Love Me Forever	1974	—	2.50	5.00
50071	(You Make Me Want to Be) A Mother/I'm Not a Has-Been	1975	—	2.50	5.00
50145	I Still Believe in Fairy Tales/Your Memory's Gone to Rest	1975	—	2.50	5.00
50196	'Til I Can Make It on My Own/Love Is Something Good for Everybody	1976	—	2.50	5.00
50264	You and Me/When Love Was All We Had	1976	—	2.50	5.00
50349	(Let's Get Together) One Last Time/Hardly a Day Goes By	1977	—	2.50	5.00
50450	One of a Kind/Loving You, I Do	1977	—	2.50	5.00
50538	I'd Like to See Jesus (On the Midnight Special)/ Love Doesn't Always Come (On the Night It's Needed)	1978	—	2.50	5.00
50574	Womanhood/50 Words or Less	1978	—	2.50	5.00
50661	They Call It Making Love/Let Me Be Me	1979	—	2.50	5.00
50722	No One Else in the World/Mama, Your Little Girl Fell	1979	—	2.50	5.00
50868	He Was There (When I Needed You)/Only the Names Have Been Changed	1980	—	2.50	5.00
50915	Starting Over/I'll Be Thinking of You	1980	—	2.50	5.00
51011	Cowboys Don't Shoot Straight (Like They Used To)/You Brought Me Back	1981	—	2.00	4.00
68570	Next to You/When a Girl Becomes a Wife	1989	—	—	3.00
68894	Thank the Cowboy for the Ride/We Called It Everything But Quits	1989	—	—	3.00
73427	Let's Call It a Day Today/When a Girl Becomes a Wife	1990	—	2.00	4.00
73579	I'm Turning You Loose/Just a Minute There	1990	—	2.00	4.00
73656	What Goes with Blue/Let's Call It a Day Today	1991	—	2.00	4.00
73958	We're Strangers Again/If You Were the Friend	1991	—	2.00	4.00
—A-side with Randy Travis					
Albums					
EPIC					
EGP 503 [(2)]	The World of Tammy Wynette	1970	6.25	12.50	25.00
LN 24305 [M]	Your Good Girl's Gonna Go Bad	1967	7.50	15.00	30.00
BN 26305 [S]	Your Good Girl's Gonna Go Bad	1967	5.00	10.00	20.00
BN 26353	Take Me to Your World	1968	5.00	10.00	20.00
BN 26392	D-I-V-O-R-C-E	1968	5.00	10.00	20.00

Number	Title (A Side/B Side)	Yr	VG	VG+	NM
BN 26423	Inspiration	1969	5.00	10.00	20.00
BN 26451	Stand By Your Man	1969	5.00	10.00	20.00
BN 26486	Tammy's Greatest Hits	1969	5.00	10.00	20.00
PE 26486	Tammy's Greatest Hits	198?	2.00	4.00	8.00
—Budget-line reissue					
BN 26519	The Ways to Love a Man	1970	5.00	10.00	20.00
BN 26549	Tammy's Touch	1970	5.00	10.00	20.00
E 30212	The First Lady	1970	5.00	10.00	20.00
E 30343	Christmas with Tammy	1970	5.00	10.00	20.00
KEG 30358 [(2)]	The First Songs of the First Lady	1970	5.00	10.00	20.00
E 30658	We Sure Can Love Each Other	1971	5.00	10.00	20.00
EQ 30658 [Q]	We Sure Can Love Each Other	1972	7.50	15.00	30.00
E 30733	Tammy's Greatest Hits, Volume II	1971	5.00	10.00	20.00
PE 30733	Tammy's Greatest Hits, Volume II	198?	2.00	4.00	8.00
—Budget-line reissue					
KE 31285	Bedtime Story	1972	3.75	7.50	15.00
KE 31717	My Man	1972	3.75	7.50	15.00
KE 31937	Kids Say the Darndest Things	1973	3.75	7.50	15.00
KE 32745	Another Lonely Song	1974	3.00	6.00	12.00
KE 33246	Woman to Woman	1975	3.00	6.00	12.00
KE 33396	Tammy's Greatest Hits, Volume III	1975	3.00	6.00	12.00
PE 33396	Tammy's Greatest Hits, Volume III	198?	2.00	4.00	8.00
—Budget-line reissue					
KE 33582	I Still Believe in Fairy Tales	1975	3.00	6.00	12.00
BG 33773 [(2)]	Stand By Your Man/Bedtime Story	1976	3.75	7.50	15.00
PE 34075	'Til I Can Make It on My Own	1976	3.00	6.00	12.00
PE 34289	You and Me	1976	3.00	6.00	12.00
PE 34694	Let's Get Together One Last Time	1977	3.00	6.00	12.00
KE 35044	One of a Kind	1977	3.00	6.00	12.00
KE 35442	Womanhood	1978	3.00	6.00	12.00
KE 35630	Tammy's Greatest Hits, Volume IV	1978	3.00	6.00	12.00
KE 36013	Just Tammy	1979	3.00	6.00	12.00
JE 36485	Only Lonely Sometimes	1980	2.50	5.00	10.00
FE 37104	You Brought Me Back	1981	2.50	5.00	10.00
FE 37344	Encore	1981	2.50	5.00	10.00
PE 37344	Encore	198?	2.00	4.00	8.00
—Budget-line reissue					
FE 37980	Soft Touch	1982	2.50	5.00	10.00
FE 38312	Biggest Hits	1984	2.50	5.00	10.00
FE 38372	Good Love and Heartbreak	1983	2.50	5.00	10.00
FE 38744	Even the Strong Get Lonely	1983	2.50	5.00	10.00
FE 39971	Sometimes When We Touch	1985	2.50	5.00	10.00
EG 40625 [(2)]	Anniversary: 20 Years of Hits	1987	3.75	7.50	15.00
FE 40832	Higher Ground	1987	2.50	5.00	10.00
FE 44498	Next to You	1989	3.00	6.00	12.00
HARMONY					
KH 30096	Send Me No Roses	1970	3.00	6.00	12.00
KH 30914	Just a Matter of Time	1971	3.00	6.00	12.00
PAIR					
PDL2-1073 [(2)]	From the Bottom of My Heart	1986	3.00	6.00	12.00

WYNTER, MARK

45s

Number	Title (A Side/B Side)	Yr	VG	VG+	NM
ARLEN					
744	Running to You/Don't Cry	1964	3.00	6.00	12.00
GUYDEN					
2115	Answer Me/Only You	1964	2.50	5.00	10.00
LONDON					
1973	Dream Girl/Two Little Girls	1961	3.75	7.50	15.00
1997	Exclusively Yours/Warm and Willing	1961	3.75	7.50	15.00
9522	Heaven's Plan/You Are Everything	1962	3.75	7.50	15.00
SCEPTER					
1299	Am I Living in a Dream/Can I Get to Know You Better	1965	2.50	5.00	10.00

X

X-CELLENTS, THE

45s

SMASH

Number	Title (A Side/B Side)	Yr	VG	VG+	NM
1996	Hey Little Willie/I'll Aways Be On Your Side	1965	5.00	10.00	20.00

X-CITERS UNLIMITED

45s

ABC

Number	Title (A Side/B Side)	Yr	VG	VG+	NM
11029	Soul to Fillie Joe/Hang On Sloopy	1967	2.50	5.00	10.00

X. LINCOLN

45s

DOT

Number	Title (A Side/B Side)	Yr	VG	VG+	NM
17101	In the Freedom of My Mind/What Am I Gonna Do Now	1968	2.50	5.00	10.00
17170	Anywhere I Happen to Be/You're Everything	1968	2.50	5.00	10.00
17267	You're My Heaven/Mama Was a Proper Lady	1969	2.50	5.00	10.00

X-TREMES, THE

45s

STAR TREK

Number	Title (A Side/B Side)	Yr	VG	VG+	NM
1221	Substitute/Facts of Life	1966	6.25	12.50	25.00

XIT

45s

MOTOWN

Number	Title (A Side/B Side)	Yr	VG	VG+	NM
1304	I Need Your Love (Git It To Me)/Movin' from the City	1974	2.00	4.00	8.00
1320	Renegade/Cement Prairie	1974	2.00	4.00	8.00

RARE EARTH

Number	Title (A Side/B Side)	Yr	VG	VG+	NM
5044	Nihaa Shil Hozho (I Am Happy About You)/End	1972	2.50	5.00	10.00
5055	Reservation of Education/Color Nature Gone	1973	2.50	5.00	10.00

Albums

CANYON

Number	Title (A Side/B Side)	Yr	VG	VG+	NM
7114	Entrance	197?	12.50	25.00	50.00
7121	Relocation	197?	10.00	20.00	40.00

RARE EARTH

Number	Title (A Side/B Side)	Yr	VG	VG+	NM
R-536	Plight of the Redman	1972	7.50	15.00	30.00
R-545	Silent Warrior	1973	7.50	15.00	30.00

Y

YA HO WA 13

Albums

HIGHER KEY

Number	Title (A Side/B Side)	Yr	VG	VG+	NM
3301	Kohoutek	1973	75.00	150.00	300.00
3302	Contraction	1974	125.00	250.00	500.00
3303	Expansion	1974	125.00	250.00	500.00
3304	All or Nothing at All	1974	100.00	200.00	400.00
—Above 4 as "Father Yod and the Spirit of '76"					
3305	Ya Ho Wa 13	1974	125.00	250.00	500.00
3306	The Savage Sons of Ya Ho Wa	1974	100.00	200.00	400.00
3307	Penetration: An Aquarian Symphony	1974	100.00	200.00	400.00
3308 [(2)]	I'm Gonna Take You Home	1975	200.00	400.00	800.00
3309	To the Principles for the Children	1975	200.00	400.00	800.00

YANCY DERRINGER

Albums

HEMISPHERE

Number	Title (A Side/B Side)	Yr	VG	VG+	NM
H-15104	Openers	1975	12.50	25.00	50.00

YANKEE DOLLAR, THE

45s

DOT

Number	Title (A Side/B Side)	Yr	VG	VG+	NM
17123	City Sidewalks/Sanctuary	1968	3.75	7.50	15.00
17155	Live and Let Live/Sanctuary	1968	3.75	7.50	15.00
17213	Mucky Truckee River/Reflections of a Shattered Mind	1969	3.75	7.50	15.00

Albums

DOT

Number	Title (A Side/B Side)	Yr	VG	VG+	NM
DLP-25874	The Yankee Dollar	1968	30.00	60.00	120.00

YANOVSKY, ZALMAN

Also see THE LOVIN' SPOONFUL.

45s

BUDDAH

Number	Title (A Side/B Side)	Yr	VG	VG+	NM
12	As Long As You're Here/Ereh Er'uoy Sa Gnol Sa	1967	2.50	5.00	10.00

Albums

BUDDAH

Number	Title (A Side/B Side)	Yr	VG	VG+	NM
BDS-5019	Alive and Well in Argentina	1968	10.00	20.00	40.00

KAMA SUTRA

Number	Title (A Side/B Side)	Yr	VG	VG+	NM
KSBS-2030	Alive and Well in Argentina	1971	5.00	10.00	20.00

YARBROUGH, GLENN

Also see THE LIMELITERS.

45s

PRIDE

Number	Title (A Side/B Side)	Yr	VG	VG+	NM
1020	Back Roads/(B-side unknown)	1972	—	2.50	5.00

RCA VICTOR

Number	Title (A Side/B Side)	Yr	VG	VG+	NM
47-8366	The Honey Wind Blows/San Francisco Bay Blues	1964	2.00	4.00	8.00
47-8447	An Acre of Gal to a Foot of Ground/Jenny's Gone And I Don't Care	1964	2.00	4.00	8.00
47-8498	Baby the Rain Must Fall/I've Been to Town	1965	2.50	5.00	10.00
47-8498 [PS]	Baby the Rain Must Fall/I've Been to Town	1965	3.75	7.50	15.00
47-8619	It's Gonna Be Fine/She	1965	2.00	4.00	8.00
47-8745	Ain't No Way/You Can't Ever Go Home Again	1965	2.00	4.00	8.00
47-8796	Lonely Things/Changing Way No. 2	1966	—	3.00	6.00
47-9019	Spin, Spin/Love Are Wine	1966	—	3.00	6.00
47-9187	Golden Under the Sun/Gently Here Beside Me	1967	—	3.00	6.00
47-9309	Honey and Wine/Ain't You Glad You're Livin', Joe	1967	—	3.00	6.00
47-9452	A Face in the Crown/Times Gone By	1968	—	3.00	6.00

STANYAN

Number	Title (A Side/B Side)	Yr	VG	VG+	NM
34	Simple Christmas/A Hand To Hold At Christmas	1974	—	2.50	5.00
—B-side by Rod McKuen					

STAX

Number	Title (A Side/B Side)	Yr	VG	VG+	NM
0185	I See America/Holy Creation	1973	—	2.50	5.00
0204	Everybody's Reaching Out for Someone/ Freedom to Stay	1974	—	2.50	5.00
0225	Ride This Road/Mary Makes Magic	1974	—	2.50	5.00

WARNER BROS.

Number	Title (A Side/B Side)	Yr	VG	VG+	NM
7196	Downtown L.A./Until You Happened to Pass By	1968	—	3.00	6.00
7247	Let Me Choose Life/I'll Catch the Sun	1968	—	3.00	6.00
7269	Somehow, Someway (I'm Gonna Get to You)/ Child of the Night Time	1969	—	3.00	6.00
7335	(Don't Let the Sun Shine On You) In Tulsa/ Wisconsin	1969	—	3.00	6.00
7382	Goodbye Girl/Sunshine Fields of Love	1970	—	2.50	5.00
7427	I Wish I Knew How It Would Feel to Be Free/ Jubilee	1970	—	2.50	5.00
7448	Gentle Hearts and Gentle People/A Friend of Jesus	1970	—	2.50	5.00
7478	Lonesome Cities/Ivy That Clings to the Wall	1971	—	2.50	5.00

Albums

ELEKTRA

Number	Title (A Side/B Side)	Yr	VG	VG+	NM
EKL-135 [M]	Here We Go, Baby	1957	10.00	20.00	40.00

FIRST AMERICAN

Number	Title (A Side/B Side)	Yr	VG	VG+	NM
7766	Just a Little Love	1981	2.50	5.00	10.00

RCA VICTOR

Number	Title (A Side/B Side)	Yr	VG	VG+	NM
ANL1-2138	Baby the Rain Must Fall	1977	2.50	5.00	10.00
—Reissue of LSP-3422					
LPM-2905 [M]	One More Round	1964	3.75	7.50	15.00
LSP-2905 [S]	One More Round	1964	5.00	10.00	20.00
LPM-3301 [M]	Come Share My Life	1965	3.75	7.50	15.00
LSP-3301 [S]	Come Share My Life	1965	5.00	10.00	20.00
LPM-3422 [M]	Baby the Rain Must Fall	1965	3.00	6.00	12.00
LSP-3422 [S]	Baby the Rain Must Fall	1965	3.75	7.50	15.00
LPM-3472 [M]	It's Gonna Be Fine	1965	3.00	6.00	12.00
LSP-3472 [S]	It's Gonna Be Fine	1965	3.75	7.50	15.00
LPM-3539 [M]	The Lonely Things	1966	3.00	6.00	12.00
LSP-3539 [S]	The Lonely Things	1966	3.75	7.50	15.00
LPM-3661 [M]	Live at the Hungry I	1966	3.00	6.00	12.00
LSP-3661 [S]	Live at the Hungry I	1966	3.75	7.50	15.00
LPM-3801 [M]	For Emily, Whenever I May Find Her	1967	3.75	7.50	15.00
LSP-3801 [S]	For Emily, Whenever I May Find Her	1967	3.75	7.50	15.00
LPM-3860 [M]	Honey and Wine	1967	5.00	10.00	20.00
LSP-3860 [S]	Honey and Wine	1967	3.75	7.50	15.00
LPM-3951 [M]	The Bitter and the Sweet	1968	7.50	15.00	30.00
LSP-3951 [S]	The Bitter and the Sweet	1968	3.75	7.50	15.00
LSP-4047	We Survived the Madness	1968	3.75	7.50	15.00
LSP-4349	The Best of Glenn Yarbrough	1970	3.00	6.00	12.00
VPS-6018 [(2)]	Glenn Yarbrough Sings the Rod McKuen Songbook	1969	3.75	7.50	15.00

STAX

Number	Title (A Side/B Side)	Yr	VG	VG+	NM
STX-5506	My Sweet Lady	1975	2.50	5.00	10.00

TRADITION

Number	Title (A Side/B Side)	Yr	VG	VG+	NM
1019 [M]	Come Sit By My Side	195?	5.00	10.00	20.00
2054	The Best of Glenn Yarbrough	1967	3.75	7.50	15.00
2095	Looking Back	1970	3.00	6.00	12.00

WARNER BROS.

Number	Title (A Side/B Side)	Yr	VG	VG+	NM
WS 1736	Each of Us Alone (The Words and Music of Rod McKuen)	1968	3.00	6.00	12.00
WS 1782	Somehow, Someway	1969	3.00	6.00	12.00
WS 1817	Yarbrough Country	1969	3.00	6.00	12.00
WS 1832	Let Me Choose Life	1969	3.00	6.00	12.00
WS 1876	Jubilee	1970	3.00	6.00	12.00
WS 1911	Bend Down and Touch Me	1971	3.00	6.00	12.00

YARDBIRDS, THE

Also see JEFF BECK; ERIC CLAPTON; JIMMY PAGE; KEITH RELF; SONNY BOY WILLIAMSON (2). Ex-members of the group formed LED ZEPPELIN and RENAISSANCE.

45s

EPIC

Number	Title (A Side/B Side)	Yr	VG	VG+	NM
9709	I Wish You Could/A Certain Girl	1964	10.00	20.00	40.00
—With typographical error on A-side					
9709	I Wish You Would/A Certain Girl	1964	12.50	25.00	50.00
—With correct A-side title					
9709	I Wish You Could/I Ain't Got You	1964	—	—	—
—Unreleased?					
9709 [PS]	I Wish You Could	1964	200.00	400.00	800.00
—Promo-only picture sleeve					
9790	For Your Love/Got to Hurry	1965	3.75	7.50	15.00
9823	Heart Full of Soul/Steeled Blues	1965	3.75	7.50	15.00
9823 [PS]	Heart Full of Soul/Steeled Blues	1965	12.50	25.00	50.00
9857	I'm a Man/Still I'm Sad	1965	3.75	7.50	15.00
9881	Shapes of Things/I'm Not Talking	1966	3.75	7.50	15.00
10006	Shapes of Things/New York City Blues	1966	5.00	10.00	20.00
10006	New York City Blues/You're a Better Man Than I	1966	—	—	—
—Unreleased					
10035	Over Under Sideways Down/Jeff's Boogie	1966	3.75	7.50	15.00
10035 [PS]	Over Under Sideways Down/Jeff's Boogie	1966	12.50	25.00	50.00
10094	Happenings Ten Years Time Ago/The Nazz Are Blue	1966	3.75	7.50	15.00
10094	Happenings Ten Years Time Ago/Psycho Daisies	1966	—	—	—
—Unreleased					
10094 [PS]	Happenings Ten Years Time Ago/The Nazz Are Blue	1966	12.50	25.00	50.00
10156	Little Games/Puzzles	1967	5.00	10.00	20.00
10204	Ha Ha Said the Clown/Tinker, Tailor, Soldier, Sailor	1967	5.00	10.00	20.00
10248	Ten Little Indians/Drinking Muddy Water	1967	5.00	10.00	20.00
10303	Goodnight Sweet Josephine/Think About It	1968	12.50	25.00	50.00

Albums

ACCORD

Number	Title (A Side/B Side)	Yr	VG	VG+	NM
SN-7143 [S]	For Your Love	1981	2.00	4.00	8.00
SN-7237 [R]	Having a Rave Up with the Yardbirds	1981	2.00	4.00	8.00

COLUMBIA

Number	Title (A Side/B Side)	Yr	VG	VG+	NM
HC 48455	Roger the Engineer	1982	62.50	125.00	250.00
—"Half-Speed Mastered" edition; regular edition evidently was canceled, but copies of this exist					

COLUMBIA SPECIAL PRODUCTS

Number	Title (A Side/B Side)	Yr	VG	VG+	NM
P 13311 [S]	Live Yardbirds Featuring Jimmy Page	1976	12.50	25.00	50.00

EPIC

Number	Title (A Side/B Side)	Yr	VG	VG+	NM
LN 24167 [DJ]	For Your Love	1965	100.00	200.00	400.00
—White label promo					
LN 24167 [M]	For Your Love	1965	75.00	150.00	300.00
LN 24177 [DJ]	Having a Rave Up with the Yardbirds	1965	100.00	200.00	400.00
—White label promo					
LN 24177 [M]	Having a Rave Up with the Yardbirds	1965	20.00	40.00	80.00
LN 24210 [DJ]	Over Under Sideways Down	1966	100.00	200.00	400.00
—White label promo					
LN 24210 [M]	Over Under Sideways Down	1966	15.00	30.00	60.00
LN 24246 [DJ]	The Yardbirds' Greatest Hits	1966	75.00	150.00	300.00
—White label promo					
LN 24246 [M]	The Yardbirds' Greatest Hits	1966	12.50	25.00	50.00
LN 24313 [DJ]	Little Games	1967	75.00	150.00	300.00
LN 24313 [M]	Little Games	1967	20.00	40.00	80.00
PE 24491 [P]	Great Hits	1977	2.50	5.00	10.00
BN 26167 [P]	For Your Love	1965	50.00	100.00	200.00
—The album is in true stereo except for "Sweet Music"					
BN 26177 [R]	Having a Rave Up with the Yardbirds	1965	12.50	25.00	50.00
BN 26177 [R]	Having a Rave Up with the Yardbirds	1973	7.50	15.00	30.00
—Reissue with orange label					
BN 26210 [P]	Over Under Sideways Down	1966	20.00	40.00	80.00
—"Over Under Sideways Down" is rechanneled					
BN 26246 [P]	The Yardbirds' Greatest Hits	1966	7.50	15.00	30.00
BN 26313 [S]	Little Games	1967	12.50	25.00	50.00
EG 30135 [(2)]	The Yardbirds Featuring Performances by Jeff Beck, Eric Clapton, Jimmy Page	1970	10.00	20.00	40.00
E 30615 [S]	Live Yardbirds Featuring Jimmy Page	1972	12.50	25.00	50.00
PE 34490 [P]	Yardbirds Favorites	1977	2.50	5.00	10.00
FE 38455 [M]	Yardbirds	1983	2.50	5.00	10.00
HE 48455 [S]	Yardbirds	1983	25.00	50.00	100.00
—Half-speed mastered edition					

Number	Title (A Side/B Side)	Yr	VG	VG+	NM
RHINO					
RNDF 253 [PD]	Afternoon Tea	1982	2.00	4.00	8.00
RNLP 70128 [M]	Greatest Hits, Volume 1: 1964-1966	1986	2.00	4.00	8.00
RNLP 70189 [M]	Five Live Yardbirds	1986	2.00	4.00	8.00
SPRINGBOARD					
SPB-4036 [R]	Eric Clapton and the Yardbirds	1972	2.50	5.00	10.00
SPB-4039 [R]	Shapes of Things	1972	2.50	5.00	10.00

YARROW, PETER

Also see PETER, PAUL AND MARY.

Number	Title (A Side/B Side)	Yr	VG	VG+	NM
45s					
WARNER BROS.					
7236	Don't Remind Me Now of Time/Teenage Fair	1968	2.00	4.00	8.00
—B-side by Rosko					
7567	Don't Ever Take Away My Freedom/Greenwood	1972	—	2.50	5.00
7587	Weave Me the Sunshine/Wings of Time	1972	—	2.50	5.00
7761	Old Father Time/Isn't That So	1973	—	2.00	4.00
8114	Wanderin'/Another Chain Unbound	1975	—	2.00	4.00
Albums					
WARNER BROS.					
BS 2599	Peter	1972	3.00	6.00	12.00
BS 2730	That's Enough for Me	1973	3.00	6.00	12.00
BS 2860	Hard Times	1975	3.00	6.00	12.00
BS 2891	Peter Yarrow	1975	3.00	6.00	12.00

YATES, BILL

Number	Title (A Side/B Side)	Yr	VG	VG+	NM
45s					
SUN					
390	Stop, Wait and Listen/Don't Step on My Dog	1964	3.75	7.50	15.00
397	Carleen/Too Late to Right My Wrong	1965	3.75	7.50	15.00
399	Big Big World/I Dropped My M & M's	1966	3.75	7.50	15.00

YATES, TOMMY

Number	Title (A Side/B Side)	Yr	VG	VG+	NM
45s					
VERVE					
10556	Darling, Something's Gotta Give/If You're Looking for a Fool	1967	6.25	12.50	25.00

YELLOW BALLOON, THE

Number	Title (A Side/B Side)	Yr	VG	VG+	NM
45s					
CANTERBURY					
508	Yellow Balloon/Noollab Wolley	1967	3.00	6.00	12.00
513	Good Feeling Time/I've Got a Feeling for Love	1967	2.50	5.00	10.00
516	Stained Glass Window/Can't Get Enough of Your Love	1967	2.50	5.00	10.00
Albums					
CANTERBURY					
CLPM-1502 [M]	The Yellow Balloon	1967	6.25	12.50	25.00
CLPS-1502 [S]	The Yellow Balloon	1967	7.50	15.00	30.00

YELLOW PAYGES, THE

Number	Title (A Side/B Side)	Yr	VG	VG+	NM
45s					
SHOWPLACE					
216	Sleeping Minds/Never See the Good in Me	1967	7.50	15.00	30.00
217	Love in the Making/Jezebel	1967	5.00	10.00	20.00
UNI					
55043	Our Time Is Running Out/Sweet Sunrise	1967	3.75	7.50	15.00
55072	Judge Carter/Childhood Friends	1968	3.75	7.50	15.00
55089	You're Just What I Was Looking For Today/Crowd Pleaser	1968	3.75	7.50	15.00
55107	The Two of Us/Never Put Away My Love for You	1969	3.75	7.50	15.00
55153	Would You Mind If I Loved You/Vanilla on My Mind	1969	3.75	7.50	15.00
55176	Slow Down/Fresco Annie	1969	3.75	7.50	15.00
55192	Little Women/Follow the Bouncing Ball	1970	3.75	7.50	15.00
55225	I'm a Man/Home Again	1970	3.75	7.50	15.00
Albums					
UNI					
73045	The Yellow Payges, Volume 1	1969	7.50	15.00	30.00

YELVINGTON, MALCOLM

Number	Title (A Side/B Side)	Yr	VG	VG+	NM
45s					
SUN					
211	Drinkin' Wine Spo-Dee-O-Dee/Just Rolling Along	1954	25.00	50.00	100.00
246	Rockin' with My Baby/It's Me Baby	1956	25.00	50.00	100.00

YES

Also see STEVE HOWE; RICK WAKEMAN.

Number	Title (A Side/B Side)	Yr	VG	VG+	NM
12-Inch Singles					
ATCO					
PR 529 [DJ]	Owner of a Lonely Heart (Edit)/Owner of a Lonely Heart (LP Version)	1983	3.00	6.00	12.00
PR 587 [DJ]	Leave It (3 versions)	1984	2.00	4.00	8.00
PR 796 [DJ]	Hold On (Edit)/Hold On (LP Version)	1985	3.00	6.00	12.00
PR 1133 [DJ]	Rhythm of Love (3 versions)	1987	2.50	5.00	10.00
PR 2088 [DJ]	Love Will Find a Way (Edit)/Love Will Find a Way (LP Version)	1987	3.00	6.00	12.00
96722	Rhythm of Love (3 versions)/City of Love (Live Edit)	1987	2.50	5.00	10.00
96964	Leave It (3 versions)	1984	2.00	4.00	8.00
96976	Owner of a Lonely Heart (Special Red & Blue Dance Version)/(Edit)/Our Song	1983	3.00	6.00	12.00
45s					
ARISTA					
2218	Lift Me Up/Give and Take	1991	—	2.00	4.00
ATCO					
99419	Rhythm of Love/City of Love	1987	—	—	3.00
99419 [PS]	Rhythm of Love/City of Love	1987	—	—	3.00
99449	Love Will Find a Way/Holy Lamb	1987	—	—	3.00
99449 [PS]	Love Will Find a Way/Holy Lamb	1987	—	—	3.00
99745	It Can Happen/It Can Happen (Live)	1984	—	—	3.00
99745 [PS]	It Can Happen/It Can Happen (Live)	1984	—	—	3.00
99787	Leave It/Leave It (Acapella)	1984	—	—	3.00
99787 [PS]	Leave It/Leave It (Acapella)	1984	—	—	3.00
99817	Owner of a Lonely Heart/Our Song	1983	—	—	3.00
99817 [PS]	Owner of a Lonely Heart/Our Song	1983	—	—	3.00
ATLANTIC					
2709	Every Little Thing/Sweetness	1970	—	3.00	6.00
2819	Your Move/Clap	1971	—	2.50	5.00
2854	Roundabout/Long Distance Runaround	1972	—	2.50	5.00
2854 [DJ]	Roundabout (mono/stereo)	1972	25.00	50.00	100.00
—Promo only on yellow vinyl					
2899	America/Total Mass Retain	1972	—	2.50	5.00
2920	And You And I (Part 1)/And You And I (Part 2)	1972	—	2.50	5.00
3242	Sound Chaser/Soon	1975	—	2.50	5.00
3416	Awaken (Part 1)/Wonderful Stories	1977	—	2.50	5.00
3534	Don't Kill the Whale/Release, Release	1978	—	2.50	5.00
3767	Into the Lens/Does It Really Happen	1980	—	2.50	5.00
3801	Run Through the Light/White Car	1981	—	2.50	5.00
Albums					
ARISTA					
AL 8643	Union	1991	5.00	10.00	20.00
—U.S. vinyl available only through Columbia House					
ATCO					
90125	90125	1984	2.00	4.00	8.00
90474	9012Live: The Solos	1985	2.00	4.00	8.00
90522	Big Generator	1987	2.00	4.00	8.00
ATLANTIC					
SD 3-100 [(3)]	Yessongs	1973	4.50	9.00	18.00
PR 260 [DJ]	Yes Solo LP Sampler	1976	6.25	12.50	25.00
PR 285 [DJ]	Yes Music: An Evening with Jon Anderson	1977	12.50	25.00	50.00
SD 2-510 [(2)]	Yesshows	1980	3.00	6.00	12.00
SD 2-908	Tales from Topographic Oceans	1974	3.75	7.50	15.00
SD 2-908 [DJ]	Tales from Topographic Oceans	1974	7.50	15.00	30.00
—Promo copies banded for airplay					
SD 7211	Fragile	1972	3.00	6.00	12.00
7244 [DJ]	Close to the Edge	1972	12.50	25.00	50.00
—White label mono copies banded for airplay					
SD 7244	Close to the Edge	1972	3.00	6.00	12.00
SD 8243	Yes	1969	3.00	6.00	12.00
SD 8273	Time and a Word	1970	3.00	6.00	12.00
SD 8283	The Yes Album	1971	3.00	6.00	12.00
SD 16019	Drama	1980	2.50	5.00	10.00
SD 18103	Yesterdays	1975	2.50	5.00	10.00
SD 18122	Relayer	1975	2.50	5.00	10.00
SD 18122 [DJ]	Relayer	1975	5.00	10.00	20.00
—Promo copies banded for airplay					
SD 19106	Going for the One	1977	2.50	5.00	10.00
SD 19131	The Yes Album	1977	2.00	4.00	8.00
SD 19132	Fragile	1977	2.00	4.00	8.00
SD 19133	Close to the Edge	1977	2.00	4.00	8.00
SD 19134	Yesterdays	1977	2.00	4.00	8.00
SD 19135	Relayer	1977	2.00	4.00	8.00
SD 19202	Tormato	1978	2.50	5.00	10.00
SD 19320	Classic Yes	1982	3.75	7.50	15.00
—Original copies include a bonus 7-inch promo single					
SD 19320	Classic Yes	1982	2.50	5.00	10.00
—With bonus single missing					
MOBILE FIDELITY					
1-077	Close to the Edge	1982	15.00	30.00	60.00
—Audiophile vinyl					

YESTER, JERRY

Also see THE LOVIN' SPOONFUL.

Number	Title (A Side/B Side)	Yr	VG	VG+	NM
45s					
DUNHILL					
4042	The Sound of Summer Showers/Ashes Have Turned	1966	2.50	5.00	10.00
4061	I Can Live Without You/Garden of Imagining	1967	2.50	5.00	10.00

YESTERDAY'S FOLK

Number	Title (A Side/B Side)	Yr	VG	VG+	NM
Albums					
BUDDAH					
BDS-5035	U.S. 69	1969	5.00	10.00	20.00

YETTI-MEN, THE / THE UPPA TRIO

Number	Title (A Side/B Side)	Yr	VG	VG+	NM
Albums					
KAL					
KB-4348	The Yetti-Men/The Uppa Trio	1967	200.00	400.00	600.00

YORK, RUSTY

Number	Title (A Side/B Side)	Yr	VG	VG+	NM
45s					
CAPITOL					
4663	That's What I Need/Just Like You	1961	3.75	7.50	15.00
CHESS					
1730	Sugaree/Red Rooster	1959	5.00	10.00	20.00
GAYLORD					
6428	Sally Was a Good Old Girl/I Might Just Walk Right Back Again	1962	3.75	7.50	15.00
KING					
5103	Peggy Sue/Shake 'Em Up Baby	1958	6.25	12.50	25.00
5511	Love Struck/Goodnight Cincinnati, Good Morning Tennessee	1961	3.75	7.50	15.00
5587	Tramblin'/Tore Up Over You	1961	3.75	7.50	15.00
NOTE					
10021	Sugaree/Red Rooster	1959	6.25	12.50	25.00
P.J.					
100	Sugaree/Red Rooster	1959	7.50	15.00	30.00
SAGE AND SAND					
266	Sadie May/Margaret Ann	1960	5.00	10.00	20.00

YOST, DENNIS, AND THE CLASSICS IV

See CLASSICS IV.

YOUNG, BARRY

Number	Title (A Side/B Side)	Yr	VG	VG+	NM
45s					
COLUMBIA					
43584	A Heart Without a Home/He'll Have to Go	1966	2.00	4.00	8.00
43723	I Love You So Much It Hurts/Cryin' Street	1966	2.00	4.00	8.00
DOT					
16756	One Has My Name (The Other Has My Heart)/ Show Me the Way	1965	2.50	5.00	10.00
16819	Since You Have Gone from Me/Nashville, Tennessee	1966	2.00	4.00	8.00
Albums					
DOT					
DLP 3672 [M]	One Has My Name	1965	5.00	10.00	20.00
DLP 25672 [S]	One Has My Name	1965	6.25	12.50	25.00

YOUNG, BOBBY

Number	Title (A Side/B Side)	Yr	VG	VG+	NM
45s					
GUYDEN					
2087	To Each His Own/The Only Girl for Me	1963	62.50	125.00	250.00

YOUNG, CATHY

Number	Title (A Side/B Side)	Yr	VG	VG+	NM
45s					
MAINSTREAM					
703	Spoonful/Circus	1969	3.75	7.50	15.00
Albums					
MAINSTREAM					
S-6121	A Spoonful of Cathy Young	1968	10.00	20.00	40.00

YOUNG, COLIN

Formerly of THE FOUNDATIONS.

Number	Title (A Side/B Side)	Yr	VG	VG+	NM
45s					
UNI					
55286	You're No Good/Amy Time at All	1971	—	3.00	6.00

YOUNG, DONNY

See JOHNNY PAYCHECK.

YOUNG, GEORGIE

Number	Title (A Side/B Side)	Yr	VG	VG+	NM
45s					
CAMEO					
150	Nine More Miles/The Sneak	1958	6.25	12.50	25.00
166	Feels So Good/Two Weeks with Pay	1959	5.00	10.00	20.00
168	Georgie Porgie/Where Is Your Heart	1959	5.00	10.00	20.00
CHANCELLOR					
1066	Autumn Lovers/Indian Summer	1960	3.75	7.50	15.00
1069	Birdland Hully Gully/Marie	1961	3.75	7.50	15.00
COLUMBIA					
42773	Supercar/Chicken Scratch	1963	7.50	15.00	30.00
FORTUNE					
524	Shakin' Shelley/Buggin' Baby	1957	6.25	12.50	25.00
MERCURY					
71259	Can't Stop Me/Come Back to Me	1958	20.00	40.00	80.00
PARKWAY					
809	Gold Rush/That's Tough	1960	5.00	10.00	20.00
SWAN					
4059	Yogi/By George	1960	3.75	7.50	15.00

YOUNG, JESSE COLIN

Also see THE YOUNGBLOODS.

Number	Title (A Side/B Side)	Yr	VG	VG+	NM
45s					
ELEKTRA					
45530	Rave On/Maui Sunrise	1978	—	2.00	4.00
46026	Sanctuary/City Boy	1979	—	2.00	4.00
WARNER BROS.					
7404	Peace Song/Pretty in the Fair	1970	—	3.00	6.00
7581	Good Times/Peace Song	1972	—	2.50	5.00
7581 [PS]	Good Times/Peace Song	1972	2.50	5.00	10.00
7618	It's a Lovely Day/Sweet Little Child	1972	—	2.50	5.00
7749	Evenin'/Morning Sun	1973	—	2.50	5.00
7816	Cuckoo/Light Shine	1974	—	2.50	5.00
8053	Susan/Barbados	1974	—	2.50	5.00
8106	Songbird/'Til You Come Back Home	1975	—	2.50	5.00
8129	Sugar Babe/Motorhome	1975	—	2.50	5.00
8225	Sunlight/Peace Song	1976	—	2.50	5.00
8352	Love on the Wing/(B-side unknown)	1977	—	2.50	5.00
8398	Fool/Higher and Higher	1977	—	2.50	5.00
Albums					
CAPITOL					
T 2070 [M]	The Soul of a City Boy	1964	12.50	25.00	50.00
ST-11267	The Soul of a City Boy	1974	3.00	6.00	12.00
—Reissue of 2070					
N-16129	The Soul of a City Boy	1981	2.00	4.00	8.00
—Budget-line reissue					
CYPRESS					
0103	The Highway Is for Heroes	1987	2.50	5.00	10.00
ELEKTRA					
6E-157	American Dreams	1978	2.50	5.00	10.00
MERCURY					
MG 21005 [M]	Young Blood	1965	7.50	15.00	30.00
SR 61005 [S]	Young Blood	1965	10.00	20.00	40.00
RACCOON					
BS 2588	Together	1972	3.00	6.00	12.00
WARNER BROS.					
BS 2734	Song for Juli	1973	2.50	5.00	10.00
BS 2790	Light Shine	1974	2.50	5.00	10.00
BS 2845	Songbird	1975	2.50	5.00	10.00
BS 2913	On the Road	1976	2.50	5.00	10.00
BS 3033	Love on the Wing	1977	2.50	5.00	10.00

YOUNG, KATHY, AND THE INNOCENTS

Also see THE INNOCENTS.

Number	Title (A Side/B Side)	Yr	VG	VG+	NM
45s					
INDIGO					
108	A Thousand Stars/Eddie My Darling	1960	7.50	15.00	30.00
115	Happy Birthday Blues/Someone to Love	1961	5.00	10.00	20.00
115 [PS]	Happy Birthday Blues/Someone to Love	1961	12.50	25.00	50.00
121	Our Parents Talked It Over/Just As Though You Were Here	1961	5.00	10.00	20.00
125	Magic Is the Night/Du Du'nt Du	1961	5.00	10.00	20.00
125 [PS]	Magic Is the Night/Du Du'nt Du	1961	12.50	25.00	50.00
137	Baby, Oh Baby/The Great Pretender	1961	5.00	10.00	20.00
141	Time/Dee Dee Di Oh	1962	5.00	10.00	20.00
146	Lonely Blue Nights/I'll Hang My Letters Out to Dry	1962	5.00	10.00	20.00
147	Send Her Away/Dream Awhile	1962	5.00	10.00	20.00
MONOGRAM					
506	Dreamboy/I'll Love That Man	1962	5.00	10.00	20.00
PORT					
3025	A Thousand Stars/Eddie My Darling	196?	—	2.50	5.00
STARFIRE					
112	Sparkle and Shine/Please Love Me Forever	1979	—	2.50	5.00
7-Inch Extended Plays					
INDIGO					
1001	Sparkle and Shine/Eddie My Darling//Happy Birthday Blues/Angel on My Shoulder	1961	50.00	100.00	200.00
1001 [PS]	Kathy Young	1961	50.00	100.00	200.00
Albums					
INDIGO					
LP-504 [M]	The Sound of Kathy Young	1961	75.00	150.00	300.00

YOUNG, LEON

Number	Title (A Side/B Side)	Yr	VG	VG+	NM
45s					
ATCO					
6274	Sea Winds/Spinning Jenny	1963	2.00	4.00	8.00
6301	John, Paul, George and Ringo/Westward Ho	1964	3.00	6.00	12.00
Albums					
ATCO					
33-163 [M]	Liverpool Sound for Strings	1964	6.25	12.50	25.00
SD 33-163 [S]	Liverpool Sound for Strings	1964	7.50	15.00	30.00

YOUNG, NEIL

Also see BUFFALO SPRINGFIELD; CROSBY, STILLS, NASH AND YOUNG; THE STILLS-YOUNG BAND.

Number	Title (A Side/B Side)	Yr	VG	VG+	NM
12-Inch Singles					
GEFFEN					
PRO-A-2373 [DJ]	Get Back to the Country (Long)/Get Back to the Country (Short)	1985	2.50	5.00	10.00
PRO-A-2528 [DJ]	Weight of the World (same on both sides)	1986	2.50	5.00	10.00
PRO-A-2623 [DJ]	People on the Street (same on both sides)	1986	2.50	5.00	10.00
PRO-A-2811 [DJ]	Too Lonely (Remix Edit) (same on both sides)	1987	2.50	5.00	10.00
REPRISE					
PRO2-901 [DJ]	Hawks & Doves/Union Man	1980	2.50	5.00	10.00
—Blue vinyl					
49895	Southern Pacific/Motor City	1982	75.00	150.00	300.00
—Picture disc, triangle-shaped					
49895	Southern Pacific/Motor City	1982	50.00	100.00	200.00
—Green vinyl, triangle-shaped					
49895	Southern Pacific/Motor City	1982	2.50	5.00	10.00
—Red vinyl, triangle-shaped					
49895	Southern Pacific/Motor City	1982	2.50	5.00	10.00
—Black vinyl, triangle-shaped					
45s					
COLUMBIA					
05566	Are There Any More Real Cowboys/I'm a Memory	1985	—	—	3.00
—A-side: Willie Nelson and Neil Young. B-side: Willie Nelson					
GEFFEN					
28196	Mideast Vacation/Long Walk Home	1987	—	—	3.00
28623	Weight of the World/Pressure	1986	—	—	3.00
28623 [PS]	Weight of the World/Pressure	1986	—	—	3.00
28753	Old Ways/Once an Angel	1986	—	—	3.00
28883	Get Back to the Country/Misfits	1985	—	—	3.00
29433	Cry, Cry, Cry/Payola Blues	1983	—	2.00	4.00
29574	Wonderin'/Payola Blues	1983	—	2.00	4.00
29574 [PS]	Wonderin'/Payola Blues	1983	—	2.00	4.00
29707	Mr. Soul/Mr. Soul	1983	—	2.00	4.00
29887	Little Thing Called Love/We Are In Control	1982	—	2.00	4.00
29887 [PS]	Little Thing Called Love/We Are In Control	1982	—	2.00	4.00
REPRISE					
0746	Only Love Can Break Your Heart/Cinnamon Girl	1971	—	—	3.00
—"Back to Back Hits" release					
0785	The Loner/Sugar Mountain	1968	30.00	60.00	120.00
0819	Everyone Knows This Is Nowhere/The Emperor of Wyoming	1969	25.00	50.00	100.00
0819 [DJ]	Everyone Knows This Is Nowhere/The Emperor of Wyoming	1969	125.00	250.00	500.00
—Alternate acoustic version of A-side					
0819 [DJ]	Everyone Knows This Is Nowhere/The Emperor of Wyoming	1969	7.50	15.00	30.00
—Standard version of A-side, with "RE-1" in trail-off wax					
0836	Down By the River/(When You're On the) Losing End	1969	12.50	25.00	50.00
0861	Oh, Lonesome Me/Sugar Mountain	1969	12.50	25.00	50.00
0898	I've Been Waiting for You/Oh, Lonesome Me	1970	12.50	25.00	50.00
0911	Cinnamon Girl/Sugar Mountain	1970	—	2.50	5.00
0958	Only Love Can Break Your Heart/Birds	1970	—	2.50	5.00
0992	When You Dance I Can Really Love/Sugar Mountain	1971	—	2.50	5.00
1023	Brave Belt/Rock and Roll Band	1971	—	2.50	5.00
—With Graham Nash					

Number	Title (A Side/B Side)	Yr	VG	VG+	NM
1065	Heart of Gold/Sugar Mountain	1971	—	2.00	4.00
—Without reference to "Harvest" LP on label					
1065	Heart of Gold/Sugar Mountain	1971	—	2.50	5.00
—With reference to "Harvest" LP on label					
1084	Old Man/The Needle and the Damage Done	1972	—	2.00	4.00
1099	War Song/The Needle and the Damage Done	1972	—	2.00	4.00
—With Graham Nash					
1152	Heart of Gold/Old Man	1972	—	—	3.00
—"Back to Back Hits" release					
1184	Time Fades Away/The Last Train to Tulsa (Live)	1973	2.50	5.00	10.00
1209	Walk On/For the Turnstiles	1974	—	2.00	4.00
1209 [DJ]	Walk On (same on both sides)	1974	3.75	7.50	15.00
—Small hole					
1209 [DJ]	Walk On (same on both sides)	1974	2.50	5.00	10.00
—Large hole					
1344	Lookin' for a Love/Sugar Mountain	1976	—	2.00	4.00
1350	Drive Back/Stupid Girl	1976	—	2.00	4.00
1390	Hey Baby/Homegrown	1977	—	2.00	4.00
1391	Like a Hurricane/Hold Back the Tears	1978	—	2.00	4.00
1393	Sugar Mountain/The Needle and the Damage Done	1978	—	2.00	4.00
1395	Comes a Time/Motorcycle Mama	1978	—	2.00	4.00
1395 [PS]	Comes a Time/Motorcycle Mama	1978	—	2.00	4.00
1396	Four Strong Winds/Human Highway	1979	—	2.00	4.00
18685	Harvest Moon/Old King	1992	—	2.00	4.00
19483	Over and Over	1990	—	—	—
—Cassette only					
22776	Rockin' in the Free World/Rockin' in the Free World (Live)	1989	—	2.00	4.00
22776 [DJ]	Rockin' in the Free World (same on both sides)	1989	2.50	5.00	10.00
22776 [PS]	Rockin' in the Free World/Rockin' in the Free World (Live)	1989	—	2.00	4.00
27848	This Note's For You (LP Version)/This Note's For You (Edited Live Version)	1988	—	2.00	4.00
27848 [PS]	This Note's For You (LP Version)/This Note's For You (Edited Live Version)	1988	—	2.00	4.00
27908	Ten Men Workin'/I'm Goin'	1988	—	—	3.00
27908 [PS]	Ten Men Workin'/I'm Goin'	1988	2.00	4.00	8.00
49031	Rust Never Sleeps (Hey Hey, My My [Into the Black])/Rust Never Sleeps (My My, Hey Hey [Out of the Blue])	1979	—	2.00	4.00
49031 [PS]	Rust Never Sleeps (Hey Hey, My My [Into the Black])/Rust Never Sleeps (My My, Hey Hey [Out of the Blue])	1979	2.50	5.00	10.00
49189	The Loner/Cinnamon Girl	1980	—	2.00	4.00
49555	Hawks and Doves/Union Man	1980	—	—	3.00
49555 [PS]	Hawks and Doves/Union Man	1980	—	—	3.00
49641	Stayin' Power/Captain America	1980	—	—	3.00
49870	Southern Pacific/Motor City	1981	—	—	3.00
50014	Opera Star/Surfer Joe and Moe the Sleaze	1982	—	—	3.00

Albums

GEFFEN

Number	Title (A Side/B Side)	Yr	VG	VG+	NM
GHS 2018	Trans	1982	3.75	7.50	15.00
—First pressings have a sticker on rear cover explaining the absence of "If You've Got Love"					
GHS 2018	Trans	1982	2.50	5.00	10.00
—Later pressings have neither sticker nor title of absent song					
GHS 2018 [DJ]	Trans	1982	5.00	10.00	20.00
—Promo on Quiex II audiophile vinyl					
GHS 4013	Everybody's Rockin'	1983	5.00	10.00	20.00
—Promo on Quiex II audiophile vinyl					
GHS 4013	Everybody's Rockin'	1983	2.50	5.00	10.00
GHS 24068	Old Ways	1985	3.00	6.00	12.00
GHS 24109	Landing on Water	1986	3.00	6.00	12.00
GHS 24154	Life	1987	3.00	6.00	12.00
R 134125	Landing on Water	1986	3.75	7.50	15.00
—RCA Music Service edition					
R 144439	Life	1987	3.75	7.50	15.00
—BMG Direct Marketing edition					
R 163233	Old Ways	1985	3.75	7.50	15.00
—RCA Music Service edition					

MOBILE FIDELITY

Number	Title (A Side/B Side)	Yr	VG	VG+	NM
1-252	Old Ways	1996	5.00	10.00	20.00
—Audiophile vinyl					

NAUTILUS

Number	Title (A Side/B Side)	Yr	VG	VG+	NM
NR-44	Harvest	1982	37.50	75.00	150.00
—Audiophile vinyl					

REPRISE

Number	Title (A Side/B Side)	Yr	VG	VG+	NM
MS 2032	Harvest	1972	3.75	7.50	15.00
—First pressings have textured cover and lyric insert					
MS 2032	Harvest	1972	2.50	5.00	10.00
M 2151 [M-DJ]	Time Fades Away	1973	25.00	50.00	100.00
—Special mono pressing for radio stations					
MS 2151	Time Fades Away	1973	2.50	5.00	10.00
MS 2151 [S-DJ]	Time Fades Away	1973	50.00	100.00	200.00
—With a cardboard inner sleeve, withdrawn after the earliest pressing					
MS 2180	On the Beach	1974	2.50	5.00	10.00
MS 2221	Tonight's the Night	1975	2.50	5.00	10.00
MS 2242	Zuma	1975	2.50	5.00	10.00
3RS 2257 [(3)]	Decade	1977	5.00	10.00	20.00
3RS 2257 [(3) DJ]	Decade	1977	125.00	250.00	500.00
—Test pressing; "Campaigner" contains extra verse deleted from the final version					
MSK 2261	American Stars 'N' Bars	1977	2.50	5.00	10.00
MSK 2266	Comes A Time	1978	2.50	5.00	10.00
—With "Peace of Mind" as the last song on side 1. Covers can list either "Lotta Love" or "Peace of Mind."					
MSK 2266	Comes A Time	1978	18.75	37.50	75.00
—With "Lotta Love" listed and playing as the last song on side 1					
MSK 2266 [DJ]	Give to the Wind	1978	250.00	500.00	1000.
—Test pressing; plain white jacket with inserts and STOCK COPY LABEL. Title changed to "Comes A Time" for commercial release.					
MSK 2277	Harvest	1978	2.00	4.00	8.00
—Brown "Reprise" label; new number					
MSK 2282	Everybody Knows This Is Nowhere	1978	2.00	4.00	8.00
—Brown "Reprise" label; new number					
MSK 2283	After the Gold Rush	1978	10.00	20.00	40.00
—Contains remixed extended version of "When You Dance I Can Really Love." Title on cover in red, "RE 2" in trail-off vinyl					
HS 2295	Rust Never Sleeps	1979	2.50	5.00	10.00
2RX 2296 [(2)]	Live Rust	1979	3.75	7.50	15.00
HS 2297	Hawks and Doves	1980	2.50	5.00	10.00
HS 2304	Re-Ac-Tor	1981	2.50	5.00	10.00
RS 6317	Neil Young	1968	50.00	100.00	200.00
—Brown and orange "Reprise/W7" label, no name on front cover, no "RE-1" in trail-off wax					
RS 6317	Neil Young	1969	15.00	30.00	60.00
—Re-release: Brown and orange "Reprise/W7" label, no name on front cover, four tracks remixed ("RE 1" in trail-off wax)					
RS 6317	Neil Young	1970	3.75	7.50	15.00
—Reissue: Brown "Reprise" label, Neil Young's name is now on front cover					
RS 6349	Everybody Knows This Is Nowhere	1969	7.50	15.00	30.00
—Brown and orange "Reprise/W7" label					
RS 6349	Everybody Knows This Is Nowhere	1970	3.75	7.50	15.00
—Brown "Reprise" label					
RS 6349 [DJ]	Everybody Knows This Is Nowhere	1969	18.75	37.50	75.00
—White label promo					
RS 6383	After the Gold Rush	1970	10.00	20.00	40.00
—Brown and orange label; photo of Marc Bolan (of T. Rex) appears erroneously in gatefold					
RS 6383	After the Gold Rush	1970	8.75	17.50	35.00
—Brown and orange label; photo of Neil Young appears erroneously printed upside down in gatefold					
RS 6383	After the Gold Rush	1970	3.75	7.50	15.00
—Brown and orange label; all photos correct					
RS 6383	After the Gold Rush	1970	2.50	5.00	10.00
—Brown "Reprise" label					
2XS 6480 [(2)]	Journey Through the Past (Soundtrack)	1972	5.00	10.00	20.00
25719	This Note's for You	1988	3.00	6.00	12.00
25899	Freedom	1989	3.75	7.50	15.00
26315	Ragged Glory	1990	5.00	10.00	20.00
45749 [(2)]	Sleeps with Angels	1994	3.75	7.50	15.00
45934 [(2)]	Mirror Ball	1995	3.75	7.50	15.00
—With Pearl Jam (uncredited)					
46291 [(2)]	Broken Arrow	1996	3.75	7.50	15.00
46652 [(2)]	Year of the Horse	1997	3.75	7.50	15.00
SMAS-94285	Harvest	1972	6.25	12.50	25.00
—Capitol Record Club edition					
R 113998	Harvest	1972	3.00	6.00	12.00
—RCA Music Service edition					
R 154182	This Note's for You	1987	3.00	6.00	12.00
—BMG Direct Marketing edition					

VAPOR

Number	Title (A Side/B Side)	Yr	VG	VG+	NM
46171 [(2)]	Dead Man (Soundtrack)	1996	3.00	6.00	12.00

WARNER BROS.

Number	Title (A Side/B Side)	Yr	VG	VG+	NM
WBMS-107 [DJ]	The Warner Bros. Music Show	1979	12.50	25.00	50.00
—Promo-only interview album					

YOUNG AMERICANS, THE

45s

ABC

Number	Title (A Side/B Side)	Yr	VG	VG+	NM
10940	Born to Be with You/One by One	1967	—	3.00	6.00
10977	Beautiful, Beautiful World/Little Girl	1967	—	3.00	6.00
10998	Here I Am (Billy Guy)/As Quiet As It's Kept	1967	—	3.00	6.00
11044	Happiness/Oh, What a Lovely Day	1968	—	3.00	6.00
11220	On the Blue Cloud Sky/Blackberry Organ	1969	—	3.00	6.00

Albums

ABC

Number	Title (A Side/B Side)	Yr	VG	VG+	NM
586 [M]	While We're Young	1967	3.75	7.50	15.00
S-586 [S]	While We're Young	1967	3.00	6.00	12.00
S-626	The Wonderful World of the Young	1968	3.00	6.00	12.00
S-659	Time for Livin'	1969	3.00	6.00	12.00

YOUNG GENERATION, THE

With Janis Siegel, pre-MANHATTAN TRANSFER.

45s

RED BIRD

Number	Title (A Side/B Side)	Yr	VG	VG+	NM
10-065	Hideaway/Hymn of Love	1966	3.75	7.50	15.00

YOUNG-HOLT UNLIMITED

45s

BRUNSWICK

Number	Title (A Side/B Side)	Yr	VG	VG+	NM
55305	Wack Wack/This Little Light of Mine	1966	2.00	4.00	8.00
—As "The Young-Holt Trio"					
55317	Ain't There Something Money Can't Buy/Mellow Yellow	1967	2.00	4.00	8.00
—As "The Young-Holt Trio"					
55338	The Beat Goes On/Doin' the Thing	1967	2.00	4.00	8.00
—As "The Young-Holt Trio"					
55356	Dig Her Walk/You Gimmie Thum	1967	2.00	4.00	8.00
55374	Soul Sister/Give It Up	1968	2.00	4.00	8.00
55391	Soulful Strut/Country Slicker Joe	1968	2.00	4.00	8.00
55400	Who's Making Love/Just Ain't No Love	1969	—	3.00	6.00
55410	Just a Melody/Young and Holtful	1969	—	3.00	6.00
55417	Straight Ahead/California Montage	1969	—	3.00	6.00
55420	Soulful Samba/Horoscope	1969	—	3.00	6.00

COTILLION

Number	Title (A Side/B Side)	Yr	VG	VG+	NM
44092	Mellow Dreaming/Got to Get My Baby Back Home	1970	—	2.50	5.00
44111	Luv Bugg/Wah Wah Man	1971	—	2.50	5.00
44120	Hot Pants/I'll Be There	1971	—	2.50	5.00

PAULA

Number	Title (A Side/B Side)	Yr	VG	VG+	NM
380	Superfly/Give Me Your Love	1973	—	2.50	5.00
382	Could It Be I'm Falling in Love/HeyPancho	1973	—	2.50	5.00

Albums

ATLANTIC

Number	Title (A Side/B Side)	Yr	VG	VG+	NM
SD 1634	Oh Girl	1973	3.00	6.00	12.00

BRUNSWICK

Number	Title (A Side/B Side)	Yr	VG	VG+	NM
BL 54121 [M]	Wack-Wack	1966	5.00	10.00	20.00
—As "Young-Holt Trio"					
BL 54125 [M]	On Stage	1967	5.00	10.00	20.00
—As "Young-Holt Trio"					

Number	Title (A Side/B Side)	Yr	VG	VG+	NM
BL 54128 [M]	The Beat Goes On	1967	7.50	15.00	30.00
BL 754121 [S]	Wack-Wack	1966	5.00	10.00	20.00
—As "Young-Holt Trio"					
BL 754125 [S]	On Stage	1967	5.00	10.00	20.00
—As "Young-Holt Trio"					
BL 754128 [S]	The Beat Goes On	1967	5.00	10.00	20.00
BL 754141	Funky But!	1968	5.00	10.00	20.00
BL 754144	Soulful Strut	1968	3.75	7.50	15.00
BL 754150	Just a Melody	1969	3.75	7.50	15.00

CADET

Number	Title (A Side/B Side)	Yr	VG	VG+	NM
LP-791 [M]	Feature Spot	1967	7.50	15.00	30.00
LPS-791 [S]	Feature Spot	1967	5.00	10.00	20.00
—As "Eldee Young and Red Holt (of the Ramsey Lewis Trio)"					

COTILLION

Number	Title (A Side/B Side)	Yr	VG	VG+	NM
SD 18001	Mellow Dreamin'	1971	3.00	6.00	12.00
SD 18004	Born Again	1972	3.00	6.00	12.00

PAULA

Number	Title (A Side/B Side)	Yr	VG	VG+	NM
LPS-4002	Super Fly	1973	5.00	10.00	20.00

YOUNG LADS, THE

45s

FELICE

Number	Title (A Side/B Side)	Yr	VG	VG+	NM
712	Graduation Kiss/Night After Night	1963	25.00	50.00	100.00

NEIL

Number	Title (A Side/B Side)	Yr	VG	VG+	NM
100	Moonlight/I'm in Love	1956	17.50	35.00	70.00

YOUNG LIONS, THE

45s

DOT

Number	Title (A Side/B Side)	Yr	VG	VG+	NM
16172	Little Girl/It Would Be	1960	12.50	25.00	50.00

YOUNG RASCALS, THE

See THE RASCALS.

YOUNG WORLD SINGERS, THE

45s

DECCA

Number	Title (A Side/B Side)	Yr	VG	VG+	NM
31660	Ringo for President/Like That	1964	3.00	6.00	12.00

YOUNGBLOODS, THE

Also see JESSE COLIN YOUNG.

45s

MERCURY

Number	Title (A Side/B Side)	Yr	VG	VG+	NM
72583	Sometimes/Rider	1966	5.00	10.00	20.00
—As "Jesse Colin and the Youngbloods"					
73068	Sometimes/Rider	1969	2.50	5.00	10.00

RCA VICTOR

Number	Title (A Side/B Side)	Yr	VG	VG+	NM
47-9015	Grizzly Bear/Tears Are Falling	1966	2.50	5.00	10.00
47-9142	Merry-Go-Round/Foolin' Around (The Waltz)	1967	2.50	5.00	10.00
47-9222	The Wine Song/Euphoria	1967	2.50	5.00	10.00
47-9264	Get Together/All My Dreams Blue	1967	3.75	7.50	15.00
47-9360	Fool Me/I Can Tell	1967	2.50	5.00	10.00
47-9422	Dreamer's Dream/Quicksand	1967	2.50	5.00	10.00
47-9752	Get Together/Beautiful	1969	2.00	4.00	8.00
74-0129	On Sir Francis Drake/Darkness, Darkness	1969	2.00	4.00	8.00
74-0270	Sunlight/Trillium	1969	2.00	4.00	8.00
74-0342	On Sir Francis Drake/Darkness, Darkness	1970	—	3.50	7.00
74-0380	On Sir Francis Drake/Darkness, Darkness	1970	—	3.00	6.00
74-0465	Reason to Believe/Sunlight	1971	—	3.00	6.00

WARNER BROS.

Number	Title (A Side/B Side)	Yr	VG	VG+	NM
7445	Hippie from Olema/Misty Roses	1970	—	2.50	5.00
7499	It's a Lovely Day/Ice Bag	1971	—	2.50	5.00
7563	Will the Circle Be Unbroken/Light Shine	1972	—	2.50	5.00
7639	Dreamboat/Kind Hearted Woman	1972	—	2.50	5.00
7660	Running Bear/Kind Hearted Woman	1972	—	2.50	5.00

Albums

MERCURY

Number	Title (A Side/B Side)	Yr	VG	VG+	NM
SR-61273	Two Trips	1970	6.25	12.50	25.00
—Gold border on cover					
SR-61273	Two Trips	1971	5.00	10.00	20.00
—Red border on cover					

RACCOON

Number	Title (A Side/B Side)	Yr	VG	VG+	NM
WS 1878	Rock Festival	1970	3.00	6.00	12.00
BS 2563	Ride the Wind	1971	3.00	6.00	12.00
BS 2566	Good and Dusty	1971	3.00	6.00	12.00
BS 2653	High on a Ridge Top	1972	3.00	6.00	12.00

RCA VICTOR

Number	Title (A Side/B Side)	Yr	VG	VG+	NM
AYL1-3680	The Best of the Youngbloods	1980	2.00	4.00	8.00
—"Best Buy Series" reissue					
LPM-3724 [M]	The Youngbloods	1967	10.00	20.00	40.00
LSP-3724	Get Together	1969	3.75	7.50	15.00
—Retitled version of "The Youngbloods"					
LSP-3724 [S]	The Youngbloods	1967	6.25	12.50	25.00
LPM-3865 [M]	Earth Music	1968	12.50	25.00	50.00
LSP-3865 [S]	Earth Music	1968	6.25	12.50	25.00
AFL1-4150	Elephant Mountain	1977	2.50	5.00	10.00
—Reissue of LSP-4150					
LSP-4150	Elephant Mountain	1969	3.75	7.50	15.00
AFL1-4399	The Best of the Youngbloods	1977	2.50	5.00	10.00
—Reissue of LSP-4399					
LSP-4399	The Best of the Youngbloods	1970	3.75	7.50	15.00
LSP-4561	Sunlight	1971	3.00	6.00	12.00
VPS-6051 [(2)]	This Is the Youngbloods	1972	3.75	7.50	15.00

YOUNGTONES, THE

45s

BRUNSWICK

Number	Title (A Side/B Side)	Yr	VG	VG+	NM
55089	Come On Baby/Oh Tell Me	1958	15.00	30.00	60.00

YUM YUM KIDS, THE

Albums

MGM

Number	Title (A Side/B Side)	Yr	VG	VG+	NM
E-4396 [M]	Yummy in Your Tummy	1966	3.75	7.50	15.00
SE-4396 [S]	Yummy in Your Tummy	1966	5.00	10.00	20.00

YUM YUMS, THE

45s

ABC-PARAMOUNT

Number	Title (A Side/B Side)	Yr	VG	VG+	NM
10697	Looky, Looky (What I Got)/Gonna Be a Big Thing	1965	5.00	10.00	20.00

YURO, TIMI

45s

LIBERTY

Number	Title (A Side/B Side)	Yr	VG	VG+	NM
55343	Hurt/I Apologize	1961	3.75	7.50	15.00
55375	Smile/She Really Loves You	1961	3.00	6.00	12.00
55400	I Believe/A Mother's Love	1961	2.50	5.00	10.00
—With Johnnie Ray					
55410	Let Me Call You Sweetheart/Satan Never Sleeps	1962	2.50	5.00	10.00
55432	I Know (I Love You)/Count Everything	1962	2.50	5.00	10.00
55469	What's a Matter Baby (Is It Hurting You)/ Thirteenth Hour	1962	3.00	6.00	12.00
55519	The Love of a Boy/I Ain't Gonna Cry No More	1962	2.50	5.00	10.00
55551	Insult to Injury/Talkin' About Hurt	1963	—	—	—
—Unreleased					
55552	Insult to Injury/Just About the Time	1963	2.50	5.00	10.00
55587	Make the World Go Away/Look Down	1963	2.50	5.00	10.00
55634	Gotta Travel On/Down in the Valley	1963	2.50	5.00	10.00
55665	Call Me/Permanently Lonely	1964	2.00	4.00	8.00
55701	A Legend in My Time/Should I Ever Love Again	1964	2.00	4.00	8.00
55747	I'm Movin' On (Part 1)/I'm Movin' On (Part 2)	1964	2.00	4.00	8.00
56049	Wrong/Something Bad on My Mind	1968	—	3.00	6.00
56061	I Must Have Been Out of My Head/Interlude	1968	—	3.00	6.00

MERCURY

Number	Title (A Side/B Side)	Yr	VG	VG+	NM
72316	If/The Masquerade Is Over	1964	2.00	4.00	8.00
72355	I Got It Bad and That Ain't Good/Johnny	1964	2.00	4.00	8.00
72391	Could This Be Magic/You Can Have Him	1965	2.00	4.00	8.00
72431	Can't Stop Running Away/Get Out of My Life	1965	2.00	4.00	8.00
72478	Big Mistake/Teardrops Till Dawn	1965	2.00	4.00	8.00
72515	Once a Day/Pretend	1966	2.00	4.00	8.00
72601	Don't Keep Me Lonely Too Long/You Took My Happy Away	1966	2.00	4.00	8.00
72628	Turn the World Around the Other Way/Just a Ribbon	1966	2.00	4.00	8.00
72674	Why Not Now/Cuttin' In	1967	2.00	4.00	8.00

PLAYBOY

Number	Title (A Side/B Side)	Yr	VG	VG+	NM
6050	Southern Lady/Lovin' You Is All I Ever Had	1975	—	2.50	5.00

UNITED ARTISTS

Number	Title (A Side/B Side)	Yr	VG	VG+	NM
0042	Hurt/What's a Matter Baby (Is It Hurting You)	1973	—	2.00	4.00
—"Silver Spotlight Series" reissue					

Albums

LIBERTY

Number	Title (A Side/B Side)	Yr	VG	VG+	NM
LRP-3208 [M]	Hurt	1961	10.00	20.00	40.00
LRP-3212 [M]	Soul	1962	3.75	7.50	15.00
LRP-3234 [M]	Let Me Call You Sweetheart	1962	3.75	7.50	15.00
LRP-3263 [M]	What's a Matter Baby?	1963	3.75	7.50	15.00
LRP-3286 [M]	The Best of Timi Yuro	1963	3.75	7.50	15.00
LRP-3319 [M]	Make the World Go Away	1963	3.75	7.50	15.00
LST-7208 [S]	Hurt	1961	12.50	25.00	50.00
LST-7212 [S]	Soul	1962	5.00	10.00	20.00
LST-7234 [S]	Let Me Call You Sweetheart	1962	5.00	10.00	20.00
LST-7263 [S]	What's a Matter Baby?	1963	5.00	10.00	20.00
LST-7286 [S]	The Best of Timi Yuro	1963	5.00	10.00	20.00
LST-7319 [S]	Make the World Go Away	1963	5.00	10.00	20.00
LST-7594	Something Bad on My Mind	1968	3.00	6.00	12.00

MERCURY

Number	Title (A Side/B Side)	Yr	VG	VG+	NM
MG-20963 [M]	The Amazing Timi Yuro	1964	3.00	6.00	12.00
SR-60963 [S]	The Amazing Timi Yuro	1964	3.75	7.50	15.00

SUNSET

Number	Title (A Side/B Side)	Yr	VG	VG+	NM
SUM-1107 [M]	Timi Yuro	1966	2.50	5.00	10.00
SUS-5107 [S]	Timi Yuro	1966	3.00	6.00	12.00

Z

ZACHARIAS AND THE TREE PEOPLE

Number	Title (A Side/B Side)	Yr	VG	VG+	NM
45s					
VIKING					
1004	We're All Paul Bearers (Part 1)/We're All Paul Bearers (Part 2)	1969	5.00	10.00	20.00

ZACHERLE, JOHN

Number	Title (A Side/B Side)	Yr	VG	VG+	NM
45s					
CAMEO					
130	Igor/Dinner with Drac	1958	10.00	20.00	40.00
130	Dinner with Drac (Part 1)/Dinner with Drac (Part 2)	1958	7.50	15.00	30.00
—Orange label					
130	Dinner with Drac (Part 1)/Dinner with Drac (Part 2)	1960	5.00	10.00	20.00
—Red and black label					
139	Lunch with Mother Goose/82 Tombstones	1958	7.50	15.00	30.00
145	I Was a Teenage Caveman/Dummy Doll	1958	7.50	15.00	30.00
COLPIX					
743	Monsters Have Problems Too/Hello Dolly	1964	6.25	12.50	25.00
PARKWAY					
853	Dinner with Drac/Hurry Bury Baby	1962	6.25	12.50	25.00
885	Clementine/Surfboard 109	1963	6.25	12.50	25.00
—As "Zacherley"					
888	Scarey Tales from Mother Goose/Monster Monkey	1963	6.25	12.50	25.00
—As "Zacherley"					
Albums					
ELEKTRA					
EKL-190 [M]	Spook Along with Zacherle	1960	15.00	30.00	60.00
EKS-7190 [S]	Spook Along with Zacherle	1960	20.00	40.00	80.00
PARKWAY					
P 7018 [M]	Monster Mash	1962	15.00	30.00	60.00
P 7023 [M]	Scary Tales	1963	15.00	30.00	60.00

ZACK, EDDIE

Number	Title (A Side/B Side)	Yr	VG	VG+	NM
45s					
DECCA					
9-46302	Beautiful Brown Eyes/Shenandoah Waltz	1951	10.00	20.00	40.00
9-46330	The Clouds Will Soon Roll By/You Remind Me of So Much	1951	10.00	20.00	40.00

ZACK, EDDIE, AND COUSIN RICHIE

Number	Title (A Side/B Side)	Yr	VG	VG+	NM
45s					
COLUMBIA					
4-21199	I've Lost Again/I Never Saw Her Again	1954	12.50	25.00	50.00
4-21261	Positively No Dancing/Dancing Country Style	1954	12.50	25.00	50.00
4-21307	You're Out of My Sight/Cryin' Tears	1954	37.50	75.00	150.00
4-21387	Rocky Road Blues/Lover, Lover	1955	37.50	75.00	150.00
4-21441	I'm Gonna Rock and Roll/Foolish Me	1955	37.50	75.00	150.00

ZAGER AND EVANS

Number	Title (A Side/B Side)	Yr	VG	VG+	NM
45s					
RCA VICTOR					
47-9816	Help One Man Today/Year 32	1969	—	2.50	5.00
74-0174	In the Year 2525 (Exordium & Terminus)/Little Kids	1969	—	3.00	6.00
74-0246	Mr. Turnkey/Cary Lynn Jones	1969	—	2.50	5.00
74-0299	Listen to the People/She Never Sleeps Beside Me	1969	—	2.50	5.00
74-0359	Plastic Park/Crutches	1970	—	2.50	5.00
TRUTH					
(# unknown)	In the Year 2525 (Exordium & Terminus)/Little Kids	1967	5.00	10.00	20.00
VANGUARD					
35125	Hydra 15,000/I Am	1971	—	2.50	5.00
Albums					
RCA VICTOR					
ANL1-1077	2525 (Exordium and Terminus)	1975	2.50	5.00	10.00
—Reissue of 4214					
LSP-4214	2525 (Exordium and Terminus)	1969	5.00	10.00	20.00
LSP-4302	Zager and Evans	1970	5.00	10.00	20.00
VANGUARD					
VSD-6568	Food for the Mind	1971	3.75	7.50	15.00
WHITE WHALE					
WWS-7123	The Early Writings of Zager and Evans	1969	5.00	10.00	20.00

ZAHND, RICKY, AND THE BLUE JEANERS

Number	Title (A Side/B Side)	Yr	VG	VG+	NM
45s					
COLUMBIA					
4-263	(I'm Getting) Nuttin' For Christmas/Something Barked On Christmas Morning	1955	3.75	7.50	15.00
—Yellow-label Children's Series edition					
40576	(I'm Getting) Nuttin' For Christmas/Something Barked On Christmas Morning	1955	3.75	7.50	15.00
40670	My Church Is My Palace/You Got to Go to Church	1956	3.00	6.00	12.00

ZANIES, THE

Number	Title (A Side/B Side)	Yr	VG	VG+	NM
45s					
DORE					
509	The Blob/Do You Dig Me, Mr. Pygmy	1958	6.25	12.50	25.00
515	The Mad Scientist/She's a Winner	1958	6.25	12.50	25.00
597	It's Lovely/Saxophone Safari	1961	5.00	10.00	20.00
632	Rockin' Chopin/Frustration	1962	5.00	10.00	20.00
638	London Rock/Stalled	1962	5.00	10.00	20.00
647	Sleepwalker/Alexander's Ragtime Band	1962	5.00	10.00	20.00
655	Comin' Down the Track/Hello Jackie	1962	5.00	10.00	20.00
658	Russian Roulette/Caught in a Ringer1	1963	5.00	10.00	20.00
683	Chicken Surfer/London Rick	1963	5.00	10.00	20.00
705	Slinky/Camel Walk	1964	3.75	7.50	15.00
734	Bless 'Em All/Last Dance at the Prom	1965	3.75	7.50	15.00
853	Will the Real Dr. Frankenstein Please Stand Up/Frankenstein's Laboratory	1971	3.75	7.50	15.00
875	Do the 1-2-3/Mr. President-to-Be	1972	2.50	5.00	10.00
889	Let Out a Scream (Part 1)/Let Out a Scream (Part 2)	1973	2.00	4.00	8.00
893	Flakey/(Instrumental)	1974	—	3.00	6.00
900	Los Angeles, Los Angeles/Let Out a Scream	1974	—	3.00	6.00
912	Frustration/Roller Coaster	1975	—	2.50	5.00
920	Old Man River/Los Angeles, Los Angeles	1976	—	2.50	5.00
957	Janie for President/Los Angeles, Los Angeles	1980	—	2.00	4.00
959	The Song of the Masochist/Special	1980	—	2.00	4.00
959	What Is a One/Louie's Market	1980	—	2.00	4.00
959	The Song of the Masochist/What Is a One	1980	—	2.00	4.00
962	Curvacious Cora and Carlos Condo/Percolator	1980	—	2.00	4.00
963	I Love Life, Men, Candy and Paree/I Love Life, Men, Candy and Paree (X-Rated Adult Version)	1981	—	2.00	4.00
968	From Peanuts to Jelly Beans/For He's a Jolly Good Fellow	1981	—	2.00	4.00
974	I Hate Baseball/Dancing with Ronnie Cey	1982	—	2.50	5.00
—With "A. Player"					
975	Just Another Day in L.A./I'll Be Waiting	1983	—	2.00	4.00
978	Is There An Echo in the Joint/Doin' the Head	1983	—	2.00	4.00
979	Gesundheit/Darlin' Come Back	1983	—	2.00	4.00
980	The Raiders, the Steelers, the Cowboys and Bills (same on both sides)	1984	—	2.00	4.00
1015	Politics, Religion, and Sin (Part 1)/Politics, Religion, and Sin (Part 2)	198?	—	2.00	4.00
Albums					
DORE					
321	The Zanies	1969	7.50	15.00	30.00
337	The Zanies	1979	3.75	7.50	15.00

ZAPPA, FRANK

Includes his work leading The Mothers of Invention. The label credit, if other than "Frank Zappa," is listed under each record. Also see BABY RAY AND THE FERNS; BOB GUY.

Number	Title (A Side/B Side)	Yr	VG	VG+	NM
12-Inch Singles					
BARKING PUMPKIN					
02616	Goblin Girl/Pink Napkins	1982	7.50	15.00	30.00
—Picture disc					
03069	Valley Girl/You Are What You Is	1982	3.75	7.50	15.00
—A-side: Frank and Moon Zappa					
ZAPPA					
MK 107 [DJ]	Joe's Garage/Central Scrutinizer	1979	10.00	20.00	40.00
45s					
BARKING PUMPKIN					
02972	Valley Girl/You Are What You Is	1982	—	—	3.00
—A-side: Frank and Moon Zappa					
02972 [PS]	Valley Girl/You Are What You Is	1982	—	3.50	7.00
—A-side: Frank and Moon Zappa					
BIZARRE					
0840	My Guitar/Dog Breath	1969	12.50	25.00	50.00
—The Mothers of Invention					
0889	Peaches En Regalia/Little Umbrellas	1970	12.50	25.00	50.00
0892	WPLJ/My Guitar	1970	12.50	25.00	50.00
—The Mothers of Invention					
0967	Tell Me You Love Me/Would You Go All the Way for the U.S.A.?	1970	12.50	25.00	50.00
1027	Tears Began to Fall/Junior Mintz Boogie	1971	12.50	25.00	50.00
—Junior Mintz					
1052	Tears Began to Fall/Junior Mintz Boogie	1971	12.50	25.00	50.00
—Frank Zappa and The Mothers of Invention					
1127	Cletus Awreetus-Awrightus/Eat That Question	1972	8.75	17.50	35.00
—The Mothers					
DISCREET					
PRO 586 [DJ]	Uncle Remus/Cozmik Debris	1974	5.00	10.00	20.00
1180	I'm the Slime/Montana	1973	6.25	12.50	25.00
—The Mothers					
1312	Don't Eat the Yellow Snow/Cosmic Debris	1974	3.75	7.50	15.00
UNITED ARTISTS					
50857	Magic Fingers/Daddy, Daddy, Daddy	1971	12.50	25.00	50.00
VERVE					
10418	How Could I Be Such a Fool/Help I'm a Rock (3rd Movement: It Can't Happen Here)	1966	50.00	100.00	200.00
—The Mothers of Invention					
10418 [DJ]	How Could I Be Such a Fool/Help I'm a Rock (3rd Movement: It Can't Happen Here)	1966	25.00	50.00	100.00
—The Mothers of Invention					
10458	Who Are the Brain Police/Trouble Comin' Every Day	1966	50.00	100.00	200.00
—The Mothers of Invention					
10458 [DJ]	Who Are the Brain Police/Trouble Comin' Every Day	1966	25.00	50.00	100.00
—The Mothers of Invention					
10513	Why Don't You Do Me Right/Big Leg Emma	1967	50.00	100.00	200.00
—The Mothers of Invention					
10513 [DJ]	Why Don't You Do Me Right/Big Leg Emma	1967	25.00	50.00	100.00
—The Mothers of Invention					
10570	Mother People/Lonely Little Girl	1967	50.00	100.00	200.00
—The Mothers of Invention					
10570 [DJ]	Mother People/Lonely Little Girl	1967	25.00	50.00	100.00
—The Mothers of Invention					
10632	Jelly Roll Gum Drop/Deseri	1968	37.50	75.00	150.00
—Ruben & The Jets					
10632	Jelly Roll Gum Drop/Any Way the Wind Blows	1968	37.50	75.00	150.00
—Ruben & The Jets					
10632 [DJ]	Jelly Roll Gum Drop/Deseri	1968	18.75	37.50	75.00
—Ruben & The Jets					
10632 [DJ]	Jelly Roll Gum Drop/Any Way the Wind Blows	1968	18.75	37.50	75.00
—Ruben & The Jets					
WARNER BROS.					
8296	Find Her Finer/Zoot Allures	1976	6.25	12.50	25.00
8342	Disco Boy/Miss Pinky	1977	6.25	12.50	25.00

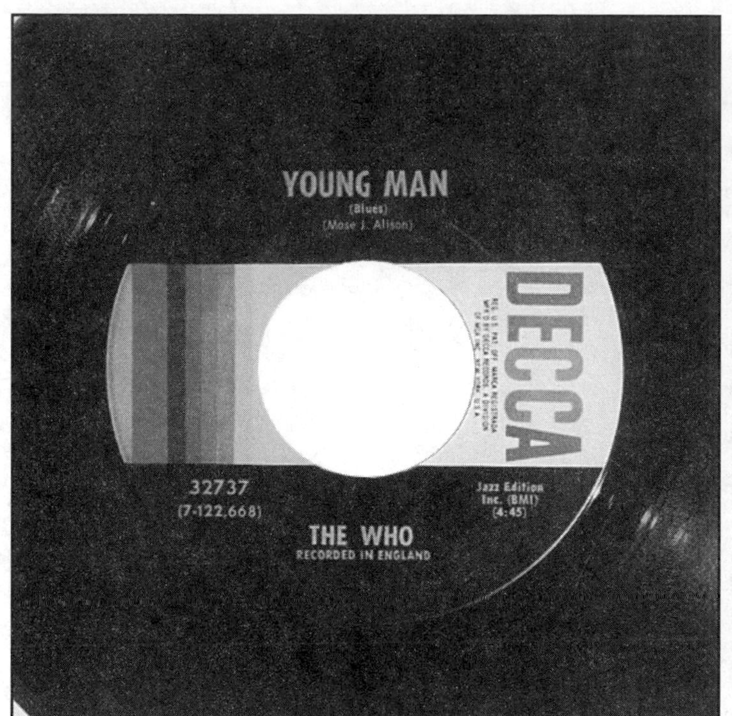

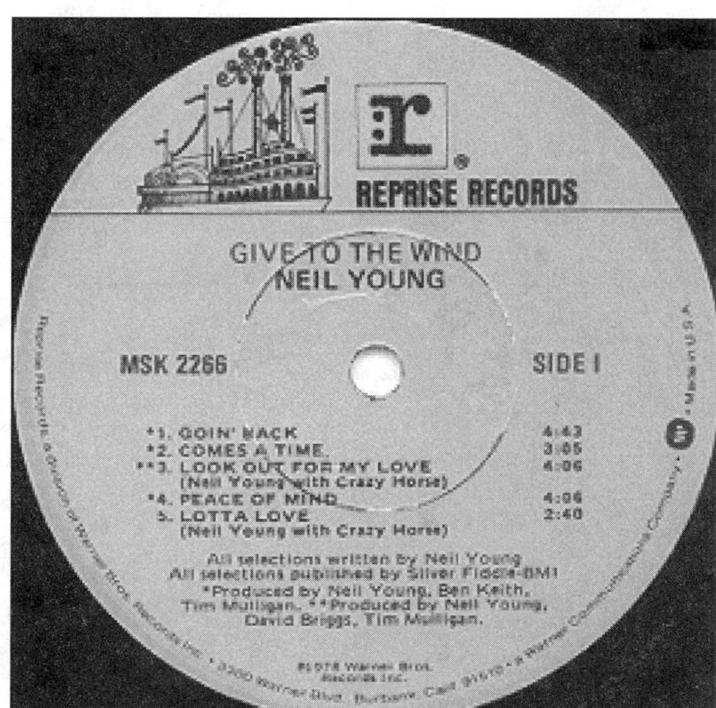

(Top left) One of the rarest of all singles by The Who was their version of "Young Man (Blues)" with "Substitute" on the other side. It was briefly released, then quickly pulled from the marketplace in1970. For a long time, stock copies were not believed to exist. (Top right) During his short life, MGM released only two full-length albums of Hank Williams' music, and both of those were in the now-extinct 10-inch format. The record label made up for lost time after that, as it released dozens of collections over the years. The first one to appear as a 12-inch LP was *Ramblin' Man* in 1955. (Bottom left) Before the album became *Comes A Time*, Neil Young's 1978 mostly acoustic album was going to be called *Give to the Wind*. It actually got to the pressing stage with this title, as illustrated here with a rare stock-copy label, but it was shelved before release. (Bottom right) The second Frank Zappa/ Mothers of Invention LP was *We're Only In It for the Money*. In addition to this front cover, it also contained a parody of the Beatles' *Sgt. Pepper* cover.

ZAPPA

Number	Title (A Side/B Side)	Yr	VG	VG+	NM
Z-10	Dancin' Fool/Baby Snakes	1979	2.50	5.00	10.00
ZR 1001	I Don't Wanna Get Drafted/Ancient Armaments (Live)	1980	—	2.00	4.00
ZR 1001 [PS]	I Don't Wanna Get Drafted/Ancient Armaments (Live)	1980	2.50	5.00	10.00
Albums					
ANGEL					
DS-38170	Boulez Conducts Zappa: The Perfect Stranger	1983	3.00	6.00	12.00
BARKING PUMPKIN					
7X4-1	The Old Masters Sampler	1984	6.25	12.50	25.00
AS 995 [DJ]	Tinsel Town Rebellion	1981	5.00	10.00	20.00
—Promo-only sampler					
BPR-1111	Shut Up 'N' Play Yer Guitar	1981	5.00	10.00	20.00
—Mail-order item only					
BPR-1112	Shut Up 'N' Play Yer Guitar Some More	1981	5.00	10.00	20.00
—Mail-order item only					
BPR-1113	Return of the Son of Shut Up 'N' Play Yer Guitar	1981	5.00	10.00	20.00
—Mail-order item only					
BPRP-1114 [PD]	Zappa	1982	3.75	7.50	15.00
—Picture disc with two songs					
BPRP-1115 [PD]	Baby Snakes	1983	3.75	7.50	15.00
—Picture disc					
AS 1294 [DJ]	You Are What You Is Special Clean Cuts Edition	1981	5.00	10.00	20.00
7777 [(8)]	The Old Masters, Box 1	1984	15.00	30.00	60.00
—Boxed set					
8888X	The Old Masters Sampler 2	1986	6.25	12.50	25.00
8888 [(8)]	The Old Masters, Box 2	1986	15.00	30.00	60.00
—Another boxed set					
9999 [(8)]	The Old Masters, Box 3	1987	15.00	30.00	60.00
—Still another boxed set					
PW2 37336 [(2)]	Tinsel Town Rebellion	1981	5.00	10.00	20.00
PW2 37537 [(2)]	You Are What You Is	1981	5.00	10.00	20.00
FW 38066	Ship Arriving Too Late to Save a Drowning Witch	1982	3.00	6.00	12.00
W3X-38290 [(3)]	Shut Up 'N' Play Yer Guitar	1982	6.25	12.50	25.00
—Box set containing all three "Shut Up 'N' Play Yer Guitar" albums					
FW 38403	Man from Utopia	1983	3.00	6.00	12.00
FW 38820	London Symphony Orchestra	1983	3.00	6.00	12.00
SVBO-74200 [(2)]	Them Or Us	1984	3.75	7.50	15.00
SWCO-74201 [(3)]	Thing-Fish	1984	5.00	10.00	20.00
ST-74202	Francesco Zappa	1985	2.50	5.00	10.00
ST-74203	Frank Zappa Meets the Mothers of Prevention	1985	2.50	5.00	10.00
ST-74205	Jazz from Hell	1986	2.50	5.00	10.00
74206 [(3)]	Joe's Garage, Acts 1, 2 and 3	1986	12.50	25.00	50.00
—Box set, two gatefolds, with insert					
SJ-74207	London Symphony Orchestra, Volume 2	1987	2.50	5.00	10.00
D1-74212 [(2)]	Guitar	1988	2.50	5.00	10.00
D1-74213 [(3)]	You Can't Do That on Stage Anymore Sampler	1988	2.50	5.00	10.00
R1 74213	You Can't Do That on Stage Anymore Sampler	1988	3.00	6.00	12.00
D1-74217 [(3)]	You Can't Do That on Stage Anymore Vol. 2	1988	2.50	5.00	10.00
D1-74218	Broadway the Hard Way	1988	2.50	5.00	10.00
BIZARRE					
MS-2024 [(2)]	Uncle Meat	1969	8.75	17.50	35.00
—Originals come with a booklet; blue label					
MS-2024 [(2)]	Uncle Meat	1973	5.00	10.00	20.00
—Reissue with brown Reprise label					
MS-2028	Weasels Ripped My Flesh	1970	6.25	12.50	25.00
—Blue label original					
MS-2028	Weasels Ripped My Flesh	1973	3.75	7.50	15.00
—Reissue with brown Reprise label					
MS-2030	Chunga's Revenge	1970	6.25	12.50	25.00
—Blue label original					
MS-2030	Chunga's Revenge	1973	3.75	7.50	15.00
—Reissue with brown Reprise label					
MS 2030 [DJ]	Chunga's Revenge	1970	12.50	25.00	50.00
—White label promo					
MS-2042	Fillmore East, June 1971	1971	6.25	12.50	25.00
—Blue label original					
MS-2042	Fillmore East, June 1971	1973	2.75	7.50	15.00
—Reissue with brown Reprise label					
MS 2075	Just Another Band from L.A.	1972	6.25	12.50	25.00
—Blue label original					
MS 2075	Just Another Band from L.A.	1973	3.75	7.50	15.00
—Reissue with brown Reprise label					
MS 2093	The Grand Wazoo	1972	6.25	12.50	25.00
—Blue label original					
MS 2093	The Grand Wazoo	1973	3.75	7.50	15.00
—Reissue with brown Reprise label					
MS 2094	Waka/Jawaka	1972	6.25	12.50	25.00
—Blue label original					
MS 2094	Waka/Jawaka	1973	3.75	7.50	15.00
—Reissue with brown Reprise label					
RS-6356	Hot Rats	1969	12.50	25.00	50.00
—Blue label original					
RS-6356	Hot Rats	1973	3.75	7.50	15.00
—Reissue with brown Reprise label					
RS-6370	Burnt Weenie Sandwich	1970	6.25	12.50	25.00
—Blue label original; with booklet					
RS-6370	Burnt Weenie Sandwich	1973	3.75	7.50	15.00
—Reissue with brown Reprise label					
COLUMBIA					
(no #) [(4) DJ]	Lather	1977	187.50	375.00	750.00
—Test pressing only; parts of this LP are on DSK 2291, 2292 and 2294; released as a whole only after Zappa's death, with vinyl only coming out in Japan					
DISCREET					
MS 2149	Over-Nite Sensation	1973	5.00	10.00	20.00
MS4 2149 [Q]	Over-Nite Sensation	1973	10.00	20.00	40.00
DS 2175	Apostrophe (')	1974	3.75	7.50	15.00
DS 2175	Apostrophe (')	1974	12.50	25.00	50.00
—White label promo					
DS4 2175 [Q]	Apostrophe (')	1974	8.75	17.50	35.00
2DS 2202 [(2)]	Roxy and Elsewhere	1974	6.25	12.50	25.00
DS 2216	One Size Fits All	1975	3.75	7.50	15.00
DS 2234	Bongo Fury	1975	3.75	7.50	15.00
DSK 2288	Over-Nite Sensation	1977	3.00	6.00	12.00
—Reissue of DiscReet 2149 with new number					
DSK 2289	Apostrophe (')	1977	3.00	6.00	12.00
—Reissue with new number					
2D 2290 [(2)]	Zappa in New York	1978	62.50	125.00	250.00
—Stock copy with "Punky's Whips" erroneously listed on jacket					
2D 2290 [(2)]	Zappa in New York	1978	5.00	10.00	20.00
2D 2290 [(2) DJ]	Zappa in New York	1978	100.00	200.00	400.00
—Test pressing with "Punky's Whips"					
DSK 2291	Studio Tan	1978	3.75	7.50	15.00
DSK 2292	Sleep Dirt	1978	3.75	7.50	15.00
DSK 2294	Orchestral Favorites	1978	3.75	7.50	15.00
FOO-EEE					
R1-70372 [(11)]	Beat the Boots #2	1992	25.00	50.00	100.00
—Legitimate box-set release by Rhino of 11 bootlegged concerts					
R1-70907 [(10)]	Beat the Boots	1991	25.00	50.00	100.00
—Legitimate box-set release by Rhino of eight bootlegged concerts					
MCA					
4183 [(2)]	200 Motels (movie soundtrack)	1986	3.75	7.50	15.00
—Reissue					
MGM					
GAS-112	The Mothers of Invention	1970	12.50	25.00	50.00
GAS-112 [DJ]	The Mothers of Invention	1970	25.00	50.00	100.00
—Yellow label promo					
SE-4754	The Worst of the Mothers	1971	12.50	25.00	50.00
SE-4754 [DJ]	The Worst of the Mothers	1971	37.50	75.00	150.00
—Yellow label promo					
RHINO/DEL-FI					
RNEP-604	Rare Meat: The Early Productions of Frank Zappa	1984	10.00	20.00	40.00
—With original cover					
RYKO ANALOGUE					
RALP 10503	We're Only in It for the Money	1995	3.00	6.00	12.00
—Vinyl reissue; Frank Zappa/The Mothers of Invention					
RALP 40500 [(2)]	Strictly Commercial: The Best of Frank Zappa	1995	5.00	10.00	20.00
—Issued with obi					
UNITED ARTISTS					
UAS-9956 [(2)]	200 Motels (movie soundtrack)	1971	12.50	25.00	50.00
VERVE					
V-5005-2 [(2) M]	Freak Out!	1966	100.00	200.00	400.00
—White label promo					
V-5005-2 [(2) M]	Freak Out!	1966	50.00	100.00	200.00
—Cover version 1: Has blurb on inside gatefold on how to get a map of "freak-out hot spots" in L.A.					
V-5005-2 [(2) M]	Freak Out!	1966	37.50	75.00	150.00
—Cover version 2: Has no blurb inside on getting a map of "freak-out hot spots"					
V6-5005-2 [(2) S]	Freak Out!	1966	75.00	150.00	300.00
—Yellow label promo					
V6-5005-2 [(2) S]	Freak Out!	1966	20.00	40.00	80.00
—Cover version 1: Has blurb on inside gatefold on how to get a map of "freak-out hot spots" in L.A.					
V6-5005-2 [(2) S]	Freak Out!	1966	15.00	30.00	60.00
—Cover version 2: Has no blurb inside on getting a map of "freak-out hot spots"					
V-5013 [M]	Absolutely Free	1967	50.00	100.00	200.00
—White label promo					
V-5013 [M]	Absolutely Free	1967	30.00	60.00	120.00
V6-5013 [S]	Absolutely Free	1967	15.00	30.00	60.00
V-5045 [M]	We're Only in It for the Money	1968	75.00	150.00	300.00
—White label promo					
V-5045 [M]	We're Only in It for the Money	1968	37.50	75.00	150.00
—With sheet of cut-outs a la "Sgt. Pepper's Lonely Hearts Club Band"					
V6-5045 [S]	We're Only in It for the Money	1968	15.00	30.00	60.00
—Un-censored version, with cut-outs					
V6-5045 [S]	We're Only in It for the Money	1968	37.50	75.00	150.00
—Censored version: the songs "Who Needs the Peace Corps?" and "Let's Make the Water Turn Black" have lines deleted					
V6-5055	Cruising with Ruben and the Jets	1968	15.00	30.00	60.00
V6-5055 [DJ]	Cruising with Ruben and the Jets	1968	37.50	75.00	150.00
—Yellow label promo					
V6-5068	Mothermania — The Best of the Mothers	1969	18.75	37.50	75.00
V6-5068 [DJ]	Mothermania — The Best of the Mothers	1969	37.50	75.00	150.00
—Yellow label promo					
V6-5074	The XXXX of the Mothers	1969	12.50	25.00	50.00
V6-5074 [DJ]	The XXXX of the Mothers	1969	37.50	75.00	150.00
—Yellow label promo					
V-8741 [M]	Lumpy Gravy	1968	75.00	150.00	300.00
—Yellow label promo; no stock copies were issued in mono					
V6-8741	Lumpy Gravy	1968	12.50	25.00	50.00
V6-8741 [DJ]	Lumpy Gravy	1968	50.00	100.00	200.00
—Yellow label promo					
WARNER BROS.					
BS-2970	Zoot Allures	1976	3.75	7.50	15.00
ZAPPA					
MK-78 [DJ]	Sheik Yerbouti Clean Cuts	1979	8.75	17.50	35.00
MK-129 [DJ]	Joe's Garage Acts I, II and III Sampler	1980	8.75	17.50	35.00
SRZ-2-1501 [(2)]	Sheik Yerbouti	1979	5.00	10.00	20.00
SRZ-2-1502 [(2)]	Joe's Garage, Acts II and III	1980	5.00	10.00	20.00
SRZ-1-1603	Joe's Garage, Act I	1979	3.75	7.50	15.00

ZAZU

Albums

Number	Title (A Side/B Side)	Yr	VG	VG+	NM
WOODEN NICKEL					
BWL1-0791	Zazu	1975	5.00	10.00	20.00

ZEBRA, THE

45s

Number	Title (A Side/B Side)	Yr	VG	VG+	NM
BLUE THUMB					
109	Christmas Morning (Part 1)/Christmas Morning (Part 2)	1969	2.50	5.00	10.00
PHILIPS					
40535	Groovy Personality/Miss Ann (Ain't That Kind of Man)	1968	3.00	6.00	12.00
WHITE WHALE					
305	Bring Me to My Knees/(B-side unknown)	1969	2.50	5.00	10.00

ZEBULONS, THE

Number	Title (A Side/B Side)	Yr	VG	VG+	NM
45s					
CUB					
9069	Falling Water/Wo-Ho-La-Tee-Da	1960	15.00	30.00	60.00

ZEE, TOMMY

Number	Title (A Side/B Side)	Yr	VG	VG+	NM
45s					
AMY					
815	Rebecca, Remember/Worlds Apart	1961	10.00	20.00	40.00

ZEKLEY, GARY

Also see THE YELLOW BALLOON.

Number	Title (A Side/B Side)	Yr	VG	VG+	NM
45s					
AVA					
151	Vagabond/When I Go to Sleep	1963	10.00	20.00	40.00
—With Dean Torrence on backing vocals					

ZELLA, DANNY

Number	Title (A Side/B Side)	Yr	VG	VG+	NM
45s					
DIAL					
100	Sapphire/You Made Me Blue	1959	50.00	100.00	200.00
FOX					
F # 1	Black Saxs/Wicked Ruby	1959	7.50	15.00	30.00
ZTSC 10056/7	Black Saxs/Wicked Ruby	1959	7.50	15.00	30.00
—Some copies of this 45 do not have a catalog number; these are the master numbers of each side					
RED ROCKET					
475	Black Saxs/Wicked Ruby	1959	10.00	20.00	40.00

ZENITHS, THE

Number	Title (A Side/B Side)	Yr	VG	VG+	NM
Albums					
ATLANTIC					
8043 [M]	Makin' the Scene	1960	25.00	50.00	100.00
SD 8043 [S]	Makin' the Scene	1960	37.50	75.00	150.00

ZENTNER, SI

Number	Title (A Side/B Side)	Yr	VG	VG+	NM
45s					
LIBERTY					
55204	Sock Hop/Two Guitars	1959	2.50	5.00	10.00
55240	Armen's Theme/The Swinging Eye	1960	2.50	5.00	10.00
55374	Up a Lazy River/Shufflin' Blues	1961	2.00	4.00	8.00
55408	Hollywood Twist/Nice 'N Easy	1962	2.00	4.00	8.00
55420 [DJ]	The Goulash (Shufflin' Blues)	1962	3.75	7.50	15.00
—One-sided promo-only release					
55476	Shadrack/Boogie Woogie Maxine	1962	2.00	4.00	8.00
55499	Desafinado/Elephant's Tango	1962	2.00	4.00	8.00
55538	Waltz in Jazz Time/A La Mode	1963	2.00	4.00	8.00
55609	Broken Date/Fink	1963	2.00	4.00	8.00
55648	James Bond Theme/Classes de Cha-Cha	1963	2.50	5.00	10.00
55675	I'm Getting Sentimental Over You/Sentimental Journey	1964	2.00	4.00	8.00
55683	From Russia with Love/James Bond Theme	1964	2.50	5.00	10.00
55941	Warning Shot/Mona Lisa	1967	—	3.00	6.00
55955	Dear John/Haven't Been to Church	1967	—	3.00	6.00
RCA VICTOR					
47-8454	Theme from Max/Spanish Rice	1964	—	3.00	6.00
47-8550	Dear Heart/In a Little Spanish Town	1965	—	3.00	6.00
47-8634	Fat Cat/My Devotion	1965	—	3.00	6.00
47-8779	Baby, Take Another Bow/Mr. Nashville	1966	—	3.00	6.00
Albums					
LIBERTY					
LRP-3197 [M]	Big Band Plays the Big Hits	1961	3.00	6.00	12.00
LRP-3216 [M]	Up a Lazy River (Big Band Plays the Big Hits: Vol. 2)	1962	3.00	6.00	12.00
LRP-3247 [M]	The Stripper and Other Big Band Hits	1962	3.00	6.00	12.00
LRP-3273 [M]	Desafinado	1963	3.00	6.00	12.00
LRP-3284 [M]	Waltz in Jazz Time	1963	3.00	6.00	12.00
LRP-3326 [M]	More	1963	3.00	6.00	12.00
LRP-3350 [M]	Big Big Band Hits	1964	3.00	6.00	12.00
LRP-3353 [M]	From Russia with Love	1964	3.00	6.00	12.00
LRP-3457 [M]	The Best of Si Zentner	1966	3.00	6.00	12.00
LST-7197 [S]	Big Band Plays the Big Hits	1961	3.75	7.50	15.00
LST-7216 [S]	Up a Lazy River (Big Band Plays the Big Hits: Vol. 2)	1962	3.75	7.50	15.00
LST-7247 [S]	The Stripper and Other Big Band Hits	1962	3.75	7.50	15.00
LST-7273 [S]	Desafinado	1963	3.75	7.50	15.00
LST-7284 [S]	Waltz in Jazz Time	1963	3.75	7.50	15.00
LST-7326 [S]	More	1963	3.75	7.50	15.00
LST-7350 [S]	Big Big Band Hits	1964	3.75	7.50	15.00
LST-7353 [S]	From Russia with Love	1964	3.75	7.50	15.00
LST-7457 [S]	The Best of Si Zentner	1966	3.00	6.00	12.00
LMM-13009 [M]	A Great Band with Great Voices	1961	3.00	6.00	12.00
LMM-13017 [M]	A Great Band with Great Voices Swing the Great Voices of the Great Bands	1962	3.00	6.00	12.00
LSS-14009 [S]	A Great Band with Great Voices	1961	3.75	7.50	15.00
LSS-14017 [S]	A Great Band with Great Voices Swing the Great Voices of the Great Bands	1962	3.75	7.50	15.00
SMASH					
MGS-27007 [M]	Presenting Si Zentner	1961	3.75	7.50	15.00
MGS-27013 [M]	Swing Fever	1962	3.75	7.50	15.00
SRS-67007 [S]	Presenting Si Zentner	1961	5.00	10.00	20.00
SRS-67013 [S]	Swing Fever	1962	5.00	10.00	20.00
SUNSET					
SUM-1110 [M]	Big Band Brilliance	196?	2.50	5.00	10.00
SUS-5110 [S]	Big Band Brilliance	196?	3.00	6.00	12.00

ZENTNER, SI AND MARTIN DENNY

Also see each artist's individual listings.

Number	Title (A Side/B Side)	Yr	VG	VG+	NM
Albums					
LIBERTY					
LMM-13020 [M]	Exotica Suite	1962	3.75	7.50	15.00
LSS-14020 [S]	Exotica Suite	1962	5.00	10.00	20.00

ZEPHYR

Also see TOMMY BOLIN.

Number	Title (A Side/B Side)	Yr	VG	VG+	NM
45s					
PROBE					
475	Sail On/Cross the River	1970	3.00	6.00	12.00
WARNER BROS.					
7444	Going Back to Colorado/Radio Song	1970	2.50	5.00	10.00
Albums					
PROBE					
4510	Zephyr	1969	12.50	25.00	50.00
WARNER BROS.					
WS 1897	Goin' Back to Colorado	1971	10.00	20.00	40.00
BS 2603	Sunset Ride	1972	5.00	10.00	20.00

ZEPHYRS, THE

Number	Title (A Side/B Side)	Yr	VG	VG+	NM
45s					
ROTATE					
5006	She's Lost You/There's Something About You	1965	3.75	7.50	15.00
5009	Let Me Love You Baby/Wonder What I'm Gonna Do	1965	3.75	7.50	15.00

ZERFAS

Number	Title (A Side/B Side)	Yr	VG	VG+	NM
Albums					
700 WEST					
730710	Zerfas	1973	200.00	400.00	800.00

ZEROES, THE

Number	Title (A Side/B Side)	Yr	VG	VG+	NM
45s					
TY-TEX					
105	Flossie Mae/Twisting with Crazee Babee	1963	50.00	100.00	200.00

ZEVON, WARREN

Number	Title (A Side/B Side)	Yr	VG	VG+	NM
12-Inch Singles					
ASYLUM					
AS 11386 [DJ]	Werewolves of London/Roland the Headless Thompson Gunner	1978	5.00	10.00	20.00
VIRGIN					
1053 [DJ]	Leave My Monkey Alone (10:31) (5:45) (5:51)	1987	2.00	4.00	8.00
2062 [DJ]	Detox Mansion/Leave My Monkey Alone	1987	—	3.00	6.00
2133 [DJ]	Boom Boom Mancini (same on both sides)	1987	—	3.00	6.00
96762	Leave My Monkey Alone (10:31) (5:45) (5:51)	1987	2.00	4.00	8.00
45s					
ASYLUM					
45356	Mohammad's Radio/Hasten Down the Wind	1976	—	2.50	5.00
45472	Werewolves of London/Roland the Headless Thompson Gunner	1978	—	2.50	5.00
45498	Lawyers, Guns and Money/Vera Cruz	1978	—	2.50	5.00
45526	Johnny Strikes Up the Band/Night Time in the Switching Yard	1978	—	2.50	5.00
46610	A Certain Girl/Empty-Handed Heart	1980	—	2.00	4.00
46641	Gorilla, You're a Desperado/Jungle Work	1980	—	2.00	4.00
47118	Lawyers, Guns and Money/Down on My Luck	1981	—	2.00	4.00
69946	Let Nothing Come Between You/The Hula Hula Boys	1982	—	2.00	4.00
69966	Looking for the Next Best Thing/The Hula Hula Boys	1982	—	2.00	4.00
ELEKTRA					
69509	Jesus Mentioned/Werewolves of London	1986	—	—	3.00
VIRGIN					
99370	Reconsider Me/Factory	1988	—	—	3.00
99370 [PS]	Reconsider Me/Factory	1988	—	—	3.00
99440	Leave My Monkey Alone/Leave My Monkey Alone (Latin Rascals Dub)	1987	—	—	3.00
99440 [PS]	Leave My Monkey Alone/Leave My Monkey Alone (Latin Rascals Dub)	1987	—	—	3.00
Albums					
ASYLUM					
6E-118	Excitable Boy	1978	2.50	5.00	10.00
5E-509	Bad Luck Streak in Dancing School	1979	2.50	5.00	10.00
5E-519	Stand in the Fire	1980	2.50	5.00	10.00
7E-1060	Warren Zevon	1976	2.50	5.00	10.00
60159	The Envoy	1982	2.50	5.00	10.00
60503	A Quiet Normal Life: The Best of Warren Zevon	1987	2.50	5.00	10.00
IMPERIAL					
LP-12456	Wanted Dead or Alive	1970	5.00	10.00	20.00
—As "Zevon"					
PICKWICK					
SPC-3715	Wanted Dead or Alive	1979	2.00	4.00	8.00
—Reissue of Imperial album					
VIRGIN					
90603	Sentimental Hygiene	1987	2.50	5.00	10.00
91068	Transverse City	1989	2.50	5.00	10.00

ZIMMERMAN, GEORGE, AND THE THRILLS

Number	Title (A Side/B Side)	Yr	VG	VG+	NM
45s					
JAB					
103	Whose Baby Are You/I Ain't Got the Money to Pay for This Drink	1956	100.00	200.00	400.00

ZINE, BEN

Number	Title (A Side/B Side)	Yr	VG	VG+	NM
45s					
PARKWAY					
994	Village of Tears/What the Heck's the Hanky Panky	1966	20.00	40.00	80.00

ZIP AND THE ZIPPERS

Number	Title (A Side/B Side)	Yr	VG	VG+	NM
45s					
PAGEANT					
607	Where You Goin' Little Boy/Gig	1963	6.25	12.50	25.00

ZIP CODES, THE

45s

Number	Title (A Side/B Side)	Yr	VG	VG+	NM
LIBERTY					
55703	Run, Little Mustang/Fancy Filly from Detroit City	1964	7.50	15.00	30.00

Albums

Number	Title (A Side/B Side)	Yr	VG	VG+	NM
LIBERTY					
LRP-3367 [M]	Mustang	1964	37.50	75.00	150.00
LST-7367 [S]	Mustang	1964	50.00	100.00	200.00

ZIRCONS, THE

Could be as many as four different groups.

45s

Number	Title (A Side/B Side)	Yr	VG	VG+	NM
AMBER					
851	One Summer Night/The Lone Stranger	1966	3.75	7.50	15.00
BAGDAD					
1007	Going Places/Surfing in the Sunset	1963	20.00	40.00	80.00
CAPITOL					
2667	Finders Keepers/You Ain't Comin' Back	1969	10.00	20.00	40.00
COOL SOUND					
1030	Silver Bells/You Are My Sunshine	1964	7.50	15.00	30.00
DOT					
15724	Only One Love/I Need It	1958	5.00	10.00	20.00
FEDERAL					
12452	No Twistin' on Sunday/Mama Wants to Drive	1962	5.00	10.00	20.00
12478	Get Up and Go to School/Mr. Jones	1962	5.00	10.00	20.00
HEIGH HO					
607	Where There's a Will/Don't Put Off for Tomorrow	1967	10.00	20.00	40.00
608/9	I Couldn't Stop Crying/Sit Down Girl	1967	10.00	20.00	40.00
645/6	Go On and Cry/Was It Meant to Be This Way	1967	10.00	20.00	40.00
MELLOMOOD					
1000	Lonely Way/Your Way	1963	5.00	10.00	20.00
OLD TIMER					
603	Stormy Weather/Sincerely	1964	3.75	7.50	15.00
SIAMESE					
403	Stormy Weather/Sincerely	1964	3.00	6.00	12.00
WINSTON					
1020	I Need It/Only One Love	1957	15.00	30.00	60.00
1022	Crazy Crazy/Return My Love	1958	20.00	40.00	80.00

Albums

Number	Title (A Side/B Side)	Yr	VG	VG+	NM
SNOWFLAKE					
1003	The Crown Kings of Acappella	196?	15.00	30.00	60.00

ZODIACS, THE

See MAURICE WILLIAMS AND THE ZODIACS.

ZOMBIES, THE

Also see ARGENT; COLIN BLUNSTONE.

45s

Number	Title (A Side/B Side)	Yr	VG	VG+	NM
COLUMBIA					
44363	Care of Cell 44/Maybe After He's Gone	1967	12.50	25.00	50.00
DATE					
1604	Time of the Season/I'll Call You Mine	1968	5.00	10.00	20.00
1612	Butcher's Tale (Western Front 1914)/This Will Be Our Year	1968	2.50	5.00	10.00
1628	Time of the Season/Friends of Mine	1968	3.00	6.00	12.00
1644	Imagine the Swan/Conversation of Floral Street	1969	2.50	5.00	10.00
1648	If It Don't Work Out/Don't Cry for Me	1969	2.50	5.00	10.00
EPIC					
11145	Time of the Season/Imagine the Swan	1974	—	2.50	5.00
PARROT					
3004	Indication/How We Were Before	1966	2.50	5.00	10.00
9695	She's Not There/You Make Me Feel So Good	1964	3.75	7.50	15.00
9723	Tell Her No/Leave Me Be	1965	3.75	7.50	15.00
9723 [PS]	Tell Her No/Leave Me Be	1965	7.50	15.00	30.00
9747	She's Coming Home/I Must Move	1965	3.00	6.00	12.00
9747 [PS]	She's Coming Home/I Must Move	1965	7.50	15.00	30.00
9769	I Want You Back Again/Once Upon a Time	1965	3.00	6.00	12.00
9786	I Love You/Whenever You're Ready	1965	3.00	6.00	12.00
9797	Just Out of Reach/Remember You	1965	3.00	6.00	12.00
9821	Don't Go Away/Is This the Dream	1966	3.00	6.00	12.00

Albums

Number	Title (A Side/B Side)	Yr	VG	VG+	NM
DATE					
TES-4013	Odessy and Oracle	1968	7.50	15.00	30.00
—With no mention of "Time of the Season" on front cover					
TES-4013	Odessy and Oracle	1969	5.00	10.00	20.00
—With "Time of the Season" mentioned on front cover					
EPIC					
KEG 32861 [(2) B]	Time of the Zombies	1974	5.00	10.00	20.00
—Record 1 is mono; Record 2 is stereo; orange labels					
PEG 32861 [(2) B]	Time of the Zombies	1979	3.75	7.50	15.00
—Later edition with blue labels					
LONDON					
PS 557 [P]	Early Days	1969	5.00	10.00	20.00
—All tracks in true stereo except "Tell Her No"					
PARROT					
PA 61001 [M]	The Zombies	1965	15.00	30.00	60.00
PAS 71001 [R]	The Zombies	1965	10.00	20.00	40.00
RHINO					
RNLP-120	Live on the BBC, 1965-67	1985	2.50	5.00	10.00
RNLP 70186 [S]	Odessy and Oracle	1986	2.00	4.00	8.00

ZOO, THE

Albums

Number	Title (A Side/B Side)	Yr	VG	VG+	NM
MERCURY					
SR-61300	The Zoo	1970	5.00	10.00	20.00
SUNBURST					
7500	The Zoo Presents the Chocolate Moose	1968	12.50	25.00	50.00

ZOO, THE (1)

45s

Number	Title (A Side/B Side)	Yr	VG	VG+	NM
SUNBURST					
775	One Night Man/(Standing On) The Sunset Strip	1968	2.50	5.00	10.00

ZOO, THE (U)

Could be group (1).

45s

Number	Title (A Side/B Side)	Yr	VG	VG+	NM
PARKWAY					
147	Good Day Sunshine/Where Have All the Good Times Gone	1967	3.00	6.00	12.00

ZZ TOP

Also see MOVING SIDEWALKS.

12-Inch Singles

Number	Title (A Side/B Side)	Yr	VG	VG+	NM
WARNER BROS.					
PRO-A-877 [DJ]	Cheap Sunglasses (LP Version)/Cheap Sunglasses (Live Version)	1979	5.00	10.00	20.00
PRO-A-2094 [DJ]	TV Dinners (same on both sides)	1983	3.00	6.00	12.00
PRO-A-2146 [DJ]	Legs (Dance Mix) (same on both sides)	1983	3.00	6.00	12.00
PRO-A-2365 [DJ]	Sleeping Bag (same on both sides)	1985	—	3.00	6.00
PRO-A-2407 [DJ]	Stages (same on both sides)	1985	—	3.00	6.00
PRO-A-2432 [DJ]	Delirious (same on both sides)	1985	—	3.00	6.00
PRO-A-2456 [DJ]	Rough Boy (same on both sides)	1985	—	3.00	6.00
PRO-A-2529 [DJ]	Velcro Fly (extended and dub versions)	1985	2.00	4.00	8.00
PRO-A-5483 [DJ]	Viva Las Vegas (5:11) (8:36)	1992	2.50	5.00	10.00
20395	Sleeping Bag (Extended Version)/Party on the Patio	1985	2.50	5.00	10.00
20524	Velcro Fly (Extended Mix) (Dub Mix)/Woke Up with Wood	1985	2.00	4.00	8.00
21840	Give It Up (4 versions)/Concrete and Steel	1990	—	3.00	6.00

45s

Number	Title (A Side/B Side)	Yr	VG	VG+	NM
LONDON					
131	Salt Lick/Miller's Farm	1970	—	3.00	6.00
138	(Somebody Else Been) Shakin' Your Tree/Neighbor, Neighbor	1970	—	3.00	6.00
179	Francene/Francene (Spanish)	1972	—	3.00	6.00
203	La Grange/Just Got Paid	1973	—	3.00	6.00
220	Tush/Blue Jean Blues	1975	—	2.50	5.00
220 [PS]	Tush/Blue Jean Blues	1975	2.00	4.00	8.00
241	It's Only Love/Asleep in the Desert	1976	—	2.00	4.00
241 [PS]	It's Only Love/Asleep in the Desert	1976	—	3.00	6.00
251	Arrested for Driving While Blind/It's Only Love	1977	—	2.00	4.00
252	Enjoy and Get It On/El Diablo	1977	—	2.00	4.00
RCA					
62812	Breakaway/Pincushion	1994	—	2.00	4.00
62928	Fuzzbox Voodoo/Girl in a T-Shirt	1994	—	2.00	4.00
SCAT					
500	Salt Lick/Miller's Farm	1969	50.00	100.00	200.00
WARNER BROS.					
18979	Viva Las Vegas/2000 Blues	1992	—	—	3.00
19812	Doubleback/Planet of Women	1990	—	—	3.00
19812 [PS]	Doubleback/Planet of Women	1990	—	3.00	6.00
28650	Velcro Fly/Woke Up with Wood	1986	—	—	3.00
28733	Rough Boy/Delicious	1986	—	—	3.00
28733 [PS]	Rough Boy/Delicious	1986	—	—	3.00
28810	Stages/Can't Stop Rockin'	1986	—	—	3.00
28810 [PS]	Stages/Can't Stop Rockin'	1986	—	—	3.00
28884	Sleeping Bag/Party on the Patio	1985	—	—	3.00
28884 [PS]	Sleeping Bag/Party on the Patio	1985	—	—	3.00
29272	Legs/Bad Girl	1984	—	2.00	4.00
29272 [PS]	Legs/Bad Girl	1984	—	2.00	4.00
29576	Sharp Dressed Man/I Got the Six	1983	—	2.00	4.00
29693	Gimme All Your Lovin/If I Could Only Flag Her Down	1983	—	2.00	4.00
29693 [PS]	Gimme All Your Lovin/If I Could Only Flag Her Down	1983	—	2.50	5.00
49163	I Thank You/Fool for Your Stockings	1980	—	2.00	4.00
49220	Cheap Sunglasses/Esther Be the One	1980	—	2.00	4.00
49782	Don't Tease Me/Leila	1981	—	2.00	4.00
49865	Tube Snake Boogie/Heaven, Hell or Houston	1981	—	2.00	4.00

Albums

Number	Title (A Side/B Side)	Yr	VG	VG+	NM
LONDON					
PS 584	ZZ Top's First Album	1971	3.00	6.00	12.00
PS 612	Rio Grande Mud	1972	3.00	6.00	12.00
XPS 631	Tres Hombres	1973	3.00	6.00	12.00
PS 656	Fandango!	1975	3.00	6.00	12.00
PS 680	Tejas	1977	3.00	6.00	12.00
PS 706	The Best of ZZ Top	1977	3.00	6.00	12.00
PS-X-1001 [DJ]	Takin' Texas to the People	1976	12.50	25.00	50.00
WARNER BROS.					
BSK 3268	ZZ Top's First Album	1979	2.00	4.00	8.00
BSK 3269	Rio Grande Mud	1979	2.00	4.00	8.00
BSK 3270	Tres Hombres	1979	2.00	4.00	8.00
BSK 3271	Fandango!	1979	2.00	4.00	8.00
BSK 3272	Tejas	1979	2.00	4.00	8.00
BSK 3273	The Best of ZZ Top	1979	2.00	4.00	8.00
HS 3361	Deguello	1979	2.50	5.00	10.00
BSK 3593	El Loco	1981	2.50	5.00	10.00
23774	Eliminator	1983	2.00	4.00	8.00
25342	Afterburner	1985	2.00	4.00	8.00
26265	Recycler	1990	3.75	7.50	15.00
26846	Greatest Hits	1992	3.75	7.50	15.00
—U.S. vinyl available only through Columbia House					

ZZEBRA

Albums

Number	Title (A Side/B Side)	Yr	VG	VG+	NM
POLYDOR					
PD-6043	Panic	1975	3.00	6.00	12.00

ORIGINAL CAST RECORDINGS

Label, Number	Yr	VG	VG+	NM
110 IN THE SHADE				
RCA Victor LOC-1085 [M]	1963	6.25	12.50	25.00
RCA Victor LSO-1085 [S]	1963	10.00	20.00	40.00
1776				
Columbia Masterworks BOS 3310	1969	7.50	15.00	30.00
—The first edition has Howard DaSilva shown as Ben Franklin in credits and synopsis, though he does not appear on the LP				
Columbia Masterworks BOS 3310	1969	3.00	6.00	12.00
—Revised (correct) edition has Rex Everhart shown as Ben Franklin in credits and synopsis				
70 GIRLS, 70				
Columbia Masterworks S 30589	1971	12.50	25.00	50.00
ALL AMERICAN				
Columbia Masterworks KOS 2160 [S]	1962	7.50	15.00	30.00
Columbia Masterworks KOL 5760 [M]	1962	6.25	12.50	25.00
ANKLES AWEIGHT				
Decca DL 9025 [M]	1955	10.00	20.00	40.00
ANNIE GET YOUR GUN				
Decca DL 8001 [M]	1949	12.50	25.00	50.00
—Original LP issue of the Broadway cast				
Decca DL 9018 [M]	1955	10.00	20.00	40.00
—Early reissue of DL 8001; black label with silver print				
Decca DL 79018 [R]	196?	3.00	6.00	12.00
RCA Victor LOC-1124 [M]	1966	3.00	6.00	12.00
RCA Victor LSO-1124 [S]	1966	3.75	7.50	15.00
—Revival cast; black label, dog on top, "Stereo Dynagroove" at bottom				
RCA Victor LSO-1124 [S]	1969	2.50	5.00	10.00
—Revival cast; orange, tan or black "dog near top" label				
ANYA				
United Artists UAL-4133 [M]	1965	5.00	10.00	20.00
United Artists UAS-5133 [S]	1965	12.50	25.00	50.00
APPLAUSE				
ABC ABCS-OC-11	1970	5.00	10.00	20.00
THE APPLE TREE				
Columbia Masterworks KOS 3020 [S]	1966	6.25	12.50	25.00
Columbia Masterworks KOL 6620 [M]	1966	5.00	10.00	20.00
ARABIAN NIGHTS				
Decca DL 9013 [M]	1954	20.00	40.00	80.00
THE ATHENIAN TOUCH				
Broadway East OCM-101 [M]	1964	37.50	75.00	150.00
Broadway East OCS-101 [S]	1964	50.00	100.00	200.00
BAJOUR				
Columbia Masterworks KOS 2700 [S]	1964	7.50	15.00	30.00
Columbia Masterworks KOL 6300 [M]	1964	6.25	12.50	25.00
BAKER STREET (A MUSICAL ADVENTURE OF SHERLOCK HOLMES)				
MGM E-7000 [M]	1965	6.25	12.50	25.00
MGM SE-7000 [S]	1965	7.50	15.00	30.00
A BALLAD FOR BIMSHIRE				
London AM 48002 [M]	1963	10.00	20.00	40.00
London AMS 78002 [S]	1963	20.00	40.00	80.00
THE BALLAD OF BABY DOE				
MGM 3GC-1 [(3) M]	1958	37.50	75.00	150.00
—Box set				
THE BAND WAGON				
"X" LVA-1001 [M]	1955	17.50	35.00	70.00
BELLS ARE RINGING				
Columbia Masterworks OS 2006 [S]	1959	6.25	12.50	25.00
—Re-recording in stereo of OL 5170				
Columbia Masterworks OL 5170 [M]	1957	7.50	15.00	30.00
—Gray and black label with six "eye" logos				
BEN FRANKLIN IN PARIS				
Capitol VAS 2191 [M]	1964	6.25	12.50	25.00
Capitol SVAS 2191 [S]	1964	7.50	15.00	30.00
BEST FOOT FORWARD				
Cadence CLP-4012 [M]	1963	5.00	10.00	20.00
Cadence CLP-24012 [S]	1963	7.50	15.00	30.00
—1963 revival of 1941 play				
BEYOND THE FRINGE				
Capitol W 1792 [M]	1962	6.25	12.50	25.00
Capitol SW 1792 [S]	1962	7.50	15.00	30.00
BEYOND THE FRINGE '64				
Capitol W 2072 [M]	1964	5.00	10.00	20.00
Capitol SW 2072 [S]	1964	6.25	12.50	25.00
THE BOY FRIEND				
RCA Victor LOC-1018 [M]	1954	7.50	15.00	30.00
—Originals have green labels				
THE BOYS IN THE BAND				
A&M SP-6001 [(2)]	1969	6.25	12.50	25.00
BRAVO, GIOVANNI				
Columbia Masterworks KOS 2200 [S]	1962	5.00	10.00	20.00

Label, Number	Yr	VG	VG+	NM
Columbia Masterworks KOL 5800 [M]	1962	3.75	7.50	15.00
BRIGADOON				
RCA Victor LOC-1001 [M]	1951	7.50	15.00	30.00
—Green front cover; green label				
RCA Victor LOC-1001 [M]	195?	5.00	10.00	20.00
—Photos of kilted dancers on front cover; black "Long Play" label				
RCA Victor LOC-1001 [M]	1963	3.75	7.50	15.00
—Drawing of kilted dancers on front cover; black "Mono" label				
RCA Victor LSO-1001(e) [R]	1963	3.00	6.00	12.00
—Black label, dog on top				
BY JUPITER				
RCA Victor LOC-1137 [M]	1967	10.00	20.00	40.00
RCA Victor LSO-1137 [S]	1967	18.75	37.50	75.00
—Above is by a revival cast				
BY THE BEAUTIFUL SEA				
Capitol S 531 [M]	1954	17.50	35.00	70.00
BYE BYE BIRDIE				
Columbia Masterworks KOS 2025 [S]	1960	7.50	15.00	30.00
—Gray and black label with six "eye" logos; with gatefold cover				
Columbia Masterworks OS 2025 [S]	196?	6.25	12.50	25.00
—Gray and black label with six "eye" logos; with regular cover				
Columbia Masterworks KOL 5510 [M]	1960	6.25	12.50	25.00
—Gray and black label with six "eye" logos; with gatefold cover				
Columbia Masterworks OL 5510 [M]	196?	5.00	10.00	20.00
—Gray and black label with six "eye" logos; with regular cover				
CABARET				
Columbia Masterworks KOS 3040 [S]	1966	5.00	10.00	20.00
Columbia Masterworks KOL 6640 [M]	1966	3.75	7.50	15.00
CABIN IN THE SKY				
Capitol W 2073 [M]	1964	7.50	15.00	30.00
Capitol SW 2073 [S]	1964	12.50	25.00	50.00
—Above is by a revival cast				
CALL ME MADAM				
RCA Victor LOC-1000 [M]	1950	20.00	40.00	80.00
—Dinah Shore sings Ethel Merman's part for contractual reasons, otherwise it's by the entire original cast				
CAMELOT				
Columbia Masterworks KOS 2031 [S]	1960	6.25	12.50	25.00
—Gray and black label with six "eye" logos; gatefold cover				
Columbia Masterworks KOL 5620 [M]	1960	5.00	10.00	20.00
—Gray and black label with six "eye" logos				
CAN-CAN				
Capitol S 452 [M]	1953	6.25	12.50	25.00
—Originals have red labels with Capitol logo at top				
Capitol W 452 [M]	195?	3.75	7.50	15.00
Capitol DW 452 [R]	196?	3.00	6.00	12.00
CANTERBURY TALES				
Capitol SW-229	1969	6.25	12.50	25.00
CAPTAIN JINKS OF THE HORSE MARINES				
RCA Victor ARL2-1727 [(2)]	1975	7.50	15.00	30.00
—Box set				
CARMEN JONES				
Decca DL 8014 [M]	1949	10.00	20.00	40.00
—Black label, gold print				
Decca DL 9021 [M]	1955	5.00	10.00	20.00
—Reissue of 8014; black label, silver print				
CARNIVAL				
MGM E-3946 [M]	1961	5.00	10.00	20.00
MGM SE-3946 [S]	1961	6.25	12.50	25.00
—Black label				
CAROUSEL				
Command RS 33-843 [M]	1962	3.75	7.50	15.00
—Studio cast				
Command RS-843 SD [M]	1962	5.00	10.00	20.00
—Studio cast witrh Alfred Drake and Roberta Peters, and Enoch Light's orchestra				
Decca DL 8003 [M]	1949	10.00	20.00	40.00
—Original LP issue of the Broadway cast				
Decca DL 9020 [M]	1955	7.50	15.00	30.00
—Early reissue of DL 8003; black label with silver print				
CHRISTINE				
Columbia Masterworks OS 2026 [S]	1960	25.00	50.00	100.00
Columbia Masterworks OL 5520 [M]	1960	15.00	30.00	60.00
CINDY				
ABC-Paramount ABC-OC-2 [M]	1964	7.50	15.00	30.00
ABC-Paramount ABC-OCS-2 [S]	1964	12.50	25.00	50.00
CLARA (BEG, BORROW OR STEAL)				
Commentary CYN-02 [M]	1960	15.00	30.00	60.00
CLOWNAROUND				
RCA Victor LSP-4741	1972	62.50	125.00	250.00
CLUB 15				
Decca DL 5155 [10]	1949	15.00	30.00	60.00
THE COACH WITH THE SIX INSIDES				
ESP-Disk' 1019 [M]	1967	6.25	12.50	25.00

Label, Number	Yr	VG	VG+	NM
COCO				
Paramount PMS-1002	1969	6.25	12.50	25.00
THE COMMITTEE				
Reprise F-2023 [M]	1964	7.50	15.00	30.00
Reprise FS-2023 [S]	1964	10.00	20.00	40.00
COMPANY				
Columbia Masterworks OS 3550	1970	3.00	6.00	12.00
Columbia Masterworks SQ 30993 [Q]	1971	7.50	15.00	30.00
—Quadraphonic version has substantially different mixes than the original stereo LP				
THE CRADLE WILL ROCK				
MGM E-4289-2 [(2) M]	1964	6.25	12.50	25.00
MGM SE-4289-2 [(2) S]	1964	7.50	15.00	30.00
—The above is by a revival cast				
THE CRITIC				
Decca DL 9154 [M]	1967	5.00	10.00	20.00
Decca DL 79154 [S]	1967	5.00	10.00	20.00
CRY FOR US ALL				
Project 3 TS-1000 SD	1970	10.00	20.00	40.00
DAMES AT SEA				
Columbia Masterworks OS 3550	1969	5.00	10.00	20.00
DAMN YANKEES				
RCA Victor LOC-1021 [M]	1955	7.50	15.00	30.00
—Green cover				
RCA Victor LOC-1021 [M]	195?	5.00	10.00	20.00
—Orange cover				
RCA Victor LSO-1021(e) [R]	1965	3.75	7.50	15.00
—Black label, dog on top, "Stereo Electronically Reprocessed" at bottom				
THE DANCERS OF BALI				
Columbia Masterworks ML 4618 [M]	1952	10.00	20.00	40.00
DARLING OF THE DAY				
RCA Victor LOC-1149 [M]	1968	10.00	20.00	40.00
RCA Victor LSO-1149 [S]	1968	15.00	30.00	60.00
DEAR WORLD				
Columbia Masterworks BOS 3260	1969	5.00	10.00	20.00
DEATH OF A SALESMAN				
Decca DX 102 [(2) M]	1951	10.00	20.00	40.00
—Two-record boxed set with contents of 9007 and 9008				
DEATH OF A SALESMAN (PART 1)				
Decca DL 9006 [M]	1951	6.25	12.50	25.00
—Black label, gold print				
DEATH OF A SALESMAN (PART 2)				
Decca DL 9007 [M]	1951	6.25	12.50	25.00
—Black label, gold print				
DESTRY RIDES AGAIN				
Decca DL 9075 [M]	1959	7.50	15.00	30.00
Decca DL 79075 [S]	1959	10.00	20.00	40.00
DO I HEAR A WALTZ?				
Columbia Masterworks KOS 2770 [S]	1965	5.00	10.00	20.00
Columbia Masterworks KOL 6370 [M]	1965	3.75	7.50	15.00
DO RE MI				
RCA Victor LOC-1105 [M]	1965	3.75	7.50	15.00
—Reissue of 2002 with standard red cover				
RCA Victor LSO-1105 [S]	1965	5.00	10.00	20.00
—Reissue of 2002 with standard red cover				
RCA Victor LOCD-2002 [M]	1961	7.50	15.00	30.00
—In black box with orange sleeve				
RCA Victor LSOD-2002 [S]	1961	10.00	20.00	40.00
—In black box with orange sleeve				
DOCTOR SELAVY'S MAGIC THEATRE				
United Artists UA-LA196-G	1974	7.50	15.00	30.00
DONNYBROOK!				
Kapp KDL-8500 [M]	1961	5.00	10.00	20.00
Kapp KD-8500-S [S]	1961	6.25	12.50	25.00
DRESSED TO THE NINES				
MGM E-3914 [M]	1960	6.25	12.50	25.00
MGM SE-3914 [S]	1960	10.00	20.00	40.00
THE EARL OF RUSTON				
Capitol ST-465	1971	10.00	20.00	40.00
ERNEST IN LOVE				
Columbia Masterworks OS 2027 [S]	1960	25.00	50.00	100.00
Columbia Masterworks OL 5530 [M]	1960	15.00	30.00	60.00
AN EVENING WITH RICHARD NIXON				
Ode SP-77015	1972	7.50	15.00	30.00
FADE OUT-FADE IN				
ABC-Paramount ABC-OC-3 [M]	1964	6.25	12.50	25.00
ABC-Paramount ABCS-OC-3 [S]	1964	7.50	15.00	30.00
A FAMILY AFFAIR				
United Artists UAL-4099 [M]	1962	7.50	15.00	30.00
United Artists UAS-5099 [S]	1962	12.50	25.00	50.00
FANNY				
RCA Victor LOC-1015 [M]	1954	6.25	12.50	25.00
—"Long Play" on label				
RCA Victor LOC-1015 [M]	196?	3.75	7.50	15.00
—"Mono" on label				
RCA Victor LSO-1015(e) [R]	196?	3.00	6.00	12.00
—"Stereo Electronically Reprocessed" on label				
THE FANTASTICKS				
MGM E-3872 [M]	1963	5.00	10.00	20.00
—Original non-gatefold cover				
MGM SE-3872 [S]	1963	6.25	12.50	25.00
—Original non-gatefold cover				
FIDDLER ON THE ROOF				
RCA Victor LOC-1093 [M]	1964	3.75	7.50	15.00
RCA Victor LSO-1093 [S]	1964	5.00	10.00	20.00
—Black label, dog on top				
FINIAN'S RAINBOW				
Columbia Masterworks OS 2080 [R]	1963	3.00	6.00	12.00
Columbia Masterworks ML 4062 [M]	1948	7.50	15.00	30.00
—Original cover with no photo; green label				
Columbia Masterworks OL 4062 [M]	196?	3.00	6.00	12.00
—Reissue cover, either pink or green; gray label				
RCA Victor LOC-1057	1960	3.00	6.00	12.00
—Revival cast; "pot of gold" cover				
RCA Victor LOC-1057	1960	2.50	5.00	10.00
—Revival cast; cover shows co-stars hiding in the trees				
RCA Victor LSO-1057	1960	3.75	7.50	15.00
—Revival cast; "pot of gold" cover				
RCA Victor LSO-1057	1960	3.00	6.00	12.00
—Revival cast; cover shows co-stars hiding in the trees				
FIORELLO!				
Capitol WAO 1321 [M]	1959	5.00	10.00	20.00
Capitol SWAO 1321 [S]	1959	6.25	12.50	25.00
FIRST IMPRESSIONS				
Columbia Masterworks OS 2014 [S]	1959	15.00	30.00	60.00
Columbia Masterworks OL 5400 [M]	1959	7.50	15.00	30.00
FLAHOOLEY				
Capitol S 284 [M]	1951	37.50	75.00	150.00
FLORA, THE RED MENACE				
RCA Victor LOC-1111 [M]	1965	6.25	12.50	25.00
RCA Victor LSO-1111 [S]	1965	7.50	15.00	30.00
FLOWER DRUM SONG				
Columbia Masterworks OS 2009 [S]	1958	6.25	12.50	25.00
—Gray and black label with six "eye" logos				
Columbia Masterworks OL 5350 [M]	1958	5.00	10.00	20.00
—Gray and black label with six "eye" logos				
FLY BLACKBIRD				
Mercury OCM-2206 [M]	1962	7.50	15.00	30.00
Mercury OCS-6206 [S]	1962	15.00	30.00	60.00
FUNNY GIRL				
Capitol VAS 2059 [M]	1964	3.75	7.50	15.00
Capitol SVAS 2059 [S]	1964	5.00	10.00	20.00
—Both Barbra Streisand and Sydney Chaplin are pictured on the back cover				
Capitol STAO 2059 [S]	196?	3.00	6.00	12.00
—Only Barbra Streisand is pictured on the back cover				
A FUNNY THING HAPPENED ON THE WAY TO THE FORUM				
Capitol WAO 1717 [M]	1962	3.75	7.50	15.00
—Gatefold cover				
Capitol SWAO 1717 [S]	1962	5.00	10.00	20.00
—Gatefold cover				
THE GAY LIFE				
Capitol WAO 1560 [M]	1961	6.25	12.50	25.00
Capitol SWAO 1560 [S]	1961	12.50	25.00	50.00
GENTLEMEN PREFER BLONDES				
Columbia Masterworks ML 4290 [M]	1949	6.25	12.50	25.00
—Original with green label				
GEORGE M!				
Columbia Masterworks KOS 3200 [S]	1968	5.00	10.00	20.00
Columbia Masterworks KOL 6800 [M]	1968	7.50	15.00	30.00
THE GIRL IN PINK TIGHTS				
Columbia Masterworks ML 4890 [M]	1954	15.00	30.00	60.00
THE GIRL WHO CAME TO SUPPER				
Columbia Masterworks KOS 2420 [S]	1963	7.50	15.00	30.00
Columbia Masterworks KOL 6020 [M]	1963	6.25	12.50	25.00
GIVE 'EM HELL, HARRY!				
United Artists UA-LA540-H2 [(2)]	1975	5.00	10.00	20.00
THE GOLDEN APPLE				
RCA Victor LOC-1014 [M]	1954	25.00	50.00	100.00
GOLDEN BOY				
Capitol VAS 2124 [M]	1964	6.25	12.50	25.00
Capitol SVAS 2124 [S]	1964	7.50	15.00	30.00
GOLDILOCKS				
Columbia Masterworks OS 2007 [S]	1958	15.00	30.00	60.00
Columbia Masterworks OL 5340 [M]	1958	6.25	12.50	25.00

Label, Number	Yr	VG	VG+	NM
GOODTIME CHARLEY				
RCA Victor ARL1-1011	1975	7.50	15.00	30.00
GREASE				
MGM 1SE-34	1972	3.00	6.00	12.00
THE GREAT WALTZ				
Capitol VAS 2426 [M]	1965	5.00	10.00	20.00
Capitol SVAS 2426 [S]	1965	6.25	12.50	25.00
GREENWICH VILLAGE U.S.A.				
20th Fox TCF-105-2 [(2) M]	1960	15.00	30.00	60.00
—With complete show				
20th Fox TCF-105-2S [(2) S]	1960	25.00	50.00	100.00
—With complete show				
20th Fox FOX-4005 [M]	1960	10.00	20.00	40.00
—With excerpts from the show				
20th Fox SFX-4005 [S]	1960	12.50	25.00	50.00
—With excerpts from the show				
GREENWILLOW				
RCA Victor LOC-2001 [M]	1960	5.00	10.00	20.00
RCA Victor LSO-2001 [S]	1960	12.50	25.00	50.00
GYPSY				
Columbia Masterworks OS 2017 [S]	1959	6.25	12.50	25.00
—Original covers are white with drawings				
Columbia Masterworks OL 5420 [M]	1959	5.00	10.00	20.00
—Original covers are white with drawings				
HAIR				
Atco SD 7002	1969	6.25	12.50	25.00
—Original London cast				
Philips PHS 600329	1969	6.25	12.50	25.00
—Original French cast				
RCA Victor LOC-1143	1967	3.75	7.50	15.00
—Off-Broadway cast				
RCA Victor LSO-1143	1967	3.00	6.00	12.00
—Off-Broadway cast; black label, dog at top, "Stereo" at bottom				
RCA Victor LOC-1150	1968	7.50	15.00	30.00
—Broadway cast				
RCA Victor LSO-1150	1968	5.00	10.00	20.00
—Broadway cast; black label, dog on top, "Stereo" at bottom				
RCA Victor LSO-1150	1968	2.50	5.00	10.00
—Broadway cast; orange label				
HALF A SIXPENCE				
RCA Victor LOC-1110 [M]	1965	5.00	10.00	20.00
RCA Victor LSO-1110 [S]	1965	6.25	12.50	25.00
HALF PAST WEDNESDAY				
Columbia CL 1917 [M]	1962	7.50	15.00	30.00
Columbia CS 8717 [S]	1962	10.00	20.00	40.00
HAMLET				
Columbia Masterworks DOL 302 [(4) M]	1964	6.25	12.50	25.00
—Boxed set with entire play (Broadway revival)				
Columbia Masterworks DOS 702 [(4) S]	1964	6.25	12.50	25.00
—Boxed set with entire play (Broadway revival)				
Columbia Masterworks OS 2620 [S]	1964	3.75	7.50	15.00
—Highlights from the box set				
Columbia Masterworks OL 6220 [M]	1964	3.75	7.50	15.00
—Highlights from the box set				
THE HAPPIEST GIRL IN THE WORLD				
Columbia Masterworks KOS 2050 [S]	1961	15.00	30.00	60.00
—Original covers are yellow				
Columbia Masterworks KOS 2050 [S]	1961	10.00	20.00	40.00
—Second covers are white				
Columbia Masterworks KOL 5650 [M]	1961	10.00	20.00	40.00
—Original covers are yellow				
Columbia Masterworks KOL 5650 [M]	1961	7.50	15.00	30.00
—Second covers are white				
HAPPY HUNTING				
RCA Victor LOC-1026 [M]	1956	10.00	20.00	40.00
HEAR! HEAR!				
Decca DL 9031 [M]	1955	12.50	25.00	50.00
HELLO, DOLLY!				
RCA Victor LOCD-1087 [M]	1964	6.25	12.50	25.00
—Original cover is black and white on back and spotlights "Come and Be My Butterfly"; this song was deleted from the show, so the cover was changed				
RCA Victor LOCD-1087 [M]	1964	3.75	7.50	15.00
—New back cover is in color and has a photo of Carol Channing; "RE" is on cover				
RCA Victor LSOD-1087 [S]	1964	7.50	15.00	30.00
—Original cover is black and white on back and spotlights "Come and Be My Butterfly"; this song was deleted from the show, so the cover was changed				
RCA Victor LSOD-1087 [S]	1964	5.00	10.00	20.00
—New back cover is in color and has a photo of Carol Channing; "RE" is on cover; black label, dog on top				
RCA Victor LSOD-1087 [S]	1969	2.50	5.00	10.00
—Orange or tan label				
HENRY, SWEET HENRY				
ABC ABC-OC-4 [M]	1967	7.50	15.00	30.00
ABC ABCS-OC-4 [S]	1967	12.50	25.00	50.00
HERE'S LOVE				
Columbia Masterworks KOS 2400 [S]	1963	10.00	20.00	40.00
Columbia Masterworks KOL 6000 [M]	1963	7.50	15.00	30.00

Label, Number	Yr	VG	VG+	NM
HIGH BUTTON SHOES				
RCA Camden CAL-457 [M]	1958	7.50	15.00	30.00
RCA Victor LOC-1107 [M]	1964	10.00	20.00	40.00
RCA Victor LSO-1107 [R]	1964	7.50	15.00	30.00
HIGH SPIRITS				
ABC-Paramount ABC-OC-1 [M]	1964	6.25	12.50	25.00
ABC-Paramount ABCS-OC-1 [S]	1964	7.50	15.00	30.00
HOUSE OF FLOWERS				
Columbia Masterworks ML 4969 [M]	1954	10.00	20.00	40.00
—Blue label original				
United Artists UAS-5180	1968	10.00	20.00	40.00
—Revival cast				
HOW NOW, DOW JONES				
RCA Victor LOC-1142 [M]	1967	6.25	12.50	25.00
RCA Victor LSO-1142 [S]	1967	7.50	15.00	30.00
HOW TO SUCCEED IN BUSINESS WITHOUT REALLY TRYING				
RCA Victor LOC-1066 [M]	1961	5.00	10.00	20.00
RCA Victor LSO-1066 [S]	1961	6.25	12.50	25.00
—Black label, dog on top				
RCA Victor LSO-1066 [S]	1969	2.50	5.00	10.00
—Orange or tan label				
HUGHIE				
Columbia Masterworks OS 2760 [S]	1965	7.50	15.00	30.00
Columbia Masterworks OL 6260 [M]	1965	6.25	12.50	25.00
I CAN GET IT FOR YOU WHOLESALE				
Columbia Masterworks KOS 2180 [S]	1962	7.50	15.00	30.00
Columbia Masterworks KOL 5780 [M]	1962	6.25	12.50	25.00
I DO! I DO!				
RCA Victor LOC-1128 [M]	1966	3.75	7.50	15.00
RCA Victor LSO-1128 [S]	1966	5.00	10.00	20.00
—Black label, dog on top				
I HAD A BALL				
Mercury OCM-2210 [M]	1964	5.00	10.00	20.00
Mercury OCM-2210 [(2) M]	1964	10.00	20.00	40.00
—Promo-only two-record set with bonus interview record MGD-2-24				
Mercury OCS-6210 [S]	1964	6.25	12.50	25.00
ICE FOLLIES				
Dot DLP-3757 [M]	1967	6.25	12.50	25.00
Dot DLP-25757 [S]	1967	7.50	15.00	30.00
ILLYA DARLING				
United Artists UAL-8901 [M]	1967	5.00	10.00	20.00
United Artists UAS-9901 [S]	1967	5.00	10.00	20.00
IRMA LA DOUCE				
Columbia Masterworks OS 2029 [S]	1960	6.25	12.50	25.00
Columbia Masterworks OL 5560 [M]	1960	5.00	10.00	20.00
JACQUES BREL IS ALIVE AND WELL AND LIVING IN PARIS				
Columbia Masterworks D2S 779 [(2)]	1968	5.00	10.00	20.00
—Box set; gray "360 Sound" labels				
JENNIE				
RCA Victor LOC-1083 [M]	1963	6.25	12.50	25.00
RCA Victor LSO-1083 [S]	1963	12.50	25.00	50.00
JESUS CHRIST SUPERSTAR				
Decca DL 71503	1971	5.00	10.00	20.00
—Not to be confused with the original studio recording (this is a one-record gatefold)				
JOSEPH AND THE AMAZING TECHNICOLOR DREAMCOAT				
Scepter SPS-588X	1968	5.00	10.00	20.00
—With gatefold cover and libretto				
Scepter SMAS-93738	197?	6.25	12.50	25.00
—Capitol Record Club edition				
JOY				
RCA Victor LSO-1166	1970	5.00	10.00	20.00
JUNO				
Columbia Masterworks OS 2013 [S]	1959	17.50	35.00	70.00
Columbia Masterworks OL 5380 [M]	1959	10.00	20.00	40.00
J.B.				
RCA Victor LD-6075 [(2) M]	1959	15.00	30.00	60.00
RCA Victor LDS-6075 [(2) S]	1959	17.50	35.00	70.00
KEAN				
Columbia Masterworks KSO 2120 [S]	1961	10.00	20.00	40.00
Columbia Masterworks KOL 5720 [M]	1961	7.50	15.00	30.00
THE KING AND I				
Decca DL 9008 [M]	1951	6.25	12.50	25.00
—Black label, gold print				
Decca DL 9008 [M]	195?	10.00	20.00	40.00
—Drawing of Gertrude Lawrence and Yul Brynner on cover, with title on three lines				
Decca DL 9008 [M]	195?	3.00	6.00	12.00
—Drawing of Gertrude Lawrence and Yul Brynner on cover, with title on two lines				
Decca DL 79008 [R]	196?	2.50	5.00	10.00
KWAMINA				
Capitol W 1645 [M]	1962	7.50	15.00	30.00
Capitol SW 1645 [S]	1962	12.50	25.00	50.00

Label, Number	Yr	VG	VG+	NM
THE LADY'S NOT FOR BURNING				
Decca DL 9508 /9 [(2) M]	1951	12.50	25.00	50.00
—Oversize box set				
LAGINAPPE '59 PRESENTS BE MY GUEST				
(no label) XCTV-10303 [M]	1959	62.50	125.00	250.00
—Custom pressing for New Trier High School, Illinois. Collectible because the future Ann-Margret sings one track on the LP!				
LET IT RIDE				
RCA Victor LOC-1064 [M]	1961	5.00	10.00	20.00
RCA Victor LSO-1064 [S]	1961	10.00	20.00	40.00
LI'L ABNER				
Columbia Masterworks OL 5150 [M]	1956	7.50	15.00	30.00
LITTLE ME				
RCA Victor LOC-1078 [M]	1962	5.00	10.00	20.00
RCA Victor LSO-1078 [S]	1962	6.25	12.50	25.00
LOOK MA, I'M DANCIN'!				
Decca DL 5231 [M]	1950	25.00	50.00	100.00
LORELEI				
MGM M3G-55	1974	7.50	15.00	30.00
—Second version, recorded with Broadway cast				
Verve MV-5097-OC	1974	6.25	12.50	25.00
—First version, recorded before the show hit Broadway				
LOST IN THE STARS				
Decca DL 8028 [M]	1949	12.50	25.00	50.00
Decca DL 9120 [M]	1965	3.75	7.50	15.00
—Reissue of 8028				
THE MAD SHOW				
Columbia Masterworks OS 2930 [S]	1965	25.00	50.00	100.00
Columbia Masterworks OL 6530 [M]	1965	12.50	25.00	50.00
MAGGIE FLYNN				
RCA Victor LSOD-2009	1968	6.25	12.50	25.00
RCA Victor LSOD-2009	1968	5.00	10.00	20.00
THE MAGIC SHOW				
Bell 9003	1974	5.00	10.00	20.00
MAME				
Columbia Masterworks KOS 3000 [S]	1966	5.00	10.00	20.00
—Gray label with "360 Sound Stereo"				
Columbia Masterworks KOL 6600 [M]	1966	3.75	7.50	15.00
MAN OF LA MANCHA				
Kapp KRL-4505 [M]	1965	3.75	7.50	15.00
Kapp KRS-4505 [S]	1965	5.00	10.00	20.00
MARK TWAIN TONIGHT!				
Columbia Masterworks OS 2019 [S]	1959	3.75	7.50	15.00
Columbia Masterworks OL 5440 [M]	1959	3.00	6.00	12.00
ME AND JULIET				
RCA Victor LOC-1012 [M]	1953	17.50	35.00	70.00
MEDEA				
Decca DLP 9000 [M]	1949	7.50	15.00	30.00
MEGILLA OF ITZIG MANGER				
Columbia Masterworks OS 3270	1968	10.00	20.00	40.00
THE MERRY WIDOW				
RCA Victor LOC-1094 [M]	1964	5.00	10.00	20.00
RCA Victor LSO-1094 [S]	1964	6.25	12.50	25.00
MEXICAN HAYRIDE				
Decca DL 5232 [10]	1950	30.00	60.00	120.00
MILK AND HONEY				
RCA Victor LOC-1065 [M]	1961	6.25	12.50	25.00
—With only credits (no picture) on front cover				
RCA Victor LOC-1065 [M]	1961	5.00	10.00	20.00
—With picture of Tommy Rall and two dancers on front cover				
RCA Victor LSO-1065 [S]	1961	7.50	15.00	30.00
—With only credits (no picture) on front cover				
RCA Victor LSO-1065 [S]	1961	6.25	12.50	25.00
—With picture of Tommy Rall and two dancers on front cover				
MISS LIBERTY				
Columbia Masterworks ML 4220 [M]	1949	7.50	15.00	30.00
—Originals have green labels				
THE MOST HAPPY FELLA				
Columbia Masterworks O3L 240 [(3) M]	1956	12.50	25.00	50.00
—Box set with entire show				
Columbia Masterworks OS 2330 [R]	196?	3.75	7.50	15.00
Columbia Masterworks OL 5118 [M]	1956	7.50	15.00	30.00
—Gray and black label with six "eye" logos				
MRS. PATTERSON				
RCA Victor LOC-1017 [M]	1954	37.50	75.00	150.00
MR. PRESIDENT				
Columbia Masterworks KOS 2270 [S]	1962	7.50	15.00	30.00
—Gatefold with shiny silver cover				
Columbia Masterworks KOL 5870 [M]	1962	5.00	10.00	20.00
—Gatefold with shiny silver cover				

Label, Number	Yr	VG	VG+	NM
MR. WONDERFUL				
Decca DL 9032 [M]	1956	12.50	25.00	50.00
THE MUSIC MAN				
Capitol WAO 990 [M]	1957	5.00	10.00	20.00
—Gatefold cover, white with credits and drawing on front; gray label				
Capitol SWAO 990 [S]	1957	6.25	12.50	25.00
—Gatefold cover, white with credits and drawing on front; gray label				
Capitol W 990 [M]	196?	3.00	6.00	12.00
—Regular cover with photo of Robert Preston as Harold Hill				
Capitol SW 990 [S]	196?	3.75	7.50	15.00
—Regular cover with photo of Robert Preston as Harold Hill				
MY FAIR LADY				
Columbia Masterworks OS 2015 [S]	1959	5.00	10.00	20.00
—Gray and black label with six "eye" logos; original London cast				
Columbia Masterworks OS 2015 [S]	1959	3.00	6.00	12.00
—Gray label, "Stereo" at bottom; original London cast				
Columbia Masterworks OL 5090 [M]	1956	6.25	12.50	25.00
—Gray and black label with six "eye" logos				
Columbia Masterworks OL 5090 [M]	1963	3.75	7.50	15.00
—Gray label with "Guaranteed High Fidelity" at bottom				
Columbia Masterworks OL 5090 [M]	1956	2.50	5.00	10.00
—Gray label, "Mono" at bottom				
MY PEOPLE				
Contact C-1 [M]	1966	5.00	10.00	20.00
Contact CS-1 [S]	1966	6.25	12.50	25.00
THE NERVOUS SET				
Columbia Masterworks OS 2018 [S]	1959	15.00	30.00	60.00
Columbia Masterworks OL 5430 [M]	1959	7.50	15.00	30.00
NEW FACES OF 1952				
RCA Victor LOC-1008 [M]	1952	6.25	12.50	25.00
NEW FACES OF 1956				
RCA Victor LOC-1025 [M]	1956	12.50	25.00	50.00
NEW FACES OF 1968				
Warner Bros. BS 2551	1968	7.50	15.00	30.00
THE NEW GIRL IN TOWN				
RCA Victor LOC-1027 [M]	1957	5.00	10.00	20.00
RCA Victor LSO-1027 [S]	1958	12.50	25.00	50.00
RCA Victor LOC-1106 [M]	1965	5.00	10.00	20.00
RCA Victor LSC-1106 [S]	1965	7.50	15.00	30.00
THE NINA, THE PINTA AND THE SANTA MARIA				
Dot DLP-9009 [M]	1960	10.00	20.00	40.00
Dot DLP-29009 [S]	1960	12.50	25.00	50.00
NO STRINGS				
Capitol O 1695 [M]	1962	5.00	10.00	20.00
Capitol SO 1695 [S]	1962	10.00	20.00	40.00
OF THEE I SING				
Capitol S 350 [M]	1952	37.50	75.00	150.00
OH, KAY!				
20th Fox FOX-4003 [M]	1960	6.25	12.50	25.00
20th Fox SFX-4003 [S]	1960	12.50	25.00	50.00
OKLAHOMA!				
Decca DLP 8000 [M]	1949	7.50	15.00	30.00
—Black label, gold print; the first 12-inch LP on Decca				
Decca DL 9017 [M]	1955	5.00	10.00	20.00
—Reissue of 8000				
Decca DL 9017 [M]	196?	5.00	10.00	20.00
—Reissue with new cover art				
Decca DL 79017 [R]	196?	3.75	7.50	15.00
Decca DL 79017 [R]	1968	5.00	10.00	20.00
—Special 25th Anniversary edition; cover has yellow drawing, inner sleeve has liner notes				
OLIVER!				
RCA Victor LOCD-2004 [M]	1962	3.75	7.50	15.00
RCA Victor LSOD-2004 [S]	1962	5.00	10.00	20.00
ON A CLEAR DAY YOU CAN SEE FOREVER				
RCA Victor LOCD-2006 [M]	1965	5.00	10.00	20.00
RCA Victor LSOD-2006 [S]	1965	6.25	12.50	25.00
ON YOUR TOES				
Decca DL 9015 [M]	1954	18.75	37.50	75.00
ONCE UPON A MATTRESS				
Kapp KDL-7004 [M]	1959	6.25	12.50	25.00
Kapp KDL-7004-S [S]	1959	7.50	15.00	30.00
ONE TOUCH OF VENUS				
Decca DL 9122 [M]	1965	6.25	12.50	25.00
Decca DL 79122 [R]	1965	6.25	12.50	25.00
OVER HERE!				
Columbia Masterworks KS 32961	1974	5.00	10.00	20.00
Columbia Masterworks SQ 32961 [Q]	1974	7.50	15.00	30.00
PAINT YOUR WAGON				
RCA Victor LOC-1006 [M]	1951	6.25	12.50	25.00
—Green label				
RCA Victor LOC-1006 [M]	1955	5.00	10.00	20.00
—Black label, dog on top, "Long Play" at bottom				

Label, Number	Yr	VG	VG+	NM
PARADE				
Kapp KDL-7005 [M]	1960	50.00	100.00	200.00
Kapp KDS-7005 [S]	1960	62.50	125.00	250.00
PARIS '90				
Columbia Masterworks ML 4619 [M]	1952	37.50	75.00	150.00
PEACE				
Metromedia MP-33001	1969	7.50	15.00	30.00
PETER PAN				
RCA Victor LOC-1019 [M]	1954	10.00	20.00	40.00
PIPE DREAM				
RCA Victor LOC-1023 [M]	1955	17.50	35.00	70.00
—With "Special Advance Edition" sticker on cover				
RCA Victor LOC-1023 [M]	1955	12.50	25.00	50.00
—Without "Special Advance Edition" sticker on cover				
PLAIN AND FANCY				
Capitol S 603 [M]	1955	6.25	12.50	25.00
—Red label				
PLAYGIRLS				
Warner Bros. W 1530 [M]	1964	6.25	12.50	25.00
Warner Bros. WS 1530 [S]	1964	7.50	15.00	30.00
PORGY AND BESS				
Decca DL 7006 [10]	1950	7.50	15.00	30.00
—Reissue of material first released on 78s				
Decca DL 8042 [M]	1950	7.50	15.00	30.00
Decca DL 9024 [M]	1955	6.25	12.50	25.00
—Reissue of 8042; drawing of Catfish Row on cover				
THE PREMISE				
Vanguard VRS-9092 [M]	1960	10.00	20.00	40.00
PURLIE				
Ampex A-40101	1970	7.50	15.00	30.00
RASHOMON				
Carlton LPX-5000 [M]	1959	6.25	12.50	25.00
Carlton STLPX-5000 [S]	1959	7.50	15.00	30.00
—Not actually the original cast recording, but the play's incidental music				
REDHEAD				
RCA Victor LOC-1048 [M]	1959	5.00	10.00	20.00
RCA Victor LSO-1048 [S]	1959	12.50	25.00	50.00
—Without "Essie's Vision"				
RCA Victor LOC-1104 [M]	1959	3.75	7.50	15.00
—Reissue of 1048				
RCA Victor LSO-1104 [M]	1965	6.25	12.50	25.00
—Reissue adds "Essie's Vision" to stereo version				
THE RIVER WIND				
London AM-48001 [M]	1962	10.00	20.00	40.00
London AMS-78001 [S]	1962	20.00	40.00	80.00
THE ROAR OF THE GREASEPAINT — THE SMELL OF THE CROWD				
RCA Victor LOC-1109 [M]	1965	3.75	7.50	15.00
RCA Victor LSO-1109 [S]	1965	5.00	10.00	20.00
THE ROTHSCHILDS				
Columbia Masterworks S 30337	1970	6.25	12.50	25.00
SAIL AWAY				
Capitol WAO 1643 [M]	1961	5.00	10.00	20.00
Capitol SWAO 1643 [S]	1961	7.50	15.00	30.00
SARATOGA				
RCA Victor LOC-1051 [M]	1959	6.25	12.50	25.00
RCA Victor LSO-1051 [S]	1959	12.50	25.00	50.00
SAY, DARLING				
RCA Victor LOC-1045 [M]	1958	10.00	20.00	40.00
RCA Victor LSO-1045 [S]	1958	15.00	30.00	60.00
SEVENTEEN				
RCA Victor LOC-1003 [M]	1951	37.50	75.00	150.00
SEVENTH HEAVEN				
Decca DL 9001 [M]	1955	37.50	75.00	150.00
SHE LOVES ME				
MGM E 4118OC-2 [(2) M]	1963	10.00	20.00	40.00
MGM SE 4118OC-2 [(2) S]	1963	12.50	25.00	50.00
SHOW BIZ (FROM VAUDE TO VIDEO)				
RCA Victor LOC-1011 [M]	1954	10.00	20.00	40.00
SHOW BOAT				
Columbia Masterworks ML 4058 [M]	1948	6.25	12.50	25.00
—From the 1946 revival; paper envelope jacket with its opening on top				
Columbia Masterworks OL 4058 [M]	195?	5.00	10.00	20.00
—From the 1946 revival; reissue of ML 4058				
SHOW GIRL				
Roulette R-80001 [M]	1961	5.00	10.00	20.00
Roulette SR-80001 [S]	1961	6.25	12.50	25.00
SILK STOCKINGS				
RCA Victor LOC-1016 [M]	1955	10.00	20.00	40.00
RCA Victor LOC-1102 [M]	1965	5.00	10.00	20.00
—Reissue; regular cover				
RCA Victor LSO-1102 [R]	1965	5.00	10.00	20.00

Label, Number	Yr	VG	VG+	NM
SIMPLY HEAVENLY				
Columbia Masterworks OL 5240 [M]	1957	6.25	12.50	25.00
SING OUT, SWEET LAND!				
Decca DL 4304 [M]	1963	5.00	10.00	20.00
Decca DL 8023 [M]	1950	12.50	25.00	50.00
Decca DL 74304 [R]	1963	5.00	10.00	20.00
SKYSCRAPER				
Capitol VAS 2422 [M]	1965	5.00	10.00	20.00
Capitol SVAS 2422 [S]	1965	6.25	12.50	25.00
SONDHEIM: A MUSICAL TRIBUTE				
Warner Bros. 2WS 2705 [(2)]	1973	5.00	10.00	20.00
SONG OF NORWAY				
Columbia CL 1328 [M]	1959	5.00	10.00	20.00
—1958 revival cast				
Columbia CS 8135 [S]	1959	12.50	25.00	50.00
—1958 revival cast				
Decca DL 8002 [M]	1949	7.50	15.00	30.00
Decca DL 9019 [M]	1955	5.00	10.00	20.00
THE SOUND OF MUSIC				
Columbia Masterworks KOS 2020 [S]	1959	6.25	12.50	25.00
—Gray and black label with six "eye" logos				
Columbia Masterworks KOS 2020 [S]	1959	3.00	6.00	12.00
—Gray label with "360 Sound Stereo" at bottom				
Columbia Masterworks KOL 5450 [M]	1959	5.00	10.00	20.00
—Gray and black label with six "eye" logos				
Columbia Masterworks KOL 5450 [M]	1963	3.00	6.00	12.00
—Gray label with "Guaranteed High Fidelity" or "360 Sound Mono" on label				
SOUTH PACIFIC				
Columbia Masterworks OS 2040 [R]	196?	2.50	5.00	10.00
—Gray label with "360 Sound Stereo"				
Columbia Masterworks ML 4180 [M]	1949	6.25	12.50	25.00
—Green or blue label; large anchor on front cover				
Columbia Masterworks OL 4180 [M]	195?	3.75	7.50	15.00
—Gray and black label with six "eye" logos; large anchor on front cover				
Columbia Masterworks OL 4180 [M]	195?	3.00	6.00	12.00
—Gray and black label with six "eye" logos; glossy gatefold cover with Ezio Pinza and Mary Martin pictured				
Columbia Masterworks OL 4180 [M]	1963	2.50	5.00	10.00
—Gray label with "Guaranteed High Fidelity" or "360 Sound Mono"				
STOP THE WORLD-I WANT TO GET OFF				
London AM 58001 [M]	1962	3.75	7.50	15.00
London AMS 88001 [S]	1962	5.00	10.00	20.00
STREET SCENE				
Columbia Masterworks ML 4139 [M]	1949	7.50	15.00	30.00
—Paper envelope jacket with its opening on top				
ST. LOUIS WOMAN				
Capitol L 355 [10]	1952	20.00	40.00	80.00
THE SUBJECT WAS ROSES				
Columbia Masterworks DOL 308 [(3) M]	1964	5.00	10.00	20.00
Columbia Masterworks DOS 708 [(3) S]	1964	7.50	15.00	30.00
SUBWAYS ARE FOR SLEEPING				
Columbia Masterworks KOS 2130 [S]	1962	10.00	20.00	40.00
Columbia Masterworks KOL 5730 [M]	1962	6.25	12.50	25.00
THE SURVIVAL OF ST. JOAN				
Paramount PAS-9000 [(2)]	1971	6.25	12.50	25.00
SWEET CHARITY				
Columbia Masterworks KOS 2900 [S]	1966	5.00	10.00	20.00
Columbia Masterworks KOL 6500 [M]	1966	3.75	7.50	15.00
TAKE ME ALONG				
RCA Victor LOC-1050 [M]	1959	3.75	7.50	15.00
RCA Victor LSO-1050 [S]	1959	5.00	10.00	20.00
—Black label				
TAMALPAIS EXCHANGE				
Atlantic SD 8263	1970	7.50	15.00	30.00
TAROT				
United Artists UAS-5563	1970	5.00	10.00	20.00
TENDERLOIN				
Capitol WAO 1492 [M]	1960	6.25	12.50	25.00
—With program				
Capitol SWAO 1492 [S]	1960	10.00	20.00	40.00
—With program				
TEVYA AND HIS DAUGHTERS				
Columbia Masterworks OL 5225 [M]	1957	7.50	15.00	30.00
TEXAS, LI'L DARLIN'				
Decca DL 5188 [10]	1950	20.00	40.00	80.00
THIS IS THE ARMY				
Decca DL 5108 [10]	1950	25.00	50.00	100.00
THIS WAS BURLESQUE				
Roulette R-25185 [M]	1962	6.25	12.50	25.00
Roulette SR-25186 [S]	1962	7.50	15.00	30.00
THREE TO MAKE MUSIC				
RCA Victor LPM-2012 [M]	1958	6.25	12.50	25.00

Label, Number	Yr	VG	VG+	NM
RCA Victor LSP-2012 [S]	1958	7.50	15.00	30.00
THREE WISHES FOR JAMIE				
Capitol S 317 [M]	1952	30.00	60.00	120.00
THE THREEPENNY OPERA				
MGM E-3121 [M]	1954	6.25	12.50	25.00
—Revival cast; yellow label				
TIME CHANGES				
ABC ABCS-681	1969	7.50	15.00	30.00
A TIME FOR SINGING				
Warner Bros. W 1639 [M]	1966	10.00	20.00	40.00
Warner Bros. WS 1639 [S]	1966	15.00	30.00	60.00
A TIME REMEMBERED				
Mercury MG-20380 [M]	1957	6.25	12.50	25.00
Mercury SR-60023 [S]	1957	10.00	20.00	40.00
—Music from the dramatic play				
TO BROADWAY WITH LOVE				
Columbia Masterworks OS 2630 [S]	1964	12.50	25.00	50.00
Columbia Masterworks OL 6030 [M]	1964	6.25	12.50	25.00
TOP BANANA				
Capitol S 308 [M]	1952	25.00	50.00	100.00
TOVARICH				
Capitol TAO 1940 [M]	1963	5.00	10.00	20.00
Capitol STAO 1940 [S]	1963	7.50	15.00	30.00
A TREE GROWS IN BROOKLYN				
Columbia Masterworks ML 4405 [M]	1951	7.50	15.00	30.00
—Blue label				
TWO'S COMPANY				
RCA Victor LOC-1009 [M]	1952	25.00	50.00	100.00
TWO BY TWO				
Columbia Masterworks S 30338	1970	5.00	10.00	20.00
TWO ON THE AISLE				
Decca DL 8040 [M]	1951	25.00	50.00	100.00
—Black label, gold print				
Decca DL 8040 [M]	1955	15.00	30.00	60.00
—Black label, silver print				
Decca DL 8040 [M]	196?	15.00	30.00	60.00
—Black label with color bars				
THE UNSINKABLE MOLLY BROWN				
Capitol WAO 1509 [M]	1960	5.00	10.00	20.00
Capitol SWAO 1509 [S]	1960	6.25	12.50	25.00
UP IN CENTRAL PARK				
Decca DL 8016 [M]	1950	10.00	20.00	40.00
—Black label, gold print				
Decca DL 8016 [M]	1955	7.50	15.00	30.00
—Black label, silver print				
WAITING FOR GODOT				
Columbia Masterworks O2L 238 [(2) M]	1956	7.50	15.00	30.00
WEST SIDE STORY				
Columbia Masterworks OS 2001 [S]	1958	7.50	15.00	30.00
—Gray and black label with six "eye" logos				
Columbia Masterworks OS 2001 [S]	1963	3.75	7.50	15.00
—Gray label with "360 Sound Stereo"				
Columbia Masterworks OL 5230 [M]	1958	6.25	12.50	25.00
—Gray and black label with six "eye" logos				
Columbia Masterworks OL 5230 [M]	1963	3.00	6.00	12.00
—Gray label with "Guaranteed High Fidelity" or "360 Sound Mono"				
Columbia Masterworks S 32603 [S]	1973	2.50	5.00	10.00
—Reissue with new number				
WHAT MAKES SAMMY RUN?				
Columbia Masterworks KSO 2440 [S]	1964	10.00	20.00	40.00
Columbia Masterworks KOL 6040 [M]	1964	7.50	15.00	30.00
WILDCAT				
RCA Victor LOC-1060 [M]	1961	6.25	12.50	25.00
RCA Victor LSO-1060 [S]	1961	10.00	20.00	40.00
WISH YOU WERE HERE				
RCA Victor LOC-1007 [M]	1952	15.00	30.00	60.00
WONDERFUL TOWN				
Decca DL 9010 [M]	1953	7.50	15.00	30.00
—Black label, gold print				
YOU'RE A GOOD MAN, CHARLIE BROWN				
MGM 1E-9 [M]	1967	5.00	10.00	20.00
MGM S1E-9 [S]	1967	5.00	10.00	20.00
YOUR OWN THING				
RCA Victor LOC-1148 [M]	1968	6.25	12.50	25.00
RCA Victor LSO-1148 [S]	1968	5.00	10.00	20.00
ZORBA				
Capitol SO-118	1969	5.00	10.00	20.00

SOUNDTRACKS

Label, Number	Yr	VG	VG+	NM
101 DALMATIONS				
Disneyland DQ-1308 [M]	1966	5.00	10.00	20.00
Disneyland ST-1908 [M]	1960	6.25	12.50	25.00
Disneyland ST-3931 [M]	1965	10.00	20.00	40.00
Disneyland ST-4903 [M]	1963	37.50	75.00	150.00
—Gatefold cover with pop-up scene in center				
1776				
Columbia S 31741	1972	5.00	10.00	20.00
40 POUNDS OF TROUBLE				
Mercury MG-20784 [M]	1963	7.50	15.00	30.00
Mercury SR-60784 [S]	1963	10.00	20.00	40.00
55 DAYS AT PEKING				
Columbia CL 2028 [M]	1963	10.00	20.00	40.00
Columbia CS 8828 [S]	1963	17.50	35.00	70.00
THE 633 SQUADRON				
United Artists UA-LA305-G	1974	6.25	12.50	25.00
THE 7TH DAWN				
United Artists UAL-4115 [M]	1964	7.50	15.00	30.00
United Artists UAS-5115 [S]	1964	10.00	20.00	40.00
THE 7TH VOYAGE OF SINBAD				
Colpix CP-504 [M]	1958	50.00	100.00	200.00
AARON SLICK FROM PUNKIN CRICK				
RCA Victor LPM-3006 [10]	1952	37.50	75.00	150.00
ADVENTURES IN PARADISE				
ABC-Paramount ABC-329 [M]	1960	7.50	15.00	30.00
ABC-Paramount ABCS-329 [S]	1960	10.00	20.00	40.00
ADVISE AND CONSENT				
RCA Victor LOC-1068 [M]	1962	7.50	15.00	30.00
RCA Victor LSO-1068 [S]	1962	15.00	30.00	60.00
AN AFFAIR TO REMEMBER				
Columbia CL 1013 [M]	1957	10.00	20.00	40.00
AFRICA ADDIO				
United Artists UAL-4141 [M]	1966	5.00	10.00	20.00
United Artists UAS-5141 [S]	1966	6.25	12.50	25.00
THE AGONY AND THE ECSTASY				
Capitol MAS 2427 [M]	1965	15.00	30.00	60.00
Capitol SMAS 2427 [S]	1965	20.00	40.00	80.00
AIRPORT				
Decca DL 79173	1970	6.25	12.50	25.00
ALAKAZAM THE GREAT				
Vee Jay LP-6000 [M]	1961	20.00	40.00	80.00
THE ALAMO				
Columbia CL 1558 [M]	1960	5.00	10.00	20.00
Columbia CS 8358 [S]	1960	6.25	12.50	25.00
ALBERT PECKINPAW'S REVENGE				
Sidewalk T 5907 [M]	1967	7.50	15.00	30.00
Sidewalk ST 5907 [S]	1967	7.50	15.00	30.00
ALEXANDER				
Polydor 24-7001	1970	10.00	20.00	40.00
ALEXANDER THE GREAT				
Mercury MG-20148 [M]	1956	62.50	125.00	250.00
ALFIE				
ABC Impulse! AS-9111 [S]	1968	3.75	7.50	15.00
Impulse! A-9111 [M]	1966	7.50	15.00	30.00
Impulse! AS-9111 [S]	1966	7.50	15.00	30.00
ALIKI, MY LOVE				
Fontana MGF-27523 [M]	1963	6.25	12.50	25.00
Fontana SRF-67523 [S]	1963	7.50	15.00	30.00
ALL NIGHT LONG				
Epic LA 16032 [M]	1962	10.00	20.00	40.00
Epic BA 17032 [S]	1962	12.50	25.00	50.00
ALL THE LOVING COUPLES				
GNP Crescendo GNPS-2051	1969	10.00	20.00	40.00
ALL THE RIGHT NOISES				
Buddah BDS-5132	1971	7.50	15.00	30.00
AN AMERICAN IN PARIS				
MGM E-93 [10]	1951	10.00	20.00	40.00
AMERICA, AMERICA				
Warner Bros. W 1527 [M]	1963	5.00	10.00	20.00
Warner Bros. WS 1527 [S]	1963	6.25	12.50	25.00
THE AMOROUS ADVENTURES OF MOLL FLANDERS				
RCA Victor LOC-1113 [M]	1965	10.00	20.00	40.00
RCA Victor LSO-1113 [S]	1965	20.00	40.00	80.00
ANASTASIA				
Decca DL 8460 [M]	1956	7.50	15.00	30.00

Label, Number	Yr	VG	VG+	NM
ANATOMY OF A MURDER				
Columbia CL 1360 [M]	1959	10.00	20.00	40.00
Columbia CS 8166 [S]	1959	12.50	25.00	50.00
AND GOD CREATED WOMAN				
Decca DL 8685 [M]	1957	30.00	60.00	120.00
THE ANDROMEDA STRAIN				
Kapp KRS-5513	1971	10.00	20.00	40.00
—Regular cover				
Kapp KRS-5513	1971	25.00	50.00	100.00
—Hexagonal cover glued onto silver cardboard				
ANGELS DIE HARD				
Uni 73091	1971	7.50	15.00	30.00
ANGELS FROM HELL				
Tower ST 5128	1968	15.00	30.00	60.00
THE ANONYMOUS VENETIAN				
United Artists UAS-5218	1971	7.50	15.00	30.00
ANOTHER TIME, ANOTHER PLACE				
Columbia CL 1180 [M]	1958	10.00	20.00	40.00
ANY WEDNESDAY				
Warner Bros. W 1669 [M]	1966	6.25	12.50	25.00
Warner Bros. WS 1669 [S]	1966	10.00	20.00	40.00
THE APARTMENT				
United Artists UAL-3105 [M]	1960	7.50	15.00	30.00
United Artists UAS-6105 [S]	1960	10.00	20.00	40.00
APRIL LOVE				
Dot DLP-9000 [M]	1957	5.00	10.00	20.00
ARMS AND THE GIRL				
Decca DL 5200 [10]	1950	25.00	50.00	100.00
AROUND THE WORLD IN 80 DAYS				
Decca DL 9046 [M]	1957	6.25	12.50	25.00
—Black label, silver print				
Decca DL 79046 [S]	1959	10.00	20.00	40.00
—Maroon label, silver print; cover has "Full Stereo" banner				
Decca DL 79046 [S]	196?	3.00	6.00	12.00
—Black label with color bars				
Decca SW-94840 [S]	197?	3.75	7.50	15.00
—Capitol Record Club edition				
AROUND THE WORLD UNDER THE SEA				
Monument MLP-8050 [M]	1966	7.50	15.00	30.00
Monument SLP-18050 [S]	1966	12.50	25.00	50.00
ARRIVIDERCI, BABY!				
RCA Victor LOC-1132 [M]	1966	5.00	10.00	20.00
RCA Victor LSO-1132 [S]	1966	10.00	20.00	40.00
AT LONG LAST LOVE				
RCA Victor ABL2-0967 [(2)]	1975	5.00	10.00	20.00
ATHENA				
Mercury MG-25202 [10]	1954	37.50	75.00	150.00
BABES IN TOYLAND				
Buena Vista BV-4022 [M]	1961	7.50	15.00	30.00
Buena Vista STER-4022 [S]	1961	10.00	20.00	40.00
BABY DOLL				
Columbia CL 958 [M]	1956	15.00	30.00	60.00
—Ads for other Columbia LPs on back cover				
Columbia CL 958 [M]	195?	12.50	25.00	50.00
—No ads for LPs on back cover				
BABY FACE NELSON				
Jubilee JLP-2021 [M]	1957	30.00	60.00	120.00
BABY, THE RAIN MUST FALL				
Ava A-53 [M]	1965	10.00	20.00	40.00
Ava AS-53 [S]	1965	12.50	25.00	50.00
Mainstream S-6056 [S]	1965	10.00	20.00	40.00
—Reissue of Ava AS-53				
Mainstream 56056 [M]	1965	7.50	15.00	30.00
—Reissue of Ava A-53				
BACK STREET				
Decca DL 9097 [M]	1961	10.00	20.00	40.00
Decca DL 79097 [S]	1961	20.00	40.00	80.00
THE BAD SEED				
RCA Victor LPM-1395 [M]	1956	75.00	150.00	300.00
BAND OF ANGELS				
RCA Victor LPM-1557 [M]	1957	25.00	50.00	100.00
THE BAND WAGON				
MGM E-3051 [M]	1953	7.50	15.00	30.00
—Yellow label				
MGM E-3051 [M]	1960	5.00	10.00	20.00
—Black label				
BARABBAS				
Colpix CP 510 [M]	1962	10.00	20.00	40.00
Colpix SCP 510 [S]	1962	20.00	40.00	80.00

Label, Number	Yr	VG	VG+	NM
BARBARELLA				
Dyno Voice DV-31908	1968	12.50	25.00	50.00
THE BARBARIAN AND THE GEISHA				
20th Fox FOX-3004 [M]	1958	62.50	125.00	250.00
BAREFOOT ADVENTURE				
Pacific Jazz PJ-35 [M]	1961	10.00	20.00	40.00
Pacific Jazz ST-35 [S]	1961	15.00	30.00	60.00
BAREFOOT IN THE PARK				
Dot DLP-3803 [M]	1967	5.00	10.00	20.00
Dot DLP-25803 [S]	1967	7.50	15.00	30.00
THE BARKLEYS OF BROADWAY				
MGM E-503 [10]	1949	20.00	40.00	80.00
BATTLE OF THE BULGE				
Warner Bros. W 1617 [M]	1965	10.00	20.00	40.00
Warner Bros. WS 1617 [S]	1965	10.00	20.00	40.00
BEACH BLANKET BINGO				
Capitol T 2323 [M]	1965	7.50	15.00	30.00
Capitol ST 2323 [S]	1965	15.00	30.00	60.00
BEAU JAMES				
Imperial LP-9041 [M]	1957	10.00	20.00	40.00
BECKET				
Decca DL 9117 [M]	1964	7.50	15.00	30.00
Decca DL 79117 [S]	1964	12.50	25.00	50.00
BEDAZZLED				
London MS-82009	1967	20.00	40.00	80.00
BEHOLD A PALE HORSE				
Colpix CP 519 [M]	1964	12.50	25.00	50.00
Colpix SCP 519 [S]	1964	17.50	35.00	70.00
BELLS ARE RINGING				
Capitol W 1435 [M]	1960	6.25	12.50	25.00
Capitol SW 1435 [S]	1960	7.50	15.00	30.00
BELL, BOOK AND CANDLE				
Colpix CP 502 [M]	1959	15.00	30.00	60.00
BEN-HUR				
MGM 1E1 [M]	1959	10.00	20.00	40.00
—Boxed edition with hardcover book				
MGM S-1E1 [S]	1959	12.50	25.00	50.00
—Boxed edition with hardcover book				
MGM 1E1 [M]	196?	3.00	6.00	12.00
—Gatefold cover, no book				
MGM S-1E1 [M]	196?	3.75	7.50	15.00
—Gatefold cover, no book; black label				
MGM S-1E1 [M]	196?	2.50	5.00	10.00
—Gatefold cover, no book; blue and gold label				
BENEATH THE PLANET OF THE APES				
Amos AAS-8001	1970	10.00	20.00	40.00
BEYOND THE GREAT WALL				
Capitol T 10401 [M]	1965	12.50	25.00	50.00
BEYOND THE VALLEY OF THE DOLLS				
20th Century Fox TFS-4211	1970	50.00	100.00	200.00
THE BIBLE				
20th Century Fox TF-3184 [M]	1966	5.00	10.00	20.00
20th Century Fox TFS-4184 [S]	1966	7.50	15.00	30.00
THE BIG COUNTRY				
United Artists UAL-4004 [M]	1958	6.25	12.50	25.00
United Artists UAS-5004 [S]	1958	12.50	25.00	50.00
THE BIG GUNDOWN				
United Artists UAS-5190	1967	10.00	20.00	40.00
THE BIGGEST BUNDLE OF THEM ALL				
MGM E-4446 [M]	1967	5.00	10.00	20.00
MGM SE-4446 [S]	1967	6.25	12.50	25.00
BILLIE				
United Artists UAL-4131 [M]	1965	5.00	10.00	20.00
United Artists UAS-5131 [S]	1965	6.25	12.50	25.00
THE BILLION DOLLAR BRAIN				
United Artists UAL-4174 [M]	1967	3.75	7.50	15.00
United Artists UAS-5174 [S]	1967	5.00	10.00	20.00
BILLY JACK				
Warner Bros. WS 1926	1971	6.25	12.50	25.00
THE BIRD WITH THE CRYSTAL PLUMAGE				
Capitol ST-642	1970	25.00	50.00	100.00
BLACK GIRL				
Fantasy F-9420	1973	17.50	35.00	70.00
THE BLACK ORCHID				
Dot DLP-3178 [M]	1959	10.00	20.00	40.00
Dot SLP-25178 [S]	1959	12.50	25.00	50.00
BLACK ORPHEUS				
Epic LN 3672 [M]	1959	10.00	20.00	40.00
Fontana MGF-27520 [M]	1963	5.00	10.00	20.00

Label, Number	Yr	VG	VG+	NM
Fontana SRF-67520 [R]	1963	3.75	7.50	15.00
BLACKBIRDS OF 1928				
Columbia Masterworks OL 6770 [M]	1968	3.75	7.50	15.00
Revue 1 [M]	196?	7.50	15.00	30.00
Sutton SU-270 [M]	196?	5.00	10.00	20.00
Sutton SSU-270 [R]	196?	3.00	6.00	12.00
BLACULA				
RCA Victor LSP-4806	1972	15.00	30.00	60.00
BLESS THE BEASTS AND CHILDREN				
A&M SP-4322	1971	6.25	12.50	25.00
BLOOD AND SAND				
Decca DL 5380 [10]	1952	20.00	40.00	80.00
BLOOMER GIRL				
Decca DL 8015 [M]	1950	7.50	15.00	30.00
BLOW-UP				
MGM E-4447 [M]	1967	10.00	20.00	40.00
MGM SE-4447 [S]	1967	12.50	25.00	50.00
THE BLUE MAX				
Mainstream S-6081 [S]	1966	20.00	40.00	80.00
Mainstream 56081 [M]	1966	10.00	20.00	40.00
BOBO				
Warner Bros. W 1711 [M]	1967	5.00	10.00	20.00
Warner Bros. WS 1711 [S]	1967	5.00	10.00	20.00
BOEING, BOEING				
RCA Victor LOC-1121 [M]	1965	6.25	12.50	25.00
RCA Victor LSO-1121 [S]	1965	7.50	15.00	30.00
BONNIE AND CLYDE				
Warner Bros. W 1742 [M]	1968	10.00	20.00	40.00
Warner Bros. WS 1742 [S]	1968	6.25	12.50	25.00
—Originals have green labels with "W7" logo in a square at top				
Warner Bros. ST-91414 [S]	1968	7.50	1.00	30.00
—Capitol Record Club issue				
BORA, BORA				
American Int'l. STA-1029	1970	7.50	15.00	30.00
BORN FREE				
MGM E-4368 [M]	1966	3.75	7.50	15.00
MGM SE-4368 [S]	1966	5.00	10.00	20.00
BORSALINO				
Paramount PAS-5019	1970	7.50	15.00	30.00
THE BOY FRIEND				
MGM 1SE-32	1971	5.00	10.00	20.00
A BOY NAMED CHARLIE BROWN				
Columbia Masterworks OS 3500	1970	5.00	10.00	20.00
BOY ON A DOLPHIN				
Decca DL 8580 [M]	1957	15.00	30.00	60.00
—Black label with silver print, or pink label with black print (promo)				
Decca DL 8580 [M]	196?	5.00	10.00	20.00
—Black label with color bars				
THE BOYS FROM SYRACUSE				
Capitol TAO 1933 [M]	1963	6.25	12.50	25.00
Capitol STAO 1933 [S]	1963	7.50	15.00	30.00
THE BRAVE ONE				
Decca DL 8344 [M]	1956	10.00	20.00	40.00
BROTHER ON THE RUN				
Perception PLP-45	1973	10.00	20.00	40.00
BUCCANEER				
Columbia CL 1278 [M]	1958	6.25	12.50	25.00
Columbia CS 8096 [S]	1958	10.00	20.00	40.00
BULLITT				
Warner Bros. WS 1777	1968	15.00	30.00	60.00
BUNDLE OF JOY				
RCA Victor LPM-1399 [M]	1956	10.00	20.00	40.00
BUNNY LAKE IS MISSING				
RCA Victor LOC-1115 [M]	1965	10.00	20.00	40.00
RCA Victor LSO-1115 [S]	1965	17.50	35.00	70.00
BUNNY O'HARE				
American Int'l. STA-1041	1971	5.00	10.00	20.00
BUONA SERA, MRS. CAMPBELL				
United Artists UAS-5192	1969	7.50	15.00	30.00
THE BURGLARS				
Bell 1105	1971	10.00	20.00	40.00
BUTTERFIELD-8				
MGM E-3952 [M]	1960	5.00	10.00	20.00
MGM SE-3952 [S]	1960	6.25	12.50	25.00
BYE BYE BIRDIE				
RCA VIctor LOC-1081 [M]	1963	6.25	12.50	25.00
—First cover without Ann-Margret on the front				
RCA Victor LOC-1081 [M]	196?	5.00	10.00	20.00
—Second cover with Ann-Margret on front, but with no credits underneath				
RCA Victor LOC-1081 [M]	196?	3.75	7.50	15.00
—Third cover with Ann-Margret on front and with credits underneath				
RCA Victor LSO-1081 [S]	1963	7.50	15.00	30.00
—First cover without Ann-Margret on the front				
RCA Victor LSO-1081 [S]	196?	6.25	12.50	25.00
—Second cover with Ann-Margret on front, but with no credits underneath				
RCA Victor LSO-1081 [S]	196?	5.00	10.00	20.00
—Third cover with Ann-Margret on front and with credits underneath				
C'MON, LET'S LIVE A LITTLE				
Liberty LRP-3430 [M]	1966	6.25	12.50	25.00
Liberty LST-7430 [S]	1966	7.50	15.00	30.00
CABARET				
ABC ABCD-752	1972	5.00	10.00	20.00
THE CAINE MUTINY				
RCA Victor LOC-1013 [M]	1954	4000.	7000.	10000.
RCA Victor LOC-1013 [M]	1993	50.00	100.00	200.00
—Very limited edition (100 copies) reproduction of the original LP				
CALL ME MADAM				
Decca DL 5465 [10]	1953	12.50	25.00	50.00
CALL ME MISTER				
Decca DLP 7005 [10]	1950	25.00	50.00	100.00
CAMELOT				
Warner Bros. B 1712 [M]	1967	6.25	12.50	25.00
Warner Bros. BS 1712 [S]	1967	5.00	10.00	20.00
Warner Bros. SW-91347	1968	6.25	12.50	25.00
—Capitol Record Club edition				
CAN-CAN				
Capitol W 1301 [M]	1960	5.00	10.00	20.00
Capitol SW 1301 [S]	1960	7.50	15.00	30.00
CANDY				
ABC ABCS-OC-9	1968	7.50	15.00	30.00
THE CARDINAL				
RCA Victor LOC-1084 [M]	1963	10.00	20.00	40.00
RCA Victor LSO-1084 [S]	1963	15.00	30.00	60.00
THE CARETAKERS				
Ava A-31 [M]	1963	5.00	10.00	20.00
Ava AS-31 [S]	1963	6.25	12.50	25.00
CAROUSEL				
Capitol W 694 [M]	1956	7.50	15.00	30.00
—Gray label				
Capitol W 694 [M]	1959	5.00	10.00	20.00
—Black colorband label, logo at left				
Capitol W 694 [M]	1962	3.75	7.50	15.00
—Black colorband label, logo at top				
Capitol SW 694 [S]	1962	5.00	10.00	20.00
—Black colorband label				
THE CARPETBAGGERS				
Ava A-45 [M]	1964	7.50	15.00	30.00
Ava AS-45 [S]	1964	10.00	20.00	40.00
CARRY IT ON				
Vanguard VSD-79313	1971	6.25	12.50	25.00
CASINO ROYALE				
Colgems COMO-5005 [M]	1967	7.50	15.00	30.00
Colgems COSO-5005 [S]	1967	25.00	50.00	100.00
A CERTAIN SMILE				
Columbia CL 1194 [M]	1958	10.00	20.00	40.00
Columbia CS 8068 [S]	1958	20.00	40.00	80.00
THE CHAIRMAN				
Tetragrammaton T-5007	1969	7.50	15.00	30.00
CHARLOTTE'S WEB				
Paramount PAS-1008	1973	7.50	15.00	30.00
THE CHASE				
Columbia Masterworks OS 2960 [S]	1966	15.00	30.00	60.00
Columbia Masterworks OL 6560 [M]	1966	10.00	20.00	40.00
CHINATOWN				
ABC ABDP-848	1974	10.00	20.00	40.00
CHITTY CHITTY BANG BANG				
United Artists UAS-5188	1968	6.25	12.50	25.00
THE CHRISTMAS THAT ALMOST WASN'T				
RCA Camden CAL-1086 [M]	1966	6.25	12.50	25.00
RCA Camden CAS-1086 [S]	1966	10.00	20.00	40.00
CINDERELLA				
Disneyland DQ-1207 [M]	1959	10.00	20.00	40.00
—Second issue, white back cover with ads for nine other LPs				
Disneyland DQ-1207 [M]	1963	7.50	15.00	30.00
—Third issue, pink back cover				
Disneyland WDL-4007 [M]	1957	50.00	100.00	200.00
—Original issue, gatefold cover				
CINDERFELLA				
Dot DLP-8001 [M]	1960	15.00	30.00	60.00

Label, Number	Yr	VG	VG+	NM
Dot SLP-38001 [S]	1960	25.00	50.00	100.00
—Gatefold cover with many extras including game board, spinner, booklet, music stand.				
CLEOPATRA				
20th Century Fox FXG-5008 [M]	1963	7.50	15.00	30.00
20th Century Fox SXG-5008 [S]	1963	10.00	20.00	40.00
CLEOPATRA JONES				
Warner Bros. BS 2719	1973	7.50	15.00	30.00
THE CLOWNS				
Columbia S 30772	1971	10.00	20.00	40.00
COFFY				
Polydor PD-5048	1973	25.00	50.00	100.00
THE COLLECTOR				
Mainstream S-6053 [S]	1965	12.50	25.00	50.00
Mainstream 56053 [M]	1965	7.50	15.00	30.00
COLLEGE CONFIDENTIAL				
Chancellor CHL-5016 [M]	1960	10.00	20.00	40.00
Chancellor CHLS-5016 [S]	1960	12.50	25.00	50.00
COMANCHE				
Coral CRL 57046 [M]	1956	100.00	200.00	400.00
COME BACK CHARLESTON BLUE				
Atco SD 7010	1972	7.50	15.00	30.00
COME BLOW YOUR HORN				
Reprise R-6071 [M]	1963	7.50	15.00	30.00
Reprise R9-6071 [S]	1963	12.50	25.00	50.00
COMETOGETHER				
Apple SW-3377	1971	5.00	10.00	20.00
THE CONNECTION				
Charlie Parker PLP-806 [M]	1962	7.50	15.00	30.00
Charlie Parker PLP-806S [S]	1962	10.00	20.00	40.00
Felsted 2512 [S]	1960	75.00	150.00	300.00
Felsted 7512 [M]	1960	50.00	100.00	200.00
COOL WORLD				
Philips PHM 200138 [M]	1964	12.50	25.00	50.00
Philips PHS 600138 [S]	1964	20.00	40.00	80.00
COOLEY HIGH				
Motown M7-840 R2 [(2)]	1975	5.00	10.00	20.00
THE CORRUPT ONES				
United Artists UAL-4158 [M]	1967	10.00	20.00	40.00
United Artists UAS-5158 [S]	1967	10.00	20.00	40.00
COTTON COMES TO HARLEM				
United Artists UAS-5211	1970	7.50	15.00	30.00
THE COURT JESTER				
Decca DL 8212 [M]	1956	17.50	35.00	70.00
—Black label, silver print, or pink label, black print promo copy				
Decca DL 8212 [M]	196?	7.50	15.00	30.00
—Black label with color bars				
THE COWBOY				
Decca DL 8684 [M]	1958	15.00	30.00	60.00
—Black label, silver print, or pink label, black print promo copy				
Decca DL 8684 [M]	196?	5.00	10.00	20.00
—Black label with color bars				
CRIME IN THE STREETS				
Decca DL 8376 [M]	1956	15.00	30.00	60.00
—Black label, silver print, or pink label, black print promo copy				
Decca DL 8376 [S]	196?	7.50	15.00	30.00
—Black label with color bars				
THE CROSS AND THE SWITCHBLADE				
Light LS-5550	1970	7.50	15.00	30.00
CUSTER OF THE WEST				
ABC ABC-OC-5 [M]	1968	20.00	40.00	80.00
ABC ABCS-OC-5 [S]	1968	25.00	50.00	100.00
CYCLE SAVAGES				
American Int'l. STA-1033	1970	7.50	15.00	30.00
CYRANO DE BERGERAC				
Capitol S 283 [M]	1951	7.50	15.00	30.00
—Originals have red labels with Capitol logo at top				
DAKTARI				
Leo the Lion CH-1043 [M]	1967	5.00	10.00	20.00
MGM CH-1043 [M]	1967	5.00	10.00	20.00
DAMN THE DEFIANT!				
Colpix CP 511 [M]	1962	7.50	15.00	30.00
Colpix SCP 511 [S]	1962	15.00	30.00	60.00
DAMN YANKEES				
RCA Victor LOC-1047 [M]	1958	10.00	20.00	40.00
—Original pressing with "Long Play" on label				
THE DAMNED				
Warner Bros. WS 1829	1969	7.50	15.00	30.00
THE DARK OF THE SUN				
MGM SE-4544	1968	10.00	20.00	40.00

Label, Number	Yr	VG	VG+	NM
DARLING LILI				
RCA Victor LSPX-1000	1969	5.00	10.00	20.00
DAY OF ANGER				
RCA Victor LSO-1165	1969	5.00	10.00	20.00
THE DAY OF THE DOLPHIN				
Avco AV-11014	1973	6.25	12.50	25.00
THE DAY THE FISH CAME OUT				
20th Century Fox TF-3194 [M]	1967	7.50	15.00	30.00
20th Century Fox TFS-4194 [S]	1967	10.00	20.00	40.00
DAYDREAMER				
Columbia Masterworks OS 2940 [S]	1966	10.00	20.00	40.00
Columbia Masterworks OL 6540 [M]	1966	7.50	15.00	30.00
DE SADE				
Tower ST-5170	1969	7.50	15.00	30.00
DEADFALL				
20th Century Fox S-4203	1968	15.00	30.00	60.00
THE DEADLY AFFAIR				
Verve V-8679 [M]	1966	6.25	12.50	25.00
Verve V6-8679 [S]	1966	7.50	15.00	30.00
DEAR JOHN				
Dunhill OCD-55001 [M]	1966	5.00	10.00	20.00
Dunhill OCDS-55001 [S]	1966	6.25	12.50	25.00
DEEP IN MY HEART				
MGM E-3153 [M]	1955	10.00	20.00	40.00
MGM E-3153 [M]	1955	12.50	25.00	50.00
DESIRE UNDER THE ELMS				
Dot DLP-3095 [M]	1958	25.00	50.00	100.00
DESTINATION MOON				
Columbia CL 6151 [10]	1950	30.00	60.00	120.00
Omega OL-3 [M]	1959	10.00	20.00	40.00
Omega OSL-3 [S]	196?	20.00	40.00	80.00
THE DEVIL'S BRIGADE				
United Artists UAS-6654	1968	5.00	10.00	20.00
THE DEVIL AT 4 O'CLOCK				
Colpix CP 509 [M]	1962	10.00	20.00	40.00
Colpix SCP 509 [S]	1962	17.50	35.00	70.00
THE DEVIL IN MISS JONES				
Janus JLS-3059	1973	6.25	12.50	25.00
DIAMOND HEAD				
Colpix CP-440 [M]	1963	7.50	15.00	30.00
Colpix SCP 440 [S]	1963	15.00	30.00	60.00
DIAMONDS ARE FOREVER				
United Artists UAS-5520	1971	5.00	10.00	20.00
THE DIARY OF ANNE FRANK				
20th Fox FOX-3012 [M]	1959	12.50	25.00	50.00
20th Fox SFX-3012 [S]	1959	20.00	40.00	80.00
DIRTY GAME				
Laurie LLP-2034 [M]	1966	6.25	12.50	25.00
Laurie SLP-2034 [S]	1966	7.50	15.00	30.00
DIVORCE AMERICAN STYLE				
United Artists UAL-4163 [M]	1967	5.00	10.00	20.00
United Artists UAS-5163 [S]	1967	5.00	10.00	20.00
DIVORCE ITALIAN STYLE				
United Artists UAL-4106 [M]	1962	10.00	20.00	40.00
United Artists UAS-5106 [S]	1962	12.50	25.00	50.00
DOCTOR DOLITTLE				
20th Century Fox TCF-5101 [M]	1967	5.00	10.00	20.00
20th Century Fox TCS-5101 [S]	1967	5.00	10.00	20.00
DOCTOR GOLDFOOT AND THE GIRL BOMBS				
Tower T 5053 [M]	1966	5.00	10.00	20.00
Tower DT 5053 [R]	1966	6.25	12.50	25.00
DOCTOR ZHIVAGO				
MGM 1E-6 [M]	1965	3.75	7.50	15.00
MGM S1E-6 ST [S]	1965	5.00	10.00	20.00
A DOG OF FLANDERS				
20th Fox FOX-3026 [M]	1959	20.00	40.00	80.00
20th Fox SFX-3026 [S]	1959	75.00	150.00	300.00
$ (DOLLARS)				
Reprise MS 2051	1971	5.00	10.00	20.00
DON'T MAKE WAVES				
MGM E-4483 [M]	1967	7.50	15.00	30.00
MGM SE-4483 [S]	1967	7.50	15.00	30.00
DRANGO				
Liberty LRP-3036 [M]	1957	37.50	75.00	150.00
A DREAM OF KINGS				
National General NG-1000	1969	7.50	15.00	30.00
DR. NO				
United Artists UAL-4108 [M]	1963	10.00	20.00	40.00

Label, Number	Yr	VG	VG+	NM
United Artists UAS-5108 [S]	1963	12.50	25.00	50.00
DR. PHIBES				
American Int'l. A-1040	1971	15.00	30.00	60.00
DUCK, YOU SUCKER				
United Artists UAS-5221	1972	10.00	20.00	40.00
DUEL AT DIABLO				
United Artists UAL-4139 [M]	1966	6.25	12.50	25.00
United Artists UAS-5139 [S]	1966	7.50	15.00	30.00
DUMBO				
Disneyland DQ-1204 [M]	1959	6.25	12.50	25.00
—Second issue, back cover has ads for nine other LPs				
Disneyland DQ-1204 [M]	1963	3.75	7.50	15.00
—Third issue, four black & white photos on back cover				
Disneyland 1204 [M]	197?	2.50	5.00	10.00
—Fourth issue, yellow rainbow label, flying Dumbo on back cover				
Disneyland WDL-4013 [M]	1957	50.00	100.00	200.00
—Original issue, gatefold cover				
Disneyland ST-4904 [M]	1963	50.00	100.00	200.00
—Special issue with pop-up figures in gatefold				
THE DUNWICH HORROR				
American Int'l. STA-1028	1970	10.00	20.00	40.00
EAST SIDE, WEST SIDE				
Columbia CL 2123 [M]	1963	6.25	12.50	25.00
Columbia CS 8923 [S]	1963	10.00	20.00	40.00
EASTER PARADE				
MGM E-502 [10]	1950	20.00	40.00	80.00
EASY RIDER				
ABC Dunhill DSX-50063	1969	6.25	12.50	25.00
ECCO				
Warner Bros. W 1600 [M]	1965	6.25	12.50	25.00
Warner Bros. WS 1600 [S]	1965	7.50	15.00	30.00
THE EDDY DUCHIN STORY				
Decca DL 8289 [M]	1956	10.00	20.00	40.00
—Original cover with Tyrone Power and Kim Novak at a piano				
Decca DL 8289 [M]	1959	5.00	10.00	20.00
—Reissue cover with Tyrone Power and Kim Novak kissing				
Decca DL 78289 [S]	1959	6.25	12.50	25.00
—Maroon label, silver print, "Full Stereo" on front cover				
THE EDUCATION OF SONNY CARSON				
Paramount PAS-1045	1974	5.00	10.00	20.00
THE EGYPTIAN				
Decca DL 9014 [M]	1954	15.00	30.00	60.00
Decca DL 79014 [R]	196?	5.00	10.00	20.00
EL CID				
MGM E-3977 [M]	1962	10.00	20.00	40.00
MGM SE-3977 [S]	1962	12.50	25.00	50.00
EL DORADO				
Epic FLM-13114 [M]	1967	12.50	25.00	50.00
Epic LFS-15114 [S]	1967	17.50	35.00	70.00
EL TOPO				
Apple SWAO-3388	1972	10.00	20.00	40.00
ELECTRA GLIDE IN BLUE				
United Artists UA-LA062-H [(2)]	1973	10.00	20.00	40.00
—With booklet and two posters				
ELEPHANT STEPS				
Columbia Masterwords M2X 33044 [(2)]	1975	5.00	10.00	20.00
ELMER GANTRY				
United Artists UAL-4069 [M]	1960	10.00	20.00	40.00
United Artists UAS-5069 [S]	1960	12.50	25.00	50.00
ENTER THE DRAGON				
Warner Bros. BS 2727	1973	15.00	30.00	60.00
EVERYTHING I HAVE IS YOURS				
MGM E-187 [10]	1953	10.00	20.00	40.00
EXODUS				
RCA Victor LOC-1058 [M]	1960	5.00	10.00	20.00
—"Long Play" on label				
RCA Victor LSO-1058 [S]	1960	6.25	12.50	25.00
—"Living Stereo" on label				
THE EXORCIST				
Warner Bros. W 2774	1974	7.50	15.00	30.00
A FACE IN THE CROWD				
Capitol W 872 [M]	1957	12.50	25.00	50.00
THE FALL OF THE ROMAN EMPIRE				
Columbia Masterworks OS 2460 [S]	1964	15.00	30.00	60.00
Columbia Masterworks OL 6060 [M]	1964	10.00	20.00	40.00
THE FAMILY WAY				
London M 76007 [M]	1967	25.00	50.00	100.00
—No promo sticker on front cover (deduct 20 percent for promo)				
London ST 82007 [S]	1967	30.00	60.00	120.00
—No promo sticker on front cover (deduct 20 percent for promo)				

Label, Number	Yr	VG	VG+	NM
FANNY				
Warner Bros. W 1416 [M]	1961	6.25	12.50	25.00
Warner Bros. WS 1416 [S]	1961	7.50	15.00	30.00
FANTASIA				
Buena Vista WDX-101 [(3) M]	1961	7.50	15.00	30.00
—Second issue, blue labels, includes 24-page booklet				
Buena Vista STER-101 [(3) S]	1961	10.00	20.00	40.00
—First stereo issue, black and yellow rainbow labels, includes 24-page booklet				
Buena Vista 101 [(2) S]	1982	5.00	10.00	20.00
—Stereo reissue, two records, no booklet				
Disneyland WDX-101 [(3)]	1957	15.00	30.00	60.00
—Original issue, maroon/red labels, includes 24-page booklet				
FANTASIA: NIGHT ON BALD MOUNTAIN; PASTORAL SYMPHONY; AVE MARIA				
Disneyland WDL-4101C [M]	1958	5.00	10.00	20.00
Disneyland STER-4101C [S]	1958	7.50	15.00	30.00
FANTASIA: RITE OF SPRING; TOCCATA AND FUGUE				
Disneyland WDL-4101A [M]	1958	5.00	10.00	20.00
Disneyland STER-4101A [S]	1959	7.50	15.00	30.00
FANTASIA: THE NUTCRACKER SUITE; DANCE OF THE HOURS				
Disneyland WDL-4101B [M]	1958	5.00	10.00	20.00
Disneyland STER-4101B [S]	1959	7.50	15.00	30.00
THE FANTASTIC PLASTIC MACHINE				
Epic BN 26469	1969	6.25	12.50	25.00
FAR FROM THE MADDING CROWD				
MGM 1E-11 [M]	1967	3.75	7.50	15.00
MGM S1E-11 [S]	1967	6.25	12.50	25.00
A FAREWELL TO ARMS				
Capitol W 918 [M]	1957	12.50	25.00	50.00
THE FASTEST GUITAR ALIVE				
MGM SE-4475	1968	7.50	15.00	30.00
FATHOM				
20th Century Fox TFM-4195 [M]	1967	10.00	20.00	40.00
20th Century Fox TFS-4195 [S]	1967	12.50	25.00	50.00
FELLINI'S ROMA				
United Artists UA-LA052-F	1972	7.50	15.00	30.00
FELLINI SATYRICON				
United Artists UAS-5208	1969	7.50	15.00	30.00
THE FEMALE PRISONER				
Columbia Masterworks OS 3320	1969	7.50	15.00	30.00
FIDDLER ON THE ROOF				
United Artists UAS-10900 [(2)]	1971	5.00	10.00	20.00
—With booklet				
THE FIGHTER				
Decca DL 5414 [10]	1952	20.00	40.00	80.00
FINIAN'S RAINBOW				
Warner Bros. BS 2550	1968	5.00	10.00	20.00
FIRE DOWN BELOW				
Decca DL 8597 [M]	1957	17.50	35.00	70.00
A FISTFUL OF DOLLARS				
RCA Victor LOC-1135 [M]	1967	5.00	10.00	20.00
RCA Victor LSO-1135 [S]	1967	7.50	15.00	30.00
—Black label, dog on top				
RCA Victor LSO-1135 [S]	1969	3.00	6.00	12.00
—Orange label, tan label, or black label with dog at 1 o'clock				
FITZWILLY				
United Artists UAL-4173 [M]	1967	5.00	10.00	20.00
United Artists UAS-5173 [S]	1967	6.25	12.50	25.00
FIVE EASY PIECES				
Epic KE 30456	1971	6.25	12.50	25.00
THE FIVE PENNIES				
Dot DLP-9500 [M]	1959	6.25	12.50	25.00
Dot DLP-29500 [S]	1959	12.50	25.00	50.00
A FLEA IN HER EAR				
20th Century Fox TFS-4200	1968	7.50	15.00	30.00
FLOWER DRUM SONG				
Decca DL 9098 [M]	1961	5.00	10.00	20.00
Decca DL 79098 [S]	1961	6.25	12.50	25.00
FOLIES BERGERE				
Decca DL 8571 [M]	1958	6.25	12.50	25.00
FOLLOW ME				
Uni 73056	1969	7.50	15.00	30.00
FOR A FEW DOLLARS MORE				
United Artists UAL-3608 [M]	1967	5.00	10.00	20.00
United Artists UAS-6608 [S]	1967	6.25	12.50	25.00
FOR LOVE OF IVY				
ABC SOC-7	1968	6.25	12.50	25.00
FOR THE FIRST TIME				
RCA Red Seal LSC-2338 [S]	1959	5.00	10.00	20.00
—"Shaded dog" and smaller "RCA Victor" lettering				

Label, Number	Yr	VG	VG+	NM
RCA Red Seal LSC-2338 [S]	1969	3.00	6.00	12.00
—Red label, no dog				
RCA Red Seal LM-2338 [M]	1959	3.75	7.50	15.00
RCA Victor Red Seal LSC-2338 [S]	1965	3.75	7.50	15.00
—"White dog" and larger "RCA Victor" lettering				
THE FOUR HORSEMEN OF THE APOCALYPSE				
MGM E-3993 [M]	1962	5.00	10.00	20.00
MGM SE-3993 [S]	1962	6.25	12.50	25.00
FOUR IN THE MORNING				
Roulette OS 805 [M]	1966	10.00	20.00	40.00
Roulette OSS 805 [S]	1966	12.50	25.00	50.00
THE FOX				
Warner Bros. W 1738 [M]	1968	10.00	20.00	40.00
Warner Bros. WS 1738 [S]	1968	6.25	12.50	25.00
FOXY BROWN				
Motown M7-811	1974	5.00	10.00	20.00
FRANCIS OF ASSISI				
20th Fox FOX-3053 [M]	1961	50.00	100.00	200.00
20th Fox SFX-3053 [S]	1961	62.50	125.00	250.00
THE FRENCH LINE				
Mercury MG-25182 [10]	1954	20.00	40.00	80.00
FRIENDLY PERSUASION				
RKO Unique LP-110 [M]	1956	18.75	37.50	75.00
FRITZ THE CAT				
Fantasy F-9406	1972	7.50	15.00	30.00
FROM RUSSIA WITH LOVE				
United Artists UAL-4114 [M]	1964	5.00	10.00	20.00
United Artists UAS-5114 [S]	1964	6.25	12.50	25.00
THE FUGITIVE KIND				
United Artists UAL-4065 [M]	1959	12.50	25.00	50.00
United Artists UAS-5065 [S]	1959	17.50	35.00	70.00
FUNERAL IN BERLIN				
RCA Victor LOC-1136 [M]	1966	7.50	15.00	30.00
RCA Victor LSO-1136 [S]	1966	12.50	25.00	50.00
FUNNY GIRL				
Columbia Masterworks BOS 3220	1968	3.75	7.50	15.00
—Gray "360 Sound" label; record is removed from inside the gatefold; liner notes on a black background				
Columbia Masterworks BOS 3220	1968	3.00	6.00	12.00
—Gray "360 Sound" label; record is removed from inside the gatefold; liner notes on a tan background				
Columbia Masterworks BOS 3220	1970	2.50	5.00	10.00
—Olive label with "Columbia" encircling the edge				
Columbia Masterworks SQ 30992	1971	10.00	20.00	40.00
A FUNNY THING HAPPENED ON THE WAY TO THE FORUM				
United Artists UAL-4144 [M]	1966	3.00	6.00	12.00
United Artists UAS-5144 [S]	1966	3.75	7.50	15.00
GAILY, GAILY				
United Artists UAS 5202	1969	6.25	12.50	25.00
THE GAME IS OVER				
Atco 33-205 [M]	1967	5.00	10.00	20.00
Atco SD 33-205 [S]	1967	6.25	12.50	25.00
THE GAMES				
Viking LPS-105	1970	50.00	100.00	200.00
GAY PURR-EE				
Warner Bros. B 1479 [M]	1963	5.00	10.00	20.00
Warner Bros. BS 1479 [S]	1963	7.50	15.00	30.00
GEISHA BOY				
Jubilee JLP-1096 [M]	1958	12.50	25.00	50.00
Jubilee JGS-1096 [S]	1959	20.00	40.00	80.00
THE GENE KRUPA STORY				
Verve MGVS-6105 [S]	1959	25.00	50.00	100.00
—Original issue				
Verve MGV-15010 [M]	1959	12.50	25.00	50.00
Verve V6-15010 [S]	1963	20.00	40.00	80.00
—Early reissue				
Verve V-15010 [M]	1961	5.00	10.00	20.00
GENGHIS KHAN				
Liberty LRP-3412 [M]	1965	10.00	20.00	40.00
Liberty LST-7412 [S]	1965	15.00	30.00	60.00
THE GENTLE RAIN				
Mercury MG-21016 [M]	1966	5.00	10.00	20.00
Mercury SR-61016 [S]	1966	6.25	12.50	25.00
GENTLEMEN MARRY BRUNETTES				
Coral CRL 57013 [M]	1955	17.50	35.00	70.00
GENTLEMEN PREFER BLONDES				
MGM E-208 [M]	1953	30.00	60.00	120.00
GET YOURSELF A COLLEGE GIRL				
MGM E-4273 [M]	1965	5.00	10.00	20.00
MGM SE-4273 [S]	1965	10.00	20.00	40.00
GETTING STRAIGHT				
Colgems COSO-5010	1970	7.50	15.00	30.00
GIANT				
Capitol W 773 [M]	1956	10.00	20.00	40.00
—Turquoise or gray label				
Capitol W 773 [M]	1959	6.25	12.50	25.00
—Black colorband label, logo at left				
Capitol W 773 [M]	1962	3.75	7.50	15.00
—Black colorband label, logo at top				
Capitol DW 773 [R]	196?	3.00	6.00	12.00
GIDGET GOES HAWAIIAN				
Colpix CP 418 [M]	1961	12.50	25.00	50.00
GIGI				
MGM E-3641 [M]	1958	5.00	10.00	20.00
—Yellow label				
MGM SE-3641 [S]	1959	6.25	12.50	25.00
—Yellow label				
MGM E-3641 [M]	1960	3.00	6.00	12.00
—Black label				
MGM SE-3641 [S]	1960	3.75	7.50	15.00
—Black label				
MGM SE-3641 [S]	1959	3.00	6.00	12.00
—Blue and gold label				
MGM W 90523 [M]	1965	3.00	6.00	12.00
—Capitol Record Club edition				
MGM SW 90523 [S]	1965	3.75	7.50	15.00
MGM SW-90523 [S]	196?	3.75	7.50	15.00
—Capitol Record Club issue				
GIGOT				
Capitol W 1754 [M]	1962	7.50	15.00	30.00
Capitol SW 1754 [S]	1962	10.00	20.00	40.00
THE GIRL IN THE BIKINI				
Poplar PLP 33-1002 [M]	1952	100.00	200.00	400.00
THE GIRL MOST LIKELY				
Capitol W 930 [M]	1957	15.00	30.00	60.00
GIRL ON A MOTORCYCLE				
Tetragrammaton T-5000	1969	7.50	15.00	30.00
THE GLENN MILLER STORY				
Decca DL 5519 [10]	1954	10.00	20.00	40.00
Decca DL 8226 [M]	1956	7.50	15.00	30.00
Decca DL 9123 [M]	196?	5.00	10.00	20.00
—Reissue of 8226				
Decca DL 79123 [R]	196?	3.75	7.50	15.00
THE GLORY STOMPERS				
Sidewalk DT 5910 [R]	1968	12.50	25.00	50.00
GOD'S LITTLE ACRE				
United Artists UAL-4002 [M]	1958	37.50	75.00	150.00
THE GODFATHER				
Paramount PAS-1003	1972	5.00	10.00	20.00
—Original cover with triple gatefold				
THE GODFATHER PART II				
ABC ABDP-856	1975	5.00	10.00	20.00
GOLD				
ABC ABCD-855	1975	7.50	15.00	30.00
GOLDEN BOY				
Colpix CP-478 [M]	1964	5.00	10.00	20.00
Colpix SCP-478 [S]	1964	6.25	12.50	25.00
THE GOLDEN BREED				
Capitol ST 2886	1967	7.50	15.00	30.00
THE GOLDEN COACH				
MGM E-3111 [M]	1954	37.50	75.00	150.00
THE GOLDEN SCREW				
Atco 33-208 [M]	1967	7.50	15.00	30.00
Atco SD 33-208 [S]	1967	10.00	20.00	40.00
GOLDFINGER				
United Artists UAL-4117 [M]	1964	3.75	7.50	15.00
United Artists UAS-5117 [S]	1964	5.00	10.00	20.00
GOLIATH AND THE BARBARIANS				
American Int'l. 1001-M [M]	1960	10.00	20.00	40.00
American Int'l. 1001-S [S]	1960	17.50	35.00	70.00
GONE WITH THE WAVE				
Colpix CP-492 [M]	1965	10.00	20.00	40.00
Colpix SCP-492 [S]	1965	15.00	30.00	60.00
GONE WITH THE WIND				
MGM 1E-10 [M]	1967	5.00	10.00	20.00
—Gatefold edition with 32-page booklet				
MGM S1E-10 [S]	1967	5.00	10.00	20.00
—Gatefold edition with 32-page booklet				
GOOD NEWS				
MGM E-504 [10]	1950	12.50	25.00	50.00
GOODBYE AGAIN				
United Artists UAL-4091 [M]	1961	7.50	15.00	30.00

Label, Number	Yr	VG	VG+	NM
United Artists UAS-5091 [S]	1961	10.00	20.00	40.00
GOODBYE, CHARLIE				
20th Century Fox TFM-3165 [M]	1964	6.25	12.50	25.00
20th Century Fox TFS-4165 [S]	1964	7.50	15.00	30.00
GOODBYE, MR. CHIPS				
MGM 1SE-19	1969	5.00	10.00	20.00
GORDON'S WAR				
Buddah BDS-5137	1973	10.00	20.00	40.00
THE GOSPEL ACCORDING TO ST. MATTHEW				
Mainstream S-4000 [S]	1966	25.00	50.00	100.00
Mainstream 54000 [M]	1966	6.25	12.50	25.00
GOYA				
Decca DL 8236 [M]	1959	37.50	75.00	150.00
GO, GO, GO WORLD				
Musicor MM-2059 [M]	1965	10.00	20.00	40.00
Musicor MS-3059 [S]	1965	15.00	30.00	60.00
GO, JOHNNY, GO!				
(No label) (no number) [DJ]	1959	250.00	500.00	1000.
—Only exists as a promo				
GRAND PRIX				
MGM 1E-8 [M]	1967	5.00	10.00	20.00
MGM 1SE-8 [S]	1967	6.25	12.50	25.00
THE GREAT ESCAPE				
United Artists UAL-4107 [M]	1963	6.25	12.50	25.00
United Artists UAS-5107 [S]	1963	7.50	15.00	30.00
THE GREAT GATSBY				
Paramount 2-3001 [(2)]	1974	5.00	10.00	20.00
THE GREATEST SHOW ON EARTH				
RCA Victor LPM-3018 [10]	1952	50.00	100.00	200.00
THE GREATEST STORY EVER TOLD				
United Artists UAL-4120 [M]	1965	6.25	12.50	25.00
United Artists UAS-5120 [S]	1965	7.50	15.00	30.00
GROUNDS FOR MARRIAGE				
MGM E-536 [M]	1950	20.00	40.00	80.00
GUESS WHO'S COMING TO DINNER				
Colgems COM-108 [M]	1968	7.50	15.00	30.00
Colgems COS-108 [S]	1968	7.50	15.00	30.00
GULLIVER'S TRAVELS BEYOND THE MOON				
Mainstream S-4001 [S]	1965	10.00	20.00	40.00
Mainstream 54001 [M]	1965	7.50	15.00	30.00
GUNS FOR SAN SEBASTIAN				
MGM SE-4565	1968	15.00	30.00	60.00
THE GUNS OF NAVARONE				
Columbia CL 1655 [M]	1961	5.00	10.00	20.00
Columbia CS 8455 [S]	1961	12.50	25.00	50.00
GURU				
RCA Victor LSO-1158	1969	5.00	10.00	20.00
GUYS AND DOLLS				
Decca DL 8036 [M]	1950	7.50	15.00	30.00
Decca DL 9023 [M]	1955	5.00	10.00	20.00
—Reissue of 8036				
GYPSY				
Warner Bros. B 1480 [M]	1962	5.00	10.00	20.00
Warner Bros. BS 1480 [S]	1962	7.50	15.00	30.00
GYPSY GIRL				
Mainstream S-6090 [S]	1966	10.00	20.00	40.00
Mainstream 56090 [M]	1966	7.50	15.00	30.00
HALLELUJAH THE HILLS				
Fontana MGF-27524 [M]	1964	6.25	12.50	25.00
Fontana SRF-67524 [S]	1964	7.50	15.00	30.00
THE HALLELUJAH TRAIL				
United Artists UAL-4127 [M]	1965	5.00	10.00	20.00
United Artists UAS-5127 [S]	1965	6.25	12.50	25.00
HAMMERHEAD				
Colgems COS-110	1968	10.00	20.00	40.00
HAMMERSMITH IS OUT				
Capitol SW-861	1972	7.50	15.00	30.00
HANG 'EM HIGH				
United Artists UAS-5179	1968	6.25	12.50	25.00
THE HAPPENING				
Colgems COMO-5006 [M]	1967	7.50	15.00	30.00
Colgems COSO-5006 [S]	1967	12.50	25.00	50.00
THE HAPPIEST MILLIONAIRE				
Buena Vista BV-5001 [M]	1967	3.75	7.50	15.00
Buena Vista STER-5001 [S]	1967	5.00	10.00	20.00
THE HARD RIDE				
Paramount PAS-6005	1971	7.50	15.00	30.00
HARPER				
Mainstream S-6078 [S]	1966	6.25	12.50	25.00
Mainstream 56078 [M]	1966	5.00	10.00	20.00
THE HARRAD EXPERIMENT				
Capitol ST-11182	1973	6.25	12.50	25.00
HARRAD SUMMER				
Capitol ST-11338	1974	6.25	12.50	25.00
HAWAII				
United Artists UAL-4143 [M]	1966	5.00	10.00	20.00
United Artists UAS-5143 [S]	1966	6.25	12.50	25.00
United Artists SW-90935 [S]	1966	7.50	15.00	30.00
—Capitol Record Club issue				
THE HEART IS A LONELY HUNTER				
Warner Bros. WS 1759	1968	7.50	15.00	30.00
HEAVY TRAFFIC				
Fantasy F-9436	1973	6.25	12.50	25.00
THE HELEN MORGAN STORY				
RCA Victor LOC-1030 [M]	1957	15.00	30.00	60.00
HELL'S ANGELS '69				
Capitol SKAO-303	1969	6.25	12.50	25.00
HELL'S ANGELS ON WHEELS				
Smash MGS-27094 [M]	1967	6.25	12.50	25.00
Smash SRS-67094 [S]	1967	7.50	15.00	30.00
HELL'S BELLS				
Sidewalk ST 5919	1969	7.50	15.00	30.00
HELL TO ETERNITY				
Warwick W 2030 [M]	1960	30.00	60.00	120.00
Warwick WST 2030 [S]	1960	50.00	100.00	200.00
HELL UP IN HARLEM				
Motown M 802V1	1974	7.50	15.00	30.00
HELLCATS				
Tower ST 5124	1968	7.50	15.00	30.00
HELLO-GOODBYE				
20th Century Fox S-4210	1970	10.00	20.00	40.00
HEMINGWAY'S ADVENTURES OF A YOUNG MAN				
RCA Victor LOC-1074 [M]	1962	10.00	20.00	40.00
RCA Victor LSO-1074 [S]	1962	17.50	35.00	70.00
THE HERO				
Capitol SW-11098	1972	5.00	10.00	20.00
HEROES OF TELEMARK				
Mainstream S-6064 [S]	1965	7.50	15.00	30.00
Mainstream 56064 [M]	1965	5.00	10.00	20.00
HEY THERE, IT'S YOGI BEAR!				
Colpix CP-472 [M]	1964	12.50	25.00	50.00
Colpix SCP-472 [S]	1964	20.00	40.00	80.00
HIGH SOCIETY				
Capitol W 750 [M]	1956	7.50	15.00	30.00
—Gray label original				
Capitol W 750 [M]	1959	5.00	10.00	20.00
—Black colorband label, logo at left				
Capitol W 750 [M]	1962	3.75	7.50	15.00
—Black colorband label, logo at top				
Capitol SW 750 [S]	1959	7.50	15.00	30.00
—Black colorband label, logo at left				
Capitol SW 750 [S]	1962	5.00	10.00	20.00
—Black colorband label, logo at top				
HOLIDAY INN				
Decca DL 4256	1962	6.25	12.50	25.00
HOOTENANNY HOOT				
MGM E-4172 [M]	1963	5.00	10.00	20.00
MGM SE-4172 [S]	1963	6.25	12.50	25.00
THE HORSE SOLDIERS				
United Artists UAL-4035 [M]	1959	15.00	30.00	60.00
United Artists UAS-5035 [S]	1959	37.50	75.00	150.00
THE HORSEMEN				
Sunflower SNF-5007	1971	10.00	20.00	40.00
THE HOT ROCK				
Prophesy SD 8055	1972	5.00	10.00	20.00
HOT ROD RUMBLE				
Liberty LRP-3048 [M]	1957	37.50	75.00	150.00
HOTEL PARADISO				
MGM E-4419 [M]	1966	5.00	10.00	20.00
MGM SE-4419 [S]	1966	6.25	12.50	25.00
THE HOUR OF THE GUN				
United Artists UAL-4166 [M]	1967	10.00	20.00	40.00
United Artists UAS-5166 [S]	1967	17.50	35.00	70.00
A HOUSE IS NOT A HOME				
Ava A-50 [M]	1964	6.25	12.50	25.00
Ava AS-50 [S]	1964	7.50	15.00	30.00

Label, Number	Yr	VG	VG+	NM
HOUSEBOAT				
Columbia CL 1222 [M]	1958	12.50	25.00	50.00
HOW SWEET IT IS				
RCA Victor LSP-4037	1968	5.00	10.00	20.00
HOW THE WEST WAS WON				
MGM 1E-5 [M]	1963	3.75	7.50	15.00
MGM S1E-5 [S]	1963	5.00	10.00	20.00
HOW TO MURDER YOUR WIFE				
United Artists UAL-4119 [M]	1965	3.75	7.50	15.00
United Artists UAS-5119 [S]	1965	5.00	10.00	20.00
HOW TO SAVE A MARRIAGE AND RUIN YOUR LIFE				
Columbia Masterworks OS 3140	1968	5.00	10.00	20.00
HOW TO STEAL A MILLION				
20th Century Fox TFM-3183 [M]	1966	10.00	20.00	40.00
20th Century Fox TFS-4183 [S]	1966	12.50	25.00	50.00
HOW TO STUFF A WILD BIKINI				
Wand 671 [M]	1965	7.50	15.00	30.00
Wand S-671 [S]	1965	10.00	20.00	40.00
HOW TO SUCCEED IN BUSINESS WITHOUT REALLY TRYING				
United Artists UAL-4151 [M]	1967	5.00	10.00	20.00
United Artists UAS-5151 [S]	1967	6.25	12.50	25.00
HURRY SUNDOWN				
RCA Victor LOC-1133 [M]	1967	7.50	15.00	30.00
RCA Victor LSO-1133 [S]	1967	10.00	20.00	40.00
THE HUSTLER				
Kapp KL-1264 [M]	1961	15.00	30.00	60.00
Kapp KS-3264 [S]	1961	30.00	60.00	120.00
I'LL NEVER FORGET WHAT'S 'IS NAME				
Decca DL 9163 [M]	1967	6.25	12.50	25.00
Decca DL 79163 [S]	1967	7.50	15.00	30.00
I LOVE MELVIN				
MGM E-190 [10]	1953	12.50	25.00	50.00
I NEVER SANG FOR MY FATHER				
Bell 1204	1970	10.00	20.00	40.00
I WANT TO LIVE				
United Artists UXL 1 [(2) M]	1958	15.00	30.00	60.00
—Combines 4005 and 4006 into one package				
United Artists UXS 51 [(2) S]	1958	20.00	40.00	80.00
—Combines 5005 and 5006 into one package				
United Artists UAL-4005 [M]	1958	6.25	12.50	25.00
—Orchestral music by Johnny Mandel				
United Artists UAS-4005 [S]	1958	10.00	20.00	40.00
—Orchestral music by Johnny Mandel				
United Artists UAL-4006 [M]	1958	7.50	15.00	30.00
—Jazz music by Gerry Mulligan, Shelly Mann and Art Farmer				
United Artists UAS-4006 [S]	1958	10.00	20.00	40.00
—Jazz music by Gerry Mulligan, Shelly Mann and Art Farmer				
ICE STATION ZEBRA				
MGM S1E-14 ST	1968	10.00	20.00	40.00
IF HE HOLLERS, LET HIM GO				
Tower ST 5152	1968	10.00	20.00	40.00
IMITATION OF LIFE				
Decca DL 8879 [M]	1959	12.50	25.00	50.00
Decca DL 78879 [S]	1959	20.00	40.00	80.00
IN HARM'S WAY				
RCA Victor LOC-1100 [M]	1965	10.00	20.00	40.00
RCA Victor LSO-1100 [S]	1965	20.00	40.00	80.00
IN LIKE FLINT				
20th Century Fox 4193 [M]	1967	10.00	20.00	40.00
20th Century Fox S-4193 [S]	1967	20.00	40.00	80.00
IN SEARCH OF THE CASTAWAYS				
Disneyland ST-3916 [M]	1962	17.50	35.00	70.00
IN THE GOOD OLD SUMMERTIME				
MGM E-169 [10]	1949	25.00	50.00	100.00
IN THE HEAT OF THE NIGHT				
United Artists UAL-4160 [M]	1967	3.75	7.50	15.00
United Artists UAS-5160 [S]	1967	5.00	10.00	20.00
THE INDISCRETION OF AN AMERICAN WIFE				
Columbia CL 6277 [10]	1954	20.00	40.00	80.00
THE INN OF THE SIXTH HAPPINESS				
20th Century Fox FOX-3011 [M]	1958	12.50	25.00	50.00
20th Century Fox SFX-3011 [S]	1958	17.50	35.00	70.00
INSIDE DAISY CLOVER				
Warner Bros. W 1616 [M]	1965	5.00	10.00	20.00
Warner Bros. WS 1616 [S]	1965	7.50	15.00	30.00
INSPECTOR CLOUSEAU				
United Artists UAS-5186	1968	7.50	15.00	30.00
INTERLUDE				
Colgems COSO-5007	1968	10.00	20.00	40.00

Label, Number	Yr	VG	VG+	NM
THE INTERNS				
Colpix CP 427 [M]	1962	7.50	15.00	30.00
Colpix SCP 427 [S]	1962	10.00	20.00	40.00
INVITATION TO THE DANCE				
MGM E-3207 [M]	1956	12.50	25.00	50.00
THE IPCRESS FILE				
Decca DL 9124 [M]	1965	7.50	15.00	30.00
Decca DL 79124 [S]	1965	10.00	20.00	40.00
IRMA LA DOUCE				
Columbia Masterworks OS 2029 [S]	1960	10.00	20.00	40.00
Columbia Masterworks OL 5560 [M]	1960	7.50	15.00	30.00
United Artists UAL-4109 [M]	1963	5.00	10.00	20.00
United Artists UAS-5109 [S]	1963	6.25	12.50	25.00
IS PARIS BURNING?				
Columbia Masterworks OS 3030 [S]	1966	10.00	20.00	40.00
Columbia Masterworks OL 6630 [M]	1966	7.50	15.00	30.00
THE ISLAND AT THE TOP OF THE WORLD				
Disneyland ST-3814	1974	6.25	12.50	25.00
ISLAND IN THE SKY				
Decca DL 7029 [10]	1953	75.00	150.00	300.00
IT'S A MAD, MAD, MAD, MAD WORLD				
United Artists UAL-4110 [M]	1963	5.00	10.00	20.00
United Artists UAS-5110 [S]	1963	6.25	12.50	25.00
IT'S ALWAYS FAIR WEATHER				
MGM E-3241 [M]	1955	12.50	25.00	50.00
IT STARTED IN NAPLES				
Dot DLP-3324 [M]	1960	15.00	30.00	60.00
Dot DLP-25324 [S]	1960	25.00	50.00	100.00
THE ITALIAN JOB				
Paramount PAS-5007	1969	10.00	20.00	40.00
JACK THE RIPPER				
RCA Victor LPM-2199 [M]	1960	7.50	15.00	30.00
RCA Victor LSP-2199 [S]	1960	12.50	25.00	50.00
JAMBOREE!				
Warner Bros. (no #) [M]	1957	300.00	600.00	1200.
—Album has been counterfeited. Originals have front cover slicks and back cover notes printed on the cardboard, and the records have "Jam 1" and "Jam 2" stamped (not etched) in the dead wax.				
THE JAMES DEAN STORY				
Capitol W 881 [M]	1957	15.00	30.00	60.00
Kimberly 2016 [M]	1960	10.00	20.00	40.00
Kimberly 11016 [S]	1960	12.50	25.00	50.00
—Reissue of World Pacific 2005				
World Pacific P-2005 [M]	1958	25.00	50.00	100.00
JAWS				
MCA 2087	1975	5.00	10.00	20.00
JEREMIAH JOHNSON				
Warner Bros. BS 2902	1972	5.00	10.00	20.00
—Green label				
JESSICA				
United Artists UAL-4096 [M]	1962	5.00	10.00	20.00
United Artists UAS-5096 [S]	1962	6.25	12.50	25.00
THE JOE LOUIS STORY				
MGM E-221 [10]	1953	20.00	40.00	80.00
JOHN PAUL JONES				
Warner Bros. W 1293 [M]	1959	15.00	30.00	60.00
Warner Bros. WS 1293 [S]	1959	30.00	60.00	120.00
JOHNNY COOL				
United Artists UAL-4111 [M]	1963	5.00	10.00	20.00
United Artists UAS-5111 [S]	1963	6.25	12.50	25.00
JOHNNY TREMAIN				
Disneyland WDL-4014 [M]	1957	12.50	25.00	50.00
JUD				
Ampex A-50101	1971	5.00	10.00	20.00
JUDGMENT AT NUREMBERG				
United Artists UAL-4095 [M]	1961	5.00	10.00	20.00
United Artists UAS-5095 [S]	1961	12.50	25.00	50.00
JUDITH				
RCA Victor LOC-1119 [M]	1966	3.75	7.50	15.00
RCA Victor LSO-1119 [S]	1966	7.50	15.00	30.00
JULIET OF THE SPIRITS				
Mainstream S-6062 [S]	1965	15.00	30.00	60.00
Mainstream 56062 [M]	1965	6.25	12.50	25.00
JULIUS CAESAR				
MGM E-3033 [M]	1953	10.00	20.00	40.00
JUMBO (BILLY ROSE'S)				
Columbia Masterworks OS 2260 [S]	1962	7.50	15.00	30.00
Columbia Masterworks OL 5860 [M]	1962	5.00	10.00	20.00
THE JUNGLE BOOK				
Buena Vista BV-4041 [M]	1967	3.75	7.50	15.00

Label, Number	Yr	VG	VG+	NM
Buena Vista STER-4041 [S]	1967	6.25	12.50	25.00
JUSTINE				
Monument SLP-18123	1969	7.50	15.00	30.00
KALEIDOSCOPE				
Warner Bros. W 1663 [M]	1966	5.00	10.00	20.00
Warner Bros. WS 1663 [S]	1966	6.25	12.50	25.00
KELLY'S HEROES				
MGM S1E-23	1970	7.50	15.00	30.00
THE KEY				
Columbia CL 1185 [M]	1958	20.00	40.00	80.00
KILLERS THREE				
Tower ST-5141	1968	5.00	10.00	20.00
THE KING AND I				
Capitol W 740 [M]	1956	6.25	12.50	25.00
—Gray label				
Capitol W 740 [M]	1959	3.75	7.50	15.00
—Black colorband label, logo at left				
Capitol W 740 [M]	1962	3.00	6.00	12.00
—Black colorband label, logo at top				
Capitol SW 740 [S]	1959	5.00	10.00	20.00
—Black colorband label, logo at left				
Capitol SW 740 [S]	1962	3.75	7.50	15.00
—Black colorband label, logo at top				
KING KONG				
Reprise MS 2260	1976	5.00	10.00	20.00
KING OF KINGS				
MGM 1E-2 [M]	1961	7.50	15.00	30.00
—Boxed version with hardbound book and four 8x10 photos				
MGM S1E-2 [S]	1961	10.00	20.00	40.00
—Boxed version with hardbound book and four 8x10 photos				
KING RAT				
Mainstream S-6061 [S]	1965	12.50	25.00	50.00
Mainstream 56061 [M]	1965	7.50	15.00	30.00
KINGS GO FORTH				
Capitol W 1063 [M]	1958	37.50	75.00	150.00
KISMET				
MGM E-3281 [M]	1955	5.00	10.00	20.00
—Yellow label				
KWAMINA				
Mercury MG-20654 [M]	1961	6.25	12.50	25.00
Mercury SR-60654 [S]	1961	7.50	15.00	30.00
LADY AND THE TRAMP				
Decca DL 5557 [10]	1955	15.00	30.00	60.00
Decca DL 8462 [M]	1957	17.50	35.00	70.00
THE LANDLORD				
United Artists UAS-5209	1970	5.00	10.00	20.00
THE LAST OF THE SECRET AGENTS				
Dot DLP-3714 [M]	1966	5.00	10.00	20.00
Dot DLP-25714 [S]	1966	6.25	12.50	25.00
THE LAST RUN				
MGM 1SE-30	1971	6.25	12.50	25.00
LAST SUMMER				
Warner Bros. WS 1791	1969	5.00	10.00	20.00
THE LAST VALLEY				
ABC-Dunhill DSX-50102	1971	10.00	20.00	40.00
LAWRENCE OF ARABIA				
Colpix CP-514 [M]	1962	5.00	10.00	20.00
Colpix SCP-514 [S]	1962	7.50	15.00	30.00
LENNY				
United Artists UA-LA359-H [(2)]	1974	5.00	10.00	20.00
THE LEOPARD				
20th Century Fox FXG-5015 [M]	1963	7.50	15.00	30.00
20th Century Fox SXG-5015 [S]	1963	10.00	20.00	40.00
LES LIAISONS DANGEREUSES				
Charlie Parker PLP-813 [M]	1962	6.25	12.50	25.00
Charlie Parker PLP-813S [S]	1962	7.50	15.00	30.00
Epic LA 16022 [M]	1961	10.00	20.00	40.00
Epic BA 17022 [S]	1961	7.50	15.00	30.00
Fontana MGF-27539 [M]	1965	5.00	10.00	20.00
Fontana SRF-67539 [R]	1965	3.75	7.50	15.00
LET'S MAKE LOVE				
Columbia CL 1527 [M]	1960	7.50	15.00	30.00
Columbia CS 8327 [S]	1960	12.50	25.00	50.00
LET THE GOOD TIMES ROLL				
Bell 9002 [(2)]	1973	6.25	12.50	25.00
LI'L ABNER				
Columbia Masterworks OS 2021 [S]	1959	10.00	20.00	40.00
—Credits within photo				
Columbia Masterworks OS 2021 [S]	196?	6.25	12.50	25.00
—Credits in red strip at bottom of photo				

Label, Number	Yr	VG	VG+	NM
Columbia Masterworks OL 5460 [M]	1959	7.50	15.00	30.00
—Credits within photo				
Columbia Masterworks OL 5460 [M]	196?	5.00	10.00	20.00
—Credits in red strip at bottom of photo				
THE LIFE AND TIMES OF JUDGE ROY BEAN				
Columbia Masterworks S 31948	1972	6.25	12.50	25.00
LIGHT FANTASTIC				
20th Century Fox FXG-5016 [M]	1963	5.00	10.00	20.00
20th Century Fox SXG-5016 [S]	1963	6.25	12.50	25.00
LILIES OF THE FIELD				
Epic LN 24094 [M]	1964	5.00	10.00	20.00
Epic BN 26094 [S]	1964	7.50	15.00	30.00
THE LION				
London M-76001 [M]	1962	100.00	200.00	400.00
THE LION IN WINTER				
Columbia Masterworks OS 3250	1969	5.00	10.00	20.00
LITTLE BIG MAN				
Columbia Masterworks S 30545	1970	5.00	10.00	20.00
LIVE AND LET DIE				
United Artists UA-LA100-G	1973	5.00	10.00	20.00
—Tan label; cover corner is not clipped off				
United Artists SWAO-95120	1973	7.50	15.00	30.00
—Longines (formerly Capitol) Record Club edition				
LIVE FOR LIFE				
United Artists UAL-4165 [M]	1967	5.00	10.00	20.00
United Artists UAS-5165 [S]	1967	5.00	10.00	20.00
THE LIVELY SET				
Decca DL 9119 [M]	1964	7.50	15.00	30.00
Decca DL 79119 [S]	1964	10.00	20.00	40.00
LOLITA				
MGM E-4050 [M]	1962	5.00	10.00	20.00
MGM SE-4050 [S]	1962	7.50	15.00	30.00
THE LOLLIPOP COVER				
Mainstream S-6067 [S]	1966	7.50	15.00	30.00
Mainstream 56067 [M]	1966	5.00	10.00	20.00
THE LONG HOT SUMMER				
Roulette R-25026 [M]	1958	18.75	37.50	75.00
LONG JOHN SILVER				
RCA Victor LPM-3279 [10]	1954	75.00	150.00	300.00
THE LONG SHIPS				
Colpix CP-517 [M]	1964	12.50	25.00	50.00
Colpix SCP-517 [S]	1964	15.00	30.00	60.00
THE LONGEST DAY				
20th Century Fox FXG-5007 [M]	1962	5.00	10.00	20.00
20th Century Fox SXG-5007 [S]	1962	6.25	12.50	25.00
LORD JIM				
Colpix CP-521 [M]	1965	6.25	12.50	25.00
Colpix SCP-521 [S]	1965	10.00	20.00	40.00
LORD LOVE A DUCK				
United Artists UAL-4137 [M]	1966	5.00	10.00	20.00
United Artists UAS-5137 [S]	1966	6.25	12.50	25.00
THE LORDS OF FLATBUSH				
ABC ABCD-828	1974	7.50	15.00	30.00
A LOSS OF INNOCENCE				
Colpix CP-508 [M]	1961	10.00	20.00	40.00
THE LOST CONTINENT				
MGM E-3635 [M]	1957	50.00	100.00	200.00
LOVE IN 4 DIMENSIONS				
Request RLP-8090 [M]	1966	6.25	12.50	25.00
Request SRLP-8090 [S]	1966	7.50	15.00	30.00
LOVE LIFE				
Heritage 600 [M]	195?	15.00	30.00	60.00
LOVERS AND OTHER STRANGERS				
ABC ABCS-OC-15	1970	5.00	10.00	20.00
ABC SW-93479	1971	6.25	12.50	25.00
—Capitol Record Club edition				
THE MAD ADVENTURES OF RABBI JACOB				
London PS 652	1974	5.00	10.00	20.00
—Price for intact copies; cut-outs go for maybe 50 percent of this				
MADAME BOVARY				
MGM E-3507 [M]	195?	37.50	75.00	150.00
THE MAGIC CHRISTIAN				
Commonwealth United CU-6004	1970	6.25	12.50	25.00
MAGNIFICENT OBSESSION				
Decca DL 8078 [M]	1954	15.00	30.00	60.00
—Black label, gold print				
Decca DL 8078 [M]	1055	12.60	25.00	50.00
—Black label, silver print				

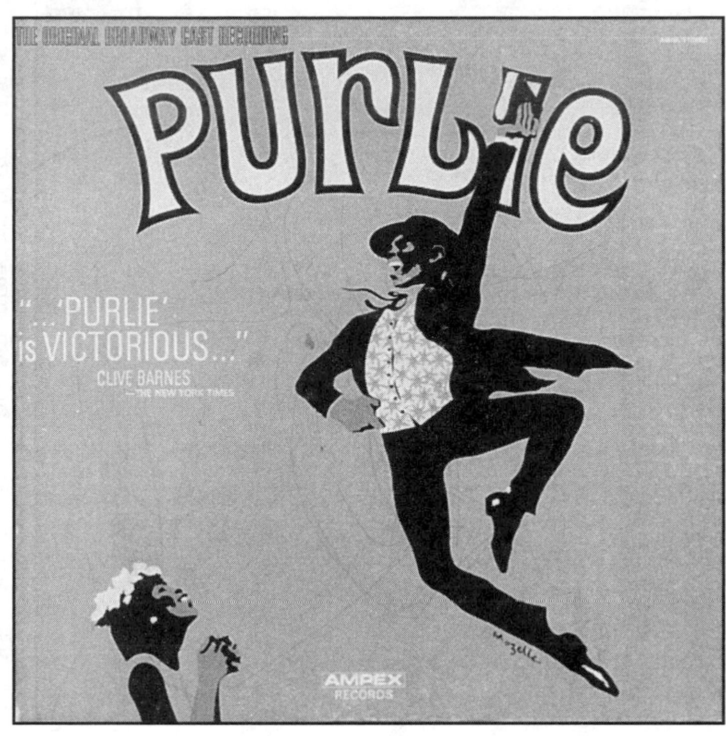

(Top left) *The Mad Show* was an attempt to turn the popular satire magazine into a stage play. It was almost as big a bomb as the one next to Alfred E. Neuman on the cover, which is one reason this LP is highly collectible today. (Top right) *Purlie* was a highly regarded early 1970s show with a cast that included Cleavon Little and Melba Moore. (Bottom left) The last album issued under Bing Crosby's exclusive record deal with Decca – all future material was leased to various record companies — was the obscure TV soundtrack *High Tor*. It also marks a very early appearance on record by Julie Andrews. (Bottom right) One of the rarest and most sought-after of all soundtracks is this one, a promo-only issue from the movie *Jamboree!* It was issued by Warner Bros. in 1957 even before there was a Warner Bros. Records. The LP has been counterfeited, but a knowledgeable collector can tell the real ones from the fakes.

Label, Number	Yr	VG	VG+	NM
Decca DL 8078 [M]	196?	7.50	1.00	30.00
—Black label with color bars				
MAJOR DUNDEE				
Columbia Masterworks OS 2780 [S]	1965	7.50	15.00	30.00
Columbia Masterworks OL 6380 [M]	1965	5.00	10.00	20.00
MAKE A WISH				
RCA Victor LOC-1002 [M]	1951	37.50	75.00	150.00
MALAMONDO				
Epic LN 24126 [M]	1964	7.50	15.00	30.00
Epic BN 26126 [S]	1964	10.00	20.00	40.00
MAME				
Warner Bros. PRO 580 [DJ]	1973	12.50	25.00	50.00
—Promo-only gatefold edition with Lucille Ball in Christmas hat on the cover				
Warner Bros. W 2773	1974	3.75	7.50	15.00
A MAN AND A WOMAN (UN HOMME ET UNE FEMME)				
United Artists UAL-4147 [M]	1966	3.75	7.50	15.00
United Artists UAS-5147 [S]	1966	5.00	10.00	20.00
A MAN CALLED ADAM				
Reprise R 6180 [M]	1966	3.75	7.50	15.00
Reprise RS 6180 [S]	1966	5.00	10.00	20.00
A MAN CALLED DAGGER				
MGM E-4516 [M]	1967	3.75	7.50	15.00
MGM SE-4516 [S]	1967	5.00	10.00	20.00
A MAN CALLED FLINTSTONE				
Hanna-Barbera HLP-2055 [M]	1967	25.00	50.00	100.00
A MAN COULD GET KILLED				
Decca DL 4750 [M]	1966	3.75	7.50	15.00
Decca DL 74750 [S]	1966	5.00	10.00	20.00
A MAN FOR ALL SEASONS				
RCA Victor VDM-116 [(2) M]	1966	7.50	15.00	30.00
MAN FROM SHAFT				
MGM SE-4836	1972	7.50	15.00	30.00
MAN IN THE MIDDLE				
20th Century Fox TFM-3128 [M]	1965	7.50	15.00	30.00
20th Century Fox TFS-4128 [S]	1965	12.50	25.00	50.00
THE MAN OF A THOUSAND FACES				
Decca DL 8623 [M]	1957	12.50	25.00	50.00
—Black label, silver print, or pink label, black print promos				
Decca DL 8623 [M]	196?	7.50	15.00	30.00
—Black label with color bars				
MAN OF LA MANCHA				
United Artists UAS-9906	1972	5.00	10.00	20.00
—Price for intact copies; cut-outs go for maybe 50 percent of this				
THE MAN WHO WOULD BE KING				
Capitol SW-11474	1975	5.00	10.00	20.00
THE MAN WITH THE GOLDEN ARM				
Decca DL 8257 [M]	1956	10.00	20.00	40.00
Decca DL 78257 [R]	196?	5.00	10.00	20.00
THE MAN WITH THE GOLDEN GUN				
United Artists UA-LA358-G	1974	5.00	10.00	20.00
MARACAIBO				
Decca DL 8756 [M]	1958	10.00	20.00	40.00
—Black label, silver print, or pink label, black print promos				
Decca DL 8756 [M]	196?	5.00	10.00	20.00
—Black label with color bars				
MARCO THE MAGNIFICENT				
Columbia Masterworks OS 2870 [S]	1966	10.00	20.00	40.00
Columbia Masterworks OL 6470 [M]	1966	6.25	12.50	25.00
MARJORIE MORNINGSTAR				
RCA Victor LOC-1044 [M]	1958	10.00	20.00	40.00
—"RE" next to label number				
RCA Victor LOC-1044 [M]	1958	15.00	30.00	60.00
—"An Original Soundtrack Recording" on spine				
MARRY ME, MARRY ME				
RCA Victor LSO-1160	1969	5.00	10.00	20.00
MARY POPPINS				
Buena Vista BV-4026 [M]	1964	3.00	6.00	12.00
—Originals have gatefold covers				
Buena Vista STER-4026 [S]	1964	3.75	7.50	15.00
—Originals have gatefold covers				
Buena Vista STER-5005 [S]	1973	2.50	5.00	10.00
—Reissue with new number and no gatefold				
RCA Victor COP-111 [M]	1964	3.75	7.50	15.00
—With gatefold; RCA Record Club edition				
RCA Victor CSO-111 [S]	1964	5.00	10.00	20.00
—With gatefold; RCA Record Club edition				
MARY, QUEEN OF SCOTS				
Decca DL 79186	1972	7.50	15.00	30.00
MASTER OF THE WORLD				
Vee Jay LP-4000 [M]	1961	6.25	12.50	25.00
Vee Jay SR-4000 [S]	1961	10.00	20.00	40.00

Label, Number	Yr	VG	VG+	NM
MCLINTOCK!				
United Artists UAL-4112 [M]	1963	15.00	30.00	60.00
United Artists UAS-5112 [S]	1963	20.00	40.00	80.00
ME AND THE COLONEL				
RCA Victor LOC-1046 [M]	1958	12.50	25.00	50.00
MEDITERRANEAN HOLIDAY				
London M-76003 [M]	1964	12.50	25.00	50.00
London MS-82003 [S]	1964	20.00	40.00	80.00
MEET ME IN ST.LOUIS				
Decca DL 8498 [M]	1957	7.50	15.00	30.00
—LP reissue of 78 rpm album from 1944; B-side of LP is "The Harvey Girls."				
MEMORIES AUX BRUXELLES				
Carlton LP-112 [M]	1959	6.25	12.50	25.00
Carlton LP-12112 [S]	1959	10.00	20.00	40.00
MEN IN WAR				
Imperial LP-9032 W [M]	1957	37.50	75.00	150.00
MERRY ANDREW				
Capitol T 1016 [M]	1958	12.50	25.00	50.00
MICKEY ONE				
MGM E-4312 [M]	1965	5.00	10.00	20.00
MGM SE-4312 [S]	1965	6.25	12.50	25.00
MIDNIGHT COWBOY				
United Artists UAS-5198	1969	5.00	10.00	20.00
A MILANESE STORY				
Atlantic 1388 [M]	1962	5.00	10.00	20.00
Atlantic SD 1388 [S]	1962	6.25	12.50	25.00
THE MINX				
Amsterdam 12007	1970	30.00	60.00	120.00
THE MISFITS				
United Artists UAL-4087 [M]	1961	12.50	25.00	50.00
United Artists UAS-5087 [S]	1961	25.00	50.00	100.00
MISS SADIE THOMPSON				
Mercury MG-20123 [M]	1956	37.50	75.00	150.00
Mercury MG-25181 [10]	1954	18.75	37.50	75.00
MOBY DICK				
RCA Victor LPM-1247 [M]	1956	30.00	60.00	120.00
MODERN TIMES				
United Artists UAL-4049 [M]	1959	6.25	12.50	25.00
MODESTY BLAISE				
20th Century Fox TFM-3182 [M]	1966	7.50	15.00	30.00
20th Century Fox TFS-4182 [S]	1966	12.50	25.00	50.00
MONDO CANE				
United Artists UAL-4105 [M]	1963	3.75	7.50	15.00
United Artists UAS-5105 [S]	1963	5.00	10.00	20.00
MONDO CANE NO. 2				
20th Century Fox TFM-3147 [M]	1964	7.50	15.00	30.00
20th Century Fox TFS-4147 [S]	1964	10.00	20.00	40.00
THE MOON SPINNERS				
Buena Vista BV-3323 [M]	1964	10.00	20.00	40.00
MR. BUDDWING				
Verve V-8638 [M]	1965	3.75	7.50	15.00
Verve V6-8638 [S]	1965	6.25	12.50	25.00
MR. MAGOO: 1001 ARABIAN NIGHTS				
Colpix CP-410 [M]	1959	12.50	25.00	50.00
Colpix SCP-410 [S]	1959	37.50	75.00	150.00
MURDER INC.				
Canadian American CALP-1003 [M]	1960	25.00	50.00	100.00
MUSCLE BEACH PARTY PLUS MERLIN JONES AND THE SCRAMBLED EGGHEAD				
Buena Vista BV-3314 [M]	1964	15.00	30.00	60.00
Buena Vista STER-3314 [S]	1964	30.00	60.00	120.00
THE MUSIC MAN				
Warner Bros. B 1459 [M]	1962	3.75	7.50	15.00
Warner Bros. BS 1459 [S]	1962	5.00	10.00	20.00
—Gold label originals				
MUTINY ON THE BOUNTY				
MGM 1E-4 [M]	1962	7.50	15.00	30.00
—Boxed set with book and painting				
MGM S1E-4 [S]	1962	10.00	20.00	40.00
—Boxed set with book and painting				
MY FAIR LADY				
Columbia Masterworks KOS 2600 [S]	1964	3.75	7.50	15.00
Columbia Masterworks KOL 8000 [M]	1964	3.00	6.00	12.00
MY GEISHA				
RCA Victor LOC-1070 [M]	1962	12.50	25.00	50.00
RCA Victor LSO-1070 [S]	1962	25.00	50.00	100.00
MY SIDE OF THE MOUNTAIN				
Capitol ST-245	1969	6.25	12.50	25.00

Label, Number	Yr	VG	VG+	NM
MY WILD IRISH ROSE				
RCA Victor LPM-3036 [10]	1952	10.00	20.00	40.00
M*A*S*H				
Columbia Masterworks OS 3520	1970	5.00	10.00	20.00
—Original copies do not have the theme song done by Ahmad Jamal				
NAKED ANGELS				
Straight STS-1056	1969	6.25	12.50	25.00
THE NAKED MAJA				
United Artists UAL-4031 [M]	1959	7.50	15.00	30.00
United Artists UAS-5031 [S]	1959	10.00	20.00	40.00
NANCY GOES TO RIO				
MGM E-508 [10]	1950	15.00	30.00	60.00
NASHVILLE				
ABC ABCD-893	1975	5.00	10.00	20.00
NAVAJO JOE				
United Artists UA-LA292-G	1974	6.25	12.50	25.00
NED KELLY				
United Artists UAS-5213	1970	6.25	12.50	25.00
NEVADA SMITH				
Dot DLP-3718 [M]	1966	6.25	12.50	25.00
Dot DLP-25718 [S]	1966	10.00	20.00	40.00
NEVER ON SUNDAY				
United Artists UAL-4070 [M]	1960	3.75	7.50	15.00
United Artists UAS-5070 [S]	1960	5.00	10.00	20.00
United Artists SW-90834 [S]	196?	5.00	10.00	20.00
—Capitol Record Club edition				
THE NEW INTERNS				
Colpix CP-473 [M]	1964	7.50	15.00	30.00
Colpix SCP-473 [S]	1964	10.00	20.00	40.00
A NEW KIND OF LOVE				
Mercury MG-20859 [M]	1963	3.75	7.50	15.00
Mercury SR-60859 [S]	1963	5.00	10.00	20.00
THE NEW MESSIAH				
Columbia KC 31713	1972	5.00	10.00	20.00
NICHOLAS AND ALEXANDRA				
Bell 1103	1971	6.25	12.50	25.00
NIGHT OF THE GENERALS				
Colgems COMO-5002 [M]	1967	10.00	20.00	40.00
Colgems COSO-5002 [S]	1967	17.50	35.00	70.00
THE NIGHT OF THE HUNTER				
RCA Victor LPM-1136 [M]	1955	62.50	125.00	250.00
NINE HOURS TO RAMA				
London M-76002 [M]	1963	75.00	150.00	300.00
NO WAY TO TREAT A LADY				
Dot DLP-25846	1968	6.25	12.50	25.00
NOT WITH MY WIFE, YOU DON'T				
Warner Bros. W 1668 [M]	1966	3.75	7.50	15.00
Warner Bros. WS 1668 [S]	1966	5.00	10.00	20.00
NOTHING BUT THE BEST				
Colpix CP-477 [M]	1964	5.00	10.00	20.00
Colpix SCP-477 [S]	1964	6.25	12.50	25.00
A NUN'S STORY				
Warner Bros. B 1306 [M]	1959	15.00	30.00	60.00
Warner Bros. BS 1306 [S]	1959	25.00	50.00	100.00
THE ODD COUPLE				
Dot DLP-25862	1968	5.00	10.00	20.00
ODDS AGAINST TOMORROW				
United Artists UAL-4061 [M]	1959	7.50	15.00	30.00
United Artists UAS-5061 [S]	1959	12.50	25.00	50.00
OF LOVE AND DESIRE				
20th Century Fox FXG-5014 [M]	1963	6.25	12.50	25.00
20th Century Fox SXG-5014 [S]	1963	7.50	15.00	30.00
OH DAD, POOR DAD, MAMMA'S HUNG YOU IN THE CLOSET AND I'M FEELIN' SO SAD				
RCA Victor LPM-3750 [M]	1967	5.00	10.00	20.00
RCA Victor LSP-3750 [S]	1967	6.25	12.50	25.00
OH, ROSALINDA!				
Mercury MG-20145 [M]	1957	12.50	25.00	50.00
OIL TOWN, U.S.A.				
RCA Victor LFM-2000 [10]	1953	15.00	30.00	60.00
OKLAHOMA!				
Capitol WAO 595 [M]	1955	6.25	12.50	25.00
—Purple or dark red label				
Capitol WAO 595 [M]	1956	5.00	10.00	20.00
—Gray label				
Capitol WAO 595 [M]	1959	3.75	7.50	15.00
—Black colorband label, logo at left				
Capitol WAO 595 [M]	1962	3.00	6.00	12.00
—Black colorband label, logo at top				

Label, Number	Yr	VG	VG+	NM
Capitol SWAO 595 [S]	1959	5.00	10.00	20.00
—Black colorband label, logo at left				
Capitol SWAO 595 [S]	1962	3.75	7.50	15.00
—Black colorband label, logo at top				
THE OLD MAN AND THE SEA				
Columbia CL 1183 [M]	1958	7.50	15.00	30.00
Columbia CS 8013 [S]	1958	15.00	30.00	60.00
OLD YELLER				
Disneyland WDL-1024 [M]	1960	10.00	20.00	40.00
—Second edition				
Disneyland 1024 [M]	1974	6.25	12.50	25.00
—Reissue with no prefix				
Disneyland WDL-3024 [M]	1957	12.50	25.00	50.00
—First edition				
ON HER MAJESTY'S SECRET SERVICE				
United Artists UAS-5204	1969	5.00	10.00	20.00
ONCE UPON A TIME IN THE WEST				
RCA Victor LSP-4736	1969	7.50	15.00	30.00
THE ONE-EYED JACKS				
Liberty LOM-16001 [M]	1961	7.50	15.00	30.00
Liberty LOS-17001 [S]	1961	12.50	25.00	50.00
THE ONE AND ONLY, GENUINE, ORIGINAL FAMILY BAND				
Buena Vista BV-5002 [M]	1968	3.75	7.50	15.00
Buena Vista STER-5002 [S]	1968	5.00	10.00	20.00
ONE FLEW OVER THE CUCKOO'S NEST				
Fantasy F-9500	1975	5.00	10.00	20.00
THE OPTIMISTS				
Paramount PAS-1015	1973	7.50	15.00	30.00
ORCHESTRA WIVES				
RCA Victor LPT-3065 [10]	1954	15.00	30.00	60.00
THE OSCAR				
Columbia Masterworks OS 2950 [S]	1966	6.25	12.50	25.00
Columbia Masterworks OL 6550 [M]	1966	5.00	10.00	20.00
OTLEY				
Colgems COS-112	1969	7.50	15.00	30.00
OUR MAN FLINT				
20th Century Fox TFM-3179 [M]	1966	10.00	20.00	40.00
20th Century Fox TFS-4179 [S]	1966	15.00	30.00	60.00
OUT OF SIGHT				
Decca DL 4751 [M]	1966	5.00	10.00	20.00
Decca DL 74751 [S]	1966	6.25	12.50	25.00
THE OUTLAW RIDERS				
MGM 1SE-26	1970	5.00	10.00	20.00
PAGAN LOVE SONG				
MGM E-534 [M]	1950	10.00	20.00	40.00
PAINT YOUR WAGON				
Paramount PMS-1001	1969	5.00	10.00	20.00
—With booklet				
THE PAJAMA GAME				
Columbia Masterworks OL 5210 [M]	1957	7.50	15.00	30.00
—Gray and black label with six "eye" logos				
PANIC BUTTON				
Musicor MM-2026 [M]	1964	20.00	40.00	80.00
Musicor MS-3026 [S]	1964	30.00	60.00	120.00
PAPER MOON				
Paramount PAS-1012	1973	5.00	10.00	20.00
PAPER TIGER				
Capitol SW-11475	1975	5.00	10.00	20.00
PAPILLON				
Capitol ST-11260	1973	5.00	10.00	20.00
THE PARENT TRAP!				
Buena Vista BV-3309 [M]	1961	10.00	20.00	40.00
Buena Vista STER-3309 [S]	1961	15.00	30.00	60.00
—B-side of the above two: Camerata Conducts Themes from Great Motion Pictures				
PARIS BLUES				
United Artists UAL-4092 [M]	1961	6.25	12.50	25.00
United Artists UAS-5092 [S]	1961	7.50	15.00	30.00
PARIS HOLIDAY				
United Artists UAL-4001 [M]	1958	12.50	25.00	50.00
PARIS WHEN IT SIZZLES				
Reprise R 6113 [M]	1964	6.25	12.50	25.00
Reprise RS 6113 [S]	1964	10.00	20.00	40.00
PARRISH				
Warner Bros. W 1413 [M]	1961	7.50	15.00	30.00
Warner Bros. WS 1413 [S]	1961	20.00	40.00	80.00
—B-side of the above two: Popular Piano Concertos by George Greeley				
A PATCH OF BLUE				
Mainstream S-6068 [S]	1965	6.25	12.50	25.00
Mainstream 56068 [M]	1965	5.00	10.00	20.00

Label, Number	Yr	VG	VG+	NM
Mainstream ST-90805 [S]	1965	7.50	15.00	30.00
—Capitol Record Club edition				
PATTON				
20th Century Fox S-4208	1970	5.00	10.00	20.00
PENELOPE				
MGM E-4426 [M]	1966	5.00	10.00	20.00
MGM SE-4426 [S]	1966	7.50	15.00	30.00
PENTHOUSE				
United Artists UAL-4170 [M]	1967	5.00	10.00	20.00
United Artists UAS-5170 [S]	1967	5.00	10.00	20.00
THE PEOPLE NEXT DOOR				
Avco AV-11002	1970	6.25	12.50	25.00
PEPE				
Colpix CP-507 [M]	1960	5.00	10.00	20.00
Colpix SCP-507 [S]	1960	6.25	12.50	25.00
PERFORMANCE				
Warner Bros. WS 1846	1970	7.50	15.00	30.00
—Original issue				
Warner Bros. BS 2554	1970	5.00	10.00	20.00
—Second issue				
PETE KELLY'S BLUES				
Columbia CL 690 [M]	1955	10.00	20.00	40.00
Decca DL 8166 [M]	1955	12.50	25.00	50.00
—Black label, silver print				
PETULIA				
Warner Bros. WS 1755	1968	6.25	12.50	25.00
PEYTON PLACE				
RCA Victor LOC-1042 [M]	1958	7.50	15.00	30.00
—"Long Play" at bottom of label				
RCA Victor LOC-1042 [M]	1965	6.25	12.50	25.00
—"Monaural" at bottom of label				
RCA Victor LSO-1042 [S]	1958	25.00	50.00	100.00
—"Living Stereo" at bottom of label				
RCA Victor LSO-1042 [S]	1965	15.00	30.00	60.00
—"Stereo" at bottom of label				
PHAEDRA				
United Artists UAL-4102 [M]	1962	5.00	10.00	20.00
United Artists UAS-5102 [S]	1962	7.50	15.00	30.00
PICNIC				
Decca DL 8320 [M]	1956	7.50	15.00	30.00
—Black label, silver print				
Decca DL 8320 [M]	196?	3.75	7.50	15.00
—Black label with color bars				
Decca DL 78320 [S]	1959	7.50	15.00	30.00
—Maroon or all-black label				
Decca DL 78320 [S]	196?	3.75	7.50	15.00
—Black label with color bars				
PINOCCHIO				
Disneyland DQ-1202 [M]	1959	7.50	15.00	30.00
—Second edition				
Disneyland DQ-1202MO [M]	1963	5.00	10.00	20.00
—Third edition				
Disneyland WDL-4002 [M]	1956	62.50	125.00	250.00
—Original edition				
Disneyland ST-4905 [M]	1963	37.50	75.00	150.00
—Gatefold cover with pop-up center graphics				
THE PIRATE				
MGM E-21 [10]	1951	17.50	35.00	70.00
PLANET OF THE APES				
Project 3 PR-5023 SD	1968	7.50	15.00	30.00
—Gatefold cover				
Project 3 PR-5023 SD	1968	5.00	10.00	20.00
—Regular cover				
THE PLEASURE SEEKERS				
RCA Victor LOC-1101 [M]	1964	12.50	25.00	50.00
RCA Victor LSO-1101 [S]	1964	25.00	50.00	100.00
POLLYANNA				
Disneyland DQ-1307 [M]	1967	6.25	12.50	25.00
Disneyland ST-1906 [M]	1960	12.50	25.00	50.00
PORGY AND BESS				
Columbia Masterworks OS 2016 [S]	1959	5.00	10.00	20.00
Columbia Masterworks OL 5410 [M]	1959	3.75	7.50	15.00
PRETTY BOY FLOYD				
Audio Fidelity AFLP-1936 [M]	1960	15.00	30.00	60.00
Audio Fidelity AFSD-5936 [S]	1960	20.00	40.00	80.00
THE PRIDE AND THE PASSION				
Capitol W 873 [M]	1957	15.00	30.00	60.00
THE PRISONER OF ZENDA				
United Artists UA-LA374-G	1974	5.00	10.00	20.00
PRIVATE HELL 36				
Coral CRL 56122 [10]	1954	25.00	50.00	100.00

Label, Number	Yr	VG	VG+	NM
THE PRODUCERS				
RCA Victor LPM-4008 [M]	1968	12.50	25.00	50.00
RCA Victor LSP-4008 [S]	1968	7.50	15.00	30.00
THE PROFESSIONALS				
Colgems COMO-5001 [M]	1966	15.00	30.00	60.00
Colgems COSO-5001 [S]	1966	37.50	75.00	150.00
A PROMISE AT DAWN				
Polydor 24-5502	1970	7.50	15.00	30.00
THE PROPER TIME				
Contemporary M-3587 [M]	1960	7.50	15.00	30.00
Contemporary S-7587 [S]	1960	10.00	20.00	40.00
PRUDENCE AND THE PILL				
20th Century Fox S-4199	1968	5.00	10.00	20.00
THE QUIET MAN				
Decca DL 5411 [10]	1952	30.00	60.00	120.00
THE QUILLER MEMORANDUM				
Columbia Masterworks OS 3060 [S]	1966	15.00	30.00	60.00
Columbia Masterworks OL 6660 [M]	1966	7.50	15.00	30.00
QUO VADIS?				
MGM E-103 [10]	1951	10.00	20.00	40.00
—Music soundtrack only				
MGM E-134 [(2) 10]	1951	15.00	30.00	60.00
—Box set of two discs; includes dialogue				
THE RAILWAY CHILDREN				
Capitol SW-871	1972	5.00	10.00	20.00
THE RAINMAKER				
RCA Victor LPM-1434 [M]	1956	25.00	50.00	100.00
RAINTREE COUNTY				
RCA Victor LOC-1038 [M]	1958	7.50	15.00	30.00
RCA Victor LSO-1038 [S]	1958	12.50	25.00	50.00
RCA Victor LOC-6000 [(2) M]	1957	30.00	60.00	120.00
THE RAT RACE				
Dot DLP-3306 [M]	1960	10.00	20.00	40.00
Dot DLP-25306 [S]	1960	12.50	25.00	50.00
RED GARTERS				
Columbia CL 6282 [10]	1954	12.50	25.00	50.00
THE RED PONY				
Columbia Masterworks ML 5983 [M]	196?	6.25	12.50	25.00
Columbia Masterworks MS 6583 [R]	196?	6.25	12.50	25.00
THE RED TENT				
Paramount PAS-6019	1971	6.25	12.50	25.00
THE REPORTER				
Columbia CL 2269 [M]	1963	7.50	15.00	30.00
Columbia CS 9069 [S]	1963	10.00	20.00	40.00
RETURN TO PARADISE				
Decca DL 5489 [10]	1953	50.00	100.00	200.00
THE REVOLUTION				
United Artists UAS-5185	1968	6.25	12.50	25.00
RHAPSODY OF STEEL				
U.S. Steel JB-502/3	1958	25.00	50.00	100.00
RICH, YOUNG AND PRETTY				
MGM E-86 [10]	1951	10.00	20.00	40.00
RIDER ON THE RAIN				
Capitol ST-584	1970	6.25	12.50	25.00
RIOT ON SUNSET STRIP				
Tower T 5065 [M]	1967	5.00	10.00	20.00
Tower DT 5065 [R]	1967	6.25	12.50	25.00
ROAD TO HONG KONG				
Liberty LOM-16002 [M]	1962	5.00	10.00	20.00
Liberty LOS-17002 [S]	1962	10.00	20.00	40.00
THE ROBE				
Decca DL 9012 [M]	1953	7.50	15.00	30.00
—Maroon label				
ROBIN AND THE SEVEN HOODS				
Reprise F 2021 [M]	1964	12.50	25.00	50.00
Reprise FS 2021 [S]	1964	15.00	30.00	60.00
ROBIN HOOD				
Disneyland ST-3810	1973	6.25	12.50	25.00
ROCK ALL NIGHT				
Mercury MG-20293 [M]	1957	25.00	50.00	100.00
ROCK, PRETTY BABY				
Decca DL 8429 [M]	1957	30.00	60.00	120.00
—Black label, silver print; also includes pink label promo				
Decca DL 8429 [M]	196?	7.50	15.00	30.00
—Black label with color bars				
ROCK, ROCK, ROCK				
Chess LP-1425 [M]	1958	50.00	100.00	200.00

Label, Number	Yr	VG	VG+	NM
(no label) (no #) [M]	1958	375.00	750.00	1500.
—Demo version, 20 tracks				
ROMANCE OF A HORSETHIEF				
Allied Artists AAS-110-100	1971	12.50	25.00	50.00
ROME ADVENTURE				
Warner Bros. W 1458 [M]	1962	5.00	10.00	20.00
Warner Bros. WS 1458 [S]	1962	6.25	12.50	25.00
ROMEO AND JULIET				
Capitol SWDR-289 [(4)]	1969	7.50	15.00	30.00
—From the 1968 Franco Zeffirelli remake; contains dialogue and music				
Capitol ST-400	1970	3.75	7.50	15.00
—From the 1968 Franco Zeffirelli remake; edited version of 289				
Capitol ST-2993	1968	3.00	6.00	12.00
—From the 1968 Franco Zeffirelli remake; contains the music; black label with colorband				
Epic LC 3126 [M]	1954	15.00	30.00	60.00
Epic FLM 13104 [M]	1966	7.50	15.00	30.00
—Reissue of 3126				
Epic FLS 15104 [R]	1966	6.25	12.50	25.00
ROOTS OF HEAVEN				
20th Fox FOX-3005 [M]	1958	75.00	150.00	300.00
ROSE MARIE				
MGM E-229 [10]	1954	10.00	20.00	40.00
THE ROSE TATTOO				
Columbia CL 727 [M]	1955	12.50	25.00	50.00
ROSEMARY'S BABY				
Dot DLP-25875	1968	5.00	10.00	20.00
THE ROYAL WEDDING				
MGM E-543 [10]	1951	12.50	25.00	50.00
THE RULING CLASS				
Avco AV-11003	1972	6.25	12.50	25.00
THE RUN OF THE ARROW				
Decca DL 8620 [M]	1957	15.00	30.00	60.00
—Black label, silver print, or pink label, black print promo				
Decca DL 8620 [M]	196?	7.50	15.00	30.00
—Black label with color bars				
RUN WILD, RUN FREE				
SGC SD 5003	1969	5.00	10.00	20.00
RUN, ANGEL, RUN				
Epic BN 26474	1969	5.00	10.00	20.00
RYAN'S DAUGHTER				
MGM 1SE-27	1970	6.25	12.50	25.00
SACCO AND VANZETTI				
RCA Victor LSP-4612	1971	5.00	10.00	20.00
THE SACRED IDOL				
Capitol T 1293 [M]	1960	6.25	12.50	25.00
Capitol ST 1293 [S]	1960	7.50	15.00	30.00
SAINT JOAN				
Capitol W 865 [M]	1957	7.50	15.00	30.00
SALLAH				
Philips PHM 200177 [M]	1965	5.00	10.00	20.00
Philips PHS 600177 [S]	1965	6.25	12.50	25.00
SALOME				
Decca DL 6026 [10]	1953	30.00	60.00	120.00
SAMSON AND DELILAH				
Decca DL 6007 [10]	1952	15.00	30.00	60.00
THE SAND CASTLE				
Columbia CL 1455 [M]	1961	3.75	7.50	15.00
Columbia CS 8249 [S]	1961	5.00	10.00	20.00
THE SAND PEBBLES				
20th Century Fox 3189 [M]	1966	7.50	15.00	30.00
20th Century Fox S-4189 [S]	1966	12.50	25.00	50.00
THE SANDPIPER				
Mercury MG-21032 [M]	1965	6.25	12.50	25.00
Mercury SR-61032 [S]	1965	7.50	15.00	30.00
SANTA AND THE 3 BEARS				
Mr. Pickwick SPC 1501	196?	5.00	10.00	20.00
—With "Santa" cutout intact				
SATAN'S SADISTS				
Smash SRS-67127	1969	7.50	15.00	30.00
SATAN IN HIGH HEELS				
Charlie Parker PLP-406 [M]	1962	12.50	25.00	50.00
—Gatefold cover				
Charlie Parker PLP-406S [S]	1962	15.00	30.00	60.00
—Gatefold cover				
Charlie Parker PLP-406 [M]	1962	7.50	15.00	30.00
—Standard cover				
Charlie Parker PLP-406S [S]	1962	10.00	20.00	40.00
—Standard cover				
THE SAVAGE SEVEN				
Atco 33-245 [M]	1968	7.50	15.00	30.00
Atco SD 33-245 [S]	1968	7.50	15.00	30.00
SAVAGE WILD				
American Int'l. STA-1032	1970	5.00	10.00	20.00
SAY ONE FOR ME				
Columbia CL 1337 [M]	1959	10.00	20.00	40.00
Columbia CS 8147 [S]	1959	20.00	40.00	80.00
SAYONARA				
RCA Victor LOC-1041 [M]	1957	12.50	25.00	50.00
RCA Victor LSO-1041 [S]	1957	17.50	35.00	70.00
THE SCALPHUNTERS				
United Artists UAL-4176 [M]	1968	7.50	15.00	30.00
United Artists UAS-5176 [S]	1968	10.00	20.00	40.00
SCENT OF MYSTERY				
Ramrod T-6001 [M]	1960	12.50	25.00	50.00
Ramrod ST-6001 [S]	1960	25.00	50.00	100.00
SCROOGE				
Columbia Masterworks S 30258	1970	7.50	15.00	30.00
SEARCH FOR PARADISE				
RCA Victor LOC-1034 [M]	1957	10.00	20.00	40.00
SEASIDE SWINGERS				
Mercury MG-21031 [M]	1965	5.00	10.00	20.00
Mercury SR-61031 [S]	1965	6.25	12.50	25.00
SEBASTIAN				
Dot DLP-25845	1968	5.00	10.00	20.00
THE SECRET OF SANTA VITTORIA				
United Artists UAS-5200	1969	7.50	15.00	30.00
SERGEANTS 3				
Reprise R-2013 [M]	1962	7.50	15.00	30.00
Reprise RS-2013 [S]	1962	12.50	25.00	50.00
SERPICO				
Paramount PAS-1016	1973	6.25	12.50	25.00
SEVEN BRIDES FOR SEVEN BROTHERS				
MGM E-244 [10]	1954	10.00	20.00	40.00
SEVEN GOLDEN MEN				
United Artists UAS-5193	1969	6.25	12.50	25.00
THE SEVEN LITTLE FOYS				
RCA Victor LPM-3275 [10]	1955	17.50	35.00	70.00
THE SEVENTH DAWN				
United Artists UAL-4115 [M]	1964	7.50	15.00	30.00
United Artists UAS-5115 [S]	1964	10.00	20.00	40.00
SEX AND THE SINGLE GIRL				
Warner Bros. W 1572 [M]	1964	3.75	7.50	15.00
Warner Bros. WS 1572 [S]	1964	5.00	10.00	20.00
SHAFT'S BIG SCORE				
MGM 1SE-36	1972	7.50	15.00	30.00
SHAFT IN AFRICA				
ABC ABCX-793	1973	7.50	15.00	30.00
SHAKE HANDS WITH THE DEVIL				
United Artists UAL-4043 [M]	1959	7.50	15.00	30.00
United Artists UAS-5043 [S]	1959	12.50	25.00	50.00
SHALAKO				
Philips PHS 600286	1968	7.50	15.00	30.00
SHEBA BABY				
Buddah BDS-5634	1975	7.50	15.00	30.00
SHENANDOAH				
Decca DL 9125 [M]	1965	7.50	15.00	30.00
Decca DL 79125 [S]	1965	10.00	20.00	40.00
THE SHOP ON MAIN STREET				
Mainstream S-6082 [S]	1966	10.00	20.00	40.00
Mainstream 56082 [M]	1966	6.25	12.50	25.00
SHOW BOAT				
MGM E-559 [10]	1951	7.50	15.00	30.00
THE SICILIAN CLAN				
20th Century Fox S-4209	1970	12.50	25.00	50.00
THE SIDEHACKERS				
Amaret ST-5004	1969	5.00	10.00	20.00
THE SILENCERS				
RCA Victor LOC-1120 [M]	1966	7.50	15.00	30.00
RCA Victor LSO-1120 [S]	1966	12.50	25.00	50.00
SILENT RUNNING				
Decca DL 79188	1972	10.00	20.00	40.00
SILK STOCKINGS				
MGM E-3542 [M]	1957	7.50	15.00	30.00
SINGIN' IN THE RAIN				
MGM E-113 [10]	1952	7.50	15.00	30.00

Label, Number	Yr	VG	VG+	NM
SINGLE ROOM FURNISHED				
Sidewalk ST-5917	1968	10.00	20.00	40.00
SKATEDANCER				
Mira LP-3004 [M]	1966	5.00	10.00	20.00
Mira LPS-3004 [S]	1966	6.25	12.50	25.00
SKI ON THE WILD SIDE				
MGM E-4439 [M]	1967	7.50	15.00	30.00
MGM SE-4439 [S]	1967	12.50	25.00	50.00
SLAUGHTER ON 10TH AVENUE				
Decca DL 8657 [M]	1957	6.25	12.50	25.00
—Black label, silver print				
Decca DL 78657 [S]	1957	7.50	15.00	30.00
—Black label, silver print				
SLAUGHTERHOUSE-FIVE				
Columbia Masterworks S 31333	1972	6.25	12.50	25.00
THE SLAVE TRADE IN THE WORLD TODAY				
London M-76006 [M]	1964	50.00	100.00	200.00
SLAVES				
Skye SK-11	1969	6.25	12.50	25.00
SLEEPING BEAUTY				
Disneyland WDL-4018 [M]	1959	7.50	15.00	30.00
Disneyland STER-4018 [S]	1959	10.00	20.00	40.00
Disneyland STER-4036 [S]	1970	5.00	10.00	20.00
—Reissue of STER-4018				
SLEUTH				
Columbia Masterworks S 32154	1973	5.00	10.00	20.00
SLIPPERY WHEN WET				
World Pacific WP-1265 [M]	1959	12.50	25.00	50.00
A SMASHING TIME				
ABC ABC-OC-6 [M]	1967	5.00	10.00	20.00
ABC ABCS-OC-6 [S]	1967	6.25	12.50	25.00
ABC SW-91399 [S]	1967	6.25	12.50	25.00
—Capitol Record Club edition				
SNOOPY COME HOME				
Columbia Masterworks S 31451	1972	5.00	10.00	20.00
THE SNOW QUEEN				
Decca DL 8977 [M]	1959	10.00	20.00	40.00
Decca DL 78977 [S]	1959	15.00	30.00	60.00
SNOW WHITE AND THE SEVEN DWARFS				
Buena Vista 102 [(3)]	1975	12.50	25.00	50.00
—Entire movie on three LPs; TV mail-order item				
Disneyland DQ-1201 [M]	1959	12.50	25.00	50.00
—Reissue of 4005; whirlpool-like designs on cover				
Disneyland DQ-1201 [M]	1968	6.25	12.50	25.00
—Reissue; with same cover as 4005, but no gatefold				
Disneyland WDL-4005 [M]	1956	50.00	100.00	200.00
—Gatefold cover				
SNOW WHITE AND THE THREE STOOGES				
Columbia CL 1650 [M]	1961	15.00	30.00	60.00
Columbia CS 8450 [S]	1961	25.00	50.00	100.00
SO THIS IS LOVE				
RCA Victor LOC-3000 [10]	1953	20.00	40.00	80.00
SO THIS IS PARIS				
Decca DL 5553 [10]	1955	12.50	25.00	50.00
SODOM AND GOMORRAH				
RCA Victor LOC-1076 [M]	1963	20.00	40.00	80.00
RCA Victor LSO-1076 [S]	1963	25.00	50.00	100.00
SOL MADRID				
MGM SE-4541 ST	1968	7.50	15.00	30.00
SOLOMON AND SHEBA				
United Artists UAL-4051 [M]	1959	12.50	25.00	50.00
—First cover with silky finish				
United Artists UAL-4051 [M]	1959	6.25	12.50	25.00
—Second, regular cover				
United Artists UAS-5051 [S]	1959	30.00	60.00	120.00
—First cover with silky finish				
United Artists UAS-5051 [S]	1959	15.00	30.00	60.00
—Second, regular cover				
SOME CAME RUNNING				
Capitol W 1109 [M]	1958	7.50	15.00	30.00
Capitol SW 1109 [S]	1958	20.00	40.00	80.00
SOME LIKE IT HOT				
United Artists UAL-4030 [M]	1959	12.50	25.00	50.00
United Artists UAS-5030 [S]	1959	18.75	37.50	75.00
SOMEBODY LOVES ME				
RCA Victor LPM-3097 [10]	1952	12.50	25.00	50.00
SONG OF THE SOUTH				
Disneyland WDL-4001 [M]	1956	75.00	150.00	300.00
—Yellow label (first pressing)				
Disneyland WDL-4001 [M]	1957	50.00	100.00	200.00
—Red/maroon label (second pressing)				
SONG OF THE SOUTH (UNCLE REMUS)				
Disneyland DQ-1205 [M]	1959	6.25	12.50	25.00
SONG WITHOUT END				
Colpix CP-506 [M]	1960	5.00	10.00	20.00
Colpix SCP-506 [S]	1960	6.25	12.50	25.00
THE SONS OF KATIE ELDER				
Columbia Masterworks OS 2820 [S]	1965	25.00	50.00	100.00
Columbia Masterworks OL 6420 [M]	1965	12.50	25.00	50.00
THE SOUL OF NIGGER CHARLEY				
MGM 1SE-46	1973	5.00	10.00	20.00
THE SOUND AND THE FURY				
Decca DL 8885 [M]	1959	7.50	15.00	30.00
Decca DL 78885 [S]	1959	17.50	35.00	70.00
THE SOUND OF MUSIC				
RCA Victor LOCD-2005 [M]	1965	3.75	7.50	15.00
—With booklet; back cover lists "I Have Confidence" as "I Have Confidence in Me"				
RCA Victor LSOD-2005 [S]	1965	5.00	10.00	20.00
—With booklet; back cover lists "I Have Confidence" as "I Have Confidence in Me"				
RCA Victor LOCD-2005 [M]	1965	3.00	6.00	12.00
—With booklet; back cover lists "I Have Confidence" correctly				
RCA Victor LSOD-2005 [S]	1965	3.75	7.50	15.00
—With booklet; back cover lists "I Have Confidence" correctly				
RCA Victor LSOD-2005 [S]	1969	3.00	6.00	12.00
—No booklet; gatefold cover, record comes out from inside; orange or tan label				
RCA Victor LSOD-2005 [S]	1977	2.50	5.00	10.00
—Gatefold cover, record comes out from outside; black label with dog at 1 o'clock				
SOUTH PACIFIC				
RCA Victor LOC-1032 [M]	1958	5.00	10.00	20.00
—"Long Play" on label				
RCA Victor LSO-1032 [S]	1958	6.25	12.50	25.00
—"Living Stereo" on label				
SOUTHERN STAR				
Colgems COSO-5009	1969	15.00	30.00	60.00
A SPANISH AFFAIR				
Dot DLP-3078 [M]	1958	25.00	50.00	100.00
SPARTACUS				
Decca DL 9092 [M]	1960	5.00	10.00	20.00
—Black label, silver print				
Decca DL 79092 [S]	1960	6.25	12.50	25.00
—Maroon label, silver print				
THE SPIRIT OF ST. LOUIS				
RCA Victor LPM-1472 [M]	1957	12.50	25.00	50.00
THE SPY WHO CAME IN FROM THE COLD				
RCA Victor LOC-1118 [M]	1965	5.00	10.00	20.00
RCA Victor LSO-1118 [S]	1965	10.00	20.00	40.00
THE SPY WITH A COLD NOSE				
Columbia Masterworks OS 3070 [S]	1966	7.50	15.00	30.00
Columbia Masterworks OL 6670 [M]	1966	5.00	10.00	20.00
STAGECOACH				
Mainstream S-6077 [S]	1966	7.50	15.00	30.00
Mainstream 56077 [M]	1966	5.00	10.00	20.00
Mainstream T-90802 [M]	1966	6.25	12.50	25.00
—Capitol Record Club edition				
Mainstream ST-90802 [S]	1966	7.50	15.00	30.00
—Capitol Record Club edition				
THE STARS AND STRIPES FOREVER				
MGM E-176 [10]	1952	7.50	15.00	30.00
STAR!				
20th Century Fox DTCS-5102	1968	5.00	10.00	20.00
STATE FAIR				
Dot DLP-9011 [M]	1962	6.25	12.50	25.00
Dot DLP-29011 [S]	1962	7.50	15.00	30.00
THE STERILE CUCKOO				
Paramount PAS-5009	1970	5.00	10.00	20.00
STILETTO				
Columbia Masterworks OS 3360	1969	5.00	10.00	20.00
THE STING				
MCA 390	1973	3.00	6.00	12.00
—Original edition				
THE STRANGE ONE				
Coral CRL 57132 [M]	1957	17.50	35.00	70.00
THE STRAWBERRY STATEMENT				
MGM 2SE-14 [(2)]	1970	6.25	12.50	25.00
A STREETCAR NAMED DESIRE				
Capitol L 289 [10]	1951	12.50	25.00	50.00
A STUDY IN TERROR				
Roulette OS-801 [M]	1965	10.00	20.00	40.00
Roulette OSS-801 [S]	1965	20.00	40.00	80.00
ST. LOUIS BLUES				
Capitol W 993 [M]	1958	12.50	25.00	50.00
—Turquoise or gray label				

Label, Number	Yr	VG	VG+	NM
Capitol W 993 [M]	1959	6.25	12.50	25.00
—Black colorband label, logo at left				
Capitol W 993 [M]	196?	5.00	10.00	20.00
—Black colorband label, logo at top				
ST. LOUIS WOMAN				
Capitol L 355 [10]	1955	20.00	40.00	80.00
THE SUBTERRANEANS				
MGM E-3812 ST [M]	1960	10.00	20.00	40.00
MGM SE-3812 ST [S]	1960	20.00	40.00	80.00
SUMMER AND SMOKE				
RCA Victor LOC-1067 [M]	1961	12.50	25.00	50.00
RCA Victor LSO-1067 [S]	1961	17.50	35.00	70.00
SUMMER HOLIDAY				
Epic LN 24063 [M]	1963	6.25	12.50	25.00
Epic BN 26063 [S]	1963	7.50	15.00	30.00
SUMMER LOVE				
Decca DL 8714 [M]	1958	15.00	30.00	60.00
—Black label, silver print, or pink label, black print promo				
Decca DL 8714 [M]	196?	7.50	15.00	30.00
—Black label with color bars				
SUMMER MAGIC				
Buena Vista BV-4025 [M]	1963	10.00	20.00	40.00
Buena Vista STER-4025 [S]	1963	15.00	30.00	60.00
SUMMER STOCK				
MGM E-519 [10]	1950	10.00	20.00	40.00
THE SUN ALSO RISES				
Kapp KDL-7001 [M]	1957	15.00	30.00	60.00
SUN VALLEY SERENADE				
RCA Victor LPT-3064 [10]	1954	15.00	30.00	60.00
THE SUNNY SIDE OF THE STREET				
Mercury MG-25100 [10]	1951	15.00	30.00	60.00
SURF PARTY				
20th Century Fox TFM-3131 [M]	1964	6.25	12.50	25.00
20th Century Fox TFS-4131 [S]	1964	7.50	15.00	30.00
THE SWAN				
MGM E-3399 [M]	1956	17.50	35.00	70.00
SWEDISH HEAVEN AND HELL				
Ariel ARS-15000	1969	6.25	12.50	25.00
SWEET CHARITY				
Decca DL 71502	1969	5.00	10.00	20.00
SWEET LOVE, BITTER				
ABC Impulse! AS-9141 [S]	1968	3.75	7.50	15.00
Impulse! A-9141 [M]	1967	10.00	20.00	40.00
Impulse! AS-9141 [S]	1967	7.50	15.00	30.00
THE SWEET RIDE				
20th Century Fox S-4198	1968	5.00	10.00	20.00
THE SWEET SMELL OF SUCCESS				
Decca DL 8610 [M]	1957	15.00	30.00	60.00
SWEET SWEETBACK'S BADASSSSSS SONG				
Stax STS-3001	1971	7.50	15.00	30.00
SWEPT AWAY				
Peters International PLD 1005	1957	10.00	20.00	40.00
THE SWIMMER				
Columbia Masterworks OS 3210	1968	6.25	12.50	25.00
SWINGER'S PARADISE				
Epic LN 24145 [M]	1965	5.00	10.00	20.00
Epic BN 26145 [S]	1965	6.25	12.50	25.00
A SWINGIN' SUMMER				
Hanna-Barbera HLP-8500 [M]	1966	6.25	12.50	25.00
Hanna-Barbera HST-9500 [S]	1966	7.50	15.00	30.00
SYLVIA				
Mercury MG-21004 [M]	1965	5.00	10.00	20.00
Mercury SR-61004 [S]	1965	7.50	15.00	30.00
TARAS BULBA				
United Artists UAL-4100 [M]	1962	7.50	15.00	30.00
United Artists UAS-5100 [S]	1962	12.50	25.00	50.00
TEENAGE REBELLION				
Sidewalk T-5903 [M]	1967	5.00	10.00	20.00
Sidewalk ST-5903 [S]	1967	6.25	12.50	25.00
TELL ME THAT YOU LOVE ME, JUNIE MOON				
Columbia Masterworks OS 3540	1970	5.00	10.00	20.00
THE TEN COMMANDMENTS				
Dot DLP-3054 [M]	1956	10.00	20.00	40.00
Dot DLP-25054 [S]	1959	6.25	12.50	25.00
—Re-recording of the original soundtrack in stereo				
Paramount PAS-1006	1973	5.00	10.00	20.00
—Re-release				

Label, Number	Yr	VG	VG+	NM
TENDER IS THE NIGHT				
20th Century Fox FOX-3054 [M]	1962	37.50	75.00	150.00
20th Century Fox SFX-3054 [S]	1962	50.00	100.00	200.00
THE TENTH VICTIM				
Mainstream S-6071 [S]	1965	12.50	25.00	50.00
Mainstream 56071 [M]	1965	10.00	20.00	40.00
THAT DARN CAT				
Buena Vista BV-3334 [M]	1965	5.00	10.00	20.00
Buena Vista STER-3334 [S]	1965	6.25	12.50	25.00
THAT MAN IN ISTANBUL				
Mainstream S-6072 [S]	1966	6.25	12.50	25.00
Mainstream 56072 [M]	1966	5.00	10.00	20.00
THERE'S NO BUSINESS LIKE SHOW BUSINESS				
Decca DL 8091 [M]	1954	10.00	20.00	40.00
—Black label, silver print				
Decca DL 8091 [M]	196?	5.00	10.00	20.00
—Black label with color bars				
Decca DL 8091 [M]	1954	7.50	15.00	30.00
—Black label with silver print				
THEY SHOOT HORSES, DON'T THEY?				
ABC ABCS-OC-10	1969	5.00	10.00	20.00
THIS COULD BE THE NIGHT				
MGM E-3530 [M]	1957	12.50	25.00	50.00
THIS EARTH IS MINE				
Decca DL 8915 [M]	1959	20.00	40.00	80.00
Decca DL 78915 [S]	1959	25.00	50.00	100.00
THIS PROPERTY IS CONDEMNED				
Verve V-8664 [M]	1966	5.00	10.00	20.00
Verve V6-8664 [S]	1966	7.50	15.00	30.00
THE THOMAS CROWN AFFAIR				
United Artists UAS-5182	1968	5.00	10.00	20.00
THOROUGHLY MODERN MILLIE				
Decca DL 1500 [M]	1967	5.00	10.00	20.00
—With bound-in booklet				
Decca DL 71500 [S]	1967	5.00	10.00	20.00
—With bound-in booklet				
THOSE GLORIOUS MGM MUSICALS: DEEP IN MY HEART/WORDS AND MUSIC				
MGM 2-SES-54-ST [(2)]	1973	5.00	10.00	20.00
THOSE GLORIOUS MGM MUSICALS: EVERYTHING I HAVE IS YOURS/SUMMER STOCK/I LOVE MELVIN				
MGM 2-SES-52-ST [(2)]	1973	5.00	10.00	20.00
THOSE GLORIOUS MGM MUSICALS: GOOD NEWS/IN THE GOOD OLD SUMMERTIME/TWO WEEKS WITH LOVE				
MGM 2-SES-49-ST [(2)]	1973	5.00	10.00	20.00
THOSE GLORIOUS MGM MUSICALS: LOVELY TO LOOK AT/BRIGADOON				
MGM 2-SES-50-ST [(2)]	1973	5.00	10.00	20.00
THOSE GLORIOUS MGM MUSICALS: NANCY GOES TO RIO/RICH, YOUNG AND PRETTY/ROYAL WEDDING				
MGM 2-SES-53-ST [(2)]	1973	5.00	10.00	20.00
THOSE GLORIOUS MGM MUSICALS: ROSE MARIE/SEVN BRIDES FOR SEVEN BROTHERS				
MGM 2-SES-41-ST [(2)]	1973	5.00	10.00	20.00
THOSE GLORIOUS MGM MUSICALS: SHOW BOAT/ANNIE GET YOUR GUN				
MGM 2-SES-42-ST [(2)]	1973	5.00	10.00	20.00
THOSE GLORIOUS MGM MUSICALS: SINGIN' IN THE RAIN/EASTER PARADE				
MGM 2-SES-40-ST [(2)]	1973	5.00	10.00	20.00
THOSE GLORIOUS MGM MUSICALS: THE BAND WAGON/KISS ME, KATE				
MGM 2-SES-44-ST [(2)]	1973	5.00	10.00	20.00
THOSE GLORIOUS MGM MUSICALS: THE BARKLEYS OF BROADWAY/LES GIRLS				
MGM 2-SES-51-ST [(2)]	1973	5.00	10.00	20.00
THOSE GLORIOUS MGM MUSICALS: THE PIRATE/PAGAN LOVE SONG/HIT THE DECK				
MGM 2-SES-43-ST [(2)]	1973	10.00	20.00	40.00
THOSE GLORIOUS MGM MUSICALS: TILL THE CLOUDS ROLL BY/THREE LITTLE WORDS				
MGM 2-SES-45-ST [(2)]	1973	5.00	10.00	20.00
THREE FOR THE SHOW				
Mercury MG-25204 [M]	1955	15.00	30.00	60.00
THREE IN THE ATTIC				
Sidewalk ST-5918	1968	7.50	15.00	30.00
THREE LITTLE WORDS				
MGM E-516 [10]	1959	15.00	30.00	60.00
THE THREE WORLDS OF GULLIVER				
Colpix CP-414 [M]	1960	15.00	30.00	60.00
THE THREEPENNY OPERA				
RCA Victor LOC-1086 [M]	1964	37.50	75.00	150.00
—With rare original cover: White background, pink and black drawing, characters underneath				

Label, Number	Yr	VG	VG+	NM
RCA Victor LOC-1086 [M]	1964	3.75	7.50	15.00
—Reissue cover: White background, orange drawing, Sammy Davis Jr. in foreground, "RE" at bottom				
RCA Victor LSO-1086 [S]	1964	50.00	100.00	200.00
—With rare original cover: White background, pink and black drawing, characters underneath				
RCA Victor LSO-1086 [S]	1964	5.00	10.00	20.00
—Reissue cover: White background, orange drawing, Sammy Davis Jr. in foreground, "RE" at bottom				
THUNDER ALLEY				
Sidewalk T-5902 [M]	1967	5.00	10.00	20.00
Sidewalk ST-5902 [S]	1967	6.25	12.50	25.00
THUNDERBALL				
United Artists UAL-4132 [M]	1965	5.00	10.00	20.00
United Artists UAS-5132 [S]	1965	7.50	15.00	30.00
United Artists SW-90820 [S]	1965	10.00	20.00	40.00
—Capitol Record Club edition				
TICK...TICK...TICK				
MGM SE-4667 [M]	1970	6.25	12.50	25.00
TILL THE CLOUDS ROLL BY				
MGM E-501 [10]	1950	12.50	25.00	50.00
A TIME TO LOVE AND A TIME TO DIE				
Decca DL 8778 [M]	1958	25.00	50.00	100.00
TO BED... OR NOT TO BED				
London M-76005 [M]	1963	10.00	20.00	40.00
TO KILL A MOCKINGBIRD				
Ava A-20 [M]	1962	6.25	12.50	25.00
Ava AS-20 [S]	1962	7.50	15.00	30.00
TO SIR, WITH LOVE				
Fontana MGF-27569 [M]	1967	5.00	10.00	20.00
Fontana SRF-67569 [S]	1967	6.25	12.50	25.00
TOKYO OLYMPIAD				
Monument MLP-8046 [M]	1966	3.75	7.50	15.00
Monument SLP-18046 [S]	1966	5.00	10.00	20.00
TOM JONES				
United Artists UAL-4113 [M]	1963	5.00	10.00	20.00
United Artists UAS-5113 [S]	1963	6.25	12.50	25.00
TOM SAWYER				
United Artists UA-LA057-F	1973	5.00	10.00	20.00
TOMMY				
Polydor PD 2-9502 [(2)]	1975	5.00	10.00	20.00
TOO MUCH TOO SOON				
Mercury MG-20381 [M]	1958	7.50	15.00	30.00
Mercury SR-60019 [S]	1958	20.00	40.00	80.00
TOPKAPI				
United Artists UAL-4118 [M]	1964	5.00	10.00	20.00
United Artists UAS-5118 [S]	1964	7.50	15.00	30.00
THE TOUCHABLES				
20th Century Fox S-4206	1969	5.00	10.00	20.00
THE TRAIN				
United Artists UAL-4122 [M]	1965	5.00	10.00	20.00
United Artists UAS-5122 [S]	1965	10.00	20.00	40.00
THE TRAP				
Atco 33-204 [M]	1966	10.00	20.00	40.00
Atco SD 33-204 [S]	1966	17.50	35.00	70.00
TRAPEZE				
Columbia CL 870 [M]	1956	6.25	12.50	25.00
THE TRAPP FAMILY				
20th Fox FOX-3044 [M]	1961	6.25	12.50	25.00
20th Fox STX-3044 [S]	1961	10.00	20.00	40.00
THE TREASURE OF SAN GENNARO				
Buddah BDS-5011	1968	10.00	20.00	40.00
THE TRIP				
Sidewalk T-5908 [M]	1967	7.50	15.00	30.00
Sidewalk ST-5908 [S]	1967	10.00	20.00	40.00
TRIPLE CROSS				
United Artists UAL-4162 [M]	1967	5.00	10.00	20.00
United Artists UAS-5162 [S]	1967	7.50	15.00	30.00
THE TROUBLE WITH ANGELS				
Mainstream S-6073 [S]	1966	20.00	40.00	80.00
Mainstream 56073 [M]	1966	10.00	20.00	40.00
TRUE GRIT				
Capitol ST-263	1969	7.50	15.00	30.00
Capitol ST-8-0263	1969	10.00	20.00	40.00
—Capitol Record Club edition				
TRUE LIFE ADVENTURES				
Disneyland WDL-4011 [M]	1957	17.50	35.00	70.00
THE TRUE STORY OF THE CIVIL WAR				
Coral CRL 59100 [M]	1958	20.00	40.00	80.00
TWO MULES FOR SISTER SARA				
Kapp KRS-5512	1970	6.25	12.50	25.00

Label, Number	Yr	VG	VG+	NM
TWO WEEKS WITH LOVE				
MGM E-530 [10]	1950	10.00	20.00	40.00
ULYSSES				
RCA Victor LOC-1138 [M]	1967	6.25	12.50	25.00
RCA Victor LSO-1138 [S]	1967	7.50	15.00	30.00
THE UMBRELLAS OF CHERBOURG (LES PARAPLUIES DE CHERBOURG)				
Philips PCC 216 [M]	1965	5.00	10.00	20.00
Philips PCC 616 [S]	1965	7.50	15.00	30.00
UNCLE TOM'S CABIN				
Philips PHS 600272	1968	10.00	20.00	40.00
THE UNFORGIVEN				
United Artists UAL-4068 [M]	1960	10.00	20.00	40.00
United Artists UAS-5068 [S]	1960	17.50	35.00	70.00
THE UNSINKABLE MOLLY BROWN				
MGM E-4232 [M]	1964	3.75	7.50	15.00
MGM SE-4232 [S]	1964	5.00	10.00	20.00
UP IN THE CELLAR				
American Int'l. A-1036	1970	5.00	10.00	20.00
UP THE DOWN STAIRCASE				
United Artists UAL-4169 [M]	1967	5.00	10.00	20.00
United Artists UAS-5169 [S]	1967	10.00	20.00	40.00
UP THE JUNCTION				
Mercury SR-61159	1968	6.25	12.50	25.00
VALLEY OF THE DOLLS				
20th Century Fox TF-4196 [M]	1968	7.50	15.00	30.00
20th Century Fox TFS-4196 [S]	1968	7.50	15.00	30.00
THE VANISHING POINT				
Amos AAS-8002	1971	5.00	10.00	20.00
THE VANISHING PRAIRIE				
Columbia CL 6332 [10]	1954	20.00	40.00	80.00
VERTIGO				
Mercury MG-20384 [M]	1958	37.50	75.00	150.00
THE VICTORS				
Colpix CP-516 [M]	1963	5.00	10.00	20.00
Colpix SCP-516 [S]	1963	7.50	15.00	30.00
THE VIKINGS				
United Artists UAL-4003 [M]	1958	7.50	15.00	30.00
United Artists UAS-5003 [S]	1958	10.00	20.00	40.00
VILLA RIDES!				
Dot DLP-25870	1968	10.00	20.00	40.00
VIVA MARIA!				
United Artists UAL-4135 [M]	1965	5.00	10.00	20.00
United Artists UAS-5135 [S]	1965	7.50	15.00	30.00
VIVA MAX!				
RCA Victor LSP-4275	1969	5.00	10.00	20.00
THE VIXEN				
Beverly Hills BHS-22	1968	12.50	25.00	50.00
VOYAGE EN BALLON				
Philips PHM 200029 [M]	1960	7.50	15.00	30.00
Philips PHS 600029 [S]	1960	10.00	20.00	40.00
THE V.I.P.S THEME				
MGM E-4184 [M]	1963	5.00	10.00	20.00
MGM SE-4184 [S]	1963	6.25	12.50	25.00
—Music by Bill Evans				
WALK DON'T RUN				
Mainstream S-6080 [S]	1966	10.00	20.00	40.00
Mainstream 56080 [M]	1966	5.00	10.00	20.00
WALK ON THE WILD SIDE				
Ava A-4-ST [M]	1962	5.00	10.00	20.00
Ava AS-4-ST [S]	1962	10.00	20.00	40.00
Choreo A-4-ST [M]	1962	7.50	15.00	30.00
Choreo AS-4-ST [S]	1962	12.50	25.00	50.00
WAR AND PEACE				
Columbia CL 930 [M]	1956	6.25	12.50	25.00
Melodiya/Capitol SWAO 2918	1968	10.00	20.00	40.00
THE WAR LORD				
Decca DL 9149 [M]	1965	6.25	12.50	25.00
Decca DL 79149 [S]	1965	12.50	25.00	50.00
WARNING SHOT				
Liberty LRP-3498 [M]	1967	7.50	15.00	30.00
Liberty LST-7498 [S]	1967	10.00	20.00	40.00
WATERLOO				
Paramount PAS-6003	1971	7.50	15.00	30.00
Paramount SW-93729	1971	7.50	15.00	30.00
—Capitol Record Club edition				
WATERMELON MAN				
Beverly Hills BHS-26	1970	7.50	15.00	30.00

Label, Number	Yr	VG	VG+	NM
WAY...WAY OUT				
20th Century Fox 3192 [M]	1966	7.50	15.00	30.00
20th Century Fox S-4192 [S]	1966	10.00	20.00	40.00
WEDDING IN MONACO				
Mercury MG-20149 [M]	1956	62.50	125.00	250.00
WEST SIDE STORY				
Columbia Masterworks OS 2070 [S]	1961	6.25	12.50	25.00
—Originals have gatefold covers and gray and black labels with six "eye" logos				
Columbia Masterworks OS 2070 [S]	1963	3.75	7.50	15.00
—Gatefold cover; gray "360 Sound Stereo" label				
Columbia Masterworks OS 2070 [S]	196?	3.00	6.00	12.00
—Regular cover; gray "360 Sound Stereo" label				
Columbia Masterworks OS 2070 [S]	1971	2.50	5.00	10.00
—Regular cover; olive label with "Columbia" continuously around edge				
Columbia Masterworks OL 5670 [M]	1961	5.00	10.00	20.00
—Originals have gatefold covers and gray and black labels with six "eye" logos				
Columbia Masterworks OL 5670 [M]	1963	3.00	6.00	12.00
—Gatefold cover; gray "360 Sound Stereo" label				
Columbia Masterworks OL 5670 [M]	196?	2.50	5.00	10.00
—Regular cover; gray "360 Sound Stereo" label				
WHAT'S NEW PUSSYCAT?				
United Artists UAL-4128 [M]	1965	5.00	10.00	20.00
United Artists UAS-5128 [S]	1965	6.25	12.50	25.00
WHAT A WAY TO GO!				
20th Century Fox TFM-3143 [M]	1964	5.00	10.00	20.00
20th Century Fox TFS-4143 [S]	1964	10.00	20.00	40.00
WHEN THE BOYS MEET THE GIRLS				
MGM E-4334 [M]	1965	3.75	7.50	15.00
MGM SE-4334 [S]	1965	7.50	15.00	30.00
WHERE'S JACK?				
Paramount PAS-5005	1969	6.25	12.50	25.00
WHERE'S POPPA?				
United Artists UAS-5216	1970	6.25	12.50	25.00
WHERE EAGLES DARE				
MGM S1E-16 ST	1969	7.50	15.00	30.00
THE WHISPERERS				
United Artists UAL-4161 [M]	1967	5.00	10.00	20.00
United Artists UAS-5161 [S]	1967	7.50	15.00	30.00
WHITE CHRISTMAS				
Decca DL 8083	1954	12.50	25.00	50.00
WHO'S AFRAID OF VIRGINIA WOOLF?				
Warner Bros. B 1656 [M]	1966	6.25	12.50	25.00
Warner Bros. BS 1656 [S]	1966	7.50	15.00	30.00
Warner Bros. 2B 1657 [(2) M]	1966	10.00	20.00	40.00
—Above (1657) is the complete film, not just the music and some dialogue				
THE WILD BUNCH				
Warner Bros. WS 1814	1969	25.00	50.00	100.00
THE WILD EYE				
RCA Victor LSP-4003	1968	6.25	12.50	25.00
WILD IN THE STREETS				
Tower SKAO 5099	1968	7.50	15.00	30.00
WILD IS THE WIND				
Columbia CL 1090 [M]	1957	6.25	12.50	25.00
WILD ON THE BEACH				
RCA Victor LPM-3441 [M]	1965	6.25	12.50	25.00
WILD ON THE BEACH				
RCA Victor LSP-3441 [S]	1965	10.00	20.00	40.00
THE WILD ONE				
Decca DL 5515 [10]	1954	20.00	40.00	80.00
Decca DL 8349 [M]	1956	10.00	20.00	40.00
THE WILD RACERS				
Sidewalk ST-5914	1968	6.25	12.50	25.00
WILD WHEELS				
RCA Victor LSO-1156	1969	5.00	10.00	20.00
WILD, WILD WINTER				
Decca DL 4699 [M]	1966	5.00	10.00	20.00
Decca DL 74699 [S]	1966	7.50	15.00	30.00
WILLIE DYNAMITE				
MCA 393	1974	5.00	10.00	20.00
WILLY WONKA AND THE CHOCOLATE FACTORY				
Paramount PAS-6012	1971	10.00	20.00	40.00
WITH A SONG IN MY HEART				
Capitol L 309 [10]	1952	10.00	20.00	40.00
Capitol T 309 [M]	195?	6.25	12.50	25.00
THE WIZARD OF OZ				
MGM E-3464 [M]	1956	12.50	25.00	50.00
—Yellow label				
MGM E-3996 [M]	1962	3.75	7.50	15.00
—Gatefold cover, black label				
MGM SE-3996 [R]	196?	3.75	7.50	15.00
—Gatefold cover, black label				
WOMEN OF THE WORLD				
Decca DL 9112 [M]	1963	5.00	10.00	20.00
Decca DL 79112 [S]	1963	7.50	15.00	30.00
WONDERFUL COUNTRY				
United Artists UAL-4050 [M]	1959	12.50	25.00	50.00
United Artists UAS-5050 [S]	1959	25.00	50.00	100.00
WONDERFUL TO BE YOUNG				
Dot DLP-3474 [M]	1962	6.25	12.50	25.00
Dot DLP-25474 [S]	1962	10.00	20.00	40.00
THE WONDERFUL WORLD OF THE BROTHERS GRIMM				
MGM 1E-3 [M]	1962	6.25	12.50	25.00
—With box and hardback book				
MGM S1E-3 [S]	1962	10.00	20.00	40.00
—With box and hardback book				
WORDS AND MUSIC				
MGM E-505 [10]	1950	12.50	25.00	50.00
THE WORLD OF SUZIE WONG				
RCA Victor LOC-1059 [M]	1960	5.00	10.00	20.00
RCA Victor LSO-1059 [S]	1960	12.50	25.00	50.00
WRITTEN ON THE WIND				
Decca DL 8424 [M]	1956	10.00	20.00	40.00
—Black label, silver print, or pink label, black print promo				
Decca DL 8424 [M]	196?	5.00	10.00	20.00
—Black label with color bars				
THE WRONG BOX				
Mainstream S-6088 [S]	1966	37.50	75.00	150.00
Mainstream 56088 [M]	1966	25.00	50.00	100.00
WUTHERING HEIGHTS				
American Int'l. A-1039	1971	7.50	15.00	30.00
W.W. AND THE DIXIE DANCEKINGS				
20th Century ST-103	1975	6.25	12.50	25.00
THE YELLOW CANARY				
Verve V-8548 [M]	1963	5.00	10.00	20.00
Verve V6-8548 [S]	1963	6.25	12.50	25.00
THE YELLOW ROLLS-ROYCE				
MGM E-4292 [M]	1965	5.00	10.00	20.00
MGM SE-4292 [S]	1965	7.50	15.00	30.00
MGM T 90424 [M]	1965	3.75	7.50	15.00
—Capitol Record Club edition				
MGM ST 90424 [S]	1965	3.75	7.50	15.00
—Capitol Record Club edition				
YESTERDAY, TODAY AND TOMORROW				
Warner Bros. W 1552 [M]	1964	10.00	20.00	40.00
Warner Bros. WS 1552 [S]	1964	12.50	25.00	50.00
YOJIMBO				
MGM E-4096 [M]	1962	25.00	50.00	100.00
MGM SE-4096 [S]	1962	37.50	75.00	150.00
YOU ARE WHAT YOU EAT				
Columbia Masterworks OS 3240	1968	5.00	10.00	20.00
YOU ONLY LIVE TWICE				
United Artists UAL-4155 [M]	1967	5.00	10.00	20.00
United Artists UAS-5155 [S]	1967	6.25	12.50	25.00
YOUNG BILLY YOUNG				
United Artists UAS-5199	1969	6.25	12.50	25.00
YOUNG FRANKENSTEIN				
ABC ABCD-870	1975	5.00	10.00	20.00
THE YOUNG GIRLS OF ROCHEFORT				
Philips PCC 2-226 [(2) M]	1968	5.00	10.00	20.00
Philips PCC 2-626 [(2) S]	1968	7.50	15.00	30.00
THE YOUNG LIONS				
Decca DL 8719 [M]	1958	7.50	15.00	30.00
Decca DL 78719 [S]	1958	20.00	40.00	80.00
YOUNG LOVERS				
Columbia Masterworks OS 2510 [S]	1964	6.25	12.50	25.00
Columbia Masterworks OL 7010 [M]	1964	5.00	10.00	20.00
YOUNG MAN WITH A HORN				
Columbia CL 582 [M]	1950	7.50	15.00	30.00
Columbia CL 6106 [10]	1950	12.50	25.00	50.00
THE YOUNG SAVAGES				
Columbia CL 1672 [M]	1961	7.50	15.00	30.00
Columbia CS 8472 [S]	1961	25.00	50.00	100.00
YOUNG WINSTON				
Angel SFO-36901	1972	6.25	12.50	25.00
YOURS, MINE AND OURS				
United Artists UAS-5181	1968	5.00	10.00	20.00
Z				
Columbia Masterworks OS 3370	1970	5.00	10.00	20.00

Label, Number	Yr	VG	VG+	NM
ZABRISKIE POINT				
MGM SE-4468	1970	5.00	10.00	20.00
ZACHARIAH				
ABC ABCS-OC-13	1970	6.25	12.50	25.00
ZORBA THE GREEK				
20th Century Fox TFM-3167 [M]	1965	5.00	10.00	20.00
20th Century Fox TFS-4167 [S]	1965	6.25	12.50	25.00
ZULU				
United Artists UAL-4116 [M]	1964	10.00	20.00	40.00
United Artists UAS-5116 [S]	1964	17.50	35.00	70.00

TELEVISION RECORDS

Label, Number	Yr	VG	VG+	NM
67 MELODY LANE				
Columbia CL 724 [M]	1955	7.50	15.00	30.00
77 SUNSET STRIP				
Warner Bros. W 1289 [M]	1959	7.50	15.00	30.00
Warner Bros. WS 1289 [S]	1959	10.00	20.00	40.00
THE ADDAMS FAMILY				
RCA Victor LPM-3421 [M]	1965	20.00	40.00	80.00
RCA Victor LSP-3421 [S]	1965	37.50	75.00	150.00
AFRICA				
MGM E-4462 [M]	1967	12.50	25.00	50.00
MGM SE-4462 [S]	1967	15.00	30.00	60.00
THE AGE OF TELEVISION — A CHRONICLE OF THE FIRST 25 YEARS				
RCA Victor LL-8	1972	5.00	10.00	20.00
—With booklet				
ALADDIN				
Columbia CL 1117 [M]	1958	12.50	25.00	50.00
ALICE THROUGH THE LOOKING GLASS				
RCA Victor LOC-1130 [M]	1966	6.25	12.50	25.00
RCA Victor LSO-1130 [S]	1966	7.50	15.00	30.00
AMAHL AND THE NIGHT VISITORS				
RCA Red Seal LM-1701 [10]	1952	12.50	25.00	50.00
—Soundtrack of the 1951 NBC-TV production				
RCA Red Seal LM-1701 [M]	1952	10.00	20.00	40.00
—Soundtrack of the 1951 NBC-TV production; 12-inch record in box with booklet				
RCA Red Seal LM-2762 [M]	1964	3.75	7.50	15.00
—Soundtrack of the 1963 NBC Opera Company TV production				
RCA Red Seal LSC-2762 [S]	1964	3.75	7.50	15.00
—Large "RCA Victor" and dog at top of label				
RCA Red Seal LSC-2762 [S]	1969	3.00	6.00	12.00
—Stereo reissue on red label without dog; no bar code on back cover				
ANDROCLES AND THE LION				
RCA Victor LOC-1141 [M]	1967	6.25	12.50	25.00
RCA Victor LSO-1141 [S]	1967	6.25	12.50	25.00
ANNIE GET YOUR GUN				
Capitol W 913 [M]	1957	7.50	15.00	30.00
—Los Angeles/San Francisco production aired on NBC-TV				
AT HOME WITH THE MUNSTERS				
Golden LP-139 [M]	1964	50.00	100.00	200.00
ATOM ANT IN MUSCLE MAGIC				
Hanna-Barbera HLP-2041 [M]	1966	37.50	75.00	150.00
THE AVENGERS				
Hanna-Barbera HLP-8506 [M]	1966	15.00	30.00	60.00
Hanna-Barbera HST-9506 [S]	1966	20.00	40.00	80.00
BATMAN				
20th Century Fox TFM-3180 [M]	1966	15.00	30.00	60.00
20th Century Fox TFS-4180 [S]	1966	25.00	50.00	100.00
THE BEVERLY HILLBILLIES				
Columbia CL 2402 [M]	1965	10.00	20.00	40.00
Columbia CS 9202 [S]	1965	15.00	30.00	60.00
THE BIG VALLEY				
ABC-Paramount ABC-527 [M]	1965	10.00	20.00	40.00
ABC-Paramount ABCS-527 [S]	1965	12.50	25.00	50.00
THE BORN LOSERS				
Tower T 5082 [M]	1967	6.25	12.50	25.00
Tower DT 5082 [R]	1967	5.00	10.00	20.00
THE BORROWERS				
Stanyan SRQ-4014 [Q]	1973	12.50	25.00	50.00
BOURBON STREET BEAT				
Warner Bros. W 1321 [M]	1960	6.25	12.50	25.00
Warner Bros. WS 1321 [S]	1960	7.50	15.00	30.00
BRIGADOON				
Columbia Special Products CSM 385	1968	5.00	10.00	20.00
—Sold through the mail by broadcast sponsor Armstrong				
BURKE'S LAW				
Liberty LRP-3374 [M]	1964	15.00	30.00	60.00
Liberty LST-7374 [S]	1964	20.00	40.00	80.00
CAROUSEL				
Columbia Special Products CSM 479	1969	5.00	10.00	20.00
—Sold through the mail by broadcast sponsor Armstrong				
CHECKMATE				
Columbia CL 1591 [M]	1960	10.00	20.00	40.00
Columbia CS 8391 [S]	1960	15.00	30.00	60.00
CINDERELLA				
Columbia Masterworks OS 2005 [S]	1959	10.00	20.00	40.00
—Stage presentation for TV starring Julie Andrews				
Columbia Masterworks OS 2730 [S]	1965	7.50	15.00	30.00
—Stage presentation for TV starring Lesley-Ann Warren				
Columbia Masterworks OL 5190 [M]	1957	7.50	15.00	30.00
Columbia Masterworks OL 6330 [M]	1965	6.25	12.50	25.00
THE COMING OF CHRIST				
Decca DL 9093 [M]	1960	10.00	20.00	40.00
Decca DL 79093 [S]	1960	12.50	25.00	50.00
THE CRICKET ON THE HEARTH				
RCA Victor LOC-1140 [M]	1967	5.00	10.00	20.00
RCA Victor LSO-1140 [S]	1967	7.50	15.00	30.00
DANGER				
MGM E-111 [10]	1951	30.00	60.00	120.00
THE DANGEROUS CHRISTMAS OF RED RIDING HOOD				
ABC-Paramount ABC-536 [M]	1965	3.75	7.50	15.00
ABC-Paramount ABCS-536 [S]	1965	6.25	12.50	25.00
DARK SHADOWS				
Philips PHS 600314	1969	7.50	15.00	30.00
—With poster				
DAVID COPPERFIELD				
GRT 10008	1970	37.50	75.00	150.00
DENNIS THE MENACE SONGS				
Golden LP-59 [M]	1960	20.00	40.00	80.00
—Black label original				
DOGGIE DADDY TELLS AUGGY DOGGIE THE STORY OF PINOCCHIO				
Hanna-Barbera HLP-2028 [M]	1965	25.00	50.00	100.00
EAST SIDE, WEST SIDE				
Columbia CL 2123 [M]	1963	7.50	15.00	30.00
Columbia CS 8923 [S]	1963	10.00	20.00	40.00
ELEVEN AGAINST THE ICE				
RCA Victor LPM-1618 [M]	1958	15.00	30.00	60.00
ELIZABETH TAYLOR IN LONDON				
Colpix CP 459 [M]	1963	7.50	15.00	30.00
Colpix SCP 459 [S]	1963	12.50	25.00	50.00
EXCITING HONG KONG				
ABC-Paramount ABC-367 [M]	1961	10.00	20.00	40.00
ABC-Paramount ABCS-367 [S]	1961	12.50	25.00	50.00
FELIX THE CAT				
Cricket CR-28 [M]	1958	25.00	50.00	100.00
FENWICK				
Fenwick FLP-621	1968	5.00	10.00	20.00
—Soundtrack to TV special; packaged in oversize (13 1/2 x 13 1/2) sleeve with color cartoon booklet; made especially for Motorola. Unbanded record; narration surrounds the following songs:				
THE FLINTSTONES				
Colpix CP-302 [M]	1961	50.00	100.00	200.00
THE FLINTSTONES' FLIP FABLES: GOLDI-ROCKS AND THE THREE BEAROSAURUSES				
Hanna-Barbera HLP-2021 [M]	1965	25.00	50.00	100.00
THE FLINTSTONES AND JOSE JIMENEZ IN THE TIME MACHINE				
Hanna-Barbera HLP-2052 [M]	1966	20.00	40.00	80.00
THE FLINTSTONES IN S.A.S.F.A.T.P.O.G.O.B.S.O.A.L.T.				
Hanna-Barbera HLP-2047 [M]	1966	25.00	50.00	100.00
THE FORD 50TH ANNIVERSARY TELEVISION SHOW				
Decca DL 7027 [10]	1953	10.00	20.00	40.00
FOUR ADVENTURES OF ZORRO				
Disneyland WDA-3601 [M]	1958	20.00	40.00	80.00
—Gatefold with booklet				
FRED FLINTSTONE AND BARNEY RUBBLE SING SONGS FROM MARY POPPINS				
Hanna-Barbera HLP-2035 [M]	1965	25.00	50.00	100.00
FROSTY THE SNOWMAN				
MGM SE-4733	1970	15.00	30.00	60.00
GENERAL ELECTRIC THEATER				
Columbia CL 1395 [M]	1959	10.00	20.00	40.00
Columbia CS 8190 [S]	1959	12.50	25.00	50.00
GENERAL MOTORS' 50TH ANNIVERSARY SHOW				
RCA Victor LOC-1037 [M]	1958	25.00	50.00	100.00
GET SMART				
United Artists UAL-3533 [M]	1965	10.00	20.00	40.00
United Artists UAS-6566 [S]	1965	15.00	30.00	60.00

Label, Number	Yr	VG	VG+	NM
THE GIFT OF LOVE				
Columbia CL 1113 [M]	1958	7.50	15.00	30.00
THE GIFT OF THE MAGI				
United Artists UAL-4013 [M]	1959	10.00	20.00	40.00
United Artists UAS-5103 [S]	1959	12.50	25.00	50.00
THE GIRL FROM U.N.C.L.E.				
MGM E-4410 [M]	1966	10.00	20.00	40.00
MGM SE-4410 [S]	1966	15.00	30.00	60.00
GOOFY'S TV SPECTACULAR				
Disneyland DQ-1252 [M]	1964	5.00	10.00	20.00
THE GREEN HORNET				
20th Century Fox TF-3186 [M]	1966	50.00	100.00	200.00
20th Century Fox S-3186 [S]	1966	62.50	125.00	250.00
HANS BRINKER				
Dot DLP-9001 [M]	1958	10.00	20.00	40.00
HANSEL AND GRETEL STARRING THE FLINTSTONES				
Hanna-Barbera HLP-2038 [M]	1965	25.00	50.00	100.00
HAWAII FIVE-O				
Capitol ST-410	1969	10.00	20.00	40.00
HAWAIIAN EYE				
Warner Bros. W 1355 [M]	1959	7.50	15.00	30.00
Warner Bros. WS 1355 [S]	1959	10.00	20.00	40.00
HECTOR, THE STOWAWAY PUP				
Disneyland ST-1921 [M]	1964	7.50	15.00	30.00
HEIDI				
Capitol SKAO 2995	1968	10.00	20.00	40.00
HENNESSEY				
Signature 1049 [M]	1959	15.00	30.00	60.00
Signature SS-1049 [S]	1959	20.00	40.00	80.00
HERE COMES HUCKLEBERRY HOUND				
Colpix CP-207 [M]	1961	45.00	90.00	180.00
HEY THERE, IT'S YOGI BEAR				
Golden LP-124 [M]	1964	10.00	20.00	40.00
HIGH TOR				
Decca DL 8272 [M]	1956	50.00	100.00	200.00
THE HILLBILLY BEARS IN HILLBILLY SHINDIG				
Hanna-Barbera HLP-2044 [M]	1966	37.50	75.00	150.00
HOGAN'S HEROES SING THE BEST OF WWII				
Sunset SUM-1137 [M]	1967	7.50	15.00	30.00
Sunset SUS-5137 [S]	1967	10.00	20.00	40.00
HONEY WEST				
ABC-Paramount ABC-532 [M]	1965	10.00	20.00	40.00
ABC-Paramount ABCS-532 [S]	1965	12.50	25.00	50.00
HOW THE GRINCH STOLE CHRISTMAS				
Leo LE-901 [M]	1966	12.50	25.00	50.00
Leo LES-901 [S]	1966	17.50	35.00	70.00
HOWL ALONG WITH HUCKLEBERRY HOUND AND YOGI BEAR				
Golden LP-55 [M]	1959	37.50	75.00	150.00
—Black label original				
HUCKLEBERRY HOUND AND THE GHOST SHIP				
Colpix CP-210 [M]	1962	25.00	50.00	100.00
HUCKLEBERRY HOUND FOR PRESIDENT				
Golden LP-60 [M]	1960	25.00	50.00	100.00
—Black label original				
HUCKLEBERRY HOUND TELLS STORIES OF UNCLE REMUS				
Hanna-Barbera HLP-2022 [M]	1965	25.00	50.00	100.00
HUCKLEBERRY HOUND, THE GREAT KELLOGG'S TV SHOW				
Colpix CP-202 [M]	1959	50.00	100.00	200.00
I SPY				
Warner Bros. W 1637 [M]	1965	7.50	15.00	30.00
Warner Bros. WS 1637 [S]	1965	10.00	20.00	40.00
I SPY, VOLUME 2				
Capitol ST 2839	1968	7.50	15.00	30.00
IT'S HOWDY DOODY TIME				
RCA Victor LSP-4546	1971	6.25	12.50	25.00
JAMES BOMB STARRING SUPER SNOOPER AND BLABBER MOUSE				
Hanna-Barbera HLP-2036 [M]	1965	25.00	50.00	100.00
JANE EYRE				
Capitol SW-749	1971	7.50	15.00	30.00
THE JETSONS				
Colpix CP-213 [M]	1962	62.50	125.00	250.00
Golden LP-98 [M]	1963	50.00	100.00	200.00
—Red cover original				
Golden LP-98 [M]	1964	30.00	60.00	120.00
—Blue cover reissue				
THE JETSONS IN FIRST FAMILY ON THE MOON				
Hanna-Barbera HLP-2037 [M]	1965	37.50	75.00	150.00

Label, Number	Yr	VG	VG+	NM
THE JIMMY DURANTE TV SHOW				
Royale 1812 [10]	1955	25.00	50.00	100.00
JONNY QUEST IN 20,000 LEAGUES UNDER THE SEA				
Hanna-Barbera HLP-2030 [M]	1965	37.50	75.00	150.00
KING KONG				
Golden LP-151 [M]	1965	10.00	20.00	40.00
KISS ME, KATE				
Columbia Special Products CSS 645	1968	6.25	12.50	25.00
—Sold through the mail by broadcast sponsor Armstrong				
A LOOK AT MONACO				
Columbia CL 2019 [M]	1963	12.50	25.00	50.00
Columbia CS 8819 [R]	1963	12.50	25.00	50.00
LOVE, AMERICAN STYLE				
Capitol ST-11250	1973	10.00	20.00	40.00
MAGILLA GORILLA AND HIS PALS				
Golden LP-120 [M]	1964	12.50	25.00	50.00
MAGILLA GORILLA TELLS OGEE THE STORY OF ALICE IN WONDERLAND				
Hanna-Barbera HLP-2024 [M]	1965	25.00	50.00	100.00
THE MAN FROM INTERPOL				
Top Rank RM-327 [M]	1962	12.50	25.00	50.00
Top Rank RS-627 [S]	1962	15.00	30.00	60.00
THE MAN FROM U.N.C.L.E.				
RCA Victor LPM-3475 [M]	1965	15.00	30.00	60.00
RCA Victor LSP-3475 [S]	1965	20.00	40.00	80.00
THE MAN FROM U.N.C.L.E. VOLUME 2				
RCA Victor LPM-3574 [M]	1966	10.00	20.00	40.00
RCA Victor LSP-3574 [S]	1966	12.50	25.00	50.00
MARK TWAIN TONIGHT!				
Columbia Masterworks OS 3080 [S]	1967	5.00	10.00	20.00
Columbia Masterworks OL 6680 [M]	1967	3.75	7.50	15.00
MERRY CHRISTMAS FROM KUKLA, FRAN AND OLLIE				
Decca DL 8192 [M]	1955	20.00	40.00	80.00
MICKEY MOUSE CLUB MOUSEKEDANCES AND OTHER MOUSEKETEER FAVORITES				
Disneyland DQ-1362 [M]	1974	5.00	10.00	20.00
—With booklet				
Disneyland STER-1362 [S]	1974	6.25	12.50	25.00
—With booklet				
MICKEY MOUSE CLUB SONG HITS				
Disneyland ST-3815	1975	10.00	20.00	40.00
—With 16-page photo album				
MICKEY MOUSE CLUB: 27 NEW SONGS FROM THE MICKEY MOUSE CLUB TV SHOW				
Mickey Mouse Club MM-14	1958	12.50	25.00	50.00
MICKEY MOUSE CLUB: A WALT DISNEY SONG FEST				
Mickey Mouse Club MM-20	1958	10.00	20.00	40.00
MICKEY MOUSE CLUB: FUN WITH MUSIC — 30 FAVORITE DISNEY SONGS				
Disneyland DQ-1209 [M]	1959	6.25	12.50	25.00
MICKEY MOUSE CLUB: HOLIDAYS WITH THE MOUSEKETEERS (A SONG FOR EVERY HOLIDAY)				
Mickey Mouse Club MM-22	1958	10.00	20.00	40.00
MICKEY MOUSE CLUB: HOW TO BE A MOUSEKETEER				
Disneyland ST-3918	1962	10.00	20.00	40.00
MICKEY MOUSE CLUB: MOUSEKETEERS TALENT ROUNDUP				
Mickey Mouse Club MM-16	1958	10.00	20.00	40.00
MICKEY MOUSE CLUB: MUSICAL HIGHLIGHTS FROM THE MICKEY MOUSE CLUB				
Disneyland DQ-1227 [M]	1962	7.50	15.00	30.00
MICKEY MOUSE CLUB: MUSICAL HIGHLIGHTS FROM THE MICKEY MOUSE CLUB TV SHOW				
Mickey Mouse Club MM-12	1958	20.00	40.00	80.00
MICKEY MOUSE CLUB: SONGS FROM ANNETTE AND OTHER WALT DISNEY SERIALS				
Mickey Mouse Club MM-24	1958	30.00	60.00	120.00
MICKEY MOUSE CLUB: SONGS FROM THE MICKEY MOUSE CLUB SERIALS				
Disneyland DQ-1229 [M]	1962	10.00	20.00	40.00
MICKEY MOUSE CLUB: WE'RE THE MOUSEKETEERS				
Mickey Mouse Club MM-18	1957	10.00	20.00	40.00
THE MIGHTY HERCULES				
Golden LP-109 [M]	1963	50.00	100.00	200.00
MIKADO				
Columbia Masterworks OS 2022 [S]	1960	25.00	50.00	100.00
Columbia Masterworks OL 5480 [M]	1960	7.50	15.00	30.00
THE MISADVENTURES OF DENNIS THE MENACE				
Colpix CP-204 [M]	1960	50.00	100.00	200.00
MR. BROADWAY				
RCA Victor LPM-1520 [M]	1957	7.50	15.00	30.00

Label, Number	Yr	VG	VG+	NM
MR. ED, THE TALKING HORSE				
Colpix CP-209 [M]	1962	75.00	150.00	300.00
MR. ED: STRAIGHT FROM THE HORSE'S MOUTH				
Golden LP-88 [M]	1962	50.00	100.00	200.00
MR. JINKS, PIXIE AND DIXIE				
Colpix CP-208 [M]	1961	25.00	50.00	100.00
THE MUNSTERS				
Decca DL 4588 [M]	1964	15.00	30.00	60.00
Decca DL 74588 [S]	1964	25.00	50.00	100.00
THE MUSIC FROM M SQUAD				
RCA Victor LPM-2062 [M]	1959	7.50	15.00	30.00
RCA Victor LSP-2062 [S]	1959	10.00	20.00	40.00
THE MUSIC FROM MARLBORO COUNTRY				
United Artists SP-107	1967	12.50	25.00	50.00
MUSIC FROM SHUBERT ALLEY				
Sinclair OSS-2250 [M]	1959	10.00	20.00	40.00
—From the NBC TV program, November 13, 1959				
NAKED CITY — A MUSICAL PORTRAIT				
Colpix CP-505 [M]	1958	10.00	20.00	40.00
Colpix SCP-505 [S]	1959	15.00	30.00	60.00
OF THEE I SING				
Columbia S 31763	1972	5.00	10.00	20.00
THE OFFICIAL ALBUM OF NBC'S BAT MASTERSON				
Sea Horse/Chancellor CSH-7002 [M]	1960	20.00	40.00	80.00
ONE STEP BEYOND				
Decca DL 8970 [M]	1960	7.50	1.00	30.00
Decca DL 78970 [S]	1960	10.00	20.00	40.00
ORIGINAL AMATEUR HOUR 25TH ANNIVERSARY ALBUM				
United Artists UXL 2 [(2) M]	1960	10.00	20.00	40.00
THE ORIGINAL TV ADVENTURES OF KING KONG				
Epic LN 24231 [M]	1966	6.25	12.50	25.00
Epic BN 26231 [S]	1966	7.50	15.00	30.00
THE OTHER WORLD OF WINSTON CHURCHILL				
Mercury MG-21033 [M]	1965	7.50	15.00	30.00
Mercury SR-61033 [S]	1965	10.00	20.00	40.00
OZZIE AND HARRIET				
Imperial LP-9049 [M]	1957	50.00	100.00	200.00
PEYTON PLACE				
Epic LN 24147 [M]	1965	7.50	15.00	30.00
Epic BN 26147 [S]	1965	10.00	20.00	40.00
THE PIED PIPER OF HAMELIN				
RCA Victor LPM-1563 [M]	1957	12.50	25.00	50.00
PINOCCHIO				
Columbia CL 1055 [M]	1957	10.00	20.00	40.00
PIXIE AND DIXIE WITH MR. JINKS TELL THE STORY OF CINDERELLA				
Hanna-Barbera HLP-2025 [M]	1965	25.00	50.00	100.00
PRECIOUS PUPP IN HOT ROD GRANNY				
Hanna-Barbera HLP-2045 [M]	1966	37.50	75.00	150.00
QUICK DRAW MCGRAW				
Colpix CP-203 [M]	1960	20.00	40.00	80.00
QUICK DRAW MCGRAW AND HUCKLEBERRY HOUND				
Golden LP-51 [M]	1959	37.50	75.00	150.00
—Black label original				
QUICK DRAW MCGRAW: THE TREASURE OF SARAH'S MATTRESS				
Colpix CP-211 [M]	1962	30.00	60.00	120.00
THE REPORTER				
Columbia CL 2269 [M]	1964	7.50	15.00	30.00
Columbia CS 9069 [S]	1964	10.00	20.00	40.00
RICHARD DIAMOND				
EmArcy MG-36162 [M]	1959	12.50	25.00	50.00
EmArcy SR-80045 [S]	1959	20.00	40.00	80.00
THE RISE AND FALL OF THE THIRD REICH				
MGM 1SE-12	1968	7.50	15.00	30.00
ROBIN HOOD STARRING TOP CAT				
Hanna-Barbera HLP-2031 [M]	1965	25.00	50.00	100.00
ROCKY AND HIS FRIENDS				
Golden LP-64 [M]	1961	50.00	100.00	200.00
—Gold label original				
THE ROGUES				
RCA Victor LPM-2976 [M]	1964	5.00	10.00	20.00
RCA Victor LSP-2976 [S]	1964	7.50	15.00	30.00
RUDOLPH THE RED-NOSED REINDEER				
Decca DL 4815 [M]	1964	15.00	30.00	60.00
Decca DL 34327 [M]	1965	10.00	20.00	40.00
—Same as DL 4815; custom products reissue				
Decca DL 74815 [S]	1964	20.00	40.00	80.00
MCA 15003	1973	5.00	10.00	20.00
—Reissue; black rainbow label				

Label, Number	Yr	VG	VG+	NM
RUFF AND READY ADVENTURES IN SPACE				
Colpix CP-201 [M]	1959	50.00	100.00	200.00
RUGGLES OF RED GAP				
Verve MGV-15000 [M]	1957	12.50	25.00	50.00
THE SAINT				
RCA Victor LPM-3631 [M]	1966	30.00	60.00	120.00
RCA Victor LSP-3631 [S]	1966	50.00	100.00	200.00
SANTA CLAUS IS COMIN' TO TOWN				
MGM SE-4732	1970	15.00	30.00	60.00
SATINS AND SPURS				
Capitol L 547 [10]	1954	17.50	35.00	70.00
SECRET AGENT				
RCA Victor LPM-3630 [M]	1966	62.50	125.00	250.00
RCA Victor LSP-3630 [S]	1966	75.00	150.00	300.00
—With correct title on label				
RCA Victor LSP-3630 [S]	1966	62.50	125.00	250.00
—With incorrect title, "Danger Man," on label				
SECRET AGENT MEETS THE SAINT				
RCA Victor LPM-3467 [M]	1965	50.00	100.00	200.00
RCA Victor LSP-3467 [S]	1965	55.00	110.00	220.00
—Music from both TV shows; pre-dates the individual albums				
SECRET SQUIRREL AND MOROCCO MOLE IN SUPER SPY				
Hanna-Barbera HLP-2046 [M]	1966	37.50	75.00	150.00
SHOTGUN SLADE				
Mercury MG-20575 [M]	1960	10.00	20.00	40.00
Mercury SR-60235 [S]	1960	15.00	30.00	60.00
SINBAD JR. IN TREASURE ISLAND				
Hanna-Barbera HLP-2039 [M]	1965	30.00	60.00	120.00
SNAGGLEPUSS TELLS THE STORY OF THE WIZARD OF OZ				
Hanna-Barbera HLP-2026 [M]	1965	25.00	50.00	100.00
SONGS OF THE FLINTSTONES				
Golden LP-66 [M]	1961	62.50	125.00	250.00
—Gold label original				
SONGS OF YOGI BEAR AND HIS PALS				
Golden LP-70 [M]	1961	20.00	40.00	80.00
—Gold label original				
THE SOUND OF JAZZ				
Columbia CL 1098 [M]	1958	6.25	12.50	25.00
Columbia CS 8040 [S]	1958	10.00	20.00	40.00
SPACE: 1999				
RCA Victor ABL1-1422	1975	5.00	10.00	20.00
SQUIDDLEY DIDDLEY IN SURFIN' SAFARI				
Hanna-Barbera HLP-2043 [M]	1966	37.50	75.00	150.00
STACCATO (MUSIC FROM JOHNNY STACCATO)				
Capitol T 1287 [M]	1959	7.50	15.00	30.00
Capitol ST 1287 [S]	1959	12.50	25.00	50.00
THE STINGIEST MAN IN TOWN				
Columbia CL 950	1956	5.00	10.00	20.00
—Music from a television play first aired on The Alcoa Hour				
Columbia Special Products P 12637	1975	2.50	5.00	10.00
—Reissue of Columbia LP; same contents				
SUPER SNOOPER AND BLABBER MOUSE IN MONSTER SHINDIG				
Hanna-Barbera HLP-2020 [M]	1965	25.00	50.00	100.00
THRILLER				
Time S-2034 [S]	1960	10.00	20.00	40.00
Time 52034 [M]	1960	7.50	15.00	30.00
TOM SAWYER				
Decca DL 8432 [M]	1957	10.00	20.00	40.00
—First aired on the U.S. Steel Hour, starring Jimmy Boyd				
TOP CAT				
Colpix CP-212 [M]	1963	75.00	150.00	300.00
TOUCHE TURTLE AND DUM-DUM IN THE RELUCTANT DRAGON				
Hanna-Barbera HLP-2029 [M]	1965	25.00	50.00	100.00
THE UNTOUCHABLES				
Capitol T 1430 [M]	1960	10.00	20.00	40.00
Capitol ST 1430 [S]	1960	12.50	25.00	50.00
UP WITH PEOPLE!				
Pace 1101	1965	5.00	10.00	20.00
—Among the many people on this LP is a young Glenn Close (first name misspelled "Gleen")				
THE VALIANT YEARS				
ABC-Paramount ABC-387 [M]	1962	7.50	15.00	30.00
ABC-Paramount ABCS-387 [S]	1962	10.00	20.00	40.00
VICTORY AT SEA				
RCA Victor LM-1779 [M]	1954	6.25	12.50	25.00
—Original recording				
RCA Victor LM-2335 [M]	1959	5.00	10.00	20.00
—Re-recording of 1779				
RCA Victor LSC-2335 [S]	1959	5.00	10.00	20.00
—Re-recording of 1779 in stereo				

Label, Number	Yr	VG	VG+	NM
VICTORY AT SEA, VOL. 2				
RCA Victor LM-2226 [M]	1958	5.00	10.00	20.00
RCA Victor LSC-2226 [S]	1958	6.25	12.50	25.00
—Original with "shaded dog" label				
VICTORY AT SEA, VOL. 3				
RCA Victor LM-2523 [M]	1961	5.00	10.00	20.00
RCA Victor LSC-2523 [S]	1961	6.25	12.50	25.00
WAGON TRAIN				
Mercury MG-20502 [M]	1959	12.50	25.00	50.00
Mercury SR-60179 [S]	1959	20.00	40.00	80.00
WALT DISNEY'S WONDERFUL WORLD OF COLOR				
Disneyland DQ-1245 [M]	1963	7.50	15.00	30.00
WIDE, WIDE WORLD				
RCA Victor LPM-1280 [M]	1956	10.00	20.00	40.00
WILMA FLINTSTONE TELLS THE STORY OF BAMBI				
Hanna-Barbera HLP-2027 [M]	1965	25.00	50.00	100.00
WINSOME WITCH IN IT'S MAGIC				
Hanna-Barbera HLP-2042 [M]	1966	37.50	75.00	150.00
WONDERFUL TOWN				
Columbia Masterworks OS 2008 [S]	1958	6.25	12.50	25.00
Columbia Masterworks OL 5360 [M]	1958	5.00	10.00	20.00
YOGI BEAR AND BOO-BOO				
Colpix CP-205 [M]	1961	30.00	60.00	120.00
YOGI BEAR AND BOO-BOO TELL STORIES OF LITTLE RED RIDING HOOD AND JACK AND THE BEANSTALK				
Hanna-Barbera HLP-2023 [M]	1965	25.00	50.00	100.00
YOGI BEAR AND THE THREE STOOGES IN THE MAD, MAD, DR. NO-NO				
Hanna-Barbera HLP-2050 [M]	1966	25.00	50.00	100.00
YOGI BEAR: HOW TO BE A BETTER THAN AVERAGE CHILD				
Golden LP-90 [M]	1962	20.00	40.00	80.00

VARIOUS ARTISTS COLLECTIONS

Label, Number	Yr	VG	VG+	NM
THE 12 GREATEST OLDIES IN THE WHOLE WORLD, EVER				
Parkway P-7031 [M]	1963	7.50	15.00	30.00
12 MILLION SELLERS				
Forum F-9057 [M]	1963	5.00	10.00	20.00
Forum SF-9057 [R]	1963	3.75	7.50	15.00
12 SONGS OF CHRISTMAS				
Reprise F-2022 [M]	1964	5.00	10.00	20.00
Reprise FS-2022 [S]	1964	3.75	7.50	15.00
12 TOP TEEN DANCES 1961-1962				
Cameo C-1016 [M]	1962	7.50	15.00	30.00
12 + 3 = 15 HITS				
End LP 310 [M]	1961	15.00	30.00	60.00
14 GOLDEN RECORDINGS FROM THE HISTORIC VAULTS OF DUKE-PEACOCK RECORDS				
ABC ABCX-784	1973	5.00	10.00	20.00
14 GOLDEN RECORDINGS FROM THE HISTORIC VAULTS OF DUKE-PEACOCK RECORDS, VOLUME 2				
ABC ABCX-789	1973	5.00	10.00	20.00
14 GREAT ALL TIME C&W WALTZES				
King 890 [M]	1964	17.50	35.00	70.00
14 HIT FLASHBACKS FROM THE GOLDEN GROUP ERA				
King 893 [M]	1964	17.50	35.00	70.00
14 MORE NEWIES BUT GOODIES				
Mercury MG-20493 [M]	1960	7.50	15.00	30.00
Mercury SR-60241 [S]	1960	10.00	20.00	40.00
14 NEWIES BUT GOODIES				
Mercury MG-20493 [M]	1960	7.50	15.00	30.00
Mercury SR-60172 [S]	1960	10.00	20.00	40.00
14 OF THE WORLD'S BEST-LOVED CHRISTMAS SONGS				
Columbia Special Products CSP 122 [M]	1963	3.75	7.50	15.00
—Sold only at Walgreens drug stores. Title on record is "Music of Christmas"; number on record is "XTV 88672" on Side 1, "XTV 88673" on Side 2				
15 FAVORITES				
Hickory LPM-105 [M]	1962	6.25	12.50	25.00
15 GOLDEN HITS				
United Artists UAL-3192 [M]	1962	6.25	12.50	25.00
United Artists UAS-6192 [S]	1962	7.50	15.00	30.00
15 HITS: THE ORIGINAL RECORDINGS (THE ORIGINAL HITS, VOLUME 5)				
Liberty LRP-3235 [M]	1962	5.00	10.00	20.00
16 GOODIES — BLASTS FROM THE PAST				
Blast LP-6805 [M]	1964	10.00	20.00	40.00
16 ORIGINAL BIG HITS, VOLUME 2				
Tamla TM 256 [M]	1964	5.00	10.00	20.00
16 ORIGINAL BIG HITS, VOLUME 3				
Motown MT 624 [M]	1965	5.00	10.00	20.00
16 ORIGINAL BIG HITS, VOLUME 4				
Motown M 633 [M]	1965	3.75	7.50	15.00
Motown MS 633 [S]	1965	5.00	10.00	20.00
16 ORIGINAL BIG HITS, VOLUME 5				
Motown M 651 [M]	1966	3.75	7.50	15.00
18 ALL TIME COUNTRY AND WESTERN HITS				
King 1027 [M]	1968	7.50	15.00	30.00
18 ALL TIME RHYTHM 'N' BLUES HITS				
King 1026 [M]	1968	7.50	15.00	30.00
18 KING-SIZE COUNTRY HITS				
Columbia CL 2668 [M]	1967	5.00	10.00	20.00
Columbia CS 9468 [R]	1967	5.00	10.00	20.00
18 KING-SIZE RHYTHM AND BLUES HITS				
Columbia CL 2667 [M]	1967	7.50	15.00	30.00
Columbia CS 9467 [R]	1967	5.00	10.00	20.00
THE 1969 WARNER/REPRISE RECORD SHOW				
Warner Bros. PRO 336 [(2)]	1969	7.50	15.00	30.00
—Originals have "W7" logos on labels				
THE 1969 WARNER/REPRISE SONGBOOK				
Warner Bros. PRO 331 [(2)]	1969	7.50	15.00	30.00
—The first of the famous Warner/Reprise "Loss Leaders" mail-order series; originals have "W7" logos on labels				
20 ALL TIME NO. 1 HITS				
Roulette R 25290 [M]	1965	5.00	10.00	20.00
Roulette SR 25290 [R]	1965	3.00	6.00	12.00
20 BIG BOSS FAVORITES: 10 GREAT HITS OF 1964 — 10 GREAT OLDIES HITS				
Roulette R 25304 [M]	1965	5.00	10.00	20.00
Roulette SR 25304 [R]	1965	3.75	7.50	15.00
—Of the 20 tracks, only "Laugh, Laugh" by the Beau Brummels and "El Watusi" by Ray Barretto are true stereo				

Label, Number	Yr	VG	VG+	NM
20 ORIGINAL WINNERS OF 1964				
Roulette R 25293 [M]	1965	5.00	10.00	20.00
Roulette SR 25293 [R]	1965	3.00	6.00	12.00
20 ORIGINAL WINNERS, VOLUME 1				
Roulette R 25249 [M]	1964	5.00	10.00	20.00
20 ORIGINAL WINNERS, VOLUME 2				
Roulette R 25251 [M]	1964	5.00	10.00	20.00
20 ORIGINAL WINNERS, VOLUME 3				
Roulette R 25263 [M]	1965	5.00	10.00	20.00
20 ORIGINAL WINNERS, VOLUME 4				
Roulette R 25264 [M]	1965	5.00	10.00	20.00
20 SOULFUL OLDIES, VOLUME 1				
Vee Jay VJVS-1001 [R]	1972	5.00	10.00	20.00
20 SOULFUL OLDIES, VOLUME 2				
Vee Jay VJVS-1002 [R]	1972	5.00	10.00	20.00
20 SOULFUL OLDIES, VOLUME 3				
Vee Jay VJVS-1003 [R]	1972	5.00	10.00	20.00
20 SOULFUL OLDIES, VOLUME 4				
Vee Jay VJVS-73-1006/7 [R]	1973	5.00	10.00	20.00
20 SOULFUL OLDIES, VOLUME 5				
Vee Jay VJVS-73-1008/9 [R]	1973	5.00	10.00	20.00
20 SOULFUL OLDIES, VOLUME 6				
Vee Jay VJVS-73-1010/11 [R]	1973	5.00	10.00	20.00
24 KARAT GOLD FOR GROOVIN'				
Verve V6-6654 [(2)]	1968	5.00	10.00	20.00
24 SACRED SONGS				
King 965 [M]	1966	12.50	25.00	50.00
25 YEARS OF COUNTRY AND WESTERN AND SACRED				
King 807 [M]	1962	25.00	50.00	100.00
25 YEARS OF C&W HITS				
King 1006 [M]	1966	7.50	15.00	30.00
25 YEARS OF POPULAR MUSIC				
King 1008 [M]	1966	7.50	15.00	30.00
25 YEARS OF R&B HITS				
King 1004 [M]	1966	7.50	15.00	30.00
25 YEARS OF R&B HITS, VOLUME 1				
King 725 [M]	1961	25.00	50.00	100.00
25 YEARS OF R&B HITS, VOLUME 2				
King 749 [M]	1961	25.00	50.00	100.00
30 FAVORITE SONGS OF CHRISTMAS WITH CHIMES AND CHORUS				
Disneyland DQ-1329 [M]	1963	5.00	10.00	20.00
—Performed by anonymous musicians				
5-STRING BANJO PICKIN' AND SINGIN'				
King 994 [M]	1966	10.00	20.00	40.00
50 YEARS OF FILM				
Warner Bros. 3XX 2737 [(3)]	1973	6.25	12.50	25.00
—Box set with 60-page booklet				
50 YEARS OF FILM MUSIC				
Warner Bros. 3XX 2736 [(3)]	1973	6.25	12.50	25.00
—Box set with 28-page booklet				
50 YEARS OF JAZZ GREATS				
Columbia Musical Treasury P3S 5932 [(3)]	197?	5.00	10.00	20.00
52ND STREET JAZZ				
Waldorf Music Hall MH 33-148 [10]	195?	25.00	50.00	100.00
60 YEARS OF MUSIC AMERICA LOVES BEST				
RCA Victor LM-6074 [(2)]	1959	7.50	15.00	30.00
60 YEARS OF MUSIC AMERICA LOVES BEST, VOLUME II				
RCA Victor LM-6088 [(2)]	1960	7.50	15.00	30.00
60 YEARS OF MUSIC AMERICA LOVES BEST, VOLUME III (POPULAR)				
RCA Victor LOP-1509	1961	5.00	10.00	20.00
$ 64,000 JAZZ				
Columbia CL 777 [M]	1955	12.50	25.00	50.00
ACCENT ON PIANO				
Urania UJLP-1207 [M]	1955	7.50	15.00	30.00
ACCENT ON TROMBONE				
Urania UJLP-1205 [M]	1955	7.50	15.00	30.00
ADD-A-PART JAZZ				
Columbia CL 908 [M]	1956	6.25	12.50	25.00
THE ADVANCE GUARD OF THE '40S				
EmArcy MG-36016 [M]	1955	12.50	25.00	50.00
AFRO-COOL				
GNP Crescendo GNP-48 [M]	1959	5.00	10.00	20.00
AFRO SUMMIT				
BASF 20675	197?	5.00	10.00	20.00

Label, Number	Yr	VG	VG+	NM
AFTER HOUR JAZZ				
Epic LN (# unk) [M]	1955	7.50	15.00	30.00
AFTER HOURS				
King 395-528 [M]	1956	125.00	250.00	500.00
AFTER HOURS BLUES, 1949				
Biograph 12010	1969	3.00	6.00	12.00
AIN'T THAT GOOD NEWS				
Specialty SPS-2115	1969	5.00	10.00	20.00
ALAN FREED'S GOLDEN PICS				
End LP-313 [M]	1961	15.00	30.00	60.00
ALAN FREED'S MEMORY LANE				
End LP-314 [M]	1962	15.00	30.00	60.00
ALAN FREED'S TOP 15				
End LP-315 [M]	1962	15.00	30.00	60.00
Roulette SR 42042 [R]	1970	3.75	7.50	15.00
—Reissue of End LP-315				
ALL-STAR DATES				
RCA Victor LPT-21 [10]	1951	12.50	25.00	50.00
ALL-TIME CHRISTMAS FAVORITES				
Capitol Special Markets SL-6931	1973	3.00	6.00	12.00
—Sold only at Sylvania dealers				
ALL DAY LONG				
Prestige PRLP-7081 [M]	1957	25.00	50.00	100.00
—Reissued as Prestige 7277; see KENNY BURRELL.				
ALL GIRL MILLION SELLERS				
Ascot AM-13007 [M]	1964	10.00	20.00	40.00
Ascot AS-16007 [P]	1964	10.00	20.00	40.00
ALL MEAT				
Warner Bros. PRO 604 [(2)]	1975	5.00	10.00	20.00
ALL NIGHT LONG				
Prestige PRLP-7073 [M]	1957	25.00	50.00	100.00
—Reissued as Prestige 7289; see KENNY BURRELL.				
ALL SINGING — ALL TALKING — ALL ROCKING				
Warner Bros. PRO 573 [(2)]	1973	6.25	12.50	25.00
ALL STAR JAZZ				
Halo 50223 [M]	195?	7.50	15.00	30.00
ALL STAR ROCK AND ROLL REVUE				
King 395-513 [M]	1956	100.00	200.00	400.00
King 638 [M]	1959	50.00	100.00	200.00
—Reissue of King 395-513				
ALL STAR SESSIONS				
Capitol M-11031	1973	3.00	6.00	12.00
ALL STAR TRIBUTE TO TATUM				
American Recording Society G-424 [M]	1957	7.50	15.00	30.00
ALL THE HITS BY ALL THE STARS				
Parkway P 7013 [M]	1962	10.00	20.00	40.00
ALL THE HITS BY ALL THE STARS, VOL. 2				
Parkway P 7016 [M]	1963	7.50	15.00	30.00
ALL THE STARS' BIGGEST HITS				
Parkway P-7033 [M]	1963	12.50	25.00	50.00
—With "pull-off pix" still intact on cover				
ALL THE STARS' BIGGEST HITS, VOLUME 2				
Parkway P-7034 [M]	1963	12.50	25.00	50.00
—With "pull-off pix" still intact on cover				
ALL THESE THINGS				
Instant LP-71000	1969	7.50	15.00	30.00
ALL TIME COUNTRY AND WESTERN HITS				
King 537 [M]	1956	37.50	75.00	150.00
King 710 [M]	1961	25.00	50.00	100.00
—Not a reissue of King 537, but a different collection				
ALL TIME HIT SACRED AND GOSPEL SONGS				
King 1023 [M]	1967	7.50	15.00	30.00
ALTERNATIVES				
Warner Bros. BS 1873	1970	3.00	6.00	12.00
ALTO ALTITUDE				
EmArcy MG-36018 [M]	1955	12.50	25.00	50.00
ALTO SAXES				
Norgran MGN-1035 [M]	1955	20.00	40.00	80.00
Verve MGV-8126 [M]	1957	7.50	15.00	30.00
Verve V-8126 [M]	1961	5.00	10.00	20.00
ALTO SUMMIT				
Prestige PRLP-7684	1969	3.75	7.50	15.00
THE AMAZING METS				
Buddah 1969	1969	6.25	12.50	25.00

Label, Number	Yr	VG	VG+	NM
AMERICA'S GREATEST JAZZMEN PLAY COLE PORTER				
Moodsville MVLP-34 [M]	1963	10.00	20.00	40.00
—Green label				
Moodsville MVST-34 [S]	1963	10.00	20.00	40.00
—Green label				
Moodsville MVLP-34 [M]	1965	5.00	10.00	20.00
—Blue label, trident logo at right				
Moodsville MVST-34 [S]	1965	5.00	10.00	20.00
—Blue label, trident logo at right				
AMERICA'S GREATEST JAZZMEN PLAY GEORGE GERSHWIN				
Moodsville MVLP-33 [M]	1963	10.00	20.00	40.00
—Green label				
Moodsville MVST-33 [S]	1963	10.00	20.00	40.00
—Green label				
Moodsville MVLP-33 [M]	1965	5.00	10.00	20.00
—Blue label, trident logo at right				
Moodsville MVST-33 [S]	1965	5.00	10.00	20.00
—Blue label, trident logo at right				
AMERICA'S GREATEST JAZZMEN PLAY RICHARD RODGERS				
Moodsville MVLP-35 [M]	1963	10.00	20.00	40.00
—Green label				
Moodsville MVST-35 [S]	1963	10.00	20.00	40.00
—Green label				
Moodsville MVLP-35 [M]	1965	5.00	10.00	20.00
—Blue label, trident logo at right				
Moodsville MVST-35 [S]	1965	5.00	10.00	20.00
—Blue label, trident logo at right				
AMERICA'S GREATEST JAZZMEN PLAY THE BROADWAY SCENE				
Moodsville MVLP-38 [M]	1963	10.00	20.00	40.00
—Green label				
Moodsville MVST-38 [S]	1963	10.00	20.00	40.00
—Green label				
Moodsville MVLP-38 [M]	1965	5.00	10.00	20.00
—Blue label, trident logo at right				
Moodsville MVST-38 [S]	1965	5.00	10.00	20.00
—Blue label, trident logo at right				
AMERICAN FOLK BLUES FESTIVAL				
Excello LPS-8029	1972	5.00	10.00	20.00
Exodus EX-302 [M]	1966	5.00	10.00	20.00
Exodus EXS-302 [S]	1966	6.25	12.50	25.00
AMERICAN JAZZ FESTIVAL AT NEWPORT '56, NO. 1				
Columbia CL 931 [M]		—	—	—
—See LOUIS ARMSTRONG.				
AMERICAN JAZZ FESTIVAL AT NEWPORT '56, NO. 2				
Columbia CL 932 [M]		—	—	—
—See DAVE BRUBECK.				
AMERICAN JAZZ FESTIVAL AT NEWPORT '56, NO. 3				
Columbia CL 933 [M]		—	—	—
—See DUKE ELLINGTON.				
AMERICAN JAZZ FESTIVAL AT NEWPORT '56, NO. 4				
Columbia CL 934 [M]		—	—	—
—See DUKE ELLINGTON.				
AMERICANS ABROAD, VOL. 1				
Pax LP-6009 [10]	1955	10.00	20.00	40.00
AMERICANS ABROAD, VOL. 2				
Pax LP-6015 [10]	1955	10.00	20.00	40.00
AMERICANS IN EUROPE, VOL. 1				
ABC Impulse! AS-36 [S]	1968	3.00	6.00	12.00
Impulse! A-36 [M]	1963	5.00	10.00	20.00
Impulse! AS-36 [S]	1963	6.25	12.50	25.00
AMERICANS IN EUROPE, VOL. 2				
ABC Impulse! AS-37 [S]	1968	3.00	6.00	12.00
Impulse! A-37 [M]	1963	5.00	10.00	20.00
Impulse! AS-37 [S]	1963	6.25	12.50	25.00
THE ANATOMY OF IMPROVISATION				
Verve MGV-8230 [M]	1958	7.50	15.00	30.00
Verve V-8230 [M]	1961	5.00	10.00	20.00
ANOTHER MONDAY NIGHT AT BIRDLAND				
Roulette R 52022 [M]	1959	7.50	15.00	30.00
Roulette SR 52022 [S]	1959	7.50	15.00	30.00
AN ANTHOLOGY OF BRITISH BLUES, VOL. 1				
Immediate Z12 52006	1968	7.50	15.00	30.00
AN ANTHOLOGY OF BRITISH BLUES, VOL. 2				
Immediate Z12 52014	1968	7.50	15.00	30.00
AN ANTHOLOGY OF CALIFORNIA MUSIC				
Jazz: West Coast JWC-500 [M]	1955	37.50	75.00	150.00
AN ANTHOLOGY OF CALIFORNIA MUSIC, VOL. 2				
Jazz: West Coast JWC-501 [M]	1956	37.50	75.00	150.00
APOLLO SATURDAY NIGHT				
Atco 33-159 [M]	1964	10.00	20.00	40.00
Atco SD 33-159 [S]	1964	12.50	25.00	50.00
APPETIZERS				
Warner Bros. PRO 569 [(2)]	1973	6.25	12.50	25.00
APPROVED BY 10,000,000				
Teem LP-5004 [M]	196?	7.50	15.00	30.00
AROUND THE CHRISTMAS TREE				
Decca DL 38170 [M]	196?	3.00	6.00	12.00
THE ART OF JAZZ PIANO				
Epic LN 3295 [M]	1956	7.50	15.00	30.00
THE ART OF THE BALLAD				
Verve VSP-17 [M]	1966	3.75	7.50	15.00
Verve VSPS-17 [R]	1966	2.50	5.00	10.00
THE ART OF THE BALLAD 2				
Verve VSP-38 [M]	1966	3.75	7.50	15.00
Verve VSPS-38 [R]	1966	2.50	5.00	10.00
ASSORTED FLAVORS OF PACIFIC JAZZ				
Pacific Jazz HFS-1 [M]	1956	12.50	25.00	50.00
AT THE HOOTENANNY				
Kapp KL-1330 [M]	1963	5.00	10.00	20.00
Kapp KS-3330 [S]	1963	6.25	12.50	25.00
AT THE HOOTENANNY, VOL. 2				
Kapp KL-1343 [M]	1963	5.00	10.00	20.00
Kapp KS-3343 [S]	1963	6.25	12.50	25.00
AT THE HOOTENANNY, VOL. 3				
Kapp KL-1344 [M]	1963	5.00	10.00	20.00
Kapp KS-3344 [S]	1963	6.25	12.50	25.00
AUTOBIOGRAPHY IN JAZZ				
Debut DEB-198 [M]	1955	37.50	75.00	150.00
AWARD ALBUM JAZZ VOCALS				
Bethlehem BCP-6060 [M]	1961	6.25	12.50	25.00
BACKGROUNDS OF JAZZ, VOL. 1: THE JUG BANDS				
"X" LX-3009 [10]	1954	20.00	40.00	80.00
BACKGROUNDS OF JAZZ, VOL. 2: COUNTRY & URBAN BLUES				
"X" LVA-3016 [10]	1954	20.00	40.00	80.00
BACKGROUNDS OF JAZZ, VOL. 3: KINGS OF THE BLUES				
"X" LVA-3032 [10]	1955	20.00	40.00	80.00
BACKWOOD BLUES				
Riverside RLP-1039 [10]	1954	20.00	40.00	80.00
BALLADS AND BREAKDOWNS OF THE GOLDEN ERA				
Columbia CS 9660	1968	5.00	10.00	20.00
BALLROOM BANDSTAND				
Columbia CL 611 [M]	1955	6.25	12.50	25.00
BANG AND SHOUT SUPER HITS				
Bang BLPS-220 [P]	1969	5.00	10.00	20.00
BANJO COUNTRY STYLE				
Audio Lab AL-1569 [M]	1962	20.00	40.00	80.00
BARGAIN DAY				
EmArcy MG-36087 [M]	1956	10.00	20.00	40.00
BARREL HOUSE PIANO				
Brunswick BL 58022 [10]	1951	15.00	30.00	60.00
A BARREL OF OLDIES				
Del-Fi DFLP-1219 [M]	1961	12.50	25.00	50.00
BARRY MANN AND CYNTHIA WEIL: SOLID GOLD				
Screen Gems/Columbia CPL-712 [DJ]	1975	5.00	10.00	20.00
—Promo-only compilation of oldies sent to radio to spur airplay on songs owned by this publishing house				
THE BASS				
ABC Impulse! AS-9284 [(3)]	197?	5.00	10.00	20.00
BATTLE OF BANDS				
Capitol H 235 [10]	1950	12.50	25.00	50.00
BATTLE OF JAZZ, VOL. 3				
Brunswick BL 58039 [10]	1953	12.50	25.00	50.00
BATTLE OF THE BIG BANDS				
Capitol T 667 [M]	1956	7.50	15.00	30.00
BATTLE OF THE GROUPS				
End LP-305 [M]	1960	15.00	30.00	60.00
BATTLE OF THE GROUPS, VOLUME 2				
End LP-309 [M]	1960	15.00	30.00	60.00
BATTLE OF THE SAXES				
Aladdin LP-701 [10]	1950	125.00	250.00	500.00
BATTLE OF THE SAXES-TENOR ALL STARS				
EmArcy MG-36023 [M]	1955	12.50	25.00	50.00
THE BE-BOP ERA				
RCA Victor LPV-519	1965	5.00	10.00	20.00
BE-BOP SINGERS				
Prestige PRST-7828	1971	3.00	6.00	12.00
BE OUR GUEST				
Gene Norman GNP-20 [M]	1955	6.25	12.50	25.00

Label, Number	Yr	VG	VG+	NM
THE BELLS OF CHRISTMAS				
Book-of-the-Month Club 90-5677 [(3)]	1973	5.00	10.00	20.00
—Sold through Book-of-the-Month Records; secondary number is "P3 11972"				
BEST COAST JAZZ				
EmArcy MG-36039 [M]	1955	20.00	40.00	80.00
BEST FROM THE WEST: MODERN SOUNDS FROM CALIFORNIA, VOL. 1				
Blue Note BLP-5059 [10]	1955	50.00	100.00	200.00
BEST FROM THE WEST: MODERN SOUNDS FROM CALIFORNIA, VOL. 2				
Blue Note BLP-5060 [10]	1955	50.00	100.00	200.00
THE BEST OF ARGO JAZZ				
Argo ALPS-1 [M]	1961	7.50	15.00	30.00
THE BEST OF BLUE NOTE, VOL. 1				
Blue Note BST-84429 [(2)]	197?	5.00	10.00	20.00
THE BEST OF BLUE NOTE, VOL. 2				
Blue Note BST-84433 [(2)]	197?	5.00	10.00	20.00
THE BEST OF CHRISTMAS				
Capitol STBB 2979 [(2)]	1968	5.00	10.00	20.00
THE BEST OF DIXIELAND				
RCA Victor LPM-2982 [M]	1965	5.00	10.00	20.00
RCA Victor LSP-2982 [R]	1965	3.00	6.00	12.00
BEST OF RHYTHM AND BLUES				
Jubilee JLP-1014 [M]	1956	125.00	250.00	500.00
—Pink label, red vinyl				
Jubilee JLP-1014 [M]	1956	50.00	100.00	200.00
—Pink label, black vinyl				
Jubilee JLP-1014 [M]	1956	37.50	75.00	150.00
—Blue label, black vinyl				
Warwick W 2026 [M]	1961	20.00	40.00	80.00
BEST OF THE BIG NAME BANDS				
RCA Camden CAL-368 [M]	1958	6.25	12.50	25.00
BEST OF THE BLUES, VOLUME 1				
Imperial LP-9257 [M]	1964	6.25	12.50	25.00
Imperial LP-12257 [R]	1964	5.00	10.00	20.00
BEST OF THE BLUES, VOLUME 2				
Imperial LP-9259 [M]	1964	6.25	12.50	25.00
Imperial LP-12259 [R]	1964	5.00	10.00	20.00
BEST OF THE GREAT SONGS OF CHRISTMAS (ALBUM 10)				
Columbia Special Products CSS 1478	1970	3.00	6.00	12.00
—Sold only at Goodyear tire dealers				
BEST OF THE MUSICAL SOUNDS OF CHRISTMAS				
Capitol Creative Products SL-6713	1971	3.00	6.00	12.00
THE BEST OF THE R AND B GROUPS				
Warwick W 2025 [M]	1961	25.00	50.00	100.00
BEST OF THE SOUNDTRACKS				
Tower ST-5148	1969	6.25	12.50	25.00
THE BEST VOCAL GROUPS IN ROCK 'N' ROLL				
Dooto DL-224 [M]	1957	25.00	50.00	100.00
—Yellow label				
Dooto DL-224 [M]	196?	7.50	15.00	30.00
—Multi-color label				
BETHLEHEM'S BEST				
Bethlehem EXLP-6 [(3) M]	1958	17.50	35.00	70.00
—Box set of 82, 83, and 84				
BETHLEHEM'S BEST, VOLUME 1				
Bethlehem BCP-82 [M]	1958	7.50	15.00	30.00
BETHLEHEM'S BEST, VOLUME 2				
Bethlehem BCP-83 [M]	1958	7.50	15.00	30.00
BETHLEHEM'S BEST, VOLUME 3				
Bethlehem BCP-84 [M]	1958	7.50	15.00	30.00
BETHLEHEM'S GRAB BAG				
Bethlehem EXLP-2 [M]	1958	10.00	20.00	40.00
THE BIG BALL				
Warner Bros. PRO 358 [(2)]	1970	6.25	12.50	25.00
—Originals have green labels				
BIG BAND CONTRAST				
Bethlehem BCP-6037 [M]	1960	7.50	15.00	30.00
BIG BAND JAZZ				
Brunswick BL 58050 [10]	1953	12.50	25.00	50.00
BIG BAND STEREO				
Capitol SW 1055 [S]	1959	6.25	12.50	25.00
BIG BANDS				
Capitol STFL-293 [(6)]	1969	7.50	15.00	30.00
—One album each by Les Brown, Glen Gray, Duke Ellington, Benny Goodman, Harry James and Woody Herman				
BIG BANDS' GREATEST HITS				
Columbia G 30009 [(2)]	1970	5.00	10.00	20.00
—Red "360 Sound" labels				
Columbia G 30009 [(2)]	1970	3.75	7.50	15.00
—Orange labels				
Columbia CG 30009 [(2)]	197?	3.00	6.00	12.00
—"CG" prefix is a reissue of "G"				
BIG BANDS' GREATEST HITS, VOL. 2				
Columbia G 31213 [(2)]	1972	3.75	7.50	15.00
Columbia CG 31213 [(2)]	197?	3.00	6.00	12.00
—"CG" prefix is a reissue of "G"				
THE BIG BANDS 1933				
Prestige PRLP-7645	1969	3.75	7.50	15.00
BIG BANDS UPTOWN, VOL. 1				
Decca DL 79242	1969	3.00	6.00	12.00
BIG COUNTRY HITS				
Pickwick JS-6166	1975	7.50	15.00	30.00
THE BIG HITS				
Columbia CL 1353 [M]	1959	7.50	15.00	30.00
Columbia CS 8161 [S]	1959	10.00	20.00	40.00
THE BIG HITS OF MID-AMERICA				
Soma MG-1245 [M]	1965	20.00	40.00	80.00
THE BIG HITS OF MID-AMERICA, VOLUME 2				
Soma MG-1246 [M]	1965	20.00	40.00	80.00
BIG NAME DIXIE				
Score SLP-4024 [M]	1958	12.50	25.00	50.00
THE BIG ONES FROM DUKE AND PEACOCK RECORDS				
Peacock PLP-2000 [M]	1967	5.00	10.00	20.00
THE BIG SOUNDS OF THE DRAGS!				
Capitol T 2001 [M]	1963	5.00	10.00	20.00
Capitol ST 2001 [S]	1963	6.25	12.50	25.00
BIG SUR FESTIVAL/ONE HAND CLAPPING				
Columbia KC 31138	1972	5.00	10.00	20.00
BIG SURF HITS				
Del-Fi DFLP-1249 [M]	1964	12.50	25.00	50.00
Del-Fi DFST-1249 [S]	1964	18.75	37.50	75.00
BILLIE HOLIDAY REVISITED				
Mainstream MRL-409	197?	3.00	6.00	12.00
BIRD'S NIGHT — THE MUSIC OF CHARLIE PARKER				
Savoy MG-12138 [M]	1958	12.50	25.00	50.00
BIRDLAND ALL STARS AT CARNEGIE HALL				
Roulette RE-127 [(2)]	197?	3.00	6.00	12.00
BIRDLAND DREAM BAND, VOL. 1				
Vik LX-1070 [M]	1957	7.50	15.00	30.00
BIRDLAND DREAM BAND, VOL. 2				
Vik LX-1077 [M]	1957	7.50	15.00	30.00
THE BIRDLAND STARS ON TOUR, VOL. 1				
RCA Victor LPM-1327 [M]	1956	10.00	20.00	40.00
THE BIRDLAND STARS ON TOUR, VOL. 2				
RCA Victor LPM-1328 [M]	1956	10.00	20.00	40.00
THE BIRDLAND STORY				
Roulette RB-2 [(2) M]	1961	10.00	20.00	40.00
Roulette SRB-2 [(2) S]	1961	10.00	20.00	40.00
THE BIRTH OF BOP, VOL. 1				
Savoy MG-9022 [10]	1953	37.50	75.00	150.00
THE BIRTH OF BOP, VOL. 2				
Savoy MG-9023 [10]	1953	37.50	75.00	150.00
THE BIRTH OF BOP, VOL. 3				
Savoy MG-9024 [10]	1953	37.50	75.00	150.00
THE BIRTH OF BOP, VOL. 4				
Savoy MG-9025 [10]	1953	37.50	75.00	150.00
THE BIRTH OF BOP, VOL. 5				
Savoy MG-9026 [10]	1953	37.50	75.00	150.00
BIRTH OF SOUL				
Decca DL 79245	1969	3.00	6.00	12.00
BLACK AND WHITE RAGTIME, 1921-39				
Biograph 12047	197?	3.00	6.00	12.00
BLOWIN' SESSIONS				
Blue Note BN-LA521-H2 [(2)]	1975	5.00	10.00	20.00
BLOWOUT AT MARDI GRAS				
Cook LP-1084 [M]	1955	10.00	20.00	40.00
BLUE NOTE CLASSICS				
Blue Note B-6509 [M]	1969	3.75	7.50	15.00
BLUE RIBBON COUNTRY				
Capitol STBB 2969 [(2)]	1968	6.25	12.50	25.00
BLUE RIBBON COUNTRY, VOL. 2				
Capitol STBB-217 [(2)]	1969	6.25	12.50	25.00

Label, Number	Yr	VG	VG+	NM
THE BLUES				
Vee Jay VJS-2-1007 [(2)]	1974	5.00	10.00	20.00
Vee Jay LP-1020 [M]	1960	10.00	20.00	40.00
BLUES 'N' FOLK				
Bethlehem BCP-6071 [M]	1963	15.00	30.00	60.00
BLUES FOR TOMORROW				
Riverside RLP 12-243 [M]	1957	10.00	20.00	40.00
BLUES FROM BIG BILL'S COPACABANA				
Chess LP 1533 [M]	1969	6.25	12.50	25.00
—Possibly a reissue of "Folk Festival of the Blues," Argo 4031				
THE BLUES IN MODERN JAZZ				
Atlantic 1337 [M]	1961	5.00	10.00	20.00
—Multicolor label, white "fan" logo at right				
Atlantic 1337 [M]	1963	3.75	7.50	15.00
—Multicolor label, black "fan" logo at right				
Atlantic SD 1337 [R]	1969	3.00	6.00	12.00
THE BLUES IN STEREO				
World Pacific ST-1021 [S]	1959	7.50	15.00	30.00
BLUES LIVE IN BATON ROUGE				
Excello LPS-8021	1971	6.25	12.50	25.00
THE BLUES PROJECT				
Elektra EKL-264 [M]	1964	6.25	12.50	25.00
Elektra EKS-7264 [S]	1964	7.50	15.00	30.00
—No relation to the band of the same name; on one track, Bob Dylan plays piano under the name "Bob Landy"				
BLUES THAT GAVE AMERICA SOUL				
ABC Duke DLPX-82 [S]	1974	3.75	7.50	15.00
Duke DLP-82 [M]	1966	5.00	10.00	20.00
Duke DLPS-82 [S]	1966	6.25	12.50	25.00
BLUES UPTOWN: URBAN BLUES, VOLUME 1				
Imperial LP-94002	1968	5.00	10.00	20.00
BLUESVILLE				
Bethlehem BCP-6038 [M]	1960	7.50	15.00	30.00
THE BLUES, VOLUME 1				
Argo LP-4026 [M]	1963	6.25	12.50	25.00
THE BLUES, VOLUME 2				
Argo LP-4027 [M]	1963	6.25	12.50	25.00
THE BLUES, VOL. 2				
Pacific Jazz JWC-502 [M]	1956	12.50	25.00	50.00
World Pacific JWC-502 [M]	1958	10.00	20.00	40.00
THE BLUES, VOL. 2: HAVE BLUES, WILL TRAVEL				
World Pacific JWC-509 [M]	1958	10.00	20.00	40.00
THE BLUES, VOLUME 3				
Argo LP-4034 [M]	1964	6.25	12.50	25.00
THE BLUES, VOL. 3: BLOWIN' THE BLUES				
World Pacific JWC-512 [M]	1958	10.00	20.00	40.00
World Pacific ST-1029 [S]	1959	7.50	15.00	30.00
THE BLUES, VOLUME 4				
Argo LP-4042 [M]	1964	6.25	12.50	25.00
THE BLUES, VOLUME 5				
Cadet LP-4051 [M]	1966	6.25	12.50	25.00
BODY AND SOUL				
RCA Victor LPV-501	1964	5.00	10.00	20.00
BONING UP ON 'BONES				
EmArcy MG-36038 [M]	1955	12.50	25.00	50.00
BOOGIE WOOGIE				
Decca DL 5248 [10]	1950	12.50	25.00	50.00
BOOGIE WOOGIE KINGS AND QUEENS				
Decca DL 5249 [10]	1950	12.50	25.00	50.00
BOOGIE WOOGIE PIANO				
Brunswick BL 58018 [10]	1950	15.00	30.00	60.00
BOOGIE WOOGIE PIANOS				
Columbia KC 32708	197?	2.50	5.00	10.00
BOOTY				
Mainstream MRL-413	197?	3.00	6.00	12.00
BOPPIN'				
Jubilee JGM-1118 [M]	1960	37.50	75.00	150.00
BOSS GOLDIES — SOUNDS FROM THE GROOVEYARD				
Columbia CL 2559 [M]	1966	5.00	10.00	20.00
Columbia CS 9339 [S]	1966	6.25	12.50	25.00
BOY MEETS GIRL				
Stax STS 2-2024 [(2)]	1969	5.00	10.00	20.00
THE BRIGHTEST STARS OF CHRISTMAS				
RCA Special Products DPL1-0086	1974	5.00	10.00	20.00
—Sold only at JCPenney department stores				
BRITISH FESTIVAL OF JAZZ CONCERT				
Decca DL 5422 [10]	1952	12.50	25.00	50.00

Label, Number	Yr	VG	VG+	NM
BRITISH JAZZ FESTIVAL				
Decca DL 5424 [10]	1952	12.50	25.00	50.00
BRUNSWICK'S GREATEST HITS				
Brunswick BL 754186	1973	5.00	10.00	20.00
BUBBLE GUM MUSIC IS THE NAKED TRUTH, VOLUME 1				
Buddah BDA 5032	1969	6.25	12.50	25.00
BUDDAH'S 360 DEGREE DIAL-A-HIT				
Buddah BDA 5039	1969	7.50	15.00	30.00
—With rotating wheel under the front LP cover				
A BUMPER CROP OF ALL STARS				
King 753 [M]	1961	25.00	50.00	100.00
BUNCH OF GOODIES				
Chess LP 1441 [DJ]	1960	150.00	300.00	600.00
—Multi-color splash vinyl				
Chess LP 1441 [M]	1960	30.00	60.00	120.00
—Black vinyl				
BURBANK				
Warner Bros. PRO 529 [(2)]	1972	6.25	12.50	25.00
—Originals have green labels				
BURBANK'S GREATEST HITS				
Warner Bros. PRO 548	1973	5.00	10.00	20.00
BUSHKIN-SAFRANSKI-WILSON GROUPS				
Allegro 1590 [10]	1955	12.50	25.00	50.00
BYE BYE BIRDIE				
Colpix CP-454 [M]	1963	20.00	40.00	80.00
Colpix SCP-454 [S]	1963	25.00	50.00	100.00
—Studio version performed by Paul Petersen, Shelley Fabares, James Darren, the Marcels and others				
CARLOAD O' HITS				
Muse M-500 [M]	1959	50.00	100.00	200.00
A CARNIVAL OF SONGS				
King 819 [M]	1963	25.00	50.00	100.00
CAROLS AND CANDLELIGHT				
Columbia Special Products P 12525	1974	2.50	5.00	10.00
—Sold only at Goodyear tire dealers				
THE CATS				
New Jazz NJLP-8217 [M]	1959	20.00	40.00	80.00
—Purple label				
New Jazz NJLP-8217 [M]	1965	7.50	15.00	30.00
—Blue label, trident logo at right				
CATS AND JAMMER KIDS				
Angel ANG-60007 [10]	1955	12.50	25.00	50.00
CATS VS. CHICKS				
MGM E-255 [10]	1954	12.50	25.00	50.00
CBS TWO-FERS ARE GREAT MUSICAL VALUES!				
CBS A2S 143/4 [(2) DJ]	1975	5.00	10.00	20.00
CHARLIE PARKER 10TH MEMORIAL CONCERT				
Limelight LM-82017 [M]	1965	3.75	7.50	15.00
Limelight LS-86017 [S]	1965	5.00	10.00	20.00
CHARLIE PARKER MEMORIAL CONCERT				
Cadet 2CA-60002 [(2)]	1971	5.00	10.00	20.00
CHART BUSTERS '62				
Capitol T 1837 [M]	1963	7.50	15.00	30.00
Capitol ST 1837 [S]	1963	10.00	20.00	40.00
CHARTBUSTERS, VOL. 2				
Capitol T 1945 [M]	1963	7.50	15.00	30.00
Capitol ST 1945 [S]	1963	10.00	20.00	40.00
CHARTBUSTERS, VOL. 3				
Capitol T 2006 [M]	1963	7.50	15.00	30.00
Capitol ST 2006 [S]	1963	10.00	20.00	40.00
CHARTBUSTERS, VOL. 4				
Capitol T 2094 [M]	1964	10.00	20.00	40.00
Capitol ST 2094 [S]	1964	15.00	30.00	60.00
CHICAGO'S BOSS TENORS				
Chess CHV-414	1970	3.75	7.50	15.00
CHICAGO AND ALL THAT JAZZ!				
Verve V-8441 [M]	1961	6.25	12.50	25.00
Verve V6-8441 [S]	1962	7.50	15.00	30.00
CHICAGO BLUES ANTHOLOGY				
Chess 2CH-60012 [(2)]	1972	5.00	10.00	20.00
CHICAGO JAZZ ALBUM				
Decca DL 8029 [M]	1954	10.00	20.00	40.00
CHICAGO JAZZ, 1923-29				
Biograph 12005	1968	3.00	6.00	12.00
CHICAGO JAZZ, VOLUME 2, 1925-29				
Biograph 12043	197?	3.00	6.00	12.00

Label, Number	Yr	VG	VG+	NM
CHICAGO SOUTH SIDE				
Historical 10	1968	2.50	5.00	10.00
CHICAGO SOUTH SIDE, VOL. 2				
Historical 30	1969	2.50	5.00	10.00
CHICAGO STYLE JAZZ				
Columbia CL 632 [M]	1955	6.25	12.50	25.00
CHICAGO / AUSTIN HIGH SCHOOL				
RCA Victor LPM-1508 [M]	1957	7.50	15.00	30.00
THE CHICAGOANS				
Decca DL 79231	1968	3.00	6.00	12.00
CHICAGO: THE LIVING LEGENDS, VOL. 1				
Riverside RLP-389 [M]	196?	5.00	10.00	20.00
Riverside RS-9389 [R]	196?	3.00	6.00	12.00
CHICAGO: THE LIVING LEGENDS, VOL. 2				
Riverside RLP-390 [M]	196?	5.00	10.00	20.00
Riverside RS-9390 [R]	196?	3.00	6.00	12.00
A CHILD'S CHRISTMAS				
Harmony HS 14563	197?	3.00	6.00	12.00
CHRISTMAS — A GIFT OF MUSIC				
Capitol Special Markets SL-6687	197?	3.00	6.00	12.00
—Reissue of "Zenith Presents Chrisrmas, A Gift of Music, Vol. 4" with almost identical cover				
CHRISTMAS — THE SEASON OF MUSIC				
Capitol Creative Products SL-6679	1970	3.00	6.00	12.00
—Reissue of "Zenith Presents Christmas, A Gift of Music, Vol. 3" with almost identical cover				
THE CHRISTMAS ALBUM				
Columbia G 30763 [(2)]	1972	3.75	7.50	15.00
CHRISTMAS AMERICA				
Capitol Special Markets SL-6884	1973	3.00	6.00	12.00
—Sold only at Firestone tire dealers (add 50% for sticker that says "Season's Greetings Firestone")				
CHRISTMAS AMERICA, ALBUM TWO				
Capitol Special Markets SL-6950	1974	3.00	6.00	12.00
—Sold only at Firestone tire dealers (add 50% for sticker that says "Season's Greetings Firestone")				
CHRISTMAS AS IT HAPPENED				
Mennonite Hour TR4H-5299/5300 [DJ]	1966	3.00	6.00	12.00
—"A series of seven 'newscasts' of the memorable events leading up to the birth of Jesus Christ"; tracks have locked grooves; possibly issued without a cover				
CHRISTMAS AT HOME				
Capitol Creative Products SL-6530	1967	3.00	6.00	12.00
CHRISTMAS AT OUR HOUSE				
Impact R 3381	1975	3.00	6.00	12.00
—Also contains narration by John T. Benson				
CHRISTMAS CAROUSEL				
Capitol SQBE-94406 [(2)]	1972	3.75	7.50	15.00
—Available only through the Capitol Record Club				
CHRISTMAS CHORUS				
Columbia Special Products CSS 932/3 [(2)]	1969	3.75	7.50	15.00
—Produced for NORM/A Step Ahead				
CHRISTMAS CLASSICS 1963				
E.F. MacDonald EFMX-63	1963	5.00	10.00	20.00
—Special album done by the E.F. MacDonald Company, Dayton, Ohio				
CHRISTMAS DAY IN THE COUNTRY				
Columbia Special Products P 11887	1973	2.50	5.00	10.00
CHRISTMAS DAY WITH COLONEL SANDERS				
RCA Victor PRS-274	1968	5.00	10.00	20.00
—Sold only at Kentucky Fried Chicken restaurants				
CHRISTMAS EVE WITH COLONEL SANDERS				
RCA Victor PRS-256	1967	5.00	10.00	20.00
—Sold only at Kentucky Fried Chicken restaurants				
CHRISTMAS FAVORITES				
RCA Victor PR-115-A [M]	1961	3.75	7.50	15.00
—Sold only at Acme markets (Mid-Atlantic states)				
A CHRISTMAS FESTIVAL				
RCA Record Club CCS-0145 [(2)]	1970	3.75	7.50	15.00
A CHRISTMAS FESTIVAL OF SONGS AND CAROLS				
RCA Victor PRM-170 [M]	1964	3.00	6.00	12.00
—Sold only at JCPenney department stores				
RCA Victor PRS-170 [S]	1964	3.75	7.50	15.00
—Sold only at JCPenney department stores				
A CHRISTMAS FESTIVAL OF SONGS AND CAROLS, VOLUME 2				
RCA Victor PRM-195 [M]	1965	3.00	6.00	12.00
—Sold only at JCPenney department stores				
RCA Victor PRS-195 [S]	1965	3.75	7.50	15.00
—Sold only at JCPenney department stores				
CHRISTMAS GIFT 'RAP				
Motown MS-725	1970	5.00	10.00	20.00
—Reissue of "Merry Christmas from Motown," MS-681				

Label, Number	Yr	VG	VG+	NM
A CHRISTMAS GIFT FOR YOU FROM PHILLES RECORDS				
Philles PHLP-4005 [M]	1963	40.00	80.00	160.00
—First pressings have blue and black labels				
Philles PHLP-4005 [M]	1964	20.00	40.00	80.00
—Second pressings have yellow and red labels				
CHRISTMAS GREETINGS				
Columbia Special Products CSS 1433	1970	2.50	5.00	10.00
Columbia Special Products CSS 1499	1970	2.50	5.00	10.00
—Sold only at A&P grocery stores				
CHRISTMAS GREETINGS FROM NASHVILLE				
RCA Victor APL1-0262	1973	3.00	6.00	12.00
CHRISTMAS GREETINGS, VOL. 2				
Columbia Special Products C 10399	1971	2.50	5.00	10.00
—Sold only at A&P grocery stores				
CHRISTMAS GREETINGS, VOL. 3				
Columbia Special Products P 11383	1972	2.50	5.00	10.00
—Sold only at A&P grocery stores				
CHRISTMAS GREETINGS, VOL. 4				
Columbia Special Products P 11987	1973	3.00	6.00	12.00
—Sold only at A&P grocery stores				
CHRISTMAS HITS FROM WARNER BROS.				
Warner Bros. 8467/8 [DJ]	1959	12.50	25.00	50.00
CHRISTMAS IN CALIFORNIA				
RCA Victor PRS-276	1968	3.00	6.00	12.00
—Available only from Bank of America				
CHRISTMAS IN ENGLAND				
Capitol T 10097 [M]	195?	3.75	7.50	15.00
CHRISTMAS IN ITALY				
Capitol T 10093 [M]	196?	3.75	7.50	15.00
Capitol SM-10093 [R]	197?	2.50	5.00	10.00
CHRISTMAS IN NEW YORK				
RCA Victor PRM-257 [M]	1967	3.00	6.00	12.00
RCA Victor PRS-257 [S]	1967	3.75	7.50	15.00
CHRISTMAS IN NEW YORK VOLUME 2				
RCA Victor PRS-270	1968	3.00	6.00	12.00
CHRISTMAS IN NORWAY				
Capitol T 10377 [M]	196?	3.75	7.50	15.00
CHRISTMAS IN SAN FRANCISCO				
Embarcadero Center EC-101	1974	3.75	7.50	15.00
—Featuring members of the San Francisco, Oakland ans San Jose Symphonies, the San Francisco and Western Operas, etc.; not all tracks have artists identified				
CHRISTMAS IN THE AIR				
RCA Special Products DPL1-0133	1975	2.50	5.00	10.00
CHRISTMAS IS...				
Columbia Special Products P 11417	1972	3.00	6.00	12.00
—Sold only at Goodyear tire dealers				
A CHRISTMAS MUSIC FESTIVAL				
Capitol Creative Products SL-6688	1970	2.50	5.00	10.00
CHRISTMAS NIGHT IN BETHLEHEM: THE MIDNIGHT CEREMONY AT ST. CATHERINE'S CHURCH				
ABC Dunhill DS-55002	1968	3.75	7.50	15.00
—Recording of the 1967 midnight Mass in the Holy Land; with 24-page booklet				
CHRISTMAS PROGRAMMING FROM RCA VICTOR				
RCA Victor SP-33-66 [DJ]	1959	250.00	500.00	1000.
—Promo-only collection; has been counterfeited, but originals have color covers				
THE CHRISTMAS SONG AND OTHER FAVORITES				
Columbia Special Products P 12446	1974	2.50	5.00	10.00
THE CHRISTMAS SOUND OF MUSIC				
Capitol Special Markets SL-6996	1975	2.50	5.00	10.00
THE CHRISTMAS SOUNDS OF MUSIC				
Capitol Creative Products SL-6643	1969	3.00	6.00	12.00
— Sold only at B.F. Goodrich tire dealers				
CHRISTMAS STARS: SUTHERLAND/TEBALDI/PRICE SING BEST LOVED CHRISTMAS FAVORITES				
London OS 26408	1974	3.00	6.00	12.00
CHRISTMAS STOCKING				
Capitol NP 90494 [M]	1965	3.75	7.50	15.00
—Available only through the Capitol Record Club				
Capitol SNP 90494 [S]	1965	3.75	7.50	15.00
—Available only through the Capitol Record Club				
CHRISTMAS THROUGH THE YEARS				
MCA Special Markets DL 734596	197?	3.00	6.00	12.00
—Produced for First Financial Marketing Group				
CHRISTMAS TIME				
Decca DL 34037 [M]	196?	3.75	7.50	15.00
CHRISTMAS TRIMMINGS				
Columbia Special Products P 12795	1975	2.50	5.00	10.00

Label, Number	Yr	VG	VG+	NM
CHRISTMAS WITH ANDY WILLIAMS AND THE WILLIAMS BROTHERS				
Columbia Special Products C 10105	1971	2.50	5.00	10.00
CHRISTMAS WITH COLONEL SANDERS				
RCA Victor PRS-291	1969	5.00	10.00	20.00
—Sold only at Kentucky Fried Chicken restaurants				
CHRISTMAS WITH EDDY ARNOLD/CHRISTMAS WITH HENRY MANCINI				
RCA Special Products DPL1-0079	1974	3.00	6.00	12.00
CHRISTMAS WITH GLEN CAMPBELL AND THE HOLLYWOOD POPS ORCHESTRA				
Capitol Creative Products SL-6699	1971	3.00	6.00	12.00
Capitol Special Markets SL-6699	197?	2.50	5.00	10.00
—Reissue on renamed label				
CHRISTMAS WITH JOHNNY MATHIS AND PERCY FAITH				
Columbia Special Products P 11805	1973	2.50	5.00	10.00
CHRISTMAS WITH JULIE ANDREWS (FEATURING THE YULETIDE CHORISTERS)				
RCA Victor PRS-290	1969	3.00	6.00	12.00
CHRISTMAS WITH NAT KING COLE AND FRED WARING & THE PENNSYLVANIANS				
Capitol Special Markets SL-6883	197?	2.50	5.00	10.00
CHRISTMAS WITH THE STARS				
Capitol Special Markets SL-6931	1973	2.50	5.00	10.00
CHRISTMASTIME IN CAROL AND SONG				
RCA Victor PRM-271 [M]	1968	5.00	10.00	20.00
RCA Victor PRS-271 [S]	1968	3.00	6.00	12.00
RCA Victor PRS-289	1969	3.00	6.00	12.00
CLAMBAKE ON BOURBON STREET				
Cook LP-1085 [10]	1955	12.50	25.00	50.00
CLASSIC BLUES ACCOMPANISTS				
Riverside RLP-1052 [10]	1955	20.00	40.00	80.00
CLASSIC JAZZ PIANO STYLES				
RCA Victor LPV-544 [M]	1967	5.00	10.00	20.00
CLASSICS IN JAZZ				
Capitol T 320 [M]	1954	7.50	15.00	30.00
CLASSICS IN JAZZ: COOL AND QUIET				
Capitol H 371 [10]	1953	12.50	25.00	50.00
CLASSICS IN JAZZ: DIXIELAND STYLISTS				
Capitol H 321 [10]	1952	12.50	25.00	50.00
CLASSICS IN JAZZ: SMALL COMBOS				
Capitol H 322 [10]	1952	12.50	25.00	50.00
CLAY COLE'S BIN OF ORIGINAL GOLDEN OLDIES				
Jubilee JGM-5026 [M]	1964	25.00	50.00	100.00
A COLLECTION OF 16 ORIGINAL BIG HITS, VOLUME 3				
Motown MS 624 [S]	1966	6.25	12.50	25.00
A COLLECTION OF 16 ORIGINAL BIG HITS, VOLUME 5				
Motown MS 651 [S]	1966	5.00	10.00	20.00
A COLLECTION OF 16 ORIGINAL BIG HITS, VOLUME 6				
Motown M 655 [M]	1967	5.00	10.00	20.00
Motown MS 655 [S]	1967	5.00	10.00	20.00
A COLLECTION OF 16 ORIGINAL BIG HITS, VOLUME 7				
Motown M 661 [M]	1967	5.00	10.00	20.00
Motown MS 661 [S]	1967	5.00	10.00	20.00
A COLLECTION OF 16 ORIGINAL BIG HITS, VOLUME 8				
Motown M 666 [M]	1967	5.00	10.00	20.00
Motown MS 666 [S]	1967	5.00	10.00	20.00
A COLLECTION OF 16 ORIGINAL BIG HITS, VOLUME 9				
Motown MS 668	1968	5.00	10.00	20.00
A COLLECTION OF 16 ORIGINAL BIG HITS, VOLUME 10				
Motown MS 684	1969	5.00	10.00	20.00
A COLLECTION OF 16 ORIGINAL BIG HITS, VOLUME 11				
Motown MS 693	1969	5.00	10.00	20.00
COLLECTORS' CHOICE				
Verve V-8408 [M]	1961	—	—	—
—Canceled				
COLLECTORS' ITEMS, 1922-30				
Historical 11	1967	2.50	5.00	10.00
COLLECTORS' ITEMS, 1925-29				
Historical 20	1968	2.50	5.00	10.00
COLLECTORS ITEMS, VOL. 2				
Riverside RLP-1040 [10]	1954	20.00	40.00	80.00
COLLEGE ALBUM				
Verve MGV-8341 [M]	1959	—	—	—
—Canceled				
COLLEGE JAZZ: DIXIELAND				
Columbia CL 736 [M]	1956	5.00	10.00	20.00
COLOR ME OBG: STATION WDRC				
Roulette R 25347 [M]	1967	5.00	10.00	20.00
COLORADO JAZZ PARTY				
BASF 25099 [(2)]	197?	5.00	10.00	20.00
COLUMBIA JAZZ FESTIVAL				
Columbia JJ-1 [M]	1959	6.25	12.50	25.00
COMBO JAZZ				
Jazztone J-1221 [M]	1956	7.50	15.00	30.00
COME CLOSER TO GOD				
Vee Jay LP-5061 [M]	1964	7.50	15.00	30.00
COMPARATIVE BLUES				
Jazztone J-1258 [M]	1957	7.50	15.00	30.00
COMPOSERS AT PLAY: HAROLD ARLEN AND COLE PORTER				
"X" LVA-1003 [M]	1955	10.00	20.00	40.00
THE COMPOSITIONS OF BENNY GOLSON				
Riverside RLP-3505 [M]	1962	3.75	7.50	15.00
Riverside RS-93505 [S]	1962	5.00	10.00	20.00
THE COMPOSITIONS OF BOBBY TIMMONS				
Riverside RLP-3512 [M]	1962	3.75	7.50	15.00
Riverside RS-93512 [S]	1962	5.00	10.00	20.00
THE COMPOSITIONS OF CHARLIE PARKER				
Riverside RLP-3506 [M]	1962	3.75	7.50	15.00
Riverside RS-93506 [S]	1962	5.00	10.00	20.00
THE COMPOSITIONS OF COLE PORTER				
Riverside RM-3515 [M]	1963	3.75	7.50	15.00
Riverside RS-93515 [S]	1963	5.00	10.00	20.00
THE COMPOSITIONS OF DIZZY GILLESPIE				
Riverside RLP-3508 [M]	1962	3.75	7.50	15.00
Riverside RS-93508 [S]	1962	5.00	10.00	20.00
THE COMPOSITIONS OF DUKE ELLINGTON				
Riverside RLP-3507 [M]	1962	3.75	7.50	15.00
Riverside RS-93507 [S]	1962	5.00	10.00	20.00
THE COMPOSITIONS OF DUKE ELLINGTON, VOL. 2				
Riverside RLP-3510 [M]	1962	3.75	7.50	15.00
Riverside RS-93510 [S]	1962	5.00	10.00	20.00
THE COMPOSITIONS OF GEORGE GERSHWIN				
Riverside RM-3517 [M]	1963	3.75	7.50	15.00
Riverside RS-93517 [S]	1963	5.00	10.00	20.00
THE COMPOSITIONS OF HAROLD ARLEN				
Riverside RM-3518 [M]	1963	3.75	7.50	15.00
Riverside RS-93518 [S]	1963	5.00	10.00	20.00
THE COMPOSITIONS OF HORACE SILVER				
Riverside RLP-3509 [M]	1962	3.75	7.50	15.00
Riverside RS-93509 [S]	1962	5.00	10.00	20.00
THE COMPOSITIONS OF IRVING BERLIN				
Riverside RM-3519 [M]	1963	3.75	7.50	15.00
Riverside RS-93519 [S]	1963	5.00	10.00	20.00
THE COMPOSITIONS OF JEROME KERN				
Riverside RM-3516 [M]	1963	3.75	7.50	15.00
Riverside RS-93516 [S]	1963	5.00	10.00	20.00
COMPOSITIONS OF LIONEL HAMPTON				
Crown CLP-5107 [M]	195?	6.25	12.50	25.00
THE COMPOSITIONS OF MILES DAVIS				
Riverside RLP-3504 [M]	1962	3.75	7.50	15.00
Riverside RS-93504 [S]	1962	5.00	10.00	20.00
THE COMPOSITIONS OF RICHARD RODGERS				
Riverside RM-3514 [M]	1963	3.75	7.50	15.00
Riverside RS-93514 [S]	1963	5.00	10.00	20.00
THE COMPOSITIONS OF TADD DAMERON				
Riverside RLP-3511 [M]	1962	3.75	7.50	15.00
Riverside RS-93511 [S]	1962	5.00	10.00	20.00
THE COMPOSITIONS OF THELONIOUS MONK				
Riverside RLP-3503 [M]	1962	3.75	7.50	15.00
Riverside RS-93503 [S]	1962	5.00	10.00	20.00
CONCEPTION				
Prestige PRLP-7013 [M]	1956	25.00	50.00	100.00
CONCERT IN JAZZ				
Tops L-1532 [M]	1958	5.00	10.00	20.00
CONCERT JAZZ				
Brunswick BL 54027 [M]	1956	7.50	15.00	30.00
COOL AND CAREFREE				
Columbia Special Products CSP 119 [M]	1963	3.00	6.00	12.00
—Sold only by Carrier air conditioner dealers				
COOL EUROPE				
MGM E-3157 [M]	1955	7.50	15.00	30.00
COOL GABRIELS				
Groove LG-1003 [M]	1956	15.00	30.00	60.00
COOL JAZZ				
Seeco CELP-465 [M]	1960	5.00	10.00	20.00

Label, Number	Yr	VG	VG+	NM
COOL JAZZ FROM HOLLAND				
Epic LN 1126 [10]	1955	10.00	20.00	40.00
COOLIN'				
New Jazz NJLP-8216 [M]	1959	15.00	30.00	60.00
—Purple label				
New Jazz NJLP-8216 [M]	1965	7.50	15.00	30.00
—Blue label, trident logo at right				
THE CORE OF JAZZ				
MGM SE-4737	1970	3.00	6.00	12.00
COUNTRY AND WESTERN JAMBOREE				
King 697 [M]	1961	37.50	75.00	150.00
COUNTRY CHRISTMAS				
Columbia CS 9888	1968	3.75	7.50	15.00
Columbia Special Products CSS 1434	1970	3.00	6.00	12.00
King 811 [M]	1962	25.00	50.00	100.00
Monument SLP-18125	1969	5.00	10.00	20.00
COUNTRY CHRISTMAS FAVORITES				
Columbia Special Products C 10876	1972	2.50	5.00	10.00
COUNTRY FAIR				
Capitol SWBB-562 [(2)]	1970	6.25	12.50	25.00
COUNTRY HOLIDAY				
Columbia Musical Treasury DS 467	1968	3.75	7.50	15.00
COUNTRY MUSIC BY THE WAYSIDE				
Wayside 1013	1968	5.00	10.00	20.00
COUNTRY MUSIC HOOTENANNY				
Capitol ST 2009 [S]	1963	7.50	15.00	30.00
Capitol T 2009 [M]	1963	6.25	12.50	25.00
COUNTRY MUSIC SPECTACULAR				
Hickory LPM-116 [M]	1963	6.25	12.50	25.00
THE COUNTRY SIDE OF CHRISTMAS/ALL-TIME FAVORITES IN THE TRADITIONAL STYLE				
Capitol Creative Products SL-6586	1968	3.00	6.00	12.00
COUNTRY SPECIAL				
Capitol STBB-402 [(2)]	1969	6.25	12.50	25.00
A COUNTRY STYLE CHRISTMAS				
Columbia Musical Treasury 3P 6316 [(3)]	1975	3.75	7.50	15.00
COUNTRY & WESTERN CLASSICS 1955				
Economic Consultants 1955	1973	5.00	10.00	20.00
COUNTRY & WESTERN CLASSICS 1956				
Economic Consultants 1956	1973	5.00	10.00	20.00
COUNTRY & WESTERN CLASSICS 1957				
Economic Consultants 1957	1973	5.00	10.00	20.00
COUNTRY & WESTERN CLASSICS 1958				
Economic Consultants 1958	1973	5.00	10.00	20.00
CRITICS' CHOICE				
Dawn DLP-1123 [M]	1958	20.00	40.00	80.00
CRUISIN'				
Jazzland JLP-7 [M]	1960	6.25	12.50	25.00
Jazzland JLP-97 [S]	1960	7.50	15.00	30.00
D'OES CRAZY OLDIES				
Oldies 33 OL-8007 [M]	1964	6.25	12.50	25.00
DANCE BAND HITS				
RCA Victor LPT-2 [10]	1951	10.00	20.00	40.00
DANCE DISCOTHEQUE				
Decca DL 4556 [M]	1964	3.75	7.50	15.00
Decca DL 4556 [M]	1964	3.75	7.50	15.00
Decca DL 74556 [S]	1964	5.00	10.00	20.00
DANCE ON THE WILD SIDE				
Chancellor CHL-5028 [M]	1962	6.25	12.50	25.00
Chancellor CHLS-5028 [S]	1962	7.50	15.00	30.00
DANCE THE ROCK & ROLL				
Atlantic 8013 [M]	1957	20.00	40.00	80.00
DANCE TO THE BANDS				
Capitol TBO 727 [(2) M]	1956	10.00	20.00	40.00
Capitol T 977 [M]	1958	5.00	10.00	20.00
DANCE TUNES FROM THE VAULT, VOLUME 2				
Chess LP 1476 [M]	1962	10.00	20.00	40.00
DANCE, BE HAPPY!				
Columbia CL 967 [M]	1957	5.00	10.00	20.00
DANCING WITH THE STARS				
Epic LN 3136 [M]	1955	7.50	15.00	30.00
DARK MUDDY BOTTOM BLUES				
Specialty SPS-2149	1971	5.00	10.00	20.00
DAS IS JAZZ!				
Decca DL 8229 [M]	1956	7.50	15.00	30.00
A DATE WITH GREATNESS				
Imperial LP-9188A [M]	1962	12.50	25.00	50.00
—Features Aladdin tracks by Coleman Hawkins, Howard McGhee and Lester Young				
Imperial LP-12188A [R]	1962	6.25	12.50	25.00
A DATE WITH RIVERSIDE				
Riverside S-4 [M]	195?	10.00	20.00	40.00
A DAY IN THE COUNTRY				
Audio Lab AL-1519 [M]	1959	20.00	40.00	80.00
DAYS OF WINE AND VINYL				
Warner Bros. PRO 540 [(2)]	1973	7.50	15.00	30.00
DECADE OF JAZZ, VOLUME 1, 1939-49				
Blue Note BN-LA158-G2 [(2)]	1974	3.75	7.50	15.00
DECADE OF JAZZ, VOLUME 2, 1949-59				
Blue Note BN-LA159-G2 [(2)]	1974	3.75	7.50	15.00
DECADE OF JAZZ, VOLUME 3, 1959-69				
Blue Note BN-LA160-G2 [(2)]	1974	3.75	7.50	15.00
DEEP EAR				
Warner Bros. PRO 591 [(2)]	1974	6.25	12.50	25.00
THE DEFINITIVE JAZZ SCENE, VOL. 1				
ABC Impulse! AS-99 [S]	1968	3.00	6.00	12.00
Impulse! A-99 [M]	1966	3.75	7.50	15.00
Impulse! AS-99 [S]	1966	5.00	10.00	20.00
THE DEFINITIVE JAZZ SCENE, VOL. 2				
ABC Impulse! AS-100 [S]	1968	3.00	6.00	12.00
Impulse! A-100 [M]	1966	3.75	7.50	15.00
Impulse! AS-100 [S]	1966	5.00	10.00	20.00
THE DEFINITIVE JAZZ SCENE, VOL. 3				
ABC Impulse! AS-9101 [S]	1968	3.00	6.00	12.00
Impulse! A-9101 [M]	1966	3.75	7.50	15.00
Impulse! AS-9101 [S]	1966	5.00	10.00	20.00
DEL-FI ALBUM SAMPLER				
Del-Fi (no #) [DJ]	1959	125.00	250.00	500.00
—Green vinyl, promo only, with paper sleeve				
DEL-FI RECORD HOP				
Del-Fi DFLP-1210 [M]	1959	20.00	40.00	80.00
DEMAND PERFORMANCES				
Monument MLP-8010 [M]	1963	6.25	12.50	25.00
Monument SLP-18010 [S]	1963	10.00	20.00	40.00
DEMONSTRATION RECORD — DISC JOCKEYS — JAN.-FEB. 1955				
Capitol PRO-213 [DJ]	1955	10.00	20.00	40.00
DIAL A HIT				
Bell 6030	1969	5.00	10.00	20.00
DICK CLARK: 20 YEARS OF ROCK N' ROLL				
Buddah BDS 5133 [(2)]	1973	5.00	10.00	20.00
—Gatefold cover with booklet and bonus 7-inch cardboard record				
Buddah BDS 5133 [(2)]	1974	2.50	5.00	10.00
—With none of the extras				
DISCO-TEEN '66				
Columbia Record Club D 155 [M]	1966	5.00	10.00	20.00
Columbia Record Club DS 155 [S]	1966	12.50	25.00	50.00
—Sought-after for its otherwise unavailable extended stereo mix of Bob Dylan's "Positively 4th Street"				
DISPLAY CASE #10				
Warner Bros. PRO 542 [(3)]	1973	7.50	15.00	30.00
DISPLAY CASE #8				
Warner Bros. PRO 532 [(2)]	1972	7.50	15.00	30.00
DISPLAY CASE #9				
Warner Bros. PRO 538 [(2)]	1972	7.50	15.00	30.00
DIXIE LAND U.S.A.				
Promenade 2134 [M]	195?	3.75	7.50	15.00
DIXIELAND — NEW ORLEANS				
Mainstream S-6003 [R]	1965	3.00	6.00	12.00
Mainstream 56003 [M]	1965	6.25	2.50	25.00
DIXIELAND AT CARNEGIE HALL				
Forum SF-9011 [S]	196?	6.25	12.50	25.00
Forum F-9011 [M]	196?	5.00	10.00	20.00
Roulette R 25038 [M]	1958	7.50	15.00	30.00
—Originals have a black label				
Roulette R 25038 [M]	1959	5.00	10.00	20.00
—Second pressings have a white label with colored spokes				
DIXIELAND AT ITS BEST				
RCA Camden CAL-838 [M]	1964	3.00	6.00	12.00
RCA Camden CAS-838 [R]	1964	2.50	5.00	10.00
DIXIELAND AT JAZZ, LTD.				
Atlantic 1261 [M]	1957	10.00	20.00	40.00
—Black label				
Atlantic 1261 [M]	1961	6.25	12.50	25.00
—Multicolor label, white "fan" logo at right				
DIXIELAND AT JAZZ, LTD., VOL. 1				
Atlantic ALS-139 [10]	1952	15.00	30.00	60.00

Label, Number	Yr	VG	VG+	NM
DIXIELAND AT JAZZ, LTD., VOL. 2				
Atlantic ALS-140 [10]	1952	15.00	30.00	60.00
DIXIELAND CLASSICS				
Jazztone J-1216 [M]	1956	7.50	15.00	30.00
DIXIELAND CONTRASTS				
Jazzman LJ-334 [M]	1954	7.50	15.00	30.00
DIXIELAND DETOUR				
Capitol H 312 [10]	1952	12.50	25.00	50.00
DIXIELAND FESTIVAL, VOL. 1				
Vik LX-1057 [M]	1956	7.50	15.00	30.00
DIXIELAND HITS				
Swingville SVLP-2040 [M]	1962	10.00	20.00	40.00
—Purple label				
Swingville SVLP-2040 [M]	1965	5.00	10.00	20.00
—Blue label, trident logo at right				
DIXIELAND IN OLD NEW ORLEANS				
Golden Crest GC-3021 [M]	1958	5.00	10.00	20.00
DIXIELAND JAZZ				
Audiophile XL-325 [M]	1954	7.50	15.00	30.00
Audiophile XL-330 [M]	1954	7.50	15.00	30.00
Grand Award GA 33-310 [M]	1955	15.00	30.00	60.00
—With wrap-around outer cover				
Grand Award GA 33-310 [M]	1955	6.25	12.50	25.00
—Without wrap-around outer cover				
DIXIELAND JAZZ GEMS				
Commodore FL-20010 [10]	1950	12.50	25.00	50.00
DIXIELAND MAIN STREAM				
Savoy MG-12213 [M]	196?	5.00	10.00	20.00
DIXIELAND RHYTHM KINGS				
Paradox LP-6002 [10]	1951	12.50	25.00	50.00
DIXIELAND SERIES, VOL. 1				
Savoy MG-15005 [10]	1952	20.00	40.00	80.00
DIXIELAND SERIES, VOL. 2				
Savoy MG-15009 [10]	1952	20.00	40.00	80.00
DIXIELAND VS. BIRDLAND				
MGM E-231 [10]	1954	12.50	25.00	50.00
DIXIE, LONDON STYLE				
London LL 1337 [M]	1956	5.00	10.00	20.00
DIZZY ATMOSPHERE				
Specialty LP-2110 [M]	1957	10.00	20.00	40.00
DOO WOP				
Specialty SPS-2114	1969	5.00	10.00	20.00
DOUBLE BARREL JAZZ				
Bethlehem BCP-87 [M]	1958	7.50	15.00	30.00
DOWN BEAT'S HALL OF FAME, VOL. 1				
Verve MGV-8320 [M]	1959	12.50	25.00	50.00
Verve V-8320 [M]	1961	5.00	10.00	20.00
DOWN BEAT CRITICS POLL WINNERS				
Clef MGC-742 [M]	1955	—	—	—
—Canceled				
DOWN BEAT JAZZ CONCERT				
Dot DLP-9003 [M]	1958	7.50	15.00	30.00
Dot DLP-29003 [S]	1958	6.25	12.50	25.00
DOWN BEAT JAZZ CONCERT, VOL. 2				
Dot DLP-3188 [M]	1959	7.50	15.00	30.00
Dot DLP-25188 [S]	1959	6.25	12.50	25.00
DOWN HOME STOMP: RURAL BLUES, VOLUME 3				
Imperial LP-94006	1968	5.00	10.00	20.00
DREAMING ON THE RIVER TO NEW ORLEANS				
Southland SLP-238	1963	3.75	7.50	15.00
THE DRUMS				
ABC Impulse! AS-9272 [(3)]	197?	5.00	10.00	20.00
DRUMS ON FIRE				
World Pacific WP-1247 [M]	1958	10.00	20.00	40.00
THE DUTCH EXPLOSION				
White Whale WWS-7130	1970	7.50	15.00	30.00
EARLY AND RARE: CLASSIC JAZZ "COLLECTORS ITEMS"				
Riverside RLP 12-134 [M]	1957	10.00	20.00	40.00
EARLY JAZZ GREATS, VOL. 1				
Jazztone J-1249 [M]	1957	7.50	15.00	30.00
EARLY JAZZ GREATS, VOL. 2				
Jazztone J-1252 [M]	1957	7.50	15.00	30.00
EARTHY!				
Prestige PRLP-7102 [M]	1957	25.00	50.00	100.00
THE EAST COAST JAZZ SCENE, VOL. 1				
Coral CRL 57035 [M]	1956	12.50	25.00	50.00

Label, Number	Yr	VG	VG+	NM
EASY LISTENING				
Audiophile AP-27 [M]	1953	7.50	15.00	30.00
Audiophile AP-38 [M]	1953	7.50	15.00	30.00
Audiophile XL-327 [M]	1954	7.50	15.00	30.00
ECHOES OF NEW ORLEANS				
Southland SLP-239	1963	3.75	7.50	15.00
EIGHT WAYS TO JAZZ				
Riverside RLP 12-272 [M]	1958	7.50	15.00	30.00
ELEKTRA'S BEST, VOLUME 1: 1966-1968				
Elektra EB-1 [(2)]	1969	6.25	12.50	25.00
—Promo only, red labels				
ENCYCLOPEDIA OF JAZZ IN THE '60'S, VOL. 1				
Verve V-8677 [M]	1966	3.75	7.50	15.00
Verve V6-8677 [S]	1966	5.00	10.00	20.00
THE ENCYCLOPEDIA OF JAZZ ON RECORDS				
Decca DXF 140 [(4) M]	1957	25.00	50.00	100.00
—Box set; individually issued as Decca 8398, 8399, 8400 and 8401				
THE ENCYCLOPEDIA OF JAZZ ON RECORDS, VOL. 1: JAZZ OF THE TWENTIES				
Decca DL 8398 [M]	1957	5.00	10.00	20.00
THE ENCYCLOPEDIA OF JAZZ ON RECORDS, VOL. 2: JAZZ OF THE THIRTIES				
Decca DL 8399 [M]	1957	5.00	10.00	20.00
THE ENCYCLOPEDIA OF JAZZ ON RECORDS, VOL. 3: JAZZ OF THE FORTIES				
Decca DL 8400 [M]	1957	5.00	10.00	20.00
THE ENCYCLOPEDIA OF JAZZ ON RECORDS, VOL. 4: JAZZ OF THE FIFTIES				
Decca DL 8401 [M]	1957	5.00	10.00	20.00
END OF AN ERA: RHYTHM 'N' BLUES, VOLUME 1				
Imperial LP-94003	1968	5.00	10.00	20.00
ENERGY ESSENTIALS				
ABC Impulse! ASD-9228 [(3)]	197?	5.00	10.00	20.00
ENGLAND'S GREATEST HIT MAKERS				
London PS 430 [R]	1965	5.00	10.00	20.00
London LL 3430 [M]	1965	6.25	12.50	25.00
ENGLAND'S GREATEST HITS				
Fontana MGF 27570 [M]	1967	12.50	25.00	50.00
—With poster				
Fontana MGF 27570 [M]	1967	10.00	20.00	40.00
—Without poster				
Fontana SRF 67570 [R]	1967	7.50	15.00	30.00
—With poster				
Fontana SRF 67570 [R]	1967	5.00	10.00	20.00
—Without poster				
ERA OF THE CLARINET				
Mainstream S-6011 [R]	1965	3.00	6.00	12.00
Mainstream 56011 [M]	1965	6.25	12.50	25.00
ESCAPADE REVIEWS THE JAZZ SCENE				
Liberty SL-9005 [M]	1957	7.50	15.00	30.00
ESCAPE				
Gene Norman GNP-27 [M]	1958	6.25	12.50	25.00
ESQUIRE'S ALL-AMERICAN HOT JAZZ				
RCA Victor LPV-544 [M]	1967	5.00	10.00	20.00
ESQUIRE'S WORLD OF JAZZ				
Capitol TBO 1970 [(2) M]	1963	5.00	10.00	20.00
Capitol STBO 1970 [(2) S]	1963	5.00	10.00	20.00
THE ESSENTIAL JAZZ VOCALS				
Verve V-8505 [M]	1963	5.00	10.00	20.00
Verve V6-8505 [S]	1963	6.25	12.50	25.00
AN EVENING OF JAZZ				
Norgran MGN-1065 [M]	1956	20.00	40.00	80.00
Verve MGV-8155 [M]	1957	7.50	15.00	30.00
Verve V-8155 [M]	1961	5.00	10.00	20.00
EVERYBODY'S FAVORITE BLUES				
King 875 [M]	1963	17.50	35.00	70.00
EVERYBODY'S GONE SURFIN'				
Parkway P-7035 [M]	1963	12.50	25.00	50.00
THE EXCELLO STORY				
Excello LPS-8025 [(2)]	1972	6.25	12.50	25.00
THE EXCITING NEW LIVERPOOL SOUND				
Columbia CL 2172 [M]	1964	7.50	15.00	30.00
EXPLOSIVE!				
Liberty MM-412 [DJ]	1962	12.50	25.00	50.00
—Promo-only release				
FABULOUS FAVORITES OF OUR TIME				
Liberty LRP-3223 [M]	1962	5.00	10.00	20.00
Liberty LST-7223 [S]	1962	6.25	12.50	25.00
FAMILY CHRISTMAS FAVORITES FROM BING CROSBY AND THE COLUMBUS BOYCHOIR				
Decca DL 34487	1967	3.75	7.50	15.00
—Sold only at Safeway grocery stores				

Label, Number	Yr	VG	VG+	NM
FAMILY PORTRAIT				
A&M SP-19002	1968	5.00	10.00	20.00
FANFARE OF HITS				
Argo LP-656 [M]	1960	6.25	12.50	25.00
FAVORITE CHRISTMAS CAROLS FROM THE VOICE OF FIRESTONE				
Firestone MLP 7005 [M]	1962	3.75	7.50	15.00
—Sold only at Firestone tire dealers; actually Volume 1 of the "Firestone Presents..." series				
FAVORITE SACRED SONGS				
King 556 [M]	1956	37.50	75.00	150.00
THE FEMININE TOUCH				
Decca DL 5486 [10]	1953	12.50	25.00	50.00
Decca DL 8316 [M]	1956	7.50	15.00	30.00
FIFTEEN STAR SAXOPHONES				
Bethlehem BCP-6035 [M]	1959	7.50	15.00	30.00
FIFTY CHRISTMAS FAVORITES				
RCA Camden CXS-9025 [(2)]	1972	3.75	7.50	15.00
FILL YOUR HEAD WITH JAZZ				
Columbia G 30217 [(2)]	1971	3.75	7.50	15.00
FILLET OF SOUL				
Stax STS 3021	1972	5.00	10.00	20.00
FILM MUSIC FROM FRANCE				
Philips PHM 200071 [M]	1962	5.00	10.00	20.00
Philips PHS 600071 [S]	1962	7.50	15.00	30.00
FINK ALONG WITH MAD				
Big Top 12-1306 [M]	1962	25.00	50.00	100.00
FIRESTONE PRESENTS YOUR CHRISTMAS FAVORITES, VOLUME 3				
Firestone MLP 7008 [M]	1964	3.75	7.50	15.00
—Sold only at Firestone tire dealers				
Firestone SLP 7008 [S]	1964	4.00	8.00	16.00
—Sold only at Firestone tire dealers				
FIRESTONE PRESENTS YOUR CHRISTMAS FAVORITES, VOLUME 7				
Firestone CSLP 7015	1968	3.00	6.00	12.00
—Sold only at Firestone tire dealers				
FIRESTONE PRESENTS YOUR FAVORITE CHRISTMAS CAROLS, VOLUME 2				
Firestone MLP 7006 [M]	1963	3.75	7.50	15.00
—Sold only at Firestone tire dealers				
Firestone SLP 7006 [S]	1963	4.00	8.00	16.00
—Sold only at Firestone tire dealers				
FIRESTONE PRESENTS YOUR FAVORITE CHRISTMAS MUSIC, VOLUME 4				
Firestone MLP 7011 [M]	1965	3.00	6.00	12.00
—Sold only at Firestone tire dealers				
Firestone SLP 7011 [S]	1965	3.75	7.50	15.00
—Sold only at Firestone tire dealers				
FIRESTONE PRESENTS YOUR FAVORITE CHRISTMAS MUSIC, VOLUME 5				
Firestone MLP 7012 [M]	1966	3.00	6.00	12.00
—Sold only at Firestone tire dealers				
Firestone SLP 7012 [S]	1966	3.75	7.50	15.00
—Sold only at Firestone tire dealers				
FIRESTONE PRESENTS YOUR FAVORITE CHRISTMAS MUSIC, VOLUME 6				
Firestone MLP 7014 [M]	1967	2.50	5.00	10.00
—Sold only at Firestone tire dealers				
Firestone SLP 7014 [S]	1967	3.00	6.00	12.00
—Sold only at Firestone tire dealers				
FIRST ALBUM OF JAZZ				
Folkways FP-712 [10]	1951	12.50	25.00	50.00
FIRST CHRISTMAS RECORD FOR CHILDREN				
Harmony HS 14554	197?	3.00	6.00	12.00
THE FIRST GREAT ROCK FESTIVALS OF THE SEVENTIES: ISLE OF WIGHT/ ATLANTA POP FESTIVAL				
Columbia G3X 30805 [(3)]	1971	6.25	12.50	25.00
FIVE FEET OF SWING				
Decca DL 8045 [M]	1954	10.00	20.00	40.00
THE FOLK BOX				
Elektra EKL-9001 [(4)]	1964	12.50	25.00	50.00
FOLK FESTIVAL				
Elektra SMP 2 [M]	1956	7.50	15.00	30.00
FOLK FESTIVAL OF THE BLUES				
Argo LP-4031 [M]	1964	10.00	20.00	40.00
FOLK POPS 'N JAZZ SAMPLER				
Elektra SMP 3 [M]	1957	6.25	12.50	25.00
FOLK SAMPLER FIVE				
Elektra SMP 5 [M]	196?	6.25	12.50	25.00
THE FOLK SCENE				
Elektra SMP 6 [M]	196?	6.25	12.50	25.00
FOLKSONG '65				
Elektra SMP 8 [M]	1965	5.00	10.00	20.00
Elektra S 78 [S]	1965	6.25	12.50	25.00

Label, Number	Yr	VG	VG+	NM
FOOTNOTES TO JAZZ, VOL. 2: ANATOMY OF A JAZZ COMPOSITION				
Folkways FP-31 [10]	1951	12.50	25.00	50.00
FOOTPRINTS IN TIME				
White Whale WWS-7125	1970	6.25	12.50	25.00
FOR A MUSICAL MERRY CHRISTMAS				
RCA Victor PR-149A [M]	1963	3.00	6.00	12.00
—Sold only at Acme Markets (Mid-Atlantic states)				
FOR A MUSICAL MERRY CHRISTMAS, VOL. TWO				
RCA Victor PRM 189 [M]	1965	3.00	6.00	12.00
—Sold only at B.F. Goodrich tire dealers				
RCA Victor PRS 189 [S]	1965	3.75	7.50	15.00
—Sold only at B.F. Goodrich tire dealers				
FOR A MUSICAL MERRY CHRISTMAS, VOLUME 3				
RCA Victor PRM-221 [M]	1966	3.00	6.00	12.00
—Sold only at B.F. Goodrich tire dealers				
RCA Victor PRS-221 [S]	1966	3.75	7.50	15.00
—Sold only at B.F. Goodrich tire dealers				
FOR A MUSICAL MERRY CHRISTMAS, VOLUME 4				
RCA Victor PRS-253	1967	3.00	6.00	12.00
—Sold only at B.F. Goodrich tire dealers				
FOR DANCERS ONLY				
Epic LN 3120 [M]	1955	7.50	15.00	30.00
FOR JAZZ LOVERS				
EmArcy MG-36086 [M]	1956	10.00	20.00	40.00
FOR TWISTERS ONLY				
Ace LP-1020 [M]	1962	17.50	35.00	70.00
THE FORCE				
Warner Bros. PRO 593	1974	5.00	10.00	20.00
Warner Bros. PRO 596 [(2)]	1974	6.25	12.50	25.00
FORD HOOTENANNY				
RCA Victor PRM-152 [M]	1964	5.00	10.00	20.00
—Sold only at Ford dealers				
FORGOTTEN MILLION SELLERS				
King 792 [M]	1962	25.00	50.00	100.00
FORTY GOSPEL GREATS				
Vee Jay VJS-2-19000 [(2)]	1975	6.25	12.50	25.00
FOUR ALTOS				
Prestige PRLP-7116 [M]	1957	25.00	50.00	100.00
FOUR FRENCH HORNS				
Savoy MG-12173 [M]	1961	12.50	25.00	50.00
THE FOUR MOST GUITARS				
ABC-Paramount ABC-109 [M]	1956	7.50	15.00	30.00
Paramount LP-109 [10]	1954	15.00	30.00	60.00
THE FOUR ROSES DANCE PARTY				
Columbia Special Products XTV 68933/4 [M]	1961	3.75	7.50	15.00
FOUR TO GO				
Columbia CL 2018 [M]	1963	5.00	10.00	20.00
Columbia CS 8818 [S]	1963	3.75	7.50	15.00
FRANK BULL AND GENE NORMAN PRESENT DIXIELAND JUBILEE				
Decca DL 7022 [10]	1952	12.50	25.00	50.00
FRENCH TOAST				
Angel ANG-60009 [10]	1956	12.50	25.00	50.00
FROM DAVID FROST AND BILLY TAYLOR...MERRY CHRISTMAS				
Bell 6053	1970	3.75	7.50	15.00
FROM UNDER THE CHRISTMAS TREE				
Capitol Creative Products SL-6589	1968	3.00	6.00	12.00
FUNKY BLUES NO. 2				
American Recording Society G-404 [M]	1956	7.50	15.00	30.00
GARDEN OF DELIGHTS				
Elektra S3 10 [(3)]	1971	5.00	10.00	20.00
—Butterfly labels, possibly promo only				
GARY MOORE PRESENTS "MY KIND OF MUSIC"				
Columbia CL 717 [M]	1956	6.25	12.50	25.00
GEMS OF JAZZ, VOL. 1				
Decca DL 5133 [10]	1950	12.50	25.00	50.00
Decca DL 8039 [M]	1954	10.00	20.00	40.00
GEMS OF JAZZ, VOL. 2				
Decca DL 5134 [10]	1950	12.50	25.00	50.00
Decca DL 8040 [M]	1954	10.00	20.00	40.00
GEMS OF JAZZ, VOL. 3				
Decca DL 5383 [10]	1952	12.50	25.00	50.00
Decca DL 8041 [M]	1954	10.00	20.00	40.00
GEMS OF JAZZ, VOL. 4				
Decca DL 5384 [10]	1952	12.50	25.00	50.00
Decca DL 8042 [M]	1954	10.00	20.00	40.00
GEMS OF JAZZ, VOL. 5				
Decca DL 8043 [M]	1954	10.00	20.00	40.00

Label, Number	Yr	VG	VG+	NM
GENE NORMAN PRESENTS JUST JAZZ				
RCA Victor LPM-3102 [10]	1953	12.50	25.00	50.00
GERRY GOFFIN AND CAROLE KING: SOLID GOLD				
Screen Gems/Columbia CPL-713 [DJ]	1975	5.00	10.00	20.00
—Promo-only compilation of oldies sent to radio to spur airplay on songs owned by this publishing house				
GET IT TOGETHER				
Mainstream MRL-350	197?	3.00	6.00	12.00
GIANTS OF BOOGIE WOOGIE				
Riverside RLP 12-106 [M]	1956	10.00	20.00	40.00
GIANTS OF JAZZ				
American Recording Society G-401 [M]	1956	7.50	15.00	30.00
Columbia CL 1970 [M]	1963	7.50	15.00	30.00
GIANTS OF JAZZ ORGAN				
King 837 [M]	1963	30.00	60.00	120.00
GIANTS OF JAZZ VOL. 2				
American Recording Society G-444 [M]	1957	7.50	15.00	30.00
GIANTS OF SMALL BAND SWING, VOL. 1				
Riverside RLP 12-143 [M]	1957	10.00	20.00	40.00
GIANTS OF SMALL BAND SWING, VOL. 2				
Riverside RLP 12-145 [M]	1957	10.00	20.00	40.00
THE GIFT OF CHRISTMAS				
Columbia Special Products C 10018	1971	3.00	6.00	12.00
—Sold only at Ace hardware stores (sticker on lower right front cover)				
Columbia Special Products P 11648	1973	2.50	5.00	10.00
—Same contents and order as "The Gift of Christmas," C 10018; oddly, the record calls this "The Gift of Christmas -- Volume II"!				
THE GIFT OF CHRISTMAS, VOLUME I				
Columbia Special Products CSS 706	1968	3.00	6.00	12.00
—Produced for First Financial Marketing Group				
THE GIRLS SING				
Savoy MG-12220 [M]	196?	5.00	10.00	20.00
THE GLORY OF CHRISTMAS				
Columbia Musical Treasury P3S 5356 [(3)]	196?	3.75	7.50	15.00
—Performed by anonymous musicians				
GOIN' UP THE COUNTRY: RURAL BLUES, VOLUME 1				
Imperial LP-94000	1968	5.00	10.00	20.00
GOLD HITS				
Warwick W 2008 [M]	1959	20.00	40.00	80.00
—Reissue of "Goodies But Oldies, Volume 2"; this title still appears on the label				
GOLD SOUL				
Stax STS 2031	1970	5.00	10.00	20.00
THE GOLDEN AGE OF RHYTHM AND BLUES				
Chess 2CH-50030 [(2)]	1972	6.25	12.50	25.00
GOLDEN ECHOES				
Arvee A-433 [M]	1962	6.25	12.50	25.00
Arvee SA-433 [S]	1962	7.50	15.00	30.00
GOLDEN ENCORES				
Cadence CLP-3043 [M]	1960	10.00	20.00	40.00
THE GOLDEN ERA OF JAZZ, VOL. 1				
Savoy MG-15015 [10]	1952	20.00	40.00	80.00
THE GOLDEN ERA OF JAZZ, VOL. 2				
Savoy MG-15018 [10]	1952	20.00	40.00	80.00
GOLDEN GASSERS				
Chess LP 1458 USA [M]	1961	30.00	60.00	120.00
—National version; see listings in this section under "KYA," "Murray the K" and "WAMO" for regional releases				
THE GOLDEN GLOW OF CHRISTMAS				
Columbia Special Products C 10925	1972	3.00	6.00	12.00
—Sold only at JCPenney department stores				
GOLDEN GOODIES OF 1963, VOL. 18				
Roulette R 25247 [M]	1964	5.00	10.00	20.00
GOLDEN GOODIES, VOL. 1				
Roulette R 25207 [M]	1963	6.25	12.50	25.00
GOLDEN GOODIES, VOL. 2				
Roulette R 25210 [M]	1963	6.25	12.50	25.00
GOLDEN GOODIES, VOL. 3				
Roulette R 25218 [M]	1963	6.25	12.50	25.00
GOLDEN GOODIES, VOL. 4: GOODIES FOR A DANCE PARTY				
Roulette R 25209 [M]	1963	6.25	12.50	25.00
GOLDEN GOODIES, VOL. 5				
Roulette R 25215 [M]	1963	6.25	12.50	25.00
GOLDEN GOODIES, VOL. 6				
Roulette R 25216 [M]	1963	6.25	12.50	25.00
GOLDEN GOODIES, VOL. 7				
Roulette R 25212 [M]	1963	6.25	12.50	25.00

Label, Number	Yr	VG	VG+	NM
GOLDEN GOODIES, VOL. 8				
Roulette R 25214 [M]	1963	6.25	12.50	25.00
GOLDEN GOODIES, VOL. 9				
Roulette R 25213 [M]	1963	6.25	12.50	25.00
GOLDEN GOODIES, VOL. 10				
Roulette R 25217 [M]	1963	6.25	12.50	25.00
GOLDEN GOODIES, VOL. 11				
Roulette R 25219 [M]	1963	6.25	12.50	25.00
GOLDEN GOODIES, VOL. 12				
Roulette R 25211 [M]	1963	6.25	12.50	25.00
GOLDEN GOODIES, VOL. 14				
Roulette R 25239 [M]	1964	5.00	10.00	20.00
GOLDEN GOODIES, VOL. 15				
Roulette R 25240 [M]	1964	5.00	10.00	20.00
GOLDEN GOODIES, VOL. 16				
Roulette R 25241 [M]	1964	5.00	10.00	20.00
GOLDEN GOODIES, VOL. 17				
Roulette R 25242 [M]	1964	5.00	10.00	20.00
GOLDEN GREATS				
Liberty LRP-3500 [M]	1967	3.75	7.50	15.00
Liberty LST-7500 [P]	1967	5.00	10.00	20.00
THE GOLDEN GROUPS				
Specialty SPS-2155	1972	5.00	10.00	20.00
GOLDEN HITS FROM THE GANG AT BANG				
Bang BLP-215 [M]	1967	5.00	10.00	20.00
Bang BLPS-215 [P]	1967	6.25	12.50	25.00
GOLDEN INSTRUMENTALS				
Dot DLP-3820 [M]	1967	6.25	12.50	25.00
Dot DLP-25820 [S]	1967	6.25	12.50	25.00
GOLDEN JAZZ INTRSUMENTALS				
Bethlehem BCP-6065 [M]	1962	6.25	12.50	25.00
GOLDEN SOUVENIRS				
United Artists UAL-3317 [M]	1963	6.25	12.50	25.00
United Artists UAS-6317 [S]	1963	7.50	15.00	30.00
GOLDEN TEEN HITS				
Liberty L-5505 [M]	1962	10.00	20.00	40.00
GOLDEN TREASURE CHEST				
United Artists UAL-3314 [M]	1963	6.25	12.50	25.00
United Artists UAS-6314 [S]	1963	7.50	15.00	30.00
GONE BUT NOT FORGOTTEN				
Class LP-5004 [M]	1959	25.00	50.00	100.00
Rendezvous M-1314 [M]	196?	10.00	20.00	40.00
—Reissue of Class 5004				
GOOD GUY JACK SPECTOR PRESENTS 22 ORIGINAL WINNERS				
Roulette R 25254 [M]	1964	5.00	10.00	20.00
THE GOOD OLD 50'S				
Atco 33-118 [M]	1960	15.00	30.00	60.00
GOODIES BUT OLDIES VOLUME 2				
Warwick W 2008 [M]	1959	30.00	60.00	120.00
—Original title of LP appears on both cover and label; reissued as "Gold Hits" -- and there was no Volume 1!				
GOSPEL HOOTENANNY				
Imperial LP-9240 [M]	1963	5.00	10.00	20.00
Imperial LP-12240 [S]	1963	6.25	12.50	25.00
GOSPEL STARS IN CONCERT				
Specialty SPS-2153	1971	5.00	10.00	20.00
GRAFFITI GOLD				
Vee Jay VJS-2-9000 [(2)]	1974	5.00	10.00	20.00
THE GREAT BANDS				
Columbia Musical Treasury P2M 5267 [(2)]	1968	5.00	10.00	20.00
GREAT BLUES				
Riverside RLP-1074 [10]	1955	20.00	40.00	80.00
GREAT BLUES SINGERS				
Riverside RLP 12-121 [M]	1957	10.00	20.00	40.00
Riverside RLP-1032 [10]	1954	20.00	40.00	80.00
THE GREAT GROUP GOODIES				
Atco 33-143 [M]	1962	20.00	40.00	80.00
GREAT GROUP OLDIES				
Oldies 33 OL-8003 [M]	1963	6.25	12.50	25.00
GREAT GROUP OLDIES, VOL. 2				
Oldies 33 OL-8006 [M]	1964	6.25	12.50	25.00
GREAT GROUPS, GREAT RECORDS				
Laurie LLP-2010 [M]	1961	7.50	15.00	30.00
GREAT GUITARS OF JAZZ				
MGM SE-4691	1970	3.00	6.00	12.00

Label, Number	Yr	VG	VG+	NM
THE GREAT HITS OF 1964 AND SOME GOLDEN OLDIES				
Vee Jay LP-1112 [M]	1965	7.50	15.00	30.00
—Not known to exist in stereo				
GREAT INSTRUMENTAL R&B HITS				
Imperial LP-9271 [M]	1964	6.25	12.50	25.00
Imperial LP-12271 [R]	1964	5.00	10.00	20.00
GREAT JAZZ				
Rondo-lette A-31 [M]	195?	6.25	12.50	25.00
GREAT JAZZ BRASS				
RCA Camden CAL-383 [M]	1958	6.25	12.50	25.00
GREAT JAZZ PIANISTS				
RCA Camden CAL-328 [M]	1958	6.25	12.50	25.00
GREAT JAZZ PIANISTS OF OUR TIME				
RCA Camden CAL-882 [M]	1965	3.75	7.50	15.00
RCA Camden CAS-882 [R]	1965	2.50	5.00	10.00
GREAT JAZZ REEDS				
RCA Camden CAL-339 [M]	1958	6.25	12.50	25.00
THE GREAT JAZZ SINGERS				
Halo 50269 [M]	1957	3.75	7.50	15.00
GREAT MOTION PICTURE THEMES				
United Artists UAL-3122 [M]	1960	3.75	7.50	15.00
United Artists UAS-6122 [S]	1960	5.00	10.00	20.00
GREAT MOTION PICTURE THEMES (MORE ORIGINAL SOUND TRACKS AND HIT MUSIC)				
United Artists UAL-3158 [M]	1961	3.75	7.50	15.00
United Artists UAS-6158 [S]	1961	5.00	10.00	20.00
THE GREAT SONGS OF CHRISTMAS				
Columbia Special Products XTV 69406/7 [M]	1961	3.75	7.50	15.00
—Sold only at Goodyear tire dealers				
Columbia Special Products XTV 69406/7 [M]	1962	3.00	6.00	12.00
—Reissue with no reference to Goodyear on the cover				
THE GREAT SONGS OF CHRISTMAS, ALBUM TWO				
Columbia Special Products XTV 86100/1 [M]	1962	3.75	7.50	15.00
—Sold only at Goodyear tire dealers				
THE GREAT SONGS OF CHRISTMAS, ALBUM THREE				
Columbia Special Products CSP 117 [M]	1963	3.75	7.50	15.00
—Sold only at Goodyear tire dealers. The number listed is on the jacket; on the record, the number is "XTV 86656" on Side 1 and "XTV 86657" on Side 2				
THE GREAT SONGS OF CHRISTMAS, ALBUM FOUR				
Columbia Special Products CSP 155M [M]	1964	3.75	7.50	15.00
—Sold only at Goodyear tire dealers				
Columbia Special Products CSP 155S [S]	1964	4.50	9.00	18.00
—Sold only at Goodyear tire dealers				
THE GREAT SONGS OF CHRISTMAS, ALBUM FIVE				
Columbia Special Products CSP 238M [M]	1965	3.00	6.00	12.00
—Sold only at Goodyear tire dealers				
Columbia Special Products CSP 238S [S]	1965	3.75	7.50	15.00
—Sold only at Goodyear tire dealers				
THE GREAT SONGS OF CHRISTMAS, ALBUM SIX				
Columbia Special Products CSM 388 [M]	1966	3.00	6.00	12.00
—Sold only at Goodyear tire dealers				
Columbia Special Products CSS 388 [S]	1966	3.75	7.50	15.00
—Sold only at Goodyear tire dealers				
THE GREAT SONGS OF CHRISTMAS, ALBUM SEVEN				
Columbia Special Products CSS 547	1967	3.00	6.00	12.00
—Sold only at Goodyear tire dealers				
THE GREAT SONGS OF CHRISTMAS, ALBUM EIGHT				
Columbia Special Products CSS 888	1968	3.00	6.00	12.00
—Sold only at Goodyear tire dealers				
GREAT SONGS OF CHRISTMAS, ALBUM NINE				
Columbia Special Products CSS 1033	1969	3.00	6.00	12.00
—Sold only at Goodyear tire dealers; version 1 has a 10 1/2-inch flap on right inner gatefold (part of record is exposed)				
Columbia Special Products CSS 1033	1969	3.00	6.00	12.00
—Sold only at Goodyear tire dealers; version 2 has a 12 1/4-inch flap on right inner gatefold (record is completely covered)				
THE GREAT SOUL HITS				
Brunswick BL 54129 [M]	1968	6.25	12.50	25.00
Brunswick BL 754129 [S]	1968	3.75	7.50	15.00
THE GREAT SWING BANDS				
Jazztone J-1245 [M]	1957	7.50	15.00	30.00
GREAT SWING BANDS OF THE FORTIES				
Audio Lab AL-1530 [M]	1959	20.00	40.00	80.00
THE GREAT TENOR JAZZMEN				
Allegro 1634 [M]	195?	10.00	20.00	40.00
GREAT TRUMPET ARTISTS				
RCA Victor LPT-26 [10]	1951	12.50	25.00	50.00
RCA Victor LPT-35 [10]	1952	12.50	25.00	50.00
THE GREATEST 15 HITS ON ACE RECORDS				
Ace LP-1012 [M]	1960	17.50	35.00	70.00

Label, Number	Yr	VG	VG+	NM
GREATEST COUNTRY & WESTERN HITS NO. 3				
Columbia CL 1816 [M]	1962	5.00	10.00	20.00
Columbia CS 8616 [S]	1962	6.25	12.50	25.00
GREATEST COUNTRY & WESTERN HITS NO. 4				
Columbia CL 2081 [M]	1963	5.00	10.00	20.00
Columbia CS 8881 [S]	1963	6.25	12.50	25.00
THE GREATEST GOLDEN GOODIES				
Laurie LLP-2014 [M]	1962	7.50	15.00	30.00
Laurie SLP-2014 [R]	196?	3.75	7.50	15.00
GREATEST GOSPEL SONGS OF OUR TIMES				
Vee Jay LP-5043 [M]	1963	7.50	15.00	30.00
GREATEST GOSPEL SONGS, VOLUME 1				
Specialty SPS-2144	1970	5.00	10.00	20.00
GREATEST GOSPEL SONGS, VOLUME 2				
Specialty SPS-2145	1970	5.00	10.00	20.00
GREATEST HITS				
Harmony HL 7255 [M]	1960	3.75	7.50	15.00
THE GREATEST HITS FROM ENGLAND				
Parrot PA 61010 [M]	1967	6.25	12.50	25.00
Parrot PAS 71010 [R]	1967	5.00	10.00	20.00
THE GREATEST HITS FROM ENGLAND, VOLUME 2				
Parrot PA 61017 [M]	1968	6.25	12.50	25.00
Parrot PAS 71017 [R]	1968	5.00	10.00	20.00
THE GREATEST ROCK & ROLL				
Atlantic 8001 [M]	1956	30.00	60.00	120.00
THE GREATEST TEENAGE HITS OF ALL TIME!				
Teem LP-5003 [M]	196?	7.50	15.00	30.00
GREATEST WESTERN HITS				
Columbia CL 1257 [M]	1959	7.50	15.00	30.00
Columbia CS 8776 [R]	1963	5.00	10.00	20.00
GREATEST WESTERN HITS NO. 2				
Columbia CL 1408 [M]	1960	7.50	15.00	30.00
Columbia CS 8777 [R]	1963	5.00	10.00	20.00
GRETSCH DRUM NIGHT AT BIRDLAND				
Roulette R 52049 [M]	1960	7.50	15.00	30.00
Roulette SR 52049 [S]	1960	7.50	15.00	30.00
GRETSCH DRUM NIGHT, VOLUME 2				
Roulette R 52067 [M]	1961	7.50	15.00	30.00
Roulette SR 52067 [S]	1961	7.50	15.00	30.00
GROOVY GOODIES				
Colpix CP-466 [M]	1964	20.00	40.00	80.00
Colpix SCP-466 [S]	1964	25.00	50.00	100.00
GROUP OF GOODIES				
Chess LP 1478 [M]	1963	12.50	25.00	50.00
Chess LPS 1478 [R]	196?	5.00	10.00	20.00
GROUP OF GOODIES, VOLUME 2				
Chess LP 1491 [M]	1965	12.50	25.00	50.00
GUARANTEED TO PLEASE				
Teem LP-5002 [M]	196?	7.50	15.00	30.00
GUIDE TO JAZZ				
RCA Victor LPM-1393 [M]	1956	7.50	15.00	30.00
GUITAR PLAYERS				
Mainstream MRL-410	197?	3.00	6.00	12.00
HANDFUL OF COOL JAZZ				
Bethlehem BCP-90 [M]	1959	7.50	15.00	30.00
HAPPY HOLIDAYS				
Columbia Special Products CSP 242 [M]	1965	3.75	7.50	15.00
—Sold only at True Value Hardware stores				
HAPPY HOLIDAYS, VOLUME II				
Columbia Special Products CSM 348 [M]	1966	3.75	7.50	15.00
—Sold only at True Value Hardware stores				
Columbia Special Products CSS 348 [S]	1966	3.00	6.00	12.00
—Sold only at True Value Hardware stores				
HAPPY HOLIDAYS, VOL. III				
RCA Victor PRS-255	1967	3.75	7.50	15.00
—Sold only at True Value Hardware stores				
HAPPY HOLIDAYS, VOLUME IV				
RCA Victor PRS-267	1968	3.75	7.50	15.00
—Sold only at True Value Hardware stores				
HAPPY HOLIDAYS, VOL. 5				
Capitol Creative Products SL-6627	1969	3.00	6.00	12.00
—Sold only at True Value Hardware stores				
HAPPY HOLIDAYS, ALBUM 6				
Capitol Creative Products SL-6669	1970	3.00	6.00	12.00
—Sold only at True Value Hardware stores				
HAPPY HOLIDAYS, ALBUM SEVEN				
Capitol Creative Products SL-6730	1971	3.00	6.00	12.00
—Sold only at True Value Hardware stores				

Label, Number	Yr	VG	VG+	NM
HAPPY HOLIDAYS, ALBUM 8				
Columbia Special Products C 11086	1972	2.50	5.00	10.00
—Sold only at True Value Hardware stores				
HAPPY HOLIDAYS, ALBUM NINE				
Columbia Special Products P 11793	1973	2.50	5.00	10.00
—Sold only at True Value Hardware stores				
HAPPY HOLIDAYS, ALBUM 10				
Columbia Special Products P 12344	1974	2.50	5.00	10.00
—Sold only at True Value Hardware stores				
HAPPY HOLLY DAYS				
Capitol Creative Products SL-6654	1969	3.00	6.00	12.00
Capitol Creative Products SL-6761	1971	2.50	5.00	10.00
HAPPY JAZZ				
Jazztone J-1215 [M]	1956	7.50	15.00	30.00
HARD GOODS				
Warner Bros. PRO 583 [(2)]	1974	6.25	12.50	25.00
THE HARD SWING				
Pacific Jazz JWC-508 [M]	1957	12.50	25.00	50.00
World Pacific JWC-508 [M]	1958	10.00	20.00	40.00
HARLEM JAZZ 1930				
Brunswick BL 58024 [10]	1951	12.50	25.00	50.00
HAVE A HAPPY HOLIDAY				
Columbia Special Products CSS 1432	1970	2.50	5.00	10.00
HAVE A JEWISH CHRISTMAS...?				
Tower T-5081 [M]	1967	3.75	7.50	15.00
—Comedy sketches narrated by Lennie Weinrib and acted by Christine Nelson, Benny Rubin, Reginald X. Carlisle and Naomi Lewis				
HAVE YOURSELF A MERRY LITTLE CHRISTMAS				
Reprise R 50001 [M]	1963	6.25	12.50	25.00
—Wreath cover; titled on back cover "Top Hollywood Stars Want You to..."				
Reprise R 50001 [M]	1963	6.25	12.50	25.00
—Christmas tree cover; titled "Frank Sinatra and His Friends Want You to..."				
Reprise R9-50001 [S]	1963	7.50	15.00	30.00
—Christmas tree cover; titled "Frank Sinatra and His Friends Want You to..."; stereo version of above				
Reprise 50001 [M]	1963	6.25	12.50	25.00
—Red and green cover with ornaments at top; titled on back cover "Top Hollywood Stars Want You to..."				
HAVING A BALL				
End LP-302 [M]	1958	125.00	250.00	500.00
—Original cover with groups pictured on a record				
HEAVY HEADS				
Chess LP 1522 [M]	1967	6.25	12.50	25.00
Chess LPS 1522 [P]	1967	6.25	12.50	25.00
HEAVY HEADS, VOYAGE 2				
Chess LP 1528 [M]	1969	5.00	10.00	20.00
HEAVY HITS!				
Columbia CS 9840	1969	3.75	7.50	15.00
HEAVY METAL (SUPERSTARS OF THE 70S, VOLUME 2)				
Warner Special Products SP-2001	1974	5.00	10.00	20.00
HEAVY SOUNDS				
Columbia CS 9952	1970	3.75	7.50	15.00
HENRY MANCINI SELECTS GREAT SONGS OF CHRISTMAS				
RCA Special Products DPL1-0148	1975	2.50	5.00	10.00
—Sold only at Goodyear tire dealers				
HERALD THE BEAT				
Herald HLP-0110 [M]	1957	75.00	150.00	300.00
—Black label				
Herald HLP-0110 [M]	195?	37.50	75.00	150.00
—Yellow label				
HERE ARE THE HITS!				
Fire FLP-100 [M]	1959	100.00	200.00	400.00
—Reissued as "Memory Lane, Hits by the Original Groups" with the same label and number				
HERE COME THE GIRLS				
Verve MGV-2036 [M]	1956	10.00	20.00	40.00
Verve V-2036 [M]	1961	5.00	10.00	20.00
HERE COME THE SWINGING BANDS				
Verve MGV-8207 [M]	1957	7.50	15.00	30.00
Verve V-8207 [M]	1961	5.00	10.00	20.00
HI-FI JAZZ				
Brunswick BL 58058 [10]	1954	12.50	25.00	50.00
HI-FI JAZZ SESSION				
Masterseal MSLP 5013 [M]	1957	6.25	12.50	25.00
A HI-FI SALUTE TO THE GREAT ONES				
MGM E-3325 [M]	1956	7.50	15.00	30.00
A HI-FI SALUTE TO THE GREAT ONES, VOL. 2				
MGM E-3354 [M]	1956	7.50	15.00	30.00
HILLBILLY HOUSE PARTY				
Imperial LP-9214 [M]	1963	6.25	12.50	25.00
Imperial LP-12214 [R]	1963	5.00	10.00	20.00

Label, Number	Yr	VG	VG+	NM
HISTORIC JAZZ CONCERT AT MUSIC INN				
Atlantic 1298 [M]	1958	10.00	20.00	40.00
—Black label				
Atlantic 1298 [M]	1961	6.25	12.50	25.00
—Multicolor label, white "fan" logo at right				
Atlantic 1298 [M]	1963	5.00	10.00	20.00
—Multicolor label, black "fan" logo at right				
HISTORY OF BRITISH BLUES, VOLUME 1				
Sire SASH-3701 [(2)]	1973	5.00	10.00	20.00
HISTORY OF BRITISH ROCK				
Sire SASH-3702 [(2)]	1974	5.00	10.00	20.00
HISTORY OF BRITISH ROCK, VOL. 2				
Sire SASH-3705 [(2)]	1974	5.00	10.00	20.00
HISTORY OF BRITISH ROCK, VOLUME 3				
Sire SASH-3712 [(2)]	1975	5.00	10.00	20.00
HISTORY OF CLASSIC JAZZ				
Riverside SDP-11 [(5) M]	1956	75.00	150.00	300.00
—Five-record set in leatherette album with booklet; records were available separately as Riverside 112, 113, 114, 115 and 116.				
HISTORY OF CLASSIC JAZZ, VOL. 1				
Riverside RLP 12-112 [M]	1957	10.00	20.00	40.00
HISTORY OF CLASSIC JAZZ, VOL. 2				
Riverside RLP 12-113 [M]	1957	10.00	20.00	40.00
HISTORY OF CLASSIC JAZZ, VOL. 3				
Riverside RLP 12-114 [M]	1957	10.00	20.00	40.00
HISTORY OF CLASSIC JAZZ, VOL. 4				
Riverside RLP 12-115 [M]	1957	10.00	20.00	40.00
HISTORY OF CLASSIC JAZZ, VOL. 5				
Riverside RLP 12-116 [M]	1957	10.00	20.00	40.00
HISTORY OF JAZZ, VOL. 1: NEW ORLEANS ORIGINS				
Capitol T 793 [M]	1956	6.25	12.50	25.00
HISTORY OF JAZZ, VOL. 1: THE SOLID SOUTH				
Capitol H 239 [10]	1950	12.50	25.00	50.00
HISTORY OF JAZZ, VOL. 2: THE GOLDEN ERA				
Capitol H 240 [10]	1950	12.50	25.00	50.00
HISTORY OF JAZZ, VOL. 2: THE TURBULENT '20S				
Capitol T 794 [M]	1956	6.25	12.50	25.00
HISTORY OF JAZZ, VOL. 3: EVERYBODY SWINGS				
Capitol T 795 [M]	1956	6.25	12.50	25.00
HISTORY OF JAZZ, VOL. 3: THEN CAME SWING				
Capitol H 241 [10]	1950	12.50	25.00	50.00
HISTORY OF JAZZ, VOL. 4: ENTER THE COOL				
Capitol H 242 [10]	1950	12.50	25.00	50.00
Capitol T 796 [M]	1956	6.25	12.50	25.00
HISTORY OF RHYTHM & BLUES, VOLUME 1/THE ROOTS 1947-52				
Atlantic SD 8161	1968	5.00	10.00	20.00
HISTORY OF RHYTHM & BLUES, VOLUME 2/THE GOLDEN YEARS 1953-55				
Atlantic SD 8162	1968	5.00	10.00	20.00
HISTORY OF RHYTHM & BLUES, VOLUME 3/ROCK & ROLL 1956-57				
Atlantic SD 8163	1968	5.00	10.00	20.00
HISTORY OF RHYTHM & BLUES, VOLUME 4/THE BIG BEAT 1958-60				
Atlantic SD 8164	1968	5.00	10.00	20.00
THE HIT MAKERS AND THEIR RECORD BREAKERS				
King 737 [M]	1961	25.00	50.00	100.00
HIT SOUNDS OF MERRIE MELODIES				
Warner Bros. PRO 550 [(2)]	1973	6.25	12.50	25.00
THE HITS ARE ON VERVE				
Verve V-201 [M]	1964	3.75	7.50	15.00
Verve V6-201 [S]	1964	5.00	10.00	20.00
HITS FROM THE SOUTH PRESENTED BY NICK CHARLES				
Stax 702 [M]	1962	25.00	50.00	100.00
—Has the same number as "Walk Right In" by Gus Cannon, but this LP doesn't have any mention of Atlantic distribution				
HITS I FORGOT TO BUY				
Swan SLP-512 [M]	1963	12.50	25.00	50.00
HITS OF THE HOPS				
Warner Bros. W 1448 [M]	1962	7.50	15.00	30.00
Warner Bros. WS 1448 [S]	1962	10.00	20.00	40.00
HITS THAT JUMPED				
Checker LP 2975 [M]	1959	30.00	60.00	120.00
HITSVILLE				
Coral CRL 57269 [M]	1959	20.00	40.00	80.00
Coral CRL 757269 [S]	1959	25.00	50.00	100.00
HITSVILLE U.S.A.				
Imperial LP-9084 [M]	1959	10.00	20.00	40.00

Label, Number	Yr	VG	VG+	NM
HITSVILLE U.S.A., VOLUME 2				
Imperial LP-9099 [M]	1960	10.00	20.00	40.00
HOLIDAY IN SAX				
EmArcy MG-26019 [10]	1954	20.00	40.00	80.00
HOLIDAY IN TRUMPET				
EmArcy MG-26015 [10]	1954	20.00	40.00	80.00
HOLIDAY MAGIC				
Capitol Creative Products SL-6728	1971	3.00	6.00	12.00
Capitol Special Markets SL-6728	197?	2.50	5.00	10.00
—Same as above, but reissue on renamed label				
HOME FOR CHRISTMAS				
Columbia Musical Treasury P3S 5608 [(3)]	1971	3.75	7.50	15.00
HOME FOR THE HOLIDAYS				
Columbia Special Products P 12014	1973	2.50	5.00	10.00
—Sold only at Big N discount department store				
HOME OF THE BLUES				
Minit LP-0001 [M]	1961	12.50	25.00	50.00
HOME OF THE BLUES, VOLUME 2				
Minit LP-0004 [M]	1963	12.50	25.00	50.00
Minit LP-24004 [R]	1964	5.00	10.00	20.00
Minit LP-40004 [M]	1964	6.25	12.50	25.00
—Reissue of 0004				
HOMESPUN HUMOR				
King 726 [M]	1961	25.00	50.00	100.00
HOT CANARIES				
Columbia CL 2534 [10]	1954	7.50	15.00	30.00
HOT CLARINETS				
Historical 25	1969	2.50	5.00	10.00
THE HOT ONES				
Columbia Special Products CSP-107 [M]	1963	5.00	10.00	20.00
—Available only from Johnson Sea Horse boat dealers				
HOT PIANOS				
Historical 29	1969	2.50	5.00	10.00
HOT PLATTERS				
Warner Bros. PRO 474 [(2)]	1971	6.25	12.50	25.00
—Originals have green labels				
HOT TRUMPETS				
Historical 28	1969	2.50	5.00	10.00
HOT VS. COOL: A BATTLE OF JAZZ				
MGM E-211 [10]	1953	12.50	25.00	50.00
HOUSE RENT PARTY				
Savoy MG-12199 [M]	1961	12.50	25.00	50.00
HOW HIGH THE MOON				
Clef MGC-Vol. 1 [M]	1955	12.50	25.00	50.00
—Reissue of 608				
Clef MGC-608 [M]	1955	10.00	20.00	40.00
—Reissue of Mercury 608				
Mercury MGC-Vol. 1 [10]	1951	15.00	30.00	60.00
—Reissue of 35001				
Mercury MGC-608 [M]	1953	20.00	40.00	80.00
—Reissue of Vol. 1				
Mercury MG-35001 [10]	1950	20.00	40.00	80.00
Verve MGV-Vol. 1 [M]	1957	7.50	15.00	30.00
—Reissue of 12-inch Clef Vol. 1				
HOW THE GRINCH STOLE CHRISTMAS				
Random House/Scholastic 0-394-05008-8	1975	3.75	7.50	15.00
—Not the original soundtrack, but placed here to avoid confusion (we hope). B-side is a condensation of Folkways FC-7750 (1956).				
HUM-N-STRUM: THE BEST OF FOLK AND COUNTRY				
Columbia Special Products CSP 309 [M]	1966	3.75	7.50	15.00
—For General Electric				
HYMNS OF FAITH				
Colpix CP-408 [M]	1959	7.50	15.00	30.00
I'M WILD ABOUT MY LOVIN'				
Historical 32	1969	2.50	5.00	10.00
I DIDN'T KNOW THEY STILL MADE RECORDS LIKE THIS				
Warner Bros. PRO 608 [(2)]	1975	5.00	10.00	20.00
I DIG ROCK AND ROLL				
Score SLP-4002 [M]	1957	50.00	100.00	200.00
—Reissue of "Rock & Roll with Rhythm & Blues," Aladdin 710				
I LIKE JAZZ!				
Columbia JZ 1 [M]	1955	7.50	15.00	30.00
IMAGINE THE JOYS OF CHRISTMAS. PRESENTED BY SYLVANIA.				
Capitol Creative Products SL-6700	1971	3.00	6.00	12.00
—Sold only at Sylvania dealers; label calls this "A Sylvania Christmas"				
IMPERIAL MOVES				
Imperial MM-428 [DJ]	1966	10.00	20.00	40.00
IMPERIAL SAMPLER				
Imperial DJLP-1 [10]	195?	25.00	50.00	100.00
—Promo-only item				
IMPULSE ARTISTS ON TOUR				
ABC Impulse! AS-9264	197?	3.00	6.00	12.00
IMPULSIVELY!				
ABC Impulse! AS-9266 [(2)]	197?	3.75	7.50	15.00
IN CONCERT				
RCA Victor CPL2-1014 [(2)]	1975	5.00	10.00	20.00
IN LOVING MEMORY				
Motown M 642 [M]	1968	62.50	125.00	250.00
—Without song titles on cover				
Motown M 642 [M]	1968	37.50	75.00	150.00
—With song titles on cover				
Motown MS 642 [S]	1968	62.50	125.00	250.00
—Without song titles on cover				
Motown MS 642 [S]	1968	37.50	75.00	150.00
—With song titles on cover				
Motown M 642 [DJ]	1969	125.00	250.00	500.00
—With custom silver cover; Loucye Gordy Wakefield Scholarship Fund benefit giveaway				
INCENSE AND OLDIES				
Buddah BDS 5014	1969	5.00	10.00	20.00
INFORMAL SESSION AT SQUIRREL'S BY THE SONS OF BIX				
Paramount LP-104 [(2) 10]	1954	20.00	40.00	80.00
THE INSTRUMENTAL CHRISTMAS FAVORITES				
Capitol STBB-349 [(2)]	1969	3.75	7.50	15.00
INSTRUMENTAL GOLDEN GOODIES, VOL. 13				
Roulette R 25238 [M]	1964	5.00	10.00	20.00
INTERCOLLEGIATE MUSIC FESTIVAL, VOL. 1				
ABC Impulse! AS-9145 [S]	1968	3.00	6.00	12.00
Impulse! A-9145 [M]	1967	5.00	10.00	20.00
Impulse! AS-9145 [S]	1967	3.75	7.50	15.00
INTERNATIONAL JAZZ WORKSHOP				
EmArcy MGE-26002 [M]	1964	6.25	12.50	25.00
EmArcy SRE-66002 [S]	1964	7.50	15.00	30.00
INTERPLAY FOR TWO TRUMPETS AND TWO TENORS				
Prestige PRLP-7112 [M]	1957	25.00	50.00	100.00
INTRODUCTION TO JAZZ				
Decca DL 8244 [M]	1956	7.50	15.00	30.00
INTRODUCTION TO RARE EARTH RECORDS				
Rare Earth RS-505 to 509 [(5) DJ]	1969	50.00	100.00	200.00
—Promo-only box set with rounded top; contains the first five LPs on the Rare Earth label				
ISLES OF JAZZ				
Discovery DL-2010 [10]	1954	12.50	25.00	50.00
IT'S CHRISTMAS				
Columbia Special Products C 10040	1971	3.00	6.00	12.00
IT'S CHRISTMASTIME!				
Columbia Special Products CSM 429 [M]	1966	3.00	6.00	12.00
—Sold only at A&P grocery stores				
IT'S DANCE TIME				
Cameo C-1068 [M]	1964	7.50	15.00	30.00
ITALIAN JAZZ STARS				
Angel ANG-60001 [10]	1955	12.50	25.00	50.00
IVY LEAGUE JAZZ				
Decca DL 8282 [M]	1956	7.50	15.00	30.00
Golden Crest GC-3039 [M]	1958	5.00	10.00	20.00
JACKPOT OF HITS				
Apollo LP-490 [M]	1959	37.50	75.00	150.00
JAM SESSION				
Clef MGC-4001/7 [(7) M]	1953	75.00	150.00	300.00
—Boxed set containing 4001-4007				
EmArcy MG-36002 [M]	1954	12.50	25.00	50.00
JAM SESSION AT CARNEGIE HALL				
Columbia CL 557 [M]	1954	7.50	15.00	30.00
JAM SESSION AT COMMODORE				
Commodore FL-30006 [M]	1951	10.00	20.00	40.00
JAM SESSION COAST TO COAST				
Columbia CL 547 [M]	1954	7.50	1.00	30.00
JAM SESSION #1				
Clef MGC-601 [M]	1954	10.00	20.00	40.00
Clef MGC-651 [M]	1955	10.00	20.00	40.00
—Reissue of 4001				
Clef MGC-4001 [M]	1953	12.50	25.00	50.00
Mercury MGC-601 [M]	1953	20.00	40.00	80.00
Verve MGV-8049 [M]	1956	7.50	15.00	30.00
—Reissue of Clef 651				
JAM SESSION #2				
Clef MGC-602 [M]	1954	10.00	20.00	40.00
Clef MGC-652 [M]	1955	10.00	20.00	40.00
—Reissue of 4002				

Label, Number	Yr	VG	VG+	NM
Clef MGC-4002 [M]	1953	12.50	25.00	50.00
Mercury MGC-602 [M]	1953	20.00	40.00	80.00
Verve MGV-8050 [M]	1956	7.50	15.00	30.00
—Reissue of Clef 652				
JAM SESSION #3				
Clef MGC-653 [M]	1955	10.00	20.00	40.00
—Reissue of 4003				
Clef MGC-4003 [M]	1953	12.50	25.00	50.00
Verve MGV-8051 [M]	1956	7.50	15.00	30.00
—Reissue of Clef 653				
JAM SESSION #4				
Clef MGC-654 [M]	1955	10.00	20.00	40.00
—Reissue of 4004				
Clef MGC-4004 [M]	1953	12.50	25.00	50.00
Verve MGV-8052 [M]	1956	7.50	15.00	30.00
—Reissue of Clef 654				
JAM SESSION #5				
Clef MGC-655 [M]	1955	10.00	20.00	40.00
—Reissue of 4005				
Clef MGC-4005 [M]	1953	12.50	25.00	50.00
Verve MGV-8053 [M]	1956	7.50	15.00	30.00
—Reissue of Clef 655				
JAM SESSION #6				
Clef MGC-656 [M]	1955	10.00	20.00	40.00
—Reissue of 4006				
Clef MGC-4006 [M]	1953	12.50	25.00	50.00
Verve MGV-8054 [M]	1956	7.50	15.00	30.00
—Reissue of Clef 656				
JAM SESSION #7				
Clef MGC-677 [M]	1955	10.00	20.00	40.00
Verve MGV-8062 [M]	1957	7.50	15.00	30.00
—Reissue of Clef 677				
JAM SESSION #8				
Clef MGC-711 [M]	1955	10.00	20.00	40.00
Verve MGV-8094 [M]	1957	7.50	15.00	30.00
—Reissue of Clef 711				
JAM SESSION #9				
Verve MGV-8196 [M]	1957	7.50	15.00	30.00
JAMES BOND — 10TH ANNIVERSARY				
United Artists UXS-91 [(2)]	1972	7.50	15.00	30.00
THE JATP ALL-STARS AT THE OPERA HOUSE				
Verve MGVS-6029 [S]	1960	7.50	15.00	30.00
Verve MGV-8267 [M]	1958	10.00	20.00	40.00
Verve V-8267 [M]	1961	5.00	10.00	20.00
Verve V6-8267 [S]	1961	3.75	7.50	15.00
Verve MGV-8284 [M]	1959	—	—	—
—Canceled				
Verve V-8489 [M]	1962	6.25	12.50	25.00
Verve V6-8489 [S]	1962	7.50	15.00	30.00
THE JATP ALL-STARS: FUNKY BLUES				
Verve V-8486 [M]	1962	6.25	12.50	25.00
Verve V6-8486 [S]	1962	7.50	15.00	30.00
THE JATP ALL STARS: HOW HIGH THE MOON				
Verve VSP-15 [M]	1966	3.75	7.50	15.00
Verve VSPS-15 [R]	1966	2.50	5.00	10.00
THE JATP ALL STARS: PERDIDO				
Verve VSP-16 [M]	1966	3.75	7.50	15.00
Verve VSPS-16 [R]	1966	2.50	5.00	10.00
JAZZ				
Halo 50242 [M]	1957	3.75	7.50	15.00
Mainstream MRL-408	197?	3.00	6.00	12.00
Royale 1883 [10]	195?	7.50	15.00	30.00
JAZZ — WEST COAST VOL. III				
Jazztone J-1274 [M]	195?	7.50	15.00	30.00
JAZZ A LA MIDNIGHT				
Jazztone J-1282 [M]	1957	7.50	15.00	30.00
JAZZ A LA MOOD				
Jazztone J-1254 [M]	1957	7.50	15.00	30.00
JAZZ AMERICANA				
Tampa TP-11 [M]	1957	25.00	50.00	100.00
—Colored vinyl				
Tampa TP-11 [M]	1958	10.00	20.00	40.00
—Black vinyl				
JAZZ ANTHOLOGY OF WEST COAST JAZZ				
Jazztone J-1243 [M]	1957	7.50	15.00	30.00
JAZZ AT CARNEGIE HALL				
Arco AL-4 [10]	1950	20.00	40.00	80.00
Mercury MG-35002 [10]	1950	20.00	40.00	80.00
—Reissue of Arco 4				
JAZZ AT CARNEGIE HALL, VOLUME 2				
Arco AL-8 [10]	195?	20.00	40.00	80.00

Label, Number	Yr	VG	VG+	NM
JAZZ AT COLUMBIA — COLLECTORS ITEMS				
Columbia CB-16 [M]	195?	5.00	10.00	20.00
—Columbia Record Club "bonus record" in generic sleeve with die-cut circle in middle				
JAZZ AT COLUMBIA — DIXIELAND				
Columbia CB-8 [M]	195?	5.00	10.00	20.00
—Columbia Record Club "bonus record" in generic sleeve with die-cut circle in middle				
JAZZ AT JAZZ LTD.				
Atlantic 1338 [M]	1961	6.25	12.50	25.00
—Multicolor label, white "fan" logo at right				
JAZZ AT PRESERVATION HALL				
Atlantic 1408 [M]	1964	3.00	6.00	12.00
Atlantic SD 1408 [S]	1964	3.75	7.50	15.00
JAZZ AT PRESERVATION HALL, VOL. 2				
Atlantic 1409 [M]	1964	3.00	6.00	12.00
Atlantic SD 1409 [S]	1964	3.75	7.50	15.00
JAZZ AT PRESERVATION HALL, VOL. 3				
Atlantic 1410 [M]	1964	3.00	6.00	12.00
Atlantic SD 1410 [S]	1964	3.75	7.50	15.00
JAZZ AT STORYVILLE				
Paradox LP-6003 [10]	1951	12.50	25.00	50.00
Savoy MG-15001 [10]	1952	20.00	40.00	80.00
Savoy MG-15014 [10]	1952	20.00	40.00	80.00
Storyville STLP-319 [10]	1955	20.00	40.00	80.00
JAZZ AT STORYVILLE, VOL. 2				
Savoy MG-15016 [10]	1952	20.00	40.00	80.00
JAZZ AT STORYVILLE, VOL. 3				
Savoy MG-15019 [10]	1953	20.00	40.00	80.00
JAZZ AT STORYVILLE, VOL. 4				
Savoy MG-15020 [10]	1953	20.00	40.00	80.00
JAZZ AT THE BOSTON ARTS FESTIVAL				
Storyville STLP-311 [10]	1954	20.00	40.00	80.00
JAZZ AT THE HOLLYWOOD BOWL				
Verve MGV-8231-2 [(2) M]	1958	12.50	25.00	50.00
Verve V-8231-2 [(2) M]	1961	6.25	12.50	25.00
JAZZ AT THE PHILHARMONIC				
Stinson SLP-23 [10]	195?	20.00	40.00	80.00
—Black vinyl				
Stinson SLP-23 [10]	195?	20.00	40.00	80.00
—Opaque red vinyl				
Stinson SLP-23 [10]	1950	30.00	60.00	120.00
—See-through red vinyl; the first pressing of the first volume to be issued				
Stinson SLP-23 [M]	195?	5.00	10.00	20.00
JAZZ AT THE PHILHARMONIC ALL STARS				
American Recording Society G-416 [M]	1957	7.50	15.00	30.00
JAZZ AT THE PHILHARMONIC IN EUROPE				
Verve V6-8823 [(2)]	197?	5.00	10.00	20.00
JAZZ AT THE PHILHARMONIC IN EUROPE, VOL. 1				
Verve V-8539 [M]	1963	5.00	10.00	20.00
Verve V6-8539 [S]	1963	6.25	12.50	25.00
JAZZ AT THE PHILHARMONIC IN EUROPE, VOL. 2				
Verve V-8540 [M]	1963	5.00	10.00	20.00
Verve V6-8540 [S]	1963	6.25	12.50	25.00
JAZZ AT THE PHILHARMONIC IN EUROPE, VOL. 3				
Verve V-8541 [M]	1963	5.00	10.00	20.00
Verve V6-8541 [S]	1963	6.25	12.50	25.00
JAZZ AT THE PHILHARMONIC IN EUROPE, VOL. 4				
Verve V-8542 [M]	1963	5.00	10.00	20.00
Verve V6-8542 [S]	1963	6.25	12.50	25.00
JAZZ AT THE PHILHARMONIC, NEW VOLUME 2				
Clef MGC-Vol. 2 [M]	1955	12.50	25.00	50.00
—Side 1 is the 10-inch Vol. 2; Side 2 is the 10-inch Vol. 3				
JAZZ AT THE PHILHARMONIC, NEW VOLUME 3				
Clef MGC-Vol. 3 [M]	1955	12.50	25.00	50.00
—Side 1 is the 10-inch Vol. 4; Side 2 is the 10-inch Vol. 5				
JAZZ AT THE PHILHARMONIC, NEW VOLUME 4				
Clef MGC-Vol. 4 [M]	1955	12.50	25.00	50.00
—Combines the 10-inch Vol. 6 and Vol. 14 on one record				
JAZZ AT THE PHILHARMONIC, NEW VOLUME 5				
Clef MGC-Vol. 5 [M]	1955	12.50	25.00	50.00
—Combines the 10-inch Vol. 7, 10 and 11 on one record				
JAZZ AT THE PHILHARMONIC, NEW VOLUME 6				
Clef MGC-Vol. 6 [M]	1955	12.50	25.00	50.00
—Combines the 10-inch Vol. 8 and Vol. 9 on one record				
JAZZ AT THE PHILHARMONIC, NEW VOLUME 7				
Clef MGC-Vol. 7 [M]	1955	12.50	25.00	50.00
—Combines the 10-inch Vol. 12 and 13 on one record				
JAZZ AT THE PHILHARMONIC, VOLUME 2				
Arco AL-1 [10]	1950	20.00	40.00	80.00
Clef MGC-Vol. 2 [10]	1953	15.00	30.00	60.00
—Reissue of Mercury Vol. 2				

Label, Number	Yr	VG	VG+	NM
Mercury MGC-Vol. 2 [10]	1951	15.00	30.00	60.00
—*Reissue of 35003*				
Mercury MG-35003 [10]	1950	20.00	40.00	80.00
—*Reissue of Arco 1*				
JAZZ AT THE PHILHARMONIC, VOL. 2				
Verve MGV-Vol. 2 [M]	1957	7.50	15.00	30.00
—*Reissue of 12-inch Clef Vol. 2*				
JAZZ AT THE PHILHARMONIC, VOLUME 3				
Arco AL-2 [10]	1950	20.00	40.00	80.00
Clef MGC-Vol. 3 [10]	1953	15.00	30.00	60.00
—*Reissue of Mercury Vol. 3*				
Mercury MGC-Vol. 3 [10]	1951	15.00	30.00	60.00
—*Reissue of 35004*				
Mercury MG-35004 [10]	1950	20.00	40.00	80.00
—*Reissue of Arco 2*				
JAZZ AT THE PHILHARMONIC, VOL. 3				
Verve MGV-Vol. 3 [M]	1957	7.50	15.00	30.00
—*Reissue of 12-inch Clef Vol. 3*				
JAZZ AT THE PHILHARMONIC, VOLUME 4				
Clef MGC-Vol. 4 [10]	1953	15.00	30.00	60.00
—*Reissue of Mercury Vol. 4*				
Mercury MGC-Vol. 4 [10]	1951	15.00	30.00	60.00
—*Reissue of 35005*				
Mercury MG-35005 [10]	1950	20.00	40.00	80.00
JAZZ AT THE PHILHARMONIC, VOL. 4				
Verve MGV-Vol. 4 [M]	1957	7.50	15.00	30.00
—*Reissue of 12-inch Clef Vol. 4*				
JAZZ AT THE PHILHARMONIC, VOLUME 5				
Clef MGC-Vol. 5 [10]	1953	15.00	30.00	60.00
—*Reissue of Mercury Vol. 5*				
Mercury MGC-Vol. 5 [10]	1951	15.00	30.00	60.00
—*Reissue of 35006*				
Mercury MG-35006 [10]	1950	20.00	40.00	80.00
JAZZ AT THE PHILHARMONIC, VOL. 5				
Verve MGV-Vol. 5 [M]	1957	7.50	15.00	30.00
—*Reissue of 12-inch Clef Vol. 5*				
JAZZ AT THE PHILHARMONIC, VOLUME 6				
Clef MGC-Vol. 6 [10]	1953	15.00	30.00	60.00
—*Reissue of Mercury Vol. 6*				
Mercury MGC-Vol. 6 [10]	1951	15.00	30.00	60.00
—*Reissue of 35007*				
Mercury MG-35007 [10]	1950	20.00	40.00	80.00
JAZZ AT THE PHILHARMONIC, VOL. 6				
Verve MGV-Vol. 6 [M]	1957	7.50	15.00	30.00
—*Reissue of 12-inch Clef Vol. 6*				
JAZZ AT THE PHILHARMONIC, VOLUME 7				
Clef MGC-Vol. 7 [10]	1953	15.00	30.00	60.00
—*Reissue of Mercury Vol. 7*				
Mercury MGC-Vol. 7 [10]	1951	15.00	30.00	60.00
—*Reissue of 35008*				
Mercury MG-35008 [10]	1950	20.00	40.00	80.00
JAZZ AT THE PHILHARMONIC, VOL. 7				
Verve MGV-Vol. 7 [M]	1957	7.50	15.00	30.00
—*Reissue of 12-inch Clef Vol. 7*				
JAZZ AT THE PHILHARMONIC, VOLUME 8				
Clef MGC-Vol. 8 [10]	1953	15.00	30.00	60.00
—*Reissue of Mercury Vol. 8*				
Mercury MGC-Vol. 8 [10]	1951	15.00	30.00	60.00
—*Reissue of 35000*				
Mercury MG-35000 [10]	1950	20.00	40.00	80.00
JAZZ AT THE PHILHARMONIC, VOL. 8				
Verve MGV-Vol. 8 [(3) M]	1957	15.00	30.00	60.00
—*Reissue of Clef Vol. 15*				
JAZZ AT THE PHILHARMONIC, VOLUME 9				
Clef MGC-Vol. 9 [10]	1953	15.00	30.00	60.00
—*Reissue of Mercury Vol. 9*				
Mercury MGC-Vol. 9 [10]	1951	15.00	30.00	60.00
—*Reissue of 35009*				
Mercury MG-35009 [10]	1950	20.00	40.00	80.00
JAZZ AT THE PHILHARMONIC, VOL. 9				
Verve MGV-Vol. 9 [(3) M]	1957	15.00	30.00	60.00
—*Reissue of Clef Vol. 16*				
JAZZ AT THE PHILHARMONIC, VOLUME 10				
Clef MGC-Vol. 10 [10]	1953	15.00	30.00	60.00
—*Reissue of Mercury Vol. 10*				
Mercury MGC-Vol. 10 [10]	1951	15.00	30.00	60.00
—*Reissue of 35010*				
Mercury MG-35010 [10]	1950	25.00	50.00	100.00
JAZZ AT THE PHILHARMONIC, VOL. 10				
Verve MGV-Vol. 10 [(3) M]	1957	15.00	30.00	60.00
—*Reissue of Clef Vol. 17*				
JAZZ AT THE PHILHARMONIC, VOLUME 11				
Clef MGC-Vol. 11 [10]	1953	15.00	30.00	60.00
—*Reissue of Mercury Vol. 11*				

Label, Number	Yr	VG	VG+	NM
Mercury MGC-Vol. 11 [10]	1951	15.00	30.00	60.00
—*Reissue of 35011*				
Mercury MG-35011 [10]	1950	20.00	40.00	80.00
JAZZ AT THE PHILHARMONIC, VOL. 11				
Verve MGV-Vol. 11 [(3) M]	1957	15.00	30.00	60.00
—*Reissue of Clef Vol. 18*				
JAZZ AT THE PHILHARMONIC, VOLUME 12				
Clef MGC-Vol. 12 [10]	1953	15.00	30.00	60.00
—*Reissue of Mercury Vol. 12*				
Mercury MGC-Vol. 12 [10]	1951	15.00	30.00	60.00
JAZZ AT THE PHILHARMONIC, VOL. 12				
Verve MGV-Vol. 12 [(2) M]	195?	—	—	—
—*Advertised, but unreleased?*				
JAZZ AT THE PHILHARMONIC, VOLUME 13				
Clef MGC-Vol. 13 [10]	1953	15.00	30.00	60.00
—*Reissue of Mercury Vol. 13*				
Mercury MGC-Vol. 13 [10]	1951	15.00	30.00	60.00
JAZZ AT THE PHILHARMONIC, VOLUME 14				
Clef MGC-Vol. 14 [10]	1953	15.00	30.00	60.00
—*Reissue of Mercury Vol. 14*				
Mercury MGC-Vol. 14 [10]	1951	15.00	30.00	60.00
JAZZ AT THE PHILHARMONIC, VOLUME 15				
Clef MGC-Vol. 15 [(3) M]	1954	20.00	40.00	80.00
—*Boxed set of new material with program*				
Clef MGC-Vol. 15 [10]	1953	15.00	30.00	60.00
—*Reissue of Mercury Vol. 15*				
Mercury MGC-Vol. 15 [10]	1951	15.00	30.00	60.00
JAZZ AT THE PHILHARMONIC, VOLUME 16				
Clef MGC-Vol. 16 [(3) M]	1954	20.00	40.00	80.00
—*Boxed set of new material with program*				
JAZZ AT THE PHILHARMONIC, VOLUME 17				
Clef MGC-Vol. 17 [(3) M]	1955	20.00	40.00	80.00
—*Boxed set of new material with photo booklet*				
JAZZ AT THE PHILHARMONIC, VOLUME 18				
Clef MGC-Vol. 18 [(3) M]	1955	20.00	40.00	80.00
—*Boxed set of new material with booklet*				
JAZZ BAND BALL				
Good Time Jazz L-12005 [M]	1954	5.00	10.00	20.00
JAZZ BANDS 1926-30				
Historical 16	1967	2.50	5.00	10.00
JAZZ CITY PRESENTS				
Bethlehem BCP-80 [M]	1957	7.50	15.00	30.00
JAZZ COMMITTEE FOR LATIN AMERICAN AFFAIRS				
FM LP-303 [M]	1963	12.50	25.00	50.00
JAZZ CONCERT				
Jazztone J-1219 [M]	1956	7.50	15.00	30.00
Mercury MGJC-1 [(2) M]	1953	30.00	60.00	120.00
—*Combines 601 and 602 in a box*				
Norgran MGN-3501-2 [(2) M]	1956	30.00	60.00	120.00
—*Reissue of Mercury MGJC-1*				
JAZZ CONCERT WEST COAST				
Savoy MG-12012 [M]	1955	20.00	40.00	80.00
Savoy MG-12196 [M]	1961	12.50	25.00	50.00
JAZZ CONFIDENTIAL				
Crown CLP-5056 [M]	1959	5.00	10.00	20.00
JAZZ CORNUCOPIA				
Coral CRL 57149 [M]	1958	7.50	15.00	30.00
JAZZ DANCE				
Jaguar JP-801 [10]	1954	12.50	25.00	50.00
JAZZ DUPLEX				
Pax LP-6006 [10]	1954	7.50	15.00	30.00
JAZZ FESTIVAL				
Imperial LP-9233 [M]	1963	5.00	10.00	20.00
Imperial LP-12233 [S]	1963	6.25	12.50	25.00
Kapp KS-1 [M]	1956	5.00	10.00	20.00
JAZZ FESTIVAL IN HI-FI: NEAR IN AND FAR OUT				
Warner Bros. W 1281 [M]	1959	6.25	12.50	25.00
JAZZ FESTIVAL IN STEREO: NEAR IN AND FAR OUT				
Warner Bros. WS 1281 [S]	1959	7.50	15.00	30.00
JAZZ FESTIVAL, VOLUME 2				
Imperial LP-9238 [M]	1963	5.00	10.00	20.00
Imperial LP-12238 [S]	1963	6.25	12.50	25.00
JAZZ FOR A SUNDAY AFTERNOON				
Solid State SS-18027	1968	3.75	7.50	15.00
JAZZ FOR A SUNDAY AFTERNOON, VOL. 2				
Solid State SS-18028	1968	3.75	7.50	15.00
JAZZ FOR A SUNDAY AFTERNOON, VOL. 3				
Solid State SS-18037	1968	3.75	7.50	15.00

Label, Number	Yr	VG	VG+	NM
JAZZ FOR A SUNDAY AFTERNOON, VOL. 4				
Solid State SS-18052	1969	3.75	7.50	15.00
JAZZ FOR ART'S SAKE				
Dotted Eighth 101 [M]	195?	10.00	20.00	40.00
JAZZ FOR HI-FI LOVERS				
Dawn DLP-1124 [M]	1958	20.00	40.00	80.00
JAZZ FOR LOVERS				
Riverside RLP 12-244 [M]	1957	10.00	20.00	40.00
JAZZ FOR PEOPLE WHO HATE JAZZ				
RCA Victor LJM-1008 [M]	1954	12.50	25.00	50.00
JAZZ FOR SURF-NIKS				
Bethlehem BCP-6073 [M]	1961	7.50	15.00	30.00
JAZZ FROM DOWN UNDER				
Jaguar JP-803 [10]	1954	12.50	25.00	50.00
JAZZ FROM NEW YORK, 1928-32				
Historical 33	1969	2.50	5.00	10.00
JAZZ FROM SWEDEN				
Discovery DL-2002 [10]	1953	12.50	25.00	50.00
JAZZ GIANTS				
Biograph 3002	196?	3.00	6.00	12.00
Norgran MGN-1056 [M]	1956	20.00	40.00	80.00
THE JAZZ GIANTS '56				
Verve MGV-8146 [M]	1957	7.50	15.00	30.00
Verve V-8146 [M]	1961	5.00	10.00	20.00
JAZZ GIANTS '58				
Verve MGV-8248 [M]	1958	12.50	25.00	50.00
Verve V-8248 [M]	1961	6.25	12.50	25.00
JAZZ GIANTS, VOL. 1				
EmArcy MG-36048 [M]	1955	10.00	20.00	40.00
JAZZ GIANTS, VOL. 2: THE PIANO PLAYERS				
EmArcy MG-36049 [M]	1955	10.00	20.00	40.00
JAZZ GIANTS, VOL. 3: REEDS, PART 1				
EmArcy MG-36050 [M]	1955	10.00	20.00	40.00
JAZZ GIANTS, VOL. 3: REEDS, PART 2				
EmArcy MG-36051 [M]	1955	10.00	20.00	40.00
JAZZ GIANTS, VOL. 4: FOLK BLUES				
EmArcy MG-36052 [M]	1955	10.00	20.00	40.00
JAZZ GIANTS, VOL. 5: BRASS				
EmArcy MG-36053 [M]	1955	10.00	20.00	40.00
JAZZ GIANTS, VOL. 6: MODERN SWEDES				
EmArcy MG-36054 [M]	1955	10.00	20.00	40.00
JAZZ GIANTS, VOL. 7: DIXIELAND				
EmArcy MG-36055 [M]	1955	10.00	20.00	40.00
JAZZ GIANTS, VOL. 8: DRUM ROLE				
EmArcy MG-36071 [M]	1956	10.00	20.00	40.00
JAZZ GOES TO BROADWAY				
Kapp KL-1007 [M]	1956	5.00	10.00	20.00
JAZZ GREATS				
Tops L-1508 [M]	1958	5.00	10.00	20.00
JAZZ GREATS!				
Allegro 737 [M]	1958	7.50	15.00	30.00
JAZZ HALL OF FAME, VOL. 2				
Design DLP-113 [M]	196?	5.00	10.00	20.00
THE JAZZ HOUR				
Savoy MG-12126 [M]	1957	12.50	25.00	50.00
JAZZ IN HOLLYWOOD				
Liberty LJH-6001 [M]	1955	7.50	15.00	30.00
JAZZ IN TRANSITION				
Transition TRLP-30 [M]	1956	50.00	100.00	200.00
—With booklet (deduct 1/4 if missing)				
JAZZ INTERPLAY				
Prestige PRLP-7341 [(2) M]	1964	10.00	20.00	40.00
Prestige PRLP-7341 [(2) R]	1964	6.25	12.50	25.00
JAZZ IS BUSTING OUT ALL OVER				
Savoy MG-12123 [M]	1957	12.50	25.00	50.00
JAZZ JAMBOREE				
Halo 50229 [M]	1957	5.00	10.00	20.00
JAZZ LAB				
Starlite ST-7003 [M]	1955	12.50	25.00	50.00
THE JAZZ LIFE				
Candid CD-8019 [M]	1960	10.00	20.00	40.00
Candid CS-9019 [S]	1960	7.50	15.00	30.00
JAZZ LTD.				
Regal LP-11 [10]	1951	12.50	25.00	50.00

Label, Number	Yr	VG	VG+	NM
THE JAZZ MAKERS				
Columbia CL 1036 [M]	1957	5.00	10.00	20.00
JAZZ MONTAGE				
Liberty LRP-3292 [M]	1963	3.75	7.50	15.00
Liberty LST-7292 [S]	1963	5.00	10.00	20.00
JAZZ MUSIC FOR BIRDS				
Bethlehem BCP-6039 [M]	1959	7.50	15.00	30.00
JAZZ MUSIC FOR PEOPLE WHO DON'T CARE ABOUT MONEY				
Bethlehem BCP-88 [M]	1958	7.50	15.00	30.00
JAZZ ODYSSEY: THE SOUND OF CHICAGO				
Columbia C3L 32 [(3) M]	1964	10.00	20.00	40.00
JAZZ ODYSSEY: THE SOUND OF HARLEM				
Columbia C2L 33 [(3)]	1964	10.00	20.00	40.00
JAZZ ODYSSEY: THE SOUND OF NEW ORLEANS				
Columbia C3L 30 [(3) M]	1964	10.00	20.00	40.00
JAZZ OF THE FORTIES, VOL. 1				
Folkways FJ-2841	197?	3.00	6.00	12.00
JAZZ OF THE ROARING 20'S				
Riverside RLP 12-801 [M]	195?	12.50	25.00	50.00
JAZZ OF THE ROARING TWENTIES: DANCE MUSIC OF THE CHARLESTON ERA				
Riverside RLP 12-108 [M]	1956	10.00	20.00	40.00
JAZZ OF THE SIXTIES				
Vee Jay VJS-2-1008 [(2)]	1974	5.00	10.00	20.00
JAZZ OF TWO DECADES				
EmArcy DEM-2 [M]	1956	10.00	20.00	40.00
JAZZ OFF THE AIR, VOL. 1				
Esoteric ESJ-2 [10]	1952	20.00	40.00	80.00
JAZZ OFF THE AIR, VOL. 2				
Esoteric ESJ-3 [10]	1952	20.00	40.00	80.00
JAZZ OMNIBUS				
Columbia CL 1020 [M]	1957	5.00	10.00	20.00
JAZZ ON THE AIR				
Brunswick BL 58048 [10]	1953	12.50	25.00	50.00
JAZZ ON THE SCREEN				
Fontana MGF-27532 [M]	1965	7.50	15.00	30.00
Fontana SRF-67532 [S]	1965	10.00	20.00	40.00
JAZZ PIANISTS GALORE				
Jazz: West Coast JWC-506 [M]	1956	37.50	75.00	150.00
THE JAZZ PIANO				
RCA Victor LPM-3499 [M]	1966	5.00	10.00	20.00
RCA Victor LSP-3499 [S]	1966	6.25	12.50	25.00
A JAZZ PIANO ANTHOLOGY				
Columbia PG 32355 [(2)]	197?	3.75	7.50	15.00
JAZZ PIANO GREATS				
Folkways FJ-2852	197?	3.00	6.00	12.00
JAZZ PIONEERS 1933-36				
Prestige PRLP-7647	1969	3.75	7.50	15.00
JAZZ POLL WINNERS				
Columbia CL 1610 [M]	1960	5.00	10.00	20.00
JAZZ POTPOURRI				
Audiophile AP-24 [M]	1953	7.50	15.00	30.00
THE JAZZ ROUND				
Verve VSP-24 [M]	1966	3.75	7.50	15.00
Verve VSPS-24 [R]	1966	2.50	5.00	10.00
A JAZZ SALUTE TO FREEDOM				
Core 100 [(2) M]	196?	6.25	12.50	25.00
THE JAZZ SCENE				
American Recording Society G-419 [M]	1957	7.50	15.00	30.00
Clef MGC-674 [M]	1955	10.00	20.00	40.00
—Reissue of 4007				
Clef MGC-4007 [M]	1953	12.50	25.00	50.00
Clef Special Edition (no #) [(2) 10]	1953	25.00	50.00	100.00
—Two 10-inch LPs in box. Buyers had the option of purchasing a collection of photos that had been used in the original 78 rpm album; add another 50 percent if these photos are included				
Verve MGV-8060 [M]	1957	7.50	15.00	30.00
—Reissue of Clef 674				
Verve V-8060 [M]	1961	5.00	10.00	20.00
JAZZ SOUL OF "CLEOPATRA"				
New Jazz NJLP-8292 [M]	1962	10.00	20.00	40.00
—Purple label				
New Jazz NJLP-8292 [M]	1965	5.00	10.00	20.00
—Blue label, trident logo at right				
THE JAZZ SOUND				
Columbia Special Products CSP 298 [M]	1966	2.50	5.00	10.00
JAZZ SOUTH PACIFIC				
Regent MG-6001 [M]	1956	12.50	25.00	50.00
Savoy MG-12205 [M]	196?	5.00	10.00	20.00

Label, Number	Yr	VG	VG+	NM
THE JAZZ STORY				
Coral CJE-100 [(3) M]	195?	25.00	50.00	100.00
—Box set; narrated by Steve Allen				
JAZZ SUPER HITS				
Atlantic SD 1528	1969	6.25	12.50	25.00
JAZZ SUPER HITS, VOL. 2				
Atlantic SD 1559	1970	5.00	10.00	20.00
JAZZ SURPRISE				
Crown CLP-5008 [M]	1957	5.00	10.00	20.00
JAZZ SWINGS BROADWAY				
Pacific Jazz PJM-404 [M]	1956	12.50	25.00	50.00
World Pacific PJM-404 [M]	1958	10.00	20.00	40.00
JAZZ TIME U.S.A. — VOLUME 1				
Brunswick BL 54000 [M]	1952	7.50	15.00	30.00
JAZZ TIME U.S.A. — VOLUME 2				
Brunswick BL 54001 [M]	1953	7.50	15.00	30.00
JAZZ TIME U.S.A. — VOLUME 3				
Brunswick BL 54002 [M]	1954	7.50	15.00	30.00
JAZZ VARIATIONS, VOL. 1				
Stinson SLP-20 [10]	195?	15.00	30.00	60.00
Stinson SLP-20 [M]	196?	6.25	12.50	25.00
JAZZ VARIATIONS, VOL. 2				
Stinson SLP-29 [M]	196?	6.25	12.50	25.00
JAZZ VIOLINS OF THE 40S				
Folkways FJ-2854	197?	3.00	6.00	12.00
JAZZ VOCALS AWARD ALBUM				
Bethlehem BCP-6068 [M]	1963	6.25	12.50	25.00
JAZZ WEST COAST, VOL. 1				
Pacific Jazz JWC-500 [M]	1956	12.50	25.00	50.00
World Pacific JWC-500 [M]	1958	10.00	20.00	40.00
JAZZ WEST COAST, VOL. 2				
Pacific Jazz JWC-501 [M]	1956	12.50	25.00	50.00
World Pacific JWC-501 [M]	1958	10.00	20.00	40.00
JAZZ WEST COAST, VOL. 3				
Pacific Jazz JWC-507 [M]	1957	12.50	25.00	50.00
World Pacific JWC-507 [M]	1958	10.00	20.00	40.00
JAZZ WEST COAST, VOL. 4				
World Pacific JWC-510 [M]	1958	10.00	20.00	40.00
World Pacific ST-1009 [S]	1959	7.50	15.00	30.00
JAZZ WEST COAST, VOL. 5				
World Pacific JWC-511 [M]	1958	10.00	20.00	40.00
THE JAZZ WORLD				
Columbia Special Products CSS 524 [S]	1967	2.50	5.00	10.00
JAZZMEN — DETROIT				
Savoy MG-12083 [M]	1956	20.00	40.00	80.00
JAZZTONE SAMPLER				
Jazztone J-SPEC-100 [10]	1955	12.50	25.00	50.00
—With booklet				
JAZZVILLE, VOL. 1				
Dawn DLP-1101 [M]	1956	20.00	40.00	80.00
JAZZ, VOL. 1: THE SOUTH				
Folkways FP-53/4 [M]	1951	6.25	12.50	25.00
Folkways FJ-2801 [M]	197?	3.00	6.00	12.00
JAZZ, VOL. 2: THE BLUES				
Folkways FP-55/6 [M]	1951	6.25	12.50	25.00
Folkways FJ-2802 [M]	197?	3.00	6.00	12.00
JAZZ, VOL. 3: NEW ORLEANS				
Folkways FP-57/8 [M]	1951	6.25	12.50	25.00
Folkways FJ-2803 [M]	197?	3.00	6.00	12.00
JAZZ, VOL. 4: JAZZ SINGERS				
Folkways FP-59/60 [M]	1951	6.25	12.50	25.00
Folkways FJ-2804 [M]	197?	3.00	6.00	12.00
JAZZ, VOL. 5: CHICAGO				
Folkways FP-63/4 [M]	1951	6.25	12.50	25.00
Folkways FJ-2805 [M]	197?	3.00	6.00	12.00
JAZZ, VOL. 6: CHICAGO #2				
Folkways FP-65/6 [M]	1951	6.25	12.50	25.00
Folkways FJ-2806 [M]	197?	3.00	6.00	12.00
JAZZ, VOL. 7: NEW YORK 1922-1934				
Folkways FP-67/8 [M]	1951	6.25	12.50	25.00
Folkways FJ-2807 [M]	197?	3.00	6.00	12.00
JAZZ, VOL. 8: BIG BANDS BEFORE 1938				
Folkways FP-69/70 [M]	1951	6.25	12.50	25.00
Folkways FJ-2808 [M]	197?	3.00	6.00	12.00
JAZZ, VOL. 9: PIANO				
Folkways FP-71/2 [M]	1951	6.25	12.50	25.00
Folkways FJ-2809 [M]	197?	3.00	6.00	12.00
JAZZ, VOL. 10: BOOGIE WOOGIE, JUMP, KANSAS CITY				
Folkways FP-73/4 [M]	1951	6.25	12.50	25.00
Folkways FJ-2810 [M]	197?	3.00	6.00	12.00
JAZZ, VOL. 11: ADDENDA				
Folkways FP-75/6 [M]	1951	6.25	12.50	25.00
Folkways FJ-2811 [M]	197?	3.00	6.00	12.00
JESUS CHRIST SUPERSTAR				
Decca DXSA 7206 [(2)]	1970	6.25	12.50	25.00
—Gatefold cover with booklet				
Decca DXA 7206 [(2)]	1970	7.50	15.00	30.00
—Box set with booklet				
MCA 2-10000 [(2)]	1973	3.00	6.00	12.00
—Gatefold cover with booklet; reissue				
JINGLE BELL JAZZ				
Columbia CL 1893 [M]	1962	5.00	10.00	20.00
Columbia CS 8693 [S]	1962	3.75	7.50	15.00
Harmony KH 32529	1973	3.00	6.00	12.00
—Reissue of CS 8693 with one track changed				
JOHN COLTRANE IN THE WINNER'S CIRCLE				
Bethlehem BCP-6066 [M]	1961	6.25	12.50	25.00
—Reissue of 6024 with new title				
JOHN HAMMOND PRESENTS "FROM SPIRITUALS TO SWING" AT CARNEGIE HALL 1938				
Vanguard VRS-8523 [M]	1959	10.00	20.00	40.00
JOHN HAMMOND PRESENTS "FROM SPIRITUALS TO SWING" AT CARNEGIE HALL 1939				
Vanguard VRS-8524 [M]	1959	10.00	20.00	40.00
THE JOY OF CHRISTMAS				
Capitol SP 8693	1968	3.00	6.00	12.00
Capitol Creative Products SL-6580	1968	3.00	6.00	12.00
Columbia Special Products P 12042	1973	3.00	6.00	12.00
—Sold only at Strawbridge & Clothier stores (Philadelphia area)				
RCA Victor PRM-197 [M]	1965	3.75	7.50	15.00
—Created for the National Tea Company				
RCA Victor PRS-429	1972	3.00	6.00	12.00
THE JOY OF CHRISTMAS, FEATURING MARTY ROBBINS AND HIS FRIENDS				
Columbia Special Products C 11087	1972	3.75	7.50	15.00
THE JOY OF CHRISTMAS, VOLUME II				
RCA Victor PRM-230 [M]	1966	3.75	7.50	15.00
—Created for the National Tea Company				
RCA Victor PRM-230-A [M]	1966	3.75	7.50	15.00
—Sold only at Acme markets (Mid-Atlantic area); same contents as PRM-230				
JOY TO THE WORLD				
Columbia Special Products P 11647	1973	2.50	5.00	10.00
THE JOYFUL SOUND OF CHRISTMAS				
RCA Record Club CSP-0601 [(2)]	1969	5.00	10.00	20.00
—Available only through the RCA Record Club				
JOYOUS CHRISTMAS, VOLUME 2				
Columbia Special Products CSS 808	1968	3.00	6.00	12.00
—Produced for the Beneficial Finance System				
JOYOUS CHRISTMAS, VOLUME 4				
Columbia Special Products CSS 1485	1970	3.00	6.00	12.00
—Produced for the Beneficial Finance System				
JOYOUS CHRISTMAS, VOLUME V				
Columbia Special Products C 10398	1971	2.50	5.00	10.00
—Produced for the Beneficial Finance System				
JOYOUS CHRISTMAS, VOLUME 6				
Columbia Special Products C 11083	1972	2.50	5.00	10.00
—Produced for the Beneficial Finance System				
JOYOUS MUSIC FOR CHRISTMAS TIME				
Reader's Digest RD 45-M [(4) M]	1963	5.00	10.00	20.00
Reader's Digest RD 45-S [(4) S]	1963	5.00	10.00	20.00
—Available only through Reader's Digest magazine by mail order				
JOYOUS NOEL				
Reader's Digest RDA-57A [(4)]	1966	5.00	10.00	20.00
—Available only through Reader's Digest magazine by mail order				
THE JOYOUS SONGS OF CHRISTMAS				
Columbia Special Products C 10400	1971	2.50	5.00	10.00
—Sold only at Goodyear tire dealers				
JOYS OF CHRISTMAS				
Capitol Creative Products SL-6610	1969	3.00	6.00	12.00
Capitol Special Markets SL-6610	197?	2.50	5.00	10.00
—Reissue with revised label name				
JUBILEE MONAURAL SAMPLER: VOCALS AND INSTRUMENTALS				
Jubilee MSJLP-803 [M]	1959	7.50	15.00	30.00
JUBILEE STEREOSONIC VOCAL SAMPLER, VOLUME 2				
Jubilee SSJLP-802 [S]	1959	10.00	20.00	40.00
JUBILEE SURPRISE PARTY				
Jubilee JGM-1107 [M]	1959	37.50	75.00	150.00
Jubilee JGS-1107 [S]	1959	50.00	100.00	200.00

Label, Number	Yr	VG	VG+	NM
JUST JAZZ				
Imperial LP-9246 [M]	1963	5.00	10.00	20.00
Imperial LP-12246 [S]	1963	6.25	12.50	25.00
K-BOX DUSTY DISCS				
Roulette R 25338 [M]	1966	5.00	10.00	20.00
KANSAS CITY IN THE '30S				
Capitol T 1057 [M]	1958	6.25	12.50	25.00
KANSAS CITY JAZZ				
Decca DL 8044 [M]	1954	10.00	20.00	40.00
KANSAS CITY PIANO				
Decca DL 9226 [M]	1967	7.50	15.00	30.00
Decca DL 79226 [R]	1967	3.00	6.00	12.00
KATS KARAVAN (OLD FAVORITES WITH JIM LOWE)				
Vee Jay LP-100 [M]	1957	12.50	25.00	50.00
—Gold label, black print				
KBIG CHOICES				
World Pacific KBIG-1 [S]	1964	6.25	12.50	25.00
KEYBOARD KINGS				
MGM E-100 [10]	1951	12.50	25.00	50.00
KEYBOARD KINGS OF JAZZ				
RCA Victor LPT-4 [10]	1951	10.00	20.00	40.00
KGFJ SOUNDS OF SUCCESS				
Roulette R 25349 [M]	1967	5.00	10.00	20.00
KINGS OF CLASSIC JAZZ				
Riverside RLP 12-131 [M]	1957	10.00	20.00	40.00
KINGS OF THE KEYBOARD				
American Recording Society G-406 [M]	1956	7.50	15.00	30.00
THE KINGS SING THE BLUES				
Teem LP-5005 [M]	196?	7.50	15.00	30.00
KNOW YOUR JAZZ				
ABC-Paramount ABC-115 [M]	1956	7.50	15.00	30.00
KPOI'S BATTLE OF THE SURFING BANDS				
Del-Fi DFST-1235 [S]	1964	25.00	50.00	100.00
—Honolulu version of the above LP				
Del-Fi DFLP-1235 [M]	1964	15.00	30.00	60.00
KTLA'S BATTLE OF THE SURFING BANDS				
Del-Fi DFLP-1235 [M]	1964	12.50	25.00	50.00
Del-Fi DFST-1235 [S]	1964	20.00	40.00	80.00
—Los Angeles version of the above LP				
KYA'S BATTLE OF THE SURFING BANDS				
Del-Fi DFLP-1235 [M]	1964	12.50	25.00	50.00
Del-Fi DFST-1235 [S]	1964	20.00	40.00	80.00
—San Francisco version of the above LP, with slightly different contents				
KYA'S MEMORIES OF THE COW PALACE				
Autumn LP 101 [M]	1963	17.50	35.00	70.00
KYA GOLDEN GATE GREATS				
Chess LP 1458 SF [M]	1961	37.50	75.00	150.00
—San Francisco version of "Golden Gassers," Chess 1458				
LATE MUSIC, VOLUME I				
Columbia CL 541 [M]	1954	6.25	12.50	25.00
LATE MUSIC, VOLUME II				
Columbia CL 542 [M]	1954	6.25	12.50	25.00
LATE MUSIC, VOLUME III				
Columbia CL 543 [M]	1954	6.25	12.50	25.00
LAURIE GOLDEN GOODIES				
Laurie LLP-2041 [M]	1967	3.75	7.50	15.00
Laurie SLLP-2041 [P]	1967	6.25	12.50	25.00
LEONARD FEATHER'S ENCYCLOPEDIA OF JAZZ OF THE '60S: BLUES BAG				
Vee Jay LP-2506 [M]	1964	5.00	10.00	20.00
LEONARD FEATHER'S ENCYCLOPEDIA OF JAZZ, VOLUME ONE: GIANTS OF THE SAXOPHONE				
Vee Jay LP-2501 [M]	1964	5.00	10.00	20.00
Vee Jay VJS-2501 [S]	1964	6.25	12.50	25.00
LESTORIAN MODE				
Savoy MG-12105 [M]		—	—	—
—See STAN GETZ.				
LET'S CELEBRATE CHRISTMAS				
Capitol Special Markets SL-6923	1973	3.00	6.00	12.00
LET'S HAVE A DANCE PARTY				
Ace LP-1019 [M]	1961	17.50	35.00	70.00
LET'S SING ABOUT FREEDOM				
Vee Jay LP-5044 [M]	1963	7.50	15.00	30.00
LIBERTY PREMIER SERIES SPECTACULAR				
Liberty L-5504 [M]	1962	5.00	10.00	20.00
Liberty S-6604 [S]	1962	7.50	15.00	30.00
LIBERTY PROUDLY PRESENTS STEREO — THE VISUAL SOUND				
Liberty LST-100 [S]	1959	10.00	20.00	40.00

Label, Number	Yr	VG	VG+	NM
THE LIFE TREASURY OF CHRISTMAS MUSIC				
Project/Capitol TL 100 [M]	1963	5.00	10.00	20.00
—Designed as a supplement to the Life Book of Christmas; selections performed by anonymous chorus and orchestra and Boy Choristers from the Church of the Transfiguration (NY)				
LIGHTS OUT SAN FRANCISCO				
Blue Thumb BT 6004	1970	6.25	12.50	25.00
LIKE 'ER RED HOT				
ABC Duke DLPX-73 [M]	1974	3.75	7.50	15.00
Duke DLP-73 [M]	1960	30.00	60.00	120.00
—Purple and yellow label				
Duke DLP-73 [M]	196?	12.50	25.00	50.00
—Orange label				
Duke DLP-73 [M]	196?	7.50	15.00	30.00
—Green label, "Distributed by ABC-Dunhill"				
LISTEN TO OUR STORY				
Brunswick BL 59001 [10]	1950	15.00	30.00	60.00
A LITTLE ROCK AND ROLL FOR EVERYBODY				
Audio Lab AL-1567 [M]	1960	50.00	100.00	200.00
THE LITTLEST ANGEL/LULLABY OF CHRISTMAS				
Decca DLP 8009 [M]	1949	10.00	20.00	40.00
LIVE AT BILL GRAHAM'S FILLMORE WEST				
Columbia CS 9893	1969	3.75	7.50	15.00
LIVE AT THE WHISKEY A-GO-GO				
Vee Jay LP-1100 [M]	1964	7.50	15.00	30.00
—Not known to exist in stereo				
THE LIVELY SOUND OF UNIVERSITY				
Capitol Custom (no #) [M]	1966	5.00	10.00	20.00
—"Mustang Sweepstakes Prize Winner" on front cover				
LOADED				
Savoy MG-12074 [M]	1956	12.50	25.00	50.00
LONDON BROIL				
Angel ANG-60004 [10]	1955	12.50	25.00	50.00
A LOOK AT YESTERDAY				
Mainstream S-6025 [R]	1965	3.00	6.00	12.00
Mainstream 56025 [M]	1965	6.25	12.50	25.00
LOOK WHO'S SURFIN' NOW!				
King 882 [M]	1964	37.50	75.00	150.00
LOONEY TUNES AND MERRIE MELODIES				
Warner Bros. PRO 423 [(3)]	1970	25.00	50.00	100.00
—Box set with booklet of liner notes; originals have green labels				
A LOT OF YARN BUT A WELL-KNITTED JAZZ ALBUM				
Bethlehem BCP-91 [M]	1958	7.50	15.00	30.00
LOVE THOSE GOODIES				
Checker LP 2973 [DJ]	1959	125.00	250.00	500.00
—White label, multi-color splash vinyl				
Checker LP 2973 [M]	1959	30.00	60.00	120.00
LULLABY OF BIRDLAND				
RCA Victor LPM-1146 [M]	1955	12.50	25.00	50.00
LUSTY MOODS				
Moodsville MVLP-37 [M]	1963	10.00	20.00	40.00
—Green label				
Moodsville MVST-37 [S]	1963	10.00	20.00	40.00
—Green label				
Moodsville MVLP-37 [M]	1965	5.00	10.00	20.00
—Blue label, trident logo at right				
Moodsville MVST-37 [S]	1965	5.00	10.00	20.00
—Blue label, trident logo at right				
New Jazz NJLP-8319 [M]	1963	—	—	—
—Canceled				
Status ST-8319 [M]	1965	7.50	15.00	30.00
MAD "TWISTS" ROCK 'N' ROLL				
Big Top 12-1305 [M]	1962	25.00	50.00	100.00
THE MAGIC HORN				
RCA Victor LPM-1332 [M]	1956	10.00	20.00	40.00
THE MAGIC OF CHRISTMAS				
Capitol SWBB-93810 [(2)]	1971	3.75	7.50	15.00
—Available only through the Capitol Record Club				
Columbia Musical Treasury P2M 5245	196?	3.75	7.50	15.00
—No artists mentioned				
Columbia Musical Treasury P3S 5806 [(3)]	1972	5.00	10.00	20.00
THE MAGIC OF CHRISTMAS WITH CHILDREN				
Capitol Creative Products L 6517 [M]	196?	3.75	7.50	15.00
—Sold only at Safeway stores (In Association with Jon M. Huntsman Inc., Continental Production Company)				
MAGNAVOX ALBUM OF CHRISTMAS MUSIC				
Columbia Special Products CSQ 11093 [Q]	1972	5.00	10.00	20.00
—Sold only at Magnavox dealers; yes, this is in quadraphonic!				
MAGNAVOX PRESENTS A REPRISE OF GREAT HITS				
Reprise PRO 578	1973	2.50	5.00	10.00

Label, Number	Yr	VG	VG+	NM
MAHALIA (JACKSON) AND FRIENDS AT CHRISTMASTIME				
Columbia Special Products P 11804	1973	3.00	6.00	12.00
—Side 2 is all rechanneled stereo; Side 1 is true stereo				
MAMBO JAZZ				
Prestige PRLP-135 [10]	1952	37.50	75.00	150.00
THE MAN WITH A HORN				
Decca DL 5191 [10]	1950	12.50	25.00	50.00
THE MANY FACES OF THE BLUES				
Savoy MG-12125 [M]	1957	12.50	25.00	50.00
THE MANY MOODS OF CHRISTMAS				
Columbia Special Products P 12013	1973	3.00	6.00	12.00
—Sold only at Goodyear tire dealers				
RCA Special Products DPL1-0085	1974	2.50	5.00	10.00
MAR Y SOL				
Atco SD-2-705 [(2)]	1972	3.75	7.50	15.00
THE MELLOW MOODS OF JAZZ				
RCA Victor LPM-1365 [M]	1956	10.00	20.00	40.00
MELLOW THE MOOD/JAZZ IN A MELLOW MOOD				
Blue Note BLP-5001 [10]	1951	50.00	100.00	200.00
MEMORABLE SESSIONS IN JAZZ				
Blue Note BLP-5026 [10]	1953	50.00	100.00	200.00
MEMORIES ARE MADE OF HITS				
Liberty LRP-3200 [M]	1961	6.25	12.50	25.00
—Reissued as "The Original Hits, Volume 4"				
MEMORY LANE, HITS BY THE ORIGINAL GROUPS				
Fire FLP-100 [M]	1959	50.00	100.00	200.00
—Reissue of "Here Are the Hits!" with the same label and number				
MEMPHIS COUNTRY				
Sun 120	1970	3.75	7.50	15.00
MEMPHIS GOLD				
Stax 710 [M]	1966	6.25	12.50	25.00
Stax S710 [S]	1966	7.50	15.00	30.00
MEMPHIS GOLD VOLUME 2				
Stax 726 [M]	1967	5.00	10.00	20.00
Stax S726 [S]	1967	6.25	12.50	25.00
MEMPHIS MILLIONS				
Stax STS 3023	1973	3.75	7.50	15.00
MERRY CHRISTMAS				
Columbia Musical Treasury 3P 6306 [(3)]	1975	3.75	7.50	15.00
Coral CRL 56080 [10]	1952	20.00	40.00	80.00
RCA Victor PRS-168	1964	3.75	7.50	15.00
MERRY CHRISTMAS BABY (CHRISTMAS MUSIC FOR YOUNG LOVERS)				
Hollywood HLP 501 [M]	1956	30.00	60.00	120.00
MERRY CHRISTMAS FROM MOTOWN				
Motown MS-681	1968	7.50	15.00	30.00
MERRY CHRISTMAS FROM SESAME STREET				
CRA CTW 25516	1975	3.00	6.00	12.00
MERRY CHRISTMAS FROM...				
King 680 [M]	1959	50.00	100.00	200.00
MERRY CHRISTMAS MUSIC/CHRISTMAS FAVORITES				
Plymouth P12-59 [M]	1952	5.00	10.00	20.00
—Artists not mentioned on jacket or label				
MERRY CHRISTMAS TO YOU				
Capitol T 9030 [M]	1955	12.50	25.00	50.00
MERRY CHRISTMAS WITH NAT KING COLE/FRED WARING AND THE PENNSYLVANIANS				
Capitol Special Markets SL-6883	1973	2.50	5.00	10.00
A MERRY MERRY CHRISTMAS				
Columbia Special Products CSP 161	1964	3.75	7.50	15.00
—Number on record is "XTV 86094" on Side 1 and "XTV 86095" on Side 2				
THE METRONOME ALL-STARS				
Columbia CL 2528 [10]	1954	7.50	15.00	30.00
Harmony HL 7044 [M]	1957	6.25	12.50	25.00
RCA Camden CAL-426 [M]	1958	6.25	12.50	25.00
METRONOME ALL STARS 1956				
Clef MGC-743 [M]	1956	10.00	20.00	40.00
Verve MGV-8030 [M]	1957	10.00	20.00	40.00
Verve V-8030 [M]	1961	5.00	10.00	20.00
MGM RECORDS PARADE OF STARS				
MGM NP 90569 [M]	1965	5.00	10.00	20.00
—Capitol Record Club sampler of 12 MGM artists and soundtracks				
MICKEY MOST PRESENTS BRITISH GO-GO				
MGM E 4306 [M]	1965	7.50	15.00	30.00
MGM SE 4306 [R]	1965	7.50	15.00	30.00
MICKEY MOST PRESENTS ENGLISH IN-GROUPS				
Metro 577 [M]	1966	5.00	10.00	20.00
Metro MS-577 [R]	1966	5.00	10.00	20.00
MIDDLE OF THE ROAD				
Warner Bros. PRO 525 [(2)]	1972	7.50	15.00	30.00
—Originals have green labels				
MIDNIGHT JAZZ AT CARNEGIE HALL				
Verve MGV-8189-2 [(2) M]	1957	12.50	25.00	50.00
Verve V-8189-2 [(2) M]	1961	6.25	12.50	25.00
THE MILLION-AIRS				
Coral CRL 57310 [M]	1959	6.25	12.50	25.00
A MILLION OR MORE				
ABC-Paramount ABC-216 [M]	1959	20.00	40.00	80.00
MILLION SELLER DANCE HITS				
Parkway P-7028 [M]	1963	7.50	15.00	30.00
THE MODERN IDIOM				
Capitol H 325 [10]	1952	12.50	25.00	50.00
MODERN JAZZ				
London LL 1185 [M]	1955	5.00	10.00	20.00
Tops L-1521 [M]	1958	5.00	10.00	20.00
MODERN JAZZ CONCERT				
Adventures in Sound WL-127 [M]	1958	10.00	20.00	40.00
MODERN JAZZ FESTIVAL				
Harmony HL 7196 [M]	1958	5.00	10.00	20.00
MODERN JAZZ GALLERY				
Kapp KXL-5001 [M]	195?	5.00	10.00	20.00
MODERN JAZZ GREATS				
Crown CLP-5212 [M]	196?	3.75	7.50	15.00
MODERN JAZZ GREATS, VOL. 2				
Crown CLP-5220 [M]	196?	3.75	7.50	15.00
MODERN JAZZ HALL OF FAME				
Design DLP-29 [M]	196?	3.00	6.00	12.00
Design DLPS-29 [R]	196?	2.00	4.00	8.00
MODERN JAZZ PIANO				
RCA Camden CAL-384 [M]	1958	6.25	12.50	25.00
MODERN JAZZ SPECTACULAR				
Jazztone J-1231 [M]	1956	7.50	15.00	30.00
MODERN JAZZ TRUMPETS				
Prestige PRLP-113 [10]	1951	50.00	100.00	200.00
MODERN MOODS				
Moodsville MVLP-2 [M]	1961	10.00	20.00	40.00
—Green label				
Moodsville MVLP-2 [M]	1965	5.00	10.00	20.00
—Blue label, trident logo at right				
MONARCH ALL STAR JAZZ, VOL. 1				
Monarch LP-201 [10]	1952	12.50	25.00	50.00
MONARCH ALL STAR JAZZ, VOL. 2				
Monarch LP-202 [10]	1952	12.50	25.00	50.00
MONARCH ALL STAR JAZZ, VOL. 3				
Monarch LP-203 [10]	1952	12.50	25.00	50.00
MONARCH ALL STAR JAZZ, VOL. 4				
Monarch LP-204 [10]	1952	12.50	25.00	50.00
MONARCH ALL STAR JAZZ, VOL. 5				
Monarch LP-205 [10]	1952	12.50	25.00	50.00
MONDAY NIGHT AT BIRDLAND				
Roulette R 52015 [M]	1958	7.50	15.00	30.00
Roulette SR 52015 [S]	1959	7.50	15.00	30.00
MONTAGE				
Savoy MG-12029 [M]	1955	20.00	40.00	80.00
MONTGOMERY WARD PRESENTS A CHRISTMAS TO REMEMBER				
Capitol Creative Products SL-6573	1968	3.00	6.00	12.00
—Sold only at Montgomery Ward stores				
MONTGOMERY WARD PRESENTS A CHRISTMAS TO REMEMBER VOL. 2				
Capitol Creative Products SL-6610	1969	3.00	6.00	12.00
—Sold only at Montgomery Ward stores				
MONTGOMERY WARD PRESENTS A CHRISTMAS TO REMEMBER VOL. 3				
Capitol Creative Products SL-6681	1970	2.50	5.00	10.00
—Sold only at Montgomery Ward stores				
MONTGOMERY WARD PRESENTS CHRISTMAS FAVORITES				
Montgomery Ward W-101	1965	3.75	7.50	15.00
—No artists mentioned on label or jacket				
MONUMENTAL COUNTRY HITS				
Monument SLP-18095	1968	5.00	10.00	20.00
MONUMENTAL POP HITS				
Monument SLP-18096	1968	5.00	10.00	20.00
MOOD IN BLUE				
Urania UJLP-1209 [M]	1955	7.50	15.00	30.00
MOOD TO BE WOOED				
Cadet LP-784 [M]	1967	5.00	10.00	20.00

Label, Number	Yr	VG	VG+	NM
Cadet LPS-784 [S]	1967	3.75	7.50	15.00
MORE DRUMS ON FIRE				
World Pacific ST-1022 [S]	1960	7.50	15.00	30.00
World Pacific WP-1261 [M]	1960	10.00	20.00	40.00
MORE FOR YOUR MONEY				
Bell 6009	1968	5.00	10.00	20.00
MORE GOLD HITS, VOLUME 2				
Warwick W 2044 [M]	1961	20.00	40.00	80.00
MORE GOLDEN GREATS				
Liberty LRP-3548 [M]	1967	5.00	10.00	20.00
Liberty LST-7548 [P]	1967	3.75	7.50	15.00
MORE GREAT HITS OF 1964 AND OTHER GOLDEN GOODIES				
Vee Jay LP-1136 [M]	1965	7.50	15.00	30.00
—Not known to exist in stereo				
MORE LIVE ECHOES OF THE SWINGING BANDS				
RCA Victor LSP-1983 [S]	1959	12.50	25.00	50.00
RCA Victor LPM-1983 [M]	1959	10.00	20.00	40.00
MORE SOLID GOLD PROGRAMMING				
Screen Gems/Columbia CPL-716/7 [(2) DJ]	1975	7.50	15.00	30.00
—Promo-only compilation of oldies sent to radio to spur airplay on songs owned by this publishing house; contains three Beatles recordings				
THE MOST				
Forum Circle FC-9079 [M]	1963	3.00	6.00	12.00
Forum Circle FCS-9079 [S]	1963	3.00	6.00	12.00
THE MOST OF THE TWIST				
Roulette R 25176 [M]	1962	6.25	12.50	25.00
—Originals have a white label with colored spokes				
THE MOST, VOLUME 1				
Roulette R 52050 [M]	1960	5.00	10.00	20.00
Roulette SR 52050 [S]	1960	6.25	12.50	25.00
THE MOST, VOLUME 2				
Roulette R 52053 [M]	1960	5.00	10.00	20.00
Roulette SR 52053 [S]	1960	6.25	12.50	25.00
THE MOST, VOLUME 3				
Roulette R 52057 [M]	1961	5.00	10.00	20.00
Roulette SR 52057 [S]	1961	6.25	12.50	25.00
THE MOST, VOLUME 4				
Roulette R 52062 [M]	1961	5.00	10.00	20.00
Roulette SR 52062 [S]	1961	6.25	12.50	25.00
THE MOST, VOLUME 5				
Roulette R 52075 [M]	1961	5.00	10.00	20.00
Roulette SR 52075 [S]	1961	6.25	12.50	25.00
THE MOTOR-TOWN REVIEW, VOL. 1				
Motown MT 609 [M]	1963	10.00	20.00	40.00
THE MOTOR-TOWN REVIEW, VOL. 2				
Motown MT 615 [M]	1964	7.50	15.00	30.00
MOTOR CITY SCENE				
Bethlehem BCP-6056 [M]	1961	12.50	25.00	50.00
THE MOTORTOWN REVIEW IN PARIS				
Tamla T 264 [M]	1965	6.25	12.50	25.00
Tamla TS 264 [S]	1965	7.50	15.00	30.00
MOTORTOWN REVIEW LIVE				
Motown MS 688	1969	3.75	7.50	15.00
THE MOTORTOWN REVUE LIVE!				
Motown MS-688	1969	6.25	12.50	25.00
MOTOWN AT THE HOLLYWOOD PALACE				
Motown MS 703	1970	3.75	7.50	15.00
Motown MS-703	1970	3.75	7.50	15.00
MOTOWN CHARTBUSTERS, VOLUME 1				
Motown MS-707	1970	3.75	7.50	15.00
MOTOWN CHARTBUSTERS, VOLUME 2				
Motown MS-715	1970	3.75	7.50	15.00
A MOTOWN CHRISTMAS				
Motown M-795V2 [(2)]	1973	5.00	10.00	20.00
MOTOWN SPECIAL				
Motown M 603 [M]	1962	20.00	40.00	80.00
THE MOTOWN STORY: THE FIRST DECADE				
Motown MS-726 [(5)]	1971	7.50	15.00	30.00
MOTOWN WINNER'S CIRCLE: #1 HITS, VOL. 1				
Gordy GS-935	1969	6.25	12.50	25.00
MOTOWN WINNER'S CIRCLE: #1 HITS, VOL. 2				
Gordy GS-936	1969	6.25	12.50	25.00
MOTOWN WINNER'S CIRCLE: #1 HITS, VOL. 3				
Gordy GS-943	1969	6.25	12.50	25.00
MOTOWN WINNER'S CIRCLE: #1 HITS, VOL. 4				
Gordy GS-946	1969	6.25	12.50	25.00
MOTOWN WINNER'S CIRCLE: #1 HITS, VOL. 5				
Gordy GS-950	1970	6.25	12.50	25.00
MOUNTAIN FROLIC				
Brunswick BL 59000 [10]	1950	15.00	30.00	60.00
MURRAY THE K'S BLASTS FROM THE PAST				
Chess LP 1461 [M]	1961	10.00	20.00	40.00
MURRAY THE K'S GASSERS FOR SUBMARINE RACE WATCHERS				
Chess LP 1470 [M]	1962	10.00	20.00	40.00
MURRAY THE K'S GOLDEN GASSERS				
Chess LP 1458 NYC [M]	1961	37.50	75.00	150.00
—New York version of "Golden Gassers," Chess 1458				
MURRAY THE K'S NINETEEN-SIXTY TWO BOSS GOLDEN GASSERS				
Scepter SP-510 [M]	1963	5.00	10.00	20.00
Scepter SPS-510 [P]	1963	6.25	12.50	25.00
MURRAY THE K — LIVE FROM THE BROOKLYN FOX				
KFM 1001 [M]	1963	10.00	20.00	40.00
MURRAY THE K PRESENTS GOLDEN GASSERS FOR A DANCE PARTY				
Roulette R 25192 [M]	1962	6.25	12.50	25.00
MURRAY THE K PRESENTS GOLDEN GASSERS FOR HAND HOLDERS				
Roulette R 25191 [M]	1962	6.25	12.50	25.00
MURRAY THE "K'S" SING ALONG WITH THE ORIGINAL GOLDEN GASSERS				
Roulette R 25159 [M]	1961	7.50	15.00	30.00
MUSIC FOR THE BOY FRIEND...HE REALLY DIGS JAZZ				
Decca DL 8314 [M]	1956	7.50	15.00	30.00
MUSIC FROM THE DANCING YEARS				
RCA Victor PR-112 [M]	1961	3.75	7.50	15.00
—Created for Dole Pineapple				
MUSIC FROM THE SOUTH, VOL. 1: COUNTRY BRASS BANDS				
Folkways FA-2650 [M]	195?	5.00	10.00	20.00
THE MUSIC OF NEW ORLEANS, VOL. 1				
Folkways FA-2461 [M]	1959	5.00	10.00	20.00
THE MUSIC OF NEW ORLEANS, VOL. 2				
Folkways FA-2462 [M]	1959	5.00	10.00	20.00
THE MUSIC OF NEW ORLEANS, VOL. 3: DANCE HALLS				
Folkways FA-2463 [M]	1959	5.00	10.00	20.00
THE MUSIC OF NEW ORLEANS, VOL. 4: THE BIRTH OF JAZZ				
Folkways FA-2464 [M]	1959	5.00	10.00	20.00
THE MUSIC OF NEW ORLEANS, VOL. 5: NEW ORLEANS JAZZ				
Folkways FA-2465 [M]	1959	5.00	10.00	20.00
THE MUSIC PEOPLE				
Columbia C3X 31280 [(3)]	1972	6.25	12.50	25.00
MUSIC TO READ JAMES BOND BY				
United Artists UAL-3415 [M]	1965	5.00	10.00	20.00
United Artists UAS-6415 [S]	1965	6.25	12.50	25.00
MUSIC TO READ JAMES BOND BY, VOL. 2				
United Artists UAL-3541 [M]	1966	5.00	10.00	20.00
United Artists UAS-6541 [S]	1966	6.25	12.50	25.00
MUSIC TO TRIM YOUR TREE BY				
RCA Victor PRM 225 [M]	1966	3.00	6.00	12.00
RCA Victor PRS 225 [S]	1966	3.75	7.50	15.00
A MUSICAL HISTORY OF JAZZ				
Grand Award GA 33-322 [M]	1955	5.00	10.00	20.00
MY FAIR LADY				
New Jazz NJLP-8315 [M]	1963	—	—	—
—Canceled				
Status ST-8315 [M]	1965	7.50	15.00	30.00
MY SON THE SURF NUT				
Capitol T 1939 [M]	1963	12.50	25.00	50.00
Capitol ST 1939 [S]	1963	15.00	30.00	60.00
THE NAMES OF DIXIELAND				
Baronet B-108 [M]	195?	5.00	10.00	20.00
NASCAR GOES COUNTRY				
MCA 474	1975	7.50	15.00	30.00
NASHVILLE BANDSTAND				
King 813 [M]	1962	25.00	50.00	100.00
NASHVILLE BANDSTAND, VOLUME 2				
King 847 [M]	1963	20.00	40.00	80.00
NATIVE NEW ORLEANS JAZZ				
Dot DLP-3009 [M]	1956	7.50	15.00	30.00
NEW BLUE HORNS				
Riverside RLP 12-294 [M]	1958	7.50	15.00	30.00
NEW CHAMBER JAZZ				
Epic LN 1124 [10]	1955	7.50	15.00	30.00
NEW FACES AT NEWPORT				
Metrojazz E-1005 [M]	1959	10.00	20.00	40.00

Label, Number	Yr	VG	VG+	NM
Metrojazz SE-1005 [S]	1959	7.50	15.00	30.00
NEW ORLEANS BOUNCE: URBAN BLUES, VOLUME 2				
Imperial LP-94004	1968	5.00	10.00	20.00
NEW ORLEANS DIXIELAND				
Southland SLP-216 [M]	1955	6.25	12.50	25.00
NEW ORLEANS ENCORE				
Riverside RLP-2503 [10]	1954	20.00	40.00	80.00
NEW ORLEANS EXPRESS				
EmArcy MG-36022 [M]	1955	12.50	25.00	50.00
NEW ORLEANS HORNS				
Riverside RLP-1005 [10]	1953	20.00	40.00	80.00
NEW ORLEANS JAZZ				
Decca DL 5483 [10]	1953	12.50	25.00	50.00
Decca DL 8283 [M]	1956	7.50	15.00	30.00
NEW ORLEANS JAZZ BABIES				
Southland SLP-214 [M]	1955	6.25	12.50	25.00
NEW ORLEANS JAZZ KINGS				
Southland SLP-217 [M]	1955	6.25	12.50	25.00
NEW ORLEANS JAZZ STARS				
Southland SLP-211 [M]	1955	6.25	12.50	25.00
NEW ORLEANS LEGENDS				
Riverside RLP 12-119 [M]	1957	10.00	20.00	40.00
NEW ORLEANS REVIVAL				
Riverside RLP-1047 [10]	1954	20.00	40.00	80.00
NEW ORLEANS STYLE				
"X" LVA-3029 [10]	1954	20.00	40.00	80.00
NEW ORLEANS TO LOS ANGELES				
Southland SLP-215 [M]	1955	6.25	12.50	25.00
NEW ORLEANS, OUR HOME TOWN				
Imperial LP-9260 [M]	1964	6.25	12.50	25.00
Imperial LP-12260 [R]	1964	5.00	10.00	20.00
NEW ORLEANS: THE LIVING LEGENDS, VOL. 1				
Riverside RLP-356 [M]	196?	5.00	10.00	20.00
Riverside RS-9356 [R]	196?	3.00	6.00	12.00
NEW ORLEANS: THE LIVING LEGENDS, VOL. 2				
Riverside RLP-357 [M]	196?	5.00	10.00	20.00
Riverside RS-9357 [R]	196?	3.00	6.00	12.00
NEW SOUNDS FROM SWEDEN, VOL. 1: THE DARING YOUNG SWEDES				
Prestige PRLP-119 [10]	1951	50.00	100.00	200.00
THE NEW SPIRIT OF CAPITOL				
Capitol NPB-6	1970	3.00	6.00	12.00
NEW VOICES				
Dawn DLP-1125 [M]	1956	20.00	40.00	80.00
THE NEW WAVE IN JAZZ				
ABC Impulse! AS-90 [S]	1968	3.00	6.00	12.00
Impulse! A-90 [M]	1966	3.75	7.50	15.00
Impulse! AS-90 [S]	1966	5.00	10.00	20.00
NEW YORK JAZZ OF THE TWENTIES				
Riverside RLP-1048 [10]	1954	20.00	40.00	80.00
NEWPORT JAZZ FESTIVAL				
RCA Victor LPM-3369 [M]	1965	3.75	7.50	15.00
RCA Victor LSP-3369 [S]	1965	5.00	10.00	20.00
NEWPORT JAZZ FESTIVAL ALL-STARS				
Atlantic 1331 [M]	1961	6.25	12.50	25.00
—Multicolor label, white "fan" logo at right				
NEWPORT JAZZ FESTIVAL ALL STARS				
Atlantic SD 1331 [S]	1961	7.50	15.00	30.00
—Multicolor label, white "fan" logo at right				
A NIGHT AT EDDIE CONDON'S				
Decca DL 8281 [M]	1956	7.50	15.00	30.00
A NIGHT AT THE BOULEVARD				
Felsted FL-7503 [M]	1960	10.00	20.00	40.00
A NIGHT AT THE FIVE SPOT: A MEMORIAL CONCERT DEDICATED TO THE MUSIC OF CHARLIE PARKER				
Signal S-1204 [M]	1957	30.00	60.00	120.00
THE NITTY GRITTY				
Vee Jay LP-1084 [M]	1964	7.50	15.00	30.00
—Not known to exist in stereo				
NO 'COUNT				
Savoy MG-12078 [M]	1956	15.00	30.00	60.00
NO ENERGY CRISIS				
ABC Impulse! AS-9267 [(2)]	1974	5.00	10.00	20.00
NO SOUR GRAPES, JUST PURE JAZZ				
Bethlehem BCP-92 [M]	1958	7.50	15.00	30.00

Label, Number	Yr	VG	VG+	NM
NON DAIRY CREAMER				
Warner Bros. PRO 443	1971	6.25	12.50	25.00
—Originals have green labels				
NORMAN GRANZ JAZZ CONCERT				
Norgran MGN-2501 [M]	1954	20.00	40.00	80.00
Norgran MGN-2502 [M]	1954	20.00	40.00	80.00
NOTHING CHEESY ABOUT THIS JAZZ				
Bethlehem BCP-85 [M]	1958	7.50	15.00	30.00
NOVA SCOTIA FOLK SONGS				
Elektra EKL-23 [10]	1954	10.00	20.00	40.00
NUGGETS				
Elektra 7E-2006 [(2)]	1972	10.00	20.00	40.00
OCTOBER '61 POP SAMPLER				
RCA Victor SPS-33-141 [DJ]	1961	150.00	300.00	600.00
—Promo-only collection.				
OCTOBER 1960 POPULAR STEREO SAMPLER				
RCA Victor SPS-33-96 [DJ]	1960	150.00	300.00	600.00
—Promo-only collection				
OCTOBER CHRISTMAS SAMPLER 59-40-41				
RCA Victor SPS-33-54 [DJ]	1959	150.00	300.00	600.00
—Promo-only collection				
OLD 'N GOLDEN				
Jamie JLPS-3031	1968	5.00	10.00	20.00
OLD AND HEAVY GOLD 1955				
Economic Consultants 1955	1973	5.00	10.00	20.00
OLD AND HEAVY GOLD 1956				
Economic Consultants 1956	1973	7.50	15.00	30.00
OLD AND HEAVY GOLD 1957				
Economic Consultants 1957	1973	7.50	15.00	30.00
OLD AND HEAVY GOLD 1958				
Economic Consultants 1958	1973	7.50	15.00	30.00
OLD AND HEAVY GOLD 1959				
Economic Consultants 1959	1973	5.00	10.00	20.00
OLD AND HEAVY GOLD 1960				
Economic Consultants 1960	1973	7.50	15.00	30.00
OLD AND HEAVY GOLD 1961				
Economic Consultants 1961	1973	7.50	15.00	30.00
OLD AND HEAVY GOLD 1962				
Economic Consultants 1962	1973	7.50	15.00	30.00
OLD AND HEAVY GOLD 1963				
Economic Consultants 1963	1973	5.00	10.00	20.00
OLD AND HEAVY GOLD 1964				
Economic Consultants 1964	1973	5.00	10.00	20.00
—Original magazine ads claimed that six Beatles tracks would appear on this LP; they were replaced before release				
OLD AND HEAVY GOLD 1965				
Economic Consultants 1965	1973	5.00	10.00	20.00
—Original magazine ads claimed that three Beatles tracks would appear on this LP; they were replaced before release				
OLD AND HEAVY GOLD 1966				
Economic Consultants 1966	1973	5.00	10.00	20.00
OLD AND HEAVY GOLD 1967				
Economic Consultants 1967	1973	5.00	10.00	20.00
—Original magazine ads claimed that a Beatles track would appear on this LP; it was replaced with another track before release				
OLD AND HEAVY GOLD 1968				
Economic Consultants 1968	1973	5.00	10.00	20.00
—Original magazine ads claimed that a Beatles track would appear on this LP; it was replaced with another track before release				
OLD AND HEAVY GOLD 1969				
Economic Consultants 1969	1973	5.00	10.00	20.00
—Original magazine ads claimed that a Beatles track would appear on this LP; it was replaced with another track before release				
OLD AND HEAVY GOLD 1970				
Economic Consultants 1970	1973	5.00	10.00	20.00
—Original magazine ads claimed that a Beatles track would appear on this LP; it was replaced with another track before release				
OLD AND HEAVY GOLD 1971				
Economic Consultants 1971	1973	5.00	10.00	20.00
—Original magazine ads claimed that a Paul McCartney track would appear on this LP; it was replaced with another track before release				
OLD TIME BANJO PROJECT				
Elektra EKL-276 [M]	1964	5.00	10.00	20.00
Elektra EKS-7276 [S]	1964	6.25	12.50	25.00
OLDIES BUT GOODIES				
Original Sound LPM-5001 [M]	1959	12.50	25.00	50.00
—Original pressing with no reference to other volumes on the back cover				

Label, Number	Yr	VG	VG+	NM
Original Sound LPM-5001 [M]	1960s	3.00	6.00	12.00
—Later editions with later volumes in the series on the back cover				
OLDIES BUT GOODIES, VOL. 2				
Original Sound LPM-5003 [M]	1960	10.00	20.00	40.00
—Original pressing with no reference to later volumes on the back cover				
Original Sound LPM-5003 [M]	1960s	3.00	6.00	12.00
—Later editions with later volumes in the series on the back cover				
OLDIES BUT GOODIES, VOL. 3				
Original Sound LPM-5004 [M]	1961	7.50	15.00	30.00
—Original pressing with no reference to later volumes on the back cover				
Original Sound LPM-5004 [M]	1960s	3.00	6.00	12.00
—Later editions with later volumes in the series on the back cover				
OLDIES BUT GOODIES, VOL. 4				
Original Sound LPM-5005 [M]	1962	7.50	15.00	30.00
—Original pressing with no reference to later volumes on the back cover				
Original Sound LPM-5005 [M]	1960s	3.00	6.00	12.00
—Later editions with later volumes in the series on the back cover				
OLDIES BUT GOODIES, VOL. 5				
Original Sound LPM-5007 [M]	1963	5.00	10.00	20.00
—Original pressing with no reference to later volumes on the back cover				
Original Sound LPM-5007 [M]	1960s	3.00	6.00	12.00
—Later editions with later volumes in the series on the back cover				
OLDIES BUT GOODIES, VOL. 6				
Original Sound LPM-5011 [M]	1963	5.00	10.00	20.00
—Original pressing with no reference to later volumes on the back cover				
Original Sound LPM-5011 [M]	1960s	3.00	6.00	12.00
—Later editions with later volumes in the series on the back cover				
OLDIES BUT GOODIES, VOL. 7				
Original Sound LPM-5012 [M]	1964	5.00	10.00	20.00
—Original pressing with no reference to later volumes on the back cover				
Original Sound LPM-5012 [M]	1960s	3.00	6.00	12.00
—Later editions with later volumes in the series on the back cover				
OLDIES BUT GOODIES, VOL. 8				
Original Sound LPM-5014 [M]	1966	3.75	7.50	15.00
—Original pressing with no reference to later volumes on the back cover				
Original Sound LPM-5014 [M]	1960s	2.50	5.00	10.00
—Later editions with later volumes in the series on the back cover				
OLDIES BY THE DOZEN				
Parkway P-7035 [M]	1963	7.50	15.00	30.00
OLDIES BY THE DOZEN, VOLUME 2				
Parkway P-7041 [M]	1964	12.50	25.00	50.00
—With bonus 45 of "The Twist" by Chubby Checker on on side and "Mashed Potato Time" by Dee Dee Sharp on the other; deduct 40 percent if missing				
OLDIES DANCE PARTY, VOLUME 1				
Oldies 33 OL-8001 [M]	1963	5.00	10.00	20.00
OLDIES DANCE PARTY, VOLUME 2				
Oldies 33 OL-8002 [M]	1963	5.00	10.00	20.00
OLDIES IN HI-FI				
Chess LP 1439 [M]	1959	75.00	150.00	300.00
—Black vinyl				
Chess LP 1439 [DJ]	1959	150.00	300.00	600.00
—Multi-color splash vinyl				
OLIO				
Prestige PRLP-7084 [M]	1957	25.00	50.00	100.00
ON-THE-ROAD JAZZ				
Riverside RLP 12-127 [M]	1957	10.00	20.00	40.00
ONE DOZEN GOLDIES				
Carlton LP 12-121 [M]	1960	12.50	25.00	50.00
ONE WORLD JAZZ				
Adventures in Sound WL-162 [M]	1959	12.50	25.00	50.00
Adventures in Sound WS-314 [S]	1959	10.00	20.00	40.00
OPUS DE BLUES				
Savoy MG-12142 [M]	1959	15.00	30.00	60.00
OPUS DE BOP				
Savoy MG-12114 [M]		—	—	—
—See STAN GETZ.				
OPUS DE JAZZ				
Savoy MG-12036 [M]	1955	20.00	40.00	80.00
OPUS IN SWING				
Savoy MG-12085 [M]	1956	15.00	30.00	60.00
THE ORCHESTRA "HOUSE OF SOUND"				
Brunswick BL 54003 [M]	1954	7.50	15.00	30.00
THE ORGAN PLAYS MUSIC FOR A MERRY CHRISTMAS				
Reader's Digest RDA 42-A [(4)]	1966	5.00	10.00	20.00
—Available only through Reader's Digest magazine by mail order				
ORIGINAL BLUE NOTE JAZZ, VOL. 1				
Blue Note B-6504	1969	5.00	10.00	20.00
ORIGINAL BLUE NOTE JAZZ, VOL. 2				
Blue Note B-6506	1970	5.00	10.00	20.00

Label, Number	Yr	VG	VG+	NM
THE ORIGINAL COUNTRY HITS #1				
Liberty LRP-3305 [M]	1963	5.00	10.00	20.00
THE ORIGINAL COUNTRY HITS #2				
Liberty LRP-3345 [M]	1964	5.00	10.00	20.00
THE ORIGINAL COUNTRY HITS #3				
Liberty LRP-3382 [M]	1964	5.00	10.00	20.00
ORIGINAL GOLDEN BLUES GREATS, VOL. 1				
Liberty LST-7572 [R]	1968	3.00	6.00	12.00
—Reissue of "The Original R&B Hits, Volume 1," Liberty 3381, in rechanneled stereo				
ORIGINAL GOLDEN COUNTRY GREATS, VOLUME 1				
Liberty LST-7569 [R]	1968	3.00	6.00	12.00
—Reissue of "The Original Country Hits #1," Liberty 3305, in rechanneled stereo				
ORIGINAL GOLDEN COUNTRY GREATS, VOLUME 2				
Liberty LST-7570 [R]	1968	3.00	6.00	12.00
—Reissue of "The Original Country Hits #2," Liberty 3345, in rechanneled stereo				
ORIGINAL GOLDEN COUNTRY GREATS, VOLUME 3				
Liberty LST-7571 [R]	1968	3.00	6.00	12.00
—Reissue of "The Original Country Hits #3," Liberty 3382, in rechanneled stereo				
ORIGINAL GOLDEN GREATS, VOLUME 3				
Liberty LST-7573 [R]	1968	3.00	6.00	12.00
—Reissue of "The Original Hits, Volume 7," Liberty 3274, in rechanneled stereo				
ORIGINAL GOLDEN GREATS, VOLUME 4				
Liberty LST-7574 [R]	1968	3.00	6.00	12.00
—Only one track, "Surf City" by Jan and Dean, is true stereo				
ORIGINAL GOLDEN GREATS, VOLUME 5				
Liberty LST-7575 [R]	1968	3.00	6.00	12.00
—Three tracks are in true stereo: "Hurt" (Timi Yuro), "Tower of Strength" (Gene McDaniels) and "The Night Has a Thousand Eyes" (Bobby Vee)				
ORIGINAL GOLDEN GREATS, VOLUME 6				
Liberty LST-7576 [R]	1968	3.00	6.00	12.00
—Four tracks are in true stereo				
ORIGINAL GOLDEN GREATS, VOLUME 7				
Liberty LST-7577 [R]	1968	3.00	6.00	12.00
—Three tracks are in true stereo				
ORIGINAL GOLDEN GREATS, VOLUME 8				
Liberty LST-7578 [R]	1968	3.00	6.00	12.00
ORIGINAL GOLDEN GREATS, VOLUME 9				
Liberty LST-7579 [R]	1968	3.00	6.00	12.00
ORIGINAL GOLDEN GREATS, VOLUME 10				
Liberty LST-7619	1969	3.75	7.50	15.00
ORIGINAL GOLDIES FROM THE FABULOUS '50S, VOLUME 1				
Josie JM-4002 [M]	1963	15.00	30.00	60.00
ORIGINAL GOLDIES FROM THE FABULOUS '50S, VOLUME 2				
Josie JM-4003 [M]	1963	15.00	30.00	60.00
ORIGINAL GOLDIES FROM THE FABULOUS '50S, VOLUME 3				
Josie JM-4004 [M]	1963	15.00	30.00	60.00
ORIGINAL HIT RECORDS				
Roulette R 25106 [M]	1960	7.50	15.00	30.00
—Originals have a white label with colored spokes				
THE ORIGINAL HITS, PAST & PRESENT				
Liberty LRP-3178 [M]	1960	5.00	10.00	20.00
THE ORIGINAL HITS, VOLUME TWO: PAST & PRESENT				
Liberty LRP-3180 [M]	1961	5.00	10.00	20.00
THE ORIGINAL HITS, VOLUME 3: PAST & PRESENT				
Liberty LRP-3187 [M]	1961	5.00	10.00	20.00
THE ORIGINAL HITS, VOLUME 4				
Liberty LRP-3200 [M]	1962	5.00	10.00	20.00
—Reissue of "Memories Are Made of Hits"; for "The Original Hits, Volume 5," see "15 Hits: The Original Recordings"				
THE ORIGINAL HITS, VOLUME 6				
Liberty LRP-3260 [M]	1962	5.00	10.00	20.00
THE ORIGINAL HITS, VOLUME 7: ALL-TIME HIT INSTRUMENTALS				
Liberty LRP-3274 [M]	1963	5.00	10.00	20.00
THE ORIGINAL HITS, VOLUME 8				
Liberty LRP-3288 [M]	1963	5.00	10.00	20.00
THE ORIGINAL HITS, VOLUME 9				
Liberty LRP-3325 [M]	1963	5.00	10.00	20.00
THE ORIGINAL HITS, VOLUME 10				
Liberty LRP-3344 [M]	1964	5.00	10.00	20.00
THE ORIGINAL HITS, VOLUME 11				
Liberty LRP-3418 [M]	1965	5.00	10.00	20.00
Liberty LST-7418 [P]	1965	5.00	10.00	20.00
THE ORIGINAL HOOTENANNY				
Crestview CRV 806 [M]	1963	5.00	10.00	20.00
Crestview CRS 7806 [S]	1963	6.25	12.50	25.00

Label, Number	Yr	VG	VG+	NM
ORIGINAL MEMPHIS ROCK AND ROLL, VOLUME 1				
Sun 116	1970	5.00	10.00	20.00
ORIGINAL MOTION PICTURE HIT THEMES				
United Artists UAL-3197 [M]	1962	3.75	7.50	15.00
United Artists UAS-6197 [S]	1962	5.00	10.00	20.00
ORIGINAL ROCK OLDIES, VOLUME 1				
Specialty SPS-2129	1970	5.00	10.00	20.00
ORIGINAL ROCK OLDIES, VOLUME 2				
Specialty SPS-2130	1970	5.00	10.00	20.00
THE ORIGINAL R&B HITS, VOLUME 1				
Liberty LRP-3381 [M]	1964	5.00	10.00	20.00
THE ORIGINAL SOUND OF THE 20'S				
Columbia C3L 35 [(3)]	1965	10.00	20.00	40.00
ORIGINAL SURFIN' HITS				
GNP Crescendo GNP-84 [M]	1963	10.00	20.00	40.00
—With bonus photos; deduct 25-50 percent if missing				
GNP Crescendo GNPS-84 [S]	1963	12.50	25.00	50.00
—With bonus photos; deduct 25-50 percent if missing				
OUR BEST				
Clef MGC-639 [M]	1955	12.50	25.00	50.00
Norgran MGN-1021 [M]	1955	20.00	40.00	80.00
OUR BEST TO YOU				
Everlast ELP-201 [M]	1960	50.00	100.00	200.00
OUR SIGNIFICANT HITS				
Specialty SP-2112 [M]	1960	30.00	60.00	120.00
—Gold and black label				
OUR SINGING HERITAGE, VOL. 1				
Elektra EKL-151 [M]	1958	6.25	12.50	25.00
OUR SINGING HERITAGE, VOL. 2				
Elektra EKL-152 [M]	1958	6.25	12.50	25.00
O. HENRY'S THE GIFT OF THE MAGI				
E.F. MacDonald EFMX-62	1962	5.00	10.00	20.00
—Special album done by the E.F. MacDonald Company, Dayton, Ohio				
A PACKAGE OF 16 BIG HITS				
Motown MT 614 [M]	1964	25.00	50.00	100.00
—"Package" cover				
Motown MT 614 [M]	1966	5.00	10.00	20.00
—No "package" on cover				
Motown MS 614 [S]	1966	7.50	15.00	30.00
—No "package" on cover; contains alternate stereo versions of "Please Mr. Postman" by the Marvelettes and "Do You Love Me" by the Contours				
PAJAMA PARTY				
Forum F-9006 [M]	196?	7.50	15.00	30.00
—Reissue of Roulette 25021				
Forum SF-9006 [R]	196?	5.00	10.00	20.00
Gee GLP-703 [M]	1959	—	—	—
—Canceled; released as Roulette R-25021 instead				
Roulette R 25021 [M]	1958	10.00	20.00	40.00
—Originals have a black label				
Roulette R 25021 [M]	1959	6.25	12.50	25.00
—Second pressings have a white label with colored spokes				
Roulette SR 25021 [R]	196?	3.00	6.00	12.00
PANORAMA OF BRITISH JAZZ				
Discovery DL-2001 [10]	1953	12.50	25.00	50.00
PARTY AFTER HOURS				
Aladdin LP-703 [10]	1950	2000.	4000.	8000.
—Red vinyl				
Aladdin LP-703 [10]	1950	1000.	2000.	4000.
—Black vinyl				
PEACE ON EARTH				
Capitol S?B?-585 [(2)]	1970	3.75	7.50	15.00
PERCUSSION UNABRIDGED				
Kimberly 2022 [M]	1963	5.00	10.00	20.00
Kimberly 11022 [S]	1963	6.25	12.50	25.00
PERFECT FOR DANCING: ALL TEMPOS				
RCA Victor LPM-1072 [M]	1954	7.50	15.00	30.00
PERFECT FOR DANCING: FOX TROTS				
RCA Victor LPM-1070 [M]	1954	7.50	15.00	30.00
PERFECT FOR DANCING: JITTERBUG OR LINDY				
RCA Victor LPM-1071 [M]	1954	7.50	15.00	30.00
PERIOD'S JAZZ DIGEST				
Period SPL-302 [M]	1956	12.50	25.00	50.00
PERIOD'S JAZZ DIGEST VOL. 2				
Period SPL-304 [M]	1955	12.50	25.00	50.00
PETAL PUSHERS				
Chess LP 1520 [M]	1967	6.25	12.50	25.00
Chess LPS 1520 [S]	1967	6.25	12.50	25.00
PHIL SPECTOR'S CHRISTMAS ALBUM				
Apple SW 3400 [M]	1972	7.50	15.00	30.00
—Reissue of "A Christmas Gift for You from Philles Records," PHLP-4005				

Label, Number	Yr	VG	VG+	NM
Warner/Spector SP 9103 [S]	1974	5.00	10.00	20.00
—Reissue of above album; though the cover says "Authentic Mono," the record is actually in 100 percent true stereo!				
PHIL SPECTOR'S GREATEST HITS				
Warner/Spector 2SP 9104 [(2)]	1977	10.00	20.00	40.00
THE PHIL SPECTOR SPECTACULAR				
Philles PHLP 100 [DJ]	197?	375.00	750.00	1500.
—Not issued with cover				
THE PHILCO ALBUM OF HOLIDAY MUSIC				
Columbia Special Products CSM 431	1966	3.75	7.50	15.00
—Sold only at Philco dealers				
PIANISTS GALORE				
Pacific Jazz JWC-506 [M]	1957	12.50	25.00	50.00
World Pacific JWC-506 [M]	1958	10.00	20.00	40.00
PIANO ARTISTRY				
Audiophile AP-28 [M]	1953	7.50	15.00	30.00
PIANO INTERPRETATIONS				
Norgran MGN-1036 [M]	1955	20.00	40.00	80.00
Verve MGV-8125 [M]	1957	7.50	15.00	30.00
Verve V-8125 [M]	1961	5.00	10.00	20.00
PIANO JAZZ, VOLUME 1				
Brunswick BL 54014 [M]	1955	7.50	15.00	30.00
PIANO JAZZ, VOLUME 2				
Brunswick BL 54015 [M]	1955	7.50	15.00	30.00
PIANO MODERN				
Verve VSP-13 [M]	1966	3.75	7.50	15.00
Verve VSPS-13 [R]	1966	2.50	5.00	10.00
PIANO MUSIC FOR PARTIES				
Columbia CL 603 [M]	1955	6.25	12.50	25.00
PIANO MUSIC FOR TWO				
Columbia CL 602 [M]	1955	6.25	12.50	25.00
PIANO ROLL HALL OF FAME				
Sounds 1202	196?	3.00	6.00	12.00
PIANO ROLL TRANSCRIPTIONS				
Riverside RLP 12-110 [M]	1956	10.00	20.00	40.00
Riverside RLP 12-126 [M]	1957	10.00	20.00	40.00
PIANO STYLISTS				
Capitol H 323 [10]	1952	12.50	25.00	50.00
PIANO VARIATIONS				
King 540 [M]	1956	37.50	75.00	150.00
PICK HITS OF THE RADIO GOOD GUYS				
Laurie LLP-2021 [M]	1963	7.50	15.00	30.00
Laurie SLP-2021 [R]	196?	3.75	7.50	15.00
PICK HITS OF THE RADIO GOOD GUYS, VOLUME 2				
Laurie LLP-2026 [M]	1964	6.25	12.50	25.00
Laurie SLP-2026 [R]	196?	3.75	7.50	15.00
PICK UP THE BEAT				
Epic LN 3127 [M]	1955	7.50	15.00	30.00
PIONEERS OF BOOGIE WOOGIE				
Riverside RLP-1009 [10]	1953	20.00	40.00	80.00
PIONEERS OF BOOGIE WOOGIE, VOL. 2				
Riverside RLP-1034 [10]	1954	20.00	40.00	80.00
PLAYBOY ALL STARS VOLUME 1				
Playboy PB-1957 [(2) M]	1957	10.00	20.00	40.00
PLAYBOY ALL STARS VOLUME 2				
Playboy PB-1958 [(2) M]	1958	10.00	20.00	40.00
PLAYBOY ALL STARS VOLUME 3				
Playboy PB-1959 [(3) M]	1959	15.00	30.00	60.00
PLAZA HOUSE PRESENTS MUSIC HALL				
Capitol Creative Products SL-6719	1971	3.00	6.00	12.00
—One side by Merle Haggard; one side by Sonny James				
POLKAS				
Audio Lab AL-1543 [M]	1959	10.00	20.00	40.00
POP HIT PARTY				
Columbia CL 1237 [M]	195?	5.00	10.00	20.00
POP ORIGINS				
Chess LP 1544 [M]	1969	6.25	12.50	25.00
POP PARADE				
MGM E-194 [10]	1953	12.50	25.00	50.00
POPULAR FAVORITES				
Columbia CL 6057 [10]	1949	10.00	20.00	40.00
THE POPULAR GOLD ALBUM				
Capitol T 972 [M]	1958	7.50	15.00	30.00
PORGY AND BESS				
Bethlehem EXLP-1 [(3) M]	1956	17.50	35.00	70.00
Bethlehem BCP-6040 [M]	1959	7.50	15.00	30.00

Label, Number	Yr	VG	VG+	NM
PORTRAITS IN JAZZ				
Reprise R-6084 [M]	1963	3.00	6.00	12.00
Reprise R9-6084 [S]	1963	3.75	7.50	15.00
A POT OF FLOWERS				
Mainstream S-6100 [S]	1967	25.00	50.00	100.00
Mainstream 56100 [M]	1967	20.00	40.00	80.00
POT OF GOLDEN GOODIES				
Herald HLP-1015 [M]	1962	37.50	75.00	150.00
A POTPOURRI OF JAZZ				
Verve MGV-2032 [M]	1956	10.00	20.00	40.00
Verve V-2032 [M]	1961	5.00	10.00	20.00
PRESTIGE GROOVY GOODIES, VOL. 1				
Prestige PRLP-7298 [M]	1964	7.50	15.00	30.00
Prestige PRST-7298 [R]	1964	5.00	10.00	20.00
PRIMITIVE PIANO				
Tone 1 [M]	195?	7.50	15.00	30.00
PROGRESSIVE PIANO				
RCA Victor LJM-3001 [10]	1952	12.50	25.00	50.00
THE PROGRESSIVES				
Columbia KG 31574 [(2)]	1973	5.00	10.00	20.00
Columbia KG 31574 [(2)]	1972	3.75	7.50	15.00
Columbia CG 31574 [(2)]	197?	3.00	6.00	12.00
—"CG" prefix is a reissue of "KG"				
RADAR BLUES				
King KLP-1050 [M]	1969	7.50	15.00	30.00
RADIO SMASH FLASHBACKS: DRIVE TIME				
Laurie LLP-2028 [M]	1964	6.25	12.50	25.00
Laurie SLP-2028 [R]	196?	3.75	7.50	15.00
RADIO SMASH FLASHBACKS: PRIME TIME				
Laurie LLP-2029 [M]	1964	6.25	12.50	25.00
Laurie SLP-2029 [R]	196?	3.75	7.50	15.00
RAGTIME PIANO ROLL, VOL. 1				
Riverside RLP-1006 [10]	1953	25.00	50.00	100.00
RAGTIME PIANO ROLL, VOL. 2				
Riverside RLP-1025 [10]	1954	20.00	40.00	80.00
RAGTIME PIANO ROLL, VOL. 3				
Riverside RLP-1049 [10]	1954	20.00	40.00	80.00
RAGTIMERS' IMMORTAL PERFORMANCES				
RCA Victor LPT-1000 [M]	1954	7.50	15.00	30.00
RAILROAD SONGS				
King 869 [M]	1963	17.50	35.00	70.00
RARE BANDS OF THE 20S, VOL. 1				
Historical ASC-3	1966	3.00	6.00	12.00
RARE BANDS OF THE 20S, VOL. 2				
Historical ASC-6	1966	3.00	6.00	12.00
RARE BANDS OF THE 20S, VOL. 3				
Historical ASC-7	1966	3.00	6.00	12.00
RARE VERTICAL JAZZ				
Historical ASC-8	1966	3.00	6.00	12.00
THE RCA VICTOR ENCYCLOPEDIA OF RECORDED JAZZ, ALBUM 1				
RCA Victor LEJ-1 [10]	1956	10.00	20.00	40.00
THE RCA VICTOR ENCYCLOPEDIA OF RECORDED JAZZ, ALBUM 2				
RCA Victor LEJ-2 [10]	1956	10.00	20.00	40.00
THE RCA VICTOR ENCYCLOPEDIA OF RECORDED JAZZ, ALBUM 3				
RCA Victor LEJ-3 [10]	1956	10.00	20.00	40.00
THE RCA VICTOR ENCYCLOPEDIA OF RECORDED JAZZ, ALBUM 4				
RCA Victor LEJ-4 [10]	1956	10.00	20.00	40.00
THE RCA VICTOR ENCYCLOPEDIA OF RECORDED JAZZ, ALBUM 5				
RCA Victor LEJ-5 [10]	1956	10.00	20.00	40.00
THE RCA VICTOR ENCYCLOPEDIA OF RECORDED JAZZ, ALBUM 6				
RCA Victor LEJ-6 [10]	1956	10.00	20.00	40.00
THE RCA VICTOR ENCYCLOPEDIA OF RECORDED JAZZ, ALBUM 7				
RCA Victor LEJ-7 [10]	1956	10.00	20.00	40.00
THE RCA VICTOR ENCYCLOPEDIA OF RECORDED JAZZ, ALBUM 8				
RCA Victor LEJ-8 [10]	1956	10.00	20.00	40.00
THE RCA VICTOR ENCYCLOPEDIA OF RECORDED JAZZ, ALBUM 9				
RCA Victor LEJ-9 [10]	1956	10.00	20.00	40.00
THE RCA VICTOR ENCYCLOPEDIA OF RECORDED JAZZ, ALBUM 10				
RCA Victor LEJ-10 [10]	1956	10.00	20.00	40.00
THE RCA VICTOR ENCYCLOPEDIA OF RECORDED JAZZ, ALBUM 11				
RCA Victor LEJ-11 [10]	1956	10.00	20.00	40.00
THE RCA VICTOR ENCYCLOPEDIA OF RECORDED JAZZ, ALBUM 12				
RCA Victor LEJ-12 [10]	1956	10.00	20.00	40.00
RCA VICTOR PRESENTS MUSIC FOR THE TWELVE DAYS OF CHRISTMAS				
RCA Victor PRS-188 [S]	1965	3.00	6.00	12.00

Label, Number	Yr	VG	VG+	NM
THE REAL AMBASSADORS				
Columbia OS 2250 [S]	1962	6.25	12.50	25.00
Columbia CL 5850 [M]	1962	5.00	10.00	20.00
THE REAL BLUES				
Excello LPS-8011 [R]	1969	5.00	10.00	20.00
RECORD HOP				
Decca DL 8067 [M]	1955	7.50	15.00	30.00
RECORDED IN NEW ORLEANS, VOL. 1				
Good Time Jazz L-12019 [M]	1955	5.00	10.00	20.00
RECORDED IN NEW ORLEANS, VOL. 2				
Good Time Jazz L-12020 [M]	1955	5.00	10.00	20.00
RED BIRD GOLDIES				
Red Bird LP 20-102 [M]	1965	20.00	40.00	80.00
RED HOT AND BLUE JAZZ				
Waldorf Music Hall MH 33-141 [10]	195?	50.00	100.00	200.00
RELAXED SAXOPHONE MOODS				
Prestige PRLP-141 [10]	1953	25.00	50.00	100.00
REMEMBER HOW GREAT, VOLUME 1				
Roulette SR 42027 [R]	1968	3.00	6.00	12.00
REMEMBER HOW GREAT, VOLUME 2				
Roulette SR 42028 [R]	1968	3.00	6.00	12.00
REMEMBER HOW GREAT, VOLUME 3				
Roulette SR 42029 [R]	1968	3.00	6.00	12.00
REMEMBER HOW GREAT, VOLUME 4				
Roulette SR 42031 [R]	1969	3.00	6.00	12.00
REMEMBER HOW GREAT, VOLUME 5				
Roulette SR 42032 [R]	1969	3.00	6.00	12.00
REMEMBER THE OLDIES				
Argo LP-649 [M]	1963	10.00	20.00	40.00
Argo LP-649 [M]	1963	100.00	200.00	400.00
—Multi-color splash vinyl; white label promo				
REQUESTED BY YOU				
Columbia CL 607 [M]	1955	6.25	12.50	25.00
RHYTHM AND BLUES				
Savoy MG-15008 [10]	1952	20.00	40.00	80.00
RHYTHM PLUS ONE				
Epic LN 3297 [M]	1956	7.50	15.00	30.00
THE RHYTHM SECTION				
Epic LN 3271 [M]	1956	7.50	15.00	30.00
RHYTHM & BLUES				
RCA Camden CAL-371 [M]	1958	6.25	12.50	25.00
RHYTHM, BLUES AND BOOGIE-WOOGIE				
Decca DL 4011 [M]	1960	7.50	15.00	30.00
RICHARD NADER/LET THE GOOD TIMES ROLL				
Bell 9002 [(2)]	1973	5.00	10.00	20.00
RINGSIDE AT CONDON'S				
Savoy MG-15029 [10]	1954	20.00	40.00	80.00
RINGSIDE AT CONDON'S VOL. 2				
Savoy MG-15030 [10]	1954	20.00	40.00	80.00
RIVERBOAT JAZZ				
Brunswick BL 58026 [10]	1951	12.50	25.00	50.00
RIVERSIDE DRIVE				
Riverside RLP 12-267 [M]	1958	7.50	15.00	30.00
RIVERSIDE MODERN JAZZ SAMPLER				
Riverside S-3 [M]	1956	10.00	20.00	40.00
ROBERT W. SARNOFF — 25 YEARS OF RCA LEADERSHIP				
RCA Victor RWS-0001 [DJ]	1973	1000.	1500.	2000.
—Souvenir record handed out at Sarnoff's retirement party				
ROCK'S GREATEST HITS				
Columbia GP 11 [(2)]	1969	5.00	10.00	20.00
ROCK-A-BALLADS				
Cadence CLP-3041 [M]	1960	10.00	20.00	40.00
ROCK-A-HITS				
Cadence CLP-3042 [M]	1960	10.00	20.00	40.00
ROCK-O-RAMA				
Abkco AB 4222 [(2)]	1972	5.00	10.00	20.00
ROCK-O-RAMA, VOLUME 2				
Abkco AB 4223 [(2)]	1972	5.00	10.00	20.00
ROCK 'N' ROLL SOCK HOP				
Score SLP-4018 [M]	1958	50.00	100.00	200.00
ROCK AND ROLL BANDSTAND				
Roulette R 25093 [M]	1959	7.50	15.00	30.00
—Originals have a white label with colored spokes				

Label, Number	Yr	VG	VG+	NM
ROCK AND ROLL DANCE PARTY				
King 536 [M]	1956	75.00	150.00	300.00
ROCK AND ROLL RECORD HOP				
Roulette R 25059 [M]	1959	7.50	15.00	30.00
—Originals have a white label with colored spokes				
ROCK AND ROLL REVUE, VOLUME 2				
King 654 [M]	1959	37.50	75.00	150.00
ROCK AND ROLL VS. RHYTHM AND BLUES				
Dooto DTL-223 [M]	1957	25.00	50.00	100.00
ROCK & ROLL FOREVER				
Atlantic 1239 [M]	1956	37.50	75.00	150.00
ROCK & ROLL JAMBOREE				
End LP-302 [M]	1959	30.00	60.00	120.00
—Second cover and title with puppet and a guitar				
ROCK & ROLL WITH RHYTHM & BLUES				
Aladdin LP-710 [M]	195?	375.00	750.00	1500.
A ROCKIN' CHRISTMAS				
Columbia Special Products P 12445	1974	3.75	7.50	15.00
ROCKIN' SLUMBER PARTY				
Famous LP-501 [M]	1961	7.50	15.00	30.00
ROCKIN' TOGETHER				
Atco 33-103 [M]	1958	25.00	50.00	100.00
RODGERS AND HART GEMS				
World Pacific JWC-504 [M]	1958	10.00	20.00	40.00
ROGERS & HART GEMS				
Pacific Jazz JWC-504 [M]	1956	12.50	25.00	50.00
RONCO PRESENTS A CHRISTMAS GIFT				
Ronco/CSP P 12430	1974	3.75	7.50	15.00
—Gatefold with pop-up manger scene				
RONCO PRESENTS A CHRISTMAS PRESENT				
Ronco/CSP P 11772	1973	3.75	7.50	15.00
—Gatefold with pop-up North Pole scene				
ROOST 5TH ANNIVERSARY ALBUM				
Roost RST-1201 [M]	1955	12.50	25.00	50.00
ROOTS OF BRITISH ROCK				
Sire SASH-3711 [(2)]	1975	5.00	10.00	20.00
ROULETTE PRESENTS A DEMONSTRATION OF THE NEW DIMENSIONAL SOUND OF DYNAMIC STEREO				
Roulette SR-100 [S]	1958	7.50	15.00	30.00
RUMBLE				
Jubilee JGM-1114 [M]	1959	37.50	75.00	150.00
SATURDAY NIGHT AT THE UPTOWN				
Atlantic 8101 [M]	1964	6.25	12.50	25.00
Atlantic SD 8101 [S]	1964	7.50	15.00	30.00
SATURDAY NIGHT FUNCTION: RURAL BLUES, VOLUME 2				
Imperial LP-94001	1968	5.00	10.00	20.00
SATURDAY NIGHT MOOD				
Columbia CL 599 [M]	1954	6.25	12.50	25.00
THE SAX SECTION				
Epic LN 3278 [M]	1956	10.00	20.00	40.00
SAX STYLISTS				
Capitol H 328 [10]	1952	12.50	25.00	50.00
SAXOMANIAC				
Apollo LP-477 [M]	1958	25.00	50.00	100.00
THE SAXOPHONE				
ABC Impulse! AS-9253 [(3)]	197?	5.00	10.00	20.00
SAXOPHONE REVOLT				
Riverside RLP 12-284 [M]	1958	7.50	15.00	30.00
SCHLAGERS!				
Warner Bros. PRO 359 [(2)]	1970	7.50	15.00	30.00
—Originals have green labels				
A SCRAPBOOK OF BRITISH JAZZ, 1926-1956				
London LL 1444 [M]	1956	5.00	10.00	20.00
SEASON'S GREETINGS FROM BARBRA STREISAND...AND FRIENDS				
Columbia Special Products CSS 1075	1969	5.00	10.00	20.00
—Created exclusively for Maxwell House Coffee				
SEASONS GREETINGS (A CHRISTMAS FESTIVAL OF STARS)				
Columbia CL 1394 [M]	1959	5.00	10.00	20.00
Columbia CS 8189 [S]	1959	6.25	12.50	25.00
SECOND SESSION AT SQUIRREL'S				
Paramount LP-108 [10]	1954	15.00	30.00	60.00
SELECTIONS FROM APRIL 1956 ALBUMS FOR RADIO-TV PROGRAM USE				
Capitol PRO-252/3 [DJ]	1956	10.00	20.00	40.00

Label, Number	Yr	VG	VG+	NM
SELECTIONS FROM FEBRUARY 1956 POPULAR ALBUMS FOR RADIO-TV PROGRAM USE				
Capitol PRO-240/1 [DJ]	1956	10.00	20.00	40.00
SELECTIONS FROM JANUARY 1956 ALBUMS FOR RADIO-TV PROGRAM USE				
Capitol PRO-238/9 [DJ]	1956	10.00	20.00	40.00
SELECTIONS FROM MARCH 1956 ALBUMS FOR RADIO-TV PROGRAM USE				
Capitol PRO-246/7 [DJ]	1956	10.00	20.00	40.00
SESSION AT MIDNIGHT				
Capitol T 707 [M]	1956	7.50	15.00	30.00
SESSION AT RIVERSIDE				
Capitol T 761 [M]	1956	7.50	15.00	30.00
THE SEVEN AGES OF JAZZ				
Metrojazz 2-E-1009 [(2) M]	1959	15.00	30.00	60.00
Metrojazz 2-SE-1009 [(2) S]	1959	12.50	25.00	50.00
SHADES OF GOSPEL SOUL				
Motown MS-701	1970	3.75	7.50	15.00
SHADES OF NEW ORLEANS				
Southland SLP-240	1963	3.75	7.50	15.00
SHOUTIN', SWINGIN' AND MAKIN' LOVE				
Chess CHV-412	1970	3.75	7.50	15.00
SHUT DOWN				
Capitol T 1918 [M]	1963	10.00	20.00	40.00
Capitol ST 1918 [S]	1963	12.50	25.00	50.00
SHUT DOWNS AND HILL CLIMBS				
Liberty LRP-3366 [M]	1964	10.00	20.00	40.00
Liberty LST-7366 [S]	1964	12.50	25.00	50.00
THE SINATRA FAMILY WISH YOU A MERRY CHRISTMAS				
Reprise FS-1026	1969	12.50	25.00	50.00
SING A SONG OF SOUL				
Checker LP 2998 [M]	1966	20.00	40.00	80.00
Checker LPS 2998 [S]	1966	25.00	50.00	100.00
THE SINGER-SONGWRITER PROJECT				
Elektra EKL-299 [M]	1965	6.25	12.50	25.00
—With 13 tracks				
Elektra EKL-299 [M]	1965	5.00	10.00	20.00
—With 11 tracks, though the label and cover claim there are 13				
Elektra EKS-7299 [S]	1965	7.50	15.00	30.00
—With 13 tracks				
Elektra EKS-7299 [S]	1965	5.00	10.00	20.00
—With 11 tracks, though the label and cover claim there are 13				
SINGIN' AND SWINGIN'				
Savoy MG-12217 [M]	196?	5.00	10.00	20.00
SITTIN' IN				
Verve MGV-8225 [M]	1958	12.50	25.00	50.00
Verve V-8225 [M]	1961	6.25	12.50	25.00
SMALL COMBO HITS				
RCA Victor LPT-3 [10]	1951	10.00	20.00	40.00
SMART, LUSCIOUS, BEAUTIFUL				
Bethlehem BCP-6034 [M]	1960	7.50	15.00	30.00
THE SMITHSONIAN COLLECTION OF CLASSIC JAZZ				
Smithsonian/CSP P6 11891 [(6)]	1973	12.50	25.00	50.00
SMOKE RINGS				
RCA Victor LPT-13 [10]	1951	10.00	20.00	40.00
SOFT PEDAL				
Columbia CL 2511 [10]	1954	7.50	15.00	30.00
SOLID GOLD HITS				
Imperial LP-9230 [M]	1963	6.25	12.50	25.00
Imperial LP-12230 [R]	1963	5.00	10.00	20.00
SOLID GOLD PROGRAMMING				
Screen Gems/Columbia CPL-711 [DJ]	1975	5.00	10.00	20.00
—Promo-only compilation of oldies sent to radio to spur airplay on songs owned by this publishing house				
Screen Gems/Columbia CPL-715 [DJ]	1975	5.00	10.00	20.00
—Same concept as above album, but completely different contents, and mostly in stereo				
SOLID GOLD SONGS INSTRUMENTALLY				
Screen Gems/Columbia CPL-714 [DJ]	1975	5.00	10.00	20.00
—Promo-only compilation of oldies sent to radio to spur airplay on songs owned by this publishing house				
SOLID GOLD SOUL				
Atlantic 8116 [M]	1966	3.75	7.50	15.00
Atlantic SD 8116 [S]	1966	5.00	10.00	20.00
SOLO FLIGHT				
Pacific Jazz JWC-505 [M]	1956	12.50	25.00	50.00
World Pacific JWC-505 [M]	1958	10.00	20.00	40.00
SOLO SPOTLIGHTS				
King 745 [M]	1961	25.00	50.00	100.00
SOME LIKE IT COOL				
United Artists X-71 [M]	1959	10.00	20.00	40.00
United Artists SX-71 [S]	1959	10.00	20.00	40.00

Label, Number	Yr	VG	VG+	NM
SOMETHING FESTIVE!				
A&M SP-19003	1968	3.75	7.50	15.00
—Sold only at B.F. Goodrich tire dealers				
SOMETHING FOR BOTH EARS				
World Pacific HFS-2 [S]	1958	10.00	20.00	40.00
—Stereo sampler				
SOMETHING NEW, SOMETHING BLUE				
Columbia CL 1388 [M]	1959	5.00	10.00	20.00
SONGS BY RODGERS AND HART AND JOHNNY GREEN				
Discovery DL-3014 [10]	1951	12.50	25.00	50.00
SONGS FOR A SUMMER NIGHT				
Columbia PM 2 [(2) M]	1963	5.00	10.00	20.00
Columbia PMS 2 [(2) S]	1963	6.25	12.50	25.00
SONGS FOR CHRISTMAS — THE OLD AND THE NEW				
RCA Victor PR-132-A [M]	1962	3.75	7.50	15.00
—Sold only at Jewel food stores				
SONGS FOR THE CHRISTMAS SEASON				
Capitol Creative Products SL-6541	1967	3.00	6.00	12.00
SONGS OF FAITH				
Audio Lab AL-1504 [M]	1959	20.00	40.00	80.00
SONGS OF FAITH VOLUME 2				
Audio Lab AL-1523 [M]	1959	20.00	40.00	80.00
SONGS OF RIVERS, OCEANS AND SEAS				
King 871 [M]	1963	17.50	35.00	70.00
SONGS OF THE HILLS				
Audio Lab AL-1515 [M]	1959	20.00	40.00	80.00
SOUL CHRISTMAS				
Atco SD 33-269	1968	7.50	15.00	30.00
SOUL EXPLOSION				
Stax STS 2-2007 [(2)]	1969	5.00	10.00	20.00
SOUL JAZZ GIANTS				
Prestige PRST-7791	1970	3.75	7.50	15.00
SOUL JAZZ, VOL. 1				
Bluesville BVLP-1009 [M]	1960	12.50	25.00	50.00
—Blue label, silver print				
Bluesville BVLP-1009 [M]	1965	6.25	12.50	25.00
—Blue label, trident logo at right				
SOUL JAZZ, VOL. 2				
Bluesville BVLP-1010 [M]	1960	12.50	25.00	50.00
—Blue label, silver print				
Bluesville BVLP-1010 [M]	1965	6.25	12.50	25.00
—Blue label, trident logo at right				
SOUL MEETING SATURDAY NIGHT HOOTENANNY STYLE				
Vee Jay LP-1074 [M]	1963	7.50	15.00	30.00
—Not known to exist in stereo				
THE SOUL OF JAZZ				
Riverside S-5 [M]	1957	10.00	20.00	40.00
World Wide MGS-20002 [S]	1958	20.00	40.00	80.00
THE SOUL OF JAZZ PERCUSSION				
Warwick W 5003 [M]	1961	7.50	15.00	30.00
Warwick W 5003ST [S]	1961	10.00	20.00	40.00
THE SOUL OF JAZZ PIANO				
Riverside 9S-7 [S]	196?	7.50	15.00	30.00
SOUL OLDIES VOLUME I				
Unart M 20022 [M]	1967	3.75	7.50	15.00
Unart S 21022 [S]	1967	3.00	6.00	12.00
SOUL OLDIES VOLUME II				
Unart M 20023 [M]	1967	3.75	7.50	15.00
Unart S 21023 [S]	1967	3.00	6.00	12.00
SOULED OUT				
Chess LPS 1546 [S]	1969	12.50	25.00	50.00
SOULFUL OLDIES				
Oldies 33 OL-8005 [M]	1964	6.25	12.50	25.00
THE SOUND OF BIG BAND JAZZ IN HI-FI				
World Pacific WP-1257 [M]	1960	10.00	20.00	40.00
THE SOUND OF BIG BAND JAZZ IN STEREO				
World Pacific ST-1015 [S]	1960	7.50	15.00	30.00
THE SOUND OF CHRISTMAS				
Capitol Creative Products SL-6515 [S]	1966	3.00	6.00	12.00
THE SOUND OF CHRISTMAS, VOL. 2				
Capitol Creative Products SL-6534	1967	3.00	6.00	12.00
THE SOUND OF CHRISTMAS, VOL. 3				
Capitol Creative Products SL-6680	1970	3.00	6.00	12.00
THE SOUND OF GENIUS				
Columbia Masterworks SGM 1 [(2) M]	1963	5.00	10.00	20.00
Columbia Masterworks SGS 1 [(2) S]	1963	6.25	12.50	25.00

Label, Number	Yr	VG	VG+	NM
THE SOUND OF JAZZ				
Columbia CL 1098 [M]	1957	5.00	10.00	20.00
THE SOUNDS OF CHRISTMAS				
Capitol STBB-93245 [(2)]	1970	3.75	7.50	15.00
—Available only through the Capitol Record Club				
Columbia Special Products P 12474	1974	3.00	6.00	12.00
—Sold only through Amway dealers				
MCA Special Markets DL 734735	197?	3.00	6.00	12.00
SOUNDS OF SUCCESS				
Jamie JLP-3017 [M]	1961	6.25	12.50	25.00
Jamie JLPS-3017 [S]	1961	7.50	15.00	30.00
SOUTH SIDE JAZZ				
Chess CHV-415	1971	3.00	6.00	12.00
SOUTHERN MEETIN'				
Kimberly 2017 [M]	1963	5.00	10.00	20.00
Kimberly 11017 [S]	1963	6.25	12.50	25.00
SOUVENIR/PROGRAMMING RECORD — DEALERS/DISC JOCKEYS — OCT.-NOV. 1955				
Capitol PRO-232 [DJ]	1955	10.00	20.00	40.00
THE SPANISH SIDE OF JAZZ				
Roulette SR-42001	1968	5.00	10.00	20.00
SPECIAL CHRISTMAS LP FOR DISC JOCKEYS				
Capitol PRO-201 [DJ]	1954	12.50	25.00	50.00
SPIN TIME WITH LIBERTY				
Liberty MM-417 [DJ]	1962	12.50	25.00	50.00
—Promo-only release				
THE SPIRIT OF CHRISTMAS				
Capitol Creative Products SL-6516	1966	3.75	7.50	15.00
Columbia Musical Treasury DS 453	1968	3.00	6.00	12.00
—Columbia Record Club exclusive				
Columbia Special Products CSP 249 [M]	1965	3.75	7.50	15.00
—Sold only at A&P grocery stores				
Columbia Special Products P 11403	1972	2.50	5.00	10.00
—Sold only by The Treasury family store and supermarket				
THE SPIRIT OF CHRISTMAS, VOLUME II				
Columbia Special Products CSS 889	1969	3.00	6.00	12.00
—Distributed by TG&Y				
THE SPIRIT OF CHRISTMAS, VOLUME III				
Columbia Special Products CSS 1463	1970	3.00	6.00	12.00
SPIRITUALS				
King 951 [M]	1966	12.50	25.00	50.00
—Reissue of "Spirituals, Volume 5," King 576				
SPIRITUALS TO SWING: JOHN HAMMOND'S 30TH ANNIVERSARY CONCERT 1967				
Columbia G 30776 [(2)]	1971	3.75	7.50	15.00
Columbia CG 30776 [(2)]	197?	3.00	6.00	12.00
—"CG" prefix is a reissue of "G"				
SPIRITUALS, VOLUME 5				
King 576 [M]	1957	37.50	75.00	150.00
STABLE MATES				
Savoy MG-12115 [M]	1957	12.50	25.00	50.00
STARS FOR A SUMMER NIGHT				
Columbia PM 1 [(2) M]	1961	6.25	12.50	25.00
Columbia PMS 1 [(2) S]	1961	7.50	15.00	30.00
THE STARS OF HEE HAW				
Capitol ST-437	1970	5.00	10.00	20.00
STARS OF JAZZ '61				
Jazzland JLP-1001 [M]	1961	6.25	12.50	25.00
STARS OF THE APOLLO				
Columbia G 30788 [(2)]	1971	3.75	7.50	15.00
Columbia CG 30788 [(2)]	197?	3.00	6.00	12.00
—"CG" prefix is a reissue of "G"				
STARS OF THE GRAND OLE OPRY 1926-1974				
RCA Victor CPL2-0466 [(2)]	1974	5.00	10.00	20.00
THE STAX/VOLT REVUE — LIVE IN LONDON				
Stax 721 [M]	1967	5.00	10.00	20.00
Stax S721 [S]	1967	6.25	12.50	25.00
THE STAX/VOLT REVUE — LIVE IN LONDON, VOLUME 2				
Stax 722 [M]	1967	5.00	10.00	20.00
Stax S722 [S]	1967	6.25	12.50	25.00
STAX...ONCE YOU'VE BEEN THERE, YOU KNOW YOU'RE HOME				
Stax STS 1 [(2) DJ]	1971	10.00	20.00	40.00
—Promo only in blank white gatefold cover				
STAY IN SCHOOL — DON'T BE A DROP OUT				
Stax A-11 [DJ]	1967	125.00	250.00	500.00
STEREOSONIC JUBILEE SAMPLER, VOLUME 1				
Jubilee SSJLP-801 [S]	1959	10.00	20.00	40.00

Label, Number	Yr	VG	VG+	NM
STERLING BALL 1971				
Motown M 739 [DJ]	1971	62.50	125.00	250.00
—Loucye Gordy Wakefield Scholarship Fund benefit giveaway				
STILL MORE GOLD HITS, VOLUME 3				
Warwick W 2048 [M]	1962	20.00	40.00	80.00
STRETCHING OUT				
United Artists UAL-4023 [M]	1959	30.00	60.00	120.00
United Artists UAS-5023 [S]	1959	25.00	50.00	100.00
STRICTLY BEBOP				
Capitol M-11059	1973	3.00	6.00	12.00
STRICTLY FROM DIXIE				
MGM E-3262 [M]	1956	7.50	15.00	30.00
THE STRING BAND PROJECT				
Elektra EKL-292 [M]	1965	5.00	10.00	20.00
Elektra EKS-7292 [S]	1965	6.25	12.50	25.00
A STRING OF SWINGIN' PEARLS				
RCA Victor LPM-1373 [M]	1956	7.50	15.00	30.00
SUMMER SOUVENIRS				
Bell 6035	1969	5.00	10.00	20.00
SUMMIT MEETING				
Vee Jay LP-3026 [M]	1961	5.00	10.00	20.00
Vee Jay SR-3026 [S]	1961	6.25	12.50	25.00
SUN'S GOLD HITS				
Sun LP-1250 [M]	1961	50.00	100.00	200.00
SUNDAY MORNING				
Vee Jay LP-5016 [M]	1961	7.50	15.00	30.00
SUPER GOLDEN HITS				
Jubilee JGS-8019	1968	25.00	50.00	100.00
—Despite the stereo prefix, this LP is mono				
SUPER GOLDEN HITS, VOLUME 2				
Jubilee JGS-8023	1969	25.00	50.00	100.00
—Reissue of "Clay Cole's Bin of Original Golden Oldies," Jubilee 5026; again, despite the stereo prefix, this LP is mono				
THE SUPER GROUPS				
Atco SD 33-279	1969	5.00	10.00	20.00
THE SUPER GROUPS FROM HOLLAND				
White Whale WWS-7129	1970	6.25	12.50	25.00
THE SUPER HITS, VOL. 2				
Atlantic SD 8188	1968	5.00	10.00	20.00
THE SUPER HITS, VOL. 3				
Atlantic SD 8203	1968	5.00	10.00	20.00
THE SUPER HITS, VOL. 4				
Atlantic SD 8224	1969	5.00	10.00	20.00
THE SUPER HITS, VOL. 5				
Atlantic SD 8274	1970	5.00	10.00	20.00
SUPER OLDIES/VOL. 1				
Capitol T 2562 [M]	1966	5.00	10.00	20.00
Capitol ST 2562 [S]	1966	6.25	12.50	25.00
SUPER OLDIES/VOL. 2				
Capitol T 2565 [M]	1966	5.00	10.00	20.00
Capitol ST 2565 [S]	1966	6.25	12.50	25.00
SUPER OLDIES/VOL. 3				
Capitol STBB 2910 [(2)]	1968	5.00	10.00	20.00
SUPER OLDIES/VOL. 4				
Capitol STBB-149 [(2)]	1969	5.00	10.00	20.00
SUPER OLDIES/VOL. 5				
Capitol STBB-216 [(2)]	1969	5.00	10.00	20.00
SUPER ROCK				
Columbia G 30121 [(2)]	1970	3.75	7.50	15.00
THE SUPER SOUL-DEES				
Capitol T 2798 [M]	1967	5.00	10.00	20.00
Capitol ST 2798 [S]	1967	5.00	10.00	20.00
THE SUPER SOUL-DEES, VOL. 2				
Capitol STBB-2911 [(2)]	1968	5.00	10.00	20.00
THE SUPER SOUL-DEES, VOL. 3				
Capitol STBB-178 [(2)]	1969	5.00	10.00	20.00
SUPERSTARS OF THE '70S				
Warner Special Products SP-4000 [(4)]	1973	10.00	20.00	40.00
—Box set with booklet of liner notes				
SURF'S UP AT BANZAI PIPELINE				
Northridge NM-101 [M]	1963	50.00	100.00	200.00
—Original pressing of LP reissued on Reprise				
Reprise R 6094 [M]	1963	25.00	50.00	100.00
Reprise RS 6094 [S]	1963	37.50	75.00	150.00
SURFIN' ON WAVE NINE				
King 855 [M]	1963	20.00	40.00	80.00

Label, Number	Yr	VG	VG+	NM
SWAMP BLUES VOLUME 1				
Excello LPS-8015 [R]	1970	5.00	10.00	20.00
SWAMP BLUES VOLUME 2				
Excello LPS-8016 [R]	1970	5.00	10.00	20.00
SWEDES FROM JAZZVILLE				
Epic LN 3309 [M]	1957	12.50	25.00	50.00
SWEDISH PASTRY				
Discovery DL-2008 [10]	1954	12.50	25.00	50.00
SWEET 'N GREASY: RHYTHM 'N' BLUES, VOLUME 2				
Imperial LP-94005	1968	5.00	10.00	20.00
SWEET ADELINES MEDALIST QUARTETS OF 1958				
Cadence CLP-3018 [M]	1959	10.00	20.00	40.00
SWEET ADELINES MEDALISTS OF 1957				
Cadence CLP-3009 [M]	1958	10.00	20.00	40.00
SWING 1946				
Prestige PRLP-7604	1969	3.75	7.50	15.00
SWING AGAIN!				
Capitol T 1386 [M]	1960	5.00	10.00	20.00
Capitol DT 1386 [R]	196?	3.00	6.00	12.00
SWING BILLIES				
Audio Lab AL-1546 [M]	1960	30.00	60.00	120.00
SWING BILLIES VOLUME 2				
Audio Lab AL-1566 [M]	1960	30.00	60.00	120.00
SWING CLASSICS 1935				
Prestige PRLP-7646	1969	3.75	7.50	15.00
THE SWING ERA, VOL. 1				
"X" LVA-3030 [10]	1955	20.00	40.00	80.00
SWING GOES DIXIE				
American Recording Society G-420 [M]	1957	7.50	15.00	30.00
SWING GUITARS				
Norgran MGN-1033 [M]	1955	20.00	40.00	80.00
Verve MGV-8124 [M]	1957	7.50	15.00	30.00
Verve V-8124 [M]	1961	5.00	10.00	20.00
SWING HI, SWING LO				
Blue Note BLP-5027 [10]	1953	50.00	100.00	200.00
Blue Note B-6507 [M]	1969	3.75	7.50	15.00
SWING LIGHTLY				
Jazztone J-1265 [M]	1957	7.50	15.00	30.00
SWING POTPOURRI				
Audiophile AP-23 [M]	1953	7.50	15.00	30.00
A SWINGIN' GIG				
Tampa TP-2 [M]	1957	25.00	50.00	100.00
—Colored vinyl				
Tampa TP-2 [M]	1958	10.00	20.00	40.00
—Black vinyl				
SWINGIN' LIKE SIXTY, VOL. 1				
World Pacific ST-1289 [S]	1960	7.50	15.00	30.00
SWINGIN' LIKE SIXTY, VOL. 2				
World Pacific ST-1290 [S]	1960	7.50	15.00	30.00
SWINGIN' LIKE SIXTY, VOL. 3				
World Pacific ST-1291 [S]	1960	7.50	15.00	30.00
SWINGIN' SOUNDS				
Columbia Special Products XTV 82030 [M]	1962	6.25	12.50	25.00
—Issued for the W.A. Sheaffer Pen Co.				
SWINGIN': BIG BAND SWING AND JAZZ FROM THE 1930S AND 1940S				
Folkways FJ-2861	1986	3.00	6.00	12.00
SWINGING BROADWAY				
Kimberly 2024 [M]	1963	5.00	10.00	20.00
Kimberly 11024 [S]	1963	6.25	12.50	25.00
SWINGING FOR THE KING				
Mercury MG-20133 [M]	1956	12.50	25.00	50.00
SWINGING SOUNDTRACK				
Kimberly 2016 [M]	1963	5.00	10.00	20.00
Kimberly 11016 [S]	1963	6.25	12.50	25.00
THE SWINGVILLE ALL-STARS				
Swingville SVLP-2010 [M]	1960	10.00	20.00	40.00
—Purple label				
Swingville SVLP-2010 [M]	1965	5.00	10.00	20.00
—Blue label, trident logo at right				
SWING... NOT SPRING!				
Savoy MG-12062 [M]	1956	12.50	25.00	50.00
SWITCHED ON BLUES				
Soul SS-720	1969	37.50	75.00	150.00
TAKE THE LIBERTY				
Liberty MM-427 [DJ]	1960	10.00	20.00	40.00

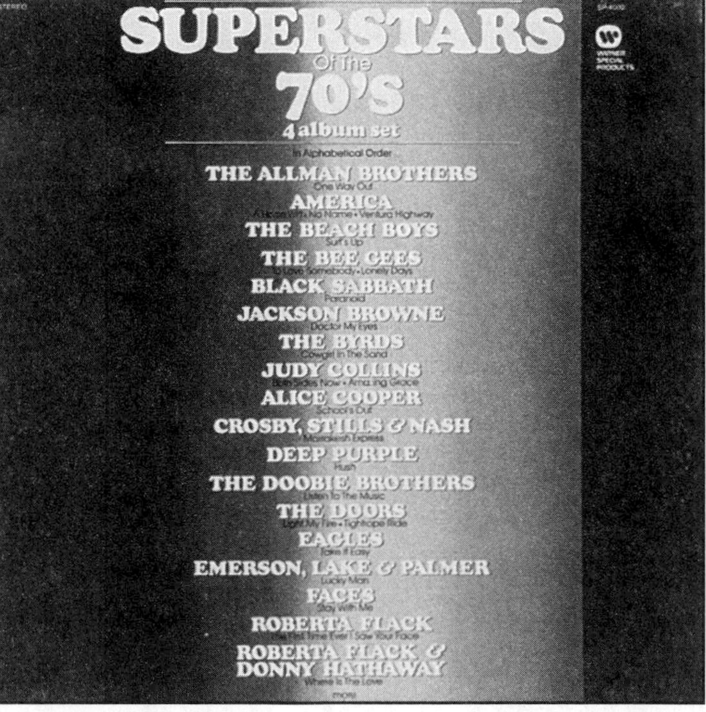

(Top left) For a nice dose of late 1960s bubblegum music, it's hard to top this Buddah compilation. But how did the Shadows of Knight get in there with the 1910 Fruitgum Company? By the way, there never was a Volume 2, as far as we know. (Top right) Dick Clark lent his name to several compilation albums over the years. This one, released in 1973 and in print for years afterward, is both the most common and the most difficult to find intact. Original issues contained, in addition to two records in a gatefold sleeve, a booklet and a cardboard record called "Inside Stories with Dick Clark." Issues without all the parts are of little interest to the collector. (Bottom left) In stereo, this otherwise ordinary Columbia Record Club compilation is noteworthy for its first true stereo mix of Bob Dylan's "Positively 4th Street," which runs longer than any other version of the song ever issued. (Bottom right) *Superstars of the 70's* was everywhere in the late fall of 1973. It was heavily advertised on TV and marketed to discount stores rather than record stores. It also spawned several follow-up albums. But the original boxed four-record set is the most collectible.

Label, Number	Yr	VG	VG+	NM
TAMLA SPECIAL #1				
Tamla TM 224 [M]	1962	37.50	75.00	150.00
—White label				
Tamla TM 224 [M]	1963	17.50	35.00	70.00
—Yellow label				
TEEN DELIGHTS				
Vee Jay LP-1021 [M]	1960	7.50	15.00	30.00
TEEN DELIGHTS, VOLUME 2				
Vee Jay LP-1036 [M]	1961	7.50	15.00	30.00
THE TEEN SOUND				
Columbia Special Products CSS 523	1967	3.00	6.00	12.00
TEENAGE PARTY				
Gee GLP-702 [M]	1958	50.00	100.00	200.00
—Red label				
Gee GLP-702 [M]	196?	15.00	30.00	60.00
—Gray label				
TEENSVILLE				
Liberty L-5503 [M]	1962	10.00	20.00	40.00
TENNESSEE				
Design DLP-611 [M]	1962	5.00	10.00	20.00
TENOR CONCLAVE				
Prestige PRLP-7074 [M]	1957	25.00	50.00	100.00
—Reissued as Prestige 7249; see JOHN COLTRANE.				
TENOR JAZZ				
Mercury MG-20016 [10]	1950	25.00	50.00	100.00
—Issued in a paper sleeve				
TENOR SAX				
Concord 3012 [M]	195?	10.00	20.00	40.00
TENOR SAX SOLOS, VOL. 1				
Savoy MG-9008 [10]	1952	37.50	75.00	150.00
TENOR SAX SOLOS, VOL. 2				
Savoy MG-9013 [10]	1952	37.50	75.00	150.00
TENOR SAX SOLOS, VOL. 3				
Savoy MG-9021 [10]	1953	37.50	75.00	150.00
TENOR SAXES				
Norgran MGN-1034 [M]	1955	20.00	40.00	80.00
Verve MGV-8127 [M]	1957	7.50	15.00	30.00
Verve V-8127 [M]	1961	5.00	10.00	20.00
TENORS ANYONE?				
Dawn DLP-1126 [M]	1958	20.00	40.00	80.00
TERRITORY BANDS 1926-31				
Historical 26	1969	2.50	5.00	10.00
TERRITORY BANDS 1929-33				
Historical 24	1968	2.50	5.00	10.00
THAT CHRISTMAS FEELING				
Columbia Special Products P 11853	1973	3.00	6.00	12.00
—Sold only at JCPenney department stores				
THAT CHRISTMAS FEELING!				
Columbia Special Products CSS 1429	1970	2.50	5.00	10.00
THEME SONGS				
Columbia CL 6016 [10]	1949	10.00	20.00	40.00
RCA Victor LPT-1 [10]	1951	10.00	20.00	40.00
THEMES LIKE OLD TIMES				
Viva 36018 [(2)]	1969	5.00	10.00	20.00
THESAURUS OF CLASSIC JAZZ				
Columbia C4L 18 [(4)]	1961	12.50	25.00	50.00
A THIRD SESSION AT SQUIRREL'S				
Paramount LP-110 [10]	1954	15.00	30.00	60.00
THIS COULD LEAD TO LOVE				
Riverside RLP 12-808 [M]	195?	12.50	25.00	50.00
THIS IS CHRISTMAS				
RCA Victor VPS-6046 [(2)]	1971	3.75	7.50	15.00
THIS IS HOW IT ALL BEGAN: THE SPECIALTY STORY, VOLUME 1				
Specialty SPS-2117	1970	5.00	10.00	20.00
THIS IS HOW IT ALL BEGAN: THE SPECIALTY STORY, VOLUME 2				
Specialty SPS-2118	1970	5.00	10.00	20.00
THIS IS SOUL				
Atlantic SD 8170	1968	5.00	10.00	20.00
THIS IS STEREO				
Liberty LST-101 [S]	1960	10.00	20.00	40.00
—Black vinyl				
Liberty LST-101 [S]	1960	30.00	60.00	120.00
—Red vinyl				
THIS IS THE BIG BAND ERA				
RCA Victor VPM-6043 [(2)]	197?	3.75	7.50	15.00
THIS IS THE BLUES				
Kimberly 2020 [M]	1963	5.00	10.00	20.00

Label, Number	Yr	VG	VG+	NM
Kimberly 11020 [S]	1963	6.25	12.50	25.00
THIS IS THE BLUES, VOL. 1				
Pacific Jazz PJ-13 [M]	1961	7.50	15.00	30.00
THIS IS THE BLUES, VOL. 2				
Pacific Jazz PJ-30 [M]	1962	6.25	12.50	25.00
Pacific Jazz ST-30 [M]	1962	7.50	15.00	30.00
THREADS OF GLORY — 200 YEARS OF AMERICA IN WORDS & MUSIC				
London Phase 4 6SP 14000 [(6)]	1975	7.50	15.00	30.00
THREE DECADES OF MUSIC, 1939-49, VOL. 1				
Blue Note BST-89902 [(2)]	1969	6.25	12.50	25.00
THREE DECADES OF MUSIC, 1949-59, VOL. 1				
Blue Note BST-89903 [(2)]	1969	6.25	12.50	25.00
THREE DECADES OF MUSIC, 1959-69, VOL. 1				
Blue Note BST-89904 [(2)]	1969	6.25	12.50	25.00
THREE ROADS TO JAZZ				
American Recording Society LP-100 [M]	1956	7.50	15.00	30.00
A TIME FOR PRAYER				
Audio Lab AL-1518 [M]	1959	20.00	40.00	80.00
' TIS THE SEASON				
Columbia Special Products C 10874	1972	2.50	5.00	10.00
TODAY'S HITS				
Philles PHLP 4004 [M]	1963	100.00	200.00	400.00
—First pressings have blue and black labels				
Philles PHLP 4004 [M]	1964	50.00	100.00	200.00
—Second pressings have yellow and red labels				
TOGETHER				
Warner Bros. PRO 486	1972	5.00	10.00	20.00
—Originals have green labels				
TOGETHER AT CHRISTMAS (READER'S DIGEST FAMILY ALBUM OF CHRISTMAS MUSIC)				
Reader's Digest RDA 151-A [(5)]	1974	5.00	10.00	20.00
—Available only through Reader's Digest magazine by mail order				
TOMORROW'S HITS				
Vee Jay LP-1042 [M]	1962	7.50	15.00	30.00
TOP HITS OF '54 VOLUME II				
Capitol H 9119 [10]	1954	12.50	25.00	50.00
TOP R&B ARTISTS SING COUNTRY SONGS				
King 884 [M]	1964	20.00	40.00	80.00
TOWN HALL CONCERT				
Mainstream S-6004 [R]	1965	3.00	6.00	12.00
Mainstream 56004 [M]	1965	6.25	12.50	25.00
TRADITIONAL CHRISTMAS SONGS				
Audio Lab AL-1517 [M]	1959	20.00	40.00	80.00
TRADITIONAL JAZZ				
London LL 1242 [M]	1955	5.00	10.00	20.00
TRADITIONAL JAZZ AT THE ROYAL FESTIVAL HALL				
London LL 1184 [M]	1955	5.00	10.00	20.00
TREASURE ALBUM				
Hickory LPS-154	1970	10.00	20.00	40.00
TREASURE CHEST GOODIES				
Stax 703 [M]	1963	10.00	20.00	40.00
—National version of "Hits from the South Presented by Nick Charles" with rearranged contents				
TREASURE CHEST OF HITS				
Swan LP-501 [M]	1960	20.00	40.00	80.00
A TREASURE CHEST OF SONG HITS				
Columbia CL 613 [M]	1955	6.25	12.50	25.00
TREASURE TUNES FROM THE VAULT (AS ADVERTISED ON WLS)				
Chess LP 1474 [M]	1962	10.00	20.00	40.00
A TREASURY OF CHRISTMAS				
Columbia Record Club P4S 5022 [(4)]	1965	7.50	15.00	30.00
A TREASURY OF GOLDEN CHRISTMAS SONGS				
Vee Jay LP-5045 [M]	1963	7.50	15.00	30.00
TRIBUTE TO CHARLIE PARKER FROM THE NEWPORT JAZZ FESTIVAL				
RCA Victor LPM-3738 [M]	1967	7.50	15.00	30.00
RCA Victor LSP-3738 [S]	1967	5.00	10.00	20.00
TROMBONE BAND STAND				
Bethlehem BCP-6036 [M]	1960	7.50	15.00	30.00
TROMBONE SCENE				
Vik LX-1087 [M]	1957	7.50	15.00	30.00
TROMBONES				
Savoy MG-12086 [M]	1956	15.00	30.00	60.00
THE TROMBONES, INC.				
Warner Bros. W 1272 [M]	1959	6.25	12.50	25.00
Warner Bros. WS 1272 [S]	1959	7.50	15.00	30.00

Label, Number	Yr	VG	VG+	NM
TRUCK DRIVER SONGS				
King 866 [M]	1963	17.50	35.00	70.00
TRUMPET BLUES 1925-29				
Historical 27	1969	2.50	5.00	10.00
TRUMPET INTERLUDE				
EmArcy MG-36017 [M]	1955	12.50	25.00	50.00
TRUMPET STYLISTS				
Capitol H 326 [10]	1952	12.50	25.00	50.00
TRUMPETER'S HOLIDAY				
Epic LN 3252 [M]	1956	7.50	15.00	30.00
TRUMPETS ALL OUT				
Savoy MG-12096 [M]	1957	15.00	30.00	60.00
TUNES TO BE REMEMBERED				
Excello LP-8001 [M]	1960	37.50	75.00	150.00
—Original cover is green with black records that list the title and artist of each selection				
TURN BACK THE CLOCK				
King 859 [M]	1963	17.50	35.00	70.00
TWISTIN' ALL NIGHT LONG				
Swan LP-506 [M]	1962	30.00	60.00	120.00
THE UNAVAILABLE 16				
Vee Jay LP-1051 [M]	1962	10.00	20.00	40.00
UNDER ONE ROOF				
EmArcy MG-36088 [M]	1956	10.00	20.00	40.00
UNDERGROUND GOLD				
Liberty LST-7625	1969	3.75	7.50	15.00
UNEXPURGATED JAZZ				
Audiophile AP-43 [M]	1953	7.50	15.00	30.00
UNFORGETTABLE OLDIES				
Unart M 20014 [M]	1967	3.75	7.50	15.00
Unart S 21014 [S]	1967	3.00	6.00	12.00
UNFORGETTABLE OLDIES — VOLUME II				
Unart M 20027 [M]	1968	3.75	7.50	15.00
Unart S 21027 [S]	1968	3.00	6.00	12.00
UNFORGETTABLE PERFORMANCES BY THE JAZZ IMMORTALS				
Dot DLP-3444 [M]	196?	3.00	6.00	12.00
UP SWING				
RCA Victor LPT-12 [10]	1951	10.00	20.00	40.00
UPRIGHT AND LOWDOWN				
Columbia CL 685 [M]	1955	5.00	10.00	20.00
A VARIETY OF COUNTRY SACRED SONGS				
Audio Lab AL-1557 [M]	1960	15.00	30.00	60.00
THE VERVE COMPENDIUM OF JAZZ, NO. 1				
Verve MGV-8194 [M]	1957	7.50	15.00	30.00
Verve V-8194 [M]	1961	5.00	10.00	20.00
THE VERVE COMPENDIUM OF JAZZ, NO. 2				
Verve MGV-8195 [M]	1957	7.50	15.00	30.00
Verve V-8195 [M]	1961	5.00	10.00	20.00
A VERY MERRY CHRISTMAS				
Columbia Special Products CSS 563	1967	5.00	10.00	20.00
—Sold only at Grants stores				
A VERY MERRY CHRISTMAS TO ALL				
Columbia Special Products CSP 159	1964	3.75	7.50	15.00
—Sold only at Acme markets (Mid-Atlantic states)				
A VERY MERRY CHRISTMAS, VOLUME TWO				
Columbia Special Products CSS 788	1968	3.00	6.00	12.00
—Sold only at Grants stores				
A VERY MERRY CHRISTMAS, VOLUME 3				
Columbia Special Products CSS 997	1969	3.00	6.00	12.00
—Sold only at Grants stores				
A VERY MERRY CHRISTMAS, VOLUME IV				
Columbia Special Products CSS 1464	1970	3.75	7.50	15.00
—Sold only at Grants stores				
A VERY MERRY CHRISTMAS, VOLUME 5				
RCA Special Products PRS-343	1971	2.50	5.00	10.00
—Sold only at Grants stores				
A VERY MERRY CHRISTMAS, VOLUME VI				
RCA Special Products PRS-427	1972	2.50	5.00	10.00
—Sold only at Grants stores				
A VERY MERRY CHRISTMAS, VOLUME VII				
RCA Special Products DPL1-0049	1973	2.50	5.00	10.00
—Sold only at Grants stores				
A VERY MERRY CHRISTMAS, VOLUME VIII				
Capitol Special Markets SL-6954	1974	2.50	5.00	10.00
—Sold only at Grants stores				
VERY SAXY				
Prestige PRLP-7167 [M]	1959	15.00	30.00	60.00

Label, Number	Yr	VG	VG+	NM
Prestige PRST-7790	1971	5.00	10.00	20.00
—Reissue of 7167				
VICEROY CIGARETTES CAMPUS JAZZ FESTIVAL				
RCA Custom KO7P-1544 [M]	1959	7.50	15.00	30.00
—Available thoruigh Viceroy cigarettes				
THE VIOLIN SUMMIT				
Prestige PRLP-7631	1969	3.75	7.50	15.00
VOICES OF HAITI				
Elektra EKL-5 [10]	1953	10.00	20.00	40.00
VOODOO DRUMS IN HI-FI				
Atlantic 1296 [M]	1958	10.00	20.00	40.00
—Black label				
Atlantic 1296 [M]	1961	6.25	12.50	25.00
—Multicolor label, white "fan" logo at right				
Atlantic 1296 [M]	1963	5.00	10.00	20.00
—Multicolor label, black "fan" logo at right				
WALKIN' BY MYSELF				
Chess LP 1446 [M]	1960	20.00	40.00	80.00
THE WALTONS' CHRISTMAS ALBUM				
Columbia KC 33193	1974	3.75	7.50	15.00
—Only one of the actors who appeared on the show appears on the album, thus it's listed here under Various Artists rather than Soundtracks or Television Albums				
WAMO'S GOLDEN GASSERS				
Chess LP 1458 PGH [M]	1961	37.50	75.00	150.00
—Pittsburgh version of "Golden Gassers," Chess 1458				
THE WARNER/REPRISE RADIO SHOW				
Warner Bros. PRO 463	1971	6.25	12.50	25.00
—Originals have green labels				
WASHBOARD RHYTHM KINGS, VOL. 1				
"X" LVA-3021 [10]	1954	20.00	40.00	80.00
WE'VE BUILT A JAZZ ALBUM FOR YOU				
Bethlehem BCP-89 [M]	1958	7.50	15.00	30.00
WE CUT THIS ALBUM FOR BREAD				
Bethlehem BCP-86 [M]	1958	7.50	15.00	30.00
WE LIKE BANDS				
Coral CRL 57229 [M]	195?	3.00	6.00	12.00
WE LIKE BOYS/GREAT BOY OLDIES				
Oldies 33 OL-8004 [M]	1964	6.25	12.50	25.00
WE SING THE BLUES				
Minit LP-0003 [M]	1962	12.50	25.00	50.00
WE WISH YOU A MERRY CHRISTMAS				
Harmony KH 31536	1972	2.50	5.00	10.00
Warner Bros. W 1337 [M]	1960	6.25	12.50	25.00
Warner Bros. WS 1337 [S]	1960	7.50	15.00	30.00
WEST COAST JAZZ, VOL. 2				
Jazztone J-(# unk) [M]	1957	7.50	15.00	30.00
WEST COAST VS. EAST COAST				
MGM E-3390 [M]	1956	7.50	15.00	30.00
WESTERN SWING				
King 876 [M]	1963	17.50	35.00	70.00
WFUN GOOD GUYS				
Roulette R 25273 [M]	1965	5.00	10.00	20.00
WHAT'S NEW? ON CAPITOL STEREO, VOL. 1				
Capitol SN-1 [S]	1959	6.25	12.50	25.00
WHAT'S SHAKIN'				
Elektra EKL-4002 [M]	1966	10.00	20.00	40.00
—Deduct 25 percent if booklet is missing				
Elektra EKS-74002 [S]	1966	12.50	25.00	50.00
—Deduct 25 percent if booklet is missing				
WHEELIN' AND DEALIN'				
Prestige PRLP-7131 [M]	1957	25.00	50.00	100.00
—Reissued as Status 8327; see JOHN COLTRANE.				
WHK GOOD GUYS				
Roulette R 25295 [M]	1965	5.00	10.00	20.00
THE WHO'S WHO OF COUNTRY AND WESTERN MUSIC				
Capitol T 2538 [M]	1966	5.00	10.00	20.00
Capitol ST 2538 [S]	1966	5.00	10.00	20.00
THE WHOLE BURBANK CATALOG				
Warner Bros. PRO 512 [(2)]	1972	5.00	10.00	20.00
—Originals have green labels				
A WHOLE LOT OF BLOWIN'				
Audio Lab AL-1539 [M]	1959	15.00	30.00	60.00
WHOPPERS				
Jubilee JGM-1119 [M]	1960	25.00	50.00	100.00
—Reissue of "Best of Rhythm and Blues," Jubilee 1014				
THE WIDE, WIDE WORLD OF JAZZ				
RCA Victor LPM-1325 [M]	1956	7.50	15.00	30.00

Label, Number	Yr	VG	VG+	NM
WILD WILDWOOD RECORDED LIVE				
Chancellor CHL-5017 [M]	1960	6.25	12.50	25.00
Chancellor CHLS-5017 [S]	1960	7.50	15.00	30.00
WILDFLOWERS: NEW YORK LOFT JAZZ 1				
Douglas 7045	1976	3.00	6.00	12.00
WILDFLOWERS: NEW YORK LOFT JAZZ 2				
Douglas 7046	1976	3.00	6.00	12.00
WILDFLOWERS: NEW YORK LOFT JAZZ 3				
Douglas 7047	1976	3.00	6.00	12.00
WILDFLOWERS: NEW YORK LOFT JAZZ 4				
Douglas 7048	1976	3.00	6.00	12.00
WILDFLOWERS: NEW YORK LOFT JAZZ 5				
Douglas 7049	1976	3.00	6.00	12.00
WING LIVELY GUYS				
Roulette R 25307 [M]	1965	5.00	10.00	20.00
WINNER'S CIRCLE				
Bethlehem BCP-6024 [M]	1958	10.00	20.00	40.00
WINNERS ALL! THE DOWN BEAT JAZZ POLL '64				
Verve V-8579 [M]	1964	5.00	10.00	20.00
Verve V6-8579 [S]	1964	6.25	12.50	25.00
WINNERS CIRCLE LIMITED EDITION				
Columbia GB-4 [M]	1959	6.25	12.50	25.00
WINTER'S WARMTH				
Columbia Special Products CSP 315/6 [(2)]	1965	3.75	7.50	15.00
—Produced for NORM/A Step Ahead				
WISHING YOU A MERRY CHRISTMAS				
RCA Victor LSP-4793	1972	3.00	6.00	12.00
WMAK JET SET-22 WINNERS				
Roulette R 25291 [M]	1965	5.00	10.00	20.00
WOL SOUL BROTHERS				
Roulette R 25337 [M]	1966	5.00	10.00	20.00
—Same LP as "WWIN Astro Jocks"				
THE WOMEN IN JAZZ				
Storyville STLP-916 [M]	1956	12.50	25.00	50.00
WONDERFUL MEMORIES FROM THE FAMILY PRAYER BOOK				
Vee Jay LP-5066 [M]	1964	7.50	15.00	30.00
THE WONDERFUL WORLD OF CHRISTMAS				
Capitol Special Markets SL-8000	1975	3.00	6.00	12.00
—Sold only at Firestone tire dealers (add 50% for sticker that says "Season's Greetings Firestone")				
WONDROUS WINTER				
Columbia Special Products CSS 708/9 [(2)]	1968	3.75	7.50	15.00
—Produced for NORM/A Step Ahead				
WOODSTOCK				
Cotillion SD 3-500 [(3)]	1970	5.00	10.00	20.00
—Pale blue labels				
WOODSTOCK TWO				
Cotillion SD 2-400 [(2)]	1971	5.00	10.00	20.00
THE WORKS				
Warner Bros. PRO 610 [(2)]	1975	6.25	12.50	25.00
WORLD'S GREATEST MUSIC SERIES POP/JAZZ				
Artia-Parliament WGM 2-AB [(10)]	196?	25.00	50.00	100.00
—Box set of material from the Roulette label. Also issued as two five-record boxes.				
Artia-Parliament WGM 2-A [(5)]	196?	10.00	20.00	40.00
—First of two five-record sets				
Artia-Parliament WGM 2-B [(5)]	196?	10.00	20.00	40.00
—Second of two five-record sets				
A WORLD OF BLUES				
Imperial LP-9210 [M]	1963	7.50	15.00	30.00

Label, Number	Yr	VG	VG+	NM
Imperial LP-12210 [R]	1963	5.00	10.00	20.00
THE WORLD OF COUNTRY MUSIC				
Capitol NPB-5 [(3)]	1965	7.50	15.00	30.00
WWIN ASTRO JOCKS				
Roulette R 25337 [M]	1966	5.00	10.00	20.00
—Same LP as "WOL Soul Brothers"				
YESTERDAY				
Mainstream MRL-364	197?	3.00	6.00	12.00
YOU'VE GOT TO HEAR IT TO BELIEVE IT				
Solid State SS-94	1966	5.00	10.00	20.00
THE YOUNG AT BOP				
EmArcy MG-26001 [10]	1954	20.00	40.00	80.00
THE YOUNG ONES OF JAZZ				
EmArcy MG-36085 [M]	1956	10.00	20.00	40.00
YOUR FAVORITE GROUPS AND THEIR GOLDEN GOODIES, VOL. 19				
Roulette R 25248 [M]	1964	5.00	10.00	20.00
YOUR FAVORITE SINGING GROUPS				
Hull 1002 [M]	1962	375.00	750.00	1500.
YOUR INTRODUCTION TO THE SOUND OF THE 'SIXTIES				
Liberty MM-403 [DJ]	1960	7.50	15.00	30.00
—Promo-only release				
YOUR OLD FAVORITES ON OLD TOWN				
Old Town LP-101 [M]	1959	50.00	100.00	200.00
YOURS				
Harmony HL 7042 [M]	1957	5.00	10.00	20.00
ZENITH PRESENTS ALL STAR HOOTENANNY				
Columbia Special Products CSP 149 [M]	1963	12.50	25.00	50.00
—With three early Bob Dylan tracks credited to "Bobby Dylan." Also has tracks by Pete Seeger (2), Orriel Smith (2) and The Clancy Brothers with Tommy Makem (3)				
ZENITH PRESENTS CHRISTMAS, A GIFT OF MUSIC				
Capitol Creative Products SL-6544 [S]	1967	3.00	6.00	12.00
—Sold only at Zenith dealers				
ZENITH PRESENTS CHRISTMAS, A GIFT OF MUSIC VOL. 2				
Columbia Special Products CSS 834	1968	3.00	6.00	12.00
—Sold only at Zenith dealers				
ZENITH PRESENTS CHRISTMAS, A GIFT OF MUSIC VOL. 3				
Capitol Creative Products SL-6659	1969	3.00	6.00	12.00
—Sold only at Zenith dealers; reissued as "Christmas -- The Season of Music" for general release				
ZENITH PRESENTS CHRISTMAS, A GIFT OF MUSIC VOL. 4				
Capitol Creative Products SL-6687	1970	3.00	6.00	12.00
—Sold only at Zenith dealers; reissued as "Christmas -- A Gift of Music" for general release				
ZENITH PRESENTS CHRISTMAS, A GIFT OF MUSIC VOL. 5				
Columbia Special Products C 10395	1971	2.50	5.00	10.00
—Sold only at Zenith dealers				
ZENITH PRESENTS CHRISTMAS, A GIFT OF MUSIC, VOL. 6 (THE CHRISTMAS HIT PARADE)				
Longines Symphonette SYS 5562	1972	2.50	5.00	10.00
—Sold only at Zenith dealers				
ZENITH PRESENTS HOOTENANNY SPECIAL				
Columbia Special Products CSP 216M [M]	1965	6.25	12.50	25.00
Columbia Special Products CSP 216S [S]	1965	7.50	151.00	30.00
ZENITH SALUTES THE SWINGIN' BANDS				
Columbia Special Products CSS 525 [M]	1967	3.75	7.50	15.00
—Available from Zenith dealers				
ZIG ZAG FESTIVAL				
Mercury SRD-2-29 [DJ]	1970	6.25	12.50	25.00

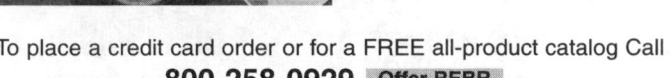

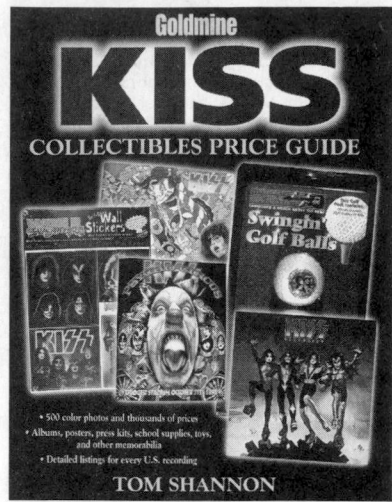

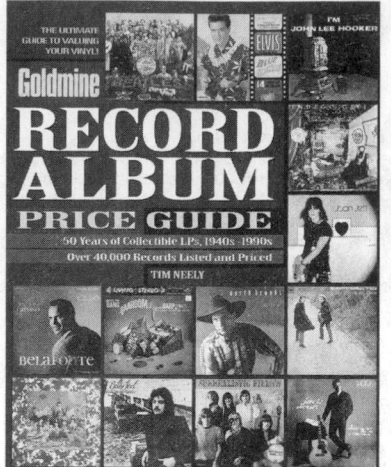

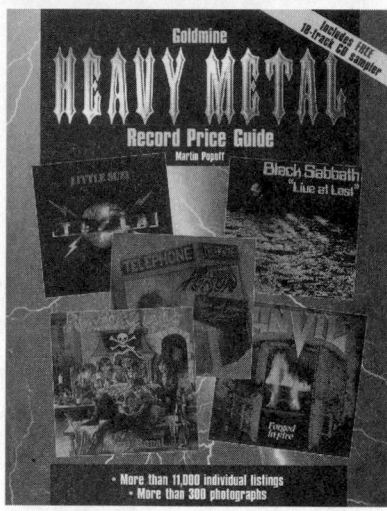

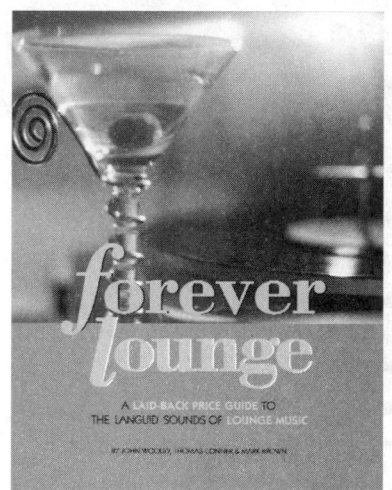

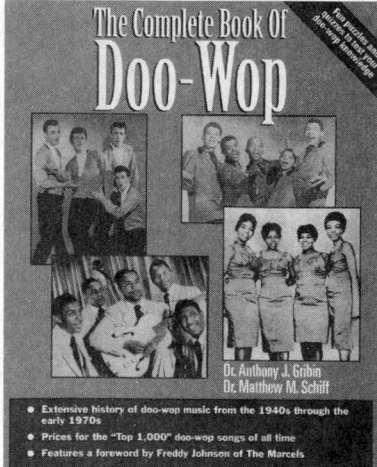

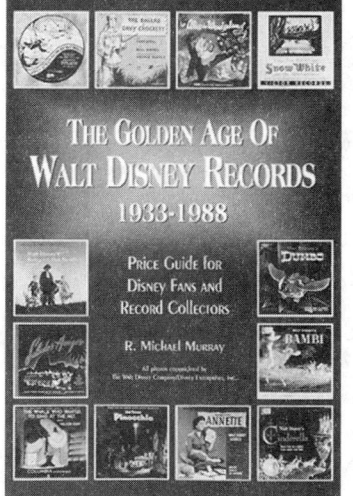